A Concordance to the Poems of

W. B. YEATS

THE CORNELL CONCORDANCES

S. M. Parrish, *General Editor*

Supervisory Committee

M. H. Abrams
Donald D. Eddy
Ephim Fogel
Alain Seznec

POEMS OF MATTHEW ARNOLD, *edited by S. M. Parrish*
POEMS OF W. B. YEATS, *edited by S. M. Parrish*
POEMS OF EMILY DICKINSON, *edited by S. P. Rosenbaum*
WRITINGS OF WILLIAM BLAKE, *edited by David V. Erdman*
BYRON'S *DON JUAN*, *edited by Charles W. Hagelman, Jr., and Robert J. Barnes*
THÉÂTRE ET POÉSIES DE JEAN RACINE, *edited by Bryant C. Freeman*
BEOWULF, *edited by J. B. Bessinger, Jr.*
PLAYS OF W. B. YEATS, *edited by Eric Domville*
POEMS OF JONATHAN SWIFT, *edited by Michael Shinagel*
PLAYS OF WILLIAM CONGREVE, *edited by David Mann*
POEMS OF SAMUEL JOHNSON, *edited by Helen Naugle*

A Concordance to the Poems of
W. B. YEATS

Edited by
STEPHEN MAXFIELD PARRISH

Programmed by
JAMES ALLAN PAINTER

Cornell University Press
ITHACA AND LONDON

First published 1963 by Cornell University Press.
Published in the United Kingdom by Cornell University Press Ltd.,
2-4 Brook Street, London W1Y 1AA.

Second printing 1966
Third printing 1973

International Standard Book Number 0-8014-0328-6
Library of Congress Catalog Card Number 63-11493

Printed in the United States of America by Valley Offset, Inc.

EDITOR'S PREFACE

TO invoke the aid of an electronic computer in mapping Yeats's private worlds of myth and symbol and Irish legend may well arouse disquiet. What humanist can remain undisturbed at the cold prospect of tabulating cones (1 occurrence), cubes (2), and gyres (14, in its various forms)— those magical designs which, Yeats tells us, "Robartes describes the Judwali Arabs as making upon the sand for the instruction of their young people, and which, according to tradition, were drawn as described in sleep by the wife of Kusta-Ben-Luka"? But the reader of Yeats who can learn to tolerate these ironies will find in this concordance (produced on an IBM 704 Electronic Data Processing Machine) information never before readily accessible. For this is, I believe, the first concordance of a symbolist poet ever undertaken. Apart from the ordinary uses of such an index, the reader has available here the means of tracing surely and in intricate detail the language patterns of a symbolist imagination.

Consider, to take an elementary instance, the advantages of cataloguing the extraordinary birds that beat, wheel, cry, hover, and keen through Yeats's poems. Birds, to be sure, warble outrageously through all English poetry; in some peculiar way they express the national genius. But a full inventory of this Irish poet's birds overwhelms the mind. I count, for a beginning, some 8 hawks, 21 owls, 6 bats, 2 kites, 6 falcons, 15 eagles, 8 ospreys, and 5 kingfishers—all birds of prey—as well as 2 robins, 2 partridges, 2 gannets, 9 swallows, 3 water-hens, 2 water-fowls, 4 moor-hens, 2 peahens, 3 moorfowl, 10 herons, 12 curlews, 3 bitterns, 6 gulls, 2 seagulls, 1 sea-mew, 10 doves, 1 ringdove, 4 pigeons, 1 crane, 2 night-ingales, 5 sparrows, 4 parrots, 2 crows, 11 cocks, 4 hens, 13 peacocks, 1 daw, 2 rooks, 1 stare, 1 nightjar, 2 lapwings, 1 jay, 1 cormorant, 1 grouse, 2 ducks, 16 swans, 6 ravens, 2 woodpeckers, 3 flamingos, 4 linnets, 2 snipes, 4 peewits, 8 geese, 1 barnacle-goose, 1 turkey, and 6 cuckoos— not to speak of the halcyon (3), the phoenix (8), or the bird that Grecian goldsmiths make. "Bird," incidentally, has 163 occurrences in all its forms, not counting such compounds as "gamebird" (2), "cattle-birds" (1), "sea-

bird" (2), and "song-bird" (2). To carry on a study of bird imagery one would, of course, have not only to complete the inventory, but also to move out through such associated words as "bill," "wing," "feather," "claw," "pinion," "perch," "nest," "cage," and "flutter." And one might appropriately hunt down Yeats's other winged creatures—wasps (1), bees (39), moths (18), grasshoppers (7), flies (27), and the like, ending perhaps with vampire (1) and muse (11).

The symbolic importance of Yeats's birds has been recognized by critics and scholars. Yeats's landscape world of images, we all agree, is a forest of trees (each with a mask hanging on the trunk), their branches alive with birds—a forest running along the edge of the sea, broken by an occasional house with a tower and a rose garden, and overhead (though not all at once) the sun, the moon, and the stars. But one might wonder whether (save for the rough beast that slouches toward Bethlehem) the animals that thickly populate this forest have aroused the interest they deserve. As the concordance reveals, savage or noxious animals (analogous, perhaps, to the birds of prey) abound: 3 leopards, 3 bears, 6 panthers, 9 wolves, 20 lions, 7 weasels, 12 foxes, 1 rat, 1 rhinoceros, 5 boars, 3 adders, 3 lynxes, 4 spiders, 4 serpents, 18 worms, 1 polecat, and 1 mole. But animals of every sort—wild and domestic, large and small, four-legged and aquatic—throng the poems. I count, loosely, 72 horses (also 2 stallions, 5 mares), 23 hares, 3 asses, 1 jackass, 2 antelopes, 33 deer (plus 17 stags, 4 roes, 2 roebucks, and 5 does), 4 badgers, 4 crickets, 18 mice, 1 haymouse, 6 oxen, 6 lambs, 17 sheep, 2 gazelles, 2 pigs, 11 otters, 9 cattle, 3 kine, 7 calves, 1 steer, 4 bulls (excluding of course, John Bull, who shows up 3 times), 10 squirrels, 5 rabbits, 1 coney, 1 lev'ret, 14 cats, 24 dogs (one, at least, is a great Dane), 3 camels, 2 stoats, 8 goats, 2 ponies, 1 monkey, 1 mackerel, 3 herring, 7 trout, 1 eel, 7 salmon, 5 dolphins, 2 goldfish, and a minnow, together with twenty-odd fish, 9 animals, and 26 just plain beasts. (Should we add dragon [11], mermaid [3], and sphinx [1]?) The profusion of animals here—both on the hoof, as it were, and in the vehicle of a metaphor—may give new force to Yeats's complaint of desertion at the waning of his inventive power:

> I sought a theme and sought for it in vain,
> I sought it daily for six weeks or so.
> Maybe at last, being but a broken man,
> I must be satisfied with my heart, although
> Winter and summer till old age began
> My circus animals were all on show.

Although these homely catalogues represent a fairly unsophisticated approach to Yeats's poetry, they will perhaps suggest the kinds of dis-

covery that are now made easier and surer. Ultimately, we hope that this concordance and others to follow (the Blake in particular) will stimulate exploration of the strange, dazzling, highly organized but often ill-charted worlds created by symbolist and mythopoeic genius.

Basic Text and Format

With the permission of The Macmillan Company and Colonel Russell K. Alspach, this concordance is based upon the superb *Variorum Edition of the Poems of W. B. Yeats,* edited by Peter Allt and Colonel Alspach (New York, 1957). The technique of preparing the text for the computer was about the same as that developed for the first volume in this series, *A Concordance to the Poems of Matthew Arnold* (Ithaca, 1959). The lines of Yeats's verse were punched on IBM cards (one line per card) and "verified"; speaker identifications, stage directions, dedications, and all like material not bearing line numbers were omitted. Page numbers and line numbers as shown in the variorum edition were added to the cards by a semiautomatic process. Lines too long for a single card were divided and punched on two (or more) cards with the same line number; the first portion of the line was followed and the last portion preceded by three spaced periods. Variant lines, with certain exceptions as noted below (see "Variants," p. ix), were put together from the Allt and Alspach collations and punched, each with a "v" preceding the line number, then interfiled by page in the main deck. A single title card for each poem, containing an abbreviated title designed to serve as identifying information (for the full list of abbreviations see pp. xv–xxvi) was placed at the head of the cards representing the poem. There was one important departure from the Arnold procedure: complete titles and variant titles of all poems, less subtitles and other prefatory matter, were punched in the same way as lines of verse, but with "т" in the line-number position, so that they could be indexed. Where digits occurred in titles, they were spelled out within brackets.

After proofreading, the material on the cards was transferred to magnetic tape. The 704 was then programmed to search the tape and index alphabetically every word on it, with some exceptions (see "Omitted Words," p. xi), by listing all lines of verse in which the word occurred, together with the identifying information: page number, abbreviated title, and line number (or т) preceded by v for variant lines or titles. The order in which the lines of verse fall under each of the index words is the order in which the cards were fed onto tape—that is, page and line order in the variorum edition. As with the Arnold concordance, the final IBM list, spaced into pages, was reproduced for publication by

an offset process, and a table of index words in order of frequency was provided in an appendix.

Several features of this volume represent sophistications of the techniques developed for Arnold (a twentieth-century poet deserves more help from modern technology than a nineteenth). Particulars of these are given in the Programmer's Preface (p. xxix), but three brief statements must be made here. First, a new print-wheel design made it possible to include punctuation symbols on the text cards and to show them on the concordance page. It might be noted that since apostrophes and single quotation marks would be indistinguishable, all quotation marks are double, even those within quotations. Second, a cross-reference routine was devised whereby the hyphen was treated in the indexing as a letter, not as a space (the computer recognizes only these two categories). Each hyphenated word thus appears as an index entry, and a cross reference is provided from the second (third, fourth, and so on) part of the word to the whole entry, under which the lines of text appear. An occasional word not hyphenated has been held together, for obvious reasons, as though it were (e.g., FOL DE ROL). Finally, the new program made it possible to exercise a certain amount of editorial judgment on an unpaged listing of the concordance text, then to incorporate changes in the final paged list. Thus partial listings of certain homographs have been provided (ART, MIGHT, and WILL) by the simple device of dropping the unimportant meanings. Conceivably, a hardier editor might in much the same way discriminate all homographs, to the limit of his discernment and endurance. But, as with nearly all other concordances, the user can make his own discriminations here (and they might not always be the same as an editor's) by looking through the quoted lines of text. For an illustration of what can be achieved with our elegant new techniques, see the ROSE entries where I have disentangled one of Yeats's important symbols from the occurrences of ROSE as a verb.

In the Appendix to this volume will be found, listed in order of frequency, the 10,465 words of Yeats's poetic vocabulary which are indexed in the concordance. The total of 10,666 (10,465 indexed, 3 partially indexed, 198 wholly omitted), like the total of 10,097 for Arnold, is somewhat inflated by the way in which hyphenated and apostrophized words have been handled, and individual frequencies are swollen by the presence of variant lines. Moreover, it may be useful to repeat here a caution set down in the Arnold Preface: since the Appendix shows raw frequencies, transcribed from the indexing tapes—MAN (456 occurrences), MAN's (54), MEN (263), and MEN's (23) are separate entries—the list cannot be compared directly with other lists of high-frequency words made up by combining variant forms.

viii

Yet these figures should offer a number of suggestive facts even to the casual reader. Among the dozen highest frequencies perhaps OLD (575) is the one surprise; the appearance of LOVE (353) and HEART (272) could have been foretold. In a lower range, parts of the body are unexpectedly prominent. BODY itself has 104 occurrences, BODIES 34, EYES 244, EYE 86, FACE 131, HAIR 138, FEET 108, FOOT 34, BREAST 76, ARMS 58, LIPS 88, and MOUTH 39. (Here, of course, the figures are occasionally padded by homographs.) At the lowest range one is struck by the abundance of nonce words in some of Yeats's most brilliant lyrics. Consider, for an example, the opening stanza of "Byzantium":

> The *unpurged* images of day *recede;*
> The *Emperor's* drunken soldiery are abed;
> Night *resonance recedes, night-walkers'* song
> After great *cathedral* gong;
> A starlit or a moonlit dome *disdains*
> All that man is,
> All mere *complexities,*
> The fury and the mire of human veins.

The italicized forms occur nowhere in Yeats outside this poem; moreover, "abed," "soldiery," "gong," "starlit," and "dome" show up elsewhere only once or twice. It is almost as though on these occasions Yeats rose to a fresh level of poetic discourse.

Variants

> The friends that have it I do wrong
> When ever I remake a song,
> Should know what issue is at stake;
> It is myself that I remake.

So sang Yeats relatively early in his career as maker and remaker of songs. The record of his lifelong struggle for perfection of the work and of the self may be read in the thousands of collations printed by Allt and Alspach. In putting together variant lines from these collations, I have followed the numbering scrupulously, with one exception: variants of a refrain line were punched once only, with REF in the line-number position (refrain lines in the main text were all given proper line numbers).

While I have striven not to leave out any important part of Yeats's self, and have thus swelled this volume and padded the frequency lists with numerous minor variants—some, alas, probably introduced by editors or

printers, not by the poet—certain omissions have seemed desirable, if only to confine the work to a volume. The following variants listed in Allt and Alspach have therefore *not* been recorded:

1) Variants involving punctuation, capitalization, italics, or accents only (for these could not be shown in the IBM print).

2) Variants involving only material not given a line number in the main text (and therefore not punched): speaker identifications, stage directions, subtitles, and the like.

3) Variants involving simply the renumbering or transposition of identical lines or portions of lines that are relatively close together—that is, on the same page of Allt and Alspach (e.g., p. 4, line 34 and var. line 35). Lines moved from one location to another, or from one poem to another, were punched in both.

4) Variants involving only the apostrophization, abbreviation, contraction, or expansion of single words (e.g., "altho' " for "although," "St." for "Saint," "Ha'pence" for "halfpence," and "H——'s" for "Horton's").

5) Variants involving the separation or joining of two words where no word concerned is "significant"—that is, included in the index. Thus "I'll" for "I will," "what's" for "what is," "he's" for "he has," and the like, were not punched ("will" as a verb is nonsignificant, as are all the other words above). But "a while" for "awhile" was punched, since both "while" and "awhile" are significant words.

6) Most variants produced by obvious misprints in one or another edition of Yeats (e.g., "beech-hole" for "beech-bole," p. 278, line 36). Identification of misprints has been conservative, with the result that some unlikely but possible readings are included. I have also thought it best to keep a few apparent misprints that have acquired currency by surviving many printings (see, for example, p. 39, var. line 158 and p. 121, var. line 6). The following misprints, however, appearing in lines which had to be punched, have been corrected silently: "hundrd" for "hundred," p. 8, var. line 85a; "unwieldly" for "unwieldy," p. 18, var. line 268; "lounging" for "lunging," p. 41, var. line 181; "langour" for "languor," p. 44, line 223; "dread-dimmed" for "dream-dimmed," p. 164, var. line 1; "Drumhair" for "Drumahair," p. 207, var. line 11; "Any" for "And," p. 273, line 64; "their" for "there," p. 279, var. line 53; "clanguor" for "clangour," p. 382, line 9; "at" for "a," p. 392, var. line 17; "An" for "And," p. 392, var. line 25; "wndow" for "window," p. 694, line 95; "howewards" for "homewards," p. 757, line 202; and "comortable" for "comfortable," p. 780, line 6.

7) Variant titles to groups of poems after the *first* listing in Allt and Alspach. Thus "Momentary Thoughts" has been punched once only, as a variant title to poem No. 105, p. 260.

8) Variant titles which are simply first lines of poems.

9) Variants involving spelling only. To introduce these would not only have required extensive cross-referencing of a kind the computer could not accomplish unaided, but might also have masked the consistency of spelling in Yeats's final text. I have, however, preserved a few variants that seemed for one reason or another to be of interest or to offer difficulties (e.g., "phantasy" for "fantasy," "faery" for "fairy," and "chaunt" for "chant"). Proper names, of course, are a special case. Most variant names vary only slightly and should give little trouble (e.g., "Hoolihan" for "Houlihan," and "Kyle-na-gno" for "Kyle-na-no"); most of those that might give trouble (e.g., "Usheen" for "Oisin") are listed helpfully on pages 1 and 105 of Allt and Alspach. The connoisseur of Irish spellings will be sorry to have lost "Coulte" and "Moharabuiee" (which occur only as variants) but will perhaps be satisfied with "Shee," "Cu," "Cann," and "Cola," which survive (a number of variant names, "Usheen" among them, show up in the concordance by reason of their occurrence in lines that contain other, significant variants).

Besides the types listed above, a very small number of miscellaneous variants have been omitted for what seemed compelling reasons. These include an occasional line all of whose variants were incorporated separately in variant lines or half-lines already punched, and an occasional curiosity such as var. line 418, p. 242: "O! O! O! But no, that is not it" for "O! O! O! O! But no, that is not it." (Actually, no matter how hard we might punch this particular line, we could not get it to show up anywhere, all words in it being nonsignificant.)

It might be worth remarking, finally, that the omissions do not include any variants of hyphenation (save for a handful of proper names). As a consequence, the user must realize, three forms of a substantial number of terms are to be found in the concordance (e.g., HARPSTRING, HARP STRING, and HARP-STRING).

Omitted Words

Our computer routines have made it possible not only to offer selective listings of the most troublesome homographs, but also to provide frequencies of the omitted words. Words in the first list, below, are indexed only in the forms shown; words in the second list are omitted from the index altogether. DOES, MAY, and WILT were listed for editing, then dropped, since neither of the first two occurs as a noun, nor does the last occur in the sense of "droop"; TILL, which has only two occurrences as a noun, none as a verb, might have been dropped or edited, but the 145 occurrences as a preposition or conjunction were thought to be of sufficient interest to warrant retaining them.

PARTIALLY LISTED

ART	(noun)	12	(12 occurrences as verb omitted)
MIGHT	(noun)	12	(74 occurrences as verb omitted)
WILL	(noun)	32	(262 occurrences as verb omitted)

OMITTED ENTIRELY

A	2841	HADST	3	ME	464	THEIR	633
AGAIN	99	HAS	364	MUST	131	THEIRS	5
AH	88	HAST	17	MY	1118	THEM	219
ALSO	11	HATH	26	MYSEL'	1	THEMSELVES	12
ALTHOUGH	48	HAVE	850	MYSELF	18	THEN	168
AM	165	HE	789	NEITHER	31	THERE	468
AN	300	HE'D	12	NO	526	THERE'S	46
AND	6023	HE'LL	5	NOR	209	THEREFORE	21
ANOTHER	51	HER	737	NOT	540	THERE'LL	5
ANOTHER'S	10	HERE	77	NOW	337	THESE	166
ARE	589	HERE'S	11	O	318	THEY	567
AT	469	HERS	10	O'	3	THEY'D	6
BE	485	HERSELF	13	OF	3320	THEY'LL	5
BECAUSE	158	HE'S	9	OH	64	THEY'RE	10
BEEN	111	HIM	289	ON	992	THEY'VE	2
BOTH	29	HIMSELF	22	OR	799	THINE	23
BUT	974	HIS	1081	OTHER	82	THIS	306
BY	514	HOW	183	OTHER'LL	1	THOSE	229
CAN	267	I	2132	OTHERS	19	THOU	107
CANNOT	65	II	1	OTHER'S	9	THOUGH	218
CANST	1	III	1	OTHERS'	1	THOUL'T	1
COULD	165	IV	2	OUR	318	THOU'RT	1
D	1	I'	2	OURS	4	THRO'	2
DE	9	I'D	57	OURSELVES	2	THROUGH	161
DID	95	IF	281	P	1	THUS	30
DIDST	1	I'LL	42	'S	1	THY	123
DID'ST	1	I'M	13	SHALL	158	THYSELF	2
DO	138	IN	2088	SHALT	14	'TIS	24
DOES	20	IN'T	2	SHE	361	TO	1751
DON'T	1	INTO	179	SHE'D	7	TOO	88
DOST	4	IS	922	SHE'LL	2	T'OTHER	3
DOTH	4	IS'T	1	SHOULD	123	T'OTHER'S	1
EACH	79	IT	713	SO	339	'TWAS	16
EITHER	10	ITS	188	'TH	3	'TWERE	12
'EM	3	IT'S	24	THAT	2357	'TWILL	2
FOR	1007	ITSELF	17	THAT'S	40	'TWOULD	3
FROM	665	I'VE	20	THE	8436	UPON	508
HAD	610	MAY	245	THEE	68	US	174

V	2	WE'VE	5	WHICH	10	WOULDST	1
WAS	344	WHAT	503	WHO	293	YE	65
WAST	1	WHAT'S	31	WHO'D	4	YOU	716
WAS'T	1	WHATE'ER	2	WHOM	32	YOU'D	5
WE	446	WHATEVER	21	WHO'S	2	YOU'LL	10
WE'D	6	WHATEVER'S	2	WHOSE	69	YOUR	362
WE'LL	11	WHEN	590	WHY	95	YOU'RE	8
WERE	330	WHERE	459	WILT	9	YOURS	4
WE'RE	4	WHERE'S	1	WITH	1079	YOURSELF	5
WERE'T	2	WHEREVER	4	WON'T	1	YOU'VE	6
WERT	4	WHETHER	27	WOULD	238		

The presence here of low-frequency words may be explained by a desire for consistency. For example, with HE (789), HIS (1,081), and HIM (289) out for obvious reasons it seemed logical to drop HIMSELF, with only 22 occurrences (regrettable as that omission may seem from the work of an Irish poet). But endless controversy might be waged over my selections. Consider the lowly preposition OF. Having observed that Yeats liked to form metaphors by connecting vehicle and tenor with "of," I listed and examined all 3,320 occurrences of the word (the computer can provide a list of any given word in about 30 minutes). Scattered through the chaff were the following images, which could not, I suppose, have been collected in any other way:

	Page		Line
THE PALE BLOSSOM OF THE MOON	20		288
THE OSPREY OF SORROW	27	V	415D
THE ANVIL OF THE WORLD	42		204
THE FIRE OF SADNESS	73		49
THE GULPH OF SLEEP	83		22
THE ROOD OF TIME	100		title
THE BOUGHS OF LOVE AND HATE	101		10
GREAT WEBS OF SORROW	104		39
THE WHARVES OF SORROW	115		27
FLAMING FOUNTS OF DUTY	124		5
THE GLASS OF OUTER WEARINESS	135		31
THE FLAMING CIRCLE OF OUR LIFE	135	V	16
THE RAVENS OF UNRESTING THOUGHT	136		34
THE NETS OF WRONG AND RIGHT	147		2
THE SHADOWY BLOSSOM OF MY HAIR	152		7
THE HORSES OF DISASTER	154		8
THE PALE FIRE OF TIME	157		6
LILIES OF DEATH-PALE HOPE, ROSES OF PASSIONATE DREAM	172		8
THE NETS OF DAY AND NIGHT	175		12

	Page	Line
THE PALE CUP OF THE SEA	175	14
THE WATERS OF SLEEP	218	25
THE BURNISHED MIRROR OF THE WORLD	228	132
THE SHIVERING CASTING-NET OF THE STARS	237	329
THE LABYRINTH OF HER DAYS	260	13
THE DIM / IMAGINATIONS OF THEIR EYES	272	27/28
THE GOLDEN TOP OF CARE	309	20
THE WICK OF YOUTH	334 V	3
THE PESTLE OF THE MOON	346	30
YELLOW-EYED HAWK OF THE MIND	349	14
THE BALLOON OF THE MIND	358	2
THE CAT-O'-NINE-TAILS OF THE MIND	374	42
THE BASIN OF THE MIND	478	34
THE HONEY-POT OF HIS MIND	481	21
THIS PRAGMATICAL, PREPOSTEROUS PIG OF A WORLD	481	26
THOSE BRANCHES OF THE NIGHT AND DAY	502	68
THE MARE OF TIME	529	5
THE FOAL OF THE WORLD	529	6
THE MATERNAL MIDNIGHT OF MY BREAST	535	7
THE MILL OF THE MIND	575	10
THE CAVERN OF THE MIND	600	2
THE FOUL RAG-AND-BONE SHOP OF THE HEART	630	40
THE BOUGHS OF TIME	756	178
THE LABYRINTH OF THE MIND	785	24

Other insignificant words in Yeats, arbitrarily omitted from this index to economize space, may be of like interest to scholars and critics. To prevent any word from being lost forever, we expect to keep on file the magnetic tapes of all texts in the Cornell series.

Abbreviated Titles

In assigning title abbreviations—as in all things—I have followed the numbering of lines in the variorum edition. Wherever a poem breaks into parts or scenes with separate sequences of numbers, separate titles have been assigned; where numbering is continuous from one section to the next, one title carries over. Yeats's longer titles have not been easy to reduce to fourteen columns of an IBM card, and I have followed no very consistent principle. I have occasionally taken the opening words; more often, I have tried to devise a catch title from words which seemed likely to have lodged in a reader's memory.

Abbreviations are listed below exactly as they appear in the concordance text. Following each abbreviation the reader will find the full title of the poem and the number of the page on which the poem begins in the variorum edition.

Abbreviation	Title	Page
ABBEY THEATRE	At the Abbey Theatre (Imitated from Ronsard)	264
ACCURSED WHO	'Accursed who brings to light of day'	779
ACRE OF GRASS	An Acre of Grass	575
ADAMS CURSE	Adam's Curse	204
AGAINST WITCH	Against Witchcraft	775
ALF POLLEXFEN	In Memory of Alfred Pollexfen	360
ALL SOUL NIGHT	All Souls' Night: Epilogue to 'A Vision'	470
ALL TEMPT ME	All Things can Tempt me	267
AM OF IRELAND	Words for Music Perhaps XX. 'I Am of Ireland'	526
ANASHU VIJAYA	Anashuya and Vijaya	71
ANCEST HOUSES	Meditations in Time of Civil War I. Ancestral Houses	417
ANNE GREGORY	For Anne Gregory	492
APPARITIONS	The Apparitions	624
APPOINTMENT	An Appointment	624
ARROW	The Arrow	199
ASKS FORGIVE	The Lover asks Forgiveness because of his Many Moods	162
AT ALGECIRAS	At Algeciras — A Meditation upon Death	493
BAILE AILLINN	Baile and Aillinn	189
BALLOON MIND	The Balloon of the Mind	358
BEFORE WORLD	A Woman Young and Old II. Before the World was Made	531
BEGGAR CRIED	Beggar to Beggar Cried	299
BELOVED DEAD	He wishes his Beloved were Dead	175
BELOVED PEACE	He bids his Beloved be at Peace	154
BELOVED RHYMES	He gives his Beloved certain Rhymes	157
BEN BULBEN	Under Ben Bulben	636
BLACK CENTAUR	On a Picture of a Black Centaur by Edmund Dulac	442
BLACK PIG	The Valley of the Black Pig	161
BLACK TOWER	The Black Tower	635
BLESS PSALTER	The Players ask for a Blessing on the Psalteries and on Themselves	212
BLESSED	The Blessed	166
BLOOD AND MOON	Blood and the Moon	480
BLOOD BOND	The Blood Bond: from the play 'Grania' by George Moore and W. B. Yeats	769
BONE OF A HARE	The Collar-Bone of a Hare	330

BOOK STORIES	The Dedication to a Book of Stories selected from The Irish Novelists	129
BRAVEST ASK	'The bravest from the gods but ask:'	788
BREAK OF DAY	Towards Break of Day	398
BROKEN DREAMS	Broken Dreams	355
BRONZE HEAD	A Bronze Head	618
BROWN PENNY	Brown Penny	268
BYZANTIUM	Byzantium	497
CAP AND BELLS	The Cap and Bells	159
CARVED STONE	To be Carved on a Stone at Thoor Ballylee	406
CAT AND MOON	The Cat and the Moon	378
CATHLEEN PARA	The Countess Cathleen in Paradise	124
CHANGE BELOVED	He mourns for the Change that has come upon him and his Beloved, and longs for the End of the World	153
CHILD DANCING	I. To a Child Dancing in the Wind	312
CHOICE	The Choice	495
CHOSEN	A Woman Young and Old VI. Chosen	534
CHURCH STATE	Church and State	553
CIRCUS ANIMALS	The Circus Animals' Desertion	629
CLOAK BOAT	The Cloak, the Boat, and the Shoes	69
CLOTHS HEAVEN	He wishes for the Cloths of Heaven	176
COAT	A Coat	320
COLD HEAVEN	The Cold Heaven	316
COLONEL MARTIN	Colonel Martin	594
COLONUS PRAISE	Colonus' Praise (from 'Oedipus at Colonus')	446
COME RIDE	'Come ride and ride to the garden' [from the play 'The Travelling Man,' by Lady Gregory]	773
COMING WISDOM	The Coming of Wisdom with Time	261
CONJUNCTIONS	Supernatural Songs X. Conjunctions	562
CONSOLATION	A Woman Young and Old V. Consolation	534
COOLE BALLYLEE	Coole Park and Ballylee, 1931	490
COOLE PARK 29	Coole Park, 1929	488
CRADLE SONG	A Cradle Song	118
CRAZED GIRL	A Crazed Girl	578
CRAZED MOON	The Crazed Moon	487
CRY OF SEDGE	He hears the Cry of the Sedge	165
CUCHULAIN COMF	Cuchulain Comforted	634
CUCHULAIN SEA	Cuchulain's Fight with the Sea	105
CURSE CROMWELL	The Curse of Cromwell	580
DANAAN QUICK	The Danaan Quicken Tree	742
DANCER CRUACH	Words for Music Perhaps XXI. The Dancer at Cruachan and Cro-Patrick	528
DANCING DAYS	Words for Music Perhaps XIX. Those Dancing Days are Gone	524

DAWN	The Dawn	344
DAWN-SONG	A Dawn-Song	705
DEATH	Death	476
DEATH OF HARE	A Man Young and Old IV. The Death of the Hare	453
DEDICATION	Dedication	790
DEEP-SWORN VOW	A Deep-sworn Vow	357
DEJECTION	Lines Written in Dejection	343
DELPHIC ORACLE	Words for Music Perhaps XXV. The Delphic Oracle upon Plotinus	530
DEMON BEAST	Demon and Beast	399
DOLLS	The Dolls	319
DOLLS DRAWINGS	Upon a Dying Lady II. Certain Artists bring her Dolls and Drawings	362
DOLLS FACES	Upon a Dying Lady III. She turns the Dolls' Faces to the Wall	363
DOR WELLESLEY	To Dorothy Wellesley	579
DRAWING-ROOM	In a Drawing-Room	685
DREAM OF DEATH	A Dream of Death	123
DREAM OF FAERY	The Man who Dreamed of Faeryland	126
DRINKING SONG	A Drinking Song	261
DRUNK SOBRIETY	A Drunken Man's Praise of Sobriety	591
DWELT SYCAMORE	She Who Dwelt among the Sycamores. A Fancy.	715
EARL PAUL	The Ballad of Earl Paul	739
EASTER 1916	Easter 1916	391
EGO DOMINUS	Ego Dominus Tuus	367
ELEMENT POWERS	The Poet-pleads with the Elemental Powers	174
EMPTY CUP	A Man Young and Old V. The Empty Cup	454
END OF DAY	Upon a Dying Lady IV. The End of Day	364
EPHEMERA	Ephemera	79
EVA GORE-BOOTH	In Memory of Eva Gore-Booth and Con Markiewicz	475
EVERLAST VOICE	The Everlasting Voices	141
EVIL OF BELOV	He thinks of those who have Spoken Evil of his Beloved	166
FAERY SONG	A Faery Song	116
FAIRY DOCTOR	The Fairy Doctor	716
FAIRY PEDANT	The Fairy Pedant	706
FALLEN MAJESTY	Fallen Majesty	314
FALLING LEAVES	The Falling of the Leaves	79
FASC DIFFICULT	The Fascination of What's Difficult	260
FATHER CHILD	A Woman Young and Old I. Father and Child	531
FATHER OHART	The Ballad of Father O'Hart	91
FERENCZ RENYI	How Ferencz Renyi Kept Silent. Hungary, 1848.	709
FERGUS DRUID	Fergus and the Druid	102
FIDDLER DOONEY	The Fiddler of Dooney	178
FIRST CONFESS	A Woman Young and Old III. A First Confession	532

FIRST LOVE	A Man Young and Old I. First Love	451
FISH	The Fish	146
FISHERMAN	The Fisherman	347
FOLLY COMFORT	The Folly of Being Comforted	199
FOR DAUGHTER	A Prayer for my Daughter	403
FOR MY SON	A Prayer for my Son	435
FORGOT BEAUTY	He remembers Forgotten Beauty	155
FOUR AGES MAN	Supernatural Songs IX. The Four Ages of Man	561
FOXHUNTER	The Ballad of the Foxhunter	97
FR GILLIGAN	The Ballad of Father Gilligan	132
FRAGMENTS	Fragments	439
FRIEND ILLNESS	A Friend's Illness	267
FRIENDS	Friends	315
FRIENDS WRONG	'The friends that have it I do wrong'	778
FRIENDS YOUTH	A Man Young and Old VII. The Friends of his Youth	455
FROM ANTIGONE	A Woman Young and Old XI. From the 'Antigone'	540
FROM JAPANESE	Imitated from the Japanese	567
FROM OEDIPUS	A Man Young and Old XI. From 'Oedipus at Colonus'	459
GALLERY REVIS	The Municipal Gallery Revisited	601
GALWAY RACES	At Galway Races	266
GARRET CELLAR	'To Garret or Cellar a wheel I send,'	787
GEORGE MOORE	'Moore once had visits from the muse'	792
GHOST ROG CASE	The Ghost of Roger Casement	583
GIRLS SONG A	Girl's Song	723
GIRLS SONG B	Words for Music Perhaps VIII. Girl's Song	515
GLOVE CLOAK	The Glove and the Cloak	744
GOES FERGUS	Who Goes with Fergus?	125
GOING THE ROAD	'I was going the road one day'	779
GRAT INSTRUCT	Gratitude to the Unknown Instructors	505
GREAT DAY	The Great Day	590
GREY ROCK	The Grey Rock	270
GREY ROUND	At the Grey Round of the Hill	782
GYRES	The Gyres	564
HANRAHANS SONG	Red Hanrahan's Song about Ireland	206
HAPPY SHEPHERD	The Song of the Happy Shepherd	64
HAPPY TOWNLAND	The Happy Townland	213
HARP OF AENGUS	The Harp of Aengus [prefixed to 1906 version of 'The Shadowy Waters: A Dramatic Poem']	219
HARUN RASHID	The Gift of Harun Al-Rashid	460
HATED PLAYBOY	On those that hated 'The Playboy of the Western World,' 1907	294
HAWK	The Hawk	349

xviii

HAWTHORN TREE	The Wicked Hawthorn Tree	788
HE AND SHE	Supernatural Songs VI. He and She	559
HEART FRIGHT	Why should the Heart take Fright?	781
HEART OF WOMAN	The Heart of the Woman	151
HEART SLEEVE	'The heart well worn upon the sleeve. . .'	790
HELEN LIVED	When Helen Lived	293
HER ANXIETY	Words for Music Perhaps X. Her Anxiety	517
HER CHRIS TREE	Upon a Dying Lady VII. Her Friends bring her a Christmas Tree	366
HER COURAGE	Upon a Dying Lady VI. Her Courage	365
HER COURTESY	Upon a Dying Lady I. Her Courtesy	362
HER DREAM	Words for Music Perhaps XIII. Her Dream	519
HER PRAISE	Her Praise	350
HER RACE	Upon a Dying Lady V. Her Race	365
HER TRIUMPH	A Woman Young and Old IV. Her Triumph	533
HER VISION	A Woman Young and Old VIII. Her Vision in the Wood	536
HERO GIRL FOOL	The Hero, The Girl, and the Fool	447
HIGH TALK	High Talk	622
HIS BARGAIN	Words for Music Perhaps XIV. His Bargain	520
HIS CONFIDENCE	Words for Music Perhaps XI. His Confidence	517
HIS DREAM	His Dream	253
HIS MEMORIES	A Man Young and Old VI. His Memories	454
HIS PHOENIX	His Phoenix	353
HIS WILDNESS	A Man Young and Old X. His Wildness	458
HOST OF AIR	The Host of the Air	143
HOSTING SIDHE	The Hosting of the Sidhe	140
HOUND VOICE	Hound Voice	621
HOUR DAWN	The Hour before Dawn	302
HOUSE SHAKEN	Upon a House shaken by the Land Agitation	264
HUDDON DUDDON	'Huddon, Duddon and Daniel O'Leary'	787
HUMAN DIGNITY	A Man Young and Old II. Human Dignity	452
IMAGE PAST	An Image from a Past Life	389
IN CHURCH	In Church	735
IN FIRELIGHT	In the Firelight	737
IN TARAS HALLS	In Tara's Halls	609
IN TIME OF WAR	A Meditation in Time of War	406
INDIAN ON GOD	The Indian upon God	76
INDIAN TO LOVE	The Indian to His Love	77
INTO TWILIGHT	Into the Twilight	147
IRISH AIRMAN	An Irish Airman Foresees his Death	328
ISLE IN WATER	To an Isle in the Water	89
ISLE INNISFREE	The Lake Isle of Innisfree	117
ISLE STAT I 1	The Island of Statues (Act I, Scene 1)	645
ISLE STAT I 2	The Island of Statues (Act I, Scene 2)	651

ISLE STAT I 3	The Island of Statues (Act I, Scene 3)	655
ISLE STAT II 1	The Island of Statues (Act II, Scene 1)	658
ISLE STAT II 2	The Island of Statues (Act II, Scene 2)	662
ISLE STAT II 3	The Island of Statues (Act II, Scene 3)	666
JANE AND JACK	Words for Music Perhaps IV. Crazy Jane and Jack the Journeyman	511
JANE BISHOP	Words for Music Perhaps I. Crazy Jane and the Bishop	507
JANE GROWN OLD	Words for Music Perhaps VIII. Crazy Jane grown old looks at the Dancers	514
JANE JUDGMENT	Words for Music Perhaps III. Crazy Jane on the Day of Judgment	510
JANE MOUNTAIN	Crazy Jane on the Mountain	628
JANE ON GOD	Words for Music Perhaps V. Crazy Jane on God	512
JANE REPROVED	Words for Music Perhaps II. Crazy Jane Reproved	509
JANE TALK BISH	Words for Music Perhaps VI. Crazy Jane talks with the Bishop	513
JOHN KINSELLA	John Kinsella's Lament for Mrs. Mary Moore	620
KANVA ON SELF	Kanva on Himself	723
KING NO KING	King and No King	258
LADYS 1ST SONG	The Lady's First Song	572
LADYS 2ND SONG	The Lady's Second Song	572
LADYS 3RD SONG	The Lady's Third Song	573
LAPIS LAZULI	Lapis Lazuli (For Harry Clifton)	565
LAST CONFESS	A Woman Young and Old IX. A Last Confession	538
LEADERS CROWD	The Leaders of the Crowd	398
LEDA AND SWAN	Leda and the Swan	441
LEGEND	A Legend. A drowned city is supposed to lie under the waters of Lough Gill.	724
LIFE	Life	686
LIVING BEAUTY	The Living Beauty	333
LOFTY THINGS	Beautiful Lofty Things	577
LONG-LEG FLY	Long-Legged Fly	617
LONG SILENCE	Words for Music Perhaps XVII. After Long Silence	523
LOSS OF LOVE	The Lover mourns for the Loss of Love	152
LOVE AND DEATH	Love and Death	680
LOVE SONG	Love Song. From the Gaelic.	717
LOVERS QUARREL	A Lover's Quarrel among the Fairies	726
LOVERS SONG	The Lover's Song	574
LOVES LONENESS	Words for Music Perhaps XII. Love's Loneliness	518
LULLABY	Words for Music Perhaps XVI. Lullaby	522
MAD AS MIST	Words for Music Perhaps XVIII. Mad as the Mist and Snow	523
MAD KING GOLL	The Madness of King Goll	81

MAGI	The Magi	318
MAGIC DRUM	Supernatural Songs VII. What Magic Drum?	559
MAID QUIET	Maid Quiet	171
MAIDS 1ST SONG	The Chambermaid's First Song	574
MAIDS 2ND SONG	The Chambermaid's Second Song	575
MAN AND ECHO	The Man and the Echo	632
MANS SONG	Words for Music Perhaps IX. Young Man's Song	516
MARCH SONGS 1	Three Marching Songs (I)	613
MARCH SONGS 2	Three Marching Songs (II)	614
MARCH SONGS 3	Three Marching Songs (III)	615
MASK	The Mask	263
MEETING	A Woman Young and Old X. Meeting	539
MEMORY	Memory	350
MEMORY YOUTH	A Memory of Youth	313
MEN IMPROVE	Men Improve with the Years	329
MERMAID	A Man Young and Old III. The Mermaid	452
MERU	Supernatural Songs XII. Meru	563
MODEL LAUREATE	A Model for the Laureate	597
MOHINI CHATTER	Mohini Chatterjee	495
MOLL MAGEE	The Ballad of Moll Magee	94
MOODS	The Moods	142
MOSADA 1	Mosada (Scene I)	690
MOSADA 2	Mosada (Scene II)	695
MOSADA 3	Mosada (Scene III)	699
MOTHER OF GOD	The Mother of God	499
MOUNTAIN TOMB	The Mountain Tomb	311
MOURN THEN ON	Mourn—and Then Onward!	737
MY DESCENDANTS	Meditations in Time of Civil War IV. My Descendants	422
MY HEART BEAT	Why does my Heart beat so?	781
MY HOUSE	Meditations in Time of Civil War II. My House	419
MY TABLE	Meditations in Time of Civil War III. My Table	421
NATIVITY	A Nativity	625
NEEDLES EYE	Supernatural Songs XI. A Needle's Eye	562
NETTLESHIP	On Mr. Nettleship's Picture at the Royal Hibernian Academy	688
NEVER GIVE ALL	Never Give all the Heart	202
NEW FACES	The New Faces	435
NEWS ORACLE	News for the Delphic Oracle	611
NIGHT COME	That the Night Come	317
NINETEEN 19	Nineteen Hundred and Nineteen	428
NINETEENTH CEN	The Nineteenth Century and After	485
NO SECOND TROY	No Second Troy	256
O DO NOT LOVE	O Do Not Love Too Long	211
OIL AND BLOOD	Oil and Blood	483

OISIN 1	The Wanderings of Oisin (Book I)	2
OISIN 2	The Wanderings of Oisin (Book II)	29
OISIN 3	The Wanderings of Oisin (Book III)	47
OLD FISHERMAN	The Meditation of the Old Fisherman	90
OLD MEMORY	Old Memory	201
OLD MEN ADMIRE	The Old Men Admiring Themselves in the Water	208
OLD MEN BE MAD	Why should not Old Men be Mad?	625
OLD MOTHER	The Song of the Old Mother	150
OLD PENSIONER	The Lamentation of the Old Pensioner	131
OLD TOM AGAIN	Words for Music Perhaps XXIV. Old Tom Again	530
OLD WICKED MAN	The Wild Old Wicked Man	587
ON GOING HOUSE	A Prayer on going into my House	371
ON WOMAN	On Woman	345
ORAHILLY	The O'Rahilly	584
OWEN AHERNE	Owen Aherne and his Dancers	449
PARDON FATHERS	Pardon, Old Fathers	269
PARN FUNERAL 1	Parnell's Funeral I	541
PARN FUNERAL 2	Parnell's Funeral II	542
PARNELL	Parnell	590
PARNELLITES	Come Gather Round Me, Parnellites	586
PARTING	A Woman Young and Old VII. Parting	535
PAST GREATNESS	He thinks of his Past Greatness when a Part of the Constellations of Heaven	177
PAUDEEN	Paudeen	291
PEACE	Peace	258
PEACOCK	II. The Peacock	310
PEOPLE	The People	351
PERFECT BEAUTY	He tells of the Perfect Beauty	164
PHANTOM HATRED	Meditations in Time of Civil War VII. I see Phantoms of Hatred and of the Heart's Fullness and of the Coming Emptiness	425
PHANTOM SHIP	The Phantom Ship	718
PHASES OF MOON	The Phases of the Moon	372
PILGRIM	The Pilgrim	592
PITY OF LOVE	The Pity of Love	119
PLAYER QUEEN	A Song from 'The Player Queen'	308
PLEADS FRIEND	The Lover pleads with his Friend for Old Friends	172
POET BELOVED	A Poet to his Beloved	157
POLIT PRISONER	On a Political Prisoner	397
POLITICS	Politics	631
PRAYER OLD AGE	A Prayer for Old Age	553
PRESENCES	Presences	358
PRIEST FAIRY	The Priest and the Fairy	728
PROPERTIUS	A Thought from Propertius	355
QUARREL IN AGE	Quarrel in Old Age	503

QUATRAIN APHOR	Quatrains and Aphorisms	734
QUEEN MAEVE	The Old Age of Queen Maeve	180
RAGGED WOOD	The Ragged Wood	210
REALISTS	The Realists	309
RECONCILIATION	Reconciliation	257
REED WHISPERER	While I, from that reed-throated whisperer	320
REMEMBRANCE	Remembrance	704
REMORSE SPEECH	Remorse for Intemperate Speech	506
REPRISALS	Reprisals	791
REPROVE CURLEW	He reproves the Curlew	155
RESULT THOUGHT	The Results of Thought	504
RIBH AT TOMB	Supernatural Songs I. Ribh at the Tomb of Baile and Aillinn	554
RIBH CHRISTIAN	Supernatural Songs V. Ribh Considers Christian Love Insufficient	558
RIBH ECSTASY	Supernatural Songs III. Ribh in Ecstasy	557
RIBH PATRICK	Supernatural Songs II. Ribh denounces Patrick	556
ROAD AT DOOR	Meditations in Time of Civil War V. The Road at my Door	423
ROBARTES DANCE	Michael Robartes and the Dancer	385
ROBERT GREGORY	In Memory of Major Robert Gregory	323
ROGER CASEMENT	Roger Casement (After Reading 'The Forged Casement Diaries' by Dr. Maloney)	581
ROSE IN HEART	The Lover tells of the Rose in his Heart	142
ROSE OF BATTLE	The Rose of Battle	113
ROSE OF PEACE	The Rose of Peace	112
ROSE OF WORLD	The Rose of the World	111
ROSE TREE	The Rose Tree	396
ROSE UPON ROOD	To the Rose upon the Rood of Time	100
ROSY CROSS	A Song of the Rosy Cross	744
ROUND TOWER	Under the Round Tower	331
RUN PARADISE	Running to Paradise	300
SAD SHEPHERD	The Sad Shepherd	67
SAIL BYZANTIUM	Sailing to Byzantium	407
SAINT HUNCH	The Saint and the Hunchback	379
SALLEY GARDENS	Down by the Salley Gardens	90
SCHOLARS	The Scholars	337
SCHOOL CHILDR	Among School Children	443
SECOND COMING	The Second Coming	401
SECRET ROSE	The Secret Rose	169
SECRETS OF OLD	A Man Young and Old IX. The Secrets of the Old	457
SEEKER	The Seeker. A Dramatic Poem—in Two Scenes.	681
SELF AND SOUL	A Dialogue of Self and Soul	477
SEPTEMBER 1913	September 1913	289
SEVEN SAGES	The Seven Sages	486

SEVEN WOODS	In the Seven Woods	198
SEVERED HEAD	Alternative Song for the Severed Head in 'The King of the Great Clock Tower'	549
SHADOW WATER A	The Shadowy Waters [first version, 1900]	747
SHADOW WATER B	The Shadowy Waters [second version, 1906]	221
SHEP GOATHERD	Shepherd and Goatherd	338
SINGING HEAD	The Singing Head and the Lady	789
SIXTEEN DEAD	Sixteen Dead Men	395
SOLOMON SHEBA	Solomon to Sheba	332
SOLOMON WITCH	Solomon and the Witch	387
SONG	A Song	334
SONG DEIRDRE 1	Queen Edaine [Songs from Deirdre I]	771
SONG DEIRDRE 2	Songs from Deirdre II	777
SONG DEIRDRE 3	Songs from Deirdre III	777
SONG FAERIES	Song of the Faeries	643
SONG OF FOOL	Another Song of a Fool	381
SONGS BURDEN 1	Three Songs to the One Burden (I)	605
SONGS BURDEN 2	Three Songs to the One Burden (II)	606
SONGS BURDEN 3	Three Songs to the One Burden (III)	608
SONGS FOOL 1	Two Songs of a Fool (I)	380
SONGS FOOL 2	Two Songs of a Fool (II)	381
SONGS PLAY 1	Two Songs from a Play (I)	437
SONGS PLAY 2	Two Songs from a Play (II)	438
SONGS REWRIT 1	Two Songs Rewritten for the Tune's Sake (I)	550
SONGS REWRIT 2	Two Songs Rewritten for the Tune's Sake (II)	552
SORROW OF LOVE	The Sorrow of Love	119
SPEAKS HEARERS	The Lover speaks to the Hearers of his Songs in Coming Days	173
SPILT MILK	Spilt Milk	484
SPINNING SONG	Spinning Song	770
SPIRIT MEDIUM	The Spirit Medium	599
SPUR	The Spur	591
STARES NEST	Meditations in Time of Civil War VI. The Stare's Nest by my Window	424
STATES HOLIDAY	The Statesman's Holiday	626
STATISTICS	Statistics	485
STATUES	The Statues	610
STICK INCENSE	A Stick of Incense	619
STOLEN CHILD	The Stolen Child	86
STONE CROSS	The Old Stone Cross	598
STREAM AND SUN	Stream and Sun at Glendalough	506
STREET DANCERS	Street Dancers	731
STUDENTS AGIT	On hearing that the Students of our New University have joined the Agitation against Immoral Literature	262

SUMMER EVENING	A Summer Evening	736
SUMMER SPRING	A Man Young and Old VIII. Summer and Spring	456
SWANS AT COOLE	The Wild Swans at Coole	322
SWEET DANCER	Sweet Dancer	568
SWIFTS EPITAPH	Swift's Epitaph	493
SYMBOLS	Symbols	484
THERE	Supernatural Songs IV. There	557
THESE CLOUDS	These are the Clouds	265
THOSE IMAGES	Those Images	600
THREE BEGGARS	The Three Beggars	294
THREE BUSHES	The Three Bushes (An Incident from the 'Historia Mei Temporis' of the Abbé Michel de Bourdeille)	569
THREE HERMITS	The Three Hermits	298
THREE MONUMENT	The Three Monuments	460
THREE MOVEMENT	The Three Movements	485
THREE THINGS	Words for Music Perhaps XV. Three Things	521
TO A FRIEND	To a Friend whose Work has come to Nothing	290
TO A POET	To a Poet, who would have me Praise certain Bad Poets, Imitators of His and Mine	262
TO A SHADE	To a Shade	292
TO A SQUIRREL	To a Squirrel at Kyle-na-no	359
TO HIS HEART	To his Heart, bidding it have no Fear	158
TO IRELAND	To Ireland in the Coming Times	137
TO SAME TUNE 1	Three Songs to the Same Tune (I)	544
TO SAME TUNE 2	Three Songs to the Same Tune (II)	545
TO SAME TUNE 3	Three Songs to the Same Tune (III)	547
TO SOME I TALK	To Some I have Talked with by the Fire	136
TO WEALTHY MAN	To a Wealthy Man who promised a Second Subscription to the Dublin Municipal Gallery if it were proved the People wanted Pictures	287
TOM CRUACHAN	Words for Music Perhaps XXIII. Tom at Cruachan	529
TOM LUNATIC	Words for Music Perhaps XXII. Tom the Lunatic	528
TOM OROUGHLEY	Tom O'Roughley	337
TOWER	The Tower	409
TRAV PASSION	The Travail of Passion	172
TWO KINGS	The Two Kings	276
TWO TITANS	The Two Titans. A Political Poem.	687
TWO TREES	The Two Trees	134
TWO YEAR LATER	II. Two Years Later	312
UNAPPEAS HOST	The Unappeasable Host	146
UNDER SATURN	Under Saturn	390
UNDER THE MOON	Under the Moon	209
UNWORTH PRAISE	Against Unworthy Praise	259

VACILLATION	Vacillation	499
VALLEY LOVERS	He tells of a Valley full of Lovers	163
VERONIC NAPKIN	Veronica's Napkin	483
VISION ROBART	The Double Vision of Michael Robartes	382
WANDER AENGUS	The Song of Wandering Aengus	149
WAR POEM	On being asked for a War Poem	359
WELL AND TREE	The Well and the Tree	780
WHAT THEN	What Then?	576
WHAT WAS LOST	What Was Lost	591
WHEEL	The Wheel	434
WHENCE COME	Supernatural Songs VIII. Whence Had They Come?	560
WHERE BOOKS GO	Where My Books Go	739
WHITE BIRDS	The White Birds	121
WISDOM	Wisdom	440
WISDOM DREAMS	Wisdom and Dreams	743
WITCH	I. The Witch	310
WITCH VIVIEN	Time and the Witch Vivien	720
WITHER BOUGHS	The Withering of the Boughs	203
WOMAN HOMER	A Woman Homer Sung	254
WOMANS BEAUTY	A Woman's Beauty is like a white frail Bird	784
WOODS OF COOLE	I walked among the Seven Woods of Coole [prefixed to 'The Shadowy Waters: A Dramatic Poem']	217
WORDS	Words	255
YOU ARE OLD	When You are Old	120
YOU ARE SAD	When you are Sad	738
YOU CONTENT	Are You Content?	604
YOUNG BEAUTY	To a Young Beauty	335
YOUNG GIRL	To a Young Girl	336
YOUR HEART	Why does your Heart beat thus?	785
YOUTH AND AGE	Youth and Age	434

Acknowledgments

The beginning of work on this volume was made possible by a grant-in-aid from the American Council of Learned Societies; at a later stage support was given from the grant-in-aid program of the Cornell Department of English; throughout, we have been dependent upon services provided by the International Business Machines Corporation, the Cornell Computing Center in Ithaca, and the Cornell Aeronautical Laboratory in Buffalo, New York.

These formal announcements scarcely reveal the warm sense of obligation I feel to the individuals who placed their confidence in this venture and gave it their help: William Andrus, now Director of Standards for IBM (who gave the Arnold concordance its start and nursed this one

along at a critical time); J. A. Kearns, University and Research Institute Representative of IBM; Robert Hoopes, formerly Vice President of the A.C.L.S. and now Dean of the Faculty at Michigan State University—Oakland; John Hastie, Coordinator of Research at Cornell University; Richard Lesser, Director of the Cornell Computing Center; and Theodore P. Wright, Chairman of the Board of Directors, Ira G. Ross, President, and John J. O'Neil, Vice President, of the Cornell Aeronautical Laboratory. The generous support given us by the Laboratory deserves particular mention: it included not only the arrangement of time on the computer together with operating services, but the purchase of print wheels for our exclusive use. This significant investment in the humanities on the part of a corporation committed to scientific research is most gratefully appreciated.

I am further indebted to Miss Laura Franklin, Associate Professor of English at Nebraska State Teachers College, Wayne, who gallantly surrendered her prior claim to the variorum text; to Colonel Alspach, first for passing the rights to me, then for continuing kindly advice; and to Marshall Cohen and George Rice at the Aeronautical Laboratory, who patiently and expertly guided our use of facilities there. In Ithaca, Samuel Miles Weber, Mrs. Marilyn Paul, and Mrs. Elizabeth Savage cheerfully undertook proofreading and editorial chores. The supervisory committee (including the late Stephen E. Whicher) stood loyally ready with counsel of many kinds. Again, I must particularly thank Professor William R. Keast, whose lively interest and encouragement made all difficulties manageable. But this time it is gratifying not to have to thank James Painter, who appears in this volume in his rightful place.

Ithaca, New York   S. M. PARRISH
September 1962

PROGRAMMER'S PREFACE

THE invitation to write this preface was rather unsettling, for my experience with the concordance project had made it clear to me that a language gap exists between the humanities and the sciences. There are in fact several languages here, some highly technical—the language of Arnold and Yeats, the language of the computer, and the language of programming—and one of them was always giving trouble either to the editor or to me. It was further clear that I would probably be an interloper in this volume, since its readers would be likely to be more interested in poetic vocabulary than in computer techniques. However, it seemed that an account of the techniques could be of interest, and I agreed to write it, taking courage from the thought that not all of my readers could have programmed the concordance for the computer.

The Computer

The computer in question was an IBM 704 Data Processing Machine (IBM stands for the International Business Machines Corporation, the manufacturer of the computer; 704 is a number arbitrarily assigned as a means of identifying the type of computer and has no other significance). The IBM 704 can do only a few (about 90) things, but it can do them very rapidly (up to speeds of 42,000 operations per second). The things which the computer can do fall under five functions: input, output, storage, arithmetic, and control.

These terms—which represent our first problem of language—can be simply explained. To begin with, the computer can receive information from the outside world and transmit information back. These functions are called, respectively, "input" and "output," or more familiarly (and anthropocentrically) reading and writing. Input or output to the 704 can make use of magnetic tape, punched cards, printed matter, or lights on the control panel which can be interpreted by the operator. Magnetic tape is usually used for reading and writing because it can be handled much faster than the other input-output media. Computer tape, which is very similar to that used in a tape recorder, is magnetized as data are

inscribed upon it. The tape can be read or written upon very rapidly (15,000 characters per second), but in one direction only. This means that when all the data have been written the reel of tape must be returned to the beginning to be read. This process, called "rewinding," is very slow, usually requiring more than a minute. "Storage" is the function of the section of the machine where data and instructions are stored or preserved for later use in the other sections. For instance, when data are read they must be entered into storage before the arithmetic section can process them. In the 704, the storage unit (or "memory" as it is often called) consists of magnetized cores. These cores are small doughnut-shaped magnets whose magnetism can be changed to represent different numbers. The 704 "memory" has 32,768 "words" of storage, a "word" being either six alphabetic characters or one instruction. The "arithmetic" section does all the addition, subtraction, multiplication, and division; moreover, it can make simple tests (e.g., to discover whether this number is larger than that number). Finally, the "control" section of the computer has the function of supervising the activities of the other four sections.

Information is furnished to a computer in the form of numbers only. It is the outside world that interprets the numbers as actual numbers, or as alphabetic information, or even as computer instructions. Where we see an "A" the computer sees "01"; where we see a "B" the computer sees "02." (This is not the actual code used, but it is analogous.) Thus the question of which comes first in sorting, "APPLE" or "ASPEN," is considered by the 704 to be the question of whether 0116161205 or 0119160514 is smaller. It follows that the 704 could add APPLE to ASPEN and get an answer. In fact this is often done as a check on the machine. A "check sum" is the result of adding certain data together, treating each piece of data only as a number. During sorting, for instance, it is apparent that no matter how the data are rearranged, their sum will be constant. The check here consists of adding all the data before and after a sort and comparing the sums. Of course, all problems do not admit of this error-detection technique. Hence another type of check commonly used on magnetic tape is called "parity" or "redundancy" checking. For this process, each number as it is written has another number added to it, and written automatically on the magnetic tape, such that the sum of the two numbers is odd. This check number is read automatically during reading operations. If the check number plus the read data does not form an odd sum, an error has occurred. Since this type of checking is built into the computer, it is called a "machine" check. The check sum must be programmed, and it is therefore called a "program" check. Both types of check were liberally used in our routines.

The Arnold Concordance Programs

Although I wish to present primarily a description of the program used for the Yeats concordance, I shall begin with a description of the Arnold program so that the changes in the Arnold routines and their motivation can be explained.

Input for the Arnold concordance consisted of magnetic tape prepared from punched cards. The program operated in three phases. The first phase scanned the input cards, each of which contained one line of poetry. It broke the line into its component words and appended an identification of the source line to each word. After all the lines of text had been scanned, the words were sorted into alphabetical order. This was phase two. Phase three retrieved the source lines, edited them, and prepared the printed output. In addition, two auxiliary programs, to be described later, were written.

Because a line of poetry together with its source identification was ordinarily too long to put on one card, two types of cards were used to carry the input information. One type was a title card which identified the following cards as being lines belonging to a specific poem. The title card contained an abbreviation of the title of the poem and a code symbol to indicate that it was a title card. The line cards contained the actual text line of poetry, the page number and line number, and information as to whether or not this was a variant line. During the first phase of the program the appropriate title was appended to the text line; the resultant line was then stored as a record in a "line directory" on a magnetic tape. (A magnetic-tape record is a collection of characters separated physically by blank tape from other similar collections.) The text line was then scanned character by character until all the words on it had been recognized and collected. As each word was collected it was checked against a table of "common" words (that is, words to be omitted from the concordance index). If the word was not "common," a record number or line number was appended to it. This record number "referenced" the corresponding tape record in the line directory. The word and its associated line number were then entered into a section of storage. When this section was filled, its contents were sorted (a very rapid and simple process) and stored on an intermediate magnetic tape in the form of "word blocks." A word block contained 625 words in sorted order, each word with its line number attached. After all words in a line card had been processed—that is, either identified as "common" or prepared for sorting—another input card was read in. This process continued until all the input tape had been exhausted. To sum it up, the first phase of the program read the data tape and produced a line-directory tape and a word-block tape.

The second phase, which was the most time-consuming, consolidated the contents of the word-block tape. The consolidation was accomplished by a series of merges. The data on the word-block tape were written string by string alternately upon two intermediate tapes. (A string is a collection of data in strictly sorted order; for example, each word block produced in the first phase is a string.) The data from two strings, one taken from each of the two tapes, were then merged, producing a single string which was written upon one of a pair of output tapes. Then the data from two more strings, one from each of the two input tapes, were merged and written as a string upon the other output tape. This process of merging two strings into one continued until all the data had been read. The result was to reduce the number of strings to one-half the previous total. The tapes were then rewound, and the merging process was resumed, the old input tapes now becoming output tapes and the old output tapes being used as input. This procedure was repeated, each time reducing the number of strings, until after the final merge only one string remained. At this point all the data had been sorted.

The third phase of the program was the retrieval and editing phase. The word-block tape having been sorted, the words from this tape comprised the index entries for the concordance; the object of this phase was to retrieve the original context of each index word. Two schemes were tried for this retrieval process. The first involved making four copies of the line directory. A count was kept for each tape to specify where the tape was positioned at any given moment. When a new line of context was required, its location as specified by the line number was compared with the present position of each tape. The nearest tape was then moved forward or backward to the proper record; this record was then prepared for printing. This scheme required a lot of useless tape passing; hence it was very slow. It had the advantage that four copies of the line directory were available to the computer at all times, so that an error on one tape could be corrected from another. It was, on the whole, a practical scheme for small volumes of data, but it became impractical at about 10,000 lines of input.

The second scheme was the one used in the actual production of the Arnold concordance. A number of items from the word-block tape were read into core storage. The line numbers associated with these items were then sorted there, and the appropriate lines were looked up in the line directory. Each line requested was read into core storage when found until the table of line numbers was exhausted. The line-directory tape was then rewound. During the time required to rewind the tape, the words from the word block were processed for output. Their context lines were available in core storage; they too were found and prepared for out-

put. The line directory was rewound by the time the editing and output of each group of items were finished. The cycle would then be restarted by bringing in a new group of items from the word-block tape. The third phase was finished when all words from the word-block tape had been processed. Output from the editing process consisted of tapes ready to be printed on the peripheral equipment associated with the computer.

The auxiliary routines mentioned above operated upon either the sorted word-block tape or the line directory. The first routine used the word-block tape to make a frequency table. It counted the number of occurrences of each word and sorted this information according to the frequency. The output from this program was thus a listing of the index words in order of frequency of occurrence. The second auxiliary routine would read the line directory and print in edited form every line containing an occurrence of a specified word. The routine was used to spot-check the main program and to examine homographs. A further, unexpected use of this routine was to prepare printed lines for correction purposes. Imperfections of several sorts occurred during the final printing, the most common arising from ink blots on the paper or from a faulty printing cycle in which an erroneous character was printed. Passes were made to collect single correctly printed lines which could be cut apart and inserted in the proper places before the output page was photographed.

I have already mentioned the system of checks which was written into the programs in an effort to eliminate processing errors in the output. The original input tape was parity-checked. From that point on all core-to-tape information transfers were accompanied by a record check sum, except for the preparation of the final output tape. At every convenient point (at an average of every ten minutes in running the program) the console switches used for program control were examined to see whether the program was running correctly. At the same time a check sum of the program itself was recomputed. If it was not correct, the program "rolled back" to the last check point; that is, the last ten minutes were run again. If the check sum was correct, the program continued.

A harder problem was the checking of data operations and transfers of information from section to section of the computer. This was accomplished both by the built-in parity checks and by the programmed check sums. The line directory was written during the first phase and read during the third. Little tape movement was involved in these operations, and the checks worked very well. During sorting, as has already been explained, the word-block tape was split onto two intermediate tapes and then these two tapes were written upon two more. This process by which two tapes produced two other tapes, continuing until the data were

sorted, involved a very large amount of tape manipulation. To ensure accuracy several precautions were taken. In addition to the record check sum carried with each record, a file check sum was generated by the first phase while the word-block tape was first being written. (A file is simply a collection of records, such as two boxes of cards or one reel of tape.) Before the internal sorting of the word-block tape was begun, a block check sum was generated. It was checked after the sorting of the block and again after the writing of the block on tape. This check sum was then added to the file check sum. During every pass upon the complete file, whether on one tape (first and last passes only) or two tapes, this check sum was recomputed and checked.

Moreover, during the last phase and before printing, a rescanning of the selected line was made to ensure that the line really contained the index word. Despite the fact that all line numbers were check-summed from the time the block was sorted until the line was selected for printing, nine instances were found where the selected line did not contain the specified word. (These nine were from the same section of input text, though not all index words from these lines were in error.) A run was made on the auxiliary selection program to prepare and print replacement lines. It is worth remarking that these nine errors were the only ones found in processing about 17,000 lines, containing over 65,000 indexed words. So far as I know, no machine or programming errors produced errors which survive in the printed Arnold volume. The same is true of the Yeats concordance.

The Yeats Concordance Programs

A critique of the Arnold programs disclosed several problem areas. First, and easiest to correct, the tape merge used during phase two was very inefficient, though it actually was improved during the late stages of production for the Arnold concordance. A second correction introduced a much-improved sorting method for use in phase one. These were, of course, technical changes only, not changes in fundamental method. The fundamental changes from a programmer's viewpoint were based upon two general conclusions. The first was that error detection and correction procedures had to be made an integral part of the entire process, instead of a controlling superstructure. The second was that the context-retrieval problem in phase three would become intolerable with a very moderate increase in the amount of text. An entirely new approach was needed here. Other modifications were also desirable from an editorial viewpoint. The improved print wheels, the cross-reference feature, and the desire for easy editorial control were the main factors to be taken account of here. These matters were negotiated with the editor on a "what is

needed—what is practical" basis, and our common experience with the Arnold procedure made agreements relatively easy to reach.

From a user's point of view, the most impressive change in the Yeats volume is the addition of punctuation to the print. Though this required a new set of type wheels, it involved relatively little programming. From the producer's viewpoint the most impressive change has been the tremendous increase in speed. The Arnold volume was produced in 38 hours of machine time, while the Yeats with one-third more text required only 12 hours. This total could have been reduced even further if the checking for errors had not been so rigorous. These figures, which purport to be the time required to produce the final text, are not all that they seem to be, for they really represent the minimum computer time that would be required if everything ran perfectly. They do not include program-testing time, nor rerun time required by errors (human and machine), nor time used by the auxiliary routines. The figures are thus more nearly indicative of a rate of speed than of a span of actual time. The improvement in speed in Yeats was brought about by improvements in sorting and merging techniques in phases one and two and by one major change in strategy. In the Arnold program, the context of each word was coded as a line number and appended to the text-word entry. This was done to reduce the volume of data sorted in phase two, but it produced a very bad retrieval problem in phase three. In Yeats, the source line itself was appended to the text-word entry and carried through the sort. This meant that the sort processed much more data, but also that the retrieval problem in phase three disappeared. What we were dealing with here was a general problem that always occurs in sorting. For small amounts of data, it is usually more effective to code the context and retrieve it after sorting. For large amounts of data, it is usually more effective to append the context and eliminate the retrieval problem, even though this means that the sort must process more data.

Based upon the Arnold experience, a completely new set of programs was written, checked out, and used to prepare the present volume. They operated in four phases, rather than the three used for Arnold. The first phase operated upon magnetic tape produced from line and title cards very similar to those of Arnold. There were relatively few changes in the input. Output from the first phase consisted of three tapes—the line directory, the word-block tape, and a cross-reference tape. The line directory was identical, except for format, to that of Arnold. The word-block tape contained both index words and their associated context lines. The cross-reference tape was analogous to the word-block tape except that it contained only portions of hyphenated words together with their complete form.

The second phase sorted the word-block tape and the cross-reference tape independently. Once again this phase took the longest time, but it was still quite an improvement over the Arnold program. The third phase merged the word-block and cross-reference tapes and produced "unpaged" printing (i.e., a listing of each line in edited form, but with no attempt made to divide the lines into pages). In addition to the edited line, a unique line number was produced for each line. This line number was used to control the desired editorial changes for the final printing. The last phase made all the changes requested by the editor that could be accomplished by the operations of "insert," "delete," and "replace" any line or lines. It also put the lines into page format, that is, reprinted the index word with (CONTINUED) if needed at the top of a page, titled the identification columns, and adjusted the number of lines per page. In addition to the four basic phases, the same two auxiliary routines (designed to print selected lines and to prepare the frequency data) were written. These were identical in function to those of the Arnold program except that, besides the frequencies of the printed words, frequencies of omitted words were also shown.

The Arnold experience, in which errors had occurred despite the check sums, prompted us to devise a more stringent system of checks for Yeats. To begin with, the first phase of the Yeats was run twice, using the same input data. Between the first and second phases a checking pass was made upon the output tapes produced by the two runs of phase one to make sure that these tapes were identical (machine errors would have produced discrepancies between them). At the end of the check pass, a check sum was punched into cards. This check sum was used as an independent check upon the tape sorting; it guaranteed that the tapes used as input to the merge were correct. The record and file check sums were used as a control during the merge. The third phase used record check sums and parity checks for its control.

With all the checking machine errors were much less troublesome for this volume than for the Arnold one. There are three things that would account for this fact. First, the 704 itself is better, since it has been in operation long enough to become a proven computer. Second, the programmed error procedures were better. Third, the machine time was much shorter, so that the 704 simply had less opportunity to fail.

Conclusion

Based upon our experiences with Arnold and Yeats, minor changes are being incorporated in the programs for future volumes—so minor as to represent my desire to change things for change's sake, rather than any significant improvement. Future volumes should be produced more and

more rapidly as this work becomes more routine. It is axiomatic that a computer should not be used for a problem unless the problem must be solved many times. Thus the preparation of one or two concordances is not efficient, but the preparation of many volumes becomes a valid application of computers. The start we have made should now make it possible to produce basic information of this sort for a whole series of authors.

My motives for participating in the project have been twofold. First, and most important, is the fact that concordances represent a technical problem which I find interesting. Secondly, I am convinced that data of this type should be available, just as data in scientific and mathematical tables are available. I probably will never need to know Yeats's uses of PAINTER. I doubt if I will ever need to know the heat of fusion of acetic acid, though I might need to know what the sine of 78° 15′ is. In any event, I am certain that a good reference library ought to have all this data available. This volume represents my attempt to help compile some of the data.

Poughkeepsie, New York   JAMES A. PAINTER
September 1962

A Concordance to the Poems of

W. B. YEATS

PAGE   TITLE   LINE

ABASHED
    I WAS ABASHED, AND NOW THEY COME TO MIND . . . . . .   353 PEOPLE   36
    AFTER NINE YEARS, I SINK MY HEAD ABASHED. . . . . . .   353 PEOPLE   37
    TIMID, ENTANGLED, EMPTY AND ABASHED, ...   368 EGO DOMINUS   16
    ABASHED BY THAT REPORT. . . . .   516 MANS SONG   13
ABBEY
    AT THE ABBEY THEATRE . . . .   264 ABBEY THEATRE   T
    MY FATHER UPON THE ABBEY STAGE, BEFORE HIM A RAGING CROWD: 577 LOFTY THINGS   2
    THEN THAT OLD ABBEY ACTOR, DUDLEY DIGGES, ...   790 DEDICATION   7
ABBOT
    AN ABBOT OR ARCHBISHOP WITH AN UPRAISED HAND . . . . .   601 GALLERY REVIS   9
ABD
    TO ABD AL-RABBAN: FELLOW-ROYSTERER ONCE, ...   460 HARUN RASHID   2
ABD-AL-RABBAN
    TO ABD-AL-RABBAN: FELLOW ROYSTERER ONCE . . . .   460 HARUN RASHID   V   2
ABEAT
    ANGERS THAT ARE LIKE NOISY CLOUDS HAVE SET OUR HEARTS   207 HANRAHANS SONG   8
      ABEAT:
    ANGERS THAT ARE LIKE BUNDLED CLOUDS HAVE SET OUR HEARTS   207 HANRAHANS SONG V   8
      ABEAT:
ABED
    THE EMPEROR'S DRUNKEN SOLDIERY ARE ABED: . . . . . .   497 BYZANTIUM   2
    BUT SHE IS STILL ABED, ...   595 COLONEL MARTIN   31
A-BED
    THE EMPEROR'S DRUNKEN SOLDIERY ARE A-BED: . . . . . .   497 BYZANTIUM   V   2
    BUT SHE IS STILL A-BED . . . .   595 COLONEL MARTIN V   31
ABIDE
    WASHES THE SHORES WHERE YE ABIDE, ...   5 OISIN 1   V   47
    BUT WE IN A LONELY LAND ABIDE . . . .   22 OISIN 1   337
    YOUTH, HERE WILL WE ABIDE, AND BE THOU KING . . . . .   679 ISLE STAT II 3   314
ABIDES
    A TOSSING LAUGH BETWEEN THEIR RED ABIDES: . . . . . .   735 QUATRAIN APHOR   22
ABLE
    I'LL HAVE ASSURANCE THAT YOU ARE ABLE . . . .   304 HOUR DAWN   51
    "I'LL HAVE MY SAY, TILL I AM ABLE . . . .   304 HOUR DAWN   V   51
    "I'D HAVE ASSURANCE THAT YOU ARE ABLE . . . .   304 HOUR DAWN   V   51
ABLOW
    FOR DREAMS ARE THE FLOWERS ABLOW, ...   743 WISDOM DREAMS   6
A-BLOWIN'
    A-BLOWIN' OF HER MORNIN' FIRE, ...   95 MOLL MAGEE   V   35
ABOARD
    WHEN SHE FINDS OUT WE HAVE BETTER MEN ABOARD . . . . .   232 SHADOW WATER B   231
    I SAW A FLAGON OF BROWN ALE ABOARD HER. . . . .   240 SHADOW WATER B   388
    WHEN YOU ARE ABOARD THE LOCHLANN GALLEY, LASH . . . . .   752 SHADOW WATER A   128
ABODE
    BOW DOWN, ARCHANGELS, IN YOUR DIM ABODE: . . . . . .   112 ROSE OF WORLD   11
    ABODE, AS BANDED ADDERS IN MY BREAST. . . . .   683 SEEKER   50
ABOLISHED
    ABOLISHED BY A MIRE OF LITTLE THINGS, ...   711 FERENCZ RENYI   36
ABOUNDING
    THE ABOUNDING GUTTER HAD BEEN HELICON . . . .   398 LEADERS CROWD   6
    THE ABOUNDING GLITTERING JET: THOUGH NOW IT SEEMS . . .   417 ANCEST HOUSES   12
    AND WHEN ABOUNDING HEDGES RING . . . .   434 WHEEL   3
    AND WHEN ABOUNDING HEDGES SING . . . .   434 WHEEL   V   3
    WHO FINDS ABOUNDING CEPHISUS . . . .   447 COLONUS PRAISE   23
    ABOUNDING FOLIAGE MOISTENED WITH THE DEW: . . . . . .   500 VACILLATION   13
ABOUT
    ABOUT HIS FADING CRIMSON BALL: . . . .   12 OISIN 1   155
    ABOUT THEM: AND THE HORSE OF FAERY SCREAMED . . . . .   30 OISIN 2   24
    JABBER AND SCREAM ABOUT HIM IN THE NIGHT: . . . . . .   34 OISIN 2   82
    MAKING A WORLD ABOUT HER IN THE AIR, ...   37 OISIN 2   122
    MAKING A WORLD ABOUT HER, PASSED FROM SIGHT . . . . .   37 OISIN 2   V   123
    SHOUTED. WITH FIRE OF HAIR ABOUT HER SWIRLED, ...   38 OISIN 2   V   134
    COULD SLEEP ON A COUCH OF RUSHES--ROUND AND ABOUT THEM   49 OISIN 3   V   32
      LAID.
    AND LONELY AND LONGING FOR NIAMH, I SHIVERED AND TURNED   60 OISIN 3   181
      ME ABOUT,
    AND SHIVERING AND LONELY, AND LONGING FOR NIAM, I TURNED   60 OISIN 3   V   181
      ME ABOUT,
    TO THOSE ABOUT, "BEAT HIM WITH THONGS OF HIDE . . . . .   106 CUCHULAIN SEA V   17A
    WHILE YOUNG STARS ABOUT HER DANCE. . . . .   125 CATHLEEN PARA V   16
    DID NOT THE WORMS THAT SPIRED ABOUT HIS BONES . . . . .   128 DREAM OF FAERY   41
    WERE NOT THE WORMS THAT SPIRED ABOUT HIS BONES . . . .   128 DREAM OF FAERY V   41
    MY HEART WOULD BRIM WITH DREAMS ABOUT THE TIMES . . . .   136 TO SOME I TALK   2
    TRAILS ALL ABOUT THE WRITTEN PAGE. . . . .   138 TO IRELAND   9
    ABOUT MY TABLE TO AND FRO, ...   138 TO IRELAND   24
    FOR ROUND ABOUT MY TABLE GO . . . .   138 TO IRELAND   V   23
    ABOUT MY TABLE TO AND FRO, ...   139 TO IRELAND   40
    THE DANCERS CROWDED ABOUT HIM . . . .   144 HOST OF AIR   17
    ABOUT THE CASTING OUT OF MY NET, ...   146 FISH   4
    OVER MY HEART, AND YOUR HAIR FALL ABOUT MY BREAST . . .   154 BELOVED PEACE V   10
    OF UNKNOWN PERISHING ARMIES BEAT ABOUT MY EARS. . . . .   161 BLACK PIG   4
    AND DREAM ABOUT THE GREAT AND THEIR PRIDE: . . . . . .   166 EVIL OF BELOV   2
    ARE SINGING ABOUT THE WOOD?" . . . .   167 BLESSED   24
    WHEN SHALL THE STARS BE BLOWN ABOUT THE SKY, ...   170 SECRET ROSE   29
    BUT THINK ABOUT OLD FRIENDS THE MOST: . . . .   173 PLEADS FRIEND   5
    ABOUT THE STARS AND MOON AND SUN: . . . .   176 BELOVED DEAD   10
    ABOUT MY THRESHOLD TO COUNSEL AND TO HELP?" . . . . .   183 QUEEN MAEVE   82
    ABOUT MY DOOR TO COUNSEL AND TO HELP." . . . .   183 QUEEN MAEVE   V   82
    FOR THERE IS NO HIGH STORY ABOUT QUEENS . . . .   186 QUEEN MAEVE   134
    ABOUT WHOSE FACE BIRDS WAGGED THEIR FIERY WINGS, ...   187 QUEEN MAEVE   145

1

		PAGE	TITLE		LINE
ABOUT   (CONTINUED)
ABOUT THE TIME WHEN CHRIST WAS BORN,		189	BAILE AILLINN		13
BEING TUMBLED AND BLOWN ABOUT		191	BAILE AILLINN		66
ABOUT THE WINDY WATER-SIDE,		192	BAILE AILLINN		93
ABOUT THE WINDY WATER SIDE		192	BAILE AILLINN	V	93
GATHERING HIS CLOAK ABOUT HIM, RUN		193	BAILE AILLINN		101
WHO PEERED ABOUT ON EVERY SIDE:		193	BAILE AILLINN	V	112
UPON THE THRONE AND CRYING ABOUT THE STREETS		198	SEVEN WOODS		7
AND LITTLE SHADOWS COME ABOUT HER EYES:		199	FOLLY COMFORT		3
AND THERE ARE LITTLE CREASES ABOUT HER EYES:		199	FOLLY COMFORT	V	3
THE FIRE THAT STIRS ABOUT HER, WHEN SHE STIRS,		200	FOLLY COMFORT		10
ABOUT THE STARS AND BROKE IN DAYS AND YEARS.		206	ADAMS CURSE		33
ABOUT THE STARN AND BROKE IN DAYS AND YEARS.		206	ADAMS CURSE	V	33
RED HANRAHAN'S SONG ABOUT IRELAND		206	HANRAHANS SONG		T
AND DO YOU GATHER ABOUT US WHEN PALE LIGHT		218	WOODS OF COOLE		37
OR CRY ABOUT ONE'S EARS. NOTHING TO FEAR.		222	SHADOW WATER B		19
OR FUMBLING IN A DREAM ABOUT THE HOUSE?		230	SHADOW WATER B		174
CARE MORE ABOUT THE KEGS OF SILVER AND GOLD		232	SHADOW WATER B		234
AND THAT IS WHY THE WORLD TOTTERS ABOUT.		233	SHADOW WATER B		238
OF THE GREAT GOLDEN NET THAT IS ABOUT US.		238	SHADOW WATER B		352
BELOVED, HAVING DRAGGED THE NET ABOUT US.		252	SHADOW WATER B		615
NOTHING TO MAKE A SONG ABOUT BUT KINGS,		257	RECONCILIATION		5
THESE ARE THE CLOUDS ABOUT THE FALLEN SUN,		265	THESE CLOUDS		1
THESE ARE THE CLOUDS ABOUT THE FALLEN SUN,		265	THESE CLOUDS		11
THEY HAVE GONE ABOUT THE WORLD LIKE WIND,		289	SEPTEMBER 1913		11
WHEN GREY GULLS FLIT ABOUT INSTEAD OF MEN,		292	TO A SHADE		6
WHEN GREY GULLS FLY ABOUT INSTEAD OF MEN,		292	TO A SHADE	V	6
ABOUT YOUR HEAD TILL THE DUST STOPS YOUR EAR,		293	TO A SHADE		20
ROUND ABOUT HELL'S GATE TO STARE		294	HATED PLAYBOY	V	3
ABOUT A FARM," THE SECOND CRIED.		296	THREE BEGGARS	V	38
AND SEEN THE RUBBISH RUN ABOUT,		297	THREE BEGGARS		65
AS THOUGH DRIED STRAW, AND IF WE TURN ABOUT		327	ROBERT GREGORY		83
SHE GOES ABOUT HER HOUSE ERECT AND CALM		340	SHEP GOATHERD		35
I HAVE GONE ABOUT THE HOUSE, GONE UP AND DOWN		350	HER PRAISE		2
IT IS ABOUT TO DIE.		367	HER CHRIS TREE		12
I LAY ABOUT ME WITH THE TAWS		379	SAINT HUNCH		8
IS MOVING ITS SLOW THIGHS, WHILE ALL ABOUT IT		402	SECOND COMING		16
THAT PITCHES COMMON THINGS ABOUT. THERE STOOD		428	NINETEEN 19		4
BUT TROD THE ROAD, OR SPLASHED ABOUT THE SHORE,		447	COLONUS PRAISE		27
AND A CLOAK WRAPPED ABOUT THE STONE,		456	FRIENDS YOUTH		7
AND PAUSE AT LAST, I WAS ABOUT TO SAY,		461	HARUN RASHID		11
AND ASKED ABOUT THE PICTURES OR THE TEXT:		466	HARUN RASHID		121
AND ASKED ABOUT THESE PICTURES OR THOSE OTHERS:		466	HARUN RASHID	V	121
AND SWEPT THE HOUSE AND SANG ABOUT HER WORK		468	HARUN RASHID		148
ON THE SOUL'S JOURNEY. HOW IT IS WHIRLED ABOUT,		472	ALL SOUL NIGHT		54
FIVE HUNDRED YEARS AGO, ABOUT IT LIE		478	SELF AND SOUL		26
I TURNED ABOUT AND LOOKED WHERE BRANCHES BREAK		490	COOLE BALLYLEE		15
I TURNED ABOUT AND LOOKED WHERE BRANCHES BROKE		490	COOLE BALLYLEE	V	15
WE SHIFT ABOUT——ALL THAT GREAT GLORY SPENT——		491	COOLE BALLYLEE		39
MAN SHIFTS ABOUT——ALL THAT GREAT GLORY SPENT——		491	COOLE BALLYLEE	V	39
WINGS BEATING ABOUT THE ROOM:		499	MOTHER OF GOD		3
CHANGE THEIR LOVES ABOUT.		520	HIS BARGAIN		6
ABOUT THE SKY: WHERE THAT IS CLEAR OF CLOUD		541	PARN FUNERAL 1		3
EMPEDOCLES HAS THROWN ALL THINGS ABOUT:		564	GYRES		6
THE GREAT STAGE CURTAIN ABOUT TO DROP,		565	LAPIS LAZULI		13
POETS AND WITS ABOUT HIM DREW:		577	WHAT THEN		14
AND THERE'S NO LUCK ABOUT A HOUSE		584	GHOST ROG CASE		27
I POKED ABOUT A VILLAGE CHURCH		584	GHOST ROG CASE		31
WHAT REMAINS TO SING ABOUT		585	ORAHILLY		28
"BECAUSE I AM MAD ABOUT WOMEN		587	OLD WICKED MAN		1
I AM MAD ABOUT THE HILLS."		587	OLD WICKED MAN		2
ALL KNOW THAT ALL THE DEAD IN THE WORLD ABOUT THAT PLACE ARE STUCK,		593	PILGRIM		11
BOUND A THONG ABOUT HIS HAND,		595	COLONEL MARTIN		25
CARRY THE GOLD ABOUT THE TOWN,		596	COLONEL MARTIN		52
I KNOCK THEIR HEADS ABOUT.		605	SONGS BURDEN 1		8
THAT SOMETHING IS ABOUT TO HAPPEN, I THINK		609	IN TARAS HALLS		4
PLOTINUS CAME AND LOOKED ABOUT,		611	NEWS ORACLE		9
I TALKED ABOUT AN APPARITION.		624	APPARITIONS		2
WITH BOYS AND GIRLS ABOUT HIM,		627	STATES HOLIDAY		27
WHAT HE TALKS ABOUT.		631	POLITICS		6
ABOUT THE SEA. BEFORE HER LIES THAT YOUTH,		687	TWO TITANS		22
ABOUT A SUN-FLUSHED DOVE-COT, COOING, CLING		710	FERENCZ RENYI		20
I KEEP SUCH THINGS ABOUT ME: THEY ARE FOOD		721	WITCH VIVIEN		37
WHAT SHALLOW THOUGHTS ABOUT DEEP THINGS:		725	LEGEND		11
WHEN HUNDREDS STOOD ABOUT TO SEE		740	EARL PAUL		27
AND PLUMED HEADS ABOUT HIM,		740	EARL PAUL		31
HOW ALL THAT DIE ARE BORNE ABOUT THE WORLD		750	SHADOW WATER A		84
AND TURN HIS GALLEY ABOUT AND BRING ME HOME.		751	SHADOW WATER A		108
THE GODS HOLD WATCH ABOUT THE WORDS OF A QUEEN.		756	SHADOW WATER A		191
GATHER ABOUT HIM, THAT THE GODS MAY NOT KNOW		758	SHADOW WATER A		231
THERE'S SO MUCH TO THINK ABOUT		772	SONG DEIRDRE 1		7
ABOVE
WE RODE IN SADNESS ABOVE LOUGH LAEN,		2	OISIN 1	V	7H
AND 'TWEEN HIS EARS, ABOVE HIS MANE,		2	OISIN 1	V	7AA
AND SET YOUR NAME ALL NAMES ABOVE,		7	OISIN 1		76
SHE SAID: "FOR HE IS FAIR ABOVE		7	OISIN 1	V	62A
BY ROOTS THAT JOINED ABOVE OUR PLUMES——		16	OISIN 1	V	224C
BENT DOWN ABOVE EACH HOOKED KNEE,		26	OISIN 1		392
HE HEARS THE STORM IN THE CHIMNEY ABOVE,		26	OISIN 1		404
BENT LOW ABOVE EACH HOOKED KNEE,		26	OISIN 1	V	392

2

ABOVE   (CONTINUED)   PAGE   TITLE   LINE
     FOG-DRIPPING, PEDESTALLED ABOVE THE TIDE, ...   31 OISIN 2   V   36
     FROM HIGH ABOVE, LIKE FEATHERS OF YOUNG BIRDS . . . . .   32 OISIN 2   V   50
     WAITED. ABOVE, IN ENDLESS CARVEN JAGS, ...   38 OISIN 2   V 144
     AND THE STARS WERE BLOTTED ABOVE US, ...   48 OISIN 3   24
     THE WOOD WAS SO SPACIOUS ABOVE THEM, ...   49 OISIN 3   37
     SO SPACIOUS THE WOOD WAS ABOVE THEM, ...   49 OISIN 3   V   37
     HIS LANGUID TAIL ABOVE US, LIT WITH MYRIAD SPOTS OF LIGHT. 77 INDIAN ON GOD   20
     YELLOW THE LEAVES OF THE ROWAN ABOVE US, ...   79 FALLING LEAVES   3
     I STOOD, KEEN STARS ABOVE ME SHONE, ...   83 MAD KING GOLL   29
     I PAUSED--THE STARS ABOVE ME FLASHED, ...   83 MAD KING GOLL V 29
     I PAUSED--THE STARS ABOVE ME SHONE   . . . .   83 MAD KING GOLL V 29
     FROM THE HILLS ABOVE GLEN-CAR, ...   88 STOLEN CHILD   29
     AND THE WAVES FLOWED ABOVE HIM AND HE DIED, ...   111 CUCHULAIN SEA V 86
     ABOVE THE TIDE OF HOURS, TROUBLE THE AIR, ...   114 ROSE OF BATTLE   3
     ABOVE THE TIDE OF HOURS, RISE ON THE AIR, ...   114 ROSE OF BATTLE V 3
     AND THE STARS ABOVE, ...   116 FAERY SONG   8
     ABOVE YOUR BED, ...   118 CRADLE SONG   2
     ABOVE YOUR WHITE BED, ...   118 CRADLE SONG   V   2
     THE CLOUDS ON THEIR JOURNEY ABOVE, ...   119 PITY OF LOVE   4
     HE PACED UPON THE MOUNTAINS FAR ABOVE, ...   121 YOU ARE OLD   V 11
     AND THEY HAD NAILED THE BOARDS ABOVE HER FACE, ...   123 DREAM OF DEATH   3
     AND RAISED ABOVE HER MOUND . . . .   123 DREAM OF DEATH   6
     AND LEFT HER TO THE INDIFFERENT STARS ABOVE . . . . .   123 DREAM OF DEATH   9
     AND GAZED UPON THE MOURNFUL STARS ABOVE, ...   123 DREAM OF DEATH V 11
     AND ABOVE THE DEEP OF HEAVEN, ...   125 CATHLEEN PARA V 15
     WHEN WE BENT DOWN ABOVE THE FADING COALS . . . . . .   136 TO SOME I TALK   3
     WHILE THE NIGHT GREW, ABOVE THE FADING COALS, ...   136 TO SOME I TALK V 3
     WHO RISE, WING ABOVE WING, FLAME ABOVE FLAME, ...   137 TO SOME I TALK 11
     WHO RISE, WING ABOVE WING, FLAME ABOVE FLAME, ...   137 TO SOME I TALK 11
     WHAT MEASURER TIME HAS LIT ABOVE, ...   139 TO IRELAND   38
     THE MARINERS OF NIGHT ABOVE, ...   139 TO IRELAND   V 38
     THE NORTH UNFOLDS ABOVE THEM CLINGING, CREEPING NIGHT, . . 154 BELOVED PEACE   3
     THE NORTH UNROLLS ABOVE THEM CLINGING, CREEPING NIGHT, . . 154 BELOVED PEACE V 3
     ABOVE THE WANDERING TIDE, ...   162 ASKS FORGIVE   14
     AND WRAPPED THE FLAMES ABOVE HIS HOLY HEAD, ...   162 ASKS FORGIVE   17
     AND GATHERED THE FLAMES ABOVE HIS HOLY HEAD, ...   162 ASKS FORGIVE V 17
     ABOVE ITS CLOUDY RIM, ...   175 ELEMENT POWERS 16
     ABOVE THE STARS AND MOON AND SUN, ...   176 BELOVED DEAD V 10
     THEY HAVE HEAPED THE STONES ABOVE HIS GRAVE . . . . .   193 BAILE AILLINN 115
     WHAT ARE YOU CALLING OUT ABOVE THE MAST? . . . . . .   243 SHADOW WATER B 437
     I WEEP--I WEEP BECAUSE BARE NIGHT'S ABOVE, ...   246 SHADOW WATER B 499
     AND KNELT ABOVE IT WITH DRAWN KNIFE. ON THE INSTANT . .   278 TWO KINGS   37
     ABOVE A WINDY PRECIPICE?" THEN HE, ...   285 TWO KINGS   195
     THE BELL-BEAT OF THEIR WINGS ABOVE MY HEAD, ...   323 SWANS AT COOLE 17
     SOMEWHERE AMONG THE CLOUDS ABOVE, ...   328 IRISH AIRMAN   2
     ABOVE THE CLOUDY SHOULDERS OF THE HORSES, ...   344 DAWN   12
     A LAMP BURNS ON ABOVE THE OPEN BOOK . . . .   367 EGO DOMINUS   V   3
     NOW SHE HAS THROWN HER ARMS ABOVE HER HEAD, ...   390 IMAGE PAST   36
     IN THE ELMS ABOVE THE FLOODED STREAM, ...   403 FOR DAUGHTER   12
     ABOVE THE MURDEROUS TREACHERY OF THE MOON, ...   428 NINETEEN 19   V   3
     ABOVE THE STAGGERING GIRL, HER THIGHS CARESSED . . . .   441 LEDA AND SWAN   2
     ABOVE A SINKING FIRE, A TALE THAT SHE . . . .   443 SCHOOL CHILDR   10
     ABOVE A SINKING FIRE, SOME TALE THAT SHE . . . . . .   443 SCHOOL CHILDR V 10
     GREAT NATIONS BLOSSOM ABOVE, ...   547 TO SAME TUNE 3   5
     FROM ABOVE TO BELOW, ...   547 TO SAME TUNE 3 V 6
     HERE IN THE PITCH-DARK ATMOSPHERE ABOVE . . . . . .   555 RIBH AT TOMB   17
     HERE IN THE PITCH DARK ATMOSPHERE ABOVE . . . . . .   555 RIBH AT TOMB V 17
     THE DOOR ABOVE HIS HEAD . . . .   585 ORAHILLY   33
     ARE SUNG ABOVE THE GLASS, ...   587 PARNELLITES   30
     ARE SUNG ABOVE A GLASS, ...   587 PARNELLITES   V 30
     GREAT NATIONS BLOSSOM ABOVE, ...   614 MARCH SONGS 2   5
     TO PROVE WHAT CAN YE DO? WHAT THINGS ABOVE . . . . .   650 ISLE STAT I 1 146
     ABOVE THESE MEN WHOSE MOUTHS WERE SEALED . . . . . .   656 ISLE STAT I 3   27
     FROM YONDER PINNACLE ABOVE THE LAKE . . . .   657 ISLE STAT I 3   63
     CAN ENTER THERE. SEE, SEE, ABOVE YON BROW . . . . .   659 ISLE STAT II 1 27
     THE AIR IS STILL ABOVE, AND STILL EACH LEAF, ...   662 ISLE STAT II 2   7
     WHERE RISE THE WALLS MAJESTICAL ABOVE . . . .   679 ISLE STAT II 3 311
     AND THE FLOWING AIR ABOVE, ...   680 LOVE AND DEATH 14
     DROPT DOWN THE VELVET DARKNESS FROM AROVE, ...   688 TWO TITANS   37
     ABOVE, SALIVA DRIPPING FROM HIS JAWS, ...   689 NETTLESHIP   4
     (SWALLOWS WERE FLASHING THEIR WHITE BREASTS ABOVE . . .   690 MOSADA 1   7
     ABOVE THE ALPUJARRAS ON THEIR THRONES, ...   691 MOSADA 1   27
     ABOVE THE FARM-HOUSE BY THE LITTLE LAKE . . . . . .   699 MOSADA 3   3
     SOON WILL THE CHURCHMEN NOD ABOVE THE CROWD, ...   699 MOSADA 3   19
     BEFORE WE TAKE OUR SEATS ABOVE THE CROWD, ...   704 MOSADA 3   134
     ABOVE, THE WOODS WHERE WITH THE SOFT MILD EYE . . . .   710 FERENCZ RENYI   26
     AND EVERY FLOWER ABOVE ITS SHADOW SITS, ...   712 FERENCZ RENYI   73
     AND EVERY FLOWER ABOVE A SHADOW SITS, ...   712 FERENCZ RENYI V 73
     WHEN WE ROWED NORTH, SINGING ABOVE THE OARS, ...   749 SHADOW WATER A 39
     HE HOVERS ABOVE THE MAST AND WAITS HIS KIND, ...   753 SHADOW WATER A 135
ABROAD
     RISES, AND SHOWERS ABROAD HIS FRAGRANT ARROWS, ...   72 ANASHU VIJAYA   27
ABSENT
     I'LL HAVE. OH, ABSENT ONE 'TIS NOT FOR DEARTH . . .   664 ISLE STAT II 2 50
ABSOLVO
     AND HAS NOT HEARD ABSOLVO TE. . . . .   656 ISLE STAT I 3   19
ABSTINENCE
     I AM SO LECHEROUS WITH ABSTINENCE . . . .   222 SHADOW WATER B V 8
ABSTRACT
     THEY DO NOT EVEN FEEL, SO ABSTRACT ARE THEY, ...   382 VISION ROBART   14

3

	PAGE	TITLE		LINE
ABSTRACT (CONTINUED)				
BECAME A BITTER, AN ABSTRACT THING,	397	POLIT PRISONER		9
IN ABSTRACT THINGS; OR BE DERIDED BY	409	TOWER		15
IT HAD BUT MADE US PINE THE MORE. THE ABSTRACT JOY,	427	PHANTOM HATRED		38
IN THE MAD ABSTRACT DARK AND GROUND IT GRAIN BY GRAIN	442	BLACK CENTAUR		8
OR OUT OF ABSTRACT HATRED, AND SHED BLOOD,	482	BLOOD AND MOON		38
AN ABSTRACT GREEK ABSURDITY HAS CRAZED THE MAN--	556	RIBH PATRICK		1
ABSTRACTIONS				
ALL THOSE ABSTRACTIONS THAT YOU FANCIED WERE	469	HARUN RASHID		182
AND THOSE ABSTRACTIONS THAT YOU FANCIED WERE	469	HARUN RASHID	V	182
ABSTRACTIONS OF THE GREEK PHILOSOPHY HAVE CRAZED THE MAN.	556	RIBH PATRICK	V	1
ABSURD				
HE SPLASHED WHERE AN ABSURD	400	DEMON BEAST		27
ABSURDITY				
WHAT SHALL I DO WITH THIS ABSURDITY--	409	TOWER		1
AN ABSTRACT GREEK ABSURDITY HAS CRAZED THE MAN--	556	RIBH PATRICK		1
ABU				
DOWN TO THE TUNE OF O'DONNELL ABU.	544	TO SAME TUNE 1		10
DOWN TO THE TUNE OF O'DONNELL ABU.	545	TO SAME TUNE 1		20
DOWN TO THE TUNE OF O'DONNELL ABU.	545	TO SAME TUNE 1		30
DOWN TO THE TUNE OF O'DONNELL ABU.	546	TO SAME TUNE 2	V	REF
DOWN TO THE TUNE OF O'DONNELL ABU.	548	TO SAME TUNE 3	V	REF
ABUNDANCE				
KING ABUNDANCE GOT HIM ON	440	WISDOM		16
UPON THE ABUNDANCE OF MY BREAST";	521	THREE THINGS		5
ABYSS				
UPON HIS WINGS. THRO' YONDER GREEN ABYSS	649	ISLE STAT I 1		114
ACACIA				
TO SCATTER THE ACACIA SPRAY	360	ALF POLLEXFEN		10
ACADEMY				
ON MR. NETTLESHIP'S PICTURE AT THE ROYAL HIBERNIAN ACADEMY.	688	NETTLESHIP		T
ACCEPT				
ACCEPT THE MIRACLES OF THE SAINTS AND HONOUR SANCTITY?	503	VACILLATION		79
ACCEPTED				
WHO HAVE ACCEPTED THE BYZANTINE FAITH,	464	HARUN RASHID		78
ACCIDENT				
IT WAS AN ACCIDENT."	319	DOLLS		20
NOR ACCIDENT OF PEACE NOR WAR	446	COLONUS PRAISE		14
ACCIDENTAL				
EVERY ACCIDENTAL CRACK OR DENT,	567	LAPIS LAZULI		44
ACCIDENTS				
THOSE UNDREAMT ACCIDENTS THAT HAVE MADE ME	321	REED WHISPERER		10
ACCLAIMING				
ACCLAIMING, PROCLAIMING, DECLAIMING HIM.	528	DANCER CRUACH		8
ACCOMPLISH				
BEFORE HE CAN ACCOMPLISH FATE,	638	BEN BULBEN		35
ACCOMPLISHED				
MIGHT BE ACCOMPLISHED. BUNCHING THE CURTAIN UP	183	QUEEN MAEVE		68
ALL WAS ACCOMPLISHED. "WHEN THIS DAY	273	GREY ROCK		70
ACCOMPLISHED HIS PREDESTINED WILL,	522	LULLABY		16
ACCOMPLISHED FINGERS BEGIN TO PLAY.	567	LAPIS LAZULI		54
ACCOMPLISHMENT				
YOUTH CAN EXCEL THEM IN ACCOMPLISHMENT,	340	SHEP GOATHERD		47
A MARVELLOUS ACCOMPLISHMENT,	421	MY TABLE		17
ACCORDING				
ACCORDING TO A DIFFERENT PLAN.	379	SAINT HUNCH		6
ACCORDING TO THE WIND, FOR ALL ARE BLIND.	433	NINETEEN 19		124
"ACCORDING TO MY BOYISH PLAN;	577	WHAT THEN		17
"GREATEST SINCE REMBRANDT," ACCORDING TO JOHN SYNGE;	602	GALLERY REVIS		26
ACCOUNT				
AND WE AND ALL THE MUSES ARE THINGS OF NO ACCOUNT.	580	CURSE CROMWELL		12
ACCOUNTED				
KNOW, THAT I WOULD ACCOUNTED BE	137	TO IRELAND		1
ACCURSED SEE MOON-ACCURSED				
MAYBE THE WEATHER WAS ACCURSED	305	HOUR DAWN		65
SO LET HER THINK OPINIONS ARE ACCURSED.	405	FOR DAUGHTER		58
IMAGINING MOON ACCURSED,	454	EMPTY CUP	V	4
OR THE FIDDLE-STRING ACCURSED,	527	AM OF IRELAND		20
OR THE FIDDLE STRING ACCURSED,	527	AM OF IRELAND	V	20
ACCURSED WHO BRINGS TO LIGHT OF DAY	779	ACCURSED WHO		1
ACCURST				
COMPANIONS LONG ACCURST AND DEAD,	11	OISIN 1		130
FOR I AND ALL MY PEOPLE WERE ACCURST	690	MOSADA 1		15
IN EVERY DANCE, BY CHILDREN SOUGHT. "ACCURST,	709	FERENCZ RENYI		12
ACCUSATION				
I THIRST FOR ACCUSATION. ALL THAT WAS SUNG,	542	PARN FUNERAL 1		25
ACCUSE				
THEY MUST TO KEEP THEIR CERTAINTY ACCUSE	398	LEADERS CROWD		1
ACCUSED SEE SELF-ACCUSED				
ACCUSING				
EVEN ACCUSING HEAVEN BECAUSE	399	BREAK OF DAY		15
COME, FIX UPON ME THAT ACCUSING EYE.	542	PARN FUNERAL 1		24
ACCUSTOMED				
NEAR NO ACCUSTOMED HAND;	123	DREAM OF DEATH		2
THAN THIS ACCUSTOMED TOIL. WHEN I WAS YOUNG,	267	ALL TEMPT ME		5
I AM ACCUSTOMED TO THEIR LACK OF BREATH,	325	ROBERT GREGORY		45
HAD SCARCELY ACCUSTOMED OUR EARS	341	SHEP GOATHERD		67
HAD SCARCELY ACCUSTOMED OUR EYES	341	SHEP GOATHERD		69
WHERE ALL'S ACCUSTOMED, CEREMONIOUS;	405	FOR DAUGHTER		74
ACH				
ACH, CALL ME WHAT YOU PLEASE!	627	STATES HOLIDAY		21

4

ACHAIANS'
    ARE STILL THE ACHAIANS' TENTED CHIEFS AT BAY? . . . . .   679 ISLE STAT II 3   910
ACHE
    FOR YOUR SOLE SAKE--THAT ALL HEART'S ACHE HAVE KNOWN, . .   355 BROKEN DREAMS   7
    AND GIVEN TO OTHERS ALL HEART'S ACHE, ...   355 BROKEN DREAMS   8
    BUT FOR YOUR SAKE--THAT ALL HEART'S ACHE HAVE KNOWN, . .   355 BROKEN DREAMS V   7
ACHILLES
    AYE, AND ACHILLES, TIMOR, BABAR, BARHAIM, ALL . . . . .   366 HER COURAGE   9
    ATHENE TAKES ACHILLES BY THE HAIR, ...   374 PHASES OF MOON   45
ACHING
    PITY, AN ACHING HEAD, ...   346 ON WOMAN   38
    NO MOON; ONLY AN ACHING HEART . . . .   421 MY TABLE   13
    HAD SUCH AN ACHING HEART . . . .   422 MY TABLE   28
    THEY FIXED OLD ACHING EYES, ...   432 NINETEEN 19   100
ACKNOWLEDGE
    YOUR COMING BROUGHT; THOUGH I ACKNOWLEDGE I HAVE GONE . .   391 UNDER SATURN V   5
ACORNS
    ACORNS GREEN, WITH EYES AWAKE. . . . .   655 ISLE STAT I 3   5
ACQUAINTANCE
    ACQUAINTANCE; COMPANION; . . . .   504 RESULT THOUGHT   1
ACRE
    AN ACRE OF STONY GROUND, ...   419 MY HOUSE   3
    AN ACRE OF GRASS . . . .   575 ACRE OF GRASS   T
    AN ACRE OF GREEN GRASS . . . .   575 ACRE OF GRASS   2
ACROPOLIS
    TO BURN THAT STUMP ON THE ACROPOLIS, ...   430 NINETEEN 19   46
ACROSS
    THY WANDERING STEPS ACROSS THE SEA? . . . .   5 OISIN 1 V   51
    ACROSS THE GLOSSY SEA." "OH, WILD . . . .   6 OISIN 1 V   58
    WE RODE ACROSS THE OILY SEA, ...   10 OISIN 1 V   114
    ACROSS YOUR WANDERING RUBY CARS . . . .   22 OISIN 1   330
    I MOUNTED, AND WE RODE ACROSS THE LONE . . . .   45 OISIN 2 V   231
    ACROSS THE BARE BOREEN. . . . .   95 MOLL MAGEE   32
    WHEN THE WIND COMES BLOWING ACROSS THE HILLY LAND; . . .   207 HANRAHANS SONG V   7
    ACROSS THE BITTER SEA." . . . .   396 ROSE TREE   6
    THE POPLARS GAZE ACROSS THE WATERS GREY, ...   653 ISLE STAT I 2   34
    HE PASSED ACROSS THE LAKE. WHEN WE TWO CAME . . . . .   658 ISLE STAT II 1   5
    HALF LIT, SO FLAPT THE WINGS ACROSS THE LAKE-- . . . .   659 ISLE STAT II 1   17
    ONE HAND BROW-SHADING, FAR ACROSS THE NIGHT, ...   663 ISLE STAT II 2   27
    HOLD FESTIVAL ACROSS THE LAND, ...   671 ISLE STAT II 3   128
    I FEEL A FINGER DRAWN ACROSS MY CHEEK! . . . .   694 MOSADA 1   96
    A FEARFUL PALENESS CREEPS ACROSS HER BREAST . . . . .   701 MOSADA 3   69
    FLAMES THE SHUTTLE OF THE LIGHTNING ACROSS THE DRIVING
       SLEET,   718 PHANTOM SHIP   1
    AN OLD HORSE LOOKED ACROSS A FENCE. . . . .   725 LEGEND   27
    TRAVELLED TO AND FRO ACROSS THE ATLANTIC. . . . . . .   790 DEDICATION   3
A-CROW
    SPOKE AND SET THE COCKS A-CROW. . . . .   637 BEN BULBEN   4
    THE STRONG MARCH BIRDS A-CROW. . . . .   783 GREY ROUND   26
ACTION
    FOR THOSE THAT LOVE THE WORLD SERVE IT IN ACTION, . . .   369 EGO DOMINUS   42
    AND SHOULD THEY PAINT OR WRITE, STILL IT IS ACTION; . . .   369 EGO DOMINUS   44
    AND SHOULD THEY PAINT OR WRITE STILL IS IT ACTION, . . .   369 EGO DOMINUS V   44
    EVERY EVENT IN ACTION OR IN THOUGHT; . . . .   479 SELF AND SOUL   66
    COUNT EVERY SIN OF ACTION OR OF THOUGHT; . . . . . .   479 SELF AND SOUL V   66
    BUT COPY SOME ONE ACTION, ...   600 SPIRIT MEDIUM   13
    "WITH ACTION ALL THE WORLD IS VEXED," . . . .   728 PRIEST FAIRY   15
ACTION'S
    AND EVIL STILL IS ACTION'S CHILD. . . . .   728 PRIEST FAIRY   14
ACTOR
    THEN THAT OLD ABBEY ACTOR, DUDLEY DIGGES, ...   790 DEDICATION   7
ACTORS
    BUT ACTORS LACKING MUSIC . . . .   599 STONE CROSS   17
ACTUAL
    BUT ACTUAL SHELLS OF ROSSES' LEVEL SHORE. . . . . . .   494 AT ALGECIRAS   12
A-CURSED
    BECAUSE THE WEATHER WAS A-CURSED . . . .   305 HOUR DAWN V   65
ADAM
    THE FIRST ADAM IN THEIR THOUGHT, ...   617 LONG-LEG FLY   22
    WHERE BUT HALF-AWAKENED ADAM . . . .   638 BEN BULBEN   47
ADAM'S
    ADAM'S CURSE . . . .   204 ADAMS CURSE   T
    SINCE ADAM'S FALL BUT NEEDS MUCH LABOURING. . . . . .   205 ADAMS CURSE   22
    BUT FOR ADAM'S SIN . . . .   621 JOHN KINSELLA   26
ADD
    AND ADD THE HALFPENCE TO THE PENCE . . . .   289 SEPTEMBER 1913   3
    AND FURTHER ADD TO THAT . . . .   415 TOWER   153
    I ADD IN COMMENTARY, ...   496 MOHINI CHATTER   16
ADDER'S
    UNTIL THIS MORN. AS ADDER'S BACK . . . .   667 ISLE STAT II 3   22
    WAS BANDED AS AN ADDER'S BACK, ...   667 ISLE STAT II 3 V   23
ADDERS
    ABODE, AS BANDED ADDERS IN MY BREAST. . . . .   683 SEEKER   50
ADDING
    ADDING FEATHER TO FEATHER . . . .   311 PEACOCK   10
ADDRESSED
    APOLOGIA ADDRESSED TO IRELAND IN THE COMING DAYS . . . .   137 TO IRELAND V   T
ADMIRED
    ADMIRED AND BEAUTIFUL, ...   472 ALL SOUL NIGHT   43
ADMIRING
    THE OLD MEN ADMIRING THEMSELVES IN THE WATER . . . . .   208 OLD MEN ADMIRE   T

		PAGE	TITLE	LINE

ADMIT
IF ON THE LOST, ADMIT YOU TURNED ASIDE . . . . . . 413 TOWER 115
NONE DARED ADMIT, IF SUCH A THOUGHT WERE HIS, ... 430 NINETEEN 19 44
I ADMIT THE BRIAR . . . . 532 FIRST CONFESS 1
ADMONISH
ADMONISH US TO CLING TO THAT . . . . 460 THREE MONUMENT 8
ADOLESCENCE
SLIM ADOLESCENCE THAT A NYMPH HAS STRIPPED, ... 612 NEWS ORACLE 25
ADORE
THAT I DO MUCH ADORE! . . . . 592 DRUNK SOBRIETY 6
ADORED
SOUL'S BEAUTY BEING MOST ADORED, ... 421 MY TABLE 22
TROY BACKED ITS HELEN! TROY DIED AND ADORED! . . . . . 547 TO SAME TUNE 3 4
TROY LOOKED ON HELEN, IT DIED AND ADORED! . . . . . 547 TO SAME TUNE 3 V 4
TROY BACKED ITS HELEN! TROY DIED AND ADORED! . . . . . 614 MARCH SONGS 2 4
ADORES
MY SOUL ADORES, ... 572 LADYS 1ST SONG 10
ADORN
CAN, TATTERED, STILL PROTECT, FADED ADORN. . . . . . 477 SELF AND SOUL 16
THAT MIGHT ADORN OLD SONGS OR COURTLY SHOWS! . . . . . 629 CIRCUS ANIMALS 14
STRANGE DRAPERIES DID ALL THE SIDES ADORN, ... 657 ISLE STAT I 3 55
ADORNING
LIKE A BRIDE BENDING OVER HER MIRROR ADORNING, ... 28 OISIN 1 V 423E
ADORNING EVERY SECRET TRACK . . . . 509 JANE REPROVED 9
SOME TAKE DELIGHT IN ADORNING A WOMAN. . . . . . . 547 TO SAME TUNE 3 V 3
ADRIFT
AND BOTH ADRIFT ON THE MIRACULOUS STREAM . . . . . 535 CHOSEN 16
ADRIP
AND SHE WITH GOBAN'S WINE ADRIP, ... 276 GREY ROCK 121
ADVANCE
SHOULD STARVE GOOD MEN AND BAD ADVANCE, ... 626 OLD MEN BE MAD 10
ADVENTURE
BUT SUMMONS TO ADVENTURE AND THE MAN . . . . . . 373 PHASES OF MOON 37
THAT THE ADVENTURE OF OLD AGE BEGINS. . . . . . . 609 IN TARAS HALLS 5
ADVERSITY
BEFITTING EMBLEMS OF ADVERSITY. . . . . 420 MY HOUSE 30
AEDH
HEARING AEDH TOUCH THE MOURNFUL STRINGS OF GOLD." . . . 35 OISIN 2 87
AEDH TELLS OF THE ROSE IN HIS HEART . . . . 142 ROSE IN HEART V T
AEDH LAMENTS THE LOSS OF LOVE . . . . 152 LOSS OF LOVE V T
AEDH GIVES HIS BELOVED CERTAIN RHYMES . . . . . . 157 BELOVED RHYMES V T
AEDH TELLS OF A VALLEY FULL OF LOVERS . . . . . . 163 VALLEY LOVERS V T
AEDH TELLS OF THE PERFECT BEAUTY . . . . 164 PERFECT BEAUTY V T
AEDH HEARS THE CRY OF THE SEDGE . . . . 165 CRY OF SEDGE V T
AEDH THINKS OF THOSE WHO HAVE SPOKEN EVIL OF HIS BELOVED 166 EVIL OF BELOV V T
AEDH WISHES HIS BELOVED WERE DEAD . . . . 175 BELOVED DEAD V T
AEDH WISHES FOR THE CLOTHS OF HEAVEN . . . . . . 176 CLOTHS HEAVEN V T
AENGUS
AENGUS AND EDAIN, MY OWN NAME . . . . 5 OISIN 1 47
AENGUS AND EDAIN, AND MY NAME . . . . 5 OISIN 1 V 47
FROM WHERE THE BIRDS OF AENGUS WING?" . . . . . . 6 OISIN 1 53
WHERE AENGUS DREAMS, FROM SUN TO SUN, ... 16 OISIN 1 218
THE SONG OF WANDERING AENGUS . . . . 149 WANDER AENGUS T
FOR I AM AENGUS, AND I AM CROSSED IN LOVE." . . . . 183 QUEEN MAEVE 84
FOR YOU HAVE BEEN, O AENGUS OF THE BIRDS, ... 185 QUEEN MAEVE 101
SAID: "AENGUS AND HIS SWEETHEART GIVE THEIR THANKS . . . 187 QUEEN MAEVE 146
THEN MAEVE: "O AENGUS, MASTER OF ALL LOVERS, ... 187 QUEEN MAEVE 149
WHILE OVER THEM BIRDS OF AENGUS FLY, ... 197 BAILE AILLINN 182
LAND-OF-THE-TOWER, WHERE AENGUS HAS THROWN THE GATES APART, 209 UNDER THE MOON 8
LAND OF THE TOWER, WHEN AENGUS HAS THROWN THE GATES APART, 209 UNDER THE MOON V 8
THE HARP OF AENGUS . . . . 219 HARP OF AENGUS T
BESIDE YOUNG AENGUS IN HIS TOWER OF GLASS, ... 219 HARP OF AENGUS 2
'TWAS AENGUS AND EDAIN, THE WANDERING LOVERS, ... 224 SHADOW WATER B 42
AS THAT WILD AENGUS. LONG BEFORE HER DAY . . . . . 224 SHADOW WATER B 47
AENGUS AND EDAIN, THOSE PASSIONATE WANDERERS, ... 228 SHADOW WATER B 138
AENGUS AND EDAIN RAN UP OUT OF THE WAVE-- . . . . . 231 SHADOW WATER B 196
IN ISLANDS WHERE THE CHILDREN OF AENGUS WIND . . . . 245 SHADOW WATER B 469
WHEN AENGUS AND HIS EDAINE WAKE FROM SLEEP . . . . . 749 SHADOW WATER A 57
AENGUS LOOKS ON YOU WHEN I LOOK: HE AWAITS . . . . 757 SHADOW WATER A 209
AENGUS LOOKS ON YOU WHEN I LOOK: HE WAITS . . . . 757 SHADOW WATER A V 209
AS THE AGELESS BIRDS OF AENGUS, OR THE BIRDS . . . . 761 SHADOW WATER A 260
O, AENGUS OF THE HERDS, WATCH OVER ME! . . . . . . 762 SHADOW WATER A 291
BESIDE YOUNG AENGUS IN HIS TOWER OF GLASS, ... 762 SHADOW WATER A 297
AND BRING ME WHERE THE CHILDREN OF AENGUS WIND . . . . 763 SHADOW WATER A 317
IN ONE ANOTHER'S ARMS. AENGUS HAS SEEN . . . . . 763 SHADOW WATER A 321
AENGUS'
OF AENGUS' BIRDS GLEAM IN THEIR APPLE BOUGHS. . . . . 751 SHADOW WATER A 103
FOR HE WHO GAVE IT CALLED IT AENGUS' HARP . . . . . 762 SHADOW WATER A 288
AEROPLANE
AEROPLANE AND ZEPPELIN WILL COME OUT, ... 565 LAPIS LAZULI 6
AERY
OF BIRDS EVEN, LONGINGS FOR AERY . . . . 708 FAIRY PEDANT 26
AFAR
"THE SOUL IS A DROP OF JOY AFAR, ... 19 OISIN 1 V 276
AFAR FROM WHERE THE YEARS ARE FLYING . . . . . . 22 OISIN 1 V 340A
WHITENED AFAR WITH SURGE, FAN-FORMED AND WIDE, ... 31 OISIN 2 28
WHITENING THE SURGE AFAR, FAN-FORMED AND WIDE, ... 31 OISIN 2 V 28
AFAR IN ANCIENT ERI. . . . . 32 OISIN 2 V 50E
BY LAKES AND MEADOW LANDS AND LAWNS AFAR, ... 32 OISIN 2 V 50F
IT DIED AFAR. GREY SLEET THOSE TOWERS HID . . . . . 46 OISIN 2 V 245
YOU HUNTER OF THE FIELDS AFAR! . . . . 75 ANASHU VIJAYA 79

6

AFAR   (CONTINUED)
    SHE MOTIONED HIM AFAR, AND ROSE AND SPOKE: . . . . . .   280 TWO KINGS   68
    ALL DREAD AFAR TILL MORNING'S BACK, ...   435 FOR MY SON   6
    MARK AND DIGEST MY TALE, CARRY IT AFAR . . . .   554 RIBH AT TOMB   3
    WE PICKED EACH OTHER FROM AFAR AND KNEW . . . .   622 HOUND VOICE   10
    AFAR, CLEAR-SHINING ON THE HERALD HILLS. . . . .   645 ISLE STAT I 1   14
    UNTIL AFAR APPEAR THE GLEAMING DRAGON-SCALES: . . . . .   651 ISLE STAT I 1   160
    WHITE LILIES, AND HER SONG FLEW FORTH AFAR . . . . . .   693 MOSADA 1   85
    AWAKE, AWAKE, AND WE WILL SAIL AFAR, ...   702 MOSADA 3   78
    AFAR ALONG THE FLEET WHITE RIVER'S FACE-- . . . .   702 MOSADA 3   79
    AFAR FROM OUR LAWN AND OUR LEVEE, ...   706 FAIRY PEDANT   1
    THE CALLING AFAR OF THE DOE AND THE DEER, ...   717 LOVE SONG   5
    IN THE BOSOM AFAR OF THE FRAGRANT WOOD, ...   717 LOVE SONG   9
    AS THERE FLOATS FROM FIELDS AFAR . . . .   732 STREET DANCERS   20
AFFABLE
    AN AFFABLE IRREGULAR, ...   423 ROAD AT DOOR   1
AFFAIR
    FOR SOME TRIVIAL AFFAIR . . . .   293 HELEN LIVED   3
    IMAGINED SUCH A FINE AFFAIR: . . . .   791 REPRISALS   14
AFFAIRS
    AND PETER THAT HAD GREAT AFFAIRS . . . .   456 FRIENDS YOUTH   13
    THE RICH MAN AND HIS AFFAIRS, ...   540 FROM ANTIGONE   3
AFFECTION
    THAT PASSION, PIETY OR AFFECTION KNOWS, ...   445 SCHOOL CHILDR   54
AFFECTIONS
    IN THE AFFECTIONS OF OUR HEART, ...   324 ROBERT GREGORY   12
AFFIRMS
    SOME PLATONIST AFFIRMS THAT IN THE STATION . . . . . .   431 NINETEEN 19   72
AFFLICT
    TO AFFLICT MANKIND, BUT NOW . . . .   431 NINETEEN 19   86
AFFRIGHTING   SEE SELF-AFFRIGHTING
A-FISHING
    WE WENT A-FISHING IN LONG BOATS . . . .   23 OISIN 1   352
AFLAME
    I WENT TO BLOW THE FIRE AFLAME, ...   149 WANDER AENGUS   10
    I BENT TO BLOW THE FIRE AFLAME: . . . .   149 WANDER AENGUS V   10
    I STOOPED TO BLOW THE FIRE AFLAME, ...   149 WANDER AENGUS V   10
A-FLAME
    I WENT TO BLOW THE FIRE A-FLAME, ...   149 WANDER AENGUS V   10
AFLASH
    YOUR EYES ARE ALL AFLASH. SHE IS NOT HERE. . . . . .   669 ISLE STAT II 3 V   68
A-FLASH
    YOUR EYES ARE ALL A-FLASH. SHE IS NOT HERE. . . . . .   669 ISLE STAT II 3   68
A-FLICKER
    OF BEAMS A-FLICKER ON YON LONELY FIR, ...   661 ISLE STAT II 1   72
AFLOAT
    WHO WHEN NIGHT THICKENS ARE AFLOAT . . . .   196 BAILE AILLINN   179
A-FLUTTER
    THEY WILL NOT HUSH, THE LEAVES A-FLUTTER ROUND ME, . . .   82 MAD KING GOLL   12
    THEY WILL NOT HUSH, THE LEAVES A-FLUTTER ROUND ME, . . .   83 MAD KING GOLL   24
    THEY WILL NOT HUSH, THE LEAVES A-FLUTTER ROUND ME, . . .   84 MAD KING GOLL   36
    THEY WILL NOT HUSH, THE LEAVES A-FLUTTER ROUND ME, . . .   84 MAD KING GOLL   48
    THEY WILL NOT HUSH, THE LEAVES A-FLUTTER ROUND ME, . . .   85 MAD KING GOLL   60
    THEY WILL NOT HUSH, THE LEAVES A-FLUTTER ROUND ME, . . .   86 MAD KING GOLL   72
    WHY ARE THEY ALL A-FLUTTER OF A SUDDEN? . . . .   243 SHADOW WATER B   436
A-FLUTTERING
    A-FLUTTERING THE PAINTED POPULACE OF LAKE . . . .   675 ISLE STAT II 3   224
AFOOT
    WHAT MATTERS WERE AFOOT AMONG THE SIDHE, ...   182 QUEEN MAEVE   61
AFORETIME
    AFORETIME, AND SHALL NOT GROW SAD . . . .   22 OISIN 1   V 340E
AFRAID
    AND DEMONS AFRAID IN THEIR DARKNESS: . . . .   62 OISIN 3   205
    AFRAID, THEIR EARS ON THE EARTH LAID, ...   62 OISIN 3   206
    BELOVED, I AM NOT AFRAID OF HER. . . . .   197 BAILE AILLINN   200
    BUT WERE YOU NOT AFRAID? WHY SHOULD I FEAR? . . . . .   224 SHADOW WATER B   41
    BUT THAT I AM AFRAID THEY MAY HAVE PASSED, ...   226 SHADOW WATER B   84
    YOUR SOUL SHALL GIVE THE KISS. I AM NOT AFRAID, . . .   238 SHADOW WATER B   346
    AND THAT IS WHY THEIR LOVERS ARE AFRAID . . . .   245 SHADOW WATER B   481
    AND I AM AFRAID THAT YOU WILL RUN . . . .   356 BROKEN DREAMS   30
    I AM AFRAID THAT YOU WILL RUN . . . .   356 BROKEN DREAMS V   30
    HE WERE AFRAID THE BIRDS, WHO CRY ALOUD . . . .   371 EGO DOMINUS   77
    BUT WHY SHOULD YOU GROW SUDDENLY AFRAID . . . .   390 IMAGE PAST   29
    I DO NOT KNOW, THAT KNOW I AM AFRAID . . . .   390 IMAGE PAST   41
    THE WEST WIND MADE IT PITIFUL, AND THE NORTH WIND AFRAID. 449 OWEN AHERNE   6
    AFRAID THEY MIGHT BE BEATEN . . . .   582 ROGER CASEMENT   5
    THE RATTLE OF THOSE ARMS MAKES US AFRAID. . . . . . .   634 CUCHULAIN COMF   15
    BE NOT AFRAID, YOU'LL SEE NO FEARFUL THING. . . . . .   693 MOSADA 1   74
    I SAW A GIRL AFRAID TO BE TOO NEAR, ...   712 FERENCZ RENYI   68
    AFRAID TO BE TOO FAR." "AY, BRING HER HERE!" . . . .   712 FERENCZ RENYI   69
    I AM AFRAID OF THE HARP. O! WINGS ON WINGS! . . . .   759 SHADOW WATER A   236
    I AM AFRAID OF HIS LOW-LAUGHING HARP. . . . .   759 SHADOW WATER A   239
    I AM AFRAID OF HIS LOW LAUGHING HARP. . . . .   759 SHADOW WATER A V 239
AFRICA
    IN AFRICA ON MOUNTAIN OF THE MOON, ...   277 TWO KINGS   V 20
AFRICAN
    AMONG THE AFRICAN MOUNTAINS OF THE MOON, ...   277 TWO KINGS   20
AFTER
    THE OSPREY OF SORROW GOES AFTER AND CLUTCHES, ...   27 OISIN 1   V 415D
    GREENISH AND SLIPPERY. TIME AFTER TIME . . . .   37 OISIN 2   V 114
    HOUR AFTER HOUR I WAITED, AND THE DOME . . . .   39 OISIN 2   V 147

7

		PAGE	TITLE		LINE
AFTER (CONTINUED)					
AND MANANNAN'S DARK TOWER, STONE AFTER STONE, ...		45	OISIN 2		236
AND THEY HAVE FALLEN OR FLED, AGE AFTER AGE.		45	OISIN 2		242
"AGE AFTER AGE I FEEL MY SOUL DECAY		45	OISIN 2	V	235
CAME TO MY TOWER AS AGE DRAGGED AFTER AGE		45	OISIN 2	V	242
AND NOW THE WARMTH OF SIGHS, AND AFTER THE QUIVER OF LIPS,		47	OISIN 3		8
. . . AND YEARS AFTER YEARS 'GAN FLOW, ...		52	OISIN 3		75
. . . AND YEARS AFTER YEARS 'GAN THEIR FLOW, ...		52	OISIN 3	V	75
NO MORE TO CRAWL ON THE SEAS WITH LONG OARS MILE AFTER MILE,		55	OISIN 3		119
CAME AFTER THE HARD GAZE OF YOUTH, OR AN OLD MAN LIFTED HIS HEAD,		59	OISIN 3		170
TO HUNGER FIERCELY AFTER TRUTH, ...		66	HAPPY SHEPHERD		24
FAR, FAR AWAY. I NAMED HIM AFTER YOU.		72	ANASHU VIJAYA		35
FAR, FAR AWAY. I'VE NAMED HIM AFTER YOU.		72	ANASHU VIJAYA	V	35
AFTER SHORT FIGHTING IN THE LEAFY SHADE, ...		109	CUCHULAIN SEA		57
AND AFTER CRIED HE, "GOD FORGIVE!		132	FR GILLIGAN		11
AFTER THE RED-ROSE-BORDERED HEM.		139	TO IRELAND		30
AFTER THE RED-ROSE-BORDERED HEM.		139	TO IRELAND		48
AFTER THE RED ROSE BORDERED HEM.		139	TO IRELAND	V	30
AFTER THE RED ROSE BORDERED HEM.		139	TO IRELAND	V	48
AFTER THE DEATHS OF MANY MEN, ...		197	BAILE AILLINN		193
AND AFTER CIRCLING WITH STRANGE CRIES AWHILE		223	SHADOW WATER B		26
BUT HE THAT GETS THEIR LOVE AFTER THE FASHION		228	SHADOW WATER B		145
THAT FOLLOWS AFTER. I UNDERSTAND YOU NOW.		237	SHADOW WATER B		341
AND AFTER RUNNING AT THE BRIM		254	HIS DREAM		9
THE NO KING CRIED WHO AFTER THAT WAS KING, ...		258	KING NO KING		2
AND AFTER SET YOUR HEART TO BEAT.		263	MASK		9
THE GIFTS THAT GOVERN MEN, AND AFTER THESE		264	HOUSE SHAKEN		10
AFTER A RAGGED HAT IN BISCAY BAY, ...		270	PARDON FATHERS		14
AND AFTER, WHEN HER BLOOD RAN WILD, ...		272	GREY ROCK		44
FOOT AFTER FOOT WAS GIVING WAY, ...		274	GREY ROCK		72
OUTRODE HIS TROOP THAT AFTER TWELVE MONTHS' WAR . . .		276	TWO KINGS	V	1
"DAY AFTER DAY YOU QUESTION ME, AND I, ...		281	TWO KINGS		99
AND AFTER HEAPED UP STONE ON STONE, ...		307	HOUR DAWN		116
AND AFTER HEAPED THE STONES AGAIN		307	HOUR DAWN	V	116
AND AFTER, DRAINED DRY, ...		310	WITCH		4
AFTER NINE YEARS, I SINK MY HEAD ABASHED.		353	PEOPLE		37
AND AFTER TWENTY YEARS THEY LAID		360	ALF POLLEXFEN		6
HE HAS FOUND, AFTER THE MANNER OF HIS KIND, ...		373	PHASES OF MOON		12
THERE IS NO MUSCLE IN THE ARM, AND AFTER, ...		374	PHASES OF MOON		52
AND AFTER THAT THE CRUMBLING OF THE MOON.		375	PHASES OF MOON		87
HE WOULD NEVER KNOW ME AFTER ALL THESE YEARS		377	PHASES OF MOON		129
DAY AFTER DAY, YET NEVER FIND THE MEANING.		377	PHASES OF MOON		135
AUGUSTUS CAESAR, AND AFTER THESE		379	SAINT HUNCH		11
AND AFTER KISSED A STONE, ...		384	VISION ROBART		64
AND AFTER THAT ARRANGED IT IN A SONG		384	VISION ROBART		65
AND SURELY AFTER TWENTY YEARS IT WAS TIME TO COME." . .		391	UNDER SATURN		14
WAS IT NEEDLESS DEATH AFTER ALL?		394	EASTER 1916		67
AND I, THAT AFTER ME		420	MY HOUSE		27
AND THERE'S BUT COMMON GREENNESS AFTER THAT. . . .		422	MY DESCENDANTS		8
MOCK MOCKERS AFTER THAT		432	NINETEEN 19		108
A SUDDEN BLAST OF DUSTY WIND AND AFTER		433	NINETEEN 19		119
AND AFTER THAT THERE'S NOTHING GOOD		434	WHEEL		5
AND AFTER BAKED IT SLOWLY IN AN OVEN, BUT NOW . . .		442	BLACK CENTAUR		9
AND AFTER, SWEPT FROM THERE, ...		453	DEATH OF HARE		10
AND AFTER KEPT IT FROM DECAY, ...		460	THREE MONUMENT		7
IN AFTER TIME THEY WILL SPEAK MUCH OF ME		462	HARUN RASHID		29
EVEN TO-DAY, AFTER SOME SEVEN YEARS		468	HARUN RASHID		161
EVEN TODAY, AFTER SOME SEVEN YEARS		468	HARUN RASHID	V	161
. . . CENTURY AFTER CENTURY, ...		481	BLOOD AND MOON		23
THE NINETEENTH CENTURY AND AFTER		485	NINETEENTH CEN		T
FOR SCHOLARS AND FOR POETS AFTER US, ...		488	COOLE PARK 29		6
AFTER GREAT CATHEDRAL GONG, ...		497	BYZANTIUM		4
SPIRIT AFTER SPIRIT! THE SMITHIES BREAK THE FLOOD, . .		498	BYZANTIUM		34
AND AFTER NAILED UPON THE NIGHT		519	HER DREAM		7
AND DID AFTER STRETCH AND YAWN", ...		521	THREE THINGS		17
AFTER LONG SILENCE		523	LONG SILENCE		T
SPEECH AFTER LONG SILENCE, IT IS RIGHT, ...		523	LONG SILENCE		1
FROM MIRROR AFTER MIRROR, ...		532	BEFORE WORLD		5
AND AFTER THAT I HELD MY FINGERS UP, ...		537	HER VISION		9
THOSE THAT COME AFTER SHALL MOCK AT O'DONNELL, . . .		546	TO SAME TUNE 2		23
THOSE THAT COME AFTER SHALL MOCK O'DONNELL, ...		546	TO SAME TUNE 2	V	23
RAVENING THROUGH CENTURY AFTER CENTURY, ...		563	MERU		5
AFTER CERTAIN YEARS HE WON		577	WHAT THEN		7
AND AFTER THAT BETRAYED?		587	PARNELLITES		28
THOSE THAT COME AFTER SHALL MOCK AT O'DONNELL, . . .		614	MARCH SONGS 1		23
GROWS MORE DEEP DAY AFTER DAY, ...		624	APPARITIONS		18
IRELAND AFTER THE REVOLUTION IV		628	JANE MOUNTAIN	V	T
I LIE AWAKE NIGHT AFTER NIGHT		632	MAN AND ECHO		9
PALMER'S PHRASE, BUT AFTER THAT		639	BEN BULBEN		66
THE HOLINESS OF MONKS, AND AFTER		640	BEN BULBEN		76
THE HOLINESS OF THE MONKS, AND AFTER		640	BEN BULBEN	V	76
NAMES AFTER ME. LADY—I COME. FORGIVE, ...		695	MOSADA 1		117
"WATCHER, WHEREFORE HAVE YE CALLED US?" EYES GO AFTER HIS LEAN HAND,		718	PHANTOM SHIP		10
WHILE THEY MURMUR, "AFTER THIS		776	AGAINST WITCH		30
FOR THE THINGS COME AFTER DEATH?		777	SONG DEIRDRE 2		12
AT DAYBREAK AFTER STORMY NIGHT		784	WOMANS BEAUTY		3
AFTERNOON					
WHEN EVERY SUNDAY AFTERNOON		607	SONGS BURDEN 2		19

8

		PAGE	TITLE		LINE
AFTERNOON (CONTINUED)					
IS STONE: OLD SLEEPER: THIS SAME AFTERNOON		657	ISLE STAT I 3		74
AFTERWARDS					
IT SOUGHT ITSELF AND AFTERWARDS THE WORLD.		376	PHASES OF MOON		95
AGAINST					
AND SUNKEN SHAPE, AGAINST MY FACE AND BREAST, ...		40	OISIN 2	V	179
SIDLED THEIR BODIES AGAINST HIM, FILLING THE SHADE WITH THEIR EYES.		50	OISIN 3		48
THEY HAVE SPOKEN AGAINST YOU EVERYWHERE, ...		166	EVIL OF BELOV		3
THAT MAKES ME FEAR TO RAISE A HAND AGAINST HIM, ...		222	SHADOW WATER B	V	16A
THIS LONG WHILE NOW: WE HAD NOT TURNED AGAINST HIM . . .		225	SHADOW WATER B		68B
THAT I WILL NEVER LIFT A HAND AGAINST YOU.		227	SHADOW WATER B		108
TOO MANY YEARS TO LIFT A HAND AGAINST YOU.		227	SHADOW WATER B		111
THAT RAISED THEIR HANDS AGAINST HIM. THERE ARE SOME . .		235	SHADOW WATER B		291
WOULD RISE AGAINST ME. NO, I AM NOT MAD—.		236	SHADOW WATER B		318
BUT NO, NO: YOUR CRY IS NOT AGAINST ME.		244	SHADOW WATER B		449
BUT I HAVE DONE SO GREAT A WRONG AGAINST YOU.		245	SHADOW WATER B		483
AGAINST UNWORTHY PRAISE		259	UNWORTH PRAISE		T
. . . HAVE JOINED THE AGITATION AGAINST IMMORAL LITERATURE		262	STUDENTS AGIT		T
. . . AGITATION AGAINST IMMORAL LITERATURE		262	STUDENTS AGIT	V	T
AGAINST A SOUL?		267	FRIEND ILLNESS		7
AGAINST THE STAG. WHEN HORN AND STEEL WERE MET		277	TWO KINGS		15
AGAINST A BEECH-BOLE, HE THREW DOWN THE BEAST		278	TWO KINGS		36
AGAINST A BEECH BOLE, HE THREW DOWN THE BEAST		278	TWO KINGS	V	36
BECAUSE THAT WERE A GUILT AGAINST HER KING, ...		280	TWO KINGS	V	74A
AND THAT WOULD BE AGAINST GOD'S PROVIDENCE.		339	SHEP GOATHERD		5
MATCHING OUR BROKEN-HEARTED WIT AGAINST HER WIT, . . .		362	HER COURTESY		7
AS I DO NOW AGAINST OLD AGE?		413	TOWER		100
FOR EMBLEMS OF THE DAY AGAINST THE TOWER		478	SELF AND SOUL		29
BUT WE OLD MEN ARE MASSED AGAINST THE WORLD.		486	SEVEN SAGES		14
BUT WE OLD MEN ARE OUT AGAINST THE WORLD.		486	SEVEN SAGES	V	14
HARRIED, AND BURKE'S GREAT MELODY AGAINST IT.		487	SEVEN SAGES		16
THE AVENGING LEAF THOSE FIELDS RAISED UP AGAINST IT. . .		487	SEVEN SAGES		20
NOW I AM IN THE TAVERN AND LEAN AGAINST THE WALL, . . .		593	PILGRIM	V	21
THOU'RT WELCOME. LIE THERE CLOSE AGAINST MY FINGERS. . .		700	MOSADA 3		44
AND MORE, IF YOU WILL WAR AGAINST THE DANES		756	SHADOW WATER A	V	190
AGAINST MY FACE AND EYES. MINE TOO ARE BEATEN.		759	SHADOW WATER A	V	233
AGAINST WITCHCRAFT		775	AGAINST WITCH	V	T
AGAMEMNON					
AND AGAMEMNON DEAD. BEING SO CAUGHT UP, ...		441	LEDA AND SWAN		11
AGATE					
OR MAYBE AN AGATE CUP.		781	MY HEART BEAT		16
AGE SEE MIDDLE-AGE					
AND FLOWING STRENGTH, WITH AGE IS SUBTLE-SOULED. . . .		35	OISIN 2	V	83
AND THEY HAVE FALLEN OR FLED, AGE AFTER AGE.		45	OISIN 2		242
AND THEY HAVE FALLEN OR FLED, AGE AFTER AGE.		45	OISIN 2		242
"AGE AFTER AGE I FEEL MY SOUL DECAY		45	OISIN 2	V	235
"AGE AFTER AGE I FEEL MY SOUL DECAY		45	OISIN 2	V	235
CAME TO MY TOWER AS AGE DRAGGED AFTER AGE		45	OISIN 2	V	242
CAME TO MY TOWER AS AGE DRAGGED AFTER AGE		45	OISIN 2	V	242
. . . I MURMURED, "IN OLD AGE THEY CEASED":		59	OISIN 3		177
. . . AND ITS GODLESS AND PASSIONATE AGE.		63	OISIN 3		216
AH ME: TO BE SHAKEN WITH COUGHING AND BROKEN WITH OLD AGE AND PAIN.		63	OISIN 3		217
. . . AND THE GODLESS FIRES OF THINE AGE.		63	OISIN 3	V	216
"HE BRINGS THE PEACEFUL AGE OF GOLD"—		82	MAD KING GOLL	V	11
"THIS YOUNG MAN BRINGS THE AGE OF GOLD."		82	MAD KING GOLL	V	11
FOR IN THE WORLD'S FIRST BLOSSOMING AGE		138	TO IRELAND	V	10
THE OLD AGE OF QUEEN MAEVE		180	QUEEN MAEVE		T
THOUGH NOW IN HER OLD AGE, IN HER YOUNG AGE		180	QUEEN MAEVE		18
THOUGH NOW IN HER OLD AGE, IN HER YOUNG AGE		180	QUEEN MAEVE		18
OF THOSE THAT, IT MAY BE, CAN NEVER AGE.		183	QUEEN MAEVE		76
IT MIGHT CALL UP A NEW AGE, CALLING TO MIND		201	OLD MEMORY		4
WHERE OLD AGE CANNOT FIND THEM: PAIRC-NA-LEE, ...		217	WOODS OF COOLE		7
THAT IS NOT NATURAL IN AN AGE LIKE THIS, ...		257	NO SECOND TROY		9
THAT COULD SHOW WHAT HOMER'S AGE		258	PEACE		2
YOUTH AND AGE		261	COMING WISDOM	V	T
MOST COURTEOUS TO SLOW AGE AND HASTY YOUTH, ...		339	SHEP GOATHERD		19
WHEN AGE MIGHT WELL HAVE CHILLED HIS BLOOD."		356	BROKEN DREAMS		19
DECREPIT AGE THAT HAS BEEN TIED TO ME		409	TOWER		3
DECREPIT AGE THAT HAS BEEN TIED UPON ME		409	TOWER	V	3
AS I DO NOW AGAINST OLD AGE?		413	TOWER		100
AND BUILDINGS THAT A HAUGHTIER AGE DESIGNED, ...		418	ANCEST HOUSES		34
YOUTH AND AGE		434	YOUTH AND AGE		T
AND WONDER IF SHE STOOD SO AT THAT AGE—		444	SCHOOL CHILDR		19
THAT IS TO AGE WHAT MILK IS TO A CHILD?		469	HARUN RASHID		174
QUARREL IN OLD AGE		503	QUARREL IN AGE		T
THAT HAD FORGIVEN OLD AGE.		504	QUARREL IN AGE		8
HIDDEN BY OLD AGE AWHILE		539	MEETING		1
AN AGE IS THE REVERSAL OF AN AGE:		541	PARN FUNERAL 1		16
AN AGE IS THE REVERSAL OF AN AGE:		541	PARN FUNERAL 1		16
A PRAYER FOR OLD AGE		553	PRAYER OLD AGE		T
OLD AGE		553	PRAYER OLD AGE	V	T
MATTER FOR OLD AGE MEET:		553	CHURCH STATE		2
SHOULD DANCE ATTENTION UPON MY OLD AGE:		591	SPUR		2
SHOULD DANCE ATTENDANCE UPON MY OLD AGE:		591	SPUR	V	2
BECAUSE THIS AGE AND THE NEXT AGE		598	STONE CROSS		9
BECAUSE THIS AGE AND THE NEXT AGE		598	STONE CROSS		9
COULD CRAZY JANE PUT OFF OLD AGE		606	SONGS BURDEN 1		19
THAT THE ADVENTURE OF OLD AGE BEGINS.		609	IN TARAS HALLS		5
BANISH AGE AND CARE, ...		620	JOHN KINSELLA		20

		PAGE	TITLE	LINE

AGE   (CONTINUED)
```
WINTER AND SUMMER TILL OLD AGE BEGAN . . . . .        629 CIRCUS ANIMALS       5
THOU WILT NOT SPEAK, AND I WITH AGE AM NEAR   . . . .  684 SEEKER              62
WHO, DREAMING TO A WONDROUS AGE, LIVED ON, . . . . .  692 MOSADA 1            52
OF MIDDLE AGE. "HIS SISTER HERE AND MOTHER." . . . .  711 FERENCZ RENYI       53
OWLS THERE BE WHOM AGE MAKES NUMB; . . . . . . .      727 LOVERS QUARREL      35
PEACE OF YOUTH AND PEACE OF AGE, . . . . . . . .      733 STREET DANCERS      46
```
AGED
```
THE WARRIOR DREAMS IN AN AGED LEISURE  . . . . . .     26 OISIN 1         V  401
SHE LIMPS ALONG IN AN AGED WHITENESS; . . . . . .      27 OISIN 1            415
SHE LIMPS ALONG IN AN AGED WHITENESS. . . . . . .      28 OISIN 1         V  423
AGED AND WISE, THEY SEEK THEIR WONTED PERCHES . . .    72 ANASHU VIJAYA      31
FOR LEADING AGED HOUNDS AND YOUNG . . . . . . .        98 FOXHUNTER          23
AND NOW WITH AGED HOUNDS AND YOUNG . . . . . .         98 FOXHUNTER       V   21
AGED HOUNDS AND YOUNG. . . . . . . . . . . .           99 FOXHUNTER          40
BOTH AGED HOUNDS AND YOUNG. . . . . . . . . .          99 FOXHUNTER       V   40
MY FATHER STANDS." "AGED, WORN OUT WITH WARS . . . .  107 CUCHULAIN SEA      29
AND THEREUPON WITH AGED, HIGH-PITCHED VOICE . . . .   375 PHASES OF MOON     84
AN AGED MAN IS BUT A PALTRY THING, . . . . . .        407 SAIL BYZANTIUM      9
CEASE TO REMEMBER THE DELIGHTS OF YOUTH, TRAVEL-WEARIED  459 FROM OEDIPUS      2
   AGED MAN;
UPON AN AGED WOMAN AND HER HOUSE, . . . . . . .       488 COOLE PARK 29       2
STRAIGHTEN AGED KNEES, . . . . . . . . . . .          505 RESULT THOUGHT     16
INFIRM AND AGED I MIGHT STAY  . . . . . . . .         605 YOU CONTENT        17
```
AGEING
```
SUFFICE THE AGEING MAN AS ONCE THE GROWING BOY. . . .  427 PHANTOM HATRED    40
TILL IT DIP AN AGEING WING . . . . . . . . . .        777 SONG DEIRDRE 2      3
```
AGELESS
```
THE AGELESS SENTINELS WHO HOLD THEIR WATCH . . . .    664 ISLE STAT II 2     45
AS THE AGELESS BIRDS OF AENGUS, OR THE BIRDS . . . .  761 SHADOW WATER A    260
```
AGE'S
```
BY AGE'S WEARINESS ARE SLAIN, . . . . . . . . .        27 OISIN 1        V 415A
```
AGES   SEE MIDDLE-AGES
```
THE FOUR AGES OF MAN  . . . . . . . . . . .           561 FOUR AGES MAN       T
DREAMER OF THE MIDDLE AGES, EMPTY EYEBALLS KNEW . . .  610 STATUES           20
AND WHEN THOU HAST THESE THINGS FOR MANY AGES FELT, . 674 ISLE STAT II 3    214
AND WHEN THOU HAST THESE THINGS FOR AGES FELT, . . .  674 ISLE STAT II 3 V  214
SHE IS LONG AGES DUST.  AH, WOE IS ME! . . . .        679 ISLE STAT II 3    313
```
AGHAST
```
BACK THE SHADOWS CREEP AGHAST—  . . . . . . . .       648 ISLE STAT I 1      98
```
AGILE
```
THE STRONG THIGH AND THE AGILE THIGH WERE MET, . . .  278 TWO KINGS         28
```
AGIN
```
AND FETCH ME HOME AGIN; . . . . . . . . . . .          96 MOLL MAGEE        42
```
AGITATION
```
. . . HAVE JOINED THE AGITATION AGAINST IMMORAL LITERATURE  262 STUDENTS AGIT   T
. . . AGITATION AGAINST IMMORAL LITERATURE . . . . .  262 STUDENTS AGIT  V   T
UPON A HOUSE SHAKEN BY THE LAND AGITATION . . . . .   264 HOUSE SHAKEN       T
```
AGLEAM
```
OUR BREASTS ARE HEAVING, OUR EYES ARE AGLEAM, . . . . 140 HOSTING SIDHE      8
```
A-GLEAM
```
FOR BREASTS ARE HEAVING AND EYES A-GLEAM; . . . . .   140 HOSTING SIDHE  V   7
OUR BREASTS ARE HEAVING, OUR EYES ARE A-GLEAM, . . .  140 HOSTING SIDHE  V   8
```
A-GLITTER
```
BEFORE THE WIND.  SAW YOU HIS EYES A-GLITTER? . . . . 683 SEEKER            35
```
AGO
```
LOOSED LONG AGO FROM HEAVEN'S GATE. . . . . . .        24 OISIN 1          362
FROM MACE AND SWORD AND POLE-AXE, LONG AGO . . . . .   31 OISIN 2           30
"HE DIED AN HOUR AGO." . . . . . . . . . . .          133 FR GILLIGAN       34
A THOUSAND YEARS AGO YOU HELD HIGH TALK . . . . .     187 QUEEN MAEVE      150
AWOKE THE HARP-STRINGS LONG AGO. . . . . . . .        190 BAILE AILLINN     37
AWOKE THE HARP STRINGS LONG AGO. . . . . . . .        190 BAILE AILLINN  V  37
BUT THE GODS LONG AGO DECREED  . . . . . . . .        194 BAILE AILLINN    119
THE QUEENS THAT WERE IMAGINED LONG AGO, . . . . .     201 OLD MEMORY         5
I KNOW THAT HE DIED A THOUSAND YEARS AGO, . . . .     241 SHADOW WATER B   392
AND THAT HE DIED A THOUSAND YEARS AGO. . . . . .      242 SHADOW WATER B   417
THAT YOU WERE BORN A THOUSAND YEARS AGO, . . . . .    245 SHADOW WATER B   468
I HAD THIS THOUGHT A WHILE AGO, . . . . . . . .       255 WORDS              1
I HAD THIS THOUGHT AWHILE AGO, . . . . . . . .        255 WORDS          V   1
WE'LL OUT, FOR THE WORLD LIVES AS LONG AGO; . . . .   257 RECONCILIATION     8
IN MOMENTARY ANGER LONG AGO; . . . . . . . . .        258 KING NO KING      10
HE HAD COUNTED, WHERE LONG YEARS AGO . . . . . .      302 HOUR DAWN          7
HE COUNTED, WHERE LONG YEARS AGO  . . . . . . .       302 HOUR DAWN      V   7
WITH THE HOT BLOOD OF YOUTH, OF LOVE CROSSED LONG AGO; . . 316 COLD HEAVEN    6
WHEN LONG AGO I SAW HER RIDE . . . . . . . . .        397 POLIT PRISONER    13
I THOUGHT IT ALL OUT TWENTY YEARS AGO; . . . . .      411 TOWER             64
WE, WHO SEVEN YEARS AGO . . . . . . . . . . .         431 NINETEEN 19       89
FIVE HUNDRED YEARS AGO, ABOUT IT LIE . . . . . .      478 SELF AND SOUL     26
THINGS SAID OR DONE LONG YEARS AGO, . . . . . .       501 VACILLATION       51
HOW MANY YEARS AGO . . . . . . . . . . . . .          524 MAD AS MIST       10
A YEAR AGO FOR THE FIRST TIME . . . . . . . .         570 THREE BUSHES      38
I MET HER ALL BUT FIFTY YEARS AGO . . . . . . .       602 GALLERY REVIS     15
IF HE DIED LONG AGO . . . . . . . . . . . .           635 BLACK TOWER       15
LONG YEARS AGO, A CHURCH STANDS NEAR, . . . . .       640 BEN BULBEN        87
LONG YEARS AGO, AND UNTO STONE CONGEALED. . . . .     656 ISLE STAT I 3     28
HE WILL BE TALLER NOW—'TWAS LONG AGO. . . . . .       699 MOSADA 3          15
BELOVED, HOW TWO LITTLE YEARS AGO . . . . . . .       713 FERENCZ RENYI     89
GOD PLANTED HIM LONG AGO. . . . . . . . . . .         743 WISDOM DREAMS      8
I HAD KILLED HIM LONG AGO, BUT THAT THE FOOL . . . .  748 SHADOW WATER A    17
HE HAS HEARD ME AND NOT YOU.  NINE DAYS AGO . . . .   752 SHADOW WATER A   113
IT PASSED BUT A MOMENT AGO. . . . . . . . . .         781 MY HEART BEAT      3
```

10

```
                                                      PAGE    TITLE            LINE
AGO    (CONTINUED)
   IT PASSED BY A MOMENT AGO. . . . . . . . . . . .   781 MY HEART BEAT   V    3
AGONY
   MY HEART'S AGONY . . . . . . . . . . . . . . . .   452 HUMAN DIGNITY       10
   AN AGONY OF TRANCE, . . . . . . . . . . . . . .    498 BYZANTIUM           31
   AN AGONY OF FLAME THAT CANNOT SINGE A SLEEVE. . .   498 BYZANTIUM           32
AGREE
   BUT I, BEING YOUNG AND FOOLISH, WITH HER WOULD NOT AGREE.   90 SALLEY GARDENS   4
AGREED
   AGREED THEIR CLOTHES TO SWOP, . . . . . . . . .    595 COLONEL MARTIN      20
A-HAWKING
   GOES HIS POPPIES NOW A-HAWKING: . . . . . . . .    705 DAWN-SONG            4
AHEAD
   HE RAN ON AHEAD, . . . . . . . . . . . . . . .     595 COLONEL MARTIN      42
AHERNE
   AHERNE LAUGHED, THINKING OF THE MAN WITHIN, . .    375 PHASES OF MOON      85
   OWEN AHERNE AND HIS DANCERS . . . . . . . . . .    449 OWEN AHERNE          T
AI
   HE SAID, "HIGH QUEEN OF CRUACHAN AND MAGH AI, . .  183 QUEEN MAEVE         77
AIBHLIN
   A FRUITFUL LAND UNDER THE AIBHLIN HILLS? . . . .   748 SHADOW WATER A V    33
AIBRIC
   I'VE THOUGHT OF THAT. WE MUST HAVE AIBRIC WITH US, .  225 SHADOW WATER B   62
   BECOME OUR CAPTAIN, AIBRIC. I AM RESOLVED . . . .  225 SHADOW WATER B      64
   BE OF YOUR TROOP! AIBRIC BE ONE OF YOU . . . . .   225 SHADOW WATER B      75
   THAT NEVER DID A HAND'S TURN? AIBRIC! AIBRIC! . .  228 SHADOW WATER B     130
   THAT NEVER DID A HAND'S TURN? AIBRIC! AIBRIC! . .  228 SHADOW WATER B     130
   FOR EVERYTHING IS GONE. COME HITHER, AIBRIC, . .   241 SHADOW WATER B     402
   AND YOU, MY AIBRIC, WHO HAVE BEEN A KING . . . .   748 SHADOW WATER A      27
   DO YOU REMEMBER, AIBRIC, HOW YOU BORE . . . . .    749 SHADOW WATER A      48
   I HAVE GOOD PILOTS, AIBRIC. WHEN MEN DIE . . . .   750 SHADOW WATER A      81
   GIVE HER TO AIBRIC, IF HE WILL. I WAIT . . . .     755 SHADOW WATER A     172
   AND I SHALL LAUGH WITH JOY. COME HITHER, AIBRIC, . 760 SHADOW WATER A     249
   AND WE GO HOME. COME, AIBRIC! END YOUR TALE . .    766 SHADOW WATER A     374
   SEEK AIBRIC ON THE LOCHLANN GALLEY, AND TELL HIM . 767 SHADOW WATER A     401
   LIVING OR DYING. BID AIBRIC TO YOUR COUNTRY, . .   768 SHADOW WATER A     413
AIBRIC'S
   I THINK THAT THERE IS LOVE IN AIBRIC'S EYES. . .   768 SHADOW WATER A     407
AID
   THUS BECKON TO OUR AID A PHANTOM FAIR . . . . .    693 MOSADA 1            76
AILED
   AND WONDER WHAT HAS AILED HIM THESE TWELVE MONTHS." . 284 TWO KINGS       163
   SOME KNEW WHAT AILED THE WORLD . . . . . . . .     627 STATES HOLIDAY       9
AILELL
   SHE SAW HER HUSBAND AILELL SLEEPING THERE, . . .   183 QUEEN MAEVE         69
   SUDDENLY AILELL SPOKE OUT OF HIS SLEEP, . . . .    183 QUEEN MAEVE         73
AILING
   AND MADE--BEING POOR, AILING AND IGNORANT, . . .   370 EGO DOMINUS         59
AILLINN
   BAILE AND AILLINN . . . . . . . . . . . . . .      188 BAILE AILLINN        T
   AILLINN, WHO WAS KING LUGAIDH'S HEIR. . . . . .    189 BAILE AILLINN        7
   BAILE AND AILLINN WOULD BE WED. . . . . . . . .    190 BAILE AILLINN       24
   TO TELL HIM HOW THE GIRL AILLINN . . . . . . .     191 BAILE AILLINN       49
   WHERE AILLINN RODE WITH WAITING-MAIDS, . . . . .   193 BAILE AILLINN      102
   WHERE AILLINN RODE WITH WAITING MAIDS . . . . .    193 BAILE AILLINN V    102
   RIBH AT THE TOMB OF BAILE AND AILLINN . . . . .    554 RIBH AT TOMB         T
   OF BAILE AND AILLINN YOU NEED NOT SPEAK, . . . .   555 RIBH AT TOMB         6
AILLINN'S
   BAILE AND AILLINN'S MARRIAGE-BED, . . . . . . .    194 BAILE AILLINN      121
   BAILE AND AILLINN'S MARRIAGE BED, . . . . . . .    194 BAILE AILLINN V    121
AILS
   OUT OF MY HEART. THERE'S SOMETHING AILS OUR COLT . 260 FASC DIFFICULT       4
   FOR HURTS AND AILS AND LOVER'S MOAN-- . . . . .    717 FAIRY DOCTOR        18
AIMED
   AIMED AT THE COMMONEST EAR. . . . . . . . . . .    347 FISHERMAN           20
   ALL MEN HAVE AIMED AT, FOUND AND LOST: . . . . .   566 LAPIS LAZULI        18
AIMLESS
   AN AIMLESS JOY IS A PURE JOY," . . . . . . . . .   338 TOM OROUGHLEY        4
   IN AIMLESS ARGUMENT: . . . . . . . . . . . . .     392 EASTER 1916   V     18
   FOR AIMLESS JOY HAD MADE ME STOP . . . . . . .     400 DEMON BEAST         22
   AND AIMLESS WANDERINGS THE WOODLANDS LONE, . . .   674 ISLE STAT II 3     209
AIMLESSNESS
   MY DAYS OUT OF THEIR AIMLESSNESS. . . . . . . .    421 MY TABLE             5
AIR
   BUT THE TALE, THOUGH WORDS BE LIGHTER THAN AIR, .    3 OISIN 1             11
   CLOSED IN THE MISTY AIR PROFOUND. . . . . . . .     10 OISIN 1       V  114D
   AND HOUNDS FOR CENTURIES DUST AND AIR. . . . . .    11 OISIN 1            131
   OR HAVE THEY BREATHED THE MORTAL AIR?" . . . . .    12 OISIN 1            147
   OF DANCERS LEAPING IN THE AIR: . . . . . . . .      18 OISIN 1            254
   LIKE TULIPS IN THE AIR A-WINGING, . . . . . . .     27 OISIN 1            417
   FANNED THE DELIGHTED AIR LIKE WINGS OF BIRDS: . .    32 OISIN 2            50
   AND WHEN THE DEW-DROWNED STARS HANG IN THE AIR . .   32 OISIN 2            54
   THAT FAN THE PULSES OF DELIGHTED AIR, . . . . .     32 OISIN 2       V    50A
   MAKING A WORLD ABOUT HER IN THE AIR, . . . . .      37 OISIN 2           122
   AND THICKENED ALL THE WHIRLING AIR. THEN DID . .     46 OISIN 2       V  245A
   CAME NOW THE SLIDING OF TEARS AND SWEEPING OF MIST-COLD
      AIR.                                             47 OISIN 3       V     7
   . . . FROM HIS MILES IN THE MIDST OF THE AIR, . .   54 OISIN 3            103
   . . . WITH ITS BELFRY IN AIR: . . . . . . . . .     61 OISIN 3            193
   THE WILD FOWL OF THE AIR INCREASED: . . . . . .     82 MAD KING GOLL        8
   AND SHEDS FAINT ODOURS THROUGH THE AIR: . . . .     85 MAD KING GOLL       64
```

11

AIR (CONTINUED)

PAGE TITLE LINE

AND SHEDS FAINT ODOUR THROUGH THE AIR; . . . . 85 MAD KING GOLL V 64
TO THE BIRDS IN THE WHITE OF THE AIR. . . . . 92 FATHER OHART 16
OVER THE DOOR-STEP INTO THE AIR, ... 97 FOXHUNTER V 3
ABOVE THE TIDE OF HOURS, TROUBLE THE AIR, ... 114 ROSE OF BATTLE 3
A SONG INTO THE AIR, AND SINGING PASSED . . . . 114 ROSE OF BATTLE 14
ABOVE THE TIDE OF HOURS, RISE ON THE AIR. . . . . . . 114 ROSE OF BATTLE V 3
A SONG INTO THE AIR, AND SINGING PAST . . . . 114 ROSE OF BATTLE V 14
THE HOST OF THE AIR . . . . 143 HOST OF AIR T
THE FOLK OF THE AIR . . . . 143 HOST OF AIR V T
FOR THESE WERE THE HOST OF THE AIR; . . . . 144 HOST OF AIR 26
FOR THESE WERE THE FOLK OF THE AIR; . . . . 144 HOST OF AIR V 26
BUT HE HEARD HIGH UP IN THE AIR . . . . 145 HOST OF AIR 41
HE KNEW NOW THE FOLK OF THE AIR, ... 145 HOST OF AIR V 40A
AND FADED THROUGH THE BRIGHTENING AIR. . . . . 150 WANDER AENGUS 16
O CURLEW, CRY NO MORE IN THE AIR, ... 155 REPROVE CURLEW 1
AND WAVED IT OFF ON THE AIR. . . . . 160 CAP AND BELLS 20
TILL STARS GREW OUT OF THE AIR. . . . . 160 CAP AND BELLS 28
AND WAVED IT OUT ON THE AIR. . . . . 160 CAP AND BELLS V 20
THE STARS GREW OUT OF THE AIR. . . . . 160 CAP AND BELLS V 28
WITH WORDS LIGHTER THAN AIR, ... 162 ASKS FORGIVE 2
I MADE IT OUT OF A MOUTHFUL OF AIR, ... 166 EVIL OF BELOV 5
AND SMOKE FROM THIS DEAD HEART DRIFTS THROUGH THE VIOLET 173 SPEAKS HEARERS 3
    AIR
O BEAST OF THE WILDERNESS, BIRD OF THE AIR, ... 177 PAST GREATNESS 11
ALTHOUGH THE RUSHES AND THE FOWL OF THE AIR . . . . . 177 PAST GREATNESS V 11
WAS THAT, THE AIR BEING HEAVY AND THE DOGS . . . . . . 182 QUEEN MAEVE 53
WITH LONG WHITE BODIES CAME OUT OF THE AIR . . . . . . 185 QUEEN MAEVE 118
UNTIL TWO LOVERS CAME OUT OF THE AIR . . . . 187 QUEEN MAEVE 143
BUT OUT OF THE DARK AIR OVER HER HEAD THERE CAME . . . 187 QUEEN MAEVE 153
IN OLD TIMES AMONG THE CLOUDS OF THE AIR. . . . . . . 194 BAILE AILLINN 133
AWAKEN WANDERINGS OF LIGHT AIR . . . . 197 BAILE AILLINN 185
FOR THE WET WINDS ARE BLOWING OUT OF THE CLINGING AIR; 207 HANRAHANS SONG 12
WHEN THE RAIN IS PELTING OUT OF THE WINTRY AIR; . . . 207 HANRAHANS SONG V 12
THEIR SUDDEN FRAGRANCES ON THE GREEN AIR; . . . . . . 217 WOODS OF COOLE 10
TO THE OTHER SIDE, AND HIGHER IN THE AIR. . . . . . . 234 SHADOW WATER B 259
I HAVE FLED TO MY BELOVED IN THE AIR, ... 234 SHADOW WATER B 262
IN THE WASTE OF THE HIGH AIR, THAT WE MAY WANDER . . . 234 SHADOW WATER B 263
BEING TOO BUSY IN THE AIR AND THE HIGH AIR. . . . . . 234 SHADOW WATER B 274
BEING TOO BUSY IN THE AIR AND THE HIGH AIR, ... 234 SHADOW WATER B 274
HE HAS FLUNG A DRUID SPELL UPON THE AIR, ... 240 SHADOW WATER B 385
THEY HAVE BEEN CIRCLING OVER OUR HEADS IN THE AIR, . . 247 SHADOW WATER B 525
DID NOT THE POET CARRY HIM WITH AN AIR . . . . 267 ALL TEMPT ME V 7
"WHO IS THE FRIEND THAT SEEMS BUT AIR . . . . 274 GREY ROCK 83
AMID THE ELABORATE WILDERNESS OF THE AIR. . . . . . . 278 TWO KINGS 31
AND CLIMBED INTO THE AIR, CRUMBLING AWAY. . . . . . . 278 TWO KINGS 42
I WAS YOUR HUSBAND WHEN YOU RODE THE AIR, ... 284 TWO KINGS 166
OUR SUDDEN PALACES IN THE STILL AIR . . . . 284 TWO KINGS 180
ONCE, WHEN MIDNIGHT SMOTE THE AIR, ... 294 HATED PLAYBOY 1
THREE OLD HERMITS TOOK THE AIR . . . . 298 THREE HERMITS 1
AND FIND MY HEALTH AGAIN IN THE SEA AIR?" . . . . . . 299 BEGGAR CRIED 2
THREW UP IN THE AIR HIS MARVELLOUS MOON. . . . . . . 314 MEMORY YOUTH V 21
A CLEAR ARTICULATION IN THE AIR, ... 320 REED WHISPERER 3
COMPANIONABLE STREAMS OR CLIMB THE AIR; . . . . 323 SWANS AT COOLE 21
"CALL DOWN THE HAWK FROM THE AIR; . . . . 349 HAWK 1
IN RAMBLING TALK WITH AN IMAGE OF AIR; . . . . 357 BROKEN DREAMS 40
SEA-BORNE, OR BALANCED ON THE AIR . . . . 397 POLIT PRISONER 19
A BIT OF BREAD THROWN UP INTO THE AIR; . . . . 400 DEMON BEAST 25
IT SEEMED THAT A DRAGON OF AIR . . . . 430 NINETEEN 19 51
SO MASTERED BY THE BRUTE BLOOD OF THE AIR. . . . . . 441 LEDA AND SWAN 12
BY HER DISTRACTED AIR . . . . 453 DEATH OF HARE 8
ONE AMONG THE BIRDS OF THE AIR. . . . . 460 THREE MONUMENT 3
AS AIR UNDER A WING, CAN GIVE BIRDS' WIT. . . . . . . 462 HARUN RASHID 28
AS AIR UNDER A WING, CAN GIVE BIRD'S WIT. . . . . . . 462 HARUN RASHID V 28
UPON THE BREATHLESS STARLIT AIR; . . . . 477 SELF AND SOUL 4
SYMBOLICAL GLORY OF THE EARTH AND AIR; . . . . 483 VERONIC NAPKIN 3
FOUND CERTAINTY UPON THE DREAMING AIR. . . . . 489 COOLE PARK 29 22
AN EVENING CHILL UPON THE AIR, ... 494 AT ALGECIRAS 14
IN A GREAT TUMULT OF THE AIR, ... 519 HER DREAM 6
BUT ALL THAT RUN IN COUPLES, ON EARTH, IN FLOOD OR AIR, 556 RIBH PATRICK 11
    . . .
BIRD SIGHS FOR THE AIR, ... 574 LOVERS SONG 1
FOR AIR AND EXERCISE; . . . . 575 ACRE OF GRASS 3
FIND IN MIDDLE AIR . . . . 601 THOSE IMAGES 13
THAT AIR IN IMMORTALITY . . . . 637 BEN BULBEN 8
AND THRO' THE ODOROUS AIR LOVE-DREAMS ARE WINGING-- . 645 ISLE STAT I 1 5
OF THIS WIDE VALE, EMBOSOMED IN THE AIR, ... 652 ISLE STAT I 2 19
OUT OF THE AIR. AND WHEN? WHEN THE SUN GOES DOWN . . 652 ISLE STAT I 2 29
THE AIR IS STILL ABOVE, AND STILL EACH LEAF, ... 662 ISLE STAT II 2 7
TO DIE FOR HER IN AIR OR GROUND. . . . . 668 ISLE STAT II 3 52
AND THE FLOWING AIR ABOVE. . . . . 680 LOVE AND DEATH 14
TO BUILD THE CIRCLING SEATS, WHERE HIGH IN AIR . . . 699 MOSADA 3 18
IN THE BOSOM OF THE AIR-- . . . . 706 DAWN-SONG 30
HANG THE MIST-THREADS FOR A LITTLE WHILE LIKE COBWEBS IN 719 PHANTOM SHIP 29
    THE AIR,
HANG THE MIST THREADS FOR A LITTLE WHILE LIKE COBWEBS IN 719 PHANTOM SHIP V 29
    THE AIR,
ONE WHOSE BREATHING SHAKES THE AIR, ... 727 LOVERS QUARREL 31
THE SUNLIGHT IN THE AIR. . . . . 736 IN CHURCH 10
AND SHAKE THEIR BIRDS UPON THE AIR; . . . . 736 SUMMER EVENING 3
AND SHAKE THEIR BIRDS UPON THE AIR. . . . . 737 SUMMER EVENING 19

```
                                                      PAGE      TITLE          LINE
AIR   (CONTINUED)
    LEAPED UP INTO THE AIR.                            741  EARL PAUL              36
    UPON CLEAR NIGHTS THEY LEAVE THE UPPER AIR         750  SHADOW WATER A        87
    TO THE OTHER SIDE AND HIGHER IN THE AIR.           753  SHADOW WATER A       149
    IN THE WASTE AIR. I WILL WANDER BY HIS SIDE        754  SHADOW WATER A       152
    HE HAS THROWN A DRUID DREAM UPON THE AIR.          759  SHADOW WATER A       237
    I HAVE HEARD IN THE NIGHT AIR                      783  GREY ROUND             6
    O, WHAT IS LIFE BUT A MOUTHFUL OF AIR?             788  HAWTHORN TREE          9
AIR-BREATH
    FOR THERE CAME AN AIR-BREATH COOL                  667  ISLE STAT II 3        27
AIRMAN
    AN IRISH AIRMAN FORESEES HIS DEATH                 328  IRISH AIRMAN           T
AIRS
    DID NOT THE POET SING IT WITH SUCH AIRS            267  ALL TEMPT ME           7
    THAT AIRS IN IMMORTALITY                           637  BEN BULBEN       V     8
    THAT AIRS AN IMMORTALITY                           637  BEN BULBEN       V     8
AIRY
    WHEN WE ARE HIGH AND AIRY HUNDREDS SAY             265  ABBEY THEATRE          2
    THAT IS AN AIRY SPOT,                              614  MARCH SONGS 2          9
    THAT IS AN AIRY SPOT,                              615  MARCH SONGS 2         19
    THAT IS AN AIRY SPOT,                              615  MARCH SONGS 2         29
    A WANDERING AIRY MUSIC!                            783  GREY ROUND             7
    A WANDERING AIRY MUSIC!                            783  GREY ROUND            17
AKIN
    THAT MAKE THE HEART AKIN TO THE DUMB STONE."       281  TWO KINGS             94
AL    SEE ABD-AL-RABBAN
ALARM
    RAISE THE DOOR-PIN WITH ALARM,                     727  LOVERS QUARREL        52
ALARMED
    WHAT CAN HAVE SUDDENLY ALARMED YOU                 389  IMAGE PAST            16
ALARMS
    WHERE THROUGH LONG WARS AND SUDDEN NIGHT ALARMS    420  MY HOUSE              24
    WHAT WERE ALL THE WORLD'S ALARMS                   522  LULLABY                3
    WHAT ARE ALL THE WORLD'S ALARMS?                   522  LULLABY          V     3
    OF WAR AND WAR'S ALARMS,                           631  POLITICS              10
ALARUMS
    WHERE THROUGH LONG WARS AND SUDDEN NIGHT ALARUMS   420  MY HOUSE         V    24
ALAS
    AND SHAKE THEIR RAGGED WINGS! ALAS!                136  TWO TREES             38
    AND WHEN THEY SHAKE THEIR WINGS--ALAS!             136  TWO TREES        V    38
    ALAS! I MAKE YOU SADDER, SHEPHERDESS.              659  ISLE STAT II 1        18
ALBAN
    AND HARRIED ALBAN TOWNS, AND OVERTHREW             749  SHADOW WATER A        40
ALCIBIADES
    THAT GREAT ROGUE ALCIBIADES.                       379  SAINT HUNCH           12
    BUT MOST TO ALCIBIADES.                            380  SAINT HUNCH           16
ALCOVE'S
    IN THE DEEP ALCOVE'S DIMNESS SMILES AND HIDES."    735  QUATRAIN APHOR        24
ALCOVES
    IN THE DEEP ALCOVES DIMNESS SMILES AND HIDES.      685  DRAWING-ROOM           4
    IN THE DEEP ALCOVES DIMNESS SMILES AND HIDES.      735  QUATRAIN APHOR V      24
ALDER
    TALL WANDS OF ALDER AND WHITE QUICKEN WANDS.       111  CUCHULAIN SEA V      82A
    AN OWL, WHO IN AN ALDER TREE                       670  ISLE STAT II 3       115
    FORTH FROM THE HOLLOW ALDER TRUNK                  670  ISLE STAT II 3       120
ALE
    I HAVE DRUNK ALE FROM THE COUNTRY OF THE YOUNG     177  PAST GREATNESS         1
    SHOOK THE ALE HORNS AND SHIELDS UPON THEIR HOOKS!  181  QUEEN MAEVE      V    38
    AND ALL THE ALE RAN OUT AT THE NEW MOON.           222  SHADOW WATER B V     11
    THE ALE CUP IS MY FATHER AND MY MOTHER.            222  SHADOW WATER B      11B
    WHEN WE HAVE NEITHER BROWN NOR YELLOW ALE?         240  SHADOW WATER B      387
    I SAW A FLAGON OF BROWN ALE ABOARD HER.            240  SHADOW WATER B      388
    WHO SAID WE HAD A SKIN OF YELLOW ALE?              759  SHADOW WATER A      243
    I SAID THE ALE WAS BROWN. I HAVE FOUND THE ALE,    759  SHADOW WATER A      244
    I SAID THE ALE WAS BROWN. I HAVE FOUND THE ALE,    759  SHADOW WATER A      244
    FORGAEL CAN DIE TO-MORROW. COME TO THE ALE.        759  SHADOW WATER A      246
    COME TO THE ALE! FOR HE CAN DIE TO-MORROW.         760  SHADOW WATER A      247
    ALE SETS THEM QUARRELLING. GIVE ME YOUR SWORDS.    766  SHADOW WATER A      372
    WHEN THE DARK HOUNDS WERE LOOSED. COME TO THE ALE. 766  SHADOW WATER A      379
    IT IS THE BROWN ALE DOES IT. GIVE ME YOUR SWORDS.  766  SHADOW WATER A V    372
    HAVE FOUND IT LIKE THE FROTH UPON THE ALE.         767  SHADOW WATER A      387
    AND TELL ITS STORY OVER THEIR BROWN ALE.           767  SHADOW WATER A      393
ALEEL
    "I AM ALEEL, THE SWINEHERD, WHOM YOU BID           105  CUCHULAIN SEA V      3A
    LOOKING ON HER, ALEEL, THE SWINEHERD, SAID!        106  CUCHULAIN SEA V       9
    ALEEL, THE SWINEHERD, WEPT AND CAST HIM DOWN       106  CUCHULAIN SEA V      14
    ALEEL, HIS COUNTESS! HANRAHAN                      550  SEVERED HEAD          15
ALE-HORNS
    SHOOK THE ALE-HORNS AND SHIELDS UPON THEIR HOOKS!  181  QUEEN MAEVE           38
ALEXANDER
    GREEK ALEXANDER FROM MY FLESH,                     379  SAINT HUNCH           10
ALEXANDER'S
    WHEN ALEXANDER'S EMPIRE PASSED, THEY SLEPT SO SOUND. 442 BLACK CENTAUR        12
    WHEN ALEXANDER'S EMPIRE PAST, THEY SLEPT SO SOUND.   442 BLACK CENTAUR  V     12
ALEXANDRIA'S
    ALEXANDRIA'S WAS A BEACON TOWER, AND BABYLON'S     480  BLOOD AND MOON        13
ALFRED
    IN MEMORY OF ALFRED POLLEXFEN                      360  ALF POLLEXFEN          T
    AND "MR. ALFRED" BE AGAIN                          361  ALF POLLEXFEN         32
    COME ALFRED NOYES AND ALL THE TROUP               582  ROGER CASEMENT V      17
```

```
                                                              PAGE    TITLE            LINE
ALGECIRAS
    AT ALGECIRAS--A MEDITATION UPON DEATH  . . . . . . .      493 AT ALGECIRAS             7
    A MEDITATION WRITTEN DURING SICKNESS AT ALGECIRAS  . . .  493 AT ALGECIRAS        V    7
    IN ALGECIRAS GARDENS, AND THERE REST . . . . . . . . .    494 AT ALGECIRAS        V    5
ALHAMBRA
    OF THE ALHAMBRA BLACK ATHWART HIS DISK1 . . . . . . .     691 MOSADA 1            V   37
ALIEN
    UNDER AN ALIEN EYELID, FOR IT WAS MY CRAFT . . . . . .    284 TWO KINGS           V  156
    AS ALIEN AS A CUCKOO IN A ROBIN'S NEST, . . . . . . .     671 ISLE STAT II 3         138
    ALIEN AS CUCKOO IN A ROBIN'S NEST, . . . . . . . . . .    671 ISLE STAT II 3 V      138
ALIENS
    EARTH'S ALIENS.  WHY SO SORROWFUL? OUR SOULS . . . . .     80 EPHEMERA            V  12A
ALIGHIERI
    DANTE ALIGHIERI, SO UTTERLY FOUND HIMSELF . . . . . .     368 EGO DOMINUS            19
ALIGHT
    AND ALIGHT AT THE COMELY TREES AND THE LAWN, . . . . .    330 BONE OF A HARE          4
    NOR A CAGE, NOR ALIGHT UPON WRIST, . . . . . . . . .      349 HAWK                    8
    ITS OPEN LIGHTED DOORWAY AND ITS WINDOWS ALL ALIGHT, . .  581 CURSE CROMWELL         26
ALIGHTED
    ALIGHTED ON THE WINDY GRASS. . . . . . . . . . . . .      195 BAILE AILLINN         138
ALIKE
    MUST WE PART, VON HUEGEL, THOUGH MUCH ALIKE, FOR WE . . . 503 VACILLATION            78
ALIT
    DOWN TO HER CELL AND THERE ALIT, . . . . . . . . . .      397 POLIT PRISONER          4
    THE HEAVENS ALL STAR-THROBBING ARE ALIT. . . . . . .     671 ISLE STAT II 3 V      143
A-LIT
    THE HEAVENS ALL STAR-THROBBING ARE A-LIT. . . . . . .     671 ISLE STAT II 3        143
ALIVE
    HAVE FACES ALIVE WITH SUCH BEAUTY BEEN KNOWN TO THE SALT   50 OISIN 3                51
      EYE OF MAN,
    ARE FACES ALIVE WITH SUCH BEAUTY MADE KNOWN TO THE SALT    50 OISIN 3            V   51
      EYE OF MAN,
    ARE FACES ALIVE WITH SUCH BEAUTY MADE KNOWN TO THE SOFT    50 OISIN 3            V   51
      EYE OF MAN,
    FOR THERE MOVES ALIVE IN YOUR FINGERS . . . . . . . .      55 OISIN 3               124
    FOR MOVETH ALIVE IN THY FINGERS THE FLUTTERING SADNESS     55 OISIN 3            V  124
      OF EARTH.
    "NO MAN ALIVE, NO MAN AMONG THE DEAD, . . . . . . . .     106 CUCHULAIN SEA          10
    "NOT ANY GOD ALIVE NOR MORTAL DEAD, . . . . . . . . .     106 CUCHULAIN SEA  V       10
    LIKE THEM THAT ARE NO MORE ALIVE. . . . . . . . . . .     197 BAILE AILLINN         207
    OF THOSE THAT ARE ALIVE FOR EVER AND EVER. . . . . . .    223 SHADOW WATER B         35
    WHERE NO SHIP SAILS, WHERE NOTHING THAT'S ALIVE . . . .   226 SHADOW WATER B         98
    HAD DROWNED ME ALSO.  BUT, BEING YET ALIVE, . . . . .     235 SHADOW WATER B        289
    FOR NONE ALIVE TO-DAY . . . . . . . . . . . . . . .       458 SECRETS OF OLD         10
    FOR NONE ALIVE TODAY . . . . . . . . . . . . . . . .      458 SECRETS OF OLD V       10
    WHEN MY BODY WAS ALIVE . . . . . . . . . . . . . . .      521 THREE THINGS           10
    TO KEEP THE SOUL OF MAN ALIVE, . . . . . . . . . . .      620 JOHN KINSELLA          19
    TO SNATCH ALIVE OUT OF THE STREAMS ALL LOVERS . . . . .   765 SHADOW WATER A        347
ALL
    YET WILL I MAKE ALL PLAIN FOR THEE. . . . . . . . . .       2 OISIN 1            V   7B
    THAT YOU THROUGH ALL THAT FOAM SHOULD RUN?" . . . . .       6 OISIN 1                61
    OF ALL THAT WISDOM AND THE FAME . . . . . . . . . . .       7 OISIN 1                66
    AND SET YOUR NAME ALL NAMES ABOVE, . . . . . . . . .        7 OISIN 1                76
    ALL MEN, AND STRONGER OF HIS HANDS, . . . . . . . . .       7 OISIN 1            V   63
    BEFORE THY FEET SHALL KNEEL DOWN ALL . . . . . . . .        7 OISIN 1            V   77
    AND THE FENIANS ALL HAD WEPT WITH ME, . . . . . . . .      10 OISIN 1               113
    ALL PEARLY WHITE, SAVE ONE RED EAR1 . . . . . . . . .      12 OISIN 1               141
    AS THOUGH THEY ALL WERE BEATING TIME, . . . . . . . .      13 OISIN 1               174
    AND SINGING, SINGING ALL TOGETHER1 . . . . . . . . .       15 OISIN 1               203
    THEIR ROBES WERE ALL OF YELLOW SILK . . . . . . . .        15 OISIN 1            V  205
    FROM ALL THEIR LIPS, AND ONCE THEY SANG . . . . . . .      16 OISIN 1               226
    AND MADE IN ALL THEIR DISTANT PARTS, . . . . . . . .       16 OISIN 1               228
    AND ROSE FROM ALL THEIR DISTANT PARTS, . . . . . . .       16 OISIN 1            V  228
    "O SADDEST HARP IN ALL THE WORLD, . . . . . . . . .        17 OISIN 1               245
    "THE SADDEST HARP IN ALL THE WORLD!" . . . . . . . .       17 OISIN 1            V  246
    A FIRWOOD HOUSE, ALL COVERED OVER . . . . . . . . .        17 OISIN 1            V  248
    AROUND A SCEPTRE OF ALL LIGHTS, . . . . . . . . . .        18 OISIN 1            V  254
    TO ALL THINGS CRIED1 "I AM A SLAVE1 . . . . . . . . .      19 OISIN 1            V  280
    BENT ALL OUR SWAYING BODIES DOWN, . . . . . . . . .        20 OISIN 1               297
    AND ALL LISTLESS HOURS FEAR US, . . . . . . . . . .        21 OISIN 1               317
    THAT HIDES US FROM ALL HUMAN SPYING. . . . . . . . .       22 OISIN 1            V 338A
    FOR LOVE THEY FOLLOWED ONE AND ALL1 . . . . . . . . .      23 OISIN 1            V 345G
    THE THINGS THAT MOST OF ALL I HATE1 . . . . . . . . .      24 OISIN 1               359
    TWO THINGS THAT 'FORE ALL ELSE I HATE, . . . . . . .       24 OISIN 1            V  359
    WITH ALL THE ANCIENT SORROW OF MEN"1 . . . . . . . .       25 OISIN 1               381
    FLOATED IN ALL HER SINGING.  HALF ENTRANCED . . . . .      30 OISIN 2            V   19
    THE SADDEST OF ALL MEN." . . . . . . . . . . . . .        33 OISIN 2                68
    HER FACE SEEMED FASHIONED ALL OF MOONLIT VAPOURS, . .      33 OISIN 2            V   70
    JABBER AND SCREAM.  YET HE, FOR ALL HIS BOLD . . . .       34 OISIN 2            V   82
    "FOR ALL MEN FLEE THE DEMONS1 BUT MOVED NOT . . . . .      36 OISIN 2                93
    ROOTED IN FOAM AND CLOUDS, AND CRIED TO ALL . . . .        38 OISIN 2               132
    AND WHEN THE SUN IN ALL HIS FLAGRANT SAFFRON STEPT, . .    41 OISIN 2            V  192
    AND ALL THE EXULTANT LABOURS OF THE STRONG, . . . . .      42 OISIN 2               195
    FOR ALL YOUR CROZIERS, THEY HAVE LEFT THE PATH . . .       42 OISIN 2               200
    ALL IS DONE NOW--I SEE THE RAVENS FLOCK-- . . . . . .      43 OISIN 2            V  212
    THAT ALL BE OVERTHROWN. . . . . . . . . . . . . . .        45 OISIN 2               239
    "BUT TILL THE MOON HAS TAKEN ALL, I WAGE . . . . . .       45 OISIN 2               240
    "WITH ALL IN ALL THE WORLD I BATTLE WAGE. . . . . . .      45 OISIN 2               240
    "WITH ALL IN ALL THE WORLD I BATTLE WAGE. . . . . . .      45 OISIN 2            V  240
    ARE EMPTY OF ALL POWER."  "AND WHICH OF THESE . . . .      46 OISIN 2               248
    AND THICKENED ALL THE WHIRLING AIR.  THEN DID . . . .      46 OISIN 2            V 245A
```

14

		PAGE	TITLE		LINE
ALL	**(CONTINUED)**				
COULD SLEEP ON A COUCH OF RUSHES, AND ALL INWROUGHT AND INLAID,		49	OISIN 3		31
COULD SLEEP ON A BED OF RUSHES, AND ALL INWROUGHT AND INLAID,		49	OISIN 3	V	31
MOVED ROUND ME, OF SEAMEN OR LANDSMEN, ALL WHO ARE WINTER TALES;		53	OISIN 3		86
IN A REVERIE FORGETFUL OF ALL THINGS, OVER THE BUBBLING GROUND.		56	OISIN 3		140
. . . . WHERE ALL IS BARREN AND GREY,		56	OISIN 3		141
IN REVERIE FORGETFUL OF ALL THINGS, OVER THE BUBBLING GROUND.		56	OISIN 3	V	140
MUCH WONDERING TO SEE UPON ALL HANDS, OF WATTLES AND WOODWORK MADE,		58	OISIN 3		162
MUCH WONDERING TO SEE UPON ALL HANDS, OF WATTLES AND WOOD-WORK MADE,		58	OISIN 3	V	162
AND DEMONS, ALL BROKEN IN PIECES, BE TRAMPLED BENEATH THEM IN DEATH.		61	OISIN 3	V	204
ALL EMPTIED OF PURPLE HOURS AS A BEGGAR'S CLOAK IN THE RAIN,		63	OISIN 3		219
OF ALL THE MANY CHANGING THINGS		65	HAPPY SHEPHERD		7
LEST ALL THY TOILING ONLY BREEDS		66	HAPPY SHEPHERD		25
AND DEAD IS ALL THEIR HUMAN TRUTH.		66	HAPPY SHEPHERD		34
THROUGH ALL THE WELL-BELOVED GLADE.		67	HAPPY SHEPHERD	V	46C
CRIED ALL HIS STORY TO THE DEWDROPS GLISTENING.		68	SAD SHEPHERD		14
HE CALLED ALOUD TO ALL THE STARS TO LEND		68	SAD SHEPHERD	V	5
CHANGED ALL HE SANG TO INARTICULATE MOAN		69	SAD SHEPHERD		27
CHANGED ALL HIS WORDS TO INARTICULATE MOAN		69	SAD SHEPHERD	V	27
O LOVELY TO SEE IN ALL MEN'S SIGHT		69	CLOAK BOAT		3
IN ALL MEN'S SIGHT."		69	CLOAK BOAT		5
O SWIFT ON THE SEAS ALL DAY AND NIGHT		70	CLOAK BOAT		8
ALL DAY AND NIGHT."		70	CLOAK BOAT		10
IN ALL MEN'S EARS OF SORROW.		70	CLOAK BOAT		14
SEND PEACE ON ALL THE LANDS AND FLICKERING CORN.—		71	ANASHU VIJAYA		1
WHO IS AMRITA? SORROW OF ALL SORROWS!		71	ANASHU VIJAYA		15
WEARY, WITH ALL HIS POPPIES GATHERED ROUND HIM,		72	ANASHU VIJAYA		25
PAINTING WITH SHADOW ALL THE MARBLE STEPS;		72	ANASHU VIJAYA		30
WITH ALL YOUR WHIRLING HAIR, AND DROP MANY AN AZURE TEAR.		73	ANASHU VIJAYA		46
THEIR FACES ARE ALL WORN, AND IN THEIR EYES		73	ANASHU VIJAYA		48
THE ICICLES THAT FAMISH ALL THE NORTH,		73	ANASHU VIJAYA		50
AND LIONESS, WITH ALL THEIR WHIMPERING CUBS,		73	ANASHU VIJAYA		53
WITH ALL YOUR WHIRLING HAIR, AND DROP THROUGH SPACE AN AZURE TEAR.		73	ANASHU VIJAYA	V	46
WITH ALL YOUR WHIRLING HAIR, AND DROP TEAR UPON AZURE TEAR.		73	ANASHU VIJAYA	V	46
WITH ALL OUR WHIRLING HAIR, AND DROP MANY AN AZURE TEAR.		73	ANASHU VIJAYA	V	46
IN THE TREE ROOTS, AND ALL THE SACRED FLOCKS		75	ANASHU VIJAYA		88
THE MERRY LAMBS AND ALL THE KINE COMPLACENT,		75	ANASHU VIJAYA		86
IN THE TREE ROOTS, AND ALL THY SACRED FLOCKS		75	ANASHU VIJAYA	V	88
ALL DRIPPING ON A GRASSY SLOPE, AND SAW THEM CEASE TO CHASE		76	INDIAN ON GOD		4
FOR I AM IN HIS IMAGE MADE, AND ALL THIS TINKLING TIDE		76	INDIAN ON GOD		11
HE IS A MONSTROUS PEACOCK, AND HE WAVETH ALL THE NIGHT		77	INDIAN ON GOD		19
AND ALL IS OVER SAVE THE MURMUR AND THE SWEETNESS.		77	INDIAN TO LOVE	V	5E
MURMURING HOW FAR AWAY ARE ALL EARTH'S FEVERISH LANDS.		78	INDIAN TO LOVE	V	10
I RULED O'ER ALL MY FAIR DOMINIONS,		82	MAD KING GOLL	V	7
WITH ALL HIS COLOURS JOURNEY-DULL,		82	MAD KING GOLL	V	13
SPLASHED ALL WITH CLAY AND JOURNEY DULL,		82	MAD KING GOLL	V	13
I SAW THIS HARP ALL SONGLESS LIE,		85	MAD KING GOLL	V	55
IN ALL HIS EVENING VAPOURS ROLLED—		86	MAD KING GOLL	V	71
WE FOOT IT ALL THE NIGHT,		87	STOLEN CHILD		16
SLEIVEENS WERE ALL HIS RACE;		92	FATHER OHART		6
ALL LOVED HIM, ONLY THE SHONEEN,		92	FATHER OHART		13
THIS WAY WERE ALL REPROVED		93	FATHER OHART		39
MY MONEY'S ALL USED UP,		96	MOLL MAGEE		38
THE SUN UPON ALL THINGS THAT GROW		98	FOXHUNTER		15
RED ROSE, PROUD ROSE, SAD ROSE OF ALL MY DAYS!		100	ROSE UPON ROOD		1
IN ALL POOR FOOLISH THINGS THAT LIVE A DAY,		101	ROSE UPON ROOD		11
RED ROSE, PROUD ROSE, SAD ROSE OF ALL MY DAYS.		101	ROSE UPON ROOD		24
AND ALL THESE THINGS WERE WONDERFUL AND GREAT!		104	FERGUS DRUID		37
BUT NOW I HAVE GROWN NOTHING, KNOWING ALL.		104	FERGUS DRUID		38
BUT NOW I HAVE GROWN NOTHING, BEING ALL!		104	FERGUS DRUID	V	38
AND RAISING ARMS ALL RADDLED WITH THE DYE,		105	CUCHULAIN SEA		7
AND ALL AROUND THE HARP-STRING TOLD HIS PRAISE,		109	CUCHULAIN SEA		44
"HE BADE ME LET ALL KNOW HE GIVES HIS NAME		109	CUCHULAIN SEA		52
OF ALL THIS HOST SO BOUND FROM CHILDHOOD ON."		109	CUCHULAIN SEA		56
AND ALL AROUND THE HARPSTRING TOLD HIS PRAISE,		109	CUCHULAIN SEA	V	44
AND ALL AROUND THE HARP STRING TOLD HIS PRAISE,		109	CUCHULAIN SEA	V	44
THEN CONCHUBAR, THE SUBTLEST OF ALL MEN,		110	CUCHULAIN SEA		75
AND THEM ARISE, AND RAVING SLAY US ALL.		110	CUCHULAIN SEA		79
FOR THESE RED LIPS, WITH ALL THEIR MOURNFUL PRIDE,		111	ROSE OF WORLD		2
AND ALL FOLK SEEING HIM BOW DOWN,		113	ROSE OF PEACE		9
SAYING ALL THINGS WERE WELL!		113	ROSE OF PEACE		14
ROSE OF ALL ROSES, ROSE OF ALL THE WORLD!		113	ROSE OF BATTLE		1
ROSE OF ALL ROSES, ROSE OF ALL THE WORLD!		113	ROSE OF BATTLE		1
BUT GATHER ALL FOR WHOM NO LOVE HATH MADE		114	ROSE OF BATTLE		12
TO THESE OLD NIGHT SHALL ALL HER MYSTERY TELL!		114	ROSE OF BATTLE		22
ROSE OF ALL ROSES, ROSE OF ALL THE WORLD!		115	ROSE OF BATTLE		25
ROSE OF ALL ROSES, ROSE OF ALL THE WORLD!		115	ROSE OF BATTLE		25
IF ALL WERE TOLD!		116	FAERY SONG		4
IF ALL WERE TOLD.		116	FAERY SONG		16
THERE MIDNIGHT'S ALL A GLIMMER, AND NOON A PURPLE GLOW,		117	ISLE INNISFREE		7
A PITY BEYOND ALL TELLING		119	PITY OF LOVE		1

15

ALL   (CONTINUED)

	PAGE	TITLE		LINE
ALL THREATEN THE HEAD THAT I LOVE.	119	PITY OF LOVE	V	8
THE BRILLIANT MOON AND ALL THE MILKY SKY,	119	SORROW OF LOVE		2
AND ALL THAT FAMOUS HARMONY OF LEAVES.	120	SORROW OF LOVE		3
AND ALL THAT LAMENTATION OF THE LEAVES.	120	SORROW OF LOVE		11
AND ALL THE SORROWS OF HER LABOURING SHIPS,	120	SORROW OF LOVE	V	7
AND ALL THE TROUBLE OF HER LABOURING SHIPS,	120	SORROW OF LOVE	V	7
AND ALL THE BURDEN OF HER MYRIAD YEARS.	120	SORROW OF LOVE	V	8
AND ALL THE TROUBLE OF HER MYRIAD YEARS.	120	SORROW OF LOVE	V	8
ALL THE HEAVY DAYS ARE OVER:	124	CATHLEEN PARA		1
CARRY ALL THAT MOURNFUL BEAUTY	124	CATHLEEN PARA		7
ALL THE HEAVENS BOW DOWN TO HEAVEN,	125	CATHLEEN PARA		15
AND ALL DISHEVELLED WANDERING STARS.	126	GOES FERGUS		12
HIS HEART HUNG ALL UPON A SILKEN DRESS.	126	DREAM OF FAERY		2
HIS MIND RAN ALL ON MONEY CARES AND FEARS,	127	DREAM OF FAERY		14
NOW THAT THE EARTH HAD TAKEN MAN AND ALL:	128	DREAM OF FAERY		40
AND ALL THEIR TROUBLE DIES INTO ITS PEACE:--	128	DREAM OF FAERY	V	35
NOW THAT OLD EARTH HAD TAKEN MAN AND ALL:	128	DREAM OF FAERY	V	40
A DRUID KINDNESS, ON ALL HEARERS FELL.	129	BOOK STORIES		4
AND ALL GREW FRIENDLY FOR A LITTLE WHILE.	129	BOOK STORIES		8
FOR ALL WHO HEARD IT DREAMED A LITTLE WHILE.	129	BOOK STORIES	V	8
AND ALL WHO HEARD GREW FRIENDLY FOR A WHILE.	129	BOOK STORIES	V	8
SPINNING AT ALL TIMES ERI'S GOOD TO-MORROW,	129	BOOK STORIES		10
THE WELL-KNOWN FACES ARE ALL GONE,	132	OLD PENSIONER	V	17
AND ALL THE TREMBLING FLOWERS THEY BEAR.	134	TWO TREES		4
REMEMBERING ALL THAT SHAKEN HAIR	135	TWO TREES		17
FOR ALL THINGS TURN TO BARRENNESS	135	TWO TREES		29
ALL THINGS TURN TO BARRENNESS	135	TWO TREES	V	29
THY TENDER EYES GROW ALL UNKIND:	136	TWO TREES		39
AND THE WHITE HUSH END ALL BUT THE LOUD BEAT	137	TO SOME I TALK		15
AND THE WHITE HUSH END ALL THINGS BUT THE BEAT	137	TO SOME I TALK	V	15
TRAILS ALL ABOUT THE WRITTEN PAGE.	138	TO IRELAND		9
AND TIME BADE ALL HIS CANDLES FLARE	138	TO IRELAND		13
AND ALL BENIGHTED THINGS THAT GO	139	TO IRELAND		39
NO PLACE FOR LOVE AND DREAM AT ALL:	139	TO IRELAND		43
AND ALL THE WIZARD THINGS THAT GO	139	TO IRELAND	V	39
ALL THINGS UNCOMELY AND BROKEN, ALL THINGS WORN OUT AND OLD,	142	ROSE IN HEART		1
ALL THINGS UNCOMELY AND BROKEN, ALL THINGS WORN OUT AND OLD,	142	ROSE IN HEART		1
ALL THINGS UNCOMELY AND BROKEN, ALL THINGS WORN AND OLD,	142	ROSE IN HEART	V	1
ALL THINGS UNCOMELY AND BROKEN, ALL THINGS WORN AND OLD,	142	ROSE IN HEART	V	1
THE EAST TELLS ALL HER SECRET JOY BEFORE DAYBREAK,	154	BELOVED PEACE	V	4
FOR HOURS WHEN ALL MUST FADE LIKE DEW,	156	FORGOT BEAUTY		20
ALL BUT THE FLAMES, AND DEEP ON DEEP,	156	FORGOT BEAUTY	V	21
AND ALL MEN'S HEARTS MUST BURN AND BEAT;	158	BELOVED RHYMES		9
AND TROUBLE WITH A SIGH FOR ALL THINGS LONGING FOR REST	163	ASKS FORGIVE		23
AND TROUBLE WITH SIGHS FOR ALL HEARTS WITHOUT REST	163	ASKS FORGIVE	V	23
TILL ALL THE VALLEYS OF THE WORLD HAVE BEEN WITHERED AWAY.	163	VALLEY LOVERS		8
THE POETS LABOURING ALL THEIR DAYS	164	PERFECT BEAUTY		2
WE POETS LABOUR ALL OUR DAYS,	164	PERFECT BEAUTY	V	2
ALL MANNER OF BLESSED SOULS,	167	BLESSED		14
"WHERE ALL ARE COMELY AND GOOD?	167	BLESSED		22
ALL MANNER OF BLESSEDEST SOULS,	167	BLESSED	V	14
FOR ALL EYES BUT THESE EYES,	173	PLEADS FRIEND		8
BEND DOWN AND PRAY FOR ALL THAT SIN I WOVE IN SONG,	173	SPEAKS HEARERS		5
AND SHE FORGET THE WANDERING AND ALL THE CRIMSON GLOOM	175	ELEMENT POWERS	V	11
AND WEEP BECAUSE I KNOW ALL THINGS NOW:	177	PAST GREATNESS		2
KNOWING ONE, OUT OF ALL THINGS, ALONE, THAT HIS HEAD	177	PAST GREATNESS		8
THEY WILL ALL COME UP TO ME,	179	FIDDLER DOONEY		18
WILL ALL COME UP TO ME,	179	FIDDLER DOONEY	V	18
IN COMFORTABLE SLEEP: ALL LIVING SLEPT	180	QUEEN MAEVE		15
THAT'S ALL BUT GONE: FOR THE PROUD HEART IS GONE,	181	QUEEN MAEVE		20
AND THE FOOL HEART OF THE COUNTING-HOUSE FEARS ALL	181	QUEEN MAEVE		21
HAD TROUBLED HIS SLEEP. BUT ALL HE HAD TO SAY	182	QUEEN MAEVE		52
FOR ALL THEIR BEAUTY'S LIKE A HOLLOW DREAM."	184	QUEEN MAEVE		88
FOR ALL THEIR BEAUTY, LIKE A HOLLOW DREAM?"	184	QUEEN MAEVE	V	89
AND ALL THAT NIGHT, AND ALL THROUGH THE NEXT DAY	185	QUEEN MAEVE		113
AND ALL THAT NIGHT, AND ALL THROUGH THE NEXT DAY	185	QUEEN MAEVE		113
HAVE ALL THAT GREATNESS, AND NOT HERS ALONE,	186	QUEEN MAEVE		133
TO MAEVE AND TO MAEVE'S HOUSEHOLD, OWING ALL	187	QUEEN MAEVE		147
THEN MAEVE: "O AENGUS, MASTER OF ALL LOVERS,	187	QUEEN MAEVE		149
THAT ALL THINGS FELL OUT HAPPILY,	189	BAILE AILLINN		22
AND THERE, FOR ALL THAT FOOLS HAD SAID,	190	BAILE AILLINN		23
WITH ALL THIS CRYING IN THE WIND,	190	BAILE AILLINN		33
YET THEY THAT KNOW ALL THINGS BUT KNOW	190	BAILE AILLINN		38
THAT ALL THIS LIFE CAN GIVE US IS	190	BAILE AILLINN		39
THAT ALL LIFE HAS TO GIVE US IS	190	BAILE AILLINN	V	39
THAT ALL LIFE HAD TO GIVE US IS	190	BAILE AILLINN	V	39
FOR ALL THAT COUNTRY HAD BEEN ASTIR	191	BAILE AILLINN		52
OF THE EBB OF ALL THINGS TO MAKE LOVE	193	BAILE AILLINN	V	109
THEY KNOW ALL WONDERS, FOR THEY PASS	196	BAILE AILLINN		160
ALL THE LOVE STORIES THAT THEY KNEW.	197	BAILE AILLINN		197
FOR ALL HER WANDERINGS OVER-SEA:	197	BAILE AILLINN		203
BECAUSE IT IS ALONE OF ALL THINGS HAPPY.	198	SEVEN WOODS		9
ALL THAT YOU NEED IS PATIENCE." HEART CRIES, "NO,	200	FOLLY COMFORT		6
WHEN ALL THE WILD SUMMER WAS IN HER GAZE."	200	FOLLY COMFORT		12
PATIENCE IS ALL THAT YOU HAVE NEED OF." NO,	200	FOLLY COMFORT	V	6
IT ALL, AND MORE THAN IT ALL, WOULD COME TO NAUGHT,	201	OLD MEMORY		8
IT ALL, AND MORE THAN IT ALL, WOULD COME TO NAUGHT,	201	OLD MEMORY		8
IT ALL, MORE THAN IT ALL, WOULD COME TO NAUGHT,	201	OLD MEMORY	V	8

16

ALL   (CONTINUED)

		PAGE	TITLE		LINE
IT ALL, MORE THAN IT ALL, WOULD COME TO NAUGHT,	. . . .	201	OLD MEMORY	V	8
NEVER GIVE ALL THE HEART	202	NEVER GIVE ALL		T
NEVER GIVE ALL THE HEART, FOR LOVE	202	NEVER GIVE ALL		1
FOR THEY, FOR ALL SMOOTH LIPS CAN SAY, ...	202	NEVER GIVE ALL		9
HE THAT MADE THIS KNOWS ALL THE COST, ...	202	NEVER GIVE ALL		13
FOR HE GAVE ALL HIS HEART AND LOST, ...	202	NEVER GIVE ALL		14
WITH WISDOM, THEY WANDER TILL ALL THE YEARS HAVE GONE BY,	204	WITHER BOUGHS		21
LIKE AN OLD PAUPER, IN ALL KINDS OF WEATHER, ...	205	ADAMS CURSE		9
IS TO WORK HARDER THAN ALL THESE, AND YET	205	ADAMS CURSE		11
THERE'S MANY A ONE SHALL FIND OUT ALL HEARTACHE	205	ADAMS CURSE		16
"THERE IS ONE THING THAT ALL WE WOMEN KNOW	205	ADAMS CURSE	V	18
THAT IT HAD ALL SEEMED HAPPY, AND YET WE'D GROWN	206	ADAMS CURSE		37
AND THROWN THE THUNDER ON THE STONES FOR ALL THAT MAEVE CAN SAY.	207	HANRAHANS SONG		7
BUT WE HAVE ALL BENT LOW AND LOW AND KISSED THE QUIET FEET	207	HANRAHANS SONG		9
"ALL THAT'S BEAUTIFUL DRIFTS AWAY	208	OLD MEN ADMIRE		8
I WILL DRIVE ALL THOSE LOVERS OUT AND CRY--	211	RAGGED WOOD		10
I'LL HOLLO ALL THOSE LOVERS OUT AND CRY--	211	RAGGED WOOD	V	10
ALL THROUGH THE YEARS OF OUR YOUTH	211	O DO NOT LOVE		5
WHEN ALL THIS HEAVY HISTORY'S DONE, ...	213	BLESS PSALTER		17
AT ALL TIMES OF THE YEAR, ...	214	HAPPY TOWNLAND		6
BUT ALL THAT ARE KILLED IN BATTLE	215	HAPPY TOWNLAND		25
I ONLY KNOW THAT ALL WE KNOW COMES FROM YOU, ...	218	WOODS OF COOLE		28
SWEET WITH ALL MUSIC, OUT OF HIS LONG HAIR, ...	219	HARP OF AENGUS		8
I COULD GIVE ALL MY HEART TO THAT RED MOLL	222	SHADOW WATER B		9
AND ALL THE ALE RAN OUT AT THE NEW MOON, ...	222	SHADOW WATER B	V	11
AT THE FULL MOON? HE PLAYED ALL THROUGH THE NIGHT. . . .	223	SHADOW WATER B		21
MY COURAGE CAME AGAIN. BUT THAT'S NOT ALL.	223	SHADOW WATER B		31
TO WHOM ALL LOVERS PRAY. BUT WHAT OF THAT?	224	SHADOW WATER B		43
THE FLAGSTONE UNDER ALL, THE FIRE OF FIRES, ...	227	SHADOW WATER B		103
IF YOU WILL GIVE ME ALL YOUR MIND AWHILE--	227	SHADOW WATER B		117
ALL, ALL, THE VERY BOTTOM OF THE BOWL--	227	SHADOW WATER B		118
ALL, ALL, THE VERY BOTTOM OF THE BOWL--	227	SHADOW WATER B		118
"YOU WILL HAVE ALL YOU HAVE WISHED FOR WHEN YOU HAVE EARNED	228	SHADOW WATER B		124
OR CREAKY SHOES. AND AT THE END OF ALL	228	SHADOW WATER B		128
FOR THAT IS WHAT THEY SAY--ALL, ALL THE SHADOWS-- . . .	228	SHADOW WATER B		137
FOR THAT IS WHAT THEY SAY--ALL, ALL THE SHADOWS-- . . .	228	SHADOW WATER B		137
AND ALL THE OTHERS, BUT IT MUST BE LOVE	228	SHADOW WATER B		139
HAD SEEMED TO BE THE GIVER OF ALL PEACE, ...	228	SHADOW WATER B		149
AND AS SOON FINISHED. ALL THAT EVER LOVED	229	SHADOW WATER B		151
THAT HE HAS BEEN ALL NIGHT UPON THE HILLS, ...	229	SHADOW WATER B		168
THAT SET HIM TO THE FANCY. ALL WOULD BE WELL	230	SHADOW WATER B		177
AND NOW THEY ALL WHEEL SUDDENLY AND FLY.	233	SHADOW WATER B		242
WAKE ALL BELOW! WHY HAVE YOU BROKEN OUR SLEEP? . . .	234	SHADOW WATER B		258
I ASK A FITTING PUNISHMENT FOR ALL	235	SHADOW WATER B		290
THAT WEIGH AND MEASURE ALL IN THESE WASTE SEAS-- . . .	235	SHADOW WATER B		292
THEY THAT HAVE ALL THE WISDOM THAT'S IN LIFE, ...	235	SHADOW WATER B		293
AND ALL THAT PROPHESYING IMAGES	235	SHADOW WATER B		294
BUT ALL THAT'S RAVING. WHO IS THERE CAN COMPEL . . .	237	SHADOW WATER B		333
FOR ALL HIS SPELLS WILL VANISH WHEN HE DIES, ...	240	SHADOW WATER B		376
AND ALL THE BIRDS ARE SCATTERED. O! O! O! O! . . .	241	SHADOW WATER B		395
THROUGH WICKED SPELLS. THAT IS NOT ALL THE TALE, . . .	242	SHADOW WATER B		408
I WILL END ALL YOUR MAGIC ON THE INSTANT.	242	SHADOW WATER B		411
IT WAS IN ALL HIS BATTLES. I WILL SPREAD MY HAIR, . . .	242	SHADOW WATER B		413
WHY ARE THEY ALL A-FLUTTER OF A SUDDEN?	243	SHADOW WATER B		436
AND ALL THAT TOSSING OF YOUR WINGS IS JOY, ...	244	SHADOW WATER B		451
AND ALL THAT MURMURING'S BUT A MARRIAGE-SONG, ...	244	SHADOW WATER B		452
BUT IT WAS ALL DECEIT, AND FLATTERY	244	SHADOW WATER B		457
OUT OF ALL RECKONING. IS IT NOT TRUE	244	SHADOW WATER B		467
AND ALL THAT MURMURING IS BUT A MARRIAGE SONG, . . .	244	SHADOW WATER B	V	452
I WILL CONFESS IT ALL. WHAT DO I CARE, ...	245	SHADOW WATER B		485
AND ALL THAT IS AND ALL THAT IS TO BE, ...	246	SHADOW WATER B		505
AND ALL THAT IS AND ALL THAT IS TO BE, ...	246	SHADOW WATER B		505
ALL THAT IS NOT THE MEETING OF OUR LIPS.	246	SHADOW WATER B		506
LEAPS UPWARD, AS IF ALL THE STREAMS O' THE WORLD . . .	249	SHADOW WATER B		560
WITH ALL THOSE SIGHTS AND ALL THAT CRYING OUT? . . .	249	SHADOW WATER B		573
WITH ALL THOSE SIGHTS AND ALL THAT CRYING OUT? . . .	249	SHADOW WATER B		573
AND ALL THE BIRDS ARE SCATTERED--O! O! O!	251	SHADOW WATER B		594
MY DARLING UNDERSTANDS IT ALL, ...	256	WORDS		10
"WERE NOT ALL HER LIFE BUT STORM, ...	259	PEACE		4
ALL THAT STERNNESS AMID CHARM, ...	259	PEACE		8
ALL THAT SWEETNESS AMID STRENGTH?"	259	PEACE		9
THAT'S ALL WE SHALL KNOW FOR TRUTH	261	DRINKING SONG		3
THROUGH ALL THE LYING DAYS OF MY YOUTH	261	COMING WISDOM		2
"O NO, MY DEAR, LET ALL THAT BE, ...	263	MASK		13
WHERE WINGS HAVE MEMORY OF WINGS, AND ALL	264	HOUSE SHAKEN		6
ALL THEIR LIVES THROUGH INTO SOME DRIFT OF WINGS. . . .	265	ABBEY THEATRE		7
AND ALL THINGS AT ONE COMMON LEVEL LIE.	265	THESE CLOUDS		6
DELIGHT MAKES ALL OF THE ONE MIND, ...	266	GALWAY RACES		2
ALL THINGS CAN TEMPT ME	267	ALL TEMPT ME		T
ALL THINGS CAN TEMPT ME FROM THIS CRAFT OF VERSE, . . .	267	ALL TEMPT ME		1
TO FIND OUT ALL THAT IS IN IT, ...	268	BROWN PENNY		11
YOU MOST OF ALL, SILENT AND FIERCE OLD MAN, ...	270	PARDON FATHERS		15
TILL YOUR BAD MASTER BLENCHED AND ALL WAS LOST, . . .	270	PARDON FATHERS	V	12
FOR ALL WERE FULL OF WINE AND MEAT.	271	GREY ROCK		17
ALL THOSE HAD LIFTED UP THE DIM	272	GREY ROCK		27
FOR HE IS THE WORST OF ALL DEAD MEN."	272	GREY ROCK		36
THAT EMPTIED ALL OUR DAYS TO COME, ...	272	GREY ROCK		40
ALL WAS ACCOMPLISHED. "WHEN THIS DAY	273	GREY ROCK		70
AND WHEN FOR ALL I'D DONE OR SAID--	275	GREY ROCK		99

ALL   (CONTINUED)

TILL ALL THE PLACE WAS BEATEN INTO MIRE. . . . . . .   278 TWO KINGS   27
TILL ALL HAD SEEMED A SHADOW OR A VISION   . . . . . .   278 TWO KINGS   43
THAN MOUND AND STONE THAT KEEP ALL VIRTUE IN, ...   281 TWO KINGS   106
I BADE HIM GO WHEN ALL HIS HOUSEHOLD SLEPT . . . . . .   282 TWO KINGS   133
TOLD HIM, THAT WHEN ORION ROSE, AND ALL . . . .   282 TWO KINGS   V 132A
ALONE WITH ALL THIS USELESS HAPPINESS?". . . . . . .   285 TWO KINGS   200
AND BADE ALL WELCOME, BEING IGNORANT. . . . .   286 TWO KINGS   218
FOR THIS THAT ALL THAT BLOOD WAS SHED, ...   290 SEPTEMBER 1913   19
ALL THAT DELIRIUM OF THE BRAVE?   . . . .   290 SEPTEMBER 1913   22
IN ALL THEIR LONELINESS AND PAIN, ...   290 SEPTEMBER 1913   27
NOW ALL THE TRUTH IS OUT, ...   290 TO A FRIEND   1
BECAUSE OF ALL THINGS KNOWN . . . .   291 TO A FRIEND   15
THAT ON THE LONELY HEIGHT WHERE ALL ARE IN GOD'S EYE, . .   291 PAUDEEN   6
"FOR ALL MY PAINS ON LEBEEN—LONE?" . . . .   295 THREE BEGGARS   7
AND LAY IT ALL UPON A HORSE"! . . . .   296 THREE BEGGARS   35
ALL SHOUTED TILL THEIR ANGER GREW . . . .   297 THREE BEGGARS   46
THEY MAULED AND BIT THROUGH ALL THAT DAY . . . . . .   297 THREE BEGGARS   50
"TIME'S UP," HE CRIED, AND ALL THE THREE . . . . . .   297 THREE BEGGARS   57
"TIME'S UP," HE CRIED, AND ALL THE THREE . . . . . .   297 THREE BEGGARS   59
WHEN ALL THOUGHTS AND DEEDS ARE RECKONED, ...   298 THREE HERMITS   15
AND ALL THAT I NEED DO IS TO WISH . . . .   300 RUN PARADISE   4
AND STUFFED WITH ALL THAT'S OLD AND BAD: . . . . . .   303 HOUR DAWN   V 25
THAT'S STUFFED WITH ALL THAT'S OLD AND BAD: . . . . . .   303 HOUR DAWN   V 25
THE BEGGAR DEAF TO ALL BUT HOPE . . . .   304 HOUR DAWN   V 44
I'LL SLEEP AWAY ALL TIME WITHIN IT: . . . .   306 HOUR DAWN   74
FOR ALL LIFE LONGS FOR THE LAST DAY . . . .   306 HOUR DAWN   98
AND SLEEP AWAY ALL TIME WITHIN IT. . . . .   306 HOUR DAWN   V 74
FOR ALL THE SLEEPER KNEW OR CARED: . . . .   307 HOUR DAWN   115
FROM MAEVE AND ALL THAT JUGGLING PLAIN, ...   307 HOUR DAWN   120
AND ALL THE WHILE HER NEEDLE PULLED . . . .   308 PLAYER QUEEN   7
ALL WISDOM SHUT INTO HIS ONYX EYES. . . . .   311 MOUNTAIN TOMB   11
ALL WISDOM SHUT INTO ITS ONYX EYES. . . . .   311 MOUNTAIN TOMB   V 11
AND ALL THE SHEAVES TO BIND. . . . .   312 CHILD DANCING   10
AND DREAM THAT ALL THE WORLD'S A FRIEND, ...   313 TWO YEAR LATER   8
AND YET FOR ALL THAT I COULD SAY, ...   313 MEMORY YOUTH   4
YET WE, FOR ALL THAT PRAISE, COULD FIND . . . .   314 MEMORY YOUTH   13
ALL TILL MY YOUTH WAS GONE . . . .   315 FRIENDS   18
AND I TOOK ALL THE BLAME OUT OF ALL SENSE AND REASON, . .   316 COLD HEAVEN   7
AND I TOOK ALL THE BLAME OUT OF ALL SENSE AND REASON, . .   316 COLD HEAVEN   7
NOW AS AT ALL TIMES I CAN SEE IN THE MIND'S EYE, . . .   318 MAGI   1
WITH ALL THEIR ANCIENT FACES LIKE RAIN-BEATEN STONES, . .   318 MAGI   4
AND ALL THEIR HELMS OF SILVER HOVERING SIDE BY SIDE, . .   318 MAGI   5
AND ALL THEIR EYES STILL FIXED, HOPING TO FIND ONCE MORE, .   318 MAGI   6
BUT THE OLDEST OF ALL THE DOLLS. . . . .   319 DOLLS   4
NOTORIOUS, TILL ALL MY PRICELESS THINGS . . . .   321 REED WHISPERER   13
ALL SUDDENLY MOUNT . . . .   322 SWANS AT COOLE   10
ALL, ALL ARE IN MY THOUGHTS TO-NIGHT BEING DEAD. . . . .   324 ROBERT GREGORY   8
ALL, ALL ARE IN MY THOUGHTS TO-NIGHT BEING DEAD. . . . .   324 ROBERT GREGORY   8
FOR ALL THAT COME INTO MY MIND ARE DEAD. . . . . . .   324 ROBERT GREGORY   16
TILL ALL HIS GREEK AND LATIN LEARNING SEEMED . . . . .   324 ROBERT GREGORY   21
AND SOLID MEN, FOR ALL THEIR PASSION, LIVE . . . . . .   325 ROBERT GREGORY   37
FOR ALL THINGS THE DELIGHTED EYE NOW SEES . . . . . .   326 ROBERT GREGORY   49
TO HAVE PUBLISHED ALL TO BE A WORLD'S DELIGHT. . . . .   327 ROBERT GREGORY   72
IN ALL LOVELY INTRICACIES OF A HOUSE . . . .   327 ROBERT GREGORY   74
ALL WORK IN METAL OR IN WOOD, ...   327 ROBERT GREGORY   76
AND ALL HE DID DONE PERFECTLY . . . .   327 ROBERT GREGORY   79
AS 'TWERE ALL LIFE'S EPITOME. . . . .   327 ROBERT GREGORY   87
ALL THOSE THAT MANHOOD TRIED, OR CHILDHOOD LOVED . . . .   327 ROBERT GREGORY   91
ALL THE COMBUSTIBLE WORLD IN ONE SMALL ROOM . . . . .   327 ROBERT GREGORY   V 82
OF THAT LATE DEATH TOOK ALL MY HEART FOR SPEECH. . . . .   328 ROBERT GREGORY   96
I BALANCED ALL, BROUGHT ALL TO MIND, ...   328 IRISH AIRMAN   13
I BALANCED ALL, BROUGHT ALL TO MIND, ...   328 IRISH AIRMAN   13
AND ALL DAY LONG I LOOK . . . .   329 MEN IMPROVE   4
AT ALL WHO MARRY IN CHURCHES, ...   330 BONE OF A HARE   15
"ALL DAY LONG FROM MID-DAY . . . .   332 SOLOMON SHEBA   3
ALL DAY LONG FROM SHADOWLESS NOON . . . .   332 SOLOMON SHEBA   5
"ALL DAY LONG FROM MIDDAY . . . .   332 SOLOMON SHEBA   V 3
AND ALL DAY LONG WE HAVE FOUND . . . .   333 SOLOMON SHEBA   22
SET ALL HER BLOOD ASTIR . . . .   336 YOUNG GIRL   10
ALL SHUFFLE THERE: ALL COUGH IN INK: . . . .   337 SCHOLARS   7
ALL SHUFFLE THERE: ALL COUGH IN INK: . . . .   337 SCHOLARS   7
ALL WEAR THE CARPET WITH THEIR SHOES: . . . .   337 SCHOLARS   8
ALL THINK WHAT OTHER PEOPLE THINK: . . . .   337 SCHOLARS   9
ALL KNOW THE MAN THEIR NEIGHBOUR KNOWS. . . . . . .   337 SCHOLARS   10
AND EVERY COUNTRY CRAFT, AND OF US ALL . . . .   339 SHEP GOATHERD   18
OLD GOATHERDS AND OLD GOATS, IF IN ALL ELSE . . . . .   340 SHEP GOATHERD   46
YOU HAVE PUT THE THOUGHT IN RHYME. I WORKED ALL DAY, . .   341 SHEP GOATHERD   58
SEED-PODS AND FLOWERS THAT ARE NOT ALL WILD POPPY. . . .   342 SHEP GOATHERD   88
THAT WERE ALL HIS BIRTHDAYS RECKONED . . . .   342 SHEP GOATHERD   90
OF ALL 'TWAS PAIN OR JOY TO LEARN, ...   342 SHEP GOATHERD   98
OF ALL THAT HE HAD MADE. . . . .   342 SHEP GOATHERD   99
SEED PODS AND FLOWERS THAT ARE NOT ALL WILD POPPY. . . .   342 SHEP GOATHERD   V 88
ALL KNOWLEDGE LOST IN TRANCE . . . .   343 SHEP GOATHERD   111
ALL THE WILD WITCHES, THOSE MOST NOBLE LADIES, ...   343 DEJECTION   4
FOR ALL THEIR BROOM-STICKS AND THEIR TEARS, ...   343 DEJECTION   5
THAT GIVES UP ALL HER MIND, ...   345 ON WOMAN   2
THAT COVERS ALL HE HAS BROUGHT . . . .   345 ON WOMAN   5
COUNT ALL THE PRAISES DUE . . . .   345 ON WOMAN   15
THAT POUNDS UP ALL ANEW . . . .   346 ON WOMAN   31
AND ALL BECAUSE OF SOME ONE . . . .   346 ON WOMAN   40

		PAGE	TITLE	LINE
ALL (CONTINUED)				
ALL DAY I'D LOOKED IN THE FACE		347	FISHERMAN		9
"WHAT HAVE I EARNED FOR ALL THAT WORK," I SAID,		351	PEOPLE		1
"FOR ALL THAT I HAVE DONE AT MY OWN CHARGE?		351	PEOPLE		2
ALL THE DISHONEST CROWD I HAD DRIVEN AWAY,		352	PEOPLE		24
COMPLAINED OF THE PEOPLE." ALL I COULD REPLY		352	PEOPLE		29
WITH ALL A WOMAN'S PASSION, A CHILD'S IMPERIOUS WAY,		354	HIS PHOENIX		14
THEY CAN SPREAD OUT WHAT SAIL THEY PLEASE FOR ALL I HAVE TO SAY,		354	HIS PHOENIX		22
. . . THROUGH ALL THE CENTURIES,		354	HIS PHOENIX		25
AND ALL THE SHAPELY BODY NO TITTLE GONE ASTRAY,		354	HIS PHOENIX		30
THERE'LL BE THAT CROWD TO MAKE MEN WILD THROUGH ALL THE CENTURIES,		354	HIS PHOENIX	V	25
FOR YOUR SOLE SAKE--THAT ALL HEART'S ACHE HAVE KNOWN,		355	BROKEN DREAMS		7
AND GIVEN TO OTHERS ALL HEART'S ACHE		355	BROKEN DREAMS		8
BUT FOR YOUR SAKE--THAT ALL HEART'S ACHE HAVE KNOWN,		355	BROKEN DREAMS	V	7
BUT IN THE GRAVE ALL, ALL, SHALL BE RENEWED,		356	BROKEN DREAMS		21
BUT IN THE GRAVE ALL, ALL, SHALL BE RENEWED.		356	BROKEN DREAMS		21
ALL DAY IN THE ONE CHAIR		357	BROKEN DREAMS		38
ALL I HAD RHYMED OF THAT MONSTROUS THING		358	PRESENCES		7
ALL I HAVE RHYMED OF THAT MONSTROUS THING		358	PRESENCES	V	7
WHEN ALL I WOULD DO		359	TO A SQUIRREL		6
AT ALL THESE DEATH-BEDS WOMEN HEARD		361	ALF POLLEXFEN		36
AT ALL THESE DEATHBEDS WOMEN HEARD		361	ALF POLLEXFEN	V	36
THE MEDITATIVE CRITIC; ALL ARE ON THEIR TOES,		363	DOLLS FACES		8
OR KEEP US ALL AWAKE WITH BAYING AT THE MOON,		364	DOLLS FACES		11
ALL BUT THE TERRORS OF THE WOODLAND FLIGHT FORGOT		366	HER COURAGE		5
AYE, AND ACHILLES, TIMOR, BABAR, BARHAIM, ALL,		366	HER COURAGE		9
ALL BUT THE PERILS OF THE WOODLAND FLIGHT FORGOT,		366	HER COURAGE	V	5
TILL ALL THE BOUGHS ARE GAY,		366	HER CHRIS TREE		5
I CALL TO MY OWN OPPOSITE, SUMMON ALL		367	EGO DOMINUS		8
SHUT OUT FROM ALL THE LUXURY OF THE WORLD,		370	EGO DOMINUS		60
AND PROVE OF ALL IMAGINABLE THINGS		371	EGO DOMINUS		73
ALL THAT I SEEK; AND WHISPER IT AS THOUGH		371	EGO DOMINUS		76
AND PROVE IF ALL IMAGINABLE THINGS		371	EGO DOMINUS	V	73
AND ON MY HEIRS, IF ALL REMAIN UNSPOILED,		371	ON GOING HOUSE		2
WHO KNOW IT ALL RING AT HIS DOOR, AND SPEAK		373	PHASES OF MOON		21
OF ALL THOSE TRUTHS THAT ARE YOUR DAILY BREAD;		373	PHASES OF MOON		24
THE FULL AND THE MOON'S DARK AND ALL THE CRESCENTS,		373	PHASES OF MOON		32
THE STRANGE REWARD OF ALL THAT DISCIPLINE.		374	PHASES OF MOON		57
ALL THOUGHT BECOMES AN IMAGE AND THE SOUL		374	PHASES OF MOON		58
BEYOND THE VISIBLE WORLD. ALL DREAMS OF THE SOUL		374	PHASES OF MOON		63
WHEN ALL IS FED WITH LIGHT AND HEAVEN IS BARE.		375	PHASES OF MOON		74
SHUDDERS IN MANY CRADLES; ALL IS CHANGED,		375	PHASES OF MOON		89
CRADLE UPON CRADLE, AND ALL IN FLIGHT AND ALL		376	PHASES OF MOON		100
CRADLE UPON CRADLE, AND ALL IN FLIGHT AND ALL		376	PHASES OF MOON		100
BECAUSE ALL DARK, LIKE THOSE THAT ARE ALL LIGHT,		376	PHASES OF MOON		104
BECAUSE ALL DARK, LIKE THOSE THAT ARE ALL LIGHT,		376	PHASES OF MOON		104
WHEN ALL THE DOUGH HAS BEEN SO KNEADED UP		377	PHASES OF MOON		114
BESIDE THE CASTLE DOOR, WHERE ALL IS STARK		377	PHASES OF MOON		126
HE WOULD NEVER KNOW ME AFTER ALL THESE YEARS		377	PHASES OF MOON		129
TO ALL THAT IN YOUR FLESH HAVE STOOD		380	SAINT HUNCH		13
HONOURED BY ALL IN THEIR DEGREES;		380	SAINT HUNCH		15
MEN THAT DO ALL BY RULE;		380	SONGS FOOL 1		14
ALTHOUGH I SAW IT ALL IN THE MIND'S EYE		383	VISION ROBART		25
GAZED UPON ALL THINGS KNOWN, ALL THINGS UNKNOWN,		383	VISION ROBART		30
GAZED UPON ALL THINGS KNOWN, ALL THINGS UNKNOWN,		383	VISION ROBART		30
BEING FIXED ON ALL THINGS LOVED, ALL THINGS UNLOVED,		383	VISION ROBART		34
BEING FIXED ON ALL THINGS LOVED, ALL THINGS UNLOVED,		383	VISION ROBART		34
AT ALL THAT IS NOT PICTURED THERE.		385	ROBARTES DANCE		17
AND ALL HIS SACRED COMPANY		386	ROBARTES DANCE		27
IMAGINED BODIES ALL THEIR DAYS		386	ROBARTES DANCE		28
THAT ALL MUST COME TO SIGHT AND TOUCH;		386	ROBARTES DANCE		31
AND THAT ALL BEAUTIFUL WOMEN MAY		387	ROBARTES DANCE		45
ALL SOUNDS BY BIRD OR ANGEL SUNG		387	SOLOMON WITCH	V	7
ALL THAT THE BRIGAND APPLE BROUGHT		388	SOLOMON WITCH		15
AYE, THOUGH ALL PASSION'S IN THE GLANCE--		388	SOLOMON WITCH		21
TILL ALL THE EDDIES GLEAM;		389	IMAGE PAST		4
OUT OF ALL LIKELIHOOD, OR REASON,		389	IMAGE PAST		9
I HAD THOUGHT THAT ALL MY DAYS WERE CAST		389	IMAGE PAST		12
ALL THAT TO THIS MOMENT CHARMED YOU?		390	IMAGE PAST		21
ALL CHANGED, CHANGED UTTERLY;		392	EASTER 1916		15
ALL THAT SHE GOT SHE SPENT,		392	EASTER 1916	V	20
THE STONE'S IN THE MIDST OF ALL.		393	EASTER 1916		56
WAS IT NEEDLESS DEATH AFTER ALL?		394	EASTER 1916		67
FOR ALL THAT IS DONE AND SAID.		394	EASTER 1916		69
FOR ALL SHE HAD DONE AND SAID.		394	EASTER 1916	V	69
"WHEN ALL THE WELLS ARE PARCHED AWAY?		396	ROSE TREE		15
WITH ALL YOUTH'S LONELY WILDNESS STIRRED,		397	POLIT PRISONER		16
ALL THAT ARE DIFFERENT OF A BASE INTENT;		398	LEADERS CROWD		2
THAT ALL MY CHILDHOOD COUNTED DEAR;		398	BREAK OF DAY		7
AND ALL LAUGH IN THE SUN.		400	DEMON BEAST		8
WELCOME, AND THE ORMONDES ALL		400	DEMON BEAST		11
FOR ALL MEN'S THOUGHTS GREW CLEAR		400	DEMON BEAST		19
FOR ALL MEN'S THOUGHT GREW CLEAR		400	DEMON BEAST	V	19
THE BEST LACK ALL CONVICTION, WHILE THE WORST		402	SECOND COMING		7
IS MOVING ITS SLOW THIGHS, WHILE ALL ABOUT IT		402	SECOND COMING		16
THAT ALL HER THOUGHTS MAY LIKE THE LINNET BE,		404	FOR DAUGHTER		42
MAY WELL BE OF ALL EVIL CHANCES CHIEF.		405	FOR DAUGHTER		53
CONSIDERING THAT, ALL HATRED DRIVEN HENCE,		405	FOR DAUGHTER		65
WHEN ALL IS RUIN ONCE AGAIN.		406	CARVED STONE		6

ALL   (CONTINUED)
                                                        PAGE   TITLE   LINE
FISH, FLESH, OR FOWL, COMMEND ALL SUMMER LONG . . . . . 407 SAIL BYZANTIUM   5
CAUGHT IN THAT SENSUAL MUSIC ALL NEGLECT   . . . . . . 407 SAIL BYZANTIUM   7
FOR I WOULD ASK A QUESTION OF THEM ALL. . . . . 410 TOWER   24
AND HELEN HAS ALL LIVING HEARTS BETRAYED. . . . . 411 TOWER   53
I THOUGHT IT ALL OUT TWENTY YEARS AGO: . . . .   411 TOWER   64
THAT ALL BUT THE ONE CARD BECAME . . . . 411 TOWER   68
AS I WOULD QUESTION ALL, COME ALL WHO CAN: . . . . . .   412 TOWER   89
AS I WOULD QUESTION ALL, COME ALL WHO CAN: . . . . . .   412 TOWER   89
DID ALL OLD MEN AND WOMEN, RICH AND POOR, ... 413 TOWER   97
FOR I NEED ALL HIS MIGHTY MEMORIES. . . . . 413 TOWER   104
ALL THAT YOU HAVE DISCOVERED IN THE GRAVE, ...   413 TOWER   107
WHEN ALL STREAMS ARE DRY. . . . . 414 TOWER   138
AYE, SUN AND MOON AND STAR, ALL, ...   415 TOWER   152
ALL THOSE THINGS WHEREOF . . . .   415 TOWER   163
THE SWEETNESS THAT ALL LONGED FOR NIGHT AND DAY, . . .   418 ANCEST HOUSES   20
FOR ALL ITS BRONZE AND MARBLE, 'S BUT A MOUSE. . . . .   418 ANCEST HOUSES   24
OR ELSE ALL JUNO FROM AN URN DISPLAYS . . . .   418 ANCEST HOUSES   27
A MIST THAT IS LIKE BLOWN SNOW IS SWEEPING OVER ALL, . . 425 PHANTOM HATRED   2
BECAUSE OF ALL THAT SENSELESS TUMULT, ALL BUT CRIED . . 426 PHANTOM HATRED   15
BECAUSE OF ALL THAT SENSELESS TUMULT, ALL BUT CRIED . . 426 PHANTOM HATRED   15
IN SOMETHING THAT ALL OTHERS UNDERSTAND OR SHARE: . . . 427 PHANTOM HATRED   35
AND ALL THE GOLDEN GRASSHOPPERS AND BEES. . . . . 428 NINETEEN 19   8
WE THOUGHT IT WOULD OUTLIVE ALL FUTURE DAYS. . . . . .   428 NINETEEN 19   14
OR ALL THAT WAYWARD EBB AND FLOW. THERE STOOD . . . .   428 NINETEEN 19   V 4
ON ALL THAT WAYWARD EBB AND FLOW. THERE STOOD . . . .   428 NINETEEN 19   V 4
AND ALL HIS GOLDEN GRASSHOPPERS AND BEES. . . . . 428 NINETEEN 19   V 8
ALL TEETH WERE DRAWN, ALL ANCIENT TRICKS UNLEARNED, . . 429 NINETEEN 19   17
ALL TEETH WERE DRAWN, ALL ANCIENT TRICKS UNLEARNED, . . 429 NINETEEN 19   17
AND YET IT LACK ALL GLORY: AND PERCHANCE . . . . 429 NINETEEN 19   23
HAS BUT ONE COMFORT LEFT: ALL TRIUMPH WOULD . . . . . . 429 NINETEEN 19   39
ALL MEN ARE DANCERS AND THEIR TREAD . . . . 430 NINETEEN 19   57
GREEKS WERE BUT LOVERS: ALL THAT COUNTRY ROUND . . . .   430 NINETEEN 19   V 43
TO END ALL THINGS, TO END . . . . 431 NINETEEN 19   81
WITH ALL THOSE CALENDARS WHEREON . . . .   432 NINETEEN 19   99
ALL BREAK AND VANISH, AND EVIL GATHERS HEAD: . . . . .   433 NINETEEN 19   117
ALL TURN WITH AMOROUS CRIES, OR ANGRY CRIES, ...   433 NINETEEN 19   123
ACCORDING TO THE WIND, FOR ALL ARE BLIND. . . . . 433 NINETEEN 19   124
DECLARE THAT WINTER'S BEST OF ALL: . . . .   434 WHEEL   4
ALL DREAD AFAR TILL MORNING'S BACK . . . .   435 FOR MY SON   6
ALL OF THAT WORST IGNOMINY . . . . 436 FOR MY SON   23
AND WHEN THROUGH ALL THE TOWN THERE RAN . . . . 436 FOR MY SON   25
AND THEN DID ALL THE MUSES SING . . . .   437 SONGS PLAY 1   6
MADE ALL PLATONIC TOLERANCE VAIN . . . . 438 SONGS PLAY 2   7
AND VAIN ALL DORIC DISCIPLINE. . . . .   438 SONGS PLAY 2   8
STRAIGHTENED ALL THAT WENT AWRY . . . . 440 WISDOM   V 4
BY THE WEBBED TOES, AND THAT ALL POWERFUL BILL . . . .   441 LEDA AND SWAN   V 3
ALL THE STRETCHED BODY'S LAID ON THE WHITE RUSH . . . . 441 LEDA AND SWAN   V 7
MY WORKS ARE ALL STAMPED DOWN INTO THE SULTRY MUD. . .   442 BLACK CENTAUR   3
I HAVE LOVED YOU BETTER THAN MY SOUL FOR ALL MY WORDS, . 442 BLACK CENTAUR   14
BETTER TO SMILE ON ALL THAT SMILE, AND SHOW . . . . .   444 SCHOOL CHILDR   31
AND THAT ALL HEAVENLY GLORY SYMBOLISE-- . . . . 445 SCHOOL CHILDR   55
AND SO REMEMBERS THAT WHEN ALL MANKIND . . . . 447 COLONUS PRAISE   26
FOR ALL MEN LOVE YOUR WORTH: AND I MUST RAGE . . . . .   447 HERO GIRL FOOL V   8
A NUN AT LEAST HAS ALL MEN'S REVERENCE . . . . 448 HERO GIRL FOOL V 12
ALL MEN HAVE PRAISED MY STRENGTH BUT NOT MY WORTH, . .   448 HERO GIRL FOOL V   9
FOR THEY AT LEAST ALL MEN'S REVERENCE . . . . 448 HERO GIRL FOOL V 12
WHEN ALL WORKS THAT HAVE . . . .   449 HERO GIRL FOOL   18
IT FEARED TO GIVE ITS LOVE A HURT WITH ALL THE TEMPEST   450 OWEN AHERNE   7
     THERE:
"YOU BUT IMAGINE LIES ALL DAY, O MURDERER," I REPLIED. . 450 OWEN AHERNE   17
"AND ALL THOSE LIES HAVE BUT ONE END, POOR WRETCHES TO   450 OWEN AHERNE   18
     BETRAY:
"SPEAK ALL YOUR MIND," MY HEART SANG OUT, ...   450 OWEN AHERNE   21
. . . "SPEAK ALL YOUR MIND: WHO CARES, ...   450 OWEN AHERNE   21
O LET HER CHOOSE A YOUNG MAN NOW AND ALL FOR HIS   450 OWEN AHERNE   24
     WILD SAKE."
BUT IS THE SAME FOR ALL . . . .   452 HUMAN DIGNITY   4
WHEN ALL BUT DEAD OF THIRST, ...   454 EMPTY CUP   2
WHEN ALL BUT DEAD WITH THIRST, ...   454 EMPTY CUP   V 2
THE FIRST OF ALL THE TRIBE LAY THERE . . . .   455 HIS MEMORIES   13
AND PUT ALL TROY TO WRECK-- . . . . 455 HIS MEMORIES   16
AND PUT ALL TROY TO WRACK-- . . . . 455 HIS MEMORIES   V 16
TOLD ALL THAT HAD BEEN SAID OR DONE . . . . 456 SUMMER SPRING   3
WHEN WE HAD ALL THE SUMMER-TIME . . . . 457 SUMMER SPRING   15
AND SHE HAD ALL THE SPRING! . . . . 457 SUMMER SPRING   16
WHEN WE HAD ALL THE SUMMER TIME . . . . 457 SUMMER SPRING   V 15
OF ALL THAT ARE GONE, ... 458 SECRETS OF OLD   14
BEING ALL ALONE I'D NURSE A STONE . . . . 459 HIS WILDNESS   11
DELIGHT BECOMES DEATH-LONGING IF ALL LONGING ELSE BE VAIN. 459 FROM OEDIPUS   3
. . . ALL ENTANGLEMENTS OF MANKIND GROW, ...   459 FROM OEDIPUS   5
. . . AT ALL NOR LOOKED INTO THE EYE OF DAY. . . . . .   459 FROM OEDIPUS   V 11
AND ALL THE POPULAR STATESMEN SAY . . . . 460 THREE MONUMENT   5
AND LET ALL BASE AMBITION BE, ... 460 THREE MONUMENT   9
THAT SPEECH WAS ALL THAT THE TOWN KNEW, BUT HE . . . .   462 HARUN RASHID   35
THAT SPEECH WAS ALL THAT THE COURT KNOW, BUT HE . . . . 462 HARUN RASHID   V 35
THAT I COMMEND TO ALL THE CHRONICLERS . . . .   463 HARUN RASHID   46
BEING ALL BRIMMED WITH LIFE?" "WERE IT BUT TRUE . . . . 465 HARUN RASHID   90
THAN ALL MY BURSTING SPRINGTIME KNEW. A GIRL . . . . .   466 HARUN RASHID   105
OF ALL THE UNCOUNTED BOOKS THAT I HAVE READ, ...   467 HARUN RASHID   139
IN CHILDISH IGNORANCE OF ALL THAT PASSED. . . . . 468 HARUN RASHID   149

ALL   (CONTINUED)
IN CHILDISH IGNORANCE OF ALL THAT PASSED. . . . . . .   468 HARUN RASHID   160
HEARD ALL THE ANXIETY OF MY PASSIONATE YOUTH. . . . .   468 HARUN RASHID   168
ITS FIRST SIMPLICITY, LOVE, VOICE AND ALL. . . . . .   469 HARUN RASHID   177
ALL MY FINE FEATHERS WOULD BE PLUCKED AWAY . . . . .   469 HARUN RASHID   178
ALL THOSE ABSTRACTIONS THAT YOU FANCIED WERE . . . .   469 HARUN RASHID   182
ALL, ALL THOSE GYRES AND CUBES AND MIDNIGHT THINGS .   469 HARUN RASHID   184
ALL, ALL THOSE GYRES AND CUBES AND MIDNIGHT THINGS .   469 HARUN RASHID   184
ITS FIRST SIMPLICITY, LOVE AND ALL. . . . .   469 HARUN RASHID   V 177
OF ALL ARABIA'S LOVERS I ALONE-- . . . .   470 HARUN RASHID   190
ALL SOULS' NIGHT . . . .   470 ALL SOUL NIGHT   T
AND IT IS ALL SOULS' NIGHT. . . . .   470 ALL SOUL NIGHT   3
IT IS ALL SOULS' NIGHT AND THE GREAT CHRIST CHURCH BELL 470 ALL SOUL NIGHT V   1
IT MAY BE ALL THAT HEAR . . . .   471 ALL SOUL NIGHT   19
FOR MAYBE ALL THAT HEAR . . . .   474 ALL SOUL NIGHT   89
TILL MEDITATION MASTER ALL ITS PARTS. . . . .   474 ALL SOUL NIGHT   92
DEAR SHADOWS, NOW YOU KNOW IT ALL. . . . .   476 EVA GORE-BOOTH   21
ALL THE FOLLY OF A FIGHT . . . .   476 EVA GORE-BOOTH   22
RUN TILL ALL THE SAGES KNOW. . . . .   476 EVA GORE-BOOTH   29
DREADING AND HOPING ALL. . . . .   476 DEATH   4
SET ALL YOUR MIND UPON THE STEEP ASCENT. . . . . .   477 SELF AND SOUL   2
THAT QUARTER WHERE ALL THOUGHT IS DONE. . . . . . .   477 SELF AND SOUL   7
HEART'S PURPLE--AND ALL THESE I SET . . . .   478 SELF AND SOUL   28
WHAT MATTER IF I LIVE IT ALL ONCE MORE? . . . . . .   478 SELF AND SOUL   43
I AM CONTENT TO LIVE IT ALL AGAIN . . . .   479 SELF AND SOUL   57
OR INTO THAT MOST FECUND DITCH OF ALL. . . . . . .   479 SELF AND SOUL   61
AND GOD-APPOINTED BERKELEY THAT PROVED ALL THINGS A DREAM, 481 BLOOD AND MOON   25
WHAT ARE ALL THOSE FISH THAT LIE GASPING ON THE STRAND? 485 THREE MOVEMENT   3
ALL HATED WHIGGERY, BUT WHAT IS WHIGGERY? . . . . .   486 SEVEN SAGES   10
WHEN SHE IN ALL HER VIRGINAL PRIDE . . . .   488 CRAZED MOON   8
FOR ALL HIS TIMID HEART, THERE THAT SLOW MAN. . . .   489 COOLE PARK 29   12
WHEN ALL THOSE ROOMS AND PASSAGES ARE GONE. . . . .   489 COOLE PARK 29   26
AND ALL THE SENSUALITY OF THE SHADE-- . . . . . .   489 COOLE PARK 29   31
NOW ALL DRY STICKS UNDER A WINTRY SUN. . . . . . .   490 COOLE BALLYLEE   10
AND ALL THE RANT'S A MIRROR OF MY MOOD. . . . . . .   490 COOLE BALLYLEE   13
AND ALL THE RANT A MIRROR OF MY MOOD. . . . .   490 COOLE BALLYLEE V   13
WE SHIFT ABOUT--ALL THAT GREAT GLORY SPENT-- . . .   491 COOLE BALLYLEE   39
MAN SHIFTS ABOUT--ALL THAT GREAT GLORY SPENT-- . .   491 COOLE BALLYLEE   39
BUT ALL IS CHANGED, THAT HIGH HORSE RIDERLESS. . . .   492 COOLE BALLYLEE   46
ALL THAT IS WRITTEN IN WHAT POETS NAME . . . . . .   492 COOLE BALLYLEE   43
WHEN ALL THAT STORY'S FINISHED, WHAT'S THE NEWS? . .   495 CHOICE   5
ALL THAT TIME DENIED-- . . . .   496 MOHINI CHATTER   18
ALL THAT MAN IS. . . . .   497 BYZANTIUM   6
ALL MERE COMPLEXITIES. . . . .   497 BYZANTIUM   7
AND ALL COMPLEXITIES OF MIRE OR BLOOD. . . . . . .   498 BYZANTIUM   24
AND ALL COMPLEXITIES OF FURY LEAVE. . . . .   498 BYZANTIUM   29
THE TERROR OF ALL TERRORS THAT I BORE . . . . . .   499 MOTHER OF GOD   4
AND GATHER ALL THE TALK? . . . .   499 MOTHER OF GOD   10
ALL THOSE ANTINOMIES . . . .   500 VACILLATION   5
IS HALF ALL GLITTERING FLAME AND HALF ALL GREEN . .   500 VACILLATION   12
IS HALF ALL GLITTERING FLAME AND HALF ALL GREEN . .   500 VACILLATION   12
AND HALF IS HALF AND YET IS ALL THE SCENE. . . . .   500 VACILLATION   14
GET ALL THE GOLD AND SILVER THAT YOU CAN. . . . . .   500 VACILLATION   19
ALL WOMEN DOTE UPON AN IDLE MAN . . . .   500 VACILLATION   23
IS HALF ALL GLITTERING FLAME AND HALF A GREEN . . .   500 VACILLATION   V   12
"LET ALL THINGS PASS AWAY." . . . .   502 VACILLATION   61
"LET ALL THINGS PASS AWAY." . . . .   502 VACILLATION   66
WHAT'S THE MEANING OF ALL SONG? . . . .   502 VACILLATION   70
"LET ALL THINGS PASS AWAY." . . . .   502 VACILLATION   71
ALL LIVES THAT HAS LIVED. . . . .   504 QUARREL IN AGE   9
ALL BY THEIR YOUTH UNDONE. . . . .   504 RESULT THOUGHT   4
ALL, ALL, BY THAT INHUMAN . . . .   504 RESULT THOUGHT   5
ALL, ALL, BY THAT INHUMAN . . . .   504 RESULT THOUGHT   5
ALL THEIR WHOLESOME STRENGTH. . . . .   505 RESULT THOUGHT   12
ALL THE WRECK AND WRACK. . . . .   505 RESULT THOUGHT V   8
ALL THINGS HANG LIKE A DROP OF DEW . . . .   505 GRAT INSTRUCT   3
AND ALL MY HEART SEEMED GAY. . . . .   507 STREAM AND SUN   3
(ALL FIND SAFETY IN THE TOMB.) . . . .   508 JANE BISHOP   3
(ALL FIND SAFETY IN THE TOMB.) . . . .   508 JANE BISHOP   10
(ALL FIND SAFETY IN THE TOMB.) . . . .   508 JANE BISHOP   17
(ALL FIND SAFETY IN THE TOMB.) . . . .   508 JANE BISHOP   24
ALL THOSE DREADFUL THUNDER-STONES. . . . .   509 JANE REPROVED   2
ALL THAT STORM THAT BLOTS THE DAY . . . .   509 JANE REPROVED   3
ALL THOSE DREADFUL THUNDERSTONES. . . . .   509 JANE REPROVED V   2
ALL THOSE STORMS THAT BLOT THE DAY . . . .   509 JANE REPROVED V   3
"LOVE IS ALL . . . .   510 JANE JUDGMENT   1
ALL COULD BE KNOWN OR SHOWN . . . .   510 JANE JUDGMENT   18
ALL THINGS REMAIN IN GOD. . . . .   512 JANE ON GOD   6
ALL THINGS REMAIN IN GOD. . . . .   512 JANE ON GOD   12
ALL THINGS REMAIN IN GOD. . . . .   512 JANE ON GOD   18
ALL THINGS REMAIN IN GOD. . . . .   512 JANE ON GOD   24
THEY HAD ALL THAT HAD THEIR HATE. . . . .   514 JANE GROWN OLD   13
AND THAT WAS ALL MY SONG-- . . . .   515 GIRLS SONG B   9
DID ALL THE FABRIC FADE. . . . .   516 MANS SONG   10
AND ALL SHALL BEND THE KNEE . . . .   516 MANS SONG   16
ALL TRUE LOVE MUST DIE. . . . .   517 HER ANXIETY   3
ALL WRONGS DONE. . . . .   518 HIS CONFIDENCE   4
ALL NIGHT'S FATHOMLESS WISDOM COME. . . . .   519 HER DREAM   2
AND ALL THE WINDINGS THERE. . . . .   520 HIS BARGAIN   12
"A CHILD FOUND ALL A CHILD CAN LACK. . . . .   521 THREE THINGS   3
FOUND ALL THE PLEASURE THAT LIFE GAVE". . . . . .   521 THREE THINGS   11

ALL   (CONTINUED)

		PAGE	TITLE	LINE
WHAT WERE ALL THE WORLD'S ALARMS		522	LULLABY	3
WHAT ARE ALL THE WORLD'S ALARMS?		522	LULLABY V	3
ALL OTHER LOVERS BEING ESTRANGED OR DEAD,		523	LONG SILENCE	2
ALL THAT SILK AND SATIN GEAR,		525	DANCING DAYS	3
OF ALL THAT RAMBLED THERE		526	AM OF IRELAND	9
"THE FIDDLERS ARE ALL THUMBS,		527	AM OF IRELAND	19
AND THE TRUMPETS ALL ARE BURST,		527	AM OF IRELAND	22
ALL THAT COULD RUN OR LEAP OR SWIM		528	DANCER CRUACH	6
ALL THAT RUN OR LEAP OR SWIM		528	DANCER CRUACH V	6
IN ALL THE VIGOUR OF ITS BLOOD:		529	TOM LUNATIC	17
AND ALL THEIR SWELLING CANVAS WEAR,		530	OLD TOM AGAIN	2
AND ALL THEIR YELLOW CANVAS WEAR,		530	OLD TOM AGAIN V	2
AND ALL THE CHOIR OF LOVE.		531	DELPHIC ORACLE	10
OF ALL GOOD MEN AND WOMEN,		531	FATHER CHILD	3
THAT HAS THE WORST OF ALL BAD NAMES:		531	FATHER CHILD	5
OR ASK IF ALL BE RIGHT		532	BEFORE WORLD	4
BLACKENS ALL OUR LOT?		534	CONSOLATION	10
BIDS ALL TRUE LOVERS REST,		536	PARTING	6
ALL STATELY WOMEN MOVING TO A SONG		537	HER VISION	17
THAT THING ALL BLOOD AND MIRE, THAT BEAST-TORN WRECK,		537	HER VISION	25
AND, THOUGH LOVE'S BITTER-SWEET HAD ALL COME BACK,		537	HER VISION	27
OF ALL THAT WITH ME LAY?		538	LAST CONFESS	2
WHAT SHUDDERS RUN THROUGH ALL THAT ANIMAL BLOOD?		541	PARN FUNERAL 1	5
I THIRST FOR ACCUSATION. ALL THAT WAS SUNG,		542	PARN FUNERAL 1	25
ALL THAT WAS SAID IN IRELAND IS A LIE		542	PARN FUNERAL 1	26
TO THIS BARE SOUL, LET ALL MEN JUDGE THAT CAN		542	PARN FUNERAL 1	30
"HEAR, GENTLEMEN, LADIES, AND ALL MANKIND:		544	TO SAME TUNE 1	2
THOSE FANATICS ALL THAT WE DO WOULD UNDO:		544	TO SAME TUNE 1	7
ALL THERE CAUGHT UP THE TUNE:		545	TO SAME TUNE 1	15
THOSE FANATICS ALL THAT WE DO WOULD UNDO:		545	TO SAME TUNE 1	17
THOSE FANATICS ALL THAT WE DO WOULD UNDO:		545	TO SAME TUNE 1	27
JUSTIFY ALL THOSE RENOWNED GENERATIONS:		545	TO SAME TUNE 2	1
"DROWN ALL THE DOGS," SAID THE FIERCE YOUNG WOMAN,		546	TO SAME TUNE 2	7
DROWN ALL THE DOGS," SAID THE FIERCE YOUNG WOMAN.		546	TO SAME TUNE 2	10
JUSTIFY ALL THOSE RENOWNED GENERATIONS,		546	TO SAME TUNE 2	11
JUSTIFY ALL THAT HAVE SUNK IN THEIR BLOOD,		546	TO SAME TUNE 2	12
JUSTIFY ALL THAT HAVE DIED ON THE SCAFFOLD,		546	TO SAME TUNE 2	13
JUSTIFY ALL THAT HAVE FLED, THAT HAVE STOOD,		546	TO SAME TUNE 2	14
"DROWN ALL THE DOGS," SAID THE FIERCE YOUNG WOMAN,		546	TO SAME TUNE 2	17
DROWN ALL THE DOGS," SAID THE FIERCE YOUNG WOMAN.		546	TO SAME TUNE 2	20
ALL THAT GREAT PAST TO A TROUBLE OF FOOLS:		546	TO SAME TUNE 2	22
THOSE FANATICS ALL THAT WE DO WOULD UNDO:		546	TO SAME TUNE 2 V	REF
JUSTIFY ALL THAT HAVE FLED OR HAVE STOOD,		546	TO SAME TUNE 2 V	14
ALL THE RENOWN THAT FELL.		547	TO SAME TUNE 2	26
"DROWN ALL THE DOGS," SAID THE FIERCE YOUNG WOMAN,		547	TO SAME TUNE 2	27
DROWN ALL THE DOGS," SAID THE FIERCE YOUNG WOMAN.		547	TO SAME TUNE 2	30
TIME FOR US ALL TO PICK OUT A GOOD TUNE,		548	TO SAME TUNE 3	13
THOSE FANATICS ALL THAT WE DO WOULD UNDO:		548	TO SAME TUNE 3 V	REF
TIME FOR US ALL BOYS, TO HIT ON A TUNE BOYS,		548	TO SAME TUNE 3 V	13
ALL THOSE TRAGIC CHARACTERS RIDE		549	SEVERED HEAD	4
AND ALL ALONE COMES RIDING THERE		550	SEVERED HEAD	18
FOR ALL MY HEART HAS HAD FOR ITS HIRE		551	SONGS REWRIT 1	3
FOR ALL MY TOIL HAS HAD FOR ITS HIRE		551	SONGS REWRIT 1 V	3
FOR ALL THAT MY HEART HAS HAD FOR ITS HIRE		551	SONGS REWRIT 1 V	3
I CRIED AND WHISTLED BUT VAIN, ALL VAIN,		551	SONGS REWRIT 1	16
FROM ALL THAT MAKES A WISE OLD MAN		553	PRAYER OLD AGE	5
THAT CAN BE PRAISED OF ALL:		553	PRAYER OLD AGE	6
ALL KNOW THEIR TALE, ALL KNOW WHAT LEAF AND TWIG,		555	RIBH AT TOMB	7
ALL KNOW THEIR TALE, ALL KNOW WHAT LEAF AND TWIG,		555	RIBH AT TOMB	7
THAT'S HOW ALL NATURAL OR SUPERNATURAL STORIES RUN.		556	RIBH PATRICK	3
YET ALL MUST COPY COPIES, ALL INCREASE THEIR KIND:		556	RIBH PATRICK	7
YET ALL MUST COPY COPIES, ALL INCREASE THEIR KIND:		556	RIBH PATRICK	7
BUT ALL THAT RUN IN COUPLES, ON EARTH, IN FLOOD OR AIR,		556	RIBH PATRICK	11
ALL HAPPINESS IN ITS OWN CAUSE OR GROUND.		557	RIBH ECSTASY	4
THERE ALL THE BARREL-HOOPS ARE KNIT,		557	THERE	1
THERE ALL THE SERPENT-TAILS ARE BIT,		557	THERE	2
THERE ALL THE GYRES CONVERGE IN ONE,		557	THERE	3
THERE ALL THE PLANETS DROP IN THE SUN.		557	THERE	4
HOW SOUL MAY WALK WHEN ALL SUCH THINGS ARE PAST,		558	RIBH CHRISTIAN	11
ALL CREATION SHIVERS		559	HE AND SHE	11
HE HOLDS HIM FROM DESIRE, ALL BUT STOPS HIS BREATHING LEST		559	MAGIC DRUM	1
ALL THE STREAM THAT'S ROARING BY		562	NEEDLES EYE	1
EMPEDOCLES HAS THROWN ALL THINGS ABOUT:		564	GYRES	6
AND ALL IT KNOWS IS THAT ONE WORD "REJOICE!"		564	GYRES	16
THE WORKMAN, NOBLE AND SAINT, AND ALL THINGS RUN		565	GYRES	23
ALL PERFORM THEIR TRAGIC PLAY.		565	LAPIS LAZULI	9
GAIETY TRANSFIGURING ALL THAT DREAD.		565	LAPIS LAZULI	17
ALL MEN HAVE AIMED AT, FOUND AND LOST:		566	LAPIS LAZULI	18
AND ALL THE DROP-SCENES DROP AT ONCE		566	LAPIS LAZULI	22
ALL THINGS FALL AND ARE BUILT AGAIN,		566	LAPIS LAZULI	35
AND ALL THE DROP SCENES DROP AT ONCE		566	LAPIS LAZULI V	22
ON ALL THE TRAGIC SCENE THEY STARE.		567	LAPIS LAZULI	52
AND MAYBE WE ARE ALL THE SAME		570	THREE BUSHES	24
AND MAYBE WE ARE ALL THE SAME		570	THREE BUSHES	26
LOOKED HALF ASLEEP ALL DAY.		570	THREE BUSHES	34
HIS LADY SAW IT ALL		571	THREE BUSHES	53
UPON ALL FOURS.		572	LADYS 1ST SONG	12
BODY WERE NOT AT ALL,		572	LADYS 2ND SONG	9
ALL THE LABOURING HEAVENS SIGH.		573	LADYS 3RD SONG	12

ALL (CONTINUED)

		PAGE	TITLE		LINE
OUT OF ALL HARM,		574	MAIDS 1ST SONG		8
ALL HIS TWENTIES CRAMMED WITH TOIL;		576	WHAT THEN		4
ALL HIS HAPPIER DREAMS CAME TRUE--		577	WHAT THEN		11
ALL THE OLYMPIANS; A THING NEVER KNOWN AGAIN.		578	LOFTY THINGS		12
ALL NEIGHBOURLY CONTENT AND EASY TALK ARE GONE,		580	CURSE CROMWELL		9
AND WE AND ALL THE MUSES ARE THINGS OF NO ACCOUNT.		580	CURSE CROMWELL		12
THAT I AM STILL THEIR SERVANT THOUGH ALL ARE UNDERGROUND.		581	CURSE CROMWELL		22
ITS OPEN LIGHTED DOORWAY AND ITS WINDOWS ALL ALIGHT,		581	CURSE CROMWELL		26
AND ALL MY FRIENDS WERE THERE AND MADE ME WELCOME TOO;		581	CURSE CROMWELL		27
THEY GAVE IT OUT TO ALL THE WORLD.		582	ROGER CASEMENT		11
COME TOM AND DICK, COME ALL THE TROOP		582	ROGER CASEMENT		17
COME ALFRED NOYES AND ALL THE TROUP		582	ROGER CASEMENT	V	17
THAT ALL MUST HANG THEIR TRUST		583	GHOST ROG CASE		16
AND ALL MUST PAY HIM HEED,		583	GHOST ROG CASE		22
ALL THOSE LEARNED HISTORIANS.		584	ORAHILLY		5
KEEPING ALL THE KERRY MEN		585	ORAHILLY		14
COME FILL UP ALL THOSE GLASSES		586	PARNELLITES		7
HE BROUGHT IT ALL TO PASS;		586	PARNELLITES		14
THAT IS ALL I ASK, MY DEAR.		587	OLD WICKED MAN		7
"KIND ARE ALL YOUR WORDS, MY DEAR,		588	OLD WICKED MAN		10
I GAVE IT ALL TO AN OLDER MAN;		588	OLD WICKED MAN		23
HID FROM ALL THOSE WARTY LADS		589	OLD WICKED MAN		43
"ALL MEN LIVE IN SUFFERING,		589	OLD WICKED MAN		46
I FORGET IT ALL AWHILE		590	OLD WICKED MAN		61
AND ALL DEAD MEN ARE DRUNK.		592	DRUNK SOBRIETY		16
AND WHAT'S THE GOOD OF WOMEN, FOR ALL THAT THEY CAN SAY		592	PILGRIM		4
I PRAYED AT ALL THE STATIONS UPON MY MARROW-BONES,		593	PILGRIM		7
AND THERE I FOUND AN OLD MAN, AND THOUGH I PRAYED ALL DAY		593	PILGRIM		8
ALL KNOW THAT ALL THE DEAD IN THE WORLD ABOUT THAT PLACE ARE STUCK,		593	PILGRIM		11
ALL KNOW THAT ALL THE DEAD IN THE WORLD ABOUT THAT PLACE ARE STUCK,		593	PILGRIM		11
I SWEAR TO GOD I QUESTIONED THEM, AND ALL THEY HAD TO SAY		593	PILGRIM		14
FOR I CAN PUT THE WHOLE LOT DOWN, AND ALL I HAVE TO SAY		593	PILGRIM		24
I PRAYED AT ALL THE STATIONS UPON MY MARROW BONES,		593	PILGRIM	V	7
I SWEAR TO GOD I QUESTIONED THEM ALL AND ALL THEY HAD TO SAY		593	PILGRIM	V	14
I SWEAR TO GOD I QUESTIONED THEM ALL AND ALL THEY HAD TO SAY		593	PILGRIM	V	14
FOR ALL TONGUES HE KNEW.		594	COLONEL MARTIN		4
SHE MAY BE ALL ALONE THERE,		594	COLONEL MARTIN		14
"TAKE ALL TO YOUR MISTRESS,"		595	COLONEL MARTIN		34
AND THERE AT ALL STREET-CORNERS		596	COLONEL MARTIN		55
AND ALL MEN HEARD THEM SWEAR		596	COLONEL MARTIN		60
DID ALL THAT FOR THE POOR.		596	COLONEL MARTIN		62
AND THERE AT ALL STREET CORNERS		596	COLONEL MARTIN	V	55
ALL SORTS OF KINGS HAVE SAT		597	MODEL LAUREATE		2
THAT MEN AND WOMEN OF ALL SORTS		597	MODEL LAUREATE		3
PUTS ALL MEN IN A FRIGHT,		597	MODEL LAUREATE		12
I MET HER ALL BUT FIFTY YEARS AGO		602	GALLERY REVIS		15
HUGH LANE, "ONLIE BEGETTER" OF ALL THESE;		602	GALLERY REVIS		22
AS THOUGH SOME BALLAD-SINGER HAD SUNG IT ALL;		602	GALLERY REVIS		24
OF ALL THAT PRIDE AND THAT HUMILITY?		602	GALLERY REVIS		29
AS THOUGH SOME BALLAD SINGER HAD SUNG IT ALL.		602	GALLERY REVIS	V	24
HONOUR HAD LIVED SO LONG, ALL LACKING FOUND,		603	GALLERY REVIS		35
ALL THAT WE DID, ALL THAT WE SAID OR SANG		603	GALLERY REVIS		42
ALL THAT WE DID, ALL THAT WE SAID OR SANG		603	GALLERY REVIS		42
OF ALL THAT SCHOLARLY GENERATIONS HAD HELD DEAR;		603	GALLERY REVIS	V	37A
CONTACT ALL THINGS ANTAEUS-LIKE GREW STRONG;		603	GALLERY REVIS	V	44
ALL THINGS DOWN TO THAT COMMON TEST AGAIN;		603	GALLERY REVIS	V	46
ALL MANNIONS COME FROM MANANNAN,		606	SONGS BURDEN 1		10
I PITY ALL THE YOUNG,		607	SONGS BURDEN 2		11
COME GATHER ROUND ME, PLAYERS ALL;		608	SONGS BURDEN 3		1
THAT ALL ATTENDANTS AND THE CASUAL CROWD MIGHT HEAR.		609	IN TARAS HALLS		13
ALL ASIATIC VAGUE IMMENSITIES,		610	STATUES		12
MIRROR ON MIRROR MIRRORED IS ALL THE SHOW.		610	STATUES		22
THERE ALL THE GOLDEN CODGERS LAY,		611	NEWS ORACLE		1
REMEMBER ALL THOSE RENOWNED GENERATIONS,		613	MARCH SONGS 1		1
ALL THAT IS FINISHED, LET IT FADE.		613	MARCH SONGS 1		10
REMEMBER ALL THOSE RENOWNED GENERATIONS,		613	MARCH SONGS 1		11
REMEMBER ALL THAT HAVE SUNK IN THEIR BLOOD,		613	MARCH SONGS 1		12
REMEMBER ALL THAT HAVE DIED ON THE SCAFFOLD,		613	MARCH SONGS 1		13
REMEMBER ALL THAT HAVE FLED, ALL THAT HAVE STOOD,		613	MARCH SONGS 1		14
AND ALL THAT'S FINISHED, LET IT FADE.		613	MARCH SONGS 1		20
REMEMBER ALL THESE RENOWNED GENERATIONS,		613	MARCH SONGS 1	V	11
ALL THAT GREAT PAST TO A TROUBLE OF FOOLS;		614	MARCH SONGS 1		22
ALL THE RENOWN THAT FELL.		614	MARCH SONGS 1		26
AND ALL THAT'S FINISHED, LET IT FADE.		614	MARCH SONGS 1		30
"HEAR, GENTLEMEN, LADIES, AND ALL MANKIND;		615	MARCH SONGS 3		2
ALL THERE CAUGHT UP THE TUNE;		616	MARCH SONGS 3		15
(SOMETHING MAY LINGER THERE THOUGH ALL ELSE DIE;)		618	BRONZE HEAD		5
NO DARK TOMB-HAUNTER ONCE; HER FORM ALL FULL		618	BRONZE HEAD		8
BUT EVEN AT THE STARTING-POST, ALL SLEEK AND NEW,		619	BRONZE HEAD		15
ALL THAT IS NOT ITSELF; I HAD GROWN WILD		619	BRONZE HEAD		20
ANCESTRAL PEARLS ALL PITCHED INTO A STY,		619	BRONZE HEAD		26
WHENCE DID ALL THAT FURY COME?		619	STICK INCENSE		1
AND YET GAVE TONGUE. "HOUND VOICES" WERE THEY ALL.		622	HOUND VOICE		9
ALL METAPHOR, MALACHI, STILTS AND ALL. A BARNACLE GOOSE		623	HIGH TALK		11
ALL METAPHOR, MALACHI, STILTS AND ALL. A BARNACLE GOOSE		623	HIGH TALK		11
BUT HE HAS NEED OF ALL THAT STRENGTH		624	APPARITIONS		20

23

ALL   (CONTINUED)

	PAGE	TITLE	LINE
A GIRL THAT KNEW ALL DANTE ONCE	626	OLD MEN BE MAD	5
MY CIRCUS ANIMALS WERE ALL ON SHOW,	629	CIRCUS ANIMALS	6
THIS DREAM ITSELF HAD ALL MY THOUGHT AND LOVE.	630	CIRCUS ANIMALS	24
HEART-MYSTERIES THERE, AND YET WHEN ALL IS SAID	630	CIRCUS ANIMALS	27
PLAYERS AND PAINTED STAGE TOOK ALL MY LOVE,	630	CIRCUS ANIMALS	31
I MUST LIE DOWN WHERE ALL THE LADDERS START,	630	CIRCUS ANIMALS	39
HEART MYSTERIES THERE, AND YET WHEN ALL IS SAID	630	CIRCUS ANIMALS V	27
ALL THAT I HAVE SAID AND DONE,	632	MAN AND ECHO	6
AND ALL SEEMS EVIL UNTIL I	632	MAN AND ECHO	17
AND, ALL WORK DONE, DISMISSES ALL	633	MAN AND ECHO	34
AND, ALL WORK DONE, DISMISSES ALL	633	MAN AND ECHO	34
"WE THREAD THE NEEDLES' EYES, AND ALL WE DO	634	CUCHULAIN COMF	16
ALL MUST TOGETHER DO." THAT DONE, THE MAN	634	CUCHULAIN COMF	17
CONVICTED COWARDS ALL, BY KINDRED SLAIN	634	CUCHULAIN COMF	21
THOUGH ALL WAS DONE IN COMMON AS BEFORE;	635	CUCHULAIN COMF	24
THAT ALL ARE OATH-BOUND MEN;	635	BLACK TOWER	5
AND ANCIENT IRELAND KNEW IT ALL.	637	BEN BULBEN	16
KNOW THAT WHEN ALL WORDS ARE SAID	638	BEN BULBEN	27
ALL OUT OF SHAPE FROM TOE TO TOP,	639	BEN BULBEN	71
NOW HER SHEEP ALL BROWSING MEET	646	ISLE STAT I 1	22
TILL ALL ELSE IS EMPTY CHAFF,	647	ISLE STAT I 1	60
WEEPING WHEN ALL OTHERS LAUGH.	647	ISLE STAT I 1	62
ALL THE WORLD IS RINGING, RINGING;	648	ISLE STAT I 1	93
ALL THE WORLD IS SINGING, SINGING.	648	ISLE STAT I 1	94
STRICKEN ALL THE NIGHT IS PAST--	648	ISLE STAT I 1	96
ALL CLAMOUR-CLOTHED--WAS'T CLAMOUR WHEN I SUNG,	649	ISLE STAT I 1	108
OF FLIGHT ARE DONE. MOST FAIR OF ALL WHO GRAZE	649	ISLE STAT I 1	118
NASCHINA, HAIL! MOST FAIR OF ALL WHO GRAZE	649	ISLE STAT I 1	120
WHERE ALL NIGHT LONG THE HEAVENS WEEP AND WEEP,	649	ISLE STAT I 1	124
WHERE ALL NIGHT LONG THE LONELY MOON, THE WHITE	650	ISLE STAT I 1	126
ALL FLAME-LIKE GUSHING FROM THE HOLLOW STONES,	650	ISLE STAT I 1	129
OF ALL ON WHOM ARCADIAN SUNS HAVE SHONE	650	ISLE STAT I 1	143
THE PALE ANEMONES. WE'VE SOUGHT ALL DAY,	651	ISLE STAT I 2	5
ALL RHAPSODY HATH SORROW FOR ITS SOUL.	652	ISLE STAT I 2	17
SOME SAY THAT ALL WHO TOUCH THE ISLAND LONE	653	ISLE STAT I 2	42
TELLS ALL HIS SINNING IN THEIR EARS.	655	ISLE STAT I 3	14
TELLS ALL HER SINNING IN THEIR EARS.	655	ISLE STAT I 3 V	14
AND THEY ARE ALL NOW STONE, AS I SHALL BE,	656	ISLE STAT I 3	35
ALL CHOICE, AND GIVE TO CHANCE FOR GUIDING CHANCE	656	ISLE STAT I 3	39
MOCKING WITH PATIENT LAUGHTER ALL THE NIGHT	657	ISLE STAT I 3	52
STRANGE DRAPERIES DID ALL THE SIDES ADORN,	657	ISLE STAT I 3	55
THE WINGED WONDER OF ALL FAERY LAND.	657	ISLE STAT I 3	57
OF THE FORESTS ALL THE PRIDE,	658	ISLE STAT I 3	84
IN ALL SUCH THINGS, PRAY LET THINE EARS BE TURNED,	660	ISLE STAT II 1	39
AND ONLY SHEEP HE LOVED OF ALL THE TROOP.	661	ISLE STAT II 1	61
ALL THINGS ARE QUIET IN THE EVE'S WIDE EYE.	662	ISLE STAT II 2	6
ALL SWIM WITH TEARS. THE FAERY BOAT'S AT HAND!	663	ISLE STAT II 2	33
OH, LOVELY TO SEE IN ALL MEN'S SIGHT	666	ISLE STAT II 3	3
IN ALL MEN'S SIGHT.	666	ISLE STAT II 3	5
O SWIFT ON THE SEAS ALL DAY AND NIGHT	666	ISLE STAT II 3	8
ALL DAY AND NIGHT,	666	ISLE STAT II 3	10
OF MY SAD HUNTER-FRIEND WILL ALL DEPART	668	ISLE STAT II 3	45
YOUR EYES ARE ALL A-FLASH. SHE IS NOT HERE.	669	ISLE STAT II 3	68
WITH YOU I AM ALL GENTLENESS; IN TRUTH,	669	ISLE STAT II 3	70
MY WORDS WERE ALL: "HERE NO LOVES WANE AND WITHER,	669	ISLE STAT II 3	84
MY WORDS WERE ALL: "O WHITHER, WHITHER, WHITHER	669	ISLE STAT II 3	87
YOUR EYES ARE ALL AFLASH. SHE IS NOT HERE.	669	ISLE STAT II 3 V	68
AND THOU WILT STAY. ALL THOUGHT OF WHAT THEY FIND	670	ISLE STAT II 3	92
HAS FENCED US ROUND FOR ALL ETERNITY.	670	ISLE STAT II 3	95
AND ALL WAS QUIET ROUND ME SPREAD,	670	ISLE STAT II 3	112
AND ALL HIS VEINS HAD NEAR RUN DRY,	670	ISLE STAT II 3	119
AND ONE ALONE OF ALL WOULD HARK,	671	ISLE STAT II 3	123
FOR EACH WITHIN HIMSELF HATH ALL,	671	ISLE STAT II 3	132
THE HEAVENS ALL STAR-THROBBING ARE A-LIT.	671	ISLE STAT II 3	143
THE HEAVENS ALL STAR-THROBBING ARE ALIT.	671	ISLE STAT II 3 V	143
AH! YOU ARE WEEPING! HERE SHOULD ALL GRIEF CEASE.	672	ISLE STAT II 3	149
AND FADED NOW IS ALL THY WONDROUS ART.	673	ISLE STAT II 3	194
YET EVER MORE, THROUGH ALL THY DAYS OF RUTH,	674	ISLE STAT II 3	206
YET EVERMORE, THROUGH ALL THY DAYS OF RUTH,	674	ISLE STAT II 3 V	206
I HURL AWAY THESE ALL UNFAERY FEARS.	675	ISLE STAT II 3	228
DOTH STILL THE WANDERER ROVE? WITH ALL HIS SHIPS	677	ISLE STAT II 3	287
IT IS THE VOICE OF ALL OUR HEARTS THAT LAUGH.	681	SEEKER	7
A CREEPING HORROR IS ALL OVER ME.	681	SEEKER	12
ARE ALL THINGS WELL WITH YOU AND WITH YOUR SHEEP?	682	SEEKER	13
YES, ALL IS VERY WELL. WHENCE COMEST THOU?	682	SEEKER	14
A COWARD IN THE FIELD; AND ALL MEN CRIED:	684	SEEKER	53
WERE ALL MY WANDERING DAYS OF NO AVAIL.	684	SEEKER	64
MINE HEART-STRINGS ARE ALL BROKEN SAVING ONE,	684	SEEKER V	69B
FOR ALL I GAVE THE VOICE, FOR ALL MY YOUTH,	685	SEEKER	78
FOR ALL I GAVE THE VOICE, FOR ALL MY YOUTH,	685	SEEKER	78
FOR ALL MY JOY--AH, WOE!	685	SEEKER	79
TO LIGHTEST OF LIGHT THINGS ALL SANCTITY.	686	DRAWING-ROOM	8
ALL THESE ARE SOULS THAT FLY FROM THEIR DREAD SELVES.	686	LIFE	4
CRAMM'D ALL HER YOUTH; AND HATES HAVE BOUGHT AND SOLD	687	TWO TITANS	13
MAKING ALL ONE O'ER ROCK AND SEA AND SKIES;	687	TWO TITANS	28
THAT ALL MEN EVERMORE MAY HUMBLY BOW	688	TWO TITANS	49
WHERE THEY ALL SUMMER FEED THEIR WANDERING FLOCKS,	690	MOSADA 1	5
FOR I AND ALL MY PEOPLE WERE ACCURST	690	MOSADA 1	15
AND ALL WAS DIMNESS, TILL A DYING LEAF	690	MOSADA 1	20
WE MEET--WE TWO. HOW MERRY ALL THESE ARE	691	MOSADA 1	31

24

ALL   (CONTINUED)

	PAGE	TITLE		LINE
AWAY FROM ALL THE OTHERS. NOW THE SUN	691	MOSADA 1		33
IN COIL ON COIL OF AZURE. ALL IS READY.	691	MOSADA 1		41
THEY SAY I AM ALL UGLINESS; LAME-FOOTED	692	MOSADA 1		60
AND ALL THE ELDERS SITTING IN THE SUN	693	MOSADA 1		69
AND CALM, ROBED ALL IN RAIMENT MOONY WHITE.	693	MOSADA 1		77
THEM ALL, AND LET THEM FIND YOU IN THE VAPOUR.	694	MOSADA 1	V	108A
TO THEIR FARM WORK; HOW SILENT ALL WILL BE!	699	MOSADA 3		8
TO THEIR FARM-WORK; HOW SILENT ALL WILL BE.	699	MOSADA 3	V	8
FOR IT ALONE OF ALL THE WORLD WILL DO	700	MOSADA 3		28
DAY'S DEAD, ALL FLAME-BEWILDERED, AND THE HILLS	702	MOSADA 3		86
ALL HEAVEN'S FLOOR, WITH VAPOURS BEDDED--	705	DAWN-SONG		11
THOUGH YOUNGEST OF ALL IN OUR GOOD BAND,	707	FAIRY PEDANT		11
THOUGH YOUNGEST OF ALL IN OUR GOOD BAND,	708	FAIRY PEDANT		39
OFTEN HE HAD BENT DOWN SOME BOUGH ALL BRIGHT	710	FERENCZ RENYI		28
OFTEN HE HAD BENT DOWN SOME BOUGH ALL BRIGHT WITH BERRIES!	710	FERENCZ RENYI	V	28
AS THOUGH THEY'D VOWED TO MEASURE ALL ITS WAYS.	711	FERENCZ RENYI		48
THERE FAR AWAY FROM ALL WE TWO WILL GO,	714	FERENCZ RENYI		99
FOR ALL SAVE HIM WHO PINING FELL,	717	FAIRY DOCTOR		19
FOR ALL SAVE HE WHO PINING FELL,	717	FAIRY DOCTOR	V	19
NOW A SCREAM FROM ALL THOSE FISHERS, FOR THERE ON DECK THERE BE	719	PHANTOM SHIP		19
ALL THE DROWNED THAT EVER WERE DROWNED FROM THAT VILLAGE BY THE SEA!	719	PHANTOM SHIP		20
AND THE GHASTLY GHOST-FLAMES GLIMMER ALL ALONG THE TAFFRAIL RAILS	719	PHANTOM SHIP		21
ALL THOSE LONG FORGOTTEN FISHERS, TILL IN THE EASTERN SKIES	719	PHANTOM SHIP	V	32
I AM DULL TO-DAY, OR YOU WERE NOW ALL LOST.	722	WITCH VIVIEN		59
ILL WORDS FOR ALL THINGS SOFT AND FAIR.	723	GIRLS SONG A		6
HAST THOU NOT KNOWN ALL SORROW AND DELIGHT	723	KANVA ON SELF		2
ALL THEIR JEALOUSY DISPLAY.	726	LOVERS QUARREL		22
"WITH ACTION ALL THE WORLD IS VEXED,"	728	PRIEST FAIRY		15
AND ALL THE SAD FAY CHIVALRY	730	PRIEST FAIRY		71
REMOTE FROM ALL THE HARD EARTH TROUBLES,	731	PRIEST FAIRY		80
HANGS O'ER ALL THE WOODED EARTH.	731	STREET DANCERS		8
ALL THE HEALING EARTH MAY-TREASURE,	733	STREET DANCERS		63
ALL THE HEALING EARTH MAY TREASURE,	733	STREET DANCERS	V	63
ALL THESE ARE SOULS WHO FLY FROM THEIR DREAD SELVES.	734	QUATRAIN APHOR		4
TO LIGHTEST OF ALL LIGHT THINGS SANCTITY.	734	QUATRAIN APHOR		8
ALL THESE ARE SOULS THAT FLY FROM THEIR DREAD SELVES.	734	QUATRAIN APHOR	V	4
TO LIGHTEST OF LIGHT THINGS ALL SANCTITY.	734	QUATRAIN APHOR	V	8
FOR ALL GOOD MEN NOW FALLEN ILL.	736	IN CHURCH		5
IN ALL ITS HONEY-THICKENED TUNE	736	SUMMER EVENING		7
MOURN ALL THE NIGHT AND DAY.	737	MOURN THEN ON		2
AND ALL HER STARLIGHT IS WITH SORROW MAD,	738	YOU ARE SAD		3
ALL THE WORDS THAT I GATHER,	739	WHERE BOOKS GO		1
AND ALL THE WORDS THAT I WRITE,	739	WHERE BOOKS GO		2
"AND ALL DOWN FROM NORTHUMBERLAND	740	EARL PAUL		9
TILL ALL THINGS ARE AT REST.	741	EARL PAUL		52
"I ASK THAT I AND ALL MY RACE,"	742	EARL PAUL		61
THAT ARE A POISON TO ALL MEN	743	DANAAN QUICK		16
OR LEAVE SOME SERVICE ALL UNDONE,	743	DANAAN QUICK		21
CAST OUT ALL HOPE, CAST OUT ALL FEAR,	743	DANAAN QUICK		25
CAST OUT ALL HOPE, CAST OUT ALL FEAR,	743	DANAAN QUICK		25
AND NOW THEY ARE ALL GONE, I FOLLOW STILL.	749	SHADOW WATER A		37
TIME AND THE WORLD AND ALL THINGS DWINDLE OUT.	749	SHADOW WATER A		47
AND WERE ALL DREAMS, IT WOULD NOT WEIGH IN THE HAND.	750	SHADOW WATER A		77
HOW ALL THAT DIE ARE BORNE ABOUT THE WORLD	750	SHADOW WATER A		84
NONE SHOULD ESCAPE MY SWORD; I WOULD SEND ALL	752	SHADOW WATER A		111
HE HAS HEARD ME BECAUSE I PROMISED ALL.	752	SHADOW WATER A		116
WAKE ALL BELOW. WHY HAVE YOU BROKEN OUR SLEEP?	753	SHADOW WATER A		132
WHEN ALL GATHER THEY WILL FLY UPON THEIR WAY.	753	SHADOW WATER A		136
AND NOW THEY ALL WHEEL SUDDENLY AND FLY	753	SHADOW WATER A		148
ENDS ALL THINGS. I HAVE SLAIN THE LOCHLANN KING.	754	SHADOW WATER A		163
YOUR HEART'S DESIRE AND THE END OF ALL OUR TROUBLE!	755	SHADOW WATER A		175
BUT NOW I WILL KILL HER. ALL COMES TO AN END.	755	SHADOW WATER A		176
FOR I HAVE ALL HIS GARDEN WISDOM. O SPEAK!	756	SHADOW WATER A		180
I WILL SWEAR BY SUN AND MOON TO PARDON ALL	756	SHADOW WATER A		183
AND TO GIVE WEALTH OF OXEN AND SHEEP TO ALL;	756	SHADOW WATER A		184
ALL THAT TIME KNOWS. SPEAK TO ME, QUEEN. O SPEAK!	756	SHADOW WATER A	V	180
BECAUSE THESE WATERS MAKE ALL WOMEN ONE.	757	SHADOW WATER A		194
THAT HAVE BUILT ALL ARE DUST ON A MOTH'S WING.	757	SHADOW WATER A		205
AND A STRONG GALLEY. I GIVE YOU ALL AS MUCH.	758	SHADOW WATER A		222
I HAVE FORGOT IT ALL. HOW SOON DREAMS FADE!	761	SHADOW WATER A		272
SWEET WITH ALL MUSIC, OUT OF HIS LONG HAIR,	762	SHADOW WATER A		303
ALL DIES AMONG THOSE STREAMS. THE FOOL HAS MADE	764	SHADOW WATER A		335
AND ALL THE WISDOM THAT OLD IMAGES,	764	SHADOW WATER A		344
AND ALL THAT PROPHESYING IMAGES	764	SHADOW WATER A	V	344A
TO SNATCH ALIVE OUT OF THE STREAMS ALL LOVERS	765	SHADOW WATER A		347
THE LOVE OF ALL UNDER THE LIGHT OF THE SUN	765	SHADOW WATER A		353
WE WILL NOT QUARREL, NOW THAT ALL IS WELL.	766	SHADOW WATER A		373
ALL THAT KNOW LOVE AMONG THE WINDS OF THE WORLD	767	SHADOW WATER A		386
AMID THE DARKNESS, NOW THAT ALL MY STARS	767	SHADOW WATER A	V	404
PUT ALL YOUR POWER ON THE THREAD	771	SPINNING SONG		12
HAD NOT ALL HIS LIMBS A STIR	772	SONG DEIRDRE 1		11
WHAT IS ALL OUR PRAISE TO THEM	773	SONG DEIRDRE 1		23
AND ALL THE GARDEN BLESS,	774	COME RIDE		10
UNTIL ALL BE RUINOUS.	775	AGAINST WITCH		4
ALL THEIR BODIES, JOINT BY JOINT,	776	AGAINST WITCH		22
ALL HIS BODY CAN BUT SHOVE	776	AGAINST WITCH		33
ALL THAT MINGLING OF OUR BREATH,	777	SONG DEIRDRE 2		10

25

ALL   (CONTINUED)
    "LIVES ALL HIS DAYS . . . . 780 WELL AND TREE   3
    THAT ALL THE VALLEY FILLS . . . . 781 MY HEART BEAT   10
    FOR ALL OUR TALKING. . . . . 785 YOUR HEART   7
    AND ALL SEEM WELL ENOUGH. . . . . 786 YOUR HEART   15
    I MOCK AT ALL SO BURNING OUT. . . . . 787 HUDDON DUDDON   15
    CASTLE DARGAN'S RUIN ALL LIT. . . . . 788 HAWTHORN TREE   3
    YET ALL THE LOVELY THINGS THAT WERE . . . . . . 788 HAWTHORN TREE   11
    MAYBE I SHALL NOT DIE AT ALL. . . . . 788 HAWTHORN TREE   16
    MAY BE I SHALL NOT DIE AT ALL. . . . . 788 HAWTHORN TREE V 16
    AND ALL MEN LIE THAT SAY THAT I . . . . 789 SINGING HEAD   3
    OF ALL THAT LOVERS SAID. . . . . 789 SINGING HEAD   10
    GAVE ALL THE LOVE THAT WOMEN KNOW! . . . . 789 SINGING HEAD   21
    OUTWEIGHED ALL OTHER YEARS, YOU SAID, ... 791 REPRISALS   6
ALLAH
    OH, ALLAH! IT WAS THUS THEY SHONE THAT NIGHT . . . . . 701 MOSADA 3   50
ALLAH'S
    I HERE ARREST THEE. IT WAS ALLAH'S WILL. . . . . . . 694 MOSADA 1   105
    I HERE ARREST THEE. IT IS ALLAH'S WILL. . . . . . . 694 MOSADA 1 V 105
    FORGIVE ME! IT WAS ALLAH'S WILL. THE CORDS. . . . . 695 MOSADA 1   109
    FORGIVE, OR I WILL DIE. 'TWAS ALLAH'S WILL. . . . . 695 MOSADA 1   118
    FORGIVE ME! IT WAS ALLAH'S WILL. NOW CORDS. . . . . 695 MOSADA 1 V 109
ALL-DESTROYING
    ALL-DESTROYING SWORD-BLADE STILL . . . . 484 SYMBOLS   3
ALLEGORICAL
    THROUGH THREE ENCHANTED ISLANDS, ALLEGORICAL DREAMS, . . 629 CIRCUS ANIMALS   11
ALLEN'S
    THE FLOOR OF ALLEN'S HOSTING HALL . . . . 13 OISIN 1 V 156
ALLEYS
    OR DOWN THE DEWY FOREST ALLEYS, ... 10 OISIN 1   120
    AND DOWN THE DEWY FOREST ALLEYS, ... 10 OISIN 1 V 120
ALLIANCES
    MARRIAGES, ALLIANCES AND FAMILIES, ... 491 COOLE BALLYLEE 36
ALL-LABOURING
    AND BY THE HEAVEN'S ALL-LABOURING BROODS! . . . . . . 164 PERFECT BEAUTY V 5
ALLOW
    ALLOW THAT HE, DESPITE . . . . 584 ORAHILLY   4
    NOT TO ALLOW HIS LOOKS TO TELL . . . . 624 APPARITIONS   13
ALLOWS
    MY TRADE ALLOWS! CHOSEN MY COMPANY, ... 352 PEOPLE   20
ALL-POWERFUL
    BY THE WEBBED TOES, AND THAT ALL-POWERFUL BILL . . . . 441 LEDA AND SWAN V 3
ALL'S
    ALL'S CHANGED SINCE I, HEARING AT TWILIGHT, ... 322 SWANS AT COOLE 15
    WHERE ALL'S ACCUSTOMED, CEREMONIOUS! . . . . . . 405 FOR DAUGHTER   74
    OR OUT OF DRUNKARD'S EYE. ALL'S WHIGGERY NOW, ... 486 SEVEN SAGES   13
    OR DRUNKARD'S EYE. ALL'S WHIGGERY NOW, ... 486 SEVEN SAGES V 13
    OR OUT OF A DRUNKARD'S EYE. ALL'S WHIGGERY NOW, ... 486 SEVEN SAGES V 13
    THAT ALL'S ARRANGED IN ONE CLEAR VIEW, ... 633 MAN AND ECHO   31
    BE ONE? I THINK ALL'S FINISHED NOW AND SEALED. . . . . 701 MOSADA 3   62
ALL-UNNEEDED
    TOLD WHERE--AH, LITTLE, ALL-UNNEEDED VOICE!-- . . . . . 127 DREAM OF FAERY V 30
ALMANACS
    REMEMBERED OUT OF BABYLONIAN ALMANACS, ... 426 PHANTOM HATRED 20
ALMHUIN
    UNDER A BEECH AT ALMHUIN AND HEARD THE THIN . . . . 44 OISIN 2   228
ALMHUIN'S
    THE FLOOR OF ALMHUIN'S HOSTING HALL . . . . . . 13 OISIN 1   156
ALMINTOR
    NAY, NAY, ALMINTOR, YONDER SONG IS GLAD. . . . . . 652 ISLE STAT I 2 23
    ALMINTOR, THOU HAST GROWN SO FULL OF RUTH, ... 652 ISLE STAT I 2 26
    ALMINTOR WITH HER LOVE. WHO ART THOU?--SPEAK, . . . 660 ISLE STAT II 1 50
    O, MY ALMINTOR, NOBLE WAS THY QUEST! . . . . . 679 ISLE STAT II 3 319
ALMINTOR'S
    YON IS THE HUNTER'S, SIR ALMINTOR'S, PAGE! . . . . 660 ISLE STAT II 1 35
    SIR PAGE, ALMINTOR'S FRIEND, AND THEREFORE LEARNED . . 660 ISLE STAT II 1 38
    BEING ALMINTOR'S PAGE. NOW JUDGE YOU HERE. . . . . 660 ISLE STAT II 1 47
    ASIDE!--THE WILD HORNS TOLD ALMINTOR'S END, ... 665 ISLE STAT II 2 68
ALMOST
    AND ALMOST WEPT BECAUSE THEY COULD NOT FIND IT. . . . 229 SHADOW WATER B 155
    AND WE ARE ALMOST ON HER! WE HAD NOT KNOWN . . . . 232 SHADOW WATER B 220
    I ALMOST LONG THAT IT WERE POSSIBLE! . . . . . . 236 SHADOW WATER B 306
    NOW THAT WE'RE ALMOST SETTLED IN OUR HOUSE . . . . 323 ROBERT GREGORY   1
    NOW THAT WE'VE ALMOST SETTLED IN OUR HOUSE . . . . 323 ROBERT GREGORY V 1
ALONE
    AND SURGING PHOSPHORUS ALONE GAVE LIGHT . . . . . 31 OISIN 2   33
    OF SURGING PHOSPHORUS ALONE GAVE LIGHT. . . . . . 31 OISIN 2 V 33
    HOPELESS FOR EVER, THEY ALONE SHALL SEEK . . . . 42 OISIN 2 V 200
    "LAST OF MY RACE, THREE THINGS I RULE ALONE-- . . . 45 OISIN 2 V 239A
    . . . REMEMBERING ALONE THAT DELIGHT . . . . . 54 OISIN 3   111
    . . . ALONE WITH REMEMBRANCE AND FEAR! . . . . . 63 OISIN 3   218
    WITHOUT LAUGHTER, A COUGHING, ALONE WITH REMEMBRANCE AND 63 OISIN 3 V 218
      FEAR!
    WORDS ALONE ARE CERTAIN GOOD. . . . . 65 HAPPY SHEPHERD 10
    FOR WORDS ALONE ARE CERTAIN GOOD! . . . . 66 HAPPY SHEPHERD 43
    AND WORDS ALONE ARE CERTAIN GOOD, ... 66 HAPPY SHEPHERD V 43
    WHILE WE ALONE HAVE ROUND US WOVEN WOODS, ... 73 ANASHU VIJAYA 56
    HOW WE ALONE OF MORTALS ARE . . . . 78 INDIAN TO LOVE 11
    BUT SEEK ALONE TO HEAR THE STRANGE THINGS SAID . . . 101 ROSE UPON ROOD 19
    BUT TELL ALONE YOUR NAME AND HOUSE TO HIM . . . . 108 CUCHULAIN SEA V 36
    AND WENT DOWN TO THE LONG SANDS ALONE, ... 111 CUCHULAIN SEA V 84

```
                                                    PAGE      TITLE            LINE
ALONE   (CONTINUED)
     AND HE WENT DOWN TO THE LONG SANDS ALONE,        111  CUCHULAIN SEA   V   84
     STOOD UP, AND CAME TO THE LONG SANDS ALONE!      111  CUCHULAIN SEA   V   84
     AND LIVE ALONE IN THE BEE-LOUD GLADE.            117  ISLE INNISFREE      4
     OF SERAPHS, BROODING, EACH ALONE,                156  FORGOT BEAUTY   V  22
     NODDING ALONE AND APART,                         171  MAID QUIET      V   6
     KNOWING ONE, OUT OF ALL THINGS, ALONE, THAT HIS HEAD  177  PAST GREATNESS  8
     HAVE ALL THAT GREATNESS, AND NOT HERS ALONE,     186  QUEEN MAEVE       133
     BECAUSE IT IS ALONE OF ALL THINGS HAPPY.         198  SEVEN WOODS         9
     ALONE AND WINGED.  OUR LOVE SHALL BE LIKE THEIRS 250  SHADOW WATER B    581
     AND I AM LEFT ALONE WITH MY BELOVED,             251  SHADOW WATER B    600
     WE ARE ALONE FOR EVER, AND I LAUGH,              251  SHADOW WATER B    602
     SHALL BE ALONE FOR EVER.  WE TWO--THIS CROWN--   251  SHADOW WATER B    605
     PALE-FACED, ALONE UPON A BENCH, EDAIN            279  TWO KINGS          61
     PALE-FACED, ALONE UPON A BENCH, HIS WIFE         279  TWO KINGS       V  61
     WHERE I MAY SPEAK TO YOU ALONE, MY CRAFT         284  TWO KINGS         159
     ALONE WITH ALL THIS USELESS HAPPINESS?"          285  TWO KINGS         200
     BUT I ALONE BEING BLESSED KEEP                   307  HOUR DAWN         104
     AND EVEN OLD MEN'S EYES GREW DIM, THIS HAND ALONE, 314  FALLEN MAJESTY   2
     AS THOUGH HE HAD BUT THAT ONE TRADE ALONE,       327  ROBERT GREGORY     80
     BEING OLD, BUT THAT THE OLD ALONE MIGHT DIE,     339  SHEP GOATHERD       4
     I LET THEM STRAY.  I THOUGHT OF RHYME ALONE,     339  SHEP GOATHERD      11
     THAT HE ALONE HAD GATHERED UP NO GEAR,           340  SHEP GOATHERD      49
     BURNING ALONE BESIDE AN OPEN BOOK,               370  EGO DOMINUS        63
     ALONE, IMPORTANT AND WISE,                       379  CAT AND MOON       26
     AND BOTH LOOK UP TO ME ALONE                     380  SONGS FOOL 1        4
     HEARTS WITH ONE PURPOSE ALONE                    393  EASTER 1916        41
     THAT HAVE AN EAR ALONE                           395  SIXTEEN DEAD       14
     AND THERE ALONE, THAT HAVE NO SOLITUDE?          398  LEADERS CROWD       9
     AND THAT ALONE: YET I, BEING DRIVEN HALF INSANE  442  BLACK CENTAUR       6
     BEING ALL ALONE I'D NURSE A STONE                459  HIS WILDNESS       11
     UNDER IT WISDOM STANDS, AND I ALONE--            469  HARUN RASHID      189
     OF ALL ARABIA'S LOVERS I ALONE--                 470  HARUN RASHID      190
     AND I ALONE, ONE IN TEN THOUSAND YEARS,          470  HARUN RASHID      190
     OUT OF TEN THOUSAND WINTERS, I ALONE--           470  HARUN RASHID    V 190
     LOVE YOU FOR YOURSELF ALONE.                     492  ANNE GREGORY        5
     MAY LOVE ME FOR MYSELF ALONE                     492  ANNE GREGORY       11
     COULD LOVE YOU FOR YOURSELF ALONE                492  ANNE GREGORY       17
     BUT WERE I LEFT TO LIE ALONE                     511  JANE AND JACK      13
     I WENT OUT ALONE                                 515  GIRLS SONG B        1
     ONE MAN, ONE MAN ALONE                           526  AM OF IRELAND       6
     ONE MAN, AND ONE MAN ALONE                       526  AM OF IRELAND   V   6
     AND ALL ALONE COMES RIDING THERE                 550  SEVERED HEAD       18
     IS WHAT I CAN WHISTLE ALONE AND ALONE.           551  SONGS REWRIT 1      4
     IS WHAT I CAN WHISTLE ALONE AND ALONE.           551  SONGS REWRIT 1      4
     ALONE AND ALONE, WITH A SPECKLED SHIN?           551  SONGS REWRIT 1      8
     ALONE AND ALONE, WITH A SPECKLED SHIN?           551  SONGS REWRIT 1      8
     ALONE AND ALONE NINE NIGHTS I LAY                551  SONGS REWRIT 1     13
     ALONE AND ALONE NINE NIGHTS I LAY                551  SONGS REWRIT 1     13
     IS DRINKING HER HEALTH WHEN LONE, ALONE--        551  SONGS REWRIT 1 V    4
     DRINKING ALONE WITH A SPECKLED SHIN?             551  SONGS REWRIT 1 V    8
     LIVE LONE, ALONE WITH A SPECKLED SHIN?           551  SONGS REWRIT 1 V    8
     HE RHYMING ALONE IN HIS BED.                     552  SONGS REWRIT 2     12
     LYING ALONE ON A BED                             552  SONGS REWRIT 2 V   10
     ALONE WITH A CRAZY HEAD.                         552  SONGS REWRIT 2 V   12
     IN THE MIND ALONE:                               553  PRAYER OLD AGE      2
     AND SHE WAS MUCH ALONE,                          594  COLONEL MARTIN     11
     SHE MAY BE ALL ALONE THERE.                      594  COLONEL MARTIN     14
     WE THREE ALONE IN MODERN TIMES HAD BROUGHT       603  GALLERY REVIS      45
     YOU THAT WOULD JUDGE ME, DO NOT JUDGE ALONE      603  GALLERY REVIS      50
     THE POST AND GARDEN-BOY ALONE                    607  SONGS BURDEN 2      7
     SHE ALONE, MY LADY, LINGERETH                    646  ISLE STAT I 1      28
     I'D BE ALONE.  WE TWO, BY THAT PALE FOUNT,       650  ISLE STAT I 1     132
     THAT NESTLES ALONE IN THE WHISTLING WIND,        657  ISLE STAT I 1      68
     DOWN TO THEIR FEET THE STARS THAT SHINE ALONE,   662  ISLE STAT II 1     80
     LAUGHS NOT.  IT DWELLS ALONE ON MORTAL LIPS!     670  ISLE STAT II 3    100
     AND ONE ALONE OF ALL WOULD HARK.                 671  ISLE STAT II 3    123
     I SPEAK ALONE WITH SERVANTS OF THE CROSS         698  MOSADA 2           48
     FOR IT ALONE OF ALL THE WORLD WILL DO            700  MOSADA 3           28
     ALONE WITH OUR OWN WHISPERS AND REPLIES--        702  MOSADA 3           80
     ALONE AMONG THE MURMURS OF THE DAWN.             702  MOSADA 3           81
     WHO WANDER AND WHISPER ALONE.                    707  FAIRY PEDANT        8
     AH! CRUEL ONES, LEAVE ME ALONE NOW               707  FAIRY PEDANT       13
     AH! CRUEL ONES, LEAVE ME ALONE                   707  FAIRY PEDANT    V  13
     GAVE TO ME ALONE THE CROSS!                      744  ROSY CROSS          3
     GAVE TO ME ALONE THE CROSS.                      744  ROSY CROSS         11
     THAT FORGAEL HAS FOLLOWED THE GREY BIRDS ALONE,  767  SHADOW WATER A    402
     FRAIL BIRD, LIKE A WHITE SEA-BIRD ALONE          784  WOMANS BEAUTY       2
ALONG
     NEIGHING ALONG THE LIFELESS WASTE!               13   OISIN 1           170
     AND ROLLS ALONG THE UNWIELDY SUN,                18   OISIN 1           267
     TRICKLING ALONG THE EARTH, I RAVE!               19   OISIN 1         V 281
     ALONG THE BLOOD-BEDABBLED PLAINS,                24   OISIN 1           371
     REMEMBERING HOW ALONG THE PLAINS,                24   OISIN 1         V 370
     SHE LIMPS ALONG IN AN AGED WHITENESS!            27   OISIN 1           415
     HIS SHADOW ALONG IN THE EVENING BLAZE,           27   OISIN 1         V 409
     SHE LIMPS ALONG IN AN AGED WHITENESS.            28   OISIN 1         V 423
     FLUTTER ALONG THE FROTH LIPS OF THE SEA,         33   OISIN 2            58
     FLUTTER ALONG THE FROTH LIPS OF THE SEA          33   OISIN 2            64
     FLUTTER ALONG THE FROTH-LIPS OF THE SEA,         33   OISIN 2         V  58
     HIS HAND ALONG THE RUNNEL'S SIDE, AS THOUGH      39   OISIN 2           162
```

		PAGE	TITLE		LINE

ALONG   (CONTINUED)
    BARKING. ALONG THE HERBLESS PLAIN, WITH BLOWS . . . . 40 OISIN 2 V 170
    . . . FLUNG LOOSELY ALONG THE DIM GROUND! . . . . . 50 OISIN 3   45
    WENT WALKING WITH SLOW STEPS ALONG THE GLEAMING . . . . 68 SAD SHEPHERD   3
    ROLLING ALONG IN DREAMS FROM HILL TO HILL. . . . . . 68 SAD SHEPHERD   11
    THEIR HAIR ALONG THE MOUNTAINS ROLLED AND FILLED . . . . 74 ANASHU VIJAYA   71
    I PASSED ALONG THE WATER'S EDGE BELOW THE HUMID TREES, . . . 76 INDIAN ON GOD   1
    ALONG THE GRASS, ALONG THE SANDS, ... 78 INDIAN TO LOVE   9
    ALONG THE GRASS, ALONG THE SANDS. . . . . 78 INDIAN TO LOVE   9
    PENSIVE THEY PACED ALONG THE FADED LEAVES, ... 80 EPHEMERA   10
    OR WHEN ALONG THE WINTRY STRANDS . . . . 84 MAD KING GOLL   41
    I LEAD ALONG THE WOODLAND DEER! . . . . 84 MAD KING GOLL   46
    OR WHERE ALONG THE WINTRY STRANDS . . . . 84 MAD KING GOLL V 41
    ALONG THE PEBBLY STREET. . . . . 94 MOLL MAGEE   12
    DRIVING THE DEER ALONG THE WOODY WAYS. . . . . . . 109 CUCHULAIN SEA V 48
    AND WHEN THE UPROAR RAN ALONG THE GRASS . . . . . . 186 QUEEN MAEVE   127
    SWINGING, SWINGING ALONG. . . . . 544 TO SAME TUNE 1 V REF
    TAKE TO THE ROADS AND GO MARCHING ALONG. . . . . . 548 TO SAME TUNE 3   14
    MARCHING, MARCHING ALONG. . . . . 549 TO SAME TUNE 3   25
    AND LAUGH'D, SO, SO ALONG THE BUBBLING RILLS . . . . 645 ISLE STAT I 1   18
    ALONG THE WOOD WITH SUBTLE TREAD AND BENDED BOWS. . . . 649 ISLE STAT I 1   111
    IF SO I MIGHT, ALONG A DEWY VALE, ... 649 ISLE STAT I 1   123
    THAT CALLS. O EVIL STARRED! IT COMES ALONG. . . . . 653 ISLE STAT I 2   49
    ALONG THE LAKE. THE CRANE HAS HOMEWARD FLED. . . . . 656 ISLE STAT I 3   23
    TO EASE THEIR WORLD-OLD THIRST ALONG THE BRINK . . . . 663 ISLE STAT II 2   41
    FAIR YOUTH, ALONG A WANDERING WAY . . . . 667 ISLE STAT II 3   38
    OF THE DREAD WOODS; ALONG THEIR RUSSET FLOOR . . . . 675 ISLE STAT II 3   243
    ALONG THE VELVET VALE I SAW HIM COME-- . . . . . . 690 MOSADA 1   10
    ALONG THE SEA: AND MANY A MAN GREW HUSHED . . . . . 693 MOSADA 1   86
    ALONG THE CORNFIELD, WHERE THE POPPIES GROW, ... 699 MOSADA 3 V   7
    I CANNOT EVEN CRAWL ALONG THE FLAGS . . . . . . 701 MOSADA 3   58
    AFAR ALONG THE FLEET WHITE RIVER'S FACE-- . . . . . 702 MOSADA 3   79
    FROM HERE, ALONG THE SHADOWY WAY THAT WINDS . . . . 703 MOSADA 3   111
    AND ALONG THE MOUNTAINS PASS, ... 705 DAWN-SONG   12
    ALONG THE TENTS, THE FIELDS, THE VILLAGE WALLS. . . . 712 FERENCZ RENYI   71
    ALONG THE TENTS, FIELD, THE VILLAGE WALLS. . . . . 712 FERENCZ RENYI V 71
    CREEPING ALONG THE HEAVENS' PURPLE CUP, ... 714 FERENCZ RENYI   112
    AY, AND SHAKES IN SEA-GREEN WAVERINGS ALONG THE FISHERS' 718 PHANTOM SHIP   2
        STREET!
    AYE AND SHAKES IN SEA GREEN WAVERINGS, ALONG THE FISHERS' 718 PHANTOM SHIP V 2
        STREET.
    AND THE GHASTLY GHOST-FLAMES GLIMMER ALL ALONG THE TAFFRAIL 719 PHANTOM SHIP   21
        RAILS
    AND THE GHASTLY GHOST FLAMES GLIMMER ALONG THE TAFFREL 719 PHANTOM SHIP V 21
        RAILS,
    WHISPERING ALONG THE SUNNY PATH! . . . . 725 LEGEND   18
    AND RUBBED ALONG THE RAIL HIS NOSE. . . . . 725 LEGEND   28
    ROLLS ALONG THE SEA SANDS WHITE. . . . . 732 STREET DANCERS   34
    ROLLS ALONG THE SEA-SANDS WHITE. . . . . 732 STREET DANCERS V 34
ALOUD
    HE CALLED ALOUD TO ALL THE STARS TO LEND . . . . . 68 SAD SHEPHERD V 5
    I LAUGHED ALOUD AND HURRIED ON . . . . 83 MAD KING GOLL   31
    WHERE HER GRANDCHILDREN SLEPT, AND CRIED ALOUD, . . . 185 QUEEN MAEVE   109
    WHERE HER GRAND-CHILDREN SLEPT, AND CRIED ALOUD . . . 185 QUEEN MAEVE V 109
    TO CRY ALOUD TO THE GREY BIRDS, AND DREAMS, ... 252 SHADOW WATER B   618
    TILL THE WILDERNESS CRIED ALOUD, ... 259 UNWORTH PRAISE   8
    CRYING ALOUD AS THE RACECOURSE IS, ... 266 GALWAY RACES   14
    CRYING ALOUD AS THE RACE-COURSE IS, ... 266 GALWAY RACES V 14
    CRYING ALOUD AS THE RACE-COURSE IS, ... 266 GALWAY RACES V 14
    FOR MEDICINE." THEREON HE CRIED ALOUD, ... 281 TWO KINGS   98
    "YOU CRY ALOUD, O WOULD 'TWERE SPRING . . . . . 306 HOUR DAWN   91
    HE WERE AFRAID THE BIRDS, WHO CRY ALOUD . . . . 371 EGO DOMINUS   77
    THE THREE OLD RASCALS LAUGH ALOUD. . . . . . 460 THREE MONUMENT   12
    OR, BY THE MOON EMBITTERED, SCORN ALOUD . . . . 498 BYZANTIUM   21
    UPON CRO-PATRICK SANG ALOUD! . . . . 528 DANCER CRUACH   5
    THE GOLDEN PLOUGH AND HARROW AND SPOKE ALOUD . . . 609 IN TARAS HALLS   12
    LAUGHS ALOUD, HIS HEART AT PEACE. . . . . . . 638 BEN BULBEN   32
ALPUJARRAS
    ABOVE THE ALPUJARRAS ON THEIR THRONES! . . . . . 691 MOSADA 1   27
AL-RABBAN
    TO ABD AL-RABBAN: FELLOW-ROYSTERER ONCE, ... 460 HARUN RASHID   2
AL-RASCHID
    DESERT GEOMETRY OR THE GIFT OF HARUN AL-RASCHID . . . 460 HARUN RASHID V T
AL-RASHID
    THE GIFT OF HARUN AL-RASHID . . . . 460 HARUN RASHID   T
    WHAT GREAT HARUN AL-RASHID, OCCUPIED . . . . . . 462 HARUN RASHID   24
ALREADY
    DAYLIGHT ALREADY FLIES . . . . 536 PARTING   9
    AMONG THE WHIMPERING GHOSTS. MATE THUS. ALREADY? . . 722 WITCH VIVIEN   68
    THERE! THERE! THEY HAVE GONE QUICKLY, FOR ALREADY . . 764 SHADOW WATER A   326
    SHE IS ALREADY FADING, AS THOUGH THE GODS . . . . 768 SHADOW WATER A V 422
ALT
    IN A CLEFT THAT'S CHRISTENED ALT . . . . 632 MAN AND ECHO   1
ALTAR
    O COLLEENS, KNEELING BY YOUR ALTAR RAILS LONG HENCE, . . 173 SPEAKS HEARERS V 1
    O, WOMEN, KNEELING BY YOUR ALTAR RAILS LONG HENCE, . . 173 SPEAKS HEARERS V 1
    HAVE WALKED TO THE ALTAR . . . . 355 PROPERTIUS   4
ALTAR-PIECE
    IN THIS ALTAR-PIECE THE KNIGHT, ... 385 ROBARTES DANCE   2
ALTAR-RAILS
    O WOMEN, KNEELING BY YOUR ALTAR-RAILS LONG HENCE, . . 173 SPEAKS HEARERS   1

28

		PAGE	TITLE	LINE

ALTER
    OR ELSE, TO ALTER PLATO'S PARABLE, ... 443 SCHOOL CHILDR 15
    ALTER AT THE BEST . . . . 517 HER ANXIETY 4
ALTERED
    AND THE WORLD'S ALTERED SINCE YOU DIED, ... 276 GREY ROCK 126
    AND DECKED AND ALTERED IT FOR A GIRL'S LOVE, ... 423 MY DESCENDANTS 22
ALTERNATIVE
    ALTERNATIVE SONG FOR THE SEVERED HEAD IN . . . . . . 549 SEVERED HEAD T
ALTERS
    "EVERYTHING ALTERS, ... 208 OLD MEN ADMIRE 2
ALTOGETHER
    AND SINGING, SINGING ALTOGETHER! . . . . 15 OISIN 1 V 203
ALWAY
    AMONG THEMSELVES LAUGH ON AND SING ALWAY! . . . . . . 68 SAD SHEPHERD 7
    OF YONDER LAKE, FROM WHOSE GREEN BANKS ALWAY . . . . . 653 ISLE STAT I 2 33
    WE TURNED AROUND THE PLACE ALWAY, ... 667 ISLE STAT II 3 40
ALWAYS
    AND FEARED ALWAYS THE BOW-STRING'S TWANGING. . . . . . 3 OISIN 1 V 7GG
    AND ALWAYS NEVER-ANXIOUS SLEEP: . . . . 8 OISIN 1 93
    BUT NAUGHT THEY HEARD, FOR THEY ARE ALWAYS LISTENING, . . 68 SAD SHEPHERD 15
    I'D ALWAYS BEEN BUT WEAKLY, ... 94 MOLL MAGEE 13
    BUT ALWAYS, AS I'M MOVIN' ROUND, ... 96 MOLL MAGEE 43
    THEY WENT FORTH TO THE BATTLE, BUT THEY ALWAYS FELL . . 113 ROSE OF BATTLE V T
    I WILL ARISE AND GO NOW, FOR ALWAYS NIGHT AND DAY . . . 117 ISLE INNISFREE 9
    AND PLANNING, PLOTTING ALWAYS THAT SOME MORROW . . . . 129 BOOK STORIES 10
    AH, WORLD-WIDE NATION, ALWAYS GROWING SORROW, ... 130 BOOK STORIES V 11
    AH, WORLDWIDE NATION, ALWAYS GROWING SORROW! . . . . . 130 BOOK STORIES V 11
    GREEN BOUGHS OF TOSSING ALWAYS, WEARY, WEARY, ... 130 BOOK STORIES V 14
    YOUR MOTHER EIRE IS ALWAYS YOUNG, ... 148 INTO TWILIGHT 5
    THY MOTHER ERI IS ALWAYS YOUNG, ... 148 INTO TWILIGHT V 5
    FOR THE GOOD ARE ALWAYS THE MERRY, ... 178 FIDDLER DOONEY 13
    HE ALWAYS WEPT THEM ON THAT DAY, ... 192 BAILE AILLINN 78
    ALWAYS IN HIS ONE SEAT, AND BID ME CARE HIM . . . . . 280 TWO KINGS 80
    THOUGH ALWAYS AT MY WORDS HIS TROUBLE GREW: . . . . . 281 TWO KINGS 91
    ALWAYS WE'D HAVE THE NEW FRIEND MEET THE OLD . . . . . 324 ROBERT GREGORY 9
    YOU SING AS ALWAYS OF THE NATURAL LIFE. . . . . . . 342 SHEP GOATHERD 75
    IN THAT MYSTERIOUS, ALWAYS BRIMMING LAKE . . . . . . 356 BROKEN DREAMS 32
    YET ALWAYS WHEN I LOOK DEATH IN THE FACE, ... 357 DEEP-SWORN VOW 3
    IS ALWAYS HAPPY LIKE A BIRD OR A BEAST! . . . . . . 373 PHASES OF MOON 38
    HAVE YOU NOT ALWAYS KNOWN IT? THE SONG WILL HAVE IT . . 374 PHASES OF MOON 65
    OF POETS THAT ARE ALWAYS GAY. . . . . 565 LAPIS LAZULI 3
    THEY ALWAYS BEAT ON THE SAME SMALL STONE. . . . . . . 591 WHAT WAS LOST 5
    I WHO HAVE ALWAYS HATED WORK, ... 605 YOU CONTENT 19
    I ALWAYS SAID YOU COULD NOT TRUST THESE MOORS. . . . . 704 MOSADA 3 V 134A
    WHY DO YOU LAUGH? I LAUGH THE LAST ALWAYS. . . . . . 721 WITCH VIVIEN 25
    I LOSE! THEY'RE LOADED DICE. TIME ALWAYS PLAYS . . . 721 WITCH VIVIEN 44
    THEY ARE ALWAYS QUARRELLING. GIVE ME YOUR SWORDS. . . 766 SHADOW WATER A 370
    EOCHA AND MAINE ARE ALWAYS QUARRELLING. . . . . . . 766 SHADOW WATER A 371
    GIVE ME YOUR SWORDS. THEY ARE ALWAYS QUARRELLING. . . 766 SHADOW WATER A V 370
AMAZED
    HE SAT WITH TIGHTENED REIN AMAZED, HIS HORSE . . . . . 277 TWO KINGS V 10
AMBASSADOR
    BEING THEIR AMBASSADOR, ... 582 ROGER CASEMENT 14
AMBASSADORS
    WITH PERSIAN WARS OR GREEK AMBASSADORS . . . . 462 HARUN RASHID V 25
AMBER
    AMONG THE GOLD, THE AMBER, AND THE RED." . . . . . . 712 FERENCZ RENYI 76
    AMONG THE BLUE, THE AMBER, AND THE RED." . . . . . . 712 FERENCZ RENYI V 76
    MY FINGERS FEEL HIS AMBER HAIR. . . . . 723 GIRLS SONG A 8
AMBERGRIS
    BUT FOR THE AMBERGRIS AND SANDALWOOD. . . . . 232 SHADOW WATER B 221
AMBERS
    HER GOLDS, HER AMBERS, AND HER BLUES, ... 13 OISIN 1 163
AMBITION
    AND LET ALL BASE AMBITION BE, ... 460 THREE MONUMENT 9
    AND EVERY BRIDE'S AMBITION SATISFIED. . . . . 491 COOLE BALLYLEE 37
    SATISFY AMBITION, ANIMATE . . . . 500 VACILLATION 20
    SATISFY AMBITION, OR ANIMATE . . . . 500 VACILLATION V 20
AMBITIONS
    OR THE AMBITIONS THAT HE SERVED, ... 342 SHEP GOATHERD 93
AMBITIOUS
    LIFE OVERFLOWS WITHOUT AMBITIOUS PAINS! . . . . 417 ANCEST HOUSES 3
    BUT O! AMBITIOUS HEART, HAD SUCH A PROOF DRAWN FORTH . . 427 PHANTOM HATRED 36
AMBLING
    WHEN AMBLING DOWN THE VALE WE MET . . . . 2 OISIN 1 V 7U
AMBUSCADE
    AND DOWNY BEES HAVE AMBUSCADE, ... 67 HAPPY SHEPHERD V 46A
AMBUSH
    AN AMBUSH! PILGRIMS AT THE WATER-SIDE! . . . . 601 GALLERY REVIS 2
    AN AMBUSH! PILGRIMS AT THE WATER SIDE! . . . . 601 GALLERY REVIS V 2
AMEND
    COULD NOT AMEND. I HAVE GOOD SPIRITS ENOUGH. . . . . 227 SHADOW WATER B 116
    THAT NOTHING CAN AMEND IT BUT THESE WATERS, ... 227 SHADOW WATER B 120
AMENDED
    AMENDED WHAT WAS TOLD AWRY . . . . 440 WISDOM 4
AMENDS
    THAT SOME AMENDS BE MADE . . . . 582 ROGER CASEMENT 22
    BUT TIME AMENDS OLD WRONG, ... 613 MARCH SONGS 1 9
    BUT TIME AMENDS OLD WRONG, ... 613 MARCH SONGS 1 19
    BUT TIME AMENDS OLD WRONG, ... 614 MARCH SONGS 1 29

AMERGIN
    AND SHOOK AT INVER AMERGIN . . . .   81 MAD KING GOLL   3
AMERICAN
    AMERICAN COLONIES, IRELAND, FRANCE AND INDIA . . . . .   487 SEVEN SAGES   15
AMETHYST
    IVORY IMAGES WITH AMETHYST EYES. . . . .   248 SHADOW WATER B   534
    THERE'S SOMEBODY I'D GIVE THE AMETHYST EYES TO. . . . .   248 SHADOW WATER B   538
AMID
    AMID THE SHADES OF NIGHT, HE CHANGED AND RAN . . . . .   40 OISIN 2   174
    SAINT, DO YOU WEEP? I HEAR AMID THE THUNDER . . . . .   43 OISIN 2   209
    SAINT, DOST THOU WEEP? I HEAR AMID THE THUNDER . . . .   43 OISIN 2   V   209
    BUT TO BE AMID SHOOTING OF FLIES AND FLOWERING OF RUSHES   55 OISIN 3   120
        AND FLAGS."
    I FEAST AMID MY PEOPLE ON THE HILL. . . . .   103 FERGUS DRUID   17
    MY FATHER STANDS AMID HIS BATTLE-CARS." . . . . . .   107 CUCHULAIN SEA   26
    "STILL TREADS THE WORLD AMID HIS ARMED MEN." . . . . .   107 CUCHULAIN SEA   V   26
    MY FATHER STANDS AMID HIS BATTLE CARS." . . . . . .   107 CUCHULAIN SEA   26
    HIS EVENING FIRE AMID THE LEAFY SHADE. . . . . . .   109 CUCHULAIN SEA   48
    AMID MEN'S SOULS, THAT WAVER AND GIVE PLACE . . . . .   112 ROSE OF WORLD   7
    AMID MEN'S SOULS THAT DAY BY DAY GIVE PLACE, ...   112 ROSE OF WORLD   V   7
    OR SIGHS AMID THE WANDERING, STARRY MIRTH, ...   114 ROSE OF BATTLE   18
    AND HID HIS FACE AMID A CROWD OF STARS. . . . . . .   121 YOU ARE OLD   12
    I DREAMED THAT I STOOD IN A VALLEY, AND AMID SIGHS, . . .   163 VALLEY LOVERS   1
    AMID THE HOVERING, PITEOUS, PENITENTIAL THRONG." . . .   173 SPEAKS HEARERS   8
    AND HURLED IT FROM ITS PLACE AMID THE PEARLY LIGHT . . .   174 ELEMENT POWERS   V   3
    WHO STOOD AMID A SILENCE BY THE THORN . . . . . .   187 QUEEN MAEVE   142
    WHO AMID LEAFY LIGHTS AND SHADES . . . .   193 BAILE AILLINN   103
    AND AMID LEAFY LIGHT HE CRIED, ...   193 BAILE AILLINN   V   113
    O HURRY TO THE WATER AMID THE TREES, ...   210 RAGGED WOOD   V   1
    O HURRY TO THE WATER AMID THE TREES. . . . . . .   211 RAGGED WOOD   V   5
    CRYING AMID THE GLITTERING SEA, ...   254 HIS DREAM   17
    ALL THAT STERNNESS AMID CHARM, ...   259 PEACE   8
    ALL THAT SWEETNESS AMID STRENGTH?" . . . .   259 PEACE   9
    AMID THE ELABORATE WILDERNESS OF THE AIR. . . . . .   278 TWO KINGS   31
    BECAUSE THERE IS SUCH A STORM AMID MY THOUGHTS . . . .   281 TWO KINGS   100
    AMID A PLACE OF STONE, ...   291 TO A FRIEND   13
    KING GUAIRE WALKED AMID HIS COURT . . . .   295 THREE BEGGARS   8
    AND HEAR AMID THE GARDEN'S NIGHTLY PEACE," . . . . .   300 BEGGAR CRIED   18
    AMID WET ROCKS AND HEATHER, ...   311 PEACOCK   8
    SHE LIES, HER LOVELY PITEOUS HEAD AMID DULL RED HAIR . .   362 HER COURTESY   2
    AMID THE DREAMS OF YOUTH; LET HER COME FACE TO FACE, . .   366 HER COURAGE   3
    AMID THAT FIRST ASTONISHMENT, WITH GRANIA'S SHADE. . .   366 HER COURAGE   4
    ESTRANGED AMID THE STRANGENESS OF THEMSELVES. . . . .   375 PHASES OF MOON   78
    AMID MOST LOVELY PLACES; SMITTEN AS THOUGH . . . . .   389 IMAGE PAST   13
    AMID THE RUSTLE OF HIS PLANTED HILLS. . . . . . .   417 ANCEST HOUSES   2
    AMID GREAT CHAMBERS AND LONG GALLERIES, LINED . . . .   418 ANCEST HOUSES   36
    AMID THE ORNAMENTAL BRONZE AND STONE. . . . . . .   428 NINETEEN 19   5
    IS LOST AMID THE LABYRINTH THAT HE HAS MADE . . . . .   431 NINETEEN 19   70
    AMID THE CLOUDY WRACK, ...   458 HIS WILDNESS   2
    ONE HAND AMID THE GOLDFISH IN THE POOL; . . . . . .   463 HARUN RASHID   44
    LIKE THIS PURE JET, NOW LOST AMID BLUE SKY, ...   464 HARUN RASHID   64
    HIDING AMID THE CARGO OF A STEAMSHIP, ...   578 CRAZED GIRL   5
    THERE SIGHED AMID HIS CHOIR OF LOVE . . . . . .   611 NEWS ORACLE   7
    AND CHANTS OF VICTORY AMID THE ENCIRCLING HOUNDS. . . .   622 HOUND VOICE   21
    THIS HEARD I WHERE, AMID THE APPLE TREES, ...   735 QUATRAIN APHOR   17
    AMID A CLOUD OF BANNERS. . . . .   741 EARL PAUL   39
    AMID THE DARKNESS, NOW THAT ALL MY STARS . . . .   767 SHADOW WATER A   V   404
    AMID THE DARK BEFORE DAY HAD BROKEN. . . . . . .   784 WOMANS BEAUTY   20
AMONG
    AMONG THE FIELDS OF WAVING FERN. . . . .   2 OISIN 1   V   7N
    AMONG THE LEAVES OF THE LAUREL WALL. . . . . . .   3 OISIN 1   V   7FF
    YOU ARE STILL WRECKED AMONG HEATHEN DREAMS. . . . .   4 OISIN 1   31
    AMONG THE WAVING FIELDS OF FERN; . . . .   4 OISIN 1   38
    AMONG UNDYING PEOPLE HAS RUN . . . .   6 OISIN 1   V   60
    AMONG THEM 'LIGHTING FROM OUR STEED, ...   14 OISIN 1   V   193
    AMONG THE WOODLAND GRASSES SWEET, ...   15 OISIN 1   V   199
    FROM BEES AMONG THEIR HONEY MARTS, ...   16 OISIN 1   V   229
    AMONG THE FOAMDROPS OF THE SEA, ...   20 OISIN 1   294
    AMONG THE RINGING HALLS A SHOUT . . . .   20 OISIN 1   V   288
    THEN ON AMONG THE WINDLESS WOODS . . . .   21 OISIN 1   V   320
    WRESTLED AMONG THE ISLAND BANDS. . . . .   23 OISIN 1   350
    THE IMMORTALS MOVED AMONG THE FOUNTAINS . . . . .   25 OISIN 1   386
    THE FAIRIES MOVED AMONG THE FOUNTAINS, ...   25 OISIN 1   V   386
    SHONE MANY TIMES AMONG THE GLIMMERING FLOWERS . . . .   30 OISIN 2   21
    A JUBILANT LIFE AMONG THE LEAVES, RETURN. . . . .   35 OISIN 2   V   89A
    AMONG THEMSELVES LAUGH ON AND SING ALWAY; . . . . .   68 SAD SHEPHERD   7
    AMONG HER WILDERING WHIRLS, FORGETTING HIM. . . . .   69 SAD SHEPHERD   28
    AMONG THE MOULDERING OF ANCIENT WOODS . . . . .   74 ANASHU VIJAYA   61
    WITH VAPOURY FOOTSOLE AMONG THE WATER'S DROWSY BLAZE. . .   78 INDIAN TO LOVE   V   20
    IN POOLS AMONG THE RUSHES . . . .   88 STOLEN CHILD   30
    "NO MAN ALIVE, NO MAN AMONG THE DEAD, ...   106 CUCHULAIN SEA   10
    "MY FATHER DWELLS AMONG THE SEA-WORN BANDS, ...   107 CUCHULAIN SEA   V   25
    AMONG THOSE FEASTING MEN CUCHULAIN DWELT, ...   108 CUCHULAIN SEA   39
    AMONG THOSE FEASTING KINGS CUCHULAIN DWELT, ...   108 CUCHULAIN SEA   V   39
    HE STOOD AMONG A CROWD AT DROMAHAIR; . . . . .   126 DREAM OF FAERY   1
    AND BRIDGET HIS BRIDE AMONG THEM, ...   144 HOST OF AIR   15
    AND WALK AMONG LONG DAPPLED GRASS, ...   150 WANDER AENGUS   21
    AMONG PALE EYELIDS, HEAVY WITH THE SLEEP . . . . .   169 SECRET ROSE   6
    WHO MET FAND WALKING AMONG FLAMING DEW . . . . .   169 SECRET ROSE   13
    DWELT AMONG WINE-STAINED WANDERERS IN DEEP WOODS; . . .   170 SECRET ROSE   21
    VOICES AMONG THE CROWD . . . .   172 PLEADS FRIEND   2

```
                                          PAGE     TITLE          LINE
AMONG    (CONTINUED)
     AMONG MY LEAVES IN TIMES OUT OF MIND;  . . . . . . .   177 PAST GREATNESS     5
     WHAT MATTERS WERE AFOOT AMONG THE SIDHE,  . . . . . .   182 QUEEN MAEVE       61
     AND PINCHES AMONG HAIL AND SNOW?  . . . . . . . . .    191 BAILE AILLINN     46
     IN OLD TIMES AMONG THE CLOUDS OF THE AIR.  . . . . .   194 BAILE AILLINN    133
     AMONG THE GIANT KINGS WHOSE HOARD,  . . . . . . .      196 BAILE AILLINN    164
     AMONG PIGEONS AND BEES, WHILE THAT GREAT ARCHER,  . .   198 SEVEN WOODS       12
     O HURRY WHERE BY WATER AMONG THE TREES  . . . . . .    210 RAGGED WOOD        1
     O HURRY WHERE BY WATER AMONG TREES.  . . . . . . .     210 RAGGED WOOD    V   1
     IS NOT KNOWN AMONG MEN,  . . . . . . . . . . .         215 HAPPY TOWNLAND    28
     I WALKED AMONG THE SEVEN WOODS OF COOLE;  . . . . .    217 WOODS OF COOLE     1
     SHINING ON WATER AND FALLEN AMONG LEAVES,  . . . . .   218 WOODS OF COOLE    38
     THAT SHE AMONG HER WINDS MIGHT KNOW HE WEPT;  . . .    220 HARP OF AENGUS    12
     THAT SHE AMONG HER WOODS MIGHT KNOW HE WEPT;  . . .    220 HARP OF AENGUS V  12
     AND HID HER AMONG FRUITS OF JEWEL-STONE  . . . . . .   224 SHADOW WATER B    49
     IF HE HAD BROUGHT US AMONG PEOPLED SEAS,  . . . . .    225 SHADOW WATER B   68C
     AMONG SUBSTANTIAL THINGS; FOR IT IS DREAMS  . . . .    230 SHADOW WATER B   181
     AMONG THE WINDY MEADOWS OF THE DAWN."  . . . . . .     234 SHADOW WATER B   264
     IT HAD WASHED AMONG THE STARS AND PUT THEM OUT,  . .   236 SHADOW WATER B   311
     THERE IS NOT ONE AMONG YOU THAT MADE LOVE  . . . . .   244 SHADOW WATER B   454
     O FLOWER OF THE BRANCH, O BIRD AMONG THE LEAVES,  . .   251 SHADOW WATER B   608
     AND WE FIND HEARTENERS AMONG MEN  . . . . . . .        266 GALWAY RACES      15
     AND FIND HEARTENERS AMONG MEN  . . . . . . . .         266 GALWAY RACES   V  15
     AMONG THE AFRICAN MOUNTAINS OF THE MOON,  . . . . .    277 TWO KINGS         20
     "I HAVE SENT AMONG THE FIELDS OR TO THE WOODS  . . .   280 TWO KINGS         69
     WESTWARD OF TARA, AMONG THE HAZEL-TREES--  . . . . .   283 TWO KINGS        135
     WENT OUT.  AMONG THE IVY-COVERED ROCKS,  . . . . . .   283 TWO KINGS        147
     WESTWARD OF TARA, AMONG THE HAZEL TREES--  . . . . .   283 TWO KINGS      V 135
     AMONG THOSE MOUTHS THAT SING THEIR SWEETHEARTS' PRAISE,   285 TWO KINGS     185
     AMONG THE STONES AND THORN-TREES, UNDER MORNING LIGHT;    291 PAUDEEN         3
     AMONG THE STONES AND THORN TREES, UNDER MORNING LIGHT, .  291 PAUDEEN     V   3
     AMONG THE OTHER GENTLEMEN,  . . . . . . . . .          296 THREE BEGGARS     34
     AMONG THE KINGS OF GREECE AND FRANCE."  . . . . . .    296 THREE BEGGARS V  32A
     UPON THE BRIMMING WATER AMONG THE STONES  . . . . .    322 SWANS AT COOLE     5
     AMONG WHAT RUSHES WILL THEY BUILD,  . . . . . . .      323 SWANS AT COOLE    27
     SOMEWHERE AMONG THE CLOUDS ABOVE;  . . . . . . .       328 IRISH AIRMAN       2
     AMONG THE STREAMS;  . . . . . . . . . . .             329 MEN IMPROVE        3
     BUT I GROW OLD AMONG DREAMS,  . . . . . . . .          329 MEN IMPROVE       16
     AMONG THE STREAMS.  . . . . . . . . . . .             329 MEN IMPROVE       18
     HE HAD OFTEN PLAYED HIS PIPES AMONG MY HILLS,  . . .   339 SHEP GOATHERD     23
     AMONG THE EVENING SHADOWS;  . . . . . . . . .          341 SHEP GOATHERD     71
     AMONG THE POOR BOTH OLD AND YOUNG GAVE HER PRAISE.  .   351 HER PRAISE        18
     OR CLIMBED AMONG THE IMAGES OF THE PAST--  . . . . .   352 PEOPLE            10
     YOUR BEAUTY CAN BUT LEAVE AMONG US  . . . . . . .      356 BROKEN DREAMS     14
     AMONG THE COARSE GRASS AND THE CAMEL-DUNG.  . . . .    369 EGO DOMINUS       31
     AMONG THE COARSE GRASS AND THE CAMEL DUNG.  . . . .    369 EGO DOMINUS    V  31
     AMONG WHIMS NOT IMPOSSIBLE, AND THOUGH SCARRED,  . .   374 PHASES OF MOON    41
     AMONG TASKS NOT IMPOSSIBLE, IT TAKES  . . . . . .      376 PHASES OF MOON    92
     AMONG THE STARRY EDDIES OF HER HAIR  . . . . . .       390 IMAGE PAST        27
     FROM COUNTER OR DESK AMONG GREY  . . . . . . . .       392 EASTER 1916        3
     IT HAD SET DOWN AMONG ITS LAWS;  . . . . . . .         399 BREAK OF DAY      16
     AMONG THE DEEPENING SHADES,  . . . . . . . .           416 TOWER            195
     SURELY AMONG A RICH MAN'S FLOWERING LAWNS,  . . . .    417 ANCEST HOUSES      1
     HAD FALLEN AMONG DANCERS, HAD WHIRLED THEM ROUND  . .   430 NINETEEN 19      52
     AMONG SCHOOL CHILDREN  . . . . . . . . . .             443 SCHOOL CHILDR      T
     AMONG SCHOOLCHILDREN  . . . . . . . . . . .            443 SCHOOL CHILDR V    T
     GLITTERING AMONG GREY-LEAVED OLIVE-TREES,  . . . .     447 COLONUS PRAISE    21
     GLITTERING AMONG GREY-LEAVED OLIVE TREES,  . . . .     447 COLONUS PRAISE V  21
     AND LIVE AMONG THE ANCIENT HOLY MEN,  . . . . . .      448 HERO GIRL FOOL V 11A
     ONE AMONG THE BIRDS OF THE AIR.  . . . . . . .         460 THREE MONUMENT     3
     AMONG DARK SKINS, AND THERE  . . . . . . . .           472 ALL SOUL NIGHT    48
     CONSPIRING AMONG THE IGNORANT,  . . . . . . . .        475 EVA GORE-BOOTH     9
     THE FINISHED MAN AMONG HIS ENEMIES?--  . . . . . .     479 SELF AND SOUL     49
     AND SAPLINGS ROOT AMONG THE BROKEN STONE,  . . . .     489 COOLE PARK 29     28
     HAD I NOT FOUND CONTENT AMONG THE SHOWS  . . . . .     499 MOTHER OF GOD      6
     AMONG BIRDS OR BEASTS OR MEN  . . . . . . . .          528 DANCER CRUACH      2
     AND THEN YOU STOOD AMONG THE DRAGON-RINGS.  . . . .    533 HER TRIUMPH        7
     AND THEN YOU STOOD AMONG THE DRAGON RINGS.  . . . .    533 HER TRIUMPH    V   7
     AMONG THE DOGS AND HORSES THAT UNDERSTAND MY TALK.  .   581 CURSE CROMWELL    30
     FROM THOSE THEY LIVE AMONG,  . . . . . . . .           607 SONGS BURDEN 2    13
     I LIVED AMONG GREAT HOUSES,  . . . . . . . .           626 STATES HOLIDAY     1
     VIOLENT AND FAMOUS, STRODE AMONG THE DEAD;  . . . .    634 CUCHULAIN COMF     2
     AMONG THOSE BIRD-LIKE THINGS CAME, AND LET FALL  . .   634 CUCHULAIN COMF     8
     AMONG THE BOUGHS, BLUE AS THE HALCYON'S WING,  . . .   683 SEEKER            38
     THIS HEARD I WHERE AMONG THE APPLE TREES,  . . . .     686 LIFE              19
     OF HIS SAD GOD; AND DOWN AMONG THE GRASS  . . . .      690 MOSADA 1          16
     AROUND MY HEAD AND DANCED AMONG THE GRASS;  . . . .    690 MOSADA 1          19
     AMONG THE FRUIT;  BUT THERE, LAME COLA CROUCHES  . .   691 MOSADA 1          32
     AMONG THE FRUIT.  BUT YON, LAME COLA CROUCHES  . . .   691 MOSADA 1       V  32
     AMONG THE PLANTS; THE FLOWERY SILENCE FELL  . . . .    692 MOSADA 1          55
     ALONE AMONG THE MURMURS OF THE DAWN.  . . . . . .      702 MOSADA 3          81
     AMONG THY NATION NONE SHALL KNOW THAT I  . . . . .     702 MOSADA 3       V  82
     HE FADES AMONG THE MISTS; HOW FAST THEY COME,  . . .   703 MOSADA 3         117
     AMONG THE GOLD, THE AMBER, AND THE RED."  . . . .      712 FERENCZ RENYI     76
     AMONG THE BLUE, THE AMBER AND THE RED."  . . . . .     712 FERENCZ RENYI V   76
     SHE WHO DWELT AMONG THE SYCAMORES,  . . . . . .        715 DWELT SYCAMORE     T
     SHE DWELT AMONG THE SYCAMORES.  . . . . . . .          715 DWELT SYCAMORE V   T
     AMONG THE WHIMPERING GHOSTS.  MATE THUS, ALREADY?  .   722 WITCH VIVIEN      68
     HAST THOU NOT RULED AMONG THE GILDED WALLS?  . . .     724 KANVA ON SELF      7
     A LOVER'S QUARREL AMONG THE FAIRIES.  . . . . .        726 LOVERS QUARREL     T
     HE'D SLEPT AMONG THE SINGING TREES,  . . . . . .       728 PRIEST FAIRY      17
```

		PAGE	TITLE	LINE

AMONG   (CONTINUED)
                AMONG THE MURMURS OF THE BEES, ...   728 PRIEST FAIRY   18
                AMONG THE HAUNTS OF BEE AND BIRD. . . . .   729 PRIEST FAIRY   42
            THIS HEARD I WHERE AMONG THE APPLE TREES, ...   735 QUATRAIN APHOR V   19
            A PATH AMONG THESE WAVES AND WEIGH THE WIND? . . . .   748 SHADOW WATER A   21
            OF PASTURE-LAND AND PLOUGH-LAND AMONG THE HILLS? . .   748 SHADOW WATER A   33
            AND PRAISED YOUR WAR AMONG THE ENDLESS SEAS, ...   749 SHADOW WATER A   35
            AND PRAISE A WAR AMONG THE ENDLESS SEAS, ...   749 SHADOW WATER A V   35
                AMONG THOSE STREAMS, OR ON THEIR CLOUDY EDGE. . .   750 SHADOW WATER A   63
            AND FALLS AMONG THE DREAMS THE DROWSY GODS . . . . .   750 SHADOW WATER A   68
                AMONG THE WATERS THAT NO PILOT KNOWS. . . . . .   750 SHADOW WATER A   80
            AND FLY AMONG THE FOAM, THRUST DOWN THE HELM, . . .   750 SHADOW WATER A   88
            A WOMAN LIES AMONG EMBROIDERIES. . . . .   752 SHADOW WATER A   120
                AMONG THESE MISTY WATERS. TWO! NOW FOUR! . . . .   753 SHADOW WATER A   138
                AMONG THE WINDY MEADOWS OF THE DAWN." . . . . .   754 SHADOW WATER A   153
            HAVE THE WINDS BLOWN YOU AMONG THESE EMPTY WATERS? . .   756 SHADOW WATER A   192
            TO CONQUER AMONG THE COUNTRIES OF THE NORTH. . . . .   757 SHADOW WATER A   200
                AMONG THE WINDS, LOOKS UNDER YOUR PALE EYELIDS. . .   757 SHADOW WATER A   211
                AMONG THE QUEENS, AND CHOSE THE MIGHTIEST . . .   757 SHADOW WATER A   213
            FOR THOSE AMONG YOUR PEOPLE THAT ARE DEAD? . . . .   758 SHADOW WATER A   224
                AMONG THE HEBRIDES. WHEN SHE AWAKENS, ...   760 SHADOW WATER A V   255
            THE STARS WOULD HURL THEIR CROWNS AMONG THE FOAM . .   761 SHADOW WATER A   265
                AMONG GREAT TREES, AND IN THE WINGS OF OWLS, . .   762 SHADOW WATER A   285
            THAT SHE AMONG HER WINDS MIGHT KNOW HE WEPT! . . .   763 SHADOW WATER A   307
            AND SHE, NO LONGER BLOWN AMONG THE WINDS, ...   763 SHADOW WATER A   323
                AMONG THE WINDS AND WATERS! AND WHEN THEY PASS . .   764 SHADOW WATER A   331
            ALL DIES AMONG THOSE STREAMS. THE FOOL HAS MADE . .   764 SHADOW WATER A   335
            WHERE TRUE-LOVE WANDERS AMONG THE HOLY WOODS. . . .   764 SHADOW WATER A   337
            WHAT WERE TRUE-LOVE AMONG THE RUSH OF HIS STREAMS? .   764 SHADOW WATER A   338
            WHERE TRUE LOVE WANDERS AMONG THE HOLY WOODS. . . .   764 SHADOW WATER A V   337
            WHAT WERE TRUE LOVE AMONG THE RUSH OF HIS STREAMS? .   764 SHADOW WATER A V   338
            THAT LIVES AMONG THE WOODS OF THE DARK HOUNDS. . . .   766 SHADOW WATER A   376
            ALL THAT KNOW LOVE AMONG THE WINDS OF THE WORLD . .   767 SHADOW WATER A   386
            BUT I AM NEW TO LOVE. GO AMONG THESE . . . . . .   767 SHADOW WATER A   391
            THAT HAVE KNOWN LOVE AMONG THE WINDS OF THE WORLD . .   767 SHADOW WATER A   392
                AMONG HIGH MOUNTAINS, AND THE MOUNTAIN ROBBERS . .   768 SHADOW WATER A   411
            SO WORTHY AMONG MEN. I FOLLOW YOU, ...   768 SHADOW WATER A V   412
            WHETHER AMONG THE COLD WINDS OF THE DEAD. . . . . .   768 SHADOW WATER A V   413
            OR AMONG WINDS THAT MOVE IN THE MEADOWS AND WOODS. .   768 SHADOW WATER A   413
            O FLOWER OF THE BRANCH, O BIRD AMONG THE LEAVES, . .   769 SHADOW WATER A   424
                AMONG HIS CHILDREN, GRANDCHILDREN AND GREAT-GRANDCHILDREN!   790 DEDICATION   6
                AMONG THE OTHER CHEATED DEAD. . . . .   791 REPRISALS   24
AMOROUS
            TRAPPED OF AN AMOROUS DEMON THING. . . . .   2 OISIN 1   V   4
            MUST I ENDURE YOUR AMOROUS CRIES? . . . .   177 PAST GREATNESS   12
            ALL TURN WITH AMOROUS CRIES, OR ANGRY CRIES, ...   433 NINETEEN 19   123
            THOSE AMOROUS CRIES THAT OUT OF QUIET COME . . . . .   557 RIBH ECSTASY   7
            THOU SHALT OUTLIVE THINE AMOROUS HAPPY TIME, ...   674 ISLE STAT II 3   203
AMPLE
            TWO MEN WHO LOVE ONE MAID HAVE AMPLE CAUSE . . . .   659 ISLE STAT II 1   30
AMRITA
            PRAYERS FOR THE LAND. I WILL WAIT HERE, AMRITA. . . .   71 ANASHU VIJAYA   • 13
            WHO IS AMRITA? SORROW OF ALL SORROWS! . . . . .   71 ANASHU VIJAYA   15
            AMRITA. DRAW YOU NEAR, AND 'NEATH YON PILLAR . . .   71 ANASHU VIJAYA V   13A
            WHO IS AMRITA? WOE! AH, WOE IS ME! . . . .   71 ANASHU VIJAYA V   15
            AMRITA, WHILE--AH ME! YOU LOVE ANOTHER, ...   74 ANASHU VIJAYA   58
            AMRITA. THIS SAME EVE SHE WATCHED ME PASS. . . . .   74 ANASHU VIJAYA V   64
A-MURMUR
            A-MURMUR LIKE YOUNG PARTRIDGE! WITH LOUD HORN . . . .   32 OISIN 2   52
ANALYTIC
            OF THE ANALYTIC MIND, CAN NEITHER CLOSE . . . . .   353 PEOPLE   33
ANARCHY
            MERE ANARCHY IS LOOSED UPON THE WORLD, ...   402 SECOND COMING   4
ANASHUYA
            ANASHUYA AND VIJAYA . . . .   70 ANASHU VIJAYA   T
            HAIL! HAIL, MY ANASHUYA. NO! BE STILL. . . . . .   71 ANASHU VIJAYA   11
            HAIL! HAIL, MY ANASHUYA. NAY! BE STILL. . . . . .   71 ANASHU VIJAYA V   11
ANBUAL'S
            AND SET THEM DIGGING INTO ANBUAL'S HILL. . . . . .   184 QUEEN MAEVE V   93
ANCESTOR
            AN ANCESTOR WAS RECTOR THERE . . . .   640 BEN BULBEN   86
ANCESTORS
            WITH FAMOUS PORTRAITS OF OUR ANCESTORS! . . . . .   418 ANCEST HOUSES   37
ANCESTRAL
            MAY SET A STONE UPON ANCESTRAL SORROW! . . . . .   130 BOOK STORIES   11
            OF THEIR RETURN TO THAT ANCESTRAL HOUSE. . . . . .   286 TWO KINGS   V 218C
            ANCESTRAL HOUSES . . . .   417 ANCEST HOUSES   T
            MEDITATIONS IN TIME OF CIVIL WAR   ANCESTRAL HOUSES . .   417 ANCEST HOUSES V   T
            THINK OF ANCESTRAL NIGHT THAT CAN, ...   478 SELF AND SOUL   20
            . . . IS MY ANCESTRAL STAIR! . . . .   480 BLOOD AND MOON   17
            ODOUR OF BLOOD ON THE ANCESTRAL STAIR! . . . . .   482 BLOOD AND MOON   40
            SEEMED ONCE MORE DEAR THAN LIFE! ANCESTRAL TREES, . .   491 COOLE BALLYLEE   34
            THROUGH THEIR ANCESTRAL PATTERNS DANCE, ...   612 NEWS ORACLE   19
            ANCESTRAL PEARLS ALL PITCHED INTO A STY, ...   619 BRONZE HEAD   26
ANCIENT
            FOR THESE WERE ANCIENT OISIN'S FATE . . . . . .   24 OISIN 1   361
            WITH ALL THE ANCIENT SORROW OF MEN"! . . . . . .   25 OISIN 1   381
            AFAR IN ANCIENT ERI, ...   32 OISIN 2   V   50E
            TO TWO OLD EAGLES, FULL OF ANCIENT PRIDE, ...   34 OISIN 2   74
            FOR THEIR DIM MINDS WERE WITH THE ANCIENT THINGS. . .   34 OISIN 2   77
            TO EAGLES TWAIN THAT, FULL OF ANCIENT PRIDE, . . .   34 OISIN 2   V   73

		PAGE	TITLE	LINE
ANCIENT (CONTINUED)				
IN SOME DIM MEMORY OR ANCIENT MOOD,		36	OISIN 2	99
MY SOUL, ONCE GLORY OF ITS ANCIENT LINE,		36	OISIN 2 V	95
HOPELESS FOR EVER! ANCIENT OISIN KNOWS,		42	OISIN 2	202
OF ANCIENT WARRIORS, THE LABOURS OF THE STRONG,		42	OISIN 2 V	195
THAT ONCE MORE MOVED IN MY BOSOM THE ANCIENT SADNESS OF MAN,		54	OISIN 3	107
AND LO! MY ANCIENT BURDEN MAY DEPART,		69	SAD SHEPHERD	24
AMONG THE MOULDERING OF ANCIENT WOODS		74	ANASHU VIJAYA	61
AND EVERY ANCIENT OLLAVE SAID,		82	MAD KING GOLL	9
FILLED FULL OF ANCIENT CHEER."		97	FOXHUNTER V	12
COME NEAR ME, WHILE I SING THE ANCIENT WAYS!		100	ROSE UPON ROOD	2
SING OF OLD EIRE AND THE ANCIENT WAYS!		101	ROSE UPON ROOD	23
FIRST AS A RAVEN ON WHOSE ANCIENT WINGS		102	FERGUS DRUID	3
EVEN AS SPRING UPON THE ANCIENT SKIES,		108	CUCHULAIN SEA	42
STARED LIKE THE SPRING UPON THE ANCIENT SKIES,		108	CUCHULAIN SEA	41
THAT YOU COME HERE TO MEET THIS ANCIENT SWORD?"		109	CUCHULAIN SEA V	61
MAY SURELY MEET THEIR ANCIENT GAZE.		139	TO IRELAND V	28
WITH A TWINKLING OF ANCIENT HANDS.		144	HOST OF AIR	24
THE ANCIENT BEARDS, THE HELMS OF RUBY AND GOLD		169	SECRET ROSE	8
IN ANY ANCIENT BOOK BUT TELLS OF YOU!		186	QUEEN MAEVE	135
IT WHIRLS INTO THE FOAM. O ANCIENT WORM,		251	SHADOW WATER B	597
. . HAVE JOINED THE ANCIENT ORDER OF HIBERNIANS AND THE . . .		262	STUDENTS AGIT V	T
BY THE ANCIENT HOLY HANDS THAT BROUGHT THEM		271	GREY ROCK V	21
NOR ON THE ANCIENT BEATEN PATHS, THAT WOUND		279	TWO KINGS	52
BECAUSE AN ANCIENT HISTORY SAID		303	HOUR DAWN	24
WITH ALL THEIR ANCIENT FACES LIKE RAIN-BEATEN STONES,		318	MAGI	4
AT KYLE-NA-NO UNDER THAT ANCIENT ROOF		321	REED WHISPERER	7
BEING BUT A PART OF ANCIENT CEREMONY--		321	REED WHISPERER	12
TO KYLE-NA-INO AND TO THAT ANCIENT ROOF		321	REED WHISPERER V	7
BESIDE A FIRE OF TURF IN TH' ANCIENT TOWER,		324	ROBERT GREGORY	3
FROM RUIN OR FROM ANCIENT TREES,		410	TOWER	23
AND WHEN THAT ANCIENT RUFFIAN'S TURN WAS ON		411	TOWER	66
AN ANCIENT BANKRUPT MASTER OF THIS HOUSE.		412	TOWER	80
AN ANCIENT BRIDGE, AND A MORE ANCIENT TOWER,		419	MY HOUSE	1
AN ANCIENT BRIDGE, AND A MORE ANCIENT TOWER,		419	MY HOUSE	1
AN ANCIENT IMAGE MADE OF OLIVE WOOD--		428	NINETEEN 19	6
ALL TEETH WERE DRAWN, ALL ANCIENT TRICKS UNLEARNED,		429	NINETEEN 19	17
THE ANCIENT HABIT STICKS.		431	NINETEEN 19	74
AND LIVE AMONG THE ANCIENT HOLY MEN,		448	HERO GIRL FOOL V	11A
NEVER HAVE LIVED IS BEST, ANCIENT WRITERS SAY!		459	FROM OEDIPUS	10
I SUMMON TO THE WINDING ANCIENT STAIR!		477	SELF AND SOUL	1
IS SATO'S ANCIENT BLADE, STILL AS IT WAS,		477	SELF AND SOUL	10
I SUMMON TO THE WINDY ANCIENT STAIR!		477	SELF AND SOUL V	1
IS SATO'S ANCIENT SWORD, STILL AS IT WAS,		477	SELF AND SOUL V	10
AND ANCIENT LINEAMENTS ARE BLOTTED OUT.		564	GYRES	4
IN ANCIENT TOMBS I SIGHED, BUT NOT AGAIN!		564	GYRES	14
THEIR ANCIENT, GLITTERING EYES, ARE GAY.		567	LAPIS LAZULI	56
SOME ANCIENT FAMOUS AUTHORS MISREPRESENT,		579	DOR WELLESLEY	15
WE IRISH, BORN INTO THAT ANCIENT SECT		611	STATUES	28
AND FIND OUR ANCIENT HOUNDS BEFORE THE DOOR,		622	HOUND VOICE	16
"OBEY OUR ANCIENT RULE AND MAKE A SHROUD!		634	CUCHULAIN COMF	13
AND ANCIENT IRELAND KNEW IT ALL.		637	BEN BULBEN	16
BY THE ROAD AN ANCIENT CROSS.		640	BEN BULBEN	88
HE WAS OUR ANCIENT GOD. IF I SPEAK LOW,		658	ISLE STAT I 3	78
THAT ANCIENT MOTHER CRIES, "SPEAK NOT, MY SON,		711	FERENCZ RENYI	56
OF ANCIENT PASSIONS AND OF ANCIENT FEARS?		724	KANVA ON SELF	16
OF ANCIENT PASSIONS AND OF ANCIENT FEARS?		724	KANVA ON SELF	16
THEREFORE IN THIS ANCIENT CUP		776	AGAINST WITCH	36
THEREFORE FROM THIS ANCIENT CUP		776	AGAINST WITCH V	36
AN ANCIENT LECHER TOOK TO GEESE		792	GEORGE MOORE	3
ANEMONES				
THE PALE ANEMONES. WE'VE SOUGHT ALL DAY,		651	ISLE STAT I 2	5
ANEW				
FLOWED ON ANEW, AND OFT, ANEW DECLINING,		33	OISIN 2 V	68D
FLOWED ON ANEW, AND OFT, ANEW DECLINING,		33	OISIN 2 V	68D
I HUNGER TO BUILD THEM ANEW AND SIT ON A GREEN KNOLL APART,		143	ROSE IN HEART	6
AND THEREFORE MY HEART BOWS DOWN ANEW,		164	PERFECT BEAUTY V	6
AND WHEN I'D WRITE IT OUT ANEW, THE WORDS,		186	QUEEN MAEVE	139
FOR WHOM THE CAIRN'S BUT HEAPED ANEW.		192	BAILE AILLINN	84
DRAW THE GLASNEVIN COVERLET ANEW		293	TO A SHADE V	19
THAT POUNDS UP ALL ANEW		346	ON WOMAN	31
SELF-BORN, BORN ANEW?		507	STREAM AND SUN	15
NOW THE HUNT BEGINS ANEW?		773	SONG DEIRDRE 1	18
ANGEL				
ALL SOUNDS BY BIRD OR ANGEL SUNG		387	SOLOMON WITCH V	7
GO ASK THE YOUNGEST ANGEL,		680	LOVE AND DEATH	29
THE ARCHANGEL AXEL, VICTOR THE ANGEL		774	COME RIDE	11
ANGELIC				
BEFORE GOD MADE THE ANGELIC CLAN,		138	TO IRELAND	8
WHEN THE FLAMING LUTE-THRONGED ANGELIC DOOR IS WIDE!		172	TRAV PASSION	1
YOU GREAT ANGELIC POWERS OF WIND, AND WAVE, AND FIRE,		174	ELEMENT POWERS V	7
THE FATHER AND HIS ANGELIC HIERARCHY		483	VERONIC NAPKIN	4
ANGELO				
A MIND MICHAEL ANGELO KNEW		576	ACRE OF GRASS	19
MICHAEL ANGELO.		618	LONG-LEG FLY	26
MICHAEL ANGELO LEFT A PROOF		638	BEN BULBEN	45
ANGELO'S				
WHILE MICHAEL ANGELO'S SISTINE ROOF,		386	ROBARTES DANCE	32

ANGELS
    BETWEEN THEM A GATEWAY OF BRASS, AND THE HOWL OF THE ANGELS 61 OISIN 3   200
        WHO FELL.
    THE ANGELS ARE STOOPING . . . . 118 CRADLE SONG   1
    THE ANGELS ARE BENDING . . . . 118 CRADLE SONG   V   1
    'MONG THE FEET OF ANGELS SEVEN . . . . 125 CATHLEEN PARA   13
    WITH WHITE FEET OF ANGELS SEVEN . . . . 125 CATHLEEN PARA V 13
    AND HER GUIDES ARE ANGELS SEVEN, ... 125 CATHLEEN PARA V 15
    SENT ONE OF HIS GREAT ANGELS DOWN . . . . 134 FR GILLIGAN   43
    FOR THE INTERCOURSE OF ANGELS IS A LIGHT . . . . . 555 RIBH AT TOMB   15
ANGER
    THE SPACIOUS LOVES, THE ANGER WITHOUT SLEEP . . . . 42 OISIN 2   V 194
    IN MOMENTARY ANGER LONG AGO: . . . . 258 KING NO KING   10
    ALL SHOUTED TILL THEIR ANGER GREW . . . . 297 THREE BEGGARS   46
    AND THEREUPON THEIR ANGER GREW, ... 297 THREE BEGGARS V 46
ANGERS
    WE SANG THE LOVES AND ANGERS WITHOUT SLEEP, ... 42 OISIN 2   194
    ANGERS THAT ARE LIKE NOISY CLOUDS HAVE SET OUR HEARTS 207 HANRAHANS SONG   8
        ABEAT:
    VEERING, FLEETING, FICKLE, OUR LOVES AND ANGERS MEET: . . 207 HANRAHANS SONG V   3
    ANGERS THAT ARE LIKE BUNDLED CLOUDS HAVE SET OUR HEARTS 207 HANRAHANS SONG V   8
        ABEAT:
ANGRY
    MY ANGRY KING—REMEMBERING SOUL ONE JOT. . . . . . . 36 OISIN 2   94
    MY ANGRY, KING REMEMBERING SOUL ONE JOT: . . . . . 36 OISIN 2   V   94
    FOR GOD HAS HEARD, AND SPEAKS HIS ANGRY MIND: . . . 42 OISIN 2   206
    DARKEN: HEAVEN IS ANGRY. CEASE: UNTO MY MIND, . . 42 OISIN 2   V 205
    AND CRIED WITH ANGRY VOICE, "IT IS NOT MEET . . . 107 CUCHULAIN SEA   20
    THE TALE DROVE HIS FINE ANGRY MOOD AWAY. . . . . . 128 DREAM OF FAERY   36
    CUMHAL THE KING, BEING ANGRY AND SAD, ... 166 BLESSED   V   1
    NOR PUBLIC MAN, NOR ANGRY CROWDS, ... 328 IRISH AIRMAN V 10
    THEIR ANGRY TEARS, ARE GONE. . . . . 344 DEJECTION   6
    WITHOUT AN ANGRY THOUGHT . . . . 366 HER CHRIS TREE   2
    FOR AN OLD BELLOWS FULL OF ANGRY WIND? . . . . . . 405 FOR DAUGHTER   64
    ALL TURN WITH AMOROUS CRIES, OR ANGRY CRIES, ... 433 NINETEEN 19   123
ANIGH
    "SAY AND THRICE ANIGH THY DOOR . . . . 730 PRIEST FAIRY   54
ANIMAL
    TROUBLED HIS ANIMAL BLOOD. . . . . 378 CAT AND MOON   8
    AND FASTENED TO A DYING ANIMAL . . . . 408 SAIL BYZANTIUM   22
    AND FASTENED TO THIS DYING ANIMAL . . . . 408 SAIL BYZANTIUM V 22
    A DYING ANIMAL: . . . . 476 DEATH   2
    WHAT SHUDDERS RUN THROUGH ALL THAT ANIMAL BLOOD? . . 541 PARN FUNERAL 1   5
    WHETHER IT BE AN ANIMAL OR A MAN. . . . . 542 PARN FUNERAL 1   31
ANIMAL'S
    THE CIRCUS ANIMAL'S DESERTION . . . . 629 CIRCUS ANIMALS V   T
ANIMALS
    MY CIRCUS ANIMALS WERE ALL ON SHOW, ... 629 CIRCUS ANIMALS   6
ANIMALS'
    THE CIRCUS ANIMALS' DESERTION . . . . 629 CIRCUS ANIMALS   T
ANIMATE
    I KNEW THAT ONE IS ANIMATE, ... 406 IN TIME OF WAR   4
    THAT ANIMATE A MOTHER'S REVERIES, ... 445 SCHOOL CHILDR   51
    SATISFY AMBITION, ANIMATE . . . . 500 VACILLATION   20
    SATISFY AMBITION, OR ANIMATE . . . . 500 VACILLATION V 20
ANKLES
    AND BROKE THE CHAIN AND SET MY ANKLES FREE, ... 533 HER TRIUMPH   9
ANNE
    FOR ANNE GREGORY . . . . 492 ANNE GREGORY   T
    ANNE GREGORY . . . . 492 ANNE GREGORY V   T
ANNIVERSARY
    HERE ON THE ANNIVERSARY OF THEIR DEATH, ... 555 RIBH AT TOMB   19
    THE ANNIVERSARY OF THEIR FIRST EMBRACE. . . . . . . 555 RIBH AT TOMB   20
ANNOTATE
    EDIT AND ANNOTATE THE LINES . . . . 337 SCHOLARS   3
ANNOUNCES
    THAT SONG ANNOUNCES DAWN. . . . . 536 PARTING   4
ANNUS
    OF MAGNUS ANNUS AT THE SPRING, ... 437 SONGS PLAY 1   7
ANODYNE
    ANODYNE FOR HIS LOVE. . . . . 471 ALL SOUL NIGHT   26
ANOINT
    WHERE A SHELL THE SEAS ANOINT, ... 732 STREET DANCERS   32
    OR GROW KIND, FOR THEY ANOINT . . . . 776 AGAINST WITCH   21
ANOINTING
    ANOINTING, TORCH JAMMED DOWN BETWEEN THE FLAGS, . . 38 OISIN 2   V 143
ANON
    MY SHEPHERD GARMENTS, AND RETURN ANON. . . . . . . 659 ISLE STAT II 1   29
ANSWER
    THEN DID YOU ANSWER, PEARL-PALE ONE, ... 6 OISIN 1   V 53
    HIS LIPS MOVED SLOWLY IN ANSWER, NO ANSWER OUT OF THEM 51 OISIN 3   66
        CAME:
    HIS LIPS MOVED SLOWLY IN ANSWER, NO ANSWER OUT OF THEM 51 OISIN 3   66
        CAME:
    "MY FATHER," MADE HE, SMILING, ANSWER THEN, ... 107 CUCHULAIN SEA V 25
    CASTS UP A SHOW AND THE WINDS ANSWER IT . . . . . . 186 QUEEN MAEVE   125
    I'LL GIVE MY ANSWER. YOU HAVE AWAKENED HIM. . . . 225 SHADOW WATER B   79
    I'LL GIVE MY ANSWER. YOU HAVE AWAKED HIM. . . . . 225 SHADOW WATER B V 79
    BY MAGIC STRINGS, I'LL MAKE THIS ANSWER TO IT: . . . 243 SHADOW WATER B   440
    MY MAGIC STRINGS, I'LL MAKE THIS ANSWER TO IT: . . . 243 SHADOW WATER B V 440
    BUT IF IT BE REPROACH, I ANSWER THIS: . . . . . . 244 SHADOW WATER B   453

	PAGE	TITLE	LINE

ANSWER   (CONTINUED)

"WHAT IS THIS TROUBLE?" HE WOULD ANSWER NOTHING,   .   .   .   281 TWO KINGS   90
BUT I HAVE FOUND AN ANSWER IN THOSE EYES   .   .   .   .   .   413 TOWER   101
I ANSWER THAT I GAVE MY SOUL   .   .   .   .   538 LAST CONFESS   3
AND THEY'LL ANSWER DEATH AND LOVE.   .   .   .   .   .   .   680 LOVE AND DEATH   16
"NOW ANSWER, IF THIS LIFE BE DEAR TO THEE, ...   713 FERENCZ RENYI   V   83
SHE WILL ANSWER NOW LIKE ANY WAITING WOMAN   .   .   .   .   757 SHADOW WATER A   193

ANSWERED

"O PLEASANT WOMAN," ANSWERED FINN, ...   5 OISIN 1   40
"O PLEASANT MAIDEN," ANSWERED FINN, ...   5 OISIN 1   V   40
YOUNG WARRIOR." "NAY," I ANSWERED, "MY HANDS BURN   .   .   35 OISIN 2   V   89B
WHILE SLOWLY ANSWERED HE WHOSE HAND HELD HERS--   .   .   .   80 EPHEMERA   V   11
AND WITH GLAD VOICE MAEVE ANSWERED HIM, "WHAT KING   .   .   183 QUEEN MAEVE   79
AND WITH GLAD VOICE MAEVE ANSWERED "MANY A TIME   .   .   .   183 QUEEN MAEVE   V   79
YET ANSWERED HIM, "I AM KING EOCHAID'S WIFE   .   .   .   .   284 TWO KINGS   173
YOUR EMPTY BED." "HOW SHOULD I LOVE," I ANSWERED,   .   .   285 TWO KINGS   186
A CURLEW ANSWERED: AND SUDDENLY THEREUPON I THOUGHT   .   .   291 PAUDEEN   5
A CURLEW ANSWERED, AND I WAS STARTLED BY THE THOUGHT   .   . 291 PAUDEEN   V   5
THEREON MY PHOENIX ANSWERED IN REPROOF, ...   352 PEOPLE   22
ANSWERED: "A CRESTED COCKEREL CREW   .   .   .   .   .   .   387 SOLOMON WITCH   V   9
ANSWERED PETER: "ENTER IN: .   .   .   .   697 MOSADA 2   30
AND ANSWERED UNTO HIM: .   .   .   .   740 EARL PAUL   18
BUT HER GOODMAN ANSWERED HER: .   .   .   .   772 SONG DEIRDRE 1   9
BUT HER GOOD MAN ANSWERED HER   .   .   .   .   772 SONG DEIRDRE 1 V   9

ANSWERING

AND THEN AN ANSWERING WHISPERING FLEW   .   .   .   .   .   15 OISIN 1   197
ERE LONG AN ANSWERING WHISPER FLEW, ...   15 OISIN 1   V   197
AND THEN AN ANSWERING WHISPER FLEW   .   .   .   .   .   .   15 OISIN 1   V   197
NOW OLD AND MOUSELIKE. FOR AN ANSWERING SIGN   .   .   .   36 OISIN 2   V   96
EACH OTHER ANSWERING. THEN BETWEEN EACH WING   .   .   .   659 ISLE STAT II 1   14

ANSWERS

ANOTHER ANSWERS, "MAYBE WE SHALL FIND   .   .   .   .   .   233 SHADOW WATER B   254
AND NEVER GET THE ANSWERS RIGHT.   .   .   .   .   .   .   632 MAN AND ECHO   10
A SOLDIER ANSWERS: "BY THE CAMP'S FAR END   .   .   .   .   712 FERENCZ RENYI   67
AND THE OTHER ANSWERS, "MAYBE WE SHALL FIND   .   .   .   .   753 SHADOW WATER A   144

ANTAEUS-LIKE

CONTACT EVERYTHING ANTAEUS-LIKE GREW STRONG.   .   .   .   .   603 GALLERY REVIS   44
CONTACT ALL THINGS ANTAEUS-LIKE GREW STRONG: .   .   .   .   603 GALLERY REVIS   V   44

ANTELOPE

THE JOYOUS FLOCKS OF DEER AND ANTELOPE, ...   75 ANASHU VIJAYA   74

ANTELOPES

THE JOYOUS FLOCKS OF DEER AND ANTELOPES, ...   75 ANASHU VIJAYA   V   74

ANTHONY

WHEN THAT EXULTANT ANTHONY   .   .   .   .   401 DEMON BEAST   46

ANTIGONE

FROM THE "ANTIGONE"   .   .   .   .   540 FROM ANTIGONE   T

ANTINOMIES

ALL THOSE ANTINOMIES   .   .   .   .   500 VACILLATION   5

ANTIQUARIAN

FOR ANTIQUARIAN MEDITATION. AY, ...   721 WITCH VIVIEN   38

ANTIQUE

AND OVER IS THEIR ANTIQUE JOY: .   .   .   .   64 HAPPY SHEPHERD   2
BY WOOD ANTIQUE, BY WAVE AND WASTE.   .   .   .   .   .   .   670 ISLE STAT II 3   109
AWAY IN THE HEART OF THE ANTIQUE WOOD: .   .   .   .   .   730 PRIEST FAIRY   64

ANTI-SELF

THE MOST UNLIKE, BEING MY ANTI-SELF, ...   371 EGO DOMINUS   74

ANTLERS

WITH ANTLERS AND THE SHAGGY SKIN   .   .   .   .   17 OISIN 1   V   249

ANTONIO

AYE, FIGHT WE MUST. TELL ME, ANTONIO, MIGHT   .   .   .   .   662 ISLE STAT II 1   77
ANTONIO, IF I RETURN NO MORE, ...   663 ISLE STAT II 2   17
OF GRIEF. AND IF THEY SAY, "ANTONIO LAUGHED,"   .   .   .   664 ISLE STAT II 2   51
ANTONIO! WE HAVE RESOLVED TO FIGHT, ...   664 ISLE STAT II 2   55

ANVIL

ON THE ANVIL OF THE WORLD. BE STILL: THE SKIES   .   .   .   42 OISIN 2   204
UPON THE ANVIL OF THE WORLD. THE SKIES   .   .   .   .   .   42 OISIN 2   V   204
HOW THE HAMMERS SPRING ON THE ANVIL, ON THE SPEARHEAD'S   52 OISIN 3   83
   BURNING SPOT:

ANXIETY

HEARD ALL THE ANXIETY OF MY PASSIONATE YOUTH, ...   468 HARUN RASHID   168
HER ANXIETY   .   .   .   .   517 HER ANXIETY   T

ANXIOUS   SEE NEVER-ANXIOUS

AND IS ANXIOUS IN ITS SLEEP.   .   .   .   .   87 STOLEN CHILD   23

ANY

SLEEK AS ANY GRANARY MOUSE   .   .   .   .   2 OISIN 1   V   7M
MORE SLEEK THAN ANY GRANARY MOUSE, ...   4 OISIN 1   36
SLEEK AS ANY GRANARY MOUSE, ...   4 OISIN 1   37
BEEN SPOKEN OF WITH ANY MAN: .   .   .   .   6 OISIN 1   56
BEEN SPOKEN OF WITH ANY ONE: .   .   .   .   6 OISIN 1   V   56
I NE'ER LOVED ANY TILL SONG BROUGHT ME   .   .   .   .   .   7 OISIN 1   V   69
OR TIRED ON ANY DAWNING MORROW, ...   23 OISIN 1   V   341
AS ANY RUDDY MOTH, LOOKED DOWN ON US: .   .   .   .   .   34 OISIN 2   72
.   .   . FOR NOWHERE IN ANY CLANN   .   .   .   .   .   .   50 OISIN 3   49
BUT IF WHEN ANY ONE DIED, ...   92 FATHER OHART   V   21
"NOT ANY GOD ALIVE NOR MORTAL DEAD, ...   106 CUCHULAIN SEA   V   10
BEFORE YOU WERE, OR ANY HEARTS TO BEAT, ...   112 ROSE OF WORLD   12
BEFORE YE WERE, OR ANY HEARTS TO BEAT, ...   112 ROSE OF WORLD   V   12
AND NO ONE ANY LEAF-CROWNED DANCER MISS   .   .   .   .   .   128 DREAM OF FAERY V   46
NOR BE I ANY LESS OF THEM, ...   137 TO IRELAND   5
AND IF ANY GAZE ON OUR RUSHING BAND, ...   141 HOSTING SIDHE   10
IN ANY ANCIENT BOOK BUT TELLS OF YOU: .   .   .   .   .   .   186 QUEEN MAEVE   135

35

ANY   (CONTINUED)
    THAN ANY WHOSE UNHAPPINESS . . . .   190 BAILE AILLINN   36
    FOR ANY GENTLE THING SHE SPAKE, ...   191 BAILE AILLINN   63
    ALTHOUGH YOU ARE MORE BEAUTIFUL THAN ANY, . . .   236 SHADOW WATER B   305
    BY ANY OTHER MEANS. YOU CALL IT PASSION, . . .   244 SHADOW WATER B   455
    FOR NEITHER I NOR ANY LIVING MAN . . . . .   250 SHADOW WATER B   588
    IF ANY MAN DREW NEAR . . . .   254 WOMAN HOMER   1
    THAT HAS NOT PASSED THROUGH ANY HUCKSTER'S LOIN,   269 PARDON FATHERS   8
    MORE HANDS IN HEIGHT THAN ANY STAG IN THE WORLD   277 TWO KINGS   9
    SHE WOULD NOT LOOK IN ANY KNOWN MAN'S FACE . .   280 TWO KINGS   73
    DEARER THAN ANY THAT THE DUMB STONE HIDES, . .   281 TWO KINGS   V   96
    "NEVER WILL I BELIEVE THERE IS ANY CHANGE . .   285 TWO KINGS   203
    FROM ANY BRAZEN THROAT, ...   291 TO A FRIEND   3
    YET NEVER HAVE I, NOW NOR ANY TIME, ...   352 PEOPLE   28
    YOU ARE MORE BEAUTIFUL THAN ANY ONE, ...   356 BROKEN DREAMS   27
    YOU WERE MORE BEAUTIFUL THAN ANY ONE, ...   356 BROKEN DREAMS V   27
    MORE PLAIN TO THE MIND'S EYE THAN ANY FACE . .   368 EGO DOMINUS   21
    NOR ANY HUMAN SIGHT WITHIN IT . . . . . .   389 SOLOMON WITCH   41
    THAT ANY NIGHT COULD BRING . . . .   390 IMAGE PAST   32
    LIKE ANY ROCK-BRED, SEA-BORNE BIRD: . . . . .   397 POLIT PRISONER   18
    MY BODILY FORM FROM ANY NATURAL THING, ...   408 SAIL BYZANTIUM   26
    BUT IS THERE ANY COMFORT TO BE FOUND? . . . .   429 NINETEEN 19   41
    I CAN EXCHANGE OPINION WITH ANY NEIGHBOURING MIND, 450 OWEN AHERNE   9
    I HAVE AS HEALTHY FLESH AND BLOOD AS ANY RHYMER'S HAD, 450 OWEN AHERNE   10
    I DID NOT FIND IN ANY CAGE THE WOMAN AT MY SIDE.   450 OWEN AHERNE   19
    O ANY OLD WORDS TO A TUNE. . . . .   548 TO SAME TUNE 3   16
    OR ANY RICH, DARK NOTHING DISINTER . . . . .   565 GYRES   22
    FROM ANY PASSING WRETCH: . . . .   598 STONE CROSS   12
    MARCH WIND, AND ANY OLD TUNE, ...   615 MARCH SONGS 2   25
    WITH ANY SORT OF CLOTHES, ...   627 STATES HOLIDAY   28
    AS FAIR AS ANY THAT ON IDA'S MOUNT . . . . .   650 ISLE STAT I 1   134
    IS SORROW IN HIS SONG, OR ANY CARE? . . . .   652 ISLE STAT I 2   20
    AND NEVER ANY MORE THE WIDE-EYED BANDS . . . .   674 ISLE STAT II 3   218
    WOULD HE TEACH ANY SIN? GAZE IN THE CLOUD . .   692 MOSADA 1   58
    OF ANY UNBLESSED EARTHLY BIRD." . . . . . .   697 MOSADA 2   33
    "NOW HATH HE KITH OR KIN, OR ANY FRIEND?" . . .   712 FERENCZ RENYI   66
    WHERE MOVES THERE ANY BEAUTIFUL AS I, ...   720 WITCH VIVIEN   1
    THAN OLD MEN'S ANY DAY, AS MERLIN FOUND. . . .   721 WITCH VIVIEN   47
    ANY THAT LIVED, AND I HAVE BROUGHT MY GALLEY   756 SHADOW WATER A V 191A
    SHE WILL ANSWER NOW LIKE ANY WAITING WOMAN . .   757 SHADOW WATER A   193
ANYBODY
    IF ANYBODY HALF AS FAIR . . . .   191 BAILE AILLINN   53
ANYONE
    BEEN SPOKEN OF WITH ANYONE: . . . .   6 OISIN 1   y   56
    BUT IF WHEN ANYONE DIED . . . .   92 FATHER OHART   21
    YOU ARE MORE BEAUTIFUL THAN ANYONE . . . . .   356 BROKEN DREAMS V   27
ANYTHING
    IS ANYTHING BETTER, ANYTHING BETTER? . . . .   116 FAERY SONG   11
    IS ANYTHING BETTER, ANYTHING BETTER? . . . .   116 FAERY SONG   11
    AND WILL BELIEVE THAT ANYTHING . . . . . .   191 BAILE AILLINN   68
    "WOULD IT WERE ANYTHING BUT MERELY VOICE!" . . .   258 KING NO KING   1
    BECAUSE HE HAD NOT HEARD OF ANYTHING . . . .   258 KING NO KING   3
    "THEY ARE NOT CHANGED TO ANYTHING, ...   299 THREE HERMITS   25
    FOR ANYTHING YOU DID OR SAID . . . . . .   306 HOUR DAWN   89
    COULD MAKE ME WISH FOR ANYTHING THIS DAY, . . .   338 SHEP GOATHERD   3
    AN IMAGE UP, OR ANYTHING . . . .   390 IMAGE PAST   33
    OR ANYTHING CALLED CONSCIENCE ONCE: . . . .   413 TOWER   118
    NOR IS THERE ANYTHING, ...   496 MOHINI CHATTER   7
    OR ANYTHING ELSE BUT A RHYMER . . . . . .   552 SONGS REWRIT 2   9
    OR ANYTHING ELSE BUT A MAN . . . .   552 SONGS REWRIT 2 V   9
    BUT WHERE IS THE BRUSH THAT COULD SHOW ANYTHING   602 GALLERY REVIS   28
    'TIS BUT TO SEE IF ANYTHING WILL STIR . . . .   669 ISLE STAT II 3   75
    WERE HE ANYTHING BY HALF, ...   772 SONG DEIRDRE 1   13
ANYWHERE
    HAD CHOSEN A HUSBAND ANYWHERE . . . .   191 BAILE AILLINN   54
AODH
    AODH TO DECTORA   THREE SONGS . . . . . .   152 LOSS OF LOVE   V   T
    AODH PLEADS WITH THE ELEMENTAL POWERS . . . .   174 ELEMENT POWERS V   T
    AODH TO DECTORA . . . .   175 BELOVED DEAD   V   T
AOIBHIN
    DEAR CRAOIBHIN AOIBHIN, LOOK INTO OUR CASE. . . .   264 ABBEY THEATRE   1
AOIFE
    ROCK-NURTURED AOIFE TOOK A PIN, ...   274 GREY ROCK   88
AOLAN
    OF GOLDEN ARMED AOLAN AND THE QUEEN . . . . .   766 SHADOW WATER A V   375
APART
    "BUT WE ARE APART IN THE GRASSY PLACES, ...   27 OISIN 1   408
    THE STREAM CHURNED, CHURNED, AND CHURNED---HIS LIPS APART,   31 OISIN 2   43
    . . . AND CHURNED. HIS LIPS WERE ROLLED APART, . . 31 OISIN 2   V   43
    SNATCHING THE BIRD IN SECRET: NOR KNEW I, EMBOSOMED APART,   57 OISIN 3   150
    . . . THE SOUND OF TWO STUMBLING APART. . . . .   60 OISIN 3   V   184
    A LITTLE FROM THE OTHER SHADES APART. . . . .   71 ANASHU VIJAYA   9
    HID UNDER QUIET BOUGHS APART, ...   78 INDIAN TO LOVE   12
    HID UNDER QUIET BOWS APART, ...   78 INDIAN TO LOVE V   12
    PENSIVELY APART. . . . .   89 ISLE IN WATER   4
    IS HEARD ON THE WATER, AS THEY WERE, THE PROUD AND APART,   91 OLD FISHERMAN   10
    ONE BLIND HOUND ONLY LIES APART . . . . .   99 FOXHUNTER   41
    OUR ARMS ARE WAVING, OUR LIPS ARE APART: . . .   140 HOSTING SIDHE   9
    "ARMS ARE A-WAVING AND LIPS APART: . . . .   140 HOSTING SIDHE V   9
    OUR ARMS ARE WEAVING, OUR LIPS ARE APART: . . .   140 HOSTING SIDHE V   9
    I HUNGER TO BUILD THEM ANEW AND SIT ON A GREEN KNOLL APART, 143 ROSE IN HEART   6

		PAGE	TITLE		LINE

APART   (CONTINUED)
NODDING ALONE AND APART. . . . . 171 MAID QUIET   V   6
LAND-OF-THE-TOWER, WHERE AENGUS HAS THROWN THE GATES APART, 209 UNDER THE MOON   8
LAND OF THE TOWER, WHEN AENGUS HAS THROWN THE GATES APART, 209 UNDER THE MOON   V   8
TOWARDS NIGHTFALL UPON CERTAIN SET APART . . . . . . 325 ROBERT GREGORY   29
THINGS FALL APART! THE CENTRE CANNOT HOLD! . . . . . . 402 SECOND COMING   3
THINGS FALL APART! THE CENTRE CAN NOT HOLD, ... 402 SECOND COMING   V   3
NO CIVIL RANCOUR TORN THE LAND APART. . . . . 542 PARN FUNERAL 2   4
AND THEN THE FAY QUEEN SOBBED APART, ... 730 PRIEST FAIRY   70
THE GHOSTS WENT BY ME WITH THEIR LIPS APART . . . . . 734 QUATRAIN APHOR   13
AND STOOD IN MY SORROW APART, ... 744 GLOVE CLOAK   2
APHORISMS
QUATRAINS AND APHORISMS. . . . . 734 QUATRAIN APHOR   T
A-PILIN'
A-PILIN' WOOD OR PILIN' TURF, ... 96 MOLL MAGEE   V   45
APOLOGIA
APOLOGIA ADDRESSED TO IRELAND IN THE COMING DAYS . . . 137 TO IRELAND   V   T
APPALLED
THE ROMAN EMPIRE STOOD APPALLED! . . . . 437 SONGS PLAY 1   13
MY CONSCIENCE OR MY VANITY APPALLED. . . . . 501 VACILLATION   56
APPAREL
SIGH, O YOU LITTLE STARS! O SIGH AND SHAKE YOUR   72 ANASHU VIJAYA   18
  BLUE APPAREL!
SIGH, OH YE LITTLE STARS! OH, SIGH AND SHAKE YOUR BLUE 72 ANASHU VIJAYA   V   18
  APPAREL!
APPARITION
THAN 'TWERE AN APPARITION. O HEART, WE ARE OLD! . . . 334 LIVING BEAUTY   8
I TALKED ABOUT AN APPARITION. . . . . 624 APPARITIONS   2
APPARITIONS
THAT YOU HAVE TALKED WITH APPARITIONS. INDEED . . . 342 SHEP GOATHERD   82
THE APPARITIONS . . . . 624 APPARITIONS   T
FIFTEEN APPARITIONS HAVE I SEEN! . . . . 624 APPARITIONS   7
FIFTEEN APPARITIONS HAVE I SEEN! . . . . 624 APPARITIONS   15
FIFTEEN APPARITIONS HAVE I SEEN! . . . . 624 APPARITIONS   23
APPEAR
APPEAR AND DISAPPEAR IN THE BLUE DEPTH OF THE SKY . . 318 MAGI   3
APPEAR AND DISAPPEAR IN THE BLUE DEPTHS OF THE SKY . . 318 MAGI   V   3
FOUL GOAT-HEAD, BRUTAL ARM APPEAR, ... 612 NEWS ORACLE   33
UNTIL AFAR APPEAR THE GLEAMING DRAGON-SCALES! . . . . 651 ISLE STAT I 1   160
APPEARED
A GREAT BLACK RAGGED BIRD APPEARED WHEN I WAS IN THE BOAT! 593 PILGRIM   16
A GREAT BLACK BIRD APPEARED WHEN I WAS IN THE BOAT, . . 593 PILGRIM   V   16
APPEARS
IN BRONZE, OR THAT IN DAZZLING MARBLE APPEARS, ... 334 LIVING BEAUTY   5
APPEARS, BUT WHEN WE HAVE GONE IS GONE AGAIN, ... 334 LIVING BEAUTY   6
APPEARS, AND WHEN WE HAVE GONE IS GONE AGAIN, ... 334 LIVING BEAUTY   V   6
YET IF NO CHANGE APPEARS . . . . 421 MY TABLE   12
APPEASING   SEE SELF-APPEASING
APPLAUD
THE YOUNG MEN EVERY NIGHT APPLAUD THEIR GABY'S LAUGHING 353 HIS PHOENIX   9
  EYE,
APPLAUD A MODERN THRONE! . . . . 597 MODEL LAUREATE   18
APPLAUSE
WHAT'S NOT FOR THEIR APPLAUSE. . . . . 259 UNWORTH PRAISE   3
"THIS LAND OF SAINTS," AND THEN AS THE APPLAUSE DIED OUT, 577 LOFTY THINGS   3
APPLE
WITH AN APPLE OF GOLD IN HER TOSSING HAND! . . . . . . 12 OISIN 1   143
AN APPLE OF GOLD IN HER TOSSING HAND! . . . . 12 OISIN 1   V   143
WITH APPLE BLOSSOM IN HER HAIR . . . . 150 WANDER AENGUS   14
WITH APPLE BLOSSOMS IN HER HAIR, ... 150 WANDER AENGUS   14
OR TWO SWEET BLOSSOMING APPLE BOUGHS . . . . 195 BAILE AILLINN   V 153
BUT A WILD APPLE HID THE GRASS . . . . 197 BAILE AILLINN   189
MADE OF THE APPLE AND THE YEW, ... 197 BAILE AILLINN   196
DELICATE IN COLOUR AS APPLE BLOSSOM. . . . . 199 ARROW   6
AND OF APPLE ISLANDS WHERE THE DANAAN KIND . . . . . . 203 WITHER BOUGHS   V   12
HE MADE A HARP WITH DRUID APPLE WOOD . . . . 220 HARP OF AENGUS V   11
A HUNGER FOR THE APPLE ON THE BOUGH . . . . 368 EGO DOMINUS   24
CREW FROM A BLOSSOMING APPLE BOUGH . . . . 387 SOLOMON WITCH   10
UPON A BLOSSOMING APPLE BOUGH . . . . 387 SOLOMON WITCH   V   10
CRIED FROM A BLOSSOMING APPLE BOUGH . . . . 387 SOLOMON WITCH   V   10
ALL THAT THE BRIGAND APPLE BROUGHT . . . . 388 SOLOMON WITCH   15
WHAT JUNCTURE OF THE APPLE AND THE YEW, ... 555 RIBH AT TOMB   8
THE TREMBLING OF THE APPLE AND THE YEW, ... 555 RIBH AT TOMB   18
THIS HEARD I WHERE AMONG THE APPLE TREES, ... 686 LIFE   19
OF APPLE BLOSSOM CIRCLES IN THE GLOOM, ... 700 MOSADA 3   V   42
AN APPLE BLOSSOM CIRCLES IN THE GLOOM, ... 700 MOSADA 3   42
WHERE SHADOW OF CHERRY, AND SHADOW OF APPLE TREES, . . 710 FERENCZ RENYI   23
THIS HEARD I WHERE, AMID THE APPLE TREES, ... 735 QUATRAIN APHOR   17
THIS HEARD I WHERE AMONG THE APPLE TREES, ... 735 QUATRAIN APHOR   19
THAT DRUIDS WRITE ON YEW AND APPLE WOOD, ... 748 SHADOW WATER A   29
OF AENGUS' BIRDS GLEAM IN THEIR APPLE BOUGHS. . . . . 751 SHADOW WATER A   103
SHOOK THE PALE APPLE BLOSSOM OVER IT! . . . . 761 SHADOW WATER A V 275
HE MADE A HARP WITH DRUID APPLE WOOD . . . . 763 SHADOW WATER A   306
UPON THIN BOARDS OF YEW AND APPLE WOOD, ... 764 SHADOW WATER A   343
OF THE GOLDEN APPLE TREE! . . . . 771 SPINNING SONG   9
PRAISE THE BLOSSOMING APPLE STEM! . . . . 773 SONG DEIRDRE 1 V   21
APPLE-BLOSSOM
WITH APPLE-BLOSSOM IN HER HAIR, ... 150 WANDER AENGUS   V   14
OF APPLE-BLOSSOM CIRCLES IN THE GLOOM, ... 700 MOSADA 3   42
SHOOK THE PALE APPLE-BLOSSOM OVER IT! . . . . 761 SHADOW WATER A   275

37

APPLE-BOUGHS
   OR TWO SWEET BLOSSOMING APPLE-BOUGHS . . . . 195 BAILE AILLINN   153
APPLED   SEE O'ER-APPLED
APPLES
   THE SILVER APPLES OF THE MOON, ... 150 WANDER AENGUS   23
   THE GOLDEN APPLES OF THE SUN. . . . . 150 WANDER AENGUS   24
   OR APPLES OF THE SUN AND MOON. . . . . 196 BAILE AILLINN   176
   AND SLEEPY BOUGHS, AND BOUGHS WHERE APPLES MADE . . . . 219 HARP OF AENGUS   5
   LIKE CHARMED APPLES MADE OF CHRYSOPRASE, ... 231 SHADOW WATER B   214
   AND SLEEPY BOUGHS, AND BOUGHS WHERE APPLES MADE . . . . 762 SHADOW WATER A   300
   O SCENT OF THE BROKEN APPLES! . . . . 774 COME RIDE   14
APPLE-STEM
   PRAISE THE BLOSSOMING APPLE-STEM. . . . . 773 SONG DEIRDRE 1   21
APPLE-WOOD
   HE MADE A HARP WITH DRUID APPLE-WOOD . . . . 220 HARP OF AENGUS   11
   HE MADE A HARP WITH DRUID APPLE-WOOD . . . . 763 SHADOW WATER A V   306
   UPON THIN BOARDS OF YEW AND APPLE-WOOD, ... 764 SHADOW WATER A V   343
APPOINTED   SEE GOD-APPOINTED
   NO GOVERNMENT APPOINTED HIM. . . . . 318 APPOINTMENT   12
APPOINTMENT
   AN APPOINTMENT . . . . 317 APPOINTMENT   T
   ON A RECENT GOVERNMENT APPOINTMENT IN IRELAND . . . . 317 APPOINTMENT   V   T
APPROACHING
   THOSE WINDS THAT CLAMOUR OF APPROACHING NIGHT. . . . . 431 NINETEEN 19   68
   HER EIGHTIETH WINTER APPROACHING! "YESTERDAY HE THREATENED 578 LOFTY THINGS   8
     MY LIFE.
APPROPRIATE
   WITH SOME APPROPRIATE COMMENTARY ON EACH! . . . . . . 328 ROBERT GREGORY   93
   APPROPRIATE TO THAT BEATING BREAST, ... 386 ROBARTES DANCE   22
   TO FIND OUT SOME APPROPRIATE PAIN-- . . . . 388 SOLOMON WITCH   20
   WILL FIND OUT SOME APPROPRIATE PAIN, ... 388 SOLOMON WITCH V   20
APPROVE
   BUT THE WILD BEDOUIN. THOUGH I APPROVE . . . . . . 462 HARUN RASHID   22
APPROVED
   OR BOYISH INTELLECT APPROVED, ... 328 ROBERT GREGORY   92
   THE SORT OF BEAUTY THAT I HAVE APPROVED, ... 405 FOR DAUGHTER   50
   APPROVED PATTERNS OF WOMEN OR OF MEN . . . . 602 GALLERY REVIS   31
APRIL
   SOFTER THAN SNOW-FLAKES IN APRIL AND PIERCING THE MARROW 51 OISIN 3   68
     LIKE FLAME.
   SOFTER THAN SNOWFLAKES IN APRIL, AND PIERCING THE MARROW 51 OISIN 3   V   68
     LIKE FLAME.
APRIL'S
   HE STOOD A MESSENGER. IN APRIL'S PRIME . . . . . . 690 MOSADA 1   6
A-QUAKE
   PEACE, PEACE, THE EARTH'S A-QUAKE. I HEAR . . . . . 656 ISLE STAT I 3   20
AQUAMARINE
   THEIR LEGS LONG, DELICATE AND SLENDER, AQUAMARINE THEIR 426 PHANTOM HATRED   17
     EYES,
   THE CLOUD-PALE UNICORNS, THE EYES OF AQUAMARINE, . . . 427 PHANTOM HATRED   25
   THE CLOUD PALE UNICORNS, THE EYES OF AQUAMARINE, . . . 427 PHANTOM HATRED V   25
AQUILINE
   MADE AQUILINE, ARE OPEN TO THAT LIGHT. . . . . . . 555 RIBH AT TOMB   24
ARAB
   AND KISSED HER ARAB EYES, ... 333 SOLOMON SHEBA   18
   AND THUS DECLARED THAT ARAB LADY! . . . . 387 SOLOMON WITCH   1
   LIKE SOME POOR ARAB TRIBESMAN AND HIS TENT. . . . . 491 COOLE BALLYLEE   40
ARABIAN
   THAT SEEMS UNNATURAL TO ARABIAN MINDS, ... 464 HARUN RASHID   79
   MUST DRIVE THE ARABIAN HOST. THE VOICE GREW STILL, . . . 467 HARUN RASHID   145
   MADE DRIVE THE ARABIAN HOST. THE VOICE GREW STILL, . . . 467 HARUN RASHID   V 145
ARABIA'S
   OF ALL ARABIA'S LOVERS I ALONE-- . . . . 470 HARUN RASHID   190
ARABS
   BUT WANDERING ARABS. I COMMEND THE ARABS . . . . . 462 HARUN RASHID   V 22
   BUT WANDERING ARABS. I COMMEND THE ARABS . . . . . 462 HARUN RASHID   V 22
ARBITER
   THINKING OF SAINTS AND OF PETRONIUS ARBITER. . . . . . 362 HER COURTESY   8
ARCADIA
   OF GREEN ARCADIA DO NOT HIDE, I TROW, ... 651 ISLE STAT I 1   166
ARCADIAN
   SONG OF THE LAST ARCADIAN . . . . 64 HAPPY SHEPHERD V   T
   OF ALL ON WHOM ARCADIAN SUNS HAVE SHONE . . . . . . 650 ISLE STAT I 1   143
   CLEAR-BROWED ARCADIAN, THOU SHALT BE OUR KING! . . . . 679 ISLE STAT II 3   318
   CLEAR-BROWED ARCADIAN, THOU SHALT BE OUR KING! . . . . 679 ISLE STAT II 3   321
ARCADIANS
   THE ARCADIANS BRING, AND BID THE STONE BE RAISED . . . . 663 ISLE STAT II 2   25
   AND ONCE A-YEAR LET THE ARCADIANS COME, ... 663 ISLE STAT II 2   29
ARCADIA'S
   WHOM MEN HAVE NAMED ARCADIA'S SWEETEST TONGUE. . . . . 649 ISLE STAT I 1   109
ARCADY
   THE WOODS OF ARCADY ARE DEAD, ... 64 HAPPY SHEPHERD   1
   THEIR SHEEP IN ARCADY, NASCHINA, HAIL! . . . . . . 649 ISLE STAT I 1   119
   THEIR SHEEP IN ARCADY, NASCHINA, HAIL! . . . . . . 649 ISLE STAT I 1   121
   POOR RACE OF LEAFY ARCADY, YOUR LOVE . . . . 650 ISLE STAT I 1   145
   O ARCADY, O ARCADY, THIS DAY . . . . 676 ISLE STAT II 3   272
   O ARCADY, O ARCADY, THIS DAY . . . . 676 ISLE STAT II 3   272
ARCHANGEL
   THE ARCHANGEL AXEL, VICTOR THE ANGEL . . . . 774 COME RIDE   11
ARCHANGELS
   BOW DOWN, ARCHANGELS, IN YOUR DIM ABODE! . . . . . . 112 ROSE OF WORLD   11

		PAGE	TITLE	LINE

ARCHANGELS   (CONTINUED)
THE ARCHANGELS STAND IN A ROW THERE . . . .   774 COME RIDE   9
ARCHBISHOP
AN ABBOT OR ARCHBISHOP WITH AN UPRAISED HAND . . . . .   601 GALLERY REVIS   9
ARCHED
A WINDING STAIR, A CHAMBER ARCHED WITH STONE, ...   419 MY HOUSE   11
ARCHER
AMONG PIGEONS AND BEES, WHILE THAT GREAT ARCHER, ...   198 SEVEN WOODS   12
YON ARCHER, HE WHO HATH THE HALCYON'S WING . . . . . .   679 ISLE STAT II 3   316
ARCHERY
SLEEPING LORD OF ARCHERY. . . . .   658 ISLE STAT I 3   81
SLEEPING LORD OF ARCHERY. . . . .   658 ISLE STAT I 3   96
ARCHES
AND UNDER THE ARCHES OF THE BRIDGE, AND SCREAM . . . .   403 FOR DAUGHTER   11
ARCHIMEDES'
OR ARCHIMEDES' GUESS, ...   784 WOMANS BEAUTY   12
ARCHITECT
CALLED ARCHITECT AND ARTIST IN, THAT THEY, ...   418 ANCEST HOUSES   18
ARDAN
"YOU BROUGHT ME WHERE YOUR BROTHER ARDAN SAT . . . . .   280 TWO KINGS   79
ARDAN, AND THOUGH I CALLED TO HIM AND TRIED . . . . .   283 TWO KINGS   142
ARGIVE
AS ARGIVE CLYTEMNESTRA SAW OUT-BURN . . . .   645 ISLE STAT I 1   12
ARGO'S
ANOTHER ARGO'S PAINTED PROW . . . .   437 SONGS PLAY 1   11
ARGOSY
AND MANNED AN ARGOSY AND SAILING DIED. . . . .   693 MOSADA 1   89
ARGUE
BUT WHO IS THERE TO ARGUE THAT . . . .   395 SIXTEEN DEAD   9
ARGUED
YOU MEAN THEY ARGUED, PUT IT SO! . . . .   385 ROBARTES DANCE   13
ARGUMENT
AND LEFT THEM TO THEIR ARGUMENT. . . . .   296 THREE BEGGARS   28
HER NIGHTS IN ARGUMENT . . . .   392 EASTER 1916   19
IN AIMLESS ARGUMENT! . . . .   392 EASTER 1916   V 18
CAN BE CONTENT WITH ARGUMENT AND DEAL . . . . . .   409 TOWER   14
BUT HEAVY FRUIT. HOW SWIFT THE ARGUMENT . . . . . .   665 ISLE STAT II 2   66
ARISE
AND THE STARS SHALL ARISE AND SAY IN THE MORNING, . . .   28 OISIN 1   V 423G
ARISE THE LEOPARD-COLOURED TREES! . . . .   84 MAD KING GOLL   40
AND THEN ARISE, AND RAVING SLAY US ALL. . . . . . .   110 CUCHULAIN SEA   79
I WILL ARISE AND GO NOW, AND GO TO INNISFREE, ...   117 ISLE INNISFREE   1
I WILL ARISE AND GO NOW, FOR ALWAYS NIGHT AND DAY . . .   117 ISLE INNISFREE   9
ARISE AND BID ME STRIKE A MATCH . . . .   476 EVA GORE-BOOTH   26
ARISE THOU AND FOLLOW! . . . .   654 ISLE STAT I 2   57
ARISE FROM THE HOLLOW, ...   654 ISLE STAT I 2   68
I SAW HER AS YOU NOW ARISE! . . . .   654 ISLE STAT I 2   73
ARISE, WORM, AND FOLLOW! . . . .   655 ISLE STAT I 2   83
THAT SHEPHERDESS! ARISE, AND BRING TO ME, ...   673 ISLE STAT II 3   191
ARISEN
A STRANGER NEW ARISEN WAIT . . . .   696 MOSADA 2   V 22
ARISTOTLE
SOLIDER ARISTOTLE PLAYED THE TAWS . . . .   445 SCHOOL CHILDR   43
ARM
STRETCHED HIS LONG ARM TO WHERE, A MISTY SMOTHER, . . .   31 OISIN 2   42
YOU HAVE THE HEAVIEST ARM UNDER THE SKY." . . . . . .   107 CUCHULAIN SEA   24
AND STRETCHING FORTH HIS ARM AND CUP . . . .   275 GREY ROCK   118
AND CROUCHED BY THE ARM OF HIS CHAIR, ...   319 DOLLS   16
THERE IS NO MUSCLE IN THE ARM: AND AFTER, ...   374 PHASES OF MOON   52
TROOPER BELABOURING TROOPER, BITING AT ARM OR AT FACE, . .   426 PHANTOM HATRED   12
THAT RULE BECAUSE A STRONG RIGHT ARM . . . .   597 MODEL LAUREATE   11
FOUL GOAT-HEAD, BRUTAL ARM APPEAR, ...   612 NEWS ORACLE   33
AND ONE ARM POINTING THUS, IN MARBLE WHITE. . . . . .   663 ISLE STAT II 2   28
I STOOD WITH HER CLOAK ON MY ARM . . . .   744 GLOVE CLOAK   5
ARMCHAIR
AND TO THE ARMCHAIR GOES, ...   98 FOXHUNTER   18
ARMED   SEE ONE-ARMED LONG-ARMED GOLDEN-ARMED
. . . WHEN THERE ENTERS THE STRONGLY ARMED GUEST! . . . .   62 OISIN 3   210
"STILL TREADS THE WORLD AMID HIS ARMED MEN." . . . . .   107 CUCHULAIN SEA   V 26
ARMED MEN HAVE COME UPON US! O I AM SLAIN! . . . . .   233 SHADOW WATER B   241
ARMED MEN HAVE COME UPON US! O I AM SLAIN! . . . . .   233 SHADOW WATER B   243
AND TAKE HER IN THE MIDDLE OF ARMED MEN, ...   282 TWO KINGS   114
UNDER IT ARMED WISDOM STANDS, A SEPARATE WISDOM . . . .   469 HARUN RASHID   V 189
CAN HEAR THE ARMED MAN SPEAK. . . . .   470 HARUN RASHID   193
THAT STORMS ARE SHAKING, HEAR THE ARMED MAN SPEAK. . . .   470 HARUN RASHID   V 193
BEST PLEASES YOU. ARMED MEN HAVE COME UPON US. . . . .   752 SHADOW WATER A   131
ARMED MEN HAVE COME UPON US. O! I AM SLAIN! . . . . .   753 SHADOW WATER A   133
OF GOLDEN ARMED AOLAN AND THE QUEEN . . . .   766 SHADOW WATER A V 375
AND SUCKLE CHILDREN NOW? ARMED MEN . . . .   791 REPRISALS   20
ARMIES
LAUGHTER AND CRIES. THE ARMIES CLASH AND SHOCK, ...   43 OISIN 2   211
HAS SLAIN SO MIGHTY ARMIES, SO GREAT KINGS, ...   106 CUCHULAIN SEA   V 10A
IN SHADOWY POOLS, WHEN ARMIES FLED! . . . .   155 FORGOT BEAUTY   5
OF UNKNOWN PERISHING ARMIES BEAT ABOUT MY EARS. . . . .   161 BLACK PIG   4
WAR-LADEN GALLEYS, AND ARMIES ON WHITE ROADS, ...   757 SHADOW WATER A   203
WAR LADEN GALLEYS, AND ARMIES ON WHITE ROADS, ...   757 SHADOW WATER A V 203
ARMIES'
OF ARMOUR--LAUGHTER AND CRIES--THE ARMIES' SHOCK. . . .   43 OISIN 2   V 211
ARMLETS
ARMLETS OF GOLD OR SHIELDS WITH GOLDEN NAILS . . . . .   749 SHADOW WATER A   43

39

	PAGE	TITLE		LINE

ARMOUR
    THE FENIAN HORSES! ARMOUR TORN ASUNDER! . . . . 43 OISIN 2   210
    OF ARMOUR--LAUGHTER AND CRIES--THE ARMIES' SHOCK. . . . 43 OISIN 2   V 211
    . . . MADE ARMOUR FOR CONOR THE OLD. . . . . 52 OISIN 3   V 80
    . . . MADE ARMOUR FOR CONHOR OF OLD. . . . . 52 OISIN 3   V 80
    . . . MADE ARMOUR FOR MIDHIR OF OLD . . . . 52 OISIN 3   V 80
    WHEN THEY FROZE THE CLOTH ON MY BODY LIKE ARMOUR RIVETED 57 OISIN 3   151
      FAST,
    "GO BRING ME MY OLD ARMOUR . . . . 740 EARL PAUL   19
    GO BRING ME MY OWN ARMOUR . . . . 740 EARL PAUL   V 19
    AND STOOD IN HIS DIM ARMOUR, ... 741 EARL PAUL   33
    WITH SHIELD AND ARMOUR WROUGHT WITH GOLD, ... 741 EARL PAUL   37
    I FOUGHT TWELVE BATTLES DRESSED IN GOLDEN ARMOUR. . . . 761 SHADOW WATER A   271
ARMOURED
    ARMOURED HORSES NEIGH . . . . 512 JANE ON GOD   9
ARM'S
    AT ARM'S LENGTH, THUS TILL DUMB ETERNITY . . . . . . 671 ISLE STAT II 3   145
ARMS   SEE MAN-AT-ARMS MEN-AT-ARMS
    WITH HER TRIUMPHING ARMS AROUND ME, ... 9 OISIN 1   107
    IN TRIUMPH WITH HER ARMS AROUND ME, ... 9 OISIN 1   V 107
    MY HUMAN SORROW HER WHITE ARMS WOUND. . . . . 11 OISIN 1   138
    MY HUMAN SADNESS FAY ARMS WOUND, ... 11 OISIN 1   V 138
    AND WAVERING ARMS AND WANDERING DANCES. . . . . . . 19 OISIN 1   275
    AND WAVING ARMS AND WANDERING DANCES. . . . . 19 OISIN 1   V 275
    UNTIL THE TOSSING ARMS GREW STILL . . . . 21 OISIN 1   322
    WITH ME IN HER WHITE ARMS A HUNDRED YEARS . . . . . 30 OISIN 2   17
    ONCE HELD BETWEEN MY ARMS, WITH LIVID CHOP . . . . . 40 OISIN 2   V 178
    BLIND AND NIGH DEAF, WITH WITHERED ARMS HE LIES . . . . 42 OISIN 2   V 203
    AND RAISING ARMS ALL RADDLED WITH THE DYE, ... 105 CUCHULAIN SEA   7
    AND STRETCHING OUT HER ARMS, RED WITH THE DYE, ... 105 CUCHULAIN SEA   V 7
    WHO LOVES YOU, NO WHITE ARMS TO WRAP YOU ROUND, . . . 109 CUCHULAIN SEA   59
    IN VAIN HER ARMS, IN VAIN HER SOFT WHITE BREAST. . . . 110 CUCHULAIN SEA   74
    MY ARMS ROUND MY OWN! . . . . 118 CRADLE SONG   V 10
    WITH ARMS ROUND MY OWN! . . . . 118 CRADLE SONG   V 10
    OUR ARMS ARE WAVING, OUR LIPS ARE APART! . . . . . . 140 HOSTING SIDHE   9
    "ARMS ARE A-WAVING AND LIPS APART . . . . 140 HOSTING SIDHE   V 9
    OUR ARMS ARE WEAVING, OUR LIPS ARE APART! . . . . . 140 HOSTING SIDHE   V 9
    HE BORE HER AWAY IN HIS ARMS, ... 145 HOST OF AIR   33
    AND HIS NECK AND HIS BREAST AND HIS ARMS . . . . . 145 HOST OF AIR   35
    WHEN MY ARMS WRAP YOU ROUND I PRESS . . . . 155 FORGOT BEAUTY   1
    WITH SHOUTING AND THE CLANG OF UNHOOKED ARMS. . . . . 185 QUEEN MAEVE   111
    HAVE BURIED NOTHING BUT MY GOLDEN ARMS. . . . . . . 243 SHADOW WATER B   431
    BUT WHEN HE THOUGHT TO TAKE HER IN HIS ARMS . . . . . 280 TWO KINGS   67
    THAT WHEN HE HAS FALLEN ASLEEP WITHIN MY ARMS, ... 285 TWO KINGS   191
    THEREON HE SEIZED ME IN HIS ARMS, BUT I . . . . . . 285 TWO KINGS   201
    WITHIN MY ARMS GREAT SOLOMON, ... 387 SOLOMON WITCH   4
    NOW SHE HAS THROWN ARMS ABOVE HER HEAD! . . . . . . 390 IMAGE PAST   36
    IN ONE ANOTHER'S ARMS, BIRDS IN THE TREES . . . . . 407 SAIL BYZANTIUM   2
    ROUGH MEN AT ARMS, CROSS-GARTERED TO THE KNEES . . . . 412 TOWER   V 82
    AND CERTAIN MEN AT ARMS THERE WERE . . . . 412 TOWER   V 84
    PLUNGES TOWARDS NOTHING, ARMS AND FINGERS SPREADING WIDE 426 PHANTOM HATRED   13
    OR EYES THAT RAGE HAS BRIGHTENED, ARMS IT HAS MADE LEAN, 427 PHANTOM HATRED   27
    OF EYES THAT RAGE HAS BRIGHTENED, ARMS IT HAS MADE LEAN, 427 PHANTOM HATRED V 27
    MY ARMS ARE LIKE THE TWISTED THORN . . . . 455 HIS MEMORIES   11
    AND FELL THE ONE IN T'OTHER'S ARMS . . . . 457 SUMMER SPRING   7
    THAT FIRST DAWN IN HELEN'S ARMS? . . . . 522 LULLABY   6
    THAT FIRST NIGHT IN HELEN'S ARMS. . . . . 522 LULLABY   V 6
    FLINGING FROM HIS ARMS I LAUGHED . . . . 538 LAST CONFESS   7
    HURRY INTO EACH OTHER'S ARMS! THESE EYES, ... 555 RIBH AT TOMB   22
    AND HELD HER IN MY ARMS! . . . . 631 POLITICS   12
    THE RATTLE OF THOSE ARMS MAKES US AFRAID. . . . . . 634 CUCHULAIN COMF   15
    SINGING OF ARMS AND BATTLES SOME OLD STAVE. . . . . . 650 ISLE STAT I 1   137
    OH, HEART! HER DIRGE! WITH RUSHING ARMS THE WAVES . . 665 ISLE STAT II 2   70
    THE SHEPHERD RAISED HIS ARMS AND SANK. . . . . . . 673 ISLE STAT II 3   187
    THE YOUTH HAD FLUNG HIS ARMS AROUND THE ROCKS, ... 688 TWO TITANS   40
    STAY, STAY, OR I WILL HOLD YOUR WHITE ARMS DOWN, . . . 694 MOSADA 1   92
    AND, WHILE THEY GATHER ROUND MY BECKONING ARMS, . . . 694 MOSADA 1   100
    WHEN MY LOST LOVER LEFT THESE ARMS. MY GOMEZ . . . . 701 MOSADA 3   51
    I TRY TO LIFT MINE ARMS--THEY FALL AGAIN. . . . . . 701 MOSADA 3   56
    AND OUT-SPREAD ARMS. BE NOT SO PALE, DEAR LOVE. . . . 701 MOSADA 3   70
    WHEN MY LOST LOVER LEFT THESE ARMS. MY VALLENCE, . . . 701 MOSADA 3   V 51
    WHY DO YOU HANG SO HEAVY IN MY ARMS? . . . . 703 MOSADA 3   108
    POOR LOVE AND SORROW, WITH THEIR ARMS THROWN ROUND . . 703 MOSADA 3   119
    HER ARMS AROUND HIS FEET. THE SIGNAL GOES . . . . . 714 FERENCZ RENYI   103
    A WOMAN IN MY ARMS, SHE SINKS AWAY . . . . 749 SHADOW WATER A   54
    IN ONE ANOTHER'S ARMS. AENGUS HAS SEEN . . . . . . 763 SHADOW WATER A   321
ARMSTRONG
    A BUTLER OR AN ARMSTRONG THAT WITHSTOOD . . . . 270 PARDON FATHERS   10
ARMY
    LIKE AN ARMY OF OLD MEN LONGING FOR REST FROM THE MOAN 48 OISIN 3   16
      OF THE SEAS.
    LIKE AN ARMY OF OLD MEN LONGING FOR REST FROM THE MOAN 57 OISIN 3   144
      OF THE SEAS.
    LIKE AN ARMY OF OLD MEN LOUNGING FOR REST FROM THE FOAM 57 OISIN 3   V 144
      OF THE SEAS.
    HE MADE FOR HER AN ARMY CEASE TO BE." . . . . 106 CUCHULAIN SEA V 16B
    AND A GREAT ARMY BUT A SHOWY THING! . . . . 429 NINETEEN 19   18
AROSE
    AROSE FROM EVERY MAID AND BOY, ... 20 OISIN 1   289
    AS THUS OUR SONG AROSE! "YOU STARS, ... 22 OISIN 1   329
    AS THUS OUR SONG AROSE! "YE STARS, ... 22 OISIN 1   V 329

	PAGE	TITLE		LINE

AROSE   (CONTINUED)
```
    LIKE WINGS OF KINGFISHERS; AND HE AROSE . . . . . .      40 OISIN 2        169
    LONG SIGHS AROSE IN OUR SPIRITS, BENEATH US BUBBLED THE  48 OISIN 3         20
       GROUND.
    A GIRL AROSE THAT HAD RED MOURNFUL LIPS . . . . . . .   120 SORROW OF LOVE    5
    AROSE, AND ON THE INSTANT CLAMOROUS EAVES, . . . . . . 120 SORROW OF LOVE    9
    NEVER STORM AROSE SO SWIFTLY; SCARCE THE CHILDREN WERE  718 PHANTOM SHIP      4
       IN BED,
    THE STORM AROSE AND SUDDENLY FELL . . . . . . . . . .  784 WOMANS BEAUTY    19
AROUND
    WITH HER TRIUMPHING ARMS AROUND ME, . . . . . . . .      9 OISIN 1         107
    IN TRIUMPH WITH HER ARMS AROUND ME, . . . . . . . .      9 OISIN 1     V   107
    AROUND A SCEPTRE OF ALL LIGHTS, . . . . . . . . . .     18 OISIN 1     V   254
    AND GAZES AROUND HER WITH EYES OF BRIGHTNESS; . . .     27 OISIN 1         413
    AND GAZES AROUND HER WITH EYES OF BRIGHTNESS; . . .     28 OISIN 1     V   421
    NOW, MAN OF CROSIERS, PHANTOMS DREW AROUND . . . .      29 OISIN 2     V     1
    SPRANG FROM A GATEWAY WALLED AROUND WITH BLACK . .      31 OISIN 2     V    29
    FEEDING WHITE MOTHS AROUND SOME EASTERN SHRINE, . .     41 OISIN 2     V   186
    FLED FOAM UNDERNEATH US, AND AROUND US, A WANDERING AND 47 OISIN 3     V     1
       MILKY SMOKE,
    IN MIDST OF AN OLD MAN'S BOSOM; OWLS RUFFLING AND PACING 50 OISIN 3        47
       AROUND
    IN THE MIDST OF AN OLD MAN'S BOSOM; OWLS RUFFLING       50 OISIN 3     V    47
       AND PACING AROUND
    LONG FLED THE FOAM-FLAKES AROUND ME, THE WINDS FLED OUT 57 OISIN 3        149
       OF THE VAST,
    AROUND ME SHONE KEEN EYES OF MEN; . . . . . . . .      83 MAD KING GOLL     30
    AND SHONE AROUND THE EYES OF MEN; . . . . . . . .      83 MAD KING GOLL V   30
    AND ALL AROUND THE HARP-STRING TOLD HIS PRAISE, . .    109 CUCHULAIN SEA    44
    AND ALL AROUND THE HARPSTRING TOLD HIS PRAISE, . .     109 CUCHULAIN SEA V  44
    AND ALL AROUND THE HARP STRING TOLD HIS PRAISE, . .    109 CUCHULAIN SEA V  44
    AROUND THE FIRE AT THE CLUB, . . . . . . . . . .       392 EASTER 1916      12
    COME SWISH AROUND, MY PRETTY PUNK; . . . . . . . .     591 DRUNK SOBRIETY    1
    AROUND ME THE IMAGES OF THIRTY YEARS; . . . . . .      601 GALLERY REVIS     1
    AND FLOWERS AROUND IN CLUSTERING THOUSANDS ARE, . .    656 ISLE STAT I 3    24
    AROUND THE FEATHERY TIP, UNTO THE SHAFT . . . . .      657 ISLE STAT I 3    71
    WE TURNED AROUND THE PLACE ALWAY, . . . . . . . .      667 ISLE STAT II 3   40
    LONG CITRON COILS THAT HANG AROUND THEE, BLOWN . .     670 ISLE STAT II 3  105
    BEHOLD, I BEND! AROUND MY BEARD IN DRIFTS . . . .      684 SEEKER           68
    BEHOLD I BOW! AROUND MY BEARD IN DRIFTS . . . . .      684 SEEKER       V   68
    AROUND THE TWITTER OF THE LIPS OF DUST . . . . . .     685 DRAWING-ROOM      1
    THE YOUTH HAD FLUNG HIS ARMS AROUND THE ROCKS, . .     688 TWO TITANS       40
    AND THRICE THE CORN AROUND THE SICKLES FLAMED, . .     690 MOSADA 1          3
    AROUND MY HEAD AND DANCED AMONG THE GRASS; . . . .     690 MOSADA 1         19
    AND IN HER SINGING WOVE AROUND HER HEAD . . . . .      693 MOSADA 1         84
    'TIS THOU, FOR THEY'VE GROWN BLUE AROUND THE NAILS. .  700 MOSADA 3         46
    I'LL DRAW MY CLOAK AROUND ME; IT IS COLD. . . . .      704 MOSADA 3        123
    HER ARMS AROUND HIS FEET. THE SIGNAL GOES . . . .      714 FERENCZ RENYI   103
    "AROUND, THE TWITTER OF THE LIPS OF DUST . . . . .     735 QUATRAIN APHOR   21
A-ROVING
    NO MORE A-ROVING SHALT THOU SEE . . . . . . . . .      658 ISLE STAT I 3    82
ARRAIGNED
    CONSTRAINED, ARRAIGNED, BAFFLED, BENT AND UNBENT . . . 382 VISION ROBART     9
ARRANGED
    AND AFTER THAT ARRANGED IT IN A SONG . . . . . .       384 VISION ROBART    65
    THAT ALL'S ARRANGED IN ONE CLEAR VIEW, . . . . .       633 MAN AND ECHO     31
ARRAYED
    AND CLOUDS ARRAYED THEIR RANK ON RANK . . . . . .      12 OISIN 1         154
    THE CLOUDS ARRAYED THEM RANK ON RANK . . . . . . .     12 OISIN 1     V   154
ARREST
    I HERE ARREST THEE. IT WAS ALLAH'S WILL. . . . .       694 MOSADA 1        105
    I HERE ARREST THEE. IT IS ALLAH'S WILL. . . . .        694 MOSADA 1     V  105
ARROGANCE
    FOR ARROGANCE AND HATRED ARE THE WARES . . . . .       406 FOR DAUGHTER     75
ARROGANT
    OR ARROGANT LOVELINESS, . . . . . . . . . . . .        390 IMAGE PAST       25
    AND MAY HAVE GROWN MORE ARROGANT BEING A GHOST. . .    473 ALL SOUL NIGHT   80
    A BLOODY, ARROGANT POWER . . . . . . . . . . . .       480 BLOOD AND MOON    3
    PALLAS ATHENE IN THAT STRAIGHT BACK AND ARROGANT HEAD; 578 LOFTY THINGS     11
ARROGANTLY
    SO ARROGANTLY PURE, A CHILD MIGHT THINK . . . . . .    491 COOLE BALLYLEE   23
ARROW
    AND BY THEM WERE ARROW AND WAR-AXE, ARROW AND SHIELD AND 49 OISIN 3        29
       BLADE;
    AND BY THEM WERE ARROW AND WAR-AXE, ARROW AND SHIELD AND 49 OISIN 3        29
       BLADE;
    WERE ARROW AND SHIELD AND WAR-AXE, ARROW AND SPEAR AND  49 OISIN 3     V   30
       BLADE,
    WERE ARROW AND SHIELD AND WAR-AXE, ARROW AND SPEAR AND  49 OISIN 3     V   30
       BLADE,
    THE ARROW . . . . . . . . . . . . . . . . . .         199 ARROW             T
    I THOUGHT OF YOUR BEAUTY, AND THIS ARROW, . . . . .    199 ARROW             1
    THE BURNING BOW THAT ONCE COULD SHOOT AN ARROW . .     377 PHASES OF MOON  119
    A WOMAN, AND AN ARROW ON A STRING; . . . . . . .       541 PARN FUNERAL 1   11
    I SENT AN ARROW. AND I SAW YOU MISS; . . . . . .       649 ISLE STAT I 1   115
    LONG ERE AN ARROW WHIZZED OR SWORD LEFT SHEATH . .     650 ISLE STAT I 1   135
    SOME CAST OF DIE, OR LET SOME ARROW GLANCE . . .       656 ISLE STAT I 3    40
    I'LL SEND MINE ARROW, NOW MY ONE RESOURCE; . . .       657 ISLE STAT I 3    64
    FICKLE THE GUIDING HIS ARROW SHALL FIND! . . . .       657 ISLE STAT I 3    66
    'TIS HERE THE ARROW FELL; THE BREEZES LAUGHED . .      657 ISLE STAT I 3    70
    A RED HOUND RUNNING FROM A SILVER ARROW. . . . .       747 SHADOW WATER A    6
```

41

ARROW   (CONTINUED)
      FOR THESE NINE YEARS? O ARROW UPON ARROW! . . . . . .   761 SHADOW WATER A   268
      FOR THESE NINE YEARS? O ARROW UPON ARROW! . . . . . .   761 SHADOW WATER A   268
ARROW'S
      UPON THE WIND, AND GUIDE MINE ARROW'S COURSE. . . . . .   657 ISLE STAT I 3   62
      GO PILOT THE COURSE OF HIS ARROW'S DECEIT! . . . . . .   657 ISLE STAT I 3   69
ARROWS
      RISES, AND SHOWERS ABROAD HIS FRAGRANT ARROWS, ...   72 ANASHU VIJAYA   27
      AH, YOU WILL KNOW MY LOVED ONE BY HIS HUNTER'S ARROWS
         TRULY,   75 ANASHU VIJAYA   80
      MY EYES ARE TROUBLED BY THE SILVER ARROWS! . . . . . .   761 SHADOW WATER A   269
ARROWY
      HAS FLUNG ITS ARROWY SHAFT UPON THE FLOOR. . . . . . .   482 BLOOD AND MOON   32
      HAD FLUNG ITS ARROWY SHAFT UPON THE FLOOR, ...   482 BLOOD AND MOON V   32
ART
      BECAUSE WE HAVE MADE OUR ART OF COMMON THINGS, ...   265 ABBEY THEATRE   5
      DELIGHT IN ART WHOSE END IS PEACE, ...   288 TO WEALTHY MAN   26
      AND GREAT ART BEATEN DOWN. . . . .   348 FISHERMAN   24
      YET SURELY THERE ARE MEN WHO HAVE MADE THEIR ART . . .   369 EGO DOMINUS   38
      THE SENTIMENTALIST HIMSELF! WHILE ART . . . .   369 EGO DOMINUS   47
      HIS ART IS HAPPY, BUT WHO KNOWS HIS MIND? . . . . . .   370 EGO DOMINUS   54
      CONCEIVES A CHANGELESS WORK OF ART. . . . .   421 MY TABLE   14
      THAT LOVED INFERIOR ART. . . . .   422 MY TABLE   27
      HAVE LOVED INFERIOR ART. . . . .   422 MY TABLE   V   27
      IN ART OR POLITICS! . . . .   431 NINETEEN 19   71
      UPON THE SUPREME THEME OF ART AND SONG! . . . .   523 LONG SILENCE   6
      AND FADED NOW IS ALL THY WONDROUS ART. . . . .   673 ISLE STAT II 3   194
ARTERY
      FOR ONE THROB OF THE ARTERY, ...   406 IN TIME OF WAR   1
ARTHUR
      WHAT NAME HAD THAT DEAD KING? ARTHUR OF BRITAIN? . . .   242 SHADOW WATER B   404
      NO, NO--NOT ARTHUR. I REMEMBER NOW. . . . .   242 SHADOW WATER B   405
      THE MARVELLOUS STAG OF ARTHUR, ...   399 BREAK OF DAY   23
      THE AUSTERE ARTHUR, RULE FROM UTHER'S CHAIR? . . . . .   678 ISLE STAT II 3   296
ARTICULATE
      FOR TO ARTICULATE SWEET SOUNDS TOGETHER . . . .   205 ADAMS CURSE   10
      YOU HAVE LACKED ARTICULATE SPEECH . . . .   436 FOR MY SON   20
ARTICULATION
      A CLEAR ARTICULATION IN THE AIR, ...   320 REED WHISPERER   3
ARTIFICE
      INTO THE ARTIFICE OF ETERNITY. . . . .   408 SAIL BYZANTIUM   24
ARTISSON
      THAT INSOLENT FIEND ROBERT ARTISSON . . . .   433 NINETEEN 19   128
ARTIST   SEE FELLOW-ARTIST
      DEAR FELLOW ARTIST WHY SO FREE . . . .   335 YOUNG BEAUTY   V   1
      WHAT PORTION IN THE WORLD CAN THE ARTIST HAVE . . . .   369 EGO DOMINUS   49
      CALLED ARCHITECT AND ARTIST IN, THAT THEY, ...   418 ANCEST HOUSES   18
ARTIST'S
      A MIMICRY OF YOUTH. AN ARTIST'S THOUGHT, ...   463 HARUN RASHID   V   62
ARTISTS
      CERTAIN ARTISTS BRING HER DOLLS AND DRAWINGS . . . . .   362 DOLLS DRAWINGS   T
AS
      SLEEK AS ANY GRANARY MOUSE . . . .   2 OISIN 1   V   7M
      AS THOUGH HE HELD AN EARTHLY MEAD . . . .   2 OISIN 1   V   7X
      HER EYES WERE SOFT AS DEWDROPS HANGING . . . .   3 OISIN 1   V   7HH
      AS HER SOFT BOSOM ROSE AND FELL. . . . .   4 OISIN 1   30
      "WHY, AS YE RIDE, DROOPS LOW EACH HEAD? . . . .   4 OISIN 1   32
      SLEEK AS ANY GRANARY MOUSE. . . . .   4 OISIN 1   V   37
      AND GLORIOUS AS ASIAN BIRDS, ...   7 OISIN 1   V   65
      AND A HUNDRED LADIES, MERRY AS BIRDS, ...   9 OISIN 1   96
      AND A HUNDRED MAIDENS, MERRY AS BIRDS, ...   9 OISIN 1   V   96
      AND I BE WITH THEE AS THY WIFE." . . . .   9 OISIN 1   V   101
      OR ARE YOU PHANTOMS WHITE AS SNOW, ...   10 OISIN 1   117
      OR ARE YE PHANTOMS WHITE AS SNOW, ...   10 OISIN 1   V   117
      SAID NIAM, AS SHE LAID THE TIP . . . .   12 OISIN 1   V   150
      AS, FULL OF LOVING FANTASY, ...   13 OISIN 1   158
      AS THOUGH THEY ALL WERE BEATING TIME, ...   13 OISIN 1   174
      AND, AS THE SUN SANK EVER LOWER, ...   13 OISIN 1   V 170A
      OR CLUNG AS CLOSE AS SWARMS OF BEES, ...   14 OISIN 1   V   181
      OR CLUNG AS CLOSE AS SWARMS OF BEES, ...   14 OISIN 1   V   181
      THEIR BROWS WERE WHITE AS FRAGRANT MILK . . . .   15 OISIN 1   204
      THEIR BROWS WERE WHITE AS THE FRAGRANT MILK . . . . .   15 OISIN 1   V   204
      AND KISSED, AS THEY WOULD NEVER CEASE. . . . .   16 OISIN 1   215
      AS WE KISSED EACH ROSE'S HEAD! . . . .   21 OISIN 1   V   307
      AS THUS OUR SONG AROSE! "YOU STARS, ...   22 OISIN 1   329
      UNCHAINABLE AS THE DIM TIDE, ...   22 OISIN 1   338
      AS THUS OUR SONG AROSE! "YE STARS, ...   22 OISIN 1   V   329
      AND, AS THEY SANG, THE PAINTED BIRDS . . . .   26 OISIN 1   396
      THE HARE GROWS OLD AS SHE PLAYS IN THE SUN . . . . . .   27 OISIN 1   412
      STROKED THE YOUNG WINDS AS THEY ROLLED ON THE PLAIN, .   27 OISIN 1   V 415C
      "OLD GROWS THE HARE AS SHE PLAYS IN THE SUN, ...   28 OISIN 1   V   420
      AS THEY GAZE AT EACH OTHER, "OH, WHERE IS THAT GREAT ONE?" 28 OISIN 1   V 423H
      YET SANG NO MORE AS WHEN, LIKE A BROWN BEE . . . . . .   30 OISIN 2   15
      HAPPY AS CHILDREN WITH UNWITHERING LIPS, ...   30 OISIN 2   V 14B
      UNLANGUID AS THE BIRDS, IN PROUD COMPANIONSHIPS! . . .   30 OISIN 2   V 14C
      BUT SANG NO MORE, AS WHEN, LIKE A BROWN BEE . . . . .   30 OISIN 2   V   15
      NO LONGER GLAD AS ON THAT MORNING, SPED . . . .   30 OISIN 2   V   16
      I LAY, AS OVER SEA THE LIGHT HOOVES GLANCED . . . . .   30 OISIN 2   V 19A
      AS THOUGH HE TOLD HIS NEVER-SLUMBERING HEART . . . . .   32 OISIN 2   44
      AS THOUGH UNTO HIS NEVER SLUMBERING HEART . . . . . .   32 OISIN 2   V   44
      AS THOUGH HE TOLD HIS NEVER SLUMBERING HEART . . . . .   32 OISIN 2   V   44

AS   (CONTINUED)

		PAGE	TITLE		LINE
OUR TREAD, AS ROSE AND FELL THE LIQUID TONES	. . . . .	33	OISIN 2	V	68B
AS ANY RUDDY MOTH, LOOKED DOWN ON US;	. . . . .	34	OISIN 2		72
AS LIKE A RUDDY MOTH THEY WAVED AND FLUTTERED.	. . . .	34	OISIN 2	V	72
WITH HOPE, MINE ENEMY. AS HE BY NIGHT	. . . .	34	OISIN 2	V	81
FOR HE IS STRONG AND CRAFTY AS THE SEAS	. . . . . .	35	OISIN 2		83
AS THOUGH HIS HOUR WERE COME. WE SOUGHT THE PART	. . .	37	OISIN 2		112
AS THOUGH HIS HOUR WERE ON HIM. TO THE PART	. . .	37	OISIN 2	V	112
A DUSKY DEMON DRY AS A WITHERED SEDGE	. . . . . .	39	OISIN 2		158
HIS HAND ALONG THE RUNNEL'S SIDE, AS THOUGH	. . . .	39	OISIN 2		162
A DUSK DEMON, DRY AS A WITHERED SEDGE,	. . . . . .	39	OISIN 2	V	158
A HUSKY DEMON, DRY AS A WITHERED SEDGE	. . . . . .	39	OISIN 2	V	158
A DEMON'S LEISURE. EYES FIRST WHITE AS SNOW,	. . . . .	40	OISIN 2	V	168
CAME TO MY TOWER AS AGE DRAGGED AFTER AGE	. . . . .	45	OISIN 2	V	242
HIGH AS THE SADDLE-GIRTH, COVERING AWAY FROM OUR GLANCES THE TIDE;		47	OISIN 3		2
HIGH AS THE SADDLE GIRTH, COVERING AWAY FROM OUR GLANCES THE TIDE;		47	OISIN 3	V	2
DRIPPING AND DOUBLING LANDWARD, AS THOUGH THEY WOULD HASTEN AWAY,		48	OISIN 3		15
FOR, AS DRIFT FROM A SAILOR SLOW DROWNING	. . . . . .	48	OISIN 3		22
IN THE ROOTS OF THE GRASSES, THE SORRELS, I LAID MY BODY AS LOW;		52	OISIN 3		73
OR MOVED AS THEY MOVED ONCE,	. . . .	53	OISIN 3		88
DARK BALOR, AS OLD AS A FOREST, CAR-BORNE, HIS MIGHTY HEAD SUNK		53	OISIN 3		91
DARK BALOR, AS OLD AS A FOREST, CAR-BORNE, HIS MIGHTY HEAD SUNK		53	OISIN 3		91
IN A LONG IRON SLEEP, AS A FISH IN THE WATER GOES DUMB AS A STONE.		53	OISIN 3		96
IN A LONG IRON SLEEP, AS A FISH IN THE WATER GOES DUMB AS A STONE.		53	OISIN 3		96
CAME CAR-BORNE BALOR, AS OLD AS A FOREST, HIS VAST FACE SUNK		53	OISIN 3	V	91
CAME CAR-BORNE BALOR, AS OLD AS A FOREST, HIS VAST FACE SUNK		53	OISIN 3	V	91
CAME BALOR, AS OLD AS A FOREST, CAR BORNE, HIS MIGHTY HEAD SUNK		53	OISIN 3	V	91
CAME BALOR, AS OLD AS A FOREST, CAR BORNE, HIS MIGHTY HEAD SUNK		53	OISIN 3	V	91
. . . WAKING WHITE AS A SHELL	. . . .	54	OISIN 3		109
O HAD YOU SEEN BEAUTIFUL NIAMH GROW WHITE AS THE WATERS ARE WHITE,		54	OISIN 3		109
AS SHE MURMURED, "O WANDERING OISIN,	. . . .	55	OISIN 3		123
BRUSH LIGHTLY AS HAYMOUSE EARTH'S PEBBLES,	. . . . . .	56	OISIN 3		128
BRUSH LIGHTLY AS HAY MOUSE EARTH'S PEBBLES,	. . . . .	56	OISIN 3	V	128
DRIPPING AND DOUBLING LANDWARD, AS THOUGH THEY WOULD HASTEN AWAY,		57	OISIN 3		143
AS MY MIND MADE THE NAMES OF THE FENIANS.	. . . . . .	57	OISIN 3		146
I RODE AWAY ON THE SURGES, WHERE, HIGH AS THE SADDLE-BOW	.	57	OISIN 3		147
I RODE AWAY ON THE SURGES, WHERE HIGH AS THE SADDLE BOW	.	57	OISIN 3	V	147
I RODE AWAY ON THE SURGES, WHERE, HIGH AS THE SADDLEBOW,	.	57	OISIN 3	V	147
IF I WERE AS I ONCE WAS,	. . . .	58	OISIN 3		157
COMING OUT OF THE SEA AS THE DAWN COMES, A CHAUNT OF LOVE ON MY LIPS,		58	OISIN 3		158
. . . THE FLESH OF HIS FACE AS DRIED GRASS,	. . . . .	59	OISIN 3		173
. . . HE SAD AS A CHILD WITHOUT MILK;	. . . . .	59	OISIN 3		174
. . . AND THEIR YOUTH, AND THEIR EYES SOFT AS SILK. . .	59	OISIN 3	V	176
HEARING HELL LOUD WITH A MURMUR, AS SHOUTING AND MOCKING WE SWEEP,		62	OISIN 3		208
MAKE CLEAN AS A BROOM CLEANS,	. . . .	62	OISIN 3		211
. . . AND MARCH ON AS OXEN MOVE OVER YOUNG GRASS;	. .	62	OISIN 3		211
ALL EMPTIED OF PURPLE HOURS AS A BEGGAR'S CLOAK IN THE RAIN,		63	OISIN 3		219
AS A HAY-COCK OUT ON THE FLOOD, OR A WOLF SUCKED UNDER A WEIR.		63	OISIN 3		220
AS A GRASS SEED CRUSHED BY A PEBBLE, AS A WOLF SUCKED UNDER A WEIR.		63	OISIN 3	V	220
AS A GRASS SEED CRUSHED BY A PEBBLE, AS A WOLF SUCKED UNDER A WEIR.		63	OISIN 3	V	220
AS IN THE WOODS HE WANDERS, IF HE LOVE	. . . . . .	71	ANASHU VIJAYA	V	3
TO MIGHTY BRAHMA, HE WHO MADE YOU MANY AS THE SANDS,	. .	72	ANASHU VIJAYA		21
TO MIGHTY BRAHMA--HE WHO MADE YE MANY AS THE SANDS,	. .	72	ANASHU VIJAYA	V	21
TO MIGHTY BRAHMA, WHO HAS MADE YOU MANY AS THE SANDS, . .	72	ANASHU VIJAYA	V	21
GATHERED IN SILENCE, DEWY AS HER EYES,	. . . . . .	80	EPHEMERA		19
AND AH, THEY KNOW NOT, AS THEY PINE AND CEASE,	. . . .	81	EPHEMERA	V	24I
BUT SLOWLY, AS I SHOUTING SLEW	. . . .	83	MAD KING GOLL		25
AS ONCE WITHIN A LITTLE TOWN	. . . .	85	MAD KING GOLL		49
TIME WAS, AS IN A LITTLE TOWN,	. . . .	85	MAD KING GOLL	V	49
AND AS I SANG MY SOUL WAS FREE	. . . .	86	MAD KING GOLL	V	65
AND SHY AS A RABBIT,	. . . .	89	ISLE IN WATER		13
SHE BID ME TAKE LOVE EASY, AS THE LEAVES GROW ON THE TREE;	90	SALLEY GARDENS		3
SHE BID ME TAKE LIFE EASY, AS THE GRASS GROWS ON THE WEIRS;	90	SALLEY GARDENS		7
SHE BID ME TAKE LOVE EASY, AS THE LEAVES GROW ON THE TREES;	90	SALLEY GARDENS	V	3
THE HERRING ARE NOT IN THE TIDES AS THEY WERE OF OLD;	. .	91	OLD FISHERMAN		5
IS HEARD ON THE WATER, AS THEY WERE, THE PROUD AND APART,	91	OLD FISHERMAN		10
AND HE GAVE THEM AS DOWERS TO HIS DAUGHTERS,	. . . .	92	FATHER OHART		7
AS HE WENT UP AND DOWN;	. . . .	92	FATHER OHART		18
BECAUSE I MUTTER AS I GO;	. . . .	94	MOLL MAGEE		3
BUT ALWAYS, AS I'M MOVIN' ROUND,	. . . .	96	MOLL MAGEE		43
FIRST AS A RAVEN ON WHOSE ANCIENT WINGS	. . . . . .	102	FERGUS DRUID		3

AS   (CONTINUED)
WITH THONGS OF LEATHER." AS SHE SPAKE IT WAS! . . . .   106 CUCHULAIN SEA V   178
EVEN AS SPRING UPON THE ANCIENT SKIES, ...   108 CUCHULAIN SEA   42
I CALL, AS THEY GO BY ME ONE BY ONE, ...   114 ROSE OF BATTLE   8
AND PROUD AS PRIAM MURDERED WITH HIS PEERS! . . . . .   120 SORROW OF LOVE   8
SHINING BRIGHT AS A NEW LANCE! . . . .   125 CATHLEEN PARA V   14
AS HE WENT BY THE SANDS OF LISADILL . . . .   127 DREAM OF FAERY V   13
AND AS IT FALLS AWAKENS LEAFY TUNES!-- . . . . . .   127 DREAM OF FAERY V   23
AS IN THE OLD DAYS LONG GONE BY, ...   131 OLD PENSIONER V   15
HE RODE NOW AS HE NEVER RODE, ...   133 FR GILLIGAN   29
AS MERRY AS A BIRD." . . . .   133 FR GILLIGAN   38
AS MERRY AS A BIRD." . . . .   133 FR GILLIGAN   38
LIFT UP BEFORE US AS THEY PASS, ...   135 TWO TREES   V   23
AND WHERE IS THERE HOPE OR DEED AS FAIR? . . . . . .   141 HOSTING SIDHE   14
AS A CLOUD FADED INTO THE SKY. . . . .   145 HOST OF AIR   V   40
AS THE TIDE WEARS THE DOVE-GREY SANDS, ...   157 POET BELOVED   4
AS THE TIDE HAS THE DOVE-GREY SANDS, ...   157 POET BELOVED   V   4
AND AS SOON AS THE MORN HAD WHITENED, ...   160 CAP AND BELLS   V   23
AND AS SOON AS THE MORN HAD WHITENED, ...   160 CAP AND BELLS   V   23
AS THE LIGHT ON THE SEA, ...   175 ELEMENT POWERS V   14
OR AS THE CHANGING SPEARS FLUNG BY THE GOLDEN STARS . . .   175 ELEMENT POWERS V   15
AS THOUGH ONE LISTENED THERE, AND HIS VOICE SANK . . .   180 QUEEN MAEVE   7
AS IF THERE WERE NO TALE BUT YOUR OWN TALE . . . . .   181 QUEEN MAEVE   32
BUT THE HORSE-BOYS SLEPT ON, AS THOUGH SOME POWER . .   181 QUEEN MAEVE   39
HAD COME AS IN THE OLD TIMES TO COUNSEL HER, ...   181 QUEEN MAEVE   42
HAD COME, AS IN OLD TIMES, TO COUNSEL HER, ...   181 QUEEN MAEVE   V   42
AS IN THE OLD DAYS WHEN THEY WOULD COME AND GO . . .   183 QUEEN MAEVE   81
AND WITH A GROAN, AS IF THE MORTAL BREATH . . . . .   185 QUEEN MAEVE   103
AS MIDDLE NIGHT GREAT CATS WITH SILVER CLAWS, ...   185 QUEEN MAEVE   115
IMAGINED, AS THEY STRUCK THE WAY . . . .   189 BAILE AILLINN   20
IF ANYBODY HALF AS FAIR . . . .   191 BAILE AILLINN   53
AS THOUGH THEIR MUSIC WERE ENOUGH . . . .   193 BAILE AILLINN   108
AS WHEN NEWLY GROWN TO BE A WOMAN, ...   199 ARROW   4
DELICATE IN COLOUR AS APPLE BLOSSOM. . . . .   199 ARROW   6
COUPLED WITH GOLDEN CHAINS, AND SING AS THEY FLY. . .   204 WITHER BOUGHS   18
A MOON, WORN AS IF IT HAD BEEN A SHELL . . . . . .   206 ADAMS CURSE   31
WASHED BY TIME'S WATERS AS THEY ROSE AND FELL . . . .   206 ADAMS CURSE   32
AS WEARY-HEARTED AS THAT HOLLOW MOON. . . . . . .   206 ADAMS CURSE   38
AS WEARY-HEARTED AS THAT HOLLOW MOON. . . . . . .   206 ADAMS CURSE   38
A MOON--MOON WORN AS IF IT HAD BEEN A SHELL . . . .   206 ADAMS CURSE   V   31
AS WEARY HEARTED AS THAT HOLLOW MOON. . . . . . .   206 ADAMS CURSE   V   38
AS WEARY HEARTED AS THAT HOLLOW MOON. . . . . . .   206 ADAMS CURSE   V   38
BUT PURE AS A TALL CANDLE BEFORE THE TRINITY . . . .   208 HANRAHANS SONG V   14
WHERE MANY HUNDRED SQUIRRELS ARE AS HAPPY . . . . .   217 WOODS OF COOLE   5
AS THOUGH THEY HAD BEEN HIDDEN BY GREEN BOUGHS . . .   217 WOODS OF COOLE   6
FROM HUMAN THOUGHT, AS HARES AND MICE AND CONEYS . .   218 WOODS OF COOLE   31
AS MEN IN THE OLD TIMES, BEFORE THE HARPS BEGAN, . .   219 WOODS OF COOLE   43
AS MEN IN THE OLD TIMES, BEFORE THE HARP BEGAN, . .   219 WOODS OF COOLE V   43
I SAW THEM ON THAT NIGHT AS WELL AS YOU. . . . . .   223 SHADOW WATER B   29
I SAW THEM ON THAT NIGHT AS WELL AS YOU. . . . . .   223 SHADOW WATER B   29
AS THAT WILD AENGUS. LONG BEFORE HER DAY . . . . .   224 SHADOW WATER B   47
HE DOES NOT HATE SEAFARERS AS HE HATES . . . . . .   224 SHADOW WATER B   53
FOR HE CAN JUDGE THE STARS AS WELL AS FORGAEL. . . .   225 SHADOW WATER B   63
FOR HE CAN JUDGE THE STARS AS WELL AS FORGAEL. . . .   225 SHADOW WATER B   63
YOU'LL BE AS GOOD A LEADER. BE OF YOUR TROOP! . . .   225 SHADOW WATER B V   73
BEING AS DOUBTFUL? I HAVE CALLED YOU MASTER . . . .   227 SHADOW WATER B   110
AS THEY HAVE KNOWN IT. NOW THE SECRET'S OUT! . . . .   228 SHADOW WATER B   140
AND AS SOON FINISHED. ALL THAT EVER LOVED . . . .   229 SHADOW WATER B   151
AS A LAMP SHADOW--NO--NO LAMP, THE SUN. . . . . .   229 SHADOW WATER B   160
MUTTER SUCH THINGS AS THEY AWAKE FROM TRANCE. . . .   229 SHADOW WATER B   163
THEY ARE BESOTTING YOU AS THEY BESOT . . . . . .   229 SHADOW WATER B   166
AS THOSE THAT CAN OUTLIVE THE MOON HAVE KNOWN IT, . .   230 SHADOW WATER B   193
AS THOSE THAT CAN OUTLIVE THE MOON HAVE SHOWN IT, . .   230 SHADOW WATER B   193
HAD YOU LOOKED ON THEM FACE TO FACE AS I DID, . . .   230 SHADOW WATER B V   193
ONE OF THE EVER-LIVING, AS I THINK-- . . . . . .   231 SHADOW WATER B   198
AS NOW. DOES WANDERING IN THESE DESOLATE SEAS . . .   231 SHADOW WATER B   210
I CAN PUT FEAR AWAY AS A QUEEN SHOULD. . . . . .   236 SHADOW WATER B   314
AS I AM DOING NOW. WHY DO YOU WEEP? . . . . . .   238 SHADOW WATER B   355
THAT I MIGHT LAY IT ON YOUR HEAD AS A CROWN. . . .   246 SHADOW WATER B   495
FLASHES AS IF IT WERE A NET OF HERRINGS. . . . . .   246 SHADOW WATER B   511
AS FOR THIS WOMAN, I THINK SHE IS COMING WITH ME. . .   248 SHADOW WATER B   536
LEAPS UPWARD, AS IF ALL THE STREAMS O' THE WORLD . .   248 SHADOW WATER B   545
AS 'TWERE UPON A CLOUD, ...   249 SHADOW WATER B   560
THAT NOBLENESS MADE SIMPLE AS A FIRE, ...   255 WOMAN HOMER   18
WE'LL OUT, FOR THE WORLD LIVES AS LONG AGO! . . . .   256 NO SECOND TROY   7
TO HAVE LIT UPON AS CLEAN AND SWEET A TALE . . . .   257 RECONCILIATION   8
WE'LL FIND SO GOOD A THING AS THAT WE HAVE LOST? . .   258 KING NO KING   8
THAT MUST, AS IF IT HAD NOT HOLY BLOOD . . . . . .   258 KING NO KING   13
AS THOUGH IT DRAGGED ROAD-METAL. MY CURSE ON PLAYS . .   260 FASC DIFFICULT   5
AS THOUGH IT DRAGGED ROAD METAL. MY CURSE ON PLAYS . .   260 FASC DIFFICULT   8
YOU SAY, AS I HAVE OFTEN GIVEN TONGUE . . . . . .   260 FASC DIFFICULT V   8
CRYING ALOUD AS THE RACECOURSE IS, ...   262 TO A POET   1
CRYING ALOUD AS THE RACE COURSE IS, ...   266 GALWAY RACES   14
CRYING ALOUD AS THE RACE-COURSE IS, ...   266 GALWAY RACES   14
WORLD, AS IT WERE A COAL. . . . .   266 GALWAY RACES   V   14
AS THOUGH TO SAY "IT IS THE SWORD ELSEWHERE," . . .   267 FRIEND ILLNESS   5
BEFORE THAT ROOMFUL OR AS GOOD. . . . .   267 ALL TEMPT ME   V   8
THE HORN RESOUNDED AS THOUGH IT HAD BEEN SILVER, . .   273 GREY ROCK   52
AS THOUGH A STAG AND UNICORN WERE MET . . . . . .   277 TWO KINGS   16
AND CAME INTO A WOOD AS THE SUN SET . . . .   277 TWO KINGS   19
AND RAN AT HIM, AND PASSED, AND AS IT PASSED . . . .   277 TWO KINGS   V   12A

44

		PAGE	TITLE		LINE
AS	(CONTINUED)				
	AND THEN, AS TERROR-STRICKEN AS A CHILD	279	TWO KINGS	V	45A
	AND THEN, AS TERROR-STRICKEN AS A CHILD	279	TWO KINGS	V	45A
	HER BEAUTY AS THE CONSTELLATIONS POUR	279	TWO KINGS	V	62B
	AND AT THESE WORDS HE PALED, AS SHE HAD PALED,	280	TWO KINGS		76
	AS ON THE BLUE LIGHT OF A SWORD, A MAN	283	TWO KINGS		148
	THAT COULD, AS HE HAD TOLD HER, WORK HIS CURE.	283	TWO KINGS	V	137
	THAT I MAY CLAIM YOU AS MY WIFE AGAIN."	284	TWO KINGS		170
	THAT MADE THE BODY SEEM AS IT WERE A STRING	284	TWO KINGS		176
	AND CALL THOSE EXILES AS THEY WERE	290	SEPTEMBER 1913		26
	HAD GIVEN BUT AS THE REST	293	HELEN LIVED		10
	"IF THAT BE TRUE AS IT SEEMS TRUE,	295	THREE BEGGARS		20
	AND THEREON, MERRY AS A BIRD	296	THREE BEGGARS		25
	I'VE STOOD AS I WERE MADE OF STONE	297	THREE BEGGARS		64
	ARE DRIVEN BY WEALTH AS BEGGARS BY THE ITCH,"	300	BEGGAR CRIED		14
	AS I CAME OVER WINDY GAP	300	RUN PARADISE		1
	AND THERE THE KING IS BUT AS THE BEGGAR,	301	RUN PARADISE		7
	AND THERE THE KING IS BUT AS THE BEGGAR,	301	RUN PARADISE		14
	AND THERE THE KING IS BUT AS THE BEGGAR,	301	RUN PARADISE		21
	AND THERE THE KING IS BUT AS THE BEGGAR,	301	RUN PARADISE		28
	CALLED CRUACHAN, AND IT WAS AS MUCH	302	HOUR DAWN		4
	AS THE ONE STURDY LEG COULD DO	302	HOUR DAWN		5
	CURSING THE WIND. IT WAS AS MUCH	302	HOUR DAWN	V	4
	AS WHEN I ALSO PLAYED THE FOOL."	306	HOUR DAWN		79
	AS IF IT WERE NOT WORTH THE DOING.	306	HOUR DAWN		84
	AND SOULS AS IF THEY WERE BUT SIGHS,	307	HOUR DAWN		102
	LOVE LOST AS SOON AS WON,	312	CHILD DANCING		8
	LOVE LOST AS SOON AS WON,	312	CHILD DANCING		8
	SUFFER AS YOUR MOTHER SUFFERED,	313	TWO YEAR LATER		9
	BE AS BROKEN IN THE END.	313	TWO YEAR LATER		10
	THE MOMENTS PASSED AS AT A PLAY;	313	MEMORY YOUTH		1
	AND SHE SEEMED HAPPY AS A KING,	313	MEMORY YOUTH	V	6
	WE SAT AS SILENT AS A STONE,	314	MEMORY YOUTH		15
	WE SAT AS SILENT AS A STONE	314	MEMORY YOUTH		15
	I SAT AS SILENT AS A STONE	314	MEMORY YOUTH	V	15
	I SAT AS SILENT AS A STONE	314	MEMORY YOUTH	V	15
	ONCE WALKED A THING THAT SEEMED, AS IT WERE, A BURNING CLOUD,	315	FALLEN MAJESTY	V	8
	THAT SEEMED AS THOUGH ICE BURNED AND WAS BUT THE MORE ICE,	316	COLD HEAVEN		2
	OUT NAKED ON THE ROADS, AS THE BOOKS SAY, AND STRICKEN	316	COLD HEAVEN		11
	BUT LIVED AS 'TWERE A KING	317	NIGHT COME		6
	NOW AS AT ALL TIMES I CAN SEE IN THE MIND'S EYE,	318	MAGI		1
	AS THOUGH THEY'D WROUGHT IT.	320	COAT		7
	WHO COMES AT NEED, ALTHOUGH NOT NOW AS ONCE	320	REED WHISPERER		2
	BUT AS THE OUTRAGEOUS STARS INCLINE	325	ROBERT GREGORY		38
	A PORTION OF MY MIND AND LIFE, AS IT WERE,	325	ROBERT GREGORY		42
	AS HE THAT PRACTISED OR THAT UNDERSTOOD	327	ROBERT GREGORY		75
	AS THOUGH HE HAD BUT THAT ONE TRADE ALONE.	327	ROBERT GREGORY		80
	AS THOUGH DRIED STRAW, AND IF WE TURN ABOUT	327	ROBERT GREGORY		83
	AS 'TWERE ALL LIFE'S EPITOME.	327	ROBERT GREGORY		87
	AS THOUGH I HAD FOUND IN A BOOK	329	MEN IMPROVE		6
	AS THOUGH I HAD FOUND IN BOOK	329	MEN IMPROVE	V	6
	IF I SHOULD LIVE AS LIVE THE NEIGHBOURS,"	331	ROUND TOWER		3
	IF I SHOULD LIVE AS LIVES THE NEIGHBOURS'	331	ROUND TOWER	V	3
	AS COMMON BEAUTIES MAY,	336	YOUNG BEAUTY		9
	CAN KNOW IT AS I KNOW,	336	YOUNG GIRL		5
	HER LABOURING MEN, AS THOUGH HER DARLING LIVED,	340	SHEP GOATHERD		38
	BUT SUCH AS I HAVE SEEN UPON HER FACE	340	SHEP GOATHERD		40
	AS OTHERS WILL, WHEN FIRST THEY TAKE POSSESSION,	341	SHEP GOATHERD		52
	BUT LEFT THE HOUSE AS IN HIS FATHER'S TIME	341	SHEP GOATHERD		53
	AS THOUGH HE KNEW HIMSELF, AS IT WERE, A CUCKOO,	341	SHEP GOATHERD		54
	AS THOUGH HE KNEW HIMSELF, AS IT WERE, A CUCKOO,	341	SHEP GOATHERD		54
	YOU SING AS ALWAYS OF THE NATURAL LIFE,	342	SHEP GOATHERD		75
	I WOULD BE IGNORANT AS THE DAWN	344	DAWN		1
	I WOULD BE IGNORANT AS THE DAWN	344	DAWN		10
	IGNORANT AND WANTON AS THE DAWN.	344	DAWN		14
	I WOULD BE AS IGNORANT AS THE DAWN,	344	DAWN	V	1
	I WOULD BE AS IGNORANT AS THE DAWN,	344	DAWN	V	1
	AS WITH HER FLESH AND BONE,	345	ON WOMAN		6
	POEM MAYBE AS COLD	348	FISHERMAN		39
	AND PASSIONATE AS THE DAWN."	348	FISHERMAN		40
	POEM MAY BE AS COLD	348	FISHERMAN	V	39
	AS A MAN DOES WHO HAS PUBLISHED A NEW BOOK,	350	HER PRAISE		3
	AS THOUGH SOME OTHER NAME RAN IN HIS HEAD.	351	HER PRAISE		9
	AND THAT PROUD LOOK AS THOUGH SHE HAD GAZED INTO THE BURNING SUN,	354	HIS PHOENIX		29
	AS IF THE HAIR STOOD UP ON MY HEAD,	358	PRESENCES		2
	AS THOUGH I'D A GUN	359	TO A SQUIRREL		4
	AS NARROW NATURES WOULD	365	HER RACE		2
	ALL THAT I SEEK; AND WHISPER IT AS THOUGH	371	EGO DOMINUS		76
	THEY HAD KEPT A STEADY PACE AS THOUGH THEIR BEDS,	372	PHASES OF MOON		5
	AS WITH THE CAT-O'-NINE-TAILS OF THE MIND,	374	PHASES OF MOON		42
	BEFORE THE FULL MOON, HELPLESS AS A WORM,	374	PHASES OF MOON		49
	IT WOULD BE THE WORLD'S SERVANT, AND AS IT SERVES,	376	PHASES OF MOON		90
	INSIPID AS THE DOUGH BEFORE IT IS BAKED,	376	PHASES OF MOON		112
	FOR, WANDER AND WAIL AS HE WOULD,	378	CAT AND MOON		6
	AS I LOOK UP TO PROVIDENCE.	380	SONGS FOOL 1		6
	AS 'TWERE A SPINNING-TOP.	384	VISION ROBART		44
	AS THOUGH I HAD BEEN UNDONE	384	VISION ROBART		55
	AMID MOST LOVELY PLACES; SMITTEN AS THOUGH	389	IMAGE PAST		13
	AS THOUGH SHE HAD BEEN FORCED TO LINGER	390	IMAGE PAST		23

45

AS   (CONTINUED)

	PAGE	TITLE		LINE
AS A MOTHER NAMES HER CHILD	394	EASTER 1916		62
O PLAIN AS PLAIN CAN BE	396	ROSE TREE		16
AND MURMUR IT WITH BATED BREATH, AS THOUGH	398	LEADERS CROWD		5
AND EVEN STRAFFORD SMILED AS THOUGH	400	DEMON BEAST		13
BEING DEAR AS MINE ARE DEAR.	400	DEMON BEAST		20
AND EVEN STAFFORD SMILED AS THOUGH	400	DEMON BEAST	V	13
YET I AM CERTAIN AS CAN BE	401	DEMON BEAST		33
A GAZE BLANK AND PITILESS AS THE SUN,	402	SECOND COMING		15
HEARTS ARE NOT HAD AS A GIFT BUT HEARTS ARE EARNED	404	FOR DAUGHTER		34
AS IN THE GOLD MOSAIC OF A WALL,	408	SAIL BYZANTIUM		18
BUT SUCH A FORM AS GRECIAN GOLDSMITHS MAKE	408	SAIL BYZANTIUM		27
AS TO A DOG'S TAIL? NEVER HAD I MORE	409	TOWER		4
AS UPON A DOG'S TAIL. NEVER HAD I MORE	409	TOWER	V	4
AS I WOULD QUESTION ALL, COME ALL WHO CAN!	412	TOWER		89
AS I DO NOW AGAINST OLD AGE?	413	TOWER		100
AS AT THE LOOPHOLE THERE	415	TOWER		166
AS THOUGH TO CHOOSE WHATEVER SHAPE IT WILLS	417	ANCEST HOUSES		6
AS IF SOME MARVELLOUS EMPTY SEA-SHELL FLUNG	417	ANCEST HOUSES		13
AS VIGOROUS OF MIND, AND YET IT SEEMS	422	MY DESCENDANTS		4
AS THOUGH TO DIE BY GUNSHOT WERE	424	ROAD AT DOOR		4
SUFFICE THE AGEING MAN AS ONCE THE GROWING BOY,	427	PHANTOM HATRED		40
MELT DOWN, AS IT WERE WAX IN THE SUN'S RAYS!	428	NINETEEN 19		12
THE NIGHT CAN SWEAT WITH TERROR AS BEFORE	429	NINETEEN 19		29
AS THOUGH GOD'S DEATH WERE BUT A PLAY,	437	SONGS PLAY 1		8
SHE STANDS BEFORE ME AS A LIVING CHILD.	444	SCHOOL CHILDR		24
HOLLOW OF CHEEK AS THOUGH IT DRANK THE WIND	444	SCHOOL CHILDR		27
AS RECOLLECTION OR THE DRUG DECIDE,	444	SCHOOL CHILDR		36
BUT THOSE THE CANDLES LIGHT ARE NOT AS THOSE	445	SCHOOL CHILDR		50
IT IS AS THOUGH YOU PRAISED ANOTHER, OR EVEN	448	HERO GIRL FOOL		3
IT IS AS THOUGH YOU PRAISE ANOTHER, OR EVEN	448	HERO GIRL FOOL	V	3
I HAVE AS HEALTHY FLESH AND BLOOD AS ANY RHYMER'S HAD,	450	OWEN AHERNE		10
I HAVE AS HEALTHY FLESH AND BLOOD AS ANY RHYMER'S HAD,	450	OWEN AHERNE		10
AS THOUGH MY SORROW WERE A SCENE	452	HUMAN DIGNITY		5
REJOICE AS LOVER SHOULD	453	DEATH OF HARE		4
BUT FOUND IT DRY AS BONE,	454	EMPTY CUP		8
AND BARREN AS A BREAKING WAVE	456	FRIENDS YOUTH		11
AS THAT OLD WANDERING BEGGAR AND THESE GOD-HATED CHILDREN KNOW.	459	FROM OEDIPUS		6
BUT BRILLIANT AS THE NIGHT'S EMBROIDERY,	461	HARUN RASHID		7
MUST KEEP THAT PERFECT, AS THEY KEEP HER SONG,	461	HARUN RASHID		18
AS AIR UNDER A WING, CAN GIVE BIRDS' WIT.	462	HARUN RASHID		28
AS AIR UNDER A WING, CAN GIVE BIRD'S WIT.	462	HARUN RASHID	V	28
"BUT SUCH AS YOU AND I DO NOT SEEM OLD"	463	HARUN RASHID		55
AS IF THAT WRITING OR THE FIGURED PAGE	466	HARUN RASHID		126
SHE MOVED HER LIMBS CONFUSEDLY AS THOUGH	466	HARUN RASHID	V 125A
AS THOUGH THE WRITTEN OR THE PICTURED PAGE	466	HARUN RASHID	V	126
AS MUMMIES IN THE MUMMY-CLOTH ARE WOUND!	471	ALL SOUL NIGHT		14
AS MUMMIES IN THE MUMMY CLOTH ARE WOUND!	471	ALL SOUL NIGHT	V	14
AS MUMMIES IN THE MUMMY-CLOTH ARE WOUND.	474	ALL SOUL NIGHT		100
AS MUMMIES IN THE MUMMY CLOTH ARE WOUND.	474	ALL SOUL NIGHT	V	100
IS SATO'S ANCIENT BLADE, STILL AS IT WAS,	477	SELF AND SOUL		10
IS SATO'S ANCIENT SWORD, STILL AS IT WAS,	477	SELF AND SOUL	V	10
AND CLAIM AS BY A SOLDIER'S RIGHT	478	SELF AND SOUL		31
WHEN SUCH AS I CAST OUT REMORSE	479	SELF AND SOUL		68
SOFT AS THE RUSTLE OF A REED FROM CLOYNE	487	SEVEN SAGES		22
MIMICKING WHAT THEY HEARD, AS CHILDREN MIMIC!	487	SEVEN SAGES		25
NOT SUCH AS ARE IN NEWTON'S METAPHOR,	494	AT ALGECIRAS		11
UNTIL THE MORNING BREAK AS ON A DARK BREAST.	494	AT ALGECIRAS	V	6
OR, AS GREAT SAGES SAY,	496	MOHINI CHATTER		27
THAT ARE NOT SUITED FOR SUCH MEN AS COME	501	VACILLATION		33
NOR SO MUCH AS PARISH PRIEST,	508	JANE BISHOP		11
NONE SO OLD AS HE AND I!	508	JANE BISHOP	V	6
AS THOUGH TO STRANGLE HER, NO SCREAM	514	JANE GROWN OLD		4
SUCH A DANCE AS THERE WAS DANCED--	515	JANE GROWN OLD		20
SHE WOULD AS BRAVELY SHOW	516	MANS SONG		9
RISE AS KINDRED SHOULD.	518	LOVES LONENESS		2
I DREAMED AS IN MY BED I LAY,	519	HER DREAM		1
AS DID THAT WILD TRISTRAM KNOW	522	LULLABY		8
SUCH A SLEEP AND SOUND AS FELL	522	LULLABY		13
BELOVED SUCH A SLEEP AS FELL	522	LULLABY	V	13
MAD AS THE MIST AND SNOW.	523	MAD AS MIST		T
MAD AS THE MIST AND SNOW.	523	MAD AS MIST		6
MAD AS THE MIST AND SNOW?	524	MAD AS MIST		12
MAD AS THE MIST AND SNOW.	524	MAD AS MIST		18
IN AS FOUL A RAG!	525	DANCING DAYS		6
CURSE AS YOU MAY I SING IT THROUGH!	525	DANCING DAYS		9
COLD AS THE MARCH WIND HIS EYES.	531	FATHER CHILD		8
AS THOUGH ON MY BELOVED,	532	BEFORE WORLD		10
NOR KNEW, DRUNKEN WITH SINGING AS WITH WINE,	537	HER VISION		30
BEAST GAVE BEAST AS MUCH.	538	LAST CONFESS		12
THAT SUCH AS I HAD SUCH A MAN	539	MEETING		9
BUT SUCH AS HE FOR SUCH AS ME--	539	MEETING		15
BUT SUCH AS HE FOR SUCH AS ME--	539	MEETING		15
AS MAN, AS BEAST, AS AN EPHEMERAL FLY BEGETS, GODHEAD BEGETS GODHEAD,	556	RIBH PATRICK		5
AS MAN, AS BEAST, AS AN EPHEMERAL FLY BEGETS, GODHEAD BEGETS GODHEAD,	556	RIBH PATRICK		5
AS MAN, AS BEAST, AS AN EPHEMERAL FLY BEGETS, GODHEAD BEGETS GODHEAD,	556	RIBH PATRICK		5

```
AS   (CONTINUED)                                              PAGE    TITLE         LINE
     AND COULD BEGET OR BEAR THEMSELVES COULD THEY BUT LOVE    556  RIBH PATRICK     12
       AS HE.
     AS THE MOON SIDLES UP . . . . . . . . . . . . . . . .     559  HE AND SHE        1
     AS TRIPS THE SCARED MOON . . . . . . . . . . . . . . .    559  HE AND SHE        3
     SHE SINGS AS THE MOON SINGS! . . . . . . . . . . . . .    559  HE AND SHE        7
     AS TRIPS THE SACRED MOON . . . . . . . . . . . . . . .    559  HE AND SHE     V  3
     DRINKING JOY AS IT WERE MILK UPON HIS BREAST. . . . .     559  MAGIC DRUM        3
     WHO HANDLED MARBLE AS IF IT WERE BRONZE, . . . . . . .    566  LAPIS LAZULI     30
     HE SHALL LOVE MY SOUL AS THOUGH . . . . . . . . . . .     572  LADYS 2ND SONG    8
     WEAK AS A WORM. . . . . . . . . . . . . . . . . . . .     574  MAIDS 1ST SONG   10
     DULL AS A WORM, . . . . . . . . . . . . . . . . . . .     575  MAIDS 2ND SONG    2
     LIMP AS A WORM, . . . . . . . . . . . . . . . . . . .     575  MAIDS 2ND SONG    4
     BLIND AS A WORM. . . . . . . . . . . . . . . . . . . .    575  MAIDS 2ND SONG    6
     "THIS LAND OF SAINTS," AND THEN AS THE APPLAUSE DIED OUT, 577  LOFTY THINGS      3
     AS THOUGH THAT HAND COULD REACH TO WHERE THEY STAND, . .  579  DOR WELLESLEY     2
     AS THOUGH TO DRAW THEM CLOSER YET.  RAMMED FULL . . . .   579  DOR WELLESLEY     5
     AS THE FOX IN THE OLD FABLE DESTROYED THE SPARTAN BOY'S,  580  CURSE CROMWELL   18
     OR SUCKED SUCH MILK AS HE. . . . . . . . . . . . . . .    584  GHOST ROG CASE   26
     I KNOW AS FEW CAN KNOW. . . . . . . . . . . . . . . .     589  OLD WICKED MAN   47
     AND WHAT'S THE ODDS IF SUCH AS THESE . . . . . . . . .    597  MODEL LAUREATE    5
     AS THOUGH SOME BALLAD-SINGER HAD SUNG IT ALL! . . . . .   602  GALLERY REVIS    24
     AS THOUGH SOME BALLAD SINGER HAD SUNG IT ALL. . . . . .   602  GALLERY REVIS  V 24
     HER LIMBS ARE DELICATE AS AN EYELID, . . . . . . . . .    612  NEWS ORACLE      27
     AS THOUGH WITH MAGNANIMITY OF LIGHT, . . . . . . . . .    618  BRONZE HEAD       9
     AS THOUGH A STERNER EYE LOOKED THROUGH HER EYE . . . .    619  BRONZE HEAD      23
     AS MY LONG-PLANNED HALF SOLITUDE, . . . . . . . . . .     624  APPARITIONS      10
     AS MY LONG PLANNED HALF SOLITUDE, . . . . . . . . . .     624  APPARITIONS    V 10
     AS THOUGH UPON A LIGHTED SCREEN, . . . . . . . . . . .    626  OLD MEN BE MAD   12
     AS THAT WHICH CLEANS MAN'S DIRTY SLATE. . . . . . . .     633  MAN AND ECHO     24
     AS THOUGH TO MEDITATE ON WOUNDS AND BLOOD. . . . . . .    634  CUCHULAIN COMF    6
     THOUGH ALL WAS DONE IN COMMON AS BEFORE, . . . . . . .    635  CUCHULAIN COMF   24
     THOUGH THEY BUT FEED AS THE GOATHERD FEEDS, . . . . .     635  BLACK TOWER       2
     AS A LEAF THAT IS OLD, AND WITHERED, AND COLD, . . . .    643  SONG FAERIES      3
     AS A LEAF THAT IS OLD, AND WITHERED, AND COLD, . . . .    644  SONG FAERIES     15
     COME FORTH! THE MORN IS FAIR! AS FROM THE PYRE . . . .    645  ISLE STAT I 1     8
     UNTO THE WANDERER'S SHIPS, OR AS DAY FILLS . . . . . .    645  ISLE STAT I 1    10
     AS ARGIVE CLYTEMNESTRA SAW OUT-BURN . . . . . . . . .     645  ISLE STAT I 1    12
     AS WHEN UPON HER CLOUD-O'ER-MUFFLED STEEP . . . . . .     645  ISLE STAT I 1    16
     AS WITHIN A CELLAR CHILLY . . . . . . . . . . . . . .     647  ISLE STAT I 1    57
     AS A TOKEN AND A SIGN, . . . . . . . . . . . . . . . .    648  ISLE STAT I 1    78
     AS THE LEAVES IN AUTUMN SCATTER. . . . . . . . . . . .    648  ISLE STAT I 1    90
     WITH SINGING SWEET AS E'ER ROUND LAKE-LULLED ISLE . .     649  ISLE STAT I 1   106
     AS FAIR AS ANY THAT ON IDA'S MOUNT . . . . . . . . . .    650  ISLE STAT I 1   134
     AS FAIR AS ANY THAT ON IDA'S MOUNT . . . . . . . . . .    650  ISLE STAT I 1   134
     AS LIES DARK WATER IN A MURMUROUS GLADE, . . . . . . .    650  ISLE STAT I 1   138
     SUCH QUESTS AS THESE, I TROW, NEED LITTLE WIT. . . . .    650  ISLE STAT I 1   150
     AS SOME DEAD MAIDEN'S SINGING IN A DREAM. . . . . . .     654  ISLE STAT I 2    59
     AS I SING NOW TO THEE! . . . . . . . . . . . . . . . .    654  ISLE STAT I 2    67
     AS I WANDERED UNSEEN, . . . . . . . . . . . . . . . .     654  ISLE STAT I 2    71
     I SAW HER AS YOU NOW ARISE! . . . . . . . . . . . . .     654  ISLE STAT I 2    73
     AS I SING NOW TO THEE! . . . . . . . . . . . . . . . .    654  ISLE STAT I 2    77
     AS I SING NOW TO THEE! . . . . . . . . . . . . . . . .    655  ISLE STAT I 2    81
     AS, CLOTHED IN CEREMONIAL GLOOM, . . . . . . . . . . .    655  ISLE STAT I 3    10
     EACH SHINING CLEAR AS SOME UNBAFFLED STAR! . . . . . .    656  ISLE STAT I 3    25
     AS I, TO CHOOSE BENEATH DAY'S DYING FLAMES! . . . . .     656  ISLE STAT I 3    34
     AND THEY ARE ALL NOW STONE, AS I SHALL BE, . . . . . .    656  ISLE STAT I 3    35
     BINDS, AS WITHIN A GIRDLE OR A RING, . . . . . . . . .    657  ISLE STAT I 3    59
     IF WRONG MY CHOICE, AS SILENT AS THOU ART. . . . . . .    657  ISLE STAT I 3    76
     IF WRONG MY CHOICE, AS SILENT AS THOU ART. . . . . . .    657  ISLE STAT I 3    76
     AS I MY WATCHING LEST YOU WAKE, . . . . . . . . . . .     658  ISLE STAT I 3    95
     I, AS A SHEPHERD DRESSED, WILL SEEK AND SEEK . . . . .    658  ISLE STAT II 1    1
     CURVING BENEATH THE PROW! AS SOME WILD DRAKE . . . . .    659  ISLE STAT II 1   16
     AS THE SEA'S FURROWS ON A SEA-TOST SHELL, . . . . . .     660  ISLE STAT II 1   51
     AS I AM STANDING NOW--AS THOUGH I GAZED, . . . . . . .    663  ISLE STAT II 2   26
     AS I AM STANDING NOW--AS THOUGH I GAZED, . . . . . . .    663  ISLE STAT II 2   26
     WITH STREAMING HAIR AS WANDERING LIGHTS . . . . . . .     667  ISLE STAT II 3   19
     UNTIL THIS MORN.  AS ADDER'S BACK . . . . . . . . . .     667  ISLE STAT II 3   22
     FILLED THEM AS THEY SAT TOGETHER! . . . . . . . . . .     667  ISLE STAT II 3   31
     AS THEY GO WITH DROOPING FEATHER. . . . . . . . . . .     667  ISLE STAT II 3   33
     IS ROLLED AS VERDANT SMOKE! O THOU WHOSE FACE . . . .     667  ISLE STAT II 3   35
     IS WORN AS THOUGH WITH FIRE. OH, GOBLIN QUEEN, . . . .    667  ISLE STAT II 3   36
     I'VE LED THEE HERE, AND AS A WHEEL, . . . . . . . . .     667  ISLE STAT II 3   39
     AS ON THOSE OTHER HEARTS WERE LAID. . . . . . . . . .     667  ISLE STAT II 3   42
     WAS BANDED AS AN ADDER'S BACK, . . . . . . . . . . . .    667  ISLE STAT II 3 V 23
     I, AS MUSIC THAT GROWS MUTE, . . . . . . . . . . . . .    668  ISLE STAT II 3   65
     AS THOUGH SHE WHOM YOU FEAR HAD CROSSED THE WIDE . . .    669  ISLE STAT II 3   77
     MY LIPS, FAIR YOUTH. IT SHALL BE AS YOU ASK. . . . . .    669  ISLE STAT II 3   80
     FAIR SHEPHERD, AS WE WANDERED HITHER. . . . . . . . .     669  ISLE STAT II 3   83
     IN SHADOWY DIMNESS. TO BE FAIR AS THEE . . . . . . . .    670  ISLE STAT II 3  106
     AS QUIET AS THE CLAY-COLD DEAD. . . . . . . . . . . .     670  ISLE STAT II 3  113
     AS QUIET AS THE CLAY-COLD DEAD. . . . . . . . . . . .     670  ISLE STAT II 3  113
     HE HOOTED AS I WANDERED BY. . . . . . . . . . . . . .     670  ISLE STAT II 3  121
     AS BLOSSOMS, WHEN THE WINDS OF MARCH . . . . . . . . .    671  ISLE STAT II 3  127
     AS ALIEN AS A CUCKOO IN A ROBIN'S NEST, . . . . . . .     671  ISLE STAT II 3  138
     AS ALIEN AS A CUCKOO IN A ROBIN'S NEST, . . . . . . .     671  ISLE STAT II 3  138
     AS MOTHS WITH BROKEN WINGS, AND AS WE SIT . . . . . .     671  ISLE STAT II 3  142
     AS MOTHS WITH BROKEN WINGS, AND AS WE SIT . . . . . .     671  ISLE STAT II 3  142
     ALIEN AS CUCKOO IN A ROBIN'S NEST, . . . . . . . . . .    671  ISLE STAT II 3 V 138
     AS THE CANKER-WORM ON A MILK-WHITE ROSE! . . . . . . .    673  ISLE STAT II 3  177
     AND DOWN I CAME AS A FALCON SWOOPS . . . . . . . . . .    673  ISLE STAT II 3  178
```

47

		PAGE	TITLE		LINE

AS   (CONTINUED)

	PAGE	TITLE		LINE
AS LIGHT OF TRIUMPH IN THY GOBLIN EYES--	674	ISLE STAT II 3		199
AND DEAD AS ARE THE LOVERS OF OLD RIME.	674	ISLE STAT II 3		204
AS AN HURT LEOPARD FILLS WITH CEASELESS MOAN,	674	ISLE STAT II 3		208
AND DEAD AS ARE THE LOVERS OF OLD RHYME.	674	ISLE STAT II 3	V	204
AS A HURT LEOPARD FILLS WITH CEASELESS MOAN	674	ISLE STAT II 3	V	208
AS A LEAF THAT IS OLD, AND WITHERED, AND COLD,	676	ISLE STAT II 3		250
AS A LEAF THAT IS OLD, AND WITHERED, AND COLD,	676	ISLE STAT II 3		262
AS FIGURES MOVING MIRRORED IN A GLASS,	676	ISLE STAT II 3		270
O WAKE! WAKE! WAKE! FOR SOFT AS A BEE SIPS,	677	ISLE STAT II 3		276
OLD WARRIOR, WAKE! FOR SOFT AS A BEE SIPS,	677	ISLE STAT II 3		284
THOSE TWAIN ARE DUST. WAKE! LIGHT AS A BEE SIPS	678	ISLE STAT II 3		290
HE IS LONG DEAD. WAKE! SOFT AS A BEE SIPS	678	ISLE STAT II 3		297
AS HERE I CAME I SAW GOD PAN. HE PLAYED	678	ISLE STAT II 3		300
NAY, HE IS GONE. WAKE! WAKE! AS A BEE SIPS	678	ISLE STAT II 3		305
AS FLAMING MINSTREL-WORD UPON HIS CREST.	679	ISLE STAT II 3		317
MY DREAMS ROUND THOUGHTS OF PLENTY, AS IN GLOOM	681	SEEKER		3
MY DREAMS O'ER THOUGHTS OF PLENTY, AS THE RED-	681	SEEKER	V	3
HIS BODY SHAKE? AY, QUIVERING AS YON SMOKE	683	SEEKER		36
AMONG THE BOUGHS, BLUE AS THE HALCYON'S WING,	683	SEEKER		38
TO MAKE US GLAD WITH WONDER AS WE SAT	683	SEEKER		41
AS WORDS OF THINE THROUGH FOURSCORE YEARS HAVE FILLED	683	SEEKER		46
ABODE, AS BANDED ADDERS IN MY BREAST.	683	SEEKER		50
WITHIN THE WOODWAYS, BLUE AS THE HALCYON'S WING,	683	SEEKER	V	38
I GO AS SOFT AS FOLLY! I AM FATE."	686	LIFE		18
I GO AS SOFT AS FOLLY! I AM FATE."	686	LIFE		18
A SIBYL, WITH FIERCE FACE AS OF A HOUND	687	TWO TITANS		9
HER SPIRIT. AS SHE MOVES, THE FOAM-GLOBES BURST	687	TWO TITANS		14
AS ROUND HER, SLOW ON FEET THAT HAVE NO BLOOD,	687	TWO TITANS		18
NOT AS HE SHAKES THE FOREST! BUT A CRY	689	NETTLESHIP		8
AS SLOWLY AUTUMN CLIMBED THE GOLDEN THRONE	690	MOSADA 1	V	1A
WITH DEW, AS THOUGH 'TWERE SEALING THEM FOR DEATH.	691	MOSADA 1		22
DRAW STAR TO STAR, AS ON THAT EVE HE PASSED	691	MOSADA 1		29
AS WITH AN AUREOLE. MY SUIT TO YOU--	697	MOSADA 2		38
AS QUIET AS THE LITTLE RIVULETS	698	MOSADA 2		57
AS QUIET AS THE LITTLE RIVULETS	698	MOSADA 2		57
SOFT AS THE WHISPERING OF A LONG-LOST FOOTSTEP	699	MOSADA 3		5
WILL BE THE FAINT FAR THUNDER-SOUND, AS THOUGH	699	MOSADA 3		10
I HEAR THE MURMUR AS THEY RAISE THE BEAMS	699	MOSADA 3		17
SOFT AS A LONG DEAD FOOTSTEP WHISPERING THROUGH	699	MOSADA 3	V	5
SOFT AS THE WHISPERING OF A LOST FOOTSTEP	699	MOSADA 3	V	5
WILL MOVE THE FAINT FAR THUNDER-SOUND, AS THOUGH	699	MOSADA 3	V	10
EACH OTHER'S NECKS, AND WHISPERING AS THEY GO,	703	MOSADA 3		120
TREMBLES AS A BELL OF GLASS .	705	DAWN-SONG		10
STRAYING AS THE HERON STRAYETH,	706	DAWN-SONG		27
AS THE MOORFOWL AND THE HARE.	706	DAWN-SONG		28
WITH BERRIES. PLACID AS A HOMEWARD BEE,	710	FERENCZ RENYI		29
AS THOUGH THEY'D VOWED TO MEASURE ALL ITS WAYS.	711	FERENCZ RENYI		48
SO LITTLE. AS THE MONTHS PASSED BY WE GREW	713	FERENCZ RENYI		93
AH! IT DWELT WITHIN THE TWILIGHT AS THE WORM WITHIN THE NUT.	718	PHANTOM SHIP		6
SLOW THE CHAPEL BELL IS TOLLING AS THOUGH THE DEAD PASSED BY.	718	PHANTOM SHIP		16
WHERE MOVES THERE ANY BEAUTIFUL AS I,	720	WITCH VIVIEN		1
THAN OLD MEN'S ANY DAY, AS MERLIN FOUND.	721	WITCH VIVIEN		47
AND AS A SLAVE BEEN WAKEFUL IN THE HALLS	724	KANVA ON SELF		5
FOR AS THINGS WERE SO SHALL THINGS EVER BE.	724	KANVA ON SELF		20
AND OUR SLAVES BE AS OF OLD.	727	LOVERS QUARREL		56
AS THE SUMMER VOICE OF THE DAYTIME CEASED,	728	PRIEST FAIRY		4
AND AS THE TIME TO DARKNESS PLODDED	728	PRIEST FAIRY		11
HE THOUGHT WISE THINGS AS HIS GREY HEAD NODDED.	728	PRIEST FAIRY		12
THREE SPANS HIGH AS HE ROSE TO HIS FEET,	729	PRIEST FAIRY		25
AND HIS HAIR WAS AS YELLOW AS WAVING WHEAT,	729	PRIEST FAIRY		26
AND HIS HAIR WAS AS YELLOW AS WAVING WHEAT.	729	PRIEST FAIRY		26
AND HIS HAIR WAS AS DARK AS A PLOVER'S EYE,	729	PRIEST FAIRY		46
AND HIS HAIR WAS AS DARK AS A PLOVER'S EYE.	729	PRIEST FAIRY		46
AS A WREATH OF SMOKE IN WIND-BLOWN FLIGHT	730	PRIEST FAIRY		61
AS THOUGH HIS DAYS WERE FULL OF RUTH.	731	PRIEST FAIRY		76
"IF I WERE FREE TO DO AS LITTLE	731	PRIEST FAIRY		77
AS DANCE UPON THE SPEAR-GRASS BRITTLE,	731	PRIEST FAIRY		78
AS THERE FLOATS FROM FIELDS AFAR	732	STREET DANCERS		20
FROM DEATH'S LATE LANGUOR AS THESE LINES I READ	734	QUATRAIN APHOR		14
I GO AS SOFT AS FOLLY! I AM FATE."	735	QUATRAIN APHOR		20
I GO AS SOFT AS FOLLY! I AM FATE."	735	QUATRAIN APHOR		20
AS THOUGH THEIR SEASON HAD NO DATE,	736	SUMMER EVENING		10
PLAYED ON HIS HARP. AND I WOULD BE AS SAD	747	SHADOW WATER A		3
AS THOUGH THE WATERS HAD FLOWED UP BETWEEN;	749	SHADOW WATER A		55
THEY ARE CHANGED AND AS GREY BIRDS FLY OUT TO SEA,	750	SHADOW WATER A		82
AND A STRING MURMURS AS THOUGH TIME WERE DEAD	752	SHADOW WATER A		124
FOR AN IMMORTAL WOMAN, AS I THINK,	755	SHADOW WATER A		173
HAS BLOSSOMED, AND I GROW AS OLD AS TIME.	756	SHADOW WATER A		179
HAS BLOSSOMED, AND I GROW AS OLD AS TIME.	756	SHADOW WATER A		179
I AWAIT YOUR WORDS AS THE BLIND GRASS AWAITS	756	SHADOW WATER A		181
BY SUN AND MOON AND A HUNDRED GODS AS WELL,	756	SHADOW WATER A		189
AND I AM OLD AS TIME, BECAUSE I KNOW	756	SHADOW WATER A	V	179
I WAIT YOUR WORDS AS THE DEAD WAIT THE LIVING.	756	SHADOW WATER A	V	182
IF YOU WOULD SERVE ME, AS YOUR WORD AND VOICE	756	SHADOW WATER A	V	183
SO MUCH OF WEALTH AS MAY BEFIT THEIR RANK!	756	SHADOW WATER A	V	186
BECAUSE I HAD HOPED TO COME, AS DREAMS FORETOLD,	757	SHADOW WATER A		197
AND A STRONG GALLEY. I GIVE YOU ALL AS MUCH.	758	SHADOW WATER A		222
I GREW AS OLD AS TIME, AND SHE GROWS YOUNG	761	SHADOW WATER A		259

```
                                                PAGE    TITLE             LINE

AS    (CONTINUED)
    I GREW AS OLD AS TIME, AND SHE GROWS YOUNG  .  .  .  .  .  .   761  SHADOW WATER A    259
    AS THE AGELESS BIRDS OF AENGUS, OR THE BIRDS  .  .  .  .  .    761  SHADOW WATER A    260
    SHE IS ALREADY FADING, AS THOUGH THE GODS  .  .  .  .  .  .    768  SHADOW WATER A  V 422
    DELIGHTED ME AS A CHILD!  .  .  .  .  .  .  .  .  .  .  .      787  HUDDON DUDDON       2
    DELIGHTED ME AS A CHILD.  .  .  .  .  .  .  .  .  .  .  .      787  HUDDON DUDDON       7
    DELIGHTED ME AS A CHILD.  .  .  .  .  .  .  .  .  .  .  .      787  HUDDON DUDDON      12
    HE, DISGUISED AS A SAILOR BEFORE THE MAST,  .  .  .  .  .  .   790  DEDICATION          2
ASCENDS
    THAT IS TO SAY, ASCENDS TO HEAVEN:  .  .  .  .  .  .  .  .     478  SELF AND SOUL      38
ASCENT
    SET ALL YOUR MIND UPON THE STEEP ASCENT,  .  .  .  .  .  .  .  477  SELF AND SOUL       2
ASH
    FLICKERING WITH ASH AND HAZEL, BUT HALF SHOWED  .  .  .  .     180  QUEEN MAEVE        12
    WHERE HAZEL AND ASH AND PRIVET BLIND THE PATHS!  .  .  .  .    217  WOODS OF COOLE      8
    AND THOUGH THEY'RE BUT THE COLOUR OF GREY ASH,  .  .  .  .     247  SHADOW WATER B    528
    DESTROY THE VIEW BY CUTTING DOWN AN ASH  .  .  .  .  .  .  .   372  ON GOING HOUSE     13
A-SHAKE
    I HEAR THE SHADOWY HORSES, THEIR LONG MANES A-SHAKE,  .  .  .  154  BELOVED PEACE       1
ASHEN
    AN ASHEN HUNTING SPEAR.  .  .  .  .  .  .  .  .  .  .  .  .     32  OISIN 2            56
ASHES
    SHEPHERDS, FAREWELL!  HE SOON WILL BE--ASHES  .  .  .  .  .    682  SEEKER             34
    THE SOUL UPON THE ASHES OF THE HEART."  .  .  .  .  .  .  .    735  QUATRAIN APHOR     16
ASH-GREY
    WHAT IS THERE BUT A TROOP OF ASH-GREY BIRDS  .  .  .  .  .     247  SHADOW WATER B    517
    SAW ON THE WOOD'S EDGE GLEAM AN ASH-GREY FEATHER!  .  .  .     715  DWELT SYCAMORE      2
    FOLLOWED A RINGDOVE'S ASH-GREY GLEAM OF FEATHER.  .  .  .  .   715  DWELT SYCAMORE      6
    FOLLOWED THE RING-DOVE'S ASH-GREY GLEAM OF FEATHER.  .  .  .   715  DWELT SYCAMORE  V   6
A-SHINING
    OR WEEDING OR PLOUGHING WITH FACES A-SHINING WITH MUCH-TOIL    58  OISIN 3           165
        WET!
    A-SHINING ON THE LITTLE CRUCIFIX  .  .  .  .  .  .  .  .  .    691  MOSADA 1        V  34
ASHORE
    HE NEVER FOUND HIS REST ASHORE,  .  .  .  .  .  .  .  .  .     361  ALF POLLEXFEN      21
ASH-TREES'
    AND 'MONG THE STUNTED ASH-TREES' DROOPING RINGS,  .  .  .  .   650  ISLE STAT I 1     128
ASHWOOD
    THAT THE SPEAR-SHAFT IS MADE OUT OF ASHWOOD,  .  .  .  .        52  OISIN 3            82
    THAT THE SPEARSHAFT IS MADE OUT OF ASHWOOD,  .  .  .  .  .      52  OISIN 3         V  82
ASH-WOOD
    AN ASH-WOOD HUNTING SPEAR.  .  .  .  .  .  .  .  .  .  .  .     32  OISIN 2         V  56
ASIAN
    THAT ARE LIKE COLOURED ASIAN BIRDS  .  .  .  .  .  .  .  .       7  OISIN 1            69
    AND GLORIOUS AS ASIAN BIRDS  .  .  .  .  .  .  .  .  .  .        7  OISIN 1         V  65
    A STORM OF BIRDS IN THE ASIAN TREES  .  .  .  .  .  .  .  .     27  OISIN 1           416
    OF ASIAN RIVERS, ROLLING ON IN LIGHT.  .  .  .  .  .  .  .     682  SEEKER             20
ASIATIC
    ALL ASIATIC VAGUE IMMENSITIES,  .  .  .  .  .  .  .  .  .  .    610  STATUES            12
ASIDE
    AND SAID, CASTING ASIDE HIS DRAGGLED HAIR,  .  .  .  .  .  .   105  CUCHULAIN SEA   V   3
    AND NO MORE TURN ASIDE AND BROOD  .  .  .  .  .  .  .  .  .    125  GOES FERGUS         7
    MERE BONE AND MUSCLE THROWN ASIDE,  .  .  .  .  .  .  .  .     273  GREY ROCK          51
    BUT THE OTHER PUSHED HIS HAND ASIDE,  .  .  .  .  .  .  .  .   304  HOUR DAWN       V  48
    IF ON THE LOST, ADMIT YOU TURNED ASIDE  .  .  .  .  .  .  .    413  TOWER             115
    WHAT BRUSHES FLY AND MOTH ASIDE?  .  .  .  .  .  .  .  .  .    625  NATIVITY            7
    MAYHAP 'TWERE BETTER THAT ASIDE I THROW .  .  .  .  .  .  .    656  ISLE STAT I 3      38
    ASIDE!--THE WILD HORNS TOLD ALMINTOR'S END.  .  .  .  .  .  .  665  ISLE STAT II 2     68
ASK
    "I ONLY ASK WHAT WAY MY JOURNEY LIES,  .  .  .  .  .  .  .  .  108  CUCHULAIN SEA      31
    SHE'LL NOT ASK A HAUGHTY DRESS!  .  .  .  .  .  .  .  .  .     124  CATHLEEN PARA       6
    THE PLAYERS ASK FOR A BLESSING ON THE PSALTERIES AND ON       212  BLESS PSALTER       T
        THEMSELVES
    THE PLAYERS ASK FOR A BLESSING ON THE PSALTERIES             212  BLESS PSALTER   V   T
        AND THEMSELVES
    AND ASK FOR SATISFACTION UPON THESE  .  .  .  .  .  .  .  .    235  SHADOW WATER B    281
    I ASK A FITTING PUNISHMENT FOR ALL  .  .  .  .  .  .  .  .     235  SHADOW WATER B    290
    FOR I WOULD ASK A QUESTION OF THEM ALL.  .  .  .  .  .  .  .   410  TOWER              24
    ENDURE WHAT LIFE GOD GIVES AND ASK NO LONGER SPAN!  .  .  .    459  FROM OEDIPUS        1
    YOU ASK WHAT MAKES ME SIGH, OLD FRIEND,  .  .  .  .  .  .  .   524  MAD AS MIST        13
    OR ASK IF ALL BE RIGHT  .  .  .  .  .  .  .  .  .  .  .  .     532  BEFORE WORLD        4
    WITH OPEN BOOK YOU ASK ME WHAT I DO.  .  .  .  .  .  .  .  .   554  RIBH AT TOMB        2
    YOU ASK WHAT I HAVE FOUND, AND FAR AND WIDE I GO!  .  .  .     580  CURSE CROMWELL      1
    THAT IS ALL I ASK, MY DEAR,  .  .  .  .  .  .  .  .  .  .  .   587  OLD WICKED MAN      7
    BUT NEVER ASKED FOR LOVE! SHOULD I ASK THAT,  .  .  .  .  .    609  IN TARAS HALLS      9
    "GOD I HAVE LOVED, BUT SHOULD I ASK RETURN  .  .  .  .  .  .   609  IN TARAS HALLS     14
    THIS THING WE ASK! MUST WE TWO FIGHT?--JUDGE THOU.  .  .  .    660  ISLE STAT II 1     41
    MY LIPS, FAIR YOUTH.  IT SHALL BE AS YOU ASK.  .  .  .  .  .   669  ISLE STAT II 3     80
    GO ASK THE SPRINGING FLOWERS,  .  .  .  .  .  .  .  .  .  .    680  LOVE AND DEATH     13
    GO ASK THE YOUNGEST ANGEL,  .  .  .  .  .  .  .  .  .  .  .    680  LOVE AND DEATH     29
    IF PETER WOULD BUT ASK HER LIFE--WHO KNOWS?  .  .  .  .  .     696  MOSADA 2           17
    "I BID HIM ASK WHAT GIFT HE WILL,  .  .  .  .  .  .  .  .  .   741  EARL PAUL          57
    "I ASK THAT I AND ALL MY RACE."  .  .  .  .  .  .  .  .  .     742  EARL PAUL          61
    THE BRAVEST FROM THE GODS BUT ASK!  .  .  .  .  .  .  .  .  .  788  BRAVEST ASK         1
ASKED
    AND I BUT ASKED THE MORE, TILL HE CRIED OUT,  .  .  .  .  .    281  TWO KINGS          92
    BUT ASKED THE MORE UNTIL HE SPOKE THESE WORDS,  .  .  .  .     281  TWO KINGS       V 92A
    ON BEING ASKED FOR A WAR POEM  .  .  .  .  .  .  .  .  .  .    359  WAR POEM            T
    AND ASKED ABOUT THE PICTURES OR THE TEXT!  .  .  .  .  .  .    466  HARUN RASHID      121
    AND ASKED ABOUT THESE PICTURES OR THOSE OTHERS!  .  .  .  .    466  HARUN RASHID    V 121
    I ASKED IF I SHOULD PRAY,  .  .  .  .  .  .  .  .  .  .  .     495  MOHINI CHATTER      1
```

49

ASKED   (CONTINUED)
          BUT NEVER ASKED FOR LOVE! SHOULD I ASK THAT, ...   609 IN TARAS HALLS   9
ASKS
     THE LOVER ASKS FORGIVENESS BECAUSE OF HIS MANY MOODS   . .   162 ASKS FORGIVE   T
     MICHAEL ROBARTES ASKS FORGIVENESS BECAUSE OF HIS MANY MOODS   162 ASKS FORGIVE   V   T
     AND THEN ONE ASKS ANOTHER HOW HE DIED, ...   234 SHADOW WATER B   256
     ONE ASKS FOR MOURNFUL MELODIES!   . . . .   567 LAPIS LAZULI   53
     AND THEN ONE ASKS ANOTHER HOW HE DIED, ...   753 SHADOW WATER A   146
ASLAUGA
     AND MEAT TO THE ASLAUGA SHEE. . . . .   743 DANAAN QUICK   17
ASLEEP
     UNTIL THE GODS AND DEMONS DROP ASLEEP, ...   35   OISIN 2   86
     WHEN THE POOR TIRED CHILD, PASSION, FALLS ASLEEP. . . .   80   EPHEMERA   7
     HE PRAYED AND FELL ASLEEP! . . . .   132 FR GILLIGAN   14
     HE KNELT, PRAYED, FELL ASLEEP! . . . .   132 FR GILLIGAN   V 14
     ASLEEP UPON A CHAIR." . . . .   134 FR GILLIGAN   48
     WHERE ONLY BODY'S LAID ASLEEP. . . . .   138 TO IRELAND   22
     HE HAD FALLEN ASLEEP, AND, THOUGH HE HAD DREAMED NOTHING,   182 QUEEN MAEVE   55
     AND I FELL ASLEEP UPON LONELY ECHTGE OF STREAMS. . . . .   203 WITHER BOUGHS   6
     TILL HE HAS FALLEN ASLEEP   . . . .   216 HAPPY TOWNLAND   51
     BUT WHEN I HAD EATEN AND DRUNK MYSELF ASLEEP   . . . . .   223 SHADOW WATER B   30
     AND OVERPOWER THE CREW WHILE YET ASLEEP! . . . . . .   233 SHADOW WATER B   240
     THE WOMEN OF HIS HOUSEHOLD WERE ASLEEP, ...   282 TWO KINGS   V 133
     THAT WHEN HE HAS FALLEN ASLEEP WITHIN MY ARMS, ...   285 TWO KINGS   191
     WHO IS FIRST ASLEEP, IF BUT HE CAN   . . . .   295 THREE BEGGARS   23
     FALL ASLEEP WHEN I SHOULD PRAY." . . . .   298 THREE HERMITS   12
     WITH HER WHITE FINGER. I LED HER HOME ASLEEP   . . . .   468 HARUN RASHID   158
     LOOKED HALF ASLEEP ALL DAY. . . . .   570 THREE BUSHES   34
     SEER OF VISIONS! NOW EVE FALLS ASLEEP, ...   691 MOSADA 1   36
     IN THE FAR ISLE SHE SANG HERSELF ASLEEP, ...   694 MOSADA 1   90
     HALF ASLEEP THE OLD COW CROPS, ...   706 DAWN-SONG   20
     THE HARE HATH LAID ASLEEP HER FROLIC WITS, ...   712 FERENCZ RENYI   72
     GAVE HIM HIS HARP. NOW THAT HE IS ASLEEP. . . . . .   748 SHADOW WATER A   18
     SO THESE WOULD HAVE KILLED FORGAEL WHILE ASLEEP   . . .   748 SHADOW WATER A   25
     BEFORE I DROPPED ASLEEP, A KINGFISHER   . . . . . .   761 SHADOW WATER A   274
     I HAVE WET THIS BRAID OF HAIR WITH TEARS WHILE ASLEEP. . .   762 SHADOW WATER A   294
ASS
     "HARNESS AN ASS AND CART, ...   596 COLONEL MARTIN   51
ASSAILS
     OF SOME FORGOTTEN FIEND. NOW NONE ASSAILS   31   OISIN 2   V 308
ASSASSIN
     SOLDIER, ASSASSIN, EXECUTIONER, ...   482 BLOOD AND MOON   36
     "ASSASSIN, MY ASSASSIN! THOU WHO LET'ST ME DIE, ...   714 FERENCZ RENYI   106
     "ASSASSIN, MY ASSASSIN! THOU WHO LET'ST ME DIE, ...   714 FERENCZ RENYI   106
ASSAULT
     ASSAULT AND BATTERY OF THE WIND   . . . .   405 FOR DAUGHTER   55
ASS-BACK
     CAMEL-BACK, HORSE-BACK, ASS-BACK, MULE-BACK, ...   566 LAPIS LAZULI   26
ASSES
     WHEELS BY MILK-WHITE ASSES DRAWN   . . . .   502 VACILLATION   62
ASSIZE
     THE JUDGE AT THE ASSIZE COURT, ...   596 COLONEL MARTIN   46
ASS'S
     BEYOND THE FLING OF THE DULL ASS'S HOOF . . . .   321 REED WHISPERER   5
ASSUAGE
     A GREATER WITH A LESSER PANG ASSUAGE . . . .   537 HER VISION   5
ASSURANCE
     I'LL HAVE ASSURANCE THAT YOU ARE ABLE . . . . . .   304 HOUR DAWN   51
     "I'D HAVE ASSURANCE THAT YOU ARE ABLE . . . .   304 HOUR DAWN   V 51
ASTIR
     FOR ALL THAT COUNTRY HAD BEEN ASTIR   . . . .   191 BAILE AILLINN   52
     SET ALL HER BLOOD ASTIR . . . .   336 YOUNG GIRL   10
     NOR FAERIES IN THE HONEY-HEART OF JUNE ASTIR. . . . .   661 ISLE STAT II 1   73
ASTONISHED
     SO PERILOUS THAT HALF THE ASTONISHED MEET   . . . . .   326 ROBERT GREGORY   61
     AND NOW WE STARE ASTONISHED AT THE SEA, ...   534 HER TRIUMPH   11
     AND WE THOUGH ASTONISHED ARE DUMB . . . .   785 YOUR HEART   11
     AND WE THOUGH ASTONISHED ARE DUMB . . . .   786 YOUR HEART   24
     AND WE THOUGH ASTONISHED ARE DUMB . . . .   786 YOUR HEART   37
ASTONISHING
     A MOST ASTONISHING THING-- . . . .   567 FROM JAPANESE   1
ASTONISHMENT
     AMID THAT FIRST ASTONISHMENT, WITH GRANIA'S SHADE, . . .   366 HER COURAGE   4
ASTRADDLE
     ASTRADDLE ON THE DOLPHIN'S MIRE AND BLOOD, ...   498 BYZANTIUM   33
ASTRAY
     AND ALL THE SHAPELY BODY NO TITTLE GONE ASTRAY. . . . .   354 HIS PHOENIX   30
     MUSIC HAD DRIVEN THEIR WITS ASTRAY-- . . . .   411 TOWER   47
     FOR THE EMBRACE OF NOTHING! AND I, MY WITS ASTRAY   . . .   426 PHANTOM HATRED   14
     "WHAT CHANGE HAS PUT MY THOUGHTS ASTRAY . . . . . .   529 TOM LUNATIC   3
     LEAD THEM GENTLY ASTRAY! . . . .   568 SWEET DANCER   11
     IN COUNTRY SHAWL OR PARIS CLOAK, HAD PUT MY WITS ASTRAY,   592 PILGRIM   3
ASTROLOGER
     HIS SON GEORGE, THE ASTROLOGER! . . . .   360 ALF POLLEXFEN   8
     WAS BURIED NEAR THE ASTROLOGER, ...   361 ALF POLLEXFEN   26
     WHERE--WROTE A LEARNED ASTROLOGER-- . . . .   535 CHOSEN   17
ASUNDER
     THE FENIAN HORSES! ARMOUR TORN ASUNDER!   43   OISIN 2   210
     THE HORSES OF THE FENIANS--TEARING ASUNDER   43   OISIN 2   V 210
ATE
     AND FROM HER FINGERS ATE ITS BIT. . . . .   397 POLIT PRISONER   6

ATE   (CONTINUED)
    THEY ATE SPREAD WIDE THAT EACH . . . .   488 CRAZED MOON   V   17
    BECAUSE THE FIRES OF PURGATORY HAVE ATE THEIR SHAPES AWAY!   593 PILGRIM   13
A-TELLING
    A-TELLING WITH THEIR LOW AND REEDY CRY . . . .   128 DREAM OF FAERY V   42
ATHEIST
    THE BISHOP MURMURED, "ATHEIST! . . . .   725 LEGEND   21
ATHENE
    ATHENE TAKES ACHILLES BY THE HAIR . . . .   374 PHASES OF MOON   45
    GO PLUCK ATHENE BY THE HAIR! . . . .   386 ROBARTES DANCE   19
    THE GREAT GREY-EYED ATHENE STARES THEREON. . . . . . .   447 COLONUS PRAISE   16
    PALLAS ATHENE IN THAT STRAIGHT BACK AND ARROGANT HEAD! . .   578 LOFTY THINGS   11
ATHENE'S
    AT PALLAS ATHENE'S SIDE, ...   355 PROPERTIUS   6
ATHENIAN
    ATHENIAN INTELLECT ITS MASTERY, ...   446 COLONUS PRAISE   11
ATHWART
    THE FAERY SHIP THAT SWIMS ATHWART THE SKY. . . . . .   663 ISLE STAT II 2   16
    OF THE ALHAMBRA BLACK ATHWART HIS DISK! . . . . . .   691 MOSADA 1   V   37
A-TIPTOE
    PASSED A-TIPTOE UP AND DOWN . . . .   20 OISIN 1   V 294
    AND PASSED A-TIPTOE UP AND DOWN, ...   85 MAD KING GOLL   51
    I PASSED A-TIPTOE UP AND DOWN, ...   85 MAD KING GOLL V   51
    THEY PASSED A-TIP-TOE EVERYWHERE, ...   667 ISLE STAT II 3   20
    THEY PASSED A-TIPTOE EVERYWHERE, ...   667 ISLE STAT II 3 V   20
    THE HOUR OF INCANTATION COMES A-TIPTOE, ...   691 MOSADA 1   37
ATLANTIC
    BRED ON THE ATLANTIC, CAN BE STAYED! . . . .   403 FOR DAUGHTER   6
    TRAVELLED TO AND FRO ACROSS THE ATLANTIC, ...   790 DEDICATION   3
ATLAS
    THAT THE WITCH OF ATLAS KNEW, ...   637 BEN BULBEN   3
ATMOSPHERE
    HERE IN THE PITCH-DARK ATMOSPHERE ABOVE . . . . . .   555 RIBH AT TOMB   17
    HERE IN THE PITCH DARK ATMOSPHERE ABOVE . . . . . .   555 RIBH AT TOMB   V   17
A-TREMBLE
    LIKE SMALL BROWN MOTHS, A-TREMBLE. "RENYI SAY . . .   713 FERENCZ RENYI   82
    LIKE SMALL BROWN MOTHS, A-TREMBLE CEASELESSLY. . . .   713 FERENCZ RENYI V   82
ATTACK
    STRICKEN WITH PANIC FROM THE ATTACK, ...   274 GREY ROCK   75
    THE ATTACK ON THE "PLAY BOY" . . . .   294 HATED PLAYBOY V   T
    THE ATTACK ON "THE PLAYBOY OF THE WESTERN WORLD" . .   294 HATED PLAYBOY V   T
ATTEMPTED
    I HAVE ATTEMPTED MANY THINGS . . . .   451 FIRST LOVE   9
ATTEND
    ATTEND UPON THEM STILL. . . . .   323 SWANS AT COOLE   24
    NOR DREAD NOR HOPE ATTEND . . . .   476 DEATH   1
ATTENDANCE
    WE, TOO, HAD GOOD ATTENDANCE ONCE, ...   266 GALWAY RACES   5
    SHOULD DANCE ATTENDANCE UPON MY OLD AGE! . . . . .   591 SPUR   V   2
ATTENDANT
    IT IS MY WHIM! BID SOME ATTENDANT SPRITE . . . . .   669 ISLE STAT II 3   72
ATTENDANTS
    THAT ALL ATTENDANTS AND THE CASUAL CROWD MIGHT HEAR. . .   609 IN TARAS HALLS   13
ATTENTION
    MADE MY ATTENTION STRAY. . . . .   507 STREAM AND SUN   5
    FOR A MAN'S ATTENTION . . . .   533 FIRST CONFESS   10
    AND WHEN I PAY ATTENTION I MUST OUT AND WALK . . . .   581 CURSE CROMWELL   29
    SHOULD DANCE ATTENTION UPON MY OLD AGE! . . . . . .   591 SPUR   2
    MY ATTENTION FIX . . . .   631 POLITICS   2
ATTIC
    IN THE VERSE OF ATTIC STORY . . . .   65 HAPPY SHEPHERD V   16
    WITH PATIENT BEAUTY YONDER ATTIC BUST . . . .   685 DRAWING-ROOM   3
    WITH PATIENT BEAUTY YONDER ATTIC BUST . . . .   735 QUATRAIN APHOR   23
ATTIS'
    AND HE THAT ATTIS' IMAGE HANGS BETWEEN . . . . . .   500 VACILLATION   16
ATTORNEY
    TILL THE ATTORNEY FOR LOST SOULS CRY HER SWEET CRY, . . .   173 SPEAKS HEARERS   6
AUDIENCE
    IN SCORN OF THIS AUDIENCE, ...   348 FISHERMAN   27
    FIT AUDIENCE FOUND, BUT CANNOT RULE . . . .   506 REMORSE SPEECH   4
    SPEAKING TO A DRUNKEN AUDIENCE HIGH NONSENSICAL WORDS! . .   577 LOFTY THINGS   6
AUGHT
    OR AUGHT REMOTE! OR HAST THOU NEVER HEARD . . . . .   672 ISLE STAT II 3   153
AUGUSTA
    AUGUSTA GREGORY SEATED AT HER GREAT ORMOLU TABLE, . . .   577 LOFTY THINGS   7
    AUGUSTA GREGORY'S SON! HER SISTER'S SON, ...   602 GALLERY REVIS   21
    MANCINI'S PORTRAIT OF AUGUSTA GREGORY, ...   602 GALLERY REVIS   25
    JOHN SYNGE, I AND AUGUSTA GREGORY, THOUGHT . . . .   603 GALLERY REVIS   41
AUGUSTUS
    AUGUSTUS CAESAR, AND AFTER THESE . . . .   379 SAINT HUNCH   11
AUNTS   SEE GREAT-AUNTS
    ON UNCLES, AUNTS, GREAT-UNCLES OR GREAT-AUNTS, . . .   604 YOU CONTENT   3
AUREOLE
    AS WITH AN AUREOLE. MY SUIT TO YOU-- . . . . . .   697 MOSADA 2   38
AUSTERE
    YET HE WHO TREADS IN AUSTERE WAYS . . . .   138 TO IRELAND   V   27
    OF SORROWFUL, AUSTERE, SWEET, LOFTY PIPE TUNES. . . .   341 SHEP GOATHERD   57
    THE AUSTERE ARTHUR, RULE FROM UTHER'S CHAIR . . . .   678 ISLE STAT II 3   296
AUSTERITY
    AUSTERITY, A PLACE SET OUT FOR WISDOM . . . . . .   377 PHASES OF MOON   127

51

PAGE   TITLE   LINE

AUSTRIAN
   THE AUSTRIAN HAYNAU HE, IN MANY LANDS • • • • • • • 709 FERENCZ RENYI   8
AUTHOR
   TRUE SONG, THOUGH SPEECH: "MINE AUTHOR SUNG IT ME." • • • 373 PHASES OF MOON   30
AUTHORITY
   A SHROUD THAT SEEMED TO HAVE AUTHORITY • • • • • • • 634 CUCHULAIN COMF   7
AUTHORS
   SOME ANCIENT FAMOUS AUTHORS MISREPRESENT, • • • • • • 579 DOR WELLESLEY   15
AUTUMN
   "I WOULD DIE LIKE A SMALL WITHERED LEAF IN THE AUTUMN,
    • • • 56 OISIN 3   131
   AUTUMN IS OVER THE LONG LEAVES THAT LOVE US, • • • • • 79 FALLING LEAVES   1
   AUTUMN WAS OVER HIM: AND NOW THEY STOOD • • • • • 80 EPHEMERA   16
   OR IN THE AUTUMN SOLITUDES • • • • • • • • • • 84 MAD KING GOLL V 39
   THE TREES ARE IN THEIR AUTUMN BEAUTY, • • • • • • 322 SWANS AT COOLE   1
   THE NINETEENTH AUTUMN HAS COME UPON ME • • • • • 322 SWANS AT COOLE   7
   BUT A RAVING AUTUMN SHEARS • • • • • • • • 475 EVA GORE-BOOTH   5
   AS THE LEAVES IN AUTUMN SCATTER. • • • • • • • 648 ISLE STAT I 1   90
   IN AUTUMN, WHEN FAR DOWN THE MOUNTAIN SLOPES • • • 690 MOSADA 1   12
   AS SLOWLY AUTUMN CLIMBED THE GOLDEN THRONE • • • 690 MOSADA 1   V 1A
AUTUMNAL
   OR IN AUTUMNAL SOLITUDES • • • • • • • • • 84 MAD KING GOLL   39
   CAN SHAKE MORE BLOSSOM FROM AUTUMNAL CHILL • • • • 465 HARUN RASHID   104
   THAT BRINGS MORE BLOSSOM TO AUTUMNAL CHILL • • • • 465 HARUN RASHID V 104
AUTUMN'S
   THEIR DREAD OF AUTUMN'S MORTAL WING, • • • • • • 736 SUMMER EVENING   2
   AND DREAD NO MORE FOUL AUTUMN'S WING, • • • • • 737 SUMMER EVENING   18
AVAIL
   WERE ALL MY WANDERING DAYS OF NO AVAIL, • • • • • 684 SEEKER   64
AVAILS
   OLD AND REMEMBERING, WHAT AVAILS THE WIND • • • • 42 OISIN 2   V 206
AVALANCHE
   SEEMS A WATER-COURSE OR AN AVALANCHE, • • • • • 567 LAPIS LAZULI   45
AVALLON
   OR AVALLON THE GRASS GREEN HOLLOW, OR JOYOUS ISLE • • 209 UNDER THE MOON V 2
AVALON
   NOR AVALON THE GRASS-GREEN HOLLOW, NOR JOYOUS ISLE, • • 209 UNDER THE MOON   2
   TALL DAMES GO WALKING IN GRASS-GREEN AVALON. • • • 627 STATES HOLIDAY   13
   TALL DAMES GO WALKING IN GRASS-GREEN AVALON. • • • 627 STATES HOLIDAY   26
   TALL DAMES GO WALKING IN GRASS-GREEN AVALON. • • • 627 STATES HOLIDAY   39
   TALL DAMES GO WALKING IN GRASS GREEN AVALON. • • • 627 STATES HOLIDAY V REF
AVE
   "AVE MARIE," MUTTERED HE • • • • • • • • • 730 PRIEST FAIRY   51
AVENGED
   AND WILL YOU SWEAR NEVER TO BE AVENGED • • • • • 758 SHADOW WATER A 223
AVENGING
   THE AVENGING LEAF THOSE FIELDS RAISED UP AGAINST IT. • • 487 SEVEN SAGES   20
AVOW
   SOME THERE ARE, FOR I AVOW • • • • • • • • 435 FOR MY SON   10
AWAIT
   MUSIC AND LOVE AND SLEEP AWAIT, • • • • • • • 9 OISIN 1   103
   "THAT WE ARE TIRED, FOR OTHER LOVES AWAIT US: • • • • 80 EPHEMERA   21
   A LITTLE STOLEN TRESS. I, TOO, AWAIT • • • • • • 170 SECRET ROSE   27
   FOR HOPE WOULD GIVE HIS LIMBS THE POWER--AND AWAIT • • 283 TWO KINGS   136
   WESTWARD OF TARA, THERE TO AWAIT A FRIEND • • • • 283 TWO KINGS   V 136
   AWAIT THE HOUR OF WAR, ENTER THE SMALL, • • • • 461 HARUN RASHID V 8
   I AWAIT YOUR WORDS AS THE BLIND GRASS AWAITS • • • 756 SHADOW WATER A 181
AWAITING
   AWAITING IN PATIENCE THE STRAW-DEATH, • • • • • • 58 OISIN 3   167
AWAITS
   OUR ISLE AWAITS US, ON EACH LEA • • • • • • • 77 INDIAN TO LOVE V 2
   WHO BUT AWAITS HIS HOUR TO SHOOT, STILL HANGS • • • 198 SEVEN WOODS   13
   A MAN AWAITS HIS END • • • • • • • • • 476 DEATH   3
   AWAITS RETURNING SPRING. • • • • • • • • 517 HER ANXIETY   2
   I AWAIT YOUR WORDS AS THE BLIND GRASS AWAITS • • • 756 SHADOW WATER A 181
   AENGUS LOOKS ON YOU WHEN I LOOK: HE AWAITS • • • • 757 SHADOW WATER A 209
AWAKE
   WHEN THEY AWAKE UPSPRINGING: WITH LOUD HORN • • • • 32 OISIN 2   V 52
   "OH, SIGH, AWAKE AND GO YOU FORTH FOR ME: • • • • 33 OISIN 2   V 57
   AND SHOOK HIM WIDE AWAKE, AND BID HIM SAY • • • 182 QUEEN MAEVE   50
   AWAKE UNSLEEPING FIRES: AND WOVE SEVEN STRINGS, • • • 219 HARP OF AENGUS   7
   MUTTER SUCH THINGS AS THEY AWAKE FROM TRANCE. • • • 229 SHADOW WATER B 163
   IT WAS THEIR HANDS THAT PLUCKED THE WINDS AWAKE • • 237 SHADOW WATER B 324
   AND THEN AT LAST BEING WIDE AWAKE • • • • • • 304 HOUR DAWN   V 40
   DO, BUT AWAKE A HOPE TO LIVE • • • • • • • 309 REALISTS   6
   DELIGHT MEN'S EYES WHEN I AWAKE SOME DAY • • • • 323 SWANS AT COOLE   29
   OR KEEP US ALL AWAKE WITH BAYING AT THE MOON, • • • 364 DOLLS FACES   11
   TO KEEP A DROWSY EMPEROR AWAKE: • • • • • • 408 SAIL BYZANTIUM   29
   AND THAT SHE DREAMED AWAKE CONTENT TO TOUCH • • • 466 HARUN RASHID V 125C
   "FOR EVER AND FOR EVER": THEN AWAKE • • • • • 560 WHENCE COME   3
   AND WIDE AWAKE KNOW THAT THE HUNT IS ON: • • • • 622 HOUND VOICE   17
   I LIE AWAKE NIGHT AFTER NIGHT • • • • • • • 632 MAN AND ECHO   9
   ACORNS GREEN, WITH EYES AWAKE. • • • • • • • 655 ISLE STAT I 3   5
   BUT WIDE AWAKE HIS TWO EYES WERE. • • • • • 655 ISLE STAT I 3   7
   SLEEPER, AWAKE! HOW LONG MY SLEEP? UNNUMBERED • • • 678 ISLE STAT II 3 307
   OH, GOD!--AWAKE! THOU SHALT NOT DIE. SHE SLEEPS, • • 701 MOSADA 3   66
   AWAKE, AWAKE, AND WE WILL SAIL AFAR, • • • • 702 MOSADA 3   78
   AWAKE, AWAKE, AND WE WILL SAIL AFAR, • • • • 702 MOSADA 3   78
   HER DREAMS ARE TALKING WITH OLD YEARS. AWAKE, • • 702 MOSADA 3   89
   SHALL AWAKE WITH LONELY BLEAT, • • • • • • • 726 LOVERS QUARREL   6
   AWAKE UNSLEEPING FIRES: AND WOVE SEVEN STRINGS, • • • 762 SHADOW WATER A 302

```
                                                          PAGE      TITLE         LINE
AWAKE   (CONTINUED)
      AND LANGUORS THAT AWAKE IN MINGLING HANDS  .  .  .  .  .  .   765 SHADOW WATER A      367
AWAKED
          HAS AWAKED IN OUR HEARTS, MY BELOVED, A SADNESS THAT MAY  122 WHITE BIRDS          4
            NOT DIE.
          HAS AWAKED IN OUR HEARTS, MY BELOVED, A SADNESS THAT NEVER 122 WHITE BIRDS   V     4
            MAY DIE.
          I'LL GIVE MY ANSWER.  YOU HAVE AWAKED HIM.  .  .  .  .  . 225 SHADOW WATER B V    79
AWAKEN
          THE WINDS AWAKEN, THE LEAVES WHIRL ROUND,  .  .  .  .  .  140 HOSTING SIDHE        6
          COULD BUT AWAKEN SADLY UPON LIPS  .  .  .  .  .  .  .  .  185 QUEEN MAEVE        104
          AWAKEN WANDERINGS OF LIGHT AIR  .  .  .  .  .  .  .  .  . 197 BAILE AILLINN      185
          AWAKEN TO LIFE AGAIN.  .  .  .  .  .  .  .  .  .  .  .  . 215 HAPPY TOWNLAND      26
          AWAKEN, AWAKEN TO NEW-BORN LUSTRE:  .  .  .  .  .  .  .  . 646 ISLE STAT I 1       43
          AWAKEN, AWAKEN TO NEW-BORN LUSTRE:  .  .  .  .  .  .  .  . 646 ISLE STAT I 1       43
AWAKENED       SEE DREAM-AWAKENED HALF-AWAKENED
          THE WINDS THAT AWAKENED THE STARS  .  .  .  .  .  .  .  . 171 MAID QUIET           3
          FOR THE WINDS THAT AWAKENED THE STAR,  .  .  .  .  .  .  . 171 MAID QUIET     V     3
          FOR THE WINDS THAT AWAKENED THE STARS  .  .  .  .  .  .  . 171 MAID QUIET     V     3
          I'LL GIVE MY ANSWER.  YOU HAVE AWAKENED HIM.  .  .  .  .  . 225 SHADOW WATER B     79
          BECAUSE I HAVE AWAKENED HER TO LOVE  .  .  .  .  .  .  .  . 243 SHADOW WATER B    439
          HAD HALF AWAKENED SOME OLD MEMORY--  .  .  .  .  .  .  .  . 284 TWO KINGS         172
          WHO HAS AWAKENED FROM THE COMMON DREAM  .  .  .  .  .  .  . 369 EGO DOMINUS        50
          HAD I BUT AWAKENED FROM SLEEP  .  .  .  .  .  .  .  .  .  . 381 SONGS FOOL 2       10
AWAKENS
          AND AS IT FALLS AWAKENS LEAFY TUNES:--  .  .  .  .  .  .  . 127 DREAM OF FAERY V   23
          AWAKENS AN OLD MEMORY, AND SAY,  .  .  .  .  .  .  .  .  . 201 OLD MEMORY          2
          AND THAT OLD HARP AWAKENS OF ITSELF  .  .  .  .  .  .  .  . 252 SHADOW WATER B    617
          AMONG THE HEBRIDES.  WHEN SHE AWAKENS,  .  .  .  .  .  .  . 760 SHADOW WATER A V  255
AWAKES
          HOW LITTLE AND REEDY A SOUND AWAKES A GOD  .  .  .  .  .  . 760 SHADOW WATER A    252
          ARE WISER WITCHCRAFT, FOR OUR PEACE AWAKES  .  .  .  .  .  . 763 SHADOW WATER A    320
AWARDED
          AWARDED HIM FOR DAMAGES  .  .  .  .  .  .  .  .  .  .  .  . 596 COLONEL MARTIN     48
AWARE
          THE DOLL-MAKER'S WIFE IS AWARE  .  .  .  .  .  .  .  .  .  . 319 DOLLS             14
A-WAVING
          "ARMS ARE A-WAVING AND LIPS APART  .  .  .  .  .  .  .  .  . 140 HOSTING SIDHE  V   9
AWAY      SEE FAR-AWAY
          DID YOUR COMPANION WANDER AWAY  .  .  .  .  .  .  .  .  .  .   6 OISIN 1           52
          "OISIN, THOU MUST AWAY WITH ME  .  .  .  .  .  .  .  .  .  .   8 OISIN 1       V   80
          AWAY, AWAY WITH ME," SHE CRIED,  .  .  .  .  .  .  .  .  .  .   8 OISIN 1       V  80B
          AWAY, AWAY WITH ME," SHE CRIED,  .  .  .  .  .  .  .  .  .  .   8 OISIN 1       V  80B
          HURRIED AWAY, AND OVER HER RAISED  .  .  .  .  .  .  .  .  .  12 OISIN 1       V 142B
          BID THEM AWAY AND HOLD THEIR PEACE:  .  .  .  .  .  .  .  .  15 OISIN 1          212
          NOW IN THE WOODS, AWAY WITH THEM  .  .  .  .  .  .  .  .  .  16 OISIN 1       V 216A
          ON IN THE WOODS, AWAY WITH THEM,  .  .  .  .  .  .  .  .  .  16 OISIN 1       V 222A
          AND CAUGHT THE SILVER HARP AWAY,  .  .  .  .  .  .  .  .  .  17 OISIN 1          240
          THE HARP AWAY.  A DOLOROUS POOL  .  .  .  .  .  .  .  .  .  17 OISIN 1       V 240
          EAT AWAY THE SLOPING SOD,  .  .  .  .  .  .  .  .  .  .  .  20 OISIN 1       V 299
          IT PASSETH AWAY, AND IS HEARD OF NO LONGER,  .  .  .  .  .  26 OISIN 1       V 399B
          AND THE MOON LIKE A PALE ROSE WITHER AWAY."  .  .  .  .  .  28 OISIN 1          427
          AND THEN AWAY, AWAY, LIKE WHIRLING FLAMES:  .  .  .  .  .  29 OISIN 2            2
          AND THEN AWAY, AWAY, LIKE WHIRLING FLAMES:  .  .  .  .  .  29 OISIN 2            2
          YET LOVE AND KISS ON DIM SHORES FAR AWAY  .  .  .  .  .  .  29 OISIN 2           13
          AND THEN AWAY, AWAY, LIKE SPIRAL FLAMES:  .  .  .  .  .  .  29 OISIN 2       V    2
          AND THEN AWAY, AWAY, LIKE SPIRAL FLAMES:  .  .  .  .  .  .  29 OISIN 2       V    2
          THEY LOVE AND KISS IN ISLANDS FAR AWAY,  .  .  .  .  .  .  29 OISIN 2       V   13
          BUT LOVE AND KISS ON DIM SHORES FAR AWAY  .  .  .  .  .  .  29 OISIN 2       V   13
          "I BRING THEE A DELIVERER FROM FAR AWAY,  .  .  .  .  .  .  34 OISIN 2       V  78A
          HIS PURPOSE DRIFTS AWAY."  .  .  .  .  .  .  .  .  .  .  .  45 OISIN 2       V  244
          HIGH AS THE SADDLE-GIRTH, COVERING AWAY FROM OUR GLANCES   47 OISIN 3            2
            THE TIDE:
          HIGH AS THE SADDLE GIRTH, COVERING AWAY FROM OUR GLANCES   47 OISIN 3       V    2
            THE TIDE:
          DRIPPING AND DOUBLING LANDWARD, AS THOUGH THEY WOULD HASTEN 48 OISIN 3          15
            AWAY,
          AND THE EARS OF THE HORSE WENT SINKING AWAY IN THE HOLLOW  48 OISIN 3          21
            NIGHT,
          OF HOLLIES, AND HAZELS, AND OAK TREES, A VALLEY WAS SLOPING 48 OISIN 3       V  26
            AWAY
          DRIPPING AND DOUBLING LANDWARD, AS THOUGH THEY WOULD HASTEN 57 OISIN 3         143
            AWAY,
          I RODE AWAY ON THE SURGES, WHERE, HIGH AS THE SADDLE-BOW,   57 OISIN 3         147
          LATER A SOUND CAME, HALF LOST IN THE SOUND OF A SHORE FAR   57 OISIN 3         155
            AWAY,
          I RODE AWAY ON THE SURGES, WHERE HIGH AS THE SADDLE BOW     57 OISIN 3       V 147
          I RODE AWAY ON THE SURGES, WHERE, HIGH AS THE SADDLEBOW,    57 OISIN 3       V 147
          I FELL ON THE PATH, AND THE HORSE WENT AWAY LIKE A SUMMER   60 OISIN 3         190
            FLY:
          YON TALL ONE EYES MY SUPPER: CHASE HIM AWAY,  .  .  .  .  .  72 ANASHU VIJAYA     34
          FAR, FAR AWAY.  I NAMED HIM AFTER YOU.  .  .  .  .  .  .  .  72 ANASHU VIJAYA     35
          FAR, FAR AWAY.  I'VE NAMED HIM AFTER YOU.  .  .  .  .  .  .  72 ANASHU VIJAYA V   35
          MURMURING HOW FAR AWAY ARE THE UNQUIET LANDS:  .  .  .  .  .  78 INDIAN TO LOVE    10
          MURMURING HOW FAR AWAY ARE ALL EARTH'S FEVERISH LANDS.  .  .  78 INDIAN TO LOVE V  10
          HOW FAR AWAY THE STARS SEEM, AND HOW FAR  .  .  .  .  .  .  80 EPHEMERA           8
          THEY PINE AWAY AND YELLOW AND WEAR OUT,  .  .  .  .  .  .  .  81 EPHEMERA     V  24H
          AND DROVE TUMULT AND WAR AWAY  .  .  .  .  .  .  .  .  .  .  82 MAD KING GOLL      5
          "HE DRIVES AWAY THE NORTHERN COLD."  .  .  .  .  .  .  .  .  82 MAD KING GOLL     11
          I PAUSED--AND FAR AWAY I DASHED  .  .  .  .  .  .  .  .  .  83 MAD KING GOLL V   31
          I PAUSED--AND FAR AWAY RUSHED ON,  .  .  .  .  .  .  .  .  .  83 MAD KING GOLL V   31
                                       53
```

AWAY   (CONTINUED)

	PAGE	TITLE		LINE
THAT HIDES AWAY THE DYING SUN	85	MAD KING GOLL		63
I MUST AWAY BY WOOD AND SEA	86	MAD KING GOLL	V	67
COME AWAY, O HUMAN CHILD!	87	STOLEN CHILD		9
COME AWAY, O HUMAN CHILD!	87	STOLEN CHILD		24
COME AWAY, O HUMAN CHILD!	88	STOLEN CHILD		38
AWAY WITH US HE'S GOING,	88	STOLEN CHILD		42
I WENT AWAY IN SILENCE,	95	MOLL MAGEE		27
I WENT AWAY IN SILENCE!	95	MOLL MAGEE		33
UPON HIS HEAD TO CAST AWAY MY SORROW.	102	FERGUS DRUID		14
UPON HIS HEAD TO CAST AWAY MY CARE.	102	FERGUS DRUID		14
I'D PUT AWAY THE FOOLISH MIGHT OF A KING,	103	FERGUS DRUID	V	21A
TO IDLE LIFE AWAY, A COMMON HERD."	107	CUCHULAIN SEA		21
TO IDLE LIFE AWAY WITH FLOCKS AND HERDS."	107	CUCHULAIN SEA	V	21
TROY PASSED AWAY IN ONE HIGH FUNERAL GLEAM,	111	ROSE OF WORLD		4
HAD HID AWAY EARTH'S OLD AND WEARY CRY.	120	SORROW OF LOVE	V	4
THE TALE DROVE HIS FINE ANGRY MOOD AWAY.	128	DREAM OF FAERY		36
IT CHARMED AWAY THE MERCHANT FROM HIS GUILE,	129	BOOK STORIES		5
AND NIAMH CALLING AWAY, COME AWAY!	140	HOSTING SIDHE		4
AND NIAMH CALLING AWAY, COME AWAY!	140	HOSTING SIDHE		4
AWAY, COME AWAY, TO THE DIM TWILIGHT.	140	HOSTING SIDHE	V	8
AWAY, COME AWAY, TO THE DIM TWILIGHT.	140	HOSTING SIDHE	V	8
AND NIAMH CALLING AWAY, COME AWAY.	141	HOSTING SIDHE		16
AND NIAMH CALLING AWAY, COME AWAY.	141	HOSTING SIDHE		16
HAS FALLEN AWAY?	142	MOODS		7
YOU PASS NOT AWAY.	142	MOODS	V	7
A PIPER PIPING AWAY,	144	HOST OF AIR		10
AWAY FROM THE MERRY BANDS,	144	HOST OF AIR		22
AWAY FROM THE MERRY DANCE,	145	HOST OF AIR		32
HE BORE HER AWAY IN HIS ARMS,	145	HOST OF AIR		33
A PIPER PIPING AWAY,	145	HOST OF AIR		42
SHE HAS GONE WEEPING AWAY.	152	LOSS OF LOVE		7
THE WEST WEEPS IN PALE DEW AND SIGHS PASSING AWAY,	154	BELOVED PEACE		5
TILL ALL THE VALLEYS OF THE WORLD HAVE BEEN WITHERED AWAY.	163	VALLEY LOVERS		8
TILL THE VALLEYS OF THE WORLD HAVE BEEN WITHERED AWAY."	163	VALLEY LOVERS	V	8
WHILE TIME AND THE WORLD ARE EBBING AWAY	168	BLESSED		39
UNTIL TIME AND THE WORLD HAVE EBBED AWAY	168	BLESSED	V	39
AND SORROW AWAY, AND CALLING BARD AND CLOWN	170	SECRET ROSE		20
AND TRAMPLED THE MOUNTAINS AWAY,	171	MAID QUIET	V	4C
AND TRAMPLED THE MOUNTAIN AWAY,	171	MAID QUIET	V	4C
AND COVERS AWAY THE SMOKE OF MYRRH AND FRANKINCENSE!	173	SPEAKS HEARERS		4
NOR WOULD YOU RISE AND HASTEN AWAY.	176	BELOVED DEAD		7
SHE TURNED AWAY! HE TURNED AGAIN TO SLEEP	182	QUEEN MAEVE		59
FOR ALTHOUGH YEARS HAD PASSED AWAY	192	BAILE AILLINN		77
WANDER WHERE EARTH WITHERS AWAY,	196	BAILE AILLINN		171
HUM IN THE LIME-TREE FLOWERS! AND PUT AWAY	198	SEVEN WOODS		3
HUM IN THE LIME TREE FLOWERS! AND PUT AWAY	198	SEVEN WOODS	V	3
AND ONE BY ONE WE DROP AWAY."	208	OLD MEN ADMIRE		3
"ALL THAT'S BEAUTIFUL DRIFTS AWAY	208	OLD MEN ADMIRE		8
OUR HANDS, OUR HANDS MUST EBB AWAY.	213	BLESS PSALTER		18
BUT BLESS OUR HANDS THAT EBB AWAY.	213	BLESS PSALTER		20
IS EDEN FAR AWAY, OR DO YOU HIDE	218	WOODS OF COOLE		30
PEACEABLE MEN THAT SHUT THE WIND AWAY,	224	SHADOW WATER B		54
I CAN PUT FEAR AWAY AS A QUEEN SHOULD.	238	SHADOW WATER B		355
TO CAST HIS DREAMS AWAY. NO OTHER'LL DO IT,	239	SHADOW WATER B		366
WHY DO YOU TURN AWAY AND HIDE YOUR FACE,	244	SHADOW WATER B		461
YOU TURN AWAY. WHY DO YOU TURN AWAY?	246	SHADOW WATER B		507
YOU TURN AWAY. WHY DO YOU TURN AWAY?	246	SHADOW WATER B		507
BUT NOW IT IS YOUR THOUGHTS THAT WANDER AWAY,	246	SHADOW WATER B		512
I TOO, I TOO. WHY DO YOU LOOK AWAY?	246	SHADOW WATER B	V	507
YOU ARE BROKEN, YOU ARE BROKEN. THE WORLD DRIFTS AWAY,	251	SHADOW WATER B		599
I MIGHT HAVE THROWN POOR WORDS AWAY	256	WORDS		15
SOME MAY HAVE BLAMED YOU THAT YOU TOOK AWAY	257	RECONCILIATION		1
TILL THE STARS HAD RUN AWAY	268	BROWN PENNY		13
NOT DOUBTING TO HAVE SHOULDERED IT AWAY,	277	TWO KINGS	V	11A
AND CLIMBED INTO THE AIR, CRUMBLING AWAY,	278	TWO KINGS		42
"YOUR STRENGTH AND NOBLENESS WILL PASS AWAY"?	285	TWO KINGS		189
THRUST HIM AWAY WITH BOTH MY HANDS AND CRIED,	285	TWO KINGS		202
THAN TRIUMPH, TURN AWAY	291	TO A FRIEND		10
AWAY, AWAY! YOU ARE SAFER IN THE TOMB.	293	TO A SHADE		24
AWAY, AWAY! YOU ARE SAFER IN THE TOMB.	293	TO A SHADE		24
HAD TUCKED HIMSELF AWAY BESIDE	303	HOUR DAWN		28
I'LL SLEEP AWAY ALL TIME WITHIN IT!	306	HOUR DAWN		74
BUT THE HOUR WHEN YOU SHALL PASS AWAY	306	HOUR DAWN		96
AND SLEEP AWAY ALL TIME WITHIN IT.	306	HOUR DAWN	V	74
"HE WENT AWAY," MY MOTHER SANG,	308	PLAYER QUEEN		5
SUDDENLY HID LOVE'S MOON AWAY.	313	MEMORY YOUTH		7
LOVE'S MOON WAS WITHERING AWAY.	313	MEMORY YOUTH	V	7
TO BUNDLE TIME AWAY	317	NIGHT COME		11
TO FIND THEY HAVE FLOWN AWAY?	323	SWANS AT COOLE		30
BROUGHT THE BARE NEWS. HE HAD THROWN THE CROOK AWAY	339	SHEP GOATHERD		21
ALL THE DISHONEST CROWD I HAD DRIVEN AWAY,	352	PEOPLE		24
HEAVEN HAS PUT AWAY THE STROKE OF HER DOOM,	356	BROKEN DREAMS		11
AND MASONS DROVE FROM MILES AWAY	360	ALF POLLEXFEN		9
WE AND OUR DOLLS BEING BUT THE WORLD WERE BEST AWAY.	364	DOLLS FACES		12
WOULD CARRY IT AWAY TO BLASPHEMOUS MEN,	371	EGO DOMINUS		79
BODY AND SOUL CAST OUT AND CAST AWAY	374	PHASES OF MOON		62
THAT, IT MAY BE, HAD DANCED HER LIFE AWAY,	383	VISION ROBART		22
THAT IT MAYBE HAD DANCED HER LIFE AWAY,	383	VISION ROBART	V	22
"WHEN ALL THE WELLS ARE PARCHED AWAY?	396	ROSE TREE		15
CONSUME MY HEART AWAY! SICK WITH DESIRE	408	SAIL BYZANTIUM		21

54

```
                                                      PAGE    TITLE            LINE
AWAY   (CONTINUED)
    I TURN AWAY AND SHUT THE DOOR, AND ON THE STAIR  .  .  .  .   427 PHANTOM HATRED      33
    AND BEAR THAT BEATING HEART AWAY!  .  .  .  .  .  .  .  .  .  437 SONGS PLAY 1         5
    LOVE'S PLEASURE DRIVES HIS LOVE AWAY,  .  .  .  .  .  .  .  .  438 SONGS PLAY 2        11
    "BECAUSE I MADE YOU TURN AWAY AND RUN FROM THAT YOUNG         450 OWEN AHERNE         14
        CHILD!
    O BUT HER HEART WOULD BREAK TO LEARN MY THOUGHTS ARE FAR      450 OWEN AHERNE         20
        AWAY."
    AND TALKED AWAY THE NIGHT,  .  .  .  .  .  .  .  .  .  .  .   456 SUMMER SPRING        2
    ARE GONE AWAY, AND SOME THAT STAY  .  .  .  .  .  .  .  .  .  458 HIS WILDNESS         5
    THE SECOND BEST'S A GAY GOODNIGHT AND QUICKLY TURN AWAY.      459 FROM OEDIPUS        12
    ALL MY FINE FEATHERS WOULD BE PLUCKED AWAY  .  .  .  .  .  .  469 HARUN RASHID       178
    AWAY FROM NEIGHBOUR OR FRIEND,  .  .  .  .  .  .  .  .  .  .  472 ALL SOUL NIGHT      47
    TO WHERE THE DAMNED HAVE HOWLED AWAY THEIR HEARTS,  .  .  .   474 ALL SOUL NIGHT      95
    SHAKESPEAREAN FISH SWAM THE SEA, FAR AWAY FROM LAND!  .  .    485 THREE MOVEMENT       1
    THE TOMB OF SWIFT WEARS IT AWAY.  A VOICE  .  .  .  .  .  .   487 SEVEN SAGES         21
    MAY THUNDER TIME AWAY,  .  .  .  .  .  .  .  .  .  .  .  .    496 MOHINI CHATTER      25
    "LET ALL THINGS PASS AWAY."  .  .  .  .  .  .  .  .  .  .  .  502 VACILLATION         61
    "LET ALL THINGS PASS AWAY."  .  .  .  .  .  .  .  .  .  .  .  502 VACILLATION         66
    "LET ALL THINGS PASS AWAY."  .  .  .  .  .  .  .  .  .  .  .  502 VACILLATION         71
    THAT TURN DULL-EYED AWAY,  .  .  .  .  .  .  .  .  .  .  .    505 RESULT THOUGHT      14
    NAKED AND HIDDEN AWAY,  .  .  .  .  .  .  .  .  .  .  .  .    510 JANE JUDGMENT       13
    THAT I HAD SHORN MY LOCKS AWAY  .  .  .  .  .  .  .  .  .  .  519 HER DREAM            3
    A MAN MAY PUT PRETENCE AWAY  .  .  .  .  .  .  .  .  .  .  .  525 DANCING DAYS        19
    AWAY MUST SHE TRIP!  .  .  .  .  .  .  .  .  .  .  .  .  .    559 HE AND SHE           4
    TO LEAD HER AWAY, DO NOT SAY  .  .  .  .  .  .  .  .  .  .  .  568 SWEET DANCER         9
    FROM TIME LONG PASSED AWAY.  .  .  .  .  .  .  .  .  .  .  .  589 OLD WICKED MAN      42
    BECAUSE THE FIRES OF PURGATORY HAVE ATE THEIR SHAPES AWAY!    593 PILGRIM             13
    SHE, PITY-CRAZED, HAD GIVEN HER SOUL AWAY,  .  .  .  .  .  .  629 CIRCUS ANIMALS      19
    AND FAR AWAY THE HERON SAILS, I WIS.  .  .  .  .  .  .  .  .  649 ISLE STAT I 1      116
    AWAY IN THE GREEN PARADISE,  .  .  .  .  .  .  .  .  .  .  .  654 ISLE STAT I 2       70
    BLEW MY CRIMSON CAP AWAY  .  .  .  .  .  .  .  .  .  .  .  .  656 ISLE STAT I 3       16
    I WOULD HAVE GONE ALSO! BUT FAR AWAY  .  .  .  .  .  .  .  .  663 ISLE STAT II 2      37
    AWAY FROM ME WHERE MISTS OF EVENING DRINK  .  .  .  .  .  .   663 ISLE STAT II 2      40
    PASS AWAY--  .  .  .  .  .  .  .  .  .  .  .  .  .  .  .  .   668 ISLE STAT II 3      67
    WILT ROAM AWAY FROM THIS RICH ISLAND REST?  .  .  .  .  .  .  669 ISLE STAT II 3      88
    HAS ROLLED AWAY THE STARS AND DRIED THE SEA  .  .  .  .  .    671 ISLE STAT II 3     146
    I HURL AWAY THESE ALL UNFAERY FEARS.  .  .  .  .  .  .  .  .  675 ISLE STAT II 3     228
    THE SINGING SHEPHERDS, TOO, HAVE PASSED AWAY.  .  .  .  .  .  676 ISLE STAT II 3     271
    I WILL DISSOLVE AWAY THE FAERIES' GUILE!  .  .  .  .  .  .  .  677 ISLE STAT II 3     282
    HOW HAVE THE YEARS IN TROIA FLOWN AWAY?  .  .  .  .  .  .  .  679 ISLE STAT II 3     309
    WANDER AWAY FROM MINE?  .  .  .  .  .  .  .  .  .  .  .  .    686 LIFE                 8
    AND LAUGH OUR LOVE AWAY.  .  .  .  .  .  .  .  .  .  .  .  .  686 LIFE                16
    HIDING AWAY THE OCEAN'S YELPING FLOCKS.  .  .  .  .  .  .  .  688 TWO TITANS          38
    I SAW HIM SIGH AND TURN AND PASS AWAY!  .  .  .  .  .  .  .   690 MOSADA 1            14
    AWAY FROM ALL THE OTHERS.  NOW THE SUN  .  .  .  .  .  .  .   691 MOSADA 1            33
    THIS HEATHEN HORDE AWAY.  YOU NEED NOT HOPE!  .  .  .  .  .   696 MOSADA 2             5
    NO USE.  AWAY!  HEAR, THOU ENDURING GOD.  .  .  .  .  .  .    698 MOSADA 2            50
    NO USE.  AWAY!  HEAR OH! THOU ENDURING GOD,  .  .  .  .  .    698 MOSADA 2         V  50
    AND FREE--'TWILL THIEVE AWAY WITH SLEEPY MOOD  .  .  .  .  .  700 MOSADA 3            30
    SHOWERED AWAY THE KEEN DEW DROPS!  .  .  .  .  .  .  .  .  .  705 DAWN-SONG           18
    COME AWAY WHILE THE MOON'S IN THE WOODLAND,  .  .  .  .  .    707 FAIRY PEDANT         9
    YOU ARE WASTING AWAY, LITTLE FAIRY.  .  .  .  .  .  .  .  .   707 FAIRY PEDANT        12
    THEN AWAY AND AWAY WILL I WANDER,  .  .  .  .  .  .  .  .  .  707 FAIRY PEDANT        16
    THEN AWAY AND AWAY WILL I WANDER,  .  .  .  .  .  .  .  .  .  707 FAIRY PEDANT        16
    YOU ARE WASTING AWAY, LITTLE FAIRY.  .  .  .  .  .  .  .  .   707 FAIRY PEDANT        20
    COME AWAY WHILE THE MOON'S IN THE WOODLAND,  .  .  .  .  .    708 FAIRY PEDANT        37
    SHE IS WASTING AWAY, LITTLE FAIRY.  .  .  .  .  .  .  .  .    708 FAIRY PEDANT        40
    SERENE.  THEY'RE LED AWAY, AND WHERE A BAND  .  .  .  .  .    712 FERENCZ RENYI       63
    THERE FAR AWAY FROM ALL WE TWO WILL GO.  .  .  .  .  .  .  .  714 FERENCZ RENYI       99
    AWAY HER CLINGING HANDS, AND TURNS.  SHE THROWS  .  .  .  .   714 FERENCZ RENYI      102
    HIS BONDS AWAY, SORE STRUGGLING.  NOW AT LAST  .  .  .  .  .  714 FERENCZ RENYI      116
    HER OFF AND TURNS AWAY.  SHE THROWS  .  .  .  .  .  .  .  .   714 FERENCZ RENYI    V 102
    AND AWAY IN THE WOODS WE WILL SCATTER THE DEW!  .  .  .  .    717 LOVE SONG            2
    .  .  . GONE AND PUFFED AWAY AND DEAD.  .  .  .  .  .  .  .   718 PHANTOM SHIP         3
    AND THE WINDS COME DOWN AND BLOW THEM WITH THE VAPOURS        719 PHANTOM SHIP        28
        FAR AWAY.
    LIFT THEIR CHINS AND TURN AWAY.  .  .  .  .  .  .  .  .  .    726 LOVERS QUARREL      24
    COME I KNOW WHERE, FAR AWAY,  .  .  .  .  .  .  .  .  .  .    727 LOVERS QUARREL      34
    AWAY IN THE HEART OF THE ANTIQUE WOOD!  .  .  .  .  .  .  .   730 PRIEST FAIRY        64
    FAR AWAY THE STARRY MIRTH  .  .  .  .  .  .  .  .  .  .  .    731 STREET DANCERS       7
    I FLING AWAY MY SWORD, BLOOD DIM,  .  .  .  .  .  .  .  .  .  743 DANAAN QUICK        20
    A WOMAN IN MY ARMS, SHE SINKS AWAY  .  .  .  .  .  .  .  .    749 SHADOW WATER A      54
    THAT SHALL BURN TIME WHEN TIMES HAVE EBBED AWAY.  .  .  .  .  750 SHADOW WATER A      61
    THEY HAVE FLOWN AWAY TOGETHER.  WE ARE NEARLY  .  .  .  .  .  754 SHADOW WATER A     154
    BREATHED OUT A DRUID VAPOUR, AND CRUMBLED AWAY  .  .  .  .    761 SHADOW WATER A     279
    HAVE COVERED THEM.  WHERE DID THEY VANISH AWAY?  .  .  .  .   764 SHADOW WATER A     328
    AND WHILE SHE FADES AND LIFE WITHERS AWAY,  .  .  .  .  .     768 SHADOW WATER A     422
    THE WRITINGS I HAVE CAST AWAY!  .  .  .  .  .  .  .  .  .  .  779 ACCURSED WHO         2
    OUR LUCK IS WITHERED AWAY,  .  .  .  .  .  .  .  .  .  .  .   783 GREY ROUND          18
    AND THE WIND BLOWS IT AWAY.  .  .  .  .  .  .  .  .  .  .  .  783 GREY ROUND          20
    IT CHASES OTHER THOUGHT AWAY.  .  .  .  .  .  .  .  .  .  .   791 REPRISALS            9
A-WEARY
    OR PERCHING ON THE TENTS, A-WEARY STILL  .  .  .  .  .  .  .  690 MOSADA 1             8
A-WEAVING
    FOR LOVE IS A-WEAVING WHEN A WOMAN'S HEART  .  .  .  .  .  .  761 SHADOW WATER A     262
AWFLESS
    OF AWFLESS BIRDS, AND ROUND THEIR STIRLESS FEET  .  .  .  .   74 ANASHU VIJAYA       73
AWFUL
    WATCHING O'ER HER AWFUL YOUNG,  .  .  .  .  .  .  .  .  .  .  658 ISLE STAT I 3       87
```

55

```
                                                          PAGE     TITLE        LINE
AWHILE
    AWHILE, AND CAME AGAIN, A SECOND LIGHT . . .          37 OISIN 2        V  124
    THAT EMPTY THE HEART. I HAVE FORGOT AWHILE . . . .    198 SEVEN WOODS        5
    WHERE ONE FOUND LANCELOT CRAZED, AND HID HIM FOR AWHILE,  209 UNDER THE MOON V  3
    AND AFTER CIRCLING WITH STRANGE CRIES AWHILE . . . . . 223 SHADOW WATER B    26
    AND LISTEN TO ME FOR AWHILE. THE SAILORS . . .       226 SHADOW WATER B  V  92
    IF YOU WILL GIVE ME ALL YOUR MIND AWHILE-- . . . . .  227 SHADOW WATER B   117
    THEY HOVER OVER THE MASTHEAD AWHILE . . . . .        233 SHADOW WATER B   246
    I HAD THIS THOUGHT AWHILE AGO. . . . . . . . .       255 WORDS          V   1
    OR HAVE LINGERED AWHILE AND SAID . . . . . . .       392 EASTER 1916        7
    SHE WALKED AWHILE AND BLUSHED AWHILE . . . . .       451 FIRST LOVE         3
    SHE WALKED AWHILE AND BLUSHED AWHILE . . . . .       451 FIRST LOVE         3
    HIDDEN BY OLD AGE AWHILE. . . . . . . . .            539 MEETING            1
    STAND UPRIGHT ON YOUR LEGS AWHILE. . . . . .         586 PARNELLITES        3
    I FORGET IT ALL AWHILE . . . . . . . . .             590 OLD WICKED MAN    61
    AND HAVING STRETCHED AND YAWNED AWHILE . . . .       612 NEWS ORACLE       11
    BE PATIENT YET AWHILE, FOR THIS NINTH MOON,          748 SHADOW WATER A  V  23
A-WHISPERING
    AND ON TIPTOE THE WINDS A-WHISPERING STOOD. .        715 DWELT SYCAMORE     8
    AND ON TIP-TOE THE WINDS A-WHISPERING STOOD. . . . . 715 DWELT SYCAMORE  V  8
A-WINGING
    LIKE TULIPS IN THE AIR A-WINGING, . . . . . . .      27 OISIN 1          417
AWOKE
    I AWOKE, THE STRANGE HORSE WITHOUT SUMMONS OUT OF    54 OISIN 3          105
        THE DISTANCE RAN,
    AND OUT OF HIS DREAM AWOKE, . . . . . . .            145 HOST OF AIR       38
    TILL VAIN FRENZY AWOKE AND HE DIED, AND HIM          169 SECRET ROSE       12
    AWOKE THE HARP-STRINGS LONG AGO. . . . . . .         190 BAILE AILLINN     37
    AWOKE THE HARP STRINGS LONG AGO. . . . . . .         190 BAILE AILLINN   V  37
    THE SLEEPER AWOKE WITH A SUDDEN START, . . . . .     729 PRIEST FAIRY      31
AWRY
    AMENDED WHAT WAS TOLD AWRY . . . . . . .             440 WISDOM             4
    STRAIGHTENED ALL THAT WENT AWRY . . . . . .          440 WISDOM         V   4
    WHAT KNOWLEDGE OR ITS LACK HAD SET AWRY, . . . . .   490 COOLE BALLYLEE    22
    WHAT KNOWLEDGE OR ITS LACK HAS SET AWRY, . . . . .   490 COOLE BALLYLEE  V  22
    I AM, ONE SHOULDER TURNED AWRY--WHY THEN . . . .     692 MOSADA 1          61
AXE     SEE POLE-AXE WAR-AXE BATTLE-AXE
AXEL
    THE ARCHANGEL AXEL, VICTOR THE ANGEL . . . . .       774 COME RIDE         11
AXES    SEE BATTLE-AXES
    BEND LOWER LEST YOUR BATTLE AXES GLIMMER. . . . . .  752 SHADOW WATER A  V 117
AXLE
    UNTIL THE AXLE BREAK . . . . . . . . .               165 CRY OF SEDGE       4
AY
    FASTING AND PRAYERS. TELL ON. AY, AY! . . . .        24 OISIN 1         V 360
    FASTING AND PRAYERS. TELL ON. AY, AY! . . . .        24 OISIN 1         V 360
    SAID NIAM. "AY, AND HUGE. WHEN YE HAVE LED          35 OISIN 2         V  89
    AY, OISIN KNOWS, FOR HE IS OF THE WEAK, . . . .      42 OISIN 2         V 202
    AY, AY. SWEAR BY THE PARENTS OF THE GODS, . . . .    74 ANASHU VIJAYA     66
    AY, AY. SWEAR BY THE PARENTS OF THE GODS, . . . .    74 ANASHU VIJAYA     66
    AY, BOY. LET'S SEE IF THAT SAME HERON'S DEAD.        651 ISLE STAT I 1    169
    THE OTTERS DREAMING LAY. NASCHINA! AY! . . . .       677 ISLE STAT II 3  V 280
    HIS BODY SHAKE? AY, QUIVERING AS YON SMOKE           683 SEEKER            36
    AFRAID TO BE TOO FAR." "AY, BRING HER HERE!"         712 FERENCZ RENYI     69
    AY, AND SHAKES IN SEA-GREEN WAVERINGS ALONG THE FISHERS'  718 PHANTOM SHIP  2
        STREET,
    FOR ANTIQUARIAN MEDITATION. AY, . . . . . .          721 WITCH VIVIEN      38
AYE
    SMOTE ON THEIR BRAINS THAT DWELT REMEMBERING AYE. . . 34 OISIN 2        V 77A
    FOR LONG ENOUGH? AYE, LONG AND LONG ENOUGH. . . . .  221 SHADOW WATER B     2
    AYE, AND WORSE WRONG THAN THESE. . . . . .           260 UNWORTH PRAISE    18
    AYE, HORSEMEN FOR COMPANIONS, . . . . . .            266 GALWAY RACES       7
    AYE, AND ACHILLES, TIMOR, BABAR, BARHAIM, ALL . . .  366 HER COURAGE        9
    AYE, THOUGH ALL PASSION'S IN THE GLANCE-- . . . .    388 SOLOMON WITCH     21
    AYE, SUN AND MOON AND STAR, ALL, . . . . . .         415 TOWER            152
    OF EVENING AND GLAD SILENCE DWELLETH AYE, . . . .    653 ISLE STAT I 2     37
    AYE, VERY LATELY, SORROW CAME TO WEEP . . . . .      659 ISLE STAT II 1    25
    IF HER YE LOVE. AYE, COLIN, WE MUST FIGHT, . . . .   662 ISLE STAT II 1    76
    AYE, FIGHT WE MUST. TELL ME, ANTONIO, MIGHT . . .    662 ISLE STAT II 1    77
    EACH ONE AT GAZE FOR AYE UPON HIS WHIRLING THRONE. . 662 ISLE STAT II 1    81
    THE OTTERS DREAMING LAY. AYE! . . . . . .            677 ISLE STAT II 3   280
    THE LIGHTNINGS PULSE--BEHOLD HER, AYE BEHOLD-- . . . 687 TWO TITANS        11
    AYE AND SHAKES IN SEA GREEN WAVERINGS, ALONG THE FISHERS'  718 PHANTOM SHIP V  2
        STREET.
A-YEAR
    AND ONCE A-YEAR LET THE ARCADIANS COME, . . . . .    663 ISLE STAT II 2    29
AZOLAR
    WE TWO, BEFORE WE DIE, FOR AZOLAR, . . . . .         691 MOSADA 1          24
AZURE
    WITH ALL YOUR WHIRLING HAIR, AND DROP MANY AN AZURE TEAR.  73 ANASHU VIJAYA  46
    WITH ALL YOUR WHIRLING HAIR, AND DROP THROUGH SPACE AN  73 ANASHU VIJAYA V 46
        AZURE TEAR.
    WITH ALL YOUR WHIRLING HAIR, AND DROP TEAR UPON AZURE TEAR.  73 ANASHU VIJAYA V 46
    WITH ALL OUR WHIRLING HAIR, AND DROP MANY AN AZURE TEAR.  73 ANASHU VIJAYA V 46
    IN COIL ON COIL OF AZURE. ALL IS READY. . . . .      691 MOSADA 1          41
    NO SIN TO SEE IN COIL ON COIL OF AZURE . . . . .     692 MOSADA 1          43
    IN THE SOUTH SEA'S AZURE MILES, . . . . .            732 STREET DANCERS    28
    IN THE SOUTH SEAS' AZURE MILES, . . . . . .          732 STREET DANCERS  V 28
AZURES
    HER GOLDS, HER AZURES, AND HER BLUES, . . . . . .    13 OISIN 1         V 163
```

BABAR
    AYE, AND ACHILLES, TIMOR, BABAR, BARHAIM, ALL . . . . . 366 HER COURAGE 9
BABBLING
    BABBLING OF FALLEN MAJESTY, RECORDS WHAT'S GONE. . . . . 314 FALLEN MAJESTY 4
    MID BABBLING LEAVES A WANDERING SONG-RAPT BIRD . . . . 672 ISLE STAT II 3 V 154
    AND SEDGY STREAM, AND IN EACH BABBLING BRAKE . . . . . 675 ISLE STAT II 3 225
BABY
    AND MY BABY WAS JUST BORN: . . . . 94 MOLL MAGEE 14
    I LAY UPON MY BABY: . . . . 95 MOLL MAGEE 17
    I LOOKED ON MY COLD BABY . . . . 95 MOLL MAGEE 19
    I'M THINKIN' OF MY BABY . . . . 96 MOLL MAGEE 47
BABYLON
    FROM THEIR PEDANTIC BABYLON . . . . 344 DAWN 6
    IN STARRY TOWERS OF BABYLON . . . . 440 WISDOM 14
    WHERE BABYLON OR NINEVEH . . . . 502 VACILLATION 63
BABYLONIAN
    WHAT MEDIAN, PERSIAN, BABYLONIAN, ... 420 MY HOUSE V 20D
    REMEMBERED OUT OF BABYLONIAN ALMANACS, ... 426 PHANTOM HATRED 20
    THE BABYLONIAN STARLIGHT BROUGHT . . . . 438 SONGS PLAY 2 4
    THE BABYLONIAN STAR-LIGHT BROUGHT . . . . 438 SONGS PLAY 2 V 4
BABYLON'S
    ALEXANDRIA'S WAS A BEACON TOWER, AND BABYLON'S . . . . 480 BLOOD AND MOON 13
BACCHANT
    BACCHANT AND MOURNFUL, PASSING TO AND FRO . . . . . . 39 OISIN 2 161
BACHELOR
    I AM SO TIRED OF BEING BACHELOR . . . . 222 SHADOW WATER B 8
BACK   SEE HORSE-BACK CAMEL-BACK MULE-BACK ASS-BACK
    A WALL BEHIND HIS BACK, OVER HIS HEAD . . . . 180 QUEEN MAEVE 5
    HE AND HIS BEST TROOPS BACK TO BACK . . . . 274 GREY ROCK 73
    HE AND HIS BEST TROOPS BACK TO BACK . . . . 274 GREY ROCK 73
    I COWERED BACK UPON THE WALL IN TERROR, ... 284 TWO KINGS 164
    SHOOK OFF THE WATER FROM HIS BACK: . . . . 400 DEMON BEAST 29
    OR THE HUMBLER WORM, I CLIMBED BEN BULBEN'S BACK . . . 409 TOWER 9
    ALL DREAD AFAR TILL MORNING'S BACK, ... 435 FOR MY SON 6
    THAT HAD SO STRAIGHT A BACK, ... 458 HIS WILDNESS 4
    OR CARRY THE RINGED MAIL UPON MY BACK, ... 463 HARUN RASHID 58
    BACK TURNED UPON THE BRIGHTNESS OF THE SUN . . . . . 489 COOLE PARK 29 30
    I CAN SUMMON BACK . . . . 505 RESULT THOUGHT 11
    I COULD SUMMON BACK . . . . 505 RESULT THOUGHT V 11
    THE HERON'S HUNCH UPON HIS BACK, ... 508 JANE BISHOP 19
    "O CRUEL DEATH, GIVE THREE THINGS BACK," . . . . . . 521 THREE THINGS 1
    BRIGHTNESS THAT I PULL BACK . . . . 533 FIRST CONFESS 13
    AND, THOUGH LOVE'S BITTER-SWEET HAD ALL COME BACK, . . 537 HER VISION 27
    SOME BACK A MARE THROWN FROM A THOROUGHBRED, ... 547 TO SAME TUNE 3 3
    SOME BACK A MARE THROWN FROM A THOROUGH-BRED, ... 547 TO SAME TUNE 3 V 3
    "OF PLASTER SAINTS" HIS BEAUTIFUL MISCHIEVOUS HEAD THROWN 577 LOFTY THINGS 4
        BACK.
    PALLAS ATHENE IN THAT STRAIGHT BACK AND ARROGANT HEAD: . 578 LOFTY THINGS 11
    HITCHED IT ON HIS BACK. . . . . 595 COLONEL MARTIN 26
    THE SMUGGLER MIDDLETON, BUTLERS FAR BACK, ... 605 YOU CONTENT 15
    STRADDLING EACH A DOLPHIN'S BACK . . . . 612 NEWS ORACLE 13
    SOME BACK A MARE THROWN FROM A THOROUGHBRED, ... 614 MARCH SONGS 2 3
    THE KHAKI FROM HIS BACK? . . . . 627 STATES HOLIDAY 17
    WITH A STIFF STRAIGHT BACK, ... 627 STATES HOLIDAY 33
    BACK IN THE HUMAN MIND AGAIN. . . . . 637 BEN BULBEN 24
    BACK THE SHADOWS CREEP AGHAST— . . . . 648 ISLE STAT I 1 98
    UNTIL THIS MORN, AS ADDER'S BACK . . . . 667 ISLE STAT II 3 22
    WAS BANDED AS AN ADDER'S BACK, ... 667 ISLE STAT II 3 V 23
    BRUSHING BACK HIS YELLOW HAIR: . . . . 729 PRIEST FAIRY 38
BACKED
    TROY BACKED ITS HELEN: TROY DIED AND ADORED: . . . . . 547 TO SAME TUNE 3 4
    TROY BACKED ITS HELEN: TROY DIED AND ADORED: . . . . . 614 MARCH SONGS 2 4
BACKGROUNDS
    ON BACKGROUNDS FOR A GOD OR SAINT . . . . 639 BEN BULBEN 54
BACKS
    MAGICAL UNICORNS BEAR LADIES ON THEIR BACKS. . . . . . 426 PHANTOM HATRED 18
BACKWARD
    UNTIL AT LAST THE DOUBLE HORNS, DRAWN BACKWARD, . . . 278 TWO KINGS 21
    HER HEAD CAST BACKWARD IN HER UNLOOSED HAIR. . . . . . 701 MOSADA 3 67
BACKWARDS
    I PLUCKED HER BACKWARDS BY HER DRESS OF GREEN. . . . . 676 ISLE STAT II 3 264
BAD
    THE BAD OLD DAYS, THOU WERT, MEN SING, ... 2 OISIN 1 V 3
    THAT IS BAD ENOUGH TO BE TRUE, IS TRUE, ... 191 BAILE AILLINN 69
    . . . CERTAIN BAD POETS, IMITATORS OF HIS AND MINE . . 262 TO A POET T
    . . . CERTAIN BAD POETS, IMITATORS OF HIS AND OF MINE . 262 TO A POET V T
    TILL YOUR BAD MASTER BLENCHED AND ALL WAS LOST: . . . 270 PARDON FATHERS V 12
    AND STUFFED WITH ALL THAT'S OLD AND BAD: . . . . . . 303 HOUR DAWN V 25
    THAT'S STUFFED WITH ALL THAT'S OLD AND BAD: . . . . . 303 HOUR DAWN 25
    IN THE BAD HOUR BEFORE THE DAWN." . . . . 304 HOUR DAWN 55
    AND THOUGH THE WINTER WIND IS BAD . . . . 306 HOUR DAWN 87
    I COUNT MY GOOD AND BAD, ... 316 FRIENDS 22
    WHAT'S GOOD OR BAD, OR WHAT IT IS TO TRIUMPH . . . . 376 PHASES OF MOON 108
    THAT HAS THE WORST OF ALL BAD NAMES: . . . . 531 FATHER CHILD 5
    SHOULD STARVE GOOD MEN AND BAD ADVANCE, ... 626 OLD MEN BE MAD 10
BADE
    SHE BADE THEM BRING US TO THE HALL . . . . 16 OISIN 1 217
    GAVE ME A HARP, AND BADE ME SING: . . . . 16 OISIN 1 V 232
    AND BADE ME SING OF EARTHLY LANDS: . . . . 17 OISIN 1 V 233
    HAD NEITHER HOPE NOR FEAR, I BADE THEM HIDE . . . . . 38 OISIN 2 139
    OF FEAR, I BADE THEM GO: AND FOR THE FIGHT . . . . . 38 OISIN 2 V 142

BADE   (CONTINUED)

```
HE BADE THEM GIVE OVER THEIR KEENING!  . . . . . . . .   93 FATHER OHART        23
AND GAVE ME MONEY, AND BADE ME GO .  . . . . . . . . .   95 MOLL MAGEE          23
"WHO BADE YOU TELL THESE THINGS UPON MY FLOOR?" . . . .  106 CUCHULAIN SEA   V   17
"WHO BADE YOU TELL THESE THINGS?" AND THEN SHE CRIED  .  106 CUCHULAIN SEA   V   17
"HE BADE ME LET ALL KNOW HE GIVES HIS NAME .  . . . . .  109 CUCHULAIN SEA       52
AT THE SWORD POINT, AND BADE ME BRING HIM ONE .  . . .  109 CUCHULAIN SEA   V   53
AND TIME BADE ALL HIS CANDLES FLARE .  . . . . . . . .  138 TO IRELAND          13
HE BADE ME OUT INTO THE GLOOM,  . . . . . . . . . . . .  151 HEART OF WOMAN       3
I BADE MY HEART BUILD THESE POOR RHYMES!  . . . . . . .  158 BELOVED RHYMES       3
HE BADE HIS SOUL RISE UPWARD .  . . . . . . . . . . . .  159 CAP AND BELLS        3
HE BADE HIS HEART GO TO HER,  . . . . . . . . . . . . .  159 CAP AND BELLS       13
THEY HAVE BADE YOU FOLLOW THE MAN-HEADED BIRDS,  . . .  231 SHADOW WATER B  V  204
I BADE HIM GO WHEN ALL HIS HOUSEHOLD SLEPT .  . . . . .  282 TWO KINGS          133
AND BADE ALL WELCOME, BEING IGNORANT.  . . . . . . . .  286 TWO KINGS          218
NOR LAW, NOR DUTY BADE ME FIGHT,  . . . . . . . . . . .  328 IRISH AIRMAN         9
I BADE, BECAUSE THE WICK AND OIL ARE SPENT .  . . . . .  333 LIVING BEAUTY        1
HE BADE THEM TAKE AND BURY HER .  . . . . . . . . . . .  571 THREE BUSHES        71
WHAT IF I BADE YOU LEAVE .  . . . . . . . . . . . . . .  600 THOSE IMAGES         1
I NEVER BADE YOU GO .  . . . . . . . . . . . . . . . . .  600 THOSE IMAGES         5
HE BADE, HIS HUNDRED AND FIRST YEAR AT END,  . . . . .  609 IN TARAS HALLS      16
I CRIED THE THING YOU BADE ME CRY,  . . . . . . . . . .  670 ISLE STAT II 3     114
BADE THAT SWORDSMAN TAKE .  . . . . . . . . . . . . . .  789 SINGING HEAD         4
I BADE THEM FETCH HIS HEAD.  . . . . . . . . . . . . . .  789 SINGING HEAD        12
```

BADGER

```
THE DEER, THE BADGER, AND THE BOAR,  . . . . . . . . .   23 OISIN 1            345
AND SLEW THE BADGER AND THE DEER,  . . . . . . . . . .   23 OISIN 1         V  345
DIM INCHY WOOD, THAT HIDES BADGER AND FOX .  . . . . .  218 WOODS OF COOLE      13
NO FOX CAN FOUL THE LAIR THE BADGER SWEPT--  . . . . .  603 GALLERY REVIS       39
```

BADGERED

```
CAN BE SO BATTERED, BADGERED AND DESTROYED .  . . . .  130 BOOK STORIES        17
```

BAFFLED

```
CONSTRAINED, ARRAIGNED, BAFFLED, BENT AND UNBENT  . .  382 VISION ROBART        9
```

BAG

```
TAKE, IF YOU MUST, THIS LITTLE BAG OF DREAMS!  . . . .  104 FERGUS DRUID        29
TAKE THEN THIS SMALL SLATE-COLOURED BAG OF DREAMS!  .  104 FERGUS DRUID    V   29
LAY HIDDEN IN THE SMALL SLATE-COLOURED BAG!  . . . . .  104 FERGUS DRUID    V   40
AND WITHERED TO A BAG OF BONES!  . . . . . . . . . . .  401 DEMON BEAST         49
THE MOON IN A SILVER BAG.  . . . . . . . . . . . . . .  525 DANCING DAYS         8
THE MOON IN A SILVER BAG.  . . . . . . . . . . . . . .  525 DANCING DAYS        16
THE MOON IN A SILVER BAG.  . . . . . . . . . . . . . .  525 DANCING DAYS        24
WITH A BAG FULL OF PENNIES,  . . . . . . . . . . . . .  627 STATES HOLIDAY      35
WELL THEN, TO BUSINESS! WHAT IS IN YOUR BAG? . . . . .  720 WITCH VIVIEN        19
```

BAGPIPES

```
AN OLD MAN PLAYS THE BAGPIPES .  . . . . . . . . . . .  214 HAPPY TOWNLAND       9
```

BAILE

```
BAILE AND AILLINN .  . . . . . . . . . . . . . . . . .  188 BAILE AILLINN        T
BAILE, WHO HAD THE HONEY MOUTH!  . . . . . . . . . . .  189 BAILE AILLINN        5
YOUNG BAILE HONEY-MOUTH, WHOM SOME .  . . . . . . . . .  189 BAILE AILLINN       16
CALLED RATHER BAILE LITTLE-LAND, .  . . . . . . . . . .  189 BAILE AILLINN       17
YOUNG BAILE HONEY MOUTH, WHOM SOME .  . . . . . . . . .  189 BAILE AILLINN   V   16
CALLED RATHER BAILE LITTLE LAND, .  . . . . . . . . . .  189 BAILE AILLINN   V   17
BAILE AND AILLINN WOULD BE WED.  . . . . . . . . . . .  190 BAILE AILLINN       24
I RUN TO BAILE HONEY-MOUTH, .  . . . . . . . . . . . .  191 BAILE AILLINN       48
I RUN TO BAILE HONEY MOUTH .  . . . . . . . . . . . . .  191 BAILE AILLINN   V   48
BAILE, THAT WAS OF RURY'S SEED, .  . . . . . . . . . .  194 BAILE AILLINN      118
BAILE AND AILLINN'S MARRIAGE-BED,  . . . . . . . . . .  194 BAILE AILLINN      121
BAILE AND AILLINN'S MARRIAGE BED, .  . . . . . . . . .  194 BAILE AILLINN   V  121
RIBH AT THE TOMB OF BAILE AND AILLINN .  . . . . . . .  554 RIBH AT TOMB         T
OF BAILE AND AILLINN YOU NEED NOT SPEAK, . . . . . . .  555 RIBH AT TOMB         6
```

BAILE'S

```
BAILE'S HEART WAS BROKEN IN TWO!  . . . . . . . . . . .  192 BAILE AILLINN       70
```

BAKE

```
AND THEN I MUST SCRUB AND BAKE AND SWEEP .  . . . . . .  150 OLD MOTHER           3
AND THEN I MUST MEND AND BAKE AND SWEEP .  . . . . . .  150 OLD MOTHER      V    3
```

BAKED

```
INSIPID AS THE DOUGH BEFORE IT IS BAKED, .  . . . . .  376 PHASES OF MOON     112
AND AFTER BAKED IT SLOWLY IN AN OVEN! BUT NOW . . . .  442 BLACK CENTAUR        9
```

BALANCE

```
IN BALANCE WITH THIS LIFE, THIS DEATH. .  . . . . . .  328 IRISH AIRMAN        16
```

BALANCED

```
THAT BALANCED WITH A WORD IS MORE THAN NOISE!  . . . .  258 KING NO KING         4
I BALANCED ALL, BROUGHT ALL TO MIND, .  . . . . . . .  328 IRISH AIRMAN        13
SEA-BORNE, OR BALANCED ON THE AIR .  . . . . . . . . .  397 POLIT PRISONER      19
```

BALD

```
YOU WHO ARE BENT, AND BALD, AND BLIND, .  . . . . . .    2 OISIN 1             1
AH, SWEET TO ME NOW WERE EVEN BALD CONAN'S SLANDEROUS   55 OISIN 3            116
   TONGUE!
BALD HEADS FORGETFUL OF THEIR SINS, .  . . . . . . . .  337 SCHOLARS             1
OLD, LEARNED, RESPECTABLE BALD HEADS .  . . . . . . .  337 SCHOLARS             2
```

BALES

```
WHERE THE BALES AND THE BASKETS LAY .  . . . . . . . .  578 CRAZED GIRL         12
```

BALL   SEE THUNDER-BALL

```
ABOUT HIS FADING CRIMSON BALL! .  . . . . . . . . . .   12 OISIN 1            155
IN SILENCE ROUND HIS CRIMSON BALL. .  . . . . . . . .   12 OISIN 1         V  155
AND THE KINGFISHER TURNS TO A BALL OF DUST, . . . . .   27 OISIN 1         V  418
AND THE KINGFISHER TURNS TO A BALL OF DUST, . . . . .   28 OISIN 1            422
```

BALLAD

```
THE BALLAD OF FATHER O'HART .  . . . . . . . . . . . .   91 FATHER OHART         T
THE BALLAD OF MOLL MAGEE .  . . . . . . . . . . . . .   94 MOLL MAGEE           T
THE BALLAD OF THE FOXHUNTER .  . . . . . . . . . . . .   97 FOXHUNTER            T
```

BALLAD   (CONTINUED)
   THE BALLAD OF THE OLD FOX-HUNTER . . . .   97 FOXHUNTER   V   T
   THE BALLAD OF THE OLD FOXHUNTER . . . .   97 FOXHUNTER   V   T
   THE BALLAD OF FATHER GILLIGAN . . . .   132 FR GILLIGAN   T
   BALLAD AND STORY, RANN AND SONG: . . . .   137 TO IRELAND   4
   AS THOUGH SOME BALLAD SINGER HAD SUNG IT ALL. . . . . .   602 GALLERY REVIS V   24
   THE BALLAD OF EARL PAUL . . . .   739 EARL PAUL   T
BALLAD-SINGER
   AS THOUGH SOME BALLAD-SINGER HAD SUNG IT ALL: . . . . .   602 GALLERY REVIS   24
BALLINAFAD
   KEENING FROM BALLINAFAD: . . . .   93 FATHER OHART   36
BALLOON
   THE BALLOON OF THE MIND . . . .   358 BALLOON MIND   T
   BRING THE BALLOON OF THE MIND . . . .   358 BALLOON MIND   2
BALLS   SEE PUFF-BALLS BOMB-BALLS EYE-BALLS
   I COUNT THOSE FEATHERED BALLS OF SOOT . . . .   424 ROAD AT DOOR   11
BALLYLEE
   TO BE CARVED ON A STONE AT THOOR BALLYLEE . . . . . .   406 CARVED STONE   T
   TO BE CARVED ON A STONE AT BALLYLEE . . . .   406 CARVED STONE   V   T
   COOLE PARK AND BALLYLEE, [NINETEEN-THIRTY-ONE] . . . .   490 COOLE BALLYLEE   T
   COOLE PARK AND BALLYLEE [NINETEEN-THIRTY-TWO] . . . .   490 COOLE BALLYLEE V   T
   COOLE AND BALLYLEE, [NINETEEN-THIRTY-ONE] . . . . . .   490 COOLE BALLYLEE V   T
BALOR
   DARK BALOR, AS OLD AS A FOREST, CAR-BORNE, HIS MIGHTY HEAD   53 OISIN 3   91
      SUNK
   CAME CAR-BORNE BALOR, AS OLD AS A FOREST, HIS VAST FACE   53 OISIN 3   V   91
      SUNK
   CAME BALOR, AS OLD AS A FOREST, CAR BORNE, HIS MIGHTY HEAD   53 OISIN 3   V   91
      SUNK
BAN
   NOR WAS HE BISHOP WHEN HIS BAN . . . .   508 JANE BISHOP   8
   THAT SHE IS UNDER BAN . . . .   531 FATHER CHILD   2
BAND
   AND FROM THE WOODS RUSHED OUT A BAND . . . .   15 OISIN 1   201
   AND FROM THE WOODS THERE RUSHED A BAND . . . .   15 OISIN 1   V 201
   AND, GATHERED IN A PANTING BAND, ...   22 OISIN 1   324
   WHILE HUSHED FROM FEAR, OR LOUD WITH HOPE, A BAND . .   114 ROSE OF BATTLE   5
   AND IF ANY GAZE ON OUR RUSHING BAND, ...   141 HOSTING SIDHE   10
   RODE OUT OF EMAIN WITH A BAND . . . .   189 BAILE AILLINN   18
   PERNING IN A BAND, ...   599 SPIRIT MEDIUM   6
   THOUGH YOUNGEST OF ALL IN OUR GOOD BAND, ...   707 FAIRY PEDANT   11
   THOUGH YOUNGEST OF ALL IN OUR GOOD BAND, ...   708 FAIRY PEDANT   39
   SERENE. THEY'RE LED AWAY, AND WHERE A BAND . . . . .   712 FERENCZ RENYI   63
   HALF DIZZY WITH THE LIGHTNING THERE RUNS A GATHERING BAND-- 718 PHANTOM SHIP   9
   NOW HALF DIZZY WITH THE LIGHTNING THERE RUNS A GATHERING   718 PHANTOM SHIP V   9
      BAND:
BANDAGING
   THEN CLEANING OUT AND BANDAGING OF WOUNDS, ...   622 HOUND VOICE   20
BANDED
   THE SKY WAS BANDED O'ER WITH WRACK. . . . .   667 ISLE STAT II 3   23
   WAS BANDED AS AN ADDER'S BACK, ...   667 ISLE STAT II 3 V   23
   ABODE, AS BANDED ADDERS IN MY BREAST. . . . .   683 SEEKER   50
BANDIT
   WITH A RAGGED BANDIT CLOAK, ...   627 STATES HOLIDAY   31
BANDS
   WRESTLED AMONG THE ISLAND BANDS. . . . .   23 OISIN 1   350
   "MY FATHER DWELLS AMONG THE SEA-WORN BANDS, ...   107 CUCHULAIN SEA V   25
   AWAY FROM THE MERRY BANDS, ...   144 HOST OF AIR   22
   AND NEVER ANY MORE THE WIDE-EYED BANDS . . . .   674 ISLE STAT II 3   218
   AND SHE IS DRAGGED TO WHERE THE WILLOW BANDS . . . . .   714 FERENCZ RENYI   108
BANDY
   UPON ITS BANDY LEGS, RUN AT THEM NOW, ...   233 SHADOW WATER B   239
BANDY-LEGGED
   YET CHOSE A BANDY-LEGGED SMITH FOR MAN. . . . .   404 FOR DAUGHTER   29
BANE   SEE STAR-BANE
   "O WHAT OF THE WORLD'S BANE?" . . . .   214 HAPPY TOWNLAND   14
   THAT IS THE WORLD'S BANE." . . . .   214 HAPPY TOWNLAND   20
   O WHAT IS THE WORLD'S BANE?, ...   214 HAPPY TOWNLAND V   REF
   "O WHAT OF THE WORLD'S BANE?" . . . .   215 HAPPY TOWNLAND   34
   THAT IS THE WORLD'S BANE." . . . .   215 HAPPY TOWNLAND   40
   "O WHAT OF THE WORLD'S BANE?" . . . .   216 HAPPY TOWNLAND   54
   THAT IS THE WORLD'S BANE." . . . .   216 HAPPY TOWNLAND   60
BANISH
   WILL BANISH EVERY THOUGHT, UNLESS . . . .   387 ROBARTES DANCE   48
   BANISH AGE AND CARE, ...   620 JOHN KINSELLA   20
BANISHED
   BANISHED HEROIC MOTHER MOON AND VANISHED, ...   344 DEJECTION   9
   THE HOLY CENTAURS OF THE HILLS ARE BANISHED: . . . .   344 DEJECTION   V   7
   BANISHED JACK THE JOURNEYMAN, ...   508 JANE BISHOP   9
   POETRY AND MUSIC I HAVE BANISHED, ...   600 SPIRIT MEDIUM   19
BANK
   UPON EUROTAS' GRASSY BANK . . . .   522 LULLABY   14
   BEFORE A DEATH, O'ER WAVE AND BANK . . . .   673 ISLE STAT II 3   185
BANKERS
   OF BANKERS, SCHOOLMASTERS, AND CLERGYMEN . . . . . .   205 ADAMS CURSE   13
BANKRUPT
   AN ANCIENT BANKRUPT MASTER OF THIS HOUSE. . . . . . .   412 TOWER   80
BANKS
   AND NOT THE BANKS OF OARS THAT SWAM UPON . . . . . .   610 STATUES   13
   OF YONDER LAKE, FROM WHOSE GREEN BANKS ALWAY . . . .   653 ISLE STAT I 2   33
   FROM WHOSE GREEN BANKS NO LIVING THING MAY ROVE, . . .   664 ISLE STAT II 2   57

		PAGE	TITLE		LINE

BANKS   (CONTINUED)
    THE BANKS ARE WORN FOR EVER • • • • • • • • •   680 LOVE AND DEATH   9
BANNER
    A WOMAN'S BEAUTY IS A STORM-TOSSED BANNER• • • • • • •   469 HARUN RASHID   188
    IS BUT A HEAVY, GOLD EMBROIDERED BANNER, • • • • • • •   469 HARUN RASHID   V 188
BANNERET
    WITH BANNERET AND PENNON, • • • • • • • • • • • •   317 NIGHT COME   8
BANNERS   SEE BATTLE-BANNERS
    FROM BATTLE BANNERS FOLD UPON PURPLE FOLD, • • • • • • •   162 ASKS FORGIVE   V   11
    THE BANNERS OF EAST AND WEST, • • • • • • • • •   165 CRY OF SEDGE   7
    WHERE BANNERS OF THE CALIPHS HANG, NIGHT-COLOURED • • • •   461 HARUN RASHID   6
    WHERE GOLD-EMBROIDERED BANNERS OF THE CALIF'S • • • •   461 HARUN RASHID   V   6
    BANNERS CHOKE THE SKY• • • • • • • • • • • •   512 JANE ON GOD   7
    THOSE BANNERS COME NOT IN• • • • • • • • • •   635 BLACK TOWER   6
    THOSE BANNERS COME TO BRIBE OR THREATEN, • • • • • •   635 BLACK TOWER   11
    AMID A CLOUD OF BANNERS, • • • • • • • • • •   741 EARL PAUL   39
BANQUET
    "THE RED BRANCH KINGS A TIRELESS BANQUET KEEP, • • • •   108 CUCHULAIN SEA V   33
    AT A BEANFEAST OR A BANQUET, • • • • • • • • •   583 GHOST ROG CASE   15
    AT A BEANFEST OR A BANQUET, • • • • • • • • •   583 GHOST ROG CASE V   15
    HIS TEMPLE AND HIS BANQUET HALL• • • • • • • •   671 ISLE STAT II 3   134
BANSHEE
    YOU WILL WITH THE BANSHEE CHAT, • • • • • • • •   726 LOVERS QUARREL   9
BAR
    TO BAR THAT FOUL STORM OUT, FOR WE • • • • • • •   432 NINETEEN 19   111
    BOLT AND BAR THE SHUTTER, • • • • • • • • • •   523 MAD AS MIST   1
BARACH
    COOK BARACH, THE TRAITOR• AND WARWARD, • • • • • • •   53 OISIN 3   90
BARB
    RECALL THE CRETAN BARB THAT PIERCED A STAR? • • • • •   541 PARN FUNERAL 1   7
BARBAROUS
    AND I SPEAK A BARBAROUS TONGUE. • • • • • • • •   313 TWO YEAR LATER   12
    THERE'LL BE THAT CROWD, THAT BARBAROUS CROWD, • • • • •   354 HIS PHOENIX   25
    GOES TO THE BARBAROUS CLANGOUR OF A GONG. • • • • • •   430 NINETEEN 19   58
    GOES TO THE BARBAROUS CLANGOUR OF GONG.• • • • • • •   430 NINETEEN 19   V   58
    SOME BARBAROUS, UN-FAERY THING DRAW NEAR. • • • • • •   656 ISLE STAT I 3   21
BARBS
    PIERCING THE TWILIGHT WITH THEIR MURMURING BARBS. • • •   72 ANASHU VIJAYA   28
BARCELONA
    AT BARCELONA • • • • • • • • • • • • • • •   578 CRAZED GIRL   V   T
BARD
    BARD OISIN, BOAST NOT OF THY DEEDS • • • • • • •   11 OISIN 1   V 129
    THAN THIS STRANGE HUMAN BARD," HE CRIED• • • • • •   17 OISIN 1   V 239
    THAN THIS STRANGE BARD," HE CRIED, AND CAUGHT • • • •   17 OISIN 1   V 239
    AND SORROW AWAY, AND CALLING BARD AND CLOWN • • • • •   170 SECRET ROSE   20
BARE   SEE THREAD-BARE CLOOTH-NA-BARE
    OVER THE BARE AND WOODY LAND, • • • • • • • •   15 OISIN 1   198
    AND ON THE RUNNEL'S STONY AND BARE EDGE • • • • • •   39 OISIN 2   157
    ACROSS THE BARE BOREEN. • • • • • • • • • • •   95 MOLL MAGEE   32
    BLUE-EYED, AND A QUICK RUNNER ON BARE FEET, • • • • •   242 SHADOW WATER B   416
    I WEEP--I WEEP BECAUSE BARE NIGHT'S ABOVE, • • • • •   246 SHADOW WATER B   499
    "AND MAKE MY SOUL BEFORE MY PATE IS BARE." • • • • •   299 BEGGAR CRIED   4
    THAT TOSSED A BARE HEEL WHEN AT SCHOOL, • • • • • •   301 RUN PARADISE   19
    THE BARE CHIMNEY IS GONE BLACK OUT • • • • • • •   327 ROBERT GREGORY   84
    BROUGHT THE BARE NEWS. HE HAD THROWN THE CROOK AWAY • •   339 SHEP GOATHERD   21
    FOR LARDER AND SPIT ARE BARE, • • • • • • • •   349 HAWK   4
    WHEN ALL IS FED WITH LIGHT AND HEAVEN IS BARE. • • • •   375 PHASES OF MOON   74
    BUT GREGORY'S WOOD AND ONE BARE HILL • • • • • • •   403 FOR DAUGHTER   4
    BUT GREGORY'S WOODS AND ONE BARE HILL • • • • • • •   403 FOR DAUGHTER   V   4
    TO THIS BARE SOUL, LET ALL MEN JUDGE THAT CAN • • • •   542 PARN FUNERAL 1   30
    THAT STRIP THE BODY BARE.• • • • • • • • • •   570 THREE BUSHES   27
    BECAUSE WE LOVE BARE HILLS AND STUNTED TREES • • • • •   621 HOUND VOICE   1
    THOSE GREAT SEA-HORSES BARE THEIR TEETH AND LAUGH AT THE   623 HIGH TALK   14
        DAWN.
    UNDER BARE BEN BULBEN'S HEAD • • • • • • • • •   640 BEN BULBEN   84
BARGAIN
    YOU HAVE TAKEN PAY AND MADE YOUR BARGAIN FOR IT• • • • •   225 SHADOW WATER B   68
    FOR THAT WAS IN THE BARGAIN WHEN WE STRUCK IT• • • • •   225 SHADOW WATER B V 68D
    THE EVER-LIVING HAVE KEPT MY BARGAIN FOR ME, • • • •   232 SHADOW WATER B   223
    HIS BARGAIN • • • • • • • • • • • • • •   520 HIS BARGAIN   T
    A BARGAIN WITH THAT HAIR • • • • • • • • • •   520 HIS BARGAIN   11
    THOUGH STIFF TO STRIKE A BARGAIN, • • • • • • •   620 JOHN KINSELLA   13
    HER BARGAIN STRUCK WE LAUGHED AND TALKED • • • • •   620 JOHN KINSELLA   15
BARHAIM
    AYE, AND ACHILLES, TIMOR, BABAR, BARHAIM, ALL • • • • •   366 HER COURAGE   9
BARK
    • • • IMMENSE IN THEIR WRINKLING BARK• • • • • •   48 OISIN 3   17
    THE WAILING GREW DISTANT• I RODE BY THE WOODS OF • • •   56 OISIN 3   137
        THE WRINKLING BARK,
    CUT OUT OUR RHYMES ON STRIPS OF NEW-TORN BARK • • • •   343 SHEP GOATHERD   115
BARKED
    HOWLED, MIAU-D, BARKED, BRAYED, BELLED, YELLED, CRIED,   387 SOLOMON WITCH   8
        CROWED,
    BUT NO DOGS BARKED, AND MIDNIGHTS CHIMED, • • • • •   570 THREE BUSHES   29
    AND NO DOGS BARKED THROUGH MIDNIGHTS CHIMED • • • •   570 THREE BUSHES   V   29
BARKING
    BARKING. WE TRAMPLED UP AND DOWN WITH BLOWS • • • •   40 OISIN 2   170
    BARKING. ALONG THE HERBLESS PLAIN, WITH BLOWS • • • •   40 OISIN 2   V 170
BARLEY
    AND BOWLS OF BARLEY, HONEY, AND WINE, • • • • • •   3 OISIN 1   8
    AND OVER THE MICE IN THE BARLEY SHEAVES• • • • • • •   79 FALLING LEAVES   2

BARLEY   (CONTINUED)
    IN THE LAST RIDGE OF THE BARLEY? DO OUR WOODS . . . . . 218 WOODS OF COOLE   33
    OF THE BARLEY SHOOTS IN THE SUN. . . . . 643 SONG FAERIES   8
    OF THE BARLEY SHOOTS IN THE SUN. . . . . 676 ISLE STAT II 3   255
    THERE'S BARLEY THERE, AND WATER THERE, ... 774 COME RIDE   7
BARNACLE   SEE GRASS-BARNACLE
    ALL METAPHOR, MALACHI, STILTS AND ALL. A BARNACLE GOOSE   623 HIGH TALK   11
BARNACLE-GEESE
    "THE WIND-BLOWN CLAMOUR OF THE BARNACLE-GEESE." . . . . 300 BEGGAR CRIED   20
BARRED
    THE BARRED WOODPECKER'S MANSION IS AND DEEP. . . . . . 659 ISLE STAT II 1   23
    FLOATING FROM YON BARRED WINDOW. SMALL NEW-COMER, . . . 700 MOSADA 3   43
    FLOATING FROM YON BARRED WINDOW. NEW COMER, ... 700 MOSADA 3   V 43
BARREL
    MADE LOCK, STOCK AND BARREL . . . . 415 TOWER   150
    I BRING FULL-FLAVOURED WINE OUT OF A BARREL FOUND . . . 442 BLACK CENTAUR   10
    I BRING FULL FLAVOURED WINE OUT OF A BARREL FOUND . . . 442 BLACK CENTAUR V   10
BARREL-HOOPS
    THERE ALL THE BARREL-HOOPS ARE KNIT, ... 557 THERE   1
BARRELS
    BETWEEN TWO BARRELS AT THE INN. . . . . 551 SONGS REWRIT 1   10
BARREN
    WITH BARREN WORDS AND FLATTERIES OF THE WEAK. . . . . . 42 OISIN 2   197
    . . . THE SEA'S EDGE BARREN AND GREY, ... 48 OISIN 3   13
    . . . WHERE ALL IS BARREN AND GREY, ... 56 OISIN 3   141
    I TORE IT FROM THE BARREN BOUGHS OF EIRE, ... 130 BOOK STORIES   15
    IN BARREN HILLS AND MARSHY LAND, ... 150 WANDER AENGUS V   18
    MY BARREN THOUGHTS HAVE CHILLED ME TO THE BONE. . . . . 257 RECONCILIATION   12
    PARDON THAT FOR A BARREN PASSION'S SAKE, ... 270 PARDON FATHERS   19
    THEY SAY THAT ON YOUR BARREN MOUNTAIN RIDGE . . . . . 342 SHEP GOATHERD   79
    THROUGH BARREN THEBAID, ... 401 DEMON BEAST   44
    AND BARREN AS A BREAKING WAVE . . . . 456 FRIENDS YOUTH   11
    WEARY OF REAPING THE BARREN NIGHT . . . . 648 ISLE STAT I 1   84
BARRENNESS
    FOR ALL THINGS TURN TO BARRENNESS . . . . 135 TWO TREES   29
    ALL THINGS TURN TO BARRENNESS . . . . 135 TWO TREES   V 29
BARRICADE
    A BARRICADE OF STONE OR OF WOOD: . . . . 425 STARES NEST   11
BARROW
    AND IN SOME GLOOMY BARROW LIE . . . . 19 OISIN 1   272
BARROWS
    FEASTED, AND WEPT THE BARROWS OF HIS DEAD: . . . . . . 170 SECRET ROSE   18
BARS
    AND BENDING DOWN BESIDE THE GLOWING BARS, ... 121 YOU ARE OLD   9
    CASEMENT UPON TRIAL, HALF HIDDEN BY THE BARS, ... 601 GALLERY REVIS   3
    WITH THREE BARS CROSSED. AND THESE FOUR WALLS MY WORLD, 700 MOSADA 3   32
    COOKING CHESTNUTS ON THE BARS-- . . . . 737 IN FIRELIGHT   2
    COOKING CHESTNUTS ON THE BARS. . . . . 737 IN FIRELIGHT   12
BARTER
    MAY SURELY BARTER GAZE FOR GAZE. . . . . 139 TO IRELAND   28
    BARTER THAT HORN AND EVERY GOOD . . . . 405 FOR DAUGHTER   62
BARTERED
    TO SEE MEN'S SOULS BARTERED AND BOUGHT. . . . . 136 TWO TREES   V 36
BASALT
    A HUNDRED HORSEMEN ON THE BASALT FLOOR . . . . 36 OISIN 2   102
BASALTIC
    BASALTIC PILLARS MARRED WITH HEW AND HACK . . . . . . 31 OISIN 2   V 30
    BASALTIC, MIGHT HAVE PACED. WE HELD OUR WAY . . . . . 36 OISIN 2   V 103
BASE
    ALL THAT ARE DIFFERENT OF A BASE INTENT: . . . . . . 398 LEADERS CROWD   2
    AND LET ALL BASE AMBITION BE, ... 460 THREE MONUMENT   9
    BASE DROVE OUT THE BETTER BLOOD, ... 626 STATES HOLIDAY   3
    BASE-BORN PRODUCTS OF BASE BEDS. . . . . 639 BEN BULBEN   73
BASE-BORN
    BASE-BORN PRODUCTS OF BASE BEDS. . . . . 639 BEN BULBEN   73
BASIN
    AND RAINS DOWN LIFE UNTIL THE BASIN SPILLS, ... 417 ANCEST HOUSES   4
    AND FALLS INTO THE BASIN OF THE MIND . . . . 478 SELF AND SOUL   34
BASKETS
    WHERE THE BALES AND THE BASKETS LAY . . . . 578 CRAZED GIRL   12
BAT
    SHOULD BE SO SIMPLE--A BAT ROSE FROM THE HAZELS . . . . 377 PHASES OF MOON   137
BATED
    AND MURMUR IT WITH BATED BREATH, AS THOUGH . . . . . . 398 LEADERS CROWD   5
    SHE WILL SAY WITH BATED BREATH, ... 680 LOVE AND DEATH   30
BATHE
    THAT SCARCE COULD BATHE A STAR, ... 88 STOLEN CHILD   31
BATHED
    BATHED IN FLAMING FOUNTS OF DUTY . . . . 124 CATHLEEN PARA   5
    BATHED IN MIRACULOUS OIL, SWEET ODOURS FROM IT COME, . . 503 VACILLATION   81
BATHING
    NOW BATHING LILY LEAF AND FISH'S SCALE, ... 464 HARUN RASHID   65
    NOW BATHING LILY LEAF AND FISHES' SCALE, ... 464 HARUN RASHID   V 65
BATS
    OUTCRY OF BATS. AND THEN YOUNG NIAMH CAME . . . . . . 44 OISIN 2   229
    OF PASSIONATE MEN, LIKE BATS IN THE DEAD TREES: . . . . 136 TO SOME I TALK   5
    WHEN THE BATS CRIED OUT NO MORE: . . . . 159 CAP AND BELLS V   14
    CRYING TO ONE ANOTHER LIKE THE BATS: . . . . 376 PHASES OF MOON   106
    I CANNOT SEE. THE BEETLES, AND THE BATS, ... 693 MOSADA 1   63
BATTER
    WE WILL TEAR OUT THE FLAMING STONES, AND BATTER THE GATEWAY   62 OISIN 3   209
      OF BRASS

BATTER   (CONTINUED)
    • • • AND WILL BATTER THE GATEWAY OF BRASS • • • • • •   62 OISIN 3   V 209
BATTERED
    "THIS DEMON SHALL BE BATTERED TILL HE DIE, • • • • • •   35 OISIN 2   90
    CAN BE SO BATTERED, BADGERED AND DESTROYED • • • • • •   130 BOOK STORIES   17
    BUT DESOLATE WATERS AND A BATTERED SHIP, • • • • • •   246 SHADOW WATER B   497
    ON GREAT-GRANDFATHER'S BATTERED TOMB." • • • • • • •   331 ROUND TOWER   6
    UPON A GREY OLD BATTERED TOMBSTONE • • • • • • • •   331 ROUND TOWER   7
    UPON THE GREY OLD BATTERED TOMBSTONE • • • • • • •   331 ROUND TOWER   V 7
    ON GREAT-GRANDFATHER'S BATTERED TOMB." • • • • • • •   332 ROUND TOWER   30
    ON GREAT GRANDFATHER'S BATTERED TOMB." • • • • • • •   332 ROUND TOWER   V 30
    A SORT'OF BATTERED KETTLE AT THE HEEL. • • • • • •   409 TOWER   16
    BATTERED TO DEATH IN A CELLAR, • • • • • • • • •   628 JANE MOUNTAIN   9
BATTERING
    A BLIND MAN BATTERING BLIND MEN; • • • • • • • • •   479 SELF AND SOUL   60
BATTERY
    ASSAULT AND BATTERY OF THE WIND • • • • • • • •   405 FOR DAUGHTER   55
BATTLE
    AND BROKE THE HEAVING RANKS OF BATTLE! • • • • • •   10 OISIN 1   124
    WHILE HIS HEART STILL DREAMS OF BATTLE AND LOVE • • •   27 OISIN 1   406
    FOR BATTLE." "FLY YE FROM A THING SO DREAD. • • • •   35 OISIN 2   90
    AND ONCE MORE TO A DAY-LONG BATTLE FELL, • • • • •   43 OISIN 2   V 218
    "WITH ALL IN ALL THE WORLD I BATTLE WAGE. • • • • •   45 OISIN 2   V 240
    HOW THE FETLOCKS DRIP BLOOD IN THE BATTLE, • • • • •   52 OISIN 3   78
    WAGE AN ETERNAL BATTLE, AND I FEEL • • • • • • •   104 FERGUS DRUID   V 38C
    HAS WON THE GOLD HIS CARS OF BATTLE BRING." • • • •   106 CUCHULAIN SEA   11
    "AND BREAKS THE RIDGE OF BATTLE WITH HIS HANDS." • •   107 CUCHULAIN SEA   V 26
    MY FATHER STANDS AMID HIS BATTLE CARS." • • • • • •   107 CUCHULAIN SEA   V 26
    AND WEARY OF THE CRASH OF BATTLE CARS." • • • • • •   107 CUCHULAIN SEA   V 30
    THE CARS OF BATTLE AND HIS OWN NAME CRIED! • • • • •   111 CUCHULAIN SEA   85
    THE ROSE OF BATTLE • • • • • • • • • • • • •   113 ROSE OF BATTLE   T
    THEY WENT FORTH TO THE BATTLE, BUT THEY ALWAYS FELL • •   113 ROSE OF BATTLE V   T
    AND HUSHED IN SLEEP THE ROARING RANKS OF BATTLE! • •   129 BOOK STORIES   7
    FROM BATTLE BANNERS FOLD UPON PURPLE FOLD, • • • • •   162 ASKS FORGIVE   V 11
    BUT ALL THAT ARE KILLED IN BATTLE • • • • • • • •   215 HAPPY TOWNLAND   25
    A LUCKY BATTLE, OR A WOMAN'S KISS • • • • • • • •   227 SHADOW WATER B   115
    WHERE THE GREAT BATTLE WAS • • • • • • • • • •   512 JANE ON GOD   10
    I WALK IN A BATTLE FOUGHT OVER AGAIN, • • • • • •   591 WHAT WAS LOST   2
    ITS GREAT BATTLE LOST, • • • • • • • • • • •   617 LONG-LEG FLY   2
    VAIN GAIETY, VAIN BATTLE, VAIN REPOSE, • • • • • •   629 CIRCUS ANIMALS   12
    IF WHEN THE BATTLE IS HALF WON, • • • • • • • •   743 DANAAN QUICK   19
    IN DAY OUT-LIVING BATTLE, ON THE BREAST • • • • •   750 SHADOW WATER A   73
    BEND LOWER LEST YOUR BATTLE AXES GLIMMER. • • • • •   752 SHADOW WATER A V 117
    THOUGH BATTLE JOY MAY BE SO DEAR • • • • • • • •   791 REPRISALS   7
BATTLE-AXE
    OF SWORD AND BRAZEN BATTLE-AXE, WHILE DAY • • • • •   40 OISIN 2   171
BATTLE-AXES
    BEND LOWER LEST YOUR BATTLE-AXES GLIMMER. • • • • •   752 SHADOW WATER A   117
BATTLE-BANNERS
    FROM BATTLE-BANNERS, FOLD UPON PURPLE FOLD, • • • • •   162 ASKS FORGIVE   11
BATTLE-BREAKING
    I CALLED MY BATTLE-BREAKING MEN • • • • • • •   83 MAD KING GOLL   17
BATTLE-CARS
    AND MY LOUD BRAZEN BATTLE-CARS • • • • • • • •   83 MAD KING GOLL   18
    MY FATHER STANDS AMID HIS BATTLE-CARS." • • • • • •   107 CUCHULAIN SEA   26
    ON FOOT, ON HORSEBACK OR IN BATTLE-CARS." • • • • •   107 CUCHULAIN SEA   30
BATTLE-HOST
    RIDING TO HURLEY, OR IN THE BATTLE-HOST • • • • • •   229 SHADOW WATER B   169
BATTLEMENT
    UPON THE BROKEN, CRUMBLING BATTLEMENT, • • • • • • •   477 SELF AND SOUL   3
BATTLEMENTS
    I PACE UPON THE BATTLEMENTS AND STARE • • • • • •   409 TOWER   17
BATTLES
    OF BATTLES BROKEN BY HIS HANDS, • • • • • • • •   7 OISIN 1   67
    THAT WE MAY MUSE IN THE STARLIGHT AND TALK OF THE BATTLES 51 OISIN 3   63
        OF OLD;
    TURN IF YOU MAY FROM BATTLES NEVER DONE, • • • • • •   114 ROSE OF BATTLE   7
    AND WAGE GOD'S BATTLES IN THE LONG GREY SHIPS. • • • •   114 ROSE OF BATTLE   20
    "FROM THE GREY SHIPS AND BATTLES NEVER WON. • • • • •   114 ROSE OF BATTLE V   8
    OUT OF THE BATTLES OF OLD TIMES. • • • • • • • •   158 BELOVED RHYMES   6
    IT WAS IN ALL HIS BATTLES. I WILL SPREAD MY HAIR, • • •   242 SHADOW WATER B   413
    SINGING OF ARMS AND BATTLES SOME OLD STAVE, • • • •   650 ISLE STAT I 1   137
    I FOUGHT TWELVE BATTLES DRESSED IN GOLDEN ARMOUR. • • •   761 SHADOW WATER A   271
BATTLE-WEARY
    AND CRIED TO BATTLE-WEARY MEN, • • • • • • • • •   502 VACILLATION   65
BATTLING
    CUCHULAIN BATTLING WITH THE BITTER TIDE; • • • • • •   100 ROSE UPON ROOD   3
BAUBLE
    DRIVE TO A FLASHIER BAUBLE YET. • • • • • • • •   437 SONGS PLAY 1   12
    YON BAUBLE OF THE HEAVENS, HE LIFTS HIS HANDS, • • • •   715 FERENCZ RENYI   119
BAWD
    NOW MY OLD BAWD IS DEAD? • • • • • • • • • • •   620 JOHN KINSELLA   12
    NOW MY OLD BAWD IS DEAD? • • • • • • • • • • •   621 JOHN KINSELLA   24
    NOW MY OLD BAWD IS DEAD? • • • • • • • • • • •   621 JOHN KINSELLA   36
BAWDY
    BAWDY TALK FOR THE FISHERMEN; • • • • • • • •   588 OLD WICKED MAN   32
BAWLS
    LOOKS AT THE CRADLE AND BAWLS; • • • • • • • • •   319 DOLLS   2
BAWN
    GOOD FELLOWS SHUFFLED CARDS IN AN OLD BAWN; • • • • •   411 TOWER   65

BAY
    NO MIGHTIER CREATURES BAY AT THE MOON! . . . .   8 OISIN 1   87
    AFTER A RAGGED HAT IN BISCAY BAY! . . . .   270 PARDON FATHERS   14
    BUT A GREAT DANE THAT CANNOT BAY THE MOON . . . . . .   579 DOR WELLESLEY   10
    UNTIL, IN SOME CLIFF-SHELTERED BAY . . . .   612 NEWS ORACLE   21
    ARE STILL THE ACHAIANS' TENTED CHIEFS AT BAY? . . . .   679 ISLE STAT II 3   310
BAYING
    WHEN WE FOLLOWED A DEER WITH OUR BAYING HOUNDS, . . .   3 OISIN 1   14
    OR KEEP US ALL AWAKE WITH BAYING AT THE MOON, ...   364 DOLLS FACES   11
    AND FOLLOWED UP THOSE BAYING CREATURES TOWARDS-- . . . 412 TOWER   72
BAYS
    DROPPING AT EVE IN CORAL BAYS . . . .   78 INDIAN TO LOVE V   19
    AND WOULD THROUGH HATRED OF THE BAYS . . . .   436 FOR MY SON   15
BEACON
    ALEXANDRIA'S WAS A BEACON TOWER, AND BABYLON'S . . . . 480 BLOOD AND MOON   13
BEADS
    HANDS THAT ARE BUSY WITH HIS BEADS . . . .   588 OLD WICKED MAN   25
    OVER THE BEADS OF HIS ROSARY. . . . .   730 PRIEST FAIRY   52
BEAK
    IN WHAT LAND DO THE POWERLESS TURN THE BEAK . . . . .   42 OISIN 2   198
    BEFORE THE INDIFFERENT BEAK COULD LET HER DROP? . . .   441 LEDA AND SWAN   14
BEAKED   SEE DARK-BEAKED
BEAM
    UNDER THE DAY'S DECLINING BEAM, AND CALL . . . . . .   410 TOWER   21
    ONE INEXTRICABLE BEAM, ...   411 TOWER   55
    WHERE THE SHAKING LEAF WITH THE BEAM WAS PLAYING, . .   728 PRIEST FAIRY   2
    A HURTING BEAM OF LIGHT, ...   741 EARL PAUL   38
BEAMS
    SCARCE SPREAD A GLORY TO THE MORNING BEAMS, ...   422 MY DESCENDANTS   6
    OF BEAMS A-FLICKER ON YON LONELY FIR, ...   661 ISLE STAT II 1   72
    THROUGH THIS NIGHT-VESTED PLACE THE RED BEAMS BREAK. . 662 ISLE STAT II 2   4
    O'ER GRIEF. THE WORLD DRINKS SORROW FROM THE BEAMS .   664 ISLE STAT II 2   46
    I HEAR THE MURMUR AS THEY RAISE THE BEAMS . . . . . .   699 MOSADA 3   17
BEAN
    NINE BEAN ROWS WILL I HAVE THERE, A HIVE FOR THE HONEY BEE 117 ISLE INNISFREE V   3
BEANFEAST
    AT A BEANFEAST OR A BANQUET, ...   583 GHOST ROG CASE   15
BEANFEST
    AT A BEANFEST OR A BANQUET, ...   583 GHOST ROG CASE V   15
BEAN-ROWS
    NINE BEAN-ROWS WILL I HAVE THERE, A HIVE FOR THE HONEY-BEE, 117 ISLE INNISFREE   3
BEAR
    THE SERVANTS BEAR THE BODY IN! . . . .   99 FOXHUNTER   47
    BEAR THE GOLD-EMBROIDERED DRESS-- . . . .   124 CATHLEEN PARA V   6
    BEAR THE GOLD EMBROIDERED DRESS-- . . . .   124 CATHLEEN PARA V   6
    I ALSO BEAR A BELL-BRANCH FULL OF EASE. . . . . . .   130 BOOK STORIES   12
    I ALSO BEAR A BELL BRANCH FULL OF EASE. . . . . . .   130 BOOK STORIES   V   12
    AND ALL THE TREMBLING FLOWERS THEY BEAR. . . . . . .   134 TWO TREES   4
    FOR WINDS WILL BEAR THEM GENTLY WHEN THE EAGLE FLIES, . 146 UNAPPEAS HOST V   3
    HOW DOES SHE BEAR HER GRIEF? THERE IS NOT A SHEPHERD . 340 SHEP GOATHERD   28
    I BEAR A BURDEN THAT MIGHT WELL TRY . . . .   380 SONGS FOOL 1   13
    BUT BEAR IN MIND YOUR LOVER'S WAGE . . . .   385 ROBARTES DANCE   14
    MAGICAL UNICORNS BEAR LADIES ON THEIR BACKS. . . . .   426 PHANTOM HATRED   18
    AND BEAR THAT BEATING HEART AWAY! . . . .   437 SONGS PLAY 1   5
    IT COULD NOT BEAR THAT BURDEN AND THEREFORE IT WENT MAD. 449 OWEN AHERNE   4
    BUT O! MY HEART COULD BEAR NO MORE WHEN THE UPLAND CAUGHT 450 OWEN AHERNE   11
        THE WIND!
    THAT IF THE SPRING BEAR OFF WHAT THE SPRING GAVE . . . 464 HARUN RASHID   76
    AND COULD BEGET OR BEAR THEMSELVES COULD THEY BUT LOVE   556 RIBH PATRICK   12
        AS HE.
    LIVE TO BEAR CHILDREN TO A DUNCE! . . . .   626 OLD MEN BE MAD   6
    LET THE SEA BEAR WITNESS, ...   770 BLOOD BOND   7
    LET THE WIND BEAR WITNESS, ...   770 BLOOD BOND   8
    LET THE EARTH BEAR WITNESS, ...   770 BLOOD BOND   9
    LET THE FIRE BEAR WITNESS, ...   770 BLOOD BOND   10
    LET THE DEW BEAR WITNESS, ...   770 BLOOD BOND   11
    LET THE STARS BEAR WITNESS! . . . .   770 BLOOD BOND   12
BEARD
    AND, PATRICK! BY YOUR BEARD, THEY WEPT, ...   17 OISIN 1   236
    OH, PATRICK, BY THY BEARD, THEY WEPT, ...   17 OISIN 1   V   236
    . . . THE SPITTLE ON HIS BEARD NEVER DRY, ...   53 OISIN 3   90
    I MUST GAZE ON THE BEARD OF FINN. . . . .   55 OISIN 3   114
    . . . WITH THE SPITTLE ON HIS BEARD NEVER DRY. . . .   60 OISIN 3   192
    WHOSE BEARD A MOONLIGHT RIVER IS, WHOSE BROW . . . .   657 ISLE STAT I 3   73
    UNTIL MY BEARD IS IN THE TWISTED LEAVES . . . . . .   683 SEEKER   44
    BEHOLD, I BEND! AROUND MY BEARD IN DRIFTS . . . . .   684 SEEKER   68
    BEHOLD I BOW! AROUND MY BEARD IN DRIFTS. . . . . .   684 SEEKER   V   68
    YET WHITER BEARD HAVE YOU THAN MERLIN HAD. . . . . .   721 WITCH VIVIEN   30
BEARDED
    A BEARDED WITCH, HER SLUGGISH HEAD LOW BENT . . . . .   685 SEEKER   72
    WHEN SOMETHING THAT WAS BEARDED LIKE A GOAT . . . . .   747 SHADOW WATER A   11
BEARDLESS
    ONE HAND UPHELD HIS BEARDLESS CHIN, ...   17 OISIN 1   250
    ONE HAND BENEATH HIS BEARDLESS CHIN, ...   17 OISIN 1   V   251
BEARDS
    THE ANCIENT BEARDS, THE HELMS OF RUBY AND GOLD . . . . 169 SECRET ROSE   8
BEARING   SEE CHILD-BEARING
BEARS
    OF WOLVES, OF BOREAL BEARS, WE QUAFFED THE WINE . . .   41 OISIN 2   V   188
    AND ON THE SKINS OF WOLVES AND BEARS WE SLEPT! . . . .   41 OISIN 2   V   191

                                                    PAGE   TITLE   LINE
BEARS   (CONTINUED)
    BECAUSE PIEBALD PONIES, LED BEARS, CAGED LIONS, MAKE BUT   623 HIGH TALK   5
        POOR SHOWS,
BEAST
    FROM GIRL AND BOY AND MAN AND BEAST: . . . .   82 MAD KING GOLL   6
    O BEAST OF THE WILDERNESS, BIRD OF THE AIR, ...   177 PAST GREATNESS   11
    AGAINST A BEECH-BOLE, HE THREW DOWN THE BEAST . . . . . .   278 TWO KINGS   36
    AGAINST A BEECH BOLE, HE THREW DOWN THE BEAST . . . . . .   278 TWO KINGS   V 36
    I WISHED BEFORE IT CEASED. NOR BIRD NOR BEAST . . . . . .   338 SHEP GOATHERD   2
    YEAR. I WISHED BEFORE IT CEASED. NOR BIRD NOR BEAST . . .   338 SHEP GOATHERD   V 2
    IS ALWAYS HAPPY LIKE A BIRD OR A BEAST: . . . .   373 PHASES OF MOON   38
    FROM TERRIFIED, INVISIBLE BEAST OR BIRD: . . . . 389 IMAGE PAST   6
    DEMON AND BEAST . . . .   399 DEMON BEAST   T
    THAT CRAFTY DEMON AND THAT LOUD BEAST . . . .   399 DEMON BEAST   2
    NOW THAT THE LOUD BEAST RAN . . . .   400 DEMON BEAST   16
    BELONGS TO BEAST OR DEMON, ... 401 DEMON BEAST   35
    AND WHAT ROUGH BEAST, ITS HOUR COME ROUND AT LAST, ... 402 SECOND COMING   21
    CRIED THAT WE LIVED LIKE BEAST AND BEAST: . . . .   508 JANE BISHOP   13
    CRIED THAT WE LIVED LIKE BEAST AND BEAST: . . . .   508 JANE BISHOP   13
    BIRD, BEAST, FISH OR MAN, ...   529 TOM LUNATIC   14
    SANG OF THE BEAST THAT GAVE THE FATAL WOUND. . . . .   537 HER VISION   16
    BEAST GAVE BEAST AS MUCH. . . . .   538 LAST CONFESS   12
    BEAST GAVE BEAST AS MUCH. . . . .   538 LAST CONFESS   12
    AS MAN, AS BEAST, AS AN EPHEMERAL FLY BEGETS, GODHEAD   556 RIBH PATRICK   5
        BEGETS GODHEAD,
    WHAT FROM THE FOREST CAME? WHAT BEAST HAS LICKED   560 MAGIC DRUM   6
        ITS YOUNG?
    LIKE A DUMB BEAST IN A SHOW, ...   572 LADYS 1ST SONG   2
    NO BETTER THAN A BEAST . . . .   572 LADYS 1ST SONG   11
    WITH EVERY NOBLE BEAST. . . . .   573 LADYS 2ND SONG   18
    OR SOME SMALL BEAST MOST WONDERFULLY FURR'D, ...   650 ISLE STAT I 1   148
BEASTS
    AMONG BIRDS OR BEASTS OR MEN . . . .   528 DANCER CRUACH   2
BEAST-TORN
    THAT THING ALL BLOOD AND MIRE, THAT BEAST-TORN WRECK, . .   537 HER VISION   25
BEAT   SEE BELL-BEAT
    BEAT TIME WITH THEIR BRIGHT WINGS AND FEET. . . . .   26 OISIN 1   V 397
    UPLIFTED GATEWAY. WITH THE FLASHING BEAT . . . .   31 OISIN 2   V 30D
    THEN TO HER SERVANTS, "BEAT HIM FROM THE DOOR . . . . . .   106 CUCHULAIN SEA   V 17A
    TO THOSE ABOUT, "BEAT HIM WITH THONGS OF HIDE . . . . . .   106 CUCHULAIN SEA   V 17A
    BEFORE YOU WERE, OR ANY HEARTS TO BEAT, ...   112 ROSE OF WORLD   12
    BEFORE YE WERE, OR ANY HEARTS TO BEAT, ... 112 ROSE OF WORLD   V 12
    AND THE WHITE HUSH END ALL BUT THE LOUD BEAT . . . .   137 TO SOME I TALK   15
    AND THE WHITE HUSH END ALL THINGS BUT THE BEAT . . . . . .   137 TO SOME I TALK   V 15
    MADE IRELAND'S HEART BEGIN TO BEAT: . . . .   138 TO IRELAND   12
    DESOLATE WINDS THAT BEAT THE DOORS OF HEAVEN, AND BEAT . .   147 UNAPPEAS HOST   9
    DESOLATE WINDS THAT BEAT THE DOORS OF HEAVEN, AND BEAT . .   147 UNAPPEAS HOST   9
    BELOVED, LET YOUR EYES HALF CLOSE, AND YOUR HEART BEAT . .   154 BELOVED PEACE   9
    AND ALL MEN'S HEARTS MUST BURN AND BEAT: . . . .   158 BELOVED RHYMES   9
    OF UNKNOWN PERISHING ARMIES BEAT ABOUT MY EARS. . . . . .   161 BLACK PIG   4
    LIKE TATTERED CLOUDS OF THE WORLD, PASSIONS CALL AND OUR   207 HANRAHANS SONG V   8
        HEARTS BEAT:
    AND BEAT THE BULWARK OF YOUR SHIP ON MINE. . . . .   236 SHADOW WATER B   312
    AND BEAT THE GOLDEN HELMET WITH THEIR SWORDS? . . . . . .   243 SHADOW WATER B   425
    AND AFTER SET YOUR HEART TO BEAT, ...   263 MASK   9
    WHAT MAKES YOUR HEART BEAT SO: . . . . 336 YOUNG GIRL   3
    FOR RHYME CAN BEAT A MEASURE OUT OF TROUBLE . . . .   339 SHEP GOATHERD   12
    A CRAZY JUICE THAT MAKES THE PULSES BEAT . . . .   384 VISION ROBART   54
    WHILE THEIR GREAT WOODEN DICE BEAT ON THE BOARD, ...   412 TOWER   88
    AND BEAT UPON THE BONE: . . . .   516 MANS SONG   6
    THE HAND AND LASH THAT BEAT DOWN FRIGID ROME? . . . . . .   560 WHENCE COME   10
    BEAT DOWN UPON THEIR NAKED BODIES, KNOW . . . .   563 MERU   12
    WHO BEAT UPON THE WALL . . . .   576 ACRE OF GRASS   17
    THEY ALWAYS BEAT ON THE SAME SMALL STONE. . . . .   591 WHAT WAS LOST   5
    AND I BEAT UP THE COMMON SORT . . . .   605 SONGS BURDEN 1   3
    BEAT OUT THEIR LIVES LAMENTING O'ER THE SAND: . . . . . .   652 ISLE STAT I 2   14
    BEAT ON IT WITH THEIR HAMMERS DAY AND NIGHT. . . . .   687 TWO TITANS   4
    WHY DOES MY HEART BEAT SO? . . . . 781 MY HEART BEAT   1
    WHY DOES YOUR HEART BEAT THUS? . . . . 785 YOUR HEART   1
    WHAT MAKES HER HEART BEAT THUS, ...   785 YOUR HEART   1
    WHAT MAKES YOUR HEART SO BEAT? . . . .   786 YOUR HEART   V 27
BEATEN   SEE WIND-BEATEN STORM-BEATEN RAIN-BEATEN
    BETWEEN THE WALLS COVERED WITH BEATEN BRONZE, ...   180 QUEEN MAEVE   10
    TILL ALL THE PLACE WAS BEATEN INTO MIRE. . . . .   278 TWO KINGS   27
    NOR ON THE ANCIENT BEATEN PATHS, THAT WOUND . . . .   279 TWO KINGS   52
    AND GREAT ART BEATEN DOWN. . . . .   348 FISHERMAN   24
    THERE HYDE BEFORE HE HAD BEATEN INTO PROSE . . . .   489 COOLE PARK 29   9
    UNTIL THE TOWN LIE BEATEN FLAT. . . . .   565 LAPIS LAZULI   8
    MY LANGUAGE BEATEN . . . .   572 LADYS 1ST SONG   5
    THE LOVERS AND THE DANCERS ARE BEATEN INTO THE CLAY, . .   580 CURSE CROMWELL   3
    AFRAID THEY MIGHT BE BEATEN . . . .   582 ROGER CASEMENT   5
    THAT WERE BEATEN INTO THE CLAY . . . .   640 BEN BULBEN   79
    AND UNDER HER HOOFS THE MARIGOLDS BEATEN. . . . .   729 PRIEST FAIRY   36
    AGAINST MY FACE AND EYES. MINE TOO ARE BEATEN. . . . . . .   759 SHADOW WATER A V   233
BEATING
    AS THOUGH THEY ALL WERE BEATING TIME, ...   13 OISIN 1   174
    BETWEEN THE PILLARS WITH A BEATING HEART . . . .   279 TWO KINGS   59
    THE BEATING DOWN OF THE WISE . . . .   348 FISHERMAN   23
    TILL I COULD HEAR THEIR HEARTS BEATING: . . . .   358 PRESENCES   11
    APPROPRIATE TO THAT BEATING BREAST, ...   386 ROBARTES DANCE   22
    AND BEAR THAT BEATING HEART AWAY: . . . .   437 SONGS PLAY 1   5

                                        64

		PAGE	TITLE	LINE
BEATING (CONTINUED)				
A SUDDEN BLOW! THE GREAT WINGS BEATING STILL		441	LEDA AND SWAN	1
BUT FEEL THE STRANGE HEART BEATING WHERE IT LIES?		441	LEDA AND SWAN	8
AND FEELS THE STRANGE HEART BEATING WHERE IT LIES!		441	LEDA AND SWAN V	8
AND HIS BEATING HEART WOULD BURST.		454	EMPTY CUP	6
SWIFT BEATING ON HIS BREAST IN SIBYLLINE FRENZY BLIND		481	BLOOD AND MOON	19
WINGS BEATING ABOUT THE ROOM!		499	MOTHER OF GOD	3
IS BEATING ON THE DOOR.		583	GHOST ROG CASE	10
IS BEATING ON THE DOOR.		583	GHOST ROG CASE	20
IS BEATING ON THE DOOR.		584	GHOST ROG CASE	30
IS BEATING ON THE DOOR.		584	GHOST ROG CASE	40
WITH OPEN MOUTH AND BEATING HEART.		729	PRIEST FAIRY	32
THE BEATING OF A LEV'RET'S HEART!		730	PRIEST FAIRY	69
WHAT SETS IT BEATING SO?		781	HEART FRIGHT	2
ITS STRANGE HEART BEATING FAST		785	YOUR HEART	6
BEATS				
THE HAND THAT WOUNDS. A WHITE BIRD BEATS HIS WINGS		758	SHADOW WATER A V	232
A WHITE BIRD BEATS HIS WINGS UPON MY FACE.		759	SHADOW WATER A	233
BEAUJOLET				
BUT THOSE OF BEAUJOLET.		336	YOUNG BEAUTY V	12
BEAUTIES				
AND YET THE BEAUTIES THAT I LOVED		131	OLD PENSIONER	15
AS COMMON BEAUTIES MAY,		336	YOUNG BEAUTY	9
SEE, I TELL THY BEAUTIES O'ER,		647	ISLE STAT I 1	56
BEAUTIFUL				
AND A BEAUTIFUL YOUNG MAN FOLLOWED BEHIND		12	OISIN 1	144
WAS A BEAUTIFUL YOUTH FROM AN UNKNOWN LAND.		12	OISIN 1 V	145
A BEAUTIFUL YOUNG MAN FOLLOWED BEHIND.		12	OISIN 1	145
A BEAUTIFUL YOUNG MAN DREAMED WITHIN.		17	OISIN 1	248
O HAD YOU SEEN BEAUTIFUL NIAMH GROW WHITE AS THE WATERS ARE WHITE,		54	OISIN 3	109
OH, HADST THOU SEEN BEAUTIFUL NIAM WAIL TO HERSELF AND BLANCH,		54	OISIN 3 V	109
O, HAD YOU SEEN BEAUTIFUL NEAVE WAIL TO HERSELF AND BLANCH,		54	OISIN 3 V	109
SHE WAS MORE BEAUTIFUL THAN THY FIRST LOVE,		123	DREAM OF DEATH	11
I HAD A BEAUTIFUL FRIEND		152	LOSS OF LOVE	2
SHE HAD BEEN BEAUTIFUL IN THAT OLD WAY		180	QUEEN MAEVE	19
AT NEED, AND MADE HER BEAUTIFUL AND FIERCE,		181	QUEEN MAEVE	29
THAT BEAUTIFUL MILD WOMAN, YOUR CLOSE FRIEND,		204	ADAMS CURSE	2
THAT BEAUTIFUL MILD WOMAN FOR WHOSE SAKE		205	ADAMS CURSE	15
THAT WE MUST LABOUR TO BE BEAUTIFUL."		205	ADAMS CURSE	20
PRECEDENTS OUT OF BEAUTIFUL OLD BOOKS!		205	ADAMS CURSE	26
THAT YOU WERE BEAUTIFUL, AND THAT I STROVE		206	ADAMS CURSE	35
"ALL THAT'S BEAUTIFUL DRIFTS AWAY .		208	OLD MEN ADMIRE	8
A BEAUTIFUL YOUNG MAN AND GIRL CAME UP		223	SHADOW WATER B	33
BUT OF A BEAUTIFUL, UNHEARD-OF KIND		228	SHADOW WATER B	142
HAS BEAUTIFUL WOMEN TO PLEASE EVERY MAN.		228	SHADOW WATER B	144
ALTHOUGH YOU ARE MORE BEAUTIFUL THAN ANY,		236	SHADOW WATER B	305
MYSTERIOUS, BEAUTIFUL!		323	SWANS AT COOLE	26
YOU ARE MORE BEAUTIFUL THAN ANY ONE,		356	BROKEN DREAMS	27
YOUR SMALL HANDS WERE NOT BEAUTIFUL,		356	BROKEN DREAMS	29
YOU WERE MORE BEAUTIFUL THAN ANY ONE,		356	BROKEN DREAMS V	27
YOU ARE MORE BEAUTIFUL THAN ANYONE		356	BROKEN DREAMS V	27
END IN A BEAUTIFUL MAN'S OR WOMAN'S BODY.		374	PHASES OF MOON	64
AND MUST NO BEAUTIFUL WOMAN BE .		386	ROBARTES DANCE	25
AND THAT ALL BEAUTIFUL WOMEN MAY		387	ROBARTES DANCE	45
WHEN, YOUNG AND BEAUTIFUL,		392	EASTER 1916	22
SWEET VOICED AND BEAUTIFUL,		392	EASTER 1916 V	22
BEING MADE BEAUTIFUL OVERMUCH,		403	FOR DAUGHTER	20
BY THOSE THAT ARE NOT ENTIRELY BEAUTIFUL!		404	FOR DAUGHTER	35
ADMIRED AND BEAUTIFUL,		472	ALL SOUL NIGHT	43
BEAUTIFUL, ONE A GAZELLE.		475	EVA GORE-BOOTH	4
BEAUTIFUL, ONE A GAZELLE.		475	EVA GORE-BOOTH	20
THE INNOCENT AND THE BEAUTIFUL		476	EVA GORE-BOOTH	24
THAT HIS HAIR IS BEAUTIFUL,		531	FATHER CHILD	7
A BEAUTIFUL SEATED BOY! A SACRED BOW!		541	PARN FUNERAL 1	10
BUT RHYMES FOR A BEAUTIFUL LADY.		552	SONGS REWRIT 2	11
BEAUTIFUL LOFTY THINGS		577	LOFTY THINGS	T
BEAUTIFUL LOFTY THINGS! O'LEARY'S NOBLE HEAD!		577	LOFTY THINGS	1
"OF PLASTER SAINTS"! HIS BEAUTIFUL MISCHIEVOUS HEAD THROWN BACK,		577	LOFTY THINGS	4
A BEAUTIFUL LOFTY THING, OR A THING		578	CRAZED GIRL	7
BEAUTIFUL AND GENTLE IN HER VENETIAN WAY.		602	GALLERY REVIS	14
BEAUTIFUL, GRACIOUS, IN HER VENETIAN WAY.		602	GALLERY REVIS V	14
A KING HAD SOME BEAUTIFUL COUSINS,		628	JANE MOUNTAIN	7
'TIS BEAUTIFUL, AND THEREFORE IT IS SAD.		652	ISLE STAT I 2	24
SHOULD I BE GOOD? BUT YOU ARE BEAUTIFUL.		692	MOSADA 1	62
UNPRUNED IS YOUR BEAUTIFUL PINION .		707	FAIRY PEDANT	7
WHERE MOVES THERE ANY BEAUTIFUL AS I,		720	WITCH VIVIEN	1
MY IMAGE YONDER? AH, MY BEAUTIFUL,		720	WITCH VIVIEN	4
I DREAMT SOME GREAT ONE. AH, MY BEAUTIFUL,		720	WITCH VIVIEN	14
A STREAM HAS TOLD ME THEY ARE BEAUTIFUL.		767	SHADOW WATER A	398
PRAISE THE BEAUTIFUL AND STRONG!		773	SONG DEIRDRE 1	19
BEAUTY				
HAVE FACES ALIVE WITH SUCH BEAUTY BEEN KNOWN TO THE SALT EYE OF MAN,		50	OISIN 3	51
ARE FACES ALIVE WITH SUCH BEAUTY MADE KNOWN TO THE SALT EYE OF MAN,		50	OISIN 3 V	51
ARE FACES ALIVE WITH SUCH BEAUTY MADE KNOWN TO THE SOFT EYE OF MAN,		50	OISIN 3 V	51
THE PHANTOM, BEAUTY, IN A MIST OF TEARS!		73	ANASHU VIJAYA	55

65

		PAGE	TITLE	LINE

BEAUTY   (CONTINUED)

	PAGE	TITLE	LINE
ETERNAL BEAUTY WANDERING ON HER WAY.	101	ROSE UPON ROOD	12
WHO DREAMED THAT BEAUTY PASSES LIKE A DREAM?	111	ROSE OF WORLD	1
BEAUTY GROWN SAD WITH ITS ETERNITY	115	ROSE OF BATTLE	29
AND LOVED YOUR BEAUTY WITH LOVE FALSE OR TRUE,	121	YOU ARE OLD	6
AND LOVED YOUR BEAUTY WILL LOVE FALSE OR TRUE:	121	YOU ARE OLD V	6
CARRY ALL THAT MOURNFUL BEAUTY	124	CATHLEEN PARA	7
FOR SHE NEEDS NOT HER SAD BEAUTY--	124	CATHLEEN PARA V	7
HE REMEMBERS FORGOTTEN BEAUTY	155	FORGOT BEAUTY	T
MICHAEL ROBARTES REMEMBERS FORGOTTEN BEAUTY	155	FORGOT BEAUTY V	T
I HEAR WHITE BEAUTY SIGHING, TOO,	156	FORGOT BEAUTY	19
I HEAR PALE BEAUTY SIGHING TOO,	156	FORGOT BEAUTY V	19
HE TELLS OF THE PERFECT BEAUTY	164	PERFECT BEAUTY	T
AEDH TELLS OF THE PERFECT BEAUTY	164	PERFECT BEAUTY V	T
TO BUILD A PERFECT BEAUTY IN RHYME,	164	PERFECT BEAUTY	3
TO BUILD THE PERFECT BEAUTY IN RHYME,	164	PERFECT BEAUTY V	3
MEN HAVE NAMED BEAUTY, THY GREAT LEAVES ENFOLD	169	SECRET ROSE	7
MEN HAVE NAMED BEAUTY, YOUR HEAVY LEAVES ENFOLD	169	SECRET ROSE	7
MEN HAVE NAMED BEAUTY, YOUR GREAT LEAVES ENFOLD	169	SECRET ROSE V	7
YOUR BEAUTY PERISH AND BE LOST	173	PLEADS FRIEND	7
AND YOUR HIGH BEAUTY FALL AND BE LOST	173	PLEADS FRIEND V	7
WITH BEAUTY HAND IN HAND?	174	ELEMENT POWERS V	6
BUT SOFT BEAUTY AND INDOLENT DESIRE.	181	QUEEN MAEVE	22
FOR ALL THEIR BEAUTY, LIKE A HOLLOW DREAM?"	184	QUEEN MAEVE V	89
I THOUGHT OF YOUR BEAUTY, AND THIS ARROW.	199	ARROW	1
TIME CAN BUT MAKE HER BEAUTY OVER AGAIN:	200	FOLLY COMFORT	8
TO DREAM OF WOMEN WHOSE BEAUTY WAS FOLDED IN DISMAY,	210	UNDER THE MOON	19
WITH BEAUTY LIKE A TIGHTENED BOW, A KIND	256	NO SECOND TROY	8
HER BEAUTY AS THE CONSTELLATIONS POUR	279	TWO KINGS V	62B
WHERE WIT AND BEAUTY LEARNED THEIR TRADE	288	TO WEALTHY MAN	16
BEAUTY THAT WE HAVE WON	293	HELEN LIVED	5
THE TREES ARE IN THEIR AUTUMN BEAUTY,	322	SWANS AT COOLE	1
UPON THIS LADY'S BEAUTY	329	MEN IMPROVE	5
A PICTURED BEAUTY,	329	MEN IMPROVE	7
THE LIVING BEAUTY	333	LIVING BEAUTY	*T
FROM BEAUTY THAT IS CAST OUT OF A MOULD	334	LIVING BEAUTY	4
THE LIVING BEAUTY IS FOR YOUNGER MEN:	334	LIVING BEAUTY	9
TO A YOUNG BEAUTY	335	YOUNG BEAUTY	T
I KNOW WHAT WAGES BEAUTY GIVES,	336	YOUNG BEAUTY	13
IF HEAD AND LIMB HAVE BEAUTY AND THE INSTEP'S HIGH AND LIGHT	354	HIS PHOENIX	21
BURDENSOME BEAUTY--FOR YOUR SOLE SAKE	356	BROKEN DREAMS	10
YOUR BEAUTY CAN BUT LEAVE AMONG US	356	BROKEN DREAMS	14
BURDENSOME BEAUTY--BUT FOR YOUR SAKE	356	BROKEN DREAMS V	10
AND YET YOUR BEAUTY HAD A FLAW:	356	BROKEN DREAMS V	28
BRING WHERE OUR BEAUTY LIES	362	DOLLS DRAWINGS	1
EVEN OUR BEAUTY WITH HER TURKISH TROUSERS ON.	364	DOLLS FACES	9
THEIR BEAUTY DROPPED OUT OF THE LONELINESS	375	PHASES OF MOON	70
EVEN TO EYES THAT BEAUTY HAD DRIVEN MAD,	390	IMAGE PAST	34
A TERRIBLE BEAUTY IS BORN.	392	EASTER 1916	16
A TERRIBLE BEAUTY IS BORN.	393	EASTER 1916	40
A TERRIBLE BEAUTY IS BORN.	394	EASTER 1916	80
THE BEAUTY OF HER COUNTRY-SIDE	397	POLIT PRISONER	15
MAY SHE BE GRANTED BEAUTY AND YET NOT	403	FOR DAUGHTER	17
BEAUTY TO MAKE A STRANGER'S EYE DISTRAUGHT,	403	FOR DAUGHTER	18
CONSIDER BEAUTY A SUFFICIENT END,	403	FOR DAUGHTER	21
THE SORT OF BEAUTY THAT I HAVE APPROVED,	405	FOR DAUGHTER	50
ARE INNOCENCE AND BEAUTY BORN?	406	FOR DAUGHTER	78
SOUL'S BEAUTY BEING MOST ADORED,	421	MY TABLE	22
NOR BEAUTY BORN OUT OF ITS OWN DESPAIR,	445	SCHOOL CHILDR	59
IF YOU ARE NO MORE STRENGTH THAN I AM BEAUTY	448	HERO GIRL FOOL	10
AND YET THERE BEAUTY LAY,	455	HIS MEMORIES	12
A WOMAN'S BEAUTY IS A STORM-TOSSED BANNER:	469	HARUN RASHID	188
THE BEAUTY OF A WOMAN'S MIND OR BODY	469	HARUN RASHID V	187
WITH 'MINISHED BEAUTY, MULTIPLIED COMMONPLACE,	472	ALL SOUL NIGHT	45
DIMINISHED BEAUTY, MULTIPLIED COMMONPLACE:	472	ALL SOUL NIGHT V	45
BEAUTY AND FOOL TOGETHER LAID.	484	SYMBOLS	6
EARTH IN BEAUTY DRESSED	517	HER ANXIETY	1
REMEMBERING A WOMAN'S BEAUTY,	552	SONGS REWRIT 2 V	11
FOR BEAUTY DIES OF BEAUTY, WORTH OF WORTH,	564	GYRES	3
FOR BEAUTY DIES OF BEAUTY, WORTH OF WORTH,	564	GYRES	3
SHALL GROW THY BEAUTY AND THY DREAMLESS TRUTH,	674	ISLE STAT II 3	207
WITH PATIENT BEAUTY YONDER ATTIC BUST	685	DRAWING-ROOM	3
WITH PATIENT BEAUTY YONDER ATTIC BUST	735	QUATRAIN APHOR	23
A WOMAN'S BEAUTY IS LIKE A WHITE	784	WOMANS BEAUTY	1
WHEN BEAUTY IS COMPLETE	786	YOUR HEART	29
HE SWORE TO SING MY BEAUTY	789	SINGING HEAD	7

BEAUTY-DRUNKEN

	PAGE	TITLE	LINE
AND BEAUTY-DRUNKEN BY THE WATER	447	COLONUS PRAISE	20

BEAUTY'S

	PAGE	TITLE	LINE
FOR ALL THEIR BEAUTY'S LIKE A HOLLOW DREAM,	184	QUEEN MAEVE	88
ALTHOUGH THEIR BEAUTY'S LIKE A HOLLOW DREAM"	184	QUEEN MAEVE V	89
THIS BEAUTY'S KINDER, YET FOR A REASON	199	ARROW	7
TO FLATTER BEAUTY'S IGNORANT EAR.	337	SCHOLARS	6
WHO IS MY BEAUTY'S EQUAL, THOUGH THAT MY HEART DENIES,	354	HIS PHOENIX	27
OF BEAUTY'S CRUELTY AND WISDOM'S CHATTER--	377	PHASES OF MOON	121
FOR BEAUTY'S VERY SELF, HAS CHARM MADE WISE,	404	FOR DAUGHTER	37
AND BRING BEAUTY'S BLIND RAMBLING CELEBRANT:	412	TOWER	91
IN BEAUTY'S MURDEROUS BROOD,	451	FIRST LOVE	2

BEAUVARLET

	PAGE	TITLE	LINE
BUT THOSE OF BEAUVARLET.	336	YOUNG BEAUTY	12

66

		PAGE	TITLE	LINE

BECAME
    I BECAME A RUSH THAT HORSES TREAD! . . . . 177 PAST GREATNESS 6
    I BECAME A MAN, A HATER OF THE WIND, ... 177 PAST GREATNESS 7
    TIME OUT OF MIND, BECAME TOO RUINOUS . . . . 264 HOUSE SHAKEN 3
    BECAME A BITTER, AN ABSTRACT THING, ... 397 POLIT PRISONER 9
    THAT ALL BUT THE ONE CARD BECAME . . . . 411 TOWER 68
BECK
    OR SERVILE SHAPE, AT OTHERS' BECK AND CALL. . . . . 417 ANCEST HOUSES 8
BECKON
    THUS, THUS I BECKON FROM HER VIEWLESS FIELDS-- . . . 693 MOSADA 1 75
    THUS BECKON TO OUR AID A PHANTOM FAIR . . . . . . 693 MOSADA 1 76
BECKONED
    BUT BECKONED TO SWEET COMPANY, ... 400 DEMON BEAST 18
BECKONING
    AND, WHILE THEY GATHER ROUND MY BECKONING ARMS, . . 694 MOSADA 1 100
BECKONS
    BLAND RHADAMANTHUS BECKONS HIM, ... 530 DELPHIC ORACLE 3
BECOME
    IT HAD BECOME A GLIMMERING GIRL . . . . 149 WANDER AENGUS 13
    IT HAD BECOME A LAUGHING GIRL, ... 149 WANDER AENGUS V 13
    BECOME OUR CAPTAIN, AIBRIC. I AM RESOLVED . . . . 225 SHADOW WATER B 64
    BECOME ONE MOVEMENT, ENERGY, DELIGHT, ... 231 SHADOW WATER B 217
    MAY SHE BECOME A FLOURISHING HIDDEN TREE . . . . . 404 FOR DAUGHTER 41
    BECOME A ROOFLESS RUIN THAT THE OWL . . . . 423 MY DESCENDANTS 14
    DID I BECOME A CHRISTIAN MAN AND CHOOSE FOR MY BELIEF . . 503 VACILLATION 85
    BECOME A STRANGER'S LEMAN! AND THAT YOU, ... 757 SHADOW WATER A 215
BECOMES
    ALL THOUGHT BECOMES AN IMAGE AND THE SOUL . . . . . 374 PHASES OF MOON 58
    BECOMES A BODY! THAT BODY AND THAT SOUL . . . . . 374 PHASES OF MOON 59
    DELIGHT BECOMES DEATH-LONGING IF ALL LONGING ELSE BE VAIN. 459 FROM OEDIPUS 3
BED   SEE DEATH-BED BRIDE-BED FEATHER-BED MARRIAGE-BED A-BED
    COULD SLEEP ON A BED OF RUSHES, AND ALL INWROUGHT 49 OISIN 3 V 31
      AND INLAID!
    ABOVE YOUR BED! . . . . 118 CRADLE SONG 2
    ABOVE YOUR WHITE BED, ... 118 CRADLE SONG V 2
    AND THE YOUNG LIE LONG AND DREAM IN THEIR BED . . . 150 OLD MOTHER 5
    WHILE THE YOUNG LIE LONG AND DREAM IN THEIR BED . . . 150 OLD MOTHER V 5
    BUT THE YOUNG LIE LONG AND DREAM IN THEIR BED . . . 150 OLD MOTHER V 5
    WHEN THEY HAD COME TO THE MARRIAGE BED! . . . . . 193 BAILE AILLINN V 106
    BAILE AND AILLINN'S MARRIAGE BED, ... 194 BAILE AILLINN V 121
    AND KEEP TO THE ONE WEARY MARRIAGE BED. . . . . . 224 SHADOW WATER B V 55
    THE BED OF LOVE, THAT IN THE IMAGINATION . . . . . 228 SHADOW WATER B 148
    UPON A GAUDY BED?" . . . . 253 HIS DREAM 8
    UPON A PAINTED BED?" . . . . 253 HIS DREAM V 8
    "I BID THEM MAKE HIS BED UNDER THIS ROOF . . . . . 280 TWO KINGS 87
    YOUR EMPTY BED." "HOW SHOULD I LOVE," I ANSWERED, . . 285 TWO KINGS 186
    "WERE IT NOT THAT WHEN THE DAWN HAS LIT MY BED . . . 285 TWO KINGS 187
    A PRETTY GIRL TO SHARE MY BED"! . . . . 296 THREE BEGGARS 31
    "WHEN I WAS BROUGHT TO BED," . . . . 308 PLAYER QUEEN 6
    CLIMB UP THE NARROW WINDING STAIR TO BED! . . . . . 324 ROBERT GREGORY 5
    AND SNUG IT IN A FEATHER BED. . . . . 332 ROUND TOWER 28
    LAID ON THE DEATH BED. . . . . 335 SONG V 16
    SLEEP DRIVEN FROM MY BED, ... 346 ON WOMAN 36
    RECOVERED HIM UPON THE BED OF DEATH. . . . . 355 BROKEN DREAMS 6
    AND SHE MAY LOOK FROM THE BED . . . . 366 HER CHRIS TREE 6
    NOR CRY, NOR TURN IN THE BED . . . . 435 FOR MY SON 3
    STORIES OF THE BED OF STRAW . . . . 458 SECRETS OF OLD 17
    OR THE BED OF DOWN. . . . . 458 SECRETS OF OLD 18
    AND SAW HER SITTING UPRIGHT ON THE BED! . . . . . 467 HARUN RASHID 134
    AND SHE LAY DOWN UPON HER BED AND SLEPT, ... 467 HARUN RASHID 146
    I SAW HER SITTING UPRIGHT ON THE BED, ... 467 HARUN RASHID V 134
    EVERY NIGHT IN BED, ... 495 MOHINI CHATTER 4
    THE GRASS MY BED! . . . . 510 JANE JUDGMENT 12
    IN AN EMPTY BED, ... 511 JANE AND JACK 14
    NOR GRAVE NOR BED DENIED, ... 513 JANE TALK BISH 10
    I DREAMED AS IN MY BED I LAY, ... 519 HER DREAM 1
    SLEEP UPON A GOLDEN BED . . . . 522 LULLABY 5
    AND SEEMED TO STAND ALTHOUGH IN BED I LAY. . . . . 535 CHOSEN 9
    HE RHYMING ALONE IN HIS BED. . . . . 552 SONGS REWRIT 2 12
    LYING ALONE ON A BED . . . . 552 SONGS REWRIT 2 V 10
    MAY CREEP INTO YOUR BED, ... 569 THREE BUSHES 11
    FROM PLEASURE OF THE BED, ... 575 MAIDS 2ND SONG 1
    IN A YOUNG MAN'S BED." . . . . 594 COLONEL MARTIN 17
    IN THE COMFORT OF A BED. . . . . 596 COLONEL MARTIN 44
    CONFUSION OF THE BED, ... 599 SPIRIT MEDIUM 4
    THROW LIKELY COUPLES INTO BED . . . . 606 SONGS BURDEN 1 25
    I SCRUB ITS FLOORS AND MAKE MY BED, ... 607 SONGS BURDEN 2 5
    AT TABLE OR IN BED. . . . . 620 JOHN KINSELLA 10
    WHETHER MAN DIE IN HIS BED . . . . 637 BEN BULBEN 17
    WITH ONLY BED AND BEDSTEAD THERE, ... 639 BEN BULBEN 51
    NEVER STORM AROSE SO SWIFTLY! SCARCE THE CHILDREN WERE 718 PHANTOM SHIP 4
      IN BED,
    "AND HALF FORGET THIS BED OF STRAW . . . . 739 EARL PAUL 5
    EARL PAUL STOOD ON THE BED OF STRAW, ... 740 EARL PAUL 17
    EAGLES HAVE GONE INTO THEIR CLOUDY BED. . . . . . 778 SONG DEIRDRE 3 6
BEDABBLED   SEE BLOOD-BEDABBLED
BEDDED
    ALL HEAVEN'S FLOOR, WITH VAPOURS BEDDED-- . . . . . 705 DAWN-SONG 11
    HAVE BEDDED WITH THEIR FANCY-MAN . . . . 789 SINGING HEAD 17
BEDFELLOW
    TO BE HIS BEDFELLOW? UNTIL YOUR LIPS . . . . . . 237 SHADOW WATER B 335

		PAGE	TITLE		LINE

BEDOUIN
    BUT THE WILD BEDOUIN. THOUGH I APPROVE . . . . 462 HARUN RASHID   22
BEDOUIN'S
    STARING UPON A BEDOUIN'S HORSE-HAIR ROOF . . . . . . 368 EGO DOMINUS   29
    MAYBE NOW A BEDOUIN'S BROOD, ... 732 STREET DANCERS   40
    BOWS THE BEDOUIN'S WHITENING HAIR-- . . . . 733 STREET DANCERS   45
BEDROWNED   SEE DEW-BEDROWNED
BEDS   SEE DEATH-BEDS
    "MY BROTHERS SPRING OUT OF THEIR BEDS AT MORN, ... 32 OISIN 2   51
    FOR HALF HIS FLOCK WERE IN THEIR BEDS, ... 132 FR GILLIGAN   3
    FOR HALF HIS FLOCK LAY IN THEIR BEDS . . . . 132 FR GILLIGAN   V   3
    O WANDERING BIRDS AND RUSHY BEDS, ... 190 BAILE AILLINN   31
    THAT YOUNG MEN, TOSSING ON THEIR BEDS, ... 337 SCHOLARS   4
    THEY HAD KEPT A STEADY PACE AS THOUGH THEIR BEDS, . . . 372 PHASES OF MOON   5
    WERE NOT OUR BEDS FAR OFF I'D RING THE BELL, ... 377 PHASES OF MOON   124
    THEY TURN DOWN THEIR BEDS. . . . . 589 OLD WICKED MAN   35
    OF SOLITARY BEDS, KNEW WHAT THEY WERE, ... 610 STATUES   5
    BASE-BORN PRODUCTS OF BASE BEDS. . . . . 639 BEN BULBEN   73
    ENCLOSE A QUIET PLACE OF BEDS BOX-BORDERED, BEES, . . . 710 FERENCZ RENYI   24
BEDSTEAD
    WITH ONLY BED AND BEDSTEAD THERE, ... 639 BEN BULBEN   61
BEE   SEE HONEY-BEE
    YET SANG NO MORE AS WHEN, LIKE A BROWN BEE . . . . . 30 OISIN 2   15
    BUT SANG NO MORE, AS WHEN, LIKE A BROWN BEE . . . . . 30 OISIN 2   V   15
    AND CHASE THE WILD BEE HOMEWARD TO HIS HIVE . . . . . 32 OISIN 2   V   50D
    NINE BEAN ROWS WILL I HAVE THERE, A HIVE FOR THE HONEY BEE, 117 ISLE INNISFREE V   3
    WITHIN THE DROWSY BLOSSOM HANGS THE BEE: . . . . . . 645 ISLE STAT I 1   2
    A NEW DAY'S TROOP OF WASP AND BEE . . . . 646 ISLE STAT I 1   44
    BY BOSKY JUNE I SWEAR, AND BY THE BEE, HER MINISTER. . . 661 ISLE STAT II 1   74
    O WAKE! WAKE! WAKE! FOR SOFT AS A BEE SIPS . . . . . 677 ISLE STAT II 3   276
    OLD WARRIOR, WAKE! FOR SOFT AS A BEE SIPS, ... 677 ISLE STAT II 3   284
    THOSE TWAIN ARE DUST. WAKE! LIGHT AS A BEE SIPS . . . 678 ISLE STAT II 3   290
    HE IS LONG DEAD. WAKE! SOFT AS A BEE SIPS . . . . . 678 ISLE STAT II 3   297
    NAY, HE IS GONE. WAKE! WAKE! AS A BEE SIPS . . . . . 678 ISLE STAT II 3   305
    WITH BERRIES. PLACID AS A HOMEWARD BEE. . . . . . . 710 FERENCZ RENYI   29
    LAPPED IN THE LEMON DAFFODILLS! A BEE . . . . 716 DWELT SYCAMORE   10
    AMONG THE HAUNTS OF BEE AND BIRD. . . . . 729 PRIEST FAIRY   42
BEECH
    UNDER A BEECH AT ALMHUIN AND HEARD THE THIN . . . . . 44 OISIN 2   228
    A BEECH BOUGH TO ME, AND MY HEART GREW SORE, ... 44 OISIN 2   V   226
    AT EMAN, 'NEATH THE BEECH TREES, ON EACH SIDE, ... 44 OISIN 2   V   228
    . . . THE BEECH LEAVES OLD. . . . . 82 MAD KING GOLL   12
    . . . THE BEECH LEAVES OLD. . . . . 83 MAD KING GOLL   24
    . . . THE BEECH LEAVES OLD. . . . . 84 MAD KING GOLL   36
    . . . THE BEECH LEAVES OLD. . . . . 84 MAD KING GOLL   48
    . . . THE BEECH LEAVES OLD. . . . . 85 MAD KING GOLL   60
    . . . THE BEECH LEAVES OLD. . . . . 86 MAD KING GOLL   72
    A CLUMP OF BEECH TREES MADE AN EMPTY SPACE . . . . . 277 TWO KINGS   V   4A
    BETWEEN THE PALE GREEN LIGHT OF THE BEECH LEAVES . . . 277 TWO KINGS   V   5
    AND WHERE BEECH TREES HAD MIXED A PALE GREEN LIGHT . . 277 TWO KINGS   V   5
    AGAINST A BEECH BOLE, HE THREW DOWN THE BEAST . . . . 278 TWO KINGS   V   36
    I GROPED MY WAY FROM BEECH TO HAZEL WOOD, ... 283 TWO KINGS   139
    CLOSE TO A CLUMP OF BEECH TREES IN THE WOOD . . . . . 283 TWO KINGS   V   135
    TILL OAK AND HAZEL CEASED AND BEECH BEGAN, ... 283 TWO KINGS   V 139A
    I STAGGERED, BUT A BEECH TREE STAYED MY FALL, ... 286 TWO KINGS   V   209
BEECH-BOLE
    AGAINST A BEECH-BOLE, HE THREW DOWN THE BEAST . . . . 278 TWO KINGS   36
BEECH-BOUGH
    A BEECH-BOUGH TO ME, AND MY HEART GREW SORE, ... 44 OISIN 2   226
BEECHEN
    UNDER OAK AND BEECHEN BOUGH, ... 522 LULLABY   11
BEECHES
    WHERE CERTAIN BEECHES MIXED A PALE GREEN LIGHT . . . . 277 TWO KINGS   V   5
    AND IN A COPSE OF BEECHES THERE I STOOD, ... 490 COOLE BALLYLEE   11
    UNDER OAK AND BEECHES BOUGH, ... 522 LULLABY   V   11
BEECH-LEAVES
    . . . THE BEECH-LEAVES OLD. . . . . 82 MAD KING GOLL V REF
BEECH-TREE
    I STAGGERED, BUT A BEECH-TREE STAYED MY FALL, ... 286 TWO KINGS   209
BEECH-TREES
    AND WHERE BEECH-TREES HAD MIXED A PALE GREEN LIGHT . . 277 TWO KINGS   5
BEE-LOUD
    AND LIVE ALONE IN THE BEE-LOUD GLADE. . . . . 117 ISLE INNISFREE   4
BEER
    WITH RED BEER AND BROWN BEER. . . . . 214 HAPPY TOWNLAND   8
    WITH RED BEER AND BROWN BEER. . . . . 214 HAPPY TOWNLAND   8
    A LADLE AND A TUB OF BEER, ... 303 HOUR DAWN   29
    INTO THE SLEEPER'S TUB OF BEER . . . . 304 HOUR DAWN   47
    "BEFORE YOU HAVE DIPPED IT IN THE BEER . . . . 304 HOUR DAWN   49
    TO VALUE BEER: NO HALF-LEGGED FOOL . . . . 304 HOUR DAWN   52
    AND WOULD HAVE DIPPED IT IN THE BEER . . . . 304 HOUR DAWN   V   47
    TO VALUE BEER--I WILL HAVE NO FOOL . . . . 304 HOUR DAWN   V   52
    "WHY, BEER IS ONLY BEER." "BUT SAY . . . . 305 HOUR DAWN   56
    "WHY, BEER IS ONLY BEER." "BUT SAY . . . . 305 HOUR DAWN   56
    YOU'VE BUT TO DRINK THE BEER AND SAY . . . . 305 HOUR DAWN   V   56
    IF YOU BUT DRINK THAT BEER AND SAY . . . . 305 HOUR DAWN   V   56
    SO STAY AT HOME AND DRINK YOUR BEER . . . . 598 STONE CROSS   5
    (O THE BROWN AND THE YELLOW BEER!) . . . . 779 GOING THE ROAD   2
    (O THE BROWN AND THE YELLOW BEER!) . . . . 779 GOING THE ROAD   6
    (O THE BROWN AND THE YELLOW BEER!) . . . . 779 GOING THE ROAD   10

BEERY
 A GREAT LAD WITH A BEERY FACE • • • • • • • • • • •   303 HOUR DAWN   27
BEE'S
 THE GIDDY BEE'S COMPLACENT CROON, • • • • • • • • • •   736 SUMMER EVENING   5
BEES   SEE HONEY-BEES
 AND IN THE BLOSSOMS HUNG THE BEES, • • • • • • • • •   2 OISIN 1   V   7G
 OR CLUNG THEREON LIKE SWARMS OF BEES, • • • • • • •   14 OISIN 1   181
 OR CLUNG AS CLOSE AS SWARMS OF BEES, • • • • • • •   14 OISIN 1   V   181
 WITH BOOM OF BEES IN HONEY-MARTS, • • • • • • • •   16 OISIN 1   229
 FROM BEES AMONG THEIR HONEY MARTS, • • • • • • • •   16 OISIN 1   229
 WITH BOOM OF BEES IN HONEY MARTS, • • • • • • • •   16 OISIN 1   V   229
 AND DOWNY BEES HAVE AMBUSCADE, • • • • • • • • •   67 HAPPY SHEPHERD V   46A
 LIKE SWARMING BEES, ONE WITH THE DOVE • • • • • •   78 INDIAN TO LOVE V   16
 WHEN SUMMER GLUTS THE GOLDEN BEES, • • • • • • • •   84 MAD KING GOLL   38
 WHERE SUMMER GLUTS THE GOLDEN BEES, • • • • • • •   84 MAD KING GOLL   V   38
 WHERE WILD BEES HIVE ON THE GREAT PLAIN, • • • • •   194 BAILE AILLINN   123
 MAKE THEIR FAINT THUNDER, AND THE GARDEN BEES • • •   198 SEVEN WOODS   2
 AMONG PIGEONS AND BEES, WHILE THAT GREAT ARCHER, • •   198 SEVEN WOODS   12
 DIM PAIRC-NA-CARRAIG, WHERE THE WILD BEES FLING • •   217 WOODS OF COOLE   9
 THE BEES BUILD IN THE CREVICES • • • • • • • • •   424 STARES NEST   1
 MY WALL IS LOOSENING, HONEY BEES • • • • • • • • •   424 STARES NEST   V   4
 AND ALL THE GOLDEN GRASSHOPPERS AND BEES, • • • •   428 NINETEEN 19   8
 AND ALL HIS GOLDEN GRASSHOPPERS AND BEES, • • • •   428 NINETEEN 19   V   8
 OR TRAFFIC IN THE GRASSHOPPERS OR BEES, • • • • •   430 NINETEEN 19   48
 OR TRAFFIC IN THE GRASSHOPPERS AND BEES? • • • • •   430 NINETEEN 19   V   48
 FOR, LOOK YOU, SAD'S THE MURMUR OF THE BEES, • • •   652 ISLE STAT I 2   9
 BEHOLD, HOW LIKE A SWARM OF FIERY BEES • • • • • •   662 ISLE STAT II 2   1
 ENCLOSE A QUIET PLACE OF BEDS BOX-BORDERED, BEES, • •   710 FERENCZ RENYI   24
 AMONG THE MURMURS OF THE BEES, • • • • • • • • •   728 PRIEST FAIRY   18
BEES'
 WILD BEES' HONEY LAID FOR THEE." • • • • • • • • •   730 PRIEST FAIRY   56
BEETLES
 I CANNOT SEE. THE BEETLES, AND THE BATS, • • • • •   693 MOSADA 1   63
BEFALL
 AND MAY SOME SUDDEN DREADFUL ILL BEFALL HER! • • • •   74 ANASHU VIJAYA   59
 AND MAY SOME DREADFUL ILL BEFALL HER QUICK! • • • •   74 ANASHU VIJAYA   V   59
 NOBODY KNOWS WHAT MAY BEFALL, • • • • • • • • • •   788 HAWTHORN TREE   13
BEFIT
 SO MUCH OF WEALTH AS MAY BEFIT THEIR RANK: • • • •   756 SHADOW WATER A V 186
BEFITTING
 BEFITTING EMBLEMS OF ADVERSITY. • • • • • • • • •   420 MY HOUSE   30
BEFORE
 BEFORE THY FEET SHALL KNEEL DOWN ALL • • • • • •   7 OISIN 1   V   77
 BEFORE THE SWIFT THINGS THAT SHE DREAMED OF WERE DONE • • 27 OISIN 1   414
 BEFORE GOD WAS OR MY OLD LINE BEGAN• • • • • • •   29 OISIN 2   8
 BEFORE THIS DAY: FOR NOW THE FALL OF TEARS • • • •   30 OISIN 2   18
 WOVEN INTO HER HAIR, BEFORE DARK TOWERS • • • •   30 OISIN 2   22
 WOVE IN HER FLOWER-LIKE HAIR, BEFORE DARK TOWERS • • •   30 OISIN 2   V   22
 PATRICK, BEFORE THY CRAFT DIES EACH OLD SONG. • • • •   42 OISIN 2   V 196
 AN ISLE LAY LEVEL BEFORE US, WITH DRIPPING HAZEL AND OAK? 47 OISIN 3   10
 AN ISLE LAY LEVEL BEFORE US, DRIPPING WITH HAZEL AND OAK? 47 OISIN 3   V   10
 AND BEFORE I WENT BY THEM SO HUGE AND SO SPEEDY WITH EYES 59 OISIN 3   V 169
   SO BRIGHT,
 WITH MIRTHFUL SONGS BEFORE THE DAWN, • • • • • • •   67 HAPPY SHEPHERD   49
 BEFORE US LIES ETERNITY: OUR SOULS • • • • • • • •   81 EPHEMERA   23
 COME NEAR: I WOULD, BEFORE MY TIME TO GO, • • • •   101 ROSE UPON ROOD   22
 AND PIERCED HIM. "SPEAK BEFORE YOUR BREATH IS DONE." • • 110 CUCHULAIN SEA   67
 BEFORE YOU WERE, OR ANY HEARTS TO BEAT, • • • • •   112 ROSE OF WORLD   12
 BEFORE HER WANDERING FEET, • • • • • • • • • •   112 ROSE OF WORLD   15
 BEFORE YE WERE, OR ANY HEARTS TO BEAT, • • • • •   112 ROSE OF WORLD   V   12
 WE TIRE OF THE FLAME OF THE METEOR BEFORE IT CAN FADE   122 WHITE BIRDS   2
   AND FLEE:
 FOR WE TIRE OF THE FLAME OF THE METEOR BEFORE IT CAN PASS 122 WHITE BIRDS   V   2
   BY AND FLEE
 WE TIRE OF THE FLAME OF THE METEOR, BEFORE IT CAN PASS   122 WHITE BIRDS   V   2
   BY AND FLEE:
 BEFORE EARTH TOOK HIM TO HER STONY CARE: • • • • •   126 DREAM OF FAERY   4
 BEFORE EARTH MADE OF HIM HER SLEEPY CARE: • • • •   126 DREAM OF FAERY V   4
 BEFORE THEY HEAPED HIS GRAVE UNDER THE HILL: • • •   127 DREAM OF FAERY   16
 BUT WHILE HE PASSED BEFORE A PLASHY PLACE, • • • •   127 DREAM OF FAERY   17
 LIFT UP BEFORE US WHEN THEY PASS, • • • • • • •   135 TWO TREES   23
 LIFT UP BEFORE US AS THEY PASS, • • • • • • • •   135 TWO TREES   V   23
 BEFORE GOD MADE THE ANGELIC CLAN, • • • • • • •   138 TO IRELAND   8
 IS COMELIER THAN CANDLES BEFORE MAURYA'S FEET, • • •   147 UNAPPEAS HOST   V   12
 THE EAST HER HIDDEN JOY BEFORE THE MORNING BREAK, • •   154 BELOVED PEACE   4
 THE EAST TELLS ALL HER SECRET JOY BEFORE DAYBREAK, • • 154 BELOVED PEACE   V   4
 BEFORE THEY DROWNED THEIR LOVERS' EYES • • • • • •   156 FORGOT BEAUTY   V 10A
 HIM WHO TREMBLES BEFORE THE FLAME AND THE FLOOD, • • • 158 TO HIS HEART   3
 WHO TREMBLES BEFORE THE FLAME AND THE FLOOD, • • •   158 TO HIS HEART   V   3
 IT TALKED BEFORE MORN WAS WHITE, • • • • • • • •   159 CAP AND BELLS   V   6
 SUDDENLY HURTLE BEFORE MY DREAM-AWAKENED EYES, • • •   161 BLACK PIG   2
 BEFORE THE UNLABOURING STARS AND YOU, • • • • • •   164 PERFECT BEAUTY   8
 BEFORE UNLABOURING STARS AND YOU, • • • • • • •   164 PERFECT BEAUTY V   8
 AND HURLED IT FROM ITS PLACE BEFORE HIS FOOTSTOOL WHITE, 174 ELEMENT POWERS V   3
 IT WAS BEFORE THE TIME OF THE GREAT WAR • • • • •   182 QUEEN MAEVE   57
 BEFORE MY THOUGHTS BEGIN TO RUN • • • • • • • •   189 BAILE AILLINN   3
 WHERE THE HOUND OF ULADH SAT BEFORE • • • • • •   192 BAILE AILLINN   73
 BEFORE HIS EYES, HE HAS TEARS FOR NONE, • • • • •   192 BAILE AILLINN   82
 BEFORE HER LOVE-WORN HEART HAD BROKE, • • • • • •   194 BAILE AILLINN   127
 WAS ROBBED BEFORE EARTH GAVE THE WHEAT: • • • • •   196 BAILE AILLINN   166
 BUT PURER THAN A TALL CANDLE BEFORE THE HOLY ROOD • • • 208 HANRAHANS SONG   14

69

BEFORE   (CONTINUED)

		PAGE	TITLE	LINE
BUT PURE AS A TALL CANDLE BEFORE THE TRINITY	. . . .	208	HANRAHANS SONG V	14
BUT PURER THAN A TALL CANDLE BEFORE THE BLESSED ROOD	. .	208	HANRAHANS SONG V	14
THAT RUN BEFORE THE REAPING-HOOK AND LIE	. . . . .	218	WOODS OF COOLE	32
THAT RUN BEFORE THE REAPING HOOK AND LIE	. . . . .	218	WOODS OF COOLE V	32
BEFORE THEY READ OF FORGAEL AND DECTORA,	. . . .	219	WOODS OF COOLE	42
AS MEN IN THE OLD TIMES, BEFORE THE HARPS BEGAN,	. . .	219	WOODS OF COOLE	43
AS MEN IN THE OLD TIMES, BEFORE THE HARP BEGAN,	. . . .	219	WOODS OF COOLE V	43
STRANGE CREATURES FLUTTER UP BEFORE ONE'S EYES,	. . . .	222	SHADOW WATER B	18
AS THAT WILD AENGUS. LONG BEFORE HER DAY	. . . .	224	SHADOW WATER B	47
THE ROOTS OF THE WORLD. SHADOWS BEFORE NOW	. . . .	227	SHADOW WATER B	104
UNTIL YOU STOOD BEFORE ME ON THE DECK--	. . . .	236	SHADOW WATER B	313
BEFORE A HAND CAN TOUCH ME. MY HANDS ARE STILL:	. . .	238	SHADOW WATER B	358
OR CALLED BEFORE HIS EYES. O CARRY ME	. . . . .	249	SHADOW WATER B	568
I SWEAR BEFORE THE DAWN COMES ROUND AGAIN	. . . .	260	FASC DIFFICULT	12
BEFORE WE GROW OLD AND DIE.	. . . .	261	DRINKING SONG	4
BEFORE THE MERCHANT AND THE CLERK	. . . . . .	266	GALWAY RACES	8
BEFORE THEIR SLEEPY EYELIDS RAN	. . . .	272	GREY ROCK	30
BEFORE THAT ROOMFUL OR AS GOOD,	. . . . . .	273	GREY ROCK	52
AND HALF THE KINGS, BEFORE SUNDOWN	. . . . . .	273	GREY ROCK	69
AND HALF HIS KINGS, BEFORE SUNDOWN	. . . . .	273	GREY ROCK V	69
WITH THE LOUD HOST BEFORE THE SEA,	. . . . . .	276	GREY ROCK	128
UNTIL HE CAME BEFORE THE PAINTED WALL,	. . . . .	279	TWO KINGS	47
BEFORE HIM OR BEHIND, BUT THAT FAR OFF	. . . . .	279	TWO KINGS	55
SAT UPRIGHT WITH A SWORD BEFORE HER FEET,	. . . .	279	TWO KINGS	62
BEFORE HIM OR BEHIND, BUT THAT FAR-OFF	. . . . .	279	TWO KINGS V	55
BEFORE HIS CHAIR AND BENDING DOWN MY HEAD	. . . .	282	TWO KINGS	132
BEFORE YOU'LL PUT YOUR GUINEAS DOWN,	. . . . .	287	TO WEALTHY MAN	5
BEFORE YOU'VE PUT YOUR GUINEAS DOWN,	. . . . .	287	TO WEALTHY MAN V	5
YOU HAD ENOUGH OF SORROW BEFORE DEATH--	. . . .	293	TO A SHADE	23
SLEEP BEFORE THE THIRD NOON SOUNDS."	. . . . .	295	THREE BEGGARS	24
BEFORE THE THREE TO END THIS TALE,	. . . . . .	297	THREE BEGGARS	55
"AND MAKE MY SOUL BEFORE MY PATE IS BARE."	. . . .	299	BEGGAR CRIED	4
THE HOUR BEFORE DAWN	. . . .	302	HOUR DAWN	T
BEFORE HIS EYES, WHERE STONES HAD BEEN,	. . . .	302	HOUR DAWN	20
"AND I WILL TALK BEFORE I SLEEP	. . . . . .	304	HOUR DAWN	44
AND DRINK BEFORE I TALK." AND HE	. . . . . .	304	HOUR DAWN	45
"BEFORE YOU HAVE DIPPED IT IN THE BEER	. . . . .	304	HOUR DAWN	49
IN THE BAD HOUR BEFORE THE DAWN."	. . . . . .	304	HOUR DAWN	55
I SAW, BEFORE I HAD WELL FINISHED,	. . . . .	322	SWANS AT COOLE	9
OR LEAVE THEM HAPPIER THAN BEFORE.	. . . . . .	328	IRISH AIRMAN	8
"BEFORE NIGHTFALL I'LL PICK A POCKET	. . . . .	332	ROUND TOWER	27
YOU HAD BEFORE THE SUN HAD THROWN	. . . . .	333	SOLOMON SHEBA	13
I WISHED BEFORE IT CEASED. NOR BIRD NOR BEAST	. . .	338	SHEP GOATHERD	2
YEAR. I WISHED BEFORE IT CEASED. NOR BIRD NOR BEAST	.	338	SHEP GOATHERD V	2
EVEN BEFORE HIS CHILDREN AND HIS WIFE?	. . . . .	340	SHEP GOATHERD	34
AND CRIED, "BEFORE I AM OLD	. . . . .	348	FISHERMAN	37
DUMBFOUNDED BEFORE A KNAVE,	. . . .	349	HAWK	16
THEIR MOMENTARY CRIES BEFORE IT IS DAWN,	. . . .	371	EGO DOMINUS	78
BEFORE THE FULL MOON, HELPLESS AS A WORM.	. . . .	374	PHASES OF MOON	49
THE COARSENESS OF THE DRUDGE. BEFORE THE FULL	. . .	376	PHASES OF MOON	94
INSIPID AS THE DOUGH BEFORE IT IS BAKED,	. . . .	376	PHASES OF MOON	112
BEFORE SHE HAD SETTLED HER MIND	. . . . . .	381	SONGS FOOL 2	8
THREE HUNDRED YEARS BEFORE THE FALL,	. . . . .	388	SOLOMON WITCH	11
BEFORE MY TIME, SEEM LIKE A VIVID MEMORY.	. . . .	391	UNDER SATURN	10
AND THOUGHT BEFORE I HAD DONE	. . . . . .	392	EASTER 1916	9
O BUT WE TALKED AT LARGE BEFORE	. . . . . .	395	SIXTEEN DEAD	1
RECALL THE YEARS BEFORE HER MIND	. . . . . .	397	POLIT PRISONER	8
OR HERS BEFORE A LOOKING-GLASS, FOR SUCH,	. . . .	403	FOR DAUGHTER	19
BEFORE THAT RUIN CAME, FOR CENTURIES,	. . . . .	412	TOWER	81
BEFORE THE INDIFFERENT GARDEN DEITIES:	. . . . .	418	ANCEST HOUSES	28
THE NIGHT CAN SWEAT WITH TERROR AS BEFORE	. . . .	429	NINETEEN 19	29
BEFORE THAT BRIEF GLEAM OF ITS LIFE BE GONE,	. . .	430	NINETEEN 19	63
BEFORE THE INDIFFERENT BEAK COULD LET HER DROP?	. . .	441	LEDA AND SWAN	14
SHE STANDS BEFORE ME AS A LIVING CHILD.	. . . .	444	SCHOOL CHILDR	24
BEFORE SHE HAD SPREAD A BOOK UPON HER KNEES	. . .	466	HARUN RASHID	120
BEFORE THEN MUCH HAD SHE RAVELLED OUT	. . . . .	472	ALL SOUL NIGHT	51
MUCH BOISTEROUS COURAGE, BEFORE LONELINESS	. . . .	473	ALL SOUL NIGHT	72
THERE HYDE BEFORE HE HAD BEATEN INTO PROSE	. . . .	489	COOLE PARK 29	9
BEFORE ME FLOATS AN IMAGE, MAN OR SHADE,	. . . .	497	BYZANTIUM	9
THAT SHONE BEFORE THESE EYES	. . . .	504	QUARREL IN AGE	15
BEFORE THEIR EYES A HOUSE	. . . .	512	JANE ON GOD	13
BEFORE THE WORLD WAS MADE."	. . . .	516	MANS SONG	12
BEFORE THE THREAD BEGAN	. . . .	520	HIS BARGAIN	8
BEFORE THE WORLD WAS MADE	. . . .	531	BEFORE WORLD	T
BEFORE THE WORLD WAS MADE.	. . . .	532	BEFORE WORLD	8
BEFORE THE WORLD WAS MADE.	. . . .	532	BEFORE WORLD	16
BEFORE I HAD MARKED HIM ON HIS NORTHERN WAY,	. . .	535	CHOSEN	8
SAVING THE RHYME RATS HEAR BEFORE THEY DIE.	. . .	542	PARN FUNERAL 1	28
BUT HE KICKED BEFORE HE DIED,	. . . . .	545	TO SAME TUNE 1	25
HOW SOUL COULD WALK BEFORE SUCH THINGS BEGAN.	. . .	558	RIBH CHRISTIAN	12
HOW SOUL HAS WALKED BEFORE SUCH THINGS BEGAN.	. . .	558	RIBH CHRISTIAN V	12
THAT DAY BRINGS ROUND THE NIGHT, THAT BEFORE DAWN	. .	563	MERU	13
MY FATHER UPON THE ABBEY STAGE, BEFORE HIM A RAGING CROWD:		577	LOFTY THINGS	2
HIS FATHERS SERVED THEIR FATHERS BEFORE CHRIST WAS		580	CURSE CROMWELL	6
CRUCIFIED.				
BEFORE THE BENCH OF TIME,	. . . .	582	ROGER CASEMENT	6
SING A "THE" BEFORE HIS NAME:	. . . . . .	584	ORAHILLY	3
"THEN WANT BEFORE YOU DIE."	. . . . .	596	COLONEL MARTIN	67
BEFORE A WOMAN'S PORTRAIT SUDDENLY I STAND,	. . .	602	GALLERY REVIS	13
BEFORE THE PAINTED SCENE.	. . . .	608	SONGS BURDEN 3	17

70

	PAGE	TITLE	LINE

BEFORE   (CONTINUED)

BUT HE KICKED BEFORE HE DIED, ... 616 MARCH SONGS 3   25
SOME DAY WE SHALL GET UP BEFORE THE DAWN . . . . . . 622 HOUND VOICE   15
AND FIND OUR ANCIENT HOUNDS BEFORE THE DOOR, ... 622 HOUND VOICE   16
THOUGH ALL WAS DONE IN COMMON AS BEFORE. . . . . 635 CUCHULAIN COMF   24
BEFORE HE CAN ACCOMPLISH FATE. . . . . 638 BEN BULBEN   35
BEFORE THE SECRET WORKING MIND! . . . . 639 BEN BULBEN   51
BEFORE HER I TROD . . . . 654 ISLE STAT I 2   74
AND THE WAVES BOWED BEFORE IT LIKE MOWN CORN, ... 657 ISLE STAT I 3   56
SAY THEN,--"A POPINJAY BEFORE GRIEF'S SHAFT . . . . . . 664 ISLE STAT II 2   52
E'EN THEN, BEFORE HER SHEPHERD HAIR . . . . 668 ISLE STAT II 3   54
HE SHRANK BEFORE MY VOICE, AND STOOD . . . . 671 ISLE STAT II 3   129
BEFORE A DEATH. O'ER WAVE AND BANK . . . . 673 ISLE STAT II 3   185
BEFORE I AM TOO WEAK, FIERCE MORTAL, LET ME FLY, . . . 675 ISLE STAT II 3   245
BEFORE I AM TOO WEAK, OH LET ME FLY, ... 675 ISLE STAT II 3 V   245
BEFORE THE WIND. SAW YOU HIS EYES A-GLITTER? . . . . . 683 SEEKER   35
BEHOLD, I BEND BEFORE THEE TO THE GROUND . . . . 683 SEEKER   43
BEHOLD, I BEND BEFORE THEE TO THE GROUND! . . . . 684 SEEKER   61
THEN LET ME SEE THY FACE BEFORE I DIE. . . . . 684 SEEKER   66
BEHOLD, I BEND BEFORE THEE TO THE GROUND! . . . . 684 SEEKER   67
BEHOLD I BOW BEFORE THEE TO THE GROUND! . . . . 684 SEEKER   V   67
WHAT, LOVER, DIE BEFORE OUR LIPS HAVE MET? . . . . . . 685 SEEKER   80
ABOUT THE SEA. BEFORE HER LIES THAT YOUTH, ... 687 TWO TITANS   22
AND HE IS DRAGGED AGAIN BEFORE HER FEET. . . . . 688 TWO TITANS   43
WE TWO, BEFORE WE DIE! FOR AZOLAR, ... 691 MOSADA 1   24
WE'LL FLY FROM THIS BEFORE THE MORNING STAR. . . . . . 702 MOSADA 3   74
SO YOU MUST GO! KISS ME BEFORE YOU GO. . . . . 702 MOSADA 3   96
BEFORE WE TAKE OUR SEATS ABOVE THE CROWD. . . . . 704 MOSADA 3   134
BEFORE HIS TENT THE GENERAL SIPS HIS WINE, ... 709 FERENCZ RENYI   6
BEFORE HIM ONE WELL GUARDED, WITH BOUND HANDS! . . . . 709 FERENCZ RENYI   10
FLINGS HER BEFORE HIM. "SAVE THYSELF AND ME. . . . . . 713 FERENCZ RENYI   86
ROUND SHE COMES IN STAYS BEFORE THEM! . . . . 719 PHANTOM SHIP   17
WHEN WERE YOU BORN? BEFORE YOUR GRANDAM EVE. . . . . . 721 WITCH VIVIEN   32
LONG BEFORE THE MORNING FIRE . . . . 727 LOVERS QUARREL   45
AND STRAIGHT BEFORE THE SLEEPING PRIEST . . . . 729 PRIEST FAIRY   23
BEFORE US IN THE GLOOM! . . . . 738 MOURN THEN ON   16
WANDERS AND WAILS BEFORE MY HEART MOST TRUE . . . . . . 738 YOU ARE SAD   8
BEFORE A SANDED PLACE! . . . . 740 EARL PAUL   32
"MAY STAND BEFORE THY RACE AND THEE . . . . 742 EARL PAUL   63
IT MAY BE, BEFORE THE WINDS OF BIRTH HAVE WAKED! . . . 750 SHADOW WATER A   86
FROM ITS FIRST SIGHS AND LAUGHTER, BEFORE THE SLEEP, . 754 SHADOW WATER A   161
AND THAT DREAM ONLY SHINE BEFORE HER FEET. . . . . . . 761 SHADOW WATER A   258
BEFORE I DROPPED ASLEEP, A KINGFISHER . . . . 761 SHADOW WATER A   274
WHERE THE DEW IS MADE BEFORE DAWN! . . . . 771 SPINNING SONG   5
THAT DIES OUT BEFORE 'TIS DAY, ... 777 SONG DEIRDRE 2   8
THE CURLEW CRY BEFORE DAWN . . . . 783 GREY ROUND   22
TO THE LOUD SANDS BEFORE DAY HAS BROKEN. . . . . 784 WOMANS BEAUTY   18
AMID THE DARK BEFORE DAY HAD BROKEN. . . . . 784 WOMANS BEAUTY   20
BUT NEVER STOOD BEFORE A STAKE . . . . 790 SINGING HEAD   23
HE, DISGUISED AS A SAILOR BEFORE THE MAST, ... 790 DEDICATION   2
YOU HAD BROUGHT DOWN BEFORE YOU DIED. . . . . 791 REPRISALS   2

BEG

AH! LEAVE ME, I PRAY YOU AND BEG. . . . . 708 FAIRY PEDANT   22

BEGAN

BEFORE GOD WAS OR MY OLD LINE BEGAN! . . . . 29 OISIN 2   8
THINGS DONE ERE GOD FIRST WAS OR MY OLD LINE BEGAN! . . 29 OISIN 2   V   8
. . . NO, NOT SINCE THE WORLD BEGAN, ... 50 OISIN 3   49
AND HE BEGAN TO GRIEVE. . . . . 132 FR GILLIGAN   8
AND STARS BEGAN TO PEEP. . . . . 133 FR GILLIGAN   16
OF HER, WHOSE HISTORY BEGAN . . . . 137 TO IRELAND   7
WHEN TIME BEGAN TO RANT AND RAGE . . . . 138 TO IRELAND   10
WHEN OWLS BEGAN TO CALL! . . . . 159 CAP AND BELLS   6
UNTIL THE PILLARED DARK BEGAN TO STIR . . . . 185 QUEEN MAEVE   110
AS MEN IN THE OLD TIMES, BEFORE THE HARPS BEGAN, . . . 219 WOODS OF COOLE   43
AS MEN IN THE OLD TIMES, BEFORE THE HARP BEGAN, ... 219 WOODS OF COOLE V   43
TILL OAK AND HAZEL CEASED AND BEECH BEGAN, ... 283 TWO KINGS   V 139A
THE BEGGAR IN A RAGE BEGAN . . . . 306 HOUR DAWN   80
SANG TILL STARS BEGAN TO FADE, ... 332 ROUND TOWER   20
IT'S LONG SINCE I BEGAN . . . . 347 FISHERMAN   6
SUDDENLY I BEGAN . . . . 348 FISHERMAN   26
WHO HAD ENDED WHERE HIS BREATH BEGAN. . . . . 360 ALF POLLEXFEN   12
O NOT SINCE LIFE BEGAN. . . . . 382 VISION ROBART   8
THAT NOTHING STRANGE! THE TRAGEDY BEGAN . . . . 411 TOWER   51
BEFORE THE THREAD BEGAN . . . . 520 HIS BARGAIN   8
HOW SOUL COULD WALK BEFORE SUCH THINGS BEGAN. . . . . . 558 RIBH CHRISTIAN   12
HOW SOUL HAS WALKED BEFORE SUCH THINGS BEGAN. . . . . . 558 RIBH CHRISTIAN V   12
KNOW WHERE ITS ROOTS BEGAN. . . . . 571 THREE BUSHES   76
WINTER AND SUMMER TILL OLD AGE BEGAN . . . . 629 CIRCUS ANIMALS   5
GREW IN PURE MIND, BUT OUT OF WHAT BEGAN? . . . . 630 CIRCUS ANIMALS   34
TOOK UP THE NEAREST AND BEGAN TO SEW. . . . . 634 CUCHULAIN COMF   18
MEASUREMENT BEGAN OUR MIGHT! . . . . 638 BEN BULBEN   42
WHAT FINGER FIRST BEGAN . . . . 783 GREY ROUND   11

BEGET

FRESH IMAGES BEGET, ... 498 BYZANTIUM   39
AND COULD BEGET OR BEAR THEMSELVES COULD THEY BUT LOVE   556 RIBH PATRICK   12
    AS HE.

BEGETS

AS MAN, AS BEAST, AS AN EPHEMERAL FLY BEGETS, GODHEAD   556 RIBH PATRICK   5
    BEGETS GODHEAD,
AS MAN, AS BEAST, AS AN EPHEMERAL FLY BEGETS, GODHEAD   556 RIBH PATRICK   5
    BEGETS GODHEAD,

	PAGE	TITLE	LINE

BEGETS (CONTINUED)
A LOUT BEGETS A LOUT, ... 605 SONGS BURDEN 1   6
BEGETTER
HUGH LANE, "ONLIE BEGETTER" OF ALL THESE: . . . . 602 GALLERY REVIS   22
BEGGAR
A BEGGAR SAID, "THEY GET THE MOST . . . . 295 THREE BEGGARS   15
"AND IF I WIN," ONE BEGGAR SAID, ... 296 THREE BEGGARS   29
ONE BEGGAR CRIED: "YOU'RE SHAMMING SLEEP," . . . . . 297 THREE BEGGARS V   45
BEGGAR TO BEGGAR CRIED . . . . 299 BEGGAR CRIED   T
BEGGAR TO BEGGAR CRIED . . . . 299 BEGGAR CRIED   T
BEGGAR TO BEGGAR CRIED, BEING FRENZY-STRUCK, ... 299 BEGGAR CRIED   3
BEGGAR TO BEGGAR CRIED, BEING FRENZY-STRUCK, ... 299 BEGGAR CRIED   3
BEGGAR TO BEGGAR CRIED, BEING FRENZY-STRUCK, ... 300 BEGGAR CRIED   7
BEGGAR TO BEGGAR CRIED, BEING FRENZY-STRUCK, ... 300 BEGGAR CRIED.   7
BEGGAR TO BEGGAR CRIED, BEING FRENZY-STRUCK, ... 300 BEGGAR CRIED   11
BEGGAR TO BEGGAR CRIED, BEING FRENZY-STRUCK, ... 300 BEGGAR CRIED   11
BEGGAR TO BEGGAR CRIED, BEING FRENZY-STRUCK, ... 300 BEGGAR CRIED   15
BEGGAR TO BEGGAR CRIED, BEING FRENZY-STRUCK, ... 300 BEGGAR CRIED   15
BEGGAR TO BEGGAR CRIED, BEING FRENZY-STRUCK, ... 300 BEGGAR CRIED   19
BEGGAR TO BEGGAR CRIED, BEING FRENZY-STRUCK, ... 300 BEGGAR CRIED   19
AND THERE THE KING IS BUT AS THE BEGGAR. . . . . . 301 RUN PARADISE   7
AND THERE THE KING IS BUT AS THE BEGGAR. . . . . . 301 RUN PARADISE   14
AND THERE THE KING IS BUT AS THE BEGGAR. . . . . . 301 RUN PARADISE   21
AND THERE THE KING IS BUT AS THE BEGGAR. . . . . . 301 RUN PARADISE   28
I HAD BEEN HURT," THE OLD BEGGAR THOUGHT . . . . . 302 HOUR DAWN V   19
THE BEGGAR DEAF TO ALL BUT HOPE . . . . . . 304 HOUR DAWN V   44
THE BEGGAR IN A RAGE BEGAN . . . . . . 306 HOUR DAWN   80
CRIED THE BEGGAR, BILLY BYRNE: . . . . . . 331 ROUND TOWER   4
SOME BEGGAR SHELTERING FROM THE WIND, AND THERE . . . . 351 HER PRAISE   13
AS THAT OLD WANDERING BEGGAR AND THESE GOD-HATED CHILDREN 459 FROM OEDIPUS   6
    KNOW.
I WOULD THAT I WERE AN OLD BEGGAR . . . . . . 552 SONGS REWRIT 2   1
A DREARY, DREEPY BEGGAR . . . . 552 SONGS REWRIT 2   5
O A BEGGAR BLIND FROM HIS BIRTH: . . . . . . 552 SONGS REWRIT 2   8
O WOULD THAT I WERE AN OLD BEGGAR . . . . . . 552 SONGS REWRIT 2 V   1
A BEGGAR BLIND FROM HIS BIRTH: . . . . . . 552 SONGS REWRIT 2 V   8
NO RAGGED BEGGAR MAN, ... 567 FROM JAPANESE V   6
AND THERE IS AN OLD BEGGAR WANDERING IN HIS PRIDE-- . 580 CURSE CROMWELL   5
A BEGGAR UPON HORSEBACK LASHES A BEGGAR ON FOOT. . . 590 GREAT DAY   2
A BEGGAR UPON HORSEBACK LASHES A BEGGAR ON FOOT. . . 590 GREAT DAY   2
A BEGGAR UPON HORSEBACK LASHES A BEGGAR UPON FOOT: . . 590 GREAT DAY V   2
A BEGGAR UPON HORSEBACK LASHES A BEGGAR UPON FOOT: . . 590 GREAT DAY V   2
BEGGAR-KINGS
SOME BOAST OF BEGGAR-KINGS AND KINGS . . . . . . 597 MODEL LAUREATE   9
BEGGARLY
THIS BEGGARLY HABILIMENT-- . . . . 539 MEETING   17
BEGGARMAN
DREAM OF THE NOBLE AND THE BEGGARMAN. . . . . . 603 GALLERY REVIS V   47
BEGGAR-MAN
HOLY JOE, THE BEGGAR-MAN, ... 529 TOM LUNATIC   8
NO RAGGED BEGGAR-MAN, ... 567 FROM JAPANESE   6
DREAM OF THE NOBLE AND THE BEGGAR-MAN. . . . . . 603 GALLERY REVIS   47
BEGGAR'S
ALL EMPTIED OF PURPLE HOURS AS A BEGGAR'S CLOAK IN THE 63 OISIN 3   219
    RAIN,
THE FRENZY OF THE BEGGAR'S MOON . . . . . . 296 THREE BEGGARS V   43
BEGGARS
THE THREE BEGGARS . . . . 294 THREE BEGGARS   T
AND THERE TO THREE OLD BEGGARS SAID, ... 295 THREE BEGGARS   10
ARE DRIVEN BY WEALTH AS BEGGARS BY THE ITCH," . . . 300 BEGGAR CRIED   14
ROADS FULL OF BEGGARS, CATTLE IN THE FIELDS, . . . 487 SEVEN SAGES   18
THE BEGGARS HAVE CHANGED PLACES, BUT THE LASH GOES ON. . 590 GREAT DAY   4
BEGGARS'
THE FRENZY OF THE BEGGARS' MOON . . . . . . 296 THREE BEGGARS   43
BEGGARY
THE EXORBITANT DREAMS OF BEGGARY, ... 296 THREE BEGGARS   39
THEY UNDERSTOOD THAT WISDOM COMES OF BEGGARY. . . . . 487 SEVEN SAGES   26
BEGIN
MADE IRELAND'S HEART BEGIN TO BEAT: . . . . . 138 TO IRELAND   12
BEFORE MY THOUGHTS BEGIN TO RUN . . . . . . 189 BAILE AILLINN   3
ONE CANNOT BEGIN IT TOO SOON. . . . . . . 268 BROWN PENNY   16
NOR BUT IN MERRIMENT BEGIN A CHASE, ... 405 FOR DAUGHTER   45
BEGIN THE PREPARATION FOR YOUR DEATH . . . . . 500 VACILLATION   28
NOW HIS WARS ON GOD BEGIN: . . . . . . 561 FOUR AGES MAN   7
ACCOMPLISHED FINGERS BEGIN TO PLAY. . . . . . 567 LAPIS LAZULI   54
RED BIRD OF MARCH, BEGIN TO CROW! . . . . . 782 HEART FRIGHT   5
RED BIRD OF MARCH, BEGIN TO CROW! . . . . . 782 HEART FRIGHT   12
RED BIRD OF MARCH, BEGIN TO CROW! . . . . . 782 HEART FRIGHT   19
BEGINNING
TILL STARS ARE BEGINNING TO BLINK AND PEEP: . . . . 150 OLD MOTHER   4
AND THAT WAS THE BEGINNING OF A JOY . . . . . . 465 HARUN RASHID V   103
BEGINS
WHEN DAY BEGINS TO BREAK . . . . 316 FRIENDS   21
RIDDLED WITH LIGHT. AH! WHEN THE GHOST BEGINS TO QUICKEN, 316 COLD HEAVEN   9
THE SOUL BEGINS TO TREMBLE INTO STILLNESS, ... 374 PHASES OF MOON   54
WHEN THE CLOCK BEGINS TO CHIME." . . . . . 570 THREE BUSHES   41
THINK WHERE MAN'S GLORY MOST BEGINS AND ENDS, . . . 604 GALLERY REVIS   54
THAT THE ADVENTURE OF OLD AGE BEGINS. . . . . 609 IN TARAS HALLS   5
NOW THE HUNT BEGINS ANEW? . . . . 773 SONG DEIRDRE 1   18
BEGONE   SEE WOE-BEGONE
MY CRUELTY MUST KEEP: AND SO BEGONE . . . . . . 448 HERO GIRL FOOL V   7

```
                                                 PAGE     TITLE              LINE
BEGOT
     NOR THOUGHT OUT OF HER MIND OR MINE BEGOT, . . . . . .    467  HARUN RASHID         140
     BEGOT:  SELF-BORN, HIGH-BORN, AND SOLITARY, . . . . . .   467  HARUN RASHID    V    141
     A DANCE-LIKE GLORY THAT THOSE WALLS BEGOT. . . . . . .    488  COOLE PARK 29          8
     GODHEAD ON GODHEAD IN SEXUAL SPASM BEGOT . . . . . . .    557  RIBH ECSTASY           5
     A FASHION WITH US MOORISH MAIDS, BEGOT . . . . . .       700  MOSADA 3              25
BEGOTTEN     SEE SELF-BEGOTTEN BLOOD-BEGOTTEN
     WHATEVER IS BEGOTTEN, BORN, AND DIES, . . . . . . .      407  SAIL BYZANTIUM         6
     WHATEVER IS BEGOTTEN BORN OR DIES, . . . . . . . .       407  SAIL BYZANTIUM  V      6
     NOR STORM DISTURBS, FLAMES BEGOTTEN OF FLAME, . . . .    498  BYZANTIUM             27
     WHERE BLOOD BEGOTTEN SPIRITS COME . . . . . . . . .      498  BYZANTIUM       V     28
     OR THOSE BEGOTTEN OR UNBEGOTTEN . . . . . . . . .        599  SPIRIT MEDIUM          5
     OR THOSE BEGOTTEN OR UNBEGOTTEN, . . . . . . . . .       599  SPIRIT MEDIUM          9
BEGUILE
     NONE MAY BEGUILE HIM, AND HIS PASSIONS COLD . . . . .     35  OISIN 2         V   83A
     YON SHEPHERD--CAME YOUR SPIRIT TO BEGUILE . . . . .      648  ISLE STAT I 1       105
BEGUILED
     YOUNG PRINCESS, WHY WERT THOU BEGUILED . . . . . . .       6  OISIN 1         V     59
     YOUNG PRINCESS, WHEN WERE YOU BEGUILED . . . . . . .       6  OISIN 1         V     59
     "AND HOW AND WHERE WERE YOU BEGUILED, . . . . . . .        6  OISIN 1         V     60
BEGUN
     NOW THAT MY BODY HAS BEGUN TO DREAM, . . . . . . .       245  SHADOW WATER B      486
     IN ITS OWN BEING, AND WHEN THAT WAR'S BEGUN . . . . .    374  PHASES OF MOON       51
     SHE HAS BEGUN FORGETTING.  WHEN SHE WAKES, . . . . .     760  SHADOW WATER A      255
     I HAVE BEGUN REMEMBERING MY DREAMS. . . . . . . .        766  SHADOW WATER A      380
     THE HARP-STRINGS HAVE BEGUN TO CRY OUT TO THE EAGLES. . . 769  SHADOW WATER A      431
     IT HAS BEGUN TO CRY OUT TO THE EAGLES. . . . . .         769  SHADOW WATER A  V   431
BEHIND
     AND FAR BEHIND US, SLOWLY ROUND . . . . . .              10  OISIN 1         V  114B
     AND A BEAUTIFUL YOUNG MAN FOLLOWED BEHIND . . . . . .    12  OISIN 1             144
     A BEAUTIFUL YOUNG MAN FOLLOWED BEHIND. . . . . . .       12  OISIN 1             145
     OF MURMURING OCEAN, AND BEHIND US . . . . . . . .        25  OISIN 1         V   384
     A WALL BEHIND HIS BACK, OVER HIS HEAD . . . . . .       180  QUEEN MAEVE           5
     NOT WHAT'S BEHIND." . . . . . . . .                     263  MASK                 10
     THE CROWD THAT CLOSES IN BEHIND: . . . . . . .          266  GALWAY RACES          4
     THE FIELD THAT CLOSES IN BEHIND. . . . . . .            266  GALWAY RACES    V     4
     BEFORE HIM OR BEHIND, BUT THAT FAR OFF . . . . . .      279  TWO KINGS            55
     BEFORE HIM OR BEHIND, BUT THAT FAR-OFF . . . . . .      279  TWO KINGS            55
     AND WHAT WAITS BEHIND THE DOOR, . . . . . . . .         298  THREE HERMITS         9
     AND LEAVE NO SMOKING WICK BEHIND, . . . . . . .         306  HOUR DAWN            97
     A WASTE OF BREATH THE YEARS BEHIND . . . . . . .        328  IRISH AIRMAN         15
     AND LEAVE A WOMAN AND A MAN BEHIND . . . . . . .        422  MY DESCENDANTS        3
     TO LEAVE A WOMAN AND A MAN BEHIND . . . . . . .         422  MY DESCENDANTS  V     3
     TO LEAVE SOME MONUMENT BEHIND, . . . . . . .            432  NINETEEN 19          96
     THE HEART BEHIND ITS RIB LAUGHED OUT. . . .             450  OWEN AHERNE          13
     HIS PROUD HEART HE LEFT BEHIND. . . . . . .             561  FOUR AGES MAN         6
     TWO CHINAMEN, BEHIND THEM A THIRD, . . . . .            566  LAPIS LAZULI         37
     HE NEVER LAY BEHIND FOUR WALLS . . . . . . .            606  SONGS BURDEN 1       12
     OR CROWD BEHIND THE BULWARK, THAT WE SEEM . . . . .     751  SHADOW WATER A       94
     I HAD THROWN IT DOWN BEHIND THIS COIL OF ROPE. . . . .  759  SHADOW WATER A      245
BEHOLD
     BEHOLD THAT GREAT PLOTINUS SWIM, . . . . . . .          530  DELPHIC ORACLE        1
     BEHOLD, HOW LIKE A SWARM OF FIERY BEES . . . . . . .    662  ISLE STAT II 2        1
     BEHOLD THE BRAZEN-GATED GLADE! . . . . . . . .          667  ISLE STAT II 3       43
     BEHOLD THE LOVING LOVELESS FLOWER OF LONE WAYS, . . .   674  ISLE STAT II 3      201
     BEHOLD THE HAPLESS SLEEPERS STANDING BY. . . . . .      677  ISLE STAT II 3      281
     BEHOLD THE FLASHING WATERS, . . . . . . .               680  LOVE AND DEATH        1
     BEHOLD, I BEND BEFORE THEE TO THE GROUND . . . . .      683  SEEKER               43
     "BEHOLD THE KNIGHT OF THE WATERFALL, WHOSE HEART . . .  684  SEEKER               54
     BEHOLD, I BEND BEFORE THEE TO THE GROUND: . . . . .     684  SEEKER               61
     BEHOLD, I BEND BEFORE THEE TO THE GROUND! . . . . .     684  SEEKER               67
     BEHOLD, I BEND!  AROUND MY BEARD IN DRIFTS . . . . .    684  SEEKER               68
     BEHOLD I BOW BEFORE THEE TO THE GROUND! . . . . .       684  SEEKER          V    67
     BEHOLD I BOW!  AROUND MY BEARD IN DRIFTS                684  SEEKER          V    68
     THE LIGHTNINGS PULSE--BEHOLD HER, AYE BEHOLD-- . . . .  687  TWO TITANS           11
     THE LIGHTNINGS PULSE--BEHOLD HER, AYE BEHOLD-- . . . .  687  TWO TITANS           11
     AND THE SALMON BEHOLD, AND THE OUSEL TOO, . . . . .     717  LOVE SONG             3
BEING
     BUT I, BEING YOUNG AND FOOLISH, WITH HER WOULD NOT AGREE.   90  SALLEY GARDENS      4
     BUT NOW I HAVE GROWN NOTHING, BEING ALL: . . . . .      104  FERGUS DRUID    V    38
     BEING WEARY OF THE WORLD'S EMPIRES, BOW DOWN TO YOU, . .  161  BLACK PIG           7
     CUMHAL THE KING, BEING ANGRY AND SAD, . . . . . .       166  BLESSED               1
     BUT I, BEING POOR, HAVE ONLY MY DREAMS: . . . . .       176  CLOTHS HEAVEN   V     6
     MAEVE WALKED, YET WITH SLOW FOOTFALL, BEING OLD, . . .  181  QUEEN MAEVE          43
     WAS THAT, THE AIR BEING HEAVY AND THE DOGS . . . . .    182  QUEEN MAEVE          53
     BEING FORBID TO MARRY ON EARTH, . . . . . . .           189  BAILE AILLINN        11
     BEING TUMBLED AND BLOWN ABOUT . . . . . . .             191  BAILE AILLINN        66
     AND HE, BEING LAID UPON GREEN BOUGHS, . . . . .         192  BAILE AILLINN        71
     WHO BEING LOVELY WAS SO WISE-- . . . . . .              193  BAILE AILLINN        98
     IN THE HID PLACE, BEING CRAZED BY LOVE. . . . .         195  BAILE AILLINN       143
     AND BEING IN GOOD HEART, BECAUSE . . . . . .            197  BAILE AILLINN       191
     THE FOLLY OF BEING COMFORTED . . . . . . .              199  FOLLY COMFORT         T
     YOU'D KNOW THE FOLLY OF BEING COMFORTED. . . . .        200  FOLLY COMFORT        14
     HEAVY LIKE STONE, THEIR WISDOM BEING HALF SILENCE. . .  218  WOODS OF COOLE       26
     I AM SO TIRED OF BEING BACHELOR . . . . . .             222  SHADOW WATER B        8
     FROM EARLIEST CHILDHOOD, BUT THAT BEING SO, . . . .     225  SHADOW WATER B  V    77
     BEING AS DOUBTFUL?  I HAVE CALLED YOU MASTER . . . .    227  SHADOW WATER B      110
     BEING TOO BUSY IN THE AIR AND THE HIGH AIR, . . . .     234  SHADOW WATER B      274
     HAD DROWNED ME ALSO.  BUT, BEING YET ALIVE, . . . .     235  SHADOW WATER B      289
     BEING DRIVEN ON BY VOICES AND BY DREAMS . . . . .       243  SHADOW WATER B      441
     THEIR HEADS BEING TURNED WITH PRAISE AND FLATTERY! . .  245  SHADOW WATER B      480
```

73

BEING   (CONTINUED)

	PAGE	TITLE	LINE
THAT HE IS BEING DRIVEN TO HIS DEATH.	248	SHADOW WATER B	551
BEING TOO HIGH, THEIR HEADY PROPHECIES	250	SHADOW WATER B	578
AND NOW, BEING GREY.	255	WOMAN HOMER	9
BEING HIGH AND SOLITARY AND MOST STERN?	257	NO SECOND TROY	10
WHY, WHAT COULD SHE HAVE DONE, BEING WHAT SHE IS?	257	NO SECOND TROY	11
WHEN, THE EARS BEING DEAFENED, THE SIGHT OF THE EYES BLIND	257	RECONCILIATION	3
YET OLD ROMANCE BEING KIND, LET HIM PREVAIL	258	KING NO KING	5
BEING FOR A WOMAN'S SAKE.	259	UNWORTH PRAISE	4
ITS FLESH BEING WILD, AND IT AGAIN	266	GALWAY RACES	13
AND BEING THANKFUL MURROUGH FOUND,	274	GREY ROCK	77
BEING BETRAYED INTO A CRADLE, AND I COME	284	TWO KINGS	169
BEING WEARIED OUT, I LOVE IN MAN THE CHILD?	285	TWO KINGS	192
AND BADE ALL WELCOME, BEING IGNORANT.	286	TWO KINGS	218
AND RIDDEN TOWARDS IT, BEING IGNORANT.	286	TWO KINGS V	218
WHAT NEED YOU, BEING COME TO SENSE.	289	SEPTEMBER 1913	1
BEING HONOUR BRED, WITH ONE	291	TO A FRIEND	5
WHO HAVE FAILED, BEING WEAK OF WILL,	298	THREE HERMITS	18
BEGGAR TO BEGGAR CRIED, BEING FRENZY-STRUCK,	299	BEGGAR CRIED	3
BEGGAR TO BEGGAR CRIED, BEING FRENZY-STRUCK,	300	BEGGAR CRIED	7
BEGGAR TO BEGGAR CRIED, BEING FRENZY-STRUCK,	300	BEGGAR CRIED	11
BEGGAR TO BEGGAR CRIED, BEING FRENZY-STRUCK,	300	BEGGAR CRIED	15
BEGGAR TO BEGGAR CRIED, BEING FRENZY-STRUCK,	300	BEGGAR CRIED	19
BEING CERTAIN IT WAS NO RIGHT ROCK	303	HOUR DAWN	23
BEING CERTAIN IT WAS NO RIGHT PLACE	303	HOUR DAWN V	23
AND THEN AT LAST BEING WIDE AWAKE	304	HOUR DAWN V	40
BUT I ALONE BEING BLESSED KEEP	307	HOUR DAWN	104
BEING YOUNG YOU HAVE NOT KNOWN	312	CHILD DANCING	6
BEING WAKEFUL FOR HER SAKE,	316	FRIENDS	23
BEING OUT OF HEART WITH GOVERNMENT	317	APPOINTMENT	1
BEING OUT OF HEART AT GOVERNMENT	317	APPOINTMENT V	1
BEING BY CALVARY'S TURBULENCE UNSATISFIED,	318	MAGI	7
WHO HAD SEEN, BEING KEPT FOR SHOW,	319	DOLLS	5
BEING BUT A PART OF ANCIENT CEREMONY--	321	REED WHISPERER	12
ALL, ALL ARE IN MY THOUGHTS TO-NIGHT BEING DEAD.	324	ROBERT GREGORY	8
BEING MORE INDIFFERENT TO OUR SOLITUDE	334	LIVING BEAUTY	7
THE WICK OF YOUTH BEING BURNED AND THE OIL SPENT,	334	LIVING BEAUTY V	3
BEING OLD, BUT THAT THE OLD ALONE MIGHT DIE,	339	SHEP GOATHERD	4
ON BEING ASKED FOR A WAR POEM	359	WAR POEM	T
WE AND OUR DOLLS BEING BUT THE WORLD WERE BEST AWAY.	364	DOLLS FACES	12
BEING MOCKED BY GUIDO FOR HIS LECHEROUS LIFE,	369	EGO DOMINUS	33
AND MADE--BEING POOR, AILING AND IGNORANT,	370	EGO DOMINUS	59
AND LOOK MOST LIKE ME, BEING INDEED MY DOUBLE,	371	EGO DOMINUS	72
THE MOST UNLIKE, BEING MY ANTI-SELF,	371	EGO DOMINUS	74
IN ITS OWN BEING, AND WHEN THAT WAR'S BEGUN	374	PHASES OF MOON	51
FOR NOW BEING DEAD IT SEEMED	383	VISION ROBART	23
BEING FIXED ON ALL THINGS LOVED, ALL THINGS UNLOVED,	383	VISION ROBART	34
BEING CAUGHT BETWEEN THE PULL	384	VISION ROBART	59
CHANCE BEING AT ONE WITH CHOICE AT LAST,	388	SOLOMON WITCH	14
YOUTH'S BITTERNESS BEING PAST,	389	IMAGE PAST	11
BEING A PORTION OF MY YOUTH, CAN MAKE ME PINE	391	UNDER SATURN V	3
BEING CERTAIN THAT THEY AND I	392	EASTER 1916	13
BEING DEAR AS MINE ARE DEAR.	400	DEMON BEAST	20
BEING NO MORE DEMONIAC	400	DEMON BEAST	30
BEING MADE BEAUTIFUL OVERMUCH,	403	FOR DAUGHTER	20
HELEN BEING CHOSEN FOUND LIFE FLAT AND DULL	404	FOR DAUGHTER	25
BEING FATHERLESS COULD HAVE HER WAY	404	FOR DAUGHTER	28
AND CERTAIN MEN, BEING MADDENED BY THOSE RHYMES,	410	TOWER	41
INTO THE LABYRINTH OF ANOTHER'S BEING;	413	TOWER	112
THAT, BEING DEAD, WE RISE,	415	TOWER	154
BEING OF THAT METAL MADE	416	TOWER	178
SOUL'S BEAUTY BEING MOST ADORED,	421	MY TABLE	22
BEING BY THE WORLD OPPRESSED,	434	YOUTH AND AGE	2
AND AGAMEMNON DEAD. BEING SO CAUGHT UP,	441	LEDA AND SWAN	11
AND THAT ALONE; YET I, BEING DRIVEN HALF INSANE	442	BLACK CENTAUR	6
BEING BUT HOLY SHOWS	454	HIS MEMORIES	2
BEING ALL ALONE I'D NURSE A STONE	459	HIS WILDNESS	11
AND SHE AND I, BEING SUNK IN HAPPINESS,	463	HARUN RASHID	51
BEING ALL BRIMMED WITH LIFE?" "WERE IT BUT TRUE	465	HARUN RASHID	90
BUT I BEING NONE CAN PRAISE ITS OPPOSITE.	465	HARUN RASHID	98
BEING SO BRIMMED WITH LIFE. "IF THAT COULD BE	465	HARUN RASHID V	90
BEING SHARPENED BY HIS DEATH,	471	ALL SOUL NIGHT	8
BEING BOTH CHANCE AND CHOICE,	472	ALL SOUL NIGHT	58
AND MAY HAVE GROWN MORE ARROGANT BEING A GHOST.	473	ALL SOUL NIGHT	80
MINE WOULD WALK, BEING DEAD.	511	JANE AND JACK V	18
WHEN, THE POTION'S WORK BEING DONE,	522	LULLABY	9
ALL OTHER LOVERS BEING ESTRANGED OR DEAD,	523	LONG SILENCE	2
BEING MENTIONED WITH A MAN	531	FATHER CHILD	4
I MOCKED, BEING CRAZY, BUT YOU MASTERED IT	533	HER TRIUMPH	8
THAT THE CRIME OF BEING BORN	534	CONSOLATION	9
THAT SHE IS HAPPY BEING CRAZY;	568	SWEET DANCER	10
BEING THEIR AMBASSADOR,	582	ROGER CASEMENT	14
SOME THAT BEING UNBEGOTTEN,	600	SPIRIT MEDIUM	11
AND BEING OLD SHE PUT A SKIN	621	JOHN KINSELLA	21
MAYBE AT LAST, BEING BUT A BROKEN MAN,	629	CIRCUS ANIMALS	3
BEING ALMINTOR'S PAGE. NOW JUDGE YOU HERE.	660	ISLE STAT II 1	47
WILL HE HAVE HAPPINESS? GREAT SOBS HER BEING SHAKE.	676	ISLE STAT II 3	247
BEING THE MOON OF BIRTH; MAY END OUR DOUBT.	748	SHADOW WATER A	24
I CEASED TO BE A WOMAN, BEING A QUEEN.	758	SHADOW WATER A	228
TO RAISE INTO BEING	784	WOMANS BEAUTY	13
BEING IMAGINED WITHIN	785	WOMANS BEAUTY	23

BEING   (CONTINUED)
    DRAGGED INTO BEING . . . .   785 WOMANS BEAUTY   27
BEINGS
    FOR THE ELEMENTAL BEINGS GO . . . .   138 TO IRELAND   V   23
    YET DREAMED THAT BEINGS HAPPIER THAN MEN . . . . . .   218 WOODS OF COOLE   18
BELABOURING
    TROOPER BELABOURING TROOPER, BITING AT ARM OR AT FACE, . .   426 PHANTOM HATRED   12
BELFRY
    . . . WITH ITS BELFRY IN AIR; . . . .   61 OISIN 3   193
    SAY WHAT RINGER RINGS AT MIDNIGHT; FOR, IN THE BELFRY HIGH,   718 PHANTOM SHIP   15
BELIEF
    DID I BECOME A CHRISTIAN MAN AND CHOOSE FOR MY BELIEF . .   503 VACILLATION   85
BELIEVE
    AND WILL BELIEVE THAT ANYTHING . . . .   191 BAILE AILLINN   68
    "NEVER WILL I BELIEVE THERE IS ANY CHANGE . . . . . .   285 TWO KINGS   203
    SWEETENED BY DEATH, BUT IF I COULD BELIEVE, ...   285 TWO KINGS   205
    BELIEVE THAT GOLD AND WOMEN TAKEN IN WAR . . . . . .   754 SHADOW WATER A   159
BELIEVED
    BELIEVED THERE WAS SOME OTHER NEAR AT HAND, ...   229 SHADOW WATER B   154
    THAT ONE BELIEVED HE HAD A SWORD UPSTAIRS; . . . . .   267 ALL TEMPT ME   8
BELIEVING
    BELIEVING EVERY WORD I SAID, ...   314 MEMORY YOUTH   8
BELL   SEE DUMB-BELL
    O PATRICK, BY YOUR BRAZEN BELL, ...   7 OISIN 1   71
    AND GOD'S BELL BUOYED TO BE THE WATER'S CARE; . . . .   114 ROSE OF BATTLE   4
    GOD'S BELL HAS CLAIMED THEM BY THE LITTLE CRY . . . .   114 ROSE OF BATTLE   23
    THE BELL THAT CALLS US ON; THE SWEET FAR THING . . .   115 ROSE OF BATTLE   28
    THERE WAS A GREEN BRANCH HUNG WITH MANY A BELL . . .   129 BOOK STORIES   1
    I ALSO BEAR A BELL BRANCH FULL OF EASE. . . . . . .   130 BOOK STORIES   V   12
    MY BELL BRANCH MURMURS; THE GAY BELLS BRING LAUGHTER, . .   130 BOOK STORIES   V   18
    CAP AND BELL . . . .   159 CAP AND BELLS V   T
    "I'VE CAP AND BELL," HE PONDERED, ...   160 CAP AND BELLS V   21
    THAN DUMB BELL AND FOIL . . . .   334 SONG   V   3
    WERE NOT OUR BEDS FAR OFF I'D RING THE BELL, ...   377 PHASES OF MOON   124
    LIKE THE CLANGOUR OF A BELL, ...   382 SONG OF FOOL   9
    MIDNIGHT HAS COME, AND THE GREAT CHRIST CHURCH BELL . . .   470 ALL SOUL NIGHT   1
    AND MANY A LESSER BELL SOUND THROUGH THE ROOM; . . .   470 ALL SOUL NIGHT   2
    IT IS ALL SOULS' NIGHT AND THE GREAT CHRIST CHURCH BELL   470 ALL SOUL NIGHT V   1
    A SLOW LOW NOTE AND AN IRON BELL. . . . .   549 SEVERED HEAD   7
    A SLOW LOW NOTE AND AN IRON BELL. . . . .   550 SEVERED HEAD   14
    A SLOW LOW NOTE AND AN IRON BELL. . . . .   550 SEVERED HEAD   21
    TREMBLES AS A BELL OF GLASS . . . .   705 DAWN-SONG   10
    SLOW THE CHAPEL BELL IS TOLLING AS THOUGH THE DEAD PASSED   718 PHANTOM SHIP   16
        BY.
    WHERE A HAND ON THE BELL . . . .   780 WELL AND TREE   4
BELL-BEAT
    THE BELL-BEAT OF THEIR WINGS ABOVE MY HEAD, ...   323 SWANS AT COOLE   17
BELL-BRANCH
    AND I GAZED ON THE BELL-BRANCH, SLEEP'S FOREBEAR, . . .   50 OISIN 3   53
    LAID HANDS ON THE BELL-BRANCH AND SWAYED IT, ...   51 OISIN 3   56
    THEN HE SWAYED IN HIS FINGERS THE BELL-BRANCH, ...   51 OISIN 3   67
    . . . THE STRENGTH OF THE BELL-BRANCH IS NAUGHT, . . .   55 OISIN 3   123
    I ALSO BEAR A BELL-BRANCH FULL OF EASE. . . . . . .   130 BOOK STORIES   12
BELLE
    AND WHO CAN SAY BUT SOME YOUNG BELLE MAY WALK AND TALK   354 HIS PHOENIX   26
        MEN WILD
    AND MAY BE THERE'LL BE SOME YOUNG BELLE WALK OUT TO MAKE   354 HIS PHOENIX   V   26
        MEN WILD
    AND MAYBE THERE'LL BE SOME YOUNG BELLE WALK OUT TO MAKE   354 HIS PHOENIX   V   26
        MEN WILD
BELLED
    HOWLED, MIAU-D, BARKED, BRAYED, BELLED, YELLED, CRIED,   387 SOLOMON WITCH   8
        CROWED,
BELLIED   SEE POT-BELLIED
BELLIES
    THAT BELLIES AND DRAGS IN THE WIND . . . .   358 BALLOON MIND   3
BELL-MOUNTED
    YOUR BELL-MOUNTED CHURCHES, ...   58 OISIN 3   163
    THY BELL-MOUNTED CHURCHES, ...   58 OISIN 3   V   163
BELL-NOTES
    . . . AH! WHAT BELL-NOTES DO THEY HEAR? . . . . . .   718 PHANTOM SHIP   14
BELLOW
    I BELLOW TO THE WINDS WHEN STORMS MAKE MOAN, ...   45 OISIN 2   V 239D
BELLOWED
    ON THE HORIZON EDGE BELLOWED THE HERDS. . . . . . .   279 TWO KINGS   56
    BELLOWED AND PRANCED IN THE ROUND TOWER; . . . . . .   331 ROUND TOWER   12
BELLOWING
    THEREON THE BELLOWING OF THE EMPOUNDED HERDS . . . . .   286 TWO KINGS   214
    BELLOWING UP AND BELLOWING ROUND, ...   331 ROUND TOWER   14
    BELLOWING UP AND BELLOWING ROUND, ...   331 ROUND TOWER   14
BELLOWS
    FOR AN OLD BELLOWS FULL OF ANGRY WIND? . . . .   405 FOR DAUGHTER   64
    OR EVERY BELLOWS BURST, BE HAPPY STILL. . . . . . .   405 FOR DAUGHTER   72
BELLS
    IN ONE WAS A BRANCH SOFT-SHINING WITH BELLS MORE MANY THAN   50 OISIN 3   46
        SIGHS
    . . . AND PRAYING, AND WROTH WITH THE BELLS, ...   58 OISIN 3   159
    THAT HE'S A LOVELESS MAN; GAY BELLS BRING LAUGHTER . .   130 BOOK STORIES   18
    GAY BELLS OR SAD, THEY BRING YOU MEMORIES . . . . .   130 BOOK STORIES   21
    MY BELL BRANCH MURMURS; THE GAY BELLS BRING LAUGHTER, . .   130 BOOK STORIES   V   18
    THE SAD BELLS BOW THE FOREHEAD ON THE HANDS. . . . .   130 BOOK STORIES   V   20

                                                            PAGE   TITLE   LINE
BELLS   (CONTINUED)
        THE CAP AND BELLS . . . .   159 CAP AND BELLS   T
        "I HAVE CAP AND BELLS," HE PONDERED, ...   160 CAP AND BELLS   21
BELLY
        DOWN LIMB AND BREAST OR DOWN THAT GLIMMERING BELLY . . . 560 MAGIC DRUM   5
        BUT THETIS' BELLY LISTENS. . . . .   612 NEWS ORACLE   29
        BELLY, SHOULDER, BUM, ...   612 NEWS ORACLE   34
        WHERE MEN FORGIVE IF THE BELLY GAIN? . . . .   615 MARCH SONGS 2   14
BELLYFUL
        BUT WHEN I HAD EATEN AND DRUNK A BELLYFUL . . . . . .   223 SHADOW WATER B V   30
BELONG
        LEAVE NOTHING BUT THE NOTHINGS THAT BELONG . . . . . .   542 PARN FUNERAL 1   29
BELONGS
        BELONGS TO BEAST OR DEMON, ...   401 DEMON BEAST   35
BELOVED   SEE WELL-BELOVED
        BELOVED IN A THOUSAND SONGS. . . . .   7 OISIN 1   V 76
        I WOULD THAT WE WERE, MY BELOVED, WHITE BIRDS ON THE FOAM 121 WHITE BIRDS   1
            OF THE SEA!
        O WOULD THAT WE WERE, MY BELOVED, WHITE BIRDS ON THE FOAM 121 WHITE BIRDS   V   1
            OF THE SEA,
        HAS AWAKED IN OUR HEARTS, MY BELOVED, A SADNESS THAT MAY 122 WHITE BIRDS   4
            NOT DIE.
        AH, DREAM NOT OF THEM, MY BELOVED, THE FLAME OF THE METEOR 122 WHITE BIRDS   6
            THAT GOES,
        WERE WE ONLY WHITE BIRDS, MY BELOVED, ...   122 WHITE BIRDS   12
        HAS AWAKED IN OUR HEARTS, MY BELOVED, A SADNESS THAT NEVER 122 WHITE BIRDS   V   4
            MAY DIE.
        BELOVED, GAZE IN THINE OWN HEART, ...   134 TWO TREES   1
        BELOVED, GAZE IN THINE OWN HEART. . . . .   135 TWO TREES   20
        . . . AND HIS BELOVED, AND LONGS FOR THE END OF THE WORLD 153 CHANGE BELOVED   T
        MONGAN LAMENTS THE CHANGE THAT HAS COME UPON HIM AND HIS 153 CHANGE BELOVED V   T
            BELOVED
        HE BIDS HIS BELOVED BE AT PEACE . . . .   154 BELOVED PEACE   T
        MICHAEL ROBARTES BIDS HIS BELOVED BE AT PEACE . . . . .   154 BELOVED PEACE V   T
        BELOVED, LET YOUR EYES HALF CLOSE, AND YOUR HEART BEAT . .   154 BELOVED PEACE   9
        A POET TO HIS BELOVED . . . .   157 POET BELOVED   T
        HE GIVES HIS BELOVED CERTAIN RHYMES . . . .   157 BELOVED RHYMES   T
        AEDH GIVES HIS BELOVED CERTAIN RHYMES . . . .   157 BELOVED RHYMES V   T
        A QUEEN WAS BELOVED BY A JESTER, ...   159 CAP AND BELLS V   1
        OF YOUR BELOVED IN SLEEP. . . . .   165 CRY OF SEDGE   10
        HE THINKS OF THOSE WHO HAVE SPOKEN EVIL OF HIS BELOVED . .   166 EVIL OF BELOV   T
        AEDH THINKS OF THOSE WHO HAVE SPOKEN EVIL OF HIS BELOVED   166 EVIL OF BELOV V T
        WHEN SONGS I WOVE FOR MY BELOVED HIDE THE PRAYER, ...   173 SPEAKS HEARERS   2
        AND CALL TO MY BELOVED AND ME: "NO LONGER FLY . . . . .   173 SPEAKS HEARERS   7
        WHEN SONG I WOVE FOR MY BELOVED HIDES THE PRAYER, . . .   173 SPEAKS HEARERS V   2
        HE WISHES HIS BELOVED WERE DEAD . . . .   175 BELOVED DEAD   T
        AEDH WISHES HIS BELOVED WERE DEAD . . . .   175 BELOVED DEAD   V   T
        O WOULD, BELOVED, THAT YOU LAY . . . .   176 BELOVED DEAD   11
        BELOVED, I AM NOT AFRAID OF HER. . . . .   197 BAILE AILLINN   200
        I HAVE FLED TO MY BELOVED IN THE AIR, ...   234 SHADOW WATER B   262
        HAVE CALLED ME THEIR BELOVED, I'LL NOT KISS THEM. . . .   237 SHADOW WATER B   336
        BUT MY BELOVED--THAT NIGHT AND DAY HAD PERISHED, ...   246 SHADOW WATER B   504
        AND I AM LEFT ALONE WITH MY BELOVED, ...   251 SHADOW WATER B   600
        BELOVED, HAVING DRAGGED THE NET ABOUT US, ...   252 SHADOW WATER B   615
        LOVED AND THOUGHT HIMSELF BELOVED, ...   404 FOR DAUGHTER   39
        BELOVED HAROUN EL RASHID, OCCUPIED . . . .   462 HARUN RASHID   V   24
        WHEN OUR BELOVED CALIPH PUT TO DEATH . . . .   462 HARUN RASHID   31
        BELOVED BOOKS THAT FAMOUS HANDS HAVE BOUND, ...   491 COOLE BALLYLEE   27
        BELOVED, MAY YOUR SLEEP BE SOUND . . . .   522 LULLABY   1
        SLEEP, BELOVED, SUCH A SLEEP . . . .   522 LULLABY   7
        BELOVED SUCH A SLEEP AS FELL . . . .   522 LULLABY   V   13
        AS THOUGH ON MY BELOVED, ...   532 BEFORE WORLD   10
        DRAW ROUND, BELOVED AND BITTER MEN, ...   584 GHOST ROG CASE   37
        PICTURED, WHERE WANDER THE BELOVED FEET . . . . . .   692 MOSADA 1   44
        BELOVED, HOW TWO LITTLE YEARS AGO . . . .   713 FERENCZ RENYI   89
        BELOVED, HEAR MY BITTER TALE!-- . . . .   742 DANAAN QUICK   1
        BELOVED, BLAME THE DANAAN WHIM, ...   743 DANAAN QUICK   22
        AND SHE CRIES OUT, "I HAVE FLED TO MY BELOVED . . . .   754 SHADOW WATER A   151
        AND CRYING, "I HAVE FLED TO MY BELOVED . . . . . .   754 SHADOW WATER A V 151
        I HAVE COMMANDED MEN IN DREAMS. BELOVED, ...   766 SHADOW WATER A   381
        OUT OF THEIR HATRED, MY BELOVED, FAREWELL. . . . .   767 SHADOW WATER A   400
BELOVED'S   SEE WELL-BELOVED'S
        "YOUR WELL BELOVED'S HAIR HAS THREADS OF GREY, ...   199 FOLLY COMFORT V   2
BELOVEDS
        OF MYRIADS OF BELOVEDS, AND ON THINE . . . .   724 KANVA ON SELF   10
BELOW
        THE FLIES BELOW THE LEAVES, AND THE YOUNG MICE . . . .   75 ANASHU VIJAYA   87
        I PASSED ALONG THE WATER'S EDGE BELOW THE HUMID TREES, . .   76 INDIAN ON GOD   1
        WAKE ALL BELOW! WHY HAVE YOU BROKEN OUR SLEEP? . . . .   233 SHADOW WATER B   242
        BUTTED BELOW THE SINGLE AND SO PIERCED . . . .   278 TWO, KINGS   22
        ONE HEARS THE RUMBLE OF IT FAR BELOW . . . .   420 MY HOUSE   V 20B
        OTTERS BELOW AND MOOR-HENS ON THE TOP, ...   490 COOLE BALLYLEE   2
        OTTERS BELOW AND MOOR HENS ON THE TOP, ...   490 COOLE BALLYLEE V   2
        A RIVERY FIELD SPREAD OUT BELOW, ...   502 VACILLATION   57
        PLATO STANDS BELOW, ...   524 MAD AS MIST   8
        FROM ABOVE TO BELOW. . . . .   547 TO SAME TUNE 3 V   6
        FOR THINGS BELOW ARE COPIES, THE GREAT SMARAGDINE TABLET   556 RIBH PATRICK   6
            SAID.
        'TIS LATE, WAIT ONE MORE DAY! BELOW THE HILLS . . . .   702 MOSADA 3   91
        HAVE NOT A MYRIAD SWAYED BELOW STRANGE TREES . . . .   724 KANVA ON SELF   11
        WAKE ALL BELOW. WHY HAVE YOU BROKEN OUR SLEEP? . . .   753 SHADOW WATER A   132

		PAGE	TITLE	LINE

BELOW   (CONTINUED)
    I HAVE HEARD FROM FAR BELOW . . . . 783 GREY ROUND   25
BELT
    SHE CAUGHT THIS BLADE OUT OF MY BELT AND DIED. . . . . . 755 SHADOW WATER A V   168
BEMOCKERS
    WORD BEMOCKERS?--BY THE ROOD . . . . 65 HAPPY SHEPHERD V   12
BE-MOCKERS
    WORD BE-MOCKERS?--BY THE ROOD, ... 65 HAPPY SHEPHERD   12
BEN
    --BEN JONSON'S PHRASE--AND FIND WHEN JUNE IS COME . . . 321 REED WHISPERER   6
    BEN JONSON'S PHRASE--AND STILL MAY TURN MY FEET . . . 321 REED WHISPERER V   6
    UNDER BEN BULBEN TO THE MEET . . . . 397 POLIT PRISONER   14
    UPON BEN BULBEN SIDE . . . . 398 BREAK OF DAY   6
    OR THE HUMBLER WORM, I CLIMBED BEN BULBEN'S BACK . . . . 409 TOWER   9
    KUSTA BEN LUKA IS MY NAME, I WRITE . . . . 460 HARUN RASHID   1
    OUT OF BEN BULBEN AND KNOCKNAREA, ... 549 SEVERED HEAD   2
    UNDER BEN BULBEN . . . . 636 BEN BULBEN   T
    WHERE BEN BULBEN SETS THE SCENE. . . . . 637 BEN BULBEN   11
    UNDER BARE BEN BULBEN'S HEAD . . . . 640 BEN BULBEN   84
BENCH
    PALE-FACED, ALONE UPON A BENCH, EDAIN . . . . 279 TWO KINGS   61
    HER HANDS ON EITHER SIDE HAD GRIPPED THE BENCH, ... 279 TWO KINGS   63
    PALE-FACED, ALONE UPON A BENCH, HIS WIFE . . . . . 279 TWO KINGS   V   61
    ON NO LONG BENCH NOR LOFTY MILKING-SHED . . . . . . 341 SHEP GOATHERD   51
    ON NO LONG BENCH NOR LOFTY MILKING SHED . . . . . . 341 SHEP GOATHERD   V   51
    A POT-HOUSE BENCH WITH OLIVER GOLDSMITH ONCE. . . . . . 486 SEVEN SAGES   3
    BEFORE THE BENCH OF TIME, ... 582 ROGER CASEMENT   6
BENCHES
    OR ON THE BENCHES UNDERNEATH THE WALLS, ... 180 QUEEN MAEVE   14
    UPON THE ROWERS' BENCHES UNDERNEATH, ... 751 SHADOW WATER A   92
BEND
    AND HE CALLED LOUDLY TO THE STARS TO BEND . . . . . . 68 SAD SHEPHERD   5
    WE WILL BEND DOWN AND LOOSEN OUR HAIR OVER YOU, ... 172 TRAV PASSION   6
    BEND DOWN AND PRAY FOR ALL THAT SIN I WOVE IN SONG, . . . 173 SPEAKS HEARERS   5
    BEND DOWN AND PRAY FOR THE GREAT SIN I WOVE IN SONG, . . . 173 SPEAKS HEARERS V   5
    YOU WOULD COME HITHER, AND BEND YOUR HEAD, ... 175 BELOVED DEAD   3
    O TUFTED REEDS, BEND LOW AND LOW IN POOLS ON THE GREEN   206 HANRAHANS SONG V   1
        LAND,
    BUT WE BEND TOGETHER AND KISS THE QUIET FEET . . . . . 207 HANRAHANS SONG V   4
    BEND LOWER, O KING, THAT I MAY CROWN YOU WITH IT. . . . . 251 SHADOW WATER B   607
    BEND LOWER, THAT I MAY COVER YOU WITH MY HAIR, ... 251 SHADOW WATER B   613
    AND ALL SHALL BEND THE KNEE . . . . 516 MANS SONG   16
    I BEND MY BODY TO THE SPADE . . . . 599 SPIRIT MEDIUM   7
    I BEND MY BODY TO THE SPADE . . . . 600 SPIRIT MEDIUM   15
    I BEND MY BODY TO THE SPADE . . . . 600 SPIRIT MEDIUM   23
    MY MEDIAEVAL KNEES LACK HEALTH UNTIL THEY BEND, ... 603 GALLERY REVIS   33
    BEHOLD, I BEND BEFORE THEE TO THE GROUND . . . . . . 683 SEEKER   43
    BEHOLD, I BEND BEFORE THEE TO THE GROUND! . . . . . . 684 SEEKER   61
    BEHOLD, I BEND BEFORE THEE TO THE GROUND! . . . . . . 684 SEEKER   67
    BEHOLD, I BEND! AROUND MY BEARD IN DRIFTS . . . . . 684 SEEKER   68
    AND THOU SHALT BEND, ENDURING GOD, THE KNEES . . . . . 698 MOSADA 2   59
    AND THOU SHALL BEND, ENDURING GOD, THE KNEES . . . . . 698 MOSADA 2   V   59
    WHERE LONG GREY GRASSES BOW AND BEND, ... 736 SUMMER EVENING   6
    AND MADE THE BRIGHT SPEAR BEND, ... 741 EARL PAUL   46
    BEND LOWER LEST YOUR BATTLE-AXES GLIMMER. . . . . . . 752 SHADOW WATER A   117
    BEND LOWER LEST YOUR BATTLE AXES GLIMMER. . . . . . . 752 SHADOW WATER A   117
    AND UNDER LOVERS' EYELIDS. BEND YOUR HEAD, ... 762 SHADOW WATER A   286
    I CROWN YOU WITH THIS CROWN. BEND LOWER, O KING, . . . 768 SHADOW WATER A   423
    BEND LOWER, THAT I MAY COVER YOU WITH MY HAIR, ... 769 SHADOW WATER A   429
BENDED
    ALONG THE WOOD WITH SUBTLE TREAD AND BENDED BOWS. . . . 649 ISLE STAT I 1   111
BENDING
    UPON THE GRASS-BLADES' BENDING TIPS, ...   3 OISIN 1   V 7II
    WITH BENDING STERNS AND BENDING BOWS, ... 14 OISIN 1   189
    WITH BENDING STERNS AND BENDING BOWS, ... 14 OISIN 1   189
    AND BENDING OVER THEM SOFTLY SAID, ... 21 OISIN 1   307
    BENDING OVER THEM IN THE DANCE, ... 21 OISIN 1   308
    WITH BENDING STERNS AND BENDING BOWS, ... 23 OISIN 1   353
    WITH BENDING STERNS AND BENDING BOWS, ... 23 OISIN 1   353
    LIKE A BRIDE BENDING OVER HER MIRROR ADORNING, ... 28 OISIN 1   V 423E
    BENDING LOW HIS PIOUS HEAD, ... 82 MAD KING GOLL   V   10
    BENDING LOW HIS FADING HEAD, ... 82 MAD KING GOLL   V   10
    THE ANGELS ARE BENDING . . . . 118 CRADLE SONG   V   1
    AND BENDING DOWN BESIDE THE GLOWING BARS, ... 121 YOU ARE OLD   9
    CUMHAL CALLED OUT, BENDING HIS HEAD, ... 166 BLESSED   1
    AND CUMHAL SAID, BENDING HIS KNEES, ... 167 BLESSED   5
    BEFORE HIS CHAIR AND BENDING DOWN MY HEAD . . . . . . 282 TWO KINGS   132
    BENDING HER FACE O'ER HIS, SHE WATCHES MEET . . . . . 688 TWO TITANS   45
    BENDING HUMBLY EVERY KNEE, ... 726 LOVERS QUARREL   14
BENDS
    AND BENDS TO THE FIRE AND SHAKES WITH THE COLD . . . . 26 OISIN 1   405
    THE LION, THE WORLD'S GREAT SOLITARY, BENDS . . . . . 689 NETTLESHIP   5
BENEATH
    ONE HAND BENEATH HIS BEARDLESS CHIN, ... 17 OISIN 1   V 251
    BENEATH HAD PACED CONTENT! WE HELD OUR WAY . . . . . 36 OISIN 2   103
    LONG SIGHS AROSE IN OUR SPIRITS, BENEATH US BUBBLED THE   48 OISIN 3   20
        GROUND.
    . . . BENEATH ME THE HOOVES IMPATIENTLY STEPT. . . . . 54 OISIN 3   V 112
    AND DEMONS BE BROKEN IN PIECES, AND TRAMPLED BENEATH THEM 61 OISIN 3   204
        IN DEATH.

	PAGE	TITLE		LINE

BENEATH   (CONTINUED)
```
    AND DEMONS, ALL BROKEN IN PIECES, BE TRAMPLED BENEATH THEM    61 OISIN 3        V  204
       IN DEATH.
    AND HOW BENEATH THOSE THREE TIMES BLESSED SKIES  . . . .     127 DREAM OF FAERY V   21
    CRIED OUT UPON THAT THING BENEATH  . . . . . . . . .         254 HIS DREAM          10
    TREMBLING BENEATH HIM, AND THEN DROVE THE SPUR  . . . .      277 TWO KINGS       V   11
    AS I, TO CHOOSE BENEATH DAY'S DYING FLAMES:  . . . . .       656 ISLE STAT I 3      34
    CURVING BENEATH THE PROW: AS SOME WILD DRAKE  . . . . .      659 ISLE STAT II 1     16
    BENEATH THE WEIGHT OF GREATER GRIEF THAN I:  . . . . .       661 ISLE STAT II 1     63
    BUT LOUD THE GRASSHOPPER THAT SITS BENEATH.  . . . . .       662 ISLE STAT II 2      8
    BENEATH THE BURTHEN OF THE INFINITE,  . . . . . . . .        674 ISLE STAT II 3    212
    BENEATH THE BURDEN OF THE INFINITE,  . . . . . . . .         674 ISLE STAT II 3  V 212
    MORE DARK BENEATH THE POPLARS, WHERE YON OWL  . . . . .      675 ISLE STAT II 3    233
    ON HER BROAD BREAST: BENEATH HER WITHERED BROWS  . . .       685 SEEKER             73
    BENEATH THE SHELTERING SHADOW OF THY CHURCH:  . . . . .      698 MOSADA 2           58
    NOW STEPS DRAW CLOSE, HE HIDES BENEATH A DRUM.  . . . .      713 FERENCZ RENYI      78
    BENEATH THE WILLOW--NAY, TO YONDER STAR,  . . . . . .        715 FERENCZ RENYI   V 118
    BENEATH THE FLAMING EYEBALLS OF THE NIGHT,  . . . . . .      723 KANVA ON SELF       4
    BENEATH A POINTED CAP OF GREEN:  . . . . . . . . . .         728 PRIEST FAIRY       22
BENIGHTED
    AND ALL BENIGHTED THINGS THAT GO  . . . . . . . . . .        139 TO IRELAND         39
    BENIGHTED TRAVELLERS  . . . . . . . . . . . . . .            419 MY HOUSE           18
BENT
    YOU WHO ARE BENT, AND BALD, AND BLIND,  . . . . . . .          2 OISIN 1             1
    BENT ALL OUR SWAYING BODIES DOWN,  . . . . . . . . .          20 OISIN 1           297
    BENT DOWN ABOVE EACH HOOKED KNEE,  . . . . . . . . .          26 OISIN 1           392
    BENT LOW ABOVE EACH HOOKED KNEE,  . . . . . . . . .           26 OISIN 1         V 392
    WHILE HE BENT DOWN HIS FADING HEAD,  . . . . . . . .          82 MAD KING GOLL      10
    WHEN WE BENT DOWN ABOVE THE FADING COALS  . . . . . .        136 TO SOME I TALK      3
    BECAUSE THEIR BLOSSOMING DREAMS HAVE NEVER BENT  . . .       136 TO SOME I TALK      8
    I BENT TO BLOW THE FIRE AFLAME:  . . . . . . . . . .         149 WANDER AENGUS   V  10
    BUT WE HAVE ALL BENT LOW AND LOW AND KISSED THE QUIET FEET   207 HANRAHANS SONG      9
    CONSTRAINED, ARRAIGNED, BAFFLED, BENT AND UNBENT  . . .      382 VISION ROBART       9
    I DREAM OF A LEDAEAN BODY, BENT  . . . . . . . . . .         443 SCHOOL CHILDR       9
    AND DEDICATE--EYES BENT UPON THE GROUND,  . . . . . .        489 COOLE PARK 29      29
    ROWER BENT IN HIS ROW-BOAT  . . . . . . . . . . .            589 OLD WICKED MAN     50
    OR WEAVER BENT AT HIS LOOM,  . . . . . . . . . . .           589 OLD WICKED MAN     51
    ROWER BENT IN HIS ROWBOAT  . . . . . . . . . . . .           589 OLD WICKED MAN  V  50
    OF THOSE STEEL TONGUES: CRASH, SWORDS! WELL THRUST!         665 ISLE STAT II 2      67
       WELL BENT
    A BEARDED WITCH, HER SLUGGISH HEAD LOW BENT  . . . . .       685 SEEKER             72
    OFTEN HE HAD BENT DOWN SOME BOUGH ALL BRIGHT  . . . .        710 FERENCZ RENYI      28
    OFTEN HE HAD BENT DOWN SOME BOUGH ALL BRIGHT WITH BERRIES!   710 FERENCZ RENYI   V  28
    BENT LOW WITH TOIL AND HOARIEST YEARS. THE OTHER  . . .      711 FERENCZ RENYI      52
BERA
    . . . FROM RACHLIN TO BERA OF SHIPS. . . . . . . . .          58 OISIN 3           160
BEREFT
    NIGH OF HIS WITS BY FEAR BEREFT. . . . . . . . . . .         730 PRIEST FAIRY       50
BERENICE'S
    THE HEAVENLY CIRCUIT: BERENICE'S HAIR:  . . . . . . .        483 VERONIC NAPKIN      1
    BERENICE'S BURNING HAIR. . . . . . . . . . . . .            519 HER DREAM           8
BERKELEY
    . . . BERKELEY AND BURKE HAVE TRAVELLED THERE.  . . . .      481 BLOOD AND MOON     18
    AND GOD-APPOINTED BERKELEY THAT PROVED ALL THINGS A DREAM,   481 BLOOD AND MOON     25
BERRIES      SEE SLOE-BERRIES
    CAME, AND MY FOREHEAD FELL LOW, AND MY TEARS LIKE BERRIES     57 OISIN 3           154
       FELL DOWN:
    AND MY TEARS WERE LARGER THAN BERRIES, AND I MURMURED,       59 OISIN 3           178
       . . .
    AND MY TEARS WERE LARGE LIKE TO BERRIES, AND I MURMURED,     59 OISIN 3         V 178
       . . .
    FULL OF BERRIES . . . . . . . . . . . . . . . .              87 STOLEN CHILD        7
    WITH BERRIES. PLACID AS A HOMEWARD BEE,  . . . . . .         710 FERENCZ RENYI      29
    OFTEN HE HAD BENT DOWN SOME BOUGH ALL BRIGHT WITH BERRIES!   710 FERENCZ RENYI   V  28
    ROASTING BERRIES STEAM AND SHAKE--  . . . . . . . .          727 LOVERS QUARREL     43
    DARK JOAN CALL THE BERRIES SWEET,  . . . . . . . . .         743 DANAAN QUICK       28
BERRY
    AND HOOKED A BERRY TO A THREAD:  . . . . . . . . . .         149 WANDER AENGUS       4
    I DROPPED THE BERRY IN A STREAM  . . . . . . . . . .         149 WANDER AENGUS       7
    AND PUT A BERRY ON A THREAD:  . . . . . . . . . .            149 WANDER AENGUS   V   4
    A BERRY THREW FOR ME--OR THEE. . . . . . . . . . .          743 DANAAN QUICK       11
BERYL
    OR CHRYSOBERYL, OR BERYL, OR CHRYSOLITE:  . . . . . .        231 SHADOW WATER B    215
    OF CHRYSOBERYL, OR BERYL, OR CHRYSOLITE:  . . . . . .        231 SHADOW WATER B  V 215
    OF CHRYSOBERYL AND BERYL AND CHRYSOLITE,  . . . . . .        765 SHADOW WATER A    357
BESEECH
    FORBID, BESEECH AND WASTE MY BREATH." THEN I:  . . . .       281 TWO KINGS         102
BESEECHING
    THOUGH FROM BESEECHING THEY DESISTED NOT,  . . . . . .        36 OISIN 2         V  93
    I KNOW YOU NOW, BESEECHING HANDS AND EYES. . . . . .         763 SHADOW WATER A    312
    BESEECHING HANDS AND MORE BESEECHING EYES? . . . . .        763 SHADOW WATER A  V 312
    BESEECHING HANDS AND MORE BESEECHING EYES? . . . . .        763 SHADOW WATER A  V 312
BESET
    THE HOUR OF THE WANING OF LOVE HAS BESET US,  . . . .        79 FALLING LEAVES      5
BESIDE
    AND STOOD BESIDE THE SEA TOGETHER:  . . . . . . . .           9 OISIN 1         V 101B
    BESIDE THE SEA, WHERE, HUSHED AND SLOW,  . . . . . .         20 OISIN 1         V 292
    HEAPED BESIDE THE GLIMMERING WAVES,  . . . . . . . .         21 OISIN 1           314
    HEAVED BESIDE THE GLIMMERING WAVES,  . . . . . . . .         21 OISIN 1         V 314
    BESIDE THE PILED-UP HUNTING SPEARS,  . . . . . . . .         23 OISIN 1           348
    BESIDE THE PILED-UP HUNTING-SPEARS,  . . . . . . . .         23 OISIN 1         V 349
```

```
                                                              PAGE     TITLE          LINE
BESIDE   (CONTINUED)
    WHEN ONCE BESIDE THE SHORE I STOOD,  . . . . . . . .       24  OISIN 1        V   364
    AND RODE AND STOOD BESIDE THE SHORE. . . . . . . . .       25  OISIN 1        V  379A
    ROLLING HIS WHEEL, WE SANG BESIDE THE DEEP . . . . .       42  OISIN 2        V   193
    OH, MAY TRANQUILLITY BESIDE HIM GO, . . . . . . . .        71  ANASHU VIJAYA  V     2
    AND I MUST WAIL BESIDE THE SEA . . . . . . . . . .         86  MAD KING GOLL  V    67
    AND HIS YOUNG SWEETHEART CLOSE BESIDE HIM KNELT, . . .    108  CUCHULAIN SEA       40
    AND HIS YOUNG DEAR ONE CLOSE BESIDE HIM KNELT, . . . .    108  CUCHULAIN SEA       40
    WEARY AND KIND ONE STOOD BESIDE HIS SEAT, . . . . . .     112  ROSE OF WORLD  V    13
    BESIDE HER CLEAN-SWEPT HEARTH, HER QUIET SHADE, . . .     114  ROSE OF BATTLE      11
    AND BENDING DOWN BESIDE THE GLOWING BARS, . . . . .       121  YOU ARE OLD          9
    WHERE PEOPLE LOVE BESIDE THE RAVELLED SEAS, . . . . .     126  DREAM OF FAERY       9
    WHERE PEOPLE LOVE BESIDE STAR-LADEN SEAS, . . . . . .     126  DREAM OF FAERY V     9
    HE MUSED BESIDE THE WELL OF SCANAVIN, . . . . . . .       127  DREAM OF FAERY      25
    BESIDE YOUNG AENGUS IN HIS TOWER OF GLASS, . . . . .      219  HARP OF AENGUS       2
    THIS SWORD IS TO LIE BESIDE HIM IN THE GRAVE. . . .       242  SHADOW WATER B     412
    BESIDE THE BRACKISH WATERS OF THE BOYNE . . . . . .       270  PARDON FATHERS      11
    HAD TUCKED HIMSELF AWAY BESIDE . . . . . . . . . .        303  HOUR DAWN           28
    IN SOME OUTLANDISH COAT BESIDE . . . . . . . . . .        303  HOUR DAWN      V    28
    BESIDE A FIRE OF TURF IN TH' ANCIENT TOWER, . . . . .     324  ROBERT GREGORY       3
    IN GLENDALOUGH BESIDE THE STREAM, . . . . . . . . .       331  ROUND TOWER          8
    AND THERE ARE--BUT NO MATTER IF THERE ARE SCORES BESIDE,  354  HIS PHOENIX         15
    ON THE GREY SAND BESIDE THE SHALLOW STREAM . . . . .      367  EGO DOMINUS          1
    A LAMP BURNS ON BESIDE THE OPEN BOOK . . . . . . . .      367  EGO DOMINUS          3
    BURNING ALONE BESIDE AN OPEN BOOK, . . . . . . . . .      370  EGO DOMINUS         63
    BESIDE THE CASTLE DOOR, WHERE ALL IS STARK . . . . .      377  PHASES OF MOON     126
    BUT SHE THAT BESIDE ME LAY . . . . . . . . . . .          399  BREAK OF DAY        21
    BESIDE THE LITTLE LAKE . . . . . . . . . . . . .          400  DEMON BEAST         23
    "SO YOU MUST LIE BESIDE HIM . . . . . . . . . . .         570  THREE BUSHES        22
    BESIDE HER LADY'S MAN, . . . . . . . . . . . . .          571  THREE BUSHES        72
    AND THAT OLD MAN BESIDE ME, NOTHING WOULD HE SAY . . .    593  PILGRIM              9
    THEN STUMBLING TO THE KILL BESIDE THE SHORE, . . . .      622  HOUND VOICE         19
    THAT STUMBLING TO THE KILL BESIDE THE SHORE, . . . .      622  HOUND VOICE    V    19
    FIERCE MORTAL, AND CROUCHED LOW BESIDE THE LAKE . . .     675  ISLE STAT II 3 V 245A
    IF ONE SHOULD RISE BESIDE THEE, . . . . . . . . .         680  LOVE AND DEATH      27
    THAT WAS BESIDE THE WATERFALL, THY WORDS . . . . . .      683  SEEKER              49
    UNDER A LEMON TREE BESIDE YOUR DOOR, . . . . . . . .      693  MOSADA 1            68
    BESIDE THE DOOR OF PETER'S GATE. . . . . . . . . .        696  MOSADA 2       V    23
    GRIEVE NOT, FOR GOMEZ KNEELS BESIDE THEE--GOMEZ, . . .    702  MOSADA 3            90
    GRIEVE NOT, FOR VALLENCE KNEELS BESIDE THEE--VALLENCE,    702  MOSADA 3       V    90
    I SAT ME DOWN BESIDE THEE, AND I KNEW . . . . . .         713  FERENCZ RENYI       92
    BESIDE THE WILLOW. NAY, TO YONDER STAR, . . . . . .       715  FERENCZ RENYI      118
    WHERE LIES THE COW AT PEACE BESIDE HER CALF, . . . .      715  FERENCZ RENYI      121
    TROTTED BESIDE HIM IN A PLAYFUL MOOD. . . . . . . .       715  DWELT SYCAMORE       4
    CRIES A VOICE AT ROARING MIDNIGHT BESIDE THE MOONLESS DEEP.  718  PHANTOM SHIP      8
    PRAYED BESIDE THE OCEAN, THE OLD MUMBLING MOTHER OF THE
        DEAD. . . . . . . . . . . . . . . . . .              719  PHANTOM SHIP   V    34
    COME, BESIDE A SANDY LAKE, . . . . . . . . . . .          727  LOVERS QUARREL      41
    OR STAY WITH ME BESIDE THE THAMES, . . . . . . . .        741  EARL PAUL           59
    BESIDE A LOCHLANN WHARF, AND THOUGH SHE HAD SWORN . .     756  SHADOW WATER A     188
    I SAT BESIDE MY FOSTER-MOTHER, AND NOW . . . . . .        762  SHADOW WATER A     292
    BESIDE YOUNG AENGUS IN HIS TOWER OF GLASS, . . . . .      762  SHADOW WATER A     297
    I SAT BESIDE MY FOSTER MOTHER, AND NOW . . . . . .        762  SHADOW WATER A V   292
    OR GO BESIDE HIM TO HIS MOUNTAIN WARS. . . . . . .        768  SHADOW WATER A     414
BESIDES
    BESIDES HER CLEAN SWEPT HEARTH, HER QUIET SHADE, . . .    114  ROSE OF BATTLE V    11
    AND TO GIVE YOU BESIDES A HUNDRED SHIELDS, . . . . .      756  SHADOW WATER A     185
BESOM
    A SORT OF BESOM THAT CAN CLEAR THE SOUL . . . . . .       558  RIBH CHRISTIAN       5
BESOT        SEE WORLD-BESOTTED
    THEY ARE BESOTTING YOU AS THEY BESOT . . . . . . .       229  SHADOW WATER B     166
BESOTTED
    WORLD BESOTTED TRAVELLER, HE . . . . . . . . . .         493  SWIFTS EPITAPH V     5
BESOTTING
    THEY ARE BESOTTING YOU AS THEY BESOT . . . . . . .       229  SHADOW WATER B     166
BESOUGHT
    "I LOVED NO MAN, THOUGH KINGS BESOUGHT, . . . . . .        7  OISIN 1             62
    "I LOVED NO MAN, THOUGH CANNS BESOUGHT, . . . . . .        7  OISIN 1        V    62
    FULL MANY BOWING KINGS BESOUGHT ME, . . . . . . .          7  OISIN 1        V    67
BEST         SEE SECOND-BEST
    FOR OUR BEST WERE DEAD ON GAVRA'S GREEN. . . . . .         2  OISIN 1        V    71
    . . . OF BEST ONES A SAD THING WERE-- . . . . . .         63  OISIN 3        V   222
    AND YET THE SADDEST CHIMES ARE BEST ENJOYED. . . . .     130  BOOK STORIES        20
    THAT I HAVE THE BEST OF PILOTS. SHADOWS, ILLUSIONS, .    249  SHADOW WATER B     565
    REMEMBERING THAT THE BEST I HAVE DONE . . . . . .        256  WORDS                7
    THAT COMES OF THE BEST KNIT TO THE BEST? ALTHOUGH .      264  HOUSE SHAKEN         7
    THAT COMES OF THE BEST KNIT TO THE BEST? ALTHOUGH .      264  HOUSE SHAKEN         7
    HE AND HIS BEST TROOPS BACK TO BACK . . . . . . .        274  GREY ROCK           73
    IMAGINES BEST TO MAKE IT THRIVE. . . . . . . . .         287  TO WEALTHY MAN       8
    THAT SOME NEW DAY MAY BREED THE BEST . . . . . . .       288  TO WEALTHY MAN      34
    NOR THE BEST LABOURER DEAD . . . . . . . . . . .         312  CHILD DANCING        9
    AND HE, THE BEST WARRIOR, DEAD . . . . . . . . .         312  CHILD DANCING  V     9
    THAT EVEN THE BEST OF LOVE MUST DIE, . . . . . . .       314  MEMORY YOUTH        17
    AND LEARN THAT THE BEST THING IS . . . . . . . .        330  BONE OF A HARE       6
    CHOOSE YOUR COMPANIONS FROM THE BEST, . . . . . .       335  YOUNG BEAUTY         4
    HE THAT WAS BEST IN EVERY COUNTRY SPORT . . . . .       339  SHEP GOATHERD       17
    AND CHOSEN WHAT SCENERY HAD PLEASED ME BEST." . . .     352  PEOPLE              21
    WE AND OUR DOLLS BEING BUT THE WORLD WERE BEST AWAY. .   364  DOLLS FACES         12
    AND, THOUGH YOU HAVE PASSED THE BEST OF LIFE, STILL TRACE,  367  EGO DOMINUS       5
    WHEREON 'TWERE BEST . . . . . . . . . . . . .           389  IMAGE PAST          17
    THE BEST LACK ALL CONVICTION, WHILE THE WORST . . .     402  SECOND COMING        7
```

79

```
                                                      PAGE    TITLE           LINE
BEST   (CONTINUED)
     THE BEST LACK CONVICTION, WHILE THE WORST  . . . . .   402 SECOND COMING V    7
     DECLARE THAT WINTER'S BEST OF ALL,  . . . . . . . .    434 WHEEL                4
     THAT COGNOMEN SOUNDED BEST  . . . . . . . . . . . .    440 WISDOM              18
     IN THE BEST MODERN WAY--THE CHILDREN'S EYES  . . . .   443 SCHOOL CHILDR        6
     NEVER TO HAVE LIVED IS BEST, ANCIENT WRITERS SAY;  .   459 FROM OEDIPUS        10
     I WOULD HAVE FOUND THE BEST THAT LIFE CAN GIVE,  . .   465 HARUN RASHID        91
     ALTER AT THE BEST  . . . . . . . . . . . . . . . .     517 HER ANXIETY          4
     OUR MINDS ARE AT THEIR BEST THIS NIGHT,  . . . . . .   523 MAD AS MIST          3
     THOSE DEEDS WERE BEST THAT GAVE THE MINUTE WINGS  . .  533 HER TRIUMPH          5
     BEST PLEASE A WANDERING MAN.  . . . . . . . . . . .    606 SONGS BURDEN 1      17
     "NOW MUST WE SING AND SING THE BEST WE CAN,  . . . .   634 CUCHULAIN COMF      19
     WE LOVE NASCHINA BOTH.  WHOM LOVES SHE BEST?  . . .    660 ISLE STAT II 1      48
     WE, TOO, HAVE SEEN OUR BRAVEST AND OUR BEST  . . . .   709 FERENCZ RENYI        1
     THREE MOONS.  IT WERE BEST TO KILL HIM, AND CHOOSE OUT 748 SHADOW WATER A      15
     BEST PLEASES YOU.  ARMED MEN HAVE COME UPON US.  . .   752 SHADOW WATER A     131
     HE THAT HAS LOVED THE BEST  . . . . . . . . . . . .    786 YOUR HEART          19
     THE HEART WELL WORN UPON THE SLEEVE MAY BE THE BEST OF 790 HEART SLEEVE         1
          SIGHTS,
BEST-ENDOWED
     THE BEST-ENDOWED, THE ELECT,  . . . . . . . . . . .    504 RESULT THOUGHT       3
BESTIAL
     THE UNCONTROLLABLE MYSTERY ON THE BESTIAL FLOOR. . . . 318 MAGI                 8
BESTIR
     I MUST BESTIR MYSELF.  BOTH DEAD FOR ME!  . . . . . .  673 ISLE STAT II 3     189
BEST'S
     THE SECOND BEST'S A GAY GOODNIGHT AND QUICKLY TURN AWAY. 459 FROM OEDIPUS       12
BETAKE
     TO HIS OWN HOUSE DID HIM BETAKE,  . . . . . . . . . .  725 LEGEND              30
BETHLEHEM
     SLOUCHES TOWARDS BETHLEHEM TO BE BORN?  . . . . . . .  402 SECOND COMING       22
BETIDE
     MOURNFUL THAT NO NEW WONDER MAY BETIDE,  . . . . . .   111 ROSE OF WORLD        3
     OF MY DEAD CHILDREN SOON, WHATE'ER BETIDE,  . . . . .  712 FERENCZ RENYI       58
BETRAY
     "AND ALL THOSE LIES HAVE BUT ONE END, POOR WRETCHES TO 450 OWEN AHERNE         18
          BETRAY,
BETRAYED
     FOR ON THAT DAY THEY HAD BEEN BETRAYED;  . . . . . .   192 BAILE AILLINN       79
     HE HAD BETRAYED ME TO HIS GRAVE,  . . . . . . . . . .  275 GREY ROCK           96
     WHY ARE THE GODS BY MEN BETRAYED?"  . . . . . . . . .  275 GREY ROCK          115
     BEING BETRAYED INTO A CRADLE, AND I COME  . . . . . .  284 TWO KINGS          169
     AND HELEN HAS ALL LIVING HEARTS BETRAYED.  . . . . .   411 TOWER               53
     HONEY OF GENERATION HAD BETRAYED,  . . . . . . . . .   444 SCHOOL CHILDR       34
     OR THAT HE IS BETRAYED?  . . . . . . . . . . . . . .   532 BEFORE WORLD        14
     AND AFTER THAT BETRAYED;  . . . . . . . . . . . . .    587 PARNELLITES         28
BETTER
     "WERE THERE NO BETTER THAN MY SON  . . . . . . . . .     6 OISIN 1             60
     IS ANYTHING BETTER, ANYTHING BETTER?  . . . . . . .    116 FAERY SONG          11
     IS ANYTHING BETTER, ANYTHING BETTER?  . . . . . . .    116 FAERY SONG          11
     A BETTER TIME HAD COME AGAIN  . . . . . . . . . . .    197 BAILE AILLINN      192
     BETTER GO DOWN UPON YOUR MARROW-BONES  . . . . . . .   204 ADAMS CURSE          7
     BETTER GO DOWN UPON YOUR MARROW BONES  . . . . . . .   204 ADAMS CURSE   V      7
     THAT I MAY DROWN MYSELF?  BETTER STEER HOME,  . . .    222 SHADOW WATER B      12
     WHETHER HE WILL OR NO; AND BETTER STILL  . . . . . .   222 SHADOW WATER B      13
     IT WOULD BE BETTER TO TURN HOME AGAIN.  . . . . . .    222 SHADOW WATER B V    12
     WE'D BETTER GO, FOR WE HAVE LOST THIS CHANCE.  . . .   226 SHADOW WATER B      80
     HOW ARE WE BETTER OFF THAN SEAGHAN THE FOOL,  . . .    228 SHADOW WATER B     129
     WE HAVE BEEN NO BETTER OFF THAN SEAGHAN THE FOOL,  .   228 SHADOW WATER B V   129
     OF THAT MORE POWERFUL LIFE?  HIS WIFE KNOWS BETTER.    230 SHADOW WATER B     172
     WHEN SHE FINDS OUT WE HAVE BETTER MEN ABOARD  . . .    232 SHADOW WATER B     231
     BETTER THAN MY OWN HANDS.  I HAVE DECEIVED YOU  . .    244 SHADOW WATER B     466
     IMAGINING 'TWOULD BETTER PLEASE  . . . . . . . . .     271 GREY ROCK            4
     THAT THINK SWORD-STROKES WERE BETTER MEANT  . . . .    276 GREY ROCK          129
     THAT THINK SWORD STROKES WERE BETTER MEANT  . . . .    276 GREY ROCK     V    129
     FOR HE KNEW BETTER HOW TO LIVE.  . . . . . . . . .     288 TO WEALTHY MAN      30
     "I HAD NO BETTER PLAN AT FIRST.  . . . . . . . . .     305 HOUR DAWN           63
     THAT LOVED HIS LEARNING BETTER THAN MANKIND,  . . .    324 ROBERT GREGORY      18
     HAD SOUNDED BETTER TO YOUR MOUNTAIN FANCY.  . . . .    341 SHEP GOATHERD       61
     I THINK IT BETTER THAT IN TIMES LIKE THESE  . . . .    359 WAR POEM             1
     I THINK IT BETTER THAT AT TIMES LIKE THESE  . . . .    359 WAR POEM      V      1
     WHAT BETTER THAN CALL A DANCE?  . . . . . . . . . .    378 CAT AND MOON        13
     I HAVE LOVED YOU BETTER THAN MY SOUL FOR ALL MY WORDS, 442 BLACK CENTAUR       14
     BETTER TO SMILE ON ALL THAT SMILE, AND SHOW  . . .     444 SCHOOL CHILDR       31
     I HAD BETTER FIND A CONVENT AND TURN NUN;  . . . .     448 HERO GIRL FOOL      11
     BETTER CONDUCT MYSELF OR HAVE MORE  . . . . . . . .    507 STREAM AND SUN       9
     MY BETTER SELF DISOWNS,  . . . . . . . . . . . . .     533 FIRST CONFESS        9
     MONEY IS GOOD AND A GIRL MIGHT BE BETTER,  . . . .     544 TO SAME TUNE 1       3
     "MONEY IS GOOD AND A GIRL MIGHT BE BETTER,  . . . .    545 TO SAME TUNE 1      21
     NO BETTER THAN A BEAST  . . . . . . . . . . . . .      572 LADYS 1ST SONG      11
     THERE'S BETTER EXERCISE  . . . . . . . . . . . . .     600 THOSE IMAGES         3
     MONEY IS GOOD AND A GIRL MIGHT BE BETTER,  . . . .     616 MARCH SONGS 3        3
     "MONEY IS GOOD AND A GIRL MIGHT BE BETTER,  . . . .    616 MARCH SONGS 3       21
     AND THAT NO BETTER CAN BE HAD,  . . . . . . . . .      626 OLD MEN BE MAD      19
     BASE DROVE OUT THE BETTER BLOOD,  . . . . . . . .      626 STATES HOLIDAY       3
     THAT KNOWING BETTER TALK HAD GONE  . . . . . . . .     627 STATES HOLIDAY       7
     SO I HAVE PICKED A BETTER TRADE  . . . . . . . . .     627 STATES HOLIDAY      11
     MAYHAP 'TWERE BETTER THAT ASIDE I THROW  . . . . .     656 ISLE STAT I         38
     COME TO THE CHESS, FOR YOUNG GIRLS' WITS ARE BETTER .  721 WITCH VIVIEN        46
     IT WERE BETTER TO PASS BY, BECAUSE THE GODS  . . .     751 SHADOW WATER A     104
     ARE BETTER THAN THE WOODS WHERE NO LOVE FADES  . .     754 SHADOW WATER A     160
```

		PAGE	TITLE		LINE

BETTERS
    I SOUGHT MY BETTERS: THOUGH IN EACH . . . .   506 REMORSE SPEECH.   6
BETWEEN
    WHEN GODS AND GIANTS WARRED. WE RODE BETWEEN . . . . .   31 OISIN 2   31
    UPON DARK THRONES. BETWEEN THE LIDS OF ONE . . . . .   31 OISIN 2   37
    OF DANAAN HOOVES WE URGED OUR WAY BETWEEN . . . . . .   31 OISIN 2   V   31
    HUGE FORMS OF STONE: BETWEEN THE LIDS OF ONE . . . . .   31 OISIN 2   V   37
    BURNING BETWEEN HER FINGERS, AND IN MINE . . . . . .   37 OISIN 2   125
    AND THRUST THE TORCH BETWEEN THE SLIMY FLAGS. . . . . .   38 OISIN 2   143
    ANOINTING, TORCH JAMMED DOWN BETWEEN THE FLAGS, ...   38 OISIN 2   V   143
    ONCE HELD BETWEEN MY ARMS, WITH LIVID CHOP . . . . . .   40 OISIN 2   V   178
    BETWEEN THEM A GATEWAY OF BRASS, AND THE HOWL OF THE ANGELS   61 OISIN 3   200
      WHO FELL.
    WHO HOLDS THE WORLD BETWEEN HIS BILL AND MADE US STRONG   76 INDIAN ON GOD   6
      OR WEAK
    IS BUT A SLIDING DROP OF RAIN BETWEEN HIS PETALS WIDE. . .   76 INDIAN ON GOD   12
    WHO HOLDS THE WORLD BETWEEN HIS BILL AND MAKES US STRONG   76 INDIAN ON GOD   V   6
      OR WEAK
    AND BROKE BETWEEN MY HANDS THE STAFF . . . .   84 MAD KING GOLL   V   33
    GO WATCH THE ROAD BETWEEN THE WOOD AND TIDE. . . . . .   105 CUCHULAIN SEA   4
    BETWEEN WOOD'S RIM AND THE HORSES OF THE SEA. . . . . .   108 CUCHULAIN SEA   34
    BETWEEN THE GAME AND THE HORSES OF THE SEA. . . . . .   108 CUCHULAIN SEA   V   34
    BETWEEN THE LAVISH SHELTER OF A WOOD . . . .   108 CUCHULAIN SEA   V   38A
    WE COME BETWEEN HIM AND THE DEED OF HIS HAND, ...   141 HOSTING SIDHE   11
    WE COME BETWEEN HIM AND THE HOPE OF HIS HEART. . . . . .   141 HOSTING SIDHE   12
    BETWEEN THE WIND AND THE WOOD. . . . .   166 BLESSED   4
    BETWEEN THE WIND AND THE WOOD. . . . .   167 BLESSED   V   4D
    BETWEEN THE WALLS COVERED WITH BEATEN BRONZE, ...   180 QUEEN MAEVE   10
    OF THE HUNTER'S MOON, THAT HUNG BETWEEN THE NIGHT AND THE   210 UNDER THE MOON   18
      DAY,
    OF THE THIRD MOON, THAT HUNG BETWEEN THE NIGHT AND THE DAY,   210 UNDER THE MOON V   18
    AND CARRIES IT BETWEEN US. HOLY FIRE . . . .   239 SHADOW WATER B   371
    THAT HE IS HOLDING UP BETWEEN US THERE, ...   240 SHADOW WATER B   378
    A SECRET BETWEEN YOU TWO, ...   259 UNWORTH PRAISE   9
    BETWEEN THE PROUD AND THE PROUD. . . . .   259 UNWORTH PRAISE   10
    BETWEEN THE DAWN AND DUSK," SHE SAID: . . . .   273 GREY ROCK   66
    BETWEEN THE WOOD OF DURAS AND MAGAI . . . .   276 TWO KINGS   V   G
    BETWEEN THE PALE GREEN LIGHT OF THE BEECH LEAVES . . . .   277 TWO KINGS   V   5
    WANDERED BETWEEN THE BLUE AND THE GREEN LEAF . . . . .   278 TWO KINGS   41
    BETWEEN THE PILLARS WITH A BEATING HEART . . . .   279 TWO KINGS   59
    "AND THE WORSE DEVIL THAT IS BETWEEN MY THIGHS." . . . .   300 BEGGAR CRIED   8
    BETWEEN ROCK AND WET HEATHER, ...   311 PEACOCK   V   8
    COULD EVER COME BETWEEN . . . .   315 FRIENDS   8
    BETWEEN THE PANTRY AND THE LINEN-CHEST, ...   340 SHEP GOATHERD   36
    BETWEEN THE PANTRY AND THE LINEN CHEST, ...   340 SHEP GOATHERD   V   36
    BETWEEN THE NIGHT AND MORNING. I MIGHT HAVE LIVED, . . .   351 PEOPLE   6
    THEY STOOD IN THE DOOR AND STOOD BETWEEN . . . .   358 PRESENCES   9
    AND RIGHT BETWEEN THESE TWO A GIRL AT PLAY . . . . . .   383 VISION ROBART   21
    O LITTLE DID THEY CARE WHO DANCED BETWEEN, ...   383 VISION ROBART   37
    BEING CAUGHT BETWEEN THE PULL . . . .   384 VISION ROBART   59
    BETWEEN MY HATRED AND DESIRE, ...   400 DEMON BEAST   6
    BETWEEN EXTREMITIES . . . .   499 VACILLATION   1
    AND HE THAT ATTIS' IMAGE HANGS BETWEEN . . . .   500 VACILLATION   16
    BETWEEN THE DARK AND DAWN. . . . .   511 JANE AND JACK   6
    BETWEEN TWO BARRELS AT THE INN. . . . .   551 SONGS REWRIT 1   10
    BETWEEN TWO BUSHES UNDER THE RAIN: . . . .   551 SONGS REWRIT 1   14
    AND I MUST LIE BETWEEN THE SHEETS . . . .   570 THREE BUSHES   40
    TO LIE BETWEEN YOUR FEET? . . . .   572 LADYS 2ND SONG   2
    AND HE PLAYS TUNES BETWEEN YOUR FEET, ...   573 LADYS 3RD SONG   2
    STANDISH O'GRADY SUPPORTING HIMSELF BETWEEN THE TABLES . . .   577 LOFTY THINGS   5
    WENT TO THE SACRED HOUSE AND STOOD BETWEEN . . . . . .   609 IN TARAS HALLS   11
    BETWEEN HIS TWO ETERNITIES, ...   637 BEN BULBEN   14
    EACH OTHER ANSWERING. THEN BETWEEN EACH WING . . . . .   659 ISLE STAT II 1   14
    LET HIM BETWEEN US JUDGE, FOR HE CAN GAUGE . . . . . .   660 ISLE STAT II 1   36
    BETWEEN THE LONELY FOREST AND THE SAND. . . . .   663 ISLE STAT II 2   22
    BETWEEN THE HORNED HILLS--SHEPHERDS, FAREWELL! . . . . .   682 SEEKER   27
    A TOSSING LAUGH BETWEEN THEIR REDNESS 'BIDES-- . . . . .   685 DRAWING-ROOM   2
    A TOSSING LAUGH BETWEEN THEIR RED ABIDES! . . . . . .   735 QUATRAIN APHOR   22
    A TOSSING LAUGH BETWEEN THEIR REDNESS 'BIDES-- . . . . .   735 QUATRAIN APHOR V   22
    AS THOUGH THE WATERS HAD FLOWED UP BETWEEN: . . . . . .   749 SHADOW WATER A   55
    THE TIDE NARROWS BETWEEN, AND ONE OLD MAN . . . . . .   752 SHADOW WATER A   118
    BETWEEN TWO FURROWS UPON THE PLOUGHED LAND: . . . . . .   784 WOMANS BEAUTY   4
    BETWEEN DARK FURROWS UPON THE PLOUGHED LAND. . . . . .   784 WOMANS BEAUTY   6
BETWIXT
    OUT OF THAT RAVING TIDE--IS DRAWN BETWIXT . . . . . .   377 PHASES OF MOON   122
    OR DARK BETWIXT THE POLECAT AND THE OWL. . . . . . .   565 GYRES   21
BEWILDER
    FRENZIES BEWILDER, REVERIES PERTURB THE MIND: . . . . .   426 PHANTOM HATRED   7
BEWILDERED   SEE MORN-BEWILDERED FLAME-BEWILDERED
    THERE, THROUGH BEWILDERED BRANCHES, GO . . . .   135 TWO TREES   V   13
    GAZING UPON HER WITH BEWILDERED EYES: . . . .   280 TWO KINGS   V   84
    BEWILDERED THEM TILL THEY DIED? . . . .   394 EASTER 1916   73
BEWILDERMENT
    THROUGH SHEER BEWILDERMENT? SHE HAD NOT PACED . . . .   466 HARUN RASHID   118
BEWITCHED
    HE SO BEWITCHED THE CARDS UNDER HIS THUMB . . . . . .   411 TOWER   67
BEWITCHMENT
    THAT HAD BUT THE ONE EYE. CAN NO BEWITCHMENT . . . . .   222 SHADOW WATER B   10
BEYOND
    BEYOND THE TUMBLING OF THIS TIDE." . . . .   5 OISIN 1   49
    WE RODE BEYOND THE FURZE AND HEATHER, ...   9 OISIN 1   V 101A

		PAGE	TITLE		LINE

BEYOND   (CONTINUED)

THE LEAST OF DOORS: BEYOND ON A DIM PLAIN . . . . . . 39 OISIN 2   155
THE LEAST OF DOORS: BEYOND THE DOOR A PLAIN, ... 39 OISIN 2   V   155
THE FLOWERS STILL GREW THERE. MOVED BEYOND HIM THE SEA'S   39 OISIN 2   V   163
   WASTE:
WHEN WE ARE DEAD, BEYOND THE SETTING SUNS, ... 71 ANASHU VIJAYA   8
IS AN UNDYING MOORFOWL, AND HE LIVES BEYOND THE SKY. . . 76 INDIAN ON GOD   7
AND THEY MARRIED BEYOND THEIR PLACE. . . . . 92 FATHER OHART   8
BEYOND OLD MARTIN'S BYRE . . . . 95 MOLL MAGEE   34
BEYOND OLD MARTIN'S WOOD, ... 95 MOLL MAGEE   V   34
A PITY BEYOND ALL TELLING . . . . 119 PITY OF LOVE   1
OR IN THE WINE-VAT, DWELL BEYOND THE STIR . . . . . 169 SECRET ROSE   4
OR IN THE WINE VAT, DWELL BEYOND THE STIR . . . . . 169 SECRET ROSE   V   4
AND THEY WERE LISTENING THERE BEYOND THE SAIL. . . . . 223 SHADOW WATER B   37
BUT DREAMS THAT HURRY FROM BEYOND THE WORLD . . . . . 230 SHADOW WATER B   185
THAT IN THE BLINDING LIGHT BEYOND THE GRAVE . . . . . 258 KING NO KING   12
THEN HE, DRIVEN BY HIS THOUGHT BEYOND HIS THOUGHT, . . . 282 TWO KINGS   122
THAT THE IMMEDICABLE MOUND'S BEYOND . . . . 282 TWO KINGS   129
OUR QUESTIONING, BEYOND OUR PITY EVEN. . . . . 282 TWO KINGS   130
THEN HE, DRIVEN BY THIS THOUGHT BEYOND HIS THOUGHT, . . . 282 TWO KINGS   V   122
THAT THE IMMEDICABLE WOUND'S BEYOND . . . . 282 TWO KINGS   V   129
QUESTION OF OURS, BEYOND OUR PITY EVEN. . . . . 282 TWO KINGS   V   130
BEYOND THE FLING OF THE DULL ASS'S HOOF . . . . . . 321 REED WHISPERER   5
AND DIED IN THE GREAT WAR BEYOND THE SEA. . . . . . . 339 SHEP GOATHERD   22
OR IMAGE, FROM BEYOND THE LOADSTONE MOUNTAIN, ... 371 ON GOING HOUSE   11
BEYOND THE VISIBLE WORLD. ALL DREAMS OF THE SOUL . . . 374 PHASES OF MOON   63
THEY ARE CAST BEYOND THE VERGE, AND IN A CLOUD, ... 376 PHASES OF MOON   105
DEFORMED BEYOND DEFORMITY, UNFORMED, ... 376 PHASES OF MOON   111
SO DEAD BEYOND OUR DEATH, ... 382 VISION ROBART   15
BEYOND THAT RIDGE LIVED MRS. FRENCH, AND ONCE . . . . 410 TOWER   25
HAD HE NOT FOUND IT CERTAIN BEYOND DREAMS . . . . . 417 ANCEST HOUSES   10
SO STRAINS TO LOOK BEYOND OUR LIFE, AN EYE . . . . . 465 HARUN RASHID   87
SO LONGS TO LOOK BEYOND OUR LIFE, AN EYE . . . . . 465 HARUN RASHID   V   87
SOMEWHERE BEYOND THE CURTAIN . . . . 504 QUARREL IN AGE   12
BEYOND A MORTAL'S YEARS. I WAIT THE SONG . . . . . 653 ISLE STAT I 2   48
BEYOND THE LAKE, WHOSE SMALLEST WAVE WAS BURDENED . . . 656 ISLE STAT I 3   31
WITH ROLLING FIRE, BEYOND THE HIGH TREES TURBANED . . . 656 ISLE STAT I 3   32
CARVED: HERE, BEYOND THE LAKE'S SLOW-MUFFLED TREAD, . . . 662 ISLE STAT II 2   11
BEYOND THE GATEWAY—BY THE SENTRIES NOW— . . . . . 720 WITCH VIVIEN   10
OF RAJAS AND MAHRAJAS BEYOND NUMBER? . . . . 724 KANVA ON SELF   6
CARE NOT IF BEYOND THE SHADOWS . . . . 737 IN FIRELIGHT   7
BEYOND WHERE THE WATERS ARE MOVING, ... 739 WHERE BOOKS GO   7
BEYOND THE SAIL A MAN WITH A RED CROWN . . . . . . 752 SHADOW WATER A   126
BEYOND A HILL AND A HILL. . . . . 774 COME RIDE   4
BEYOND A HILL AND A HILL THERE . . . . 774 COME RIDE   16
BEYOND EAGLE OR MOLE, ... 784 WOMANS BEAUTY   10
BEYOND HEARING OR SEEING, ... 784 WOMANS BEAUTY   11

BIBLE

IT'S PLAIN THE BIBLE MEANS . . . . 345 ON WOMAN   10
THE BIBLE PROMISED US, ... 472 ALL SOUL NIGHT   39

BID

AND BID ME STAY, WITH MANY A TEAR: . . . . 10 OISIN 1   113
BID THEM AWAY AND HOLD THEIR PEACE: . . . . 15 OISIN 1   212
GAVE ME A HARP, AND BID ME SING, ... 16 OISIN 1   232
AND BID THE STARS DROP DOWN FROM THE SKY, ... 28 OISIN 1   426
AND STAY A LITTLE WHILE, AND BID THEM WEEP: . . . . . 33 OISIN 2   60
SHE BID ME TAKE LOVE EASY, AS THE LEAVES GROW ON THE TREE: 90 SALLEY GARDENS   3
SHE BID ME TAKE LIFE EASY, AS THE GRASS GROWS ON THE WEIRS: 90 SALLEY GARDENS   7
SHE BID ME TAKE LOVE EASY, AS THE LEAVES GROW ON THE TREES: 90 SALLEY GARDENS V   3
AND SAID, "I AM THAT SWINEHERD WHOM YOU BID . . . . . 105 CUCHULAIN SEA   3
"I AM ALEEL, THE SWINEHERD, WHOM YOU BID . . . . . 105 CUCHULAIN SEA   V   3A
WHOSE BLADE COMPELS, AND BID THEM SEND YOU ONE . . . 108 CUCHULAIN SEA   V   37
AND GOD WOULD BID HIS WARFARE CEASE, ... 113 ROSE OF PEACE   13
AND GOD WOULD BID MAN'S WARFARE CEASE, ... 113 ROSE OF PEACE   V   13
FOR GOD HAS BID THEM SHARE AN EQUAL FATE: . . . . 115 ROSE OF BATTLE   32
AND BID THEM WANDER OBEYING YOUR WILL, ... 141 EVERLAST VOICE   3
I CRIED IN MY DREAM, O WOMEN, BID THE YOUNG MEN LAY . . 163 VALLEY LOVERS   5
AND I CRIED IN MY DREAM "O WOMEN, BID THE YOUNG MEN LAY 163 VALLEY LOVERS   V   5
HAVE I NOT BID YOU TELL OF THAT GREAT QUEEN . . . . 181 QUEEN MAEVE   34
AND SHOOK HIM WIDE AWAKE, AND BID HIM SAY . . . . . 182 QUEEN MAEVE   50
"I AM FROM THOSE RIVERS AND I BID YOU CALL . . . . 184 QUEEN MAEVE   91
"I COME FROM THE UNDIMMED RIVERS TO BID YOU CALL . . . 184 QUEEN MAEVE   V   91
"I AM FROM THE UNDIMMED RIVERS. I BID YOU CALL . . . 184 QUEEN MAEVE   V   91
AND DID THOSE WATCHERS BID YOU TAKE ME CAPTIVE? . . . 236 SHADOW WATER B   322
ALWAYS IN HIS ONE SEAT, AND BID ME CARE HIM . . . . 280 TWO KINGS   80
"I BID THEM MAKE HIS BED UNDER THIS ROOF . . . . . 280 TWO KINGS   87
WHAT CARED DUKE ERCOLE, THAT BID . . . . 287 TO WEALTHY MAN   9
HANDS, DO WHAT YOU'RE BID: . . . . 358 BALLOON MIND   1
IT SEEMS THAT I MUST BID THE MUSE GO PACK, ... 409 TOWER   11
BID A STRONG GHOST STAND AT THE HEAD . . . . . . 435 FOR MY SON   1
BID THE GHOST HAVE SWORD IN FIST: . . . . 435 FOR MY SON   9
BID THE GHOST HAVE SWORD IN HAND: . . . . 435 FOR MY SON   V   9
O BID ME MOUNT AND SAIL UP THERE . . . . 458 HIS WILDNESS   1
ARISE AND BID ME STRIKE A MATCH . . . . 476 EVA GORE-BOOTH   26
BID ME STRIKE A MATCH AND BLOW. . . . . 476 EVA GORE-BOOTH   32
BID IMAGINATION RUN . . . . 494 AT ALGECIRAS   15
WHAT CAN SHE KNOW UNTIL HE BID HER KNOW: . . . . . 558 RIBH CHRISTIAN   23
THEN BID THEM RAISE MY STATUE ON THE SHORE: . . . . 663 ISLE STAT II 2   18
THE ARCADIANS BRING, AND BID THE STONE BE RAISED . . . 663 ISLE STAT II 2   25
IT IS MY WHIM: BID SOME ATTENDANT SPRITE . . . . . 669 ISLE STAT II 3   72
I BID THEE STAY, RENOUNCING THY MAD QUEST." . . . . 669 ISLE STAT II 3   89

82

```
                                                          PAGE   TITLE          LINE
BID    (CONTINUED)
    I CRIED THE WORDS YOU BID ME CRY. . . . . . . . . .   673 ISLE STAT II 3    186
    "I BID HIM ASK WHAT GIFT HE WILL. . . . . . . . . .   741 EARL PAUL          57
    WALKED ON THE WATERS AND BID FORGAEL SEEK . . . . .   747 SHADOW WATER A     12
    AND BID THEM HIDE IN SHADOW OF THE SAIL. . . . . .    751 SHADOW WATER A     93
    HAVE BID ME HOPE, SAIL TO THE LOCHLANN SHORE . . .    756 SHADOW WATER A V  184
    THAT I WOULD BID MY PEOPLE PUT TO DEATH. . . . . .    760 SHADOW WATER A V  254
    AND BID HIM TO YOUR COUNTRY. I SHOULD WANDER . . .    767 SHADOW WATER A    403
    LIVING OR DYING. BID AIBRIC TO YOUR COUNTRY, . . .    768 SHADOW WATER A    413
BIDDEN
    THOUGH WE WERE BIDDEN TO SING, CRY NOTHING LOUD. . .  778 SONG DEIRDRE 3      2
BIDDING
    TO HIS HEART, BIDDING IT HAVE NO FEAR . . . . . . .   158 TO HIS HEART        T
    TO MY HEART, BIDDING IT HAVE NO FEAR . . . . . . .    158 TO HIS HEART    V   T
    MY BIDDING. NOW 'TIS DONE, AND I AM GLAD . . . . .    700 MOSADA 3           29
BIDDY
    WISE BIDDY EARLY CALLED THE WICKED WOOD! . . . . .    218 WOODS OF COOLE     15
BIDDY'S
    BY BIDDY'S HALFPENNIES HAVE LAIN . . . . . . . . .    287 TO WEALTHY MAN      3
    BY BIDDY'S HALF-PENNIES HAVE LAIN . . . . . . . .     287 TO WEALTHY MAN V    3
'BIDES
    A TOSSING LAUGH BETWEEN THEIR REDNESS 'BIDES-- . . .  685 DRAWING-ROOM        2
    A TOSSING LAUGH BETWEEN THEIR REDNESS 'BIDES-- . . .  735 QUATRAIN APHOR V   22
BIDS
    OLD SILENCE BIDS ITS CHOSEN RACE REJOICE, . . . . .   127 DREAM OF FAERY     31
    OLD SILENCE BIDS A LONELY FOLK REJOICE, . . . . . .   127 DREAM OF FAERY V   31
    HE BIDS HIS BELOVED BE AT PEACE . . . . . . . . .     154 BELOVED PEACE       T
    MICHAEL ROBARTES BIDS HIS BELOVED BE AT PEACE . . .   154 BELOVED PEACE   V   T
    AND BIDS MY HAIR STAND UP? . . . . . . . . . . . .    499 MOTHER OF GOD      15
    WHAT BIDS ME LIVE LIKE THESE THAT SEEM . . . . . .    507 STREAM AND SUN V   14
    AND BIDS ME TO THE OAK, FOR HE . . . . . . . . .      508 JANE BISHOP        23
    AND BIDS ME TO THAT OAK, FOR HE, . . . . . . . . .    508 JANE BISHOP     V  23
    BIDS ALL TRUE LOVERS REST. . . . . . . . . . . . .    536 PARTING             6
    AND HER DIM WAVE BIDS MAN BE NO MORE GLAD, . . . .    738 YOU ARE SAD        11
    SHE BIDS US FOLLOW HER. I HAVE GROWN WEARY . . . .    758 SHADOW WATER A    218
BIER
    TO FIND IT WHEN NIGHT FALLS LAID ON A GOLDEN BIER. . 209 UNDER THE MOON     10
BIG
    WITH SKELPING HIS BIG BRAWLING LOUT, . . . . . . .    301 RUN PARADISE        9
    AH! IT IS SO VERY BIG, . . . . . . . . . . . . .      726 LOVERS QUARREL     17
BIGOT
    INCENDIARY OR BIGOT COULD BE FOUND . . . . . . . .    430 NINETEEN 19        45
BILL
    HE RUFFLES WITH HIS BILL THE MINNOWED STREAMS. . . .   73 ANASHU VIJAYA      37
    WHO HOLDS THE WORLD BETWEEN HIS BILL AND MADE US STRONG 76 INDIAN ON GOD      6
        OR WEAK
    WHO HOLDS THE WORLD BETWEEN HIS BILL AND MAKES US STRONG 76 INDIAN ON GOD V   6
        OR WEAK
    AND THE GREY BIRD WITH CROOKED BILL . . . . . . .    192 BAILE AILLINN      89
    BY THE DARK WEBS, HER NAPE CAUGHT IN HIS BILL, . .    441 LEDA AND SWAN       3
    BY THE WEBBED TOES, AND THAT ALL-POWERFUL BILL . .    441 LEDA AND SWAN      3
    BY THE WEBBED TOES, AND THAT ALL POWERFUL BILL . .    441 LEDA AND SWAN   V   3
BILLED        SEE HERON-BILLED
BILLOWS
    TRANSFORM THESE RASCAL BILLOWS INTO WOMEN . . . . .   222 SHADOW WATER B     11
BILLY
    CRIED THE BEGGAR, BILLY BYRNE! . . . . . . . . .      331 ROUND TOWER         4
    THAT RAMBLING JAILBIRD BILLY SAID: . . . . . . . .    332 ROUND TOWER        26
    PITCH LIKE KING BILLY BOMB-BALLS IN . . . . . . .    565 LAPIS LAZULI        7
BIND
    AND BIND UP EVERY WANDERING TRESS! . . . . . . . .    157 BELOVED RHYMES      2
    AND BIND UP YOUR LONG HAIR AND SIGH! . . . . . . .    158 BELOVED RHYMES      8
    THAT NOBODY CAN BUY OR BIND! . . . . . . . . . .      301 RUN PARADISE       27
    AND ALL THE SHEAVES TO BIND. . . . . . . . . . .     312 CHILD DANCING      10
    NOW THAT NO FINGERS BIND, . . . . . . . . . . .      390 IMAGE PAST         39
    NO NEED TO BIND MY HANDS. WHERE ARE YE, SIRS? . . .   695 MOSADA 1          110
BINDING
    SQUARE LEAVES OF THE IVY MOVED OVER US, BINDING US DOWN 52 OISIN 3           76
        TO OUR REST.
    HAVE WITNESSED THE BINDING. . . . . . . . . . . .    770 BLOOD BOND         15
BINDS
    BINDS, AS WITHIN A GIRDLE OR A RING, . . . . . . .    657 ISLE STAT I 3      59
BIRCH
    OF HIS GREAT BIRCH AND HIS GREAT BOOK. . . . . . .    381 SONG OF FOOL        8
    BUT A BIRCH TREE STOOD MY JACK! . . . . . . . . .     508 JANE BISHOP     V  20
BIRCH-TREE
    BUT A BIRCH-TREE STOOD MY JACK! . . . . . . . . .     508 JANE BISHOP        20
BIRD        SEE SEA-BIRD GAME-BIRD
    IN MURMURS, LIKE A FRIGHTED BIRD. . . . . . . . .     25 OISIN 1           376
    BUT, THE BIRD IN MY FINGERS, I MOUNTED, . . . . .     54 OISIN 3           111
    BUT, THE BIRD IN MY FINGERS, I MOUNTED, MINDFUL ONLY TO 54 OISIN 3         V 111
        LAUNCH
    SNATCHING THE BIRD IN SECRET! NOR KNEW I, EMBOSOMED APART, 57 OISIN 3       150
    "WITH HIM IS ONE SWEET-THROATED LIKE A BIRD." . . .  106 CUCHULAIN SEA      16
    "WITH HIM IS ONE SWEET THROATED LIKE A BIRD, . . .   106 CUCHULAIN SEA   V  16
    AS MERRY AS A BIRD." . . . . . . . . . . . . . .     133 FR GILLIGAN        38
    O BEAST OF THE WILDERNESS, BIRD OF THE AIR, . . .    177 PAST GREATNESS     11
    AND THE GREY BIRD WITH CROOKED BILL . . . . . . .    192 BAILE AILLINN      89
    LET RUSH AND BIRD CRY OUT THEIR FILL . . . . . . .    197 BAILE AILLINN     198
    BUT I'D HAVE BIRD AND RUSH FORGET . . . . . . . .    197 BAILE AILLINN     204
    WHERE THE DEAD DRIFTED, I COULD SEE A BIRD . . . .    223 SHADOW WATER B     23
```

	PAGE	TITLE	LINE
BIRD (CONTINUED)			
O FLOWER OF THE BRANCH, O BIRD AMONG THE LEAVES, • • • •	251	SHADOW WATER B	608
A SQUIRREL WHINNIED AND A BIRD SCREAMED OUT! • • • •	278	TWO KINGS	34
AND THEREON, MERRY AS A BIRD • • • • • • • • • •	296	THREE BEGGARS	25
SANG UNNOTICED LIKE A BIRD! • • • • • • • • • • •	298	THREE HERMITS	7
SANG UNNOTICED LIKE A BIRD. • • • • • • • • • • •	299	THREE HERMITS	32
LOVE AND THE BIRD • • • • • • • • • • • • • •	313	MEMORY YOUTH V	T
OF A MOST RIDICULOUS LITTLE BIRD • • • • • • • • •	314	MEMORY YOUTH	20
AND NOT A GLOOMY BIRD OF PREY. • • • • • • • • •	338	TOM OROUGHLEY	8
I WISHED BEFORE IT CEASED. NOR BIRD NOR BEAST • • • •	338	SHEP GOATHERD	2
YEAR. I WISHED BEFORE IT CEASED. NOR BIRD NOR BEAST •	338	SHEP GOATHERD	2
"LIKE THE SPECKLED BIRD THAT STEERS • • • • • • • •	341	SHEP GOATHERD	62
THAT SHE MIGHT BE THAT SPRIGHTLY GIRL TRODDEN BY A BIRD!	353	HIS PHOENIX	4
THAT SHE MIGHT BE THAT SPRIGHTLY GIRL WHO HAD MARRIED WITH	353	HIS PHOENIX V	4
A BIRD!			
THAT SHE MIGHT BE THAT SPRIGHTLY GIRL WHO WAS TRODDEN BY	353	HIS PHOENIX V	4
A BIRD!			
A VISIONARY WHITE SEA BIRD • • • • • • • • • • •	361	ALF POLLEXFEN V	37
IS ALWAYS HAPPY LIKE A BIRD OR A BEAST! • • • • • •	373	PHASES OF MOON	38
ALL SOUNDS BY BIRD OR ANGEL SUNG • • • • • • • •	387	SOLOMON WITCH V	7
FROM TERRIFIED, INVISIBLE BEAST OR BIRD! • • • • • •	389	IMAGE PAST	6
LIKE ANY ROCK-BRED, SEA-BORNE BIRD! • • • • • • • •	397	POLIT PRISONER	18
PORTLY GREEN-PATED BIRD • • • • • • • • • • • •	400	DEMON BEAST	28
THE MOTHER BIRD WILL REST • • • • • • • • • • •	415	TOWER	170
THE BIRD DESCENDS, AND HER FRAIL THIGHS ARE PRESSED • •	441	LEDA AND SWAN V	2
OLD CLOTHES UPON OLD STICKS TO SCARE A BIRD. • • • •	445	SCHOOL CHILDR	48
LET THE CAGE BIRD AND THE CAGE BIRD MATE • • • • •	450	OWEN AHERNE	16
LET THE CAGE BIRD AND THE CAGE BIRD MATE • • • • •	450	OWEN AHERNE	16
• • • AND THE WILD BIRD MATE IN THE WILD." • • • •	450	OWEN AHERNE	16
TO PASSING BIRD, BUT I AM DUMB • • • • • • • • •	452	HUMAN DIGNITY	11
GAME BIRD, OR WOMAN DOES THE SAME THING TWICE! • • •	463	HARUN RASHID V	60
THE HERON-BILLED PALE CATTLE BIRD, • • • • • • • •	493	AT ALGECIRAS V	1
MIRACLE, BIRD OR GOLDEN HANDIWORK, • • • • • • • •	497	BYZANTIUM	17
MORE MIRACLE THAN BIRD OR HANDIWORK, • • • • • • •	497	BYZANTIUM	18
MIRACLE, BIRD OR GOLDEN HANDY-WORK, • • • • • • •	497	BYZANTIUM V	17
MORE MIRACLE THAN BIRD OR HANDY-WORK • • • • • • •	497	BYZANTIUM V	18
COMMON BIRD OR PETAL • • • • • • • • • • • • •	498	BYZANTIUM	23
WHEN THE HOLY BIRD, THAT THERE • • • • • • • • •	522	LULLABY	15
BIRD, BEAST, FISH OR MAN, • • • • • • • • • • •	529	TOM LUNATIC	14
AND A MIRACULOUS STRANGE BIRD SHRIEKS AT US. • • • •	534	HER TRIUMPH	12
NO, NIGHT'S BIRD AND LOVE'S • • • • • • • • • •	536	PARTING	5
THAT BIRD • • • LET HIM SING ON, • • • • • • • •	536	PARTING	12
THERE'S NOT A BIRD OF DAY THAT DARE • • • • • • •	538	LAST CONFESS	23
OVER THEM FLIES A LONG-LEGGED BIRD, • • • • • • •	566	LAPIS LAZULI	39
BIRD SIGHS FOR THE AIR, • • • • • • • • • • • •	574	LOVERS SONG	1
A GREAT BLACK RAGGED BIRD APPEARED WHEN I WAS IN THE BOAT!	593	PILGRIM	16
A GREAT BLACK BIRD APPEARED WHEN I WAS IN THE BOAT. • •	593	PILGRIM V	16
SHEEP-GUIDING, OR THE BRINGING SOME STRANGE BIRD, • • •	650	ISLE STAT I 1	147
DOTH NOT YON BIRD, YON QUIVERING BIRD, REJOICE? • • • •	652	ISLE STAT I 2	21
DOTH NOT YON BIRD, YON QUIVERING BIRD, REJOICE? • • • •	652	ISLE STAT I 2	21
NO OTHER BIRD MAY ENTER IN. WELL? LATE— • • • •	659	ISLE STAT II 1	24
MID BUBBLING LEAVES A WANDERING SONG-RAPT BIRD • • • •	672	ISLE STAT II 3	154
MID BABBLING LEAVES A WANDERING SONG-RAPT BIRD • • • •	672	ISLE STAT II 3 V	154
OF ANY UNBLESSED EARTHLY BIRD." • • • • • • • •	697	MOSADA 2	33
REITERANT. A BIRD GOES BY THE TENT, • • • • • • •	711	FERENCZ RENYI	46
AND THE BIRD IN THE BRANCHES WILL CRY FOR US CLEAR, • •	717	LOVE SONG	6
A BIRD WALK ON THE DOORSTEP. CHECK ONCE MORE. • • •	722	WITCH VIVIEN	64
AMONG THE HAUNTS OF BEE AND BIRD. • • • • • • • •	729	PRIEST FAIRY	42
THE BREATHING OF THE SMALLEST BIRD, • • • • • • •	730	PRIEST FAIRY	68
A GREY BIRD HAS FLOWN BY. HE HAS FLOWN UPWARD. • • •	753	SHADOW WATER A	134
THE HAND THAT WOUNDS. A WHITE BIRD BEATS HIS WINGS • •	758	SHADOW WATER A V	232
A WHITE BIRD BEATS HIS WINGS UPON MY FACE. • • • • •	759	SHADOW WATER A	233
A WHITE BIRD HAS TORN ME WITH HIS SILVER CLAWS. • • •	759	SHADOW WATER A	234
O FLOWER OF THE BRANCH, O BIRD AMONG THE LEAVES, • • •	769	SHADOW WATER A	424
RED BIRD OF MARCH, BEGIN TO CROW! • • • • • • • •	782	HEART FRIGHT	5
RED BIRD OF MARCH, BEGIN TO CROW! • • • • • • • •	782	HEART FRIGHT	12
RED BIRD OF MARCH, BEGIN TO CROW! • • • • • • • •	782	HEART FRIGHT	19
AND THE EDDYING CAT-HEADED BIRD! • • • • • • • •	783	GREY ROUND	23
FRAIL BIRD, LIKE A WHITE SEA-BIRD ALONE • • • • • •	784	WOMANS BEAUTY	2
BIRD-CLAWS			
GOLDEN THE NAILS OF HIS BIRD-CLAWS, • • • • • • •	50	OISIN 3	45
BIRD-LIKE			
AMONG THOSE BIRD-LIKE THINGS CAME, AND LET FALL • • •	634	CUCHULAIN COMF	8
BIRDLY			
AND BIRDLY ITERATION IS • • • • • • • • • • •	67	HAPPY SHEPHERD V	46B
BIRD'S			
OR A BIRD'S SLEEPY CRY • • • • • • • • • • •	416	TOWER	194
AS AIR UNDER A WING, CAN GIVE BIRD'S WIT. • • • • •	462	HARUN RASHID V	28
HUMAN, SUPERHUMAN, A BIRD'S ROUND EYE, • • • • • •	618	BRONZE HEAD	2
HUMAN, SUPER-HUMAN, A BIRD'S ROUND EYE, • • • • • •	618	BRONZE HEAD V	2
BIRDS SEE SONG-BIRDS CATTLE-BIRDS			
AND BIRDS THAT ON THE SEVEN SEAS RANGE. • • • • • •	4	OISIN 1 V	27A
FROM WHERE THE BIRDS OF AENGUS WING?" • • • • • •	6	OISIN 1	53
THAT ARE LIKE COLOURED ASIAN BIRDS • • • • • • •	7	OISIN 1	69
AND GLORIOUS AS ASIAN BIRDS • • • • • • • • • •	7	OISIN 1 V	65
AND A HUNDRED LADIES, MERRY AS BIRDS, • • • • • •	9	OISIN 1	96
AND SWEETER OF VOICE THAN THE PLEASANT BIRDS, • • • •	9	OISIN 1 V	95
AND A HUNDRED MAIDENS, MERRY AS BIRDS, • • • • • •	9	OISIN 1 V	96
SUNG OF THE BIRDS. OUR TOIL WAS DONE! • • • • • •	14	OISIN 1 V	177
THE MURMURING BIRDS IN SOLEMN POMP • • • • • • •	20	OISIN 1 V	293
AND, AS THEY SANG, THE PAINTED BIRDS • • • • • • •	26	OISIN 1	396

```
                                                          PAGE    TITLE             LINE
BIRDS   (CONTINUED)
      A STORM OF BIRDS IN THE ASIAN TREES  . . . . . . . . . .   27  OISIN 1             416
      UNLANGUID AS THE BIRDS, IN PROUD COMPANIONSHIPS! . . . .   30  OISIN 2        V    14C
      FANNED THE DELIGHTED AIR LIKE WINGS OF BIRDS! . . . . .    32  OISIN 2              50
      FROM HIGH ABOVE, LIKE FEATHERS OF YOUNG BIRDS  . . . . .   32  OISIN 2        V     50
      . . . THEIR HANDS WERE THE CLAWS OF BIRDS, . . . . . . .   49  OISIN 3              34
      OF AWELESS BIRDS, AND ROUND THEIR STIRLESS FEET  . . . .   74  ANASHU VIJAYA        73
      I LAUGHED BECAUSE BIRDS FLUTTERED BY, . . . . . . . . .    84  MAD KING GOLL        33
      TO THE BIRDS IN THE WHITE OF THE AIR. . . . . . . . . .    92  FATHER OHART         16
      THE BIRDS, FOR HE OPENED THEIR CAGES . . . . . . . . . .   92  FATHER OHART         17
      THE BIRDS FROM KNOCKNAREA  . . . . . . . . . . . . . .     93  FATHER OHART         30
      THE YOUNG BIRDS AND OLD BIRDS  . . . . . . . . . . . .     93  FATHER OHART         33
      THE YOUNG BIRDS AND OLD BIRDS  . . . . . . . . . . . .     93  FATHER OHART         33
      THE WHITE BIRDS  . . . . . . . . . . . . . . . . . . .    121  WHITE BIRDS          T
      I WOULD THAT WE WERE, MY BELOVED, WHITE BIRDS ON THE FOAM 121  WHITE BIRDS          1
         OF THE SEA!
      O WOULD THAT WE WERE, MY BELOVED, WHITE BIRDS ON THE FOAM 121  WHITE BIRDS     V     1
         OF THE SEA.
      FOR I WOULD WE WERE CHANGED TO WHITE BIRDS . . . . . .    122  WHITE BIRDS          8
      WERE WE ONLY WHITE BIRDS, MY BELOVED, . . . . . . . . .   122  WHITE BIRDS          12
      THAT YOU CALL IN BIRDS, IN WIND ON THE HILL, . . . . .    141  EVERLAST VOICE       6
      THOUGH YOU HAVE THE WILL OF THE WILD BIRDS, . . . . . .   176  BELOVED DEAD         8
      WHILE BIRDS GREW SILENT ONE BY ONE. . . . . . . . . . .   176  BELOVED DEAD    V    13
      FOR YOU HAVE BEEN, O AENGUS OF THE BIRDS, . . . . . . .   185  QUEEN MAEVE         101
      ABOUT WHOSE FACE BIRDS WAGGED THEIR FIERY WINGS, . . .    187  QUEEN MAEVE         145
      O WANDERING BIRDS AND RUSHY BEDS . . . . . . . . . . .    190  BAILE AILLINN        31
      AND IN THE LIGHT BODIES OF BIRDS . . . . . . . . . . .    190  BAILE AILLINN        44
      OR BIRDS LOST IN THE ONE CLEAR SPACE . . . . . . . . .    195  BAILE AILLINN       149
      OR BIRDS LOST IN ONE CLEAR SPACE . . . . . . . . . . .    195  BAILE AILLINN   V   149
      WHILE OVER THEM BIRDS OF AENGUS FLY, . . . . . . . . .    197  BAILE AILLINN       182
      BUT I'D HAVE BIRDS AND RUSH FORGET . . . . . . . . . .    197  BAILE AILLINN   V   204
      I CRIED WHEN THE MOON WAS MURMURING TO THE BIRDS! . . .   203  WITHER BOUGHS        1
      HAVE THE BIRDS PASSED US?  I COULD HEAR YOUR VOICE, . .   226  SHADOW WATER B      81
      HAS EVER COME BUT THOSE MAN-HEADED BIRDS, . . . . . . .   226  SHADOW WATER B      99
      THEY HAVE MADE YOU FOLLOW THE MAN-HEADED BIRDS, . . . .   231  SHADOW WATER B     204
      THEY HAVE BADE YOU FOLLOW THE MAN-HEADED BIRDS, . . . .   231  SHADOW WATER B  V  204
      "HOW LIGHT WE ARE, NOW WE ARE CHANGED TO BIRDS!" . . .    233  SHADOW WATER B     253
      THAT CANNOT BE THE MEANING OF THE BIRDS. . . . . . . .    235  SHADOW WATER B     278
      AND ALL THE BIRDS ARE SCATTERED.  O! O! O! . . . . . .    241  SHADOW WATER B     395
      THESE THOUSAND YEARS.  WHAT ARE THE BIRDS AT THERE? . .   243  SHADOW WATER B     435
      WHAT IS THERE BUT A TROOP OF ASH-GREY BIRDS  . . . . .    247  SHADOW WATER B     517
      WHAT IS THERE BUT THE CRYING OF THE BIRDS? . . . . . .    247  SHADOW WATER B     519
      THAT YOU MAY NEVER HEAR THE CRY OF THE BIRDS, . . . . .   250  SHADOW WATER B     575
      LET THE BIRDS SCATTER, FOR THE TREE IS BROKEN, . . . .    250  SHADOW WATER B     584
      AND ALL THE BIRDS ARE SCATTERED--O! O! O! . . . . . .     251  SHADOW WATER B     594
      TO CRY ALOUD TO THE GREY BIRDS, AND DREAMS, . . . . . .   252  SHADOW WATER B     618
      HE WERE AFRAID THE BIRDS, WHO CRY ALOUD  . . . . . . .    371  EGO DOMINUS         77
      THE RIDER, THE BIRDS THAT RANGE  . . . . . . . . . . .    393  EASTER 1916         46
      REEL SHADOWS OF THE INDIGNANT DESERT BIRDS. . . . . . .   402  SECOND COMING       17
      WIND SHADOWS OF THE INDIGNANT DESERT BIRDS. . . . . . .   402  SECOND COMING   V   17
      IN ONE ANOTHER'S ARMS, BIRDS IN THE TREES  . . . . . .    407  SAIL BYZANTIUM       2
      THE MOTHER BIRDS BRING GRUBS AND FLIES. . . . . . . . .   424  STARES NEST          3
      UNWEARIED EYES UPON THOSE HORRIBLE GREEN BIRDS.  . . .    442  BLACK CENTAUR       16
      ONE AMONG THE BIRDS OF THE AIR,  . . . . . . . . . . .    460  THREE MONUMENT       3
      THAT THIS UNCONQUERABLE LABYRINTH OF THE BIRDS, . . . .   481  BLOOD AND MOON      23
      THE HERON-BILLED PALE CATTLE BIRDS. . . . . . . . . . .   493  AT ALGECIRAS    V    1
      AMONG BIRDS OR BEASTS OR MEN  . . . . . . . . . . . .     528  DANCER CRUACH        2
      THEY HAD CHANGED THEIR THROATS AND HAD THE THROATS       635  CUCHULAIN COMF      25
         OF BIRDS.
      CATCHING SMALL BIRDS IN THE DEW OF THE MORN  . . . . .    636  BLACK TOWER         22
      THE BIRDS THAT NESTLE IN THE LEAVES ARE SAD, . . . . .    652  ISLE STAT I 2       15
      LIES TORN AND ROTTING.  THE FIERCE KESTREL BIRDS . . .    675  ISLE STAT II 3     234
      WHERE TO THEMSELVES INNUMERABLE BIRDS  . . . . . . . .    682  SEEKER              25
      OF BIRDS EVEN, LONGINGS FOR AERY . . . . . . . . . . .    708  FAIRY PEDANT        26
      AND SHAKE THEIR BIRDS UPON THE AIR,  . . . . . . . . .    736  SUMMER EVENING       3
      AND SHAKE THEIR BIRDS UPON THE AIR,  . . . . . . . . .    737  SUMMER EVENING      19
      THEY ARE CHANGED AND AS GREY BIRDS FLY OUT TO SEA, . .    750  SHADOW WATER A      82
      OF AENGUS' BIRDS GLEAM IN THEIR APPLE BOUGHS. . . . . .   751  SHADOW WATER A     103
      "HOW LIGHT WE ARE NOW WE ARE CHANGED TO BIRDS!" . . .     753  SHADOW WATER A     143
      I LINGER WHILE THE BIRDS ARE ON THE WING,  . . . . . .    754  SHADOW WATER A  V  157
      AS THE AGELESS BIRDS OF AENGUS, OR THE BIRDS . . . . .    761  SHADOW WATER A     260
      AS THE AGELESS BIRDS OF AENGUS, OR THE BIRDS . . . . .    761  SHADOW WATER A     260
      THAT FORGAEL HAS FOLLOWED THE GREY BIRDS ALONE, . . . .   767  SHADOW WATER A     402
      THE STRONG MARCH BIRDS A-CROW. . . . . . . . . . . . .    783  GREY ROUND          26
BIRDS'
      AS AIR UNDER A WING, CAN GIVE BIRDS' WIT. . . . . . . .   462  HARUN RASHID        28
BIRTH
      THERE WERE AN END OF CHANGE AND BIRTH, . . . . . . . .    18  OISIN 1             270
      AND TIME AND BIRTH AND CHANGE ARE HURRYING BY. . . . .   153  CHANGE BELOVED       9
      PASS THE DOOR OF BIRTH AGAIN, . . . . . . . . . . . .    298  THREE HERMITS       19
      BRINGS ME TO BIRTH AGAIN-- . . . . . . . . . . . . .     346  ON WOMAN            32
      A COMPENSATION FOR THE PANG OF HIS BIRTH, . . . . . . .   444  SCHOOL CHILDR       39
      DELIVER FROM THE CRIME OF DEATH AND BIRTH. . . . . . .    478  SELF AND SOUL       24
      BIRTH IS HEAPED ON BIRTH . . . . . . . . . . . . . .     496  MOHINI CHATTER      23
      BIRTH IS HEAPED ON BIRTH . . . . . . . . . . . . . .     496  MOHINI CHATTER      23
      O A BEGGAR BLIND FROM HIS BIRTH! . . . . . . . . . . .   552  SONGS REWRIT 2       8
      A BEGGAR BLIND FROM HIS BIRTH! . . . . . . . . . . . .   552  SONGS REWRIT 2  V    8
      BEING THE MOON OF BIRTH, MAY END OUR DOUBT. . . . . . .   748  SHADOW WATER A      24
      IT MAY BE, BEFORE THE WINDS OF BIRTH HAVE WAKED! . . .    750  SHADOW WATER A      86
BIRTHDAY
      FROM OUR BIRTHDAY, UNTIL WE DIE, . . . . . . . . . . .   139  TO IRELAND          35
```

		PAGE	TITLE	LINE

BIRTHDAYS
    THAT WERE ALL HIS BIRTHDAYS RECKONED • • • • • • • • • 342 SHEP GOATHERD 90
    AND BIRTHDAYS AND HOLIDAYS SUCH PRAISES CAN BE HEARD • • 353 HIS PHOENIX 2
BIRTH-HOUR
    BIRTH-HOUR AND DEATH-HOUR MEET, • • • • • • • • • 496 MOHINI CHATTER 26
BISCAY
    AFTER A RAGGED HAT IN BISCAY BAY! • • • • • • • • • 270 PARDON FATHERS 14
BISHOP
    DRANK TAR-WATER WITH THE BISHOP OF CLOYNE. • • • • • • 486 SEVEN SAGES 5
    GOLDSMITH AND BURKE, SWIFT AND THE BISHOP OF CLOYNE • • • 486 SEVEN SAGES 9
    CRAZY JANE AND THE BISHOP • • • • • • • • • • • 507 JANE BISHOP T
    FOUR POEMS CRACKED MARY AND THE BISHOP • • • • • • • 507 JANE BISHOP V T
    EIGHT POEMS CRAZY JANE AND THE BISHOP • • • • • • • 507 JANE BISHOP V T
    NOR WAS HE BISHOP WHEN HIS BAN • • • • • • • • • • 508 JANE BISHOP 8
    THE BISHOP HAS A SKIN, GOD KNOWS, • • • • • • • • • 508 JANE BISHOP 15
    CRAZY JANE TALKS WITH THE BISHOP • • • • • • • • • 513 JANE TALK BISH T
    I MET THE BISHOP ON THE ROAD • • • • • • • • • • 513 JANE TALK BISH 1
    I AM TIRED OF CURSING THE BISHOP, • • • • • • • • • 628 JANE MOUNTAIN 1
    THE BISHOP CAME WITH OPEN BOOK, • • • • • • • • • • 725 LEGEND 17
    THE BISHOP MURMURED, "ATHEIST! • • • • • • • • • • 725 LEGEND 21
BISHOPS
    THE BISHOPS AND THE PARTY • • • • • • • • • • • 587 PARNELLITES 25
BIT
    THEY MAULED AND BIT THE WHOLE NIGHT THROUGH! • • • • • 297 THREE BEGGARS 48
    THEY MAULED AND BIT TILL THE DAY SHONE! • • • • • • 297 THREE BEGGARS 49
    THEY MAULED AND BIT THROUGH ALL THAT DAY • • • • • • 297 THREE BEGGARS 50
    TO THROW ME A BIT OF SALTED FISH! • • • • • • • 301 RUN PARADISE 6
    SHE PULLED THE THREAD AND BIT THE THREAD • • • • • • 308 PLAYER QUEEN 9
    HE RODE A RACE WITHOUT A BIT? • • • • • • • • • • 326 ROBERT GREGORY 63
    AND FROM HER FINGERS ATE ITS BIT. • • • • • • • • • 397 POLIT PRISONER 6
    A BIT OF BREAD THROWN UP INTO THE AIR! • • • • • • 400 DEMON BEAST 25
    A BIT OF AN EMBROIDERED DRESS • • • • • • • • • • 421 MY TABLE 6
    POSEIDON GAVE IT BIT AND OAR, • • • • • • • • • • 447 COLONUS PRAISE 28
    OF THAT OAR AND OF THAT BIT! • • • • • • • • • • 447 COLONUS PRAISE 30
    SO LIKE A BIT OF STONE I LIE • • • • • • • • • • 452 HUMAN DIGNITY 7
    THERE ALL THE SERPENT-TAILS ARE BIT, • • • • • • • • 557 THERE 2
    COME SPEAK YOUR BIT IN PUBLIC • • • • • • • • • • 582 ROGER CASEMENT 21
    ARE BLOWN COLD DUST OR A BIT OF BONE. • • • • • • • 788 HAWTHORN TREE 8
BITE
    NOR STAYED FOR BITE OR SUP! • • • • • • • • • • • 93 FATHER OHART 38
    SHE GIVES ME BITE AND SUP. • • • • • • • • • • • 96 MOLL MAGEE 40
BITING
    TROOPER BELABOURING TROOPER, BITING AT ARM OR AT FACE, • • 426 PHANTOM HATRED 12
BITS
    A CROSS THEY HAD MADE OUT OF TWO BITS OF WOOD, • • • • 123 DREAM OF DEATH 7
    OR BREAK IN BITS THE FAMOUS IVORIES • • • • • • • • 430 NINETEEN 19 47
BITTEN   SEE STORM-BITTEN
    BUT HAVE NOT BITTEN YET. I AM A QUEEN, • • • • • • 235 SHADOW WATER B 280
    THEY'D MAULED AND BITTEN THE NIGHT THROUGH, • • • • • 297 THREE BEGGARS V 48
BITTER
    THROUGH BITTER TIDE ON FOAM-WET FEET? • • • • • • • 5 OISIN 1 51
    CUCHULAIN BATTLING WITH THE BITTER TIDE! • • • • • • 100 ROSE UPON ROOD 3
    FOR HE WHO MADE YOU BITTER MADE YOU WISE." • • • • • 108 CUCHULAIN SEA 32
    FOR GOD WHO MADE YOU BITTER MADE YOU WISE." • • • • • 108 CUCHULAIN SEA V 32
    FOR FOUR DAYS WARRED HE WITH THE BITTER TIDE, • • • • 111 CUCHULAIN SEA V 85
    UPON LOVE'S BITTER MYSTERY! • • • • • • • • • • • 125 GOES FERGUS 8
    GAZE NO MORE IN THE BITTER GLASS • • • • • • • • 135 TWO TREES 21
    GAZE NO MORE IN THE BITTER GLASS. • • • • • • • • 136 TWO TREES 40
    AND BLAME YOU WITH MANY BITTER WORDS. • • • • • • • 146 FISH 8
    WILL HIDE US FROM THE BITTER STORM. • • • • • • • • 152 HEART OF WOMAN 8
    SHALL HIDE US FROM THE BITTER STORM. • • • • • • • 152 HEART OF WOMAN V 8
    CROWDED WITH BITTER FACES, THE WOUNDS IN PALM AND SIDE, • 172 TRAV PASSION 4
    TIME'S BITTER FLOOD WILL RISE, • • • • • • • • • • 173 PLEADS FRIEND 6
    UNDER A BITTER BLACK WIND THAT BLOWS FROM THE LEFT HAND! • 206 HANRAHANS SONG 2
    UNDER THE BITTER BLACK WINDS BLOWING OUT OF THE LEFT HAND! • 206 HANRAHANS SONG V 2
    BUT O! 'TWAS BITTER WRONG • • • • • • • • • • • 255 WOMAN HOMER 5
    IN THIS BLIND BITTER LAND." • • • • • • • • • • • 256 WORDS 4
    THE BITTER SWEETNESS OF FALSE FACES? • • • • • • • 275 GREY ROCK 113
    I HAD THOUGHT, SEEING HOW BITTER IS THAT WIND • • • • • 327 ROBERT GREGORY 89
    AT THE OLD BITTER WORLD WHERE THEY MARRY IN CHURCHES, • • 330 BONE OF A HARE 13
    LESS BITTER. THEY HAVE BROUGHT ME FROM THAT RIDGE • • • 342 SHEP GOATHERD 87
    TO CLIMB THAT STAIR AND EAT THAT BITTER BREAD, • • • • 369 EGO DOMINUS 35
    HE HAD DONE MOST BITTER WRONG • • • • • • • • • • 393 EASTER 1916 33
    ACROSS THE BITTER SEA." • • • • • • • • • • • • 396 ROSE TREE 6
    BECAME A BITTER, AN ABSTRACT THING, • • • • • • • • 397 POLIT PRISONER 9
    OUT OF HIS BITTER SOUL, • • • • • • • • • • • • 415 TOWER 151
    SOME VIOLENT BITTER MAN, SOME POWERFUL MAN • • • • • • 418 ANCEST HOUSES 17
    BITTER AND VIOLENT MEN, MIGHT REAR IN STONE • • • • • 418 ANCEST HOUSES 19
    AND OTHER COMFORT WERE A BITTER WOUND! • • • • • • • 429 NINETEEN 19 V 41
    DRUNK WITH THE BITTER SWEETNESS OF HER YOUTH. • • • • 469 HARUN RASHID 186
    BREAK BITTER FURIES OF COMPLEXITY, • • • • • • • • 498 BYZANTIUM 37
    IN THIS BLIND BITTER TOWN, • • • • • • • • • • • 504 QUARREL IN AGE 3
    BITTER GLORY WRECKED. • • • • • • • • • • • • • 504 RESULT THOUGHT 6
    OVERCOME—O BITTER SWEETNESS, • • • • • • • • • • 540 FROM ANTIGONE 1
    PLUCKED BITTER WISDOM THAT ENRICHED HIS BLOOD. • • • • 543 PARN FUNERAL 2 12
    ESCAPED FROM BITTER YOUTH, • • • • • • • • • • • 568 SWEET DANCER 4
    DRAW ROUND, BELOVED AND BITTER MEN, • • • • • • • • 584 GHOST ROG CASE 37
    HE FIXED A BITTER LOOK • • • • • • • • • • • • 585 ORAHILLY 24
    I NEVER KNEW A NIGHT SO BITTER COLD. • • • • • • • 704 MOSADA 3 124
    THROUGH THE LONG BITTER WAY. • • • • • • • • • • 738 MOURN THEN ON 4
    BELOVED, HEAR MY BITTER TALE!— • • • • • • • • • 742 DANAAN QUICK 1

86

	PAGE	TITLE	LINE

BITTER   (CONTINUED)
THE BITTER SWEETNESS OF THE NIGHT • • • • • • • • •   781 HEART FRIGHT   3
DRY BONES THAT DREAM ARE BITTER, • • • • • • • • •   783 GREY ROUND   14
O BITTER REWARD • • • • • • • • • • • • • • • •   785 YOUR HEART   9
O BITTER REWARD • • • • • • • • • • • • • • • •   786 YOUR HEART   22
O BITTER REWARD • • • • • • • • • • • • • • • •   786 YOUR HEART   35
BITTERER
HAD WATCHED IN BITTERER SLEEP • • • • • • • • • •   399 BREAK OF DAY   22
BITTEREST
FROM BITTEREST HOURS! • • • • • • • • • • • • •   293 HELEN LIVED   6
BITTERLY
AND WRING MY HANDS, AND WAIL HIM BITTERLY, • • • • •   242 SHADOW WATER B   414
SO BITTERLY, YOU'D DREAM THEY LONGED TO LOOK • • • •   265 ABBEY THEATRE   6
HIDING MY FACE, I CRIED LONG, BITTERLY. • • • • •   690 MOSADA 1   17
UPRAISED THEIR VOICES BITTERLY. • • • • • • • •   730 PRIEST FAIRY   72
BITTERN
AND SAID, "YON BITTERN CRIES, IN TRUTH, • • • • •   731 PRIEST FAIRY   75
BITTERNESS
WE AND OUR BITTERNESS HAVE LEFT NO TRACES • • • •   130 BOOK STORIES   23
THE UNAVAILING OUTCRIES AND THE OLD BITTERNESS • • •   198 SEVEN WOODS   4
A MAN THAT FINDS GREAT BITTERNESS • • • • • • •   379 SAINT HUNCH   2
YOUTH'S BITTERNESS BEING PAST, • • • • • • • •   389 IMAGE PAST   11
BUT TAKE OUR GREATNESS WITH OUR BITTERNESS? • • • •   418 ANCEST HOUSES   40
THEIR BITTERNESS AND FIND THE HONEYCOMB. • • • • •   463 HARUN RASHID   48
BITTERNS
OF BITTERNS, AND FISH-EATING STOATS, • • • • • •   14 OISIN 1   191
OF BITTERNS AND FISH-EATING STOATS. • • • • • •   23 OISIN 1   355
BITTER-SWEET
AND, THOUGH LOVE'S BITTER-SWEET HAD ALL COME BACK, • • •   537 HER VISION   27
BITTER-SWEETNESS
DRUNK WITH THE BITTER-SWEETNESS OF HER YOUTH. • • • • •   469 HARUN RASHID   V 186
BLACK   SEE COAL-BLACK
SPRANG FROM A GATEWAY WALLED AROUND WITH BLACK • • • •   31 OISIN 2   V   29
THE VALLEY OF THE BLACK PIG • • • • • • • • • •   161 BLACK PIG   T
UNDER A BITTER BLACK WIND THAT BLOWS FROM THE LEFT HAND!   206 HANRAHANS SONG   2
UNDER THE BITTER BLACK WINDS BLOWING OUT OF THE LEFT HAND!   206 HANRAHANS SONG V   2
OUR COURAGE BREAKS LIKE AN OLD TREE IN A BLACK WIND AND   207 HANRAHANS SONG   3
   DIES,
LIKE TUFTED REEDS OUR COURAGE DROOPS IN A BLACK WIND AND   207 HANRAHANS SONG V   3
   DIES!
THE BARE CHIMNEY IS GONE BLACK OUT • • • • • • •   327 ROBERT GREGORY   84
BLACK MINNALOUSHE STARED AT THE MOON, • • • • • •   378 CAT AND MOON   5
ON A PICTURE OF A BLACK CENTAUR BY EDMUND DULAC • • •   442 BLACK CENTAUR   T
SUGGESTED BY A PICTURE OF A BLACK CENTAUR • • • • •   442 BLACK CENTAUR   V   T
YOUR HOOVES HAVE STAMPED AT THE BLACK MARGIN OF THE WOOD,   442 BLACK CENTAUR   1
BROWN, OR BLACK, OR CARROT, • • • • • • • • •   492 ANNE GREGORY   9
NOR CAN HE HIDE IN HOLY BLACK • • • • • • • • •   508 JANE BISHOP   18
THAT BLACK DAY"! • • • • • • • • • • • • •   510 JANE JUDGMENT   14
BLACK OUT! HEAVEN BLAZING INTO THE HEAD! • • • • •   566 LAPIS LAZULI   19
OR OUT OF HER BLACK CLOUD. • • • • • • • • •   568 SWEET DANCER   6
A GREAT BLACK RAGGED BIRD APPEARED WHEN I WAS IN THE BOAT!   593 PILGRIM   16
A GREAT BLACK BIRD APPEARED WHEN I WAS IN THE BOAT, • • •   593 PILGRIM   V   16
OF RASCALS BLACK AND WHITE • • • • • • • • •   597 MODEL LAUREATE   10
THE BLACK TOWER • • • • • • • • • • • • • •   635 BLACK TOWER   T
SAY THAT THE MEN OF THE OLD BLACK TOWER, • • • • •   635 BLACK TOWER   1
AND FIGHT FOR THE BLACK SLOE-BERRIES, • • • • •   644 SONG FAERIES   13
AND FIGHT FOR THE BLACK SLOE-BERRIES, • • • • •   676 ISLE STAT II 3   260
TWO FIGURES CROUCHING ON THE BLACK ROCK, BOUND • • • •   687 TWO TITANS   5
OF THE ALHAMBRA BLACK ATHWART HIS DISK! • • • • • •   691 MOSADA 1   V   37
BLACKBIRDS
COULD LIKE A BRACE OF BLACKBIRDS SING. • • • • • •   332 ROUND TOWER   24
BLACKENED
BROKEN BOUGHS AND BLACKENED LEAVES. • • • • • • •   135 TWO TREES   28
WITH BROKEN BOUGHS AND BLACKENED LEAVES • • • • • •   135 TWO TREES   V   26
AND HIS HEART WAS BLACKENED BY DREAD, • • • • • •   145 HOST OF AIR   V 40B
OVER THE BLACKENED EARTH • • • • • • • • • •   496 MOHINI CHATTER   21
AND BLACKENED HIS GOOD NAME. • • • • • • • • •   582 ROGER CASEMENT   8
BLACKENS
BLACKENS ALL OUR LOT? • • • • • • • • • • • •   534 CONSOLATION   10
BLACKER
THERE IN THE TOMB THE DARK GROWS BLACKER, • • • • •   636 BLACK TOWER   27
BLACKNESS
AND BLACKNESS IN THE DARK. THE SEA ROLLED ROUND, • • •   30 OISIN 2   V   23
AND WHEN THE WHITE STEED SAW WHAT BLACKNESS GLEAMED, • •   30 OISIN 2   V   24
AND YONDER HUDDLING BLACKNESS DRAWETH NIGH-- • • • •   663 ISLE STAT II 2   15
BLADDERED   SEE GREAT-BLADDERED
GREAT BLADDERED EMER SAT, • • • • • • • • • •   628 JANE MOUNTAIN   V   15
BLADE   SEE SWORD-BLADE
WITH BOWED HEAD, TREMBLING WHEN THE WHITE BLADE SHONE, • •   38 OISIN 3   137
AND BY THEM WERE ARROW AND WAR-AXE, ARROW AND SHIELD AND   49 OISIN 3   29
   BLADE!
WERE ARROW AND SHIELD AND WAR-AXE, ARROW AND SPEAR AND   49 OISIN 3   V   30
   BLADE,
WHOSE BLADE COMPELS, AND WAIT TILL THEY HAVE FOUND • • •   108 CUCHULAIN SEA   37
WHOSE BLADE COMPELS, AND BID THEM SEND YOU ONE • • • •   108 CUCHULAIN SEA   V   37
AND THROUGH THAT NEW BLADE'S GUARD THE OLD BLADE BROKE, • •   110 CUCHULAIN SEA   66
AND THROUGH THE OTHER'S SHIELD HIS LONG BLADE BROKE, • •   110 CUCHULAIN SEA   V   66
AND SAYS! "A SWORD BLADE PIERCED ME IN MY SLEEP." • • •   234 SHADOW WATER B V 257
THE CONSECRATED BLADE UPON MY KNEES • • • • • • •   477 SELF AND SOUL   9
IS SATO'S ANCIENT BLADE, STILL AS IT WAS, • • • • •   477 SELF AND SOUL   10
GOLD-SOWN SILK ON THE SWORD BLADE! • • • • • • •   484 SYMBOLS   V   5

		PAGE	TITLE		LINE

BLADE   (CONTINUED)
    THAT NOBLE BLADE THE MUSES BUCKLED ON, ... 489 COOLE PARK 29   10
    UPON A BLADE OF GRASS. . . . . 505 GRAT INSTRUCT   4
    HO! HO! HO! THE MERRY BLADE!—— . . . . 727 LOVERS QUARREL   26
    AND SAYS, "A SWORD BLADE PIERCED ME IN MY SLEEP." . . 753 SHADOW WATER A V 147
    THIS BLADE OUT OF MY HAND AND DIED OF A SUDDEN. . . . 755 SHADOW WATER A   168
    SHE CAUGHT THIS BLADE OUT OF MY BELT AND DIED. . . . 755 SHADOW WATER A V 168
BLADE'S
    DEEP SUNKEN ON THE BLADE'S LENGTH, "MANANAN!" . . . 38 OISIN 2   V 128
    AND THROUGH THAT NEW BLADE'S GUARD THE OLD BLADE BROKE, 110 CUCHULAIN SEA   66
    BRIGHT ON A GRASS BLADE'S UNDER SIDE, MIGHT HEAR, . . . 689 NETTLESHIP   10
BLADES   SEE GRASS-BLADES' SWORD-BLADES
    AND WITH THE CLASHING OF THEIR SWORD BLADES MAKE . . . 137 TO SOME I TALK V 13
    ON THEIR SWAYING BLADES OF GRASS, ... 705 DAWN-SONG   14
    MAY THE SWORD BLADES DRINK THEIR FILL . . . . . 776 AGAINST WITCH V 37
BLAKE
    OR THAT WILLIAM BLAKE . . . . 576 ACRE OF GRASS   16
    CALVERT AND WILSON, BLAKE AND CLAUDE, ... 639 BEN BULBEN   64
    AND WILSON, BLAKE AND CALVERT, CLAUDE, ... 639 BEN BULBEN   V 64
BLAME
    AND BLAME YOU WITH MANY BITTER WORDS. . . . . . 146 FISH   8
    FOR WHEN WE HAVE BLAMED THE WIND WE CAN BLAME LOVE! . . 201 OLD MEMORY   10
    WHY SHOULD I BLAME HER THAT SHE FILLED MY DAYS . . . 256 NO SECOND TROY   1
    AND I TOOK ALL THE BLAME OUT OF ALL SENSE AND REASON, . 316 COLD HEAVEN   7
    THOUGH SHE HAD YOUNG MEN'S PRAISE AND OLD MEN'S BLAME, . 351 HER PRAISE   17
    A LAW INDIFFERENT TO BLAME OR PRAISE, ... 428 NINETEEN 19   10
    BELOVED, BLAME THE DANAAN WHIM, ... 743 DANAAN QUICK   22
    AND BLAME THE SNARE THEY SET FOR ME. . . . . . 743 DANAAN QUICK   23
BLAMED
    FOR WHEN WE HAVE BLAMED THE WIND WE CAN BLAME LOVE! . . 201 OLD MEMORY   10
    SOME MAY HAVE BLAMED YOU THAT YOU TOOK AWAY . . . 257 RECONCILIATION   1
    I SHOULD BE BLAMED, YOUNG MAN. . . . . . . 569 THREE BUSHES   6
    FOR WHILE I BLAMED THEM I COULD HEAR . . . . . 743 DANAAN QUICK   27
BLANAID
    CAME BLANAID, MAC NESSA, TALL FERGUS WHO FEASTWARD OF OLD 53 OISIN 3   89
      TIME SLUNK,
BLANCH
    OH, HADST THOU SEEN BEAUTIFUL NIAM WAIL TO HERSELF AND   54 OISIN 3   V 109
      BLANCH,
    O, HAD YOU SEEN BEAUTIFUL NEAVE WAIL TO HERSELF AND BLANCH, 54 OISIN 3   V 109
BLANCHED   SEE DEW-BLANCHED LILY-BLANCHED
    A LILY BLANCHED PLACE, SHE SAT AND SANG, ... 693 MOSADA 1   V 83
BLAND
    BLAND RHADAMANTHUS BECKONS HIM, ... 530 DELPHIC ORACLE   3
BLANID
    CAME BLANID, MAC NESSA, CUCHULIN! . . . . 53 OISIN 3   V 89
    CAME BLANID, MAC NESSA, AND FERGUS WHO FEASTWARD OF OLD   53 OISIN 3   V 89
      TIME SLUNK,
BLANK
    UNDER BLANK EYES AND FINGERS NEVER STILL . . . . . 382 VISION ROBART   5
    A GAZE BLANK AND PITILESS AS THE SUN, ... 402 SECOND COMING   15
BLASPHEMOUS
    WOULD CARRY IT AWAY TO BLASPHEMOUS MEN. . . . . . 371 EGO DOMINUS   79
BLAST
    THIS BLAST HAS CHILLED ME TO THE BONE." . . . . . 305 HOUR DAWN   62
    A LONG BLAST UPON THE HORN THAT BROUGHT . . . . . 324 ROBERT GREGORY 22
    A SUDDEN BLAST OF DUSTY WIND AND AFTER . . . . . 433 NINETEEN 19   119
    IF HONOUR FIND HIM IN THE WINTRY BLAST? . . . . . 479 SELF AND SOUL   56
    O MARCHING WIND, O A BLAST OF THE WIND, ... 548 TO SAME TUNE 3 24
    OR WHERE THAT SNOW AND WINTER'S DREADFUL BLAST . . . 563 MERU   11
    A BLAST OF THE WIND, O A MARCHING WIND, ... 615 MARCH SONGS 2   24
    A BLAST OF WIND, O A MARCHING WIND, ... 615 MARCH SONGS 2 V 24
BLASTED
    BRING ME TO THE BLASTED OAK . . . . 507 JANE BISHOP   1
BLASTS
    TILL WINTER BLASTS WERE GONE, BUT SPEAK OF HER . . . 340 SHEP GOATHERD   33
BLAZE
    WATCHED WHERE THE SUN IN A SAFFRON BLAZE . . . . . 26 OISIN 1   394
    "AN OLD MAN STIRS THE FIRE TO A BLAZE, ... 26 OISIN 1   400
    HALF SLUMBERED WITH HIS SAFFRON BLAZE! . . . . . 26 OISIN 1   V 395
    AND BLOWS ON HIS HANDS IN THE FIRE'S WARM BLAZE! . . . 26 OISIN 1   V 404
    HIS SHADOW ALONG IN THE EVENING BLAZE, ... 27 OISIN 1   V 409
    WITH VAPOURY FOOTSOLE BY THE WATER'S DROWSY BLAZE. . . 78 INDIAN TO LOVE 20
    A VAPOURY FOOTFALL ON THE OCEAN'S SLEEPY BLAZE. . . 78 INDIAN TO LOVE V 20
    AND DROP A VAPOURY FOOTFALL IN THE WATER'S DROWSY BLAZE. 78 INDIAN TO LOVE V 20
    WITH VAPOURY FOOTSOLE AMONG THE WATER'S DROWSY BLAZE. . 78 INDIAN TO LOVE V 20
    DROPPING A VAPOURY FOOTSOLE ON THE TIDE'S DROWSY BLAZE. 78 INDIAN TO LOVE V 20
    THE BRAZEN SKY, SO BLAZE THE DAFFODILS! . . . . . 645 ISLE STAT I 1   11
    IN VALE AND DELL SO BLAZE THE DAFFODILS! . . . . . 645 ISLE STAT I 1   15
    IN LEMON-TINTED LINES, SO BLAZE THE DAFFODILS. . . . 645 ISLE STAT I 1   19
BLAZED
    MY BODY OF A SUDDEN BLAZED! . . . . 501 VACILLATION   41
BLAZING
    BLACK OUT! HEAVEN BLAZING INTO THE HEAD! . . . . . 566 LAPIS LAZULI   19
    THAT FILL THE BLAZING HOLLOWS OF MY HEART. . . . . 684 SEEKER   V 69D
BLEAK
    WHEREON THE BLEAK NORTH BLOWS, ... 454 HIS MEMORIES   4
BLEAR-EYED
    NOR BLEAR-EYED WISDOM OUT OF MIDNIGHT OIL. . . . . 446 SCHOOL CHILDR   60
BLEAT
    BUT FAINTER THAN A YOUNG LAMB'S BLEAT. . . . . . 26 OISIN 1   399

		PAGE	TITLE		LINE
BLEAT	(CONTINUED)				
	AND FAINTER THAN A YOUNG LAMB'S BLEAT.	26	OISIN 1	V	399
	SHALL AWAKE WITH LONELY BLEAT,	726	LOVERS QUARREL		6
BLEATING					
	AND THE SHEEP BLEATING AT THE WIND	306	HOUR DAWN		78
BLEED					
	FOR SOULS WHO TIRE AND BLEED,	134	FR GILLIGAN		42
BLEEDING					
	WAS MOVING. BLEEDING NOW, HIS GRASP UNLOCKS,	688	TWO TITANS		42
	THEREFORE, O NATION OF THE BLEEDING BREAST,	709	FERENCZ RENYI		4
BLEMISH					
	AND SMOOTH OUT STAIN AND BLEMISH WITH THE ELEGANCE OF HIS MIND:	353	HIS PHOENIX		7
BLENCH					
	WHY MUST YOU BLENCH AND SHAKE FROM FOOT TO CROWN?"	106	CUCHULAIN SEA		13
BLENCHED					
	TILL YOUR BAD MASTER BLENCHED AND ALL WAS LOST:	270	PARDON FATHERS	V	12
	OUR HANDS ARE BLENCHED, OUR FINGERS SEEM	488	CRAZED MOON		14
	BLENCHED BY THAT MALICIOUS DREAM	488	CRAZED MOON		16
BLENCHING					
	MY BLENCHING AND TREMBLING,	532	FIRST CONFESS		4
	BLENCHING ON HIGH THE DULL STARS SICKEN	646	ISLE STAT I 1		46
BLENDING					
	O'ER HER NEST THE LIGHTS ARE BLENDING:	646	ISLE STAT I 1		36
BLENT					
	TOLD, AND IT SEEMED THAT OUR TWO NATURES BLENT	443	SCHOOL CHILDR		13
BLESS					
	TO BLESS THAT ISLE WITH HONEY IN HIS TONES,	128	DREAM OF FAERY	V	44
	HURRY TO BLESS THE HANDS THAT PLAY,	212	BLESS PSALTER		1
	O KINSMEN, BLESS THE HANDS THAT PLAY.	213	BLESS PSALTER		15
	BUT BLESS OUR HANDS THAT EBB AWAY.	213	BLESS PSALTER		20
	STAND UP AND LIFT YOUR HAND AND BLESS	379	SAINT HUNCH		1
	I SHALL NOT CEASE TO BLESS BECAUSE	379	SAINT HUNCH		7
	CONSIDER MOST TO MAGNIFY, OR TO BLESS,	418	ANCEST HOUSES		39
	THE BOOK OF THE PEOPLE: WHATEVER MOST CAN BLESS	492	COOLE BALLYLEE		44
	THAT I WAS BLESSED AND COULD BLESS.	501	VACILLATION		44
	WHEN GONG AND CONCH DECLARE THE HOUR TO BLESS	611	STATUES		23
	AND ALL THE GARDEN BLESS,	774	COME RIDE		10
BLESSED					
	WATCHING THE BLESSED ONES MOVE FAR OFF, AND THE SMILE ON GOD'S FACE,	61	OISIN 3		199
	IT WERE SAD TO GAZE ON THE BLESSED AND NO MAN I LOVED OF OLD THERE:	63	OISIN 3		221
	IT WAS SAD TO GAZE ON THE BLESSED AND NO MAN I LOVED OF OLD THERE:	63	OISIN 3	V	221
	UNDER THE BLESSED MOONLIGHT,	94	MOLL MAGEE		11
	HOME IN THE BLESSED MOONLIGHT	94	MOLL MAGEE	V	11
	A DREAM OF A BLESSED SPIRIT	124	CATHLEEN PARA	V	T
	AND HOW BENEATH THOSE THREE TIMES BLESSED SKIES	127	DREAM OF FAERY	V	21
	THE BLESSED	166	BLESSED		T
	TO THE CAVE, WHERE DATHI THE BLESSED HAD GONE,	166	BLESSED	V	3
	ALL MANNER OF BLESSED SOULS,	167	BLESSED		14
	BUT PURER THAN A TALL CANDLE BEFORE THE BLESSED ROOD	208	HANRAHANS SONG	V	14
	BUT I ALONE BEING BLESSED KEEP	307	HOUR DAWN		104
	AND BLESSED, I GIVE MY GRATITUDE,	380	SAINT HUNCH		14
	THEREFORE A BLESSED MOON LAST NIGHT	388	SOLOMON WITCH		31
	AND WHERE THE BLESSED DANCE:	474	ALL SOUL NIGHT		96
	BLESSED BE THIS PLACE,	480	BLOOD AND MOON		1
	MORE BLESSED STILL THIS TOWER:	480	BLOOD AND MOON		2
	THAT I WAS BLESSED AND COULD BLESS.	501	VACILLATION		44
	A REVOLUTIONARY SOLDIER KNEELING TO BE BLESSED:	601	GALLERY REVIS		8
	THE BLESSED GOD WAS GOOD TO SEND US SUCH,	683	SEEKER		40
	BUT BLESSED HE THAT STIRS THEM NOT	779	ACCURSED WHO		3
BLESSEDEST					
	THE BLESSEDEST SOULS THAT WALK IN THE WORLD	167	BLESSED		19
	"AND WHICH IS THE BLESSEDEST," CUMHAL SAID,	167	BLESSED		21
	ALL MANNER OF BLESSEDEST SOULS,	167	BLESSED	V	14
	"AND WHO IS THE BLESSEDEST," CUMHAL SAID,	167	BLESSED	V	21
	I SEE THE BLESSEDEST SOUL IN THE WORLD	168	BLESSED		31
	AND HAVE SEEN THE BLESSEDEST SOUL IN THE WORLD,	168	BLESSED	V	31
BLESSEDNESS					
	TO GATHER THE HALF OF YOUR BLESSEDNESS	167	BLESSED		7
	"AND BLESSEDNESS GOES WHERE THE WIND GOES,	168	BLESSED		29
	"O BLESSEDNESS COMES IN THE NIGHT AND THE DAY	168	BLESSED		33
	LIVE IN UNCOMPOSITE BLESSEDNESS,	387	ROBARTES DANCE		46
BLESSING					
	THE PLAYERS ASK FOR A BLESSING ON THE PSALTERIES AND ON THEMSELVES	212	BLESS PSALTER		T
	THE PLAYERS ASK FOR A BLESSING ON THE PSALTERIES AND THEMSELVES	212	BLESS PSALTER	V	T
	BUT MAYBE SOME OLD GAFFER MUTTERS A BLESSING	355	BROKEN DREAMS		4
	GOD GRANT A BLESSING ON THIS TOWER AND COTTAGE	371	ON GOING HOUSE		1
	BLESSING THE TRICOLOUR. "THIS IS NOT," I SAY,	601	GALLERY REVIS		10
BLESSINGS					
	SO GET YOU GONE, VON HUEGEL, THOUGH WITH BLESSINGS ON YOUR HEAD.	503	VACILLATION		89
BLEST					
	HAND LIFTED UP THAT BLEST:	383	VISION ROBART		20
	THAT BLEST SOULS ARE NOT COMPOSITE,	387	ROBARTES DANCE		44
	WE ARE BLEST BY EVERYTHING,	479	SELF AND SOUL		71
	EVERYTHING WE LOOK UPON IS BLEST.	479	SELF AND SOUL		72

```
                                                        PAGE      TITLE          LINE

BLEST   (CONTINUED)
    WHICH IS THE MORE BLEST? . . . . . . . . . . . .    573   LADYS 2ND SONG        20
    SHE CARES NO WHIT FOR EITHER, BUT HAS BLEST . . . . .   660   ISLE STAT II 1     49
BLEW
    AND NIAMH BLEW THREE MERRY NOTES . . . . . . . . .    14   OISIN 1             195
    BLEW ONE LONG NOTE. FROM OVER REED . . . . . . . .    14   OISIN 1        V    195
    SNATCHING THE HORN OF NIAMH, I BLEW A LONG LINGERING NOTE:   51   OISIN 3          57
    SNATCHING THE HORN OF NIAM, I BLEW FORTH A LINGERING NOTE:   51   OISIN 3     V     57
    SNATCHING THE HORN OF NIAM, I BLEW A LINGERING NOTE: . .   51   OISIN 3     V     57
    BY A GREY SHORE WHERE THE WIND NEVER BLEW, . . . . .   170   SECRET ROSE        14
    AND BLEW ME HITHER TO MY LASTING SORROW. . . . . .   235   SHADOW WATER B    288
    AND BLEW YOU HITHER; AND THEIR MOUTHS HAVE PROMISED .   237   SHADOW WATER B    325
    BLEW MY CRIMSON CAP AWAY . . . . . . . . . . . . .   656   ISLE STAT I 3      16
BLIND
    YOU WHO ARE BENT, AND BALD, AND BLIND, . . . . . .     2   OISIN 1              1
    WHY THOU OUTLIVEST, BLIND AND HOARY, . . . . . . .     2   OISIN 1        V     2
    HAVE BORNE ME WHERE THE TEMPESTS BLIND . . . . . .     6   OISIN 1        V    58
    I BURST THE CHAIN: STILL EARLESS, NERVELESS, BLIND, .    36   OISIN 2             97
    STILL EARLESS, NERVELESS, BLIND, THE EAGLES STOOD. .    36   OISIN 2            100
    STILL EARLESS, NERVELESS, BLIND, THE EAGLES DREAMED.    36   OISIN 2        V   100
    FOR HE IS WEAK AND POOR AND BLIND, AND LIES . . . .    42   OISIN 2            203
    BLIND AND NIGH DEAF, WITH WITHERED ARMS HE LIES . .    42   OISIN 2        V   203
    WITH HER OLD FATHER THE BLIND WOOD-CUTTER: . . . .    74   ANASHU VIJAYA      63
    ONE BLIND HOUND ONLY LIES APART . . . . . . . . .    99   FOXHUNTER          41
    THE BLIND HOUND WITH A MOURNFUL DIN . . . . . . .    99   FOXHUNTER          45
    "WITH THE SECRETS OF GOD HALF BLIND, . . . . . . .   168   BLESSED            26
    BODIES OF SHADOW AND BLIND EYES LIKE PEARLS, . . .   185   QUEEN MAEVE       116
    BY ITS OWN BLIND IMAGINING, . . . . . . . . . . .   191   BAILE AILLINN      67
    IF DEAF AND DUMB AND BLIND WITH LOVE? . . . . . .   202   NEVER GIVE ALL     12
    HAS MADE THEM SO HAPPY AND HOPELESS, SO DEAF AND SO BLIND   204   WITHER BOUGHS      20
    WHERE HAZEL AND ASH AND PRIVET BLIND THE PATHS: . .   217   WOODS OF COOLE      8
    IN THIS BLIND BITTER LAND." . . . . . . . . . . .   256   WORDS               4
    WHEN, THE EARS BEING DEAFENED, THE SIGHT OF THE EYES BLIND   257   RECONCILIATION      3
    ARE WHAT THE BLIND AND IGNORANT TOWN . . . . . . .   287   TO WEALTHY MAN      7
    OF OUR OLD PAUDEEN IN HIS SHOP, I STUMBLED BLIND . .   291   PAUDEEN             2
    OWN NOTHING BUT THEIR BLIND, STUPEFIED HEARTS. . .   370   EGO DOMINUS        69
    BLIND AND LEADER OF THE BLIND . . . . . . . . . .   397   POLIT PRISONER     11
    BLIND AND LEADER OF THE BLIND . . . . . . . . . .   397   POLIT PRISONER     11
    STRANGE, BUT THE MAN WHO MADE THE SONG WAS BLIND: .   411   TOWER              49
    WITH HOMER THAT WAS A BLIND MAN, . . . . . . . . .   411   TOWER              52
    AND BRING BEAUTY'S BLIND RAMBLING CELEBRANT: . . .   412   TOWER              91
    ACCORDING TO THE WIND, FOR ALL ARE BLIND. . . . .   433   NINETEEN 19       124
    NOT BLIND WITH GOLD, NOR DAZZLED BY THE GOLD . . .   470   HARUN RASHID   V  191
    AND I GROW HALF CONTENTED TO BE BLIND! . . . . . .   473   ALL SOUL NIGHT     70
    THAT MAN IS STRICKEN DEAF AND DUMB AND BLIND, . . .   478   SELF AND SOUL      35
    A LIVING MAN IS BLIND AND DRINKS HIS DROP. . . . .   478   SELF AND SOUL      41
    THAT MAN IS DEAF AND DRUNK AND BLIND . . . . . . .   478   SELF AND SOUL  V   35
    WHAT MATTER IF A BLIND MAN DRINK HIS DROP? . . . .   478   SELF AND SOUL  V   41
    INTO THE FROG-SPAWN OF A BLIND MAN'S DITCH, . . . .   479   SELF AND SOUL      59
    A BLIND MAN BATTERING BLIND MEN: . . . . . . . . .   479   SELF AND SOUL      60
    A BLIND MAN BATTERING BLIND MEN: . . . . . . . . .   479   SELF AND SOUL      60
    SWIFT BEATING ON HIS BREAST IN SIBYLLINE FRENZY BLIND   481   BLOOD AND MOON     19
    WHETHER FOR DAILY PITTANCE OR IN BLIND FEAR . . .   482   BLOOD AND MOON     37
    A BLIND HERMIT RINGS THE HOUR. . . . . . . . . . .   484   SYMBOLS             2
    THAT STARING FURY AND THE BLIND LUSH LEAF . . . .   500   VACILLATION        17
    IN THIS BLIND BITTER TOWN, . . . . . . . . . . . .   504   QUARREL IN AGE      3
    ROLLING A BLIND PEARL EYE, . . . . . . . . . . . .   552   SONGS REWRIT 2      2
    O A BEGGAR BLIND FROM HIS BIRTH: . . . . . . . . .   552   SONGS REWRIT 2      8
    A BEGGAR BLIND FROM HIS BIRTH: . . . . . . . . . .   552   SONGS REWRIT 2 V    8
    "HIS LIGHT HAD STRUCK ME BLIND . . . . . . . . . .   559   HE AND SHE          5
    BLIND AS A WORM. . . . . . . . . . . . . . . . . .   575   MAIDS 2ND SONG      6
    AND WHEN THE FOOL AND BLIND MAN STOLE THE BREAD . .   630   CIRCUS ANIMALS     25
    SOMETHING DROPS FROM EYES LONG BLIND, . . . . . .   638   BEN BULBEN         29
    SEE THE DARKNESS SLOW DISGORGING A VESSEL BLIND WITH   718   PHANTOM SHIP       12
        SQUALL.
    I AWAIT YOUR WORDS AS THE BLIND GRASS AWAITS . . .   756   SHADOW WATER A    181
    I AM BLIND AND DEAF BECAUSE OF THE WHITE WINGS. . .   759   SHADOW WATER A    235
BLINDED
    COME NEAR, THAT NO MORE BLINDED BY MAN'S FATE, . .   101   ROSE UPON ROOD      9
    LOVE HAS BLINDED HIM WITH TEARS: . . . . . . . . .   612   NEWS ORACLE        28
    I AM HALF BLINDED. I AM HALF BLINDED, TOO. . . . .   759   SHADOW WATER A V  235
    I AM HALF BLINDED. I AM HALF BLINDED, TOO. . . . .   759   SHADOW WATER A V  235
    HAS MADE MY FEET UNSTEADY, AND BLINDED ME. . . . .   767   SHADOW WATER A    406
BLINDER
    BLINDER SORROWS, HARDER WAGE-- . . . . . . . . . .   733   STREET DANCERS     58
BLINDING
    INTO THE BLINDING NIGHT.-- . . . . . . . . . . . .   174   ELEMENT POWERS V    4
    THAT IN THE BLINDING LIGHT BEYOND THE GRAVE . . .   258   KING NO KING       12
BLINDS
    PULL DOWN THE BLINDS, BRING FIDDLE AND CLARIONET . .   311   MOUNTAIN TOMB       5
    THE BLINDS DRAWN UP": MAUD GONNE AT HOWTH STATION WAITING   578   LOFTY THINGS       10
        A TRAIN,
BLINK
    AND UNDER THE BLINK O' THE MORNING STAR, . . . . .    83   MAD KING GOLL  V   20
    TILL STARS ARE BEGINNING TO BLINK AND PEEP: . . .   150   OLD MOTHER          4
    WITH A BLINK IN HIS EYES, AT THE CAVE-MOUTH, . . .   166   BLESSED             3
    WITH A BLINK IN HIS EYES AT THE CAVE MOUTH, . . . .   166   BLESSED        V    3
    OF SWORD-BLUE WAVES OF CALM: WHILE O'ER HEAD BLINK .   663   ISLE STAT II 2     42
BLINKED
    THAT BLINKED AND SAW THEM IN A SHROUD. . . . . . .   529   TOM LUNATIC        12
    HE BLINKED AND BLINKED HIS EYES . . . . . . . . .   740   EARL PAUL          22
```

BLINKED (CONTINUED)
    HE BLINKED AND BLINKED HIS EYES • • • • • • • • •   740 EARL PAUL   22
BLINKING
    AND UNDER THE BLINKING OF THE STARS • • • • • • • •   83 MAD KING GOLL   20
    WITH BLINKING EYES, AT THE CAVE'S EDGE, • • • • • • • 167 BLESSED   V   4C
    "MY EYES ARE BLINKING," DATHI SAID, • • • • • • • •   168 BLESSED   25
BLITHER
    I'D GLAD FOLKS' HEARTS WITH BLITHER SONG." • • • • • 731 PRIEST FAIRY   82
BLOCKS
    SALT BLOOD BLOCKS HIS EYES. • • • • • • • • • • • •   530 DELPHIC ORACLE   5
BLONDE
    THAT BLONDE GIRL THERE IS MY HEART'S DESIRE, • • • • 550 SONGS REWRIT 1 V   1
BLOOD
    UNDER A CROWN OF THORNS AND DARK WITH BLOOD, • • • •   38 OISIN 2   135
    HOW THE FETLOCKS DRIP BLOOD IN THE BATTLE, • • • • •   52 OISIN 3   78
    WHO WASTES HIS BLOOD TO BE ANOTHER'S DREAM. • • • •   103 FERGUS DRUID   28
    ARE BLOWING THROUGH MY BLOOD. • • • • • • • • • • •   171 MAID QUIET   4
    LIKE HEAVY FLOODED WATERS OUR BODIES AND OUR BLOOD; • • 208 HANRAHANS SONG   13
    LIKE HEAVY SWOLLEN WATERS ARE OUR BODIES AND OUR BLOOD; 208 HANRAHANS SONG V 13
    AND NOW THAT TIME PUTS WATER IN MY BLOOD, • • • • •   222 SHADOW WATER B V   11A
    FOR SHE HAD FIERY BLOOD • • • • • • • • • • • • •   255 WOMAN HOMER   15
    THAT MUST, AS IF IT HAD NOT HOLY BLOOD • • • • • •   260 FASC DIFFICULT   5
    MERCHANT AND SCHOLAR WHO HAVE LEFT ME BLOOD • • • •   269 PARDON FATHERS   7
    TRADERS OR SOLDIERS WHO HAVE LEFT ME BLOOD • • • •   269 PARDON FATHERS V   7
    NOTHING BUT THAT TO PROVE YOUR BLOOD AND MINE. • • • 270 PARDON FATHERS   22
    AND AFTER, WHEN HER BLOOD RAN WILD, • • • • • • •   272 GREY ROCK   44
    LED BY A FOOTSOLE DIPPED IN BLOOD • • • • • • • •   274 GREY ROCK   78
    LED BY A FOOT-SOLE DIPPED IN BLOOD • • • • • • • •   274 GREY ROCK   V   78
    BUT FOR THE TRODDEN MIRE, THE POOL OF BLOOD, • • • • 278 TWO KINGS   44
    FOR THIS THAT ALL THAT BLOOD WAS SHED, • • • • • •   290 SEPTEMBER 1913   19
    LIKE GENTLE BLOOD, HAS BEEN DRIVEN FROM THE PLACE, • • 292 TO A SHADE   14
    THEY WERE COMMINGLING LICE AND BLOOD. • • • • • •   297 THREE BEGGARS   56
    WITH THE HOT BLOOD OF YOUTH, OF LOVE CROSSED LONG AGO; • • 316 COLD HEAVEN   6
    AND FROZEN ARE THE CHANNELS OF THE BLOOD. • • • • •   333 LIVING BEAUTY   2
    SEEING THAT TIME HAS FROZEN UP THE BLOOD • • • • •   333 LIVING BEAUTY V   2
    SET ALL HER BLOOD ASTIR • • • • • • • • • • • • •   336 YOUNG GIRL   10
    WHEN AGE MIGHT WELL HAVE CHILLED HIS BLOOD." • • • • 356 BROKEN DREAMS   19
    TROUBLED HIS ANIMAL BLOOD. • • • • • • • • • • • •   378 CAT AND MOON   8
    THERE'S NOTHING BUT OUR OWN RED BLOOD • • • • • •   396 ROSE TREE   17
    CHILLED BLOOD, THIS SWEETNESS BROUGHT; • • • • • •   401 DEMON BEAST   39
    SLOW DECAY OF BLOOD, • • • • • • • • • • • • • •   416 TOWER   185
    THAT DEAD YOUNG SOLDIER IN HIS BLOOD; • • • • • •   425 STARES NEST   14
    TO CRAWL IN HER OWN BLOOD, AND GO SCOT-FREE; • • •   429 NINETEEN 19   28
    NOR KNOW THAT WHAT DISTURBS OUR BLOOD • • • • • •   434 WHEEL   7
    ODOUR OF BLOOD WHEN CHRIST WAS SLAIN • • • • • •   438 SONGS PLAY 2   6
    SO MASTERED BY THE BRUTE BLOOD OF THE AIR, • • • •   441 LEDA AND SWAN   12
    I HAVE AS HEALTHY FLESH AND BLOOD AS ANY RHYMER'S HAD, • • 450 OWEN AHERNE   10
    A HEART OF FLESH AND BLOOD. • • • • • • • • • • •   451 FIRST LOVE   6
    AT THE MANTLING OF THE BLOOD. • • • • • • • • • •   453 DEATH OF HARE   6
    OR MANTLING OF THE BLOOD. • • • • • • • • • • • •   453 DEATH OF HARE V   6
    WHEN MY BLOOD WAS STRONG, • • • • • • • • • • • •   457 SECRETS OF OLD   4
    "AND YET THE JASMINE SEASON WARMS OUR BLOOD." • • • • 464 HARUN RASHID   73
    BLOOD AND THE MOON • • • • • • • • • • • • • • •   480 BLOOD AND MOON   T
    THE STRENGTH THAT GIVES OUR BLOOD AND STATE MAGNANIMITY 481 BLOOD AND MOON   29
        • • •
    THE BLOOD OF INNOCENCE HAS LEFT NO STAIN. • • • • •   482 BLOOD AND MOON   34
    OR OUT OF ABSTRACT HATRED, AND SHED BLOOD, • • • •   482 BLOOD AND MOON   38
    ODOUR OF BLOOD ON THE ANCESTRAL STAIR; • • • • • •   482 BLOOD AND MOON   40
    LIKE EVERYTHING THAT HAS THE STAIN OF BLOOD, • • •   482 BLOOD AND MOON   51
    THERE, ON BLOOD SATURATED GROUND, HAVE STOOD • • •   482 BLOOD AND MOON V   35
    OIL AND BLOOD • • • • • • • • • • • • • • • • • •   483 OIL AND BLOOD   T
    LIE BODIES OF THE VAMPIRES FULL OF BLOOD; • • • • •   483 OIL AND BLOOD   5
    A PATTERN ON A NAPKIN DIPPED IN BLOOD. • • • • • •   483 VERONIC NAPKIN   8
    BUT NEVER SAW THE TREFOIL STAINED WITH BLOOD, • • •   487 SEVEN SAGES   19
    AND ALL COMPLEXITIES OF MIRE OR BLOOD. • • • • • •   498 BYZANTIUM   24
    ASTRADDLE ON THE DOLPHIN'S MIRE AND BLOOD, • • • •   498 BYZANTIUM   33
    WHERE BLOOD BEGOTTEN SPIRITS COME • • • • • • • •   498 BYZANTIUM   V   28
    A STRADDLE ON THE DOLPHIN'S MIRE AND BLOOD • • • •   498 BYZANTIUM   V   33
    THIS LOVE THAT MAKES MY HEART'S BLOOD STOP • • • •   499 MOTHER OF GOD   13
    THAT PROTECT YOUR BLOOD. • • • • • • • • • • • •   518 LOVES LONENESS   6
    IN ALL THE VIGOUR OF ITS BLOOD; • • • • • • • • •   529 TOM LUNATIC   17
    SALT BLOOD BLOCKS HIS EYES. • • • • • • • • • • •   530 DELPHIC ORACLE   5
    AND MY BLOOD BE COLD THE WHILE • • • • • • • • •   532 BEFORE WORLD   11
    OR BUT TO FIND IF WITHERED VEIN RAN BLOOD, • • • •   537 HER VISION   6
    THAT THING ALL BLOOD AND MIRE, THAT BEAST-TORN WRECK, 537 HER VISION   25
    WHAT SHUDDERS RUN THROUGH ALL THAT ANIMAL BLOOD? • • 541 PARN FUNERAL 1   5
    PLUCKED BITTER WISDOM THAT ENRICHED HIS BLOOD. • • • 543 PARN FUNERAL 2   12
    JUSTIFY ALL THAT HAVE SUNK IN THEIR BLOOD, • • • •   546 TO SAME TUNE 2   12
    HOW CAN SHE LIVE TILL IN HER BLOOD HE LIVE; • • •   558 RIBH CHRISTIAN   24
    IRRATIONAL STREAMS OF BLOOD ARE STAINING EARTH; • •   564 GYRES   5
    AND BLOOD AND MIRE THE SENSITIVE BODY STAIN? • • •   564 GYRES   10
    HE CHRISTENED HIMSELF WITH BLOOD. • • • • • • • •   585 ORAHILLY   8
    R.I.P." WRIT IN BLOOD. • • • • • • • • • • • • •   585 ORAHILLY   35
    WHEN AN OLD MAN'S BLOOD GROWS COLD? • • • • • • •   588 OLD WICKED MAN   13
    MUST IRELAND'S BLOOD BE SHED. • • • • • • • • • •   608 SONGS BURDEN 3   26
    REMEMBER ALL THAT HAVE SUNK IN THEIR BLOOD, • • • •   613 MARCH SONGS 1   12
    THOSE IMAGES THAT WAKEN IN THE BLOOD. • • • • • •   622 HOUND VOICE   14
    BASE DROVE OUT THE BETTER BLOOD, • • • • • • • •   626 STATES HOLIDAY   3
    AS THOUGH TO MEDITATE ON WOUNDS AND BLOOD. • • • •   634 CUCHULAIN COMF   6
    AS ROUND HER, SLOW ON FEET THAT HAVE NO BLOOD, • •   687 TWO TITANS   18
    I FLING AWAY MY SWORD, BLOOD DIM, • • • • • • • •   743 DANAAN QUICK   20

	PAGE	TITLE	LINE

BLOOD   (CONTINUED)
   THE BLOOD BOND • • • • • • • • • • • • • • • • • •   769 BLOOD BOND   T
BLOOD—BEDABBLED
   ALONG THE BLOOD—BEDABBLED PLAINS, • • • • • •   24 OISIN 1   371
   I STARED UPON HIS BLOOD—BEDABBLED BREAST • • • • •   537 HER VISION   23
   I STARED UPON MY BLOOD—BEDABBLED BREAST • • • • • •   537 HER VISION   V   23
BLOOD—BEGOTTEN
   WHERE BLOOD—BEGOTTEN SPIRITS COME • • • • • • •   498 BYZANTIUM   28
BLOOD—DARK
   STUMBLING UPON THE BLOOD—DARK TRACK ONCE MORE, • •   622 HOUND VOICE   18
   A STAR—LIT RAPIER, HALF BLOOD—DARK, • • • • • •   671 ISLE STAT II 3   125
BLOOD—DIMMED
   THE BLOOD—DIMMED TIDE IS LOOSED, AND EVERYWHERE • • • •   402 SECOND COMING   5
BLOODLESS
   I CANNOT GO INTO THE BLOODLESS LAND • • • • • • •   722 WITCH VIVIEN   67
BLOOD—RED
   WHERE THE BLOOD—RED BLOSSOM BLOWS • • • • • • •   744 ROSY CROSS   4
BLOOD—SATURATED
   THERE, ON BLOOD—SATURATED GROUND, HAVE STOOD • • • •   482 BLOOD AND MOON   35
BLOOD—SHOT
   NONE CLOSED HIS BLOOD—SHOT EYES BUT SOUGHT • • • • •   296 THREE BEGGARS   44
   THEY 'CLOSED THEIR BLOOD—SHOT EYES FOR NAUGHT. • • • • •   296 THREE BEGGARS   V   44
   WITH BLOOD—SHOT EYES UPON HIM STARED. • • • • • •   297 THREE BEGGARS   58
BLOOD—SODDEN
   BECAUSE THE HEART IN HIS BLOOD—SODDEN BREAST • • • • •   481 BLOOD AND MOON   20
   FROM MAN'S BLOOD—SODDEN HEART ARE SPRUNG • • • • •   502 VACILLATION   67
BLOODY
   OR FROM SOME BLOODY WHIP IN THEIR OWN HANDS. • • • • •   375 PHASES OF MOON   68
   A BLOODY, ARROGANT POWER • • • • • • • • •   480 BLOOD AND MOON   3
   THEIR SHROUDS ARE BLOODY AND THEIR LIPS ARE WET. • •   483 OIL AND BLOOD   6
   A BLOODY AND A SUDDEN END, • • • • • • • •   620 JOHN KINSELLA   1
   WHAT WOUNDS, WHAT BLOODY PRESS, • • • • • • •   785 WOMANS BEAUTY   26
BLOOM
   THE DAMASK ROSES, BLOOM ON BLOOM, • • • • • •   21 OISIN 1   305
   THE DAMASK ROSES, BLOOM ON BLOOM, • • • • • •   21 OISIN 1   305
   AND SANG WE LIGHTLY TO EACH BLOOM • • • • • •   21 OISIN 1   V 306B
   BRING ROSES IF THE ROSE BE YET IN BLOOM: • • • • •   311 MOUNTAIN TOMB   2
   WHERE GOLDEN CROCUS AND NARCISSUS BLOOM, • • •   447 COLONUS PRAISE   18
   HER LOVE: TO HER WHO WEARS THAT BLOOM COMES TRUTH. • •   653 ISLE STAT I 2   46
   AND FULL OF WISDOM IS EACH BLOOM, • • • • • •   655 ISLE STAT I 3   9
   FOR GUIDING OF THE GODS. THE SACRED BLOOM • • • •   656 ISLE STAT I 3   41
   A SCARLET BLOOM. WHY RAISEST THOU, PALE ONE, • •   673 ISLE STAT II 3   196
   THE FALLING HAWTHORN BLOOM. BY MERE AND BROOK •   677 ISLE STAT II 3   279
BLOSSOM   SEE APPLE—BLOSSOM
   BLOSSOM IN SOME NEW CRIMSON FLOWER, • • • • •   16 OISIN 1   224
   AND THE PALE BLOSSOM OF THE MOON, • • • • • •   20 OISIN 1   288
   WITH APPLE BLOSSOM IN HER HAIR • • • • • •   150 WANDER AENGUS   14
   THE SHADOWY BLOSSOM OF MY HAIR • • • • • •   152 HEART OF WOMAN   7
   THEN COVER THE PALE BLOSSOM OF YOUR BREAST • • • •   163 ASKS FORGIVE   V   21
   WITH ITS SWEET BLOSSOM WHERE HERS WAS: • • • • •   197 BAILE AILLINN   190
   DELICATE IN COLOUR AS APPLE BLOSSOM. • • • • •   199 ARROW   6
   BLOSSOM PALE, SHE PULLED DOWN THE PALE BLOSSOM • •   199 ARROW   V   5
   BLOSSOM PALE, SHE PULLED DOWN THE PALE BLOSSOM • •   199 ARROW   V   5
   BOUGHS HAVE THEIR FRUIT AND BLOSSOM • • • • •   214 HAPPY TOWNLAND   5
   WHERE BOUGHS HAVE FRUIT AND BLOSSOM • • • • •   214 HAPPY TOWNLAND V   5
   AND SHAKE THE BLOSSOM FROM THE BUD • • • • •   396 ROSE TREE   11
   ARE YOU THE LEAF, THE BLOSSOM OR THE BOLE? • • •   446 SCHOOL CHILDR   62
   CAN SHAKE MORE BLOSSOM FROM AUTUMNAL CHILL • • •   465 HARUN RASHID   104
   THAT BRINGS MORE BLOSSOM TO AUTUMNAL CHILL • • •   465 HARUN RASHID   V   104
   BLOSSOM FROM THE SUMMER'S WREATH: • • • • •   475 EVA GORE—BOOTH   6
   GREAT NATIONS BLOSSOM ABOVE: • • • • • •   547 TO SAME TUNE 3   5
   OF ROOT, SHOOT, BLOSSOM OR CLAY • • • • •   600 SPIRIT MEDIUM   21
   GREAT NATIONS BLOSSOM ABOVE. • • • • • •   614 MARCH SONGS 2   5
   WITHIN THE DROWSY BLOSSOM HANGS THE BEE: • • • •   645 ISLE STAT I 1   2
   THE NIGHEST BLOSSOM WHERE IT FALLS I'LL TAKE. • • •   657 ISLE STAT I 3   65
   THIS BLOSSOM IS MOST NEAR. STATUE! OH, THOU • •   657 ISLE STAT I 3   72
   FIERCE THRUST! A TARDY BLOSSOM HAD THE SEED, • • •   665 ISLE STAT II 2   65
   THE FAERY BLOSSOM LIES UPON THY LIPS. • • • •   677 ISLE STAT II 3   285
   THE FAERY BLOSSOM LIES UPON THY LIPS: • • • •   678 ISLE STAT II 3   291
   THE FAERY BLOSSOM BROODS UPON THY LIPS. • • • • •   678 ISLE STAT II 3   306
   MY BLOSSOM, I AM DYING. AND THE STARS • • • •   700 MOSADA 3   47
   OF APPLE BLOSSOM CIRCLES IN THE GLOOM, • • • •   700 MOSADA 3   V   42
   AN APPLE BLOSSOM CIRCLES IN THE GLOOM, • • • •   700 MOSADA 3   V   42
   WHERE THE BLOOD—RED BLOSSOM BLOWS • • • • •   744 ROSY CROSS   4
   THE TOPMOST BLOSSOM ON THE BOUGHS OF TIME • • •   756 SHADOW WATER A   178
   AND THE PALE BLOSSOM: BUT I WOKE INSTEAD • • • •   761 SHADOW WATER A   281
   SHOOK THE PALE APPLE BLOSSOM OVER IT: • • • •   761 SHADOW WATER A V 275
BLOSSOMED
   THEY BLOSSOMED TO IMMORTAL MIRTH. • • • • • •   189 BAILE AILLINN   12
   HAS BLOSSOMED, AND I GROW AS OLD AS TIME. • • • •   756 SHADOW WATER A   179
BLOSSOMER
   O CHESTNUT—TREE, GREAT—ROOTED BLOSSOMER, • • • •   446 SCHOOL CHILDR   61
   O CHESTNUT TREE, GREAT ROOTED BLOSSOMER, • • • •   446 SCHOOL CHILDR   V   61
BLOSSOMING
   BECAUSE THEIR BLOSSOMING DREAMS HAVE NEVER BENT • • •   136 TO SOME I TALK   8
   FOR IN THE WORLD'S FIRST BLOSSOMING AGE • • • •   138 TO IRELAND   V   10
   OR TWO SWEET BLOSSOMING APPLE—BOUGHS • • • •   195 BAILE AILLINN   153
   OR TWO SWEET BLOSSOMING APPLE BOUGHS • • • •   195 BAILE AILLINN   V   153
   CREW FROM A BLOSSOMING APPLE BOUGH • • • • •   387 SOLOMON WITCH   10
   UPON A BLOSSOMING APPLE BOUGH • • • • • •   387 SOLOMON WITCH   V   10
   CRIED FROM A BLOSSOMING APPLE BOUGH • • • •   387 SOLOMON WITCH   V   10

	PAGE	TITLE	LINE
BLOSSOMING (CONTINUED)			
LABOUR IS BLOSSOMING OR DANCING WHERE	445	SCHOOL CHILDR	57
AND WHAT A BLOSSOMING,	457	SUMMER SPRING	14
PRAISE THE BLOSSOMING APPLE-STEM.	773	SONG DEIRDRE 1	21
PRAISE THE BLOSSOMING APPLE STEM;	773	SONG DEIRDRE 1 V	21
BLOSSOMS			
AND IN THE BLOSSOMS HUNG THE BEES.	2	OISIN 1 V	7G
ARE WRONGING YOUR IMAGE THAT BLOSSOMS A ROSE	143	ROSE IN HEART	4
FOR MY DREAMS OF YOUR IMAGE THAT BLOSSOMS A ROSE	143	ROSE IN HEART	8
WITH APPLE BLOSSOMS IN HER HAIR,	150	WANDER AENGUS V	14
AND COVER THE PALE BLOSSOMS OF YOUR BREAST	163	ASKS FORGIVE	21
BLOSSOMS OPEN DEWY LIPS;	647	ISLE STAT I 1	65
AS BLOSSOMS, WHEN THE WINDS OF MARCH	671	ISLE STAT II 3	127
THE FALLING BLOSSOMS, AND THE DEAD THE LIVING.	756	SHADOW WATER A	182
BLOT			
TILL THE FAR DOORWAY GREW A BURNING BLOT	39	OISIN 2 V	152
CAN BLOT OUT OF MY MEMORY THIS LIFE	285	TWO KINGS	204
ALL THOSE STORMS THAT BLOT THE DAY	509	JANE REPROVED V	3
NOISE! AND A FLASH, A MOMENTARY BLOT.	714	FERENCZ RENYI	110
NOISE! UPROAR! AND A MOMENTARY BLOT.	714	FERENCZ RENYI V	110
AND HEAVEN'S A CLOUDY BLOT.	782	HEART FRIGHT	17
BLOTCH			
AND PENETRATION OF THEIR EYES. WHERE YONDER BLOTCH	664	ISLE STAT II 2	47
BLOTS			
ALL THAT STORM THAT BLOTS THE DAY	509	JANE REPROVED	3
BLOTTED			
AND THE STARS WERE BLOTTED ABOVE US,	48	OISIN 3	24
HAD BLOTTED OUT MAN'S IMAGE AND HIS CRY.	120	SORROW OF LOVE	4
THIS HUMAN LIFE BLOTTED FROM MEMORY.	285	TWO KINGS	198
UNDER ECLIPSE AND THE DAY BLOTTED OUT.	414	TOWER	120
AND ANCIENT LINEAMENTS ARE BLOTTED OUT.	564	GYRES	4
BLOW			
IT SEEMED TO BLOW FROM THE DYING FLAME,	13	OISIN 1	167
SHALL BLOW INTO RUIN OUR MUSICAL DAYS,	28	OISIN 1 V	425
BURST FROM A GREAT DOOR MARRED BY MANY A BLOW	31	OISIN 1	29
"HUNTSMAN RODY, BLOW THE HORN,"	98	FOXHUNTER	25
"NOW HUNTSMAN RODY, BLOW THY HORN,	98	FOXHUNTER V	REF
"MY HUNTSMAN RODY, BLOW THE HORN,	98	FOXHUNTER V	REF
"HUNTSMAN RODY, BLOW THE HORN,	99	FOXHUNTER	33
"I CANNOT BLOW UPON MY HORN,	99	FOXHUNTER	35
THE DOORS OF HELL AND BLOW THERE MANY A WHIMPERING GHOST!	147	UNAPPEAS HOST	10
I WENT TO BLOW THE FIRE AFLAME,	149	WANDER AENGUS	10
I BENT TO BLOW THE FIRE AFLAME;	149	WANDER AENGUS V	10)
I WENT TO BLOW THE FIRE A-FLAME,	149	WANDER AENGUS V	10
I STOOPED TO BLOW THE FIRE AFLAME,	149	WANDER AENGUS V	10
I RISE IN THE DAWN, AND I KNEEL AND BLOW	150	OLD MOTHER	1
I RISE AT THE DAWN, AND I KNEEL AND BLOW	150	OLD MOTHER V	1
AND THE WINDS THAT BLOW THROUGH THE STARRY WAYS,	158	TO HIS HEART	4
AND BLOW A LITTLE NOISE	215	HAPPY TOWNLAND	43
I'LL STRIKE A BLOW FOR HIM TO GIVE HIM TIME	239	SHADOW WATER B	365
THAT WINDS OF WINTER BLOW	431	NINETEEN 19	87
A SUDDEN BLOW! THE GREAT WINGS BEATING STILL	441	LEDA AND SWAN	1
BID ME STRIKE A MATCH AND BLOW.	476	EVA GORE-BOOTH	32
FOR THE FOUL WINDS BLOW!	523	MAD AS MIST	2
WHERE THE MEADOW-SAFFRONS BLOW,	680	LOVE AND DEATH	6
AND THE WINDS COME DOWN AND BLOW THEM WITH THE VAPOURS FAR AWAY.	719	PHANTOM SHIP	28
I AND THAT MIGHTY KING A SUDDEN BLOW	757	SHADOW WATER A	195
THAT BLOW WHEN HEAVEN AND EARTH ARE WITHERING,	767	SHADOW WATER A	395
BECAUSE THE NIGHT WINDS BLOW	782	HEART FRIGHT	16
BLOWIN' SEE A-BLOWIN'			
BLOWIN' HER MORNIN' FIRE.	95	MOLL MAGEE	36
BLOWING			
THE COLD WET WINDS EVER BLOWING,	119	PITY OF LOVE	5
AND THE COLD WET WINDS EVER BLOWING,	119	PITY OF LOVE V	7
AND THE WINDS BLOWING THROUGH THE STARRY WAYS,	158	TO HIS HEART V	4
AND BLOWING US EVIL AND GOOD;	158	TO HIS HEART V	4A
ARE BLOWING THROUGH MY BLOOD.	171	MAID QUIET	4
UNDER THE BITTER BLACK WINDS BLOWING OUT OF THE LEFT HAND!	206	HANRAHANS SONG V	2
FOR THE WET WINDS ARE BLOWING OUT OF THE CLINGING AIR;	207	HANRAHANS SONG	12
WHEN THE WIND COMES BLOWING ACROSS THE HILLY LAND!	207	HANRAHANS SONG V	7
FOR THE GREY WINDS ARE BLOWING UP, OUT OF THE CLINGING SEAS!	207	HANRAHANS SONG V	12
AND WINDS BLOWING FROM FLOWERS, AND WHIRR OF FEATHERS	219	WOODS OF COOLE	39
IF A GOOD EASTER WIND WERE BLOWING,	306	HOUR DAWN	86
AND A COLD WIND IS BLOWING IN MY HAIR.	761	SHADOW WATER A	277
BLOWN SEE WIND-BLOWN			
WITH BLOWN, SPRAY-DABBLED HAIR GATHER AT HAND.	114	ROSE OF BATTLE	6
THE THRONGS WITH BLOWN WET HAIR ARE GATHERING NEAR.	114	ROSE OF BATTLE V	6
WHEN SHALL THE STARS BE BLOWN ABOUT THE SKY,	170	SECRET ROSE	29
LIKE THE SPARKS BLOWN OUT OF A SMITHY, AND DIE?	170	SECRET ROSE	30
BEING TUMBLED AND BLOWN ABOUT	191	BAILE AILLINN	66
A CLOUD BLOWN FROM THE CUT-THROAT NORTH	313	MEMORY YOUTH	6
AND QUARRELS ARE BLOWN UP UPON THAT HEAD!	324	ROBERT GREGORY	13
AND YET THEY SPEAK WHAT'S BLOWN INTO THE MIND!	376	PHASES OF MOON	110
THE COLD BLOWN SPRAY IN MY NOSTRIL.	399	BREAK OF DAY	20
A MIST THAT IS LIKE BLOWN SNOW IS SWEEPING OVER ALL,	425	PHANTOM HATRED	2
A BUNDLE OF TEMPESTUOUS CLOUD IS BLOWN	541	PARN FUNERAL 1	2
LONG CITRON COILS THAT HANG AROUND THEE, BLOWN	670	ISLE STAT II 3	105
AND NO MAN KILL ME! FOR SOME WIND HAS BLOWN	751	SHADOW WATER A	97
HAVE THE WINDS BLOWN YOU AMONG THESE EMPTY WATERS?	756	SHADOW WATER A	192

93

		PAGE	TITLE		LINE

BLOWN   (CONTINUED)
```
    AND SHE, NO LONGER BLOWN AMONG THE WINDS,  . . . . . .    763  SHADOW WATER A        323
    ARE BLOWN COLD DUST OR A BIT OF BONE.  . . . . . .        788  HAWTHORN TREE           8
BLOWS
    AND BLOWS ON HIS HANDS IN THE FIRE'S WARM BLAZE;          26  OISIN 1          V    404
    BARKING. WE TRAMPLED UP AND DOWN WITH BLOWS  . . . . .    40  OISIN 2               170
    BARKING. ALONG THE HERBLESS PLAIN, WITH BLOWS  . . . .    40  OISIN 2          V    170
    SURELY THINE HOUR HAS COME, THY GREAT WIND BLOWS,  . . .  170  SECRET ROSE            31
    THE POWERS, NOT KIND LIKE YOU, CAME WHERE GOD'S GARDEN    174  ELEMENT POWERS   V      1
        BLOWS,
    UNDER A BITTER BLACK WIND THAT BLOWS FROM THE LEFT HAND;  206  HANRAHANS SONG          2
    THAT THEY WOULD COME TO BLOWS,  . . . . . . . . . .       214  HAPPY TOWNLAND         22
    THAT THEY MUST COME TO BLOWS  . . . . . . . . . . . .     214  HAPPY TOWNLAND   V     22
    OR MAYBE BUT A WIND THAT BLOWS  . . . . . . . . . . .     396  ROSE TREE               5
    OF EVERY WIND THAT BLOWS;  . . . . . . . . . . . . .      419  MY HOUSE                7
    WHEREON THE BLEAK NORTH BLOWS,  . . . . . . . . . . .     454  HIS MEMORIES            4
    BUT GOOD STRONG BLOWS ARE DELIGHTS TO THE MIND."         544  TO SAME TUNE 1          4
    BUT A GOOD STRONG CAUSE AND BLOWS ARE DELIGHT."  . . .    545  TO SAME TUNE 1         14
    BUT A GOOD STRONG CAUSE AND THE BLOWS ARE DELIGHT."  .    545  TO SAME TUNE 1   V     14
    BUT GOOD STRONG BLOWS ARE DELIGHTS TO THE MIND."         616  MARCH SONGS 3           4
    BUT A GOOD STRONG CAUSE AND BLOWS ARE DELIGHT."  . . .    616  MARCH SONGS 3          14
    THE LONG LILY BLOWS,  . . . . . . . . . . . . . .        672  ISLE STAT II 3        165
    WHERE THE BLOOD-RED BLOSSOM BLOWS  . . . . . . . . .      744  ROSY CROSS              4
    AND THE WIND BLOWS IT AWAY.  . . . . . . . . . . . .      783  GREY ROUND             20
BLUE      SEE STEEL-BLUE SWORD-BLUE
    WILD FLAMES OF RED AND GOLD AND BLUE,  . . . . . . .      18  OISIN 1               252
    IF THEY STILL SLUMBER, TOUCH THEIR EYELIDS BLUE,  . . .   33  OISIN 2          V     61
    AH, TOUCH THEIR BLUE VEINED EYELIDS IF THEY SLEEP,  . .   33  OISIN 2          V     61
    SIGH, O YOU LITTLE STARS! O SIGH AND SHAKE YOUR          72  ANASHU VIJAYA          18
        BLUE APPAREL!
    SIGH, OH YE LITTLE STARS! OH, SIGH AND SHAKE YOUR BLUE   72  ANASHU VIJAYA    V     18
        APPAREL!
    AND THE FLAME OF THE BLUE STAR OF TWILIGHT,  . . . . .    122  WHITE BIRDS            3
    OR THE FLAME OF THE BLUE STAR THAT LINGERS  . . . . .     122  WHITE BIRDS            7
    OF THE MATCHING OF RIBBONS THE BLUE AND THE RED,  . . .   151  OLD MOTHER       V      6
    IT ROSE IN A STRAIGHT BLUE GARMENT,  . . . . . . . .      159  CAP AND BELLS          5
    IN A LONG AND STRAIGHT BLUE GARMENT  . . . . . . . .      159  CAP AND BELLS    V      5
    TO HER LEFT HAND CAME THE BLUE.  . . . . . . . . . .      160  CAP AND BELLS         32
    THE BLUE AND THE DIM AND THE DARK CLOTHS  . . . . . .     176  CLOTHS HEAVEN          3
    CAER, HIS BLUE EYED DAUGHTER THAT I LOVE.  . . . . .      184  QUEEN MAEVE      V     96
    QUEENS, THEIR EYES BLUE LIKE THE ICE,  . . . . . . .      214  HAPPY TOWNLAND        11
    TREMBLING IN THE BLUE HEAVENS LIKE A WHITE FAWN  . . .    251  SHADOW WATER B       611
    WITH THE GROUND-IVY'S BLUE, HE SAW A STAG  . . . . .      277  TWO KINGS              6
    WANDERED BETWEEN THE BLUE AND THE GREEN LEAF  . . . .     278  TWO KINGS             41
    AS ON THE BLUE LIGHT OF A SWORD, A MAN  . . . . . .       289  TWO KINGS            148
    APPEAR AND DISAPPEAR IN THE BLUE DEPTH OF THE SKY  . .    318  MAGI                   3
    APPEAR AND DISAPPEAR IN THE BLUE DEPTHS OF THE SKY  .     318  MAGI             V      3
    LIKE THIS PURE JET, NOW LOST AMID BLUE SKY,  . . . .      464  HARUN RASHID          64
    THE MOBS OF STARS IN GOLD AND GREEN AND BLUE,  . . .      663  ISLE STAT II 2        43
    AMONG THE BOUGHS, BLUE AS THE HALCYON'S WING,  . . .      683  SEEKER                38
    WITHIN THE WOODWAYS, BLUE AS THE HALCYON'S WING,  . .     683  SEEKER           V     38
    'TIS THOU, FOR THEY'VE GROWN BLUE AROUND THE NAILS. . .   700  MOSADA 3              46
    AMONG THE BLUE, THE AMBER AND THE RED.  . . . . . .       712  FERENCZ RENYI    V     76
    THE GRASS AND THE BLUE SHADOW ON THE STREAM  . . . .      761  SHADOW WATER A       280
    TREMBLING IN THE BLUE HEAVENS LIKE A WHITE FAWN  . . .    769  SHADOW WATER A       427
BLUE-EYED
    HOW THE SLOW, BLUE-EYED OXEN OF FINN LOW SADLY AT EVENING  52  OISIN 3               84
        TIDE.
    CAER, HIS BLUE-EYED DAUGHTER THAT I LOVE.  . . . . .      184  QUEEN MAEVE           96
    AND THE WOOD-WOMAN, WHOSE LOVER WAS CHANGED TO A BLUE-EYED  209  UNDER THE MOON       13
        HAWK;
    AND THE WOOD WOMAN, WHOSE LOVER WAS CHANGED TO A BLUE-EYED  209  UNDER THE MOON V     13
        HAWK;
    BLUE-EYED, AND A QUICK RUNNER ON BARE FEET,  . . . . .    242  SHADOW WATER B       416
BLUE-GREEN
    AND IN THE TREMBLING BLUE-GREEN OF THE SKY  . . . . .     206  ADAMS CURSE           30
BLUER
    AND THE GROUND IVY'S BLUER LIGHT, A STAG  . . . . . .     277  TWO KINGS        V      6
BLUES
    HER GOLDS, HER AMBERS, AND HER BLUES,  . . . . . . .      13  OISIN 1               163
    HER GOLDS, HER AZURES, AND HER BLUES,  . . . . . . .      13  OISIN 1          V    163
BLUE-VEINED
    AH, TOUCH THEIR BLUE-VEINED EYELIDS IF THEY SLEEP,  . .   33  OISIN 2               61
BLUSHED
    SHE WALKED AWHILE AND BLUSHED AWHILE  . . . . . . .       451  FIRST LOVE             3
BLUSHES
    AND THE BLUSHES OF FIRST LOVE NEVER HAVE FLOWN;  . . .    8  OISIN 1                85
BOAR
    THE DEER, THE BADGER, AND THE BOAR.  . . . . . . .       23  OISIN 1               345
    A HUNDRED YEARS I CHASED THE BOAR,  . . . . . . . .      23  OISIN 1          V    344
    THE WILD BOAR KNOWS ME, BY ONE EAR  . . . . . . . .      84  MAD KING GOLL    V     45
    I WOULD THAT THE BOAR WITHOUT BRISTLES HAD COME FROM THE  153  CHANGE BELOVED        10
        WEST
    AND SO WITH WOLF, AND BOAR, AND STEER.  . . . . . . .     671  ISLE STAT II 3       122
BOARD
    THEY WROTE ON TABLETS OF THIN BOARD,  . . . . . . .      197  BAILE AILLINN        195
    THE GODS WERE SITTING AT THE BOARD  . . . . . . . .      271  GREY ROCK             14
    WHILE THEIR GREAT WOODEN DICE BEAT ON THE BOARD.  . .     412  TOWER                 88
    TWO HEAVY TRESTLES, AND A BOARD  . . . . . . . . .       421  MY TABLE               1
    SHE HEARS ME STRIKE THE BOARD AND SAY  . . . . . . .     531  FATHER CHILD           1
    WHEN ONE HAS LEAPT ON BOARD. NO, FOR I HAVE HOPE  . .     751  SHADOW WATER A       106
```

BOARD   (CONTINUED)
    FORGAEL MAY FIND HIS HEART'S DESIRE ON BOARD . . . . .   751 SHADOW WATER A   107
BOARDED   SEE CEDAR-BOARDED
    CHRYSELEPHANTINE, CEDAR BOARDED, ...   440 WISDOM   V   10
BOARDS
    AND THEY HAD NAILED THE BOARDS ABOVE HER FACE, ...   123 DREAM OF DEATH   3
    BUT NOW LIES UNDER BOARDS. . . . .   123 DREAM OF DEATH   12
    WITH OLD MILL BOARDS AND SEA-GREEN SLATES, ...   406 CARVED STONE   2
    UPON THIN BOARDS OF YEW AND APPLE WOOD, ...   764 SHADOW WATER A   343
    UPON THIN BOARDS OF YEW AND APPLE-WOOD, ...   764 SHADOW WATER A V   343
BOAST
    BOAST NOT, NOR MOURN WITH DROOPING HEAD . . . .   11 OISIN 1   129
    BARD OISIN, BOAST NOT OF THY DEEDS . . . .   11 OISIN 1   V 129
    "LET OTHERS BOAST THEIR FILL," SAID I, ...   539 MEETING   7
    "BUT NEVER DARE TO BOAST . . . .   539 MEETING   8
    "A LOONY'D BOAST OF SUCH A LOVE," . . . .   539 MEETING   13
    SOME BOAST OF BEGGAR-KINGS AND KINGS . . . .   597 MODEL LAUREATE   9
BOASTING
    HELD TO THE TOWERS WITH BOASTING SONGS AND GAY. . . . .   41 OISIN 2   V 184C
BOASTS
    ANOTHER BOASTS, "I PICK AND CHOOSE AND HAVE BUT TWO OR   354 HIS PHOENIX   20
        THREE."
BOAT   SEE ROW-BOAT
    THE CLOAK, THE BOAT, AND THE SHOES . . . .   69 CLOAK BOAT   T
    "I BUILD A BOAT FOR SORROW! . . . .   70 CLOAK BOAT   7
    A BOAT I BUILD FOR SORROW! . . . .   70 CLOAK BOAT   V   7
    ON DAPPLED SKINS IN A GLASS BOAT, ...   196 BAILE AILLINN   180
    A GREAT BLACK RAGGED BIRD APPEARED WHEN I WAS IN THE BOAT! 593 PILGRIM   16
    A GREAT BLACK BIRD APPEARED WHEN I WAS IN THE BOAT, . .   593 PILGRIM   V 16
    OF THOSE VAST WOODS! AND THEN I SAW THE BOAT, ...   657 ISLE STAT I 3   53
    THE BOAT DRAWS NEAR AND NEAR. YOU HEED ME NOT! . . . .   663 ISLE STAT II 2   23
    SLOW WATERS, AND THE BOAT AND MAIDEN SINK . . . . . .   663 ISLE STAT II 2   39
    A BOAT I BUILD FOR SORROW. . . . .   666 ISLE STAT II 3   7
BOATMAN
    BUT I NEVER STOPPED TO QUESTION, WHAT COULD THE BOATMAN SAY 593 PILGRIM   19
BOAT'S
    THE BOAT'S PROW GRATED ON THE SHALLOW SAND, ...   659 ISLE STAT II 1   11
    ALL SWIM WITH TEARS. THE FAERY BOAT'S AT HAND! . . . .   663 ISLE STAT II 2   33
BOATS
    AND ON THE SHORES WERE MANY BOATS . . . .   14 OISIN 1   188
    WE WENT A-FISHING IN LONG BOATS . . . .   23 OISIN 1   352
BOB
    OR SEE THE BROWN MICE BOB . . . .   88 STOLEN CHILD   48
BOBBIN
    FOR HADES' BOBBIN BOUND IN MUMMY-CLOTH . . . .   497 BYZANTIUM   11
    FOR HADES' BOBBIN BOUND IN MUMMY CLOTH . . . .   497 BYZANTIUM   V 11
BODES
    "BODES ME LITTLE GOOD." . . . .   539 MEETING   6
BODICES
    THEIR BODICES IN SOME DIM PLACE . . . .   193 BAILE AILLINN   105
BODIED   SEE GREAT-BODIED
    AND YET HAD BEEN GREAT BODIED AND GREAT LIMBED, ...   181 QUEEN MAEVE   V 25
BODIES
    BENT ALL OUR SWAYING BODIES DOWN, ...   20 OISIN 1   297
    THEIR NAKED AND GLEAMING BODIES POURED OUT AND HEAPED IN   48 OISIN 3   28
        THE WAY.
    THEIR MIGHTY AND NAKED AND GLEAMING BODIES . . . . . .   48 OISIN 3   V 28
    THE BREATHING CAME FROM THOSE BODIES, ...   49 OISIN 3   36
    SIDLED THEIR BODIES AGAINST HIM, FILLING THE SHADE WITH   50 OISIN 3   48
        THEIR EYES.
    . . . WITH BODIES UNGLORIOUS, THEIR CHIEFTAINS STOOD, . .   58 OISIN 3   166
    BODIES OF SHADOW AND BLIND EYES LIKE PEARLS, ...   185 QUEEN MAEVE   116
    WITH LONG WHITE BODIES CAME OUT OF THE AIR, ...   185 QUEEN MAEVE   118
    WITH BODIES MADE OUT OF SOFT FIRE. THE ONE, ...   187 QUEEN MAEVE   144
    BECAUSE THEIR BODIES HAD GROWN OLD. . . . .   189 BAILE AILLINN   10
    AND IN THE LIGHT BODIES OF BIRDS . . . .   190 BAILE AILLINN   44
    LIKE HEAVY FLOODED WATERS OUR BODIES AND OUR BLOOD! . .   208 HANRAHANS SONG   13
    DARK AND DULL AND EARTHY OUR SOULS AND BODIES BE! . . .   208 HANRAHANS SONG V   13
    LIKE HEAVY SWOLLEN WATERS ARE OUR BODIES AND OUR BLOOD!   208 HANRAHANS SONG V   13
    ARE YOU NOT HAPPY WINGED BODIES NOW? . . . .   234 SHADOW WATER B   273
    NOW THAT YOU HAVE HAPPY WINGED BODIES? . . . .   234 SHADOW WATER B V   273
    THE ROUND GREEN EYES AND THE LONG WAVERING BODIES . . .   343 DEJECTION   2
    THEY CHANGE THEIR BODIES AT A WORD. AND THEN? . . . .   376 PHASES OF MOON   113
    IMAGINED BODIES ALL THEIR DAYS . . . .   386 ROBARTES DANCE   28
    OF THEIR OWN SWEETNESS, BODIES OF THEIR LOVELINESS. . .   426 PHANTOM HATRED   24
    AND BODIES BROKEN LIKE A THORN . . . .   454 HIS MEMORIES   3
    BODIES OF HOLY MEN AND WOMEN EXUDE . . . .   483 OIL AND BLOOD   2
    LIE BODIES OF THE VAMPIRES FULL OF BLOOD! . . . . . .   483 OIL AND BLOOD   5
    THOSE BODIES FROM A PICTURE OR A COIN . . . .   537 HER VISION   28
    DID BUT OUR BODIES TOUCH, ...   538 LAST CONFESS   10
    THEY LEFT THEIR BODIES TO FATTEN THE WOLVES, ...   545 TO SAME TUNE 2   2
    BEEN BONE AND SINEW! WHEN SUCH BODIES JOIN . . . . .   555 RIBH AT TOMB   12
    BEAT DOWN UPON THEIR NAKED BODIES, KNOW . . . . . .   563 MERU   12
    THAT BY THEIR BODIES LAY. . . . .   589 OLD WICKED MAN   44
    THEY LEFT THEIR BODIES TO FATTEN THE WOLVES, ...   613 MARCH SONGS 1   2
    BODIES THAT CAN NEVER TIRE . . . .   776 AGAINST WITCH   20
    ALL THEIR BODIES, JOINT BY JOINT, ...   776 AGAINST WITCH   22
    BURN THEIR BODIES UP FOR NOUGHT, ...   787 HUDDON DUDDON   14
    GAVE THEIR BODIES, EMPTIED PURSES . . . .   789 SINGING HEAD   19
BODILY
    AND BODILY TENDERNESS, AND FINDS THAT EVEN . . . . . .   228 SHADOW WATER B   147

BODILY   (CONTINUED)
    MY BODILY FORM FROM ANY NATURAL THING, ...   408 SAIL BYZANTIUM   26
    MY BODILY HEIRS MAY FIND, ...   420 MY HOUSE   28
    LEARNED IN BODILY LOWLINESS . . . .   513 JANE TALK BISH   11
    OR BODILY MOVEMENT DID I DARE. . . . .   514 JANE GROWN OLD   5
    BODILY DECREPITUDE IS WISDOM; YOUNG . . . .   523 LONG SILENCE   7
    THAT I LOVED BODILY. . . . .   538 LAST CONFESS   6
    A BODILY OR MENTAL FURNITURE. . . . .   558 RIBH CHRISTIAN   20
    AND BODILY TENDERNESS TO THE SOFT FIRE . . . .   750 SHADOW WATER A   60
    AND BODILY TENDERNESS; AND HE WHO LONGS . . . .   750 SHADOW WATER A   66
    AND BODILY TENDERNESS; BUT LOVE IS MADE . . . .   765 SHADOW WATER A   355
BODKIN
    IN A BODKIN OR DISEASE, ...   632 MAN AND ECHO   22
BODY
    AND THE WHITE BODY THAT LAY BY MINE; . . . .   3 OISIN 1   10
    AND HER BRIGHT BODY, SANG OF FAERY AND MAN . . . . .   29 OISIN 2   7
    AND HER BRIGHT BODY--NOW OF FAY AND MAN; . . . . . .   29 OISIN 2   V 7
    OF A DROWNED DRIPPING BODY TO MY BREAST; . . . . . .   40 OISIN 2   179
    GO CAST YOUR BODY ON THE STONES AND PRAY, ...   42 OISIN 2   207
    IN THE ROOTS OF THE GRASSES, THE SORRELS, I LAID MY BODY   52 OISIN 3   73
        AS LOW;
    WHEN THEY FROZE THE CLOTH ON MY BODY LIKE ARMOUR RIVETED   57 OISIN 3   151
        FAST,
    I WOULD LEAVE NO SAINT'S HEAD ON HIS BODY . . . . . .   58 OISIN 3   160
    . . . WHEN LIFE IN MY BODY HAS CEASED, ...   63 OISIN 3   222
    THE SERVANTS BEAR THE BODY IN; . . . .   99 FOXHUNTER   47
    THIS BODY TREMBLING LIKE A WIND-BLOWN REED. . . . . .   103 FERGUS DRUID   25
    WHEN EARTHY NIGHT HAD DRUNK HIS BODY IN; . . . . . .   127 DREAM OF FAERY   28
    NOW THAT DEEP EARTH HAS DRUNK HIS BODY IN; . . . . .   127 DREAM OF FAERY V   28
    MY BODY SPAKE, NOT I!" . . . .   132 FR GILLIGAN   12
    AND THOUGHT OF DAYS WHEN HE'D HAD A STRAIGHT BODY, . .   183 QUEEN MAEVE   70
    THEY KNEW HIM; HIS CHANGED BODY WAS . . . .   195 BAILE AILLINN   139
    A YEW-TREE WHERE HIS BODY LAY; . . . .   197 BAILE AILLINN   188
    A YEW TREE WHERE HIS BODY LAY. . . . .   197 BAILE AILLINN V   188
    WE'RE IN THE BODY THAT'S IMPOSSIBLE. . . . .   230 SHADOW WATER B   190
    THAN A STRONG BODY AND A READY HAND. . . . .   232 SHADOW WATER B   236
    UNTIL MY BODY GIVE YOU KISS FOR KISS. . . . .   238 SHADOW WATER B   345
    NOW THAT MY BODY HAS BEGUN TO DREAM, ...   245 SHADOW WATER B   486
    WHAT THING HER BODY WAS." . . . .   255 WOMAN HOMER   14
    WHEN NEITHER SOUL NOR BODY HAS BEEN CROSSED. . . . .   258 KING NO KING   16
    THAT MADE THE BODY SEEM AS IT WERE A STRING . . . .   284 TWO KINGS   176
    I PRAISED HER BODY AND HER MIND . . . .   314 MEMORY YOUTH   9
    TO KEEP THE BODY YOUNG. . . . .   334 SONG   4
    I THOUGHT 'TWOULD BURN MY BODY . . . .   335 SONG   15
    AND ALL THE SHAPELY BODY NO TITTLE GONE ASTRAY. . . .   354 HIS PHOENIX   30
    AND YET YOUR BODY HAD A FLAW. . . . .   356 BROKEN DREAMS   28
    HIS BODY MOULDED FROM WITHIN HIS BODY . . . .   374 PHASES OF MOON   43
    HIS BODY MOULDED FROM WITHIN HIS BODY . . . .   374 PHASES OF MOON   43
    BECOMES A BODY; THAT BODY AND THAT SOUL . . . . . .   374 PHASES OF MOON   59
    BECOMES A BODY; THAT BODY AND THAT SOUL . . . . . .   374 PHASES OF MOON   59
    BODY AND SOUL CAST OUT AND CAST AWAY . . . .   374 PHASES OF MOON   62
    END IN A BEAUTIFUL MAN'S OR WOMAN'S BODY. . . . . .   374 PHASES OF MOON   64
    OF BODY AND SOUL. THE LOVER'S HEART KNOWS THAT. . .   375 PHASES OF MOON   71
    WHO SHUDDER AND HURRY BY; BODY AND SOUL . . . . . .   375 PHASES OF MOON   77
    UPON THE BODY AND UPON THE SOUL . . . .   376 PHASES OF MOON   93
    DEFORMITY OF BODY AND OF MIND. . . . .   377 PHASES OF MOON   123
    BODY PERFECTION BROUGHT, ...   383 VISION ROBART   40
    THERE IS GREAT DANGER IN THE BODY. . . . .   386 ROBARTES DANCE   38
    GIVE MAN HIS THOUGHT OR HIS MERE BODY? . . . .   386 ROBARTES DANCE   40
    A SHAPE WITH LION BODY AND THE HEAD OF A MAN, . . .   402 SECOND COMING   14
    TILL THE WRECK OF BODY, ...   416 TOWER   184
    WHERE WE SHOULD CAST OFF BODY AND TRADE . . . . . .   431 NINETEEN 19   73
    AND HOW CAN BODY, LAID IN THAT WHITE RUSH, ...   441 LEDA AND SWAN   7
    I DREAM OF A LEDAEAN BODY, BENT . . . .   443 SCHOOL CHILDR   9
    THE BODY IS NOT BRUISED TO PLEASURE SOUL, ...   445 SCHOOL CHILDR   58
    O BODY SWAYED TO MUSIC, O BRIGHTENING GLANCE, . . .   446 SCHOOL CHILDR   63
    O BODY SWAYED TO MUSIC BRIGHTENING GLANCE . . . . .   446 SCHOOL CHILDR V   63
    UNTIL I THOUGHT HER BODY BORE . . . .   451 FIRST LOVE   5
    PRESSED HER BODY TO HIS BODY, ...   453 MERMAID   3
    PRESSED HER BODY TO HIS BODY, ...   453 MERMAID   3
    "IF BUT THE SHIRT UPON MY BODY KNEW IT . . . .   462 HARUN RASHID   33
    THAT SPRINGS FROM BODY AND IN BODY FALLS . . . . . .   463 HARUN RASHID   63
    THAT SPRINGS FROM BODY AND IN BODY FALLS . . . . . .   463 HARUN RASHID   63
    ARE NEARER TO THE SURFACE OF THE BODY . . . .   464 HARUN RASHID   67
    ARE BUT A NEW EXPRESSION OF HER BODY . . . .   469 HARUN RASHID   185
    THE BEAUTY OF A WOMAN'S MIND OR BODY . . . .   469 HARUN RASHID V   187
    THE BODY CALLS IT DEATH. . . . .   500 VACILLATION   7
    MY BODY OF A SUDDEN BLAZED; . . . .   501 VACILLATION   41
    THE BODY OF SAINT TERESA LIES UNDECAYED IN TOMB, . .   503 VACILLATION   80
    ETERNALISED THE BODY OF A MODERN SAINT THAT ONCE . .   503 VACILLATION   83
    THAT PIERCED MY BODY THROUGH? . . . .   507 STREAM AND SUN   13
    BODY AND SOUL"; . . . .   510 JANE JUDGMENT   4
    MY BODY IN THE TOMB-- . . . .   511 JANE AND JACK   10
    MY BODY MAKES NO MOAN . . . .   512 JANE ON GOD   22
    MY BODY HAS NOT MOANED . . . .   512 JANE ON GOD   V   22
    SUCH BODY LOVERS HAVE, ...   517 HER ANXIETY   7
    WHEN MY BODY WAS ALIVE . . . .   521 THREE THINGS   10
    WRAPPING THAT FOUL BODY UP . . . .   525 DANCING DAYS   5
    BUT STRETCH THAT BODY FOR A WHILE . . . .   534 CONSOLATION   3
    SCARCE DID HE MY BODY TOUCH, ...   535 CHOSEN   4
    I TORE MY BODY THAT ITS WINE MIGHT COVER . . . . . .   537 HER VISION   7

```
                                                            PAGE    TITLE          LINE

BODY   (CONTINUED)
     NOR SAW MY BODY FALL NOR HEARD IT SHRIEK,  . . . . . .   537 HER VISION        29
     BUT WHEN THIS SOUL, ITS BODY OFF, . . . . . . . . . .    538 LAST CONFESS      15
     . . . DAMPED BY THE BODY OR THE MIND, . . . . . . .      556 RIBH PATRICK       8
     WHAT SACRED DRAMA THROUGH HER BODY HEAVED . . . . . .    560 WHENCE COME       11
     HE WITH BODY WAGED A FIGHT, . . . . . . . . . . . . .    561 FOUR AGES MAN      1
     BUT BODY WON: IT WALKS UPRIGHT. . . . . . . . . . . .    561 FOUR AGES MAN      2
     AND BLOOD AND MIRE THE SENSITIVE BODY STAIN? . . . . .   564 GYRES             10
     THAT STRIP THE BODY BARE." . . . . . . . . . . . . .     570 THREE BUSHES      27
     WASH! MAKE YOUR BODY SWEET! . . . . . . . . . . . . .    572 LADYS 2ND SONG     4
     BODY WERE NOT AT ALL, . . . . . . . . . . . . . . .      572 LADYS 2ND SONG     9
     HE SHALL LOVE YOUR BODY . . . . . . . . . . . . . .      572 LADYS 2ND SONG    10
     IF SOUL MAY LOOK AND BODY TOUCH, . . . . . . . . . .     573 LADYS 2ND SONG    19
     NOR THINK THAT BODY IS THE WHOLE, . . . . . . . . . .    573 LADYS 3RD SONG     4
     KNOW WORSE EVIL OF THE BODY! . . . . . . . . . . . .     573 LADYS 3RD SONG     6
     NOW STRENGTH OF BODY GOES! . . . . . . . . . . . . .     575 ACRE OF GRASS      4
     I BEND MY BODY TO THE SPADE . . . . . . . . . . . .      599 SPIRIT MEDIUM      7
     I BEND MY BODY TO THE SPADE . . . . . . . . . . . .      600 SPIRIT MEDIUM     15
     I BEND MY BODY TO THE SPADE . . . . . . . . . . . .      600 SPIRIT MEDIUM     23
     AND MIND AND BODY SHRANK. . . . . . . . . . . . . .      626 STATES HOLIDAY     4
     WHILE MAN CAN STILL HIS BODY KEEP . . . . . . . . . .    633 MAN AND ECHO      25
     HAS BODY AND ITS STUPIDITY, . . . . . . . . . . . .      633 MAN AND ECHO      28
     BUT BODY GONE HE SLEEPS NO MORE, . . . . . . . . . .     633 MAN AND ECHO      29
     HIS BODY SHAKE? AY, QUIVERING AS YON SMOKE . . . . . .   683 SEEKER            36
     CLOSELY ROUND US, BODY AND MIND-- . . . . . . . . .      717 FAIRY DOCTOR      23
     IS NOT THY BODY BUT THE GARNERED RUST . . . . . .        724 KANVA ON SELF     15
     IS THIS POOR BODY THAT REDDENS AND GROWS PALE. . . . .   764 SHADOW WATER A   341
     LOOK ON THIS BODY AND THIS HEAVY HAIR: . . . . . .       767 SHADOW WATER A   397
     ALL HIS BODY CAN BUT SHOVE . . . . . . . . . . . .       776 AGAINST WITCH     33
     HIS HEAD FROM OFF HIS BODY . . . . . . . . . . . .       789 SINGING HEAD       5
BODY'S
     LEAVE THE BODY'S COLOURED PRIDE . . . . . . . . . .      124 CATHLEEN PARA      2
     WHERE ONLY BODY'S LAID ASLEEP. . . . . . . . . . . .     138 TO IRELAND        22
     ALL THE STRETCHED BODY'S LAID ON THE WHITE RUSH . . . .  441 LEDA AND SWAN  V   7
     THE SOUL'S OWN YOUTH AND NOT THE BODY'S YOUTH . . . .    464 HARUN RASHID      69
BOG
     AND ONE WAS DROWNED IN THE GREAT BOG OF CLOONE. . . . .  411 TOWER             48
BOG'S
     THE MAN DROWNED IN A BOG'S MIRE, . . . . . . . . .       413 TOWER             95
BOILED
     AND THAT IS CURED BY A BOILED LIQUORICE ROOT. . . . .    227 SHADOW WATER B V 116B
BOILING
     TO STIR THE BOILING POT? . . . . . . . . . . . . .       395 SIXTEEN DEAD       6
BOISTEROUS
     MUCH BOISTEROUS COURAGE, BEFORE LONELINESS . . . . . .   473 ALL SOUL NIGHT    72
BOLD      SEE OVER-BOLD
     JABBER AND SCREAM. YET HE, FOR ALL HIS BOLD . . . . .     34 OISIN 2       V  82
     "IS HE SO DREADFUL?" "BE NOT OVER BOLD, . . . . . .       35 OISIN 2       V  88
     THESE HANDS SLEW MANY WARRIORS BOLD-- . . . . . . .       83 MAD KING GOLL V  23
     THESE HANDS SLEW MANY ROBBERS BOLD-- . . . . . . .        83 MAD KING GOLL V  23
     THESE HANDS SLEW MANY A SEAMAN BOLD. . . . . . . . .      83 MAD KING GOLL V  23
     THE HARES RUN BY ME GROWING BOLD. . . . . . . . . .       84 MAD KING GOLL V  47
     THE HARE RUNS BY ME GROWING BOLD-- . . . . . . . .        84 MAD KING GOLL V  47
     AND HARES RUN NEAR ME GROWING BOLD. . . . . . . . .       84 MAD KING GOLL V  47
     "O NO, MY DEAR, YOU MAKE SO BOLD . . . . . . . . .       263 MASK               3
     FOR I AM NOT SO BOLD . . . . . . . . . . . . . .         346 ON WOMAN          26
     WHETHER IT BE BOLD OR SLY. . . . . . . . . . . . .       624 APPARITIONS        6
BOLE      SEE BEECH-BOLE
     AGAINST A BEECH BOLE, HE THREW DOWN THE BEAST . . . . .  278 TWO KINGS      V  36
     ARE YOU THE LEAF, THE BLOSSOM OR THE BOLE? . . . . .     446 SCHOOL CHILDR     62
BOLT
     AND PUSHED THE BRASS BOLT DOWN. . . . . . . . . . .      159 CAP AND BELLS  V  12
     I'LL FIND THE STABLE AND PULL OUT THE BOLT. . . . . .    260 FASC DIFFICULT    13
     BOLT AND BAR THE SHUTTER, . . . . . . . . . . . . .      523 MAD AS MIST        1
BOLTS
     SHE SNICKED THE BRASS BOLTS DOWN. . . . . . . . . .      159 CAP AND BELLS  V  12
BOMB-BALLS
     PITCH LIKE KING BILLY BOMB-BALLS IN . . . . . . . . .    565 LAPIS LAZULI       7
BOND
     HE HOLDS YOU WITH AN IRON BOND, . . . . . . . . . .       22 OISIN 1          333
     THE BLOOD BOND . . . . . . . . . . . . . . . . .         769 BLOOD BOND         T
     THIS BOND HAS BOUND US . . . . . . . . . . . . . .       769 BLOOD BOND     V   1
BONDS
     HIS BONDS AWAY, SORE STRUGGLING.  NOW AT LAST . . . .    714 FERENCZ RENYI    116
     YOUNG FERENCZ RENYI BURSTS HIS BONDS--AT LAST, . . . .   714 FERENCZ RENYI  V 116
     WHAT BONDS NO MAN COULD UNBIND, . . . . . . . . . .      785 WOMANS BEAUTY     22
BONE      SEE COLLAR-BONE MARROW-BONE RAG-AND-BONE
     . . . AND FILLED ME FULL TO THE BONE. . . . . . . .       52 OISIN 3           72
     AND GRANIA, WALKING AND SMILING, SEWED WITH HER NEEDLE
        OF BONE,                                               53 OISIN 3           94
     MY BARREN THOUGHTS HAVE CHILLED ME TO THE BONE. . . . .  257 RECONCILIATION    12
     AND KNOW THEM TO THE BONE! IMPART TO US-- . . . . .      265 ABBEY THEATRE      9
     MERE BONE AND MUSCLE THROWN ASIDE, . . . . . . . .       273 GREY ROCK         51
     YOU HAVE DRIED THE MARROW FROM THE BONE? . . . . . .     289 SEPTEMBER 1913     5
     THIS BLAST HAS CHILLED ME TO THE BONE." . . . . . .      305 HOUR DAWN         62
     THAT FLESH AND BONE MAY DISAPPEAR, . . . . . . . .       307 HOUR DAWN        101
     THROUGH THE WHITE THIN BONE OF A HARE. . . . . . . .     330 BONE OF A HARE    16
     AS WITH HER FLESH AND BONE, . . . . . . . . . . . .      345 ON WOMAN           6
     WERE DEAD YET FLESH AND BONE. . . . . . . . . . . .      384 VISION ROBART     48
     THAT CONVERSE BONE TO BONE? . . . . . . . . . . . .      395 SIXTEEN DEAD      18
     THAT CONVERSE BONE TO BONE? . . . . . . . . . . . .      395 SIXTEEN DEAD      18
```

97

```
                                                        PAGE    TITLE            LINE
BONE   (CONTINUED)
    OF FLESH AND BONE;  . . . . . . . . . . . . . . .   436 FOR MY SON           24
    BUT FOUND IT DRY AS BONE,  . . . . . . . . . . .    454 EMPTY CUP             8
    HE KNOWS DEATH TO THE BONE--  . . . . . . . . . .   476 DEATH                11
    BUT SLENDER NEEDLES OF BONE;  . . . . . . . . . .   488 CRAZED MOON          15
    I TREMBLE TO THE BONE,  . . . . . . . . . . . . .   511 JANE AND JACK         2
    AND BEAT UPON THE BONE;  . . . . . . . . . . . .    516 MANS SONG             6
    SANG A BONE UPON THE SHORE;  . . . . . . . . . .    521 THREE THINGS          2
    A BONE WAVE-WHITENED AND DRIED IN THE WIND.  . .    521 THREE THINGS          6
    SANG A BONE UPON THE SHORE;  . . . . . . . . . .    521 THREE THINGS          8
    A BONE WAVE-WHITENED AND DRIED IN THE WIND.  . .    521 THREE THINGS         12
    SANG A BONE UPON THE SHORE,  . . . . . . . . . .    521 THREE THINGS         14
    A BONE WAVE-WHITENED AND DRIED IN THE WIND.  . .    521 THREE THINGS         18
    AND I AM SHRUNKEN TO SKIN AND BONE,  . . . . . .    550 SONGS REWRIT 1        2
    YET I AM SHRUNKEN TO SKIN AND BONE  . . . . . .     550 SONGS REWRIT 1 V      2
    YET AM I SHRUNKEN TO SKIN AND BONE,  . . . . . .    550 SONGS REWRIT 1 V      2
    BUT I AM SHRUNKEN TO SKIN AND BONE,  . . . . . .    550 SONGS REWRIT 1 V      2
    THOUGH I AM SHRUNKEN TO BONE AND SKIN,  . . . .     551 SONGS REWRIT 1 V      8
    THINKS IN A MARROW BONE;  . . . . . . . . . .       553 PRAYER OLD AGE        4
    BEEN BONE, AND SINEW; WHEN SUCH BODIES JOIN  . .    555 RIBH AT TOMB         12
    CONSUMING ITS RAG AND BONE,  . . . . . . . . .      575 ACRE OF GRASS        11
    IN THE FOUL RAG AND BONE SHOP OF THE HEART.  . .    630 CIRCUS ANIMALS V     40
    ARE BLOWN COLD DUST OR A BIT OF BONE.  . . . . .    788 HAWTHORN TREE         8
BONES       SEE MARROW-BONES
    DID NOT THE WORMS THAT SPIRED ABOUT HIS BONES  .    128 DREAM OF FAERY       41
    WERE NOT THE WORMS THAT SPIRED ABOUT HIS BONES .    128 DREAM OF FAERY V     41
    BETTER GO DOWN UPON YOUR MARROW BONES  . . . . .    204 ADAMS CURSE    V      7
    "STRETCH BONES TILL THE DAYLIGHT COME  . . . . .    331 ROUND TOWER           5
    HE STRETCHED HIS BONES AND FELL IN A DREAM  . .     331 ROUND TOWER          10
    LAID HIS STRONG BONES DOWN IN DEATH  . . . . . .    360 ALF POLLEXFEN         3
    LAID HIS STRONG BONES IN DEATH  . . . . . . . .     360 ALF POLLEXFEN V       3
    AND WITHERED TO A BAG OF BONES;  . . . . . . . .    401 DEMON BEAST          49
    EVEN THOSE TRUTHS THAT WHEN MY BONES ARE DUST  .    467 HARUN RASHID        144
    TRUTHS THAT WHEN MY VERY BONES ARE DUST  . . . .    467 HARUN RASHID   V    144
    OR STRIKES A SUDDEN CHILL INTO MY BONES  . . . .    499 MOTHER OF GOD        14
    TO THE CRAVING IN MY BONES.  . . . . . . . . . .    533 FIRST CONFESS        12
    SURMOUNT THEIR BONES; BUT SPEAK WHAT NONE HAVE HEARD.  555 RIBH AT TOMB       9
    SURMOUNTS THEIR BONES; BUT SPEAK WHAT NONE HAVE HEARD.  555 RIBH AT TOMB V    9
    THINGS HID IN THEIR MARROW BONES  . . . . . . .     589 OLD WICKED MAN V     41
    I PRAYED AT ALL THE STATIONS UPON MY MARROW BONES, 593 PILGRIM        V      7
    OLD IRON, OLD BONES, OLD RAGS, THAT RAVING SLUT    630 CIRCUS ANIMALS       37
    OLD BONES UPON THE MOUNTAIN SHAKE.  . . . . . .     635 BLACK TOWER          10
    OLD BONES UPON THE MOUNTAIN SHAKE.  . . . . . .     636 BLACK TOWER          20
    OLD BONES UPON THE MOUNTAIN SHAKE.  . . . . . .     636 BLACK TOWER          30
    WOULD END THIS PEACEFUL LIFE THAT ROTS THE BONES,  752 SHADOW WATER A      110
    FROM THE DRY BONES OF THE DEAD?  . . . . . . . .    781 MY HEART BEAT         8
    THE DREAMING BONES CRY OUT  . . . . . . . . . .     782 HEART FRIGHT         15
    DRY BONES THAT DREAM ARE BITTER,  . . . . . . .     783 GREY ROUND           14
BONY
    O DEATH'S OLD BONY FINGER  . . . . . . . . . .      213 HAPPY TOWNLAND V      1
    MACDONAGH'S BONY THUMB?  . . . . . . . . . . . .    395 SIXTEEN DEAD         12
BOOK       SEE PICTURE-BOOK PRAYER-BOOK LOG-BOOK
    FROM THE BOOK OF KAURI THE INDIAN-- SECTION V. ON THE   76 INDIAN ON GOD V   T
       NATURE OF GOD
    AND NODDING BY THE FIRE, TAKE DOWN THIS BOOK,  . .  120 YOU ARE OLD           2
    THE DEDICATION TO A BOOK OF STORIES SELECTED FROM THE IRISH  129 BOOK STORIES  T
       NOVELISTS
    I READ IN MY BOOK OF SONGS  . . . . . . . . . .     178 FIDDLER DOONEY        7
    THEY READ IN A BOOK OF PRAYER,  . . . . . . . .     178 FIDDLER DOONEY V      6
    I READ IN A BOOK OF SONGS  . . . . . . . . . . .    178 FIDDLER DOONEY V      7
    IN ANY ANCIENT BOOK BUT TELLS OF YOU;  . . . . .    186 QUEEN MAEVE         135
    YOU'VE DANDLED THEM AND FED THEM FROM THE BOOK  .    265 ABBEY THEATRE         8
    I HAVE NO CHILD, I HAVE NOTHING BUT A BOOK,  . .     270 PARDON FATHERS       21
    OUT OF SOME OLD PICTURE BOOK;  . . . . . . . . .    325 ROBERT GREGORY V     44
    AS THOUGH I HAD FOUND IN A BOOK  . . . . . . . .    329 MEN IMPROVE           6
    AS THOUGH I HAD FOUND IN BOOK  . . . . . . . . .    329 MEN IMPROVE    V      6
    AND NO KNAVE BROUGHT TO BOOK  . . . . . . . . .     347 FISHERMAN            17
    AS A MAN DOES WHO HAS PUBLISHED A NEW BOOK,  . .     350 HER PRAISE            3
    A LAMP BURNS ON BESIDE THE OPEN BOOK  . . . . .     367 EGO DOMINUS           3
    A LAMP BURNS ON ABOVE THE OPEN BOOK  . . . . . .     367 EGO DOMINUS    V      3
    BURNING ALONE BESIDE AN OPEN BOOK,  . . . . . .     370 EGO DOMINUS          63
    BECAUSE I SEEK AN IMAGE, NOT A BOOK.  . . . . .     370 EGO DOMINUS          67
    BOOK I   WHAT THE CALIPH PARTLY LEARNED  . . . .    372 PHASES OF MOON        T
    AND NOW HE SEEKS IN BOOK OR MANUSCRIPT  . . . .     373 PHASES OF MOON       19
    AND NEVER WROTE A BOOK, YOUR THOUGHT IS CLEAR.  .    376 PHASES OF MOON       97
    OF HIS GREAT BIRCH AND HIS GREAT BOOK.  . . . .     381 SONG OF FOOL          8
    FOR WHAT MERE BOOK CAN GRANT A KNOWLEDGE  . . .     386 ROBARTES DANCE       20
    BOOK III   DOVE OR SWAN   I.   LEDA  . . . . . .    441 LEDA AND SWAN  V      T
    BOOK V:   DOVE OR SWAN   I   LEDA  . . . . . . .    441 LEDA AND SWAN  V      T
    BOOK IV   THE GATES OF PLUTO   I.   THE FOOL BY THE ROADSIDE  447 HERO GIRL FOOL V  T
    BOOK II   WHAT THE CALIPH REFUSED TO LEARN  . .     460 HARUN RASHID   V      T
    AT THE GREAT BOOK OF SAPPHO'S SONG; BUT NO,  . .    461 HARUN RASHID         12
    IF YOU SHOULD HIDE MY PARCHMENT IN THAT BOOK  .     461 HARUN RASHID   V     13
    BEFORE SHE HAD SPREAD A BOOK UPON HER KNEES  . .    466 HARUN RASHID        120
    TRUTHS WITHOUT FATHER CAME, TRUTHS THAT NO BOOK    467 HARUN RASHID        138
    . . . A LOG BOOK OF THE SUN'S JOURNEY AND THE MOON'S,  480 BLOOD AND MOON V   14
    THE BOOK OF THE PEOPLE; WHATEVER MOST CAN BLESS .    492 COOLE BALLYLEE       44
    AN OPEN BOOK AND EMPTY CUP  . . . . . . . . . .     501 VACILLATION          38
    YET HE, AN OLD BOOK IN HIS FIST,  . . . . . . .     508 JANE BISHOP          12
    WITH OPEN BOOK YOU ASK ME WHAT I DO.  . . . . .     554 RIBH AT TOMB          2
    I TURN THE PAGES OF MY HOLY BOOK.  . . . . . . .    555 RIBH AT TOMB         27
```

BOOK   (CONTINUED)
   PICTURE AND BOOK REMAIN, ...   575 ACRE OF GRASS   1
   THIS BOOK OR THAT, COME TO THIS HALLOWED PLACE . . . .   604 GALLERY REVIS   51
   THE PRIESTS HAVE GOT A BOOK THAT SAYS . . . .   621 JOHN KINSELLA   25
   TO LOVE EACH OTHER. IN MY PRAYER BOOK STILL . . . . .   713 FERENCZ RENYI   V   94
   THE BISHOP CAME WITH OPEN BOOK, ...   725 LEGEND   17
BOOKS   SEE READING-BOOKS
   FOR HE WAS A MAN OF BOOKS. . . . .   93 FATHER OHART   24
   THE BOOKS OF MY NUMBERLESS DREAMS, ...   157 POET BELOVED   2
   WOMEN AND CHILDREN, YOUNG MEN WITH BOOKS, ...   167 BLESSED   15
   THEY READ IN THEIR BOOKS OF PRAYER: . . . .   178 FIDDLER DOONEY   6
   PRECEDENTS OUT OF BEAUTIFUL OLD BOOKS: . . . .   205 ADAMS CURSE   26
   IF BOOKS SPEAK TRUTH, IN SLIEVENAMON-- . . . . . .   271 GREY ROCK   V   15
   WHAT CAN BOOKS OF MEN THAT WIVE . . . .   309 REALISTS   2
   OUT NAKED ON THE ROADS, AS THE BOOKS SAY, AND STRICKEN . . 316 COLD HEAVEN   11
   I WILL TALK NO MORE OF BOOKS OR THE LONG WAR . . . . .   351 HER PRAISE   11
   TO STUDY READING BOOKS AND HISTORY . . . .   443 SCHOOL CHILDR   V   4
   TO STUDY READING BOOKS AND HISTORIES, ...   443 SCHOOL CHILDR   V   4
   PASS BOOKS OF LEARNING FROM BYZANTIUM . . . .   461 HARUN RASHID   9
   OF ALL THE UNCOUNTED BOOKS THAT I HAVE READ, ...   467 HARUN RASHID   139
   THAT FIRST UNNATURAL INTEREST IN MY BOOKS. . . . . .   468 HARUN RASHID   165
   THAT FIRST STRANGE INTEREST IN MY BOOKS AND STUDIES. . . 468 HARUN RASHID   V 165
   BELOVED BOOKS THAT FAMOUS HANDS HAVE BOUND, ...   491 COOLE BALLYLEE   27
   CLIMB TO YOUR CHAMBER FULL OF BOOKS AND WAIT, ...   579 DOR WELLESLEY   8
   NO BOOKS UPON THE KNEE, AND NO ONE THERE . . . . . .   579 DOR WELLESLEY   9
   AND WHEN THEY KNOW WHAT OLD BOOKS TELL, ...   626 OLD MEN BE MAD   18
   NINE BOOKS OR NINE HATS . . . .   628 JANE MOUNTAIN   3
   WHERE MY BOOKS GO. . . . .   739 WHERE BOOKS GO   T
BOOM
   WITH BOOM OF BEES IN HONEY-MARTS, ...   16 OISIN 1   229
   WITH BOOM OF BEES IN HONEY MARTS, ...   16 OISIN 1   V 229
BOOTH   SEE GORE-BOOTH
BOOTS
   HAD TROD THE UNEVEN ROAD. THEIR BOOTS WERE SOILED, . . . 372 PHASES OF MOON   3
BORDA
   TO EMER OF BORDA, IN HER CLAY-PILED DUN, ...   105 CUCHULAIN SEA   V   2
BORDER
   AND SHAKES O'ER THE WIDTH OF THE SEA-WORLD BORDER . . .   28 OISIN 1   V 423C
   YOU LIVE, AND ON THE VILLAGE BORDER SHE, ...   74 ANASHU VIJAYA   62
   YOU LIVE, AND ON THE BORDER OF THE VILLAGE SHE, . . .   74 ANASHU VIJAYA   V   62
   BY THE LONE BORDER OF THE LAKE ONCE MORE, ...   79 EPHEMERA   5
   STAND BY THE BORDER OF THE LAKE ONCE MORE. . . . . .   79 EPHEMERA   V   5
   ON THE LONE BORDER OF THE LAKE ONCE MORE: . . . . . .   80 EPHEMERA   17
   ON THE LONE BORDER OF THE SULLEN LAKE. . . . .   80 EPHEMERA   V   17
   IN THE WHITE BORDER OF THE MURMURING SEA: . . . . . .   103 FERGUS DRUID   19
   UPON THE MISTY BORDER OF THE WOOD. . . . .   251 SHADOW WATER B   612
   UPON THE BORDER OF THAT LAKE'S A WOOD . . . .   490 COOLE BALLYLEE   9
   UNTO THE DOLOROUS BORDER OF THE FAIRY LAKE. . . . . .   655 ISLE STAT I 2   85
   UPON THE MISTY BORDER OF THE WOOD,-- . . . .   769 SHADOW WATER A   428
BORDERED   SEE WILLOW-BORDERED RED-ROSE-BORDERED BOX-BORDERED
   BECAUSE THE RED ROSE BORDERED HEM . . . .   137 TO IRELAND   V   6
   AFTER THE RED ROSE BORDERED HEM. . . . .   139 TO IRELAND   V   30
   AFTER THE RED ROSE BORDERED HEM. . . . .   139 TO IRELAND   V   48
   SHANWALLA, WHERE A WILLOW BORDERED POND . . . . . .   217 WOODS OF COOLE V   2
BORDERS
   AND MARTEN-CAT, AND BORDERS THAT OLD WOOD . . . . . .   218 WOODS OF COOLE   14
   AND MARTIN CAT, AND BORDERS THAT OLD WOOD . . . . .   218 WOODS OF COOLE V   14
BORE
   I STOOD UPON THE STAIR: THE SURGES BORE . . . .   44 OISIN 2   225
   THEY BORE IT WITH STAGGERING AND SWEATING, ...   60 OISIN 3   186
   AND BORE IT TO THE WOODS WITH ME; . . . .   85 MAD KING GOLL   57
   WHILE DAY ITS BURDEN ON TO EVENING BORE, ...   110 CUCHULAIN SEA   70
   UNTIL ONE BORE BRIDGET HIS BRIDE . . . .   145 HOST OF AIR   31
   HE BORE HER AWAY IN HIS ARMS, ...   145 HOST OF AIR   33
   THE DEW-COLD LILIES LADIES BORE . . . .   156 FORGOT BEAUTY   11
   KING EOCHAID SAID, AND HE THAT BORE HIS SHIELD . . . .   276 TWO KINGS   V   B
   UNTIL I THOUGHT HER BODY BORE . . . .   451 FIRST LOVE   5
   THE TERROR OF ALL TERRORS THAT I BORE . . . .   499 MOTHER OF GOD   4
   BUT SOMETHING BORE THEM OUT OF SIGHT . . . .   519 HER DREAM   5
   IT BORE ME SOFTLY WHERE THE SHALLOW SAND . . . . . .   657 ISLE STAT I 3   58
   DO YOU REMEMBER, AIBRIC, HOW YOU BORE . . . .   749 SHADOW WATER A   48
BOREAL
   OF WOLVES, OF BOREAL BEARS, WE QUAFFED THE WINE . . . .   41 OISIN 2   V 188
BOREDOM
   ITS BOREDOM OF THE DESK OR OF THE SPADE, BECAUSE . . . . 621 HOUND VOICE   3
BOREEN
   ACROSS THE BARE BOREEN. . . . .   95 MOLL MAGEE   32
BORN   SEE SELF-BORN HIGH-BORN SEA-BORN FIRE-BORN ROCK-BORN TWIN-BORN NEW-BORN BASE-BORN
   A SWIFTER CREATURE NEVER WAS BORN, ...   2 OISIN 1   V   7Q
   AND WAS BORN WHERE THE SUN DROPS DOWN IN THE TIDE, . . .   5 OISIN 1   V   49
   "WERE THESE TWO BORN IN THE DANAAN LAND, ...   12 OISIN 1   146
   AND MY BABY WAS JUST BORN: . . . .   94 MOLL MAGEE   14
   ABOUT THE TIME WHEN CHRIST WAS BORN, ...   189 BAILE AILLINN   13
   REPLIED: "TO BE BORN WOMAN IS TO KNOW-- . . . . . .   205 ADAMS CURSE   18
   THAT YOU WERE BORN A THOUSAND YEARS AGO, ...   245 SHADOW WATER B   468
   WHERE NO CHILD'S BORN BUT TO OUTLIVE THE MOON." . . . .   247 SHADOW WATER B   531
   FOR MEN WERE BORN TO PRAY AND SAVE: . . . .   289 SEPTEMBER 1913   6
   WAS BORN TO WEAR A CROWN. . . . .   308 PLAYER QUEEN   12
   WE DREAMED THAT A GREAT PAINTER HAD BEEN BORN . . . .   326 ROBERT GREGORY   65
   BORN UNDER THE SKIES . . . .   333 SOLOMON SHEBA   20
   WHO WERE NOT BORN TO KEEP IN TRIM . . . .   336 YOUNG BEAUTY   10

	PAGE	TITLE		LINE
BORN (CONTINUED)				
HECTOR IS IN THE DUST, NIETZSCHE IS BORN,	374	PHASES OF MOON		46
AND YET, TWICE BORN, TWICE BURIED, GROW HE MUST,	374	PHASES OF MOON		48
HAS CALLED UP THE COLD SPIRITS THAT ARE BORN	382	VISION ROBART		2
A TERRIBLE BEAUTY IS BORN.	392	EASTER 1916		16
A TERRIBLE BEAUTY IS BORN.	393	EASTER 1916		40
A TERRIBLE BEAUTY IS BORN.	394	EASTER 1916		80
SLOUCHES TOWARDS BETHLEHEM TO BE BORN?	402	SECOND COMING		22
HAVE I NOT SEEN THE LOVELIEST WOMAN BORN	405	FOR DAUGHTER		59
ARE INNOCENCE AND BEAUTY BORN?	406	FOR DAUGHTER		78
WHATEVER IS BEGOTTEN, BORN, AND DIES.	407	SAIL BYZANTIUM		6
WHATEVER IS BEGOTTEN BORN OR DIES,	407	SAIL BYZANTIUM	V	6
NOR BEAUTY BORN OUT OF ITS OWN DESPAIR,	445	SCHOOL CHILDR		59
MORE WOMEN BORN THAN MEN."	485	STATISTICS		4
FOR CHILDREN BORN OF HER PAIN.	487	CRAZED MOON		6
WHAT, BE A SINGER BORN AND LACK A THEME?	502	VACILLATION		73
SELF-BORN, BORN ANEW?	507	STREAM AND SUN		15
THAT THE CRIME OF BEING BORN	534	CONSOLATION		9
WE IRISH, BORN INTO THAT ANCIENT SECT	611	STATUES		28
WERE WE NOT BORN IN THE PEASANT'S COT	615	MARCH SONGS 2		13
WE WERE NOT BORN IN THE PEASANT'S COT	615	MARCH SONGS 2	V	13
WHEN WERE YOU BORN? BEFORE YOUR GRANDAM EVE.	721	WITCH VIVIEN		32
BORN OUT OF IMMODERATE THOUGHT:	772	SONG DEIRDRE 1		12
BORNE SEE SEA-BORNE CAR-BORNE				
HAVE BORNE ME WHERE THE TEMPESTS BLIND	6	OISIN 1	V	58
CAME BALOR, AS OLD AS A FOREST, CAR BORNE, HIS MIGHTY HEAD SUNK	53	OISIN 3	V	91
WINGED LOVES BORNE ON IN GENTLE STRIFE,	135	TWO TREES	V	14
EVEN IN AN OLD STORY, IS A BURDEN NOT TO BE BORNE.	210	UNDER THE MOON		20
THAT IDLENESS HAD BORNE TO PRIDE,	296	THREE BEGGARS		40
HAVE BORNE YOU THROUGH THE SMOOTH AND ROUGH	436	FOR MY SON	V	29
HOW ALL THAT DIE ARE BORNE ABOUT THE WORLD	750	SHADOW WATER A		84
BORROW				
FOR NOON AND MIDNIGHT FROM EACH OTHER BORROW,	735	QUATRAIN APHOR		26
BOSKY				
BY BOSKY JUNE I SWEAR, AND BY THE BEE, HER MINISTER.	661	ISLE STAT II 1		74
BOSOM				
AS HER SOFT BOSOM ROSE AND FELL.	4	OISIN 1		30
AND ON MY BOSOM LAID HER WEEPING HEAD.	46	OISIN 2		250
IN MIDST OF AN OLD MAN'S BOSOM: OWLS RUFFLING AND PACING AROUND	50	OISIN 3		47
IN THE MIDST OF AN OLD MAN'S BOSOM: OWLS RUFFLING AND PACING AROUND	50	OISIN 3	V	47
THRUSTING HIS NOSE TO MY SHOULDER: HE KNEW IN HIS BOSOM DEEP	54	OISIN 3		106
THAT ONCE MORE MOVED IN MY BOSOM THE ANCIENT SADNESS OF MAN,	54	OISIN 3		107
IN BOSOM AND HAIR. "AH, DO NOT MOURN," HE SAID,	80	EPHEMERA		20
IN BOSOM AND HAIR. THEN HE! "LET US NOT MOURN	80	EPHEMERA	V	20
OF THE MATCHING OF RIBBONS FOR BOSOM AND HEAD,	151	OLD MOTHER		6
SHE LAID THEM UPON HER BOSOM,	160	CAP AND BELLS		25
SHE TOOK THEM INTO HER BOSOM,	160	CAP AND BELLS	V	25
TALL AND NOBLE BUT WITH FACE AND BOSOM	199	ARROW		5
AT THE MOTH HOUR AND HID IT IN HER BOSOM.	199	ARROW	V	6
I, STARVED FOR THE BOSOM OF HIS FAERY BRIDE?	629	CIRCUS ANIMALS		16
IN THE BOSOM OF THE AIR--	706	DAWN-SONG		30
DROPS ON HIS BOSOM, SOMBRE, MOIST AND SLOW.	711	FERENCZ RENYI		40
UPON HIS BOSOM, SOMBRE, MOIST AND SLOW.	711	FERENCZ RENYI	V	40
IN THE BOSOM AFAR OF THE FRAGRANT WOOD.	717	LOVE SONG		9
BOTTLE				
AND PASS THE BOTTLE ROUND.	586	PARNELLITES		8
SO PASS THE BOTTLE ROUND.	587	PARNELLITES		24
FOR PASSING ROUND THE BOTTLE WITH GIRLS IN RAGS OR SILK,	592	PILGRIM		2
FOR PASSING ROUND THE BOTTLE WITH GIRLS IN RAG OR SILK,	592	PILGRIM	V	2
BOTTLES				
OLD KETTLES, OLD BOTTLES, AND A BROKEN CAN,	630	CIRCUS ANIMALS		36
BOTTLING				
AND THOUGH AT BOTTLING OF YOUR WINE	271	GREY ROCK		9
THOUGH AT THE BOTTLING OF YOUR WINE	271	GREY ROCK	V	9
BOTTOM				
ALL, ALL, THE VERY BOTTOM OF THE BOWL--	227	SHADOW WATER B		118
MANACLE HIS SOUL UPON THE RED SEA BOTTOM.	372	ON GOING HOUSE		16
UPON THE BOTTOM OF A KING OF KINGS:	445	SCHOOL CHILDR		44
AT THE BOTTOM OF A PIT	632	MAN AND ECHO		3
AT THE BOTTOM OF A LETTER, FIFTY MEN.	790	DEDICATION		10
BOUGH SEE BEECH-BOUGH YEW-BOUGH				
A BEECH BOUGH TO ME, AND MY HEART GREW SORE,	44	OISIN 2	V	226
FROM A BOUGH OVERHEAD,	215	HAPPY TOWNLAND		42
THE YEW BOUGH HAS BEEN BROKEN INTO TWO,	241	SHADOW WATER B		593
THE YEW BOUGH HAS BEEN BROKEN INTO TWO,	251	SHADOW WATER B	V	593
THE YEW BOUGH HAS BEEN BROKEN IN TWO,	251	SHADOW WATER B	V	593
AND THREW HIM UP TO LAUGH ON THE BOUGH:	318	APPOINTMENT		11
A HUNGER FOR THE APPLE ON THE BOUGH	368	EGO DOMINUS		24
CREW FROM A BLOSSOMING APPLE BOUGH	387	SOLOMON WITCH		10
UPON A BLOSSOMING APPLE BOUGH	387	SOLOMON WITCH	V	10
CRIED FROM A BLOSSOMING APPLE BOUGH	387	SOLOMON WITCH	V	10
OR SET UPON A GOLDEN BOUGH TO SING	408	SAIL BYZANTIUM		30
WHEN EVENING STIRS THE JASMINE BOUGH, AND YET	463	HARUN RASHID		53
PLANTED ON THE STAR-LIT GOLDEN BOUGH;	497	BYZANTIUM		19
PLANTED ON THE STARLIT GOLDEN BOUGH,	497	BYZANTIUM	V	19
A TREE THERE IS THAT FROM ITS TOPMOST BOUGH	500	VACILLATION		11

100

		PAGE	TITLE		LINE
BOUGH	**(CONTINUED)**				
	UNDER OAK AND BEECHEN BOUGH,	522	LULLABY		11
	UNDER OAK AND BEECHES BOUGH,	522	LULLABY	V	11
	OFTEN HE HAD BENT DOWN SOME BOUGH ALL BRIGHT	710	FERENCZ RENYI		28
	OFTEN HE HAD BENT DOWN SOME BOUGH ALL BRIGHT WITH BERRIES,	710	FERENCZ RENYI	V	28
BOUGHS	**SEE APPLE-BOUGHS**				
	AND GREAT BOUGHS DROP TRANQUILLITY,	77	INDIAN TO LOVE		2
	HID UNDER QUIET BOUGHS APART,	78	INDIAN TO LOVE		12
	THE HEAVY BOUGHS, THE BURNISHED DOVE	78	INDIAN TO LOVE		16
	THE GREAT BOUGHS, AND THE BURNISHED DOVE	78	INDIAN TO LOVE		16
	AND GREAT BOUGHS, AND THE BURNISHED DOVE,	78	INDIAN TO LOVE	V	16
	I FIND UNDER THE BOUGHS OF LOVE AND HATE,	101	ROSE UPON ROOD		10
	UNDER THAT WOVEN CHANGELESS ROOF OF BOUGHS,	126	DREAM OF FAERY		11
	UNDER THE WOVEN ROOFS OF QUICKEN BOUGHS,--	126	DREAM OF FAERY	V	11
	I TORE IT FROM GREEN BOUGHS WINDS TORE AND TOSSED	130	BOOK STORIES		13
	I TORE IT FROM THE BARREN BOUGHS OF EIRE,	130	BOOK STORIES		15
	I TORE IT FROM GREEN BOUGHS WINDS TOSSED AND HURLED,	130	BOOK STORIES	V	13
	GREEN BOUGHS OF TOSSING ALWAYS, WEARY, WEARY,	130	BOOK STORIES	V	14
	I TORE IT FROM THE GREEN BOUGHS OF OLD ERI,	130	BOOK STORIES	V	15
	BROKEN BOUGHS AND BLACKENED LEAVES.	135	TWO TREES		28
	WITH BROKEN BOUGHS AND BLACKENED LEAVES	135	TWO TREES	V	26
	IN SHAKEN BOUGHS, IN TIDE ON THE SHORE?	141	EVERLAST VOICE		7
	AND HE, BEING LAID UPON GREEN BOUGHS,	192	BAILE AILLINN		71
	OR TWO SWEET BLOSSOMING APPLE BOUGHS	195	BAILE AILLINN	V	153
	THE WITHERING OF THE BOUGHS	203	WITHER BOUGHS		T
	NO BOUGHS HAVE WITHERED BECAUSE OF THE WINTRY WIND,	203	WITHER BOUGHS		7
	THE BOUGHS HAVE WITHERED BECAUSE I HAVE TOLD THEM MY DREAMS.	203	WITHER BOUGHS		8
	NO BOUGHS HAVE WITHERED BECAUSE OF THE WINTRY WIND,	203	WITHER BOUGHS		15
	THE BOUGHS HAVE WITHERED BECAUSE I HAVE TOLD THEM MY DREAMS.	203	WITHER BOUGHS		16
	NO BOUGHS HAVE WITHERED BECAUSE OF THE WINTRY WIND,	204	WITHER BOUGHS		23
	THE BOUGHS HAVE WITHERED BECAUSE I HAVE TOLD THEM MY DREAMS.	204	WITHER BOUGHS		24
	BOUGHS HAVE THEIR FRUIT AND BLOSSOM	214	HAPPY TOWNLAND		5
	WHERE BOUGHS HAVE FRUIT AND BLOSSOM	214	HAPPY TOWNLAND	V	5
	FROM GOLDEN AND SILVER BOUGHS,	215	HAPPY TOWNLAND		24
	FROM THE GOLDEN AND SILVER BOUGHS.	215	HAPPY TOWNLAND	V	24
	AS THOUGH THEY HAD BEEN HIDDEN BY GREEN BOUGHS	217	WOODS OF COOLE		6
	AND DRUID MOONS, AND MURMURING OF BOUGHS,	219	HARP OF AENGUS		4
	AND SLEEPY BOUGHS, AND BOUGHS WHERE APPLES MADE	219	HARP OF AENGUS		5
	AND SLEEPY BOUGHS, AND BOUGHS WHERE APPLES MADE	219	HARP OF AENGUS		5
	I GROPED MY WAY THROUGH BOUGHS, AND OVER ROOTS,	283	TWO KINGS	V	139
	TILL ALL THE BOUGHS ARE GAY,	366	HER CHRIS TREE		5
	AMONG THE BOUGHS, BLUE AS THE HALCYON'S WING,	683	SEEKER		38
	OF AENGUS' BIRDS GLEAM IN THEIR APPLE BOUGHS.	751	SHADOW WATER A		103
	THE TOPMOST BLOSSOM ON THE BOUGHS OF TIME	756	SHADOW WATER A		178
	AND DRUID MOONS, AND MURMURING OF BOUGHS,	762	SHADOW WATER A		299
	AND SLEEPY BOUGHS, AND BOUGHS WHERE APPLES MADE	762	SHADOW WATER A		300
	AND SLEEPY BOUGHS, AND BOUGHS WHERE APPLES MADE	762	SHADOW WATER A		300
	IMPERISHABLE FIRE UNDER THE BOUGHS	765	SHADOW WATER A		356
	WHERE ARE THESE BOUGHS? WHERE ARE THE HOLY WOODS	765	SHADOW WATER A		359
	AND MINGLING HAIR FALL FROM THE FIERY BOUGHS,	765	SHADOW WATER A		368
	AND ONE LIVES UNDER THE BOUGHS	771	SPINNING SONG		8
BOUGHT					
	TO SEE MEN'S SOULS BARTERED AND BOUGHT.	136	TWO TREES	V	36
	I BOUGHT AT THE SLIGO FAIR.	178	FIDDLER DOONEY		8
	AND HERE AND THERE HAVE BOUGHT	366	HER CHRIS TREE		4
	(FOR SINCE THE HORIZON'S BOUGHT STRANGE DOGS ARE STILL)	579	DOR WELLESLEY		7
	AND BOUGHT THE GRANDEST JEWELRY	595	COLONEL MARTIN		21
	THOSE CHEERS THAT CAN BE BOUGHT OR SOLD,	598	MODEL LAUREATE		19
	CRAMM'D ALL HER YOUTH, AND HATES HAVE BOUGHT AND SOLD	687	TWO TITANS		13
BOUND	**SEE SPELL-BOUND OATH-BOUND SLUMBER-BOUND**				
	AND IT WAS BOUND WITH A PEARL-PALE SHELL	4	OISIN 1		28
	FOR BROOCH 'TWAS BOUND WITH A BRIGHT SEA-SHELL,	4	OISIN 1		28
	AND IT WAS BOUND WITH A PEARL PALE SHELL	4	OISIN 1	V	28
	AND CAPTIVES BOUND WITH LEATHERN THONGS	7	OISIN 1		77
	MY CAPTIVES, BOUND IN LEATHERN THONGS,	8	OISIN 1	V	78
	AND THEN I MOUNTED AND SHE BOUND ME	9	OISIN 1		106
	LIES FAR." I MOUNTED, AND SHE BOUND ME	9	OISIN 1	V	106
	SOME FEASTING MAN THAT THE SAME OATH HAS BOUND."	108	CUCHULAIN SEA		38
	SOME FEATING MAN THAT THE SAME OATH HAS BOUND."	108	CUCHULAIN SEA	V	38
	SOME FEASTING MAN THAT THE SAME OATH HAS BOUND."	109	CUCHULAIN SEA		54
	OF ALL THIS HOST SO BOUND FROM CHILDHOOD ON."	109	CUCHULAIN SEA		56
	"SOME FEATING MAN THAT THE SAME OATH HAS BOUND."	109	CUCHULAIN SEA	V	54
	BUT KNOW YOUR HAIR WAS BOUND AND WOUND	176	BELOVED DEAD		9
	BUT KNOW YOUR HAIR WAS BOUND AND BOUND	176	BELOVED DEAD	V	9
	BUT KNOW YOUR HAIR WAS BOUND AND BOUND	176	BELOVED DEAD	V	9
	AND SO TO THE OTHER TREE AT A BOUND.	318	APPOINTMENT		7
	BOUND NEITHER TO CAUSE NOR TO STATE,	414	TOWER		129
	SUCH THOUGHT, THAT IN IT BOUND	474	ALL SOUL NIGHT		97
	THE WOODEN SCABBARD BOUND AND WOUND,	477	SELF AND SOUL		15
	BELOVED BOOKS THAT FAMOUS HANDS HAVE BOUND,	491	COOLE BALLYLEE		27
	FOR HADES' BOBBIN BOUND IN MUMMY-CLOTH	497	BYZANTIUM		11
	FOR HADES' BOBBIN BOUND IN MUMMY CLOTH	497	BYZANTIUM	V	11
	THE SKEIN SO BOUND US GHOST TO GHOST	511	JANE AND JACK		15
	BOUND A THONG ABOUT HIS HAND,	595	COLONEL MARTIN		25
	OUR VOICES CARRY, AND THOUGH SLUMBER BOUND,	622	HOUND VOICE		5
	OH, BOY, I'M BOUND ON A MOST FEARFUL QUEST,	653	ISLE STAT I 2		31
	TWO FIGURES CROUCHING ON THE BLACK ROCK, BOUND	687	TWO TITANS		5
	WITH PITILESS MAGIC HAS BOUND YOU--	708	FAIRY PEDANT		31

BOUND   (CONTINUED)

BEFORE HIM ONE WELL GUARDED, WITH BOUND HANDS:	709	FERENCZ RENYI	10
I HAVE CUT THE ROPE THAT BOUND THIS GALLEY TO OURS, . . .	768	SHADOW WATER A	421
THIS SOD HAS BOUND US	769	BLOOD BOND	1
THIS BOND HAS BOUND US	769	BLOOD BOND V	1

BOUNDS

THAT SPRING FIVE PACES IN THEIR BOUNDS, ...	8	OISIN 1 V	86A
FROM THESE EARTHLY BOUNDS."	97	FOXHUNTER	12
HER CHARITY HAD NO BOUNDS:	392	EASTER 1916 V	21

BOUNTIFUL

BE PASSIONATE, NOT BOUNTIFUL	335	YOUNG BEAUTY	8

BOUNTY

OR THOSE WHO NEED HIS BOUNTY OR HIS LAW, ...	462	HARUN RASHID V	25A
AND THEREUPON HIS BOUNTY GAVE WHAT NOW	465	HARUN RASHID	103

BOW   SEE SADDLE-BOW FIDDLE-BOW

AH, FENIANS, WITH THE SHIELD AND BOW?	10	OISIN 1	116
TELL ON, NOR BOW THY HEATHEN CREST	11	OISIN 1 V	131A
I RODE AWAY ON THE SURGES, WHERE HIGH AS THE SADDLE BOW	57	OISIN 3 V	147
THE SORROWS OF THE WORLD BOW DOWN MY HEAD, ...	104	FERGUS DRUID V	38A
I HAVE OFTEN HEARD THE SWEET SOUND OF HIS BOW.	109	CUCHULAIN SEA	50
I OFTEN HEAR THE SWEET SOUND OF HIS BOW.	109	CUCHULAIN SEA V	50
BOW DOWN, ARCHANGELS, IN YOUR DIM ABODE!	112	ROSE OF WORLD	11
AND FOLK SEEING HIM BOW DOWN, ...	113	ROSE OF PEACE	9
ALL THE HEAVENS BOW DOWN TO HEAVEN, ...	125	CATHLEEN PARA	15
THE SAD BELLS BOW THE FOREHEAD ON THE HANDS.	130	BOOK STORIES V	20
BEING WEARY OF THE WORLD'S EMPIRES, BOW DOWN TO YOU, . .	161	BLACK PIG	7
AND THEREFORE MY HEART WILL BOW, WHEN DEW	164	PERFECT BEAUTY	6
WITH BEAUTY LIKE A TIGHTENED BOW, A KIND	256	NO SECOND TROY	8
UNDER A BOW, HE CRIED, "WHAT HAPPINESS	284	TWO KINGS	177
THE BURNING BOW THAT COULD SHOOT AN ARROW	377	PHASES OF MOON	119
A BEAUTIFUL SEATED BOY: A SACRED BOW:	541	PARN FUNERAL 1	10
A HOARY HUNTER LEANING ON HIS BOW.	672	ISLE STAT II 3	157
BEHOLD I BOW BEFORE THEE TO THE GROUND!	684	SEEKER V	67
BEHOLD I BOW! AROUND MY BEARD IN DRIFTS	684	SEEKER V	68
THAT ALL MEN EVERMORE MAY HUMBLY BOW	688	TWO TITANS	49
HIS MOODS BOW LOW HIS SOMBRE CREST, ...	723	GIRLS SONG A	2
WHERE LONG GREY GRASSES BOW AND BEND, ...	736	SUMMER EVENING	6
AND MADE THE TYRANT BOW.	738	MOURN THEN ON	12

BOWED

AND SIGHING BOWED HER GENTLE HEAD, ...	12	OISIN 1	149
WITH BOWED HEAD, TREMBLING WHEN THE WHITE BLADE SHONE, . .	38	OISIN 2	137
ARE BOWED IN SORROW UNDER PENDULOUS LIDS, ...	79	EPHEMERA	2
ARE BOWED IN SORROW UNDER THEIR TREMBLING LIDS, ...	79	EPHEMERA V	2
WITH HEAD BOWED ON HIS KNEES CUCHULAIN STAYED:	110	CUCHULAIN SEA	71
WITH HEAD BOWED ON HIS KNEES, CUCHULLIN STAID, ...	110	CUCHULAIN SEA V	71
AND THOUGH THE SEVEN LIGHTS BOWED IN THEIR DANCE AND WEPT,	174	ELEMENT POWERS	3
HIS FACE BOWED LOW TO WEEP THE END	192	BAILE AILLINN	75
AND HARPERS PONDERING WITH BOWED HEAD	193	BAILE AILLINN V	107
CROW UPON TARA." KING EOCHAID BOWED HIS HEAD	286	TWO KINGS	211
WHAT'S BOWED YOUR SHOULDER AND MADE PALE YOUR CHEEK": . .	467	HARUN RASHID	133
AND THE WAVES BOWED BEFORE IT LIKE MOWN CORN, ...	657	ISLE STAT II 3	56
LOW BOWED AND DUMB UPON THE SAND.	671	ISLE STAT II 3	130

BOWELS

TILL HER BOWELS ARE IN HEAT, ...	638	BEN BULBEN	49

BOWERS

COME FORTH, FOR IN A THOUSAND BOWERS	647	ISLE STAT I 1	64
AND HANGING O'ER THE HUSH OF WILLOW BOWERS, ...	705	REMEMBRANCE	8

BOWING

FULL MANY BOWING KINGS BESOUGHT ME, ...	7	OISIN 1 V	67
CUMHAL CALLED OUT, BOWING HIS HEAD, ...	167	BLESSED V	4A
BOWING NATIONS, PLUMED WARS--	737	IN FIRELIGHT	10

BOWL

ALL, ALL, THE VERY BOTTOM OF THE BOWL--	227	SHADOW WATER B	118
IT SEEMED A GOLD-FISH SWIMMING IN A BOWL.	472	ALL SOUL NIGHT	40

BOW-LEGGED

THE BOW-LEGGED GOBAN HAD NO SAY:	271	GREY ROCK V	10

BOWLS   SEE DRINKING-BOWLS

AND BOWLS OF BARLEY, HONEY, AND WINE, ...	3	OISIN 1	8
I PROMISE YOU A HUNDRED DRINKING BOWLS, ...	756	SHADOW WATER A V	187

BOWS

AND A HUNDRED SPEARS AND A HUNDRED BOWS, ...	8	OISIN 1	91
AND A HUNDRED SWORDS AND A HUNDRED BOWS:	8	OISIN 1	91
WITH BENDING STERNS AND BENDING BOWS, ...	14	OISIN 1	189
WITH BENDING STERNS AND BENDING BOWS, ...	23	OISIN 1	353
HID UNDER QUIET BOWS APART, ...	78	INDIAN TO LOVE V	12
AND THEREFORE MY HEART BOWS DOWN ANEW, ...	164	PERFECT BEAUTY V	6
A SLAVE BOWS DOWN TO A SLAVE.	547	TO SAME TUNE 3	6
A SLAVE BOWS DOWN TO A SLAVE.	614	MARCH SONGS 2	6
ALONG THE WOOD WITH SUBTLE TREAD AND BENDED BOWS. . . .	649	ISLE STAT I 1	111
BOWS THE BEDOUIN'S WHITENING HAIR--	733	STREET DANCERS	45
YOU HAVE DONE WELL, BECAUSE MY BOWS ARE TURNED	755	SHADOW WATER A	164

BOW-STRING'S

AND FEARED ALWAYS THE BOW-STRING'S TWANGING.	3	OISIN 1 V	7GG

BOWSTRINGS

. . . AND THE QUIVER OF STRETCHED BOWSTRINGS, ...	62	OISIN 3	207

BOX-BORDERED

ENCLOSE A QUIET PLACE OF BEDS BOX-BORDERED, BEES, . . .	710	FERENCZ RENYI	24

BOXES

TREASURE ON TREASURE. BOXES OF PRECIOUS SPICE.	247	SHADOW WATER B	533
TREASURE AND TREASURE. BOXES OF PRECIOUS SPICE.	247	SHADOW WATER B V	533
FOR PAINTED FORMS OR BOXES OF MAKE-UP	564	GYRES	13

BOY   SEE PLAY-BOY SHEPHERD-BOY GARDEN-BOY
UNTIL ONE CAME, A TEARFUL BOY! . . . . 17 OISIN 1 237
AND ONE CAME CLOSE, A TEARFUL BOY. . . . . . . 17 OISIN 1 V 237
WITH ONE LONG GLANCE FOR GIRL AND BOY . . . . . 19 OISIN 1 287
WITH ONE LONG GLANCE ON MAID AND BOY . . . . . 19 OISIN 1 V 287
AROSE FROM EVERY MAID AND BOY, ... 20 OISIN 1 V 289
FROM GIRL AND BOY AND MAN AND BEAST! . . . . . . 82 MAD KING GOLL 6
A GRACIOUS, GENTLE, KINGLY BOY. . . . . 82 MAD KING GOLL V 8
PEACE-MAKING, MILD, A KINGLY BOY. . . . . 82 MAD KING GOLL V 8
WHEN I WAS A BOY WITH NEVER A CRACK IN MY HEART. . . . 91 OLD FISHERMAN 4
WHEN I WAS A BOY WITH NEVER A CRACK IN MY HEART. . . . 91 OLD FISHERMAN 8
WHEN I WAS A BOY WITH NEVER A CRACK IN MY HEART. . . . 91 OLD FISHERMAN 12
A BOY OF TWENTY YEARS!--A MOUND AND STONE . . . . 276 TWO KINGS V F
WHERE HELEN WALKED WITH HER BOY, ... 293 HELEN LIVED 9
THE ATTACK ON THE "PLAY BOY" . . . . 294 HATED PLAYBOY V T
AND EVERY MAN AND MAID AND BOY . . . . 337 TOM OROUGHLEY 2
IS DEAD. THE BOY THAT BRINGS MY GRIDDLE-CAKE . . . 339 SHEP GOATHERD 20
IS DEAD. THE BOY THAT BRINGS MY GRIDDLE CAKE . . . 339 SHEP GOATHERD V 20
I SEE A SCHOOL BOY WHEN I THINK OF HIM . . . . . 370 EGO DOMINUS V 55
SUFFICE THE AGEING MAN AS ONCE THE GROWING BOY. . . . 427 PHANTOM HATRED 40
OFTEN AT EVENING WHEN A BOY . . . . 494 AT ALGECIRAS 7
A BEAUTIFUL SEATED BOY! A SACRED BOW! . . . . . 541 PARN FUNERAL 1 10
A PIERCED BOY, IMAGE OF A STAR LAID LOW. . . . . 541 PARN FUNERAL 1 12
STAMPED BOY AND TREE UPON SICILIAN COIN. . . . . 541 PARN FUNERAL 1 15
ETERNITY IS PASSION, GIRL OR BOY . . . . 560 WHENCE COME 1
SEVENTY YEARS MAN AND BOY, ... 567 FROM JAPANESE 8
AY, BOY. LET'S SEE IF THAT SAME HERON'S DEAD. . . . 651 ISLE STAT I 1 169
OH, BOY, I'M BOUND ON A MOST FEARFUL QUEST! . . . 653 ISLE STAT I 2 31
AND, BOY, SAW YOU, WHEN THROUGH THE FOREST WE . . . 662 ISLE STAT II 2 9
BUT, FOR A BOY, HOW LONG THINE HAIR HAS GROWN! . . . 670 ISLE STAT II 3 104
TOUCH NOT THIS BOY, FOR HE IS INNOCENT. . . . . 694 MOSADA 1 106
REITERANT. A BOY GOES BY THE TENT. . . . . . . 711 FERENCZ RENYI V 46
A LITTLE BOY OUTSIDE THE SYCAMORE WOOD . . . . . 715 DWELT SYCAMORE 1
A LITTLE BOY INSIDE THE SYCAMORE WOOD . . . . . 715 DWELT SYCAMORE 5
A BOY AND GIRL HOLD ONE ANOTHER'S HANDS! . . . . 752 SHADOW WATER A 122
BOYHOOD
NO, NOT IN BOYHOOD WHEN WITH ROD AND FLY, ... 409 TOWER 8
THE IGNOMINY OF BOYHOOD! THE DISTRESS . . . . . 478 SELF AND SOUL 45
OF BOYHOOD CHANGING INTO MAN! . . . . 479 SELF AND SOUL 46
EVEN FROM BOYHOOD, IN MY FATHER'S HOUSE, ... 683 SEEKER 48
BOYISH
MY FANCY, AND SET MY BOYISH LIPS TO SAY, ... 270 PARDON FATHERS 17
OR BOYISH INTELLECT APPROVED, ... 328 ROBERT GREGORY 92
"ACCORDING TO MY BOYISH PLAN! . . . . 577 WHAT THEN 17
BOYNE
BESIDE THE BRACKISH WATERS OF THE BOYNE . . . . 270 PARDON FATHERS 11
BOY'S
OR, IT MAY BE, LIKE A BOY'S. . . . . 363 DOLLS DRAWINGS 9
FOR SHOULD YOU LEAVE MY LETTER THERE, A BOY'S . . . 461 HARUN RASHID 13
A BOY'S LOVELORN INDIFFERENT HANDS MIGHT FIND . . . 461 HARUN RASHID V 14
A BOY'S TURBULENT DAYS . . . . 496 MOHINI CHATTER 13
AS THE FOX IN THE OLD FABLE DESTROYED THE SPARTAN BOY'S, 580 CURSE CROMWELL 18
BOYS   SEE HORSE-BOYS
TIME FOR US ALL BOYS, TO HIT ON A TUNE BOYS, . . . 548 TO SAME TUNE 3 V 13
TIME FOR US ALL BOYS, TO HIT ON A TUNE BOYS, . . . 548 TO SAME TUNE 3 V 13
BUT BOYS AND GIRLS, PALE FROM THE IMAGINED LOVE . . . 610 STATUES 4
WITH BOYS AND GIRLS ABOUT HIM, ... 627 STATES HOLIDAY 27
THOSE STILTED BOYS, THAT BURNISHED CHARIOT, . . . 629 CIRCUS ANIMALS 7
AND LITTLE BOYS PLAYED PITCH AND TOSS. . . . . . 725 LEGEND 4
THE BOYS, THE WOMEN, AND OLD MEN, ... 725 LEGEND 7
AND DROVE THE BOYS AND WOMEN OFF. . . . . . . 725 LEGEND 24
BRACE
COULD LIKE A BRACE OF BLACKBIRDS SING. . . . . . 332 ROUND TOWER 24
BRACE ME AND MAKE ME STRONG! . . . . 607 SONGS BURDEN 2 24
BRACKISH
BESIDE THE BRACKISH WATERS OF THE BOYNE . . . . 270 PARDON FATHERS 11
BRAHMA
TO MIGHTY BRAHMA, HE WHO MADE YOU MANY AS THE SANDS, . 72 ANASHU VIJAYA 21
TO MIGHTY BRAHMA--HE WHO MADE YE MANY AS THE SANDS, . 72 ANASHU VIJAYA V 21
TO MIGHTY BRAHMA, WHO HAS MADE YOU MANY AS THE SANDS, . 72 ANASHU VIJAYA V 21
WHOM BRAHMA, TOUCHING WITH HIS FINGER, PRAISES, FOR YOU
   HOLD . . . 73 ANASHU VIJAYA 42
WHOM BRAHMA, TOUCHING WITH HIS FINGER, PRAISES, FOR YE HOLD 73 ANASHU VIJAYA V 42
PRAYERS FOR THE LAND. O BRAHMA, GUARD IN SLEEP . . . 75 ANASHU VIJAYA 85
BRAHMA'S
BY MIGHTY BRAHMA'S EVER-RUSTLING ROBE, ... 71 ANASHU VIJAYA 14
STAND YOU. BY BRAHMA'S EVER-RUSTLING ROBE, . . . 71 ANASHU VIJAYA V 14
BY MIGHTY BRAHMA'S EVER RUSTLING ROBE, ... 71 ANASHU VIJAYA V 14
ON BRAHMA'S GATEWAY, "THEY WITHIN HAVE FED . . . 735 QUATRAIN APHOR 15
BRAHMIN
BUT THE BRAHMIN SAID, ... 495 MOHINI CHATTER 2
BRAID
HOW THEREFORE COULD SHE HELP BUT BRAID . . . . . 309 PLAYER QUEEN 17
I HAVE WET THIS BRAID OF HAIR WITH TEARS WHILE ASLEEP. . 762 SHADOW WATER A 294
BRAIN
IN EVERY BRAIN A WIZARD GLOW. . . . . 20 OISIN 1 V 291A
SHADOWS AND SHOWS THAT CAN BUT TURN THE BRAIN." . . . 281 TWO KINGS 108
NOR THE TAME WILL, NOR TIMID BRAIN, ... 318 APPOINTMENT 8
ON THAT WOMAN'S REELING BRAIN? . . . . 632 MAN AND ECHO 14
ON MY POOR BRAIN YOUR BUSY TUMULTS CROWD. . . . . 648 ISLE STAT I 1 100
MY SINKING BRAIN!--CEASE!--CEASE! HEARD YE YON SOUND? . 665 ISLE STAT II 2 73

BRAIN   (CONTINUED)
    LAUGHTER-LIPPED, BUT FOR HER BRAIN . . . . 668 ISLE STAT II 3   58
    THAT DREAMS. SHE MOVETH, FEELING IN HER BRAIN . . . . 687 TWO TITANS   10
    CIRCLING THE BRAIN? MY BROTHERS WILL PASS DOWN . . . . 699 MOSADA 3   6
    THE BRAIN. MY BROTHERS WILL BE PASSING DOWN . . . . . 699 MOSADA 3   V   6
    CIRCLING THE BRAIN? MY BROTHERS NOW PASS DOWN . . . . 699 MOSADA 3   V   6
    SO ENDS A BRAIN--A WORLD! THE SMOKE GOES UP, ... 714 FERENCZ RENYI   111
    OF FIRE. SO ENDS A BRAIN--A WORLD! THE SMOKE FLOATS UP, 714 FERENCZ RENYI V 111
    SORROWS SAPPING BRAIN AND HEART. . . . . 733 STREET DANCERS   60
BRAINS
    SMOTE ON THEIR BRAINS THAT DWELT REMEMBERING AYE. . . . 34 OISIN 2   V   77A
BRAKE
    AND SEDGY STREAM, AND IN EACH BABBLING BRAKE . . . . . 675 ISLE STAT II 3   225
BRAN
    BRAN, SGEOLAN, AND LOMAIR, ... 2 OISIN 1   V   7D
    AND BRAN, SGEOLAN, AND LOMAIR, ... 2 OISIN 1   V   7R
    WITH BRAN, SCEOLAN, AND LOMAIR, ... 3 OISIN 1   15
    AND BRAN, SCEOLAN, AND LOMAIR, ... 11 OISIN 1   125
    I MUSED ON THE CHASE WITH THE FENIANS, AND BRAN, SCEOLAN, 47 OISIN 3   5
      LOMAIR,
    WHEN THE FENIANS MADE FORAY AT MORNING WITH BRAN, SCEOLAN, 54 OISIN 3   104
      LOMAIR,
    WHAT PLACE HAVE CAOILTE AND CONAN, AND BRAN, SCEOLAN, 61 OISIN 3   195
      LOMAIR?
    WHAT PLACE HAVE CAOLTE AND FIN, AND BRAN, SGEOLAN, LOMAIR? 61 OISIN 3   V   195
    I WILL GO TO CAOILTE, AND CONAN, AND BRAN, SCEOLAN, LOMAIR, 63 OISIN 3   223
    TO FIN, CAOLTE, AND CONAN, AND BRAN, SGEOLAN, LOMAIR. . . 63 OISIN 3   V   224
BRANCH   SEE BELL-BRANCH CHERRY-BRANCH
    ROUND EVERY BRANCH THE SONG-BIRDS FLEW, ... 14 OISIN 1   180
    FOR ROUND EACH BRANCH THE SONG-BIRDS FLEW, ... 14 OISIN 1   V   180
    IN ONE WAS A BRANCH SOFT-SHINING WITH BELLS MORE MANY THAN 50 OISIN 3   46
      SIGHS
    CAME BY ME THE KINGS OF THE RED BRANCH, ... 53 OISIN 3   87
    CAME BY ME THE CANNS OF THE RED BRANCH . . . . 53 OISIN 3   V   87
    WHAT WOULD YOU, KING OF THE PROUD RED BRANCH KINGS? . . 102 FERGUS DRUID   8
    WHAT WOULD YOU, KING OF THE PROUD RED BRANCH KINGS? . . 102 FERGUS DRUID   15
    WHAT WOULD YOU, KING OF THE PROUD RED BRANCH KINGS? . . 103 FERGUS DRUID   V   21
    "THE RED BRANCH CAMP IN A GREAT COMPANY . . . . . . 108 CUCHULAIN SEA   33
    "THE RED BRANCH KINGS A TIRELESS BANQUET KEEP, ... 108 CUCHULAIN SEA   V   33
    "THE RED BRANCH GATHER A GREAT COMPANY . . . . . . 108 CUCHULAIN SEA   V   33
    AND THE GREY TIDE, THE RED BRANCH MULTITUDE . . . . . 108 CUCHULAIN SEA   V   38B
    AND CONCHUBAR, THE RED BRANCH KING OF KINGS, ... 109 CUCHULAIN SEA   45
    "I ONLY OF THE RED BRANCH HOSTED NOW," . . . . . . 109 CUCHULAIN SEA   V   55
    THERE WAS A GREEN BRANCH HUNG WITH MANY A BELL . . . . 129 BOOK STORIES   1
    I ALSO BEAR A BELL BRANCH FULL OF EASE. . . . . . . 130 BOOK STORIES   V   12
    MY BELL BRANCH MURMURS! THE GAY BELLS BRING LAUGHTER, . 130 BOOK STORIES   V   12
    O FLOWER OF THE BRANCH, O BIRD AMONG THE LEAVES, . . . 251 SHADOW WATER B   608
    O FLOWER OF THE BRANCH, O BIRD AMONG THE LEAVES, . . . 769 SHADOW WATER A   424
BRANCHES
    FROM JOY THE HOLY BRANCHES START, ... 134 TWO TREES   3
    THERE, THROUGH THE BROKEN BRANCHES, GO . . . . 135 TWO TREES   33
    THERE, THROUGH BEWILDERED BRANCHES, GO . . . . 135 TWO TREES   V   13
    I TURNED ABOUT AND LOOKED WHERE BRANCHES BREAK . . . . 490 COOLE BALLYLEE   15
    I TURNED ABOUT AND LOOKED WHERE BRANCHES BROKE . . . . 490 COOLE BALLYLEE V   15
    THOSE BRANCHES OF THE NIGHT AND DAY . . . . 502 VACILLATION   68
    A FRENZIED CROWD, AND WHERE THE BRANCHES SPRANG . . . 541 PARN FUNERAL 1   9
    EYES STARED OUT OF THE BRANCHES AND WERE GONE. . . . . 634 CUCHULAIN COMF   3
    AND THE BIRD IN THE BRANCHES WILL CRY FOR US CLEAR, . . 717 LOVE SONG   6
BRANCHING
    BUT THE STAG STOOPED ITS HEAVY BRANCHING HORNS, ... 277 TWO KINGS   V   12
BRAND
    A BRAND, OR FLAMING BREATH, ... 500 VACILLATION   3
BRAND-NEW
    UPON SOME BRAND-NEW HAPPY DAY! . . . . 432 NINETEEN 19   V   106
BRANWEN
    THEREIN ARE MANY QUEENS LIKE BRANWEN AND GUINEVERE: . . 209 UNDER THE MOON   11
BRASS
    BETWEEN THEM A GATEWAY OF BRASS, AND THE HOWL OF THE ANGELS 61 OISIN 3   200
      WHO FELL.
    WE WILL TEAR OUT THE FLAMING STONES, AND BATTER THE GATEWAY 62 OISIN 3   209
      OF BRASS
    . . . AND WILL BATTER THE GATEWAY OF BRASS . . . . . 62 OISIN 3   V   209
    SHE SNICKED THE BRASS BOLTS DOWN. . . . . 159 CAP AND BELLS V   12
    AND PUSHED THE BRASS BOLT DOWN. . . . . 159 CAP AND BELLS   12
    A HUNDRED SHIELDS OF BRASS, A HUNDRED SWORDS, ... 756 SHADOW WATER A V   188
BRATTA
    AND WHEN THEY SAW THAT THE BRATTA I WORE . . . . . . 15 OISIN 1   V   207
BRATTAS
    THEIR BRATTAS MADE OUT OF YELLOW SILK, ... 15 OISIN 1   V   205
BRAVE
    ALL THAT DELIRIUM OF THE BRAVE? . . . . 290 SEPTEMBER 1913   22
    COULD TRUMPETER MICHAEL BE SO BRAVE?" . . . . 338 TOM OROUGHLEY   13
    FLY! FLY! SO THESE BRAVE SHEPHERDS BOTH ARE GONE: . . . 649 ISLE STAT I 1   112
BRAVED
    BRAVED LIONS FOR MY SAKE, ... 789 SINGING HEAD   2
BRAVELY
    SHE WOULD AS BRAVELY SHOW . . . . 516 MANS SONG   9
BRAVEST
    WE, TOO, HAVE SEEN OUR BRAVEST AND OUR BEST . . . . . 709 FERENCZ RENYI   1
    THE BRAVEST FROM THE GODS BUT ASK! . . . . 788 BRAVEST ASK   1

		PAGE	TITLE	LINE

BRAWLING
THE BRAWLING OF A SPARROW IN THE EAVES, ... 119 SORROW OF LOVE 1
WITH SKELPING HIS BIG BRAWLING LOUT, ... 301 RUN PARADISE 9
WHAT ONE OF MAEVE'S NINE BRAWLING SONS . . . . . . 303 HOUR DAWN 36
HAS ONE OF MAEVE'S NINE BRAWLING SONS . . . . . . 303 HOUR DAWN V 36
"I TOOK YOU FOR A BRAWLING GHOST, ... 304 HOUR DAWN V 41
BRAY
TO HEAR A JACKASS BRAY; . . . . 455 HIS MEMORIES 10
BRAYED
HOWLED, MIAU-D, BARKED, BRAYED, BELLED, YELLED, CRIED, 387 SOLOMON WITCH 8
CROWED,
BRAZEN
O PATRICK, BY YOUR BRAZEN BELL, ... 7 OISIN 1 71
OF SWORD AND BRAZEN BATTLE-AXE, WHILE DAY . . . . . 40 OISIN 2 171
AND MY LOUD BRAZEN BATTLE-CARS . . . . 83 MAD KING GOLL 18
WITH HIS OWN FINGERS TOUCHED THE BRAZEN STRINGS. . . . 109 CUCHULAIN SEA 46
WITH HIS OWN FINGER TOUCHED THE BRAZEN STRINGS. . . . 109 CUCHULAIN SEA V 46
FOR FERGUS RULES THE BRAZEN CARS, ... 126 GOES FERGUS 9
THE BRAZEN PILLARS OF HIS DOOR, ... 192 BAILE AILLINN 74
FROM ANY BRAZEN THROAT, ... 291 TO A FRIEND 3
TO BRAZEN HAWKS, NOR SELF-DELIGHTING REVERIE, ... 427 PHANTOM HATRED 29
THE BRAZEN SKY, SO BLAZE THE DAFFODILS; . . . . . 645 ISLE STAT I 1 11
BRAZEN-GATED
BEHOLD THE BRAZEN-GATED GLADE! . . . . 667 ISLE STAT II 3 43
OF HIM ON YONDER BRAZEN-GATED SPOT, ... 675 ISLE STAT II 3 240
BREAD
THOSE TWO CAME CARRYING WINE AND MEAT AND BREAD, . . . 41 OISIN 2 184
HOPING AND FEARING, BROUGHT ME WINE AND BREAD. . . . 41 OISIN 2 V 184A
AND A YOUNG GIRL WHITE BREAD. . . . . 144 HOST OF AIR 20
THE BREAD AND THE WINE HAD A DOOM, ... 144 HOST OF AIR 25
TO CLIMB THAT STAIR AND EAT THAT BITTER BREAD, . . . 369 EGO DOMINUS 35
OF ALL THOSE TRUTHS THAT ARE YOUR DAILY BREAD! . . . 373 PHASES OF MOON 24
DID GOD IN PORTIONING WINE AND BREAD . . . . . 386 ROBARTES DANCE 39
A BIT OF BREAD THROWN UP INTO THE AIR; . . . . . 400 DEMON BEAST 25
MIND'S BREAD GROW SWEET. . . . . 554 CHURCH STATE 6
BREAD TASTE SOUR. . . . . 554 CHURCH STATE 12
I FASTED FOR SOME FORTY DAYS ON BREAD AND BUTTERMILK, 592 PILGRIM 1
THAT PLUCKS THE TREES FOR BREAD? . . . . 621 JOHN KINSELLA 34
AND WHEN THE FOOL AND BLIND MAN STOLE THE BREAD . . . 630 CIRCUS ANIMALS 25
BREAK   SEE DAY-BREAK HEART-BREAK
. . . WHO COULD BREAK UP THE WORLD IN THEIR RAGE; . . . 62 OISIN 3 214
A RAPTUROUS MUSIC, TILL THE MORNING BREAK . . . . 137 TO SOME I TALK 14
CONTINUAL MUSIC TILL THE MORNING BREAK, ... 137 TO SOME I TALK V 14
THE EAST HER HIDDEN JOY BEFORE THE MORNING BREAK, . . . 154 BELOVED PEACE 4
UNTIL THE AXLE BREAK . . . . 165 CRY OF SEDGE 4
AND SCRUB A KITCHEN PAVEMENT, OR BREAK STONES . . . 204 ADAMS CURSE 8
THE OLD BROWN THORN-TREES BREAK IN TWO HIGH OVER CUMMEN 206 HANRAHANS SONG 1
STRAND,
THE OLD BROWN THORN TREES BREAK IN TWO HIGH OVER CUMANN'S 206 HANRAHANS SONG V 1
STRAND,
WHOSE HEART WOULD BREAK IN TWO, ... 213 HAPPY TOWNLAND 2
FOR NEITHER I NOR YOU CAN BREAK A MESH . . . . . 238 SHADOW WATER B 351
NOR KNAVE NOR DOLT CAN BREAK . . . . 259 UNWORTH PRAISE 2
WHAT DOES HE CARE IF MY HEART BREAK? . . . . . 275 GREY ROCK 104
I HAVE STOOD HERE FROM BREAK OF DAY, ... 294 THREE BEGGARS 2
WHEN DAY BEGINS TO BREAK . . . . 316 FRIENDS 21
TO HIS SPEECH AT THE BREAK OF DAY, ... 341 SHEP GOATHERD 68
OR SICKNESS BREAK HER WILL . . . . 365 HER RACE 10
IMAGES CAN BREAK THE SOLITUDE . . . . 375 PHASES OF MOON 82
TOWARDS BREAK OF DAY . . . . 398 BREAK OF DAY T
I DREAMED TOWARDS BREAK OF DAY, ... 399 BREAK OF DAY 19
TO BREAK UPON A SLEEPER'S REST . . . . 412 TOWER 87
WHERE THE SYMBOLIC ROSE CAN BREAK IN FLOWER, . . . 419 MY HOUSE 4
BUT BREAK UPON HIS GHOSTLY SOLITUDE . . . . . . 429 NINETEEN 19 40
OR BREAK IN BITS THE FAMOUS IVORIES . . . . . 430 NINETEEN 19 47
ALL BREAK AND VANISH, AND EVIL GATHERS HEAD; . . . 433 NINETEEN 19 117
WHERE WE WROUGHT THAT SHALL BREAK THE TEETH OF TIME. . 435 NEW FACES 4
AND YET THEY TOO BREAK HEARTS—O PRESENCES . . . . 445 SCHOOL CHILDR 53
O BUT HER HEART WOULD BREAK TO LEARN MY THOUGHTS ARE FAR 450 OWEN AHERNE 20
AWAY."
I TURNED ABOUT AND LOOKED WHERE BRANCHES BREAK . . . 490 COOLE BALLYLEE 15
TILL THE DAWN BREAK UPON THOSE MINGLED SEAS. . . . 494 AT ALGECIRAS 6
UNTIL THE MORNING BREAK AS ON A DARK BREAST, . . . 494 AT ALGECIRAS V 6
SPIRIT AFTER SPIRIT! THE SMITHIES BREAK THE FLOOD, . . 498 BYZANTIUM 34
BREAK BITTER FURIES OF COMPLEXITY, ... 498 BYZANTIUM 37
I MADE, AND MAY NOT BREAK IT . . . . 520 HIS BARGAIN 9
TO-MORROW NIGHT I WILL BREAK DOWN THE DOOR. . . . 551 SONGS REWRIT 1 6
TO-MORROW NIGHT I WILL BREAK DOWN THE DOOR. . . . 551 SONGS REWRIT 1 12
TO-MORROW NIGHT I WILL BREAK DOWN THE DOOR. . . . 551 SONGS REWRIT 1 18
TOMORROW NIGHT I WILL BREAK DOWN THE DOOR. . . . 551 SONGS REWRIT 1 V REF
TO-MORROW NIGHT I WILL BREAK IN THE DOOR. . . . 551 SONGS REWRIT 1 V REF
DO NOT BREAK UP THEIR LINES TO WEEP. . . . . . 565 LAPIS LAZULI 15
"IRELAND SHALL GET HER FREEDOM AND YOU STILL BREAK STONE." 590 PARNELL 2
THROUGH THIS NIGHT-VESTED PLACE THE RED BEAMS BREAK. . 662 ISLE STAT II 2 4
"SHIELD BREAKER, BREAK A SHIELD TO-DAY, ... 739 EARL PAUL 1
SHIELD-BREAKER, BREAK A SHIELD TO-DAY, ... 739 EARL PAUL V 1
O! I WOULD BREAK THIS NET THE GODS HAVE WOVEN . . . 765 SHADOW WATER A 361
BREAKER   SEE PROMISE-BREAKER SHIELD-BREAKER
"SHIELD BREAKER, BREAK A SHIELD TO-DAY, ... 739 EARL PAUL 1
MEN CRY "BRING PAUL, SHIELD BREAKER, ... 740 EARL PAUL 11
"SHIELD BREAKER, GREAT SHIELD BREAKER," . . . . 740 EARL PAUL 25

<table>
<tr><td></td><td>PAGE</td><td>TITLE</td><td>LINE</td></tr>
</table>

BREAKER   (CONTINUED)
"SHIELD BREAKER, GREAT SHIELD BREAKER," . . . .   740 EARL PAUL   25
BREAKERS
BE BUT THE BREAKERS OF MEN'S HEARTS OR ENGINES OF DELIGHT!   354 HIS PHOENIX   23
BREAKING   SEE BATTLE-BREAKING
IN A WHITE BREAKING WAVE! THEY HAD THE LOOK . . . . .   223 SHADOW WATER B   34
AND BARREN AS A BREAKING WAVE . . . .   456 FRIENDS YOUTH   11
BREAKS
"AND BREAKS THE RIDGE OF BATTLE WITH HIS HANDS." . . . .   107 CUCHULAIN SEA V 26
OUR COURAGE BREAKS LIKE AN OLD TREE IN A BLACK WIND AND   207 HANRAHANS SONG   3
    DIES.
. . . NIGHT SPLITS AND THE DAWN BREAKS LOOSE! . . . . .   623 HIGH TALK   12
THE DIM SPEAR BREAKS THE BRIGHT SHIELD . . . .   741 EARL PAUL   49
LET HIM WHO BREAKS IT . . . .   770 BLOOD BOND   4
BREAST
OF A DROWNED DRIPPING BODY TO MY BREAST! . . . . . .   40 OISIN 2   179
AND SUNKEN SHAPE, AGAINST MY FACE AND BREAST, ...   40 OISIN 2   V 179
AND DRIPPING AND SUNKEN SHAPE, TO FACE AND BREAST, . . .   40 OISIN 2   V 179
. . . HER BROW ON THE MIDST OF MY BREAST! . . . . . .   52 OISIN 3   74
SAD NIAM CAME NEAR ME, AND LAID HER BROWS ON THE MIDST   52 OISIN 3   V   74
    OF MY BREAST
AND PEARL-PALE NEAVE LAY BY ME, HER BROW ON THE MIDST OF   52 OISIN 3   V   74
    MY BREAST!
. . . FOR BREAST UNTO BREAST . . . .   56 OISIN 3   131
. . . FOR BREAST UNTO BREAST . . . .   56 OISIN 3   131
SING PEACE INTO HIS BREAST, ...   88 STOLEN CHILD   47
IN VAIN HER ARMS, IN VAIN HER SOFT WHITE BREAST. . . . .   110 CUCHULAIN SEA   74
AND THE WHITE BREAST OF THE DIM SEA . . . .   126 GOES FERGUS   11
AND HIS NECK AND HIS BREAST AND HIS ARMS . . . . . .   145 HOST OF AIR   35
I KISS MY WAILING CHILD AND PRESS IT TO MY BREAST, . . .   147 UNAPPEAS HOST   5
AND MY BREAST LIES UPON HIS BREAST. . . . .   151 HEART OF WOMAN   4
AND MY BREAST LIES UPON HIS BREAST. . . . .   151 HEART OF WOMAN   4
AND MY WHITE BREAST ON HIS HE LAID. . . . .   151 HEART OF WOMAN V   4
OVER MY HEART, AND YOUR HAIR FALL OVER MY BREAST, ...   154 BELOVED PEACE   10
OVER MY HEART, AND YOUR HAIR FALL ABOUT MY BREAST . . .   154 BELOVED PEACE V 10
THAT WAS SHAKEN OUT OVER MY BREAST! . . . .   155 REPROVE CURLEW   5
FOR THAT PALE BREAST AND LINGERING HAND . . . . . .   156 FORGOT BEAUTY   15
AND COVER THE PALE BLOSSOMS OF YOUR BREAST . . . . .   163 ASKS FORGIVE   21
THEN COVER THE PALE BLOSSOM OF YOUR BREAST . . . . .   163 ASKS FORGIVE   V 21
YOUR BREAST WILL NOT LIE BY THE BREAST . . . . . .   165 CRY OF SEDGE   9
YOUR BREAST WILL NOT LIE BY THE BREAST . . . . . .   165 CRY OF SEDGE   9
YOUR BREAST WILL NOT LIE ON THE BREAST . . . . . .   165 CRY OF SEDGE   V   9
YOUR BREAST WILL NOT LIE ON THE BREAST . . . . . .   165 CRY OF SEDGE   V   9
AND I WOULD LAY MY HEAD ON YOUR BREAST! . . . .   175 BELOVED DEAD   4
MAY NOT LIE ON THE BREAST NOR HIS LIPS ON THE HAIR . . .   177 PAST GREATNESS   9
WOULD NOT LIE ON THE BREAST, OR HIS LIPS ON THE HAIR, . .   177 PAST GREATNESS V   9
LIKE A GREY GULL UPON THE BREAST OF EACH. . . . . . .   223 SHADOW WATER B   24
A SPHINX WITH WOMAN BREAST AND LION PAW, ...   383 VISION ROBART   18
APPROPRIATE TO THAT BEATING BREAST, ...   386 ROBARTES DANCE   22
WHILE UNDER ITS STORM-BEATEN BREAST . . . .   397 POLIT PRISONER   23
COME WITH LOUD CRY AND PANTING BREAST . . . .   412 TOWER   86
THE BREAST THRUST OUT IN PRIDE . . . .   430 NINETEEN 19   66
DROVE HORROR FROM HIS MOTHER'S BREAST. . . . .   440 WISDOM   20
HE HOLDS HER HELPLESS BREAST UPON HIS BREAST. . . . . .   441 LEDA AND SWAN   4
HE HOLDS HER HELPLESS BREAST UPON HIS BREAST. . . . . .   441 LEDA AND SWAN   4
HAS LAID HER HELPLESS FACE UPON HIS BREAST. . . . . . .   441 LEDA AND SWAN V   4
A STONE UPON HER BREAST, ...   456 FRIENDS YOUTH   6
SO GREAT A SWEETNESS FLOWS INTO THE BREAST . . . . .   479 SELF AND SOUL   69
SWIFT BEATING ON HIS BREAST IN SIBYLLINE FRENZY BLIND . .   481 BLOOD AND MOON   19
BECAUSE THE HEART IN HIS BLOOD-SODDEN BREAST . . . . .   481 BLOOD AND MOON   20
CANNOT LACERATE HIS BREAST. . . . .   493 SWIFTS EPITAPH   3
UNTIL THE MORNING BREAK AS ON A DARK BREAST. . . . . .   494 AT ALGECIRAS   V   6
AND YET UPON MY BREAST . . . .   496 MOHINI CHATTER   10
UPON THE ABUNDANCE OF MY BREAST"! . . . .   521 THREE THINGS   5
ON THE MATERNAL MIDNIGHT OF MY BREAST . . . .   535 CHOSEN   7
I STARED UPON HIS BLOOD-BEDABBLED BREAST . . . . . .   537 HER VISION   23
I STARED UPON MY BLOOD-BEDABBLED BREAST . . . . . .   537 HER VISION   V 23
AND LAUGHED UPON HIS BREAST TO THINK . . . .   538 LAST CONFESS   11
DRINKING JOY AS IT WERE MILK UPON HIS BREAST. . . . . .   559 MAGIC DRUM   3
DOWN LIMB AND BREAST OR DOWN THAT GLIMMERING BELLY . . .   560 MAGIC DRUM   5
ON BREAST OF MARS THE GODDESS SIGHED. . . . .   562 CONJUNCTIONS   4
PROPER TO MY BREAST, ...   573 LADYS 2ND SONG   16
WITH EVERY NOBLE BREAST. . . . .   573 LADYS 2ND SONG V 18
ON MY COLD BREAST? . . . .   574 MAIDS 1ST SONG   4
UPON A WOMAN'S BREAST." . . . .   590 OLD WICKED MAN   62
THE SALT-FLAKES ON HIS BREAST, ...   612 NEWS ORACLE   10
THE SALT FLAKES ON HIS BREAST, ...   612 NEWS ORACLE   V 10
JOY'S BROTHER, FEAR, DWELLS EVER IN EACH BREAST-- . . .   651 ISLE STAT I 1   155
FOR SO SHE WILLED--THOU HEARD'ST? UPON THE BREAST . .   653 ISLE STAT I 2   32
ABODE, AS BANDED ADDERS IN MY BREAST. . . . .   683 SEEKER   50
ON HER BROAD BREAST! BENEATH HER WITHERED BROWS . . . .   685 SEEKER   73
MADONNA FROM MY BREAST? . . . .   686 LIFE   12
I WAVE THEM HITHER, MY BREAST HEAVES WITH JOY. . . . .   694 MOSADA 1   98
A FEARFUL PALENESS CREEPS ACROSS HER BREAST . . . . .   701 MOSADA 3   69
HANGS ON MY BREAST! LISTEN, WE SHALL BE SAFE. . . . . .   701 MOSADA 3   73
SAFE ON THE BREAST OF GOMEZ LIES THY HEAD, ...   703 MOSADA 3   101
SAFE ON THE BREAST OF VALLENCE IS THY HEAD . . . . .   703 MOSADA 3   V 101
SAFE ON THE BREAST OF GOMEZ IS THY HEAD, ...   703 MOSADA 3   V 101
THEREFORE, O NATION OF THE BLEEDING BREAST, ...   709 FERENCZ RENYI   4
AND HE SHALL SLUMBER ON MY BREAST. . . . .   723 GIRLS SONG A   4
AND PIERCED THE MIRTHFUL BREAST, ...   741 EARL PAUL   50

BREAST   (CONTINUED)
    IN DAY OUT-LIVING BATTLE, ON THE BREAST . . . .   750 SHADOW WATER A   73
    HIS TOO HUMAN BREAST. . . . .   786 YOUR HEART   21
BREASTPLATE
    SAID THE MAN IN THE GOLDEN BREASTPLATE . . . .   598 STONE CROSS   7
    SAID THE MAN IN THE GOLDEN BREASTPLATE . . . .   599 STONE CROSS   15
    SAID THE MAN IN THE GOLDEN BREASTPLATE . . . .   599 STONE CROSS   23
    SAID THE OLD MAN IN THE GOLDEN BREASTPLATE . . . . .   599 STONE CROSS   V   23
BREASTS
    OUR BREASTS ARE HEAVING, OUR EYES ARE AGLEAM, ...   140 HOSTING SIDHE   8
    FOR BREASTS ARE HEAVING AND EYES A-GLEAM. . . . . . .   140 HOSTING SIDHE   V   7
    OUR BREASTS ARE HEAVING, OUR EYES ARE A-GLEAM, . . .   140 HOSTING SIDHE   V   8
    "THOSE BREASTS ARE FLAT AND FALLEN NOW, ...   513 JANE TALK BISH   3
    (SWALLOWS WERE FLASHING THEIR WHITE BREASTS ABOVE . .   690 MOSADA 1   7
BREATH   SEE ROSE-BREATH AIR-BREATH WINE-BREATH
    BUT ONLY KIND AND MERRY BREATH, ...   19 OISIN 1   285
    WERE THE WINDS LESS SOFT THAN THE BREATH OF A PIGEON . . .   56 OISIN 3   134
    . . . THEY WILL RISE, MAKING CLOUDS WITH THEIR BREATH, . .   61 OISIN 3   202
    HE CAUGHT HIS BREATH AND CAST HIM WEEPING DOWN . . .   106 CUCHULAIN SEA   V   14
    AND PIERCED HIM. "SPEAK BEFORE YOUR BREATH IS DONE." . .   110 CUCHULAIN SEA   67
    MY BREATH IS MIXED INTO HIS BREATH. . . . .   152 HEART OF WOMAN   12
    MY BREATH IS MIXED INTO HIS BREATH. . . . .   152 HEART OF WOMAN   12
    AND WITH A GROAN, AS IF THE MORTAL BREATH . . . . .   185 QUEEN MAEVE   103
    THAT HAPPIER BREATH HAD MOVED, HER HUSBAND TURNED . .   185 QUEEN MAEVE   105
    I AM A WOMAN, I DIE AT EVERY BREATH. . . . .   250 SHADOW WATER B   583
    NAMING IT WITH ECSTATIC BREATH, ...   254 HIS DREAM   18
    BREATHED ON THE WORLD WITH TIMID BREATH. . . . . . .   266 GALWAY RACES   9
    THOUGH YOU MAY THINK I WASTE MY BREATH . . . .   271 GREY ROCK   6
    TOWARD PEOPLED TARA, NOR STOOD TO DRAW HIS BREATH . .   279 TWO KINGS   46
    ON PEOPLED TARA, NOR STOOD TO DRAW HIS BREATH . . .   279 TWO KINGS   V   46
    TOWARDS PEOPLED TARA, NOR STOOD TO DRAW HIS BREATH .   279 TWO KINGS   V   46
    FORBID, BESEECH AND WASTE MY BREATH." THEN I. . . .   281 TWO KINGS   102
    TO DRINK OF THAT SALT BREATH OUT OF THE SEA . . . .   292 TO A SHADE   5
    THE TIME FOR YOU TO TASTE OF THAT SALT BREATH . . .   293 TO A SHADE   21
    I AM ACCUSTOMED TO THEIR LACK OF BREATH, ...   325 ROBERT GREGORY   45
    THE YEARS TO COME SEEMED WASTE OF BREATH, ...   328 IRISH AIRMAN   14
    A WASTE OF BREATH THE YEARS BEHIND . . . .   328 IRISH AIRMAN   15
    YOUNG MEN NO LONGER SUDDENLY CATCH THEIR BREATH . .   355 BROKEN DREAMS   2
    WHO HAD ENDED WHERE HIS BREATH BEGAN. . . . .   360 ALF POLLEXFEN   12
    WHO HAD MURMURED OF GIORGIONE AT HIS LATEST BREATH-- .   366 HER COURAGE   8
    OBEDIENT TO SOME HIDDEN MAGICAL BREATH. . . . . . .   382 VISION ROBART   13
    "MAYBE A BREATH OF POLITIC WORDS . . . .   396 ROSE TREE   3
    AND MURMUR IT WITH BATED BREATH, AS THOUGH . . . .   398 LEADERS CROWD   5
    THAT MADE A CATCH IN THE BREATH-- . . . .   416 TOWER   191
    CHAUCER HAD NOT DRAWN BREATH . . . .   421 MY TABLE   8
    BUT VANISH WITH OUR BREATH . . . .   431 NINETEEN 19   76
    NEVER TO HAVE DRAWN THE BREATH OF LIFE, ...   459 FROM OEDIPUS   11
    NEVER TO HAVE DRUNK THE BREATH OF LIFE, ...   459 FROM OEDIPUS   V   11
    WORDS WERE BUT WASTED BREATH. . . . .   471 ALL SOUL NIGHT   27
    SUPERSESSION OF BREATH. . . . .   476 DEATH   10
    A MOUTH THAT HAS NO MOISTURE AND NO BREATH . . . .   497 BYZANTIUM   13
    A BRAND, OR FLAMING BREATH, ...   500 VACILLATION   3
    AND CALL THOSE WORKS EXTRAVAGANCE OF BREATH . . .   501 VACILLATION   32
    SUCH EXACTING BREATH, ...   517 HER ANXIETY   8
    LAY IN THE COFFIN, STOPPED HIS BREATH AND DIED. . .   609 IN TARAS HALLS   20
    PROFOUND MCTAGGART THOUGHT SO, AND IN A BREATH . .   619 BRONZE HEAD   13
    SHE WILL SAY WITH BATED BREATH, ...   680 LOVE AND DEATH   30
    ALL THAT MINGLING OF OUR BREATH, ...   777 SONG DEIRDRE 2   10
BREATHE
    BREATHE ON THE BURNISHED MIRROR OF THE WORLD . . . .   228 SHADOW WATER B   132
    BREATHE ON THE BURNISHED MIRROR OF THE WORLD . . . .   750 SHADOW WATER A   69
BREATHED
    OR HAVE THEY BREATHED THE MORTAL AIR?" . . . . . .   12 OISIN 1   147
    BREATHED ON THE WORLD WITH TIMID BREATH. . . . . .   266 GALWAY RACES   9
    BREATHED OUT A DRUID VAPOUR, AND CRUMBLED AWAY . .   761 SHADOW WATER A   279
BREATHES
    WHEN AN IMMORTAL PASSION BREATHES IN MORTAL CLAY. . .   172 TRAV PASSION   2
BREATHING
    THE BREATHING CAME FROM THOSE BODIES, ...   49 OISIN 3   36
    HE HOLDS HIM FROM DESIRE, ALL BUT STOPS HIS BREATHING LEST   559 MAGIC DRUM   1
    ONE WHOSE BREATHING SHAKES THE AIR, ...   727 LOVERS QUARREL   31
    THE BREATHING OF THE SMALLEST BIRD. . . . .   730 PRIEST FAIRY   68
BREATHLESS
    AND NOW THEIR BREATHLESS FACES SEEM TO LOOK . . . .   325 ROBERT GREGORY   43
    AND THEIR BREATHLESS FACES SEEM TO LOOK . . . . . .   325 ROBERT GREGORY V   43
    UPON THE BREATHLESS STARLIT AIR, ...   477 SELF AND SOUL   4
    BREATHLESS MOUTHS MAY SUMMON. . . . .   497 BYZANTIUM   14
BRED   SEE COARSE-BRED PURE-BRED MIRACLE-BRED ILL-BRED ROCK-BRED THOROUGH-BRED
    BRED TO BE A HERO'S WAGE. . . . .   258 PEACE   3
    BEING HONOUR BRED, WITH ONE . . . .   291 TO A FRIEND   5
    BRED TO A HARDER THING . . . .   291 TO A FRIEND   9
    BRED THAT FIERCE TOOTH AND CLEANLY LIMB . . . . . .   318 APPOINTMENT   10
    BRED ON THE ATLANTIC, CAN BE STAYED. . . . .   403 FOR DAUGHTER   6
    HOW COULD SHE MATE WITH FIFTY YEARS THAT WAS SO WILDLY   450 OWEN AHERNE   15
        BRED?
    BRED OUT OF THE CONTAGION OF THE THRONG, ...   542 PARN FUNERAL 1   27
BREECHED
    THAT HE MIGHT BE NOBLY BREECHED . . . .   440 WISDOM   13
BREED
    TO BREED THE LIDLESS EYE THAT LOVES THE SUN? . . . .   264 HOUSE SHAKEN   4
    THAT SOME NEW DAY MAY BREED THE BEST . . . .   288 TO WEALTHY MAN   34

		PAGE	TITLE		LINE
BREED	(CONTINUED)				
	THAT NONE OF ANOTHER BREED • • • • • • • • • •	583	GHOST ROG CASE		24
BREEDING	SEE WOLF-BREEDING				
BREEDS					
	LEST ALL THY TOILING ONLY BREEDS • • • • • • •	66	HAPPY SHEPHERD		25
	THE COMMON BREEDS THE COMMON, • • • • • • • • •	605	SONGS BURDEN 1		5
BREEZE					
	BUT NOW A WANDERING LAND BREEZE CAME • • • • • •	13	OISIN 1		165
	AND HEARD THE MOURNFUL BREEZE. • • • • • • • • •	123	DREAM OF DEATH	V	12
	THE SOUTH BREEZE NOW IN DYING FEARS • • • • • •	655	ISLE STAT I 3		13
	HAD FELT THE ISLAND BREEZE, MY LORE • •• • • • •	668	ISLE STAT II 3		55
	HAD LEFT THE ISLAND BREEZE, MY LORE • • • • • •	668	ISLE STAT II 3	V	55
BREEZES					
	'TIS HERE THE ARROW FELL' THE BREEZES LAUGHED • •	657	ISLE STAT I 3		70
BRESSEL					
	BRESSEL THE FISHERMAN • • • • • • • • • • • • •	146	FISH	V	T
BRETHREN					
	AND CAME TO WHERE HIS BRETHREN STOOD, • • • • • •	730	PRIEST FAIRY		63
BREW	SEE HOME-BREW				
BREWED					
	BREWED' BY THE SEA-GODS, FROM HUGE CUPS THAT LAY • • •	41	OISIN 2		189
	BREWED OF THE SEA-GODS, FROM HUGE CUPS THAT LAY • • •	41	OISIN 2	V	189
	BREWED BY THE SEA GODS, FROM HUGE CUPS THAT LAY • • •	41	OISIN 2	V	189
	THAT SACRED GOBAN BREWED," HE CRIED • • • • • • •	304	HOUR DAWN	V	50
BREWS					
	TO HOLD THE SACRED STUFF HE BREWS • • • • • • •	272	GREY ROCK		24
BRIAR					
	I ADMIT THE BRIAR • • • • • • • • • • • • • •	532	FIRST CONFESS		1
BRIBE					
	TO BRIBE OR THREAT' HABITS THAT MADE OLD WRONG • • • •	428	NINETEEN 19		11
	THOSE BANNERS COME TO BRIBE OR THREATEN, • • • • •	635	BLACK TOWER		11
BRIDE					
	LIKE A BRIDE BENDING OVER HER MIRROR ADORNING, • • • •	28	OISIN 1	V	423E
	THE STOLEN BRIDE • • • • • • • • • • • • • •	143	HOST OF AIR	V	T
	OF BRIDGET HIS BRIDE. • • • • • • • • • • • • •	144	HOST OF AIR		8
	AND BRIDGET HIS BRIDE AMONG THEM, • • • • • • • •	144	HOST OF AIR		15
	UNTIL ONE BORE BRIDGET HIS BRIDE • • • • • • • •	145	HOST OF AIR		31
	AND FLINGS HERSELF OUT OF THE ROOM WHEN JULIET WOULD BE BRIDE	354	HIS PHOENIX		13
	AND FLINGS HERSELF OUT OF THE ROOM WHEN JULIET WOULD BE A BRIDE	354	HIS PHOENIX	V	13
	THE BRIDE IS CARRIED TO THE BRIDEGROOM'S CHAMBER • • • •	459	FROM OEDIPUS		8
	"I HAVE BROUGHT A SLENDER BRIDE INTO THE HOUSE' • • •	463	HARUN RASHID		49
	YOU KNOW THE SAYING, "CHANGE THE BRIDE WITH SPRING," • •	463	HARUN RASHID		50
	THINK WHEN I CHOOSE A BRIDE I CHOOSE FOR EVER' • • •	464	HARUN RASHID		80
	BY SOME NEW-MARRIED BRIDE, I TAKE • • • • • • • •	535	CHOSEN		13
	BY SOME NEW MARRIED BRIDE I TAKE • • • • • • • •	535	CHOSEN	V	13
	THOUGHT IS A GARMENT AND THE SOUL'S A BRIDE • • • •	558	RIBH CHRISTIAN		16
	I, STARVED FOR THE BOSOM OF HIS FAERY BRIDE? • • • •	629	CIRCUS ANIMALS		16
BRIDE-BED					
	IN OWING THEM THE BRIDE-BED THAT GIVES PEACE." • • • •	187	QUEEN MAEVE		148
	MAYBE THE BRIDE-BED BRINGS DESPAIR, • • • • • • •	388	SOLOMON WITCH		25
BRIDEGROOM					
	AND MAY HER BRIDEGROOM BRING HER TO A HOUSE • • • • •	405	FOR DAUGHTER		73
BRIDE-GROOM					
	AND MAY HER BRIDE-GROOM BRING HER TO A HOUSE • • • •	405	FOR DAUGHTER	V	73
BRIDEGROOM'S					
	THE BRIDE IS CARRIED TO THE BRIDEGROOM'S CHAMBER • • • •	459	FROM OEDIPUS		8
BRIDELESS					
	ARE BRIDELESS." "I AM FALLING INTO YEARS." • • • • •	463	HARUN RASHID		54
BRIDE'S					
	AND EVERY BRIDE'S AMBITION SATISFIED. • • • • • • •	491	COOLE BALLYLEE		37
BRIDGE					
	THAT CAST THEIR SHADOWS UPON ROAD AND BRIDGE' • • • •	326	ROBERT GREGORY		51
	AN OLD MAN COCKED HIS EAR UPON A BRIDGE' • • • • •	372	PHASES OF MOON		1
	WE ARE ON THE BRIDGE' THAT SHADOW IS THE TOWER, • • •	372	PHASES OF MOON		10
	AND UNDER THE ARCHES OF THE BRIDGE, AND SCREAM • • •	403	FOR DAUGHTER		11
	AN ANCIENT BRIDGE, AND A MORE ANCIENT TOWER, • • • •	419	MY HOUSE		1
	THE WOMEN-SLINGERS ON THE NARROW BRIDGE, • • • • •	749	SHADOW WATER A		41
	A CAPTIVE WOMAN FROM THE NARROW BRIDGE, • • • • • •	749	SHADOW WATER A		49
	THE WOMEN SLINGERS ON THE NARROW BRIDGE, • • • • •	749	SHADOW WATER A	V	41
BRIDGET					
	OF BRIDGET HIS BRIDE. • • • • • • • • • • • • •	144	HOST OF AIR		8
	AND BRIDGET HIS BRIDE AMONG THEM, • • • • • • • •	144	HOST OF AIR		15
	BUT BRIDGET DREW HIM BY THE SLEEVE • • • • • • •	144	HOST OF AIR		21
	UNTIL ONE BORE BRIDGET HIS BRIDE • • • • • • • •	145	HOST OF AIR		31
BRIDLE					
	ON A HORSE WITH BRIDLE OF FINDRINNY' • • • • • • •	3	OISIN 1		21
	IS THERE A BRIDLE FOR THIS PROTEUS • • • • • • •	265	ABBEY THEATRE		11
BRIDLED					
	AND FOUND THE HORSE AND BRIDLED HIM, • • • • • • •	25	OISIN 1		378
BRIDLE-PATH					
	MAKING WAY FROM THE KINDLING SURGES, I RODE ON A BRIDLE-PATH	58	OISIN 3		161
BRIEF					
	BUT A BRIEF, DREAMY, KIND DELIGHT. • • • • • • •	202	NEVER GIVE ALL		7
	FOR THAT BRIEF SIGHING. IF YOU HAD LOVED SOME WOMAN-- • •	228	SHADOW WATER B		135
	LOVES IN BRIEF LONGING AND DECEIVING HOPE • • • • •	228	SHADOW WATER B		146
	IS THAT WE GIVE, ALTHOUGH IT BE BRIEF GIVING, • • • •	282	TWO KINGS		120
	FOR WHAT IS DOUBLY BRIEF." AND NOW THE SHAPE • • • •	285	TWO KINGS		207
	FOR WHAT IS DOUBLY BRIEF." "BUT NOW THE SHAPE, • • • •	285	TWO KINGS	V	207

BRIEF   (CONTINUED)
    BEFORE THAT BRIEF GLEAM OF ITS LIFE BE GONE, ...   430 NINETEEN 19   63
    A BRIEF PARTING FROM THOSE DEAR   . . . .   637 BEN BULBEN   19
    AND TURN BRIEF LONGING AND DECEIVING HOPE   . . . . .   750 SHADOW WATER A   59
    THAN IN BRIEF LONGING AND DECEIVING HOPE   . . . . . .   750 SHADOW WATER A   65
    IS BUT BRIEF LONGING, AND DECEIVING HOPE, ...   765 SHADOW WATER A   354
    THEIR BRIEF LIVES I NEVER KNEW.   . . . .   787 HUDDON DUDDON   5
BRIGAND
    ALL THAT THE BRIGAND APPLE BROUGHT   . . . .   388 SOLOMON WITCH   15
BRIGHT
    FOR BROOCH 'TWAS BOUND WITH A BRIGHT SEA-SHELL, ...   4 OISIN 1   V   28
    KEPT TIME WITH THEIR BRIGHT WINGS AND FEET: . . . . .   26 OISIN 1   397
    BEAT TIME WITH THEIR BRIGHT WINGS AND FEET.   . . . . .   26 OISIN 1   V   397
    AND KISSED MY EYES, AND, SWAYING HER BRIGHT HEAD   . . .   29 OISIN 2   6
    AND HER BRIGHT BODY, SANG OF FAERY AND MAN   . . . . .   29 OISIN 2   7
    AND NOW SANG NIAM, SWAYING HER BRIGHT HEAD   . . . . .   29 OISIN 2   V   6
    AND HER BRIGHT BODY--NOW OF FAY AND MAN: . . . . . .   29 OISIN 2   V   7
    SO SANG YOUNG NIAM, SWAYING HER BRIGHT HEAD, ...   30 OISIN 2   V   15
    LIKE DRIFTS OF LEAVES, IMMOVABLE AND BRIGHT, ...   40 OISIN 2   166
    LIKE DRIFTS OF LAUREL LEAVES, IMMOVABLE AND BRIGHT   . . .   40 OISIN 2   V 166
    AND BECAUSE I WENT BY THEM SO HUGH AND SO SPEEDY WITH EYES   59 OISIN 3   169
        SO BRIGHT,
    AND BEFORE I WENT BY THEM SO HUGE AND SO SPEEDY WITH EYES   59 OISIN 3   V 169
        SO BRIGHT,
    "WHAT DO YOU MAKE SO FAIR AND BRIGHT?"   . . . .   69 CLOAK BOAT   1
    "WHAT DO YOU WEAVE SO SOFT AND BRIGHT?"   . . . .   69 CLOAK BOAT   V   1
    "WHAT DO YOU WEAVE SO FAIR AND BRIGHT?"   . . . .   69 CLOAK BOAT   V   1
    BY GOD TO THE BRIGHT HEARTS OF THOSE LONG DEAD, ...   101 ROSE UPON ROOD   20
    SHINING BRIGHT AS A NEW LANCE: . . . .   125 CATHLEEN PARA   V   14
    "AND BROOD NO MORE WHERE THE FIRE IS BRIGHT   . . . . .   140 HOSTING SIDHE   V   5
    TILL PRIDE HAD MADE HER EYES GROW BRIGHT, ...   314 MEMORY YOUTH   10
    SHOWS THROUGH OUR LINEAMENTS. MY CANDLE'S BRIGHT,   . . .   464 HARUN RASHID   70
    AND IF HER EYE SHOULD NOT GROW BRIGHT FOR MINE   . . . .   464 HARUN RASHID   81
    THAT NEVER KNEW THAT STRAIN WOULD SCARCE SEEM BRIGHT,   . .   465 HARUN RASHID   88
    AND THE EYES MORE BRIGHT   . . . .   531 BEFORE WORLD   2
    SLEEPILY CLOSE HER ROUND BRIGHT EYNE: . . . .   646 ISLE STAT I 1   35
    AND THINE EYES MORE BRIGHT THAN FAERY'S, ...   647 ISLE STAT I 1   53
    NASCHINA, WHEREFORE ARE YOUR EYES SO BRIGHT   . . . . .   650 ISLE STAT I 1   141
    WHAT DO YOU WEAVE SO FAIR AND BRIGHT?   . . . . . .   666 ISLE STAT II 3   1
    THY SOUL SHALL BE, THOUGH PITILESS AND BRIGHT   . . . .   674 ISLE STAT II 3   210
    AND WHEREFORE SHOULD THY BRIGHT BROW ROAM   . . . . . .   686 LIFE   11
    BRIGHT ON A GRASS BLADE'S UNDER SIDE, MIGHT HEAR,   . . .   689 NETTLESHIP   10
    A LITTLE NEARER THOSE BRIGHT STARS. TELL ME, ...   701 MOSADA 3   59
    WHILE O'ER THE BUDS, AND O'ER THE GRASS-BLADES, BRIGHT . .   704 REMEMBRANCE   3
    OFTEN HE HAD BENT DOWN SOME BOUGH ALL BRIGHT   . . . . .   710 FERENCZ RENYI   28
    OFTEN HE HAD BENT DOWN SOME BOUGH ALL BRIGHT WITH BERRIES: 710 FERENCZ RENYI   V   28
    IT SEEMS TO FONDLE, WITH A FINGER BRIGHT   . . . . . .   714 FERENCZ RENYI   114
    CHECK. AH! HOW BRIGHT YOUR EYES. HOW SWIFT YOUR MOVES.   722 WITCH VIVIEN   61
    AND FOR HIM MAKE ME WISE AND BRIGHT.   . . . .   723 GIRLS SONG A   12
    ARE TWO RAGGED CHILDREN BRIGHT--   . . . .   731 STREET DANCERS   4
    STORM DARKENED OR STARRY BRIGHT.   . . . .   739 WHERE BOOKS GO   8
    THE DIM SPEAR MET THE BRIGHT SPEAR, ...   741 EARL PAUL   45
    AND MADE THE BRIGHT SPEAR BEND, ...   741 EARL PAUL   46
    THE DIM SPEAR BREAKS THE BRIGHT SHIELD   . . . .   741 EARL PAUL   49
    THE DIM SPEAR MET THE BRIGHT SPEAR   . . . .   741 EARL PAUL   V   49
BRIGHTEN
    OR BRIGHTEN ONLY FOR SOME YOUNGER EYE, ...   464 HARUN RASHID   82
BRIGHTENED
    OR EYES THAT RAGE HAS BRIGHTENED, ARMS IT HAS MADE LEAN,   427 PHANTOM HATRED   27
    OF EYES THAT RAGE HAS BRIGHTENED, ARMS IT HAS MADE LEAN,   427 PHANTOM HATRED V   27
BRIGHTENING
    AND FADED THROUGH THE BRIGHTENING AIR.   . . . .   150 WANDER AENGUS   16
    SHE DREW IN THE BRIGHTENING CASEMENT, ...   159 CAP AND BELLS   V   11
    THE CLOUDS WERE BRIGHTENING WITH THE DAWN.   . . . . . .   307 HOUR DAWN   122
    O BODY SWAYED TO MUSIC, O BRIGHTENING GLANCE, ...   446 SCHOOL CHILDR   63
    O BODY SWAYED TO MUSIC BRIGHTENING GLANCE   . . . . .   446 SCHOOL CHILDR   V   63
    MY THOUGHTS, AND YONDER BRIGHTENING PATCH OF SKY   . . .   700 MOSADA 3   31
BRIGHTER
    BRIGHTNESS REMAINS: A BRIGHTER STAR SHOOTS DOWN: . . . .   541 PARN FUNERAL 1   4
BRIGHT-EYED
    YONDER HE COMES: BRIGHT-EYED, AND HOLLOW-CHEEKED   . . .   697 MOSADA 2   35
BRIGHTNESS
    OF MILKY BRIGHTNESS TO AND FRO   . . . .   22 OISIN 1   328
    AND GAZES AROUND HER WITH EYES OF BRIGHTNESS: . . . . .   27 OISIN 1   413
    AND GAZES AROUND HER WITH EYES OF BRIGHTNESS: . . . . .   28 OISIN 1   V 421
    BUT THEY MISTOOK THE BRIGHTNESS OF THE MOON   . . . . .   411 TOWER   45
    BACK TURNED UPON THE BRIGHTNESS OF THE SUN   . . . . . .   489 COOLE PARK 29   30
    BRIGHTNESS THAT I PULL BACK   . . . .   533 FIRST CONFESS   13
    BRIGHTNESS REMAINS: A BRIGHTER STAR SHOOTS DOWN: . . . .   541 PARN FUNERAL 1   4
    AH! WOE FOR YOUR EYES AND THEIR BRIGHTNESS--   . . . . .   708 FAIRY PEDANT   35
BRILLIANT
    THE BRILLIANT MOON AND ALL THE MILKY SKY, ...   119 SORROW OF LOVE   2
    I HAVE LOOKED UPON THOSE BRILLIANT CREATURES   . . . . .   322 SWANS AT COOLE   13
    I HAVE LOOKED UPON THESE BRILLIANT CREATURES   . . . . .   322 SWANS AT COOLE V   13
    OF EVERY BRILLIANT EYE   . . . .   416 TOWER   190
    BUT BRILLIANT AS THE NIGHT'S EMBROIDERY, ...   461 HARUN RASHID   7
    ONE DEAR BRILLIANT WOMAN: . . . .   504 RESULT THOUGHT   2
    A FAMOUS, A BRILLIANT FIGURE   . . . .   608 SONGS BURDEN 3   16
BRIM
    MY HEART WOULD BRIM WITH DREAMS ABOUT THE TIMES   . . . .   136 TO SOME I TALK   2
    O HEAVY SWOLLEN WATERS, BRIM THE FALL OF THE OAK TREES,   207 HANRAHANS SONG V   11

	PAGE	TITLE		LINE

BRIM   (CONTINUED)
AND AFTER RUNNING AT THE BRIM . . . .   254 HIS DREAM   9
AND FISHES, BUBBLING TO THE BRIM, ...   254 HIS DREAM   V 9
A HORSE-HOOF SLIDES ON THE BRIM, ...   393 EASTER 1916   51
BRIMFUL
BRIMFUL OF STARLIGHT, AND HE SAID: THE STAMPER OF   76 INDIAN ON GOD   14
THE SKIES,
BRIMMED
THAT WAS BRIMMED UP WITH PRAYER AND REST: . . . . .   151 HEART OF WOMAN   2
THAT IS BRIMMED FROM THE PALE FIRE OF TIME: . . . . .   157 POET BELOVED   6
BEING ALL BRIMMED WITH LIFE?" "WERE IT BUT TRUE . .   465 HARUN RASHID   90
BEING SO BRIMMED WITH LIFE. "IF THAT COULD BE . .   465 HARUN RASHID   V 90
AND TWO LONG GLASSES BRIMMED WITH MUSCATEL . . . .   470 ALL SOUL NIGHT   4
BRIMMING
UPON THE BRIMMING WATER AMONG THE STONES . . . . .   322 SWANS AT COOLE   5
IN THAT MYSTERIOUS, ALWAYS BRIMMING LAKE . . . . .   356 BROKEN DREAMS   32
BRING
OF THE YOUNG. "YOUNG MAIDEN, WHAT MAY BRING . . . .   5 OISIN 1   V 50
O WORN DEED-DOER." "WHAT MAY BRING . . . .   5 OISIN 1   V 50
SHE BADE THEM BRING US TO THE HALL . . . .   16 OISIN 1   217
"I BRING DELIVERANCE," PEARL-PALE NIAMH SAID. . . .   34 OISIN 2   78
"I BRING.THEE A DELIVERER FROM FAR AWAY, ...   34 OISIN 2   V 78A
BRING WHAT IS THERE TO BRING: . . . .   97 FOXHUNTER   6
BRING WHAT IS THERE TO BRING: . . . .   97 FOXHUNTER   6
BRING RODY AND HIS HOUNDS. . . . .   97 FOXHUNTER   10
AND SOME ONE FROM THE STABLE BRING . . . .   97 FOXHUNTER   5
AND SOME ONE FROM THE STABLES BRING . . . .   97 FOXHUNTER   V 5
BRING MY BROWN HUNTER NEAR, ...   97 FOXHUNTER   V 6
BRING HOUND AND HUNTSMAN HERE, ...   97 FOXHUNTER   V 10
HAS WON THE GOLD HIS CARS OF BATTLE BRING." . . . .   106 CUCHULAIN SEA   11
AT THE SWORD POINT, AND BADE ME BRING HIM ONE . . . .   109 CUCHULAIN SEA V 53
THAT HE'S A LOVELESS MAN: GAY BELLS BRING LAUGHTER . .   130 BOOK STORIES   18
GAY BELLS OR SAD, THEY BRING YOU MEMORIES . . . . .   130 BOOK STORIES   21
MY BELL BRANCH MURMURS: THE GAY BELLS BRING LAUGHTER,   130 BOOK STORIES   V 18
THEY BRING YOU MEMORIES OF OLD VILLAGE FACES, ...   130 BOOK STORIES   V 22
I BRING YOU WITH REVERENT HANDS . . . .   157 POET BELOVED   1
I BRING YOU MY PASSIONATE RHYME. . . . .   157 POET BELOVED   8
"I CAN BRING YOU SALMON OUT OF THE STREAMS . . . . .   167 BLESSED   9
AND BRING US INTO POPULOUS SEAS AGAIN? . . . . . .   225 SHADOW WATER B   74
BRING MADNESS? QUEEN, I AM NOT MAD. YET SAY . . . .   236 SHADOW WATER B 316
AND MEASURE OUT A COURSE AND BRING US HOME, ...   238 SHADOW WATER B 362
AND THAT YOU'LL BRING ME THERE? I HAVE DECEIVED YOU: 245 SHADOW WATER B 471
TO FANCY THAT SHE'D BRING YOU HOME AGAIN. . . . . .   248 SHADOW WATER B 549
FOR HE WILL SHELTER YOU AND BRING YOU HOME. . . . .   250 SHADOW WATER B 590
PLEASURE ITSELF CAN BRING NO WEARINESS, ...   284 TWO KINGS   181
AND DO NOT KNOW THAT YOU WOULD BRING, ...   306 HOUR DAWN   93
BRING ROSES IF THE ROSE BE YET IN BLOOM: . . . . .   311 MOUNTAIN TOMB   2
PULL DOWN THE BLINDS, BRING FIDDLE AND CLARIONET . .   311 MOUNTAIN TOMB   5
I HAD THE WISDOM LOVE CAN BRING, ...   313 MEMORY YOUTH   V 2
FOR WHAT PROUD DEATH MAY BRING . . . .   317 NIGHT COME   3
THE MAN AND THE WOMAN BRING . . . .   319 DOLLS   10
BUT NOT A FRIEND THAT I WOULD BRING . . . .   324 ROBERT GREGORY   14
NO LIKELY END COULD BRING THEM LOSS . . . .   328 IRISH AIRMAN   7
BRING THE BALLOON OF THE MIND . . . .   358 BALLOON MIND   2
CERTAIN ARTISTS BRING HER DOLLS AND DRAWINGS . . . .   362 DOLLS DRAWINGS   T
BRING WHERE OUR BEAUTY LIES . . . .   362 DOLLS DRAWINGS   1
HER FRIENDS BRING HER A CHRISTMAS TREE . . . . . .   366 HER CHRIS TREE   T
HER FRIENDS BRING HER A CHRISTMAS-TREE . . . . . .   366 HER CHRIS TREE V T
THAT ANY NIGHT COULD BRING . . . .   390 IMAGE PAST   32
AND MAY HER BRIDEGROOM BRING HER TO A HOUSE . . . .   405 FOR DAUGHTER   73
AND MAY HER BRIDE-GROOM BRING HER TO A HOUSE . . . .   405 FOR DAUGHTER   V 73
AND BRING BEAUTY'S BLIND RAMBLING CELEBRANT: . . . .   412 TOWER   91
BRING UP OUT OF THAT DEEP CONSIDERING MIND . . . .   413 TOWER   106
THE MOTHER BIRDS BRING GRUBS AND FLIES. . . . . .   424 STARES NEST   3
AND PLANNED TO BRING THE WORLD UNDER A RULE, ...   429 NINETEEN 19   31
THAT IMAGE CAN BRING WILDNESS, BRING A RAGE . . . .   431 NINETEEN 19   80
THAT IMAGE CAN BRING WILDNESS, BRING A RAGE . . . .   431 NINETEEN 19   80
BRING THAT TO NOUGHT. . . . .   436 FOR MY SON   16
I BRING FULL-FLAVOURED WINE OUT OF A BARREL FOUND . .   442 BLACK CENTAUR   10
I BRING FULL FLAVOURED WINE OUT OF A BARREL FOUND . .   442 BLACK CENTAUR V 10
AND PRIDE BRING IN IMPURITY: . . . .   460 THREE MONUMENT   11
NOTHING COULD BRING HIM, WHEN HIS LADY DIED, ...   471 ALL SOUL NIGHT   25
BRING ME TO THE BLASTED OAK . . . .   507 JANE BISHOP   1
HATRED OF GOD MAY BRING THE SOUL TO GOD. . . . . .   558 RIBH CHRISTIAN   18
AND I AM IN DESPAIR THAT TIME MAY BRING . . . . . .   602 GALLERY REVIS   30
THAT PASSION COULD BRING CHARACTER ENOUGH, ...   610 STATUES   6
BRING THE SOUL OF MAN TO GOD, ...   638 BEN BULBEN   40
I'LL BRING THAT FLOWER TO HER, AND SO MAY EARN . . .   653 ISLE STAT I 2   45
AND SHOREWARD WAVES, WE NIGH HAVE FOUGHT: WAVES BRING   660 ISLE STAT II 1   44
THE ARCADIANS BRING, AND BID THE STONE BE RAISED . .   663 ISLE STAT II 2   25
THAT SHEPHERDESS: ARISE, AND BRING TO ME, ...   673 ISLE STAT II 3 191
FOR THIS DID THE ETERNAL DARKNESS BRING . . . . .   688 TWO TITANS   51
I SAW HIS JOVIAL MOOD BRING ONCE A SMILE . . . . .   696 MOSADA 2   14
OH, CAN MY KISSES BRING A FLUSH NO MORE . . . . .   701 MOSADA 3   71
AFRAID TO BE TOO FAR." "AY, BRING HER HERE!" . . .   712 FERENCZ RENYI   69
THAT MAIDEN BRING THEY. WHEN THE TALL RED DEER . .   713 FERENCZ RENYI   79
"BRING THE ROPES NOW: STAND YE BY NOW: . . . . .   718 PHANTOM SHIP   13
I DO NOT NEED YOUR SCYTHE. MAY THAT BRING PEACE . .   721 WITCH VIVIEN   26
WE WILL BRING A CROWN OF GOLD, ...   726 LOVERS QUARREL   13
MEN CRY "BRING PAUL, SHIELD BREAKER, ...   740 EARL PAUL   11
"GO BRING ME MY OLD ARMOUR . . . .   740 EARL PAUL   19

```
                                                    PAGE   TITLE              LINE
BRING   (CONTINUED)
    MEN CRY:  "BRING PAUL, SHIELD-BREAKER, . . . . . . .   740 EARL PAUL        V   11
    GO BRING ME MY OWN ARMOUR . . . . . . . . . . . .     740 EARL PAUL        V   19
    AND TURN HIS GALLEY ABOUT AND BRING ME HOME. . . .    751 SHADOW WATER A      108
    AND BRING HER TO HER KINGDOM AND HER PEOPLE. . . . .  755 SHADOW WATER A      170
    WE BRING YOU THIS GREAT QUEEN. . . . . . . . . . .    755 SHADOW WATER A V    166
    AND BRING ME TO MY PEOPLE.  I PROMISED THESE . . . .  756 SHADOW WATER A      185
    AND BRING ME WHERE THE CHILDREN OF AENGUS WIND . . .  763 SHADOW WATER A      317
    THAT THE VAST TROUBLED WATERS BRING . . . . . . .     784 WOMANS BEAUTY        17
BRINGING
    BRINGING ME HONEYED, WANDERING THOUGHT . . . . . . .    7 OISIN 1         V   65
    SHEEP-GUIDING, OR THE BRINGING SOME STRANGE BIRD,  . .  650 ISLE STAT I 1      147
BRINGS
    IT BRINGS NO SHAME UPON A HUMAN HEAD . . . . . . .     35 OISIN 2         V 90A
    "HE BRINGS THE PEACEFUL AGE OF GOLD"-- . . . . . . .   82 MAD KING GOLL   V   11
    "THIS YOUNG MAN BRINGS THE AGE OF GOLD," . . . . . .   82 MAD KING GOLL   V   11
    NOR WON THE GOLD THAT NOW CUCHULAIN BRINGS." . . . .  106 CUCHULAIN SEA   V   11
    BECAUSE YOUR CRYING BRINGS TO MY MIND . . . . . .    155 REPROVE CURLEW       3
    KNOWING THAT SILENCE BRINGS NO GOOD TO KINGS, . . . .  279 TWO KINGS          57
    I HAD THE WISDOM LOVE BRINGS FORTH: . . . . . . .    313 MEMORY YOUTH         2
    IS DEAD.  THE BOY THAT BRINGS MY GRIDDLE-CAKE . . .  339 SHEP GOATHERD       20
    IS DEAD.  THE BOY THAT BRINGS MY GRIDDLE CAKE . . .  339 SHEP GOATHERD   V   20
    BRINGS ME TO BIRTH AGAIN-- . . . . . . . . . . . .   346 ON WOMAN            32
    MAYBE THE BRIDE-BED BRINGS DESPAIR, . . . . . . .    388 SOLOMON WITCH       25
    FOR EACH AN IMAGINED IMAGE BRINGS . . . . . . . .    388 SOLOMON WITCH       26
    AND THAT MERE GROWING OLD, THAT BRINGS . . . . . .   401 DEMON BEAST         38
    THAT BRINGS MORE BLOSSOM TO AUTUMNAL CHILL . . . . .  465 HARUN RASHID    V  104
    BRINGS SUCH SATISFACTION . . . . . . . . . . . . .   533 FIRST CONFESS       11
    THAT DAY BRINGS ROUND THE NIGHT, THAT BEFORE DAWN  . .  563 MERU               13
    THE BROWN WEED BURDEN, SO THE SWORD BRINGS FEAR . . .  660 ISLE STAT II 1     45
    HE DIGS HIS CABBAGES.  HE BRINGS TO MIND . . . . .    696 MOSADA 2           18
    HALF HID.  HE BRINGS THE PEASANT'S ONLY KIN, . . . .  711 FERENCZ RENYI      50
    ACCURSED WHO BRINGS TO LIGHT OF DAY . . . . . . .     779 ACCURSED WHO        1
BRINK
    UPON THE STARRY BRINK. . . . . . . . . . . . . .     216 HAPPY TOWNLAND      52
    TO EASE THEIR WORLD-OLD THIRST ALONG THE BRINK . . .  663 ISLE STAT II 2     41
BRISTLES
    I WOULD THAT THE BOAR WITHOUT BRISTLES HAD COME FROM THE   153 CHANGE BELOVED    10
        WEST
BRITAIN
    WHAT NAME HAD THAT DEAD KING?  ARTHUR OF BRITAIN? . . .  242 SHADOW WATER B    404
BRITISH
    UPON THE BRITISH EMPIRE, . . . . . . . . . . . . .   583 GHOST ROG CASE      17
BRITTLE
    AS DANCE UPON THE SPEAR-GRASS BRITTLE, . . . . . . .  731 PRIEST FAIRY       78
BROACHED
    "IF YOU HAD BROACHED A MATTER . . . . . . . . . .    333 SOLOMON SHEBA       11
BROAD
    ON CREVROE OR BROAD KNOCKFEFIN, WITH MANY OF OLD THEY FEAST   59 OISIN 3      179
    ON CREVROE OR ON BROAD KNOCKFEFIN, WITH MANY OF OLD THEY      59 OISIN 3    V 179
        FAST
    BY A BROAD WATER-LILY LEAF: . . . . . . . . . . .    195 BAILE AILLINN      146
    THAT BROAD NOON HAS NEVER LIT, . . . . . . . . . .   632 MAN AND ECHO         4
    ON HER BROAD BREAST: BENEATH HER WITHERED BROWS . . .  685 SEEKER             73
    DANCING ON THE MOON'S BROAD STAIN, . . . . . . .     731 STREET DANCERS      15
    YE ON THE BROAD HIGH MOUNTAINS OF OLD ERI, . . . .    737 MOURN THEN ON        1
BROKE
    AND BROKE THE HEAVING RANKS OF BATTLE: . . . . . .    10 OISIN 1            124
    . . . FROM THE FOAM-PALE DISTANCE BROKE: . . . . .    47 OISIN 3              3
    . . . FROM THE DISTANCE BROKE: . . . . . . . . . .    47 OISIN 3         V    3
    AND BROKE BETWEEN MY HANDS THE STAFF . . . . . . .    84 MAD KING GOLL   V   33
    AND THROUGH THAT NEW BLADE'S GUARD THE OLD BLADE BROKE,   110 CUCHULAIN SEA   66
    AND THROUGH THE OTHER'S SHIELD HIS LONG BLADE BROKE,  110 CUCHULAIN SEA   V   66
    BROKE FROM HIS PARTED LIPS AND BROKE AGAIN, . . . .  182 QUEEN MAEVE         48
    BROKE FROM HIS PARTED LIPS AND BROKE AGAIN, . . . .  182 QUEEN MAEVE         48
    BEFORE HER LOVE-WORN HEART HAD BROKE, . . . . . .    194 BAILE AILLINN      127
    ABOUT THE STARS AND BROKE IN DAYS AND YEARS. . . .   206 ADAMS CURSE         33
    ABOUT THE STARN AND BROKE IN DAYS AND YEARS. . . .   206 ADAMS CURSE     V   33
    A SHELTER TILL THE DAYLIGHT BROKE. . . . . . . .    302 HOUR DAWN           15
    WHO BROKE MY HEART FOR HER . . . . . . . . . . .    336 YOUNG GIRL           6
    I TURNED ABOUT AND LOOKED WHERE BRANCHES BROKE . . .  490 COOLE BALLYLEE  V   15
    I BROKE MY HEART IN TWO . . . . . . . . . . . .     518 HIS CONFIDENCE       7
    AND BROKE THE CHAIN AND SET MY ANKLES FREE, . . . .  533 HER TRIUMPH          9
BROKEN       SEE WIND-BROKEN STORM-BROKEN
    OF BATTLES BROKEN BY HIS HANDS, . . . . . . . . .      7 OISIN 1            67
    WHERE BROKEN FAITH HAS NEVER BEEN KNOWN, . . . . .     8 OISIN 1            84
    FROM SOME DEAD WARRIOR'S BROKEN LANCE: . . . . . .    24 OISIN 1           367
    AND DEMONS BE BROKEN IN PIECES, AND TRAMPLED BENEATH THEM   61 OISIN 3       204
        IN DEATH.
    AND DEMONS, ALL BROKEN IN PIECES, BE TRAMPLED BENEATH THEM   61 OISIN 3    V 204
        IN DEATH.
    AH ME: TO BE SHAKEN WITH COUGHING AND BROKEN WITH OLD AGE   63 OISIN 3      217
        AND PAIN,
    UNDER A BROKEN TREE . . . . . . . . . . . . . .    131 OLD PENSIONER        2
    UPON A BROKEN TREE, . . . . . . . . . . . . . .    131 OLD PENSIONER       14
    BROKEN BOUGHS AND BLACKENED LEAVES. . . . . . . .   135 TWO TREES           28
    THERE, THROUGH THE BROKEN BRANCHES, GO . . . . . .   135 TWO TREES           33
    WITH BROKEN BOUGHS AND BLACKENED LEAVES . . . . .   135 TWO TREES       V   26
    ALL THINGS UNCOMELY AND BROKEN, ALL THINGS WORN OUT AND   142 ROSE IN HEART    1
        OLD,
    ALL THINGS UNCOMELY AND BROKEN, ALL THINGS WORN AND OLD,   142 ROSE IN HEART V  1
```

		PAGE	TITLE	LINE

BROKEN   (CONTINUED)
```
      BECAUSE EARTH, CRAZY FOR ITS BROKEN POWER, . . . . . . .   186 QUEEN MAEVE       124
      ARE TRODDEN AND BROKEN BY THE HERDS, . . . . . . . . . .   190 BAILE AILLINN      43
      BAILE'S HEART WAS BROKEN IN TWO: . . . . . . . . . . .    192 BAILE AILLINN      70
      WANDERING FROM BROKEN STREET TO STREET . . . . . . . .    196 BAILE AILLINN     167
      WAKE ALL BELOW!  WHY HAVE YOU BROKEN OUR SLEEP? . . . .   233 SHADOW WATER B    242
      THE YEW-BOUGH HAS BEEN BROKEN INTO TWO, . . . . . . .    241 SHADOW WATER B    394
      THE YEW BOUGH HAS BEEN BROKEN INTO TWO, . . . . . . .    241 SHADOW WATER B V  394
      LET THE BIRDS SCATTER, FOR THE TREE IS BROKEN, . . . .   250 SHADOW WATER B    584
      THE YEW-BOUGH HAS BEEN BROKEN INTO TWO, . . . . . . .    251 SHADOW WATER B    593
      YOU ARE BROKEN, YOU ARE BROKEN.  THE WORLD DRIFTS AWAY,  251 SHADOW WATER B    599
      YOU ARE BROKEN, YOU ARE BROKEN.  THE WORLD DRIFTS AWAY,  251 SHADOW WATER B    599
      THE YEW BOUGH HAS BEEN BROKEN INTO TWO, . . . . . . .    251 SHADOW WATER B V  593
      THE YEW BOUGH HAS BEEN BROKEN IN TWO, . . . . . . . .    251 SHADOW WATER B V  593
      BE AS BROKEN IN THE END. . . . . . . . . . . . . . .     313 TWO YEAR LATER     10
      I TOOK A BROKEN ROOT TO FLING . . . . . . . . . . .      317 APPOINTMENT         2
      AND SCATTER WHEELING IN GREAT BROKEN RINGS . . . . . .   322 SWANS AT COOLE     11
      "IT'S CERTAIN THAT MY LUCK IS BROKEN," . . . . . . .     332 ROUND TOWER        25
      IN THE BROKEN MIST . . . . . . . . . . . . . . . . .     349 HAWK               11
      BROKEN DREAMS . . . . . . . . . . . . . . . . . . . .    355 BROKEN DREAMS       T
      WILL SCARCELY FIND FOR HIM A BROKEN CRUST . . . . . .    373 PHASES OF MOON     23
      AND HAD BUT BROKEN KNEES FOR HIRE . . . . . . . . . .    411 TOWER              62
      TILL IT WAS BROKEN BY . . . . . . . . . . . . . . .      416 TOWER             179
      A PEAR-TREE BROKEN BY THE STORM. . . . . . . . . . .     424 ROAD AT DOOR       10
      A PEAR TREE BROKEN BY THE STORM. . . . . . . . . . .     424 ROAD AT DOOR    V  10
      I CLIMB TO THE TOWER-TOP AND LEAN UPON BROKEN STONE, . . 425 PHANTOM HATRED      1
      I CLIMB TO THE TOWER TOP AND LEAN UPON BROKEN STONE, . . 425 PHANTOM HATRED  V   1
      THE BROKEN WALL, THE BURNING ROOF AND TOWER . . . . .    441 LEDA AND SWAN      10
      UNDER A BROKEN TREE. . . . . . . . . . . . . . . . .     452 HUMAN DIGNITY       8
      AND BODIES BROKEN LIKE A THORN . . . . . . . . . . .     454 HIS MEMORIES        3
      FORGET ITS BROKEN TOYS . . . . . . . . . . . . . . .     473 ALL SOUL NIGHT     59
      UPON THE BROKEN, CRUMBLING BATTLEMENT, . . . . . . .     477 SELF AND SOUL       3
      AND SAPLINGS ROOT AMONG THE BROKEN STONE, . . . . . .    489 COOLE PARK 29      28
      THOUGH SOMEWHAT BROKEN BY THE LEAVES, THAT LIGHT . . .   555 RIBH AT TOMB       25
      IN BROKEN SENTENCES.  MY SOUL HAD FOUND . . . . . . .    557 RIBH ECSTASY        3
      FROM MARBLE OF A BROKEN SEPULCHRE, . . . . . . . . .     565 GYRES              20
      HER KNEE-CAP BROKEN, THAT GIRL I DECLARE . . . . . .     578 CRAZED GIRL         6
      HER KNEE CAP BROKEN: THAT GIRL I DECLARE . . . . . .     578 CRAZED GIRL     V   6
      MAYBE AT LAST, BEING BUT A BROKEN MAN, . . . . . . .     629 CIRCUS ANIMALS      3
      OLD KETTLES, OLD BOTTLES, AND A BROKEN CAN, . . . . .    630 CIRCUS ANIMALS     36
      UNDER BROKEN STONE I HALT . . . . . . . . . . . . .      632 MAN AND ECHO        2
      WAS BROKEN IN HIS QUIVERING HAND. . . . . . . . . .      671 ISLE STAT II 3    126
      AS MOTHS WITH BROKEN WINGS, AND AS WE SIT . . . . . .    671 ISLE STAT II 3    142
      MINE HEART-STRINGS ARE ALL BROKEN SAVING ONE, . . . .    684 SEEKER          V 69B
      WAKE ALL BELOW.  WHY HAVE YOU BROKEN OUR SLEEP? . . .    753 SHADOW WATER A    132
      O SCENT OF THE BROKEN APPLES! . . . . . . . . . . .      774 COME RIDE          14
      TO THE LOUD SANDS BEFORE DAY HAS BROKEN. . . . . . .     784 WOMANS BEAUTY      18
      AMID THE DARK BEFORE DAY HAD BROKEN. . . . . . . . .     784 WOMANS BEAUTY      20
BROKENHEARTED
      BROKENHEARTED, HAVING LOST HIS QUEEN . . . . . . . . .   242 SHADOW WATER B V  407
BROKEN-HEARTED
      BROKEN-HEARTED, HAVING LOST HIS QUEEN . . . . . . . .    242 SHADOW WATER B    407
      MATCHING OUR BROKEN-HEARTED WIT AGAINST HER WIT, . . .   362 HER COURTESY        7
BRONZE
      . . . WITH BRONZE AND SILVER AND GOLD. . . . . . . .      49 OISIN 3           32
      BETWEEN THE WALLS COVERED WITH BEATEN BRONZE, . . . .    180 QUEEN MAEVE        10
      THE POSTS OF POLISHED YEW, CIRCLED WITH BRONZE, . . .    279 TWO KINGS          48
      IN BRONZE, OR THAT IN DAZZLING MARBLE APPEARS, . . .     334 LIVING BEAUTY       5
      FOR ALL ITS BRONZE AND MARBLE, 'S BUT A MOUSE. . . .     418 ANCEST HOUSES      24
      AMID THE ORNAMENTAL BRONZE AND STONE . . . . . . . .     428 NINETEEN 19         5
      BUT KEEP A MARBLE OR A BRONZE REPOSE. . . . . . . .      445 SCHOOL CHILDR      52
      WHO HANDLED MARBLE AS IF IT WERE BRONZE, . . . . . .     566 LAPIS LAZULI       30
      IN MARBLE OR IN BRONZE, LACKED CHARACTER. . . . . . .    610 STATUES             3
      A BRONZE HEAD . . . . . . . . . . . . . . . . . . .      618 BRONZE HEAD         T
      HERE AT RIGHT OF THE ENTRANCE THIS BRONZE HEAD, . . .    618 BRONZE HEAD         1
BRONZED
      BRONZED PEACOCK FEATHERS, RED COMBS OF HER COCKS. . . .  433 NINETEEN 19       130
BRONZE-RINGED
      ROSE ROUND THE WALLS, AND THROUGH THE BRONZE-RINGED DOOR 286 TWO KINGS         215
BROOCH
      FOR BROOCH 'TWAS BOUND WITH A BRIGHT SEA-SHELL, . . . .    4 OISIN 1         V  28
      WITH THE PIN OF A BROOCH, . . . . . . . . . . . . .      344 DAWN                4
BROOD
      SPAKE THUS: "CUCHULAIN WILL DWELL THERE AND BROOD . . .  110 CUCHULAIN SEA      77
      AND CRIED, "CUCHULLIN WILL DWELL THERE AND BROOD, . . .  110 CUCHULLIN SEA   V  77
      AND BROOD ON HOPES AND FEAR NO MORE. . . . . . . . .     125 GOES FERGUS         6
      AND NO MORE TURN ASIDE AND BROOD . . . . . . . . . .     125 GOES FERGUS         7
      AND BROOD ON HOPES AND FEARS NO MORE. . . . . . . . .    125 GOES FERGUS     V   6
      AND MAY THE THOUGHTS OF IRELAND BROOD . . . . . . .      138 TO IRELAND         15
      AND STILL THE THOUGHTS OF IRELAND BROOD, . . . . . .     138 TO IRELAND      V  15
      "AND BROOD NO MORE WHERE THE FIRE IS BRIGHT . . . . .    140 HOSTING SIDHE   V   5
      BROOD HER HIGH LONELY MYSTERIES. . . . . . . . . . .     156 FORGOT BEAUTY      24
      AND BY THE UNLABOURING BROOD OF THE SKIES! . . . . .     164 PERFECT BEAUTY      5
      HAVE WRONG TO BROOD UPON--ENOUGH OF THAT, . . . . . .    444 SCHOOL CHILDR   V  30
      IN BEAUTY'S MURDEROUS BROOD, . . . . . . . . . . .       451 FIRST LOVE          2
      AND ROVE UNCEASING ROUND THEIR DREADFUL BROOD. . . .     681 SEEKER              5
      AND TRAILING CRIMSON VANS, A MUMBLING BROOD, . . . .     687 TWO TITANS         20
      WHY THEY WHO WILL THE HIGHEST SOMETIMES BROOD, . . .     711 FERENCZ RENYI      34
      MAYBE NOW A BEDOUIN'S BROOD, . . . . . . . . . . .       732 STREET DANCERS     40
      MINE WHERE WATERS BROOD AND TOSS! . . . . . . . . .      744 ROSY CROSS          7
```

```
                                             PAGE    TITLE          LINE
BROODED
    BROODED UPON SANCTITY . . . . . . . . . . . .   324 ROBERT GREGORY    20
BROODING
    IN BROODING MEMORY, NOR WEEP. . . . . . . .     11 OISIN 1      V 131B
    BROODING NO MORE UPON GOD'S WARS . . . . . .    113 ROSE OF PEACE      5
    OF SERAPHS, BROODING, EACH ALONE, . . . . . .   156 FORGOT BEAUTY  V  22
    WHERE GODS ARE BROODING IN A MOUNTAINOUS PLACE . . . .   757 SHADOW WATER A   198
BROODS
    AND SANG UNTO THE STARRY BROODS. . . . . . .     22 OISIN 1         326
    AND BY THE HEAVEN'S ALL-LABOURING BROODS: . . . . . .   164 PERFECT BEAUTY V   5
    AND BY THE HEAVEN'S UN-LABOURING BROODS: . . . . . .   164 PERFECT BEAUTY V   5
    THE FAERY BLOSSOM BROODS UPON THY LIPS. . . . . . .   678 ISLE STAT II 3   306
BROOK
    AND YOUNG HARES BROOK MY HARMLESS HOLD-- . . . . . .    84 MAD KING GOLL  V  47
    THE FALLING HAWTHORN BLOOM. BY MERE AND BROOK . . . .   677 ISLE STAT II 3   279
BROOM
    MAKE CLEAN AS A BROOM CLEANS, . . . . . . . .    62 OISIN 3         211
BROOM-STICKS
    FOR ALL THEIR BROOM-STICKS AND THEIR TEARS, . . . . .   343 DEJECTION        5
BROTHER
    EACH ONE WOVEN TO HIS BROTHER . . . . . . . .    22 OISIN 1         335
    IN THE HOUSE OF A CHILD, OF A FRIEND, OF A BROTHER. . . .    26 OISIN 1         401
    IN THE HOUSE OF HIS FRIEND, OF HIS KIN, OF HIS BROTHER,   26 OISIN 1      V 405
    TRUE BROTHER OF A COMPANY . . . . . . . . . .   137 TO IRELAND         2
    TRUE BROTHER OF THAT COMPANY . . . . . . . .    137 TO IRELAND     V   2
    MY BROTHER IN MOCHARABUIEE. . . . . . . . . .   178 FIDDLER DOONEY     4
    I PASSED MY BROTHER AND COUSIN: . . . . . . .   178 FIDDLER DOONEY     5
    MY BROTHER IS PRIEST OF KILBARNET, . . . . .    178 FIDDLER DOONEY V   3
    MY BROTHER IS PRIEST IN KILVARNET, . . . . .    178 FIDDLER DOONEY V   3
    "YOU BROUGHT ME WHERE YOUR BROTHER ARDAN SAT . . . .   280 TWO KINGS       79
    AND THANKED HER FOR HER KINDNESS TO HIS BROTHER, . . . .   286 TWO KINGS      212
    AND IN THE MIDST KING EOCHAID'S BROTHER STOOD, . . . .   286 TWO KINGS      217
    "I THANK YOU FOR YOUR KINDNESS TO MY BROTHER, . . . .   286 TWO KINGS    V 212
    MY BROTHER MOURTEEN IS WORN OUT . . . . . . .   301 RUN PARADISE       8
    BROTHER AND BROTHER, FRIEND AND FRIEND, . . . . .   540 FROM ANTIGONE    10
    BROTHER AND BROTHER, FRIEND AND FRIEND, . . . . .   540 FROM ANTIGONE    10
    JOY'S BROTHER, FEAR, DWELLS EVER IN EACH BREAST-- . . . .   651 ISLE STAT I 1   155
    JOY'S BROTHER, FEAR, LURKS IN EACH LEAFY WAY. . . . .   651 ISLE STAT I 1   156
    HARK! HE'S DEAD--MY DROWSY BROTHER, . . . . .    656 ISLE STAT I 3    18
    O BROTHER, LAY THY FLUTE UPON THY LIPS: . . . . .   681 SEEKER           6
    STAR-ENVIOUS. HE WAS A SPIRIT, BROTHER. . . . .   683 SEEKER          39
    WHERE IS OUR BROTHER PETER? WHEN YOU'RE NIGH, . . . .   696 MOSADA 2        12
    HE LOVES OUR BROTHER PETER IN HIS HEART. . . . .   696 MOSADA 2        16
    SEE YOU, BROTHER, CRANBERRY FRUIT-- . . . . .    727 LOVERS QUARREL    25
    LIKE BROTHER TO BROTHER, . . . . . . . . . .    769 BLOOD BOND         2
    LIKE BROTHER TO BROTHER, . . . . . . . . . .    769 BLOOD BOND         2
BROTHERHOOD
    AND DIE A PEARLY BROTHERHOOD: . . . . . . . .    66 HAPPY SHEPHERD    42
    FOR RUTH AND JOY HAVE BROTHERHOOD, . . . . .     66 HAPPY SHEPHERD V  42
    FOR THERE THE MYSTICAL BROTHERHOOD . . . . .    148 INTO TWILIGHT     10
    FOR THERE LIVE THE MYSTIC BROTHERHOOD . . . .   148 INTO TWILIGHT  V  10
BROTHER'S
    WITH HER DEAD BROTHER'S VALOUR . . . . . . .    365 HER RACE          11
BROTHERS
    TO JOIN HIS BROTHERS IN THE HOME OF YEARS . . . .    30 OISIN 2      V  17
    "MY BROTHERS SPRING OUT OF THEIR BEDS AT MORN, . . . .    32 OISIN 2        51
    "MY BROTHERS AND MY SISTERS LIVE AND THRIVE, . . . .    32 OISIN 2      V 50C
    CIRCLING THE BRAIN? MY BROTHERS WILL PASS DOWN . . . .   699 MOSADA 3         6
    THE BRAIN. MY BROTHERS WILL BE PASSING DOWN . . . .   699 MOSADA 3     V   6
    CIRCLING THE BRAIN? MY BROTHERS NOW PASS DOWN . . . .   699 MOSADA 3     V   6
BROUGHT
    UNTIL THE DANAAN POETS BROUGHT . . . . . . .      7 OISIN 1         63
    LOVE, TILL THE DANAAN POETS BROUGHT . . . . .     7 OISIN 1         63
    I NE'ER LOVED ANY TILL SONG BROUGHT ME . . . .     7 OISIN 1         69
    WHO BROUGHT US FOUND A TORCH, AND, WITH ITS FLARE . . .    37 OISIN 2      V 122
    HOPING AND FEARING, BROUGHT ME WINE AND BREAD. . . . .    41 OISIN 2      V 184A
    VIJAYA, I HAVE BROUGHT MY EVENING RICE: . . . .    72 ANASHU VIJAYA    23
    AND A YOUNG MAN BROUGHT HIM RED WINE . . . .    144 HOST OF AIR       19
    IF HE HAD BROUGHT US AMONG PEOPLED SEAS, . . . .   225 SHADOW WATER B V 68C
    WHERE DO YOU COME FROM? WHO BROUGHT YOU TO THIS PLACE?   235 SHADOW WATER B   284
    YOU DID NOT KNOW WHAT BROUGHT HIM TO HIS END, . . . .   240 SHADOW WATER B   382
    I DREAM THAT I HAVE BROUGHT . . . . . . . . .   255 WOMAN HOMER       10
    SICKNESS BROUGHT ME THIS . . . . . . . . . .    267 FRIEND ILLNESS     1
    BY THE ANCIENT HOLY HANDS THAT BROUGHT THEM . . . .   271 GREY ROCK    V  21
    "YOU BROUGHT ME WHERE YOUR BROTHER ARDAN SAT . . . .   280 TWO KINGS       79
    OF YOUR OWN PASSIONATE SERVING KIND WHO HAD BROUGHT . . . .   292 TO A SHADE       10
    OF YOUR OWN PASSIONATE SERVING KIND WHO HAS BROUGHT . . . .   292 TO A SHADE   V  10
    AND WHEN THE SECOND TWILIGHT BROUGHT . . . .    296 THREE BEGGARS     42
    I HAD BEEN HURT": AND TOPPLING BROUGHT . . . .   302 HOUR DAWN         19
    "WHEN I WAS BROUGHT TO BED," . . . . . . . .    308 PLAYER QUEEN       6
    TO BE BROUGHT . . . . . . . . . . . . . . .     310 WITCH              5
    A LONG BLAST UPON THE HORN THAT BROUGHT . . . .   324 ROBERT GREGORY    22
    THAT SHAKES THE SHUTTER, TO HAVE BROUGHT TO MIND . . . .   327 ROBERT GREGORY    90
    UNTIL IMAGINATION BROUGHT . . . . . . . . . .   328 ROBERT GREGORY    94
    I BALANCED ALL, BROUGHT ALL TO MIND, . . . .    328 IRISH AIRMAN      13
    LET THE YOUNG WISH. BUT WHAT HAS BROUGHT YOU HERE? . . .   339 SHEP GOATHERD      6
    BROUGHT THE BARE NEWS. HE HAD THROWN THE CROOK AWAY . . . .   339 SHEP GOATHERD     21
    LESS BITTER. THEY HAVE BROUGHT ME FROM THAT RIDGE . . . .   342 SHEP GOATHERD     87
    THAT COVERS ALL HE HAS BROUGHT . . . . . . .    345 ON WOMAN           5
    AND NO KNAVE BROUGHT TO BOOK . . . . . . . .    347 FISHERMAN         17
    SINBAD THE SAILOR'S BROUGHT A PAINTED CHEST, . . . .   371 ON GOING HOUSE    10
```

113

	PAGE	TITLE		LINE

BROUGHT   (CONTINUED)
BODY PERFECTION BROUGHT, ...   383 VISION ROBART   40
TO SUCH A PITCH OF FOLLY I AM BROUGHT, ...   384 VISION ROBART   58
ALL THAT THE BRIGAND APPLE BROUGHT . . . .   388 SOLOMON WITCH   15
OF THE HOVERING THING NIGHT BROUGHT ME. . . . . . .   390 IMAGE PAST   42
FOR HOW SHOULD I FORGET THE WISDOM THAT YOU BROUGHT, . . .   391 UNDER SATURN   4
YOUR COMING BROUGHT: THOUGH I ACKNOWLEDGE I HAVE GONE . .   391 UNDER SATURN   V   5
CHILLED BLOOD, THIS SWEETNESS BROUGHT: . . . . . .   401 DEMON BEAST   39
AND BROUGHT THEM IN A LITTLE COVERED DISH. . . . . . .   410 TOWER   32
TO WHOM THE LOVE-LORN LADY KYTELER BROUGHT . . . .   433 NINETEEN 19   129
THE BABYLONIAN STARLIGHT BROUGHT . . . .   438 SONGS PLAY 2   4
THE BABYLONIAN STAR-LIGHT BROUGHT . . . .   438 SONGS PLAY 2   V   4
THE SOUTH WIND BROUGHT IT LONGING, AND THE EAST WIND   449 OWEN AHERNE   5
    DESPAIR,
THE SOUTH WIND BROUGHT IT LONGING, AND THE EAST BROUGHT   449 OWEN AHERNE   V   5
    IN DESPAIR,
THE SOUTH WIND BROUGHT IT LONGING, AND THE EAST BROUGHT   449 OWEN AHERNE   V   5
    IN DESPAIR,
THE SOUTH WIND BROUGHT IT LONGING, AND THE EAST BROUGHT   449 OWEN AHERNE   V   5
    IT DESPAIR,
THE SOUTH WIND BROUGHT IT LONGING, AND THE EAST BROUGHT   449 OWEN AHERNE   V   5
    IT DESPAIR,
SHE WHO HAD BROUGHT GREAT HECTOR DOWN . . . . . .   455 HIS MEMORIES   15
"I HAVE BROUGHT A SLENDER BRIDE INTO THE HOUSE: . . . .   463 HARUN RASHID   49
BROUGHT FACE TO FACE WITH HIS OWN CLUMSINESS: . . . . .   479 SELF AND SOUL   48
THEY BROUGHT TO PASS: . . . .   505 GRAT INSTRUCT   2
THAT THEY HAD BROUGHT NO FABULOUS SYMBOL THERE . . . .   537 HER VISION   31
STRONG DRINK I HAD, AND IT BROUGHT ME TO SORROW, ...   544 TO SAME TUNE 1   13
WHAT BROUGHT THEM THERE SO FAR FROM THEIR HOME, ...   549 SEVERED HEAD   8
CIVILIZATION IS HOOPED TOGETHER, BROUGHT . . . . . .   563 MERU   1
SOMETHING TO PERFECTION BROUGHT": . . . .   577 WHAT THEN   19
HE BROUGHT IT ALL TO PASS: . . . .   586 PARNELLITES   14
WE THREE ALONE IN MODERN TIMES HAD BROUGHT . . . . .   603 GALLERY REVIS   45
STRONG DRINK I HAD, AND IT BROUGHT ME TO SORROW, ...   616 MARCH SONGS 3   13
HAD SHATTERED HER SOUL. PROPINQUITY HAD BROUGHT . . . .   619 BRONZE HEAD   18
AND THIS BROUGHT FORTH A DREAM AND SOON ENOUGH . . . .   630 CIRCUS ANIMALS   23
I HAVE BROUGHT HIS CROWN. AND I HAVE BROUGHT HIS QUEEN.   755 SHADOW WATER A   166
I HAVE BROUGHT HIS CROWN. AND I HAVE BROUGHT HIS QUEEN.   755 SHADOW WATER A   166
ANY THAT LIVED, AND I HAVE BROUGHT MY GALLEY . . . . .   756 SHADOW WATER A V 191A
YOU HAD BROUGHT DOWN BEFORE YOU DIED. . . . . . .   791 REPRISALS   2
BROW
. . . HER BROW ON THE MIDST OF MY BREAST: . . . . . .   52 OISIN 3   74
AND PEARL-PALE NEAVE LAY BY ME, HER BROW ON THE MIDST OF   52 OISIN 3   V   74
    MY BREAST:
FOR FAIR ARE POPPIES ON THE BROW: . . . .   67 HAPPY SHEPHERD   56
WITH A KISS AND A TEAR ON THY DROOPING BROW. . . . . .   79 FALLING LEAVES   8
YOUNG MAN, LIFT UP YOUR RUSSET BROW, ...   125 GOES FERGUS   4
PALE BROW, STILL HANDS, AND DIM HAIR. . . . . . .   152 LOSS OF LOVE   V   1
FOR THAT DIM BROW AND LINGERING HAND . . . .   156 FORGOT BEAUTY   V   15
NOR HEAVY KNITTING OF THE BROW . . . .   318 APPOINTMENT   9
WHOSE BEARD A MOONLIGHT RIVER IS, WHOSE BROW . . . .   657 ISLE STAT I 3   73
CAN ENTER THERE. SEE: SEE: ABOVE YON BROW . . . . .   659 ISLE STAT II 1   27
AND WHEREFORE SHOULD THY BRIGHT BROW ROAM . . . . .   686 LIFE   11
TO PLACE A KISS OF FIRE ON THE DIM BROW . . . . . .   688 TWO TITANS   47
FROM THE GREAT PAINTED WINDOW WRAPS HIS BROW, ...   697 MOSADA 2   37
UPON THE MOUNTAIN'S BROW. YONDER HE TREADS . . . .   703 MOSADA 3   114
FLED FROM HIS BROW WHERE THE HAIR WAS GREY: . . . .   728 PRIEST FAIRY   10
BROWED   SEE CLEAR-BROWED PLACID-BROWED
SORROW-WORN, YET PLACID BROWED. . . . .   733 STREET DANCERS V   56
BROWN   SEE SQUIRREL-BROWN
AND NOW A MAID, ON A SWIFT BROWN STEED . . . . . .   12 OISIN 1   V 142
YET SANG NO MORE AS WHEN, LIKE A BROWN BEE . . . . .   30 OISIN 2   15
BUT SANG NO MORE, AS WHEN, LIKE A BROWN BEE . . . . .   30 OISIN 2   V   15
. . . AND LATER THE SHORE-WEEDS BROWN. . . . . . .   57 OISIN 3   156
OR SEE THE BROWN MICE BOB . . . .   88 STOLEN CHILD   48
THE LINES ARE NOT HEAVY, NOR HEAVY THE LONG NETS BROWN--   91 OLD FISHERMAN V   5
BRING MY BROWN HUNTER NEAR, ...   97 FOXHUNTER   V   6
MY DERMOT DEAR AND BROWN, ...   97 FOXHUNTER   V   6
BROWN LOLLARD TREADS UPON THE LAWN, ...   98 FOXHUNTER   17
HE SMOOTHS THE LONG BROWN NOSE. . . . .   98 FOXHUNTER   20
BROWN DERMOT TREADS UPON THE LAWN. . . . .   98 FOXHUNTER   V   17
OVER THE WHITE-HORNED BULL AND THE BROWN BULL. . . . .   182 QUEEN MAEVE   58
AND THE BROWN BULL HAD NOT YET COME, ...   189 BAILE AILLINN   15
THE OLD BROWN THORN-TREES BREAK IN TWO HIGH OVER CUMMEN   206 HANRAHANS SONG   1
    STRAND,
THE OLD BROWN THORN TREES BREAK IN TWO HIGH OVER CUMANN'S   206 HANRAHANS SONG V   1
    STRAND,
WITH RED BEER AND BROWN BEER. . . . .   214 HAPPY TOWNLAND   8
WHEN WE HAVE NEITHER BROWN NOR YELLOW ALE? . . . .   240 SHADOW WATER B   387
I SAW A FLAGON OF BROWN ALE ABOARD HER. . . . . .   240 SHADOW WATER B   388
BROWN PENNY . . . .   268 BROWN PENNY   T
AH, PENNY, BROWN PENNY, BROWN PENNY, ...   268 BROWN PENNY   7
AH, PENNY, BROWN PENNY, BROWN PENNY, ...   268 BROWN PENNY   7
AH, PENNY, BROWN PENNY, BROWN PENNY, ...   268 BROWN PENNY   15
AH, PENNY, BROWN PENNY, BROWN PENNY, ...   268 BROWN PENNY   15
WHERE THE BROWN HARE MIGHT BE, ...   381 SONGS FOOL 2   4
A BROWN LIEUTENANT AND HIS MEN, ...   424 ROAD AT DOOR   6
BROWN, OR BLACK, OR CARROT, ...   492 ANNE GREGORY   9
OVER THE CROWN OF THE WILLOWS BROWN. . . . . . .   653 ISLE STAT I 2   30
OVER THE CROWN OF THE WILLOWS BROWN. . . . . . .   653 ISLE STAT I 2   51
THE BROWN WEED BURDEN, SO THE SWORD BRINGS FEAR . . . .   660 ISLE STAT II 1   45

114

BROWN   (CONTINUED)
A LONG, BROWN GRASSHOPPER OF MAIDS! PEACE, SIR! . . .   661 ISLE STAT II 1   69
HE NUMBERS. HE A BROWN FARM-HOUSE SEES, ...   710 FERENCZ RENYI   22
RINGED ROUND AND FONDLED, A BROWN FARM HOUSE SEES.   710 FERENCZ RENYI V   23
LIKE SMALL BROWN MOTHS, A-TREMBLE. "RENYI SAY . . .   713 FERENCZ RENYI   82
LIKE SMALL BROWN MOTHS, A-TREMBLE CEASELESSLY. . .   713 FERENCZ RENYI V   82
NESTED 'MONG THE VAPOURS BROWN. . . . .   731 STREET DANCERS   6
I SAID THE ALE WAS BROWN. I HAVE FOUND THE ALE, . .   759 SHADOW WATER A   244
IT IS THE BROWN ALE DOES IT. GIVE ME YOUR SWORDS.   766 SHADOW WATER A V   372
AND TELL ITS STORY OVER THEIR BROWN ALE. . . . .   767 SHADOW WATER A   393
(O THE BROWN AND THE YELLOW BEER!) . . . . . .   779 GOING THE ROAD   2
(O THE BROWN AND THE YELLOW BEER!) . . . . . .   779 GOING THE ROAD   6
(O THE BROWN AND THE YELLOW BEER!) . . . . . .   779 GOING THE ROAD   10
BROWNING
WHAT ROBERT BROWNING MEANT . . . .   605 YOU CONTENT   22
BROWS
THEIR BROWS WERE WHITE AS FRAGRANT MILK, ...   15 OISIN 1   204
THEIR BROWS WERE WHITE AS THE FRAGRANT MILK . . . .   15 OISIN 1 V   204
AND, GATHERING ON OUR BROWS A FROWN, ...   20 OISIN 1   296
AND, GATHERING ON OUR BROWS A FROWN, ...   20 OISIN 1 V   297
SAD NIAM CAME NEAR ME, AND LAID HER BROWS ON THE MIDST   52 OISIN 3 V   74
  OF MY BREAST
AND CHAPLET THEIR CALM BROWS WITH LEAFAGE DIM, . .   127 DREAM OF FAERY V   32
AND CHAPLET THEIR CALM BROWS WITH LEAFAGE COOL! .   127 DREAM OF FAERY V   32
PALE BROWS, STILL HANDS AND DIM HAIR, ...   152 LOSS OF LOVE   1
ON HER BROAD BREAST! BENEATH HER WITHERED BROWS . .   685 SEEKER   73
BROWSE
WHERE MY GOATS BROWSE ON THE SCARCE GRASS OR LEAP . . .   339 SHEP GOATHERD   8
BROW-SHADING
ONE HAND BROW-SHADING, FAR ACROSS THE NIGHT, ...   663 ISLE STAT II 2   27
BROWSING
AND HIS OWN FLOCK WAS BROWSING AT THE DOOR. . . .   340 SHEP GOATHERD   27
NOW HER SHEEP ALL BROWSING MEET . . . .   646 ISLE STAT I 1   22
BRUISE
AND FILL ME WITH THY RAGE, THAT I MAY BRUISE . . . .   698 MOSADA 2   54
BRUISED
THE BODY IS NOT BRUISED TO PLEASURE SOUL, ...   445 SCHOOL CHILDR   58
BRUISING
BRUISING THE DARKNESS WITH THEIR CRACKLING LIGHT! . . .   687 TWO TITANS   2
BRUSH
BRUSH LIGHTLY AS HAYMOUSE EARTH'S PEBBLES, ...   56 OISIN 3   128
BRUSH LIGHTLY AS HAY MOUSE EARTH'S PEBBLES, . . .   56 OISIN 3 V   128
WHETHER WE HAVE CHOSEN CHISEL, PEN OR BRUSH, . . .   368 EGO DOMINUS   14
THE PAINTER'S BRUSH CONSUMES HIS DREAMS! . . . .   438 SONGS PLAY 2   12
BUT WHERE IS THE BRUSH THAT COULD SHOW ANYTHING . .   602 GALLERY REVIS   28
BRUSHED
WHEN BRUSHED WITH THE WINGS OF THE OWLS, ...   53 OISIN 3   98
BRUSHES
WHAT BRUSHES FLY AND MOTH ASIDE? . . . .   625 NATIVITY   7
BRUSHING
BRUSHING BACK HIS YELLOW HAIR! . . . .   729 PRIEST FAIRY   38
BRUTAL
THE HEART'S GROWN BRUTAL FROM THE FARE! . . . . .   425 STARES NEST   17
THE HEART GROWS BRUTAL FROM THE FARE, ...   425 STARES NEST V   17
FOUL GOAT-HEAD, BRUTAL ARM APPEAR, ...   612 NEWS ORACLE   33
BRUTE
SO MASTERED BY THE BRUTE BLOOD OF THE AIR, ...   441 LEDA AND SWAN   12
AND THE BRUTE DOLPHINS PLUNGE . . . .   612 NEWS ORACLE   20
BRYCELINDE
I HAVE NO HAPPINESS IN DREAMING OF BRYCELINDE, . . .   209 UNDER THE MOON   1
I FIND NO HAPPINESS IN SHADY BRYCELINDE . . . . .   209 UNDER THE MOON V   1
BUAL'S
AND SET THEM DIGGING UNDER BUAL'S HILL. . . . . .   184 QUEEN MAEVE   93
BUAN'S
ON THE HEIR OF ULADH, BUAN'S SON, ...   189 BAILE AILLINN   4
BUBBLE
BUBBLE UPON THE TABLE. A GHOST MAY COME! . . . .   470 ALL SOUL NIGHT   5
AND NOW AND THEN A BUBBLE RISE. I HEAR . . . . .   722 WITCH VIVIEN   63
BUBBLED
LONG SIGHS AROSE IN OUR SPIRITS, BENEATH US BUBBLED THE   48 OISIN 3   20
  GROUND.
BUBBLES
LIKE BUBBLES IN A FROZEN POND! . . . .   22 OISIN 1   336
AND CHASE THE FROTHY BUBBLES, ...   87 STOLEN CHILD   21
"OR SEEK WHERE SWEETEST WATER BUBBLES, ...   731 PRIEST FAIRY   79
BUBBLING
A LITTLE RUNNEL MADE A BUBBLING STRAIN, ...   39 OISIN 2   156
DUSKY AND HERBLESS, WHERE A BUBBLING STRAIN . . .   39 OISIN 2 V   156
IN A REVERIE FORGETFUL OF ALL THINGS, OVER THE BUBBLING   56 OISIN 3   140
  GROUND.
IN REVERIE FORGETFUL OF ALL THINGS, OVER THE BUBBLING   56 OISIN 3 V   140
  GROUND.
AND TRAMPLED IN THE BUBBLING MIRE, ...   83 MAD KING GOLL   26
AND TRAMPLED ON THE BUBBLING MIRE, ...   83 MAD KING GOLL V   26
AND FISHES, BUBBLING TO THE BRIM, ...   254 HIS DREAM V   9
AND LAUGH'D, SO, SO ALONG THE BUBBLING RILLS . . .   645 ISLE STAT I 1   18
TO WANDER BY THE BUBBLING SHORE. . . . .   668 ISLE STAT II 3   57
MID BUBBLING LEAVES A WANDERING SONG-RAPT BIRD . .   672 ISLE STAT II 3   154
BUCKET
WHO DRAWS A BUCKET WITH THE REST . . . .   335 YOUNG BEAUTY   5

BUCKLED
    THAT NOBLE BLADE THE MUSES BUCKLED ON, ...   489 COOLE PARK 29   10
BUCKLERS
    AND HEARD THE FOEMEN'S BUCKLERS RATTLE, ...   10 OISIN 1   123
    AND HEARD THE FOEMAN'S BUCKLERS RATTLE, ...   10 OISIN 1   V 123
BUCKSKIN
    FOR NATURE'S PULLED HER TRAGIC BUCKSKIN ON . . . . . .   490 COOLE BALLYLEE V   12
BUD
    AND SHAKE THE BLOSSOM FROM THE BUD . . . .   396 ROSE TREE   11
BUDDHA
    A BUDDHA, HAND AT REST, ...   383 VISION ROBART   19
BUDDHA'S
    GRIMALKIN CRAWLS TO BUDDHA'S EMPTINESS. . . . .   611 STATUES   24
BUDDING
    AND STIRS THE YOUNG KID'S BUDDING HORN, ...   18 OISIN 1   264
BUDS
    WHILE O'ER THE BUDS, AND O'ER THE GRASS-BLADES, BRIGHT . .   704 REMEMBRANCE   3
BUFFETED
    BUFFETED BY SUCH SEAS! . . . .   530 DELPHIC ORACLE   2
BUGLE
    THUS FOR ANOTHER'S BUGLE CALL! . . . .   671 ISLE STAT II 3   136
BUILD
    "WHAT DO YOU BUILD WITH SAILS FOR FLIGHT?" . . . .   69 CLOAK BOAT   6
    "I BUILD A BOAT FOR SORROW! . . . .   70 CLOAK BOAT   7
    A BOAT I BUILD FOR SORROW! . . . .   70 CLOAK BOAT   V   7
    AND A SMALL CABIN BUILD THERE, OF CLAY AND WATTLES MADE!   117 ISLE INNISFREE   2
    I HUNGER TO BUILD THEM ANEW AND SIT ON A GREEN KNOLL APART,   143 ROSE IN HEART   6
    I BADE MY HEART BUILD THESE POOR RHYMES! . . . .   158 BELOVED RHYMES   3
    TO BUILD A PERFECT BEAUTY IN RHYME . . . .   164 PERFECT BEAUTY   3
    TO BUILD THE PERFECT BEAUTY IN RHYME, ...   164 PERFECT BEAUTY V   3
    MUST END AT THE DUMB STONE? BUT WHERE WE BUILD . . . .   284 TWO KINGS   179
    AMONG WHAT RUSHES WILL THEY BUILD, ...   323 SWANS AT COOLE   27
    MAY BUILD IN THE CRACKED MASONRY AND CRY . . . . . .   423 MY DESCENDANTS   15
    THE BEES BUILD IN THE CREVICES . . . .   424 STARES NEST   1
    COME BUILD IN THE EMPTY HOUSE OF THE STARE. . . . . .   424 STARES NEST   5
    COME BUILD IN THE EMPTY HOUSE OF THE STARE. . . . . .   425 STARES NEST   10
    COME BUILD IN THE EMPTY HOUSE OF THE STARE. . . . . .   425 STARES NEST   15
    COME BUILD IN THE EMPTY HOUSE OF THE STARE. . . . . .   425 STARES NEST   20
    AND THOSE THAT BUILD THEM AGAIN ARE GAY. . . . . . .   566 LAPIS LAZULI   36
    HERE WHERE THE ROUND WAVES COME, HERE LET THEM BUILD, . .   663 ISLE STAT II 2   19
    WHAT DO YOU BUILD WITH SAILS FOR FLIGHT? . . . . . .   666 ISLE STAT II 3   6
    A BOAT I BUILD FOR SORROW. . . . .   666 ISLE STAT II 3   7
    TO BUILD THE CIRCLING SEATS, WHERE HIGH IN AIR . . . .   699 MOSADA 3   18
BUILDED
    OF STORIES BUILDED BY HIS WORDS . . . .   7 OISIN 1   68
    . . . THE OWLS HAD BUILDED THEIR NESTS IN THEIR LOCKS, . .   49 OISIN 3   39
BUILDER
    (I WONDER IF THE BUILDER HAS BEEN PAID) . . . .   292 TO A SHADE   3
BUILDING
    BUILDING A SORROWFUL LOVELINESS . . . .   158 BELOVED RHYMES   5
    BUILDING YARD AND STORMY SHORE, ...   530 OLD TOM AGAIN V   5
BUILDINGS
    AND BUILDINGS THAT A HAUGHTIER AGE DESIGNED, ...   418 ANCEST HOUSES   34
BUILDING-YARD
    BUILDING-YARD AND STORMY SHORE, ...   530 OLD TOM AGAIN   5
BUILDS
    SHE BUILDS HER NEST UPON A NARROW LEDGE . . . . . .   285 TWO KINGS   194
BUILT   SEE HEAVILY-BUILT
    OUT OF THE SEVENFOLD SEAS, BUILT THE DARK HALL . . . .   38 OISIN 2   131
    OUT OF THE SEVEN-FOLD SEAS, BUILT THE DARK HALL . . . .   38 OISIN 2   V 131
    AND A SMALL CABIN BUILT THERE, OF CLAY AND WATTLES MADE!   117 ISLE INNISFREE V 2
    I HELPED YOUR FATHERS WHEN THEY BUILT THESE WALLS, . . .   184 QUEEN MAEVE   97
    HE RAN TOWARDS THE HOUSE HIS FATHERS BUILT . . . . .   279 TWO KINGS   V 45E
    A HEAVILY BUILT FALSTAFFAN MAN, ...   423 ROAD AT DOOR   V 2
    THAT PURITY BUILT UP THE STATE . . . .   460 THREE MONUMENT   6
    WE THE GREAT GAZEBO BUILT, ...   476 EVA GORE-BOOTH 30
    ALL THINGS FALL AND ARE BUILT AGAIN, ...   566 LAPIS LAZULI   35
    THAT HAVE BUILT ALL ARE DUST ON A MOTH'S WING. . . . .   757 SHADOW WATER A   205
BULBEN
    UNDER BEN BULBEN TO THE MEET, ...   397 POLIT PRISONER 14
    UPON BEN BULBEN SIDE . . . .   398 BREAK OF DAY   6
    OUT OF BEN BULBEN AND KNOCKNAREA, ...   549 SEVERED HEAD   2
    UNDER BEN BULBEN . . . .   636 BEN BULBEN   T
    WHERE BEN BULBEN SETS THE SCENE. . . . .   637 BEN BULBEN   11
BULBEN'S
    OR THE HUMBLER WORM, I CLIMBED BEN BULBEN'S BACK . . . .   409 TOWER   9
    UNDER BARE BEN BULBEN'S HEAD . . . .   640 BEN BULBEN   84
BULK
    AND HIS LOOSE BULK BE THROWN IN THE LOUD TIDE." . . . .   35 OISIN 2   91
    CAST THE LOOSE BULK, LEST NIAM FEAR HIM DEAD! . . . .   41 OISIN 2   V 183
BULL
    OVER THE WHITE-HORNED BULL AND THE BROWN BULL. . . . .   182 QUEEN MAEVE   58
    OVER THE WHITE-HORNED BULL AND THE BROWN BULL. . . . .   182 QUEEN MAEVE   58
    AND THE BROWN BULL HAD NOT YET COME, ...   189 BAILE AILLINN   15
    THAT CHANGED A LOVER FOR A BULL. . . . .   509 JANE REPROVED   6
    JOHN BULL AND THE SEA ARE FRIENDS! . . . .   583 GHOST ROG CASE   4
    JOHN BULL HAS STOOD FOR PARLIAMENT, ...   583 GHOST ROG CASE 11
    JOHN BULL HAS GONE TO INDIA . . . .   583 GHOST ROG CASE 21
BULLETS
    WHERE WORM THE REBELS, OR MY BULLETS LAY . . . . . .   713 FERENCZ RENYI   83

BULLO
    LULLABULLOO, BULOO, BULOO, LULLABULLOO, BULLO. • • • • 594 COLONEL MARTIN V REF
BULOO
    LULLABULLOO, BULOO, BULOO, LULLABULLOO, BULLO. • • • • 594 COLONEL MARTIN V REF
    LULLABULLOO, BULOO, BULOO, LULLABULLOO, BULLO. • • • • 594 COLONEL MARTIN V REF
BULWARK
    AND BEAT THE BULWARK OF YOUR SHIP ON MINE, • • • • • • 236 SHADOW WATER B 312
    OR CROWD BEHIND THE BULWARK, THAT WE SEEM • • • • • • 751 SHADOW WATER A 94
    BULWARK TO BULWARK, AND SQUARE HER SAIL BY OURS. • • • • 752 SHADOW WATER A 129
    BULWARK TO BULWARK, AND SQUARE HER SAIL BY OURS. • • • • 752 SHADOW WATER A 129
BUM
    BELLY, SHOULDER, BUM, • • • • • • • • • • • • 612 NEWS ORACLE 34
BUNCH
    OUT OF A NEIGHBOURING BUNCH OF HEATHER; • • • • • • 728 PRIEST FAIRY 20
BUNCHES
    SEE! OH, SEE! THE DEW-DROWNED BUNCHES • • • • • • • 655 ISLE STAT I 3 1
BUNCHING
    MIGHT BE ACCOMPLISHED. BUNCHING THE CURTAIN UP • • • • 183 QUEEN MAEVE 68
BUNDLE
    A BUNDLE OF RAGS UPON A CRUTCH, • • • • • • • • • 302 HOUR DAWN 2
    TO BUNDLE TIME AWAY • • • • • • • • • • • • 317 NIGHT COME 11
    A BUNDLE OF TEMPESTUOUS CLOUD IS BLOWN • • • • • • • 541 PARN FUNERAL 1 2
    A BUNDLE OF LINEN. SHROUDS BY TWO AND THREE • • • • • 634 CUCHULAIN COMF 9
BUNDLED
    THE WIND HAS BUNDLED UP THE CLOUDS HIGH OVER KNOCKNAREA, 207 HANRAHANS SONG 6
    THE WINDS HAVE BUNDLED UP THE CLOUDS HIGH OVER KNOCKNAREA 207 HANRAHANS SONG V 6
    ANGERS THAT ARE LIKE BUNDLED CLOUDS HAVE SET OUR HEARTS 207 HANRAHANS SONG V 8
      ABEAT;
BUOYED
    AND GOD'S BELL BUOYED TO BE THE WATER'S CARE; • • • • • 114 ROSE OF BATTLE 4
    • • • BUOYED OUT ON THE FOAM OF THE SEA! • • • • • • 122 WHITE BIRDS 12
BURDEN
    • • • BUT FELL WITH THEIR BURDEN AT LENGTH. • • • • • 60 OISIN 3 186
    AND LO! MY ANCIENT BURDEN MAY DEPART. • • • • • • • 69 SAD SHEPHERD 24
    AND WHAT TO ME WAS BURDEN WITHOUT END, • • • • • • • 102 FERGUS DRUID 12
    WHILE DAY ITS BURDEN ON TO EVENING BORE, • • • • • • 110 CUCHULAIN SEA 70
    AND ALL THE BURDEN OF HER MYRIAD YEARS. • • • • • • 120 SORROW OF LOVE V 8
    EVEN IN AN OLD STORY, IS A BURDEN NOT TO BE BORNE. • • 210 UNDER THE MOON 20
    I BEAR A BURDEN THAT MIGHT WELL TRY • • • • • • • 380 SONGS FOOL 1 13
    SHOULD FIND NO BURDEN BUT ITSELF AND YET SHOULD BE WORN 449 OWEN AHERNE 3
      OUT.
    IT COULD NOT DEAR THAT BURDEN AND THEREFORE IT WENT MAD. 449 OWEN AHERNE 4
    THREE SONGS TO THE ONE BURDEN • • • • • • • • • 605 SONGS BURDEN 1 T
    THE BROWN WEED BURDEN, SO THE SWORD BRINGS FEAR • • • • 660 ISLE STAT II 1 45
    BENEATH THE BURDEN OF THE INFINITE; • • • • • • • 674 ISLE STAT II 3 V 212
    LAY DOWN THE BURDEN OF THY RACE, • • • • • • • • • 736 SUMMER EVENING 14
BURDENED
    BEYOND THE LAKE, WHOSE SMALLEST WAVE WAS BURDENED • • • 656 ISLE STAT I 3 31
BURDENS
    NOR LANDS THAT SEEM TOO DIM TO BE BURDENS ON THE HEART! 209 UNDER THE MOON 5
    OR LANDS THAT SEEMED TOO OLD TO BE BURDENS ON THE HEART, 209 UNDER THE MOON V 5
    THAT HAD SUCH BURDENS ON THE MIND. • • • • • • • • 432 NINETEEN 19 94
    THEY PITCH THEIR BURDENS OFF. • • • • • • • • • • 612 NEWS ORACLE 24
BURDENSOME
    BURDENSOME BEAUTY--FOR YOUR SOLE SAKE • • • • • • • 356 BROKEN DREAMS 10
    BURDENSOME BEAUTY--BUT FOR YOUR SAKE • • • • • • • • 356 BROKEN DREAMS V 10
BURGHERS
    THE BURGHERS OF THE NIGHT FADE ONE BY ONE. • • • • • • 700 MOSADA 3 40
BURIAL
    AND PASSING THE FIRBOLGS' BURIAL MOUNDS, • • • • • • 3 OISIN 1   V 16
    WHERE MEN HAVE HEAPED NO BURIAL MOUNDS, • • • • • • 8 OISIN 1   V 82
    AND SHOULD HE DIE TO HEAP HIS BURIAL MOUND • • • • • • 280 TWO KINGS   V 82
BURIAL-MOUND
    AND SHOULD HE DIE TO HEAP HIS BURIAL-MOUND • • • • • • 280 TWO KINGS 82
BURIAL-MOUNDS
    AND PASSING THE FIRBOLGS' BURIAL-MOUNDS, • • • • • • 3 OISIN 1 16
    WHERE MEN HAVE HEAPED NO BURIAL-MOUNDS, • • • • • • 8 OISIN 1 82
BURIED
    BURIED AND MIGHTY. WHEN THROUGH THE GREAT DOOR • • • • 39 OISIN 2 151
    BURIED AND MIGHTY. THENCE I JOURNEYED NOT • • • • • 39 OISIN 2   V 151
    BURIED UNDER THE SLEEPY GROUND, • • • • • • • • • 67 HAPPY SHEPHERD 48
    (WHO'S BURIED IN THE SLEEPY GROUND), • • • • • • • 67 HAPPY SHEPHERD 48
    WHO HAS BEEN BURIED SOME TWO THOUSAND YEARS? • • • • • 181 QUEEN MAEVE 35
    HAVE BURIED NOTHING BUT MY GOLDEN ARMS. • • • • • • 243 SHADOW WATER B 431
    WHERE THE O'BYRNES AND BYRNES ARE BURIED, • • • • • 331 ROUND TOWER 9
    WAS BURIED NEAR THE ASTROLOGER. • • • • • • • • 361 ALF POLLEXFEN 26
    AND YET, TWICE BORN, TWICE BURIED, GROW HE MUST, • • • 374 PHASES OF MOON 48
    BUT WHEN THE MASTER'S BURIED MICE CAN PLAY, • • • • 418 ANCEST HOUSES 22
    TO THINK OF BURIED HECTOR • • • • • • • • • • 455 HIS MEMORIES 5
    TIME I WERE BURIED," SAID THE OLD, OLD MAN. • • • • 548 TO SAME TUNE 3 10
    TIME I WERE BURIED," SAID THE OLD, OLD MAN. • • • • 548 TO SAME TUNE 3 20
    TIME I WERE BURIED," SAID THE OLD, OLD MAN. • • • • 549 TO SAME TUNE 3 30
    THEY BUT THRUST THEIR BURIED MEN • • • • • • • 637 BEN BULBEN 23
    "WE BURIED LATE IN A HAZEL DELL • • • • • • • • 729 PRIEST FAIRY 43
BURKE
    THE PEOPLE OF BURKE AND OF GRATTAN • • • • • • • 414 TOWER 132
    • • • BERKELEY AND BURKE HAVE TRAVELLED THERE. • • • 481 BLOOD AND MOON 18
    AND HAUGHTIER-HEADED BURKE THAT PROVED THE STATE A TREE, 481 BLOOD AND MOON 22
    AND HAUGHTIER HEADED BURKE THAT PROVED THE STATE A TREE 481 BLOOD AND MOON V 22
    MY GREAT-GRANDFATHER SPOKE TO EDMUND BURKE • • • • • 486 SEVEN SAGES 1
    BURKE WAS A WHIG. WHETHER THEY KNEW OR NOT, • • • • 486 SEVEN SAGES 8

	PAGE	TITLE		LINE
BURKE (CONTINUED)				
GOLDSMITH AND BURKE, SWIFT AND THE BISHOP OF CLOYNE • • •	486	SEVEN SAGES		9
BURKE'S				
HARRIED, AND BURKE'S GREAT MELODY AGAINST IT. • • • • • •	487	SEVEN SAGES		16
BURN SEE OUT-BURN				
YOUNG WARRIOR." "NAY," I ANSWERED; "MY HANDS BURN • • •	35	OISIN 2	V	89B
DREAM, UNTIL GOD BURN NATURE WITH A KISS? • • • • • •	128	DREAM OF FAERY		47
UNTIL HE BURN UP NATURE WITH A KISS;— • • • • • • •	128	DREAM OF FAERY	V	47
AND ALL MEN'S HEARTS MUST BURN AND BEAT; • • • • • •	158	BELOVED RHYMES		9
IS DROPPING SLEEP, UNTIL GOD BURN TIME, • • • • • •	164	PERFECT BEAUTY		7
AT HUSH OF EVENING TILL GOD BURN TIME • • • • • • •	164	PERFECT BEAUTY	V	7
TO BURN US TO THE MARROW IF WE STRIKE. • • • • • •	239	SHADOW WATER B		372
WAS THERE ANOTHER TROY FOR HER TO BURN? • • • • • •	257	NO SECOND TROY		12
SOME BURN DAMP FAGGOTS, OTHERS MAY CONSUME • • • • •	327	ROBERT GREGORY		81
I THOUGHT 'TWOULD BURN MY BODY • • • • • • • • •	335	SONG		15
TO BURN THAT STUMP ON THE ACROPOLIS, • • • • • • •	430	NINETEEN 19		46
CAN BURN OUT THAT SUFFERING • • • • • • • • • •	589	OLD WICKED MAN		57
THUS DO I BURN THESE PRECIOUS HERBS, WHOSE SMOKE • • •	691	MOSADA 1		39
THEY SAID I'D BURN IN HELL UNLESS I TOLD. • • • • •	694	MOSADA 1		108
SO SHE MUST BURN, YOU SAY? SHE MUST IN TRUTH. • • •	696	MOSADA 2		2
I WILL BURN HERESY FROM THIS MAD EARTH, • • • • • •	697	MOSADA 2		40
THAT SHALL BURN TIME WHEN TIMES HAVE EBBED AWAY. • • •	750	SHADOW WATER A		61
BURN THEIR BODIES UP FOR NOUGHT, • • • • • • • •	787	HUDDON DUDDON		14
BURNED				
A DEMON'S LEISURE: EYES, FIRST WHITE, NOW BURNED • • •	40	OISIN 2		168
WHEN WINDS HAVE GATHERED AND SUN AND MOON BURNED DIM • •	175	ELEMENT POWERS		15
THOUGH FLAME HAD BURNED THE WHOLE • • • • • • • •	267	FRIEND ILLNESS		4
THE MOTHS ARE WHEN THEY ARE BURNED? • • • • • • •	313	TWO YEAR LATER		4
THAT SEEMED AS THOUGH ICE BURNED AND WAS BUT THE MORE ICE,	316	COLD HEAVEN		2
THE WICK OF YOUTH BEING BURNED AND THE OIL SPENT, • • •	334	LIVING BEAUTY	V	3
WHEN OIL AND WICK ARE BURNED IN ONE; • • • • • • •	388	SOLOMON WITCH		30
A MAN IS KILLED, OR A HOUSE BURNED, • • • • • • •	425	STARES NEST		8
THOUGHT THAT UNLESS A LITTLE POWDER BURNED • • • • •	429	NINETEEN 19		21
OR BURNED GREAT CITIES DOWN, • • • • • • • • • •	789	SINGING HEAD		16
BURNING				
BURNING BETWEEN HER FINGERS, AND IN MINE • • • • • •	37	OISIN 2		125
TILL THE FAR DOORWAY GREW A BURNING BLOT • • • • • •	39	OISIN 2	V	152
HOW THE HAMMERS SPRING ON THE ANVIL, ON THE SPEARHEAD'S	52	OISIN 3		83
BURNING SPOT:				
• • • ON THE SPEAR-HEAD'S BURNING SPOT: • • • • •	52	OISIN 3	V	83
• • • ON THE BURNING STONES IS THEIR PLACE: • • • •	61	OISIN 3		197
• • • ON THE BURNING STONES OF WIDE HELL, • • • • •	61	OISIN 3		198
A METEOR OF THE BURNING HEART, • • • • • • • • •	78	INDIAN TO LOVE		14
CAOILTE TOSSING HIS BURNING HAIR, • • • • • • • •	140	HOSTING SIDHE		3
CAOILTE TOSSING HIS BURNING HAIR, • • • • • • • •	141	HOSTING SIDHE		15
BURNING IN FIRES OF A SLANDEROUS TONGUE. • • • • • •	148	INTO TWILIGHT		8
BUT WITH THE BURNING, LIVE, UNSHAKEN VOICE • • • • • •	183	QUEEN MAEVE		75
AND YOU HAVE GROWN TO BE A BURNING SOD • • • • • •	245	SHADOW WATER B		487
"PUT OFF THAT MASK OF BURNING GOLD • • • • • • •	263	MASK		1
THE MAJESTY THAT SHUTS HIS BURNING EYE: • • • • • •	265	THESE CLOUDS		2
THE MAJESTY THAT SHUTS HIS BURNING EYE. • • • • • •	265	THESE CLOUDS		12
WOMEN CAN FIND." WITH A MOST BURNING VOICE • • • • •	284	TWO KINGS	V	175
WHEREON A THING ONCE WALKED THAT SEEMED A BURNING CLOUD.	315	FALLEN MAJESTY		8
ONCE WALKED A THING THAT SEEMED, AS IT WERE, A BURNING	315	FALLEN MAJESTY	V	8
CLOUD.				
WHEN I HAD MY BURNING YOUTH! • • • • • • • • • •	329	MEN IMPROVE		15
AND THAT PROUD LOOK AS THOUGH SHE HAD GAZED INTO	354	HIS PHOENIX		29
THE BURNING SUN,				
BURNING ALONE BESIDE AN OPEN BOOK, • • • • • • • •	370	EGO DOMINUS		63
THE BURNING BOW THAT ONCE COULD SHOOT AN ARROW • • • •	377	PHASES OF MOON		119
WHO NEVER GAVE THE BURNING TOWN A THOUGHT; • • • • •	384	VISION ROBART		57
THE BROKEN WALL, THE BURNING ROOF AND TOWER • • • • •	441	LEDA AND SWAN		10
THE BURNING TREE • • • • • • • • • • • • • •	499	VACILLATION	V	T
BERENICE'S BURNING HAIR. • • • • • • • • • • • •	519	HER DREAM		8
THE SKIES MORE DIM, THOUGH BURNING LIKE A SHIELD, • • •	656	ISLE STAT I 3		26
OR HER EVER BURNING EYES, • • • • • • • • • •	658	ISLE STAT I 3		85
THIS VISION OF PETER AND THE BURNING GATE. • • • • •	696	MOSADA 2		21
OF HOLY PETER OF THE BURNING GATE: • • • • • • •	696	MOSADA 2	V	20
HIS MEMORY NOW IS A TALL PILLAR, BURNING • • • • • •	738	MOURN THEN ON		15
AT THE BURNING WHEEL OF LOVE • • • • • • • • •	776	AGAINST WITCH		34
I MOCK AT ALL SO BURNING OUT. • • • • • • • • •	787	HUDDON DUDDON		15
BUT HOW THEY MOCK US BURNING OUT. • • • • • • • •	787	HUDDON DUDDON	V	15
BURNISHED				
THE HEAVY BOUGHS, THE BURNISHED DOVE • • • • • • •	78	INDIAN TO LOVE		16
THE GREAT BOUGHS, AND THE BURNISHED DOVE • • • • • •	78	INDIAN TO LOVE	V	16
AND GREAT BOUGHS, AND THE BURNISHED DOVE • • • • • •	78	INDIAN TO LOVE	V	16
BREATHE ON THE BURNISHED MIRROR OF THE WORLD • • • • •	228	SHADOW WATER B		132
THOSE STILTED BOYS, THAT BURNISHED CHARIOT, • • • • •	629	CIRCUS ANIMALS		7
BREATHE ON THE BURNISHED MIRROR OF THE WORLD • • • • •	750	SHADOW WATER A		69
BURNS				
AT HUSH OF EVENING TILL GOD BURNS TIME • • • • • • •	164	PERFECT BEAUTY	V	7
BURNS BUT MORE CLEARLY. O SHE HAD NOT THESE WAYS • • •	200	FOLLY COMFORT		11
A LAMP BURNS ON BESIDE THE OPEN BOOK • • • • • • •	367	EGO DOMINUS		3
A LAMP BURNS ON ABOVE THE OPEN BOOK • • • • • • •	367	EGO DOMINUS	V	3
BURNT				
LIKE A CANDLE BURNT OUT, • • • • • • • • • •	142	MOODS		2
THAT THE TOPLESS TOWERS BE BURNT • • • • • • • •	617	LONG-LEG FLY		11
BURROW				
I CHOSE THIS BURROW UNDER GROUND. • • • • • • • •	305	HOUR DAWN		73
BURROWING				
WHO'S BURROWING SOMEWHERE IN THE GROUND, • • • • • •	272	GREY ROCK		33

118

BURST
>BURST FROM A GREAT DOOR MARRED BY MANY A BLOW . . . . .   31 OISIN 2   29
>I BURST THE CHAIN; STILL EARLESS, NERVELESS, BLIND, . . .   36 OISIN 2   97
>THERE IS NO MEASURE THAT IT WOULD NOT BURST. . . . . .   245 SHADOW WATER B   484
>AND HAVING SAID IT, BURST IN TEARS. . . . .   273 GREY ROCK   48
>OR EVERY BELLOWS BURST, BE HAPPY STILL. . . . . . .   405 FOR DAUGHTER   72
>THE TRUMPETERS MIGHT BURST WITH TRUMPETING . . . . .   429 NINETEEN 19   22
>AND HIS BEATING HEART WOULD BURST. . . . .   454 EMPTY CUP   6
>AND THE TRUMPETS ALL ARE BURST, ...   527 AM OF IRELAND   22
>HER SPIRIT. AS SHE MOVES, THE FOAM-GLOBES BURST . . . .   687 TWO TITANS   14
BURSTING
>THAT UNDER BURSTING DAWN . . . .   416 TOWER   176
>O WHAT A BURSTING OUT THERE WAS, ...   457 SUMMER SPRING   13
>THAN ALL MY BURSTING SPRINGTIME KNEW. A GIRL . . . .   466 HARUN RASHID   105
BURSTS
>YOUNG FERENCZ RENYI BURSTS HIS BONDS--AT LAST, ...   714 FERENCZ RENYI   V 116
BURTHEN
>AND LO--MY HEAVY BURTHEN MAY DEPART!" . . . . . .   69 SAD SHEPHERD   V 24
>IS THE BURTHEN AND PERSISTENCE . . . .   647 ISLE STAT I 1   75
>BENEATH THE BURTHEN OF THE INFINITE, ...   674 ISLE STAT II 3   212
>FOR LONG THE BURTHEN OF THEIR TALKING GRIEFS. . . . .   693 MOSADA 1   71
>THE BURTHEN OF THY TRUTH. REACH DOWN THY HANDS . . .   698 MOSADA 2   53
BURY
>HE BADE THEM TAKE AND BURY HER . . . .   571 THREE BUSHES   71
BUSH
>THROUGH BUSH THEY PLUNGED AND OVER IVIED ROOT, ...   278 TWO KINGS   32
BUSHES   SEE CURRANT-BUSHES
>BETWEEN TWO BUSHES UNDER THE RAIN: . . . .   551 SONGS REWRIT 1   14
>THE THREE BUSHES . . . .   569 THREE BUSHES   T
>AND THERE TWO BUSHES PLANTED . . . .   571 THREE BUSHES   59
>HIVES, CURRANT BUSHES. THERE HIS KIN ARE. HIGH . . .   710 FERENCZ RENYI   25
BUSINESS
>THEATRE BUSINESS, MANAGEMENT OF MEN. . . . .   260 FASC DIFFICULT   11
>AND HAVE NO BUSINESS BUT DISPENSING ROUND . . . . .   404 FOR DAUGHTER   43
>MEN AND THEIR BUSINESS TOOK . . . .   421 MY TABLE   23
>THROUGH TOO MUCH BUSINESS WITH THE PASSING HOUR, . . .   423 MY DESCENDANTS   11
>WELL THEN, TO BUSINESS; WHAT IS IN YOUR BAG? . . . .   720 WITCH VIVIEN   19
BUSKIN
>FOR NATURE'S PULLED HER TRAGIC BUSKIN ON . . . . .   490 COOLE BALLYLEE   12
>FOR NATURE'D PULLED HER TRAGIC BUSKIN ON . . . . .   490 COOLE BALLYLEE V   12
BUST
>WITH PATIENT BEAUTY YONDER ATTIC BUST . . . . . .   685 DRAWING-ROOM   3
>WITH PATIENT BEAUTY YONDER ATTIC BUST . . . . . .   735 QUATRAIN APHOR   23
BUSTLE
>THAT SCARES WITH HIS BUSTLE THE DELICATE NIGHT, ...   28 OISIN 1   V 423B
BUSY
>AND NEW FRIENDS BUSY WITH YOUR PRAISE, ...   173 PLEADS FRIEND   3
>THEY ARE TOO BUSY WITH EACH OTHER. LOOK! . . . . .   232 SHADOW WATER B   229
>BEING TOO BUSY IN THE AIR AND THE HIGH AIR, ...   234 SHADOW WATER B   274
>HANDS THAT ARE BUSY WITH HIS BEADS . . . . . .   588 OLD WICKED MAN   25
>ON MY POOR BRAIN YOUR BUSY TUMULTS CROWD. . . . .   648 ISLE STAT I 1   100
>IN BUSY FLAKES; RE-SHINING FROM THE LAKE, ...   662 ISLE STAT II 2   3
>THE MEN ARE BUSY IN THE GLIMMERING SQUARE. . . . .   699 MOSADA 3   16
>OH, WOULD THE BUSY MINUTES MIGHT FOLD UP . . . . .   702 MOSADA 3   97
>NOW MAKING BUSY WITH THE OAR, ...   742 DANAAN QUICK   2
BUTLER
>A BUTLER OR AN ARMSTRONG THAT WITHSTOOD . . . . .   270 PARDON FATHERS   10
BUTLERS
>OLD BUTLERS WHEN YOU TOOK TO HORSE AND STOOD . . . .   270 PARDON FATHERS V   10
>THE SMUGGLER MIDDLETON, BUTLERS FAR BACK, ...   605 YOU CONTENT   15
BUTT   SEE WATER-BUTT
>THE BUTT END OF A STEERING OAR, ...   253 HIS DREAM   V   2
>DROWN, DROWN IN THE WATER BUTT, ...   546 TO SAME TUNE 2 V REF
BUTTED
>BUTTED BELOW THE SINGLE AND SO PIERCED . . . . . .   278 TWO KINGS   22
BUTT-END
>THE BUTT-END OF A STEERING-OAR, ...   253 HIS DREAM   2
BUTTERFLIES
>TORTOISESHELL BUTTERFLIES, PEACOCK BUTTERFLIES, ...   482 BLOOD AND MOON   45
>TORTOISESHELL BUTTERFLIES, PEACOCK BUTTERFLIES, ...   482 BLOOD AND MOON   45
>NOT GOOD; BUT YOU ARE LIKE THE BUTTERFLIES. . . . .   693 MOSADA 1   65
BUTTERFLY
>"AND WISDOM IS A BUTTERFLY . . . .   338 TOM OROUGHLEY   7
>THIS GREAT PURPLE BUTTERFLY, ...   381 SONG OF FOOL   1
>BUT EVERY BUTTERFLY TO A FRIEND. . . . .   787 GARRET CELLAR   2
BUTTERMILK
>I FASTED FOR SOME FORTY DAYS ON BREAD AND BUTTERMILK, . .   592 PILGRIM   1
BUTTING
>HIS ROD AND ITS BUTTING HEAD . . . .   575 MAIDS 2ND SONG   3
BUY
>THAT ONLY GODS MAY BUY OF HIM. . . . .   272 GREY ROCK   25
>TO HOLD THE WINE THEY BUY OF HIM. . . . .   272 GREY ROCK   V 25
>THAT NOBODY CAN BUY OR BIND! . . . .   301 RUN PARADISE   27
>IT SEEMS I MUST BUY KNOWLEDGE WITH MY PEACE. . . . .   468 HARUN RASHID   169
>UNDYING LOVE TO BUY . . . .   517 HIS CONFIDENCE   1
>COME HERE. BE SEATED NOW! I'D BUY OF YOU. . . . .   720 WITCH VIVIEN   17
>SOME DAY YOU'LL BUY THEM, MAYBE. NEVER! NEVER? . . .   721 WITCH VIVIEN   24
>I'D BUY YOUR GLASS. MY GLASS I WILL NOT SELL. . . .   721 WITCH VIVIEN   28
BUYING
>THE FOLK WHO ARE BUYING AND SELLING, ...   119 PITY OF LOVE   3

			PAGE	TITLE	LINE
BYE	SEE HUSH-A-BYE GOOD-BYE				
BYRE					
	BEYOND OLD MARTIN'S BYRE		95	MOLL MAGEE	34
BYRNE					
	CRIED THE BEGGAR, BILLY BYRNE:		331	ROUND TOWER	4
BYRNES					
	WHERE THE O'BYRNES AND BYRNES ARE BURIED,		331	ROUND TOWER	9
BYZANTINE					
	GATHERED A CROWD IN SOME BYZANTINE LANE,		180	QUEEN MAEVE	2
	WHO HAVE ACCEPTED THE BYZANTINE FAITH,		464	HARUN RASHID	78
	SHARED THE BYZANTINE CROWN?		789	SINGING HEAD	14
BYZANTIUM					
	SAILING TO BYZANTIUM		407	SAIL BYZANTIUM	T
	TO THE HOLY CITY OF BYZANTIUM.		408	SAIL BYZANTIUM	16
	TO LORDS AND LADIES OF BYZANTIUM		408	SAIL BYZANTIUM	31
	PASS BOOKS OF LEARNING FROM BYZANTIUM		461	HARUN RASHID	9
	BYZANTIUM		497	BYZANTIUM	T
CABBAGE					
	GROUNDS WHERE PLUM AND CABBAGE GREW,		577	WHAT THEN	13
CABBAGES					
	HE DIGS HIS CABBAGES. HE BRINGS TO MIND		696	MOSADA 2	18
CABIN					
	AND A SMALL CABIN BUILD THERE, OF CLAY AND WATTLES MADE:		117	ISLE INNISFREE	2
	AND A SMALL CABIN BUILT THERE, OF CLAY AND WATTLES MADE:		117	ISLE INNISFREE V	2
CABINS					
	CABINS GONE NOW, OLD WELL-SIDES, OLD DEAR PLACES,		130	BOOK STORIES V	23
CAER					
	CAER, HIS BLUE-EYED DAUGHTER THAT I LOVE.		184	QUEEN MAEVE	96
	CAER, HIS BLUE EYED DAUGHTER THAT I LOVE.		184	QUEEN MAEVE V	96
CAESAR					
	A ROMAN CAESAR IS HELD DOWN		379	SAINT HUNCH	4
	AUGUSTUS CAESAR, AND AFTER THESE		379	SAINT HUNCH	11
	OUR MASTER CAESAR IS IN THE TENT		617	LONG-LEG FLY	5
CAESARS					
	WHAT HAD THE CAESARS BUT THEIR THRONES?		401	DEMON BEAST	50
CAGE					
	NOR A CAGE, NOR ALIGHT UPON WRIST,		349	HAWK	8
	LET THE CAGE BIRD AND THE CAGE BIRD MATE		450	OWEN AHERNE	16
	LET THE CAGE BIRD AND THE CAGE BIRD MATE		450	OWEN AHERNE	16
	I DID NOT FIND IN ANY CAGE THE WOMAN AT MY SIDE.		450	OWEN AHERNE	19
CAGED					
	LET HIM BE HOODED OR CAGED		349	HAWK	2
	BECAUSE PIEBALD PONIES, LED BEARS, CAGED LIONS, MAKE BUT POOR SHOWS,		623	HIGH TALK	5
CAGES					
	THE BIRDS, FOR HE OPENED THEIR CAGES		92	FATHER OHART	17
CAIRN					
	. . . AND GUARDLESS THE SACRED CAIRN AND THE RATH,		58	OISIN 3	163
	THE GREY CAIRN ON THE HILL, WHEN DAY SINKS DROWNED IN DEW,		161	BLACK PIG	6
	UNDER A CAIRN OF SLEEPY STONE		192	BAILE AILLINN	81
	O TATTERED CLOUDS OF THE WORLD, CALL FROM THE HIGH CAIRN OF MAIVE,		207	HANRAHANS SONG V	6
	A HIGH, GREY CAIRN. WHAT MORE IS TO BE SAID?		778	SONG DEIRDRE 3	5
CAIRN-HEAPED					
	CAME TO THE CAIRN-HEAPED GRASSY HILL		3	OISIN 1	17
CAIRN'S					
	FOR WHOM THE CAIRN'S BUT HEAPED ANEW.		192	BAILE AILLINN	84
CAKE	SEE GRIDDLE-CAKE				
	IS DEAD. THE BOY THAT BRINGS MY GRIDDLE CAKE		339	SHEP GOATHERD V	20
CALAMITY					
	HEAVEN KNOWS WHAT CALAMITY:		193	BAILE AILLINN	112
	THAT IN THE SAME CALAMITY		540	FROM ANTIGONE	9
	CALAMITY CAN HAVE ITS FLING.		782	HEART FRIGHT	18
CALCULATION					
	WHAT CALCULATION, NUMBER, MEASUREMENT, REPLIED?		611	STATUES	27
CALCULATIONS					
	CALCULATIONS THAT LOOK BUT CASUAL FLESH, PUT DOWN		610	STATUES	11
CALENDARS					
	WITH ALL THOSE CALENDARS WHEREON		432	NINETEEN 19	99
CALF					
	WHERE LIES THE COW AT PEACE BESIDE HER CALF,		715	FERENCZ RENYI	121
	CURES FOR CALF WITH 'PLAINING THROAT,		717	FAIRY DOCTOR V	15
CALIF'S					
	FOR THE GREAT CALIF'S TREASURER AND MY FRIEND,		460	HARUN RASHID V	2
	WHERE GOLD-EMBROIDERED BANNERS OF THE CALIF'S		461	HARUN RASHID V	6
CALIPH					
	BOOK I WHAT THE CALIPH PARTLY LEARNED		372	PHASES OF MOON V	T
	BOOK II WHAT THE CALIPH REFUSED TO LEARN		460	HARUN RASHID V	T
	WHEN OUR BELOVED CALIPH PUT TO DEATH		462	HARUN RASHID	31
CALIPH'S					
	NOW THE GOOD CALIPH'S LEARNED TREASURER,		461	HARUN RASHID	3
CALIPHS					
	WHERE BANNERS OF THE CALIPHS HANG, NIGHT-COLOURED		461	HARUN RASHID	6
	AND HIDE IT THERE, FOR CALIPHS TO WORLD'S END		461	HARUN RASHID	17
CALL	SEE HUNTING-CALL				
	I CALL, AS THEY GO BY ME ONE BY ONE,		114	ROSE OF BATTLE	8
	"TURN IF YE MAY," I CALL OUT TO EACH ONE,		114	ROSE OF BATTLE V	7
	THAT YOU CALL IN BIRDS, IN WIND ON THE HILL,		141	EVERLAST VOICE	6
	WHEN OWLS BEGAN TO CALL:		159	CAP AND BELLS	6
	AND CALL TO MY BELOVED ME: "NO LONGER FLY		173	SPEAKS HEARERS	7
	BUT CALL ME FIRST THROUGH THE GATE:		178	FIDDLER DOONEY	12

120

CALL   (CONTINUED)
    "I AM FROM THOSE RIVERS AND I BID YOU CALL . . . . .   184 QUEEN MAEVE   91
    "I COME FROM THE UNDIMMED RIVERS TO BID YOU CALL . . .   184 QUEEN MAEVE   91
    "I AM FROM THE UNDIMMED RIVERS. I BID YOU CALL . . . .   184 QUEEN MAEVE   V   91
    "I AM FROM THOSE RIVERS AND WOULD HAVE YOU CALL . . . .   184 QUEEN MAEVE   V   91
    WHAT SHALL I CALL THEM? FISH THAT SWIM. . . . . . .   195 BAILE AILLINN   144
    IT MIGHT CALL UP A NEW AGE, CALLING TO MIND . . . . .   201 OLD MEMORY   4
    "LET PEEWIT CALL AND CURLEW CRY WHERE THEY WILL. . . .   203 WITHER BOUGHS   2
    THE MARTYRS CALL THE WORLD." AND THEREUPON . . . . .   205 ADAMS CURSE   14
    THE MARTYRS CALL THE WORLD." THAT WOMAN THEN . . . .   205 ADAMS CURSE   V   14
    O TATTERED CLOUDS OF THE WORLD, CALL FROM THE HIGH CAIRN   207 HANRAHANS SONG V   6
        OF MAIVE.
    LIKE TATTERED CLOUDS OF THE WORLD, PASSIONS CALL AND OUR   207 HANRAHANS SONG V   8
        HEARTS BEAT!
    LIKE PLOVERS THAT HAVE HEARD THE CALL. . . . . . .   213 BLESS PSALTER   13
    WHAT DO YOU CALL IT?--THAT OLD PROMISE-BREAKER, ...   228 SHADOW WATER B   122
    A MAGIC THAT CAN CALL A DEMON UP, ...   238 SHADOW WATER B   344
    WHAT NAME TO CALL HIM BY? COME TO HIS SHIP. . . . .   240 SHADOW WATER B   390
    BY ANY OTHER MEANS. YOU CALL IT PASSION. . . . . .   244 SHADOW WATER B   455
    AND WORDS OBEY MY CALL"! . . . .   256 WORDS   12
    I CALL FOR SPADE AND HORSE AND HOUND . . . .   275 GREY ROCK   105
    AND CALL THOSE EXILES AS THEY WERE . . . .   290 SEPTEMBER 1913   26
    BUT I'LL HAVE NO MAN CALL ME GHOST." . . . .   304 HOUR DAWN   41
    THERE IS NOT A FOOL CAN CALL ME FRIEND. . . . . . .   336 YOUNG BEAUTY   16
    THAT NOT A FOOL CAN CALL ME FRIEND. . . . .   336 YOUNG BEAUTY   V   16
    TO CALL UP TO THE EYES . . . .   347 FISHERMAN   7
    "CALL DOWN THE HAWK FROM THE AIR! . . . .   349 HAWK   1
    I CALL TO MY OWN OPPOSITE, SUMMON ALL . . . .   367 EGO DOMINUS   8
    I CALL TO THE MYSTERIOUS ONE WHO YET . . . .   371 EGO DOMINUS   70
    WHAT BETTER THAN CALL A DANCE? . . . .   378 CAT AND MOON   13
    AND HENS TO MOOR-COCKS CALL! . . . .   393 EASTER 1916   54
    UNDER THE DAY'S DECLINING BEAM, AND CALL . . . . . .   410 TOWER   21
    OR SERVILE SHAPE, AT OTHERS' BECK AND CALL. . . . . .   417 ANCEST HOUSES   8
    THROUGH WINTER-TIME WE CALL ON SPRING. . . . . . .   434 WHEEL   1
    AND THROUGH THE SPRING ON SUMMER CALL. . . . . . .   434 WHEEL   2
    EVEN WHERE HORRIBLE GREEN PARROTS CALL AND SWING. . . .   442 BLACK CENTAUR   2
    EVEN WHERE THE HORRIBLE GREEN PARROTS CALL AND SWING. . .   442 BLACK CENTAUR V   2
    IF KINDNESS I MAY CALL . . . .   452 HUMAN DIGNITY   2
    AND SPEAK BUT LIES. CALL UP TO MEMORY . . . .   462 HARUN RASHID   V   30
    HORTON'S THE FIRST I CALL. HE LOVED STRANGE THOUGHT .   471 ALL SOUL NIGHT   21
    ON FLORENCE EMERY I CALL THE NEXT, ...   472 ALL SOUL NIGHT   41
    AND I CALL UP MACGREGOR FROM THE GRAVE, ...   473 ALL SOUL NIGHT   61
    I CALL MACGREGOR MATHERS FROM HIS GRAVE. . . . . . .   473 ALL SOUL NIGHT V   61
    I CALL IT DEATH-IN-LIFE AND LIFE-IN-DEATH. . . . . .   497 BYZANTIUM   16
    AND CALL THOSE WORKS EXTRAVAGANCE OF BREATH . . . . .   501 VACILLATION   32
    MAY CALL DOWN CURSES ON HIS HEAD . . . .   508 JANE BISHOP   4
    MAY CALL A CURSE OUT OF THE SKY . . . .   508 JANE BISHOP   V   4
    TILL TRUTH OBEYED HIS CALL! . . . .   576 ACRE OF GRASS   18
    CALL THE MUSES HOME. . . . .   600 THOSE IMAGES   8
    I CALL ON THOSE THAT CALL ME SON, ...   604 YOU CONTENT   1
    I CALL ON THOSE THAT CALL ME SON, ...   604 YOU CONTENT   1
    AND IN THAT TERROR'S NAME OBEYED THE CALL, ...   622 HOUND VOICE   12
    ACH, CALL ME WHAT YOU PLEASE! . . . .   627 STATES HOLIDAY   21
    THE FAIRY'S CALL . . . .   654 ISLE STAT I 2 V   T
    NO, NO! WHEN THAT SHALL BE, THEN MEN MAY CALL . . . .   662 ISLE STAT II 1   79
    FOR SUCH A CALL. LET THE WILD WORD BE CRIED . . . .   669 ISLE STAT II 3   76
    THUS FOR ANOTHER'S BUGLE CALL! . . . .   671 ISLE STAT II 3   136
    I SOUGHT THEE NOT. MEN CALL ME INFAMY. . . . . . .   685 SEEKER   75
    DARK JOAN CALL THE BERRIES SWEET, ...   743 DANAAN QUICK   28
    AND I HAVE HEARD THEM CALL FROM WIND TO WIND . . . .   750 SHADOW WATER A   83
    GIVE ME THE HELM! CALL HITHER THOSE WHO LIE . . . . .   751 SHADOW WATER A   91
    WE WILL GO CALL THESE SAILORS, AND ESCAPE . . . . . .   766 SHADOW WATER A   382
    CAN CALL THE MILCH COWS . . . .   780 WELL AND TREE   5
    CAN CALL THE MILCH-COWS . . . .   780 WELL AND TREE V   5
CALLED
    NOW, MAN OF CROZIERS, SHADOWS CALLED OUR NAMES . . . .   29 OISIN 2   1
    HALF LOST IN VAPOUR, SHADOWS CALLED OUR NAMES, ...   29 OISIN 2   V   3
    AND CALLED HIM SWEETEST NAMES AND SOOTHED HIS FEARS. . .   30 OISIN 2   V   27
    HOLDING THAT HORSE, AND SADLY CALLED MY NAME! . . . .   44 OISIN 2   230
    AND HE CALLED LOUDLY TO THE STARS TO BEND . . . . . .   68 SAD SHEPHERD   5
    HE CALLED ALOUD TO ALL THE STARS TO LEND . . . . . .   68 SAD SHEPHERD   V   5
    I CALLED MY BATTLE-BREAKING MEN . . . .   83 MAD KING GOLL   17
    AND CALLED OUT TO HIM, "SON IT IS NOT MEET . . . . .   107 CUCHULAIN SEA V   20
    AND SOME ONE CALLED ME BY MY NAME! . . . .   149 WANDER AENGUS   12
    AND SOMEONE CALLED ME BY MY NAME. . . . .   149 WANDER AENGUS V   12
    WHO CALLED ME BY MY NAME AND RAN . . . .   150 WANDER AENGUS   15
    THAT CALLED ME BY MY NAME AND RAN . . . .   150 WANDER AENGUS V   15
    WHEN THE OWLS CALLED OUT NO MORE! . . . .   159 CAP AND BELLS   14
    CUMHAL CALLED OUT, BENDING HIS HEAD, ...   166 BLESSED   1
    CUMHAL CALLED OUT, BOWING HIS HEAD, ...   167 BLESSED   V   4A
    NOW WORDS THAT CALLED UP THE LIGHTNING . . . .   171 MAID QUIET   7
    FOR THE WORDS THAT CALLED UP THE LIGHTNING . . . . .   171 MAID QUIET   V   7
    SHE COULD HAVE CALLED OVER THE RIM OF THE WORLD . . . .   181 QUEEN MAEVE   23
    TILL MAEVE CALLED OUT, "THESE ARE BUT COMMON MEN. . . .   186 QUEEN MAEVE   122
    CALLED RATHER BAILE LITTLE-LAND, ...   189 BAILE AILLINN   17
    CALLED RATHER BAILE LITTLE LAND, ...   189 BAILE AILLINN V   17
    WISE BIDDY EARLY CALLED THE WICKED WOOD! . . . . . .   218 WOODS OF COOLE   15
    BEING AS DOUBTFUL? I HAVE CALLED YOU MASTER . . . . .   227 SHADOW WATER B   110
    HAVE CALLED ME THEIR BELOVED, I'LL NOT KISS THEM. . . .   237 SHADOW WATER B   336
    OR CALLED BEFORE HIS EYES. O CARRY ME . . . .   249 SHADOW WATER B   568
    ARDAN, AND THOUGH I CALLED TO HIM AND TRIED . . . . .   283 TWO KINGS   142

```
                                                              PAGE      TITLE        LINE

CALLED   (CONTINUED)
    CALLED CRUACHAN, AND IT WAS AS MUCH . . . . . . . . . .    302  HOUR DAWN            4
    AND CALLED THE PLEASURES EVIL . . . . . . . . . . .        365  HER RACE             3
    AND CALLED HER NAME, SHE HAD HEARD, . . . . . . . . .      381  SONGS FOOL 2        11
    HAS CALLED UP THE COLD SPIRITS THAT ARE BORN . . . . .     382  VISION ROBART        2
    NEVER TO LEAVE THAT VALLEY HIS FATHERS CALLED THEIR HOME.  391  UNDER SATURN        16
    OR ANYTHING CALLED CONSCIENCE ONCE: . . . . . . . . .      413  TOWER              118
    CALLED ARCHITECT AND ARTIST IN, THAT THEY, . . . . . .     418  ANCEST HOUSES       18
    OUT OF THE FABULOUS DARKNESS CALLED. . . . . . . . .       437  SONGS PLAY 1        16
    . . . "YOU HAVE CALLED ME MAD," IT SAID, . . . . . .       450  OWEN AHERNE         13
    THAT'S CALLED PLATONIC LOVE. . . . . . . . . . . . .       471  ALL SOUL NIGHT      23
    . . . THOUGHT'S CROWNED POWERS HE CALLED THEM ONCE. . .    480  BLOOD AND MOON      15
    I HAD THOUGHT TO HAVE CALLED HER OUT TO THE DOOR, . . .    551  SONGS REWRIT 1  V   15
    BUT THAT I CALLED ON HIM? . . . . . . . . . . . . .        658  ISLE STAT I 3       80
    MY LORD, YOU CALLED? NOT I. THIS MAID IS DEAD. . . . .     704  MOSADA 3           125
    "WATCHER, WHEREFORE HAVE YE CALLED US?" EYES GO AFTER      718  PHANTOM SHIP        10
        HIS LEAN HAND,
    FOR HE WHO GAVE IT CALLED IT AENGUS' HARP . . . . . .      762  SHADOW WATER A     288
    HAVE CALLED HIM MIGHTY. I WILL FOLLOW YOU . . . . . .      768  SHADOW WATER A     412
    WE CALLED IT A GOOD DEATH. TODAY . . . . . . . . . .       791  REPRISALS            3
CALLED'ST
    THOU CALLED'ST ME FORTH. AND HOW THOU MADEST ME . . . .    683  SEEKER              52
CALLEN
    YOUNG NIAM, AND THOU SHALT BE CALLEN . . . . . . . .        7  OISIN 1         V   75
CALLIMACHUS
    NO HANDIWORK OF CALLIMACHUS, . . . . . . . . . . . .       566  LAPIS LAZULI        29
CALLING
    FROM THE GREAT GRASS-BARNACLE CALLING, . . . . . . .       57   OISIN 3            156
    AND NIAMH CALLING AWAY, COME AWAY! . . . . . . . .         140  HOSTING SIDHE        4
    AND NIAMH CALLING AWAY, COME AWAY. . . . . . . . .         141  HOSTING SIDHE       16
    AND HEAR THE NARROW GRAVES CALLING MY CHILD AND ME. . .    147  UNAPPEAS HOST        6
    DO YOU NOT HEAR ME CALLING, WHITE DEER WITH NO HORNS?      153  CHANGE BELOVED       1
    AND NOW MY CALLING IS BUT THE CALLING OF A HOUND. . .      153  CHANGE BELOVED       8
    AND NOW MY CALLING IS BUT THE CALLING OF A HOUND: . .      153  CHANGE BELOVED       8
    AND SORROW AWAY, AND CALLING BARD AND CLOWN . . . . .      170  SECRET ROSE         20
    ARE CALLING THROUGH MY HEART. . . . . . . . . .            171  MAID QUIET      V    8
    IT MIGHT CALL UP A NEW AGE, CALLING TO MIND . . . . .      201  OLD MEMORY           4
    WHAT ARE YOU CALLING OUT ABOVE THE MAST? . . . . . .       243  SHADOW WATER B     437
    YOU'LL HEAR THEM CALLING OUT TO ONE ANOTHER . . . .        247  SHADOW WATER B     521
    A VOICE CAME CALLING ME TO THIS YOUR LAND, . . . . .       682  SEEKER              22
    THE CALLING AFAR OF THE DOE AND THE DEER. . . . . .        717  LOVE SONG            5
    AH, WELL! THEY ARE CALLING ME--THEY ARE CALLING ME.        760  SHADOW WATER A     251
    AH, WELL! THEY ARE CALLING ME--THEY ARE CALLING ME. .      760  SHADOW WATER A     251
    WHEN THE WINDS ARE CALLING THERE, . . . . . . . . .        772  SONG DEIRDRE 1       4
    OR THE GANNETS CALLING OUT . . . . . . . . . . . .         772  SONG DEIRDRE 1       5
CALLS
    THE BELL THAT CALLS US ON: THE SWEET FAR THING. . . .      115  ROSE OF BATTLE      28
    WHAT THE EXULTANT HEART CALLS GOOD . . . . . . . .         288  TO WEALTHY MAN      33
    THE BODY CALLS IT DEATH, . . . . . . . . . . . . .         500  VACILLATION          7
    THAT CALLS. O EVIL STARRED! IT COMES ALONG . . . .         653  ISLE STAT I 2       49
    HUSH'D THE FISHERS, TILL A MOTHER CALLS BY NAME HER DROWNED 719 PHANTOM SHIP        23
        SON:
    THEN EACH WIFE AND MAID AND MOTHER CALLS BY NAME           719  PHANTOM SHIP        24
        SOME DROWNED ONE.
CALM
    THE VAN OF WANDERING QUIET: ERE YOU BE TOO CALM AND OLD,   73   ANASHU VIJAYA   V   43
    THE VAN OF WANDERING QUIET: ERE YE BE TOO CALM AND OLD,    73   ANASHU VIJAYA   V   43
    AND CHAPLET THEIR CALM BROWS WITH LEAFAGE DIM, . . . .     127  DREAM OF FAERY  V   32
    AND CHAPLET THEIR CALM BROWS WITH LEAFAGE COOL: . . .      127  DREAM OF FAERY  V   32
    AND FROM ITS MURMURING GREENNESS, CALM OF FAERY, . . .     129  BOOK STORIES         3
    O HOW COULD I BE SO CALM . . . . . . . . . . . . .         171  MAID QUIET           5
    SHE GOES ABOUT HER HOUSE ERECT AND CALM . . . . . .        340  SHEP GOATHERD       35
    OF SWORD-BLUE WAVES OF CALM: WHILE O'ER HEAD BLINK . .     663  ISLE STAT II 2      42
    IN THEIR COILING CALM AND SLOW. . . . . . . . . .          680  LOVE AND DEATH       8
    AND CALM, ROBED ALL IN RAIMENT MOONY WHITE. . . . . .      693  MOSADA 1            77
CALUMNY
    OR CALUMNY A SONG. HOW CAN THEY KNOW . . . . . . .         398  LEADERS CROWD        7
CALVARY'S
    BEING BY CALVARY'S TURBULENCE UNSATISFIED, . . . . . .     318  MAGI                 7
CALVERT
    CALVERT AND WILSON, BLAKE AND CLAUDE, . . . . . . .        639  BEN BULBEN          64
    AND WILSON, BLAKE AND CALVERT, CLAUDE. . . . . . .         639  BEN BULBEN      V   64
CALVES
    AND A HUNDRED CALVES AND A HUNDRED SHEEP . . . . . .        8   OISIN 1             89
    OF THE CALVES ON THE WARM HILLSIDE . . . . . . . .         88   STOLEN CHILD        45
    OF THE CALVES ON THE WARM HILL SIDE. . . . . . . .         88   STOLEN CHILD    V   45
    OF THE CALVES ON THE WARM HILL-SIDE. . . . . . . .         88   STOLEN CHILD    V   45
    CURES FOR CALVES WITH 'PLAINING THROAT, . . . . . .        717  FAIRY DOCTOR        15
CAME
    CAME TO THE CAIRN-HEAPED GRASSY HILL . . . . . . .         3    OISIN 1             17
    "WHAT DREAM CAME WITH YOU THAT YOU CAME . . . . . .         5   OISIN 1             50
    "WHAT DREAM CAME WITH YOU THAT YOU CAME . . . . . .         5   OISIN 1             50
    UNTIL THE DANAAN POETS CAME, . . . . . . . . . . .         7    OISIN 1         V   64
    CAOILTE, CONAN, AND FINN CAME NEAR, . . . . . . . .        10   OISIN 1            111
    BUT NOW A WANDERING LAND BREEZE CAME . . . . . . .         13   OISIN 1            165
    WHEN ROUND US SUDDENLY THERE CAME . . . . . . . .          13   OISIN 1         V  165
    UNTIL ONE CAME, A TEARFUL BOY: . . . . . . . . . .         17   OISIN 1            237
    AND NOW, STILL SAD, WE CAME TO WHERE . . . . . . .         17   OISIN 1            247
    AND ONE CAME CLOSE, A TEARFUL BOY. . . . . . . . .         17   OISIN 1         V  237
    THAT FROM THE SAFFRON MORNING CAME, . . . . . . . .        19   OISIN 1            277
    AND CAME TO WHERE THE DEWDROPS FALL . . . . . . .          20   OISIN 1            293
```

122

CAME (CONTINUED)

	PAGE	TITLE		LINE
A SEA-WORN WAIF CAME FLOATING BY.	24	OISIN 1	V	365
THEREON YOUNG NIAMH SOFTLY CAME	25	OISIN 1		373
THEN SOFTLY TO ME NIAM CAME, ...	25	OISIN 1	V	373
LIKE DROPS OF HONEY CAME THEIR WORDS, ...	26	OISIN 1		398
NEARER THE CASTLE CAME WE. A VAST TIDE, ...	31	OISIN 2	V	27A
CAME SWIMMING SADLY DOWN THE MIGHTY STAIR.	32	OISIN 2	V	50B
AND TELL ME HOW YOU CAME TO ONE UNBID, ...	33	OISIN 2	V	67
LIKE A SMALL RIVER, AND WHERE FEET TOUCHED CAME . .	37	OISIN 2		117
AND CAME AGAIN, HOLDING A SECOND LIGHT	37	OISIN 2		124
AND WHERE OUR FOOTFALL 'LIGHTED LAST THERE CAME . . .	37	OISIN 2	V	119
AWHILE, AND CAME AGAIN, A SECOND LIGHT	37	OISIN 2	V	124
AND AT HIS CRY THERE CAME NO MILK-PALE FACE	38	OISIN 2		134
THE DAWN CAME IN, AND GLIMMERED ON THE FLOOR . . .	39	OISIN 2		152
THOSE TWO CAME CARRYING WINE AND MEAT AND BREAD, . . .	41	OISIN 2		184
OUTCRY OF BATS. AND THEN YOUNG NIAMH CAME . . .	44	OISIN 2		229
THE HARE LEAPED IN THE GRASS. YOUNG NIAMH CAME . . .	44	OISIN 2	V	229
AND DRIFTING GREYNESS. CAME THIS MONOTONE . . .	45	OISIN 2	V	232
CAME TO MY TOWER AS AGE DRAGGED AFTER AGE	45	OISIN 2	V	242
CAME NOW THE SLIDING OF TEARS AND SWEEPING OF MIST-COLD HAIR,	47	OISIN 3		7
CAME NOW THE SLIDING OF TEARS AND SWEEPING OF MIST-COLD AIR,	47	OISIN 3	V	7
CAME NOW THE SLIDING OF TEARS AND SWEEPING OF MIST COLD HAIR,	47	OISIN 3	V	7
THE BREATHING CAME FROM THOSE BODIES, ...	49	OISIN 3		36
AND OVER THE LIMBS AND THE VALLEY THE SLOW OWLS WANDERED AND CAME,	49	OISIN 3		41
CAME SOUND FROM THOSE MONSTROUS SLEEPERS, ...	51	OISIN 3		58
HIS LIPS MOVED SLOWLY IN ANSWER, NO ANSWER OUT OF THEM CAME:	51	OISIN 3		66
AND A SOFTNESS CAME FROM THE STARLIGHT	52	OISIN 3		72
SAD NIAM CAME NEAR ME, AND LAID HER BROWS ON THE MIDST OF MY BREAST	52	OISIN 3	V	74
CAME BY ME THE KINGS OF THE RED BRANCH, ...	53	OISIN 3		87
CAME BLANAID, MAC NESSA, TALL FERGUS WHO FEASTWARD OF OLD TIME SLUNK,	53	OISIN 3		89
CAME BY ME THE CANNS OF THE RED BRANCH	53	OISIN 3	V	87
CAME BLANID, MAC NESSA, CUCHULIN:	53	OISIN 3	V	89
. . . CAME FERGUS WHO FEASTWARD SAD SLUNK, ...	53	OISIN 3	V	89
CAME BLANID, MAC NESSA, AND FERGUS WHO FEASTWARD OF OLD TIME SLUNK,	53	OISIN 3	V	89
CAME CAR-BORNE BALOR, AS OLD AS A FOREST, HIS VAST FACE SUNK	53	OISIN 3	V	91
CAME BALOR, AS OLD AS A FOREST, CAR BORNE, HIS MIGHTY HEAD SUNK	53	OISIN 3	V	91
CAME, AND MY FOREHEAD FELL LOW, AND MY TEARS LIKE BERRIES FELL DOWN:	57	OISIN 3		154
LATER A SOUND CAME, HALF LOST IN THE SOUND OF A SHORE FAR AWAY,	57	OISIN 3		155
CAME AFTER THE HARD GAZE OF YOUTH, OR AN OLD MAN LIFTED HIS HEAD:	59	OISIN 3		170
A HERDSMAN CAME FROM INLAND VALLEYS, ...	82	MAD KING GOLL		14
I CAME UPON A LITTLE TOWN	85	MAD KING GOLL		49
WITH EYES OF SADNESS CAME TO HEAR	85	MAD KING GOLL	V	62
CAME KEENERS HOARSER THAN ROOKS, ...	92	FATHER OHART		22
PEOPLE CAME INTO COLOONEY:	93	FATHER OHART		27
CAME KEENING IN THAT DAY.	93	FATHER OHART		32
CAME FLYING, HEAVY AND SAD:	93	FATHER OHART		34
A MAN CAME SLOWLY FROM THE SETTING SUN, ...	105	CUCHULAIN SEA		1
HERDED THE CATTLE CAME WITH STUMBLING FEET, ...	106	CUCHULAIN SEA		19
WAS DRIVING CATTLE CAME SHE WITH SWIFT FEET, ...	106	CUCHULAIN SEA	V	19
SEEK OUT WHAT MAN HE IS." ONE WENT AND CAME. . . .	109	CUCHULAIN SEA		51
STOOD UP, AND CAME TO THE LONG SANDS ALONE: . . .	111	CUCHULAIN SEA	V	84
A WOVEN SILENCE, OR BUT CAME TO CAST	114	ROSE OF BATTLE		13
AND THEN YOU CAME WITH THOSE RED MOURNFUL LIPS, . . .	120	SORROW OF LOVE	V	5
AND WITH YOU CAME THE WHOLE OF THE WORLD'S TEARS, . . .	120	SORROW OF LOVE	V	6
I CAME AND WROTE UPON A CROSS OF WOOD--	123	DREAM OF DEATH	V	7
WHEN THE MOTHS CAME ONCE MORE, ...	133	FR GILLIGAN		22
WHEN MOTHS CAME ONCE MORE, ...	133	FR GILLIGAN	V	22
A MAN WITH A HAZEL WAND CAME WITHOUT SOUND: . . .	153	CHANGE BELOVED		6
A MAN WITH A WAND OF HAZEL CAME WITHOUT SOUND! . . .	153	CHANGE BELOVED	V	6
AND THE HEART AND THE SOUL CAME THROUGH, ...	160	CAP AND BELLS		30
TO HER RIGHT HAND CAME THE RED ONE, ...	160	CAP AND BELLS		31
TO HER LEFT HAND CAME THE BLUE.	160	CAP AND BELLS		32
THE HEART AND THE SOUL CAME THROUGH:	160	CAP AND BELLS	V	30
THAT MURMURING AND LONGING CAME	162	ASKS FORGIVE		8
THAT LONGING AND MURMURING CAME	162	ASKS FORGIVE	V	8
AND I DREAMED MY LOST LOVE CAME STEALTHILY OUT OF THE WOOD	163	VALLEY LOVERS		3
TILL DATHI CAME AND STOOD, ...	166	BLESSED		2
CAME BY THE WOODY WAY	166	BLESSED	V	2
TILL DATHI CAME AND STOOD, ...	167	BLESSED	V	4B
THE POWERS, NOT KIND LIKE YOU, CAME WHERE GOD'S GARDEN BLOWS,	174	ELEMENT POWERS	V	1
CAME TO THE THRESHOLD OF THE PAINTED HOUSE	185	QUEEN MAEVE		108
CAME UP OUT OF THE HOLE, AND RED-EARED HOUNDS . . .	185	QUEEN MAEVE		117
WITH LONG WHITE BODIES CAME OUT OF THE AIR	185	QUEEN MAEVE		118
UNTIL TWO LOVERS CAME OUT OF THE AIR	187	QUEEN MAEVE		143
BUT OUT OF THE DARK AIR OVER HER HEAD THERE CAME . . .	187	QUEEN MAEVE		153
HE RAN AND LAUGHED UNTIL HE CAME	194	BAILE AILLINN		128
TWO SWANS CAME FLYING UP TO HIM, ...	194	BAILE AILLINN		135

CAME   (CONTINUED)
          AND HURRYING TO THE SOUTH HE CAME . . . .   194 BAILE AILLINN   V   128
          EDAIN CAME OUT OF MIDHIR'S HILL, AND LAY . . . . .   219 HARP OF AENGUS   1
          MY COURAGE CAME AGAIN. BUT THAT'S NOT ALL. . . . .   223 SHADOW WATER B   31
          A BEAUTIFUL YOUNG MAN AND GIRL CAME UP . . . . . .   223 SHADOW WATER B   33
          AND IF YOU SAY THAT SHE CAME WILLINGLY-- . . . . .   244 SHADOW WATER B   460
          AND YOU SAY THAT SHE CAME WILLINGLY-- . . . . . .   244 SHADOW WATER B V 460
          CAME WHEN TIME HAD TOUCHED HER FORM. . . . . . .   259 PEACE   11
          AND THESE THINGS CAME, SO MUCH THE MORE THEREBY . .   265 THESE CLOUDS   8
          'TWAS ROUNDLY SPOKE, BUT WHEN NIGHT CAME . . . .   275 GREY ROCK   95
          KING EOCHAID CAME AT SUNDOWN TO A WOOD . . . . .   276 TWO KINGS   1
          AND CAME INTO A WOOD AS THE SUN SET . . . . . .   277 TWO KINGS   V   3
          UNTIL HE CAME BEFORE THE PAINTED WALL, ...   279 TWO KINGS   47
          AND WHEN OLD GUAIRE CAME AND STOOD . . . .   297 THREE BEGGARS   54
          AS I CAME OVER WINDY GAP . . . .   300 RUN PARADISE   1
          HE CAME, BUT MAN IS A FOOL." . . . .   341 SHEP GOATHERD   74
          "HUNCHBACK AND SAINT AND FOOL," AND THAT THEY CAME . .   377 PHASES OF MOON   132
          BEFORE THAT RUIN CAME, FOR CENTURIES, ...   412 TOWER   81
          OUT OF NOTHING IT CAME, ...   439 FRAGMENTS   7
          CAME TO THE LEAST CONSIDERED OF HIS COURTIERS! . .   462 HARUN RASHID   42
          TRUTHS WITHOUT FATHER CAME, TRUTHS THAT NO BOOK . .   467 HARUN RASHID   138
          BUT MINE SAW STELLA ONCE. WHENCE CAME OUR THOUGHT? . .   486 SEVEN SAGES   6
          MINE SAW STELLA ONCE. WHENCE CAME OUR THOUGHT? . .   486 SEVEN SAGES   V   6
          MINE SAW STELLA ONCE. WHEN CAME OUR THOUGHT? . .   486 SEVEN SAGES   V   6
          THEY CAME LIKE SWALLOWS AND LIKE SWALLOWS WENT, . .   489 COOLE PARK 29   17
          OR OUT OF FOLLY INTO FOLLY CAME. . . . .   491 COOLE BALLYLEE   32
          CAME TO SO DEEP A THOUGHT . . . .   505 RESULT THOUGHT   10
          CAME WHEN HE WOULD, ...   512 JANE ON GOD   2
          ANOTHER CAME IN SIGHT . . . .   515 GIRLS SONG B   5
          CAME WHERE YOU STOOD, ...   518 LOVES LONENESS   4
          I DID THE DRAGON'S WILL UNTIL YOU CAME . . . . .   533 HER TRIUMPH   1
          WHAT FROM THE FOREST CAME? WHAT BEAST HAS LICKED
            ITS YOUNG?   560 MAGIC DRUM   6
          CAME OUT OF A NEEDLE'S EYE . . . .   562 NEEDLES EYE   2
          ON THEIR OWN FEET THEY CAME, OR ON SHIPBOARD, . . .   566 LAPIS LAZULI   25
          "BECAUSE MY LADY CAME . . . .   570 THREE BUSHES   37
          THE PRIEST CAME WHERE SHE WAS! . . . .   571 THREE BUSHES   65
          HOW CAME THIS RANGER . . . .   574 MAIDS 1ST SONG   1
          ALL HIS HAPPIER DREAMS CAME TRUE-- . . . .   577 WHAT THEN   11
          I CAME ON A GREAT HOUSE IN THE MIDDLE OF THE NIGHT, . .   581 CURSE CROMWELL   25
          PARNELL CAME DOWN THE ROAD, HE SAID TO A CHEERING MAN! . .   590 PARNELL   1
          AND HE CAME SAILING HOME. . . . .   594 COLONEL MARTIN   6
          AND WHEN THEY CAME TO THE TOP STAIR . . . . . .   595 COLONEL MARTIN   41
          PRAISE EVERY MAN THAT CAME AGAIN, ...   608 SONGS BURDEN 3   7
          PLOTINUS CAME AND LOOKED ABOUT, ...   611 NEWS ORACLE   9
          CAME AND WERE GONE. HE LEANT UPON A TREE . . . .   634 CUCHULAIN COMF   5
          AMONG THOSE BIRD-LIKE THINGS CAME, AND LET FALL . .   634 CUCHULAIN COMF   8
          CAME CREEPING UP BECAUSE THE MAN WAS STILL. . . .   634 CUCHULAIN COMF   10
          LOVE FROM HEAVEN CAME OF YORE . . . .   648 ISLE STAT I 1   77
          AND TROUBLED EYES CAME MORNING'S FIRST-BORN GLOW! . .   648 ISLE STAT I 1   103
          YON SHEPHERD--CAME YOUR SPIRIT TO BEGUILE . . . .   648 ISLE STAT I 1   105
          AND, OH! THE WONDER OF THE THING! EACH CAME . . .   656 ISLE STAT I 3   29
          WITH CLINGING MIST, EACH STAR-FOUGHT WANDERER CAME . .   656 ISLE STAT I 3   33
          AND THEN NEW MURMURS CAME NEW UTTERING . . . . .   657 ISLE STAT I 3   50
          HE PASSED ACROSS THE LAKE. WHEN WE TWO CAME . .   658 ISLE STAT II 1   5
          AYE, VERY LATELY, SORROW CAME TO WEEP . . . . .   659 ISLE STAT II 1   25
          EACH CAME ONE MORN, WITH WELCOMING OF SONG, . . .   660 ISLE STAT II 1   42
          TWO CAME, HIS NAME AND MINE ON MANY A TREE . . .   662 ISLE STAT II 2   10
          YONDER'S THE ISLE IN SEARCH WHEREOF WE CAME! . . .   662 ISLE STAT II 2   13
          FOR THERE CAME AN AIR-BREATH COOL . . . .   667 ISLE STAT II 3   27
          AND DOWN I CAME AS A FALCON SWOOPS . . . .   673 ISLE STAT II 3   178
          AS HERE I CAME I SAW GOD PAN. HE PLAYED . . . .   678 ISLE STAT II 3   300
          SHEPHERDS, I CAME THIS MORNING TO YOUR LAND . . .   682 SEEKER   15
          A VOICE CAME CALLING ME TO THIS YOUR LAND, . . .   682 SEEKER   22
          WHEN FLASH ON FLASH ONCE MORE THE LIGHTNING CAME, .   688 TWO TITANS   39
          I CAME THE FIRST TIME TO THY VILLAGE SCHOOL? . . .   713 FERENCZ RENYI   90
          CAME OLIVE FIRES OF MORNING AND ON THE DARKNESS FED, .   719 PHANTOM SHIP   33
          CAME THE OLIVE FIRE OF MORNING, AND ON THE DARKNESS FED, .   719 PHANTOM SHIP   V   33
          THE MAYOR CAME, LEANING HIS DEAF EAR-- . . . . .   725 LEGEND   13
          THE BISHOP CAME WITH OPEN BOOK, ...   725 LEGEND   17
          A COCK CAME BY UPON HIS TOES! . . . .   725 LEGEND   26
          HE CAME TO THE HOME OF THE FOREST PEOPLE . . . .   728 PRIEST FAIRY   5
          AND CAME TO WHERE HIS BRETHREN STOOD, ...   730 PRIEST FAIRY   63
          EARL PAUL CAME WHERE THE KING SAT, ...   740 EARL PAUL   29
          AND CAME AND DWELT IN HIS OWN HOUSE, ...   742 EARL PAUL   67
          HIS FACE HAD NEVER GLADDENED SINCE HE CAME . . .   747 SHADOW WATER A   1
          AND WHEN YOU CAME, THE NORTH UNDER YOUR SAILS, . .   749 SHADOW WATER A   34
          AND WHEN YOU CAME TO SCORN OUR LITTLE WARS . . .   749 SHADOW WATER A V   34
          THE FOOL THAT CAME OUT OF THE WINTRY WOOD . . . .   750 SHADOW WATER A   75
          WHERE I HAD HEARD NO FEET BUT THE GODS' CAME. . .   756 SHADOW WATER A V 191B
          EDAINE CAME OUT OF MIDHER'S HILL, AND LAY . . . .   762 SHADOW WATER A   296
CAMEL
          AMONG THE COARSE GRASS AND THE CAMEL DUNG. . . . .   369 EGO DOMINUS   V   31
CAMEL-BACK
          CAMEL-BACK, HORSE-BACK, ASS-BACK, MULE-BACK, . . .   566 LAPIS LAZULI   26
CAMEL-DUNG
          AMONG THE COARSE GRASS AND THE CAMEL-DUNG. . . . .   369 EGO DOMINUS   31
CAMEL'S
          PAST THE CAMEL'S DREAMING EYE. . . . .   733 STREET DANCERS   43
CAMP
          "THE RED BRANCH CAMP IN A GREAT COMPANY . . . . .   108 CUCHULAIN SEA   33

		PAGE	TITLE		LINE

CAMP   (CONTINUED)
GO THERE, AND CAMP UPON THE FOREST'S RIM: . . . . . .   108 CUCHULAIN SEA   V   35
GO THERE, AND LIGHT A CAMP FIRE AT WOOD'S RIM: . . . .   108 CUCHULAIN SEA   V   35
CAMP-FIRE
GO THERE, AND LIGHT A CAMP-FIRE AT WOOD'S RIM: . . . .   108 CUCHULAIN SEA   35
CAMPING
. . . THERE CAMPING IN GRASSES DEEP, ...   50 OISIN 3   54
LIKE SOME LAST COURTIER AT A GYPSY CAMPING PLACE . . . .   314 FALLEN MAJESTY V   3
CAMPING-PLACE
LIKE SOME LAST COURTIER AT A GYPSY CAMPING-PLACE . . . .   314 FALLEN MAJESTY   3
CAMP'S
A SOLDIER ANSWERS: "BY THE CAMP'S FAR END . . . . .   712 FERENCZ RENYI   67
CANDLE
LIKE A CANDLE BURNT OUT, ...   142 MOODS   2
BUT PURER THAN A TALL CANDLE BEFORE THE HOLY ROOD . . .   208 HANRAHANS SONG   14
BUT PURE AS A TALL CANDLE BEFORE THE TRINITY . . . . .   208 HANRAHANS SONG V   14
BUT PURER THAN A TALL CANDLE BEFORE THE BLESSED ROOD . .   208 HANRAHANS SONG V   14
BECAUSE, IT MAY BE, OF THE CANDLE LIGHT . . . .   373 PHASES OF MOON V   14
HIS SLEEPLESS CANDLE AND LABORIOUS PEN. . . . .   375 PHASES OF MOON   86
A CANDLE AND WRITTEN PAGE. . . . .   419 MY HOUSE   13
HAVE SEEN HIS MIDNIGHT CANDLE GLIMMERING. . . . . . .   420 MY HOUSE   20
HAD SEEN HIS MIDNIGHT CANDLE GLIMMERING . . . .   420 MY HOUSE   V   20
TOWER WHERE A CANDLE GLEAMS, ...   420 MY HOUSE   V 20I
AND WROTE BY CANDLE LIGHT: BUT HER FORM MOVED . . . . .   467 HARUN RASHID   V 129
DAYBREAK AND A CANDLE END. . . . .   588 OLD WICKED MAN V REF
DAY-BREAK AND A CANDLE END. . . . .   588 OLD WICKED MAN V REF
CANDLE-END
DAYBREAK AND A CANDLE-END. . . . .   588 OLD WICKED MAN   9
DAYBREAK AND A CANDLE-END. . . . .   588 OLD WICKED MAN   18
DAYBREAK AND A CANDLE-END. . . . .   588 OLD WICKED MAN   27
DAYBREAK AND A CANDLE-END. . . . .   589 OLD WICKED MAN   36
DAYBREAK AND A CANDLE-END. . . . .   589 OLD WICKED MAN   45
DAYBREAK AND A CANDLE-END. . . . .   589 OLD WICKED MAN   54
DAYBREAK AND A CANDLE-END. . . . .   590 OLD WICKED MAN   63
CANDLE-LIGHT
BECAUSE, IT MAY BE, OF THE CANDLE-LIGHT . . . .   373 PHASES OF MOON   14
AND WROTE BY CANDLE-LIGHT: BUT HER FORM MOVED, ...   467 HARUN RASHID   129
CANDLE-LIKE
AND CANDLE-LIKE FOAM ON THE DIM SAND, ...   158 BELOVED RHYMES   10
CANDLE'S
SHOWS THROUGH OUR LINEAMENTS. MY CANDLE'S BRIGHT, . . .   464 HARUN RASHID   70
CANDLES
SHE CARRIES IN THE CANDLES, ...   89 ISLE IN WATER   9
GOD LIGHTS THE STARS, HIS CANDLES, ...   96 MOLL MAGEE   51
AND TIME BADE ALL HIS CANDLES FLARE . . . .   138 TO IRELAND   13
AND STILL THE STARRY CANDLES FLARE . . . .   138 TO IRELAND   V   13
IS COMELIER THAN CANDLES AT MOTHER MARY'S FEET. . . . .   147 UNAPPEAS HOST   12
IS COMELIER THAN CANDLES BEFORE MAURYA'S FEET. . . . .   147 UNAPPEAS HOST   V   12
BUT THOSE THE CANDLES LIGHT ARE NOT AS THOSE . . . . .   445 SCHOOL CHILDR   50
"HAVE NO LIT CANDLES IN YOUR ROOM," . . . .   569 THREE BUSHES   8
WHERE NO CANDLES ARE. . . . .   570 THREE BUSHES   25
WHERE NO LIT CANDLES ARE, ...   570 THREE BUSHES   V   25
CANDLESTICK
WHEN EVERY SILVER CANDLESTICK OR SCONCE . . . .   410 TOWER   26
CANKER-WORM
AS THE CANKER-WORM ON A MILK-WHITE ROSE: . . . . . .   673 ISLE STAT II 3   177
CANN
. . . NO, NEITHER IN HOUSE OF A CANN . . . .   50 OISIN 3   V   49
I CRIED, "COME OUT OF THE SHADOW, CANN OF THE NAILS OF   51 OISIN 3   V   61
GOLD!
CANNON
THOUGH HE'D BUT CANNON--WHEREAS WE THAT HAD THOUGHT . .   258 KING NO KING   7
AND THE OUTRAGEOUS CANNON, ...   317 NIGHT COME   10
WHAT MATTER THAT NO CANNON HAD BEEN TURNED . . . . . .   429 NINETEEN 19   19
I NEED SOME MIND THAT, IF THE CANNON SOUND . . . . . .   471 ALL SOUL NIGHT   11
HURRAH FOR REVOLUTION AND CANNON COME AGAIN! . . . . .   590 GREAT DAY   3
HURRAH FOR REVOLUTION AND MORE CANNON SHOT: . . . . .   590 GREAT DAY   V   1
CANNONADE
THAT SUCH CANNONADE . . . .   496 MOHINI CHATTER   24
CANNON-SHOT
HURRAH FOR REVOLUTION AND MORE CANNON-SHOT! . . . . .   590 GREAT DAY   1
CANNS
"I LOVED NO MAN, THOUGH CANNS BESOUGHT, ...   7 OISIN 3   V   62
CAME BY THE CANNS OF THE RED BRANCH . . . .   53 OISIN 3   V   87
CANOPY
UPON THE CLOUDY CANOPY, ...   397 POLIT PRISONER   22
THAT SLEEPS UNDER THE CANOPY: . . . .   528 TOM LUNATIC   2
AND RULE TOGETHER UNDER A CANOPY. . . . .   767 SHADOW WATER A   385
CANTERED
WE CANTERED TO THE SHORE, AND KNEW . . . .   14 OISIN 1   178
CANVAS
AND ALL THEIR SWELLING CANVAS WEAR, ...   530 OLD TOM AGAIN   2
AND ALL THEIR YELLOW CANVAS WEAR, ...   530 OLD TOM AGAIN   V   2
GOD! THEY'RE MAD TO FLY SUCH CANVAS!" . . . .   718 PHANTOM SHIP   14
CAOILTE
CAOILTE, AND CONAN, AND FINN WERE THERE, ...   3 OISIN 1   13
CAOILTE, CONAN, AND FINN CAME NEAR, ...   10 OISIN 1   111
WHAT PLACE HAVE CAOILTE AND CONAN, AND BRAN, SCEOLAN,   61 OISIN 3   195
LOMAIR?
I WILL GO TO CAOILTE, AND CONAN, AND BRAN, SCEOLAN, LOMAIR,   63 OISIN 3   223
CAOILTE TOSSING HIS BURNING HAIR, ...   140 HOSTING SIDHE   3

125

CAOILTE   (CONTINUED)
     CAOILTE TOSSING HIS BURNING HAIR, ...   141 HOSTING SIDHE   15
CAOLTE
     WHAT PLACE HAVE CAOLTE AND FIN, AND BRAN, SGEOLAN, LOMAIR?   61 OISIN 3   V   195
     TO FIN, CAOLTE, AND CONAN, AND BRAN, SGEOLAN, LOMAIR. . .   63 OISIN 3   V   224
     . . . FINVARRA, FEACRA, AND CAOLTE . . . .   174 ELEMENT POWERS V   T
CAP   SEE KNEE-CAP
     AND FOR THE PEEWIT PAINTS HIS CAP, ...   18 OISIN 1   266
     THE CAP AND BELLS . . . .   159 CAP AND BELLS   T
     CAP AND BELL . . . .   159 CAP AND BELLS V   T
     "I HAVE CAP AND BELLS," HE PONDERED, ...   160 CAP AND BELLS   21
     "I'VE CAP AND BELL," HE PONDERED, ...   160 CAP AND BELLS V   21
     THEY THREW A HALFPENNY INTO MY CAP, ...   300 RUN PARADISE   2
     HER KNEE CAP BROKEN: THAT GIRL I DECLARE . . . . .   578 CRAZED GIRL   V   6
     BLEW MY CRIMSON CAP AWAY . . . .   656 ISLE STAT I 3   16
     BENEATH A POINTED CAP OF GREEN: . . . .   728 PRIEST FAIRY   22
     HE DREW FROM HIS CAP A FEATHER GREY, ...   729 PRIEST FAIRY   29
CAPS
     IN THEIR DOWNY CAPS, AND STARTLE THE NAPS . . . . .   644 SONG FAERIES   11
     IN THEIR DOWNY CAPS, AND STARTLE THE NAPS . . . . .   676 ISLE STAT II 3   258
CAPTAIN
     IF HE WERE DEAD: BUT WHO WILL BE OUR CAPTAIN, . . .   224 SHADOW WATER B   60
     BECOME OUR CAPTAIN, AIBRIC. I AM RESOLVED . . . .   225 SHADOW WATER B   64
     THE SOLDIER TAKES PRIDE IN SALUTING HIS CAPTAIN, . . .   547 TO SAME TUNE 3   1
     SOLDIERS TAKE PRIDE IN SALUTING THEIR CAPTAIN, . . .   547 TO SAME TUNE 3 V   1
     SOLDIERS TAKE PRIDE IN SALUTING THEIR CAPTAIN, . . .   548 TO SAME TUNE 3   21
     THE SOLDIER TAKES PRIDE IN SALUTING HIS CAPTAIN, . . .   614 MARCH SONGS 2   1
CAPTAIN'S
     AND TAKE THE CAPTAIN'S SHARE OF EVERYTHING . . . .   225 SHADOW WATER B   73
     YOU'LL HAVE THE CAPTAIN'S SHARE OF EVERYTHING. . . .   225 SHADOW WATER B V 67A
CAPTAINS
     WHERE ARE THE CAPTAINS THAT GOVERN MANKIND? . . . .   548 TO SAME TUNE 3   22
     WHERE ARE THE CAPTAINS THAT GOVERN MANKIND? . . . .   615 MARCH SONGS 2   22
CAPTIVE
     SPRANG DRIPPING, AND, WITH CAPTIVE DEMONS SENT . . .   38 OISIN 2   130
     AND DID THOSE WATCHERS BID YOU TAKE ME CAPTIVE? . . .   236 SHADOW WATER B   322
     THE CAPTIVE FROM KINSALE. . . . .   740 EARL PAUL   28
     A CAPTIVE WOMAN FROM THE NARROW BRIDGE, ...   749 SHADOW WATER A   49
CAPTIVE'S
     THE CAPTIVE'S JOURNEYS TO AND FRO WERE WRIT . . . .   37 OISIN 2   116
CAPTIVES
     AND CAPTIVES BOUND WITH LEATHERN THONGS . . . . .   7 OISIN 1   77
     MY CAPTIVES, BOUND IN LEATHERN THONGS, ...   8 OISIN 1   V   78
CAPTIVES'
     THE CAPTIVES' JOURNEYS TO AND FRO WERE WRIT . . . .   37 OISIN 2   V 116
     THE CAPTIVES' FOOTSTEPS WRITTEN TO AND FRO: . . . .   37 OISIN 2   V 118
CAR   SEE GLEN-CAR
     CAME BALOR, AS OLD AS A FOREST, CAR BORNE, HIS MIGHTY HEAD   53 OISIN 3   V   91
          SUNK
     . . . AND O'ER YOUR CAR HEADS PEER . . . .   73 ANASHU VIJAYA V   45
CAR-BORNE
     DARK BALOR, AS OLD AS A FOREST, CAR-BORNE, HIS MIGHTY HEAD   53 OISIN 3   91
          SUNK
     CAME CAR-BORNE BALOR, AS OLD AS A FOREST, HIS VAST FACE   53 OISIN 3   V   91
          SUNK
CARD
     THAT ALL BUT THE ONE CARD BECAME . . . .   411 TOWER   68
CARDINAL
     THAT MADE HER DIARMUID DEAR, AND SOME OLD CARDINAL . . .   366 HER COURAGE   6
     AND THAT MADE HER DERMUID DEAR, AND SOME OLD CARDINAL . .   366 HER COURAGE   V   6
CARDS
     TO OLD MEN PLAYING AT CARDS . . . .   144 HOST OF AIR   23
     O'DRISCOLL SCATTERED THE CARDS . . . .   145 HOST OF AIR   37
     AND SCATTERED THE CARDS WITH A CRY, ...   145 HOST OF AIR   V   38
     GOOD FELLOWS SHUFFLED CARDS IN AN OLD BAWN: . . . .   411 TOWER   65
     HE SO BEWITCHED THE CARDS UNDER HIS THUMB . . . .   411 TOWER   67
     A PACK OF HOUNDS AND NOT A PACK OF CARDS, ...   411 TOWER   69
CARE
     WHERE CARE CANNOT TROUBLE THE LEAST OF OUR DAYS, . . .   27 OISIN 1   409
     UPON HIS HEAD TO CAST AWAY MY CARE. . . . . . .   102 FERGUS DRUID   V   14
     AND FOUND HER DYEING CLOTH WITH SUBTLE CARE . . .   105 CUCHULAIN SEA V   2A
     AND GOD'S BELL BUOYED TO BE THE WATER'S CARE: . . .   114 ROSE OF BATTLE   4
     BEFORE EARTH TOOK HIM TO HER STONY CARE: . . . .   126 DREAM OF FAERY   4
     BEFORE EARTH MADE OF HIM HER SLEEPY CARE: . . . .   126 DREAM OF FAERY V   4
     AND RODE WITH LITTLE CARE. . . . .   133 FR GILLIGAN   28
     WITH PLANETS IN HIS CARE, ...   134 FR GILLIGAN   46
     THINE EYES GROW FULL OF TENDER CARE: . . . . . .   135 TWO TREES   19
     O WHAT TO ME MY MOTHER'S CARE, ...   151 HEART OF WOMAN   5
     THAT MY OLD CARE MAY CEASE: . . . .   174 ELEMENT POWERS   10
     THEIR LOVE WAS NEVER DROWNED IN CARE . . . . . .   189 BAILE AILLINN   8
     CARE MORE ABOUT THE KEGS OF SILVER AND GOLD . . .   232 SHADOW WATER B   234
     I WILL CONFESS IT ALL. WHAT DO I CARE, ...   245 SHADOW WATER B   485
     WHAT DOES HE CARE IF MY HEART BREAK? . . . . . .   275 GREY ROCK   104
     MY MARRIED SISTER PUT INTO MY CARE . . . . . .   276 TWO KINGS   V   E
     HAVE BEEN THE MEASURE OF THAT CARE." BUT. EOCHAID, . .   276 TWO KINGS   V   H
     ALWAYS IN HIS ONE SEAT, AND BID ME CARE HIM . . .   280 TWO KINGS   80
     IF BUT I DO NOT SEEM TO CARE." . . . .   297 THREE BEGGARS   68
     "WHAT CARE I IF YOU SLEEP OR WAKE? . . . .   304 HOUR DAWN   40
     THE GOLDEN TOP OF CARE? . . . .   309 PLAYER QUEEN   20
     WHAT NEED HAVE YOU TO CARE . . . .   312 CHILD DANCING   2
     BY TENDERNESS AND CARE, ...   346 ON WOMAN   37

```
                                              PAGE     TITLE        LINE
CARE   (CONTINUED)
    O LITTLE DID THEY CARE WHO DANCED BETWEEN,  . . .    383 VISION ROBART      37
    SO THE CROWD COME THEY CARE NOT WHAT MAY COME.  . . . .   398 LEADERS CROWD      10
    BUT WHAT CARE I THAT LONG FOR A MAN'S LOVE?  . . . .   448 HERO GIRL FOOL     17
    GAVE BUT MORE REASON FOR A WOMAN'S CARE.  . . . . .   466 HARUN RASHID      111
    PERPLEXED HER FANTASY AND PLANNED HER CARE?  . . . .   466 HARUN RASHID      114
    PERPLEXED HER PHANTASY AND PLANNED HER CARE?  . . . .   466 HARUN RASHID    V 114
    THAT STIRRED HER FANTASY AND PLANNED HER CARE,  . . . .   466 HARUN RASHID    V 114
    BUT NAMES ARE NOTHING.  I CARE NOT WHO IT BE.  . . .   473 ALL SOUL NIGHT  V  81
    I CARE NOT WHAT THE SAILORS SAY!  . . . . . .   509 JANE REPROVED       1
    CARE NOT A THRANEEN FOR WHAT CHANCED  . . . . .   514 JANE GROWN OLD  V  18
    BUT NOT FROM HER PROTECTING CARE.  . . . . . .   522 LULLABY           18
    "WHO'D CARE TO DIG 'EM," SAID THE OLD, OLD MAN,  . .   548 TO SAME TUNE 3     7
    "WHO'D CARE TO DIG 'EM," SAID THE OLD, OLD MAN,  . .   548 TO SAME TUNE 3    17
    "WHO'D CARE TO DIG 'EM," SAID THE OLD, OLD MAN,  . .   549 TO SAME TUNE 3    27
    BANISH AGE AND CARE,  . . . . . . . . .   620 JOHN KINSELLA     20
    IS SORROW IN HIS SONG, OR ANY CARE?  . . . .   652 ISLE STAT I 2     20
    GROWETH THE GOBLIN FLOWER OF JOY, HER CARE,  . . .   653 ISLE STAT I 2     39
    AND NEVER HEARD OF GRIEF OR CARE  . . . . .   667 ISLE STAT II 3    21
    LEAD THEY ONE WITH FOOLISH CARE,  . . . . . .   727 LOVERS QUARREL    29
    THE LIVING WOODS FOREGO THEIR CARE,  . . . . .   736 SUMMER EVENING     1
    CARE NOT IF BEYOND THE SHADOWS  . . . . . .   737 IN FIRELIGHT       7
CARED
    THE VERSES THAT THEY CARED FOR ON THE DAY  . . . .   257 RECONCILIATION V   2
    WHAT CARED DUKE ERCOLE, THAT BID  . . . . . .   287 TO WEALTHY MAN     9
    FOR ALL THE SLEEPER KNEW OR CARED!  . . . . .   307 HOUR DAWN        115
    CARED NOT A THRANEEN FOR WHAT CHANCED  . . . .   514 JANE GROWN OLD    18
    BUT WHAT CARED I THAT SET HIM ON TO RIDE,  . . . .   629 CIRCUS ANIMALS    15
CAREFUL
    WHOSE CAREFUL PASTERN PRESSED THE SOD  . . . . .     2 OISIN 1         V  7W
    A CAREFUL FIELD-MOUSE FINDS A FALLEN CRUMB!  . . .   713 FERENCZ RENYI     77
    I MUST BE CAREFUL NOW.  I HAVE SUCH PLOTS--  . . .   722 WITCH VIVIEN      65
CARELESS
    THE PROUD AND CARELESS NOTES LIVE ON,  . . . .   213 BLESS PSALTER     19
    THE CARELESS PLANETS IN THEIR COURSES,  . . . . .   344 DAWN               7
    WHAT A STAR SANG AND CARELESS MUSES HEARD!  . . . .   445 SCHOOL CHILDR     47
CARES
    IMMEDIATE, MOURNFUL, WHITE WITH SUDDEN CARES,  . . .    44 OISIN 2      V 229A
    HIS MIND RAN ALL ON MONEY CARES AND FEARS,  . . . .   127 DREAM OF FAERY    14
    NOR THOSE UNPASSING CARES,  . . . . . . .   315 FRIENDS            5
    . . . "SPEAK ALL YOUR MIND! WHO CARES,  . . . . .   450 OWEN AHERNE       21
    CARES WHAT KING SETS UP HIS RULE.  . . . . .   635 BLACK TOWER       14
    SHE CARES NO WHIT FOR EITHER, BUT HAS BLEST  . . . .   660 ISLE STAT II 1    49
CARESSED
    BUT NIAM WITH HER HANDS CARESSED HIS EARS,  . . . .    30 OISIN 2         V  26
    AND SHE, TO WIN HIM, HIS GREY HAIR CARESSED!  . . .   110 CUCHULAIN SEA     73
    ABOVE THE STAGGERING GIRL, HER THIGHS CARESSED  . .   441 LEDA AND SWAN      2
CARGO
    HIDING AMID THE CARGO OF A STEAMSHIP,  . . . . . .   578 CRAZED GIRL        5
CARHEADS
    . . . AND FROM YOUR CARHEADS PEER,  . . . . . .    73 ANASHU VIJAYA     45
CARICATURE
    O HEART, O TROUBLED HEART--THIS CARICATURE,  . . . .   409 TOWER              2
CAROL
    SING, O YOU LITTLE STARS! O SING AND RAISE YOUR RAPTUROUS     72 ANASHU VIJAYA     20
        CAROL
    SING, OH YE LITTLE STARS! OH, SING, AND RAISE YOUR     72 ANASHU VIJAYA  V  20
        RAPTUROUS CAROL
CARP
    SAVE, WITH THE LITTLE GOLDEN GREEDY CARP,  . . . . .   720 WITCH VIVIEN       2
    HOW STILL IT IS!  I HEAR THE CARP GO SPLASH,  . . . .   722 WITCH VIVIEN      62
CARPENTER      SEE WORKING-CARPENTER
CARPENTERS
    SET CARPENTERS TO WORK ON NO WIDE TABLE,  . . . . .   340 SHEP GOATHERD     50
    AND DIRTY NAILS OF CARPENTERS.  . . . . . . .   440 WISDOM          V   7
    DIGGERS AND CARPENTERS MAKE GRAVE AND COFFIN!  . . .   609 IN TARAS HALLS    17
CARPET
    ALL WEAR THE CARPET WITH THEIR SHOES!  . . . . .   337 SCHOLARS           8
    WEAR OUT THE CARPET WITH THEIR SHOES  . . . . .   337 SCHOLARS        V   8
CARRAIG        SEE PAIRC-NA-CARRAIG
CARRIAGE
    CARRIAGE AND VOICE HAD HE!  . . . . . . . .   608 SONGS BURDEN 3    13
    THERE IN A TWO-HORSED CARRIAGE  . . . . . . .   628 JANE MOUNTAIN     13
    THERE IN A TWO HORSED CARRIAGE  . . . . . . .   628 JANE MOUNTAIN   V  13
CARRIED
    . . . TWO CARRIED A SACK FULL OF SAND,  . . . . .    60 OISIN 3          185
    THAT CARRIED THE TAKE TO SLIGO TOWN TO BE SOLD,  . . .    91 OLD FISHERMAN      7
    THAT CARRIED THE FISH FOR THE SALE IN THE FAR-AWAY TOWN,    91 OLD FISHERMAN  V   7
    WAS CARRIED TO THE GOODLY HOUSE  . . . . . .   192 BAILE AILLINN     72
    HE CARRIED EDAIN OFF FROM A KING'S HOUSE,  . . . .   224 SHADOW WATER B    48
    AND CARRIED HIM HIS FOOD WITH MY OWN HANDS,  . . .   280 TWO KINGS         88
    I SHALL BE CARRIED IN THE GUST, COMMAND,  . . . .   281 TWO KINGS        101
    WHO CARRIED IN THEIR MEMORY.  . . . . . . .   361 ALF POLLEXFEN     34
    WE'VE CARRIED IN OUR TREE.  . . . . . . . .   366 HER CHRIS TREE     3
    THE BRIDE IS CARRIED TO THE BRIDEGROOM'S CHAMBER  . . . .   459 FROM OEDIPUS       8
    CARRIED BY THE WANDERING FOOL.  . . . . . . .   484 SYMBOLS            4
CARRIER        SEE LINEN-CARRIER
CARRIES
    SHE CARRIES IN THE DISHES,  . . . . . . . .    89 ISLE IN WATER      5
    SHE CARRIES IN THE CANDLES,  . . . . . . . .    89 ISLE IN WATER      9
    AND CARRIES IT BETWEEN US.  HOLY FIRE  . . . . .   239 SHADOW WATER B   371
```

```
                                                        PAGE    TITLE              LINE
CARRIES   (CONTINUED)
    AND SO A HUNTER CARRIES IN THE EYE   . . . . . . . .   463 HARUN RASHID          61
    CARRIES A MUSICAL INSTRUMENT. . . . . . . . . . . . .   566 LAPIS LAZULI         42
CARROT
    BROWN, OR BLACK, OR CARROT, . . . . . . . . . . . . .   492 ANNE GREGORY          9
CARRY
    CARRY ME, YE FOUR, . . . . . . . . . . . . . . . . .    97 FOXHUNTER             2
    AND CARRY ME YE FOUR, . . . . . . . . . . . . . . .    97 FOXHUNTER        V     2
    AND CARRY ME, YOU FOUR, . . . . . . . . . . . . . .    97 FOXHUNTER        V     2
    CARRY ALL THAT MOURNFUL BEAUTY . . . . . . . . . .     124 CATHLEEN PARA         7
    WILL OVERTHROW HIS SHADOWS AND CARRY OFF . . . . .     184 QUEEN MAEVE          95
    TO TAKE HIM WHILE HE SLEEPS AND CARRY HIM . . . .      222 SHADOW WATER B       14
    A SHADOW DOES NOT CARRY SWORD OR SPEAR. . . . . .      224 SHADOW WATER B       44
    THAT EVERY MAN SHOULD CARRY HIS OWN SOUL . . . .       235 SHADOW WATER B      299
    OR CALLED BEFORE HIS EYES.  O CARRY ME . . . . .       249 SHADOW WATER B      568
    DID NOT THE POET CARRY HIM WITH AN AIR . . . . .       267 ALL TEMPT ME     V     7
    AND DREAM THAT I SHOULD CARRY . . . . . . . . . .      309 PLAYER QUEEN         19
    WOULD CARRY IT AWAY TO BLASPHEMOUS MEN. . . . . .      371 EGO DOMINUS          79
    AND FOR NO EAR BUT HIS.  CARRY THIS LETTER . . .       461 HARUN RASHID          4
    OR CARRY THE RINGED MAIL UPON MY BACK, . . . . .       463 HARUN RASHID         58
    WOULD I CARRY TO A FRIEND-- . . . . . . . . . . .      494 AT ALGECIRAS          8
    I WOULD CARRY TO A FRIEND-- . . . . . . . . . . .      494 AT ALGECIRAS     V     8
    I CARRY FROM MY MOTHER'S WOMB . . . . . . . . . .      506 REMORSE SPEECH       14
    I CARRY THE SUN IN A GOLDEN CUP, . . . . . . . .       525 DANCING DAYS          7
    I CARRY THE SUN IN A GOLDEN CUP, . . . . . . . .       525 DANCING DAYS         15
    I CARRY THE SUN IN A GOLDEN CUP, . . . . . . . .       525 DANCING DAYS         23
    MARK AND DIGEST MY TALE, CARRY IT AFAR . . . . .       554 RIBH AT TOMB          3
    CARRY THE GOLD ABOUT THE TOWN, . . . . . . . . .       596 COLONEL MARTIN       52
    OUR VOICES CARRY; AND THOUGH SLUMBER-BOUND, . .        622 HOUND VOICE           5
    OUR VOICES CARRY; AND THOUGH SLUMBER BOUND, . .        622 HOUND VOICE      V     5
    CARRY IT! SUDDENLY IT IS STILL. . . . . . . . .        783 GREY ROUND            5
CARRYING
    THOSE TWO CAME CARRYING WINE AND MEAT AND BREAD, . . .  41 OISIN 2             184
    ALTHOUGH HE IS CARRYING STONE, BUT TWO . . . . . . .   192 BAILE AILLINN        83
CARS       SEE BATTLE-CARS
    ACROSS YOUR WANDERING RUBY CARS . . . . . . . . .      22 OISIN 1             330
    SING, TURNING IN YOUR CARS, . . . . . . . . . . .      73 ANASHU VIJAYA        44
    HAS WON THE GOLD HIS CARS OF BATTLE BRING." . . .     106 CUCHULAIN SEA        11
    MY FATHER STANDS AMID HIS BATTLE CARS." . . . . .     107 CUCHULAIN SEA     V  26
    AND WEARY OF THE CRASH OF BATTLE CARS." . . . . .     107 CUCHULAIN SEA     V  30
    THE CARS OF BATTLE AND HIS OWN NAME CRIED; . . .      111 CUCHULAIN SEA        85
    FOR FERGUS RULES THE BRAZEN CARS, . . . . . . . .     126 GOES FERGUS           9
    OUT OF THEIR WHIRLING CARS, . . . . . . . . . . .     175 ELEMENT POWERS    V  16
CART
    MY SORROW! FOR MANY A CREAK GAVE THE CREEL IN THE CART . .  91 OLD FISHERMAN    6
    AH WOE! FULL MANY A CREAK GAVE THE CREEL IN THE CART . .    91 OLD FISHERMAN  V  6
    AH ME! FULL MANY A CREAK GAVE THE CREEL IN THE CART . . .   91 OLD FISHERMAN  V  6
    THE CRY OF A CHILD BY THE ROADWAY, THE CREAK OF A LUMBERING  142 ROSE IN HEART   2
        CART,
    THERE, STANDING ON THE CART, . . . . . . . . . .      544 TO SAME TUNE 1        5
    "HARNESS AN ASS AND CART, . . . . . . . . . . . .     596 COLONEL MARTIN       51
    THERE, STANDING ON THE CART, . . . . . . . . . .      616 MARCH SONGS 3         5
CART-HORSE
    SHE KNOWS THAT IT WAS BUT THE CART-HORSE COUGHING  . .  230 SHADOW WATER B    176
CARVE
    OR CARVE A DREADFUL SPEAR. . . . . . . . . . . .       32 OISIN 2          V   56
    AND CARVE HIS NAME IN OGHAM." EOCHAID SAID, . . .     280 TWO KINGS            83
CARVED
    UNTIL I CARVED THESE WORDS: . . . . . . . . . .       123 DREAM OF DEATH       10
    TO BE CARVED ON A STONE AT THOOR BALLYLEE . . . .     406 CARVED STONE          T
    TO BE CARVED ON A STONE AT BALLYLEE . . . . . . .     406 CARVED STONE     V    T
    ARE CARVED IN LAPIS LAZULI, . . . . . . . . . . .     566 LAPIS LAZULI         38
    HE CARVED ON TREES, AND WITH A SUN-DRY WEED . . .     659 ISLE STAT II 1        8
    CARVED: HERE, BEYOND THE LAKE'S SLOW-MUFFLED TREAD, . .  662 ISLE STAT II 2    11
CARVEN
    AND CARVEN FIGURES ON THEIR PROWS . . . . . . . .      14 OISIN 1             190
    AND CARVEN FIGURES ON THEIR PROWS . . . . . . . .      23 OISIN 1             354
    A DOME MADE OUT OF ENDLESS CARVEN JAGS, . . . . .      38 OISIN 2             144
    WAITED.  ABOVE, IN ENDLESS CARVEN JAGS, . . . . .      38 OISIN 2          V  144
    LIFTED THE DOME, WHERE FACE IN CARVEN FACE . . .       39 OISIN 2          V  145
    IN MOULDED PLASTER OR IN CARVEN STONE? . . . . .      327 ROBERT GREGORY       77
    AND GONE ARE PHIDIAS' CARVEN IVORIES. . . . . . .     428 NINETEEN 19      V    7
CASE
    DEAR CRAOIBHIN AOIBHIN, LOOK INTO OUR CASE. . . .     264 ABBEY THEATRE         1
    "THAT'S CERTAINLY THE CASE," SAID HE. . . . . . .     510 JANE JUDGMENT        10
    "THAT'S CERTAINLY THE CASE," SAID HE. . . . . . .     510 JANE JUDGMENT        20
    "THAT'S CERTAINLY THE CASE," SAID SHE. . . . . .      510 JANE JUDGMENT    V   10
    AND UNDERSTOOD HER CASE. . . . . . . . . . . . .      571 THREE BUSHES         69
CASEMENT
    SHE DREW IN THE HEAVY CASEMENT . . . . . . . . .      159 CAP AND BELLS        11
    SHE DREW IN THE BRIGHTENING CASEMENT, . . . . . .     159 CAP AND BELLS    V   11
    ROGER CASEMENT . . . . . . . . . . . . . . . . .      581 ROGER CASEMENT        T
    I SAY THAT ROGER CASEMENT . . . . . . . . . . . .     581 ROGER CASEMENT        1
    THE GHOST OF ROGER CASEMENT . . . . . . . . . . .     583 GHOST ROG CASE        T
    THE GHOST OF ROGER CASEMENT . . . . . . . . . . .     583 GHOST ROG CASE        9
    THE GHOST OF ROGER CASEMENT . . . . . . . . . . .     583 GHOST ROG CASE       19
    THE GHOST OF ROGER CASEMENT . . . . . . . . . . .     584 GHOST ROG CASE       29
    THE GHOST OF ROGER CASEMENT . . . . . . . . . . .     584 GHOST ROG CASE       39
    CASEMENT UPON TRIAL, HALF HIDDEN BY THE BARS, . .     601 GALLERY REVIS         3
CASHEL
    ON THE GREY ROCK OF CASHEL THE MIND'S EYE . . . .     382 VISION ROBART         1
```

```
                                                     PAGE   TITLE          LINE
CASHEL  (CONTINUED)
     ON THE GREY ROCK OF CASHEL I SUDDENLY SAW . . . . . .   383 VISION ROBART    17
CASKET
     . . . REMADE, LIKE A CASKET OF GOLD . . . . . . . .     143 ROSE IN HEART     7
     . . . RE-MADE LIKE A CASKET OF GOLD . . . . . . . .     143 ROSE IN HEART  V  7
CAST
     THROUGH HEART AND SPINE; AND CAST HIM IN THE WAVE . . .  41 OISIN 2        182
     CAST THE LOOSE BULK, LEST NIAM FEAR HIM DEAD; . . . .    41 OISIN 2      V 183
     GO CAST YOUR BODY ON THE STONES AND PRAY, . . . . . .    42 OISIN 2        207
     WHO CAST ROUND FERGUS DREAMS, AND RUIN UNTOLD; . . . .  101 ROSE UPON ROOD   5
     UPON HIS HEAD TO CAST AWAY MY SORROW. . . . . . . . .   102 FERGUS DRUID    14
     UPON HIS HEAD TO CAST AWAY MY CARE. . . . . . . . . .   102 FERGUS DRUID  V 14
     THEN EMER CAST THE WEB UPON THE FLOOR, . . . . . . .    105 CUCHULAIN SEA    6
     THEREON HE SHOOK THE MORE AND CAST HIM DOWN . . . . .   106 CUCHULAIN SEA   14
     ALEEL, THE SWINEHERD, WEPT AND CAST HIM DOWN . . . . .  106 CUCHULAIN SEA V 14
     HE CAUGHT HIS BREATH AND CAST HIM WEEPING DOWN . . . .  106 CUCHULAIN SEA V 14
     GO, CAST ON HIM DELUSIONS MAGICAL, . . . . . . . . .    111 CUCHULAIN SEA   80
     A WOVEN SILENCE, OR BUT CAME TO CAST . . . . . . . .    114 ROSE OF BATTLE  13
     I CAST MY HEART INTO MY RHYMES, . . . . . . . . . .     139 TO IRELAND      45
     LET GO MY HANDS! WHY DO YOU CAST A SHADOW? . . . . .    235 SHADOW WATER B 283
     TO CAST HIS DREAMS AWAY. NO OTHER'LL DO IT. . . . .     239 SHADOW WATER B 366
     THE IMMORTAL MOCKERS HAVE CAST INTO HIS MIND, . . . .   249 SHADOW WATER B 567
     SOLDIERS THAT GAVE, WHATEVER DIE WAS CAST; . . . . .    269 PARDON FATHERS   9
     SHE CAST HERSELF UPON THE GROUND . . . . . . . . . .    275 GREY ROCK      107
     THEREON SHE CAST HERSELF UPON THE GROUND, . . . . . .   275 GREY ROCK    V 107
     THAT CAST THEIR SHADOWS UPON ROAD AND BRIDGE; . . . .   326 ROBERT GREGORY  51
     WOULD I COULD CAST A SAIL ON THE WATER . . . . . . .    330 BONE OF A HARE   1
     FROM BEAUTY THAT IS CAST OUT OF A MOULD . . . . . . .   334 LIVING BEAUTY    4
     AT DAWN TO CAST HIS FLIES, . . . . . . . . . . . .      347 FISHERMAN        5
     BODY AND SOUL CAST OUT AND CAST AWAY . . . . . . . .    374 PHASES OF MOON  62
     BODY AND SOUL CAST OUT AND CAST AWAY . . . . . . . .    374 PHASES OF MOON  62
     THEY ARE CAST BEYOND THE VERGE, AND IN A CLOUD, . . .   376 PHASES OF MOON 105
     I HAD THOUGHT THAT ALL MY DAYS WERE CAST . . . . . .    389 IMAGE PAST      12
     DROP THEIR CAST AT THE SIDE . . . . . . . . . . . .     414 TOWER          125
     LIFE SCARCE CAN CAST A FRAGRANCE ON THE WIND, . . . .   422 MY DESCENDANTS   5
     WHERE WE SHOULD CAST OFF BODY AND TRADE . . . . . . .   431 NINETEEN 19     73
     WHEN SUCH AS I CAST OUT REMORSE . . . . . . . . . .     479 SELF AND SOUL   68
     CAST BUT DEAD LEAVES TO MATHEMATICAL EQUALITY; . . . .  481 BLOOD AND MOON  24
     BUT COULD NOT CAST A SINGLE JET THEREON. . . . . . .    482 BLOOD AND MOON  39
     CAST YOUR MIND ON OTHER DAYS . . . . . . . . . . .      640 BEN BULBEN      81
     CAST A COLD EYE . . . . . . . . . . . . . . . . .       640 BEN BULBEN      92
     SOME CAST OF DIE, OR LET SOME ARROW GLANCE . . . . .    656 ISLE STAT I 3   40
     CAST ON THE SOUND, ON. ON. THIS NIGHT OF GRAVES, . . .  665 ISLE STAT II 2  71
     HAVE LIT LONE TAPERS. NOW THE NIGHT WAS CAST, . . . .   687 TWO TITANS      27
     CAST OFF THY HERESIES, AND SAVE THY SOUL . . . . . .    701 MOSADA 3        64
     HER HEAD CAST BACKWARD IN HER UNLOOSED HAIR. . . . .    701 MOSADA 3        67
     AND SOFT, ONE GLIMMERING STAR. RENYI HAS CAST . . . .   714 FERENCZ RENYI  115
     CAST OUT ALL HOPE, CAST OUT ALL FEAR, . . . . . . .     743 DANAAN QUICK    25
     CAST OUT ALL HOPE, CAST OUT ALL FEAR, . . . . . . .     743 DANAAN QUICK    25
     THE WRITINGS I HAVE CAST AWAY! . . . . . . . . . .      779 ACCURSED WHO     2
CASTAWAYS
     HIS DWINDLING SCORE AND HE SEEMED CASTAWAYS . . . . .   420 MY HOUSE        25
CAST-A-WAYS
     HIS DWINDLING SCORE AND HE SEEMED CAST-A-WAYS . . . .   420 MY HOUSE     V  25
CASTING
     AND SAID, CASTING ASIDE HIS DRAGGLED HAIR, . . . . .    105 CUCHULAIN SEA V  3
     ABOUT THE CASTING OUT OF MY NET, . . . . . . . . .      146 FISH             4
     CRIED, CASTING OFF THE MOUNTAIN SNOW, . . . . . . .     502 VACILLATION     60
     OR THAN THE SHIVERING CASTING NET OF THE STARS. . . .   762 SHADOW WATER A V 290
CASTING-NET
     OR THAN THE SHIVERING CASTING-NET OF THE STARS, . . .   237 SHADOW WATER B 329
     OR THAN THE SHIVERING CASTING-NET OF THE STARS. . . .   762 SHADOW WATER A 290
CASTLE
     NEARER THE CASTLE CAME WE. A VAST TIDE, . . . . . .      31 OISIN 2      V 27A
     FROM CASTLE TAYLOR TO THE ROXBOROUGH SIDE . . . . .     326 ROBERT GREGORY  58
     BESIDE THE CASTLE DOOR, WHERE ALL IS STARK . . . . .    377 PHASES OF MOON 126
     CASTLE DARGAN'S RUIN ALL LIT. . . . . . . . . . . .     788 HAWTHORN TREE    3
CASTLE'S
     AND EVEN THE SUN, THE DAY CASTLE'S WARDER, . . . . .     28 OISIN 1     V 423A
CASTS
     CASTS UP A SHOW AND THE WINDS ANSWER IT . . . . . .     186 QUEEN MAEVE    125
     THEY WOULD NOT SEND ME ONE THAT CASTS A SHADOW. . . .   235 SHADOW WATER B 285
     CASTS DERISION UPON . . . . . . . . . . . . . . .       476 DEATH            9
     CASTS UPON HIS EYES UNTIL AT LAST . . . . . . . . .     479 SELF AND SOUL   53
     CASTS BUT DEAD LEAVES TO MATHEMATICAL EQUALITY; . . .   481 BLOOD AND MOON V 24
     IMAGINATION TO THAT PITCH WHERE IT CASTS OUT . . . .    619 BRONZE HEAD     19
CASUAL
     SO WILD THAT EVERY CASUAL THOUGHT OF THAT AND THIS . .  316 COLD HEAVEN      4
     IN THE CASUAL COMEDY; . . . . . . . . . . . . . .       393 EASTER 1916     37
     BECAUSE I HAD FANCIED LOVE A CASUAL . . . . . . . .     533 HER TRIUMPH      2
     THAT ALL ATTENDANTS AND THE CASUAL CROWD MIGHT HEAR. .  609 IN TARAS HALLS  13
     CALCULATIONS THAT LOOK BUT CASUAL FLESH, PUT DOWN . .   610 STATUES         11
CAT      SEE MARTEN-CAT
     AND MARTIN CAT, AND BORDERS THAT OLD WOOD . . . . .     218 WOODS OF COOLE V 14
     SHE WILL BE LIKE A WILD CAT! FOR THESE QUEENS . . . .   232 SHADOW WATER B 233
     THE CAT AND THE MOON . . . . . . . . . . . . . .        378 CAT AND MOON     T
     THE CAT WENT HERE AND THERE . . . . . . . . . . .       378 CAT AND MOON     1
     THE CREEPING CAT, LOOKED UP. . . . . . . . . . . .      378 CAT AND MOON     4
     A SPECKLED CAT AND A TAME HARE . . . . . . . . . .      380 SONGS FOOL 1     1
     THE SPECKLED CAT SLEPT ON MY KNEE; . . . . . . . .      381 SONGS FOOL 2     2
     "THEY KILLED MY GOOSE AND A CAT. . . . . . . . . .      546 TO SAME TUNE 2   8
```

129

	PAGE	TITLE		LINE
CAT (CONTINUED)				
"THEY KILLED MY GOOSE AND A CAT.	546	TO SAME TUNE 2		18
"THEY KILLED MY GOOSE AND A CAT.	547	TO SAME TUNE 2		28
THAT CAN MAKE A CAT LAUGH, OR	589	OLD WICKED MAN		39
CATALPA				
NEITHER CATALPA TREE NOR SCENTED LIME	435	NEW FACES	V	2
CATALPA-TREE				
NEITHER CATALPA-TREE NOR SCENTED LIME	435	NEW FACES		2
CATARACT				
THE CATARACT SMOKES UPON THE MOUNTAIN SIDE, ...	311	MOUNTAIN TOMB		3
IN VAIN, IN VAIN: THE CATARACT STILL CRIES:	311	MOUNTAIN TOMB		9
THE CATARACT SMOKES ON THE MOUNTAIN SIDE.	311	MOUNTAIN TOMB	V	3
CATCH				
YES, VOICES: BUT I DO NOT CATCH THE WORDS.	233	SHADOW WATER B		251
THE CATCH CRIES OF THE CLOWN.	347	FISHERMAN	V	22
YOUNG MEN NO LONGER SUDDENLY CATCH THEIR BREATH . . .	355	BROKEN DREAMS		2
THAT MADE A CATCH IN THE BREATH--	416	TOWER		191
AND STRIKE ANOTHER TILL TIME CATCH:	476	EVA GORE-BOOTH		27
CATCH-CRIES				
THE CATCH-CRIES OF THE CLOWN, ...	347	FISHERMAN		22
CATCHERS SEE FLY-CATCHERS				
CATCHES				
PROCESSIONS THAT LACK HIGH STILTS HAVE NOTHING THAT CATCHES	622	HIGH TALK		1
THE EYE.				
CATCHING				
CATCHING SMALL BIRDS IN THE DEW OF THE MORN	636	BLACK TOWER		22
CAT-HEADED				
AND THE EDDYING CAT-HEADED BIRD:	783	GREY ROUND		23
CATHEDRAL				
AFTER GREAT CATHEDRAL GONG:	497	BYZANTIUM		4
CATHLEEN				
THE COUNTESS CATHLEEN IN PARADISE	124	CATHLEEN PARA		T
OF CATHLEEN, THE DAUGHTER OF HOULIHAN.	207	HANRAHANS SONG		5
OF CATHLEEN, THE DAUGHTER OF HOULIHAN.	207	HANRAHANS SONG		10
IS CATHLEEN, THE DAUGHTER OF HOULIHAN.	208	HANRAHANS SONG		15
THE COUNTESS CATHLEEN WAS THE NAME I GAVE IT:	629	CIRCUS ANIMALS		18
CAT-O'-NINE-TAILS				
AS WITH THE CAT-O'-NINE-TAILS OF THE MIND, ...	374	PHASES OF MOON		42
CATS				
FROM THE WIVES, AND THE CATS, AND THE CHILDREN, . . .	92	FATHER OHART		15
FROM THEIR WIVES, AND THEIR CATS, AND THEIR CHILDREN, . .	92	FATHER OHART	V	15
AS MIDDLE NIGHT GREAT CATS WITH SILVER CLAWS, ...	185	QUEEN MAEVE		115
CATTLE				
HERDED THE CATTLE CAME WITH STUMBLING FEET, ...	106	CUCHULAIN SEA		19
WAS DRIVING CATTLE CAME SHE WITH SWIFT FEET, ...	106	CUCHULAIN SEA	V	19
AND TURNED THE FARMER'S MEMORY FROM HIS CATTLE, . . .	129	BOOK STORIES		6
TOILED WITH EMPOUNDED CATTLE THROUGH THE MIRE, ...	276	TWO KINGS	V	2
THAT WITH EMPOUNDED CATTLE TROD THE MIRE, ...	277	TWO KINGS		4
THE FORD WHERE DRINKING CATTLE MAKE A STIR	326	ROBERT GREGORY		53
ROADS FULL OF BEGGARS, CATTLE IN THE FIELDS, ...	487	SEVEN SAGES		18
THE HERON-BILLED PALE CATTLE BIRD, ...	493	AT ALGECIRAS	V	1
THE HERON-BILLED PALE CATTLE BIRDS, ...	493	AT ALGECIRAS	V	1
CATTLE-BIRDS				
THE HERON-BILLED PALE CATTLE-BIRDS	493	AT ALGECIRAS		1
CATULLUS				
DID THEIR CATULLUS WALK THAT WAY?	337	SCHOLARS		12
SHOULD THEIR CATULLUS WALK THAT WAY:	337	SCHOLARS	V	12
CAUGHT				
AND CAUGHT THE SILVER HARP AWAY, ...	17	OISIN 1		240
THAN THIS STRANGE BARD," HE CRIED, AND CAUGHT	17	OISIN 1	V	239
AND CAUGHT MY HANDS, BUT SPAKE NO WORD	25	OISIN 1		374
AND CAUGHT MY HANDS AND SPAKE NO WORD	25	OISIN 1	V	374
. . . CROZIERED ONE, CAUGHT IN YOUR NET:	58	OISIN 3		167
. . . CROZIERED ONE, CAUGHT IN THY NET--	58	OISIN 3	V	167
. . . CROZIERED ONE, CAUGHT IN THEIR NET:	58	OISIN 3	V	167
HE CAUGHT HIS BREATH AND CAST HIM WEEPING DOWN	106	CUCHULAIN SEA	V	14
AND CAUGHT A LITTLE SILVER TROUT.	149	WANDER AENGUS		8
AND CAUGHT THAT CAUGHT FIRE LIKE THE DRIED FLAX, ...	181	QUEEN MAEVE		28
AN OLD MAN CAUGHT THE HORSE'S HEAD	191	BAILE AILLINN		57
HE HAS CAUGHT THE CRESCENT MOON OUT OF THE SKY, . . .	239	SHADOW WATER B		370
CAUGHT AND CRACKED HIS FLEA, THE THIRD, ...	299	THREE HERMITS		30
BUT THE FOOLS CAUGHT IT, ...	320	COAT		5
CAUGHT UP IN CONTEMPLATION, THE MIND'S EYE	375	PHASES OF MOON		79
I'D STAND AND MUTTER THERE UNTIL HE CAUGHT	377	PHASES OF MOON		131
BEING CAUGHT BETWEEN THE PULL	384	VISION ROBART		59
CAUGHT IN THAT SENSUAL MUSIC ALL NEGLECT	407	SAIL BYZANTIUM		7
CAUGHT BY AN OLD MAN'S JUGGLERIES	411	TOWER		60
MIND FROM MIND HAS CAUGHT;	420	MY HOUSE	V	20G
AND TURN TOWARDS MY CHAMBER, CAUGHT	424	ROAD AT DOOR		14
BY THE DARK WEBS, HER NAPE CAUGHT IN HIS BILL, ...	441	LEDA AND SWAN		3
AND AGAMEMNON DEAD. BEING SO CAUGHT UP, ...	441	LEDA AND SWAN		11
BUT O! MY HEART COULD BEAR NO MORE WHEN THE UPLAND CAUGHT	450	OWEN AHERNE		11
THE WIND:				
NO LONGER IN LETHEAN FOLIAGE CAUGHT	500	VACILLATION		27
TILL SUDDENLY IN GRIEF'S CONTAGION CAUGHT, ...	537	HER VISION		22
ALL THERE CAUGHT UP THE TUNE:	545	TO SAME TUNE 1		15
ALL THERE CAUGHT UP THE TUNE:	616	MARCH SONGS 3		15
I WOULD HAVE SPARED HER HANDMAID, BUT SHE CAUGHT . . .	755	SHADOW WATER A		167
SHE CAUGHT THIS BLADE OUT OF MY BELT AND DIED.	755	SHADOW WATER A	V	168
I AM CAUGHT IN WOVEN NETS OF ENCHANTMENT. LOOK! . . .	762	SHADOW WATER A		293

CAULDRON
    CAULDRON AND SPEAR AND STONE AND SWORD, • • • • • • • 196 BAILE AILLINN   165
CAUSE
    AND MEN WHO LOVED THE CAUSE THAT NEVER DIES. • • • • • 130 BOOK STORIES V 24
    NOR GAVE LOUD SERVICE TO A CAUSE • • • • • • • • • 273 GREY ROCK   57
    BOUND NEITHER TO CAUSE NOR TO STATE, • • • • • • • 414 TOWER   129
    BUT A GOOD STRONG CAUSE AND BLOWS ARE DELIGHT." • • • 545 TO SAME TUNE 1   14
    BUT A GOOD STRONG CAUSE"--THE ROPE GAVE A JERK THERE, • • 545 TO SAME TUNE 1   23
    BUT A GOOD STRONG CAUSE AND THE BLOWS ARE DELIGHT." • • 545 TO SAME TUNE 1 V 14
    ALL HAPPINESS IN ITS OWN CAUSE OR GROUND. • • • • • 557 RIBH ECSTASY   4
    BUT A GOOD STRONG CAUSE AND BLOWS ARE DELIGHT." • • • 616 MARCH SONGS 3   14
    BUT A GOOD STRONG CAUSE"--THE ROPE GAVE A JERK THERE, • • 616 MARCH SONGS 3   23
    TWO MEN WHO LOVE ONE MAID HAVE AMPLE CAUSE • • • • 659 ISLE STAT II 1   30
    UPON THE CAUSE YOU SERVED, THAT WE • • • • • • • • 791 REPRISALS   13
CAVE
    THE WEAK WORM HIDING DOWN IN ITS SMALL CAVE, • • • • • 101 ROSE UPON ROOD   16
    TO THE CAVE, WHERE DATHI THE BLESSED HAD GONE, • • • • 166 BLESSED   V 3
    WITH A BLINK IN HIS EYES AT THE CAVE MOUTH, • • • • • 166 BLESSED   V 3
CAVE-MOUTH
    WITH A BLINK IN HIS EYES, AT THE CAVE-MOUTH, • • • • • 166 BLESSED   3
CAVERN
    I WILL FIND OUT SOME CAVERN IN THE HILLS • • • • • 448 HERO GIRL FOOL V 11
    IN CAVERN, CREVICE, HOLE, • • • • • • • • • • 546 TO SAME TUNE 2   5
    IN CAVERN, CREVICE OR HOLE, • • • • • • • • • • 546 TO SAME TUNE 2 V   5
    WHAT MATTER? OUT OF CAVERN COMES A VOICE, • • • • • 564 GYRES   15
    WHAT MATTER? OUT OF CAVERN COME A VOICE • • • • • 564 GYRES   V 15
    THE CAVERN OF THE MIND? • • • • • • • • • • • 600 THOSE IMAGES   2
    FROM WHERE PAN'S CAVERN IS • • • • • • • • • • 612 NEWS ORACLE   31
    IN CAVERN, CREVICE, OR HOLE, • • • • • • • • • 613 MARCH SONGS 1   5
    WHEN SHE IN A CAVERN LIES, • • • • • • • • • • 658 ISLE STAT I 3   86
CAVERNED
    CAVERNED IN NIGHT UNDER THE DRIFTED SNOW, • • • • • • 563 MERU   10
CAVERN-GLOOMS
    WHERE TREES MADE SUDDEN CAVERN-GLOOMS • • • • • • • 16 OISIN 1   V 224B
CAVERNS
    EYED PANTHERS IN THEIR DESERT CAVERNS ROVE • • • • • 681 SEEKER   V   4
CAVE'S
    WITH BLINKING EYES, AT THE CAVE'S EDGE, • • • • • • 167 BLESSED   V 4C
CAVES   SEE DESERT-CAVES
    AND TOSS AND TURN IN NARROW CAVES: • • • • • • • 19 OISIN 1   281
    I PASSED BY MANY CAVES OF DRIPPING STONE, • • • • • 657 ISLE STAT I 3   47
CEASE
    AND KISSED, AS THEY WOULD NEVER CEASE, • • • • • • 16 OISIN 1   215
    AND THEY CEASE WITH A SIGH OF "UNJUST! UNJUST!" • • • • 27 OISIN 1   V 416
    DARKEN: HEAVEN IS ANGRY. CEASE! UNTO MY MIND, • • • 42 OISIN 2   V 205
    AND LIGHTNING FLASH FOR EVER? CEASE AND HEAR. • • • 42 OISIN 2   V 207
    CEASE, CEASE, O MOURNFUL, LAUGHING FENIAN HORN! • • 43 OISIN 2   213
    CEASE, CEASE, O MOURNFUL, LAUGHING FENIAN HORN! • • 43 OISIN 2   V 213
    AH, CEASE, THOU MOURNFUL, LAUGHING FENIAN HORN! • • 43 OISIN 2   V 213
    AH, CEASE, YOU MOURNFUL, LAUGHING FENIAN HORN! • • • • 43 OISIN 2   V 213
    ALL DRIPPING ON A GRASSY SLOPE, AND SAW THEM CEASE TO CHASE 76 INDIAN ON GOD   4
    AND AH, THEY KNOW NOT, AS THEY PINE AND CEASE, • • • 81 EPHEMERA   V 24I
    HE MADE FOR HER AN ARMY CEASE TO BE." • • • • • • 106 CUCHULAIN SEA V 16B
    AND GOD WOULD BID HIS WARFARE CEASE, • • • • • • • 113 ROSE OF PEACE   13
    AND GOD WOULD BID MAN'S WARFARE CEASE, • • • • • • 113 ROSE OF PEACE V 13
    FOR HIM WHO HEARS LOVE SING AND NEVER CEASE, • • • • 114 ROSE OF BATTLE   10
    OR HOPES THAT IN MERE HOPING FLICKER AND CEASE: • • • 162 ASKS FORGIVE   3
    AND HOPES THAT IN MERE HOPING FLICKER AND CEASE: • • • 162 ASKS FORGIVE V 3
    THAT MY OLD CARE MAY CEASE: • • • • • • • • • • 174 ELEMENT POWERS   10
    I SHALL NOT CEASE TO BLESS BECAUSE • • • • • • • 379 SAINT HUNCH   7
    CEASE TO REMEMBER THE DELIGHTS OF YOUTH, TRAVEL-WEARIED 459 FROM OEDIPUS   2
        AGED MAN:
    AND HE, DESPITE HIS TERROR, CANNOT CEASE • • • • • 563 MERU   4
    OH, CEASE YOUR SINGING! WILD AND SHRILL AND LOUD, • • • 648 ISLE STAT I 1   99
    WITH THEIR UNHUMAN SORROWS. CEASE! NO MORE! • • • 661 ISLE STAT II 1 58
    CEASE! THERNOT'S WOUNDED, CEASE! THEY WILL NOT HEED. • • 665 ISLE STAT II 2 64
    CEASE! THERNOT'S WOUNDED, CEASE! THEY WILL NOT HEED. • 665 ISLE STAT II 2 64
    MY SINKING BRAIN!--CEASE!--CEASE! HEARD YE YON SOUND? • • 665 ISLE STAT II 2 73
    MY SINKING BRAIN!--CEASE!--CEASE! HEARD YE YON SOUND? • 665 ISLE STAT II 2 73
    THE DIRGE OF HER YE LOVE. CEASE!--CEASE! • • • • • 665 ISLE STAT II 2 74
    THE DIRGE OF HER YE LOVE. CEASE!--CEASE! • • • • • 665 ISLE STAT II 2 74
    AH! YOU ARE WEEPING; HERE SHOULD ALL GRIEF CEASE. • • • 672 ISLE STAT II 3 149
    SAD LADY, CEASE! • • • • • • • • • • • • • 672 ISLE STAT II 3 160
    • • • CEASE THE WINDS, AND ON THEIR POLES • • • • 719 PHANTOM SHIP   17
    CEASE THE SAILS THEIR FLAPPING UPROAR, AND THE HULL NO 719 PHANTOM SHIP   18
        LONGER ROLLS.
    CEASE THE SAILS, THEIR FLAPPING UPROAR TO THE HULL 719 PHANTOM SHIP V 18
        NO LONGER ROLLS.
CEASED
    AND LOVE, IN THE HOURS WHEN YOUTH HAS CEASED: • • • • 2 OISIN 1   V 7A
    NOR CEASED UNTIL WHITE NIAMH STROKED HIS EARS • • • • 30 OISIN 2   26
    AN ENDLESS WAR. THE HUNDRED YEARS HAD CEASED: • • • • 44 OISIN 2   224
    AN ENDLESS WAR. THE HUNDREDTH YEAR HAD CEASED. • • • 44 OISIN 2   V 224
    CEASED ON OUR HANDS AND OUR FACES, ON HAZEL AND OAK LEAF, 48 OISIN 3   23
        THE LIGHT,
    • • • I MURMURED, "IN OLD AGE THEY CEASED": • • • • 59 OISIN 3   177
    • • • WHEN LIFE IN MY BODY HAS CEASED, • • • • • 63 OISIN 3   222
    TILL OAK AND HAZEL CEASED AND BEECH BEGAN, • • • • 283 TWO KINGS   V 139A
    I WISHED BEFORE IT CEASED. NOR BIRD NOR BEAST • • • • 338 SHEP GOATHERD   2
    YEAR. I WISHED BEFORE IT CEASED. NOR BIRD NOR BEAST • • 338 SHEP GOATHERD V 2
    AS THE SUMMER VOICE OF THE DAYTIME CEASED, • • • • • 728 PRIEST FAIRY   4

	PAGE	TITLE		LINE

CEASED   (CONTINUED)
I CEASED TO BE A WOMAN, BEING A QUEEN. . . . .   758 SHADOW WATER A   228
CEASELESS
AS AN HURT LEOPARD FILLS WITH CEASELESS MOAN, ...   674 ISLE STAT II 3   208
AS A HURT LEOPARD FILLS WITH CEASELESS MOAN . . . . .   674 ISLE STAT II 3 V 208
OF CEASELESS LONELINESS AND HIGH REGRET . . . .   705 REMEMBRANCE   9
CEASELESSLY
AND THEY WERE TREMBLING CEASELESSLY, ...   13 OISIN 1   173
LIKE SMALL BROWN MOTHS, A-TREMBLE CEASELESSLY. . . . .   713 FERENCZ RENYI V 82
CEDAR
CHRYSELEPHANTINE, CEDAR BOARDED, ...   440 WISDOM   V 10
CEDAR-BOARDED
CHRYSELEPHANTINE, CEDAR-BOARDED, ...   440 WISDOM   10
CEILING
WHAT MADE THE CEILING WATERPROOF? . . . .   625 NATIVITY   5
CELEBRANT
AND BRING BEAUTY'S BLIND RAMBLING CELEBRANT; . . . . .   412 TOWER   91
CELEBRATE
I CELEBRATE THE SILENT KISS THAT ENDS SHORT LIFE OR LONG.   450 FROM OEDIPUS   9
CELL
DOWN TO HER CELL AND THERE ALIT, ...   397 POLIT PRISONER   4
CELLAR
THEN DARKENING THROUGH "DARK" RAFTERY'S "CELLAR" DROP, . .   490 COOLE BALLYLEE   4
BATTERED TO DEATH IN A CELLAR, ...   628 JANE MOUNTAIN   9
AS WITHIN A CELLAR CHILLY . . . .   647 ISLE STAT I 1   57
TO GARRET OR CELLAR A WHEEL I SEND, ...   787 GARRET CELLAR   1
CELTIC
THE CELTIC TWILIGHT . . . .   147 INTO TWILIGHT V T
CENTAUR
OR BEEN FIT SPOIL FOR A CENTAUR . . . .   355 PROPERTIUS   7
ON A PICTURE OF A BLACK CENTAUR BY EDMUND DULAC . . . .   442 BLACK CENTAUR   T
SUGGESTED BY A PICTURE OF A BLACK CENTAUR . . . . . .   442 BLACK CENTAUR V T
CENTAURS
THE HOLY CENTAURS OF THE HILLS ARE VANISHED; . . . . .   344 DEJECTION   7
THE HOLY CENTAURS OF THE HILLS ARE BANISHED; . . . . .   344 DEJECTION   V 7
CENTO   SEE QUINTO-CENTO QUATTRO-CENTO
CENTRAL
OF THE GREAT ROUND SUN, FROM HIS CENTRAL FIRES. . . . .   13 OISIN 1   V 168
UPON THE WOODY CENTRAL HILL; . . . .   22 OISIN 1   323
TILL ON THE CENTRAL HILL WE HUSHED . . . .   22 OISIN 1   V 323
THE SAGE, WHO DEEP IN CENTRAL NATURE DELVES, ...   686 LIFE   2
THE SAGE WHO DEEP IN CENTRAL NATURE DELVES, ...   734 QUATRAIN APHOR   2
CENTRE
UPON THE CENTRE OF THE SUN, ...   14 OISIN 1   175
THINGS FALL APART; THE CENTRE CANNOT HOLD; . . . . . .   402 SECOND COMING   3
THINGS FALL APART; THE CENTRE CAN NOT HOLD, ...   402 SECOND COMING V 3
CENTRES
IN THE DEEP CENTRES OF THE SECRET WOODS. . . . . . .   661 ISLE STAT II 1   54
CENTURIES
HAVE KNOWN THREE CENTURIES, POETS SING, ...   2 OISIN 1   3
AND HOUNDS FOR CENTURIES DUST AND AIR. . . . .   11 OISIN 1   131
FOR CENTURIES, AND STARS HAD DAWNED AND SET. . . . . .   31 OISIN 2   V 40
NO CENTURIES COULD DIM, AND A WORD RAN . . . .   38 OISIN 2   127
NOT LOADED CENTURIES MIGHT VAPOUR. RAN . . . . . .   38 OISIN 2   V 127
THE MOIL OF MY CENTURIES FILLED ME; AND GONE LIKE   51 OISIN 3   70
A SEA-COVERED STONE
MY SLEEP WERE NOW NINE CENTURIES . . . .   306 HOUR DAWN   75
. . . THROUGH ALL THE CENTURIES, ...   354 HIS PHOENIX   25
THERE'LL BE THAT CROWD TO MAKE MEN WILD THROUGH ALL THE   354 HIS PHOENIX   V 25
CENTURIES,
THROUGHOUT SO MANY VARYING CENTURIES . . . .   371 ON GOING HOUSE   8
THAT TWENTY CENTURIES OF STONY SLEEP . . . .   402 SECOND COMING   19
THAT THIRTY CENTURIES OF STONY SLEEP . . . .   402 SECOND COMING V 19
BEFORE THAT RUIN CAME, FOR CENTURIES, ...   412 TOWER   81
AND THROUGH THE CENTURIES RAN . . . .   421 MY TABLE   20
UNSPOTTED BY THE CENTURIES; . . . .   477 SELF AND SOUL   12
SEVEN CENTURIES HAVE PASSED AND IT IS PURE, ...   482 BLOOD AND MOON   33
THROUGH SEVEN HEROIC CENTURIES; . . . .   640 BEN BULBEN   80
HOW MANY CENTURIES SPENT . . . .   784 WOMANS BEAUTY   7
CENTURY   SEE EIGHTEENTH-CENTURY
AND, MAN OF THE MANY WHITE CROZIERS, A CENTURY THERE I   52 OISIN 3   77
FORGOT
AND, MAN OF THE MANY WHITE CROZIERS, A CENTURY THERE I   52 OISIN 3   81
FORGOT
. . . AT THE HEEL OF A CENTURY FELL, ...   54 OISIN 3   102
I'LL SLEEP ANOTHER CENTURY." . . . .   304 HOUR DAWN   43
. . . CENTURY AFTER CENTURY, ...   481 BLOOD AND MOON   23
. . . CENTURY AFTER CENTURY, ...   481 BLOOD AND MOON   23
THE NINETEENTH CENTURY AND AFTER . . . .   485 NINETEENTH CEN   T
RAVENING THROUGH CENTURY AFTER CENTURY, ...   563 MERU   5
RAVENING THROUGH CENTURY AFTER CENTURY, ...   563 MERU   5
CEPHISUS
WHO FINDS ABOUNDING CEPHISUS . . . .   447 COLONUS PRAISE   23
CEREMONIAL
AS, CLOTHED IN CEREMONIAL GLOOM, ...   655 ISLE STAT I 3   10
CEREMONIOUS
FOR PROUD, SOFT, CEREMONIOUS PROOF . . . .   386 ROBARTES DANCE   30
WHERE ALL'S ACCUSTOMED, CEREMONIOUS; . . . .   405 FOR DAUGHTER   74
CEREMONY
BEING BUT A PART OF ANCIENT CEREMONY-- . . . .   321 REED WHISPERER   12
THE CEREMONY OF INNOCENCE IS DROWNED; . . . .   402 SECOND COMING   6

CEREMONY   (CONTINUED)
```
    HOW BUT IN CUSTOM AND IN CEREMONY . . . . . .        406 FOR DAUGHTER          77
    WITH THE GREAT TOIL AND CEREMONY OF STATE, . . . . . .  462 HARUN RASHID     V    25
CEREMONY'S
    CEREMONY'S A NAME FOR THE RICH HORN, . . . . . . .    406 FOR DAUGHTER          79
CERTAIN
    WORDS ALONE ARE CERTAIN GOOD. . . . . . . . .          65 HAPPY SHEPHERD        10
    FOR WORDS ALONE ARE CERTAIN GOOD, . . . . . . .        66 HAPPY SHEPHERD        43
    AND WORDS ALONE ARE CERTAIN GOOD, . . . . . . .        66 HAPPY SHEPHERD   V    43
    HE GIVES HIS BELOVED CERTAIN RHYMES . . . . . .       157 BELOVED RHYMES        T
    AEDH GIVES HIS BELOVED CERTAIN RHYMES . . . . . .     157 BELOVED RHYMES   V    T
    A CERTAIN POET IN OUTLANDISH CLOTHES . . . . . .      180 QUEEN MAEVE           1
    CERTAIN, AND THEY NEVER DREAM . . . . . . . .         202 NEVER GIVE ALL        4
    I SAID: "IT'S CERTAIN THERE IS NO FINE THING . .      205 ADAMS CURSE          21
    IT'S CERTAIN I'D SLEEP EASIER O' NIGHTS . . . .       224 SHADOW WATER B       59
    YOU'RE CERTAIN OF IT?  I NEVER WAKE FROM SLEEP        226 SHADOW WATER B       83
    IT'S CERTAIN THEY ARE LEADING YOU TO DEATH. . . .     231 SHADOW WATER B      201
    THAT MUCH IS CERTAIN.  I SHALL FIND A WOMAN, . .      231 SHADOW WATER B      209
    I DO NOT KNOW FOR CERTAIN, BUT I KNOW . . . .         249 SHADOW WATER B      564
    . . . CERTAIN BAD POETS, IMITATORS OF HIS AND MINE    262 TO A POET             T
    . . . CERTAIN BAD POETS, IMITATORS OF HIS AND OF MINE 262 TO A POET        V    T
    TO A CERTAIN COUNTRY HOUSE IN TIME OF CHANGE . .      264 HOUSE SHAKEN     V    T
    WHERE CERTAIN BEECHES MIXED A PALE GREEN LIGHT . .    277 TWO KINGS        V    5
    IT'S CERTAIN THERE ARE TROUT SOMEWHERE . . . .       297 THREE BEGGARS        66
    BEING CERTAIN IT WAS NO RIGHT ROCK . . . . . .       303 HOUR DAWN            23
    BEING CERTAIN IT WAS NO RIGHT PLACE . . . . . .       303 HOUR DAWN        V   23
    TOWARDS NIGHTFALL UPON CERTAIN SET APART . . . .     325 ROBERT GREGORY       29
    "IT'S CERTAIN THAT MY LUCK IS BROKEN," . . . . .     332 ROUND TOWER          25
    AND CERTAIN LOST COMPANIONS OF MY OWN. . . . . .     342 SHEP GOATHERD        78
    CERTAIN ARTISTS BRING HER DOLLS AND DRAWINGS . .     362 DOLLS DRAWINGS        T
    BEING CERTAIN THAT THEY AND I . . . . . . . .        392 EASTER 1916          13
    FOR CERTAIN MINUTES AT THE LEAST . . . . . . .       399 DEMON BEAST           1
    YET I AM CERTAIN AS CAN BE . . . . . . . . .         401 DEMON BEAST          33
    IT'S CERTAIN THAT FINE WOMEN EAT . . . . . . .       404 FOR DAUGHTER         30
    AND CERTAIN MEN, BEING MADDENED BY THOSE RHYMES,     410 TOWER                41
    AND CERTAIN MEN-AT-ARMS THERE WERE . . . . . .       412 TOWER                84
    AND CERTAIN MEN AT ARMS THERE WERE . . . . . .       412 TOWER            V   84
    FOR IT IS CERTAIN THAT YOU HAVE . . . . . .          413 TOWER               108
    HAD HE NOT FOUND IT CERTAIN BEYOND DREAMS . . .      417 ANCEST HOUSES        10
    THE EXTRAVAGANCE OF SPRING; OR CERTAIN TIMES . .     466 HARUN RASHID     V  125
    A CERTAIN MARVELLOUS THING . . . . . . . . .         471 ALL SOUL NIGHT       16
    SO MUCH IS CERTAIN; . . . . . . . . . . .            504 QUARREL IN AGE       10
    LIVES; THAT MUCH IS CERTAIN; . . . . . . . .         504 QUARREL IN AGE   V   10
    AFTER CERTAIN YEARS HE WON . . . . . . . . .         577 WHAT THEN             7
    CERTAIN MEN THE ENGLISH SHOT? . . . . . . . .        632 MAN AND ECHO         12
    THEN CERTAIN SHROUDS THAT MUTTERED HEAD TO HEAD       634 CUCHULAIN COMF        4
    FOR I AM CERTAIN SOMEBODY IS DEAD. . . . . . .       760 SHADOW WATER A      254
    TILL CERTAIN SECOND THOUGHTS HAVE COME . . . . .     791 REPRISALS            12
CERTAINLY
    FOR CERTAINLY HE SANK INTO HIS GRAVE . . . . . .     370 EGO DOMINUS          57
    "THAT'S CERTAINLY THE CASE," SAID HE. . . . . .      510 JANE JUDGMENT        10
    "THAT'S CERTAINLY THE CASE," SAID HE. . . . . .      510 JANE JUDGMENT        20
    "THAT'S CERTAINLY THE CASE," SAID SHE. . . . .       510 JANE JUDGMENT    V   10
    A GREAT EBULLIENT PORTRAIT CERTAINLY; . . . . .      602 GALLERY REVIS        27
    AN EBULLIENT GREAT PORTRAIT CERTAINLY; . . . . .     602 GALLERY REVIS    V   27
CERTAINTY
    THE CERTAINTY THAT I SHALL SEE THAT LADY . . . .     356 BROKEN DREAMS        22
    THEY MUST TO KEEP THEIR CERTAINTY ACCUSE . . . .     398 LEADERS CROWD         1
    FOUND CERTAINTY UPON THE DREAMING AIR, . . . .       489 COOLE PARK 29        22
CHAFF
    TILL ALL ELSE IS EMPTY CHAFF, . . . . . . . .        647 ISLE STAT I 1        60
CHAIN
    AND SHE WITH A WAVE-RUSTED CHAIN WAS TIED . . . .     34 OISIN 2              73
    WITH CHAIN SEA-ROTTED, ROUND HER MIDDLE TIED, . .     34 OISIN 2          V   75
    I BURST THE CHAIN; STILL EARLESS, NERVELESS, BLIND,   36 OISIN 2              97
    I THROW DOWN THE CHAIN OF SMALL STONES! . . . .       63 OISIN 3             222
    LINKED BY A GOLD CHAIN EACH TO EACH, . . . . .       194 BAILE AILLINN       136
    AND BROKE THE CHAIN AND SET MY ANKLES FREE, . .      533 HER TRIUMPH           9
    WITH A MONKEY ON A CHAIN, . . . . . . . . .          627 STATES HOLIDAY       36
    TO ONE ANOTHER WITH A COILING CHAIN; . . . . .       687 TWO TITANS            6
    I SAW HIM STAGGER WITH THE CLANKING CHAIN, . . .     687 TWO TITANS           31
CHAINED
    CHAINED WAS SHE.  ON THEIR WINGS THE HUNDREDTH YEAR   34 OISIN 2          V   76
CHAINS
    COUPLED WITH GOLDEN CHAINS, AND SING AS THEY FLY.    204 WITHER BOUGHS        18
CHAIR
    MINE WAS A CHAIR OF SKINS AND GOLD, . . . . . .       81 MAD KING GOLL    V    1
    "LAY ME IN A CUSHIONED CHAIR; . . . . . . . .         97 FOXHUNTER             1
    "PUT THE CHAIR UPON THE GRASS; . . . . . . .          97 FOXHUNTER             9
    "NOW LAY ME IN A CUSHIONED CHAIR . . . . . . .        97 FOXHUNTER        V    1
    "NOW LEAVE THE CHAIR DOWN ON THE GRASS, . . . .       97 FOXHUNTER        V    9
    "NOW LEAVE THE CHAIR UPON THE GRASS, . . . . .        97 FOXHUNTER        V    9
    AND BY THE CHAIR HE GOES, . . . . . . . . .           98 FOXHUNTER        V   18
    A KING SITTING UPON A CHAIR OF GOLD-- . . . . .      104 FERGUS DRUID         36
    MY CHAIR WAS NEAREST TO THE FIRE . . . . . . .       131 OLD PENSIONER         3
    I HAD A CHAIR AT EVERY HEARTH; . . . . . . .         131 OLD PENSIONER    V    1
    ONCE, WHILE HE NODDED ON A CHAIR, . . . . . .        132 FR GILLIGAN           5
    HE KNELT, AND LEANING ON THE CHAIR . . . . . .       132 FR GILLIGAN          13
    AND THEN, HALF-LYING ON THE CHAIR, . . . . . .       132 FR GILLIGAN      V   13
    WHILE I SLEPT ON THE CHAIR"; . . . . . . . .         133 FR GILLIGAN          26
    ASLEEP UPON A CHAIR." . . . . . . . . . .            134 FR GILLIGAN          48
```

PAGE   TITLE   LINE

CHAIR   (CONTINUED)
    BEFORE HIS CHAIR AND BENDING DOWN MY HEAD . . . . . . 282 TWO KINGS   132
    AND CROUCHED BY THE ARM OF HIS CHAIR, ... 319 DOLLS   16
    ALL DAY IN THE ONE CHAIR . . . . 357 BROKEN DREAMS   38
    NO TABLE OR CHAIR OR STOOL NOT SIMPLE ENOUGH . . . . 371 ON GOING HOUSE   3
    FROM SOMEBODY THAT TOILS FROM CHAIR TO CHAIR; . . . . 491 COOLE BALLYLEE   26
    FROM SOMEBODY THAT TOILS FROM CHAIR TO CHAIR; . . . . 491 COOLE BALLYLEE   26
    THE AUSTERE ARTHUR, RULE FROM UTHER'S CHAIR? . . . . . 678 ISLE STAT II 3   296
CHAIRED
    CHAIRED IN THE CUSHIONED OTTER SKIN, ... 82 MAD KING GOLL   V 5
    CHAIRED IN A CUSHIONED OTTER-SKIN . . . . 82 MAD KING GOLL   V 5
CHALK
    "THOSE SIX FEET MARKED IN CHALK? . . . . 548 TO SAME TUNE 3   8
    "THOSE SIX FEET MARKED IN CHALK? . . . . 548 TO SAME TUNE 3   18
    "THOSE SIX FEET MARKED IN CHALK? . . . . 549 TO SAME TUNE 3   28
CHAMBER
    TO THAT SMALL CHAMBER BY THE OUTER GATE. . . . . . . 181 QUEEN MAEVE   44
    TO THE CHAMBER WHERE . . . . 310 WITCH   6
    A WINDING STAIR, A CHAMBER ARCHED WITH STONE, ... 419 MY HOUSE   11
    IN SOME LIKE CHAMBER, SHADOWING FORTH . . . . 419 MY HOUSE   15
    AND TURN TOWARDS MY CHAMBER, CAUGHT . . . . 424 ROAD AT DOOR   14
    THE BRIDE IS CARRIED TO THE BRIDEGROOM'S CHAMBER . . . . 459 FROM OEDIPUS   8
    TAKE THIS LIGHT PARCHMENT, PASS THROUGH THE GREAT CHAMBER 461 HARUN RASHID   V   5
    CLIMB TO YOUR CHAMBER FULL OF BOOKS AND WAIT, ... 579 DOR WELLESLEY   8
CHAMBERMAID
    DEAR CHAMBERMAID," SAID SHE. . . . . 569 THREE BUSHES   16
    BUT HEAVED A SIGH IF THE CHAMBERMAID . . . . 570 THREE BUSHES   33
    THE CHAMBERMAID LIVED LONG, AND TOOK . . . . 571 THREE BUSHES   57
CHAMBERMAID'S
    THE CHAMBERMAID'S FIRST SONG . . . . 574 MAIDS 1ST SONG   T
    THE CHAMBERMAID'S SECOND SONG . . . . 575 MAIDS 2ND SONG   T
CHAMBERS
    AMID GREAT CHAMBERS AND LONG GALLERIES, LINED . . . . . 418 ANCEST HOUSES   36
CHANCE
    WE MOCKED AT TIME AND FATE AND CHANCE . . . . 20 OISIN 1   291
    EQUAL TO GOOD OR GRIEVOUS CHANCE; . . . . 24 OISIN 1   372
    EQUAL TO GOOD OR EVIL CHANCE . . . . 24 OISIN 1   V 371
    AND THOUGHT NOT OF EVIL CHANCE, ... 145 HOST OF AIR   30
    SAVE BY AN EVIL CHANCE, ... 178 FIDDLER DOONEY   14
    I'D DROWN HIM WHILE WE HAVE THE CHANCE TO DO IT. . . . . 224 SHADOW WATER B   58
    I'D KILL HIM WHILE WE HAVE THE CHANCE TO DO IT. . . . . 224 SHADOW WATER B V 58
    WE'D BETTER GO, FOR WE HAVE LOST THIS CHANCE. . . . . 226 SHADOW WATER B   80
    PERVERSE CREATURE OF CHANCE, ... 346 ON WOMAN   41
    CHANCE BEING AT ONE WITH CHOICE AT LAST, ... 388 SOLOMON WITCH   14
    WITH CRUELTIES OF CHOICE AND CHANCE; . . . . 388 SOLOMON WITCH   23
    BEING BOTH CHANCE AND CHOICE, ... 472 ALL SOUL NIGHT   58
    SOME THINK IT A MATTER OF COURSE THAT CHANCE . . . . . 626 OLD MEN BE MAD   9
    SOME THINK IT MATTER OF COURSE THAT CHANCE . . . . . 626 OLD MEN BE MAD V   9
    ALL CHOICE, AND GIVE TO CHANCE FOR GUIDING CHANCE . . . 656 ISLE STAT I 3   39
    ALL CHOICE, AND GIVE TO CHANCE FOR GUIDING CHANCE . . . 656 ISLE STAT I 3   39
    WITH LOADED DICE. ANOTHER CHANCE! COME, FATHER; . . . 721 WITCH VIVIEN   45
    CHANCE, AND NOT SKILL, HAS FAVOURED YOU, OLD FATHER! . . 722 WITCH VIVIEN   60
    CHANCE HATH A SKILL; . . . . 722 WITCH VIVIEN   69
CHANCED
    CARED NOT A THRANEEN FOR WHAT CHANCED . . . . 514 JANE GROWN OLD   18
    CARE NOT A THRANEEN FOR WHAT CHANCED . . . . 514 JANE GROWN OLD V 18
CHANCELLOR
    AM I A GREAT LORD CHANCELLOR . . . . 627 STATES HOLIDAY   14
CHANCES
    MAY WELL BE OF ALL EVIL CHANCES CHIEF. . . . . 405 FOR DAUGHTER   53
    AT CHANCES AND AT MOMENTS WITH MANKIND. . . . . . . 721 WITCH VIVIEN   35
CHANGE
    WHERE THE VOICE OF CHANGE IS THE VOICE OF A TUNE, . . . 8 OISIN 1   V 82
    THERE WERE AN END OF CHANGE AND BIRTH, ... 18 OISIN 1   270
    AND HERE THERE IS NOR CHANGE NOR DEATH, ... 19 OISIN 1   284
    FOR NEITHER DEATH NOR CHANGE COMES NEAR US, ... 21 OISIN 1   316
    FOR CHANGE AND DEATH THEY COME NOT NEAR US, ... 21 OISIN 1   V 316
    NOR EVER CHANGE OR FEEL THE CLUTCHES . . . . 23 OISIN 1   V 341A
    FROM CHANGE TO CHANGE; I HAVE BEEN MANY THINGS-- . . . 104 FERGUS DRUID   32
    FROM CHANGE TO CHANGE; I HAVE BEEN MANY THINGS-- . . . 104 FERGUS DRUID   32
    HE MOURNS FOR THE CHANGE THAT HAS COME UPON HIM . . . 153 CHANGE BELOVED   T
    MONGAN LAMENTS THE CHANGE THAT HAS COME UPON HIM AND HIS 153 CHANGE BELOVED V   T
       BELOVED
    AND TIME AND BIRTH AND CHANGE ARE HURRYING BY. . . . . 153 CHANGE BELOVED   9
    O PITEOUS HEARTS, CHANGING TILL CHANGE BE DEAD . . . . 163 ASKS FORGIVE   19
    AND NIAMH AND LABAN AND FAND, WHO COULD CHANGE TO AN OTTER 209 UNDER THE MOON   12
       OR FAWN,
    AND FAND, AND NIAM, AND LABAN, WHO COULD CHANGE TO AN OTTER 209 UNDER THE MOON V 12
       OR FAWN,
    TO A CERTAIN COUNTRY HOUSE IN TIME OF CHANGE . . . . . 264 HOUSE SHAKEN   V   T
    HEARING THE WHOLE EARTH CHANGE ITS TUNE, ... 266 GALWAY RACES   12
    "NEVER WILL I BELIEVE THERE IS ANY CHANGE . . . . . . 285 TWO KINGS   203
    THE WATER-HEN MUST CHANGE HER GROUND. . . . . 326 ROBERT GREGORY   55
    THE WATERHEN MUST CHANGE HER GROUND; . . . . 326 ROBERT GREGORY V 55
    TO CHANGE MY LOVES WHILE DANCING . . . . 330 BONE OF A HARE   7
    BUT FOR HER GRANDSON NOW; THERE IS NO CHANGE . . . . . 340 SHEP GOATHERD   39
    THEY CHANGE THEIR BODIES AT A WORD. AND THEN? . . . . 376 PHASES OF MOON   113
    WILL PASS FROM CHANGE TO CHANGE, ... 379 CAT AND MOON   22
    WILL PASS FROM CHANGE TO CHANGE, ... 379 CAT AND MOON   22
    MINUTE BY MINUTE THEY CHANGE; . . . . 393 EASTER 1916   48
    MINUTE BY MINUTE CHANGE. . . . . 393 EASTER 1916   V 48

134

	PAGE	TITLE	LINE

CHANGE   (CONTINUED)
YET IF NO CHANGE APPEARS . . . . 421 MY TABLE 12
YOU KNOW THE SAYING, "CHANGE THE BRIDE WITH SPRING," . . . 463 HARUN RASHID 50
AND WHAT IF MIND SEEMED CHANGE . . . . 473 ALL SOUL NIGHT V 66
MUST VANISH ON THE INSTANT IF THE MIND BUT CHANGE 481 BLOOD AND MOON 27
   ITS THEME:
"SHE WILL CHANGE," I CRIED. . . . . 516 MANS SONG 1
CHANGE THEIR LOVES ABOUT. . . . . 520 HIS BARGAIN 6
"WHAT CHANGE HAS PUT MY THOUGHTS ASTRAY . . . . 529 TOM LUNATIC 3
I COOK AND CHANGE MY PLATE. . . . . 607 SONGS BURDEN 2 6
OF HIS DEATH AND CHANGE MALIGN. . . . . 648 ISLE STAT I 1 80
A DEAL OF EVIL AND OF CHANGE HATH CROSSED . . . . . . 676 ISLE STAT II 3 273
MAKE GALLEYS OUT OF WIND THAT CHANGE TO WIND . . . . . 751 SHADOW WATER A 105
ENDS TIME AND CHANGE. . . . . 754 SHADOW WATER A V 163
THAT CAN CHANGE LOVE TO IMPERISHABLE FIRE? . . . . . . 765 SHADOW WATER A 360
THEY WOULD CHANGE THEM INTO HOUNDS . . . . 775 AGAINST WITCH 15
THOUGH THE CHANGE WERE BUT A WHIM; . . . . 775 AGAINST WITCH 17
THOUGH THEIR CHANGE WERE BUT A WHIM; . . . . 775 AGAINST WITCH V 17
CHANGED
AMID THE SHADES OF NIGHT, HE CHANGED AND RAN . . . . . 40 OISIN 2 174
OF A GREAT EEL; IT CHANGED, AND I BUT SMOTE . . . . . 40 OISIN 2 176
CHANGED ALL HE SANG TO INARTICULATE MOAN . . . . . . 69 SAD SHEPHERD 27
CHANGED ALL HIS WORDS TO INARTICULATE MOAN . . . . . . 69 SAD SHEPHERD V 27
AND YOU HAVE CHANGED AND FLOWED FROM SHAPE TO SHAPE, . . 102 FERGUS DRUID 2
FOR I WOULD WE WERE CHANGED TO WHITE BIRDS . . . . . . 122 WHITE BIRDS 8
I HAVE BEEN CHANGED TO A HOUND WITH ONE RED EAR; . . . 153 CHANGE BELOVED 2
HE CHANGED ME SUDDENLY; I WAS LOOKING ANOTHER WAY; . . 153 CHANGE BELOVED 7
THEY KNEW HIM; HIS CHANGED BODY WAS . . . . 195 BAILE AILLINN 139
AND THE WOOD-WOMAN, WHOSE LOVER WAS CHANGED TO A BLUE-EYED 209 UNDER THE MOON 13
   HAWK;
AND THE WOOD WOMAN, WHOSE LOVER WAS CHANGED TO A BLUE-EYED 209 UNDER THE MOON V 13
   HAWK;
BUT O, IN A MINUTE SHE CHANGED-- . . . . 212 O DO NOT LOVE 9
WHEN MIDHIR'S WIFE HAD CHANGED HER TO A FLY, ... 220 HARP OF AENGUS 10
AND WHEN ONE CHANGED HER TO A SILVER FLY, ... 220 HARP OF AENGUS V 10
"HOW LIGHT WE ARE, NOW WE ARE CHANGED TO BIRDS!" . . . 233 SHADOW WATER B 253
TILL THEY HAD CHANGED US TO LIKE STRENGTH?" . . . . . 259 PEACE V 9
"THEY ARE NOT CHANGED TO ANYTHING, ... 299 THREE HERMITS 25
SO CHANGED ME THAT I LIVE . . . . 315 FRIENDS 15
ALL'S CHANGED SINCE I, HEARING AT TWILIGHT, ... 322 SWANS AT COOLE 15
WHEN MY LUCK CHANGED AND THEY DARED MEET MY FACE, . . . 352 PEOPLE 25
WHEN MY LUCK CHANGED AND THEY DARED TO MEET MY FACE, . . 352 PEOPLE V 25
SHUDDERS IN MANY CRADLES; ALL IS CHANGED, ... 375 PHASES OF MOON 89
ALL CHANGED, CHANGED UTTERLY; . . . . 392 EASTER 1916 15
ALL CHANGED, CHANGED UTTERLY; . . . . 392 EASTER 1916 15
HE, TOO, HAS BEEN CHANGED IN HIS TURN, ... 393 EASTER 1916 38
ARE CHANGED, CHANGED UTTERLY; . . . . 394 EASTER 1916 79
ARE CHANGED, CHANGED UTTERLY; . . . . 394 EASTER 1916 79
AND THAT HE CHANGED INTO A HARE. . . . . 412 TOWER 70
THAT CHANGED SOME CHILDISH DAY TO TRAGEDY-- . . . . . 443 SCHOOL CHILDR 12
HAVE CHANGED THEIR SILK FOR SACK. . . . . 458 HIS WILDNESS 6
AND WHAT IF MIND SEEM CHANGED. . . . . 473 ALL SOUL NIGHT 66
AND IT SEEM CHANGED WITH THE MIND, ... 473 ALL SOUL NIGHT 67
AND IT SEEMED CHANGED WITH THE MIND, ... 473 ALL SOUL NIGHT V 67
BUT ALL IS CHANGED, THAT HIGH HORSE RIDERLESS, ... 492 COOLE BALLYLEE 46
BUT FASHION'S CHANGED, THAT HIGH-HORSE RIDERLESS . . . 492 COOLE BALLYLEE V 46
THAT CHANGED A LOVER FOR A BULL, ... 509 JANE REPROVED 6
THE ZODIAC IS CHANGED INTO A SPHERE. . . . . 535 CHOSEN 18
BUT THE DARK CHANGED TO RED, AND TORCHES SHONE, . . . 537 HER VISION 12
THE BEGGARS HAVE CHANGED PLACES, BUT THE LASH GOES ON. . 590 GREAT DAY 4
THEY HAD CHANGED THEIR THROATS AND HAD THE THROATS 635 CUCHULAIN COMF 25
   OF BIRDS.
ARE CHANGED FOR EVER INTO MOON-WHITE STONE. . . . . . 653 ISLE STAT I 2 43
YOUR HOOD IS THREADBARE--SEE THAT IT BE CHANGED . . . 704 MOSADA 3 133
BUT THAT THE WIND CHANGED; FOR I FOLLOWED HIM . . . . 747 SHADOW WATER A 4
THEY ARE CHANGED AND AS GREY BIRDS FLY OUT TO SEA, . . 750 SHADOW WATER A 82
"HOW LIGHT WE ARE NOW WE ARE CHANGED TO BIRDS!" . . . 753 SHADOW WATER A 143
WHEN MIDHER'S WIFE HAD CHANGED HER TO A FLY . . . . . 763 SHADOW WATER A 305
AND WHEN ONE CHANGED HER TO A SILVER FLY, ... 763 SHADOW WATER A V 305
CHANGELESS
UNDER THAT WOVEN CHANGELESS ROOF OF BOUGHS; . . . . . 126 DREAM OF FAERY 11
IN CHANGELESS OGHAM LETTERS WRIT-- . . . . 194 BAILE AILLINN 117
WHERE PASSION GROWS TO BE A CHANGELESS THING, ... 231 SHADOW WATER B 213
WHEN WE HAVE PUT THEIR CHANGELESS IMAGE ON. . . . . . 250 SHADOW WATER B 582
WHERE SATO'S GIFT, A CHANGELESS SWORD, ... 421 MY TABLE 2
CONCEIVES A CHANGELESS WORK OF ART. . . . . 421 MY TABLE 14
IS A MAN'S MOCKERY OF THE CHANGELESS SOUL." . . . . . 465 HARUN RASHID 102
IN GLORY OF CHANGELESS METAL . . . . 498 BYZANTIUM 22
CHANGERS   SEE SHAPE-CHANGERS
THE SHAPE CHANGERS THAT CAN PUT . . . . 775 AGAINST WITCH V 2
CHANGES
THAT TURNS AND CHANGES LIKE HIS DRAUGHTY SEAS? . . . . 265 ABBEY THEATRE 12
SING ME THE CHANGES OF THE MOON ONCE MORE; . . . . . 373 PHASES OF MOON 29
CHANGES MINUTE BY MINUTE; . . . . 393 EASTER 1916 50
CHANGING   SEE MANY-CHANGING
OF ALL THE MANY CHANGING THINGS . . . . 65 HAPPY SHEPHERD 7
AND LOVED THE SORROWS OF YOUR CHANGING FACE; . . . . . 121 YOU ARE OLD 8
THE CHANGING COLOURS OF ITS FRUIT . . . . 134 TWO TREES 5
AND THE CHANGING MOON WORK OUT THEIR WILL. . . . . . 148 INTO TWILIGHT V 12
O WINDS, OLDER THAN CHANGING OF NIGHT AND DAY, ... 162 ASKS FORGIVE 7
O WINDS, ELDER THAN CHANGING OF NIGHT AND DAY, ... 162 ASKS FORGIVE V 7

```
                                                          PAGE     TITLE            LINE
CHANGING   (CONTINUED)
      O PITEOUS HEARTS, CHANGING TILL CHANGE BE DEAD  . . . .    163 ASKS FORGIVE          19
      OR AS THE CHANGING SPEARS FLUNG BY THE GOLDEN STARS . . .  175 ELEMENT POWERS V     15
      AND WONDERING WHO OF THE MANY CHANGING SIDHE . . . . . .   181 QUEEN MAEVE     V    41
      THAT LIFT US TO THE FLOWING, CHANGING WORLD  . . . . . .   230 SHADOW WATER B      182
      AND LIFTS TO THE CHANGING MOON . . . . . . . . . . . .     379 CAT AND MOON         27
      HIS CHANGING EYES. . . . . . . . . . . . . . . . . . .     379 CAT AND MOON         28
      OF BOYHOOD CHANGING INTO MAN: . . . . . . . . . . . .      479 SELF AND SOUL        46
CHANNELS
      AND FROZEN ARE THE CHANNELS OF THE BLOOD, . . . . . . .    333 LIVING BEAUTY         2
CHANT
      . . . I WILL GO TO THE FENIANS, THOU CLERIC, AND CHANT . .  61 OISIN 3         V   201
      AND LEARN TO CHANT A TONGUE MEN DO NOT KNOW. . . . . .     101 ROSE UPON ROOD V     21
CHANTED
      THE DRUIDS CHANTED, SWAYING IN THEIR HANDS . . . . . .     111 CUCHULAIN SEA   V    82
      AND CHANTED FOR THREE DAYS. CUCHULAIN STIRRED, . . . . .   111 CUCHULAIN SEA   V    83
CHANTING
      AND THE LOUD CHANTING OF THE UNQUIET LEAVES, . . . . . .   120 SORROW OF LOVE V     11
CHANTS
      AND CHANTS OF VICTORY AMID THE ENCIRCLING HOUNDS. . . . .  622 HOUND VOICE          21
CHAPEL
      SHUT THE DOOR OF THE POPE'S CHAPEL, . . . . . . . . . .    618 LONG-LEG FLY         23
      ON THE SISTINE CHAPEL ROOF, . . . . . . . . . . . . .     638 BEN BULBEN           46
      SLOW THE CHAPEL BELL IS TOLLING AS THOUGH THE DEAD PASSED  718 PHANTOM SHIP         16
         BY.
CHAPLET
      A CHAPLET FOR YOUR HEAD. . . . . . . . . . . . . . . .     113 ROSE OF PEACE         8
      AND CHAPLET THEIR CALM BROWS WITH LEAFAGE DIM, . . . . .   127 DREAM OF FAERY V     32
      AND CHAPLET THEIR CALM BROWS WITH LEAFAGE COOL: . . . .    127 DREAM OF FAERY V     32
CHARACTER
      AND YET A WOMAN'S POWERFUL CHARACTER . . . . . . . . .     489 COOLE PARK 29        18
      HE HAD SUCH CHARACTER. . . . . . . . . . . . . . . . .     606 SONGS BURDEN 1       13
      IN MARBLE OR IN BRONZE, LACKED CHARACTER. . . . . . . .    610 STATUES               3
      THAT PASSION COULD BRING CHARACTER ENOUGH, . . . . . . .   610 STATUES               6
      CHARACTER ISOLATED BY A DEED . . . . . . . . . . . .      630 CIRCUS ANIMALS       29
      BUT FIRST YOU MUST BE TOLD OUR CHARACTER: . . . . . . .    634 CUCHULAIN COMF       20
CHARACTERS
      AND TRACE THESE CHARACTERS UPON THE SANDS? . . . . . .     370 EGO DOMINUS          64
      AND TRACE THESE CHARACTERS UPON THE SAND? . . . . . .      370 EGO DOMINUS     V    64
      AND, STANDING BY THESE CHARACTERS, DISCLOSE . . . . . .    371 EGO DOMINUS          75
      AND MAY THESE CHARACTERS REMAIN . . . . . . . . . . .      406 CARVED STONE          5
      ALL THOSE TRAGIC CHARACTERS RIDE . . . . . . . . . . .     549 SEVERED HEAD          4
CHARGE
      WHAT TURNED SO GOOD A SHEPHERD FROM HIS CHARGE. . . . .    339 SHEP GOATHERD        16
      "FOR ALL THAT I HAVE DONE AT MY OWN CHARGE? . . . . . .    351 PEOPLE                2
      THEIR GRAVES INTO HER CHARGE, . . . . . . . . . . . .      571 THREE BUSHES         58
CHARGERS
      THE GUARDSMEN'S DROWSY CHARGERS WOULD NOT PRANCE. . . . .  429 NINETEEN 19          24
CHARIOT
      AND PACE THE WOODS, AND DRIVE MY CHARIOT WHEELS . . . .    103 FERGUS DRUID    V    18
      THOSE STILTED BOYS, THAT BURNISHED CHARIOT, . . . . . .    629 CIRCUS ANIMALS        7
CHARIOT-WHEELS
      AND PACE THE WOODS, AND DRIVE MY CHARIOT-WHEELS . . . .    103 FERGUS DRUID         18
CHARITY
      HER CHARITY HAD NO BOUNDS: . . . . . . . . . . . . .      392 EASTER 1916     V    21
      "COME OUT OF CHARITY, . . . . . . . . . . . . . . . .     526 AM OF IRELAND         4
      "COME OUT OF CHARITY, . . . . . . . . . . . . . . . .     527 AM OF IRELAND        17
      "COME OUT OF CHARITY, . . . . . . . . . . . . . . . .     527 AM OF IRELAND        30
CHARLEMAGNE
      WHEN WORLD-TRANSFORMING CHARLEMAGNE WAS CONCEIVED? . . .   560 WHENCE COME          12
CHARM
      ALL THAT STERNNESS AMID CHARM, . . . . . . . . . . . .     259 PEACE                 8
      SO MUCH STERNNESS AND SUCH CHARM." . . . . . . . . . .     259 PEACE           V     8
      AND TWO OR THREE HAD CHARM, . . . . . . . . . . . . .      350 MEMORY                2
      BUT CHARM AND FACE WERE IN VAIN . . . . . . . . . . .      350 MEMORY                3
      AND RUTH ST. DENIS HAD MORE CHARM ALTHOUGH SHE HAD POOR    353 HIS PHOENIX          10
         LUCK:
      FOR BEAUTY'S VERY SELF, HAS CHARM MADE WISE, . . . . .     404 FOR DAUGHTER         37
CHARMED
      IT CHARMED AWAY THE MERCHANT FROM HIS GUILE, . . . . .     129 BOOK STORIES          5
      LIKE CHARMED APPLES MADE OF CHRYSOPRASE, . . . . . . .     231 SHADOW WATER B      214
      ALL THAT TO THIS MOMENT CHARMED YOU? . . . . . . . .      390 IMAGE PAST           21
      WELL NIGH IMMORTAL IN THIS CHARMED CLIME, . . . . . .      674 ISLE STAT II 3      202
      WELL-NIGH IMMORTAL IN THIS CHARMED CLIME: . . . . . .      674 ISLE STAT II 3 V    202
      UNTIL WE DIE WITHIN THE CHARMED RING . . . . . . . .      679 ISLE STAT II 3      322
CHARTER
      A CHARTER TO COMMIT THE CRIME ONCE MORE. . . . . . . .     478 SELF AND SOUL        32
CHASE
      THE STAG YE CHASE IS NOT MORE SAD, . . . . . . . . .        4 OISIN 1         V    35
      OF WAR, AND THE CHASE, AND HUNTING, AND PLEASURE: . . .     26 OISIN 1         V   403
      THEY CHASE THE NOONTIDE DEER: . . . . . . . . . . . .       32 OISIN 2              53
      AND CHASE THE WILD BEE HOMEWARD TO HIS HIVE . . . . .       32 OISIN 2         V  50D
      THEY CHASE AT NOON THE DEER. . . . . . . . . . . . .        32 OISIN 2         V    53
      THEY CHASE THE NOON-TIDE DEER: . . . . . . . . . . .        32 OISIN 2         V    53
      I MUSED ON THE CHASE WITH THE FENIANS, AND BRAN, SCEOLAN,   47 OISIN 3               5
         LOMAIR,
      YON TALL ONE EYES MY SUPPER: CHASE HIM AWAY, . . . . .      72 ANASHU VIJAYA        34
      YON TALL ONE EYES MY SUPPER: SWIFTLY CHASE HIM . . . .      72 ANASHU VIJAYA   V    34
      ALL DRIPPING ON A GRASSY SLOPE, AND SAW THEM CEASE TO CHASE 76 INDIAN ON GOD         4
      AND CHASE THE FROTHY BUBBLES, . . . . . . . . . . . .       87 STOLEN CHILD         21
      NOR BUT IN MERRIMENT BEGIN A CHASE, . . . . . . . . .      405 FOR DAUGHTER         45
```

CHASED
    THE STAG WE CHASED WAS NOT MORE SAD, ...   2 OISIN 1   V   7J
    THAN THE HORNLESS DEER WE CHASED THAT MORN, ...   2 OISIN 1   V   7P
    I CHASED AT MORN THE FLYING DEER, ...   10 OISIN 1   121
    I CHASED WITH HOUNDS THE FLYING DEER, ...   10 OISIN 1   V   121
    PASSED BY US, CHASED BY A PHANTOM HOUND . . . .   11 OISIN 1   140
    PASSED BY US, CHASED OF A PHANTOM HOUND . . . .   11 OISIN 1   V   140
    I CHASED UPON THAT WOODY SHORE . . . .   23 OISIN 1   344
    A HUNDRED YEARS I CHASED THE BOAR, ...   23 OISIN 1   V   344
    SHAKING AND WAVING, VAPOUR VAPOUR CHASED, ...   39 OISIN 2   164
    SHAKING AND WAVING, VAPOURS VAPOURS CHASED; . . . . .   39 OISIN 2   V   164
CHASES
    "BUT NEVER WITH US WHERE THE WILD FOWL CHASES . . . . .   27 OISIN 1   V   408
    THE CHILD WHO CHASES LIZARDS IN THE GRASS, ...   734 QUATRAIN APHOR   1
    IT CHASES OTHER THOUGHT AWAY, ...   791 REPRISALS   9
CHASTITY
    IF I LOST MY CHASTITY? . . . .   570 THREE BUSHES   20
CHAT
    YOU WILL WITH THE BANSHEE CHAT, ...   726 LOVERS QUARREL   9
CHATTER
    OF BEAUTY'S CRUELTY AND WISDOM'S CHATTER-- . . . . . .   377 PHASES OF MOON   121
    THE DAWS CHATTER AND SCREAM, ...   415 TOWER   167
CHATTERING
    A CHATTERING WISE AND SWEET, ...   161 CAP AND BELLS   34
    THE WATERS OF SLEEP CAN MAKE A CHATTERING TONGUE . . . .   218 WOODS OF COOLE   25
    PIERCED THROUGH, CHATTERING FROM HABIT IN THE SUN; . . .   664 ISLE STAT II 2   53
CHATTERJEE
    MOHINI CHATTERJEE . . . .   495 MOHINI CHATTER   T
    MOHINI CHATTERJEE . . . .   496 MOHINI CHATTER   14
CHAUCER
    CHAUCER HAD NOT DRAWN BREATH . . . .   421 MY TABLE   8
CHAUNT
    COMING OUT OF THE SEA AS THE DAWN COMES, A CHAUNT OF LOVE   58 OISIN 3   158
      ON MY LIPS,
    . . FOR I GO TO THE FENIANS, O CLERIC, TO CHAUNT . . .   61 OISIN 3   201
    AND LEARN TO CHAUNT A TONGUE MEN DO NOT KNOW. . . . .   101 ROSE UPON ROOD   21
    CHAUNT IN HIS EAR DELUSIONS MAGICAL, ...   111 CUCHULAIN SEA   80
CHAUNTED
    AND CHAUNTED FOR THREE DAYS. CUCHULAIN STIRRED, ...   111 CUCHULAIN SEA   83
    THE DRUIDS CHAUNTED, SWAYING IN THEIR HANDS . . . . .   111 CUCHULAIN SEA   V   82
CHAUNTING
    AND THE LOUD CHAUNTING OF THE UNQUIET LEAVES, ...   120 SORROW OF LOVE V   11
CHEATED
    AMONG THE OTHER CHEATED DEAD. . . . .   791 REPRISALS   24
CHECK
    I TRAP YOU. CHECK. I DO MISCALCULATE. . . . .   722 WITCH VIVIEN   58
    CHECK. AH! HOW BRIGHT YOUR EYES. HOW SWIFT YOUR MOVES.   722 WITCH VIVIEN   61
    A BIRD WALK ON THE DOORSTEP. CHECK ONCE MORE. . . . .   722 WITCH VIVIEN   64
CHECKED
    COULD MY SPOKEN WORDS HAVE CHECKED . . . .   632 MAN AND ECHO   15
CHEEK
    NOR CAN TIME WASTE THE CHEEK, NOR IS THERE FOOT . . . .   284 TWO KINGS   182
    AND HAD THAT COLOUR UPON CHEEK OR HAIR, ...   444 SCHOOL CHILDR   22
    HOLLOW OF CHEEK AS THOUGH IT DRANK THE WIND . . . . .   444 SCHOOL CHILDR   27
    WERE SOME DEAR CHEEK. UPON A MOONLESS NIGHT . . . .   466 HARUN RASHID   127
    WHAT'S BOWED YOUR SHOULDER AND MADE PALE YOUR CHEEK"! .   467 HARUN RASHID   133
    INHABITANT OF THE SOFT CHEEK OF A GIRL-- . . . . . .   540 FROM ANTIGONE   2
    SAD HISTORIES ARE LETTERED ON THY CHEEK. . . . . . .   660 ISLE STAT II 1   52
    I FEEL A FINGER DRAWN ACROSS MY CHEEK! . . . . . .   694 MOSADA 1   96
CHEEKED   SEE HOLLOW-CHEEKED
CHEEKS
    LOOK ON MY THIN GREY HAIR AND HOLLOW CHEEKS . . . . .   103 FERGUS DRUID   23
    OUR CHEEKS ARE PALE, OUR HAIR IS UNBOUND, ...   140 HOSTING SIDHE   7
    AND PLEASURE MADE HER CHEEKS GROW RED, ...   314 MEMORY YOUTH   11
    A GREY-HAIRED YOUTH, WHOSE CHEEKS HAD NEVER FOUND, . . .   687 TWO TITANS   7
CHEER
    FILLED FULL OF ANCIENT CHEER." . . . .   97 FOXHUNTER   V   12
    WHO HAS WON A DRUNKEN CHEER, ...   347 FISHERMAN   18
    COULD, HE WAS SO HARRIED, CHEER! . . . .   412 TOWER   76
    COULD, SO HE WAS HARRIED, CHEER! . . . .   412 TOWER   V   76
    AND FULL HIS EYES OF FAIRY CHEER. . . . .   716 FAIRY DOCTOR   12
CHEERING
    NOR PUBLIC MEN, NOR CHEERING CROWDS, ...   328 IRISH AIRMAN   10
    NOR PUBLIC MAN, NOR CHEERING CROWDS, ...   328 IRISH AIRMAN   V   10
    PARNELL CAME DOWN THE ROAD, HE SAID TO A CHEERING MAN! .   590 PARNELL   1
CHEERS
    THOSE CHEERS THAT CAN BE BOUGHT OR SOLD, ...   598 MODEL LAUREATE   19
CHEESE
    COMPANIONS OF THE CHESHIRE CHEESE, ...   270 GREY ROCK   2
CHERRIES
    AND OF REDDEST STOLEN CHERRIES. . . . .   87 STOLEN CHILD   8
CHERRY
    WHERE SHADOW OF CHERRY, AND SHADOW OF APPLE TREES, . . .   710 FERENCZ RENYI   23
CHERRY-BRANCH
    THOUGH DOUBTLESS PLUM OR CHERRY-BRANCH . . . .   567 LAPIS LAZULI   47
CHERUBIM
    WITH OLD EZEKIEL'S CHERUBIM . . . .   336 YOUNG BEAUTY   11
CHESHIRE
    COMPANIONS OF THE CHESHIRE CHEESE, ...   270 GREY ROCK   2
CHESS
    THAT SAT SO STILL AND PLAYED AT THE CHESS? . . . . . .   550 SEVERED HEAD   12

		PAGE	TITLE		LINE

CHESS (CONTINUED)
    COME TO THE CHESS, FOR YOUNG GIRLS' WITS ARE BETTER • • •   721 WITCH VIVIEN   46
CHESSBOARDS
    IN THE FENIANS' DWELLINGS OF WATTLE LEAN ON THE CHESSBOARDS 55 OISIN 3   115
        AND PLAY,
CHEST   SEE LINEN-CHEST OATMEAL-CHEST
    ROUND AND ROUND THE OATMEAL CHEST• • • • • • • • • • • 88 STOLEN CHILD V 49
    BETWEEN THE PANTRY AND THE LINEN CHEST, • • • • • • • • 340 SHEP GOATHERD V 36
    SINBAD THE SAILOR'S BROUGHT A PAINTED CHEST, • • • • • 371 ON GOING HOUSE 10
CHESTNUT
    O CHESTNUT TREE, GREAT ROOTED BLOSSOMER, • • • • • • • 446 SCHOOL CHILDR V 61
CHESTNUTS
    COOKING CHESTNUTS ON THE BARS-- • • • • • • • • • • 737 IN FIRELIGHT 2
    COOKING CHESTNUTS ON THE BARS• • • • • • • • • • • • 737 IN FIRELIGHT 12
CHESTNUT-TREE
    O CHESTNUT-TREE, GREAT-ROOTED BLOSSOMER, • • • • • • • 446 SCHOOL CHILDR 61
CHIDE
    OUR HEARTS CAN HEAR THE VOICES CHIDE• • • • • • • • • 192 BAILE AILLINN 94
    OUR HEART CAN HEAR THE VOICES CHIDE• • • • • • • • • 192 BAILE AILLINN V 94
CHIEF
    AND THE CHIEF OF THE HUGE WHITE CREATURES, • • • • • • 50 OISIN 3 43
    THE CHIEF IMAGINATION OF CHRISTENDOM, • • • • • • • 368 EGO DOMINUS 18
    MAY WELL BE OF ALL EVIL CHANCES CHIEF• • • • • • • • 405 FOR DAUGHTER 53
    WHAT IS IT, FRIEND? HE LOST I' THE WOODS THE CHIEF • • • 661 ISLE STAT II 1 60
CHIEFLY
    IN COURTESY I'D HAVE HER CHIEFLY LEARNED; • • • • • • 404 FOR DAUGHTER 33
CHIEFS
    ARE STILL THE ACHAIANS' TENTED CHIEFS AT BAY? • • • • • 679 ISLE STAT II 3 310
CHIEFTAINS
    • • • WITH BODIES UNGLORIOUS, THEIR CHIEFTAINS STOOD, • • 58 OISIN 3 166
CHILD
    "I AM NEAVE, A CHILD OF THE MIGHTY SHEE, • • • • • • • 5 OISIN 1 V 48
    IN THE HOUSE OF A CHILD, OF A FRIEND, OF A BROTHER• • • • 26 OISIN 1 401
    AND DEW-BLANCHED HORNS, IN WHOSE HOLLOW A CHILD OF THREE 49 OISIN 3 30
        YEARS OLD
    AND DEW-BLANCHED HORNS, IN WHOSE HOLLOWS A CHILD OF THREE 49 OISIN 3 V 31
        YEARS OLD
    • • • HE SAD AS A CHILD WITHOUT MILK; • • • • • • • 59 OISIN 3 174
    WHEN THE POOR TIRED CHILD, PASSION, FALLS ASLEEP• • • • 80 EPHEMERA 7
    A GENTLE YET A KINGLY CHILD; • • • • • • • • • • • 82 MAD KING GOLL V 8
    THE STOLEN CHILD • • • • • • • • • • • • • • • • 86 STOLEN CHILD T
    COME AWAY, O HUMAN CHILD; • • • • • • • • • • • • 87 STOLEN CHILD 9
    COME AWAY, O HUMAN CHILD; • • • • • • • • • • • • 87 STOLEN CHILD 24
    COME AWAY, O HUMAN CHILD; • • • • • • • • • • • • 88 STOLEN CHILD 38
    FOR HE COMES, THE HUMAN CHILD, • • • • • • • • • • 88 STOLEN CHILD 50
    COME, O HUMAN CHILD; • • • • • • • • • • • • • • 88 STOLEN CHILD V 38
    THE CRY OF A CHILD BY THE ROADWAY, THE CREAK OF A LUMBERING 142 ROSE IN HEART 2
        CART,
    I KISS MY WAILING CHILD AND PRESS IT TO MY BREAST, • • • 147 UNAPPEAS HOST 5
    AND HEAR THE NARROW GRAVES CALLING MY CHILD AND ME• • • 147 UNAPPEAS HOST 6
    HALF LION, HALF CHILD, IS AT PEACE• • • • • • • • • 260 UNWORTH PRAISE 20
    I HAVE NO CHILD, I HAVE NOTHING BUT A BOOK, • • • • • 270 PARDON FATHERS 21
    BECAUSE SHE DREAMED WHEN BUT A CHILD • • • • • • • • 272 GREY ROCK 42
    AND THEN, AS TERROR-STRICKEN AS A CHILD • • • • • • • 279 TWO KINGS V 45A
    BEING WEARIED OUT, I LOVE IN MAN THE CHILD? • • • • • 285 TWO KINGS 192
    TO A CHILD DANCING IN THE WIND • • • • • • • • • • 312 CHILD DANCING T
    TO A CHILD DANCING UPON THE SHORE • • • • • • • • • 312 CHILD DANCING V T
    BUT NOT THE EXACT LIKENESS, THE SIMPLICITY OF A CHILD, • • 354 HIS PHOENIX 28
    ONE IS A HARLOT, AND ONE A CHILD • • • • • • • • • 358 PRESENCES 12
    SHE IS PLAYING LIKE A CHILD • • • • • • • • • • • 364 END OF DAY 1
    AS A MOTHER NAMES HER CHILD • • • • • • • • • • • 394 EASTER 1916 62
    I WOULD HAVE TOUCHED IT LIKE A CHILD • • • • • • • • 399 BREAK OF DAY 12
    MY CHILD SLEEPS ON• THERE IS NO OBSTACLE • • • • • • 403 FOR DAUGHTER 3
    I HAVE WALKED AND PRAYED FOR THIS YOUNG CHILD AN HOUR • • 403 FOR DAUGHTER 9
    I LOOK UPON ONE CHILD OR T'OTHER THERE • • • • • • 443 SCHOOL CHILDR 18
    SHE STANDS BEFORE ME AS A LIVING CHILD• • • • • • • • 444 SCHOOL CHILDR 24
    "BECAUSE I MADE YOU TURN AWAY AND RUN FROM THAT YOUNG 450 OWEN AHERNE 14
        CHILD;
    NOW THAT YOUR TONGUE CANNOT PERSUADE THE CHILD TILL SHE 450 OWEN AHERNE 22
        MISTAKE
    THINKS THAT THE STONE'S A CHILD• • • • • • • • • • 456 FRIENDS YOUTH 12
    SHE SEEMED THE LEARNED MAN AND I THE CHILD; • • • • • 467 HARUN RASHID 137
    THAT IS TO AGE WHAT MILK IS TO A CHILD? • • • • • • 469 HARUN RASHID 174
    SO ARROGANTLY PURE, A CHILD MIGHT THINK • • • • • • • 491 COOLE BALLYLEE 23
    "A CHILD FOUND ALL A CHILD CAN LACK, • • • • • • • • 521 THREE THINGS 3
    "A CHILD FOUND ALL A CHILD CAN LACK, • • • • • • • • 521 THREE THINGS 3
    FATHER AND CHILD • • • • • • • • • • • • • • • 531 FATHER CHILD T
    A WOMAN YOUNG AND OLD I FATHER AND CHILD • • • • • 531 FATHER CHILD V T
    AND YET I WEEP--OEDIPUS' CHILD • • • • • • • • • • 540 FROM ANTIGONE 15
    • • • MAN, WOMAN, CHILD (A DAUGHTER OR A SON), • • • • 556 RIBH PATRICK 2
    RECALL HIS TRINITY. A FATHER, MOTHER, CHILD (A DAUGHTER 556 RIBH PATRICK V 2
        OR A SON),
    PRIMORDIAL MOTHERHOOD FORSAKE HIS LIMBS, THE CHILD 559 MAGIC DRUM 2
        NO LONGER REST,
    OR CHILD HID IN THE WOMB• • • • • • • • • • • • 589 OLD WICKED MAN 53
    THE HARLOT AND THE CHILD• • • • • • • • • • • • • 601 THOSE IMAGES 12
    SHE THINKS, PART WOMAN, THREE PARTS A CHILD, • • • • • 617 LONG-LEG FLY 15
    AND WANDERED MURMURING EVERYWHERE, "MY CHILD, MY CHILD!" 619 BRONZE HEAD 21
    AND WANDERED MURMURING EVERYWHERE, "MY CHILD, MY CHILD!" 619 BRONZE HEAD 21
    FROM COLLAR TO COLLAR, FROM STILT TO STILT, FROM FATHER 623 HIGH TALK 10
        TO CHILD•

```
                                                      PAGE    TITLE           LINE
CHILD   (CONTINUED)
    MY PRETTY CHILD, SINCE HE HAS GONE, OH SAY  . .   658 ISLE STAT II 1        3
    THE CHILD PURSUING LIZARDS IN THE GRASS, . . . . . 686 LIFE                 1
    HUNG ON HIS DOUBLET--DEAR AND MOURNFUL CHILD, . .  691 MOSADA 1            35
    THE VISION.  YOU ARE PALE AND WEEPING.  CHILD.     693 MOSADA 1            73
    AND KNOW YOU NOT SHE KISSED THAT PIOUS CHILD  . .  696 MOSADA 2             6
    A WEAK, THIN CHILD, WHEN LAST I SAW HIM THERE. . . 699 MOSADA 3           14
    AND EVIL STILL IS ACTION'S CHILD . . . . . . . .   728 PRIEST FAIRY       14
    THE CHILD WHO CHASES LIZARDS IN THE GRASS, . . .   734 QUATRAIN APHOR      1
    THE CHILD PURSUING LIZARDS IN THE GRASS, . . . .   734 QUATRAIN APHOR V    1
    THE LITTLE OLD GLOVE OF A CHILD! . . . . . . . .   744 GLOVE CLOAK         9
    DELIGHTED ME AS A CHILD! . . . . . . . . . . . .   787 HUDDON DUDDON       2
    DELIGHTED ME AS A CHILD. . . . . . . . . . . . .   787 HUDDON DUDDON       7
    DELIGHTED ME AS A CHILD. . . . . . . . . . . . .   787 HUDDON DUDDON      12
CHILD-BEARING
    CRAZED THROUGH MUCH CHILD-BEARING . . . . . . .    487 CRAZED MOON         1
CHILDER
    COME ROUND ME, LITTLE CHILDER! . . . . . . . . .    94 MOLL MAGEE          1
    YE LITTLE CHILDER DEAR, . . . . . . . . . . . .     95 MOLL MAGEE         18
    SO NOW, YE LITTLE CHILDER, . . . . . . . . . . .    96 MOLL MAGEE         53
CHILDHOOD
    OF ALL THIS HOST SO BOUND FROM CHILDHOOD ON." . .  109 CUCHULAIN SEA      56
    AND HE MY MASTER FROM MY CHILDHOOD UP! . . . . .   225 SHADOW WATER B     77
    FROM EARLIEST CHILDHOOD, BUT THAT BEING SO, . . .  225 SHADOW WATER B V   77
    ALL THOSE THAT MANHOOD TRIED, OR CHILDHOOD LOVED,  327 ROBERT GREGORY     91
    HIS CHILDHOOD AND HIS FAMILY. . . . . . . . . . .  361 ALF POLLEXFEN      35
    FROM CHILDHOOD ON, HAD NOW SO MUCH  . . . . . . .  397 POLIT PRISONER      2
    THAT ALL MY CHILDHOOD COUNTED DEAR! . . . . . . .  398 BREAK OF DAY        7
    AND CHILDHOOD A DELIGHT FOR EVERY SENSE, . . . .   418 ANCEST HOUSES      31
    THAT FROM CHILDHOOD STOOD . . . . . . . . . . . .  512 JANE ON GOD        14
CHILDISH
    THE NAMES THAT STILLED YOUR CHILDISH PLAY, . . .   289 SEPTEMBER 1913     10
    BY CHILDISH MEMORIES OF AN OLD CROSS POLLEXFEN, .   391 UNDER SATURN        7
    SO MANY TIMES CHILDISH DELIGHT. . . . . . . . .    399 BREAK OF DAY       11
    THAT CHANGED SOME CHILDISH DAY TO TRAGEDY--  . . . 443 SCHOOL CHILDR      12
    HER CHILDISH GRATITUDE FOR LOVE AND MATCH YOUR FIFTY YEARS? 450 OWEN AHERNE 23
    HAD SPOKEN OF THEIR CHILDISH DAYS . . . . . . .    457 SUMMER SPRING      11
    IN CHILDISH IGNORANCE OF ALL THAT PASSED. . . .    468 HARUN RASHID      149
    IN CHILDISH IGNORANCE OF ALL THAT PASSED. . . .    468 HARUN RASHID      160
CHILDLESS
    CHILDLESS I THOUGHT, "MY CHILDREN MAY FIND HERE    603 GALLERY REVIS      36
    CHILDLESS, I THOUGHT, "MY CHILDREN MAY LEARN HERE  603 GALLERY REVIS V    36
CHILDREN   SEE GRAND-CHILDREN
    HAPPY AS CHILDREN WITH UNWITHERING LIPS, . . . .    30 OISIN 2        V  14B
    WITHOUT LAUGHTER, A SHOW UNTO CHILDREN, . . . . .   63 OISIN 3        V  218
    AH ME! TO BE OLD WITHOUT SUCCOUR, A SHOW UNTO CHILDREN,  63 OISIN 3   V  217
        A STAIN,
    BUT O, SICK CHILDREN OF THE WORLD, . . . . . . .    65 HAPPY SHEPHERD      6
    YOU WAVES, THOUGH YOU DANCE BY MY FEET LIKE CHILDREN AT  90 OLD FISHERMAN  1
        PLAY,
    YE WAVES, THOUGH YE DANCE 'FORE MY FEET LIKE CHILDREN AT  90 OLD FISHERMAN V 1
        PLAY,
    FROM THE WIVES, AND THE CATS, AND THE CHILDREN, .   92 FATHER OHART       15
    FROM THEIR WIVES, AND THEIR CATS, AND THEIR CHILDREN, .  92 FATHER OHART V  15
    AND USNA'S CHILDREN DIED. . . . . . . . . . . . .  111 ROSE OF WORLD       5
    GIVE TO THESE CHILDREN, NEW FROM THE WORLD, . . .  116 FAERY SONG          5
    GIVE TO THESE CHILDREN, NEW FROM THE WORLD, . . .  116 FAERY SONG          9
    THE DANAAN CHILDREN LAUGH, IN CRADLES OF WROUGHT GOLD,  146 UNAPPEAS HOST   1
    THE FAERY CHILDREN LAUGH IN CRADLES OF WROUGHT GOLD, .  146 UNAPPEAS HOST V 1
    THEIR CHILDREN'S CHILDREN SHALL SAY THEY HAVE LIED. .  166 EVIL OF BELOV   6
    WOMEN AND CHILDREN, YOUNG MEN WITH BOOKS, . . . .  167 BLESSED            15
    CHILDREN AND WOMEN AND TONSURED YOUNG MEN, . . .   167 BLESSED        V   15
    FASHIONED TO BE THE MOTHER OF STRONG CHILDREN! . . 181 QUEEN MAEVE        26
    THE CHILDREN OF THE MAINES OUT OF SLEEP, . . . . . 184 QUEEN MAEVE        92
    THE MAINES' CHILDREN DROPPED THEIR SPADES, AND STOOD  185 QUEEN MAEVE    120
    THE MAINES' CHILDREN HAVE NOT DROPPED THEIR SPADES . . 186 QUEEN MAEVE   123
    THAT WOULD BE HARSH FOR CHILDREN THAT HAVE STRAYED. .  201 OLD MEMORY     12
    THAT HAD BEEN HARSH FOR CHILDREN THAT HAVE STRAYED. .  201 OLD MEMORY V   12
    LAND FOR YOUR CHILDREN OR MONEY IN A POT." . . . . 228 SHADOW WATER B    125
    IN ISLANDS WHERE THE CHILDREN OF AENGUS WIND . . . 245 SHADOW WATER B    469
    ALTHOUGH IT BE FOR CHILDREN THAT YOU SIGH! . . .   265 THESE CLOUDS       10
    HAPPINESS TO CHILDREN AND TO MEN." . . . . . . .   282 TWO KINGS         121
    HAD GIVEN THEIR CHILDREN'S CHILDREN LOFTIER THOUGHT, . 292 TO A SHADE     12
    EVEN BEFORE HIS CHILDREN AND HIS WIFE? . . . . . . 340 SHEP GOATHERD      34
    AND CHILDREN WHEN THEY SPRING UP SHOULDER-HIGH. .   343 SHEP GOATHERD     119
    AND CHILDREN WHEN THEY SPRING UP SHOULDER HIGH. . . 343 SHEP GOATHERD V   119
    AMONG SCHOOL CHILDREN  . . . . . . . . . . . . .   443 SCHOOL CHILDR       T
    THE CHILDREN LEARN TO CIPHER AND TO SING, . . . .  443 SCHOOL CHILDR       3
    AS THAT OLD WANDERING BEGGAR AND THESE GOD-HATED CHILDREN  459 FROM OEDIPUS 6
        KNOW.
    MIMICKING WHAT THEY HEARD, AS CHILDREN MIMIC! . .  487 SEVEN SAGES        25
    FOR CHILDREN BORN OF HER PAIN. . . . . . . . . .   487 CRAZED MOON         6
    CHILDREN DAZED OR DEAD! . . . . . . . . . . . .    488 CRAZED MOON         7
    GREAT ROOMS WHERE TRAVELLED MEN AND CHILDREN FOUND .  491 COOLE BALLYLEE  29
    ALTHOUGH THEIR CHILDREN NEED A RICH ESTATE! . . .  500 VACILLATION        24
    THE CHILDREN THAT HE GAVE. . . . . . . . . . . .   525 DANCING DAYS       12
    CHILDLESS I THOUGHT, "MY CHILDREN MAY FIND HERE .   603 GALLERY REVIS      36
    CHILDLESS, I THOUGHT, "MY CHILDREN MAY LEARN HERE  603 GALLERY REVIS V    36
    KEEP THOSE CHILDREN OUT. . . . . . . . . . . . .   618 LONG-LEG FLY       24
    BECAUSE CHILDREN DEMAND DADDY-LONG-LEGS UPON HIS TIMBER  623 HIGH TALK     6
        TOES,
```

139

CHILDREN   (CONTINUED)
```
    LIVE TO BEAR CHILDREN TO A DUNCE!  . . . . . . . . . .   626 OLD MEN BE MAD        6
    AND FLOWERS AND LITTLE CHILDREN.  SUDDENLY . . . . . .   688 TWO TITANS          36
    ONE SHOULDER TWISTED, AND THE CHILDREN CRY . . . . . .   695 MOSADA 1           116
    MURMURS OF HER CHILDREN TALKING-- . . . . . . . . . .    705 DAWN-SONG            6
    IN EVERY DANCE, BY CHILDREN SOUGHT.  "ACCURST, . . . .   709 FERENCZ RENYI       12
    OF MY DEAD CHILDREN SOON, WHATE'ER BETIDE, . . . . . .   712 FERENCZ RENYI       58
    NEVER STORM AROSE SO SWIFTLY! SCARCE THE CHILDREN WERE   718 PHANTOM SHIP         4
      IN BED,
    DOWN THE VAPOURS FALL AND HIDE THEM FROM THE CHILDREN OF  719 PHANTOM SHIP       27
      A DAY,
    ARE TWO RAGGED CHILDREN BRIGHT-- . . . . . . . . . .     731 STREET DANCERS       4
    CHILDREN SING IN TWOS AND THREES. . . . . . . . . . .    732 STREET DANCERS      17
    DANCE THE SAVAGE CHILDREN SMALL, . . . . . . . . . .     732 STREET DANCERS      29
    AND BRING ME WHERE THE CHILDREN OF AENGUS WIND . . . .   763 SHADOW WATER A     317
    BUT CHILDREN AND DOGS ON THE FLOOR. . . . . . . . . .    780 WELL AND TREE       14
    AMONG HIS CHILDREN, GRANDCHILDREN AND GREAT-GRANDCHILDREN! 790 DEDICATION         6
    AND SUCKLE CHILDREN NOW?  ARMED MEN . . . . . . . . .    791 REPRISALS           20
CHILDREN'S
    THEIR CHILDREN'S CHILDREN SHALL SAY THEY HAVE LIED. . .  166 EVIL OF BELOV        6
    HAD GIVEN THEIR CHILDREN'S CHILDREN LOFTIER THOUGHT, . . 292 TO A SHADE          12
    IN THE BEST MODERN WAY--THE CHILDREN'S EYES . . . . .    443 SCHOOL CHILDR        6
    OF CHILDREN'S GRATITUDE OR WOMAN'S LOVE. . . . . . .     500 VACILLATION         26
    OF SOME MILD WOMAN, OR IN CHILDREN'S WAYS. . . . . .     750 SHADOW WATER A      74
CHILD'S
    A CHILD'S LAUGHTER, A WOMAN'S KISS. . . . . . . . .      190 BAILE AILLINN       40
    WHERE NO CHILD'S BORN BUT TO OUTLIVE THE MOON." . . .    247 SHADOW WATER B     531
    WITH ALL A WOMAN'S PASSION, A CHILD'S IMPERIOUS WAY,     354 HIS PHOENIX         14
    I AM THINKING OF A CHILD'S VOW SWORN IN VAIN . . . .     391 UNDER SATURN        15
CHILL
    CAN SHAKE MORE BLOSSOM FROM AUTUMNAL CHILL . . . . .     465 HARUN RASHID       104
    THAT BRINGS MORE BLOSSOM TO AUTUMNAL CHILL . . . . .     465 HARUN RASHID   V   104
    AN EVENING CHILL UPON THE AIR, . . . . . . . . . .      494 AT ALGECIRAS        14
    OR STRIKES A SUDDEN CHILL INTO MY BONES . . . . . .     499 MOTHER OF GOD       14
    TO DEATH.  HIS DARKNESS AND HIS CHILL I FEEL. . . . .    684 SEEKER              63
    MY SOUL.  HIS DARKNESS AND HIS CHILL I FEEL. . . . .     684 SEEKER         V   63B
CHILLED
    MY BARREN THOUGHTS HAVE CHILLED ME TO THE BONE. . . .    257 RECONCILIATION      12
    THIS BLAST HAS CHILLED ME TO THE BONE." . . . . . .     305 HOUR DAWN           62
    WHEN AGE MIGHT WELL HAVE CHILLED HIS BLOOD." . . . .     356 BROKEN DREAMS       19
    CHILLED BLOOD, THIS SWEETNESS BROUGHT! . . . . . . .     401 DEMON BEAST         39
CHILLING
    THE WARMTH OF LIFE IS CHILLING, AND THE SHADOWS GROW  . . 675 ISLE STAT II 3    232
CHILLS
    THIS SULLEN PEASANT CHILLS THE GOOD SUNSHINE. . . . .    711 FERENCZ RENYI  V    42
CHILLY
    AS WITHIN A CELLAR CHILLY  . . . . . . . . . . . .      647 ISLE STAT I 1       57
    LIES A CHILLY FINGER TIP, . . . . . . . . . . . .       732 STREET DANCERS      19
CHIMAERAS
    CHRONICLING CHIMAERAS FLED. . . . . . . . . . . .        65 HAPPY SHEPHERD V     17
CHIME
    AND THROUGH THE CHIME SHE'D SAY, . . . . . . . . .      570 THREE BUSHES        30
    WHEN THE CLOCK BEGINS TO CHIME." . . . . . . . . .      570 THREE BUSHES        41
CHIMED
    BUT NO DOGS BARKED, AND MIDNIGHTS CHIMED, . . . . .     570 THREE BUSHES        29
    AND NO DOGS BARKED THROUGH MIDNIGHTS CHIMED . . . .     570 THREE BUSHES   V    29
CHIMES
    AND YET THE SADDEST CHIMES ARE BEST ENJOYED. . . . .    130 BOOK STORIES        20
CHIMNEY     SEE LAMP-CHIMNEY
    HE HEARS THE STORM IN THE CHIMNEY ABOVE, . . . . . .     26 OISIN 1            404
    THE BARE CHIMNEY IS GONE BLACK OUT  . . . . . . . .     327 ROBERT GREGORY      84
    CHIMNEY CORNER, GARDEN WALK, . . . . . . . . . . .      499 MOTHER OF GOD        8
    HIS LONG LAMP CHIMNEY SHAPED LIKE THE STEM . . . . .    566 LAPIS LAZULI   V    33
CHIN
    ONE HAND UPHELD HIS BEARDLESS CHIN, . . . . . . . .      17 OISIN 1            250
    ONE HAND BENEATH HIS BEARDLESS CHIN. . . . . . . .       17 OISIN 1        V   251
    THE SUN HAS LAID HIS CHIN ON THE GREY WOOD, . . . .      72 ANASHU VIJAYA       24
    THE SUN HATH LAID HIS CHIN ON THE GREY WOOD, . . . .     72 ANASHU VIJAYA  V    24
CHINA
    THERE IS A QUEEN IN CHINA  . . . . . . . . . . .        353 HIS PHOENIX    V     T
    THERE IS A QUEEN IN CHINA, OR MAYBE IT'S IN SPAIN, . .   353 HIS PHOENIX         1
    THERE IS A QUEEN IN CHINA, OR MAY BE IT'S IN SPAIN, . .  353 HIS PHOENIX    V     1
    ON THRONES FROM CHINA TO PERU . . . . . . . . . .       597 MODEL LAUREATE      1
CHINAMEN
    TWO CHINAMEN, BEHIND THEM A THIRD, . . . . . . . .      566 LAPIS LAZULI        37
    THOSE CHINAMEN CLIMB TOWARDS, AND I . . . . . . . .     567 LAPIS LAZULI        49
CHINESE
    WHEN LOIE FULLER'S CHINESE DANCERS ENWOUND . . . . .    430 NINETEEN 19         49
CHINS
    LIFT THEIR CHINS AND TOSS THEIR CURLS, . . . . . . .    726 LOVERS QUARREL      23
    LIFT THEIR CHINS AND TURN AWAY. . . . . . . . . .       726 LOVERS QUARREL      24
CHIRP     SEE SPARROW-CHIRP
    UPON THE TIME OF SPARROW CHIRP, . . . . . . . . .       133 FR GILLIGAN    V    21
CHISEL
    WHETHER WE HAVE CHOSEN CHISEL, PEN OR BRUSH, . . . .    368 EGO DOMINUS         14
    HE SET HIS CHISEL TO THE HARDEST STONE. . . . . . .     369 EGO DOMINUS         32
    THAT WITH A MALLET OR A CHISEL MODELLED THESE . . . .   610 STATUES             10
    THAT PATCHING OLD HEELS THEY MAY SHRIEK, I TAKE TO CHISEL 623 HIGH TALK           8
      AND PLANE.
CHIVALRY
    AND MEASURE OUT THE WAYS OF CHIVALRY. . . . . . . .     660 ISLE STAT II 1      37
```

		PAGE	TITLE		LINE
CHIVALRY (CONTINUED)					
AND ALL THE SAD FAY CHIVALRY	· · · · · · · · · · ·	730	PRIEST FAIRY		71
CHOICE					
CHANCE BEING AT ONE WITH CHOICE AT LAST,	· · · · · ·	388	SOLOMON WITCH		14
WITH CRUELTIES OF CHOICE AND CHANCE:	· · · · · · ·	388	SOLOMON WITCH		23
BEING BOTH CHANCE AND CHOICE,	· · · · · · · · ·	472	ALL SOUL NIGHT		58
THE CHOICE	· · · · · · · · · · · · · · · ·	495	CHOICE		T
THE CHOICE	· · · · · · · · · · · · · · · ·	534	CHOSEN	V	T
SOME FEW HALF WAKE AND HALF RENEW THEIR CHOICE,	· ·	622	HOUND VOICE		6
IN THIS MY CHOICE. SOME GOD MIGHT HELP: IF SO	· ·	656	ISLE STAT I 3		37
ALL CHOICE, AND GIVE TO CHANCE FOR GUIDING CHANCE	· ·	656	ISLE STAT I 3		39
IF WRONG MY CHOICE, AS SILENT AS THOU ART.	· · · ·	657	ISLE STAT I 3		76
CHOIR					
WITH YOUR HARMONIOUS CHOIR	· · · · · · · · · ·	174	ELEMENT POWERS		8
AND ALL THE CHOIR OF LOVE.	· · · · · · · · · ·	531	DELPHIC ORACLE		10
THERE SIGHED AMID HIS CHOIR OF LOVE	· · · · · · ·	611	NEWS ORACLE		7
WHERE WADES THE CHOIR OF LOVE	· · · · · · · · ·	612	NEWS ORACLE		22
WHERE WADE THE CHOIR OF LOVE	· · · · · · · · · ·	612	NEWS ORACLE	V	22
CHOIRS					
A FAR VAGUE SOUND OF FEATHERY CHOIRS.	· · · · · · ·	13	OISIN 1	V	166
CHOKE					
BANNERS CHOKE THE SKY:	· · · · · · · · · · · ·	512	JANE ON GOD		7
CHOKED					
ARE CHOKED WITH THUNDER, LIGHTNING, AND FIERCE WIND,	· ·	42	OISIN 2		205
YET KNOWS THAT TO BE CHOKED WITH HATE	· · · · · ·	405	FOR DAUGHTER		52
CHOOSE					
YET NOW I CHOOSE, FOR THESE FOUR FEET	· · · · · · ·	6	OISIN 1		57
CHOOSE YOUR COMPANIONS FROM THE BEST:	· · · · · · ·	335	YOUNG BEAUTY		4
ANOTHER BOASTS, "I PICK AND CHOOSE AND HAVE BUT TWO OR		354	HIS PHOENIX		20
THREE."					
SAID I WAS DEAD: AND DEAD I CHOOSE TO BE.	· · · · ·	373	PHASES OF MOON		28
CHOOSE PLATO AND PLOTINUS FOR A FRIEND	· · · · · ·	409	TOWER		12
I CHOOSE UPSTANDING MEN,	· · · · · · · · · · ·	414	TOWER		122
AS THOUGH TO CHOOSE WHATEVER SHAPE IT WILLS	· · · ·	417	ANCEST HOUSES		6
O LET HER CHOOSE A YOUNG MAN NOW AND ALL FOR HIS		450	OWEN AHERNE		24
WILD SAKE."					
THINK WHEN I CHOOSE A BRIDE I CHOOSE FOR EVER:	· · ·	464	HARUN RASHID		80
THINK WHEN I CHOOSE A BRIDE I CHOOSE FOR EVER:	· · ·	464	HARUN RASHID		80
THE INTELLECT OF MAN IS FORCED TO CHOOSE	· · · · ·	491	COOLE BALLYLEE	V	40A
THE INTELLECT OF MAN IS FORCED TO CHOOSE	· · · · · ·	495	CHOICE		1
DID I BECOME A CHRISTIAN MAN AND CHOOSE FOR MY BELIEF	·	503	VACILLATION		85
I CHOOSE ANOTHER MARK,	· · · · · · · · · · · ·	588	OLD WICKED MAN		29
I CHOOSE THE SECOND-BEST,	· · · · · · · · · · ·	590	OLD WICKED MAN		60
AND WERE THE LAST TO CHOOSE THE SETTLED GROUND,	· · ·	621	HOUND VOICE		2
KNOW HIS WORK OR CHOOSE HIS MATE.	· · · · · · · ·	638	BEN BULBEN		36
AS I, TO CHOOSE BENEATH DAY'S DYING FLAMES:	· · · ·	656	ISLE STAT I 3		34
"CHOOSE:" RESTLESS HAYNAU'S FINGERS TAPPING GO.	· · ·	711	FERENCZ RENYI		41
THREE MOONS. IT WERE BEST TO KILL HIM, AND CHOOSE OUT	· ·	748	SHADOW WATER A		15
CHOOSES					
THAT CHOOSES RIGHT, AND NEVER FIND A FRIEND.	· · · ·	404	FOR DAUGHTER		24
CHOOSING					
CHOOSING WHATEVER TASK'S MOST DIFFICULT	· · · · · ·	376	PHASES OF MOON		91
CHOP					
AND THEREUPON I DREW THE LIVID CHOP	· · · · · · ·	40	OISIN 2		178
ONCE HELD BETWEEN MY ARMS, WITH LIVID CHOP	· · · · ·	40	OISIN 2	V	178
I HELD A DRIPPING CORPSE, WITH LIVID CHOP	· · · · ·	40	OISIN 2	V	178
AND I BUT HELD A CORPSE, WITH LIVID CHOP	· · · · ·	40	OISIN 2	V	178
CHOPPERS SEE LOGIC-CHOPPERS					
"THOUGH LOGIC CHOPPERS RULE THE TOWN,	· · · · · ·	337	TOM OROUGHLEY	V	1
CHORUS					
CHORUS FOR A PLAY	· · · · · · · · · · · · · ·	771	SONG DEIRDRE 1	V	T
CHOSE					
SOUGHT ONCE AGAIN THE SHORE, AND CHOSE A SHELL	· · · ·	68	SAD SHEPHERD	V	18
I CHOSE THIS BURROW UNDER GROUND.	· · · · · · · ·	305	HOUR DAWN		73
THAT DYING CHOSE THE LIVING WORLD FOR TEXT	· · · · ·	324	ROBERT GREGORY		26
SAID I WAS DEAD: AND DEAD I CHOSE TO BE.	· · · · ·	373	PHASES OF MOON	V	28
YET CHOSE A BANDY-LEGGED SMITH FOR MAN.	· · · · · ·	404	FOR DAUGHTER		29
WHEN MOCKING MUSES CHOSE THE COUNTRY WENCH.	· · · ·	413	TOWER		96
FOR AN OLD NEIGHBOUR'S FRIENDSHIP CHOSE THE HOUSE	· · ·	423	MY DESCENDANTS		21
TWO CONTEMPLATING PASSIONS CHOSE ONE THEME	· · · · ·	466	HARUN RASHID		117
WE WERE THE LAST ROMANTICS—CHOSE FOR THEME	· · · · ·	491	COOLE BALLYLEE		41
I CHOSE IT FOR MY LOT: IF QUESTIONED ON	· · · · ·	535	CHOSEN		11
AMONG THE QUEENS, AND CHOSE THE MIGHTIEST	· · · · ·	757	SHADOW WATER A		213
CHOSEN					
OLD SILENCE BIDS ITS CHOSEN RACE REJOICE,	· · · · ·	127	DREAM OF FAERY		31
HAD CHOSEN A HUSBAND ANYWHERE	· · · · · · · · · ·	191	BAILE AILLINN		54
MY TRADE ALLOWS: CHOSEN MY COMPANY,	· · · · · · ·	352	PEOPLE		20
AND CHOSEN WHAT SCENERY HAD PLEASED ME BEST."	· · · ·	352	PEOPLE		21
WHETHER WE HAVE CHOSEN CHISEL, PEN OR BRUSH,	· · · ·	368	EGO DOMINUS		14
MERE IMAGES: CHOSEN THIS PLACE TO LIVE IN	· · · · ·	373	PHASES OF MOON		13
HELEN BEING CHOSEN FOUND LIFE FLAT AND DULL	· · · · ·	404	FOR DAUGHTER		25
DANCING WITH HER CHOSEN YOUTH,	· · · · · · · · ·	514	JANE GROWN OLD		2
CHOSEN	· · · · · · · · · · · · · · · · ·	534	CHOSEN		T
THE LOT OF LOVE IS CHOSEN. I LEARNT THAT MUCH	· · ·	534	CHOSEN		1
HIS CHOSEN COMRADES THOUGHT AT SCHOOL	· · · · · ·	576	WHAT THEN		1
AND PRAISE OUR CHOSEN MAN:	· · · · · · · · · · ·	586	PARNELLITES		2
CHOU					
IN HIS NOSTRILS, THE GREAT LORD OF CHOU	· · · · · ·	502	VACILLATION		59
CHRIST					
ABOUT THE TIME WHEN CHRIST WAS BORN,	· · · · · · ·	189	BAILE AILLINN		13
BUT THAT OF CHRIST. AND DID HE FIND HIMSELF	· · · · ·	368	EGO DOMINUS		22

141

CHRIST (CONTINUED)
    ODOUR OF BLOOD WHEN CHRIST WAS SLAIN • • • • • • •   438 SONGS PLAY 2   6
    MIDNIGHT HAS COME, AND THE GREAT CHRIST CHURCH BELL • • •   470 ALL SOUL NIGHT   1
    IT IS ALL SOULS' NIGHT AND THE GREAT CHRIST CHURCH BELL   470 ALL SOUL NIGHT V   1
    HIS FATHERS SERVED THEIR FATHERS BEFORE CHRIST WAS   580 CURSE CROMWELL   6
        CRUCIFIED.
    UPON THE CHURCH OF CHRIST. • • • • • • • • • • •   583 GHOST ROG CASE   18
CHRISTENDOM
    THE CHIEF IMAGINATION OF CHRISTENDOM, • • • • • • •   368 EGO DOMINUS   18
CHRISTENED
    HE CHRISTENED HIMSELF WITH BLOOD. • • • • • • • • •   585 ORAHILLY   8
    IN A CLEFT THAT'S CHRISTENED ALT • • • • • • • • •   632 MAN AND ECHO   1
CHRISTIAN
    DID I BECOME A CHRISTIAN MAN AND CHOOSE FOR MY BELIEF • •   503 VACILLATION   85
    RIBH CONSIDERS CHRISTIAN LOVE INSUFFICIENT • • • • • •   558 RIBH CHRISTIAN   T
    WITH CHRISTIAN AND WITH INFIDEL, • • • • • • • • •   594 COLONEL MARTIN   3
CHRISTMAS
    HER FRIENDS BRING HER A CHRISTMAS TREE • • • • • • •   366 HER CHRIS TREE   T
CHRISTMAS-TREE
    HER FRIENDS BRING HER A CHRISTMAS-TREE • • • • • • •   366 HER CHRIS TREE V   T
CHRONICLER
    A MYSTERY THAT ELSE HAD FOUND NO CHRONICLER • • • • •   461 HARUN RASHID   21
CHRONICLERS
    THAT I COMMEND TO ALL THE CHRONICLERS • • • • • • •   463 HARUN RASHID   46
CHRONICLING
    CHRONICLING CHIMAERAS FLED. • • • • • • • • • • •   65 HAPPY SHEPHERD V   17
CHRONOS
    TO THE CRACKED TUNE THAT CHRONOS SINGS, • • • • • • •   65 HAPPY SHEPHERD   9
    TO THE OLD CRACKED TUNE THAT CHRONOS SINGS, • • • • •   65 HAPPY SHEPHERD V   9
CHRYSELEPHANTINE
    CHRYSELEPHANTINE, CEDAR-BOARDED, • • • • • • • • • •   440 WISDOM   10
    CHRYSELEPHANTINE, CEDAR BOARDED, • • • • • • • • • V   440 WISDOM   V   10
CHRYSOBERYL
    OR CHRYSOBERYL, OR BERYL, OR CHRYSOLITE; • • • • • •   231 SHADOW WATER B   215
    OF CHRYSOBERYL, OR BERYL, OR CHRYSOLITE; • • • • • •   231 SHADOW WATER B V   215
    OF CHRYSOBERYL AND BERYL AND CHRYSOLITE, • • • • • •   765 SHADOW WATER A   357
CHRYSOLITE
    OF OPAL AND RUBY AND PALE CHRYSOLITE • • • • • • • •   219 HARP OF AENGUS   6
    OR CHRYSOBERYL, OR BERYL, OR CHRYSOLITE; • • • • • •   231 SHADOW WATER B   215
    OF CHRYSOBERYL, OR BERYL, OR CHRYSOLITE; • • • • • •   231 SHADOW WATER B V   215
    OF OPAL AND RUBY AND PALE CHRYSOLITE • • • • • • • •   762 SHADOW WATER A   301
    OF CHRYSOBERYL AND BERYL AND CHRYSOLITE, • • • • • •   765 SHADOW WATER A   357
CHRYSOPRASE
    LIKE CHARMED APPLES MADE OF CHRYSOPRASE, • • • • • •   231 SHADOW WATER B   214
    AND CHRYSOPRASE AND RUBY AND SARDONYX. • • • • • • •   765 SHADOW WATER A   358
CHUBBY
    LIES A CHUBBY FINGER-TIP, • • • • • • • • • • • •   732 STREET DANCERS V   19
CHURCH
    HOW THE MEN OF THE SAND-SACK SHOWED ME A CHURCH • • • • •   61 OISIN 3   193
    MIDNIGHT HAS COME, AND THE GREAT CHRIST CHURCH BELL • • •   470 ALL SOUL NIGHT   1
    IT IS ALL SOULS' NIGHT AND THE GREAT CHRIST CHURCH BELL   470 ALL SOUL NIGHT V   1
    CHURCH AND STATE • • • • • • • • • • • • • • •   553 CHURCH STATE   T
    MIGHT OF THE CHURCH AND THE STATE, • • • • • • • •   554 CHURCH STATE   3
    WHAT IF THE CHURCH AND THE STATE • • • • • • • • •   554 CHURCH STATE   9
    UPON THE CHURCH OF CHRIST. • • • • • • • • • • •   583 GHOST ROG CASE   18
    I POKED ABOUT A VILLAGE CHURCH • • • • • • • • • •   584 GHOST ROG CASE   31
    LONG YEARS AGO, A CHURCH STANDS NEAR, • • • • • • •   640 BEN BULBEN   87
    BENEATH THE SHELTERING SHADOW OF THY CHURCH; • • • • •   698 MOSADA 2   58
    IN CHURCH • • • • • • • • • • • • • • • • • •   735 IN CHURCH   T
    IN THE HOLY CHURCH OF GOD • • • • • • • • • • • •   735 IN CHURCH   4
    IN THE HOLY CHURCH OF GOD. • • • • • • • • • • •   736 IN CHURCH   16
CHURCHES
    YOUR BELL-MOUNTED CHURCHES, • • • • • • • • • • • •   58 OISIN 3   163
    THY BELL-MOUNTED CHURCHES, • • • • • • • • • • • • V   58 OISIN 3   V   163
    AT THE OLD BITTER WORLD WHERE THEY MARRY IN CHURCHES, • •   330 BONE OF A HARE   13
    AT ALL WHO MARRY IN CHURCHES, • • • • • • • • • •   330 BONE OF A HARE   15
CHURCHMEN
    SOON WILL THE CHURCHMEN NOD ABOVE THE CROWD. • • • • •   699 MOSADA 3   19
CHURCH'S
    TAKEN IN MAGIC, IN THE CHURCH'S NAME • • • • • • • •   694 MOSADA 1   104
CHURCHYARD
    IN DRUMCLIFF CHURCHYARD YEATS IS LAID. • • • • • • •   640 BEN BULBEN   85
CHURNED
    THE STREAM CHURNED, CHURNED, AND CHURNED--HIS LIPS APART,   31 OISIN 2   43
    THE STREAM CHURNED, CHURNED, AND CHURNED--HIS LIPS APART,   31 OISIN 2   43
    THE STREAM CHURNED, CHURNED, AND CHURNED--HIS LIPS APART,   31 OISIN 2   43
    THE STREAM CHURNED, CHURNED, • • • • • • • • • • •   31 OISIN 2   V   43
    THE STREAM CHURNED, CHURNED, • • • • • • • • • • •   31 OISIN 2   V   43
    • • • AND CHURNED. HIS LIPS WERE ROLLED APART, • • • •   31 OISIN 2   V   43
CICERO
    THAT EVEN CICERO • • • • • • • • • • • • • • •   524 MAD AS MIST   16
CIDER
    WORK AT THE CIDER PRESS. • • • • • • • • • • • • •   774 COME RIDE   12
CINCTURE
    AND GATHERED IN A SILVER CINCTURE; • • • • • • • •   3 OISIN 1   V   24A
CINNAMON
    NO; BUT OPOPONAX AND CINNAMON. • • • • • • • • • •   232 SHADOW WATER B   222
CIPHER
    THE CHILDREN LEARN TO CIPHER AND TO SING, • • • • • •   443 SCHOOL CHILDR   3
CIRCLE
    THERE THE LOVES A CIRCLE GO, • • • • • • • • • • •   135 TWO TREES   13

```
                                                 PAGE     TITLE            LINE
CIRCLE   (CONTINUED)
    THE FLAMING CIRCLE OF OUR DAYS,     . . . . . . .     135 TWO TREES            14
    THE FLAMING CIRCLE OF OUR LIFE.     . . . . . . .     135 TWO TREES        V   16
    PROTECTED FROM THE CIRCLE OF THE MOON . . . . . .     428 NINETEEN 19          3
    LIES IN A CIRCLE ON THE GRASS; THEREIN . . . . .      555 RIBH AT TOMB        26
    WILL CIRCLE ROUND THE WORLD UPON A QUEST, . . . .     651 ISLE STAT I 1      159
    THE FLAMING CIRCLE OF THE OUTER LAW, . . . . . .      689 NETTLESHIP          13
CIRCLED    SEE ORCHARD-CIRCLED
    THE POSTS OF POLISHED YEW, CIRCLED WITH BRONZE, . . . 279 TWO KINGS           48
    AND CIRCLED ROUND HIM WITH ITS SQUEAKY CRY, . . . . . 377 PHASES OF MOON     138
CIRCLES
    EACH OTHER ROUND IN CIRCLES, AND HEARD THE ELDEST SPEAK!  76 INDIAN ON GOD     5
    EACH OTHER ROUND IN CIRCLES! AND I HEARD THE ELDEST       76 INDIAN ON GOD V   5
        SPEAK!--
    HAS MADE THE VERY OWLS IN CIRCLES MOVE! . . . , . .   423 MY DESCENDANTS      18
    OF APPLE-BLOSSOM CIRCLES IN THE GLOOM, . . . . . .    700 MOSADA 3            42
    OF APPLE BLOSSOM CIRCLES IN THE GLOOM, . . . . . .    700 MOSADA 3        V   42
    AN APPLE BLOSSOM CIRCLES IN THE GLOOM, . . . . . .    700 MOSADA 3        V   42
    AND THROB WITHIN THE CIRCLES OF GREEN DAWN. . . . .   701 MOSADA 3            54
CIRCLING
    OF MISTY DAWN; WHEN, CIRCLING ROUND THE HALL, . . .    39 OISIN 2         V  153
    AND AFTER CIRCLING WITH STRANGE CRIES AWHILE . . . .  223 SHADOW WATER B      26
    CIRCLING AND CIRCLING OVER THE MASTHEAD? . . . . .    234 SHADOW WATER B     266
    CIRCLING AND CIRCLING OVER THE MASTHEAD? . . . . .    234 SHADOW WATER B     266
    A MEANING IN THAT CIRCLING OVERHEAD? . . . . . .      234 SHADOW WATER B     270
    THEY HAVE BEEN CIRCLING OVER OUR HEADS IN THE AIR,    247 SHADOW WATER B     525
    I SLEPT, 'TWAS SULTRY, AND SCARCE CIRCLING SHOOK . .  677 ISLE STAT II 3     278
    SLID CIRCLING DOWN AND SOFTLY TOUCHED MY LIPS . . .   690 MOSADA 1            21
    CIRCLING THE BRAIN?  MY BROTHERS WILL PASS DOWN . .   699 MOSADA 3             6
    TO BUILD THE CIRCLING SEATS, WHERE HIGH IN AIR . .    699 MOSADA 3            18
    CIRCLING THE BRAIN? MY BROTHERS NOW PASS DOWN . . .   699 MOSADA 3        V    6
CIRCUIT
    THAN THE HEAVENLY CIRCUIT OF ITS STARS . . . . .      451 FIRST LOVE          17
    THAN HEAVENLY CIRCUIT OF ITS STARS . . . . . .        451 FIRST LOVE      V   17
    THE HEAVENLY CIRCUIT! BERENICE'S HAIR! . . . . .      483 VERONIC NAPKIN       1
    STOOD IN THE CIRCUIT OF A NEEDLE'S EYE. . . . . .     483 VERONIC NAPKIN       6
CIRCUS
    THE CIRCUS ANIMALS' DESERTION . . . . . . . .         629 CIRCUS ANIMALS       T
    THE CIRCUS ANIMAL'S DESERTION . . . . . . . .         629 CIRCUS ANIMALS V     T
    MY CIRCUS ANIMALS WERE ALL ON SHOW, . . . . . .       629 CIRCUS ANIMALS       6
CISTERN
    OR ROCKY CISTERN WHERE WE TREAD THE CLOTHES  . . . .  499 MOTHER OF GOD        9
CITIES
    FROM MARBLE CITIES LOUD WITH TABORS OF OLD . . . .    162 ASKS FORGIVE         9
    GIRLS THAT HAVE GOVERNED CITIES, . . . . . . .        789 SINGING HEAD        15
    OR BURNED GREAT CITIES DOWN, . . . . . . . .          789 SINGING HEAD        16
CITRON
    A CITRON COLOUR GLOOMED IN HER HAIR, . . . . . .        3 OISIN 1             24
    HER HAIR WAS OF A CITRON TINCTURE, . . . . . .          3 OISIN 1         V   24
    LONG CITRON COILS THAT HANG AROUND THEE, BLOWN        670 ISLE STAT II 3     105
CITY
    TO THE HOLY CITY OF BYZANTIUM. . . . . . . .          408 SAIL BYZANTIUM      16
    CITY AND CITY MAY CONTEND, . . . . . . . .            540 FROM ANTIGONE       12
    CITY AND CITY MAY CONTEND, . . . . . . . .            540 FROM ANTIGONE       12
    OR ROUND THE CITY HALL, . . . . . . . . .            608 SONGS BURDEN 3       6
    CLOSE TO THE CITY HALL HE DIED; . . . . . . .         608 SONGS BURDEN 3      12
    AND ON THAT CITY DROPPED A TEAR, . . . . . . .        725 LEGEND              31
    AND NOW THAT CITY IS A LAKE. . . . . . . . .          725 LEGEND              32
CIVIL
    MEDITATIONS IN TIME OF CIVIL WAR   ANCESTRAL HOUSES  . .  417 ANCEST HOUSES V   T
    COMES CRACKING JOKES OF CIVIL WAR . . . . . . .       423 ROAD AT DOOR         3
    SOME FOURTEEN DAYS OF CIVIL WAR; . . . . . . .        425 STARES NEST         12
    NO CIVIL RANCOUR TORN THE LAND APART. . . . . .       542 PARN FUNERAL 2       4
CIVILISATION
    THAT CIVILISATION MAY NOT SINK, . . . . . . .         617 LONG-LEG FLY         1
CIVILISATIONS
    OLD CIVILISATIONS PUT TO THE SWORD. . . . . . .       566 LAPIS LAZULI        27
CIVILIZATION
    CIVILIZATION IS HOOPED TOGETHER, BROUGHT . . . . .    563 MERU                 1
CLAIM
    SOME OTHER WOMAN HAS A CLAIM ON YOU, . . . . . .      245 SHADOW WATER B     474
    THAT I MAY CLAIM YOU AS MY WIFE AGAIN." . . . . .     284 TWO KINGS          170
    AND CLAIM AS BY A SOLDIER'S RIGHT . . . . . . .       478 SELF AND SOUL       31
CLAIMED
    GOD'S BELL HAS CLAIMED THEM BY THE LITTLE CRY . . . . 114 ROSE OF BATTLE      23
    HE CLAIMED HIS COUNTRY'S NEED WAS MOST, . . . . .     275 GREY ROCK          101
CLAMBER
    WHEN I CLAMBER TO THE HEIGHTS OF SLEEP, . . . . .     357 DEEP-SWORN VOW       4
    THE TOWER'S OLD COOK THAT MUST CLIMB AND CLAMBER . . . 636 BLACK TOWER        21
CLAMBERING
    TILL, CLAMBERING AT THE CRADLE-SIDE, . . . . . .      343 SHEP GOATHERD      109
    TILL, CLAMBERING AT THE CRADLE SIDE, . . . . . .      343 SHEP GOATHERD  V   109
CLAMOROUS
    AROSE, AND ON THE INSTANT CLAMOROUS EAVES, . . . . .  120 SORROW OF LOVE       9
    UPON THEIR CLAMOROUS WINGS. . . . . . . . .           322 SWANS AT COOLE      12
CLAMOUR
    CRIED FROM THE PORTER'S LODGE, AND WITH LONG CLAMOUR  . . 181 QUEEN MAEVE     37
    AND YET YOU MAKE A CLAMOUR OF REPROACH. . . . . .     243 SHADOW WATER B     444
    "THE WIND-BLOWN CLAMOUR OF THE BARNACLE-GEESE." . . . 300 BEGGAR CRIED       20
    THOSE WINDS THAT CLAMOUR OF APPROACHING NIGHT. . . .  431 NINETEEN 19         68
    AND CLAMOUR IN DRUNKEN FRENZY FOR THE MOON. . . . .   482 BLOOD AND MOON      42
```

```
                                                    PAGE      TITLE            LINE
CLAMOUR   (CONTINUED)
    ALL CLAMOUR-CLOTHED--WAS'T CLAMOUR WHEN I SUNG,  . . . .   649 ISLE STAT I 1     108
    CLAMOUR OF THE LONE NIGHTJAR. . . . . . . . . .   732 STREET DANCERS     21
CLAMOUR-CLOTHED
    ALL CLAMOUR-CLOTHED--WAS'T CLAMOUR WHEN I SUNG,  . . . .   649 ISLE STAT I 1     108
CLAN
    MINE WERE CLAN MORNA'S TRIBES UNTOLD, . . . . . . . . .    81 MAD KING GOLL V     3
    BEFORE GOD MADE THE ANGELIC CLAN. . . . . . . . .   138 TO IRELAND          8
CLANG
    WITH SHOUTING AND THE CLANG OF UNHOOKED ARMS. . . . . .   185 QUEEN MAEVE       111
    WITH A CLANG OF HIS DIM MAIL, . . . . . . . . .   742 EARL PAUL          66
CLANGING
    IN CLANGING SPACE A MOMENT HEARD, . . . . . . . . .    65 HAPPY SHEPHERD     20
    'MID CLANGING SPACE A MOMENT HEARD . . . . . . . .    65 HAPPY SHEPHERD V   20
    AND WITH THE CLANGING OF THEIR SWORD-BLADES MAKE . . . .   137 TO SOME I TALK V   13
    THE INNUMERABLE CLANGING WINGS THAT HAVE PUT OUT THE MOON.   427 PHANTOM HATRED     32
CLANGOUR
    INTO THE CLANGOUR OF THE WIND AND SEA. . . . . . . . .    45 OISIN 2           234
    LIKE THE CLANGOUR OF A BELL. . . . . . . . . .   382 SONG OF FOOL        9
    GOES TO THE BARBAROUS CLANGOUR OF A GONG. . . . . . .   430 NINETEEN 19        58
    GOES TO THE BARBAROUS CLANGOUR OF GONG. . . . . . .   430 NINETEEN 19     V   58
CLANKING
    I SAW HIM STAGGER WITH THE CLANKING CHAIN, . . . . . .   687 TWO TITANS         31
CLANN
    . . . FOR NOWHERE IN ANY CLANN . . . . . . . . . .    50 OISIN 3         V   49
CLAP      SEE THUNDER-CLAP
    AND CLAP THEIR HANDS TOGETHER, AND HALF CLOSE THEIR EYES,   146 UNAPPEAS HOST       2
    SOUL CLAP ITS HANDS AND SING, AND LOUDER SING . . . . .   407 SAIL BYZANTIUM     11
    THAT GATHERS VOLUME; NOW A THUNDER CLAP. . . . . . .   487 SEVEN SAGES     V   23
    UP WITH THE NECK AND CLAP THE WING, . . . . . . . .   782 HEART FRIGHT        6
    UP WITH THE NECK AND CLAP THE WING, . . . . . . . .   782 HEART FRIGHT       13
    UP WITH THE NECK AND CLAP THE WING, . . . . . . . .   782 HEART FRIGHT       20
    STRETCH NECK AND CLAP THE WING, . . . . . . . . .   783 GREY ROUND         27
CLAPPED
    "I WILL NOT BE CLAPPED IN A HOOD, . . . . . . . . .   349 HAWK                7
CLARE
    TO COLD CLARE ROCK AND GALWAY ROCK AND THORN, . . . . .   326 ROBERT GREGORY     66
CLARE-GALWAY
    THE WINDS OUT OF CLARE-GALWAY . . . . . . . . . .   783 GREY ROUND          4
CLARIONET
    PULL DOWN THE BLINDS, BRING FIDDLE AND CLARIONET . . . .   311 MOUNTAIN TOMB       5
CLASH
    LAUGHTER AND CRIES. THE ARMIES CLASH AND SHOCK, . . . .    43 OISIN 2           211
    AND THEN THE CLASH OF FALLEN HORSEMEN AND THE CRIES . . .   161 BLACK PIG           3
CLASHING
    AND WITH THE CLASHING OF THEIR SWORD-BLADES MAKE . . . .   137 TO SOME I TALK     13
    AND WITH THE CLASHING OF THEIR SWORD BLADES MAKE . . . .   137 TO SOME I TALK V   13
    AND FLUNG DOWN CLASHING ON THE FLOOR . . . . . . .   740 EARL PAUL          15
CLASPING
    HELP THEM THAT WANDER WITH HAND CLASPING HAND, . . . . .   184 QUEEN MAEVE        86
CLATTER
    TO MAKE A CLATTER IN THE HOLE . . . . . . . . . .   304 HOUR DAWN       V   54
CLAUDE
    CALVERT AND WILSON, BLAKE AND CLAUDE, . . . . . . .   639 BEN BULBEN         64
    AND WILSON, BLAKE AND CALVERT, CLAUDE, . . . . . . .   639 BEN BULBEN      V   64
CLAW
    NOR SORROW WITH HER OSPREY CLAW. . . . . . . . . .    19 OISIN 1         V  285
    CRUEL CLAW AND HUNGRY THROAT. . . . . . . . . .   136 TWO TREES          36
    NOTHING BUT GRIP OF CLAW, AND THE EYE'S COMPLACENCY, . .   427 PHANTOM HATRED     31
CLAWS     SEE BIRD-CLAWS
    . . . THEIR HANDS WERE THE CLAWS OF BIRDS, . . . . . .    49 OISIN 3            34
    AS MIDDLE NIGHT GREAT CATS WITH SILVER CLAWS, . . . . .   185 QUEEN MAEVE       115
    THEY HAD HANDS LIKE CLAWS, AND THEIR KNEES . . . . . .   208 OLD MEN ADMIRE      4
    AND DUG ITS CLAWS AND SHRIEKED AND FOUGHT. . . . . .   385 ROBARTES DANCE      8
    A WHITE BIRD HAS TORN ME WITH HIS SILVER CLAWS. . . . .   759 SHADOW WATER A    234
CLAY
    A HOUSE OF WATTLES, CLAY, AND SKIN; . . . . . . . .    17 OISIN 1           249
    INNUMERABLE, SINGING, EXULTANT: THE CLAY UNDERNEATH THEM    61 OISIN 3           203
        SHALL PANT,
    SPLASHED ALL WITH CLAY AND JOURNEY DULL, . . . . . .    82 MAD KING GOLL V    13
    AND A SMALL CABIN BUILD THERE, OF CLAY AND WATTLES MADE;   117 ISLE INNISFREE V    2
    AND A SMALL CABIN BUILT THERE, OF CLAY AND WATTLES MADE;   117 ISLE INNISFREE      2
    IN FLOOD AND FIRE AND CLAY AND WIND, . . . . . . .   138 TO IRELAND      V   25
    THE HORSES OF DISASTER PLUNGE IN THE HEAVY CLAY; . . . .   154 BELOVED PEACE       8
    THE HORSES OF DISASTER PLUNGE IN THE DESOLATE CLAY. . . .   154 BELOVED PEACE   V    8
    WHEN AN IMMORTAL PASSION BREATHES IN MORTAL CLAY; . . . .   172 TRAV PASSION        2
    BUT UNDER HEAVY LOADS OF TRAMPLED CLAY . . . . . . .   483 OIL AND BLOOD       4
    THE LOVERS AND THE DANCERS ARE BEATEN INTO THE CLAY, . .   580 CURSE CROMWELL      3
    OF ROOT, SHOOT, BLOSSOM OR CLAY . . . . . . . . .   600 SPIRIT MEDIUM      21
    THAT WERE BEATEN INTO THE CLAY . . . . . . . . .   640 BEN BULBEN         79
    MADE THEM OF FIRE AND CLAY. . . . . . . . . .   680 LOVE AND DEATH     12
    CLOGGED IN A MARSH WHERE THE SLOW MARSH CLAY CLINGS, . .   711 FERENCZ RENYI      35
    WITH LIGHT IMAGES OF CLAY . . . . . . . . . .   775 AGAINST WITCH      12
CLAY-COLD
    AS QUIET AS THE CLAY-COLD DEAD. . . . . . . . . .   670 ISLE STAT II 3    113
CLAY-PILED
    TO EMER OF BORDA, IN HER CLAY-PILED DUN, . . . . . .   105 CUCHULAIN SEA V     2
CLEAN
    MAKE CLEAN AS A BROOM CLEANS, . . . . . . . . .    62 OISIN 3           211
    BESIDES HER CLEAN SWEPT HEARTH, HER QUIET SHADE; . . . .   114 ROSE OF BATTLE V   11
    TO HAVE LIT UPON AS CLEAN AND SWEET A TALE . . . . . .   258 KING NO KING        8
```

144

	PAGE	TITLE	LINE

CLEAN   (CONTINUED)
SHE SEEMED TO HAVE GROWN CLEAN AND SWEET . . . . . . 397 POLIT PRISONER   17
CLEANING
THEN CLEANING OUT AND BANDAGING OF WOUNDS, ... 622 HOUND VOICE   20
CLEANLY
BRED THAT FIERCE TOOTH AND CLEANLY LIMB . . . . 318 APPOINTMENT   10
CLEANS
MAKE CLEAN AS A BROOM CLEANS, ...   62 OISIN 3   211
AS THAT WHICH CLEANS MAN'S DIRTY SLATE. . . . . 633 MAN AND ECHO   24
CLEAN-SWEPT
BESIDE HER CLEAN-SWEPT HEARTH, HER QUIET SHADE; . . . . 114 ROSE OF BATTLE   11
CLEAR
CLEAR FLUTED THEN THAT GOBLIN RARE-- . . . .   6 OISIN 1   V   54
WITH A CLEAR VOICE THE YOUNG MAN CRIED, ...   18 OISIN 1   V   260
WHEN THE MORN GREW FROSTY AND CLEAR. . . . .   95 MOLL MAGEE   20
IN THE FROSTY MORNIN' CLEAR. . . . .   95 MOLL MAGEE   V   20
COME CLEAR OF THE NETS OF WRONG AND RIGHT; . . . . . . 147 INTO TWILIGHT   2
COME CLEAR OFF THE NETS OF WRONG AND RIGHT; . . . . . . 147 INTO TWILIGHT V   2
OR BIRDS LOST IN THE ONE CLEAR SPACE . . . . 195 BAILE AILLINN   149
OR BIRDS LOST IN ONE CLEAR SPACE . . . . 195 BAILE AILLINN V   149
THAT WERE CLEAR MESSAGES FROM THE EVER-LIVING, ... 243 SHADOW DANCER B   442
A CLEAR ARTICULATION IN THE AIR, ...   320 REED WHISPERER   3
AND NEVER WROTE A BOOK, YOUR THOUGHT IS CLEAR. . . . . 376 PHASES OF MOON   97
FOR ALL MEN'S THOUGHTS GREW CLEAR . . . .   400 DEMON BEAST   19
FOR ALL MEN'S THOUGHT GREW CLEAR . . . .   400 DEMON BEAST   V   19
YET NO CLEAR FACT TO BE DISCERNED; . . . .   425 STARES NEST   9
ABOUT THE SKY; WHERE THAT IS CLEAR OF CLOUD . . . . . 541 PARN FUNERAL 1   3
A SORT OF BESOM THAT CAN CLEAR THE SOUL . . . . 558 RIBH CHRISTIAN   5
THAT ALL'S ARRANGED IN ONE CLEAR VIEW, ... 633 MAN AND ECHO   31
EACH SHINING CLEAR AS SOME UNBAFFLED STAR; . . . . . . 656 ISLE STAT I 3   25
AND NOT TOO CLEAR, HOW WILL THE NEW GOD KNOW . . . . . 658 ISLE STAT I 3   79
'TIS CLEAR THAT YOU HAVE SEEN HER NOT. THE CROWN . . . 661 ISLE STAT II 1   70
I COULD GAZE, GAZE UPON THINE EYES' CLEAR GREY; . . . . 671 ISLE STAT II 3   147
AGAIN THE WOODLAND LAUGHTER, AND THE CLEAR . . . . . . 674 ISLE STAT II 3   221
AND THE BIRD IN THE BRANCHES WILL CRY FOR US CLEAR, . . 717 LOVE SONG   6
. . . SEE, SHE ROUNDS THE HARBOUR CLEAR. . . . . . . 718 PHANTOM SHIP   13
UPON CLEAR NIGHTS THEY LEAVE THE UPPER AIR . . . . . . 750 SHADOW WATER A   87
CLEAR-BROWED
CLEAR-BROWED ARCADIAN, THOU SHALT BE OUR KING! . . . . 679 ISLE STAT II 3   318
CLEAR-BROWED ARCADIAN, THOU SHALT BE OUR KING! . . . . 679 ISLE STAT II 3   321
CLEARED
UNTIL MY THOUGHTS CLEARED UP AGAIN, ...   256 WORDS   6
CLEARLY
BURNS BUT MORE CLEARLY. O SHE HAD NOT THESE WAYS . . . 200 FOLLY COMFORT   11
CLEAR-SHINING
AFAR, CLEAR-SHINING ON THE HERALD HILLS, ... 645 ISLE STAT I 1   14
CLEAVE
AND MORE I MAY NOT WRITE OF, FOR THEY THAT CLEAVE . . 218 WOODS OF COOLE   24
AND MORE I MAY NOT WRITE OF, FOR THEM THAT CLEAVE . . 218 WOODS OF COOLE V   24
"WHAT TUMBLING CLOUD DID YOU CLEAVE, ...   349 HAWK   13
CLEFT
LIKE SOME OLD RABBIT TO MY CLEFT . . . .   307 HOUR DAWN   105
IN A CLEFT THAT'S CHRISTENED ALT . . . .   632 MAN AND ECHO   1
CLENCHED
WITHIN HIS CLENCHED TEETH A SWORD. . . . .   673 ISLE STAT II 3   182
CLERGYMEN
OF BANKERS, SCHOOLMASTERS, AND CLERGYMEN . . . . . . 205 ADAMS CURSE   13
CLERIC
. . . FOR I GO TO THE FENIANS, O CLERIC, TO CHAUNT . . 61 OISIN 3   201
. . . I WILL GO TO THE FENIANS, THOU CLERIC, AND CHANT . . 61 OISIN 3   V   201
CLERICS
BUT NOW THE LYING CLERICS MURDER SONG . . . .   42 OISIN 2   196
CLERK
BEFORE THE MERCHANT AND THE CLERK . . . .   266 GALWAY RACES   8
CLEVER
THE CLEVER MAN WHO CRIES . . . .   347 FISHERMAN   21
AND O HE WAS A CLEVER MAN, ...   595 COLONEL MARTIN   39
CLIFF
FROM DOORED AND WINDOWED CLIFF, OR HALF UPTURNED . . . 368 EGO DOMINUS   30
ON THE CLIFF BY THE SEA, ...   739 EARL PAUL   4
ON THE CLIFF OF KINSALE. . . . .   742 EARL PAUL   68
CLIFF-ENCIRCLED
HERE IS THE PLACE, THE CLIFF-ENCIRCLED WOOD; . . . . . 651 ISLE STAT I 2   3
CLIFFS
GO DWELL UPON THE SEA CLIFFS, VAPOUR HID, ... 105 CUCHULAIN SEA V   4
GO DWELL UPON THE SEA CLIFFS, VAPOUR-HID, ... 105 CUCHULAIN SEA V   4
GO DWELL UPON THE CLIFFS AND WATCH THE TIDE; . . . . . 105 CUCHULAIN SEA V   4
CLIFF-SHELTERED
UNTIL, IN SOME CLIFF-SHELTERED BAY . . . .   612 NEWS ORACLE   21
CLIMB
COMPANIONABLE STREAMS OR CLIMB THE AIR; . . . . 323 SWANS AT COOLE   21
CLIMB UP THE NARROW WINDING STAIR TO BED; . . . . . . 324 ROBERT GREGORY   5
TO CLIMB THAT STAIR AND EAT THAT BITTER BREAD, ... 369 EGO DOMINUS   35
THAT CLIMB THE STREAMS UNTIL . . . .   414 TOWER   123
THAT CLIMB THE MOUNTAIN SIDE, ...   416 TOWER   V   175
I CLIMB TO THE TOWER-TOP AND LEAN UPON BROKEN STONE, . . 425 PHANTOM HATRED   1
I CLIMB TO THE TOWER TOP AND LEAN UPON BROKEN STONE, . . 425 PHANTOM HATRED V   1
SHOULD THE CONFLAGRATION CLIMB, ...   476 EVA GORE-BOOTH   28
THOSE CHINAMEN CLIMB TOWARDS, AND I . . . . 567 LAPIS LAZULI   49
CLIMB TO YOUR CHAMBER FULL OF BOOKS AND WAIT, ... 579 DOR WELLESLEY   8
CLIMB TO OUR PROPER DARK, THAT WE MAY TRACE . . . . . 611 STATUES   31

145

CLIMB   (CONTINUED)
         CLIMB ON A WAGONETTE TO SCREAM. . . . .   626 OLD MEN BE MAD   8
         THE TOWER'S OLD COOK THAT MUST CLIMB AND CLAMBER . . . . 636 BLACK TOWER   21
         "IF I DO BUT CLIMB THE STAIR . . . .   771 SONG DEIRDRE 1   2
CLIMBED
         HALF IN THE UNVESSELLED SEA, WE CLIMBED THE STAIR . . .   32 OISIN 2   47
         AND CLIMBED SO LONG, I THOUGHT THE LAST STEPS WERE . . . 32 OISIN 2   48
         HALF IN THE UNVESSELLED SEA, WE CLIMBED THE STAIRS . . . 32 OISIN 2   V 47
         AND THEN WE CLIMBED THE STAIR TO A HIGH DOOR; . . . . .   36 OISIN 2   101
         THAT OLD MAN CLIMBED; THE DAY GREW DIM. . . . .   194 BAILE AILLINN   134
         AND CLIMBED INTO THE AIR, CRUMBLING AWAY, ...   278 TWO KINGS   42
         OR CLIMBED AMONG THE IMAGES OF THE PAST-- . . . .   352 PEOPLE   10
         CLIMBED UP MY CREAKING STAIR. THEY HAD READ . . . . .   358 PRESENCES   6
         OR THE HUMBLER WORM, I CLIMBED BEN BULBEN'S BACK . . . . 409 TOWER   9
         OR SHOD IN IRON, CLIMBED THE NARROW STAIRS, ...   412 TOWER   83
         AND BOTH CLIMBED UP THE STAIR, ...   595 COLONEL MARTIN   38
         AS SLOWLY AUTUMN CLIMBED THE GOLDEN THRONE . . . . . .   690 MOSADA 1   V 1A
CLIMBING
         A CLIMBING MOON UPON AN EMPTY SKY, ...   120 SORROW OF LOVE   10
         AND STARS CLIMBING THE DEW-DROPPING SKY, ...   158 BELOVED RHYMES   11
         CLIMBING UP TO A PLACE . . . .   348 FISHERMAN   31
         CLIMBING THE MOUNTAIN-SIDE, ...   416 TOWER   175
         CLIMBING, FALLING SHE KNEW NOT WHERE, ...   578 CRAZED GIRL   4
CLIMBS
         WHERE I WOULD BE WHEN THE WHITE MOON CLIMBS, ...   9 OISIN 1   104
         AND NOW LIES SUNK IN SLEEP. WHAT CLIMBS THE STAIR? . . . 579 DOR WELLESLEY   11
         BUT NOW LIES SUNK IN SLEEP. WHAT CLIMBS THE STAIR? . . . 579 DOR WELLESLEY   V 11
CLIME
         LIAR AND FLATTERER OF THE WEAK, IN WHAT STRANGE CLIME . . 42 OISIN 2   V 198
         WELL NIGH IMMORTAL IN THIS CHARMED CLIME, ...   674 ISLE STAT II 3   202
         WELL-NIGH IMMORTAL IN THIS CHARMED CLIME; . . . . . .   674 ISLE STAT II 3 V 202
         THE SUNFLOWERS WEAVE A GOLDEN CLIME, ...   736 SUMMER EVENING   9
CLING
         BUT, DEAR, CLING CLOSE TO ME; SINCE YOU WERE GONE, . . . 257 RECONCILIATION   11
         ADMONISH US TO CLING TO THAT . . . .   460 THREE MONUMENT   8
         UPON THE DUSTY, GLITTERING WINDOWS CLING, ...   482 BLOOD AND MOON   43
         AND SEEM TO CLING UPON THE MOONLIT SKIES, ...   482 BLOOD AND MOON   44
         CLOSE AND CLING SO TIGHT, ...   538 LAST CONFESS   22
         ABOUT A SUN-FLUSHED DOVE-COT, COOING, CLING . . . . .   710 FERENCZ RENYI   20
CLINGETH
         WHERE THE FLESH OF THE FOOTSOLE CLINGETH . . . . .   61 OISIN 3   197
         WHEN THE FLESH OF THE FOOTSOLE CLINGETH . . . .   61 OISIN 3   V 197
CLINGING
         AND WANDER IN THE STORMS AND CLINGING SNOWS, ...   42 OISIN 2   201
         THE NORTH UNFOLDS ABOVE THEM CLINGING, CREEPING NIGHT, . . 154 BELOVED PEACE   3
         THE NORTH UNROLLS ABOVE THEM CLINGING, CREEPING NIGHT, . . 154 BELOVED PEACE   V 3
         FOR THE WET WINDS ARE BLOWING OUT OF THE CLINGING AIR! . . 207 HANRAHANS SONG   12
         FOR THE GREY WINDS ARE BLOWING UP, OUT OF THE CLINGING   207 HANRAHANS SONG V 12
             SEAS!
         AND CLINGING TO IT I COULD HEAR THE COCKS . . . . .   286 TWO KINGS   210
         WITH CLINGING MIST, EACH STAR-FOUGHT WANDERER CAME . .   656 ISLE STAT I 3   33
         AND CLINGING WITH THE DEW OF ODOROUS SHOWERS, ...   704 REMEMBRANCE   4
         AWAY HER CLINGING HANDS, AND TURNS. SHE THROWS . . . .   714 FERENCZ RENYI   102
CLINGS
         CLOGGED IN A MARSH WHERE THE SLOW MARSH CLAY CLINGS, . . 711 FERENCZ RENYI   35
         AND BE SO HAPPY." TO HIS HANDS SHE CLINGS, ...   714 FERENCZ RENYI   100
         AND BE SO HAPPY." TO HIS HAND SHE CLINGS, ...   714 FERENCZ RENYI   V 100
CLIP
         FOR THEY SHOULD CLIP AND CLIP AGAIN . . . .   194 BAILE AILLINN   122
         FOR THEY SHOULD CLIP AND CLIP AGAIN . . . .   194 BAILE AILLINN   122
CLIPPED
         CLIPPED AN INSOLENT FARMER'S EARS . . . .   410 TOWER   31
         NOR MUSIC NOR AN ENEMY'S CLIPPED EAR . . . .   412 TOWER   75
CLOAK
         AND WHEN THEY SAW THE CLOAK I WORE . . . .   15 OISIN 1   207
         ALL EMPTIED OF PURPLE HOURS AS A BEGGAR'S CLOAK IN THE   63 OISIN 3   219
             RAIN,
         THE CLOAK, THE BOAT, AND THE SHOES . . . .   69 CLOAK BOAT   T
         "I MAKE THE CLOAK OF SORROW! . . . .   69 CLOAK BOAT   2
         SHALL BE THE CLOAK OF SORROW! . . . .   69 CLOAK BOAT   4
         THE CLOAK I WEAVE OF SORROW! . . . .   69 CLOAK BOAT   V 2
         HE HAD HALF A CLOAK TO KEEP HIM DRY, ...   190 BAILE AILLINN   29
         GATHERING HIS CLOAK ABOUT HIM, RUN . . . .   193 BAILE AILLINN   101
         AND THERE'S A PLAYER IN THE STATES WHO GATHERS UP HER CLOAK 354 HIS PHOENIX   12
         AND THERE'S THE PLAYER IN THE STATES WHO GATHERS UP HER   354 HIS PHOENIX   V 12
             CLOAK
         AND A CLOAK WRAPPED ABOUT THE STONE, ...   456 FRIENDS YOUTH   7
         I WRAPPED HER IN A HOODED CLOAK, AND SHE, ...   468 HARUN RASHID   154
         I WRAPPED HER IN A HEAVY HOODED CLOAK, ...   468 HARUN RASHID   V 154
         I WRAPPED HER IN A HEAVY HOODED CLOAK, AND SHE . . . .   468 HARUN RASHID   V 154
         IN MASKER'S CLOAK AND HOOD, ...   539 MEETING   2
         IN COUNTRY SHAWL OR PARIS CLOAK, HAD PUT MY WITS ASTRAY, 592 PILGRIM   3
         SO COME IN RAGS OR COME IN SILK, IN CLOAK OR COUNTRY SHAWL, 593 PILGRIM   22
         SO COME IN RAG OR COME IN SILK, IN CLOAK OR COUNTRY SHAWL, 593 PILGRIM   V 22
         WITH A RAGGED BANDIT CLOAK, ...   627 STATES HOLIDAY   31
         THE CLOAK I WEAVE OF SORROW, ...   666 ISLE STAT II 3   2
         SHALL BE THE CLOAK OF SORROW, ...   666 ISLE STAT II 3   4
         I'LL DRAW MY CLOAK AROUND ME; IT IS COLD. . . . . . .   704 MOSADA 3   123
         THE GLOVE AND THE CLOAK . . . .   744 GLOVE CLOAK   T
         I STOOD WITH HER CLOAK ON MY ARM . . . .   744 GLOVE CLOAK   5
         AND MURMURED: "O LONG GREY CLOAK, ...   744 GLOVE CLOAK   11

CLOAKS
    THEIR CLOAKS MADE OUT OF YELLOW SILK, ...   15 OISIN 1   205
CLOCK
    SHOULD LAUGH AND WEEP AN HOUR UPON THE CLOCK. . . . . .   471 ALL SOUL NIGHT   20
    SHOULD LAUGH AND WEEP AN HOUR UPON THE CLOCK. . . . . .   474 ALL SOUL NIGHT   90
    SHOULD WEEP AND LAUGH AN HOUR UPON THE CLOCK. . . . . .   474 ALL SOUL NIGHT V   90
    NOON UPON THE CLOCK, ...   525 DANCING DAYS   18
    . . . "THE KING OF THE GREAT CLOCK TOWER" . . . .   549 SEVERED HEAD   T
    WHAT SAYS THE CLOCK IN THE GREAT CLOCK TOWER? . . . . .   549 SEVERED HEAD   3
    WHAT SAYS THE CLOCK IN THE GREAT CLOCK TOWER? . . . . .   549 SEVERED HEAD   3
    WHAT SAYS THE CLOCK IN THE GREAT CLOCK TOWER? . . . . .   550 SEVERED HEAD   10
    WHAT SAYS THE CLOCK IN THE GREAT CLOCK TOWER? . . . . .   550 SEVERED HEAD   10
    WHAT SAYS THE CLOCK IN THE GREAT CLOCK TOWER? . . . . .   550 SEVERED HEAD   17
    WHAT SAYS THE CLOCK IN THE GREAT CLOCK TOWER? . . . . .   550 SEVERED HEAD   17
    "THAT I AT MIDNIGHT BY THE CLOCK . . . .   569 THREE BUSHES   10
    WHEN THE CLOCK BEGINS TO CHIME." . . . .   570 THREE BUSHES   41
    "BECAUSE I HELPED TO WIND THE CLOCK . . . .   585 ORAHILLY   25
    "TILL THE SUN GOES DOWN AND AN HOUR OF THE CLOCK" . . .   779 GOING THE ROAD   7
    "FOR A YEAR AND A DAY BY THE CLOCK OF THE SUN" . . . .   779 GOING THE ROAD   11
CLOGGED
    CLOGGED IN A MARSH WHERE THE SLOW MARSH CLAY CLINGS, . .   711 FERENCZ RENYI   35
CLOONE
    AND ONE WAS DROWNED IN THE GREAT BOG OF CLOONE. . . . .   411 TOWER   48
CLOOTH-NA-BARE
    AND OVER THE GRAVE OF CLOOTH-NA-BARE: . . . .   140 HOSTING SIDHE   2
    THE YELLOW POOL HAS OVERFLOWED HIGH UP ON CLOOTH-NA-BARE,   207 HANRAHANS SONG   11
    THE YELLOW POOL HAS OVERFLOWED HIGH UPON CLOOTH-NA-BARE,   207 HANRAHANS SONG V   11
CLOSE
    OR CLUNG AS CLOSE AS SWARMS OF BEES, ...   14 OISIN 1   V 181
    AND ONE CAME CLOSE, A TEARFUL BOY. . . . .   17 OISIN 1   V 237
    AND GO YOU CLOSE TO THEM. . . . .   33 OISIN 2   V 59
    HIS EYELIDS CLOSE, HIS HEAD DROOPS LOW, ...   98 FOXHUNTER   V 13
    YOUNG SUBTLE CONCHUBAR SAT CLOSE BY ME . . . .   102 FERGUS DRUID   10
    AND HIS YOUNG SWEETHEART CLOSE BESIDE HIM KNELT, ...   108 CUCHULAIN SEA   40
    AND HIS YOUNG DEAR ONE CLOSE BESIDE HIM KNELT, ...   108 CUCHULAIN SEA   40
    AND CLAP THEIR HANDS TOGETHER, AND HALF CLOSE THEIR EYES,   146 UNAPPEAS HOST   2
    BELOVED, LET YOUR EYES HALF CLOSE, AND YOUR HEART BEAT .   154 BELOVED PEACE   9
    THAT ONLY GOD'S EYES DID NOT CLOSE: . . . .   156 FORGOT BEAUTY   14
    THAT ONLY THE GODS' EYES DID NOT CLOSE: . . . .   156 FORGOT BEAUTY   14
    HALF CLOSE YOUR EYELIDS, LOOSEN YOUR HAIR, ...   166 EVIL OF BELOV   1
    WHEN WE COME AT THE CLOSE OF TIME . . . .   178 FIDDLER DOONEY V   9
    THAT BEAUTIFUL MILD WOMAN, YOUR CLOSE FRIEND, ...   204 ADAMS CURSE   2
    BUT, DEAR, CLING CLOSE TO ME: SINCE YOU WERE GONE, . . .   257 RECONCILIATION   11
    ALTHOUGH I HAVE COME CLOSE ON FORTY-NINE, ...   270 PARDON FATHERS   20
    WHEN CUPS WENT ROUND AT CLOSE OF DAY-- . . . .   271 GREY ROCK   12
    CLOSE TO A CLUMP OF BEECH TREES IN THE WOOD . . . . . .   283 TWO KINGS   V 135
    WHEN CLOSE TO HIS RIGHT HAND A HEAP . . . .   302 HOUR DAWN   11
    THEY WERE MY CLOSE COMPANIONS MANY A YEAR, ...   325 ROBERT GREGORY   41
    HANDS GRIPPED IN HANDS, TOES CLOSE TOGETHER, ...   332 ROUND TOWER   21
    OF THE ANALYTIC MIND, CAN NEITHER CLOSE . . . .   353 PEOPLE   33
    WHEN TWO CLOSE KINDRED MEET, ...   378 CAT AND MOON   12
    I HAVE MET THEM AT CLOSE OF DAY . . . .   391 EASTER 1916   1
    THE LADIES CLOSE THEIR MUSING EYES. NO PROPHECIES, . . .   426 PHANTOM HATRED   19
    CLOSE AND CLING SO TIGHT. . . . .   538 LAST CONFESS   22
    IN HATING GOD SHE MAY CREEP CLOSE TO GOD. . . . . . .   558 RIBH CHRISTIAN V   10
    THOSE HANDS TO CLOSE THESE EYES. . . . .   587 OLD WICKED MAN   6
    CAN NEVER CLOSE THOSE EYES." . . . .   588 OLD WICKED MAN   26
    CLOSE TO THE CITY HALL HE DIED: . . . .   608 SONGS BURDEN 3   12
    SLEEPILY CLOSE HER ROUND BRIGHT EYNE: . . . .   646 ISLE STAT I 1   35
    WHEN HIS SINEWY WINGS TOGETHER CLOSE. . . . .   673 ISLE STAT II 3   179
    THOU'RT WELCOME. LIE THERE CLOSE AGAINST MY FINGERS, . .   700 MOSADA 3   44
    NOW STEPS DRAW CLOSE, HE HIDES BENEATH A DRUM. . . . . .   713 FERENCZ RENYI   78
    CLOSE AND MORE CLOSE--I FEEL HIM IN MY HEART-- . . . . .   720 WITCH VIVIEN   11
    CLOSE AND MORE CLOSE--I FEEL HIM IN MY HEART-- . . . . .   720 WITCH VIVIEN   11
    YE BY THE WAVES THAT CLOSE IN OUR SAD NATION, ...   738 MOURN THEN ON   5
    YET ONE JOY HAVE I: HID CLOSE, ...   744 ROSY CROSS   8
    THEN CLOSE YOUR EARS WITH DUST AND LIE . . . .   791 REPRISALS   23
CLOSE-CROPPED
    OR ON THE CLOSE-CROPPED GRASS . . . .   343 SHEP GOATHERD   103
CLOSED   SEE HALF-CLOSED
    CLOSED IN THE MISTY AIR PROFOUND. . . . .   10 OISIN 1   V 114D
    THE MIST CLOSED ROUND US: PEARLY LIGHT . . . .   28 OISIN 1   V 427C
    NONE CLOSED HIS BLOOD-SHOT EYES BUT SOUGHT . . . . . .   296 THREE BEGGARS   44
    THEY CLOSED THEIR BLOOD-SHOT EYES FOR NAUGHT. . . . . .   296 THREE BEGGARS V   44
    WE ARE CLOSED IN, AND THE KEY IS TURNED . . . .   425 STARES NEST   6
    WE ARE CLOSED IN, AND THE KEY TURNED . . . .   425 STARES NEST   V 6
    HAVE CLOSED THE LADIES' EYES, THEIR MINDS ARE BUT A POOL   426 PHANTOM HATRED   21
    FOR CLOSED IN DARKNESS NOW . . . .   738 MOURN THEN ON   10
CLOSELY
    LULLED WEARINESS: AND CLOSELY ROUND . . . .   11 OISIN 1   V 137
    IF YOU'LL BUT LISTEN CLOSELY TO THAT CRYING . . . . .   247 SHADOW WATER B   520
    CLOSELY ROUND US, BODY AND MIND-- . . . .   717 FAIRY DOCTOR   23
CLOSER
    BUT THE TREES GREW TALLER AND CLOSER, ...   48 OISIN 3   17
    BUT TALLER THE TREES GREW AND CLOSER, ...   48 OISIN 3   V 17
    AS THOUGH TO DRAW THEM CLOSER YET. RAMMED FULL . . . .   579 DOR WELLESLEY   5
    SHIVERING CLOSER TO THEIR DAMS . . . .   726 LOVERS QUARREL   7
CLOSES
    THE CROWD THAT CLOSES IN BEHIND: . . . .   266 GALWAY RACES   4
    THE FIELD THAT CLOSES IN BEHIND. . . . .   266 GALWAY RACES   V 4

		PAGE	TITLE	LINE
CLOSING				
CLOSING RHYMES • • • • • • • • • • • • • •		320	REED WHISPERER V	T
CLOSING RHYME • • • • • • • • • • • •		320	REED WHISPERER V	T
CLOTH SEE MUMMY-CLOTH				
WHEN THEY FROZE THE CLOTH ON MY BODY LIKE ARMOUR RIVETED FAST,		57	OISIN 3	151
AND FOUND HER DYEING CLOTH WITH SUBTLE CARE • • • • •		105	CUCHULAIN SEA V	2A
BY DREAMING LADIES UPON CLOTH • • • • • • • •		156	FORGOT BEAUTY	7
AND GREY CONNEMARA CLOTH, • • • • • • • • • •		348	FISHERMAN	30
THEIR CONNEMARA CLOTH WORN OUT OF SHAPE: • • • • • •		372	PHASES OF MOON	4
A SHINING WEB, A FLOATING RIBBON OF CLOTH, • • • • • •		430	NINETEEN 19	50
I ROSE THAT I MIGHT SCREEN IT WITH A CLOTH. • • • • •		467	HARUN RASHID	131
AS MUMMIES IN THE MUMMY CLOTH ARE WOUND: • • • • •		471	ALL SOUL NIGHT V	14
AS MUMMIES IN THE MUMMY CLOTH ARE WOUND. • • • • •		474	ALL SOUL NIGHT V	100
FOR HADES' BOBBIN BOUND IN MUMMY CLOTH • • • • • •		497	BYZANTIUM V	11
CLOTHED SEE CLAMOUR-CLOTHED				
AND STOOD WITHIN: CLOTHED IN A MISTY RAY • • • • • •		36	OISIN 2	104
IN DAMASK CLOTHED AND ON A SEAT • • • • • • •		440	WISDOM	9
AS, CLOTHED IN CEREMONIAL GLOOM, • • • • • • •		655	ISLE STAT I 3	10
HAVE CLOTHED THEIR TONGUES WITH SONG OF SONGLESS DAYS? • •		666	ISLE STAT II 3	17
CLOTHES SEE SWADDLING-CLOTHES				
A CERTAIN POET IN OUTLANDISH CLOTHES • • • • • • •		180	QUEEN MAEVE	1
AND RENT HER CLOTHES AND MADE HER MOAN: • • • • •		275	GREY ROCK	108
SHE MAY HAVE WORN SILK CLOTHES, OR WORN A CROWN, • • • •		282	TWO KINGS	117
IN THEIR STIFF, PAINTED CLOTHES, THE PALE UNSATISFIED ONES		318	MAGI	2
IN GREY CONNEMARA CLOTHES • • • • • • • • • •		347	FISHERMAN	4
FOR SILKEN CLOTHES AND STATELY WALK, • • • • • • •		422	MY TABLE	30
OLD CLOTHES UPON OLD STICKS TO SCARE A BIRD. • • • •		445	SCHOOL CHILDR	48
OR ROCKY CISTERN WHERE WE TREAD THE CLOTHES • • • •		499	MOTHER OF GOD	9
WINDING-SHEET AND SWADDLING CLOTHES. • • • • • • •		530	OLD TOM AGAIN V	6
THAT STEPPED OUT OF THEIR CLOTHES, • • • • • • •		538	LAST CONFESS	14
AGREED HER CLOTHES TO SWOP, • • • • • • • • •		595	COLONEL MARTIN	20
A ROOF, GOOD CLOTHES, PASSION, LOVE PERHAPS, • • • •		609	IN TARAS HALLS	8
WITH ANY SORT OF CLOTHES, • • • • • • • • •		627	STATES HOLIDAY	28
CLOTHING				
CLOTHING HIM ROUND, I SAW A SEAGULL FLOAT • • • • • •		36	OISIN 2 V	105
CLOTHS				
HE WISHES FOR THE CLOTHS OF HEAVEN • • • • • • •		176	CLOTHS HEAVEN	T
AEDH WISHES FOR THE CLOTHS OF HEAVEN • • • • • •		176	CLOTHS HEAVEN V	T
HAD I THE HEAVENS' EMBROIDERED CLOTHS, • • • • • •		176	CLOTHS HEAVEN	1
THE BLUE AND THE DIM AND THE DARK CLOTHS • • • • • •		176	CLOTHS HEAVEN	3
I WOULD SPREAD THE CLOTHS UNDER YOUR FEET: • • • • •		176	CLOTHS HEAVEN	5
HAD I THE HEAVEN'S EMBROIDERED CLOTHS, • • • • • •		176	CLOTHS HEAVEN V	1
CLOTTED				
WHEN LOW THE SUN SANK DOWN IN CLOTTED FLAME • • • •		656	ISLE STAT I 3	30
LIE STREWN THE YELLOW LEAVES--THE CLOTTED LEAVES. • • •		684	SEEKER	69
LIE STREWN THE CLOTTED LEAVES--THE DEAD OLD LEAVES. • • •		684	SEEKER V	69
CLOUD				
THE DARKNESS COMES. A CLOUD HANGS OVERHEAD-- • • • •		43	OISIN 2 V	208A
HIS OLD EYES CLOUD WITH DREAMS: • • • • • • • •		98	FOXHUNTER	14
AS A CLOUD FADED INTO THE SKY. • • • • • • • •		145	HOST OF AIR V	40
UNDER A CLOUD OF HER HAIR, • • • • • • • • •		160	CAP AND BELLS	26
AS 'TWERE UPON A CLOUD, • • • • • • • • • •		255	WOMAN HOMER	18
NOR ON OLYMPUS LEAPED FROM CLOUD TO CLOUD, • • • • •		260	FASC DIFFICULT	6
NOR ON OLYMPUS LEAPED FROM CLOUD TO CLOUD, • • • • •		260	FASC DIFFICULT	6
NOR ON AN OLYMPUS LEAPED FROM CLOUD TO CLOUD, • • • •		260	FASC DIFFICULT V	6
NOR ON AN OLYMPUS LEAPED FROM CLOUD TO CLOUD, • • • •		260	FASC DIFFICULT V	6
A CLOUD BLOWN FROM THE CUT-THROAT NORTH • • • • • •		313	MEMORY YOUTH	6
WHEREON A THING ONCE WALKED THAT SEEMED A BURNING CLOUD.		315	FALLEN MAJESTY	8
ONCE WALKED A THING THAT SEEMED, AS IT WERE, A BURNING CLOUD.		315	FALLEN MAJESTY V	8
OR TUMBLING CLOUD." • • • • • • • • • • •		349	HAWK	12
"WHAT TUMBLING CLOUD DID YOU CLEAVE, • • • • • • •		349	HAWK	13
THEY ARE CAST BEYOND THE VERGE, AND IN A CLOUD, • • • •		376	PHASES OF MOON	105
FROM CLOUD TO TUMBLING CLOUD, • • • • • • • •		393	EASTER 1916	47
FROM CLOUD TO TUMBLING CLOUD, • • • • • • • •		393	EASTER 1916	47
A SHADOW OF CLOUD ON THE STREAM • • • • • • • •		393	EASTER 1916	49
"VENGENCE FOR JACQUES MOLAY." IN CLOUD PALE RAGS, OR IN LACE,		426	PHANTOM HATRED V	10
THE QUIVERING HALF-CLOSED EYELIDS, THE RAGS OF CLOUD OR OF LACE,		427	PHANTOM HATRED	26
THE CLOUD PALE UNICORNS, THE EYES OF AQUAMARINE, • • • •		427	PHANTOM HATRED V	25
WHEN IT HAS LOOKED IN GLORY FROM A CLOUD. • • • • •		482	BLOOD AND MOON	54
ALTHOUGH THAT WESTERN CLOUD IS LUMINOUS, • • • • •		488	COOLE PARK 29	4
WHETHER IN WOOD, WATER OR CLOUD, • • • • • • •		528	DANCER CRUACH	7
A BUNDLE OF TEMPESTUOUS CLOUD IS BLOWN • • • • • •		541	PARN FUNERAL 1	2
ABOUT THE SKY: WHERE THAT IS CLEAR OF CLOUD • • • • •		541	PARN FUNERAL 1	3
OR OUT OF HER BLACK CLOUD. • • • • • • • • •		568	SWEET DANCER	6
WOULD HE TEACH ANY SIN? GAZE IN THE CLOUD • • • • •		692	MOSADA 1	58
THAT YOU SHALL SEE ON YONDER GLOWING CLOUD • • • • •		692	MOSADA 1 V	43
"ON THIS EMBROIDERED CLOUD," THE SUN HATH SAID, • • • •		712	FERENCZ RENYI	74
AMID A CLOUD OF BANNERS, • • • • • • • • •		741	EARL PAUL	39
MY HEAD IS IN A CLOUD: • • • • • • • • • •		782	HEART FRIGHT	8
CLOUDLESS				
FLOWERS AND GRASS AND CLOUDLESS SKY, • • • • • • •		639	BEN BULBEN	57
CLOUDLETS				
WHILE HIGH FRAIL CLOUDLETS, FED WITH A GREEN LIGHT, • • •		40	OISIN 2	165
HUNG THE FRAIL LOFTIER CLOUDLETS. TURNED HE SLOW-- • • •		40	OISIN 2 V	167
CLOUD-O'ER-MUFFLED				
AS WHEN UPON HER CLOUD-O'ER-MUFFLED STEEP • • • • • •		645	ISLE STAT I 1	16

148

	PAGE	TITLE		LINE
CLOUD-PALE				
WITH HER CLOUD-PALE EYELIDS FALLING ON DREAM-DIMMED EYES:	163	VALLEY LOVERS		4
WITH HER CLOUD-PALE EYELIDS HALF COVERING HER DIM EYES:	163	VALLEY LOVERS	V	4
O CLOUD-PALE EYELIDS, DREAM-DIMMED EYES,	164	PERFECT BEAUTY		1
"VENGEANCE FOR JACQUES MOLAY." IN CLOUD-PALE RAGS, OR IN LACE,	426	PHANTOM HATRED		10
THE CLOUD-PALE UNICORNS, THE EYES OF AQUAMARINE, ...	427	PHANTOM HATRED		25
CLOUDS				
AND CLOUDS ARRAYED THEIR RANK ON RANK	12	OISIN 1		154
THE CLOUDS ARRAYED THEM RANK ON RANK	12	OISIN 1	V	154
OR OF THE FLAKED CLOUDS?" "NOT SO, FOR WE	34	OISIN 2	V	78C
ROOTED IN FOAM AND CLOUDS, AND CRIED TO ALL	38	OISIN 2		132
ROOTED IN FOAM AND CLOUDS. THERE MIGHTIER MASTERS MET . .	38	OISIN 2	V	132
. . . "WHERE WHITE CLOUDS LIE SPREAD	59	OISIN 3		178
. . . THEY WILL RISE, MAKING CLOUDS WITH THEIR BREATH, . .	61	OISIN 3		202
AND STARLIGHT GLEAMED, AND CLOUDS FLEW HIGH, ...	84	MAD KING GOLL		34
THE CLOUDS ON THEIR JOURNEY ABOVE, ...	119	PITY OF LOVE		4
WHERE SUCH GREY CLOUDS OF INCENSE ROSE	156	FORGOT BEAUTY		13
IN OLD TIMES AMONG THE CLOUDS OF THE AIR.	194	BAILE AILLINN		133
THE WIND HAS BUNDLED UP THE CLOUDS HIGH OVER KNOCKNAREA,	207	HANRAHANS SONG		6
ANGERS THAT ARE LIKE NOISY CLOUDS HAVE SET OUR HEARTS ABEAT:	207	HANRAHANS SONG		8
O TATTERED CLOUDS OF THE WORLD, CALL FROM THE HIGH CAIRN OF MAIVE,	207	HANRAHANS SONG	V	6
THE WINDS HAVE BUNDLED UP THE CLOUDS HIGH OVER KNOCKNAREA	207	HANRAHANS SONG	V	6
LIKE TATTERED CLOUDS OF THE WORLD, PASSIONS CALL AND OUR HEARTS BEAT:	207	HANRAHANS SONG	V	8
ANGERS THAT ARE LIKE BUNDLED CLOUDS HAVE SET OUR HEARTS ABEAT:	207	HANRAHANS SONG	V	8
THESE ARE THE CLOUDS	265	THESE CLOUDS		T
THESE ARE THE CLOUDS ABOUT THE FALLEN SUN, ...	265	THESE CLOUDS		1
THESE ARE THE CLOUDS ABOUT THE FALLEN SUN, ...	265	THESE CLOUDS		11
THE CLOUDS WERE BRIGHTENING WITH THE DAWN.	307	HOUR DAWN		122
TORE FROM THE CLOUDS HIS MARVELLOUS MOON.	314	MEMORY YOUTH		21
SOMEWHERE AMONG THE CLOUDS ABOVE:	328	IRISH AIRMAN		2
DROVE TO THIS TUMULT IN THE CLOUDS:	328	IRISH AIRMAN		12
SEEM BUT THE CLOUDS OF THE SKY	416	TOWER		192
THAT CAN PIERCE THE CLOUDS, ...	576	ACRE OF GRASS		20
CLOUDY				
ABOVE ITS CLOUDY RIM:	175	ELEMENT POWERS		16
A CLOUDY QUIVER OVER PAIRC-NA-LEE.	198	SEVEN WOODS		14
ABOVE THE CLOUDY SHOULDERS OF THE HORSES:	344	DAWN		12
UPON THE CLOUDY CANOPY, ...	397	POLIT PRISONER		22
AMID THE CLOUDY WRACK, ...	458	HIS WILDNESS		2
CLOUDY LEAFAGE OF THE SKY, ...	501	VACILLATION		46
AMONG THOSE STREAMS, OR ON THEIR CLOUDY EDGE.	750	SHADOW WATER A		63
THE CLOUDY WATERS AND THE GLIMMERING WINDS	764	SHADOW WATER A		327
WHERE THE MOON MAKES A CLOUDY LIGHT IN THE MIST.	764	SHADOW WATER A		329
EAGLES HAVE GONE INTO THEIR CLOUDY BED.	778	SONG DEIRDRE 3		6
AND HEAVEN'S A CLOUDY BLOT.	782	HEART FRIGHT		17
CLOVEN				
HAS CLOVEN AND RENT THEIR HEARTS IN TWAIN.	66	HAPPY SHEPHERD		33
MY DREAMS WERE CLOVEN BY VOICES AND BY FIRES:	218	WOODS OF COOLE		20
TREAD AND TREAD THEIR CLOVEN FEET	646	ISLE STAT I 1		24
I SEE WITHIN A CLOVEN ROCK DISPART	673	ISLE STAT II 3		195
A CLOVEN, DANCING JET, ...	680	LOVE AND DEATH		2
WHY HAVE YOU CLOVEN ME WITH A MORTAL LOVE?	768	SHADOW WATER A		419
CLOVER				
WE PASSED BY WOODS, AND LAWNS OF CLOVER, ...	25	OISIN 1		377
BY WOODS OF MOSS, BY LAWNS OF CLOVER, ...	25	OISIN 1	V	377
UNDERNEATH THE GRASS AND CLOVER, ...	124	CATHLEEN PARA		3
CLOWN				
AND SORROW AWAY, AND CALLING BARD AND CLOWN	170	SECRET ROSE		20
THE CATCH-CRIES OF THE CLOWN, ...	347	FISHERMAN		22
THE CATCH CRIES OF THE CLOWN, ...	347	FISHERMAN	V	22
DOWN THE FANATIC, DOWN THE CLOWN:	544	TO SAME TUNE 1		8
DOWN THE FANATIC, DOWN THE CLOWN:	545	TO SAME TUNE 1		18
DOWN THE FANATIC, DOWN THE CLOWN:	545	TO SAME TUNE 1		28
DOWN THE FANATIC, DOWN THE CLOWN:	546	TO SAME TUNE 2	V	REF
DOWN THE FANATIC, DOWN THE CLOWN:	548	TO SAME TUNE 3	V	REF
HEROIC REVERIE MOCKED BY CLOWN AND KNAVE, ...	619	BRONZE HEAD		27
WITHOUT MY GLASS I'D BE A SORRY CLOWN.	721	WITCH VIVIEN		29
WHETHER A KING OR CLOWN:	789	SINGING HEAD		18
FOR PRAISE OF CLOWN OR KING, ...	789	SINGING HEAD		20
CLOYNE				
DRANK TAR-WATER WITH THE BISHOP OF CLOYNE.	486	SEVEN SAGES		5
GOLDSMITH AND BURKE, SWIFT AND THE BISHOP OF CLOYNE . . .	486	SEVEN SAGES		9
SOFT AS THE RUSTLE OF A REED FROM CLOYNE	487	SEVEN SAGES		22
CLUB				
AROUND THE FIRE AT THE CLUB, ...	392	EASTER 1916		12
CLUMP				
WE TIED THE HORSE IN A LEAFY CLUMP, ...	14	OISIN 1		194
AND RIVER, FERN AND FLOWERY CLUMP, ...	15	OISIN 1	V	196
A CLUMP OF BEECH TREES MADE AN EMPTY SPACE	277	TWO KINGS	V	4A
CLOSE TO A CLUMP OF BEECH TREES IN THE WOOD	283	TWO KINGS	V	135
CLUMSINESS				
BROUGHT FACE TO FACE WITH HIS OWN CLUMSINESS:	479	SELF AND SOUL		48
CLUNG				
OR CLUNG THEREON LIKE SWARMING BEES:	14	OISIN 1		181
OR CLUNG AS CLOSE AS SWARMS OF BEES, ...	14	OISIN 1	V	181

149

```
                                                          PAGE    TITLE           LINE
CLUSTER      SEE GRAPE-CLUSTER
CLUSTERING
    AND FLOWERS AROUND IN CLUSTERING THOUSANDS ARE,  .  .  .  .   656 ISLE STAT I 3      24
CLUSTERS
    THE HEAVY CLUSTERS OF THE GRAPES WERE FULL,  .  .  .  .  .   690 MOSADA 1           13
CLUTCHES
    NOR EVER CHANGE OR FEEL THE CLUTCHES .  .  .  .  .  .  .  .    23 OISIN 1       V 341A
    THE OSPREY OF SORROW GOES AFTER AND CLUTCHES,  .  .  .  .     27 OISIN 1       V 415D
CLYTEMNESTRA
    AS ARGIVE CLYTEMNESTRA SAW OUT-BURN  .  .  .  .  .  .  .  .   645 ISLE STAT I 1      12
COACH
    THAT MERELY STOOD, ROCKING THE GLITTERING COACH  .  .  .  .   344 DAWN               11
    YET DID BUT LOOK, ROCKING THE GLITTERING COACH  .  .  .  .    344 DAWN          V    11
COAGULATE
    COAGULATE OF STUFF .  .  .  .  .  .  .  .  .  .  .  .  .  .   449 HERO GIRL FOOL     26
COAL
    WORLD, AS IT WERE A COAL,  .  .  .  .  .  .  .  .  .  .  .    267 FRIEND ILLNESS      5
    ISAIAH'S COAL, WHAT MORE CAN MAN DESIRE?  .  .  .  .  .  .    502 VACILLATION        74
    EZEKIEL'S COAL, WHAT MORE CAN MAN DESIRE?  .  .  .  .  .  .   502 VACILLATION   V    74
COAL-BLACK
    BUT WHEN HE WOUND HER COAL-BLACK HAIR  .  .  .  .  .  .  .    514 JANE GROWN OLD      3
COALS
    WHEN WE BENT DOWN ABOVE THE FADING COALS  .  .  .  .  .  .    136 TO SOME I TALK      3
    WHILE THE NIGHT GREW, ABOVE THE FADING COALS,  .  .  .  .     136 TO SOME I TALK V    3
COARSE
    AMONG THE COARSE GRASS AND THE CAMEL-DUNG.  .  .  .  .  .  .   369 EGO DOMINUS        31
    AMONG THE COARSE GRASS AND THE CAMEL DUNG.  .  .  .  .  .  .   369 EGO DOMINUS   V    31
    CONDUCT AND WORK GROW COARSE, AND COARSE THE SOUL,  .  .  .   564 GYRES              17
    CONDUCT AND WORK GROW COARSE, AND COARSE THE SOUL,  .  .  .   564 GYRES              17
    BUT A COARSE OLD MAN AM I,  .  .  .  .  .  .  .  .  .  .  .   590 OLD WICKED MAN     59
COARSE-BRED
    THE COARSE-BRED SON OF A LIVERY-STABLE KEEPER--  .  .  .  .   370 EGO DOMINUS        61
COARSENESS
    THE COARSENESS OF THE DRUDGE.  BEFORE THE FULL  .  .  .  .    376 PHASES OF MOON     94
COAST
    HELP! HELP! AND HURL HIM FROM OUR COAST .  .  .  .  .  .  .    83 MAD KING GOLL V    17
COAT
    IN SOME OUTLANDISH COAT BESIDE .  .  .  .  .  .  .  .  .  .   303 HOUR DAWN     V    28
    A COAT .  .  .  .  .  .  .  .  .  .  .  .  .  .  .  .  .  .   320 COAT               T
    I MADE MY SONG A COAT .  .  .  .  .  .  .  .  .  .  .  .  .   320 COAT                1
    A TATTERED COAT UPON A STICK, UNLESS .  .  .  .  .  .  .  .   407 SAIL BYZANTIUM     10
    AND WEAR A COAT IN FASHION,  .  .  .  .  .  .  .  .  .  .  .   607 SONGS BURDEN 2     21
    THE WORST A COAT UPON A COAT-HANGER.  .  .  .  .  .  .  .  .   624 APPARITIONS         8
    THE WORST A COAT UPON A COAT-HANGER.  .  .  .  .  .  .  .  .   624 APPARITIONS        16
    THE WORST A COAT UPON A COAT-HANGER.  .  .  .  .  .  .  .  .   624 APPARITIONS        24
    A COAT OF GILDED MAIL.  .  .  .  .  .  .  .  .  .  .  .  .    740 EARL PAUL          16
COATED       SEE LEATHER-COATED
COAT-HANGER
    THE WORST A COAT UPON A COAT-HANGER.  .  .  .  .  .  .  .  .   624 APPARITIONS         8
    THE WORST A COAT UPON A COAT-HANGER.  .  .  .  .  .  .  .  .   624 APPARITIONS        16
    THE WORST A COAT UPON A COAT-HANGER.  .  .  .  .  .  .  .  .   624 APPARITIONS        24
COBWEB
    THAT SHAKES A MOULDERING COBWEB FROM THE RAFTER!  .  .  .  .   130 BOOK STORIES       19
    LEAPING TO SHAKE A COBWEB FROM THE RAFTER!  .  .  .  .  .  .   130 BOOK STORIES  V    19
    AND SHAKE A MOULDERING COBWEB FROM THE RAFTER,  .  .  .  .    130 BOOK STORIES  V    19
    AT MORN, AND WITH HER FEET EACH COBWEB RENDS,  .  .  .  .     670 ISLE STAT II 3     99
COBWEBS
    HANG THE MIST-THREADS FOR A LITTLE WHILE LIKE COBWEBS IN      719 PHANTOM SHIP       29
        THE AIR!
    HANG THE MIST THREADS FOR A LITTLE WHILE LIKE COBWEBS IN      719 PHANTOM SHIP  V    29
        THE AIR,
COCK        SEE HAY-COCK
    MARE OR STALLION, COCK OR HEN,  .  .  .  .  .  .  .  .  .  .   529 TOM LUNATIC        15
    A COCK CAME BY UPON HIS TOES!  .  .  .  .  .  .  .  .  .  .    725 LEGEND             26
    RED COCK, AND CROW!  .  .  .  .  .  .  .  .  .  .  .  .  .     782 HEART FRIGHT        7
    RED COCK, AND CROW!  .  .  .  .  .  .  .  .  .  .  .  .  .     782 HEART FRIGHT       14
    RED COCK, AND CROW!  .  .  .  .  .  .  .  .  .  .  .  .  .     782 HEART FRIGHT       21
COCK-A-DOODLE-DOODLE-DO
    "COCK-A-DOODLE-DOODLE-DO!"  .  .  .  .  .  .  .  .  .  .  .    697 MOSADA 2           29
COCKED
    AN OLD MAN COCKED HIS EAR UPON A BRIDGE!  .  .  .  .  .  .     372 PHASES OF MOON      1
    WERE DISTANT STILL.  AN OLD MAN COCKED HIS EAR.  .  .  .  .    372 PHASES OF MOON      7
    WERE DISTANT.  AN OLD MAN COCKED HIS EAR.  .  .  .  .  .  .    372 PHASES OF MOON V    7
    AND COCKED A MALICIOUS EYE,  .  .  .  .  .  .  .  .  .  .  .   527 AM OF IRELAND      25
COCKEREL
    THEREON REPLIED!  "A COCKEREL  .  .  .  .  .  .  .  .  .  .    387 SOLOMON WITCH       9
    ANSWERED!  "A CRESTED COCKEREL CREW  .  .  .  .  .  .  .  .    387 SOLOMON WITCH V     9
    THEREON EXPLAINED!  "A COCKEREL  .  .  .  .  .  .  .  .  .     387 SOLOMON WITCH V     9
    YOUR COCKEREL FOUND US IN THE WRONG  .  .  .  .  .  .  .  .    388 SOLOMON WITCH      34
COCK'S
    WITH A GREAT COCK'S FEATHER,  .  .  .  .  .  .  .  .  .  .     627 STATES HOLIDAY     37
COCKS       SEE MOOR-COCKS
    AND CLINGING TO IT I COULD HEAR THE COCKS  .  .  .  .  .  .    286 TWO KINGS         210
    AND THERE'S NO MAN BUT COCKS HIS EAR .  .  .  .  .  .  .  .    306 HOUR DAWN          99
    BRONZED PEACOCK FEATHERS, RED COMBS OF HER COCKS.  .  .  .     433 NINETEEN 19       130
    CAN LIKE THE COCKS OF HADES CROW  .  .  .  .  .  .  .  .  .    498 BYZANTIUM          20
    SPOKE AND SET THE COCKS A-CROW.  .  .  .  .  .  .  .  .  .     637 BEN BULBEN          4
    RED COCKS, AND CROW!  .  .  .  .  .  .  .  .  .  .  .  .  .    783 GREY ROUND         28
CODGERS
    THERE ALL THE GOLDEN CODGERS LAY,  .  .  .  .  .  .  .  .  .   611 NEWS ORACLE         1
```

COFFIN
    DIGGERS AND CARPENTERS MAKE GRAVE AND COFFIN! . . . . .   609 IN TARAS HALLS   17
    SAW THAT THE GRAVE WAS DEEP, THE COFFIN SOUND, ...   609 IN TARAS HALLS   18
    LAY IN THE COFFIN, STOPPED HIS BREATH AND DIED. . . . .   609 IN TARAS HALLS   20
COGENT
    AND HERE'S A COGENT REASON, ...   586 PARNELLITES   9
COGNOMEN
    THAT COGNOMEN SOUNDED BEST . . . .   440 WISDOM   18
COIL
    THAT JUGGLING NATURE MOUNTS, HER COIL IN THEIR EMBRACES   556 RIBH PATRICK   9
        TWINED.
    IN COIL ON COIL OF AZURE. ALL IS READY. . . . . . .   691 MOSADA 1   41
    IN COIL ON COIL OF AZURE. ALL IS READY. . . . . . .   691 MOSADA 1   41
    NO SIN TO SEE IN COIL ON COIL OF AZURE . . . . . .   692 MOSADA 1   43
    NO SIN TO SEE IN COIL ON COIL OF AZURE . . . . . .   692 MOSADA 1   43
    I HAD THROWN IT DOWN BEHIND THIS COIL OF ROPE. . . . .   759 SHADOW WATER A   245
COILING
    IN THEIR COILING CALM AND SLOW. . . . .   680 LOVE AND DEATH   8
    TO ONE ANOTHER WITH A COILING CHAIN! . . . .   687 TWO TITANS   6
COILS
    LONG CITRON COILS THAT HANG AROUND THEE, BLOWN . . . .   670 ISLE STAT II 3   105
COIN
    THOSE BODIES FROM A PICTURE OR A COIN . . . .   537 HER VISION   28
    STAMPED BOY AND TREE UPON SICILIAN COIN. . . . . . .   541 PARN FUNERAL 1   15
COLA
    AMONG THE FRUIT! BUT THERE, LAME COLA CROUCHES . . . .   691 MOSADA 1   32
    AND COLA, SEEING, KNOWS THE SIGN AND COMES. . . . . .   691 MOSADA 1   38
    AMONG THE FRUIT. BUT YON, LAME COLA CROUCHES . . . .   691 MOSADA 1   V 32
    AND COLA, SEEING, KNOWS THE SIGN AND RISES. . . . . .   691 MOSADA 1   V 38
COLA'S
    OF SILVER HANGING ROUND LAME COLA'S NECK-- . . . . .   691 MOSADA 1   V 35
COLD   SEE MIST-COLD DEW-COLD CLAY-COLD
    AND BENDS TO THE FIRE AND SHAKES WITH THE COLD . . . .   26 OISIN 1   405
    NONE MAY BEGUILE HIM, AND HIS PASSIONS COLD . . . . .   35 OISIN 2   V 83A
    CAME NOW THE SLIDING OF TEARS AND SWEEPING OF MIST COLD   47 OISIN 3   V 7
        HAIR,
    NO WORD OF THEIRS--THE COLD STAR-BANE . . . .   66 HAPPY SHEPHERD   32
    "HE DRIVES AWAY THE NORTHERN COLD." . . . .   82 MAD KING GOLL   11
    THROUGH SUMMER'S HEAT AND WINTER'S COLD. . . . . . .   86 MAD KING GOLL   71
    I LOOKED ON MY COLD BABY . . . .   95 MOLL MAGEE   19
    THE COLD WET WINDS EVER BLOWING, ...   119 PITY OF LOVE   5
    AND THE COLD WET WINDS EVER BLOWING, ...   119 PITY OF LOVE   V 7
    UNDER THAT COLD AND VAPOUR-TURBANED STEEP, ...   128 DREAM OF FAERY   39
    WITH HEAVY WHITENING WINGS, AND A HEART FALLEN COLD! . .   147 UNAPPEAS HOST   4
    AND THE SEED OF THE FIRE GETS FEEBLE AND COLD. . . . .   151 OLD MOTHER   10
    BUT THE SEED OF THE FIRE GETS FEEBLE AND COLD, ...   151 OLD MOTHER   V 9
    WERE YOU BUT LYING COLD AND DEAD, ...   175 BELOVED DEAD   1
    NOR THE COLD NORTH HAS TROUBLED?" HE REPLIED, ...   184 QUEEN MAEVE   90
    OF THIS OR THAT THING, NOR GREW COLD . . . .   189 BAILE AILLINN   9
    OF THIS OR THAT THING, OR GREW COLD . . . .   189 BAILE AILLINN   V 9
    "FROM HEAT AND COLD AND WIND AND WAVE! . . . .   193 BAILE AILLINN   114
    WRUNG FROM THE COLD WOMEN OF THE SEA-- . . . .   237 SHADOW WATER B   343
    AND YET NOT COLD." . . . .   263 MASK   5
    HER EYES WERE COLD AND STEADY, HER LIPS TIGHT. . . . .   279 TWO KINGS   64
    BY A COLD AND DESOLATE SEA, ...   298 THREE HERMITS   2
    THE COLD HEAVEN . . . .   316 COLD HEAVEN   T
    SUDDENLY I SAW THE COLD AND ROOK-DELIGHTING HEAVEN . .   316 COLD HEAVEN   1
    SUDDENLY I SAW THE COLD AND ROOK DELIGHTING HEAVEN . .   316 COLD HEAVEN   V 1
    THEY PADDLE IN THE COLD . . . .   323 SWANS AT COOLE   20
    AND WE ARE HURT IF EITHER FRIEND SEEM COLD, ...   324 ROBERT GREGORY   10
    TO COLD CLARE ROCK AND GALWAY ROCK AND THORN, ...   326 ROBERT GREGORY   66
    POEM MAYBE AS COLD . . . .   348 FISHERMAN   39
    POEM MAY BE AS COLD . . . .   348 FISHERMAN   V 39
    THE PURE COLD LIGHT IN THE SKY . . . .   378 CAT AND MOON   7
    HAS CALLED UP THE COLD SPIRITS THAT ARE BORN . . . .   382 VISION ROBART   2
    UNDER THE FIRST COLD GLEAM OF DAY? . . . .   398 BREAK OF DAY   4
    COLD STONE AND WATER. I GREW WILD, ...   399 BREAK OF DAY   14
    THE COLD BLOWN SPRAY IN MY NOSTRIL. . . . .   399 BREAK OF DAY   20
    IN THE COLD SNOWS OF A DREAM. . . . .   424 ROAD AT DOOR   15
    COLD AS THE MARCH WIND HIS EYES. . . . .   531 FATHER CHILD   8
    AND MY BLOOD BE COLD THE WHILE . . . .   532 BEFORE WORLD   11
    ON MY COLD BREAST? . . . .   574 MAIDS 1ST SONG   4
    WHEN AN OLD MAN'S BLOOD GROWS COLD? . . . .   588 OLD WICKED MAN   13
    NO MAN GROWS OLD, NO GIRL GROWS COLD, ...   621 JOHN KINSELLA   31
    CAST A COLD EYE . . . .   640 BEN BULBEN   92
    AS A LEAF THAT IS OLD, AND WITHERED, AND COLD, ...   643 SONG FAERIES   3
    AS A LEAF THAT IS OLD, AND WITHERED, AND COLD, ...   644 SONG FAERIES   15
    AS A LEAF THAT IS OLD, AND WITHERED, AND COLD, ...   676 ISLE STAT II 3   250
    AS A LEAF THAT IS OLD, AND WITHERED, AND COLD, ...   676 ISLE STAT II 3   262
    I'M WEARY--WEARY, AND 'TIS VERY COLD. . . . . . .   703 MOSADA 3   122
    I'LL DRAW MY CLOAK AROUND ME! IT IS COLD. . . . . .   704 MOSADA 3   123
    I NEVER KNEW A NIGHT SO BITTER COLD. . . . . . .   704 MOSADA 3   124
    IN THE COLD STREAMS, AND WAKE TO THEIR DESIRE, ...   750 SHADOW WATER A   85
    AND UNFORGOTTEN NAMES, AND THE COLD STARS . . . . .   757 SHADOW WATER A   204
    AND A COLD WIND IS BLOWING IN MY HAIR. . . . . . .   761 SHADOW WATER A   277
    WHETHER AMONG THE COLD WINDS OF THE DEAD. . . . . .   768 SHADOW WATER A V   413
    ARE BLOWN COLD DUST OR A BIT OF BONE. . . . . . .   788 HAWTHORN TREE   8
COLDER
    COLDER AND DUMBER AND DEAFER THAN A FISH. . . . . . .   267 ALL TEMPT ME   10
COLIN
    IF HER YE LOVE. AYE, COLIN, WE MUST FIGHT. . . . . .   662 ISLE STAT II 1   76

		PAGE	TITLE	LINE

COLLAR
    FROM COLLAR TO COLLAR, FROM STILT TO STILT, FROM FATHER   623 HIGH TALK   10
        TO CHILD.
    FROM COLLAR TO COLLAR, FROM STILT TO STILT, FROM FATHER   623 HIGH TALK   10
        TO CHILD.
COLLAR-BONE
    THE COLLAR-BONE OF A HARE . . . .   330 BONE OF A HARE   T
    THE COLLAR-BONE OF A HARE . . . .   330 BONE OF A HARE   10
COLLEENS
    O COLLEENS, KNEELING BY YOUR ALTAR RAILS LONG HENCE, . .   173 SPEAKS HEARERS V   1
COLLEGE
    MAY I NOT PUT MYSELF TO COLLEGE? . . . .   385 ROBARTES DANCE   18
COLLOQUY
    AND THEREUPON A COLLOQUY TOOK PLACE . . . .   463 HARUN RASHID   45
    THAT THEREUPON A COLLOQUY TOOK PLACE . . . .   463 HARUN RASHID V   45
COLONEL
    COLONEL MARTIN . . . .   594 COLONEL MARTIN   T
    THE COLONEL WENT OUT SAILING, ...   594 COLONEL MARTIN   1
    THE COLONEL WENT OUT SAILING. . . . .   594 COLONEL MARTIN   9
    THE COLONEL WENT OUT SAILING. . . . .   594 COLONEL MARTIN   18
    THE COLONEL MET A PEDLAR, ...   595 COLONEL MARTIN   19
    THE COLONEL WENT OUT SAILING. . . . .   595 COLONEL MARTIN   27
    THE COLONEL KNOCKED ON THE RICH MAN'S DOOR, ...   595 COLONEL MARTIN   28
    THE COLONEL WENT OUT SAILING. . . . .   595 COLONEL MARTIN   36
    THE COLONEL KNOCKED ON A RICH MAN'S DOOR. . . . . . .   595 COLONEL MARTIN V   28
    THE COLONEL WENT OUT SAILING, ...   596 COLONEL MARTIN   45
    THE COLONEL SAID TO TOM HIS MAN, ...   596 COLONEL MARTIN   50
    THE COLONEL WENT OUT SAILING. . . . .   596 COLONEL MARTIN   54
    TO SHOOT THE COLONEL DEAD! . . . .   596 COLONEL MARTIN   58
    THE COLONEL WENT OUT SAILING. . . . .   596 COLONEL MARTIN   63
    THE COLONEL WENT OUT SAILING. . . . .   597 COLONEL MARTIN   72
COLONIES
    AMERICAN COLONIES, IRELAND, FRANCE AND INDIA . . . . .   487 SEVEN SAGES   15
COLONUS
    EVERY COLONUS LAD OR LASS DISCOURSES . . . .   447 COLONUS PRAISE   29
    FROM "OEDIPUS AT COLONUS" . . . .   459 FROM OEDIPUS   T
COLONUS'
    COLONUS' PRAISE . . . .   446 COLONUS PRAISE   T
    COME PRAISE COLONUS' HORSES, AND COME PRAISE . . . . .   446 COLONUS PRAISE   1
COLOONEY
    PEOPLE CAME INTO COLOONEY! . . . .   93 FATHER OHART   27
COLOONY
    THE PRIEST OF COLOONY . . . .   91 FATHER OHART V   T
COLOUR
    A CITRON COLOUR GLOOMED IN HER HAIR, ...   3 OISIN 1   24
    KINGFISHER COLOUR GREW WITH RAGE. HE ROSE . . . . . .   40 OISIN 2   V 169
    DELICATE IN COLOUR AS APPLE BLOSSOM. . . . .   199 ARROW   6
    AND THOUGH THEY'RE BUT THE COLOUR OF GREY ASH, ...   247 SHADOW WATER B   528
    TO THAT STERN COLOUR AND THAT DELICATE LINE . . . . .   326 ROBERT GREGORY   67
    AND PRAISED THE COLOUR OF HER FACE, ...   410 TOWER   36
    AND HAD THAT COLOUR UPON CHEEK OR HAIR, ...   444 SCHOOL CHILDR   22
    AND SET SUCH COLOUR THERE, ...   492 ANNE GREGORY   8
COLOURED   SEE LEOPARD-COLOURED SLATE-COLOURED MANY-COLOURED GRASS-COLOURED HONEY-COLOURED
    THAT ARE LIKE COLOURED ASIAN BIRDS . . . .   7 OISIN 1   69
    LEAVE THE BODY'S COLOURED PRIDE . . . .   124 CATHLEEN PARA   2
COLOURS
    WITH ALL HIS COLOURS JOURNEY-DULL, ...   82 MAD KING GOLL V   13
    THE CHANGING COLOURS OF ITS FRUIT . . . .   134 TWO TREES   5
COLT
    OUT OF MY HEART. THERE'S SOMETHING AILS OUR COLT . . .   260 FASC DIFFICULT   4
COLTSFOOT
    COME YOU, COLTSFOOT, MOUSETAIL, COME! . . . .   727 LOVERS QUARREL   33
COMB   SEE HONEY-COMB
    WHAT MADE US DREAM THAT HE COULD COMB GREY HAIR? . . . .   327 ROBERT GREGORY   88
COMBS
    BRONZED PEACOCK FEATHERS, RED COMBS OF HER COCKS. . . .   433 NINETEEN 19   130
COMBUSTIBLE
    THE ENTIRE COMBUSTIBLE WORLD IN ONE SMALL ROOM . . . .   327 ROBERT GREGORY   82
    ALL THE COMBUSTIBLE WORLD IN ONE SMALL ROOM . . . . .   327 ROBERT GREGORY V   82
COME
    FOR CHANGE AND DEATH THEY COME NOT NEAR US, ...   21 OISIN 1   V 316
    WHEN GOD SHALL COME FROM THE SEA WITH A SIGH . . . . .   28 OISIN 1   425
    COME FROM THE ISLE OF THE LIVING." "THEN GET YE . . . .   34 OISIN 2   V 79
    AS THOUGH HIS HOUR WERE COME. WE SOUGHT THE PART . . .   37 OISIN 2   112
    I CRIED, "COME OUT OF THE SHADOW, KING OF THE NAILS OF   51 OISIN 3   61
        GOLD!
    I CRIED, "COME OUT OF THE SHADOW, CANN OF THE NAILS OF   51 OISIN 3   V 61
        GOLD!
    AND SOFTLY COME TO YOUR NIAMH OVER THE TOPS OF THE TIDE!   55 OISIN 3   126
    AND SOFTLY COME TO THY NIAM OVER THE TOPS OF THE TIDE! . .   52 OISIN 3   V 126
    . . . YOU WILL COME NO MORE TO MY SIDE. . . . .   56 OISIN 3   128
    "IN THE ISLES OF THE FARTHEST SEAS WHERE ONLY THE SPIRITS   56 OISIN 3   133
        COME.
    SEE HOW THE SACRED OLD FLAMINGOES COME, ...   72 ANASHU VIJAYA   29
    MAYBE YOU HAVE NOT HEARD OF US, YOU HAVE COME FORTH SO   75 ANASHU VIJAYA   78
        NEWLY,
    HATH COME A SEA-KING MASTERFUL, ...   82 MAD KING GOLL V   15
    COME AWAY, O HUMAN CHILD! . . . .   87 STOLEN CHILD   9
    COME AWAY, O HUMAN CHILD! . . . .   87 STOLEN CHILD   24
    COME AWAY, O HUMAN CHILD! . . . .   88 STOLEN CHILD   38
    COME, O HUMAN CHILD! . . . .   88 STOLEN CHILD V 38

152

COME   (CONTINUED)

	PAGE	TITLE		LINE
COME ROUND ME, LITTLE CHILDER;	94	MOLL MAGEE		1
SHE SAYS MY MAN WILL SURELY COME,	96	MOLL MAGEE		41
SHE SAYS MY HUSBAND SURE WILL COME	96	MOLL MAGEE	V	41
COME NEAR ME, WHILE I SING THE ANCIENT WAYS;	100	ROSE UPON ROOD		2
COME NEAR, THAT NO MORE BLINDED BY MAN'S FATE,	101	ROSE UPON ROOD		9
COME NEAR, COME NEAR, COME NEAR--AH, LEAVE ME STILL	101	ROSE UPON ROOD		13
COME NEAR, COME NEAR, COME NEAR--AH, LEAVE ME STILL	101	ROSE UPON ROOD		13
COME NEAR, COME NEAR, COME NEAR--AH, LEAVE ME STILL	101	ROSE UPON ROOD		13
COME NEAR; I WOULD, BEFORE MY TIME TO GO,	101	ROSE UPON ROOD		22
THAT YOU HAVE COME AND DARED ME TO MY FACE?"	109	CUCHULAIN SEA		61
THAT YOU COME HERE TO MEET THIS ANCIENT SWORD?"	109	CUCHULAIN SEA	V	61
WOULD COME AT LAST TO GOD'S GREAT TOWN,	113	ROSE OF PEACE		11
YOU, TOO, HAVE COME WHERE THE DIM TIDES ARE HURLED	115	ROSE OF BATTLE		26
WHERE TIME WOULD SURELY FORGET US, AND SORROW COME NEAR US NO MORE;	122	WHITE BIRDS		10
WHERE SURELY TIME WOULD FORGET US AND SORROW COME NEAR US NO MORE;	122	WHITE BIRDS	V	10
"FATHER! YOU COME AGAIN!"	133	FR GILLIGAN		32
AND NIAMH CALLING AWAY, COME AWAY;	140	HOSTING SIDHE		4
AWAY, COME AWAY, TO THE DIM TWILIGHT.	140	HOSTING SIDHE	V	8
WE COME BETWEEN HIM AND THE DEED OF HIS HAND,	141	HOSTING SIDHE		11
WE COME BETWEEN HIM AND THE HOPE OF HIS HEART.	141	HOSTING SIDHE		12
AND NIAMH CALLING AWAY, COME AWAY.	141	HOSTING SIDHE		16
COME CLEAR OF THE NETS OF WRONG AND RIGHT;	147	INTO TWILIGHT		2
COME CLEAR OFF THE NETS OF WRONG AND RIGHT;	147	INTO TWILIGHT	V	2
COME, HEART, WHERE HILL IS HEAPED UPON HILL;	148	INTO TWILIGHT		9
HE MOURNS FOR THE CHANGE THAT HAS COME UPON HIM	153	CHANGE BELOVED		T
MONGAN LAMENTS THE CHANGE THAT HAS COME UPON HIM AND HIS BELOVED	153	CHANGE BELOVED	V	T
I WOULD THAT THE BOAR WITHOUT BRISTLES HAD COME FROM THE WEST	153	CHANGE BELOVED		10
COME FROM A MORE DREAM-HEAVY LAND,	156	FORGOT BEAUTY		16
"I HAVE COME BY THE WINDY WAY	167	BLESSED		6
"I COME BY THE WINDY WAY	167	BLESSED	V	6
SURELY THINE HOUR HAS COME, THY GREAT WIND BLOWS,	170	SECRET ROSE		31
I WOULD THE PALE DEER HAD COME	171	MAID QUIET	V	4A
HAD COME THROUGH THE MOUNTAIN SIDE,	171	MAID QUIET	V	4B
YOU WOULD COME HITHER, AND BEND YOUR HEAD,	175	BELOVED DEAD		3
WHEN WE COME AT THE END OF TIME	178	FIDDLER DOONEY		9
WHEN WE COME AT THE CLOSE OF TIME	178	FIDDLER DOONEY	V	9
THEY WILL ALL COME UP TO ME,	179	FIDDLER DOONEY		18
WILL ALL COME UP TO ME,	179	FIDDLER DOONEY	V	18
HAD COME AS IN THE OLD TIMES TO COUNSEL HER,	181	QUEEN MAEVE		42
HAD COME, AS IN OLD TIMES, TO COUNSEL HER,	181	QUEEN MAEVE	V	42
OF THE FAR-WANDERING SHADOWS HAS COME TO ME	183	QUEEN MAEVE		80
AS IN THE OLD DAYS WHEN THEY WOULD COME AND GO	183	QUEEN MAEVE		81
OF THE FAR WANDERING SHADOWS HAS COME TO ME,	183	QUEEN MAEVE	V	80
KINGS OF THE GREAT PLAIN HAVE COME AND GONE	183	QUEEN MAEVE	V	81
"I COME FROM THE UNDIMMED RIVERS TO BID YOU CALL	184	QUEEN MAEVE	V	91
AND THE BROWN BULL HAD NOT YET COME,	189	BAILE AILLINN		15
WHEN THEY HAD COME TO THE MARRIAGE-BED;	193	BAILE AILLINN		106
WHEN THEY HAD COME TO THE MARRIAGE BED;	193	BAILE AILLINN	V	106
THEY COME WHERE SOME HUGE WATCHER IS,	196	BAILE AILLINN		168
A BETTER TIME HAD COME AGAIN	197	BAILE AILLINN		192
AND LITTLE SHADOWS COME ABOUT HER EYES;	199	FOLLY COMFORT		3
IT ALL, AND MORE THAN IT ALL, WOULD COME TO NAUGHT,	201	OLD MEMORY		8
IT ALL, MORE THAN IT ALL, WOULD COME TO NAUGHT,	201	OLD MEMORY	V	8
WHO COME WITH THEIR CROWNS OF PEARL AND THEIR SPINDLES OF WOOL,	203	WITHER BOUGHS		10
THAT THEY WOULD COME TO BLOWS,	214	HAPPY TOWNLAND		22
THAT THEY MUST COME TO BLOWS	214	HAPPY TOWNLAND	V	22
GABRIEL WILL COME FROM THE WATER	215	HAPPY TOWNLAND		45
AND THAT YOU COME FROM EDEN ON FLYING FEET.	218	WOODS OF COOLE		29
WE HAVE NOT COME UPON A SHORE OR SHIP	222	SHADOW WATER B		3
I'D NEVER COME UPON THE HAPPINESS	226	SHADOW WATER B		87
HAS EVER COME BUT THOSE MAN-HEADED BIRDS,	226	SHADOW WATER B		99
AND THE HIGH FAME THAT COME TO THEM IN MARRIAGE,	232	SHADOW WATER B		235
ARMED MEN HAVE COME UPON US! O I AM SLAIN!	233	SHADOW WATER B		241
ARMED MEN HAVE COME UPON US! O I AM SLAIN!	233	SHADOW WATER B		243
THERE! THERE THEY COME! GULL, GANNET, OR DIVER,	233	SHADOW WATER B		244
TO WAIT THEIR FRIENDS! BUT WHEN THEIR FRIENDS HAVE COME	233	SHADOW WATER B		247
WHERE DO YOU COME FROM? WHO BROUGHT YOU TO THIS PLACE?	235	SHADOW WATER B		284
HAS COME INTO THE JEWELS OF THE HARP	239	SHADOW WATER B	V	371A
WHAT NAME TO CALL HIM BY? COME TO HIS SHIP.	240	SHADOW WATER B		390
HIS NAME WILL COME INTO OUR THOUGHTS IN A MINUTE.	241	SHADOW WATER B		391
FOR EVERYTHING IS GONE. COME HITHER, AIBRIC,	241	SHADOW WATER B		402
BUT HARRY US WITH HOPES THAT COME TO NOTHING,	250	SHADOW WATER B		579
BECAUSE I HAVE COME INTO MY STRENGTH,	256	WORDS		11
ALTHOUGH I HAVE COME CLOSE ON FORTY-NINE,	270	PARDON FATHERS		20
"COME OUT AND DIG FOR A DEAD MAN,	272	GREY ROCK		32
THAT EMPTIED ALL OUR DAYS TO COME.	272	GREY ROCK		40
BEING BETRAYED INTO A CRADLE, AND I COME	284	TWO KINGS		169
"SEEING THAT WHEN YOU COME TO THE DEATHBED	285	TWO KINGS		196
"SEEING THAT WHEN YOU COME TO THE DEATH-BED	285	TWO KINGS	V	196
WHAT NEED YOU, BEING COME TO SENSE,	289	SEPTEMBER 1913		1
TO A FRIEND WHOSE WORK HAS COME TO NOTHING	290	TO A FRIEND		T
AND LISTEN AT THE CORNERS HAS NOT COME;	293	TO A SHADE		22
COULD EVER COME BETWEEN	315	FRIENDS		8
THAT THE NIGHT COME	317	NIGHT COME		T
THAT THE NIGHT COME.	317	NIGHT COME		12

153

	PAGE	TITLE	LINE

COME (CONTINUED)

	PAGE	TITLE	LINE
--BEN JONSON'S PHRASE--AND FIND WHEN JUNE IS COME	321	REED WHISPERER	6
THE NINETEENTH AUTUMN HAS COME UPON ME	322	SWANS AT COOLE	7
FOR ALL THAT COME INTO MY MIND ARE DEAD.	324	ROBERT GREGORY	16
BUT THAT, LONG TRAVELLING, HE HAD COME	325	ROBERT GREGORY	28
THE YEARS TO COME SEEMED WASTE OF BREATH,	328	IRISH AIRMAN	14
"STRETCH BONES TILL THE DAYLIGHT COME	331	ROUND TOWER	5
AND NOW THAT I HAVE COME TO FIFTY YEARS	344	DEJECTION	10
MANAGE THE TALK UNTIL HER NAME COME ROUND.	351	HER PRAISE	14
MANAGE TO TALK UNTIL HER NAME COME ROUND.	351	HER PRAISE	V	14
I WAS ABASHED, AND NOW THEY COME TO MIND	353	PEOPLE	36
COME PLAY WITH ME;	359	TO A SQUIRREL	1
NOW THAT HIS FIFTIETH YEAR HAD COME,	361	ALF POLLEXFEN	31
WILL COME FROM THE HOUSE, AND SAY--	364	END OF DAY	6
"COME IN AND LEAVE THE PLAY."	364	END OF DAY	8
AMID THE DREAMS OF YOUTH) LET HER COME FACE TO FACE,	366	HER COURAGE	3
COULD THE IMPOSSIBLE COME TO PASS	385	ROBARTES DANCE	9
THAT ALL MUST COME TO SIGHT AND TOUCH;	386	ROBARTES DANCE	31
NO, NO, NOT SAID, BUT CRIED IT OUT--"YOU HAVE COME AGAIN,	391	UNDER SATURN	13
AND SURELY AFTER TWENTY YEARS IT WAS TIME TO COME."	391	UNDER SATURN	14
WHEN SLEEP AT LAST HAS COME	394	EASTER 1916	63
"TO MAKE THE GREEN COME OUT AGAIN	396	ROSE TREE	9
SO THE CROWD COME THEY CARE NOT WHAT MAY COME.	398	LEADERS CROWD	10
SO THE CROWD COME THEY CARE NOT WHAT MAY COME.	398	LEADERS CROWD	10
AND WHAT ROUGH BEAST, ITS HOUR COME ROUND AT LAST,	402	SECOND COMING	21
THAT THE FUTURE YEARS HAD COME,	403	FOR DAUGHTER	14
AND THEREFORE I HAVE SAILED THE SEAS AND COME	408	SAIL BYZANTIUM	15
COME FROM THE HOLY FIRE, PERNE IN A GYRE,	408	SAIL BYZANTIUM	19
OF WHAT IS PAST, OR PASSING, OR TO COME.	408	SAIL BYZANTIUM	32
AND THEREFORE HAVE I SAILED THE SEAS AND COME	408	SAIL BYZANTIUM V	15
COME WITH LOUD CRY AND PANTING BREAST	412	TOWER	86
AS I WOULD QUESTION ALL, COME ALL WHO CAN;	412	TOWER	89
COME OLD, NECESSITOUS, HALF-MOUNTED MAN;	412	TOWER	90
OR WHAT WORSE EVIL COME--	416	TOWER	188
COME BUILD IN THE EMPTY HOUSE OF THE STARE.	424	STARES NEST	5
COME BUILD IN THE EMPTY HOUSE OF THE STARE.	425	STARES NEST	10
COME BUILD IN THE EMPTY HOUSE OF THE STARE.	425	STARES NEST	15
COME BUILD IN THE EMPTY HOUSE OF THE STARE.	425	STARES NEST	20
NOR HATE OF WHAT'S TO COME, NOR PITY FOR WHAT'S GONE,	427	PHANTOM HATRED	30
COME LET US MOCK AT THE GREAT	432	NINETEEN 19	93
COME LET US MOCK AT THE WISE;	432	NINETEEN 19	98
COME LET US MOCK AT THE GOOD	432	NINETEEN 19	103
BECAUSE THE SPRING-TIME HAS NOT COME--	434	WHEEL	6
TILL HIS MORNING MEAL COME ROUND;	435	FOR MY SON	4
COME PRAISE COLONUS' HORSES, AND COME PRAISE	446	COLONUS PRAISE	1
COME PRAISE COLONUS' HORSES, AND COME PRAISE	446	COLONUS PRAISE	1
WHO COMES INTO THIS COUNTRY, AND HAS COME	447	COLONUS PRAISE	17
A STRANGE THING SURELY THAT MY HEART, WHEN LOVE HAD COME UNSOUGHT	449	OWEN AHERNE	1
LOVE-LORN, INDIFFERENT HANDS MIGHT COME UPON IT	461	HARUN RASHID	14
MIDNIGHT HAS COME, AND THE GREAT CHRIST CHURCH BELL	470	ALL SOUL NIGHT	1
BUBBLE UPON THE TABLE. A GHOST MAY COME;	470	ALL SOUL NIGHT	5
CAN COME UPON THE VISAGE OF THE MOON	482	BLOOD AND MOON	53
WHERE BLOOD-BEGOTTEN SPIRITS COME	498	BYZANTIUM	28
WHERE BLOOD BEGOTTEN SPIRITS COME	498	BYZANTIUM	V	28
THAT ARE NOT SUITED FOR SUCH MEN AS COME	501	VACILLATION	33
MY FIFTIETH YEAR HAD COME AND GONE,	501	VACILLATION	35
BATHED IN MIRACULOUS OIL, SWEET ODOURS FROM IT COME,	503	VACILLATION	81
OUT OF IRELAND HAVE WE COME.	506	REMORSE SPEECH	11
BUT SHOULD THAT OTHER COME, I SPIT!	509	JANE BISHOP	27
THAT TO GOD SHALL COME!	511	JANE AND JACK	8
MEN COME, MEN GO.	512	JANE ON GOD	5
ALL NIGHT'S FATHOMLESS WISDOM COME,	519	HER DREAM	2
COME, LET ME SING INTO YOUR EAR;	524	DANCING DAYS	1
"COME OUT OF CHARITY,	526	AM OF IRELAND	4
COME DANCE WITH ME IN IRELAND."	526	AM OF IRELAND	5
"COME OUT OF CHARITY,	527	AM OF IRELAND	17
"COME OUT OF CHARITY,	527	AM OF IRELAND	30
AND, THOUGH LOVE'S BITTER-SWEET HAD ALL COME BACK,	537	HER VISION	27
COME, FIX UPON ME THAT ACCUSING EYE.	542	PARN FUNERAL 1	24
COME MARCH, SINGING THIS SONG,	544	TO SAME TUNE 1 V	REF
THOSE THAT COME AFTER SHALL MOCK AT O'DONNELL,	546	TO SAME TUNE 2	23
THOSE THAT COME AFTER SHALL MOCK O'DONNELL,	546	TO SAME TUNE 2 V	23
WHAT MADE THEM MOUNT AND WHAT MADE THEM COME,	549	SEVERED HEAD	V	8
THOSE AMOROUS CRIES THAT OUT OF QUIET COME	557	RIBH ECSTASY	7
WHENCE HAD THEY COME?	560	WHENCE COME	T
WHAT MASTER MADE THE LASH. WHENCE HAD THEY COME,	560	WHENCE COME	9
RAVENING, RAGING, AND UPROOTING THAT HE MAY COME	563	MERU	6
WHAT MATTER? OUT OF CAVERN COME A VOICE	564	GYRES	V	15
AEROPLANE AND ZEPPELIN WILL COME OUT,	565	LAPIS LAZULI	6
IF STRANGE MEN COME FROM THE HOUSE	568	SWEET DANCER	8
STRANGE NIGHT HAS COME;	574	MAIDS 1ST SONG	6
COME TOM AND DICK, COME ALL THE TROOP	582	ROGER CASEMENT	17
COME TOM AND DICK, COME ALL THE TROOP	582	ROGER CASEMENT	17
COME FROM THE FORGER AND HIS DESK,	582	ROGER CASEMENT	19
COME SPEAK YOUR BIT IN PUBLIC	582	ROGER CASEMENT	21
COME ALFRED NOYES AND ALL THE TROUP	582	ROGER CASEMENT V	17
I COME TO HEAR IT STRIKE."	585	ORAHILLY	26
COME GATHER ROUND ME, PARNELLITES	586	PARNELLITES	T
COME GATHER ROUND ME, PARNELLITES,	586	PARNELLITES	1
COME FILL UP ALL THOSE GLASSES	586	PARNELLITES	7

154

COME   (CONTINUED)

	PAGE	TITLE		LINE
HURRAH FOR REVOLUTION AND CANNON COME AGAIN!	590	GREAT DAY		3
COME SWISH AROUND, MY PRETTY PUNK,	591	DRUNK SOBRIETY		1
SO COME IN RAGS OR COME IN SILK, IN CLOAK OR COUNTRY SHAWL,	593	PILGRIM		22
SO COME IN RAGS OR COME IN SILK, IN CLOAK OR COUNTRY SHAWL,	593	PILGRIM		22
AND COME WITH LEARNED LOVERS OR WITH WHAT MEN YOU MAY,	593	PILGRIM		23
SO COME IN RAG OR COME IN SILK, IN CLOAK OR COUNTRY SHAWL,	593	PILGRIM	V	22
SO COME IN RAG OR COME IN SILK, IN CLOAK OR COUNTRY SHAWL,	593	PILGRIM	V	22
AND COME WITH LEARNED LOVERS OR WITH WHAT MAN YOU MAY,	593	PILGRIM	V	23
THOSE WORDS COME TRUE IN THE END	597	COLONEL MARTIN	V	69
THAT COME INTO MY SOUL AND ESCAPE	599	SPIRIT MEDIUM		3
AND NOW THAT END HAS COME I HAVE NOT WEPT!	603	GALLERY REVIS		38
MUST COME FROM CONTACT WITH THE SOIL, FROM THAT	603	GALLERY REVIS		43
BUT NOW THAT END HAS COME I HAVE NOT WEPT!	603	GALLERY REVIS	V	38
THIS BOOK OR THAT, COME TO THIS HALLOWED PLACE	604	GALLERY REVIS		51
ALL MANNIONS COME FROM MANANNAN,	606	SONGS BURDEN 1		10
COME GATHER ROUND ME, PLAYERS ALL!	608	SONGS BURDEN 3		1
COME PRAISE NINETEEN-SIXTEEN,	608	SONGS BURDEN 3		2
AND YET WHO KNOWS WHAT'S YET TO COME?	608	SONGS BURDEN 3		2
COME PRAISE NINETEEN SIXTEEN,	608	SONGS BURDEN 3	V	2
OF GOD OR WOMAN, THE TIME WERE COME TO DIE."	609	IN TARAS HALLS		15
THOSE THAT COME AFTER SHALL MOCK AT O'DONNELL,	614	MARCH SONGS 1		23
WHENCE DID ALL THAT FURY COME?	619	STICK INCENSE		1
THOSE BANNERS COME NOT IN.	635	BLACK TOWER		6
BUT WINDS COME UP FROM THE SHORE!	635	BLACK TOWER		8
THOSE BANNERS COME TO BRIBE OR THREATEN,	635	BLACK TOWER		11
BUT WINDS COME UP FROM THE SHORE!	636	BLACK TOWER	V	REF
MAIDEN, COME FORTH! THE WOODS KEEP WATCH FOR THEE!	645	ISLE STAT I 1		1
COME FORTH! THE MORN IS FAIR! AS FROM THE PYRE	645	ISLE STAT I 1		8
COME FORTH, COME FORTH, MY MUSIC FLOWS FOR THEE,	645	ISLE STAT I 1		20
COME FORTH, COME FORTH, MY MUSIC FLOWS FOR THEE,	645	ISLE STAT I 1		20
SHEPHERD, TO MAR THE MORNING HAST THOU COME?	646	ISLE STAT I 1		30
COME THOU, COME, AND TO THIS STRING--	646	ISLE STAT I 1		37
COME THOU, COME, AND TO THIS STRING--	646	ISLE STAT I 1		37
COME FORTH, FOR IN A THOUSAND BOWERS	647	ISLE STAT I 1		64
AND WHEREFORE HAVE WE COME? A SONG TO HEAR.	652	ISLE STAT I 2		27
COME FOLLOW! COME FOLLOW!	654	ISLE STAT I 2		79
COME FOLLOW! COME FOLLOW!	654	ISLE STAT I 2		79
OF HILL TWO SHEPHERDS COME. FAREWELL! I'LL DON	659	ISLE STAT II 1		28
HERE WHERE THE ROUND WAVES COME, HERE LET THEM BUILD,	663	ISLE STAT II 2		19
AND ONCE A-YEAR LET THE ARCADIANS COME,	663	ISLE STAT II 2		29
ONCE MORE THOSE SHEPHERDS COME. MAYHAP SOME MIRTH	664	ISLE STAT II 2		49
THENCE HAVE I COME WINGING!	672	ISLE STAT II 3		170
NOW HERE I COME WINGING!	672	ISLE STAT II 3	V	170
A ROVER I, WHO COME FROM WHERE MEN'S EARS	678	ISLE STAT II 3		293
ALONG THE VELVET VALE I SAW HIM COME--	690	MOSADA 1		10
THE DARK STILL MAN, HAS COME AND SAYS 'TIS SIN.	692	MOSADA 1		47
THE PHANTOMS COME! HA! HA! THEY COME, THEY COME!	694	MOSADA 1		97
THE PHANTOMS COME! HA! HA! THEY COME, THEY COME!	694	MOSADA 1		97
THE PHANTOMS COME! HA! HA! THEY COME, THEY COME!	694	MOSADA 1		97
THE PHANTOMS COME! THEY COME, THEY COME, THEY COME!	694	MOSADA 1		97
THE PHANTOMS COME! THEY COME, THEY COME, THEY COME!	694	MOSADA 1	V	97
THE PHANTOMS COME! THEY COME, THEY COME, THEY COME!	694	MOSADA 1	V	97
THE PHANTOMS COME! THEY COME, THEY COME, THEY COME!	694	MOSADA 1	V	97
NAMES AFTER ME. LADY--I COME. FORGIVE,	695	MOSADA 1		117
YOU'RE FULL OF WORDINESS. COME, HEAR MY SONG.	696	MOSADA 2		8
AND NOT COME THENCE! FOR HERE IN THIS SMALL RING--	699	MOSADA 3		22
HE FADES AMONG THE MISTS! HOW FAST THEY COME,	703	MOSADA 3		117
COME AWAY WHILE THE MOON'S IN THE WOODLAND,	707	FAIRY PEDANT		9
COME AWAY WHILE THE MOON'S IN THE WOODLAND,	708	FAIRY PEDANT		37
HAYNAU! THINE HOUR HAS COME, THY FOLLOWERS FAR	715	FERENCZ RENYI		117
AND DEATH, OH MY FAIR ONE, WILL NEVER COME NEAR	717	LOVE SONG		8
AND THE WINDS COME DOWN AND BLOW THEM WITH THE VAPOURS FAR AWAY.	719	PHANTOM SHIP		28
COME HERE. BE SEATED NOW! I'D BUY OF YOU.	720	WITCH VIVIEN		17
COME, FATHER. LADY, I NOR REST NOR SIT.	720	WITCH VIVIEN		18
WITH LOADED DICE. ANOTHER CHANCE! COME, FATHER!	721	WITCH VIVIEN		45
COME TO THE CHESS, FOR YOUNG GIRLS' WITS ARE BETTER	721	WITCH VIVIEN		46
AND THEN THE GREAT ONES COME, AND LAST THE KING.	722	WITCH VIVIEN		54
COME YOU, COLTSFOOT, MOUSETAIL, COME!	727	LOVERS QUARREL		33
COME YOU, COLTSFOOT, MOUSETAIL, COME!	727	LOVERS QUARREL		33
COME I KNOW WHERE, FAR AWAY.	727	LOVERS QUARREL		34
COME AND TEASE THEM TILL THE DAY.	727	LOVERS QUARREL		36
COME, BESIDE A SANDY LAKE,	727	LOVERS QUARREL		41
AND COME KNEELING ON ONE KNEE,	727	LOVERS QUARREL		53
COME AND DREAM OF KINGS AND KINGDOMS,	737	IN FIRELIGHT		1
TILL THEY COME WHERE YOUR SAD, SAD HEART IS,	739	WHERE BOOKS GO		5
FOR A KNIGHT, COME FROM NORMANDY	740	EARL PAUL		7
BEST PLEASES YOU. ARMED MEN HAVE COME UPON US.	752	SHADOW WATER A		131
ARMED MEN HAVE COME UPON US. O! I AM SLAIN!	753	SHADOW WATER A		133
BECAUSE I HAD HOPED TO COME, AS DREAMS FORETOLD,	757	SHADOW WATER A		197
I HAVE COME HITHER BECAUSE I HOPED TO COME	757	SHADOW WATER A		197
I HAVE COME HITHER BECAUSE I HOPED TO COME	757	SHADOW WATER A	V	197
FORGAEL CAN DIE TO-MORROW. COME TO THE ALE.	759	SHADOW WATER A		246
COME TO THE ALE! FOR HE CAN DIE TO-MORROW.	760	SHADOW WATER A		247
AND I SHALL LAUGH WITH JOY. COME HITHER, AIBRIC,	760	SHADOW WATER A		249
THAT MY TRUE-LOVE WOULD COME IN A SHIP OF PEARL	763	SHADOW WATER A		315
BUT FAITHFUL LOVERS. WHITHER HAVE YOU COME,	763	SHADOW WATER A		309
THAT MY TRUE LOVE WOULD COME IN A SHIP OF PEARL	763	SHADOW WATER A	V	315
AND WE GO HOME. COME, AIBRIC! END YOUR TALE.	766	SHADOW WATER A		374
WHEN THE DARK HOUNDS WERE LOOSED. COME TO THE ALE.	766	SHADOW WATER A		379

155

COME   (CONTINUED)
    FOR LOVE IS KIND AND HAPPY. O COME WITH ME! . . . . . .   767 SHADOW WATER A   396
    COME RIDE AND RIDE TO THE GARDEN, ...   773 COME RIDE   1
    COME RIDE AND RIDE WITH A WILL! . . . .   773 COME RIDE   2
    COME RIDE AND RIDE TO THE GARDEN, ...   774 COME RIDE   5
    COME RIDE LIKE THE MARCH WIND! . . . .   774 COME RIDE   6
    COME RIDE AND RIDE TO THE GARDEN, ...   774 COME RIDE   13
    COME RIDE AND RIDE TO THE GARDEN, ...   774 COME RIDE   18
    FOR THE THINGS COME AFTER DEATH? . . . .   777 SONG DEIRDRE 2   12
    TILL CERTAIN SECOND THOUGHTS HAVE COME . . . .   791 REPRISALS   12
COMEDIAN'S
    UNDER THE GREAT COMEDIAN'S TOMB THE CROWD. . . . . . .   541 PARN FUNERAL 1   1
COMEDIES
    FOR THE ITALIAN COMEDIES? . . . .   287 TO WEALTHY MAN   13
COMEDY
    IN THE CASUAL COMEDY! . . . .   393 EASTER 1916   37
COMELIER
    IS COMELIER THAN CANDLES AT MOTHER MARY'S FEET. . . . .   147 UNAPPEAS HOST   12
    IS COMELIER THAN CANDLES BEFORE MAURYA'S FEET. . . . .   147 UNAPPEAS HOST V 12
    GROWS COMELIER. ELEVEN PASS, AND THEN . . . . . .   374 PHASES OF MOON   44
COMELY
    AND MORE COMELY THAN MAN CAN MAKE THEM . . . .   49 OISIN 3   32
    MORE COMELY THAN MAN MAY MAKE THEM, INLAID WITH SILVER   49 OISIN 3   V 29
      AND GOLD,
    "WHERE ALL ARE COMELY AND GOOD? . . . .   167 BLESSED   22
    "AND THOUGH I'D MARRY WITH A COMELY LASS, ...   300 BEGGAR CRIED   9
    SHE NEED NOT BE TOO COMELY--LET IT PASS," . . . . .   300 BEGGAR CRIED   10
    AND ALIGHT AT THE COMELY TREES AND THE LAWN, ...   330 BONE OF A HARE   4
COMER   SEE NEW-COMER
    FLOATING FROM YON BARRED WINDOW. NEW COMER, ...   700 MOSADA 3   V 43
COMES
    "HOW COMES IT, PRINCESS, THAT YOUR MIND . . . .   6 OISIN 1   V 59A
    FOR NEITHER DEATH NOR CHANGE COMES NEAR US, ...   21 OISIN 1   316
    THE DARKNESS COMES. A CLOUD HANGS OVERHEAD-- . . . . .   43 OISIN 2   V 208A
    YOUR QUESTIONER, OISIN, IS WORTHY, HE COMES FROM THE FENIAN   51 OISIN 3   64
      LANDS."
    COMING OUT OF THE SEA AS THE DAWN COMES, A CHAUNT OF LOVE   58 OISIN 3   158
      ON MY LIPS.
    COMES A SEA-KING MASTERFUL . . . .   82 MAD KING GOLL V 15
    FOR HE COMES, THE HUMAN CHILD, ...   88 STOLEN CHILD   50
    "BUT IF YOUR MASTER COMES HOME TRIUMPHING . . . . . .   106 CUCHULAIN SEA   12
    OR COMES IN LAUGHTER FROM THE SEA'S SAD LIPS, ...   114 ROSE OF BATTLE   19
    AND I SHALL HAVE SOME PEACE THERE, FOR PEACE COMES DROPPING   117 ISLE INNISFREE   5
      SLOW,
    A WEARINESS COMES FROM THOSE DREAMERS, ...   122 WHITE BIRDS   5
    AND A WEARINESS COMES FROM THOSE DREAMERS . . . . . .   122 WHITE BIRDS   V   5
    "O BLESSEDNESS COMES IN THE NIGHT AND THE DAY . . . . .   168 BLESSED   33
    WHEN THE WIND COMES BLOWING ACROSS THE HILLY LAND! . . .   207 HANRAHANS SONG V   7
    I ONLY KNOW THAT ALL WE KNOW COMES FROM YOU, ...   218 WOODS OF COOLE   28
    THE COZENING FORTUNE-TELLER THAT COMES WHISPERING, . . .   228 SHADOW WATER B   123
    COMES CRYING, "I HAVE RUN UPON THE SWORD. . . . . . .   234 SHADOW WATER B   261
    AH, BUT PEACE THAT COMES AT LENGTH, ...   259 PEACE   10
    I SWEAR BEFORE THE DAWN COMES ROUND AGAIN . . . . . .   260 FASC DIFFICULT   12
    WINE COMES IN AT THE MOUTH . . . .   261 DRINKING SONG   1
    AND LOVE COMES IN AT THE EYE! . . . .   261 DRINKING SONG   2
    THAT COMES OF THE BEST KNIT TO THE BEST? ALTHOUGH . . .   264 HOUSE SHAKEN   7
    NOW NOTHING BUT COMES READIER TO THE HAND . . . . . .   267 ALL TEMPT ME   4
    FOR ONLY RUBBISH COMES MY WAY. . . . .   295 THREE BEGGARS   4
    WHO COMES AT NEED, ALTHOUGH NOT NOW AS ONCE . . . . .   320 REED WHISPERER   2
    LIONEL JOHNSON COMES THE FIRST TO MIND, ...   324 ROBERT GREGORY   17
    AND THAT ENQUIRING MAN JOHN SYNGE COMES NEXT, ...   324 ROBERT GREGORY   25
    THE STARS FADE OUT WHERE THE MOON COMES, ...   344 DAWN   8
    PLEASURE THAT COMES WITH SLEEP, ...   345 ON WOMAN   22
    AND THEREUPON THERE COMES THAT SCREAM . . . .   389 IMAGE PAST   5
    THE HORSE THAT COMES FROM THE ROAD, ...   393 EASTER 1916   45
    COMES CRACKING JOKES OF CIVIL WAR . . . .   423 ROAD AT DOOR   3
    WHO COMES INTO THIS COUNTRY, AND HAS COME . . . . . .   447 COLONUS PRAISE   17
    FOR THAT OLD MADGE COMES DOWN THE LANE, ...   456 FRIENDS YOUTH   5
    THEY UNDERSTOOD THAT WISDOM COMES OF BEGGARY. . . . . .   487 SEVEN SAGES   26
    MAY REND WHAT COMES IN REACH. . . . .   488 CRAZED MOON   18
    COMES TO DESTROY . . . .   500 VACILLATION   4
    AND ALL ALONE COMES RIDING THERE . . . .   550 SEVERED HEAD   18
    AND PRAYER COMES ROUND AGAIN-- . . . .   553 PRAYER OLD AGE   10
    WHAT MATTER? OUT OF CAVERN COMES A VOICE, ...   564 GYRES   15
    WHAT HOUR OF TERROR COMES TO TEST THE SOUL, ...   622 HOUND VOICE   11
    BUT WIND COMES UP FROM THE SHORE! . . . .   636 BLACK TOWER   18
    BUT WIND COMES UP FROM THE SHORE! . . . .   636 BLACK TOWER   28
    HER LOVE! TO HER WHO WEARS THAT BLOOM COMES TRUTH. . . .   653 ISLE STAT I 2   46
    THAT CALLS. O EVIL STARRED! IT COMES ALONG . . . . .   653 ISLE STAT I 2   49
    THE HOUR OF INCANTATION COMES A-TIPTOE, ...   691 MOSADA 1   37
    AND COLA, SEEING, KNOWS THE SIGN AND COMES. . . . . .   691 MOSADA 1   38
    YONDER HE COMES! BRIGHT-EYED, AND HOLLOW-CHEEKED . . .   697 MOSADA 2   35
    IS IT YOUR MESSAGE, STARS, THAT WHEN DEATH COMES . . . .   701 MOSADA 3   60
    FOR NIGHT COMES FAST. LOOK DOWN ON ME, MY LOVE, ...   703 MOSADA 3   103
    THE FAIRY DOCTOR COMES OUR WAY . . . .   716 FAIRY DOCTOR   1
    ROUND SHE COMES IN STAYS BEFORE THEM! . . . . . .   719 PHANTOM SHIP   17
    THEY ARE STILL WAITING! AND NOW THE LAGGARD COMES, . . .   754 SHADOW WATER A   150
    WHOSE SHADOW IS THE SLEEP THAT COMES WITH LOVE, ...   754 SHADOW WATER A   162
    THEY ARE STILL WAITING! AND A LAGGARD COMES, ...   754 SHADOW WATER A V 150
    BUT NOW I WILL KILL HER. ALL COMES TO AN END. . . . .   755 SHADOW WATER A   176
    THAT COMES WITH LOVE, COMES MURMURING OF AN HOUR . . . .   765 SHADOW WATER A   365

		PAGE	TITLE	LINE

COMES   (CONTINUED)
THAT COMES WITH LOVE, COMES MURMURING OF AN HOUR . . . . .   765 SHADOW WATER A   365
FOR THE FLOWER COMES WITH THE FRUIT THERE . . . . . .   774 COME RIDE   3
TILL THE SIDE OF HATE COMES UP. . . . .   776 AGAINST WITCH   35
COMEST
YES, ALL IS VERY WELL. WHENCE COMEST THOU? . . . . . .   682 SEEKER   14
COMETH
OR DEATH THAT COMETH WITH THE NEXT LIFE-KEY? . . . . . .   724 KANVA ON SELF   18
COMFORT
FROM THEIR PALE THRONES AND COMFORT HIM, BUT THEY . . . .   68 SAD SHEPHERD   6
THEIR HEARING, AND SOME COMFORT GIVE, BUT THEY . . . . .   68 SAD SHEPHERD   V   6
THE MAN HAS FOUND NO COMFORT IN THE GRAVE. . . . . . .   128 DREAM OF FAERY   48
I HAVE NOT A CRUMB OF COMFORT, NOT A GRAIN. . . . . . .   200 FOLLY COMFORT   7
BUT HEART THERE IS NO COMFORT, NOT A GRAIN: . . . . . .   200 FOLLY COMFORT   V   7
THE COMFORT THAT YOU MADE? ALTHOUGH MY WITS HAVE GONE . . .   391 UNDER SATURN   5
AND SO FORGET THE COMFORT THAT NO WORDS CAN TELL . . . .   391 UNDER SATURN   V   4
AND FIND A COMFORT IN IT? MAY THIS TOWER . . . .   423 MY DESCENDANTS   V   13
HAS BUT ONE COMFORT LEFT: ALL TRIUMPH WOULD . . . . . .   429 NINETEEN 19   39
BUT IS THERE ANY COMFORT TO BE FOUND? . . . .   429 NINETEEN 19   41
AND OTHER COMFORT WERE A BITTER WOUND: . . . .   429 NINETEEN 19   V   41
IN THE COMFORT OF A BED. . . . .   596 COLONEL MARTIN   44
COMFORTABLE
IN COMFORTABLE SLEEP: ALL LIVING SLEPT . . . .   180 QUEEN MAEVE   15
"AND GET A COMFORTABLE WIFE AND HOUSE . . . .   299 BEGGAR CRIED   5
AND EVERY COMFORTABLE THING, ...   307 HOUR DAWN   111
THERE IS A COMFORTABLE KIND OF OLD SCARECROW. . . . . .   444 SCHOOL CHILDR   32
TO THE COMFORTABLE DOOR OF HIS HOUSE. . . . .   780 WELL AND TREE   6
COMFORTED
THE FOLLY OF BEING COMFORTED . . . .   199 FOLLY COMFORT   T
YOU'D KNOW THE FOLLY OF BEING COMFORTED. . . . .   200 FOLLY COMFORT   14
WHERE MAN IS COMFORTED. . . . .   534 CONSOLATION   6
CUCHULAIN COMFORTED . . . .   634 CUCHULAIN COMF   T
COMFORTERS
AND THEY THY COMFORTERS WILL BE, ...   66 HAPPY SHEPHERD   38
COMFORTING
AND MY OWN WHISPERING WORDS BE COMFORTING, ...   68 SAD SHEPHERD   23
AND MINE OWN WHISPERING WORDS BE COMFORTING, ...   68 SAD SHEPHERD   V   23
COMING
COMING OUT OF THE SEA AS THE DAWN COMES, A CHAUNT OF LOVE   58 OISIN 3   158
ON MY LIPS,
COMING FORTH FROM THE SEA LIKE THE MORNING . . . . . .   58 OISIN 3   V   158
TO IRELAND IN THE COMING TIMES . . . .   137 TO IRELAND   T
APOLOGIA ADDRESSED TO IRELAND IN THE COMING DAYS . . . .   137 TO IRELAND   V   T
THAT YOU, IN THE DIM COMING TIMES, ...   139 TO IRELAND   46
AT THE COMING OF NIGHT-TIDE, ...   144 HOST OF AIR   6
AT THE COMING OF NIGHT TIDE, ...   144 HOST OF AIR   V   6
THE PEOPLE OF COMING DAYS WILL KNOW . . . .   146 FISH   3
THE LOVER SPEAKS TO THE HEARERS OF HIS SONGS IN COMING DAYS   173 SPEAKS HEARERS   T
HANRAHAN SPEAKS TO THE LOVERS OF HIS SONGS IN COMING DAYS   173 SPEAKS HEARERS   V   T
A LOVER SPEAKS TO THE HEARERS OF HIS SONGS IN COMING DAYS   173 SPEAKS HEARERS   V   T
AS FOR THIS WOMAN, I THINK SHE IS COMING WITH ME. . . . .   248 SHADOW WATER B   545
THAT COMING TIME CAN SAY, ...   255 WOMAN HOMER   12
THE COMING OF WISDOM WITH TIME . . . .   261 COMING WISDOM   T
YOUR COMING BROUGHT: THOUGH I ACKNOWLEDGE I HAVE GONE . .   391 UNDER SATURN   V   5
COMING WITH VIVID FACES . . . .   391 EASTER 1916   2
WAS COMING INTO HIS FORCE: . . . .   392 EASTER 1916   27
THE SECOND COMING . . . .   401 SECOND COMING   T
SURELY THE SECOND COMING IS AT HAND. . . . .   402 SECOND COMING   10
THE SECOND COMING: HARDLY ARE THOSE WORDS OUT . . . . .   402 SECOND COMING   11
. . . FULLNESS AND OF THE COMING EMPTINESS . . . . . .   425 PHANTOM HATRED   T
ROMANTIC FISH SWAM IN NETS COMING TO THE HAND: . . . . .   485 THREE MOVEMENT   2
WHAT SORT OF MAN IS COMING . . . .   572 LADYS 2ND SONG   1
THAT WE IN COMING DAYS MAY BE . . . .   640 BEN BULBEN   82
COMMAND
I SHALL BE CARRIED IN THE GUST, COMMAND, ...   281 TWO KINGS   101
IS NOT AT MY COMMAND. . . . .   588 OLD WICKED MAN   22
BY HIS COMMAND THESE WORDS ARE CUT: . . . .   640 BEN BULBEN   91
COMMANDED
I HAVE COMMANDED MEN IN DREAMS. BELOVED, ...   766 SHADOW WATER A   381
COMMANDING
COMMANDING OFFICER THAT TORE . . . .   627 STATES HOLIDAY   16
COMMENCED
ERE YONDER PALM COMMENCED HIS THOUSAND YEARS? . . . . .   724 KANVA ON SELF   14
COMMEND
FISH, FLESH, OR FOWL, COMMEND ALL SUMMER LONG . . . . .   407 SAIL BYZANTIUM   5
BUT WANDERING ARABS. I COMMEND THE ARABS . . . . . .   462 HARUN RASHID   V   22
THAT I COMMEND TO ALL THE CHRONICLERS . . . .   463 HARUN RASHID   46
DID AN OLDER MIND COMMEND-- . . . .   494 AT ALGECIRAS   10
COMMENDED
A PEASANT GIRL COMMENDED BY A SONG, ...   410 TOWER   34
COMMENTARY
WITH SOME APPROPRIATE COMMENTARY ON EACH: . . . . . .   328 ROBERT GREGORY   93
I ADD IN COMMENTARY, ...   496 MOHINI CHATTER   16
COMMINGLING
THEY WERE COMMINGLING LICE AND BLOOD. . . . .   297 THREE BEGGARS   56
COMMIT
A CHARTER TO COMMIT THE CRIME ONCE MORE. . . . . . .   478 SELF AND SOUL   32
COMMITTED
BUT WHERE THE CRIME'S COMMITTED . . . .   534 CONSOLATION   11
COMMON
LEST I NO MORE HEAR COMMON THINGS THAT CRAVE: . . . . .   101 ROSE UPON ROOD   15

157

COMMON   (CONTINUED)
    TO IDLE LIFE AWAY, A COMMON HERD." . . . .   107 CUCHULAIN SEA   21'
    TILL MAEVE CALLED OUT, "THESE ARE BUT COMMON MEN. . . . .   186 QUEEN MAEVE   122
    NO COMMON LOVE IS TO OUR MIND, ...   190 BAILE AILLINN   34
    THE HOURLY KINDNESS, THE DAY'S COMMON SPEECH, ...   258 KING NO KING   14
    BECAUSE WE HAVE MADE OUR ART OF COMMON THINGS, ...   265 ABBEY THEATRE   5
    AND ALL THINGS AT ONE COMMON LEVEL LIE. . . . .   265 THESE CLOUDS   6
    THE COMMON GOOD OF LIFE. . . . .   317 NIGHT COME   5
    AS COMMON BEAUTIES MAY, ...   336 YOUNG BEAUTY   9
    UPON THE LIPS OF COMMON MEN . . . .   361 ALF POLLEXFEN   33
    OR RANK, RAISED FROM A COMMON . . . .   365 HER RACE   7
    WHO HAS AWAKENED FROM THE COMMON DREAM . . . .   369 EGO DOMINUS   50
    AND THERE'S BUT COMMON GREENNESS AFTER THAT. . . . . . .   422 MY DESCENDANTS   8
    THAT PITCHES COMMON THINGS ABOUT. THERE STOOD . . . . .   428 NINETEEN 19   4
    WITH A COMMON WRONG OR RIGHT. . . . .   476 EVA GORE-BOOTH   23
    COMMON BIRD OR PETAL . . . .   498 BYZANTIUM   23
    EVERY COMMON WOMAN KNOWS, ...   499 MOTHER OF GOD   7
    SENSE THAN A COMMON MAN? . . . .   507 STREAM AND SUN   10
    AND MUST THE COMMON ROUND OF DAY RESUME. . . . .   557 RIBH ECSTASY   8
    LIMBS A LOVE IN COMMON . . . .   573 LADYS 2ND SONG   17
    NO COMMON INTELLIGIBLE SOUND . . . .   578 CRAZED GIRL   13
    NOTHING THAT COMMON WOMEN PONDER ON . . . .   579 DOR WELLESLEY   12
    (AN IMAGE OUT OF SPENSER AND THE COMMON TONGUE). . . . .   603 GALLERY REVIS   40
    ALL THINGS DOWN TO THAT COMMON TEST AGAIN, ...   603 GALLERY REVIS   V 46
    AND I BEAT UP THE COMMON SORT . . . .   605 SONGS BURDEN 1   3
    THE COMMON BREEDS THE COMMON, ...   605 SONGS BURDEN 1   5
    THE COMMON BREEDS THE COMMON, ...   605 SONGS BURDEN 1   5
    THOUGH ALL WAS DONE IN COMMON AS BEFORE: . . . .   635 CUCHULAIN COMF   24
    AND COMMON MEN THAT SLEEP. . . . .   736 IN CHURCH   8
COMMONEST
    AIMED AT THE COMMONEST EAR, ...   347 FISHERMAN   20
COMMONNESS
    TARA UPROOTED, AND NEW COMMONNESS . . . .   198 SEVEN WOODS   6
    THE COMMONNESS OF THOUGHT AND IMAGES . . . .   384 VISION ROBART   61
COMMONPLACE
    WITH 'MINISHED BEAUTY, MULTIPLIED COMMONPLACE, ...   472 ALL SOUL NIGHT   45
    DIMINISHED BEAUTY, MULTIPLIED COMMONPLACE: . . . .   472 ALL SOUL NIGHT   V 45
COMMUNE
    HE HOLDS DEEP COMMUNE WITH HIS HEART: . . . .   99 FOXHUNTER   43
COMMUNIST
    AND TO HIMSELF CRIED, "COMMUNIST!" . . . .   725 LEGEND   15
COMPANIES
    AND OF THE WAYWARD TWILIGHT COMPANIES . . . .   136 TO SOME I TALK   6
    AND OF THE WANDERING TWILIGHT COMPANIES . . . .   136 TO SOME I TALK   V   6
COMPANION
    DID YOUR COMPANION WANDER AWAY. . . . .   6 OISIN 1   52
    IS THY COMPANION GONE FROM THEE?" . . . .   6 OISIN 1   V 52
    HAVE YOU MADE GREATNESS YOUR COMPANION, ...   265 THESE CLOUDS   9
    TO PLEASE A COMPANION . . . .   392 EASTER 1916   11
    SEMELE'S LAD A GAY COMPANION. . . . .   446 COLONUS PRAISE   8
    ACQUAINTANCE: COMPANION: . . . .   504 RESULT THOUGHT   1
COMPANIONABLE
    COMPANIONABLE STREAMS OR CLIMB THE AIR: . . . .   323 SWANS AT COOLE   21
    AND THAT A SLIGHT COMPANIONABLE GHOST. . . . .   472 ALL SOUL NIGHT   35
COMPANIONED
    SO MANY YEARS COMPANIONED BY A HOUND, ...   621 HOUND VOICE   4
COMPANIONING
    COMPANIONING THE RIVER'S PILGRIM TORCH. . . . .   703 MOSADA 3   112
COMPANIONS
    COMPANIONS LONG ACCURST AND DEAD, ...   11 OISIN 1   130
    NOR THY COMPANIONS. LET THEM REST, ...   11 OISIN 1   V 130
    REMEMBERING ITS LONG-OARED COMPANIONS, ...   55 OISIN 3   118
    AYE, HORSEMEN FOR COMPANIONS, ...   266 GALWAY RACES   7
    COMPANIONS OF THE CHESHIRE CHEESE, ...   270 GREY ROCK   2
    BUT INWARDLY, SURMISE COMPANIONS . . . .   320 REED WHISPERER   4
    OR MERE COMPANIONS OF MY YOUTH, ...   324 ROBERT GREGORY   7
    THEY WERE MY CLOSE COMPANIONS MANY A YEAR, ...   325 ROBERT GREGORY   41
    CHOOSE YOUR COMPANIONS FROM THE BEST: . . . .   335 YOUNG BEAUTY   4
    AND CERTAIN LOST COMPANIONS OF MY OWN. . . . .   342 SHEP GOATHERD   78
    MY COMPANIONS, TWO AND TWO, ...   705 DAWN-SONG   7
COMPANIONSHIP
    COMPANIONSHIP IN THOSE MYSTERIOUS THINGS . . . .   465 HARUN RASHID   92
COMPANIONSHIPS
    UNLANGUID AS THE BIRDS, IN PROUD COMPANIONSHIPS: . . . .   30 OISIN 2   V 14C
COMPANY
    "THE RED BRANCH CAMP IN A GREAT COMPANY . . . .   108 CUCHULAIN SEA   33
    "THE RED BRANCH GATHER A GREAT COMPANY . . . .   108 CUCHULAIN SEA   V 33
    IN EVERY COMPANY . . . .   131 OLD PENSIONER   4
    TRUE BROTHER OF A COMPANY . . . .   137 TO IRELAND   2
    TRUE BROTHER OF THAT COMPANY . . . .   137 TO IRELAND   V   2
    HAS TIRED OF HIS OWN COMPANY? . . . .   303 HOUR DAWN   35
    GROWN TIRED OF HIS OWN COMPANY? . . . .   303 HOUR DAWN   V 37
    WITH EVERY SORT OF COMPANY, ...   335 YOUNG BEAUTY   2
    MY TRADE ALLOWS: CHOSEN MY COMPANY, ...   352 PEOPLE   20
    AND ALL HIS SACRED COMPANY . . . .   386 ROBARTES DANCE   27
    BUT BECKONED TO SWEET COMPANY, ...   400 DEMON BEAST   18
    A COMPANY OF FRIENDS, A CONSCIENCE SET AT EASE, ...   427 PHANTOM HATRED   37
    A SCENE WELL SET AND EXCELLENT COMPANY. . . . .   489 COOLE PARK 29   16
    THAT THE SWORDSMEN AND THE LADIES CAN STILL KEEP COMPANY, . 581 CURSE CROMWELL   20
    IN SOME GOOD COMPANY, ...   605 YOU CONTENT   18
    THAT PALE, LONG-VISAGED COMPANY . . . .   637 BEN BULBEN   7

```
                                                         PAGE     TITLE              LINE
COMPANY   (CONTINUED)
    THAT PALE, LONG VISAGED COMPANY  . . . . . . . .     637 BEN BULBEN       V    7
    BY THOSE WAN STARS THAT SIT IN COMPANY . . . . . .   691 MOSADA 1             26
    I'M NOT OF THAT PALE COMPANY WHOSE FEET . . . . .    699 MOSADA 3             20
COMPARES
    COMPARES THE SOLITARY SOUL TO A SWAN;  . . . . . .   430 NINETEEN 19          60
COMPASS
    THAT SEEMED TO WHIRL UPON A COMPASS POINT, . . . .   489 COOLE PARK 29   V   21
COMPASS-POINT
    THAT SEEMED TO WHIRL UPON A COMPASS-POINT, . . . .   489 COOLE PARK 29       21
COMPEL
    BUT ALL THAT'S RAVING.  WHO IS THERE CAN COMPEL . . .237 SHADOW WATER B      333
COMPELLING
    COMPELLING IT TO STUDY  . . . . . . . . . . . .      416 TOWER               182
COMPELS
    WHOSE BLADE COMPELS, AND WAIT TILL THEY HAVE FOUND . 108 CUCHULAIN SEA        37
    WHOSE BLADE COMPELS, AND BID THEM SEND YOU ONE  . . .108 CUCHULAIN SEA   V   37
COMPENSATION
    A COMPENSATION FOR THE PANG OF HIS BIRTH, . . . . .  444 SCHOOL CHILDR        39
COMPETE
    FOR HOW CAN YOU COMPETE, . . . . . . . . . . .       291 TO A FRIEND          4
COMPLACENCY
    NOTHING BUT GRIP OF CLAW, AND THE EYE'S COMPLACENCY, . 427 PHANTOM HATRED     31
COMPLACENT
    THE MERRY LAMBS AND THE COMPLACENT KINE, . . . . .    75 ANASHU VIJAYA        86
    THE MERRY LAMBS AND ALL THE KINE COMPLACENT, . . .    75 ANASHU VIJAYA   V   86
    THE GIDDY BEE'S COMPLACENT CROON, . . . . . . . .    736 SUMMER EVENING        5
COMPLAIN
    I'VE NOTHING TO COMPLAIN OF BUT HEARTBURN, . . . .   227 SHADOW WATER B  V 116A
    STAND AT MY DOOR, AND I COMPLAIN . . . . . . . .     424 ROAD AT DOOR          8
COMPLAINED
    COMPLAINED OF THE PEOPLE."  ALL I COULD REPLY . . . . 352 PEOPLE             29
COMPLAINING
    BUT THERE'S NO GOOD COMPLAINING, FOR MONEY'S RANT IS ON. 580 CURSE CROMWELL   10
COMPLETE
    THOSE MASTERFUL IMAGES BECAUSE COMPLETE . . . . . .  630 CIRCUS ANIMALS       33
    WHEN BEAUTY IS COMPLETE . . . . . . . . . . . . .    786 YOUR HEART           29
COMPLETED
    FOR PERFECTED, COMPLETED, AND IMMOVABLE . . . . . .  375 PHASES OF MOON V     81
COMPLETENESS
    COMPLETENESS OF THEIR PASSIONS WON; . . . . . . .    637 BEN BULBEN            9
COMPLETES
    HE COMPLETES HIS PARTIAL MIND, . . . . . . . . .     638 BEN BULBEN           30
COMPLEXION
    COMPLEXION AND FORM PROVE SUPERHUMAN,  . . . . . .   637 BEN BULBEN            6
COMPLEXITIES
    ALL MERE COMPLEXITIES, . . . . . . . . . . . . .     497 BYZANTIUM            7
    AND ALL COMPLEXITIES OF MIRE OR BLOOD. . . . . . .   498 BYZANTIUM            24
    AND ALL COMPLEXITIES OF FURY LEAVE, . . . . . . .    498 BYZANTIUM            29
COMPLEXITY
    BREAK BITTER FURIES OF COMPLEXITY, . . . . . . .     498 BYZANTIUM            37
COMPLIMENT
    AND WHEN I PASS A COMPLIMENT . . . . . . . . . .     453 DEATH OF HARE         3
COMPOSE
    COULD BUT COMPOSE MAN'S IMAGE AND HIS CRY. . . . . . 120 SORROW OF LOVE      12
COMPOSITE
    THAT BLEST SOULS ARE NOT COMPOSITE, . . . . . . .    387 ROBARTES DANCE       44
    OR MAYBE SUBSTANCE CAN BE COMPOSITE, . . . . . . .   619 BRONZE HEAD          12
    OR MAY BE SUBSTANCE CAN BE COMPOSITE, . . . . . .    619 BRONZE HEAD     V   12
COMPOUNDED
    SO MUCH COMPOUNDED OF HIGH COURTESY . . . . . . .    205 ADAMS CURSE          24
COMPREHENSION
    WHAT HAS NO COMPREHENSION IN'T, . . . . . . . . .    452 HUMAN DIGNITY         3
    WHAT HAS NOT COMPREHENSION IN'T; . . . . . . . .     452 HUMAN DIGNITY   V    3
COMRADE
    AND HE, OF HIS HIGH COMRADE SORROW DREAMING, . . . .  67 SAD SHEPHERD         2
COMRADES
    SINCE, TAVERN COMRADES, YOU HAVE DIED, . . . . . .   273 GREY ROCK            49
    FOR THOSE NEW COMRADES THEY HAVE FOUND, . . . . .    395 SIXTEEN DEAD         15
    HIS CHOSEN COMRADES THOUGHT AT SCHOOL  . . . . . .   576 WHAT THEN             1
    SLEW THEE, POOR SIBYL!  COMRADES THOU AND I; . . .   675 ISLE STAT II 3      235
CON
    IN MEMORY OF EVA GORE-BOOTH AND CON MARKIEWICZ  . . .475 EVA GORE-BOOTH       T
CONAN
    CAOILTE, AND CONAN, AND FINN WERE THERE, . . . . .     3 OISIN 1             13
    CAOILTE, CONAN, AND FINN CAME NEAR, . . . . . . .     10 OISIN 1            111
    FIN, CONAN, OSCAR, MANY MORE, THE TIDE . . . . . .    44 OISIN 2          V 228A
    WHAT PLACE HAVE CAOILTE AND CONAN, AND BRAN, SCEOLAN, 61 OISIN 3           195
        LOMAIR?
    I WILL GO TO CAOILTE, AND CONAN, AND BRAN, SCEOLAN, LOMAIR, 63 OISIN 3      223
    TO FIN, CAOLTE, AND CONAN, AND BRAN, SGEOLAN, LOMAIR. . . 63 OISIN 3     V 224
CONAN'S
    AH, SWEET TO ME NOW WERE EVEN BALD CONAN'S SLANDEROUS 55 OISIN 3           116
        TONGUE!
CONCEIVE
    CONCEIVE A THING SO SAD AND SOFT, A GENTLE THING LIKE ME?  77 INDIAN ON GOD  16
CONCEIVED
    WHEN WORLD-TRANSFORMING CHARLEMAGNE WAS CONCEIVED? . . . 560 WHENCE COME    12
CONCEIVES
    CONCEIVES A CHANGELESS WORK OF ART. . . . . . . . .  421 MY TABLE            14
```

159

CONCENTRATION
    BUT SEEMS A CONCENTRATION OF THE SKY;   . . . . 490 COOLE BALLYLEE   18
CONCERNING
    TWO POEMS CONCERNING PEASANT VISIONARIES A CRADLE SONG 146 UNAPPEAS HOST V T
    TWO POEMS BY O'SULLIVAN THE RED CONCERNING MARY LAVELL. 157 POET BELOVED V T
CONCH
    WHEN GONG AND CONCH DECLARE THE HOUR TO BLESS . . . . . 611 STATUES   23
CONCHUBAR
    YOUNG SUBTLE CONCHUBAR SAT CLOSE BY ME . . . . 102 FERGUS DRUID   10
    AND CONCHUBAR, THE RED BRANCH KING OF KINGS, ... 109 CUCHULAIN SEA   45
    THEN CONCHUBAR SENT THAT SWEET-THROATED MAID, ... 110 CUCHULAIN SEA   72
    THEN CONCHUBAR, THE SUBTLEST OF ALL MEN, ... 110 CUCHULAIN SEA   75
CONCHUBAR'S
    . . . MADE CONCHUBAR'S SWORD-BLADE OF OLD. . . . . . . 52 OISIN 3   80
CONCOBAR
    THEN CONCOBAR SENT THAT SWEET THROATED MAID . . . . . 110 CUCHULAIN SEA V 72
CONDEMNED
    THE OLDER IS CONDEMNED TO DEATH, ... 475 EVA GORE-BOOTH   7
CONDUCT
    BETTER CONDUCT MYSELF OR HAVE MORE . . . . 507 STREAM AND SUN   9
    CONDUCT AND WORK GROW COARSE, AND COARSE THE SOUL, . . . 564 GYRES   17
CONES
    THOSE CONES AND CUBES AND GYRES, THOSE MIDNIGHT THINGS, 469 HARUN RASHID V 184
CONEYS
    FROM HUMAN THOUGHT, AS HARES AND MICE AND CONEYS . . . . 218 WOODS OF COOLE   31
CONFER
    SO GREAT A GLORY DID THE SONG CONFER. . . . . 410 TOWER   40
CONFESS
    I WILL CONFESS IT ALL. WHAT DO I CARE, ... 245 SHADOW WATER B   485
CONFESSION
    A FIRST CONFESSION . . . . 532 FIRST CONFESS   T
    A LAST CONFESSION . . . . 538 LAST CONFESS   T
    SHE MADE A FULL CONFESSION. . . . . 571 THREE BUSHES   66
CONFIDENCE
    HER CONFIDENCE IN MINE, OR EVEN LOSE . . . . 469 HARUN RASHID   176
    CAN WITH A FITTING CONFIDENCE REPLY. . . . . 494 AT ALGECIRAS   18
    HIS CONFIDENCE . . . . 517 HIS CONFIDENCE   T
CONFLAGRATION
    SHOULD THE CONFLAGRATION CLIMB, ... 476 EVA GORE-BOOTH   28
    WHEN THE CONFLAGRATION OF THEIR PASSION SINKS, ... 556 RIBH PATRICK   8
CONFRONTING
    CONFRONTING MURDEROUS MEN . . . . 476 DEATH   8
CONFUSEDLY
    A MAN CONFUSEDLY IN A HALF DREAM . . . . 351 HER PRAISE   8
    SHE MOVED HER LIMBS CONFUSEDLY AS THOUGH . . . . . . 466 HARUN RASHID V 125A
CONFUSION
    THERE CANNOT BE, CONFUSION OF OUR SOUND FORGOT, ... 291 PAUDEEN   7
    CONFUSION OF THE DEATH-BED OVER, IS IT SENT . . . . . 316 COLD HEAVEN   10
    IN THE CONFUSION OF ITS NIGHT-DARK FOLDS, ... 470 HARUN RASHID   192
    CONFUSION OF THE BED, ... 599 SPIRIT MEDIUM   4
    CONFUSION FELL UPON OUR THOUGHT. . . . . 639 BEN BULBEN   67
CONGEALED
    LONG YEARS AGO, AND UNTO STONE CONGEALED. . . . . . . 656 ISLE STAT I 3   28
CONHOR
    . . . MADE ARMOUR FOR CONHOR OF OLD. . . . . 52 OISIN 3 V 80
CONJUNCTIONS
    CONJUNCTIONS . . . . 562 CONJUNCTIONS   T
CONNACHT
    WELL KNOWN FOR HORSEMANSHIP TO CONNACHT MEN . . . . . 325 ROBERT GREGORY V 34
CONNEMARA
    ON MUNSTER GRASS AND CONNEMARA SKIES. . . . . 130 BOOK STORIES   24
    ON MUNSTER GRASS, OR CONNEMARA SKIES. . . . . 130 BOOK STORIES V 24
    IN GREY CONNEMARA CLOTHES . . . . 347 FISHERMAN   4
    AND GREY CONNEMARA CLOTH, ... 348 FISHERMAN   30
    THEIR CONNEMARA CLOTH WORN OUT OF SHAPE; . . . . . . 372 PHASES OF MOON   4
CONNOLLY
    AND CONNOLLY AND PEARSE . . . . 394 EASTER 1916   76
    SAID PEARSE TO CONNOLLY, ... 396 ROSE TREE   2
    JAMES CONNOLLY REPLIED, ... 396 ROSE TREE   8
    SAID PEARSE TO CONNOLLY, ... 396 ROSE TREE   14
    HE TOLD PEARSE AND CONNOLLY . . . . 585 ORAHILLY   12
    THEN ON PEARSE AND CONNOLLY . . . . 585 ORAHILLY   23
    THE PLAYER CONNOLLY, ... 608 SONGS BURDEN 3   11
CONOR
    . . . MADE ARMOUR FOR CONOR THE OLD. . . . . 52 OISIN 3 V 80
CONQUER
    TO CONQUER AMONG THE COUNTRIES OF THE NORTH. . . . . . 757 SHADOW WATER A   200
CONQUERED
    AND DROWNED THE TREASURES OF NINE CONQUERED NATIONS, . . 235 SHADOW WATER B   287
CONQUEROR
    ROSE: SOME CONQUEROR DREW REIN . . . . 502 VACILLATION   64
CONQUERORS
    CONQUERORS . . . . 499 VACILLATION V T
CONQUEST
    PASSION OR CONQUEST, WANDER WHERE THEY WILL, ... 323 SWANS AT COOLE   23
CONSCIENCE
    A STERNER CONSCIENCE AND A FRIENDLIER HOME, ... 321 REED WHISPERER   8
    OR ANYTHING CALLED CONSCIENCE ONCE; . . . . 413 TOWER   118
    A COMPANY OF FRIENDS, A CONSCIENCE SET AT EASE, ... 427 PHANTOM HATRED   37
    THAT NONE MIGHT KNOW THAT HE WAS CONSCIENCE STRUCK, . . . 462 HARUN RASHID V 38
    CONSCIENCE . . . . 499 VACILLATION V T

		PAGE	TITLE	LINE

CONSCIENCE (CONTINUED)
MY CONSCIENCE OR MY VANITY APPALLED. . . . . 501 VACILLATION   56
NOR SATISFIED CONSCIENCE, BUT THAT GREAT FAMILY . . . . 579 DOR WELLESLEY   14
CONSCIENCE-STRUCK
THAT NONE MIGHT KNOW THAT HE WAS CONSCIENCE-STRUCK-- . . 462 HARUN RASHID   38
CONSECRATED
THE CONSECRATED BLADE UPON MY KNEES . . . . 477 SELF AND SOUL   9
THE CONSECRATED SWORD UPON MY KNEES . . . . 477 SELF AND SOUL   V   9
CONSIDER
CONSIDER BEAUTY A SUFFICIENT END, ... 403 FOR DAUGHTER   21
CONSIDER MOST TO MAGNIFY, OR TO BLESS, ... 418 ANCEST HOUSES   39
CONSIDERATION
CONSIDERATION, GENEROSITY, ... 244 SHADOW WATER B   456
CONSIDERED
YET, NOW I HAVE CONSIDERED IT, I FIND . . . . . . 411 TOWER   50
CAME TO THE LEAST CONSIDERED OF HIS COURTIERS; . . . . 462 HARUN RASHID   42
CONSIDERING
CONSIDERING THAT, ALL HATRED DRIVEN HENCE, ... 405 FOR DAUGHTER   65
BRING UP OUT OF THAT DEEP CONSIDERING MIND . . . . . 413 TOWER   106
CONSIDERING WHAT WILD INFANCY . . . . 440 WISDOM   19
CONSIDERS
RIBH CONSIDERS CHRISTIAN LOVE INSUFFICIENT . . . . . 558 RIBH CHRISTIAN   T
CONSOLATION
THE CONSOLATION . . . . 255 WORDS   V   T
CONSOLATION . . . . 534 CONSOLATION   T
CONSPIRACY
FOR SOME CONSPIRACY, ... 131 OLD PENSIONER   8
CONSPIRING
CONSPIRING AMONG THE IGNORANT. . . . . 475 EVA GORE-BOOTH   9
CONSTELLATIONS
. . . WHEN A PART OF THE CONSTELLATIONS OF HEAVEN . . . 177 PAST GREATNESS   T
HER BEAUTY AS THE CONSTELLATIONS POUR . . . . . . 279 TWO KINGS   V 62B
CONSTITUTE
THAT CONSTITUTE THE WILD, ... 601 THOSE IMAGES   10
CONSTRAINED
CONSTRAINED, ARRAIGNED, BAFFLED, BENT AND UNBENT . . . . 382 VISION ROBART   9
CONSTRUCTED
GREAT WORKS CONSTRUCTED THERE IN NATURE'S SPITE . . . . 488 COOLE PARK 29   5
CONSUME
SOME BURN DAMP FAGGOTS, OTHERS MAY CONSUME . . . . 327 ROBERT GREGORY   81
CONSUME MY HEART AWAY; SICK WITH DESIRE . . . . . 408 SAIL BYZANTIUM   21
AND HALF AND HALF CONSUME WHAT THEY RENEW, ... 500 VACILLATION   15
CONSUMED
EVERYTHING THAT IS NOT GOD CONSUMED WITH INTELLECTUAL FIRE. 481 BLOOD- AND MOON   30
WHERE FOR ITS MOMENT BOTH SEEM LOST, CONSUMED. . . . 555 RIBH AT TOMB   16
CONSUMES
THE PAINTER'S BRUSH CONSUMES HIS DREAMS; . . . . . 438 SONGS PLAY 2   12
CONSUMING
IN TRUTH'S CONSUMING ECSTASY, ... 139 TO IRELAND   42
CONSUMING ITS RAG AND BONE, ... 575 ACRE OF GRASS   11
CONSUMMATION
A MEASURELESS CONSUMMATION THAT HE DREAMED. . . . . 324 ROBERT GREGORY   24
CONTACT
MUST COME FROM CONTACT WITH THE SOIL, FROM THAT . . . 603 GALLERY REVIS   43
CONTACT EVERYTHING ANTAEUS-LIKE GREW STRONG. . . . . 603 GALLERY REVIS   44
CONTACT ALL THINGS ANTAEUS-LIKE GREW STRONG; . . . . 603 GALLERY REVIS   V   44
CONTAGION
TILL SUDDENLY IN GRIEF'S CONTAGION CAUGHT, ... 537 HER VISION   22
BRED OUT OF THE CONTAGION OF THE THRONG, ... 542 PARN FUNERAL 1   27
CONTEMPLATING
TWO CONTEMPLATING PASSIONS CHOSE ONE THEME . . . . 466 HARUN RASHID   117
CONTEMPLATION
CAUGHT UP IN CONTEMPLATION, THE MIND'S EYE . . . . 375 PHASES OF MOON   79
IN CONTEMPLATION HAD THOSE THREE SO WROUGHT . . . . 384 VISION ROBART   45
WHERE SLIPPERED CONTEMPLATION FINDS HIS EASE . . . . 418 ANCEST HOUSES   30
CONTEMPLATIONS
MY CONTEMPLATIONS ARE OF TIME . . . . 131 OLD PENSIONER   11
CONTEMPLATIVE
HAVING GROWN SLUGGISH AND CONTEMPLATIVE. . . . . . 325 ROBERT GREGORY   40
CONTEND
CITY AND CITY MAY CONTEND, ... 540 FROM ANTIGONE   12
CONTENT
BENEATH HAD PACED CONTENT; WE HELD OUR WAY . . . . 36 OISIN 2   103
SHOUTED AND HAILED HIM. STILL HE HUNG CONTENT, . . . 36 OISIN 2   V 107
THAT SEA-GOD'S NAME, WHO IN A DEEP CONTENT . . . . 38 OISIN 2   129
SEA-GOD, THAT ONCE, TO GIVE HIS SLAVES CONTENT, . . . 38 OISIN 2   V 129
THAT SEA GOD'S NAME, WHO IN A DEEP CONTENT . . . . 38 OISIN 2   V 129
IS THE ISLAND OF CONTENT?" "NONE KNOW," SHE SAID; . . . 46 OISIN 2   249
WHO SIGH WITH MINGLED SORROW AND CONTENT, ... 136 TO SOME I TALK   7
TO FILL YOUR HEART WITH CONTENT." . . . . . . 167 BLESSED   20
HOW COULD WE BE SO SOON CONTENT, ... 193 BAILE AILLINN   95
AND BEEN CONTENT TO LIVE. . . . . 256 WORDS   16
THE HABITUAL CONTENT OF EACH WITH EACH . . . . . 258 KING NO KING   15
SPONTANEOUS JOY AND NATURAL CONTENT . . . . . . 260 FASC DIFFICULT   3
SO THAT THE WANDERING FOOT'S CONTENT. . . . . . 276 GREY ROCK   131
LET THESE CONTENT YOU AND BE GONE AGAIN; . . . . 292 TO A SHADE   8
I'LL SAY AND MAYBE DREAM I HAVE DRAWN CONTENT, . . . 333 LIVING BEAUTY   V   1
MY DISCONTENTED HEART TO DRAW CONTENT . . . . . 334 LIVING BEAUTY   3
CAN BE CONTENT WITH ARGUMENT AND DEAL . . . . . 409 TOWER   14
I AM CONTENT WITH THAT, ... 430 NINETEEN 19   V   61
AND THAT SHE DREAMED AWAKE CONTENT TO TOUCH . . . . 466 HARUN RASHID   V 125C

161

		PAGE	TITLE		LINE

CONTENT   (CONTINUED)
    I AM CONTENT TO LIVE IT ALL AGAIN • • • • • • • • • 479 SELF AND SOUL   57
    I AM CONTENT TO FOLLOW TO ITS SOURCE • • • • • • • 479 SELF AND SOUL   65
    CONTENT TO TRACE THAT MISERY TO ITS SOURCE, • • • • 479 SELF AND SOUL   V 65
    CONTENT OR JOY; A LAST INHERITOR • • • • • • • • • 491 COOLE BALLYLEE   30
    HAD I NOT FOUND CONTENT AMONG THE SHOWS • • • • • • 499 MOTHER OF GOD   6
    IF YOU ARE WORTH MY HOPE; NEITHER CONTENT • • • • • 579 DOR WELLESLEY   13
    ALL NEIGHBOURLY CONTENT AND EASY TALK ARE GONE, • • 580 CURSE CROMWELL   9
    I AM CONTENT TO STAND AND SING • • • • • • • • • • 582 ROGER CASEMENT V 21
    OR STAY CONTENT ON THE LOW, • • • • • • • • • • • 589 OLD WICKED MAN   49
    ARE YOU CONTENT? • • • • • • • • • • • • • • • • 604 YOU CONTENT   T
    I CANNOT, BUT I AM NOT CONTENT. • • • • • • • • • 604 YOU CONTENT   8
    BUT I AM NOT CONTENT. • • • • • • • • • • • • • • 605 YOU CONTENT   24
    FORGAEL, SEEK OUT CONTENT, WHERE OTHER MEN • • • • 750 SHADOW WATER A   71
    AND CAN NEVER BE CONTENT • • • • • • • • • • • • 777 SONG DEIRDRE 2   2
CONTENTED
    THAT I MAY CONTENTED PASS • • • • • • • • • • • • 97 FOXHUNTER   11
    I AM CONTENTED, FOR I KNOW THAT QUIET • • • • • • 198 SEVEN WOODS   10
    SINCE HE WHO HAD BEEN CONTENTED LONG, • • • • • • 361 ALF POLLEXFEN   28
    CONTENTED THAT A TROUBLED MIRROR SHOW IT, • • • • 430 NINETEEN 19   V 62
    AND I GROW HALF CONTENTED TO BE BLIND! • • • • • 473 ALL SOUL NIGHT   70
CONTEST
    THE SHEPHERDS' CONTEST OF SONG • • • • • • • • • 646 ISLE STAT I 1 V T
CONTINUAL
    ARE LOVE, AND A CONTINUAL FAREWELL." • • • • • • 81 EPHEMERA   24
    CONTINUAL MUSIC TILL THE MORNING BREAK, • • • • • 137 TO SOME I TALK V 14
CONTINUALLY
    AND NIAMH SANG CONTINUALLY • • • • • • • • • • • 11 OISIN 1   134
    FOR FAIRY SONGS CONTINUALLY • • • • • • • • • • • 11 OISIN 1   V 134
    FOR NEAVE SANG CONTINUALLY • • • • • • • • • • • 11 OISIN 1   V 134
CONTRADICT
    HE CANNOT CONTRADICT ME. IS THAT TRUE? • • • • • 249 SHADOW WATER B V 563
CONTRAPUNTAL
    A CONTRAPUNTAL SERPENT HISS, • • • • • • • • • • 573 LADYS 3RD SONG 10
CONTROL
    FOR THAT'S A PASSION IN MY OWN CONTROL, • • • • • 558 RIBH CHRISTIAN 4
CONVENT
    I HAD BETTER FIND A CONVENT AND TURN NUN! • • • • 448 HERO GIRL FOOL 11
CONVENTIONAL
    NO MARBLE, NO CONVENTIONAL PHRASE! • • • • • • • 640 BEN BULBEN   89
CONVERGE
    THERE ALL THE GYRES CONVERGE IN ONE, • • • • • • 557 THERE   3
CONVERSE
    THEN FEAST, MAKING CONVERSE OF WARS, • • • • • • 62 OISIN 3   212
    THEN FEAST, MAKING CONVERSE OF EIRE, OF WARS, • • 62 OISIN 3   V 212
    THAT CONVERSE BONE TO BONE? • • • • • • • • • • 395 SIXTEEN DEAD   18
CONVICTED
    THEY CONVICTED US OF GUILT! • • • • • • • • • • 476 EVA GORE-BOOTH 31
    CONVICTED COWARDS ALL, BY KINDRED SLAIN • • • • • 634 CUCHULAIN COMF 21
CONVICTION
    THE BEST LACK ALL CONVICTION, WHILE THE WORST • • 402 SECOND COMING   7
    THE BEST LACK CONVICTION, WHILE THE WORST • • • • 402 SECOND COMING V 7
CONVINCE
    I TOOK NO TROUBLE TO CONVINCE, • • • • • • • • • 624 APPARITIONS   3
COOING
    ABOUT A SUN-FLUSHED DOVE-COT, COOING, CLING • • • 710 FERENCZ RENYI   20
COOK
    COOK BARACH, THE TRAITOR! AND WARWARD, • • • • • 53 OISIN 3   90
    THE OLD COOK ENRAGED, • • • • • • • • • • • • • 349 HAWK   5
    THAT IT CAN TAKE WHAT FORM COOK NATURE FANCIES • 377 PHASES OF MOON 115
    THAT IT CAN TAKE WHAT FORM COOK NATURE FANCY • • 377 PHASES OF MOON V 115
    I COOK AND CHANGE MY PLATE, • • • • • • • • • • 607 SONGS BURDEN 2 6
    THE TOWER'S OLD COOK THAT MUST CLIMB AND CLAMBER • 636 BLACK TOWER   21
COOKING
    COOKING CHESTNUTS ON THE BARS-- • • • • • • • • 737 IN FIRELIGHT   2
    COOKING CHESTNUTS ON THE BARS. • • • • • • • • • 737 IN FIRELIGHT   12
COOL
    LAY 'NEATH US! OF ITS HOLLOW COOL • • • • • • • 17 OISIN 1   V 241
    AND CHAPLET THEIR CALM BROWS WITH LEAFAGE COOL! • 127 DREAM OF FAERY V 32
    WIND AND UNWIND THEIR DANCES WHEN THE LIGHT GROWS COOL • • 203 WITHER BOUGHS 13
    WIND AND UNWIND DANCING WHEN THE LIGHT GROWS COOL • • 203 WITHER BOUGHS V 13
    FOR THERE CAME AN AIR-BREATH COOL • • • • • • • 667 ISLE STAT II 3 27
COOLE
    I WALKED AMONG THE SEVEN WOODS OF COOLE! • • • • 217 WOODS OF COOLE 1
    THE WILD SWANS AT COOLE • • • • • • • • • • • • 322 SWANS AT COOLE T
    COOLE PARK, [NINETEEN-TWENTY-NINE] • • • • • • • 488 COOLE PARK 29   T
    COOLE PARK • • • • • • • • • • • • • • • • • • 488 COOLE PARK 29 V T
    COOLE PARK AND BALLYLEE, [NINETEEN-THIRTY-ONE] • • 490 COOLE BALLYLEE T
    COOLE PARK AND BALLYLEE [NINETEEN-THIRTY-TWO] • • 490 COOLE BALLYLEE V T
    COOLE AND BALLYLEE, [NINETEEN-THIRTY-ONE] • • • • 490 COOLE BALLYLEE V T
    IN COOLE DEMESNE, AND THERE TO FINISH UP • • • • 490 COOLE BALLYLEE 6
COPIED
    HER DOMINO, HER PANNIERED SKIRT COPIED FROM LONGHI! • • 363 DOLLS FACES   7
    AND COPIED OUT WHAT I COULD READ • • • • • • • 584 GHOST ROG CASE 33
COPIES
    FOR THINGS BELOW ARE COPIES, THE GREAT SMARAGDINE TABLET 556 RIBH PATRICK 6
        SAID.
    YET ALL MUST COPY COPIES, ALL INCREASE THEIR KIND! • • • 556 RIBH PATRICK 7
COPSE
    AND IN A COPSE OF BEECHES THERE I STOOD, • • • • • • 490 COOLE BALLYLEE 11

	PAGE	TITLE	LINE

COPULATE
    COPULATE IN THE FOAM. . . . . 612 NEWS ORACLE 36
COPY
    AND COPY THEIR PROUD STEADY GAZE. . . . . 273 GREY ROCK 64
    YET ALL MUST COPY COPIES, ALL INCREASE THEIR KIND! . . . 556 RIBH PATRICK 7
    BUT COPY SOME ONE ACTION, ... 600 SPIRIT MEDIUM 13
COQUETRY
    NOTHING BUT COQUETRY. . . . . 532 FIRST CONFESS 6
CORAL
    DROPPING AT EVE IN CORAL BAYS . . . . 78 INDIAN TO LOVE V 19
CORBETS
    SANDYMOUNT CORBETS, THAT NOTABLE MAN . . . . 604 YOU CONTENT 13
CORD
    UNLOOSE THE CORD, AND THEY WILL WRAP YOU ROUND. . . . . 104 FERGUS DRUID 30
CORDELIA
    THAT'S OPHELIA, THAT CORDELIA! . . . . 565 LAPIS LAZULI 11
CORDS
    OVER THE LITTLE SILVER CORDS, ... 146 FISH 6
    FORGIVE ME! IT WAS ALLAH'S WILL. THE CORDS. . . . . . 695 MOSADA 1 109
    FORGIVE ME! IT WAS ALLAH'S WILL. NOW CORDS. . . . . 695 MOSADA 1 V 109
    I HAVE CUT THE CORDS THAT HELD THIS GALLEY TO OURS. . . 768 SHADOW WATER A V 421
CORE
    I HEAR IT IN THE DEEP HEART'S CORE. . . . . 117 ISLE INNISFREE 12
    SHALL LIGHT UPON A PLACE IN THE WORLD'S CORE, ... 231 SHADOW WATER B 212
    YOU ARE NOT THE WORLD'S CORE. O NO, NO, NO! . . . . 234 SHADOW WATER B 277
    YOU ARE NOT ITS CORE. MY TEETH ARE IN THE WORLD, . . . 235 SHADOW WATER B 279
CORMAC'S
    IN CORMAC'S RUINED HOUSE. . . . . 384 VISION ROBART 68
CORMORANTS
    THE CORMORANTS SHIVER ON THEIR ROCKS! . . . . 84 MAD KING GOLL 42
CORN
    AND WAKES THE SLUGGARD SEEDS OF CORN, ... 18 OISIN 1 263
    CRIES TO THE SLUGGARD SEEDS OF CORN, ... 18 OISIN 1 V 263
    SEND PEACE ON ALL THE LANDS AND FLICKERING CORN.-- . . . 71 ANASHU VIJAYA 1
    THAT MEN THRESHED CORN AT MIDNIGHT BY A TRESS, ... 170 SECRET ROSE 26
    AND THE WAVES BOWED BEFORE IT LIKE MOWN CORN, ... 657 ISLE STAT I 3 56
    AND THRICE THE CORN AROUND THE SICKLES FLAMED, ... 690 MOSADA 1 3
CORNER
    CHIMNEY CORNER, GARDEN WALK, ... 499 MOTHER OF GOD 8
    WHEN SEA-WIND SWEPT THE CORNER, STANDS! . . . . 566 LAPIS LAZULI 32
CORNERS   SEE STREET-CORNERS
    AND LISTEN AT THE CORNERS HAS NOT COME! . . . . . . 293 TO A SHADE 22
    THE CORNERS OF THIS EYE . . . . 518 HIS CONFIDENCE 3
    AND THERE AT ALL STREET CORNERS . . . . 596 COLONEL MARTIN V 55
CORNFIELD
    QUITE SOON THE CORNFIELD, WHERE THE POPPIES GROW, . . . 699 MOSADA 3 7
    ALONG THE CORNFIELD, WHERE THE POPPIES GROW, ... 699 MOSADA 3 V 7
CORPSE
    I HELD A DRIPPING CORPSE, WITH LIVID CHOP . . . . . 40 OISIN 2 V 178
    AND I BUT HELD A CORPSE, WITH LIVID CHOP . . . . . . 40 OISIN 2 V 178
    AND SUNKEN SHAPE, A NINE DAYS' CORPSE SEA-DASHED-- . . . 40 OISIN 2 V 179
CORRIDOR
    THROUGH MANY A SACRED CORRIDOR . . . . 156 FORGOT BEAUTY 12
COSGRAVE
    HAD COSGRAVE EATEN PARNELL'S HEART, THE LAND'S . . . . 543 PARN FUNERAL 2 5
COSIMO
    AND WHEN THEY DROVE OUT COSIMO, ... 288 TO WEALTHY MAN 20
COSSETING
    THEY'D SOONER LEAVE THEIR COSSETING . . . . 455 HIS MEMORIES 9
COST
    HE THAT MADE THIS KNOWS ALL THE COST, ... 202 NEVER GIVE ALL 13
    PARDON, AND YOU THAT DID NOT WEIGH THE COST, ... 269 PARDON FATHERS V 9
COT   SEE DOVE-COT
    WERE WE NOT BORN IN THE PEASANT'S COT . . . . 615 MARCH SONGS 2 13
    WE WERE NOT BORN IN THE PEASANT'S COT . . . . 615 MARCH SONGS 2 V 13
COTTAGE
    GOD GRANT A BLESSING ON THIS TOWER AND COTTAGE . . . . 371 ON GOING HOUSE 1
    THAT SHADES THE ROAD, OR SETTING UP A COTTAGE . . . . 372 ON GOING HOUSE 14
COTTAGES
    FROM SOMEWHERE IN THE NEIGHBOURING COTTAGES. . . . . 411 TOWER 59
    STORM-BEATEN COTTAGES-- . . . . 480 BLOOD AND MOON 7
    STORMBEATEN COTTAGES. . . . . 480 BLOOD AND MOON V 7
COUCH
    COULD SLEEP ON A COUCH OF RUSHES, AND ALL INWROUGHT AND 49 OISIN 3 31
      INLAID.
    COULD SLEEP ON A COUCH OF RUSHES--ROUND AND ABOUT THEM 49 OISIN 3 V 32
      LAID.
COUGH
    ALL SHUFFLE THERE! ALL COUGH IN INK! . . . . 337 SCHOLARS 7
    THEY'LL COUGH IN THE INK TO THE WORLD'S END! . . . . 337 SCHOLARS V 7
COUGHING
    NOT COUGHING, MY HEAD ON MY KNEES, ... 58 OISIN 3 159
    AH ME! TO BE SHAKEN WITH COUGHING AND BROKEN WITH OLD AGE 63 OISIN 3 217
      AND PAIN,
    WITHOUT LAUGHTER, A COUGHING, ALONE WITH REMEMBRANCE AND 63 OISIN 3 V 218
      FEAR!
    SHE KNOWS THAT IT WAS BUT THE CART-HORSE COUGHING . . . 230 SHADOW WATER B 176
COUNCIL
    AND SPOKEN IN THE COUNCIL, AND HEARD TALES . . . . . 748 SHADOW WATER A 28
COUNCILS
    YOU KNOW THE COUNCILS OF THE EVER-LIVING, ... 244 SHADOW WATER B V 450

163

```
                                                          PAGE      TITLE             LINE
COUNSEL
     HAD COME AS IN THE OLD TIMES TO COUNSEL HER,   . . . . .    181 QUEEN MAEVE          42
     HAD COME, AS IN OLD TIMES, TO COUNSEL HER,     . . . . .    181 QUEEN MAEVE      V   42
     ABOUT MY THRESHOLD TO COUNSEL AND TO HELP?"    . . . . .    183 QUEEN MAEVE          82
     ABOUT MY DOOR TO COUNSEL AND TO HELP."         . . . . .    183 QUEEN MAEVE      V  -82
     OUR GIVER OF GOOD COUNSEL AND GOOD LUCK."      . . . . .    185 QUEEN MAEVE         102
COUNSELLED
     WHAT OTHER COULD SO WELL HAVE COUNSELLED US    . . . . .    327 ROBERT GREGORY       73
COUNSELS
     YOU KNOW THE COUNSELS OF THE EVER-LIVING,      . . . . .    244 SHADOW WATER B      450
COUNT
     I COUNT MY GOOD AND BAD,  . . . . . . . . . . . . . .       316 FRIENDS              22
     SINCE I FIRST MADE MY COUNT,  . . . . . . . . . . . .       322 SWANS AT COOLE        8
     COUNT ALL THE PRAISES DUE  . . . . . . . . . . . . .        345 ON WOMAN             15
     AND I, THAT COUNT MYSELF MOST PROSPEROUS,  . . . . . .      423 MY DESCENDANTS       19
     I COUNT THOSE FEATHERED BALLS OF SOOT  . . . . . . .        424 ROAD AT DOOR         11
     COUNT EVERY SIN OF ACTION OR OF THOUGHT;  . . . . . .       479 SELF AND SOUL    V   66
COUNTED
     NOR MAY I LESS BE COUNTED ONE  . . . . . . . . . . .        138 TO IRELAND           17
     HE HAD COUNTED, WHERE LONG YEARS AGO  . . . . . . . .       302 HOUR DAWN             7
     HE COUNTED, WHERE LONG YEARS AGO  . . . . . . . . .         302 HOUR DAWN        V    7
     THEY SAY HE COUNTED GRASS,  . . . . . . . . . . . .         345 ON WOMAN             14
     THAT ALL MY CHILDHOOD COUNTED DEAR;  . . . . . . . .        398 BREAK OF DAY          7
     THE GARDEN PATHS, NOR COUNTED UP THE ROOMS,  . . . . .      466 HARUN RASHID        119
COUNTENANCE
     LACKING THE COUNTENANCE OF OUR FRIENDS. AND YET  . . . .    368 EGO DOMINUS          17
     KEVIN O'HIGGINS' COUNTENANCE THAT WEARS  . . . . . .        601 GALLERY REVIS         5
COUNTENANCES
     THEN THE STARS GROW OUT OF HEAVEN WITH THEIR COUNTENANCES   719 PHANTOM SHIP         30
        FAIR.
COUNTER
     FROM COUNTER OR DESK AMONG GREY  . . . . . . . . . .        392 EASTER 1916           3
COUNTER-TRUTH
     AND THEN A COUNTER-TRUTH FILLED OUT ITS PLAY,  . . . . .    629 CIRCUS ANIMALS       17
COUNTESS
     THE COUNTESS CATHLEEN IN PARADISE  . . . . . . . . .        124 CATHLEEN PARA         T
     ALEEL, HIS COUNTESS; HANRAHAN  . . . . . . . . . .          550 SEVERED HEAD         15
     THE COUNTESS CATHLEEN WAS THE NAME I GAVE IT;  . . . .      629 CIRCUS ANIMALS       18
COUNTING-HOUSE
     AND THE FOOL HEART OF THE COUNTING-HOUSE FEARS ALL  . . .   181 QUEEN MAEVE          21
COUNTLESS
     ON OUR DARK PATHWAY, TILL A COUNTLESS FLIGHT  . . . . .      31 OISIN 2              34
COUNTRIES
     FLED TO FAR COUNTRIES, OR SHELTERED THEMSELVES  . . . .     546 TO SAME TUNE 2        4
     FLED TO FAR COUNTRIES, OR SHELTERED THEMSELVES  . . . .     613 MARCH SONGS 1         4
     TO CONQUER AMONG THE COUNTRIES OF THE NORTH.  . . . . .     757 SHADOW WATER A      200
COUNTRY
     AND FROM WHAT COUNTRY DO YOU RIDE?"  . . . . . . . .          5 OISIN 1              45
     NIAMH, AND MY COUNTRY FAR  . . . . . . . . . . . .            5 OISIN 1              48
     THY NAME, THY KIN, AND THY COUNTRY,"  . . . . . . .           5 OISIN 1          V   44
     AND INTO WHAT COUNTRY DO YOU RIDE?"  . . . . . . . .          5 OISIN 1          V   45
     HIS SUDDEN VENGEANCE WERE A COUNTRY TALE,  . . . . . .      127 DREAM OF FAERY       27
     THAT COUNTRY WHERE A MAN CAN BE SO CROSSED;  . . . . .      130 BOOK STORIES         16
     I HAVE DRUNK ALE FROM THE COUNTRY OF THE YOUNG  . . . .     177 PAST GREATNESS        1
     TALKED OF HIS COUNTRY AND ITS PEOPLE, SANG  . . . . .       180 QUEEN MAEVE           3
     RODE FROM THE COUNTRY OF HER KIN,  . . . . . . . . .        191 BAILE AILLINN        50
     FOR ALL THAT COUNTRY HAD BEEN ASTIR  . . . . . . . .        191 BAILE AILLINN        52
     I KNOW OF THE SLEEPY COUNTRY, WHERE SWANS FLY ROUND  . . .  204 WITHER BOUGHS         7
     TOWARDS THE COUNTRY OF THE DEAD. WHAT MATTER  . . . .       231 SHADOW WATER B      206
     WHAT ARE THEY?  UNTO WHAT COUNTRY DO THEY FLY?  . . . .     247 SHADOW WATER B      523
     "THERE IS A COUNTRY AT THE END OF THE WORLD  . . . . .      247 SHADOW WATER B      530
     WE WOULD RETURN TO OUR OWN COUNTRY, FORGAEL,  . . . . .     248 SHADOW WATER B      539
     IT SHALL BE IN THE COUNTRY OF THE DEAD,  . . . . . .        249 SHADOW WATER B      557
     IF THERE BE SUCH A COUNTRY.  NO, NOT THERE,  . . . . .      249 SHADOW WATER B      558
     TO SOME SURE COUNTRY, SOME FAMILIAR PLACE.  . . . . . .     249 SHADOW WATER B      569
     TO A CERTAIN COUNTRY HOUSE IN TIME OF CHANGE  . . . . .     264 HOUSE SHAKEN     V    T
     OLD COUNTRY SCHOLAR, ROBERT EMMET'S FRIEND,  . . . . .      269 PARDON FATHERS        5
     AND COUNTRY SCHOLAR, ROBERT EMMET'S FRIEND,  . . . . .      269 PARDON FATHERS V      5
     MY COUNTRY IS KILTARTAN CROSS,  . . . . . . . . . .         328 IRISH AIRMAN          5
     HE THAT WAS BEST IN EVERY COUNTRY SPORT  . . . . . .        339 SHEP GOATHERD        17
     AND EVERY COUNTRY CRAFT, AND OF US ALL  . . . . . .         339 SHEP GOATHERD        18
     ARE MET ON THE WASTE HILLS BY COUNTRY MEN  . . . . . .      375 PHASES OF MOON V     76
     BUT TAKE ME FOR SOME DRUNKEN COUNTRY MAN;  . . . . . .      377 PHASES OF MOON V    130
     THAT IS NO COUNTRY FOR OLD MEN.  THE YOUNG  . . . . .       407 SAIL BYZANTIUM        1
     WHEN MOCKING MUSES CHOSE THE COUNTRY WENCH.  . . . . .      413 TOWER                96
     WHAT MORE IS THERE TO SAY?  THAT COUNTRY ROUND  . . . .     430 NINETEEN 19          43
     GREEKS WERE BUT LOVERS; ALL THAT COUNTRY ROUND  . . . .     430 NINETEEN 19      V   43
     WHO COMES INTO THIS COUNTRY, AND HAS COME  . . . . . .      447 COLONUS PRAISE       17
     BECAUSE THIS COUNTRY HAS A PIOUS MIND  . . . . . . .        447 COLONUS PRAISE       25
     THE COUNTRY THINKS NO END OF HIM,  . . . . . . . . .        583 GHOST ROG CASE       13
     AND PARNELL LOVED HIS COUNTRY,  . . . . . . . . . .         587 PARNELLITES          31
     IN COUNTRY SHAWL OR PARIS CLOAK, HAD PUT MY WITS ASTRAY,    592 PILGRIM               3
     SO COME IN RAGS OR COME IN SILK, IN CLOAK OR COUNTRY SHAWL, 593 PILGRIM              22
     SO COME IN RAG OR COME IN SILK, IN CLOAK OR COUNTRY SHAWL,  593 PILGRIM          V   22
     "I KEPT HER MUCH IN THE COUNTRY  . . . . . . . . .          594 COLONEL MARTIN       10
     ON COUNTRY AND ON TOWN,  . . . . . . . . . . . . .          606 SONGS BURDEN 1       24
     HARD-RIDING COUNTRY GENTLEMEN,  . . . . . . . . . .         639 BEN BULBEN           75
     THE SISTER:  "SELL THY COUNTRY, AND THE SHAME  . . . . .    712 FERENCZ RENYI        60
     TOWARDS A COUNTRY WHERE THERE ARE NO KINGS.  . . . . .      755 SHADOW WATER A      165
     THERE--THERE--BY THE OAR.  THE CROWN OF A FAR COUNTRY.  .   763 SHADOW WATER A      310
     AND BID HIM TO YOUR COUNTRY.  I SHOULD WANDER  . . . . .    767 SHADOW WATER A      403
```

PAGE   TITLE   LINE

COUNTRY   (CONTINUED)
   LIVING OR DYING. BID AIBRIC TO YOUR COUNTRY, ...   768 SHADOW WATER A   413
COUNTRYMAN
   BUT TAKE ME FOR SOME DRUNKEN COUNTRYMAN: . . . .   377 PHASES OF MOON   130
   FOUR SONGS FROM THE YOUNG COUNTRYMAN . . . .   451 FIRST LOVE   V   T
   THE YOUNG COUNTRYMAN . . . .   451 FIRST LOVE   V   T
   TWO SONGS FROM THE OLD COUNTRYMAN . . . .   454 EMPTY CUP   V   T
   THE OLD COUNTRYMAN . . . .   454 EMPTY CUP   V   T
   MORE SONGS OF AN OLD COUNTRYMAN . . . .   454 HIS MEMORIES   V   T
COUNTRYMEN
   MY COUNTRYMEN KILTARTAN'S POOR, ...   328 IRISH AIRMAN   6
   ARE MET ON THE WASTE HILLS BY COUNTRYMEN . . . . . .   375 PHASES OF MOON   76
COUNTRY'S
   HE CLAIMED HIS COUNTRY'S NEED WAS MOST, ...   275 GREY ROCK   101
   THAT HE, ALTHOUGH A COUNTRY'S TALK . . . .   422 MY TABLE   29
COUNTRYSIDE
   WHAT STIR RAN THROUGH THE COUNTRYSIDE . . . .   488 CRAZED MOON   10
COUNTRY-SIDE
   THE BEAUTY OF HER COUNTRY-SIDE . . . .   397 POLIT PRISONER   15
COUNTY
   THAT RED-HEADED RECTOR IN COUNTY DOWN, ...   604 YOU CONTENT   11
COUPLE
   ONE--AND ONE--A COUPLE--FIVE TOGETHER: . . . .   233 SHADOW WATER B   249
   A COUPLE OF NIGHT-MOTHS ARE ON THE WING, ...   482 BLOOD AND MOON   46
   A COUPLE OF NIGHT MOTHS ARE ON THE WING, ...   482 BLOOD AND MOON V   46
COUPLED
   COUPLED WITH GOLDEN CHAINS, AND SING AS THEY FLY. . . . .   204 WITHER BOUGHS   18
COUPLES
   THOSE MERRY COUPLES DANCING IN TUNE, ...   3 OISIN 1   9
   BUT ALL THAT RUN IN COUPLES, ON EARTH, IN FLOOD OR AIR,   556 RIBH PATRICK   11
    . . .
   THROW LIKELY COUPLES INTO BED . . . .   606 SONGS BURDEN 1   25
COURAGE
   WITH EQUAL COURAGE IN THAT WHIRLING ROUT: . . . .   186 QUEEN MAEVE   131
   OUR COURAGE BREAKS LIKE AN OLD TREE IN A BLACK WIND AND   207 HANRAHANS SONG   3
     DIES,
   LIKE TUFTED REEDS OUR COURAGE DROOPS IN A BLACK WIND AND   207 HANRAHANS SONG V   3
     DIES:
   WEAK AND WORN AND WEARY OUR COURAGE DROOPS AND DIES . . .   207 HANRAHANS SONG V   8
   MY COURAGE CAME AGAIN. BUT THAT'S NOT ALL. . . . . .   223 SHADOW WATER B   31
   HAD THEY BUT COURAGE EQUAL TO DESIRE? . . . .   256 NO SECOND TROY   5
   HER COURAGE . . . .   365 HER COURAGE   T
   MUCH BOISTEROUS COURAGE, BEFORE LONELINESS . . . . .   473 ALL SOUL NIGHT   72
   SUSTAINS HIS SOUL IN COURAGE OR IN MIGHT. . . . . .   650 ISLE STAT I 1   144
   WAS FORGAEL'S COURAGE THAT THE MUSIC KILLED. . . . .   747 SHADOW WATER A   9
COURAGEOUS
   COURAGEOUS MIRACLES: THE SUNLIGHT SHONE . . . . . .   649 ISLE STAT I 1   113
COURSE   SEE RACE-COURSE WATER-COURSE
   JUDGE OF THE STARS, AND FIND A COURSE FOR US? . . . .   224 SHADOW WATER B   61
   AND MEASURE OUT A COURSE AND BRING US HOME, ...   238 SHADOW WATER B   362
   THERE WHERE THE COURSE IS, ...   266 GALWAY RACES   1
   OUT YONDER, WHERE THE RACE COURSE IS, ...   266 GALWAY RACES   V   1
   CRYING ALOUD AS THE RACE COURSE IS, ...   266 GALWAY RACES   V   14
   THE THIRD: "I'LL HURRY TO THE COURSE . . . .   296 THREE BEGGARS   33
   BUT THE THIRD CRIED: "I'LL TO THE COURSE . . . . . .   296 THREE BEGGARS V   33
   MAN RUNS HIS COURSE: . . . .   499 VACILLATION   2
   LOVE LEAPS UPON ITS COURSE. . . . .   518 HIS CONFIDENCE   12
   SOME THINK IT A MATTER OF COURSE THAT CHANCE . . . .   626 OLD MEN BE MAD   9
   SOME THINK IT MATTER OF COURSE THAT CHANCE . . . . .   626 OLD MEN BE MAD V   9
   UPON THE WIND, AND GUIDE MINE ARROW'S COURSE. . . . .   657 ISLE STAT I 3   62
   GO PILOT THE COURSE OF HIS ARROW'S DECEIT! . . . . .   657 ISLE STAT I 3   69
COURSES   SEE RACE-COURSES
   THE CARELESS PLANETS IN THEIR COURSES, ...   344 DAWN   7
   BUT WEARIED RUNNING ROUND AND ROUND IN THEIR COURSES . .   433 NINETEEN 19   116
   BUT, WEARY RUNNING ROUND AND ROUND IN THEIR COURSES, . .   433 NINETEEN 19   V   116
COURT
   KING GUAIRE WALKED AMID HIS COURT . . . .   295 THREE BEGGARS   8
   COURT HIS SHEPHERD LASS, ...   343 SHEP GOATHERD   104
   THAT SPEECH WAS ALL THAT THE COURT KNOW, BUT HE . . .   462 HARUN RASHID   V   35
   OR COURT A WOMAN: NEITHER ENEMY, ...   463 HARUN RASHID   59
   THE JUDGE AT THE ASSIZE COURT, ...   596 COLONEL MARTIN   46
   THEN TURNED HE FROM THE KING'S COURT, ...   742 EARL PAUL   65
COURTEOUS
   THOUGH COURTEOUS TO THE WORST: MUCH FALLING HE . . . .   324 ROBERT GREGORY   19
   MOST COURTEOUS TO SLOW AGE AND HASTY YOUTH, ...   339 SHEP GOATHERD   19
   NOW BE COURTEOUS, NOW BE KIND, ...   717 FAIRY DOCTOR   21
   GREET HIM COURTEOUS, GREET HIM KIND, ...   717 FAIRY DOCTOR   V   21
COURTESIES
   THAT GRAMMAR SCHOOL OF COURTESIES . . . .   288 TO WEALTHY MAN   15
   --PEDANT IN PASSION, LEARNED IN OLD COURTESIES, . . .   363 DOLLS FACES   4
COURTESY
   SO MUCH COMPOUNDED OF HIGH COURTESY . . . .   205 ADAMS CURSE   24
   COURTESY AND PASSION INTO ONE LIKE THOSE . . . . . .   352 PEOPLE   17
   HER COURTESY . . . .   362 HER COURTESY   T
   IN COURTESY I'D HAVE HER CHIEFLY LEARNED: . . . . .   404 FOR DAUGHTER   33
COURTIER
   LIKE SOME LAST COURTIER AT A GYPSY CAMPING-PLACE . . . .   314 FALLEN MAJESTY   3
   LIKE SOME LAST COURTIER AT A GYPSY CAMPING PLACE . . . .   314 FALLEN MAJESTY V   3
COURTIERS
   AND "WAKEN, COURTIERS OF THE MORN!" . . . .   18 OISIN 1   V 262
   CAME TO THE LEAST CONSIDERED OF HIS COURTIERS: . . . .   462 HARUN RASHID   42

		PAGE	TITLE		LINE

COURT-LADIES'
    FROM SOME COURT-LADIES' DRESS AND ROUND . . . . 477 SELF AND SOUL V 14
COURT-LADY'S
    FROM SOME COURT-LADY'S DRESS AND ROUND . . . . 477 SELF AND SOUL 14
COURTLY
    THE UNPERTURBED AND COURTLY IMAGES-- . . . . 352 PEOPLE 11
    TIRED OF THAT COURTLY FASHION, ... 378 CAT AND MOON 15
    TIRED OF HER COURTLY FASHION, ... 378 CAT AND MOON V 15
    THAT MIGHT ADORN OLD SONGS OR COURTLY SHOWS: . . . . . 629 CIRCUS ANIMALS 14
COUSIN
    MY COUSIN IS PRIEST IN KILVARNET, ... 178 FIDDLER DOONEY 3
    I PASSED MY BROTHER AND COUSIN: . . . . 178 FIDDLER DOONEY 5
    MY COUSIN OF ROSNAREE. . . . . 178 FIDDLER DOONEY V 4
    MY COUSIN IN ROSNAREE. . . . . 178 FIDDLER DOONEY V 4
COUSINS
    MY COUSINS BY THE SCORE, ... 620 JOHN KINSELLA 6
    A KING HAD SOME BEAUTIFUL COUSINS, ... 628 JANE MOUNTAIN 7
COVER
    THE SOUTH WOULD COVER THEM WITH ROSES OF CRIMSON FIRE: . . . 154 BELOVED PEACE V 6
    COVER OVER AND HIDE, FOR HE HAS NO PART . . . . 158 TO HIS HEART 6
    AND COVER YOUR LIPS WITH ODOROUS TWILIGHT AND SAY, . . . 162 ASKS FORGIVE 5
    COVER YOUR LIPS WITH ROSE-HEAVY TWILIGHT, AND SAY: . . . 162 ASKS FORGIVE V 5
    AND COVER THE PALE BLOSSOMS OF YOUR BREAST . . . . . . 163 ASKS FORGIVE 21
    THEN COVER THE PALE BLOSSOM OF YOUR BREAST . . . . . . 163 ASKS FORGIVE V 21
    UNFOLD YOUR FLAMING WINGS AND COVER OUT OF SIGHT . . . . 175 ELEMENT POWERS 11
    AND WINDS AND PONDS COVER MORE QUIET WOODS, ... 218 WOODS OF COOLE 34
    I LOVED HIM: I WOULD COVER UP MY EARS, ... 246 SHADOW WATER B 494
    BUT I WILL COVER UP YOUR EYES AND EARS, ... 250 SHADOW WATER B 574
    BEND LOWER, THAT I MAY COVER YOU WITH MY HAIR, ... 251 SHADOW WATER B 613
    I TORE MY BODY THAT ITS WINE MIGHT COVER . . . . . . 537 HER VISION 7
    COVER YOUR EARS: FOR ONCE WE HAD MOORED OUR GALLEY . . . 756 SHADOW WATER A 187
    COVER THEIR FACES WITH THEIR HAIR AND WEEP. . . . . . 764 SHADOW WATER A 333
    BEND LOWER, THAT I MAY COVER YOU WITH MY HAIR, ... 769 SHADOW WATER A 429
COVERED   SEE RAVEN-COVERED SEAWEED-COVERED MIST-COVERED SEA-COVERED IVY-COVERED
        SORREL-COVERED
    A FIRWOOD HOUSE, ALL COVERED OVER . . . . 17 OISIN 1 V 248
    AND GOD COVERED THE WORLD WITH SHADE, ... 133 FR GILLIGAN 19
    BETWEEN THE WALLS COVERED WITH BEATEN BRONZE, ... 180 QUEEN MAEVE 10
    THE MIST HAS COVERED THE HEAVENS, AND YOU AND I . . . . 251 SHADOW WATER B 604
    COVERED WITH EMBROIDERIES . . . . 320 COAT 2
    AND BROUGHT THEM IN A LITTLE COVERED DISH. . . . . . 410 TOWER 32
    MY HEART RECOVERING WITH COVERED EYES: . . . . 602 GALLERY REVIS 18
    AND KEEP A COVERED HEAD." . . . . 742 EARL PAUL 64
    KEEP HIDDEN AND COVERED HER HEART!" . . . . 744 GLOVE CLOAK 12
    HAVE COVERED THEM. WHERE DID THEY VANISH AWAY? . . . . 764 SHADOW WATER A 328
COVERING
    HIGH AS THE SADDLE-GIRTH, COVERING AWAY FROM OUR GLANCES 47 OISIN 3 2
        THE TIDE:
    HIGH AS THE SADDLE GIRTH, COVERING AWAY FROM OUR GLANCES 47 OISIN 3 V 2
        THE TIDE:
    WITH HER CLOUD-PALE EYELIDS HALF COVERING HER DIM EYES: 163 VALLEY LOVERS V 4
COVERLET
    AND SHAKE THEIR COVERLET. . . . . 33 OISIN 2 62
    TO STIR THEIR COVERLET AND THEIR HAIR. . . . . 197 BAILE AILLINN 186
    AND GATHER THE GLASNEVIN COVERLET . . . . 293 TO A SHADE 19
    DRAW THE GLASNEVIN COVERLET ANEW . . . . 293 TO A SHADE V 19
COVERLET'S
    AND SHAKE THEIR COVERLET'S HEM, ... 33 OISIN 2 V 62
COVERLID
    UNDER THIS CRADLE-HOOD AND COVERLID . . . . 403 FOR DAUGHTER 2
COVERS
    AND COVERS AWAY THE SMOKE OF MYRRH AND FRANKINCENSE: . . 173 SPEAKS HEARERS 4
    THAT COVERS ALL HE HAS BROUGHT . . . . 345 ON WOMAN 5
    COVERS ITS WOODEN SHEATH. . . . . 421 MY TABLE 7
COW
    HALF ASLEEP THE OLD COW CROPS, ... 706 DAWN-SONG 20
    WHERE LIES THE COW AT PEACE BESIDE HER CALF, ... 715 FERENCZ RENYI 121
    CURES HE HATH FOR COW OR GOAT . . . . 716 FAIRY DOCTOR 13
    HE HAD DREAMED THE COW HAD GOT WITHIN . . . . 729 PRIEST FAIRY 33
COWARD
    A COWARD IN THE FIELD: AND ALL MEN CRIED: . . . . . . 684 SEEKER 53
COWARDICE
    COWARDICE, SOME SILLY OVER-SUBTLE THOUGHT . . . . . . 413 TOWER 117
    COWARDICE, OVER SOME SILLY SUBTLE THOUGHT . . . . . . 413 TOWER V 117
COWARDLY
    THAT WERE A COWARDLY SONG, ... 554 CHURCH STATE 7
COWARDS
    CONVICTED COWARDS ALL, BY KINDRED SLAIN . . . . . . 634 CUCHULAIN COMF 21
COWER
    AND IN THE FLAMING FORESTS COWER THE LION . . . . . . 73 ANASHU VIJAYA 52
    THEY SEE IN FLAMING FORESTS COWER THE LION . . . . . 73 ANASHU VIJAYA V 52
COWERED
    I COWERED BACK UPON THE WALL IN TERROR, ... 284 TWO KINGS 164
COWS   SEE MILCH-COWS
    WHIPS TO THE SEA THE COWS AND SWINE." . . . . 82 MAD KING GOLL V 16
    TO FILL WITH COWS HIS HOLLOW GALLEYS." . . . . . . 82 MAD KING GOLL V 16
    SCARED BY THE SPLASHING OF A DOZEN COWS: . . . . . . 419 MY HOUSE 10
    SCARED BY THE SPLASHING OF A HUNDRED COWS. . . . . . 419 MY HOUSE V 10
    TO MIND HIS COWS AND SWINE BY THE RED LAKE. . . . . . 752 SHADOW WATER A 112
    CAN CALL THE MILCH COWS . . . . 780 WELL AND TREE 5

		PAGE	TITLE	LINE

COXCOMB
COXCOMB WAS THE LEAST HE SAID, ... 508 JANE BISHOP 6
THE SOLID MAN AND THE COXCOMB. . . . . 508 JANE BISHOP 7
THE SOLID MAN AND THE COXCOMB. . . . . 508 JANE BISHOP 14
THE SOLID MAN AND THE COXCOMB. . . . . 508 JANE BISHOP 21
THE SOLID MAN AND THE COXCOMB. . . . . 509 JANE BISHOP 28
COY
THE PROUDEST OR MOST COY OF SPIRIT THINGS, ... 720 WITCH VIVIEN 7
COZENING
THE COZENING FORTUNE-TELLER THAT COMES WHISPERING, . . . 228 SHADOW WATER B 123
CRABBED
YOUR THIRST FOR THOSE OLD CRABBED MYSTERIES, ... 465 HARUN RASHID 86
CRACK
WHEN I WAS A BOY WITH NEVER A CRACK IN MY HEART. . . . . 91 OLD FISHERMAN 4
WHEN I WAS A BOY WITH NEVER A CRACK IN MY HEART. . . . . 91 OLD FISHERMAN 8
WHEN I WAS A BOY WITH NEVER A CRACK IN MY HEART. . . . . 91 OLD FISHERMAN 12
AND THEN I'D STAGGER OUT. HE'D CRACK HIS WITS . . . . 377 PHASES OF MOON 134
AND PUT THAT CRACK IN IT, ... 455 FRIENDS YOUTH 2
MADE THE JOINTS OF HEAVEN CRACK, ... 509 JANE REPROVED 11
EVERY ACCIDENTAL CRACK OR DENT, ... 567 LAPIS LAZULI 44
CRACKED
TO THE CRACKED TUNE THAT CHRONOS SINGS, ... 65 HAPPY SHEPHERD 9
TO THE OLD CRACKED TUNE THAT CHRONOS SINGS, ... 65 HAPPY SHEPHERD V 9
CAUGHT AND CRACKED HIS FLEA, THE THIRD, ... 299 THREE HERMITS 30
MAY BUILD IN THE CRACKED MASONRY AND CRY . . . . . . 423 MY DESCENDANTS 15
FOUR POEMS CRACKED MARY AND THE BISHOP . . . . . . 507 JANE BISHOP V T
CRACKED MARY REPROVED . . . . 509 JANE REPROVED V T
CRACKED MARY AND THE DANCERS . . . . 514 JANE GROWN OLD V T
NOR HEARD THIS VOICE THAT NINETY YEARS HAVE CRACKED. . . 555 RIBH AT TOMB 5
CRACKING
COMES CRACKING JOKES OF CIVIL WAR . . . . 423 ROAD AT DOOR 3
CRACKLE
HEARING THE HARPERS PLAY, THE PINE-WOOD CRACKLE, . . . 759 SHADOW WATER A 241
HEARING THE HARPERS PLAY, THE PINE WOOD CRACKLE, . . . 759 SHADOW WATER A V 241
CRACKLING
BRUISING THE DARKNESS WITH THEIR CRACKLING LIGHT, . . . 687 TWO TITANS 2
CRACK-PATED
LEARN THAT WE WERE CRACK-PATED WHEN WE DREAMED. . . . . 431 NINETEEN 19 88
CRADLE
A CRADLE SONG . . . . 118 CRADLE SONG T
TWO POEMS CONCERNING PEASANT VISIONARIES A CRADLE SONG 146 UNAPPEAS HOST V T
BEING BETRAYED INTO A CRADLE, AND I COME . . . . . 284 TWO KINGS 169
AND MADE A GOLDEN CRADLE . . . . 308 PLAYER QUEEN 3
LOOKS AT THE CRADLE AND BAWLS, ... 319 DOLLS 2
TILL, CLAMBERING AT THE CRADLE SIDE, ... 343 SHEP GOATHERD V 109
TOO PERFECT AT THE FULL TO LIE IN A CRADLE, ... 374 PHASES OF MOON 60
THEY RAN FROM CRADLE TO CRADLE TILL AT LAST . . . . . 375 PHASES OF MOON 69
THEY RAN FROM CRADLE TO CRADLE TILL AT LAST . . . . . 375 PHASES OF MOON 69
CRADLE UPON CRADLE, AND ALL IN FLIGHT AND ALL . . . . 376 PHASES OF MOON 100
CRADLE UPON CRADLE, AND ALL IN FLIGHT AND ALL . . . . 376 PHASES OF MOON 100
WERE VEXED TO NIGHTMARE BY A ROCKING CRADLE, ... 402 SECOND COMING 20
FROM CRADLE RUN TO GRAVE . . . . 449 HERO GIRL FOOL 19
FROM GRAVE TO CRADLE RUN INSTEAD, ... 449 HERO GIRL FOOL 20
WHEN CRADLE AND SPOOL ARE PAST . . . . 449 HERO GIRL FOOL 24
CRADLED
AND CRADLED ME HERE WHERE ARE SUNG, ... 708 FAIRY PEDANT 25
CRADLE-HOOD
UNDER THIS CRADLE-HOOD AND COVERLID . . . . 403 FOR DAUGHTER 2
CRADLES
THE DANAAN CHILDREN LAUGH, IN CRADLES OF WROUGHT GOLD, . . 146 UNAPPEAS HOST 1
THE FAERY CHILDREN LAUGH IN CRADLES OF WROUGHT GOLD, . . 146 UNAPPEAS HOST V 1
THE CRADLES THAT A MAN MUST NEEDS BE ROCKED IN, ... 373 PHASES OF MOON 34
SHUDDERS IN MANY CRADLES, ALL IS CHANGED, ... 375 PHASES OF MOON 89
MAKE HIM FILL THE CRADLES RIGHT. . . . . 638 BEN BULBEN 41
CRADLE-SIDE
TILL, CLAMBERING AT THE CRADLE-SIDE, ... 343 SHEP GOATHERD 109
CRAFT
PATRICK, BEFORE THY CRAFT DIES EACH OLD SONG. . . . . 42 OISIN 2 V 196
YOU HAVE A DRUID CRAFT OF WICKED SOUND . . . . . . 237 SHADOW WATER B 342
YOU HAVE A DRUID CRAFT, WICKED SOUND . . . . 237 SHADOW WATER B V 342
ALL THINGS CAN TEMPT ME FROM THIS CRAFT OF VERSE, . . . 267 ALL TEMPT ME 1
UNDER THE EYELIDS OF ANOTHER, FOR IT WAS MY CRAFT . . . 284 TWO KINGS 156
WHERE I MAY SPEAK TO YOU ALONE, MY CRAFT . . . . . . 284 TWO KINGS 159
UNDER AN ALIEN EYELID, FOR IT WAS MY CRAFT . . . . . 284 TWO KINGS V 156
AND EVERY COUNTRY CRAFT, AND OF US ALL . . . . . . 339 SHEP GOATHERD 18
CRAFTY
FOR HE IS STRONG AND CRAFTY AS THE SEAS . . . . . . 35 OISIN 2 83
NOW HAD THAT OLD GAUNT CRAFTY ONE, ... 193 BAILE AILLINN 100
THAT CRAFTY DEMON AND THAT LOUD BEAST . . . . . . 399 DEMON BEAST 2
CRAM
LOVE CRAM LOVE'S TWO DIVISIONS . . . . 573 LADYS 2ND SONG 12
CRAMM'D
CRAMM'D ALL HER YOUTH, AND HATES HAVE BOUGHT AND SOLD . . 687 TWO TITANS 13
CRAMMED
ALL HIS TWENTIES CRAMMED WITH TOIL, ... 576 WHAT THEN 4
CRANBERRY
SEE YOU, BROTHER, CRANBERRY FRUIT-- . . . . 727 LOVERS QUARREL 25
CRANE
MUTTERED THE OLD CRANE OF GORT. . . . . 295 THREE BEGGARS 6
NOW THEY ARE SILENT," SAID THE CRANE. . . . . . . 297 THREE BEGGARS 62
ALONG THE LAKE. THE CRANE HAS HOMEWARD FLED. . . . . 656 ISLE STAT I 3 23

167

PAGE   TITLE   LINE

CRAOIBHIN
    DEAR CRAOIBHIN AOIBHIN, LOOK INTO OUR CASE. • • • • • • • 264 ABBEY THEATRE   1
CRASH
    AND WEARY OF THE CRASH OF BATTLE CARS." • • • • • • • • 107 CUCHULAIN SEA V   30
    OF THOSE STEEL TONGUES! CRASH, SWORDS! WELL THRUST! 665 ISLE STAT II 2   67
       WELL BENT
CRASHED
    CRASHED ON THE STONES, UPON THE GLIMMERING STONES, • • • 33 OISIN 2   V 68A
CRASHING   SEE LOUD-CRASHING
    OF THE LOUD CRASHING AND EARTH SHAKING FIGHT • • • • • 38 OISIN 2   V 141
CRAVE
    LEST I NO MORE HEAR COMMON THINGS THAT CRAVE! • • • • • 101 ROSE UPON ROOD   15
CRAVEN
    THE CRAVEN MAN IN HIS SEAT, • • • • • • • • • • • • 347 FISHERMAN   15
    "AM I SUCH A CRAVEN THAT • • • • • • • • • • • • • 585 ORAHILLY   19
CRAVING
    TO THE CRAVING IN MY BONES. • • • • • • • • • • • • 533 FIRST CONFESS   12
CRAWL
    NO MORE TO CRAWL ON THE SEAS WITH LONG OARS MILE AFTER 55 OISIN 3   119
       MILE,
    TO CRAWL IN HER OWN BLOOD, AND GO SCOT-FREE! • • • • • 429 NINETEEN 19   28
    I CANNOT EVEN CRAWL ALONG THE FLAGS • • • • • • • • • 701 MOSADA 3   58
CRAWLED
    HE CRAWLED INTO THAT PLEASANT NOOK. • • • • • • • • • 303 HOUR DAWN   32
    CRAWLED FROM OBSCURITY, AND SET UPON ME • • • • • • • 352 PEOPLE   26
CRAWLING
    THE NETTED MARKS OF CRAWLING SCALES SEA-SPRUNG • • • • 37 OISIN 2   V 115
    BUT TURN FROM ROSSES' CRAWLING TIDE, • • • • • • • • 549 SEVERED HEAD   5
CRAWLS
    GRIMALKIN CRAWLS TO BUDDHA'S EMPTINESS. • • • • • • • 611 STATUES   24
    A LIZARD CRAWLS--THE TWO MEN GAZE INTENT, • • • • • • 711 FERENCZ RENYI   47
    TIME GOES. THE FLAKED FIRE OF EVENING CRAWLS • • • • • 712 FERENCZ RENYI   70
    TIME GOES. THE FLICKED FIRE OF EVENING CRAWLS • • • • 712 FERENCZ RENYI V 70
    FROM WHERE THE OLD IVY CRAWLS ROUND THE OLD STEEPLE, • • 728 PRIEST FAIRY   6
CRAZED   SEE PITY-CRAZED
    CRAZED WITH ITS OWN INTERMINABLE SOUND, • • • • • • • 30 OISIN 2   V 23A
    IN THE HID PLACE, BEING CRAZED BY LOVE. • • • • • • • 195 BAILE AILLINN   143
    WHERE ONE FOUND LANCELOT CRAZED AND HID HIM FOR A WHILE! 209 UNDER THE MOON   3
    WHERE ONE FOUND LANCELOT CRAZED, AND HID HIM FOR AWHILE, 209 UNDER THE MOON V 3
    AND FOR THAT REASON AM I CRAZED • • • • • • • • • • 454 EMPTY CUP   9
    HAD DRIVEN HIM CRAZED! • • • • • • • • • • • • • 473 ALL SOUL NIGHT   73
    THE CRAZED MOON • • • • • • • • • • • • • • • 487 CRAZED MOON   T
    CRAZED THROUGH MUCH CHILD-BEARING • • • • • • • • • 487 CRAZED MOON   1
    AN ABSTRACT GREEK ABSURDITY HAS CRAZED THE MAN-- • • • • 556 RIBH PATRICK   1
    ABSTRACTIONS OF THE GREEK PHILOSOPHY HAVE CRAZED THE MAN, 556 RIBH PATRICK V 1
    A CRAZED GIRL • • • • • • • • • • • • • • • • 578 CRAZED GIRL   T
    THAT CRAZED GIRL IMPROVISING HER MUSIC, • • • • • • • 578 CRAZED GIRL   1
CRAZY
    AND CRAZY RASCALS RAGE THEIR FILL • • • • • • • • • 131 OLD PENSIONER   9
    BECAUSE EARTH, CRAZY FOR ITS BROKEN POWER, • • • • • • 186 QUEEN MAEVE   124
    HALF CRAZY WITH THE THOUGHT, SHE TOO HAS WEPT! • • • • 186 QUEEN MAEVE   140
    THE CRAZY HERDSMAN THAT WILL TELL HIS FELLOWS • • • • • 229 SHADOW WATER B 167
    THE CRAZY NOTHING THAT I THINK IT IS, • • • • • • • 248 SHADOW WATER B 556
    A CRAZY JUICE THAT MAKES THE PULSES BEAT • • • • • • 384 VISION ROBART   54
    A CRAZY SALAD WITH THEIR MEAT • • • • • • • • • • 404 FOR DAUGHTER   31
    AND SHOULD SOME CRAZY HAND DARE TOUCH A DAUGHTER • • • • 433 NINETEEN 19   122
    A CRAZY MAN THAT FOUND A CUP, • • • • • • • • • • 454 EMPTY CUP   1
    CRAZY JANE AND THE BISHOP • • • • • • • • • • • • 507 JANE BISHOP   T
    EIGHT POEMS CRAZY JANE AND THE BISHOP • • • • • • • 507 JANE BISHOP   V T
    CRAZY JANE REPROVED • • • • • • • • • • • • • • 509 JANE REPROVED   T
    CRAZY JANE ON THE DAY OF JUDGMENT • • • • • • • • • 510 JANE JUDGMENT   T
    CRAZY JANE AND JACK THE JOURNEYMAN • • • • • • • • • 511 JANE AND JACK   T
    CRAZY JANE ON GOD • • • • • • • • • • • • • • 512 JANE ON GOD   T
    CRAZY JANE TALKS WITH THE BISHOP • • • • • • • • • 513 JANE TALK BISH   T
    CRAZY JANE GROWN OLD LOOKS AT THE DANCERS • • • • • • 514 JANE GROWN OLD   T
    CRAZY JANE AND THE DANCERS • • • • • • • • • • • 514 JANE GROWN OLD V T
    I MOCKED, BEING CRAZY, BUT YOU MASTERED IT • • • • • • 533 HER TRIUMPH   8
    ALONE WITH A CRAZY HEAD. • • • • • • • • • • • • 552 SONGS REWRIT 2 V 12
    THAT SHE IS HAPPY BEING CRAZY! • • • • • • • • • • 568 SWEET DANCER   10
    OUT OF THAT CRAZY FIGHT! • • • • • • • • • • • • 585 ORAHILLY   15
    COULD CRAZY JANE PUT OFF OLD AGE • • • • • • • • • 606 SONGS BURDEN 1 19
    CRAZY JANE ON THE MOUNTAIN • • • • • • • • • • • 628 JANE MOUNTAIN   T
    (SAID CRAZY JANE) • • • • • • • • • • • • • • 628 JANE MOUNTAIN   2
    (SAID CRAZY JANE) • • • • • • • • • • • • • • 628 JANE MOUNTAIN   12
    O! WHY IS LOVE SO CRAZY THAT IT LONGS • • • • • • • 765 SHADOW WATER A 363
    THOSE CRAZY FINGERS PLAY • • • • • • • • • • • • 783 GREY ROUND   16
CREAK
    MY SORROW! FOR MANY A CREAK GAVE THE CREEL IN THE CART • • 91 OLD FISHERMAN   6
    AH WOE! FULL MANY A CREAK GAVE THE CREEL IN THE CART • • 91 OLD FISHERMAN V 6
    AH ME! FULL MANY A CREAK GAVE THE CREEL IN THE CART • • • 91 OLD FISHERMAN V 6
    THE CRY OF A CHILD BY THE ROADWAY, THE CREAK OF A LUMBERING 142 ROSE IN HEART   2
       CART,
CREAKING
    CLIMBED UP MY CREAKING STAIR. THEY HAD READ • • • • • 358 PRESENCES   6
    WITHIN THE FOLD TO HEAR THE CREAKING GATE-- • • • • • 646 ISLE STAT I 1   41
CREAKY
    OR CREAKY SHOES. AND AT THE END OF ALL • • • • • • • 228 SHADOW WATER B 128
CREAMY
    WILD FLAMES OF RED AND CREAMY WHITES, • • • • • • • 18 OISIN 1   V 255
CREASES
    AND THERE ARE LITTLE CREASES ABOUT HER EYES! • • • • • 199 FOLLY COMFORT V 3

168

		PAGE	TITLE	LINE

CREATE
  WE ARE BUT CRITICS, OR BUT HALF CREATE, ... 368 EGO DOMINUS 15
  DREAM AND SO CREATE . . . . 415 TOWER 155
CREATED
  AND I MYSELF CREATED HANRAHAN . . . . 411 TOWER 57
  MAN HAS CREATED DEATH. . . . . 476 DEATH 12
CREATION
  ALL CREATION SHIVERS . . . . 559 HE AND SHE 11
CREATURE
  A SWIFTER CREATURE NEVER WAS BORN, ... 2 OISIN 1 V 7Q
  OF MANY A FIGURED CREATURE STRANGE, ... 4 OISIN 1 V 27
  "A SADDER CREATURE NEVER STEPT . . . . 17 OISIN 1 238
  NO CREATURE HAD FAMILIAR THOUGHT . . . . 17 OISIN 1 242
  THE POWERS WHOSE NAME AND SHAPE NO LIVING CREATURE KNOWS 174 ELEMENT POWERS 1
  PERVERSE CREATURE OF CHANCE, ... 346 ON WOMAN 41
  A STUPID HAPPY CREATURE . . . . 400 DEMON BEAST 31
CREATURES
  NO MIGHTIER CREATURES BAY AT THE MOON! . . . . . . 8 OISIN 1 87
  FOR NO LIVE CREATURES LIVED THERE, NO WEASELS MOVED IN 48 OISIN 3 19
    THE DARK,
  AND EACH OF THE HUGE WHITE CREATURES WAS HUGER THAN 49 OISIN 3 33
    FOURSCORE MEN
  AND EACH OF THE HUGE WHITE CREATURES WAS HUGER THAN 49 OISIN 3 V 33
    FOUR-SCORE MEN,
  AND THE CHIEF OF THE HUGE WHITE CREATURES, ... 50 OISIN 3 43
  . . . WITH CREATURES OF DREAMS, ... 53 OISIN 3 95
  FOR NO LIVE CREATURES LIVE THERE, NO WEASELS MOVE IN THE 56 OISIN 3 139
    DARK!
  FOR THE ELEMENTAL CREATURES GO . . . . 138 TO IRELAND 23
  STRANGE CREATURES FLUTTER UP BEFORE ONE'S EYES, ... 222 SHADOW WATER B 18
  I HAVE LOOKED UPON THOSE BRILLIANT CREATURES, ... 322 SWANS AT COOLE 13
  I HAVE LOOKED UPON THESE BRILLIANT CREATURES . . . . 322 SWANS AT COOLE V 13
  WHEN THE MOON'S FULL THOSE CREATURES OF THE FULL . . . 375 PHASES OF MOON 75
  AND FOLLOWED UP THOSE BAYING CREATURES TOWARDS— . . . . 412 TOWER 72
  WITH CREATURES OF OUR HEAVY NIGHT, ... 743 DANAAN QUICK 10
  SIX HOLY CREATURES, ... 770 BLOOD BOND 14
CREEL
  MY SORROW! FOR MANY A CREAK GAVE THE CREEL IN THE CART . . 91 OLD FISHERMAN 6
  AH WOE! FULL MANY A CREAK GAVE THE CREEL IN THE CART . . . 91 OLD FISHERMAN V 6
  AH ME! FULL MANY A CREAK GAVE THE CREEL IN THE CART . . . 91 OLD FISHERMAN V 6
CREEP
  IN HATING GOD SHE MAY CREEP CLOSE TO GOD. . . . . . . 558 RIBH CHRISTIAN V 18
  MAY CREEP INTO YOUR BED, ... 569 THREE BUSHES 11
  FOR IF I SAW MYSELF CREEP IN . . . . 569 THREE BUSHES 12
  BACK THE SHADOWS CREEP AGHAST— . . . . 648 ISLE STAT I 1 98
CREEPERS
  AND TANGLED CREEPERS EVERY HOUR . . . . 16 OISIN 1 223
  WHERE TANGLING CREEPERS EVERY HOUR . . . . 16 OISIN 1 V 223
CREEPING
  A CREEPING OLD MAN, FULL OF SLEEP, ... 60 OISIN 3 192
  THE NORTH UNFOLDS ABOVE THEM CLINGING, CREEPING NIGHT, . . 154 BELOVED PEACE 3
  THE NORTH UNROLLS ABOVE THEM CLINGING, CREEPING NIGHT, . . 154 BELOVED PEACE V 3
  THE CREEPING CAT, LOOKED UP. . . . . 378 CAT AND MOON 4
  CAME CREEPING UP BECAUSE THE MAN WAS STILL. . . . . . 634 CUCHULAIN COMF 10
  A CREEPING HORROR IS ALL OVER ME. . . . . 681 SEEKER 12
  CREEPING ALONG THE HEAVENS' PURPLE CUP, ... 714 FERENCZ RENYI 112
CREEPS
  MINNALOUSHE CREEPS THROUGH THE GRASS . . . . 378 CAT AND MOON 17
  MINNALOUSHE CREEPS THROUGH THE GRASS . . . . 379 CAT AND MOON 25
  A FEARFUL PALENESS CREEPS ACROSS HER BREAST . . . . . 701 MOSADA 3 69
CRESCENT
  A GOLDEN CRESCENT LIT THE PLAIN, ... 2 OISIN 1 V 7BB
  AND THE THIN CRESCENT OF THE MOON, ... 20 OISIN 1 V 288
  HE HAS CAUGHT THE CRESCENT MOON OUT OF THE SKY, ... 239 SHADOW WATER B 370
  FROM THE FIRST CRESCENT TO THE HALF, THE DREAM . . . . 373 PHASES OF MOON 36
  BECAUSE THE HERO'S CRESCENT IS THE TWELFTH. . . . . . 374 PHASES OF MOON 47
  BECAUSE THE HEROES' CRESCENT IS THE TWELFTH. . . . . . 374 PHASES OF MOON V 47
  THAT THE LAST SERVILE CRESCENT HAS SET FREE? . . . . . 376 PHASES OF MOON 103
  THE FIRST THIN CRESCENT IS WHEELED ROUND ONCE MORE. . . . 377 PHASES OF MOON 116
  AND THAT FROM ROUND TO CRESCENT, ... 379 CAT AND MOON 23
  FROM CRESCENT TO ROUND THEY RANGE? . . . . . . 379 CAT AND MOON 24
  OF RHYME: REMEMBERING THEE, THIS CRESCENT NIGHT, ... 704 REMEMBRANCE 2
CRESCENTS
  THE FULL AND THE MOON'S DARK AND ALL THE CRESCENTS, . . 373 PHASES OF MOON 32
  HUNCHBACK AND SAINT AND FOOL ARE THE LAST CRESCENTS. . . 377 PHASES OF MOON 118
  UNDER THE THREE LAST CRESCENTS OF THE MOON, ... 377 PHASES OF MOON 133
CREST
  TELL ON, NOR BOW THY HEATHEN CREST . . . . 11 OISIN 1 V 131A
  FROM MOUNTAIN CREST TO CREST. . . . . 536 PARTING 10
  FROM MOUNTAIN CREST TO CREST. . . . . 536 PARTING 10
  AS FLAMING MINSTREL-WORD UPON HIS CREST. . . . . . . 679 ISLE STAT II 3 317
  WHERE HOMES ONCE WHITENED VALE AND MOUNTAIN CREST! . . . 709 FERENCZ RENYI 3
  HIS MOODS BOW LOW HIS SOMBRE CREST, ... 723 GIRLS SONG A 2
CRESTED   SEE GOLDEN-CRESTED
  ANSWERED: "A CRESTED COCKEREL CREW . . . . 387 SOLOMON WITCH V 9
CRETAN
  RECALL THE CRETAN BARB THAT PIERCED A STAR? . . . . . 541 PARN FUNERAL 1 7
CREVICE
  IN CAVERN, CREVICE, HOLE, ... 546 TO SAME TUNE 2 5
  IN CAVERN, CREVICE OR HOLE, ... 546 TO SAME TUNE 2 V 5
  IN CAVERN, CREVICE, OR HOLE, ... 613 MARCH SONGS 1 5

169

	PAGE	TITLE		LINE

CREVICED
IN CREVICED ROCKS, AND LAUGHED TO THE OLD SEA, ... 688 TWO TITANS 34
CREVICES
THE BEES BUILD IN THE CREVICES . . . . 424 STARES NEST 1
CREVROE
ON CREVROE OR BROAD KNOCKFEFIN, WITH MANY OF OLD THEY FEAST 59 OISIN 3 179
ON CREVROE OR ON BROAD KNOCKFEFIN, WITH MANY OF OLD THEY 59 OISIN 3 V 179
    FAST
CREW
AND OVERPOWER THE CREW WHILE YET ASLEEP! . . . . . . 233 SHADOW WATER B 240
CREW FROM A BLOSSOMING APPLE BOUGH . . . . 387 SOLOMON WITCH 10
ANSWERED: "A CRESTED COCKEREL CREW . . . . 387 SOLOMON WITCH V 9
AND NEVER CREW AGAIN TILL NOW. . . . . 388 SOLOMON WITCH 12
NOTHING BUT CROMWELL'S HOUSE AND CROMWELL'S MURDEROUS CREW, 580 CURSE CROMWELL 2
THEN THE STRANGER SOFTLY CREW— . . . . 697 MOSADA 2 28
BUT WHERE THAT ROARING, RANTING CREW . . . . 787 HUDDON DUDDON 3
CRICKET
DROPPING FROM THE VEILS OF THE MORNING TO WHERE THE CRICKET 117 ISLE INNISFREE 6
    SINGS:
'TWAS EVENING, AND THE CRICKET NATION SANG . . . . . . 690 MOSADA 1 18
A NEIGHBOURING CRICKET LIFTS HIS SHRILLY SHOUT . . . . 711 FERENCZ RENYI 45
CRICKETS
THEY SET UP A NOISE LIKE CRICKETS, ... 161 CAP AND BELLS 33
CRIED
CRIED FIN: AND CRIED SHE, "MEN OF FAME, ... 5 OISIN 1 V 45
CRIED FIN: AND CRIED SHE, "MEN OF FAME, ... 5 OISIN 1 V 45
"YOU ONLY WILL I WED," I CRIED, ... 7 OISIN 1 74
IN LOVE. I CRIED, "THEE WILL I WED, ... 7 OISIN 1 V 74
AWAY, AWAY WITH ME," SHE CRIED, ... 8 OISIN 1 V 80B
THAN THIS STRANGE HUMAN BARD," HE CRIED: . . . . 17 OISIN 1 239
THAN THIS STRANGE BARD," HE CRIED, AND CAUGHT . . . . . 17 OISIN 1 V 239
WITH A CLEAR VOICE THE YOUNG MAN CRIED, ... 18 OISIN 1 V 260
TO ALL THINGS CRIED: "I AM A SLAVE! . . . . 19 OISIN 1 V 280
"FLEE FROM HIM," PEARL-PALE NIAMH WEEPING CRIED, . . . 35 OISIN 2 92
ROOTED IN FOAM AND CLOUDS, AND CRIED TO ALL . . . . . 38 OISIN 2 132
I CRIED, "COME OUT OF THE SHADOW, KING OF THE NAILS OF 51 OISIN 3 61
    GOLD!
I CRIED, "THOU ART SURELY A WARRIOR, FORGETTING HIS FAMOUS 51 OISIN 3 V 61
    LINE,
I CRIED, "COME OUT OF THE SHADOW, CANN OF THE NAILS OF 51 OISIN 3 V 61
    GOLD!
I CRIED, "O NIAMH! O WHITE ONE! IF ONLY A TWELVE-HOURED 55 OISIN 3 113
    DAY,
AND I RODE AND I RODE, AND I CRIED OUT, ... 59 OISIN 3 171
SO SLEEP THEE BY DAYTIME." A VOICE CRIED, ... 59 OISIN 3 172
. . . HE CRIED, "NO, THE GODS A LONG TIME ARE DEAD." . 59 OISIN 3 180
SO SLEEP THEY BY DAYTIME." A VOICE CRIED, ... 59 OISIN 3 V 172
. . . HE CRIED, "NAY, THE GODS A LONG TIME ARE DEAD." 59 OISIN 3 V 180
CRIED OUT, DIM SEA, HEAR MY MOST PITEOUS STORY! . . . . 68 SAD SHEPHERD 9
THE SEA SWEPT ON AND CRIED HER OLD CRY STILL, ... 68 SAD SHEPHERD 10
CRIED ALL HIS STORY TO THE DEWDROPS GLISTENING, ... 68 SAD SHEPHERD 14
THEN CRIED THE MAN WHOM SORROW NAMED HIS FRIEND: . . . 68 SAD SHEPHERD V 8
THERE CRIED A HERALD, "TO OUR VALLEYS . . . . 82 MAD KING GOLL V 14
CRIED A HERALD, "PEACE WITH THINE! . . . . 82 MAD KING GOLL V 14
CRIED A HERALD, "TO OUR VALLEYS . . . . 82 MAD KING GOLL V 14
UPON THE WEB-HEAPED FLOOR, AND CRIED HIS WORD: . . . . 106 CUCHULAIN SEA 15
"WHO BADE YOU TELL THESE THINGS?" AND THEN SHE CRIED . 106 CUCHULAIN SEA V 17
AND CRIED WITH ANGRY VOICE, "IT IS NOT MEET . . . . . 107 CUCHULAIN SEA 20
AND CRIED OUT TO HIM, "SON IT IS NOT MEET . . . . . . 107 CUCHULAIN SEA V 20
CUCHULAIN CRIED, "I AM THE ONLY MAN . . . . 109 CUCHULAIN SEA 55
CUCHULAIN CRIED, "HAVE MADE AND KEEP THAT VOW." . . . . 109 CUCHULAIN SEA V 56
AND CRIED, "CUCHULLIN WILL DWELL THERE AND BROOD, . . . 110 CUCHULAIN SEA V 77
THE CARS OF BATTLE AND HIS OWN NAME CRIED: . . . . . . 111 CUCHULAIN SEA 85
AND AFTER CRIED HE, "GOD FORGIVE! . . . . 132 FR GILLIGAN 11
"AND IS THE POOR MAN DEAD?" HE CRIED. . . . . 133 FR GILLIGAN 33
WHEN THE BATS CRIED OUT NO MORE: . . . . 159 CAP AND BELLS V 14
I CRIED IN MY DREAM, O WOMEN, BID THE YOUNG MEN LAY . . 163 VALLEY LOVERS 5
AND I CRIED IN MY DREAM "O WOMEN, BID THE YOUNG MEN LAY 163 VALLEY LOVERS V 5
CRIED FROM THE PORTER'S LODGE, AND WITH LONG CLAMOUR . . 181 QUEEN MAEVE 37
WHERE HER GRANDCHILDREN SLEPT, AND CRIED ALOUD, ... 185 QUEEN MAEVE 109
WHERE HER GRAND-CHILDREN SLEPT, AND CRIED ALOUD . . . . 185 QUEEN MAEVE V 109
A YOUNG MAN CRIED AND KISSED HER HAND, ... 191 BAILE AILLINN 60
"ANOTHER'S HURRIED OFF," CRIED HE, ... 193 BAILE AILLINN 113
AND AMID LEAFY LIGHT HE CRIED, ... 193 BAILE AILLINN V 113
I CRIED WHEN THE MOON WAS MURMURING TO THE BIRDS: . . . 203 WITHER BOUGHS 1
CRIED OUT UPON THAT THING BENEATH . . . . 254 HIS DREAM 10
CRIED OUT THE WHOLE NIGHT LONG, ... 254 HIS DREAM 16
THAT EVERY YEAR I HAVE CRIED, "AT LENGTH . . . . . . 256 WORDS 9
THE NO KING CRIED WHO AFTER THAT WAS KING, ... 258 KING NO KING 2
TILL THE WILDERNESS CRIED ALOUD, ... 259 UNWORTH PRAISE 8
AND I BUT ASKED THE MORE, TILL HE CRIED OUT, ... 281 TWO KINGS 92
FOR MEDICINE." THEREON HE CRIED ALOUD, ... 281 TWO KINGS 98
UNDER A BOW, HE CRIED, "WHAT HAPPINESS . . . . 284 TWO KINGS 177
THRUST HIM AWAY WITH BOTH MY HANDS AND CRIED, ... 285 TWO KINGS 202
UNTIL A CURLEW CRIED AND IN THE LUMINOUS WIND . . . . . 291 PAUDEEN 4
AN OLD FOUL MOUTH THAT ONCE CRIED OUT ON YOU . . . . . 292 TO A SHADE V 17
WE HAVE CRIED IN OUR DESPAIR . . . . 293 HELEN-LIVED 1
ONE TO ANOTHER SIGHED AND CRIED: . . . . 296 THREE BEGGARS 38
BUT THE THIRD CRIED: "I'LL TO THE COURSE . . . . . . 296 THREE BEGGARS V 33
ABOUT A FARM," THE SECOND CRIED. . . . . 296 THREE BEGGARS V 38
"TIME'S UP," HE CRIED, AND ALL THE THREE . . . . . . 297 THREE BEGGARS 57

170

CRIED   (CONTINUED)
    "TIME'S UP," HE CRIED, AND ALL THE THREE   .   .   .   .   297 THREE BEGGARS   59
    ONE BEGGAR CRIED: "YOU'RE SHAMMING SLEEP,"   .   .   .   .   .   .   297 THREE BEGGARS   V   45
    BEGGAR TO BEGGAR CRIED   .   .   .   .   299 BEGGAR CRIED   T
    BEGGAR TO BEGGAR CRIED, BEING FRENZY-STRUCK, ...   299 BEGGAR CRIED   3
    BEGGAR TO BEGGAR CRIED, BEING FRENZY-STRUCK, ...   300 BEGGAR CRIED   7
    BEGGAR TO BEGGAR CRIED, BEING FRENZY-STRUCK, ...   300 BEGGAR CRIED   11
    BEGGAR TO BEGGAR CRIED, BEING FRENZY-STRUCK, ...   300 BEGGAR CRIED   15
    BEGGAR TO BEGGAR CRIED, BEING FRENZY-STRUCK, ...   300 BEGGAR CRIED   19
    THAT SACRED GOBAN BREWED," HE CRIED   .   .   .   .   304 HOUR DAWN   V   50
    BUT THE OTHER CRIED, "YOU LONG FOR SPRING   .   .   .   .   .   .   306 HOUR DAWN   V   91
    UNTIL I CRIED AND TREMBLED AND ROCKED TO AND FRO,   .   .   .   316 COLD HEAVEN   8
    CRIED THE BEGGAR, BILLY BYRNE: .   .   .   .   331 ROUND TOWER   4
    THE EXULTATION OF THEIR STONE, THAT CRIED   .   .   .   .   .   .   339 SHEP GOATHERD   25
    AND CRIED, "BEFORE I AM OLD   .   .   .   .   348 FISHERMAN   37
    I SUDDENLY CRIED OUT IN A STRANGE TONGUE   .   .   .   .   .   387 SOLOMON WITCH   5
    HOWLED, MIAU-D, BARKED, BRAYED, BELLED, YELLED, CRIED,   .   387 SOLOMON WITCH   8
        CROWED,
    CRIED FROM A BLOSSOMING APPLE BOUGH   .   .   .   .   387 SOLOMON WITCH   V   10
    NO, NO, NOT SAID, BUT CRIED IT OUT--"YOU HAVE COME AGAIN,   391 UNDER SATURN   13
    CRIED OUT THE HOLLOWS OF THE SEA.   .   .   .   .   397 POLIT PRISONER   24
    BECAUSE OF ALL THAT SENSELESS TUMULT, ALL BUT CRIED   .   .   426 PHANTOM HATRED   15
    THAT SHE CRIED INTO THIS EAR, ...   455 HIS MEMORIES   17
    CRIED, CASTING OFF THE MOUNTAIN SNOW, ...   502 VACILLATION   60
    AND CRIED TO BATTLE-WEARY MEN, ...   502 VACILLATION   65
    CRIED THAT WE LIVED LIKE BEAST AND BEAST: .   .   .   .   .   508 JANE BISHOP   13
    AND FAIR NEEDS FOUL," I CRIED.   .   .   .   .   513 JANE TALK BISH   8
    I SAT AND CRIED.   .   .   .   .   515 GIRLS SONG B   8
    "SHE WILL CHANGE," I CRIED, ...   516 MANS SONG   1
    AND TIME RUNS ON," CRIED SHE.   .   .   .   .   526 AM OF IRELAND   3
    AND TIME RUNS ON," CRIED SHE.   .   .   .   .   527 AM OF IRELAND   16
    AND THE TROMBONE," CRIED HE: .   .   .   .   527 AM OF IRELAND   23
    AND TIME RUNS ON," CRIED SHE.   .   .   .   .   527 AM OF IRELAND   29
    I CRIED AND WHISTLED BUT VAIN, ALL VAIN.   .   .   .   .   .   551 SONGS REWRIT 1   V   16
    THAT CRIED IT FAR AND WIDE, ...   582 ROGER CASEMENT   18
    AND I CRIED TEARS DOWN.   .   .   .   .   628 JANE MOUNTAIN   22
    AND, LEAPING TO THEIR FEET, FAR ECHOES CRIED, ...   659 ISLE STAT II 1   13
    FOR SUCH A CALL, LET THE WILD WORD BE CRIED   .   .   .   .   669 ISLE STAT II 3   76
    I CRIED THE THING YOU BADE ME CRY.   .   .   .   .   670 ISLE STAT II 3   114
    I CRIED THE WORDS YOU BID ME CRY.   .   .   .   .   673 ISLE STAT II 3   186
    A COWARD IN THE FIELD: AND ALL MEN CRIED: .   .   .   .   .   684 SEEKER   53
    HIDING MY FACE, I CRIED LONG, BITTERLY.   .   .   .   .   .   .   690 MOSADA 1   17
    THY SACRED DOOR:" BUT PETER CRIED, ...   697 MOSADA 2   25
    A GREY PROFESSOR PASSING CRIED, ...   725 LEGEND   9
    AND TO HIMSELF CRIED, "COMMUNIST!"   .   .   .   .   725 LEGEND   15
    "THEY ARE LOST, THEY ARE LOST, EACH ONE," CRIED HE.   .   .   730 PRIEST FAIRY   58
    WAS CRIED IN STREET AND LANE   .   .   .   .   740 EARL PAUL   26
    THE PEOPLE CRIED "SHIELD-BREAKER!"   .   .   .   .   741 EARL PAUL   53
CRIES   SEE CATCH-CRIES
    CRIES TO THE SLUGGARD SEEDS OF CORN, ...   18 OISIN 1   V   263
    LAUGHTER AND CRIES.   THE ARMIES CLASH AND SHOCK,   .   .   .   43 OISIN 2   211
    OF ARMOUR--LAUGHTER AND CRIES--THE ARMIES' SHOCK.   .   .   .   43 OISIN 2   V   211
    AND THEN THE CLASH OF FALLEN HORSEMEN AND THE CRIES   .   .   161 BLACK PIG   3
    WHERE WIND CRIES IN THE SEDGE: .   .   .   .   165 CRY OF SEDGE   3
    MUST I ENDURE YOUR AMOROUS CRIES?   .   .   .   .   177 PAST GREATNESS   12
    CRY OF HIS LOVE WITH THEIR PITIFUL CRIES.   .   .   .   .   .   177 PAST GREATNESS   V   12
    ALL THAT YOU NEED IS PATIENCE."   HEART CRIES, "NO,   .   .   .   200 FOLLY COMFORT   6
    AND AFTER CIRCLING WITH STRANGE CRIES AWHILE   .   .   .   .   223 SHADOW WATER B   26
    THE LAPWING AT THEIR FOOLISH CRIES   .   .   .   .   306 HOUR DAWN   77
    TO KNOW WHEN MICHAEL'S TRUMPET CRIES   .   .   .   .   .   .   307 HOUR DAWN   100
    IN VAIN, IN VAIN: THE CATARACT STILL CRIES: .   .   .   .   .   311 MOUNTAIN TOMB   9
    THE CLEVER MAN WHO CRIES   .   .   .   .   347 FISHERMAN   21
    THE CATCH CRIES OF THE CLOWN, ...   347 FISHERMAN   V   22
    THEIR MOMENTARY CRIES BEFORE IT IS DAWN, ...   371 EGO DOMINUS   78
    ALL TURN WITH AMOROUS CRIES, OR ANGRY CRIES, ...   433 NINETEEN 19   123
    ALL TURN WITH AMOROUS CRIES, OR ANGRY CRIES, ...   433 NINETEEN 19   123
    FOR THE HEART CRIES THAT WHAT DECEPTION WINS   .   .   .   .   448 HERO GIRL FOOL   6
    THOSE AMOROUS CRIES THAT OUT OF QUIET COME   .   .   .   .   557 RIBH ECSTASY   7
    THEIR CRIES ARE SWEET AND STRANGE, ...   612 NEWS ORACLE   18
    WILD CRIES, GROWN SWEET WITH LULLS AND LINGERINGS LONG.   674 ISLE STAT II 3   222
    WITH LITTLE CRIES OF JOY HE KISSED THE RAIN   .   .   .   .   688 TWO TITANS   33
    THAT ANCIENT MOTHER CRIES, "SPEAK NOT, MY SON.   .   .   .   711 FERENCZ RENYI   56
    WITH CRIES AND MURMURS.   SUDDENLY HE FLINGS   .   .   .   .   714 FERENCZ RENYI   101
    CRIES A VOICE AT ROARING MIDNIGHT BESIDE THE MOONLESS DEEP.   718 PHANTOM SHIP   8
    "PRAY FOR THE SOULS IN PURGATORY," THE PALE PRIEST   719 PHANTOM SHIP   31
        TREMBLING CRIES.
    AND SAID, "YON BITTERN CRIES, IN TRUTH, ...   731 PRIEST FAIRY   75
    AND SHE CRIES OUT, "I HAVE FLED TO MY BELOVED   .   .   .   .   754 SHADOW WATER A   151
    UPON THIS WORLD NO LONGER.   THE HARP CRIES OUT.   .   .   .   769 SHADOW WATER A V   430
    CRIES OUT THE EMPTY WELL, ...   780 WELL AND TREE   2
    CRIES OUT THE LEAFLESS TREE, ...   780 WELL AND TREE   10
CRIETH
    LOUD FOR THEE THE MORNING CRIETH, ...   648 ISLE STAT I 1   86
CRIME
    DELIVER FROM THE CRIME OF DEATH AND BIRTH.   .   .   .   .   478 SELF AND SOUL   24
    A CHARTER TO COMMIT THE CRIME ONCE MORE.   .   .   .   .   478 SELF AND SOUL   32
    THAT THE CRIME OF BEING BORN   .   .   .   .   534 CONSOLATION   9
    THE CRIME CAN BE FORGOT.   .   .   .   .   534 CONSOLATION   12
CRIME'S
    BUT WHERE THE CRIME'S COMMITTED   .   .   .   .   534 CONSOLATION   11

CRIMSON
    AND WITH THE GLIMMERING CRIMSON GLOWED . . . .   3 OISIN 1   26
    AND WITH THE WOVEN CRIMSON GLOWED . . . .   3 OISIN 1   V   26
    ABOUT HIS FADING CRIMSON BALL! . . . .   12 OISIN 1   155
    IN SILENCE ROUND HIS CRIMSON BALL. . . . .   12 OISIN 1   V   155
    AND TRIMMED WITH MANY A CRIMSON FEATHER! . . . .   15 OISIN 1   206
    TRIMMED ROUND WITH MANY A CRIMSON FEATHER! . . . . . .   15 OISIN 1   V   206
    BLOSSOM IN SOME NEW CRIMSON FLOWER, ...   16 OISIN 1   224
    LIKE CRIMSON METEORS HANG IN THE GLOOM, ...   21 OISIN 1   306
    THE PEA-HENS DANCE, IN CRIMSON FEATHER . . . .   77 INDIAN TO LOVE V   3
    THE SOUTH IS POURING DOWN ROSES OF CRIMSON FIRE! . . . .   154 BELOVED PEACE   6
    THE SOUTH WOULD COVER THEM WITH ROSES OF CRIMSON FIRE! . . 154 BELOVED PEACE V   6
    AND STOLE THE CRIMSON ROSE, ...   174 ELEMENT POWERS V   2
    AND SHE FORGET THE WANDERING AND ALL THE CRIMSON GLOOM . . 175 ELEMENT POWERS V   11
    AND SHE FORGET THE WANDERING AND THE CRIMSON GLOOM . . .   175 ELEMENT POWERS V   11
    OVER THEM CRIMSON VAPOURS WINGING. . . . .   648 ISLE STAT I 1   92
    BLEW MY CRIMSON CAP AWAY . . . .   656 ISLE STAT I 3   16
    AND TRAILING CRIMSON VANS, A MUMBLING BROOD, ...   687 TWO TITANS   20
CRITIC
    THE MEDITATIVE CRITIC! ALL ARE ON THEIR TOES, ...   363 DOLLS FACES   8
CRITICS
    WE ARE BUT CRITICS, OR BUT HALF CREATE, ...   368 EGO DOMINUS   15
CROAGH
    UPON CROAGH PATRICK SANG IT LOUD! . . . .   528 DANCER CRUACH V   5
CROCUS
    WHERE GOLDEN CROCUS AND NARCISSUS BLOOM, ...   447 COLONUS PRAISE   18
CROMLECH
    WE WHO STILL LABOUR BY THE CROMLECH ON THE SHORE, . . .   161 BLACK PIG   5
    WE, WHO ARE LABOURING BY THE CROMLECH ON THE SHORE, . . . 161 BLACK PIG   V   5
CROMWELL
    THE CURSE OF CROMWELL . . . .   580 CURSE CROMWELL   T
CROMWELL'S
    NOTHING BUT CROMWELL'S HOUSE AND CROMWELL'S MURDEROUS CREW, 580 CURSE CROMWELL   2
    NOTHING BUT CROMWELL'S HOUSE AND CROMWELL'S MURDEROUS CREW, 580 CURSE CROMWELL   2
CRONE
    "INTO A WITHERED CRONE." . . . .   516 MANS SONG   2
    NO WITHERED CRONE I SAW . . . .   516 MANS SONG   11
CROOK
    BROUGHT THE BARE NEWS. HE HAD THROWN THE CROOK AWAY . . 339 SHEP GOATHERD   21
    AND THOUGH I HAVE TURNED THE TALK BY HOOK OR CROOK . . .   350 HER PRAISE   5
CROOKED
    THE PILOT STAR AND THE CROOKED PLOUGH . . . .   177 PAST GREATNESS   4
    AND THE GREY BIRD WITH CROOKED BILL . . . .   192 BAILE AILLINN   89
    O LOVE IS THE CROOKED THING, ...   268 BROWN PENNY   9
    SAID THE WICKED, CROOKED, HAWTHORN TREE! . . . .   788 HAWTHORN TREE   6
    SAID THE WICKED, CROOKED, HAWTHORN TREE. . . . . . .   788 HAWTHORN TREE   14
CROON
    THE GIDDY BEE'S COMPLACENT CROON, ...   736 SUMMER EVENING   5
CROONING
    SWAYED, CROONING TO HIMSELF AN UNKNOWN TONGUE! . . . .   39 OISIN 2   159
CROP
    WHAT A CROP OF MUMMY WHEAT! . . . .   562 CONJUNCTIONS   2
CRO-PATRICK
    THE DANCER AT CRUACHAN AND CRO-PATRICK . . . .   528 DANCER CRUACH   T
    UPON CRO-PATRICK SANG ALOUD! . . . .   528 DANCER CRUACH   5
CROPPED   SEE CLOSE-CROPPED
CROPS
    HALF ASLEEP THE OLD COW CROPS, ...   706 DAWN-SONG   20
CROSIERED
    . . . CROSIERED ONE, CAUGHT IN THY NET-- . . . .   58 OISIN 3   V   167
    THE REST THOU HAST HEARD OF, THOU CROSIERED ONE-- . . .   60 OISIN 3   V   189
CROSIERS
    NOW, MAN OF CROSIERS, PHANTOMS DREW AROUND . . . . . .   29 OISIN 2   V   1
    LORD OF THE CROSIERS, THOU EVEN HADST LIFTED THY HANDS
        AND WEPT!   54 OISIN 3   V   110
CROSS
    A CROSS THEY HAD MADE OUT OF TWO BITS OF WOOD, ...   123 DREAM OF DEATH   7
    I CAME AND WROTE UPON A CROSS OF WOOD-- . . . . . .   123 DREAM OF DEATH V   7
    AND THOUGH THEY HAVE TO CROSS THE LOUGHLAN WATERS . . .   282 TWO KINGS   113
    AND THOUGH THEY HAVE TO CROSS THE LOUGHLAN SEAS . . . .   282 TWO KINGS   V   113
    MY COUNTRY IS KILTARTAN CROSS, ...   328 IRISH AIRMAN   5
    BY CHILDISH MEMORIES OF AN OLD CROSS POLLEXFEN, ...   391 UNDER SATURN   7
    THAT CUT THROUGH TIME OR CROSS IT WITHERSHINS. . . . .   489 COOLE PARK 29   24
    THAT CAN CROSS TIME AND CUT IT WITHERSHINS. . . . . .   489 COOLE PARK 29 V   24
    CROSS THE NARROW STRAITS TO LIGHT . . . .   494 AT ALGECIRAS   4
    CROSS THOSE NARROW STRAITS TO LIGHT . . . .   494 AT ALGECIRAS   V   4
    THE SWORD'S A CROSS! THEREON HE DIED! . . . .   562 CONJUNCTIONS   3
    THE OLD STONE CROSS . . . .   598 STONE CROSS   T
    UNDER THE OLD STONE CROSS. . . . .   598 STONE CROSS   8
    UNDER THE OLD STONE CROSS. . . . .   599 STONE CROSS   16
    UNDER THE OLD STONE CROSS. . . . .   599 STONE CROSS   24
    SET UP THE OLD STONE CROSS, ...   604 YOU CONTENT   10
    BY THE ROAD AN ANCIENT CROSS. . . . .   640 BEN BULBEN   88
    I SPEAK ALONE WITH SERVANTS OF THE CROSS . . . . . .   698 MOSADA 2   48
    SAT UNDERNEATH THE MARKET CROSS, ...   724 LEGEND   2
    A SONG OF THE ROSY CROSS . . . .   744 ROSY CROSS   T
    GAVE TO ME ALONE THE CROSS! . . . .   744 ROSY CROSS   3
    GAVE TO ME ALONE THE CROSS. . . . .   744 ROSY CROSS   11
    FLIT TO KILTARTAN CROSS AND STAY . . . .   791 REPRISALS   11
CROSS'D
    FROM WASTE SEAS CROSS'D, YET EVER GARRULOUS) . . . . .   690 MOSADA 1   9

172

	PAGE	TITLE	LINE

CROSSED
  THAT HAS DRUNK FULL, SHE CROSSED THE MISTY SEA . . . . 30 OISIN 2   16
  THAT COUNTRY WHERE A MAN CAN BE SO CROSSED: . . . . . 130 BOOK STORIES   16
  FOR I AM AENGUS, AND I AM CROSSED IN LOVE." . . . . . 183 QUEEN MAEVE   84
  WHEN NEITHER SOUL NOR BODY HAS BEEN CROSSED. . . . . . 258 KING NO KING   16
  JAMES AND HIS IRISH WHEN THE DUTCHMAN CROSSED: . . . . 270 PARDON FATHERS   12
  WITH THE HOT BLOOD OF YOUTH, OF LOVE CROSSED LONG AGO: . 316 COLD HEAVEN   6
  IT NEVER CROSSED THE SEA BECAUSE . . . . 583 GHOST ROG CASE   3
  ONE IMAGE CROSSED THE MANY-HEADED, SAT . . . . . . 610 STATUES   17
  TO SEEK NOT HOPELESS HAVE I CROSSED THE GLOOM, ... 656 ISLE STAT I 3   42
  AS THOUGH SHE WHOM YOU FEAR HAD CROSSED THE WIDE . . . 669 ISLE STAT II 3   77
  A DEAL OF EVIL AND OF CHANGE HATH CROSSED . . . . . 676 ISLE STAT II 3   273
  WITH THREE BARS CROSSED, AND THESE FOUR WALLS MY WORLD, 700 MOSADA 3   32
CROSSES
  CROSSES THE NARROW STRAITS TO LIGHT . . . . 494 AT ALGECIRAS   V   4
CROSS-GARTERED
  ROUGH MEN-AT-ARMS, CROSS-GARTERED TO THE KNEES . . . . 412 TOWER   82
  ROUGH MEN AT ARMS, CROSS-GARTERED TO THE KNEES . . . . 412 TOWER   V   82
CROSSING
  CROSSING STREAM AGAIN . . . . 419 MY HOUSE   9
CROUCH
  CROUCH UPON A STONE, ... 525 DANCING DAYS   4
  AND CROUCH IN SOME FAR STILLNESS OF THE ISLE, AND DIE. . 675 ISLE STAT II 3   246
CROUCHED
  AND CROUCHED BY THE ARM OF HIS CHAIR, ... 319 DOLLS   16
  FIERCE MORTAL, AND CROUCHED LOW BESIDE THE LAKE . . . 675 ISLE STAT II 3 V 245A
CROUCHES
  AMONG THE FRUIT! BUT THERE, LAME COLA CROUCHES . . . . 691 MOSADA 1   32
  AMONG THE FRUIT. BUT YON, LAME COLA CROUCHES . . . . 691 MOSADA 1   V   32
CROUCHING
  TWO FIGURES CROUCHING ON THE BLACK ROCK, BOUND . . . . 687 TWO TITANS   5
  WHY NOT? HE IS HER OWN! AND CROUCHING NIGH . . . . . 688 TWO TITANS   44
CROW   SEE A-CROW
  CROW UPON TARA." KING EOCHAID BOWED HIS HEAD . . . . 286 TWO KINGS   211
  CROW UPON TARA." SHE HAD FIXED HER EYES . . . . . 286 TWO KINGS   V   211
  ALTHOUGH HE THOUGHT IT WORTH A CROW. . . . . . . 388 SOLOMON WITCH   35
  ANOTHER LINEAGE FEED THE CROW, ... 437 SONGS PLAY 1   10
  CAN LIKE THE COCKS OF HADES CROW, ... 498 BYZANTIUM   20
  BUT YONDER THING, YON IDLE NOISE, YON CROW, ... 648 ISLE STAT I 1   104
  RED BIRD OF MARCH, BEGIN TO CROW! . . . . 782 HEART FRIGHT   5
  RED COCK, AND CROW! . . . . 782 HEART FRIGHT   7
  RED BIRD OF MARCH, BEGIN TO CROW! . . . . 782 HEART FRIGHT   12
  RED COCK, AND CROW! . . . . 782 HEART FRIGHT   14
  RED BIRD OF MARCH, BEGIN TO CROW! . . . . 782 HEART FRIGHT   19
  RED COCK, AND CROW! . . . . 782 HEART FRIGHT   21
  RED COCKS, AND CROW! . . . . 783 GREY ROUND   28
CROWD
  AND HID HIS FACE AMID A CROWD OF STARS. . . . . . 121 YOU ARE OLD   12
  HE STOOD AMONG A CROWD AT DROMAHAIR: . . . . . . 126 DREAM OF FAERY   1
  VOICES AMONG THE CROWD . . . . 172 PLEADS FRIEND   2
  AND THE TONGUES OF THE CROWD . . . . 172 PLEADS FRIEND   V   2
  GATHERED A CROWD IN SOME BYZANTINE LANE, ... 180 QUEEN MAEVE   2
  ARE DANCING IN A CROWD. . . . . 214 HAPPY TOWNLAND   12
  ARE DANCING IN THE CROWD. . . . . 214 HAPPY TOWNLAND V   12
  A CROWD UPON A SHORE. . . . . 253 HIS DREAM   4
  AND THOUGH I WOULD HAVE HUSHED THE CROWD, ... 253 HIS DREAM   5
  AND RUNNING CROWD AND GAUDY SHIP . . . . 254 HIS DREAM   15
  AND FISH AND CROWD AND PAINTED SHIP, ... 254 HIS DREAM   V   15
  AND FISH AND CROWD AND GAUDY SHIP . . . . 254 HIS DREAM   V   15
  THE CROWD THAT CLOSES IN BEHIND: . . . . 266 GALWAY RACES   4
  THESE, THESE REMAIN, BUT I RECORD WHAT'S GONE. A CROWD 315 FALLEN MAJESTY   6
  ALL THE DISHONEST CROWD I HAD DRIVEN AWAY. . . . . 352 PEOPLE   24
  THERE'LL BE THAT CROWD, THAT BARBAROUS CROWD. . . . . 354 HIS PHOENIX   25
  THERE'LL BE THAT CROWD, THAT BARBAROUS CROWD, ... 354 HIS PHOENIX   25
  THERE'LL BE THAT CROWD TO MAKE MEN WILD THROUGH ALL THE 354 HIS PHOENIX   V   25
    CENTURIES,
  THE LEADERS OF THE CROWD . . . . 398 LEADERS CROWD   T
  SO THE CROWD COME THEY CARE NOT WHAT MAY COME. . . . 398 LEADERS CROWD   10
  UNDER THE GREAT COMEDIAN'S TOMB THE CROWD. . . . . 541 PARN FUNERAL 1   1
  A FRENZIED CROWD, AND WHERE THE BRANCHES SPRANG . . . 541 PARN FUNERAL 1   9
  THEIR SCHOOL A CROWD, HIS MASTER SOLITUDE! . . . . 543 PARN FUNERAL 2   10
  THEIR SCHOOL THE CROWD, HIS MASTER SOLITUDE, ... 543 PARN FUNERAL 2 V   10
  THEIR SCHOOL A CROWD, HIS MASTER'S SOLITUDE: . . . . 543 PARN FUNERAL 2 V   10
  ESCAPED OUT OF HER CROWD, ... 568 SWEET DANCER   5
  MY FATHER UPON THE ABBEY STAGE, BEFORE HIM A RAGING CROWD! 577 LOFTY THINGS   2
  THAT ALL ATTENDANTS AND THE CASUAL CROWD MIGHT HEAR. . 609 IN TARAS HALLS   13
  ON MY POOR BRAIN YOUR BUSY TUMULTS CROWD. . . . . . 648 ISLE STAT I 1   100
  SOON WILL THE CHURCHMEN NOD ABOVE THE CROWD. . . . . 699 MOSADA 3   19
  BEFORE WE TAKE OUR SEATS ABOVE THE CROWD. . . . . . 704 MOSADA 3   134
  OR CROWD BEHIND THE BULWARK, THAT WE SEEM . . . . . 751 SHADOW WATER A   94
CROWDED   SEE MACKEREL-CROWDED
  THE DANCERS CROWDED ABOUT HIM . . . . 144 HOST OF AIR   17
  CROWDED WITH BITTER FACES, THE WOUNDS IN PALM AND SIDE, 172 TRAV PASSION   4
  OUR HEARTS ENDURE THE PLAITED THORN, THE CROWDED WAY, . 172 TRAV PASSION   V   3
  ON EVERY CROWDED STREET TO STARE . . . . 294 HATED PLAYBOY   3
  IN A CROWDED LONDON SHOP, ... 501 VACILLATION   37
CROWDS
  AND ARE PLAGUED BY CROWDS, UNTIL . . . . 298 THREE HERMITS   20
  ALTHOUGH CROWDS GATHERED ONCE IF SHE BUT SHOWED HER FACE, 314 FALLEN MAJESTY   1
  NOR PUBLIC MEN, NOR CHEERING CROWDS, ... 328 IRISH AIRMAN   10
  NOR PUBLIC MAN, NOR ANGRY CROWDS, ... 328 IRISH AIRMAN   V   10

	PAGE	TITLE		LINE

CROWDS   (CONTINUED)
NOR PUBLIC MAN, NOR CHEERING CROWDS, ...   328 IRISH AIRMAN   V   10
CROWDS JOSTLED AT THE FAIR . . . .   410 TOWER   V   39
CROWED
HOWLED, MIAU-D, BARKED, BRAYED, BELLED, YELLED, CRIED,   387 SOLOMON WITCH   8
   CROWED,
HE THAT CROWED OUT ETERNITY . . . .   388 SOLOMON WITCH   17
THOUGHT TO HAVE CROWED IT IN AGAIN. . . . .   388 SOLOMON WITCH   18
CROWN
UNDER A CROWN OF THORNS AND DARK WITH BLOOD, ...   38 OISIN 2   135
TO HIM SEEMED EASY, SO I LAID THE CROWN . . . .   102 FERGUS DRUID   13
AND STILL I FEEL THE CROWN UPON MY HEAD. . . . . . .   103 FERGUS DRUID   20
BUT STILL I FEEL THE CROWN UPON MY HEAD. . . . . . .   103 FERGUS DRUID   V   20
WHY MUST YOU BLENCH AND SHAKE FROM FOOT TO CROWN?" . .   106 CUCHULAIN SEA   13
"WHY DO YOU TREMBLE THUS FROM FEET TO CROWN?" . . . .   106 CUCHULAIN SEA   V   13
WHY ARE YOU PALE AND SHAKE FROM FOOT TO CROWN?" . . .   106 CUCHULAIN SEA   V   13
AND THE PROUD DREAMING KING WHO FLUNG THE CROWN . . .   170 SECRET ROSE   19
THAT I MIGHT LAY IT ON YOUR HEAD AS A CROWN. . . . .   246 SHADOW WATER B   511
SHALL BE ALONE FOR EVER. WE TWO--THIS CROWN-- . . .   251 SHADOW WATER B   605
BEND LOWER, O KING, THAT I MAY CROWN YOU WITH IT. . .   251 SHADOW WATER B   607
SHE MAY HAVE WORN SILK CLOTHES, OR WORN A CROWN, . .   282 TWO KINGS   117
WAS BORN TO WEAR A CROWN. . . . .   308 PLAYER QUEEN   12
OVER THE CROWN OF THE WILLOWS BROWN. . . . .   653 ISLE STAT I 2   30
OVER THE CROWN OF THE WILLOWS BROWN. . . . .   653 ISLE STAT I 2   51
'TIS CLEAR THAT YOU HAVE SEEN HER NOT. THE CROWN . .   661 ISLE STAT II 1   70
OF FAILURE, AND TO CROWN HER CROWNLESS HEAD, ...   688 TWO TITANS   48
WE WILL BRING A CROWN OF GOLD, ...   726 LOVERS QUARREL   13
BEYOND THE SAIL A MAN WITH A RED CROWN . . . .   752 SHADOW WATER A   126
I HAVE BROUGHT HIS CROWN. AND I HAVE BROUGHT HIS QUEEN.   755 SHADOW WATER A   166
THERE--THERE--BY THE OAR. THE CROWN OF A FAR COUNTRY. .   763 SHADOW WATER A   310
THAT CROWN WAS IN MY DREAMS--NO, NO--IN A RHYME. . .   763 SHADOW WATER A   311
I CROWN YOU WITH THIS CROWN. BEND LOWER, O KING, . .   768 SHADOW WATER A   423
I CROWN YOU WITH THIS CROWN. BEND LOWER, O KING, . .   768 SHADOW WATER A   423
SHARED THE BYZANTINE CROWN? . . . .   789 SINGING HEAD   14
CROWNED   SEE LEAF-CROWNED
HIS SHOUTING DAYS WITH MIRTH WERE CROWNED. . . . . .   67 HAPPY SHEPHERD   50
OF THE CROWNED MAGI; AND THE KING WHOSE EYES . . . .   169 SECRET ROSE   9
OF THE CROWNED MAGI; AND THE HOUND OF CU . . . . . .   169 SECRET ROSE   V   9
OF THE CROWNED MAGI; AND THE KINGS WHOSE EYES . . . .   169 SECRET ROSE   V   9
. . . THOUGHT'S CROWNED POWERS HE CALLED THEM ONCE. . .   480 BLOOD AND MOON   15
CROWNLESS
OF FAILURE, AND TO CROWN HER CROWNLESS HEAD, ...   688 TWO TITANS   48
CROWNS
THE JEWELLED CROWNS THAT KINGS HAVE HURLED . . . . .   155 FORGOT BEAUTY   4
WHO COME WITH THEIR CROWNS OF PEARL AND THEIR SPINDLES   203 WITHER BOUGHS   10
   OF WOOL,
HURL HELMETS, CROWNS, AND SWORDS INTO THE PIT. . . .   257 RECONCILIATION   10
THE CROWNS OF NINEVEH. . . . .   439 FRAGMENTS   10
PROFFERING ITS SACRED LAUREL CROWNS, ...   612 NEWS ORACLE   23
THE STARS WOULD HURL THEIR CROWNS AMONG THE FOAM . .   761 SHADOW WATER A   265
CROZIER
. . . THE CROZIER GLEAMS! . . . .   61 OISIN 3   194
. . . THAT CROZIER GLEAMS! . . . .   61 OISIN 3   V   194
CROZIERED
. . . CROZIERED ONE, CAUGHT IN YOUR NET! . . . . .   58 OISIN 3   167
. . . CROZIERED ONE, CAUGHT IN THEIR NET! . . . . .   58 OISIN 3   V   167
THE REST YOU HAVE HEARD OF, O CROZIERED MAN! . . . .   60 OISIN 3   189
CROZIERS
NOW, MAN OF CROZIERS, SHADOWS CALLED OUR NAMES . . .   29 OISIN 2   1
FOR ALL YOUR CROZIERS, THEY HAVE LEFT THE PATH . . .   42 OISIN 2   200
AND, MAN OF THE MANY WHITE CROZIERS, A CENTURY THERE I   52 OISIN 3   77
   FORGOT
AND, MAN OF THE MANY WHITE CROZIERS, A CENTURY THERE I   52 OISIN 3   81
   FORGOT
BUT IN DREAMS, MILD MAN OF THE CROZIERS, ...   53 OISIN 3   85
SO WATCHED I WHEN, MAN OF THE CROZIERS, ...   54 OISIN 3   101
LORD OF THE CROZIERS, YOU EVEN HAD LIFTED YOUR HANDS AND   54 OISIN 3   110
   WEPT!
AND OLD MEN WITH CROZIERS AND STOLES. . . . .   167 BLESSED   16
CRUACHAN
IN HER HIGH HOUSE AT CRUACHAN; THE LONG HEARTH, . . .   180 QUEEN MAEVE   11
HE SAID, "HIGH QUEEN OF CRUACHAN AND MAGH AI, ...   183 QUEEN MAEVE   77
HE SAID "QUEEN OF UNSHELTERED CRUACHAN, ...   183 QUEEN MAEVE   V   77
QUEEN OF HIGH CRUACHAN." "I OBEY YOUR WILL . . . . .   184 QUEEN MAEVE   99
WITH THE FIRST KINGS OF MANY-PILLARED CRUACHAN. . . .   187 QUEEN MAEVE   151
WITH THE FIRST KINGS OF MANY PILLARED CRUACHAN . . .   187 QUEEN MAEVE   V   151
CALLED CRUACHAN, AND IT WAS AS MUCH . . . .   302 HOUR DAWN   4
STUMBLED ON WINDY CRUACHAN . . . .   302 HOUR DAWN   V   3
BUT THE HELL MOUTH AT CRUACHAN . . . .   303 HOUR DAWN   V   24
FROM THE HELL MOUTH AT CRUACHAN . . . .   307 HOUR DAWN   V   120
THE DANCER AT CRUACHAN AND CRO-PATRICK . . . .   528 DANCER CRUACH   T
TOM AT CRUACHAN . . . .   529 TOM CRUACHAN   T
OLD TOM AT CRUACHAN . . . .   529 TOM CRUACHAN   V   T
CRUACHAN'S
DANCED ON CRUACHAN'S WINDY PLAIN, ...   528 DANCER CRUACH   4
DANCED IT ON CRUACHAN'S WINDY PLAIN, ...   528 DANCER CRUACH   V   4
ON CRUACHAN'S PLAIN SLEPT HE . . . .   529 TOM CRUACHAN   1
CRUCIFIED
HIS FATHERS SERVED THEIR FATHERS BEFORE CHRIST WAS   580 CURSE CROMWELL   6
   CRUCIFIED.

		PAGE	TITLE		LINE

CRUCIFIX
   SINKS, SHINING ON THE LITTLE CRUCIFIX • • • • • • •   691 MOSADA 1   34
   A-SHINING ON THE LITTLE CRUCIFIX • • • • • • • •   691 MOSADA 1   V 34
CRUEL
   SANG WHERE--UNNECESSARY CRUEL VOICE-- • • • • •   127 DREAM OF FAERY   30
   CRUEL CLAW AND HUNGRY THROAT, • • • • • • • •   136 TWO TREES   36
   FORGOT IN CRUEL HAPPINESS • • • • • • • • •   453 MERMAID   5
   "O CRUEL DEATH, GIVE THREE THINGS BACK," • • • •   521 THREE THINGS   1
   WHY SHOULD HE THINK ME CRUEL • • • • • • • •   532 BEFORE WORLD   13
   THOU WILT NOT SPEAK, OH CRUEL ART THOU YET! • • •   684 SEEKER   V 69A
   AH! CRUEL ONES, LEAVE ME ALONE NOW • • • • • •   707 FAIRY PEDANT   13
   AH! CRUEL ONES, LEAVE ME ALONE • • • • • • •   707 FAIRY PEDANT   V 13
   AND LOVE WENCH WISDOM'S CRUEL FACE. • • • • • •   787 HUDDON DUDDON   10
   AND LOVE WENCH--WISDOM'S CRUEL FACE. • • • • • •   787 HUDDON DUDDON   V 10
CRUELTIES
   WITH CRUELTIES OF CHOICE AND CHANCE! • • • • •   388 SOLOMON WITCH   23
CRUELTY
   OF BEAUTY'S CRUELTY AND WISDOM'S CHATTER-- • • • •   377 PHASES OF MOON   121
   CRUELTY MUST KEEP; THEREFORE BE WARNED AND GO • • •   448 HERO GIRL FOOL   7
   AND NEEDS NO CRUELTY. I HAVE HEARD ONE SAY • • •   448 HERO GIRL FOOL   13
   MY CRUELTY MUST KEEP! AND SO BEGONE • • • • •   448 HERO GIRL FOOL   V 7
   AND HAVE NO NEED OF CRUELTY TO KEEP • • • • • •   448 HERO GIRL FOOL   V 12A
   OR IN MERE WOMAN'S CRUELTY • • • • • • • • •   789 SINGING HEAD   11
CRUISE
   A GOOD ROUND SUM UPON THIS CRUISE, AND TURN-- • • • •   222 SHADOW WATER B   5
CRUMB
   I HAVE NOT A CRUMB OF COMFORT, NOT A GRAIN. • • • •   200 FOLLY COMFORT   7
   A CAREFUL FIELD-MOUSE FINDS A FALLEN CRUMB! • • •   713 FERENCZ RENYI   77
CRUMBLED
   BREATHED OUT A DRUID VAPOUR, AND CRUMBLED AWAY • • • •   761 SHADOW WATER A   279
CRUMBLING
   THE CRUMBLING MOON, THE WHITE STARS IN THE SKY, • • • •   120 SORROW OF LOVE V   10
   AND CLIMBED INTO THE AIR, CRUMBLING AWAY, • • • • •   278 TWO KINGS   42
   AND AFTER THAT THE CRUMBLING OF THE MOON. • • • • •   375 PHASES OF MOON   87
   UPON THE BROKEN, CRUMBLING BATTLEMENT, • • • • • •   477 SELF AND SOUL   3
CRUMPLE
   CRUMPLE THE ROSE IN YOUR HAIR! • • • • • • • •   162 ASKS FORGIVE   4
CRUMPLED
   AND CRUMPLED IN MY HANDS THE STAFF • • • • • • •   84 MAD KING GOLL   V 33
CRUNCHES
   THERE WHERE YONDER SQUIRREL CRUNCHES • • • • • • •   655 ISLE STAT I 3   4
CRUSH
   CRUSH THE ROSE IN YOUR HAIR, • • • • • • • • •   162 ASKS FORGIVE   V 4
CRUSHED
   AS A GRASS SEED CRUSHED BY A PEBBLE, AS A WOLF SUCKED UNDER   63 OISIN 3   V 220
     A WEIR.
   BUT THE CRUSHED GRASS WHERE WE HAVE LAIN! • • • • •   389 SOLOMON WITCH   42
CRUSHING
   • • • THE STRONG HOOFS CRUSHING THE SAND AND THE SHELLS,   58 OISIN 3   157
   • • • THE GOLD HOOVES CRUSHING THE SANDS AND THE SHELLS   58 OISIN 3   V 157
   • • • THE STRONG HOOFS CRUSHING THE SANDS AND THE SHELLS   58 OISIN 3   V 157
   ARE 'NEATH ITS PROW, AND CRUSHING SHELLS. • • • • •   663 ISLE STAT II 2   35
CRUST
   WILL SCARCELY FIND FOR HIM A BROKEN CRUST • • • • •   373 PHASES OF MOON   23
CRUTCH
   A BUNDLE OF RAGS UPON A CRUTCH, • • • • • • •   302 HOUR DAWN   2
   WERE HERE, HE WOULD TURN DEATH INTO A CRUTCH! • • • •   711 FERENCZ RENYI   38
CRUTCHES
   OF GRIEVOUS TIME ON HIS OLD CRUTCHES, • • • • • •   23 OISIN 1   V 341B
   GREY HAIRS AND CRUTCHES, CRUTCHES AND GREY HAIRS, • • •   721 WITCH VIVIEN   20
   GREY HAIRS AND CRUTCHES, CRUTCHES AND GREY HAIRS, • • •   721 WITCH VIVIEN   20
CRY
   BUT NOW HEARTS CRY THAT HEARTS ARE SLAVES, • • • • •   19 OISIN 1   280
   AND THE CRY OF THE HOUNDS ON THE HILLS OF OLD. • • • •   27 OISIN 1   407
   FOR NO MAN'S CRY SHALL EVER MOUNT SO FAR! • • • • •   36 OISIN 2   108
   FOR NEVER MORTAL CRY SO FAR HATH SENT. • • • • • •   36 OISIN 2   V 108
   NOR NO MAN'S CRY SHALL EVER MOUNT SO FAR! • • • • •   36 OISIN 2   V 108
   AND AT HIS CRY THERE CAME NO MILK-PALE FACE • • • • •   38 OISIN 2   134
   THE SEA SWEPT ON AND CRIED HER OLD CRY STILL, • • • •   68 SAD SHEPHERD   10
   I KNOW THE WORD THEY CRY, "ETERNITY!" • • • • • •   81 EPHEMERA   V 24F
   NOT THEY ARE THE ETERNAL--'TIS THE CRY." • • • • •   81 EPHEMERA   V 24J
   A GAY WANDERING CRY. • • • • • • • • • • •   98 FOXHUNTER   28
   A GAY AND WANDERING CRY. • • • • • • • • • •   98 FOXHUNTER   V 28
   PARTED HER LIPS WITH A LOUD SUDDEN CRY. • • • • •   105 CUCHULAIN SEA   8
   GOD'S BELL HAS CLAIMED THEM BY THE LITTLE CRY • • • •   114 ROSE OF BATTLE   23
   WE SHALL NO LONGER HEAR THE LITTLE CRY • • • • • •   115 ROSE OF BATTLE   35
   HAD BLOTTED OUT MAN'S IMAGE AND HIS CRY. • • • • •   120 SORROW OF LOVE   4
   COULD BUT COMPOSE MAN'S IMAGE AND HIS CRY. • • • • •   120 SORROW OF LOVE   12
   HAD HID AWAY EARTH'S OLD AND WEARY CRY. • • • • •   120 SORROW OF LOVE V   4
   ARE SHAKEN WITH EARTH'S OLD AND WEARY CRY. • • • • •   120 SORROW OF LOVE V   12
   PROCLAIM WITH THAT UNWEARIED, REEDY CRY • • • • • •   128 DREAM OF FAERY   42
   A-TELLING WITH THEIR LOW AND REEDY CRY • • • • • •   128 DREAM OF FAERY V   42
   PROCLAIMING WITH A LOW AND REEDY CRY, • • • • • •   128 DREAM OF FAERY V   42
   AND, LIKE A STORM, CRY THE INEFFABLE NAME, • • • • •   137 TO SOME I TALK   12
   THE CRY OF A CHILD BY THE ROADWAY, THE CREAK OF A LUMBERING   142 ROSE IN HEART   2
     CART,
   AND SCATTERED THE CARDS WITH A CRY, • • • • • •   145 HOST OF AIR   V 38
   DESOLATE WINDS THAT CRY OVER THE WANDERING SEA! • • •   147 UNAPPEAS HOST   7
   O CURLEW, CRY NO MORE IN THE AIR, • • • • • • •   155 REPROVE CURLEW   1
   HE HEARS THE CRY OF THE SEDGE • • • • • • • • •   165 CRY OF SEDGE   T
   AEDH HEARS THE CRY OF THE SEDGE • • • • • • • •   165 CRY OF SEDGE   V T

175

CRY   (CONTINUED)

	PAGE	TITLE		LINE
TILL THE ATTORNEY FOR LOST SOULS CRY HER SWEET CRY,	173	SPEAKS HEARERS		6
TILL THE ATTORNEY FOR LOST SOULS CRY HER SWEET CRY,	173	SPEAKS HEARERS		6
TILL MAURYA OF THE WOUNDED HEART CRY A SWEET CRY,	173	SPEAKS HEARERS	V	6
TILL MAURYA OF THE WOUNDED HEART CRY A SWEET CRY,	173	SPEAKS HEARERS	V	6
CRY OF HIS LOVE WITH THEIR PITIFUL CRIES,	177	PAST GREATNESS	V	12
I HARDLY HEAR THE CURLEW CRY,	189	BAILE AILLINN		1
LET RUSH AND BIRD CRY OUT THEIR FILL	197	BAILE AILLINN		198
"LET PEEWIT CALL AND CURLEW CRY WHERE THEY WILL,	203	WITHER BOUGHS		2
A QUEEN-WOMAN DRESSED OUT IN SILVER, CRY	210	RAGGED WOOD	V	2
I WILL DRIVE ALL THOSE LOVERS OUT AND CRY--	211	RAGGED WOOD		10
FOR THERE THE TALL DEER AND HIS LEMAN CRY	211	RAGGED WOOD	V	6
I WILL DRIVE OUT THE DEER AND MOON AND CRY--	211	RAGGED WOOD	V	10
I'LL HOLLO ALL THOSE LOVERS OUT AND CRY--	211	RAGGED WOOD		10
OR CRY ABOUT ONE'S EARS. NOTHING TO FEAR.	222	SHADOW WATER B		19
AND LISTENING TO THE CRY OF WIND AND WAVE	236	SHADOW WATER B		315
AND LISTENING TO THE CRY OF THE WIND AND WAVE	236	SHADOW WATER B	V	315
BUT NO, NO, NO! YOUR CRY IS NOT AGAINST ME.	244	SHADOW WATER B		449
THAT YOU MAY NEVER HEAR THE CRY OF THE BIRDS,	250	SHADOW WATER B		575
TO CRY ALOUD TO THE GREY BIRDS, AND DREAMS,	252	SHADOW WATER B		618
IT VANISHED LIKE A SHADOW, AND A CRY	278	TWO KINGS		38
SO MOURNFUL THAT IT SEEMED THE CRY OF ONE	278	TWO KINGS		39
YOU'D CRY, "SOME WOMAN'S YELLOW HAIR	290	SEPTEMBER 1913		28
A SINGLE SOUL THAT LACKS A SWEET CRYSTALLINE CRY.	291	PAUDEEN		8
"YOU CRY ALOUD, O WOULD 'TWERE SPRING	306	HOUR DAWN		91
"I HEARD A SEA-MEW CRY,	308	PLAYER QUEEN		14
"I HEARD A SEAMEW CRY,	308	PLAYER QUEEN	V	14
WERE IT NOT THAT LOVE UPON THE CRY	314	MEMORY YOUTH		19
FROM NINETEEN HUNDRED NINE OR TEN, PAVLOVA'S HAD THE CRY,	354	HIS PHOENIX		11
AND WITH THAT CRY I HAVE RAISED MY CRY.	361	ALF POLLEXFEN		39
AND WITH THAT CRY I HAVE RAISED MY CRY,	361	ALF POLLEXFEN		39
HE WERE AFRAID THE BIRDS, WHO CRY ALOUD	371	EGO DOMINUS		77
AND CIRCLED ROUND HIM WITH ITS SQUEAKY CRY,	377	PHASES OF MOON		138
COME WITH LOUD CRY AND PANTING BREAST	412	TOWER		86
AND CRY IN PLATO'S TEETH,	415	TOWER		147
OR A BIRD'S SLEEPY CRY	416	TOWER		194
MAY BUILD IN THE CRACKED MASONRY AND CRY	423	MY DESCENDANTS		15
"VENGEANCE UPON THE MURDERERS," THE CRY GOES UP,	426	PHANTOM HATRED		9
NOR CRY, NOR TURN IN THE BED	435	FOR MY SON		3
THE HERALD'S CRY, THE SOLDIER'S TREAD	438	SONGS PLAY 2		13
I'D HAVE A PEACOCK CRY,	458	HIS WILDNESS		8
WITH THAT SWEET CRY.	559	HE AND SHE		12
CRY AT THE ONSET OF THEIR SEXUAL JOY	560	WHENCE COME		2
CRY AT THE ONSET OF THE SEXUAL JOY	560	WHENCE COME	V	2
AND ITS CRY DISTRACTS MY THOUGHT.	633	MAN AND ECHO		46
AND ITS CRY DISTRACTS MY THOUGHTS.	633	MAN AND ECHO	V	46
OF THINE CRY OVER WOLD AND WATER WHITE,	669	ISLE STAT II 3		73
I CRIED THE THING YOU BADE ME CRY.	670	ISLE STAT II 3		114
I CRIED THE WORDS YOU BID ME CRY.	673	ISLE STAT II 3		186
MAKE MOAN AND CRY. WITHIN YON SUNLESS VALLEY,	682	SEEKER		26
THITHER THY DUST, AND KNEAD IT WITH A CRY,	688	TWO TITANS		52
NOT AS HE SHAKES THE FOREST! BUT A CRY	689	NETTLESHIP		8
NOR HEEDS THE OLD, DIM PROTEST AND THE CRY	689	NETTLESHIP		14
ONE SHOULDER TWISTED, AND THE CHILDREN CRY	695	MOSADA 1		116
AND SEIZE HER, AND THUS FLOATS HER QUIVERING CRY!	714	FERENCZ RENYI		105
AND THE BIRD IN THE BRANCHES WILL CRY FOR US CLEAR,	717	LOVE SONG		6
MEN CRY "BRING PAUL, SHIELD BREAKER,	740	EARL PAUL		11
MEN CRY! "BRING PAUL, SHIELD-BREAKER,	740	EARL PAUL	V	11
THOUGH THE GLAD CRY "SHIELD-BREAKER,"	741	EARL PAUL		35
TO CRY HIS FOLDING CRY! NO, NO, BE SILENT,	760	SHADOW WATER A		253
TO CRY HIS FOLDING CRY! NO, NO, BE SILENT,	760	SHADOW WATER A		253
TO CRY HIS FOLDING CRY. THERE IS SOME MAN	760	SHADOW WATER A	V	253
TO CRY HIS FOLDING CRY. THERE IS SOME MAN	760	SHADOW WATER A	V	253
THE HARP-STRINGS HAVE BEGUN TO CRY OUT TO THE EAGLES.	769	SHADOW WATER A		431
IT HAS BEGUN TO CRY OUT TO THE EAGLES.	769	SHADOW WATER A	V	431
THAT I CRY, THAT I CRY?"	772	SONG DEIRDRE 1		8
THAT I CRY, THAT I CRY?"	772	SONG DEIRDRE 1		8
HAVE TO CRY, HAVE TO CRY."	772	SONG DEIRDRE 1		16
HAVE TO CRY, HAVE TO CRY."	772	SONG DEIRDRE 1		16
THOUGH WE WERE BIDDEN TO SING, CRY NOTHING LOUD.	778	SONG DEIRDRE 3		2
THE DREAMING BONES CRY OUT	782	HEART FRIGHT		15
THE CURLEW CRY BEFORE DAWN	783	GREY ROUND		22

CRYING

	PAGE	TITLE		LINE
CRYING, THE PIRATES DROVE HIS SWINE	82	MAD KING GOLL		15
FLYING, CRYING, TO AND FRO,	136	TWO TREES		35
BECAUSE YOUR CRYING BRINGS TO MY MIND	155	REPROVE CURLEW		3
THERE IS ENOUGH EVIL IN THE CRYING OF WIND.	155	REPROVE CURLEW		6
WITH ALL THIS CRYING IN THE WIND,	190	BAILE AILLINN		33
UPON THE THRONE AND CRYING ABOUT THE STREETS	198	SEVEN WOODS		7
COMES CRYING, "I HAVE RUN UPON THE SWORD.	234	SHADOW WATER B		261
WHAT IS THERE BUT THE CRYING OF THE BIRDS?	247	SHADOW WATER B		519
IF YOU'LL BUT LISTEN CLOSELY TO THAT CRYING	247	SHADOW WATER B		520
THEY'RE CRYING OUT, COULD YOU BUT HEAR THEIR WORDS,	247	SHADOW WATER B		529
WITH ALL THOSE SIGHTS AND ALL THAT CRYING OUT?	249	SHADOW WATER B		573
CRYING AMID THE GLITTERING SEA,	254	HIS DREAM		17
CRYING ALOUD AS THE RACECOURSE IS,	266	GALWAY RACES		14
CRYING ALOUD AS THE RACE COURSE IS,	266	GALWAY RACES	V	14
CRYING ALOUD AS THE RACE-COURSE IS,	266	GALWAY RACES	V	14
THE MONSTROUS CRYING OF WIND?	312	CHILD DANCING		12
CRYING TO ONE ANOTHER LIKE THE BATS!	376	PHASES OF MOON		106
"A LAUGHING, CRYING, SACRED SONG,	570	THREE BUSHES		43

CRYING   (CONTINUED)
   A STRICKEN RABBIT IS CRYING OUT, ...   633 MAN AND ECHO   45
   AND CRYING, "I HAVE FLED TO MY BELOVED . . . . .   754 SHADOW WATER A V 151
   AND NOW THE WAVES ARE CRYING IN MY EARS, ...   761 SHADOW WATER A   276
CRY'S
   THAT CRY'S FROM THE FIRST CUCKOO OF THE YEAR. . . . .   338 SHEP GOATHERD   1
   THAT CRY'S FROM THE FIRST CUCKOO OF THE . . . .   338 SHEP GOATHERD   V   1
CRYSTALLINE
   A SINGLE SOUL THAT LACKS A SWEET CRYSTALLINE CRY. . . .   291 PAUDEEN   8
CU
   OF THE CROWNED MAGI, AND THE HOUND OF CU . . . . . .   169 SECRET ROSE   V   9
CUB
   BUT HERE THE LIONESS LICKS HER SOFT CUB. . . . .   688 NETTLESHIP   2
CUBES
   ALL, ALL THOSE GYRES AND CUBES AND MIDNIGHT THINGS . .   469 HARUN RASHID   184
   THOSE CONES AND CUBES AND GYRES, THOSE MIDNIGHT THINGS,   469 HARUN RASHID   V 184
CUBS
   AND LIONESS, WITH ALL THEIR WHIMPERING CUBS; . . . .   73 ANASHU VIJAYA   53
CUCHULAIN
   CUCHULAIN BATTLING WITH THE BITTER TIDE; . . . .   100 ROSE UPON ROOD   3
   THE DEATH OF CUCHULAIN . . . . . .   105 CUCHULAIN SEA V   T
   NOR WON THE GOLD THAT NOW CUCHULAIN BRINGS." . . .   106 CUCHULAIN SEA V 11
   "NAY, YOU ARE TALLER THAN CUCHULAIN, SON." . .   107 CUCHULAIN SEA V 27
   AMONG THOSE FEASTING MEN CUCHULAIN DWELT, .   108 CUCHULAIN SEA V 39
   FEASTED, AND WITH THEM OLD CUCHULAIN DWELT, . . .   108 CUCHULAIN SEA V 39
   AMONG THOSE FEASTING KINGS CUCHULAIN DWELT, . .   108 CUCHULAIN SEA V 39
   AT LAST CUCHULAIN SPAKE, "SOME MAN HAS MADE .   109 CUCHULAIN SEA   47
   CUCHULAIN CRIED, "I AM THE ONLY MAN . . . .   109 CUCHULAIN SEA   55
   AT LAST CUCHULAIN SPAKE, "A YOUNG MAN STRAYS .   109 CUCHULAIN SEA V 47
   CUCHULAIN CRIED, "HAVE MADE AND KEEP THAT VOW."   109 CUCHULAIN SEA V 56
   BUT NOW THE WAR-RAGE IN CUCHULAIN WOKE, . .   110 CUCHULAIN SEA   65
   "CUCHULAIN I, MIGHTY CUCHULAIN'S SON." . .   110 CUCHULAIN SEA   68
   WITH HEAD BOWED ON HIS KNEES CUCHULAIN STAYED;   110 CUCHULAIN SEA   71
   SPAKE THUS: "CUCHULAIN WILL DWELL THERE AND BROOD   110 CUCHULAIN SEA   77
   BUT NOW THE WAR RAGE IN CUCHULAIN WOKE, . .   110 CUCHULAIN SEA V 65
   AND CHAUNTED FOR THREE DAYS. CUCHULAIN STIRRED,   111 CUCHULAIN SEA   83
   IN THREE DAYS' TIME, CUCHULAIN WITH A MOAN .   111 CUCHULAIN SEA V 83
   AND CHANTED FOR THREE DAYS. CUCHULAIN STIRRED,   111 CUCHULAIN SEA V 83
   CUCHULAIN THE GIRL AND THE FOOL . . .   447 HERO GIRL FOOL V   T
   CUCHULAIN THAT FOUGHT NIGHT LONG WITH THE FOAM,   549 SEVERED HEAD   9
   WHEN PEARSE SUMMONED CUCHULAIN TO HIS SIDE, .   611 STATUES   25
   CUCHULAIN SAT AT HER SIDE; . . . . .   628 JANE MOUNTAIN   17
   CUCHULAIN FOUGHT THE UNGOVERNABLE SEA; . .   630 CIRCUS ANIMALS   26
   CUCHULAIN COMFORTED . . . . .   634 CUCHULAIN COMF   T
CUCHULAIN'S
   CUCHULAIN'S FIGHT WITH THE SEA . . . .   105 CUCHULAIN SEA   T
   "CUCHULAIN I, MIGHTY CUCHULAIN'S SON." . . .   110 CUCHULAIN SEA   68
   "I AM FINMOLE, MIGHTY CUCHULAIN'S SON." . .   110 CUCHULAIN SEA V 68
CUCHULIN
   CAME BLANID, MAC NESSA, CUCHULIN; . . . .   53 OISIN 3   V 89
CUCHULLIN
   WITH HEAD BOWED ON HIS KNEES, CUCHULLIN STAID; .   110 CUCHULAIN SEA V 71
   AND CRIED, "CUCHULLIN WILL DWELL THERE AND BROOD,   110 CUCHULAIN SEA V 77
   NEAR TO CUCHULLIN, ROUND A QUICKEN TREE, . .   111 CUCHULAIN SEA V 81A
CUCKOO
   THAT CRY'S FROM THE FIRST CUCKOO OF THE YEAR. .   338 SHEP GOATHERD   1
   THAT CRY'S FROM THE FIRST CUCKOO OF THE . . .   338 SHEP GOATHERD   V   1
   AS THOUGH HE KNEW HIMSELF, AS IT WERE, A CUCKOO, .   341 SHEP GOATHERD   54
   AS ALIEN AS A CUCKOO IN A ROBIN'S NEST, . .   671 ISLE STAT II 3   138
   ALIEN AS CUCKOO IN A ROBIN'S NEST, . . .   671 ISLE STAT II 3 V 138
   AND THE CUCKOO UNSEEN IN HIS FESTIVAL MOOD; . .   717 LOVE SONG   7
CUFF
   NOW CUFF HIM OFF. HE'S OFF! A KISS FOR YOU, . .   73 ANASHU VIJAYA   39
CUMANN'S
   THE OLD BROWN THORN TREES BREAK IN TWO HIGH OVER CUMANN'S 206 HANRAHANS SONG V   1
     STRAND,
CUMBERED   SEE DEW-CUMBERED
   HE HAD SAT DOWN AND SIGHED WITH CUMBERED HEART, . .   37 OISIN 2   111
   HE HAD GONE WHISPERING FORTH WITH CUMBERED HEART, . .   37 OISIN 2   V 111
CUMBROUS
   . . . FOR, CUMBROUS WITH STEMS OF THE HAZEL AND OAK, . .   48 OISIN 3   25
CUMHAL
   CUMHAL CALLED OUT, BENDING HIS HEAD, ...   166 BLESSED   1
   CUMHAL THE KING, BEING ANGRY AND SAD, ...   166 BLESSED   V   1
   AND CUMHAL SAID, BENDING HIS KNEES, ...   167 BLESSED   5
   AND CUMHAL SAW LIKE A DRIFTING SMOKE, . . .   167 BLESSED   13
   "AND WHICH IS THE BLESSEDEST," CUMHAL SAID, . .   167 BLESSED   21
   CUMHAL CALLED OUT, BOWING HIS HEAD, ...   167 BLESSED   V 4A
   "AND WHO IS THE BLESSEDEST," CUMHAL SAID, . . .   167 BLESSED   V 21
CUMMEN
   THE OLD BROWN THORN-TREES BREAK IN TWO HIGH OVER CUMMEN 206 HANRAHANS SONG   1
     STRAND,
   WEAK AND WORN AND WEARY THE WAVES OF CUMMEN STRAND, . .   207 HANRAHANS SONG V   6
CUP   SEE WINE-CUP
   AND FILLS WITH STARS NIGHT'S PURPLE CUP, ...   18 OISIN 1   262
   LIKE THE PALE CUP OF THE SEA, ...   175 ELEMENT POWERS   14
   THEIR HEARTS WOULD BE LIKE A CUP . . . .   215 HAPPY TOWNLAND   31
   FOR THEIR HEARTS WOULD BE LIKE A CUP . . .   215 HAPPY TOWNLAND V 31
   THE ALE CUP IS MY FATHER AND MY MOTHER. . .   222 SHADOW WATER B   11B
   A MELANCHOLY THAT A CUP OF WINE, ...   227 SHADOW WATER B   114
   IS NO MORE THAN A WINE CUP IN THE TASTING, . .   229 SHADOW WATER B V 150

```
                                              PAGE    TITLE              LINE
CUP   (CONTINUED)
         OR ON SOME STILL UNEMPTIED CUP  . . . . . . . .    271  GREY ROCK            21
         AND STRETCHING FORTH HIS ARM AND CUP  . . . . . .  275  GREY ROCK            118
         THE EMPTY CUP  . . . . . . . . . . . . . . . . .   454  EMPTY CUP            T
         A CRAZY MAN THAT FOUND A CUP,  . . . . . . . . .   454  EMPTY CUP            1
         AN OPEN BOOK AND EMPTY CUP  . . . . . . . . . .    501  VACILLATION          38
         I CARRY THE SUN IN A GOLDEN CUP,  . . . . . . .    525  DANCING DAYS         7
         I CARRY THE SUN IN A GOLDEN CUP,  . . . . . . .    525  DANCING DAYS         15
         I CARRY THE SUN IN A GOLDEN CUP,  . . . . . . .    525  DANCING DAYS         23
         MORN-BEWILDERED, AND THE CUP  . . . . . . . . .    646  ISLE STAT I 1        47
         CREEPING ALONG THE HEAVENS' PURPLE CUP,  . . . .   714  FERENCZ RENYI        112
         THEREFORE IN THIS ANCIENT CUP  . . . . . . . . .   776  AGAINST WITCH        36
         THEREFORE FROM THIS ANCIENT CUP  . . . . . . .     776  AGAINST WITCH   V    36
         A GREY-GREEN CUP OF JADE,  . . . . . . . . . . .   781  MY HEART BEAT        15
         OR MAYBE AN AGATE CUP.  . . . . . . . . . . . .    781  MY HEART BEAT        16
CUPBOARDS
         I HAVE CUPBOARDS OF DRIED FRAGRANCE,  . . . . . .  572  LADYS 2ND SONG       5
CUPS
         BREWED BY THE SEA-GODS, FROM HUGE CUPS THAT LAY  . . . .  41  OISIN 2         189
         BREWED BY THE SEA-GODS, FROM HUGE CUPS THAT LAY  . . . .  41  OISIN 2    V    189
         BREWED BY THE SEA GODS, FROM HUGE CUPS THAT LAY  . . . .  41  OISIN 2    V    189
         WHEN CUPS WENT ROUND AT CLOSE OF DAY--  . . . . .  271  GREY ROCK            12
         FROM MURMURING MURIAS: ON CUPS--  . . . . . . .    271  GREY ROCK       V    22
CUR
         BUT A THIEVING RASCALLY CUR--  . . . . . . . . .   552  SONGS REWRIT 2       7
CURD-PALE
         THE CURD-PALE MOON, THE WHITE STARS IN THE SKY,  . . . .  120  SORROW OF LOVE V  10
CURDS
         . . . LONG WARLESS, GROWN WHITER THAN CURDS.  . . . . .  49  OISIN 3         36
         . . . LONG-WARLESS, GROWN WHITER THAN CURDS.  . . . . .  49  OISIN 3    V    36
         WHITER THAN CURDS, ITS EYES THE TINT OF THE SEA.  . . .  277  TWO KINGS      7
CURE
         SIGHED, "YOU, EVEN YOU YOURSELF, COULD WORK THE CURE!"  .  282  TWO KINGS     124
         A FRIEND THAT COULD, HE HAD TOLD HER, WORK HIS CURE  . .  283  TWO KINGS     137
         THAT COULD, AS HE HAD TOLD HER, WORK HIS CURE,  . . . .  283  TWO KINGS  V   137
CURED
         AND THAT IS CURED BY A BOILED LIQUORICE ROOT.  . . . .   227  SHADOW WATER B V 116B
CURES
         CURES HE HATH FOR COW OR GOAT  . . . . . . . . .   716  FAIRY DOCTOR         13
         CURES FOR CALVES WITH 'PLAINING THROAT,  . . . .   717  FAIRY DOCTOR         15
         CURES FOR CALF WITH 'PLAINING THROAT,  . . . . .   717  FAIRY DOCTOR    V    15
CURLEW
         HE REPROVES THE CURLEW  . . . . . . . . . . . .    155  REPROVE CURLEW       T
         WINDLE-STRAWS  I.  O'SULLIVAN RUA TO THE CURLEW  . . . .  155  REPROVE CURLEW V  T
         HANRAHAN REPROVES THE CURLEW  . . . . . . . . .    155  REPROVE CURLEW  V    T
         O CURLEW, CRY NO MORE IN THE AIR,  . . . . . . .   155  REPROVE CURLEW       1
         I HARDLY HEAR THE CURLEW CRY,  . . . . . . . . .   189  BAILE AILLINN        1
         "LET PEEWIT CALL AND CURLEW CRY WHERE THEY WILL,  . . .  203  WITHER BOUGHS    2
         I KNOW, AND THE CURLEW AND PEEWIT ON ECHTGE OF STREAMS.  204  WITHER BOUGHS   22
         AND THE CURLEW AND PEEWIT KNOW ON ECHTGE OF STREAMS.  .  204  WITHER BOUGHS V  22
         UNTIL A CURLEW CRIED AND IN THE LUMINOUS WIND  . . . .   291  PAUDEEN          4
         A CURLEW ANSWERED; AND SUDDENLY THEREUPON I THOUGHT  . .  291  PAUDEEN         5
         A CURLEW ANSWERED, AND I WAS STARTLED BY THE THOUGHT  .  291  PAUDEEN    V    5
         THE CURLEW CRY BEFORE DAWN  . . . . . . . . . .    783  GREY ROUND           22
CURLS
         THE ODOROUS WEIGHT OF HIS CURLS OF LIGHT,  . . .   28   OISIN 1         V 423D
         LIFT THEIR CHINS AND TOSS THEIR CURLS.  . . . .    726  LOVERS QUARREL       23
CURRANT
         HIVES, CURRANT BUSHES.  THERE HIS KIN ARE.  HIGH  . . .  710  FERENCZ RENYI   25
         HE NUMBERS.  HE, WITH FLOWERING CURRANT TREES,  . . . .  710  FERENCZ RENYI V  22
CURRANT-BUSHES
         HIVES, CURRANT-BUSHES.  THERE HIS KIN ARE.  HIGH  . . .  710  FERENCZ RENYI V  25
CURSE
         AND GAVE HIS CURSE TO ME:  . . . . . . . . . . .   95   MOLL MAGEE           26
         ADAM'S CURSE  . . . . . . . . . . . . . . . . .    204  ADAMS CURSE          T
         AS THOUGH IT DRAGGED ROAD-METAL.  MY CURSE ON PLAYS  . .  260  FASC DIFFICULT   8
         AS THOUGH IT DRAGGED ROAD METAL.  MY CURSE ON PLAYS  . .  260  FASC DIFFICULT V  8
         THOSE WINE-DRENCHED EYES, AND CURSE OUR LUCK  . . . . .  272  GREY ROCK       39
         AND THOSE FIERCE EYES, AND CURSE OUR LUCK  . . . .  272  GREY ROCK       V    39
         'TWAS WINE OR WOMEN, OR SOME CURSE--  . . . . . .   273  GREY ROCK            54
         AND MURMURED "MAY GOD CURSE THE NIGHT  . . . . .   303  HOUR DAWN       V 32B
         "THOSE PLATONISTS ARE A CURSE," HE SAID,  . . . .  485  STATISTICS           1
         MAY CALL A CURSE OUT OF THE SKY  . . . . . . . .   508  JANE BISHOP     V    4
         CURSE AS YOU MAY I SING IT THROUGH:  . . . . . .   525  DANCING DAYS         9
         THE CURSE OF CROMWELL  . . . . . . . . . . . . .   580  CURSE CROMWELL       T
         I CURSE THEE--CURSE THEE!"  RENYI SILENT STANDS,  . . .  714  FERENCZ RENYI   107
         I CURSE THEE--CURSE THEE!"  RENYI SILENT STANDS,  . . .  714  FERENCZ RENYI   107
CURSED     SEE A-CURSED
         TO KEEP HIM UPRIGHT WHILE HE CURSED.  . . . . . .  302  HOUR DAWN            6
         AND THEN, GROWN WEARY, PRAYED AND CURSED  . . . .  307  HOUR DAWN            117
         AND PRAYED AND CURSED AND CURSED AND FLED  . . .   307  HOUR DAWN            119
         AND PRAYED AND CURSED AND CURSED AND FLED  . . .   307  HOUR DAWN            119
         AND CURSED AND PRAYED, AND PRAYED AND CURSED  . .  307  HOUR DAWN       V    117
         AND CURSED AND PRAYED, AND PRAYED AND CURSED  . .  307  HOUR DAWN       V    117
CURSES
         MAY CALL DOWN CURSES ON HIS HEAD  . . . . . . . .  508  JANE BISHOP
CURSING
         A CURSING ROGUE WITH A MERRY FACE,  . . . . . . .  302  HOUR DAWN            1
         CURSING THE WIND.  IT WAS AS MUCH  . . . . . . .   302  HOUR DAWN       V    4
         I AM TIRED OF CURSING THE BISHOP,  . . . . . . .   628  JANE MOUNTAIN        1
```

CURTAIN
  LIFTED THE CURTAIN OF HER SLEEPING-ROOM, ...   182 QUEEN MAEVE   63
  LIFTED THE CURTAIN OF HER SLEEPING ROOM, ...   182 QUEEN MAEVE   V   63
  MIGHT BE ACCOMPLISHED. BUNCHING THE CURTAIN UP . . . .   183 QUEEN MAEVE   68
  SOMEWHERE BEYOND THE CURTAIN . . . .   504 QUARREL IN AGE   12
  THE GREAT STAGE CURTAIN ABOUT TO DROP, ...   565 LAPIS LAZULI   13
CURTAINED
  AND LIGHTS THE CURTAINED ROOM, ...   89 ISLE IN WATER   10
CURTAINS
  THE CURTAINS DRAWN UPON UNFRIENDLY NIGHT, ...   523 LONG SILENCE   4
CURVED
  TO ONE VAST FOOT, FROTH-SPLASHED, WITH CURVED TOES LYING   32 OISIN 2   V   46A
  CURVED LIKE NEW MOON, MOON-LUMINOUS, ...   421 MY TABLE   10
  CURVED LIKE NEW MOON, MOON LUMINOUS, ...   421 MY TABLE   V   10
CURVING
  CURVING BENEATH THE PROW: AS SOME WILD DRAKE . . . .   659 ISLE STAT II 1   16
CUSHIONED
  I SAT ON CUSHIONED OTTER-SKIN: . . . .   81 MAD KING GOLL   1
  I SAT ON CUSHIONED OTTER SKIN: . . . .   81 MAD KING GOLL   V   1
  CHAIRED IN THE CUSHIONED OTTER SKIN, ...   82 MAD KING GOLL   V   5
  CHAIRED IN A CUSHIONED OTTER-SKIN . . . .   82 MAD KING GOLL   V   5
  *LAY ME IN A CUSHIONED CHAIR: . . . .   97 FOXHUNTER   1
  *NOW LAY ME IN A CUSHIONED CHAIR, ...   97 FOXHUNTER   V   1
  SERVANTS ROUND HIS CUSHIONED PLACE . . . .   99 FOXHUNTER   37
  THE SERVANTS ROUND HIS CUSHIONED PLACE . . . .   99 FOXHUNTER   V   37
CUSHIONS
  WITH CUSHIONS HERE AND CUSHIONS THERE, ...   97 FOXHUNTER   3
  WITH CUSHIONS HERE AND CUSHIONS THERE, ...   97 FOXHUNTER   3
CUSHLA
  WAKE, MA CUSHLA, SLEEPY-HEADED: . . . .   705 DAWN-SONG   9
CUSTOM
  HOW BUT IN CUSTOM AND IN CEREMONY . . . .   406 FOR DAUGHTER   77
  AND CUSTOM FOR THE SPREADING LAUREL TREE. . . . . .   406 FOR DAUGHTER   80
CUSTOMARY
  FAR FROM THE CUSTOMARY SKIES, ...   360 ALF POLLEXFEN   14
CUSTOMS
  WHO DIG OLD CUSTOMS UP. . . . .   93 FATHER OHART   40
CUT
  AND CUT AND PEELED A HAZEL WAND, ...   149 WANDER AENGUS   3
  AND CUT AND PEELED A HAZEL ROD . . . .   149 WANDER AENGUS   V   3
  AND I WILL FOLLOW YOU AND CUT THE ROPE . . . . . .   250 SHADOW WATER B   586
  AND CUT THE ROPE, FOR I GO ON WITH FORGAEL. . . . .   250 SHADOW WATER B   592
  CUT OUT OUR RHYMES ON STRIPS OF NEW-TORN BARK . . .   343 SHEP GOATHERD   115
  CUT IN THE TURKISH FASHION, ...   363 DOLLS DRAWINGS   8
  TO CUT AND SEW, BE NEAT IN EVERYTHING . . . . . .   443 SCHOOL CHILDR   5
  THAT CUT THROUGH TIME OR CROSS IT WITHERSHINS. . . .   489 COOLE PARK 29   24
  THAT CAN CROSS TIME AND CUT IT WITHERSHINS, ...   489 COOLE PARK 29   V   24
  THAT CUT THROUGH TIME AND CUT IT WITHERSHINS, . . .   489 COOLE PARK 29   V   24
  THAT CUT THROUGH TIME AND CUT IT WITHERSHINS . . . .   489 COOLE PARK 29   V   24
  CUT OUT HIS HEART. SOME MASTER OF DESIGN . . . . .   541 PARN FUNERAL 1   14
  BY HIS COMMAND THESE WORDS ARE CUT: . . . .   640 BEN BULBEN   91
  *AND CUT NO WOOD THE WHOLE DAY LONG, ...   731 PRIEST FAIRY   81
  I HAVE CUT THE ROPE THAT BOUND THIS GALLEY TO OURS, . .   768 SHADOW WATER A   421
  I HAVE CUT THE CORDS THAT HELD THIS GALLEY TO OURS. . .   768 SHADOW WATER A   V 421
CUTTER   SEE WOOD-CUTTER
CUT-THROAT
  A CLOUD BLOWN FROM THE CUT-THROAT NORTH . . . . . .   313 MEMORY YOUTH   6
CUTTING
  DESTROY THE VIEW BY CUTTING DOWN AN ASH . . . . . .   372 ON GOING HOUSE   13
CYPRESS
  AND PLANTED CYPRESS ROUND: . . . .   123 DREAM OF DEATH   8
  A CYPRESS AND A YEW. . . . .   123 DREAM OF DEATH   V   6
  WHERE CYPRESS IS AND OOZY PINE, ...   670 ISLE STAT II 3   110
DA
  DA VINCI: FINGER SO HAD FASHIONED IT . . . .   444 SCHOOL CHILDR   V   26
DABBLE
  THE FEET OF SUMMER DABBLE . . . .   680 LOVE AND DEATH   7
DABBLED   SEE DEW-DABBLED SPRAY-DABBLED
  . . . DEW DABBLED, THE LILY AND ROSE: . . . .   122 WHITE BIRDS   V   5
DAD   SEE GRAND-DAD
DADDY-LONG-LEGS
  BECAUSE CHILDREN DEMAND DADDY-LONG-LEGS UPON HIS TIMBER   623 HIGH TALK   6
    TOES,
DAEMONIC
  HOW THE DAEMONIC RAGE . . . .   419 MY HOUSE   16
  THE HALF-READ WISDOM OF DAEMONIC IMAGES, ...   427 PHANTOM HATRED   39
  THE HALF READ WISDOM OF DAEMONIC IMAGES, ...   427 PHANTOM HATRED V   39
DAEMONS
  AND IN MY HEART THE DAEMONS AND THE GODS . . . . . .   104 FERGUS DRUID   V 38B
DAFFODIL
  WHERE DAFFODIL AND LILY WAVE, ...   67 HAPPY SHEPHERD   46
DAFFODILLS
  THE BRAZEN SKY, SO BLAZE THE DAFFODILLS: . . . . . .   645 ISLE STAT I 1   11
  IN VALE AND DELL SO BLAZE THE DAFFODILLS: . . . . .   645 ISLE STAT I 1   15
  IN LEMON-TINTED LINES, SO BLAZE THE DAFFODILLS. . . .   645 ISLE STAT I 1   19
  LAPPED IN THE LEMON DAFFODILLS: A BEE . . . .   716 DWELT SYCAMORE   10
DAILY
  QUIET'S WILD HEART, LIKE DAILY MEAT: . . . .   196 BAILE AILLINN   178
  BECAUSE THE DAILY SPECTACLE THAT STIRRED . . . . .   270 PARDON FATHERS   16
  MY DAILY THOUGHTS SINCE THE FIRST STUPOR OF YOUTH . .   342 SHEP GOATHERD   83
  THE DAILY SPITE OF THIS UNMANNERLY TOWN, ...   351 PEOPLE   3

179

DAILY   (CONTINUED)
    OF ALL THOSE TRUTHS THAT ARE YOUR DAILY BREAD; . . . . .   373 PHASES OF MOON   24
    MY HEART COULD NEVER TURN FROM DAILY RUIN, ...   464 HARUN RASHID   83
    MY HEART MUST LOOK UPON A DAILY RUIN . . . .   464 HARUN RASHID   V   83
    HAD WATCHED MY DAILY PASSAGE TO AND FRO; . . . .   466 HARUN RASHID   107
    WHETHER FOR DAILY PITTANCE OR IN BLIND FEAR . . . . . .   482 BLOOD AND MOON   37
    I SOUGHT IT DAILY FOR SIX WEEKS OR SO. . . . .   629 CIRCUS ANIMALS   2
DAIRY
    WE'LL DANCE AND THEN FEAST IN A DAIRY. . . . .   707 FAIRY PEDANT   10
    WE'LL DANCE AND THEN FEAST IN A DAIRY. . . . .   708 FAIRY PEDANT   38
DAISY
    DEWY-TONGUED, THE DAISY TOPS-- . . . .   706 DAWN-SONG   22
DALLIANCE
    OF DALLIANCE WITH A DEMON THING. . . . .   2 OISIN 1   4
DAMAGES
    AWARDED HIM FOR DAMAGES . . . .   596 COLONEL MARTIN   48
DAMASK
    THE DAMASK ROSES, BLOOM ON BLOOM, ...   21 OISIN 1   305
    SHALL FALL THE LEAVES OF DAMASK ROSES. . . . .   21 OISIN 1   315
    DAMASK ROSES IN THE NIGHT, ...   21 OISIN 1   V 306A
    IN DAMASK CLOTHED AND ON A SEAT . . . .   440 WISDOM   9
DAMES
    TALL DAMES GO WALKING IN GRASS-GREEN AVALON. . . . .   627 STATES HOLIDAY   13
    TALL DAMES GO WALKING IN GRASS-GREEN AVALON. . . . .   627 STATES HOLIDAY   26
    TALL DAMES GO WALKING IN GRASS-GREEN AVALON. . . . .   627 STATES HOLIDAY   39
    TALL DAMES GO WALKING IN GRASS GREEN AVALON. . . . .   627 STATES HOLIDAY   V   REF
DAMNED
    TO WHERE THE DAMNED HAVE HOWLED AWAY THEIR HEARTS, ...   474 ALL SOUL NIGHT   95
DAMP
    SOME BURN DAMP FAGGOTS, OTHERS MAY CONSUME . . . . . .   327 ROBERT GREGORY   81
DAMPED
    . . . DAMPED BY THE BODY OR THE MIND, ...   556 RIBH PATRICK   8
DAMS
    SHIVERING CLOSER TO THEIR DAMS . . . .   726 LOVERS QUARREL   7
DAN
    DAN AND JERRY LOUT . . . .   520 HIS BARGAIN   5
    DAN AND JERRY TOUT, ...   520 HIS BARGAIN   V   5
DANAAN
    UNTIL THE DANAAN POETS BROUGHT . . . .   7 OISIN 1   63
    LOVE, TILL THE DANAAN POETS BROUGHT . . . .   7 OISIN 1   V   63
    UNTIL THE DANAAN POETS CAME, ...   7 OISIN 1   V   64
    AND YOU SHALL KNOW THE DANAAN LEISURE; . . . . . .   9 OISIN 1   100
    DANAAN SONGS, AND THEIR DEWY SHOWERS . . . .   11 OISIN 1   135
    "WERE THESE TWO BORN IN THE DANAAN LAND, ...   12 OISIN 1   146
    THAT SLOPING GREEN DE DANAAN SOD . . . .   20 OISIN 1   299
    OF DANAAN HOOVES WE URGED OUR WAY BETWEEN . . . .   31 OISIN 2   V   31
    THAT FEED WHITE MOTHS BY SOME DE DANAAN SHRINE; . . . .   41 OISIN 2   186
    I AM HAUNTED BY NUMBERLESS ISLANDS, AND MANY A DANAAN
        SHORE,   122 WHITE BIRDS   9
    A DANAAN FRUITAGE MAKES A SHOWER OF MOONS, ...   127 DREAM OF FAERY   V   22
    WHILE I WROUGHT OUT THESE FITFUL DANAAN RHYMES, . . .   136 TO SOME I TALK   1
    I DEDICATE THESE FITFUL DANAAN RHYMES . . . . . .   136 TO SOME I TALK   V   1
    THE DANAAN CHILDREN LAUGH, IN CRADLES OF WROUGHT GOLD, . .   146 UNAPPEAS HOST   1
    I KNOW WHERE A DIM MOON DRIFTS, WHERE THE DANAAN KIND . .   203 WITHER BOUGHS   12
    AND I KNOW OF THE ISLES WHERE THE DANAAN KIND . . . .   203 WITHER BOUGHS   V   12
    AND OF APPLE ISLANDS WHERE THE DANAAN KIND . . . . .   203 WITHER BOUGHS   V   12
    THE DANAAN QUICKEN TREE . . . .   742 DANAAN QUICK   T
    (AH, MOURNFUL DANAAN QUICKEN TREE!) . . . .   742 DANAAN QUICK   6
    (AH, MOURNFUL DANAAN QUICKEN TREE!) . . . .   743 DANAAN QUICK   12
    (AH, MOURNFUL DANAAN QUICKEN TREE!) . . . .   743 DANAAN QUICK   18
    BELOVED, BLAME THE DANAAN WHIM, ...   743 DANAAN QUICK   22
    (AH, MOURNFUL DANAAN QUICKEN TREE!) . . . .   743 DANAAN QUICK   24
    (AH, MOURNFUL DANAAN QUICKEN TREE!) . . . .   743 DANAAN QUICK   30
DANCE
    WHO WHEN THEY DANCE TO A FITFUL MEASURE . . . . . .   9 OISIN 1   97
    AND IN A WILD AND SUDDEN DANCE, ...   20 OISIN 1   290
    BENDING OVER THEM IN THE DANCE, ...   21 OISIN 1   308
    THE DANCE WOUND THROUGH THE WINDLESS WOODS; . . . .   21 OISIN 1   320
    SANG WE SOFTLY IN THE DANCE, ...   21 OISIN 1   V 308
    THE PEAHENS DANCE ON A SMOOTH LAWN, ...   77 INDIAN TO LOVE   3
    THE PEA-HENS DANCE, IN CRIMSON FEATHER . . . . . .   77 INDIAN TO LOVE   V   3
    YOU WAVES, THOUGH YOU DANCE BY MY FEET LIKE CHILDREN AT
        PLAY,   90 OLD FISHERMAN   1
    YE WAVES, THOUGH YE DANCE 'FORE MY FEET LIKE CHILDREN AT
        PLAY,   90 OLD FISHERMAN   V   1
    WHILE YOUNG STARS ABOUT HER DANCE. . . . .   125 CATHLEEN PARA   V   16
    AND DANCE UPON THE LEVEL SHORE? . . . .   125 GOES FERGUS   3
    AND DREAMING HOW THEY DANCE AND DART, ...   135 TWO TREES   V   18
    AWAY FROM THE MERRY DANCE. . . . .   145 HOST OF AIR   32
    AND THOUGH THE SEVEN LIGHTS BOWED IN THEIR DANCE AND WEPT, .   174 ELEMENT POWERS   3
    FOLK DANCE LIKE A WAVE OF THE SEA; . . . .   178 FIDDLER DOONEY   2
    AND THE MERRY LOVE TO DANCE! . . . .   179 FIDDLER DOONEY   16
    AND DANCE LIKE A WAVE OF THE SEA. . . . .   179 FIDDLER DOONEY   20
    THAT HAS GROWN WEARY OF THE WANDERING DANCE, ...   285 TWO KINGS   183
    THAT HAS GROWN WEARY OF THE WHIRLING DANCE, ...   285 TWO KINGS   V 183
    POUR WINE AND DANCE IF MANHOOD STILL HAVE PRIDE, . . .   311 MOUNTAIN TOMB   1
    POUR WINE AND DANCE, IF MANKIND STILL HAVE PRIDE, . . .   311 MOUNTAIN TOMB   V   1
    DANCE THERE UPON THE SHORE; . . . .   312 CHILD DANCING   1
    I'D DANCE A MEASURE ON HIS GRAVE." . . . .   338 TOM OROUGHLEY   16
    THAT SHEBA LED A DANCE. . . . .   346 ON WOMAN   43
    DO YOU DANCE, MINNALOUSHE, DO YOU DANCE? . . . . .   378 CAT AND MOON   11

180

	PAGE	TITLE		LINE

DANCE   (CONTINUED)
```
    DO YOU DANCE, MINNALOUSHE, DO YOU DANCE?  . . . . . . .   378 CAT AND MOON        11
    WHAT BETTER THAN CALL A DANCE?  . . . . . . . . . . . .   378 CAT AND MOON        13
    A NEW DANCE TURN. . . . . . . . . . . . . . . . . . . .   378 CAT AND MOON        16
    A NEW DANCE TUNE. . . . . . . . . . . . . . . . . . . .   378 CAT AND MOON      V 16
    AND NEW DANCE TURN. . . . . . . . . . . . . . . . . . .   378 CAT AND MOON      V 16
    AND LITTLE SHE BY WHOM HER DANCE WAS SEEN . . . . . . .   383 VISION ROBART       38
    HOW CAN WE KNOW THE DANCER FROM THE DANCE?  . . . . . .   446 SCHOOL CHILDR       64
    AND WHERE THE BLESSED DANCE!  . . . . . . . . . . . . .   474 ALL SOUL NIGHT      96
    WHAT MANHOOD LED THE DANCE!   . . . . . . . . . . . . .   488 CRAZED MOON         12
    MEN DANCE ON DEATHLESS FEET."   . . . . . . . . . . . .   496 MOHINI CHATTER      28
    DYING INTO A DANCE. . . . . . . . . . . . . . . . . . .   498 BYZANTIUM           30
    SUCH A DANCE AS THERE WAS DANCED--  . . . . . . . . . .   515 JANE GROWN OLD      20
    COME DANCE WITH ME IN IRELAND."   . . . . . . . . . . .   526 AM OF IRELAND        5
    AND DANCE WITH ME IN IRELAND."  . . . . . . . . . . . .   527 AM OF IRELAND       18
    AND DANCE WITH ME IN IRELAND."  . . . . . . . . . . . .   527 AM OF IRELAND       31
    LET HER FINISH HER DANCE, . . . . . . . . . . . . . . .   568 SWEET DANCER        12
    LET HER FINISH HER DANCE. . . . . . . . . . . . . . . .   568 SWEET DANCER        13
    A DANCE FOR THE FISHER-LADS!  . . . . . . . . . . . . .   589 OLD WICKED MAN      33
    A DANCE FOR THE FISHER LADS!  . . . . . . . . . . . . .   589 OLD WICKED MAN    V 33
    SHOULD DANCE ATTENTION UPON MY OLD AGE!  . . . . . . . .  591 SPUR                 2
    SHOULD DANCE ATTENDANCE UPON MY OLD AGE!  . . . . . . .   591 SPUR              V  2
    THROUGH THEIR ANCESTRAL PATTERNS DANCE, . . . . . . . .   612 NEWS ORACLE         19
    SO LET US DANCE WHERE THE YELLOW LANCE  . . . . . . . .   643 SONG FAERIES         7
    SO LET US DANCE ON FRINGED WAVES, . . . . . . . . . . .   644 SONG FAERIES         9
    SO LET US DANCE WHERE THE YELLOW LANCE  . . . . . . . .   676 ISLE STAT II 3     254
    SO LET US DANCE ON THE FRINGED WAVES. . . . . . . . . .   676 ISLE STAT II 3     256
    AND UNTO IT WE'LL DANCE UPON THE SWARD. . . . . . . . .   681 SEEKER              10
    THOU KNOWEST THIS, AND HOW FROM 'MID THE DANCE  . . . .   683 SEEKER              51
    WE'LL DANCE AND THEN FEAST IN A DAIRY.  . . . . . . . .   707 FAIRY PEDANT        10
    WE'LL DANCE AND THEN FEAST IN A DAIRY.  . . . . . . . .   708 FAIRY PEDANT        38
    IN EVERY DANCE, BY CHILDREN SOUGHT.   "ACCURST, . . . .   709 FERENCZ RENYI       12
    SO WE DANCE A FAIRY JIG . . . . . . . . . . . . . . . .   726 LOVERS QUARREL      19
    "THE SWIFTEST HE TO DANCE OR FLY. . . . . . . . . . . .   729 PRIEST FAIRY        45
    AS DANCE UPON THE SPEAR-GRASS BRITTLE,  . . . . . . . .   731 PRIEST FAIRY        78
    DANCE THE SAVAGE CHILDREN SMALL,  . . . . . . . . . . .   732 STREET DANCERS      29
    THE FLIES THAT DANCE IN THREES, IN TWOS,  . . . . . . .   736 IN CHURCH           11
DANCED
    WE DANCED TO WHERE IN THE WINDING THICKET . . . . . . .    20 OISIN 1            304
    WE DANCED TO WHERE WITHIN THE GLOOM . . . . . . . . . .    21 OISIN 1          V 305
    SOME DANCED LIKE SHADOWS ON THE MOUNTAINS,  . . . . . .    25 OISIN 1            388
    WHO DANCED ON A LEVEL PLACE,  . . . . . . . . . . . . .   144 HOST OF AIR         14
    DANCED IN THE WHIRLING FOAM AND IN THE DUST,  . . . . .   284 TWO KINGS          167
    THAT, IT MAY BE, HAD DANCED HER LIFE AWAY,  . . . . . .   383 VISION ROBART       22
    O LITTLE DID THEY CARE WHO DANCED BETWEEN,  . . . . . .   383 VISION ROBART       37
    THAT IT MAYBE HAD DANCED HER LIFE AWAY. . . . . . . . .   383 VISION ROBART     V 22
    SO THAT SHE DANCED. NO THOUGHT, . . . . . . . . . . . .   383 VISION ROBART     V 39
    I SAID THAT SHE HAD DANCED HEART'S TRUTH, . . . . . . .   514 JANE GROWN OLD       9
    SUCH A DANCE AS THERE WAS DANCED--  . . . . . . . . . .   515 JANE GROWN OLD      20
    DANCED ON CRUACHAN'S WINDY PLAIN. . . . . . . . . . . .   528 DANCER CRUACH        4
    DANCED IT ON CRUACHAN'S WINDY PLAIN,  . . . . . . . . .   528 DANCER CRUACH     V  4
    AND NEVER HAVE I DANCED FOR JOY,  . . . . . . . . . . .   567 FROM JAPANESE        9
    AROUND MY HEAD AND DANCED AMONG THE GRASS!  . . . . . .   690 MOSADA 1            19
    DANCED, LAUGHED, LOVED, FOUGHT THROUGH  . . . . . . . .   787 HUDDON DUDDON        4
    WHAT THOUGH THEY DANCED!  THOSE DAYS ARE GONE,  . . . .   788 HAWTHORN TREE        5
DANCE-LIKE
    A DANCE-LIKE GLORY THAT THOSE WALLS BEGOT.  . . . . . .   488 COOLE PARK 29        8
DANCER
    WHAT A DANCER GLIMMERING!   . . . . . . . . . . . . . .   125 CATHLEEN PARA       14
    THAT IF A DANCER STAYED HIS HUNGRY FOOT . . . . . . . .   127 DREAM OF FAERY      22
    UPON THE DANCER BY THE DREAMLESS WAVE.  . . . . . . . .   128 DREAM OF FAERY      45
    AND NO ONE LEAF-CROWNED DANCER MISS . . . . . . . . . .   128 DREAM OF FAERY    V 46
    MICHAEL ROBARTES AND THE DANCER . . . . . . . . . . . .   385 ROBARTES DANCE       T
    HOW CAN WE KNOW THE DANCER FROM THE DANCE?  . . . . . .   446 SCHOOL CHILDR       64
    THE DANCER AT CRUACHAN AND CRO-PATRICK  . . . . . . . .   528 DANCER CRUACH        T
    SWEET DANCER  . . . . . . . . . . . . . . . . . . . . .   568 SWEET DANCER         T
    AH, DANCER, AH, SWEET DANCER! . . . . . . . . . . . . .   568 SWEET DANCER         7
    AH, DANCER, AH, SWEET DANCER! . . . . . . . . . . . . .   568 SWEET DANCER         7
    AH, DANCER, AH, SWEET DANCER! . . . . . . . . . . . . .   568 SWEET DANCER        14
    AH, DANCER, AH, SWEET DANCER! . . . . . . . . . . . . .   568 SWEET DANCER        14
    AND UNDER EVERY DANCER  . . . . . . . . . . . . . . . .   592 DRUNK SOBRIETY      11
DANCERS
    OF DANCERS LEAPING IN THE AIR!  . . . . . . . . . . . .    18 OISIN 1            254
    THE MANY-COLOURED DANCERS RUSHED, . . . . . . . . . . .    21 OISIN 1          V 322
    THE DANCERS CROWDED ABOUT HIM . . . . . . . . . . . . .   144 HOST OF AIR         17
    BUT THE OLD MEN AND DANCERS WERE GONE,  . . . . . . . .   145 HOST OF AIR       V 39
    WHEN LOIE FULLER'S CHINESE DANCERS ENWOUND  . . . . . .   430 NINETEEN 19         49
    HAD FALLEN AMONG DANCERS, HAD WHIRLED THEM ROUND  . . .   430 NINETEEN 19         52
    ALL MEN ARE DANCERS AND THEIR TREAD . . . . . . . . . .   430 NINETEEN 19         57
    OWEN AHERNE AND HIS DANCERS . . . . . . . . . . . . . .   449 OWEN AHERNE          T
    IN THE LONG ECHOING STREET THE LAUGHING DANCERS THRONG,   459 FROM OEDIPUS         7
    IN THE LONG ECHOING STREETS THE LAUGHING DANCERS THRONG, 459 FROM OEDIPUS      V  7
    CRAZY JANE GROWN OLD LOOKS AT THE DANCERS . . . . . . .   514 JANE GROWN OLD       T
    CRACKED MARY AND THE DANCERS  . . . . . . . . . . . . .   514 JANE GROWN OLD    V  T
    CRAZY JANE AND THE DANCERS  . . . . . . . . . . . . . .   514 JANE GROWN OLD    V  T
    THE LOVERS AND THE DANCERS ARE BEATEN INTO THE CLAY,  .   580 CURSE CROMWELL       3
    STREET DANCERS  . . . . . . . . . . . . . . . . . . . .   731 STREET DANCERS       T
DANCE'S
    SWEPT ON THE DANCE'S LINKED FLOW, . . . . . . . . . . .    20 OISIN 1          V 291
    ONCE MORE THE DANCE'S LINKED FLOW,  . . . . . . . . . .    22 OISIN 1          V 323A
```

```
                                                              PAGE     TITLE        LINE
DANCES
     AND WAVERING ARMS AND WANDERING DANCES.  . . . . . .      19  OISIN 1           275
     AND WAVING ARMS AND WANDERING DANCES.  . . . . . . .      19  OISIN 1        V  275
     WEAVING OLDEN DANCES,  . . . . . . . . . . . . . . .      87  STOLEN CHILD       17
     WIND AND UNWIND THEIR DANCES WHEN THE LIGHT GROWS COOL .  203  WITHER BOUGHS      13
     IN HAPPY DANCES UNDER A WINDY MOON,  . . . . . . . .     245  SHADOW WATER B    470
     IN HAPPY DANCES, UNDER A WINDY MOON:  . . . . . . . .     763  SHADOW WATER A    318
DANCING
     THOSE MERRY COUPLES DANCING IN TUNE,  . . . . . . . .       3  OISIN 1            9
     AND FEET OF MAIDENS DANCING IN TUNE,  . . . . . . . .       3  OISIN 1        V   9
     THE FLOOR OF EMAN'S DANCING HALL  . . . . . . . . . .      13  OISIN 1        V  156
     THE ISLANDS OF DANCING AND OF VICTORIES  . . . . . .      46  OISIN 2           247
     IN DREARY DANCING PAST US WHIRLED,  . . . . . . . . .      65  HAPPY SHEPHERD     8
     IN DANCING SILVER-SANDALLED ON THE SEA,  . . . . . .     101  ROSE UPON ROOD     7
     IN DANCING SILVER SANDALLED ON THE SEA,  . . . . . .     101  ROSE UPON ROOD V   7
     AH, FAERIES, DANCING UNDER THE MOON,  . . . . . . . .     139  TO IRELAND        31
     WIND AND UNWIND DANCING WHEN THE LIGHT GROWS COOL  .     203  WITHER BOUGHS  V  13
     ARE DANCING IN A CROWD.  . . . . . . . . . . . . . .     214  HAPPY TOWNLAND    12
     ARE DANCING IN THE CROWD.  . . . . . . . . . . . . .     214  HAPPY TOWNLAND V  12
     TO A CHILD DANCING IN THE WIND  . . . . . . . . . . .     312  CHILD DANCING      T
     TO A CHILD DANCING UPON THE SHORE  . . . . . . . . .     312  CHILD DANCING  V   T
     THE PLAYING UPON PIPES AND THE DANCING,  . . . . . .     330  BONE OF A HARE     5
     TO CHANGE MY LOVES WHILE DANCING  . . . . . . . . . .     330  BONE OF A HARE     7
     THAT SHE OF DANCING DREAMED.  . . . . . . . . . . . .     383  VISION ROBART     24
     DANCING TO A FRENZIED DRUM,  . . . . . . . . . . . .     403  FOR DAUGHTER      15
     LABOUR IS BLOSSOMING OR DANCING WHERE  . . . . . . .     445  SCHOOL CHILDR     57
     MARBLES OF THE DANCING FLOOR  . . . . . . . . . . . .     498  BYZANTIUM         36
     DANCING WITH HER CHOSEN YOUTH,  . . . . . . . . . . .     514  JANE GROWN OLD     2
     THOSE DANCING DAYS ARE GONE  . . . . . . . . . . . .     524  DANCING DAYS       T
     THOSE DANCING DAYS ARE GONE,  . . . . . . . . . . . .     524  DANCING DAYS       2
     THE GIRL GOES DANCING THERE  . . . . . . . . . . . .     568  SWEET DANCER       1
     HER POETRY, DANCING UPON THE SHORE,  . . . . . . . .     578  CRAZED GIRL        2
     AND KEEP ME DANCING STILL  . . . . . . . . . . . . .     591  DRUNK SOBRIETY     2
     AND THEREFORE KEEP ME DANCING  . . . . . . . . . . .     592  DRUNK SOBRIETY     7
     KEEP DANCING LIKE A WAVE,  . . . . . . . . . . . . .     592  DRUNK SOBRIETY    10
     DANCING IN SOME MOONY PLACE,  . . . . . . . . . . . .     647  ISLE STAT I 1     54
     THE LIGHT IS DANCING O'ER THE KNOTTED TREES,  . . . .     662  ISLE STAT II 2     2
     A CLOVEN, DANCING JET,  . . . . . . . . . . . . . . .     680  LOVE AND DEATH     2
     DANCING ON THE MOON'S BROAD STAIN,  . . . . . . . . .     731  STREET DANCERS    15
     DANCING IN THE FEEBLE GLOW,  . . . . . . . . . . . .     733  STREET DANCERS    49
     LOVELY LADIES DANCING IN IT.  . . . . . . . . . . . .     788  HAWTHORN TREE      4
     LIVE, FOR I SAW THEM DANCING THERE.  . . . . . . . .     788  HAWTHORN TREE     12
DANCING-PLACE
     WHEN HER SOUL FLIES TO THE PREDESTINED DANCING-PLACE  .   365  HER COURAGE        1
DANDLED
     YOU'VE DANDLED THEM AND FED THEM FROM THE BOOK  . . .     265  ABBEY THEATRE      8
     MY MOTHER DANDLED ME AND SANG,  . . . . . . . . . . .     308  PLAYER QUEEN       1
DANE
     BUT A GREAT DANE THAT CANNOT BAY THE MOON  . . . . .     579  DOR WELLESLEY     10
DANES
     HAD PERISHED THERE, BUT THE DANES RAN,  . . . . . . .     274  GREY ROCK         74
     AND MORE, IF YOU WILL WAR AGAINST THE DANES  . . . .     756  SHADOW WATER A V 190
DANGER
     DANGER NO REFUGE HOLDS, AND WAR NO PEACE,  . . . . .     114  ROSE OF BATTLE     9
     THERE IS GREAT DANGER IN THE BODY.  . . . . . . . . .     386  ROBARTES DANCE    38
     PROTECTING, TILL THE DANGER PAST,  . . . . . . . . .     436  FOR MY SON        31
     AND DANGER NOT BE DIMINISHED:  . . . . . . . . . . .     786  YOUR HEART        31
DANGEROUS
     OF THE EVER-LIVING HALF SO DANGEROUS  . . . . . . . .     224  SHADOW WATER B    46
     AND HAS BEEN DANGEROUS TO HIM.  I HAVE HEARD  . . . .     224  SHADOW WATER B    52
DANGLING
     BUT NEVER, NEVER DANGLING LEAVE THE LIVER AND THE LIGHTS.  790  HEART SLEEVE       2
DANIEL
     "HUDDON AND DUDDON AND DANIEL O'LEARY,  . . . . . . .     529  TOM LUNATIC        7
     HUDDON, DUDDON AND DANIEL O'LEARY  . . . . . . . . .     787  HUDDON DUDDON      1
     HUDDON, DUDDON AND DANIEL O'LEARY  . . . . . . . . .     787  HUDDON DUDDON      6
     HUDDON, DUDDON AND DANIEL O'LEARY  . . . . . . . . .     787  HUDDON DUDDON     11
DANISH
     "THE DANISH TROOP WAS DRIVEN OUT  . . . . . . . . . .     273  GREY ROCK         65
DANTE
     DANTE ALIGHIERI, SO UTTERLY FOUND HIMSELF  . . . . .     368  EGO DOMINUS       19
     A GIRL THAT KNEW ALL DANTE ONCE  . . . . . . . . . .     626  OLD MEN BE MAD     5
DAPHNE
     A DAPHNE AND A MARY WHO LIVE IN PRIVACY:  . . . . . .     354  HIS PHOENIX       18
DAPPLED
     AND WALK AMONG LONG DAPPLED GRASS,  . . . . . . . . .     150  WANDER AENGUS     21
     ON DAPPLED SKINS IN A GLASS BOAT,  . . . . . . . . .     196  BAILE AILLINN    180
DARE
     "YOU DARE ME TO MY FACE," AND THEREUPON  . . . . . .     106  CUCHULAIN SEA     17
     AND DROP HIM FROM THE GUNNEL.  I DARE NOT DO IT.  . .     222  SHADOW WATER B    15
     DARE MATCH IN LEARNING WITH US TWO,  . . . . . . . .     333  SOLOMON SHEBA     21
     AND SHOULD SOME CRAZY HAND DARE TOUCH A DAUGHTER  . .     433  NINETEEN 19      122
     IMITATE HIM IF YOU DARE,  . . . . . . . . . . . . . .     493  SWIFTS EPITAPH     4
     BUT WHAT AM I THAT DARE  . . . . . . . . . . . . . .     507  STREAM AND SUN     7
     OR BODILY MOVEMENT DID I DARE,  . . . . . . . . . . .     514  JANE GROWN OLD     5
     THERE'S NOT A BIRD OF DAY THAT DARE  . . . . . . . .     538  LAST CONFESS      23
     "BUT NEVER DARE TO BOAST  . . . . . . . . . . . . . .     539  MEETING            8
DARED
     THAT YOU HAVE COME AND DARED ME TO MY FACE?"  . . . .     109  CUCHULAIN SEA     61
     TO GRASP THE WOMAN.  YOU HAVE DARED TO TOUCH HER?  .     223  SHADOW WATER B    39
     WHEN MY LUCK CHANGED AND THEY DARED MEET MY FACE,  .     352  PEOPLE            25
```

182

DARED   (CONTINUED)
    WHEN MY LUCK CHANGED AND THEY DARED TO MEET MY FACE, • • •   352 PEOPLE   V   25
    NONE DARED ADMIT, IF SUCH A THOUGHT WERE HIS, • • • • •   430 NINETEEN 19   44
    HARDLY DARED TO WET HIS MOUTH • • • • • • • • •   454 EMPTY CUP   3
    MADGE TELLS ME WHAT I DARED NOT THINK • • • • • •   457 SECRETS OF OLD   3
    DARED I STOP". • • • • • • • • • • • • • • •   559 HE AND SHE   6
    NO SHEPHERD FOOT HAS EVER DARED ITS DEPTHS. • • • •   682 SEEKER   32
DARGAN'S
    CASTLE DARGAN'S RUIN ALL LIT, • • • • • • • • • •   788 HAWTHORN TREE   3
DARING
    HAS NO ONE SAID THOSE DARING • • • • • • • • •   312 TWO YEAR LATER   1
    SO DARING AND SWEET HIS THOUGHT. • • • • • • • •   393 EASTER 1916   30
DARK   SEE WINE-DARK BLOOD-DARK PITCH-DARK NIGHT-DARK
    OF OUR STRONG STEEDS WAS DARK WITH SWEAT, • • • •   2 OISIN 1   V   7T
    TOGETHER, WHILE THE DARK WOODS RANG, • • • • • •   16 OISIN 1   227
    WOVEN INTO HER HAIR, BEFORE DARK TOWERS • • • •   30 OISIN 2   22
    WOVE IN HER FLOWER-LIKE HAIR, BEFORE DARK TOWERS •   30 OISIN 2   V   22
    AND BLACKNESS IN THE DARK. THE SEA ROLLED ROUND, •   30 OISIN 2   V   23
    ON OUR DARK PATHWAY, TILL A COUNTLESS FLIGHT • • •   31 OISIN 2   34
    DARK STATUES GLIMMERED OVER THE PALE TIDE • • • •   31 OISIN 2   36
    UPON DARK THRONES. BETWEEN THE LIDS OF ONE • • •   31 OISIN 2   37
    OUT OF THE SEVENFOLD SEAS, BUILT THE DARK HALL • •   38 OISIN 2   131
    UNDER A CROWN OF THORNS AND DARK WITH BLOOD, • • •   38 OISIN 2   135
    OUT OF THE SEVEN-FOLD SEAS, BUILT THE DARK HALL • •   38 OISIN 2   V   131
    AND MANANNAN'S DARK TOWER, STONE AFTER STONE, • • •   45 OISIN 2   236
    AND MANANAN'S DARK TOWER, STONE BY STONE. • • • •   45 OISIN 2   V   236
    AND TRAMPLE MY DARK ISLE. • • • • • • • • • • • •   45 OISIN 2   V   239E
    FOR NO LIVE CREATURES LIVED THERE, NO WEASELS MOVED IN   48 OISIN 3   19
        THE DARK:
    DARK BALOR, AS OLD AS A FOREST, CAR-BORNE, HIS MIGHTY HEAD   53 OISIN 3   91
        SUNK
    FOR NO LIVE CREATURES LIVE THERE, NO WEASELS MOVE IN THE   56 OISIN 3   139
        DARK:
    ORCHIL SHAKES OUT HER LONG DARK HAIR • • • • • •   85 MAD KING GOLL   62
    AND TALKED OF THE DARK FOLK WHO LIVE IN SOULS • • •   136 TO SOME I TALK   4
    OF THAT DARK FOLK WHO GATHER IN THE SOULS • • • •   136 TO SOME I TALK V   4
    AND HE SAW HOW THE REEDS GREW DARK • • • • • • •   144 HOST OF AIR   5
    THE BLUE AND THE DIM AND THE DARK CLOTHS • • • •   176 CLOTHS HEAVEN   3
    UNTIL THE PILLARED DARK BEGAN TO STIR • • • • • •   185 QUEEN MAEVE   110
    BUT OUT OF THE DARK AIR OVER HER HEAD THERE CAME • •   187 QUEEN MAEVE   153
    DARK AND DULL AND EARTHY THE STREAM OF DRUMAHAIR • •   207 HANRAHANS SONG V   11
    DARK AND DULL AND EARTHY OUR SOULS AND BODIES BE: • •   208 HANRAHANS SONG V   13
    A DARK DEEP HOLLOW IN THE ROCK. • • • • • • • • •   303 HOUR DAWN   21
    A DARK DEEP HOLE IN THE ROCK'S FACE. • • • • • • •   303 HOUR DAWN   V   21
    OF THE DARK LEOPARDS OF THE MOON? • • • • • • •   343 DEJECTION   3
    WHERE STONE IS DARK UNDER FROTH, • • • • • • • •   348 FISHERMAN   32
    WHERE STONE IS DARK WITH FROTH, • • • • • • • •   348 FISHERMAN   V   32
    THE FULL AND THE MOON'S DARK AND ALL THE CRESCENTS, •   373 PHASES OF MOON   32
    FOR THERE'S NO HUMAN LIFE AT THE FULL OR THE DARK. • •   373 PHASES OF MOON   35
    BECAUSE ALL DARK, LIKE THOSE THAT ARE ALL LIGHT, • •   376 PHASES OF MOON   104
    OF THE DARK MOON AND THE FULL. • • • • • • • • •   384 VISION ROBART   60
    ON THE DARK STREAM, • • • • • • • • • • • • • •   389 IMAGE PAST   3
    LIT UP THE DARK MAHOGANY AND THE WINE, • • • • •   410 TOWER   27
    OUT OF THE OBSCURE DARK OF THE RICH STREAMS, • • •   417 ANCEST HOUSES   14
    OUT OF DARK NIGHT WHERE LAY • • • • • • • • • •   439 FRAGMENTS   9
    BY THE DARK WEBS, HER NAPE CAUGHT IN HIS BILL, • • •   441 LEDA AND SWAN   3
    IN THE MAD ABSTRACT DARK AND GROUND IT GRAIN BY GRAIN   442 BLACK CENTAUR   8
    THE WINE DARK OF THE WOOD'S INTRICACIES, • • • •   446 COLONUS PRAISE V   2
    AMONG DARK SKINS, AND THERE • • • • • • • • • •   472 ALL SOUL NIGHT   48
    THEN DARKENING THROUGH "DARK" RAFTERY'S "CELLAR" DROP.   490 COOLE BALLYLEE   4
    A HEAVENLY MANSION, RAGING IN THE DARK, • • • •   491 COOLE BALLYLEE V   40D
    UNTIL THE MORNING BREAK AS ON A DARK BREAST. • • •   494 AT ALGECIRAS   V   6
    A HEAVENLY MANSION, RAGING IN THE DARK. • • • •   495 CHOICE   6
    BETWEEN THE DARK AND DAWN. • • • • • • • • • • •   511 JANE AND JACK   6
    IF I MAKE THE LASHES DARK. • • • • • • • • • • •   531 BEFORE WORLD   1
    MY DARK DECLIVITIES. • • • • • • • • • • • • •   536 PARTING   14
    STARED AT THE WINE-DARK NAIL, OR DARK THAT RAN • •   537 HER VISION   10
    BUT THE DARK CHANGED TO RED, AND TORCHES SHONE, • •   537 HER VISION   12
    THROUGH JONATHAN SWIFT'S DARK GROVE HE PASSED, AND THERE   543 PARN FUNERAL 2   11
    BECAUSE YOU HAVE IT IN THE PITCH DARK NIGHT • • •   554 RIBH AT TOMB   V   1
    BECAUSE YOU HAVE FOUND ME IN THE PITCH DARK NIGHT • •   554 RIBH AT TOMB   V   1
    HERE IN THE PITCH DARK ATMOSPHERE ABOVE, • • • •   555 RIBH AT TOMB   V   17
    OR DARK BETWIXT THE POLECAT AND THE OWL, • • • •   565 GYRES   21
    OR ANY RICH, DARK NOTHING DISINTER • • • • • • •   565 GYRES   22
    WHO UNDERSTAND THE DARK: • • • • • • • • • • •   588 OLD WICKED MAN   31
    WHEN DARK HANGS UPON THE WATER • • • • • • • •   589 OLD WICKED MAN   34
    "A YOUNG MAN IN THE DARK AM I, • • • • • • • •   589 OLD WICKED MAN   37
    CLIMB TO OUR PROPER DARK, THAT WE MAY TRACE • • •   611 STATUES   31
    NO DARK TOMB-HAUNTER ONCE: HER FORM ALL FULL • •   618 BRONZE HEAD   8
    THERE IN THE TOMB THE DARK GROWS BLACKER, • • • •   636 BLACK TOWER   27
    OH, MORE DARK THY GLEAMING HAIR IS • • • • • • •   647 ISLE STAT I 1   51
    AS LIES DARK WATER IN A MURMUROUS GLADE, • • • •   650 ISLE STAT I 1   138
    IN THE NEVER-LIFTING DARK. • • • • • • • • • • •   658 ISLE STAT I 3   89
    MORE DARK BENEATH THE POPLARS, WHERE YON OWL • •   675 ISLE STAT II 3   233
    IN ENDLESS DARK, AND BY THE WEEDY MARGE • • • •   682 SEEKER   19
    FEET OF DARK GOMEZ, WHERE NOW WANDER YE? • • • •   690 MOSADA 1   11
    THE DARK STILL MAN, HAS COME AND SAYS 'TIS SIN. • •   692 MOSADA 1   47
    THE FOOT-WORN WAY IS LONG, AND IT GROWS DARK. • •   702 MOSADA 3   92
    THE FOOTWORN WAY IS LONG, AND IT GROWS DARK. • •   702 MOSADA 3   V   92
    AND HIS HAIR WAS AS DARK AS A PLOVER'S EYE. • • •   729 PRIEST FAIRY   46
    DARK JOAN CALL THE BERRIES SWEET, • • • • • • • •   743 DANAAN QUICK   28

		PAGE	TITLE	LINE
DARK	(CONTINUED)			
	THAT LIVES AMONG THE WOODS OF THE DARK HOUNDS.	766	SHADOW WATER A	376
	WHEN THE DARK HOUNDS WERE LOOSED. COME TO THE ALE.	766	SHADOW WATER A	379
	BETWEEN DARK FURROWS UPON THE PLOUGHED LAND.	784	WOMANS BEAUTY	6
	AMID THE DARK BEFORE DAY HAD BROKEN.	784	WOMANS BEAUTY	20
DARK-BEAKED				
	TO FILL THEIR DARK-BEAKED HOLLOW GALLEYS.	82	MAD KING GOLL	16
DARKEN				
	DARKEN: HEAVEN IS ANGRY. CEASE! UNTO MY MIND,	42	OISIN 2	V 205
	THEY DREAM AND DARKEN OUR SUN.	783	GREY ROUND	15
DARKENED				
	STORM DARKENED OR STARRY BRIGHT.	739	WHERE BOOKS GO	8
DARKENING	SEE DAYLIGHT-DARKENING			
	IN PITY FOR MAN'S DARKENING THOUGHT	438	SONGS PLAY 2	1
	THEN DARKENING THROUGH "DARK" RAFTERY'S "CELLAR" DROP,	490	COOLE BALLYLEE	4
	WHERE THE SWAN DRIFTS UPON A DARKENING FLOOD.	492	COOLE BALLYLEE	48
DARKER				
	A DARKER KNOWLEDGE AND IN HATRED TURN	558	RIBH CHRISTIAN	14
DARKEST				
	IT IS THE DARKEST EVE I EVER KNEW.	702	MOSADA 3	93
DARKNESS				
	ROSE IN THE DARKNESS, AND THE WHITE SURF GLEAMED	30	OISIN 2	23
	THE DARKNESS COMES. A CLOUD HANGS OVERHEAD--	43	OISIN 2	V 208A
	AND DEMONS AFRAID IN THEIR DARKNESS:	62	OISIN 3	205
	AND LAY IN THE DARKNESS, GRUNTING, AND TURNING TO HIS REST.	153	CHANGE BELOVED	12
	HE HAS PUT A SUDDEN DARKNESS OVER THE MOON.	239	SHADOW WATER B	367
	NOTHING BUT DARKNESS OVERHEAD.	314	MEMORY YOUTH	14
	THE DARKNESS DROPS AGAIN: BUT NOW I KNOW	402	SECOND COMING	18
	OUT OF THE FABULOUS DARKNESS CALLED.	437	SONGS PLAY 1	16
	A FABULOUS, FORMLESS DARKNESS IN:	438	SONGS PLAY 2	5
	WHO CAN DISTINGUISH DARKNESS FROM THE SOUL?	477	SELF AND SOUL	8
	TO DEATH. HIS DARKNESS AND HIS CHILL I FEEL.	684	SEEKER	63
	MY SOUL. HIS DARKNESS AND HIS CHILL I FEEL.	684	SEEKER	V 63B
	BRUISING THE DARKNESS WITH THEIR CRACKLING LIGHT:	687	TWO TITANS	2
	DROPT DOWN THE VELVET DARKNESS FROM ABOVE,	688	TWO TITANS	37
	FOR THIS DID THE ETERNAL DARKNESS BRING	688	TWO TITANS	51
	THE DARKNESS OF THE WHIRLWIND SHATTERED DEEP.	688	TWO TITANS	58
	SEE THE DARKNESS SLOW DISGORGING A VESSEL BLIND WITH SQUALL.	718	PHANTOM SHIP	12
	CAME OLIVE FIRES OF MORNING AND ON THE DARKNESS FED,	719	PHANTOM SHIP	33
	CAME THE OLIVE FIRE OF MORNING, AND ON THE DARKNESS FED,	719	PHANTOM SHIP	V 33
	AND AS THE TIME TO DARKNESS PLODDED	728	PRIEST FAIRY	11
	FOR CLOSED IN DARKNESS NOW	738	MOURN THEN ON	10
	LOVE WAS NOT MADE FOR DARKNESS AND THE WINDS	767	SHADOW WATER A	394
	AMID THE DARKNESS, NOW THAT ALL MY STARS	767	SHADOW WATER A	V 404
DARLING				
	"MY DARLING CANNOT UNDERSTAND	255	WORDS	2
	MY DARLING UNDERSTANDS IT ALL,	256	WORDS	10
	AND MANY A DARLING WIT'S GROWN DULL	301	RUN PARADISE	18
	HER LABOURING MEN, AS THOUGH HER DARLING LIVED,	340	SHEP GOATHERD	38
	"ON, ON, MY DARLING MAN"	545	TO SAME TUNE 1	16
	"ON, ON, MY DARLING MAN."	616	MARCH SONGS 3	16
	"OH, ON, MY DARLING MAN."	616	MARCH SONGS 3	V 16
DART				
	ONE WITH THE TIDE THAT GLEAMS, THE WINGS THAT GLEAM AND DART,	78	INDIAN TO LOVE	15
	ONE WITH THE WAVES THAT SOFTLY ROUND US LAUGH AND DART.	78	INDIAN TO LOVE V	15
	. . . THE WINGS THAT GLIMMER AND GLEAM AND DART;	78	INDIAN TO LOVE V	15
	. . . AND WINGS, THAT GLIMMER AND GLEAM AND DART,	78	INDIAN TO LOVE V	15
	THOUGH YOU GLOW AND YOU GLANCE, THOUGH YOU PURR AND YOU DART:	90	OLD FISHERMAN	2
	THOUGH YE GLOW AND YE GLANCE, THOUGH YE PURR AND YE DART,	90	OLD FISHERMAN V	2
	AND HOW THE WINGED SANDALS DART,	135	TWO TREES	18
	AND DREAMING HOW THEY DANCE AND DART,	135	TWO TREES V	18
DARTING				
	DARTING YOU WAVE THEM, DARTING IN THE VAPOUR.	694	MOSADA 1	94
	DARTING YOU WAVE THEM, DARTING IN THE VAPOUR.	694	MOSADA 1	94
DASHED	SEE SEA-DASHED			
	I PAUSED--AND FAR AWAY I DASHED	83	MAD KING GOLL V	31
DATE				
	WILD INDOLENCE AND MUSIC HAVE NO DATE.	686	LIFE	20
	WILD INDOLENCE AND MUSIC HAVE NO DATE,	735	QUATRAIN APHOR	18
	AS THOUGH THEIR SEASON HAD NO DATE,	736	SUMMER EVENING	10
DATELESS				
	FROM DATELESS PAIN. SHE SLEEPS--MOSADA--THOU--	701	MOSADA 3	V 65
DATHI				
	TILL DATHI CAME AND STOOD,	166	BLESSED	2
	TO THE CAVE, WHERE DATHI THE BLESSED HAD GONE,	166	BLESSED	V 3
	BUT DATHI FOLDED HIS HANDS AND SMILED	167	BLESSED	11
	"PRAISE GOD AND GOD'S MOTHER," DATHI SAID,	167	BLESSED	17
	TILL DATHI CAME AND STOOD,	167	BLESSED	V 4B
	"MY EYES ARE BLINKING," DATHI SAID,	168	BLESSED	25
DAUGHTER				
	IS NIAM, DAUGHTER OF THE KING	5	OISIN 1 V	49
	THE DAUGHTER OF THE GREY OLD WOOD-CUTTER,	74	ANASHU VIJAYA V	63
	TO FORGAIL'S DAUGHTER, EMER, IN HER DUN,	105	CUCHULAIN SEA	2
	O DAUGHTER OF THE ISLAND OF WOODS:	164	PERFECT BEAUTY V	1
	CAER, HIS BLUE-EYED DAUGHTER THAT I LOVE.	184	QUEEN MAEVE	96
	CAER, HIS BLUE EYED DAUGHTER THAT I LOVE.	184	QUEEN MAEVE	96
	OF THE HARPER'S DAUGHTER AND HER FRIEND.	192	BAILE AILLINN	76
	OF THE HARPER'S DAUGHTER IF THEY WILL,	197	BAILE AILLINN	199

DAUGHTER   (CONTINUED)
    OF CATHLEEN, THE DAUGHTER OF HOULIHAN. . . . .   207 HANRAHANS SONG   5
    OF CATHLEEN, THE DAUGHTER OF HOULIHAN. . . . .   207 HANRAHANS SONG   10
    IS CATHLEEN, THE DAUGHTER OF HOULIHAN. . . . .   208 HANRAHANS SONG   15
    THE DAUGHTER AND THE GRANDDAUGHTER OF KINGS . . . . .   237 SHADOW WATER B   334
    THE DAUGHTER AND GRANDDAUGHTER OF KINGS . . . . . .   237 SHADOW WATER B V   334
    AND MANY A KING'S DAUGHTER, ...   330 BONE OF A HARE   3
    MANY A SON AND DAUGHTER LIES . . . .   360 ALF POLLEXFEN   13
    A PRAYER FOR MY DAUGHTER . . . .   403 FOR DAUGHTER   T
    AND SHOULD SOME CRAZY HAND DARE TOUCH A DAUGHTER . . .   433 NINETEEN 19   122
    WHERE THE GREAT MOTHER, MOURNING FOR HER DAUGHTER . . .   447 COLONUS PRAISE   19
    . . . MAN, WOMAN, CHILD (A DAUGHTER OR A SON), ...   556 RIBH PATRICK   2
    RECALL HIS TRINITY. A FATHER, MOTHER, CHILD (A DAUGHTER   556 RIBH PATRICK   V   2
      OR A SON),
    A SMALL OLD HOUSE, WIFE, DAUGHTER, SON, ...   577 WHAT THEN   12
    IN THY WAN FACE? HEAR THOU, O DAUGHTER OF THE DAYS, . .   674 ISLE STAT II 3   200
    IN THOSE FAR YEARS, O DAUGHTER OF THE DAYS. . . . .   674 ISLE STAT II 3   213
    IN THY WAN FACE? HEAR, DAUGHTER OF THE DAYS. . . . .   674 ISLE STAT II 3 V   200
    IN THOSE FAIR YEARS, O DAUGHTER OF THE DAYS. . . . .   674 ISLE STAT II 3 V   213
    O WHAT INNKEEPER'S DAUGHTER . . . .   789 SINGING HEAD   13
DAUGHTERS
    AND HE GAVE THEM AS DOWERS TO HIS DAUGHTERS, ...   92 FATHER OHART   7
    HERODIAS' DAUGHTERS HAVE RETURNED AGAIN, ...   433 NINETEEN 19   118
    FOR EVEN DAUGHTERS OF THE SWAN CAN SHARE . . . . .   444 SCHOOL CHILDR   20
DAVIS
    WITH DAVIS, MANGAN, FERGUSON, ...   138 TO IRELAND   18
DAWN
    AND THINGS THAT FEAR THE DAWN OF THE MORROW . . . .   20 OISIN 1   302
    THE DAWN CAME IN, AND GLIMMERED ON THE FLOOR . . . .   39 OISIN 2   152
    OF MISTY DAWN; WHEN, CIRCLING ROUND THE HALL, . . .   39 OISIN 2   V   153
    HUNG IN THE PASSIONATE DAWN. HE SLOWLY TURNED; . . .   40 OISIN 2   167
    DAWN PASSIONED; FED WITH A FAINT GREEN LIGHT, . . .   40 OISIN 2   V   165
    FOR HE HAS WROUGHT MIDNIGHT AND DAWN AND DAY. . . .   43 OISIN 2   208
    AND MANY PATER NOSTERS SAID SINCE DAWN. . . . . .   43 OISIN 2   V 208D
    COMING OUT OF THE SEA AS THE DAWN COMES, A CHAUNT OF LOVE   58 OISIN 3   158
      ON MY LIPS,
    WITH MIRTHFUL SONGS BEFORE THE DAWN. . . . .   67 HAPPY SHEPHERD   49
    WITH MIRTHFUL SONGS TILL RISE THE DAWN. . . . . .   67 HAPPY SHEPHERD V   49
    THE ISLAND DREAMS UNDER THE DAWN . . . .   77 INDIAN TO LOVE   1
    TO SMILE ON THE PALE DAWN; AND GATHER YOU . . . .   114 ROSE OF BATTLE   15
    I RISE IN THE DAWN, AND I KNEEL AND BLOW . . . . .   150 OLD MOTHER   1
    I RISE AT THE DAWN, AND I KNEEL AND BLOW . . . . .   150 OLD MOTHER   V   1
    AND WOOD-OF-WONDERS, WHERE ONE KILLS AN OX AT DAWN, . .   209 UNDER THE MOON   9
    GATHERS THE WILD DUCK FROM THE WINTER DAWN; . . . .   217 WOODS OF COOLE   3
    AMONG THE WINDY MEADOWS OF THE DAWN." . . . . . .   234 SHADOW WATER B   264
    I SWEAR BEFORE THE DAWN COMES ROUND AGAIN . . . . .   260 FASC DIFFICULT   12
    BETWEEN THE DAWN AND DUSK," SHE SAID; . . . . . .   273 GREY ROCK   66
    "WERE IT NOT THAT WHEN THE DAWN HAS LIT MY BED . . .   285 TWO KINGS   187
    THE HOUR BEFORE DAWN . . . .   302 HOUR DAWN   T
    "NIGHT GROWS UNEASY NEAR THE DAWN . . . .   303 HOUR DAWN   33
    THAT'S GROWN UNEASY NEAR THE DAWN . . . .   303 HOUR DAWN   V   33
    IN THE BAD HOUR BEFORE THE DAWN." . . . .   304 HOUR DAWN   55
    THE CLOUDS WERE BRIGHTENING WITH THE DAWN. . . . .   307 HOUR DAWN   122
    THE DAWN . . . .   344 DAWN   T
    I WOULD BE IGNORANT AS THE DAWN . . . .   344 DAWN   1
    I WOULD BE IGNORANT AS THE DAWN . . . .   344 DAWN   10
    IGNORANT AND WANTON AS THE DAWN. . . . .   344 DAWN   14
    I WOULD BE AS IGNORANT AS THE DAWN, ...   344 DAWN   V   1
    AT DAWN TO CAST HIS FLIES, ...   347 FISHERMAN   5
    AND PASSIONATE AS THE DAWN." . . . .   348 FISHERMAN   40
    IN THEIR GREAT WINDOW LOOKING AT THE DAWN; . . . .   352 PEOPLE   15
    THAT SAW THE WICKS GROW YELLOW IN THE DAWN; . . . .   352 PEOPLE   18
    THEIR MOMENTARY CRIES BEFORE IT IS DAWN, ...   371 EGO DOMINUS   78
    AND DROVE HIM DRUNK OR SOBER THROUGH THE DAWN . . .   411 TOWER   58
    THE FOUNTAIN LEAP, AND AT DAWN . . . .   414 TOWER   124
    THAT UNDER BURSTING DAWN . . . .   416 TOWER   176
    TILL THE DAWN BREAK UPON THOSE MINGLED SEAS. . . .   494 AT ALGECIRAS   6
    BETWEEN THE DARK AND DAWN. . . . .   511 JANE AND JACK   6
    THAT FIRST DAWN IN HELEN'S ARMS? . . . .   522 LULLABY   6
    THAT SONG ANNOUNCES DAWN. . . . .   536 PARTING   4
    THAT DAY BRINGS ROUND THE NIGHT, THAT BEFORE DAWN . .   563 MERU   13
    SOME DAY WE SHALL GET UP BEFORE THE DAWN . . . . .   622 HOUND VOICE   15
    . . . NIGHT SPLITS AND THE DAWN BREAKS LOOSE; . . .   623 HIGH TALK   12
    THOSE GREAT SEA-HORSES BARE THEIR TEETH AND LAUGH AT THE   623 HIGH TALK   14
      DAWN.
    NOW THEY RIDE THE WINTRY DAWN . . . .   637 BEN BULBEN   10
    FOR THE DAWN THE FOLIAGE FINGERETH, ...   646 ISLE STAT I 1   26
    FOR THE DAWN OF FOLIAGE FINGERETH, ...   646 ISLE STAT I 1   V   26
    IN THE HEART OF THE DAWN THE RIVERS ARE SINGING, . .   648 ISLE STAT I 1   91
    AND RULE THE SHADOWS OF THE EVE AND DAWN? . . . .   678 ISLE STAT II 3   304
    AND THROB WITHIN THE CIRCLES OF GREEN DAWN. . . . .   701 MOSADA 3   54
    ALONE AMONG THE MURMURS OF THE DAWN. . . . .   702 MOSADA 3   81
    AMONG THE WINDY MEADOWS OF THE DAWN." . . . . . .   754 SHADOW WATER A   153
    WHERE THE DEW IS MADE BEFORE DAWN; . . . .   771 SPINNING SONG   5
    THE CURLEW CRY BEFORE DAWN . . . .   783 GREY ROUND   22
DAWNED
    AND THE FIXED STARS HAD DAWNED AND SHONE AND SET, . .   31 OISIN 2   40
    FOR CENTURIES, AND STARS HAD DAWNED AND SET. . . .   31 OISIN 2   V   40
    FOR YEARS HIS DAYS HAD DAWNED AND FADED THUS . . . .   692 MOSADA 1   54
DAWNING
    AND WE FEAR NO DAWNING MORROW, ...   21 OISIN 1   318

DAWNING (CONTINUED)

OR TIRED ON ANY DAWNING MORROW, ... 23 OISIN 1   V 341
WENT IN THE DAWNING LIGHT . . . . 512 JANE ON GOD   3
THAT WILL BE LATER, DAY IS SCARCELY DAWNING. . . . . 699 MOSADA 3   12
THAT WILL BE LATER, DAY IS DAWNING. . . . . 699 MOSADA 3   V 12

DAWNS

THE HUMAN SADNESS DAWNS ONCE MORE;" . . . . 25 OISIN 1   V 381

DAWN-SONG

A DAWN-SONG. . . . . 705 DAWN-SONG   T

DAWS

THE DAWS CHATTER AND SCREAM, ... 415 TOWER   167

DAY   SEE TO-DAY MARRIAGE-DAY MID-DAY WELL-A-DAY

WHEN ONE DAY BY THE TIDE I STOOD, ... 24 OISIN 1   364
WHEN ONE DAY BY THE SHORE I STOOD, ... 24 OISIN 1   V 364
BUT THE LOVE-DEW DIMS OUR EYES TILL THE DAY . . . . 28 OISIN 1   424
AND EVEN THE SUN, THE DAY CASTLE'S WARDER, ... 28 OISIN 1   V 423A
BEFORE THIS DAY; FOR NOW THE FALL OF TEARS . . . . . 30 OISIN 2   18
THOSE WARRIORS OF A LONG-FORGOTTEN DAY, ... 30 OISIN 2   V 14A
AND THROUGH THEIR EYES NO LIGHT OF MOON OR DAY . . . 34 OISIN 2   V   77
OF SWORD AND BRAZEN BATTLE-AXE, WHILE DAY . . . . . 40 OISIN 2   171
MINGLING OF SWORD AND WAR-AXE, WHILE THE DAY . . . . 40 OISIN 2   V 171
UPON THE LIPS OF SEA-GODS IN THEIR DAY; . . . . . . 41 OISIN 2   190
FOR HE HAS WROUGHT MIDNIGHT AND DAWN AND DAY. . . . . 43 OISIN 2   208
TO LIE THERE 'TILL THE FOURTH DAY SAW EMERGE . . . . 44 OISIN 2   V 220
AND THE MOON GOAD THE WATERS NIGHT AND DAY, ... 45 OISIN 2   238
I CRIED, "O NIAMH! O WHITE ONE! IF ONLY A TWELVE-HOURED 55 OISIN 3   113
    DAY,
O SWIFT ON THE SEAS ALL DAY AND NIGHT . . . . . . 70 CLOAK BOAT   8
ALL DAY AND NIGHT." . . . . 70 CLOAK BOAT   10
THE FIELDS GREW FATTER DAY BY DAY, ... 82 MAD KING GOLL   7
THE FIELDS GREW FATTER DAY BY DAY, ... 82 MAD KING GOLL   7
HOW I HAVE FOLLOWED, NIGHT AND DAY, ... 85 MAD KING GOLL   53
CAME KEENING IN THAT DAY, ... 93 FATHER OHART   32
THE WHOLE OF THE LONG DAY, ... 94 MOLL MAGEE   8
A NEIGHBOUR MINDED HER BY DAY, ... 94 MOLL MAGEE   15
IN ALL POOR FOOLISH THINGS THAT LIVE A DAY, ... 101 ROSE UPON ROOD   11
THIS WHOLE DAY HAVE I FOLLOWED IN THE ROCKS, ... 102 FERGUS DRUID   1
THE WHOLE DAY HAVE I FOLLOWED IN THE ROCKS, ... 102 FERGUS DRUID   V   1
WHILE DAY ITS BURDEN ON TO EVENING BORE, ... 110 CUCHULAIN SEA   70
AMID MEN'S SOULS THAT DAY BY DAY GIVE PLACE, ... 112 ROSE OF WORLD   V   7
AMID MEN'S SOULS THAT DAY BY DAY GIVE PLACE, ... 112 ROSE OF WORLD   V   7
I WILL ARISE AND GO NOW, FOR ALWAYS NIGHT AND DAY . . 117 ISLE INNISFREE   9
AND SANG HOW DAY A DRUID TWILIGHT SHEDS . . . . . . 126 DREAM OF FAERY V   7
OR STORMY SILVER FRET THE GOLD OF DAY, ... 128 DREAM OF FAERY   33
AND HOW, WHEN FADES THE SEA-STREWN ROSE OF DAY, . . . 128 DREAM OF FAERY V 33
WAS WEARY NIGHT AND DAY, ... 132 FR GILLIGAN   2
THE HOST IS RUSHING 'TWIXT NIGHT AND DAY, ... 141 HOSTING SIDHE   13
HAVE THEIR DAY, HAVE THEIR DAY; . . . . 142 MOODS   4
HAVE THEIR DAY, HAVE THEIR DAY; . . . . 142 MOODS   4
AND THEIR DAY GOES OVER IN IDLENESS, ... 151 OLD MOTHER   7
SHE LOOKED IN MY HEART ONE DAY . . . . 152 LOSS OF LOVE   5
UNDER MY FEET THAT THEY FOLLOW YOU NIGHT AND DAY. . . 153 CHANGE BELOVED   5
UNDER MY FEET, THAT I FOLLOW YOU, NIGHT AND DAY. . . 153 CHANGE BELOVED V   5
IT WORKED AT THEM, DAY OUT, DAY IN, ... 158 BELOVED RHYMES   4
IT WORKED AT THEM, DAY OUT, DAY IN, ... 158 BELOVED RHYMES   4
THE GREY CAIRN ON THE HILL, WHEN DAY SINKS DROWNED IN DEW, 161 BLACK PIG   6
O WINDS, OLDER THAN CHANGING OF NIGHT AND DAY, . . . 162 ASKS FORGIVE   7
O WINDS, ELDER THAN CHANGING OF NIGHT AND DAY, . . . 162 ASKS FORGIVE   V   7
TO HIDE FROM THE TROUBLED DAY. . . . . 166 BLESSED   V   4
"O BLESSEDNESS COMES IN THE NIGHT AND THE DAY . . . 168 BLESSED   33
THE NETS OF DAY AND NIGHT. . . . . 175 ELEMENT POWERS   12
AND ALL THAT NIGHT, AND ALL THROUGH THE NEXT DAY . . 185 QUEEN MAEVE   113
BUT WHERE IT COULD SEE HER EVERY DAY. . . . . . . 191 BAILE AILLINN   55
HE ALWAYS WEPT THEM ON THAT DAY, ... 192 BAILE AILLINN   78
FOR ON THAT DAY THEY HAD BEEN BETRAYED; . . . . . 192 BAILE AILLINN   79
THAT OLD MAN CLIMBED; THE DAY GREW DIM; . . . . . 194 BAILE AILLINN   134
O THOUGHT, FLY TO HER WHEN THE END OF DAY . . . . . 201 OLD MEMORY   1
I THOUGHT TO FLY TO HER WHEN THE END OF DAY . . . . 201 OLD MEMORY   1
THOUGHT FLY TO HER WHEN THE END OF DAY . . . . . . 201 OLD MEMORY   V   1
WHEN IN RAGGED VAPOUR THEY MUTTER NIGHT AND DAY, . . 206 HANRAHANS SONG V   2
OF THE HUNTER'S MOON, THAT HUNG BETWEEN THE NIGHT AND THE 210 UNDER THE MOON   18
    DAY,
OF THE THIRD MOON, THAT HUNG BETWEEN THE NIGHT AND THE DAY, 210 UNDER THE MOON V 18
AS THAT WILD AENGUS, LONG BEFORE HER DAY . . . . . 224 SHADOW WATER B   47
AND IN A TOWER OF GLASS, AND FROM THAT DAY . . . . 224 SHADOW WATER B   50
BUT MY BELOVED--THAT NIGHT AND DAY HAD PERISHED, . . 246 SHADOW WATER B   504
THE VERSES THAT COULD MOVE THEM ON THE DAY . . . . 257 RECONCILIATION   2
THE VERSES THAT THEY CARED FOR ON THE DAY . . . . 257 RECONCILIATION V   2
WHILE THOSE SAME HUNDREDS MOCK ANOTHER DAY . . . . 265 ABBEY THEATRE   4
BUT SOME DAY AND AT SOME NEW MOON . . . . . . 266 GALWAY RACES   V 10
WHEN CUPS WENT ROUND AT CLOSE OF DAY-- . . . . . 271 GREY ROCK   12
ALL WAS ACCOMPLISHED. "WHEN THIS DAY . . . . . 273 GREY ROCK   70
THE MEANING OF THAT MONSTROUS DAY. THEN SHE; . . . 280 TWO KINGS   78
"DAY AFTER DAY YOU QUESTION ME, AND I, ... 281 TWO KINGS   99
"DAY AFTER DAY YOU QUESTION ME, AND I, ... 281 TWO KINGS   99
THAT SOME NEW DAY MAY BREED THE BEST . . . . . . 288 TO WEALTHY MAN   34
OR HAPPIER-THOUGHTED WHEN THE DAY IS SPENT . . . . 292 TO A SHADE   4
OR HAPPIER THOUGHTED WHEN THE DAY IS SPENT . . . . 292 TO A SHADE   V   4
I HAVE STOOD HERE FROM BREAK OF DAY, ... 294 THREE BEGGARS   2
THEY MAULED AND BIT TILL THE DAY SHONE; . . . . . 297 THREE BEGGARS   49
THEY MAULED AND BIT THROUGH ALL THAT DAY . . . . . 297 THREE BEGGARS   50

DAY   (CONTINUED)

	PAGE	TITLE		LINE
THREE TIMES IN A SINGLE DAY	298	THREE HERMITS		10
OR MAYBE TO MIDSUMMER DAY,"	305	HOUR DAWN		58
FOR ALL LIFE LONGS FOR THE LAST DAY	306	HOUR DAWN		98
WHEN DAY BEGINS TO BREAK	316	FRIENDS		21
THAT PACKED HIS MARRIAGE DAY	317	NIGHT COME		7
DELIGHT MEN'S EYES WHEN I AWAKE SOME DAY	323	SWANS AT COOLE		29
AND ALL DAY LONG I LOOK	329	MEN IMPROVE		4
"ALL DAY LONG FROM MID-DAY	332	SOLOMON SHEBA		3
ALL DAY LONG FROM SHADOWLESS NOON	332	SOLOMON SHEBA		5
"ALL DAY LONG FROM MIDDAY	332	SOLOMON SHEBA	V	3
AND ALL DAY LONG WE HAVE FOUND	333	SOLOMON SHEBA		22
COULD MAKE ME WISH FOR ANYTHING THIS DAY,	338	SHEP GOATHERD		3
YOU HAVE PUT THE THOUGHT IN RHYME. I WORKED ALL DAY	341	SHEP GOATHERD		58
TO HIS SPEECH AT THE BREAK OF DAY,	341	SHEP GOATHERD		68
I MIGHT HAVE WISHED ON THE DAY	341	SHEP GOATHERD		73
I HAD WISHED A DEAR THING ON THAT DAY	341	SHEP GOATHERD	V	73
ALL DAY I'D LOOKED IN THE FACE	347	FISHERMAN		9
WHERE EVERY DAY MY FOOTFALL SHOULD HAVE LIT	352	PEOPLE		8
I KNEW A PHOENIX IN MY YOUTH, SO LET THEM HAVE THEIR DAY.	353	HIS PHOENIX		8
I KNEW A PHOENIX IN MY YOUTH, SO LET THEM HAVE THEIR DAY.	354	HIS PHOENIX		16
I KNEW A PHOENIX IN MY YOUTH, SO LET THEM HAVE THEIR DAY.	354	HIS PHOENIX		24
I KNEW A PHOENIX IN MY YOUTH, SO LET THEM HAVE THEIR DAY.	354	HIS PHOENIX		32
ALL DAY IN THE ONE CHAIR	357	BROKEN DREAMS		38
BECAUSE THE PRIEST MUST HAVE LIKE EVERY DOG HIS DAY	364	DOLLS FACES		10
THE END OF DAY	364	END OF DAY		T
BECAUSE THE END OF DAY	364	END OF DAY		4
DAY AFTER DAY, YET NEVER FIND THE MEANING.	377	PHASES OF MOON		135
DAY AFTER DAY, YET NEVER FIND THE MEANING.	377	PHASES OF MOON		135
SOME DAY I MAY FORGET	380	SONGS FOOL 1		8
DO NOT BECAUSE THIS DAY I HAVE GROWN SATURNINE	390	UNDER SATURN		1
I HAVE MET THEM AT CLOSE OF DAY	391	EASTER 1916		1
THEY HAVE LOUD MUSIC, HOPE EVERY DAY RENEWED	398	LEADERS CROWD		11
TOWARDS BREAK OF DAY	398	BREAK OF DAY		T
UNDER THE FIRST COLD GLEAM OF DAY?	398	BREAK OF DAY		4
I DREAMED TOWARDS BREAK OF DAY,	399	BREAK OF DAY		19
THAT PLAGUE ME DAY AND NIGHT	399	DEMON BEAST		3
TO MAKE IT LINGER HALF A DAY.	401	DEMON BEAST		42
AND HAD THE LIVELONG SUMMER DAY TO SPEND.	409	TOWER		10
FOR THE PROSAIC LIGHT OF DAY—	411	TOWER		46
WHEN HE FINISHED HIS DOG'S DAY!	412	TOWER		79
UNDER ECLIPSE AND THE DAY BLOTTED OUT.	414	TOWER		120
THE SWEETNESS THAT ALL LONGED FOR NIGHT AND DAY,	418	ANCEST HOUSES		20
UPON SOME BRAND-NEW HAPPY DAY!	432	NINETEEN 19	V	106
IN THE OLD ROOMS! NIGHT CAN OUTBALANCE DAY,	435	NEW FACES		6
FROM NOTHING EVERY DAY, AND TEACH	436	FOR MY SON		18
ENDURES A MOMENT OR A DAY.	438	SONGS PLAY 2		10
THAT CHANGED SOME CHILDISH DAY TO TRAGEDY—	443	SCHOOL CHILDR		12
SUMMER AND WINTER, DAY AND NIGHT,	447	COLONUS PRAISE		31
"YOU BUT IMAGINE LIES ALL DAY, O MURDERER," I REPLIED.	450	OWEN AHERNE		17
. . . NEVER TO HAVE LOOKED INTO THE EYE OF DAY;	459	FROM OEDIPUS		11
. . . AT ALL NOR LOOKED INTO THE EYE OF DAY.	459	FROM OEDIPUS	V	11
LIKE MEN WHO LIVE BY HABIT. EVERY DAY	463	HARUN RASHID		56
BUT WOKE AT THE FIRST GLEAM OF DAY, ROSE UP	467	HARUN RASHID		147
THAT DAY BY DAY I STUDY AND MARVEL AT,	468	HARUN RASHID		157
THAT DAY BY DAY I STUDY AND MARVEL AT,	468	HARUN RASHID		157
FOR EMBLEMS OF THE DAY AGAINST THE TOWER	478	SELF AND SOUL		29
THE UNPURGED IMAGES OF DAY RECEDE;	497	BYZANTIUM		1
OF DAY AND NIGHT!	500	VACILLATION		6
WEIGH ME DOWN, AND NOT A DAY	501	VACILLATION		54
THOSE BRANCHES OF THE NIGHT AND DAY	502	VACILLATION		68
ALL THAT STORM THAT BLOTS THE DAY	509	JANE REPROVED		3
ALL THOSE STORMS THAT BLOT THE DAY	509	JANE REPROVED	V	3
CRAZY JANE ON THE DAY OF JUDGMENT	510	JANE JUDGMENT		T
THAT BLACK DAY"!	510	JANE JUDGMENT		14
I THOUGHT IT OUT THIS VERY DAY,	525	DANCING DAYS		17
THE MURDEROUS STEALTH OF DAY.	536	PARTING		8
THERE'S NOT A BIRD OF DAY THAT DARE	538	LAST CONFESS		23
NO LOOSE-LIPPED DEMAGOGUE HAD WON THE DAY,	542	PARN FUNERAL 2		3
NO LOOSE LIPPED DEMAGOGUE HAD WON THE DAY,	542	PARN FUNERAL 2	V	3
AND MUST THE COMMON ROUND OF DAY RESUME.	557	RIBH ECSTASY		8
THAT DAY BRINGS ROUND THE NIGHT, THAT BEFORE DAWN	563	MERU		13
OF A SLENDER PALM, STOOD BUT A DAY!	566	LAPIS LAZULI		34
LOOKED HALF ASLEEP ALL DAY.	570	THREE BUSHES		34
NO, BUT THAT DAY THEY DID.	570	THREE BUSHES		46
A DOG MUST HAVE HIS DAY,	582	ROGER CASEMENT	V	18
A DOG MUST HAVE HIS DAY,	583	GHOST ROG CASE		12
THE GREAT DAY	590	GREAT DAY		T
FRAGMENTS THE GREAT DAY	590	GREAT DAY	V	T
AND THERE I FOUND AN OLD MAN, AND THOUGH I PRAYED ALL DAY	593	PILGRIM		8
THEIR DRINK, THEIR PITCH-AND-TOSS BY DAY,	607	SONGS BURDEN 2		14
THEIR DRINK, THEIR PITCH AND TOSS BY DAY,	607	SONGS BURDEN 2	V	14
WHO WAS THE FIRST MAN SHOT THAT DAY?	608	SONGS BURDEN 3		10
SOME DAY WE SHALL GET UP BEFORE THE DAWN	622	HOUND VOICE		15
GROWS MORE DEEP DAY AFTER DAY,	624	APPARITIONS		18
GROWS MORE DEEP DAY AFTER DAY,	624	APPARITIONS		18
UNTO THE WANDERER'S SHIPS, OR AS DAY FILLS	645	ISLE STAT I 1		10
BY DAY AND NIGHT A LONELY FOUNTAIN SINGS,	650	ISLE STAT I 1		130
THE PALE ANEMONES. WE'VE SOUGHT ALL DAY,	651	ISLE STAT I 2		5
O'ER THE LAKE THIS VERY DAY.	656	ISLE STAT I 3		17
ONCE MORE HOW ON THAT MISERABLE DAY	658	ISLE STAT II 1		4

187

	PAGE	TITLE		LINE
DAY (CONTINUED)				
O SWIFT ON THE SEAS ALL DAY AND NIGHT	666	ISLE STAT II 3		8
ALL DAY AND NIGHT.	666	ISLE STAT II 3		10
AND THE HAPPY WINGED DAY.	668	ISLE STAT II 3		64
IT IS, YET SHALL IT FAIL THEE DAY AND NIGHT.	674	ISLE STAT II 3		211
O ARCADY, O ARCADY, THIS DAY	676	ISLE STAT II 3		272
AND WOE-BEGONE. FOR THEM NO EVIL DAY!	677	ISLE STAT II 3		275
BEAT ON IT WITH THEIR HAMMERS DAY AND NIGHT.	687	TWO TITANS		4
THAT WILL BE LATER, DAY IS SCARCELY DAWNING.	699	MOSADA 3		12
THAT WILL BE LATER, DAY IS DAWNING.	699	MOSADA 3	V	12
'TIS LATE, WAIT ONE MORE DAY! BELOW THE HILLS	702	MOSADA 3		91
AND POUR UPON THE WORLD! AH! WELL A DAY!	703	MOSADA 3	V	118
DOWN THE VAPOURS FALL AND HIDE THEM FROM THE CHILDREN OF A DAY,	719	PHANTOM SHIP		27
SOME DAY YOU'LL BUY THEM, MAYBE. NEVER! NEVER?	721	WITCH VIVIEN		24
THAN OLD MEN'S ANY DAY, AS MERLIN FOUND.	721	WITCH VIVIEN		47
COME AND TEASE THEM TILL THE DAY.	727	LOVERS QUARREL		36
THE TANGLED THOUGHTS OF THE FINISHED DAY	728	PRIEST FAIRY		9
"AND CUT NO WOOD THE WHOLE DAY LONG,	731	PRIEST FAIRY		81
LONG THOU FOR NOTHING, NEITHER NIGHT NOR DAY!	734	QUATRAIN APHOR		10
MOURN ALL THE NIGHT AND DAY,	737	MOURN THEN ON		2
TILL DAY AND NIGHT TIME END.	741	EARL PAUL		48
IN DAY OUT-LIVING BATTLE, ON THE BREAST	750	SHADOW WATER A		73
THAT DIES OUT BEFORE 'TIS DAY.	777	SONG DEIRDRE 2		8
I WAS GOING THE ROAD ONE DAY	779	GOING THE ROAD		1
"FOR A YEAR AND A DAY BY THE CLOCK OF THE SUN"	779	GOING THE ROAD		11
ACCURSED WHO BRINGS TO LIGHT OF DAY	779	ACCURSED WHO		1
TO THE LOUD SANDS BEFORE DAY HAS BROKEN.	784	WOMANS BEAUTY		18
AMID THE DARK BEFORE DAY HAD BROKEN.	784	WOMANS BEAUTY		20
DAYBREAK				
THE EAST TELLS ALL HER SECRET JOY BEFORE DAYBREAK,	154	BELOVED PEACE	V	4
"SAY WHAT YOU PLEASE, BUT FROM DAYBREAK	304	HOUR DAWN		42
I STRUGGLED WITH THE HORROR OF DAYBREAK,	535	CHOSEN		10
DAYBREAK AND A CANDLE-END.	588	OLD WICKED MAN		9
DAYBREAK AND A CANDLE-END.	588	OLD WICKED MAN		18
DAYBREAK AND A CANDLE-END.	588	OLD WICKED MAN		27
DAYBREAK AND A CANDLE END.	588	OLD WICKED MAN	V	REF
DAYBREAK AND A CANDLE-END.	589	OLD WICKED MAN		36
DAYBREAK AND A CANDLE-END.	589	OLD WICKED MAN		45
DAYBREAK AND A CANDLE-END.	589	OLD WICKED MAN		54
DAYBREAK AND A CANDLE-END.	590	OLD WICKED MAN		63
HOW MANY HOURS TO DAYBREAK, BECAUSE LOVE	767	SHADOW WATER A		405
AT DAYBREAK AFTER STORMY NIGHT	784	WOMANS BEAUTY		3
DAY-BREAK				
"SAY WHAT YOU PLEASE, BUT FROM DAY-BREAK	304	HOUR DAWN	V	42
DAY-BREAK AND A CANDLE END.	588	OLD WICKED MAN	V	REF
DAYLIGHT				
"WHETHER UNDER ITS DAYLIGHT OR ITS STARS	107	CUCHULAIN SEA		25
"NO, SOMEWHERE UNDER DAYLIGHT OR THE STARS	107	CUCHULAIN SEA	V	25
"WHETHER UNDER ITS DAYLIGHT OR THE STARS	107	CUCHULAIN SEA	V	25
WE SAW THE LAST EMBERS OF DAYLIGHT DIE,	205	ADAMS CURSE		29
A SHELTER TILL THE DAYLIGHT BROKE.	302	HOUR DAWN		15
"STRETCH BONES TILL THE DAYLIGHT COME	331	ROUND TOWER		5
AND MAKE THE DAYLIGHT SWEET ONCE MORE! BUT WHEN	339	SHEP GOATHERD		13
THE NIGHTINGALE THAT DEAFENS DAYLIGHT THERE,	446	COLONUS PRAISE		3
IF DAYLIGHT EVER VISIT WHERE,	446	COLONUS PRAISE		4
DAYLIGHT ALREADY FLIES	536	PARTING		9
FOR I THAT AM HIS DAYLIGHT LADY	573	LADYS 3RD SONG		5
DAYLIGHT-DARKENING				
AND NOW THE DAYLIGHT-DARKENING RAVENS FLOCK.	43	OISIN 2		212
DAY-LONG				
AND ONCE MORE TO A DAY-LONG BATTLE FELL,	43	OISIN 2		218
DAY'S				
I SANG HOW, WHEN DAY'S TOIL IS DONE,	85	MAD KING GOLL		61
THE HOURLY KINDNESS, THE DAY'S COMMON SPEECH,	258	KING NO KING		14
ON THE DAY'S WAR WITH EVERY KNAVE AND DOLT,	260	FASC DIFFICULT		10
UNDER THE DAY'S DECLINING BEAM, AND CALL	410	TOWER		21
OR THE DAY'S VANITY, THE NIGHT'S REMORSE.	491	COOLE BALLYLEE	V	40H
OR THE DAY'S VANITY, THE NIGHT'S REMORSE.	495	CHOICE		8
A NEW DAY'S TROOP OF WASP AND BEE	646	ISLE STAT I 1		44
AS I, TO CHOOSE BENEATH DAY'S DYING FLAMES!	656	ISLE STAT I 3		34
DAY'S DEAD, ALL FLAME-BEWILDERED, AND THE HILLS	702	MOSADA 3		86
DAYS				
THE BAD OLD DAYS. THOU WERT, MEN SING,	2	OISIN 1	V	3
AND THE DAYS PASS BY LIKE A WAYWARD TUNE,	8	OISIN 1		83
I KNOW NOT IF DAYS PASSED OR HOURS,	11	OISIN 1		133
I KNEW NOT IF DAYS PASSED OR HOURS,	11	OISIN 1	V	133
A DRUID DREAM OF THE END OF DAYS	16	OISIN 1		219
FOR HIS LAST DAYS TO LIE IN WAIT.	24	OISIN 1		363
HE HAS OVER-LINGERED HIS WELCOME! THE DAYS,	26	OISIN 1		402
WHERE CARE CANNOT TROUBLE THE LEAST OF OUR DAYS,	27	OISIN 1		409
HE HATH OVER LINGERED HIS WELCOME! THE DAYS,	27	OISIN 1	V	406
WILL SCATTER IN RUIN THE LEAST OF OUR DAYS,	27	OISIN 1	V	419B
SHALL BLOW INTO RUIN OUR MUSICAL DAYS.	28	OISIN 1	V	425
ON THE OLD SORROWS OF HIS HUMAN DAYS.	29	OISIN 2	V	12
TROUBLED HER SONG. I DO NOT KNOW IF DAYS	30	OISIN 2		19
FLASHING—I KNOW NOT WERE IT HOURS OR DAYS,	30	OISIN 2	V	19B
WAS LOADED WITH THE MEMORY OF DAYS	39	OISIN 2		150
WE FEASTED FOR THREE DAYS. ON THE FOURTH MORN	43	OISIN 2		214
THREE DAYS WE FEASTED, WHEN ON THE FOURTH MORN	43	OISIN 2	V	214
REMEMBERING HOW I PACED IN DAYS GONE O'ER,	44	OISIN 2	V	227

188

DAYS   (CONTINUED)

	PAGE	TITLE		LINE
WERE WE DAYS LONG OR HOURS LONG IN RIDING,	47	OISIN 3		9
HIS SHOUTING DAYS WITH MIRTH WERE CROWNED;	67	HAPPY SHEPHERD		50
THAT MOANS AND SIGHS A HUNDRED DAYS;	78	INDIAN TO LOVE		17
IN PENAL DAYS RODE OUT	91	FATHER OHART		2
RED ROSE, PROUD ROSE, SAD ROSE OF ALL MY DAYS;	100	ROSE UPON ROOD		1
RED ROSE, PROUD ROSE, SAD ROSE OF ALL MY DAYS.	101	ROSE UPON ROOD		24
AND PONDERED ON THE GLORY OF HIS DAYS;	108	CUCHULAIN SEA		43
AND PONDERED ON THE WONDER OF HIS DAYS.	108	CUCHULAIN SEA	V	43
FOR THREE DAYS MORE IN DREADFUL QUIETUDE,	110	CUCHULAIN SEA		78
AND CHAUNTED FOR THREE DAYS. CUCHULAIN STIRRED,	111	CUCHULAIN SEA		83
AND CHANTED FOR THREE DAYS. CUCHULAIN STIRRED,	111	CUCHULAIN SEA	V	83
FOR FOUR DAYS WARRED HE WITH THE BITTER TIDE,	111	CUCHULAIN SEA	V	85
ALL THE HEAVY DAYS ARE OVER;	124	CATHLEEN PARA		1
AS IN THE OLD DAYS LONG GONE BY,	131	OLD PENSIONER	V	15
THE FLAMING CIRCLE OF OUR DAYS,	135	TWO TREES		14
APOLOGIA ADDRESSED TO IRELAND IN THE COMING DAYS	137	TO IRELAND	V	T
THE PEOPLE OF COMING DAYS WILL KNOW	146	FISH		3
OUT OF THE OLD DAYS	158	TO HIS HEART	V	T
REMEMBER THE WISDOM OUT OF THE OLD DAYS;	158	TO HIS HEART		2
THE POETS LABOURING ALL THEIR DAYS	164	PERFECT BEAUTY		2
WE POETS LABOUR ALL OUR DAYS.	164	PERFECT BEAUTY	V	2
THOUGH YOU ARE IN YOUR SHINING DAYS,	172	PLEADS FRIEND		1
ALTHOUGH YOU ARE IN YOUR SHINING DAYS,	172	PLEADS FRIEND	V	1
THE LOVER SPEAKS TO THE HEARERS OF HIS SONGS IN COMING DAYS	173	SPEAKS HEARERS		T
HANRAHAN SPEAKS TO THE LOVERS OF HIS SONGS IN COMING DAYS	173	SPEAKS HEARERS	V	T
A LOVER SPEAKS TO THE HEARERS OF HIS SONGS IN COMING DAYS	173	SPEAKS HEARERS	V	T
AND THOUGHT OF DAYS WHEN HE'D HAD A STRAIGHT BODY,	183	QUEEN MAEVE		70
AS IN THE OLD DAYS WHEN THEY WOULD COME AND GO	183	QUEEN MAEVE		81
THROUGH THE LONG DAYS OF YOUTH, AND WHO WOULD HAVE THOUGHT	201	OLD MEMORY	V	7
ABOUT THE STARS AND BROKE IN DAYS AND YEARS.	206	ADAMS CURSE		33
ABOUT THE STARN AND BROKE IN DAYS AND YEARS.	206	ADAMS CURSE	V	33
THESE MANY DAYS; AND YET THERE MUST BE MANY	226	SHADOW WATER B		89
WHY SHOULD I BLAME HER THAT SHE FILLED MY DAYS	256	NO SECOND TROY		1
THE LABYRINTH OF HER DAYS	260	UNWORTH PRAISE		13
THROUGH ALL THE LYING DAYS OF MY YOUTH	261	COMING WISDOM		2
THAT EMPTIED ALL OUR DAYS TO COME.	272	GREY ROCK		40
AND FOR NINE DAYS HE HAD FOOD FROM OTHER HANDS,	282	TWO KINGS		126
AND FOR NINE DAYS MY MIND WENT WHIRLING ROUND	282	TWO KINGS		127
BUT WHEN NINE DAYS HAD GONE I STOOD AGAIN	282	TWO KINGS		131
IN DAYS YOU HAVE NOT KEPT IN MEMORY,	284	TWO KINGS		168
WHAT JOY IS IN MY DAYS;	315	FRIENDS		3
AND BE WELL PLEASED REMEMBERING IT, FOR IN THE OLD DAYS,	351	HER PRAISE		16
HAPPIER DAYS THOUGHT GOOD;	365	HER RACE		4
IMAGINED BODIES ALL THEIR DAYS	386	ROBARTES DANCE		28
I HAD THOUGHT THAT ALL MY DAYS WERE CAST	389	IMAGE PAST		12
THAT WOMAN'S DAYS WERE SPENT	392	EASTER 1916		17
GATHERED A SCORE OF HORSE AND SPENT HIS DAYS	420	MY HOUSE		22
MY DAYS OUT OF THEIR AIMLESSNESS.	421	MY TABLE		5
SOME FOURTEEN DAYS OF CIVIL WAR;	425	STARES NEST		12
WE THOUGHT IT WOULD OUTLIVE ALL FUTURE DAYS.	428	NINETEEN 19		14
NOW DAYS ARE DRAGON-RIDDEN, THE NIGHTMARE	429	NINETEEN 19		25
NOW DAYS ARE DRAGON RIDDEN, THE NIGHTMARE	429	NINETEEN 19	V	25
THAT WAITS UPON HIS FUTURE DAYS;	436	FOR MY SON		14
WHEN MY DAYS THAT HAVE	449	HERO GIRL FOOL	V	18
HAD SPOKEN OF THEIR CHILDISH DAYS	457	SUMMER SPRING		11
AND OFTEN THOSE FIRST DAYS I SAW HER STARE	466	HARUN RASHID		122
A BOY'S TURBULENT DAYS	496	MOHINI CHATTER		13
THE TRIVIAL DAYS AND RAM THEM WITH THE SUN,	500	VACILLATION		21
OF DISTORTING DAYS	504	QUARREL IN AGE		13
THOSE DANCING DAYS ARE GONE	524	DANCING DAYS		T
THOSE DANCING DAYS ARE GONE,	524	DANCING DAYS		2
I FASTED FOR SOME FORTY DAYS ON BREAD AND BUTTERMILK,	592	PILGRIM		1
CAST YOUR MIND ON OTHER DAYS	640	BEN BULBEN		81
THAT WE IN COMING DAYS MAY BE	640	BEN BULBEN		82
NAY, NAY, I MISS'D HIM NOT; HIS DAYS	649	ISLE STAT I 1		117
HAVE CLOTHED THEIR TONGUES WITH SONG OF SONGLESS DAYS?	666	ISLE STAT II 3		17
IN THY WAN FACE? HEAR THOU, O DAUGHTER OF THE DAYS,	674	ISLE STAT II 3		200
YET EVER MORE, THROUGH ALL THY DAYS OF RUTH,	674	ISLE STAT II 3		206
IN THOSE FAR YEARS, O DAUGHTER OF THE DAYS.	674	ISLE STAT II 3		213
IN THY WAN FACE? HEAR, DAUGHTER OF THE DAYS,	674	ISLE STAT II 3 V		200
YET EVERMORE, THROUGH ALL THY DAYS OF RUTH,	674	ISLE STAT II 3 V		206
IN THOSE FAIR YEARS, O DAUGHTER OF THE DAYS.	674	ISLE STAT II 3 V		213
AND PEACE BE WITH YOU, PEACE AND WEALTH OF DAYS.	682	SEEKER		28
WERE ALL MY WANDERING DAYS OF NO AVAIL,	684	SEEKER		64
FOR YEARS HIS DAYS HAD DAWNED AND FADED THUS	692	MOSADA 1		54
LIKE HAPPY THOUGHTS GROWN SAD IN EVIL DAYS.	703	MOSADA 3		116
AND DREAM OF THE END OF THEIR DAYS,	707	FAIRY PEDANT		4
AND NUMBER THEIR DAYS AND THEIR HOURS--	707	FAIRY PEDANT		19
IN THEIR DAYS OF YOUTHFUL MIRTH!	727	LOVERS QUARREL		40
AS THOUGH HIS DAYS WERE FULL OF RUTH.	731	PRIEST FAIRY		76
HE HAS HEARD ME AND NOT YOU. NINE DAYS AGO	752	SHADOW WATER A		113
"LIVES ALL HIS DAYS	780	WELL AND TREE		3
WHAT THOUGH THEY DANCED! THOSE DAYS ARE GONE,	788	HAWTHORN TREE		5

DAYS'

	PAGE	TITLE		LINE
AND SUNKEN SHAPE, A NINE DAYS' CORPSE SEA-DASHED--	40	OISIN 2	V	179
IN THREE DAYS' TIME HE STOOD UP WITH A MOAN,	111	CUCHULAIN SEA	V	83
IN THREE DAYS' TIME, CUCHULAIN WITH A MOAN .	111	CUCHULAIN SEA	V	83

DAYSPRING

	PAGE	TITLE		LINE
TO HIS OWN DAYSPRING,	342	SHEP GOATHERD		96

189

		PAGE	TITLE		LINE

DAYTIME
    SO SLEEP THEE BY DAYTIME." A VOICE CRIED, ... 59 OISIN 3   172
    SO SLEEP THEY BY DAYTIME." A VOICE CRIED, ... 59 OISIN 3   V   172
    TILL DAYTIME, PLAYTIME SEEM THE SAME: . . . . 343 SHEP GOATHERD   106
    OR RUN WHERE LADS REFORM OUR DAYTIME . . . . 343 SHEP GOATHERD   V   105
    AS THE SUMMER VOICE OF THE DAYTIME CEASED, ... 728 PRIEST FAIRY   4
DAZED
    WE SHOULD BE DAZED AND TERROR-STRUCK, ... 272 GREY ROCK   37
    WE SHOULD BE DAZED AND TERROR STRUCK . . . . . . 272 GREY ROCK   V   37
    OF THE STARK MYSTERY THAT HAS DAZED MY SIGHT, ... 466 HARUN RASHID   113
    CHILDREN DAZED OR DEAD! . . . . 488 CRAZED MOON   7
DAZZLED
    NOR DAZZLED BY THE EMBROIDERY, NOR LOST . . . . . . 470 HARUN RASHID   191
    NOT BLIND WITH GOLD, NOR DAZZLED BY THE GOLD . . . . . 470 HARUN RASHID   V   191
DAZZLING
    IN BRONZE, OR THAT IN DAZZLING MARBLE APPEARS, ... 334 LIVING BEAUTY   5
DEAD   SEE HALF-DEAD MUMMY-DEAD
    FOR OUR BEST WERE DEAD ON GAVRA'S GREEN. . . . . . . 2 OISIN 1   V   71
    COMPANIONS LONG ACCURST AND DEAD, ... 11 OISIN 1   130
    FROM DEWY EYES! "UPON THE DEAD . . . . 21 OISIN 1   310
    ON THE DEAD DIM EARTH ENCLOSES! . . . . 21 OISIN 1   312
    SANG WE SOFTLY, "ON THE DEAD, ... 21 OISIN 1   V   310
    ON THE DEAD THE EARTH ENCLOSES, ... 21 OISIN 1   V   312
    FROM SOME DEAD WARRIOR'S BROKEN LANCE! . . . . 24 OISIN 1   367
    IT WAS OF SOME DEAD WARRIOR'S LANCE. . . . . 24 OISIN 1   V   367
    "NEITHER THE LIVING, NOR THE UNLABOURING DEAD, ... 34 OISIN 2   79
    THE DEAD GOD'S SWORD, TO MANY FORMS HE GREW, ... 40 OISIN 2   V   175
    CAST THE LOOSE BULK, LEST NIAM FEAR HIM DEAD! . . . . . 41 OISIN 2   V   183
    A HUSH! AH, ME! IT HANGS TO STRIKE US DEAD. . . . . . 43 OISIN 2   V   208B
    . . . "THE FENIANS A LONG TIME ARE DEAD." . . . . . 59 OISIN 3   172
    . . . HE CRIED, "NO, THE GODS A LONG TIME ARE DEAD." . . . 59 OISIN 3   180
    . . . HE CRIED, "NAY, THE GODS A LONG TIME ARE DEAD." . . . 59 OISIN 3   V   180
    THE WOODS OF ARCADY ARE DEAD, ... 64 HAPPY SHEPHERD   1
    THE KINGS OF THE OLD TIME ARE DEAD! . . . . 65 HAPPY SHEPHERD   17
    AND DEAD IS ALL THEIR HUMAN TRUTH. . . . . 66 HAPPY SHEPHERD   34
    WHEN WE ARE DEAD, BEYOND THE SETTING SUNS, ... 71 ANASHU VIJAYA   8
    TURNING, HE SAW THAT SHE HAD THRUST DEAD LEAVES . . . . 80 EPHEMERA   18
    THE HOUNDS WAIL FOR THE DEAD. . . . . 99 FOXHUNTER   48
    THE HOUNDS KEEN FOR THE DEAD. . . . . 99 FOXHUNTER   V   48
    BY GOD TO THE BRIGHT HEARTS OF THOSE LONG DEAD, ... 101 ROSE UPON ROOD   20
    "NO MAN ALIVE, NO MAN AMONG THE DEAD, ... 106 CUCHULAIN SEA   10
    "NOT ANY GOD ALIVE NOR MORTAL DEAD, ... 106 CUCHULAIN SEA   V   10
    WITH THE WHIMPERING DEAD. . . . . 118 CRADLE SONG   4
    THE SOULS OF THE DEAD. . . . . 118 CRADLE SONG   V   4
    "AND IS THE POOR MAN DEAD?" HE CRIED. . . . . . . 133 FR GILLIGAN   33
    OF PASSIONATE MEN, LIKE BATS IN THE DEAD TREES! . . . . 136 TO SOME I TALK   5
    OLD WOMEN WERE KEENING THE DEAD! . . . . 145 HOST OF AIR   V   40D
    O PITEOUS HEARTS, CHANGING TILL CHANGE BE DEAD . . . . . 163 ASKS FORGIVE   19
    AND WHEN IT IS GONE WE ARE DEAD; . . . . 168 BLESSED   30
    FEASTED, AND WEPT THE BARROWS OF HIS DEAD! . . . . . 170 SECRET ROSE   18
    AND SMOKE FROM THIS DEAD HEART DRIFTS THROUGH THE VIOLET
       AIR . . . . 173 SPEAKS HEARERS   3
    HE WISHES HIS BELOVED WERE DEAD . . . . 175 BELOVED DEAD   T
    AEDH WISHES HIS BELOVED WERE DEAD . . . . 175 BELOVED DEAD   V   T
    WERE YOU BUT LYING COLD AND DEAD, ... 175 BELOVED DEAD   1
    FORGIVING ME, BECAUSE YOU WERE DEAD! . . . . 175 BELOVED DEAD   6
    WHERE THE DEAD DRIFTED, I COULD SEE A BIRD . . . . . 223 SHADOW WATER B   23
    IF HE WERE DEAD! BUT WHO WILL BE OUR CAPTAIN, ... 224 SHADOW WATER B   60
    NONE BUT THE DEAD, OR THOSE THAT NEVER LIVED. . . . . 231 SHADOW WATER B   202
    TOWARDS THE COUNTRY OF THE DEAD. WHAT MATTER . . . . 231 SHADOW WATER B   206
    UNTIL THE OVERBURTHENED MOON IS DEAD. . . . . . . 231 SHADOW WATER B   218
    NOW THAT HE'S DEAD I HAVE NO NEED OF IT, ... 241 SHADOW WATER B   401
    WHAT NAME HAD THAT DEAD KING? ARTHUR OF BRITAIN? . . . 242 SHADOW WATER B   404
    THAT YOU ARE WEEPING FOR. NO, FOR HE IS DEAD. . . . . 243 SHADOW WATER B   427
    IT SHALL BE IN THE COUNTRY OF THE DEAD, ... 249 SHADOW WATER B   557
    "COME OUT AND DIG FOR A DEAD MAN, ... 272 GREY ROCK   32
    FOR HE IS THE WORST OF ALL DEAD MEN." . . . . . . 272 GREY ROCK   36
    ALTHOUGH THE KING OF IRELAND'S DEAD . . . . 273 GREY ROCK   68
    FOR HE AND THE KING'S SON WERE DEAD. . . . . . . 275 GREY ROCK   97
    TOWARDS THE HOUR FOR SPEAKING OF THE DEAD? . . . . . 276 TWO KINGS   V   D
    ROMANTIC IRELAND'S DEAD AND GONE, ... 289 SEPTEMBER 1913   7
    ROMANTIC IRELAND'S DEAD AND GONE, ... 289 SEPTEMBER 1913   15
    ROMANTIC IRELAND'S DEAD AND GONE, ... 290 SEPTEMBER 1913   23
    BUT LET THEM BE, THEY'RE DEAD AND GONE, ... 290 SEPTEMBER 1913   31
    NOR THE BEST LABOURER DEAD . . . . 312 CHILD DANCING   9
    AND HE, THE BEST WARRIOR, DEAD . . . . 312 CHILD DANCING   V   9
    ALL, ALL ARE IN MY THOUGHTS TO-NIGHT BEING DEAD. . . . 324 ROBERT GREGORY   8
    FOR ALL THAT COME INTO MY MIND ARE DEAD. . . . . . 324 ROBERT GREGORY   16
    "AND IF MY DEAREST FRIEND WERE DEAD . . . . 338 TOM OROUGHLEY   15
    IS DEAD. THE BOY THAT BRINGS MY GRIDDLE-CAKE . . . . 339 SHEP GOATHERD   20
    IS DEAD. THE BOY THAT BRINGS MY GRIDDLE CAKE . . . . 339 SHEP GOATHERD   V   20
    THE DEAD MAN THAT I LOVED, ... 347 FISHERMAN   14
    TO STRIKE YOU DEAD? . . . . 359 TO A SQUIRREL   5
    WITH HER DEAD BROTHER'S VALOUR . . . . 365 HER RACE   11
    SAID I WAS DEAD! AND DEAD I CHOOSE TO BE. . . . . . 373 PHASES OF MOON   28
    SAID I WAS DEAD! AND DEAD I CHOOSE TO BE. . . . . . 373 PHASES OF MOON   28
    SAID I WAS DEAD! AND DEAD I CHOSE TO BE. . . . . . 373 PHASES OF MOON   28
    SAID I WAS DEAD! AND DEAD I CHOSE TO BE. . . . . . 373 PHASES OF MOON V   28
    SO DEAD BEYOND OUR DEATH, ... 382 VISION ROBART   15
    FOR NOW BEING DEAD IT SEEMED . . . . 383 VISION ROBART   23
    WERE DEAD YET FLESH AND BONE. . . . . 384 VISION ROBART   48

DEAD   (CONTINUED)

AND THIS FOUL WORLD WERE DEAD AT LAST.   388 SOLOMON WITCH   16
TO KNOW THEY DREAMED AND ARE DEAD!   394 EASTER 1916   71
SIXTEEN DEAD MEN   395 SIXTEEN DEAD   T
WHILE THOSE DEAD MEN ARE LOITERING THERE   395 SIXTEEN DEAD   5
THAT, BEING DEAD, WE RISE.   415 TOWER   154
THAT DEAD YOUNG SOLDIER IN HIS BLOOD!   425 STARES NEST   14
IF YOU, THAT HAVE GROWN OLD, WERE THE FIRST DEAD,   435 NEW FACES   1
AND AGAMEMNON DEAD. BEING SO CAUGHT UP,   441 LEDA AND SWAN   11
WHEN ALL BUT DEAD OF THIRST,   454 EMPTY CUP   2
WHEN ALL BUT DEAD WITH THIRST,   454 EMPTY CUP   V   2
ONLY THE DEAD CAN BE FORGIVEN!   478 SELF AND SOUL   39
HALF DEAD AT THE TOP.   480 BLOOD AND MOON   12
CAST BUT DEAD LEAVES TO MATHEMATICAL EQUALITY!   481 BLOOD AND MOON   24
CASTS BUT DEAD LEAVES TO MATHEMATICAL EQUALITY!   481 BLOOD AND MOON   V   24
HALF DEAD AT THE TOP? NO MATTER WHAT I SAID,   482 BLOOD AND MOON   48
FOR WISDOM IS THE PROPERTY OF THE DEAD.   482 BLOOD AND MOON   49
CHILDREN DAZED OR DEAD!   488 CRAZED MOON   7
BECAUSE OF MY DEAR JACK THAT'S DEAD.   508 JANE BISHOP   5
MINE MUST WALK WHEN DEAD.   511 JANE AND JACK   18
MINE WOULD WALK, BEING DEAD.   511 JANE AND JACK   V   18
DREW A KNIFE TO STRIKE HIM DEAD,   514 JANE GROWN OLD   10
ALL OTHER LOVERS BEING ESTRANGED OR DEAD,   523 LONG SILENCE   2
HECTOR IS DEAD AND THERE'S A LIGHT IN TROY!   564 GYRES   7
I THINK I SHOULD DROP DEAD."   569 THREE BUSHES   13
"I KNOW THAT I MUST DROP DOWN DEAD   569 THREE BUSHES   17
YET WHAT COULD I BUT DROP DOWN DEAD   569 THREE BUSHES   19
SHAKE THE DEAD IN THEIR SHROUDS!   576 ACRE OF GRASS   22
A DEAD MAN IN HIS GRAVE.   592 DRUNK SOBRIETY   12
A DRUNKARD IS A DEAD MAN,   592 DRUNK SOBRIETY   15
AND ALL DEAD MEN ARE DRUNK.   592 DRUNK SOBRIETY   16
ALL KNOW THAT ALL THE DEAD IN THE WORLD ABOUT THAT PLACE   593 PILGRIM   11
   ARE STUCK,
TO SHOOT THE COLONEL DEAD!   596 COLONEL MARTIN   58
BECAUSE OF THOSE NEW DEAD   599 SPIRIT MEDIUM   2
"THE DEAD IRELAND OF MY YOUTH, BUT AN IRELAND   602 GALLERY REVIS   11
NOW MY OLD BAWD IS DEAD?   620 JOHN KINSELLA   12
NOW MY OLD BAWD IS DEAD?   621 JOHN KINSELLA   24
NOW MY OLD BAWD IS DEAD?   621 JOHN KINSELLA   36
VIOLENT AND FAMOUS, STRODE AMONG THE DEAD!   634 CUCHULAIN COMF   2
THERE IN THE TOMB STAND THE DEAD UPRIGHT,   635 BLACK TOWER   7
OR THE RIFLE KNOCKS HIM DEAD,   637 BEN BULBEN   18
OR THE RIFLE KNOCK HIM DEAD,   637 BEN BULBEN   V   18
AY, BOY. LET'S SEE IF THAT SAME HERON'S DEAD.   651 ISLE STAT I 1   169
AS SOME DEAD MAIDEN'S SINGING IN A DREAM.   654 ISLE STAT I 2   59
HARK! HE'S DEAD--MY DROWSY BROTHER,   656 ISLE STAT I 3   18
AS QUIET AS THE CLAY-COLD DEAD.   670 ISLE STAT II 3   113
A MAN WHO BY A DEAD MAN STOOD.   671 ISLE STAT II 3   124
I MUST BESTIR MYSELF. BOTH DEAD FOR ME!   673 ISLE STAT II 3   189
BOTH DEAD!--NO TIME TO THINK. I AM SHE,   673 ISLE STAT II 3   190
BOTH DEAD!--NO TIME FOR THINKING. I AM SHE,   673 ISLE STAT II 3 V   190
AND DEAD AS ARE THE LOVERS OF OLD RIME   674 ISLE STAT II 3   204
AND DEAD AS ARE THE LOVERS OF OLD RHYME   674 ISLE STAT II 3 V   204
SAVING A GREEN FROG DEAD UPON THE GRASS.   676 ISLE STAT II 3   269
HE IS LONG DEAD. WAKE! SOFT AS A BEE SIPS   678 ISLE STAT II 3   297
LIE STREWN THE CLOTTED LEAVES--THE DEAD OLD LEAVES.   684 SEEKER   V   69
DOWN TO THE MOTHER OF THE FOILED AND DEAD.   688 TWO TITANS   50
SOFT AS A LONG DEAD FOOTSTEP WHISPERING THROUGH   699 MOSADA 3   V   5
DAY'S DEAD, ALL FLAME-BEWILDERED, AND THE HILLS   702 MOSADA 3   86
THE PATH O'ER-MUFFLED WITH THE LEAVES--DEAD LEAVES,   703 MOSADA 3   115
THE PATH O'ER MUFFLED WITH THE LEAVES--DEAD LEAVES,   703 MOSADA 3   V   115
MY LORD, YOU CALLED? NOT I. THIS MAID IS DEAD.   704 MOSADA 3   125
SILENCE! THOU SHALT BE DEAD!" NOW SUDDENLY   710 FERENCZ RENYI   16
OF MY DEAD CHILDREN SOON, WHATE'ER BETIDE,   712 FERENCZ RENYI   58
. . . GONE AND PUFFED AWAY AND DEAD.   718 PHANTOM SHIP   3
SLOW THE CHAPEL BELL IS TOLLING AS THOUGH THE DEAD PASSED   718 PHANTOM SHIP   16
   BY.
BY THE SLOW HEAVING OCEAN--MUMBLING MOTHER OF THE DEAD.   719 PHANTOM SHIP   34
PRAYED BESIDE THE OCEAN, THE OLD MUMBLING MOTHER OF THE   719 PHANTOM SHIP   V   34
   DEAD.
AND THEN HIS HEART GREW WELL-NIGH DEAD   730 PRIEST FAIRY   59
AND A STRING MURMURS AS THOUGH TIME WERE DEAD   752 SHADOW WATER A   124
THE FALLING BLOSSOMS, AND THE DEAD THE LIVING.   756 SHADOW WATER A   182
I WAIT YOUR WORDS AS THE DEAD WAIT THE LIVING.   756 SHADOW WATER A V   182
FOR THOSE AMONG YOUR PEOPLE THAT ARE DEAD?   758 SHADOW WATER A   224
FOR I AM CERTAIN SOMEBODY IS DEAD.   760 SHADOW WATER A   254
WHETHER AMONG THE COLD WINDS OF THE DEAD.   768 SHADOW WATER A V   413
FROM THE DRY BONES OF THE DEAD?   781 MY HEART BEAT   8
AND HEARD THE DEAD LIPS SING.   790 SINGING HEAD   24
A MEMORY, EVEN TO THE DEAD,   791 REPRISALS   8
AMONG THE OTHER CHEATED DEAD.   791 REPRISALS   24

DEADLY

FRIEND! BUT 'TWERE A DEADLY SIN   697 MOSADA 2   31

DEAF

BLIND AND NIGH DEAF, WITH WITHERED ARMS HE LIES   42 OISIN 2   V   203
IF DEAF AND DUMB AND BLIND WITH LOVE?   202 NEVER GIVE ALL   12
HAS MADE THEM SO HAPPY AND HOPELESS, SO DEAF AND SO BLIND   204 WITHER BOUGHS   20
THE BEGGAR DEAF TO ALL BUT HOPE   304 HOUR DAWN   V   44
NOW PEARSE IS DEAF AND DUMB?   395 SIXTEEN DEAD   10
THAT MAN IS STRICKEN DEAF AND DUMB AND BLIND,   478 SELF AND SOUL   35
THAT MAN IS DEAF AND DRUNK AND BLIND   478 SELF AND SOUL   V   35

```
                                                               PAGE    TITLE               LINE

DEAF   (CONTINUED)
    THE MAYOR CAME, LEANING HIS DEAF EAR--  . . . . . . .      725 LEGEND                 13
    I AM BLIND AND DEAF BECAUSE OF THE WHITE WINGS. . . . .    759 SHADOW WATER A   235
DEAFENED
    WHEN, THE EARS BEING DEAFENED, THE SIGHT OF THE EYES BLIND 257 RECONCILIATION          3
DEAFENING
    AND DEAFENING MUSIC SHOOK THE LEAVES: A TROOP . . . . .    537 HER VISION             13
    DEAFENING US WITH IDLE SOUND-- . . . . . . . . . . .       727 LOVERS QUARREL         30
DEAFENS
    THE NIGHTINGALE THAT DEAFENS DAYLIGHT THERE, . . . . .     446 COLONUS PRAISE          3
DEAFER
    COLDER AND DUMBER AND DEAFER THAN A FISH. . . . . . .      267 ALL TEMPT ME           10
DEAL
    ON PAINTED PILLARS, ON A DEAL . . . . . . . . . . .        271 GREY ROCK        V     19
    A DEAL I'D SWEAT AND LITTLE EARN . . . . . . . . .         331 ROUND TOWER             2
    CAN BE CONTENT WITH ARGUMENT AND DEAL . . . . . . .        409 TOWER                  14
    A DEAL OF EVIL AND OF CHANGE HATH CROSSED . . . . . .      676 ISLE STAT II 3        273
DEAN
    THAT GOLDSMITH AND THE DEAN, . . . . . . . . . .           481 BLOOD AND MOON         18
DEAR
    YE LITTLE CHILDER DEAR, . . . . . . . . . .                 95 MOLL MAGEE             18
    MY DERMOT DEAR AND BROWN, . . . . . . . . . .               97 FOXHUNTER        V      6
    MY LOLLARD OLD AND DEAR. . . . . . . . . . . . .            97 FOXHUNTER        V      8
    AND HIS YOUNG DEAR ONE CLOSE BESIDE HIM KNELT, . . .       108 CUCHULAIN SEA    V     40
    MY DEAR, WHEN YOU'RE GROWN! . . . . . . . . .              118 CRADLE SONG      V     12
    WHEN, DEAR, YOU HAVE GROWN. . . . . . . . . .              118 CRADLE SONG      V     12
    CABINS GONE NOW, OLD WELL-SIDES, OLD DEAR PLACES, . . .    130 BOOK STORIES     V     23
    AND HOPE IS LESS DEAR THAN THE DEW OF THE MORN. . . .      148 INTO TWILIGHT          16
    AND THAT DEAR WORDS MEANT NOTHING?" BUT ENOUGH, . . .      201 OLD MEMORY              9
    I THOUGHT, "HE HOLDS HER DEAR," . . . . . . . .            254 WOMAN HOMER             3
    BUT, DEAR, CLING CLOSE TO ME: SINCE YOU WERE GONE, . . .   257 RECONCILIATION         11
    "O NO, MY DEAR, YOU MAKE SO BOLD . . . . . . . .           263 MASK                    3
    "O NO, MY DEAR, LET ALL THAT BE: . . . . . . . .           263 MASK                   13
    DEAR CRAOIBHIN AOIBHIN, LOOK INTO OUR CASE. . . . .        264 ABBEY THEATRE           1
    HOPELESS AND DEAR, OR TERRIBLE TO THINK ON, . . . .        281 TWO KINGS              96
    "MY DEAR, MY DEAR, O DEAR, . . . . . . . . . .             319 DOLLS                  19
    "MY DEAR, MY DEAR, O DEAR, . . . . . . . . . .             319 DOLLS                  19
    "MY DEAR, MY DEAR, O DEAR, . . . . . . . . . .             319 DOLLS                  19
    BUT NOT THAT MY DEAR FRIEND'S DEAR SON, . . . . .          325 ROBERT GREGORY         46
    BUT NOT THAT MY DEAR FRIEND'S DEAR SON, . . . . .          325 ROBERT GREGORY         46
    DEAR FELLOW-ARTIST, WHY SO FREE . . . . . . . .            335 YOUNG BEAUTY            1
    DEAR FELLOW ARTIST WHY SO FREE . . . . . . . .             335 YOUNG BEAUTY     V      1
    MY DEAR, MY DEAR, I KNOW . . . . . . . . . .               336 YOUNG GIRL              1
    MY DEAR, MY DEAR, I KNOW . . . . . . . . . .               336 YOUNG GIRL              1
    I HAD WISHED A DEAR THING ON THAT DAY . . . . . .          341 SHEP GOATHERD    V     73
    TO HOPE A THING SO DEAR . . . . . . . . . .                346 ON WOMAN               27
    THAT MADE HER DIARMUID DEAR, AND SOME OLD CARDINAL . .     366 HER COURAGE             6
    AND THAT MADE HER DERMUID DEAR, AND SOME OLD CARDINAL . .  366 HER COURAGE      V      6
    THAT ALL MY CHILDHOOD COUNTED DEAR: . . . . . . .          398 BREAK OF DAY            7
    I COULD NOT FIND A THING SO DEAR." . . . . . . .           398 BREAK OF DAY            9
    BEING DEAR AS MINE ARE DEAR. . . . . . . . . .             400 DEMON BEAST            20
    BEING DEAR AS MINE ARE DEAR. . . . . . . . . .             400 DEMON BEAST            20
    ROOTED IN ONE DEAR PERPETUAL PLACE. . . . . . . .          405 FOR DAUGHTER           48
    WERE SOME DEAR CHEEK. UPON A MOONLESS NIGHT . . . .        466 HARUN RASHID          127
    WERE SOME DEAR FACE. UPON A MOONLESS NIGHT . . . .         466 HARUN RASHID     V    127
    ONE DEAR HOPE HAD HE: . . . . . . . . . .                  471 ALL SOUL NIGHT         28
    DEAR SHADOWS, NOW YOU KNOW IT ALL, . . . . . . .           476 EVA GORE-BOOTH         21
    SEEMED ONCE MORE DEAR THAN LIFE: ANCESTRAL TREES, . . .    491 COOLE BALLYLEE         34
    THAT ONLY GOD, MY DEAR, . . . . . . . . . .                492 ANNE GREGORY           16
    ONE DEAR BRILLIANT WOMAN: . . . . . . . . .                504 RESULT THOUGHT          2
    BECAUSE OF MY DEAR JACK THAT'S DEAD. . . . . . .           508 JANE BISHOP             5
    "THREE DEAR THINGS THAT WOMEN KNOW," . . . . . .           521 THREE THINGS            7
    DEAR, I MUST BE GONE . . . . . . . . . .                   535 PARTING                 1
    WHAT MATTER? THOSE THAT ROCKY FACE HOLDS DEAR, . . .       564 GYRES                  18
    O MY DEAR, O MY DEAR. . . . . . . . . .                    569 THREE BUSHES            7
    O MY DEAR, O MY DEAR. . . . . . . . . .                    569 THREE BUSHES            7
    O MY DEAR, O MY DEAR. . . . . . . . . .                    569 THREE BUSHES           14
    O MY DEAR, O MY DEAR. . . . . . . . . .                    569 THREE BUSHES           14
    DEAR CHAMBERMAID," SAID SHE. . . . . . . . . .             569 THREE BUSHES           16
    O MY DEAR, O MY DEAR. . . . . . . . . .                    570 THREE BUSHES           21
    O MY DEAR, O MY DEAR. . . . . . . . . .                    570 THREE BUSHES           21
    O MY DEAR, O MY DEAR. . . . . . . . . .                    570 THREE BUSHES           28
    O MY DEAR, O MY DEAR. . . . . . . . . .                    570 THREE BUSHES           28
    O MY DEAR, O MY DEAR. . . . . . . . . .                    570 THREE BUSHES           35
    O MY DEAR, O MY DEAR. . . . . . . . . .                    570 THREE BUSHES           35
    O MY DEAR, O MY DEAR. . . . . . . . . .                    570 THREE BUSHES           42
    O MY DEAR, O MY DEAR. . . . . . . . . .                    570 THREE BUSHES           42
    O MY DEAR, O MY DEAR. . . . . . . . . .                    571 THREE BUSHES           49
    O MY DEAR, O MY DEAR. . . . . . . . . .                    571 THREE BUSHES           49
    O MY DEAR, O MY DEAR. . . . . . . . . .                    571 THREE BUSHES           56
    O MY DEAR, O MY DEAR. . . . . . . . . .                    571 THREE BUSHES           56
    O MY DEAR, O MY DEAR. . . . . . . . . .                    571 THREE BUSHES           63
    O MY DEAR, O MY DEAR. . . . . . . . . .                    571 THREE BUSHES           63
    O MY DEAR, O MY DEAR. . . . . . . . . .                    571 THREE BUSHES           70
    O MY DEAR, O MY DEAR. . . . . . . . . .                    571 THREE BUSHES           70
    O MY DEAR, O MY DEAR. . . . . . . . . .                    571 THREE BUSHES           77
    O MY DEAR, O MY DEAR. . . . . . . . . .                    571 THREE BUSHES           77
    THAT IS ALL I ASK, MY DEAR, . . . . . . . .                587 OLD WICKED MAN          7
    "KIND ARE ALL YOUR WORDS, MY DEAR, . . . . . .             588 OLD WICKED MAN         10
    WHO CAN KNOW THE YEAR, MY DEAR, . . . . . .                588 OLD WICKED MAN         12
    OF ALL THAT SCHOLARLY GENERATIONS HAD HELD DEAR: . . . .   603 GALLERY REVIS    V    37A
```

```
                                              PAGE    TITLE          LINE
DEAR    (CONTINUED)
    BUT MY DEAR MARY MOORE,  . . . . . . . . . . .    620 JOHN KINSELLA      8
    I THOUGHT MY DEAR MUST HER OWN SOUL DESTROY, . . . . . .    630 CIRCUS ANIMALS    21
    A BRIEF PARTING FROM THOSE DEAR  . . . . . . . .    637 BEN BULBEN        19
    I LAUGHED?  AND WHY IS THAT A THING SO DEAR? . . . .    670 ISLE STAT II 3    97
    SO BE THOU STILL, DEAR HEART, A LITTLE WHILE! . . . .    677 ISLE STAT II 3   283
    HUNG ON HIS DOUBLET--DEAR AND MOURNFUL CHILD, . . . .    691 MOSADA 1          35
    AND OUT-SPREAD ARMS.  BE NOT SO PALE, DEAR LOVE. . . .    701 MOSADA 3          70
    DEAR HEART, THERE IS A SECRET WAY THAT LEADS . . .    702 MOSADA 3          75
    "NOW ANSWER, IF THIS LIFE BE DEAR TO THEE, . . . .    713 FERENCZ RENYI  V   83
    SHE PRAYS FOR FATHER, MOTHER DEAR,  . . . . . . .    735 IN CHURCH          1
    HER PRAYER FOR FATHER, MOTHER DEAR, . . . . . . .    736 IN CHURCH         13
    (O MY DEAR, MY DEAR). . . . . . . . . . . . .    779 GOING THE ROAD     4
    (O MY DEAR, MY DEAR). . . . . . . . . . . . .    779 GOING THE ROAD     4
    (O MY DEAR, MY DEAR). . . . . . . . . . . . .    779 GOING THE ROAD     8
    (O MY DEAR, MY DEAR). . . . . . . . . . . . .    779 GOING THE ROAD     8
    (O MY DEAR, MY DEAR). . . . . . . . . . . . .    779 GOING THE ROAD    12
    (O MY DEAR, MY DEAR). . . . . . . . . . . . .    779 GOING THE ROAD    12
    O MY DEAR, O MY DEAR! . . . . . . . . . . . .    779 GOING THE ROAD V   4
    O MY DEAR, O MY DEAR! . . . . . . . . . . . .    779 GOING THE ROAD V   4
    THOUGH BATTLE JOY MAY BE SO DEAR  . . . . . . .    791 REPRISALS          7
DEARER
    DEARER THAN ANY THAT THE DUMB STONE HIDES, . . . . .    281 TWO KINGS      V   96
    YET HAVE NO DEARER THOUGHT  . . . . . . . . .    401 DEMON BEAST       40
    I HOLD HIM DEARER THAN THE GLAD, . . . . . . . .    723 GIRLS SONG A       3
    I HOLD HIM DEARER THAN THE GOOD, . . . . . . . .    723 GIRLS SONG A       7
    I HOLD HIM DEARER THAN THE WISE, . . . . . . . .    723 GIRLS SONG A      11
DEAREST
    "AND IF MY DEAREST FRIEND WERE DEAD . . . . . . .    338 TOM OROUGHLEY     15
    THERE'S LITTLE I'D REFUSE THEE, DEAREST YOUTH. . . .    669 ISLE STAT II 3    71
DEARTH
    I'LL HAVE.  OH, ABSENT ONE 'TIS NOT FOR DEARTH . . . .    664 ISLE STAT II 2    50
DEATH    SEE STRAW-DEATH LIFE-IN-DEATH
    THEN MOCK AT DEATH AND TIME WITH GLANCES  . . . . .     19 OISIN 1          274
    AND HERE THERE IS NOR CHANGE NOR DEATH, . . . . . .     19 OISIN 1          284
    FOR NEITHER DEATH NOR CHANGE COMES NEAR US, . . . .     21 OISIN 1          316
    FOR CHANGE AND DEATH THEY COME NOT NEAR US, . . . .     21 OISIN 1        V 316
    SINCE GOD MADE TIME AND DEATH AND SLEEP! THE OTHER . . .     31 OISIN 2           41
    AND DEMONS BE BROKEN IN PIECES, AND TRAMPLED BENEATH THEM     61 OISIN 3          204
       IN DEATH.
    AND DEMONS, ALL BROKEN IN PIECES, BE TRAMPLED BENEATH THEM     61 OISIN 3        V 204
       IN DEATH.
    THE DEATH OF CUCHULAIN  . . . . . . . . . . .    105 CUCHULAIN SEA  V   T
    A DREAM OF DEATH  . . . . . . . . . . . . .    123 DREAM OF DEATH     T
    I AM NO MORE WITH LIFE AND DEATH, . . . . . . . .    152 HEART OF WOMAN    10
    ARE PLOTTING FOR YOUR DEATH.  HAVE I NOT GIVEN . . .    226 SHADOW WATER B    93
    TO DEATH: FOR THEY THAT PROMISED TO ME LOVE . . .    230 SHADOW WATER B   192
    IT'S CERTAIN THEY ARE LEADING YOU TO DEATH. . . . .    231 SHADOW WATER B   201
    IF I AM GOING TO MY DEATH?--FOR THERE, . . . . . .    231 SHADOW WATER B   207
    WE'LL PUT THIS MAN TO DEATH.  I PROMISE IT. . . .    238 SHADOW WATER B   363
    TO HIM THAT WOUNDS HIM TO THE DEATH.  I'LL DO IT. . .    240 SHADOW WATER B   375
    THAT HE IS BEING DRIVEN TO HIS DEATH. . . . . . .    248 SHADOW WATER B   551
    HE KNOWS THAT HE IS TAKING YOU TO DEATH! . . . .    249 SHADOW WATER B   562
    BY THE SWEET NAME OF DEATH. . . . . . . . . .    254 HIS DREAM         12
    BY THE SWEET NAME OF DEATH. . . . . . . . . .    254 HIS DREAM         20
    WE'LL LEARN THAT SLEEPING IS NOT DEATH, . . . . .    266 GALWAY RACES      11
    THAT HAS MORE LIFE IN IT THAN DEATH, . . . . . .    271 GREY ROCK          8
    SWEETENED BY DEATH, BUT IF I COULD BELIEVE, . . . .    285 TWO KINGS        205
    YOU HAD ENOUGH OF SORROW BEFORE DEATH-- . . . . .    293 TO A SHADE        23
    "THOUGH THE DOOR OF DEATH IS NEAR . . . . . . .    298 THREE HERMITS      8
    FOR WHAT PROUD DEATH MAY BRING  . . . . . . . .    317 NIGHT COME         3
    COULD SHARE IN THAT DISCOURTESY OF DEATH. . . . . .    325 ROBERT GREGORY    48
    OF THAT LATE DEATH TOOK ALL MY HEART FOR SPEECH. . . .    328 ROBERT GREGORY    96
    AN IRISH AIRMAN FORESEES HIS DEATH  . . . . . .    328 IRISH AIRMAN       T
    IN BALANCE WITH THIS LIFE, THIS DEATH. . . . . . .    328 IRISH AIRMAN      16
    LAID ON THE DEATH BED. . . . . . . . . . . .    335 SONG           V  16
    RECOVERED HIM UPON THE BED OF DEATH. . . . . . .    355 BROKEN DREAMS      6
    YET ALWAYS WHEN I LOOK DEATH IN THE FACE, . . . . .    357 DEEP-SWORN VOW     3
    LAID HIS STRONG BONES DOWN IN DEATH . . . . . .    360 ALF POLLEXFEN      3
    LAID HIS STRONG BONES IN DEATH  . . . . . . . .    360 ALF POLLEXFEN  V   3
    WE HAVE NAUGHT FOR DEATH BUT TOYS. . . . . . . .    363 DOLLS DRAWINGS    11
    WHO HAVE LIVED IN JOY AND LAUGHED INTO THE FACE OF DEATH.    366 HER COURAGE       10
    WHO LIVED IN SHAMELESS JOY AND LAUGHED INTO THE FACE OF    366 HER COURAGE    V  10
       DEATH.
    THAT LIVED IN JOY AND LAUGHED INTO THE FACE OF DEATH. . .    366 HER COURAGE    V  10
    WHO HAVE LIVED IN JOY AND LAUGHED IN THE FACE OF DEATH.    366 HER COURAGE    V  10
    FROM DEATH, AND WOUNDS, OR ON SINAI'S TOP, . . . . .    375 PHASES OF MOON    67
    SO DEAD BEYOND OUR DEATH, . . . . . . . . . .    382 VISION ROBART  V  15
    NO, NO, NOT NIGHT BUT DEATH: . . . . . . . . .    394 EASTER 1916       66
    WAS IT NEEDLESS DEATH AFTER ALL? . . . . . . . .    394 EASTER 1916       67
    DEATH AND LIFE WERE NOT  . . . . . . . . . .    415 TOWER            148
    THE DEATH OF FRIENDS, OR DEATH  . . . . . . . .    416 TOWER            189
    THE DEATH OF FRIENDS, OR DEATH  . . . . . . . .    416 TOWER            189
    THAT WERE A LUCKY DEATH, . . . . . . . . . .    431 NINETEEN 19       77
    AS THOUGH GOD'S DEATH WERE BUT A PLAY. . . . . .    437 SONGS PLAY 1       8
    THE DEATH OF THE HARE  . . . . . . . . . . .    453 DEATH OF HARE      T
    AT THE DEATH OF THE HARE. . . . . . . . . . .    453 DEATH OF HARE     12
    DEATH, DESPAIR, DIVISION OF FAMILIES, . . . . . .    459 FROM OEDIPUS       5
    WHEN OUR BELOVED CALIPH PUT TO DEATH . . . . . .    462 HARUN RASHID      31
    BEING SHARPENED BY HIS DEATH, . . . . . . . . .    471 ALL SOUL NIGHT     8
    OF THAT OR THE NEXT WINTER WOULD BE DEATH. . . . .    471 ALL SOUL NIGHT    30
```

193

DEATH   (CONTINUED)
    THE OLDER IS CONDEMNED TO DEATH, ...   475 EVA GORE-BOOTH   7
    DEATH . . . .   476 DEATH   T
    HE KNOWS DEATH TO THE BONE-- . . . .   476 DEATH   11
    MAN HAS CREATED DEATH . . . .   476 DEATH   12
    DELIVER FROM THE CRIME OF DEATH AND BIRTH. . . . . .   478 SELF AND SOUL   24
    AT ALGECIRAS--A MEDITATION UPON DEATH . . . .   493 AT ALGECIRAS   T
    MEDITATIONS UPON DEATH . . . .   493 AT ALGECIRAS   V   T
    THE BODY CALLS IT DEATH, ...   500 VACILLATION   7
    BEGIN THE PREPARATION FOR YOUR DEATH . . . .   500 VACILLATION   28
    LOVE IS NEARER DEATH. . . . .   517 HER ANXIETY   11
    "O CRUEL DEATH, GIVE THREE THINGS BACK," . . . . .   521 THREE THINGS   1
    THE MIRACLE THAT GAVE THEM SUCH A DEATH . . . . . .   555 RIBH AT TOMB   10
    HERE ON THE ANNIVERSARY OF THEIR DEATH, ...   555 RIBH AT TOMB   19
    BUT OF THE DEATH HE MET . . . .   585 ORAHILLY   29
    EYES SPIRITUALISED BY DEATH CAN JUDGE, ...   604 YOU CONTENT   7
    THOSE INNOCENTS RE-LIVE THEIR DEATH, ...   612 NEWS ORACLE   15
    THESE INNOCENTS RELIVE THEIR DEATH, ...   612 NEWS ORACLE   V   15
    STOOD, TOOK DEATH LIKE A TUNE . . . .   613 MARCH SONGS 1   15
    A MOUTHFUL HELD THE EXTREME OF LIFE AND DEATH. . . .   619 BRONZE HEAD   14
    A MOUTHFUL HOLD THE EXTREME OF LIFE AND DEATH. . . .   619 BRONZE HEAD   V   14
    FOR DEATH WHO TAKES WHAT MAN WOULD KEEP, ...   620 JOHN KINSELLA   3
    BATTERED TO DEATH IN A CELLAR, ...   628 JANE MOUNTAIN   9
    ON LIFE, ON DEATH. . . . .   640 BEN BULBEN   93
    OF HIS DEATH AND CHANGE MALIGN. . . . .   648 ISLE STAT I 1   80
    BEFORE A DEATH, O'ER WAVE AND BANK . . . .   673 ISLE STAT II 3   185
    OH DEATH IS HORRIBLE! AND FOUL, FOUL, FOUL! . . . .   675 ISLE STAT II 3   238
    LOVE AND DEATH. . . . .   680 LOVE AND DEATH   T
    AND THEY'LL ANSWER DEATH AND LOVE. . . . .   680 LOVE AND DEATH   16
    ARE THE SPIRITS LOVE AND DEATH. . . . .   680 LOVE AND DEATH   32
    TO DEATH. HIS DARKNESS AND HIS CHILL I FEEL. . . .   684 SEEKER   63
    TO DEATH. HIS LIPS ARE GLUED, WITH QUIVERING TOUCH,   684 SEEKER   V   63
    WITH DEW, AS THOUGH 'TWERE SEALING THEM FOR DEATH. .   691 MOSADA 1   22
    THE WAGES OF SIN IS DEATH. NO USE. NO GOOD. . . .   697 MOSADA 2   42
    THE WAGE OF SIN IS DEATH. NO USE. NO USE. . . . .   697 MOSADA 2   V   42
    TOO LATE, TOO LATE, FOR I AM NEAR TO DEATH. . . . .   701 MOSADA 3   55
    THIS DEATH IS HEAVY IN MY VEINS LIKE SLEEP. . . . .   701 MOSADA 3   57
    IS IT YOUR MESSAGE, STARS, THAT WHEN DEATH COMES . .   701 MOSADA 3   60
    WERE HERE, HE WOULD TURN DEATH INTO A CRUTCH; . . .   711 FERENCZ RENYI   38
    THE MAN WHOSE HOUR OF DEATH DRAWS NIGH, ...   716 FAIRY DOCTOR   6
    AND DEATH, OH MY FAIR ONE, WILL NEVER COME NEAR . .   717 LOVE SONG   8
    DEFEAT IS DEATH. SHOULD MY PLOTS FAIL I'D DIE. . .   722 WITCH VIVIEN   52
    OR DEATH THAT COMETH WITH THE NEXT LIFE-KEY? . . .   724 KANVA ON SELF   18
    THAT I WOULD BID MY PEOPLE PUT TO DEATH. . . . . .   760 SHADOW WATER A V   254
    FOR THE THINGS COME AFTER DEATH? . . . .   777 SONG DEIRDRE 2   12
    WHAT DEATH? WHAT DISCIPLINE? . . . .   784 WOMANS BEAUTY   21
    THOUGH DEATH ITSELF FORBADE. . . . .   789 SINGING HEAD   8
    WE CALLED IT A GOOD DEATH. TODAY . . . .   791 REPRISALS   3
DEATHBED
    "SEEING THAT WHEN YOU COME TO THE DEATHBED . . . . .   285 TWO KINGS   196
DEATH-BED
    "SEEING THAT WHEN YOU COME TO THE DEATH-BED . . . .   285 TWO KINGS   V 196
    CONFUSION OF THE DEATH-BED OVER, IS IT SENT . . . .   316 COLD HEAVEN   10
    LAID ON THE DEATH-BED, ...   335 SONG   16
DEATHBEDS
    AT ALL THESE DEATHBEDS WOMEN HEARD . . . .   361 ALF POLLEXFEN V   36
DEATH-BEDS
    AT ALL THESE DEATH-BEDS WOMEN HEARD . . . .   361 ALF POLLEXFEN   36
DEATHFUL
    I HEARD THE DEATHFUL MONOTONE, ...   673 ISLE STAT II 3   183
DEATH-HOUR
    BIRTH-HOUR AND DEATH-HOUR MEET, ...   496 MOHINI CHATTER   26
DEATH-IN-LIFE
    I CALL IT DEATH-IN-LIFE AND LIFE-IN-DEATH. . . . . .   497 BYZANTIUM   16
DEATHLESS
    MEN DANCE ON DEATHLESS FEET." . . . .   496 MOHINI CHATTER   28
    SIX THAT ARE DEATHLESS, ...   770 BLOOD BOND   13
DEATH-LONGING
    DELIGHT BECOMES DEATH-LONGING IF ALL LONGING ELSE BE VAIN.   459 FROM OEDIPUS   3
DEATH-MAKING
    HELPLESS, MEN LIFTING THE LIDS OF HIS WEARY   53 OISIN 3   92
        AND DEATH-MAKING EYE.
DEATH-PALE
    I WOULD THAT THE DEATH-PALE DEER . . . .   171 MAID QUIET   V   4A
    LILIES OF DEATH-PALE HOPE, ROSES OF PASSIONATE DREAM. . .   172 TRAV PASSION   8
DEATH-POURING
    HELPLESS, MEN LIFTING THE LIDS OF HIS WEARY   53 OISIN 3   V   92
        AND DEATH-POURING EYE.
DEATH'S
    O DEATH'S OLD BONY FINGER . . . .   213 HAPPY TOWNLAND V   1
    THE GLITTERING EYES IN A DEATH'S HEAD . . . . . .   400 DEMON BEAST   9
    FROM DEATH'S LATE LANGUOR AS THESE LINES I READ . .   734 QUATRAIN APHOR   14
DEATHS
    AFTER THE DEATHS OF MANY MEN, ...   197 BAILE AILLINN   193
DECAY
    "I HEAR MY SOUL DROP DOWN INTO DECAY, ...   45 OISIN 2   235
    "AGE AFTER AGE I FEEL MY SOUL DECAY . . . .   45 OISIN 2   V 235
    TIME DROPS IN DECAY, ...   142 MOODS   1
    THOUGH HOPE FALL FROM YOU AND LOVE DECAY, ...   148 INTO TWILIGHT   7
    THOUGH HOPE FALL FROM THEE OR LOVE DECAY . . . . .   148 INTO TWILIGHT V   7
    SLOW DECAY OF BLOOD, ...   416 TOWER   185

DECAY   (CONTINUED)
    AND AFTER KEPT IT FROM DECAY: . . . .   460 THREE MONUMENT   7
    GAZE ON TILL RAGGED TIME HIMSELF DECAY. . . . .   672 ISLE STAT II 3   148
    THEY WOULD MAKE A PRINCE DECAY . . . .   775 AGAINST WITCH   11
DECAYETH
    WHILE THE MORNING STAR DECAYETH . . . .   706 DAWN-SONG   29
DECEIT   SEE HALF-DECEIT
    BUT IT WAS ALL DECEIT, AND FLATTERY . . . .   244 SHADOW WATER B   457
    LOVE OR DECEIT." . . . .   263 MASK   7
    GO PILOT THE COURSE OF HIS ARROW'S DECEIT! . . . . . .   657 ISLE STAT I 3   69
DECEITLESS
    AND LOVE IS KINDLY AND DECEITLESS, ...   77 INDIAN TO LOVE V   5D
DECEIVE
    THE RHETORICIAN WOULD DECEIVE HIS NEIGHBOURS, ...   369 EGO DOMINUS   46
DECEIVED
    BETTER THAN MY OWN HANDS. I HAVE DECEIVED YOU . . . . .   244 SHADOW WATER B   466
    AND THAT YOU'LL BRING ME THERE? I HAVE DECEIVED YOU: . . .   245 SHADOW WATER B   471
    I HAVE DECEIVED YOU UTTERLY. HOW CAN THAT BE? . . . . .   245 SHADOW WATER B   472
    OLD SAGES WERE NOT DECEIVED! . . . .   504 QUARREL IN AGE   11
DECEIVING
    LOVES IN BRIEF LONGING AND DECEIVING HOPE . . . .   228 SHADOW WATER B   146
    AND TURN BRIEF LONGING AND DECEIVING HOPE . . . .   750 SHADOW WATER A   59
    THAN IN BRIEF LONGING AND DECEIVING HOPE . . . .   750 SHADOW WATER A   65
    IS BUT BRIEF LONGING, AND DECEIVING HOPE, ...   765 SHADOW WATER A   354
DECENT
    FOR THINGS LIKE THESE WHAT DECENT MAN . . . .   598 MODEL LAUREATE   22
DECEPTION
    FOR THE HEART CRIES THAT WHAT DECEPTION WINS . . . . . .   448 HERO GIRL FOOL   6
    WHAT NO DECEPTION WON. I HAVE HEARD THEM SAY . . . . .   448 HERO GIRL FOOL V   13
    FROM TERROR AND DECEPTION FREED IT CAN . . . .   558 RIBH CHRISTIAN   9
DECIDE
    AS RECOLLECTION OR THE DRUG DECIDE, ...   444 SCHOOL CHILDR   36
DECIDED
    DECIDED HE WOULD JOURNEY HOME, ...   361 ALF POLLEXFEN   30
    DECIDED HE MUST JOURNEY HOME, ...   361 ALF POLLEXFEN V   30
DECK
    THERE IS A KING AND QUEEN UPON HER DECK, ...   232 SHADOW WATER B   226
    UNTIL YOU STOOD BEFORE ME ON THE DECK-- . . . .   236 SHADOW WATER B   313
    NOW A SCREAM FROM ALL THOSE FISHERS, FOR THERE ON DECK   719 PHANTOM SHIP   19
        THERE BE
DECKED
    AND DECKED AND ALTERED IT FOR A GIRL'S LOVE, ...   423 MY DESCENDANTS   22
DECLAIMING
    ACCLAIMING, PROCLAIMING, DECLAIMING HIM. . . . .   528 DANCER CRUACH   8
DECLARE
    OF DRIPPING STONE: I DECLARE . . . .   414 TOWER   126
    AND I DECLARE MY FAITH: . . . .   414 TOWER   145
    DECLARE THAT WINTER'S BEST OF ALL: . . . .   434 WHEEL   4
    I DECLARE THIS TOWER IS MY SYMBOL: I DECLARE . . . . .   480 BLOOD AND MOON   16
    I DECLARE THIS TOWER IS MY SYMBOL: I DECLARE . . . . .   480 BLOOD AND MOON   16
    BUT YESTERNIGHT DECLARE . . . .   492 ANNE GREGORY   14
    HER KNEE-CAP BROKEN, THAT GIRL I DECLARE . . . .   578 CRAZED GIRL   6
    HER KNEE CAP BROKEN: THAT GIRL I DECLARE . . . .   578 CRAZED GIRL   V   6
    WHEN GONG AND CONCH DECLARE THE HOUR TO BLESS . . . . .   611 STATUES   23
    AND WHEN IT'S VANISHED STILL DECLARE, ...   639 BEN BULBEN   60
DECLARED
    AND THUS DECLARED THAT ARAB LADY: . . . .   387 SOLOMON WITCH   1
    ROSE FROM THE TABLE AND DECLARED IT RIGHT . . . .   410 TOWER   43
    HE IN HIS RAGE DECLARED: . . . .   539 MEETING   14
DECLENSION
    THROUGH NATURAL DECLENSION OF THE SOUL, ...   423 MY DESCENDANTS   10
DECLINE
    AND KNOW WHATEVER FLOURISH AND DECLINE . . . .   423 MY DESCENDANTS   23
    ON THIS FOUL WORLD IN ITS DECLINE AND FALL: . . . . .   619 BRONZE HEAD   24
DECLINING
    FLOWED ON ANEW, AND OFT, ANEW DECLINING, ...   33 OISIN 2   V   68D
    UNDER THE DAY'S DECLINING BEAM, AND CALL . . . .   410 TOWER   21
DECLIVITIES
    MY DARK DECLIVITIES. . . . .   536 PARTING   14
DECREED
    BUT THE GODS LONG AGO DECREED . . . .   194 BAILE AILLINN   119
    THE STAR-TAUGHT MOOR, SAID THUS IT WAS DECREED . . . . .   691 MOSADA 1   25
DECREES
    WHERE FASHION OR MERE FANTASY DECREES . . . .   491 COOLE BALLYLEE   38
DECREPIT
    DECREPIT AGE THAT HAS BEEN TIED TO ME . . . .   409 TOWER   3
    DECREPIT AGE THAT HAS BEEN TIED UPON ME . . . .   409 TOWER   V   3
DECREPITUDE
    OR DULL DECREPITUDE, ...   416 TOWER   187
    BODILY DECREPITUDE IS WISDOM: YOUNG . . . .   523 LONG SILENCE   7
DECTORA
    AODH TO DECTORA   THREE SONGS . . . .   152 LOSS OF LOVE   V   T
    AODH TO DECTORA . . . .   175 BELOVED DEAD   V   T
    OF FORGAEL AND DECTORA AND THE EMPTY WATERS . . . . . .   218 WOODS OF COOLE   22
    BEFORE THEY READ OF FORGAEL AND DECTORA, ...   219 WOODS OF COOLE   42
DEDICATE
    I DEDICATE THESE FITFUL DANAAN RHYMES . . . .   136 TO SOME I TALK V   1
    AND DEDICATE--EYES BENT UPON THE GROUND, ...   489 COOLE PARK 29   29
DEDICATION
    THE DEDICATION TO A BOOK OF STORIES SELECTED FROM THE IRISH   129 BOOK STORIES   T
        NOVELISTS

		PAGE	TITLE		LINE
DEDICATION (CONTINUED)					
DEDICATION	129	BOOK STORIES	V	T
DEDICATION OF "IRISH TALES"	129	BOOK STORIES	V	T
DEDICATION TO THE "SHADOWY WATERS"	217	WOODS OF COOLE	V	T
DEDICATION	790	DEDICATION		T
DEED					
WE COME BETWEEN HIM AND THE DEED OF HIS HAND, ...	141	HOSTING SIDHE		11
AND WHERE IS THERE HOPE OR DEED AS FAIR?	141	HOSTING SIDHE		14
WAS: "YOU, THAT HAVE NOT LIVED IN THOUGHT BUT DEED, . . .	353	PEOPLE		30
OF SOME MOST HAUGHTY DEED OR THOUGHT	436	FOR MY SON		13
CHARACTER ISOLATED BY A DEED	630	CIRCUS ANIMALS		29
THE NOISY WORLD DIVIDES. HOW SOON A DEED	700	MOSADA 3		34
DEED-DOER					
O WORN DEED-DOER." "WHAT MAY BRING	5	OISIN 1	V	50
DEED-DOERS					
YE WORN DEED-DOERS, AND MY NAME	5	OISIN 1	V	48
DEEDS					
BARD OISIN, BOAST NOT OF THY DEEDS	11	OISIN 1	V	129
THEN NOWISE WORSHIP DUSTY DEEDS, ...	65	HAPPY SHEPHERD		22
THEN NO WISE WORSHIP DUSTY DEEDS, ...	65	HAPPY SHEPHERD		22
HE WOULD HIS DEEDS FORGET.	112	ROSE OF PEACE		4
WHEN ALL THOUGHTS AND DEEDS ARE RECKONED, ...	298	THREE HERMITS		15
THOSE DEEDS WERE BEST THAT GAVE THE MINUTE WINGS . . .	533	HER TRIUMPH		5
DEEM					
YET DIMLY DEEM I THAT THE MORNING RAYS	30	OISIN 2	V	20
DEEP					
THEN, MOUNTED ON A HERON, O'ER THE DEEP	33	OISIN 2	V	64
THAT SEA-GOD'S NAME, WHO IN A DEEP CONTENT	38	OISIN 2	V	129
DEEP SUNKEN ON THE BLADE'S LENGTH, "MANANAN!"	38	OISIN 2	V	128
THAT SEA GOD'S NAME, WHO IN A DEEP CONTENT	38	OISIN 2	V	129
AND FOUND A DOOR DEEP SUNKEN IN THE WALL, ...	39	OISIN 2		154
ROLLING HIS FLAGRANT WHEEL OUT OF THE DEEP, ...	42	OISIN 2		193
ROLLING HIS WHEEL, WE SANG BESIDE THE DEEP	42	OISIN 2	V	193
. . . THERE CAMPING IN GRASSES DEEP, ...	50	OISIN 3		54
THRUSTING HIS NOSE TO MY SHOULDER; HE KNEW IN HIS BOSOM DEEP	54	OISIN 3		106
. . . DEEP HORROR OF EYES AND OF WINGS, ...	62	OISIN 3		205
FELL ON THE PIRATES BY THE DEEP, ...	83	MAD KING GOLL		21
FELL ON THE ROBBERS BY THE DEEP, ...	83	MAD KING GOLL		21
FELL ON THE PIRATES BY THE DEEP, ...	83	MAD KING GOLL	V	21
HE HOLDS DEEP COMMUNE WITH HIS HEART:	99	FOXHUNTER		43
WHERE THE SUN FALLS INTO THE WESTERN DEEP.	108	CUCHULAIN SEA	V	34
I HEAR IT IN THE DEEP HEART'S CORE.	117	ISLE INNISFREE		12
YOUR EYES HAD ONCE, AND OF THEIR SHADOWS DEEP;	121	YOU ARE OLD		4
AND ABOVE THE DEEP OF HEAVEN, ...	125	CATHLEEN PARA	V	15
AND PIERCE THE DEEP WOOD'S WOVEN SHADE, ...	125	GOES FERGUS		2
NOW THAT DEEP EARTH HAS DRUNK HIS BODY IN;	127	DREAM OF FAERY	V	28
OF THINGS DISCOVERED IN THE DEEP, ...	138	TO IRELAND		21
OF THE DIM WISDOMS OLD AND DEEP, ...	138	TO IRELAND	V	21
DROWNING LOVE'S LONELY HOUR IN DEEP TWILIGHT OF REST, . .	154	BELOVED PEACE		11
BUT FLAME ON FLAME, AND DEEP ON DEEP, ...	156	FORGOT BEAUTY		21
BUT FLAME ON FLAME, AND DEEP ON DEEP, ...	156	FORGOT BEAUTY		21
BUT FLAME ON FLAME, DEEP UNDER DEEP, ...	156	FORGOT BEAUTY		21
BUT FLAME ON FLAME, DEEP UNDER DEEP, ...	156	FORGOT BEAUTY	V	21
ALL BUT THE FLAMES, AND DEEP ON DEEP, ...	156	FORGOT BEAUTY	V	21
ALL BUT THE FLAMES, AND DEEP ON DEEP, ...	156	FORGOT BEAUTY	V	21
AND HANDS HURL IN THE DEEP	165	CRY OF SEDGE		6
AND TUMULT OF DEFEATED DREAMS; AND DEEP	169	SECRET ROSE		5
DWELT AMONG WINE-STAINED WANDERERS IN DEEP WOODS: . . .	170	SECRET ROSE		21
HIS HEAVY RINGS UNCOILED FROM GLIMMERING DEEP TO DEEP: . .	174	ELEMENT POWERS		5
HIS HEAVY RINGS UNCOILED FROM GLIMMERING DEEP TO DEEP: . .	174	ELEMENT POWERS		5
ON OLD DEEP SILVER ROLLING THERE	271	GREY ROCK		20
A DARK DEEP HOLLOW IN THE ROCK.	303	HOUR DAWN		21
A DARK DEEP HOLE IN THE ROCK'S FACE, ...	303	HOUR DAWN	V	21
HAD DIPPED THE WOODEN LADLE DEEP	304	HOUR DAWN		46
A DEEP SWORN VOW	357	DEEP-SWORN VOW	V	T
THAT DEEP SWORN VOW, HAVE BEEN FRIENDS OF MINE, . . .	357	DEEP-SWORN VOW	V	2
BRING UP OUT OF THAT DEEP CONSIDERING MIND	413	TOWER		106
CAME TO SO DEEP A THOUGHT	505	RESULT THOUGHT		10
HOW COULD PASSION RUN SO DEEP	534	CONSOLATION		7
"FORGETTING HUMAN WORDS," A GRAVE DEEP FACE.	603	GALLERY REVIS		49
WHAT DEEP ROOTS ARE," AND NEVER FORESAW THE END . . .	603	GALLERY REVIS	V	37
SAW THAT THE GRAVE WAS DEEP, THE COFFIN SOUND, . . .	609	IN TARAS HALLS		18
GROWS MORE DEEP DAY AFTER DAY, ...	624	APPARITIONS		18
SADNESS, SOUL OF JOY MOST DEEP	647	ISLE STAT I 1		74
SAD LADY OF THE DEEP, POURS DOWN HER LIGHT:	650	ISLE STAT I 1		127
LONE REGENT OF THE WOODS, DEEP MUTTERING, ...	657	ISLE STAT I 3		49
THE BARRED WOODPECKER'S MANSION IS AND DEEP, ...	659	ISLE STAT II 1		23
OF THE WIDE WOODS. AND THE DEEP EARTH GATHERED THEM. . .	660	ISLE STAT II 1		33
IN THE DEEP CENTRES OF THE SECRET WOODS.	661	ISLE STAT II 1		54
FROM THE DEEP EARTH UNTO THE LURID SKY	662	ISLE STAT II 2		5
AND WHEN THE SUMMER'S DEEP, THEN TO THIS SPOT	663	ISLE STAT II 2		24
WAS MY SLEEP LONG, OH, YOUTH? LONG, LONG AND DEEP. . .	678	ISLE STAT II 3		299
IN THE DEEP ALCOVES DIMNESS SMILES AND HIDES, ...	685	DRAWING-ROOM		4
THE SAGE, WHO DEEP IN CENTRAL NATURE DELVES, ...	686	LIFE		2
THE DARKNESS OF THE WHIRLWIND SHATTERED DEEP.	688	TWO TITANS		58
DEEP IN HIS SOUL, LIKE RAIN UPON A SOIL	692	MOSADA 1		56
DEEP IN THE WOODLAND PAUSED THEY, THE SIX FEET	716	DWELT SYCAMORE		9
DEEP IN THE WOODLAND PASSED THEY. THE SIX FEET . . .	716	DWELT SYCAMORE	V	9
CRIES A VOICE AT ROARING MIDNIGHT BESIDE THE MOONLESS DEEP.	718	PHANTOM SHIP		8
WHAT SHALLOW THOUGHTS ABOUT DEEP THINGS!	725	LEGEND		11

196

```
                                           PAGE   TITLE            LINE
DEEP   (CONTINUED)
     THE SAGE WHO DEEP IN CENTRAL NATURE DELVES,  . . . . .   734 QUATRAIN APHOR      2
     IN THE DEEP ALCOVE'S DIMNESS SMILES AND HIDES."  . . . .  735 QUATRAIN APHOR     24
     AND JOY, IN GROWING DEEPER AND MORE DEEP,  . . . . .  .   735 QUATRAIN APHOR     27
     IN THE DEEP ALCOVES DIMNESS SMILES AND HIDES. . . . . .   735 QUATRAIN APHOR V   24
DEEPENED
     AND WOULD BE NO HARSH FRIEND.  WHEN NIGHT HAD DEEPENED,   283 TWO KINGS         138
DEEPENING
     AMONG THE DEEPENING SHADES. . . . . . . . . . . .  .      416 TOWER             195
DEEPER
     TO WATCH THEE PASS?  YET DEEPER THAN MEN KNOW . . . . .   672 ISLE STAT II 3    158
     DEEPER THAN THE DEEPEST WELL." . . . . . . . . . .  .     697 MOSADA 2           27
     AND JOY, IN GROWING DEEPER AND MORE DEEP, . . . . . .     735 QUATRAIN APHOR     27
DEEPEST
     UNDER THE DEEPEST SHADOWS OF THE HALL  . . . . . . .       37 OISIN 2          119
     WHEN NIGHT WAS AT ITS DEEPEST, A WILD GOOSE  . . . . .    181 QUEEN MAEVE        36
     "NO, THY HOME IS DEEPEST HELL, . . . . . . . . .  .  .    697 MOSADA 2           26
     DEEPER THAN THE DEEPEST WELL." . . . . . . . . . . .      697 MOSADA 2           27
DEEP-EYED
     DEEP-EYED, SLOW-FOOTING DOWN THE EMPTY GLADE. . . . .     653 ISLE STAT I 2      55
DEEP-ROOTED
     DEEP-ROOTED THINGS," BUT NEVER FORESAW ITS END,  . . .    603 GALLERY REVIS      37
     A GUERDON OF DEEP-ROOTED PAIN. . . . . . . . . .  .  .    668 ISLE STAT II 3     59
DEEPS
     PIERCED WITH SOFT LIGHT THE SHALLOWING DEEPS. . . . .      13 OISIN 1          164
     AND TOLD THE PURPLE DEEPS THEIR PRIDE, . . . . . .  .      14 OISIN 1          186
     . . . IN THE DEEPS OF MY HEART. . . . . . . . .  .  .     143 ROSE IN HEART       4
     . . . IN THE DEEPS OF MY HEART. . . . . . . . .  .  .     143 ROSE IN HEART       8
     AND THEIR SECRET SMILE, OUT OF THE DEEPS OF THE LAKE, . . 203 WITHER BOUGHS V    11
DEEP-SUNKEN
     I FOUND A DOOR DEEP-SUNKEN IN THE WALL, . . . . . . .      39 OISIN 2        V 154
DEEP-SWORN
     A DEEP-SWORN VOW . . . . . . . . . . . . . . .  .  .      357 DEEP-SWORN VOW      T
     THAT DEEP-SWORN VOW HAVE BEEN FRIENDS OF MINE, . . . .    357 DEEP-SWORN VOW      2
DEER
     THAN THE HORNLESS DEER WE CHASED THAT MORN, . . . . .  .    2 OISIN 1        V  7P
     WHEN WE FOLLOWED A DEER WITH OUR BAYING HOUNDS, . . . .     3 OISIN 1           14
     THE HORNLESS DEER IS NOT MORE SAD . . . . . . . .  .  .     4 OISIN 1           34
     I CHASED AT MORN THE FLYING DEER, . . . . . . .  .  .      10 OISIN 1          121
     I CHASED WITH HOUNDS THE FLYING DEER, . . . . . .  .       10 OISIN 1        V 121
     YOU GO NOT WHERE THE RED DEER FEEDS, . . . . . . .  .      11 OISIN 1          127
     WE GALLOPED, NOW A HORNLESS DEER . . . . . . . .  .  .     11 OISIN 1          139
     YE GO NOT WHERE THE RED DEER FEEDS, . . . . . .  .  .      11 OISIN 1        V 127
     ON, ON, AND NOW A HORNLESS DEER . . . . . . . .  .  .      11 OISIN 1        V 139
     SAVE DEER TOWARDS NOON THAT WATER SOUGHT. . . . . . .      17 OISIN 1        V 243
     THE DEER, THE BADGER, AND THE BOAR, . . . . . .  .  .      23 OISIN 1          345
     AND SLEW THE BADGER AND THE DEER, . . . . . . . .  .       23 OISIN 1        V 345
     THE YOUTH AND LADY AND THE DEER AND HOUND, . . . .  .      29 OISIN 2            4
     ONCE MORE—THE YOUTH AND LADY, DEER AND HOUND, . . . .      29 OISIN 2        V   2
     THEY CHASE THE NOONTIDE DEER, . . . . . . . . . .  .       32 OISIN 2           53
     THEY CHASE AT NOON THE DEER. . . . . . . . . .  .  .       32 OISIN 2        V  53
     THEY CHASE THE NOON-TIDE DEER, . . . . . . . . .  .  .     32 OISIN 2        V  53
     THE DEER AND THE HOUND, AND THE LADY AND YOUTH, . . . .    47 OISIN 3        V   3
     THE JOYOUS FLOCKS OF DEER AND ANTELOPE, . . . . . .  .     75 ANASHU VIJAYA     74
     THE JOYOUS FLOCKS OF DEER AND ANTELOPES, . . . . . .      75 ANASHU VIJAYA     74
     I LEAD ALONG THE WOODLAND DEER, . . . . . . . . .  .      84 MAD KING GOLL     46
     DRIVING THE DEER ALONG THE WOODY WAYS. . . . . . .  .     109 CUCHULAIN SEA V   48
     DO YOU NOT HEAR ME CALLING, WHITE DEER WITH NO HORNS?  .  153 CHANGE BELOVED     1
     I WOULD THE PALE DEER HAD COME . . . . . . . . . .  .     171 MAID QUIET     V  4A
     I WOULD THAT THE DEATH-PALE DEER . . . . . . . .  .  .    171 MAID QUIET     V  4A
     FOR THERE THE TALL DEER AND HIS LEMAN SIGH . . . .  . .   210 RAGGED WOOD    V   2
     FOR THERE THE TALL DEER AND HIS LEMAN CRY . . . . .  .    211 RAGGED WOOD    V   6
     I WILL DRIVE OUT THE DEER AND MOON AND CRY— . . . .  .    211 RAGGED WOOD    V  10
     THAT MAIDEN BRING THEY,  WHEN THE TALL RED DEER . . . .   713 FERENCZ RENYI     79
     THE CALLING AFAR OF THE DOE AND THE DEER. . . . . . .     717 LOVE SONG          5
     A RED-EARED HOUND FOLLOWS A HORNLESS DEER. . . . . .  .   764 SHADOW WATER A   325
     THE PALE HOUND AND THE DEER WANDER FOR EVER . . . . .     764 SHADOW WATER A   330
     THE PALE HOUND AND THE DEER WANDER FOREVER . . . . . .    764 SHADOW WATER A V 330
DEER-HOUNDS
     THE FENIANS.  LET THEIR DEER-HOUNDS SLEEP. . . . . . .     11 OISIN 1        V 131
DEFAMED
     WHERE WHO HAS SERVED THE MOST IS MOST DEFAMED, . . . .    351 PEOPLE             4
DEFEAT
     BE SECRET AND TAKE DEFEAT . . . . . . . . . . . .  .      290 TO A FRIEND        2
     THE HEART NEED SUFFER NO DEFEAT, BUT I . . . .  .  .  .   464 HARUN RASHID      77
     DEFEAT IS DEATH.  SHOULD MY PLOTS FAIL I'D DIE. . . . .   722 WITCH VIVIEN      52
DEFEATED
     AND WHEN AT LAST, DEFEATED IN HIS WARS, . . . . . . .     115 ROSE OF BATTLE    33
     AND TUMULT OF DEFEATED DREAMS, AND DEEP . . . . . .  .    169 SECRET ROSE        5
     HAVE BEEN DEFEATED BY THAT PLEDGE YOU GAVE . . . . .  .   258 KING NO KING       9
DEFENCE
     FOR LEARNING AND DEFENCE . . . . . . . . . . . .  .  .    380 SONGS FOOL 1       5
DEFENDING
     DEFENDING IRELAND'S SOUL. . . . . . . . . . . . .  .      546 TO SAME TUNE 2     6
     DEFENDING IRELAND'S SOUL. . . . . . . . . . . . .  .      613 MARCH SONGS 1      6
DEFILE
     ARE BUT A POST THE PASSING DOGS DEFILE. . . . . . .  .    321 REED WHISPERER    14
DEFILED
     WE KNOW WHAT RASCAL MIGHT HAS DEFILED, . . . . . . .  .   614 MARCH SONGS 2     11
DEFILING
     THAT DEFILING AND DISFIGURED SHAPE . . . . . . . .  .     479 SELF AND SOUL     51
```

197

			PAGE	TITLE	LINE

DEFINITIONS
BUT I, WHOSE VIRTUES ARE THE DEFINITIONS • • • • • • 353 PEOPLE 32
DEFORMED
DEFORMED BECAUSE THERE IS NO DEFORMITY • • • • • • • 376 PHASES OF MOON 101
DEFORMED BEYOND DEFORMITY, UNFORMED, • • • • • • • • 376 PHASES OF MOON 111
DEFORMITY
DEFORMED BECAUSE THERE IS NO DEFORMITY • • • • • • • 376 PHASES OF MOON 101
DEFORMED BEYOND DEFORMITY, UNFORMED, • • • • • • • • 376 PHASES OF MOON 111
DEFORMITY OF BODY AND OF MIND• • • • • • • • • • • • 377 PHASES OF MOON 123
DEGREES
HONOURED BY ALL IN THEIR DEGREES, • • • • • • • • • 380 SAINT HUNCH 15
DEIGN
AND SHALL BE DONE, IF YOU WILL DEIGN TO KISS • • • • 669 ISLE STAT II 3 79
DEIRDRE
REMEMBER DEIRDRE AND HER MAN; • • • • • • • • • • • 192 BAILE AILLINN 91
THE PRAISE OF DEIRDRE • • • • • • • • • • • • • • • 771 SONG DEIRDRE 1 V T
THE ENTRANCE OF DEIRDRE • • • • • • • • • • • • • • 771 SONG DEIRDRE 1 V T
SONGS FROM DEIRDRE • • • • • • • • • • • • • • • • • 771 SONG DEIRDRE 1 V T
DEIRDRE'S
AND THEY HAVE NEWS OF DEIRDRE'S EYES, • • • • • • • 193 BAILE AILLINN 97
DEITIES
BEFORE THE INDIFFERENT GARDEN DEITIES; • • • • • • • 418 ANCEST HOUSES 28
DEJECTION
LINES WRITTEN IN DEJECTION • • • • • • • • • • • • • 343 DEJECTION T
DELACROIX
NOT A MAN BUT DELACROIX• • • • • • • • • • • • • • • 625 NATIVITY 4
DELIBERATE
REMEMBER HIS DELIBERATE HAPPINESS• • • • • • • • • • 370 EGO DOMINUS 53
DELIBERATELY
GOLDSMITH DELIBERATELY SIPPING AT THE HONEY-POT OF HIS 481 BLOOD AND MOON 21
MIND,
GOLDSMITH DELIBERATELY SIPPING AT THE HONEY POT OF HIS 481 BLOOD AND MOON V 21
MIND;
DELICATE
THAT SCARES WITH HIS BUSTLE THE DELICATE NIGHT, • • • • 28 OISIN 1 V 423B
DELICATE IN COLOUR AS APPLE BLOSSOM• • • • • • • • • 199 ARROW 6
THE DELICATE STEPPING STAG AND HIS LADY SIGH • • • • 210 RAGGED WOOD V 2
"SUCH A DELICATE HIGH HEAD, • • • • • • • • • • 259 PEACE 7
TO THAT STERN COLOUR AND THAT DELICATE LINE • • • • 326 ROBERT GREGORY 67
LIFTING HIS DELICATE FEET• • • • • • • • • • • • • • 378 CAT AND MOON 10
AND LIFTS HIS DELICATE FEET• • • • • • • • • • • • • 378 CAT AND MOON V 10
WITH DELICATE FEET UPON OLD TERRACES, • • • • • • • 418 ANCEST HOUSES 26
THEIR LEGS LONG, DELICATE AND SLENDER, AQUAMARINE THEIR 426 PHANTOM HATRED 17
EYES,
ON DELICATE SENSITIVE EAR OR TOSSING MANE, • • • • • 433 NINETEEN 19 115
WITH THE DELICATE MOTHER-OF-PEARL, • • • • • • • • • 509 JANE REPROVED 10
HER LIMBS ARE DELICATE AS AN EYELID, • • • • • • • • 612 NEWS ORACLE 27
DELICATE-STEPPING
THE DELICATE-STEPPING STAG AND HIS LADY SIGH, • • • • 210 RAGGED WOOD 2
DELIGHT SEE SELF-DELIGHT
AND MURMURED SNATCHES OF DELIGHT; • • • • • • • • • 14 OISIN 1 187
• • • REMEMBERING ALONE THAT DELIGHT • • • • • • • • 54 OISIN 3 111
BUT A BRIEF, DREAMY, KIND DELIGHT • • • • • • • • • 202 NEVER GIVE ALL 7
BECOME ONE MOVEMENT, ENERGY, DELIGHT, • • • • • • • 231 SHADOW WATER B 217
DELIGHT MAKES ALL OF THE ONE MIND, • • • • • • • • • 266 GALWAY RACES 2
DELIGHT IN ART WHOSE END IS PEACE, • • • • • • • • • 288 TO WEALTHY MAN 26
TAKING DELIGHT THAT HE COULD SPRING; • • • • • • • • 317 APPOINTMENT 4
DELIGHT MEN'S EYES WHEN I AWAKE SOME DAY • • • • • • 323 SWANS AT COOLE 29
TO HAVE PUBLISHED ALL TO BE A WORLD'S DELIGHT• • • • 327 ROBERT GREGORY 72
A LONELY IMPULSE OF DELIGHT • • • • • • • • • • • • 328 IRISH AIRMAN 11
BE BUT THE BREAKERS OF MEN'S HEARTS OR ENGINES OF DELIGHT; 354 HIS PHOENIX 23
SO MANY TIMES CHILDISH DELIGHT• • • • • • • • • • • 399 BREAK OF DAY 11
THAT OUT OF LIFE'S OWN SELF DELIGHT HAD SPRUNG • • • 417 ANCEST HOUSES V 11
AND CHILDHOOD A DELIGHT FOR EVERY SENSE, • • • • • • 418 ANCEST HOUSES 31
DELIGHT BECOMES DEATH-LONGING IF ALL LONGING ELSE BE VAIN. 459 FROM OEDIPUS 3
EVEN THAT DELIGHT MEMORY TREASURES SO, • • • • • • • 459 FROM OEDIPUS 4
AND SINK INTO ITS OWN DELIGHT AT LAST• • • • • • • • 473 ALL SOUL NIGHT 60
THERE'S KEEN DELIGHT IN WHAT WE HAVE; • • • • • • • 485 NINETEENTH CEN 2
EXTINGUISH THAT DELIGHT• • • • • • • • • • • • • • • 538 LAST CONFESS 24
BUT A GOOD STRONG CAUSE AND BLOWS ARE DELIGHT." • • • 545 TO SAME TUNE 1 14
BUT A GOOD STRONG CAUSE AND THE BLOWS ARE DELIGHT•" • • 545 TO SAME TUNE 1 V 14
SOME TAKE DELIGHT IN ADORNING A WOMAN• • • • • • • • 547 TO SAME TUNE 3 V 3
DELIGHT TO IMAGINE THEM SEATED THERE; • • • • • • • 567 LAPIS LAZULI 50
BUT A GOOD STRONG CAUSE AND BLOWS ARE DELIGHT•" • • • 616 MARCH SONGS 3 14
AND I DELIGHT TO SING; • • • • • • • • • • • • • • • 627 STATES HOLIDAY 25
HAST THOU NOT KNOWN ALL SORROW AND DELIGHT • • • • • 723 KANVA ON SELF 2
HAVE FOUND DELIGHT, IN THE RESOUNDING OARS, • • • • • 750 SHADOW WATER A 72
DELIGHTED
A RUMOUR OF DELIGHTED HEARTS• • • • • • • • • • • • 16 OISIN 1 230
FANNED THE DELIGHTED AIR LIKE WINGS OF BIRDS; • • • • 32 OISIN 2 50
THAT FAN THE PULSES OF DELIGHTED AIR, • • • • • • • 32 OISIN 2 V 50A
MIND AND DELIGHTED MIND; • • • • • • • • • • • • • • 315 FRIENDS 9
HEART AND DELIGHTED HEART; • • • • • • • • • • • • • 315 FRIENDS V 9
FOR ALL THINGS THE DELIGHTED EYE NOW SEES • • • • • 326 ROBERT GREGORY 49
DELIGHTED TO BE BUT WISE, • • • • • • • • • • • • • 329 MEN IMPROVE 10
DELIGHTED ME AS A CHILD; • • • • • • • • • • • • • • 787 HUDDON DUDDON 2
DELIGHTED ME AS A CHILD• • • • • • • • • • • • • • • 787 HUDDON DUDDON 7
DELIGHTED ME AS A CHILD• • • • • • • • • • • • • • • 787 HUDDON DUDDON 12
DELIGHTFUL
DELIGHTFUL TO THE TOUCH; TIGHTEN THAT HAND • • • • • 579 DOR WELLESLEY 4

			PAGE	TITLE	LINE

DELIGHTING   SEE ROOK-DELIGHTING SELF-DELIGHTING
SUDDENLY I SAW THE COLD AND ROOK DELIGHTING HEAVEN . . . 316 COLD HEAVEN V 1
DELIGHTS
CEASE TO REMEMBER THE DELIGHTS OF YOUTH, TRAVEL-WEARIED 459 FROM OEDIPUS   2
    AGED MAN:
BUT GOOD STRONG BLOWS ARE DELIGHTS TO THE MIND." . . . . 544 TO SAME TUNE 1 4
BUT GOOD STRONG BLOWS ARE DELIGHTS TO THE MIND." . . . . 616 MARCH SONGS 3 4
DELIRIUM
ALL THAT DELIRIUM OF THE BRAVE? . . . . 290 SEPTEMBER 1913 22
TESTY DELIRIUM . . . . 416 TOWER 186
DELIVER
DELIVER FROM THE CRIME OF DEATH AND BIRTH. . . . . . . 478 SELF AND SOUL 24
DELIVERANCE
"I BRING DELIVERANCE," PEARL-PALE NIAMH SAID. . . . . . 34 OISIN 2 78
DELIVERED
THEN MY DELIVERED SOUL HERSELF SHALL LEARN . . . . . 558 RIBH CHRISTIAN 13
DELIVERER
"I BRING THEE A DELIVERER FROM FAR AWAY, ... 34 OISIN 2 V 78A
DELL
IN VALE AND DELL SO BLAZE THE DAFFODILLS: . . . . . 645 ISLE STAT I 1 15
WERE FURLED THE WINGS OF SHIPS. THERE IN A DELL, . . . 693 MOSADA 1 82
"WE BURIED LATE IN A HAZEL DELL . . . . 729 PRIEST FAIRY 43
DELLS
AND HATH HER HOME BY MANY-FOLDED DELLS. . . . . . . 657 ISLE STAT I 3 46
DELPHIC
THE DELPHIC ORACLE UPON PLOTINUS . . . . 530 DELPHIC ORACLE T
NEWS FOR THE DELPHIC ORACLE . . . . 611 NEWS ORACLE T
DELUSION
ENTHRALLED BY THE UNCONQUERABLE DELUSION, ... 367 EGO DOMINUS 6
DELUSIONS
CHAUNT IN HIS EAR DELUSIONS MAGICAL, ... 111 CUCHULAIN SEA 80
GO, CAST ON HIM DELUSIONS MAGICAL, ... 111 CUCHULAIN SEA V 80
DELVES
THE SAGE, WHO DEEP IN CENTRAL NATURE DELVES, ... 686 LIFE 2
THE SAGE WHO DEEP IN CENTRAL NATURE DELVES, ... 734 QUATRAIN APHOR 2
DEMAGOGUE
NO LOOSE-LIPPED DEMAGOGUE HAD WON THE DAY, ... 542 PARN FUNERAL 2 3
NO LOOSE LIPPED DEMAGOGUE HAD WON THE DAY, ... 542 PARN FUNERAL 2 V 3
DEMAND
MAKES NO DEMAND. . . . . 600 SPIRIT MEDIUM 22
BECAUSE CHILDREN DEMAND DADDY-LONG-LEGS UPON HIS TIMBER 623 HIGH TALK 6
    TOES,
BECAUSE WOMEN IN THE UPPER STOREYS DEMAND A FACE AT THE 623 HIGH TALK 7
    PANE.
DEMESNE
IN COOLE DEMESNE, AND THERE TO FINISH UP . . . . . . 490 COOLE BALLYLEE 6
I HAVE A SMALL DEMESNE, ... 606 SONGS BURDEN 2 2
DEMON
THE WANDERINGS OF OISIN AND HOW A DEMON TRAPPED HIM . . . 1 OISIN 1 V T
OF DALLIANCE WITH A DEMON THING. . . . . 2 OISIN 1 4
TRAPPED OF AN AMOROUS DEMON THING. . . . . 2 OISIN 1 V 4
"THIS DEMON SHALL BE BATTERED TILL HE DIE, ... 35 OISIN 2 90
"THIS DEMON SHALL BE PIERCED AND DROP AND DIE, ... 35 OISIN 2 V 90
A DUSKY DEMON DRY AS A WITHERED SEDGE . . . . . . 39 OISIN 2 158
A DUSK DEMON, DRY AS A WITHERED SEDGE, ... 39 OISIN 2 V 158
A HUSKY DEMON, DRY AS A WITHERED SEDGE . . . . . . 39 OISIN 2 V 158
THROUGH HEART AND DEMON SPINE, AND IN THE WAVE . . . . 41 OISIN 2 V 182
THAT DEMON DULL AND UNSUBDUABLE: . . . . 43 OISIN 2 217
AND THE NAME OF THE DEMON WHOSE HAMMER . . . . . . 52 OISIN 3 80
THROUGH THE DEMON LOVE OF ITS YOUTH . . . . 63 OISIN 3 216
A MAGIC THAT CAN CALL A DEMON UP, ... 238 SHADOW WATER B 344
DEMON AND BEAST . . . . 399 DEMON BEAST T
THAT CRAFTY DEMON AND THAT LOUD BEAST . . . . . . 399 DEMON BEAST 2
BELONGS TO BEAST OR DEMON, ... 401 DEMON BEAST 35
AND OVERTURNED THE DEMON WITH A SOUND . . . . . . 762 SHADOW WATER A 283
DEMONIAC
BEING NO MORE DEMONIAC . . . . 400 DEMON BEAST 30
DEMONIC
HOW THE DEMONIC RAGE . . . . 419 MY HOUSE V 16
THE HALF-READ WISDOM OF DEMONIC IMAGES . . . . . . 427 PHANTOM HATRED V 39
DEMON'S
A DEMON'S LEISURE: EYES, FIRST WHITE, NOW BURNED . . . . 40 OISIN 2 168
A DEMON'S LEISURE. EYES FIRST WHITE AS SNOW, ... 40 OISIN 2 V 168
DEMONS
MY ENEMY AND HOPE: DEMONS FOR FRIGHT . . . . 34 OISIN 2 81
THE DEMONS OF THE WILDS AND WINDS FOR FRIGHT . . . . . 34 OISIN 2 V 81B
UNTIL THE GODS AND DEMONS DROP ASLEEP. . . . . . . 35 OISIN 2 86
"FOR ALL MEN FLEE THE DEMONS": BUT MOVED NOT . . . . 36 OISIN 2 93
SPRANG DRIPPING, AND, WITH CAPTIVE DEMONS SENT . . . . 38 OISIN 2 130
. . . NOR IN GLAMOURS BY DEMONS FLUNG, ... 50 OISIN 3 50
. . . OR IN GLAMOURS BY DEMONS FLUNG, ... 50 OISIN 3 V 50
OF THE HIGH PEOPLE OF SORACA NOR IN GLAMOUR BY DEMONS 50 OISIN 3 V 50
    FLUNG,
AND THE NAMES OF THE DEMONS WHOSE HAMMERS . . . . . 52 OISIN 3 V 80
WHERE THE DEMONS WHIP THEM WITH WIRES . . . . . . 61 OISIN 3 198
AND DEMONS BE BROKEN IN PIECES, AND TRAMPLED BENEATH THEM 61 OISIN 3 204
    IN DEATH.
AND DEMONS, ALL BROKEN IN PIECES, BE TRAMPLED BENEATH THEM 61 OISIN 3 V 204
    IN DEATH.
AND DEMONS AFRAID IN THEIR DARKNESS: . . . . 62 OISIN 3 205

		PAGE	TITLE	LINE

DEMONS (CONTINUED)
FOR THY YOUTH WITHOUT PEACE, AND THY YEARS WITH THE DEMONS,   63 OISIN 3   V 216
    • • •
    THE DEMONS, WITH THEIR SUBTLE GUILE, • • • • • • • • •   135 TWO TREES   22
    IN THE DIM GLASS THE DEMONS HOLD, • • • • • • • • • • •   135 TWO TREES   30
DEMONSTRATE
    OR DEMONSTRATE IN MY OWN LIFE • • • • • • • • • • • • •   605 YOU CONTENT   21
DENIED
    ALL THAT TIME DENIED-- • • • • • • • • • • • • • • • •   496 MOHINI CHATTER   18
    NOR GRAVE NOR BED DENIED, • • • • • • • • • • • • • •   513 JANE TALK BISH   10
DENIES
    THAT SHE DENIES • • • • • • • • • • • • • • • • • • •   336 YOUNG GIRL   8
    THOUGH PEDANTRY DENIES, • • • • • • • • • • • • • • •   345 ON WOMAN   9
    WHO IS MY BEAUTY'S EQUAL, THOUGH THAT MY HEART DENIES, • •   354 HIS PHOENIX   27
    NO ONE DENIES TO KEATS LOVE OF THE WORLD; • • • • • •   370 EGO DOMINUS   52
    NO RIGHT-TAUGHT MAN DENIES. • • • • • • • • • • • • •   590 OLD WICKED MAN   58
    NO RIGHT TAUGHT MAN DENIES. • • • • • • • • • • • • •   590 OLD WICKED MAN   V 58
DENIS
    AND RUTH ST. DENIS HAD MORE CHARM ALTHOUGH SHE HAD POOR   353 HIS PHOENIX   10
        LUCK;
DENOUNCES
    RIBH DENOUNCES PATRICK • • • • • • • • • • • • • • •   556 RIBH PATRICK   T
DENT
    EVERY ACCIDENTAL CRACK OR DENT, • • • • • • • • • • •   567 LAPIS LAZULI   44
DENY
    SPEAK--HE WILL NOT DENY IT. IS THAT TRUE? • • • • • •   249 SHADOW WATER B   563
    DO NOT DENY HIS RIGHT; • • • • • • • • • • • • • • •   584 ORAHILLY   2
DENYING
    WITH A STARK, DENYING LOOK; • • • • • • • • • • • • •   381 SONG OF FOOL   6
DEPART
    AND LO! MY ANCIENT BURDEN MAY DEPART. • • • • • • • •   69 SAD SHEPHERD   24
    AND LO--MY HEAVY BURTHEN MAY DEPART;" • • • • • • • •   69 SAD SHEPHERD   V 24
    WHEN SHE ROSE UP TO DEPART? • • • • • • • • • • • • •   171 MAID QUIET   6
    INNOCENCE AND PEACE DEPART. • • • • • • • • • • • • •   561 FOUR AGES MAN   4
    OF MY SAD HUNTER-FRIEND WILL ALL DEPART • • • • • • •   668 ISLE STAT II 3   45
    I SAW HIM FROM SAD DIDO'S SHORES DEPART, • • • • • • •   677 ISLE STAT II 3   288
DEPARTING
    AND MAY DEPARTING TWILIGHT KEEP • • • • • • • • • •   435 FOR MY SON   5
DEPTH
    MORE MOURNFUL THAN THE DEPTH OF STARRY SKIES, • • • • •   108 CUCHULAIN SEA   V 42
    APPEAR AND DISAPPEAR IN THE BLUE DEPTH OF THE SKY • • •   318 MAGI   3
DEPTHS
    AND THEIR SECRET SMILE, OUT OF THE DEPTHS OF THE LAKE; • •   203 WITHER BOUGHS   11
    APPEAR AND DISAPPEAR IN THE BLUE DEPTHS OF THE SKY • • •   318 MAGI   V 3
    NO SHEPHERD FOOT HAS EVER DARED ITS DEPTHS. • • • • • •   682 SEEKER   32
DERG'S
    ROUND LOUGH DERG'S HOLY ISLAND I WENT UPON THE STONES, • •   593 PILGRIM   6
DERIDED
    DERIDED AND DERIDING, DRIVEN OUT • • • • • • • • • •   369 EGO DOMINUS   34
    IN ABSTRACT THINGS; OR BE DERIDED BY • • • • • • • •   409 TOWER   15
    IS HE WHO LABOURED ON, DERIDED, HATED, • • • • • • • •   738 MOURN THEN ON   11
DERIDING
    DERIDED AND DERIDING, DRIVEN OUT • • • • • • • • • •   369 EGO DOMINUS   34
DERISION
    CASTS DERISION UPON • • • • • • • • • • • • • • • •   476 DEATH   9
    BECAUSE THERE IS SAFETY IN DERISION • • • • • • • • •   624 APPARITIONS   1
DERMOT
    MY DERMOT DEAR AND BROWN, • • • • • • • • • • • • •   97 FOXHUNTER   V 6
    BROWN DERMOT TREADS UPON THE LAWN, • • • • • • • • •   98 FOXHUNTER   V 17
DERMUID
    AND THAT MADE HER DERMUID DEAR, AND SOME OLD CARDINAL • •   366 HER COURAGE   V 6
DESCANT
    THAT WE DESCANT AND YET AGAIN DESCANT • • • • • • •   523 LONG SILENCE   5
    THAT WE DESCANT AND YET AGAIN DESCANT • • • • • • •   523 LONG SILENCE   5
DESCEND
    MY LORD, IF IT MUST BE, I PRAY DESCEND • • • • • • •   697 MOSADA 2   43
DESCENDANTS
    MY DESCENDANTS • • • • • • • • • • • • • • • • • • •   422 MY DESCENDANTS   T
    AND WHAT IF MY DESCENDANTS LOSE THE FLOWER • • • • • •   423 MY DESCENDANTS   9
DESCENDS
    THE BIRD DESCENDS, AND HER FRAIL THIGHS ARE PRESSED • • •   441 LEDA AND SWAN   V 2
    DESCENDS INTO THE LOVELESS DUST. • • • • • • • • • •   540 FROM ANTIGONE   16
DESERT
    THAT MEN DESERT, • • • • • • • • • • • • • • • • • •   293 HELEN LIVED   2
    TROUBLES MY SIGHT; SOMEWHERE IN SANDS OF THE DESERT • • •   402 SECOND COMING   13
    REEL SHADOWS OF THE INDIGNANT DESERT BIRDS. • • • • • •   402 SECOND COMING   17
    TROUBLES MY SIGHT; A WASTE OF DESERT SAND; • • • • • •   402 SECOND COMING   V 13
    WIND SHADOWS OF THE INDIGNANT DESERT BIRDS. • • • • •   402 SECOND COMING   V 17
    DESERT GEOMETRY OR THE GIFT OF HARUN AL-RASCHID • • • •   460 HARUN RASHID   V T
    THAT WANDERING IN A DESERT, FEATURELESS • • • • • • •   462 HARUN RASHID   27
    WANDERING IN A DESERT FEATURELESS • • • • • • • • • •   462 HARUN RASHID   V 27
    HALF RUNNING, DROPPED AT THE FIRST RIDGE OF THE DESERT • •   468 HARUN RASHID   155
    MURMURED THE WISDOM OF THE DESERT DJINNS, • • • • • •   468 HARUN RASHID   163
    HAS SPOKEN THE WISDOM OF THE DESERT DJINS, • • • • • •   468 HARUN RASHID   V 163
    HAS MURMURED WISDOM OF THE DESERT DJINNS, • • • • • •   468 HARUN RASHID   V 163
    DESERT THE PERJURER'S SIDE; • • • • • • • • • • • •   582 ROGER CASEMENT   20
    EYED PANTHERS IN THEIR DESERT CAVERNS ROVE • • • • • •   681 SEEKER   V 4
DESERT-CAVES
    OF DESERT-CAVES THE RED-EYED PANTHERS ROVE • • • • • •   681 SEEKER   4
DESERTED
    DESERTED ON A DOORWAY SEAT, • • • • • • • • • • • •   85 MAD KING GOLL   56

200

DESERTED   (CONTINUED)
        DESERTED IN A DOORWAY SEAT, ...   85 MAD KING GOLL V   56
DESERTION
        THE CIRCUS ANIMALS' DESERTION . . . .   629 CIRCUS ANIMALS   T
        THE CIRCUS ANIMAL'S DESERTION . . . .   629 CIRCUS ANIMALS V   T
DESIGN
        CUT OUT HIS HEART. SOME MASTER OF DESIGN . . . . .   541 PARN FUNERAL 1   14
DESIGNED
        AND BUILDINGS THAT A HAUGHTIER AGE DESIGNED, ... 418 ANCEST HOUSES   34
DESIRE
        THE IMMORTAL DESIRE OF IMMORTALS WE SAW IN THEIR FACES,   47 OISIN 3   4
            AND SIGHED.
        THE DESIRE OF MAN AND OF WOMAN . . . .   153 CHANGE BELOVED V   T
        FOR SOMEBODY HID HATRED AND HOPE AND DESIRE AND FEAR . . 153 CHANGE BELOVED   4
        AND I HAVE HATRED AND HOPE AND DESIRE AND FEAR . . . . 153 CHANGE BELOVED V   4
        O VANITY OF SLEEP, HOPE, DREAM, ENDLESS DESIRE, ... 154 BELOVED PEACE   7
        AND THE SWEETNESS OF DESIRE, ...   168 BLESSED   38
        THE HEAVINESS OF DESIRE, ...   168 BLESSED   V   38
        BUT SOFT BEAUTY AND INDOLENT DESIRE. . . . .   181 QUEEN MAEVE   22
        OUR HEART'S DESIRE NOW THAT WE ARE SO LIGHT." . . . . 233 SHADOW WATER B   255
        WHAT POWER THAT IS MORE MIGHTY THAN DESIRE . . . . . . 234 SHADOW WATER B   267
        WHY LINGER? RUN TO YOUR DESIRE, ...   234 SHADOW WATER B   272
        WHY DO YOU NOT RUN TO YOUR DESIRE, ...   234 SHADOW WATER B V 272
        HAD THEY BUT COURAGE EQUAL TO DESIRE? . . . . 256 NO SECOND TROY   5
        DO MEN WHO LEAST DESIRE GET MOST, ... 295 THREE BEGGARS   13
        OR GET THE MOST WHO MOST DESIRE?" . . . . 295 THREE BEGGARS   14
        UNLESS DESIRE HAD MADE THEM SO?" . . . .   295 THREE BEGGARS   18
        HER SOUL HAD SUCH DESIRE . . . .   317 NIGHT COME   2
        I HAVE NOT LOST DESIRE . . . .   335 SONG   13
        HARSHNESS OF THEIR DESIRE . . . . 345 ON WOMAN   20
        THAT NEVER LOOKED UPON MAN WITH DESIRE, ... 358 PRESENCES   13
        AND HAVING NO DESIRE THEY CANNOT TELL . . . . 376 PHASES OF MOON   107
        BUT HAVING NO DESIRE THEY CANNOT TELL . . . . 376 PHASES OF MOON V 107
        BETWEEN MY HATRED AND DESIRE, ... 400 DEMON BEAST   6
        CONSUME MY HEART AWAY; SICK WITH DESIRE . . . . 408 SAIL BYZANTIUM   21
        AND HORRIBLE SPLENDOUR OF DESIRE; . . . . 411 TOWER   63
        . . . OF ITS OWN DESIRE; . . . .   481 BLOOD AND MOON   29
        ISAIAH'S COAL, WHAT MORE CAN MAN DESIRE? . . . . . .   502 VACILLATION   74
        EZEKIEL'S COAL, WHAT MORE CAN MAN DESIRE? . . . . . . 502 VACILLATION   V   74
        MY PAISTIN FINN IS MY SOLE DESIRE, ...   550 SONGS REWRIT 1   1
        MY PRETTY PAISTIN IS MY HEART'S DESIRE, ... 550 SONGS REWRIT 1 V   1
        THAT BLONDE GIRL THERE IS MY HEART'S DESIRE, ... 550 SONGS REWRIT 1 V   1
        HE HOLDS HIM FROM DESIRE, ALL BUT STOPS HIS BREATHING LEST 559 MAGIC DRUM   1
        HIS HEART'S DESIRE WHERE THE WORLD DWINDLES OUT? . . . 747 SHADOW WATER A   13
        IN THE COLD STREAMS, AND WAKE TO THEIR DESIRE, . . .   750 SHADOW WATER A   85
        FORGAEL MAY FIND HIS HEART'S DESIRE ON BOARD . . . . . 751 SHADOW WATER A   107
        OUR HEARTS' DESIRE NOW THAT WE ARE SO LIGHT. . . . .   753 SHADOW WATER A   145
        YOUR HEART'S DESIRE AND THE END OF ALL OUR TROUBLE; . . 755 SHADOW WATER A 175
        AND NONE KNOWS WHEREFORE; BUT THE HEART'S DESIRE . . . 764 SHADOW WATER A   340
        FOLDING THEIR HEARTS' DESIRE TO THEIR GLAD HEARTS. . . . 765 SHADOW WATER A 349
        THAT HE FOLLOW WITH DESIRE . . . .   776 AGAINST WITCH   19
DESISTED
        THOUGH FROM BESEECHING THEY DESISTED NOT, ...   36 OISIN 2   V   93
DESK
        FROM COUNTER OR DESK AMONG GREY . . . . 392 EASTER 1916   3
        COME FROM THE FORGER AND HIS DESK, ...   582 ROGER CASEMENT   19
        ITS BOREDOM OF THE DESK OR OF THE SPADE, BECAUSE . . . 621 HOUND VOICE   3
DESOLATE
        GROWN DESOLATE, WHISPER AND SIGH TO EACH OTHER; . . . .   26 OISIN 1   403
        GROWN DESOLATE, WHISPER AND SIGH TO EACH OTHER; . . . .   27 OISIN 1   V   407
        DESOLATE WINDS THAT CRY OVER THE WANDERING SEA; . . . . 147 UNAPPEAS HOST   7
        DESOLATE WINDS THAT HOVER IN THE FLAMING WEST; . . . . 147 UNAPPEAS HOST   8
        DESOLATE WINDS THAT BEAT THE DOORS OF HEAVEN, AND BEAT . 147 UNAPPEAS HOST   9
        THE HORSES OF DISASTER PLUNGE IN THE DESOLATE CLAY. . . . 154 BELOVED PEACE V 8
        AND LINGERED IN THE HIDDEN DESOLATE PLACE . . . . . . 162 ASKS FORGIVE   15
        OF THIS DESOLATE LAKE . . . . 165 CRY OF SEDGE   2
        AS NOW. DOES WANDERING IN THESE DESOLATE SEAS . . . . 236 SHADOW WATER B   314
        BUT DESOLATE WATERS AND A BATTERED SHIP. . . . . 246 SHADOW WATER B   497
        BY A COLD AND DESOLATE SEA, ... 298 THREE HERMITS   2
        AND DESOLATE THREE ROCK . . . . 310 PEACOCK   5
        AND DESOLATE THREE-ROCK . . . . 310 PEACOCK   V   5
        IN A MOST DESOLATE STONY PLACE, ... 325 ROBERT GREGORY   30
        HER DESOLATION TO THE DESOLATE SKY. . . . . 423 MY DESCENDANTS   16
        THE SWAN HAS LEAPED INTO THE DESOLATE HEAVEN; . . . . 431 NINETEEN 19   79
        OUT OF A DESOLATE SOURCE, ... 518 HIS CONFIDENCE   11
        AND THE DESOLATE SHUDDERING SEA. . . . . 648 ISLE STAT I 1   85
DESOLATION
        HER DESOLATION TO THE DESOLATE SKY. . . . . 423 MY DESCENDANTS   16
        INTO THE DESOLATION OF REALITY; . . . . 563 MERU   7
DESPAIR
        A KING AND PROUD! AND THAT IS MY DESPAIR. . . . . . . 103 FERGUS DRUID   16
        AND DREAMED THAT THE OLD DESPAIR . . . . 152 LOSS OF LOVE   3
        WE HAVE CRIED IN OUR DESPAIR . . . . 293 HELEN LIVED   1
        WITH DESPAIR? . . . . 310 WITCH   8
        RHYMED OUT IN LOVE'S DESPAIR . . . . 337 SCHOLARS   5
        GNASHING OF TEETH, DESPAIR; . . . . 346 ON WOMAN   39
        BUT DISSIPATION AND DESPAIR? AND YET . . . . 369 EGO DOMINUS   51
        MAYBE THE BRIDE-BED BRINGS DESPAIR, ... 388 SOLOMON WITCH   25
        NOR BEAUTY BORN OUT OF ITS OWN DESPAIR, ... 445 SCHOOL CHILDR   59
        THE SOUTH WIND BROUGHT IT LONGING, AND THE EAST WIND   449 OWEN AHERNE   5
            DESPAIR,

		PAGE	TITLE		LINE

DESPAIR   (CONTINUED)
THE SOUTH WIND BROUGHT IT LONGING, AND THE EAST BROUGHT   449 OWEN AHERNE   V   5
IN DESPAIR,
THE SOUTH WIND BROUGHT IT LONGING, AND THE EAST BROUGHT   449 OWEN AHERNE   V   5
IT DESPAIR,
DEATH, DESPAIR, DIVISION OF FAMILIES, ...   459 FROM OEDIPUS   5
THROWN INTO DESPAIR . . . .   492 ANNE GREGORY   2
THAT YOUNG MEN IN DESPAIR . . . .   492 ANNE GREGORY   10
AND I AM IN DESPAIR THAT TIME MAY BRING . . . . . .   602 GALLERY REVIS   30
THAT DESPAIR AND KEEP THE PACE . . . .   787 HUDDON DUDDON   9
DESPAIRING
OR WARNED YOU HOW DESPAIRING . . . .   313 TWO YEAR LATER   3
I HAVE FOUND OUT HOW DESPAIRING . . . .   313 TWO YEAR LATER V   3
MOON-STRUCK BY THE DESPAIRING . . . .   487 CRAZED MOON   3
DESPERATE
INTO A DESPERATE GULPH OF LOVE! . . . .   7 OISIN 1   73
SHE STOOD IN DESPERATE MUSIC WOUND, ...   578 CRAZED GIRL   10
DESPITE
TO WIN A WOMAN IN HER OWN DESPITE, ...   244 SHADOW WATER B   458
TO WIN A WOMAN IS IN HER OWN DESPITE, ...   244 SHADOW WATER B V   458
DESPITE A DWINDLING AND LATE-RISEN MOON, ...   372 PHASES OF MOON   6
DESPITE A DWINDLING AND LATE RISEN MOON, ...   372 PHASES OF MOON V   6
UNTIL THAT GLANCE RUN IN THE WORLD'S DESPITE . . . .   474 ALL SOUL NIGHT   94
AND HE, DESPITE HIS TERROR, CANNOT CEASE . . . . .   563 MERU   4
ALLOW THAT HE, DESPITE . . . .   584 ORAHILLY   4
DESTINY
AND ON THIS LOOM I WEAVE THY DESTINY." . . . . . .   716 DWELT SYCAMORE   14
DESTROY
DESTROY THE VIEW BY CUTTING DOWN AN ASH . . . . . .   372 ON GOING HOUSE   13
COMES TO DESTROY . . . .   500 VACILLATION   4
I THOUGHT MY DEAR MUST HER OWN SOUL DESTROY, ...   630 CIRCUS ANIMALS   21
DESTROYED
CAN BE SO BATTERED, BADGERED AND DESTROYED . . . . .   130 BOOK STORIES   17
LAUGHTER NOT TIME DESTROYED MY VOICE . . . .   455 FRIENDS YOUTH   1
AS THE FOX IN THE OLD FABLE DESTROYED THE SPARTAN BOY'S,   580 CURSE CROMWELL   18
DESTROYING   SEE ALL-DESTROYING
DESTROYS
BUT THERE'S ANOTHER KNOWLEDGE THAT MY HEART DESTROYS, . .   580 CURSE CROMWELL   17
DEVIL
WHOM MAN OR DEVIL CANNOT TIRE, ...   295 THREE BEGGARS   16
TO RID ME OF THE DEVIL IN MY SHOES," . . . .   299 BEGGAR CRIED   6
"AND THE WORSE DEVIL THAT IS BETWEEN MY THIGHS," . . . .   300 BEGGAR CRIED   8
"BUT THERE'S A DEVIL IN A LOOKING-GLASS." . . . . . .   300 BEGGAR CRIED   12
THAT DREAM IS A NORM! AND SHOULD SOME LIMB OF THE DEVIL   372 ON GOING HOUSE   12
AND MAY THE DEVIL TAKE THE REST. . . . .   386 ROBARTES DANCE   24
DEVILISH
SUCH DEVILISH THINGS EXIST, ...   436 FOR MY SON   11
DEVIL'S
HE TAKES THE DEVIL'S PAY. . . . .   582 ROGER CASEMENT V   20
I KNOW WHAT DEVIL'S TRADE THEY LEARN . . . .   607 SONGS BURDEN 2   12
DEVILS
WHOM THE DEVILS HAVE BY THE HAIR, ...   92 FATHER OHART   14
DEVIOUS
WITHIN THE TEMPLE, DEVIOUS WALKING, MADE . . . . . .   72 ANASHU VIJAYA   32
DEVOTEE
THE DEVOTEE PROFFERS A KNEE TO HIS LORD, ...   547 TO SAME TUNE 3   2
THE DEVOTEE PROFFERS A KNEE TO HIS LORD, ...   614 MARCH SONGS 2   2
DEVOUR
BUT NOW TWO THINGS DEVOUR MY LIFE! . . . .   24 OISIN 1   358
DEVOURED
UPON A PAINTED STAGE WHEN WE DEVOURED HIS HEART. . . . .   542 PARN FUNERAL 1   23
DEVOUTLY
AND LEAN YOUR LIPS DEVOUTLY TO THIS HARP, ...   762 SHADOW WATER A   287
DEW   SEE LOVE-DEW
WHERE DROPS OF DEW IN MYRIADS FALL, ...   16 OISIN 1   222
"JOY DROWNS THE TWILIGHT IN THE DEW, ...   18 OISIN 1   261
WALKING GHOSTLY IN THE DEW, ...   67 HAPPY SHEPHERD   52
WALKING GHOSTLY 'MONG THE DEW, ...   67 HAPPY SHEPHERD V   52
THE DEW DROPS, FOR THE SOUND OF THEIR OWN DROPPING-- . .   68 SAD SHEPHERD   V   16
IT QUENCHED, WITH SOUND LIKE FALLING DEW, ...   86 MAD KING GOLL   66
OF DEW ON THE YOUNG STREAMS. . . . .   88 STOLEN CHILD   V   37
WHO HAVE SOUGHT MORE THAN IS IN RAIN OR DEW . . . . .   114 ROSE OF BATTLE   16
. . . HUNG LOW IN THE FALL OF THE DEW! . . . . . .   122 WHITE BIRDS   7
. . . DEW DABBLED, THE LILY AND ROSE! . . . .   122 WHITE BIRDS   V   5
SIGH, HEART, AGAIN IN THE DEW OF THE MORN. . . . . . .   147 INTO TWILIGHT   4
DEW EVER SHINING AND TWILIGHT GREY! . . . .   148 INTO TWILIGHT   6
AND HOPE IS LESS DEAR THAN THE DEW OF THE MORN. . . . .   148 INTO TWILIGHT   16
THE WEST WEEPS IN PALE DEW AND SIGHS PASSING AWAY, . . .   154 BELOVED PEACE   5
FOR HOURS WHEN ALL MUST FADE LIKE DEW, ...   156 FORGOT BEAUTY   20
THE GREY CAIRN ON THE HILL, WHEN DAY SINKS DROWNED IN DEW,   161 BLACK PIG   6
THE DEW DROPS SLOWLY! THE DREAMS GATHER! UNKNOWN SPEARS   161 BLACK PIG   V   1
AND THEREFORE MY HEART WILL BOW, WHEN DEW . . . . . .   164 PERFECT BEAUTY   6
IN TWILIGHTS OF DEW AND OF FIRE." . . . .   168 BLESSED   40
IN TWILIGHTS OF DEW AND FIRE!" . . . .   168 BLESSED   V   40
WHO MET FAND WALKING AMONG FLAMING DEW . . . .   169 SECRET ROSE   13
THAT IT MAY DROP FAINT PERFUME, AND BE HEAVY WITH DEW, . .   172 TRAV PASSION   7
ABOUNDING FOLIAGE MOISTENED WITH THE DEW! . . . . . .   500 VACILLATION   13
ALL THINGS HANG LIKE A DROP OF DEW . . . .   505 GRAT INSTRUCT   3
THERE THE SILVER DEW . . . .   611 NEWS ORACLE   2
CATCHING SMALL BIRDS IN THE DEW OF THE MORN . . . . .   636 BLACK TOWER   22
WITH DEW, AS THOUGH 'TWERE SEALING THEM FOR DEATH. . . .   691 MOSADA 1   22

	PAGE	TITLE	LINE
DEW (CONTINUED)			
AND SEE HOW THICK THE DEW LIES ON MY FACE.	703	MOSADA 3	104
AND CLINGING WITH THE DEW OF ODOROUS SHOWERS, ...	704	REMEMBRANCE	4
GATHERING MUSHROOMS IN THE DEW.	705	DAWN-SONG	8
GATHERING MUSHROOMS IN THE DEW.	705	DAWN-SONG	16
SHOWERED AWAY THE KEEN DEW DROPS:	705	DAWN-SONG	18
GATHERING MUSHROOMS IN THE DEW.	706	DAWN-SONG	24
GATHERING MUSHROOMS IN THE DEW.	706	DAWN-SONG	32
AND AWAY IN THE WOODS WE WILL SCATTER THE DEW:	717	LOVE SONG	2
FOR GOD IS WALKING IN THE DEW, ...	736	SUMMER EVENING	15
AND TEARS OF FIRE FALL GENTLY IN THE DEW.	738	YOU ARE SAD	4
IN A WOOD OF DEW AND MOSS, ...	744	ROSY CROSS	5
LET THE DEW BEAR WITNESS.	770	BLOOD BOND	11
WHERE THE DEW IS MADE BEFORE DAWN:	771	SPINNING SONG	5
DEW-BEDROWNED			
I NEVER KNEW A NIGHT SO DEW-BEDROWNED.	703	MOSADA 3	105
DEW-BLANCHED			
AND DEW-BLANCHED HORNS, IN WHOSE HOLLOW A CHILD OF THREE	49	OISIN 3	30
YEARS OLD			
AND DEW-BLANCHED HORNS, IN WHOSE HOLLOWS A CHILD OF THREE	49	OISIN 3	V 31
YEARS OLD			
DEW-COLD			
THE DEW-COLD LILIES LADIES BORE	156	FORGOT BEAUTY	11
DEW-CUMBERED			
. . . NOR GO FROM HIS DEW-CUMBERED SKIES:	49	OISIN 3	38
DEW-DABBLED			
. . . DEW-DABBLED, THE LILY AND ROSE:	122	WHITE BIRDS	5
DEW-DRENCH'D			
'TIS MORN, AND FROM THE DEW-DRENCH'D WOOD I'VE SPED . . .	645	ISLE STAT I 1	6
DEW-DROP			
LOW, LONG AND MUSICAL. A DEW-DROP HUNG	689	NETTLESHIP	9
DEW-DROPPING			
AND THE LONG DEW-DROPPING HOURS OF THE NIGHT, ...	116	FAERY SONG	7
AND STARS CLIMBING THE DEW-DROPPING SKY, ...	158	BELOVED RHYMES	11
DEWDROPS			
HER EYES WERE SOFT AS DEWDROPS HANGING	3	OISIN 1	V 7HH
WHERE WHITE DEWDROPS IN MILLIONS FALL:	16	OISIN 1	V 222
AND CAME TO WHERE THE DEWDROPS FALL	20	OISIN 1	293
CRIED ALL HIS STORY TO THE DEWDROPS GLISTENING.	68	SAD SHEPHERD	14
THE DEWDROPS, FOR THE SOUND OF THEIR OWN DROPPING. . . .	68	SAD SHEPHERD	16
DEW-DROWNED			
AND WHEN THE DEW-DROWNED STARS HANG IN THE AIR	32	OISIN 2	54
SEE! OH, SEE! THE DEW-DROWNED BUNCHES	655	ISLE STAT I 3	1
DEWS			
. . . THEIR DIMNESS, THEIR DEWS DROPPING SLEEP.	54	OISIN 3	108
THE DEWS DROP SLOWLY AND DREAMS GATHER: UNKNOWN SPEARS . .	161	BLACK PIG	1
DEW-WASHED			
WHEN THE EARLIEST DEW-WASHED STAR FROM EVE HATH LEANT, . .	32	OISIN 2	V 54
DEWY			
OR DOWN THE DEWY FOREST ALLEYS, ...	10	OISIN 1	120
AND DOWN THE DEWY FOREST ALLEYS, ...	10	OISIN 1	V 120
DANAAN SONGS, AND THEIR DEWY SHOWERS	11	OISIN 1	135
SANG NIAM, AND THEIR DEWY SHOWERS	11	OISIN 1	V 135
FROM DEWY EYES: "UPON THE DEAD	21	OISIN 1	310
OR WRESTLE WITH THEIR PEERS IN DEWY VALLEYS.	30	OISIN 2	V 14E
GATHERED IN SILENCE, DEWY AS HER EYES, ...	80	EPHEMERA	19
O HIDING HAIR AND DEWY EYES, ...	152	HEART OF WOMAN	9
BLOSSOMS OPEN DEWY LIPS:	647	ISLE STAT I 1	65
IF SO I MIGHT, ALONG A DEWY VALE, ...	649	ISLE STAT I 1	123
WITH QUIET SHADE ITS EVER DEWY SPOT, ...	714	FERENCZ RENYI	V 109
WITH QUIET SHADE ITS EVER DEWY PLOT.	714	FERENCZ RENYI	V 109
DEWY-PLOT			
WITH QUIET SHADE ITS EVER DEWY-PLOT.	714	FERENCZ RENYI	109
DEWY-TONGUED			
DEWY-TONGUED, THE DAISY TOPS--	706	DAWN-SONG	22
DIAGRAM			
A DIAGRAM HUNG THERE INSTEAD, ...	485	STATISTICS	3
DIALOGUE			
A DIALOGUE OF SELF AND SOUL	477	SELF AND SOUL	T
A DIALOGUE	499	VACILLATION	V T
DIARMUID			
THAT MADE HER DIARMUID DEAR, AND SOME OLD CARDINAL . . .	366	HER COURAGE	6
DICE			
WHILE THEIR GREAT WOODEN DICE BEAT ON THE BOARD.	412	TOWER	88
I LOSE! THEY'RE LOADED DICE. TIME ALWAYS PLAYS	721	WITCH VIVIEN	44
WITH LOADED DICE. ANOTHER CHANCE! COME, FATHER! . . .	721	WITCH VIVIEN	45
DICK			
COME TOM AND DICK, COME ALL THE TROOP	582	ROGER CASEMENT	17
DIDO			
OF SAD QUEEN DIDO SHONE THE LAPPING FIRE	645	ISLE STAT I 1	9
DIDO'S			
I SAW HIM FROM SAD DIDO'S SHORES DEPART, ...	677	ISLE STAT II 3	288
DIE			
SLEEP THERE TILL THE MOON AND THE STARS DIE!"	17	OISIN 1	246
AND EARTH AND HEAVEN AND HELL WOULD DIE, ...	19	OISIN 1	271
THE UNIVERSE HERSELF WOULD DIE, ...	19	OISIN 1	V 271
O'ER MEN WHO SLEEP, AND WAKE, AND DIE, ...	22	OISIN 1	V 340B
OR LOVE'S FIRST TENDERNESS DIE IN OUR GAZE.	27	OISIN 1	411
OR LOVE'S FIRST TENDERNESS DIE IN OUR GAZE.	27	OISIN 1	V 419D
OR LOVE'S FIRST TENDERNESS DIE IN OUR GAZE."	28	OISIN 1	V 427
"THIS DEMON SHALL BE BATTERED TILL HE DIE, ...	35	OISIN 2	90

	PAGE	TITLE		LINE

DIE   (CONTINUED)

	PAGE	TITLE		LINE
"THIS DEMON SHALL BE PIERCED AND DROP AND DIE,	35	OISIN 2	V	90
"I WOULD DIE LIKE A SMALL WITHERED LEAF IN THE AUTUMN, . . .	56	OISIN 3		131
AND DIE A PEARLY BROTHERHOOD!	66	HAPPY SHEPHERD		42
HOW WHEN WE DIE OUR SHADES WILL ROVE,	78	INDIAN TO LOVE		18
HOW WHEN WE DIE OUR SHADES MAY ROVE,	78	INDIAN TO LOVE	V	18
DIE OFF THE FEEBLE SOUNDS!	99	FOXHUNTER	V	42
BUT WHEREFORE NOW?" "THERE IS A MAN TO DIE!	107	CUCHULAIN SEA		23
OF THEIR SAD HEARTS, THAT MAY NOT LIVE NOR DIE.	114	ROSE OF BATTLE		24
OF OUR SAD HEARTS, THAT MAY NOT LIVE NOR DIE.	115	ROSE OF BATTLE		36
HAS AWAKED IN OUR HEARTS, MY BELOVED, A SADNESS THAT MAY NOT DIE.	122	WHITE BIRDS		4
HAS AWAKED IN OUR HEARTS, MY BELOVED, A SADNESS THAT NEVER MAY DIE.	122	WHITE BIRDS	V	4
FOR PEOPLE DIE AND DIE",	132	FR GILLIGAN		10
FOR PEOPLE DIE AND DIE",	132	FR GILLIGAN		10
FROM OUR BIRTHDAY, UNTIL WE DIE,	139	TO IRELAND		35
"I WILL SEND THEM TO HER AND DIE"!	160	CAP AND BELLS		22
AND WHEN IT IS GONE WE DIE!	168	BLESSED	V	30
LIKE THE SPARKS BLOWN OUT OF A SMITHY, AND DIE?	170	SECRET ROSE		30
"SHE WILL GROW OLD AND DIE, AND SHE HAS WEPT!"	186	QUEEN MAEVE		138
WE SAW THE LAST EMBERS OF DAYLIGHT DIE,	205	ADAMS CURSE		29
I AM A WOMAN, I DIE AT EVERY BREATH.	250	SHADOW WATER B		583
BEFORE WE GROW OLD AND DIE.	261	DRINKING SONG		4
SOLDIERS THAT GAVE, WHATEVER DIE WAS CAST!	269	PARDON FATHERS		9
HER LOVE, AND WOULD NOT HAVE ME DIE,	274	GREY ROCK		87
AND SHOULD HE DIE TO HEAP HIS BURIAL-MOUND	280	TWO KINGS		82
AND SHOULD HE DIE TO HEAP HIS BURIAL MOUND	280	TWO KINGS	V	82
LIVE HE OR DIE	310	PEACOCK		7
THAT EVEN THE BEST OF LOVE MUST DIE,	314	MEMORY YOUTH		17
BEING OLD, BUT THAT THE OLD ALONE MIGHT DIE,	339	SHEP GOATHERD		4
LAMENTING THAT A MAN SHOULD DIE!	361	ALF POLLEXFEN		38
IT IS ABOUT TO DIE.	367	HER CHRIS TREE		12
TO DIE INTO THE LABYRINTH OF ITSELF!	374	PHASES OF MOON		55
THERE CAN BE NOTHING SOLIDER TILL I DIE!	383	VISION ROBART		26
AS THOUGH TO DIE BY GUNSHOT WERE	424	ROAD AT DOOR		4
ERE THE ONE OR T'OTHER DIE.	508	JANE BISHOP	V	5
DID HE DIE OR DID SHE DIE?	514	JANE GROWN OLD		15
DID HE DIE OR DID SHE DIE?	514	JANE GROWN OLD		15
SEEMED TO DIE OR DIED THEY BOTH?	514	JANE GROWN OLD		16
SEEM TO DIE OR DIED THEY BOTH?	514	JANE GROWN OLD	V	16
ALL TRUE LOVE MUST DIE,	517	HER ANXIETY		3
IN THAT FAITH I LIVE OR DIE.	529	TOM LUNATIC		18
SAVING THE RHYME RATS HEAR BEFORE THEY DIE.	542	PARN FUNERAL 1		28
THAT I MAY SEEM, THOUGH I DIE OLD,	553	PRAYER OLD AGE		11
WHAT CAN THEY KNOW THAT WE KNOW THAT KNOW THE TIME TO DIE?	580	CURSE CROMWELL		14
"NOT TO DIE ON THE STRAW AT HOME,	587	OLD WICKED MAN		5
"THEN WANT BEFORE YOU DIE."	596	COLONEL MARTIN		67
TO FOLLOW IS TO DIE!	600	SPIRIT MEDIUM		18
BUT HAD GONE OUT TO DIE	608	SONGS BURDEN		20
OF GOD OR WOMAN, THE TIME WERE COME TO DIE."	609	IN TARAS HALLS		15
(SOMETHING MAY LINGER THERE THOUGH ALL ELSE DIE!)	618	BRONZE HEAD		5
SLEEPLESS WOULD LIE DOWN AND DIE.	632	MAN AND ECHO		18
LIE DOWN AND DIE. THAT WERE TO SHIRK	632	MAN AND ECHO		19
"OR DRIVEN FROM HOME AND LEFT TO DIE IN FEAR."	635	CUCHULAIN COMF		22
WHETHER MAN DIE IN HIS BED	637	BEN BULBEN		17
SOME CAST OF DIE, OR LET SOME ARROW GLANCE	656	ISLE STAT I 3		40
TO DIE FOR HER IN AIR OR GROUND,	668	ISLE STAT II 3		52
THAT ONE SHALL DIE, UNLESS ONE DIE FOR HER.	669	ISLE STAT II 3		74
THAT ONE SHALL DIE, UNLESS ONE DIE FOR HER.	669	ISLE STAT II 3		74
I DREAM!--I CANNOT DIE!--NO! NO!	675	ISLE STAT II 3		227
AND CROUCH IN SOME FAR STILLNESS OF THE ISLE, AND DIE.	675	ISLE STAT II 3		246
I DREAM!--I CANNOT DIE!--NOT DIE! NO! NO!	675	ISLE STAT II 3	V	227
I DREAM!--I CANNOT DIE!--NOT DIE! NO! NO!	675	ISLE STAT II 3	V	227
IN A FAR STILLNESS OF THE ISLAND DIE.	675	ISLE STAT II 3	V	246
UNTIL WE DIE WITHIN THE CHARMED RING	679	ISLE STAT II 3		322
THEN LET ME SEE THY FACE BEFORE I DIE.	684	SEEKER		66
WHAT, LOVER, DIE BEFORE OUR LIPS HAVE MET?	685	SEEKER		80
WE TWO, BEFORE WE DIE! FOR AZOLAR,	691	MOSADA 1		24
FORGIVE, OR I WILL DIE. 'TWAS ALLAH'S WILL.	695	MOSADA 1		118
I WILL NOT HEAR! THE MOORISH GIRL MUST DIE.	697	MOSADA 2		39
OH, GOD!--AWAKE! THOU SHALT NOT DIE. SHE SLEEPS,	701	MOSADA 3		66
LOVE, WILL YOU DIE WHEN WE HAVE MET? ONE LOOK	703	MOSADA 3		109
WE GATHERED. FERENCZ, NAY, I MUST NOT DIE!	713	FERENCZ RENYI		96
WE GATHERED. FERENCZ, DO NOT LET ME DIE.	713	FERENCZ RENYI	V	96
"ASSASSIN, MY ASSASSIN! THOU WHO LET'ST ME DIE,	714	FERENCZ RENYI		106
DEFEAT IS DEATH. SHOULD MY PLOTS FAIL I'D DIE.	722	WITCH VIVIEN		52
I HAVE GOOD PILOTS, AIBRIC. WHEN MEN DIE	750	SHADOW WATER A		81
HOW ALL THAT DIE ARE BORNE ABOUT THE WORLD	750	SHADOW WATER A		84
BE PULLERS OF THE OAR UNTIL YOU DIE?	757	SHADOW WATER A		217
WITH ONE YOU HAVE KILLED AND DIE! FOR WHEN I LEFT	758	SHADOW WATER A		226
WITH SOME YOU HAVE KILLED AND DIE! FOR WHEN I LEFT	758	SHADOW WATER A	V	226
FORGAEL CAN DIE TO-MORROW. COME TO THE ALE.	759	SHADOW WATER A		246
COME TO THE ALE! FOR HE CAN DIE TO-MORROW.	760	SHADOW WATER A		247
MAYBE I SHALL NOT DIE AT ALL.	788	HAWTHORN TREE		16
MAY BE I SHALL NOT DIE AT ALL.	788	HAWTHORN TREE	V	16

DIED

	PAGE	TITLE		LINE
UNDER THE SHADOWS TILL THE TUMULTS DIED	38	OISIN 2		140
IT DIED AFAR. GREY SLEET THOSE TOWERS HID	46	OISIN 2	V	245
BUT IF WHEN ANYONE DIED	92	FATHER OHART		21

204

PAGE   TITLE   LINE

DIED (CONTINUED)
BUT IF WHEN ANY ONE DIED,   92 FATHER OHART   V   21
FOR HE'D DIED AT NINETY-FOUR.   93 FATHER OHART   28
AND THE WAVES FLOWED ABOVE HIM AND HE DIED.   111 CUCHULAIN SEA   V   86
AND USNA'S CHILDREN DIED.   111 ROSE OF WORLD   5
I DREAMED THAT ONE HAD DIED IN A STRANGE PLACE   123 DREAM OF DEATH   1
"MAVRONE, MAVRONE! THE MAN HAS DIED   133 FR GILLIGAN   25
"HE DIED AN HOUR AGO."   133 FR GILLIGAN   34
"WHEN YOU WERE GONE, HE TURNED AND DIED   133 FR GILLIGAN   37
"OCHONE, OCHONE! THE MAN HAS DIED,   133 FR GILLIGAN   V   25
WHERE THE LAST PHOENIX DIED,   162 ASKS FORGIVE   16
TILL VAIN FRENZY AWOKE AND HE DIED! AND HIM   169 SECRET ROSE   12
TILL IT DIED OUT WHERE AN OLD THORN-TREE STOOD.   186 QUEEN MAEVE   129
AND WHEN I'VE HEARD HOW THEY GREW OLD AND DIED,   186 QUEEN MAEVE   136
TILL IT DIED OUT WHERE AN OLD THORN TREE STOOD.   186 QUEEN MAEVE   V 129
SHE FELL AND DIED OF THE HEART-BREAK."   191 BAILE AILLINN   64
AND THEN ONE ASKS ANOTHER HOW HE DIED,   234 SHADOW WATER B   256
MY HUSBAND AND MY KING DIED AT MY FEET,   237 SHADOW WATER B   337
I KNOW THAT HE DIED A THOUSAND YEARS AGO,   241 SHADOW WATER B   392
IT WAS GOLDEN-ARMED IOLLAN, AND HE DIED   242 SHADOW WATER B   406
AND THAT HE DIED A THOUSAND YEARS AGO.   242 SHADOW WATER B   417
SINCE, TAVERN COMRADES, YOU HAVE DIED,   273 GREY ROCK   49
AND THE WORLD'S ALTERED SINCE YOU DIED,   276 GREY ROCK   126
FOR THIS EDWARD FITZGERALD DIED,   290 SEPTEMBER 1913   20
AND DIED IN THE GREAT WAR BEYOND THE SEA.   339 SHEP GOATHERD   22
AND OF A RED-HAIRED YEATS WHOSE LOOKS, ALTHOUGH HE DIED   391 UNDER SATURN   9
BEWILDERED THEM TILL THEY DIED?   394 EASTER 1916   73
THAT THE WORST ROGUES AND RASCALS HAD DIED OUT.   428 NINETEEN 19   16
WHERE HOLY DIONYSUS DIED,   437 SONGS PLAY 1   2
THE GARDEN DIED!   439 FRAGMENTS   2
NOTHING COULD BRING HIM, WHEN HIS LADY DIED,   471 ALL SOUL NIGHT   25
MANY TIMES HE DIED,   476 DEATH   5
A SPOT WHEREON THE FOUNDERS LIVED AND DIED   491 COOLE BALLYLEE   33
SEEMED TO DIE OR DIED THEY BOTH?   514 JANE GROWN OLD   16
SEEM TO DIE OR DIED THEY BOTH?   514 JANE GROWN OLD V   16
O'HIGGINS ITS SOLE STATESMAN HAD NOT DIED.   543 PARN FUNERAL 2   8
BUT HE KICKED BEFORE HE DIED,   545 TO SAME TUNE 1   25
JUSTIFY ALL THAT HAVE DIED ON THE SCAFFOLD,   546 TO SAME TUNE 2   13
TROY BACKED ITS HELEN! TROY DIED AND ADORED!   547 TO SAME TUNE 3   4
TROY LOOKED ON HELEN, IT DIED AND ADORED!   547 TO SAME TUNE 3 V   4
THE SWORD'S A CROSS! THEREON HE DIED!   562 CONJUNCTIONS   3
HE DROPPED UPON HIS HEAD AND DIED.   571 THREE BUSHES   52
AND DROPPED AND DIED THEREON, FOR SHE   571 THREE BUSHES   54
"THIS LAND OF SAINTS," AND THEN AS THE APPLAUSE DIED OUT,   577 LOFTY THINGS   3
HE DIED UPON THE GALLOWS.   581 ROGER CASEMENT   3
"HERE DIED THE O'RAHILLY.   585 ORAHILLY   34
CLOSE TO THE CITY HALL HE DIED!   608 SONGS BURDEN 3   12
LAY IN THE COFFIN, STOPPED HIS BREATH AND DIED.   609 IN TARAS HALLS   20
REMEMBER ALL THAT HAVE DIED ON THE SCAFFOLD,   613 MARCH SONGS 1   13
TROY BACKED ITS HELEN! TROY DIED AND ADORED!   614 MARCH SONGS 2   4
BUT HE KICKED BEFORE HE DIED,   616 MARCH SONGS 3   25
IF HE DIED LONG AGO   635 BLACK TOWER   15
AND MANNED AN ARGOSY AND SAILING DIED.   693 MOSADA 1   89
HOW MANY MOONS HAVE DIED FROM THE FULL MOON   747 SHADOW WATER A   10
AND THEN ONE ASKS ANOTHER HOW HE DIED,   753 SHADOW WATER A   146
THIS BLADE OUT OF MY HAND AND DIED OF A SUDDEN.   755 SHADOW WATER A   168
SHE CAUGHT THIS BLADE OUT OF MY BELT AND DIED.   755 SHADOW WATER A V   168
UNTIL HE HAD DIED OF HIS WOUNDS,   775 AGAINST WITCH   16
YOUR OWN THOUGHT WILL HAVE DIED   786 YOUR HEART   30
HER OWN THOUGHT WILL HAVE DIED   786 YOUR HEART   V   30
YOU HAD BROUGHT DOWN BEFORE YOU DIED.   791 REPRISALS   2
DIES
UPON THE LIFE THAT FADES AND FLICKERS AND DIES,   29 OISIN 2   12
PATRICK, BEFORE THY CRAFT DIES EACH OLD SONG.   42 OISIN 2   V 196
HIS PURPOSE DRIFTS AND DIES."   45 OISIN 2   244
AND WHEN THE WANDERING MUSIC DIES   99 FOXHUNTER   31
AND ALL THEIR TROUBLE DIES INTO ITS PEACE!—   128 DREAM OF FAERY V   35
AND MEN WHO LOVED THE CAUSE THAT NEVER DIES.   130 BOOK STORIES   V   24
OF THE WOMAN THAT HE LOVES, UNTIL HE DIES.   177 PAST GREATNESS   10
OUR COURAGE BREAKS LIKE AN OLD TREE IN A BLACK WIND AND   207 HANRAHANS SONG   3
    DIES,
LIKE TUFTED REEDS OUR COURAGE DROOPS IN A BLACK WIND AND   207 HANRAHANS SONG V   3
    DIES!
WEAK AND WORN AND WEARY OUR COURAGE DROOPS AND DIES   207 HANRAHANS SONG V   8
FOR ALL HIS SPELLS WILL VANISH WHEN HE DIES,   240 SHADOW WATER B   376
THE LAST STROKE OF MIDNIGHT DIES.   357 BROKEN DREAMS   37
WHATEVER IS BEGOTTEN, BORN, AND DIES.   407 SAIL BYZANTIUM   6
WHATEVER IS BEGOTTEN BORN OR DIES,   407 SAIL BYZANTIUM V   6
FOR BEAUTY DIES OF BEAUTY, WORTH OF WORTH,   564 GYRES   3
MANY TIMES MAN LIVES AND DIES   637 BEN BULBEN   13
BUT SOULLESS A FAIRY DIES,   643 SONG FAERIES   2
FOR SOULLESS A FAIRY DIES,   644 SONG FAERIES   14
BUT SOULLESS A FAERY DIES,   676 ISLE STAT II 3   249
FOR SOULLESS A FAERY DIES,   676 ISLE STAT II 3   261
THE VERY SQUIRREL DIES THAT ENTERS THERE.   682 SEEKER   33
THE VERY SQUIRREL DIES THAT ENTERS IT.   682 SEEKER   V   33
A LITTLE WHILE AND—RED EVE DIES—   686 LIFE   13
ALL DIES AMONG THOSE STREAMS. THE FOOL HAS MADE   764 SHADOW WATER A   335
THAT DIES OUT BEFORE 'TIS DAY,   777 SONG DEIRDRE 2   8
DIETH
AND MY SOUL IN WAITING DIETH,   648 ISLE STAT I 1   87

205

DIETH (CONTINUED)
    EVER DIETH, DIETH, DIETH. . . . . 648 ISLE STAT I 1   88
    EVER DIETH, DIETH, DIETH. . . . . 648 ISLE STAT I 1   88
    EVER DIETH, DIETH, DIETH. . . . . 648 ISLE STAT I 1   88
    THAT DIETH SLOW WITH SUNSICK DOOM. . . . . 655 ISLE STAT I 3   12
DIFFERENT
    YET THEY WERE OF A DIFFERENT KIND. . . . . 289 SEPTEMBER 1913   9
    SO WE SPEAK A DIFFERENT TONGUE. . . . . 313 TWO YEAR LATER   6
    ACCORDING TO A DIFFERENT PLAN. . . . . 379 SAINT HUNCH   6
    THEY SAY SUCH DIFFERENT THINGS AT SCHOOL. . . . . 387 ROBARTES DANCE   52
    ALL THAT ARE DIFFERENT OF A BASE INTENT; . . . . . 398 LEADERS CROWD   2
    SOME FOUND A DIFFERENT POLE, AND WHERE IT STOOD . . . . 483 VERONIC NAPKIN   7
DIFFERENTLY
    I'LL SHOW YOU THAT I AM MADE DIFFERENTLY, ... 227 SHADOW WATER B   119
DIFFICULT
    THAT WORK TOO DIFFICULT FOR MORTAL HANDS . . . . . 182 QUEEN MAEVE   67
    THE FASCINATION OF WHAT'S DIFFICULT . . . . 260 FASC DIFFICULT   T
    THE FASCINATION OF WHAT'S DIFFICULT . . . . 260 FASC DIFFICULT   1
    THAT IS MOST DIFFICULT. . . . . 291 TO A FRIEND   16
    HE FOLLOWS WHATEVER WHIM'S MOST DIFFICULT . . . . . 374 PHASES OF MOON   40
    CHOOSING WHATEVER TASK'S MOST DIFFICULT . . . . . . 376 PHASES OF MOON   91
DIG
    WHO DIG OLD CUSTOMS UP. . . . . 93 FATHER OHART   40
    "COME OUT AND DIG FOR A DEAD MAN, ... 272 GREY ROCK   32
    "WHO'D CARE TO DIG 'EM," SAID THE OLD, OLD MAN, ... 548 TO SAME TUNE 3   7
    "WHO'D CARE TO DIG 'EM," SAID THE OLD, OLD MAN, ... 548 TO SAME TUNE 3   17
    "WHO'D CARE TO DIG 'EM," SAID THE OLD, OLD MAN, ... 549 TO SAME TUNE 3   27
DIGEST
    MARK AND DIGEST MY TALE, CARRY IT AFAR . . . . . . 554 RIBH AT TOMB   3
DIGGERS   SEE GRAVE-DIGGERS GRAVE-DIGGERS'
    DIGGERS AND CARPENTERS MAKE GRAVE AND COFFIN; . . . . . 609 IN TARAS HALLS   17
DIGGES
    THEN THAT OLD ABBEY ACTOR, DUDLEY DIGGES, ... 790 DEDICATION   7
DIGGING
    AND SET THEM DIGGING UNDER BUAL'S HILL. . . . . . 184 QUEEN MAEVE   93
    AND SET THEM DIGGING INTO ANBUAL'S HILL. . . . . . 184 QUEEN MAEVE V 93
    AND SET THEM DIGGING IN THE WEST OF THE HILL. . . . . 184 QUEEN MAEVE V 93
DIGNITY
    --IT HAD SUCH DIGNITY OF LIMB-- . . . . 254 HIS DREAM   11
    BECAUSE IT HAD SUCH DIGNITY. . . . . 254 HIS DREAM   19
    A FARMER HAS MORE DIGNITY." . . . . 296 THREE BEGGARS   37
    THERE IS A SOLID DIGNITY . . . . 296 THREE BEGGARS V 37
    HUMAN DIGNITY . . . . 452 HUMAN DIGNITY   T
    FROM HUMAN DIGNITY. . . . . 452 HUMAN DIGNITY   12
DIGS
    HE DIGS HIS CABBAGES. HE BRINGS TO MIND . . . . . . 696 MOSADA 2   18
DILIGENCE
    I STUDY HATRED WITH GREAT DILIGENCE, ... 558 RIBH CHRISTIAN   3
DIM
    TO THIS DIM SHORE THOSE GENTLE FEET? . . . . 5 OISIN 1 V 51
    TO THIS DIM SHORE ON FOAM WET FEET? . . . . 5 OISIN 1 V 51
    TO THIS DIM SHORE ON FOAM-WET FEET? . . . . 5 OISIN 1 V 51
    THE RED SUN FALLS AND THE WORLD GROWS DIM." . . . . 9 OISIN 1   105
    WAS DIM WITH MIRE OF A MORTAL SHORE, ... 15 OISIN 1   208
    WAS DIM WITH THE MIRE OF A MORTAL SHORE, ... 15 OISIN 1 V 208
    THAT KEPT DIM WATERS FROM THE SKY; . . . . 17 OISIN 1   243
    AND SHOWED THEIR EYES WITH TEARDROPS DIM, ... 18 OISIN 1   256
    ON THE DEAD DIM EARTH ENCLOSES; . . . . 21 OISIN 1   312
    UNCHAINABLE AS THE DIM TIDE, ... 22 OISIN 1   338
    I HEARD ONE SAY, "HIS EYES GROW DIM . . . . 25 OISIN 1   380
    YET LOVE AND KISS ON DIM SHORES FAR AWAY . . . . . 29 OISIN 2   13
    BUT LOVE AND KISS ON DIM SHORES FAR AWAY . . . . . 29 OISIN 2 V 13
    THAT WITH DIM EYEBALLS STOOD ON EITHER SIDE. . . . 34 OISIN 2   75
    FOR THEIR DIM MINDS WERE WITH THE ANCIENT THINGS. . 34 OISIN 2   77
    STOOD LONELY, WITH DIM EYEBALLS ON EACH SIDE, . . . 34 OISIN 2 V 74
    IN SOME DIM MEMORY OR ANCIENT MOOD, ... 36 OISIN 2   99
    WRAPT ROUND IN SOME DIM MEMORY, IT SEEMED-- . . . . 36 OISIN 2 V 99
    PASSED UNDER THE DIM DOORWAY, OUT OF SIGHT, ... 37 OISIN 2   123
    PASSED UNDER A DIM DOORWAY, OUT OF SIGHT, ... 37 OISIN 2 V 123
    NO CENTURIES COULD THIN, AND A WORD RAN . . . . . 38 OISIN 2   127
    THE LEAST OF DOORS; BEYOND ON A DIM PLAIN . . . . . 39 OISIN 2   155
    THEN IN THAT HALL, LIT BY THE DIM SEA-SHINE, . . . 41 OISIN 2   187
    THEN IN THAT HALL, LIT BY THE DIM SEA SHINE, . . . 41 OISIN 2 V 187
    . . . FLUNG LOOSELY ALONG THE DIM GROUND; . . . . 50 OISIN 3   45
    SORRY PLACE, WHERE FOR SWING OF THE WAR-AXE IN MY DIM EYES   61 OISIN 3   194
    . . .
    CRIED OUT, DIM SEA, HEAR MY MOST PITEOUS STORY! . . . . 68 SAD SHEPHERD   9
    RAGING AT HIS OWN IMAGE IN THE DIM ENAMELLED SEA . . . . 77 INDIAN TO LOVE V 5
    THE DIM GREY SANDS WITH LIGHT, ... 87 STOLEN CHILD   14
    OR DO YOU LONG FOR THE DIM SLEEPY GROUND, ... 109 CUCHULAIN SEA   60
    BOW DOWN, ARCHANGELS, IN YOUR DIM ABODE! . . . . . 112 ROSE OF WORLD   11
    YOU, TOO, HAVE COME WHERE THE DIM TIDES ARE HURLED . . . 115 ROSE OF BATTLE   26
    MADE YOU OF US, AND OF THE DIM GREY SEA. . . . . . 115 ROSE OF BATTLE   30
    AND THE WHITE BREAST OF THE DIM SEA . . . . 126 GOES FERGUS   11
    UPON A DIM, GREEN, WELL-BELOVED ISLE, ... 126 DREAM OF FAERY V 8
    AND CHAPLET THEIR CALM BROWS WITH LEAFAGE DIM, ... 127 DREAM OF FAERY V 32
    IN THE DIM GLASS THE DEMONS HOLD, ... 135 TWO TREES   30
    OF THE DIM WISDOMS OLD AND DEEP, ... 138 TO IRELAND V 21
    THAT YOU, IN THE DIM COMING TIMES, ... 139 TO IRELAND   46
    AND DREAMED OF THE LONG DIM HAIR . . . . 144 HOST OF AIR   7
    OF HER LONG DIM HAIR. . . . . 145 HOST OF AIR   28

	PAGE	TITLE	LINE

DIM   (CONTINUED)

WERE DROWNED IN HER LONG DIM HAIR.	145	HOST OF AIR	36
PALE BROWS, STILL HANDS AND DIM HAIR,	152	LOSS OF LOVE	1
PALE BROW, STILL HANDS, AND DIM HAIR,	152	LOSS OF LOVE V	1
FOR THAT DIM BROW AND LINGERING HAND .	156	FORGOT BEAUTY V	15
AND CANDLE-LIKE FOAM ON THE DIM SAND,	158	BELOVED RHYMES	10
WITH YOUR DIM HEAVY HAIR,	163	ASKS FORGIVE	22
WITH YOUR DIM SHADOWY HAIR,	163	ASKS FORGIVE V	22
WITH HER CLOUD-PALE EYELIDS HALF COVERING HER DIM EYES!	163	VALLEY LOVERS V	4
IN DRUID VAPOUR AND MAKE THE TORCHES DIM!	169	SECRET ROSE	11
DIM POWERS OF DROWSY THOUGHT, LET HER NO LONGER BE	175	ELEMENT POWERS	13
WHEN WINDS HAVE GATHERED AND SUN AND MOON BURNED DIM	175	ELEMENT POWERS	15
THE BLUE AND THE DIM AND THE DARK CLOTHS	176	CLOTHS HEAVEN	3
THEIR BODICES IN SOME DIM PLACE	193	BAILE AILLINN	105
THAT OLD MAN CLIMBED! THE DAY GREW DIM!	194	BAILE AILLINN	134
SCALE RUBBING SCALE WHERE LIGHT IS DIM	195	BAILE AILLINN	145
OF MORNING LIGHT IN A DIM SKY,	195	BAILE AILLINN	150
I KNOW WHERE A DIM MOON DRIFTS, WHERE THE DANAAN KIND	203	WITHER BOUGHS	12
NOR LANDS THAT SEEM TOO DIM TO BE BURDENS ON THE HEART!	209	UNDER THE MOON	5
DIM PAIRC-NA-CARRAIG, WHERE THE WILD BEES FLING	217	WOODS OF COOLE	9
DIM PAIRC-NA-TARAV, WHERE ENCHANTED EYES	217	WOODS OF COOLE	11
DIM INCHY WOOD, THAT HIDES BADGER AND FOX	218	WOODS OF COOLE	13
MADE OF DIM GOLD RAVE OUT IN SECRET TOMBS!	235	SHADOW WATER B	295
ALL THOSE HAD LIFTED UP THE DIM	272	GREY ROCK	27
AND EVEN OLD MEN'S EYES GREW DIM, THIS HAND ALONE,	314	FALLEN MAJESTY	2
BUT THE GOLDEN RACE LOOKS DIM,	530	DELPHIC ORACLE	4
THE SKIES MORE DIM, THOUGH BURNING LIKE A SHIELD,	656	ISLE STAT I 3	26
NOURISH THE PANTHERS IN DIM SOLITUDES!	657	ISLE STAT I 3	44
FROM THE DIM WOOD'S FOUNDATION--	672	ISLE STAT II 3	162
TO PLACE A KISS OF FIRE ON THE DIM BROW	688	TWO TITANS	47
NOR HEEDS THE OLD, DIM PROTEST AND THE CRY	689	NETTLESHIP	14
AND YON FEW STARS GROWN DIM, LIKE EYES OF LOVERS	700	MOSADA 3	33
AND HER DIM WAVE BIDS MAN BE NO MORE GLAD,	738	YOU ARE SAD	11
THAT THE RED RUST MAKES DIM."	740	EARL PAUL	20
AND STOOD IN HIS DIM ARMOUR,	741	EARL PAUL	33
THE DIM SPEAR MET THE BRIGHT SPEAR,	741	EARL PAUL	45
THE DIM SPEAR BREAKS THE BRIGHT SHIELD	741	EARL PAUL	49
THE DIM SPEAR MET THE BRIGHT SPEAR	741	EARL PAUL V	49
WITH A CLANG OF HIS DIM MAIL,	742	EARL PAUL	66
I FLING AWAY MY SWORD, BLOOD DIM,	743	DANAAN QUICK	20
MADE OF DIM GOLD, RAVE OUT IN SECRET TOMBS,	765	SHADOW WATER A	345

DIMINISHED

DIMINISHED BEAUTY, MULTIPLIED COMMONPLACE!	472	ALL SOUL NIGHT V	45
AND DANGER NOT BE DIMINISHED!	786	YOUR HEART	31

DIMLY

YET DIMLY DEEM I THAT THE MORNING RAYS	30	OISIN 2 V	20

DIMMED   SEE BLOOD-DIMMED PASSION-DIMMED DREAM-DIMMED

BY RIVERS WHERE THE RAIN HAS NEVER DIMMED	184	QUEEN MAEVE V	87
BY RIVERS WHERE NOR RAIN NOR HAIL HAS DIMMED	184	QUEEN MAEVE V	87
DIMMED AT THREE-QUARTER LIGHT,	786	YOUR HEART	32
DIMMED AT THREE QUARTER LIGHT	786	YOUR HEART V	32

DIMNESS

FILLING THE FIBROUS DIMNESS WITH LONG GENERATIONS OF EYES.	49	OISIN 3	40
. . . IN THE DIMNESS THEY LOVE GOING BY!	53	OISIN 3	98
. . . THEIR DIMNESS, THEIR DEWS DROPPING SLEEP.	54	OISIN 3	108
IN SHADOWY DIMNESS. TO BE FAIR AS THEE	670	ISLE STAT II 3	106
IN THE DEEP ALCOVES DIMNESS SMILES AND HIDES.	685	DRAWING-ROOM	4
AND ALL WAS DIMNESS, TILL A DYING LEAF	690	MOSADA 1	20
IN THE DEEP ALCOVE'S DIMNESS SMILES AND HIDES."	735	QUATRAIN APHOR	24
IN THE DEEP ALCOVES DIMNESS SMILES AND HIDES.	735	QUATRAIN APHOR V	24

DIMS

BUT THE LOVE-DEW DIMS OUR EYES TILL THE DAY	28	OISIN 1	424
LEAPS AND TIME'S OLD LANTHORN DIMS.	777	SONG DEIRDRE 2	5

DIN

WHILE THE WOOD-PECKER MADE A MERRY DIN,	44	OISIN 2 V	228
THE BLIND HOUND WITH A MOURNFUL DIN	99	FOXHUNTER	45
THE OLDEST HOUND WITH MOURNFUL DIN,	99	FOXHUNTER V	45
HE'D HEARD THAT DIN ON THE HORIZON'S EDGE	286	TWO KINGS	V 217A

DINE

AND I MAY DINE AT JOURNEY'S END	336	YOUNG BEAUTY	17
THAT I MAY DINE AT JOURNEY'S END	336	YOUNG BEAUTY V	17

DIONYSUS

WHERE HOLY DIONYSUS DIED,	437	SONGS PLAY 1	2

DIP

SHALL DIP HIS NOSE INTO MY LADLE	304	HOUR DAWN	53
TILL IT DIP AN AGEING WING	777	SONG DEIRDRE 2	3

DIPPED

LED BY A FOOTSOLE DIPPED IN BLOOD	274	GREY ROCK	78
LED BY A FOOT-SOLE DIPPED IN BLOOD	274	GREY ROCK V	78
HAD DIPPED THE WOODEN LADLE DEEP	304	HOUR DAWN	46
"BEFORE YOU HAVE DIPPED IT IN THE BEER	304	HOUR DAWN	49
AND WOULD HAVE DIPPED IT IN THE BEER	304	HOUR DAWN V	47
HE DIPPED HIS LADLE IN THE TUB	307	HOUR DAWN	107
A PATTERN ON A NAPKIN DIPPED IN BLOOD.	483	VERONIC NAPKIN	8

DIPPING

DIPPING HIS NOSE INTO MY LADLE	304	HOUR DAWN V	53

DIPS

WHERE DIPS THE ROCKY HIGHLAND	86	STOLEN CHILD	1

DIRGE

OH, HEART! HER DIRGE! WITH RUSHING ARMS THE WAVES	665	ISLE STAT II 2	70
THE DIRGE OF HER YE LOVE. CEASE!--CEASE!	665	ISLE STAT II 2	74

```
                                                   PAGE     TITLE           LINE
DIRT
    I KNELT IN THE DIRT. . . . . . . . . . . . . .  516 MANS SONG            15
    I LAY STRETCHED OUT IN THE DIRT  . . . . . . .  628 JANE MOUNTAIN        21
DIRTY
    AND DIRTY NAILS OF CARPENTERS. . . . . . . . .  440 WISDOM          V    7
    OR GROPE WITH A DIRTY HAND. . . . . . . . . . . 599 SPIRIT MEDIUM        8
    OR GROPE WITH A DIRTY HAND. . . . . . . . . . . 600 SPIRIT MEDIUM       16
    OR GROPE WITH A DIRTY HAND. . . . . . . . . . . 600 SPIRIT MEDIUM       24
    AS THAT WHICH CLEANS MAN'S DIRTY SLATE. . . . . 633 MAN AND ECHO        24
DISAPPEAR
    THAT FLESH AND BONE MAY DISAPPEAR, . . . . . .  307 HOUR DAWN          101
    APPEAR AND DISAPPEAR IN THE BLUE DEPTH OF THE SKY  . . .  318 MAGI        3
    APPEAR AND DISAPPEAR IN THE BLUE DEPTHS OF THE SKY  . . .  318 MAGI   V   3
DISASTER
    THE HORSES OF DISASTER PLUNGE IN THE HEAVY CLAY! . . . . 154 BELOVED PEACE   8
    THE HORSES OF DISASTER PLUNGE IN THE DESOLATE CLAY. . . . 154 BELOVED PEACE V 8
    NO MATTER WHAT DISASTER OCCURRED  . . . . . . .  578 CRAZED GIRL         9
DISASTROUS
    THE ONE DISASTROUS ZODIAC, MUTTERING . . . . .  282 TWO KINGS          128
DISCARD
    COULD WE BOTH DISCARD . . . . . . . . . . . . . 539 MEETING             16
DISCERNED
    SO IT'S PLAIN TO BE DISCERNED . . . . . . . . . 298 THREE HERMITS       16
    YET NO CLEAR FACT TO BE DISCERNED! . . . . . .  425 STARES NEST          9
DISCERNING
    OR THE DISCERNING EARS, . . . . . . . . . . . . 329 MEN IMPROVE          9
DISCIPLINE
    THAT ARE OUR SECRET DISCIPLINE . . . . . . . .  326 ROBERT GREGORY      68
    THE STRANGE REWARD OF ALL THAT DISCIPLINE. . .  374 PHASES OF MOON      57
    AND VAIN ALL DORIC DISCIPLINE. . . . . . . . .  438 SONGS PLAY 2         8
    AND VAIN THE DORIC DISCIPLINE. . . . . . . . .  438 SONGS PLAY 2    V    8
    IN VAIN THE DORIC DISCIPLINE. . . . . . . . . . 438 SONGS PLAY 2    V    8
    WHAT DEATH? WHAT DISCIPLINE? . . . . . . . . .  784 WOMANS BEAUTY       21
DISCLOSE
    AND, STANDING BY THESE CHARACTERS, DISCLOSE  . . . . . . 371 EGO DOMINUS    75
    HIS "MORNING" AND HIS "NIGHT" DISCLOSE . . . .  386 ROBARTES DANCE      33
    THE PARCHMENT WILL DISCLOSE TO SOME LEARNED MAN  . . . . 461 HARUN RASHID  20
DISCOLORATION
    EVERY DISCOLORATION OF THE STONE, . . . . . . . 567 LAPIS LAZULI        43
DISCONTENTED
    MY DISCONTENTED HEART TO DRAW CONTENT  . . . .  334 LIVING BEAUTY        3
DISCORD
    AND DISCORD FOLLOW UPON UNISON, . . . . . . . . 265 THESE CLOUDS         5
DISCOURSE
    FROM A DISCOURSE IN FIGURATIVE SPEECH  . . . .  472 ALL SOUL NIGHT      52
DISCOURSES
    EVERY COLONUS LAD OR LASS DISCOURSES . . . . .  447 COLONUS PRAISE      29
DISCOURTESY
    COULD SHARE IN THAT DISCOURTESY OF DEATH. . . . 325 ROBERT GREGORY      48
DISCOVER
    DISCOVER IMPURITIES, CAN SHOW AT LAST  . . . .  558 RIBH CHRISTIAN      10
DISCOVERED
    OF THINGS DISCOVERED IN THE DEEP, . . . . . . . 138 TO IRELAND          21
    DISCOVERED THAT MY THOUGHTS, NOT IT, . . . . .  333 SOLOMON SHEBA       15
    ALL THAT YOU HAVE DISCOVERED IN THE GRAVE, . .  413 TOWER              107
    THE TRUE FAITH DISCOVERED WAS . . . . . . . . . 440 WISDOM               1
DISCOVERERS
    DISCOVERERS OF FORGOTTEN TRUTH . . . . . . . .  324 ROBERT GREGORY       6
DISDAINS
    A STARLIT OR A MOONLIT DOME DISDAINS . . . . .  497 BYZANTIUM            5
DISEASE
    IN A BODKIN OR DISEASE, . . . . . . . . . . . . 632 MAN AND ECHO        22
DISEMBOWELLED
    THE DISEMBOWELLED HORSE. KING EOCHAID RAN . .  278 TWO KINGS           45
    THE DISEMBOWELLED HORSE. KING EOCHAID GAZED, .  278 TWO KINGS      V    45
DISFIGURED
    THAT DEFILING AND DISFIGURED SHAPE  . . . . . . 479 SELF AND SOUL       51
DISFIGURING
    LIVED AT MY SIDE: THOUGHT TIME'S DISFIGURING TOUCH . . . 466 HARUN RASHID   110
    LIVED AT MY SIDE; THAT TIME'S DISFIGURING TOUCH . . . . 466 HARUN RASHID  V 110
DISGORGING
    SEE THE DARKNESS SLOW DISGORGING A VESSEL BLIND WITH
        SQUALL.                                     718 PHANTOM SHIP        12
DISGRACE
    AND FOR HIS OPEN-HANDEDNESS, DISGRACE: . . . .  292 TO A SHADE          16
    HITHER, TO OUR DISGRACE, . . . . . . . . . . . 319 DOLLS               11
DISGUISED
    HE, DISGUISED AS A SAILOR BEFORE THE MAST, . .  790 DEDICATION           2
DISH
    AND SOMEBODY PUTS HIS HAND IN THE DISH . . . .  301 RUN PARADISE         5
    AND BROUGHT THEM IN A LITTLE COVERED DISH. . .  410 TOWER               32
DISHES
    SHE CARRIES IN THE DISHES, . . . . . . . . . .   89 ISLE IN WATER        5
DISHEVELLED
    FEW FEATHERS WERE ON THEIR DISHEVELLED WINGS, .   34 OISIN 2             76
    AND ALL DISHEVELLED WANDERING STARS. . . . . .  126 GOES FERGUS         12
DISHONEST
    ALL THE DISHONEST CROWD I HAD DRIVEN AWAY, . .  352 PEOPLE              24
DISINTER
    OR ANY RICH, DARK NOTHING DISINTER  . . . . . . 565 GYRES               22
```

208

```
                                                    PAGE    TITLE         LINE
DISK
    OF THE ALHAMBRA BLACK ATHWART HIS DISK:  . . . . . . .  691 MOSADA 1      V   37
DISLIKE
    ON THOSE WHO DISLIKE THE PLAYBOY  . . . . . . . . .     294 HATED PLAYBOY V    T
DISMAY
    TO DREAM OF WOMEN WHOSE BEAUTY WAS FOLDED IN DISMAY,  . .  210 UNDER THE MOON    19
    HEARD THE VOICE OF THEIR DISMAY,  . . . . . . . . . .   730 PRIEST FAIRY      74
DISMAYED
    WHY SHOULD I BE DISMAYED . . . . . . . . . . . . .     267 FRIEND ILLNESS     3
DISMISSES
    AND, ALL WORK DONE, DISMISSES ALL . . . . . . . .     633 MAN AND ECHO      34
DISOWNS
    MY BETTER SELF DISOWNS,  . . . . . . . . . . . .      533 FIRST CONFESS      9
DISPART
    I SEE WITHIN A CLOVEN ROCK DISPART  . . . . . . . .    673 ISLE STAT II 3   195
DISPENSING
    AND HAVE NO BUSINESS BUT DISPENSING ROUND . . . . . .   404 FOR DAUGHTER      43
DISPLAY
    WITH FLOPPING AND WITH FLAPPING IT MADE A GREAT DISPLAY,   593 PILGRIM           18
    WITH THEIR FLOPPING AND THEIR FLAPPING IT MADE A GREAT     593 PILGRIM       V   18
        DISPLAY
    ALL THEIR JEALOUSY DISPLAY,  . . . . . . . . . . .    726 LOVERS QUARREL    22
DISPLAYED
    NO VANITY'S DISPLAYED:  . . . . . . . . . . . .       532 BEFORE WORLD       6
DISPLAYS
    OR ELSE ALL JUNO FROM AN URN DISPLAYS  . . . . . . .   418 ANCEST HOUSES     27
DISPLEASE
    MY MEN, WHETHER IT PLEASE HER OR DISPLEASE,  . . . . .  281 TWO KINGS        112
DISPORTED
    AND HAD DISPORTED IN THE STILLY JET,  . . . . . . .    31 OISIN 2           39
    AND HAD DISPORTED IN THE EYES STILL JET . . . . . . .   31 OISIN 2       V   39
DISSEMBLING
    NOTHING BUT DISSEMBLING,  . . . . . . . . . . . .     532 FIRST CONFESS      5
DISSIPATION
    BUT DISSIPATION AND DESPAIR?  AND YET  . . . . . . .   369 EGO DOMINUS       51
DISSOLVE
    I WILL DISSOLVE AWAY THE FAERIES' GUILE:  . . . . . .  677 ISLE STAT II 3   282
DISTAFF
    FROM THE DISTAFF OF THE MOON.  . . . . . . . . . .    743 WISDOM DREAMS      4
DISTAINS
    A STARLIGHT OR A MOONLIT DOME DISTAINS  . . . . . . .  497 BYZANTIUM     V    5
DISTANCE
    . . . FROM THE FOAM-PALE DISTANCE BROKE:  . . . . . .   47 OISIN 3            3
    . . . FROM THE DISTANCE BROKE:  . . . . . . . . . .    47 OISIN 3       V    3
    AND THE HORSE WAS GONE IN THE DISTANCE, . . . . . . .   52 OISIN 3           75
    I AWOKE: THE STRANGE HORSE WITHOUT SUMMONS OUT OF       54 OISIN 3          105
        THE DISTANCE RAN,
    FORTH, PIERCING THE DISTANCE-- . . . . . . . . . .     54 OISIN 3       V  112
DISTANT
    AND MADE IN ALL THEIR DISTANT PARTS, . . . . . . . .   16 OISIN 1          228
    AND ROSE FROM ALL THEIR DISTANT PARTS,  . . . . . . .   16 OISIN 1       V  228
    THAT WAS MOST DISTANT FROM THE DOOR: GREEN SLIME . . . .  37 OISIN 2          113
    MOST DISTANT STRODE WE.  ON THE FLOOR LAY SLIME, . . . .  37 OISIN 2       V  113
    SURLY AND DISTANT, MIXED INSEPARABLY . . . . . . . .    45 OISIN 2          233
    SURLY AND DISTANT, WITH THE WINDS AND SEA:-- . . . . .   45 OISIN 2       V  234
    I SAW FROM A DISTANT SADDLE: FROM THE EARTH SHE MADE HER  56 OISIN 3          130
        MOAN:
    THE WAILING GREW DISTANT: I RODE BY THE WOODS OF        56 OISIN 3          137
        THE WRINKLING BARK,
    HAS MARKED A DISTANT OBJECT DOWN, . . . . . . . . .    337 TOM OROUGHLEY      3
    WERE DISTANT STILL.  AN OLD MAN COCKED HIS EAR. . . . .  372 PHASES OF MOON     7
    WERE DISTANT.  AN OLD MAN COCKED HIS EAR. . . . . . .   372 PHASES OF MOON V   7
    TO A DISTANT POST:  . . . . . . . . . . . . . .      617 LONG-LEG FLY       4
    WHAT GREAT TOMB-HAUNTER SWEEPS THE DISTANT SKY  . . . .  618 BRONZE HEAD        4
DISTINGUISH
    WHO CAN DISTINGUISH DARKNESS FROM THE SOUL?  . . . . .  477 SELF AND SOUL      8
DISTINGUISHED
    WITH THE OLD KINDNESS, THE OLD DISTINGUISHED GRACE, . .  362 HER COURTESY       1
DISTORTING
    OF DISTORTING DAYS . . . . . . . . . . . . . . .      504 QUARREL IN AGE    13
DISTRACTED
    BY HER DISTRACTED AIR . . . . . . . . . . . . . .     453 DEATH OF HARE      8
    DISTRACTED GENTLENESS THAT CANNOT HIDE  . . . . . . .  601 GALLERY REVIS V    6
DISTRACTION
    DISTRACTION  . . . . . . . . . . . . . . . . . .      267 ALL TEMPT ME  V    T
DISTRACTS
    AND ITS CRY DISTRACTS MY THOUGHT. . . . . . . . . .    633 MAN AND ECHO      46
    AND ITS CRY DISTRACTS MY THOUGHTS. . . . . . . . . .   633 MAN AND ECHO  V   46
DISTRAUGHT       SEE GRIEF-DISTRAUGHT
    BEAUTY TO MAKE A STRANGER'S EYE DISTRAUGHT,  . . . . .  403 FOR DAUGHTER      18
    WITH LOOSENED HAIR OR FOREHEADS GRIEF DISTRAUGHT, . . .  537 HER VISION    V   18
DISTRESS
    BUT NIAMH WITH A SWIFT DISTRESS . . . . . . . . . .    15 OISIN 1          211
    BUT NIAM, WITH A SAD DISTRESS, . . . . . . . . . .     15 OISIN 1       V  211
    BUT LITTLE NEED THE GRAVE DISTRESS. . . . . . . . .    338 TOM OROUGHLEY     10
    AND LITTLE NEED THE GRAVE DISTRESS. . . . . . . . .    338 TOM OROUGHLEY V   10
    FROM VAGUE DISTRESS  . . . . . . . . . . . . . .      390 IMAGE PAST        24
    THE IGNOMINY OF BOYHOOD: THE DISTRESS  . . . . . . .   478 SELF AND SOUL     45
DISTRUSTFUL
    DISTRUSTFUL OF THAT POPULAR EYE  . . . . . . . . . .   624 APPARITIONS        5
```

209

```
                                                          PAGE      TITLE              LINE
DISTURB
    CAN DISTURB GLOBE-TROTTING MADAM  . . . . . . . . .   638 BEN BULBEN             48
DISTURBED
    AND FEARING THAT MY LIGHT DISTURBED HER SLEEP . . . . . 467 HARUN RASHID        130
DISTURBS
    NOR KNOW THAT WHAT DISTURBS OUR BLOOD . . . . . . .   434 WHEEL                   7
    NOR STORM DISTURBS, FLAMES BEGOTTEN OF FLAME, . . . . . 498 BYZANTIUM            27
DITCH
    DRINKING THE FOUL DITCH WHERE THEY LIE? . . . . . .   397 POLIT PRISONER         12
    INTO THE FROG-SPAWN OF A BLIND MAN'S DITCH, . . . .   479 SELF AND SOUL          59
    OR INTO THAT MOST FECUND DITCH OF ALL, . . . . . .   479 SELF AND SOUL          61
    ENGENDER IN THE DITCH, . . . . . . . . . . . . .     598 STONE CROSS            10
DITCHES
    WHAT MATTER IF THE DITCHES ARE IMPURE? . . . . . .   478 SELF AND SOUL          42
DIVE
    THE LONG-LEGGED MOOR-HENS DIVE, . . . . . . . .      393 EASTER 1916            53
    WHERE LONG-LEGGED MOOR-HENS DIVE, . . . . . . .      393 EASTER 1916     V      53
DIVER
    THERE! THERE THEY COME! GULL, GANNET, OR DIVER, . . . . 233 SHADOW WATER B      244
DIVIDED
    . . . HOW, WHEN DIVIDED THE GIRTH, . . . . . . . .    60 OISIN 3              189
DIVIDES
    THE NOISY WORLD DIVIDES. HOW SOON A DEED . . . . .   700 MOSADA 3               34
DIVINE
    IN HIS DIVINE HOMESTEAD, . . . . . . . . . . . .     113 ROSE OF PEACE           6
    REMEMBERING THAT SHE TOO HAD SEEMED DIVINE . . . . .   182 QUEEN MAEVE          64
    A SERVING-MAN, THAT COULD DIVINE . . . . . . . .     410 TOWER                  28
    A SERVING MAN THAT COULD DIVINE . . . . . . . .      410 TOWER           V      28
DIVINITY
    WILD WITH DIVINITY, . . . . . . . . . . . . .        472 ALL SOUL NIGHT         36
DIVISION
    DEATH, DESPAIR, DIVISION OF FAMILIES, . . . . . .    459 FROM OEDIPUS            5
    HER SOUL IN DIVISION FROM ITSELF . . . . . . . .     578 CRAZED GIRL             3
DIVISIONS
    LOVE CRAM LOVE'S TWO DIVISIONS . . . . . . . . .     573 LADYS 2ND SONG         12
DIZZY
    AND NOW I AM DIZZY WITH THE THOUGHT . . . . . . .      7 OISIN 1               65
    AND MOUNTS MORE DIZZY HIGH THE MORE IT RAINS . . . . . 417 ANCEST HOUSES         5
    DIZZY WITH HARMONIOUS SOUND, . . . . . . . . .       446 COLONUS PRAISE          7
    HALF DIZZY WITH THE LIGHTNING THERE RUNS A GATHERING BAND--  718 PHANTOM SHIP    9
    NOW HALF DIZZY WITH THE LIGHTNING THERE RUNS A GATHERING     718 PHANTOM SHIP  V  9
        BAND!
    THAT DIZZY DREAMS CAN SPRING . . . . . . . . . .     781 MY HEART BEAT           7
DJIN
    I SAY THAT A DJIN SPOKE. A LIVE LONG HOUR . . . . .   467 HARUN RASHID    V    136
DJINN
    OR WAS IT SHE THAT SPOKE OR SOME GREAT DJINN? . . . . . 467 HARUN RASHID      135
    I SAY THAT A DJINN SPOKE. A LIVELONG HOUR . . . .    467 HARUN RASHID         136
DJINNS
    MURMURED THE WISDOM OF THE DESERT DJINNS, . . . . .   468 HARUN RASHID        163
    HAS MURMURED WISDOM OF THE DESERT DJINNS, . . . . .   468 HARUN RASHID    V   163
DJINS
    HAS SPOKEN THE WISDOM OF THE DESERT DJINS, . . . .   468 HARUN RASHID    V   163
DOCK-LEAVES
    UNDER THE DOCK-LEAVES IN THE GROUND, . . . . . .     176 BELOVED DEAD           12
DOCTOR
    THE FAIRY DOCTOR. . . . . . . . . . . . . . .        716 FAIRY DOCTOR            T
    THE FAIRY DOCTOR COMES OUR WAY . . . . . . . .       716 FAIRY DOCTOR            1
DOE
    THE WILD STAG AND THE DOE! THAT MOUTH TO MOUTH  . . . . 465 HARUN RASHID       101
    ROE COULD RUN OR DOE COULD LEAP  . . . . . . .       522 LULLABY                10
    ROE COULD LEAP OR DOE COULD RUN! . . . . . . .       522 LULLABY                12
    IN TROUBLE IS, THE DOE WILL LINGER NEAR. . . . .     713 FERENCZ RENYI          80
    THE CALLING AFAR OF THE DOE AND THE DEER. . . . .    717 LOVE SONG               5
DOER      SEE DEED-DOER
DOERS     SEE DEED-DOERS
DOG
    BUT WAS THERE EVER DOG THAT PRAISED HIS FLEAS?  . . . . 262 TO A POET           4
    BUT WHERE'S THE WILD DOG THAT HAS PRAISED HIS FLEAS? . . . 262 TO A POET   V    4
    BUT HAVE YOU KNOWN A DOG TO PRAISE HIS FLEAS? . . . . . 262 TO A POET     V     4
    AND THOUGH HE KEEP A DOG AND A GUN, . . . . . .      301 RUN PARADISE           12
    BECAUSE THE PRIEST MUST HAVE LIKE EVERY DOG HIS DAY . . . 364 DOLLS FACES      10
    A DOG MUST HAVE HIS DAY, . . . . . . . . . .         582 ROGER CASEMENT V       18
    A DOG MUST HAVE HIS DAY, . . . . . . . . . .         583 GHOST ROG CASE         12
    QUIET THE DOG, TETHER THE PONY . . . . . . . .       617 LONG-LEG FLY            3
DOG'S
    AS TO A DOG'S TAIL? NEVER HAD I MORE  . . . . . .     409 TOWER                  4
    AS UPON A DOG'S TAIL. NEVER HAD I MORE . . . . .     409 TOWER           V      4
    WHEN HE FINISHED HIS DOG'S DAY! . . . . . . . .      412 TOWER                  79
DOGS
    WAS THAT, THE AIR BEING HEAVY AND THE DOGS  . . . . . 182 QUEEN MAEVE           53
    ARE BUT A POST THE PASSING DOGS DEFILE. . . . . .    321 REED WHISPERER         14
    "DROWN ALL THE DOGS," SAID THE FIERCE YOUNG WOMAN. . . . 546 TO SAME TUNE 2     7
    DROWN ALL THE DOGS, SAID THE FIERCE YOUNG WOMAN. . . . . 546 TO SAME TUNE 2    10
    "DROWN ALL THE DOGS," SAID THE FIERCE YOUNG WOMAN. . . . 546 TO SAME TUNE 2    17
    DROWN ALL THE DOGS, SAID THE FIERCE YOUNG WOMAN, . . . . 546 TO SAME TUNE 2    20
    "DROWN ALL THE DOGS," SAID THE FIERCE YOUNG WOMAN, . . . 547 TO SAME TUNE 2    27
    DROWN ALL THE DOGS, SAID THE FIERCE YOUNG WOMAN, . . . . 547 TO SAME TUNE 2    30
    BUT NO DOGS BARKED, AND MIDNIGHTS CHIMED, . . . . .   570 THREE BUSHES        29
    AND NO DOGS BARKED THROUGH MIDNIGHTS CHIMED  . . . .  570 THREE BUSHES    V   29
    (FOR SINCE THE HORIZON'S BOUGHT STRANGE DOGS ARE STILL)  579 DOR WELLESLEY      7
```

210

DOGS   (CONTINUED)
    AMONG THE DOGS AND HORSES THAT UNDERSTAND MY TALK. . . .   581 CURSE CROMWELL   30
    BUT CHILDREN AND DOGS ON THE FLOOR. . . . .   780 WELL AND TREE   14
DOING
    AS I AM DOING NOW. WHY DO YOU WEEP? . . . .   246 SHADOW WATER B   495
    AS IF IT WERE NOT WORTH THE DOING. . . . .   306 HOUR DAWN   84
DOLL
    A DOLL IN THE DOLL-MAKER'S HOUSE . . . .   319 DOLLS   1
    A NEW MODELLED DOLL, OR DRAWING, ...   362 DOLLS DRAWINGS   2
    NOW THY GREAT WHITE DOLL TO HOLD-- . . . .   726 LOVERS QUARREL   15
DOLL-MAKER'S
    A DOLL IN THE DOLL-MAKER'S HOUSE . . . .   319 DOLLS   1
    THE DOLL-MAKER'S WIFE IS AWARE . . . .   319 DOLLS   14
DOLLS
    THE DOLLS . . . .   319 DOLLS   T
    BUT THE OLDEST OF ALL THE DOLLS, ...   319 DOLLS   4
    CERTAIN ARTISTS BRING HER DOLLS AND DRAWINGS . . . .   362 DOLLS DRAWINGS   T
    WE AND OUR DOLLS BEING BUT THE WORLD WERE BEST AWAY. . .   364 DOLLS FACES   12
DOLLS'
    SHE TURNS THE DOLLS' FACES TO THE WALL . . . .   363 DOLLS FACES   T
DOLOROUS
    THE HARP AWAY. A DOLOROUS POOL . . . .   17 DOLOROUS POOL   V   240
    UNTO THE DOLOROUS BORDER OF THE FAIRY LAKE. . . . . .   655 ISLE STAT I 2   85
    WE SAW THE DOLOROUS LAKE! AND THEN THY NAME . . . . .   659 ISLE STAT II 1   7
DOLPHIN
    PAINTINGS OF THE DOLPHIN DRAWN: . . . .   309 REALISTS   V   4
DOLPHIN-DRAWN
    PAINTINGS OF THE DOLPHIN-DRAWN . . . .   309 REALISTS   4
DOLPHIN'S
    ASTRADDLE ON THE DOLPHIN'S MIRE AND BLOOD, ...   498 BYZANTIUM   33
    A STRADDLE ON THE DOLPHIN'S MIRE AND BLOOD . . . . .   498 BYZANTIUM   V   33
    STRADDLING EACH A DOLPHIN'S BACK . . . .   612 NEWS ORACLE   13
DOLPHINS
    AND THE BRUTE DOLPHINS PLUNGE . . . .   612 NEWS ORACLE   20
DOLPHIN-TORN
    THAT DOLPHIN-TORN, THAT GONG-TORMENTED SEA. . . . . .   498 BYZANTIUM   40
DOLT
    NOR KNAVE NOR DOLT CAN BREAK . . . .   259 UNWORTH PRAISE   2
    FROM SELF-SAME DOLT AND KNAVE: . . . .   260 UNWORTH PRAISE   17
    ON THE DAY'S WAR WITH EVERY KNAVE AND DOLT, ...   260 FASC DIFFICULT   10
    WHAT HURRIES OUT THE KNAVE AND DOLT? . . . .   625 NATIVITY   9
DOME
    A DOME MADE OUT OF ENDLESS CARVEN JAGS, ...   38 OISIN 2   144
    I WAITED HOUR BY HOUR, AND THE HIGH DOME, ...   39 OISIN 2   147
    LIFTED THE DOME, WHERE FACE IN CARVEN FACE . . . . .   39 OISIN 2   V   145
    HOUR AFTER HOUR I WAITED, AND THE DOME . . . . . .   39 OISIN 2   V   147
    A STARLIT OR A MOONLIT DOME DISDAINS . . . .   497 BYZANTIUM   5
    A STARLIGHT OR A MOONLIT DOME DISTAINS . . . . . .   497 BYZANTIUM   V   5
DOMINATE
    TO ENGROSS THE PRESENT AND DOMINATE MEMORY. . . . . .   630 CIRCUS ANIMALS   30
DOMINION
    YOU MOVE IN ANOTHER DOMINION . . . .   707 FAIRY PEDANT   5
DOMINIONS
    I RULED O'ER ALL MY FAIR DOMINIONS, ...   82 MAD KING GOLL   V   7
DOMINO
    HER DOMINO, HER PANNIERED SKIRT COPIED FROM LONGHI: . .   363 DOLLS FACES   7
DOMINUS
    EGO DOMINUS TUUS . . . .   367 EGO DOMINUS   T
DON
    OF HILL TWO SHEPHERDS COME. FAREWELL! I'LL DON . . . .   659 ISLE STAT II 1   28
DONE   SEE HALF-DONE
    YOUR MORTAL SHORES TILL TIME IS DONE!" . . . .   6 OISIN 1   V   59
    AND, NOW OUR WANDERING HOURS WERE DONE, ...   14 OISIN 1   177
    SUNG OF THE BIRDS. OUR TOIL WAS DONE: . . . .   14 OISIN 1   V 177
    WHEN THE STARS ARE TO WANE AND THE WORLD BE DONE. . . .   16 OISIN 1   220
    BEFORE THE SWIFT THINGS THAT SHE DREAMED OF WERE DONE . . 27 OISIN 1   414
    ERE HALF THE SWIFT THINGS THAT SHE DREAMT ON WERE DONE, . 28 OISIN 1   V 422
    MAY SLEEP IN THE END WITH THE WHOLE OF HIS FATE DONE, . . 28 OISIN 1   V 423F
    THINGS DONE ERE GOD FIRST WAS OR MY OLD LINE BEGAN: . . . 29 OISIN 2   V   8
    ALL IS DONE NOW--I SEE THE RAVENS FLOCK-- . . . . . .   43 OISIN 2   V 212
    I SANG HOW, WHEN DAY'S TOIL IS DONE, ...   85 MAD KING GOLL   61
    FOR MY REMEMBERING HOUR IS DONE: . . . .   86 MAD KING GOLL   V   69
    AND PIERCED HIM. "SPEAK BEFORE YOUR BREATH IS DONE." . . 110 CUCHULAIN SEA   67
    TURN IF YOU MAY FROM BATTLES NEVER DONE, ...   114 ROSE OF BATTLE   7
    AND PLUCK TILL TIME AND TIMES ARE DONE . . . . . .   150 WANDER AENGUS   22
    WHEN ALL THIS HEAVY HISTORY'S DONE: . . . .   213 BLESS PSALTER   17
    OR WAVE TO DROWN. BUT I HAVE DONE WITH WORDS, ...   238 SHADOW WATER B   348
    I HAVE DONE RIGHT. WHAT COULD I BUT OBEY? . . . . .   243 SHADOW WATER B   443
    BUT I HAVE DONE SO GREAT A WRONG AGAINST YOU, ...   245 SHADOW WATER B   483
    WHAT I HAVE DONE, OR WHAT WOULD DO . . . .   256 WORDS   3
    REMEMBERING THAT THE BEST I HAVE DONE . . . .   256 WORDS   7
    WAS DONE TO MAKE IT PLAIN: . . . .   256 WORDS   8
    THAT HAD SHE DONE SO WHO CAN SAY . . . .   256 WORDS   13
    WHY, WHAT COULD SHE HAVE DONE, BEING WHAT SHE IS? . . .   257 NO SECOND TROY   11
    THE WEAK LAY HAND ON WHAT THE STRONG HAS DONE, ...   265 THESE CLOUDS   3
    AND WHEN FOR ALL I'D DONE OR SAID-- . . . .   275 GREY ROCK   99
    AND EVIL MUST IT BE, IF DONE 'TWERE WORSE . . . . .   281 TWO KINGS   105
    AND ALL HE DID DONE PERFECTLY . . . .   327 ROBERT GREGORY   79
    REMEMBERING KINDNESS DONE, AND HOW CAN I, ...   340 SHEP GOATHERD   30
    AND TILL THAT'S DONE CAN NEITHER WORK NOR WAIT. . . . .   340 SHEP GOATHERD   45
    AND WHEN 'TWAS DONE SO LITTLE HAD I DONE . . . . .   341 SHEP GOATHERD   59

211

DONE (CONTINUED)
 AND WHEN 'TWAS DONE SO LITTLE HAD I DONE . . . . . . 341 SHEP GOATHERD 59
 "FOR ALL THAT I HAVE DONE AT MY OWN CHARGE? . . . . . . 351 PEOPLE   2
 I MOURN FOR THAT MOST LONELY THING; AND YET GOD'S WILL 354 HIS PHOENIX 31
  BE DONE!
 A YOUNG MAN, WHEN THE OLD MEN ARE DONE TALKING . . . . . 356 BROKEN DREAMS 16
 THOUGH PLAY IS BUT HALF DONE— . . . . 364 END OF DAY   7
 AND THOUGHT BEFORE I HAD DONE . . . . 392 EASTER 1916 9
 HE HAD DONE MOST BITTER WRONG . . . . 393 EASTER 1916 33
 FOR ALL THAT IS DONE AND SAID. . . . . 394 EASTER 1916 69
 FOR ALL SHE HAD DONE AND SAID. . . . . 394 EASTER 1916 V 69
 AND NOT A THING IS DONE, ... 451 FIRST LOVE 10
 TOLD ALL THAT HAD BEEN SAID OR DONE . . . . 456 SUMMER SPRING 3
 THAT QUARTER WHERE ALL THOUGHT IS DONE! . . . . . . 477 SELF AND SOUL 7
 WE THAT HAVE DONE AND THOUGHT, ... 484 SPILT MILK 1
 THAT HAVE THOUGHT AND DONE, ... 484 SPILT MILK 2
 THINGS SAID OR DONE LONG YEARS AGO, ... 501 VACILLATION 51
 NOTHING SAID OR DONE CAN REACH . . . . 506 REMORSE SPEECH 9
 SOME STUPID THING THAT I HAD DONE . . . . 507 STREAM AND SUN 4
 ALL WRONGS DONE. . . . . 518 HIS CONFIDENCE 4
 WHEN, THE POTION'S WORK BEING DONE, ... 522 LULLABY   9
 THAT IF NOTHING DRASTIC IS DONE . . . . 565 LAPIS LAZULI 5
 THAT IF NOTHING DRASTIC CAN BE DONE . . . . 565 LAPIS LAZULI V 5
 "THE WORK IS DONE," GROWN OLD HE THOUGHT, ... 577 WHAT THEN 16
 TO JUDGE WHAT I HAVE DONE. . . . . 604 YOU CONTENT 4
 ALL THAT I HAVE SAID AND DONE, ... 632 MAN AND ECHO 6
 AND, ALL WORK DONE, DISMISSES ALL . . . . 633 MAN AND ECHO 34
 ALL MUST TOGETHER DO." THAT DONE, THE MAN . . . . . 634 CUCHULAIN COMF 17
 THOUGH ALL WAS DONE IN COMMON AS BEFORE! . . . . . . 635 CUCHULAIN COMF 24
 AND OUR LAUGHTER OVER AND DONE! . . . . 643 SONG FAERIES 6
 OF FLIGHT ARE DONE. MOST FAIR OF ALL WHO GRAZE . . . 649 ISLE STAT I 1 118
 HAVE DONE THIS PHRASING, AND SAY WHY, IN SOOTH, . . . 652 ISLE STAT I 2 25
 TILL HIS LAST WRETCHEDNESS WAS O'ER AND DONE." . . . 664 ISLE STAT II 2 54
 AND SHALL BE DONE, IF YOU WILL DEIGN TO KISS . . . . 669 ISLE STAT II 3 79
 AND OUR LAUGHTER OVER AND DONE! . . . . 676 ISLE STAT II 3 253
 BUT NOW MY WANDERING SHALL BE DONE, I KNOW. . . . . 682 SEEKER   21
 BUT SOON MY WANDERING SHALL BE DONE I KNOW. . . . . 682 SEEKER V 21
 MY BIDDING. NOW 'TIS DONE, AND I AM GLAD . . . . . 700 MOSADA 3 29
 YOU HAVE DONE WELL, BECAUSE MY BOWS ARE TURNED . . . 755 SHADOW WATER A 164
DONNE
 WITH LANDOR AND WITH DONNE. . . . . 336 YOUNG BEAUTY 18
DOODLE SEE COCK-A-DOODLE-DOODLE-DO
DOOM
 "GOD ONLY SEES WHAT DOOM FOR ME LIES STORED." . . . . 110 CUCHULAIN SEA V 62
 THE BREAD AND THE WINE HAD A DOOM, ... 144 HOST OF AIR 25
 OF THE ROSE IN ITS DOOM. . . . . 175 ELEMENT POWERS V 12
 HEAVEN HAS PUT AWAY THE STROKE OF HER DOOM, ... 356 BROKEN DREAMS 11
 THAT DIETH SLOW WITH SUNSICK DOOM. . . . . 655 ISLE STAT I 3 12
DOOMED
 A STORMY SUNSET ON DOOMED SHIPS! . . . . 3 OISIN 1   23
 A STORMY SUNSET O'ER DOOMED SHIPS. . . . . 3 OISIN 1 V 23
 DOOMED LIKE ODYSSEUS AND THE LABOURING SHIPS . . . . 120 SORROW OF LOVE 7
 HOW THEY WHO SEEK ARE EVER DOOMED TO FAIL. . . . . . 653 ISLE STAT I 2 41
DOOMS
 "THE DOOMS OF MEN ARE IN GOD'S HIDDEN PLACE." . . . . 110 CUCHULAIN SEA 62
 "THE DOOMS OF MEN ARE IN GOD'S HIDDEN HOARD." . . . . 110 CUCHULAIN SEA V 62
DOONEY
 THE FIDDLER OF DOONEY . . . . 178 FIDDLER DOONEY T
 WHEN I PLAY ON MY FIDDLE IN DOONEY, ... 178 FIDDLER DOONEY 1
 WITH "HERE IS THE FIDDLER OF DOONEY!" . . . . 179 FIDDLER DOONEY 19
DOOR
 BURST FROM A GREAT DOOR MARRED BY MANY A BLOW . . . . 31 OISIN 2   29
 AND THEN WE CLIMBED THE STAIR TO A HIGH DOOR! . . . . 36 OISIN 2   101
 AND UP THE STAIR WE TOILED TO A HIGH DOOR, ... 36 OISIN 2 V 101
 THAT WAS MOST DISTANT FROM THE DOOR; GREEN SLIME . . . 37 OISIN 2   113
 BURIED AND MIGHTY. WHEN THROUGH THE GREAT DOOR . . . 39 OISIN 2   151
 AND FOUND A DOOR DEEP SUNKEN IN THE WALL, ... 39 OISIN 2   154
 I FOUND A DOOR DEEP-SUNKEN IN THE WALL, ... 39 OISIN 2 V 154
 THE LEAST OF DOORS! BEYOND THE DOOR A PLAIN, ... 39 OISIN 2 V 155
 I SAW HER STANDING IN HER DOOR BUT NOW, ... 74 ANASHU VIJAYA 64
 HE DROVE ME OUT AND SHUT THE DOOR, ... 95 MOLL MAGEE 25
 HE DROVE ME FORTH AND SHUT THE DOOR, ... 95 MOLL MAGEE V 25
 WHEN, OPENIN' WIDE HIS DOOR, ... 96 MOLL MAGEE 50
 THEN TO HER SERVANTS, "BEAT HIM FROM THE DOOR . . . . 106 CUCHULAIN SEA V 17A
 AND DRIVE HIM FROM THE DOOR." AND THUS IT WAS! . . . 106 CUCHULAIN SEA V 17B
 THE SICK MAN'S WIFE OPENED THE DOOR . . . . 133 FR GILLIGAN 31
 AND HE RAN TO THE DOOR OF HIS HOUSE! . . . . 145 HOST OF AIR V 40C
 IT SANG TO HER THROUGH THE DOOR. . . . . 160 CAP AND BELLS 16
 SHE OPENED HER DOOR AND HER WINDOW, ... 160 CAP AND BELLS 29
 MASTER OF THE STILL STARS AND OF THE FLAMING DOOR. . . 161 BLACK PIG   8
 WHEN THE FLAMING LUTE-THRONGED ANGELIC DOOR IS WIDE! 172 TRAV PASSION 1
 HAD PACED FROM DOOR TO FIRE AND FIRE TO DOOR, ... 180 QUEEN MAEVE 17
 HAD PACED FROM DOOR TO FIRE AND FIRE TO DOOR. . . . . 180 QUEEN MAEVE 17
 ABOUT MY DOOR TO COUNSEL AND TO HELP." . . . . . . 183 QUEEN MAEVE V 82
 THE BRAZEN PILLARS OF HIS DOOR, ... 192 BAILE AILLINN 74
 OR THE DOOR PILLARS OF ONE HOUSE, ... 195 BAILE AILLINN V 152
 BECAUSE OF THAT OLD DRAUGHT UNDER THE DOOR, ... 228 SHADOW WATER B 127
 OF THE GREAT DOOR; BUT THOUGH THE HANGING LAMPS . . . 279 TWO KINGS 49
 NOR DOOR, NOR MOUTH, NOR SLIPPER MADE A NOISE, . . . 279 TWO KINGS 51
 IN THE HALF LIGHT, AND RUNS TO ITS OWN DOOR . . . . 279 TWO KINGS V 45C
 ROSE ROUND THE WALLS, AND THROUGH THE BRONZE-RINGED DOOR 286 TWO KINGS 215

	PAGE	TITLE	LINE
DOOR (CONTINUED)			
"THOUGH THE DOOR OF DEATH IS NEAR	298	THREE HERMITS	8
AND WHAT WAITS BEHIND THE DOOR,	298	THREE HERMITS	9
PASS THE DOOR OF BIRTH AGAIN,	298	THREE HERMITS	19
AND HIS OWN FLOCK WAS BROWSING AT THE DOOR.	340	SHEP GOATHERD	27
BUT PUT NO NAME AND LEAVE THEM AT HER DOOR.	343	SHEP GOATHERD	116
THEY STOOD IN THE DOOR AND STOOD BETWEEN	358	PRESENCES	9
WHO KNOW IT ALL RING AT HIS DOOR, AND SPEAK	373	PHASES OF MOON	21
BESIDE THE CASTLE DOOR, WHERE ALL IS STARK	377	PHASES OF MOON	126
OR, THE HOUSE DOOR LEFT UNSHUT,	380	SONGS FOOL 1	10
AND WHETHER THE DOOR WERE SHUT.	381	SONGS FOOL 2	5
WHO TROD UPON THESE ROCKS OR PASSED THIS DOOR,	413	TOWER	98
KNOWING THAT NONE COULD PASS HEAVEN'S DOOR	422	MY TABLE	26
KNOWING THAT NONE WHO PASS HEAVEN'S DOOR	422	MY TABLE	26
KNOWING THAT NONE CAN PASS HEAVEN'S DOOR	422	MY TABLE V	26
THE ROAD AT MY DOOR	423	ROAD AT DOOR	T
STAND AT MY DOOR, AND I COMPLAIN	424	ROAD AT DOOR	8
I TURN AWAY AND SHUT THE DOOR, AND ON THE STAIR	427	PHANTOM HATRED	33
CAN LEAVE THE MOTHER, MURDERED AT HER DOOR,	429	NINETEEN 19	27
THE MORE I LEAVE THE DOOR UNLATCHED	511	JANE AND JACK	3
FROM DOOR TO TOP!	512	JANE ON GOD	17
TO-MORROW NIGHT I WILL BREAK DOWN THE DOOR.	551	SONGS REWRIT 1	6
TO-MORROW NIGHT I WILL BREAK DOWN THE DOOR.	551	SONGS REWRIT 1	12
TO-MORROW NIGHT I WILL BREAK DOWN THE DOOR.	551	SONGS REWRIT 1	18
TO-MORROW NIGHT I WILL BREAK IN THE DOOR.	551	SONGS REWRIT 1 V	REF
TOMORROW NIGHT I WILL BREAK DOWN THE DOOR.	551	SONGS REWRIT 1 V	REF
I HAD THOUGHT TO HAVE CALLED HER OUT TO THE DOOR,	551	SONGS REWRIT 1 V	15
ARE THE MOB THAT HOWLS AT THE DOOR!	554	CHURCH STATE	10
IS BEATING ON THE DOOR.	583	GHOST ROG CASE	10
IS BEATING ON THE DOOR.	583	GHOST ROG CASE	20
IS BEATING ON THE DOOR.	584	GHOST ROG CASE	30
IS BEATING ON THE DOOR.	584	GHOST ROG CASE	40
THE DOOR ABOVE HIS HEAD	585	ORAHILLY	33
THE COLONEL KNOCKED ON THE RICH MAN'S DOOR,	595	COLONEL MARTIN	28
THE COLONEL KNOCKED ON A RICH MAN'S DOOR.	595	COLONEL MARTIN V	28
SHUT THE DOOR OF THE POPE'S CHAPEL,	618	LONG-LEG FLY	23
AND FIND OUR ANCIENT HOUNDS BEFORE THE DOOR,	622	HOUND VOICE	16
UNTO HER DOOR; FOR THIS, WHERE NOD THE LONG	660	ISLE STAT II 1	43
BY THE DOOR OF MARY'S GARDEN	680	LOVE AND DEATH	31
TENDING THE ROSES ROUND HIS LATTICE DOOR.	692	MOSADA 1	53
UNDER A LEMON TREE BESIDE YOUR DOOR!	693	MOSADA 1	68
BY THE DOOR OF PETER'S GATE,	696	MOSADA 2	23
BESIDE THE DOOR OF PETER'S GATE.	696	MOSADA 2 V	23
THY SACRED DOOR!" BUT PETER CRIED,	697	MOSADA 2	25
OF DREAMING AND OF WATCHING BY THE DOOR	700	MOSADA 3	26
AND HURRIED TO THE GUARD-HOUSE DOOR.	725	LEGEND	16
"SAY AND THRICE ANIGH THY DOOR	730	PRIEST FAIRY	54
THE HANDMAIDS LAUGH AND WHISPER IN THE DOOR.	759	SHADOW WATER A	242
TO THE COMFORTABLE DOOR OF HIS HOUSE.	780	WELL AND TREE	6
ALTHOUGH THE DOOR BE SHUT	786	YOUR HEART	14
DOORED			
FROM DOORED AND WINDOWED CLIFF, OR HALF UPTURNED	368	EGO DOMINUS	30
DOORMAT			
WHERE THE MOSS WAS SPREAD LIKE HIS OWN DOORMAT.	728	PRIEST FAIRY	8
DOOR-PILLARS			
OR THE DOOR-PILLARS OF ONE HOUSE,	195	BAILE AILLINN	152
DOOR-PIN			
RAISE THE DOOR-PIN WITH ALARM,	727	LOVERS QUARREL	52
DOOR-POST			
LOOKED DOWN ON YOU FROM HEAVEN'S DOOR-POST	112	ROSE OF PEACE	3
DOOR-POSTS			
LOOKED DOWN ON YOU FROM HEAVEN'S DOOR-POSTS,	112	ROSE OF PEACE V	3
DOORS			
AND THROUGH THE DOORS, A RUSTLING ROUT,	20	OISIN 1 V	290
THE LEAST OF DOORS! BEYOND ON A DIM PLAIN	39	OISIN 2	155
THE LEAST OF DOORS! BEYOND THE DOOR A PLAIN,	39	OISIN 2 V	155
THE WINDOWS AND THE DOORS WERE SHUT,	95	MOLL MAGEE	29
WITHOUT DOORS OR WITHIN,	96	MOLL MAGEE	44
DESOLATE WINDS THAT BEAT THE DOORS OF HEAVEN, AND BEAT	147	UNAPPEAS HOST	9
THE DOORS OF HELL AND BLOW THERE MANY A WHIMPERING GHOST!	147	UNAPPEAS HOST	10
WHAT IF THE GLORY OF ESCUTCHEONED DOORS,	418	ANCEST HOUSES	33
SCARCE THE OLD AND WIZEN HOUSES HAD THEIR DOORS AND WINDOWS SHUT.	718	PHANTOM SHIP	5
SCARCE THE OLD AND WIZENED HOUSES HAD THEIR DOORS AND WINDOWS SHUT.	718	PHANTOM SHIP V	5
THE HARVEST'S IN! THE GRANARY DOORS ARE SHUT!	755	SHADOW WATER A	177
DOORSTEP			
A BIRD WALK ON THE DOORSTEP. CHECK ONCE MORE.	722	WITCH VIVIEN	64
DOOR-STEP			
OVER THE DOOR-STEP INTO THE AIR,	97	FOXHUNTER V	3
DOORWAY			
PASSED UNDER THE DIM DOORWAY, OUT OF SIGHT,	37	OISIN 2	123
PASSED UNDER A DIM DOORWAY, OUT OF SIGHT,	37	OISIN 2 V	123
TILL THE FAR DOORWAY GREW A BURNING BLOT	39	OISIN 2 V	152
DESERTED ON A DOORWAY SEAT,	85	MAD KING GOLL	56
DESERTED IN A DOORWAY SEAT,	85	MAD KING GOLL V	56
SHY IN THE DOORWAY	89	ISLE IN WATER	11
ITS OPEN LIGHTED DOORWAY AND ITS WINDOWS ALL ALIGHT,	581	CURSE CROMWELL	26
STRETCHED UNDER A DOORWAY	585	ORAHILLY	30
DORIC			
AND VAIN ALL DORIC DISCIPLINE.	438	SONGS PLAY 2	8

DORIC   (CONTINUED)
    AND VAIN THE DORIC DISCIPLINE. • • • • • • • • • •   438 SONGS PLAY 2   V   '8
    IN VAIN THE DORIC DISCIPLINE. • • • • • • • • • • •   438 SONGS PLAY 2   V   8
DOROTHY
    THERE'S MARGARET AND MARJORIE AND DOROTHY AND NAN, • • • •   354 HIS PHOENIX   17
    TO DOROTHY WELLESLEY • • • • • • • • • • • • • •   579 DOR WELLESLEY   T
DORTHA   SEE KYLE-DORTHA
DOTE
    ALL WOMEN DOTE UPON AN IDLE MAN • • • • • • • • •   500 VACILLATION   23
DOUBLE
    UNTIL AT LAST THE DOUBLE HORNS, DRAWN BACKWARD, • • • •   278 TWO KINGS   21
    THAT WERE A DOUBLE HUNGER IN MY LIPS • • • • • • •   285 TWO KINGS   206
    THAT WERE A DOUBLE HUNGER ON MY LIPS • • • • • • •   285 TWO KINGS   V   206
    AND LOOK MOST LIKE ME, BEING INDEED MY DOUBLE, • • • •   371 EGO DOMINUS   72
    THE DOUBLE VISION OF MICHAEL ROBARTES • • • • • •   382 VISION ROBART   T
    WAS IT THE DOUBLE OF MY DREAM • • • • • • • • • •   398 BREAK OF DAY   1
    DOUBLE SIXES! • • • • • • • • • • • • • • • • •   721 WITCH VIVIEN   43
DOUBLES
    WHEREIN THE GAZING HEART DOUBLES HER MIGHT. • • • • • •   326 ROBERT GREGORY   69
DOUBLET
    HUNG ON HIS DOUBLET--DEAR AND MOURNFUL CHILD, • • • • •   691 MOSADA 1   35
DOUBLING
    DRIPPING AND DOUBLING LANDWARD, AS THOUGH THEY WOULD HASTEN   48 OISIN 3   15
    AWAY,
    DRIPPING AND DOUBLING LANDWARD, AS THOUGH THEY WOULD HASTEN   57 OISIN 3   143
    AWAY,
DOUBLY
    FOR WHAT IS DOUBLY BRIEF." AND NOW THE SHAPE • • • • •   285 TWO KINGS   207
    FOR WHAT IS DOUBLY BRIEF." "BUT NOW THE SHAPE, • • • •   285 TWO KINGS   V   207
DOUBT
    DO YOU, TOO, DOUBT ME? HAVE YOU JOINED THEIR PLOT? • • •   227 SHADOW WATER B   106
    MAYBE IT IS BUT NATURAL TO DOUBT ME. • • • • • • •   227 SHADOW WATER B   112
    YOU'D NEVER DOUBT THAT IT WAS LIFE THEY PROMISED • • • •   231 SHADOW WATER B   197
    "ALTHOUGH THE EVENT WAS LONG IN DOUBT, • • • • • • •   273 GREY ROCK   67
    BEING THE MOON OF BIRTH, MAY END OUR DOUBT. • • • • •   748 SHADOW WATER A   24
    I DOUBT YOUR WISDOM, BUT DO NOT DOUBT MY LOVE. • • • •   748 SHADOW WATER A   31
    I DOUBT YOUR WISDOM, BUT DO NOT DOUBT MY LOVE. • • • •   748 SHADOW WATER A   31
    ALTHOUGH I DOUBT YOUR WISDOM, DO NOT DOUBT • • • • •   748 SHADOW WATER A   V   31
    ALTHOUGH I DOUBT YOUR WISDOM, DO NOT DOUBT • • • • •   748 SHADOW WATER A   V   31
DOUBTFUL
    BEING AS DOUBTFUL? I HAVE CALLED YOU MASTER • • • • •   227 SHADOW WATER B   110
    ARE DOUBTFUL LIKE THESE PULLERS OF THE OAR! • • • • •   748 SHADOW WATER A   30
DOUBTING
    NOT DOUBTING TO HAVE SHOULDERED IT AWAY. • • • • • •   277 TWO KINGS   V   11A
DOUBTLESS
    DOUBTLESS I SPOKE OR SANG WHAT I HAD HEARD • • • • • •   557 RIBH ECSTASY   2
    THE THIRD, DOUBTLESS A SERVING-MAN. • • • • • • • •   566 LAPIS LAZULI   41
    THOUGH DOUBTLESS PLUM OR CHERRY-BRANCH • • • • • • •   567 LAPIS LAZULI   47
DOUBTS
    BUT WOULD TURN HOME AGAIN. NO MAN HAD DOUBTS • • • • •   749 SHADOW WATER A   38
DOUGH
    IS BUT HALF YOURS; HE KNEADED IN THE DOUGH • • • • • •   201 OLD MEMORY   6
    INSIPID AS THE DOUGH BEFORE IT IS BAKED, • • • • • •   376 PHASES OF MOON   112
    WHEN ALL THE DOUGH HAS BEEN SO KNEADED UP • • • • • •   377 PHASES OF MOON   114
DOVE
    THE HEAVY BOUGHS, THE BURNISHED DOVE • • • • • • • •   78 INDIAN TO LOVE   16
    LIKE SWARMING BEES, ONE WITH THE DOVE • • • • • • •   78 INDIAN TO LOVE   V   16
    ONE WITH THE LEAVES: ONE WITH THE DOVE • • • • • • •   78 INDIAN TO LOVE   V   16
    THE GREAT BOUGHS, AND THE BURNISHED DOVE • • • • • •   78 INDIAN TO LOVE   V   16
    AND GREAT BOUGHS, AND THE BURNISHED DOVE • • • • • •   78 INDIAN TO LOVE   V   16
    BOOK III DOVE OR SWAN I LEDA • • • • • • • • •   441 LEDA AND SWAN   V   T
    BOOK V: DOVE OR SWAN I LEDA • • • • • • • • • •   441 LEDA AND SWAN   V   T
DOVE-COT
    ABOUT A SUN-FLUSHED DOVE-COT, COOING, CLING • • • • • •   710 FERENCZ RENYI   20
DOVE-GREY
    AND FOUND ON THE DOVE-GREY EDGE OF THE SEA • • • • • •   3 OISIN 1   19
    AS THE TIDE WEARS THE DOVE-GREY SANDS, • • • • • • •   157 POET BELOVED   4
    AS THE TIDE HAS THE DOVE-GREY SANDS, • • • • • • • •   157 POET BELOVED   V   4
    IN DOVE-GREY FAERY LANDS! • • • • • • • • • • •   162 ASKS FORGIVE   10
DOVE'S   SEE RING-DOVE'S
DOVES
    THAN DOVES THAT MOANED ROUND EMAN'S HALL • • • • • •   3 OISIN 1   V   7EE
    THE DOVES WHOSE GROWING FORMS HE'D WATCHED. NOT THESE • •   710 FERENCZ RENYI   21
    THE DOVES WHOSE GROWING FORM HE'D WATCHED. NOT THESE • •   710 FERENCZ RENYI   V   21
DOWERED
    HAVE DOWERED THE STARS WITH MERRY LIGHT! • • • • • •   134 TWO TREES   6
DOWERS
    AND HE GAVE THEM AS DOWERS TO HIS DAUGHTERS, • • • • •   92 FATHER OHART   7
DOWN   SEE GOING-DOWN
    WHEN AMBLING DOWN THE VALE WE MET • • • • • • • •   2 OISIN 1   V   7U
    BUT DOWN TO HER FEET WHITE VESTURE FLOWED, • • • • •   3 OISIN 1   25
    DOWN TO HER FEET WHITE VESTURE FLOWED, • • • • • •   3 OISIN 1   V   25
    AND WAS BORN WHERE THE SUN DROPS DOWN IN THE TIDE, • • •   5 OISIN 1   49
    BEFORE THY FEET SHALL KNEEL DOWN ALL • • • • • • •   7 OISIN 1   V   77
    OR DOWN THE DEWY FOREST ALLEYS, • • • • • • • • •   10 OISIN 1   120
    AND DOWN THE DEWY FOREST ALLEYS, • • • • • • • •   10 OISIN 1   V   120
    IT DOWN IN A LEAF-HID, HOLLOW PLACE • • • • • • •   17 OISIN 1   242
    BENT ALL OUR SWAYING BODIES DOWN, • • • • • • • •   20 OISIN 1   297
    PASSED A-TIPTOE UP AND DOWN • • • • • • • • • • •   20 OISIN 1   V   294
    BENT DOWN ABOVE EACH HOOKED KNEE, • • • • • • • •   26 OISIN 1   392
    AND BID THE STARS DROP DOWN FROM THE SKY, • • • • •   28 OISIN 1   426

```
                                                          PAGE      TITLE          LINE
DOWN   (CONTINUED)
    CAME SWIMMING SADLY DOWN THE MIGHTY STAIR. . . . . . .    32 OISIN 2       V   50B
    DOWN ON US WITH HER EYES LIKE FUNERAL TAPERS. . . . . .   33 OISIN 2       V   69
    AS ANY RUDDY MOTH, LOOKED DOWN ON US: . . . . . .  .      34 OISIN 2           72
    NOT EVEN YOUR GOD COULD HAVE THROWN DOWN THAT HALL! . . . 36 OISIN 2           109
    NOT E'EN THY GOD COULD HAVE THROWN DOWN THAT HALL: . . .  36 OISIN 2           109
    HE HAD SAT DOWN AND SIGHED WITH CUMBERED HEART, . . . .   37 OISIN 2           111
    SHOWED PRINTS OF SEA-BORN SCALES, WHILE DOWN THROUGH IT   37 OISIN 2           115
    ANOINTING, TORCH JAMMED DOWN BETWEEN THE FLAGS, . . . .   38 OISIN 2       V   143
    LOOKED DOWN ON ME: AND IN THE SELF-SAME PLACE . . . . .   39 OISIN 2           146
    BARKING.  WE TRAMPLED UP AND DOWN WITH BLOWS . . . . .    40 OISIN 2           170
    WHEN I HAD TORN IT DOWN: BUT WHEN THE WEST . . . . . .    41 OISIN 2       V   180
    WHEN I TORE DOWN THE TREE: BUT WHEN THE WEST . . . . .    41 OISIN 2       V   180
    WHEN I'D TORE DOWN THAT TREE: BUT WHEN THE WEST . . . .   41 OISIN 2       V   180
    WHEN I TORE DOWN THAT TREE: BUT WHEN THE WEST . . . . .   41 OISIN 2       V   180
    "I HEAR MY SOUL DROP DOWN INTO DECAY, . . . . . . .      45 OISIN 2           235
    A VALLEY FLOWED DOWN FROM HIS HOOFS, AND THERE IN THE LONG 48 OISIN 3          26
       GRASS LAY,
    SQUARE LEAVES OF THE IVY MOVED OVER US, BINDING US DOWN   52 OISIN 3           76
       TO OUR REST.
    CAME, AND MY FOREHEAD FELL LOW, AND MY TEARS LIKE BERRIES 57 OISIN 3          154
    FELL DOWN:
    LEANING DOWN FROM THE GEM-STUDDED SADDLE, . . . . . .     60 OISIN 3           187
    I THROW DOWN THE CHAIN OF SMALL STONES! . . . . . . .     63 OISIN 3           222
    A RABBIT OLD AND LAME LIMPED DOWN THE PATH: . . . . .     80 EPHEMERA          15
    WHILE HE BENT DOWN HIS FADING HEAD, . . . . . . . .       82 MAD KING GOLL     10
    AND SONG THAT DOWN THE VALLEYS ROLLED-- . . . . . . .     84 MAD KING GOLL V   35
    AND SONG THAT DOWN THE VALLEY ROLLED-- . . . . . . .      84 MAD KING GOLL V   35
    THAT DOWN THE ECHOING VALLEYS ROLLED. . . . . . . .       84 MAD KING GOLL V   35
    AND PASSED A-TIPTOE UP AND DOWN, . . . . . . . . .        85 MAD KING GOLL     51
    I PASSED A TIP-TOE UP AND DOWN, . . . . . . . . . .       85 MAD KING GOLL V   51
    I PASSED A-TIPTOE UP AND DOWN, . . . . . . . . . .        85 MAD KING GOLL V   51
    DOWN BY THE SALLEY GARDENS . . . . . . . . . . .          90 SALLEY GARDENS    T
    DOWN BY THE SALLEY GARDENS MY LOVE AND I DID MEET! . . .  90 SALLEY GARDENS    1
    AND FATHER JOHN WENT DOWN! . . . . . . . . . . .          92 FATHER OHART      10
    AS HE WENT UP AND DOWN: . . . . . . . . . . . .           92 FATHER OHART      18
    AND SLOWLY UP AND DOWN. . . . . . . . . . . . .           97 FOXHUNTER     V   8
    AND GENTLY UP AND DOWN. . . . . . . . . . . . .           97 FOXHUNTER     V   8
    "NOW LEAVE THE CHAIR DOWN ON THE GRASS, . . . . . .       97 FOXHUNTER     V   9
    THE WEAK WORM HIDING DOWN IN ITS SMALL CAVE, . . . . .   101 ROSE UPON ROOD    16
    THE SORROWS OF THE WORLD BOW DOWN MY HEAD, . . . . . .   104 FERGUS DRUID  V   38A
    AND THE WHOLE WORLD WEIGHS DOWN UPON MY HEART-- . . . .  104 FERGUS DRUID  V   38A
    THEREON HE SHOOK THE MORE AND CAST HIM DOWN . . . . .    106 CUCHULAIN SEA     14
    ALEEL, THE SWINEHERD, WEPT AND CAST HIM DOWN . . . . .   106 CUCHULAIN SEA V   14
    HE CAUGHT HIS BREATH AND CAST HIM WEEPING DOWN . . . .   106 CUCHULAIN SEA V   14
    AND WENT DOWN TO THE LONG SANDS ALONE, . . . . . . .    111 CUCHULAIN SEA V   84
    AND HE WENT DOWN TO THE LONG SANDS ALONE, . . . . . .   111 CUCHULAIN SEA V   84
    BOW DOWN, ARCHANGELS, IN YOUR DIM ABODE! . . . . . .    112 ROSE OF WORLD     11
    LOOKED DOWN ON YOU FROM HEAVEN'S DOOR-POST . . . . .    112 ROSE OF PEACE     3
    LOOKED DOWN ON YOU FROM HEAVEN'S DOOR-POSTS, . . . . .  112 ROSE OF PEACE V   3
    AND ALL FOLK SEEING HIM BOW DOWN. . . . . . . . .      113 ROSE OF PEACE     9
    THEY HAVE GONE DOWN UNDER THE SAME WHITE STARS, . . .  115 ROSE OF BATTLE    34
    AND NODDING BY THE FIRE, TAKE DOWN THIS BOOK, . . . .  120 YOU ARE OLD       2
    AND BENDING DOWN BESIDE THE GLOWING BARS, . . . . .    121 YOU ARE OLD       9
    ALL THE HEAVENS BOW DOWN TO HEAVEN, . . . . . . .     125 CATHLEEN PARA     15
    SHE GOES DOWN THE FLOOR OF HEAVEN. . . . . . . .      125 CATHLEEN PARA V   13
    SENT ONE OF HIS GREAT ANGELS DOWN . . . . . . . .     134 FR GILLIGAN       43
    WHEN WE BENT DOWN ABOVE THE FADING COALS . . . . . .   136 TO SOME I TALK    3
    HE SAT DOWN AND PLAYED IN A DREAM . . . . . . . . .    145 HOST OF AIR   V   27
    THE SOUTH IS POURING DOWN ROSES OF CRIMSON FIRE: . . .  154 BELOVED PEACE     6
    AND PUSHED THE LATCHES DOWN. . . . . . . . . . .      159 CAP AND BELLS     12
    SHE SNICKED THE BRASS BOLTS DOWN. . . . . . . . .     159 CAP AND BELLS     12
    AND PUSHED THE BRASS BOLT DOWN. . . . . . . . . .     159 CAP AND BELLS V   12
    BEING WEARY OF THE WORLD'S EMPIRES, BOW DOWN TO YOU,  . 161 BLACK PIG         7
    AND THEREFORE MY HEART BOWS DOWN ANEW: . . . . . . .   164 PERFECT BEAUTY V  6
    WE WILL BEND DOWN AND LOOSEN OUR HAIR OVER YOU, . . .  172 TRAV PASSION      6
    BEND DOWN AND PRAY FOR ALL THAT SIN I WOVE IN SONG,  . 173 SPEAKS HEARERS    5
    BEND DOWN AND PRAY FOR THE GREAT SIN I WOVE IN SONG,  . 173 SPEAKS HEARERS V  5
    BLOSSOM PALE, SHE PULLED DOWN THE PALE BLOSSOM . . . .  199 ARROW         V   5
    BETTER GO DOWN UPON YOUR MARROW-BONES . . . . . . .    204 ADAMS CURSE       7
    BETTER GO DOWN UPON YOUR MARROW BONES . . . . . . .    204 ADAMS CURSE   V   7
    AND SHAKE DOWN THUNDER ON THE STONES BECAUSE THE RED WINDS 207 HANRAHANS SONG V  7
    RAVE!
    O! LAY THE SHRILLY TRUMPET DOWN, . . . . . . . . .    212 BLESS PSALTER     4
    O NO, O NO! THEY HURRY DOWN . . . . . . . . . .       213 BLESS PSALTER     12
    HE HAS STOOPED DOWN AND KISSED HER ON THE LIPS. . . .  232 SHADOW WATER B    230
    AGAINST A BEECH-BOLE, HE THREW DOWN THE BEAST . . . .  278 TWO KINGS         36
    AGAINST A BEECH BOLE, HE THREW DOWN THE BEAST . . . .  278 TWO KINGS     V   36
    BUT FINDING HIM STILL SILENT I STOOPED DOWN . . . . .  281 TWO KINGS         109
    BEFORE HIS CHAIR AND BENDING DOWN MY HEAD . . . . .    282 TWO KINGS         132
    BEFORE YOU'LL PUT YOUR GUINEAS DOWN, . . . . . . .     287 TO WEALTHY MAN    5
    BEFORE YOU'VE PUT YOUR GUINEAS DOWN, . . . . . . .     287 TO WEALTHY MAN V  5
    FELL DOWN UPON THE DUST AND SNORED. . . . . . . .     297 THREE BEGGARS     60
    WENT DOWN UPON A HAND AND KNEE . . . . . . . . .      304 HOUR DAWN     V   45
    I SHOULD NOT BE TOO DOWN IN THE MOUTH . . . . . . .    306 HOUR DAWN         88
    PULL DOWN THE BLINDS, BRING FIDDLE AND CLARIONET . . . 311 MOUNTAIN TOMB     5
    SOON TOPPLES DOWN THE HILL. . . . . . . . . . .       335 YOUNG BEAUTY      6
    HAS MARKED A DISTANT OBJECT DOWN, . . . . . . . .     337 TOM OROUGHLEY     3
    THAT HAS LOOKED DOWN . . . . . . . . . . . .          344 DAWN              2
    THE BEATING DOWN OF THE WISE . . . . . . . . . .      348 FISHERMAN         23
    AND GREAT ART BEATEN DOWN. . . . . . . . . . . .      348 FISHERMAN         24
```

215

DOWN   (CONTINUED)

	PAGE	TITLE		LINE
AND THE DOWN TURN OF HIS WRIST	348	FISHERMAN	V	33
"CALL DOWN THE HAWK FROM THE AIR;	349	HAWK		1
I HAVE GONE ABOUT THE HOUSE, GONE UP AND DOWN	350	HER PRAISE		2
FROM GOING DOWN OF THE SUN I HAVE DREAMED	358	PRESENCES	V	3
LAID HIS STRONG BONES DOWN IN DEATH	360	ALF POLLEXFEN		3
DESTROY THE VIEW BY CUTTING DOWN AN ASH	372	ON GOING HOUSE		13
OUT OF THE UP AND DOWN, THE WAGON-WHEEL	377	PHASES OF MOON		120
OUT OF THE UP AND DOWN, THE WAGON WHEEL	377	PHASES OF MOON	V	120
A ROMAN CAESAR IS HELD DOWN	379	SAINT HUNCH		4
DOWN TO HER CELL AND THERE ALIT,	397	POLIT PRISONER		4
PULL DOWN ESTABLISHED HONOUR; HAWK FOR NEWS	398	LEADERS CROWD		3
IT HAD SET DOWN AMONG ITS LAWS;	399	BREAK OF DAY		16
NOW GYRING DOWN AND PERNING THERE	400	DEMON BEAST		26
AND RAINS DOWN LIFE UNTIL THE BASIN SPILLS,	417	ANCEST HOUSES		4
LAST NIGHT THEY TRUNDLED DOWN THE ROAD	425	STARES NEST		13
MELT DOWN, AS IT WERE WAX IN THE SUN'S RAYS;	428	NINETEEN 19		12
MY WORKS ARE ALL STAMPED DOWN INTO THE SULTRY MUD.	442	BLACK CENTAUR		3
LAUGHED; AND PLUNGING DOWN	453	MERMAID		4
AM SET DOWN STANDING IN THE WOOD	453	DEATH OF HARE		11
SHE WHO HAD BROUGHT GREAT HECTOR DOWN	455	HIS MEMORIES		15
FOR THAT OLD MADGE COMES DOWN THE LANE,	456	FRIENDS YOUTH		5
AND THEN I LAUGH TILL TEARS RUN DOWN	456	FRIENDS YOUTH		17
OR THE BED OF DOWN.	458	SECRETS OF OLD		18
SAT DOWN UPON THE FOUNTAIN'S MARBLE EDGE,	463	HARUN RASHID		43
AND SHE LAY DOWN UPON HER BED AND SLEPT,	467	HARUN RASHID		146
. . . HAD DRAGGED HIM DOWN INTO MANKIND,	481	BLOOD AND MOON		20
RESPONSIBILITY SO WEIGHS ME DOWN.	501	VACILLATION		50
WEIGH ME DOWN, AND NOT A DAY	501	VACILLATION		54
MAY CALL DOWN CURSES ON HIS HEAD	508	JANE BISHOP		4
AND LAY DOWN THAT HEAD	534	CONSOLATION		4
DOWN EVERY WITHERED FINGER FROM THE TOP;	537	HER VISION		11
BRIGHTNESS REMAINS; A BRIGHTER STAR SHOOTS DOWN;	541	PARN FUNERAL 1		4
HYSTERICA PASSIO DRAGGED THIS QUARRY DOWN.	542	PARN FUNERAL 1		21
DOWN THE FANATIC, DOWN THE CLOWN;	544	TO SAME TUNE 1		8
DOWN THE FANATIC, DOWN THE CLOWN;	544	TO SAME TUNE 1		8
DOWN, DOWN, HAMMER THEM DOWN,	544	TO SAME TUNE 1		9
DOWN, DOWN, HAMMER THEM DOWN,	544	TO SAME TUNE 1		9
DOWN, DOWN, HAMMER THEM DOWN,	544	TO SAME TUNE 1		9
DOWN TO THE TUNE OF O'DONNELL ABU.	544	TO SAME TUNE 1		10
DOWN THE FANATIC, DOWN THE CLOWN;	545	TO SAME TUNE 1		18
DOWN THE FANATIC, DOWN THE CLOWN;	545	TO SAME TUNE 1		18
DOWN, DOWN, HAMMER THEM DOWN,	545	TO SAME TUNE 1		19
DOWN, DOWN, HAMMER THEM DOWN,	545	TO SAME TUNE 1		19
DOWN, DOWN, HAMMER THEM DOWN,	545	TO SAME TUNE 1		19
DOWN TO THE TUNE OF O'DONNELL ABU.	545	TO SAME TUNE 1		20
DOWN THE FANATIC, DOWN THE CLOWN;	545	TO SAME TUNE 1		28
DOWN THE FANATIC, DOWN THE CLOWN;	545	TO SAME TUNE 1		28
DOWN, DOWN, HAMMER THEM DOWN,	545	TO SAME TUNE 1		29
DOWN, DOWN, HAMMER THEM DOWN,	545	TO SAME TUNE 1		29
DOWN, DOWN, HAMMER THEM DOWN,	545	TO SAME TUNE 1		29
DOWN TO THE TUNE OF O'DONNELL ABU.	545	TO SAME TUNE 1		30
DOWN THE FANATIC, DOWN THE CLOWN;	546	TO SAME TUNE 2	V	REF
DOWN THE FANATIC, DOWN THE CLOWN;	546	TO SAME TUNE 2	V	REF
DOWN, DOWN, HAMMER THEM DOWN,	546	TO SAME TUNE 2	V	REF
DOWN, DOWN, HAMMER THEM DOWN,	546	TO SAME TUNE 2	V	REF
DOWN, DOWN, HAMMER THEM DOWN,	546	TO SAME TUNE 2	V	REF
DOWN TO THE TUNE OF O'DONNELL ABU.	546	TO SAME TUNE 2	V	REF
A SLAVE BOWS DOWN TO A SLAVE.	547	TO SAME TUNE 3		6
DOWN THE FANATIC, DOWN THE CLOWN;	548	TO SAME TUNE 3	V	REF
DOWN THE FANATIC, DOWN THE CLOWN;	548	TO SAME TUNE 3	V	REF
DOWN, DOWN, HAMMER THEM DOWN,	548	TO SAME TUNE 3	V	REF
DOWN, DOWN, HAMMER THEM DOWN,	548	TO SAME TUNE 3	V	REF
DOWN, DOWN, HAMMER THEM DOWN,	548	TO SAME TUNE 3	V	REF
DOWN TO THE TUNE OF O'DONNELL ABU.	548	TO SAME TUNE 3	V	REF
TO-MORROW NIGHT I WILL BREAK DOWN THE DOOR.	551	SONGS REWRIT 1		6
TO-MORROW NIGHT I WILL BREAK DOWN THE DOOR.	551	SONGS REWRIT 1		12
I THOUGHT TO HAVE WHISTLED HER DOWN THAT WAY,	551	SONGS REWRIT 1		15
TO-MORROW NIGHT I WILL BREAK DOWN THE DOOR.	551	SONGS REWRIT 1		18
TOMORROW NIGHT I WILL BREAK DOWN THE DOOR.	551	SONGS REWRIT 1	V	REF
DOWN LIMB AND BREAST OR DOWN THAT GLIMMERING BELLY	560	MAGIC DRUM		5
DOWN LIMB AND BREAST OR DOWN THAT GLIMMERING BELLY	560	MAGIC DRUM		5
THE HAND AND LASH THAT BEAT DOWN FRIGID ROME?	560	WHENCE COME		10
BEAT DOWN UPON THEIR NAKED BODIES, KNOW	563	MERU		12
"I KNOW THAT I MUST DROP DOWN DEAD	569	THREE BUSHES		17
YET WHAT COULD I BUT DROP DOWN DEAD	569	THREE BUSHES		19
GIRLS DOWN ON THE SEASHORE	588	OLD WICKED MAN		30
THEY TURN DOWN THEIR BEDS.	589	OLD WICKED MAN		35
PARNELL CAME DOWN THE ROAD, HE SAID TO A CHEERING MAN;	590	PARNELL		1
FOR I CAN PUT THE WHOLE LOT DOWN, AND ALL I HAVE TO SAY	593	PILGRIM		24
BUT THEY THREW DOWN THEIR PISTOLS	596	COLONEL MARTIN		59
HEART-SMITTEN WITH EMOTION I SINK DOWN,	602	GALLERY REVIS		17
HEART SMITTEN WITH EMOTION, I SINK DOWN,	602	GALLERY REVIS	V	17
EVERYTHING DOWN TO THAT SOLE TEST AGAIN,	603	GALLERY REVIS		46
ALL THINGS DOWN TO THAT COMMON TEST AGAIN,	603	GALLERY REVIS	V	46
THAT RED-HEADED RECTOR IN COUNTY DOWN,	604	YOU CONTENT		11
AND KNOCK THE OTHERS DOWN.	606	SONGS BURDEN 1		26
CALCULATIONS THAT LOOK BUT CASUAL FLESH, PUT DOWN	610	STATUES		11
DOWN THE MOUNTAIN WALLS	612	NEWS ORACLE		30
A SLAVE BOWS DOWN TO A SLAVE.	614	MARCH SONGS 2		6
WHAT MARCHES DOWN THE MOUNTAIN PASS?	615	MARCH SONGS 2		17

	PAGE	TITLE		LINE
DOWN (CONTINUED)				
WHAT TEARS DOWN A TREE THAT HAS NOTHING WITHIN IT?	615	MARCH SONGS 2		23
WHAT MARCHES DOWN THE MOUNTAIN PASS?	615	MARCH SONGS 2		27
WHAT TEARS DOWN A TREE HAS NOTHING WITHIN IT?	615	MARCH SONGS 2	V	23
BUT HE TOOK DOWN THE MOON	616	MARCH SONGS 3		8
BUT HE TOOK DOWN THE MOON	616	MARCH SONGS 3		18
BUT HE TOOK DOWN THE MOON	616	MARCH SONGS 3		28
AND I CRIED TEARS DOWN.	628	JANE MOUNTAIN		22
I MUST LIE DOWN WHERE ALL THE LADDERS START,	630	CIRCUS ANIMALS		39
SLEEPLESS WOULD LIE DOWN AND DIE.	632	MAN AND ECHO		18
LIE DOWN AND DIE. THAT WERE TO SHIRK	632	MAN AND ECHO		19
'TIS MORN! THY SHEEP ARE WANDERING DOWN THE VALE--	645	ISLE STAT I 1		3
SAD LADY OF THE DEEP, POURS DOWN HER LIGHT!	650	ISLE STAT I 1		127
OUT OF THE AIR. AND WHEN? WHEN THE SUN GOES DOWN	652	ISLE STAT I 2		29
THE WIND- AT EVENING WHEN THE SUN GOES DOWN.	653	ISLE STAT I 2		50
DEEP-EYED, SLOW-FOOTING DOWN THE EMPTY GLADE.	653	ISLE STAT I 2		55
WHEN LOW THE SUN SANK DOWN IN CLOTTED FLAME	656	ISLE STAT I 3		30
DOWN TO THEIR FEET THE STARS THAT SHINE ALONE,	662	ISLE STAT II 1		80
AND WHO WILL THROW HIS MANSION DOWN	671	ISLE STAT II 3		135
AND DOWN I CAME AS A FALCON SWOOPS	673	ISLE STAT II 3		178
GO UP AND DOWN, AND RAISE THEIR HEADS AND SING	682	SEEKER		30
DROPT DOWN THE VELVET DARKNESS FROM ABOVE,	688	TWO TITANS		37
DOWN TO THE MOTHER OF THE FOILED AND DEAD.	688	TWO TITANS		50
FAILURE FOR GLORY DOWN ON THEE, AND MOULD	688	TWO TITANS		54
DOWN LOW THE HEAD OF HIS MAGNIFICENCE	689	NETTLESHIP	V	6
IN AUTUMN, WHEN FAR DOWN THE MOUNTAIN SLOPES	690	MOSADA 1		12
OF HIS SAD GOD; AND DOWN AMONG THE GRASS	690	MOSADA 1		16
SLID CIRCLING DOWN AND SOFTLY TOUCHED MY LIPS	690	MOSADA 1		21
DOWN THE LONG VALLEYS FROM MY PEOPLE'S TENTS,	691	MOSADA 1		30
SINKS DOWN AT LAST WITH YONDER MINARET.	691	MOSADA 1	V	36
STAY, STAY, OR I WILL HOLD YOUR WHITE ARMS DOWN.	694	MOSADA 1		92
FROM FASTING--SEE, THE RED LIGHT SLANTING DOWN	697	MOSADA 2		36
THE BURTHEN OF THY TRUTH. REACH DOWN THY HANDS	698	MOSADA 2		53
CIRCLING THE BRAIN? MY BROTHERS WILL PASS DOWN	699	MOSADA 3		6
THE BRAIN. MY BROTHERS WILL BE PASSING DOWN	699	MOSADA 3	V	6
CIRCLING THE BRAIN? MY BROTHERS NOW PASS DOWN	699	MOSADA 3	V	6
WHERE SHALL I LAY ME DOWN? THAT QUESTION IS	700	MOSADA 3		36
NAY HERE, I'LL LAY ME DOWN WHERE I CAN WATCH	700	MOSADA 3		39
FOR NIGHT COMES FAST. LOOK DOWN ON ME, MY LOVE,	703	MOSADA 3		103
OFTEN HE HAD BENT DOWN SOME BOUGH ALL BRIGHT	710	FERENCZ RENYI		28
OFTEN HE HAD BENT DOWN SOME BOUGH ALL BRIGHT WITH BERRIES!	710	FERENCZ RENYI	V	28
I SAT ME DOWN BESIDE THEE, AND I KNEW	713	FERENCZ RENYI		92
DOWN THE VAPOURS FALL AND HIDE THEM FROM THE CHILDREN OF A DAY,	719	PHANTOM SHIP		27
AND THE WINDS COME DOWN AND BLOW THEM WITH THE VAPOURS FAR AWAY.	719	PHANTOM SHIP		28
LAY DOWN THE BURDEN OF THY RACE.	736	SUMMER EVENING		14
"AND ALL DOWN FROM NORTHUMBERLAND	740	EARL PAUL		9
AND FLUNG DOWN CLASHING ON THE FLOOR	740	EARL PAUL		15
AND FLY AMONG THE FOAM. THRUST DOWN THE HELM,	750	SHADOW WATER A		88
I SWEAR IT, THOUGH I GLADLY WOULD LIE DOWN	758	SHADOW WATER A		225
I HAD THROWN IT DOWN BEHIND THIS COIL OF ROPE.	759	SHADOW WATER A		245
"TILL THE SUN GOES DOWN AND AN HOUR OF THE CLOCK"	779	GOING THE ROAD		7
OR BURNED GREAT CITIES DOWN,	789	SINGING HEAD		16
YOU HAD BROUGHT DOWN BEFORE YOU DIED.	791	REPRISALS		2
DOWNS				
THAT HAS LESS UPS AND DOWNS THAN ROBBERY.	222	SHADOW WATER B		7
NO UPS AND DOWNS, MY PRETTY,	592	DRUNK SOBRIETY		13
DOWN-TURN				
AND THE DOWN-TURN OF HIS WRIST	348	FISHERMAN		33
DOWNWARD				
FACE DOWNWARD, TOSSING IN A TROUBLED SLEEP!	185	QUEEN MAEVE		106
DOWNY				
AND DOWNY BEES HAVE AMBUSCADE,	67	HAPPY SHEPHERD	V	46A
IN THEIR DOWNY CAPS, AND STARTLE THE NAPS	644	SONG FAERIES		11
IN THEIR DOWNY CAPS, AND STARTLE THE NAPS	676	ISLE STAT II 3		258
DOWSON				
DOWSON AND JOHNSON MOST I PRAISE--	273	GREY ROCK		62
DOZEN				
THESE DOZEN WEEKS. AND I HAD THOUGHT TO MAKE	222	SHADOW WATER B		4
AND FOR A DOZEN HOURS HAVE BEEN A PART	230	SHADOW WATER B		171
SCARED BY THE SPLASHING OF A DOZEN COWS!	419	MY HOUSE		10
A DOZEN NIGHTS OF NATURAL SLEEP, AND THEN	468	HARUN RASHID		150
AND HALF A DOZEN IN FORMATION THERE,	489	COOLE PARK 29		20
DRAG				
I SCARCE COULD DRAG MY FEET,	94	MOLL MAGEE		10
DRAGGED				
CAME TO MY TOWER AS AGE DRAGGED AFTER AGE	45	OISIN 2	V	242
BELOVED, HAVING DRAGGED THE NET ABOUT US,	252	SHADOW WATER B		615
AS THOUGH IT DRAGGED ROAD-METAL. MY CURSE ON PLAYS	260	FASC DIFFICULT		8
AS THOUGH IT DRAGGED ROAD METAL. MY CURSE ON PLAYS	260	FASC DIFFICULT	V	8
I DRAGGED FROM GOBAN'S MOUNTAIN-TOP	304	HOUR DAWN		50
. . . HAD DRAGGED HIM DOWN INTO MANKIND,	481	BLOOD AND MOON		20
HYSTERICA PASSIO DRAGGED THIS QUARRY DOWN.	542	PARN FUNERAL 1		21
AND HE IS DRAGGED AGAIN BEFORE HER FEET.	688	TWO TITANS		43
AND SHE IS DRAGGED TO WHERE THE WILLOW BANDS	714	FERENCZ RENYI		108
DRAGGED INTO BEING	785	WOMANS BEAUTY		27
DRAGGLED				
AND SAID, CASTING ASIDE HIS DRAGGLED HAIR,	105	CUCHULAIN SEA	V	3
DRAGON				
THE POLAR DRAGON SLEPT,	174	ELEMENT POWERS		4

```
                                                            PAGE    TITLE        LINE
DRAGON   (CONTINUED)
      DRAGON THAT LOVED THE WORLD AND HELD US TO IT,  . . . .     251 SHADOW WATER B    598
      THAT DRAGON THROUGH THE FADING LIGHT,  . . . . . . .        385 ROBARTES DANCE      4
      THE HALF-DEAD DRAGON WAS HER THOUGHT,  . . . . . .          385 ROBARTES DANCE      6
      MY WRETCHED DRAGON IS PERPLEXED.  . . . . . . . . .         386 ROBARTES DANCE     41
      NOW DAYS ARE DRAGON RIDDEN, THE NIGHTMARE  . . . . .        429 NINETEEN 19    V   25
      IT SEEMED THAT A DRAGON OF AIR . . . . . . . . . .          430 NINETEEN 19        51
      AND THEN YOU STOOD AMONG THE DRAGON RINGS. . . . . .        533 HER TRIUMPH    V    7
DRAGON-GUARDED
      IN A DRAGON-GUARDED LAND,  . . . . . . . . . . .            309 REALISTS            3
DRAGON-RIDDEN
      NOW DAYS ARE DRAGON-RIDDEN, THE NIGHTMARE  . . . . .        429 NINETEEN 19        25
DRAGON-RINGS
      AND THEN YOU STOOD AMONG THE DRAGON-RINGS. . . . . .        533 HER TRIUMPH         7
DRAGON'S
      I DID THE DRAGON'S WILL UNTIL YOU CAME . . . . . . .        533 HER TRIUMPH         1
DRAGONS
      DRAGONS WITH EYES OF RUBY.  THE WHOLE SHIP . . . . .        248 SHADOW WATER B    535
      WITH THE DRAGONS? . . . . . . . . . . . . . .              309 REALISTS            8
DRAGON-SCALES
      UNTIL AFAR APPEAR THE GLEAMING DRAGON-SCALES! . . . .       651 ISLE STAT I 1     160
DRAGS
      AND DRAGS HIM THROUGH THE SEA.  WELL, NET OR NONE,  . .     224 SHADOW WATER B     57
      THAT BELLIES AND DRAGS IN THE WIND . . . . . . .           358 BALLOON MIND        3
      PARDONED, DRAGS OUT LONELY YEARS . . . . . . . .           475 EVA GORE-BOOTH      8
DRAIN
      UNLESS WE DRAIN MORE FLAGONS IN A YEAR . . . . . . .        225 SHADOW WATER B     70
DRAINED
      AND AFTER, DRAINED DRY, . . . . . . . . . . .              310 WITCH               4
DRAKE
      THE WILD DUCK AND THE DRAKE . . . . . . . . . .            143 HOST OF AIR         2
      CURVING BENEATH THE PROW; AS SOME WILD DRAKE . . . . .      659 ISLE STAT II 1     16
DRAMA
      WHAT SACRED DRAMA THROUGH HER BODY HEAVED . . . . . .       560 WHENCE COME        11
DRAMATIC
      INTRODUCTION TO A DRAMATIC POEM  . . . . . . . . .          217 WOODS OF COOLE V    T
DRAMATIS
      IGNORANT WHAT DRAMATIS PERSONAE SPAKE! . . . . . . .        560 WHENCE COME         4
DRAMATIST
      IGNORANT WHAT THAT DRAMATIST ENJOINS, . . . . . . .        560 WHENCE COME         8
DRANK
      WE LAY ON SKINS OF OTTERS, AND DRANK WINE, . . . . .        41 OISIN 2           188
      I SAT AND MUSED AND DRANK SWEET WINE; . . . . . .          82 MAD KING GOLL      13
      AND DRANK AND YAWNED AND STRETCHED HIM OUT, . . . . .       307 HOUR DAWN         108
      WHO KNOWS HOW SHE DRANK THE WIND . . . . . .               381 SONGS FOOL 2        6
      HOLLOW OF CHEEK AS THOUGH IT DRANK THE WIND . . . . .       444 SCHOOL CHILDR      27
      DRANK TAR-WATER WITH THE BISHOP OF CLOYNE. . . . . .        486 SEVEN SAGES         5
      I WOULD THAT I DRANK WITH MY LOVE ON MY KNEE, . . . .       551 SONGS REWRIT 1      9
DRAPERIES
      MADE DRAPERIES THAT SEEMED TO RISE  . . . . . . .          566 LAPIS LAZULI       31
      STRANGE DRAPERIES DID ALL THE SIDES ADORN, . . . . .       657 ISLE STAT I 3      55
DRAPERY
      TENT-POLE OF EDEN; THE TENT'S DRAPERY; . . . . . .         483 VERONIC NAPKIN      2
      TENT POLE OF EDEN; THE TENT'S DRAPERY; . . . . . .         483 VERONIC NAPKIN V    2
      WHAT MADE THE DRAPERY GLISTEN SO? . . . . . . . .          625 NATIVITY            3
DRASTIC
      THAT IF NOTHING DRASTIC IS DONE  . . . . . . . .           565 LAPIS LAZULI        5
      THAT IF NOTHING DRASTIC CAN BE DONE . . . . . . . .        565 LAPIS LAZULI   V    5
DRAUGHT
      BECAUSE OF THAT OLD DRAUGHT UNDER THE DOOR, . . . . .       228 SHADOW WATER B    127
DRAUGHTY
      THAT TURNS AND CHANGES LIKE HIS DRAUGHTY SEAS? . . . .      265 ABBEY THEATRE      12
DRAVE
      HAD SURGED UP IN A PLUMY FIRE, I DRAVE . . . . . .         41 OISIN 2           181
      WITH SURGE OF PLUMY FIRE, LUNGING I DRAVE . . . . .        41 OISIN 2        V  181
      SURGED UP IN PLUMY FIRE, I LUNGED AND DRAVE . . . .        41 OISIN 2        V  181
DRAW
      AMRITA.  DRAW YOU NEAR, AND 'NEATH YON PILLAR . . . .      71 ANASHU VIJAYA  V  13A
      IF YOU WILL DRAW THAT SWORD OUT OF ITS SCABBARD . . .     225 SHADOW WATER B     78
      TOWARD PEOPLED TARA, NOR STOOD TO DRAW HIS BREATH . . .   279 TWO KINGS          46
      ON PEOPLED TARA, NOR STOOD TO DRAW HIS BREATH . . .      279 TWO KINGS      V   46
      TOWARDS PEOPLED TARA, NOR STOOD TO DRAW HIS BREATH . .    279 TWO KINGS      V   46
      WHENCE TURBULENT ITALY SHOULD DRAW . . . . . . .          288 TO WEALTHY MAN     25
      DRAW THE GLASNEVIN COVERLET ANEW . . . . . . . .          293 TO A SHADE     V   19
      MY DISCONTENTED HEART TO DRAW CONTENT . . . . . .         334 LIVING BEAUTY       3
      "BUT WHERE CAN WE DRAW WATER," . . . . . . . .           396 ROSE TREE          13
      AS THOUGH TO DRAW THEM CLOSER YET.  RAMMED FULL . . .     579 DOR WELLESLEY       5
      DRAW ROUND, BELOVED AND BITTER MEN, . . . . . . .        584 GHOST ROG CASE     37
      DRAW ROUND AND RAISE A SHOUT; . . . . . . . .            584 GHOST ROG CASE     38
      SOME BARBAROUS, UN-FAERY THING DRAW NEAR. . . . . .       656 ISLE STAT I 3      21
      OF WONDERS! EVE OF PRODIGIES! DRAW! DRAW! . . . .         664 ISLE STAT II 2     62
      OF WONDERS! EVE OF PRODIGIES! DRAW! DRAW! . . . .         664 ISLE STAT II 2     62
      DRAW STAR TO STAR, AS ON THAT EVE HE PASSED . . . .       691 MOSADA 1           29
      I'LL DRAW MY CLOAK AROUND ME; IT IS COLD. . . . .         704 MOSADA 3          123
      NOW STEPS DRAW CLOSE, HE HIDES BENEATH A DRUM. . . .      713 FERENCZ RENYI      78
      FROM HAYNAU'S LIFTED FINGERS--TWO DRAW NIGH . . . .       714 FERENCZ RENYI     104
      I SWEAR IT.  LET EVERY MAN DRAW OUT HIS SWORD. . . .      758 SHADOW WATER A    230
DRAWETH
      AND YONDER HUDDLING BLACKNESS DRAWETH NIGH-- . . . .      663 ISLE STAT II 2     15
DRAWING
      A NEW MODELLED DOLL, OR DRAWING, . . . . . . . .         362 DOLLS DRAWINGS      2
```

DRAWING-ROOM
    IN A DRAWING-ROOM. . . . . 685 DRAWING-ROOM   T
    IN A DRAWING-ROOM . . . . L . . . . . . 734 QUATRAIN APHOR V   T
DRAWINGS
    CERTAIN ARTISTS BRING HER DOLLS AND DRAWINGS . . . . . . 362 DOLLS DRAWINGS   T
DRAWN   SEE DOLPHIN-DRAWN
    UNTIL AT LAST THE DOUBLE HORNS, DRAWN BACKWARD, ... 278 TWO KINGS   21
    AND KNELT ABOVE IT WITH DRAWN KNIFE. ON THE INSTANT . 278 TWO KINGS   37
    AND WHEN I HAD GOT MY WILL AND DRAWN YOU HERE, ... 284 TWO KINGS   158
    PAINTINGS OF THE DOLPHIN DRAWN: . . . . 309 REALISTS   V   4
    I'LL SAY AND MAYBE DREAM I HAVE DRAWN CONTENT, . . . 333 LIVING BEAUTY V   1
    OUT OF THAT RAVING TIDE--IS DRAWN BETWIXT . . . . . . 377 PHASES OF MOON 122
    CHAUCER HAD NOT DRAWN BREATH . . . . 421 MY TABLE   8
    BUT O! AMBITIOUS HEART, HAD SUCH A PROOF DRAWN FORTH . 427 PHANTOM HATRED 36
    ALL TEETH WERE DRAWN, ALL ANCIENT TRICKS UNLEARNED, . . 429 NINETEEN 19   17
    NEVER TO HAVE DRAWN THE BREATH OF LIFE, ... 459 FROM OEDIPUS   11
    DRAWN THROUGH THE WANDERING VEGETATIVE DREAM, ... 467 HARUN RASHID 143
    AND I LEFT SHIVERING. THE VOICE HAS DRAWN . . . . 469 HARUN RASHID 179
    WHEELS BY MILK-WHITE ASSES DRAWN . . . . 502 VACILLATION   62
    THE CURTAINS DRAWN UPON UNFRIENDLY NIGHT, ... 523 LONG SILENCE   4
    THE BLINDS DRAWN UP": MAUD GONNE AT HOWTH STATION WAITING 578 LOFTY THINGS   10
      A TRAIN,
    NASCHINA'S GONE, DRAWN BY A THIRST OF LOVE, ... 664 ISLE STAT II 2   59
    I FEEL A FINGER DRAWN ACROSS MY CHEEK! . . . . . 694 MOSADA 1   96
    OF SOLDIERS DRAWN IS ON A GRASSY SPOT. . . . . . 712 FERENCZ RENYI V 64
DRAWS
    WHO DRAWS A BUCKET WITH THE REST . . . . 335 YOUNG BEAUTY   5
    THE BOAT DRAWS NEAR AND NEAR. YOU HEED ME NOT! . . . 663 ISLE STAT II 2   23
    THE MAN WHOSE HOUR OF DEATH DRAWS NIGH. . . . . . 716 FAIRY DOCTOR   6
DREAD
    "FRET NOT WITH SPEECH THE PHANTOMS DREAD," . . . . . 12 OISIN 1   V 148
    "THESE FORMS?" "VEX NOT WITH SPEECH THE PHANTOMS DREAD." 29 OISIN 2   V   5
    LONG WHILE, ARE WHIPS OF STEEL. "IS HE SO DREAD?" . . 35 OISIN 2   V 88
    FOR BATTLE." "FLY YE FROM A THING SO DREAD. . . . 35 OISIN 2   V 90
    LEST NIAMH SHUDDER. FULL OF HOPE AND DREAD . . . . 41 OISIN 2   183
    DREAD OATH, WHO DWELL ON SACRED HIMALAY, ... 74 ANASHU VIJAYA   67
    AND HIS HEART WAS BLACKENED BY DREAD, ... 145 HOST OF AIR V 40B
    WHAT NEED HAVE YOU TO DREAD . . . . 312 CHILD DANCING   11
    WHAT NEED THAT YOU SHOULD DREAD . . . . 312 CHILD DANCING V 11
    ALL DREAD AFAR TILL MORNING'S BACK, ... 435 FOR MY SON   6
    AND WHEN I WAKE TOWARDS MORN I DREAD MYSELF, ... 448 HERO GIRL FOOL   5
    NOR DREAD NOR HOPE ATTEND . . . . 476 DEATH   1
    DREAD HAS FOLLOWED LONGING, ... 519 LOVES LONENESS 11
    GAIETY TRANSFIGURING ALL THAT DREAD. . . . . . . 565 LAPIS LAZULI   17
    I SING WHAT WAS LOST AND DREAD WHAT WAS WON, ... 591 WHAT WAS LOST   1
    MORE DREAD THE LIFE THAT WE LIVE, ... 615 MARCH SONGS 2   15
    WHY DO YOU DREAD US SO? . . . . 635 BLACK TOWER   16
    OF THE DREAD WOODS: ALONG THEIR RUSSET FLOOR . . . . 675 ISLE STAT II 3 243
    ALL THESE ARE SOULS THAT FLY FROM THEIR DREAD SELVES. . 686 LIFE   4
    ALL THESE ARE SOULS WHO FLY FROM THEIR DREAD SELVES. . 734 QUATRAIN APHOR 4
    ALL THESE ARE SOULS THAT FLY FROM THEIR DREAD SELVES. . 734 QUATRAIN APHOR V 4
    THEIR DREAD OF AUTUMN'S MORTAL WING, ... 736 SUMMER EVENING   2
    AND DREAD NO MORE FOUL AUTUMN'S WING, ... 737 SUMMER EVENING 18
DREADFUL
    OR CARVE A DREADFUL SPEAR. . . . . 32 OISIN 2   V 56
    "IS HE SO DREADFUL?" "BE NOT OVER-BOLD, ... 35 OISIN 2   88
    "IS HE SO DREADFUL?" "BE NOT OVER-BOLD, ... 35 OISIN 2   V 88
    LEST THEY SHOULD LOOK UPON SOME DREADFUL SIGHT: . . . 38 OISIN 2   142
    AND MAY SOME SUDDEN DREADFUL ILL BEFALL HER! . . . . 74 ANASHU VIJAYA   59
    AND MAY SOME DREADFUL ILL BEFALL HER QUICK! . . . . 74 ANASHU VIJAYA V 59
    FOR THREE DAYS MORE IN DREADFUL QUIETUDE. . . . . . 110 CUCHULAIN SEA   78
    ALL THOSE DREADFUL THUNDER-STONES, ... 509 JANE REPROVED   2
    ALL THOSE DREADFUL THUNDERSTONES, ... 509 JANE REPROVED V 2
    OR WHERE THAT SNOW AND WINTER'S DREADFUL BLAST . . . 563 MERU   11
    AND ROVE UNCEASING ROUND THEIR DREADFUL BROOD. . . . 681 SEEKER   5
DREADING
    DREADING AND HOPING ALL: . . . . 476 DEATH   4
DREADS
    HE DREADS THE WEIGHT OF MORTAL HOURS. . . . . . . 212 BLESS PSALTER 11
DREAM
    "WHAT DREAM CAME WITH YOU THAT YOU CAME . . . . . 5 OISIN 1   50
    A DRUID DREAM OF THE END OF DAYS . . . . 16 OISIN 1   219
    AND STILL I DREAM HE TREADS THE LAWN, ... 67 HAPPY SHEPHERD 51
    BUT AH! SHE DREAMS NOT NOW! DREAM THOU! . . . . . 67 HAPPY SHEPHERD 55
    DREAM, DREAM, FOR THIS IS ALSO SOOTH. . . . . . 67 HAPPY SHEPHERD 57
    DREAM, DREAM, FOR THIS IS ALSO SOOTH. . . . . . 67 HAPPY SHEPHERD 57
    WHO WASTES HIS BLOOD TO BE ANOTHER'S DREAM. . . . 103 FERGUS DRUID   28
    BECAUSE I BE NOT OF THE THINGS I DREAM. . . . . . 103 FERGUS DRUID V 26A
    TO DO AND DO AND DO AND NEVER DREAM. . . . . . . 103 FERGUS DRUID V 28
    WHO DREAMED THAT BEAUTY PASSES LIKE A DREAM? . . . . 111 ROSE OF WORLD   1
    AND SLOWLY READ, AND DREAM OF THE SOFT LOOK . . . . 121 YOU ARE OLD   3
    AH, DREAM NOT OF THEM, MY BELOVED, THE FLAME OF THE METEOR 122 WHITE BIRDS   6
      THAT GOES,
    A DREAM OF DEATH . . . . 123 DREAM OF DEATH   T
    A DREAM OF A BLESSED SPIRIT . . . . 124 CATHLEEN PARA V T
    DREAM, UNTIL GOD BURN NATURE WITH A KISS? . . . . 128 DREAM OF FAERY 47
    THE LOVE I LIVED, THE DREAM I KNEW. . . . . . . 139 TO IRELAND   34
    NO PLACE FOR LOVE AND DREAM AT ALL: . . . . . . 139 TO IRELAND   43
    EMPTY YOUR HEART OF ITS MORTAL DREAM. . . . . . 140 HOSTING SIDHE   5
    FILLING THY HEART WITH A MORTAL DREAM, ... 140 HOSTING SIDHE V 6
    HE SAT AND PLAYED IN A DREAM . . . . 145 HOST OF AIR   27

```
                                                          PAGE    TITLE             LINE
DREAM   (CONTINUED)
     AND OUT OF HIS DREAM AWOKE:  . . . . . . . . . . .   145 HOST OF AIR            38
     HE SAT DOWN AND PLAYED IN A DREAM . . . . . . . .    145 HOST OF AIR        V   27
     AND THE YOUNG LIE LONG AND DREAM IN THEIR BED . . .  150 OLD MOTHER              5
     WHILE THE YOUNG LIE LONG AND DREAM IN THEIR BED . .  150 OLD MOTHER         V    5
     BUT THE YOUNG LIE LONG AND DREAM IN THEIR BED . . .  150 OLD MOTHER         V    5
     O VANITY OF SLEEP, HOPE, DREAM, ENDLESS DESIRE, . .  154 BELOVED PEACE           7
     I CRIED IN MY DREAM, O WOMEN, BID THE YOUNG MEN LAY  163 VALLEY LOVERS          5
     AND I CRIED IN MY DREAM "O WOMEN, BID THE YOUNG MEN LAY  163 VALLEY LOVERS  V    5
     AND DREAM ABOUT THE GREAT AND THEIR PRIDE: . . . .   166 EVIL OF BELOV          2
     LILIES OF DEATH-PALE HOPE, ROSES OF PASSIONATE DREAM. 172 TRAV PASSION          8
     FOR ALL THEIR BEAUTY'S LIKE A HOLLOW DREAM. . . .    184 QUEEN MAEVE           88
     FOR ALL THEIR BEAUTY, LIKE A HOLLOW DREAM?" . . .    184 QUEEN MAEVE        V  89
     ALTHOUGH THEIR BEAUTY'S LIKE A HOLLOW DREAM" . . .   184 QUEEN MAEVE        V  89
     CERTAIN, AND THEY NEVER DREAM . . . . . . . . . .    202 NEVER GIVE ALL         4
     TO DREAM OF WOMEN WHOSE BEAUTY WAS FOLDED IN DISMAY, 210 UNDER THE MOON        19
     AND LET THE DREAM GO BY.  IT'S NOT A DREAM, . . .    229 SHADOW WATER B       158
     AND LET THE DREAM GO BY.  IT'S NOT A DREAM, . . .    229 SHADOW WATER B       158
     OR FUMBLING IN A DREAM ABOUT THE HOUSE? . . . . .    230 SHADOW WATER B       174
     COULD WE BUT MIX OURSELVES INTO A DREAM, . . . .     230 SHADOW WATER B       188
     NOW THAT MY BODY HAS BEGUN TO DREAM, . . . . . .     245 SHADOW WATER B       486
     HIS DREAM . . . . . . . . . . . . . . . . . . .      253 HIS DREAM              T
     A DREAM . . . . . . . . . . . . . . . . . . . .      253 HIS DREAM          V   T
     I DREAM THAT I HAVE BROUGHT . . . . . . . . . . .    255 WOMAN HOMER           10
     BUT AN HEROIC DREAM. . . . . . . . . . . . . . .     255 WOMAN HOMER           21
     A DREAM THAT A LION HAD DREAMED . . . . . . . .      259 UNWORTH PRAISE         7
     SO BITTERLY, YOU'D DREAM THEY LONGED TO LOOK . . .   265 ABBEY THEATRE          6
     AND DREAM THAT I SHOULD CARRY . . . . . . . . . .    309 PLAYER QUEEN          19
     AND DREAM THAT ALL THE WORLD'S A FRIEND, . . . .     313 TWO YEAR LATER         8
     WHAT MADE US DREAM THAT HE COULD COMB GREY HAIR? .   327 ROBERT GREGORY        88
     IS THIS MY DREAM, OR THE TRUTH? . . . . . . . .      329 MEN IMPROVE           13
     HE STRETCHED HIS BONES AND FELL IN A DREAM . . .     331 ROUND TOWER           10
     I'LL SAY AND MAYBE DREAM I HAVE DRAWN CONTENT, . .   333 LIVING BEAUTY      V   1
     A MAN WHO IS BUT A DREAM: . . . . . . . . . . .      348 FISHERMAN             36
     A MAN CONFUSEDLY IN A HALF DREAM . . . . . . . .     351 HER PRAISE             8
     A MAN--SO VAGUELY THAT HE SEEMED TO DREAM-- . . .    351 HER PRAISE         V   8
     FROM DREAM TO DREAM AND RHYME TO RHYME I HAVE RANGED 357 BROKEN DREAMS         39
     FROM DREAM TO DREAM AND RHYME TO RHYME I HAVE RANGED 357 BROKEN DREAMS         39
     WHO HAS AWAKENED FROM THE COMMON DREAM . . . . .     369 EGO DOMINUS           50
     WE TAKE IT FOR THE NORM: YET SHOULD I DREAM . . .    371 ON GOING HOUSE         9
     THAT DREAM IS A NORM: AND SHOULD SOME LIMB OF THE DEVIL  372 ON GOING HOUSE    12
     FROM THE FIRST CRESCENT TO THE HALF, THE DREAM . .   373 PHASES OF MOON        36
     BUT SAVES US FROM A DREAM.  AND WHAT OF THOSE . .    376 PHASES OF MOON       102
     WE KNOW THEIR DREAM: ENOUGH . . . . . . . . . .      394 EASTER 1916           70
     HOW COULD YOU DREAM THEY'D LISTEN . . . . . . .      395 SIXTEEN DEAD          13
     WAS IT THE DOUBLE OF MY DREAM . . . . . . . . .      398 BREAK OF DAY           1
     DREAMED, OR DID WE HALVE A DREAM . . . . . . . .     398 BREAK OF DAY           3
     DREAM AND SO CREATE . . . . . . . . . . . . . .      415 TOWER                155
     MIRROR-RESEMBLING DREAM. . . . . . . . . . . .       415 TOWER                165
     IN THE COLD SNOWS OF A DREAM. . . . . . . . . .      424 ROAD AT DOOR          15
     FEW DREAM THAT THEY EXIST, . . . . . . . . . . .     436 FOR MY SON         V  11
     DREAM OF SHAVINGS ON A FLOOR . . . . . . . . . .     440 WISDOM             V   6
     I DREAM OF A LEDAEAN BODY, BENT . . . . . . . .      443 SCHOOL CHILDR          9
     THAT THEY HAVE WELCOMED IN THEIR TENTS THE DREAM .   462 HARUN RASHID       V  23
     DRAWN THROUGH THE WANDERING VEGETATIVE DREAM, . .    467 HARUN RASHID         143
     DREAM THAT I LOVE HER ONLY FOR THE VOICE, . . .      469 HARUN RASHID         171
     DREAM THAT I LOVE HER ONLY FOR THAT VOICE, . . .     469 HARUN RASHID       V 171
     AND GOD-APPOINTED BERKELEY THAT PROVED ALL THINGS A DREAM,  481 BLOOD AND MOON 25
     BLENCHED BY THAT MALICIOUS DREAM . . . . . . . .     488 CRAZED MOON           16
     HER DREAM . . . . . . . . . . . . . . . . . . .      519 HER DREAM              T
     DREAM OF THE NOBLE AND THE BEGGAR-MAN. . . . . .     603 GALLERY REVIS         47
     DREAM OF THE NOBLE AND THE BEGGARMAN. . . . . .      603 GALLERY REVIS      V  47
     A HELEN OF SOCIAL WELFARE DREAM, . . . . . . . .     626 OLD MEN BE MAD         7
     AND THIS BROUGHT FORTH A DREAM AND SOON ENOUGH . .   630 CIRCUS ANIMALS        23
     THIS DREAM ITSELF HAD ALL MY THOUGHT AND LOVE. . .   630 CIRCUS ANIMALS        24
     IT WAS THE DREAM ITSELF ENCHANTED ME: . . . . .      630 CIRCUS ANIMALS        28
     ITS JOY OR NIGHT SEEM BUT A DREAM: . . . . . . .     633 MAN AND ECHO          42
     ITS JOY OR NIGHT SEEMS BUT A DREAM. . . . . . .      633 MAN AND ECHO       V  42
     WHEN SLEEPERS WAKE AND YET STILL DREAM, . . . .      639 BEN BULBEN            59
     WHEN THAT GREATER DREAM HAD GONE . . . . . . . .     639 BEN BULBEN            63
     AS SOME DEAD MAIDEN'S SINGING IN A DREAM. . . . .    654 ISLE STAT I 2         59
     I DREAM!--I CANNOT DIE!--NO! NO! . . . . . . . .     675 ISLE STAT II 3       227
     I DREAM!--I CANNOT DIE!--NOT DIE!  NO! NO! . . .     675 ISLE STAT II 3 V     227
     AND DREAM OF THE END OF THEIR DAYS, . . . . . .      707 FAIRY PEDANT           4
     COME AND DREAM OF KINGS AND KINGDOMS, . . . . .      737 IN FIRELIGHT           1
     OF FOLLOWING FORGAEL'S DREAM FROM WIND TO WIND. . .  758 SHADOW WATER A       219
     HE HAS THROWN A DRUID DREAM UPON THE AIR. . . .      759 SHADOW WATER A       237
     AND THAT DREAM ONLY SHINE BEFORE HER FEET. . . .     761 SHADOW WATER A       258
     THEY DREAM THAT LAUGHED IN THE SUN. . . . . . .      783 GREY ROUND            13
     DRY BONES THAT DREAM ARE BITTER, . . . . . . . .     783 GREY ROUND            14
     THEY DREAM AND DARKEN OUR SUN. . . . . . . . . .     783 GREY ROUND            15
DREAM-AWAKENED
     SUDDENLY HURTLE BEFORE MY DREAM-AWAKENED EYES, . . . 161 BLACK PIG              2
DREAM-DIMMED
     WITH HER CLOUD-PALE EYELIDS FALLING ON DREAM-DIMMED EYES:  163 VALLEY LOVERS   4
     O CLOUD-PALE EYELIDS, DREAM-DIMMED EYES, . . . . .   164 PERFECT BEAUTY         1
DREAMED
     A BEAUTIFUL YOUNG MAN DREAMED WITHIN . . . . . . .   17 OISIN 1              248
     BEFORE THE SWIFT THINGS THAT SHE DREAMED OF WERE DONE . .  27 OISIN 1         414
     STILL EARLESS, NERVELESS, BLIND, THE EAGLES DREAMED.  36 OISIN 2          V 100
     WHO DREAMED THAT BEAUTY PASSES LIKE A DREAM? . . .   111 ROSE OF WORLD          1

                                    220
```

DREAMED   (CONTINUED)
    I DREAMED THAT ONE HAD DIED IN A STRANGE PLACE . . . . .   123 DREAM OF DEATH   1
    THE MAN WHO DREAMED OF FAERYLAND . . . .   126 DREAM OF FAERY   T
    A MAN WHO DREAMED OF FAIRYLAND . . . .   126 DREAM OF FAERY V   T
    FOR ALL WHO HEARD IT DREAMED A LITTLE WHILE. . . . . .   129 BOOK STORIES   V   8
    AND DREAMED OF THE LONG DIM HAIR . . . .   144 HOST OF AIR   7
    HE HEARD WHILE HE SANG AND DREAMED . . . .   144 HOST OF AIR   9
    AND DREAMED THAT THE OLD DESPAIR . . . .   152 LOSS OF LOVE   3
    I DREAMED THAT I STOOD IN A VALLEY, AND AMID SIGHS, ... 163 VALLEY LOVERS   1
    AND I DREAMED MY LOST LOVE CAME STEALTHILY OUT OF THE WOOD 163 VALLEY LOVERS   3
    HE HAD FALLEN ASLEEP, AND, THOUGH HE HAD DREAMED NOTHING,   182 QUEEN MAEVE   55
    DREAMED OF THE HANDS THAT WOULD UNLACE . . . .   193 BAILE AILLINN   104
    YET DREAMED THAT BEINGS HAPPIER THAN MEN . . . . . .   218 WOODS OF COOLE   18
    A DREAM THAT A LION HAD DREAMED . . . .   259 UNWORTH PRAISE   7
    BECAUSE SHE DREAMED WHEN BUT A CHILD . . . .   272 GREY ROCK   42
    A MEASURELESS CONSUMMATION THAT HE DREAMED. . . . . .   324 ROBERT GREGORY   24
    WE DREAMED THAT A GREAT PAINTER HAD BEEN BORN . . . .   326 ROBERT GREGORY   65
    BECAUSE OF WHAT HE HAD DREAMED, ...   342 SHEP GOATHERD   92
    FROM GOING-DOWN OF THE SUN I HAVE DREAMED . . . . . .   358 PRESENCES   3
    FROM GOING DOWN OF THE SUN I HAVE DREAMED . . . . . .   358 PRESENCES   V   3
    THAT SHE OF DANCING DREAMED. . . . .   383 VISION ROBART   24
    THIS OTHER MAN I HAD DREAMED . . . .   393 EASTER 1916   31
    TO KNOW THEY DREAMED AND ARE DEAD; . . . .   394 EASTER 1916   71
    DREAMED, OR DID WE HALVE A DREAM . . . .   398 BREAK OF DAY   3
    I DREAMED TOWARDS BREAK OF DAY, ...   399 BREAK OF DAY   19
    O BUT WE DREAMED TO MEND . . . .   431 NINETEEN 19   84
    LEARN THAT WE WERE CRACK-PATED WHEN WE DREAMED. . . .   431 NINETEEN 19   88
    AND THAT SHE DREAMED AWAKE CONTENT TO TOUCH . . . .   466 HARUN RASHID   V   125C
    I DREAMED AS IN MY BED I LAY, ...   519 HER DREAM   1
    HE HAD DREAMED THE COW HAD GOT WITHIN . . . . . .   729 PRIEST FAIRY   33
    WHEN SHE DREAMED FIRST OF LOVE, SHALL FLICKER OUT . . .   760 SHADOW WATER A V   257
    THEY DREAMED THAT LAUGHED IN THE SUN. . . . . . .   783 GREY ROUND   V   13
DREAMER
    DREAMER OF THE MIDDLE AGES, EMPTY EYEBALLS KNEW . . . .   610 STATUES   20
    DREAMER OF THE MIDDLE-AGES, EMPTY EYE-BALLS KNEW . . . .   610 STATUES   V   20
    SCHOOLMASTER HE, A DREAMER, FIDDLER, FIRST . . . . . .   709 FERENCZ RENYI   11
DREAMERS
    A WEARINESS COMES FROM THOSE DREAMERS, ...   122 WHITE BIRDS   5
    AND A WEARINESS COMES FROM THOSE DREAMERS . . . . . .   122 WHITE BIRDS   V   5
DREAM-FED
    WHERE DREAM-FED PASSION IS AND PEACE ENCLOSES, ...   669 ISLE STAT II 3   85
DREAM-HEAVY
    COME FROM A MORE DREAM-HEAVY LAND, ...   156 FORGOT BEAUTY   16
    A MORE DREAM-HEAVY HOUR THAN THIS; . . . .   156 FORGOT BEAUTY   17
DREAMING
    DREAMING OF HER OWN MELTING HUES, ...   13 OISIN 1   162
    OF OLD THE WORLD ON DREAMING FED; . . . .   64 HAPPY SHEPHERD   3
    AND HE, OF HIS HIGH COMRADE SORROW DREAMING, ...   67 SAD SHEPHERD   2
    AND HE, OF HIS HIGH KINSMAN SORROW DREAMING, ...   67 SAD SHEPHERD   V   2
    BUT LEARN THE DREAMING WISDOM THAT IS YOURS. . . . .   103 FERGUS DRUID   22
    AND DREAMING HOW THEY DANCE AND DART, ...   135 TWO TREES   V   18
    BY DREAMING LADIES UPON CLOTH . . . .   156 FORGOT BEAUTY   7
    IT HAD GROWN SWEET-TONGUED BY DREAMING . . . . . .   160 CAP AND BELLS   17
    THE TONGUE OF IT SWEET WITH DREAMING . . . .   160 CAP AND BELLS   V   17
    AND THE PROUD DREAMING KING WHO FLUNG THE CROWN . .   170 SECRET ROSE   19
    I HAVE NO HAPPINESS IN DREAMING OF BRYCELINDE, . . .   209 UNDER THE MOON   1
    AND SET YOU DREAMING. HOW CAN WE HAVE A WAKE . . . .   240 SHADOW WATER B   386
    AND HOW WHAT HER DREAMING GAVE . . . .   260 UNWORTH PRAISE   15
    THAT VIGOROUS THIGH, THAT DREAMING EYE? . . . . . .   386 ROBARTES DANCE   23
    FOUND CERTAINTY UPON THE DREAMING AIR, ...   489 COOLE PARK 29   22
    OF THE DREAMING WATER-FOWLS, ...   644 SONG FAERIES   12
    DREAMING IN THEIR SOFT ODOUR-LADEN SLEEP; . . . . .   650 ISLE STAT I 1   125
    DREAMING THE LIVE-LONG SUMMER IN THE SHADE, ...   650 ISLE STAT I 1   139
    DREAMING OF FLASHING FLIGHT AND OF THE PLUMED WAVE. . .   650 ISLE STAT I 1   140
    OF THE DREAMING WATER-FOWLS, ...   676 ISLE STAT II 3   259
    THE OTTERS DREAMING LAY. AYE; . . . .   677 ISLE STAT II 3   280
    THE OTTERS DREAMING LAY. NASCHINA! AY! . . . . . .   677 ISLE STAT II 3 V   280
    WHO, DREAMING TO A WONDROUS AGE, LIVED ON, ...   692 MOSADA 1   52
    THE WORLD WERE DREAMING IN ITS SUMMER SLEEP; . . . .   699 MOSADA 3   11
    OF DREAMING AND OF WATCHING BY THE DOOR . . . . . .   700 MOSADA 3   26
    PAST THE CAMEL'S DREAMING EYE. . . . .   733 STREET DANCERS   43
    WEIGH THEM IN AN HOUR OF DREAMING, ...   737 IN FIRELIGHT   11
    AND LEAVE HER DREAMING. WHEN I LOOKED ON HER, . . .   761 SHADOW WATER A V   258
    THE DREAMING BONES CRY OUT . . . .   782 HEART FRIGHT   15
DREAM-LED
    FROM THREESCORE YEARS OF DREAM-LED WANDERING . . . . .   682 SEEKER   16
DREAMLESS
    UPON THE DANCER BY THE DREAMLESS WAVE. . . . . . .   128 DREAM OF FAERY   45
    SHALL GROW THY BEAUTY AND THY DREAMLESS TRUTH, ...   674 ISLE STAT II 3   207
    OF LOVE FROM OUT A DREAMLESS RACE FOR STRIFE, ...   684 SEEKER   58
    HAST THOU NOT KNOWN A RAJA'S DREAMLESS SLUMBER? . . . .   724 KANVA ON SELF   8
DREAMS   SEE LOVE-DREAMS
    YOU ARE STILL WRECKED AMONG HEATHEN DREAMS. . . . .   4 OISIN 1   31
    AND DREAMS OF HER OWN MELTING HUES, ...   13 OISIN 1   V   162
    WHERE AENGUS DREAMS, FROM SUN TO SUN, ...   16 OISIN 1   218
    AND WRAPPED IN DREAMS RODE OUT AGAIN . . . .   25 OISIN 1   382
    OR SAT IN DREAMS ON THE PALE STRAND, ...   25 OISIN 1   390
    MY DREAMS WERE LIVING. NOW THE HOOF . . . .   25 OISIN 1   V   382
    THE WARRIOR DREAMS IN AN AGED LEISURE . . . . . .   26 OISIN 1   V   401
    WHILE HIS HEART STILL DREAMS OF BATTLE AND LOVE . . . .   27 OISIN 1   406
    SO WARRED, SO FEASTED, WITH NOR DREAMS NOR FEARS, . . .   44 OISIN 2   222

DREAMS   (CONTINUED)

	PAGE	TITLE		LINE
SO WARRED, SO FEASTED WE. NO DREAMS, NO FEARS,	44	OISIN 2	V	222
. . DULL WITH THE SMOKE OF THEIR DREAMS;	51	OISIN 3		65
BUT IN DREAMS, MILD MAN OF THE CROZIERS,	53	OISIN 3		85
. . . WITH CREATURES OF DREAMS,	53	OISIN 3		95
AND THE DREAMS OF THE ISLANDS WERE GONE,	59	OISIN 3		175
AND THE DREAMS OF THE ISLANDS WENT OUT OF ME,	59	OISIN 3	V	175
. . . AN OLD MAN SURROUNDED WITH DREAMS.	61	OISIN 3		196
NEW DREAMS, NEW DREAMS! THERE IS NO TRUTH	66	HAPPY SHEPHERD		26
NEW DREAMS, NEW DREAMS! THERE IS NO TRUTH	66	HAPPY SHEPHERD		26
BUT AH! SHE DREAMS NOT NOW! DREAM THOU!	67	HAPPY SHEPHERD		55
ROLLING ALONG IN DREAMS FROM HILL TO HILL.	68	SAD SHEPHERD		11
ON THEIR VAST FACES MYSTERY AND DREAMS!	74	ANASHU VIJAYA		70
TROUBLE HIS SLEEPING! GIVE HIM DREAMS OF ME.	75	ANASHU VIJAYA		91
THE ISLAND DREAMS UNDER THE DAWN	77	INDIAN TO LOVE		1
GIVE THEM UNQUIET DREAMS!	88	STOLEN CHILD		34
WE GIVE THEM EVIL DREAMS,	88	STOLEN CHILD	V	34
HIS OLD EYES CLOUD WITH DREAMS!	98	FOXHUNTER		14
AND NOW THE OLD MAN'S DREAMS ARE GONE,	98	FOXHUNTER		19
WHO CAST ROUND FERGUS DREAMS, AND RUIN UNTOLD!	101	ROSE UPON ROOD		5
TAKE, IF YOU MUST, THIS LITTLE BAG OF DREAMS!	104	FERGUS DRUID		29
TAKE THEN THIS SMALL SLATE-COLOURED BAG OF DREAMS!	104	FERGUS DRUID	V	29
MY HEART WOULD BRIM WITH DREAMS ABOUT THE TIMES	136	TO SOME I TALK		2
BECAUSE THEIR BLOSSOMING DREAMS HAVE NEVER BENT	136	TO SOME I TALK		8
FOR MY DREAMS OF YOUR IMAGE THAT BLOSSOMS A ROSE	143	ROSE IN HEART		8
THE BOOKS OF MY NUMBERLESS DREAMS,	157	POET BELOVED		2
WHITE WOMAN WITH NUMBERLESS DREAMS,	157	POET BELOVED		7
THE DEWS DROP SLOWLY AND DREAMS GATHER! UNKNOWN SPEARS	161	BLACK PIG		1
THE DEW DROPS SLOWLY! THE DREAMS GATHER! UNKNOWN SPEARS	161	BLACK PIG	V	1
AND TUMULT OF DEFEATED DREAMS! AND DEEP	169	SECRET ROSE		5
BUT I, BEING POOR, HAVE ONLY MY DREAMS!	176	CLOTHS HEAVEN		6
I HAVE SPREAD MY DREAMS UNDER YOUR FEET!	176	CLOTHS HEAVEN		7
TREAD SOFTLY BECAUSE YOU TREAD ON MY DREAMS.	176	CLOTHS HEAVEN		8
HE COULD REMEMBER WHEN HE HAD HAD FINE DREAMS.	182	QUEEN MAEVE		56
THE BOUGHS HAVE WITHERED BECAUSE I HAVE TOLD THEM MY DREAMS.	203	WITHER BOUGHS		8
THE BOUGHS HAVE WITHERED BECAUSE I HAVE TOLD THEM MY DREAMS.	203	WITHER BOUGHS		16
THE BOUGHS HAVE WITHERED BECAUSE I HAVE TOLD THEM MY DREAMS.	204	WITHER BOUGHS		24
AND WHETHER I GO IN MY DREAMS BY WOODLAND, OR DUN, OR SHORE,	210	UNDER THE MOON		14
MY DREAMS WERE CLOVEN BY VOICES AND BY FIRES!	218	WOODS OF COOLE		20
WE HAVE FALLEN IN THE DREAMS THE EVER-LIVING	228	SHADOW WATER B		131
COULD WE BUT GIVE US WHOLLY TO THE DREAMS,	230	SHADOW WATER B		178
AMONG SUBSTANTIAL THINGS; FOR IT IS DREAMS	230	SHADOW WATER B		181
BUT DREAMS THAT HURRY FROM BEYOND THE WORLD	230	SHADOW WATER B		185
TO CAST HIS DREAMS AWAY. NO OTHER'LL DO IT.	239	SHADOW WATER B		366
BEING DRIVEN ON BY VOICES AND BY DREAMS ,	243	SHADOW WATER B		441
AND IF THAT HAPPINESS BE MORE THAN DREAMS,	248	SHADOW WATER B		554
I HALF REMEMBER. IT HAS BEEN IN MY DREAMS.	251	SHADOW WATER B		606
TO CRY ALOUD TO THE GREY BIRDS, AND DREAMS,	252	SHADOW WATER B		618
THAT HAVE HAD DREAMS FOR FATHER, LIVE IN US.	252	SHADOW WATER B		619
IF WE BUT SAW IN DREAMS THAT ROOM,	272	GREY ROCK		38
AND LOOSEN ON US DREAMS THAT WASTE OUR LIFE,	281	TWO KINGS		107
THE EXORBITANT DREAMS OF BEGGARY.	296	THREE BEGGARS		39
I AM WORN OUT WITH DREAMS!	329	MEN IMPROVE		1
BUT I GROW OLD AMONG DREAMS,	329	MEN IMPROVE		16
HE DREAMS HIMSELF HIS MOTHER'S PRIDE,	343	SHEP GOATHERD		110
BROKEN DREAMS	355	BROKEN DREAMS		T
AMID THE DREAMS OF YOUTH; LET HER COME FACE TO FACE,	366	HER COURAGE		3
BEYOND THE VISIBLE WORLD. ALL DREAMS OF THE SOUL	374	PHASES OF MOON		63
OR ELSE MY DREAMS THAT FLY	384	VISION ROBART		51
MIRROR RESEMBLING DREAMS.	415	TOWER	V	165
MERE DREAMS, MERE DREAMS! YET HOMER HAD NOT SUNG	417	ANCEST HOUSES		9
MERE DREAMS, MERE DREAMS! YET HOMER HAD NOT SUNG	417	ANCEST HOUSES		9
HAD HE NOT FOUND IT CERTAIN BEYOND DREAMS	417	ANCEST HOUSES		10
BUT THAT HE FOUND MORE SUBSTANCE THERE THAN DREAMS,	417	ANCEST HOUSES	V	10
FROM MY OLD FATHERS, I MUST NOURISH DREAMS	422	MY DESCENDANTS		2
THE PAINTER'S BRUSH CONSUMES HIS DREAMS!	438	SONGS PLAY 2		12
I KNOW NOT WHAT THE YOUNGER DREAMS--	475	EVA GORE-BOOTH		10
WANDER IN DREAMS NO MORE!	554	CHURCH STATE		8
ALL HIS HAPPIER DREAMS CAME TRUE--	577	WHAT THEN		11
GAVE WOMEN DREAMS AND DREAMS THEIR LOOKING-GLASS.	610	STATUES		16
GAVE WOMEN DREAMS AND DREAMS THEIR LOOKING-GLASS.	610	STATUES		16
GAVE WOMEN DREAMS AND DREAMS THEIR LOOKING GLASS.	610	STATUES	V	16
GAVE WOMEN DREAMS AND DREAMS THEIR LOOKING GLASS.	610	STATUES	V	16
THROUGH THREE ENCHANTED ISLANDS, ALLEGORICAL DREAMS,	629	CIRCUS ANIMALS		11
MY DREAMS ROUND THOUGHTS OF PLENTY, AS IN GLOOM	681	SEEKER		3
MY DREAMS O'ER THOUGHTS OF PLENTY, AS THE RED-	681	SEEKER	V	3
THAT DREAMS. SHE MOVETH, FEELING IN HER BRAIN	687	TWO TITANS		10
HER DREAMS ARE TALKING WITH OLD YEARS. AWAKE,	702	MOSADA 3		89
FIRST DREAMS, AND GOBLINS, AND THE LESSER SPRITES,	722	WITCH VIVIEN		56
WISDOM AND DREAMS	743	WISDOM DREAMS		T
WISDOM AND DREAMS ARE ONE,	743	WISDOM DREAMS		5
FOR DREAMS ARE THE FLOWERS ABLOW,	743	WISDOM DREAMS		6
BECAUSE A GOD HAS MADE HIM WISE WITH DREAMS!	748	SHADOW WATER A		26
WOULD OVERCOME YOUR SORROW AND YOUR DREAMS.	749	SHADOW WATER A		52
AND FALLS AMONG THE DREAMS THE DROWSY GODS	750	SHADOW WATER A		68
AND WERE ALL DREAMS, IT WOULD NOT WEIGH IN THE HAND.	750	SHADOW WATER A		77
BECAUSE I HAD HOPED TO COME, AS DREAMS FORETOLD,	757	SHADOW WATER A		197

```
                                                    PAGE    TITLE              LINE
DREAMS    (CONTINUED)
    I HAVE FORGOT IT ALL.  HOW SOON DREAMS FADE!  . . . . .    761 SHADOW WATER A      272
    THAT CROWN WAS IN MY DREAMS---NO, NO--IN A RHYME. . . . .  763 SHADOW WATER A      311
    OF VOICES AND OF DREAMS.  O HEART, BE STILL!  . . . . .    765 SHADOW WATER A      362
    I HAVE BEGUN REMEMBERING MY DREAMS. . . . . . . . .        766 SHADOW WATER A      380
    I HAVE COMMANDED MEN IN DREAMS.  BELOVED, . . . . . .      766 SHADOW WATER A      381
    AND EDDY TO EDDY.  MASTERS OF OUR DREAMS, . . . . . .      768 SHADOW WATER A      418
    THAT DIZZY DREAMS CAN SPRING  . . . . . . . . . .          781 MY HEART BEAT         7
    WITH THOSE FANTASTIC DREAMS. . . . . . . . . . .           781 MY HEART BEAT        11
DREAMT
    ERE HALF THE SWIFT THINGS THAT SHE DREAMT ON WERE DONE,     28 OISIN 1          V  422
    AND WEPT BECAUSE SHE HAD DREAMT THAT I . . . . . . .       308 PLAYER QUEEN         11
    I DREAMT SOME GREAT ONE.  AH, MY BEAUTIFUL, . . . . .      720 WITCH VIVIEN         14
    WHEN SHE DREAMT FIRST OF LOVE, SHALL FLICKER OUT  . . . .  760 SHADOW WATER A      257
DREAMY
    OF DREAMY FOAM A STAFF OF WOOD . . . . . . . . . .          24 OISIN 1             366
    AND SANG, AND WITH A DREAMY GAZE  . . . . . . . . .         26 OISIN 1             393
    MY SONGS OF OLD EARTH'S DREAMY YOUTH! . . . . . . .         67 HAPPY SHEPHERD       54
    THERE DREAMY TIME LETS FALL HIS SICKLE  . . . . . . .       77 INDIAN TO LOVE  V   5A
    VEILED IN A DREAMY SORROW FOR THEIR LOVE  . . . . . .       79 EPHEMERA        V   2A
    BUT A BRIEF, DREAMY, KIND DELIGHT.  . . . . . . .          202 NEVER GIVE ALL        7
    THAT THE GRAVE-DIGGERS IN A DREAMY FRENZY . . . . . .      243 SHADOW WATER B      430
    YOUTH'S DREAMY LOAD, TILL SHE . . . . . . . . . .          315 FRIENDS              14
DREAR
    OF THE DREAR HART LAKE. . . . . . . . . . . . .            143 HOST OF AIR           4
DREARY
    IN DREARY DANCING PAST US WHIRLED, . . . . . . . .          65 HAPPY SHEPHERD        8
    A DREARY, DREEPY BEGGAR . . . . . . . . . . . .            552 SONGS REWRIT 2        5
DREEPY
    A DREARY, DREEPY BEGGAR . . . . . . . . . . . .            552 SONGS REWRIT 2        5
DRENCH'D       SEE DEW-DRENCH'D
DRENCHED       SEE WINE-DRENCHED
    SUDDENLY DRENCHED HER TO THE SKIN! . . . . . . . .         275 GREY ROCK           120
DRESS
    AND WHEN THEY SAW MY EARTHLY DRESS, . . . . . . . .         15 OISIN 1          V  207
    HER PEARL-PALE HAND AND THE HEM OF HER DRESS. . . . .       16 OISIN 1             216
    SHE'LL NOT ASK A HAUGHTY DRESS! . . . . . . . . .          124 CATHLEEN PARA         6
    BEAR THE GOLD-EMBROIDERED DRESS-- . . . . . . . . .        124 CATHLEEN PARA   V     6
    BEAR THE GOLD EMBROIDERED DRESS-- . . . . . . . . .        124 CATHLEEN PARA   V     6
    HIS HEART HUNG ALL UPON A SILKEN DRESS, . . . . . . .      126 DREAM OF FAERY        2
    OVER SOME SILKEN DRESS  . . . . . . . . . .                363 DOLLS DRAWINGS        7
    FOR EVERY TATTER IN ITS MORTAL DRESS, . . . . . . .        407 SAIL BYZANTIUM       12
    A BIT OF AN EMBROIDERED DRESS . . . . . . . . . .          421 MY TABLE              6
    FROM SOME COURT-LADY'S DRESS AND ROUND  . . . . . .        477 SELF AND SOUL        14
    FROM SOME COURT-LADIES' DRESS AND ROUND . . . . . . .      477 SELF AND SOUL   V    14
    I PLUCKED HER BACKWARDS BY HER DRESS OF GREEN. . . . .     676 ISLE STAT II 3      264
DRESSED
    A QUEEN-WOMAN DRESSED OUT IN SILVER, CRY  . . . . . .      210 RAGGED WOOD     V     2
    OR A YOUNG GIRL DRESSED OUT IN HER NEW GOWN, . . . . .     350 HER PRAISE            4
    HALF DRESSED IN NATIONAL UNIFORM, . . . . . . . . .        424 ROAD AT DOOR          7
    EARTH IN BEAUTY DRESSED . . . . . . . . . . . .            517 HER ANXIETY           1
    I, AS A SHEPHERD DRESSED, WILL SEEK AND SEEK  . . . . .    658 ISLE STAT II 1        1
    I FOUGHT TWELVE BATTLES DRESSED IN GOLDEN ARMOUR.  . . .   761 SHADOW WATER A      271
DREW
    AND NOW STILL SAD OUR TROOP DREW NIGH  . . . . . . .        17 OISIN 1          V  247
    AND NIGH UNTO HIM EACH ONE DREW, . . . . . . . . .          18 OISIN 1          V  257
    I DREW OUT OF THE NUMBERLESS  . . . . . . . . . .           24 OISIN 1          V  365
    I DREW IT FORTH! THE STAFF OF WOOD, . . . . . . . .         24 OISIN 1          V  366
    NOW, MAN OF CROSIERS, PHANTOMS DREW AROUND  . . . . . .     29 OISIN 2          V    1
    AND THEREUPON I DREW THE LIVID CHOP . . . . . . . .         40 OISIN 2             178
    LAY LOOSE IN A PLACE OF SHADOW! WE DREW THE REINS BY HIS    50 OISIN 3              44
        SIDE.
    I DREW AT EVENING MY MAILED MEN, . . . . . . . . .          83 MAD KING GOLL   V    19
    SHE DREW FROM ME MY STORY-- . . . . . . . . . .             96 MOLL MAGEE           37
    BUT BRIDGET DREW HIM BY THE SLEEVE  . . . . . . . .        144 HOST OF AIR          21
    SHE DREW IN THE HEAVY CASEMENT . . . . . . . . . .         159 CAP AND BELLS        11
    SHE DREW IN THE BRIGHTENING CASEMENT, . . . . . . .        159 CAP AND BELLS   V    11
    IF ANY MAN DREW NEAR  . . . . . . . . . . . .             254 WOMAN HOMER           1
    THEN DREW HIS SWORD TO HOLD ITS LEVELLED POINT  . . . .    277 TWO KINGS            14
    BUT DREW HIS SWORD, AND THOUGHT WITH LEVELLED POINT  . .   277 TWO KINGS       V    14
    ROSE! SOME CONQUEROR DREW REIN. . . . . . . . . .         502 VACILLATION          64
    DREW A KNIFE TO STRIKE HIM DEAD, . . . . . . . . .         514 JANE GROWN OLD       10
    POETS AND WITS ABOUT HIM DREW! . . . . . . . . .          577 WHAT THEN            14
    MY MOTHER DREW FORTH FROM THE LONG GRASS  . . . . . .      708 FAIRY PEDANT         23
    HE DREW FROM HIS CAP A FEATHER GREY, . . . . . . . .       729 PRIEST FAIRY         29
    I DREW MY SWORD TO FLING IT IN A POOL,-- . . . . . .       747 SHADOW WATER A        7
DRIED
    . . . THE FLESH OF HIS FACE AS DRIED GRASS, . . . .         59 OISIN 3             173
    AND WISDOM THAT CAUGHT FIRE LIKE THE DRIED FLAX, . . . .   181 QUEEN MAEVE          28
    HAS DRIED THE SAP OUT OF MY VEINS, AND RENT  . . . . .     260 FASC DIFFICULT        2
    YOU HAVE DRIED THE MARROW FROM THE BONE? . . . . . .       289 SEPTEMBER 1913        5
    AS THOUGH DRIED STRAW, AND IF WE TURN ABOUT  . . . . .     327 ROBERT GREGORY       83
    PROSPER BUT LITTLE, HAS DRIED UP OF LATE, . . . . . .      405 FOR DAUGHTER         51
    A BONE WAVE-WHITENED AND DRIED IN THE WIND. . . . . .      521 THREE THINGS          6
    A BONE WAVE-WHITENED AND DRIED IN THE WIND. . . . . .      521 THREE THINGS         12
    A BONE WAVE-WHITENED AND DRIED IN THE WIND. . . . . .      521 THREE THINGS         18
    I HAVE CUPBOARDS OF DRIED FRAGRANCE, . . . . . . .         572 LADYS 2ND SONG        5
    HAS ROLLED AWAY THE STARS AND DRIED THE SEA . . . . .      671 ISLE STAT II 3      146
DRIFT
    I SAW A FOAM-WHITE SEAGULL DRIFT AND FLOAT . . . . . .      36 OISIN 2             105
    FOR, AS DRIFT FROM A SAILOR SLOW DROWNING . . . . . .       48 OISIN 3              22
```

223

		PAGE	TITLE	LINE

DRIFT (CONTINUED)
```
      ALL THEIR LIVES THROUGH INTO SOME DRIFT OF WINGS.  . . .   265 ABBEY THEATRE        7
      BUT NOW THEY DRIFT ON THE STILL WATER,  . . . . . . . .   323 SWANS AT COOLE      25
      DRIFT AND FLOAT LIKE SILVER SHIPS:  . . . . . . . . . .   647 ISLE STAT I 1       67
DRIFTED
      WHERE THE DEAD DRIFTED, I COULD SEE A BIRD  . . . . . .   223 SHADOW WATER B      23
      CAVERNED IN NIGHT UNDER THE DRIFTED SNOW.  . . . . . .    563 MERU                10
DRIFTING
      DRIFTING ON HIGH, AND WITH A STRAINING THROAT . . . . .    36 OISIN 2        V  106
      AND DRIFTING GREYNESS, WHILE THIS MONOTONE,  . . . . .     45 OISIN 2           232
      AND DRIFTING GREYNESS.  CAME THIS MONOTONE.  . . . . .     45 OISIN 2        V  232
      I SEE MY LIFE GO DRIFTING LIKE A RIVER  . . . . . . . .   104 FERGUS DRUID        31
      WERE GONE LIKE A DRIFTING SMOKE:  . . . . . . . . . .     145 HOST OF AIR         40
      AND CUMHAL SAW LIKE A DRIFTING SMOKE  . . . . . . . .     167 BLESSED             13
DRIFTS
      LIKE DRIFTS OF LEAVES, IMMOVABLE AND BRIGHT,  . . . . .    40 OISIN 2           166
      LIKE DRIFTS OF LAUREL LEAVES, IMMOVABLE AND BRIGHT . . .   40 OISIN 2        V  166
      HIS PURPOSE DRIFTS AND DIES."  . . . . . . . . . . . .     45 OISIN 2           244
      HIS PURPOSE DRIFTS AWAY."  . . . . . . . . . . . . . .     45 OISIN 2        V  244
      AND SMOKE FROM THIS DEAD HEART DRIFTS THROUGH THE VIOLET  173 SPEAKS HEARERS       3
          AIR
      I KNOW WHERE A DIM MOON DRIFTS, WHERE THE DANAAN KIND . .  203 WITHER BOUGHS       12
      "ALL THAT'S BEAUTIFUL DRIFTS AWAY  . . . . . . . . . .    208 OLD MEN ADMIRE       8
      YOU ARE BROKEN, YOU ARE BROKEN.  THE WORLD DRIFTS AWAY,   251 SHADOW WATER B     599
      WHERE THE SWAN DRIFTS UPON A DARKENING FLOOD. . . . . .   492 COOLE BALLYLEE      48
      BEHOLD, I BEND!  AROUND MY BEARD IN DRIFTS .  . . . . .   684 SEEKER              68
      BEHOLD I BOW!  AROUND MY BEARD IN DRIFTS  . . . . . .     684 SEEKER         V   68
DRINK
      OF HAMMERED SILVER, AND DRINK  . . . . . . . . . . . .    215 HAPPY TOWNLAND      50
      TO MAKE LOW LAUGHTER MORE THAN MEAT AND DRINK,  . . . .   230 SHADOW WATER B     186
      TO DRINK OF THAT SALT BREATH OUT OF THE SEA  . . . . .    292 TO A SHADE           5
      AND DRINK BEFORE I TALK."  AND HE . . . . . . . . . .     304 HOUR DAWN           45
      AND DRINK, AND YOU WILL SLEEP THAT LENGTH."  . . . . .    305 HOUR DAWN           59
      YOU'VE BUT TO DRINK THE BEER AND SAY . . . . . . . . .    305 HOUR DAWN      V   56
      IF YOU BUT DRINK THAT BEER AND SAY  . . . . . . . . .     305 HOUR DAWN      V   56
      THEIR FOOD AND DRINK:  . . . . . . . . . . . . . . . .    380 SONGS FOOL 1         9
      TO DRINK FROM THE WINE-BREATH  . . . . . . . . . . . .    471 ALL SOUL NIGHT       9
      WHILE OUR GROSS PALATES DRINK FROM THE WHOLE WINE,  . .   471 ALL SOUL NIGHT      10
      NO LIVING MAN CAN DRINK FROM THE WHOLE WINE.  . . . . .   474 ALL SOUL NIGHT      85
      WHAT MATTER IF A BLIND MAN DRINK HIS DROP?  . . . . .     478 SELF AND SOUL  V   41
      STRONG DRINK I HAD, AND IT BROUGHT ME TO SORROW,  . . .   544 TO SAME TUNE 1      13
      COULD I BUT DRINK, MY LOVE ON MY KNEE,  . . . . . . .     551 SONGS REWRIT 1 V    9
      O COULD I DRINK, MY LOVE ON MY KNEE,  . . . . . . . .     551 SONGS REWRIT 1 V    9
      ALTHOUGH I DRINK MY FILL.  . . . . . . . . . . . . .      592 DRUNK SOBRIETY       4
      SO STAY AT HOME AND DRINK YOUR BEER  . . . . . . . . .    598 STONE CROSS          5
      WE'D DRINK A CAN OR TWO,  . . . . . . . . . . . . . .     606 SONGS BURDEN 1      22
      THEIR DRINK, THEIR PITCH-AND-TOSS BY DAY,  . . . . . .    607 SONGS BURDEN 2      14
      THEIR DRINK, THEIR PITCH AND TOSS BY DAY,  . . . . . .    607 SONGS BURDEN 2  V   14
      STRONG DRINK I HAD, AND IT BROUGHT ME TO SORROW,  . . .   616 MARCH SONGS 3       13
      AWAY FROM ME WHERE MISTS OF EVENING DRINK  . . . . . .    663 ISLE STAT II 2      40
      AND TELL ME A LOVE-STORY WHILE I DRINK.  . . . . . . .    760 SHADOW WATER A     250
      AND TELL ME A LOVE STORY WHILE I DRINK.  . . . . . . .    760 SHADOW WATER A  V  250
      I WILL DRINK OUT OF THE STREAM.  THE STREAM IS GONE!     761 SHADOW WATER A     273
      MAY THE SWORD-BLADES DRINK THEIR FILL  . . . . . . .     776 AGAINST WITCH       37
      MAY THE SWORD BLADES DRINK THEIR FILL  . . . . . . .     776 AGAINST WITCH   V   37
DRINKERS'     SEE PORTER-DRINKERS'
DRINKING
      A DRINKING SONG . . . . . . . . . . . . . . . . . . .    261 DRINKING SONG        T
      THE FORD WHERE DRINKING CATTLE MAKE A STIR  . . . . .     326 ROBERT GREGORY      53
      DRINKING THE FOUL DITCH WHERE THEY LIE?  . . . . . . .    397 POLIT PRISONER      12
      WENCHING, DRINKING, STILL REMAIN  . . . . . . . . . .     529 TOM LUNATIC          9
      IS DRINKING HER HEALTH WHEN LONE, ALONE--  . . . . . .    551 SONGS REWRIT 1 V    4
      DRINKING ALONE WITH A SPECKLED SHIN?  . . . . . . . .     551 SONGS REWRIT 1 V    8
      DRINKING JOY AS IT WERE MILK UPON HIS BREAST.  . . . .    559 MAGIC DRUM           3
      I PROMISE YOU A HUNDRED DRINKING BOWLS,  . . . . . . .    756 SHADOW WATER A  V  187
DRINKING-BOWLS
      A HUNDRED SWORDS, A HUNDRED DRINKING-BOWLS.  . . . . .    756 SHADOW WATER A     186
DRINKS
      A LIVING MAN IS BLIND AND DRINKS HIS DROP.  . . . . .     478 SELF AND SOUL       41
      O'ER GRIEF.  THE WORLD DRINKS SORROW FROM THE BEAMS . .   664 ISLE STAT II 2      46
DRIP
      HOW THE FETLOCKS DRIP BLOOD IN THE BATTLE,  . . . . .      52 OISIN 3             78
DRIPPED
      DRIPPED ON THE EARTH! BUT SOON, AH! SOON,  . . . . . .     19 OISIN 1        V  279
DRIPPING     SEE FOG-DRIPPING
      SPRANG DRIPPING, AND, WITH CAPTIVE DEMONS SENT  . . . .    38 OISIN 2           130
      OF A DROWNED DRIPPING BODY TO MY BREAST!  . . . . . .      40 OISIN 2           179
      I HELD A DRIPPING CORPSE, WITH LIVID CHOP  . . . . . .     40 OISIN 2        V  178
      AND DRIPPING AND SUNKEN SHAPE, TO FACE AND BREAST,  . .    40 OISIN 2        V  179
      AN ISLE LAY LEVEL BEFORE US, WITH DRIPPING HAZEL AND OAK?  47 OISIN 3            10
      AN ISLE LAY LEVEL BEFORE US, DRIPPING WITH HAZEL AND OAK?  47 OISIN 3        V   10
      GREY SAND ON THE GREEN OF THE GRASSES AND OVER THE DRIPPING 48 OISIN 3           14
          TREES,
      DRIPPING AND DOUBLING LANDWARD, AS THOUGH THEY WOULD HASTEN 48 OISIN 3           15
          AWAY,
      GREY SANDS ON THE GREEN OF THE GRASSES AND OVER THE        48 OISIN 3        V   14
          DRIPPING TREES,
      GREY SAND ON THE GREEN OF THE GRASSES AND OVER THE DRIPPING 57 OISIN 3          142
          TREES,
      DRIPPING AND DOUBLING LANDWARD, AS THOUGH THEY WOULD HASTEN 57 OISIN 3          143
          AWAY,
```

224

```
                                                        PAGE    TITLE           LINE
DRIPPING   (CONTINUED)
     GREY SANDS ON THE GREEN OF THE GRASSES AND OVER THE    57 OISIN 3       V 142
          DRIPPING TREES,
     ALL DRIPPING ON A GRASSY SLOPE, AND SAW THEM CEASE TO CHASE  76 INDIAN ON GOD      4
     THE RAINS ARE FROM HIS DRIPPING WING, THE MOONBEAMS FROM     76 INDIAN ON GOD      8
          HIS EYE.
     I SEE MY LIFE GO DRIPPING LIKE A STREAM . . . . . . .  104 FERGUS DRUID    V  31
     OF DRIPPING STONE; I DECLARE  . . . . . . . . . . .    414 TOWER             126
     I PASSED BY MANY CAVES OF DRIPPING STONE,  . . . . .   657 ISLE STAT I 3     47
     ABOVE, SALIVA DRIPPING FROM HIS JAWS,  . . . . . . .   689 NETTLESHIP         4
     HE TURNS WHERE, HUNG LIKE DROPS OF DRIPPING GOLD,  . . .  710 FERENCZ RENYI    18
     AND THE FISHER MEN AND WOMEN FROM THE DRIPPING HARBOUR WALL  718 PHANTOM SHIP    11
DRIVE
     AND PACE THE WOODS, AND DRIVE MY CHARIOT-WHEELS  . . . .  103 FERGUS DRUID     18
     AND PACE THE WOODS, AND DRIVE MY CHARIOT-WHEELS  . . . .  103 FERGUS DRUID   V  18
     AND DRIVE HIM FROM THE DOOR." AND THUS IT WAS!  . . .   106 CUCHULAIN SEA  V 17B
     WHO WILL GO DRIVE WITH FERGUS NOW,  . . . . . . . . .   125 GOES FERGUS        1
     I WILL DRIVE ALL THOSE LOVERS OUT AND CRY--  . . . . .  211 RAGGED WOOD       10
     I WILL DRIVE OUT THE DEER AND MOON AND CRY--  . . . .   211 RAGGED WOOD    V  10
     DRIVE TO A FLASHIER BAUBLE YET.  . . . . . . . . . . .  437 SONGS PLAY 1      12
     MUST DRIVE THE ARABIAN HOST. THE VOICE GREW STILL,  . .  467 HARUN RASHID     145
     MADE DRIVE THE ARABIAN HOST. THE VOICE GREW STILL,  . .  467 HARUN RASHID   V 145
     NASCHINA, HAIL! I'D DRIVE THY WOOLLY SHEEP,  . . . . .  649 ISLE STAT I 1    122
     GATHER ON THE WIND AND DRIVE  . . . . . . . . . . . .   775 AGAINST WITCH      7
DRIVEN     SEE RAGE-DRIVEN FOOL-DRIVEN PASSION-DRIVEN
     DRIVEN BY A STORM THAT EVER GRIEVES. . . . . . . . . .  135 TWO TREES      V  28
     HAVE DRIVEN TRAVELLERS MAD FOR THEIR OWN SPORT. . . . .  227 SHADOW WATER B   105
     MAY NOT HAVE DRIVEN YOU MAD FOR THEIR OWN SPORT? . . .  227 SHADOW WATER B V 105
     BEING DRIVEN ON BY VOICES AND BY DREAMS  . . . . . . .  243 SHADOW WATER B   441
     THAT HE IS BEING DRIVEN TO HIS DEATH. . . . . . . . .   248 SHADOW WATER B   551
     "THE DANISH TROOP WAS DRIVEN OUT  . . . . . . . . . .   273 GREY ROCK         65
     THEN HE, DRIVEN BY HIS THOUGHT BEYOND HIS THOUGHT,  . .  282 TWO KINGS        122
     THEN HE, DRIVEN BY THIS THOUGHT BEYOND HIS THOUGHT,  . .  282 TWO KINGS      V 122
     LIKE GENTLE BLOOD, HAS BEEN DRIVEN FROM THE PLACE,  . .  292 TO A SHADE        14
     ARE DRIVEN BY WEALTH AS BEGGARS BY THE ITCH,"  . . . .  300 BEGGAR CRIED      14
     AND THEREUPON IMAGINATION AND HEART WERE DRIVEN  . . .  316 COLD HEAVEN        3
     I HAD DRIVEN EVERY RHYME INTO ITS PLACE  . . . . . . .  339 SHEP GOATHERD     14
     UNTIL I AM DRIVEN MAD,  . . . . . . . . . . . . . .     346 ON WOMAN          35
     SLEEP DRIVEN FROM MY BED,  . . . . . . . . . . . . .    346 ON WOMAN          36
     ALL THE DISHONEST CROWD I HAD DRIVEN AWAY,  . . . . . .  352 PEOPLE            24
     DERIDED AND DERIDING, DRIVEN OUT  . . . . . . . . . .   369 EGO DOMINUS       34
     EVEN TO EYES THAT BEAUTY HAD DRIVEN MAD,  . . . . . .   390 IMAGE PAST        34
     CONSIDERING THAT, ALL HATRED DRIVEN HENCE,  . . . . .   405 FOR DAUGHTER      65
     MUSIC HAD DRIVEN THEIR WITS ASTRAY--  . . . . . . . .   411 TOWER             47
     THE RAGE DRIVEN, RAGE TORMENTED, AND RAGE HUNGRY TROOP,  426 PHANTOM HATRED V  11
     AND THAT ALONE; YET I, BEING DRIVEN HALF INSANE  . . .  442 BLACK CENTAUR      6
     AND THEREUPON MY HEART IS DRIVEN WILD!  . . . . . . .   444 SCHOOL CHILDR     23
     HAD DRIVEN HIM CRAZED!  . . . . . . . . . . . . . .     473 ALL SOUL NIGHT    73
     BY THAT GREAT GLORY DRIVEN WILD. . . . . . . . . . .    540 FROM ANTIGONE     13
     "OR DRIVEN FROM HOME AND LEFT TO DIE IN FEAR."  . . .   635 CUCHULAIN COMF    22
     HAD DRIVEN HER FORTH, FOR EVER MORE  . . . . . . . .    668 ISLE STAT II 3    56
     HAD DRIVEN HER FORTH, FOR EVERMORE  . . . . . . . . .   668 ISLE STAT II 3 V  56
     BE DRIVEN FROM THE THRESHOLD  . . . . . . . . . . . .   770 BLOOD BOND         5
     BE DRIVEN FROM THE THRESHOLDS  . . . . . . . . . . . .  770 BLOOD BOND     V   4
     MAY THIS FIRE HAVE DRIVEN OUT  . . . . . . . . . . . .  775 AGAINST WITCH      1
     MAY THIS FLAME HAVE DRIVEN OUT  . . . . . . . . . . .   775 AGAINST WITCH  V   1
DRIVES
     "HE DRIVES AWAY THE NORTHERN COLD."  . . . . . . . . .   82 MAD KING GOLL     11
     LOVE'S PLEASURE DRIVES HIS LOVE AWAY,  . . . . . . . .  438 SONGS PLAY 2      11
DRIVING
     . . . DRIVING THE DUST WITH THEIR THRONGS,  . . . . .    53 OISIN 3           85
     WAS DRIVING CATTLE CAME SHE WITH SWIFT FEET,  . . . .   106 CUCHULAIN SEA  V  19
     DRIVING THE DEER ALONG THE WOODY WAYS. . . . . . . .    109 CUCHULAIN SEA  V  48
     FLAMES THE SHUTTLE OF THE LIGHTNING ACROSS THE DRIVING  718 PHANTOM SHIP       1
          SLEET,
DROMAHAIR
     HE STOOD AMONG A CROWD AT DROMAHAIR!  . . . . . . . .   126 DREAM OF FAERY     1
DROOP
     "AND EVERY HERO DROOP HIS HEAD?  . . . . . . . . . .      4 OISIN 1           33
     HIS EYELIDS DROOP, HIS HEAD FALLS LOW,  . . . . . . .    98 FOXHUNTER         13
     IN THE LONG GRASS--FOUR EYES DROOP LOW--A SEAT  . . .   716 DWELT SYCAMORE    11
DROOPED
     GLIMMERING IN HER DROOPED EYES, SAW HER LIPS MOVE  . .   81 EPHEMERA       V 24D
DROOPETH
     DROOPETH NOW HIS FOREHEAD LOW  . . . . . . . . . . .    711 FERENCZ RENYI  V  39
DROOPING
     BOAST NOT, NOR MOURN WITH DROOPING HEAD . . . . . . .    11 OISIN 1          129
     WITH A KISS AND A TEAR ON THY DROOPING BROW. . . . . .   79 FALLING LEAVES     8
     AT THE DROOPING OF AN EYE,  . . . . . . . . . . . . .   453 DEATH OF HARE      5
     AND 'MONG THE STUNTED ASH-TREES' DROOPING RINGS, . . .  650 ISLE STAT I 1    128
     AS THEY GO WITH DROOPING FEATHER. . . . . . . . . . .   667 ISLE STAT II 3    33
DROOPS
     "WHY, AS YE RIDE, DROOPS LOW EACH HEAD?  . . . . . . .    4 OISIN 1        V  32
     HIS EYELIDS CLOSE, HIS HEAD DROOPS LOW,  . . . . . . .   98 FOXHUNTER      V  13
     LIKE TUFTED REEDS OUR COURAGE DROOPS IN A BLACK WIND AND  207 HANRAHANS SONG V  3
          DIES!
     WEAK AND WORN AND WEARY OUR COURAGE DROOPS AND DIES . .  207 HANRAHANS SONG V  8
DROP     SEE TEAR-DROP FROTH-DROP DEW-DROP
     "THE SOUL IS A DROP OF JOY AFAR.  . . . . . . . . . .    19 OISIN 1        V 276
     AND BID THE STARS DROP DOWN FROM THE SKY,  . . . . . .   28 OISIN 1          426
     UNTIL THE GODS AND DEMONS DROP ASLEEP,  . . . . . . .    35 OISIN 2           86
```

		PAGE	TITLE		LINE

DROP   (CONTINUED)

"THIS DEMON SHALL BE PIERCED AND DROP AND DIE, ...   35 OISIN 2   V   90
"I HEAR MY SOUL DROP DOWN INTO DECAY, ...   45 OISIN 2   235
WITH ALL YOUR WHIRLING HAIR, AND DROP MANY AN AZURE TEAR.   73 ANASHU VIJAYA   46
WITH ALL YOUR WHIRLING HAIR, AND DROP THROUGH SPACE AN
    AZURE TEAR.   73 ANASHU VIJAYA   V   46
WITH ALL YOUR WHIRLING HAIR, AND DROP TEAR UPON AZURE TEAR.   73 ANASHU VIJAYA   V   46
WITH ALL OUR WHIRLING HAIR, AND DROP MANY AN AZURE TEAR.   73 ANASHU VIJAYA   V   46
IS BUT A SLIDING DROP OF RAIN BETWEEN HIS PETALS WIDE. . .   76 INDIAN ON GOD   12
IS BUT A SLIDING DROP OF RAIN WITHIN HIS PETALS WIDE."   . .   76 INDIAN ON GOD   V   12
AND GREAT BOUGHS DROP TRANQUILLITY;   . . . .   77 INDIAN TO LOVE   2
AND DROP A VAPOURY FOOTFALL IN THE WATER'S DROWSY BLAZE.   78 INDIAN TO LOVE   V   20
FROM FERNS THAT DROP THEIR TEARS   . . . .   88 STOLEN CHILD   36
FROM FERNS THAT DROP THEIR TEAR   . . . .   88 STOLEN CHILD   V   36
A GREEN DROP IN THE SURGE, A GLEAM OF LIGHT   . . . . .   104 FERGUS DRUID   33
THE DEWS DROP SLOWLY AND DREAMS GATHER; UNKNOWN SPEARS   161 BLACK PIG   1
"THE ROSE THAT MUST DROP, OUT OF SWEET LEAVES, ...   168 BLESSED   V   37
THAT IT MAY DROP FAINT PERFUME, AND BE HEAVY WITH DEW,   . .   172 TRAV PASSION   7
AND ONE BY ONE WE DROP AWAY."   . . . .   208 OLD MEN ADMIRE   3
AND DROP HIM FROM THE GUNNEL. I DARE NOT DO IT. . . . .   222 SHADOW WATER B   15
WHEN THE FLIES DROP IN THE STREAM;   . . . .   348 FISHERMAN   34
DROP THEIR CAST AT THE SIDE   . . . .   414 TOWER   125
AND DROP TWIGS LAYER UPON LAYER. . . . .   415 TOWER   168
THEY MAY DROP A FLY;   . . . .   416 TOWER   177
BEFORE THE INDIFFERENT BEAK COULD LET HER DROP?   . . . .   441 LEDA AND SWAN   14
A LIVING MAN IS BLIND AND DRINKS HIS DROP. . . . . . .   478 SELF AND SOUL   41
WHAT MATTER IF A BLIND MAN DRINK HIS DROP?   . . . . .   478 SELF AND SOUL   V   41
THEN DARKENING THROUGH "DARK" RAFTERY'S "CELLAR" DROP, . .   490 COOLE BALLYLEE   4
SPREAD TO A LAKE AND DROP INTO A HOLE. . . . .   490 COOLE BALLYLEE   7
ALL THINGS HANG LIKE A DROP OF DEW   . . . .   505 GRAT INSTRUCT   3
MAY SING, AND SING UNTIL HE DROP, ...   525 DANCING DAYS   21
THERE ALL THE PLANETS DROP IN THE SUN.   . . . . . .   557 THERE   4
WHAT MATTER? HEAVE NO SIGH, LET NO TEAR DROP, ...   564 GYRES   11
THE GREAT STAGE CURTAIN ABOUT TO DROP, ...   565 LAPIS LAZULI   13
AND ALL THE DROP-SCENES DROP AT ONCE   . . . . . .   566 LAPIS LAZULI   22
AND ALL THE DROP SCENES DROP AT ONCE   . . . . . .   566 LAPIS LAZULI   V   22
AND ALL THE DROP SCENES DROP AT ONCE   . . . . . .   566 LAPIS LAZULI   V   22
I THINK I SHOULD DROP DEAD."   . . . .   569 THREE BUSHES   13
"I KNOW THAT I MUST DROP DOWN DEAD   . . . .   569 THREE BUSHES   17
YET WHAT COULD I BUT DROP DOWN DEAD   . . . .   569 THREE BUSHES   19
A POISON DROP. A TOY, A FANCY ONCE, ...   700 MOSADA 3   24
A POISON DROP. THE TOY OF FANCY ONCE, ...   700 MOSADA 3   V   24

DROPPED

I DROPPED THE BERRY IN A STREAM   . . . .   149 WANDER AENGUS   7
THE MAINES' CHILDREN DROPPED THEIR SPADES, AND STOOD   . .   185 QUEEN MAEVE   120
THE MAINES' CHILDREN HAVE NOT DROPPED THEIR SPADES . . .   186 QUEEN MAEVE   123
THAT DROPPED UPON MY THIGH."   . . . .   309 PLAYER QUEEN   16
THEIR BEAUTY DROPPED OUT OF THE LONELINESS   . . . . .   375 PHASES OF MOON   70
IT DROPPED THE REINS OF PEACE AND WAR   . . . . . .   437 SONGS PLAY 1   14
HALF RUNNING, DROPPED AT THE FIRST RIDGE OF THE DESERT . .   468 HARUN RASHID   155
HE DROPPED UPON HIS HEAD AND DIED. . . . .   571 THREE BUSHES   52
AND DROPPED AND DIED THEREON, FOR SHE   . . . . . .   571 THREE BUSHES   54
AND ON THAT CITY DROPPED A TEAR, ...   725 LEGEND   31
BEFORE I DROPPED ASLEEP, A KINGFISHER   . . . . . .   761 SHADOW WATER A   274

DROPPING   SEE DEW-DROPPING

GOES DROPPING FROM HIS EYES A LANGUID LIGHT, ...   34 OISIN 2   V   81A
I FOUND, DROPPING SEA-FOAM ON THE WIDE STAIR, ...   43 OISIN 2   V   215
I FOUND, DROPPING SEA FOAM ON THE WIDE STAIR, ...   43 OISIN 2   V   215
DROPPING; A MURMUROUS DROPPING; OLD SILENCE AND THAT ONE
    SOUND;   48 OISIN 3   18
DROPPING; A MURMUROUS DROPPING; OLD SILENCE AND THAT ONE
    SOUND;   48 OISIN 3   18
. . . SLOW DROPPING A SOUND IN FAINT STREAMS   . . . .   51 OISIN 3   67
. . . THEIR DIMNESS, THEIR DEWS DROPPING SLEEP. . . . .   54 OISIN 3   108
WHERE EVER IS MURMUROUS DROPPING, OLD SILENCE AND THAT
    ONE SOUND;   56 OISIN 3   138
THE DEWDROPS, FOR THE SOUND OF THEIR OWN DROPPING. . . .   68 SAD SHEPHERD   16
THE DEW DROPS, FOR THE SOUND OF THEIR OWN DROPPING--   . .   68 SAD SHEPHERD   V   16
DROPPING AT EVE IN CORAL BAYS   . . . .   78 INDIAN TO LOVE   V   19
DROPPING A VAPOURY FOOTSOLE ON THE TIDE'S DROWSY BLAZE. . .   78 INDIAN TO LOVE   V   20
AND I SHALL HAVE SOME PEACE THERE, FOR PEACE COMES DROPPING   117 ISLE INNISFREE   5
    SLOW,
DROPPING FROM THE VEILS OF THE MORNING TO WHERE THE CRICKET   117 ISLE INNISFREE   6
    SINGS;
IS DROPPING SLEEP, UNTIL GOD BURN TIME, ...   164 PERFECT BEAUTY   7
THE ENTRAILS OF THE HORSE. DROPPING HIS SWORD . . . . .   278 TWO KINGS   23
THROUGH THE ENTRAILS OF THE HORSE. DROPPING HIS SWORD . .   278 TWO KINGS   V   23
DROPPING OUT OF SKY OR ROCK, ...   633 MAN AND ECHO   44
DROPPING LIQUID RAINBOW LIGHT, ...   732 STREET DANCERS   33

DROPS   SEE MIST-DROPS

AND WAS BORN WHERE THE SUN DROPS DOWN IN THE TIDE, . . .   5 OISIN 1   V   49
AND DROPS OF HONEY ARE HIS WORDS, ...   7 OISIN 1   V   64
LIKE DROPS OF FROZEN RAINBOW LIGHT, ...   14 OISIN 1   183
WHERE DROPS OF DEW IN MYRIADS FALL, ...   16 OISIN 1   222
"MEN'S HEARTS OF OLD WERE DROPS OF FLAME   . . . . .   19 OISIN 1   276
OR DROPS OF SILVER JOY THAT FELL . . . .   19 OISIN 1   278
LIKE DROPS OF HONEY CAME THEIR WORDS, ...   26 OISIN 1   398
THE DEW DROPS, FOR THE SOUND OF THEIR OWN DROPPING-- . .   68 SAD SHEPHERD   V   16
TIME DROPS IN DECAY, ...   142 MOODS   1
THE DEW DROPS SLOWLY; THE DREAMS GATHER; UNKNOWN SPEARS   161 BLACK PIG   V   1
"THAT DROWSILY DROPS FAINT LEAVES ON HIM   . . . . .   168 BLESSED   37

DROPS   (CONTINUED)
    THAT THE SALT DROPS HAVE WET, ...   312 CHILD DANCING   5
    THE DARKNESS DROPS AGAIN, BUT NOW I KNOW . . . . .   402 SECOND COMING   18
    BUT NOW WIND DROPS, DUST SETTLES, THEREUPON . . . . 433 NINETEEN 19   125
    THERE IN THE TOMB DROPS THE FAINT MOONLIGHT, ... 636 BLACK TOWER   17
    SOMETHING DROPS FROM EYES LONG BLIND, ... 638 BEN BULBEN   29
    SHOWERED AWAY THE KEEN DEW DROPS, ... 705 DAWN-SONG   18
    HE TURNS WHERE, HUNG LIKE DROPS OF DRIPPING GOLD, . 710 FERENCZ RENYI   18
    HE TURNS WHERE, HUNG LIKE DROPS OF LIQUID GOLD, . . 710 FERENCZ RENYI V   18
    BUT THIS ONE--THIS ONE. NOW HIS HEAD DROPS LOW, . . 711 FERENCZ RENYI   39
    DROPS ON HIS BOSOM, SOMBRE, MOIST AND SLOW. . . . . 711 FERENCZ RENYI   40
DROP-SCENES
    AND ALL THE DROP-SCENES DROP AT ONCE . . . . 566 LAPIS LAZULI   22
DROPT
    DROPT DOWN THE VELVET DARKNESS FROM ABOVE, ... 688 TWO TITANS   37
    THE FATHER DROPT HIS ROSARY-- . . . . 730 PRIEST FAIRY   57
DROUGHT
    WHEN LOVE LONGING IS BUT DROUGHT . . . . 777 SONG DEIRDRE 2 V   11
DROUTH
    WHEN LOVE-LONGING IS BUT DROUTH . . . . 777 SONG DEIRDRE 2   11
DROVE
    AND DROVE TUMULT AND WAR AWAY . . . .   82 MAD KING GOLL   5
    CRYING, THE PIRATES DROVE HIS SWINE . . . .   82 MAD KING GOLL   15
    HE DROVE ME OUT AND SHUT THE DOOR, ... 95 MOLL MAGEE   25
    HE DROVE ME FORTH AND SHUT THE DOOR, ... 95 MOLL MAGEE   V   25
    THE TALE DROVE HIS FINE ANGRY MOOD AWAY. . . . . . . 128 DREAM OF FAERY   36
    O'DRISCOLL DROVE WITH A SONG . . . . 143 HOST OF AIR   1
    AND HIM WHO DROVE THE GODS OUT OF THEIR LISS, . . . 170 SECRET ROSE   16
    THAT DROVE YOU TO IT, AND I FOOL ENOUGH . . . . . . 248 SHADOW WATER B   548
    UPON HIS TREMBLING HORSE, THEN DROVE THE SPUR, . . . 277 TWO KINGS   11
    TREMBLING BENEATH HIM, AND THEN DROVE THE SPUR . . . 277 TWO KINGS   V   11
    AND WHEN THEY DROVE OUT COSIMO, ... 288 TO WEALTHY MAN   20
    DROVE TO THIS TUMULT IN THE CLOUDS, ... 328 IRISH AIRMAN   12
    AND MASONS DROVE FROM MILES AWAY . . . . 360 ALF POLLEXFEN   9
    AND DROVE HIM DRUNK OR SOBER THROUGH THE DAWN . . . 411 TOWER   58
    DROVE HORROR FROM HIS MOTHER'S BREAST. . . . . . . 440 WISDOM   20
    RICHES DROVE OUT RANK, ... 626 STATES HOLIDAY   2
    BASE DROVE OUT THE BETTER BLOOD, ... 626 STATES HOLIDAY   3
    AND DROVE THE BOYS AND WOMEN OFF. . . . . 725 LEGEND   24
DROWN
    AND SLEEP DROWN SUN AND MOON AND STAR." . . . . . .   5 OISIN 1   V   49
    THEIR HEADS ON YOUR KNEES, AND DROWN THEIR EYES WITH YOUR 163 VALLEY LOVERS   6
        HAIR,
    THAT I MAY DROWN MYSELF? BETTER STEER HOME, ... 222 SHADOW WATER B   12
    I'D DROWN HIM WHILE WE HAVE THE CHANCE TO DO IT. . . 224 SHADOW WATER B   58
    OR WAVE TO DROWN. BUT I HAVE DONE WITH WORDS, . . . 238 SHADOW WATER B   348
    NO NEED TO DROWN, FOR, IF YOU WILL PARDON US . . . 238 SHADOW WATER B   361
    THAT EVEN LOVERS DROWN. . . . . 453 MERMAID   6
    "DROWN ALL THE DOGS," SAID THE FIERCE YOUNG WOMAN, . 546 TO SAME TUNE 2   7
    DROWN, DROWN IN THE WATER-BUTT, ... 546 TO SAME TUNE 2   9
    DROWN, DROWN IN THE WATER-BUTT, ... 546 TO SAME TUNE 2   9
    DROWN ALL THE DOGS," SAID THE FIERCE YOUNG WOMAN. . 546 TO SAME TUNE 2   10
    "DROWN ALL THE DOGS," SAID THE FIERCE YOUNG WOMAN, . 546 TO SAME TUNE 2   17
    DROWN, DROWN IN THE WATER-BUTT, ... 546 TO SAME TUNE 2   19
    DROWN, DROWN IN THE WATER-BUTT, ... 546 TO SAME TUNE 2   19
    DROWN ALL THE DOGS," SAID THE FIERCE YOUNG WOMAN. . 546 TO SAME TUNE 2   20
    DROWN, DROWN IN THE WATER BUTT, ... 546 TO SAME TUNE 2 V   REF
    DROWN, DROWN IN THE WATER-BUTT, ... 546 TO SAME TUNE 2 V   REF
    "DROWN ALL THE DOGS," SAID THE FIERCE YOUNG WOMAN, . 547 TO SAME TUNE 2   27
    DROWN, DROWN IN THE WATER-BUTT, ... 547 TO SAME TUNE 2   29
    DROWN, DROWN IN THE WATER-BUTT, ... 547 TO SAME TUNE 2   29
    DROWN ALL THE DOGS," SAID THE FIERCE YOUNG WOMAN. . 547 TO SAME TUNE 2   30
    WITH FIERY SONG I'LL DROWN YON PUNY VOICE. . . . . 648 ISLE STAT I 1   81
    TO DROWN IN ITS OWN IMAGE? EVEN THAT SLEEP . . . . 765 SHADOW WATER A   364
DROWNED   SEE DEW-DROWNED
    OF A DROWNED DRIPPING BODY TO MY BREAST, ...   40 OISIN 2   179
    WERE DROWNED IN HER LONG DIM HAIR. . . . . 145 HOST OF AIR   36
    BEFORE THEY DROWNED THEIR LOVERS' EYES . . . . . . 156 FORGOT BEAUTY V   10A
    THE GREY CAIRN ON THE HILL, WHEN DAY SINKS DROWNED IN DEW, 161 BLACK PIG   6
    THEIR LOVE WAS NEVER DROWNED IN CARE . . . . 189 BAILE AILLINN   8
    WHERE TIME IS DROWNED IN ODOUR-LADEN WINDS . . . . 219 HARP OF AENGUS   3
    AND DROWNED THE TREASURES OF NINE CONQUERED NATIONS, . 235 SHADOW WATER B 287
    HAD DROWNED ME ALSO. BUT, BEING YET ALIVE, ... 235 SHADOW WATER B   289
    THE CEREMONY OF INNOCENCE IS DROWNED, ... 402 SECOND COMING   6
    AND ONE WAS DROWNED IN THE GREAT BOG OF CLOONE. . . 411 TOWER   48
    THE MAN DROWNED IN A BOG'S MIRE, ... 413 TOWER   95
    AND WHAT HAD DROWNED A LOVER ONCE . . . . 457 SECRETS OF OLD   5
    TO SEE THEM DROWNED BY THOSE VAST SOLITUDES, . . . 661 ISLE STAT II 1   57
    ALL THE DROWNED THAT EVER WERE DROWNED FROM THAT VILLAGE 719 PHANTOM SHIP   20
        BY THE SEA,
    ALL THE DROWNED THAT EVER WERE DROWNED FROM THAT VILLAGE 719 PHANTOM SHIP   20
        BY THE SEA,
    ON THE DROWNED MEN'S HANDS AND FACES, ON THE SPARS AND 719 PHANTOM SHIP   22
        ON THE SAILS.
    HUSH'D THE FISHERS, TILL A MOTHER CALLS BY NAME HER DROWNED 719 PHANTOM SHIP 23
        SON,
    THEN EACH WIFE AND MAID AND MOTHER CALLS BY NAME . 719 PHANTOM SHIP   24
        SOME DROWNED ONE.
    WHERE TIME IS DROWNED IN ODOUR-LADEN WINDS . . . . 762 SHADOW WATER A   298
DROWNING
    FOR, AS DRIFT FROM A SAILOR SLOW DROWNING . . . . .   48 OISIN 3   22

		PAGE	TITLE	LINE

DROWNING   (CONTINUED)
  DROWNING LOVE'S LONELY HOUR IN DEEP TWILIGHT OF REST,   . .   154 BELOVED PEACE   11
DROWNS
  "JOY DROWNS THE TWILIGHT IN THE DEW, ...   18 OISIN 1   261
  WHERE EVEN LONGING DROWNS UNDER ITS OWN EXCESS: . . . . 426 PHANTOM HATRED   22
DROWSILY
  "THAT DROWSILY DROPS FAINT LEAVES ON HIM . . . .   168 BLESSED   37
DROWSY
  WITH VAPOURY FOOTSOLE BY THE WATER'S DROWSY BLAZE. . . .   78 INDIAN TO LOVE   20
  AND DROP A VAPOURY FOOTFALL IN THE WATER'S DROWSY BLAZE.   78 INDIAN TO LOVE V   20
  WITH VAPOURY FOOTSOLE AMONG THE WATER'S DROWSY BLAZE. . . 78 INDIAN TO LOVE V   20
  DROPPING A VAPOURY FOOTSOLE ON THE TIDE'S DROWSY BLAZE.   78 INDIAN TO LOVE V   20
  THE DROWSY WATER-RATS: . . . .   87 STOLEN CHILD   5
  THE DROWSY WATER RATS: . . . .   87 STOLEN CHILD   V   5
  DIM POWERS OF DROWSY THOUGHT, LET HER NO LONGER BE . . . 175 ELEMENT POWERS   13
  THEY SANG A DROWSY SONG, OR SNORED, ...   271 GREY ROCK   16
  AND SANG A DROWSY SONG, OR SNORED, ...   271 GREY ROCK   V   16
  TO KEEP A DROWSY EMPEROR AWAKE: . . . .   408 SAIL BYZANTIUM   29
  THE GUARDSMEN'S DROWSY CHARGERS WOULD NOT PRANCE. . . .   429 NINETEEN 19   24
  WITHIN THE DROWSY BLOSSOM HANGS THE BEE: . . . . . .   645 ISLE STAT I 1   2
  HARK! HE'S DEAD--MY DROWSY BROTHER, ...   656 ISLE STAT I 3   18
  FAR OFF IN DROWSY VALLEYS . . . .   680 LOVE AND DEATH   5
  AND FALLS AMONG THE DREAMS THE DROWSY GODS . . . . .   750 SHADOW WATER A   68
DRUDGE
  THE COARSENESS OF THE DRUDGE. BEFORE THE FULL . . . .   376 PHASES OF MOON   94
DRUDGERY
  RENOUNCE THAT DRUDGERY, ...   600 THOSE IMAGES   7
DRUG
  AS RECOLLECTION OR THE DRUG DECIDE, ...   444 SCHOOL CHILDR   36
  WINE OR LOVE DRUG HIM TO SLEEP, ...   633 MAN AND ECHO   26
DRUGS
  WINE OR LOVE DRUGS HIM TO SLEEP, ...   633 MAN AND ECHO   V   26
DRUID
  A DRUID DREAM OF THE END OF DAYS . . . .   16 OISIN 1   219
  HE FELL INTO A DRUID SWOON. . . . .   20 OISIN 1   289
  WHO WEDDED MEN WITH RINGS OF DRUID GOLD: . . . . . .   29 OISIN 2   10
  THE DRUID SWORD OF MANANAN, HE GREW . . . .   40 OISIN 2   V 174
  AND EVERY WHISPERING DRUID SAID: . . . .   82 MAD KING GOLL   V   9
  THE DRUID, GREY, WOOD-NURTURED, QUIET-EYED, ...   101 ROSE UPON ROOD   4
  THE DRUID, GREY, WOOD NURTURED, QUIET EYED, ...   101 ROSE UPON ROOD V   4
  FERGUS AND THE DRUID . . . .   102 FERGUS DRUID   T
  AH! DRUID, DRUID, HOW GREAT WEBS OF SORROW . . . . .   104 FERGUS DRUID   39
  AH! DRUID, DRUID, HOW GREAT WEBS OF SORROW . . . . .   104 FERGUS DRUID   39
  AND SANG HOW DAY A DRUID TWILIGHT SHEDS . . . . . .   126 DREAM OF FAERY V   7
  A DRUID KINDNESS, ON ALL HEARERS FELL. . . . . . .   129 BOOK STORIES   4
  A DRUID LAND, A DRUID TUNE! . . . .   139 TO IRELAND   32
  A DRUID LAND, A DRUID TUNE! . . . .   139 TO IRELAND   32
  IN DRUID VAPOUR AND MAKE THE TORCHES DIM: . . . . .   169 SECRET ROSE   11
  HAD FILLED THE HOUSE WITH DRUID HEAVINESS: . . . . .   181 QUEEN MAEVE   40
  AND DRUID MOONS, AND MURMURING OF BOUGHS, ...   219 HARP OF AENGUS   4
  HE MADE A HARP WITH DRUID APPLE-WOOD . . . .   220 HARP OF AENGUS   11
  HE MADE A HARP WITH DRUID APPLE WOOD . . . .   220 HARP OF AENGUS V   11
  YOU HAVE A DRUID CRAFT OF WICKED SOUND . . . . . .   237 SHADOW WATER B   342
  YOU HAVE A DRUID CRAFT, WICKED SOUND . . . .   237 SHADOW WATER B   342
  HE HAS FLUNG A DRUID SPELL UPON THE AIR, ...   240 SHADOW WATER B   385
  HE HAS THROWN A DRUID DREAM UPON THE AIR. . . . . .   759 SHADOW WATER A   237
  BREATHED OUT A DRUID VAPOUR, AND CRUMBLED AWAY . . . .   761 SHADOW WATER A   279
  AND DRUID MOONS, AND MURMURING OF BOUGHS, ...   762 SHADOW WATER A   299
  HE MADE A HARP WITH DRUID APPLE WOOD . . . .   763 SHADOW WATER A   306
  HE MADE A HARP WITH DRUID APPLE-WOOD . . . .   763 SHADOW WATER A V   306
DRUIDS
  RANKING HIS DRUIDS ROUND HIM TEN BY TEN, ...   110 CUCHULAIN SEA   76
  SENT FOR HIS DRUIDS TWENTY SCORE AND TEN, ...   110 CUCHULAIN SEA   V   76
  THE DRUIDS TOOK THEM TO THEIR MYSTERY, ...   111 CUCHULAIN SEA   82
  THE DRUIDS CHANTED, SWAYING IN THEIR HANDS . . . . .   111 CUCHULAIN SEA   82
  THE DRUIDS CHAUNTED, SWAYING IN THEIR HANDS . . . .   111 CUCHULAIN SEA   V   82
  MUST BE SUBSTANTIAL SOMEWHERE. I HAVE HEARD THE DRUIDS   229 SHADOW WATER B   162
  THAT DRUIDS WRITE ON YEW AND APPLE WOOD, ...   748 SHADOW WATER A   29
  AND HEARS THE ROAR OF THE STREAMS WHERE, DRUIDS SAY, . . 749 SHADOW WATER A   46
DRUM
  . . . THE SOUND OF THE SEA'S VAGUE DRUM? . . . . . .   56 OISIN 3   135
  TO DRUM WITH HER HEEL AND TO LEAP? . . . .   381 SONGS FOOL 2   9
  DANCING TO A FRENZIED DRUM, ...   403 FOR DAUGHTER   15
  WHAT MAGIC DRUM? . . . .   559 MAGIC DRUM   T
  THROUGH LIGHT-OBLITERATING GARDEN FOLIAGE WHAT MAGIC DRUM? 560 MAGIC DRUM   4
  NOW STEPS DRAW CLOSE, HE HIDES BENEATH A DRUM. . . . .   713 FERENCZ RENYI   78
DRUMAHAIR
  DARK AND DULL AND EARTHY THE STREAM OF DRUMAHAIR . . .   207 HANRAHANS SONG V   11
DRUMCLIFF
  HE THAT IN SLIGO AT DRUMCLIFF . . . .   604 YOU CONTENT   9
  IN DRUMCLIFF CHURCHYARD YEATS IS LAID. . . . . . .   640 BEN BULBEN   85
DRUMS
  THE DRUMS AND THE KETTLEDRUMS . . . .   527 AM OF IRELAND   21
  THE DRUMS AND THE KETTLE DRUMS . . . .   527 AM OF IRELAND   V   21
  THE DRUMS AND THE KETTLE DRUMS . . . .   527 AM OF IRELAND   V   21
DRUNK   SEE HALF-DRUNK
  THAT HAS DRUNK FULL, SHE CROSSED THE MISTY SEA . . . .   30 OISIN 2   16
  WHEN EARTHY NIGHT HAD DRUNK HIS BODY IN: . . . . .   127 DREAM OF FAERY   28
  NOW THAT DEEP EARTH HAS DRUNK HIS BODY IN: . . . . .   127 DREAM OF FAERY V   28
  AND DRUNK UP THE MURMURING TIDE: . . . .   171 MAID QUIET   V   40
  I HAVE DRUNK ALE FROM THE COUNTRY OF THE YOUNG . . . .   177 PAST GREATNESS   1

DRUNK (CONTINUED)
    THAT SOMEBODY HAD DRUNK DRY. . . . .   215 HAPPY TOWNLAND   32
    BUT WHEN I HAD EATEN AND DRUNK MYSELF ASLEEP . . . .   223 SHADOW WATER B   30
    BUT WHEN I HAD EATEN AND DRUNK A BELLYFUL . . . . .   223 SHADOW WATER B V   30
    DRUNK WITH THE UNMIXED WINE. . . . .   355 PROPERTIUS   8
    DRUNK WITH THE UN-MIXED WINE. . . . .   355 PROPERTIUS   V   8
    AND DROVE HIM DRUNK OR SOBER THROUGH THE DAWN . . . .   411 TOWER   58
    NEVER TO HAVE DRUNK THE BREATH OF LIFE. . . . . . .   459 FROM OEDIPUS   V   11
    DRUNK WITH THE BITTER SWEETNESS OF HER YOUTH. . . . .   469 HARUN RASHID   186
    DRUNK WITH THE BITTER-SWEETNESS OF HER YOUTH. . . . .   469 HARUN RASHID   V   186
    THAT MAN IS DEAF AND DRUNK AND BLIND . . . .   478 SELF AND SOUL V   35
    AND ALL DEAD MEN ARE DRUNK. . . . .   592 DRUNK SOBRIETY   16
    AND DRUNK OR SOBER LIVE AT EASE . . . .   597 MODEL LAUREATE   13
DRUNKARD
    A DRUNKARD IS A DEAD MAN, ...   592 DRUNK SOBRIETY   15
DRUNKARD'S
    OR OUT OF DRUNKARD'S EYE. ALL'S WHIGGERY NOW, ...   486 SEVEN SAGES   13
    OR DRUNKARD'S EYE. ALL'S WHIGGERY NOW, ...   486 SEVEN SAGES   V   13
    OR OUT OF A DRUNKARD'S EYE. ALL'S WHIGGERY NOW, . . .   486 SEVEN SAGES   V   13
DRUNKARDS
    "THE DRUNKARDS, PILFERERS OF PUBLIC FUNDS, ...   352 PEOPLE   23
    THOUGH DRUNKARDS LIE AND SNORE. . . . .   592 DRUNK SOBRIETY   8
DRUNKEN   SEE BEAUTY-DRUNKEN
    AND HE NODS A DRUNKEN HEAD. . . . .   168 BLESSED   32
    THOUGH DRUNKEN WITH THE FLAGS THAT SWAY . . . . . .   212 BLESS PSALTER   5
    AND WAIT HIM IN A DRUNKEN SLEEP." . . . .   307 HOUR DAWN   106
    WHO HAS WON A DRUNKEN CHEER, ...   347 FISHERMAN   18
    BUT TAKE ME FOR SOME DRUNKEN COUNTRYMAN: . . . . . .   377 PHASES OF MOON   130
    BUT TAKE ME FOR SOME DRUNKEN COUNTRY MAN: . . . . . .   377 PHASES OF MOON V   130
    A DRUNKEN, VAINGLORIOUS LOUT. . . . .   393 EASTER 1916   32
    A DRUNKEN, VAIN-GLORIOUS LOUT. . . . .   393 EASTER 1916   V   32
    RIDES UPON SLEEP: A DRUNKEN SOLDIERY . . . .   429 NINETEEN 19   26
    AND CLAMOUR IN DRUNKEN FRENZY FOR THE MOON. . . . . .   482 BLOOD AND MOON   42
    THE EMPEROR'S DRUNKEN SOLDIERY ARE ABED: . . . . . .   497 BYZANTIUM   2
    THE EMPEROR'S DRUNKEN SOLDIERY ARE A-BED: . . . . . .   497 BYZANTIUM   V   2
    NOR KNEW, DRUNKEN WITH SINGING AS WITH WINE, ...   537 HER VISION   30
    SPEAKING TO A DRUNKEN AUDIENCE HIGH NONSENSICAL WORDS: .   577 LOFTY THINGS   6
    A DRUNKEN MAN'S PRAISE OF SOBRIETY . . . .   591 DRUNK SOBRIETY   T
    TURN TO A DRUNKEN JOURNALIST: . . . .   626 OLD MEN BE MAD   4
DRY   SEE SUN-DRY
    A DUSKY DEMON DRY AS A WITHERED SEDGE . . . .   39 OISIN 2   158
    A DUSK DEMON, DRY AS A WITHERED SEDGE, ...   39 OISIN 2   V   158
    A HUSKY DEMON, DRY AS A WITHERED SEDGE . . . .   39 OISIN 2   V   158
    . . . THE SPITTLE ON HIS BEARD NEVER DRY. . . . . .   53 OISIN 3   90
    . . . WITH THE SPITTLE ON HIS BEARD NEVER DRY. . . .   60 OISIN 3   192
    HE HAD HALF A CLOAK TO KEEP HIM DRY, ...   190 BAILE AILLINN   29
    THAT SOMEBODY HAD DRUNK DRY. . . . .   215 HAPPY TOWNLAND   32
    AND AFTER, DRAINED DRY. . . . .   310 WITCH   4
    THE WOODLAND PATHS ARE DRY, ...   322 SWANS AT COOLE   2
    BUT WALK BY THE DRY THORN UNTIL I HAVE FOUND . . . .   351 HER PRAISE   12
    WHEN ALL STREAMS ARE DRY, ...   414 TOWER   138
    BUT FOUND IT DRY AS BONE, ...   454 EMPTY CUP   8
    ON OLD DRY WRITING IN A LEARNED TONGUE, ...   466 HARUN RASHID   123
    ON OLD DRY FAGGOTS THAT COULD NEVER PLEASE . . . . .   466 HARUN RASHID   124
    NOW ALL DRY STICKS UNDER A WINTRY SUN, ...   490 COOLE BALLYLEE   10
    THOSE VEINS MUST SOON BE DRY: . . . .   513 JANE TALK BISH   4
    DRY TIMBER UNDER THAT RICH FOLIAGE, ...   536 HER VISION   1
    ON GANGLING STOCKS GROWN GREAT, GREAT STOCKS RUN DRY, .   619 BRONZE HEAD   25
    AND ALL HIS VEINS HAD NEAR RUN DRY. . . . .   670 ISLE STAT II 3   119
    WITH FAIRY-SMITTEN UDDERS DRY-- . . . .   716 FAIRY DOCTOR   14
    PAST THE SPEARS AND PALM-STEMS DRY, ...   733 STREET DANCERS   42
    WERE HIS MEASURE RUNNING DRY. . . . .   772 SONG DEIRDRE 1   14
    WERE HIS MEASURES RUNNING DRY. . . . .   772 SONG DEIRDRE 1 V   14
    DRY STONES IN A WELL?" . . . .   780 WELL AND TREE   8
    FROM THE DRY BONES OF THE DEAD? . . . .   781 MY HEART BEAT   8
    DRY BONES THAT DREAM ARE BITTER. . . . .   783 GREY ROUND   14
DUACH'S
    NOT I, NOR MAINE THERE, NOR DUACH'S SON. . . . . . .   748 SHADOW WATER A   22
DUBLIN
    OLD DUBLIN MERCHANT "FREE OF TEN AND FOUR" . . . . .   269 PARDON FATHERS   3
    OLD DUBLIN MERCHANT "FREE OF THE TEN AND FOUR" . . . .   269 PARDON FATHERS V   3
    . . . TO THE DUBLIN MUNICIPAL GALLERY IF IT WERE PROVED   287 TO WEALTHY MAN   T
        . . .
DUCHESS
    TO WHERE THE DUCHESS AND HER PEOPLE TALKED . . . . .   352 PEOPLE   13
DUCHESSES
    AND THERE'S A SCORE OF DUCHESSES, SURPASSING WOMANKIND,   353 HIS PHOENIX   5
    AND THERE'S A SCORE OF DUCHESSES, SURPASSING WOMAN-KIND,   353 HIS PHOENIX   V   5
DUCK
    THE WILD DUCK AND THE DRAKE . . . .   143 HOST OF AIR   2
    GATHERS THE WILD DUCK FROM THE WINTER DAWN: . . . . .   217 WOODS OF COOLE   3
DUDDON
    "HUDDON AND DUDDON AND DANIEL O'LEARY. . . . .   529 TOM LUNATIC   7
    HUDDON, DUDDON AND DANIEL O'LEARY. . . . .   787 HUDDON DUDDON   1
    HUDDON, DUDDON AND DANIEL O'LEARY. . . . .   787 HUDDON DUDDON   6
    HUDDON, DUDDON AND DANIEL O'LEARY. . . . .   787 HUDDON DUDDON   11
DUDLEY
    THEN THAT OLD ABBEY ACTOR, DUDLEY DIGGES, ...   790 DEDICATION   7
DUE
    COUNT ALL THE PRAISES DUE . . . .   345 ON WOMAN   15

229

```
                                                  PAGE     TITLE           LINE
DUG
    TO MIDDLE NIGHT, THEY DUG INTO THE HILL. . . . . . . .    185 QUEEN MAEVE          114
    AND DUG ITS CLAWS AND SHRIEKED AND FOUGHT. . . . . . .    385 ROBARTES DANCE         8
DUGS
    BY SUCKING AT THE DUGS OF GREECE. . . . . . . . . . .    288 TO WEALTHY MAN        28
DUKE
    WHAT CARED DUKE ERCOLE, THAT BID . . . . . . . . . .    287 TO WEALTHY MAN         9
DULAC
    ON A PICTURE OF A BLACK CENTAUR BY EDMUND DULAC . . . .    442 BLACK CENTAUR          T
DULL        SEE JOURNEY-DULL
    THAT DEMON DULL AND UNSUBDUABLE;  . . . . . . . . . .     43 OISIN 2              217
    . . . DULL WITH THE SMOKE OF THEIR DREAMS; . . . . . .     51 OISIN 3               65
    SPLASHED ALL WITH CLAY AND JOURNEY DULL, . . . . . . .     82 MAD KING GOLL   V    13
    DARK AND DULL AND EARTHY THE STREAM OF DRUMAHAIR . . .    207 HANRAHANS SONG V    11
    DARK AND DULL AND EARTHY OUR SOULS AND BODIES BE; . .    208 HANRAHANS SONG V    13
    AND MANY A DARLING WIT'S GROWN DULL  . . . . . . . . .    301 RUN PARADISE         18
    BEYOND THE FLING OF THE DULL ASS'S HOOF . . . . . . .    321 REED WHISPERER        5
    SHE LIES, HER LOVELY PITEOUS HEAD AMID DULL RED HAIR .    362 HER COURTESY          2
    OF DULL RED HAIR WAS FLOWING  . . . . . . . . . . . .    363 DOLLS DRAWINGS        6
    HELEN BEING CHOSEN FOUND LIFE FLAT AND DULL  . . . . .    404 FOR DAUGHTER         25
    OR DULL DECREPITUDE,  . . . . . . . . . . . . . . . .    416 TOWER               187
    DULL AS A WORM,  . . . . . . . . . . . . . . . . . .    575 MAIDS 2ND SONG        2
    BLENCHING ON HIGH THE DULL STARS SICKEN . . . . . . .    646 ISLE STAT I 1        46
    I'LL SILENCE THIS DULL SINGER--  . . . . . . . . . .    647 ISLE STAT I 1        50
    THAT DULL AND FADED ARE.  . . . . . . . . . . . . . .    680 LOVE AND DEATH       26
    SHINE DULL UNMOVING EYES. WHAT THING ART THOU? . . . .    685 SEEKER               74
    UNQUENCHABLE STILL GLOWS IN HER DULL STARE, . . . . .    687 TWO TITANS           17
    I AM DULL TO-DAY, OR YOU WERE NOW ALL LOST. . . . . .    722 WITCH VIVIEN         59
DULL-EYED
    THAT TURN DULL-EYED AWAY, . . . . . . . . . . . . . .    505 RESULT THOUGHT       14
DULL-WITTED
    DULL-WITTED THING, WITH FACE RED SQUIRREL-BROWN. . . .    661 ISLE STAT II 1       68
DUMB
    IN A LONG IRON SLEEP, AS A FISH IN THE WATER GOES DUMB     53 OISIN 3               96
        AS A STONE.
    IF DEAF AND DUMB AND BLIND WITH LOVE? . . . . . . . .    202 NEVER GIVE ALL       12
    THAT MAKE THE HEART AKIN TO THE DUMB STONE." . . . . .    281 TWO KINGS            94
    DEARER THAN ANY THAT THE DUMB STONE HIDES, . . . . . .    281 TWO KINGS       V    96
    MUST END AT THE DUMB STONE? BUT WHERE WE BUILD . . . .    284 TWO KINGS           179
    THAN DUMB BELL AND FOIL . . . . . . . . . . . . . . .    334 SONG            V     3
    NOW PEARSE IS DEAF AND DUMB? . . . . . . . . . . . . .    395 SIXTEEN DEAD         10
    TO PASSING BIRD, BUT I AM DUMB . . . . . . . . . . . .    452 HUMAN DIGNITY        11
    THOUGH MARGERY IS STRICKEN DUMB . . . . . . . . . . .    457 SECRETS OF OLD        7
    THAT MAN IS STRICKEN DEAF AND DUMB AND BLIND, . . . .    478 SELF AND SOUL        35
    STRUCK DUMB IN THE SIMPLICITY OF FIRE! . . . . . . . .    502 VACILLATION          75
    LIKE A DUMB BEAST IN A SHOW, . . . . . . . . . . . . .    572 LADYS 1ST SONG        2
    HEAR ME, AND, SHEPHERD, HEARING ME, GROW DUMB. . . . .    646 ISLE STAT I 1        31
    I AM NOT DUMB; I'D SOONER SILENT WAIT . . . . . . . .    646 ISLE STAT I 1        40
    A WHITE, DUMB THING OF TEARS, HERE LET IT STAND, . . .    663 ISLE STAT II 2       21
    LOW BOWED AND DUMB UPON THE SAND. . . . . . . . . . .    671 ISLE STAT II 3      130
    AT ARM'S LENGTH, THUS TILL DUMB ETERNITY . . . . . . .    671 ISLE STAT II 3      145
    AND WE THOUGH ASTONISHED ARE DUMB . . . . . . . . . .    785 YOUR HEART           11
    AND WE THOUGH ASTONISHED ARE DUMB . . . . . . . . . .    786 YOUR HEART           24
    AND WE THOUGH ASTONISHED ARE DUMB . . . . . . . . . .    786 YOUR HEART           37
DUMB-BELL
    THAN DUMB-BELL AND FOIL . . . . . . . . . . . . . . .    334 SONG                  3
DUMBER
    COLDER AND DUMBER AND DEAFER THAN A FISH. . . . . . .    267 ALL TEMPT ME         10
DUMBFOUNDED
    DUMBFOUNDED BEFORE A KNAVE, . . . . . . . . . . . . .    349 HAWK                 16
DUN
    AT EVENING IN MY WESTERN DUN." . . . . . . . . . . . .      8 OISIN 1               79
    TO EMER, RADDLING RAIMENT IN HER DUN, . . . . . . . .    105 CUCHULAIN SEA         2
    TO EMER OF BORDA, IN HER CLAY-PILED DUN, . . . . . . .    105 CUCHULAIN SEA   V     2
    TO FORGAIL'S DAUGHTER, EMER, IN HER DUN, . . . . . . .    105 CUCHULAIN SEA   V     2
    "HE IS THE MIGHTIEST MAN IN SHIP OR DUN." . . . . . .    107 CUCHULAIN SEA   V    28
    WHO HAS A LIKE VOW FROM THEIR TRIPLE DUN." . . . . . .    108 CUCHULAIN SEA   V    38
    WHO HAD A LIKE VOW FROM OUR TRIPLE DUN." . . . . . . .    109 CUCHULAIN SEA   V    54
    AND WHETHER I GO IN MY DREAMS BY WOODLAND, OR DUN,       210 UNDER THE MOON       14
        OR SHORE,
DUNCE
    LIVE TO BEAR CHILDREN TO A DUNCE; . . . . . . . . . .    626 OLD MEN BE MAD        6
DUNG        SEE CAMEL-DUNG
    AMONG THE COARSE GRASS AND THE CAMEL DUNG. . . . . . .    369 EGO DOMINUS     V    31
DUNGEON
    YOURSELF INTO THE DUNGEON 'NEATH OUR FEET . . . . . .    697 MOSADA 2             44
DURAS
    BETWEEN THE WOOD OF DURAS AND MAGAI . . . . . . . . .    276 TWO KINGS       V     G
DURING
    A MEDITATION WRITTEN DURING SICKNESS AT ALGECIRAS . . .    493 AT ALGECIRAS    V     T
DUSK
    A DUSK DEMON, DRY AS A WITHERED SEDGE, . . . . . . . .     39 OISIN 2         V   158
    BETWEEN THE DAWN AND DUSK," SHE SAID; . . . . . . . .    273 GREY ROCK            66
DUSKY
    A DUSKY DEMON DRY AS A WITHERED SEDGE . . . . . . . .     39 OISIN 2             158
    DUSKY AND HERBLESS, WHERE A BUBBLING STRAIN . . . . .     39 OISIN 2         V   156
    AND KISSED HER DUSKY FACE, . . . . . . . . . . . . . .    332 SOLOMON SHEBA         2
    I'LL SING THE SONGS THE DUSKY LOVERS SING, . . . . . .    694 MOSADA 1            101
DUST
    AND HOUNDS FOR CENTURIES DUST AND AIR. . . . . . . . .     11 OISIN 1             131
    AND THE KINGFISHER TURNS TO A BALL OF DUST, . . . . .     27 OISIN 1         V   418

                                230
```

	PAGE	TITLE	LINE

DUST (CONTINUED)
AND THE KINGFISHER TURNS TO A BALL OF DUST, ... 28 OISIN 1 422
. . . DRIVING THE DUST WITH THEIR THRONGS, ... 53 OISIN 3 85
ARE DUST ON THE MOTH'S WING! THAT NOTHING MATTERS . . . . 235 SHADOW WATER B 297
DANCED IN THE WHIRLING FOAM AND IN THE DUST, ... 284 TWO KINGS 167
ABOUT YOUR HEAD TILL THE DUST STOPS YOUR EAR, ... 293 TO A SHADE 20
FELL DOWN UPON THE DUST AND SNORED. . . . . 297 THREE BEGGARS 60
HECTOR IS IN THE DUST, NIETZSCHE IS BORN, ... 374 PHASES OF MOON 46
BUT NOW WIND DROPS, DUST SETTLES! THEREUPON . . . . . . 433 NINETEEN 19 125
EVEN THOSE TRUTHS THAT WHEN MY BONES ARE DUST . . . . . 467 HARUN RASHID 144
TRUTHS THAT WHEN MY VERY BONES ARE DUST . . . . 467 HARUN RASHID V 144
DESCENDS INTO THE LOVELESS DUST. . . . . 540 FROM ANTIGONE 16
MOULDING IT OF DUST OR SAND, ... 600 SPIRIT MEDIUM 14
THOSE TWAIN ARE DUST. WAKE! LIGHT AS A BEE SIPS . . . . 678 ISLE STAT II 3 290
SHE IS LONG AGES DUST. AH, WOE IS ME! . . . . 679 ISLE STAT II 3 313
AROUND THE TWITTER OF THE LIPS OF DUST . . . . 685 DRAWING-ROOM 1
THITHER THY DUST, AND KNEAD IT WITH A CRY, ... 688 TWO TITANS 52
BY TABLES THAT WERE FALLEN INTO DUST . . . . 724 KANVA ON SELF 13
"AROUND, THE TWITTER OF THE LIPS OF DUST . . . . 735 QUATRAIN APHOR 21
THAT HAVE BUILT ALL ARE DUST ON A MOTH'S WING. . . . . 757 SHADOW WATER A 205
ARE BLOWN COLD DUST OR A BIT OF BONE. . . . . 788 HAWTHORN TREE 8
THEN CLOSE YOUR EARS WITH DUST AND LIE . . . . 791 REPRISALS 23
DUSTWHIRL
MORE THAN THE FROTH, THE FEATHER, THE DUSTWHIRL, ... 248 SHADOW WATER B V 555
DUST-WHIRL
MORE THAN THE FROTH, THE FEATHER, THE DUST-WHIRL, . . . 248 SHADOW WATER B 555
DUSTY
THEN NOWISE WORSHIP DUSTY DEEDS, ... 65 HAPPY SHEPHERD 22
THEN NO WISE WORSHIP DUSTY DEEDS, ... 65 HAPPY SHEPHERD V 22
A SUDDEN BLAST OF DUSTY WIND AND AFTER . . . . 433 NINETEEN 19 119
UPON THE DUSTY, GLITTERING WINDOWS CLING, ... 482 BLOOD AND MOON 43
DUTCHMAN
JAMES AND HIS IRISH WHEN THE DUTCHMAN CROSSED! . . . . 270 PARDON FATHERS 12
DUTIFUL
DUTIFUL HUSBAND, HONEST WIFE BY TURN, ... 376 PHASES OF MOON 99
DUTY
BATHED IN FLAMING FOUNTS OF DUTY . . . . 124 CATHLEEN PARA 5
ONE WITH HER ARE MIRTH AND DUTY! . . . . 124 CATHLEEN PARA V 5
NOR LAW, NOR DUTY BADE ME FIGHT, ... 328 IRISH AIRMAN 9
DWELL
AND DWELL IN THE HOUSE OF THE FENIANS, BE THEY IN FLAMES 63 OISIN 3 224
  OR AT FEAST,
DREAD OATH, WHO DWELL ON SACRED HIMALAY, ... 74 ANASHU VIJAYA 67
GO DWELL UPON THE SEA CLIFFS, VAPOUR HID, ... 105 CUCHULAIN SEA V 4
GO DWELL UPON THE SEA CLIFFS, VAPOUR-HID, ... 105 CUCHULAIN SEA V 4
GO DWELL UPON THE CLIFFS AND WATCH THE TIDE! . . . . . 105 CUCHULAIN SEA V 4
GO THERE AND DWELL ON THE GREEN FOREST RIM. . . . . . 108 CUCHULAIN SEA V 35
SPAKE THUS: "CUCHULAIN WILL DWELL THERE AND BROOD . . . 110 CUCHULAIN SEA 77
AND CRIED, "CUCHULLIN WILL DWELL THERE AND BROOD, . . . 110 CUCHULAIN SEA V 77
OR IN THE WINE-VAT, DWELL BEYOND THE STIR . . . . . . 169 SECRET ROSE 4
OR IN THE WINE VAT, DWELL BEYOND THE STIR . . . . . . 169 SECRET ROSE V 4
DOES THE IMAGINATION DWELL THE MOST . . . . 413 TOWER 113
DOTH HE STILL DWELL WITHIN THE WOODY SHADE, ... 678 ISLE STAT II 3 303
WHERE DWELL THE MINDS OF OLD MEN HAVING PEACE, ... 721 WITCH VIVIEN 22
AND THOU CANST DWELL IN THINE OWN HOME, ... 739 EARL PAUL 3
DWELLER
BUT THE SAD DWELLER BY THE SEA-WAYS LONE . . . . . . 69 SAD SHEPHERD 26
BUT THE SAD DWELLER BY THE SEAWAYS LONE . . . . 69 SAD SHEPHERD V 26
DWELLETH
OF EVENING AND GLAD SILENCE DWELLETH AYE, ... 653 ISLE STAT I 2 37
DWELLING
WHOSE DWELLING WAS A TREE-WRAPT ISLAND, LULLED . . . . 693 MOSADA 1 79
DWELLINGS
IN THE FENIANS' DWELLINGS OF WATTLE LEAN ON THE CHESSBOARDS 55 OISIN 3 115
  AND PLAY,
DWELLS
"MY FATHER DWELLS AMONG THE SEA-WORN BANDS, ... 107 CUCHULAIN SEA V 25
JOY'S BROTHER, FEAR, DWELLS EVER IN EACH BREAST-- . . . 651 ISLE STAT I 1 155
VAST GREENNESS, WHERE ETERNAL RUMOUR DWELLS, ... 657 ISLE STAT I 3 45
LAUGHS NOT. IT DWELLS ALONE ON MORTAL LIPS! . . . . . 670 ISLE STAT II 3 100
THERE DWELLS A LITTLE FAIR-HAIRED MAID I LOVE. . . . . 679 ISLE STAT II 3 V 312
DWELT
SMOTE ON THEIR BRAINS THAT DWELT REMEMBERING AYE. . . . 34 OISIN 2 V 77A
AMONG THOSE FEASTING MEN CUCHULAIN DWELT, ... 108 CUCHULAIN SEA 39
FEASTED, AND WITH THEM OLD CUCHULAIN DWELT, ... 108 CUCHULAIN SEA V 39
AMONG THOSE FEASTING KINGS CUCHULAIN DWELT, ... 108 CUCHULAIN SEA V 39
THERE DWELT A GAY, EXULTING, GENTLE RACE . . . . . . 127 DREAM OF FAERY 20
DWELT AMONG WINE-STAINED WANDERERS IN DEEP WOODS! . . . 170 SECRET ROSE 21
THE RED SQUIRREL SHALL REAR HER YOUNG WHERE THOU 674 ISLE STAT II 3 215
  HAST DWELT--
SHE WHO DWELT AMONG THE SYCAMORES. . . . . 715 DWELT SYCAMORE T
SHE DWELT AMONG THE SYCAMORES. . . . . 715 DWELT SYCAMORE V T
AH! IT DWELT WITHIN THE TWILIGHT AS THE WORM WITHIN THE 718 PHANTOM SHIP 6
  NUT.
AND CAME AND DWELT IN HIS OWN HOUSE, ... 742 EARL PAUL 67
DWINDLE
ETERNITY MAY DWINDLE, ... 520 HIS BARGAIN 3
TIME AND THE WORLD AND ALL THINGS DWINDLE OUT. . . . . 749 SHADOW WATER A 47
DWINDLES
HIS HEART'S DESIRE WHERE THE WORLD DWINDLES OUT? . . . . 747 SHADOW WATER A 13

231

		PAGE	TITLE	LINE

DWINDLING
    DESPITE A DWINDLING AND LATE-RISEN MOON, ... 372 PHASES OF MOON 6
    DESPITE A DWINDLING AND LATE RISEN MOON, ... 372 PHASES OF MOON V 6
    HIS DWINDLING SCORE AND HE SEEMED CASTAWAYS . . . . . 420 MY HOUSE 25
    HIS DWINDLING SCORE AND HE SEEMED CAST-A-WAYS . . . . 420 MY HOUSE V 25
DYE   SEE HAIR-DYE
    AND RAISING ARMS ALL RADDLED WITH THE DYE, ... 105 CUCHULAIN SEA 7
    AND STRETCHING OUT HER ARMS, RED WITH THE DYE, ... 105 CUCHULAIN SEA V 7
DYEING
    AND FOUND HER DYEING CLOTH WITH SUBTLE CARE . . . . . 105 CUCHULAIN SEA V 2A
DYING
    TO SHORES WHERE DYING HAS NEVER BEEN KNOWN, ... 8 OISIN 1 V 84
    IT SEEMED TO BLOW FROM THE DYING FLAME, ... 13 OISIN 1 167
    THAT HIDES AWAY THE DYING SUN . . . . . . 85 MAD KING GOLL 63
    DYING AT EVERY MOMENT IN THE WORLD, ... 226 SHADOW WATER B 90
    THAT DYING CHOSE THE LIVING WORLD FOR TEXT . . . . . 324 ROBERT GREGORY 26
    WHAT'S DYING BUT A SECOND WIND? . . . . 338 TOM OROUGHLEY 11
    SEVEN POEMS I UPON A DYING LADY . . . . . . 362 HER COURTESY V T
    --THOSE DYING GENERATIONS--AT THEIR SONG, ... 407 SAIL BYZANTIUM 3
    AND FASTENED TO A DYING ANIMAL . . . . . . 408 SAIL BYZANTIUM 22
    AND FASTENED TO THIS DYING ANIMAL . . . . . . 408 SAIL BYZANTIUM V 22
    A DYING ANIMAL. . . . . 476 DEATH 2
    DYING INTO A DANCE, ... 498 BYZANTIUM 30
    WHEN SHE WAS OLD AND DYING, ... 571 THREE BUSHES 64
    HAZEL LAVERY LIVING AND DYING, THAT TALE . . . . 602 GALLERY REVIS 23
    THE SOUTH BREEZE NOW IN DYING FEARS . . . . . 655 ISLE STAT I 3 13
    AS I, TO CHOOSE BENEATH DAY'S DYING FLAMES. . . . 656 ISLE STAT I 3 34
    OH FAMOUS DYING MINION OF THE SUN, ... 673 ISLE STAT II 3 197
    I'M DYING. OH, FORGIVE ME IF I TOUCH . . . . . 684 SEEKER 70
    AND ALL WAS DIMNESS, TILL A DYING LEAF . . . . 690 MOSADA 1 20
    AND DYING MEN--AND YET--BUT NO, FAREWELL. . . . 698 MOSADA 2 49
    MY BLOSSOM, I AM DYING, AND THE STARS . . . . 700 MOSADA 3 47
    ARE DYING TOO. THEY WERE FULL SEVEN STARS. . . . 700 MOSADA 3 48
    LIVING OR DYING. BID AIBRIC TO YOUR COUNTRY, . . . 768 SHADOW WATER A 413
EADES'S
    THE MALL AND EADES'S GRAMMAR SCHOOL, ... 360 ALF POLLEXFEN 15
EAGER
    YON EAGER LARK, THAT FILLS WITH SONG THE WHOLE . . . 652 ISLE STAT I 2 18
    AND PART HIS FOAMING MOUTH WITH EAGER EYE-- . . . . 688 TWO TITANS 46
EAGERLY
    O'ER HER YOUNG SO EAGERLY . . . . . . 658 ISLE STAT I 3 93
EAGLE   SEE GER-EAGLE GIER-EAGLE
    FOR WINDS WILL BEAR THEM GENTLY WHEN THE EAGLE FLIES, . . 146 UNAPPEAS HOST V 3
    AND THE SWEET LAUGHING EAGLE THOUGHTS THAT GROW . . . 264 HOUSE SHAKEN 5
    WHAT EAGLE LOOK STILL SHOWS, ... 316 FRIENDS 25
    AN OLD MAN'S EAGLE MIND. . . . . 576 ACRE OF GRASS 24
    AN EAGLE ON THE WING, ... 601 THOSE IMAGES 14
    BEYOND EAGLE OR MOLE, ... 784 WOMANS BEAUTY 10
EAGLE'S
    BUT THE RIGHT TWIGS FOR AN EAGLE'S NEST. . . . . . 288 TO WEALTHY MAN 36
EAGLES
    TO TWO OLD EAGLES, FULL OF ANCIENT PRIDE, ... 34 OISIN 2 74
    TO EAGLES TWAIN THAT, FULL OF ANCIENT PRIDE, ... 34 OISIN 2 V 73
    STILL EARLESS, NERVELESS, BLIND, THE EAGLES STOOD. . . 36 OISIN 2 100
    STILL EARLESS, NERVELESS, BLIND, THE EAGLES DREAMED. . . 36 OISIN 2 V 100
    HAS TOLD ME THAT THE UNDYING SEND THEIR EAGLES . . . 765 SHADOW WATER A 346
    THE HARP-STRINGS HAVE BEGUN TO CRY OUT TO THE EAGLES. . 769 SHADOW WATER A 431
    IT HAS BEGUN TO CRY OUT TO THE EAGLES. . . . . . 769 SHADOW WATER A V 431
    EAGLES HAVE GONE INTO THEIR CLOUDY BED. . . . . . 778 SONG DEIRDRE 3 6
EAR   SEE WHEAT-EAR
    ALL PEARLY WHITE, SAVE ONE RED EAR. . . . . . . 12 OISIN 1 141
    THE GREY WOLF KNOWS ME. BY ONE EAR . . . . . . 84 MAD KING GOLL 45
    THE WILD BOAR KNOWS ME, BY ONE EAR . . . . . . 84 MAD KING GOLL V 45
    CHAUNT IN HIS EAR DELUSIONS MAGICAL, ... 111 CUCHULAIN SEA 80
    I HAVE BEEN CHANGED TO A HOUND WITH ONE RED EAR. . . 153 CHANGE BELOVED 2
    ABOUT YOUR HEAD TILL THE DUST STOPS YOUR EAR, . . . 293 TO A SHADE 20
    AND THERE'S NO MAN BUT COCKS HIS EAR . . . . . 306 HOUR DAWN 99
    SHE MURMURS INTO HIS EAR, ... 319 DOLLS 17
    TO FLATTER BEAUTY'S IGNORANT EAR. . . . . . . 337 SCHOLARS 6
    AIMED AT THE COMMONEST EAR. . . . . 347 FISHERMAN 20
    AN OLD MAN COCKED HIS EAR UPON A BRIDGE. . . . . 372 PHASES OF MOON 1
    WERE DISTANT STILL. AN OLD MAN COCKED HIS EAR. . . 372 PHASES OF MOON 7
    WERE DISTANT. AN OLD MAN COCKED HIS EAR. . . . 372 PHASES OF MOON V 7
    FOR WHAT BUT EYE AND EAR SILENCE THE MIND . . . . 384 VISION ROBART 41
    THAT HAVE AN EAR ALONE . . . . 395 SIXTEEN DEAD 14
    IMAGINATION, NOR AN EAR AND EYE . . . . . . 409 TOWER 6
    UNTIL IMAGINATION, EAR AND EYE, ... 409 TOWER 13
    NOR MUSIC NOR AN ENEMY'S CLIPPED EAR . . . . . 412 TOWER 75
    GIFTED WITH SO FINE AN EAR. . . . . . . 412 TOWER 94
    ON DELICATE SENSITIVE EAR OR TOSSING MANE, ... 433 NINETEEN 19 115
    THAT SHE CRIED INTO THIS EAR, ... 455 HIS MEMORIES 17
    AND FOR NO EAR BUT HIS. CARRY THIS LETTER . . . . 461 HARUN RASHID 4
    FARISTAH, AND NO LIVING EAR BUT HIS. . . . . . 461 HARUN RASHID V 4
    OLD FELLOW-STUDENT, WHOSE MOST PATIENT EAR . . . . 468 HARUN RASHID 167
    OLD FELLOW STUDENT, WHOSE MOST PATIENT EAR . . . . 468 HARUN RASHID V 167
    THOUGH NOT FOR SOBER EAR. . . . . 471 ALL SOUL NIGHT 18
    THOUGH NOT FOR SOBER EAR, ... 474 ALL SOUL NIGHT 88
    RAMPARTS AT YOUR EAR, ... 492 ANNE GREGORY 4
    THROUGH THE HOLLOW OF AN EAR. . . . . . . 499 MOTHER OF GOD 2
    COME, LET ME SING INTO YOUR EAR. . . . . . . 524 DANCING DAYS 1
    THOUGH NOT FOR THE PRIEST'S EAR, ... 620 JOHN KINSELLA 18

232

	PAGE	TITLE	LINE

EAR   (CONTINUED)
ANOTHER STAR HAS SHOT AN EAR. . . . .   625 NATIVITY   2
A KID, HELD BY ONE SOFT WHITE EAR FOR TETHER, . . .   715 DWELT SYCAMORE   3
THE MAYOR CAME, LEANING HIS DEAF EAR-- . . . . . .   725 LEGEND   13
EARED   SEE RED-EARED
EARL
THE BALLAD OF EARL PAUL . . . .   739 EARL PAUL   T
TO THE EARL OF KINSALE, ...   740 EARL PAUL   14
EARL PAUL STOOD ON THE BED OF STRAW, ...   740 EARL PAUL   17
EARL PAUL CAME WHERE THE KING SAT, ...   740 EARL PAUL   29
SAYING "EARL PAUL IS PARDONED . . . .   741 EARL PAUL   55
THE EARL OF KINSALE SAID, ...   742 EARL PAUL   62
EARLESS
I BURST THE CHAIN: STILL EARLESS, NERVELESS, BLIND, . . .   36 OISIN 2   97
STILL EARLESS, NERVELESS, BLIND, THE EAGLES STOOD. . .   36 OISIN 2   100
STILL EARLESS, NERVELESS, BLIND, THE EAGLES DREAMED. . .   36 OISIN 2   V   100
EARLIEST
WHEN THE EARLIEST DEW-WASHED STAR FROM EVE HATH LEANT, . .   32 OISIN 2   V   54
FROM EARLIEST CHILDHOOD, BUT THAT BEING SO, ...   225 SHADOW WATER B V   77
EARLY
WISE BIDDY EARLY CALLED THE WICKED WOOD: . . . . .   218 WOODS OF COOLE   15
THAT IN THE EARLY SUMMER OF THE YEAR. . . . . . .   462 HARUN RASHID   40
THAT IN THE EARLY SUMMER OF THAT YEAR . . . . . .   462 HARUN RASHID   V   40
EARN
"ONLY THE WASTEFUL VIRTUES EARN THE SUN": . . . . .   270 PARDON FATHERS   18
A DEAL I'D SWEAT AND LITTLE EARN . . . .   331 ROUND TOWER   2
I'LL BRING THAT FLOWER TO HER, AND SO MAY EARN . . .   653 ISLE STAT I 2   45
EARNED
"YOU WILL HAVE ALL YOU HAVE WISHED FOR WHEN YOU HAVE EARNED   228 SHADOW WATER B   124
EARNED SLANDER, INGRATITUDE, ...   260 UNWORTH PRAISE   16
AND THEREFORE EARNED THE RIGHT--AND YET . . . . . .   273 GREY ROCK   61
"WE'RE BUT GIVEN WHAT WE HAVE EARNED . . . .   298 THREE HERMITS   14
"WHAT HAVE I EARNED FOR ALL THAT WORK," I SAID. . . .   351 PEOPLE   1
HEARTS ARE NOT HAD AS A GIFT BUT HEARTS ARE EARNED . .   404 FOR DAUGHTER   34
EARNING
EARNING RESPECT: HAVE NO STRANGE FRIEND: . . . . .   337 SCHOLARS   V   9
EAR-PIERCING
MAEVE WAITED, AND WHEN THAT EAR-PIERCING NOISE . . .   182 QUEEN MAEVE   47
EARS
AND 'TWEEN HIS EARS, ABOVE HIS MANE, ...   2 OISIN 1   V 7AA
NOR CEASED UNTIL WHITE NIAMH STROKED HIS EARS . . .   30 OISIN 2   26
BUT NIAM WITH HER HANDS CARESSED HIS EARS, ...   30 OISIN 2   V   26
AND THE EARS OF THE HORSE WENT SINKING AWAY IN THE HOLLOW   48 OISIN 3   21
NIGHT,
THE TOPS OF THEIR EARS WERE FEATHERED, ...   49 OISIN 3   34
AFRAID, THEIR EARS ON THE EARTH LAID, ...   62 OISIN 3   206
IN ALL MEN'S EARS OF SORROW. . . . .   70 CLOAK BOAT   14
IN EACH MAN'S EARS OF SORROW-- . . . .   70 CLOAK BOAT   V   14
AND WHISPERING IN THEIR EARS . . . .   88 STOLEN CHILD   33
OF UNKNOWN PERISHING ARMIES BEAT ABOUT MY EARS. . . .   161 BLACK PIG   4
I HAD A THOUGHT FOR NO ONE'S BUT YOUR EARS: . . . .   206 ADAMS CURSE   34
I HAD A THOUGHT FOR NO ONE BUT YOUR EARS! . . . . .   206 ADAMS CURSE   V   34
OR CRY ABOUT ONE'S EARS. NOTHING TO FEAR. . . . .   222 SHADOW WATER B   19
I LOVED HIM: I WOULD COVER UP MY EARS, ...   246 SHADOW WATER B   494
BUT I WILL COVER UP YOUR EYES AND EARS, ...   250 SHADOW WATER B   574
WHEN, THE EARS BEING DEAFENED, THE SIGHT OF THE EYES BLIND   257 RECONCILIATION   3
YOUR EARS THAN STORIES NOW IN FASHION, ...   271 GREY ROCK   5
OR THE DISCERNING EARS, ...   329 MEN IMPROVE   9
HAD SCARCELY ACCUSTOMED OUR EARS . . . .   341 SHEP GOATHERD   67
WHEN HE VANISHED FROM EARS AND EYES. . . . .   341 SHEP GOATHERD   72
CLIPPED AN INSOLENT FARMER'S EARS . . . .   410 TOWER   31
TELLS ALL HIS SINNING IN THEIR EARS. . . . .   655 ISLE STAT I 3   14
TELLS ALL HER SINNING IN THEIR EARS. . . . .   655 ISLE STAT I 3 V   14
IN ALL SUCH THINGS, PRAY LET THINE EARS BE TURNED, . .   660 ISLE STAT II 1   39
IN EACH MAN'S EARS OF SORROW. . . . .   666 ISLE STAT II 3   14
A ROVER I, WHO COME FROM WHERE MEN'S EARS . . . . .   678 ISLE STAT II 3   293
FOR THERE ARE SUDDEN VOICES IN MY EARS. . . . . . .   753 SHADOW WATER A   141
COVER YOUR EARS: FOR ONCE WE HAD MOORED OUR GALLEY . .   756 SHADOW WATER A   187
AND NOW THE WAVES ARE CRYING IN MY EARS, ...   761 SHADOW WATER A   276
THEN CLOSE YOUR EARS WITH DUST AND LIE . . . . . .   791 REPRISALS   23
EAR-SHOT
SOMEWHERE IN EAR-SHOT FOR THE STORY'S END, ...   269 PARDON FATHERS   2
EARTH
AND IF JOY WERE NOT ON THE EARTH, ...   18 OISIN 1   269
IF JOY WERE NOWHERE ON THE EARTH . . . .   18 OISIN 1   V 269
AND EARTH AND HEAVEN AND HELL WOULD DIE, ...   19 OISIN 1   271
DRIPPED ON THE EARTH: BUT SOON, AH! SOON, ...   19 OISIN 1   V 279
TRICKLING ALONG THE EARTH, I RAVE: . . . .   19 OISIN 1   V 281
ON THE DEAD DIM EARTH ENCLOSES: . . . .   21 OISIN 1   312
ON THE DEAD THE EARTH ENCLOSES. . . . .   21 OISIN 1   V 312
OF THE LOUD CRASHING AND EARTH SHAKING FIGHT . . . .   38 OISIN 2   V 141
WRAPT IN THE WAVE OF THAT MUSIC, WITH WEARINESS MORE THAN   51 OISIN 3   69
OF EARTH,
. . . THE FLUTTERING SADNESS OF EARTH. . . . . . .   55 OISIN 3   124
FOR MOVETH ALIVE IN THY FINGERS THE FLUTTERING SADNESS   55 OISIN 3   V 124
OF EARTH.
I SAW FROM A DISTANT SADDLE: FROM THE EARTH SHE MADE HER   56 OISIN 3   130
MOAN:
. . . AND I ROSE, AND WALKED ON THE EARTH, ...   60 OISIN 3   191
AFRAID, THEIR EARS ON THE EARTH LAID, ...   62 OISIN 3   206
THE WANDERING EARTH HERSELF MAY BE . . . .   65 HAPPY SHEPHERD   18

233

EARTH   (CONTINUED)
   OR IN THE SUN AND MOON, OR ON THE EARTH, ...   114 ROSE OF BATTLE   17
   BEFORE EARTH TOOK HIM TO HER STONY CARE!   . . . . . .   126 DREAM OF FAERY   4
   BEFORE EARTH MADE OF HIM HER SLEEPY CARE!   . . . . . .   126 DREAM OF FAERY V   4
   NOW THAT DEEP EARTH HAS DRUNK HIS BODY IN!   . . . . . .   127 DREAM OF FAERY V   28
   NOW THAT THE EARTH HAD TAKEN MAN AND ALL!   . . . . . .   128 DREAM OF FAERY   40
   NOW THAT OLD EARTH HAD TAKEN MAN AND ALL!   . . . . . .   128 DREAM OF FAERY V   40
   WITH THE EARTH AND THE SKY AND THE WATER, ...   143 ROSE IN HEART   7
   BECAUSE EARTH, CRAZY FOR ITS BROKEN POWER, ...   186 QUEEN MAEVE   124
   BEING FORBID TO MARRY ON EARTH, ...   189 BAILE AILLINN   11
   WAS ROBBED BEFORE EARTH GAVE THE WHEAT!   . . . . . .   196 BAILE AILLINN   166
   WANDER WHERE EARTH WITHERS AWAY, ...   196 BAILE AILLINN   171
   HEARING THE WHOLE EARTH CHANGE ITS TUNE, ...   266 GALWAY RACES   12
   TREE, LIKE A SOOTY FINGER, STARTS FROM THE EARTH!   . . .   410 TOWER   19
   IF BUT IMAGINATION SCORN THE EARTH   . . . .   478 SELF AND SOUL   21
   SYMBOLICAL GLORY OF THE EARTH AND AIR!   . . . . . .   483 VERONIC NAPKIN   3
   OVER THE BLACKENED EARTH   . . . .   496 MOHINI CHATTER   21
   EARTH IN BEAUTY DRESSED   . . . .   517 HER ANXIETY   1
   HEAVEN AND EARTH OUT OF THEIR PLACES, ...   540 FROM ANTIGONE   8
   WITHOUT A FRIEND ON THE EARTH   . . . .   552 SONGS REWRIT 2   6
   WITHOUT A FRIEND ON THIS EARTH   . . . .   552 SONGS REWRIT 2 V   6
   BUT ALL THAT RUN IN COUPLES, ON EARTH, IN FLOOD OR AIR,   556 RIBH PATRICK   11
      . . .
   IRRATIONAL STREAMS OF BLOOD ARE STAINING EARTH!   . . .   564 GYRES   5
   OF THE WIDE WOODS. AND THE DEEP EARTH GATHERED THEM.   . .   660 ISLE STAT II 1   33
   FROM THE DEEP EARTH UNTO THE LURID SKY   . . . . .   662 ISLE STAT II 2   5
   SHOUTED A MOMENT 'TWEEN THE EARTH AND SKY.   . . . . .   675 ISLE STAT II 3   237
   I WILL BURN HERESY FROM THIS MAD EARTH, ...   697 MOSADA 2   40
   FROM THE HILLS OF EARTH HAVE PEALED   . . . . . .   705 DAWN-SONG   5
   JOYS AND FEARS IN THEIR GREY FACES THAT THE LIVE EARTH   719 PHANTOM SHIP   26
      KNOWETH NOT!
   SCOFF THEY AT THE MODERN EARTH——   . . . .   727 LOVERS QUARREL   38
   REMOTE FROM ALL THE HARD EARTH TROUBLES, ...   731 PRIEST FAIRY   80
   HANGS O'ER ALL THE WOODED EARTH.   . . . .   731 STREET DANCERS   8
   OTHERS KNOW THE HEALING EARTH, ...   733 STREET DANCERS   53
   ALL THE HEALING EARTH MAY-TREASURE, ...   733 STREET DANCERS   63
   ALL THE HEALING EARTH MAY TREASURE, ...   733 STREET DANCERS V   63
   AND HAVE BEEN WOOED BY THE TWELVE KINGS OF THE EARTH,   . .   757 SHADOW WATER A   214
   WHEN EARTH AND HEAVEN HAVE BEEN FOLDED UP!   . . . .   765 SHADOW WATER A   366
   THAT BLOW WHEN HEAVEN AND EARTH ARE WITHERING,   . . .   767 SHADOW WATER A   395
   LET THE EARTH BEAR WITNESS, ...   770 BLOOD BOND   9
EARTH-ENKINDLED
   POOR EARTH-ENKINDLED PAIR, ...   680 LOVE AND DEATH   22
EARTHLY
   AS THOUGH HE HELD AN EARTHLY MEAD   . . . .   2 OISIN 1   V   7X
   AND WHEN THEY SAW MY EARTHLY DRESS, ...   15 OISIN 1   V   207
   AND BADE ME SING OF EARTHLY LANDS!   . . . . . .   17 OISIN 1   V   233
   WEDDING THE QUEENS OF EARTHLY LANDS WITH RINGS   . . .   29 OISIN 2   V   10
   FROM THESE EARTHLY BOUNDS."   . . . .   97 FOXHUNTER   12
   OF ANY UNBLESSED EARTHLY BIRD."   . . . .   697 MOSADA 2   33
   DO NOT FEAR US, EARTHLY MAID!   . . . .   726 LOVERS QUARREL   1
EARTH'S
   BRUSH LIGHTLY AS HAYMOUSE EARTH'S PEBBLES, ...   56 OISIN 3   128
   BRUSH LIGHTLY AS HAY MOUSE EARTH'S PEBBLES, ...   56 OISIN 3   V   128
   MY SONGS OF OLD EARTH'S DREAMY YOUTH!   . . . . . .   67 HAPPY SHEPHERD   54
   MURMURING HOW FAR AWAY ARE ALL EARTH'S FEVERISH LANDS. .   78 INDIAN TO LOVE V   10
   HID IN THE EARTH'S MOST HIDDEN PART, ...   78 INDIAN TO LOVE   V   12
   EARTH'S ALIENS. WHY SO SORROWFUL? OUR SOULS   . . . .   80 EPHEMERA   V   12A
   HAD HID AWAY EARTH'S OLD AND WEARY CRY.   . . . . .   120 SORROW OF LOVE V   4
   ARE SHAKEN WITH EARTH'S OLD AND WEARY CRY.   . . . .   120 SORROW OF LOVE V   12
   FULL OF EARTH'S OLD TIMID GRACE.   . . . .   124 CATHLEEN PARA   12
   PEACE, PEACE, THE EARTH'S A-QUAKE.   I HEAR   . . . .   656 ISLE STAT I 3   20
EARTH-SHAKING
   OF THE LOUD-CRASHING AND EARTH-SHAKING FIGHT, ...   38 OISIN 2   141
EARTHY
   WHEN EARTHY NIGHT HAD DRUNK HIS BODY IN!   . . . .   127 DREAM OF FAERY   28
   WE SHADOWS, WHILE THEY UPROOT HIS EARTHY HOUSE,   . . .   184 QUEEN MAEVE   94
   WE SHADOWS, WHILE THEY UPROOT THE EARTHY HOUSE   . . .   184 QUEEN MAEVE   94
   DARK AND DULL AND EARTHY THE STREAM OF DRUMAHAIR   . .   207 HANRAHANS SONG V   11
   DARK AND DULL AND EARTHY OUR SOULS AND BODIES BE!   . .   208 HANRAHANS SONG V   13
EASE
   THE SINGING SHOOK HIM OUT OF HIS NEW EASE.   . . . . .   126 DREAM OF FAERY   12
   I ALSO BEAR A BELL-BRANCH FULL OF EASE.   . . . . .   130 BOOK STORIES   12
   I ALSO BEAR A BELL BRANCH FULL OF EASE.   . . . . .   130 BOOK STORIES   V   12
   WROUGHT OF HIGH LAUGHTER, LOVELINESS AND EASE?   . . .   264 HOUSE SHAKEN   12
   "AND THERE I'LL GROW RESPECTED AT MY EASE, ...   300 BEGGAR CRIED   17
   BUT PRAY TO GOD THAT HE EASE   . . . .   380 SONGS FOOL 1   17
   WHERE SLIPPERED CONTEMPLATION FINDS HIS EASE   . . . .   418 ANCEST HOUSES   30
   A COMPANY OF FRIENDS, A CONSCIENCE SET AT EASE,   . . .   427 PHANTOM HATRED   37
   AND DRUNK OR SOBER LIVE AT EASE   . . . .   597 MODEL LAUREATE   13
   FOR AN INSTANT STANDS AT EASE, ...   638 BEN BULBEN   31
   GARDENS WHERE A SOUL'S AT EASE!   . . . .   639 BEN BULBEN   55
   TO EASE THEIR WORLD-OLD THIRST ALONG THE BRINK   . . .   663 ISLE STAT II 2   41
   WILL WONDERING LISTEN, AND THIS TALE SHALL EASE   . . .   693 MOSADA 1   70
   HE NOW GETS NOVELS AT HIS EASE.   . . . .   792 GEORGE MOORE   4
EASIER
   TIME CAN BUT MAKE IT EASIER TO BE WISE   . . . . .   200 FOLLY COMFORT   4
   IT'S CERTAIN I'D SLEEP EASIER O' NIGHTS   . . . . .   224 SHADOW WATER B   59
EAST
   SANG HOW SOMEWHERE TO NORTH OR EAST OR SOUTH   . . . .   127 DREAM OF FAERY V   19
   THE EAST HER HIDDEN JOY BEFORE THE MORNING BREAK,   . . .   154 BELOVED PEACE   4

	PAGE	TITLE		LINE

EAST   (CONTINUED)
    THE EAST TELLS ALL HER SECRET JOY BEFORE DAYBREAK, . . . 154 BELOVED PEACE   V   4
    THE BANNERS OF EAST AND WEST, ... 165 CRY OF SEDGE   7
    A GLITTERING SWORD OUT OF THE EAST.   A PUFF OF WIND . . . 426 PHANTOM HATRED   5
    THE SOUTH WIND BROUGHT IT LONGING, AND THE EAST WIND   449 OWEN AHERNE   5
      DESPAIR,
    THE SOUTH WIND BROUGHT IT LONGING, AND THE EAST BROUGHT   449 OWEN AHERNE   V   5
      IN DESPAIR,
    THE SOUTH WIND BROUGHT IT LONGING, AND THE EAST BROUGHT   449 OWEN AHERNE   V   5
      IT DESPAIR,
    ENFOLDEN IN THE SHADOWS OF THE EAST, ... 705 REMEMBRANCE   11
    SHE OFFERS GREAT REWARDS IF WE TURN EAST . . . . . . 755 SHADOW WATER A   169
EASTER
    IF A GOOD EASTER WIND WERE BLOWING, ... 306 HOUR DAWN   86
    EASTER [NINETEEN-SIXTEEN] . . . . 391 EASTER 1916   T
EASTERN
    FEEDING WHITE MOTHS AROUND SOME EASTERN SHRINE, ...   41 OISIN 2   V 186
    PRAYED THOSE FORGOTTEN FISHERS, TILL IN THE EASTERN SKIES   719 PHANTOM SHIP   32
    ALL THOSE LONG FORGOTTEN FISHERS, TILL IN THE EASTERN SKIES   719 PHANTOM SHIP   V   32
EASTERN-HEARTED
    AH! NOW I'M EASTERN-HEARTED ONCE AGAIN, ... 694 MOSADA 1   99
EASY
    SHE BID ME TAKE LOVE EASY, AS THE LEAVES GROW ON THE TREE;   90 SALLEY GARDENS   3
    SHE BID ME TAKE LIFE EASY, AS THE GRASS GROWS ON THE WEIRS;   90 SALLEY GARDENS   7
    SHE BID ME TAKE LOVE EASY, AS THE LEAVES GROW ON THE TREE;   90 SALLEY GARDENS V   3
    TO HIM SEEMED EASY, SO I LAID THE CROWN . . . . 102 FERGUS DRUID   13
    ALL NEIGHBOURLY CONTENT AND EASY TALK ARE GONE, ... 580 CURSE CROMWELL   9
    A STATESMAN IS AN EASY MAN, ... 598 STONE CROSS   1
EAT
    EAT AWAY THE SLOPING SOD, ...   20 OISIN 1   V 299
    WHAT WERE OUR PRAISE TO THEM? THEY EAT . . . . 196 BAILE AILLINN   177
    I HAVE NOT FOUND A THING TO EAT, ... 294 THREE BEGGARS   3
    TO CLIMB THAT STAIR AND EAT THAT BITTER BREAD, ... 369 EGO DOMINUS   35
    EAT AT MY HEARTHSTONE . . . . 380 SONGS FOOL 1   2
    IT'S CERTAIN THAT FINE WOMEN EAT . . . . 404 FOR DAUGHTER   30
    WHAT WHOLESOME SUN HAS RIPENED IS WHOLESOME FOOD TO EAT,   442 BLACK CENTAUR   5
EATEN
    BUT WHEN I HAD EATEN AND DRUNK MYSELF ASLEEP . . . . . 223 SHADOW WATER B   30
    BUT WHEN I HAD EATEN AND DRUNK A BELLYFUL . . . . . . 223 SHADOW WATER B V   30
    AND THE SHADOWS EATEN THE MOON, ... 268 BROWN PENNY   14
    HAD DE VALERA EATEN PARNELL'S HEART . . . . 542 PARN FUNERAL 2   2
    HAD COSGRAVE EATEN PARNELL'S HEART, THE LAND'S . . . . . 543 PARN FUNERAL 2   5
    AND MANY A PURPLE GILLYFLOWER EATEN, ... 729 PRIEST FAIRY   35
EATING   SEE FISH-EATING
    WANDERS LAUGHING AND EATING HER WILD HEART . . . . . . 198 SEVEN WOODS   11
    NO HAMLET THIN FROM EATING FLIES, A FAT . . . . 610 STATUES   19
EAVES
    THE BRAWLING OF A SPARROW IN THE EAVES, ... 119 SORROW OF LOVE   1
    THE QUARREL OF THE SPARROWS IN THE EAVES, ... 119 SORROW OF LOVE V   1
    AROSE, AND ON THE INSTANT CLAMOROUS EAVES, ... 120 SORROW OF LOVE   9
    AND NOW THE SPARROWS WARRING IN THE EAVES, ... 120 SORROW OF LOVE V   9
EBB
    ALTHOUGH YOU HIDE IN THE EBB AND FLOW . . . . 146 FISH   1
    OF THE EBB OF ALL THINGS TO MAKE LOVE . . . . 193 BAILE AILLINN   V 109
    OUR HANDS, OUR HANDS MUST EBB AWAY. . . . . 213 BLESS PSALTER   18
    BUT BLESS OUR HANDS THAT EBB AWAY, ... 213 BLESS PSALTER   20
    OR ALL THAT WAYWARD EBB AND FLOW.   THERE STOOD . . . . 428 NINETEEN 19   V   4
    ON ALL THAT WAYWARD EBB AND FLOW.   THERE STOOD . . . . 428 NINETEEN 19   V   4
    HAVE I NOT SEEN A THOUSAND SEASONS EBB AND FLOW . . . . 675 ISLE STAT II 3   229
EBBED
    UNTIL TIME AND THE WORLD HAVE EBBED AWAY . . . . . . 168 BLESSED   V   39
    THAT SHALL BURN TIME WHEN TIMES HAVE EBBED AWAY. . . . . 750 SHADOW WATER A   61
EBBING
    WHILE TIME AND THE WORLD ARE EBBING AWAY . . . . . . 168 BLESSED   39
EBREMAR
    WHY THESE NEW FEARS?   THE GREAT MONK EBREMAR, ... 692 MOSADA 1   46
    WHEN THERE ARE MANY? EBREMAR WILL STAMP . . . . . . 696 MOSADA 2   4
    BE STILL! I HEAR THE STEP OF EBREMAR. . . . . 697 MOSADA 2   34
    WAS EBREMAR, WHOSE THOUGHTS WERE FIXED ON GOD, ... 702 MOSADA 3   83
EBREMAR'S
    TO SAINTED EBREMAR'S SAD EYES. I THINK . . . . 696 MOSADA 2   15
EBULLIENT
    A GREAT EBULLIENT PORTRAIT CERTAINLY: . . . . 602 GALLERY REVIS   27
    AN EBULLIENT GREAT PORTRAIT CERTAINLY: . . . . 602 GALLERY REVIS   V   27
ECHO
    THE MAN AND THE ECHO . . . . 632 MAN AND ECHO   T
    MAN AND THE ECHO . . . . 632 MAN AND ECHO   V   T
    AND HEARD EACH UNSEEN ECHO ON HER THRONE, ... 657 ISLE STAT I 3   48
ECHOES
    OR SAD SEA-SHELLS WHERE LITTLE ECHOES SIT? . . . . . . 650 ISLE STAT I 1   149
    AND, LEAPING TO THEIR FEET, FAR ECHOES CRIED, ... 659 ISLE STAT II 1   13
ECHO-HARBOURING
    SOME TWISTED, ECHO-HARBOURING SHELL, ...   66 HAPPY SHEPHERD   36
ECHOING   SEE RE-ECHOING
    THAT DOWN THE ECHOING VALLEYS ROLLED. . . . .   84 MAD KING GOLL   V   35
    IN THE LONG ECHOING STREET THE LAUGHING DANCERS THRONG,   459 FROM OEDIPUS   7
    IN THE LONG ECHOING STREETS THE LAUGHING DANCERS THRONG,   459 FROM OEDIPUS   V   7
    MY ECHOING HEART. NOW RAISE THY VOICE AND SPEAK! . . . 683 SEEKER   47
ECHTGE
    ECHTGE OF STREAMS . . . . 203 WITHER BOUGHS   V   T
    AND I FELL ASLEEP UPON LONELY ECHTGE OF STREAMS. . . . . 203 WITHER BOUGHS   6

235

ECHTGE   (CONTINUED)
    I KNOW, AND THE CURLEW AND PEEWIT ON ECHTGE OF STREAMS.   204 WITHER BOUGHS   22
    AND THE CURLEW AND PEEWIT KNOW ON ECHTGE OF STREAMS.   . .   204 WITHER BOUGHS V   22
ECLIPSE
    UNDER ECLIPSE AND THE DAY BLOTTED OUT. . . . .   414 TOWER   120
ECSTACY
    GIVE TO HIS SHARPENED PALATE ECSTACY . . . .   474 ALL SOUL NIGHT V   84
ECSTASY
    IN TRUTH'S CONSUMING ECSTASY, ...   139 TO IRELAND   47
    MIRACLE, ECSTASY, THE IMPOSSIBLE HOPE, ...   227 SHADOW WATER B   102
    CAN KNOW THAT ECSTASY. FORGAEL! FORGAEL! . . . . . .   231 SHADOW WATER B   203
    LABOURING IN ECSTASY. . . . .   315 FRIENDS   16
    CAN GIVE HIS SHARPENED PALATE ECSTASY . . . .   474 ALL SOUL NIGHT   84
    RIBH IN ECSTASY . . . .   557 RIBH ECSTASY   T
ECSTATIC
    NAMING IT WITH ECSTATIC BREATH, ...   254 HIS DREAM   18
    THE ECSTATIC WATERS LAUGH BECAUSE . . . .   612 NEWS ORACLE   17
EDAIN
    AENGUS AND EDAIN, MY OWN NAME . . . .   5 OISIN 1   47
    AENGUS AND EDAIN, AND MY NAME . . . .   5 OISIN 1   V   47
    THAT EDAIN, MIDHIR'S WIFE, HAD WOVE . . . .   195 BAILE AILLINN   142
    EDAIN CAME OUT OF MIDHIR'S HILL, AND LAY . . . . . .   219 HARP OF AENGUS   1
    'TWAS AENGUS AND EDAIN, THE WANDERING LOVERS, ...   224 SHADOW WATER B   42
    HE CARRIED EDAIN OFF FROM A KING'S HOUSE, ...   224 SHADOW WATER B   48
    AENGUS AND EDAIN, THOSE PASSIONATE WANDERERS, ...   228 SHADOW WATER B   138
    AENGUS AND EDAIN RAN UP OUT OF THE WAVE-- . . . . . .   231 SHADOW WATER B   196
    HAVING NO THOUGHT BUT FOR HIS QUEEN EDAIN, ...   276 TWO KINGS   V   I
    PALE-FACED, ALONE UPON A BENCH, EDAIN . . . .   279 TWO KINGS   61
    "WHY IS IT," QUEEN EDAIN SAID, ...   771 SONG DEIRDRE 1   1
    BUT IS EDAIN WORTH A SONG . . . .   773 SONG DEIRDRE 1   17
EDAINE
    WHEN AENGUS AND HIS EDAINE WAKE FROM SLEEP . . . . .   749 SHADOW WATER A   57
    TILL HIS EDAINE, NO LONGER A GOLDEN FLY . . . . . .   757 SHADOW WATER A   210
    TILL HIS EDAINE, NO MORE A SILVER FLY . . . .   757 SHADOW WATER A V 210
    EDAINE CAME OUT OF MIDHER'S HILL, AND LAY . . . . . .   762 SHADOW WATER A   296
    QUEEN EDAINE . . . .   771 SONG DEIRDRE 1 V   T
EDDIES
    TILL ALL THE EDDIES GLEAM! . . . .   389 IMAGE PAST   4
    AMONG THE STARRY EDDIES OF HER HAIR . . . .   390 IMAGE PAST   27
EDDY
    AND EDDY TO EDDY. MASTERS OF OUR DREAMS, ...   768 SHADOW WATER A   418
    AND EDDY TO EDDY. MASTERS OF OUR DREAMS, ...   768 SHADOW WATER A   418
EDDYING
    AND THE EDDYING CAT-HEADED BIRD! . . . .   783 GREY ROUND   23
EDEN
    AND THAT YOU COME FROM EDEN ON FLYING FEET. . . . . .   218 WOODS OF COOLE   29
    IS EDEN FAR AWAY, OR DO YOU HIDE . . . .   218 WOODS OF COOLE   30
    IS EDEN OUT OF TIME AND OUT OF SPACE? . . . .   218 WOODS OF COOLE   36
    TENT-POLE OF EDEN, THE TENT'S DRAPERY! . . . .   483 VERONIC NAPKIN   2
    TENT POLE OF EDEN, THE TENT'S DRAPERY! . . . .   483 VERONIC NAPKIN V   2
EDEN'S
    EDEN'S GARDEN WOULD BE THERE . . . .   621 JOHN KINSELLA   27
EDEN-SOD
    O'ER THE GREEN EDEN-SOD! . . . .   654 ISLE STAT I 2   65
    O'ER THE GREEN EDEN-SOD, ...   654 ISLE STAT I 2   75
EDGE
    AND FOUND ON THE DOVE-GREY EDGE OF THE SEA . . . . .   3 OISIN 1   19
    AND ON THE RUNNEL'S STONY AND BARE EDGE . . . . . .   39 OISIN 2   157
    ROSE FROM A LITTLE RUNNEL ON WHOSE EDGE . . . . . .   39 OISIN 2   V 157
    AND WE STOOD ON A SEA'S EDGE WE SAW NOT! . . . . . .   47 OISIN 3   11
    AND WE RODE ON THE PLAINS OF THE SEA'S EDGE! . . . . .   48 OISIN 3   13
    . . . THE SEA'S EDGE BARREN AND GREY, ...   48 OISIN 3   13
    AND I RODE BY THE PLAINS OF THE SEA'S EDGE, ...   56 OISIN 3   141
    AND THE WINDS MADE THE SANDS ON THE SEA'S EDGE . . . .   57 OISIN 3   145
    I PASSED ALONG THE WATER'S EDGE BELOW THE HUMID TREES, . .   76 INDIAN ON GOD   1
    I WANDER BY THE EDGE . . . .   165 CRY OF SEDGE   1
    WITH BLINKING EYES, AT THE CAVE'S EDGE, ...   167 BLESSED   V   4C
    ON THE HORIZON EDGE BELLOWED THE HERDS. . . . . . .   279 TWO KINGS   56
    HE'D HEARD THAT DIN ON THE HORIZON'S EDGE . . . . .   286 TWO KINGS   V 217A
    AND NOT A HOUSE TO THE PLAIN'S EDGE, ...   302 HOUR DAWN   10
    BY THE WOOD'S EDGE WHERE ONLY EQUALS MEET, ...   321 REED WHISPERER V   8
    BY WHAT LAKE'S EDGE OR POOL . . . .   323 SWANS AT COOLE   28
    THE TOWER SET ON THE STREAM'S EDGE! . . . .   326 ROBERT GREGORY   52
    THE TOWER SET BY THE STREAM'S EDGE! . . . .   326 ROBERT GREGORY   52
    I WOULD FIND BY THE EDGE OF THAT WATER . . . . . .   330 BONE OF A HARE   9
    SHALL WALK THE WET SANDS BY THE EDGE OF THE STREAM . .   371 EGO DOMINUS   71
    SHALL WALK THE WET SAND BY THE WATER'S EDGE, ...   371 EGO DOMINUS   V   71
    SAT DOWN UPON THE FOUNTAIN'S MARBLE EDGE, ...   463 HARUN RASHID   43
    I RIDE WITH FALCON TO THE RIVER'S EDGE . . . . . .   463 HARUN RASHID   57
    I RIDE WITH FALCON TO THE WATER'S EDGE . . . . . .   463 HARUN RASHID   V   57
    BY THE SINGING WATERS' EDGE, ...   646 ISLE STAT I 1   23
    SAW ON THE WOOD'S EDGE GLEAM AN ASH-GREY FEATHER! . . .   715 DWELT SYCAMORE   2
    AMONG THOSE STREAMS, OR ON THEIR CLOUDY EDGE. . . . .   750 SHADOW WATER A   63
EDIT
    EDIT AND ANNOTATE THE LINES . . . .   337 SCHOLARS   3
EDMUND
    ON A PICTURE OF A BLACK CENTAUR BY EDMUND DULAC . . . .   442 BLACK CENTAUR   T
    MY GREAT-GRANDFATHER SPOKE TO EDMUND BURKE . . . . .   486 SEVEN SAGES   1
EDWARD
    FOR THIS EDWARD FITZGERALD DIED, ...   290 SEPTEMBER 1913   20
    LORD EDWARD AND WOLFE TONE, ...   395 SIXTEEN DEAD   16

EEL
   OF A GREAT EEL; IT CHANGED, AND I BUT SMOTE . . . . .   40 OISIN 2   176
E'EN
   NOT E'EN THY GOD COULD HAVE THROWN DOWN THAT HALL; . . .   36 OISIN 2   V   109
   E'EN THEN, BEFORE HER SHEPHERD HAIR . . . .   668 ISLE STAT II 3   54
   FROM THEE I SNATCHED IT; E'EN THE FAY THAT TRIPS . . .   670 ISLE STAT II 3   98
   E'EN THOUGH HIS WINGS WERE PLUMELESS STUMPS, ...   670 ISLE STAT II 3   118
E'ER
   WITH SINGING SWEET AS E'ER ROUND LAKE-LULLED ISLE . . .   649 ISLE STAT I 1   106
EGG
   A PIECE OF A NIGHTINGALE'S EGG, ...   708 FAIRY PEDANT   24
EGGED
   'TWAS YOU THAT EGGED HIM TO IT, FOR YOU KNOW . . . . .   248 SHADOW WATER B   550
EGO
   EGO DOMINUS TUUS . . . .   367 EGO DOMINUS   T
EGYPT
   EGYPT AND GREECE, GOOD-BYE, AND GOOD-BYE, ROME! . . . .   563 MERU   8
EGYPTIAN
   FORMS A STARK EGYPTIAN THOUGHT, ...   638 BEN BULBEN   43
EIGHT   SEE TWENTY-AND-EIGHT
   EIGHT POEMS CRAZY JANE AND THE BISHOP . . . . . .   507 JANE BISHOP   V   T
EIGHTEENTH-CENTURY
   EIGHTEENTH-CENTURY HOUSES. . . . .   392 EASTER 1916   4
EIGHTIETH
   HER EIGHTIETH WINTER APPROACHING; "YESTERDAY HE THREATENED   578 LOFTY THINGS   8
      MY LIFE.
EIRE
   THEN FEAST, MAKING CONVERSE OF EIRE, OF WARS, ...   62 OISIN 3   V   212
   SING OF OLD EIRE AND THE ANCIENT WAYS; . . . . . .   101 ROSE UPON ROOD   23
   WHEN HER OWN PEOPLE RULED THIS TRAGIC EIRE; . . . . .   129 BOOK STORIES   2
   I TORE IT FROM THE BARREN BOUGHS OF EIRE, ...   130 BOOK STORIES   15
   YOUR MOTHER EIRE IS ALWAYS YOUNG, ...   148 INTO TWILIGHT   5
EL
   BELOVED HAROUN EL RASHID, OCCUPIED . . . .   462 HARUN RASHID   V   24
   THAT YEAR WHEN GREAT HAROUN EL RASHID KILLED . . . .   462 HARUN RASHID   V   31
ELABORATE
   AMID THE ELABORATE WILDERNESS OF THE AIR. . . . . .   278 TWO KINGS   31
   THE ELABORATE STARLIGHT THROWS A REFLECTION . . . . .   389 IMAGE PAST   2
   THE ELABORATE STAR-LIGHT HAS THROWN REFLECTIONS . . . .   389 IMAGE PAST   V   2
   TO ROUND THAT SHELL'S ELABORATE WHORL, ...   509 JANE REPROVED   8
ELBOW
   O MAY TRANQUILLITY WALK BY HIS ELBOW . . . .   71 ANASHU VIJAYA   2
ELBOWS
   LEANS ON HIS ELBOWS, GAZING AT THE SEA. . . . . . .   752 SHADOW WATER A   127
ELDER
   O WINDS, ELDER THAN CHANGING OF NIGHT AND DAY, . . .   162 ASKS FORGIVE   V   7
   SAW THE PIERCED HANDS AND ROOD OF ELDER RISE . . . .   169 SECRET ROSE   10
ELDERS
   AND ALL THE ELDERS SITTING IN THE SUN . . . .   693 MOSADA 1   69
ELDEST
   EACH OTHER ROUND IN CIRCLES, AND HEARD THE ELDEST SPEAK;   76 INDIAN ON GOD   5
   EACH OTHER ROUND IN CIRCLES; AND I HEARD THE ELDEST   76 INDIAN ON GOD   V   5
      SPEAK!--
ELECT
   THE BEST-ENDOWED, THE ELECT, ...   504 RESULT THOUGHT   3
   THE ENDOWED, THE ELECT; . . . .   504 RESULT THOUGHT V   3
ELEGANCE
   AND SMOOTH OUT STAIN AND BLEMISH WITH THE ELEGANCE OF HIS   353 HIS PHOENIX   7
      MIND;
   IF FOLLY LINK WITH ELEGANCE . . . .   598 STONE CROSS   13
   IF FOLLY LINKS WITH ELEGANCE . . . .   598 STONE CROSS   V   13
ELEMENT
   HIS ELEMENT IS SO FINE . . . .   470 ALL SOUL NIGHT   7
   WHERE SOME LAUGHING ELEMENT . . . .   777 SONG DEIRDRE 2   4
ELEMENTAL
   FOR THE ELEMENTAL CREATURES GO . . . .   138 TO IRELAND   23
   FOR THE ELEMENTAL BEINGS GO . . . .   138 TO IRELAND   V   23
   THE POET PLEADS WITH THE ELEMENTAL POWERS . . . . .   174 ELEMENT POWERS   T
   AODH PLEADS WITH THE ELEMENTAL POWERS . . . . . .   174 ELEMENT POWERS V   T
   GREAT ELEMENTAL POWERS OF WIND, AND WAVE, AND FIRE, . .   174 ELEMENT POWERS V   7
ELEMENTS
   A MYSTICAL PRAYER TO THE MASTERS OF THE ELEMENTS, . . .   174 ELEMENT POWERS V   T
   SO THAT HIS ELEMENTS HAVE GROWN SO FINE . . . . . .   473 ALL SOUL NIGHT   82
ELEVATE
   THE MIND OF MAN OR ELEVATE A RHYME; . . . .   492 COOLE BALLYLEE   45
ELEVEN
   GROWS COMELIER. ELEVEN PASS, AND THEN . . . . . .   374 PHASES OF MOON   44
ELF
   REPLY LIKE MOANING OF IMPRISONED ELF; . . . . . .   652 ISLE STAT I 2   11
ELFIN-SIGHTS
   AND THEY WILL WAR, 'MID WONDROUS ELFIN-SIGHTS; . . . .   651 ISLE STAT I 1   164
ELIZABETH
   BY HIS WIFE ELIZABETH . . . .   360 ALF POLLEXFEN   4
ELMS
   IN THE ELMS ABOVE THE FLOODED STREAM; . . . . . .   403 FOR DAUGHTER   12
   OLD RAGGED ELMS, OLD THORNS INNUMERABLE, ...   419 MY HOUSE   5
   VALLEY, RIVER, AND ELMS, UNDER THE LIGHT OF A MOON . .   426 PHANTOM HATRED   3
   VALLEY, RIVER, ELMS, UNDER THE LIGHT OF A MOON . . . .   426 PHANTOM HATRED V   3
ELSE
   TWO THINGS THAT 'FORE ALL ELSE I HATE, ...   24 OISIN 1   V   359
   HE IS A GENTLE ROEBUCK; FOR HOW ELSE, I PRAY, COULD HE . .   76 INDIAN ON GOD   15

		PAGE	TITLE	LINE

ELSE   (CONTINUED)
OR ELSE THEY STAND AND SNIFF THE WIND, ...   136 TWO TREES   37
OR ELSE AT MEADOW OR AT GRAZING OVERLOOKS   . . . . . .   340 SHEP GOATHERD   37
OLD GOATHERDS AND OLD GOATS, IF IN ALL ELSE   . . . . .   340 SHEP GOATHERD   46
WHAT ELSE HE GIVE OR KEEP   . . . .   346 ON WOMAN   24
OR ELSE MY DREAMS THAT FLY   . . . .   384 VISION ROBART   51
OR ELSE BY TOASTING HER A SCORE OF TIMES, ...   410 TOWER   42
OR ELSE ALL JUNO FROM AN URN DISPLAYS   . . . .   418 ANCEST HOUSES   27
OR ELSE, TO ALTER PLATO'S PARABLE, ...   443 SCHOOL CHILDR   15
DELIGHT BECOMES DEATH-LONGING IF ALL LONGING ELSE BE VAIN.   459 FROM OEDIPUS   3
A MYSTERY THAT ELSE HAD FOUND NO CHRONICLER   . . . . .   461 HARUN RASHID   21
SAINT GEORGE OR ELSE A PAGAN PERSEUS!   . . . .   533 HER TRIUMPH   10
OR ANYTHING ELSE BUT A RHYMER   . . . .   552 SONGS REWRIT 2   9
OR ANYTHING ELSE BUT A MAN   . . . .   552 SONGS REWRIT 2 V   9
FOR EVERYBODY KNOWS OR ELSE SHOULD KNOW   . . . . . .   565 LAPIS LAZULI   4
FORGOTTEN ELSE BY MANKIND, ...   576 ACRE OF GRASS   23
WHAT ELSE HAVE I TO SPUR ME INTO SONG?   . . . . . .   591 SPUR   4
EVERYTHING ELSE WITHERED AND MUMMY-DEAD.   . . . . . .   618 BRONZE HEAD   3
(SOMETHING MAY LINGER THERE THOUGH ALL ELSE DIE!)   . .   618 BRONZE HEAD   5
OR ELSE I THOUGHT HER SUPERNATURAL!   . . . .   619 BRONZE HEAD   22
TILL ALL ELSE IS EMPTY CHAFF, ...   647 ISLE STAT I 1   60
ELSEWHERE
AS THOUGH TO SAY "IT IS THE SWORD ELSEWHERE,"   . . . .   267 ALL TEMPT ME   V   8
ELVISH
AND ELVISH WISDOM, AND LONG YEARS OF YOUTH   . . . . .   653 ISLE STAT I 2   47
EMAIN
MY WORD WAS LAW FROM ITH TO EMAIN, ...   81 MAD KING GOLL   2
RODE OUT OF EMAIN WITH A BAND   . . . .   189 BAILE AILLINN   18
EMAN
AT EMAN, 'NEATH THE BEECH TREES, ON EACH SIDE, ...   44 OISIN 3   V 228
WOLF-BREEDING MOUNTAINS, GALLERIED EMAN, ...   81 MAD KING GOLL   V   2
EMAN'S
THAN DOVES THAT MOANED ROUND EMAN'S HALL   . . . . . .   3 OISIN 1   V 7EE
THE FLOOR OF EMAN'S DANCING HALL   . . . .   13 OISIN 1   V 156
MINE WAS THE THRONE IN EMAN'S HALL, ...   81 MAD KING GOLL   V   2
EMBASSY
WITH PERSIAN EMBASSY OR GRECIAN WAR, ...   462 HARUN RASHID   25
EMBATTLED
AND OF THE EMBATTLED FLAMING MULTITUDE   . . . .   137 TO SOME I TALK   10
AND OF THE PROUD EMBATTLED MULTITUDE   . . . .   137 TO SOME I TALK V   10
EMBERS
WE SAW THE LAST EMBERS OF DAYLIGHT DIE, ...   205 ADAMS CURSE   29
EMBITTERED
I HAVE NOTHING BUT THE EMBITTERED SUN!   . . . .   344 DEJECTION   8
OR, BY THE MOON EMBITTERED, SCORN ALOUD   . . . . . .   498 BYZANTIUM   21
THEMES OF THE EMBITTERED HEART, OR SO IT SEEMS,   . . .   629 CIRCUS ANIMALS   13
EMBLEM
A POWERFUL EMBLEM UP, ...   480 BLOOD AND MOON   9
ANOTHER EMBLEM THERE!   THAT STORMY WHITE   . . . . .   490 COOLE BALLYLEE   17
EMBLEMATICAL
EMBLEMATICAL OF LOVE AND WAR?   . . . .   477 SELF AND SOUL   19
EMBLEMATICAL OF THE NIGHT, ...   478 SELF AND SOUL   30
EMBLEMS
BEFITTING EMBLEMS OF ADVERSITY.   . . . .   420 MY HOUSE   30
AND THERE MARKED OUT THOSE EMBLEMS ON THE SAND   . . .   468 HARUN RASHID   156
AND THERE MARKED OUT EMBLEMS ON THE SAND   . . . . .   468 HARUN RASHID   V 156
FOR EMBLEMS OF THE DAY AGAINST THE TOWER   . . . . .   478 SELF AND SOUL   29
AND NOT THOSE THINGS THAT THEY WERE EMBLEMS OF.   . . .   630 CIRCUS ANIMALS   32
EMBOSOMED   **SEE LAKE-EMBOSOMED**
SNATCHING THE BIRD IN SECRET! NOR KNEW I, EMBOSOMED APART,   57 OISIN 3   150
OF THIS WIDE VALE, EMBOSOMED IN THE AIR, ...   652 ISLE STAT I 2   19
EMBRACE
FOR THE EMBRACE OF NOTHING! AND I, MY WITS ASTRAY   . .   426 PHANTOM HATRED   14
THE ANNIVERSARY OF THEIR FIRST EMBRACE, ...   555 RIBH AT TOMB   20
EMBRACED
THOSE WILD HANDS THAT HAVE EMBRACED   . . . .   776 AGAINST WITCH   32
EMBRACES
THAT JUGGLING NATURE MOUNTS, HER COIL IN THEIR EMBRACES   556 RIBH PATRICK   9
   TWINED.
EMBROIDERED   **SEE GOLD-EMBROIDERED**
BEAR THE GOLD EMBROIDERED DRESS--   . . . .   124 CATHLEEN PARA   V   6
HAD I THE HEAVENS' EMBROIDERED CLOTHS, ...   176 CLOTHS HEAVEN   1
HAD I THE HEAVEN'S EMBROIDERED CLOTHS, ...   176 CLOTHS HEAVEN   V   1
A BIT OF AN EMBROIDERED DRESS   . . . .   421 MY TABLE   6
IS BUT A HEAVY, GOLD EMBROIDERED BANNER, ...   469 HARUN RASHID   V 188
"ON THIS EMBROIDERED CLOUD," THE SUN HATH SAID,   . . .   712 FERENCZ RENYI   74
EMBROIDERIES
COVERED WITH EMBROIDERIES   . . . .   320 COAT   2
A WOMAN LIES AMONG EMBROIDERIES.   . . . .   752 SHADOW WATER A   120
EMBROIDERY
OF MANY A FIGURED EMBROIDERY!   . . . .   4 OISIN 1   27
BUT BRILLIANT AS THE NIGHT'S EMBROIDERY, ...   461 HARUN RASHID   7
NOR DAZZLED BY THE EMBROIDERY, NOR LOST   . . . . . .   470 HARUN RASHID   191
THAT FLOWERING, SILKEN, OLD EMBROIDERY, TORN   . . . .   477 SELF AND SOUL   13
FLOWERS FROM I KNOW NOT WHAT EMBROIDERY--   . . . . .   478 SELF AND SOUL   27
EMEN'S
THE FLOOR OF EMEN'S HOISTING HALL   . . . .   13 OISIN 1   V 156
EMER
TO EMER, RADDLING RAIMENT IN HER DUN, ...   105 CUCHULAIN SEA   2
THEN EMER CAST THE WEB UPON THE FLOOR, ...   105 CUCHULAIN SEA   6
TO EMER OF BORDA, IN HER CLAY-PILED DUN, ...   105 CUCHULAIN SEA   V   2

```
                                                        PAGE    TITLE           LINE

EMER   (CONTINUED)
    TO FORGAIL'S DAUGHTER, EMER, IN HER DUN, . . . . . .     105  CUCHULAIN SEA   V    2
    AND LOST THE WORLD AND EMER FOR A KISS! . . . . . . .    170  SECRET ROSE         15
    GREAT-BLADDERED EMER SAT, . . . . . . . . . . . .        628  JANE MOUNTAIN       15
    GREAT BLADDERED EMER SAT, . . . . . . . . . . . .        628  JANE MOUNTAIN   V   15
EMERALD
    WITH EMERALD EYES." . . . . . . . . . . . . . .         263  MASK                 2
EMERGE
    TO LIE UNTIL THE FOURTH MORN SAW EMERGE . . . . . .       44  OISIN 2            220
    TO LIE THERE 'TILL THE FOURTH DAY SAW EMERGE . . . . .    44  OISIN 2         V  220
    TO LIE UNTIL THE FOURTH MORN SUN EMERGE . . . . . .       44  OISIN 2         V  220
EMERY
    ON FLORENCE EMERY I CALL THE NEXT, . . . . . . . . .     472  ALL SOUL NIGHT      41
EMMET
    AND ROBERT EMMET AND WOLFE TONE, . . . . . . . . .      290  SEPTEMBER 1913      21
    WHEN STRANGERS MURDERED EMMET, FITZGERALD, TONE, . . .   541  PARN FUNERAL 1      17
    MOCK EMMET, MOCK PARNELL! . . . . . . . . . . . .       547  TO SAME TUNE 2      25
    MOCK EMMET, MOCK PARNELL, . . . . . . . . . . . .       614  MARCH SONGS 1       25
EMMET'S
    OLD COUNTRY SCHOLAR, ROBERT EMMET'S FRIEND, . . . . .    269  PARDON FATHERS       5
    AND COUNTRY SCHOLAR, ROBERT EMMET'S FRIEND, . . . . .    269  PARDON FATHERS  V    5
EMOTION
    SWEETER EMOTION, WORKING IN THEIR VEINS . . . . . .     292  TO A SHADE          13
    HEART-SMITTEN WITH EMOTION I SINK DOWN, . . . . . . .    602  GALLERY REVIS       17
    HEART SMITTEN WITH EMOTION, I SINK DOWN, . . . . . .     602  GALLERY REVIS   V   17
EMPEDOCLES
    EMPEDOCLES HAS THROWN ALL THINGS ABOUT! . . . . . . .    564  GYRES                6
EMPEROR
    TO KEEP A DROWSY EMPEROR AWAKE! . . . . . . . . . .      408  SAIL BYZANTIUM      29
    THE GOLDEN SMITHIES OF THE EMPEROR! . . . . . . . .      498  BYZANTIUM           35
EMPEROR'S
    THE EMPEROR'S DRUNKEN SOLDIERY ARE ABED! . . . . . .     497  BYZANTIUM            2
    THE EMPEROR'S DRUNKEN SOLDIERY ARE A-BED! . . . . . .    497  BYZANTIUM       V    2
    AT MIDNIGHT ON THE EMPEROR'S PAVEMENT FLIT . . . . .     498  BYZANTIUM           25
EMPIRE
    THE ROMAN EMPIRE STOOD APPALLED! . . . . . . . . .      437  SONGS PLAY 1        13
    WHEN ALEXANDER'S EMPIRE PASSED, THEY SLEPT SO SOUND.     442  BLACK CENTAUR       12
    WHEN ALEXANDER'S EMPIRE PAST, THEY SLEPT SO SOUND. . .   442  BLACK CENTAUR   V   12
    UPON THE BRITISH EMPIRE, . . . . . . . . . . . .        583  GHOST ROG CASE      17
EMPIRES
    BEING WEARY OF THE WORLD'S EMPIRES, BOW DOWN TO YOU,  .  161  BLACK PIG            7
EMPOUNDED
    TOILED WITH EMPOUNDED CATTLE THROUGH THE MIRE, . . . .   276  TWO KINGS       V    2
    THAT WITH EMPOUNDED CATTLE TROD THE MIRE, . . . . . .    277  TWO KINGS            4
    THEREON THE BELLOWING OF THE EMPOUNDED HERDS . . . . .   286  TWO KINGS          214
EMPTIED
    ALL EMPTIED OF PURPLE HOURS AS A BEGGAR'S CLOAK IN THE    63  OISIN 3            219
       RAIN,
    THAT EMPTIED ALL OUR DAYS TO COME. . . . . . . . .      272  GREY ROCK           40
    AND EMPTIED MANY A CAN! . . . . . . . . . . . . .       620  JOHN KINSELLA       16
    EMPTIED, RUINED, WRACKED, AND LOST, . . . . . . . .     776  AGAINST WITCH       27
    GAVE THEIR BODIES, EMPTIED PURSES . . . . . . . . .     789  SINGING HEAD        19
EMPTIER
    EMPTIER OF THOUGHT . . . . . . . . . . . . . . .        451  FIRST LOVE          16
EMPTINESS
    . . . FULLNESS AND OF THE COMING EMPTINESS . . . . . .   425  PHANTOM HATRED       T
    GRIMALKIN CRAWLS TO BUDDHA'S EMPTINESS. . . . . . . .    611  STATUES             24
    HYSTERICA PASSIO OF ITS OWN EMPTINESS? . . . . . . .     618  BRONZE HEAD          7
    HYSTERICO-PASSIO OF ITS OWN EMPTINESS? . . . . . . .     618  BRONZE HEAD     V    7
EMPTY
    ARE EMPTY OF ALL POWER." "AND WHICH OF THESE . . . . .    46  OISIN 2            248
    WE SHALL MINGLE NO MORE, NOR OUR GAZES EMPTY THEIR        56  OISIN 3            132
       SWEETNESS LONE
    A CLIMBING MOON UPON AN EMPTY SKY, . . . . . . . .      120  SORROW OF LOVE      10
    EMPTY YOUR HEART OF ITS MORTAL DREAM. . . . . . . .     140  HOSTING SIDHE        5
    THAT EMPTY THE HEART. I HAVE FORGOT AWHILE . . . . .     198  SEVEN WOODS          5
    OF FORGAEL AND DECTORA AND THE EMPTY WATERS . . . . .    218  WOODS OF COOLE      22
    A CLUMP OF BEECH TREES MADE AN EMPTY SPACE . . . . .     277  TWO KINGS       V   4A
    TO AN OLD EMPTY WOODMAN'S HOUSE THAT'S HIDDEN . . . .    282  TWO KINGS          134
    YOUR EMPTY BED." "HOW SHOULD I LOVE," I ANSWERED, . .    285  TWO KINGS          186
    TIMID, ENTANGLED, EMPTY AND ABASHED, . . . . . . .      368  EGO DOMINUS         16
    AS IF SOME MARVELLOUS EMPTY SEA-SHELL FLUNG . . . . .    417  ANCEST HOUSES       13
    COME BUILD IN THE EMPTY HOUSE OF THE STARE. . . . . .    424  STARES NEST          5
    COME BUILD IN THE EMPTY HOUSE OF THE STARE. . . . . .    425  STARES NEST         10
    COME BUILD IN THE EMPTY HOUSE OF THE STARE. . . . . .    425  STARES NEST         15
    COME BUILD IN THE EMPTY HOUSE OF THE STARE. . . . . .    425  STARES NEST         20
    THE EMPTY CUP . . . . . . . . . . . . . . . .          454  EMPTY CUP            T
    AND FOLLOWED THROUGH THE EMPTY STREET, AND SHE, . . .    468  HARUN RASHID    V 154A
    THAT OLD PERPLEXITY AN EMPTY PURSE, . . . . . . . .     491  COOLE BALLYLEE  V  40G
    THAT OLD PERPLEXITY AN EMPTY PURSE, . . . . . . . .     495  CHOICE               7
    AN OPEN BOOK AND EMPTY CUP . . . . . . . . . . .        501  VACILLATION         38
    IN AN EMPTY BED, . . . . . . . . . . . . . . .          511  JANE AND JACK       14
    IF EMPTY NIGHT REPLIES? . . . . . . . . . . . .         533  FIRST CONFESS       18
    WHEN NATIONS ARE EMPTY UP THERE AT THE TOP, . . . . .    548  TO SAME TUNE 3      11
    AND FOUND AN EMPTY ROOM. . . . . . . . . . . . .        594  COLONEL MARTIN       8
    DREAMER OF THE MIDDLE AGES. EMPTY EYEBALLS KNEW . . .    610  STATUES             20
    DREAMER OF THE MIDDLE-AGES. EMPTY EYE-BALLS KNEW . . .   610  STATUES         V   20
    FROM EMPTY TOMB OR VIRGIN WOMB? . . . . . . . . .       619  STICK INCENSE        2
    HIS EMPTY HEART IS FULL AT LENGTH, . . . . . . . .      624  APPARITIONS         19
    TILL ALL ELSE IS EMPTY CHAFF, . . . . . . . . . .       647  ISLE STAT I 1       60
    DEEP-EYED, SLOW-FOOTING DOWN THE EMPTY GLADE. . . . .    653  ISLE STAT I 2       55

                                   239
```

		PAGE	TITLE	LINE

EMPTY   (CONTINUED)
```
     THE PLACE WAS EMPTY NOW OF PEOPLE.  . . . . . . . . . .    725 LEGEND                 25
     HAVE THE WINDS BLOWN YOU AMONG THESE EMPTY WATERS?  . . .   756 SHADOW WATER A        192
     I HAVE FOUND NOTHING BUT THESE EMPTY WATERS!  . . . . . .   757 SHADOW WATER A        201
     CRIES OUT THE EMPTY WELL,  . . . . . . . . . . . . . .      780 WELL AND TREE           2
EMPTYING
     BUT WILL IT HOLD WHILE WE ARE EMPTYING HER?  . . . . .      754 SHADOW WATER A        156
EMPYREAN
     OVERCOME THE EMPYREAN! HURL . . . . . . . . . . . . .       540 FROM ANTIGONE           7
ENAMELLED
     RAGING AT HIS OWN IMAGE IN THE ENAMELLED SEA. . . . . .      77 INDIAN TO LOVE          5
     RAGES AT HIS OWN IMAGE IN THE ENAMELLED SEA . . . . . .      77 INDIAN TO LOVE  V       5
     RAGING AT HIS OWN IMAGE IN THE DIM ENAMELLED SEA . . .       77 INDIAN TO LOVE  V       5
ENAMELLING
     OF HAMMERED GOLD AND GOLD ENAMELLING . . . . . . . . .      408 SAIL BYZANTIUM         28
ENAMOURED
     ENAMOURED OF THE WAVES' IMPETUOUS LIPS. . . . . . . . .     677 ISLE STAT II 3        289
ENCHANTED
     DIM PAIRC-NA-TARAV, WHERE ENCHANTED EYES . . . . . . .      217 WOODS OF COOLE         11
     I HAD NOT EYES LIKE THOSE ENCHANTED EYES, . . . . . . .     218 WOODS OF COOLE         17
     ENCHANTED TO A STONE . . . . . . . . . . . . . . . . .      393 EASTER 1916            43
     THROUGH THREE ENCHANTED ISLANDS, ALLEGORICAL DREAMS, . .    629 CIRCUS ANIMALS         11
     IT WAS THE DREAM ITSELF ENCHANTED ME! . . . . . . . . .     630 CIRCUS ANIMALS         28
     IF ON HIS LIPS THE ENCHANTED FLOWER BE LAID! . . . . .      668 ISLE STAT II 3         46
     THE ENCHANTED FLOWER WERE, . . . . . . . . . . . . . .      668 ISLE STAT II 3         62
ENCHANTER
     WILL STRUGGLE. OR HE'LL SEEK ENCHANTER OLD, . . . . . .     651 ISLE STAT I 1         162
ENCHANTMENT
     I AM CAUGHT IN WOVEN NETS OF ENCHANTMENT. LOOK! . . . .     762 SHADOW WATER A        293
ENCHANTRESS
     FOR THERE THE GREAT ENCHANTRESS LIVES. AND THERE . . .      653 ISLE STAT I 2          38
     SHE WAS A GREAT ENCHANTRESS ONCE OF YORE, . . . . . .       693 MOSADA 1               78
ENCIRCLE
     ENCIRCLE HER I LOVE AND SING HER INTO PEACE, . . . . .      174 ELEMENT POWERS          9
ENCIRCLED        SEE CLIFF-ENCIRCLED
ENCIRCLING
     AND CHANTS OF VICTORY AMID THE ENCIRCLING HOUNDS. . . .     622 HOUND VOICE            21
ENCLOSE
     ENCLOSE A QUIET PLACE OF BEDS BOX-BORDERED, BEES, . . .     710 FERENCZ RENYI          24
ENCLOSES
     ON THE DEAD DIM EARTH ENCLOSES! . . . . . . . . . . .        21 OISIN 1               312
     ON THE DEAD THE EARTH ENCLOSES. . . . . . . . . . . .         21 OISIN 1               312
     WHERE DREAM-FED PASSION IS AND PEACE ENCLOSES, . . . .      669 ISLE STAT II 3         85
     FROM FLOOD-TIME ENCLOSES . . . . . . . . . . . . . . .      672 ISLE STAT II 3        167
END      SEE BUTT-END CANDLE-END
     A DRUID DREAM OF THE END OF DAYS . . . . . . . . . . .       16 OISIN 1               219
     THERE WERE AN END OF CHANGE AND BIRTH, . . . . . . . .       18 OISIN 1               270
     MAY SLEEP IN THE END WITH THE WHOLE OF HIS FATE DONE, . .     28 OISIN 1             V 423F
     I THOUGHT THE END HAD RESTED, WHEN THESE WORDS . . . .       32 OISIN 1             V  49
     MAY PANTHERS END HIM.--HEAR, AND LOAD OUR KING . . . .       71 ANASHU VIJAYA           6
     AND WHAT TO ME WAS BURDEN WITHOUT END, . . . . . . . .      102 FERGUS DRUID           12
     AND THE WHITE HUSH END ALL BUT THE LOUD BEAT . . . . .      137 TO SOME I TALK         15
     AND THE WHITE HUSH END ALL THINGS BUT THE BEAT . . . .      137 TO SOME I TALK  V      15
     WOULD END IN LOVE IN THE END! . . . . . . . . . . . .       152 LOSS OF LOVE            4
     WOULD END IN LOVE IN THE END! . . . . . . . . . . . .       152 LOSS OF LOVE            4
     MIGHT FADE IN LOVE IN THE END! . . . . . . . . . . . .      152 LOSS OF LOVE    V       4
     . . . AND HIS BELOVED, AND LONGS FOR THE END OF THE WORLD   153 CHANGE BELOVED          T
     WHEN WE COME AT THE END OF TIME . . . . . . . . . . .       178 FIDDLER DOONEY          9
     HIS FACE BOWED LOW TO WEEP THE END . . . . . . . . . .      192 BAILE AILLINN          75
     HAVE HAPPINESS WITHOUT AN END, . . . . . . . . . . . .      195 BAILE AILLINN         158
     THOUGH NOW IT'S HARD, TILL TROUBLE IS AT AN END! . . .      200 FOLLY COMFORT   V       5
     O THOUGHT, FLY TO HER WHEN THE END OF DAY . . . . . .       201 OLD MEMORY              1
     I THOUGHT TO FLY TO HER WHEN THE END OF DAY . . . . .       201 OLD MEMORY      V       1
     THOUGHT FLY TO HER WHEN THE END OF DAY . . . . . . .        201 OLD MEMORY      V       1
     WE SAT TOGETHER AT ONE SUMMER'S END, . . . . . . . . .      204 ADAMS CURSE             1
     TO MAKE AN END WHILE HE IS SLEEPING THERE. . . . . . .      222 SHADOW WATER B  V      14
     TO MAKE AN END OF FORGAEL WHILE HE SLEEPS. . . . . . .      225 SHADOW WATER B         65
     KNOWING IT FOR THE WORLD'S END? WHERE THE WORLD ENDS . .    226 SHADOW WATER B        100
     OR CREAKY SHOES. AND AT THE END OF ALL . . . . . . . .      228 SHADOW WATER B        128
     SHE MAY NOT BE TOO SORRY IN THE END. . . . . . . . . .      232 SHADOW WATER B        232
     AND FOR THIS END THEY GAVE ME MY OLD HARP . . . . . .       237 SHADOW WATER B        327
     YOU DID NOT KNOW WHAT BROUGHT HIM TO HIS END, . . . .       240 SHADOW WATER B        382
     I WILL END ALL YOUR MAGIC ON THE INSTANT. . . . . . .       242 SHADOW WATER B        411
     "THERE IS A COUNTRY AT THE END OF THE WORLD . . . . .       247 SHADOW WATER B        530
     I CANNOT--I AM GOING ON TO THE END. . . . . . . . . .       248 SHADOW WATER B        544
     THE BUTT END OF A STEERING OAR, . . . . . . . . . . .       253 HIS DREAM       V       2
     SOMEWHERE IN EAR-SHOT FOR THE STORY'S END, . . . . . .      269 PARDON FATHERS          2
     MUST END AT THE DUMB STONE? BUT WHERE WE BUILD . . . .      284 TWO KINGS             179
     DELIGHT IN ART WHOSE END IS PEACE, . . . . . . . . . .      288 TO WEALTHY MAN         26
     BEFORE THE THREE TO END THIS TALE, . . . . . . . . . .      297 THREE BEGGARS          55
     AND WHEN AT ONE YEAR'S END I FOUND . . . . . . . . . .      305 HOUR DAWN              71
     BE AS BROKEN IN THE END. . . . . . . . . . . . . . . .      313 TWO YEAR LATER         10
     NO LIKELY END COULD BRING THEM LOSS . . . . . . . . .       328 IRISH AIRMAN            7
     AND I MAY DINE AT JOURNEY'S END . . . . . . . . . . .       336 YOUNG BEAUTY           17
     THAT I MAY DINE AT JOURNEY'S END . . . . . . . . . . .      336 YOUNG BEAUTY    V      17
     THEY'LL COUGH IN THE INK TO THE WORLD'S END! . . . . .      337 SCHOLARS        V       7
     THE END OF DAY . . . . . . . . . . . . . . . . . . .        364 END OF DAY              T
     BECAUSE THE END OF DAY . . . . . . . . . . . . . . . .      364 END OF DAY              4
     SING OUT THE SONG! SING TO THE END, AND SING . . . . .      374 PHASES OF MOON         56
     END IN A BEAUTIFUL MAN'S OR WOMAN'S BODY. . . . . . .       374 PHASES OF MOON         64
     HE MIGHT HAVE WON FAME IN THE END, . . . . . . . . . .      392 EASTER 1916            28
```

                                        240

		PAGE	TITLE	LINE

END   (CONTINUED)
    CONSIDER BEAUTY A SUFFICIENT END, ...   403 FOR DAUGHTER   21
    TO END ALL THINGS, TO END   . . . .   431 NINETEEN 19   81
    TO END ALL THINGS, TO END   . . . .   431 NINETEEN 19   81
    "AND ALL THOSE LIES HAVE BUT ONE END, POOR WRETCHES TO   450 OWEN AHERNE   18
      BETRAY;
    AND HIDE IT THERE, FOR CALIPHS TO WORLD'S END . . . . .   461 HARUN RASHID   17
    HIDDEN FROM EYESIGHT TO THE UNNOTICED END. . . . . . .   472 ALL SOUL NIGHT   50
    BEFORE THAT END MUCH HAD SHE RAVELLED OUT . . . . . .   472 ALL SOUL NIGHT   51
    A MAN AWAITS HIS END . . . .   476 DEATH   3
    WINE SHALL RUN THICK TO THE END, ...   554 CHURCH STATE   11
    HERE AT LIFE'S END . . . .   575 ACRE OF GRASS   8
    THE COUNTRY THINKS NO END OF HIM, ...   583 GHOST ROG CASE   13
    DAYBREAK AND A CANDLE END. . . . .   588 OLD WICKED MAN V REF
    DAY-BREAK AND A CANDLE END. . . . .   588 OLD WICKED MAN V REF
    SAW THE STORY'S END, ...   597 COLONEL MARTIN   69
    THOSE WORDS COME TRUE IN THE END . . . .   597 COLONEL MARTIN V 69
    DEEP-ROOTED THINGS," BUT NEVER FORESAW ITS END, . . .   603 GALLERY REVIS   37
    AND NOW THAT END HAS COME I HAVE NOT WEPT; . . . . .   603 GALLERY REVIS   38
    WHAT DEEP ROOTS ARE," AND NEVER FORESAW THE END . . .   603 GALLERY REVIS V 37
    BUT NOW THAT END HAS COME I HAVE NOT WEPT; . . . . .   603 GALLERY REVIS V 38
    MY HUNDREDTH YEAR IS AT AN END. I THINK . . . . . .   609 IN TARAS HALLS   3
    HE BADE, HIS HUNDRED AND FIRST YEAR AT END, ...   609 IN TARAS HALLS   16
    A BLOODY AND A SUDDEN END, ...   620 JOHN KINSELLA   1
    ASIDE!--THE WILD HORNS TOLD ALMINTOR'S END, ...   665 ISLE STAT II 2   68
    AND DREAM OF THE END OF THEIR DAYS. . . . . . .   707 FAIRY PEDANT   4
    A SOLDIER ANSWERS; "BY THE CAMP'S FAR END . . . . .   712 FERENCZ RENYI   67
    HAS NO WORD OF THE SULPHUROUS END. . . . . . .   736 SUMMER EVENING   8
    TILL DAY AND NIGHT TIME END. . . . .   741 EARL PAUL   48
    BEING THE MOON OF BIRTH, MAY END OUR DOUBT. . . . .   748 SHADOW WATER A   24
    WOULD END THIS PEACEFUL LIFE THAT ROTS THE BONES, . .   752 SHADOW WATER A   110
    YOUR HEART'S DESIRE AND THE END OF ALL OUR TROUBLE; .   755 SHADOW WATER A   175
    BUT NOW I WILL KILL HER. ALL COMES TO AN END. . . .   755 SHADOW WATER A   176
    AND WE GO HOME. COME, AIBRIC; END YOUR TALE . . .   766 SHADOW WATER A   374
    SHOULD LOOK UPON HIS EYES WITH LOVE, IN THE END . .   768 SHADOW WATER A   409
    SHOULD LOOK UPON HIS EYES WITH LOVE UNTO THE END . . .   768 SHADOW WATER A V 409
ENDAPPLED   SEE LIGHT-ENDAPPLED
ENDED
    WHO HAD ENDED WHERE HIS BREATH BEGAN. . . . . . .   360 ALF POLLEXFEN   12
ENDLESS
    A DOME MADE OUT OF ENDLESS CARVEN JAGS, ...   38 OISIN 2   144
    WAITED. ABOVE, IN ENDLESS CARVEN JAGS, ...   38 OISIN 2   V 144
    NOR LANGUOR NOR FATIGUE; AN ENDLESS FEAST, ...   44 OISIN 2   223
    AN ENDLESS WAR. THE HUNDRED YEARS HAD CEASED; . . .   44 OISIN 2   224
    NO LANGUOR, NO FATIGUE; AN ENDLESS FEAST, ...   44 OISIN 2   V 223
    NOR LANGUOR NOR FATIGUE; AND ENDLESS FEAST, ...   44 OISIN 2   V 223
    AN ENDLESS WAR. THE HUNDREDTH YEAR HAD CEASED. . . .   44 OISIN 2   V 224
    TROUBLING THE ENDLESS REVERIE, ...   65 HAPPY SHEPHERD   21
    O VANITY OF SLEEP, HOPE, DREAM, ENDLESS DESIRE, . .   154 BELOVED PEACE   7
    IN ENDLESS DARK, AND BY THE WEEDY MARGE . . . . .   682 SEEKER   19
    HER SOUL FROM SEAS OF ENDLESS FLAME IN HELL. . . .   698 MOSADA 2   47
    ROUND US THE WHITE ROADS ARE ENDLESS. . . . . .   737 IN FIRELIGHT   3
    AND PRAISED YOUR WAR AMONG THE ENDLESS SEAS, . . .   749 SHADOW WATER A   35
    AND PRAISE A WAR AMONG THE ENDLESS SEAS, ...   749 SHADOW WATER A V 35
ENDLESSLY
    WHEN YOU HAVE TOLD HOW I WEEP ENDLESSLY, ...   33 OISIN 2   63
ENDOWED   SEE BEST-ENDOWED
    THE ENDOWED, THE ELECT; . . . .   504 RESULT THOUGHT V   3
ENDS
    KNOWING IT FOR THE WORLD'S END? WHERE THE WORLD ENDS . .   226 SHADOW WATER B   100
    YOU HAD TO FACE YOUR ENDS WHEN YOUNG-- . . . . . .   273 GREY ROCK   53
    AND UNREPENTING FACED YOUR ENDS, ...   273 GREY ROCK   60
    YET THE WORLD ENDS WHEN THESE TWO THINGS, ...   388 SOLOMON WITCH   28
    I CELEBRATE THE SILENT KISS THAT ENDS SHORT LIFE OR LONG.   459 FROM OEDIPUS   9
    AND TOLD HIM SO, BUT FRIENDSHIP NEVER ENDS; . . . .   473 ALL SOUL NIGHT   65
    THINK WHERE MAN'S GLORY MOST BEGINS AND ENDS, . . .   604 GALLERY REVIS   54
    NO PLEASING HABIT ENDS, ...   621 JOHN KINSELLA   30
    TALKED OF ODDS AND ENDS. . . . .   627 STATES HOLIDAY   8
    SO ENDS A BRAIN--A WORLD; THE SMOKE GOES UP, . . .   714 FERENCZ RENYI   111
    OF FIRE. SO ENDS A BRAIN--A WORLD; THE SMOKE FLOATS UP,   714 FERENCZ RENYI V 111
    ENDS ALL THINGS. I HAVE SLAIN THE LOCHLANN KING. . .   754 SHADOW WATER A   163
    ENDS TIME AND CHANGE. . . . .   754 SHADOW WATER A V 163
    THEY LURE US TO THE STREAMS WHERE THE WORLD ENDS. . .   764 SHADOW WATER A   334
    TO LEAD US TO THE STREAMS WHERE THE WORLD ENDS. . .   765 SHADOW WATER A   369
    WHERE THE WORLD ENDS, OR RUNS FROM WIND TO WIND . . .   768 SHADOW WATER A   417
ENDURE
    AND I MUST NEEDS ENDURE AND HATE AND WEEP, ...   35 OISIN 2   85
    OUR HEARTS ENDURE THE SCOURGE, THE PLAITED THORNS, THE WAY   172 TRAV PASSION   3
    OUR HEARTS ENDURE THE PLAITED THORN, THE CROWDED WAY, . .   172 TRAV PASSION   V 3
    MUST I ENDURE YOUR AMOROUS CRIES? . . . .   177 PAST GREATNESS   12
    THAT IT COULD NOT ENDURE . . . .   317 NIGHT COME   4
    I MUST ENDURE THE TIMID SUN. . . . .   344 DEJECTION   11
    ENDURE WHAT LIFE GOD GIVES AND ASK NO LONGER SPAN; . .   459 FROM OEDIPUS   1
    CANNOT ENDURE TO THINK YOU TREAD THESE PATHS, ...   463 HARUN RASHID   52
    ENDURE THAT TOIL OF GROWING UP; . . . .   478 SELF AND SOUL   44
    AT STROKE OF MIDNIGHT SOUL CANNOT ENDURE . . . .   558 RIBH CHRISTIAN   19
ENDURED
    AND THERE ENDURED HER FINGERS' TOUCH . . . . . .   397 POLIT PRISONER   5
    AND THERE ENDURED HER FINGER'S TOUCH . . . . . .   397 POLIT PRISONER V 5
ENDURES
    ENDURES A MOMENT OR A DAY. . . . .   438 SONGS PLAY 2   10

		PAGE	TITLE		LINE
ENDURING					
	NO USE. AWAY! HEAR, THOU ENDURING GOD,	698	MOSADA 2		50
	AND THOU SHALT BEND, ENDURING GOD, THE KNEES	698	MOSADA 2		59
	NO USE. AWAY! HEAR OH! THOU ENDURING GOD,	698	MOSADA 2	V	50
	AND THOU SHALL BEND, ENDURING GOD, THE KNEES	698	MOSADA 2	V	59
ENEMIES					
	THE FINISHED MAN AMONG HIS ENEMIES?--	479	SELF AND SOUL		49
ENEMY					
	MY ENEMY AND HOPE, DEMONS FOR FRIGHT	34	OISIN 2		81
	WITH HOPE, MINE ENEMY. AS HE BY NIGHT	34	OISIN 2	V	81
	MY ENEMY? I LOOKED UPON THE MOON,	246	SHADOW WATER B		509
	"BUT LEST YOU ARE MY ENEMY,	263	MASK		11
	YOUR ENEMY, AN OLD FOUL MOUTH, HAD SET	292	TO A SHADE		17
	PARDON, GREAT ENEMY,	366	HER CHRIS TREE		1
	THE SERVANTS OF YOUR ENEMY,	436	FOR MY SON		26
	OR COURT A WOMAN! NEITHER ENEMY,	463	HARUN RASHID		59
	HAVE NO ENEMY BUT TIME!	476	EVA GORE-BOOTH		25
ENEMY'S					
	WITH A FRIEND'S OR AN ENEMY'S	362	DOLLS DRAWINGS		3
	NOR MUSIC NOR AN ENEMY'S CLIPPED EAR	412	TOWER		75
ENERGY					
	BECOME ONE MOVEMENT, ENERGY, DELIGHT,	231	SHADOW WATER B		217
ENFOLD					
	AND MIDNIGHT THERE ENFOLD THEM LIKE A FLEECE	128	DREAM OF FAERY		34
	ENFOLD ME IN MY HOUR OF HOURS! WHERE THOSE	169	SECRET ROSE		2
	MEN HAVE NAMED BEAUTY. THY GREAT LEAVES ENFOLD	169	SECRET ROSE		7
	MEN HAVE NAMED BEAUTY. YOUR HEAVY LEAVES ENFOLD	169	SECRET ROSE	V	7
	MEN HAVE NAMED BEAUTY. YOUR GREAT LEAVES ENFOLD	169	SECRET ROSE	V	7
ENFOLDEN					
	ENFOLDEN IN THE SHADOWS OF THE EAST,	705	REMEMBRANCE		11
ENGAGED					
	"IT WAS THE MASK ENGAGED YOUR MIND,	263	MASK		8
ENGENDER					
	ENGENDER IN THE DITCH,	598	STONE CROSS		10
ENGENDERS					
	A SHUDDER IN THE LOINS ENGENDERS THERE	441	LEDA AND SWAN		9
ENGINES					
	BE BUT THE BREAKERS OF MEN'S HEARTS OR ENGINES OF DELIGHT!	354	HIS PHOENIX		23
ENGLAND					
	FOR ENGLAND MAY KEEP FAITH	394	EASTER 1916		68
	HE FOUGHT THE MIGHT OF ENGLAND	586	PARNELLITES		11
ENGLISH					
	CERTAIN MEN THE ENGLISH SHOT?	632	MAN AND ECHO		12
ENGRAVED					
	THE LONELY LIGHT THAT SAMUEL PALMER ENGRAVED,	373	PHASES OF MOON		17
ENGROSS					
	TO ENGROSS THE PRESENT AND DOMINATE MEMORY.	630	CIRCUS ANIMALS		30
ENJOINS					
	IGNORANT WHAT THAT DRAMATIST ENJOINS,	560	WHENCE COME		8
ENJOYED					
	AND YET THE SADDEST CHIMES ARE BEST ENJOYED.	130	BOOK STORIES		20
ENKINDLED	SEE EARTH-ENKINDLED				
ENMITIES					
	MORE SUBSTANCE IN OUR ENMITIES	425	STARES NEST		18
ENMITY					
	HER THOUGHT SOME POPULAR ENMITY!	397	POLIT PRISONER		10
	FOR THOUGHT SOME POPULAR ENMITY,	397	POLIT PRISONER	V	10
ENORMOUS					
	ON THE FAR GOLDEN PEAK! ENORMOUS SHAPES,	74	ANASHU VIJAYA		68
	THE WAVES, ENORMOUS WANDERERS OF THE WORLD,	687	TWO TITANS		3
ENOUGH					
	THERE IS ENOUGH EVIL IN THE CRYING OF WIND.	155	REPROVE CURLEW		6
	THAT IS BAD ENOUGH TO BE TRUE, IS TRUE,	191	BAILE AILLINN		69
	AS THOUGH THEIR MUSIC WERE ENOUGH	193	BAILE AILLINN		108
	A MUSIC THAT HAD THOUGHT ENOUGH,	193	BAILE AILLINN	V	108
	AND THAT DEAR WORDS MEANT NOTHING?" BUT ENOUGH,	201	OLD MEMORY		9
	AND WHO COULD PLAY IT WELL ENOUGH	202	NEVER GIVE ALL		11
	AND WHO CAN PLAY IT WELL ENOUGH	202	NEVER GIVE ALL	V	11
	YET NOW IT SEEMS AN IDLE TRADE ENOUGH."	205	ADAMS CURSE		27
	FOR LONG ENOUGH? AYE, LONG AND LONG ENOUGH.	221	SHADOW WATER B		2
	FOR LONG ENOUGH? AYE, LONG AND LONG ENOUGH.	221	SHADOW WATER B		2
	COULD NOT AMEND. I HAVE GOOD SPIRITS ENOUGH.	227	SHADOW WATER B		116
	THAT DROVE YOU TO IT, AND I FOOL ENOUGH	248	SHADOW WATER B		548
	ENOUGH IF THE WORK HAS SEEMED,	259	UNWORTH PRAISE		5
	HOW SHOULD THEIR LUCK RUN HIGH ENOUGH TO REACH	264	HOUSE SHAKEN		9
	AND THEN, "I AM OLD ENOUGH"!	268	BROWN PENNY		2
	THERE IS NOBODY WISE ENOUGH	268	BROWN PENNY		10
	UNTIL ENOUGH OF PAUDEEN'S PENCE	287	TO WEALTHY MAN		2
	YOU HAD ENOUGH OF SORROW BEFORE DEATH--	293	TO A SHADE		23
	I'D HAVE A MERRY LIFE ENOUGH	306	HOUR DAWN		85
	IF THERE BE RAGS ENOUGH HE WILL KNOW HER NAME	351	HER PRAISE		15
	HE HAS HAD ENOUGH OF MEDDLING WHO CAN PLEASE	359	WAR POEM		4
	NO TABLE OR CHAIR OR STOOL NOT SIMPLE ENOUGH	371	ON GOING HOUSE		3
	JUST TRUTH ENOUGH TO SHOW THAT HIS WHOLE LIFE	373	PHASES OF MOON		22
	OR MAYBE IS NOT STRONG ENOUGH."	388	SOLOMON WITCH		37
	WE KNOW THEIR DREAM! ENOUGH	394	EASTER 1916		70
	O TOWARDS I HAVE FORGOTTEN WHAT--ENOUGH!	412	TOWER		73
	SEEING THAT LOVE AND FRIENDSHIP ARE ENOUGH,	423	MY DESCENDANTS		20
	HAD PRETTY PLUMAGE ONCE--ENOUGH OF THAT,	444	SCHOOL CHILDR		30
	HAVE WRONG TO BROOD UPON--ENOUGH OF THAT,	444	SCHOOL CHILDR	V	30
	BUT THAT'S A TRAITOR'S THOUGHT. ENOUGH FOR ME	462	HARUN RASHID		39

242

ENOUGH   (CONTINUED)
    IT SEEMS ENOUGH THAT I AM THERE: AND YET, ...   468 HARUN RASHID   166
    NO MAN HAS EVER LIVED THAT HAD ENOUGH . . . .   500 VACILLATION   25
    I HAD FORGIVEN ENOUGH . . . .   504 QUARREL IN AGE   7
    WHAT PAYMENT WERE ENOUGH . . . .   518 HIS CONFIDENCE   5
    WHAT PAYMENTS WERE ENOUGH . . . .   518 HIS CONFIDENCE V 5
    TILL EITHER NEITHER HAVE ENOUGH, ...   573 LADYS 3RD SONG   8
    THAT PASSION COULD BRING CHARACTER ENOUGH, ...   610 STATUES   6
    AND THIS BROUGHT FORTH A DREAM AND SOON ENOUGH . . .   630 CIRCUS ANIMALS   23
    AND SAID: "SHE HAS FOOLED ME ENOUGH," . . . .   744 GLOVE CLOAK   3
    HAD I NOT GOLD AND SILVER, AND ENOUGH . . . .   748 SHADOW WATER A   32
    THEY ARE GONE, THEY ARE GONE. WHISPERING WERE ENOUGH. . .   778 SONG DEIRDRE 3   3
    AND ALL SEEM WELL ENOUGH, ...   786 YOUR HEART   15
ENQUIRE
    I MUST ENQUIRE." . . . .   263 MASK   12
    WE NEVER THOUGHT TO ENQUIRE . . . , ...   381 SONGS FOOL 2   3
ENQUIRING
    AND THAT ENQUIRING MAN JOHN SYNGE COMES NEXT, ...   324 ROBERT GREGORY   25
ENRAGED
    THE OLD COOK ENRAGED, ...   349 HAWK   5
ENRICHED
    PLUCKED BITTER WISDOM THAT ENRICHED HIS BLOOD. . . . .   543 PARN FUNERAL 2   12
ENSLAVE
    SO DID FANATICISM AND HATE ENSLAVE IT, ...   630 CIRCUS ANIMALS   22
ENTANGLED
    READING SOME ENTANGLED STORY: . . . .   65 HAPPY SHEPHERD   16
    TIMID, ENTANGLED, EMPTY AND ABASHED, ...   368 EGO DOMINUS   16
    ENTANGLED IN MY HAIR . . . .   532 FIRST CONFESS   2
ENTANGLEMENTS
    . . . ALL ENTANGLEMENTS OF MANKIND GROW, ...   459 FROM OEDIPUS   5
ENTER
    AND ENTER, AND NONE SAYETH "NO" . . . .   62 OISIN 3   210
    AND ENTER, AND NONE SAYETH "NAY" . . . .   62 OISIN 3   V 210
    AWAIT THE HOUR OF WAR, ENTER THE SMALL, ...   461 HARUN RASHID V 8
    NO OTHER BIRD MAY ENTER IN. WELL? LATE-- . . . . .   659 ISLE STAT II 1   24
    CAN ENTER THERE. SEE: SEE: ABOVE YON BROW . . . . .   659 ISLE STAT II 1   27
    ANSWERED PETER: "ENTER IN, ...   697 MOSADA 2   30
ENTERPRISE
    FOR THERE'S MORE ENTERPRISE . . . .   320 COAT   9
    O SELF-BORN MOCKERS OF MAN'S ENTERPRISE: . . . . . .   445 SCHOOL CHILDR   56
ENTERS
    . . . WHEN THERE ENTERS THE STRONGLY ARMED GUEST: . . .   62 OISIN 3   210
    THE VERY SQUIRREL DIES THAT ENTERS THERE. . . . . . .   682 SEEKER   33
    THE VERY SQUIRREL DIES THAT ENTERS IT. . . . .   682 SEEKER V 33
ENTHRALLED
    ENTHRALLED BY THE UNCONQUERABLE DELUSION, ...   367 EGO DOMINUS   6
ENTIRE
    THE ENTIRE COMBUSTIBLE WORLD IN ONE SMALL ROOM . . .   327 ROBERT GREGORY   82
ENTIRELY
    BY THOSE THAT ARE NOT ENTIRELY BEAUTIFUL: . . . . . .   404 FOR DAUGHTER   35
ENTRAILS
    THE ENTRAILS OF THE HORSE. DROPPING HIS SWORD . . . .   278 TWO KINGS   23
    THROUGH THE ENTRAILS OF THE HORSE. DROPPING HIS SWORD . .   278 TWO KINGS V 23
ENTRANCE
    HERE AT RIGHT OF THE ENTRANCE THIS BRONZE HEAD, ...   618 BRONZE HEAD   1
    THE ENTRANCE OF DEIRDRE . . . .   771 SONG DEIRDRE 1 V T
ENTRANCED
    FLOATED IN ALL HER SINGING. HALF ENTRANCED . . . . .   30 OISIN 2 V 19
ENTWINED
    OF LANGUID EVENING THAT ENTWINED US. . . . .   25 OISIN 1   V 385A
ENUMERATE
    WHAT CAN I BUT ENUMERATE OLD THEMES? . . . .   629 CIRCUS ANIMALS   9
ENVIOUS   SEE STAR-ENVIOUS
ENVY
    TO SILENCE THE ENVY IN MY THOUGHT: . . . .   424 ROAD AT DOOR   13
ENWOUND
    AND WHISPERING TO HERSELF ENWOUND ME: . . . .   9 OISIN 1   108
    AND WHEN TUMULTUOUS FEET ENWOUND ME . . . .   83 MAD KING GOLL V 20
    WHEN LOIE FULLER'S CHINESE DANCERS ENWOUND . . . . .   430 NINETEEN 19   49
ENWROUGHT
    BUT LET A GENTLE SILENCE ENWROUGHT WITH MUSIC FLOW . . .   175 ELEMENT POWERS V 17
    ENWROUGHT WITH GOLDEN AND SILVER LIGHT, ...   176 CLOTHS HEAVEN   2
EOCHA
    EOCHA AND MAINE ARE ALWAYS QUARRELLING. . . . .   766 SHADOW WATER A   371
EOCHAID
    KING EOCHAID CAME AT SUNDOWN TO A WOOD . . . .   276 TWO KINGS   1
    KING EOCHAID SAID, AND HE THAT BORE HIS SHIELD . . . .   276 TWO KINGS V B
    HAVE BEEN THE MEASURE OF THAT CARE." BUT EOCHAID, . . .   276 TWO KINGS V H
    RENDING THE HORSE'S FLANK. KING EOCHAID REELED, . . .   277 TWO KINGS   13
    RIPPED THROUGH THE HORSE'S FLANKS. KING EOCHAID REELED,   277 TWO KINGS V 13
    KING EOCHAID SEIZED THE HORNS IN HIS STRONG HANDS . . .   278 TWO KINGS   24
    THE DISEMBOWELLED HORSE. KING EOCHAID RAN . . . . .   278 TWO KINGS   45
    EOCHAID SEIZED BOTH THE HORNS IN HIS STRONG HANDS . .   278 TWO KINGS V 24
    THE DISEMBOWELLED HORSE. KING EOCHAID GAZED, ...   278 TWO KINGS V 45
    AND CARVE HIS NAME IN OGHAM." EOCHAID SAID, ...   280 TWO KINGS   83
    AND RAISE HIS PILLAR STONE." KING EOCHAID SAID, . . .   280 TWO KINGS V 83
    CROW UPON TARA." KING EOCHAID BOWED HIS HEAD . . . .   286 TWO KINGS   211
EOCHAID'S
    YET ANSWERED HIM, "I AM KING EOCHAID'S WIFE . . . . .   284 TWO KINGS   173
    AND IN THE MIDST KING EOCHAID'S BROTHER STOOD, ...   286 TWO KINGS   217
    UPON KING EOCHAID'S FACE, WHO LOWERED HIS FACE . . . .   286 TWO KINGS   V 211A

EPHEMERA
    EPHEMERA •   79 EPHEMERA   T
EPHEMERAL
    AS MAN, AS BEAST, AS AN EPHEMERAL FLY BEGETS, GODHEAD   556 RIBH PATRICK   5
        BEGETS GODHEAD,
EPHESIAN
    WHERE SEVEN EPHESIAN TOPERS SLEPT AND NEVER KNEW • • • •   442 BLACK CENTAUR   11
EPILOGUE
    AN EPILOGUE TO "THE ISLAND OF STATUES" AND "THE SEEKER"   64 HAPPY SHEPHERD V   T
EPITAPH
    AN EPITAPH • • • • • • • • • • • • • • • • • • •   123 DREAM OF DEATH V   T
    SWIFT'S EPITAPH • • • • • • • • • • • • • • • •   493 SWIFTS EPITAPH   T
EPITOME
    AS 'TWERE ALL LIFE'S EPITOME• • • • • • • • • • • •   327 ROBERT GREGORY   87
EQUAL
    EQUAL TO GOOD OR GRIEVOUS CHANCE! • • • • • • • • •   24 OISIN 1   372
    EQUAL TO GOOD OR EVIL CHANCE • • • • • • • • • •   24 OISIN 1   V   371
    FOR GOD HAS BID THEM SHARE AN EQUAL FATE! • • • •   115 ROSE OF BATTLE   32
    WITH EQUAL COURAGE IN THAT WHIRLING ROUT! • • • •   186 QUEEN MAEVE   131
    HAD THEY BUT COURAGE EQUAL TO DESIRE? • • • • • •   256 NO SECOND TROY   5
    WHO IS MY BEAUTY'S EQUAL, THOUGH THAT MY HEART DENIES, • •   354 HIS PHOENIX   27
    IN SPACE, MADE EQUAL WITH A SIGH, WE MET• • • • • •   705 REMEMBRANCE   14
    OF EQUAL POWER IN SPELLS AND SECRET RITES• • • • • •   720 WITCH VIVIEN   6
EQUALITY
    CAST BUT DEAD LEAVES TO MATHEMATICAL EQUALITY! • • •   481 BLOOD AND MOON   24
    CASTS BUT DEAD LEAVES TO MATHEMATICAL EQUALITY! • • • •   481 BLOOD AND MOON V   24
    WHAT'S EQUALITY?--MUCK IN THE YARD! • • • • • • • •   547 TO SAME TUNE 3 V   4
EQUALS
    BY THE WOOD'S EDGE WHERE ONLY EQUALS MEET, • • • • •   321 REED WHISPERER V   8
ERCOLE
    WHAT CARED DUKE ERCOLE, THAT BID • • • • • • • • •   287 TO WEALTHY MAN   9
ERE
    ERE LONG AN ANSWERING WHISPER FLEW, • • • • • • • •   15 OISIN 1   V   197
    ERE HALF THE SWIFT THINGS THAT SHE DREAMT ON WERE DONE,   28 OISIN 1   V   422
    THINGS DONE ERE GOD FIRST WAS OR MY OLD LINE BEGAN! • • •   29 OISIN 2   V   8
    THE VAN OF WANDERING QUIET! ERE YOU BE TOO CALM AND OLD,   73 ANASHU VIJAYA   43
    THE VAN OF WANDERING QUIET! ERE YE BE TOO CALM AND OLD,   73 ANASHU VIJAYA V   43
    LET US PART, ERE THE SEASON OF PASSION FORGET US, • • •   79 FALLING LEAVES   7
    ERE FALL OF EVENING, MY MAILED HOST, • • • • • • •   83 MAD KING GOLL V   19
    ERE TIME TRANSFIGURED ME• • • • • • • • • • • •   131 OLD PENSIONER   6
    IT TALKED, ERE THE MORN GREW WHITE• • • • • • • • •   159 CAP AND BELLS V   6
    ERE THE ONE OR T'OTHER DIE, • • • • • • • • • • •   508 JANE BISHOP   V   5
    LONG ERE AN ARROW WHIZZED OR SWORD LEFT SHEATH • • • •   650 ISLE STAT I 1   135
    OR LONG ERE THIS HAD LOST THEIR RUDDY STAIN, • • • •   687 TWO TITANS   8
    ERE LONG SHALL FALTER THROUGH THE NOISY SQUARE, • • •   699 MOSADA 3   21
    ERE YONDER PALM COMMENCED HIS THOUSAND YEARS? • • • •   724 KANVA ON SELF   14
ERECT
    SHE GOES ABOUT HER HOUSE ERECT AND CALM • • • • • •   340 SHEP GOATHERD   35
    WITH MOTIONLESS HEAD ERECT• • • • • • • • • • • •   383 VISION ROBART   32
    HORSEMAN ERECT UPON HORSEBACK • • • • • • • • • •   589 OLD WICKED MAN   52
ERI
    AFAR IN ANCIENT ERI, • • • • • • • • • • • • • •   32 OISIN 2   V 50E
    SAY HOW HE WEEPS IN ERI•" • • • • • • • • • • • •   33 OISIN 2   V   68
    WHEN HER OWN PEOPLE RULED IN WAVE-WORN ERI, • • • •   129 BOOK STORIES   V   2
    I TORE IT FROM THE GREEN BOUGHS OF OLD ERI, • • • •   130 BOOK STORIES   V   15
    THY MOTHER ERI IS ALWAYS YOUNG, • • • • • • • • •   148 INTO TWILIGHT V   5
    YE ON THE BROAD HIGH MOUNTAINS OF OLD ERI, • • • • •   737 MOURN THEN ON   1
    MOURN YE ON GRASS-GREEN PLAINS OF ERI FATED, • • • •   738 MOURN THEN ON   9
ERI'S
    SPINNING AT ALL TIMES ERI'S GOOD TO-MORROW, • • • • •   129 BOOK STORIES   V   10
ERROR
    FOR GREAT OUR ERROR, GREAT OUR GUILT•" • • • • • •   43 OISIN 2   V 208H
ESCAPE
    THEY'VE THE PASSION TO ESCAPE•" • • • • • • • • •   299 THREE HERMITS   21
    BUT THE ESCAPE! THE SONG'S NOT FINISHED YET• • • • •   377 PHASES OF MOON   117
    AND THAT MUST SLEEP, SHRIEK, STRUGGLE TO ESCAPE • • •   444 SCHOOL CHILDR   35
    HOW IN THE NAME OF HEAVEN CAN HE ESCAPE • • • • • •   479 SELF AND SOUL   50
    AND WHAT'S THE GOOD OF AN ESCAPE • • • • • • • • •   479 SELF AND SOUL   55
    THAT COME INTO MY SOUL AND ESCAPE • • • • • • • • •   599 SPIRIT MEDIUM   3
    SO THEY ESCAPE FROM HELL• BUT, PARDON ME, • • • • •   704 MOSADA 3   132
    NONE SHOULD ESCAPE MY SWORD! I WOULD SEND ALL • • •   752 SHADOW WATER A   111
    I PROMISED HIM THAT NONE SHOULD ESCAPE MY SWORD • • •   752 SHADOW WATER A   114
    WE WILL GO CALL THESE SAILORS, AND ESCAPE • • • • •   766 SHADOW WATER A   382
ESCAPED
    ESCAPED FROM BITTER YOUTH, • • • • • • • • • • •   568 SWEET DANCER   4
    ESCAPED OUT OF HER CROWD, • • • • • • • • • • • •   568 SWEET DANCER   5
ESCUTCHEONED
    WHAT IF THE GLORY OF ESCUTCHEONED DOORS, • • • • • •   418 ANCEST HOUSES   33
ESERKELLY
    AND ESERKELLY PLAINS, FEW KEPT HIS PACE! • • • • • •   326 ROBERT GREGORY V   59
    OR ESERKELLY PLAINS, FEW KEPT HIS PACE! • • • • • •   326 ROBERT GREGORY V   59
ESSERKELLY
    OR ESSERKELLY PLAIN, FEW KEPT HIS PACE! • • • • • •   326 ROBERT GREGORY   59
ESTABLISHED
    PULL DOWN ESTABLISHED HONOUR! HAWK FOR NEWS • • • •   398 LEADERS CROWD   3
    FOUND PRIDE ESTABLISHED IN HUMILITY, • • • • • • •   489 COOLE PARK 29   15
    ESTABLISHED IT FOR GOOD! • • • • • • • • • • • •   584 ORAHILLY   6
ESTATE
    ALTHOUGH THEIR CHILDREN NEED A RICH ESTATE! • • • • •   500 VACILLATION   24
ESTEEMS
    EVERYTHING THAT MAN ESTEEMS • • • • • • • • • • •   438 SONGS PLAY 2   9

ESTRANGED
    ESTRANGED AMID THE STRANGENESS OF THEMSELVES, ... 375 PHASES OF MOON   78
    ALTHOUGH OF LATE ESTRANGED. . . . . 473 ALL SOUL NIGHT   63
    ALL OTHER LOVERS BEING ESTRANGED OR DEAD, ... 523 LONG SILENCE   2
ETERNAL
    NOT THEY ARE THE ETERNAL--'TIS THE CRY." . . . . . . 81 EPHEMERA   V 24J
    ETERNAL BEAUTY WANDERING ON HER WAY. . . . . 101 ROSE UPON ROOD   12
    WAGE AN ETERNAL BATTLE, AND I FEEL . . . . 104 FERGUS DRUID V 38C
    VAST GREENNESS, WHERE ETERNAL RUMOUR DWELLS, ... 657 ISLE STAT I 3   45
    FOR THIS DID THE ETERNAL DARKNESS BRING . . . . . . 688 TWO TITANS   51
    GIVES FORTH. HE, THE ETERNAL, WORKS HIS WILL. . . . . 689 NETTLESHIP   16
ETERNALISED
    ETERNALISED THE BODY OF A MODERN SAINT THAT ONCE . . . . 503 VACILLATION   83
ETERNITIES
    BETWEEN HIS TWO ETERNITIES, ... 637 BEN BULBEN   14
ETERNITY
    BEFORE US LIES ETERNITY! OUR SOULS . . . . 81 EPHEMERA   23
    THAT WORD OF THE SOUL'S PEACE--"ETERNITY." . . . . . 81 EPHEMERA V 24B
    I KNOW THE WORD THEY CRY, "ETERNITY!" . . . . 81 EPHEMERA V 24F
    BEAUTY GROWN SAD WITH ITS ETERNITY . . . . 115 ROSE OF BATTLE   29
    HE THAT CROWED OUT ETERNITY . . . . 388 SOLOMON WITCH   17
    INTO THE ARTIFICE OF ETERNITY. . . . . 408 SAIL BYZANTIUM   24
    ETERNITY MAY DWINDLE, ... 520 HIS BARGAIN   3
    "THE STALLION ETERNITY . . . . 529 TOM CRUACHAN   4
    ETERNITY IS PASSION, GIRL OR BOY . . . . 560 WHENCE COME   1
    HAS FENCED US ROUND FOR ALL ETERNITY. . . . . 670 ISLE STAT II 3   95
    AT ARM'S LENGTH, THUS TILL DUMB ETERNITY . . . . . . 671 ISLE STAT II 3   145
EUNUCHS
    EUNUCHS RAN THROUGH HELL AND MET . . . . 294 HATED PLAYBOY   2
EUROPA
    GREAT EUROPA PLAYED THE FOOL . . . . 509 JANE REPROVED   5
EUROPE
    EUROPE PUT OFF THAT FOAM WHEN PHIDIAS . . . . 610 STATUES   15
EUROTAS'
    UPON EUROTAS' GRASSY BANK . . . . 522 LULLABY   14
EVA
    IN MEMORY OF EVA GORE-BOOTH AND CON MARKIEWICZ . . . . 475 EVA GORE-BOOTH   T
EVADING
    EVADING, TURNING! ONCE DID I HEW AND HEW . . . . . 40 OISIN 2 V 176
EVE
    WHEN THE EARLIEST DEW-WASHED STAR FROM EVE HATH LEANT, . . 32 OISIN 2 V 54
    GAVE TO THE NOON, AND NOON TO EVE GAVE WAY, ... 40 OISIN 2 V 172
    AND IN THE EVE I THREW HIM IN THE SURGE. . . . . . . 44 OISIN 2 V 219
    AMRITA. THIS SAME EVE SHE WATCHED ME PASS. . . . . . 74 ANASHU VIJAYA V 64
    WHEN EVE HAS HUSHED THE FEATHERED WAYS, ... 78 INDIAN TO LOVE   19
    DROPPING AT EVE IN CORAL BAYS . . . . 78 INDIAN TO LOVE   19
    WHERE EVE HAS HUSHED THE FEATHERED WAYS, ... 78 INDIAN TO LOVE V 19
    WHO PACED IN THE EVE BY THE NETS ON THE PEBBLY SHORE, . . 91 OLD FISHERMAN   11
    AT THE MOTH-HOUR OF EVE, ... 132 FR GILLIGAN   6
    OF WONDERS! EVE OF PRODIGIES! DRAW! DRAW! . . . . . 664 ISLE STAT II 2   62
    AND RULE THE SHADOWS OF THE EVE AND DAWN? . . . . . 678 ISLE STAT II 3   304
    A LITTLE WHILE AND--RED EVE DIES-- . . . . 686 LIFE   13
    DRAW STAR TO STAR, AS ON THAT EVE HE PASSED . . . . . 691 MOSADA 1   29
    SEER OF VISIONS! NOW EVE FALLS ASLEEP, ... 691 MOSADA 1   36
    THIS EVE, TO-MORROW, OR TO-MORROW NIGHT . . . . . . 699 MOSADA 3   2
    I NEVER KNEW AN EVE SO MARVELLOUS STILL. . . . . . . 702 MOSADA 3   88
    IT IS THE DARKEST EVE I EVER KNEW. . . . . 702 MOSADA 3   93
    WHEN WERE YOU BORN? BEFORE YOUR GRANDAM EVE. . . . . 721 WITCH VIVIEN   32
EVEN
    AND EVEN THE SUN, THE DAY CASTLE'S WARDER, ... 28 OISIN 1 V 423A
    NOT EVEN YOUR GOD COULD HAVE THROWN DOWN THAT HALL! . . 36 OISIN 2   109
    AND EVEN THE NAMES OF HIS FATHERS, AND EVEN THE WORKS OF
        HIS HANDS? . . . . 51 OISIN 3 V 62
    AND EVEN THE NAMES OF HIS FATHERS, AND EVEN THE WORKS OF
        HIS HANDS? . . . . 51 OISIN 3 V 62
    LORD OF THE CROZIERS, YOU EVEN HAD LIFTED YOUR HANDS AND
        WEPT! . . . . 54 OISIN 3   110
    LORD OF THE CROSIERS, THOU EVEN HADST LIFTED THY HANDS
        AND WEPT! . . . . 54 OISIN 3 V 110
    AH, SWEET TO ME NOW WERE EVEN BALD CONAN'S SLANDEROUS
        TONGUE! . . . . 55 OISIN 3   116
    EVEN AS SPRING UPON THE ANCIENT SKIES, ... 108 CUCHULAIN SEA   42
    EVEN IN AN OLD STORY, IS A BURDEN NOT TO BE BORNE. . . 210 UNDER THE MOON   20
    EVEN IF FORGAEL HAD NOT BEEN MY MASTER . . . . . . 225 SHADOW WATER B V 76
    AND BODILY TENDERNESS, AND FINDS THAT EVEN . . . . . 228 SHADOW WATER B 147
    EVEN THOUGH IT BE THE LIGHTEST OF LIGHT LOVE, ... 230 SHADOW WATER B 184
    SIGHED, "YOU, EVEN YOU YOURSELF, COULD WORK THE CURE!" . . 282 TWO KINGS 124
    OUR QUESTIONING, BEYOND OUR PITY EVEN. . . . . . . 282 TWO KINGS 130
    QUESTION OF OURS, BEYOND OUR PITY EVEN, ... 282 TWO KINGS V 130
    EVEN LIKE THESE TO RAIL AND SWEAT . . . . 294 HATED PLAYBOY   5
    TILL EVEN I SLEEP LIGHT! BUT WHO . . . . 303 HOUR DAWN   34
    SO THAT IT SEEMS EVEN I SLEEP LIGHT! . . . . 303 HOUR DAWN V 34
    EVEN A HALF-HOUR'S NOTHINGNESS, ... 305 HOUR DAWN   70
    EVEN A HALF HOUR'S NOTHINGNESS, ... 305 HOUR DAWN V 70
    THAT EVEN THE BEST OF LOVE MUST DIE, ... 314 MEMORY YOUTH   17
    AND EVEN OLD MEN'S EYES GREW DIM, THIS HAND ALONE, . . 314 FALLEN MAJESTY   2
    I CAN FORGIVE EVEN THAT WRONG OF WRONGS, ... 321 REED WHISPERER   9
    NOT EVEN YOUR OWN MOTHER . . . . 336 YOUNG GIRL   4
    EVEN BEFORE HIS CHILDREN AND HIS WIFE? . . . . . . 340 SHEP GOATHERD   34
    THEY HAD A PRIEST SAY MASS, AND EVEN THE JAPANESE, . . 363 DOLLS FACES   2
    EVEN OUR BEAUTY WITH HER TURKISH TROUSERS ON. . . . . 364 DOLLS FACES   9

EVEN   (CONTINUED)
THEY DO NOT EVEN FEEL, SO ABSTRACT ARE THEY, ... 382 VISION ROBART   14
EVEN FROM THE FOOT-SOLE THINK IT TOO, ... 387 ROBARTES DANCE   51
EVEN TO EYES THAT BEAUTY HAD DRIVEN MAD, ... 390 IMAGE PAST   34
EVEN ACCUSING HEAVEN BECAUSE . . . . 399 BREAK OF DAY   15
AND EVEN STRAFFORD SMILED AS THOUGH . . . . . . 400 DEMON BEAST   13
AND EVEN STAFFORD SMILED AS THOUGH . . . . . . 400 DEMON BEAST V   13
WHERE EVEN LONGING DROWNS UNDER ITS OWN EXCESS: . . 426 PHANTOM HATRED   22
WHAT MY LABORIOUS LIFE IMAGINED, EVEN . . . . . 431 NINETEEN 19   82
EVEN WHERE HORRIBLE GREEN PARROTS CALL AND SWING, . . 442 BLACK CENTAUR   2
EVEN WHERE THE HORRIBLE GREEN PARROTS CALL AND SWING, . . 442 BLACK CENTAUR V   2
FOR EVEN DAUGHTERS OF THE SWAN CAN SHARE . . . . 444 SCHOOL CHILDR   20
EVEN THE GREY-LEAVED OLIVE-TREE . . . . . . 446 COLONUS PRAISE   12
EVEN THE GREY-LEAVED OLIVE TREE . . . . . . 446 COLONUS PRAISE V 12
IT IS AS THOUGH YOU PRAISED ANOTHER, OR EVEN . . . 448 HERO GIRL FOOL   3
IT IS AS THOUGH YOU PRAISE ANOTHER, OR EVEN . . . 448 HERO GIRL FOOL V   3
THAT EVEN LOVERS DROWN. . . . . 453 MERMAID   6
EVEN FROM THAT DELIGHT MEMORY TREASURES SO, . . . 459 FROM OEDIPUS   4
EVEN THOSE TRUTHS THAT WHEN MY BONES ARE DUST . . 467 HARUN RASHID   144
EVEN TO-DAY, AFTER SOME SEVEN YEARS . . . . . 468 HARUN RASHID   161
EVEN TODAY, AFTER SOME SEVEN YEARS . . . . . 468 HARUN RASHID V 161
HER CONFIDENCE IN MINE, OR EVEN LOSE . . . . . 469 HARUN RASHID   176
THAT EVEN CICERO . . . . 524 MAD AS MIST   16
HAD EVEN O'DUFFY--BUT I NAME NO MORE-- . . . . 543 PARN FUNERAL 2   9
BUT EVEN AT THE STARTING-POST, ALL SLEEK AND NEW, . . 619 BRONZE HEAD   15
EVEN THE WISEST MAN GROWS TENSE . . . . . . 638 BEN BULBEN   33
AND EVEN SHE SHALL NEVER HOLD . . . . . . 668 ISLE STAT II 3   50
EVEN FROM BOYHOOD, IN MY FATHER'S HOUSE, ... 683 SEEKER   48
I CANNOT EVEN CRAWL ALONG THE FLAGS . . . . . 701 MOSADA 3   58
OF BIRDS EVEN, LONGINGS FOR AERY . . . . . . 708 FAIRY PEDANT   26
NOT EVEN "I LONG TO SEE THY LONGING OVER," . . . 734 QUATRAIN APHOR   11
EVEN THE WANDERING ISLANDS OF THE GODS, ... 749 SHADOW WATER A   45
TO DROWN IN ITS OWN IMAGE? EVEN THAT SLEEP . . . 765 SHADOW WATER A   364
A MEMORY, EVEN TO THE DEAD, ... 791 REPRISALS   8
EVENING
AT EVENING IN THEIR RAINLESS LANDS." . . . .   7 OISIN 1   70
AT EVENING IN THEIR RAINLESS LANDS. . . . . . .   7 OISIN 1 V   66
AT EVENING IN MY WESTERN DUN." . . . .   8 OISIN 1   79
AT EVENING ON THE GLIMMERING SANDS, ... 23 OISIN 1   347
UNDER THE GOLDEN EVENING LIGHT, ... 25 OISIN 1   385
OF LANGUID EVENING THAT ENTWINED US. . . . . . 25 OISIN 1 V 385A
HIS SHADOW ALONG IN THE EVENING BLAZE, ... 27 OISIN 1 V 409
SO MUCH REMAINED THAT ON THE EVENING STAR . . . 32 OISIN 2 V   48
HOW THE SLOW, BLUE-EYED OXEN OF FINN LOW SADLY AT EVENING   52 OISIN 3   84
    TIDE.
AND LAID YOU ON THE GATES OF EVENING WITH HIS QUIET HANDS. 72 ANASHU VIJAYA   22
VIJAYA, I HAVE BROUGHT MY EVENING RICE: . . . . 72 ANASHU VIJAYA   23
AND LAID YE ON THE GATES OF EVENING WITH HIS QUIET HANDS. 72 ANASHU VIJAYA V 22
MY SPIRIT ROCKED IN EVENING LIGHT, THE RUSHES ROUND MY   76 INDIAN ON GOD   2
    KNEES,
THE LITTLE WAVES THAT WALKED IN EVENING WHITENESS, . . 81 EPHEMERA V   24C
ERE FALL OF EVENING, MY MAILED HOST, ... 83 MAD KING GOLL V   19
I DREW AT EVENING MY MAILED MEN, ... 83 MAD KING GOLL V   19
IN ALL HIS EVENING VAPOURS ROLLED-- . . . . . 86 MAD KING GOLL V   71
HIS EVENING FIRE AMID THE LEAFY SHADE. . . . . 109 CUCHULAIN SEA   48
WHILE DAY ITS BURDEN ON TO EVENING BORE, ... 110 CUCHULAIN SEA   70
AND EVENING FULL OF THE LINNET'S WINGS. . . . . 117 ISLE INNISFREE   8
AND EVENING FULL OF THE LINNETS' WINGS. . . . . 117 ISLE INNISFREE V   8
AND SANG WHAT GOLD MORNING OR EVENING SHEDS . . . 126 DREAM OF FAERY   7
AT HUSH OF EVENING TILL GOD BURNS TIME . . . . 164 PERFECT BEAUTY V   7
AT HUSH OF EVENING TILL GOD BURN TIME . . . . 164 PERFECT BEAUTY V   7
AMONG THE EVENING SHADOWS, ... 341 SHEP GOATHERD   71
LAST EVENING? THAT I, WHO HAD SAT . . . . . 349 HAWK   15
EVENING AND MORNING, THE STEEP STREET OF URBINO . . 352 PEOPLE   12
EVENING AND MORN, THE STEEP STREET OF URBINO . . . 352 PEOPLE V   12
WHEN EVENING STIRS THE JASMINE BOUGH, AND YET . . . 463 HARUN RASHID   53
WHEN EVENING STIRS THE JASMINE, AND YET . . . . 463 HARUN RASHID V   53
THE LIGHT OF EVENING, LISSADELL, ... 475 EVA GORE-BOOTH   1
OFTEN AT EVENING WHEN A BOY . . . . 494 AT ALGECIRAS   7
AN EVENING CHILL UPON THE AIR, ... 494 AT ALGECIRAS   14
FROM MORN THE TWAIN UNTIL THE EVENING PALES . . . 651 ISLE STAT I 1   161
OF EVENING AND GLAD SILENCE DWELLETH AYE, . . . 653 ISLE STAT I 2   37
THE WIND AT EVENING WHEN THE SUN GOES DOWN . . . 653 ISLE STAT I 2   50
THE EVENING GLEAMS ARE GREEN AND GOLD AND RED . . 656 ISLE STAT I 3   22
AWAY FROM ME WHERE MISTS OF EVENING DRINK . . . 663 ISLE STAT II 2   40
'TWAS EVENING, AND THE CRICKET NATION SANG . . . 690 MOSADA 1   18
RETURNS THAT SOLDIER IN THE EVENING RAYS . . . . 711 FERENCZ RENYI   49
TIME GOES. THE FLAKED FIRE OF EVENING CRAWLS . . . 712 FERENCZ RENYI   70
TIME GOES. THE FLICKED FIRE OF EVENING CRAWLS . . 712 FERENCZ RENYI V 70
HIGHER AND HIGHER GOLD WITH EVENING LIGHT: . . . 714 FERENCZ RENYI   113
A SUMMER EVENING . . . . 736 SUMMER EVENING   T
AN EVENING PRESENCE FILLS THE PLACE. . . . . . 736 SUMMER EVENING   16
EVENING'S
MY SPIRIT ROCKED IN EVENING'S HUSH, THE RUSHES ROUND MY   76 INDIAN ON GOD V   2
    KNEES,
EVENINGS
SHALL FEED. I SHALL NOT IN THE EVENINGS HEAR . . . . 674 ISLE STAT II 3 220
EVENT
"ALTHOUGH THE EVENT WAS LONG IN DOUBT, ... 273 GREY ROCK   67
TOLD OF A HARSH REPROOF, OR TRIVIAL EVENT . . . . 443 SCHOOL CHILDR   11
EVERY EVENT IN ACTION OR IN THOUGHT: . . . . . 479 SELF AND SOUL   66

EVENT   (CONTINUED)
  WHY DO I HATE MAN, WOMAN OR EVENT? . . . .   558 RIBH CHRISTIAN   7
EVENTS
  WHERE I AM RID OF LIFE--THE EVENTS OF THE WORLD-- . . . 227 SHADOW WATER B   121
EVER
  ROSE EVER OUT OF THE WARM SEA. . . . .   13 OISIN 1   172
  AND, AS THE SUN SANK EVER LOWER, ...   13 OISIN 1   V 170A
  ROSE EVER FROM THE SEA'S WARM FLOOR, ...   13 OISIN 1   V 172
  AND EVER NEARER, NEARER GREW. . . . .   15 OISIN 1   200
  THE EVER SUMMERED SOLITUDES, ...   21 OISIN 1   V 321
  NOR EVER CHANGE OR FEEL THE CLUTCHES . . . .   23 OISIN 1   V 341A
  SOME WANDERED EVER HAND IN HAND. . . . .   25 OISIN 1   389
  FOR NO MAN'S CRY SHALL EVER MOUNT SO FAR. . . . .   36 OISIN 2   108
  NOR NO MAN'S CRY SHALL EVER MOUNT SO FAR. . . . .   36 OISIN 2   V 108
  HOPELESS FOR EVER, ANCIENT OISIN KNOWS, ...   42 OISIN 2   202
  HOPELESS FOR EVER, THEY ALONE SHALL SEEK . . . . .   42 OISIN 2   200
  AND LIGHTNING FLASH FOR EVER? CEASE AND HEAR. . . .   42 OISIN 2   V 207
  WHERE EVER IS MURMUROUS DROPPING, OLD SILENCE AND THAT
    ONE SOUND.   56 OISIN 3   138
  BUT NAUGHT THEY HEARD, FOR THEY ARE EVER LISTENING, . . . 68 SAD SHEPHERD   V 15
  BY MIGHTY BRAHMA'S EVER RUSTLING ROBE, ...   71 ANASHU VIJAYA   V 14
  AND, EVER PACING ON THE VERGE OF THINGS, ...   73 ANASHU VIJAYA   54
  SHOOT ON HIM SHAFTS OF QUIETNESS, THAT HE MAY EVER KEEP   75 ANASHU VIJAYA 81
  AND WANDER EVER WITH WOVEN HANDS, ...   78 INDIAN TO LOVE   7
  THE COLD WET WINDS EVER BLOWING, ...   119 PITY OF LOVE   5
  AND THE COLD WET WINDS EVER BLOWING, ...   119 PITY OF LOVE   7
  DRIVEN BY A STORM THAT EVER GRIEVES. . . . .   135 TWO TREES   V 28
  MAN EVER JOURNEYS ON WITH THEM . . . .   139 TO IRELAND   29
  DEW EVER SHINING AND TWILIGHT GREY. . . . .   148 INTO TWILIGHT   6
  AND TIME AND THE WORLD ARE EVER IN FLIGHT. . . . .   148 INTO TWILIGHT   14
  NO WAITING-MAID SHOULD EVER SPREAD . . . .   194 BAILE AILLINN   120
  NO WAITING MAID SHOULD EVER SPREAD . . . .   194 BAILE AILLINN   V 120
  ONE THAT IS EVER KIND SAID YESTERDAY. . . . . . .   199 FOLLY COMFORT   1
  WOULD NONE HAD EVER LOVED BUT YOU AND I. . . . . .   210 RAGGED WOOD   4
  O THAT NONE EVER LOVED BUT YOU AND I. . . . . . .   210 RAGGED WOOD   V   4
  O THAT NONE EVER LOVED BUT YOU AND I. . . . . . .   211 RAGGED WOOD   8
  NO ONE HAS EVER LOVED BUT YOU AND I. . . . .   211 RAGGED WOOD   12
  OF THOSE THAT ARE ALIVE FOR EVER AND EVER. . . . .   223 SHADOW WATER B   35
  OF THOSE THAT ARE ALIVE FOR EVER AND EVER. . . . .   223 SHADOW WATER B   35
  MORE RICHES THAN THEY EVER HOPED TO FIND? . . . .   226 SHADOW WATER B   94
  HAS EVER COME BUT THOSE MAN-HEADED BIRDS. . . . .   226 SHADOW WATER B   99
  AND AS SOON FINISHED. ALL THAT EVER LOVED . . . .   229 SHADOW WATER B   151
  THAT I WOULD LOOK UPON FOR EVER? MY GRIEF. . . . .   244 SHADOW WATER B   462
  WHO CANNOT PUT ME FROM HIS SIGHT FOR EVER. . . . .   251 SHADOW WATER B   601
  WE ARE ALONE FOR EVER, AND I LAUGH, ...   251 SHADOW WATER B   602
  SHALL BE ALONE FOR EVER. WE TWO--THIS CROWN-- . .   251 SHADOW WATER B   605
  BUT WAS THERE EVER DOG THAT PRAISED HIS FLEAS? . .   262 TO A POET   4
  COULD EVER COME BETWEEN . . . .   315 FRIENDS   8
  THE GENTLENESS NONE THERE HAD EVER KNOWN. . . . .   418 ANCEST HOUSES   21
  WHAT EVER MISCHIEF SEEMED . . . .   431 NINETEEN 19   V 85
  IF DAYLIGHT EVER VISIT WHERE, ...   446 COLONUS PRAISE   4
  THINK WHEN I CHOOSE A BRIDE I CHOOSE FOR EVER. . .   464 HARUN RASHID   80
  NO MAN HAS EVER LIVED THAT HAD ENOUGH . . . . . .   500 VACILLATION   25
  IF EVER LOVER'S LONELINESS . . . .   518 LOVES LONENESS   3
  WHY SHOULD THEY THINK THAT ARE FOR EVER YOUNG? . .   537 HER VISION   21
  "FOR EVER AND FOR EVER". THEN AWAKE . . . .   560 WHENCE COME   3
  "FOR EVER AND FOR EVER". THEN AWAKE . . . .   560 WHENCE COME   3
  DID EVER MEN HEAR SUCH A SONG? . . . .   570 THREE BUSHES   45
  DID EVER MAN RIDE SUCH A RACE? . . . .   570 THREE BUSHES   47
  NOR EVER MADE AN IRON RED . . . .   606 SONGS BURDEN 1   14
  EVER RINGING, RINGING, RINGING, ...   647 ISLE STAT I 1   68
  EVER DIETH, DIETH, DIETH, ...   648 ISLE STAT I 1   88
  AND THERE TO ITS OWN HEART FOR EVER MOANS. . . . .   650 ISLE STAT I 1   131
  JOY'S BROTHER, FEAR, DWELLS EVER IN EACH BREAST-- .   651 ISLE STAT I 1   155
  HOW THEY WHO SEEK ARE EVER DOOMED TO FAIL. . . . .   653 ISLE STAT I 2   41
  ARE CHANGED FOR EVER INTO MOON-WHITE STONE. . . .   653 ISLE STAT I 2   43
  SAD FAERY TONES. 'TIS THUS THEY EVER SEEM, ...   654 ISLE STAT I 2   58
  OR HER EVER BURNING EYES, ...   658 ISLE STAT I 3   85
  THAT OF OLD WERT MOVING EVER, ...   658 ISLE STAT I 3   91
  MORE GRIEF IS MINE. NO MAN SHALL EVER STOOP . . .   661 ISLE STAT II 1   62
  HAD DRIVEN HER FORTH, FOR EVER MORE . . . .   668 ISLE STAT II 3   56
  I' FAITH THOU EVER WAST A WORDY SPIRIT. . . . . .   673 ISLE STAT II 3   175
  YET EVER MORE, THROUGH ALL THY DAYS OF RUTH, . . .   674 ISLE STAT II 3   206
  FOR EVER FOAM AND FRET. . . . .   680 LOVE AND DEATH   4
  THE BANKS ARE WORN FOR EVER . . . .   680 LOVE AND DEATH   9
  NO SHEPHERD FOOT HAS EVER DARED ITS DEPTHS. . . .   682 SEEKER   32
  THAT FROM THE FIRE IS EVER POURING UP . . . . . .   683 SEEKER   37
  THROUGH MISERIES UNHUMAN EVER ON . . . .   684 SEEKER   59
  THROUGH HIS SAD SOUL FOR EVER OLD AND YOUNG, . . .   687 TWO TITANS   25
  FOR EVER ROUND THY WAKING AND THY SLEEP . . . . .   688 TWO TITANS   57
  RE-SHINING IN HIS EYES. SO EVER MOVES . . . . . .   689 NETTLESHIP   12
  FROM WASTE SEAS CROSS'D, YET EVER GARRULOUS) . . .   690 MOSADA 1   9
  EVER MORE TO SPEAK A WORD . . . .   697 MOSADA 2   32
  IT IS THE DARKEST EVE I EVER KNEW. . . . .   702 MOSADA 3   93
  FLASHING AND FLICKERING, WITH EVER UNDULANT WING, . . . 710 FERENCZ RENYI V 19
  OF TRAITOR EVER MORE IS ON OUR NAME." . . . . . .   712 FERENCZ RENYI   V 61
  WITH QUIET SHADE ITS EVER DEWY-PLOT. . . . .   714 FERENCZ RENYI   109
  WITH QUIET SHADE ITS EVER DEWY SPOT. . . . .   714 FERENCZ RENYI   V 109
  WITH QUIET SHADE ITS EVER DEWY PLOT. . . . .   714 FERENCZ RENYI   V 109
  ALL THE DROWNED THAT EVER WERE DROWNED FROM THAT VILLAGE
    BY THE SEA.   719 PHANTOM SHIP   20

247

EVER   (CONTINUED)
    FOR AS THINGS WERE SO SHALL THINGS EVER BE. • • • • •   724 KANVA ON SELF   20.
    "OF OUR GREAT QUEEN IS EVER HEARD • • • • • • •   729 PRIEST FAIRY   41
    AND HER OLD WIND THAT NO MIRTH EVER HAD, • • • • •   738 YOU ARE SAD   7
    I PRAY THAT I EVER BE WEAVING • • • • • • • •   743 WISDOM DREAMS   1
    THE WINDS AND WATERS TO BE YOUR HOME FOR EVER: • • •   762 SHADOW WATER A   282
    THE PALE HOUND AND THE DEER WANDER FOR EVER • • • •   764 SHADOW WATER A   330
    WHEN EVER I REMAKE A SONG, • • • • • • • • •   778 FRIENDS WRONG   2
EVEREST
    HERMITS UPON MOUNT MERU OR EVEREST, • • • • • • •   563 MERU   9
EVERLASTING
    THE EVERLASTING VOICES • • • • • • • • • •   141 EVERLAST VOICE   T
    EVERLASTING VOICES • • • • • • • • • • • •   141 EVERLAST VOICE V   T
    O SWEET EVERLASTING VOICES, BE STILL: • • • • • •   141 EVERLAST VOICE   1
    O SWEET EVERLASTING VOICES, BE STILL. • • • • • •   141 EVERLAST VOICE   8
    THE EVERLASTING TAPER LIGHTS THE GLOOM: • • • • • •   311 MOUNTAIN TOMB   10
EVER-LAUGHING
    THAT THE SHAPE-CHANGERS, THE EVER-LAUGHING ONES, • • •   249 SHADOW WATER B   566
EVER-LIVING
    OF THE EVER-LIVING HALF SO DANGEROUS • • • • • •   224 SHADOW WATER B   46
    WE HAVE FALLEN IN THE DREAMS THE EVER-LIVING • • • •   228 SHADOW WATER B   131
    IT MAY BE THAT THE EVER-LIVING KNOW IT-- • • • • •   229 SHADOW WATER B   164
    WITH THE EVER-LIVING. WHAT IF HE SPEAK THE TRUTH, • • •   229 SHADOW WATER B   170
    ONE OF THE EVER-LIVING, AS I THINK-- • • • • • •   231 SHADOW WATER B   210
    THE EVER-LIVING HAVE KEPT MY BARGAIN FOR ME, • • • •   232 SHADOW WATER B   223
    WITHHOLDS THEM NOW? HAVE THE EVER-LIVING ONES • • • •   234 SHADOW WATER B   269
    THE EVER-LIVING HOLD US. DO WHAT YOU WILL, • • • •   238 SHADOW WATER B   359
    THAT WERE CLEAR MESSAGES FROM THE EVER-LIVING, • • • •   243 SHADOW WATER B   442
    YOU KNOW THE COUNSELS OF THE EVER-LIVING, • • • • •   244 SHADOW WATER B   450
    YOU KNOW THE COUNCILS OF THE EVER-LIVING, • • • • •   244 SHADOW WATER B V   450
    THE EVER-LIVING HAVE MADE YOU MAD: BUT NO, • • • • •   248 SHADOW WATER B   546
EVER-LONGING
    TO THE EVER-LONGING AND MOURNFUL SPIRIT SAY. • • • • •   734 QUATRAIN APHOR   12
EVERMORE
    HAD DRIVEN HER FORTH, FOR EVERMORE • • • • • • •   668 ISLE STAT II 3 V   56
    YET EVERMORE, THROUGH ALL THY DAYS OF RUTH, • • • • •   674 ISLE STAT II 3 V   206
    THAT ALL MEN EVERMORE MAY HUMBLY BOW • • • • •   688 TWO TITANS   49
    OF TRAITOR EVERMORE IS ON OUR NAME." • • • • • •   712 FERENCZ RENYI   61
EVER-MOVING
    FROM THE EVER-MOVING PINIONS • • • • • • • •   667 ISLE STAT II 3   28
EVER-RUSTLING
    BY MIGHTY BRAHMA'S EVER-RUSTLING ROBE, • • • • • •   71 ANASHU VIJAYA   14
    STAND YOU. BY BRAHMA'S EVER-RUSTLING ROBE, • • • • •   71 ANASHU VIJAYA V   14
EVER-SINGING
    AND THE LOUD SONG OF THE EVER-SINGING LEAVES • • • • •   120 SORROW OF LOVE V   3
EVER-SUMMERED
    THE EVER-SUMMERED SOLITUDES: • • • • • • • • •   21 OISIN 1   321
EVER-TREMBLING
    PRESSED ON THE EVER-TREMBLING ROOF • • • • • • •   25 OISIN 1   V 383
EVER-UNDULANT
    FLASHING AND FLICKERING WITH EVER-UNDULANT WING • • • •   710 FERENCZ RENYI   19
EVER-WINDING
    THE EVER-WINDING WAKEFUL SEA, • • • • • • • • •   22 OISIN 1   V 338
EVERY
    "AND EVERY HERO DROOP HIS HEAD? • • • • • • • •   4 OISIN 1   33
    ROUND EVERY BRANCH THE SONG-BIRDS FLEW, • • • • • •   14 OISIN 1   180
    AND KNELT THERE, EVERY GIRL AND MAN, • • • • • • •   15 OISIN 1   214
    AND KNELT THEM, EVERY MAID AND MAN, • • • • • • •   15 OISIN 1   V 214
    AND TANGLED CREEPERS EVERY HOUR • • • • • • • •   16 OISIN 1   223
    WHERE TANGLING CREEPERS EVERY HOUR • • • • • • •   16 OISIN 1   V 223
    THEY HUSHED THEM, EVERY MAN AND MAID. • • • • • •   17 OISIN 1   V 235
    AROSE FROM EVERY MAID AND BOY, • • • • • • • •   20 OISIN 1   V 289
    IN EVERY BRAIN A WIZARD GLOW. • • • • • • • •   20 OISIN 1   V 291A
    OF EVERY FOAMDROP ON ITS MISTY WAY. • • • • • • •   32 OISIN 2   45
    HE TOLD OF EVERY FROTH-DROP HISSING, FLYING. • • • • •   32 OISIN 2   V   45
    AND SING FROM SHORE TO SHORE, AND EVERY YEAR • • • • •   81 EPHEMERA   V 24G
    AND EVERY ANCIENT OLLAVE SAID, • • • • • • • •   82 MAD KING GOLL   9
    AND MINE WAS EVERY TROPHIED WALL, • • • • • • •   82 MAD KING GOLL V   4
    AND EVERY WHISPERING DRUID SAID, • • • • • • •   82 MAD KING GOLL V   9
    AND EVERY MUMBLING OLD MAN SAID, • • • • • • •   82 MAD KING GOLL V   9
    AND EVERY WHISPERING OLD MAN SAID, • • • • • • •   82 MAD KING GOLL V   9
    AND TOADS AND EVERY OUTLAWED THING • • • • • • •   85 MAD KING GOLL V   61
    IN EVERY COMPANY • • • • • • • • • • • •   131 OLD PENSIONER   4
    I HAD A CHAIR AT EVERY HEARTH, • • • • • • • •   131 OLD PENSIONER V   1
    AND BIND UP EVERY WANDERING TRESS: • • • • • • •   157 BELOVED RHYMES   2
    BUT WHERE IT COULD SEE HER EVERY DAY. • • • • • •   191 BAILE AILLINN   55
    WHO PEERED ABOUT ON EVERY SIDE: • • • • • • •   193 BAILE AILLINN V   112
    HAS HATED EVERY MAN THAT'S NOT IN LOVE, • • • • • •   224 SHADOW WATER B   51
    DYING AT EVERY MOMENT IN THE WORLD, • • • • • • •   226 SHADOW WATER B   90
    HAS BEAUTIFUL WOMEN TO PLEASE EVERY MAN. • • • • • •   228 SHADOW WATER B   144
    THAT EVERY MAN SHOULD CARRY HIS OWN SOUL • • • • •   235 SHADOW WATER B   299
    I AM A WOMAN, I DIE AT EVERY BREATH. • • • • • • •   250 SHADOW WATER B   583
    THAT EVERY YEAR I HAVE CRIED, "AT LENGTH • • • • •   256 WORDS   9
    ON THE DAY'S WAR WITH EVERY KNAVE AND DOLT, • • • • •   260 FASC DIFFICULT   10
    BUT THEREON EVERY GOD STOOD UP • • • • • • •   275 GREY ROCK   116
    ITS TERROR GROWING WILDER AT EVERY FOOT-FALL, • • • • •   279 TWO KINGS   V   45D
    ITS TERROR GROWING WILDER AT EVERY FOOTFALL • • • • •   279 TWO KINGS   V   45D
    AND WITH HIM HAVE FOUND EVERY HAPPINESS • • • • • •   284 TWO KINGS   174
    THE GREY WING UPON EVERY TIDE: • • • • • • • •   290 SEPTEMBER 1913   18
    HAS MADDENED EVERY MOTHER'S SON": • • • • • • •   290 SEPTEMBER 1913   29
    ON EVERY CROWDED STREET TO STARE • • • • • • •   294 HATED PLAYBOY   3

EVERY   (CONTINUED)

	PAGE	TITLE	LINE
MY LIFE OF EVERY PLEASANT THOUGHT	307	HOUR DAWN	110
AND EVERY COMFORTABLE THING,	307	HOUR DAWN	111
BELIEVING EVERY WORD I SAID,	314	MEMORY YOUTH	8
SO WILD THAT EVERY CASUAL THOUGHT OF THAT AND THIS	316	COLD HEAVEN	4
WITH EVERY SORT OF COMPANY,	335	YOUNG BEAUTY	2
WITH EVERY JACK AND JILL?	335	YOUNG BEAUTY	3
AND EVERY MAN AND MAID AND BOY	337	TOM OROUGHLEY	2
I HAD DRIVEN EVERY RHYME INTO ITS PLACE	339	SHEP GOATHERD	14
HE THAT WAS BEST IN EVERY COUNTRY SPORT	339	SHEP GOATHERD	17
AND EVERY COUNTRY CRAFT, AND OF US ALL	339	SHEP GOATHERD	18
"HE GROWS YOUNGER EVERY SECOND	342	SHEP GOATHERD	89
WHERE EVERY DAY MY FOOTFALL SHOULD HAVE LIT	352	PEOPLE	8
THE YOUNG MEN EVERY NIGHT APPLAUD THEIR GABY'S LAUGHING EYE,	353	HIS PHOENIX	9
BECAUSE THE PRIEST MUST HAVE LIKE EVERY DOG HIS DAY	364	DOLLS FACES	10
THAT EVERY MORNING ROSE AGAIN	385	ROBARTES DANCE	7
WILL BANISH EVERY THOUGHT, UNLESS	387	ROBARTES DANCE	48
FOR EVERY NERVE, AND TESTS A LOVER	388	SOLOMON WITCH	22
FOR EVERY NERVE: LOVER TESTS LOVER	388	SOLOMON WITCH V	22
AND THE MOON IS WILDER EVERY MINUTE.	389	SOLOMON WITCH	43
AND SPREAD ON EVERY SIDE,	396	ROSE TREE	10
THEY HAVE LOUD MUSIC, HOPE EVERY DAY RENEWED	398	LEADERS CROWD	11
THAT EVERY NATURAL VICTORY	401	DEMON BEAST	34
BARTER THAT HORN AND EVERY GOOD	405	FOR DAUGHTER	62
SHE CAN, THOUGH EVERY FACE SHOULD SCOWL	405	FOR DAUGHTER	70
AND EVERY WINDY QUARTER HOWL	405	FOR DAUGHTER	71
OR EVERY BELLOWS BURST, BE HAPPY STILL.	405	FOR DAUGHTER	72
FOR EVERY TATTER IN ITS MORTAL DRESS,	407	SAIL BYZANTIUM	12
WHEN EVERY SILVER CANDLESTICK OR SCONCE	410	TOWER	26
THAT MOST RESPECTED LADY'S EVERY WISH,	410	TOWER	29
OLD LECHER WITH A LOVE ON EVERY WIND,	413	TOWER	105
RECKONED UP EVERY UNFOREKNOWN, UNSEEING	413	TOWER	109
OF EVERY BRILLIANT EYE	416	TOWER	190
AND CHILDHOOD A DELIGHT FOR EVERY SENSE,	418	ANCEST HOUSES	31
OF EVERY WIND THAT BLOWS:	419	MY HOUSE	7
FROM NOTHING EVERY DAY, AND TEACH	436	FOR MY SON	18
SOMETHING OF EVERY PADDLER'S HERITAGE--	444	SCHOOL CHILDR	21
EVERY COLONUS LAD OR LASS DISCOURSES	447	COLONUS PRAISE	29
FOR EVERY HAND IS LUNATIC	451	FIRST LOVE	11
LIKE MEN WHO LIVE BY HABIT. EVERY DAY	463	HARUN RASHID	56
EVERY PHILOSOPHER SHOULD PRAISE THAT LOVE.	465	HARUN RASHID	97
WHEN MAYBE THRICE IN EVERY MOON HER MOUTH	468	HARUN RASHID	162
THAT EVERY GIFT AND EVERY WORD OF PRAISE	469	HARUN RASHID	172
THAT EVERY GIFT AND EVERY WORD OF PRAISE	469	HARUN RASHID	172
FOR EVERY SEPARATE QUALITY OF LOVE:	469	HARUN RASHID V	189A
FROM EVERY QUARTER OF THE WORLD, CAN STAY	471	ALL SOUL NIGHT	12
FIX EVERY WANDERING THOUGHT UPON	477	SELF AND SOUL	6
EVERY EVENT IN ACTION OR IN THOUGHT:	479	SELF AND SOUL	66
COUNT EVERY SIN OF ACTION OR OF THOUGHT:	479	SELF AND SOUL V	66
IS EVERY MODERN NATION LIKE THE TOWER,	482	BLOOD AND MOON	47
IS EVERY NATION LIKE THE TOWER	482	BLOOD AND MOON V	47
WHERE EVERY FOOT OBEYED HER GLANCE!	488	CRAZED MOON	11
AND EVERY BRIDE'S AMBITION SATISFIED.	491	COOLE BALLYLEE	37
EVERY NIGHT IN BED,	495	MOHINI CHATTER	4
EVERY COMMON WOMAN KNOWS,	499	MOTHER OF GOD	7
TEST EVERY WORK OF INTELLECT OR FAITH,	501	VACILLATION	30
EVERY THING THAT HAS LIVED	504	QUARREL IN AGE V	9
ADORNING EVERY SECRET TRACK	509	JANE REPROVED	9
EVERY TOUCH THEY GIVE,	517	HER ANXIETY	10
DOWN EVERY WITHERED FINGER FROM THE TOP:	537	HER VISION	11
LIFT, EVERY MOTHER'S SON,	548	TO SAME TUNE 3 V	15
FROM EVERY THOUGHT OF GOD MANKIND HAS HAD.	558	RIBH CHRISTIAN	15
EVERY DISCOLORATION OF THE STONE,	567	LAPIS LAZULI	43
EVERY ACCIDENTAL CRACK OR DENT,	567	LAPIS LAZULI	44
WITH EVERY NOBLE BEAST.	573	LADYS 2ND SONG	18
WITH EVERY NOBLE BREAST.	573	LADYS 2ND SONG V	18
EVERY MAN THAT SINGS A SONG	586	PARNELLITES	19
AND UNDER EVERY DANCER	592	DRUNK SOBRIETY	11
THROW IT IN EVERY PART."	596	COLONEL MARTIN	53
THOUGH RICH ON EVERY SHORE	606	SONGS BURDEN 1	11
WHEN EVERY SUNDAY AFTERNOON	607	SONGS BURDEN 2	19
PRAISE EVERY MAN THAT CAME AGAIN,	608	SONGS BURDEN 3	7
PRAISE EVERY MAN THAT FELL.	608	SONGS BURDEN 3	8
THAT IN EVERY GENERATION	608	SONGS BURDEN 3	25
HIS SLEUTH-HOUNDS FOLLOW EVERY FAERY THING.	675	ISLE STAT II 3	244
IN EVERY DANCE, BY CHILDREN SOUGHT. "ACCURST,	709	FERENCZ RENYI	12
AND EVERY FLOWER ABOVE ITS SHADOW SITS.	712	FERENCZ RENYI	73
AND EVERY FLOWER ABOVE A SHADOW SITS.	712	FERENCZ RENYI V	73
SUCH WAR PLOTS, PEACE PLOTS, LOVE PLOTS--EVERY SIDE:	722	WITCH VIVIEN	66
BENDING HUMBLY EVERY KNEE,	726	LOVERS QUARREL	14
TEASING EVERY WILFUL MAID.	727	LOVERS QUARREL	28
"EVERY SUMMER WILT THOU SEE	730	PRIEST FAIRY	55
HUSH! HUSH! HUSH! ON EVERY LIP	732	STREET DANCERS	18
SHE PRAYS FOR EVERY FALLING TEAR	735	IN CHURCH	3
A PRAYER FOR EVERY FALLING TEAR	736	IN CHURCH	15
I SWEAR IT. LET EVERY MAN DRAW OUT HIS SWORD.	758	SHADOW WATER A	230
BUT EVERY BUTTERFLY TO A FRIEND.	787	GARRET CELLAR	2

EVERYBODY

	PAGE	TITLE	LINE
FOR EVERYBODY KNOWS OR ELSE SHOULD KNOW	565	LAPIS LAZULI	4

		PAGE	TITLE	LINE

EVERYTHING
    EVERYTHING THAT'S SAD IS WICKED-- . . . . 20 OISIN 1 V 301
    EVERYTHING THAT FEARS TO-MORROW . . . . 20 OISIN 1 V 302
    FOR EVERYTHING THAT'S LOVELY IS . . . . 202 NEVER GIVE ALL 6
    "EVERYTHING ALTERS, ... 208 OLD MEN ADMIRE 2
    AND TAKE THE CAPTAIN'S SHARE OF EVERYTHING . . . . . . 225 SHADOW WATER B 73
    YOU'LL HAVE THE CAPTAIN'S SHARE OF EVERYTHING. . . . . 225 SHADOW WATER B V 67A
    FOR EVERYTHING IS GONE. COME HITHER, AIBRIC, ... 241 SHADOW WATER B 402
    HAVE WE NOT EVERYTHING THAT LIFE CAN GIVE . . . . . . 249 SHADOW WATER B 570
    TO MOCK AT EVERYTHING I LOVE . . . . 306 HOUR DAWN 83
    IMAGINED EVERYTHING. . . . . 419 MY HOUSE 17
    THOUGH YOU CAN FASHION EVERYTHING . . . . 436 FOR MY SON 17
    EVERYTHING THAT MAN ESTEEMS . . . . 438 SONGS PLAY 2 9
    TO CUT AND SEW, BE NEAT IN EVERYTHING . . . . 443 SCHOOL CHILDR 5
    WE ARE BLEST BY EVERYTHING, ... 479 SELF AND SOUL 71
    EVERYTHING WE LOOK UPON IS BLEST. . . . . 479 SELF AND SOUL 72
    EVERYTHING THAT IS NOT GOD CONSUMED WITH INTELLECTUAL FIRE. 481 BLOOD AND MOON 30
    LIKE EVERYTHING THAT HAS THE STAIN OF BLOOD, ... 482 BLOOD AND MOON 51
    AND EVERYTHING THAT YOUR OWN HANDS HAVE WROUGHT, . . . 501 VACILLATION 31
    WHEN EVERYTHING IS TOLD, ... 515 GIRLS SONG B 10
    THAT EVERYTHING OUTSIDE US IS . . . . 523 MAD AS MIST 5
    OF EVERYTHING THAT IS NOT MIND OR SENSE. . . . . . . 558 RIBH CHRISTIAN 6
    EVERYTHING HE WROTE WAS READ, ... 577 WHAT THEN 7
    CONTACT EVERYTHING ANTAEUS-LIKE GREW STRONG. . . . . 603 GALLERY REVIS 44
    EVERYTHING DOWN TO THAT SOLE TEST AGAIN, ... 603 GALLERY REVIS 46
    AND GIVEN EVERYTHING A WOMAN NEEDS, ... 609 IN TARAS HALLS 7
    EVERYTHING ELSE WITHERED AND MUMMY-DEAD. . . . . . . 618 BRONZE HEAD 3
    ON EVERYTHING SHE SAID. . . . . 621 JOHN KINSELLA 22
    WHERE EVERYTHING THAT MEETS THE EYE, ... 639 BEN BULBEN 56
    FORGIVE! FOR I HAVE TOLD THEM EVERYTHING. . . . . . 694 MOSADA 1 107
EVERYWHERE
    THEY HAVE SPOKEN AGAINST YOU EVERYWHERE, ... 166 EVIL OF BELOV 3
    AND EVERYWHERE THAT I COULD TURN . . . . 253 HIS DREAM V 3
    THE BLOOD-DIMMED TIDE IS LOOSED, AND EVERYWHERE . . . 402 SECOND COMING 5
    OLD MARBLE HEADS, OLD PICTURES EVERYWHERE! . . . . . 491 COOLE BALLYLEE 28
    I EVERYWHERE PROCLAIMED THERE IS . . . . 528 DANCER CRUACH V 1
    AND WANDERED MURMURING EVERYWHERE, "MY CHILD, MY CHILD!" 619 BRONZE HEAD 21
    THEY PASSED A-TIP-TOE EVERYWHERE, ... 667 ISLE STAT II 3 20
    THEY PASSED A-TIPTOE EVERYWHERE, ... 667 ISLE STAT II 3 V 20
EVE'S
    FOR MOTHER EVE'S WINNING . . . . 654 ISLE STAT I 2 61
    ALL THINGS ARE QUIET IN THE EVE'S WIDE EYE. . . . . 662 ISLE STAT II 2 6
EVE-SOOTHED
    EVE-SOOTHED IN SOME FAR LEAFY REST, ... 686 LIFE 10
EVIDENCE
    TO BE "SOME SORT OF EVIDENCE", ... 287 TO WEALTHY MAN 4
EVIL
    EQUAL TO GOOD OR EVIL CHANCE . . . . 24 OISIN 1 V 371
    WE GIVE THEM EVIL DREAMS, ... 88 STOLEN CHILD V 34
    UNDER THE FRUIT OF EVIL AND OF GOOD: . . . . 137 TO SOME I TALK 9
    AND THOUGHT NOT OF EVIL CHANCE, ... 145 HOST OF AIR 30
    THERE IS ENOUGH EVIL IN THE CRYING OF WIND. . . . . 155 REPROVE CURLEW 6
    AND BLOWING US EVIL AND GOOD: . . . . 158 TO HIS HEART V 4A
    HE THINKS OF THOSE WHO HAVE SPOKEN EVIL OF HIS BELOVED . 166 EVIL OF BELOV T
    AEDH THINKS OF THOSE WHO HAVE SPOKEN EVIL OF HIS BELOVED 166 EVIL OF BELOV V T
    SAVE BY AN EVIL CHANCE. . . . . 178 FIDDLER DOONEY 14
    WHAT MAN YOU HAVE LOST, WHAT EVIL YOU HAVE FOUND." . . 280 TWO KINGS 86
    "ALTHOUGH THE THING THAT YOU HAVE HID WERE EVIL, . . . 281 TWO KINGS 103
    AND EVIL MUST IT BE, IF DONE 'TWERE WORSE . . . . . 281 TWO KINGS 105
    EVIL OF THIS PLACE, ... 319 DOLLS 9
    AND CALLED THE PLEASURES EVIL . . . . 365 HER RACE 3
    KNOWING NOT EVIL AND GOOD: . . . . 382 VISION ROBART 12
    MAY WELL BE OF ALL EVIL CHANCES CHIEF. . . . . . . 405 FOR DAUGHTER 53
    OR WHAT WORSE EVIL COME— . . . . 416 TOWER 188
    ALL BREAK AND VANISH, AND EVIL GATHERS HEAD! . . . . 433 NINETEEN 19 117
    SPEAK NO EVIL OF THE SOUL, ... 573 LADYS 3RD SONG 3
    KNOW WORSE EVIL OF THE BODY! . . . . 573 LADYS 3RD SONG 6
    AND ALL SEEMS EVIL UNTIL I . . . . 632 MAN AND ECHO 17
    THAT CALLS. O EVIL STARRED! IT COMES ALONG . . . . 653 ISLE STAT I 2 49
    A DEAL OF EVIL AND OF CHANGE HATH CROSSED . . . . . 676 ISLE STAT II 3 273
    AND WOE-BEGONE. FOR THEM NO EVIL DAY! . . . . . . 677 ISLE STAT II 3 275
    THE PREACHER WATCHING FOR THE EVIL HOUR TO PASS, . . . 686 LIFE 3
    IN TRUTH, AN EVIL RACE. WHY STRIVE FOR HER, ... 696 MOSADA 2 9
    LIKE HAPPY THOUGHTS GROWN SAD IN EVIL DAYS. . . . . 703 MOSADA 3 116
    MY LOVE HATH MANY AN EVIL MOOD, ... 723 GIRLS SONG A 5
    AND EVIL STILL IS ACTION'S CHILD. . . . . 728 PRIEST FAIRY 14
    THE PREACHER WATCHING FOR THE EVIL HOUR TO PASS, . . . 734 QUATRAIN APHOR V 3
    AND EVIL FORTUNE HAVE OVERTHROWN SAILED HITHER . . . 757 SHADOW WATER A 196
EVIL-STARRED
    I, TOO, WILL FOLLOW FOR THIS EVIL-STARRED ONE'S SAKE . . 655 ISLE STAT I 2 84
EWES
    WHEN I HAVE SHUT THESE EWES AND THIS OLD RAM . . . . . 343 SHEP GOATHERD 113
EXACT
    BUT NOT THE EXACT LIKENESS, THE SIMPLICITY OF A CHILD, . . 354 HIS PHOENIX 28
EXACTING
    SUCH EXACTING BREATH, ... 517 HER ANXIETY 8
EXALT
    TO EXALT A LONELY MIND, ... 420 MY HOUSE 29
EXALTED
    THE MOST EXALTED LADY LOVED BY A MAN. . . . . 369 EGO DOMINUS 37

250

```
                                                     PAGE      TITLE            LINE
EXAMPLE
    FOR AN EXAMPLE STILL? . . . . . . . . . . . .    365 HER RACE               12
    HOMER IS MY EXAMPLE AND HIS UNCHRISTENED HEART. . . . .   503 VACILLATION    87
EXCEL
    YOUTH CAN EXCEL THEM IN ACCOMPLISHMENT, . . . . . . .    340 SHEP GOATHERD   47
EXCELLENCE
    BUT NOT THAT SELFSAME EXCELLENCE AGAIN. . . . . . . .    602 GALLERY REVIS   32
    BUT NOT THAT SELF-SAME EXCELLENCE AGAIN. . . . . . .     602 GALLERY REVIS V 32
EXCELLENT
    A SCENE WELL SET AND EXCELLENT COMPANY. . . . . . . .    489 COOLE PARK 29   16
EXCESS
    AND WHAT IF EXCESS OF LOVE . . . . . . . . . .          394 EASTER 1916      72
    WHERE EVEN LONGING DROWNS UNDER ITS OWN EXCESS: . . . .   426 PHANTOM HATRED 22
EXCHANGE
    I CAN EXCHANGE OPINION WITH ANY NEIGHBOURING MIND, . . .   450 OWEN AHERNE    9
EXCITE
    DO MOST EXCITE MY SPLEEN, . . . . . . . . . . .         599 STONE CROSS      18
EXCITED
    OR WHEN I GROW EXCITED WITH WINE, . . . . . . . .       357 DEEP-SWORN VOW    5
    IMAGINING IN EXCITED REVERIE . . . . . . . . .         403 FOR DAUGHTER      13
    EXCITED, PASSIONATE, FANTASTICAL . . . . . . . . .     409 TOWER              5
EXCITING
    ALTHOUGH YOUR LAST EXCITING YEAR . . . . . . . .       791 REPRISALS          5
EXCREMENT
    THE PLACE OF EXCREMENT: . . . . . . . . . . .          513 JANE TALK BISH    16
EXECUTIONER
    SOLDIER, ASSASSIN, EXECUTIONER, . . . . . . . .        482 BLOOD AND MOON    36
EXERCISE
    FOR AIR AND EXERCISE, . . . . . . . . . . . .          575 ACRE OF GRASS      3
    THERE'S BETTER EXERCISE . . . . . . . . . . .          600 THOSE IMAGES       3
EXHAUST
    EXHAUST HIS GLORY AND HIS MIGHT: . . . . . . . .       438 SONGS PLAY 2      14
EXILES
    AH, EXILES WANDERING OVER LANDS AND SEAS, . . . . .    129 BOOK STORIES       9
    AH, EXILES, WANDERING OVER MANY SEAS, . . . . . .     129 BOOK STORIES  V    9
    AH, EXILES, WANDERING OVER MANY LANDS, . . . . . .    130 BOOK STORIES  V   17
    AND CALL THOSE EXILES AS THEY WERE . . . . . .        290 SEPTEMBER 1913    26
EXIST
    A MAN WHO DOES NOT EXIST, . . . . . . . . . .          348 FISHERMAN         35
    SUCH DEVILISH THINGS EXIST, . . . . . . . . . .        436 FOR MY SON        11
    FEW DREAM THAT THEY EXIST, . . . . . . . . . .         436 FOR MY SON   V    11
EXISTENCE
    JOY AND LOVE ARE ONE EXISTENCE. . . . . . . . .        647 ISLE STAT I 1     71
    LOVE AND SORROW, ONE EXISTENCE, . . . . . . . .        647 ISLE STAT I 1     73
EXORBITANT
    THE EXORBITANT DREAMS OF BEGGARY, . . . . . . . .      296 THREE BEGGARS     39
EXPECTATION
    NO EXPECTATION FAILS THERE, . . . . . . . . . .        621 JOHN KINSELLA     29
EXPECTED
    THAT MORE EXPECTED THE IMPOSSIBLE-- . . . . . . .      409 TOWER              7
EXPENSE
    HE'D GONE TO GREAT EXPENSE . . . . . . . . . .         585 ORAHILLY          13
EXPLAINED
    THEREON EXPLAINED: "A COCKEREL . . . . . . . .         387 SOLOMON WITCH V    9
EXPLORE
    YOU, SHOULD HAND EXPLORE A THIGH, . . . . . . . .      573 LADYS 3RD SONG    11
EXPOUND
    I HEARD HER VOICE, "TURN THAT I MAY EXPOUND . . . . .   467 HARUN RASHID    132
EXPRESSION
    ARE BUT A NEW EXPRESSION OF HER BODY . . . . . . .     469 HARUN RASHID     185
EXQUISITE
    A FRAGILE, EXQUISITE, PALE SHELL, . . . . . . . .      784 WOMANS BEAUTY     16
EXTINGUISH
    EXTINGUISH THAT DELIGHT. . . . . . . . . . .           538 LAST CONFESS      24
EXTRAVAGANCE
    THE EXTRAVAGANCE OF SPRING: OR MOVE A HAND . . . .     466 HARUN RASHID     125
    THE EXTRAVAGANCE OF SPRING: OR CERTAIN TIMES . . . .   466 HARUN RASHID V   125
    AND CALL THOSE WORKS EXTRAVAGANCE OF BREATH . . . .    501 VACILLATION       32
EXTRAVAGANT
    HE WROTE OF ME IN THAT EXTRAVAGANT STYLE . . . . .     373 PHASES OF MOON    26
EXTREME
    A MOUTHFUL HELD THE EXTREME OF LIFE AND DEATH. . . . .   619 BRONZE HEAD     14
    A MOUTHFUL HOLD THE EXTREME OF LIFE AND DEATH. . . . .   619 BRONZE HEAD  V  14
EXTREMITIES
    BETWEEN EXTREMITIES . . . . . . . . . . . .           499 VACILLATION        1
EXTREMITY
    AND KNEW THAT SWEET EXTREMITY OF PRIDE . . . . . .     471 ALL SOUL NIGHT    22
EXUDE
    BODIES OF HOLY MEN AND WOMEN EXUDE . . . . . . .       483 OIL AND BLOOD      2
EXULT
    BE SECRET AND EXULT, . . . . . . . . . . . .          291 TO A FRIEND       14
EXULTANT
    AND SWANS WITH THEIR EXULTANT THROATS: . . . .         14 OISIN 1          192
    WARS SHADOWY, VAST, EXULTANT: FAERIES OF OLD . . . .    29 OISIN 2            9
    WARS SHADOWY, VAST, EXULTANT: FAIRY KINGS . . . . .    29 OISIN 2      V     9
    BUT ONLY EXULTANT FACES. NIAMH STOOD . . . . .        38 OISIN 2          136
    AND ALL THE EXULTANT LABOURS OF THE STRONG. . . . .    42 OISIN 2          195
    INNUMERABLE, SINGING, EXULTANT: THE CLAY UNDERNEATH THEM   61 OISIN 3       203
        SHALL PANT,
    WHAT THE EXULTANT HEART CALLS GOOD . . . . . . .      288 TO WEALTHY MAN    33
    WHEN THAT EXULTANT ANTHONY . . . . . . . . . .        401 DEMON BEAST       46
```

PAGE TITLE LINE

EXULTANT (CONTINUED)
A PASSION-DRIVEN EXULTANT MAN SINGS OUT . . . . . . 560 WHENCE COME 5
EXULTATION
THE EXULTATION OF THEIR STONE, THAT CRIED . . . . . 339 SHEP GOATHERD 25
WHERE IN WHITE EXULTATION . . . . 672 ISLE STAT II 3 164
EXULTING
THERE DWELT A GAY, EXULTING, GENTLE RACE . . . . . 127 DREAM OF FAERY 20
EYE
HAVE FACES ALIVE WITH SUCH BEAUTY BEEN KNOWN TO THE SALT
EYE OF MAN, 50 OISIN 3 51
ARE FACES ALIVE WITH SUCH BEAUTY MADE KNOWN TO THE SALT
EYE OF MAN, 50 OISIN 3 V 51
ARE FACES ALIVE WITH SUCH BEAUTY MADE KNOWN TO THE SOFT
EYE OF MAN, 50 OISIN 3 V 51
HELPLESS, MEN LIFTING THE LIDS OF HIS WEARY
AND DEATH-MAKING EYE. 53 OISIN 3 92
HELPLESS, MEN LIFTING THE LIDS OF HIS WEARY
AND DEATH-POURING EYE. 53 OISIN 3 V 92
THE RAINS ARE FROM HIS DRIPPING WING, THE MOONBEAMS FROM
HIS EYE. 76 INDIAN ON GOD 8
AND STILL, WITH PITYIN', SCORNIN' EYE, ... 96 MOLL MAGEE 39
IS BUT THE WINKING OF AN EYE; . . . . 139 TO IRELAND 36
ALTHOUGH HE HAD A SQUIRREL'S EYE. . . . . 190 BAILE AILLINN 30
OR, IT MAY BE, THE EYELIDS OF ONE EYE, ... 195 BAILE AILLINN 151
THAT HAD BUT THE ONE EYE. CAN NO BEWITCHMENT . . . 222 SHADOW WATER B 10
FOR THAT RED MOLL THAT HAD BUT THE ONE EYE. . . . . 222 SHADOW WATER B V 10
WITH AN INDIFFERENT EYE. . . . . 255 WOMAN HOMER 7
AND LOVE COMES IN AT THE EYE; . . . . 261 DRINKING SONG 2
TO BREED THE LIDLESS EYE THAT LOVES THE SUN? . . . 264 HOUSE SHAKEN 4
THE MAJESTY THAT SHUTS HIS BURNING EYE; . . . . . 265 THESE CLOUDS 2
THE MAJESTY THAT SHUTS HIS BURNING EYE; . . . . . 265 THESE CLOUDS 12
THEREON A YOUNG MAN MET HIS EYE, ... 274 GREY ROCK 85
AND STARED INTO THE SEA-GREEN EYE, AND SO . . . . 278 TWO KINGS 25
LOOK UP IN THE SUN'S EYE AND GIVE . . . . 288 TO WEALTHY MAN 32
THAT ON THE LONELY HEIGHT WHERE ALL ARE IN GOD'S EYE, 291 PAUDEEN 6
WITH THE PRIDE OF HIS EYE? . . . . 310 PEACOCK 3
FOR THE PRIDE OF HIS EYE. . . . . 311 PEACOCK 11
NOW AS AT ALL TIMES I CAN SEE IN THE MIND'S EYE, . . 318 MAGI 1
WORE IT IN THE WORLD'S EYE . . . . 320 COAT V 6
FOR ALL THINGS THE DELIGHTED EYE NOW SEES . . . . 326 ROBERT GREGORY 49
TILL THE YELLOW EYE HAS GROWN MILD, ... 349 HAWK 3
THE EYE OF THE MIND NOR KEEP MY TONGUE FROM SPEECH." 353 PEOPLE 34
THE YOUNG MEN EVERY NIGHT APPLAUD THEIR GABY'S LAUGHING
EYE, 353 HIS PHOENIX 9
WHAT IF A LAUGHING EYE . . . . 367 HER CHRIS TREE 10
MORE PLAIN TO THE MIND'S EYE THAN ANY FACE . . . . 368 EGO DOMINUS 21
CAUGHT UP IN CONTEMPLATION, THE MIND'S EYE . . . . 375 PHASES OF MOON 79
HAS A LEARNING IN HIS EYE . . . . 381 SONG OF FOOL 3
ON THE GREY ROCK OF CASHEL THE MIND'S EYE . . . . 382 VISION ROBART 1
ALTHOUGH I SAW IT ALL IN THE MIND'S EYE . . . . . 383 VISION ROBART 25
FOR WHAT BUT EYE AND EAR SILENCE THE MIND . . . . 384 VISION ROBART 41
IF I SHOULD RUB AN EYE, ... 384 VISION ROBART 52
THAT VIGOROUS THIGH, THAT DREAMING EYE? . . . . . 386 ROBARTES DANCE 23
FOR THOUGH LOVE HAS A SPIDER'S EYE . . . . 388 SOLOMON WITCH 19
A LOVER WITH A SPIDER'S EYE . . . . 388 SOLOMON WITCH V 19
BEAUTY TO MAKE A STRANGER'S EYE DISTRAUGHT, . . . 403 FOR DAUGHTER 18
IMAGINATION, NOR AN EAR AND EYE . . . . 409 TOWER 6
UNTIL IMAGINATION, EAR AND EYE, ... 409 TOWER 13
PLUNGE, LURED BY A SOFTENING EYE, ... 413 TOWER 110
WHEN THE SWAN MUST FIX HIS EYE . . . . 414 TOWER 140
OF EVERY BRILLIANT EYE . . . . 416 TOWER 190
MONSTROUS FAMILIAR IMAGES SWIM TO THE MIND'S EYE. . 426 PHANTOM HATRED 8
AT THE DROOPING OF AN EYE, ... 453 DEATH OF HARE 5
. . . NEVER TO HAVE LOOKED INTO THE EYE OF DAY; . . 459 FROM OEDIPUS 11
. . . AT ALL NOR LOOKED INTO THE EYE OF DAY, . . . 459 FROM OEDIPUS V 11
AND SO A HUNTER CARRIES IN THE EYE . . . . 463 HARUN RASHID 61
AND IF HER EYE SHOULD NOT GROW BRIGHT FOR MINE . . 464 HARUN RASHID 81
OR BRIGHTEN ONLY FOR SOME YOUNGER EYE, ... 464 HARUN RASHID 82
SO STRAINS TO LOOK BEYOND OUR LIFE, AN EYE . . . . 465 HARUN RASHID 87
SO LONGS TO LOOK BEYOND OUR LIFE, AN EYE . . . . . 465 HARUN RASHID V 87
BUT THINK THAT HIS MIND'S EYE, ... 471 ALL SOUL NIGHT 33
STOOD IN THE CIRCUIT OF A NEEDLE'S EYE. . . . . . 483 VERONIC NAPKIN 6
THAT NEVER LOOKED OUT OF THE EYE OF A SAINT . . . 486 SEVEN SAGES 12
OR OUT OF DRUNKARD'S EYE. ALL'S WHIGGERY NOW, . . 486 SEVEN SAGES 13
OR DRUNKARD'S EYE. ALL'S WHIGGERY NOW, ... 486 SEVEN SAGES V 13
OR OUT OF A DRUNKARD'S EYE. ALL'S WHIGGERY NOW, . 486 SEVEN SAGES V 13
GLANCES OF HER WANDERING EYE . . . . 487 CRAZED MOON 4
THE CORNERS OF THIS EYE . . . . 518 HIS CONFIDENCE 3
AND COCKED A MALICIOUS EYE, ... 527 AM OF IRELAND 25
STANDS IN GOD'S UNCHANGING EYE . . . . 529 TOM LUNATIC 16
HALF TURNED AND FIXED A GLAZING EYE ON MINE, . . . 537 HER VISION 26
COME, FIX UPON ME THAT ACCUSING EYE. . . . . . . 542 PARN FUNERAL 1 24
ROLLING A BLIND PEARL EYE, ... 552 SONGS REWRIT 2 2
A NEEDLE'S EYE . . . . 562 NEEDLES EYE T
CAME OUT OF A NEEDLE'S EYE; . . . . 562 NEEDLES EYE 2
FROM NEEDLE'S EYE STILL GOAD IT ON. . . . . 562 NEEDLES EYE 4
HUMAN, SUPERHUMAN, A BIRD'S ROUND EYE, ... 618 BRONZE HEAD 2
HUMAN, SUPER-HUMAN, A BIRD'S ROUND EYE, ... 618 BRONZE HEAD V 2
AS THOUGH A STERNER EYE LOOKED THROUGH HER EYE . . 619 BRONZE HEAD 23
AS THOUGH A STERNER EYE LOOKED THROUGH HER EYE . . 619 BRONZE HEAD 23

252

		PAGE	TITLE		LINE

EYE   (CONTINUED)
```
      PROCESSIONS THAT LACK HIGH STILTS HAVE NOTHING THAT CATCHES    622 HIGH TALK              1
         THE EYE.
      DISTRUSTFUL OF THAT POPULAR EYE   . . . . . . . .              624 APPARITIONS            5
      WITH AN EYE LIKE A HAWK, . . . . . . . . . .                   627 STATES HOLIDAY        32
      WHERE EVERYTHING THAT MEETS THE EYE, . . . . . .               639 BEN BULBEN            56
      CAST A COLD EYE . . . . . . . . . . . . .                      640 BEN BULBEN            92
      ALL THINGS ARE QUIET IN THE EYE'S WIDE EYE.  . . . . .         662 ISLE STAT II 2         6
      AND PART HIS FOAMING MOUTH WITH EAGER EYE--  . . . . .         688 TWO TITANS            46
      ABOVE, THE WOODS WHERE WITH THE SOFT MILD EYE  . . . .         710 FERENCZ RENYI         26
      STAGGERING WITH LANGUID EYE. . . . . . . .                     717 FAIRY DOCTOR       V  16
      AND HIS HAIR WAS AS DARK AS A PLOVER'S EYE.  . . . . .         729 PRIEST FAIRY          46
      PAST THE CAMEL'S DREAMING EYE. . . . . .                       733 STREET DANCERS        43
EYEBALLS
      THAT WITH DIM EYEBALLS STOOD ON EITHER SIDE.  . . . .           34 OISIN 2              75
      STOOD LONELY, WITH DIM EYEBALLS ON EACH SIDE.  . . . .          34 OISIN 2           V  74
      THEIR MOTIONLESS EYEBALLS OF SPIRITS . . . . .                  55 OISIN 3             121
      THAT OTHER'S MOONLIT EYEBALLS NEVER MOVED, . . . . .           383 VISION ROBART        33
      SOMETHING MADE THESE EYEBALLS WEARY . . . . .                  529 TOM LUNATIC          11
      DREAMER OF THE MIDDLE AGES.  EMPTY EYEBALLS KNEW  . . .        610 STATUES              20
      BENEATH THE FLAMING EYEBALLS OF THE NIGHT, . . . . .           723 KANVA ON SELF         4
EYE-BALLS
      DREAMER OF THE MIDDLE-AGES.  EMPTY EYE-BALLS KNEW  . . .       610 STATUES           V  20
EYED    SEE YELLOW-EYED ONE-EYED BLEAR-EYED GREY-EYED SOLEMN-EYED BLUE-EYED
        QUIET-EYED DEEP-EYED BRIGHT-EYED GRAVE-EYED RED-EYED WIDE-EYED
        OPEN-EYED DULL-EYED
      THE DRUID, GREY, WOOD NURTURED, QUIET EYED,  . . . . .         101 ROSE UPON ROOD    V   4
      CAER, HIS BLUE EYED DAUGHTER THAT I LOVE.  . . . . .           184 QUEEN MAEVE       V  96
EYELID
      UNDER AN ALIEN EYELID, FOR IT WAS MY CRAFT  . . . . .          284 TWO KINGS         V 156
      OR EYELID SHOT THE GLEAM . . . . . . . . .                     507 STREAM AND SUN       12
      HER LIMBS ARE DELICATE AS AN EYELID, . . . . . .               612 NEWS ORACLE          27
EYELIDS
      AH, TOUCH THEIR BLUE-VEINED EYELIDS IF THEY SLEEP, . . .        33 OISIN 2             61
      IF THEY STILL SLUMBER, TOUCH THEIR EYELIDS BLUE, . . .          33 OISIN 2             61
      AH, TOUCH THEIR BLUE VEINED EYELIDS IF THEY SLEEP, . . .        33 OISIN 2           V 61
      HALF WAKENING, WE LIFTED OUR EYELIDS. . . . .                   54 OISIN 3            100
      HALF-WAKENING, WE LIFTED OUR EYELIDS, . . . . .                 54 OISIN 3           V 100
      HIS EYELIDS DROOP, HIS HEAD FALLS LOW, . . . .                  98 FOXHUNTER           13
      HIS EYELIDS CLOSE, HIS HEAD DROOPS LOW, . . . .                 98 FOXHUNTER         V 13
      AND LIFT YOUR TENDER EYELIDS, MAID, . . . . .                  125 GOES FERGUS          5
      WITH HER CLOUD-PALE EYELIDS FALLING ON DREAM-DIMMED EYES!      163 VALLEY LOVERS        4
      WITH HER CLOUD-PALE EYELIDS HALF COVERING HER DIM EYES!        163 VALLEY LOVERS     V  4
      O CLOUD-PALE EYELIDS, DREAM-DIMMED EYES.  . . . . .            164 PERFECT BEAUTY       1
      HALF CLOSE YOUR EYELIDS, LOOSEN YOUR HAIR, . . . .             166 EVIL OF BELOV        1
      AMONG PALE EYELIDS, HEAVY WITH THE SLEEP  . . . .              169 SECRET ROSE          6
      OR, IT MAY BE, THE EYELIDS OF ONE EYE, . . . . .              195 BAILE AILLINN      151
      BEFORE THEIR SLEEPY EYELIDS RAN . . . . . .                   272 GREY ROCK           30
      UNDER THE EYELIDS OF ANOTHER, FOR IT WAS MY CRAFT  . . .       284 TWO KINGS          156
      PACING WITH HALF-CLOSED EYELIDS IN A SUNNY SPOT  . . . .       366 HER COURAGE          7
      THE QUIVERING HALF-CLOSED EYELIDS, THE RAGS OF CLOUD OR        427 PHANTOM HATRED      26
         OF LACE,
      EYES UNDER EYELIDS DID SO GLEAM! . . . . .                     514 JANE GROWN OLD       6
      LOOK ON ME ONCE.  WHY SINK YOUR EYELIDS THUS?  . . . .         703 MOSADA 3           107
      LOOK ON ME ONCE.  WHY SINK YOUR EYELIDS SO?  . . . .           703 MOSADA 3         V 107
      AMONG THE WINDS, LOOKS UNDER YOUR PALE EYELIDS.  . . .         757 SHADOW WATER A     211
      HER EYELIDS TREMBLE AND THE WHITE FOAM FADES! . . . .          761 SHADOW WATER A     264
      AND UNDER LOVERS' EYELIDS.  BEND YOUR HEAD  . . . .            762 SHADOW WATER A     286
EYE'S
      NOTHING BUT GRIP OF CLAW, AND THE EYE'S COMPLACENCY,  . .      427 PHANTOM HATRED      31
EYES
      HER EYES WERE SOFT AS DEWDROPS HANGING . . . .                  3 OISIN 1           V 7HH
      AND WITH QUENCHLESS EYES AND FLUTTERING HAIR  . . . .          12 OISIN 1           V 144
      AND SHOWED THEIR EYES WITH TEARDROPS DIM, . . . .              18 OISIN 1            256
      FROM DEWY EYES! "UPON THE DEAD . . . . . .                     21 OISIN 1            310
      IN OUR RAISED EYES THERE FLASHED A GLOW . . . .                22 OISIN 1            327
      I HEARD ONE SAY, "HIS EYES GROW DIM . . . . .                  25 OISIN 1            380
      I HEARD ONE SAY, "WITHIN HIS EYES . . . . .                    25 OISIN 1           V 380
      AND GAZES AROUND HER WITH EYES OF BRIGHTNESS! . . . .          27 OISIN 1            413
      BUT THE LOVE-DEW DIMS OUR EYES TILL THE DAY  . . . .           28 OISIN 1            424
      AND GAZES AROUND HER WITH EYES OF BRIGHTNESS! . . . .          28 OISIN 1           V 421
      AND KISSED MY EYES, AND, SWAYING HER BRIGHT HEAD . . .         29 OISIN 2              6
      AND HOW THOSE LOVERS NEVER TURN THEIR EYES  . . . .            29 OISIN 2             11
      AND HAD DISPORTED IN THE EYES STILL JET . . . .                31 OISIN 2          V 39
      A LADY WITH SOFT EYES LIKE FUNERAL TAPERS, . . . .             33 OISIN 2             69
      DOWN ON US WITH HER EYES LIKE FUNERAL TAPERS, . . . .          33 OISIN 2          V 69
      A MAIDEN WITH SOFT EYES LIKE FUNERAL TAPERS, . . . .           33 OISIN 2          V 69
      AND THROUGH THEIR EYES NO LIGHT OF MOON OR DAY  . . . .        34 OISIN 2          V 77
      GOES DROPPING FROM HIS EYES A LANGUID LIGHT, . . . .           34 OISIN 2          V 81A
      A DEMON'S LEISURE! EYES, FIRST WHITE, NOW BURNED  . . .        40 OISIN 2            168
      A DEMON'S LEISURE.  EYES FIRST WHITE AS SNOW, . . . .          40 OISIN 2          V 168
      FILLING THE FIBROUS DIMNESS WITH LONG GENERATIONS OF EYES.     49 OISIN 3             40
      SIDLED THEIR BODIES AGAINST HIM, FILLING THE SHADE WITH        50 OISIN 3             48
         THEIR EYES.
      WATCHED ME WITH MOURNFUL WONDER OUT OF THE WELLS OF HIS        51 OISIN 3             60
         EYES.
      HALF OPEN HIS EYES WERE, AND HELD ME, . . . . . .              51 OISIN 3             65
      AND BECAUSE I WENT BY THEM SO HUGH AND SO SPEEDY WITH EYES     59 OISIN 3            169
         SO BRIGHT,
      AND IN FOLDS ROUND HIS EYES AND HIS MOUTH, . . . . .           59 OISIN 3            174
      . . . AND THEIR EYES THAT GLIMMER LIKE SILK. . . . . .         59 OISIN 3            176
```

253

	PAGE	TITLE		LINE

EYES (CONTINUED)

AND BEFORE I WENT BY THEM SO HUGE AND SO SPEEDY WITH EYES
   SO BRIGHT,   59 OISIN 3 V 169
. . . AND THEIR YOUTH, AND THEIR EYES SOFT AS SILK. . . . 59 OISIN 3 V 176
SORRY PLACE, WHERE FOR SWING OF THE WAR-AXE IN MY DIM EYES 61 OISIN 3   194
  . . .
. . . DEEP HORROR OF EYES AND OF WINGS, ... 62 OISIN 3   205
FOR LONELY TO MOVE 'MONG THE SOFT EYES . . . . . . 63 OISIN 3 V 222
YON TALL ONE EYES MY SUPPER! CHASE HIM AWAY, ... 72 ANASHU VIJAYA 34
YON TALL ONE EYES MY SUPPER! SWIFTLY CHASE HIM . . . . 72 ANASHU VIJAYA V 34
THEIR FACES ARE ALL WORN, AND IN THEIR EYES . . . . . 73 ANASHU VIJAYA 48
A LITTLE WAY WITHIN THE GLOOM A ROEBUCK RAISED HIS EYES 76 INDIAN ON GOD 13
"YOUR EYES THAT ONCE WERE NEVER WEARY OF MINE . . . . 79 EPHEMERA 1
GATHERED IN SILENCE, DEWY AS HER EYES, ... 80 EPHEMERA 19
GLIMMERING IN HER DROOPED EYES, SAW HER LIPS MOVE . . . 81 EPHEMERA V 24D
AROUND ME SHONE KEEN EYES OF MEN! . . . . 83 MAD KING GOLL 30
AND SHONE AROUND THE EYES OF MEN! . . . . 83 MAD KING GOLL 30
WITH EYES OF SADNESS CAME TO HEAR . . . . 85 MAD KING GOLL V 62
WITH EYES OF SADNESS ROSE TO HEAR, ... 85 MAD KING GOLL V 62
HIS OLD EYES CLOUD WITH DREAMS! . . . . 98 FOXHUNTER 14
FIRE IS IN THE OLD MAN'S EYES, ... 98 FOXHUNTER 29
A FIRE IS IN THE OLD MAN'S EYES, ... 98 FOXHUNTER V 29
STARED ON THE MOURNFUL WONDER OF HIS EYES, ... 108 CUCHULAIN SEA 41
AND GAZED UPON THE WISDOM OF HIS EYES, ... 108 CUCHULAIN SEA V 41
UPON THE MOURNFUL WONDER OF HIS EYES, ... 108 CUCHULAIN SEA V 42
YOUR EYES HAD ONCE, AND OF THEIR SHADOWS DEEP! . . . 121 YOU ARE OLD 4
THINE EYES GROW FULL OF TENDER CARE! . . . . . . 135 TWO TREES 19
THY TENDER EYES GROW ALL UNKIND! . . . . 136 TWO TREES 39
OUR BREASTS ARE HEAVING, OUR EYES ARE AGLEAM, ... 140 HOSTING SIDHE 8
FOR BREASTS ARE HEAVING AND EYES A-GLEAM, ... 140 HOSTING SIDHE V 7
OUR BREASTS ARE HEAVING, OUR EYES ARE A-GLEAM, . . . 140 HOSTING SIDHE V 8
AND CLAP THEIR HANDS TOGETHER, AND HALF CLOSE THEIR EYES, 146 UNAPPEAS HOST 2
O HIDING HAIR AND DEWY EYES, ... 152 HEART OF WOMAN 9
THEIR HOOFS HEAVY WITH TUMULT, THEIR EYES GLIMMERING WHITE! 154 BELOVED PEACE 2
BELOVED, LET YOUR EYES HALF CLOSE, AND YOUR HEART BEAT . . 154 BELOVED PEACE 9
PASSION-DIMMED EYES AND LONG HEAVY HAIR . . . . . . 155 REPROVE CURLEW 4
THAT ONLY GOD'S EYES DID NOT CLOSE! . . . . 156 FORGOT BEAUTY 14
BEFORE THEY DROWNED THEIR LOVERS' EYES . . . . . . 156 FORGOT BEAUTY V 10A
THAT ONLY THE GODS' EYES DID NOT CLOSE! . . . . . 156 FORGOT BEAUTY V 14
SUDDENLY HURTLE BEFORE MY DREAM-AWAKENED EYES, ... 161 BLACK PIG 2
WITH HER CLOUD-PALE EYELIDS FALLING ON DREAM-DIMMED EYES! 163 VALLEY LOVERS 4
THEIR HEADS ON YOUR KNEES, AND DROWN THEIR EYES WITH YOUR
   HAIR,   163 VALLEY LOVERS 6
WITH HER CLOUD-PALE EYELIDS HALF COVERING HER DIM EYES! 163 VALLEY LOVERS V 4
O CLOUD-PALE EYELIDS, DREAM-DIMMED EYES, ... 164 PERFECT BEAUTY 1
WITH A BLINK IN HIS EYES, AT THE CAVE-MOUTH, ... 166 BLESSED 3
WITH A BLINK IN HIS EYES AT THE CAVE MOUTH, ... 166 BLESSED V 3
WITH THE SECRETS OF GOD IN HIS EYES. . . . . . . 167 BLESSED 12
WITH BLINKING EYES, AT THE CAVE'S EDGE, ... 167 BLESSED V 4C
"MY EYES ARE BLINKING," DATHI SAID, ... 168 BLESSED 25
OF THE CROWNED MAGI! AND THE KING WHOSE EYES . . . . 169 SECRET ROSE 9
OF THE CROWNED MAGI! AND THE KINGS WHOSE EYES . . . . 169 SECRET ROSE V 9
FOR ALL EYES BUT THESE EYES, ... 173 PLEADS FRIEND 8
FOR ALL EYES BUT THESE EYES. . . . . 173 PLEADS FRIEND 8
AND SHE'D HAD LUCKY EYES AND A HIGH HEART, ... 181 QUEEN MAEVE 27
WITH STILL AND STONY LIMBS AND OPEN EYES, ... 182 QUEEN MAEVE 46
TO MANY THOUSAND EYES, AND TO HER OWN . . . . . . 182 QUEEN MAEVE 65
BODIES OF SHADOW AND BLIND EYES LIKE PEARLS, ... 185 QUEEN MAEVE 116
BEFORE HIS EYES, HE HAS TEARS FOR NONE, ... 192 BAILE AILLINN 82
AND THEY HAVE NEWS OF DEIRDRE'S EYES, ... 193 BAILE AILLINN 97
AND LITTLE SHADOWS COME ABOUT HER EYES! . . . . . 199 FOLLY COMFORT 3
AND THERE ARE LITTLE CREASES ABOUT HER EYES! . . . . 199 FOLLY COMFORT V 3
BUT WE HAVE HIDDEN IN OUR HEARTS THE FLAME OUT OF THE EYES 207 HANRAHANS SONG 4
BUT OUR HEARTS ARE LIGHTED FROM THE FLAME IN THE EYES . . 207 HANRAHANS SONG V 9
QUEENS, THEIR EYES BLUE LIKE THE ICE, ... 214 HAPPY TOWNLAND 11
DIM PAIRC-NA-TARAV, WHERE ENCHANTED EYES . . . . . 217 WOODS OF COOLE 11
I HAD NOT EYES LIKE THOSE ENCHANTED EYES, ... 218 WOODS OF COOLE 17
I HAD NOT EYES LIKE THOSE ENCHANTED EYES, ... 218 WOODS OF COOLE 17
STRANGE CREATURES FLUTTER UP BEFORE ONE'S EYES, . . . 222 SHADOW WATER B 18
AND HAVING SUCH WIDE-OPEN, SHINING EYES. . . . . . 231 SHADOW WATER B 200
WHY ARE YOU STANDING WITH YOUR EYES UPON ME? . . . . 234 SHADOW WATER B 276
IS IT THAT THOUGH YOUR EYES ARE FULL OF LOVE . . . . 245 SHADOW WATER B 473
I WEEP BECAUSE I'VE NOTHING FOR YOUR EYES . . . . . 246 SHADOW WATER B 496
O WHY DO YOU NOT LIFT YOUR EYES TO MINE? . . . . . 246 SHADOW WATER B 498
IVORY IMAGES WITH AMETHYST EYES. . . . . 248 SHADOW WATER B 534
DRAGONS WITH EYES OF RUBY. THE WHOLE SHIP . . . . . 248 SHADOW WATER B 535
THERE'S SOMEBODY I'D GIVE THE AMETHYST EYES TO. . . . 248 SHADOW WATER B 538
OR CALLED BEFORE HIS EYES. O CARRY ME . . . . . . 249 SHADOW WATER B 568
BUT I WILL COVER UP YOUR EYES AND EARS, ... 250 SHADOW WATER B 574
WHEN, THE EARS BEING DEAFENED, THE SIGHT OF THE EYES BLIND 257 RECONCILIATION 3
WITH EMERALD EYES." . . . . 263 MASK 2
IMAGINATIONS OF THEIR EYES, ... 272 GREY ROCK 28
THOSE WINE-DRENCHED EYES, AND CURSE OUR LUCK . . . . 272 GREY ROCK 39
AND THOSE FIERCE EYES, AND CURSE OUR LUCK . . . . . 272 GREY ROCK V 39
AND THESE IMMORTAL EYES SHED TEARS-- . . . . . . 275 GREY ROCK 100
WHITER THAN CURDS, ITS EYES THE TINT OF THE SEA. . . . 277 TWO KINGS 7
AND STARED INTO THE SEA-GREEN EYES, AND SO . . . . . 278 TWO KINGS V 25
HER EYES WERE COLD AND STEADY, HER LIPS TIGHT. . . . 279 TWO KINGS 64
GAZING UPON HER WITH BEWILDERED EYES! . . . . . . 280 TWO KINGS V 84
WHO HAD UNNATURAL MAJESTY, AND EYES . . . . 283 TWO KINGS 149
LIKE THE EYES OF SOME GREAT KITE SCOURING THE WOODS, . . 283 TWO KINGS 150

EYES   (CONTINUED)

PUSH OUT HIS VIGOROUS LIMBS AND RUB HIS EYES, • • • • • • 284 TWO KINGS 162
CROW UPON TARA." SHE HAD FIXED HER EYES • • • • • 286 TWO KINGS V 211
NOR IN HIS NEIGHBOURS' EYES? • • • • • • • • 291 TO A FRIEND 8
NONE CLOSED HIS BLOOD-SHOT EYES BUT SOUGHT • • • • • 296 THREE BEGGARS 44
THEY CLOSED THEIR BLOOD-SHOT EYES FOR NAUGHT. • • • • • 296 THREE BEGGARS V 44
WITH BLOOD-SHOT EYES UPON HIM STARED. • • • • • • 297 THREE BEGGARS 58
BEFORE HIS EYES, WHERE STONES HAD BEEN, • • • • • • • 302 HOUR DAWN 20
ALL WISDOM SHUT INTO HIS ONYX EYES. • • • • • • • 311 MOUNTAIN TOMB 11
ALL WISDOM SHUT INTO ITS ONYX EYES. • • • • • 311 MOUNTAIN TOMB V 11
KIND EYES SHOULD BE MORE LEARN'D? • • • • • • • • 312 TWO YEAR LATER 2
TILL PRIDE HAD MADE HER EYES GROW BRIGHT, • • • • • 314 MEMORY YOUTH 10
AND EVEN OLD MEN'S EYES GREW DIM, THIS HAND ALONE, • • • 314 FALLEN MAJESTY 2
AND ALL THEIR EYES STILL FIXED, HOPING TO FIND ONCE MORE, • 318 MAGI 6
WORE IT IN THE WORLD'S EYES • • • • • • • • 320 COAT 6
DELIGHT MEN'S EYES WHEN I AWAKE SOME DAY • • • • • 323 SWANS AT COOLE 29
HAD SHUT THEIR EYES, AND WHERE WAS IT • • • • • • 326 ROBERT GREGORY 62
PLEASED TO HAVE FILLED THE EYES • • • • • • • 329 MEN IMPROVE 8
AND KISSED HER ARAB EYES, • • • • • • • • 333 SOLOMON SHEBA 18
AND GLITTERED IN HER EYES. • • • • • • • • 336 YOUNG GIRL 11
HAD SCARCELY ACCUSTOMED OUR EYES • • • • • • • 341 SHEP GOATHERD 69
WHEN HE VANISHED FROM EARS AND EYES. • • • • • • 341 SHEP GOATHERD 72
WHEN IT HAS VANISHED FROM OUR NATURAL EYES, • • • • • 342 SHEP GOATHERD 81
THE ROUND GREEN EYES AND THE LONG WAVERING BODIES • • • 343 DEJECTION 2
TO CALL UP TO THE EYES • • • • • • • • • 347 FISHERMAN 7
AND WITH THE FERVOUR OF MY YOUTHFUL EYES, • • • • • 356 BROKEN DREAMS 25
AND WHEN SHE MEETS OUR GAZE HER EYES ARE LAUGHTER-LIT, • • 362 HER COURTESY 5
AND WHEN SHE MEETS OUR GAZE HER EYES ARE LAUGHTER LIT • 362 HER COURTESY V 5
MAY HANDLE NOTHING AND SET EYES ON NOTHING • • • • 371 ON GOING HOUSE 6
IT MUST BE THAT THE TERROR IN THEIR EYES • • • • • 375 PHASES OF MOON 72
OF LOVELY, SATISFIED, INDIFFERENT EYES. • • • • • • 375 PHASES OF MOON 83
HIS CHANGING EYES. • • • • • • • • • 379 CAT AND MOON 28
UNDER BLANK EYES AND FINGERS NEVER STILL • • • • • 382 VISION ROBART 5
ONE LASHED HER TAIL, HER EYES LIT BY THE MOON • • • • 383 VISION ROBART 29
SHE WOULD HAVE TIME TO TURN HER EYES, • • • • • 385 ROBARTES DANCE 10
WHY HAVE YOU LAID YOUR HANDS UPON MY EYES? • • • • • 389 IMAGE PAST 15
MY EYES SHOULD NEVER REST? • • • • • • • • 389 IMAGE PAST 18
EVEN TO EYES THAT BEAUTY HAD DRIVEN MAD, • • • • • 390 IMAGE PAST 34
THE GLITTERING EYES IN A DEATH'S HEAD • • • • • • 400 DEMON BEAST 9
FROM A GLAD KINDNESS CANNOT TAKE HIS EYES. • • • • • 404 FOR DAUGHTER 40
BUT I HAVE FOUND AN ANSWER IN THOSE EYES • • • • • 413 TOWER 101
THEIR LEGS LONG, DELICATE AND SLENDER, AQUAMARINE THEIR 426 PHANTOM HATRED 17
  EYES,
THE LADIES CLOSE THEIR MUSING EYES. NO PROPHECIES, • • • 426 PHANTOM HATRED 19
HAVE CLOSED THE LADIES' EYES, THEIR MINDS ARE BUT A POOL • 426 PHANTOM HATRED 21
THE CLOUD-PALE UNICORNS, THE EYES OF AQUAMARINE, • • • 427 PHANTOM HATRED 25
OR EYES THAT RAGE HAS BRIGHTENED, ARMS IT HAS MADE LEAN, • 427 PHANTOM HATRED 27
THE CLOUD PALE UNICORNS, THE EYES OF AQUAMARINE, • • • 427 PHANTOM HATRED V 25
OF EYES THAT RAGE HAS BRIGHTENED, ARMS IT HAS MADE LEAN, • 427 PHANTOM HATRED V 27
THEY FIXED OLD ACHING EYES, • • • • • • • • 432 NINETEEN 19 100
THERE LURCHES PAST, HIS GREAT EYES WITHOUT THOUGHT • • • 433 NINETEEN 19 126
UNWEARIED EYES UPON THOSE HORRIBLE GREEN BIRDS. • • • • 442 BLACK CENTAUR 16
IN THE BEST MODERN WAY—THE CHILDREN'S EYES • • • • • 443 SCHOOL CHILDR 6
WE SHOULD BE HIDDEN FROM THEIR EYES, • • • • • • 454 HIS MEMORIES 1
SHE ROSE, AND WITH HER EYES SHUT FAST IN SLEEP • • • • 468 HARUN RASHID 152
THE MIRROR OF MALICIOUS EYES • • • • • • • 479 SELF AND SOUL 52
CASTS UPON HIS EYES UNTIL AT LAST • • • • • • 479 SELF AND SOUL 53
AND DEDICATE—EYES BENT UPON THE GROUND, • • • • • 489 COOLE PARK 29 29
THAT SHONE BEFORE THESE EYES • • • • • • • 504 QUARREL IN AGE 15
BEFORE THEIR EYES A HOUSE • • • • • • • • 512 JANE ON GOD 13
EYES UNDER EYELIDS DID SO GLEAM, • • • • • • 514 JANE GROWN OLD 6
"UPLIFT THOSE EYES AND THROW • • • • • • • 516 MANS SONG 7
AND EYES THAT HAD SO KEEN A SIGHT? • • • • • • 529 TOM LUNATIC 4
SALT BLOOD BLOCKS HIS EYES. • • • • • • • • 530 DELPHIC ORACLE 5
COLD AS THE MARCH WIND HIS EYES. • • • • • • 531 FATHER CHILD 8
AND THE EYES MORE BRIGHT • • • • • • • • 531 BEFORE WORLD 2
WHY THOSE QUESTIONING EYES • • • • • • • 533 FIRST CONFESS 15
WHILE NIGHT SHUTS THE EYES • • • • • • • • 535 PARTING 2
HURRY INTO EACH OTHER'S ARMS, THESE EYES, • • • • • 555 RIBH AT TOMB 22
THEIR EYES MID MANY WRINKLES, THEIR EYES, • • • • • 567 LAPIS LAZULI 55
THEIR EYES MID MANY WRINKLES, THEIR EYES, • • • • • 567 LAPIS LAZULI 55
THEIR ANCIENT, GLITTERING EYES, ARE GAY. • • • • • 567 LAPIS LAZULI 56
THOSE HANDS TO CLOSE THESE EYES, • • • • • • • 587 OLD WICKED MAN 6
CAN NEVER CLOSE THOSE EYES." • • • • • • • 588 OLD WICKED MAN 26
MY HEART RECOVERING WITH COVERED EYES, • • • • • 602 GALLERY REVIS 18
EYES SPIRITUALISED BY DEATH CAN JUDGE, • • • • • • 604 YOU CONTENT 7
HIS EYES FIXED UPON NOTHING, • • • • • • • 617 LONG-LEG FLY 7
EYES STARED OUT OF THE BRANCHES AND WERE GONE. • • • • 634 CUCHULAIN COMF 3
"WE THREAD THE NEEDLES' EYES, AND ALL WE DO • • • • 634 CUCHULAIN COMF 16
SOMETHING DROPS FROM EYES LONG BLIND, • • • • • 638 BEN BULBEN 29
'TIS MORN, LIKE OLD MEN'S EYES THE STARS ARE PALE, • • • 645 ISLE STAT I 1 4
AND THINE EYES MORE BRIGHT THAN FAERY'S, • • • • • 647 ISLE STAT I 1 53
AND TROUBLED EYES CAME MORNING'S FIRST-BORN GLOW, • • • 648 ISLE STAT I 1 103
NASCHINA, WHEREFORE ARE YOUR EYES SO BRIGHT • • • • 650 ISLE STAT I 1 141
ACORNS GREEN, WITH EYES AWAKE. • • • • • • • 655 ISLE STAT I 3 5
BUT WIDE AWAKE HIS TWO EYES WERE. • • • • • • 655 ISLE STAT I 3 7
OR HER OWN BURNING EYES, • • • • • • • • 658 ISLE STAT I 3 85
AND LET THEM TELL SAD HISTORIES, TILL THEIR EYES • • • 663 ISLE STAT II 2 32
AND PENETRATION OF THEIR EYES. WHERE YONDER BLOTCH • • 664 ISLE STAT II 3 47
AND IN HER EYES A LIGHTLESS STARE, • • • • • • 668 ISLE STAT II 3 60
YOUR EYES ARE ALL A-FLASH. SHE IS NOT HERE. • • • • • 669 ISLE STAT II 3 68

EYES   (CONTINUED)
YOUR EYES ARE ALL AFLASH. SHE IS NOT HERE. . . . . .   669 ISLE STAT II 3 V   68
I COULD GAZE, GAZE UPON THINE EYES OF GREY; . . . . .   671 ISLE STAT II 3 V 147
BUT ART THOU HAPPY? THOSE GREY EYES OF THINE . . . . .   672 ISLE STAT II 3   151
HAVE THEY NE'ER SEEN THE EYES OF LYNX OR KINE, ...   672 ISLE STAT II 3   152
AS LIGHT OF TRIUMPH IN THY GOBLIN EYES-- . . . .   674 ISLE STAT II 3   199
WHOSE INSOLENT EYES UNUSED TO TEARS WOULD WEEP. . . . .   678 ISLE STAT II 3   302
BEFORE THE WIND. SAW YOU HIS EYES A-GLITTER? . . . . .   683 SEEKER   35
SHINE DULL UNMOVING EYES. WHAT THING ART THOU? . . . .   685 SEEKER   74
AND WHEREFORE, THEN, SHOULD THY GREY EYES . . . .   686 LIFE   7
AH, LET US KISS EACH OTHER'S EYES. . . . .   686 LIFE   15
TILL THEIR FIERCE MISERIES WITHIN HIS EYES . . . .   687 TWO TITANS   26
AND IN THE SIBYL'S EYES A LANGUID FLAME . . . .   688 TWO TITANS   41
RE-SHINING IN HIS EYES. SO EVER MOVES . . . .   689 NETTLESHIP   12
TO SAINTED EBREMAR'S SAD EYES. I THINK . . . .   696 MOSADA 2   15
AND YON FEW STARS GROWN DIM, LIKE EYES OF LOVERS . . . .   700 MOSADA 3   33
THE FLAME THAT SHONE WITHIN HIS EYES BUT NOW . . . . .   704 MOSADA 3   128
AH! WOE FOR YOUR EYES AND THEIR BRIGHTNESS-- . . . . .   708 FAIRY PEDANT   35
A PEASANT PALE AND PRETTY, HER EYES FOR FEAR, ...   713 FERENCZ RENYI   81
A PEASANT YOUNG AND FAIR, HER EYES FOR FEAR . . . . . .   713 FERENCZ RENYI V   81
A PEASANT, PALE AND PRETTY, HER EYES FROM FEAR, ...   713 FERENCZ RENYI V   81
IN THE LONG GRASS--FOUR EYES DROOP LOW--A SEAT . . . .   716 DWELT SYCAMORE   11
AND FULL HIS EYES OF FAIRY CHEER. . . . .   716 FAIRY DOCTOR   12
"WATCHER, WHEREFORE HAVE YE CALLED US?" EYES GO AFTER   718 PHANTOM SHIP   10
   HIS LEAN HAND,
CHECK. AH! HOW BRIGHT YOUR EYES. HOW SWIFT YOUR MOVES.   722 WITCH VIVIEN   61
NO TENDER WISDOM FLOODS THE EYES . . . .   723 GIRLS SONG A   9
HE BLINKED AND BLINKED HIS EYES . . . .   740 EARL PAUL   22
AND GAZE ON ONE ANOTHER THROUGH OUR EYES, ...   749 SHADOW WATER A   58
A TRADING GALLEY IN HER HELMSMAN'S EYES. . . . .   751 SHADOW WATER A   95
I HAVE TURNED HOMEWARDS. IN THE EYES OF THE GODS, . . .   757 SHADOW WATER A   202
AGAINST MY FACE AND EYES. MINE TOO ARE BEATEN. . . . .   759 SHADOW WATER A V 233
MY EYES ARE TROUBLED BY THE SILVER ARROWS! . . . . . .   761 SHADOW WATER A   269
I KNOW YOU NOW, BESEECHING HANDS AND EYES. . . . . . .   763 SHADOW WATER A   312
HIS WELL-BELOVED THROUGH A MORTAL'S EYES! . . . .   763 SHADOW WATER A   322
IS LAUGHING THROUGH A MORTAL'S EYES. O LOOK! . . . . .   763 SHADOW WATER A   324
BESEECHING HANDS AND MORE BESEECHING EYES . . . .   763 SHADOW WATER A V 312
I THINK THAT THERE IS LOVE IN AIBRIC'S EYES. . . . . .   768 SHADOW WATER A   407
I KNOW HE WILL OBEY YOU; AND IF YOUR EYES . . . .   768 SHADOW WATER A   408
SHOULD LOOK UPON HIS EYES WITH LOVE, IN THE END . . . .   768 SHADOW WATER A   409
PITY THESE WEEPING EYES! I WILL FOLLOW YOU. . . . . .   768 SHADOW WATER A   420
SHOULD LOOK UPON HIS EYES WITH LOVE UNTO THE END . . . .   768 SHADOW WATER A V 409
THAT HAVE ONE ANOTHER'S EYES? . . . .   773 SONG DEIRDRE 1   24
EYES'
I COULD GAZE, GAZE UPON THINE EYES' CLEAR GREY! . . . .   671 ISLE STAT II 3   147
EYESIGHT
HIDDEN FROM EYESIGHT TO THE UNNOTICED END. . . . . . .   472 ALL SOUL NIGHT   50
EYNE
SLEEPILY CLOSE HER ROUND BRIGHT EYNE; . . . .   646 ISLE STAT I 1   35
EZEKIEL'S
WITH OLD EZEKIEL'S CHERUBIM . . . .   336 YOUNG BEAUTY   11
EZEKIEL'S COAL, WHAT MORE CAN MAN DESIRE? . . . . . .   502 VACILLATION   V   74
FABLE
AS THE FOX IN THE OLD FABLE DESTROYED THE SPARTAN BOY'S,   580 CURSE CROMWELL   18
FABRIC
DID ALL THE FABRIC FADE! . . . .   516 MANS SONG   10
FABULOUS
IF SOMETHING THAT'S MOST FABULOUS WERE TRUE-- . . . . .   245 SHADOW WATER B   489
A FIGURE THAT HAS GROWN SO FABULOUS . . . .   412 TOWER   77
OR THAT OF THE FABULOUS HORN, ...   414 TOWER   136
OUT OF THE FABULOUS DARKNESS CALLED. . . . .   437 SONGS PLAY 1   16
A FABULOUS, FORMLESS DARKNESS IN! . . . .   438 SONGS PLAY 2   5
THAT THEY HAD BROUGHT NO FABULOUS SYMBOL THERE . . . .   537 HER VISION   31
FACE
A SORROW WRAPPED EACH MERRY FACE, ...   17 OISIN 1   235
AND FACE THAT SEEMED WROUGHT OUT OF MOONLIT VAPOURS, . .   33 OISIN 2   70
HER FACE SEEMED FASHIONED ALL OF MOONLIT VAPOURS, . . .   33 OISIN 2   V   70
AND AT HIS CRY THERE CAME NO MILK-PALE FACE . . . . . .   38 OISIN 2   134
WHERE SHADOWY FACE FLOWED INTO SHADOWY FACE, ...   39 OISIN 2   145
WHERE SHADOWY FACE FLOWED INTO SHADOWY FACE, ...   39 OISIN 2   V 145
LIFTED THE DOME, WHERE FACE IN CARVEN FACE . . . .   39 OISIN 2   145
LIFTED THE DOME, WHERE FACE IN CARVEN FACE . . . .   39 OISIN 2   V 145
AND SUNKEN SHAPE, AGAINST MY FACE AND BREAST, ...   40 OISIN 2   V 179
AND DRIPPING AND SUNKEN SHAPE, TO FACE AND BREAST, . . .   40 OISIN 2   V 179
CAME CAR-BORNE BALOR, AS OLD AS A FOREST, HIS VAST FACE   53 OISIN 3   V   91
   SUNK
. . . THE FLESH OF HIS FACE AS DRIED GRASS, ...   59 OISIN 3   173
AND WRAPPING MY FACE IN MY HAIR, ...   59 OISIN 3   177
WATCHING THE BLESSED ONES MOVE FAR OFF, AND THE SMILE ON   61 OISIN 3   199
   GOD'S FACE,
HOUNDS ARE GAZING ON HIS FACE, ...   99 FOXHUNTER   39
THE HOUNDS ARE GAZING ON HIS FACE, ...   99 FOXHUNTER   V   39
AND HOUNDS ARE GAZING ON HIS FACE, ...   99 FOXHUNTER   V   39
THAT SWINEHERD STARED UPON HER FACE AND SAID, ...   106 CUCHULAIN SEA   9
"YOU DARE ME TO MY FACE," AND THEREUPON . . . .   106 CUCHULAIN SEA   17
THAT YOU HAVE COME AND DARED ME TO MY FACE?" . . . . .   109 CUCHULAIN SEA   61
LIVES ON THIS LONELY FACE. . . . .   112 ROSE OF WORLD   10
MORE FLEETING THAN THE SEA'S FOAM-FICKLE FACE, ...   112 ROSE OF WORLD V   8
MORE FLEETING THAN THE SEA'S FOAM FICKLE FACE, ...   112 ROSE OF WORLD V   8
AND LOVED THE SORROWS OF YOUR CHANGING FACE! . . . . .   121 YOU ARE OLD   8
AND HID HIS FACE AMID A CROWD OF STARS. . . . .   121 YOU ARE OLD   12

FACE   (CONTINUED)

	PAGE	TITLE		LINE
AND THEY HAD NAILED THE BOARDS ABOVE HER FACE,	123	DREAM OF DEATH		3
PUT THAT MUSIC IN HER FACE?	124	CATHLEEN PARA		10
THE LONG HAIR IS ON HER FACE;	124	CATHLEEN PARA	V	10
THE LONG HAIR SHADOWS HER FACE;	124	CATHLEEN PARA	V	10
THERE'S NOT A WOMAN TURNS HER FACE	131	OLD PENSIONER		13
I SPIT INTO THE FACE OF TIME	132	OLD PENSIONER		17
WITH A SAD AND A GAY FACE.	144	HOST OF AIR		16
THAT SAW YOUNG NIAMH HOVER WITH LOVE-LORN FACE	162	ASKS FORGIVE		13
OR REMEMBERING HERS THEY WILL FIND NO OTHER FACE FAIR	163	VALLEY LOVERS		7
OR, REMEMBERING HERS, THEY WILL HOLD NO OTHER FACE FAIR	163	VALLEY LOVERS	V	7
FACE DOWNWARD, TOSSING IN A TROUBLED SLEEP;	185	QUEEN MAEVE		106
ABOUT WHOSE FACE BIRDS WAGGED THEIR FIERY WINGS,	187	QUEEN MAEVE		145
AND WHEN NO FACE GREW PITEOUS	191	BAILE AILLINN		62
HIS FACE BOWED LOW TO WEEP THE END	192	BAILE AILLINN		75
TALL AND NOBLE BUT WITH FACE AND BOSOM	199	ARROW		5
HAD YOU LOOKED ON THEM FACE TO FACE AS I DID,	231	SHADOW WATER B		198
HAD YOU LOOKED ON THEM FACE TO FACE AS I DID,	231	SHADOW WATER B		198
AND I WOULD HAVE YOU LOOK INTO MY FACE	238	SHADOW WATER B		349
FOOL, FOOL! ALTHOUGH YOU HAVE LOOKED INTO MY FACE	238	SHADOW WATER B		356
AND YOU WILL RECOLLECT MY FACE AND VOICE,	243	SHADOW WATER B		433
WHY DO YOU TURN AWAY AND HIDE YOUR FACE,	244	SHADOW WATER B		461
I DO NOT UNDERSTAND. I KNOW YOUR FACE	244	SHADOW WATER B		465
WILL LOOK UPON HIS FACE AGAIN. GO WITH HIM,	250	SHADOW WATER B		589
ONE TIME IT WAS A WOMAN'S FACE, OR WORSE--	267	ALL TEMPT ME		2
AND MOCK HIM TO HIS FACE AND THEN	272	GREY ROCK		34
YOU HAD TO FACE YOUR ENDS WHEN YOUNG--	273	GREY ROCK		53
SHE WOULD NOT LOOK IN ANY KNOWN MAN'S FACE	280	TWO KINGS		73
WOULD NEVER LOOK AGAIN ON KNOWN MAN'S FACE."	280	TWO KINGS		75
WILL NEVER LOOK AGAIN ON KNOWN MAN'S FACE."	280	TWO KINGS	V	75
UPON KING EOCHAID'S FACE, WHO LOWERED HIS FACE	286	TWO KINGS	V	211A
UPON KING EOCHAID'S FACE, WHO LOWERED HIS FACE	286	TWO KINGS	V	211A
A CURSING ROGUE WITH A MERRY FACE,	302	HOUR DAWN		1
A GREAT LAD WITH A BEERY FACE	303	HOUR DAWN		27
A DARK DEEP HOLE IN THE ROCK'S FACE,	303	HOUR DAWN	V	21
ALTHOUGH CROWDS GATHERED ONCE IF SHE BUT SHOWED HER FACE,	314	FALLEN MAJESTY		1
AND KISSED HER DUSKY FACE,	332	SOLOMON SHEBA		2
BUT SUCH AS I HAVE SEEN UPON HER FACE	340	SHEP GOATHERD		40
ALL DAY I'D LOOKED IN THE FACE	347	FISHERMAN		9
AND HIS SUN-FRECKLED FACE,	348	FISHERMAN		29
ONE HAD A LOVELY FACE,	350	MEMORY		1
BUT CHARM AND FACE WERE IN VAIN	350	MEMORY		3
WHEN MY LUCK CHANGED AND THEY DARED MEET MY FACE,	352	PEOPLE		25
WHEN MY LUCK CHANGED AND THEY DARED TO MEET MY FACE,	352	PEOPLE	V	25
YET ALWAYS WHEN I LOOK DEATH IN THE FACE,	357	DEEP-SWORN VOW		3
SUDDENLY I MEET YOUR FACE.	357	DEEP-SWORN VOW		6
PROPPED UPON PILLOWS, ROUGE ON THE PALLOR OF HER FACE.	362	HER COURTESY		3
HEEL UP AND WEIGHT ON TOE, MUST FACE THE WALL	363	DOLLS FACES		3
NO RED AND WHITE OF A FACE,	365	HER RACE		6
AMID THE DREAMS OF YOUTH) LET HER COME FACE TO FACE,	366	HER COURAGE		3
AMID THE DREAMS OF YOUTH) LET HER COME FACE TO FACE,	366	HER COURAGE		3
WHO HAVE LIVED IN JOY AND LAUGHED INTO THE FACE OF DEATH.	366	HER COURAGE		10
WHO LIVED IN SHAMELESS JOY AND LAUGHED INTO THE FACE OF DEATH.	366	HER COURAGE	V	10
THAT LIVED IN JOY AND LAUGHED INTO THE FACE OF DEATH.	366	HER COURAGE	V	10
WHO HAVE LIVED IN JOY AND LAUGHED IN THE FACE OF DEATH.	366	HER COURAGE	V	10
HAVE LOOKED INTO YOUR FACE?	367	HER CHRIS TREE		11
THAT HE HAS MADE THAT HOLLOW FACE OF HIS	368	EGO DOMINUS		20
MORE PLAIN TO THE MIND'S EYE THAN ANY FACE	368	EGO DOMINUS		21
AN IMAGE THAT MIGHT HAVE BEEN A STONY FACE	368	EGO DOMINUS		28
WITH FACE AND NOSE PRESSED TO A SWEET-SHOP WINDOW,	370	EGO DOMINUS		56
WITH FACE AND NOSE PRESSED TO A SWEETSHOP WINDOW.	370	EGO DOMINUS	V	56
SHE CAN, THOUGH EVERY FACE SHOULD SCOWL	405	FOR DAUGHTER		70
AND PRAISED THE COLOUR OF HER FACE,	410	TOWER		36
TROOPER BELABOURING TROOPER, BITING AT ARM OR AT FACE,	426	PHANTOM HATRED		12
HAS LAID HER HELPLESS FACE UPON HIS BREAST.	441	LEDA AND SWAN	V	4
WERE SOME DEAR FACE. UPON A MOONLESS NIGHT	466	HARUN RASHID	V	127
WHO FINDING THE FIRST WRINKLES ON A FACE	472	ALL SOUL NIGHT		42
BROUGHT FACE TO FACE WITH HIS OWN CLUMSINESS;	479	SELF AND SOUL		48
BROUGHT FACE TO FACE WITH HIS OWN CLUMSINESS;	479	SELF AND SOUL		48
RUN FOR A MILE UNDIMMED IN HEAVEN'S FACE	490	COOLE BALLYLEE		3
FACE TO FACE MY RIGHTFUL MAN	521	THREE THINGS		16
FACE TO FACE MY RIGHTFUL MAN	521	THREE THINGS		16
I'M LOOKING FOR THE FACE I HAD	532	BEFORE WORLD		7
FACE TO FACE WE STOOD;	539	MEETING		4
FACE TO FACE WE STOOD;	539	MEETING		4
THE GYRES! THE GYRES! OLD ROCKY FACE, LOOK FORTH;	564	GYRES		1
WHAT MATTER? THOSE THAT ROCKY FACE HOLDS DEAR,	564	GYRES		18
LONG LOOKED HE IN HER FACE,	571	THREE BUSHES		67
"FORGETTING HUMAN WORDS," A GRAVE DEEP FACE.	603	GALLERY REVIS		49
LIVE LIPS UPON A PLUMMET-MEASURED FACE.	610	STATUES		8
THE LINEAMENTS OF A PLUMMET-MEASURED FACE.	611	STATUES		32
AND MEN RECALL THAT FACE,	617	LONG-LEG FLY		12
BECAUSE WOMEN IN THE UPPER STOREYS DEMAND A FACE AT THE PANE,	623	HIGH TALK		7
WHAT DO WE KNOW BUT THAT WE FACE	633	MAN AND ECHO		39
THAN THE PEEPING PANSY'S FACE,	647	ISLE STAT I 1		52
DULL-WITTED THING, WITH FACE RED SQUIRREL-BROWN.	661	ISLE STAT II 1		68
IS ROLLED AS VERDANT SMOKE! O THOU WHOSE FACE	667	ISLE STAT II 3		35
IS IN THY FACE, AND LIPS TOGETHER PRESSED;	671	ISLE STAT II 3		139
IN THY WAN FACE? HEAR THOU, O DAUGHTER OF THE DAYS,	674	ISLE STAT II 3		200

257

FACE   (CONTINUED)
        IN THY WAN FACE? HEAR, DAUGHTER OF THE DAYS. . . . . .   674 ISLE STAT II 3 V 200
        THEN LET ME SEE THY FACE BEFORE I DIE. . . . .   684 SEEKER   66
        A SIBYL, WITH FIERCE FACE AS OF A HOUND . . . .   687 TWO TITANS   9
        BENDING HER FACE O'ER HIS, SHE WATCHES MEET . . . . .   688 TWO TITANS   45
        HIDING MY FACE, I CRIED LONG, BITTERLY. . . . .   690 MOSADA 1   17
        UPON THY FACE? HOW HEAVILY THY HEAD . . . .   701 MOSADA 3   72
        AFAR ALONG THE FLEET WHITE RIVER'S FACE-- . . . . . .   702 MOSADA 3   79
        AND SEE HOW THICK THE DEW LIES ON MY FACE. . . . . .   703 MOSADA 3   104
        AH! WOE FOR THE LOSS OF YOUR FACE, ...   708 FAIRY PEDANT   32
        AND NOW WITH FATHER TIME I'M FACE TO FACE. . . . . .   722 WITCH VIVIEN   57
        AND NOW WITH FATHER TIME I'M FACE TO FACE. . . . . .   722 WITCH VIVIEN   57
        AND THEN A POINTED FACE WAS SEEN . . . .   728 PRIEST FAIRY   21
        WITH MANY A LOVELY FACE . . . .   740 EARL PAUL   30
        HIS FACE HAS NEVER GLADDENED SINCE HE CAME . . . .   747 SHADOW WATER A   1
        A WHITE BIRD BEATS HIS WINGS UPON MY FACE. . . . .   759 SHADOW WATER A   233
        AGAINST MY FACE AND EYES. MINE TOO ARE BEATEN. . . .   759 SHADOW WATER A V   233
        AND LOVE WENCH WISDOM'S CRUEL FACE. . . . .   787 HUDDON DUDDON   10
        AND LOVE WENCH-WISDOM'S CRUEL FACE. . . . .   787 HUDDON DUDDON V   10
FACED   SEE PALE-FACED
        AND UNREPENTING FACED YOUR ENDS, ...   273 GREY ROCK   60
FACES
        OR THE SOFTNESS OF YOUTH BE GONE FROM OUR FACES, ...   27 OISIN 1   410
        WILL THE SOFTNESS OF YOUTH BE GONE FROM OUR FACES, . . .   27 OISIN 1   V 410
        OR THE SOFTNESS OF YOUTH BE GONE FROM OUR FACES, ...   27 OISIN 1   V 419C
        OR THE SOFTNESS OF YOUTH BE GONE FROM OUR FACES, ...   28 OISIN 1   V 426
        BUT ONLY EXULTANT FACES. NIAMH STOOD . . . .   38 OISIN 2   136
        OF FACES, WAITED; AND THE LEISURED GAZE . . . . . .   39 OISIN 2   149
        OF FACES, WATCHED ME, AND THE LEISURED GAZE . . . .   39 OISIN 2   V 149
        THE SEASHINE ON OUR FACES, WE OUR WAY . . . . . .   41 OISIN 2   V 184B
        THE IMMORTAL DESIRE OF IMMORTALS WE SAW IN THEIR FACES,   47 OISIN 3   4
            AND SIGHED.
        CEASED ON OUR HANDS AND OUR FACES, ON HAZEL AND OAK LEAF, 48 OISIN 3   23
            THE LIGHT,
        HAVE FACES ALIVE WITH SUCH BEAUTY BEEN KNOWN TO THE SALT   50 OISIN 3   51
            EYE OF MAN,
        ARE FACES ALIVE WITH SUCH BEAUTY MADE KNOWN TO THE SALT   50 OISIN 3   V 51
            EYE OF MAN,
        ARE FACES ALIVE WITH SUCH BEAUTY MADE KNOWN TO THE SOFT   50 OISIN 3   V 51
            EYE OF MAN,
        WATCHED HER THOSE SEAMLESS FACES FROM THE VALLEY'S   55 OISIN 3   122
            GLIMMERING GIRTH;
        WATCHED HER THOSE SEAMLESS FACES FROM THE VALLEY'S MURAL   55 OISIN 3   V 122
            GIRTH
        OR WEEDING OR PLOUGHING WITH FACES A-SHINING WITH MUCH-TOIL 58 OISIN 3   165
            WET;
        THEIR FACES ARE ALL WORN, AND IN THEIR EYES . . . . .   73 ANASHU VIJAYA   48
        ON THEIR VAST FACES MYSTERY AND DREAMS; . . . . .   74 ANASHU VIJAYA   70
        THEY BRING YOU MEMORIES OF OLD VILLAGE FACES, ...   130 BOOK STORIES   V   22
        THE WELL-KNOWN FACES ARE ALL GONE, ...   132 OLD PENSIONER   V   17
        CROWDED WITH BITTER FACES, THE WOUNDS IN PALM AND SIDE, 172 TRAV PASSION   4
        WITH QUAKING JOINTS AND TERROR-STRICKEN FACES, ...   185 QUEEN MAEVE   121
        WITH QUAKING JOINTS AND TERROR STRUCKEN FACES, ...   185 QUEEN MAEVE   121
        WITH QUAKING JOINTS AND TERROR-STRUCKEN FACES, ...   185 QUEEN MAEVE   V 121
        THE BITTER SWEETNESS OF FALSE FACES? . . . .   275 GREY ROCK   113
        WITH ALL THEIR ANCIENT FACES LIKE RAIN-BEATEN STONES, . . 318 MAGI   4
        AND NOW THEIR BREATHLESS FACES SEEM TO LOOK . . . .   325 ROBERT GREGORY   43
        AND THEIR BREATHLESS FACES SEEM TO LOOK . . . . . .   325 ROBERT GREGORY V   43
        SHE TURNS THE DOLLS' FACES TO THE WALL . . . . . .   363 DOLLS FACES   T
        HE AND HIS FRIEND, THEIR FACES TO THE SOUTH, ...   372 PHASES OF MOON   2
        COMING WITH VIVID FACES . . . .   391 EASTER 1916   2
        THE NEW FACES . . . .   435 NEW FACES   T
        LET THE NEW FACES PLAY WHAT TRICKS THEY WILL . . . . .   435 NEW FACES   5
        ON THE DROWNED MEN'S HANDS AND FACES, ON THE SPARS AND   719 PHANTOM SHIP   22
            ON THE SAILS.
        JOYS AND FEARS IN THEIR GREY FACES THAT THE LIVE EARTH   719 PHANTOM SHIP   26
            KNOWETH NOT;
        COVER THEIR FACES WITH THEIR HAIR AND WEEP. . . . . .   764 SHADOW WATER A   333
FACING
        HERE, FACING TO THE LAKE, AND NO NAME GILD; . . . . .   663 ISLE STAT II 2   20
FACT
        YET NO CLEAR FACT TO BE DISCERNED; . . . .   425 STARES NEST   9
FACTION
        WHEN ORDER HAS WEAKENED OR FACTION IS STRONG, ... 548 TO SAME TUNE 3   12
FADE
        TILL THEY SHALL SINGING FADE IN RUTH . . . .   66 HAPPY SHEPHERD   41
        WE TIRE OF THE FLAME OF THE METEOR, BEFORE IT CAN FADE 122 WHITE BIRDS   2
            AND FLEE;
        MIGHT FADE IN LOVE IN THE END; . . . .   152 LOSS OF LOVE   V   4
        FOR HOURS WHEN ALL MUST FADE LIKE DEW, ...   156 FORGOT BEAUTY   20
        OF THOSE THAT IT MAY BE SHALL NEVER FADE. . . . . .   183 QUEEN MAEVE   V   76
        THEIR HAUGHTY IMAGES THAT CANNOT FADE, ...   184 QUEEN MAEVE   V   88
        SANG TILL STARS BEGAN TO FADE; . . . .   332 ROUND TOWER   20
        THE OUTRAGEOUS WAR SHALL FADE; . . . .   342 SHEP GOATHERD   100
        THE STARS FADE OUT WHERE THE MOON COMES, ...   344 DAWN   8
        DID ALL THE FABRIC FADE! . . . .   516 MANS SONG   10
        ALL THAT IS FINISHED, LET IT FADE. . . . .   613 MARCH SONGS 1   10
        AND ALL THAT'S FINISHED, LET IT FADE. . . . . . .   613 MARCH SONGS 1   20
        AND ALL THAT'S FINISHED, LET IT FADE. . . . . . .   614 MARCH SONGS 1   30
        I FADE, AND SHALL NOT SEE THE MORNINGS WAKE, ...   674 ISLE STAT II 3   223
        THE BURGHERS OF THE NIGHT FADE ONE BY ONE. . . . . .   700 MOSADA 3   40

		PAGE	TITLE	LINE

FADE (CONTINUED)
STRIKE QUICKLY, IT WILL FADE OUT WHEN YOU STRIKE. • • • 759 SHADOW WATER A 238
I HAVE FORGOT IT ALL. HOW SOON DREAMS FADE! • • • • • 761 SHADOW WATER A 272
FADED
YET WEARY WITH PASSIONS THAT FADED • • • • • • • • • 50 OISIN 3 52
PENSIVE THEY PACED ALONG THE FADED LEAVES, • • • • • • 80 EPHEMERA 10
AS A CLOUD FADED INTO THE SKY. • • • • • • • • • • 145 HOST OF AIR V 40
AND FADED THROUGH THE BRIGHTENING AIR. • • • • • • • 150 WANDER AENGUS 16
THAT HAS LONG FADED FROM THE WORLD! • • • • • • • • 155 FORGOT BEAUTY 3
THAT HAS LONG FADED IN THE WORLD! • • • • • • • • • 155 FORGOT BEAUTY V 3
CAN, TATTERED, STILL PROTECT, FADED ADORN. • • • • • 477 SELF AND SOUL 16
AND FADED NOW IS ALL THY WONDROUS ART. • • • • • • • 673 ISLE STAT II 3 194
FADED AND VANISHED, NOTHING NOW IS SEEN, • • • • • • 676 ISLE STAT II 3 268
THAT DULL AND FADED ARE. • • • • • • • • • • • • • 680 LOVE AND DEATH 26
THE PHANTOMS OF HER FADED PLEASURES WALK! • • • • • • 687 TWO TITANS 19
FOR YEARS HIS DAYS HAD DAWNED AND FADED THUS • • • • • 692 MOSADA 1 54
FADES
UPON THE LIFE THAT FADES AND FLICKERS AND DIES, • • • • 29 OISIN 2 12
MY SINGING FADES, THE STRINGS ARE TORN, • • • • • • • 86 MAD KING GOLL V 66
AND HOW, WHEN FADES THE SEA-STREWN ROSE OF DAY, • • • • 128 DREAM OF FAERY V 33
THAT IT FADES OUT FROM KISS TO KISS! • • • • • • • • 202 NEVER GIVE ALL 5
WHEN THE HORIZON FADES, • • • • • • • • • • • • • • 416 TOWER 193
HE FADES AMONG THE MISTS! HOW FAST THEY COME, • • • • • 703 MOSADA 3 117
REMEMBERING THEE, I MUSE, WHILE FADES IN FLIGHT • • • • 705 REMEMBRANCE 6
ARE BETTER THAN THE WOODS WHERE NO LOVE FADES • • • • • 754 SHADOW WATER A 160
HER EYELIDS TREMBLE AND THE WHITE FOAM FADES! • • • • • 761 SHADOW WATER A 264
AND WHILE SHE FADES AND LIFE WITHERS AWAY, • • • • • • 768 SHADOW WATER A 422
FADETH
SLOWLY, SLOWLY FADETH SHE, • • • • • • • • • • • • 648 ISLE STAT I 1 83
FADING
ABOUT HIS FADING CRIMSON BALL! • • • • • • • • • • 12 OISIN 1 155
"THOUGH OUR SAD LOVE IS FADING, LET US YET • • • • • • 79 EPHEMERA V 4
WHILE HE BENT DOWN HIS FADING HEAD, • • • • • • • • • 82 MAD KING GOLL 10
BENDING LOW HIS FADING HEAD, • • • • • • • • • • • 82 MAD KING GOLL V 10
WHEN WE BENT DOWN ABOVE THE FADING COALS, • • • • • • 136 TO SOME I TALK 3
WHILE THE NIGHT GREW, ABOVE THE FADING COALS, • • • • • 136 TO SOME I TALK V 3
THAT DRAGON THROUGH THE FADING LIGHT, • • • • • • • • 385 ROBARTES DANCE 4
WHAT IS THERE BUT THE SLOWLY FADING WEST, • • • • • • 390 IMAGE PAST 19
UPON A FADING GLEAM, • • • • • • • • • • • • • • • 414 TOWER 141
WHERE SAT OLD SUMMER FADING INTO SONG, • • • • • • • 690 MOSADA 1 V 18
SHE IS ALREADY FADING, AS THOUGH THE GODS • • • • • • 768 SHADOW WATER A V 422
FAERIES
WARS SHADOWY, VAST, EXULTANT! FAERIES OF OLD • • • • • 29 OISIN 2 9
AH, FAERIES, DANCING UNDER THE MOON, • • • • • • • • 139 TO IRELAND 31
SONG OF THE FAERIES • • • • • • • • • • • • • • • • 643 SONG FAERIES V T
NOR FAERIES IN THE HONEY-HEART OF JUNE ASTIR. • • • • • 661 ISLE STAT II 1 73
FAERIES'
I WILL DISSOLVE AWAY THE FAERIES' GUILE! • • • • • • 677 ISLE STAT II 3 282
AND TASTE WITH ME THE FAERIES' MEAT, • • • • • • • • 743 DANAAN QUICK 26
FAERY SEE UN-FAERY
AND MANY A MILE IS THE FAERY STATE, • • • • • • • • 9 OISIN 1 V 103
AND HER BRIGHT BODY, SANG OF FAERY AND MAN • • • • • • 29 OISIN 2 7
ABOUT THEM! AND THE HORSE OF FAERY SCREAMED • • • • • 30 OISIN 2 24
THERE WE'VE HID OUR FAERY VATS, • • • • • • • • • • 87 STOLEN CHILD 6
WITH A FAERY, HAND IN HAND, • • • • • • • • • • • • 87 STOLEN CHILD 11
WITH A FAERY, HAND IN HAND, • • • • • • • • • • • • 87 STOLEN CHILD 26
WITH A FAERY, HAND IN HAND, • • • • • • • • • • • • 88 STOLEN CHILD 40
WITH A FAERY, HAND IN HAND, • • • • • • • • • • • • 89 STOLEN CHILD 52
WITH A FAERY, HAND AND HAND, • • • • • • • • • • • • 89 STOLEN CHILD V 52
A FAERY SONG • • • • • • • • • • • • • • • • • • 115 FAERY SONG T
HOW TIME MAY NEVER MAR THEIR FAERY VOWS • • • • • • • 126 DREAM OF FAERY V 10
AND FROM ITS MURMURING GREENNESS, CALM OF FAERY, • • • • 129 BOOK STORIES 3
THE FAERY HOST • • • • • • • • • • • • • • • • • • 140 HOSTING SIDHE V T
THE FAERY CHILDREN LAUGH IN CRADLES OF WROUGHT GOLD, • • 146 UNAPPEAS HOST V 1
IN DOVE-GREY FAERY LANDS! • • • • • • • • • • • • • 162 ASKS FORGIVE 10
I, STARVED FOR THE BOSOM OF HIS FAERY BRIDE? • • • • • 629 CIRCUS ANIMALS 16
SAD FAERY TONES. 'TIS THUS THEY EVER SEEM, • • • • • 654 ISLE STAT I 2 58
THE WINGED WONDER OF ALL FAERY LAND. • • • • • • • • 657 ISLE STAT I 3 57
THE FAERY SHIP THAT SWIMS ATHWART THE SKY. • • • • • • 663 ISLE STAT II 2 16
ALL SWIM WITH TEARS. THE FAERY BOAT'S AT HAND! • • • • 663 ISLE STAT II 2 33
THE FAERY THING FLEW WITH HER O'ER THE GRAY • • • • • 663 ISLE STAT II 2 38
I'D GIVE MY FAERY FLEETNESS, THOUGH I BE • • • • • • 670 ISLE STAT II 3 107
HIS SLEUTH-HOUNDS FOLLOW EVERY FAERY THING. • • • • • 675 ISLE STAT II 3 244
BUT SOULLESS A FAERY DIES, • • • • • • • • • • • • 676 ISLE STAT II 3 249
FOR SOULLESS A FAERY DIES, • • • • • • • • • • • • 676 ISLE STAT II 3 261
THE FAERY FLOWER LIES UPON THY LIPS. • • • • • • • • 677 ISLE STAT II 3 277
THE FAERY BLOSSOM LIES UPON THY LIPS. • • • • • • • • 677 ISLE STAT II 3 285
THE FAERY BLOSSOM LIES UPON THY LIPS! • • • • • • • • 678 ISLE STAT II 3 291
THE FAERY BLOSSOM BROODS UPON THY LIPS. • • • • • • • 678 ISLE STAT II 3 306
A MURMURING FAERY MULTITUDE, • • • • • • • • • • • • 742 DANAAN QUICK 7
FAERYLAND
THE MAN WHO DREAMED OF FAERYLAND • • • • • • • • • • 126 DREAM OF FAERY T
FAERY'S
AND THINE EYES MORE BRIGHT THAN FAERY'S, • • • • • • • 647 ISLE STAT I 1 53
FAGGOT
FLAMES THAT NO FAGGOT FEEDS, NOR STEEL HAS LIT, • • • • 498 BYZANTIUM 26
FAGGOTS
SOME BURN DAMP FAGGOTS, OTHERS MAY CONSUME • • • • • • 327 ROBERT GREGORY 81
ON OLD DRY FAGGOTS THAT COULD NEVER PLEASE • • • • • • 466 HARUN RASHID 124
FAIL
HE MUSED UPON HIS MOCKERS! WITHOUT FAIL • • • • • • • 127 DREAM OF FAERY 26

259

		PAGE	TITLE	LINE

FAIL (CONTINUED)
AND HOW SHOULD HER HEART FAIL HER . . . .   365 HER RACE   9
NOR SHALL THE SELF-BEGOTTEN FAIL . . . .   530 OLD TOM AGAIN   3
FAIL, AND THAT HISTORY TURNS INTO RUBBISH, ...   546 TO SAME TUNE 2   21
FAIL, AND THAT HISTORY TURNS INTO RUBBISH, ...   614 MARCH SONGS 1   21
HOW THEY WHO SEEK ARE EVER DOOMED TO FAIL. . . . . . .   653 ISLE STAT I 2   41
IT IS, YET SHALL IT FAIL THEE DAY AND NIGHT . . . . .   674 ISLE STAT II 3   211
DEFEAT IS DEATH. SHOULD MY PLOTS FAIL I'D DIE. . . . .   722 WITCH VIVIEN   52
FAILED
WHO HAVE FAILED, BEING WEAK OF WILL, ...   298 THREE HERMITS   18
FAILS
NO EXPECTATION FAILS THERE, ...   621 JOHN KINSELLA   29
FAILURE
OF FAILURE, AND TO CROWN HER CROWNLESS HEAD, ...   688 TWO TITANS   48
FAILURE FOR GLORY DOWN ON THEE, AND MOULD . . . . . .   688 TWO TITANS   54
FAIN
I FAIN HAD BEEN THE FIRST OF SINGING THINGS . . . . .   648 ISLE STAT I 1   101
FAINT
DAWN PASSIONED, FED WITH A FAINT GREEN LIGHT, ...   40 OISIN 2   V   165
. . . SLOW DROPPING A SOUND IN FAINT STREAMS . . . . .   51 OISIN 3   67
FELL LIKE FAINT METEORS IN THE GLOOM, AND ONCE . . . .   80 EPHEMERA   14
AND SHEDS FAINT ODOURS THROUGH THE AIR! . . . .   85 MAD KING GOLL   64
AND SHEDS FAINT ODOUR THROUGH THE AIR! . . . .   85 MAD KING GOLL   V   64
ONE STAR SHONE FAINT AND GREEN, ...   95 MOLL MAGEE   30
"THAT DROWSILY DROPS FAINT LEAVES ON HIM . . . . . .   168 BLESSED   37
THAT IT MAY DROP FAINT PERFUME, AND BE HEAVY WITH DEW, .   172 TRAV PASSION   7
MAKE THE FAINT THUNDER, AND THE GARDEN BEES . . . . .   198 SEVEN WOODS   2
SHOWED THEIR FAINT LIGHT THROUGH THE UNSHUTTERED WINDOWS, .   279 TWO KINGS   50
I AM NO LONGER FAINT . . . .   335 SONG   9
THERE IN THE TOMB DROPS THE FAINT MOONLIGHT, ...   636 BLACK TOWER   17
WILL BE THE FAINT FAR THUNDER-SOUND, AS THOUGH . . . .   699 MOSADA 3   10
WILL MOVE THE FAINT FAR THUNDER-SOUND, AS THOUGH . . .   699 MOSADA 3   V   10
REMEMBERING THEE, I SEARCH OUT THESE FAINT FLOWERS . .   704 REMEMBRANCE   1
FAINTER
BUT FAINTER THAN A YOUNG LAMB'S BLEAT. . . . .   26 OISIN 1   399
AND FAINTER THAN A YOUNG LAMB'S BLEAT. . . . .   26 OISIN 1   V   399
FAIR
ON A MORNING MISTY AND MILD AND FAIR. . . . .   2 OISIN 1   V   7E
HIS MISTRESS WAS MORE MILD AND FAIR . . . .   3 OISIN 1   V   7DD
SHE SAID, "FOR HE IS FAIR ABOVE . . . .   7 OISIN 1   V   62A
FOR FAIR ARE POPPIES ON THE BROW! . . . .   67 HAPPY SHEPHERD   56
"WHAT DO YOU MAKE SO FAIR AND BRIGHT?" . . . .   69 CLOAK BOAT   1
"WHAT DO YOU WEAVE SO FAIR AND BRIGHT?" . . . .   69 CLOAK BOAT   1
I RULED O'ER ALL MY FAIR DOMINIONS, ...   82 MAD KING GOLL   V   7
AND AH, YOU PROUD MAIDEN, YOU ARE NOT SO FAIR WHEN HIS OAR   91 OLD FISHERMAN   9
PROUD MAIDEN, YE ARE NOT SO FAIR, WHEN HIS OAR . . . .   91 OLD FISHERMAN   V   9
AND, AH, YE PROUD MAIDENS, YE ARE NOT SO FAIR, WHEN HIS OAR   91 OLD FISHERMAN   V   9
AND WHERE IS THERE HOPE OR DEED AS FAIR? . . . .   141 HOSTING SIDHE   14
OR REMEMBERING HERS THEY WILL FIND NO OTHER FACE FAIR . .   163 VALLEY LOVERS   7
OR, REMEMBERING HERS, THEY WILL HOLD NO OTHER FACE FAIR .   163 VALLEY LOVERS   V   7
I BOUGHT AT THE SLIGO FAIR. . . . .   178 FIDDLER DOONEY   8
IF ANYBODY HALF AS FAIR . . . .   191 BAILE AILLINN   53
BUT WITH A MAN'S HEAD, OR A FAIR WOMAN'S, ...   233 SHADOW WATER B   245
IF THE LADY BE YOUNG AND FAIR." . . . .   268 BROWN PENNY   6
FARMERS JOSTLED AT THE FAIR . . . .   410 TOWER   39
CROWDS JOSTLED AT THE FAIR . . . .   410 TOWER   V   39
"FAIR AND FOUL ARE NEAR OF KIN, ...   513 JANE TALK BISH   7
AND FAIR NEEDS FOUL," I CRIED. . . . .   513 JANE TALK BISH   8
COME FORTH! THE MORN IS FAIR! AS FROM THE PYRE . . .   645 ISLE STAT I 1   8
OF FLIGHT ARE DONE. MOST FAIR OF ALL WHO GRAZE . . .   649 ISLE STAT I 1   118
NASCHINA, HAIL! MOST FAIR OF ALL WHO GRAZE . . . . .   649 ISLE STAT I 1   120
AS FAIR AS ANY THAT ON IDA'S MOUNT . . . .   650 ISLE STAT I 1   134
IS NOT MORE FAIR AND JOYOUS THAN SHE IS . . . .   661 ISLE STAT II 1   71
WHAT DO YOU WEAVE SO FAIR AND BRIGHT? . . . .   666 ISLE STAT II 3   1
FAIR YOUTH, ALONG A WANDERING WAY . . . .   667 ISLE STAT II 3   38
MY LIPS, FAIR YOUTH. IT SHALL BE AS YOU ASK. . . . .   669 ISLE STAT II 3   80
FAIR SHEPHERD, AS WE WANDERED HITHER. . . . .   669 ISLE STAT II 3   83
IN SHADOWY DIMNESS. TO BE FAIR AS THEE . . . .   670 ISLE STAT II 3   106
IN THOSE FAIR YEARS, O DAUGHTER OF THE DAYS, ...   674 ISLE STAT II 3 V   213
THUS BECKON TO OUR AID A PHANTOM FAIR . . . .   693 MOSADA 1   76
A PEASANT YOUNG AND FAIR, HER EYES FOR FEAR . . . . .   713 FERENCZ RENYI   V   81
AND DEATH, OH MY FAIR ONE, WILL NEVER COME NEAR . . .   717 LOVE SONG   8
THEN THE STARS GROW OUT OF HEAVEN WITH THEIR COUNTENANCES   719 PHANTOM SHIP   30
FAIR.
ILL WORDS FOR ALL THINGS SOFT AND FAIR, ...   723 GIRLS SONG A   6
FAIR-HAIRED
THE PLAIN, A LITTLE FAIR-HAIRED MAID I LOVE. . . . . .   679 ISLE STAT II 3   312
THERE DWELLS A LITTLE FAIR-HAIRED MAID I LOVE. . . . .   679 ISLE STAT II 3 V   312
FAIRIES
THE FAIRIES MOVED AMONG THE FOUNTAINS, ...   25 OISIN 1   V   386
GLAMOURED BY FAIRIES FOR THEIR OWN. . . . .   717 FAIRY DOCTOR   20
A LOVER'S QUARREL AMONG THE FAIRIES. . . . .   726 LOVERS QUARREL   T
WHERE THE SOULS OF FAIRIES GO?" . . . .   729 PRIEST FAIRY   48
FAIRIES'
THE FAIRIES' HERALD SPAKE ONCE MORE! . . . .   730 PRIEST FAIRY   53
FAIRS
FROM MARKETS AND FROM FAIRS . . . .   420 MY HOUSE   19
FAIRY
MOUNT MY WHITE STEED, FOR THE FAIRY STATE . . . . . .   9 OISIN 1   V   103
FOR FAIRY SONGS CONTINUALLY. . . . .   11 OISIN 1   V   134
WARS SHADOWY, VAST, EXULTANT! FAIRY KINGS . . . . . .   29 OISIN 2   V   9

FAIRY   (CONTINUED)
    OF SEA-SPRUNG PEARL, AND QUEENS OF FAIRY LANDS . . . .   29 OISIN 2   V 10A
    BUT SOULLESS A FAIRY DIES, ...   643 SONG FAERIES   2
    FOR SOULLESS A FAIRY DIES, ...   644 SONG FAERIES   14
    UNTO THE DOLOROUS BORDER OF THE FAIRY LAKE. . . . . .   655 ISLE STAT I 2   85
    THE FAIRY VOICES . . . .   655 ISLE STAT I 3   V   T
    THE FAIRY PEDANT. . . . .   706 FAIRY PEDANT   T
    THE SOLITARY FAIRY . . . .   706 FAIRY PEDANT   V   T
    YOU ARE WASTING AWAY, LITTLE FAIRY. . . . .   707 FAIRY PEDANT   12
    YOU ARE WASTING AWAY, LITTLE FAIRY. . . . .   707 FAIRY PEDANT   20
    YOU ARE WASTING AWAY, LITTLE FAIRY. . . . .   708 FAIRY PEDANT   28
    SHE IS WASTING AWAY, LITTLE FAIRY. . . . .   708 FAIRY PEDANT   40
    THE FAIRY DOCTOR. . . . .   716 FAIRY DOCTOR   T
    THE FAIRY DOCTOR COMES OUR WAY . . . .   716 FAIRY DOCTOR   1
    HE SEES THE FAIRY HOSTING MOVE . . . .   716 FAIRY DOCTOR   9
    AND FULL HIS EYES OF FAIRY CHEER. . . . .   716 FAIRY DOCTOR   12
    SO WE DANCE A FAIRY JIG . . . .   726 LOVERS QUARREL   19
    YONDER SEE THE FAIRY GIRLS . . . .   726 LOVERS QUARREL   21
    THE PRIEST AND THE FAIRY. . . . .   728 PRIEST FAIRY   T
    NOW, WHAT HAS A FAIRY TO DO WITH A PRIEST . . . . .   729 PRIEST FAIRY   27
    A FAIRY WHOM WE LOVED FULL WELL. . . . .   729 PRIEST FAIRY   44
    THE FAIRY VANISHED FROM HIS SIGHT, ...   730 PRIEST FAIRY   62
    WERE YOU A FAIRY YOU'D HAVE HEARD . . . .   730 PRIEST FAIRY   67
FAIRY-HAUNTED
    IN THE FAIRY-HAUNTED RATH, ...   706 DAWN-SONG   21
FAIRYLAND
    A MAN WHO DREAMED OF FAIRYLAND . . . .   126 DREAM OF FAERY V   T
FAIRY'S
    THE FAIRY'S CALL . . . .   654 ISLE STAT I 2   V   T
FAIRY-SMITTEN
    WITH FAIRY-SMITTEN UDDERS DRY-- . . . .   716 FAIRY DOCTOR   14
FAITH
    WHERE BROKEN FAITH HAS NEVER BEEN KNOWN, ...   8 OISIN 1   84
    AND I THAT HAVE NOT YOUR FAITH, HOW SHALL I KNOW . . . 258 KING NO KING   11
    I HAVE KEPT MY FAITH, THOUGH FAITH WAS TRIED, ...   276 GREY ROCK   124
    I HAVE KEPT MY FAITH, THOUGH FAITH WAS TRIED, ...   276 GREY ROCK   124
    FOR ENGLAND MAY KEEP FAITH . . . .   394 EASTER 1916   68
    AND I DECLARE MY FAITH. . . . .   414 TOWER   145
    I LEAVE BOTH FAITH AND PRIDE . . . .   416 TOWER   173
    THE TRUE FAITH DISCOVERED WAS . . . .   440 WISDOM   1
    WHO HAVE ACCEPTED THE BYZANTINE FAITH, ...   464 HARUN RASHID   78
    TEST EVERY WORK OF INTELLECT OR FAITH, ...   501 VACILLATION   30
    IN THAT FAITH I LIVE OR DIE." . . . .   529 TOM LUNATIC   18
    I' FAITH THOU EVER WAST A WORDY SPIRIT! . . . . . .   673 ISLE STAT II 3   175
    SHE WOULD WEAVE A NET TO TAKE US. SHE MIGHT KEEP FAITH! 756 SHADOW WATER A   190
FAITHFUL
    BUT FAITHFUL LOVERS. . . . .   220 HARP OF AENGUS   14
    WHY SHOULD YOU BE MORE FAITHFUL THAN THE REST, . . .   227 SHADOW WATER B   109
    A FAITHFUL LOVE, A FAITHFUL LOVE. . . . .   449 HERO GIRL FOOL   29
    A FAITHFUL LOVE, A FAITHFUL LOVE. . . . .   449 HERO GIRL FOOL   29
    HE WATCHES OVER NONE BUT FAITHFUL LOVERS. . . . . .   762 SHADOW WATER A   295
    BUT FAITHFUL LOVERS. SOMETHING GLITTERS THERE-- . . . . 763 SHADOW WATER A   309
    BUT FAITHFUL LOVERS. WHITHER HAVE YOU COME, ...   763 SHADOW WATER A V   309
FAITHFULLEST
    WHY SHOULD THE FAITHFULLEST HEART MOST LOVE . . . . .   275 GREY ROCK   112
FAITHLESS
    "WHY ARE THEY FAITHLESS WHEN THEIR MIGHT . . . . . .   275 GREY ROCK   109
FALCON
    HOW THE FALCONER FOLLOWS THE FALCON IN THE WEEDS OF THE   52 OISIN 3   79
        HERON'S PLOT,
    THE FALCON CANNOT HEAR THE FALCONER: . . . .   401 SECOND COMING   2
    THE FALCON CAN NOT HEAR THE FALCONER: . . . .   401 SECOND COMING   V   2
    I RIDE WITH FALCON TO THE RIVER'S EDGE . . . . . .   463 HARUN RASHID   57
    I RIDE WITH FALCON TO THE WATER'S EDGE . . . . . .   463 HARUN RASHID   V 57
    AND DOWN I CAME AS A FALCON SWOOPS . . . .   673 ISLE STAT II 3   178
FALCONER
    HOW THE FALCONER FOLLOWS THE FALCON IN THE WEEDS OF THE   52 OISIN 3   79
        HERON'S PLOT,
    THE FALCON CANNOT HEAR THE FALCONER: . . . .   401 SECOND COMING   2
    THE FALCON CAN NOT HEAR THE FALCONER: . . . .   401 SECOND COMING   V   2
FALIAS
    AND FINDRIAS AND FALIAS, ...   196 BAILE AILLINN   162
FALL   SEE FOOT-FALL
    IT SEEMED TO FALL FROM THE VERY FLAME . . . .   13 OISIN 1   V 167
    WHERE DROPS OF DEW IN MYRIADS FALL, ...   16 OISIN 1   222
    WHERE WHITE DEWDROPS IN MILLIONS FALL: . . . .   16 OISIN 1   V 222
    AND CAME TO WHERE THE DEWDROPS FALL . . . .   20 OISIN 1   293
    FALL THE LEAVES OF OTHER ROSES, ...   21 OISIN 1   311
    SHALL FALL THE LEAVES OF DAMASK ROSES. . . . .   21 OISIN 1   315
    BEFORE THIS DAY: FOR NOW THE FALL OF TEARS . . . . .   30 OISIN 2   18
    TREMBLING, ON THE FLAGS WE FALL, ...   43 OISIN 2   V 208E
    GATHER SEA-SLIME AND FALL THE SEAWARD WAY, ...   45 OISIN 2   237
    GATHER SEA SLIME AND FALL THE SEAWARD WAY, ...   45 OISIN 2   V 237
    MY PILLARS TOWARDS THEIR FALL. . . . .   44 OISIN 2   V 239
    THERE DREAMY TIME LETS FALL HIS SICKLE . . . . . .   77 INDIAN TO LOVE V   5A
    ERE FALL OF EVENING, MY MAILED HOST, ...   83 MAD KING GOLL V   19
    . . . HUNG LOW IN THE FALL OF THE DEW: . . . .   122 WHITE BIRDS   7
    WHATEVER RAVELLED WATERS RISE AND FALL . . . . . .   127 DREAM OF FAERY   32
    THE LIGHT FALL OF HER FLYING FEET . . . .   138 TO IRELAND   V 11
    THOUGH HOPE FALL FROM YOU AND LOVE DECAY, ...   148 INTO TWILIGHT   7
    THOUGH HOPE FALL FROM THEE OR LOVE DECAY . . . . .   148 INTO TWILIGHT   V   7

		PAGE	TITLE		LINE

FALL   (CONTINUED)
```
OVER MY HEART, AND YOUR HAIR FALL OVER MY BREAST,    . . .   154 BELOVED PEACE        10
OVER MY HEART, AND YOUR HAIR FALL ABOUT MY BREAST    . . .   154 BELOVED PEACE     V  10
AND YOUR HIGH BEAUTY FALL AND BE LOST  . . . . . . .        173 PLEADS FRIEND     V   7
SINCE ADAM'S FALL BUT NEEDS MUCH LABOURING,  . . . . .      205 ADAMS CURSE          22
O HEAVY SWOLLEN WATERS, BRIM THE FALL OF THE OAK TREES,     207 HANRAHANS SONG    V  11
MEAN ROOF-TREES WERE THE STURDIER FOR ITS FALL,  . . . .    264 HOUSE SHAKEN          8
I STAGGERED, BUT A BEECH-TREE STAYED MY FALL,  . . . .      286 TWO KINGS           209
I STAGGERED, BUT A BEECH TREE STAYED MY FALL,  . . . .      286 TWO KINGS         V 209
FALL ASLEEP WHEN I SHOULD PRAY."  . . . . . . . . .         298 THREE HERMITS        12
THREE HUNDRED YEARS BEFORE THE FALL,  . . . . . . . .       388 SOLOMON WITCH        11
THINGS FALL APART! THE CENTRE CANNOT HOLD!  . . . . .       402 SECOND COMING         3
THINGS FALL APART! THE CENTRE CAN NOT HOLD,  . . . . .      402 SECOND COMING     V   3
AND LET IT FALL UNNOTICED TO THE FLOOR.  . . . . . . .      461 HARUN RASHID         15
AND IT WOULD FALL UNNOTICED ON THE FLOOR.  . . . . . .      461 HARUN RASHID      V  15
THAT FOLLOWED IF I LET THE KERCHIEF FALL!  . . . . . .      533 HER TRIUMPH           4
NOR SAW MY BODY FALL NOR HEARD IT SHRIEK,  . . . . . .      537 HER VISION           29
NO MATTER WHAT HAPPENS AND WHO TAKES THE FALL,  . . . .     545 TO SAME TUNE 1       22
NO MATTER WHAT HAPPENS OR WHO TAKES THE FALL,  . . . . .    545 TO SAME TUNE 1    V  22
ALL THINGS FALL AND ARE BUILT AGAIN,  . . . . . . .         566 LAPIS LAZULI         35
NO MATTER WHAT HAPPENS AND WHO TAKES THE FALL,  . . . . .   616 MARCH SONGS 3        22
ON THIS FOUL WORLD IN ITS DECLINE AND FALL!  . . . . .      619 BRONZE HEAD          24
AMONG THOSE BIRD-LIKE THINGS CAME, AND LET FALL  . . . .    634 CUCHULAIN COMF        8
THEY GET THEM SWORDS, AND BOTH OR EITHER FALL?  . . . .     662 ISLE STAT II 1       78
NOR TREMBLE TO ITS FALL.   THE FIRE SWEEPS ROUND  . . .     689 NETTLESHIP           11
I TRY TO LIFT MINE ARMS—THEY FALL AGAIN.  . . . . . .       701 MOSADA 3             56
DOWN THE VAPOURS FALL AND HIDE THEM FROM THE CHILDREN OF    719 PHANTOM SHIP         27
   A DAY,
TO THE FIDDLE'S RISE AND FALL. . . . . . . . . . .         726 LOVERS QUARREL       20
AND TEARS OF FIRE FALL GENTLY IN THE DEW. . . . . . .       738 YOU ARE SAD           4
AND MINGLING HAIR FALL FROM THE FIERY BOUGHS,  . . . .      765 SHADOW WATER A      368
AND, HURRYING HOMEWARD, FALL UPON SOME LAND  . . . . .      767 SHADOW WATER A      384
```
FALLEN
```
NO LIMB OF ME THAT WAS NOT FALLEN  . . . . . . . .           7 OISIN 1           V  72
AND NOW HAVE FALLEN ON MY LIFE  . . . . . . . . . .          24 OISIN 1           V 358
AND THEY HAVE FALLEN OR FLED, AGE AFTER AGE. . . . . .        45 OISIN 2             242
. . . WHEN THE FALLEN ON FALLEN LIE ROLLED!  . . . . .        52 OISIN 3              78
. . . WHEN THE FALLEN ON FALLEN LIE ROLLED!  . . . . .        52 OISIN 3              78
FROM POND AND FALLEN TREE—ME SING  . . . . . . . .           85 MAD KING GOLL     V  63
HAS FALLEN AWAY?  . . . . . . . . . . . . . . .             142 MOODS                 7
WITH HEAVY WHITENING WINGS, AND A HEART FALLEN COLD!  . .   147 UNAPPEAS HOST         4
THE GARDEN HAD FALLEN STILL!  . . . . . . . . . .           159 CAP AND BELLS         2
AND THEN THE CLASH OF FALLEN HORSEMEN AND THE CRIES . . .   161 BLACK PIG             3
HE HAD FALLEN ASLEEP, AND, THOUGH HE HAD DREAMED NOTHING,   182 QUEEN MAEVE          55
TILL HE HAS FALLEN ASLEEP  . . . . . . . . . . .            216 HAPPY TOWNLAND       51
SHINING ON WATER AND FALLEN AMONG LEAVES, . . . . . . .     218 WOODS OF COOLE       38
WE HAVE FALLEN IN THE DREAMS THE EVER-LIVING  . . . . .     228 SHADOW WATER B      131
THESE ARE THE CLOUDS ABOUT THE FALLEN SUN, . . . . . .      265 THESE CLOUDS          1
THESE ARE THE CLOUDS ABOUT THE FALLEN SUN, . . . . . .      265 THESE CLOUDS         11
THAT WHEN HE HAS FALLEN ASLEEP WITHIN MY ARMS, . . . . .    285 TWO KINGS           191
FALLEN MAJESTY  . . . . . . . . . . . . . . . .            314 FALLEN MAJESTY        T
BABBLING OF FALLEN MAJESTY, RECORDS WHAT'S GONE. . . . .    314 FALLEN MAJESTY        4
"THE NIGHT HAS FALLEN! NOT A SOUND  . . . . . . . .         389 SOLOMON WITCH        38
HAD FALLEN AMONG DANCERS, HAD WHIRLED THEM ROUND . . . .    430 NINETEEN 19          52
THE THREEFOLD TERROR OF LOVE! A FALLEN FLARE  . . . . .     499 MOTHER OF GOD         1
THIS FALLEN STAR MY MILK SUSTAINS, . . . . . . . . .        499 MOTHER OF GOD        12
THE THREE-FOLD TERROR OF LOVE! A FALLEN FLARE  . . . . .    499 MOTHER OF GOD     V   1
"THOSE BREASTS ARE FLAT AND FALLEN NOW,  . . . . . . .      513 JANE TALK BISH        3
A CAREFUL FIELD-MOUSE FINDS A FALLEN CRUMB!  . . . . .      713 FERENCZ RENYI        77
BY TABLES THAT WERE FALLEN INTO DUST  . . . . . . .         724 KANVA ON SELF        13
FOR ALL GOOD MEN NOW FALLEN ILL,  . . . . . . . .          736 IN CHURCH             5
HAVE FALLEN AND MY SUN AND MOON GONE OUT. . . . . . .       767 SHADOW WATER A    V 405
```
FALLING
```
RISING AND FALLING, MIXED INSEPARABLY, . . . . . . .         45 OISIN 2           V 233
THE FALLING OF THE LEAVES  . . . . . . . . . . .            79 FALLING LEAVES        T
FALLING OF THE LEAVES  . . . . . . . . . . . .              79 FALLING LEAVES    V   T
IT QUENCHED, WITH SOUND LIKE FALLING DEW, . . . . . .        86 MAD KING GOLL        66
WITH HER CLOUD-PALE EYELIDS FALLING ON DREAM-DIMMED EYES!   163 VALLEY LOVERS         4
GREAT POWERS OF FALLING WAVE AND WIND AND WINDY FIRE, . .   174 ELEMENT POWERS        7
THOUGH COURTEOUS TO THE WORST! MUCH FALLING HE  . . . .     324 ROBERT GREGORY       19
ARE BRIDELESS."  "I AM FALLING INTO YEARS." . . . . .       463 HARUN RASHID         54
CLIMBING, FALLING SHE KNEW NOT WHERE,  . . . . . . .        578 CRAZED GIRL           4
THE FALLING HAWTHORN BLOOM.  BY MERE AND BROOK  . . . .     677 ISLE STAT II 3      279
SHE PRAYS FOR EVERY FALLING TEAR  . . . . . . . .          735 IN CHURCH             3
A PRAYER FOR EVERY FALLING TEAR  . . . . . . . .           736 IN CHURCH            15
KINGDOMS RISING, KINGDOMS FALLING, . . . . . . . .         737 IN FIRELIGHT          9
THE FALLING BLOSSOMS, AND THE DEAD THE LIVING. . . . .      756 SHADOW WATER A      182
```
FALLS   SEE SALMON-FALLS
```
THE RED SUN FALLS AND THE WORLD GROWS DIM."  . . . . .        9 OISIN 1             105
AND THE ROOF FALLS IN OF HIS TUNNELLED HOUSE. . . . . .       27 OISIN 1           V 419
AND THE ROOF FALLS IN OF HIS TUNNELLED HOUSE. . . . . .       28 OISIN 1             423
WHEN THE POOR TIRED CHILD, PASSION, FALLS ASLEEP. . . .       80 EPHEMERA             7
HIS EYELIDS DROOP, HIS HEAD FALLS LOW, . . . . . . .         98 FOXHUNTER            13
FALLS IN SLEEPY STREAMS. . . . . . . . . . . .              98 FOXHUNTER            16
WHERE THE SUN FALLS INTO THE WESTERN DEEP. . . . . . .      108 CUCHULAIN SEA     V  34
AND AS IT FALLS AWAKENS LEAFY TUNES!—  . . . . . .         127 DREAM OF FAERY    V  23
TO FIND IT WHEN NIGHT FALLS LAID ON A GOLDEN BIER. . . .    209 UNDER THE MOON       10
THE ROPE'S IN TWO—IT FALLS INTO THE SEA,  . . . . . .       251 SHADOW WATER B      596
THE SALMON FALLS, THE MACKEREL-CROWDED SEAS, . . . . .      407 SAIL BYZANTIUM    V   4
THAT SPRINGS FROM BODY AND IN BODY FALLS  . . . . . .       463 HARUN RASHID         63
AND FALLS INTO THE BASIN OF THE MIND . . . . . . . .       478 SELF AND SOUL        34
```

262

		PAGE	TITLE		LINE

FALLS   (CONTINUED)
    INTOLERABLE MUSIC FALLS. . . . . 612 NEWS ORACLE   32
    THE NIGHEST BLOSSOM WHERE IT FALLS I'LL TAKE. . . . . 657 ISLE STAT I 3   65
    SEER OF VISIONS! NOW EVE FALLS ASLEEP, ... 691 MOSADA 1   36
    AND FALLS AMONG THE DREAMS THE DROWSY GODS . . . . 750 SHADOW WATER A   68
FALSE
    AND LOVED YOUR BEAUTY WITH LOVE FALSE OR TRUE, ... 121 YOU ARE OLD   6
    AND LOVED YOUR BEAUTY WILL LOVE FALSE OR TRUE! . . . . . 121 YOU ARE OLD   V   6
    THE BITTER SWEETNESS OF FALSE FACES? . . . . 275 GREY ROCK   113
FALSTAFFAN
    A HEAVILY BUILT FALSTAFFAN MAN, ... 423 ROAD AT DOOR   V   2
FALSTAFFIAN
    A HEAVILY-BUILT FALSTAFFIAN MAN, ... 423 ROAD AT DOOR   2
FALTER
    ERE LONG SHALL FALTER THROUGH THE NOISY SQUARE, ... 699 MOSADA 3   21
FALTERS
    AND "MY SPEED IS A WEARINESS," FALTERS THE MOUSE, . . . 28 OISIN 1   421
FAME
    CRIED FIN! AND CRIED SHE, "MEN OF FAME, ... 5 OISIN 1   V   45
    OF ALL THAT WISDOM AND THE FAME . . . . 7 OISIN 1   66
    OF NOBLE OISIN AND HIS FAME, ... 7 OISIN 1   V   66
    TO PEAK AND PINE O'ER OISIN'S FAME." . . . . 7 OISIN 1   V   70
    AND THE HIGH FAME THAT COME TO THEM IN MARRIAGE, ... 232 SHADOW WATER B   235
    --SEEING THAT FAME HAS PERISHED THIS LONG WHILE, ... 321 REED WHISPERER   11
    HE MIGHT HAVE WON FAME IN THE END, ... 392 EASTER 1916   28
    SO GREAT ITS FAME. WHEN FITTING TIME HAS PASSED . . . 461 HARUN RASHID   19
    WHERE NONE HAS REIGNED THAT LACKED A NAME AND FAME . . . 491 COOLE BALLYLEE   31
    BUT FAME AND VIRTUE ROT. . . . . 584 GHOST ROG CASE   36
FAMED
    IN SILENCE, THAT FAMED FLOWER OF WIZARDRY, ... 673 ISLE STAT II 3   192
FAMILIAR
    NO CREATURE HAD FAMILIAR THOUGHT . . . . 17 OISIN 1   V   242
    TO SOME SURE COUNTRY, SOME FAMILIAR PLACE. . . . . . 249 SHADOW WATER B   569
    MONSTROUS FAMILIAR IMAGES SWIM TO THE MIND'S EYE. . . . 426 PHANTOM HATRED   8
FAMILIES
    DEATH, DESPAIR, DIVISION OF FAMILIES, ... 459 FROM OEDIPUS   5
    MARRIAGES, ALLIANCES AND FAMILIES, ... 491 COOLE BALLYLEE   36
FAMILY
    HIS CHILDHOOD AND HIS FAMILY. . . . . 361 ALF POLLEXFEN   35
    MONTASHIGI, THIRD OF HIS FAMILY, FASHIONED IT . . . . 478 SELF AND SOUL   25
    FAMILY AND FAMILY, ... 540 FROM ANTIGONE   11
    FAMILY AND FAMILY, ... 540 FROM ANTIGONE   11
    NOR SATISFIED CONSCIENCE, BUT THAT GREAT FAMILY . . . 579 DOR WELLESLEY   14
    AND FOUND HIS FAMILY TOMB . . . . 584 GHOST ROG CASE   32
FAMISH
    THE ICICLES THAT FAMISH ALL THE NORTH, ... 73 ANASHU VIJAYA   50
FAMISHED
    BECAUSE OF SOMETHING TOLD UNDER THE FAMISHED HORN . . . 210 UNDER THE MOON   17
    HE HAD FAMISHED IN A WILDERNESS, ... 789 SINGING HEAD   1
FAMOUS   SEE WORLD-FAMOUS
    OISIN, TELL ME THE FAMOUS STORY . . . . 2 OISIN 1   V   1
    I CRIED, "THOU ART SURELY A WARRIOR, FORGETTING HIS FAMOUS   51 OISIN 3   V   61
      LINE,
    HE IS A FAMOUS FISHER! HOUR BY HOUR . . . . 73 ANASHU VIJAYA   36
    AND ALL THAT FAMOUS HARMONY OF LEAVES, ... 120 SORROW OF LOVE   3
    AND OF THAT FAMOUS FERGUS, NESSA'S HUSBAND, ... 183 QUEEN MAEVE   71
    WITH FAMOUS PORTRAITS OF OUR ANCESTORS! . . . . . . 418 ANCEST HOUSES   37
    AND GONE ARE PHIDIAS' FAMOUS IVORIES . . . . 428 NINETEEN 19   7
    OR BREAK IN BITS THE FAMOUS IVORIES . . . . 430 NINETEEN 19   47
    BELOVED BOOKS THAT FAMOUS HANDS HAVE BOUND, ... 491 COOLE BALLYLEE   27
    HE MUST GROW A FAMOUS MAN! . . . . 576 WHAT THEN   2
    AND THEY BUT FAMOUS OLD UPHOLSTERIES . . . . 579 DOR WELLESLEY   3
    SOME ANCIENT FAMOUS AUTHORS MISREPRESENT, ... 579 DOR WELLESLEY   15
    FOUND MANY A FAMOUS MAN THERE! . . . . 584 GHOST ROG CASE   35
    A FAMOUS, A BRILLIANT FIGURE . . . . 608 SONGS BURDEN 3   16
    VIOLENT AND FAMOUS, STRODE AMONG THE DEAD! . . . . 634 CUCHULAIN COMF   2
    OH FAMOUS DYING MINION OF THE SUN, ... 673 ISLE STAT II 3   197
    FAMOUS, A MAN OF RULES, A VICTOR. STANDS . . . . . 709 FERENCZ RENYI   9
FAN
    THAT FAN THE PULSES OF DELIGHTED AIR, ... 32 OISIN 2   V   50A
    BUT SHE TOOK UP HER FAN FROM THE TABLE . . . . . . 160 CAP AND BELLS   19
    BUT SHE TOOK HER FAN FROM THE TABLE, ... 160 CAP AND BELLS   V   19
    OF OCEAN FAN THEE INTO LIFE, AND FOLD . . . . . . 688 TWO TITANS   56
FANATIC
    MY FANATIC HEART. . . . . 506 REMORSE SPEECH   5
    MY FANATIC HEART, ... 506 REMORSE SPEECH   10
    A FANATIC HEART. . . . . 506 REMORSE SPEECH   15
    DOWN THE FANATIC, DOWN THE CLOWN! . . . . 544 TO SAME TUNE 1   8
    DOWN THE FANATIC, DOWN THE CLOWN! . . . . 545 TO SAME TUNE 1   18
    DOWN THE FANATIC, DOWN THE CLOWN! . . . . 545 TO SAME TUNE 1   28
    DOWN THE FANATIC, DOWN THE CLOWN! . . . . 546 TO SAME TUNE 2 V   REF
    DOWN THE FANATIC, DOWN THE CLOWN! . . . . 548 TO SAME TUNE 3 V   REF
FANATICISM
    SO DID FANATICISM AND HATE ENSLAVE IT, ... 630 CIRCUS ANIMALS   22
FANATICS
    WHAT FANATICS INVENT . . . . 503 QUARREL IN AGE   2
    THOSE FANATICS ALL THAT WE DO WOULD UNDO! . . . . 544 TO SAME TUNE 1   7
    THOSE FANATICS ALL THAT WE DO WOULD UNDO! . . . . 545 TO SAME TUNE 1   17
    THOSE FANATICS ALL THAT WE DO WOULD UNDO! . . . . 545 TO SAME TUNE 1   27
    THOSE FANATICS ALL THAT WE DO WOULD UNDO! . . . . 546 TO SAME TUNE 2 V   REF
    THOSE FANATICS ALL THAT WE DO WOULD UNDO! . . . . 548 TO SAME TUNE 3 V   REF

		PAGE	TITLE		LINE

FANCIED

		PAGE	TITLE		LINE
THAT FANCIED GOODNESS MIGHT BE GAY,		432	NINETEEN 19		104
ALL THOSE ABSTRACTIONS THAT YOU FANCIED WERE		469	HARUN RASHID		182
AND THOSE ABSTRACTIONS THAT YOU FANCIED WERE		469	HARUN RASHID	V	182
BECAUSE I HAD FANCIED LOVE A CASUAL		533	HER TRIUMPH		2
HE FANCIED THAT I GAVE A SOUL		538	LAST CONFESS		9

FANCIES

| THAT IT CAN TAKE WHAT FORM COOK NATURE FANCIES | | 377 | PHASES OF MOON | | 115 |

FANCY

WHATEVER WOMAN'S LOVER HAD HIT HER FANCY,		181	QUEEN MAEVE		24
THE ONLY RICHES THAT HAVE HIT MY FANCY.		226	SHADOW WATER B		96
THAT SET HIM TO THE FANCY. ALL WOULD BE WELL		230	SHADOW WATER B		177
TO FANCY THAT SHE'D BRING YOU HOME AGAIN,		248	SHADOW WATER B		549
MY FANCY, AND SET MY BOYISH LIPS TO SAY,		270	PARDON FATHERS		17
TO TAKE MY FANCY LIKE THE WIND		301	RUN PARADISE		26
HAD SOUNDED BETTER TO YOUR MOUNTAIN FANCY.		341	SHEP GOATHERD		61
THAT IT CAN TAKE WHAT FORM COOK NATURE FANCY		377	PHASES OF MOON	V	115
TO TEST THEIR FANCY BY THEIR SIGHT:		410	TOWER		44
FANCY THAT I CAN		507	STREAM AND SUN		8
MY FANCY ON A MAN,		515	GIRLS SONG B		3
A POISON DROP. A TOY, A FANCY ONCE,		700	MOSADA 3		24
A POISON DROP. THE TOY OF FANCY ONCE,		700	MOSADA 3	V	24

FANCY-MAN

| HAVE BEDDED WITH THEIR FANCY-MAN | | 789 | SINGING HEAD | | 17 |

FAND

WHO MET FAND WALKING AMONG FLAMING DEW		169	SECRET ROSE		13
AND NIAMH AND LABAN AND FAND, WHO COULD CHANGE TO AN OTTER OR FAWN,		209	UNDER THE MOON		12
AND FAND, AND NIAM, AND LABAN, WHO COULD CHANGE TO AN OTTER OR FAWN,		209	UNDER THE MOON	V	12

FAN-FORMED

| WHITENED AFAR WITH SURGE, FAN-FORMED AND WIDE, | | 31 | OISIN 2 | | 28 |
| WHITENING THE SURGE AFAR, FAN-FORMED AND WIDE, | | 31 | OISIN 2 | V | 28 |

FANGLED   SEE NEW-FANGLED

FANNED

| FANNED THE DELIGHTED AIR LIKE WINGS OF BIRDS! | | 32 | OISIN 2 | | 50 |

FANTASIES

| WE HAD FED THE HEART ON FANTASIES, | | 425 | STARES NEST | | 16 |
| WE HAVE FED THE HEART ON FANTASIES, | | 425 | STARES NEST | V | 16 |

FANTASTIC

PLEASE A FANTASTIC HEAD,		366	HER CHRIS TREE		8
ON A FANTASTIC RIDE, MY HORSE'S FLANKS ARE SPURRED		391	UNDER SATURN		6
ON A FANTASTIC RIDE I SWEAR MY HORSE'S FLANKS WERE SPURRED		391	UNDER SATURN	V	6
THOUGH FANTASTIC MEN SUPPOSE		530	OLD TOM AGAIN		4
WITH THOSE FANTASTIC DREAMS.		781	MY HEART BEAT		11

FANTASTICAL

| FANTASTICAL AND WILD | | 364 | END OF DAY | | 3 |
| EXCITED, PASSIONATE, FANTASTICAL | | 409 | TOWER | | 5 |

FANTASY

AS, FULL OF LOVING FANTASY,		13	OISIN 1		158
WHATEVER THEIR LOOSE FANTASY INVENT		398	LEADERS CROWD		4
MANKIND INANIMATE FANTASY.		406	IN TIME OF WAR	V	5
AND SPEAK BUT FANTASY. RECALL THE YEAR		462	HARUN RASHID		30
PERPLEXED HER FANTASY AND PLANNED HER CARE?		466	HARUN RASHID		114
THAT STIRRED HER FANTASY AND PLANNED HER CARE,		466	HARUN RASHID	V	114
WHERE FASHION OR MERE FANTASY DECREES		491	COOLE BALLYLEE		38
FANTASY OR INCIDENT		504	QUARREL IN AGE		4

FAR

NIAMH, AND MY COUNTRY FAR		5	OISIN 1		48
MY HOME IS FAR FROM WHERE THE TIDE		5	OISIN 1	V	46
LIES FAR." I MOUNTED, AND SHE BOUND ME		9	OISIN 1	V	106
IN WHAT FAR KINGDOM DO YOU GO,		10	OISIN 1		115
AND FAR BEHIND US, SLOWLY ROUND		10	OISIN 1	V	114B
IN WHAT FAR KINGDOM DO YE GO,		10	OISIN 1	V	115
AND A FAR SOUND OF FEATHERY QUIRES:		13	OISIN 1		166
A FAR VAGUE SOUND OF FEATHERY CHOIRS.		13	OISIN 1	V	166
THUS ON THE WATERS, FAR AND SWEET,		26	OISIN 1	V	398A
YET LOVE AND KISS ON DIM SHORES FAR AWAY		29	OISIN 2		13
THEY LOVE AND KISS IN ISLANDS FAR AWAY,		29	OISIN 2	V	13
BUT LOVE AND KISS ON DIM SHORES FAR AWAY		29	OISIN 2	V	13
HALF IN THE UNVESSELLED SEA. WE'D MOUNTED FAR:		32	OISIN 2	V	47
"I BRING THEE A DELIVERER FROM FAR AWAY,		34	OISIN 2	V	78A
FOR NO MAN'S CRY SHALL EVER MOUNT SO FAR:		36	OISIN 2		108
FOR NEVER MORTAL CRY SO FAR HATH SENT.		36	OISIN 2	V	108
NOR NO MAN'S CRY SHALL EVER MOUNT SO FAR:		36	OISIN 2	V	108
THE STRANGER WATCHED THE SWORD: BUT NIAM FAR,		38	OISIN 2	V	136
THE FLOWERS STILL GREW THERE: FAR ON THE SEA'S WASTE		39	OISIN 2		163
TILL THE FAR DOORWAY GREW A BURNING BLOT		39	OISIN 2	V	152
'TIS OVER: FAR WITH MEMORY I SWAY AND ROCK.		43	OISIN 2	V	212
. . . FAR SUNG BY THE SENNACHIES.		50	OISIN 3		53
. . . FAR SUNG OF THE SENNACHIES.		50	OISIN 3	V	53
"LIKE ME WERE SOME GALLEY FORSAKEN FAR OFF IN MERIDIAN ISLE,		55	OISIN 3		117
. . . FAR FROM THE HAZEL AND OAK,		57	OISIN 3		146
LATER A SOUND CAME, HALF LOST IN THE SOUND OF A SHORE FAR AWAY,		57	OISIN 3		155
WATCHING THE BLESSED ONES MOVE FAR OFF, AND THE SMILE ON GOD'S FACE,		61	OISIN 3		199
FAR, FAR AWAY. I NAMED HIM AFTER YOU.		72	ANASHU VIJAYA		35
FAR, FAR AWAY. I NAMED HIM AFTER YOU.		72	ANASHU VIJAYA		35
FAR, FAR AWAY. I'VE NAMED HIM AFTER YOU.		72	ANASHU VIJAYA	V	35

	PAGE	TITLE		LINE
FAR (CONTINUED)				
FAR, FAR AWAY. I'VE NAMED HIM AFTER YOU.	72	ANASHU VIJAYA	V	35
ON THE FAR GOLDEN PEAK: ENORMOUS SHAPES,	74	ANASHU VIJAYA		68
MURMURING HOW FAR AWAY ARE THE UNQUIET LANDS:	78	INDIAN TO LOVE		10
MURMURING HOW FAR AWAY ARE ALL EARTH'S FEVERISH LANDS.	78	INDIAN TO LOVE		10
MURMURING GENTLY HOW FAR OFF ARE THE UNQUIET LANDS:	78	INDIAN TO LOVE	V	10
HOW FAR AWAY THE STARS SEEM, AND HOW FAR	80	EPHEMERA		8
HOW FAR AWAY THE STARS SEEM, AND HOW FAR	80	EPHEMERA		8
WITH HORSEMEN HURRYING NEAR AND FAR,	83	MAD KING GOLL	V	18
I PAUSED--AND FAR AWAY I DASHED	83	MAD KING GOLL	V	31
I PAUSED--AND FAR AWAY RUSHED ON,	83	MAD KING GOLL		31
FAR OFF BY FURTHEST ROSSES	87	STOLEN CHILD		15
THE BELL THAT CALLS US ON: THE SWEET FAR THING.	115	ROSE OF BATTLE		28
REST FAR FROM MEN.	116	FAERY SONG		10
HE PACED UPON THE MOUNTAINS FAR ABOVE,	121	YOU ARE OLD	V	11
SOON FAR FROM THE ROSE AND THE LILY	122	WHITE BIRDS		11
FAR OFF, MOST SECRET, AND INVIOLATE ROSE,	169	SECRET ROSE	V	1
FAR OFF, MOST SECRET, AND INVIOLATE ROSE?	170	SECRET ROSE	V	32
OF THE FAR WANDERING SHADOWS HAS COME TO ME,	183	QUEEN MAEVE	V	80
FAR OUT UNDER A WINDLESS SKY!	197	BAILE AILLINN		181
IS EDEN FAR AWAY, OR DO YOU HIDE	218	WOODS OF COOLE		30
STRAYING TOO FAR INTO THE NORTH OR SOUTH,	226	SHADOW WATER B		86
BEFORE HIM OR BEHIND, BUT THAT FAR OFF	279	TWO KINGS		55
"YOU THAT HAVE WANDERED FAR AND WIDE	295	THREE BEGGARS		11
"YOU HAVE WANDERED FAR AND WIDE,	295	THREE BEGGARS	V	11
FAR FROM THE CUSTOMARY SKIES,	360	ALF POLLEXFEN		14
FROM THE FAR TOWER WHERE MILTON'S PLATONIST	373	PHASES OF MOON		15
WERE NOT OUR BEDS FAR OFF I'D RING THE BELL,	377	PHASES OF MOON		124
WERE I TO TRAVEL FAR AND WIDE	398	BREAK OF DAY		8
ONE HEARS THE RUMBLE OF IT FAR BELOW	420	MY HOUSE	V	20B
O BUT HER HEART WOULD BREAK TO LEARN MY THOUGHTS ARE FAR AWAY."	450	OWEN AHERNE		20
SHAKESPEAREAN FISH SWAM THE SEA, FAR AWAY FROM LAND:	485	THREE MOVEMENT		1
FLED TO FAR COUNTRIES, OR SHELTERED THEMSELVES	546	TO SAME TUNE 2		4
WHAT BROUGHT THEM THERE SO FAR FROM THEIR HOME,	549	SEVERED HEAD		8
YOU ASK WHAT I HAVE FOUND, AND FAR AND WIDE I GO:	580	CURSE CROMWELL		1
THAT CRIED IT FAR AND WIDE,	582	ROGER CASEMENT		18
THE SMUGGLER MIDDLETON, BUTLERS FAR BACK,	605	YOU CONTENT		15
FLED TO FAR COUNTRIES, OR SHELTERED THEMSELVES	613	MARCH SONGS 1		4
FAR UP IN THE STRETCHES OF NIGHT:	623	HIGH TALK		12
FAR THE MORNING VAPOURS SHATTER,	648	ISLE STAT I 1		89
AND FAR AWAY THE HERON SAILS, I WIS.	649	ISLE STAT I 1		116
AND, LEAPING TO THEIR FEET, FAR ECHOES CRIED,	659	ISLE STAT II 1		13
ONE HAND BROW-SHADING, FAR ACROSS THE NIGHT,	663	ISLE STAT II 2		27
I WOULD HAVE GONE ALSO: BUT FAR AWAY	663	ISLE STAT II 2		37
IN THE FAR WORLD WILL VANISH FROM THY MIND,	670	ISLE STAT II 3		93
FAR FLEETER THAN THE MILLION-FOOTED SEA.	670	ISLE STAT II 3		108
FOR I AM MIGHTIER NOW BY FAR THAN THEE,	673	ISLE STAT II 3		193
IN THOSE FAR YEARS, O DAUGHTER OF THE DAYS.	674	ISLE STAT II 3		213
AND CROUCH IN SOME FAR STILLNESS OF THE ISLE, AND DIE.	675	ISLE STAT II 3		246
IN A FAR STILLNESS OF THE ISLAND DIE.	675	ISLE STAT II 3	V	246
FAR OFF IN DROWSY VALLEYS	680	LOVE AND DEATH		5
THE OTHER IS NOT FAR.	680	LOVE AND DEATH		28
EVE-SOOTHED IN SOME FAR LEAFY REST,	686	LIFE		10
IN AUTUMN, WHEN FAR DOWN THE MOUNTAIN SLOPES	690	MOSADA 1		12
FAR OUT UPON THE WATER WORLD AND RINGED	693	MOSADA 1		80
HEARING THE FAR OFF SINGING GUILE AND GROANED,	693	MOSADA 1	V	88
IN THE FAR ISLE SHE SANG HERSELF ASLEEP,	694	MOSADA 1		90
HE IS NOT FAR. I'D HAVE HIM SPEAK FOR HER.	696	MOSADA 2		13
WILL BE THE FAINT FAR THUNDER-SOUND, AS THOUGH	699	MOSADA 3		10
WILL MOVE THE FAINT FAR THUNDER-SOUND, AS THOUGH	699	MOSADA 3	V	10
JUST NOW MY SOUL ROSE UP AND TOUCHED IT, FAR	705	REMEMBRANCE		13
SLEEP IN SOME FAR OTHER FIELD	705	DAWN-SONG		3
A SOLDIER ANSWERS: "BY THE CAMP'S FAR END	712	FERENCZ RENYI		67
AFRAID TO BE TOO FAR." "AY, BRING HER HERE!"	712	FERENCZ RENYI		69
AND LOST AND FAR IN YONDER HILLS I KNOW:	713	FERENCZ RENYI		98
THERE FAR AWAY FROM ALL WE TWO WILL GO,	714	FERENCZ RENYI		99
HAYNAU, THINE HOUR HAS COME, THY FOLLOWERS FAR	715	FERENCZ RENYI		17
AND THE WINDS COME DOWN AND BLOW THEM WITH THE VAPOURS FAR AWAY.	719	PHANTOM SHIP		28
COME I KNOW WHERE, FAR AWAY,	727	LOVERS QUARREL		34
FAR AWAY THE STARRY MIRTH	731	STREET DANCERS		7
MAYBE NOW IN SOME FAR LANE,	731	STREET DANCERS		14
THERE--THERE--BY THE OAR. THE CROWN OF A FAR COUNTRY.	763	SHADOW WATER A		310
I HAVE HEARD FROM FAR BELOW.	783	GREY ROUND		25
FAR-AWAY				
THAT CARRIED THE FISH FOR THE SALE IN THE FAR-AWAY TOWN,	91	OLD FISHERMAN	V	7
FARE				
THE HEART'S GROWN BRUTAL FROM THE FARE:	425	STARES NEST		17
THE HEART GROWS BRUTAL FROM THE FARE,	425	STARES NEST	V	17
FAREWELL				
FAREWELL: I MUST BE GONE I-WIS,	67	HAPPY SHEPHERD	V	46D
FAREWELL, VIJAYA. NAY, NO WORD, NO WORD:	75	ANASHU VIJAYA		83
ARE LOVE, AND A CONTINUAL FAREWELL."	81	EPHEMERA		24
WHEN I HAVE SAID FAREWELL TO THIS MAN HERE,	250	SHADOW WATER B		587
FAREWELL! FAREWELL! THE SWORD IS IN THE ROPE--	251	SHADOW WATER B		595
FAREWELL! FAREWELL! THE SWORD IS IN THE ROPE--	251	SHADOW WATER B		595
OF HILL TWO SHEPHERDS COME. FAREWELL! I'LL DON	659	ISLE STAT II 1		28
BETWEEN THE HORNED HILLS--SHEPHERDS, FAREWELL!	682	SEEKER		27
SHEPHERDS, FAREWELL! HE SOON WILL BE--ASHES	682	SEEKER		34
AND DYING MEN--AND YET--BUT NO, FAREWELL.	698	MOSADA 2		49

265

		PAGE	TITLE	LINE
FAREWELL (CONTINUED)				
OUT OF THEIR HATRED, MY BELOVED, FAREWELL.	. . . . .	767	SHADOW WATER A	400
FARISTAH				
FARISTAH, AND NO LIVING EAR BUT HIS.	. . . . . .	461	HARUN RASHID V	4
FARM				
THE MILKING-PLACE, THE SHELTERED FARM?	. . . . . .	151	HEART OF WOMAN V	6
ABOUT A FARM," THE SECOND CRIED.	. . . . . .	296	THREE BEGGARS V	38
TO THEIR FARM WORK! HOW SILENT ALL WILL BE!	. . . .	699	MOSADA 3	8
RINGED ROUND AND FONDLED, A BROWN FARM HOUSE SEES.	. .	710	FERENCZ RENYI V	23
TO THE ORCHARD-CIRCLED FARM!	. . . .	727	LOVERS QUARREL	50
FARMER				
THERE'S MANY A STRONG FARMER	. . . .	213	HAPPY TOWNLAND	1
A FARMER HAS MORE DIGNITY."	. . . .	296	THREE BEGGARS	37
FARMER'S				
AND TURNED THE FARMER'S MEMORY FROM HIS CATTLE,	. . . .	129	BOOK STORIES	6
CLIPPED AN INSOLENT FARMER'S EARS	. . . .	410	TOWER	31
WHATEVER GOOD A FARMER'S GOT	. . . .	586	PARNELLITES	13
FARMERS				
FOR O, THE STRONG FARMERS	. . . .	215	HAPPY TOWNLAND	29
FARMERS JOSTLED AT THE FAIR	. . . .	410	TOWER	39
FARMHOUSE				
A FARMHOUSE THAT IS SHELTERED BY ITS WALL,	. . . . .	419	MY HOUSE	2
FARM-HOUSE				
A FARM-HOUSE THAT IS SHELTERED BY ITS WALL,	. . . . .	419	MY HOUSE V	2
ABOVE THE FARM-HOUSE BY THE LITTLE LAKE	. . . . .	699	MOSADA 3	3
HE NUMBERS. HE A BROWN FARM-HOUSE SEES.	. . . .	710	FERENCZ RENYI	22
FARM-WORK				
TO THEIR FARM-WORK! HOW SILENT ALL WILL BE.	. . . . .	699	MOSADA 3 V	8
FAR-OFF				
AND THEY WHO TO A FAR-OFF PLACE HAD FLED,	. . . . .	41	OISIN 2 V	184
AND, IN A FAR-OFF, GENTLE VALLEY STOPPING,	. . . . .	68	SAD SHEPHERD	13
HE FLED, AND IN A FAR-OFF VALLEY STOPPING,	. . . . .	68	SAD SHEPHERD V	13
FAR-OFF, MOST SECRET, AND INVIOLATE ROSE,	. . . . .	169	SECRET ROSE	1
FAR-OFF, MOST SECRET, AND INVIOLATE ROSE?	. . . . .	170	SECRET ROSE	32
BEFORE HIM OR BEHIND, BUT THAT FAR-OFF	. . . . .	279	TWO KINGS V	55
HEARING THE FAR-OFF SINGING GUILE, AND GROANED,	. . . .	693	MOSADA 1	88
FARRELL				
THEN FARRELL, STEEL KING, MASTER OF MEN,	. . . . .	790	DEDICATION	5
FARROW				
. . . ITS FARROW THAT SO SOLID SEEM,	. . . . . .	481	BLOOD AND MOON	26
FARTHEST				
"IN THE ISLES OF THE FARTHEST SEAS WHERE ONLY THE SPIRITS COME.		56	OISIN 3	133
FAR-WANDERING				
OF THE FAR-WANDERING SHADOWS HAS COME TO ME	. . . .	183	QUEEN MAEVE	80
FASCINATION				
THE FASCINATION OF WHAT'S DIFFICULT	. . . . . .	260	FASC DIFFICULT	T
THE FASCINATION OF WHAT'S DIFFICULT	. . . . . .	260	FASC DIFFICULT	1
FASHION				
AND GREW TO BE OUT OF FASHION	. . . .	211	O DO NOT LOVE	3
OR YOU WILL GROW OUT OF FASHION	. . . .	212	O DO NOT LOVE	11
BUT HE THAT GETS THEIR LOVE AFTER THE FASHION	. . . .	228	SHADOW WATER B	145
I SHALL HAVE LOVE IN THEIR IMMORTAL FASHION!	. . . .	237	SHADOW WATER B	326
YOUR EARS THAN STORIES NOW IN FASHION,	. . . . .	271	GREY ROCK	5
CUT IN THE TURKISH FASHION,	. . . .	363	DOLLS DRAWINGS	8
TIRED OF THAT COURTLY FASHION,	. . . . . .	378	CAT AND MOON	15
TIRED OF HER COURTLY FASHION,	. . . .	378	CAT AND MOON V	15
THOUGH YOU CAN FASHION EVERYTHING	. . . . . .	436	FOR MY SON	17
DID QUATTROCENTO FINGER FASHION IT	. . . . . .	444	SCHOOL CHILDR	26
WHERE FASHION OR MERE FANTASY DECREES	. . . . .	491	COOLE BALLYLEE	38
AND WEAR A COAT IN FASHION.	. . . .	607	SONGS BURDEN 2	21
WITH A HAT OUT OF FASHION,	. . . .	627	STATES HOLIDAY	29
A FASHION WITH US MOORISH MAIDS, BEGOT	. . . . .	700	MOSADA 3	25
FASHIONED				
HER FACE SEEMED FASHIONED ALL OF MOONLIT VAPOURS,	. . .	33	OISIN 2 V	70
FASHIONED TO BE THE MOTHER OF STRONG CHILDREN!	. . .	181	QUEEN MAEVE	26
I THINK HE FASHIONED FROM HIS OPPOSITE	. . . . .	368	EGO DOMINUS	27
THE PRIMUM MOBILE THAT FASHIONED US	. . . . .	423	MY DESCENDANTS	17
WHAT QUINTO-CENTO FINGER FASHIONED IT,	. . . . .	444	SCHOOL CHILDR V	26
DA VINCI' FINGER SO HAD FASHIONED IT	. . . . .	444	SCHOOL CHILDR	26
MONTASHIGI, THIRD OF HIS FAMILY, FASHIONED IT	. . . .	478	SELF AND SOUL	25
MONTASHIGI OF OSAFUME FASHIONED IT	. . . . . .	478	SELF AND SOUL V	25
FASHION'S				
BUT FASHION'S CHANGED, THAT HIGH-HORSE RIDERLESS	. . . .	492	COOLE BALLYLEE	46
I PRAY--FOR FASHION'S WORD IS OUT	. . . . . .	553	PRAYER OLD AGE	9
FAST				
WHEN THEY FROZE THE CLOTH ON MY BODY LIKE ARMOUR RIVETED FAST,		57	OISIN 3	151
ON CREVROE OR ON BROAD KNOCKFEFIN, WITH MANY OF OLD THEY FAST		59	OISIN 3 V	179
TO MAKE HER FAST WHILE WE ARE PLUNDERING HER.	. . . .	232	SHADOW WATER B	225
THAT GIRL MY UNREMEMBERING NIGHTS HOLD FAST	. . . .	384	VISION ROBART	50
SHE ROSE, AND WITH HER EYES SHUT FAST IN SLEEP	. . .	468	HARUN RASHID	152
AND THERE, FREE AND YET FAST,	. . . .	472	ALL SOUL NIGHT	57
AND WHITHER, UNCOUTH HUNTER? WHY SO FAST?	. . . .	651	ISLE STAT I 2	1
FOR NIGHT COMES FAST. LOOK DOWN ON ME, MY LOVE,	. . .	703	MOSADA 3	103
HE FADES AMONG THE MISTS! HOW FAST THEY COME,	. . .	703	MOSADA 3	117
ITS STRANGE HEART BEATING FAST	. . . .	785	YOUR HEART	6
FASTED				
I FASTED FOR SOME FORTY DAYS ON BREAD AND BUTTERMILK,	. .	592	PILGRIM	1

FASTEN
    FASTEN YOUR HAIR WITH A GOLDEN PIN, ... 157 BELOVED RHYMES   1
FASTENED
    AND FASTENED TO A DYING ANIMAL . . . . 408 SAIL BYZANTIUM   22
    AND FASTENED TO THIS DYING ANIMAL . . . . 408 SAIL BYZANTIUM V 22
FASTING
    FASTING AND PRAYERS. TELL ON. YES, YES, ... 24 OISIN 1   360
    FASTING AND PRAYERS. TELL ON. AY, AY! . . . . . . 24 OISIN 1   V 360
    A SAINT OF MUNSTER, WHEN MUCH FASTING, SAW . . . . 696 MOSADA 2   20
    FROM FASTING--SEE, THE RED LIGHT SLANTING DOWN . . . . 697 MOSADA 2   36
FAT
    THAT HAS MADE FAT THE MURDEROUS MOTH; . . . . . . 156 FORGOT BEAUTY   8
    THE FAT FLOCKS AND THE FIELDS' FATNESS, ... 540 FROM ANTIGONE   4
    NO HAMLET THIN FROM EATING FLIES, A FAT . . . . . . 610 STATUES   19
FATAL
    FOR THERE A FATAL IMAGE GROWS . . . . 135 TWO TREES   25
    SANG OF THE BEAST THAT GAVE THE FATAL WOUND. . . . . 537 HER VISION   16
FATE
    WE MOCKED AT TIME AND FATE AND CHANCE . . . . . . 20 OISIN 1   291
    FOR THESE WERE ANCIENT OISIN'S FATE . . . . . . 24 OISIN 1   361
    MAY SLEEP IN THE END WITH THE WHOLE OF HIS FATE DONE, . . 28 OISIN 1   V 423F
    COME NEAR, THAT NO MORE BLINDED BY MAN'S FATE, . . . 101 ROSE UPON ROOD   9
    FOR GOD HAS BID THEM SHARE AN EQUAL FATE; . . . . . 115 ROSE OF BATTLE   32
    I KNOW THAT I SHALL MEET MY FATE . . . . 328 IRISH AIRMAN   1
    I COULD BUT LEAVE HIM TO HIS FATE; . . . . 514 JANE GROWN OLD   11
    BEFORE HE CAN ACCOMPLISH FATE, ... 638 BEN BULBEN   35
    I GO AS SOFT AS FOLLY; I AM FATE." . . . . . . 686 LIFE   18
    I GO AS SOFT AS FOLLY; I AM FATE." . . . . . . 735 QUATRAIN APHOR 20
FATED
    MOURN YE ON GRASS-GREEN PLAINS OF ERI FATED, ... 738 MOURN THEN ON   9
FATHER
    "MY FATHER AND MY MOTHER ARE . . . . 5 OISIN 1   46
    HAD KISSED MY FATHER, LONG-ARMED FIN, ... 10 OISIN 1   V 112B
    WITH HER OLD FATHER THE BLIND WOOD-CUTTER; . . . . 74 ANASHU VIJAYA   63
    THE BALLAD OF FATHER O'HART . . . . 91 FATHER OHART   T
    FATHER O'HART . . . . 91 FATHER OHART V   T
    GOOD FATHER JOHN O'HART . . . . 91 FATHER OHART   1
    BUT FATHER JOHN WENT UP, ... 92 FATHER OHART   9
    AND FATHER JOHN WENT DOWN; . . . . 92 FATHER OHART   10
    MY FATHER STANDS AMID HIS BATTLE-CARS." . . . . . 107 CUCHULAIN SEA   26
    MY FATHER STANDS." "AGED, WORN OUT WITH WARS . . . . 107 CUCHULAIN SEA   29
    "MY FATHER," MADE HE, SMILING, ANSWER THEN, ... 107 CUCHULAIN SEA V 25
    "MY FATHER DWELLS AMONG THE SEA-WORN BANDS, ... 107 CUCHULAIN SEA V 25
    MY FATHER STANDS AMID HIS BATTLE CARS." . . . . . 107 CUCHULAIN SEA V 26
    THE BALLAD OF FATHER GILLIGAN . . . . 132 FR GILLIGAN   T
    FATHER GILLIGAN . . . . 132 FR GILLIGAN V   T
    "FATHER! YOU COME AGAIN!" . . . . 133 FR GILLIGAN   32
    THE ALE CUP IS MY FATHER AND MY MOTHER. . . . . . 222 SHADOW WATER B V 11B
    THAT HAVE HAD DREAMS FOR FATHER, LIVE IN US. . . . . 252 SHADOW WATER B 619
    OUR FATHER ROSICROSS IS IN HIS TOMB. . . . . . . 311 MOUNTAIN TOMB   4
    OUR FATHER ROSICROSS IS IN HIS TOMB. . . . . . . 311 MOUNTAIN TOMB   8
    OUR FATHER ROSICROSS SLEEPS IN HIS TOMB. . . . . . 311 MOUNTAIN TOMB 12
    FROM FATHER UNTO SON . . . . 421 MY TABLE   19
    TRUTHS WITHOUT FATHER CAME, TRUTHS THAT NO BOOK . . . 467 HARUN RASHID   138
    THE FATHER AND HIS ANGELIC HIERARCHY . . . . . . 483 VERONIC NAPKIN   4
    MY GREAT-GRANDFATHER'S FATHER TALKED OF MUSIC, . . . 486 SEVEN SAGES   4
    MY GREAT-GRANDFATHER'S FATHER TALKED OF MUSIC AND PAINTING, 486 SEVEN SAGES V   4
    FATHER AND CHILD . . . . 531 FATHER CHILD   T
    A WOMAN YOUNG AND OLD I FATHER AND CHILD . . . . . 531 FATHER CHILD V   T
    RECALL HIS TRINITY. A FATHER, MOTHER, CHILD (A DAUGHTER 556 RIBH PATRICK V   2
      OR A SON)
    MY FATHER UPON THE ABBEY STAGE, BEFORE HIM A RAGING CROWD; 577 LOFTY THINGS   2
    MY FATHER SANG THAT SONG, ... 613 MARCH SONGS 1   8
    MY FATHER SANG THAT SONG, ... 613 MARCH SONGS 1   18
    MY FATHER SANG THAT SONG, ... 614 MARCH SONGS 1   28
    FROM COLLAR TO COLLAR, FROM STILT TO STILT, FROM FATHER 623 HIGH TALK   10
      TO CHILD.
    YET 'TIS NO SIN; MY FATHER TAUGHT IT ME. . . . . . 692 MOSADA 1   50
    COME, FATHER. LADY, I NOR REST NOR SIT. . . . . . 720 WITCH VIVIEN   18
    AND--NO! I'LL NONE OF THESE, OLD FATHER WRINKLES. . . 721 WITCH VIVIEN   23
    WITH LOADED DICE. ANOTHER CHANCE! COME, FATHER! . . 721 WITCH VIVIEN   45
    AND NOW WITH FATHER TIME I'M FACE TO FACE. . . . . 722 WITCH VIVIEN   57
    CHANCE, AND NOT SKILL, HAS FAVOURED YOU, OLD FATHER! . 722 WITCH VIVIEN   60
    THE FATHER DROPT HIS ROSARY. . . . . 730 PRIEST FAIRY   57
    SHE PRAYS FOR FATHER, MOTHER DEAR, ... 735 IN CHURCH   1
    HER PRAYER FOR FATHER, MOTHER DEAR, ... 736 IN CHURCH   13
    LIKE SON TO FATHER . . . . 769 BLOOD BOND V   2
    LIKE SON TO FATHER. . . . . 770 BLOOD BOND   3
    MEN THAT REVERE YOUR FATHER YET . . . . 791 REPRISALS   17
FATHERLESS
    BEING FATHERLESS COULD HAVE HER WAY . . . . . . 404 FOR DAUGHTER   28
FATHER'S
    BUT LEFT THE HOUSE AS IN HIS FATHER'S TIME . . . . . 341 SHEP GOATHERD   53
    THAT IT WAS MADE IN YOUR GREAT FATHER'S REIGN." . . . 464 HARUN RASHID   72
    EVEN FROM BOYHOOD, IN MY FATHER'S HOUSE, ... 683 SEEKER   48
FATHERS
    AND EVEN THE NAMES OF HIS FATHERS, AND EVEN THE WORKS OF 51 OISIN 3   V 62
      HIS HANDS?
    I HELPED YOUR FATHERS WHEN THEY BUILT THESE WALLS, . . . 184 QUEEN MAEVE   97
    PARDON, OLD FATHERS, IF YOU STILL REMAIN . . . . . . 269 PARDON FATHERS   1
    HE RAN TOWARDS THE HOUSE HIS FATHERS BUILT . . . . . 279 TWO KINGS V 45E

FATHERS   (CONTINUED)
        NEVER TO LEAVE THAT VALLEY HIS FATHERS CALLED THEIR HOME.   391 UNDER SATURN   16
        FROM MY OLD FATHERS, I MUST NOURISH DREAMS . . . .   422 MY DESCENDANTS   2
        OLD FATHERS, GREAT-GRANDFATHERS, ...   518 LOVES LONENESS   1
        OLD FATHERS, GREAT GRANDFATHERS, ...   518 LOVES LONENESS V   1
        HIS FATHERS SERVED THEIR FATHERS BEFORE CHRIST WAS   580 CURSE CROMWELL   6
            CRUCIFIED.
        HIS FATHERS SERVED THEIR FATHERS BEFORE CHRIST WAS   580 CURSE CROMWELL   6
            CRUCIFIED.
FATHOMLESS
        ALL NIGHT'S FATHOMLESS WISDOM COME, ...   519 HER DREAM   2
FATIGUE
        NOR LANGUOR NOR FATIGUE! AN ENDLESS FEAST, ...   44 OISIN 2   223
        NO LANGUOR, NO FATIGUE! AN ENDLESS FEAST, ...   44 OISIN 2   V   223
        NOR LANGUOR NOR FATIGUE! AND ENDLESS FEAST, ...   44 OISIN 2   223
FATNESS
        THE FAT FLOCKS AND THE FIELDS' FATNESS, ...   540 FROM ANTIGONE   4
FATTEN
        THEY LEFT THEIR BODIES TO FATTEN THE WOLVES, ...   545 TO SAME TUNE 2   2
        THEY LEFT THEIR HOMESTEADS TO FATTEN THE FOXES, ...   546 TO SAME TUNE 2   3
        THEY LEFT THEIR BODIES TO FATTEN THE WOLVES, ...   613 MARCH SONGS 1   2
        THEY LEFT THEIR HOMESTEADS TO FATTEN THE FOXES, ...   613 MARCH SONGS 1   3
FATTENING
        TILL, FATTENING THE WINDS OF THE MORNING, AN ODOUR   57 OISIN 3   153
            OF NEW-MOWN HAY
        FIELDS FATTENING SLOW, MEN WISE IN JOY, ...   82 MAD KING GOLL   V   6
FATTER
        THE FIELDS GREW FATTER DAY BY DAY, ...   82 MAD KING GOLL   7
FAUN
        AND I WOULD PLEASE THE HAPLESS FAUN, ...   67 HAPPY SHEPHERD   47
        THAT I MAY SOOTHE THAT HAPLESS FAUN, ...   67 HAPPY SHEPHERD V   47
        AN OATEN PIPE UNTO A LISTENING FAUN, ...   678 ISLE STAT II 3 V   301
FAVOURED
        CHANCE, AND NOT SKILL, HAS FAVOURED YOU, OLD FATHER! . .   722 WITCH VIVIEN   60
FAVOURITE
        WE WILL FIND HER FAVOURITE LAIR, ...   706 DAWN-SONG   26
FAWN
        AND NIAMH AND LABAN AND FAND, WHO COULD CHANGE TO AN OTTER   209 UNDER THE MOON   12
            OR FAWN,
        AND FAND, AND NIAM, AND LABAN, WHO COULD CHANGE TO AN OTTER   209 UNDER THE MOON V   12
            OR FAWN,
        TREMBLING IN THE BLUE HEAVENS LIKE A WHITE FAWN . . . .   251 SHADOW WATER B   611
        AN OATEN PIPE UNTO A LISTENING FAWN, ...   678 ISLE STAT II 3   301
        TREMBLING IN THE BLUE HEAVENS LIKE A WHITE FAWN . . . .   769 SHADOW WATER A   427
FAY
        MY HUMAN SADNESS FAY ARMS WOUND. . . . .   11 OISIN 1   V   138
        AND HER BRIGHT BODY--NOW OF FAY AND MAN! . . . . . .   29 OISIN 2   V   7
        AND MAY NO RESTLESS FAY WITH FIDGET FINGER . . . . .   75 ANASHU VIJAYA   90
        MAY NEVER RESTLESS FAY WITH FIDGET FINGER . . . . . .   75 ANASHU VIJAYA   V   90
        FROM THEE I SNATCHED IT! E'EN THE FAY THAT TRIPS . . .   670 ISLE STAT II 3   98
        AND THEN THE FAY QUEEN SOBBED APART, ...   730 PRIEST FAIRY   70
        AND ALL THE SAD FAY CHIVALRY . . . .   730 PRIEST FAIRY   71
FEACRA
        . . . FINVARRA, FEACRA, AND CAOLTE . . . .   174 ELEMENT POWERS V   T
FEAR
        AND THINGS THAT FEAR THE DAWN OF THE MORROW . . . . .   20 OISIN 1   302
        AND ALL LISTLESS HOURS FEAR US, ...   21 OISIN 1   317
        AND WE FEAR NO DAWNING MORROW, ...   21 OISIN 1   318
        AND WE NEVER FEAR THE MORROW . . . .   21 OISIN 1   V   318
        OR FEAR THE WILD GREY OSPREY SORROW." . . . .   23 OISIN 1   V   342
        AND A SAD MOUTH, THAT FEAR MADE TREMULOUS . . . . . .   34 OISIN 2   71
        HAD NEITHER HOPE NOR FEAR. I BADE THEM HIDE . . . . .   38 OISIN 2   139
        OF FEAR! I BADE THEM GO! AND FOR THE FIGHT. . . . . .   38 OISIN 2   142
        CAST THE LOOSE BULK, LEST NIAM FEAR HIM DEAD! . . . .   41 OISIN 2   V   183
        . . . ALONE WITH REMEMBRANCE AND FEAR! . . . .   63 OISIN 3   218
        WITHOUT LAUGHTER, A COUGHING, ALONE WITH REMEMBRANCE AND   63 OISIN 3   V   218
            FEAR!
        THE SONG OF OUTLAWS AND THEIR FEAR! . . . .   85 MAD KING GOLL   V   64
        WHILE HUSHED FROM FEAR, OR LOUD WITH HOPE, A BAND . . .   114 ROSE OF BATTLE   5
        AND PRESSING ON, OR LINGERING SLOW WITH FEAR, ...   114 ROSE OF BATTLE V   5
        AND BROOD ON HOPES AND FEAR NO MORE. . . . .   125 GOES FERGUS   6
        FOR SOMEBODY HID HATRED AND HOPE AND DESIRE AND FEAR   153 CHANGE BELOVED   4
        AND I HAVE HATRED AND HOPE AND DESIRE AND FEAR . . . .   153 CHANGE BELOVED V   4
        TO HIS HEART, BIDDING IT HAVE NO FEAR . . . .   158 TO HIS HEART   T
        TO MY HEART, BIDDING IT HAVE NO FEAR . . . .   158 TO HIS HEART   T
        OR CRY ABOUT ONE'S EARS. NOTHING TO FEAR. . . . . . .   222 SHADOW WATER B   19
        THAT MAKES ME FEAR TO RAISE A HAND AGAINST HIM, ...   222 SHADOW WATER B V   16A
        BUT WERE YOU NOT AFRAID? WHY SHOULD I FEAR? . . . . .   224 SHADOW WATER B   41
        THERE'S NOTHING IN THE WORLD THAT'S WORTH A FEAR. . . .   238 SHADOW WATER B   353
        I CAN PUT FEAR AWAY AS A QUEEN SHOULD. . . . .   238 SHADOW WATER B   355
        AM I TO FEAR THE WAVES, OR IS THE MOON . . . .   246 SHADOW WATER B   508
        AND SHOOK WITH HATE AND FEAR. . . . .   254 WOMAN HOMER   4
        SO WITH A LAUGH AT HIS OWN FEAR . . . .   303 HOUR DAWN   31
        A STRING OF SCHOLARS WENT IN FEAR . . . .   381 SONG OF FOOL   7
        A GREY GULL LOST ITS FEAR AND FLEW . . . .   397 POLIT PRISONER   3
        WHETHER FOR DAILY PITTANCE OR IN BLIND FEAR . . . . .   482 BLOOD AND MOON   37
        "OR DRIVEN FROM HOME AND LEFT TO DIE IN FEAR." . . . .   635 CUCHULAIN COMF   22
        IS THE WORST MAN HAS TO FEAR. . . . .   637 BEN BULBEN   20
        JOY'S BROTHER, FEAR, DWELLS EVER IN EACH BREAST-- . . .   651 ISLE STAT I 1   155
        JOY'S BROTHER, FEAR, LURKS IN EACH LEAFY WAY. . . . .   651 ISLE STAT I 1   156
        THE BROWN WEED BURDEN, SO THE SWORD BRINGS FEAR . . . .   660 ISLE STAT II 1   45

FEAR   (CONTINUED)

I'D KILL HER IF SHE WERE. NAY, DO NOT FEAR! • • • •   669 ISLE STAT II 3   69
AS THOUGH SHE WHOM YOU FEAR HAD CROSSED THE WIDE • • • •   669 ISLE STAT II 3   77
TO QUESTION HER——OH NO, I DID NOT FEAR, • • • • • • •   676 ISLE STAT II 3   265
A PEASANT PALE AND PRETTY, HER EYES FOR FEAR, • • • •   713 FERENCZ RENYI   81
A PEASANT YOUNG AND FAIR, HER EYES FOR FEAR • • • • •   713 FERENCZ RENYI V 81
A PEASANT, PALE AND PRETTY, HER EYES FROM FEAR, • • •   713 FERENCZ RENYI V 81
THEN WHEREFORE FEAR THE USURY OF TIME, • • • • • • •   724 KANVA ON SELF   17
DO NOT FEAR US, EARTHLY MAID! • • • • • • • • • • •   726 LOVERS QUARREL   1
NIGH OF HIS WITS BY FEAR BEREFT. • • • • • • • • •   730 PRIEST FAIRY   50
CAST OUT ALL HOPE, CAST OUT ALL FEAR, • • • • • • •   743 DANAAN QUICK   25

FEARED

AND FEARED ALWAYS THE BOW-STRING'S TWANGING. • • • •   3 OISIN 1   V 7GG
IT FEARED TO GIVE ITS LOVE A HURT WITH ALL THE TEMPEST   450 OWEN AHERNE   7
     THERE!
IT FEARED THE HURT THAT SHE COULD GIVE AND THEREFORE IT   450 OWEN AHERNE   8
     WENT MAD.

FEARFUL

FEARFUL OF THE THUNDER-BALL. • • • • • • • • • • •   43 OISIN 2   V 208F
INTO SOME MOST FEARFUL SHAPE. • • • • • • • • • • •   299 THREE HERMITS   23
OH, BOY, I'M BOUND ON A MOST FEARFUL QUEST! • • • •   653 ISLE STAT I 2   31
WITH LITTLE VOICES SONGS OF FEARFUL THINGS. • • • •   682 SEEKER   31
BE NOT AFRAID, YOU'LL SEE NO FEARFUL THING. • • • •   693 MOSADA 1   74
A FEARFUL PALENESS CREEPS ACROSS HER BREAST • • • •   701 MOSADA 3   69

FEARING

HOPING AND FEARING, BROUGHT ME WINE AND BREAD. • • •   41 OISIN 2   V 184A
THEN FEARING THAT SOME LABOURER, ON HIS WAY • • • •   283 TWO KINGS   145
AND FEARING THAT MY LIGHT DISTURBED HER SLEEP • • •   467 HARUN RASHID   130
BUT FEARING THAT SHE WOULD REFUSE • • • • • • • •   792 GEORGE MOORE   2

FEARLESS

AND KNOW THAT IT IS FEARLESS. DO WHAT YOU WILL, • • •   238 SHADOW WATER B   350
TENDER AND FEARLESS ON HER FUNERAL PYRE! • • • • •   688 NETTLESHIP   3

FEARS

EVERYTHING THAT FEARS TO-MORROW • • • • • • • • •   20 OISIN 1   V 302
FOLDED IN LOVE THAT FEARS NO MORROW. • • • • • • •   23 OISIN 1   341
AND SHIVERED, KNOWING THE ISLE OF MANY FEARS. • • •   30 OISIN 2   25
AND CALLED HIM SWEETEST NAMES AND SOOTHED HIS FEARS. •   30 OISIN 2   V 27
SO WARRED, SO FEASTED, WITH NOR DREAMS NOR FEARS, • •   44 OISIN 2   222
SO WARRED, SO FEASTED WE. NO DREAMS, NO FEARS, • • •   44 OISIN 2   V 222
AND BROOD ON HOPES AND FEARS NO MORE. • • • • • •   125 GOES FERGUS   V 6
HIS MIND RAN ALL ON MONEY CARES AND FEARS, • • • •   127 DREAM OF FAERY   14
AND THE FOOL HEART OF THE COUNTING-HOUSE FEARS ALL •   181 QUEEN MAEVE   21
THE SOUTH BREEZE NOW IN DYING FEARS • • • • • • •   655 ISLE STAT I 3   13
I HURL AWAY THESE ALL UNFAERY FEARS. • • • • • • •   675 ISLE STAT II 3   228
DOTH STILL THE MAN WHOM EACH STERN ROVER FEARS, • •   678 ISLE STAT II 3   295
WHY THESE NEW FEARS? THE GREAT MONK EBREMAR, • • •   692 MOSADA 1   46
WHY THESE NEW FEARS? THE SERVANT OF THE LORD, • • •   692 MOSADA 1   V 46
JOYS AND FEARS IN THEIR GREY FACES THAT THE LIVE EARTH   719 PHANTOM SHIP   26
     KNOWETH NOT!
OF ANCIENT PASSIONS AND OF ANCIENT FEARS? • • • • •   724 KANVA ON SELF   16
BE FULL OF SUDDEN FEARS, • • • • • • • • • • • •   738 MOURN THEN ON   6

FEAST

THE LONG-HAIRED WARRIORS, THE SPREAD FEAST! • • • •   2 OISIN 1   V 7
NOR LANGUOR NOR FATIGUE! AN ENDLESS FEAST, • • • •   44 OISIN 2   223
NO LANGUOR, NO FATIGUE! AN ENDLESS FEAST, • • • •   44 OISIN 2   V 223
NOR LANGUOR NOR FATIGUE! AND ENDLESS FEAST, • • • •   44 OISIN 2   V 223
ON CREVROE OR BROAD KNOCKFEFIN, WITH MANY OF OLD THEY FEAST   59 OISIN 3   179
THEN FEAST, MAKING CONVERSE OF WARS, • • • • • •   62 OISIN 3   212
THEN FEAST, MAKING CONVERSE OF EIRE, OF WARS, • • •   62 OISIN 3   V 212
AND DWELL IN THE HOUSE OF THE FENIANS, BE THEY IN FLAMES   63 OISIN 3   224
     OR AT FEAST.
I WILL GO TO THE HOUSE OF THE FENIANS, BE THEY IN FLAMES   63 OISIN 3   V 223
     OR AT FEAST,
I FEAST AMID MY PEOPLE ON THE HILL, • • • • • • •   103 FERGUS DRUID   17
AND SILENCE HOLDING REVELRY AND FEAST! • • • • • •   705 REMEMBRANCE   12
WE'LL DANCE AND THEN FEAST IN A DAIRY. • • • • • •   707 FAIRY PEDANT   10
WE'LL DANCE AND THEN FEAST IN A DAIRY. • • • • • •   708 FAIRY PEDANT   38

FEASTED

WE FEASTED FOR THREE DAYS. ON THE FOURTH MORN • • •   43 OISIN 2   214
THREE DAYS WE FEASTED, WHEN ON THE FOURTH MORN • • •   43 OISIN 2   V 214
SO WARRED, SO FEASTED, WITH NOR DREAMS NOR FEARS, • •   44 OISIN 2   222
SO WARRED, SO FEASTED WE. NO DREAMS, NO FEARS, • • •   44 OISIN 2   V 222
FEASTED, AND WITH THEM OLD CUCHULAIN DWELT, • • • •   108 CUCHULAIN SEA V 39
FEASTED, AND WEPT THE BARROWS OF HIS DEAD! • • • •   170 SECRET ROSE   18

FEASTING

SOME FEASTING MAN THAT THE SAME OATH HAS BOUND." • •   108 CUCHULAIN SEA   38
AMONG THOSE FEASTING MEN CUCHULAIN DWELT, • • • • •   108 CUCHULAIN SEA   39
AMONG THOSE FEASTING KINGS CUCHULAIN DWELT, • • • •   108 CUCHULAIN SEA V 39
SOME FEASTING MAN THAT THE SAME OATH HAS BOUND." • •   109 CUCHULAIN SEA   54

FEASTWARD

CAME BLANAID, MAC NESSA, TALL FERGUS WHO FEASTWARD OF OLD   53 OISIN 3   89
     TIME SLUNK,
• • • CAME FERGUS WHO FEASTWARD SAD SLUNK, • • • •   53 OISIN 3   V 89
CAME BLANID, MAC NESSA, AND FERGUS WHO FEASTWARD OF OLD   53 OISIN 3   V 89
     TIME SLUNK,

FEATHER

AND TRIMMED WITH MANY A CRIMSON FEATHER! • • • • •   15 OISIN 1   206
TRIMMED ROUND WITH MANY A CRIMSON FEATHER! • • • •   15 OISIN 1   V 206
SCARCE LEFT A WHITENING FEATHER, GREY AND SERE! • • •   34 OISIN 2   V 76A
THE PEA-HENS DANCE, IN CRIMSON FEATHER • • • • •   77 INDIAN TO LOVE V 3
SCARCELY A FEATHER LINGERED, THEN YOU SEEMED • • •   102 FERGUS DRUID   4

```
                                                        PAGE     TITLE              LINE
FEATHER    (CONTINUED)
    MORE THAN THE FROTH, THE FEATHER, THE DUST-WHIRL,    .   .   .   248 SHADOW WATER B       555
    MORE THAN THE FROTH, THE FEATHER, THE DUSTWHIRL,     .   .   .   248 SHADOW WATER B  V    555
    ADDING FEATHER TO FEATHER    .   .   .   .   .   .   .   .   .   311 PEACOCK              10
    ADDING FEATHER TO FEATHER    .   .   .   .   .   .   .   .   .   311 PEACOCK              10
    AND SNUG IT IN A FEATHER BED.    .   .   .   .   .   .   .   .   332 ROUND TOWER          28
    WITH A GREAT COCK'S FEATHER,    .   .   .   .   .   .   .   .   627 STATES HOLIDAY       37
    AS THEY GO WITH DROOPING FEATHER.   .   .   .   .   .   .   .   667 ISLE STAT II 3       33
    SAW ON THE WOOD'S EDGE GLEAM AN ASH-GREY FEATHER;    .   .   .   715 DWELT SYCAMORE        2
    FOLLOWED A RINGDOVE'S ASH-GREY GLEAM OF FEATHER,     .   .   .   715 DWELT SYCAMORE        6
    FOLLOWED THE RING-DOVE'S ASH-GREY GLEAM OF FEATHER,  .   .   .   715 DWELT SYCAMORE  V     6
    A FULL HOUR LONG, WHEN ROSE A FEATHER   .   .   .   .   .   .   728 PRIEST FAIRY         19
    HE DREW FROM HIS CAP A FEATHER GREY,    .   .   .   .   .   .   729 PRIEST FAIRY         29
FEATHER-BED
    AND SNUG IT IN A FEATHER-BED,    .   .   .   .   .   .   .   .   332 ROUND TOWER     V    28
FEATHERED
    THE TOPS OF THEIR EARS WERE FEATHERED,   .   .   .   .   .   .    49 OISIN 3              34
    WHEN EVE HAS HUSHED THE FEATHERED WAYS,  .   .   .   .   .   .    78 INDIAN TO LOVE       19
    WHERE EVE HAS HUSHED THE FEATHERED WAYS,    .   .   .   .   .     78 INDIAN TO LOVE       19
    I COUNT THOSE FEATHERED BALLS OF SOOT    .   .   .   .   .   .   424 ROAD AT DOOR         11
    THE FEATHERED GLORY FROM HER LOOSENING THIGHS?   .   .   .   .   441 LEDA AND SWAN         6
FEATHERS
    FROM HIGH ABOVE, LIKE FEATHERS OF YOUNG BIRDS,   .   .   .   .    32 OISIN 2         V    50
    FEW FEATHERS WERE ON THEIR DISHEVELLED WINGS,    .   .   .   .    34 OISIN 2              76
    WHO MADE THE GRASS AND MADE THE WORMS AND MADE MY FEATHERS       77 INDIAN ON GOD        18
        GAY,
    AND WINDS BLOWING FROM FLOWERS, AND WHIRR OF FEATHERS   .   .   219 WOODS OF COOLE       39
    "THOUGH TO MY FEATHERS IN THE WET,   .   .   .   .   .   .   .   294 THREE BEGGARS         1
    "THOUGH TO MY FEATHERS IN THE WET   .   .   .   .   .   .   .   297 THREE BEGGARS        63
    BRONZED PEACOCK FEATHERS, RED COMBS OF HER COCKS.   .   .   .   433 NINETEEN 19         130
    ALL MY FINE FEATHERS WOULD BE PLUCKED AWAY   .   .   .   .   .   469 HARUN RASHID        178
    BECAUSE HE HAD FEATHERS INSTEAD OF HAIR.    .   .   .   .   .   550 SEVERED HEAD         20
FEATHERY
    AND A FAR SOUND OF FEATHERY QUIRES;   .   .   .   .   .   .   .    13 OISIN 1             166
    A FAR VAGUE SOUND OF FEATHERY CHOIRS.    .   .   .   .   .   .    13 OISIN 1         V   166
    AROUND THE FEATHERY TIP. UNTO THE SHAFT    .   .   .   .   .   657 ISLE STAT I 3        71
FEATING
    SOME FEATING MAN THAT THE SAME OATH HAS BOUND."   .   .   .   .   108 CUCHULAIN SEA  V    38
    "SOME FEATING MAN THAT THE SAME OATH HAS BOUND."   .   .   .   109 CUCHULAIN SEA  V    54
FEATURELESS
    THAT WANDERING IN A DESERT, FEATURELESS    .   .   .   .   .   .   462 HARUN RASHID        27
    WANDERING IN A DESERT FEATURELESS   .   .   .   .   .   .   .   462 HARUN RASHID        27
FEATURES
    FEATURES, OR MAYBE SHOWING   .   .   .   .   .   .   .   .   .   363 DOLLS DRAWINGS        4
    HER FEATURES WHEN A TRESS    .   .   .   .   .   .   .   .   .   363 DOLLS DRAWINGS        5
    FEATURES, OR MAY BE SHOWING  .   .   .   .   .   .   .   .   .   363 DOLLS DRAWINGS V      4
    PICK OUT MY FEATURES IN SUCH LIGHT AND SHADE   .   .   .   .   466 HARUN RASHID        116
FECUND
    OR INTO THAT MOST FECUND DITCH OF ALL,   .   .   .   .   .   .   479 SELF AND SOUL        61
FED        SEE DREAM-FED
    WHILE HIGH FRAIL CLOUDLETS, FED WITH A GREEN LIGHT,   .   .   .    40 OISIN 2             165
    DAWN PASSIONED; FED WITH A FAINT GREEN LIGHT,    .   .   .   .    40 OISIN 2        V    165
    .  .  AND FED OF UNHUMAN SLEEP.    .   .   .   .   .   .   .   .    51 OISIN 3              56
    OF OLD THE WORLD ON DREAMING FED;    .   .   .   .   .   .   .    64 HAPPY SHEPHERD        3
    YOU'VE DANDLED THEM AND FED THEM FROM THE BOOK   .   .   .   .   265 ABBEY THEATRE         8
    THOSE I HAD SERVED AND SOME THAT I HAD FED;   .   .   .   .   .   352 PEOPLE               27
    WHEN ALL IS FED WITH LIGHT AND HEAVEN IS BARE.   .   .   .   .   375 PHASES OF MOON       74
    WE HAD FED THE HEART ON FANTASIES,   .   .   .   .   .   .   .   425 STARES NEST          16
    WE HAVE FED THE HEART ON FANTASIES,   .   .   .   .   .   .   .   425 STARES NEST    V     16
    MAN'S OWN RESINOUS HEART HAS FED.   .   .   .   .   .   .   .   438 SONGS PLAY 2         16
    THAT HAVE FOUND IT WHERE YOU FED.   .   .   .   .   .   .   .   522 LULLABY               2
    CAME OLIVE FIRES OF MORNING AND ON THE DARKNESS FED,   .   .   .   719 PHANTOM SHIP         33
    CAME THE OLIVE FIRE OF MORNING, AND ON THE DARKNESS FED,   .   719 PHANTOM SHIP    V    33
    ON BRAHMA'S GATEWAY, "THEY WITHIN HAVE FED   .   .   .   .   .   735 QUATRAIN APHOR       15
FEE
    OH I WOULD THINK THAT I HAD MY FEE,   .   .   .   .   .   .   .   551 SONGS REWRIT 1 V      7
FEEBLE
    AND A SMALL AND A FEEBLE POPULACE STOOPING WITH MATTOCK          58 OISIN 3             164
        AND SPADE,
    AND A SMALL AND A FEEBLE RACE STOOPING WITH MATTOCK AND          58 OISIN 3        V   164
        SPADE.
    AND A SMALL AND FEEBLE RACE STOOPING WITH MATTOCK               58 OISIN 3        V   164
        AND SPADE.
    DIE OFF THE FEEBLE SOUNDS;    .   .   .   .   .   .   .   .   .    99 FOXHUNTER      V    42
    AND THE SEED OF THE FIRE GETS FEEBLE AND COLD.   .   .   .   .   151 OLD MOTHER           10
    BUT THE SEED OF THE FIRE GETS FEEBLE AND COLD,   .   .   .   .   151 OLD MOTHER     V     9
    BUT MAEVE, AND NOT WITH A SLOW FEEBLE FOOT,   .   .   .   .   .   185 QUEEN MAEVE         107
    BY A WINDOW'S FEEBLE LIGHT    .   .   .   .   .   .   .   .   .   731 STREET DANCERS        3
    FOOTING IN THE FEEBLE GLOW,   .   .   .   .   .   .   .   .   .   731 STREET DANCERS       10
    FOOTING IN THE FEEBLE GLOW,   .   .   .   .   .   .   .   .   .   732 STREET DANCERS       23
    FOOTING IN THE FEEBLE GLOW,   .   .   .   .   .   .   .   .   .   732 STREET DANCERS       36
    DANCING IN THE FEEBLE GLOW,   .   .   .   .   .   .   .   .   .   733 STREET DANCERS       49
    FOOTING IN THE FEEBLE GLOW,   .   .   .   .   .   .   .   .   .   733 STREET DANCERS       62
    FOOTING IN THE FEEBLE GLOW,   .   .   .   .   .   .   .   .   .   733 STREET DANCERS V     49
FEEBLER
    FEEBLER AND FEEBLER SHONE THE MISTY GLARE.   .   .   .   .   .    37 OISIN 2        V   121
    FEEBLER AND FEEBLER SHONE THE MISTY GLARE.   .   .   .   .   .    37 OISIN 2        V   121
FEEBLY
    THEY HEAR HIM FEEBLY SAY,    .   .   .   .   .   .   .   .   .    99 FOXHUNTER            32
FEED
    THAT FEED WHITE MOTHS BY SOME DE DANAAN SHRINE;   .   .   .   .    41 OISIN 2             186
```

FEED   (CONTINUED)
    ANOTHER LINEAGE FEED THE CROW, ...   437 SONGS PLAY 1   10
    THAT FEED ON SOME FOUL PARASITE   . . . .   493 AT ALGECIRAS   2
    THOUGH THEY BUT FEED AS THE GOATHERD FEEDS, ...   635 BLACK TOWER   2
    SHALL FEED. I SHALL NOT IN THE EVENINGS HEAR . . . . .   674 ISLE STAT II 3   220
    WHERE THEY ALL SUMMER FEED THEIR WANDERING FLOCKS, . .   690 MOSADA 1   5
    FEED A FIRE WITH STEMS OF GRASS!   . . . .   727 LOVERS QUARREL   42
FEEDING
    FEEDING WHITE MOTHS AROUND SOME EASTERN SHRINE,   . . .   41 OISIN 2   V   186
    NAY, GRIEF IN FEEDING ON OLD GRIEF GROWS LESS. . . . .   659 ISLE STAT II 1   19
    GRIEF NEEDS MUCH FEEDING THEN.   OF HIM I SWEAR . . . . 659 ISLE STAT II 1   20
FEEDS
    YOU GO NOT WHERE THE RED DEER FEEDS, ...   11 OISIN 1   127
    YE GO NOT WHERE THE RED DEER FEEDS, ...   11 OISIN 1   V   127
    THAT FEEDS ON SOME FOUL PARASITE   . . . .   493 AT ALGECIRAS   V   2
    FLAMES THAT NO FAGGOT FEEDS, NOR STEEL HAS LIT, ... 498 BYZANTIUM   26
    THOUGH THEY BUT FEED AS THE GOATHERD FEEDS, ...   635 BLACK TOWER   2
FEEL
    NOR EVER CHANGE OR FEEL THE CLUTCHES   . . . .   23 OISIN 1   V 341A
    "AGE AFTER AGE I FEEL MY SOUL DECAY . . . .   45 OISIN 2   V   235
    AND FEEL THE SOFTNESS OF EACH OTHER'S HAND, ...   74 ANASHU VIJAYA   57
    AND FEEL THE SOFTNESS OF EACH OTHER'S HANDS, ...   74 ANASHU VIJAYA   V   57
    AND STILL I FEEL THE CROWN UPON MY HEAD. . . . . . .   103 FERGUS DRUID   20
    BUT STILL I FEEL THE CROWN UPON MY HEAD. . . . . . .   103 FERGUS DRUID   V   20
    WAGE AN ETERNAL BATTLE, AND I FEEL   . . . .   104 FERGUS DRUID   V   38C
    THAT NONE MAY FEEL THE POWER OF SQUALL AND WAVE, . . .   128 DREAM OF FAERY V   45
    THEY DO NOT EVEN FEEL, SO ABSTRACT ARE THEY, ...   382 VISION ROBART   14
    BUT FEEL THE STRANGE HEART BEATING WHERE IT LIES? . . . 441 LEDA AND SWAN   8
    TO DEATH. HIS DARKNESS AND HIS CHILL I FEEL. . . . . .   684 SEEKER   63
    MY SOUL. HIS DARKNESS AND HIS CHILL I FEEL. . . . . .   684 SEEKER   V   63B
    I FEEL A FINGER DRAWN ACROSS MY CHEEK! . . . .   694 MOSADA 1   96
    CLOSE AND MORE CLOSE--HE LIKE HIM IN MY HEART-- . . . . 720 WITCH VIVIEN   11
    MY FINGERS FEEL HIS AMBER HAIR. . . . .   723 GIRLS SONG A   8
    THE HOLLOW WOODLANDS FEEL HIM THERE, ...   737 SUMMER EVENING   17
FEELING
    A GENTLE FEELING WRAPS THEM LIKE A FLEECE. . . . . . .   128 DREAM OF FAERY V   34
    THAT DREAMS. SHE MOVETH, FEELING IN HER BRAIN . . . .   687 TWO TITANS   10
FEELS
    AND FEELS THE STRANGE HEART BEATING WHERE IT LIES! . .   441 LEDA AND SWAN   V   8
FEET
    BUT DOWN TO HER FEET WHITE VESTURE FLOWED, ...   3 OISIN 1   25
    AND FEET OF MAIDENS DANCING IN TUNE, ...   3 OISIN 1   V   9
    DOWN TO HER FEET WHITE VESTURE FLOWED, ...   3 OISIN 1   V   25
    THROUGH BITTER TIDE ON FOAM-WET FEET? . . . .   5 OISIN 1   51
    TO THIS DIM SHORE THOSE GENTLE FEET? . . . .   5 OISIN 1   V   51
    TO THIS DIM SHORE ON FOAM WET FEET? . . . .   5 OISIN 1   V   51
    TO THIS DIM SHORE ON FOAM-WET FEET? . . . .   5 OISIN 1   V   51
    YET NOW I CHOOSE, FOR THESE FOUR FEET . . . .   6 OISIN 1   57
    FOR LOVE OF USHEEN MY FEET RAN . . . .   6 OISIN 1   V   57
    FOR LOVE OF OISIN FOAM WET FEET   . . . .   6 OISIN 1   V   57
    FOR LOVE OF OISIN FOAM-WET FEET . . . .   6 OISIN 1   V   57
    BEFORE THY FEET SHALL KNEEL DOWN ALL . . . .   7 OISIN 1   V   77
    A WHISPER OF IMPETUOUS FEET, ...   15 OISIN 1   199
    KEPT TIME WITH THEIR BRIGHT WINGS AND FEET! . . . . .   26 OISIN 1   397
    BEAT TIME WITH THEIR BRIGHT WINGS AND FEET. . . . . .   26 OISIN 1   V   397
    HIS TOOTHLESS HOUND AT HIS NERVELESS FEET, ...   26 OISIN 1   V   400
    THAT OLD, SEA-WEEDY, SQUARED, THREE HUNDRED FEET . . .   31 OISIN 2   V   30C
    SOBBED INTO SILENCE. WE HAD MOUNTED FEET . . . . . .   33 OISIN 2   V   68E
    LIKE A SMALL RIVER, AND WHERE FEET TOUCHED CAME . . .   37 OISIN 2   117
    OF AWELESS BIRDS, AND ROUND THEIR STIRLESS FEET . . .   74 ANASHU VIJAYA   73
    AND WHEN TUMULTUOUS FEET ENWOUND ME . . . .   83 MAD KING GOLL   V   20
    A TRAMPING OF TREMENDOUS FEET, ...   85 MAD KING GOLL   V   54
    THE TRAMPING OF TREMENDOUS FEET, ...   85 MAD KING GOLL   V   54
    SHE PASSED THE SALLEY GARDENS WITH LITTLE SNOW-WHITE FEET. 90 SALLEY GARDENS   2
    YOU WAVES, THOUGH YOU DANCE BY MY FEET LIKE CHILDREN AT   90 OLD FISHERMAN   1
       PLAY,
    YE WAVES, THOUGH YE DANCE 'FORE MY FEET LIKE CHILDREN AT   90 OLD FISHERMAN   V   1
       PLAY,
    I SCARCE COULD DRAG MY FEET, ...   94 MOLL MAGEE   10
    HERDED THE CATTLE CAME WITH STUMBLING FEET, ...   106 CUCHULAIN SEA   19
    "WHY DO YOU TREMBLE THUS FROM FEET TO CROWN?" . . . .   106 CUCHULAIN SEA   V   13
    WAS DRIVING CATTLE CAME SHE WITH SWIFT FEET, ...   106 CUCHULAIN SEA   V   19
    BEFORE HER WANDERING FEET. . . . .   112 ROSE OF WORLD   15
    WITH THE FEET LAID SIDE BY SIDE. . . . .   124 CATHLEEN PARA   4
    'MONG THE FEET OF ANGELS SEVEN . . . .   125 CATHLEEN PARA   13
    WITH WHITE FEET OF ANGELS SEVEN . . . .   125 CATHLEEN PARA   V   13
    HER WHITE FEET GO GLIMMERING! . . . .   125 CATHLEEN PARA   V   14
    OF THEIR LONG WINGS, THE FLASH OF THEIR WHITE FEET. . . 137 TO SOME I TALK   16
    OF THEIR LONG WINGS, THE FLASH OF THEIR SWIFT FEET. . . 137 TO SOME I TALK V   16
    THE MEASURE OF HER FLYING FEET . . . .   138 TO IRELAND   11
    THE LIGHT FALL OF HER FLYING FEET . . . .   138 TO IRELAND   V   11
    IS COMELIER THAN CANDLES AT MOTHER MARY'S FEET. . . . . 147 UNAPPEAS HOST   12
    IS COMELIER THAN CANDLES BEFORE MAURYA'S FEET. . . . .   147 UNAPPEAS HOST   V   12
    UNDER MY FEET THAT THEY FOLLOW YOU NIGHT AND DAY. . . . 153 CHANGE BELOVED   5
    UNDER MY FEET, THAT I FOLLOW YOU, NIGHT AND DAY. . . .   153 CHANGE BELOVED V   5
    AND HIDING THEIR TOSSING MANES AND THEIR TUMULTUOUS FEET. 154 BELOVED PEACE   12
    AND HIDE THEIR TOSSING MANES AND THEIR TUMULTUOUS FEET.   154 BELOVED PEACE   V   12
    LIVE BUT TO LIGHT YOUR PASSING FEET. . . . .   158 BELOVED RHYMES   12
    AND THE QUIET OF LOVE IN HER FEET. . . . .   161 CAP AND BELLS   36
    I WOULD SPREAD THE CLOTHS UNDER YOUR FEET! . . . . . .   176 CLOTHS HEAVEN   5
    I HAVE SPREAD MY DREAMS UNDER YOUR FEET! . . . .   176 CLOTHS HEAVEN   7

FEET   (CONTINUED)
WITH SPEEDY FEET AND A MOST THANKFUL HEART, ...   185 QUEEN MAEVE   100
ON THE ISLAND LAWNS, THEIR FEET WHERE THE PALE FOAM GLEAMS.   203 WITHER BOUGHS   14
BUT WE HAVE ALL BENT LOW AND LOW AND KISSED THE QUIET FEET   207 HANRAHANS SONG   4
BUT WE BEND TOGETHER AND KISS THE QUIET FEET . . . . .   207 HANRAHANS SONG V   4
AND THAT YOU COME FROM EDEN ON FLYING FEET, ...   218 WOODS OF COOLE   29
WITH SO RED LIPS, AND RUNNING ON SUCH FEET, ...   231 SHADOW WATER B   199
MY HUSBAND AND MY KING DIED AT MY FEET, ...   237 SHADOW WATER B   337
BLUE-EYED, AND A QUICK RUNNER ON BARE FEET, ...   242 SHADOW WATER B   416
THEY KILLED HIM AT MY FEET. O! O! O! O! . . . . .   242 SHADOW WATER B   420
AND KILLED A LOVER OR HUSBAND AT MY FEET--   . . . . .   246 SHADOW WATER B   491
SAT UPRIGHT WITH A SWORD BEFORE HER FEET. . . . . .   279 TWO KINGS   62
BEN JONSON'S PHRASE--AND STILL MAY TURN MY FEET . . .   321 REED WHISPERER V   6
AND YET HIS MIND OUTRAN THE HORSES' FEET. . . . . .   326 ROBERT GREGORY   64
HAVE FOUND THE PATH MY GOATS' FEET CANNOT FIND. . . .   342 SHEP GOATHERD   84
HAVE FOUND THE PATH MY GOAT'S FEET CANNOT FIND. . . .   342 SHEP GOATHERD V   84
LIFTING HIS DELICATE FEET. . . . .   378 CAT AND MOON   10
AND LIFTS HIS DELICATE FEET. . . . .   378 CAT AND MOON   V   10
WITH DELICATE FEET UPON OLD TERRACES, ...   418 ANCEST HOUSES   26
THUNDER OF FEET, TUMULT OF IMAGES, ...   433 NINETEEN 19   120
SHOULD HEAR MY LIVING FEET, NOR WOULD I TREAD . . . .   435 NEW FACES   3
MEN DANCE ON DEATHLESS FEET." . . . .   496 MOHINI CHATTER   28
"THOSE SIX FEET MARKED IN CHALK? . . . .   548 TO SAME TUNE 3   8
"THOSE SIX FEET MARKED IN CHALK? . . . .   548 TO SAME TUNE 3   18
"THOSE SIX FEET MARKED IN CHALK? . . . .   549 TO SAME TUNE 3   28
THEIR MOBS PUT UNDER THEIR FEET. . . . .   554 CHURCH STATE   4
ON THEIR OWN FEET THEY CAME, OR ON SHIPBOARD, ...   566 LAPIS LAZULI   25
TO LIE BETWEEN YOUR FEET? . . . .   572 LADYS 2ND SONG   2
AND HE PLAYS TUNES BETWEEN YOUR FEET, ...   573 LADYS 3RD SONG   2
FEET TO THE RISING AND SETTING MAY RUN, ...   591 WHAT WAS LOST   4
O MIND YOUR FEET, O MIND YOUR FEET, ...   592 DRUNK SOBRIETY   9
O MIND YOUR FEET, O MIND YOUR FEET, ...   592 DRUNK SOBRIETY   9
SOME TWENTY FEET FROM TIP TO TIP HAD IT STRETCHED RIGHTLY   593 PILGRIM   17
    OUT,
SOME TWENTY FEET FROM TIP TO TIP HAD ITS WINGS STRETCHED   593 PILGRIM   V   17
    RIGHTLY OUT,
THAT NOBODY LOOKS, HER FEET . . . .   617 LONG-LEG FLY   16
TREAD AND TREAD THEIR CLOVEN FEET . . . .   646 ISLE STAT I 1   24
AND, LEAPING TO THEIR FEET, FAR ECHOES CRIED, ...   659 ISLE STAT II 1   13
DOWN TO THEIR FEET THE STARS THAT SHINE ALONE, . . .   662 ISLE STAT II 1   80
AT THEIR FEET THE WAVES IN RINGS . . . .   667 ISLE STAT II 3   25
AT MORN, AND WITH HER FEET EACH COBWEB RENDS, ...   670 ISLE STAT II 3   99
THE FEET OF SUMMER DABBLE . . . .   680 LOVE AND DEATH   7
AS ROUND HER, SLOW ON FEET THAT HAVE NO BLOOD, . . .   687 TWO TITANS   18
AND HE IS DRAGGED AGAIN BEFORE HER FEET. . . . . .   688 TWO TITANS   43
FEET OF DARK GOMEZ, WHERE NOW WANDER YE? . . . . .   690 MOSADA 1   11
PICTURED, WHERE WANDER THE BELOVED FEET . . . . . .   692 MOSADA 1   44
YOURSELF INTO THE DUNGEON 'NEATH OUR FEET . . . . .   697 MOSADA 2   44
I'M NOT OF THAT PALE COMPANY WHOSE FEET . . . . . .   699 MOSADA 3   20
FOR YOUR FEET THE MORNING PRAYETH, ...   706 DAWN-SONG   25
IN TERROR FLINGS HER AT HER LOVER'S FEET. . . . . .   713 FERENCZ RENYI V   85
HER ARMS AROUND HIS FEET. THE SIGNAL GOES . . . . .   714 FERENCZ RENYI   103
DEEP IN THE WOODLAND PAUSED THEY, THE SIX FEET . . .   716 DWELT SYCAMORE   9
DEEP IN THE WOODLAND PASSED THEY. THE SIX FEET . . .   716 DWELT SYCAMORE V   9
FROM THE RUSTLING OF OUR FEET. . . . .   726 LOVERS QUARREL   8
THREE SPANS HIGH AS HE ROSE TO HIS FEET, ...   729 PRIEST FAIRY   25
WHO IS SIX FEET HIGH IN HIS SOCKS AT LEAST? . . . .   729 PRIEST FAIRY   28
TO THE RHYTHM OF THEIR FEET, ...   731 STREET DANCERS   2
FELL AT MY FEET ON THE FLOOR,-- . . . .   744 GLOVE CLOAK   8
WHERE I HAD HEARD NO FEET BUT THE GODS' CAME. . . . .   756 SHADOW WATER A V 191B
AND THAT DREAM ONLY SHINE BEFORE HER FEET. . . . . .   761 SHADOW WATER A   258
HAS MADE MY FEET UNSTEADY, AND BLINDED ME. . . . . .   767 SHADOW WATER A   406
FELL
AS HER SOFT BOSOM ROSE AND FELL. . . . .   4 OISIN 1   30
THERE WAS NO LIMB OF MINE BUT FELL . . . .   7 OISIN 1   72
OR DROPS OF SILVER JOY THAT FELL . . . .   19 OISIN 1   278
IT FELL, OR FROM THE TWISTED MOON . . . .   19 OISIN 1   V   278
HE FELL INTO A DRUID SWOON. . . . .   20 OISIN 1   289
OUR TREAD, AS ROSE AND FELL THE LIQUID TONES . . . .   33 OISIN 2   V 68B
AND ONCE MORE TO A DAY-LONG BATTLE FELL, ...   43 OISIN 2   218
AND WE ONCE MORE UNTO OUR FIGHTING FELL. . . . . .   43 OISIN 2   V   218
. . . AT THE HEEL OF A CENTURY FELL, ...   54 OISIN 3   102
CAME, AND MY FOREHEAD FELL LOW, AND MY TEARS LIKE BERRIES   57 OISIN 3   154
    FELL DOWN,
CAME, AND MY FOREHEAD FELL LOW, AND MY TEARS LIKE BERRIES   57 OISIN 3   154
    FELL DOWN,
. . . BUT FELL WITH THEIR BURDEN AT LENGTH. . . . .   60 OISIN 3   186
I FELL ON THE PATH, AND THE HORSE WENT AWAY LIKE A SUMMER   60 OISIN 3   190
    FLY,
AND MY YEARS THREE HUNDRED FELL ON ME, ...   60 OISIN 3   191
BETWEEN THEM A GATEWAY OF BRASS, AND THE HOWL OF THE ANGELS   61 OISIN 3   200
    WHO FELL.
FELL LIKE FAINT METEORS IN THE GLOOM, AND ONCE . . . .   80 EPHEMERA   14
FELL ON THE PIRATES BY THE DEEP, ...   83 MAD KING GOLL   21
FELL ON THE ROBBERS BY THE DEEP, ...   83 MAD KING GOLL V   21
FELL ON THE PIRATES OF THE DEEP, ...   83 MAD KING GOLL V   21
THEY WENT FORTH TO THE BATTLE, BUT THEY ALWAYS FELL . .   113 ROSE OF BATTLE V   T
A DRUID KINDNESS, ON ALL HEARERS FELL. . . . . . .   129 BOOK STORIES   4
HE PRAYED AND FELL ASLEEP, ...   132 FR GILLIGAN   14
HE KNELT, PRAYED, FELL ASLEEP, ...   132 FR GILLIGAN   V   14
OR FELL INTO UNHAPPINESS, I'VE SAID, ...   186 QUEEN MAEVE   137

272

FELL (CONTINUED)
   THAT ALL THINGS FELL OUT HAPPILY, ...   189 BAILE AILLINN   22
   SHE FELL AND DIED OF THE HEART-BREAK." . . . .   191 BAILE AILLINN   64
   AND I FELL ASLEEP UPON LONELY ECHTGE OF STREAMS. . . . .   203 WITHER BOUGHS   6
   WASHED BY TIME'S WATERS AS THEY ROSE AND FELL . . . . .   206 ADAMS CURSE   32
   WHERE IS MY SWORD THAT FELL OUT OF MY HAND . . . .   241 SHADOW WATER B   397
   FELL DOWN UPON THE DUST AND SNORED. . . . .   297 THREE BEGGARS   60
   HE STRETCHED HIS BONES AND FELL IN A DREAM . . . .   331 ROUND TOWER   10
   AND FELL THE ONE IN T'OTHER'S ARMS   . . . .   457 SUMMER SPRING   7
   WHEN UPWARD TURNED, ON ONE SOLE IMAGE FELL: . . . . . .   471 ALL SOUL NIGHT   34
   WHEN UPWARD TURNED ON ONE SOUL IMAGE FELL, ...   471 ALL SOUL NIGHT V   34
   SUCH A SLEEP AND SOUND AS FELL . . . .   522 LULLABY   13
   BELOVED SUCH A SLEEP AS FELL . . . .   522 LULLABY   V   13
   ALL THE RENOWN THAT FELL. . . . .   547 TO SAME TUNE 2   26
   GODHEAD. SOME SHADOW FELL. MY SOUL FORGOT . . . . . .   557 RIBH ECSTASY   6
   PRAISE EVERY MAN THAT FELL. . . . .   608 SONGS BURDEN 3   8
   ALL THE RENOWN THAT FELL. . . . .   614 MARCH SONGS 1   26
   CONFUSION FELL UPON OUR THOUGHT. . . . .   639 BEN BULBEN   67
   'TIS HERE THE ARROW FELL: THE BREEZES LAUGHED . . . . .   657 ISLE STAT I 3   70
   AMONG THE PLANTS: THE FLOWERY SILENCE FELL . . . . . .   692 MOSADA 1   55
   FOR ALL SAVE HIM WHO PINING FELL, ...   717 FAIRY DOCTOR   19
   FOR ALL SAVE HE WHO PINING FELL, ...   717 FAIRY DOCTOR V   19
   FELL AT MY FEET ON THE FLOOR,—. . . . .   744 GLOVE CLOAK   8
   THE STORM AROSE AND SUDDENLY FELL . . . .   784 WOMANS BEAUTY   19
FELLOW
   WITH "LOOK AT THAT OLD FELLOW THERE: . . . .   131 OLD PENSIONER V   3
   THOUGH IT BUT SET US SIGHING. FELLOW WANDERER . . . . .   230 SHADOW WATER B V   187
   DEAR FELLOW ARTIST WHY SO FREE . . . .   335 YOUNG BEAUTY V   1
   TO ABD-AL-RABBAN: FELLOW ROYSTERER ONCE . . . .   460 HARUN RASHID V   2
   OLD FELLOW STUDENT, WHOSE MOST PATIENT EAR . . . . . .   468 HARUN RASHID V   167
FELLOW-ARTIST
   DEAR FELLOW-ARTIST, WHY SO FREE . . . .   335 YOUNG BEAUTY   1
FELLOW-ROYSTERER
   TO ABD AL-RABBAN: FELLOW-ROYSTERER ONCE, ...   460 HARUN RASHID   2
FELLOWS
   THE CRAZY HERDSMAN THAT WILL TELL HIS FELLOWS . . . . .   229 SHADOW WATER B   167
   TO KEEP HIS FELLOWS FROM THEIR SLEEP: . . . .   297 THREE BEGGARS   45
   GOOD FELLOWS SHUFFLED CARDS IN AN OLD BAWN: . . . . . .   411 TOWER   65
FELLOW-STUDENT
   OLD FELLOW-STUDENT, WHOSE MOST PATIENT EAR . . . . . .   468 HARUN RASHID   167
FELLOW-WANDERER
   THOUGH IT BUT SET US SIGHING? FELLOW-WANDERER, ...   230 SHADOW WATER B   187
FELT
   BUT WHEN THE HORSE HAD FELT MY WEIGHT, ...   9 OISIN 1   109
   AND WHEN THE WHITE STEED FELT MY WEIGHT, ...   9 OISIN 1   V   109
   HAD FELT THE ISLAND BREEZE, MY LORE . . . .   668 ISLE STAT II 3   55
   AND WHEN THOU HAST THESE THINGS FOR MANY AGES FELT, . .   674 ISLE STAT II 3   214
   AND WHEN THOU HAST THESE THINGS FOR AGES FELT, ...   674 ISLE STAT II 3 V   214
   I FELT A SUDDEN TEAR START, ...   744 GLOVE CLOAK   10
FEN
   BY ROCKY SHORE AND RUSHY FEN: . . . .   83 MAD KING GOLL   32
   O'ER HILL AND HEATH AND SPONGY FEN, ...   83 MAD KING GOLL V   32
   OVER THE HEATH AND SPONGY FEN, ...   83 MAD KING GOLL V   32
   BY ROCKY LANE AND FEN: . . . .   133 FR GILLIGAN   30
FENCE
   SOME ROGUE OF THE WORLD STOLE THEM TO PATCH UP A FENCE   623 HIGH TALK   4
    OR A FIRE.
   AN OLD HORSE LOOKED ACROSS A FENCE, ...   725 LEGEND   27
FENCED
   HAS FENCED US ROUND FOR ALL ETERNITY. . . . .   670 ISLE STAT II 3   95
FENIAN
   THE FENIAN HORSES: ARMOUR TORN ASUNDER: . . . .   43 OISIN 2   210
   CEASE, CEASE, O MOURNFUL, LAUGHING FENIAN HORN: . . . .   43 OISIN 2   213
   AH, CEASE, THOU MOURNFUL, LAUGHING FENIAN HORN! . . . .   43 OISIN 2   V   213
   AH, CEASE, YOU MOURNFUL, LAUGHING FENIAN HORN! . . . .   43 OISIN 2   V   213
   YOUR QUESTIONER, OISIN, IS WORTHY, HE COMES FROM THE FENIAN 51 OISIN 3   64
    LANDS."
   WORTHY'S THY QUESTIONER, OISIN, HE FROM THE FENIAN LANDS." 51 OISIN 3   V   64
FENIANS
   AH, FENIANS, WITH THE SHIELD AND BOW? . . . .   10 OISIN 1   116
   NEAR BY, THE FENIANS SAW, AND KNEW . . . .   10 OISIN 1   V   111
   AND THE FENIANS ALL HAD WEPT WITH ME, ...   10 OISIN 1   V   113
   THE FENIANS ON THE HUMAN GROUND . . . .   10 OISIN 1   V 114C
   THE FENIANS. LET THEIR DEER-HOUNDS SLEEP. . . . .   11 OISIN 1   V   131
   REMEMBERING HOW THE FENIANS STEPT . . . .   24 OISIN 1   370
   IN WAR, THE NOBLE FENIANS STEPT. . . . .   24 OISIN 1   V   372
   THE HORSES OF THE FENIANS—TEARING ASUNDER . . . . . .   43 OISIN 2   V   210
   I MUSED ON THE CHASE WITH THE FENIANS, AND BRAN, SCEOLAN, 47 OISIN 3   5
    LOMAIR,
   AND BY ME, IN SOFT RED RAIMENT, THE FENIANS MOVED IN LOUD 53 OISIN 3   93
    STREAMS,
   WHEN THE FENIANS MADE FORAY AT MORNING WITH BRAN, SCEOLAN, 54 OISIN 3   104
    LOMAIR,
   AS MY MIND MADE THE NAMES OF THE FENIANS. . . . .   57 OISIN 3   146
   . . . "THE FENIANS HUNT WOLVES IN THE NIGHT, ...   59 OISIN 3   171
   . . . "THE FENIANS A LONG TIME ARE DEAD." . . . . . .   59 OISIN 3   172
   . . . FOR I GO TO THE FENIANS, O CLERIC, TO CHAUNT . .   61 OISIN 3   201
   . . . I WILL GO TO THE FENIANS, THOU CLERIC, AND CHANT .   61 OISIN 3   V   201
   . . . THE LIMBS OF THE FENIANS ARE TOST: . . . . . .   62 OISIN 3   213
   AND DWELL IN THE HOUSE OF THE FENIANS, BE THEY IN FLAMES   63 OISIN 3   224
    OR AT FEAST.

	PAGE	TITLE		LINE

FENIANS   (CONTINUED)
- I WILL GO TO THE HOUSE OF THE FENIANS, BE THEY IN FLAMES   63 OISIN 3   V   223
  OR AT FEAST,

FENIANS'
- IN THE FENIANS' DWELLINGS OF WATTLE LEAN ON THE CHESSBOARDS   55 OISIN 3   115
  AND PLAY,
- . . . A SOB FOR THE FENIANS' OLD STRENGTH. . . . . . .   60 OISIN 3   188

FERENCZ
- HOW FERENCZ RENYI KEPT SILENT. . . . .   709 FERENCZ RENYI   T
- THY NAME IS?" "FERENCZ RENYI." "OF?" "THIS VILLAGE."   709 FERENCZ RENYI   V   13
  "GOOD!
- SPEAK, FERENCZ, SPEAK. WE LOVE EACH OTHER. SEE, . . .   713 FERENCZ RENYI   87
- WE GATHERED. FERENCZ, NAY, I MUST NOT DIE! . . . . .   713 FERENCZ RENYI   96
- "AH, FERENCZ, SPEAK AND SAVE THYSELF AND ME! . . . . .   713 FERENCZ RENYI   V   86
- WE GATHERED. FERENCZ, DO NOT LET ME DIE. . . . . . .   713 FERENCZ RENYI   V   96
- YOUNG FERENCZ RENYI BURSTS HIS BONDS--AT LAST, ...   714 FERENCZ RENYI   V   116

FERGUS
- CAME BLANAID, MAC NESSA, TALL FERGUS WHO FEASTWARD OF OLD   53 OISIN 3   89
  TIME SLUNK,
- . . . CAME FERGUS WHO FEASTWARD SAD SLUNK, ...   53 OISIN 3   V   89
- CAME BLANID, MAC NESSA, AND FERGUS WHO FEASTWARD OF OLD   53 OISIN 3   V   89
  TIME SLUNK,
- WHO CAST ROUND FERGUS DREAMS, AND RUIN UNTOLD! . . . .   101 ROSE UPON ROOD   5
- FERGUS AND THE DRUID . . . .   102 FERGUS DRUID   T
- WHAT WOULD YOU, FERGUS? BE NO MORE A KING, ...   103 FERGUS DRUID   21
- WHO GOES WITH FERGUS? . . . .   125 GOES FERGUS   T
- WHO WILL GO DRIVE WITH FERGUS NOW, ...   125 GOES FERGUS   1
- FOR FERGUS RULES THE BRAZEN CARS, ...   126 GOES FERGUS   9
- AND OF THAT FAMOUS FERGUS, NESSA'S HUSBAND, ...   183 QUEEN MAEVE   71

FERGUSON
- WITH DAVIS, MANGAN, FERGUSON, ...   138 TO IRELAND   18

FERN
- AMONG THE FIELDS OF WAVING FERN. . . . .   2 OISIN 1   V   7N
- AMONG THE WAVING FIELDS OF FERN! . . . .   4 OISIN 1   38
- AND RIVER, FERN AND FLOWERY CLUMP, ...   15 OISIN 1   V   196

FERNS
- AND MAKES THE INFANT FERNS UNWRAP, ...   18 OISIN 1   265
- FROM FERNS THAT DROP THEIR TEARS . . . .   88 STOLEN CHILD   36
- FROM FERNS THAT DROP THEIR TEAR . . . .   88 STOLEN CHILD   V   36

FERRARA
- IN THE GREEN SHADOW OF FERRARA WALL! . . . .   352 PEOPLE   9
- IN THE GREEN SHADOW ON FERRARA WALL! . . . .   352 PEOPLE   V   9

FERTILE
- AND THROUGH THE FERTILE AND WASTE, ...   436 FOR MY SON   30

FERVOUR
- AND WITH THE FERVOUR OF MY YOUTHFUL EYES, ...   356 BROKEN DREAMS   25

FESTIVAL
- BECAUSE TO-DAY IS SOME RELIGIOUS FESTIVAL . . . . . .   363 DOLLS FACES   1
- HOLD FESTIVAL ACROSS THE LAND, ...   671 ISLE STAT II 3   128
- AND THE CUCKOO UNSEEN IN HIS FESTIVAL MOOD! . . . . .   717 LOVE SONG   7

FETCH
- AND FETCH ME HOME AGIN! . . . .   96 MOLL MAGEE   42
- I BADE THEM FETCH HIS HEAD. . . . .   789 SINGING HEAD   12

FETLOCKS
- HOW THE FETLOCKS DRIP BLOOD IN THE BATTLE, ...   52 OISIN 3   78

FEVER
- A FEVER AND A WHIRLING FIRE! . . . .   83 MAD KING GOLL   V   28
- MY SINGING SANG ME FEVER FREE, ...   86 MAD KING GOLL   V   65
- OF FEVER. NOW THE STRINGS ARE TORN . . . .   86 MAD KING GOLL   V   66

FEVER-FREE
- MY SINGING SANG ME FEVER-FREE! . . . .   86 MAD KING GOLL   V   65

FEVERISH
- MURMURING HOW FAR AWAY ARE ALL EARTH'S FEVERISH LANDS. . .   78 INDIAN TO LOVE   V   10

FEW
- FEW FEATHERS WERE ON THEIR DISHEVELLED WINGS, ...   34 OISIN 2   76
- SING YOU OF HER, O FIRST FEW STARS, ...   73 ANASHU VIJAYA   41
- SING YE OF HER, OH FIRST FEW STARS, ...   73 ANASHU VIJAYA   V   41
- IF HE BUT SHIFTED A FEW STONES, ...   302 HOUR DAWN   14
- OR ESSERKELLY PLAIN, FEW KEPT HIS PACE! . . . . . .   326 ROBERT GREGORY   59
- AND ESERKELLY PLAINS, FEW KEPT HIS PACE! . . . . . .   326 ROBERT GREGORY   V   59
- OR ESERKELLY PLAINS, FEW KEPT HIS PACE! . . . . . .   326 ROBERT GREGORY   V   59
- SOME FEW REMEMBERED STILL WHEN I WAS YOUNG . . . . .   410 TOWER   33
- SOME FEW HAVE HANDSOME RIDERS, ARE GARLANDED . . . . .   432 NINETEEN 19   114
- FEW DREAM THAT THEY EXIST, ...   436 FOR MY SON   V   11
- THOUGH BUT A FEW LEARNED MEN SHALL LOOK WITHIN, . . .   461 HARUN RASHID   V   18A
- I KNOW AS FEW CAN KNOW, ...   589 OLD WICKED MAN   47
- SOME FEW HALF WAKE AND HALF RENEW THEIR CHOICE, ...   622 HOUND VOICE   6
- AND YON FEW STARS GROWN DIM, LIKE EYES OF LOVERS . . . .   700 MOSADA 3   33
- "HOW FEW THE MIND'S INTEMPERANCE RULE! . . . . . .   725 LEGEND   10

FIBROUS
- FILLING THE FIBROUS DIMNESS WITH LONG GENERATIONS OF EYES.   49 OISIN 3   40

FICKLE   SEE FOAM-FICKLE
- AND SLEEK YOUNG JOY IS NO MORE FICKLE, ...   77 INDIAN TO LOVE   V   5C
- MORE FLEETING THAN THE SEA'S FOAM FICKLE FACE, ...   112 ROSE OF WORLD   V   8
- VEERING, FLEETING, FICKLE, THE WINDS OF KNOCKNAREA, . . .   206 HANRAHANS SONG   V   1
- VEERING, FLEETING, FICKLE, OUR LOVES AND ANGERS MEET! . .   207 HANRAHANS SONG   V   3
- FICKLE THE GUIDING HIS ARROW SHALL FIND! . . . . .   657 ISLE STAT I 3   66

FIDDLE
- WHEN I PLAY ON MY FIDDLE IN DOONEY, ...   178 FIDDLER DOONEY   1
- AND THE MERRY LOVE THE FIDDLE, ...   179 FIDDLER DOONEY   15
- PULL DOWN THE BLINDS, BRING FIDDLE AND CLARIONET . . . .   311 MOUNTAIN TOMB   5

274

		PAGE	TITLE		LINE
FIDDLE	**(CONTINUED)**				
	FINGERED UPON A FIDDLE STICK OR STRING	445	SCHOOL CHILDR	V	46
	OR THE FIDDLE STRING ACCURSED,	527	AM OF IRELAND	V	20
	CAN PAY THE POET FOR A VERSE AND HEAR THE FIDDLE SOUND,	581	CURSE CROMWELL		21
FIDDLE-BOW					
	THEY ARE SICK OF THE PALETTE AND FIDDLE-BOW,	565	LAPIS LAZULI		2
FIDDLER					
	THE FIDDLER OF DOONEY	178	FIDDLER DOONEY		T
	WITH "HERE IS THE FIDDLER OF DOONEY!"	179	FIDDLER DOONEY		19
	SCHOOLMASTER HE, A DREAMER, FIDDLER, FIRST	709	FERENCZ RENYI		11
FIDDLERS					
	"THE FIDDLERS ARE ALL THUMBS,	527	AM OF IRELAND		19
FIDDLE'S					
	TO THE FIDDLE'S RISE AND FALL.	726	LOVERS QUARREL		20
FIDDLES					
	OF FIDDLES AND OF FLUTES HUNG THERE	271	GREY ROCK	V	20
FIDDLE-STICK					
	FINGERED UPON A FIDDLE-STICK OR STRINGS	445	SCHOOL CHILDR		46
FIDDLE-STRING					
	OR THE FIDDLE-STRING ACCURSED,	527	AM OF IRELAND		20
FIDGET					
	AND MAY NO RESTLESS FAY WITH FIDGET FINGER	75	ANASHU VIJAYA	V	90
	MAY NEVER RESTLESS FAY WITH FIDGET FINGER	75	ANASHU VIJAYA	V	90
	AND MAY NO RESTLESS PITRI'S FIDGET FINGER	75	ANASHU VIJAYA	V	90
FIELD					
	IN A FIELD BY THE RIVER MY LOVE AND I DID STAND,	90	SALLEY GARDENS		5
	THE FIELD MOUSE RUNNING BY ME IN THE GRASS,	101	ROSE UPON ROOD	V	17
	THE FIELD THAT CLOSES IN BEHIND.	266	GALWAY RACES	V	4
	OR WINTRY MOONLIGHT SINK THE FIELD	501	VACILLATION		47
	A RIVERY FIELD SPREAD OUT BELOW,	502	VACILLATION		57
	"WHATEVER STANDS IN FIELD OR FLOOD,	529	TOM LUNATIC		13
	A COWARD IN THE FIELD! AND ALL MEN CRIED!	684	SEEKER		53
	SLEEP IN SOME FAR OTHER FIELD	705	DAWN-SONG		3
	ALONG THE TENTS, FIELD, THE VILLAGE WALLS.	712	FERENCZ RENYI	V	71
FIELD-MOUSE					
	THE FIELD-MOUSE RUNNING BY ME IN THE GRASS,	101	ROSE UPON ROOD		17
	A CAREFUL FIELD-MOUSE FINDS A FALLEN CRUMB!	713	FERENCZ RENYI		77
FIELDS					
	AMONG THE FIELDS OF WAVING FERN.	2	OISIN 1	V	7N
	AMONG THE WAVING FIELDS OF FERN!	4	OISIN 1		38
	YOU HUNTER OF THE FIELDS AFAR!	75	ANASHU VIJAYA		79
	THE FIELDS GREW FATTER DAY BY DAY,	82	MAD KING GOLL		7
	FIELDS FATTENING SLOW, MEN WISE IN JOY,	82	MAD KING GOLL	V	6
	AND THE MOTH-HOUR WENT FROM THE FIELDS,	133	FR GILLIGAN		15
	"I HAVE SENT AMONG THE FIELDS OR TO THE WOODS	280	TWO KINGS		69
	"I HAVE SENT OUT INTO THE FIELDS AND WOODS	280	TWO KINGS	V	69
	ROADS FULL OF BEGGARS, CATTLE IN THE FIELDS,	487	SEVEN SAGES		18
	THE AVENGING LEAF THOSE FIELDS RAISED UP AGAINST IT.	487	SEVEN SAGES		20
	A MAN HAS THE FIELDS OF HEAVEN.	643	SONG FAERIES		1
	THUS, THUS I BECKON FROM HER VIEWLESS FIELDS—	693	MOSADA 1		75
	ALONG THE TENTS, THE FIELDS, THE VILLAGE WALLS.	712	FERENCZ RENYI		71
	AND OVER TILLAGE FIELDS AND PASTURE LANDS	715	FERENCZ RENYI		120
	AND FOLLOWING O'ER THE FIELDS AND PASTURE LANDS,	715	FERENCZ RENYI	V	120
	AS THERE FLOATS FROM FIELDS AFAR	732	STREET DANCERS		20
	WELL SHELTERED FROM THE WINDS, AND FRUITFUL FIELDS,	758	SHADOW WATER A		221
FIELDS'					
	THE FAT FLOCKS AND THE FIELDS' FATNESS,	540	FROM ANTIGONE		4
FIEND					
	OF SOME FORGOTTEN FIEND. NOW NONE ASSAILS	31	OISIN 2	V	30B
	THAT INSOLENT FIEND ROBERT ARTISSON	433	NINETEEN 19		128
FIERCE					
	ARE CHOKED WITH THUNDER, LIGHTNING, AND FIERCE WIND,	42	OISIN 3		205
	AT NEED, AND MADE HER BEAUTIFUL AND FIERCE,	181	QUEEN MAEVE		29
	"YOUR STRENGTH, THAT IS SO LOFTY AND FIERCE AND KIND,	201	OLD MEMORY		3
	YOU MOST OF ALL, SILENT AND FIERCE OLD MAN,	270	PARDON FATHERS		15
	AND THOSE FIERCE EYES, AND CURSE OUR LUCK	272	GREY ROCK	V	39
	BRED THAT FIERCE TOOTH AND CLEANLY LIMB	318	APPOINTMENT		10
	WHEN THAT FIERCE VIRGIN AND HER STAR	437	SONGS PLAY 1		15
	WHEN THE FIERCE VIRGIN AND HER STAR	437	SONGS PLAY 1	V	15
	"DROWN ALL THE DOGS," SAID THE FIERCE YOUNG WOMAN,	546	TO SAME TUNE 2		7
	DROWN ALL THE DOGS," SAID THE FIERCE YOUNG WOMAN.	546	TO SAME TUNE 2		10
	"DROWN ALL THE DOGS," SAID THE FIERCE YOUNG WOMAN.	546	TO SAME TUNE 2		17
	DROWN ALL THE DOGS," SAID THE FIERCE YOUNG WOMAN.	546	TO SAME TUNE 2		20
	"DROWN ALL THE DOGS," SAID THE FIERCE YOUNG WOMAN.	547	TO SAME TUNE 2		27
	DROWN ALL THE DOGS," SAID THE FIERCE YOUNG WOMAN.	547	TO SAME TUNE 2		30
	FROM MOUNTAIN TO MOUNTAIN RIDE THE FIERCE HORSEMEN.	605	SONGS BURDEN 1		9
	FROM MOUNTAIN TO MOUNTAIN RIDE THE FIERCE HORSEMEN.	606	SONGS BURDEN 1		18
	FROM MOUNTAIN TO MOUNTAIN RIDE THE FIERCE HORSEMEN.	606	SONGS BURDEN 1		27
	FROM MOUNTAIN TO MOUNTAIN RIDE THE FIERCE HORSEMEN.	607	SONGS BURDEN 2		9
	FROM MOUNTAIN TO MOUNTAIN RIDE THE FIERCE HORSEMEN.	607	SONGS BURDEN 2		18
	FROM MOUNTAIN TO MOUNTAIN RIDE THE FIERCE HORSEMEN.	607	SONGS BURDEN 2		27
	FROM MOUNTAIN TO MOUNTAIN RIDE THE FIERCE HORSEMEN.	608	SONGS BURDEN 3		9
	FROM MOUNTAIN TO MOUNTAIN RIDE THE FIERCE HORSEMEN.	608	SONGS BURDEN 3		18
	FROM MOUNTAIN TO MOUNTAIN RIDE THE FIERCE HORSEMEN.	608	SONGS BURDEN 3		27
	FIERCE THRUST! A TARDY BLOSSOM HAD THE SEED,	665	ISLE STAT II 2		65
	LIES TORN AND ROTTING. THE FIERCE KESTREL BIRDS	675	ISLE STAT II 3		234
	BEFORE I AM TOO WEAK, FIERCE MORTAL, LET ME FLY,	675	ISLE STAT II 3		245
	FIERCE MORTAL, AND CROUCHED LOW BESIDE THE LAKE	675	ISLE STAT II 3	V	245A
	A SIBYL, WITH FIERCE FACE AS OF A HOUND.	687	TWO TITANS		9
	TILL THEIR FIERCE MISERIES WITHIN HIS EYES	687	TWO TITANS		26
	WORN BY THE SOLSTICE FIERCE, AND MADE IT PURE.	692	MOSADA 1		57

FIERCE   (CONTINUED)
    THE WORLD TO ITS FIERCE INFANCY AGAIN. . . . .   698 MOSADA 2   61
    OBEYS. SOME FIERCE MAGICIAN FLIES OR WALKS . . . . .   720 WITCH VIVIEN   9
FIERCELY
    TO HUNGER FIERCELY AFTER TRUTH, ...   66 HAPPY SHEPHERD   24
FIERY
    ABOUT WHOSE FACE BIRDS WAGGED THEIR FIERY WINGS, ...   187 QUEEN MAEVE   145
    FOR SHE HAD FIERY BLOOD . . . .   255 WOMAN HOMER   15
    WITH FIERY SONG I'LL DROWN YON PUNY VOICE. . . . . . .   648 ISLE STAT I 1   81
    BEHOLD, HOW LIKE A SWARM OF FIERY BEES . . . .   662 ISLE STAT II 2   1
    THAT WITH THEIR FIERY RUIN FILL THE HALL, ...   683 SEEKER   45
    AND MINGLING HAIR FALL FROM THE FIERY BOUGHS, ...   765 SHADOW WATER A   368
FIFTEEN
    NO, NOT IN THESE FIFTEEN . . . .   315 FRIENDS   6
    AND MINE WERE BUT FIFTEEN FOOT, NO MODERN STALKS
      UPON HIGHER,   623 HIGH TALK   3
    FIFTEEN APPARITIONS HAVE I SEEN: . . . .   624 APPARITIONS   7
    FIFTEEN APPARITIONS HAVE I SEEN: . . . .   624 APPARITIONS   15
    FIFTEEN APPARITIONS HAVE I SEEN: . . . .   624 APPARITIONS   23
FIFTEENTH
    NOW AT ITS FIFTEENTH NIGHT. . . . .   383 VISION ROBART   28
FIFTIETH
    NOW THAT HIS FIFTIETH YEAR HAD COME, ...   361 ALF POLLEXFEN   31
    MY FIFTIETH YEAR HAD COME AND GONE, ...   501 VACILLATION   35
FIFTY   SEE NINE-AND-FIFTY
    THAT HAVE TO BE SET UP IN FIFTY WAYS, ...   260 FASC DIFFICULT   9
    ARE NINE AND FIFTY SWANS. . . . .   322 SWANS AT COOLE V   6
    AND NOW THAT I HAVE COME TO FIFTY YEARS . . . . . .   344 DEJECTION   10
    HOW COULD SHE MATE WITH FIFTY YEARS THAT WAS SO WILDLY
      BRED?   450 OWEN AHERNE   15
    HER CHILDISH GRATITUDE FOR LOVE AND MATCH YOUR FIFTY YEARS?   450 OWEN AHERNE   23
    I MET HER ALL BUT FIFTY YEARS AGO . . . .   602 GALLERY REVIS   15
    AT THE BOTTOM OF A LETTER, FIFTY MEN. . . . .   790 DEDICATION   10
FIGHT
    NOR THE HIGH GODS WHO NEVER LIVED, MAY FIGHT . . . . .   34 OISIN 2   80
    ONCE MORE UNTO YOUR FLOWERS, FOR NONE MAY FIGHT, . . .   34 OISIN 2   V 80
    OF THE LOUD-CRASHING AND EARTH-SHAKING FIGHT, ...   38 OISIN 2   141
    OF THE LOUD CRASHING AND EARTH SHAKING FIGHT . . . . .   38 OISIN 2   V 141
    OF FEAR, I BADE THEM GO: AND FOR THE FIGHT . . . . .   38 OISIN 2   V 142
    CUCHULAIN'S FIGHT WITH THE SEA . . . .   105 CUCHULAIN SEA   T
    THAT HE MAY FIGHT THE HORSES OF THE SEA." . . . . . .   111 CUCHULAIN SEA   81
    THAT HE MAY FIGHT THE WAVES OF THE LOUD SEA." . . . .   111 CUCHULAIN SEA   V 81
    THAT HE MIGHT FIGHT THE WAVES OF THE LOUD SEA." . . .   111 CUCHULAIN SEA   V 81
    THOSE THAT I FIGHT I DO NOT HATE, ...   328 IRISH AIRMAN   3
    NOR LAW, NOR DUTY BADE ME FIGHT, ...   328 IRISH AIRMAN   9
    ALL THE FOLLY OF A FIGHT . . . .   476 EVA GORE-BOOTH   22
    HE WITH BODY WAGED A FIGHT, ...   561 FOUR AGES MAN   1
    OUT OF THAT CRAZY FIGHT: . . . .   585 ORAHILLY   15
    AND FIGHT FOR THE BLACK SLOE-BERRIES, ...   644 SONG FAERIES   13
    THIS THING WE ASK: MUST WE TWO FIGHT?--JUDGE THOU. . .   660 ISLE STAT II 1   41
    FOR THIS THING FIGHT--WE LOVE ONE MAID? HER NAME? . .   661 ISLE STAT II 1   66
    THERE IS NO WAY BUT THAT YE FIGHT I WIS. . . . . . .   662 ISLE STAT II 1   75
    IF HER YE LOVE. AYE, COLIN, WE MUST FIGHT. . . . . .   662 ISLE STAT II 1   76
    AYE, FIGHT WE MUST. TELL ME, ANTONIO, MIGHT . . . . .   662 ISLE STAT II 1   77
    ANTONIO! WE HAVE RESOLVED TO FIGHT. . . . .   664 ISLE STAT II 2   55
    AND FIGHT FOR THE BLACK SLOE-BERRIES, ...   676 ISLE STAT II 3   260
FIGHTING
    AND WE ONCE MORE UNTO OUR FIGHTING FELL. . . . . . .   43 OISIN 2   V 218
    AFTER SHORT FIGHTING IN THE LEAFY SHADE, ...   109 CUCHULAIN SEA   57
    THAT I LOVED ONCE." AGAIN THE FIGHTING SPED, ...   110 CUCHULAIN SEA   64
    AND THAT LONG FIGHTING AT THE FORD, ...   197 BAILE AILLINN   194
    THE FIGHTING MEN AND SERVANTS OF THIS HOUSE, ...   280 TWO KINGS   V 70
    WHO ARE BUT WEASELS FIGHTING IN A HOLE. . . . . . .   429 NINETEEN 19   32
    AND A MAN IS FIGHTING MAD, ...   638 BEN BULBEN   28
FIGHTING-MEN
    THE FIGHTING-MEN AND SERVANTS OF THIS HOUSE, ...   280 TWO KINGS   70
FIGURATIVE
    FROM A DISCOURSE IN FIGURATIVE SPEECH . . . .   472 ALL SOUL NIGHT   52
FIGURE
    "WHAT IS THE FIGURE IN A SHROUD . . . .   253 HIS DREAM   7
    A FIGURE THAT HAS GROWN SO FABULOUS . . . .   412 TOWER   77
    A FAMOUS, A BRILLIANT FIGURE . . . .   608 SONGS BURDEN 3   16
FIGURED
    OF MANY A FIGURED EMBROIDERY: . . . .   4 OISIN 1   27
    OF MANY A FIGURED CREATURE STRANGE, ...   4 OISIN 1   V 27
    AS IF THAT WRITING OR THE FIGURED PAGE . . . .   466 HARUN RASHID   126
    THAT IF THEIR NEIGHBOURS FIGURED PLAIN, ...   626 OLD MEN BE MAD   11
FIGURES
    AND CARVEN FIGURES ON THEIR PROWS . . . .   14 OISIN 1   190
    AND CARVEN FIGURES ON THEIR PROWS . . . .   23 OISIN 1   354
    AS FIGURES MOVING MIRRORED IN A GLASS, ...   676 ISLE STAT II 3   270
    TWO FIGURES CROUCHING ON THE BLACK ROCK, BOUND . . . .   687 TWO TITANS   5
FILL
    TO FILL THEIR DARK-BEAKED HOLLOW GALLEYS. . . . . . .   82 MAD KING GOLL   16
    THAT HE MAY FILL HIS HOLLOW GALLEYS. . . . .   82 MAD KING GOLL   V 16
    TO FILL WITH COWS HIS HOLLOW GALLEYS." . . . .   82 MAD KING GOLL   V 16
    A LITTLE SPACE FOR THE ROSE-BREATH TO FILL: . . . . .   101 ROSE UPON ROOD   14
    AND CRAZY RASCALS RAGE THEIR FILL . . . .   131 OLD PENSIONER   9
    TO FILL YOUR HEART WITH CONTENT." . . . .   167 BLESSED   20
    LET RUSH AND BIRD CRY OUT THEIR FILL . . . .   197 BAILE AILLINN   198
    WOULD HAVE HIS FILL OUT OF MY LADLE . . . .   304 HOUR DAWN   V 53

FILL   (CONTINUED)
  ONE'S HAD HER FILL OF LOVERS, ANOTHER'S HAD BUT ONE, . . . 354 HIS PHOENIX   19
  HER FILL OF SLEEP. . . . . 435 FOR MY SON   8
  "LET OTHERS BOAST THEIR FILL," SAID I, ... 539 MEETING   7
  COME FILL UP ALL THOSE GLASSES . . . . 586 PARNELLITES   7
  ALTHOUGH I DRINK MY FILL. . . . . 592 DRUNK SOBRIETY   4
  MAKE HIM FILL THE CRADLES RIGHT. . . . . 638 BEN BULBEN   41
  THAT WITH THEIR FIERY RUIN FILL THE HALL, ... 683 SEEKER   45
  THAT FILL THE BLAZING HOLLOWS OF MY HEART. . . . . . 684 SEEKER   V 69D
  AND FILL ME WITH THY RAGE, THAT I MAY BRUISE . . . . 698 MOSADA 2   54
  MAY THE SWORD-BLADES DRINK THEIR FILL . . . . . . 776 AGAINST WITCH   37
  MAY THE SWORD BLADES DRINK THEIR FILL . . . . . . 776 AGAINST WITCH V 37
FILLED
  THE MOIL OF MY CENTURIES FILLED ME; AND GONE LIKE   51 OISIN 3   70
    A SEA-COVERED STONE
  . . . AND FILLED ME FULL TO THE BONE. . . . . . . 52 OISIN 3   72
  THEIR HAIR ALONG THE MOUNTAINS ROLLED AND FILLED . . 74 ANASHU VIJAYA   71
  FILLED FULL OF ANCIENT CHEER." . . . . 97 FOXHUNTER   V 12
  HAD FILLED THE HOUSE WITH DRUID HEAVINESS; . . . . . 181 QUEEN MAEVE   40
  WHY SHOULD I BLAME HER THAT SHE FILLED MY DAYS . . . 256 NO SECOND TROY   1
  NOW IT HAS FILLED AN OLD SOCK FULL! . . . . 301 RUN PARADISE   20
  PLEASED TO HAVE FILLED THE EYES . . . . 329 MEN IMPROVE   8
  AND THEN A COUNTER-TRUTH FILLED OUT ITS PLAY, ... 629 CIRCUS ANIMALS   17
  FILLED THEM AS THEY SAT TOGETHER; . . . . 667 ISLE STAT II 3   31
  AS WORDS OF THINE THROUGH FOURSCORE YEARS HAVE FILLED . . 683 SEEKER   46
FILLING
  FILLING THE FIBROUS DIMNESS WITH LONG GENERATIONS OF EYES. 49 OISIN 3   40
  SIDLED THEIR BODIES AGAINST HIM, FILLING THE SHADE WITH 50 OISIN 3   48
    THEIR EYES.
  FILLING THY HEART WITH A MORTAL DREAM, ... 140 HOSTING SIDHE V 6
FILLS
  AND FILLS WITH STARS NIGHT'S PURPLE CUP, ... 18 OISIN 1   262
  ANOTHER FILLS YOUR MIND. MY MOTHER'S NAME. . . . . 71 ANASHU VIJAYA   16
  SOME OTHER FILLS YOUR MIND. MY MOTHER'S NAME. . . . 71 ANASHU VIJAYA V 16
  UNTO THE WANDERER'S SHIPS, OR AS DAY FILLS . . . . 645 ISLE STAT I 1   10
  YON EAGER LARK, THAT FILLS WITH SONG THE WHOLE . . . 652 ISLE STAT I 2   18
  AS AN HURT LEOPARD FILLS WITH CEASELESS MOAN, . . . 674 ISLE STAT II 3 208
  AS A HURT LEOPARD FILLS WITH CEASELESS MOAN. . . . 674 ISLE STAT II 3 V 208
  AND THEN HIS HEART FILLS FULL OF LOVE, ... 716 FAIRY DOCTOR   11
  AN EVENING PRESENCE FILLS THE PLACE. . . . . 736 SUMMER EVENING 16
  THAT ALL THE VALLEY FILLS . . . . 781 MY HEART BEAT   10
  LIKE WINE THAT FILLS TO THE TOP . . . . 781 MY HEART BEAT   14
FILTHY
  A NOISY AND FILTHY THING." . . . . 319 DOLLS   12
  OR SHIFT TIME'S FILTHY LOAD, ... 505 RESULT THOUGHT   15
  BUT THROWN UPON THIS FILTHY MODERN TIDE . . . . . . 611 STATUES   29
FIN
  CRIED FIN; AND CRIED SHE, "MEN OF FAME, ... 5 OISIN 1   V 45
  HAD KISSED MY FATHER, LONG-ARMED FIN, ... 10 OISIN 1   V 112B
  FIN, CONAN, OSCAR, MANY MORE, THE TIDE . . . . . . 44 OISIN 2   V 228A
  WHAT PLACE HAVE CAOLTE AND FIN, AND BRAN, SGEOLAN, LOMAIR? 61 OISIN 3 V 195
  TO FIN, CAOLTE, AND CONAN, AND BRAN, SGEOLAN, LOMAIR. . . 63 OISIN 3 V 224
  AND STEADIED BY A FIN, ... 612 NEWS ORACLE   14
FINAL
  THE FINAL PARADISE. . . . . 415 TOWER   V 156
  AND HERE'S A FINAL REASON. . . . . 586 PARNELLITES   17
  YOUNG MOORISH GIRL, THY FINAL HOUR IS HERE; . . . . 701 MOSADA 3   63
FIND
  WENT WE TO FIND THEIR PRINCE'S HALL-- . . . . 16 OISIN 1   V 217
  AND NEVER FIND, THOUGH YE IN MUSIC SPEAK. . . . . . 42 OISIN 2   V 201
  I FIND UNDER THE BOUGHS OF LOVE AND HATE. . . . . . 101 ROSE UPON ROOD 10
  I WILL FIND OUT WHERE SHE HAS GONE, ... 150 WANDER AENGUS   19
  I WILL FIND OUT WHERE SHE IS GONE . . . . 150 WANDER AENGUS V 19
  OR REMEMBERING HERS THEY WILL FIND NO OTHER FACE FAIR . . 163 VALLEY LOVERS   7
  THERE'S MANY A ONE SHALL FIND OUT ALL HEARTACHE . . . 205 ADAMS CURSE   16
  TO FIND IT WHEN NIGHT FALLS LAID ON A GOLDEN BIER. . . 209 UNDER THE MOON 10
  I FIND NO HAPPINESS IN SHADY BRYCELINDE . . . . . . 209 UNDER THE MOON V 1
  WILL NEVER FIND US THERE . . . . 213 HAPPY TOWNLAND V 2
  WHERE OLD AGE CANNOT FIND THEM; PAIRC-NA-LEE, . . . 217 WOODS OF COOLE   7
  JUDGE OF THE STARS, AND FIND A COURSE FOR US? . . . 224 SHADOW WATER B 61
  MORE RICHES THAN THEY EVER HOPED TO FIND? . . . . . 226 SHADOW WATER B 94
  WHAT RICHES CAN YOU FIND IN THIS WASTE SEA . . . . 226 SHADOW WATER B 97
  AND FIND THEIR LAUGHTER SWEETER TO THE TASTE . . . . 228 SHADOW WATER B 134
  AND ALMOST WEPT BECAUSE THEY COULD NOT FIND IT. . . . 229 SHADOW WATER B 155
  OR SOMEWHERE, I SHALL FIND THE LOVE THEY HAVE PROMISED. 231 SHADOW WATER B 208
  THAT MUCH IS CERTAIN. I SHALL FIND A WOMAN, ... 231 SHADOW WATER B 209
  ANOTHER ANSWERS, "MAYBE WE SHALL FIND . . . . . . 233 SHADOW WATER B 254
  WITH LIGHTNING, YOU WENT FROM ME, AND I COULD FIND . . 257 RECONCILIATION   4
  WE'LL FIND SO GOOD A THING AS THAT WE HAVE LOST? . . 258 KING NO KING   13
  I'LL FIND THE STABLE AND PULL OUT THE BOLT. . . . . 260 FASC DIFFICULT 13
  TO FIND IF HEARTS BE WILD AND WISE, ... 263 MASK   4
  "I WOULD BUT FIND WHAT'S THERE TO FIND, ... 263 MASK   6
  "I WOULD BUT FIND WHAT'S THERE TO FIND, ... 263 MASK   6
  AND WE FIND HEARTENERS AMONG MEN . . . . 266 GALWAY RACES   15
  AND FIND HEARTENERS AMONG MEN . . . . 266 GALWAY RACES V 15
  TO FIND OUT IF I MIGHT LOVE. . . . . 268 BROWN PENNY   4
  TO FIND OUT ALL THAT IS IN IT, ... 268 BROWN PENNY   11
  KNOWING THAT HE SHOULD FIND UPON HER LIPS . . . . . 280 TWO KINGS   77
  AND I, THAT I MIGHT FIND AND STUB IT OUT, ... 281 TWO KINGS   V 92
  WOMEN CAN FIND." WITH A MOST MASTERFUL VOICE, . . . 284 TWO KINGS   175
  WOMEN CAN FIND." WITH A MOST BURNING VOICE . . . . 284 TWO KINGS   V 175

		PAGE	TITLE	LINE

FIND   (CONTINUED)

AND FIND MY HEALTH AGAIN IN THE SEA AIR," . . . . 299 BEGGAR CRIED   2
THAT I MAY FIND THE SLEEP I HAVE LOST." . . . . 303 HOUR DAWN   39
I HAVE TO FIND THE SLEEP I HAVE LOST." . . . . 303 HOUR DAWN   V 39
BUT FOR THOSE MORNINGS WHEN I FIND . . . . 306 HOUR DAWN   76
YET WE, FOR ALL THAT PRAISE, COULD FIND . . . . . . 314 MEMORY YOUTH   13
AND ALL THEIR EYES STILL FIXED, HOPING TO FIND ONCE MORE, 318 MAGI   6
--BEN JONSON'S PHRASE--AND FIND WHEN JUNE IS COME . . . 321 REED WHISPERER   6
TO FIND THEY HAVE FLOWN AWAY? . . . . 323 SWANS AT COOLE   30
I WOULD FIND BY THE EDGE OF THAT WATER . . . . 330 BONE OF A HARE   9
I CANNOT FIND THE PEACE OF HOME . . . . 332 ROUND TOWER   29
HAVE FOUND THE PATH MY GOATS' FEET CANNOT FIND. . . . . 342 SHEP GOATHERD   84
HAVE FOUND THE PATH MY GOAT'S FEET CANNOT FIND. . . . . 342 SHEP GOATHERD V 84
A MAN MAY FIND IN NO MAN . . . . 345 ON WOMAN   3
TO FIND WHAT ONCE I HAD . . . . 346 ON WOMAN   33
AND I WOULD FIND MYSELF AND NOT AN IMAGE. . . . . . . 367 EGO DOMINUS   10
BUT THAT OF CHRIST.   AND DID HE FIND HIMSELF . . . . . 368 EGO DOMINUS   22
WHAT HE SHALL NEVER FIND.   WHY SHOULD NOT YOU . . . . . 373 PHASES OF MOON   20
WILL SCARCELY FIND FOR HIM A BROKEN CRUST . . . . . . 373 PHASES OF MOON   23
THAT HE WILL NEVER FIND! I'D PLAY A PART! . . . . . . 377 PHASES OF MOON 128
DAY AFTER DAY, YET NEVER FIND THE MEANING. . . . . . . 377 PHASES OF MOON 135
TO FIND OUT SOME APPROPRIATE PAIN-- . . . . 388 SOLOMON WITCH   20
WILL FIND OUT SOME APPROPRIATE PAIN, ... 388 SOLOMON WITCH V 20
OR BUT TO FIND, ... 390 IMAGE PAST   38
I COULD NOT FIND A THING SO DEAR." . . . . 398 BREAK OF DAY   9
THAN THAT I MAY FIND OUT A WAY . . . . 401 DEMON BEAST   41
THAT CHOOSES RIGHT, AND NEVER FIND A FRIEND. . . . . . 404 FOR DAUGHTER   24
YET, NOW I HAVE CONSIDERED IT, I FIND . . . . 411 TOWER   50
MY BODILY HEIRS MAY FIND, ... 420 MY HOUSE   28
AND FIND A COMFORT IN IT? MAY THIS TOWER . . . . . . 423 MY DESCENDANTS V 13
I HAD BETTER FIND A CONVENT AND TURN NUN! . . . . . . 448 HERO GIRL FOOL   11
I WILL FIND OUT SOME CAVERN IN THE HILLS . . . . . . 448 HERO GIRL FOOL V 11
I THINK THAT I MAY FIND . . . . 449 HERO GIRL FOOL   28
SHOULD FIND NO BURDEN BUT ITSELF AND YET SHOULD BE WORN   449 OWEN AHERNE   3
     OUT.
I DID NOT FIND IN ANY CAGE THE WOMAN AT MY SIDE. . . . . 450 OWEN AHERNE   19
A BOY'S LOVELORN INDIFFERENT HANDS MIGHT FIND . . . . . 461 HARUN RASHID   V 14
THEIR BITTERNESS AND FIND THE HONEYCOMB. . . . . . . 463 HARUN RASHID   48
NOR FIND A REMEDY." "BUT WHAT IF I . . . . 464 HARUN RASHID   84
AND FIND NO REMEDY. "BUT WHAT IF I . . . . 464 HARUN RASHID   V 84
IF HONOUR FIND HIM IN THE WINTRY BLAST? . . . . 479 SELF AND SOUL   56
HAD SCOOPED OUT PHARAOH'S MUMMY. I--THOUGH HEART MIGHT   503 VACILLATION   84
     FIND RELIEF
(ALL FIND SAFETY IN THE TOMB.) . . . . 508 JANE BISHOP   3
(ALL FIND SAFETY IN THE TOMB.) . . . . 508 JANE BISHOP   10
(ALL FIND SAFETY IN THE TOMB.) . . . . 508 JANE BISHOP   17
(ALL FIND SAFETY IN THE TOMB.) . . . . 508 JANE BISHOP   24
OR BUT TO FIND IF WITHERED VEIN RAN BLOOD, ... 537 HER VISION   6
HE IT HAS FOUND SHALL FIND THEREIN . . . . 538 LAST CONFESS   17
"I THINK THAT I SHALL FIND HER . . . . 594 COLONEL MARTIN   16
FIND IN MIDDLE AIR . . . . 601 THOSE IMAGES   13
CHILDLESS I THOUGHT, "MY CHILDREN MAY FIND HERE . . . . 603 GALLERY REVIS   36
THAT GIRLS AT PUBERTY MAY FIND . . . . 617 LONG-LEG FLY   21
AND FIND OUR ANCIENT HOUNDS BEFORE THE DOOR, ... 622 HOUND VOICE   16
NO SINGLE STORY WOULD THEY FIND . . . . 626 OLD MEN BE MAD   13
FICKLE THE GUIDING HIS ARROW SHALL FIND! . . . . . . 657 ISLE STAT I 3   66
UNTIL I FIND HIM. WHAT A WEARY WEEK, ... 658 ISLE STAT II 1   2
WHO SEEK MAY FIND, SAVE ONLY ONE, ... 668 ISLE STAT II 3   48
AND THOU WILT STAY. ALL THOUGHT OF WHAT THEY FIND . . . 670 ISLE STAT II 3   92
THEM ALL, AND LET THEM FIND YOU IN THE VAPOUR. . . . . 694 MOSADA 1   V 108A
WE WILL FIND HER FAVOURITE LAIR, ... 706 DAWN-SONG   26
AND WILL FIND HER GOOD AT HEART, ... 726 LOVERS QUARREL   10
HE'D FIND FOR THIS SOME HOLY TEXT. . . . . 728 PRIEST FAIRY   16
THE FOOL FORETOLD ME I WOULD FIND THIS LOVE . . . . . 750 SHADOW WATER A   62
FORGAEL MAY FIND HIS HEART'S DESIRE ON BOARD . . . . . 751 SHADOW WATER A 107
NOW RUSH UPON HER AND FIND OUT WHAT PREY . . . . . . 752 SHADOW WATER A 130
I SHALL FIND OUT IF I HAVE LOST MY WAY . . . . . . 753 SHADOW WATER A 137
AND THE OTHER ANSWERS, "MAYBE WE SHALL FIND . . . . . 753 SHADOW WATER A 144
I SHALL FIND OUT IF I HAVE LOST THE WAY . . . . . . 753 SHADOW WATER A V 137
WE WILL FIND OUT VALLEYS AND WOODS AND MEADOWS . . . . 767 SHADOW WATER A 388

FINDING

ON FINDING THAT HER VOICE IS SWEET AND LOW . . . . . . 205 ADAMS CURSE   17
IN FINDING THAT IT'S YOUNG AND MILD AND LOW. . . . . . 205 ADAMS CURSE   V 17
BUT FINDING HIM STILL SILENT I STOOPED DOWN . . . . . 281 TWO KINGS   109
WHO FINDING THE FIRST WRINKLES ON A FACE . . . . . . 472 ALL SOUL NIGHT   42

FINDRIAS

AND FINDRIAS AND FALIAS. . . . . 196 BAILE AILLINN   162

FINDRINNY

ON A HORSE WITH BRIDLE OF FINDRINNY! . . . .   3 OISIN 1   21
WITH HOOFS OF THE PALE FINDRINNY . . . .   25 OISIN 1   383
WITH HOOFS OF THE RUDDY FINDRINNY . . . .   25 OISIN 1   V 383

FINDS

THE SOUL IS FREE, AND FINDS NO FLAW, ...   19 OISIN 1   V 284
THE MIND IS MADE UNCHANGING, FOR IT FINDS . . . . . . 227 SHADOW WATER B 101
AND BODILY TENDERNESS, AND FINDS THAT EVEN . . . . . 228 SHADOW WATER B 147
WHEN SHE FINDS OUT WE HAVE BETTER MEN ABOARD . . . . . 232 SHADOW WATER B 231
WHEN SHE FINDS OUT I WILL NOT LET HER GO-- . . . . . 236 SHADOW WATER B 302
A MAN THAT FINDS GREAT BITTERNESS . . . . 379 SAINT HUNCH   2
AND FINDS A REAL IMAGE THERE! . . . . 388 SOLOMON WITCH   27
WHERE SLIPPERED CONTEMPLATION FINDS HIS EASE . . . . . 418 ANCEST HOUSES   30
WHO FINDS ABOUNDING CEPHISUS . . . . 447 COLONUS PRAISE   23

FINDS   (CONTINUED)
    AND FINDS THERE NOTHING TO MAKE ITS TERROR LESS . . . . .   618 BRONZE HEAD   6
    A CAREFUL FIELD-MOUSE FINDS A FALLEN CRUMB! . . . . . .   713 FERENCZ RENYI   77
    FOR HAPPIER LOVE BUT FINDS UNHAPPINESS! . . . .   750 SHADOW WATER A   67
FINE
    THE TALE DROVE HIS FINE ANGRY MOOD AWAY. . . . .   128 DREAM OF FAERY   36
    HE COULD REMEMBER WHEN HE HAD HAD FINE DREAMS. . . . . .   182 QUEEN MAEVE   56
    I SAID! "IT'S CERTAIN THERE IS NO FINE THING . . . . . .   205 ADAMS CURSE   21
    AND YET COULD GIVE SO FINE A STROKE?" . . . .   274 GREY ROCK   84
    IT'S CERTAIN THAT FINE WOMEN EAT . . . .   404 FOR DAUGHTER   30
    GIFTED WITH SO FINE AN EAR! . . . .   412 TOWER   94
    O WHAT FINE THOUGHT WE HAD BECAUSE WE THOUGHT . . . . . .   428 NINETEEN 19   15
    O WHAT FINE THOUGHTS WE HAD BECAUSE WE THOUGHT . . . . . .   428 NINETEEN 19   V 15
    ALL MY FINE FEATHERS WOULD BE PLUCKED AWAY . . . .   469 HARUN RASHID   178
    HIS ELEMENT IS SO FINE . . . .   470 ALL SOUL NIGHT   7
    SO THAT HIS ELEMENTS HAVE GROWN SO FINE . . . .   473 ALL SOUL NIGHT   82
    FINE MANNERS, LIBERAL SPEECH, ...   506 REMORSE SPEECH   7
    IMAGINED SUCH A FINE AFFAIR! . . . .   791 REPRISALS   14
FINEST
    THE FINEST PLAY UNDER THE SUN. . . . .   424 ROAD AT DOOR   5
FINGER
    OF ONE LONG FINGER ON MY LIP. . . . .   12 OISIN 1   151
    WHOM BRAHMA, TOUCHING WITH HIS FINGER, PRAISES, FOR YOU   73 ANASHU VIJAYA   42
        HOLD
    WHOM BRAHMA, TOUCHING WITH HIS FINGER, PRAISES, FOR YE HOLD 73 ANASHU VIJAYA V 42
    AND MAY NO RESTLESS FAY WITH FIDGET FINGER . . . . . .   75 ANASHU VIJAYA V 90
    MAY NEVER RESTLESS FAY WITH FIDGET FINGER . . . .   75 ANASHU VIJAYA V 90
    AND MAY NO RESTLESS PITRI'S FIDGET FINGER . . . .   75 ANASHU VIJAYA V 90
    WITH HIS OWN FINGER TOUCHED THE BRAZEN STRINGS. . . . .   109 CUCHULAIN SEA V 46
    WHERE THAT WISE HARPER'S FINGER RAN. . . . .   195 BAILE AILLINN   156
    O DEATH'S OLD BONY FINGER . . . .   213 HAPPY TOWNLAND   1
    THOUGH I'D MY FINGER ON MY LIP, ...   254 HIS DREAM   13
    UPON THE PALENESS OF A FINGER. . . . .   390 IMAGE PAST   28
    BUT KNEW MY FINGER COULD BUT HAVE TOUCHED . . . .   399 BREAK OF DAY   13
    BUT KNEW MY FINGER WOULD HAVE TOUCHED . . . .   399 BREAK OF DAY   V 13
    TREE, LIKE A SOOTY FINGER, STARTS FROM THE EARTH! . . . .   410 TOWER   19
    DID QUATTROCENTO FINGER FASHION IT . . . .   444 SCHOOL CHILDR   26
    WHAT QUINTO-CENTO FINGER FASHIONED IT, ...   444 SCHOOL CHILDR V 26
    DA VINCI' FINGER SO HAD FASHIONED IT . . . .   444 SCHOOL CHILDR V 26
    WITH HER WHITE FINGER. I LED HER HOME ASLEEP . . . . . .   468 HARUN RASHID   158
    DOWN EVERY WITHERED FINGER FROM THE TOP! . . . .   537 HER VISION   11
    BUT LIKED THE WAY HIS FINGER SMELT. . . . .   619 STICK INCENSE   4
    AND JOY, THE TOUCHING OF WHOSE FINGER LENDS . . . . . .   686 DRAWING-ROOM   7
    I FEEL A FINGER DRAWN ACROSS MY CHEEK! . . . .   694 MOSADA 1   96
    IT SEEMS TO FONDLE, WITH A FINGER BRIGHT . . . .   714 FERENCZ RENYI   114
    LIES A CHILLY FINGER TIP. . . . .   732 STREET DANCERS   19
    AND JOY, THE TOUCHING OF WHOSE FINGER LENDS . . . . . .   734 QUATRAIN APHOR   7
    WHAT FINGER FIRST BEGAN . . . .   783 GREY ROUND   11
FINGERED
    THEY FINGERED IT AND GAZED ON ME . . . .   15 OISIN 1   209
    THEY FINGERED IT AND GAZED AT ME. . . . .   15 OISIN 1   V 209
    FINGERED UPON A FIDDLE-STICK OR STRINGS . . . .   445 SCHOOL CHILDR   46
    FINGERED UPON A FIDDLE STICK OR STRING . . . .   445 SCHOOL CHILDR V 46
FINGERETH
    FOR THE DAWN THE FOLIAGE FINGERETH, ...   646 ISLE STAT I 1   26
    FOR THE DAWN OF FOLIAGE FINGERETH, ...   646 ISLE STAT I 1 V 26
FINGER'S
    AND THERE ENDURED HER FINGER'S TOUCH . . . .   397 POLIT PRISONER V   5
FINGERS
    LIKE SOOTY FINGERS, MANY A TREE . . . .   13 OISIN 1   171
    HER FINGERS AND HER GARMENTS' HEM. . . . .   16 OISIN 1   V 216
    BURNING BETWEEN HER FINGERS, AND IN MINE . . . .   37 OISIN 2   125
    COULD FONDLE THE LEAVES WITH HIS FINGERS, ...   49 OISIN 3   38
    THEN HE SWAYED IN HIS FINGERS THE BELL-BRANCH, ...   51 OISIN 3   67
    BUT, THE BIRD IN MY FINGERS, I MOUNTED, ...   54 OISIN 3   111
    BUT, THE BIRD IN MY FINGERS, I MOUNTED, MINDFUL ONLY TO   54 OISIN 3   V 111
        LAUNCH
    FOR THERE MOVES ALIVE IN YOUR FINGERS . . . .   55 OISIN 3   124
    FOR MOVETH ALIVE IN THY FINGERS THE FLUTTERING SADNESS   55 OISIN 3   V 124
        OF EARTH.
    HIS FINGERS MOVE AND SWAY, ...   98 FOXHUNTER   30
    WITH HIS OWN FINGERS TOUCHED THE BRAZEN STRINGS. . . . .   109 CUCHULAIN SEA   46
    THAT GOD HAS LAID HIS FINGERS ON THE SKY, ...   128 DREAM OF FAERY   43
    THAT FROM THOSE FINGERS GLITTERING SUMMER RUNS . . . . .   128 DREAM OF FAERY   44
    WHERE THAT WISE HARPER'S FINGERS RAN. . . . .   195 BAILE AILLINN V 156
    WHEREON MAD FINGERS PLAY . . . .   291 TO A FRIEND   12
    UNDER HIS FINGERS. I HAD IT FROM HIS MOTHER, ...   339 SHEP GOATHERD   26
    THAT THOSE THAT WE HAVE LOVED GOT THEIR LONG FINGERS . . .   375 PHASES OF MOON   66
    UNDER BLANK EYES AND FINGERS NEVER STILL . . . .   382 VISION ROBART   5
    NOW THAT NO FINGERS BIND, ...   390 IMAGE PAST   39
    AND FROM HER FINGERS ATE ITS BIT. . . . .   397 POLIT PRISONER   6
    PLUNGES TOWARDS NOTHING, ARMS AND FINGERS SPREADING WIDE   426 PHANTOM HATRED   13
    HOW CAN THOSE TERRIFIED VAGUE FINGERS PUSH . . . . . .   441 LEDA AND SWAN   5
    OUR HANDS ARE BLENCHED, OUR FINGERS SEEM . . . .   488 CRAZED MOON   14
    AND AFTER THAT I HELD MY FINGERS UP, ...   537 HER VISION   9
    ACCOMPLISHED FINGERS BEGIN TO PLAY. . . . .   567 LAPIS LAZULI   54
    WITH INFANTINE FINGERS . . . .   672 ISLE STAT II 3 168
    THOU'RT WELCOME. LIE THERE CLOSE AGAINST MY FINGERS. . .   700 MOSADA 3   44
    "CHOOSE!" RESTLESS HAYNAU'S FINGERS TAPPING GO. . . . .   711 FERENCZ RENYI   41
    FROM HAYNAU'S LIFTED FINGERS—TWO DRAW NIGH . . . . . .   714 FERENCZ RENYI   104
    WHAT ROSEATE FINGERS! NO! NOR IS THERE ONE . . . . . .   720 WITCH VIVIEN   5

		PAGE	TITLE	LINE

FINGERS   (CONTINUED)
```
      WHAT ROSEATE FINGERS!  HA, HA! HA, HA, HA!  . . . . . .    720 WITCH VIVIEN        15
      MY FINGERS FEEL HIS AMBER HAIR. . . . . . . . . . .        723 GIRLS SONG A         8
      THOSE CRAZY FINGERS PLAY . . . . . . . . . . . . . .       783 GREY ROUND          16
FINGERS'
      AND THERE ENDURED HER FINGERS' TOUCH . . . . . . . .       397 POLIT PRISONER       5
FINGER-TIP
      LIES A CHUBBY FINGER-TIP, . . . . . . . . . . . . .        732 STREET DANCERS V    19
FINGER-TIPS
      AND TOUCHED IT WITH THEIR FINGER-TIPS. . . . . . . .        18 OISIN 1            259
      AND TOUCHED IT WITH HIS FINGER-TIPS. . . . . . . . .        18 OISIN 1          V 259
      AND NEVER A SONG SANG NIAMH, AND OVER MY FINGER-TIPS  . .   47 OISIN 3              6
FINISH
      IN COOLE DEMESNE, AND THERE TO FINISH UP . . . . . .      490 COOLE BALLYLEE        6
      LET HER FINISH HER DANCE. . . . . . . . . . . . . .       568 SWEET DANCER         12
      LET HER FINISH HER DANCE. . . . . . . . . . . . . .       568 SWEET DANCER         13
      A FINISH WORTHY OF THE START. . . . . . . . . . . .       626 OLD MEN BE MAD       15
FINISHED
      AND AS SOON FINISHED. ALL THAT EVER LOVED . . . . . .     229 SHADOW WATER B      151
      I SAW, BEFORE I HAD WELL FINISHED, . . . . . . . .        322 SWANS AT COOLE        9
      BECAUSE THE WORK HAD FINISHED IN THAT FLARE. . . . .      327 ROBERT GREGORY       85
      BUT THE ESCAPE! THE SONG'S NOT FINISHED YET. . . . .      377 PHASES OF MOON      117
      WHEN HE FINISHED HIS DOG'S DAY! . . . . . . . . . .       412 TOWER                79
      THE FINISHED MAN AMONG HIS ENEMIES?-- . . . . . . .       479 SELF AND SOUL        49
      AND WHEN THE STORY'S FINISHED, WHAT'S THE NEWS? . . .     491 COOLE BALLYLEE V    40E
      WHEN ALL THAT STORY'S FINISHED, WHAT'S THE NEWS? . . .    495 CHOICE                5
      ALL THAT IS FINISHED, LET IT FADE. . . . . . . . .        613 MARCH SONGS 1        10
      AND ALL THAT'S FINISHED, LET IT FADE. . . . . . . .       613 MARCH SONGS 1        20
      AND ALL THAT'S FINISHED, LET IT FADE. . . . . . . .       614 MARCH SONGS 1        30
      BE ONE?  I THINK ALL'S FINISHED NOW AND SEALED. . . .     701 MOSADA 3             62
      THE TANGLED THOUGHTS OF THE FINISHED DAY . . . . . .      728 PRIEST FAIRY          9
      WHEN MOON'S ROUND IS FINISHED . . . . . . . . . .         786 YOUR HEART           33
FINMOLE
      AND WHERE HER SON, FINMOLE, ON THE SMOOTH GRASS  . . . .  106 CUCHULAIN SEA V     18
      "I AM FINMOLE, MIGHTY CUCHULAIN'S SON." . . . . . .       110 CUCHULAIN SEA V     68
FINN
      CAOILTE, AND CONAN, AND FINN WERE THERE, . . . . . .        3 OISIN 1             13
      "O PLEASANT WOMAN," ANSWERED FINN, . . . . . . . .          5 OISIN 1             40
      "O PLEASANT MAIDEN," ANSWERED FINN, . . . . . . . .         5 OISIN 1          V  40
      CAOILTE, CONAN, AND FINN CAME NEAR. . . . . . . . .        10 OISIN 1            111
      REMEMBERING HOW I HAD STOOD BY WHITE-HAIRED FINN . . . .   44 OISIN 2            227
      REMEMBERING HOW I STOOD BY WHITE-HAIRED FINN . . . . . .   44 OISIN 2          V 227
      HOW THE SLOW, BLUE-EYED OXEN OF FINN LOW SADLY AT EVENING  52 OISIN 3             84
          TIDE.
      I MUST GAZE ON THE BEARD OF FINN, . . . . . . . . .       55 OISIN 3            114
      MY PAISTIN FINN IS MY SOLE DESIRE, . . . . . . . .       550 SONGS REWRIT 1        1
FINVARRA
      . . . FINVARRA, FEACRA, AND CAOLTE  . . . . . . . .      174 ELEMENT POWERS V     T
FIR
      A FIR TREE ROARING IN ITS LEAFLESS TOP, . . . . . .       40 OISIN 2          V 177
      UPON A SWORD, A FIR TREE ON A HILL, . . . . . . . .      104 FERGUS DRUID     V  34
      OF BEAMS A-FLICKER ON YON LONELY FIR, . . . . . . .      661 ISLE STAT II 1      72
FIRBOLGS'
      AND PASSING THE FIRBOLGS' BURIAL-MOUNDS, . . . . . .        3 OISIN 1             16
      AND PASSING THE FIRBOLGS' BURIAL MOUNDS, . . . . . .        3 OISIN 1          V  16
FIRE      SEE STAR-FIRE CAMP-FIRE
      "AN OLD MAN STIRS THE FIRE TO A BLAZE, . . . . . .        26 OISIN 1            400
      AND BENDS TO THE FIRE AND SHAKES WITH THE COLD  . . .     26 OISIN 1            405
      SHOUTED.  WITH FIRE OF HAIR ABOUT HER SWIRLED, . . .      38 OISIN 2          V 134
      HAD SURGED UP IN A PLUMY FIRE, I DRAVE . . . . . .        41 OISIN 2            181
      WITH SURGE OF PLUMY FIRE, LUNGING I DRAVE . . . . .       41 OISIN 2          V 181
      SURGED UP IN PLUMY FIRE, I LUNGED AND DRAVE . . . .       41 OISIN 2          V 181
      FLASHES THE FIRE OF SADNESS, FOR THEY SEE . . . . .       73 ANASHU VIJAYA       49
      A WHIRLING AND A WANDERING FIRE! . . . . . . . . .        83 MAD KING GOLL       28
      A FEVER AND A WHIRLING FIRE! . . . . . . . . . . .        83 MAD KING GOLL    V  28
      THE WHIRLING AND THE WANDERING FIRE! . . . . . . .        86 MAD KING GOLL       67
      BLOWIN' HER MORNIN' FIRE. . . . . . . . . . . . .         95 MOLL MAGEE          36
      A-BLOWIN' OF HER MORNIN' FIRE. . . . . . . . . . .        95 MOLL MAGEE       V  35
      FIRE IS IN THE OLD MAN'S EYES, . . . . . . . . . .        98 FOXHUNTER           29
      A FIRE IS IN THE OLD MAN'S EYES, . . . . . . . . .        98 FOXHUNTER        V  29
      GO THERE, AND LIGHT A CAMP FIRE AT WOOD'S RIM! . . .     108 CUCHULAIN SEA V     35
      HIS EVENING FIRE AMID THE LEAFY SHADE. . . . . . .       109 CUCHULAIN SEA       48
      AND NODDING BY THE FIRE, TAKE DOWN THIS BOOK, . . .      120 YOU ARE OLD          2
      MY CHAIR WAS NEAREST TO THE FIRE . . . . . . . . .       131 OLD PENSIONER        3
      TO SOME I HAVE TALKED WITH BY THE FIRE . . . . . .       136 TO SOME I TALK       T
      IN FLOOD AND FIRE AND CLAY AND WIND, . . . . . . .       138 TO IRELAND       V  25
      "AND BROOD NO MORE WHERE THE FIRE IS BRIGHT . . . .      140 HOSTING SIDHE V      5
      BECAUSE A FIRE WAS IN MY HEAD, . . . . . . . . . .       149 WANDER AENGUS        2
      I WENT TO BLOW THE FIRE AFLAME, . . . . . . . . .        149 WANDER AENGUS       10
      I BENT TO BLOW THE FIRE AFLAME! . . . . . . . . .        149 WANDER AENGUS    V  10
      I WENT TO BLOW THE FIRE A-FLAME, . . . . . . . . .       149 WANDER AENGUS    V  10
      I STOOPED TO BLOW THE FIRE AFLAME, . . . . . . . .       149 WANDER AENGUS    V  10
      TILL THE SEED OF THE FIRE FLICKER AND GLOW! . . . .      150 OLD MOTHER           2
      AND THE SEED OF THE FIRE GETS FEEBLE AND COLD. . . .     151 OLD MOTHER          10
      BUT THE SEED OF THE FIRE GETS FEEBLE AND COLD, . . .     151 OLD MOTHER       V   9
      THE SOUTH IS POURING DOWN ROSES OF CRIMSON FIRE! . . .   154 BELOVED PEACE        6
      THE SOUTH WOULD COVER THEM WITH ROSES OF CRIMSON FIRE! . .154 BELOVED PEACE V      6
      THAT IS BRIMMED FROM THE PALE FIRE OF TIME! . . . .      157 POET BELOVED         6
      IN TWILIGHTS OF DEW AND OF FIRE." . . . . . . . .        168 BLESSED             40
      IN TWILIGHTS OF DEW AND FIRE!" . . . . . . . . . .       168 BLESSED          V  40
      GREAT POWERS OF FALLING WAVE AND WIND AND WINDY FIRE, . . 174 ELEMENT POWERS       7
```

```
                                                        PAGE    TITLE           LINE

FIRE    (CONTINUED)
      YOU GREAT ANGELIC POWERS OF WIND, AND WAVE, AND FIRE,  . .   174  ELEMENT POWERS V    7
      GREAT ELEMENTAL POWERS OF WIND, AND WAVE, AND FIRE, . . .    174  ELEMENT POWERS V    7
      HAD PACED FROM DOOR TO FIRE AND FIRE TO DOOR. . . . . .      180  QUEEN MAEVE        17
      HAD PACED FROM DOOR TO FIRE AND FIRE TO DOOR. . . . . .      180  QUEEN MAEVE        17
      AND WISDOM THAT CAUGHT FIRE LIKE THE DRIED FLAX, . . . .     181  QUEEN MAEVE        28
      WITH BODIES MADE OUT OF SOFT FIRE.  THE ONE, . . . . . .     187  QUEEN MAEVE       144
      THE FIRE THAT STIRS ABOUT HER, WHEN SHE STIRS, . . . . .     200  FOLLY COMFORT      10
      THE FLAGSTONE UNDER ALL, THE FIRE OF FIRES, . . . . . .      227  SHADOW WATER B    103
      AND CARRIES IT BETWEEN US.  HOLY FIRE . . . . . . . .        239  SHADOW WATER B    371
      THAT NOBLENESS MADE SIMPLE AS A FIRE, . . . . . . . .        256  NO SECOND TROY      7
      WHAT MATTER, SO THERE IS BUT FIRE . . . . . . . . . .        263  MASK               14
      AND WHERE THE STONE STRUCK FIRE, WHILE IN THE LEAVES  . .    278  TWO KINGS          33
      BESIDE A FIRE OF TURF IN TH' ANCIENT TOWER, . . . . . .      324  ROBERT GREGORY      3
      NEW WELCOME AND OLD WISDOM AT HER FIRE . . . . . . . .       340  SHEP GOATHERD      32
      WHEN FROM THE SMITHY FIRE  . . . . . . . . . . . .           345  ON WOMAN           18
      MY GREAT WOOD LECTERN AND THE FIRE  . . . . . . . . .        358  PRESENCES          10
      I SLEPT ON MY THREE-LEGGED STOOL BY THE FIRE, . . . . .      381  SONGS FOOL 2        1
      AROUND THE FIRE AT THE CLUB, . . . . . . . . . . .           392  EASTER 1916        12
      O SAGES STANDING IN GOD'S HOLY FIRE . . . . . . . .          408  SAIL BYZANTIUM     17
      COME FROM THE HOLY FIRE, PERNE IN A GYRE, . . . . . .        408  SAIL BYZANTIUM     19
      ABOVE A SINKING FIRE, A TALE THAT SHE  . . . . . . .         443  SCHOOL CHILDR      10
      ABOVE A SINKING FIRE, SOME TALE THAT SHE  . . . . . .        443  SCHOOL CHILDR  V   10
      I'D TEAR IT OFF AND THROW IT IN THE FIRE." . . . . . .       462  HARUN RASHID       34
      EVERYTHING THAT IS NOT GOD CONSUMED WITH INTELLECTUAL FIRE.  481  BLOOD AND MOON     30
      "GOD'S FIRE UPON THE WANE, . . . . . . . . . . . .           485  STATISTICS          2
      STRUCK DUMB IN THE SIMPLICITY OF FIRE! . . . . . . .         502  VACILLATION        75
      LOOK ON THAT FIRE, SALVATION WALKS WITHIN. . . . . . .       502  VACILLATION        76
      SOME ROGUE OF THE WORLD STOLE THEM TO PATCH UP A FENCE       623  HIGH TALK           4
          OR A FIRE.
      OF SAD QUEEN DIDO SHONE THE LAPPING FIRE  . . . . . .        645  ISLE STAT I 1       9
      WITH ROLLING FIRE, BEYOND THE HIGH TREES TURBANED  . .       656  ISLE STAT I 3      32
      IS WORN AS THOUGH WITH FIRE.  OH, GOBLIN QUEEN, . . . .      667  ISLE STAT II 3     36
      MADE THEM OF FIRE AND CLAY. . . . . . . . . . . . .          680  LOVE AND DEATH     12
      THAT FROM THE FIRE IS EVER POURING UP . . . . . . .          683  SEEKER             37
      WEARY OF WATCHING ROUND THE FIRE AT NIGHT. . . . . . .       683  SEEKER             42
      TO PLACE A KISS OF FIRE ON THE DIM BROW . . . . . .          688  TWO TITANS         47
      NOR TREMBLE TO ITS FALL.  THE FIRE SWEEPS ROUND . . . .      689  NETTLESHIP         11
      TIME GOES.  THE FLAKED FIRE OF EVENING CRAWLS . . . . .      712  FERENCZ RENYI      70
      TIME GOES.  THE FLICKED FIRE OF EVENING CRAWLS . . . .       712  FERENCZ RENYI  V   70
      OF FIRE.  SO ENDS A BRAIN--A WORLD!  THE SMOKE FLOATS UP,    714  FERENCZ RENYI  V  111
      CAME THE OLIVE FIRE OF MORNING, AND ON THE DARKNESS FED,     719  PHANTOM SHIP   V   33
      FEED A FIRE WITH STEMS OF GRASS, . . . . . . . . . .         727  LOVERS QUARREL     42
      LONG BEFORE THE MORNING FIRE  . . . . . . . . . . .          727  LOVERS QUARREL     45
      AND TEARS OF FIRE FALL GENTLY IN THE DEW. . . . . . .        738  YOU ARE SAD         4
      AND BODILY TENDERNESS TO THE SOFT FIRE  . . . . . . .        750  SHADOW WATER A     60
      IMPERISHABLE FIRE UNDER THE BOUGHS . . . . . . . . .         765  SHADOW WATER A    356
      THAT CAN CHANGE LOVE TO IMPERISHABLE FIRE? . . . . . .       765  SHADOW WATER A    360
      LET THE FIRE BEAR WITNESS, . . . . . . . . . . . .          770  BLOOD BOND         10
      MAY THIS FIRE HAVE DRIVEN OUT . . . . . . . . . . .          775  AGAINST WITCH       1
FIRE-BORN
      OF THE FIRE-BORN MOODS  . . . . . . . . . . . . .           142  MOODS               6
FIRED
      THAT SHE MAY QUENCH THE RICK SHE HAS FIRED, AND THOUGH  . .  282  TWO KINGS         116
FIRELIGHT
      SHE MOVES IN THE FIRELIGHT . . . . . . . . . . . .           89  ISLE IN WATER       3
      IN THE FIRELIGHT  . . . . . . . . . . . . . . . .           737  IN FIRELIGHT        T
FIRELIT
      "O, WHAT TO ME THE FIRELIT ROOM, . . . . . . . . . .        151  HEART OF WOMAN V    1
FIREPLACE
      A GREY STONE FIREPLACE WITH AN OPEN HEARTH, . . . . .       419  MY HOUSE       V   12
FIRE-PLACE
      A GREY STONE FIRE-PLACE WITH AN OPEN HEARTH, . . . . .      419  MY HOUSE           12
FIRE'S
      AND BLOWS ON HIS HANDS IN THE FIRE'S WARM BLAZE, . . . .     26  OISIN 1        V  404
FIRES       SEE STAR-FIRES
      THEY SEEMED TO SING IN THE SMOULDERING FIRES. . . . . .      13  OISIN 1           168
      OF THE GREAT ROUND SUN, FROM HIS CENTRAL FIRES. . . . .      13  OISIN 1        V  168
      . . . AND THE GODLESS FIRES OF THINE AGE. . . . . . .        63  OISIN 3        V  216
      BURNING IN FIRES OF A SLANDEROUS TONGUE. . . . . . . .      148  INTO TWILIGHT       8
      MY DREAMS WERE CLOVEN BY VOICES AND BY FIRES, . . . . .     218  WOODS OF COOLE     20
      MOVED ROUND ME IN THE VOICES AND THE FIRES, . . . . .       218  WOODS OF COOLE     23
      AWAKE UNSLEEPING FIRES, AND WOVE SEVEN STRINGS, . . . .     219  HARP OF AENGUS      7
      THE FLAGSTONE UNDER ALL, THE FIRE OF FIRES, . . . . . .     227  SHADOW WATER B    103
      BECAUSE THE FIRES OF PURGATORY HAVE ATE THEIR SHAPES AWAY,   593  PILGRIM            13
      OENONE SAW THE FIRES OF TROIA LEAP, . . . . . . . .         645  ISLE STAT I 1      17
      CAME OLIVE FIRES OF MORNING AND ON THE DARKNESS FED, . .    719  PHANTOM SHIP       33
      AWAKE UNSLEEPING FIRES, AND WOVE SEVEN STRINGS, . . . .     762  SHADOW WATER A    302
FIRM
      NOR SHOOK MY FIRM AND SPACIOUS SOUL ONE JOT, . . . . .       36  OISIN 2        V   94
FIRST
      AND THE BLUSHES OF FIRST LOVE NEVER HAVE FLOWN, . . . .       8  OISIN 1            85
      AND THE FLUSHES OF FIRST LOVE NEVER HAVE FLOWN, . . . .       8  OISIN 1        V   85
      OR LOVE'S FIRST TENDERNESS DIE IN OUR GAZE. . . . . .        27  OISIN 1           411
      OR LOVE'S FIRST TENDERNESS DIE IN OUR GAZE. . . . . .        27  OISIN 1        V 419D
      OR LOVE'S FIRST TENDERNESS DIE IN OUR GAZE." . . . . .       28  OISIN 1        V  427
      THINGS DONE ERE GOD FIRST WAS OR MY OLD LINE BEGAN, . . .    29  OISIN 2        V    8
      A DEMON'S LEISURE, EYES, FIRST WHITE, NOW BURNED . . . .     40  OISIN 2           168
      A DEMON'S LEISURE, EYES FIRST WHITE AS SNOW, . . . . .       40  OISIN 2        V  168
      SING YOU OF HER, O FIRST FEW STARS, . . . . . . . .         73  ANASHU VIJAYA      41
      SING YE OF HER, OH FIRST FEW STARS, . . . . . . . .         73  ANASHU VIJAYA  V   41
```

FIRST   (CONTINUED)
    IS OUR FIRST KISS, AND AH, HOW OLD MY HEART!" . . . . .   80 EPHEMERA   9
    FIRST AS A RAVEN ON WHOSE ANCIENT WINGS . . . . . .   102 FERGUS DRUID   3
    SHE WAS MORE BEAUTIFUL THAN THY FIRST LOVE, ...   123 DREAM OF DEATH   11
    FOR IN THE WORLD'S FIRST BLOSSOMING AGE . . . . . .   138 TO IRELAND   V 10
    BUT CALL ME FIRST THROUGH THE GATE: . . . .   178 FIDDLER DOONEY   12
    WITH THE FIRST KINGS OF MANY-PILLARED CRUACHAN, . . .   187 QUEEN MAEVE   151
    WITH THE FIRST KINGS OF MANY PILLARED CRUACHAN, . . .   187 QUEEN MAEVE   V 151
    TO HIM THAT STRIKES HIM FIRST! I WILL STRIKE HIM FIRST. 239 SHADOW WATER B   369
    TO HIM THAT STRIKES HIM FIRST! I WILL STRIKE HIM FIRST. 239 SHADOW WATER B   369
    WHEN I FIRST HEARD THE NEWS? AH, THERE IT IS! . . . .   241 SHADOW WATER B   398
    WHO IS FIRST ASLEEP, IF BUT HE CAN . . . .   295 THREE BEGGARS   23
    FIRST WAS MUTTERING A PRAYER, ...   298 THREE HERMITS   3
    SO THE FIRST, BUT NOW THE SECOND! . . . .   298 THREE HERMITS   13
    "I HAD NO BETTER PLAN AT FIRST. . . . .   305 HOUR DAWN   63
    AND SO IT WILL BE. AT THE FIRST . . . .   305 HOUR DAWN   V 59
    YOU WILL SLEEP THAT LENGTH; AND AT THE FIRST . . . .   305 HOUR DAWN   V 59
    SINCE I FIRST MADE MY COUNT! . . . .   322 SWANS AT COOLE   8
    THE FIRST TIME ON THIS SHORE, ...   323 SWANS AT COOLE   16
    LIONEL JOHNSON COMES THE FIRST TO MIND, ...   324 ROBERT GREGORY   17
    THAT CRY'S FROM THE FIRST CUCKOO OF THE YEAR, ...   338 SHEP GOATHERD   1
    THAT CRY'S FROM THE FIRST CUCKOO OF THE . . . . . .   338 SHEP GOATHERD   V   1
    AS OTHERS WILL, WHEN FIRST THEY TAKE POSSESSION, . . .   341 SHEP GOATHERD   52
    I HEARD HIM FIRST, BUT MAN IS A FOOL." . . . . . .   341 SHEP GOATHERD   V 74
    MY DAILY THOUGHTS SINCE THE FIRST STUPOR OF YOUTH . . . 342 SHEP GOATHERD   83
    IN THE FIRST LOVELINESS OF WOMANHOOD, ...   356 BROKEN DREAMS   24
    AMID THAT FIRST ASTONISHMENT, WITH GRANIA'S SHADE, . .   366 HER COURAGE   4
    FROM THE FIRST CRESCENT TO THE HALF, THE DREAM . . . .   373 PHASES OF MOON   36
    THE FIRST THIN CRESCENT IS WHEELED ROUND ONCE MORE. . . 377 PHASES OF MOON   116
    WHEN FIRST IT SPRANG OUT OF THE NEST . . . .   397 POLIT PRISONER   20
    UNDER THE FIRST COLD GLEAM OF DAY? . . . .   398 BREAK OF DAY   4
    IF YOU, THAT HAVE GROWN OLD, WERE THE FIRST DEAD, . . . 435 NEW FACES   1
    FIRST LOVE . . . .   451 FIRST LOVE   T
    A MAN YOUNG AND OLD FIRST LOVE . . . .   451 FIRST LOVE   V   T
    THE FIRST OF ALL THE TRIBE LAY THERE . . . .   455 HIS MEMORIES   13
    SINCE FIRST WE SAW THE LIGHT, ...   456 SUMMER SPRING   4
    AND OFTEN THOSE FIRST DAYS I SAW HER STARE . . . . .   466 HARUN RASHID   122
    BUT WOKE AT THE FIRST GLEAM OF DAY, ROSE UP . . . .   467 HARUN RASHID   147
    HALF RUNNING, DROPPED AT THE FIRST RIDGE OF THE DESERT   468 HARUN RASHID   155
    THAT FIRST UNNATURAL INTEREST IN MY BOOKS. . . . . .   468 HARUN RASHID   165
    THAT FIRST STRANGE INTEREST IN MY BOOKS AND STUDIES. . . 468 HARUN RASHID   V 165
    ITS FIRST SIMPLICITY, LOVE, VOICE AND ALL, ...   469 HARUN RASHID   177
    ITS FIRST SIMPLICITY, LOVE AND ALL, ...   469 HARUN RASHID   V 177
    HORTON'S THE FIRST I CALL. HE LOVED STRANGE THOUGHT . . 471 ALL SOUL NIGHT   21
    WHO FINDING THE FIRST WRINKLES ON A FACE . . . . .   472 ALL SOUL NIGHT   42
    FOR IN MY FIRST HARD SPRINGTIME WE WERE FRIENDS, . . .   473 ALL SOUL NIGHT   62
    FOR IN MY FIRST HARD SPRING-TIME WE WERE FRIENDS, . . . 473 ALL SOUL NIGHT   V 62
    FIRST TROD ON THE MOUNTAIN'S HEAD . . . .   488 CRAZED MOON   9
    COULD KEEP A SWALLOW TO ITS FIRST INTENT! . . . . .   489 COOLE PARK 29   19
    THAT FIRST DAWN IN HELEN'S ARMS? . . . .   522 LULLABY   6
    THAT FIRST NIGHT IN HELEN'S ARMS. . . . .   522 LULLABY   V   6
    A FIRST CONFESSION . . . .   532 FIRST CONFESS   T
    FIRST SONG . . . .   545 TO SAME TUNE 2   V   T
    THE ANNIVERSARY OF THEIR FIRST EMBRACE, ...   555 RIBH AT TOMB   20
    A YEAR AGO FOR THE FIRST TIME . . . .   570 THREE BUSHES   38
    THE LADY'S FIRST SONG . . . .   572 LADYS 1ST SONG   T
    THE CHAMBERMAID'S FIRST SONG . . . .   574 MAIDS 1ST SONG   T
    WHO WAS THE FIRST MAN SHOT THAT DAY? . . . . . .   608 SONGS BURDEN 3   10
    HE BADE, HIS HUNDRED AND FIRST YEAR AT END, ...   609 IN TARAS HALLS   16
    THE FIRST ADAM IN THEIR THOUGHT, ...   617 LONG-LEG FLY   22
    FIRST THAT SEA-RIDER OISIN LED BY THE NOSE . . . . .   629 CIRCUS ANIMALS   10
    BUT FIRST YOU MUST BE TOLD OUR CHARACTER! . . . . .   634 CUCHULAIN COMF   20
    I FAIN HAD BEEN THE FIRST OF SINGING THINGS . . . .   648 ISLE STAT I 1   101
    SCHOOLMASTER HE, A DREAMER, FIDDLER, FIRST . . . . .   709 FERENCZ RENYI   11
    I CAME THE FIRST TIME TO THY VILLAGE SCHOOL? . . . .   713 FERENCZ RENYI   90
    THUS PLAY WE FIRST WITH PAWNS, POOR THINGS AND WEAK; . . 722 WITCH VIVIEN   53
    FIRST DREAMS, AND GOBLINS, AND THE LESSER SPRITES, . .   722 WITCH VIVIEN   56
    FROM ITS FIRST SIGHS AND LAUGHTER, BEFORE THE SLEEP, . . 754 SHADOW WATER A   161
    WHEN SHE DREAMT FIRST OF LOVE, SHALL FLICKER OUT . . .   760 SHADOW WATER A   257
    WHEN SHE DREAMED FIRST OF LOVE, SHALL FLICKER OUT . . . 760 SHADOW WATER A V   257
    WHAT FINGER FIRST BEGAN . . . .   783 GREY ROUND   11
    FIRST I GREET MACCARTAN, REVOLUTIONARY LEADER. . . .   790 DEDICATION   1
FIRST-BORN
    AND TROUBLED EYES CAME MORNING'S FIRST-BORN GLOW; . . . 648 ISLE STAT I 1   103
FIR-TREE
    A FIR-TREE ROARING IN ITS LEAFLESS TOP: . . . . . .   40 OISIN 2   177
    UPON A SWORD, A FIR-TREE ON A HILL, ...   104 FERGUS DRUID   34
FIRWOOD
    A FIRWOOD HOUSE, ALL COVERED OVER . . . .   17 OISIN 1   V 248
FISH   SEE GOLD-FISH
    IN A LONG IRON SLEEP, AS A FISH IN THE WATER GOES DUMB   53 OISIN 3   96
      AS A STONE.
    THAT CARRIED THE FISH FOR THE SALE IN THE FAR-AWAY TOWN, 91 OLD FISHERMAN   V   7
    BUT WHEN A MAN POURED FISH INTO A PILE, ...   126 DREAM OF FAERY   5
    THE FISH . . . .   146 FISH   T
    WHAT SHALL I CALL THEM? FISH THAT SWIM, ...   195 BAILE AILLINN   144
    WITH A FISH TAIL, AND TALK . . . .   215 HAPPY TOWNLAND V   46
    O SILVER FISH THAT MY TWO HANDS HAVE TAKEN . . . . .   251 SHADOW WATER B   609
    AND FISH AND CROWD AND PAINTED SHIP, ...   254 HIS DREAM   V 15
    AND FISH AND CROWD AND GAUDY SHIP . . . .   254 HIS DREAM   V 15
    COLDER AND DUMBER AND DEAFER THAN A FISH. . . . . .   267 ALL TEMPT ME   10

		PAGE	TITLE		LINE

FISH (CONTINUED)
TO THROW ME A BIT OF SALTED FISH . . . . 301 RUN PARADISE 6
FISH, FLESH, OR FOWL, COMMEND ALL SUMMER LONG . . . . . 407 SAIL BYZANTIUM 5
THOUGH MARGERY IS LIKE A FISH . . . . 457 SECRETS OF OLD V 7
SHAKESPEAREAN FISH SWAM THE SEA, FAR AWAY FROM LAND& . . . 485 THREE MOVEMENT 1
ROMANTIC FISH SWAM IN NETS COMING TO THE HAND& . . . . . 485 THREE MOVEMENT 2
WHAT ARE ALL THOSE FISH THAT LIE GASPING ON THE STRAND? . . 485 THREE MOVEMENT 3
BIRD, BEAST, FISH OR MAN, ... 529 TOM LUNATIC 14
O SILVER FISH THAT MY TWO HANDS HAVE TAKEN . . . . . . 769 SHADOW WATER A 425
FISH-EATING
OF BITTERNS, AND FISH-EATING STOATS, ... 14 OISIN 1 191
OF BITTERNS AND FISH-EATING STOATS. . . . . 23 OISIN 1 355
FISHER
HE IS A FAMOUS FISHER& HOUR BY HOUR . . . . 73 ANASHU VIJAYA 36
MY MAN WAS A POOR FISHER . . . . 94 MOLL MAGEE 5
MY HUSBAND WAS A FISHER POOR . . . . 94 MOLL MAGEE V 5
A DANCE FOR THE FISHER LADS& . . . . 589 OLD WICKED MAN V 33
AND THE FISHER MEN AND WOMEN FROM THE DRIPPING HARBOUR WALL 718 PHANTOM SHIP 11
FISHER-LADS
A DANCE FOR THE FISHER-LADS& . . . . 589 OLD WICKED MAN 33
FISHERMAN
THE MEDITATION OF THE OLD FISHERMAN . . . . 90 OLD FISHERMAN T
BRESSEL THE FISHERMAN . . . . 146 FISH V T
THE FISHERMAN . . . . 146 FISH V T
THE FISHERMAN . . . . 347 FISHERMAN T
FISHERMEN
BAWDY TALK FOR THE FISHERMEN& . . . . 588 OLD WICKED MAN 32
FISHER'S   SEE FLY-FISHER'S
THAT HAD A SOUND FLY FISHER'S WRIST . . . . 625 OLD MEN BE MAD V 3
FISHERS
"WAKEN, WAKEN, SLEEPY FISHERS& NO HOUR IS THIS FOR SLEEP," 718 PHANTOM SHIP 7
NOW A SCREAM FROM ALL THOSE FISHERS, FOR THERE ON DECK 719 PHANTOM SHIP 19
THERE BE
HUSH'D THE FISHERS, TILL A MOTHER CALLS BY NAME HER DROWNED 719 PHANTOM SHIP 23
SON&
PRAYED THOSE FORGOTTEN FISHERS, TILL IN THE EASTERN SKIES 719 PHANTOM SHIP 32
ALL THOSE LONG FORGOTTEN FISHERS, TILL IN THE EASTERN SKIES 719 PHANTOM SHIP V 32
FISHERS'
AY, AND SHAKES IN SEA-GREEN WAVERINGS ALONG THE FISHERS' 718 PHANTOM SHIP 2
STREET&
AYE AND SHAKES IN SEA GREEN WAVERINGS, ALONG THE FISHERS' 718 PHANTOM SHIP V 2
STREET.
FISHES
AND FISHES, BUBBLING TO THE BRIM, ... 254 HIS DREAM V 9
FISHES'
NOW BATHING LILY LEAF AND FISHES' SCALE, ... 464 HARUN RASHID V 65
FISHING   SEE A-FISHING
FISHING-LINES
LOOK TO LONG FISHING-LINES, OR POINT AND PARE . . . . . 32 OISIN 2 55
FISHLIKE
FLASH FISHLIKE& NYMPHS AND SATYRS . . . . 612 NEWS ORACLE 35
FISH'S
NOW BATHING LILY LEAF AND FISH'S SCALE, ... 464 HARUN RASHID 65
FISH-TAIL
WITH A FISH-TAIL, AND TALK . . . . 215 HAPPY TOWNLAND 46
FIST
SHE SMOTE WITH RADDLED FIST, AND WHERE HER SON . . . . 106 CUCHULAIN SEA 18
BID THE GHOST HAVE SWORD IN FIST& . . . . 435 FOR MY SON 9
YET HE, AN OLD BOOK IN HIS FIST, ... 508 JANE BISHOP 12
FIT
AND WHILE WE'RE IN OUR LAUGHING, WEEPING FIT, ... 257 RECONCILIATION 9
OR BEEN FIT SPOIL FOR A CENTAUR . . . . 355 PROPERTIUS 7
AND THERE IS NONE SO FIT TO KEEP A WATCH AND KEEP . . . 442 BLACK CENTAUR 15
AND THINKING OF THAT FIT OF GRIEF OR RAGE . . . . . . 443 SCHOOL CHILDR 17
I GET A LAUGHING FIT, ... 455 FRIENDS YOUTH 4
FIT AUDIENCE FOUND, BUT CANNOT RULE . . . . 506 REMORSE SPEECH 4
FITFUL
WHO WHEN THEY DANCE TO A FITFUL MEASURE . . . . 9 OISIN 1 97
MURMURING, TO A FITFUL TUNE, ... 85 MAD KING GOLL 52
WHILE I WROUGHT OUT THESE FITFUL DANAAN RHYMES, ... 136 TO SOME I TALK 1
I DEDICATE THESE FITFUL DANAAN RHYMES . . . . 136 TO SOME I TALK V 1
FITS
YOUR WEEPING FITS& LOOK YOU, SO VERY STRAIT . . . . . 659 ISLE STAT II 1 22
FITTER
A FITTER WELCOME& BUT A THOUGHT . . . . 328 ROBERT GREGORY 95
FITTING
I ASK A FITTING PUNISHMENT FOR ALL . . . . 235 SHADOW WATER B 290
SO GREAT ITS FAME. WHEN FITTING TIME HAS PASSED . . . . 461 HARUN RASHID 19
CAN WITH A FITTING CONFIDENCE REPLY. . . . . 494 AT ALGECIRAS 18
FITZGERALD
FOR THIS EDWARD FITZGERALD DIED, ... 290 SEPTEMBER 1913 20
WHEN STRANGERS MURDERED EMMET, FITZGERALD, TONE, ... 541 PARN FUNERAL 1 17
FIVE
THAT SPRING FIVE PACES IN THEIR BOUNDS, ... 8 OISIN 1 V 86A
. . . I FLUNG IT FIVE YARDS WITH MY HAND, ... 60 OISIN 3 187
ONE--AND ONE--A COUPLE--FIVE TOGETHER& . . . . 233 SHADOW WATER B 249
FIVE AND TWENTY YEARS HAVE GONE . . . . 360 ALF POLLEXFEN V 1
IT LAY FIVE HUNDRED YEARS. . . . . 421 MY TABLE 11
FIVE HUNDRED YEARS AGO, ABOUT IT LIE . . . . 478 SELF AND SOUL 26
RECOGNIZE THE FIVE . . . . 601 THOSE IMAGES 15

FIVE-AND-TWENTY
    FIVE-AND-TWENTY YEARS HAVE GONE   . . . .   360 ALF POLLEXFEN   1
FIVE-SIX
    FIVE-SIX. HA, TIME! . . . .   721 WITCH VIVIEN   42
FIX
    WHEN THE SWAN MUST FIX HIS EYE . . . .   414 TOWER   140
    FIX EVERY WANDERING THOUGHT UPON . . . .   477 SELF AND SOUL   6
    COME, FIX UPON ME THAT ACCUSING EYE. . . . . . .   542 PARN FUNERAL 1   24
    MY ATTENTION FIX . . . .   631 POLITICS   2
FIXED
    AND THE FIXED STARS HAD DAWNED AND SHONE AND SET, . . .   31 OISIN 2   40
    THROUGH THAT STRANGE ILLNESS THAT HAD FIXED HIM THERE, . . . 280 TWO KINGS   81
    CROW UPON TARA." SHE HAD FIXED HER EYES . . . . .   286 TWO KINGS   V 211
    AND ALL THEIR EYES STILL FIXED, HOPING TO FIND ONCE MORE, 318 MAGI   6
    FIXED UPON IMAGES THAT ONCE WERE THOUGHT; . . . . . 375 PHASES OF MOON   80
    BEING FIXED ON ALL THINGS LOVED, ALL THINGS UNLOVED, . . 383 VISION ROBART 34
    THEY FIXED OLD ACHING EYES, ...   432 NINETEEN 19   100
    THAT ARE FIXED UPON ME? . . . .   533 FIRST CONFESS   16
    HALF TURNED AND FIXED A GLAZING EYE ON MINE, . . .   537 HER VISION   26
    HE FIXED A BITTER LOOK; . . . .   585 ORAHILLY   24
    HIS EYES FIXED ON NOTHING, ...   617 LONG-LEG FLY   7
    WAS EBREMAR, WHOSE THOUGHTS WERE FIXED ON GOD, . .   702 MOSADA 3   83
    OF HER HE LOVED FIXED ON HIM FULL OF LIGHT, . . .   710 FERENCZ RENYI   27
FLAG
    UNDER A MARBLE FLAG? . . . .   525 DANCING DAYS   14
    AND THIS HARD FLAG OF STONE, ...   739 EARL PAUL   6
    A GALLEY FROM THE LOCHLANN SEAS; HER FLAG . . . .   751 SHADOW WATER A   98
FLAGELLANT
    THE FLAGELLANT LASHES THOSE SUBMISSIVE LOINS . . . . 560 WHENCE COME   7
FLAGON
    I SAW A FLAGON OF BROWN ALE ABOARD HER. . . . . .   240 SHADOW WATER B   388
FLAGONS
    UNLESS WE DRAIN MORE FLAGONS IN A YEAR . . . . .   225 SHADOW WATER B   70
FLAGRANT
    AND WHEN THE SUN IN ALL HIS FLAGRANT SAFFRON STEPT, . . .   41 OISIN 2   V 192
    ROLLING HIS FLAGRANT WHEEL OUT OF THE DEEP, ... 42 OISIN 2   193
    THE FLAGRANT SIGNAL OF HER LORD'S RETURN, ... 645 ISLE STAT I 1   13
FLAGS
    AND THRUST THE TORCH BETWEEN THE SLIMY FLAGS. . . . . 38 OISIN 2   143
    ANOINTING, TORCH JAMMED DOWN BETWEEN THE FLAGS, . . . 38 OISIN 2   V 143
    TREMBLING, ON THE FLAGS WE FALL, ...   43 OISIN 2   V 208E
    BUT TO BE AMID SHOOTING OF FLIES AND FLOWERING OF RUSHES 55 OISIN 3   120
        AND FLAGS."
    . . . AND THE FLOWERING OF RUSHES AND FLAGS." . . . 55 OISIN 3   V 120
    BUT KNEEL AND WEAR OUT THE FLAGS AND PRAY FOR YOUR SOUL 63 OISIN 3   215
        THAT IS LOST
    BUT WEEP THOU, AND WEAR THOU THE FLAGS WITH THY KNEES, 63 OISIN 3   V 215
        . . .
    BUT WEEP YOU, AND WEAR YOU THE FLAGS WITH YOUR KNEES, . . . 63 OISIN 3 V 215
    BUT WEEP YOU AND KNEEL; WEAR OUT THE FLAGS; . . . . 63 OISIN 3   V 215
    KNEEL, USHEEN, WEAR OUT THE FLAGS AND PRAY FOR YOUR SOUL 63 OISIN 3   V 215
        THAT IS LOST
    THOUGH DRUNKEN WITH THE FLAGS THAT SWAY . . . . . . 212 BLESS PSALTER   5
    I CANNOT EVEN CRAWL ALONG THE FLAGS . . . . . .   701 MOSADA 3   58
FLAGSTONE
    THE FLAGSTONE UNDER ALL, THE FIRE OF FIRES, ... 227 SHADOW WATER B   103
FLAKE
    AND SAW A FLAKE OF THE YELLOW FOAM . . . .   309 PLAYER QUEEN   15
    I SAW A FLAKE OF YELLOW FOAM . . . .   309 PLAYER QUEEN   V 15
FLAKED
    OR OF THE FLAKED CLOUDS?" "NOT SO, FOR WE . . . . .   34 OISIN 2   V 78C
    TIME GOES. THE FLAKED FIRE OF EVENING CRAWLS . . . 712 FERENCZ RENYI   70
FLAKES   SEE FOAM-FLAKES SNOW-FLAKES SALT-FLAKES
    THE SALT FLAKES ON HIS BREAST, ...   612 NEWS ORACLE   V 10
    IN BUSY FLAKES; RE-SHINING FROM THE LAKE, ... 662 ISLE STAT II 2   3
FLAME   SEE STAR-FLAME A-FLAME
    IT SEEMED TO BLOW FROM THE DYING FLAME, ...   13 OISIN 1   167
    IT SEEMED TO FALL FROM THE VERY FLAME . . . . . .   13 OISIN 1   V 167
    "MEN'S HEARTS OF OLD WERE DROPS OF FLAME . . . . .   19 OISIN 1   276
    A MOMENTARY GLEAM OF PHOSPHORUS FLAME. . . . . . .   37 OISIN 2   118
    A MOMENTARY GLIMMER OF VAGUE PHOSPHORUS FLAME. . . . 37 OISIN 2   V 120
    SOFTER THAN SNOW-FLAKES IN APRIL AND PIERCING THE MARROW 51 OISIN 3   68
        LIKE FLAME.
    SOFTER THAN SNOWFLAKES IN APRIL, AND PIERCING THE MARROW 51 OISIN 3   V 68
        LIKE FLAME.
    SHALL WARM THEIR LIVES AT MANY A RUSTLING FLAME." . . .   80 EPHEMERA V 12B
    WE TIRE OF THE FLAME OF THE METEOR, BEFORE IT CAN FADE   122 WHITE BIRDS   2
        AND FLEE;
    AND THE FLAME OF THE BLUE STAR OF TWILIGHT, ... 122 WHITE BIRDS   3
    AH, DREAM NOT OF THEM, MY BELOVED, THE FLAME OF THE METEOR 122 WHITE BIRDS 6
        THAT GOES,
    OR THE FLAME OF THE BLUE STAR THAT LINGERS . . . . . 122 WHITE BIRDS   7
    FOR WE TIRE OF THE FLAME OF THE METEOR BEFORE IT CAN PASS 122 WHITE BIRDS V 2
        BY AND FLEE
    WE TIRE OF THE FLAME OF THE METEOR, BEFORE IT CAN PASS 122 WHITE BIRDS V 2
        BY AND FLEE;
    FLAME TO FLAME AND WING TO WING. . . . .   125 CATHLEEN PARA   16
    FLAME TO FLAME AND WING TO WING. . . . .   125 CATHLEEN PARA   16
    FLAME ON FLAME AND WING ON WING. . . . .   125 CATHLEEN PARA V 16
    FLAME ON FLAME AND WING ON WING. . . . .   125 CATHLEEN PARA V 16
    WHO RISE, WING ABOVE WING, FLAME ABOVE FLAME, . . . 137 TO SOME I TALK   11

		PAGE	TITLE	LINE
FLAME	**(CONTINUED)**			
WHO RISE, WING ABOVE WING, FLAME ABOVE FLAME,		137	TO SOME I TALK	11
FLAME UNDER FLAME, TILL TIME BE NO MORE:		141	EVERLAST VOICE	4
FLAME UNDER FLAME, TILL TIME BE NO MORE:		141	EVERLAST VOICE	4
OF THE FLOOD AND FLAME, OF THE HEIGHT AND WOOD,		148	INTO TWILIGHT V	11
BUT FLAME ON FLAME, AND DEEP ON DEEP,		156	FORGOT BEAUTY	21
BUT FLAME ON FLAME, AND DEEP ON DEEP,		156	FORGOT BEAUTY	21
BUT FLAME ON FLAME, DEEP UNDER DEEP,		156	FORGOT BEAUTY V	21
BUT FLAME ON FLAME, DEEP UNDER DEEP,		156	FORGOT BEAUTY V	21
HIM WHO TREMBLES BEFORE THE FLAME AND THE FLOOD,		158	TO HIS HEART	3
LET THE STARRY WINDS AND THE FLAME AND THE FLOOD		158	TO HIS HEART	5
WHO TREMBLES BEFORE THE FLAME AND THE FLOOD,		158	TO HIS HEART V	3
"O HEARTS OF WIND-BLOWN FLAME!		162	ASKS FORGIVE	6
BUT WE HAVE HIDDEN IN OUR HEARTS THE FLAME OUT OF THE EYES		207	HANRAHANS SONG	4
BUT OUR HEARTS ARE LIGHTED FROM THE FLAME IN THE EYES		207	HANRAHANS SONG V	9
THOUGH FLAME HAD BURNED THE WHOLE		267	FRIEND ILLNESS	4
NOR STORM DISTURBS, FLAMES BEGOTTEN OF FLAME,		498	BYZANTIUM	27
AN AGONY OF FLAME THAT CANNOT SINGE A SLEEVE,		498	BYZANTIUM	32
IS HALF ALL GLITTERING FLAME AND HALF ALL GREEN		500	VACILLATION	12
IS HALF ALL GLITTERING FLAME AND HALF A GREEN		500	VACILLATION V	12
WHEN LOW THE SUN SANK DOWN IN CLOTTED FLAME		656	ISLE STAT I 3	30
FROM THE WOOD'S WAYS, THEN, LIKE A SILVER FLAME,		658	ISLE STAT II 1	6
THE WHITE WAVES WRAP IT IN A SHEET OF FLAME,		662	ISLE STAT II 2	14
AND IN THE SIBYL'S EYES A LANGUID FLAME		688	TWO TITANS	41
HER SOUL FROM SEAS OF ENDLESS FLAME IN HELL,		698	MOSADA 2	47
THE FLAME THAT SHONE WITHIN HIS EYES BUT NOW		704	MOSADA 3	128
MAY THIS FLAME HAVE DRIVEN OUT		775	AGAINST WITCH V	1
FLAME-BEWILDERED				
DAY'S DEAD, ALL FLAME-BEWILDERED, AND THE HILLS		702	MOSADA 3	86
FLAMED				
AND THRICE THE CORN AROUND THE SICKLES FLAMED,		690	MOSADA 1	3
FLAME-LIKE				
ALL FLAME-LIKE GUSHING FROM THE HOLLOW STONES,		650	ISLE STAT I 1	129
FLAMES	**SEE GHOST-FLAMES**			
WILD FLAMES OF RED AND GOLD AND BLUE,		18	OISIN 1	252
WILD FLAMES OF RED AND CREAMY WHITES,		18	OISIN 1 V	255
AND THEN AWAY, AWAY, LIKE WHIRLING FLAMES!		29	OISIN 2	2
AND THEN AWAY, AWAY, LIKE SPIRAL FLAMES:		29	OISIN 2 V	2
AND DWELL IN THE HOUSE OF THE FENIANS, BE THEY IN FLAMES OR AT FEAST.		63	OISIN 3	224
I WILL GO TO THE HOUSE OF THE FENIANS, BE THEY IN FLAMES OR AT FEAST,		63	OISIN 3 V	223
. . . AND FRET OF THE FLAMES WOULD WE BE,		122	WHITE BIRDS	11
. . . AND FREE OF THE FLAMES WOULD WE BE,		122	WHITE BIRDS V	11
ALL BUT THE FLAMES, AND DEEP ON DEEP,		156	FORGOT BEAUTY V	21
AND WRAPPED THE FLAMES ABOVE HIS HOLY HEAD:		162	ASKS FORGIVE	17
AND GATHERED THE FLAMES ABOVE HIS HOLY HEAD,		162	ASKS FORGIVE V	17
WHATEVER FLAMES UPON THE NIGHT		438	SONGS PLAY 2	15
FLAMES THAT NO FAGGOT FEEDS, NOR STEEL HAS LIT,		498	BYZANTIUM	26
NOR STORM DISTURBS, FLAMES BEGOTTEN OF FLAME,		498	BYZANTIUM	27
AS I, TO CHOOSE BENEATH DAY'S DYING FLAMES:		656	ISLE STAT I 3	34
MY SOUL SHALL TOUCH WITH HIS, AND THE TWO FLAMES		701	MOSADA 3	61
FLAMES THE SHUTTLE OF THE LIGHTNING ACROSS THE DRIVING SLEET,		718	PHANTOM SHIP	1
AND THE GHASTLY GHOST FLAMES GLIMMER ALONG THE TAFFREL RAILS,		719	PHANTOM SHIP V	21
FLAMING				
"O FLAMING LION OF THE WORLD, O WHEN WILL YOU TURN TO YOUR REST?"		56	OISIN 3	129
O FLAMING LION OF THE WORLD, O WHEN WILL YOU TURN TO YOUR REST?"		56	OISIN 3	136
"OH, FLAMING LION OF THE WORLD, OH, WHEN WILT THOU TURN TO THY REST?"		56	OISIN 3 V	129
WE WILL TEAR OUT THE FLAMING STONES, AND BATTER THE GATEWAY OF BRASS		62	OISIN 3	209
ON THE FLAMING STONES, WITHOUT REFUGE,		62	OISIN 3	213
WE WILL TEAR OUT THE RED FLAMING STONES,		62	OISIN 3 V	209
WE WILL TEAR THE RED FLAMING STONES OUT,		62	OISIN 3 V	209
ON THE RED FLAMING STONES WITHOUT REFUGE		62	OISIN 3 V	213
ONLY A SUDDEN FLAMING WORD,		65	HAPPY SHEPHERD	19
AND IN THE FLAMING FORESTS COWER THE LION		73	ANASHU VIJAYA	52
THEY SEE IN FLAMING FORESTS COWER THE LION		73	ANASHU VIJAYA V	52
BATHED IN FLAMING FOUNTS OF DUTY		124	CATHLEEN PARA	5
THE FLAMING CIRCLE OF OUR DAYS,		135	TWO TREES	14
THE FLAMING CIRCLE OF OUR LIFE.		135	TWO TREES V	16
AND OF THE EMBATTLED FLAMING MULTITUDE		137	TO SOME I TALK	10
DESOLATE WINDS THAT HOVER IN THE FLAMING WEST:		147	UNAPPEAS HOST	8
MASTER OF THE STILL STARS AND OF THE FLAMING DOOR.		161	BLACK PIG	8
WHO MET FAND WALKING AMONG FLAMING DEW		169	SECRET ROSE	13
WHEN THE FLAMING LUTE-THRONGED ANGELIC DOOR IS WIDE:		172	TRAV PASSION	1
UNFOLD YOUR FLAMING WINGS AND COVER OUT OF SIGHT		175	ELEMENT POWERS	11
A BRAND, OR FLAMING BREATH,		500	VACILLATION	3
AS FLAMING MINSTREL-WORD UPON HIS CREST.		679	ISLE STAT II 3	317
THE FLAMING CIRCLE OF THE OUTER LAW,		689	NETTLESHIP	13
BENEATH THE FLAMING EYEBALLS OF THE NIGHT,		723	KANVA ON SELF	4
FLAMINGO				
OF RED FLAMINGO: AND MY LOVE, VIJAYA,		75	ANASHU VIJAYA V	89
FLAMINGOES				
SEE HOW THE SACRED OLD FLAMINGOES COME,		72	ANASHU VIJAYA	29
OF RED FLAMINGOES: AND MY LOVE, VIJAYA:		75	ANASHU VIJAYA	89

```
                                              PAGE    TITLE              LINE
FLANK
    RENDING THE HORSE'S FLANK.  KING EOCHAID REELED, · · · · ·   277 TWO KINGS            13
FLANKS
    RIPPED THROUGH THE HORSE'S FLANKS.  KING EOCHAID REELED,     277 TWO KINGS          V 13
    BUT WHEN AT LAST HE FORCED THOSE SINEWY FLANKS  · · · ·      278 TWO KINGS            35
    ON A FANTASTIC RIDE, MY HORSE'S FLANKS ARE SPURRED · · ·     391 UNDER SATURN          6
    ON A FANTASTIC RIDE I SWEAR MY HORSE'S FLANKS WERE SPURRED   391 UNDER SATURN        V 6
FLAP
    THE TALL THOUGHT-WOVEN SAILS, THAT FLAP UNFURLED · · · ·     113 ROSE OF BATTLE        2
FLAPPING
    WHERE FLAPPING HERONS WAKE · · · · · · · · · · ·             86 STOLEN CHILD           4
    WITH FLOPPING AND WITH FLAPPING IT MADE A GREAT DISPLAY,     593 PILGRIM               18
    WITH THEIR FLOPPING AND THEIR FLAPPING IT MADE A GREAT       593 PILGRIM             V 18
        DISPLAY
    CEASE THE SAILS THEIR FLAPPING UPROAR, AND THE HULL NO       719 PHANTOM SHIP          18
        LONGER ROLLS.
    CEASE THE SAILS, THEIR FLAPPING UPROAR TO THE HULL           719 PHANTOM SHIP        V 18
        NO LONGER ROLLS.
    LOOK! THERE SHE LIES UNDER A FLAPPING SAIL. · · · · · ·      751 SHADOW WATER A       90
FLAPT
    AND LOUDLY TWICE THE LIVING WINGS FLAPT WIDE, · · · · ·      659 ISLE STAT II 1       12
    HALF LIT, SO FLAPT THE WINGS ACROSS THE LAKE-- · · · ·      659 ISLE STAT II 1       17
FLARE
    AND IN THE RING A TORCH, AND WITH ITS FLARE · · · · ·        37 OISIN 2             121
    WHO BROUGHT US FOUND A TORCH, AND, WITH ITS FLARE · · ·      37 OISIN 2           V 122
    AND TIME BADE ALL HIS CANDLES FLARE · · · · · · · ·          138 TO IRELAND            13
    AND STILL THE STARRY CANDLES FLARE · · · · · · · ·           138 TO IRELAND          V 13
    BECAUSE THE WORK HAD FINISHED IN THAT FLARE. · · · · ·       327 ROBERT GREGORY       85
    THE THREEFOLD TERROR OF LOVE! A FALLEN FLARE · · · ·         499 MOTHER OF GOD         1
    THE THREE-FOLD TERROR OF LOVE! A FALLEN FLARE · · · ·        499 MOTHER OF GOD       V 1
    LOVE STORM! AND STAINED WITH MIST THE NEW MOONS FLARE. · ·   678 ISLE STAT II 3      294
    LOVE STORM AND STAINED WITH MIST THE NEW MOON'S FLARE  ·     678 ISLE STAT II 3 V 294
FLASH       SEE A-FLASH
    AND LIGHTNING FLASH FOR EVER?  CEASE AND HEAR. · · · ·       42 OISIN 2           V 207
    OF THEIR LONG WINGS, THE FLASH OF THEIR WHITE FEET. · · ·    137 TO SOME I TALK       16
    OF THEIR LONG WINGS, THE FLASH OF THEIR SWIFT FEET. · · ·    137 TO SOME I TALK V    16
    FLASH FISHLIKE! NYMPHS AND SATYRS · · · · · · · ·            612 NEWS ORACLE          35
    WHEN FLASH ON FLASH ONCE MORE THE LIGHTNING CAME, · · ·      688 TWO TITANS           39
    WHEN FLASH ON FLASH ONCE MORE THE LIGHTNING CAME, · · ·      688 TWO TITANS           39
    NOISE! AND A FLASH, A MOMENTARY BLOT. · · · · · ·            714 FERENCZ RENYI       110
FLASHED
    IN OUR RAISED EYES THERE FLASHED A GLOW · · · · · ·          22 OISIN 1             327
    THE IMAGED METEORS HAD FLASHED AND RUN · · · · · ·           31 OISIN 2              38
    FORMS WITHOUT NUMBER!  WHEN THE LIVE WEST FLASHED · · ·      41 OISIN 2           V 180
    I PAUSED--THE STARS ABOVE ME FLASHED, · · · · · ·            83 MAD KING GOLL  V     29
FLASHES
    FLASHES THE FIRE OF SADNESS, FOR THEY SEE · · · · · ·        73 ANASHU VIJAYA        49
    FLASHES AS IF IT WERE A NET OF HERRINGS. · · · · · ·         248 SHADOW WATER B      536
FLASHIER
    DRIVE TO A FLASHIER BAUBLE YET. · · · · · · · · ·            437 SONGS PLAY 1         12
FLASHING
    AND ONE A SCEPTRE FLASHING OUT · · · · · · · · ·             17 OISIN 1             251
    HE HELD THAT FLASHING SCEPTRE UP. · · · · · · · ·            18 OISIN 1             260
    FLASHING--I KNOW NOT WERE IT HOURS OR DAYS, · · · ·          30 OISIN 2           V 198
    UPLIFTED GATEWAY. WITH THE FLASHING BEAT · · · · ·           31 OISIN 2           V 300
    THE RIVER IMAGING THE FLASHING SKIES, · · · · · ·            390 IMAGE PAST           20
    DREAMING OF FLASHING FLIGHT AND OF THE PLUMED WAVE. · ·      650 ISLE STAT I 1      140
    BEHOLD THE FLASHING WATERS, · · · · · · · · · ·              680 LOVE AND DEATH        1
    (SWALLOWS WERE FLASHING THEIR WHITE BREASTS ABOVE  · ·       690 MOSADA 1              7
    FLASHING AND FLICKERING WITH EVER-UNDULANT WING · · ·        710 FERENCZ RENYI        19
    FLASHING AND FLICKERING, WITH EVER UNDULANT WING, · · ·      710 FERENCZ RENYI  V    19
FLAT
    HELEN BEING CHOSEN FOUND LIFE FLAT AND DULL  · · · ·         404 FOR DAUGHTER         25
    "THOSE BREASTS ARE FLAT AND FALLEN NOW, · · · · · ·          513 JANE TALK BISH        3
    UNTIL THE TOWN LIE BEATEN FLAT. · · · · · · · · ·            565 LAPIS LAZULI          8
FLATTER
    TO FLATTER BEAUTY'S IGNORANT EAR. · · · · · · · ·            337 SCHOLARS              6
    NAY, RISE AND FLATTER HER WITH GOLDEN RHYME, · · · ·         724 KANVA ON SELF        19
FLATTERER
    LIAR AND FLATTERER OF THE WEAK, IN WHAT STRANGE CLIME  · ·   42 OISIN 2           V 198
FLATTERIES
    WITH BARREN WORDS AND FLATTERIES OF THE WEAK. · · · ·        42 OISIN 2             197
FLATTERING
    BUT NOW WITH FLATTERING TONGUE · · · · · · · · ·             434 YOUTH AND AGE         3
FLATTERY
    BUT IT WAS ALL DECEIT, AND FLATTERY · · · · · · ·            244 SHADOW WATER B      457
    THEIR HEADS BEING TURNED WITH PRAISE AND FLATTERY! · ·       245 SHADOW WATER B      480
FLAVOUR
    THAT HAS THE HEADY FLAVOUR OF NEW WINE, · · · · · ·          240 SHADOW WATER B      374
FLAVOURED      SEE FULL-FLAVOURED
    I BRING FULL FLAVOURED WINE OUT OF A BARREL FOUND  · · ·     442 BLACK CENTAUR  V    10
FLAW
    THE SOUL IS FREE, AND FINDS NO FLAW, · · · · · · ·           19 OISIN 1           V 284
    AND YET YOUR BODY HAD A FLAW! · · · · · · · · ·              356 BROKEN DREAMS        28
    AND YET YOUR BEAUTY HAD A FLAW! · · · · · · · ·              356 BROKEN DREAMS  V    28
FLAX
    AND WISDOM THAT CAUGHT FIRE LIKE THE DRIED FLAX, · · · ·     181 QUEEN MAEVE          28
FLEA
    SECOND RUMMAGED FOR A FLEA! · · · · · · · · · · ·            298 THREE HERMITS         4
    CAUGHT AND CRACKED HIS FLEA, THE THIRD, · · · · · · ·        299 THREE HERMITS        30
```

286

	PAGE	TITLE		LINE

FLEAS
BUT WAS THERE EVER DOG THAT PRAISED HIS FLEAS? . . . . 262 TO A POET 4
BUT WHERE'S THE WILD DOG THAT HAS PRAISED HIS FLEAS? . . 262 TO A POET V 4
BUT HAVE YOU KNOWN A DOG TO PRAISE HIS FLEAS? . . . . 262 TO A POET V 4
FLED
AND NOW FLED BY, MIST-COVERED, WITHOUT SOUND, ... 29 OISIN 2 3
AND THEY WHO TO A FAR-OFF PLACE HAD FLED, ... 41 OISIN 2 V 184
AND THEY HAVE FALLEN OR FLED, AGE AFTER AGE. . . . . . 45 OISIN 2 242
FLED FOAM UNDERNEATH US, AND ROUND US, A WANDERING AND 47 OISIN 3 1
   MILKY SMOKE,
AND THOSE THAT FLED, AND THAT FOLLOWED, ... 47 OISIN 3 3
FLED FOAM UNDERNEATH US, AND ROUND US, A WANDERING AND 47 OISIN 3 12
   MILKY SMOKE.
FLED FOAM UNDERNEATH US, AND AROUND US, A WANDERING AND 47 OISIN 3 V 1
   MILKY SMOKE.
FLED FOAM UNDERNEATH ME, AND ROUND ME, A WANDERING AND 57 OISIN 3 148
   MILKY SMOKE.
LONG FLED THE FOAM-FLAKES AROUND ME, THE WINDS FLED OUT 57 OISIN 3 149
   OF THE VAST,
LONG FLED THE FOAM-FLAKES AROUND ME, THE WINDS FLED OUT 57 OISIN 3 149
   OF THE VAST.
CHRONICLING CHIMAERAS FLED. . . . . 65 HAPPY SHEPHERD V 17
THE KINGS OF THE OLD TIME ARE FLED. . . . . 65 HAPPY SHEPHERD V 17
HE FLED THE PERSECUTION OF HER GLORY . . . . 68 SAD SHEPHERD 12
HE FLED, AND IN A FAR-OFF VALLEY STOPPING, ... 68 SAD SHEPHERD V 13
MURMUR, A LITTLE SADLY, HOW LOVE FLED . . . . 121 YOU ARE OLD 10
MURMUR, A LITTLE SAD, "FROM US FLED LOVE. . . . . . . 121 YOU ARE OLD 10
IN SHADOWY POOLS, WHEN ARMIES FLED; . . . . 155 FORGOT BEAUTY 5
I HAVE FLED TO MY BELOVED IN THE AIR, ... 234 SHADOW WATER B 262
HE GAVE A GASP AND THOUGHT TO HAVE FLED, ... 303 HOUR DAWN 22
AND PRAYED AND CURSED AND CURSED AND FLED . . . . . . 307 HOUR DAWN 119
IN FURY AND IN PANIC FLED . . . . 307 HOUR DAWN V 119
FLED TO FAR COUNTRIES, OR SHELTERED THEMSELVES . . . . 546 TO SAME TUNE 2 4
JUSTIFY ALL THAT HAVE FLED, THAT HAVE STOOD, ... 546 TO SAME TUNE 2 14
JUSTIFY ALL THAT HAVE FLED OR HAVE STOOD, ... 546 TO SAME TUNE 2 V 14
HIS SPIRIT THAT HAS FLED . . . . 575 MAIDS 2ND SONG 5
FLED TO FAR COUNTRIES, OR SHELTERED THEMSELVES . . . . 613 MARCH SONGS 1 4
REMEMBER ALL THAT HAVE FLED, THAT HAVE STOOD, ... 613 MARCH SONGS 1 14
ALONG THE LAKE. THE CRANE HAS HOMEWARD FLED. . . . . 656 ISLE STAT I 3 23
FLED FROM HIS BROW WHERE THE HAIR WAS GREY; . . . . . 728 PRIEST FAIRY 10
AND SHE CRIES OUT, "I HAVE FLED TO MY BELOVED . . . . 754 SHADOW WATER A 151
AND CRYING, "I HAVE FLED TO MY BELOVED . . . . 754 SHADOW WATER A V 151
WERE THEY BUT LIFTED UP. THE RED HOUND IS FLED. . . . 761 SHADOW WATER A 266
FLEE
"FLEE FROM HIM," PEARL-PALE NIAMH WEEPING CRIED, ... 35 OISIN 2 92
BUT FLEE WHILE YOU STILL MAY." THEN I! . . . . 35 OISIN 2 V 89
BUT FLEE WHILE YOU MAY FLEE FROM HIM." THEN I! . . . . 35 OISIN 2 V 89
BUT FLEE WHILE YOU MAY FLEE FROM HIM." THEN I! . . . . 35 OISIN 2 V 89
"FOR ALL MEN FLEE THE DEMONS"; BUT MOVED NOT . . . . 36 OISIN 2 93
WE TIRE OF THE FLAME OF THE METEOR, BEFORE IT CAN FADE 122 WHITE BIRDS 2
   AND FLEE;
FOR WE TIRE OF THE FLAME OF THE METEOR BEFORE IT CAN PASS 122 WHITE BIRDS V 2
   BY AND FLEE
WE TIRE OF THE FLAME OF THE METEOR, BEFORE IT CAN PASS 122 WHITE BIRDS V 2
   BY AND FLEE;
FLEECE
. . . FOR WHITER THAN NEW-WASHED FLEECE . . . . . . 47 OISIN 3 11
AND MIDNIGHT THERE ENFOLD THEM LIKE A FLEECE . . . . . 128 DREAM OF FAERY 34
A GENTLE FEELING WRAPS THEM LIKE A FLEECE; . . . . . . 128 DREAM OF FAERY V 34
HERE WHERE LABURNUM HANGS HER GOLDEN FLEECE; . . . . . 670 ISLE STAT II 3 102
FLEEING
WHAT PURSUING OR FLEEING, ... 785 WOMANS BEAUTY 25
FLEET
SOME GOBLIN, MY SERVANT, ON WINGS THAT ARE FLEET, . . . 657 ISLE STAT I 3 67
AFAR ALONG THE FLEET WHITE RIVER'S FACE— . . . . . . 702 MOSADA 3 79
WOULD THEY FOOT SO FLEET A MEASURE? . . . . 731 STREET DANCERS 12
WOULD THEY FOOT SO FLEET A MEASURE? . . . . 732 STREET DANCERS 25
WOULD THEY FOOT SO FLEET A MEASURE? . . . . 732 STREET DANCERS 38
WOULD THEY FOOT SO FLEET A MEASURE? . . . . 733 STREET DANCERS 51
WOULD THEY FOOT SO FLEET A MEASURE? . . . . 733 STREET DANCERS 64
FLEETER
FAR FLEETER THAN THE MILLION-FOOTED SEA. . . . . . . 670 ISLE STAT II 3 108
FLEETING
MORE FLEETING THAN THE SEA'S FOAM-FICKLE FACE, ... 112 ROSE OF WORLD V 8
MORE FLEETING THAN THE SEA'S FOAM FICKLE FACE, ... 112 ROSE OF WORLD V 8
VEERING, FLEETING, FICKLE, THE WINDS OF KNOCKNAREA, . . 206 HANRAHANS SONG V 1
VEERING, FLEETING, FICKLE, OUR LOVES AND ANGERS MEET! . 207 HANRAHANS SONG V 3
FLEETNESS
AND LIFE THE SANDALS OF HER FLEETNESS, ... 77 INDIAN TO LOVE V 5B
I'D GIVE MY FAERY FLEETNESS, THOUGH I BE . . . . . . 670 ISLE STAT II 3 107
FLESH
LIKE ROTTED FLESH, AND STONE BY STONE MY HALL . . . . 45 OISIN 2 V 236
. . . THE FLESH OF HIS FACE AS DRIED GRASS, ... 59 OISIN 3 173
WHERE THE FLESH OF THE FOOTSOLE CLINGETH . . . . . . 61 OISIN 3 197
WHEN THE FLESH OF THE FOOTSOLE CLINGETH . . . . 61 OISIN 3 V 197
ITS FLESH BEING WILD, AND IT AGAIN . . . . 266 GALWAY RACES 13
FLESH WILD AGAIN, AND IT AGAIN . . . . 266 GALWAY RACES V 13
THAT FLESH AND BONE MAY DISAPPEAR, ... 307 HOUR DAWN 101
AS WITH HER FLESH AND BONE. . . . . 345 ON WOMAN 6
GREEK ALEXANDER FROM MY FLESH, ... 379 SAINT HUNCH 10
TO ALL THAT IN YOUR FLESH HAVE STOOD . . . . 380 SAINT HUNCH 13

287

FLESH   (CONTINUED)
    WERE DEAD YET FLESH AND BONE. . . . .   384 VISION ROBART   48
    FISH, FLESH, OR FOWL, COMMEND ALL SUMMER LONG . . . . . 407 SAIL BYZANTIUM   9
    OF FLESH AND BONE; . . . .   436 FOR MY SON   24
    I HAVE AS HEALTHY FLESH AND BLOOD AS ANY RHYMER'S HAD, . . 450 OWEN AHERNE   10
    A HEART OF FLESH AND BLOOD. . . . .   451 FIRST LOVE   6
    WHAT IS THIS FLESH I PURCHASED WITH MY PAINS. . . . . 499 MOTHER OF GOD   11
    CALCULATIONS THAT LOOK BUT CASUAL FLESH, PUT DOWN . . 610 STATUES   11
    OVER HER SPOTTED FLESH AND FLYING HAIR . . . . . . 687 TWO TITANS   15
FLEW
    ROUND EVERY BRANCH THE SONG-BIRDS FLEW, ...   14 OISIN 1   180
    FOR ROUND EACH BRANCH THE SONG-BIRDS FLEW, ...   14 OISIN 1   V 180
    AND THEN AN ANSWERING WHISPERING FLEW . . . . . .   15 OISIN 1   197
    ERE LONG AN ANSWERING WHISPER FLEW, ...   15 OISIN 1   V 197
    AND THEN AN ANSWERING WHISPER FLEW . . . .   15 OISIN 1   V 197
    AND STARLIGHT GLEAMED, AND CLOUDS FLEW HIGH, ...   84 MAD KING GOLL   34
    FLEW WESTWARD; AND MANY A TIME SINCE THEN . . . .   223 SHADOW WATER B   27
    A GREY GULL LOST ITS FEAR AND FLEW . . . .   397 POLIT PRISONER   3
    WHERE IS THE OWL THAT LATELY FLEW . . . . . .   646 ISLE STAT I 1   32
    THE FAERY THING FLEW WITH HER O'ER THE GRAY . . . .   663 ISLE STAT II 2   38
    WHITE LILIES, AND HER SONG FLEW FORTH AFAR . . . . .   693 MOSADA 1   85
FLICKED
    TIME GOES. THE FLICKED FIRE OF EVENING CRAWLS . . .   712 FERENCZ RENYI V   70
FLICKER   SEE A-FLICKER
    TILL THE SEED OF THE FIRE FLICKER AND GLOW; . . . .   150 OLD MOTHER   2
    OR HOPES THAT IN MERE HOPING FLICKER AND CEASE; . . .   162 ASKS FORGIVE   3
    AND HOPES THAT IN MERE HOPING FLICKER AND CEASE; . . .   162 ASKS FORGIVE   V   3
    WHEN SHE DREAMT FIRST OF LOVE, SHALL FLICKER OUT . .   760 SHADOW WATER A   257
    WHEN SHE DREAMED FIRST OF LOVE, SHALL FLICKER OUT . .   760 SHADOW WATER A V 257
FLICKERED
    HAS FLICKERED AND GONE OUT. I AM NOT WELL. . . . .   704 MOSADA 3   129
FLICKERING
    SEND PEACE ON ALL THE LANDS AND FLICKERING CORN.— . .   71 ANASHU VIJAYA   1
    AND MOTH-LIKE STARS WERE FLICKERING OUT, ...   149 WANDER AENGUS   6
    FLICKERING WITH ASH AND HAZEL, BUT HALF SHOWED . . .   180 QUEEN MAEVE   12
    FLICKERING UNDER THE WHITE MOONSHINE? . . . . . .   646 ISLE STAT I 1   33
    GOES FLICKERING IN REVERBERATED LIGHT. . . . . .   653 ISLE STAT I 2   53
    NODDING BY THE FLICKERING LAKE, ...   655 ISLE STAT I 3   3
    THY FLICKERING HAND? WHAT MEAN THE LIGHTS THAT RISE .   674 ISLE STAT II 3   198
    TRAILING AND SHINING 'NEATH THE FLICKERING GLARE. . .   688 TWO TITANS   32
    FLASHING AND FLICKERING WITH EVER-UNDULANT WING, . .   710 FERENCZ RENYI   19
    FLASHING AND FLICKERING, WITH EVER UNDULANT WING, . .   710 FERENCZ RENYI V 19
    THE SUNLIGHT FLICKERING ON THE PEWS. . . . . . .   736 IN CHURCH   9
FLICKERS
    UPON THE LIFE THAT FADES AND FLICKERS AND DIES, . . .   29 OISIN 2   12
FLIES   SEE HALF-FLIES
    . . . A SOUND LIKE THE STIRRING OF FLIES. . . . . .   51 OISIN 3   58
    BUT TO BE AMID SHOOTING OF FLIES AND FLOWERING OF RUSHES
        AND FLAGS." . . . .   55 OISIN 3   120
    BUT TO BE 'MID THE SHOOTING OF FLIES . . . . . .   55 OISIN 3   V 120
    THE FLIES BELOW THE LEAVES, AND THE YOUNG MICE . . .   75 ANASHU VIJAYA   87
    FOR THEY WILL RIDE THE NORTH WHEN THE GER-EAGLE FLIES, .   146 UNAPPEAS HOST   3
    FOR WINDS WILL BEAR THEM GENTLY WHEN THE EAGLE FLIES, .   146 UNAPPEAS HOST V   3
    FOR THEY WILL RIDE THE WINDS WHEN THE GIER-EAGLE FLIES .   146 UNAPPEAS HOST V   3
    AT DAWN TO CAST HIS FLIES, ...   347 FISHERMAN   5
    WHEN THE FLIES DROP IN THE STREAM; . . . . . .   348 FISHERMAN   34
    WHEN HER SOUL FLIES TO THE PREDESTINED DANCING-PLACE . .   365 HER COURAGE   1
    THE MOTHER BIRDS BRING GRUBS AND FLIES. . . . . . .   424 STARES NEST   3
    DAYLIGHT ALREADY FLIES . . . .   536 PARTING   9
    OVER THEM FLIES A LONG-LEGGED BIRD, ...   566 LAPIS LAZULI   39
    NO HAMLET THIN FROM EATING FLIES, A FAT . . . . . .   610 STATUES   19
    WAVES OFF THE FLIES, AND WARMS HIM IN THE SHINE. . . .   709 FERENCZ RENYI   7
    OBEYS. SOME FIERCE MAGICIAN FLIES OR WALKS . . . .   720 WITCH VIVIEN   9
    THE FLIES THAT DANCE IN THREES, IN TWOS, ...   736 IN CHURCH   11
FLIETH
    FLIETH FORTUNE'S FURIOUS WHEEL. . . . .   737 IN FIRELIGHT   8
FLIGHT
    ON OUR DARK PATHWAY, TILL A COUNTLESS FLIGHT . . . .   31 OISIN 2   34
    AT LAST THE MOON AND STARS SHONE, AND A FLIGHT . . .   31 OISIN 2   V 34
    "WHAT DO YOU BUILD WITH SAILS FOR FLIGHT?" . . . . .   69 CLOAK BOAT   6
    TILL THE MOON HAS TAKEN FLIGHT; . . . .   87 STOLEN CHILD   19
    AND TIME AND THE WORLD ARE EVER IN FLIGHT; . . . . .   148 INTO TWILIGHT   14
    THAT IF WE HOLD THAT FLIGHT THEY'LL LEAVE THE PLACE, . .   265 ABBEY THEATRE   3
    ALL BUT THE TERRORS OF THE WOODLAND FLIGHT FORGOT . .   366 HER COURAGE   5
    ALL BUT THE PERILS OF THE WOODLAND FLIGHT FORGOT, . .   366 HER COURAGE   V   5
    CRADLE UPON CRADLE, AND ALL IN FLIGHT AND ALL . . . .   376 PHASES OF MOON   100
    THE WINGS HALF SPREAD FOR FLIGHT, ...   430 NINETEEN 19   65
    I MEDITATE UPON A SWALLOW'S FLIGHT . . . . . .   488 COOLE PARK 29   1
    OF FLIGHT ARE DONE. MOST FAIR OF ALL WHO GRAZE . . .   649 ISLE STAT I 1   118
    DREAMING OF FLASHING FLIGHT AND OF THE PLUMED WAVE. . .   650 ISLE STAT I 1   140
    WHAT DO YOU BUILD WITH SAILS FOR FLIGHT? . . . . .   666 ISLE STAT II 3   6
    REMEMBERING THEE, I MUSE, WHILE FADES IN FLIGHT . . .   705 REMEMBRANCE   6
    AS A WREATH OF SMOKE IN WIND-BLOWN FLIGHT . . . . .   730 PRIEST FAIRY   61
    AND NEVER REST IN THEIR FLIGHT. . . . .   739 WHERE BOOKS GO   4
FLING
    OR FLING MY LAUGHTER TO THE SUN . . . .   86 MAD KING GOLL V 69
    AND FLING MY LAUGHTER TO THE SUN . . . . . .   86 MAD KING GOLL V 69
    THERE, DON'T FLING STONES AT ME . . . .   94 MOLL MAGEE   2
    YE WON'T FLING STONES AT ME; . . . .   96 MOLL MAGEE   54
    DIM PAIRC-NA-CARRAIG, WHERE THE WILD BEES FLING . . .   217 WOODS OF COOLE   9
    I TOOK A BROKEN ROOT TO FLING . . . .   317 APPOINTMENT   2

		PAGE	TITLE		LINE

FLING (CONTINUED)

BEYOND THE FLING OF THE DULL ASS'S HOOF	321	REED WHISPERER		5
AND YET IN FLYING FLING INTO MY MEAT	384	VISION ROBART		53
THE SUMMERS FLING THEIR SCENTS? AH, SUBTILE AND SLOW, . .	675	ISLE STAT II 3		231
GATHERED ON HER OWN LIPS, OH YOUTH, AND FLING	688	TWO TITANS		53
I FLING AWAY MY SWORD, BLOOD DIM, ...	743	DANAAN QUICK		20
I DREW MY SWORD TO FLING IT IN A POOL,—	747	SHADOW WATER A		7
CALAMITY CAN HAVE ITS FLING.	782	HEART FRIGHT		18
O THEY HAD THEIR FLING, ...	790	SINGING HEAD		22

FLINGING

| FLINGING FROM HIS ARMS I LAUGHED . . . . | 538 | LAST CONFESS | | 7 |
| NOW FLINGING LOOSE THE SLANTING SAIL, ... | 742 | DANAAN QUICK | | 3 |

FLINGS

AND FLINGS HERSELF OUT OF THE ROOM WHEN JULIET WOULD BE BRIDE	354	HIS PHOENIX		13
AND FLINGS HERSELF OUT OF THE ROOM WHEN JULIET WOULD BE A BRIDE	354	HIS PHOENIX	V	13
FLINGS HER BEFORE HIM. "SAVE THYSELF AND ME.	713	FERENCZ RENYI		86
IN TERROR FLINGS HER AT HER LOVER'S FEET.	713	FERENCZ RENYI	V	85
WITH CRIES AND MURMURS. SUDDENLY HE FLINGS	714	FERENCZ RENYI		101

FLIT

WHEN GREY GULLS FLIT ABOUT INSTEAD OF MEN, ...	292	TO A SHADE		6
AT MIDNIGHT ON THE EMPEROR'S PAVEMENT FLIT	498	BYZANTIUM		25
FLIT TO KILTARTAN CROSS AND STAY	791	REPRISALS		11

FLITTING

| WITHIN HIS OTHER HAND WERE FLITTING . . . . | 18 | OISIN 1 | V | 253 |

FLOAT

I SAW A FOAM-WHITE SEAGULL DRIFT AND FLOAT	36	OISIN 2		105
CLOTHING HIM ROUND, I SAW A SEAGULL FLOAT	36	OISIN 2	V	105
FLOAT OUT UPON A LONG	414	TOWER		142
DRIFT AND FLOAT LIKE SILVER SHIPS;	647	ISLE STAT I 1		67
LIVING, WIDE WINGED, ON THE WATERS FLOAT.	657	ISLE STAT I 3		54

FLOATED

| FLOATED IN ALL HER SINGING. HALF ENTRANCED . . . . . | 30 | OISIN 2 | V | 19 |
| AND RODE ON TILL OVER THE WORLD'S RIM FLOATED THE SEA'S OLD SHOUT, | 60 | OISIN 3 | V | 183 |

FLOATING

THE HORSEMEN WITH THEIR FLOATING HAIR, ...	2	OISIN 1		7
A SEA-WORN WAIF CAME FLOATING BY.	24	OISIN 1	V	365
A SHINING WEB, A FLOATING RIBBON OF CLOTH, ...	430	NINETEEN 19		50
FLOATING FROM YON BARRED WINDOW. SMALL NEW-COMER, . . .	700	MOSADA 3		43
FLOATING FROM YON BARRED WINDOW. NEW COMER, ...	700	MOSADA 3	V	43

FLOATING-HAIRED

| AND FLOATING-HAIRED AND PROUD IN STRIFE; . . . . . . | 9 | OISIN 1 | V | 99 |

FLOATS

A SWEETHEART FROM ANOTHER LIFE FLOATS THERE	390	IMAGE PAST		22
HER PRESENT IMAGE FLOATS INTO THE MIND—	444	SCHOOL CHILDR		25
BEFORE ME FLOATS AN IMAGE, MAN OR SHADE, ...	497	BYZANTIUM		9
POURS UP AND FLOATS IN FRAGRANCE ROUND MY HEAD	691	MOSADA 1		40
POURS UP AND FLOATS IN FRAGRANCE O'ER MY HEAD	691	MOSADA 1	V	40
AND SEIZE HER, AND THUS FLOATS HER QUIVERING CRY; . . .	714	FERENCZ RENYI		105
OF FIRE. SO ENDS A BRAIN—A WORLD! THE SMOKE FLOATS UP,	714	FERENCZ RENYI	V	111
AS THERE FLOATS FROM FIELDS AFAR	732	STREET DANCERS		20

FLOCK

AND NOW THE DAYLIGHT-DARKENING RAVENS FLOCK.	43	OISIN 2		212
ALL IS DONE NOW—I SEE THE RAVENS FLOCK—	43	OISIN 2	V	212
THAT YOU STAY IDLING HERE WITH FLOCK AND HERDS." . . .	107	CUCHULAIN SEA	V	21
FOR HALF HIS FLOCK WERE IN THEIR BEDS.	132	FR GILLIGAN		3
FOR HALF HIS FLOCK LAY IN THEIR BEDS	132	FR GILLIGAN	V	3
AND HIS OWN FLOCK WAS BROWSING AT THE DOOR.	340	SHEP GOATHERD		27
OF A MOROCCAN FLOCK OR HERD.	493	AT ALGECIRAS	V	3

FLOCKS

. . . THAT HE WHO HAS STARS FOR HIS FLOCKS	49	OISIN 3		37
. . . THAT HE WHO HAD STARS FOR HIS FLOCKS	49	OISIN 3	V	37
NO OTHER.—HEAR, AND MAY THE INDOLENT FLOCKS	71	ANASHU VIJAYA		4
THE JOYOUS FLOCKS OF DEER AND ANTELOPE, ...	75	ANASHU VIJAYA		74
IN THE TREE ROOTS, AND ALL THE SACRED FLOCKS	75	ANASHU VIJAYA		88
THE JOYOUS FLOCKS OF DEER AND ANTELOPES, ...	75	ANASHU VIJAYA	V	74
IN THE TREE ROOTS, AND ALL THY SACRED FLOCKS	75	ANASHU VIJAYA	V	88
THAT YOU STAY IDLING HERE WITH FLOCKS AND HERDS." . . .	107	CUCHULAIN SEA	V	21
TO IDLE LIFE AWAY WITH FLOCKS AND HERDS."	107	CUCHULAIN SEA	V	21
OF THE MOROCCAN FLOCKS AND HERDS	493	AT ALGECIRAS		3
THE FAT FLOCKS AND THE FIELDS' FATNESS, ...	540	FROM ANTIGONE		4
HIDING AWAY THE OCEAN'S YELPING FLOCKS.	688	TWO TITANS		38
WHERE THEY ALL SUMMER FEED THEIR WANDERING FLOCKS, . . .	690	MOSADA 1		5
WHO MIGHT HAVE FLOCKS AND HERDS AND MANY THRALLS, . . .	757	SHADOW WATER A		216

FLOOD

TWO WALLS, A ROOF, A FLOOD! THERE TREMBLING GREEN . .	31	OISIN 2	V	32
AS A HAY-COCK OUT ON THE FLOOD, OR A WOLF SUCKED UNDER A WEIR.	63	OISIN 3		220
TO RANT AND RAGE IN FLOOD AND WIND;	138	TO IRELAND		26
IN FLOOD AND FIRE AND CLAY AND WIND, ...	138	TO IRELAND	V	25
OF THE FLOOD AND FLAME, OF THE HEIGHT AND WOOD, . . .	148	INTO TWILIGHT	V	11
HIM WHO TREMBLES BEFORE THE FLAME AND THE FLOOD, . . .	158	TO HIS HEART		3
LET THE STARRY WINDS AND THE FLAME AND THE FLOOD . . .	158	TO HIS HEART		5
WHO TREMBLES BEFORE THE FLAME AND THE FLOOD, ...	158	TO HIS HEART	V	3
TIME'S BITTER FLOOD WILL RISE, ...	173	PLEADS FRIEND		6
WHERE THE SWAN DRIFTS UPON A DARKENING FLOOD.	492	COOLE BALLYLEE		48
SPIRIT AFTER SPIRIT! THE SMITHIES BREAK THE FLOOD, . .	498	BYZANTIUM		34
"WHATEVER STANDS IN FIELD OR FLOOD, ...	529	TOM LUNATIC		13

289

		PAGE	TITLE		LINE

FLOOD (CONTINUED)
BUT ALL THAT RUN IN COUPLES, ON EARTH, IN FLOOD OR AIR,   556 RIBH PATRICK   11
• • •

FLOODED
LIKE HEAVY FLOODED WATERS OUR BODIES AND OUR BLOOD;   208 HANRAHANS SONG   13
IN THE ELMS ABOVE THE FLOODED STREAM;   403 FOR DAUGHTER   12
THE GLITTERING REACHES OF THE FLOODED LAKE.   490 COOLE BALLYLEE   16

FLOODS
NO TENDER WISDOM FLOODS THE EYES   723 GIRLS SONG A   9

FLOOD-TIME
FROM FLOOD-TIME ENCLOSES   672 ISLE STAT II 3   167

FLOOR
THE FLOOR OF ALMHUIN'S HOSTING HALL   13 OISIN 1   156
THE FLOOR OF EMAN'S DANCING HALL   13 OISIN 1   V   156
THE FLOOR OF EMEN'S HOISTING HALL   13 OISIN 1   V   156
THE FLOOR OF ALLEN'S HOSTING HALL   13 OISIN 1   V   156
ROSE EVER FROM THE SEA'S WARM FLOOR,   13 OISIN 1   V   172
A HUNDRED HORSEMEN ON THE BASALT FLOOR   36 OISIN 2   102
WHERETHROUGH A HUNDRED HORSEMEN ON THE FLOOR   36 OISIN 2   V   102
MOST DISTANT STRODE WE. ON THE FLOOR LAY SLIME,   37 OISIN 2   V   113
THE DAWN CAME IN, AND GLIMMERED ON THE FLOOR   39 OISIN 2   152
THEN EMER CAST THE WEB UPON THE FLOOR,   105 CUCHULAIN SEA   6
UPON THE WEB-HEAPED FLOOR, AND CRIED HIS WORD;   106 CUCHULAIN SEA   15
UPON THE WEB-HEAPED FLOOR, AND THUS HIS WORD,   106 CUCHULAIN SEA   V   15
"WHO BADE YOU TELL THESE THINGS UPON MY FLOOR?"   106 CUCHULAIN SEA   V   17
SHE GOES DOWN THE FLOOR OF HEAVEN,   125 CATHLEEN PARA   V   13
STOOD UPRIGHT ON THE FLOOR.   133 FR GILLIGAN   24
WHEN I HAD LAID IT ON THE FLOOR   149 WANDER AENGUS   9
BUT SOMETHING RUSTLED ON THE FLOOR,   149 WANDER AENGUS   11
THE UNCONTROLLABLE MYSTERY ON THE BESTIAL FLOOR.   318 MAGI   8
SWEPT THE SAWDUST FROM THE FLOOR   440 WISDOM   6
DREAM OF SHAVINGS ON A FLOOR   440 WISDOM   V   6
IMAGINED HIM UPON THE FLOOR   440 WISDOM   V   6
AND LET IT FALL UNNOTICED TO THE FLOOR.   461 HARUN RASHID   15
AND IT WOULD FALL UNNOTICED ON THE FLOOR.   461 HARUN RASHID   V   15
HAS FLUNG ITS ARROWY SHAFT UPON THE FLOOR,   482 BLOOD AND MOON   32
HAD FLUNG ITS ARROWY SHAFT UPON THE FLOOR,   482 BLOOD AND MOON V   32
SOUND OF A STICK UPON THE FLOOR, A SOUND   491 COOLE BALLYLEE   25
MARBLES OF THE DANCING FLOOR   498 BYZANTIUM   36
OF THE DREAD WOODS; ALONG THEIR RUSSET FLOOR   675 ISLE STAT II 3   243
ALL HEAVEN'S FLOOR, WITH VAPOURS BEDDED—   705 DAWN-SONG   11
AND FLUNG DOWN CLASHING ON THE FLOOR   740 EARL PAUL   15
FELL AT MY FEET ON THE FLOOR;—   744 GLOVE CLOAK   8
BUT CHILDREN AND DOGS ON THE FLOOR.   780 WELL AND TREE   14

FLOORS
ON THE FLOORS OF THE GODS."   59 OISIN 3   180
THE PACING TO AND FRO ON POLISHED FLOORS   418 ANCEST HOUSES   35
I SCRUB ITS FLOORS AND MAKE MY BED,   607 SONGS BURDEN 2   5

FLOPPING
WITH FLOPPING AND WITH FLAPPING IT MADE A GREAT DISPLAY,   593 PILGRIM   18
WITH THEIR FLOPPING AND THEIR FLAPPING IT MADE A GREAT   593 PILGRIM   V   18
DISPLAY

FLORENCE
ON FLORENCE EMERY I CALL THE NEXT,   472 ALL SOUL NIGHT   41

FLOURISH
AND KNOW WHATEVER FLOURISH AND DECLINE   423 MY DESCENDANTS   23

FLOURISHES
TRUTH FLOURISHES WHERE THE STUDENT'S LAMP HAS SHONE,   398 LEADERS CROWD   8

FLOURISHING
MAY SHE BECOME A FLOURISHING HIDDEN TREE   404 FOR DAUGHTER   41

FLOUT
WHETHER SHE THREW THEM UP TO FLOUT ME,   390 IMAGE PAST   37

FLOW
SWEPT ON THE DANCE'S LINKED FLOW,   20 OISIN 1   V   291
WHISPERED TO THE SEA WHOSE FLOW   20 OISIN 1   V   298
ONCE MORE THE DANCE'S LINKED FLOW,   22 OISIN 1   V 323A
GREY IN THE MIDST LIKE A SMALL RIVULET'S FLOW,   37 OISIN 2   V   117
• • • AND YEARS AFTER YEARS 'GAN FLOW;   52 OISIN 3   75
• • • AND YEARS AFTER YEARS 'GAN THEIR FLOW;   52 OISIN 3   V   75
ALTHOUGH YOU HIDE IN THE EBB AND FLOW   146 FISH   1
BUT LET A GENTLE SILENCE WROUGHT WITH MUSIC FLOW   175 ELEMENT POWERS   17
BUT LET A GENTLE SILENCE ENWROUGHT WITH MUSIC FLOW   175 ELEMENT POWERS V   17
OR ALL THAT WAYWARD EBB AND FLOW. THERE STOOD   428 NINETEEN 19   4
ON ALL THAT WAYWARD EBB AND FLOW. THERE STOOD   428 NINETEEN 19   V   4
HAVE I NOT SEEN A THOUSAND SEASONS EBB AND FLOW   675 ISLE STAT II 3   229
UPON THEIR THRONES. THE LIVES OF MEN SHALL FLOW   698 MOSADA 2   56

FLOWED
BUT DOWN TO HER FEET WHITE VESTURE FLOWED,   3 OISIN 1   25
DOWN TO HER FEET WHITE VESTURE FLOWED,   3 OISIN 1   V   25
FLOWED ON ANEW, AND OFT, ANEW DECLINING,   33 OISIN 2   V 68D
WHERE SHADOWY FACE FLOWED INTO SHADOWY FACE,   39 OISIN 2   145
MELTED AND FLOWED; AND IN THE SELF-SAME PLACE   39 OISIN 2   V   146
A VALLEY FLOWED DOWN FROM HIS HOOFS, AND THERE IN THE LONG   48 OISIN 3   26
GRASS LAY,
AND YOU HAVE CHANGED AND FLOWED FROM SHAPE TO SHAPE,   102 FERGUS DRUID   2
AND THE WAVES FLOWED ABOVE HIM AND HE DIED.   111 CUCHULAIN SEA V   86
AS THOUGH THE WATERS HAD FLOWED UP BETWEEN;   749 SHADOW WATER A   55

FLOWER
BLOSSOM IN SOME NEW CRIMSON FLOWER,   16 OISIN 1   224
AND HER HAIR WAS A FOLDED FLOWER   161 CAP AND BELLS   35
O FLOWER OF THE BRANCH, O BIRD AMONG THE LEAVES,   251 SHADOW WATER B   608

			PAGE	TITLE		LINE

FLOWER   (CONTINUED)
```
    WHERE THE SYMBOLIC ROSE CAN BREAK IN FLOWER,    • • • • •   419 MY HOUSE               4
    AND WHAT IF MY DESCENDANTS LOSE THE FLOWER • • • • • •     423 MY DESCENDANTS        9
    HAS PLUCKED A FLOWER AND SUNG HER LOSS: • • • • • • •      447 COLONUS PRAISE        22
    GROWETH THE GOBLIN FLOWER OF JOY, HER CARE, • • • • • •    653 ISLE STAT I 2         39
    THAT FLOWER I SEEK.  THOU NEVER WILT RETURN. • • • • •     653 ISLE STAT I 2         44
    I'LL BRING THAT FLOWER TO HER, AND SO MAY EARN • • • •     653 ISLE STAT I 2         45
    OF THE HAPPY FLOWER MINIONS. • • • • • • • • • • •         667 ISLE STAT II 3        29
    IF ON HIS LIPS THE ENCHANTED FLOWER BE LAID: • • • • •     668 ISLE STAT II 3        46
    O LET ME PASS:  THAT FLOWER NONE • • • • • • • • • •       668 ISLE STAT II 3        47
    THE FLOWER, SAVE SOME THING BE FOUND • • • • • • • •       668 ISLE STAT II 3        51
    THE ENCHANTED FLOWER WERE, • • • • • • • • • • • •         668 ISLE STAT II 3        62
    IN SILENCE, THAT FAMED FLOWER OF WIZARDRY, • • • • •       673 ISLE STAT II 3        192
    BEHOLD THE LOVING LOVELESS FLOWER OF LONE WAYS, • • •      674 ISLE STAT II 3        201
    THE FAERY FLOWER LIES UPON THY LIPS. • • • • • • • •       677 ISLE STAT II 3        277
    THE GOBLIN FLOWER LIETH ON THY LIPS. • • • • • • • •       678 ISLE STAT II 3        298
    AND EVERY FLOWER ABOVE ITS SHADOW SITS. • • • • • • •      712 FERENCZ RENYI         73
    AND EVERY FLOWER ABOVE A SHADOW SITS. • • • • • • • •      712 FERENCZ RENYI    V    73
    O FLOWER OF THE BRANCH, O BIRD AMONG THE LEAVES, • • •     769 SHADOW WATER A        424
    FOR THE FLOWER COMES WITH THE FRUIT THERE • • • • • •      774 COME RIDE             3
FLOWERED
    AND TILL A HUNDRED MORNS HAD FLOWERED RED • • • • • •      170 SECRET ROSE           17
FLOWERING
    BUT TO BE AMID SHOOTING OF FLIES AND FLOWERING OF RUSHES   55 OISIN 3               120
        AND FLAGS."
    • • • AND THE FLOWERING OF RUSHES AND FLAGS." • • • •      55 OISIN 3          V    120
    SURELY AMONG A RICH MAN'S FLOWERING LAWNS, • • • • •       417 ANCEST HOUSES         1
    THAT FLOWERING, SILKEN, OLD EMBROIDERY, TORN • • • • •     477 SELF AND SOUL         13
    HE NUMBERS.  HE, WITH FLOWERING CURRANT TREES, • • • •     710 FERENCZ RENYI    V    22
FLOWER-LIKE
    WOVE IN HER FLOWER-LIKE HAIR, BEFORE DARK TOWERS • • • •   30 OISIN 2          V    22
    OF A FLUTTER OF FLOWER-LIKE HAIR: • • • • • • • • • •      160 CAP AND BELLS         18
    ON A FLUTTER OF FLOWER-LIKE HAIR: • • • • • • • • • •      160 CAP AND BELLS    V    18
FLOWERS    SEE WATER-FLOWERS
    WHITE FLOWERS OF THE FOAM A STAFF OF WOOD • • • • • •      24 OISIN 1          V    366
    SHONE MANY TIMES AMONG THE GLIMMERING FLOWERS • • • •      30 OISIN 2               21
    ONCE MORE UNTO YOUR FLOWERS, FOR NONE MAY FIGHT, • • •     34 OISIN 2          V    80
    THE FLOWERS STILL GREW THERE: FAR ON THE SEA'S WASTE  • •  39 OISIN 2               163
    THE FLOWERS STILL GREW THERE.  MOVED BEYOND HIM THE SEA'S  39 OISIN 2          V    163
        WASTE:
    AND HEALED MY WOUNDS WITH UNGUENTS OUT OF FLOWERS   • • •  41 OISIN 2               185
    WITH WITCHERY AND UNGUENTS FROM THE FLOWERS • • • • •      41 OISIN 2          V    185
    AND ALL THE TREMBLING FLOWERS THEY BEAR. • • • • • • •     134 TWO TREES             4
    THE VINEGAR-HEAVY SPONGE, THE FLOWERS BY KEDRON STREAM:    172 TRAV PASSION          5
    THE HISSOP-HEAVY SPONGE, THE FLOWERS BY KIDRON STREAM: • • 172 TRAV PASSION     V    5
    HUM IN THE LIME-TREE FLOWERS: AND PUT AWAY • • • • • •     198 SEVEN WOODS           3
    AND HANGING ITS PAPER FLOWERS FROM POST TO POST, • • • •   198 SEVEN WOODS           8
    HUM IN THE LIME TREE FLOWERS: AND PUT AWAY • • • • • •     198 SEVEN WOODS      V    3
    AND WINDS BLOWING FROM FLOWERS, AND WHIRR OF FEATHERS • •  219 WOODS OF COOLE        39
    I SWAYED MY LEAVES AND FLOWERS IN THE SUN: • • • • •      261 COMING WISDOM         3
    SEED-PODS AND FLOWERS THAT ARE NOT ALL WILD POPPY. • • •   342 SHEP GOATHERD         88
    SEED PODS AND FLOWERS THAT ARE NOT ALL WILD POPPY. • • •   342 SHEP GOATHERD    V    88
    FLOWERS FROM I KNOW NOT WHAT EMBROIDERY-- • • • • • •      478 SELF AND SOUL         27
    (HURRAH FOR THE FLOWERS OF SPRING, • • • • • • • • •       567 FROM JAPANESE         3
    FLOWERS AND GRASS AND CLOUDLESS SKY, • • • • • • • •       639 BEN BULBEN            57
    AND FLOWERS AROUND IN CLUSTERING THOUSANDS ARE, • • •      656 ISLE STAT I 3         24
    GO ASK THE SPRINGING FLOWERS, • • • • • • • • • • •        680 LOVE AND DEATH        13
    WITH WREATHS OF WITHERED FLOWERS • • • • • • • • • •       680 LOVE AND DEATH        17
    WITH WREATHS OF WITHERED FLOWERS, • • • • • • • • • •      680 LOVE AND DEATH        19
    STILL STARING AT THEIR FLOWERS, • • • • • • • • • •        680 LOVE AND DEATH        25
    AND FLOWERS AND LITTLE CHILDREN.  SUDDENLY • • • • • •     688 TWO TITANS            36
    REMEMBERING THEE, I SEARCH OUT THESE FAINT FLOWERS  • • •  704 REMEMBRANCE           1
    AND MEASURE THE MINDS OF THE FLOWERS, • • • • • • • •      707 FAIRY PEDANT          17
    FOR DREAMS ARE THE FLOWERS ABLOW, • • • • • • • • •        743 WISDOM DREAMS         6
FLOWERS'
    THEY ARE THE FLOWERS' GUARDIAN SPRIGHTS: • • • • • •       666 ISLE STAT II 3        18
FLOWERY
    AND RIVER, FERN AND FLOWERY CLUMP, • • • • • • • •         15 OISIN 1          V    196
    WHAT ARE THE VOICES THAT IN FLOWERY WAYS • • • • • •       666 ISLE STAT II 3        16
    AMONG THE PLANTS: THE FLOWERY SILENCE FELL. • • • • •      692 MOSADA 1              55
FLOWING
    AND FLOWING STRENGTH, WITH AGE IS SUBTLE-SOULED. • • •     35 OISIN 2          V    83
    WHERE MOUSE-GREY WATERS ARE FLOWING, • • • • • • • •       119 PITY OF LOVE          7
    THE MOUSE-GREY WATERS ON FLOWING, • • • • • • • • •        119 PITY OF LOVE     V    7
    THAT LIFT US TO THE FLOWING, CHANGING WORLD • • • •       230 SHADOW WATER B        182
    THE LONG FLOWING LINE, • • • • • • • • • • • • •           355 PROPERTIUS            3
    OF DULL RED HAIR WAS FLOWING • • • • • • • • • • •         363 DOLLS DRAWINGS        6
    AND THE FLOWING AIR ABOVE, • • • • • • • • • • • •         680 LOVE AND DEATH        14
FLOWN
    AND THE BLUSHES OF FIRST LOVE NEVER HAVE FLOWN: • • • •    8 OISIN 1                85
    AND THE FLUSHES OF FIRST LOVE NEVER HAVE FLOWN: • • • •    8 OISIN 1          V    85
    TO FIND THEY HAVE FLOWN AWAY? • • • • • • • • • •          323 SWANS AT COOLE        30
    HOW HAVE THE YEARS IN TROIA FLOWN AWAY? • • • • • •        679 ISLE STAT II 3        309
    A GREY BIRD HAS FLOWN BY.  HE HAS FLOWN UPWARD. • • • •    753 SHADOW WATER A        134
    A GREY BIRD HAS FLOWN BY.  HE HAS FLOWN UPWARD. • • • •    753 SHADOW WATER A        134
    THEY HAVE FLOWN AWAY TOGETHER.  WE ARE NEARLY • • • •      754 SHADOW WATER A        154
FLOWS
    WHOSE LONG WOOL WHITER THAN SEA-FROTH FLOWS, • • • • •     8 OISIN 1                90
    WHOSE LONG WOOL WHITER THAN SEA FROTH FLOWS, • • • • •     8 OISIN 1          V    90
    SO GREAT A SWEETNESS FLOWS • • • • • • • • • • • •         316 FRIENDS               27
    SO GREAT A SWEETNESS FLOWS INTO THE BREAST • • • • •       479 SELF AND SOUL         69
```

291

	PAGE	TITLE	LINE
FLOWS (CONTINUED)			
COME FORTH, COME FORTH, MY MUSIC FLOWS FOR THEE, • • • •	645	ISLE STAT I 1	20
FLUNG			
WE FLUNG ON HIGH EACH WAVING HAND, • • • • • • • •	22	OISIN 1	325
FLUNG ON HIGH EACH WAVING HAND, • • • • • • • • •	22	OISIN 1 V	325
AND FLUNG THE JOYOUS HUNTING-SPEAR! • • • • • • • •	23	OISIN 1 V	345A
• • • FLUNG LOOSELY ALONG THE DIM GROUND! • • • • • •	50	OISIN 3	45
• • • NOR IN GLAMOURS BY DEMONS FLUNG, • • • • • •	50	OISIN 3	50
• • • OR IN GLAMOURS BY DEMONS FLUNG, • • • • • • •	50	OISIN 3 V	50
OF THE HIGH PEOPLE OF SORACA NOR IN GLAMOUR BY DEMONS FLUNG,	50	OISIN 3 V	50
• • • I FLUNG IT FIVE YARDS WITH MY HAND, • • • • • •	60	OISIN 3	187
AND THE PROUD DREAMING KING WHO FLUNG THE CROWN • • • •	170	SECRET ROSE	19
OR AS THE CHANGING SPEARS FLUNG BY THE GOLDEN STARS • • •	175	ELEMENT POWERS V	15
HE HAS FLUNG A DRUID SPELL UPON THE AIR, • • • • • •	240	SHADOW WATER B	385
AS IF SOME MARVELLOUS EMPTY SEA-SHELL FLUNG • • • • •	417	ANCEST HOUSES	13
HAS FLUNG ITS ARROWY SHAFT UPON THE FLOOR, • • • • •	482	BLOOD AND MOON	32
HAD FLUNG ITS ARROWY SHAFT UPON THE FLOOR, • • • • •	482	BLOOD AND MOON V	32
THE YOUTH HAD FLUNG HIS ARMS AROUND THE ROCKS, • • • •	688	TWO TITANS	40
AND FLUNG DOWN CLASHING ON THE FLOOR • • • • • • •	740	EARL PAUL	15
FLUSH			
OH, CAN MY KISSES BRING A FLUSH NO MORE • • • • • •	701	MOSADA 3	71
FLUSHED SEE SUN-FLUSHED			
AND THRICE THE PEACHES FLUSHED UPON THE WALLS, • • • •	690	MOSADA 1	2
FLUSHES			
AND THE FLUSHES OF FIRST LOVE NEVER HAVE FLOWN! • • • •	8	OISIN 1 V	85
FLUTE			
HE'LL PRACTISE ON THE SHEPHERD'S FLUTE, • • • • • • •	343	SHEP GOATHERD	102
O BROTHER, LAY THY FLUTE UPON THY LIPS! • • • • • • •	681	SEEKER	6
FLUTED			
CLEAR FLUTED THEN THAT GOBLIN RARE-- • • • • • • • •	6	OISIN 1 V	54
IN THE POPPY-HUNG HOUSE OF THE TWILIGHT FLUTED! • • • •	8	OISIN 1 V	83
FLUTES			
OF FIDDLES AND OF FLUTES HUNG THERE • • • • • • • •	271	GREY ROCK V	20
FLUTINGS			
GOING THE FOREST THROUGH, WITH FLUTINGS WEAK! • • • • •	672	ISLE STAT II 3	155
FLUTTER SEE A-FLUTTER			
FLUTTER ALONG THE FROTH LIPS OF THE SEA, • • • • • •	33	OISIN 2	58
FLUTTER ALONG THE FROTH LIPS OF THE SEA • • • • • • •	33	OISIN 2	64
FLUTTER ALONG THE FROTH-LIPS OF THE SEA, • • • • • •	33	OISIN 2 V	58
(THEY WILL NOT HUSH, THE LEAVES THAT ROUND ME FLUTTER--	82	MAD KING GOLL V	REF
OF A FLUTTER OF FLOWER-LIKE HAIR! • • • • • • • • •	160	CAP AND BELLS	18
ON A FLUTTER OF FLOWER-LIKE HAIR! • • • • • • • • •	160	CAP AND BELLS V	18
STRANGE CREATURES FLUTTER UP BEFORE ONE'S EYES, • • • •	222	SHADOW WATER B	18
FLUTTERED			
AS LIKE A RUDDY MOTH THEY WAVED AND FLUTTERED• • • • •	34	OISIN 2 V	72
I LAUGHED BECAUSE BIRDS FLUTTERED BY, • • • • • • •	84	MAD KING GOLL	33
HIS RUEFUL SPIRIT FLUTTERED BY• • • • • • • • • •	673	ISLE STAT II 3	188
FLUTTERING SEE A-FLUTTERING			
WITH QUENCHLESS GAZE AND FLUTTERING HAIR• • • • • • •	12	OISIN 1	145
AND WITH QUENCHLESS EYES AND FLUTTERING HAIR • • • • •	12	OISIN 1 V	144
O SIGH, O FLUTTERING SIGH, BE KIND TO ME! • • • • • •	33	OISIN 2	57
• • • THE FLUTTERING SADNESS OF EARTH. • • • • • • •	55	OISIN 3	124
FOR MOVETH ALIVE IN THY FINGERS THE FLUTTERING SADNESS OF EARTH.	55	OISIN 3 V	124
FLUTTERS			
HER RAVEN FLUTTERS. ROB HIM OF HIS FOOD • • • • • •	751	SHADOW WATER A	100
FLY			
FOLDED LIKE A FROZEN FLY! • • • • • • • • • • •	19	OISIN 1	273
BUT FLY WHILE STILL YOU MAY." AND THEREON I! • • • • •	35	OISIN 2	89
FOR BATTLE." "FLY YE FROM A THING SO DREAD• • • • • •	35	OISIN 2 V	90
TO FLY A SPIRIT," NIAM WEEPING SAID• • • • • • • •	35	OISIN 2 V	92
I FELL ON THE PATH, AND THE HORSE WENT AWAY LIKE A SUMMER FLY!	60	OISIN 3	190
WITH HER WOULD I FLY• • • • • • • • • • • • •	89	ISLE IN WATER	16
AND CALL TO MY BELOVED AND ME! "NO LONGER FLY • • • •	173	SPEAKS HEARERS	7
WHILE OVER THEM BIRDS OF AENGUS FLY • • • • • • • •	197	BAILE AILLINN	182
O THOUGHT, FLY TO HER WHEN THE END OF DAY • • • • •	201	OLD MEMORY	1
I THOUGHT TO FLY TO HER WHEN THE END OF DAY • • • • •	201	OLD MEMORY V	1
THOUGHT FLY TO HER WHEN THE END OF DAY • • • • • •	201	OLD MEMORY V	1
I KNOW OF THE SLEEPY COUNTRY, WHERE SWANS FLY ROUND • • •	204	WITHER BOUGHS	17
COUPLED WITH GOLDEN CHAINS, AND SING AS THEY FLY• • • •	204	WITHER BOUGHS	18
WHEN MIDHIR'S WIFE HAD CHANGED HER TO A FLY, • • • • •	220	HARP OF AENGUS	10
AND WHEN ONE CHANGED HER TO A SILVER FLY• • • • • •	220	HARP OF AENGUS V	10
THEY'LL FLY UPON THAT SECRET WAY OF THEIRS• • • • • •	233	SHADOW WATER B	248
AND NOW THEY ALL WHEEL SUDDENLY AND FLY • • • • • •	234	SHADOW WATER B	258
THAT FLY INTO THE WEST? BUT LISTEN, LISTEN! • • • • •	247	SHADOW WATER B	518
WHAT ARE THEY? UNTO WHAT COUNTRY DO THEY FLY? • • • •	247	SHADOW WATER B	523
WHEN GREY GULLS FLY ABOUT INSTEAD OF MEN, • • • • • •	292	TO A SHADE V	6
THE STRUGGLE OF THE FLY IN MARMALADE. • • • • • • •	369	EGO DOMINUS	45
OR ELSE MY DREAMS THAT FLY • • • • • • • • • • •	384	VISION ROBART	51
NO, NOT IN BOYHOOD WHEN WITH ROD AND FLY, • • • • •	409	TOWER	8
THEY MAY DROP A FLY! • • • • • • • • • • • • •	416	TOWER	177
AS MAN, AS BEAST, AS AN EPHEMERAL FLY BEGETS, GODHEAD BEGETS GODHEAD,	556	RIBH PATRICK	5
THE FURTHER THAT I FLY". • • • • • • • • • • • •	559	HE AND SHE	10
LONG-LEGGED FLY • • • • • • • • • • • • • •	617	LONG-LEG FLY	T
LIKE A LONG-LEGGED FLY UPON THE STREAM • • • • • • •	617	LONG-LEG FLY	9
LIKE A LONG-LEGGED FLY UPON THE STREAM • • • • • • •	617	LONG-LEG FLY	19
LIKE A LONG-LEGGED FLY UPON THE STREAM • • • • • • •	618	LONG-LEG FLY	29

FLY   (CONTINUED)
   WHAT BRUSHES FLY AND MOTH ASIDE? • • • • • • • • • •   625 NATIVITY   7
   THAT HAD A SOUND FLY FISHER'S WRIST • • • • • • • •   625 OLD MEN BE MAD V   3
   FLY! FLY! SO THESE BRAVE SHEPHERDS BOTH ARE GONE! • • •   649 ISLE STAT I 1   112
   FLY! FLY! SO THESE BRAVE SHEPHERDS BOTH ARE GONE! • • •   649 ISLE STAT I 1   112
   BEFORE I AM TOO WEAK, FIERCE MORTAL, LET ME FLY, • • • •   675 ISLE STAT II 3   245
   BEFORE I AM TOO WEAK, OH LET ME FLY, • • • • • • • •   675 ISLE STAT II 3 V   245
   ALL THESE ARE SOULS THAT FLY FROM THEIR DREAD SELVES. • •   686 LIFE   4
   OH, SWALLOWS, SWALLOWS, SWALLOWS, WILL YE FLY • • • • •   699 MOSADA 3   1
   WE'LL FLY FROM THIS BEFORE THE MORNING STAR. • • • • •   702 MOSADA 3   74
   GOD! THEY'RE MAD TO FLY SUCH CANVAS!" • • •   718 PHANTOM SHIP   14
   "THE SWIFTEST HE TO DANCE OR FLY, • • • • • • • • •   729 PRIEST FAIRY   45
   ALL THESE ARE SOULS WHO FLY FROM THEIR DREAD SELVES. • •   734 QUATRAIN APHOR   4
   ALL THESE ARE SOULS THAT FLY FROM THEIR DREAD SELVES. • •   734 QUATRAIN APHOR V   4
   THEY ARE CHANGED AND AS GREY BIRDS FLY OUT TO SEA, • • •   750 SHADOW WATER A   82
   AND FLY AMONG THE FOAM. THRUST DOWN THE HELM, • • • •   750 SHADOW WATER A   88
   WHEN ALL GATHER THEY WILL FLY UPON THEIR WAY. • • • •   753 SHADOW WATER A   136
   AND NOW THEY ALL WHEEL SUDDENLY AND FLY • • • • • •   753 SHADOW WATER A   148
   TILL HIS EDAINE, NO LONGER A GOLDEN FLY • • • • • •   757 SHADOW WATER A   210
   TILL HIS EDAINE, NO MORE A SILVER FLY • • • • • • •   757 SHADOW WATER A V   210
   WHEN MIDHER'S WIFE HAD CHANGED HER TO A FLY • • • • •   763 SHADOW WATER A   305
   AND WHEN ONE CHANGED HER TO A SILVER FLY, • • • • •   763 SHADOW WATER A V   305
FLY-CATCHERS
   FLY-CATCHERS OF THE MOON, • • • • • • • • • • • •   488 CRAZED MOON   13
FLY-FISHER'S
   THAT HAD A SOUND FLY-FISHER'S WRIST • • • • • • • •   625 OLD MEN BE MAD   3
FLYING
   I CHASED AT MORN THE FLYING DEER, • • • • • • • • •   10 OISIN 1   121
   I CHASED WITH HOUNDS THE FLYING DEER, • • • • • • •   10 OISIN 1   V 121
   AFAR FROM WHERE THE YEARS ARE FLYING • • • • • • •   22 OISIN 1   V 340A
   HE TOLD OF EVERY FROTH-DROP HISSING, FLYING. • • • •   32 OISIN 2   V 45
   CAME FLYING, HEAVY AND SAD! • • • • • • • • • • •   93 FATHER OHART   34
   FLYING, CRYING, TO AND FRO, • • • • • • • • • • •   136 TWO TREES   35
   PEERING AND FLYING TO AND FRO, • • • • • • • • •   136 TWO TREES   V 35
   THE MEASURE OF HER FLYING FEET • • • • • • • • • •   138 TO IRELAND   11
   THE LIGHT FALL OF HER FLYING FEET • • • • • • • •   138 TO IRELAND   V 11
   TWO SWANS CAME FLYING UP TO HIM, • • • • • • • •   194 BAILE AILLINN   135
   AND THAT YOU COME FROM EDEN ON FLYING FEET. • • • •   218 WOODS OF COOLE   29
   AND FLYING TOWARDS THEIR PEACE. PUT BY THESE THOUGHTS,   226 SHADOW WATER B   91
   AND YET IN FLYING FLING INTO MY MEAT • • • • • • •   384 VISION ROBART   53
   OVER HER SPOTTED FLESH AND FLYING HAIR • • • • • •   687 TWO TITANS   15
   WHEN FLYING TO THE HEART OF LIGHT • • • • • • • •   742 DANAAN QUICK   8
FOAL
   'GAT THE FOAL OF THE WORLD." • • • • • • • • • • •   529 TOM CRUACHAN   6
FOAM   SEE SEA-FOAM
   TO THIS DIM SHORE ON FOAM WET FEET? • • • • • • • •   5 OISIN 1   V 51
   RAN THROUGH THE FOAM AND RAN TO THIS • • • • • • •   6 OISIN 1   58
   THAT YOU THROUGH ALL THAT FOAM SHOULD RUN?" • • • •   6 OISIN 1   61
   FOR LOVE OF OISIN FOAM WET FEET • • • • • • • • •   6 OISIN 1   V 57
   OF DREAMY FOAM A STAFF OF WOOD • • • • • • • • • •   24 OISIN 1   366
   WHITE FLOWERS OF THE FOAM A STAFF OF WOOD • • • • •   24 OISIN 1   V 366
   ROOTED IN FOAM AND CLOUDS, AND CRIED TO ALL • • • •   38 OISIN 2   132
   ROOTED IN FOAM AND CLOUDS. THERE MIGHTIER MASTERS MET • •   38 OISIN 2   V 132
   I FOUND, DROPPING SEA FOAM ON THE WIDE STAIR, • • • •   43 OISIN 2   V 215
   FLED FOAM UNDERNEATH US, AND ROUND US, A WANDERING AND   47 OISIN 3   1
     MILKY SMOKE,
   FLED FOAM UNDERNEATH US, AND ROUND US, A WANDERING AND   47 OISIN 3   12
     MILKY SMOKE.
   FLED FOAM UNDERNEATH US, AND AROUND US, A WANDERING AND   47 OISIN 3   V   1
     MILKY SMOKE.
   FLED FOAM UNDERNEATH ME, AND ROUND ME, A WANDERING AND   57 OISIN 3   148
     MILKY SMOKE.
   LIKE AN ARMY OF OLD MEN LOUNGING FOR REST FROM THE FOAM   57 OISIN 3   V 144
     OF THE SEAS.
   UNDER THE PASSING STARS, FOAM OF THE SKY, • • • • •   112 ROSE OF WORLD   9
   MORE FLEETING THAN THE SEA'S FOAM FICKLE FACE, • • • •   112 ROSE OF WORLD V   8
   I WOULD THAT WE WERE, MY BELOVED, WHITE BIRDS ON THE FOAM   121 WHITE BIRDS   1
     OF THE SEA!
   O WOULD THAT WE WERE, MY BELOVED, WHITE BIRDS ON THE FOAM   121 WHITE BIRDS   V   1
     OF THE SEA,
   • • • ON THE WANDERING FOAM! I AND YOU! • • • • • •   122 WHITE BIRDS   8
   • • • BUOYED OUT ON THE FOAM OF THE SEA! • • • • • •   122 WHITE BIRDS   12
   AND CANDLE-LIKE FOAM ON THE DIM SAND, • • • • • •   158 BELOVED RHYMES   10
   ON THE ISLAND LAWNS, THEIR FEET WHERE THE PALE FOAM GLEAMS.   203 WITHER BOUGHS   14
   IT WHIRLS INTO THE FOAM. O ANCIENT WORM! • • • • •   251 SHADOW WATER B   597
   DANCED IN THE WHIRLING FOAM AND IN THE DUST, • • • •   284 TWO KINGS   167
   AND SAW A FLAKE OF THE YELLOW FOAM • • • • • • •   309 PLAYER QUEEN   15
   I SAW A FLAKE OF YELLOW FOAM • • • • • • • • • •   309 PLAYER QUEEN   V 15
   CUCHULAIN THAT FOUGHT NIGHT LONG WITH THE FOAM, • • • •   549 SEVERED HEAD   9
   THE MANY-HEADED FOAM AT SALAMIS. • • • • • • • •   610 STATUES   14
   EUROPE PUT OFF THAT FOAM WHEN PHIDIAS • • • • • •   610 STATUES   15
   COPULATE IN THE FOAM. • • • • • • • • • • • • •   612 NEWS ORACLE   36
   FOR EVER FOAM AND FRET! • • • • • • • • • • • •   680 LOVE AND DEATH   4
   AND FLY AMONG THE FOAM. THRUST DOWN THE HELM, • • • •   750 SHADOW WATER A   88
   THE WHITE FOOL MAKES AT MORNING OUT OF FOAM! • • • •   761 SHADOW WATER A   261
   HER EYELIDS TREMBLE AND THE WHITE FOAM FADES! • • • •   761 SHADOW WATER A   264
   THE STARS WOULD HURL THEIR CROWNS AMONG THE FOAM • • •   761 SHADOW WATER A   265
FOAMDROP
   OF EVERY FOAMDROP ON ITS MISTY WAY. • • • • • • • •   32 OISIN 2   45
FOAMDROPS
   AMONG THE FOAMDROPS OF THE SEA, • • • • • • • • •   20 OISIN 1   294

		PAGE	TITLE		LINE

FOAM-FICKLE
    MORE FLEETING THAN THE SEA'S FOAM-FICKLE FACE, ... 112 ROSE OF WORLD V 8
FOAM-FLAKES
    LONG FLED THE FOAM-FLAKES AROUND ME, THE WINDS FLED OUT 57 OISIN 3 149
        OF THE VAST,
FOAM-GLOBES
    HER SPIRIT. AS SHE MOVES, THE FOAM-GLOBES BURST . . . . 687 TWO TITANS 14
FOAMING
    AND NAMED HIM BY SWEET NAMES. A FOAMING TIDE . . . . . 30 OISIN 2 27
    AND PART HIS FOAMING MOUTH WITH EAGER EYE-- . . . . . 688 TWO TITANS 46
FOAM-OOZY
    I FOUND, FOAM-OOZY ON THE VASTY STAIR, ... 43 OISIN 2 V 215
FOAM-PALE
    . . . FROM THE FOAM-PALE DISTANCE BROKE: . . . . . . 47 OISIN 3 3
FOAM-WET
    THROUGH BITTER TIDE ON FOAM-WET FEET? . . . . 5 OISIN 1 51
    TO THIS DIM SHORE ON FOAM-WET FEET? . . . . 5 OISIN 1 V 51
    FOR LOVE OF OISIN FOAM-WET FEET . . . . 6 OISIN 1 V 57
FOAM-WHITE
    I SAW A FOAM-WHITE SEAGULL DRIFT AND FLOAT . . . . . . 36 OISIN 2 105
FOE
    THY WITHERED FOE, AND WITH THE PURPLE WING . . . . . . 688 TWO TITANS 55
FOEMAN'S
    AND HEARD THE FOEMAN'S BUCKLERS RATTLE, ... 10 OISIN 1 V 123
FOEMEN
    NOR TEAR THE FOEMEN FROM THEIR STEEDS. . . . . 11 OISIN 1 128
FOEMEN'S
    AND HEARD THE FOEMEN'S BUCKLERS RATTLE, ... 10 OISIN 1 123
FOG
    FOR I HAVE SEEN A SHIP HID IN THE FOG. . . . . 751 SHADOW WATER A 89
FOG-DRIPPING
    FOG-DRIPPING, PEDESTALLED ABOVE THE TIDE, ... 31 OISIN 2 V 36
FOIL
    THAN DUMB-BELL AND FOIL . . . . 334 SONG 3
    THAN DUMB BELL AND FOIL . . . . 334 SONG V 3
FOILED
    DOWN TO THE MOTHER OF THE FOILED AND DEAD. . . . . . . 688 TWO TITANS 50
FOLD   SEE SEVEN-FOLD THREE-FOLD
    HE, SHAKING THE FOLD OF HIS LIPS, ... 51 OISIN 3 59
    GO TO THE GUARDS OF THE HEAVENLY FOLD . . . . 141 EVERLAST VOICE 2
    FROM BATTLE-BANNERS, FOLD UPON PURPLE FOLD, ... 162 ASKS FORGIVE 11
    FROM BATTLE-BANNERS, FOLD UPON PURPLE FOLD, ... 162 ASKS FORGIVE 11
    FROM BATTLE BANNERS FOLD UPON PURPLE FOLD, ... 162 ASKS FORGIVE V 11
    FROM BATTLE BANNERS FOLD UPON PURPLE FOLD, ... 162 ASKS FORGIVE V 11
    INTO THE FOLD, WE'LL TO THE WOODS AND THERE . . . . . 343 SHEP GOATHERD 114
    WITHIN THE FOLD TO HEAR THE CREAKING GATE-- . . . . . 646 ISLE STAT I 1 41
    OF OCEAN FAN THEE INTO LIFE, AND FOLD . . . . 688 TWO TITANS 56
    OH, WOULD THE BUSY MINUTES MIGHT FOLD UP . . . . . . 702 MOSADA 3 97
    LEST HE MAY SOME GLAMOUR FOLD . . . . 717 FAIRY DOCTOR 22
    LEST SOME GLAMOUR HE MAY FOLD . . . . 717 FAIRY DOCTOR V 22
FOLDED   SEE MANY-FOLDED
    FOLDED LIKE A FROZEN FLY: . . . . 19 OISIN 1 273
    FOLDED IN LOVE THAT FEARS NO MORROW, ... 23 OISIN 1 341
    AND HER HAIR WAS A FOLDED FLOWER . . . . 161 CAP AND BELLS 35
    BUT DATHI FOLDED HIS HANDS AND SMILED . . . . 167 BLESSED 11
    TO DREAM OF WOMEN WHOSE BEAUTY WAS FOLDED IN DISMAY, . . 210 UNDER THE MOON 19
    THE WORLD, WITHIN HIS FOLDED HEART, ... 671 ISLE STAT II 3 133
    WHEN SOMETHING FOLDED AND SMALL . . . . 744 GLOVE CLOAK 7
    WHEN EARTH AND HEAVEN HAVE BEEN FOLDED UP: . . . . . 765 SHADOW WATER A 366
FOL DE ROL
    FOL DE ROL, FOL DE ROL. . . . . 509 JANE REPROVED 7
    FOL DE ROL, FOL DE ROL. . . . . 509 JANE REPROVED 7
    FOL DE ROL, FOL DE ROL. . . . . 509 JANE REPROVED 14
    FOL DE ROL, FOL DE ROL. . . . . 509 JANE REPROVED 14
    IS FOL DE ROL DE ROLLY O. . . . . 592 PILGRIM 5
    BUT FOL DE ROL DE ROLLY O. . . . . 593 PILGRIM 10
    WAS FOL DE ROL DE ROLLY O. . . . . 593 PILGRIM 15
    BUT FOL DE ROL DE ROLLY O. . . . . 593 PILGRIM 20
    IS FOL DE ROL DE ROLLY O. . . . . 593 PILGRIM 25
FOLDING
    IS FOLDING AND UNFOLDING, AND IN ITS FOLDS, ... 751 SHADOW WATER A 99
    TO CRY HIS FOLDING CRY! NO, NO, BE SILENT, ... 760 SHADOW WATER A 253
    TO CRY HIS FOLDING CRY. THERE IS SOME MAN . . . . . 760 SHADOW WATER A V 253
    FOLDING THEIR HEARTS' DESIRE TO THEIR GLAD HEARTS. . . . 765 SHADOW WATER A 349
FOLDS
    HE, SHAKING THE FOLDS OF HIS LIPS . . . . 51 OISIN 3 V 59
    AND IN FOLDS ROUND HIS EYES AND HIS MOUTH, ... 59 OISIN 3 174
    IN THE CONFUSION OF ITS NIGHT-DARK FOLDS, ... 470 HARUN RASHID 192
    THE HEART OF NOON FOLDS SILENCE AND FOLDS SLEEP, . . . 735 QUATRAIN APHOR 25
    THE HEART OF NOON FOLDS SILENCE AND FOLDS SLEEP, . . . 735 QUATRAIN APHOR 25
    IS FOLDING AND UNFOLDING, AND IN ITS FOLDS . . . . . 751 SHADOW WATER A 99
FOLIAGE
    ABOUNDING FOLIAGE MOISTENED WITH THE DEW: . . . . . 500 VACILLATION 13
    NO LONGER IN LETHEAN FOLIAGE CAUGHT . . . . 500 VACILLATION 27
    DRY TIMBER UNDER THAT RICH FOLIAGE, ... 536 HER VISION 1
    RICH FOLIAGE THAT THE STARLIGHT GLITTERED THROUGH, . . . 541 PARN FUNERAL 1 8
    THROUGH LIGHT-OBLITERATING GARDEN FOLIAGE WHAT MAGIC DRUM? 560 MAGIC DRUM 4
    FOR THE DAWN THE FOLIAGE FINGERETH, ... 646 ISLE STAT I 1 26
    FOR THE DAWN OF FOLIAGE FINGERETH, ... 646 ISLE STAT I 1 V 26
FOLK
    UNDER THE STARLIGHT AND SHADOW, A MONSTROUS SLUMBERING 48 OISIN 3 27
        FOLK,

		PAGE	TITLE		LINE

FOLK (CONTINUED)

FROM HIS HOOVES IN THE HEAVY GRASSES, WITH MONSTROUS SLUMBERING FOLK, — 48 OISIN 3 V 27
AND ALL FOLK SEEING HIM BOW DOWN, — 113 ROSE OF PEACE 9
THE FOLK WHO ARE BUYING AND SELLING, — 119 PITY OF LOVE 3
OLD SILENCE BIDS A LONELY FOLK REJOICE, — 127 DREAM OF FAERY V 31
AND TALKED OF THE DARK FOLK WHO LIVE IN SOULS — 136 TO SOME I TALK 4
OF THAT DARK FOLK WHO GATHER IN THE SOULS — 136 TO SOME I TALK V 4
THE FOLK OF THE AIR — 143 HOST OF AIR V T
FOR THESE WERE THE FOLK OF THE AIR, — 144 HOST OF AIR V 26
HE KNEW NOW THE FOLK OF THE AIR, — 145 HOST OF AIR V 40A
FOLK DANCE LIKE A WAVE OF THE SEA, — 178 FIDDLER DOONEY 2
AND WHEN THE FOLK THERE SPY ME, — 179 FIDDLER DOONEY 17
AND THE FOLK THERE WHEN THEY SPY ME — 179 FIDDLER DOONEY V 17

FOLKS

AND WHEN THE FOLKS THERE SPY ME, — 179 FIDDLER DOONEY V 17

FOLKS'

I'D GLAD FOLKS' HEARTS WITH BLITHER SONG." — 731 PRIEST FAIRY 82

FOLLOW

SHALL FOLLOW YOUR HORN AND OBEY YOUR WHIM, — 9 OISIN 1 99
WHO FOLLOW WITH THE OPTIC GLASS — 66 HAPPY SHEPHERD 29
UNDER MY FEET THAT THEY FOLLOW YOU NIGHT AND DAY, — 153 CHANGE BELOVED 5
UNDER MY FEET, THAT I FOLLOW YOU, NIGHT AND DAY, — 153 CHANGE BELOVED V 5
AND FOLLOW THE WAY OF THE WIND, — 168 BLESSED 28
AND NOW THEY WILL NOT FOLLOW, WHILE I SEEK — 226 SHADOW WATER B 95
THEY HAVE MADE YOU FOLLOW THE MAN-HEADED BIRDS, — 231 SHADOW WATER B 204
THEY HAVE BADE YOU FOLLOW THE MAN-HEADED BIRDS, — 231 SHADOW WATER B V 204
WE HAVE TO FOLLOW, FOR THEY ARE OUR PILOTS, — 247 SHADOW WATER B 527
AND I WILL FOLLOW YOU AND CUT THE ROPE — 250 SHADOW WATER B 586
AND DISCORD FOLLOW UPON UNISON, — 265 THESE CLOUDS 5
I AM CONTENT TO FOLLOW TO ITS SOURCE — 479 SELF AND SOUL 65
TO FOLLOW IS TO DIE, — 600 SPIRIT MEDIUM 18
ARISE THOU AND FOLLOW, — 654 ISLE STAT I 2 57
AND FOLLOW, AND FOLLOW, — 654 ISLE STAT I 2 69
AND FOLLOW, AND FOLLOW, — 654 ISLE STAT I 2 69
COME FOLLOW, COME FOLLOW, — 654 ISLE STAT I 2 79
COME FOLLOW, COME FOLLOW, — 654 ISLE STAT I 2 79
ARISE, WORM, AND FOLLOW, — 655 ISLE STAT I 2 83
I, TOO, WILL FOLLOW FOR THIS EVIL-STARRED ONE'S SAKE — 655 ISLE STAT I 2 84
HIS SLEUTH-HOUNDS FOLLOW EVERY FAERY THING. — 675 ISLE STAT II 3 244
DID I NOT FOLLOW WITH A SCORE OF SHIPS? — 749 SHADOW WATER A 36
AND NOW THEY ARE ALL GONE, I FOLLOW STILL. — 749 SHADOW WATER A 37
OR BE HIS FOOD, I FOLLOW THE GREY WINGS, — 751 SHADOW WATER A 101
SHE BIDS US FOLLOW HER. I HAVE GROWN WEARY — 758 SHADOW WATER A 218
HAVE CALLED HIM MIGHTY. I WILL FOLLOW YOU — 768 SHADOW WATER A 412
I WILL FOLLOW YOU. I WILL HAVE NONE OF YOU. — 768 SHADOW WATER A 415
PITY THESE WEEPING EYES, I WILL FOLLOW YOU. — 768 SHADOW WATER A 420
SO WORTHY AMONG MEN. I FOLLOW YOU, — 768 SHADOW WATER A V 412
THAT HE FOLLOW WITH DESIRE — 776 AGAINST WITCH 19
THAT THEY FOLLOW, FOR AT MOST — 776 AGAINST WITCH 28

FOLLOWED

WHEN WE FOLLOWED A DEER WITH OUR BAYING HOUNDS, — 3 OISIN 1 14
AND A BEAUTIFUL YOUNG MAN FOLLOWED BEHIND — 12 OISIN 1 144
A BEAUTIFUL YOUNG MAN FOLLOWED BEHIND. — 12 OISIN 1 V 145
THAT FOLLOWED MY KEEN HUNTING-CALL-- — 23 OISIN 1 V 345F
FOR LOVE THEY FOLLOWED ONE AND ALL, — 23 OISIN 1 V 345G
AND THOSE THAT FLED, AND THAT FOLLOWED, — 47 OISIN 3 3
I TURNED AND RODE TO THE WESTWARD, AND FOLLOWED THE SEA'S OLD SHOUT — 60 OISIN 3 183
HOW I HAVE FOLLOWED, NIGHT AND DAY, — 85 MAD KING GOLL 53
THIS WHOLE DAY HAVE I FOLLOWED IN THE ROCKS, — 102 FERGUS DRUID 1
THE WHOLE DAY HAVE I FOLLOWED IN THE ROCKS, — 102 FERGUS DRUID V 1
SHE FOLLOWED WITH LIGHT FOOTFALL IN THE MIDST, — 186 QUEEN MAEVE 128
AND FOLLOWED UP THOSE BAYING CREATURES TOWARDS-- — 412 TOWER 72
AND FOLLOWED THROUGH THE EMPTY STREET, AND SHE, — 468 HARUN RASHID V 154A
DREAD HAS FOLLOWED LONGING, — 519 LOVES LONENESS 11
THAT FOLLOWED IF I LET THE KERCHIEF FALL, — 533 HER TRIUMPH 4
"A GIRL I HAD, BUT SHE FOLLOWED ANOTHER, — 544 TO SAME TUNE 1 11
"A GIRL I HAD, BUT SHE FOLLOWED ANOTHER, — 616 MARCH SONGS 3 11
I FOLLOWED HIM FROM MY GREEN LAIR, — 655 ISLE STAT I 3 6
FOLLOWED A RINGDOVE'S ASH-GREY GLEAM OF FEATHER. — 715 DWELT SYCAMORE 6
FOLLOWED THE RING-DOVE'S ASH-GREY GLEAM OF FEATHER. — 715 DWELT SYCAMORE 6
BUT THAT THE WIND CHANGED, FOR I FOLLOWED HIM — 747 SHADOW WATER A 4
WHY DID YOU SAY THAT I HAVE FOLLOWED HIM — 761 SHADOW WATER A 267
THAT FORGAEL HAS FOLLOWED THE GREY BIRDS ALONE, — 767 SHADOW WATER A 402

FOLLOWERS

HAYNAU, THINE HOUR HAS COME, THY FOLLOWERS FAR — 715 FERENCZ RENYI 117

FOLLOWING

AND FOLLOWING HER AT A HEADLONG SPEED — 12 OISIN 1 V 144
AND FOLLOWING O'ER THE FIELDS AND PASTURE LANDS, — 715 FERENCZ RENYI V 120
OF FOLLOWING FORGAEL'S DREAM FROM WIND TO WIND. — 758 SHADOW WATER A 219

FOLLOWS

HOW THE FALCONER FOLLOWS THE FALCON IN THE WEEDS OF THE HERON'S PLOT, — 52 OISIN 3 79
THAT FOLLOWS AFTER. I UNDERSTAND YOU NOW. — 237 SHADOW WATER B 341
HE FOLLOWS WHATEVER WHIM'S MOST DIFFICULT — 374 PHASES OF MOON 40
IT FOLLOWS FROM THIS LATIN TEXT — 386 ROBARTES DANCE 43
MUST NEEDS BE IN THIS LIFE AND IN WHAT FOLLOWS — 465 HARUN RASHID 95
A RED-EARED HOUND FOLLOWS A HORNLESS DEER. — 764 SHADOW WATER A 325

FOLLY

YOU PUT SUCH FOLLY IN OUR HEADS — 190 BAILE AILLINN 32

295

		PAGE	TITLE	LINE

FOLLY   (CONTINUED)
```
    THE FOLLY OF BEING COMFORTED  . . . . . . . . .    199 FOLLY COMFORT        T
    YOU'D KNOW THE FOLLY OF BEING COMFORTED. . . . .    200 FOLLY COMFORT       14
    TO SUCH A PITCH OF FOLLY I AM BROUGHT, . . . . .    384 VISION ROBART       58
    ALL THE FOLLY OF A FIGHT . . . . . . . . . . . .    476 EVA GORE-BOOTH      22
    THE FOLLY THAT MAN DOES  . . . . . . . . . . . .    479 SELF AND SOUL       62
    OR OUT OF FOLLY INTO FOLLY CAME. . . . . . . . .    491 COOLE BALLYLEE      32
    OR OUT OF FOLLY INTO FOLLY CAME. . . . . . . . .    491 COOLE BALLYLEE      32
    IF FOLLY LINK WITH ELEGANCE  . . . . . . . . . .    598 STONE CROSS         13
    IF FOLLY LINKS WITH ELEGANCE . . . . . . . . . .    598 STONE CROSS     V   13
    I GO AS SOFT AS FOLLY; I AM FATE." . . . . . . .    686 LIFE                18
    I GO AS SOFT AS FOLLY; I AM FATE." . . . . . . .    735 QUATRAIN APHOR      20
FOND
    OF KNITTED MUSIC.  OFT THE FOND REPINING . . . . .   33 OISIN 2         V  68C
FONDER
    BUT IMAGES TO MAKE ME FONDER? . . . . . . . . .    390 IMAGE PAST          35
FONDLE
    COULD FONDLE THE LEAVES WITH HIS FINGERS, . . . .   49 OISIN 3             38
    IT SEEMS TO FONDLE, WITH A FINGER BRIGHT . . . .   714 FERENCZ RENYI      114
FONDLED
    HE SPAKE ONCE MORE AND FONDLED WITH HIS LIPS . . .  81 EPHEMERA        V  24A
    RINGED ROUND AND FONDLED, A BROWN FARM HOUSE SEES. . 710 FERENCZ RENYI   V   23
FOOD
    AND CARRIED HIM HIS FOOD WITH MY OWN HANDS, . . .  280 TWO KINGS           88
    AND FOR NINE DAYS HE HAD FOOD FROM OTHER HANDS, .  282 TWO KINGS          126
    THEIR FOOD AND DRINK; . . . . . . . . . . . . .   380 SONGS FOOL 1         9
    WHAT WHOLESOME SUN HAS RIPENED IS WHOLESOME FOOD TO EAT, 442 BLACK CENTAUR    5
    A LOVE THAT LACKS ITS PROPER FOOD; . . . . . . .   569 THREE BUSHES         3
    I KEEP SUCH THINGS ABOUT ME; THEY ARE FOOD . . .   721 WITCH VIVIEN        37
    HER RAVEN FLUTTERS.  ROB HIM OF HIS FOOD . . . .   751 SHADOW WATER A     100
    OR BE HIS FOOD, I FOLLOW THE GREY WINGS, . . . .   751 SHADOW WATER A     101
FOOL
    AND THE FOOL HEART OF THE COUNTING-HOUSE FEARS ALL  181 QUEEN MAEVE        21
    HOW ARE WE BETTER OFF THAN SEAGHAN THE FOOL, . .   228 SHADOW WATER B    129
    WE HAVE BEEN NO BETTER OFF THAN SEAGHAN THE FOOL,  228 SHADOW WATER B  V 129
    FOOL, FOOL! ALTHOUGH YOU HAVE LOOKED INTO MY FACE  238 SHADOW WATER B    356
    FOOL, FOOL! ALTHOUGH YOU HAVE LOOKED INTO MY FACE  238 SHADOW WATER B    356
    THAT DROVE YOU TO IT, AND I FOOL ENOUGH . . . .   248 SHADOW WATER B    548
    TO VALUE BEER; NO HALF-LEGGED FOOL . . . . . . .   304 HOUR DAWN           52
    TO JUDGE IF A LIGHT SLEEPING FOOL . . . . . . .   304 HOUR DAWN       V   52
    TO VALUE BEER--I WILL HAVE NO FOOL . . . . . . .   304 HOUR DAWN       V   52
    AS WHEN I ALSO PLAYED THE FOOL." . . . . . . . .   306 HOUR DAWN           79
    THERE IS NOT A FOOL CAN CALL ME FRIEND, . . . .   336 YOUNG BEAUTY        16
    THAT NOT A FOOL CAN CALL ME FRIEND, . . . . . .   336 YOUNG BEAUTY    V   16
    HE CAME, BUT MAN IS A FOOL." . . . . . . . . . .   341 SHEP GOATHERD       74
    I HEARD HIM FIRST, BUT MAN IS A FOOL." . . . . .   341 SHEP GOATHERD       74
    HAS SET ME MUTTERING LIKE A FOOL. . . . . . . .   356 BROKEN DREAMS       26
    HUNCHBACK AND SAINT AND FOOL ARE THE LAST CRESCENTS. 377 PHASES OF MOON  118
    "HUNCHBACK AND SAINT AND FOOL," AND THAT THEY CAME  377 PHASES OF MOON  132
    TWO SONGS OF A FOOL  . . . . . . . . . . . . . .   380 SONGS FOOL 1         T
    THAT AM A WANDERING-WITTED FOOL . . . . . . . .   380 SONGS FOOL 1        16
    THAT AM A WANDERING WITTED FOOL . . . . . . . .   380 SONGS FOOL 1    V   16
    ANOTHER SONG OF A FOOL . . . . . . . . . . . . .   381 SONG OF FOOL         T
    NOT A POOR FOOL UNDERSTANDS. . . . . . . . . . .   381 SONG OF FOOL         4
    AND LATER HAD MUCH TROUBLE FROM A FOOL, . . . .   404 FOR DAUGHTER        26
    YET MANY, THAT HAVE PLAYED THE FOOL . . . . . .   404 FOR DAUGHTER        36
    THROUGH TOO MUCH PLAY, OR MARRIAGE WITH A FOOL? .  423 MY DESCENDANTS      12
    THE HERO, THE GIRL AND THE FOOL . . . . . . . .   447 HERO GIRL FOOL       T
    CUCHULAIN THE GIRL AND THE FOOL . . . . . . . .   447 HERO GIRL FOOL  V    T
    BOOK IV  THE GATES OF PLUTO  I.  THE FOOL BY THE ROADSIDE 447 HERO GIRL FOOL V T
    WHEN THOUGHTS THAT A FOOL . . . . . . . . . . .   449 HERO GIRL FOOL      21
    CARRIED BY THE WANDERING FOOL. . . . . . . . . .   484 SYMBOLS              4
    BEAUTY AND FOOL TOGETHER LAID. . . . . . . . . .   484 SYMBOLS              6
    FOOL, RASCAL, KNAVE, . . . . . . . . . . . . . .   496 MOHINI CHATTER       8
    I RANTED TO THE KNAVE AND FOOL, . . . . . . . .   506 REMORSE SPEECH       1
    GREAT EUROPA PLAYED THE FOOL . . . . . . . . . .   509 JANE REPROVED        5
    FOR THE SONG'S SAKE A FOOL? . . . . . . . . . .   553 PRAYER OLD AGE       8
    BUT NOTHING SATISFIED THE FOOL . . . . . . . . .   620 JOHN KINSELLA        7
    AND WHEN THE FOOL AND BLIND MAN STOLE THE BREAD .  630 CIRCUS ANIMALS      25
    OR WHISPER THAT A MAN'S A FOOL . . . . . . . . .   635 BLACK TOWER         12
    THE WORLD GROWS OLD AND PLAYS THE FOOL." . . . .   725 LEGEND              12
    OUT OF THAT ISLAND WHERE THE FOOL OF THE WOOD . .  747 SHADOW WATER A       2
    NINE MOONS.  AND FROM THE HARPING OF THE FOOL? .  747 SHADOW WATER A      14
    I HAD KILLED HIM LONG AGO, BUT THAT THE FOOL . .  748 SHADOW WATER A      17
    THE FOOL FORETOLD ME I WOULD FIND THIS LOVE . .   750 SHADOW WATER A      62
    THE FOOL THAT CAME OUT OF THE WINTRY WOOD . . .   750 SHADOW WATER A      75
    IT WAS A FOOL THAT GAVE IT, AND MAY BE . . . .   750 SHADOW WATER A      78
    THE WHITE FOOL MAKES AT MORNING OUT OF FOAM; . .  761 SHADOW WATER A     261
    ALL DIES AMONG THOSE STREAMS.  THE FOOL HAS MADE  764 SHADOW WATER A     335
    THE FOOL, WHO HAS MADE THE WISDOM THAT MEN WRITE  764 SHADOW WATER A     342
FOOL-DRIVEN
    THE SEEMING NEEDS OF MY FOOL-DRIVEN LAND; . . . .  267 ALL TEMPT ME         3
FOOLED
    AND SAID:  "SHE HAS FOOLED ME ENOUGH," . . . . .   744 GLOVE CLOAK          3
FOOLISH
    BUT I, BEING YOUNG AND FOOLISH, WITH HER WOULD NOT AGREE. 90 SALLEY GARDENS  4
    BUT I WAS YOUNG AND FOOLISH, AND NOW AM FULL OF TEARS. . 90 SALLEY GARDENS  8
    IN ALL POOR FOOLISH THINGS THAT LIVE A DAY, . .   101 ROSE UPON ROOD      11
    A KING IS BUT A FOOLISH LABOURER . . . . . . . .   103 FERGUS DRUID        27
    I'D PUT AWAY THE FOOLISH MIGHT OF A KING, . . . .  103 FERGUS DRUID    V  21A
    A WILD AND FOOLISH LABOURER IS A KING . . . . .   103 FERGUS DRUID    V   27
```

                                        296

FOOLISH   (CONTINUED)
   THE LAPWING AT THEIR FOOLISH CRIES . . . . 306 HOUR DAWN 77
   A FOOLISH, PASSIONATE MAN. . . . . 553 PRAYER OLD AGE 12
   A FOOLISH WORD THOU GAVEST ME! . . . . 671 ISLE STAT II 3 131
   OH, I AM WEARY OF THAT FOOLISH TALE. . . . . 721 WITCH VIVIEN 33
   LEAD THEY ONE WITH FOOLISH CARE, ... 727 LOVERS QUARREL 29
   YONDER FOOLISH ONES WILL TIRE . . . . 727 LOVERS QUARREL 47
FOOL'S
   THE FOOL'S TRIUMPH, NOR YET . . . . 312 CHILD DANCING 7
FOOLS
   AND THERE, FOR ALL THAT FOOLS HAD SAID, ... 190 BAILE AILLINN 23
   ALL THAT GREAT PAST TO A TROUBLE OF FOOLS! . . . . . 546 TO SAME TUNE 2 22
   LET THE FOOLS RAGE, I SWERVED IN NAUGHT, ... 577 WHAT THEN 18
   THAT OFFICE FOOLS HAVE RUN, ... 598 MODEL LAUREATE 20
   ALL THAT GREAT PAST TO A TROUBLE OF FOOLS! . . . . . 614 MARCH SONGS 1 22
   AND I MUST LOSE MORE TIME BECAUSE THESE FOOLS . . . 754 SHADOW WATER A 158
FOOT
   TYING THE HORSE TO HIS VAST FOOT THAT LAY . . . . . 32 OISIN 2 46
   TO ONE VAST FOOT, FROTH-SPLASHED, WITH CURVED TOES LYING 32 OISIN 2 V 46A
   AND THERE AT THE FOOT OF THE MOUNTAIN, ... 60 OISIN 3 185
   WE FOOT IT ALL THE NIGHT, ... 87 STOLEN CHILD 16
   WHY MUST YOU BLENCH AND SHAKE FROM FOOT TO CROWN?" . 106 CUCHULAIN SEA 13
   WHY ARE YOU PALE AND SHAKE FROM FOOT TO CROWN?" . . 106 CUCHULAIN SEA V 13
   ON FOOT, ON HORSEBACK OR IN BATTLE-CARS." . . . . . 107 CUCHULAIN SEA 30
   THAT IF A DANCER STAYED HIS HUNGRY FOOT . . . . . . 127 DREAM OF FAERY 22
   TO HELP HER LIGHT FOOT HERE AND THERE, ... 138 TO IRELAND V 14
   BUT MAEVE, AND NOT WITH A SLOW FEEBLE FOOT, ... 185 QUEEN MAEVE 107
   FOOT AFTER FOOT WAS GIVING WAY, ... 274 GREY ROCK 72
   FOOT AFTER FOOT WAS GIVING WAY, ... 274 GREY ROCK 72
   TO THAT ROCK-BORN, ROCK-WANDERING FOOT, ... 276 GREY ROCK 125
   SOME PASSION HAD MADE HER STONE. HEARING A FOOT . . 279 TWO KINGS 65
   SHE STARTED AND THEN KNEW WHOSE FOOT IT WAS; . . . . 280 TWO KINGS 66
   STOOD ON MY PATH. TREMBLING FROM HEAD TO FOOT . . . 283 TWO KINGS 151
   STOOD ON MY PATH. TREMBLING FROM HAND TO FOOT . . . 283 TWO KINGS V 151
   NOR CAN TIME WASTE THE CHEEK, NOR IS THERE FOOT . . 284 TWO KINGS 182
   THAT THERE BE NO FOOT SILENT IN THE ROOM . . . . . 311 MOUNTAIN TOMB 6
   LET THERE BE NO FOOT SILENT IN THE ROOM, ... 311 MOUNTAIN TOMB V 6
   I SHAKE FROM HEAD TO FOOT. . . . . 316 FRIENDS 28
   WHERE EVERY FOOT OBEYED HER GLANCE! . . . . 488 CRAZED MOON 11
   WHERE VERY FOOT OBEYED HER GLANCE! . . . . 488 CRAZED MOON V 11
   WRINKLED LIKE THE FOOT OF A GOOSE, ... 508 JANE BISHOP 16
   A BEGGAR UPON HORSEBACK LASHES A BEGGAR ON FOOT. . . 590 GREAT DAY 2
   A BEGGAR UPON HORSEBACK LASHES A BEGGAR UPON FOOT! . 590 GREAT DAY V 2
   WHAT IF MY GREAT-GRANDDAD HAD A PAIR THAT WERE TWENTY FOOT 622 HIGH TALK 2
      HIGH,
   AND MINE WERE BUT FIFTEEN FOOT, NO MODERN STALKS 623 HIGH TALK 3
      UPON HIGHER,
   NO SHEPHERD FOOT HAS EVER DARED ITS DEPTHS. . . . . . 682 SEEKER 32
   WOULD THEY FOOT SO FLEET A MEASURE? . . . . 731 STREET DANCERS 12
   WOULD THEY FOOT SO FLEET A MEASURE? . . . . 732 STREET DANCERS 25
   WOULD THEY FOOT SO FLEET A MEASURE? . . . . 732 STREET DANCERS 38
   WOULD THEY FOOT SO FLEET A MEASURE? . . . . 733 STREET DANCERS 51
   WOULD THEY FOOT SO FLEET A MEASURE? . . . . 733 STREET DANCERS 64
FOOTED   SEE RESTLESS-FOOTED TUMULTUOUS-FOOTED MILLION-FOOTED LAME-FOOTED
FOOTFALL
   AND WHERE OUR FOOTFALL 'LIGHTED LAST THERE CAME . . . 37 OISIN 2 V 119
   SOUNDLESS SHALL BE THE FOOTFALL LIGHT . . . . 70 CLOAK BOAT 13
   A VAPOURY FOOTFALL ON THE OCEAN'S SLEEPY BLAZE. . . . 78 INDIAN TO LOVE V 20
   AND DROP A VAPOURY FOOTFALL IN THE WATER'S DROWSY BLAZE. 78 INDIAN TO LOVE V 20
   FOR GOD GOES BY WITH WHITE FOOTFALL. . . . . 139 TO IRELAND 44
   OF A QUIET AND LIGHT FOOTFALL; . . . . 159 CAP AND BELLS 8
   OF A FOOTFALL HUSHED AND LIGHT . . . . 159 CAP AND BELLS V 8
   MAEVE WALKED, YET WITH SLOW FOOTFALL, BEING OLD, . . 181 QUEEN MAEVE 43
   SHE FOLLOWED WITH LIGHT FOOTFALL IN THE MIDST, . . . 186 QUEEN MAEVE 128
   ITS TERROR GROWING WILDER AT EVERY FOOTFALL . . . . 279 TWO KINGS V 45D
   AND VANITY HER FOOTFALL LIGHT, ... 314 MEMORY YOUTH 12
   WHERE EVERY DAY MY FOOTFALL SHOULD HAVE LIT . . . . 352 PEOPLE 8
   SOUNDLESS SHALL BE THE FOOTFALL LIGHT . . . . 666 ISLE STAT II 3 13
   WHOSE FOOTFALL I HAVE LONGED FOR, THREE SAD SUMMERS. . 692 MOSADA 1 45
   ONE WHOSE FOOTFALL SHAKES THE GROUND. . . . . 727 LOVERS QUARREL 32
   SINGING TO THEIR LIGHT FOOTFALL. . . . . 732 STREET DANCERS 30
FOOT-FALL
   FOR GOD GOES BY WITH WHITE FOOT-FALL. . . . . 139 TO IRELAND V 44
   ON A FOOT-FALL HUSHED AND LIGHT, ... 159 CAP AND BELLS V 8
   OF A QUIET AND LIGHT FOOT-FALL! . . . . 159 CAP AND BELLS V 8
   ITS TERROR GROWING WILDER AT EVERY FOOT-FALL, . . . 279 TWO KINGS V 45D
FOOTING   SEE SLOW-FOOTING
   FOOTING IN THE FEEBLE GLOW, ... 731 STREET DANCERS 10
   FOOTING IN THE FEEBLE GLOW, ... 732 STREET DANCERS 23
   FOOTING IN THE FEEBLE GLOW, ... 732 STREET DANCERS 36
   FOOTING IN THE FEEBLE GLOW, ... 733 STREET DANCERS 62
   FOOTING IN THE FEEBLE GLOW, ... 733 STREET DANCERS V 49
FOOT'S
   SO THAT THE WANDERING FOOT'S CONTENT. . . . . 276 GREY ROCK 131
FOOTSOLE
   WHERE THE FLESH OF THE FOOTSOLE CLINGETH . . . . . . 61 OISIN 3 197
   WHEN THE FLESH OF THE FOOTSOLE CLINGETH . . . . . . 61 OISIN 3 V 197
   WITH VAPOURY FOOTSOLE BY THE WATER'S DROWSY BLAZE. . 78 INDIAN TO LOVE 20
   WITH VAPOURY FOOTSOLE AMONG THE WATER'S DROWSY BLAZE. 78 INDIAN TO LOVE V 20
   DROPPING A VAPOURY FOOTSOLE ON THE TIDE'S DROWSY BLAZE. 78 INDIAN TO LOVE V 20
   LED BY A FOOTSOLE DIPPED IN BLOOD . . . . 274 GREY ROCK 78

FOOT-SOLE
    LED BY A FOOT-SOLE DIPPED IN BLOOD . . . . 274 GREY ROCK   V   78
    EVEN FROM THE FOOT-SOLE THINK IT TOO. . . . . 387 ROBARTES DANCE   51
FOOTSORE
    YET SOMEWHERE IN THE FOOTSORE WORLD WE MEET, ... 691 MOSADA 1   23
FOOTSTEP
    YET SHE GOES WITH FOOTSTEP WARY, ... 124 CATHLEEN PARA   11
    SOFT AS THE WHISPERING OF A LONG-LOST FOOTSTEP . . . . 699 MOSADA 3   5
    SOFT AS A LONG DEAD FOOTSTEP WHISPERING THROUGH . . . 699 MOSADA 3   V   5
    SOFT AS THE WHISPERING OF A LOST FOOTSTEP . . . . . . 699 MOSADA 3   V   5
FOOTSTEPS
    THE CAPTIVES' FOOTSTEPS WRITTEN TO AND FRO; . . . . . 37 OISIN 2   V 118
    STILL SHE GOES WITH FOOTSTEPS WARY, ... 124 CATHLEEN PARA   V 11
    WHITHER HER FOOTSTEPS GO. . . . . 175 ELEMENT POWERS   18
    WHERE HER SOFT FOOTSTEPS GO. . . . . 175 ELEMENT POWERS V 18
FOOTSTOOL
    UPON HIS KNEES BY MY FOOTSTOOL . . . . 82 MAD KING GOLL   V 13
    AND HURLED IT FROM ITS PLACE BEFORE HIS FOOTSTOOL WHITE, 174 ELEMENT POWERS V   3
FOOTWORN
    THE FOOTWORN WAY IS LONG, AND IT GROWS DARK. . . . . . 702 MOSADA 3   V 92
FOOT-WORN
    THE FOOT-WORN WAY IS LONG, AND IT GROWS DARK. . . . . . 702 MOSADA 3   92
FORAY
    WHEN THE FENIANS MADE FORAY AT MORNING WITH BRAN, SCEOLAN, 54 OISIN 3   104
    LOMAIR.
FORBADE
    THOUGH DEATH ITSELF FORBADE. . . . . 789 SINGING HEAD   8
FORBID
    BEING FORBID TO MARRY ON EARTH, ... 189 BAILE AILLINN   11
    FORBID, BESEECH AND WASTE MY BREATH." THEN I; . . . . 281 TWO KINGS   102
FORBIDDEN
    IN THE FORBIDDEN SACRED GROVE . . . . 389 SOLOMON WITCH   39
FORCE
    CAN HAVE THE PURITY OF A NATURAL FORCE, ... 353 PEOPLE   31
    WAS COMING INTO HIS FORCE; . . . . 392 EASTER 1916   27
FORCED
    BUT WHEN AT LAST HE FORCED THOSE SINEWY FLANKS . . . . 278 TWO KINGS   35
    AS THOUGH SHE HAD BEEN FORCED TO LINGER . . . . 390 IMAGE PAST   23
    THE INTELLECT OF MAN IS FORCED TO CHOOSE . . . . 491 COOLE BALLYLEE V 40A
    THE INTELLECT OF MAN IS FORCED TO CHOOSE . . . . 495 CHOICE   1
FORD
    AND THAT LONG FIGHTING AT THE FORD, ... 197 BAILE AILLINN   194
    THE FORD WHERE DRINKING CATTLE MAKE A STIR . . . . . . 326 ROBERT GREGORY   53
'FORE
    TWO THINGS THAT 'FORE ALL ELSE I HATE, ... 24 OISIN 1   V 359
    YE WAVES, THOUGH YE DANCE 'FORE MY FEET LIKE CHILDREN AT 90 OLD FISHERMAN V   1
    PLAY,
    'FORE PARADISE'S GATE. . . . . 680 LOVE AND DEATH   20
FOREBEAR
    AND I GAZED ON THE BELL-BRANCH, SLEEP'S FOREBEAR, . . . 50 OISIN 3   53
FOREFATHERS
    WHAT HIS GREAT FOREFATHERS DID, ... 638 BEN BULBEN   39
FOREGATHER
    AND WHO FOREGATHER IN THE SKY. . . . . 716 FAIRY DOCTOR   8
FOREGO
    THE LIVING WOODS FOREGO THEIR CARE, ... 736 SUMMER EVENING   1
FOREHEAD
    EACH FOREHEAD LIKE AN OBSCURE STAR . . . . 26 OISIN 1   391
    CAME; AND MY FOREHEAD FELL LOW, AND MY TEARS LIKE BERRIES 57 OISIN 3   154
    FELL DOWN;
    THE SAD BELLS BOW THE FOREHEAD ON THE HANDS. . . . . . 130 BOOK STORIES V 20
    AND TOUCHED HER FOREHEAD WITH HIS LIPS AND SAID; . . . 286 TWO KINGS V 211B
    DROOPETH NOW HIS FOREHEAD LOW . . . . 711 FERENCZ RENYI V 39
FOREHEADS
    WITH LOOSENED HAIR OR FOREHEADS GRIEF-DISTRAUGHT, . . . 537 HER VISION   18
    WITH LOOSENED HAIR OR FOREHEADS GRIEF DISTRAUGHT, . . . 537 HER VISION V 18
FOREKNOWLEDGE
    IS MEMORY OR FOREKNOWLEDGE OF THE HOUR . . . . 375 PHASES OF MOON   73
    AND BY FOREKNOWLEDGE OF THE FUTURE VEXED; . . . . . . 472 ALL SOUL NIGHT V 44
FOREMOST
    SHE IS FOREMOST OF THOSE THAT I WOULD HEAR PRAISED. . . 350 HER PRAISE   1
    SHE IS FOREMOST OF THOSE THAT I WOULD HEAR PRAISED. . . 351 HER PRAISE   10
FORESAW
    DEEP-ROOTED THINGS;" BUT NEVER FORESAW ITS END, ... 603 GALLERY REVIS   37
    WHAT DEEP ROOTS ARE," AND NEVER FORESAW THE END . . . . 603 GALLERY REVIS V 37
FORESEES
    AN IRISH AIRMAN FORESEES HIS DEATH . . . . 328 IRISH AIRMAN   T
FOREST
    IN HIS OWN LEAFY FOREST HOUSE, ... 2 OISIN 1   V 7L
    IN HIS OWN LEAFY FOREST HOUSE . . . . 4 OISIN 1   37
    OR DOWN THE DEWY FOREST ALLEYS, ... 10 OISIN 1   120
    AND DOWN THE DEWY FOREST ALLEYS, ... 10 OISIN 1   V 120
    OF MANY A SLAUGHTERED FOREST ROVER. . . . . 17 OISIN 1   V 249A
    DARK BALOR, AS OLD AS A FOREST, CAR-BORNE, HIS MIGHTY HEAD 53 OISIN 3   91
    SUNK
    CAME CAR-BORNE BALOR, AS OLD AS A FOREST, HIS VAST FACE 53 OISIN 3   V 91
    SUNK
    CAME BALOR, AS OLD AS A FOREST, CAR BORNE, HIS MIGHTY HEAD 53 OISIN 3   V 91
    SUNK
    WHEN WANDERING IN THE FOREST, IF HE LOVE . . . . 71 ANASHU VIJAYA   3
    GO THERE AND DWELL ON THE GREEN FOREST RIM. . . . . . 108 CUCHULAIN SEA V 35

```
                                                    PAGE     TITLE              LINE
FOREST   (CONTINUED)
     OUT OF THE FOREST LOAM,  . . . . . . . . .     439 FRAGMENTS              8
     WHAT FROM THE FOREST CAME?  WHAT BEAST HAS LICKED   560 MAGIC DRUM         6
         ITS YOUNG?
     SUCH MAY I LOVE.  THE SHUDDERING FOREST LIGHTS  . . . .  651 ISLE STAT I 1   165
     BY MANY SOUGHT, AND 'TIS A FOREST TALE, . . . .  . . .   653 ISLE STAT I 2    40
     AND, BOY, SAW YOU, WHEN THROUGH THE FOREST WE . . . . .  662 ISLE STAT II 2    9
     BETWEEN THE LONELY FOREST AND THE SAND. . . . . . . . .  663 ISLE STAT II 2   22
     GOING THE FOREST THROUGH, WITH FLUTINGS WEAK: . . . . .  672 ISLE STAT II 3  155
     WHERE LIES THE LONG-LOST FOREST OF THE SPRITE,  . . . .  682 SEEKER           23
     THERE LIES THE LONG-LOST FOREST OF THE SPRITE,  . . . .  682 SEEKER        V  23
     NOT AS HE SHAKES THE FOREST: BUT A CRY  . . . . . . . .  689 NETTLESHIP        8
     HE CAME TO THE HOME OF THE FOREST PEOPLE  . . . . . . .  728 PRIEST FAIRY      5
FOREST'S
     GO THERE, AND CAMP UPON THE FOREST'S RIM: . . . . . .   108 CUCHULAIN SEA  V  35
FORESTS
     AND IN THE FLAMING FORESTS COWER THE LION . . . . . .    73 ANASHU VIJAYA    52
     THEY SEE IN FLAMING FORESTS COWER THE LION  . . . . .    73 ANASHU VIJAYA    52
     OF THE FORESTS ALL THE PRIDE. . . . . . . . . . . . .   658 ISLE STAT I 3    84
     WANDERING OF YORE IN FORESTS RUMOROUS,  . . . . . . .   723 KANVA ON SELF     3
FORETOLD
     O WHO COULD HAVE FORETOLD  . . . . . . . . . . . . .    334 SONG              5
     O WHO COULD HAVE FORETOLD  . . . . . . . . . . . . .    335 SONG             11
     FOR WHO COULD HAVE FORETOLD  . . . . . . . . . . . .    335 SONG             17
     BUT WHO COULD HAVE FORETOLD  . . . . . . . . . . . .    335 SONG          V  17
     A SHEPHERDESS LONG YEARS FORETOLD: . . . . . . . . .    668 ISLE STAT II 3   49
     THE FOOL FORETOLD ME I WOULD FIND THIS LOVE  . . . .    750 SHADOW WATER A   62
     BECAUSE I HAD HOPED TO COME, AS DREAMS FORETOLD, . .    757 SHADOW WATER A  197
FOREVER
     THE WINDS AND WATERS TO BE YOUR HOME FOREVER: . . . .   762 SHADOW WATER A V 282
     THE PALE HOUND AND THE DEER WANDER FOREVER . . . . .    764 SHADOW WATER A V 330
FORGAEL
     OF FORGAEL AND DECTORA AND THE EMPTY WATERS  . . . .    218 WOODS OF COOLE   22
     BEFORE THEY READ OF FORGAEL AND DECTORA, . . . . . .    219 WOODS OF COOLE   42
     I SAW THEM, TOO, ONE NIGHT.  FORGAEL WAS PLAYING, . .   223 SHADOW WATER B   36
     I THINK THAT HE HAS FORGAEL IN HIS NET, . . . . . . .   224 SHADOW WATER B   56
     FOR HE CAN JUDGE THE STARS AS WELL AS FORGAEL. . . .    225 SHADOW WATER B   63
     TO MAKE AN END OF FORGAEL WHILE HE SLEEPS. . . . . .    225 SHADOW WATER B   65
     AND FORGAEL IN THE OTHER SCALE: KILL FORGAEL, . . . .   225 SHADOW WATER B   76
     AND FORGAEL IN THE OTHER SCALE: KILL FORGAEL, . . . .   225 SHADOW WATER B   76
     EVEN IF FORGAEL HAD NOT BEEN MY MASTER  . . . . . .     225 SHADOW WATER B V  76
     CAN KNOW THAT ECSTASY.  FORGAEL! FORGAEL! . . . . . .   231 SHADOW WATER B  203
     CAN KNOW THAT ECSTASY.  FORGAEL! FORGAEL! . . . . . .   231 SHADOW WATER B  203
     WE WOULD RETURN TO OUR OWN COUNTRY, FORGAEL, . . . .    248 SHADOW WATER B  539
     AND CUT THE ROPE, FOR I GO ON WITH FORGAEL. . . . . .   250 SHADOW WATER B  592
     FORGAEL, BECAUSE YOU CANNOT PUT ME FROM YOU. . . . .    251 SHADOW WATER B  603
     WALKED ON THE WATERS AND BID FORGAEL SEEK  . . . . .    747 SHADOW WATER A   12
     SO THESE WOULD HAVE KILLED FORGAEL WHILE ASLEEP . . .   748 SHADOW WATER A   25
     FORGAEL, SEEK OUT CONTENT, WHERE OTHER MEN  . . . . .   750 SHADOW WATER A   71
     FORGAEL MAY FIND HIS HEART'S DESIRE ON BOARD . . . .    751 SHADOW WATER A  107
     FORGAEL CAN DIE TO-MORROW.  COME TO THE ALE. . . . .    759 SHADOW WATER A  246
     THAT FORGAEL HAS FOLLOWED THE GREY BIRDS ALONE, . . .   767 SHADOW WATER A  402
FORGAEL'S
     SILENCE! FOR YOU HAVE TAKEN FORGAEL'S PAY. . . . . .    225 SHADOW WATER B V  68
     WHEN FORGAEL'S IN THE OTHER SCALE.  I'D SAY IT  . . .   225 SHADOW WATER B V  75
     WAS FORGAEL'S COURAGE THAT THE MUSIC KILLED. . . . .    747 SHADOW WATER A    9
     OF FOLLOWING FORGAEL'S DREAM FROM WIND TO WIND. . . .   758 SHADOW WATER A  219
FORGAIL'S
     TO FORGAIL'S DAUGHTER, EMER, IN HER DUN,  . . . . . .   105 CUCHULAIN SEA  V   2
FORGATHERED
     A STARLING LIKE THEM THAT FORGATHERED 'NEATH A MOON . . .  54 OISIN 3      103
FORGE
     AND SMITHY WORK FROM THE GORT FORGE, . . . . . . . .    406 CARVED STONE      3
FORGED
     WHEN IT WAS FORGED.  IN SATO'S HOUSE,  . . . . . . .    421 MY TABLE          9
     THAT WHEN AND WHERE 'TWAS FORGED  . . . . . . . . . .   421 MY TABLE         16
FORGER
     COME FROM THE FORGER AND HIS DESK,  . . . . . . . . .   582 ROGER CASEMENT   19
FORGERY
     THEY TURNED A TRICK BY FORGERY . . . . . . . . . . .    582 ROGER CASEMENT    7
     TO PROVE THEIR FORGERY TRUE: . . . . . . . . . . . .    582 ROGER CASEMENT   10
     THEY TURNED A TRICK OF FORGERY . . . . . . . . . . .    582 ROGER CASEMENT V  7
FORGET
     LET US PART, ERE THE SEASON OF PASSION FORGET US, . .    79 FALLING LEAVES    7
     HE WOULD HIS DEEDS FORGET. . . . . . . . . . . . . .    112 ROSE OF PEACE     4
     WHERE TIME WOULD SURELY FORGET US, AND SORROW COME NEAR  122 WHITE BIRDS      10
         US NO MORE:
     WHERE SURELY TIME WOULD FORGET US AND SORROW COME NEAR  122 WHITE BIRDS    V 10
         US NO MORE:
     AND SHE FORGET THE WANDERING AND ALL THE CRIMSON GLOOM . .  175 ELEMENT POWERS V 11
     AND SHE FORGET THE WANDERING AND THE CRIMSON GLOOM . .  175 ELEMENT POWERS V 11
     BUT I'D HAVE BIRD AND RUSH FORGET . . . . . . . . .     197 BAILE AILLINN   204
     BUT I'D HAVE BIRDS AND RUSH FORGET . . . . . . . . .    197 BAILE AILLINN V 204
     SOME DAY I MAY FORGET . . . . . . . . . . . . . . .     380 SONGS FOOL 1      8
     FOR HOW SHOULD I FORGET THE WISDOM THAT YOU BROUGHT, . .  391 UNDER SATURN    4
     AND SO FORGET THE COMFORT THAT NO WORDS CAN TELL . . . . .  391 UNDER SATURN V  4
     FORGET ITS BROKEN TOYS  . . . . . . . . . . . . . .     473 ALL SOUL NIGHT   59
     I FORGET IT ALL AWHILE  . . . . . . . . . . . . . .     590 OLD WICKED MAN   61
     "AND HALF FORGET THIS BED OF STRAW . . . . . . . . .    739 EARL PAUL         5
FORGETFUL
     IN A REVERIE FORGETFUL OF ALL THINGS, OVER THE BUBBLING  56 OISIN 3         140
         GROUND.
```

299

FORGETFUL   (CONTINUED)
    IN REVERIE FORGETFUL OF ALL THINGS, OVER THE BUBBLING   56 OISIN 3   V 140
        GROUND.
    BALD HEADS FORGETFUL OF THEIR SINS, ...   337 SCHOLARS   1
FORGETFULNESS
    I FOUND IN THAT FORGETFULNESS . . . .   24 OISIN 1   365
    TO THE ISLAND OF FORGETFULNESS, FOR LO! . . . .   46 OISIN 2   246
    THE ISLAND OF FORGETFULNESS . . . .   47 OISIN 3   V   T
FORGETTING
    I CRIED, "THOU ART SURELY A WARRIOR, FORGETTING HIS FAMOUS   51 OISIN 3   V 61
        LINE,
    AMONG HER WILDERING WHIRLS, FORGETTING HIM. . . . . . .   69 SAD SHEPHERD   28
    WITHIN HER WILDERING WHIRLS--FORGETTING HIM. . . . . . .   69 SAD SHEPHERD V   28
    FORGETTING AND FORGOT! . . . .   420 MY HOUSE   26
    "FORGETTING HUMAN WORDS," A GRAVE DEEP FACE. . . . . . .   603 GALLERY REVIS   49
    SHE HAS BEGUN FORGETTING. WHEN SHE WAKES, ...   760 SHADOW WATER A   255
FORGIVE
    AND AFTER CRIED HE, "GOD FORGIVE! . . . .   132 FR GILLIGAN   11
    I CAN FORGIVE EVEN THAT WRONG OF WRONGS, ...   321 REED WHISPERER   9
    "GREAT PRINCE, FORGIVE THE FREEDOM OF MY SPEECH! . . . .   464 HARUN RASHID   74
    MEASURE THE LOT! FORGIVE MYSELF THE LOT! . . . .   479 SELF AND SOUL   67
    WHERE MEN FORGIVE IF THE BELLY GAIN? . . . .   615 MARCH SONGS 2   14
    HOW CAN THE MIND FORGIVE? . . . .   615 MARCH SONGS 2   16
    I'M DYING! OH, FORGIVE ME IF I TOUCH . . . .   684 SEEKER   70
    FORGIVE! FOR I HAVE TOLD THEM EVERYTHING. . . . .   694 MOSADA 1   107
    FORGIVE ME! IT WAS ALLAH'S WILL. THE CORDS. . . . . . .   695 MOSADA 1   109
    NAMES AFTER ME. LADY--I COME. FORGIVE, ...   695 MOSADA 1   117
    FORGIVE, OR I WILL DIE. 'TWAS ALLAH'S WILL. . . . . . .   695 MOSADA 1   118
    FORGIVE ME! IT WAS ALLAH'S WILL. NOW CORDS. . . . . . .   695 MOSADA 1   V 109
FORGIVEN
    I HAVE FORGIVEN, O NEW STAR! . . . .   75 ANASHU VIJAYA   77
    ONLY THE DEAD CAN BE FORGIVEN! . . . .   478 SELF AND SOUL   39
    I HAD .FORGIVEN ENOUGH . . . .   504 QUARREL IN AGE   7
    THAT HAD FORGIVEN OLD AGE. . . . .   504 QUARREL IN AGE   8
FORGIVENESS
    THE LOVER ASKS FORGIVENESS BECAUSE OF HIS MANY MOODS . .   162 ASKS FORGIVE   T
    THE TWILIGHT OF FORGIVENESS . . . .   162 ASKS FORGIVE   V   T
    MICHAEL ROBARTES ASKS FORGIVENESS BECAUSE OF HIS MANY MOODS   162 ASKS FORGIVE   V   T
FORGIVING
    FORGIVING ME, BECAUSE YOU WERE DEAD! . . . .   175 BELOVED DEAD   6
FORGO
    GAVE ME SUCH PLEASURE I'D FORGO . . . .   305 HOUR DAWN   69
FORGOT
    AND, MAN OF THE MANY WHITE CROZIERS, A CENTURY THERE I   52 OISIN 3   77
        FORGOT
    AND, MAN OF THE MANY WHITE CROZIERS, A CENTURY THERE I   52 OISIN 3   81
        FORGOT
    AND OUR MOTHER OF PEACE HAS FORGOT ME . . . .   171 MAID QUIET   V   7
    THAT EMPTY THE HEART. I HAVE FORGOT AWHILE . . . . . .   198 SEVEN WOODS   5
    SOMEWHERE OR SOMEHOW THAT I HAVE FORGOT, ...   258 KING NO KING   6
    TO TROOP WITH THOSE THE WORLD'S FORGOT, ...   273 GREY ROCK   63
    THERE CANNOT BE, CONFUSION OF OUR SOUND FORGOT, ...   291 PAUDEEN   7
    AND HAS FORGOT, ...   336 YOUNG GIRL   9
    ALL BUT THE TERRORS OF THE WOODLAND FLIGHT FORGOT . . .   366 HER COURAGE   5
    ALL BUT THE PERILS OF THE WOODLAND FLIGHT FORGOT, . . .   366 HER COURAGE   V   5
    FORGETTING AND FORGOT! . . . .   420 MY HOUSE   26
    FORGOT IN CRUEL HAPPINESS . . . .   453 MERMAID   5
    NOR HAD FORGOT THE STRANGENESS OF MY PRESENCE . . . . .   466 HARUN RASHID   V 119A
    THE CRIME CAN BE FORGOT. . . . .   534 CONSOLATION   12
    GODHEAD. SOME SHADOW FELL. MY SOUL FORGOT . . . . . .   557 RIBH ECSTASY   6
    I HAVE FORGOT IT ALL. HOW SOON DREAMS FADE! . . . . .   761 SHADOW WATER A   272
FORGOTTEN   SEE HALF-FORGOTTEN LONG-FORGOTTEN WORLD-FORGOTTEN
    OF SOME FORGOTTEN FIEND. NOW NONE ASSAILS . . . . . .   31 OISIN 2   V 30B
    HE REMEMBERS FORGOTTEN BEAUTY . . . .   155 FORGOT BEAUTY   T
    MICHAEL ROBARTES REMEMBERS FORGOTTEN BEAUTY . . . . . .   155 FORGOT BEAUTY V   T
    FORGOTTEN AT THE THRESHING-PLACE! . . . .   195 BAILE AILLINN   148
    FORGOTTEN AT THE THRESHING PLACE! . . . .   195 BAILE AILLINN V 148
    I HAD FORGOTTEN THAT WE MUST GO WAKE HIM. . . . .   240 SHADOW WATER B   384
    DISCOVERERS OF FORGOTTEN TRUTH . . . .   324 ROBERT GREGORY   6
    BECAUSE YOU ARE FORGOTTEN, HALF OUT OF LIFE, ...   376 PHASES OF MOON   96
    O TOWARDS I HAVE FORGOTTEN WHAT--ENOUGH! . . . .   412 TOWER   73
    FORGOTTEN ELSE BY MANKIND, ...   576 ACRE OF GRASS   23
    A SMALL FORGOTTEN HOUSE THAT'S SET . . . .   606 SONGS BURDEN 2   3
    WHO, WHEN HIS OWN RIGHT KING'S FORGOTTEN, ...   635 BLACK TOWER   13
    ON A GIRL'S FORGOTTEN LUTE. . . . .   668 ISLE STAT IT 3   66
    THOU HAST FORGOTTEN. ON THE OAKEN STOOL . . . .   713 FERENCZ RENYI   91
    PRAYED THOSE FORGOTTEN FISHERS, TILL IN THE EASTERN SKIES   719 PHANTOM SHIP   32
    ALL THOSE LONG FORGOTTEN FISHERS, TILL IN THE EASTERN SKIES 719 PHANTOM SHIP   V 32
    I HAVE FORGOTTEN WHEREFORE. THE RED HOUND . . . . . .   747 SHADOW WATER A   8
FORLORN
    OR PACE AND WEEP IN WOODS FORLORN, ...   86 MAD KING GOLL V 68
    AND LIFT AN ULULU FORLORN, ...   86 MAD KING GOLL V 68
    BUT THE MAN IS THRICE FORLORN, ...   776 AGAINST WITCH   26
    BUT THE MAN IS TWICE FORLORN, ...   776 AGAINST WITCH V 26
FORM
    AH, THAT TIME COULD TOUCH A FORM . . . .   258 PEACE   · 1
    AH, BUT TIME HAS TOUCHED A FORM . . . .   258 PEACE   V   1
    WOULD NOT PAINTERS PAINT A FORM . . . .   259 PEACE   5
    CAME WHEN TIME HAD TOUCHED HER FORM. . . . .   259 PEACE   11
    CANNOT BUT KEEP THE FORM . . . .   350 MEMORY   5
    THAT IT CAN TAKE WHAT FORM COOK NATURE FANCIES . . . .   377 PHASES OF MOON   115

FORM   (CONTINUED)
   THAT IT CAN TAKE WHAT FORM COOK NATURE FANCY . . . . .   377 PHASES OF MOON V   115
   MY BODILY FORM FROM ANY NATURAL THING, ...   408 SAIL BYZANTIUM   26
   BUT SUCH A FORM AS GRECIAN GOLDSMITHS MAKE . . . .   408 SAIL BYZANTIUM   27
   I SAT WHERE I COULD WATCH HER SLEEPING FORM, ...   467 HARUN RASHID   128
   AND WROTE BY CANDLE-LIGHT! BUT HER FORM MOVED, ...   467 HARUN RASHID   129
   AND WROTE BY CANDLE LIGHT! BUT HER FORM MOVED, ...   467 HARUN RASHID V   129
   NO DARK TOMB-HAUNTER ONCE! HER FORM ALL FULL . . . . .   618 BRONZE HEAD   8
   COMPLEXION AND FORM PROVE SUPERHUMAN, ...   637 BEN BULBEN   6
   THE DOVES WHOSE GROWING FORM HE'D WATCHED. NOT THESE .   710 FERENCZ RENYI V   21
FORMATION
   AND HALF A DOZEN IN FORMATION THERE, ...   489 COOLE PARK 29   20
FORMED   SEE FAN-FORMED
FORMLESS
   A FABULOUS, FORMLESS DARKNESS IN! . . . .   438 SONGS PLAY 2   5
   AND BY ITS FORMLESS SPAWNING FURY WRECKED, ...   611 STATUES   30
FORMS
   "THESE FORMS?" "VEX NOT WITH SPEECH THE PHANTOMS DREAD."   29 OISIN 2   V   5
   HUGE FORMS OF STONE! BETWEEN THE LIDS OF ONE . . . .   31 OISIN 2   V   37
   THE DEAD GOD'S SWORD, TO MANY FORMS HE GREW, ...   40 OISIN 2   V   175
   FORMS WITHOUT NUMBER! WHEN THE LIVE WEST FLASHED . .   41 OISIN 2   V   180
   FOR PAINTED FORMS OR BOXES OF MAKE-UP . . . . . .   564 GYRES   13
   WHICH OF HER FORMS HAS SHOWN HER SUBSTANCE RIGHT? . . .   618 BRONZE HEAD   11
   FORMS A STARK EGYPTIAN THOUGHT, ...   638 BEN BULBEN   43
   FORMS THAT GENTLER PHIDIAS WROUGHT, ...   638 BEN BULBEN   44
   RESEMBLE FORMS THAT ARE OR SEEM . . . .   639 BEN BULBEN   58
   THE DOVES WHOSE GROWING FORMS HE'D WATCHED. NOT THESE . .   710 FERENCZ RENYI   21
FORSAKE
   PRIMORDIAL MOTHERHOOD FORSAKE HIS LIMBS, THE CHILD   559 MAGIC DRUM   2
     NO LONGER REST,
FORSAKEN   SEE GOD-FORSAKEN
   "LIKE ME WERE SOME GALLEY FORSAKEN FAR OFF IN MERIDIAN   55 OISIN 3   117
     ISLE,
FORSWEAR
   THAT SHE FORSWEAR HER HERESIES AND SAVE . . . .   698 MOSADA 2   46
FORSWEARS
   FORSWEARS HIS WANDERING 'MONG THE PINE, ...   686 LIFE   6
FORTH
   I DREW IT FORTH! THE STAFF OF WOOD, ...   24 OISIN 1   V   366
   "OH, SIGH, AWAKE AND GO YOU FORTH FOR ME! . . . . . .   33 OISIN 2   V   57
   HE HAD GONE WHISPERING FORTH WITH CUMBERED HEART, . . .   37 OISIN 2   V   111
   SNATCHING THE HORN OF NIAM, I BLEW FORTH A LINGERING NOTE!   51 OISIN 3   V   57
   FORTH, PIERCING THE DISTANCE--- . . . .   54 OISIN 3   V   112
   COMING FORTH FROM THE SEA LIKE THE MORNING . . . . . .   58 OISIN 3   V   158
   LEANING FORTH FROM THE GEM-STUDDED SADDLE, ...   60 OISIN 3   V   187
   MAYBE YOU HAVE NOT HEARD OF US, YOU HAVE COME FORTH SO   75 ANASHU VIJAYA   78
     NEWLY,
   HE DROVE ME FORTH AND SHUT THE DOOR, ...   95 MOLL MAGEE   V   25
   THEY WENT FORTH TO THE BATTLE, BUT THEY ALWAYS FELL . .   113 ROSE OF BATTLE V   T
   AND STRETCHING FORTH HIS ARM AND CUP . . . .   275 GREY ROCK   118
   I HAD THE WISDOM LOVE BRINGS FORTH! . . . .   313 MEMORY YOUTH   2
   AND SEND IMAGINATION FORTH . . . .   410 TOWER   20
   IN SOME LIKE CHAMBER, SHADOWING FORTH . . . .   419 MY HOUSE   15
   BUT O! AMBITIOUS HEART, HAD SUCH A PROOF DRAWN FORTH . .   427 PHANTOM HATRED   36
   OR THE UNCERTAINTY OF HIS SETTING FORTH? . . . . . .   444 SCHOOL CHILDR   40
   THE GYRES! THE GYRES! OLD ROCKY FACE, LOOK FORTH! . . .   564 GYRES   1
   AND THIS BROUGHT FORTH A DREAM AND SOON ENOUGH . . . .   630 CIRCUS ANIMALS   23
   MAIDEN, COME FORTH! THE WOODS KEEP WATCH FOR THEE! . .   645 ISLE STAT I 1   1
   COME FORTH! THE MORN IS FAIR! AS FROM THE PYRE . . . .   645 ISLE STAT I 1   8
   COME FORTH, COME FORTH, MY MUSIC FLOWS FOR THEE, . . .   645 ISLE STAT I 1   20
   COME FORTH, COME FORTH, MY MUSIC FLOWS FOR THEE, . . .   645 ISLE STAT I 1   20
   COME FORTH, FOR IN A THOUSAND BOWERS . . . .   647 ISLE STAT I 1   64
   HAD DRIVEN HER FORTH, FOR EVER MORE . . . .   668 ISLE STAT II 3   56
   HAD DRIVEN HER FORTH, FOR EVERMORE . . . .   668 ISLE STAT II 3 V   56
   FORTH! FORTH! O SPIRITS, YE HAVE HEARD YOUR TASK! . . .   669 ISLE STAT II 3   81
   FORTH! FORTH! O SPIRITS, YE HAVE HEARD YOUR TASK! . . .   669 ISLE STAT II 3   81
   FORTH FROM THE HOLLOW ALDER TRUNK . . . .   670 ISLE STAT II 3   120
   THOU CALLED'ST ME FORTH. AND HOW THOU MADEST ME . . .   683 SEEKER   52
   TO MINE, AND HE IS SLOWLY SUCKING FORTH . . . . . .   684 SEEKER   V   63A
   GIVES FORTH. HE, THE ETERNAL, WORKS HIS WILL. . . .   689 NETTLESHIP   16
   WHITE LILIES, AND HER SONG FLEW FORTH AFAR . . . . .   693 MOSADA 1   85
   MY MOTHER DREW FORTH FROM THE LONG GRASS . . . . . .   708 FAIRY PEDANT   23
   NOR, GAZING FORTH WHERE LIFE'S SAD SICKLES REAP, . . .   710 FERENCZ RENYI   31
FORTIETH
   AND FROM THE FORTIETH WINTER BY THAT THOUGHT . . . . .   501 VACILLATION   29
FORTUNE
   THE FORTUNE THAT HAD BEEN MY SHAME . . . .   274 GREY ROCK   93
   AND EVIL FORTUNE HAVE OVERTHROWN SAILED HITHER . . . .   757 SHADOW WATER A   196
FORTUNE'S
   FLIETH FORTUNE'S FURIOUS WHEEL. . . . .   737 IN FIRELIGHT   8
FORTUNE-TELLER
   THE COZENING FORTUNE-TELLER THAT COMES WHISPERING, . . .   228 SHADOW WATER B   123
FORTY
   WHY MUST I LIVE SOME THIRTY, FORTY YEARS, ...   285 TWO KINGS   199
   FORTY YEARS LATER . . . .   542 PARN FUNERAL 2 V   T
   I FASTED FOR SOME FORTY DAYS ON BREAD AND BUTTERMILK, . .   592 PILGRIM   1
FORTY-NINE
   ALTHOUGH I HAVE COME CLOSE ON FORTY-NINE, ...   270 PARDON FATHERS   20
FOSTER
   MY FOSTER MOTHER'S GARDEN IN THE SOUTH . . . . . .   758 SHADOW WATER A V   227
   I SAT BESIDE MY FOSTER MOTHER, AND NOW . . . . . .   762 SHADOW WATER A V   292

			PAGE	TITLE		LINE

FOSTER   (CONTINUED)
   MY FOSTER MOTHER SANG IN AN OLD RHYME • • • • • • • • 763 SHADOW WATER A V 314
FOSTER-MOTHER
   I SAT BESIDE MY FOSTER-MOTHER, AND NOW • • • • • • 762 SHADOW WATER A   292
   MY FOSTER-MOTHER SANG IN AN OLD RHYME • • • • • • 763 SHADOW WATER A   314
FOSTER-MOTHER'S
   MY FOSTER-MOTHER'S GARDEN IN THE SOUTH • • • • • • 758 SHADOW WATER A   227
FOUGHT   SEE STAR-FOUGHT
   AND FOUGHT WITH THE INVULNERABLE TIDE. • • • • • 111 CUCHULAIN SEA   86
   AND DUG ITS CLAWS AND SHRIEKED AND FOUGHT. • • • • 385 ROBARTES DANCE   8
   CUCHULAIN THAT FOUGHT NIGHT LONG WITH THE FOAM, • • 549 SEVERED HEAD   9
   HE FOUGHT THE MIGHT OF ENGLAND • • • • • • • 586 PARNELLITES   11
   I WALK IN A BATTLE FOUGHT OVER AGAIN, • • • • • 591 WHAT WAS LOST   2
   THAT FOUGHT IN THE POST OFFICE • • • • • • 608 SONGS BURDEN 3   5
   CUCHULAIN FOUGHT THE UNGOVERNABLE SEA: • • • • 630 CIRCUS ANIMALS   26
   FOUGHT ONCE FOR SELF-SAME REASON ON THE HEM • • 660 ISLE STAT II 1   32
   AND SHOREWARD WAVES, WE NIGH HAVE FOUGHT: WAVES BRING • 660 ISLE STAT II 1   44
   I FOUGHT TWELVE BATTLES DRESSED IN GOLDEN ARMOUR. • • 761 SHADOW WATER A   271
   DANCED, LAUGHED, LOVED, FOUGHT THROUGH • • • • • 787 HUDDON DUDDON   4
FOUL
   YOUR ENEMY, AN OLD FOUL MOUTH, HAD SET • • 292 TO A SHADE   17
   AN OLD FOUL MOUTH THAT ONCE CRIED OUT ON YOU • • • 292 TO A SHADE V 17
   AN OLD FOUL MOUTH THAT SLANDERED YOU HAD SET • • 292 TO A SHADE V 17
   WITH A FOUL WITCH • • • • • • • • • 310 WITCH   3
   AND THIS FOUL WORLD WERE DEAD AT LAST. • • • • • 388 SOLOMON WITCH   16
   DRINKING THE FOUL DITCH WHERE THEY LIE? • • • • 397 POLIT PRISONER   12
   OF THE FOUL WEATHER, HAIL AND RAIN, • • • • • • 424 ROAD AT DOOR   9
   TO BAR THAT FOUL STORM OUT, FOR WE • • • • • 432 NINETEEN 19   111
   PERMIT FOUL YEARS TO WEAR • • • • • • • 472 ALL SOUL NIGHT   49
   THAT FEED ON SOME FOUL PARASITE • • • • • • 493 AT ALGECIRAS   2
   THAT FEEDS ON SOME FOUL PARASITE • • • • • • 493 AT ALGECIRAS V 2
   NOT IN SOME FOUL STY." • • • • • • • • 513 JANE TALK BISH   6
   "FAIR AND FOUL ARE NEAR OF KIN, • • • • • • 513 JANE TALK BISH   7
   AND FAIR NEEDS FOUL," I CRIED. • • • • • • 513 JANE TALK BISH   8
   FOR THE FOUL WINDS BLOW: • • • • • • • 523 MAD AS MIST   2
   WRAPPING THAT FOUL BODY UP • • • • • • • 525 DANCING DAYS   5
   IN AS FOUL A RAG: • • • • • • • • • 525 DANCING DAYS   6
   NO FOX CAN FOUL THE LAIR THE BADGER SWEPT-- • • 603 GALLERY REVIS   39
   FOUL GOAT-HEAD, BRUTAL ARM APPEAR, • • • • • 612 NEWS ORACLE   33
   ON THIS FOUL WORLD IN ITS DECLINE AND FALL: • • • 619 BRONZE HEAD   24
   WITH AN OLD FOUL TUNE. • • • • • • • • 627 STATES HOLIDAY   38
   IN THE FOUL RAG-AND-BONE SHOP OF THE HEART. • • • 630 CIRCUS ANIMALS   40
   IN THE FOUL RAG AND BONE SHOP OF THE HEART. • • • 630 CIRCUS ANIMALS V 40
   OH DEATH IS HORRIBLE! AND FOUL, FOUL, FOUL! • • • 675 ISLE STAT II 3   238
   OH DEATH IS HORRIBLE! AND FOUL, FOUL, FOUL! • • • 675 ISLE STAT II 3   238
   OH DEATH IS HORRIBLE! AND FOUL, FOUL, FOUL! • • • 675 ISLE STAT II 3   238
   AND DREAD NO MORE FOUL AUTUMN'S WING. • • • • • 737 SUMMER EVENING   18
FOUND
   AND FOUND ON THE DOVE-GREY EDGE OF THE SEA • • • • 3 OISIN 1   19
   I FOUND IN THAT FORGETFULNESS • • • • • • 24 OISIN 1   365
   AND FOUND THE HORSE AND BRIDLED HIM, • • • • • 25 OISIN 1   378
   AND TELL ME THAT YOU FOUND A MAN UNBID, • • • • 33 OISIN 2   67
   THAT WOMAN FOUND A RING HUNG ON THE WALL, • • • 37 OISIN 2   120
   THAT MAIDEN FOUND A RING HUNG ON THE WALL, • • • 37 OISIN 2 V 120
   WHO BROUGHT US FOUND A TORCH, AND, WITH ITS FLARE • • 37 OISIN 2 V 122
   AND FOUND A DOOR DEEP SUNKEN IN THE WALL. • • • 39 OISIN 2   154
   I FOUND A DOOR DEEP-SUNKEN IN THE WALL, • • • • 39 OISIN 2 V 154
   I FOUND, DROPPING SEA-FOAM ON THE WIDE STAIR, • • • 43 OISIN 2   215
   I FOUND, FOAM-OOZY ON THE VASTY STAIR, • • • • 43 OISIN 2 V 215
   I FOUND, DROPPING SEA FOAM ON THE WIDE STAIR, • • • 43 OISIN 2 V 215
   SOUGHT ONCE AGAIN THE SHORE, AND FOUND A SHELL, • • • 68 SAD SHEPHERD   18
   AND FOUND HER DYEING CLOTH WITH SUBTLE CARE • • • 105 CUCHULAIN SEA V 2A
   WHOSE BLADE COMPELS, AND WAI, ILL HE HA E FO.ND • • 108 CUCHULAIN SEA   37
   AT THE SWORD-POINT, AND WAITS TILL WE HAVE FOUND • • 109 CUCHULAIN SEA   53
   AT THE SWORD POINT, AND WAITS TILL WE HAVE FOUND • • 109 CUCHULAIN SEA V 53
   THE MAN HAS FOUND NO COMFORT IN THE GRAVE. • • • • 128 DREAM OF FAERY   48
   IN HER HEART SHE FOUND A TUNE, • • • • • • 160 CAP AND BELLS V 26
   BUT I HAVE FOUND WHERE THE WIND GOES • • • • • 168 BLESSED   27
   UNTIL HE FOUND, WITH LAUGHTER AND WITH TEARS, • • • 170 SECRET ROSE   24
   THEY FOUND AN OLD MAN RUNNING THERE: • • • • • 190 BAILE AILLINN   25
   AND POETS FOUND, OLD WRITERS SAY, • • • • • • 197 BAILE AILLINN   187
   WHERE ONE FOUND LANCELOT CRAZED AND HID HIM FOR A WHILE: 209 UNDER THE MOON   3
   WHERE ONE FOUND LANCELOT CRAZED, AND HID HIM FOR AWHILE, 209 UNDER THE MOON V   3
   FOR WE HAVE FOUND A TREASURE THAT'S SO GREAT • • • 248 SHADOW WATER B   540
   AND BEING THANKFUL MURROUGH FOUND, • • • • • 274 GREY ROCK   77
   WHAT MAN YOU HAVE LOST, WHAT EVIL YOU HAVE FOUND." • • 280 TWO KINGS   86
   FOUND THAT OLD HOUSE, A SPUTTERING TORCH WITHIN, • • • 283 TWO KINGS   140
   AND FOUND THE HOUSE, A SPUTTERING TORCH WITHIN, • • • 283 TWO KINGS V 140
   AND WITH HIM HAVE FOUND EVERY HAPPINESS • • • • 284 TWO KINGS   174
   I HAVE NOT FOUND A THING TO EAT, • • • • • • 294 THREE BEGGARS   3
   BUT YEAR BY YEAR I FOUND THAT LESS • • • • • 305 HOUR DAWN   68
   AND WHEN AT ONE YEAR'S END I FOUND • • • • • 305 HOUR DAWN   71
   I HAVE FOUND OUT HOW DESPAIRING • • • • • • 313 TWO YEAR LATER V   3
   AS THOUGH I HAD FOUND IN A BOOK • • • • • • 329 MEN IMPROVE   6
   AS THOUGH I HAD FOUND IN BOOK • • • • • • 329 MEN IMPROVE V 6
   AND ALL DAY LONG WE HAVE FOUND • • • • • • 333 SOLOMON SHEBA   22
   THAT FOUND WHEN I HAD NEITHER GOAT NOR GRAZING • • • 340 SHEP GOATHERD   31
   IS HOT TO SHOW WHATEVER IT HAS FOUND, • • • • • 340 SHEP GOATHERD   44
   HAVE FOUND THE PATH MY GOATS' FEET CANNOT FIND. • • • 342 SHEP GOATHERD   84
   HAVE FOUND THE PATH MY GOAT'S FEET CANNOT FIND. • • • 342 SHEP GOATHERD V 84
   BUT WALK BY THE DRY THORN UNTIL I HAVE FOUND • • • 351 HER PRAISE   12

FOUND   (CONTINUED)

	PAGE	TITLE	LINE
OR WHO HAVE FOUND A PAINTER TO MAKE THEM SO FOR PAY	353	HIS PHOENIX	6
HE NEVER FOUND HIS REST ASHORE,	361	ALF POLLEXFEN	21
DANTE ALIGHIERI, SO UTTERLY FOUND HIMSELF	368	EGO DOMINUS	19
HE FOUND THE UNPERSUADABLE JUSTICE, HE FOUND	369	EGO DOMINUS	36
HE FOUND THE UNPERSUADABLE JUSTICE, HE FOUND	369	EGO DOMINUS	36
AND SING WHEN THEY HAVE FOUND IT. NO, NOT SING,	369	EGO DOMINUS	41
A STYLE IS FOUND BY SEDENTARY TOIL	370	EGO DOMINUS	65
HE HAS FOUND, AFTER THE MANNER OF HIS KIND,	373	PHASES OF MOON	12
THE HARE MAY RUN TILL IT'S FOUND	380	SONGS FOOL 1	11
THAT NOW, IT MAY BE, HAS FOUND	381	SONGS FOOL 2	13
YOUR COCKEREL FOUND US IN THE WRONG	388	SOLOMON WITCH	34
FOR THOSE NEW COMRADES THEY HAVE FOUND,	395	SIXTEEN DEAD	15
HELEN BEING CHOSEN FOUND LIFE FLAT AND DULL	404	FOR DAUGHTER	25
BUT I HAVE FOUND AN ANSWER IN THOSE EYES	413	TOWER	101
HAD HE NOT FOUND IT CERTAIN BEYOND DREAMS	417	ANCEST HOUSES	10
BUT THAT HE FOUND MORE SUBSTANCE THERE THAN DREAMS,	417	ANCEST HOUSES V	10
TWO MEN HAVE FOUND IT HERE. A MAN-AT-ARMS	420	MY HOUSE V	21
BUT IS THERE ANY COMFORT TO BE FOUND?	429	NINETEEN 19	41
INCENDIARY OR BIGOT COULD BE FOUND	430	NINETEEN 19	45
I BRING FULL-FLAVOURED WINE OUT OF A BARREL FOUND	442	BLACK CENTAUR	10
I BRING FULL FLAVOURED WINE OUT OF A BARREL FOUND	442	BLACK CENTAUR V	10
HAS FOUND THE LOVELIEST SPECTACLE THERE IS.	447	COLONUS PRAISE	24
AND FOUND A HEART OF STONE	451	FIRST LOVE	8
A MERMAID FOUND A SWIMMING LAD,	452	MERMAID	1
A CRAZY MAN THAT FOUND A CUP,	454	EMPTY CUP	1
OCTOBER LAST I FOUND IT TOO	454	EMPTY CUP	7
BUT FOUND IT DRY AS BONE.	454	EMPTY CUP	8
A MYSTERY THAT ELSE HAD FOUND NO CHRONICLER	461	HARUN RASHID	21
I WOULD HAVE FOUND THE BEST THAT LIFE CAN GIVE,	465	HARUN RASHID	91
SOME FOUND A DIFFERENT POLE, AND WHERE IT STOOD	483	VERONIC NAPKIN	7
FOUND PRIDE ESTABLISHED IN HUMILITY,	489	COOLE PARK 29	15
FOUND CERTAINTY UPON THE DREAMING AIR,	489	COOLE PARK 29	22
GREAT ROOMS WHERE TRAVELLED MEN AND CHILDREN FOUND	491	COOLE BALLYLEE	29
THAT HE HAD FOUND A TEXT TO PROVE	492	ANNE GREGORY	15
HAD I NOT FOUND CONTENT AMONG THE SHOWS	499	MOTHER OF GOD	6
FIT AUDIENCE FOUND, BUT CANNOT RULE	506	REMORSE SPEECH	4
I FOUND THAT IVORY IMAGE THERE	514	JANE GROWN OLD	1
"A CHILD FOUND ALL A CHILD CAN LACK,	521	THREE THINGS	3
FOUND ALL THE PLEASURE THAT LIFE GAVE"!	521	THREE THINGS	11
THAT HAVE FOUND IT WHERE YOU FED,	522	LULLABY	2
TO MIGHTY PARIS WHEN HE FOUND	522	LULLABY	4
WHAT WERE THEY WHEN PARIS FOUND	522	LULLABY V	4
OR FOUND A SUBTERRANEAN REST	535	CHOSEN	6
HE IT HAS FOUND SHALL FIND THEREIN	538	LAST CONFESS	17
HAD FOUND A SWEETER WORD.	539	MEETING	18
BECAUSE YOU HAVE FOUND ME IN THE PITCH-DARK NIGHT	554	RIBH AT TOMB	1
BECAUSE YOU HAVE FOUND ME IN THE PITCH DARK NIGHT	554	RIBH AT TOMB V	1
IN BROKEN SENTENCES, MY SOUL HAD FOUND	557	RIBH ECSTASY	3
ALL MEN HAVE AIMED AT, FOUND AND LOST!	566	LAPIS LAZULI	18
HEROICALLY LOST, HEROICALLY FOUND.	578	CRAZED GIRL	8
YOU ASK WHAT I HAVE FOUND, AND FAR AND WIDE I GO!	580	CURSE CROMWELL	1
AND FOUND HIS FAMILY TOMB	584	GHOST ROG CASE	32
FOUND MANY A FAMOUS MAN THERE!	584	GHOST ROG CASE	35
THEY THAT FOUND HIM FOUND UPON	585	ORAHILLY	32
THEY THAT FOUND HIM FOUND UPON	585	ORAHILLY	32
AND THERE I FOUND AN OLD MAN, AND THOUGH I PRAYED ALL DAY	593	PILGRIM	8
AND FOUND AN EMPTY ROOM.	594	COLONEL MARTIN	8
HIS WIFE HE FOUND AND THE RICH MAN	595	COLONEL MARTIN	43
HONOUR HAD LIVED SO LONG, ALL LACKING FOUND.	603	GALLERY REVIS	35
HONOUR HAD LIVED SO LONG, THEIR HEALTH I FOUND.	603	GALLERY REVIS V	35
I HAVE FOUND NOTHING HALF SO GOOD	624	APPARITIONS	9
I HAVE FOUND SOMETHING WORSE	628	JANE MOUNTAIN	5
AND FOUND. 'TIS WELL!—ANOTHER MILE OF WAY	651	ISLE STAT I 2	6
THE FLOWER, SAVE SOME THING BE FOUND	668	ISLE STAT II 3	51
THE TALKING WINDS HAVE FOUND THEIR HOME,	686	LIFE	9
A GREY-HAIRED YOUTH, WHOSE CHEEKS HAD NEVER FOUND,	687	TWO TITANS	7
THAN OLD MEN'S ANY DAY, AS MERLIN FOUND.	721	WITCH VIVIEN	47
HAVE FOUND DELIGHT, IN THE RESOUNDING OARS,	750	SHADOW WATER A	72
I LEFT HER LIVING, THINKING THAT I HAD FOUND	755	SHADOW WATER A	174
I HAVE FOUND NOTHING BUT THESE EMPTY WATERS!	757	SHADOW WATER A	201
I SAID THE ALE WAS BROWN. I HAVE FOUND THE ALE,	759	SHADOW WATER A	244
HAVE FOUND IT LIKE THE FROTH UPON THE ALE.	767	SHADOW WATER A	387

FOUNDATION

	PAGE	TITLE	LINE
FROM THE DIM WOOD'S FOUNDATION--	672	ISLE STAT II 3	162

FOUNDATIONS

	PAGE	TITLE	LINE
ON THE FOUNDATIONS OF A HOUSE, OR WHERE	409	TOWER	18

FOUNDED

	PAGE	TITLE	LINE
TWO MEN HAVE FOUNDED HERE. A MAN-AT-ARMS	420	MY HOUSE	21

FOUNDERS

	PAGE	TITLE	LINE
A SPOT WHEREON THE FOUNDERS LIVED AND DIED	491	COOLE BALLYLEE	33

FOUNT

	PAGE	TITLE	LINE
I'D BE ALONE. WE TWO, BY THAT PALE FOUNT,	650	ISLE STAT I 1	132

FOUNTAIN

	PAGE	TITLE	LINE
HAD RUN INTO ONE FOUNTAIN. SPEAK TO HIM.	249	SHADOW WATER B	561
THE FOUNTAIN LEAP, AND AT DAWN	414	TOWER	124
AND NOT A FOUNTAIN, WERE THE SYMBOL WHICH	418	ANCEST HOUSES	15
AND YET HERSELF CAN SEEM YOUTH'S VERY FOUNTAIN,	465	HARUN RASHID	89
BY DAY AND NIGHT A LONELY FOUNTAIN SINGS,	650	ISLE STAT I 1	130

FOUNTAIN'S

	PAGE	TITLE	LINE
SAT DOWN UPON THE FOUNTAIN'S MARBLE EDGE,	463	HARUN RASHID	43

		PAGE	TITLE		LINE
FOUNTAINS					
THE IMMORTALS MOVED AMONG THE FOUNTAINS • • • • • • •		25	OISIN 1		386
THE FAIRIES MOVED AMONG THE FOUNTAINS, • • • • • • •		25	OISIN 1	V	386
FOUNTS					
BATHED IN FLAMING FOUNTS OF DUTY • • • • • • • • •		124	CATHLEEN PARA		5
FOUR SEE NINETY-FOUR					
YET NOW I CHOOSE, FOR THESE FOUR FEET • • • • • • •		6	OISIN 1		57
CARRY ME, YE FOUR, • • • • • • • • • • • • • •		97	FOXHUNTER		2
AND CARRY ME YE FOUR, • • • • • • • • • • • • •		97	FOXHUNTER	V	2
AND CARRY ME, YOU FOUR, • • • • • • • • • • • • •		97	FOXHUNTER	V	2
FOR FOUR DAYS WARRED HE WITH THE BITTER TIDE, • • • • •		111	CUCHULAIN SEA	V	85
OLD DUBLIN MERCHANT "FREE OF TEN AND FOUR" • • • • • •		269	PARDON FATHERS		3
OLD DUBLIN MERCHANT "FREE OF THE TEN AND FOUR" • • • • •		269	PARDON FATHERS	V	3
FOUR SONGS FROM THE YOUNG COUNTRYMAN • • • • • • • •		451	FIRST LOVE	V	T
FROM FOUR GREAT MINDS THAT HATED WHIGGERY. • • • • • •		486	SEVEN SAGES		7
WHAT SCHOOLING HAD THESE FOUR? THEY WALKED THE ROADS • •		487	SEVEN SAGES		24
FOUR POEMS CRACKED MARY AND THE BISHOP • • • • • • •		507	JANE BISHOP	V	T
THE FOUR AGES OF MAN • • • • • • • • • • • • • •		561	FOUR AGES MAN		T
HE NEVER LAY BEHIND FOUR WALLS • • • • • • • • • •		606	SONGS BURDEN 1		12
WITH THREE BARS CROSSED, AND THESE FOUR WALLS MY WORLD,		700	MOSADA 3		32
IN THE LONG GRASS--FOUR EYES DROOP LOW--A SEAT • • • •		716	DWELT SYCAMORE		11
AMONG THESE MISTY WATERS. TWO! NOW FOUR! • • • • • •		753	SHADOW WATER A		138
NOW FOUR TOGETHER! I SHALL HEAR THEIR WORDS • • • • •		753	SHADOW WATER A		139
FOURS					
UPON ALL FOURS. • • • • • • • • • • • • • • • •		572	LADYS 1ST SONG		12
FOURSCORE					
AND EACH OF THE HUGE WHITE CREATURES WAS HUGER THAN FOURSCORE MEN!		49	OISIN 3		33
AS WORDS OF THINE THROUGH FOURSCORE YEARS HAVE FILLED • •		683	SEEKER		46
FOUR-SCORE					
AND EACH OF THE HUGE WHITE CREATURES WAS HUGER THAN FOUR-SCORE MEN!		49	OISIN 3	V	33
FOUR-SIX					
FOUR-SIX. • • • • • • • • • • • • • • • • • •		721	WITCH VIVIEN		41
FOURTEEN					
SOME FOURTEEN DAYS OF CIVIL WAR! • • • • • • • • •		425	STARES NEST		12
FOURTEENTH					
UNDER THE FRENZY OF THE FOURTEENTH MOON, • • • • • •		374	PHASES OF MOON		53
FOURTH					
WE FEASTED FOR THREE DAYS. ON THE FOURTH MORN • • • •		43	OISIN 2		214
THREE DAYS WE FEASTED, WHEN ON THE FOURTH MORN • • • •		43	OISIN 2	V	214
TO LIE UNTIL THE FOURTH MORN SAW EMERGE • • • • • • •		44	OISIN 2		220
TO LIE THERE 'TILL THE FOURTH DAY SAW EMERGE • • • • •		44	OISIN 2	V	220
TO LIE UNTIL THE FOURTH MORN SUN EMERGE • • • • • • •		44	OISIN 2	V	220
FOWL					
"BUT NEVER WITH US WHERE THE WILD FOWL CHASES • • • • •		27	OISIN 1	V	408
THE WILD FOWL OF THE AIR INCREASED! • • • • • • • •		82	MAD KING GOLL		8
ALTHOUGH THE RUSHES AND THE FOWL OF THE AIR • • • • •		177	PAST GREATNESS	V	11
FISH, FLESH, OR FOWL, COMMEND ALL SUMMER LONG • • • • •		407	SAIL BYZANTIUM		5
FOWLS SEE WATER-FOWLS					
FOX					
THE LITTLE FOX HE MURMURED, • • • • • • • • • • •		214	HAPPY TOWNLAND		13
BUT THE LITTLE RED FOX MURMURED, • • • • • • • • •		214	HAPPY TOWNLAND		17
THE LITTLE FOX HE MURMURED, • • • • • • • • • • •		215	HAPPY TOWNLAND		33
BUT THE LITTLE RED FOX MURMURED, • • • • • • • • •		215	HAPPY TOWNLAND		37
THE LITTLE FOX HE MURMURED, • • • • • • • • • • •		216	HAPPY TOWNLAND		53
BUT THE LITTLE RED FOX MURMURED, • • • • • • • • •		216	HAPPY TOWNLAND		57
DIM INCHY WOOD, THAT HIDES BADGER AND FOX • • • • • •		218	WOODS OF COOLE		13
AS THE FOX IN THE OLD FABLE DESTROYED THE SPARTAN BOY'S,		580	CURSE CROMWELL		18
NO FOX CAN FOUL THE LAIR THE BADGER SWEPT-- • • • • •		603	GALLERY REVIS		39
FOXES					
THEY LEFT THEIR HOMESTEADS TO FATTEN THE FOXES, • • • •		546	TO SAME TUNE 2		3
THEY LEFT THEIR HOMESTEADS TO SHELTER THE FOXES, • • • •		546	TO SAME TUNE 2	V	3
THEY LEFT THEIR HOMESTEADS TO FATTEN THE FOXES, • • • •		613	MARCH SONGS 1		3
FOXGLOVE					
WHERE REVEL OF FOXGLOVE IS AND REVEL OF ROSES." • • • •		669	ISLE STAT II 3	V	86
FOX-GLOVE					
WHERE REVEL OF FOX-GLOVE IS AND REVEL OF ROSES." • • • •		669	ISLE STAT II 3		86
FOXHOUNDS					
WHEN WITH THE GALWAY FOXHOUNDS HE WOULD RIDE • • • • •		326	ROBERT GREGORY		57
FOXHUNTER					
THE BALLAD OF THE FOXHUNTER • • • • • • • • • • •		97	FOXHUNTER		T
THE BALLAD OF THE OLD FOXHUNTER • • • • • • • • •		97	FOXHUNTER	V	T
FOX-HUNTER					
THE BALLAD OF THE OLD FOX-HUNTER • • • • • • • • •		97	FOXHUNTER	V	T
FRAGILE					
A FRAGILE, EXQUISITE, PALE SHELL, • • • • • • • • •		784	WOMANS BEAUTY		16
FRAGMENT					
ISLAND OF STATUES A FRAGMENT • • • • • • • • • •		666	ISLE STAT II 3	V	T
FRAGMENTS					
AND THOSE WHITE GLIMMERING FRAGMENTS OF THE MIST SWEEP BY.		426	PHANTOM HATRED		6
FRAGMENTS • • • • • • • • • • • • • • • • • •		439	FRAGMENTS		T
FRAGMENTS THE GREAT DAY • • • • • • • • • • • •		590	GREAT DAY	V	T
FRAGRANCE					
LIFE SCARCE CAN CAST A FRAGRANCE ON THE WIND, • • • • •		422	MY DESCENDANTS		5
I HAVE CUPBOARDS OF DRIED FRAGRANCE, • • • • • • • •		572	LADYS 2ND SONG		5
POURS UP AND FLOATS IN FRAGRANCE ROUND MY HEAD • • • •		691	MOSADA 1		40
POURS UP AND FLOATS IN FRAGRANCE O'ER MY HEAD • • • • •		691	MOSADA 1	V	40
FRAGRANCES					
THEIR SUDDEN FRAGRANCES ON THE GREEN AIR! • • • • • •		217	WOODS OF COOLE		10

	PAGE	TITLE		LINE
FRAGRANT				
THE MIST-DROPS HUNG ON THE FRAGRANT TREES,	2	OISIN 1	V	7F
THEIR BROWS WERE WHITE AS FRAGRANT MILK,	15	OISIN 1	V	204
THEIR BROWS WERE WHITE AS THE FRAGRANT MILK	15	OISIN 1	V	204
RISES, AND SHOWERS ABROAD HIS FRAGRANT ARROWS,	72	ANASHU VIJAYA		27
IN THE BOSOM AFAR OF THE FRAGRANT WOOD.	717	LOVE SONG		9
FRAIL				
WHILE HIGH FRAIL CLOUDLETS, FED WITH A GREEN LIGHT,	40	OISIN 2		165
HUNG THE FRAIL LOFTIER CLOUDLETS. TURNED HE SLOW--	40	OISIN 2	V	167
THE BIRD DESCENDS, AND HER FRAIL THIGHS ARE PRESSED	441	LEDA AND SWAN	V	2
FRAIL BIRD, LIKE A WHITE SEA-BIRD ALONE	784	WOMANS BEAUTY		2
FRANCE				
AMONG THE KINGS OF GREECE AND FRANCE.	296	THREE BEGGARS	V	32A
AMERICAN COLONIES, IRELAND, FRANCE AND INDIA	487	SEVEN SAGES		15
FRANKINCENSE				
AND COVERS AWAY THE SMOKE OF MYRRH AND FRANKINCENSE:	173	SPEAKS HEARERS		4
FRAY				
THUNDERING, AND THE WIDE USELESS WATERS FRAY	45	OISIN 2	V	238
FRECKLED SEE SUN-FRECKLED				
THE FRECKLED MAN WHO GOES	347	FISHERMAN		2
FREE SEE SCOT-FREE FEVER-FREE				
THE SOUL IS FREE, AND FINDS NO FLAW,	19	OISIN 1	V	284
BUT WE, OH ROLLING STARS, ARE FREE.	22	OISIN 1	V	337
IS NOT SO FREE, SO FREE, SO FREE.	22	OISIN 1	V	338B
IS NOT SO FREE, SO FREE, SO FREE.	22	OISIN 1	V	338B
IS NOT SO FREE, SO FREE, SO FREE.	22	OISIN 1	V	338B
AND AS I SANG MY SOUL WAS FREE	86	MAD KING GOLL	V	65
MY SINGING SANG ME FEVER FREE,	86	MAD KING GOLL	V	65
TO A SHONEEN WHO HAD FREE LANDS	92	FATHER OHART		3
. . . AND FREE OF THE FLAMES WOULD WE BE,	122	WHITE BIRDS	V	11
OLD DUBLIN MERCHANT "FREE OF TEN AND FOUR"	269	PARDON FATHERS		3
OLD DUBLIN MERCHANT "FREE OF THE TEN AND FOUR"	269	PARDON FATHERS	V	3
HE GAVE THE HOURS THEY HAD SET FREE	288	TO WEALTHY MAN		22
DEAR FELLOW-ARTIST, WHY SO FREE	335	YOUNG BEAUTY		1
DEAR FELLOW ARTIST WHY SO FREE	335	YOUNG BEAUTY	V	1
THAT THE LAST SERVILE CRESCENT HAS SET FREE?	376	PHASES OF MOON		103
THAT GAVE, THOUGH FREE TO REFUSE--	414	TOWER		133
AND THERE, FREE AND YET FAST,	472	ALL SOUL NIGHT		57
AND BROKE THE CHAIN AND SET MY ANKLES FREE,	533	HER TRIUMPH		9
AND FREE--'TWILL THIEVE AWAY WITH SLEEPY MOOD	700	MOSADA 3		30
OR YONDER MOUNTAIN. WHERE? THOU SHALT BE FREE--	710	FERENCZ RENYI		15
OR YONDER MOUNTAIN. WHERE? THOU SHALT BE FREE--	710	FERENCZ RENYI	V	15
"IF I WERE FREE TO DO AS LITTLE	731	PRIEST FAIRY		77
FREED				
FROM TERROR AND DECEPTION FREED IT CAN	558	RIBH CHRISTIAN		9
FREEDOM				
I SAW MY FREEDOM WON	400	DEMON BEAST		7
"GREAT PRINCE, FORGIVE THE FREEDOM OF MY SPEECH:	464	HARUN RASHID		74
"IRELAND SHALL GET HER FREEDOM AND YOU STILL BREAK STONE."	590	PARNELL		2
FREELANDS				
TO A SHONEEN IN HIS FREELANDS,	92	FATHER OHART	V	3
FREEMAN				
THAT NEVER YET HAD FREEMAN	401	DEMON BEAST		36
FRENCH				
BEYOND THAT RIDGE LIVED MRS. FRENCH, AND ONCE	410	TOWER		25
THROUGH GOD-FORSAKEN MEADOWS: MRS. FRENCH,	412	TOWER		93
FRENZIED				
DANCING TO A FRENZIED DRUM,	403	FOR DAUGHTER		15
A FRENZIED CROWD, AND WHERE THE BRANCHES SPRANG	541	PARN FUNERAL 1		9
FRENZIES				
FRENZIES BEWILDER, REVERIES PERTURB THE MIND:	426	PHANTOM HATRED		7
FRENZY				
TILL VAIN FRENZY AWOKE AND HE DIED: AND HIM	169	SECRET ROSE		12
THAT THE GRAVE-DIGGERS IN A DREAMY FRENZY	243	SHADOW WATER B		430
THAT HE, WHEN FRENZY STIRRED HIS THEWS,	271	GREY ROCK		22
THE FRENZY OF THE BEGGARS' MOON	296	THREE BEGGARS		43
THE FRENZY OF THE BEGGAR'S MOON	296	THREE BEGGARS	V	43
UNDER THE FRENZY OF THE FOURTEENTH MOON,	374	PHASES OF MOON		53
THAT HAVE THE FRENZY OF OUR WESTERN SEAS,	384	VISION ROBART		62
HANRAHAN ROSE IN FRENZY THERE	412	TOWER		71
SWIFT BEATING ON HIS BREAST IN SIBYLLINE FRENZY BLIND	481	BLOOD AND MOON		19
AND CLAMOUR IN DRUNKEN FRENZY FOR THE MOON	482	BLOOD AND MOON		42
GRANT ME AN OLD MAN'S FRENZY,	576	ACRE OF GRASS		13
OR INSPIRED BY FRENZY	576	ACRE OF GRASS		21
FRENZY-STRUCK				
BEGGAR TO BEGGAR CRIED, BEING FRENZY-STRUCK,	299	BEGGAR CRIED		3
BEGGAR TO BEGGAR CRIED, BEING FRENZY-STRUCK,	300	BEGGAR CRIED		7
BEGGAR TO BEGGAR CRIED, BEING FRENZY-STRUCK,	300	BEGGAR CRIED		11
BEGGAR TO BEGGAR CRIED, BEING FRENZY-STRUCK,	300	BEGGAR CRIED		15
BEGGAR TO BEGGAR CRIED, BEING FRENZY-STRUCK,	300	BEGGAR CRIED		19
FRESH				
FRESH IMAGES BEGET,	498	BYZANTIUM		39
HERE IS FRESH MATTER, POET,	553	CHURCH STATE		1
FRESHET				
NOAH'S FRESHET NEVER REACHED.	440	WISDOM		15
FRET				
"FRET NOT WITH SPEECH THE PHANTOMS DREAD,"	12	OISIN 1	V	148
. . . AND FRET OF THE FLAMES WOULD WE BE,	122	WHITE BIRDS		11
OR STORMY SILVER FRET THE GOLD OF DAY,	128	DREAM OF FAERY		33
AND THE FRET IS ON ME.	131	OLD PENSIONER	V	6
AND THE FRET LIES ON ME.	131	OLD PENSIONER	V	6

305

PAGE   TITLE   LINE

FRET   (CONTINUED)
    AND THE FRET IS ON ME. . . . . 132 OLD PENSIONER V   18
    AND THE FRET LIES ON ME. . . . . 132 OLD PENSIONER V   18
    FOR EVER FOAM AND FRET: . . . . 680 LOVE AND DEATH   4
FRETFUL
    THY FRETFUL WORDS A LITTLE WHILE, ... 66 HAPPY SHEPHERD   40
FRIEND   SEE HUNTER-FRIEND
    IN THE HOUSE OF A CHILD, OF A FRIEND, OF A BROTHER. . . . 26 OISIN 1   401
    IN THE HOUSE OF HIS KIN, OF HIS BROTHER, . . . 26 OISIN 1   V 405
    THERE WAS A MAN WHOM SORROW NAMED HIS FRIEND. . 67 SAD SHEPHERD   1
    AND THEN THE MAN WHOM SORROW NAMED HIS FRIEND . 68 SAD SHEPHERD   8
    AND THEN THE MAN WHOM SORROW NAMED HIS FRIEND . 68 SAD SHEPHERD   17
    THEN CRIED THE MAN WHOM SORROW NAMED HIS FRIEND: 68 SAD SHEPHERD   V   8
    I HAD A BEAUTIFUL FRIEND . . . . 152 LOSS OF LOVE   2
    THE LOVER PLEADS WITH HIS FRIEND FOR OLD FRIENDS . . . 172 PLEADS FRIEND   T
    THE POET PLEADS WITH HIS FRIEND FOR OLD FRIENDS . . . 172 PLEADS FRIEND V T
    OF ONE WHO IS NO FRIEND TO ME OR TO MINE, . . . 184 QUEEN MAEVE   V 94A
    FRIEND OF THESE MANY YEARS, YOU TOO HAD STOOD . 186 QUEEN MAEVE   130
    FRIEND OF THESE MANY YEARS, YOU TO HAVE STOOD . 186 QUEEN MAEVE   V 130
    OF THE HARPER'S DAUGHTER AND HER FRIEND. . . . 192 BAILE AILLINN   76
    BECAUSE THEY HAVE MADE SO GOOD A FRIEND. . . . 195 BAILE AILLINN   159
    AND SO BE PATIENT: BE WISE AND PATIENT FRIEND." 200 FOLLY COMFORT V   6
    THAT BEAUTIFUL MILD WOMAN, YOUR CLOSE FRIEND, . 204 ADAMS CURSE   2
    AND THEREFORE, FRIEND, IF YOUR GREAT RACE WERE RUN . . 265 THESE CLOUDS   7
    OLD COUNTRY SCHOLAR, ROBERT EMMET'S FRIEND, . . 269 PARDON FATHERS   5
    AND COUNTRY SCHOLAR, ROBERT EMMET'S FRIEND, . . 269 PARDON FATHERS V   5
    "WHO IS THE FRIEND THAT SEEMS BUT AIR . . . . . 274 GREY ROCK   83
    OF A NEW FRIEND HE HAS TURNED A GHOST. . . . . 275 GREY ROCK   103
    A FRIEND THAT COULD, HE HAD TOLD HER, WORK HIS CURE . . 283 TWO KINGS   137
    AND WOULD BE NO HARSH FRIEND. WHEN NIGHT HAD DEEPENED, 283 TWO KINGS   138
    WESTWARD OF TARA, THERE TO AWAIT A FRIEND . . . 283 TWO KINGS   V   136
    TO A FRIEND WHOSE WORK HAS COME TO NOTHING . . . 290 TO A FRIEND   T
    YET NEVER HAVE I LIT ON A FRIEND . . . . 301 RUN PARADISE   25
    AND DREAM THAT ALL THE WORLD'S A FRIEND, . . . 313 TWO YEAR LATER   8
    ALWAYS WE'D HAVE THE NEW FRIEND MEET THE OLD . . 324 ROBERT GREGORY   9
    AND WE ARE HURT IF EITHER FRIEND SEEM COLD, . . 324 ROBERT GREGORY   10
    BUT NOT A FRIEND THAT I WOULD BRING . . . . . . 324 ROBERT GREGORY   14
    THERE IS NOT A FOOL CAN CALL ME FRIEND, ... 336 YOUNG BEAUTY   16
    THAT NOT A FOOL CAN CALL ME FRIEND, ... 336 YOUNG BEAUTY V   16
    EARNING RESPECT: HAVE NO STRANGE FRIEND: . . . 337 SCHOLARS   V   9
    "AND IF MY DEAREST FRIEND WERE DEAD . . . . . . 338 TOM OROUGHLEY   15
    SHOULD GIVE TO MY FRIEND . . . . 349 HAWK   17
    I MIGHT HAVE HAD NO FRIEND THAT COULD NOT MIX . 352 PEOPLE   16
    HE AND HIS FRIEND, THEIR FACES TO THE SOUTH, . . 372 PHASES OF MOON   2
    THIS OTHER HIS HELPER AND FRIEND . . . . 392 EASTER 1916   26
    THAT CHOOSES RIGHT, AND NEVER FIND A FRIEND. . . 404 FOR DAUGHTER   24
    CHOOSE PLATO AND PLOTINUS FOR A FRIEND . . . . 409 TOWER   12
    FOR THE GREAT CALIF'S TREASURER AND MY FRIEND, . 460 HARUN RASHID V   2
    AWAY FROM NEIGHBOUR OR FRIEND, ... 472 ALL SOUL NIGHT   47
    WOULD I CARRY TO A FRIEND-- . . . . 494 AT ALGECIRAS   8
    I WOULD CARRY TO A FRIEND-- . . . . 494 AT ALGECIRAS   V   8
    YOU ASK WHAT MAKES ME SIGH, OLD FRIEND, ... 524 MAD AS MIST   13
    BROTHER AND BROTHER, FRIEND AND FRIEND, ... 540 FROM ANTIGONE   10
    BROTHER AND BROTHER, FRIEND AND FRIEND, ... 540 FROM ANTIGONE   10
    WITHOUT A FRIEND ON THE EARTH . . . . 552 SONGS REWRIT 2   6
    WITHOUT A FRIEND ON THIS EARTH . . . . 552 SONGS REWRIT 2 V   6
    TO A FRIEND . . . . 579 DOR WELLESLEY V   T
    WITH SOME FRIEND THAT HAS THE WIT . . . . 624 APPARITIONS   12
    WITH SOME FRIEND WHO HAS THE WIT . . . . 624 APPARITIONS   V   12
    SIR PAGE, ALMINTOR'S FRIEND, AND THEREFORE LEARNED . . 660 ISLE STAT II 1   38
    WHAT IS IT, FRIEND? HE LOST I' THE WOODS THE CHIEF . . 661 ISLE STAT II 1   60
    SHE WAS MY ONLY FRIEND: I'M LAME, YOU KNOW-- . . 695 MOSADA 2   115
    I HAD A SISTER LIKE HER ONCE, MY FRIEND. . . . 696 MOSADA 2   11
    FRIEND: BUT 'TWERE A DEADLY SIN . . . . 697 MOSADA 2   31
    "NOW HATH HE KITH OR KIN, OR ANY FRIEND?" . . . 712 FERENCZ RENYI   66
    BUT EVERY BUTTERFLY TO A FRIEND. . . . . 787 GARRET CELLAR   2
FRIENDLIER
    A STERNER CONSCIENCE AND A FRIENDLIER HOME, ... 321 REED WHISPERER   8
FRIENDLY
    WITH A SWIFT AND FRIENDLY GLANCE . . . . 21 OISIN 1   309
    AND ALL GREW FRIENDLY FOR A LITTLE WHILE. . . . 129 BOOK STORIES   8
    AND ALL WHO HEARD GREW FRIENDLY FOR A WHILE. . . 129 BOOK STORIES V   8
FRIEND'S
    A FRIEND'S ILLNESS . . . . 267 FRIEND ILLNESS   T
    BUT NOT THAT MY DEAR FRIEND'S DEAR SON, ... 325 ROBERT GREGORY   46
    WITH A FRIEND'S OR AN ENEMY'S . . . . 362 DOLLS DRAWINGS   3
FRIENDS
    THE LOVER PLEADS WITH HIS FRIEND FOR OLD FRIENDS . . . 172 PLEADS FRIEND   T
    THE POET PLEADS WITH HIS FRIEND FOR OLD FRIENDS . . . 172 PLEADS FRIEND V T
    AND NEW FRIENDS BUSY WITH YOUR PRAISE, ... 173 PLEADS FRIEND   3
    BUT THINK ABOUT OLD FRIENDS THE MOST: . . . . . 173 PLEADS FRIEND   5
    AND OF NEW FRIENDS ARE GLAD WITH YOUR PRAISE, . 173 PLEADS FRIEND V   3
    BUT THINK OF YOUR OLD FRIENDS THE MOST: . . . . 173 PLEADS FRIEND V   5
    TO WAIT THEIR FRIENDS: BUT WHEN THEIR FRIENDS HAVE COME 233 SHADOW WATER B   247
    TO WAIT THEIR FRIENDS: BUT WHEN THEIR FRIENDS HAVE COME 233 SHADOW WATER B   247
    THAT YOU MIGHT HAVE A TROOP OF FRIENDS. . . . . 273 GREY ROCK   58
    FRIENDS . . . . 315 FRIENDS   T
    I'LL NAME THE FRIENDS THAT CANNOT SUP WITH US . 323 ROBERT GREGORY   2
    THAT DEEP-SWORN VOW HAVE BEEN FRIENDS OF MINE: . 357 DEEP-SWORN VOW   2
    THAT DEEP SWORN VOW, HAVE BEEN FRIENDS OF MINE, . 357 DEEP-SWORN VOW V   2
    HER FRIENDS BRING HER A CHRISTMAS TREE . . . . 366 HER CHRIS TREE   T

306

```
                                                            PAGE    TITLE              LINE
FRIENDS   (CONTINUED)
    HER FRIENDS BRING HER A CHRISTMAS-TREE  . . . . . .     366 HER CHRIS TREE V      T
    LACKING THE COUNTENANCE OF OUR FRIENDS.  AND YET  . . . 368 EGO DOMINUS          17
    THE DEATH OF FRIENDS, OR DEATH . . . . . . . . . .      416 TOWER               189
    A COMPANY OF FRIENDS, A CONSCIENCE SET AT EASE,  . . .  427 PHANTOM HATRED       37
    THE FRIENDS OF HIS YOUTH . . . . . . . . . . . .        455 FRIENDS YOUTH         T
    OF FRIENDS THAT ARE GONE. . . . . . . . . . . . .       458 SECRETS OF OLD V     14
    SEEMED SO ON PURPOSE, MUTTERED JAFFER'S FRIENDS, . . .  462 HARUN RASHID         37
    FOR IN MY FIRST HARD SPRINGTIME WE WERE FRIENDS, . . .  473 ALL SOUL NIGHT       62
    FOR IN MY FIRST HARD SPRING-TIME WE WERE FRIENDS, . . . 473 ALL SOUL NIGHT V     62
    "MY FRIENDS ARE GONE, BUT THAT'S A TRUTH . . . . .      513 JANE TALK BISH        9
    FRIENDS THAT HAVE BEEN FRIENDS INDEED! . . . . . .      577 WHAT THEN             9
    FRIENDS THAT HAVE BEEN FRIENDS INDEED! . . . . . .      577 WHAT THEN             9
    AND ALL MY FRIENDS WERE THERE AND MADE ME WELCOME TOO!  581 CURSE CROMWELL       27
    JOHN BULL AND THE SEA ARE FRIENDS! . . . . . . . .      583 GHOST ROG CASE        4
    AND SAY MY GLORY WAS I HAD SUCH FRIENDS. . . . . . .    604 GALLERY REVIS        55
    BUT FRIENDS WALK BY FRIENDS. . . . . . . . . . .        621 JOHN KINSELLA        32
    BUT FRIENDS WALK BY FRIENDS. . . . . . . . . . .        621 JOHN KINSELLA        32
    BUT I'D A TROOP OF FRIENDS . . . . . . . . . . .        626 STATES HOLIDAY        6
    FOR PEACE AND LAUGHTER HAVE BEEN SELDOM FRIENDS. . .    670 ISLE STAT II 3      103
    TWO SPIRIT THINGS A MAN HATH FOR HIS FRIENDS! . . . .   686 DRAWING-ROOM          5
    AND SPIDERS ARE MY FRIENDS! I'M THEIRS, AND THEY ARE .  693 MOSADA 1             64
    TWO SPIRIT-THINGS A MAN HATH FOR HIS FRIENDS-- . . .    734 QUATRAIN APHOR        5
    TWO SPIRIT THINGS A MAN HATH FOR HIS FRIENDS! . . . .   734 QUATRAIN APHOR V      5
    THE HAND THAT WOUNDS HIM, BECAUSE THE GODS ARE HIS FRIENDS. 758 SHADOW WATER A   232
    THE FRIENDS THAT HAVE IT I DO WRONG . . . . . . .      778 FRIENDS WRONG         1
FRIENDS'
    WHERE MY FRIENDS' PORTRAITS HANG AND LOOK THEREON! . . 604 GALLERY REVIS        52
FRIENDSHIP
    A FRIENDSHIP OF HER KIND . . . . . . . . . . . .        345 ON WOMAN              4
    SEEING THAT LOVE AND FRIENDSHIP ARE ENOUGH, . . . .     423 MY DESCENDANTS       20
    FOR AN OLD NEIGHBOUR'S FRIENDSHIP CHOSE THE HOUSE  . .  423 MY DESCENDANTS       21
    AND TOLD HIM SO, BUT FRIENDSHIP NEVER ENDS! . . . .     473 ALL SOUL NIGHT       65
FRIGHT
    MY ENEMY AND HOPE! DEMONS FOR FRIGHT . . . . . .         34 OISIN 2             81
    THE DEMONS OF THE WILDS AND WINDS FOR FRIGHT  . . . .    34 OISIN 2           V 81B
    PUTS ALL MEN IN A FRIGHT, . . . . . . . . . . .         597 MODEL LAUREATE       12
    THAT OPENS HER MYSTERY AND FRIGHT. . . . . . . .        624 APPARITIONS          22
    YE SAID THAT YE WOULD FRIGHT HER FROM HER SIN-- . .     695 MOSADA 1            113
    WHY SHOULD THE HEART TAKE FRIGHT? . . . . . . . .       781 HEART FRIGHT          1
FRIGHTED
    IN MURMURS, LIKE A FRIGHTED BIRD. . . . . . . . .        25 OISIN 1            376
FRIGID
    THE HAND AND LASH THAT BEAT DOWN FRIGID ROME? . . .     560 WHENCE COME          10
FRINGED
    SO LET US DANCE ON FRINGED WAVES, . . . . . . . .       644 SONG FAERIES          9
    SO LET US DANCE ON THE FRINGED WAVES, . . . . . .       676 ISLE STAT II 3      256
FRO
    OF MILKY BRIGHTNESS TO AND FRO . . . . . . . . .         22 OISIN 1            328
    THE CAPTIVE'S JOURNEYS TO AND FRO WERE WRIT . . . .      37 OISIN 2            116
    THE CAPTIVES' JOURNEYS TO AND FRO WERE WRIT . . . .      37 OISIN 2           V 116
    THE CAPTIVES' FOOTSTEPS WRITTEN TO AND FRO! . . . .      37 OISIN 2           V 118
    BACCHANT AND MOURNFUL, PASSING TO AND FRO . . . . .      39 OISIN 2            161
    WE TRAMPLED TO AND FRO. WHEN HIS MIND KNEW . . . .       40 OISIN 2           V 173
    TO AND FRO WE LEAP . . . . . . . . . . . . . .          87 STOLEN CHILD         20
    LEAD MY LOLLARD TO AND FRO, . . . . . . . . . .          97 FOXHUNTER             7
    AND LEAD HIM SLOWLY TO AND FRO, . . . . . . . .          97 FOXHUNTER         V   7
    I HAVE OFTEN HEARD HIM SINGING TO AND FRO, . . . .      109 CUCHULAIN SEA        49
    I OFTEN HEAR HIM SINGING TO AND FRO, . . . . . .        109 CUCHULAIN SEA     V  49
    IN GRIEF SWAYED TO AND FRO. . . . . . . . . . .         133 FR GILLIGAN          36
    GYRING, SPIRING TO AND FRO . . . . . . . . . .          135 TWO TREES            15
    TOSSING AND TOSSING TO AND FRO . . . . . . . . .        135 TWO TREES         V  15
    FLYING, CRYING, TO AND FRO. . . . . . . . . . .         136 TWO TREES            35
    PEERING AND FLYING TO AND FRO! . . . . . . . . .        136 TWO TREES         V  35
    ABOUT MY TABLE TO AND FRO, . . . . . . . . . .          138 TO IRELAND           24
    THE MAGICAL POWERS TO AND FRO. . . . . . . . . .        138 TO IRELAND        V  24
    ABOUT MY TABLE TO AND FRO, . . . . . . . . . .          139 TO IRELAND           40
    MAEVE THE GREAT QUEEN WAS PACING TO AND FRO, . . . .    180 QUEEN MAEVE           9
    THE NORTH WIND TUMBLES TO AND FRO . . . . . . .         191 BAILE AILLINN        45
    THAT NORTH WIND TUMBLES TO AND FRO . . . . . . .        191 BAILE AILLINN     V  45
    AND WAVING WHITE WINGS TO AND FRO . . . . . . .         197 BAILE AILLINN       184
    HITHER AND THITHER TO AND FRO THEY TROD . . . . .       278 TWO KINGS            26
    HAD SENT NO RUNNERS TO AND FRO . . . . . . . . .        288 TO WEALTHY MAN       18
    UNTIL I CRIED AND TREMBLED AND ROCKED TO AND FRO, . .   316 COLD HEAVEN           8
    HE STUMBLED, TUMBLED, FUMBLED TO AND FRO . . . .        411 TOWER                61
    THE PACING TO AND FRO ON POLISHED FLOORS . . . .        418 ANCEST HOUSES        35
    HAD WATCHED MY DAILY PASSAGE TO AND FRO! . . . .        466 HARUN RASHID        107
    HIS HAND MOVES TO AND FRO. . . . . . . . . . .          618 LONG-LEG FLY         28
    AND, NODDING TO AND FRO, SANG SONGS OF LOVE, . . .      688 TWO TITANS           35
    TRAVELLED TO AND FRO ACROSS THE ATLANTIC, . . . . .     790 DEDICATION            3
FROG
    SAVING A GREEN FROG DEAD UPON THE GRASS. . . . . .      676 ISLE STAT II 3      269
FROG-SPAWN
    INTO THE FROG-SPAWN OF A BLIND MAN'S DITCH, . . . .     479 SELF AND SOUL        59
FROLIC
    THE HARE HATH LAID ASLEEP HER FROLIC WITS, . . . .      712 FERENCZ RENYI        72
FROSTY
    WHEN THE MORN GREW FROSTY AND CLEAR. . . . . . .         95 MOLL MAGEE           20
    IN THE FROSTY MORNIN' CLEAR. . . . . . . . . .           95 MOLL MAGEE        V  20
FROTH     SEE SEA-FROTH
    WHOSE LONG WOOL WHITER THAN SEA FROTH FLOWS, . . . .      8 OISIN 1           V  90
```

307

```
                                                             PAGE    TITLE              LINE
FROTH    (CONTINUED)
     FLUTTER ALONG THE FROTH LIPS OF THE SEA,   . . . . . .  .   33 OISIN 2               58
     AND SHORES THE FROTH LIPS WET. . . . . . . . . . . . . .    33 OISIN 2               59
     FLUTTER ALONG THE FROTH LIPS OF THE SEA  . . . . . . . .    33 OISIN 2               64
     MORE THAN THE FROTH, THE FEATHER, THE DUST-WHIRL,  . . .   248 SHADOW WATER B       555
     MORE THAN THE FROTH, THE FEATHER, THE DUSTWHIRL, . . . .   248 SHADOW WATER B V     555
     WHERE STONE IS DARK UNDER FROTH,  . . . . . . . . . . .    348 FISHERMAN             32
     WHERE STONE IS DARK WITH FROTH,   . . . . . . . . . . .    348 FISHERMAN      V      32
     HAVE FOUND IT LIKE THE FROTH UPON THE ALE. . . . . . . .   767 SHADOW WATER A       387
FROTH-DROP
     HE TOLD OF EVERY FROTH-DROP HISSING, FLYING. . . . . . .    32 OISIN 2        V      45
FROTH-LIPS
     FLUTTER ALONG THE FROTH-LIPS OF THE SEA,  . . . . . . .     33 OISIN 2        V      58
FROTH-SPLASHED
     TO ONE VAST FOOT, FROTH-SPLASHED, WITH CURVED TOES LYING    32 OISIN 2        V     46A
FROTHY
     AND CHASE THE FROTHY BUBBLES, . . . . . . . . . . . . .     87 STOLEN CHILD          21
FROWN
     AND, GATHERING ON OUR BROWS A FROWN, . . . . . . . . . .    20 OISIN 1              296
     AND, GATHERING ON OUR BROWS A FROWN, . . . . . . . . . .    20 OISIN 1        V     297
     AND HE WENT HIS WAY WITH A FROWN. . . . . . . . . . . .     92 FATHER OHART          20
     AND WENT ON HIS WAY WITH A FROWN. . . . . . . . . . . .     92 FATHER OHART   V      20
     AND WENT HIS WAY WITH A FROWN. . . . . . . . . . . . . .    92 FATHER OHART   V      20
FROZE
     WHEN THEY FROZE THE CLOTH ON MY BODY LIKE ARMOUR RIVETED    57 OISIN 3             151
       FAST,
FROZEN
     LIKE DROPS OF FROZEN RAINBOW LIGHT, . . . . . . . . . .     14 OISIN 1              183
     FOLDED LIKE A FROZEN FLY. . . . . . . . . . . . . . . .     19 OISIN 1              273
     LIKE BUBBLES IN A FROZEN POND. . . . . . . . . . . . . .    22 OISIN 1              336
     WHERE MEN LIE FROZEN IN THE GLIMMERING SNOW. . . . . . .    73 ANASHU VIJAYA         51
     AND FROZEN ARE THE CHANNELS OF THE BLOOD, . . . . . . .    333 LIVING BEAUTY          2
     SEEING THAT TIME HAS FROZEN UP THE BLOOD . . . . . . . .   333 LIVING BEAUTY  V       2
FRUIT
     IT SEEMED THE SUN AND MOON WERE IN THE FRUIT. . . . . .    127 DREAM OF FAERY        23
     THE CHANGING COLOURS OF ITS FRUIT . . . . . . . . . . .    134 TWO TREES              5
     UNDER THE FRUIT OF EVIL AND OF GOOD. . . . . . . . . . .   137 TO SOME I TALK         9
     BUT FRUIT THAT IS OF PRECIOUS STONE, . . . . . . . . . .   196 BAILE AILLINN        175
     BOUGHS HAVE THEIR FRUIT AND BLOSSOM . . . . . . . . . .    214 HAPPY TOWNLAND         5
     WHERE BOUGHS HAVE FRUIT AND BLOSSOM . . . . . . . . . .    214 HAPPY TOWNLAND V       5
     I'LL GIVE A GOLDEN GALLEY FULL OF FRUIT, . . . . . . . .   240 SHADOW WATER B       373
     BUT HEAVY FRUIT. HOW SWIFT THE ARGUMENT  . . . . . . .     665 ISLE STAT II 2        66
     AMONG THE FRUIT! BUT THERE, LAME COLA CROUCHES  . . . .    691 MOSADA 1              32
     AMONG THE FRUIT. BUT YON, LAME COLA CROUCHES . . . . .     691 MOSADA 1       V      32
     SEE YOU, BROTHER, CRANBERRY FRUIT-- . . . . . . . . . .    727 LOVERS QUARREL        25
     AND THEREON GREW THE RUDDY FRUIT . . . . . . . . . . . .   743 DANAAN QUICK          15
     AND WISDOM THE FRUIT OF THE GARDEN. . . . . . . . . . .    743 WISDOM DREAMS          7
     FOR THE FLOWER COMES WITH THE FRUIT THERE  . . . . . .     774 COME RIDE              3
FRUITAGE
     A DANAAN FRUITAGE MAKES A SHOWER OF MOONS, . . . . . . .   127 DREAM OF FAERY V      22
FRUITFUL
     A FRUITFUL LAND UNDER THE AIBHLIN HILLS?  . . . . . . .    748 SHADOW WATER A V      33
     WELL SHELTERED FROM THE WINDS, AND FRUITFUL FIELDS,  . .   758 SHADOW WATER A       221
FRUITS
     AND HID HER AMONG FRUITS OF JEWEL-STONE . . . . . . . .    224 SHADOW WATER B        49
     AND PLUCKED SMALL FRUITS ON INNISFREE. . . . . . . . . .   742 DANAAN QUICK           5
FULL
     FULL MANY BOWING KINGS BESOUGHT ME, . . . . . . . . . .      7 OISIN 1        V      67
     AS, FULL OF LOVING FANTASY, . . . . . . . . . . . . . .     13 OISIN 1              158
     THAT HAS DRUNK FULL, SHE CROSSED THE MISTY SEA  . . . .     30 OISIN 2               16
     FULL MANY MORE, WHEN PEERED A MAIDEN SWEET . . . . . .      33 OISIN 2        V     68F
     TO TWO OLD EAGLES, FULL OF ANCIENT PRIDE, . . . . . . .     34 OISIN 2               74
     TO EAGLES TWAIN THAT, FULL OF ANCIENT PRIDE, . . . . .      34 OISIN 2        V      73
     LEST NIAMH SHUDDER. FULL OF HOPE AND DREAD . . . . . . .    41 OISIN 2              183
     . . . AND FILLED ME FULL TO THE BONE. . . . . . . . . .     52 OISIN 3               72
     . . . TWO CARRIED A SACK FULL OF SAND, . . . . . . . .      60 OISIN 3              185
     A CREEPING OLD MAN, FULL OF SLEEP, . . . . . . . . . . .    60 OISIN 3              192
     . . . THEY LIFTED AND SHOULDERED A SACK FULL OF SAND, . .   60 OISIN 3        V     185
     THE HOUR WHEN KAMA, FULL OF SLEEPY LAUGHTER, . . . . . .    72 ANASHU VIJAYA         26
     FULL OF BERRIES . . . . . . . . . . . . . . . . . . . .     87 STOLEN CHILD           7
     FOR THE WORLD'S MORE FULL OF WEEPING THAN YOU CAN           87 STOLEN CHILD          12
       UNDERSTAND.
     WHILE THE WORLD IS FULL OF TROUBLES  . . . . . . . . .      87 STOLEN CHILD          22
     FOR THE WORLD'S MORE FULL OF WEEPING THAN YOU CAN           87 STOLEN CHILD          27
       UNDERSTAND.
     FOR THE WORLD'S MORE FULL OF WEEPING THAN YOU CAN           88 STOLEN CHILD          41
       UNDERSTAND.
     FROM A WORLD MORE FULL OF WEEPING THAN HE CAN UNDERSTAND.   89 STOLEN CHILD          53
     FOR THE WORLD'S MORE FULL OF WEEPING THAN HE CAN UNDERSTAND 89 STOLEN CHILD   V      53
     BUT I WAS YOUNG AND FOOLISH, AND NOW AM FULL OF TEARS. . .  90 SALLEY GARDENS         8
     AH WOE! FULL MANY A CREAK GAVE THE CREEL IN THE CART . . .  91 OLD FISHERMAN  V       6
     AH ME! FULL MANY A CREAK GAVE THE CREEL IN THE CART  . . .  91 OLD FISHERMAN  V       6
     FILLED FULL OF ANCIENT CHEER." . . . . . . . . . . . . .    97 FOXHUNTER      V      12
     AND EVENING FULL OF THE LINNET'S WINGS. . . . . . . . .    117 ISLE INNISFREE         8
     AND EVENING FULL OF THE LINNETS' WINGS. . . . . . . . .    117 ISLE INNISFREE V       8
     THE FULL ROUND MOON AND THE STAR-LADEN SKY, . . . . . .    119 SORROW OF LOVE V       2
     WHEN YOU ARE OLD AND GREY AND FULL OF SLEEP, . . . . . .   120 YOU ARE OLD            1
     FULL OF EARTH'S OLD TIMID GRACE. . . . . . . . . . . . .   124 CATHLEEN PARA         12
     I ALSO BEAR A BELL-BRANCH FULL OF EASE. . . . . . . . .    130 BOOK STORIES          12
     I ALSO BEAR A BELL BRANCH FULL OF EASE. . . . . . . . .    130 BOOK STORIES   V      12
     THINE EYES GROW FULL OF TENDER CARE. . . . . . . . . . .   135 TWO TREES             19
```

FULL   (CONTINUED)
    HE TELLS OF A VALLEY FULL OF LOVERS . . . .   163 VALLEY LOVERS   T
    AEDH TELLS OF A VALLEY FULL OF LOVERS   . . . .   163 VALLEY LOVERS   V   T
    SO FULL OF THAT THING AND OF THIS, ...   192 BAILE AILLINN   86
    AT THE FULL MOON? HE PLAYED ALL THROUGH THE NIGHT. . .   223 SHADOW WATER B   21
    I'LL GIVE A GOLDEN GALLEY FULL OF FRUIT, ...   240 SHADOW WATER B   373
    THAT I SHOULD KEEN HIM FROM THE FULL OF THE MOON . . .   243 SHADOW WATER B   446
    IS IT THAT THOUGH YOUR EYES ARE FULL OF LOVE . . . .   245 SHADOW WATER B   473
    THE HOLD IS FULL OF TREASURE. FULL TO THE HATCHES. . .   247 SHADOW WATER B   532
    THE HOLD IS FULL OF TREASURE. FULL TO THE HATCHES. . .   247 SHADOW WATER B   532
    FOR ALL WERE FULL OF WINE AND MEAT . . . .   271 GREY ROCK   17
    IN HIS FULL HANDS WHAT, HAD THEY ONLY KNOWN, ...   292 TO A SHADE   11
    NOW IT HAS FILLED AN OLD SOCK FULL! . . . .   301 RUN PARADISE   20
    GROW RICH, POPULAR AND FULL OF INFLUENCE, ...   369 EGO DOMINUS   43
    THE FULL AND THE MOON'S DARK AND ALL THE CRESCENTS, .   373 PHASES OF MOON   32
    FOR THERE'S NO HUMAN LIFE AT THE FULL OR THE DARK, . .   373 PHASES OF MOON   35
    BUT WHILE THE MOON IS ROUNDING TOWARDS THE FULL . . .   373 PHASES OF MOON   39
    BEFORE THE FULL MOON, HELPLESS AS A WORM. . . . . . .   374 PHASES OF MOON   49
    TOO PERFECT AT THE FULL TO LIE IN A CRADLE, ...   374 PHASES OF MOON   60
    WHEN THE MOON'S FULL THOSE CREATURES OF THE FULL . . .   375 PHASES OF MOON   75
    WHEN THE MOON'S FULL THOSE CREATURES OF THE FULL . . .   375 PHASES OF MOON   75
    THE COARSENESS OF THE DRUDGE. BEFORE THE FULL . . . .   376 PHASES OF MOON   94
    OF THE DARK MOON AND THE FULL, ...   384 VISION ROBART   60
    WHEN THE LONG LOOKING-GLASS IS FULL, ...   387 ROBARTES DANCE   50
    ARE FULL OF PASSIONATE INTENSITY, ...   402 SECOND COMING   8
    FOR AN OLD BELLOWS FULL OF ANGRY WIND? . . . .   405 FOR DAUGHTER   64
    NOTHING BUT STILLNESS CAN REMAIN WHEN HEARTS ARE FULL   426 PHANTOM HATRED   23
    I BRING FULL FLAVOURED WINE OUT OF A BARREL FOUND . .   442 BLACK CENTAUR   V   10
    WHEN THE FULL MOON SWAM TO ITS GREATEST HEIGHT   . . .   468 HARUN RASHID   151
    LIE BODIES OF THE VAMPIRES FULL OF BLOOD, ...   483 OIL AND BLOOD   5
    ROADS FULL OF BEGGARS, CATTLE IN THE FIELDS, ...   487 SEVEN SAGES   18
    SHE MADE A FULL CONFESSION. . . . .   571 THREE BUSHES   66
    AS THOUGH TO DRAW THEM CLOSER YET. RAMMED FULL . . .   579 DOR WELLESLEY   5
    CLIMB TO YOUR CHAMBER FULL OF BOOKS AND WAIT, ...   579 DOR WELLESLEY   8
    NO DARK TOMB-HAUNTER ONCE! HER FORM ALL FULL . . . .   618 BRONZE HEAD   8
    HIS EMPTY HEART IS FULL AT LENGTH, ...   624 APPARITIONS   19
    WITH A BAG FULL OF PENNIES, ...   627 STATES HOLIDAY   35
    ALMINTOR, THOU HAST GROWN SO FULL OF RUTH, ...   652 ISLE STAT I 2   26
    SMALL ISLAND, WHERE THE FULL SOFT SHEEN . . . .   653 ISLE STAT I 2   36
    AND FULL OF WISDOM IS EACH BLOOM, ...   655 ISLE STAT I 3   9
    THE HEAVY CLUSTERS OF THE GRAPES WERE FULL, ...   690 MOSADA 1   13
    THEN HAS THIS ONE BEEN SINNED FULL MANY TIMES. . . .   692 MOSADA 1   49
    YOU'RE FULL OF WORDINESS. COME, HEAR MY SONG. . . .   696 MOSADA 2   8
    ARE DYING TOO. THEY WERE FULL SEVEN STARS! . . . . .   700 MOSADA 3   48
    OF HER HE LOVED FIXED ON HIM FULL OF LIGHT, ...   710 FERENCZ RENYI   27
    AND THEN HIS HEART FILLS FULL OF LOVE, ...   716 FAIRY DOCTOR   11
    AND FULL HIS EYES OF FAIRY CHEER. . . . .   716 FAIRY DOCTOR   12
    AND THEN HIS HEART IS FULL OF LOVE, ...   716 FAIRY DOCTOR   V   11
    FULL MOODY IS MY LOVE AND SAD, ...   723 GIRLS SONG A   1
    A FULL HOUR LONG, WHEN ROSE A FEATHER . . . .   728 PRIEST FAIRY   19
    A FAIRY WHOM WE LOVED FULL WELL, ...   729 PRIEST FAIRY   44
    AS THOUGH HIS DAYS WERE FULL OF RUTH. . . . .   731 PRIEST FAIRY   76
    BE FULL OF SUDDEN FEARS, ...   738 MOURN THEN ON   6
    HOW MANY MOONS HAVE DIED FROM THE FULL MOON . . . .   747 SHADOW WATER A   10
FULLER'S
    WHEN LOIE FULLER'S CHINESE DANCERS ENWOUND . . . . . .   430 NINETEEN 19   49
FULL-FLAVOURED
    I BRING FULL-FLAVOURED WINE OUT OF A BARREL FOUND . . .   442 BLACK CENTAUR   10
FULLNESS
    . . . FULLNESS AND OF THE COMING EMPTINESS . . . . .   425 PHANTOM HATRED   T
    SUCH FULLNESS IN THAT QUARTER OVERFLOWS . . . .   478 SELF AND SOUL   33
FUMBLE
    BUT FUMBLE IN A GREASY TILL . . . .   289 SEPTEMBER 1913   2
FUMBLED
    BUT WHILE HE FUMBLED WITH THE STONES . . . .   302 HOUR DAWN   16
    HE STUMBLED, TUMBLED, FUMBLED TO AND FRO . . . . . .   411 TOWER   61
FUMBLING
    OR FUMBLING IN A DREAM ABOUT THE HOUSE? . . . .   230 SHADOW WATER B   174
    INDIGNANT AT THE FUMBLING WITS, THE OBSCURE SPITE . . .   291 PAUDEEN   1
FUME
    THE FUME OF MUSCATEL . . . .   473 ALL SOUL NIGHT   83
FUNDS
    "THE DRUNKARDS, PILFERERS OF PUBLIC FUNDS, ...   352 PEOPLE   23
FUNERAL
    A LADY WITH SOFT EYES LIKE FUNERAL TAPERS, ...   33 OISIN 2   69
    DOWN ON US WITH HER EYES LIKE FUNERAL TAPERS. . . . .   33 OISIN 2   V   69
    A MAIDEN WITH SOFT EYES LIKE FUNERAL TAPERS, ...   33 OISIN 2   V   69
    TROY PASSED AWAY IN ONE HIGH FUNERAL GLEAM, ...   111 ROSE OF WORLD   4
    PARNELL'S FUNERAL . . . .   541 PARN FUNERAL 1   T
    A PARNELLITE AT PARNELL'S FUNERAL . . . .   541 PARN FUNERAL 1 V   T
    TENDER AND FEARLESS ON HER FUNERAL PYRE! . . . . . .   688 NETTLESHIP   3
FUNEREAL
    AND IN SOME URN FUNEREAL LIE . . . .   19 OISIN 1   V   272
FURIES
    BREAK BITTER FURIES OF COMPLEXITY, ...   498 BYZANTIUM   37
    THE PROUD FURIES EACH WITH HER TORCH ON HIGH. . . . .   579 DOR WELLESLEY   16
FURIOUS
    OR HURRIED THEM OFF ON ITS OWN FURIOUS PATH! . . . .   430 NINETEEN 19   53
    FLIETH FORTUNE'S FURIOUS WHEEL. . . . .   737 IN FIRELIGHT   8
FURLED
    TO YONDER ISLE, WHERE NEVER SAIL WAS FURLED, ...   664 ISLE STAT II 2   56

FURLED   (CONTINUED)
   WERE FURLED THE WINGS OF SHIPS. THERE IN A DELL, . . .   693 MOSADA 1   82
FURNITURE
   A BODILY OR MENTAL FURNITURE. . . . .   558 RIBH CHRISTIAN   20
FURR'D
   OR SOME SMALL BEAST MOST WONDERFULLY FURR'D, ...   650 ISLE STAT I 1   148
FURROWS
   AS THE SEA'S FURROWS ON A SEA-TOST SHELL, ...   660 ISLE STAT II 1   51
   BETWEEN TWO FURROWS UPON THE PLOUGHED LAND! . . . .   784 WOMANS BEAUTY   4
   BETWEEN DARK FURROWS UPON THE PLOUGHED LAND. . . . .   784 WOMANS BEAUTY   6
FURTHER
   I PASSED A LITTLE FURTHER ON AND HEARD A LOTUS TALK! . .   76 INDIAN ON GOD   9
   I PACED A LITTLE FURTHER ON AND HEARD A LOTUS TALK!-- .   76 INDIAN ON GOD V   9
   I PASSED A LITTLE FURTHER ON AND HEARD A PEACOCK SAY! .   77 INDIAN ON GOD   17
   I PACED A LITTLE FURTHER AND I HEARD A PEACOCK SAY!-- .   77 INDIAN ON GOD V   17
   I PASSED A LITTLE FURTHER AND I HEARD A PEACOCK SAY!-- .   77 INDIAN ON GOD V   17
   AND FURTHER ADD TO THAT . . . .   415 TOWER   153
   THE FURTHER THAT I FLY". . . . .   559 HE AND SHE   10
FURTHEST
   FAR OFF BY FURTHEST ROSSES . . . .   87 STOLEN CHILD   15
FURY
   IN FURY AND IN PANIC FLED . . . .   307 HOUR DAWN   V 119
   THE FURY AND THE MIRE OF HUMAN VEINS. . . . .   497 BYZANTIUM   8
   AND ALL COMPLEXITIES OF FURY LEAVE, ...   498 BYZANTIUM   29
   THAT STARING FURY AND THE BLIND LUSH LEAF . . . .   500 VACILLATION   17
   AND BY ITS FORMLESS SPAWNING FURY WRECKED, ...   611 STATUES   30
   WHENCE DID ALL THAT FURY COME? . . . .   619 STICK INCENSE   1
FURZE
   WE RODE BEYOND THE FURZE AND HEATHER, ...   9 OISIN 1   V 101A
FUTURE
   THAT THE FUTURE YEARS HAD COME, ...   403 FOR DAUGHTER   14
   WE THOUGHT IT WOULD OUTLIVE ALL FUTURE DAYS. . . .   428 NINETEEN 19   14
   THAT WAITS UPON HIS FUTURE DAYS, ...   436 FOR MY SON   14
   AND KNOWING THAT THE FUTURE WOULD BE VEXED . . .   472 ALL SOUL NIGHT   44
   AND BY FOREKNOWLEDGE OF THE FUTURE VEXED! . . . .   472 ALL SOUL NIGHT V 44
GABHRA'S
   ON GABHRA'S RAVEN-COVERED PLAIN! . . . .   5 OISIN 1   43
GABRIEL
   . . . MICHAEL, GABRIEL, AND RAPHAEL . . . . . .   174 ELEMENT POWERS V   T
   GABRIEL WILL COME FROM THE WATER . . . .   215 HAPPY TOWNLAND   45
GABY'S
   THE YOUNG MEN EVERY NIGHT APPLAUD THEIR GABY'S LAUGHING   353 HIS PHOENIX   9
      EYE,
GAFFER
   BUT MAYBE SOME OLD GAFFER MUTTERS A BLESSING . . . .   355 BROKEN DREAMS   4
GAIETY
   GAIETY TRANSFIGURING ALL THAT DREAD. . . . .   565 LAPIS LAZULI   17
   VAIN GAIETY, VAIN BATTLE, VAIN REPOSE, ...   629 CIRCUS ANIMALS   12
GAIN
   WHERE MEN FORGIVE IF THE BELLY GAIN? . . . . . .   615 MARCH SONGS 2   14
   HE WHO MEASURES GAIN AND LOSS, ...   744 ROSY CROSS   1
   HE WHO MEASURES GAIN AND LOSS, ...   744 ROSY CROSS   9
GAINSAY
   WHERE NONE GAINSAY THEIR RIGHT, ...   597 MODEL LAUREATE   14
GALILEAN
   IN GALILEAN TURBULENCE! . . . .   438 SONGS PLAY 2   3
GALILEE
   FOR SHEPHERD LADS IN GALILEE! AND GRANT . . . ,   371 ON GOING HOUSE   4
GALLANT
   TO THIS MOST GALLANT GENTLEMAN . . . .   582 ROGER CASEMENT   23
   LOVELY LADY OR GALLANT MAN . . . .   788 HAWTHORN TREE   7
   LOVELY LADY AND GALLANT MAN . . . .   788 HAWTHORN TREE V 7
GALLERIED
   WOLF-BREEDING MOUNTAINS, GALLERIED EMAN, ...   81 MAD KING GOLL V   2
GALLERIES
   AMID GREAT CHAMBERS AND LONG GALLERIES, LINED . . .   418 ANCEST HOUSES   36
GALLERY
   . . . TO THE DUBLIN MUNICIPAL GALLERY IF IT WERE PROVED   287 TO WEALTHY MAN   T
   . . .
   THERE WAS NO PORTRAIT IN THE GALLERY . . . .   400 DEMON BEAST   17
   THROUGH THE GREAT GALLERY OF THE TREASURE HOUSE . .   461 HARUN RASHID   5
   AND WAIT WAR'S MUSIC! PASS THE LITTLE GALLERY! . . .   461 HARUN RASHID   8
   THE MUNICIPAL GALLERY REVISITED . . . .   601 GALLERY REVIS   T
   THE MUNICIPAL GALLERY RE-VISITED . . . .   601 GALLERY REVIS V T
   THOSE FROM THE PIT AND GALLERY . . . .   608 SONGS BURDEN 3   3
GALLEY
   "LIKE ME WERE SOME GALLEY FORSAKEN FAR OFF IN MERIDIAN   55 OISIN 3   117
      ISLE,
   DO YOU REMEMBER WHEN WE SANK THAT GALLEY . . . .   223 SHADOW WATER B   20
   I'LL GIVE A GOLDEN GALLEY FULL OF FRUIT, ...   240 SHADOW WATER B   373
   A TRADING GALLEY IN HER HELMSMAN'S EYES. . . . . .   751 SHADOW WATER A   95
   A GALLEY FROM THE LOCHLANN SEAS! HER FLAG . . . .   751 SHADOW WATER A   98
   AND TURN HIS GALLEY ABOUT AND BRING ME HOME. . . .   751 SHADOW WATER A   108
   WHEN YOU ARE ABOARD THE LOCHLANN GALLEY, LASH . . .   752 SHADOW WATER A   128
   COVER YOUR EARS! FOR ONCE WE HAD MOORED OUR GALLEY . .   756 SHADOW WATER A   187
   ANY THAT LIVED, AND I HAVE BROUGHT MY GALLEY . . .   756 SHADOW WATER A V 191A
   AND A STRONG GALLEY. I GIVE YOU ALL AS MUCH. . . .   758 SHADOW WATER A   222
   SEEK AIBRIC ON THE LOCHLANN GALLEY, AND TELL HIM . .   767 SHADOW WATER A   401
   I HAVE CUT THE ROPE THAT BOUND THIS GALLEY TO OURS, . .   768 SHADOW WATER A   421
   I HAVE CUT THE CORDS THAT HELD THIS GALLEY TO OURS. . .   768 SHADOW WATER A V 421

		PAGE	TITLE		LINE
GALLEYS					
	THEY WALK ON SHORES UNSEEN OF OARING GALLEYS,	30	OISIN 2	V	14D
	TO FILL THEIR DARK-BEAKED HOLLOW GALLEYS.	82	MAD KING GOLL		16
	THAT HE MAY FILL HIS HOLLOW GALLEYS,	82	MAD KING GOLL	V	16
	TO FILL WITH COWS HIS HOLLOW GALLEYS."	82	MAD KING GOLL	V	16
	MAKE GALLEYS OUT OF WIND THAT CHANGE TO WIND	751	SHADOW WATER A		105
	WAR-LADEN GALLEYS, AND ARMIES ON WHITE ROADS,	757	SHADOW WATER A		203
	WAR LADEN GALLEYS, AND ARMIES ON WHITE ROADS,	757	SHADOW WATER A	V	203
GALLIVANTING					
	GO GALLIVANTING BY!	552	SONGS REWRIT 2		4
GALLOPED					
	WE GALLOPED OVER THE GLOSSY SEA!	11	OISIN 1		132
	WE GALLOPED! NOW A HORNLESS DEER	11	OISIN 1		139
	ON, ON, WE GALLOPED O'ER THE SEA.	11	OISIN 1	V	132
	WHILE THAT GREAT JUAN GALLOPED BY!	294	HATED PLAYBOY	V	4
GALLOPING					
	THE RIDERS UPON THE GALLOPING HORSES,	266	GALWAY RACES		3
	THE RIDERS AND THE GALLOPING HORSES,	266	GALWAY RACES	V	3
GALLOWS					
	GRANDFATHER SANG IT UNDER THE GALLOWS!	544	TO SAME TUNE 1		1
	HE DIED UPON THE GALLOWS,	581	ROGER CASEMENT		3
	GRANDFATHER SANG IT UNDER THE GALLOWS!	615	MARCH SONGS 3		1
GALWAY	SEE CLARE-GALWAY				
	AT GALWAY RACES	266	GALWAY RACES		T
	GALWAY RACES	266	GALWAY RACES	V	T
	OR TRADING OUT OF GALWAY INTO SPAIN!	269	PARDON FATHERS		4
	WHEN WITH THE GALWAY FOXHOUNDS HE WOULD RIDE	326	ROBERT GREGORY		57
	TO COLD CLARE ROCK AND GALWAY ROCK AND THORN,	326	ROBERT GREGORY		66
	IN A GALWAY SHOP,	595	COLONEL MARTIN		22
GAMBLER					
	THEY SAY YOU ARE A GAMBLER AND A PLAYER	721	WITCH VIVIEN		34
GAME					
	BETWEEN THE GAME AND THE HORSES OF THE SEA.	108	CUCHULAIN SEA	V	34
	OR PUT HIS HEART INTO SOME GAME	343	SHEP GOATHERD		105
	GAME BIRD, OR WOMAN DOES THE SAME THING TWICE!	463	HARUN RASHID	V	60
	THAN SOULS THAT START NO GAME AND TURN NO RHYME!	464	HARUN RASHID		68
	IMPROVISATION, OR A SETTLED GAME	533	HER TRIUMPH		3
GAMEBIRD					
	GAMEBIRD, NOR WOMAN DOES THE SAME THING TWICE!	463	HARUN RASHID	V	60
GAME-BIRD					
	GAME-BIRD, NOR WOMAN DOES THE SAME THING TWICE!	463	HARUN RASHID		60
'GAN					
	. . . AND YEARS AFTER YEARS 'GAN FLOW!	52	OISIN 3		75
	. . . AND YEARS AFTER YEARS 'GAN THEIR FLOW!	52	OISIN 3	V	75
	THEN 'GAN TO SPEAK THAT GOBLIN RARE,	729	PRIEST FAIRY		37
GANGLING					
	ON GANGLING STOCKS GROWN GREAT, GREAT STOCKS RUN DRY,	619	BRONZE HEAD		25
GANNET					
	THERE! THERE THEY COME! GULL, GANNET, OR DIVER,	233	SHADOW WATER B		244
GANNETS					
	OR THE GANNETS CALLING OUT	772	SONG DEIRDRE 1		5
GAP					
	AS I CAME OVER WINDY GAP	300	RUN PARADISE		1
	I HAVE STOOD SO LONG BY A GAP IN THE WALL	788	HAWTHORN TREE		15
	I HAVE STOPPED SO LONG A GAP IN THE WALL	788	HAWTHORN TREE	V	15
GAPE					
	AND NOW BUT GAPE AT THE SUN.	432	NINETEEN 19		102
GARDEN					
	THE JESTER WALKED IN THE GARDEN!	159	CAP AND BELLS		1
	THE GARDEN HAD FALLEN STILL!	159	CAP AND BELLS		2
	THE POWERS, NOT KIND LIKE YOU, CAME WHERE GOD'S GARDEN BLOWS,	174	ELEMENT POWERS	V	1
	MAKE THEIR FAINT THUNDER, AND THE GARDEN BEES	198	SEVEN WOODS		2
	WHO HAS SEEN A GARDEN IMAGE OR TWISTED TREE	279	TWO KINGS	V	45B
	RAN AND WITH THE GARDEN SHEARS	410	TOWER		30
	BEFORE THE INDIFFERENT GARDEN DEITIES!	418	ANCEST HOUSES		28
	BUT THE TORN PETALS STREW THE GARDEN PLOT!	422	MY DESCENDANTS		7
	WHEN THE TORN PETALS STREW THE GARDEN PLOT!	422	MY DESCENDANTS	V	7
	OUR SHADOWS ROVE THE GARDEN GRAVEL STILL,	435	NEW FACES		7
	THE GARDEN DIED!	439	FRAGMENTS		2
	AND YONDER IN THE GYMNASTS' GARDEN THRIVES	446	COLONUS PRAISE		9
	THE GARDEN PATHS, NOR COUNTED UP THE ROOMS,	466	HARUN RASHID		119
	IN THE RICH MIDNIGHT OF THE GARDEN TREES	494	AT ALGECIRAS		5
	IN THE RICH MIDNIGHT OF THE GARDEN TREE	494	AT ALGECIRAS	V	5
	CHIMNEY CORNER, GARDEN WALK,	499	MOTHER OF GOD		8
	THROUGH LIGHT-OBLITERATING GARDEN FOLIAGE WHAT MAGIC DRUM?	560	MAGIC DRUM		4
	GRASS PLOT OF THE GARDEN!	568	SWEET DANCER		3
	EDEN'S GARDEN WOULD BE THERE	621	JOHN KINSELLA		27
	BY THE DOOR OF MARY'S GARDEN	680	LOVE AND DEATH		31
	HIS GARDEN RINGED WITH JESSAMINE,	729	PRIEST FAIRY		34
	AND WISDOM THE FRUIT OF THE GARDEN!	743	WISDOM DREAMS		7
	FOR I HAVE ALL HIS GARDEN WISDOM. O SPEAK!	756	SHADOW WATER A		180
	MY FOSTER-MOTHER'S GARDEN IN THE SOUTH	758	SHADOW WATER A		227
	MY FOSTER MOTHER'S GARDEN IN THE SOUTH	758	SHADOW WATER A	V	227
	COME RIDE AND RIDE TO THE GARDEN,	773	COME RIDE		1
	COME RIDE AND RIDE TO THE GARDEN,	774	COME RIDE		5
	AND ALL THE GARDEN BLESS,	774	COME RIDE		10
	COME RIDE AND RIDE TO THE GARDEN,	774	COME RIDE		13
	COME RIDE AND RIDE TO THE GARDEN,	774	COME RIDE		18
GARDEN-BOY					
	THE POST AND GARDEN-BOY ALONE	607	SONGS BURDEN 2		7

GARDEN'S
    AND HEAR AMID THE GARDEN'S NIGHTLY PEACE," . . . . . .   300 BEGGAR CRIED   18
    TO BE THE GARDEN'S PRIDE." . . . .   396 ROSE TREE   12
GARDENS
    DOWN BY THE SALLEY GARDENS . . . .   90 SALLEY GARDENS   T
    DOWN BY THE SALLEY GARDENS MY LOVE AND I DID MEET: . . .   90 SALLEY GARDENS   1
    SHE PASSED THE SALLEY GARDENS WITH LITTLE SNOW-WHITE FEET. 90 SALLEY GARDENS   2
    O WHAT IF GARDENS WHERE THE PEACOCK STRAYS . . . . . .   418 ANCEST HOUSES   25
    OR GARDENS RICH IN MEMORY GLORIFIED . . . .   491 COOLE BALLYLEE   35
    IN ALGECIRAS GARDENS, AND THERE REST . . . .   494 AT ALGECIRAS   V   5
    GARDENS WHERE A SOUL'S AT EASE: . . . .   639 BEN BULBEN   55
GARLANDED
    SOME FEW HAVE HANDSOME RIDERS, ARE GARLANDED . . . . .   432 NINETEEN 19   114
GARMENT
    IT ROSE IN A STRAIGHT BLUE GARMENT, ...   159 CAP AND BELLS   5
    IN A LONG AND STRAIGHT BLUE GARMENT . . . .   159 CAP AND BELLS   V   5
    IN A RED AND QUIVERING GARMENT . . . .   160 CAP AND BELLS   15
    IN A GARMENT RED AND QUIVERING, ...   160 CAP AND BELLS   V   15
    THOUGHT IS A GARMENT AND THE SOUL'S A BRIDE . . . . .   558 RIBH CHRISTIAN   16
GARMENT'S
    THY GARMENT'S HEM, THOU VISIONARY ONE! . . . .   684 SEEKER   V   71
GARMENTS
    MY SHEPHERD GARMENTS, AND RETURN ANON. . . . .   659 ISLE STAT II 1   29
GARMENTS'
    HER FINGERS AND HER GARMENTS' HEM. . . . .   16 OISIN 1   V 216
    THY GARMENTS' HEM, THOU VISIONARY ONE! . . . .   684 SEEKER   71
GARNERED
    IS NOT THY BODY BUT THE GARNERED RUST . . . .   724 KANVA ON SELF   15
GARRET
    TO GARRET OR CELLAR A WHEEL I SEND, ...   787 GARRET CELLAR   1
GARRULOUS
    FROM WASTE SEAS CROSS'D, YET EVER GARRULOUS) . . . . .   690 MOSADA 1   9
GARTERED   SEE CROSS-GARTERED
GASP
    HE GAVE A GASP AND THOUGHT TO HAVE FLED, ...   303 HOUR DAWN   22
    HE GAVE A GASP AND THOUGHT TO RUN, ...   303 HOUR DAWN   V   22
GASPED
    TREMBLED AND GASPED AND SHOULD HAVE RUN . . . .   303 HOUR DAWN   V   22
GASPING
    WHAT ARE ALL THOSE FISH THAT LIE GASPING ON THE STRAND?   485 THREE MOVEMENT   3
'GAT
    'GAT THE FOAL OF THE WORLD." . . . .   529 TOM CRUACHAN   6
GATE
    LOOSED LONG AGO FROM HEAVEN'S GATE, ...   24 OISIN 1   362
    BUT CALL ME FIRST THROUGH THE GATE: . . . .   178 FIDDLER DOONEY   12
    TO THAT SMALL CHAMBER BY THE OUTER GATE. . . . . . .   181 QUEEN MAEVE   44
    ROUND ABOUT HELL'S GATE TO STARE . . . .   294 HATED PLAYBOY   V   3
    HAVE KEYS TO MY OLD GATE. . . . .   607 SONGS BURDEN 2   8
    THOUGH I HAVE LOCKED MY GATE ON THEM, ...   607 SONGS BURDEN 2   10
    WITHIN THE FOLD TO HEAR THE CREAKING GATE-- . . . . .   646 ISLE STAT 1 1   41
    'FORE PARADISE'S GATE. . . . .   680 LOVE AND DEATH   20
    THIS VISION OF PETER AND THE BURNING GATE. . . . . .   696 MOSADA 2   21
    BY THE DOOR OF PETER'S GATE, ...   696 MOSADA 2   23
    OF HOLY PETER OF THE BURNING GATE! . . . .   696 MOSADA 2   V   20
    BESIDE THE DOOR OF PETER'S GATE. . . . .   696 MOSADA 2   V   23
GATED   SEE BRAZEN-GATED
GATES
    . . . KEENED IN THE GATES OF MY HEART. . . . .   57 OISIN 3   152
    AND LAID YOU ON THE GATES OF EVENING WITH HIS QUIET HANDS. 72 ANASHU VIJAYA   22
    AND LAID YE ON THE GATES OF EVENING WITH HIS QUIET HANDS. 72 ANASHU VIJAYA   V   22
    THE TOWERY GATES OF GORIAS, ...   196 BAILE AILLINN   161
    LAND-OF-THE-TOWER, WHERE AENGUS HAS THROWN THE GATES APART, 209 UNDER THE MOON   8
    LAND OF THE TOWER, WHEN AENGUS HAS THROWN THE GATES APART, 209 UNDER THE MOON V   8
    BOOK IV   THE GATES OF PLUTO I. THE FOOL BY THE ROADSIDE 447 HERO GIRL FOOL V   T
GATEWAY
    SPRANG FROM A GATEWAY WALLED AROUND WITH BLACK . . . .   31 OISIN 2   V   29
    UPLIFTED GATEWAY. WITH THE FLASHING BEAT . . . . . .   31 OISIN 2   V 30D
    BETWEEN THEM A GATEWAY OF BRASS, AND THE HOWL OF THE ANGELS 61 OISIN 3   200
    WHO FELL.
    WE WILL TEAR OUT THE FLAMING STONES, AND BATTER THE GATEWAY 62 OISIN 3   209
    OF BRASS
    . . . AND WILL BATTER THE GATEWAY OF BRASS . . . . . .   62 OISIN 3   V 209
    BEYOND THE GATEWAY--BY THE SENTRIES NOW-- . . . . . .   720 WITCH VIVIEN   10
    ON BRAHMA'S GATEWAY, "THEY WITHIN HAVE FED . . . . . .   735 QUATRAIN APHOR   15
GATHER
    GATHER SEA-SLIME AND FALL THE SEAWARD WAY, ...   45 OISIN 2   237
    GATHER SEA SLIME AND FALL THE SEAWARD WAY, ...   45 OISIN 2   V 237
    GO GATHER BY THE HUMMING SEA . . . .   66 HAPPY SHEPHERD   35
    GO GATHER BY THE HUMMING-SEA . . . .   66 HAPPY SHEPHERD   V   35
    BUT GATHER WITH YOUR SHININ' LOOKS . . . .   96 MOLL MAGEE   55
    "THE RED BRANCH GATHER A GREAT COMPANY . . . . . .   108 CUCHULAIN SEA   V   33
    WITH BLOWN, SPRAY-DABBLED HAIR GATHER AT HAND. . . . .   114 ROSE OF BATTLE   6
    BUT GATHER ALL FOR WHOM NO LOVE HATH MADE . . . . . .   114 ROSE OF BATTLE   12
    TO SMILE ON THE PALE DAWN: AND GATHER YOU . . . . . .   114 ROSE OF BATTLE   15
    TO SMILE UPON HER STARS: AND GATHER YOU, ...   114 ROSE OF BATTLE   V   15
    OF THAT DARK FOLK WHO GATHER IN THE SOULS . . . . . .   136 TO SOME I TALK   V   4
    THE DEWS DROP SLOWLY AND DREAMS GATHER: UNKNOWN SPEARS . . 161 BLACK PIG   1
    THE DEW DROPS SLOWLY: THE DREAMS GATHER: UNKNOWN SPEARS   161 BLACK PIG   V   1
    TO GATHER THE HALF OF YOUR BLESSEDNESS . . . .   167 BLESSED   7
    AND DO YOU GATHER ABOUT US WHEN PALE LIGHT . . . . . .   218 WOODS OF COOLE   37
    AND GATHER THE GLASNEVIN COVERLET . . . .   293 TO A SHADE   19

```
                                                    PAGE     TITLE          LINE

GATHER   (CONTINUED)
    WILL GATHER, AND NOT KNOW IT WALKS THE VERY STREET  . . .   315 FALLEN MAJESTY        7
    WILL GATHER AND NOT KNOW THAT THROUGH ITS VERY STREET . .   315 FALLEN MAJESTY V      7
    IT KNOWS NOT WHAT IT IS! AND GATHER ME . . . . . . .   408 SAIL BYZANTIUM       23
    IT KNOWS NOT WHAT IT IS! GATHER ME . . . . . . . .   408 SAIL BYZANTIUM V     23
    AND WE THAT HAVE SHED NONE MUST GATHER THERE . . . .   482 BLOOD AND MOON       41
    AND GATHER ALL THE TALK? . . . . . . . . . . . .   499 MOTHER OF GOD        10
    COME GATHER ROUND ME, PARNELLITES . . . . . . . .   586 PARNELLITES           T
    COME GATHER ROUND ME, PARNELLITES . . . . . . . .   586 PARNELLITES           1
    COME GATHER ROUND ME, PLAYERS ALL! . . . . . . .   608 SONGS BURDEN 3        1
    AND, WHILE THEY GATHER ROUND MY BECKONING ARMS, . . .   694 MOSADA 1            100
    ALL THE WORDS THAT I GATHER, . . . . . . . . . .   739 WHERE BOOKS GO        1
    WHEN ALL GATHER THEY WILL FLY UPON THEIR WAY. . . . .   753 SHADOW WATER A      136
    GATHER ABOUT HIM, THAT THE GODS MAY NOT KNOW . . . .   758 SHADOW WATER A      231
    AND GATHER ROUND HIM, THAT NO GOD MAY KNOW . . . . .   758 SHADOW WATER A V    231
    GATHER ON THE WIND AND DRIVE . . . . . . . . . .   775 AGAINST WITCH         7
GATHERED
    AND GATHERED IN A SILVER CINCTURE! . . . . . . . .     3 OISIN 1          V  24A
    MOURNFUL, AND GATHERED ON THE SANDS! . . . . . . .    10 OISIN 1          V 111B
    AND, GATHERED IN A PANTING BAND, . . . . . . . .    22 OISIN 1             324
    WEARY, WITH ALL HIS POPPIES GATHERED ROUND HIM. . . .    72 ANASHU VIJAYA        25
    GATHERED IN SILENCE, DEWY AS HER EYES, . . . . . .    80 EPHEMERA             19
    TO HIS OWN ICE!"  I GATHERED ROUND ME, . . . . . .    83 MAD KING GOLL    V   18
    AND GATHERED THE FLAMES ABOVE HIS HOLY HEAD, . . . .   162 ASKS FORGIVE     V   17
    WHEN WINDS HAVE GATHERED AND SUN AND MOON BURNED DIM  . .   175 ELEMENT POWERS       15
    GATHERED A CROWD IN SOME BYZANTINE LANE, . . . . .   180 QUEEN MAEVE           2
    HAD THE WORLD'S TOTAL LIFE GATHERED UP, IT SEEMED, . .   231 SHADOW WATER B      194
    THE HANDS THAT GATHERED UP THE MIGHT OF THE WORLD, . . .   278 TWO KINGS            29
    ALTHOUGH CROWDS GATHERED ONCE IF SHE BUT SHOWED HER FACE,   314 FALLEN MAJESTY        1
    THAT HE ALONE HAD GATHERED UP NO GEAR, . . . . . .   340 SHEP GOATHERD        49
    GATHERED A SCORE OF HORSE AND SPENT HIS DAYS . . . .   420 MY HOUSE             22
    BECAUSE OF SOME GREEN WING, GATHERED OLD MUMMY WHEAT  . .   442 BLACK CENTAUR         7
    OF THE WIDE WOODS.  AND THE DEEP EARTH GATHERED THEM, .   660 ISLE STAT II 1       33
    HEAVY WITH WOOL THE SHEEP ARE GATHERED IN, . . . . .   681 SEEKER                1
    GATHERED ON HER OWN LIPS, OH YOUTH, AND FLING . . .   688 TWO TITANS           53
    WE GATHERED. FERENCZ, NAY, I MUST NOT DIE! . . . .   713 FERENCZ RENYI        96
    WE GATHERED, DO NOT LET ME DIE. . . . . . . . .   713 FERENCZ RENYI V      96
GATHERING
    AND, GATHERING ON OUR BROWS A FROWN, . . . . . . .    20 OISIN 1             296
    AND, GATHERING ON OUR BROWS A FROWN, . . . . . . .    20 OISIN 1          V  297
    A THIN GREY MAN HALF LOST IN GATHERING NIGHT. . . .   102 FERGUS DRUID          7
    A THIN, GREY MAN, HALF-LOST IN GATHERING NIGHT. . . .   102 FERGUS DRUID     V    7
    THE THRONGS WITH BLOWN WET HAIR ARE GATHERING NEAR. . .   114 ROSE OF BATTLE V      6
    GATHERING HIS CLOAK ABOUT HIM, RUN . . . . . . .   193 BAILE AILLINN       101
    GATHERING MUSHROOMS IN THE DEW. . . . . . . . .   705 DAWN-SONG             8
    GATHERING MUSHROOMS IN THE DEW. . . . . . . . .   705 DAWN-SONG            16
    GATHERING MUSHROOMS IN THE DEW. . . . . . . . .   706 DAWN-SONG            24
    GATHERING MUSHROOMS IN THE DEW. . . . . . . . .   706 DAWN-SONG            32
    HALF DIZZY WITH THE LIGHTNING THERE RUNS A GATHERING BAND--   718 PHANTOM SHIP         9
    NOW HALF DIZZY WITH THE LIGHTNING THERE RUNS A GATHERING     718 PHANTOM SHIP V       9
         BAND!
GATHERS
    GATHERS SEA-SLIME AND GOES THE SEAWARD WAY, . . . .    45 OISIN 2          V  237
    ONE GATHERS UP HIS PURPLE GOWN! . . . . . . . .   212 BLESS PSALTER         9
    GATHERS THE WILD DUCK FROM THE WINTER DAWN! . . . .   217 WOODS OF COOLE        3
    AND THERE'S A PLAYER IN THE STATES WHO GATHERS UP HER CLOAK   354 HIS PHOENIX          12
    AND THERE'S THE PLAYER IN THE STATES WHO GATHERS UP HER     354 HIS PHOENIX    V     12
         CLOAK
    ALL BREAK AND VANISH, AND EVIL GATHERS HEAD! . . . .   433 NINETEEN 19         117
    THAT GATHERS VOLUME! NOW A THUNDER-CLAP. . . . . .   487 SEVEN SAGES          23
    THAT GATHERS VOLUME! NOW A THUNDER CLAP. . . . . .   487 SEVEN SAGES    V     23
GAUDY
    I SWAYED UPON THE GAUDY STERN . . . . . . . . .   253 HIS DREAM             1
    UPON A GAUDY BED?" . . . . . . . . . . . . .   253 HIS DREAM             8
    AND RUNNING CROWD AND GAUDY SHIP . . . . . . . .   254 HIS DREAM            15
    AND FISH AND CROWD AND GAUDY SHIP . . . . . . . .   254 HIS DREAM      V     15
    WHERE THE GAUDY MOON IS HUNG. . . . . . . . . .   502 VACILLATION          69
GAUGE
    LET HIM BETWEEN US JUDGE, FOR HE CAN GAUGE . . . . .   660 ISLE STAT II 1       36
GAUNT        SEE SKELETON-GAUNT
    NOW HAD THAT OLD GAUNT CRAFTY ONE, . . . . . . .   193 BAILE AILLINN       100
    AND THE GAUNT HOUSES PUT ON MAJESTY! . . . . . . .   292 TO A SHADE            7
GAVE
    GAVE ME A HARP, AND BID ME SING, . . . . . . . .    16 OISIN 1             232
    GAVE ME A HARP, AND BADE ME SING, . . . . . . . .    16 OISIN 1          V  232
    AND SURGING PHOSPHORUS ALONE GAVE LIGHT . . . . . .    31 OISIN 2              33
    OF SURGING PHOSPHORUS ALONE GAVE LIGHT. . . . . . .    31 OISIN 2          V   33
    GAVE TO HIGH NOON AND NOON TO NIGHT GAVE WAY! . . . .    40 OISIN 2             172
    GAVE TO HIGH NOON AND NOON TO NIGHT GAVE WAY! . . . .    40 OISIN 2             172
    GAVE TO THE NOON, AND NOON TO EVE GAVE WAY, . . . .    40 OISIN 2          V  172
    GAVE TO THE NOON, AND NOON TO EVE GAVE WAY, . . . .    40 OISIN 2          V  172
    TILL THE HORSE GAVE A WHINNY! . . . . . . . . .    48 OISIN 3              25
    MY SORROW! FOR MANY A CREAK GAVE THE CREEL IN THE CART .    91 OLD FISHERMAN         6
    AH WOE! FULL MANY A CREAK GAVE THE CREEL IN THE CART . .    91 OLD FISHERMAN V       6
    AH ME! FULL MANY A CREAK GAVE THE CREEL IN THE CART . .    91 OLD FISHERMAN V       6
    AND HE GAVE THEM AS DOWERS TO HIS DAUGHTERS, . . . .    92 FATHER OHART          7
    AND GAVE ME MONEY, AND BADE ME GO . . . . . . . .    95 MOLL MAGEE           23
    AND GAVE HIS CURSE TO ME! . . . . . . . . . .    95 MOLL MAGEE           26
    WHEN I GAVE JUDGMENT, AND HIS WORDS WERE WISE, . . .   102 FERGUS DRUID         11
    WAS ROBBED BEFORE EARTH GAVE THE WHEAT! . . . . . .   196 BAILE AILLINN       166
    FOR HE GAVE ALL HIS HEART AND LOST. . . . . . . .   202 NEVER GIVE ALL       14

                                 313
```

GAVE (CONTINUED)

AND FOR THIS END THEY GAVE ME MY OLD HARP . . . . . . 237 SHADOW WATER B   327
THEY GAVE ME THAT OLD HARP OF THE NINE SPELLS . . . . . 237 SHADOW WATER B V 327
HAVE BEEN DEFEATED BY THAT PLEDGE YOU GAVE . . . . . . 258 KING NO KING   9
AND HOW WHAT HER DREAMING GAVE . . . . 260 UNWORTH PRAISE   15
SOLDIERS THAT GAVE, WHATEVER DIE WAS CAST! . . . . . 269 PARDON FATHERS   9
NOR GAVE LOUD SERVICE TO A CAUSE . . . . 273 GREY ROCK   57
PRAISED THEIR GREAT VICTORIES AND GAVE THEM JOY . . . . 286 TWO KINGS V 218B
YOU GAVE, BUT WILL NOT GIVE AGAIN . . . . 287 TO WEALTHY MAN   1
HE GAVE THE HOURS THEY HAD SET FREE . . . . 288 TO WEALTHY MAN   22
BECAUSE YOU GAVE, NOT WHAT THEY WOULD, ... 288 TO WEALTHY MAN   35
THEY WEIGHED SO LIGHTLY WHAT THEY GAVE. . . . . . . 290 SEPTEMBER 1913   30
HE GAVE A GASP AND THOUGHT TO HAVE FLED, ... 303 HOUR DAWN   22
HE GAVE A GASP AND THOUGHT TO RUN, ... 303 HOUR DAWN V 22
GAVE ME SUCH PLEASURE I'D FORGO . . . . 305 HOUR DAWN   69
HE GAVE HIM A GREAT PUMMELLING, ... 307 HOUR DAWN   113
NOR GAVE GOD THANKS TILL OVERHEAD . . . . 307 HOUR DAWN   121
AND GAVE GOD THANKS THAT OVERHEAD . . . . 307 HOUR DAWN V 121
AMONG THE POOR BOTH OLD AND YOUNG GAVE HER PRAISE. . . . 351 HER PRAISE   18
WHO NEVER GAVE THE BURNING TOWN A THOUGHT! . . . . . 384 VISION ROBART   57
GAVE SHEBA TO HER SOLOMON." . . . . 388 SOLOMON WITCH   32
THAT GAVE, THOUGH FREE TO REFUSE-- . . . . . . 414 TOWER   133
POSEIDON GAVE IT BIT AND OAR, ... 447 COLONUS PRAISE   28
THAT IF THE SPRING BEAR OFF WHAT THE SPRING GAVE . . . . 464 HARUN RASHID   76
AND THEREUPON HIS BOUNTY GAVE WHAT NOW . . . . . . 465 HARUN RASHID   103
GAVE BUT MORE REASON FOR A WOMAN'S CARE. . . . . . 466 HARUN RASHID   111
FOUND ALL THE PLEASURE THAT LIFE GAVE"! . . . . . . 521 THREE THINGS   11
THE CHILDREN THAT HE GAVE, ... 525 DANCING DAYS   12
THOSE DEEDS WERE BEST THAT GAVE THE MINUTE WINGS . . . . 533 HER TRIUMPH   5
AND HEAVENLY MUSIC IF THEY GAVE IT WIT! . . . . . . 533 HER TRIUMPH   6
SANG OF THE BEAST THAT GAVE THE FATAL WOUND. . . . . 537 HER VISION   16
I ANSWER THAT I GAVE MY SOUL . . . . 538 LAST CONFESS   3
HE FANCIED THAT I GAVE A SOUL . . . . 538 LAST CONFESS   9
BEAST GAVE BEAST AS MUCH. . . . . 538 LAST CONFESS   12
I GAVE WHAT OTHER WOMEN GAVE . . . . 538 LAST CONFESS   13
I GAVE WHAT OTHER WOMEN GAVE . . . . 538 LAST CONFESS   13
BUT A GOOD STRONG CAUSE"--THE ROPE GAVE A JERK THERE, . . 545 TO SAME TUNE 1   23
THE MIRACLE THAT GAVE THEM SUCH A DEATH . . . . . . 555 RIBH AT TOMB   10
THEY GAVE IT OUT TO ALL THE WORLD, ... 582 ROGER CASEMENT   11
WHAT GAVE THAT ROAR OF MOCKERY, ... 583 GHOST ROG CASE   7
I GAVE IT ALL TO AN OLDER MAN! . . . . 588 OLD WICKED MAN   23
GAVE WOMEN DREAMS AND DREAMS THEIR LOOKING-GLASS. . . . 610 STATUES   16
GAVE WOMEN DREAMS AND DREAMS THEIR LOOKING GLASS. . . . 610 STATUES V 16
BUT A GOOD STRONG CAUSE"--THE ROPE GAVE A JERK THERE, . . 616 MARCH SONGS 3   23
AND YET GAVE TONGUE. "HOUND VOICES" WERE THEY ALL. . . 622 HOUND VOICE   9
THE COUNTESS CATHLEEN WAS THE NAME I GAVE IT! . . . . 629 CIRCUS ANIMALS   18
THE SPIRITS STOLE, AND GAVE HIM IN ITS STEAD . . . . 684 SEEKER   55
FOR ALL I GAVE THE VOICE, FOR ALL MY YOUTH, ... 685 SEEKER   78
WHEN HE GAVE TO THEE THE ROSE, ... 744 ROSY CROSS   2
GAVE TO ME ALONE THE CROSS! . . . . 744 ROSY CROSS   3
WHEN HE GAVE TO THEE THE ROSE, ... 744 ROSY CROSS   10
GAVE TO ME ALONE THE CROSS. . . . . 744 ROSY CROSS   11
GAVE HIM HIS HARP. NOW THAT HE IS ASLEEP, ... 748 SHADOW WATER A   18
AND, THOUGH YOU LOVED HER, GAVE HER UP TO ME? . . . 749 SHADOW WATER A   50
TAUGHT ME WISE MUSIC, AND GAVE ME THIS OLD HARP! . . . 750 SHADOW WATER A   76
IT WAS A FOOL THAT GAVE IT, AND MAY BE . . . . . 750 SHADOW WATER A   78
FOR HE WHO GAVE IT CALLED IT AENGUS' HARP . . . . 762 SHADOW WATER A   288
GAVE THEIR BODIES, EMPTIED PURSES, ... 789 SINGING HEAD   19
GAVE ALL THE LOVE THAT WOMEN KNOW! . . . . . . 789 SINGING HEAD   21

GAVEST
A FOOLISH WORD THOU GAVEST ME! . . . . 671 ISLE STAT II 3   131

GAVRA
AND THOSE ON GAVRA LYING LOW, ... 5 OISIN 1 V 41

GAVRA'S
FOR OUR BEST WERE DEAD ON GAVRA'S GREEN. . . . . . 2 OISIN 1 V 71

GAY
HELD TO THE TOWERS WITH BOASTING SONGS AND GAY. . . . 41 OISIN 2 V 184C
WHO MADE THE GRASS AND MADE THE WORMS AND MADE MY FEATHERS
GAY,
. . . THE WAVES WERE MORE GAY, ... 91 OLD FISHERMAN   3
A GAY WANDERING CRY. . . . . 98 FOXHUNTER   28
A GAY AND WANDERING CRY. . . . . 98 FOXHUNTER V 28
WE WHO ARE OLD, OLD AND GAY, ... 116 FAERY SONG   1
US WHO ARE OLD, OLD AND GAY, ... 116 FAERY SONG   13
ARE GAY WITH HIS MOOD. . . . . 118 CRADLE SONG   8
GROW GAY WITH HIS MOOD. . . . . 118 CRADLE SONG V 8
THERE DWELT A GAY, EXULTING, GENTLE RACE . . . . 127 DREAM OF FAERY   20
THAT HE'S A LOVELESS MAN! GAY BELLS BRING LAUGHTER . . 130 BOOK STORIES   18
GAY BELLS OR SAD, THEY BRING YOU MEMORIES . . . . 130 BOOK STORIES   21
MY BELL BRANCH MURMURS! THE GAY BELLS BRING LAUGHTER, . 130 BOOK STORIES V 18
AND NEVER WAS PIPING SO GAY. . . . . 144 HOST OF AIR   12
WITH A SAD AND A GAY FACE. . . . . 144 HOST OF AIR   16
AND NEVER WAS PIPING SO GAY. . . . . 145 HOST OF AIR   44
HIS GHOST WILL BE GAY. . . . . 311 PEACOCK   9
TILL ALL THE BOUGHS ARE GAY, ... 366 HER CHRIS TREE   5
THAT FANCIED GOODNESS MIGHT BE GAY; . . . . . 432 NINETEEN 19   104
SEMELE'S LAD A GAY COMPANION. . . . . 446 COLONUS PRAISE   8
THE SECOND BEST'S A GAY GOODNIGHT AND QUICKLY TURN AWAY. . 459 FROM OEDIPUS   12
AND ALL MY HEART SEEMED GAY! . . . . 507 STREAM AND SUN   3
OF POETS THAT ARE ALWAYS GAY, ... 565 LAPIS LAZULI   3
THEY KNOW THAT HAMLET AND LEAR ARE GAY! . . . . 565 LAPIS LAZULI   16

		PAGE	TITLE		LINE

GAY (CONTINUED)
```
    AND THOSE THAT BUILD THEM AGAIN ARE GAY.  . . . . . .      566  LAPIS LAZULI           36
    THEIR ANCIENT, GLITTERING EYES, ARE GAY.  . . . . . .      567  LAPIS LAZULI           56
    MY LOVER LOOKED SO GAY". . . . . . . . . . . . .          570  THREE BUSHES           32
    MY LOVER LOOKS SO GAY." . . . . . . . . . . . . .         570  THREE BUSHES     V     32
    THE POETS HAVE IMAGINED, TERRIBLE AND GAY."  . . . .      602  GALLERY REVIS          12
    SING THE LORDS AND LADIES GAY  . . . . . . . . .          640  BEN BULBEN             78
    BY A PEOPLE SADLY GAY:  . . . . . . . . . . . .           680  LOVE AND DEATH         10
    NOW SADLY, NOW UNEARTHLY GAY,  . . . . . . . . .          716  FAIRY DOCTOR            3
    LONG THOU FOR NOTHING, NEITHER SAD NOR GAY;  . . . .      734  QUATRAIN APHOR          9
GAYEST
    GAYEST WANDERERS, I AND YOU,  . . . . . . . . . .         706  DAWN-SONG              31
GAZE
    WITH QUENCHLESS GAZE AND FLUTTERING HAIR. . . . . .        12  OISIN 1              145
    AND SANG, AND WITH A DREAMY GAZE . . . . . . . .           26  OISIN 1              393
    OR LOVE'S FIRST TENDERNESS DIE IN OUR GAZE. . . . .        27  OISIN 1              411
    OR LOVE'S FIRST TENDERNESS DIE IN OUR GAZE, . . . .        27  OISIN 1          V   419D
    AS THEY GAZE AT EACH OTHER, "OH, WHERE IS THAT GREAT ONE?"  28  OISIN 1        V   423H
    OR LOVE'S FIRST TENDERNESS DIE IN OUR GAZE."  . . .        28  OISIN 1          V   427
    "GAZE NO MORE ON THE PHANTOMS," NIAMH SAID,  . . . .       29  OISIN 2                5
    HOW SUCH A WARRIOR NEVER TURNED HIS GAZE . . . . .         29  OISIN 2          V    11
    WHERE GOES TO GAZE THE RESTLESS-FOOTED STAR  . . . .       32  OISIN 2          V   50G
    OF FACES, WAITED; AND THE LEISURED GAZE . . . . . .        39  OISIN 2              149
    OF FACES, WATCHED ME, AND THE LEISURED GAZE  . . . .       39  OISIN 2          V   149
    AND MY GAZE WAS THRONGED WITH THE SLEEPERS; . . . .        50  OISIN 3               49
    I MUST GAZE ON THE BEARD OF FINN, . . . . . . . .          55  OISIN 3              114
    CAME AFTER THE HARD GAZE OF YOUTH, OR AN OLD MAN LIFTED    59  OISIN 3              170
        HIS HEAD:
    IT WERE SAD TO GAZE ON THE BLESSED AND NO MAN I LOVED OF   63  OISIN 3              221
        OLD THERE:
    IT WAS SAD TO GAZE ON THE BLESSED AND NO MAN I LOVED OF    63  OISIN 3          V   221
        OLD THERE;
    BELOVED, GAZE IN THINE OWN HEART, . . . . . . . .         134  TWO TREES              1
    BELOVED, GAZE IN THINE OWN HEART. . . . . . . . .         135  TWO TREES             20
    GAZE NO MORE IN THE BITTER GLASS  . . . . . . . .         135  TWO TREES             21
    OR ONLY GAZE A LITTLE WHILE;  . . . . . . . . .          135  TWO TREES             24
    GAZE NO MORE IN THE BITTER GLASS. . . . . . . . .         136  TWO TREES             40
    MAY SURELY BARTER GAZE FOR GAZE.  . . . . . . . .         139  TO IRELAND            28
    MAY SURELY BARTER GAZE FOR GAZE.  . . . . . . . .         139  TO IRELAND            28
    MAY SURELY MEET THEIR ANCIENT GAZE. . . . . . . .         139  TO IRELAND       V    28
    AND IF ANY GAZE ON OUR RUSHING BAND,  . . . . . .        141  HOSTING SIDHE         10
    ARE OVERTHROWN BY A WOMAN'S GAZE  . . . . . . . .         164  PERFECT BEAUTY         4
    STILL OVERTHROWN BY A WOMAN'S GAZE,  . . . . . .          164  PERFECT BEAUTY V       4
    WHEN ALL THE WILD SUMMER WAS IN HER GAZE."  . . . .       200  FOLLY COMFORT         12
    FOR WE WILL GAZE UPON THIS WORLD NO LONGER. . . . .       251  SHADOW WATER B       614
    FOR HE WILL GAZE UPON THIS WORLD NO LONGER. . . . .       251  SHADOW WATER B V     614
    FOR WE WILL GAZE UPON THE WORLD NO LONGER.  . . . .       251  SHADOW WATER B V     614
    AND COPY THEIR PROUD STEADY GAZE. . . . . . . . .         273  GREY ROCK             64
    AND WHEN SHE MEETS OUR GAZE HER EYES ARE LAUGHTER-LIT,   362  HER COURTESY           5
    AND WHEN SHE MEETS OUR GAZE HER EYES ARE LAUGHTER LIT    362  HER COURTESY     V     5
    A GAZE BLANK AND PITILESS AS THE SUN. . . . . . .         402  SECOND COMING         15
    THE POPLARS GAZE ACROSS THE WATERS GREY,  . . . . .       653  ISLE STAT I 2         34
    EACH ONE AT GAZE FOR AYE UPON HIS WHIRLING THRONE. . . .  662  ISLE STAT II 1        81
    BUT ART THOU HAPPY? LET ME GAZE ON THEE . . . . .         671  ISLE STAT II 3       144
    I COULD GAZE, GAZE UPON THINE EYES' CLEAR GREY; . . .     671  ISLE STAT II 3       147
    I COULD GAZE, GAZE UPON THINE EYES' CLEAR GREY; . . .     671  ISLE STAT II 3       147
    I COULD GAZE, GAZE UPON THINE EYES OF GREY; . . . .       671  ISLE STAT II 3 V     147
    I COULD GAZE, GAZE UPON THINE EYES OF GREY; . . . .       671  ISLE STAT II 3 V     147
    GAZE ON TILL RAGGED TIME HIMSELF DECAY. . . . . .         672  ISLE STAT II 3       148
    WOULD HE TEACH ANY SIN?  GAZE IN THE CLOUD  . . . .       692  MOSADA 1              58
    O SISTER OF SORROWFUL GAZE! . . . . . . . . . .           706  FAIRY PEDANT           2
    AND GAZE ON THE MEADOW-MICE WARY, . . . . . . . .         707  FAIRY PEDANT          18
    A LIZARD CRAWLS—THE TWO MEN GAZE INTENT,  . . . .         711  FERENCZ RENYI         47
    AND GAZE ON ONE ANOTHER THROUGH OUR EYES, . . . .         749  SHADOW WATER A        58
    FOR WE WILL GAZE UPON THIS WORLD NO LONGER. . . . .       769  SHADOW WATER A       430
    I HIDE YOU WITH MY HAIR, THAT WE MAY GAZE . . . .         769  SHADOW WATER A V     429
GAZEBO
    WE THE GREAT GAZEBO BUILT,  . . . . . . . . . .          476  EVA GORE-BOOTH        30
GAZED
    THEY FINGERED IT AND GAZED ON ME  . . . . . . . .         15  OISIN 1              209
    THEY FINGERED IT AND GAZED AT ME, . . . . . . . .         15  OISIN 1          V   209
    AND I GAZED ON THE BELL-BRANCH, SLEEP'S FOREBEAR, . . .   50  OISIN 3               53
    . . . AND GAZED ON THE GRASS WITH A SIGH. . . . . .       54  OISIN 3              100
    AND GAZED UPON THE WISDOM OF HIS EYES, . . . . .         108  CUCHULAIN SEA  V      41
    AND GAZED UPON THE MOURNFUL STARS ABOVE, . . . . .       123  DREAM OF DEATH V      11
    AND THOUGH WHEN HE GAZED HERE AND THERE, . . . . .       274  GREY ROCK             81
    HE HAD BUT GAZED ON THORN-TREES, SPOKE, . . . . .        274  GREY ROCK             82
    HE HAD BUT GAZED ON THORN TREES, SPOKE; . . . . .        274  GREY ROCK        V    82
    THE DISEMBOWELLED HORSE.  KING EOCHAID GAZED, . . .      278  TWO KINGS        V    45
    I GAZED AT HIM LIKE GROUSE UPON A KITE; . . . . .        283  TWO KINGS            152
    AND THAT PROUD LOOK AS THOUGH SHE HAD GAZED INTO        354  HIS PHOENIX           29
        THE BURNING SUN,
    GAZED UPON ALL THINGS KNOWN, ALL THINGS UNKNOWN, . .    383  VISION ROBART         30
    WHILE ON THE SHOP AND STREET I GAZED  . . . . . .        501  VACILLATION           40
    AS I AM STANDING NOW—AS THOUGH I GAZED, . . . . .        663  ISLE STAT II 2        26
GAZELLE
    BEAUTIFUL, ONE A GAZELLE. . . . . . . . . . . .          475  EVA GORE-BOOTH         4
    BEAUTIFUL, ONE A GAZELLE. . . . . . . . . . . .          475  EVA GORE-BOOTH        20
GAZES
    AND GAZES AROUND HER WITH EYES OF BRIGHTNESS; . . .       27  OISIN 1              413
    AND GAZES AROUND HER WITH EYES OF BRIGHTNESS; . . .       28  OISIN 1          V   421
```

315

PAGE   TITLE   LINE

GAZES   (CONTINUED)
    WE SHALL MINGLE NO MORE, NOR OUR GAZES EMPTY THEIR   56 OISIN 3   132
        SWEETNESS LONE
GAZING
    HOUNDS ARE GAZING ON HIS FACE, ...   99 FOXHUNTER   39
    THE HOUNDS ARE GAZING ON HIS FACE, ...   99 FOXHUNTER   V   39
    AND HOUNDS ARE GAZING ON HIS FACE, ...   99 FOXHUNTER   V   39
    AND GAZING ON HIS VISAGE WORN, ...   99 FOXHUNTER   V   43
    GAZING UPON HER WITH BEWILDERED EYES: . . . .   280 TWO KINGS   V   84
    WHEREIN THE GAZING HEART DOUBLES HER MIGHT. . . . . . .   326 ROBERT GREGORY   69
    IN LIST'NING SILENCE GAZING ON OUR GRIEF. . . . . . .   702 MOSADA 3   87
    NOR, GAZING FORTH WHERE LIFE'S SAD SICKLES REAP, . . .   710 FERENCZ RENYI   31
    LEANS ON HIS ELBOWS, GAZING AT THE SEA. . . . .   752 SHADOW WATER A   127
GEAR
    THAT HE ALONE HAD GATHERED UP NO GEAR, ...   340 SHEP GOATHERD   49
    ALL THAT SILK AND SATIN GEAR: . . . .   525 DANCING DAYS   3
    IN THAT OUTLANDISH GEAR, ...   526 AM OF IRELAND   7
GEESE   SEE BARNACLE-GEESE
    WAS IT FOR THIS THE WILD GEESE SPREAD . . . .   290 SEPTEMBER 1913   17
    AN ANCIENT LECHER TOOK TO GEESE . . . .   792 GEORGE MOORE   3
GEM-STUDDED
    LEANING DOWN FROM THE GEM-STUDDED SADDLE, ...   60 OISIN 3   187
    LEANING FORTH FROM THE GEM-STUDDED SADDLE, ...   60 OISIN 3   V 187
GENERAL
    BEFORE HIS TENT THE GENERAL SIPS HIS WINE, ...   709 FERENCZ RENYI   6
GENERATED
    WHAT'S WATER BUT THE GENERATED SOUL? . . . .   490 COOLE BALLYLEE   8
GENERATION
    HONEY OF GENERATION HAD BETRAYED, ...   444 SCHOOL CHILDR   34
    THAT IN EVERY GENERATION . . . .   608 SONGS BURDEN 3   25
GENERATIONS
    FILLING THE FIBROUS DIMNESS WITH LONG GENERATIONS OF EYES.   49 OISIN 3   40
    ONE THAT THE GENERATIONS HAD LONG WAITED . . . . . .   182 QUEEN MAEVE   66
    GENERATIONS OF HIS SORT, ...   319 DOLLS   6
    --THOSE DYING GENERATIONS--AT THEIR SONG, ...   407 SAIL BYZANTIUM   3
    JUSTIFY ALL THOSE RENOWNED GENERATIONS: . . . .   545 TO SAME TUNE 2   1
    JUSTIFY ALL THOSE RENOWNED GENERATIONS: . . . .   546 TO SAME TUNE 2   11
    OF ALL THAT SCHOLARLY GENERATIONS HAD HELD DEAR: . . . .   603 GALLERY REVIS   V 37A
    SUMMONED THE GENERATIONS OF HIS HOUSE, ...   609 IN TARAS HALLS   19
    REMEMBER ALL THOSE RENOWNED GENERATIONS, ...   613 MARCH SONGS 1   1
    REMEMBER ALL THOSE RENOWNED GENERATIONS, ...   613 MARCH SONGS 1   11
    REMEMBER ALL THESE RENOWNED GENERATIONS, ...   613 MARCH SONGS 1   V 11
GENEROSITY
    CONSIDERATION, GENEROSITY, ...   244 SHADOW WATER B   456
GENEROUS
    ON GENEROUS THINGS THAT HE DID . . . .   473 ALL SOUL NIGHT   69
GENII
    AND WHEN ONCE MORE THE LIGHTNING GENII PASSED, ...   687 TWO TITANS   29
GENTLE
    TO THIS DIM SHORE THOSE GENTLE FEET? . . . .   5 OISIN 1   V 51
    AND SIGHING BOWED HER GENTLE HEAD, ...   12 OISIN 1   149
    THE GENTLE NIAMH WAS MY WIFE: . . . .   24 OISIN 1   357
    AND THE GENTLE WAVES OF THE SUMMER SEAS, ...   27 OISIN 1   418
    AND, IN A FAR-OFF, GENTLE VALLEY STOPPING, ...   68 SAD SHEPHERD   13
    HE IS A GENTLE ROEBUCK: FOR HOW ELSE, I PRAY, COULD HE .   76 INDIAN ON GOD   15
    CONCEIVE A THING SO SAD AND SOFT, A GENTLE THING LIKE ME?   77 INDIAN ON GOD   16
    A GENTLE YET A KINGLY CHILD: . . . .   82 MAD KING GOLL   V 8
    A GRACIOUS, GENTLE, KINGLY BOY. . . . .   82 MAD KING GOLL   V 8
    LED ON BY GENTLE WAYS: . . . .   113 ROSE OF PEACE   12
    THERE DWELT A GAY, EXULTING, GENTLE RACE . . . . .   127 DREAM OF FAERY   20
    A GENTLE FEELING WRAPS THEM LIKE A FLEECE, ...   128 DREAM OF FAERY   V 34
    WINGED LOVES BORNE ON IN GENTLE STRIFE, ...   135 TWO TREES   V 14
    BUT LET A GENTLE SILENCE WROUGHT WITH MUSIC FLOW . . . .   175 ELEMENT POWERS   17
    BUT LET A GENTLE SILENCE ENWROUGHT WITH MUSIC FLOW . . .   175 ELEMENT POWERS   V 17
    FOR ANY GENTLE THING SHE SPAKE, ...   191 BAILE AILLINN   63
    GROW GENTLE WITHOUT SORROWING, ...   193 BAILE AILLINN   110
    GROW GENTLE WITHOUT SORROWINGS: . . . .   193 BAILE AILLINN   V 110
    LIKE GENTLE BLOOD, HAS BEEN DRIVEN FROM THE PLACE, . . .   292 TO A SHADE   14
    BUT GROWS MORE GENTLE WHEN HE SPEAKS HER NAME, . . .   340 SHEP GOATHERD   29
    WE HAVE LIT UPON THE GENTLE, SENSITIVE MIND . . . . .   368 EGO DOMINUS   12
    A GENTLE QUESTIONING LOOK THAT CANNOT HIDE . . . . . .   601 GALLERY REVIS   6
    BEAUTIFUL AND GENTLE IN HER VENETIAN WAY. . . . . . .   602 GALLERY REVIS   14
    YET A MOST GENTLE WOMAN: WHO CAN TELL . . . .   618 BRONZE HEAD   10
GENTLEMAN
    TO THIS MOST GALLANT GENTLEMAN . . . .   582 ROGER CASEMENT   23
GENTLEMEN
    AMONG THE OTHER GENTLEMEN, ...   296 THREE BEGGARS   34
    "HEAR, GENTLEMEN, LADIES, AND ALL MANKIND: . . . . .   544 TO SAME TUNE 1   2
    "HEAR, GENTLEMEN, LADIES, AND ALL MANKIND: . . . . .   615 MARCH SONGS 3   2
    HARD-RIDING COUNTRY GENTLEMEN, ...   639 BEN BULBEN   75
GENTLENESS
    TOGETHER IN THAT HOUR OF GENTLENESS . . . .   80 EPHEMERA   6
    THE GENTLENESS NONE THERE HAD EVER KNOWN: . . . . . .   418 ANCEST HOUSES   21
    DISTRACTED GENTLENESS THAT CANNOT HIDE . . . .   601 GALLERY REVIS   V 6
    WITH YOU I AM ALL GENTLENESS: IN TRUTH, ...   669 ISLE STAT II 3   70
GENTLER
    FORMS THAT GENTLER PHIDIAS WROUGHT. . . . .   638 BEN BULBEN   44
GENTLY
    THEN SHE SIGHED GENTLY, "IT GROWS LATE. . . . . . .   9 OISIN 1   102
    MURMURING GENTLY HOW FAR OFF ARE THE UNQUIET LANDS: . . .   78 INDIAN TO LOVE   V 10
    OR GENTLY IN A RING. . . . .   97 FOXHUNTER   8

316

GENTLY (CONTINUED)
AND LEAD HIM GENTLY IN A RING, ... 97 FOXHUNTER V 7
AND GENTLY UP AND DOWN. . . . . 97 FOXHUNTER V 8
FOR WINDS WILL BEAR THEM GENTLY WHEN THE EAGLE FLIES, . . 146 UNAPPEAS HOST V 3
LEAD THEM GENTLY ASTRAY! . . . . 568 SWEET DANCER 11
MOVE MOST GENTLY IF MOVE YOU MUST . . . . 617 LONG-LEG FLY 13
GENTLY SHOOK THEIR MOTH-LIKE WINGS! . . . . 667 ISLE STAT II 3 26
AND TEARS OF FIRE FALL GENTLY IN THE DEW. . . . . . . 738 YOU ARE SAD 4

GEOMETRY
DESERT GEOMETRY OR THE GIFT OF HARUN AL-RASCHID . . . . 460 HARUN RASHID V T

GEORGE
AND THEN I THINK OF OLD GEORGE POLLEXFEN, ... 325 ROBERT GREGORY 33
HIS SON GEORGE, THE ASTROLOGER; . . . . 360 ALF POLLEXFEN 8
RESTORED THIS TOWER FOR MY WIFE GEORGE; . . . . . . 406 CARVED STONE 4
SAINT GEORGE OR ELSE A PAGAN PERSEUS; . . . . 533 HER TRIUMPH 10
ON GEORGE MOORE! . . . . 792 GEORGE MOORE T

GEORGIAN
OF THAT OLD GEORGIAN MANSION, MIX . . . . 475 EVA GORE-BOOTH 16

GER-EAGLE
FOR THEY WILL RIDE THE NORTH WHEN THE GER-EAGLE FLIES, . . 146 UNAPPEAS HOST 3

GERMAN
SOME NINETEEN GERMAN PLANES, THEY SAY, ... 791 REPRISALS 1

GERMANY'S
TILL GERMANY'S OVERCOME! . . . . 395 SIXTEEN DEAD 8

GET
COME FROM THE ISLE OF THE LIVING." "THEN GET YE . . . . 34 OISIN 2 V 79
AND GET INTO THEIR WORLD THAT TO THE SENSE . . . . . . 230 SHADOW WATER B 179
DO MEN WHO LEAST DESIRE GET MOST? . . . . 295 THREE BEGGARS 13
OR GET THE MOST WHO MOST DESIRE?" . . . . 295 THREE BEGGARS 14
A BEGGAR SAID, "THEY GET THE MOST . . . . 295 THREE BEGGARS 15
"AND GET A COMFORTABLE WIFE AND HOUSE . . . . 299 BEGGAR CRIED 5
I GET A LAUGHING FIT, ... 455 FRIENDS YOUTH 4
AND SHE CAN GET NO REST . . . . 456 FRIENDS YOUTH 8
"BUT I CAN GET A HAIR-DYE . . . . 492 ANNE GREGORY 7
GET ALL THE GOLD AND SILVER THAT YOU CAN, ... 500 VACILLATION 19
SO GET YOU GONE, VON HUEGEL, THOUGH WITH BLESSINGS ON YOUR 503 VACILLATION 89
    HEAD.
I SHOULD NOT GET THE WORD . . . . 585 ORAHILLY 20
"IRELAND SHALL GET HER FREEDOM AND YOU STILL BREAK STONE." 590 PARNELL 2
SOME DAY WE SHALL GET UP BEFORE THE DAWN . . . . . . 622 HOUND VOICE 15
AND NEVER GET THE ANSWERS RIGHT. . . . . 632 MAN AND ECHO 10
WE MUST GET SWORDS. IS'T THE ONLY WAY? OH, SEE, . . . 660 ISLE STAT II 1 34
THEY GET THEM SWORDS, AND BOTH OR EITHER FALL? . . . . 662 ISLE STAT II 1 78

GETS
AND THE SEED OF THE FIRE GETS FEEBLE AND COLD. . . . . 151 OLD MOTHER 10
BUT THE SEED OF THE FIRE GETS FEEBLE AND COLD, ... 151 OLD MOTHER V 9
BUT HE THAT GETS THEIR LOVE AFTER THE FASHION . . . . . 228 SHADOW WATER B 145
HE NOW GETS NOVELS AT HIS EASE. . . . . 792 GEORGE MOORE 4

GETTING
FOR I AM GETTING ON IN LIFE--TO SOMETHING . . . . . . 222 SHADOW WATER B 6

GHASTLY
AND THE GHASTLY GHOST-FLAMES GLIMMER ALL ALONG THE TAFFRAIL 719 PHANTOM SHIP 21
    RAILS
AND THE GHASTLY GHOST FLAMES GLIMMER ALONG THE TAFFREL 719 PHANTOM SHIP V 21
    RAILS,

GHOST
THE DOORS OF HELL AND BLOW THERE MANY A WHIMPERING GHOST! 147 UNAPPEAS HOST 10
OF A NEW FRIEND HE HAS TURNED A GHOST. . . . . 275 GREY ROCK 103
BUT I'LL HAVE NO MAN CALL ME GHOST." . . . . 304 HOUR DAWN 41
"I TOOK YOU FOR A BRAWLING GHOST, ... 304 HOUR DAWN V 41
HIS GHOST WILL BE GAY . . . . 311 PEACOCK 9
RIDDLED WITH LIGHT. AH! WHEN THE GHOST BEGINS TO QUICKEN, 316 COLD HEAVEN 9
BID A STRONG GHOST STAND AT THE HEAD . . . . 435 FOR MY SON 1
BID THE GHOST HAVE SWORD IN FIST! . . . . 435 FOR MY SON 9
BID THE GHOST HAVE SWORD IN HAND! . . . . 435 FOR MY SON V 9
BUBBLE UPON THE TABLE. A GHOST MAY COME; . . . . . . 470 ALL SOUL NIGHT 5
AND THAT A SLIGHT COMPANIONABLE GHOST, ... 472 ALL SOUL NIGHT 35
AND MAY HAVE GROWN MORE ARROGANT BEING A GHOST. . . . . 473 ALL SOUL NIGHT 80
A LONELY GHOST THE GHOST IS . . . . 511 JANE AND JACK 7
A LONELY GHOST THE GHOST IS . . . . 511 JANE AND JACK 7
THE SKEIN SO BOUND US GHOST TO GHOST . . . . 511 JANE AND JACK 15
THE SKEIN SO BOUND US GHOST TO GHOST . . . . 511 JANE AND JACK 15
"WHAT THEN?" SANG PLATO'S GHOST. "WHAT THEN?" . . . . 576 WHAT THEN 5
"WHAT THEN?" SANG PLATO'S GHOST. "WHAT THEN?" . . . . 577 WHAT THEN 10
"WHAT THEN?" SANG PLATO'S GHOST. "WHAT THEN?" . . . . 577 WHAT THEN 15
BUT LOUDER SANG THAT GHOST, "WHAT THEN?" . . . . . . 577 WHAT THEN 20
THE GHOST OF ROGER CASEMENT . . . . 583 GHOST ROG CASE T
THE GHOST OF ROGER CASEMENT . . . . 583 GHOST ROG CASE 9
THE GHOST OF ROGER CASEMENT . . . . 583 GHOST ROG CASE 19
THE GHOST OF ROGER CASEMENT . . . . 584 GHOST ROG CASE 29
THE GHOST OF ROGER CASEMENT . . . . 584 GHOST ROG CASE 39
AND THE GHASTLY GHOST FLAMES GLIMMER ALONG THE TAFFREL 719 PHANTOM SHIP V 21
    RAILS,
CAN GHOST OR MAN BE SATISFIED? . . . . 791 REPRISALS 4

GHOST-FLAMES
AND THE GHASTLY GHOST-FLAMES GLIMMER ALL ALONG THE TAFFRAIL 719 PHANTOM SHIP 21
    RAILS

GHOST-LOVER
A GHOST-LOVER HE WAS . . . . 473 ALL SOUL NIGHT 79

GHOSTLY
WALKING GHOSTLY IN THE DEW, ... 67 HAPPY SHEPHERD 52

GHOSTLY (CONTINUED)

	PAGE	TITLE		LINE
WALKING GHOSTLY 'MONG THE DEW, ...	67	HAPPY SHEPHERD	V	52
BUT BREAK UPON HIS GHOSTLY SOLITUDE.	429	NINETEEN 19		40
UPON A GHOSTLY PARADIGM OF THINGS;	445	SCHOOL CHILDR		42
UPON THE GHOSTLY IMAGES OF THINGS	445	SCHOOL CHILDR	V	42

GHOST'S

| FOR IT IS A GHOST'S RIGHT, ... | 470 | ALL SOUL NIGHT | | 6 |
| AN OLD GHOST'S THOUGHTS ARE LIGHTNING, ... | 600 | SPIRIT MEDIUM | | 17 |

GHOSTS

GHOSTS OF HER VANISHED GLORIES, MUSE AND STALK . . .	687	TWO TITANS		21
AMONG THE WHIMPERING GHOSTS. MATE THUS. ALREADY? . .	722	WITCH VIVIEN		68
THE GHOSTS WENT BY ME WITH THEIR LIPS APART	734	QUATRAIN APHOR		13

GIANT

| AMONG THE GIANT KINGS WHOSE HOARD, ... | 196 | BAILE AILLINN | | 164 |

GIANTS

| WHEN GODS AND GIANTS WARRED. WE RODE BETWEEN . . . | 31 | OISIN 2 | | 31 |

GIBE

| OF A MOCKING TALE OR A GIBE . . . . | 392 | EASTER 1916 | | 10 |

GIDDY

GIDDY WITH HIS HUNDREDTH YEAR, ...	298	THREE HERMITS		6
GIDDY WITH HIS HUNDREDTH YEAR, ...	299	THREE HERMITS		31
THE GIDDY BEE'S COMPLACENT CROON, ...	736	SUMMER EVENING		5

GIER-EAGLE

| FOR THEY WILL RIDE THE WINDS WHEN THE GIER-EAGLE FLIES . | 146 | UNAPPEAS HOST | V | 3 |

GIFT

TO GRADUAL TIME'S LAST GIFT, A WRITTEN SPEECH . . .	264	HOUSE SHAKEN		11
THE GIFT	287	TO WEALTHY MAN	V	T
WE HAVE NO GIFT TO SET A STATESMAN RIGHT;	359	WAR POEM		3
HEARTS ARE NOT HAD AS A GIFT BUT HEARTS ARE EARNED .	404	FOR DAUGHTER		34
WHERE SATO'S GIFT, A CHANGELESS SWORD, ...	421	MY TABLE		2
THE GIFT OF HARUN AL-RASHID	460	HARUN RASHID		T
DESERT GEOMETRY OR THE GIFT OF HARUN AL-RASCHID . .	460	HARUN RASHID	V	T
THAT EVERY GIFT AND EVERY WORD OF PRAISE	469	HARUN RASHID		172
"I BID HIM ASK WHAT GIFT HE WILL, ...	741	EARL PAUL		57

GIFTED

| GIFTED WITH SO FINE AN EAR; . . . . | 412 | TOWER | | 94 |

GIFTS

| THE GIFTS THAT GOVERN MEN, AND AFTER THESE . . . . | 264 | HOUSE SHAKEN | | 10 |

GIGANTIC

| AND HER GIGANTIC LIMBS. THE WEARY THIRST . . . . | 687 | TWO TITANS | | 16 |

GILD

| ALTHOUGH THE SUMMER SUNLIGHT GILD . . . . . . | 501 | VACILLATION | | 45 |
| HERE, FACING TO THE LAKE, AND NO NAME GILD; . . . | 663 | ISLE STAT II 2 | | 20 |

GILDED

| HAST THOU NOT RULED AMONG THE GILDED WALLS? . . . | 724 | KANVA ON SELF | | 7 |
| A COAT OF GILDED MAIL. . . . . | 740 | EARL PAUL | | 16 |

GILLIGAN

THE BALLAD OF FATHER GILLIGAN	132	FR GILLIGAN		T
FATHER GILLIGAN	132	FR GILLIGAN	V	T
THE OLD PRIEST PETER GILLIGAN	132	FR GILLIGAN		1
THE OLD PRIEST PETER GILLIGAN	133	FR GILLIGAN		23
THE OLD PRIEST PETER GILLIGAN	133	FR GILLIGAN		35
THE OLD PRIEST PETER GILLIGAN	133	FR GILLIGAN		39

GILLYFLOWER

| AND MANY A PURPLE GILLYFLOWER EATEN, ... | 729 | PRIEST FAIRY | | 35 |

GIMLET

| AND PIERCE IT THROUGH WITH A GIMLET, AND STARE . . . | 330 | BONE OF A HARE | | 12 |

GIORGIONE

| WHO HAD MURMURED OF GIORGIONE AT HIS LATEST BREATH-- . | 366 | HER COURAGE | | 8 |

GIRDLE

| AND THE GIRDLE OF LIGHT IS UNBOUND, ... | 165 | CRY OF SEDGE | | 8 |
| BINDS, AS WITHIN A GIRDLE OR A RING, ... | 657 | ISLE STAT I 3 | | 59 |

GIRL

AND KNELT THERE, EVERY GIRL AND MAN, ...	15	OISIN 1		214
WITH ONE LONG GLANCE FOR GIRL AND BOY	19	OISIN 1		287
FROM GIRL AND BOY AND MAN AND BEAST;	82	MAD KING GOLL		6
A GIRL AROSE THAT HAD RED MOURNFUL LIPS	120	SORROW OF LOVE		5
AND A YOUNG GIRL WHITE BREAD.	144	HOST OF AIR		20
IT HAD BECOME A GLIMMERING GIRL	149	WANDER AENGUS		13
IT HAD BECOME A LAUGHING GIRL, ...	149	ANDER AENGUS	V	13
TO TELL HIM HOW THE GIRL AILLINN	191	BAILE AILLINN		49
FOR THIS YOUNG GIRL AND THIS YOUNG MAN	195	BAILE AILLINN		157
A BEAUTIFUL YOUNG MAN AND GIRL CAME UP	223	SHADOW WATER B		33
A PRETTY GIRL TO SHARE MY BED";	296	THREE BEGGARS		31
TO A YOUNG GIRL	336	YOUNG GIRL		T
OR A YOUNG GIRL DRESSED OUT IN HER NEW GOWN, . .	350	HER PRAISE		4
THAT SHE MIGHT BE THAT SPRIGHTLY GIRL TRODDEN BY A BIRD;	353	HIS PHOENIX		4
THAT SHE MIGHT BE THAT SPRIGHTLY GIRL WHO HAD MARRIED WITH A BIRD;	353	HIS PHOENIX	V	4
THAT SHE MIGHT BE THAT SPRIGHTLY GIRL WHO WAS TRODDEN BY A BIRD;	353	HIS PHOENIX	V	4
A YOUNG GIRL IN THE INDOLENCE OF HER YOUTH, ...	359	WAR POEM		5
AND RIGHT BETWEEN THESE TWO A GIRL AT PLAY . . .	383	VISION ROBART		21
THAT GIRL MY UNREMEMBERING NIGHTS HOLD FAST . . .	384	VISION ROBART		50
A PEASANT GIRL COMMENDED BY A SONG, ...	410	TOWER		34
ABOVE THE STAGGERING GIRL, HER THIGHS CARESSED . .	441	LEDA AND SWAN		2
THE HERO, THE GIRL, AND THE FOOL	447	HERO GIRL FOOL		T
CUCHULAIN THE GIRL AND THE FOOL	447	HERO GIRL FOOL	V	T
THAN ALL MY BURSTING SPRINGTIME KNEW. A GIRL . .	466	HARUN RASHID		105
INHABITANT OF THE SOFT CHEEK OF A GIRL--	540	FROM ANTIGONE		2
MONEY IS GOOD AND A GIRL MIGHT BE BETTER, . . .	544	TO SAME TUNE 1		3

	PAGE	TITLE	LINE

GIRL (CONTINUED)
"A GIRL I HAD, BUT SHE FOLLOWED ANOTHER,   544 TO SAME TUNE 1   11
"MONEY IS GOOD AND A GIRL MIGHT BE BETTER,   545 TO SAME TUNE 1   21
THAT BLONDE GIRL THERE IS MY HEART'S DESIRE,   550 SONGS REWRIT 1 V   1
ETERNITY IS PASSION, GIRL OR BOY   560 WHENCE COME   1
THE GIRL GOES DANCING THERE   568 SWEET DANCER   1
A CRAZED GIRL   578 CRAZED GIRL   T
THAT CRAZED GIRL IMPROVISING HER MUSIC,   578 CRAZED GIRL   1
HER KNEE-CAP BROKEN, THAT GIRL I DECLARE   578 CRAZED GIRL   6
HER KNEE CAP BROKEN! THAT GIRL I DECLARE   578 CRAZED GIRL   V   6
MONEY IS GOOD AND A GIRL MIGHT BE BETTER,   616 MARCH SONGS 3   3
"A GIRL I HAD, BUT SHE FOLLOWED ANOTHER,   616 MARCH SONGS 3   11
"MONEY IS GOOD AND A GIRL MIGHT BE BETTER,   616 MARCH SONGS 3   21
NO MAN GROWS OLD, NO GIRL GROWS COLD,   621 JOHN KINSELLA   31
A GIRL THAT KNEW ALL DANTE ONCE   626 OLD MEN BE MAD   5
HOW CAN I, THAT GIRL STANDING THERE,   631 POLITICS   1
A LOTUS IN THEIR HANDS--YOUNG MOORISH GIRL   694 MOSADA 1   103
A LITTLE MOORISH GIRL? SMALL WORTH. MY SONG--   696 MOSADA 2   10
I WILL NOT HEAR! THE MOORISH GIRL MUST DIE.   697 MOSADA 2   39
YOUNG MOORISH GIRL, THY FINAL HOUR IS HERE!   701 MOSADA 3   63
I SAW A GIRL AFRAID TO BE TOO NEAR.   712 FERENCZ RENYI   68
A BOY AND GIRL HOLD ONE ANOTHER'S HANDS!   752 SHADOW WATER A   122
GIRLHOOD'S
FROM MEAGRE GIRLHOOD'S PUTTING ON   356 BROKEN DREAMS   9
GIRL'S
AND DECKED AND ALTERED IT FOR A GIRL'S LOVE,   423 MY DESCENDANTS   22
GIRL'S SONG   515 GIRLS SONG B   T
SEVEN POEMS GIRL'S SONG   515 GIRLS SONG B   V   T
ON A GIRL'S FORGOTTEN LUTE,   668 ISLE STAT II 3   66
GIRL'S SONG   723 GIRLS SONG A   V   T
GIRLS
AND HE SAW YOUNG MEN AND YOUNG GIRLS   144 HOST OF AIR   13
OLD MEN AND YOUNG MEN AND YOUNG GIRLS   145 HOST OF AIR   39
TWO GIRLS IN SILK KIMONOS, BOTH   475 EVA GORE-BOOTH   3
TWO GIRLS IN SILK KIMONOS, BOTH   475 EVA GORE-BOOTH   19
GIRLS DOWN ON THE SEASHORE   588 OLD WICKED MAN   30
FOR PASSING ROUND THE BOTTLE WITH GIRLS IN RAGS OR SILK,   592 PILGRIM   2
FOR PASSING ROUND THE BOTTLE WITH GIRLS IN RAG OR SILK,   592 PILGRIM   V   2
BUT BOYS AND GIRLS, PALE FROM THE IMAGINED LOVE   610 STATUES   4
THAT GIRLS AT PUBERTY MAY FIND   617 LONG-LEG FLY   21
WHAT SHALL I DO FOR PRETTY GIRLS   620 JOHN KINSELLA   11
WHAT SHALL I DO FOR PRETTY GIRLS   621 JOHN KINSELLA   23
WHAT SHALL I DO FOR PRETTY GIRLS   621 JOHN KINSELLA   35
WITH BOYS AND GIRLS ABOUT HIM,   627 STATES HOLIDAY   27
YONDER SEE THE FAIRY GIRLS   726 LOVERS QUARREL   21
GIRLS THAT HAVE GOVERNED CITIES,   789 SINGING HEAD   15
GIRLS'
COME TO THE CHESS, FOR YOUNG GIRLS' WITS ARE BETTER   721 WITCH VIVIEN   46
GIRTH   SEE SADDLE-GIRTH
HIGH AS THE SADDLE GIRTH, COVERING AWAY FROM OUR GLANCES THE TIDE!   47 OISIN 3   V   2
WATCHED HER THOSE SEAMLESS FACES FROM THE VALLEY'S GLIMMERING GIRTH!   55 OISIN 3   122
WATCHED HER THOSE SEAMLESS FACES FROM THE VALLEY'S MURAL GIRTH   55 OISIN 3   V   122
HOW, WHEN DIVIDED THE GIRTH,   60 OISIN 3   189
GIST
HERE'S THE GIST OF WHAT THEY MEAN.   637 BEN BULBEN   12
GIVE
AND THERE I WILL GIVE YOU A HUNDRED HOUNDS!   8 OISIN 1   86
SEA-GOD, THAT ONCE, TO GIVE HIS SLAVES CONTENT,   38 OISIN 2   V   129
THEIR HEARING, AND SOME COMFORT GIVE, BUT THEY   68 SAD SHEPHERD   V   6
TROUBLE HIS SLEEPING! GIVE HIM DREAMS OF ME,   75 ANASHU VIJAYA   91
GIVE THEM UNQUIET DREAMS!   88 STOLEN CHILD   34
WE GIVE THEM EVIL DREAMS,   88 STOLEN CHILD   V   34
HE BADE THEM GIVE OVER THEIR KEENING!   93 FATHER OHART   23
AMID MEN'S SOULS, THAT WAVER AND GIVE PLACE   112 ROSE OF WORLD   7
AMID MEN'S SOULS THAT DAY BY DAY GIVE PLACE,   112 ROSE OF WORLD   V   7
GIVE TO THESE CHILDREN, NEW FROM THE WORLD,   116 FAERY SONG   5
GIVE TO THESE CHILDREN, NEW FROM THE WORLD,   116 FAERY SONG   9
SAID, "AENGUS AND HIS SWEETHEART GIVE THEIR THANKS   187 QUEEN MAEVE   146
THAT ALL THIS LIFE CAN GIVE US IS   190 BAILE AILLINN   39
THAT ALL LIFE HAS TO GIVE US IS   190 BAILE AILLINN   V   39
THAT ALL LIFE HAD TO GIVE US IS   190 BAILE AILLINN   V   39
NEVER GIVE ALL THE HEART   202 NEVER GIVE ALL   T
NEVER GIVE ALL THE HEART, FOR LOVE   202 NEVER GIVE ALL   1
O NEVER GIVE THE HEART OUTRIGHT,   202 NEVER GIVE ALL   8
WHERE LOVE'S TO GIVE AND TO SPARE!   214 HAPPY TOWNLAND V   4
I COULD GIVE ALL MY HEART TO THAT RED MOLL   222 SHADOW WATER B   9
I'D GIVE THE PROFIT OF NINE VOYAGES   222 SHADOW WATER B V   9
I'LL GIVE MY ANSWER. YOU HAVE AWAKENED HIM.   225 SHADOW WATER B   79
I'LL GIVE MY ANSWER. YOU HAVE AWAKED HIM.   225 SHADOW WATER B V   79
IF YOU WILL GIVE ME ALL YOUR MIND AWHILE--   227 SHADOW WATER B   117
NO MORTAL CAN. YES! IF THEY GIVE US HELP.   229 SHADOW WATER B   165
COULD WE BUT GIVE US WHOLLY TO THE DREAMS,   230 SHADOW WATER B   178
AND I WOULD KNOW IF YOU WILL GIVE ME VENGEANCE.   235 SHADOW WATER B   301
UNTIL MY BODY GIVE YOU KISS FOR KISS.   238 SHADOW WATER B   345
YOUR SOUL SHALL GIVE THE KISS. I AM NOT AFRAID.   238 SHADOW WATER B   346
I'LL STRIKE A BLOW FOR HIM TO GIVE HIM TIME   239 SHADOW WATER B   365
I'LL GIVE A GOLDEN GALLEY FULL OF FRUIT,   240 SHADOW WATER B   373
QUEEN, GIVE IT ME. NO, I HAVE NEED OF IT.   241 SHADOW WATER B   399

GIVE   (CONTINUED)

	PAGE	TITLE	LINE
I'LL NEVER GIVE ANOTHER THOUGHT TO IT:	245	SHADOW WATER B	477
LET'S HOME: I'D GIVE SOME RUBIES TO A WOMAN.	248	SHADOW WATER B	537
THERE'S SOMEBODY I'D GIVE THE AMETHYST EYES TO.	248	SHADOW WATER B	538
HAVE WE NOT EVERYTHING THAT LIFE CAN GIVE	249	SHADOW WATER B	570
THAT LONG TO GIVE THEMSELVES FOR WAGE,	262	STUDENTS AGIT	2
AND YET COULD GIVE SO FINE A STROKE?"	274	GREY ROCK	84
IS THAT WE GIVE, ALTHOUGH IT BE BRIEF GIVING,	282	TWO KINGS	120
TO GO--FOR HOPE WOULD GIVE HIS LIMBS THE POWER--	282	TWO KINGS V	133A
FOR HOPE WOULD GIVE HIS LIMBS THE POWER--AND AWAIT	283	TWO KINGS	136
YOU GAVE, BUT WILL NOT GIVE AGAIN	287	TO WEALTHY MAN	1
THAT THINGS IT WERE A PRIDE TO GIVE	287	TO WEALTHY MAN	6
LOOK UP IN THE SUN'S EYE AND GIVE	288	TO WEALTHY MAN	32
WHAT ELSE HE GIVE OR KEEP	346	ON WOMAN	24
SHOULD GIVE TO MY FRIEND	349	HAWK	17
GIVE HER A LITTLE GRACE,	367	HER CHRIS TREE	9
AND BLESSED, I GIVE MY GRATITUDE,	380	SAINT HUNCH	14
GIVE MAN HIS THOUGHT OR HIS MERE BODY?	386	ROBARTES DANCE	40
BUT WHO CAN TALK OF GIVE AND TAKE,	395	SIXTEEN DEAD	3
OR MEDDLE WITH OUR GIVE AND TAKE	395	SIXTEEN DEAD	17
GIVE PLACE TO AN INDIFFERENT MULTITUDE, GIVE PLACE	427	PHANTOM HATRED	28
GIVE PLACE TO AN INDIFFERENT MULTITUDE, GIVE PLACE	427	PHANTOM HATRED	28
IT FEARED TO GIVE ITS LOVE A HURT WITH ALL THE TEMPEST THERE:	450	OWEN AHERNE	7
IT FEARED THE HURT THAT SHE COULD GIVE AND THEREFORE IT WENT MAD.	450	OWEN AHERNE	8
AS AIR UNDER A WING, CAN GIVE BIRDS' WIT.	462	HARUN RASHID	28
AS AIR UNDER A WING, CAN GIVE BIRD'S WIT.	462	HARUN RASHID V	28
I WOULD HAVE FOUND THE BEST THAT LIFE CAN GIVE,	465	HARUN RASHID	91
CAN GIVE HIS SHARPENED PALATE ECSTASY	474	ALL SOUL NIGHT	84
GIVE TO HIS SHARPENED PALATE ECSTACY	474	ALL SOUL NIGHT V	84
EVERY TOUCH THEY GIVE,	517	HER ANXIETY	10
"O CRUEL DEATH, GIVE THREE THINGS BACK,"	521	THREE THINGS	1
AND GIVE HIS OWN AND TAKE HIS OWN	538	LAST CONFESS	19
WHAT CAN SHE TAKE UNTIL HER MASTER GIVE:	558	RIBH CHRISTIAN	21
"LOVE TO GIVE OR TO WITHHOLD."	588	OLD WICKED MAN	21
GIVE TONGUE, PROCLAIM THEIR HIDDEN NAME--"HOUND VOICE."	622	HOUND VOICE	7
ALL CHOICE, AND GIVE TO CHANCE FOR GUIDING CHANCE	656	ISLE STAT I 3	39
I'D GIVE MY FAERY FLEETNESS, THOUGH I BE	670	ISLE STAT II 3	107
NAY, GIVE IT ME, AND I WILL SOUND A MEASURE:	681	SEEKER	9
HER HANGING MANSION. GIVE TO ME, I PRAY,	698	MOSADA 2	52
GIVE TO THY GOMEZ. GOMEZ--HE HAS GONE	703	MOSADA 3	110
GIVE TO THY VALLENCE. VALLENCE--HE HAS GONE	703	MOSADA 3 V	110
THEN GIVE ME TRIUMPH IN MY MANY PLOTS.	722	WITCH VIVIEN	51
AND YET, THERE IS A LOVE THAT THE GODS GIVE,	749	SHADOW WATER A	56
GIVE ME THE HELM: CALL HITHER THOSE WHO LIE	751	SHADOW WATER A	91
GIVE HER TO AIBRIC, IF HE WILL. I WAIT	755	SHADOW WATER A	172
AND TO GIVE WEALTH OF OXEN AND SHEEP TO ALL:	756	SHADOW WATER A	184
AND TO GIVE YOU BESIDES A HUNDRED SHIELDS,	756	SHADOW WATER A	185
GIVE ME A HUNDRED SHEEP. GIVE ME A HOUSE	758	SHADOW WATER A	220
GIVE ME A HUNDRED SHEEP. GIVE ME A HOUSE	758	SHADOW WATER A	220
AND A STRONG GALLEY. I GIVE YOU ALL AS MUCH.	758	SHADOW WATER A	222
THEY ARE ALWAYS QUARRELLING. GIVE ME YOUR SWORDS.	766	SHADOW WATER A	370
ALE SETS THEM QUARRELLING. GIVE ME YOUR SWORDS.	766	SHADOW WATER A	372
GIVE ME YOUR SWORDS. THEY ARE ALWAYS QUARRELLING.	766	SHADOW WATER A V	370
IT IS THE BROWN ALE DOES IT. GIVE ME YOUR SWORDS.	766	SHADOW WATER A V	372
THEY WILL GIVE HIM KISS FOR KISS	776	AGAINST WITCH	29
"GIVE ME YOUR WIFE," SAID HE,	779	GOING THE ROAD	5
OR GIVE BUT A SIGH AND A WORD,	786	YOUR HEART	12
A MAN BUT WILL GIVE YOU HIS LOVE	786	YOUR HEART	17
OR GIVE BUT A SIGH AND A WORD,	786	YOUR HEART	25
OR GIVE BUT A SIGH AND A WORD,	786	YOUR HEART	38

GIVEN

HAS GIVEN THE WAVES THEIR MELODY,	134	TWO TREES	10
HAVE GIVEN THEIR HEARTS UP TO THE PLAY.	202	NEVER GIVE ALL	10
ARE PLOTTING FOR YOUR DEATH. HAVE I NOT GIVEN	226	SHADOW WATER B	93
IT WAS SO GIVEN OUT, BUT I WILL PROVE	243	SHADOW WATER B	429
YOU SAY, AS I HAVE OFTEN GIVEN TONGUE	262	TO A POET	1
I HAD NOT GIVEN A PENNY FOR A SONG	267	ALL TEMPT ME	6
HE THOUGHT TO HAVE GIVEN HIS HORSE THE SPUR, BUT SAW	277	TWO KINGS V	48
TILL JUDGMENT HAS BEEN GIVEN, AND IF GUILTY,	280	TWO KINGS	74
HAD GIVEN THEIR CHILDREN'S CHILDREN LOFTIER THOUGHT,	292	TO A SHADE	12
HAD GIVEN BUT AS THE REST	293	HELEN LIVED	10
"WE'RE BUT GIVEN WHAT WE HAVE EARNED.	298	THREE HERMITS	14
AND GIVEN TO OTHERS ALL HEART'S ACHE,	355	BROKEN DREAMS	8
WE HAVE GIVEN THE WORLD OUR PASSION,	363	DOLLS DRAWINGS	10
AND GIVEN EVERYTHING A WOMAN NEEDS,	609	IN TARAS HALLS	7
SHE, PITY-CRAZED, HAD GIVEN HER SOUL AWAY,	629	CIRCUS ANIMALS	19

GIVER

OUR GIVER OF GOOD COUNSEL AND GOOD LUCK."	185	QUEEN MAEVE	102
HAD SEEMED TO BE THE GIVER OF ALL PEACE,	228	SHADOW WATER B	149

GIVES

BE PLENTY.--IF HE GIVES ANOTHER LOVE,	71	ANASHU VIJAYA V	5
SHE GIVES ME BITE AND SUP.	96	MOLL MAGEE	40
"HE BADE ME LET ALL KNOW HE GIVES HIS NAME	109	CUCHULAIN SEA	52
THAT GOD GIVES UNTO MAN IN SLEEP.	138	TO IRELAND V	22
HE GIVES HIS BELOVED CERTAIN RHYMES	157	BELOVED RHYMES	T
AEDH GIVES HIS BELOVED CERTAIN RHYMES	157	BELOVED RHYMES V	T
IN OWING THEM THE BRIDE-BED THAT GIVES PEACE."	187	QUEEN MAEVE	148
I KNOW WHAT WAGES BEAUTY GIVES,	336	YOUNG BEAUTY	13
THAT GIVES UP ALL HER MIND,	345	ON WOMAN	2

320

	PAGE	TITLE	LINE

GIVES (CONTINUED)
THE SELF-SOWN, SELF-BEGOTTEN SHAPE THAT GIVES . . . . .   446 COLONUS PRAISE   10
ENDURE WHAT LIFE GOD GIVES AND ASK NO LONGER SPAN! . . .   459 FROM OEDIPUS   1
THE STRENGTH THAT GIVES OUR BLOOD AND STATE MAGNANIMITY   481 BLOOD AND MOON   29
. . .
SORROW THAT GIVES FOR GUERDON LIBERTY . . . .   686 DRAWING-ROOM   6
GIVES FORTH. HE, THE ETERNAL, WORKS HIS WILL. . . . . .   689 NETTLESHIP   16
SORROW, THAT GIVES FOR GUERDON LIBERTY, ...   734 QUATRAIN APHOR   6
FOR GOD GIVES POWER TO THE SAD . . . .   741 EARL PAUL   47
FOR GOD GIVES POWER TO THE SAD . . . .   741 EARL PAUL   51
GIVETH
WHO GIVETH TO THE GOLDEN-CRESTED WREN . . . .   698 MOSADA 2   51
GIVING
FOOT AFTER FOOT WAS GIVING WAY, ...   274 GREY ROCK   72
IS THAT WE GIVE, ALTHOUGH IT BE BRIEF GIVING, ...   282 TWO KINGS   120
GIVING HIS HAND TO THAT MAN AND TO THIS, ...   286 TWO KINGS   V 218A
GLAD
THE HUNTING OF HEROES SHOULD BE GLAD." . . . .   4 OISIN 1   39
"THE HUNTING OF HEROES SHOULD BE GLAD! . . . .   4 OISIN 1   V 32
"FOR HUNTING HEROES SHOULD BE GLAD. . . . .   4 OISIN 1   V 34
WE ONLY KNOW THAT WE WERE GLAD . . . .   22 OISIN 1   V 340D
NO LONGER GLAD AS ON THAT MORNING, SPED . . . .   30 OISIN 2   V 16
PIERCED BY MY GLAD SINGING THROUGH, ...   67 HAPPY SHEPHERD   53
HOW MANY LOVED YOUR MOMENTS OF GLAD GRACE, ...   121 YOU ARE OLD   5
AND OF NEW FRIENDS ARE GLAD WITH YOUR PRAISE, ...   173 PLEADS FRIEND V   3
AND WITH GLAD VOICE MAEVE ANSWERED HIM, "WHAT KING . .   183 QUEEN MAEVE   79
AND WITH GLAD VOICE MAEVE ANSWERED "MANY A TIME . . .   183 QUEEN MAEVE   V 79
WITH HOLY SHADOWS." HER HIGH HEART WAS GLAD, ...   186 QUEEN MAEVE   126
THERE'S NOT A MAN BUT WILL BE GLAD OF IT . . . .   225 SHADOW WATER B   66
FROM A GLAD KINDNESS CANNOT TAKE HIS EYES. . . . . . .   404 FOR DAUGHTER   40
HERE IN THE SHADE. WHY? WHY? FOR WHAT IS GLAD? . . .   652 ISLE STAT I 2   8
POOR SAD WOOD-RHAPSODISTS. NOT SO! THEY'RE GLAD. . .   652 ISLE STAT I 2   16
NAY, NAY, ALMINTOR, YONDER SONG IS GLAD. . . . . . .   652 ISLE STAT I 2   23
OF EVENING AND GLAD SILENCE DWELLETH AYE, ...   653 ISLE STAT I 2   37
(HOW GLAD WAS HER MIEN!), ...   654 ISLE STAT I 2   72
TO MAKE US GLAD WITH WONDER AS WE SAT . . . .   683 SEEKER   41
MY BIDDING. NOW 'TIS DONE, AND I AM GLAD . . . . . .   700 MOSADA 3   29
GLAD, SIMPLE—NAY, HE SOUGHT NOT MYSTERY, ...   710 FERENCZ RENYI   30
I HOLD HIM DEARER THAN THE GLAD, ...   723 GIRLS SONG A   3
I'D GLAD FOLKS' HEARTS WITH BLITHER SONG." . . . . .   731 PRIEST FAIRY   82
AND HER DIM WAVE BIDS MAN BE NO MORE GLAD, ...   738 YOU ARE SAD   11
THOUGH THE GLAD CRY "SHIELD-BREAKER," . . . .   741 EARL PAUL   35
FOLDING THEIR HEARTS' DESIRE TO THEIR GLAD HEARTS. . .   765 SHADOW WATER A 349
GLADDENED
HIS FACE HAS NEVER GLADDENED SINCE HE CAME . . . . . .   747 SHADOW WATER A   1
GLADE   SEE WILLOW-GLADE
THROUGH ALL THE WELL-BELOVED GLADE. . . . .   67 HAPPY SHEPHERD V 46C
AND LIVE ALONE IN THE BEE-LOUD GLADE. . . . .   117 ISLE INNISFREE   4
AS LIES DARK WATER IN A MURMUROUS GLADE. . . . . . .   650 ISLE STAT I 1   138
DEEP-EYED, SLOW-FOOTING DOWN THE EMPTY GLADE. . . . .   653 ISLE STAT I 2   55
BEHOLD THE BRAZEN-GATED GLADE! . . . .   667 ISLE STAT II 3   43
BY THE WILLOWS IN THE GLADE, ...   726 LOVERS QUARREL   3
GLADLY
I SWEAR IT, THOUGH I GLADLY WOULD LIE DOWN . . . . . .   758 SHADOW WATER A 225
GLAMOUR
OF THE HIGH PEOPLE OF SORACA NOR IN GLAMOUR BY DEMONS   50 OISIN 3   V 50
   FLUNG,
LEST HE MAY SOME GLAMOUR FOLD . . . .   717 FAIRY DOCTOR   22
LEST SOME GLAMOUR HE MAY FOLD . . . .   717 FAIRY DOCTOR V 22
GLAMOURED
GLAMOURED BY FAIRIES FOR THEIR OWN. . . . .   717 FAIRY DOCTOR   20
GLAMOURS
. . . NOR IN GLAMOURS BY DEMONS FLUNG, ...   50 OISIN 3   50
. . . OR IN GLAMOURS BY DEMONS FLUNG, ...   50 OISIN 3   V 50
GLANCE
WITH ONE LONG GLANCE FOR GIRL AND BOY . . . .   19 OISIN 1   287
WITH ONE LONG GLANCE ON MAID AND BOY . . . .   19 OISIN 1   V 287
WITH A SWIFT AND FRIENDLY GLANCE . . . .   21 OISIN 1   309
WITH NO RETURNING GLANCE, IN WORDLESS MOOD . . . . . .   44 OISIN 2   V 230A
THOUGH YOU GLOW AND YOU GLANCE, THOUGH YOU PURR AND YOU   90 OLD FISHERMAN   2
   DART!
THOUGH YE GLOW AND YE GLANCE, THOUGH YE PURR AND YE DART,   90 OLD FISHERMAN V   2
A LATTICED WINDOW. HIS GLANCE WENT UP AT TIMES . . . .   180 QUEEN MAEVE   6
AYE, THOUGH ALL PASSION'S IN THE GLANCE— . . . . . .   388 SOLOMON WITCH   21
O BODY SWAYED TO MUSIC, O BRIGHTENING GLANCE, ...   446 SCHOOL CHILDR   63
O BODY SWAYED TO MUSIC BRIGHTENING GLANCE . . . . . .   446 SCHOOL CHILDR V 63
NOTHING CAN STAY MY GLANCE . . . .   474 ALL SOUL NIGHT   93
UNTIL THAT GLANCE RUN IN THE WORLD'S DESPITE . . . . .   474 ALL SOUL NIGHT   94
WHERE EVERY FOOT OBEYED HER GLANCE! . . . .   488 CRAZED MOON   11
WHERE VERY FOOT OBEYED HER GLANCE! . . . .   488 CRAZED MOON   V 11
SOME CAST OF DIE, OR LET SOME ARROW GLANCE . . . . . .   656 ISLE STAT I 3   40
GLANCED
I LAY, AS OVER SEA THE LIGHT HOOVES GLANCED . . . . .   30 OISIN 2   V 19A
GLANCES
THEN MOCK AT DEATH AND TIME WITH GLANCES . . . . . .   19 OISIN 1   274
HIGH AS THE SADDLE-GIRTH, COVERING AWAY FROM OUR GLANCES   47 OISIN 3   2
   THE TIDE!
HIGH AS THE SADDLE GIRTH, COVERING AWAY FROM OUR GLANCES   47 OISIN 3   V   2
   THE TIDE!
MINGLING HANDS AND MINGLING GLANCES . . . .   87 STOLEN CHILD   18
GLANCES OF HER WANDERING EYE . . . .   487 CRAZED MOON   4

321

GLANCES   (CONTINUED)
   THOSE GLANCES UNAFRAID! . . . . 516 MANS SONG   8
GLARE
   FEEBLER AND FEEBLER SHONE THE MISTY GLARE. . . . . . 37 OISIN 2   V 121
   THE SMOKY TORCHES MADE A GLARE . . . . 271 GREY ROCK   18
   AND SMOKY TORCHES MADE A GLARE . . . . 271 GREY ROCK   V 18
   TRAILING AND SHINING 'NEATH THE FLICKERING GLARE. . . . 688 TWO TITANS   32
GLASNEVIN
   AND GATHER THE GLASNEVIN COVERLET . . . . 293 TO A SHADE   19
   DRAW THE GLASNEVIN COVERLET ANEW . . . . 293 TO A SHADE   V 19
GLASS   SEE WINDOW-GLASS LOOKING-GLASS HOUR-GLASS
   WHO FOLLOW WITH THE OPTIC GLASS . . . . 66 HAPPY SHEPHERD   29
   GAZE NO MORE IN THE BITTER GLASS . . . . 135 TWO TREES   21
   IN THE DIM GLASS THE DEMONS HOLD, ... 135 TWO TREES   30
   THE GLASS OF OUTER WEARINESS, ... 135 TWO TREES   31
   GAZE NO MORE IN THE BITTER GLASS. . . . . 136 TWO TREES   40
   ON DAPPLED SKINS IN A GLASS BOAT . . . . 196 BAILE AILLINN 180
   BESIDE YOUNG AENGUS IN HIS TOWER OF GLASS, ... 219 HARP OF AENGUS   2
   AND IN A TOWER OF GLASS, AND FROM THAT DAY . . . . . 224 SHADOW WATER B   50
   "HE SHADOWED IN A GLASS . . . . 255 WOMAN HOMER   13
   I LIFT THE GLASS TO MY MOUTH, ... 261 DRINKING SONG   5
   HER LOVER THOUGHT, UPON THE GLASS . . . . 385 ROBARTES DANCE   11
   I RAGE AT MY OWN IMAGE IN THE GLASS . . . . 447 HERO GIRL FOOL   1
   THE GLASS BECAUSE MY GLASS! . . . . 473 ALL SOUL NIGHT   78
   THE GLASS BECAUSE MY GLASS! . . . . 473 ALL SOUL NIGHT   78
   STILL RAZOR-KEEN, STILL LIKE A LOOKING GLASS . . . . 477 SELF AND SOUL V 11
   ARE SUNG ABOVE THE GLASS, ... 587 PARNELLITES   30
   ARE SUNG ABOVE A GLASS! . . . . 587 PARNELLITES V 30
   GAVE WOMEN DREAMS AND DREAMS THEIR LOOKING GLASS. . . 610 STATUES   V 16
   AS FIGURES MOVING MIRRORED IN A GLASS, ... 676 ISLE STAT II 3 270
   TREMBLES AS A BELL OF GLASS . . . . 705 DAWN-SONG   10
   I'D BUY YOUR GLASS. MY GLASS I WILL NOT SELL. . . . 721 WITCH VIVIEN   28
   I'D BUY YOUR GLASS. MY GLASS I WILL NOT SELL. . . . 721 WITCH VIVIEN   28
   WITHOUT MY GLASS I'D BE A SORRY CLOWN. . . . . 721 WITCH VIVIEN   29
   FOR OTHER STAKES WE PLAY. YOU LOST THE GLASS. . . . 722 WITCH VIVIEN   50
   BESIDE YOUNG AENGUS IN HIS TOWER OF GLASS, ... 762 SHADOW WATER A 297
GLASSES
   AND TWO LONG GLASSES BRIMMED WITH MUSCATEL . . . . . 470 ALL SOUL NIGHT   4
   COME FILL UP ALL THOSE GLASSES . . . . 586 PARNELLITES   7
GLASS-MOSAIC
   GLASS-MOSAIC, WINDOW-GLASS, ... 440 WISDOM   3
GLAZING
   HALF TURNED AND FIXED A GLAZING EYE ON MINE, ... 537 HER VISION   26
GLEAM   SEE A-GLEAM
   A MOMENTARY GLEAM OF PHOSPHORUS FLAME. . . . . 37 OISIN 2   118
   ONE WITH THE TIDE THAT GLEAMS, THE WINGS THAT GLEAM AND 78 INDIAN TO LOVE   15
     DART,
   . . . THE WINGS THAT GLIMMER AND GLEAM AND DART! . . 78 INDIAN TO LOVE V 15
   . . . AND WINGS, THAT GLIMMER AND GLEAM AND DART, . . 78 INDIAN TO LOVE V 15
   A GREEN DROP IN THE SURGE, A GLEAM OF LIGHT . . . . 104 FERGUS DRUID   33
   TROY PASSED AWAY IN ONE HIGH FUNERAL GLEAM, ... 111 ROSE OF WORLD   4
   TILL ALL THE EDDIES GLEAM! . . . . 389 IMAGE PAST   4
   UNDER THE FIRST COLD GLEAM OF DAY? . . . . 398 BREAK OF DAY   4
   UPON A FADING GLEAM, ... 414 TOWER   141
   BEFORE THAT BRIEF GLEAM OF ITS LIFE BE GONE, ... 430 NINETEEN 19   63
   BUT WOKE AT THE FIRST GLEAM OF DAY, ROSE UP . . . . 467 HARUN RASHID   147
   OR EYELID SHOT THE GLEAM . . . . 507 STREAM AND SUN   12
   EYES UNDER EYELIDS DID SO GLEAM! . . . . 514 JANE GROWN OLD   6
   SAW ON THE WOOD'S EDGE GLEAM AN ASH-GREY FEATHER! . . 715 DWELT SYCAMORE   2
   FOLLOWED A RINGDOVE'S ASH-GREY GLEAM OF FEATHER. . . 715 DWELT SYCAMORE   6
   FOLLOWED THE RING-DOVE'S ASH-GREY GLEAM OF FEATHER. . 715 DWELT SYCAMORE V 6
   GOLD UNTO GOLD, A GLEAM IN ITS LONG HAIR, ... 720 WITCH VIVIEN   3
   A HURTING GLEAM OF LIGHT, ... 741 EARL PAUL   V 38
   I SAW HER GLITTER AND GLEAM, ... 744 GLOVE CLOAK   1
   OF AENGUS' BIRDS GLEAM IN THEIR APPLE BOUGHS. . . . 751 SHADOW WATER A 103
GLEAMED
   ROSE IN THE DARKNESS, AND THE WHITE SURF GLEAMED . . 30 OISIN 2   23
   AND WHEN THE WHITE STEED SAW WHAT BLACKNESS GLEAMED, . 30 OISIN 2   V 24
   AND STARLIGHT GLEAMED, AND CLOUDS FLEW HIGH, ... 84 MAD KING GOLL   34
GLEAMING
   THEIR NAKED AND GLEAMING BODIES POURED OUT AND HEAPED IN 48 OISIN 3   28
     THE WAY.
   THEIR MIGHTY AND NAKED AND GLEAMING BODIES . . . . . 48 OISIN 3   V 28
   WENT WALKING WITH SLOW STEPS ALONG THE GLEAMING . . 68 SAD SHEPHERD   3
   OH, MORE DARK THY GLEAMING HAIR IS . . . . 647 ISLE STAT I 1   51
   UNTIL AFAR APPEAR THE GLEAMING DRAGON-SCALES! . . . 651 ISLE STAT I 1 160
GLEAMS
   . . . THE GLEAMS OF THE WORLD AND THE SUN, ... 48 OISIN 3   22
   . . . THE CROZIER GLEAMS! . . . . 61 OISIN 3   194
   . . . THAT CROZIER GLEAMS! . . . . 61 OISIN 3   V 194
   ONE WITH THE TIDE THAT GLEAMS, THE WINGS THAT GLEAM AND 78 INDIAN TO LOVE   15
     DART,
   BUT LIGHT FROM THE PALE STARS, AND GLEAMS . . . . . 196 BAILE AILLINN 173
   ON THE ISLAND LAWNS, THEIR FEET WHERE THE PALE FOAM GLEAMS. 203 WITHER BOUGHS   14
   TOWER WHERE A CANDLE GLEAMS, ... 420 MY HOUSE   V 201
   THE EVENING GLEAMS ARE GREEN AND GOLD AND RED . . . 656 ISLE STAT I 3   22
   OF LILAC O'ER THE PULSING WATER GLEAMS, ... 664 ISLE STAT II 2   48
GLEN
   . . . AND THE LEAVES OF THE MURAL GLEN . . . . 49 OISIN 3   35
   FROM ROLLING VALE AND RIVERY GLEN! . . . . 83 MAD KING GOLL   19
   FROM ROLLING VALLEY AND RIVERY GLEN, ... 83 MAD KING GOLL V 17

		PAGE	TITLE		LINE

GLEN-CAR
    FROM THE HILLS ABOVE GLEN-CAR, ... 88 STOLEN CHILD 29
GLENDALOUGH
    IN GLENDALOUGH BESIDE THE STREAM, ... 331 ROUND TOWER 8
    STREAM AND SUN AT GLENDALOUGH . . . . 506 STREAM AND SUN T
GLIDE
    WHO HAD SEEMED TO GLIDE TO SOME INTRIGUE IN HER RED SHOES, 363 DOLLS FACES 6
GLIDING
    STREAM AND GLIDING SUN . . . . 506 STREAM AND SUN 2
GLIMMER
    AND TO THE WAVES THAT GLIMMER BY . . . . 20 OISIN 1 298
    A MOMENTARY GLIMMER OF VAGUE PHOSPHORUS FLAME. . . . 37 OISIN 2 V 120
    . . . AND THEIR EYES THAT GLIMMER LIKE SILK. . . . . 59 OISIN 3 176
    . . . THE WINGS THAT GLIMMER AND GLEAM AND DART; . . 78 INDIAN TO LOVE V 15
    . . . AND WINGS, THAT GLIMMER AND GLEAM AND DART, . . 78 INDIAN TO LOVE V 15
    THERE MIDNIGHT'S ALL A GLIMMER, AND NOON A PURPLE GLOW, 117 ISLE INNISFREE 7
    AND THE GHASTLY GHOST-FLAMES GLIMMER ALL ALONG THE TAFFRAIL 719 PHANTOM SHIP 21
        RAILS
    AND THE GHASTLY GHOST FLAMES GLIMMER ALONG THE TAFFREL 719 PHANTOM SHIP V 21
        RAILS,
    BEND LOWER LEST YOUR BATTLE-AXES GLIMMER. . . . . . 752 SHADOW WATER A 117
    BEND LOWER LEST YOUR BATTLE AXES GLIMMER. . . . . . 752 SHADOW WATER A V 117
GLIMMERED
    OF MOONLIT STEPS GLIMMERED; AND LEFT AND RIGHT . . . 31 OISIN 2 35
    DARK STATUES GLIMMERED OVER THE PALE TIDE . . . . . 31 OISIN 2 36
    THE DAWN CAME IN, AND GLIMMERED ON THE FLOOR . . . . 39 OISIN 2 152
GLIMMERING   SEE STAR-GLIMMERING
    AND WITH THE GLIMMERING CRIMSON GLOWED . . . . . . 3 OISIN 1 26
    HEAPED BESIDE THE GLIMMERING WAVES, ... 21 OISIN 1 314
    HEAVED BESIDE THE GLIMMERING WAVES, ... 21 OISIN 1 V 314
    AT EVENING ON THE GLIMMERING SANDS, ... 23 OISIN 1 347
    OVER THE GLIMMERING PURPLE SEA. . . . . 25 OISIN 1 384
    SHONE MANY TIMES AMONG THE GLIMMERING FLOWERS . . . . 30 OISIN 2 21
    CRASHED ON THE STONES, UPON THE GLIMMERING STONES, . . 33 OISIN 2 V 68A
    WATCHED HER THOSE SEAMLESS FACES FROM THE VALLEY'S 55 OISIN 3 122
        GLIMMERING GIRTH;
    WHERE MEN LIE FROZEN IN THE GLIMMERING SNOW; . . . . 73 ANASHU VIJAYA 51
    ONE WITH THE GLIMMERING TIDE, ... 78 INDIAN TO LOVE V 15
    GLIMMERING IN HER DROOPED EYES, SAW HER LIPS MOVE . . 81 EPHEMERA V 24D
    WHAT A DANCER GLIMMERING! . . . . 125 CATHLEEN PARA 14
    HER WHITE FEET GO GLIMMERING; . . . . 125 CATHLEEN PARA V 14
    IT HAD BECOME A GLIMMERING GIRL . . . . 149 WANDER AENGUS 13
    THEIR HOOFS HEAVY WITH TUMULT, THEIR EYES GLIMMERING WHITE; 154 BELOVED PEACE 2
    QUEENS WROUGHT WITH GLIMMERING HANDS; . . . . 162 ASKS FORGIVE 12
    HIS HEAVY RINGS UNCOILED FROM GLIMMERING DEEP TO DEEP; . 174 ELEMENT POWERS 5
    HAVE SEEN HIS MIDNIGHT CANDLE GLIMMERING. . . . . . 420 MY HOUSE 20
    HAD SEEN HIS MIDNIGHT CANDLE GLIMMERING . . . . . . 420 MY HOUSE V 20
    AND THOSE WHITE GLIMMERING FRAGMENTS OF THE MIST SWEEP BY. 426 PHANTOM HATRED 6
    DOWN LIMB AND BREAST OR DOWN THAT GLIMMERING BELLY . . 560 MAGIC DRUM 5
    THE MEN ARE BUSY IN THE GLIMMERING SQUARE. . . . . 699 MOSADA 3 16
    AND SOFT, ONE GLIMMERING STAR. RENYI HAS CAST . . . 714 FERENCZ RENYI 115
    AND SOFT, ONE GLIMMERING STAR—WITH POWER VAST; . . . 714 FERENCZ RENYI V 115
    THE CLOUDY WATERS AND THE GLIMMERING WINDS . . . . . 764 SHADOW WATER A 327
GLISTEN
    WHAT MADE THE DRAPERY GLISTEN SO? . . . . 625 NATIVITY 3
GLISTENING
    CRIED ALL HIS STORY TO THE DEWDROPS GLISTENING. . . . 68 SAD SHEPHERD 14
GLITTER   SEE A-GLITTER
    I SAW HER GLITTER AND GLEAM, ... 744 GLOVE CLOAK 1
GLITTERED
    AND GLITTERED IN HER EYES. . . . . 336 YOUNG GIRL 11
    RICH FOLIAGE THAT THE STARLIGHT GLITTERED THROUGH, . . 541 PARN FUNERAL 1 8
GLITTERING
    SCARED OF ITS GLITTERING LIKE A METEOR STAR, ... 38 OISIN 2 V 137
    THAT FROM THOSE FINGERS GLITTERING SUMMER RUNS . . . 128 DREAM OF FAERY 44
    O MASTERS OF THE GLITTERING TOWN! . . . . 212 BLESS PSALTER 3
    CRYING AMID THE GLITTERING SEA, ... 254 HIS DREAM 17
    THAT MERELY STOOD, ROCKING THE GLITTERING COACH . . . 344 DAWN 11
    YET DID BUT LOOK, ROCKING THE GLITTERING COACH . . . 344 DAWN V 11
    THE GLITTERING EYES IN A DEATH'S HEAD . . . . 400 DEMON BEAST 9
    LAST REACH OF GLITTERING STREAM . . . . 414 TOWER 143
    THE ABOUNDING GLITTERING JET; THOUGH NOW IT SEEMS . . 417 ANCEST HOUSES 12
    A GLITTERING SWORD OUT OF THE EAST. A PUFF OF WIND . . 426 PHANTOM HATRED 5
    GLITTERING AMONG GREY-LEAVED OLIVE-TREES, ... 447 COLONUS PRAISE 21
    GLITTERING AMONG GREY-LEAVED OLIVE TREES, ... 447 COLONUS PRAISE V 21
    UPON THE DUSTY, GLITTERING WINDOWS CLING, ... 482 BLOOD AND MOON 43
    THE GLITTERING REACHES OF THE FLOODED LAKE. . . . . 490 COOLE BALLYLEE 16
    IS HALF ALL GLITTERING FLAME AND HALF ALL GREEN . . . 500 VACILLATION 12
    IS HALF ALL GLITTERING FLAME AND HALF A GREEN . . . . 500 VACILLATION V 12
    THEIR ANCIENT, GLITTERING EYES, ARE GAY. . . . . . 567 LAPIS LAZULI 56
GLITTERS
    BUT FAITHFUL LOVERS. SOMETHING GLITTERS THERE— . . . 763 SHADOW WATER A 309
GLOBES   SEE FOAM-GLOBES
GLOBE-TROTTING
    CAN DISTURB GLOBE-TROTTING MADAM . . . . 638 BEN BULBEN 48
GLOOM
    LIKE CRIMSON METEORS HANG IN THE GLOOM, ... 21 OISIN 1 306
    WE DANCED TO WHERE WITHIN THE GLOOM . . . . 21 OISIN 1 V 305
    A LITTLE WAY WITHIN THE GLOOM A ROEBUCK RAISED HIS EYES 76 INDIAN ON GOD 13
    FELL LIKE FAINT METEORS IN THE GLOOM, AND ONCE . . . 80 EPHEMERA 14
    AND SHY IN THE GLOOM; . . . . 89 ISLE IN WATER 12

GLOOM   (CONTINUED)

	PAGE	TITLE		LINE
HE BADE ME OUT INTO THE GLOOM,	151	HEART OF WOMAN		3
AND SHE FORGET THE WANDERING AND ALL THE CRIMSON GLOOM	175	ELEMENT POWERS V		11
AND SHE FORGET THE WANDERING AND THE CRIMSON GLOOM	175	ELEMENT POWERS V		11
THE EVERLASTING TAPER LIGHTS THE GLOOM;	311	MOUNTAIN TOMB		10
BECAUSE OF THE GREAT GLOOM THAT IS IN MY MIND.	403	FOR DAUGHTER		8
IN THAT RELIGIOUS GLOOM;	584	GHOST ROG CASE		34
AS, CLOTHED IN CEREMONIAL GLOOM,	655	ISLE STAT I 3		10
TO SEEK NOT HOPELESS HAVE I CROSSED THE GLOOM,	656	ISLE STAT I 3		42
MY DREAMS ROUND THOUGHTS OF PLENTY, AS IN GLOOM	681	SEEKER		3
OF APPLE-BLOSSOM CIRCLES IN THE GLOOM,	700	MOSADA 3		42
OF APPLE BLOSSOM CIRCLES IN THE GLOOM,	700	MOSADA 3	V	42
AN APPLE BLOSSOM CIRCLES IN THE GLOOM,	700	MOSADA 3	V	42
BEFORE US IN THE GLOOM!	738	MOURN THEN ON		16

GLOOMED

A CITRON COLOUR GLOOMED IN HER HAIR,	3	OISIN 1		24

GLOOMS   SEE CAVERN-GLOOMS

GLOOMY

AND IN SOME GLOOMY BARROW LIE	19	OISIN 1		272
AND NOT A GLOOMY BIRD OF PREY.	338	TOM OROUGHLEY		8

GLORIES

GHOSTS OF HER VANISHED GLORIES, MUSE AND STALK	687	TWO TITANS		21

GLORIFIED

OR GARDENS RICH IN MEMORY GLORIFIED	491	COOLE BALLYLEE		35

GLORIOUS   SEE VAIN-GLORIOUS

AND GLORIOUS AS ASIAN BIRDS	7	OISIN 1	V	65

GLORY

MY SOUL, ONCE GLORY OF ITS ANCIENT LINE,	36	OISIN 2	V	95
AN IDLE WORD IS NOW THEIR GLORY,	65	HAPPY SHEPHERD		14
HE FLED THE PERSECUTION OF HER GLORY	68	SAD SHEPHERD		12
AND FROM THE PERSECUTION OF HER GLORY	68	SAD SHEPHERD	V	12
AND PONDERED ON THE GLORY OF HIS DAYS;	108	CUCHULAIN SEA		43
SO GREAT A GLORY DID THE SONG CONFER.	410	TOWER		40
SHADOWS THE INHERITED GLORY OF THE RICH.	418	ANCEST HOUSES		16
WHAT IF THE GLORY OF ESCUTCHEONED DOORS,	418	ANCEST HOUSES		33
SCARCE SPREAD A GLORY TO THE MORNING BEAMS,	422	MY DESCENDANTS		6
AND YET IT LACK ALL GLORY! AND PERCHANCE	429	NINETEEN 19		23
EXHAUST HIS GLORY AND HIS MIGHT!	438	SONGS PLAY 2		14
THE FEATHERED GLORY FROM HER LOOSENING THIGHS?	441	LEDA AND SWAN		6
AND THAT ALL HEAVENLY GLORY SYMBOLISE--	445	SCHOOL CHILDR		55
WHEN IT HAS LOOKED IN GLORY FROM A CLOUD.	482	BLOOD AND MOON		54
SYMBOLICAL GLORY OF THE EARTH AND AIR!	483	VERONIC NAPKIN		3
THAT MADE THE MAGNITUDE AND GLORY THERE.	483	VERONIC NAPKIN		5
A DANCE-LIKE GLORY THAT THOSE WALLS BEGOT.	488	COOLE PARK 29		8
WE SHIFT ABOUT--ALL THAT GREAT GLORY SPENT--	491	COOLE BALLYLEE		39
MAN SHIFTS ABOUT--ALL THAT GREAT GLORY SPENT--	491	COOLE BALLYLEE V		39
GREATER GLORY IN THE SUN,	494	AT ALGECIRAS		13
IN GLORY OF CHANGELESS METAL	498	BYZANTIUM		22
BITTER GLORY WRECKED.	504	RESULT THOUGHT		6
BY THAT GREAT GLORY DRIVEN WILD.	540	FROM ANTIGONE		13
HIS GLORY AND HIS MONUMENTS ARE GONE.	563	MERU		14
THINK WHERE MAN'S GLORY MOST BEGINS AND ENDS,	604	GALLERY REVIS		54
AND SAY MY GLORY WAS I HAD SUCH FRIENDS.	604	GALLERY REVIS		55
FAILURE FOR GLORY DOWN ON THEE, AND MOULD	688	TWO TITANS		54
AND MADE THEIR GLORY NAUGHT.	741	EARL PAUL		44

GLOSSES

WHERE THE WAVE OF MOONLIGHT GLOSSES	87	STOLEN CHILD		13

GLOSSY

ACROSS THE GLOSSY SEA." "OH, WILD	6	OISIN 1	V	58
OVER THE GLOSSY SEA." "O, WILD	6	OISIN 1	V	58
WE GALLOPED OVER THE GLOSSY SEA!	11	OISIN 1		132

GLOVE   SEE FOX-GLOVE

THE GLOVE AND THE CLOAK	744	GLOVE CLOAK		T
THE LITTLE OLD GLOVE OF A CHILD!	744	GLOVE CLOAK		9

GLOW

WHOSE LIPS HAD LIFE'S MOST PROSPEROUS GLOW?	10	OISIN 1		118
IN EVERY BRAIN A WIZARD GLOW.	20	OISIN 1	V	291A
IN OUR RAISED EYES THERE FLASHED A GLOW	22	OISIN 1		327
THOUGH YOU GLOW AND YOU GLANCE, THOUGH YOU PURR AND YOU DART!	90	OLD FISHERMAN		2
THOUGH YE GLOW AND YE GLANCE, THOUGH YE PURR AND YE DART,	90	OLD FISHERMAN V		2
THERE MIDNIGHT'S ALL A GLIMMER, AND NOON A PURPLE GLOW,	117	ISLE INNISFREE		7
TILL THE SEED OF THE FIRE FLICKER AND GLOW!	150	OLD MOTHER		2
AND TROUBLED EYES CAME MORNING'S FIRST-BORN GLOW!	648	ISLE STAT I 1		103
FOOTING IN THE FEEBLE GLOW!	731	STREET DANCERS		10
FOOTING IN THE FEEBLE GLOW,	732	STREET DANCERS		23
FOOTING IN THE FEEBLE GLOW,	732	STREET DANCERS		36
DANCING IN THE FEEBLE GLOW,	733	STREET DANCERS		49
FOOTING IN THE FEEBLE GLOW,	733	STREET DANCERS		62
FOOTING IN THE FEEBLE GLOW,	733	STREET DANCERS V		49

GLOWED

AND WITH THE GLIMMERING CRIMSON GLOWED	3	OISIN 1		26
AND WITH THE WOVEN CRIMSON GLOWED	3	OISIN 1	V	26

GLOWING

AND BENDING DOWN BESIDE THE GLOWING BARS,	121	YOU ARE OLD		9
THAT YOU SHALL SEE ON YONDER GLOWING CLOUD	692	MOSADA 1	V	43

GLOWS

UNQUENCHABLE STILL GLOWS IN HER DULL STARE,	687	TWO TITANS		17

GLOW-WORM

WHEN A GLOW-WORM WAS GREEN ON A GRASS-LEAF,	53	OISIN 3		99
WHEN A GLOW-WORM WAS GREEN ON A GRASS LEAF,	53	OISIN 3	V	99

		PAGE	TITLE		LINE

GLUED
    TO DEATH. HIS LIPS ARE GLUED, WITH QUIVERING TOUCH, . . . 684 SEEKER V 63
GLUTS
    WHEN SUMMER GLUTS THE GOLDEN BEES, ... 84 MAD KING GOLL 38
    WHERE SUMMER GLUTS THE GOLDEN BEES, ... 84 MAD KING GOLL V 38
GNASHING
    GNASHING OF TEETH, DESPAIR, ... 346 ON WOMAN 39
GO
    WHERE ROUND AND ROUND THE RAVENS GO. . . . . 5 OISIN 1 V 42
    IN WHAT FAR KINGDOM DO YOU GO, ... 10 OISIN 1 115
    THAT I WOULD GO WITH HER, THEY GREW . . . . 10 OISIN 1 V 111A
    IN WHAT FAR KINGDOM DO YE GO, ... 10 OISIN 1 V 115
    YOU GO NOT WHERE THE RED DEER FEEDS, ... 11 OISIN 1 127
    YE GO NOT WHERE THE RED DEER FEEDS, ... 11 OISIN 1 V 127
    "OH, SIGH, AWAKE AND GO YOU FORTH FOR ME, ... 33 OISIN 2 V 57
    AND GO YOU CLOSE TO THEM. . . . . 33 OISIN 2 V 59
    AND ONE WHOM YOU WILL GO TO WITHOUT TELLING, ... 33 OISIN 2 V 67
    OF FEAR, I BADE THEM GO, AND FOR THE FIGHT . . . . . . 38 OISIN 2 V 142
    GO CAST YOUR BODY ON THE STONES AND PRAY, ... 42 OISIN 2 207
    AND THEN LOST NIAMH MURMURED, "LOVE, WE GO . . . . . . 46 OISIN 2 245
    LOST NIAM MOURN AND SAY, "AH, LOVE, WE GO . . . . . . 46 OISIN 2 V 245B
    . . . NOR GO FROM HIS DEW-CUMBERED SKIES, ... 49 OISIN 3 38
    "THEN GO THROUGH THE LANDS IN THE SADDLE AND SEE WHAT THE 55 OISIN 3 125
        MORTALS DO,
    . . . TURNING AND TURNING GO, ... 57 OISIN 3 145
    . . . FOR I GO TO THE FENIANS, O CLERIC, TO CHAUNT . . . 61 OISIN 3 201
    . . . I WILL GO TO THE FENIANS, THOU CLERIC, AND CHANT . . 61 OISIN 3 V 201
    I WILL GO TO CAOILTE, AND CONAN, AND BRAN, SCEOLAN, LOMAIR, 63 OISIN 3 223
    I WILL GO TO THE HOUSE OF THE FENIANS, BE THEY IN FLAMES 63 OISIN 3 V 223
        OR AT FEAST,
    GO GATHER BY THE HUMMING SEA . . . . 66 HAPPY SHEPHERD 35
    GO GATHER BY THE HUMMING-SEA . . . . 66 HAPPY SHEPHERD V 35
    OH, MAY TRANQUILLITY BESIDE HIM GO, ... 71 ANASHU VIJAYA V 2
    WITH HER WOULD I GO. . . . . 89 ISLE IN WATER 8
    BECAUSE I MUTTER AS I GO, ... 94 MOLL MAGEE 3
    AND GAVE ME MONEY, AND BADE ME GO . . . . 95 MOLL MAGEE 23
    "TO STABLE AND TO KENNEL GO, ... 97 FOXHUNTER 5
    "AND OF MY SERVANTS SOME ONE GO, ... 97 FOXHUNTER V 5
    COME NEAR, I WOULD, BEFORE MY TIME TO GO, ... 101 ROSE UPON ROOD 22
    I SEE MY LIFE GO DRIFTING LIKE A RIVER . . . . 104 FERGUS DRUID 31
    I SEE MY LIFE GO DRIPPING LIKE A STREAM . . . . 104 FERGUS DRUID V 31
    GO WATCH THE ROAD BETWEEN THE WOOD AND TIDE, ... 105 CUCHULAIN SEA 4
    GO DWELL UPON THE SEA CLIFFS, VAPOUR HID, ... 105 CUCHULAIN SEA V 4
    GO DWELL UPON THE SEA CLIFFS, VAPOUR-HID, ... 105 CUCHULAIN SEA V 4
    GO DWELL UPON THE CLIFFS AND WATCH THE TIDE, ... 105 CUCHULAIN SEA V 4
    GO THERE, AND LIGHT A CAMP-FIRE AT WOOD'S RIM, ... 108 CUCHULAIN SEA 35
    GO THERE AND DWELL ON THE GREEN FOREST RIM. . . . . . 108 CUCHULAIN SEA V 35
    GO THERE, AND CAMP UPON THE FOREST'S RIM, ... 108 CUCHULAIN SEA V 35
    GO THERE, AND LIGHT A CAMP FIRE AT WOOD'S RIM, ... 108 CUCHULAIN SEA V 35
    GO, CAST ON HIM DELUSIONS MAGICAL, ... 111 CUCHULAIN SEA V 80
    HE WOULD GO WEAVE OUT OF THE STARS . . . . 113 ROSE OF PEACE 7
    I CALL, AS THEY GO BY ME ONE BY ONE, ... 114 ROSE OF BATTLE 8
    I WILL ARISE AND GO NOW, AND GO TO INNISFREE, ... 117 ISLE INNISFREE 1
    I WILL ARISE AND GO NOW, AND GO TO INNISFREE, ... 117 ISLE INNISFREE 1
    I WILL ARISE AND GO NOW, FOR ALWAYS NIGHT AND DAY . . . 117 ISLE INNISFREE 9
    HER WHITE FEET GO GLIMMERING, ... 125 CATHLEEN PARA V 14
    WHO WILL GO DRIVE WITH FERGUS NOW, ... 125 GOES FERGUS 1
    THERE THE LOVES A CIRCLE GO, ... 135 TWO TREES 13
    THERE, THROUGH THE BROKEN BRANCHES, GO . . . . 135 TWO TREES 33
    THERE, THROUGH BEWILDERED BRANCHES, GO . . . . 135 TWO TREES V 13
    FOR THE ELEMENTAL CREATURES GO . . . . 138 TO IRELAND 23
    FOR ROUND ABOUT MY TABLE GO . . . . 138 TO IRELAND V 23
    FOR THE ELEMENTAL BEINGS GO . . . . 138 TO IRELAND V 23
    AND ALL BENIGHTED THINGS THAT GO . . . . 139 TO IRELAND 39
    AND ALL THE WIZARD THINGS THAT GO . . . . 139 TO IRELAND V 39
    GO TO THE GUARDS OF THE HEAVENLY FOLD . . . . 141 EVERLAST VOICE 2
    HE BADE HIS HEART GO TO HER, ... 159 CAP AND BELLS 13
    HE MADE HIS SOUL GO UPWARD . . . . 159 CAP AND BELLS V 3
    WHITHER HER FOOTSTEPS GO. . . . . 175 ELEMENT POWERS 18
    WHERE HER SOFT FOOTSTEPS GO. . . . . 175 ELEMENT POWERS V 18
    AS IN THE OLD DAYS WHEN THEY WOULD COME AND GO . . . . 183 QUEEN MAEVE 81
    BETTER GO DOWN UPON YOUR MARROW-BONES . . . . 204 ADAMS CURSE 7
    BETTER GO DOWN UPON YOUR MARROW BONES . . . . 204 ADAMS CURSE V 7
    AND WHETHER I GO IN MY DREAMS BY WOODLAND, OR DUN, . . . 210 UNDER THE MOON 14
        OR SHORE,
    WE'D BETTER GO, FOR WE HAVE LOST THIS CHANCE. . . . . 226 SHADOW WATER B 80
    AND LET THE DREAM GO BY. IT'S NOT A DREAM, ... 229 SHADOW WATER B 158
    LET GO MY HANDS! WHY DO YOU CAST A SHADOW? . . . . . 235 SHADOW WATER B 283
    WHEN SHE FINDS OUT I WILL NOT LET HER GO-- . . . . . 236 SHADOW WATER B 302
    THAT YOU'LL NOT LET ME GO? I AM A QUEEN. . . . . . . 236 SHADOW WATER B 304
    I HAD FORGOTTEN THAT WE MUST GO WAKE HIM. . . . . . . 240 SHADOW WATER B 384
    WILL LOOK UPON HIS FACE AGAIN. GO WITH HIM, ... 250 SHADOW WATER B 589
    AND CUT THE ROPE, FOR I GO ON WITH FORGAEL. . . . . . 250 SHADOW WATER B 592
    "GO AND LOVE, GO AND LOVE, YOUNG MAN, ... 268 BROWN PENNY 5
    "GO AND LOVE, GO AND LOVE, YOUNG MAN, ... 268 BROWN PENNY 5
    I BADE HIM GO WHEN ALL HIS HOUSEHOLD SLEPT . . . . . 282 TWO KINGS 133
    TO GO--FOR HOPE WOULD GIVE HIS LIMBS THE POWER-- . . . 282 TWO KINGS V 133A
    THE PACK UPON HIM. GO, UNQUIET WANDERER, ... 292 TO A SHADE 18
    "TIME TO PUT OFF THE WORLD AND GO SOMEWHERE . . . . . 299 BEGGAR CRIED 1
    AND LET YOU GO. . . . . 359 TO A SQUIRREL 8
    GO PLUCK ATHENE BY THE HAIR! . . . . 386 ROBARTES DANCE 19

```
                                                    PAGE     TITLE              LINE
GO   (CONTINUED)
      IT SEEMS THAT I MUST BID THE MUSE GO PACK, . . . . . .   409 TOWER               11
      GO THEREFORE; BUT LEAVE HANRAHAN, . . . . . . . . .      413 TOWER              103
      TO CRAWL IN HER OWN BLOOD, AND GO SCOT-FREE; . . . . .   429 NINETEEN 19         28
      CRUELTY MUST KEEP; THEREFORE BE WARNED AND GO . . . .    448 HERO GIRL FOOL       7
      MEN COME, MEN GO, . . . . . . . . . . . . . .           512 JANE ON GOD          5
      TAKE TO THE ROADS AND GO MARCHING ALONG. . . . . .      548 TO SAME TUNE 3      14
      GO GALLIVANTING BY; . . . . . . . . . . . .            552 SONGS REWRIT 2       4
      NOR WHERE I GO, . . . . . . . . . . . . . .            572 LADYS 1ST SONG       4
      YOU ASK WHAT I HAVE FOUND, AND FAR AND WIDE I GO;       580 CURSE CROMWELL       1
      "GO YOUR WAYS, O GO YOUR WAYS, . . . . . . . .          588 OLD WICKED MAN      28
      "GO YOUR WAYS, O GO YOUR WAYS, . . . . . . . .          588 OLD WICKED MAN      28
      I NEVER BADE YOU GO . . . . . . . . . . . .            600 THOSE IMAGES         5
      HOW CAN THE YOUNG GO STRAIGHT? . . . . . . . .         607 SONGS BURDEN 2      17
      HE LACKED THOSE YEARS THAT GO WITH SKILL, . . . .      608 SONGS BURDEN 3      14
      TALL DAMES GO WALKING IN GRASS-GREEN AVALON. . . .     627 STATES HOLIDAY      13
      TALL DAMES GO WALKING IN GRASS-GREEN AVALON. . . .     627 STATES HOLIDAY      26
      TALL DAMES GO WALKING IN GRASS-GREEN AVALON. . . .     627 STATES HOLIDAY      39
      TALL DAMES GO WALKING IN GRASS GREEN AVALON. . . .     627 STATES HOLIDAY V   REF
      I COULD NOT GO. LET'S TALK, AND LET'S BE SAD, . . .    651 ISLE STAT I 2        7
      GO PILOT THE COURSE OF HIS ARROW'S DECEIT! . . . .     657 ISLE STAT I 3       69
      AS THEY GO WITH DROOPING FEATHER. . . . . .            667 ISLE STAT II 3      33
      AH, WOE IS ME! I GO FROM SUN AND SHADE, . . . .       674 ISLE STAT II 3     216
      GO ASK THE SPRINGING FLOWERS, . . . . . . . .          680 LOVE AND DEATH      13
      GO ASK THE YOUNGEST ANGEL. . . . . . . . . .          680 LOVE AND DEATH      29
      GO UP AND DOWN, AND RAISE THEIR HEADS AND SING . .     682 SEEKER              30
      I GO AS SOFT AS FOLLY; I AM FATE." . . . . . .        686 LIFE                18
      SO YOU MUST GO; KISS ME BEFORE YOU GO. . . . .        702 MOSADA 3            96
      SO YOU MUST GO; KISS ME BEFORE YOU GO. . . . .        702 MOSADA 3            96
      THERE IS NO LEAVE-TAKING. I GO NO MORE. . . . .       702 MOSADA 3           100
      THERE IS NO LEAVE TAKING. I GO NO MORE. . . . .       702 MOSADA 3         V 100
      UNHAPPY ONE. GO NOT, GO NOT, GO NOT; . . . . .        703 MOSADA 3           102
      UNHAPPY ONE. GO NOT, GO NOT, GO NOT; . . . . .        703 MOSADA 3           102
      UNHAPPY ONE. GO NOT, GO NOT, GO NOT; . . . . .        703 MOSADA 3           102
      EACH OTHER'S NECKS, AND WHISPERING AS THEY GO, . .     703 MOSADA 3           120
      TO PRISONS GO, AND MOSSY RUIN REST . . . . . .         709 FERENCZ RENYI        2
      TO PRISON GO, AND MOSSY RUIN REST . . . . . .          709 FERENCZ RENYI  V     2
      "CHOOSE!" RESTLESS HAYNAU'S FINGERS TAPPING GO. . .    711 FERENCZ RENYI       41
      THERE FAR AWAY FROM ALL WE TWO WILL GO, . . . .        714 FERENCZ RENYI       99
      MY LOVE, WE WILL GO, WE WILL GO. I AND YOU, . . .      717 LOVE SONG            1
      MY LOVE, WE WILL GO, WE WILL GO. I AND YOU, . . .      717 LOVE SONG            1
      "WATCHER, WHEREFORE HAVE YE CALLED US?" EYES GO AFTER  718 PHANTOM SHIP        10
           HIS LEAN HAND,
      HOW STILL IT IS! I HEAR THE CARP GO SPLASH, . . .     722 WITCH VIVIEN        62
      I CANNOT GO INTO THE BLOODLESS LAND . . . . .          722 WITCH VIVIEN        67
      WHERE THE SOULS OF FAIRIES GO?" . . . . . . .          729 PRIEST FAIRY        48
      I GO AS SOFT AS FOLLY! I AM FATE." . . . . .          735 QUATRAIN APHOR      20
      WHERE MY BOOKS GO. . . . . . . . . . . . .            739 WHERE BOOKS GO       T
      "GO BRING ME MY OLD ARMOUR . . . . . . . .            740 EARL PAUL           19
      GO BRING ME MY OWN ARMOUR . . . . . . . .             740 EARL PAUL        V  19
      THEN GO TO HIS OWN LAND, . . . . . . . .              741 EARL PAUL           58
      IT MAY BE NOW THAT I CAN GO MY WAY . . . .            751 SHADOW WATER A      96
      IF I GO NEARER TO THE WINDWARD SIDE, . . . .          753 SHADOW WATER A     140
      AND WE GO HOME. COME, AIBRIC; END YOUR TALE . .       766 SHADOW WATER A     374
      WE WILL GO CALL THESE SAILORS, AND ESCAPE . . .       766 SHADOW WATER A     382
      BUT I AM NEW TO LOVE. GO AMONG THESE . . . .          767 SHADOW WATER A     391
      OR GO BESIDE HIM TO HIS MOUNTAIN WARS. . . . .        768 SHADOW WATER A     414
      I'D LET THE WHOLE WORLD GO; . . . . . . . .           782 HEART FRIGHT         9
GOAD
      AND THE MOON GOAD THE WATERS NIGHT AND DAY, . . .      45 OISIN 2            238
      FROM NEEDLE'S EYE STILL GOAD IT ON. . . . . .         562 NEEDLES EYE          4
GOAT
      THAT FOUND WHEN I HAD NEITHER GOAT NOR GRAZING . .     340 SHEP GOATHERD       31
      CURES HE HATH FOR COW OR GOAT . . . . . . .           716 FAIRY DOCTOR        13
      WHEN SOMETHING THAT WAS BEARDED LIKE A GOAT . .       747 SHADOW WATER A      11
      WHEN SOMETHING, HALF A LAMB AND HALF A GOAT, . .      747 SHADOW WATER A V    11
GOAT-HEAD
      FOUL GOAT-HEAD, BRUTAL ARM APPEAR, . . . . .          612 NEWS ORACLE         33
GOATHERD
      SHEPHERD AND GOATHERD . . . . . . . . . .             338 SHEP GOATHERD        T
      THOUGH THEY BUT FEED AS THE GOATHERD FEEDS, . . .     635 BLACK TOWER          2
GOATHERDS
      OLD GOATHERDS AND OLD GOATS, IF IN ALL ELSE . . .     340 SHEP GOATHERD       46
GOAT'S
      HAVE FOUND THE PATH MY GOAT'S FEET CANNOT FIND. . .   342 SHEP GOATHERD  V   84
GOATS
      WHERE MY GOATS BROWSE ON THE SCARCE GRASS OR LEAP . . 339 SHEP GOATHERD        8
      OLD GOATHERDS AND OLD GOATS, IF IN ALL ELSE . . .     340 SHEP GOATHERD       46
GOATS'
      HAVE FOUND THE PATH MY GOATS' FEET CANNOT FIND. . .   342 SHEP GOATHERD       84
GOBAN
      OLD WHOLESOME GOBAN HAD NO SAY; . . . . . .           271 GREY ROCK           10
      THE BOW-LEGGED GOBAN HAD NO SAY; . . . . .            271 GREY ROCK      V    10
      OLD GOBAN HAMMERED THEM AND WROUGHT THEM, . . .       271 GREY ROCK      V    23
      THAT SACRED GOBAN BREWED," HE CRIED . . . . .         304 HOUR DAWN      V    50
GOBAN'D
      ON METAL GOBAN'D HAMMERED AT, . . . . . . .           271 GREY ROCK           19
GOBAN'S
      AND SHE WITH GOBAN'S WINE ADRIP, . . . . . .          276 GREY ROCK          121
      I DRAGGED FROM GOBAN'S MOUNTAIN-TOP . . . . .         304 HOUR DAWN           50
```

		PAGE	TITLE	LINE

GOBLIN
CLEAR FLUTED THEN THAT GOBLIN RARE-- . . . . 6 OISIN 1 V 54
GROWETH THE GOBLIN FLOWER OF JOY, HER CARE, ... 653 ISLE STAT I 2 39
IN SONG, FROM GOBLIN WATERS SWAYING WHITE, ... 657 ISLE STAT I 3 51
SOME GOBLIN, MY SERVANT, ON WINGS THAT ARE FLEET, . . . 657 ISLE STAT I 3 67
IS WORN AS THOUGH WITH FIRE. OH, GOBLIN QUEEN, ... 667 ISLE STAT II 3 36
AS LIGHT OF TRIUMPH IN THY GOBLIN EYES-- . . . . . . 674 ISLE STAT II 3 199
UPON MY NECKLACE. BUT THE GOBLIN QUEEN . . . . 676 ISLE STAT II 3 267
THE GOBLIN FLOWER LIETH ON THY LIPS. . . . . 678 ISLE STAT II 3 298
THE YEARS OF GOBLIN SLEEP. AH! WHILE I SLUMBERED, . . 679 ISLE STAT II 3 308
SEEK NOT THAT WOOD, FOR THERE THE GOBLIN SNAKES . . . 682 SEEKER 29
THEN 'GAN TO SPEAK THAT GOBLIN RARE, ... 729 PRIEST FAIRY 37
GOBLINS
FIRST DREAMS, AND GOBLINS, AND THE LESSER SPRITES, . . . 722 WITCH VIVIEN 56
GOD   SEE SEA-GOD
FOR JOY IS GOD AND GOD IS JOY." . . . . 19 OISIN 1 286
FOR JOY IS GOD AND GOD IS JOY." . . . . 19 OISIN 1 286
SANG, "GOD IS JOY AND JOY IS GOD, ... 20 OISIN 1 300
SANG, "GOD IS JOY AND JOY IS GOD, ... 20 OISIN 1 300
SHAKE THE LOOSE REINS! YOU SLAVES OF GOD, ... 22 OISIN 1 331
SHAKE THE LOOSE REINS! YE SLAVES OF GOD, ... 22 OISIN 1 V 331
WHEN GOD SHALL COME FROM THE SEA WITH A SIGH . . . . 28 OISIN 1 425
BEFORE GOD WAS OR MY OLD LINE BEGAN; . . . . 29 OISIN 2 8
THINGS DONE ERE GOD FIRST WAS OR MY OLD LINE BEGAN; . . 29 OISIN 2 V 8
SINCE GOD MADE TIME AND DEATH AND SLEEP! THE OTHER . . . 31 OISIN 2 41
NOT EVEN YOUR GOD COULD HAVE THROWN DOWN THAT HALL! . . 36 OISIN 2 109
NOT E'EN THY GOD COULD HAVE THROWN DOWN THAT HALL! . . 36 OISIN 2 V 109
FOR GOD HAS HEARD, AND SPEAKS HIS ANGRY MIND! . . . . 42 OISIN 2 206
GOD SHAKES THE WORLD WITH RESTLESS HANDS. MORE NEAR . . 43 OISIN 2 V 208
THE INDIAN UPON GOD . . . . 76 INDIAN ON GOD T
FROM THE BOOK OF KAURI THE INDIAN-- SECTION V. ON THE . 76 INDIAN ON GOD V T
NATURE OF GOD
KANVA, THE INDIAN, ON GOD . . . . 76 INDIAN ON GOD V T
GOD LIGHTS THE STARS, HIS CANDLES, ... 96 MOLL MAGEE 51
BY GOD TO THE BRIGHT HEARTS OF THOSE LONG DEAD, ... 101 ROSE UPON ROOD 20
"NOT ANY GOD ALIVE NOR MORTAL DEAD, ... 106 CUCHULAIN SEA V 10
FOR GOD WHO MADE YOU BITTER MADE YOU WISE." . . . . . 108 CUCHULAIN SEA V 32
"GOD ONLY SEES WHAT DOOM FOR ME LIES STORED." . . . . 110 CUCHULAIN SEA V 62
AND GOD WOULD BID HIS WARFARE CEASE, ... 113 ROSE OF PEACE 13
AND GOD WOULD BID MAN'S WARFARE CEASE, ... 113 ROSE OF PEACE V 13
FOR GOD HAS BID THEM SHARE AN EQUAL FATE! . . . . . . 115 ROSE OF BATTLE 32
GOD SMILES IN HIGH HEAVEN . . . . 118 CRADLE SONG V 5
THE STARS OF GOD WHERE THEY MOVE, ... 119 PITY OF LOVE V 4
THAT GOD HAS LAID HIS FINGERS ON THE SKY, ... 128 DREAM OF FAERY 43
DREAM, UNTIL GOD BURN NATURE WITH A KISS? . . . . . . 128 DREAM OF FAERY 47
OF HOW GOD LEANS HIS HANDS OUT OF THE SKY, ... 128 DREAM OF FAERY V 43
THAT GOD HAD LEANED HIS HANDS OUT OF THE SKY, ... 128 DREAM OF FAERY V 43
THAT GOD HAD LEANT HIS HANDS OUT OF THE SKY, ... 128 DREAM OF FAERY V 43
AND AFTER CRIED HE, "GOD FORGIVE! . . . . 132 FR GILLIGAN 11
AND GOD COVERED THE WORLD WITH SHADE, ... 133 FR GILLIGAN 19
MADE WHEN GOD SLEPT IN TIMES OF OLD. . . . . 135 TWO TREES 32
BEFORE GOD MADE THE ANGELIC CLAN. . . . . 138 TO IRELAND 8
THAT GOD GIVES UNTO MAN IN SLEEP. . . . . 138 TO IRELAND V 22
FOR GOD GOES BY WITH WHITE FOOTFALL. . . . . 139 TO IRELAND 44
FOR GOD GOES BY WITH WHITE FOOT-FALL. . . . . 139 TO IRELAND V 44
AND GOD STANDS WINDING HIS LONELY HORN, ... 148 INTO TWILIGHT 13
IS DROPPING SLEEP, UNTIL GOD BURN TIME, ... 164 PERFECT BEAUTY 7
AT HUSH OF EVENING TIME GOD BURNS TIME . . . . 164 PERFECT BEAUTY V 7
AT HUSH OF EVENING TILL GOD BURN TIME . . . . 164 PERFECT BEAUTY V 7
WITH THE SECRETS OF GOD IN HIS EYES. . . . . 167 BLESSED 12
"PRAISE GOD AND GOD'S MOTHER," DATHI SAID, ... 167 BLESSED 17
"FOR GOD AND GOD'S MOTHER HAVE SENT . . . . 167 BLESSED 18
"WITH THE SECRETS OF GOD HALF BLIND, ... 168 BLESSED 26
THAT NO GOD TROUBLED NOW, AND, WONDERING . . . . . . 182 QUEEN MAEVE 60
SOME GOD OR KING HAD MADE THE LAWS . . . . 194 BAILE AILLINN 131
BUT THEREON EVERY GOD STOOD UP . . . . 275 GREY ROCK 116
AND WHAT, GOD HELP US, COULD THEY SAVE? . . . . 289 SEPTEMBER 1913 14
HAVING LOVED GOD ONCE, BUT MAYBE . . . . 299 THREE HERMITS 26
AND MURMURED "MAY GOD CURSE THE NIGHT . . . . 303 HOUR DAWN V 32B
AND THERE BE NOTHING BUT GOD LEFT! . . . . 307 HOUR DAWN 103
NOR GAVE GOD THANKS TILL OVERHEAD . . . . 307 HOUR DAWN 121
"OH GOD IF HE GOT LOOSE!" AND THEN . . . . 307 HOUR DAWN V 118
AND GAVE GOD THANKS THAT OVERHEAD . . . . 307 HOUR DAWN V 121
MAY GOD BE PRAISED FOR WOMAN . . . . 345 ON WOMAN 1
GOD GRANT ME--NO, NOT HERE. . . . . 346 ON WOMAN 25
GOD GRANT A BLESSING ON THIS TOWER AND COTTAGE . . . . 371 ON GOING HOUSE 1
UNDER THIS HUMP. GOD TRIES EACH MAN . . . . 379 SAINT HUNCH 5
BUT PRAY TO GOD THAT HE EASE . . . . 380 SONGS FOOL 1 17
DID GOD IN PORTIONING WINE AND BREAD . . . . 386 ROBARTES DANCE 39
GOD TOOK THE SPINNING-JENNY . . . . 439 FRAGMENTS 3
THAT ONLY GOD HAS LOVED US FOR OURSELVES. . . . . . . 448 HERO GIRL FOOL 16
AND NOT THEIR WORTH. GOD LOVES US FOR OUR WORTH; . . . 448 HERO GIRL FOOL V 15
ENDURE WHAT LIFE GOD GIVES AND ASK NO LONGER SPAN; . . 459 FROM OEDIPUS 1
WHETHER OF HER OR GOD HE THOUGHT THE MOST, ... 471 ALL SOUL NIGHT 32
EVERYTHING THAT IS NOT GOD CONSUMED WITH INTELLECTUAL FIRE. 481 BLOOD AND MOON 30
THAT ONLY GOD, MY DEAR, ... 492 ANNE GREGORY 16
THE MOTHER OF GOD . . . . 499 MOTHER OF GOD T
THE BISHOP HAS A SKIN, GOD KNOWS, ... 508 JANE BISHOP 15
THAT TO GOD SHALL COME! . . . . 511 JANE AND JACK 8
CRAZY JANE ON GOD . . . . 512 JANE ON GOD T
ALL THINGS REMAIN IN GOD. . . . . 512 JANE ON GOD 6

327

		PAGE	TITLE		LINE
GOD (CONTINUED)					
ALL THINGS REMAIN IN GOD.		512	JANE ON GOD		12
ALL THINGS REMAIN IN GOD.		512	JANE ON GOD		18
ALL THINGS REMAIN IN GOD.		512	JANE ON GOD		24
GOD BE WITH THE TIMES WHEN I		514	JANE GROWN OLD		17
GOD GUARD ME FROM THOSE THOUGHTS MEN THINK		553	PRAYER OLD AGE		1
. . . SHARE GOD THAT IS BUT THREE.		556	RIBH PATRICK		11
IT IS OF GOD AND PASSES HUMAN WIT.		558	RIBH CHRISTIAN		2
FROM EVERY THOUGHT OF GOD MANKIND HAS HAD.		558	RIBH CHRISTIAN		15
HATRED OF GOD MAY BRING THE SOUL TO GOD.		558	RIBH CHRISTIAN		18
HATRED OF GOD MAY BRING THE SOUL TO GOD.		558	RIBH CHRISTIAN		18
IN HATING GOD SHE MAY CREEP CLOSE TO GOD.		558	RIBH CHRISTIAN	V	18
IN HATING GOD SHE MAY CREEP CLOSE TO GOD.		558	RIBH CHRISTIAN	V	18
NOW HIS WARS ON GOD BEGIN.		561	FOUR AGES MAN		7
AT STROKE OF MIDNIGHT GOD SHALL WIN.		561	FOUR AGES MAN		8
WHO TRAVELS WHERE GOD WILLS.		587	OLD WICKED MAN		4
I SWEAR TO GOD I QUESTIONED THEM, AND ALL THEY HAD TO SAY		593	PILGRIM		14
I SWEAR TO GOD I QUESTIONED THEM ALL AND ALL THEY HAD TO SAY		593	PILGRIM	V	14
COULD THAT OLD GOD RISE UP AGAIN		606	SONGS BURDEN 1		21
"GOD I HAVE LOVED, BUT SHOULD I ASK RETURN		609	IN TARAS HALLS		14
OF GOD OR WOMAN, THE TIME WERE COME TO DIE."		609	IN TARAS HALLS		15
BRING THE SOUL OF MAN TO GOD,		638	BEN BULBEN		40
ON BACKGROUNDS FOR A GOD OR SAINT		639	BEN BULBEN		54
PREPARED A REST FOR THE PEOPLE OF GOD,		639	BEN BULBEN		65
UNLESS SOME PITYING GOD SHALL SUCCOUR ME		656	ISLE STAT I 3		36
IN THIS MY CHOICE. SOME GOD MIGHT HELP! IF SO		656	ISLE STAT I 3		37
SHALL NOT SO HOPELESS PROVE! SOME GOD MAY REST		657	ISLE STAT I 3		61
HE WAS OUR ANCIENT GOD. IF I SPEAK LOW,		658	ISLE STAT I 3		78
AND NOT TOO CLEAR, HOW WILL THE NEW GOD KNOW		658	ISLE STAT I 3		79
AS HERE I CAME I SAW GOD PAN. HE PLAYED		678	ISLE STAT II 3		300
THE BLESSED GOD WAS GOOD TO SEND US SUCH,		683	SEEKER		40
OF HIS SAD GOD; AND DOWN AMONG THE GRASS		690	MOSADA 1		16
THE VAPOUR IS MUCH THICKER. GOD! THE STAKE!		695	MOSADA 1		112
NO USE. AWAY! HEAR, THOU ENDURING GOD,		698	MOSADA 2		50
AND THOU SHALT BEND, ENDURING GOD, THE KNEES		698	MOSADA 2		59
NO USE. AWAY! HEAR OH! THOU ENDURING GOD,		698	MOSADA 2	V	50
AND THOU SHALL BEND, ENDURING GOD, THE KNEES		698	MOSADA 2	V	59
OH, GOD!--AWAKE! THOU SHALT NOT DIE. SHE SLEEPS,		701	MOSADA 3		66
WAS EBREMAR, WHOSE THOUGHTS WERE FIXED ON GOD,		702	MOSADA 3		83
GOD! THEY'RE MAD TO FLY SUCH CANVAS!"		718	PHANTOM SHIP		14
THERE WAS SOME TALKING OF MAN'S GOD,		725	LEGEND		19
HIS GOD OF STUPOR AND OF WRATH.		725	LEGEND		20
IN THE HOLY CHURCH OF GOD.		735	IN CHURCH		4
IN THE HOLY CHURCH OF GOD.		736	IN CHURCH		16
FOR GOD IS WALKING IN THE DEW,		736	SUMMER EVENING		15
FOR GOD GIVES POWER TO THE SAD		741	EARL PAUL		47
FOR GOD GIVES POWER TO THE SAD		741	EARL PAUL		51
GOD PLANTED HIM LONG AGO.		743	WISDOM DREAMS		8
HE CANNOT WAKE THE GOD THAT HIDES IN IT.		748	SHADOW WATER A		19
BECAUSE A GOD HAS MADE HIM WISE WITH DREAMS;		748	SHADOW WATER A		26
I SWORE BUT YESTERDAY IF THE RED GOD		751	SHADOW WATER A		109
OR A GOD HID THEM UNDER THE SHADOW OF WINGS.		752	SHADOW WATER A		125
AND GATHER ROUND HIM, THAT NO GOD MAY KNOW		758	SHADOW WATER A	V	231
HOW LITTLE AND REEDY A SOUND AWAKES A GOD		760	SHADOW WATER A		252
GOD-APPOINTED					
AND GOD-APPOINTED BERKELEY THAT PROVED ALL THINGS A DREAM,		481	BLOOD AND MOON		25
GODDESS					
ON BREAST OF MARS THE GODDESS SIGHED.		562	CONJUNCTIONS		4
GOD-FORSAKEN					
THROUGH GOD-FORSAKEN MEADOWS; MRS. FRENCH,		412	TOWER		93
GOD-HATED					
AS THAT OLD WANDERING BEGGAR AND THESE GOD-HATED CHILDREN KNOW.		459	FROM OEDIPUS		6
GODHEAD					
AS MAN, AS BEAST, AS AN EPHEMERAL FLY BEGETS, GODHEAD BEGETS GODHEAD,		556	RIBH PATRICK		5
AS MAN, AS BEAST, AS AN EPHEMERAL FLY BEGETS, GODHEAD BEGETS GODHEAD,		556	RIBH PATRICK		5
GODHEAD ON GODHEAD IN SEXUAL SPASM BEGOT		557	RIBH ECSTASY		5
GODHEAD ON GODHEAD IN SEXUAL SPASM BEGOT		557	RIBH ECSTASY		5
GODHEAD. SOME SHADOW FELL. MY SOUL FORGOT		557	RIBH ECSTASY		6
GOD-KIND					
OF GOD-KIND AND MAN-KIND.		770	BLOOD BOND		6
GODLESS					
. . . AND ITS GODLESS AND PASSIONATE AGE.		63	OISIN 3		216
. . . AND THE GODLESS FIRES OF THINE AGE.		63	OISIN 3	V	216
GOD'S SEE SEA-GOD'S					
THAT SEA GOD'S NAME, WHO IN A DEEP CONTENT		38	OISIN 2	V	129
THE DEAD GOD'S SWORD, TO MANY FORMS HE GREW,		40	OISIN 2	V	175
WATCHING THE BLESSED ONES MOVE FAR OFF, AND THE SMILE ON GOD'S FACE,		61	OISIN 3		199
"THE DOOMS OF MEN ARE IN GOD'S HIDDEN PLACE."		110	CUCHULAIN SEA		62
"THE DOOMS OF MEN ARE IN GOD'S HIDDEN HOARD."		110	CUCHULAIN SEA	V	62
IF MICHAEL, LEADER OF GOD'S HOST		112	ROSE OF PEACE		1
IF MICHAEL, LEADER OF GOD'S HOSTS		112	ROSE OF PEACE	V	1
BROODING NO MORE UPON GOD'S WARS		113	ROSE OF PEACE		5
WOULD COME AT LAST TO GOD'S GREAT TOWN,		113	ROSE OF PEACE		11
AND GOD'S BELL BUOYED TO BE THE WATER'S CARE;		114	ROSE OF BATTLE		4
AND WAGE GOD'S BATTLES IN THE LONG GREY SHIPS.		114	ROSE OF BATTLE		20
GOD'S BELL HAS CLAIMED THEM BY THE LITTLE CRY		114	ROSE OF BATTLE		23

328

		PAGE	TITLE	LINE
GOD'S	**(CONTINUED)**			
GOD'S LAUGHING IN HEAVEN		118	CRADLE SONG	5
THAT ONLY GOD'S EYES DID NOT CLOSE:		156	FORGOT BEAUTY	14
"PRAISE GOD AND GOD'S MOTHER," DATHI SAID, ...		167	BLESSED	17
"FOR GOD AND GOD'S MOTHER HAVE SENT		167	BLESSED	18
THE POWERS, NOT KIND LIKE YOU, CAME WHERE GOD'S GARDEN BLOWS,		174	ELEMENT POWERS V	1
THAT ON THE LONELY HEIGHT WHERE ALL ARE IN GOD'S EYE, . .		291	PAUDEEN	6
AND THAT WOULD BE AGAINST GOD'S PROVIDENCE.		339	SHEP GOATHERD	5
I MOURN FOR THAT MOST LONELY THING: AND YET GOD'S WILL BE DONE:		354	HIS PHOENIX	31
O SAGES STANDING IN GOD'S HOLY FIRE		408	SAIL BYZANTIUM	17
AS THOUGH GOD'S DEATH WERE BUT A PLAY.		437	SONGS PLAY 1	8
"GOD'S FIRE UPON THE WANE, ...		485	STATISTICS	2
STANDS IN GOD'S UNCHANGING EYE		529	TOM LUNATIC	16
GOD'S LOVE HAS HIDDEN HIM		574	MAIDS 1ST SONG	7
GODS	**SEE SEA-GODS**			
WHEN GODS AND GIANTS WARRED. WE RODE BETWEEN		31	OISIN 2	31
NOR THE HIGH GODS WHO NEVER LIVED, MAY FIGHT		34	OISIN 2	80
UNTIL THE GODS AND DEMONS DROP ASLEEP, ...		35	OISIN 2	86
BREWED BY THE SEA GODS, FROM HUGE CUPS THAT LAY		41	OISIN 2 V	189
ON THE FLOORS OF THE GODS."		59	OISIN 3	180
. . . HE CRIED, "NO, THE GODS A LONG TIME ARE DEAD." . .		59	OISIN 3	180
. . . HE CRIED, "NAY, THE GODS A LONG TIME ARE DEAD." . .		59	OISIN 3 V	180
AY, AY. SWEAR BY THE PARENTS OF THE GODS, ...		74	ANASHU VIJAYA	66
SWEAR! BY THE PARENTS OF THE GODS, I SWEAR.		75	ANASHU VIJAYA	76
AND IN MY HEART THE DAEMONS AND THE GODS		104	FERGUS DRUID V	38B
AND HIM WHO DROVE THE GODS OUT OF THEIR LISS, ...		170	SECRET ROSE	16
BUT THE GODS LONG AGO DECREED		194	BAILE AILLINN	119
PROTECT ME NOW, GODS THAT MY PEOPLE SWEAR BY.		241	SHADOW WATER B	396
THE GODS WERE SITTING AT THE BOARD		271	GREY ROCK	14
BUT LET THAT BE--THE GODS WERE STILL		271	GREY ROCK V	16
THAT ONLY GODS MAY BUY OF HIM.		272	GREY ROCK	25
WHY ARE THE GODS BY MEN BETRAYED?"		275	GREY ROCK	115
STARED AT THE GODS WITH LAUGHING LIP.		276	GREY ROCK	123
OVERCOME GODS UPON PARNASSUS;		540	FROM ANTIGONE	6
BY AN OLD HUNTER TALKING WITH GODS;		605	YOU CONTENT	23
FOR GUIDING OF THE GODS. THE SACRED BLOOM		656	ISLE STAT I 3	41
EVEN THE WANDERING ISLANDS OF THE GODS, ...		749	SHADOW WATER A	45
AND YET, THERE IS A LOVE THAT THE GODS GIVE, ...		749	SHADOW WATER A	56
AND FALLS AMONG THE DREAMS THE DROWSY GODS		750	SHADOW WATER A	68
IT WERE BETTER TO PASS BY, BECAUSE THE GODS		751	SHADOW WATER A	104
BECAUSE THE UNAMBITIOUS THAT HATE THE GODS		754	SHADOW WATER A V	158
BY SUN AND MOON AND A HUNDRED GODS AS WELL, ...		756	SHADOW WATER A	189
THE GODS HOLD WATCH ABOUT THE WORDS OF A QUEEN. . . .		756	SHADOW WATER A	191
WHERE GODS ARE BROODING IN A MOUNTAINOUS PLACE		757	SHADOW WATER A	198
I HAVE TURNED HOMEWARDS. IN THE EYES OF THE GODS, . .		757	SHADOW WATER A	202
GATHER ABOUT HIM, THAT THE GODS MAY NOT KNOW		758	SHADOW WATER A	231
THE HAND THAT WOUNDS HIM, BECAUSE THE GODS ARE HIS FRIENDS.		758	SHADOW WATER A	232
THE MOUNTAIN OF THE GODS, THE UNAPPEASABLE GODS . . .		764	SHADOW WATER A	332
THE MOUNTAIN OF THE GODS, THE UNAPPEASABLE GODS . . .		764	SHADOW WATER A	332
THE GODS WEAVE NETS, AND TAKE US IN THEIR NETS, . . .		764	SHADOW WATER A	339
O! I WOULD BREAK THIS NET THE GODS HAVE WOVEN		765	SHADOW WATER A	361
THE NETS THE GODS HAVE WOVEN AND OUR OWN HEARTS, . . .		766	SHADOW WATER A	383
THE GODS HATE HAPPINESS, AND WEAVE THEIR NETS		767	SHADOW WATER A	399
SHE IS ALREADY FADING, AS THOUGH THE GODS		768	SHADOW WATER A V	422
THE BRAVEST FROM THE GODS BUT ASK!		788	BRAVEST ASK	1
GODS'				
THAT ONLY THE GODS' EYES DID NOT CLOSE!		156	FORGOT BEAUTY V	14
WHERE I HAD HEARD NO FEET BUT THE GODS' CAME.		756	SHADOW WATER A V	191B
GOES				
THE OSPREY OF SORROW GOES AFTER AND CLUTCHES, ...		27	OISIN 1 V	415D
WHERE GOES TO GAZE THE RESTLESS-FOOTED STAR		32	OISIN 2 V	50G
GOES DROPPING FROM HIS EYES A LANGUID LIGHT, ...		34	OISIN 2 V	81A
GATHERS SEA-SLIME AND GOES THE SEAWARD WAY, ...		45	OISIN 2 V	237
IN A LONG IRON SLEEP, AS A FISH IN THE WATER GOES DUMB AS A STONE.		53	OISIN 3	96
NO LIVE MAN GOES THITHER, ...		62	OISIN 3 V	214
AND TO THE ARMCHAIR GOES, ...		98	FOXHUNTER	18
AND BY THE CHAIR HE GOES, ...		98	FOXHUNTER V	18
AH, DREAM NOT OF THEM, MY BELOVED, THE FLAME OF THE METEOR THAT GOES,		122	WHITE BIRDS	6
YET SHE GOES WITH FOOTSTEP WARY, ...		124	CATHLEEN PARA	11
STILL SHE GOES WITH FOOTSTEPS WARY, ...		124	CATHLEEN PARA V	11
SHE GOES DOWN THE FLOOR OF HEAVEN, ...		125	CATHLEEN PARA V	13
WHO GOES WITH FERGUS?		125	GOES FERGUS	T
FOR GOD GOES BY WITH WHITE FOOTFALL, ...		139	TO IRELAND	44
FOR GOD GOES BY WITH WHITE FOOT-FALL.		139	TO IRELAND V	44
AND THEIR DAY GOES OVER IN IDLENESS, ...		151	OLD MOTHER	7
BUT I CAN SEE WHERE THE WIND GOES		168	BLESSED	27
"AND BLESSEDNESS GOES WHERE THE WIND GOES, ...		168	BLESSED	29
"AND BLESSEDNESS GOES WHERE THE WIND GOES, ...		168	BLESSED	29
BUT I HAVE FOUND WHERE THE WIND GOES		168	BLESSED V	27
SHE GOES ABOUT HER HOUSE ERECT AND CALM		340	SHEP GOATHERD	35
THE FRECKLED MAN WHO GOES		347	FISHERMAN	2
"VENGEANCE UPON THE MURDERERS," THE CRY GOES UP, . . .		426	PHANTOM HATRED	9
GOES TO THE BARBAROUS CLANGOUR OF A GONG.		430	NINETEEN 19	58
GOES TO THE BARBAROUS CLANGOUR OF GONG.		430	NINETEEN 19 V	58
NAKED TO NAKED GOES, ...		538	LAST CONFESS	16
THE GIRL GOES DANCING THERE		568	SWEET DANCER	1
NOW STRENGTH OF BODY GOES!		575	ACRE OF GRASS	4

329

	PAGE	TITLE		LINE

GOES   (CONTINUED)

	PAGE	TITLE		LINE
HOW GOES THE WEATHER?	585	ORAHILLY		9
HOW GOES THE WEATHER?	585	ORAHILLY		18
HOW GOES THE WEATHER?	585	ORAHILLY		27
HOW GOES THE WEATHER?	585	ORAHILLY		36
THE BEGGARS HAVE CHANGED PLACES, BUT THE LASH GOES ON.	590	GREAT DAY		4
A HORN! SOME TROOP OF ROBBERS WINDING GOES	649	ISLE STAT I 1		110
YON WIND GOES SADLY, AND THE GRASS AND TREES	652	ISLE STAT I 2		10
OUT OF THE AIR. AND WHEN? WHEN THE SUN GOES DOWN	652	ISLE STAT I 2		29
THE WIND AT EVENING WHEN THE SUN GOES DOWN	653	ISLE STAT I 2		50
GOES FLICKERING IN REVERBERATED LIGHT.	653	ISLE STAT I 2		53
GOES HIS POPPIES NOW A-HAWKING!	705	DAWN-SONG		4
HE WHISPERS TO A SOLDIER, WHO GOES OUT--	711	FERENCZ RENYI		44
REITERANT. A BIRD GOES BY THE TENT,	711	FERENCZ RENYI		46
REITERANT. A BOY GOES BY THE TENT,	711	FERENCZ RENYI	V	46
TIME GOES. THE FLAKED FIRE OF EVENING CRAWLS	712	FERENCZ RENYI		70
TIME GOES. THE FLICKED FIRE OF EVENING CRAWLS	712	FERENCZ RENYI	V	70
HER ARMS AROUND HIS FEET. THE SIGNAL GOES	714	FERENCZ RENYI		103
SO ENDS A BRAIN--A WORLD! THE SMOKE GOES UP,	714	FERENCZ RENYI		111
LAUGHING GOES IN WILDEST MOOD,	732	STREET DANCERS		41
THERE THY WANDERING PATHWAY GOES,	744	ROSY CROSS		6
"TILL THE SUN GOES DOWN AND AN HOUR OF THE CLOCK"	779	GOING THE ROAD		7

GOIN'

	PAGE	TITLE		LINE
OR GOIN' TO THE WELL,	96	MOLL MAGEE		46

GOING

	PAGE	TITLE		LINE
. . . IN THE DIMNESS THEY LOVE GOING BY!	53	OISIN 3		98
AWAY WITH US HE'S GOING,	88	STOLEN CHILD		42
IF I AM GOING TO MY DEATH?--FOR THERE,	231	SHADOW WATER B		207
I CANNOT--I AM GOING ON TO THE END.	248	SHADOW WATER B		544
FROM GOING DOWN OF THE SUN I HAVE DREAMED	358	PRESENCES	V	3
A PRAYER ON GOING INTO MY HOUSE	371	ON GOING HOUSE		T
GOING THE FOREST THROUGH, WITH FLUTINGS WEAK!	672	ISLE STAT II 3		155
I WAS GOING THE ROAD ONE DAY	779	GOING THE ROAD		1

GOING-DOWN

	PAGE	TITLE		LINE
FROM GOING-DOWN OF THE SUN I HAVE DREAMED	358	PRESENCES		3

GOLD

	PAGE	TITLE		LINE
FOR GOLD HIS HOOVES AND SILK HIS REIN,	2	OISIN 1	V	72
WITH AN APPLE OF GOLD IN HER TOSSING HAND!	12	OISIN 1		143
AN APPLE OF GOLD IN HER TOSSING HAND!	12	OISIN 1	V	143
WILD FLAMES OF RED AND GOLD AND BLUE,	18	OISIN 1		252
WHO WEDDED MEN WITH RINGS OF DRUID GOLD!	29	OISIN 2		10
HEARING AEDH TOUCH THE MOURNFUL STRINGS OF GOLD."	35	OISIN 2		87
. . . WITH BRONZE AND SILVER AND GOLD.	49	OISIN 3		32
MORE COMELY THAN MAN MAY MAKE THEM, INLAID WITH SILVER AND GOLD,	49	OISIN 3	V	29
I CRIED, "COME OUT OF THE SHADOW, KING OF THE NAILS OF GOLD!	51	OISIN 3		61
I CRIED, "COME OUT OF THE SHADOW, CANN OF THE NAILS OF GOLD!	51	OISIN 3	V	61
. . . WHEN THE SUN WAS ON SILVER OR GOLD!	53	OISIN 3		97
. . . THE GOLD HOOVES CRUSHING THE SANDS AND THE SHELLS	58	OISIN 3	V	157
MINE WAS A CHAIR OF SKINS AND GOLD,	81	MAD KING GOLL	V	1
OF PURPLE AND OF HEAVY GOLD!	81	MAD KING GOLL	V	3
"HE BRINGS THE PEACEFUL AGE OF GOLD"--	82	MAD KING GOLL	V	11
"THIS YOUNG MAN BRINGS THE AGE OF GOLD."	82	MAD KING GOLL		11
THESE HANDS WON MANY A TORQUE OF GOLD.	83	MAD KING GOLL		23
A KING SITTING UPON A CHAIR OF GOLD--	104	FERGUS DRUID		36
HAS WON THE GOLD HIS CARS OF BATTLE BRING."	106	CUCHULAIN SEA		11
NOR WON THE GOLD THAT NOW CUCHULAIN BRINGS."	106	CUCHULAIN SEA	V	11
BEAR THE GOLD EMBROIDERED DRESS--	124	CATHLEEN PARA	V	6
AND SANG WHAT GOLD MORNING OR EVENING SHEDS	126	DREAM OF FAERY		7
OR STORMY SILVER FRET THE GOLD OF DAY,	128	DREAM OF FAERY		33
. . . REMADE, LIKE A CASKET OF GOLD	143	ROSE IN HEART		7
. . . RE-MADE LIKE A CASKET OF GOLD	143	ROSE IN HEART	V	7
THE DANAAN CHILDREN LAUGH, IN CRADLES OF WROUGHT GOLD,	146	UNAPPEAS HOST		1
THE FAERY CHILDREN LAUGH IN CRADLES OF WROUGHT GOLD,	146	UNAPPEAS HOST	V	1
THE ANCIENT BEARDS, THE HELMS OF RUBY AND GOLD	169	SECRET ROSE		8
LINKED BY A GOLD CHAIN EACH TO EACH,	194	BAILE AILLINN		136
IN A GOLD AND SILVER WOOD,	214	HAPPY TOWNLAND	V	10
CARE MORE ABOUT THE KEGS OF SILVER AND GOLD	232	SHADOW WATER B		234
MADE OF DIM GOLD RAVE OUT IN SECRET TOMBS!	235	SHADOW WATER B		295
AND NOT A ROOF OF IVORY AND GOLD.	246	SHADOW WATER B		500
"PUT OFF THAT MASK OF BURNING GOLD	263	MASK		1
THE GOLD AND SILVER THREAD.	308	PLAYER QUEEN		8
THE GOLD INTO MY HAIR,	309	PLAYER QUEEN		18
THE GOLD UPON MY HAIR,	309	PLAYER QUEEN	V	18
AS IN THE GOLD MOSAIC OF A WALL,	408	SAIL BYZANTIUM		18
OF HAMMERED GOLD AND GOLD ENAMELLING	408	SAIL BYZANTIUM		28
OF HAMMERED GOLD AND GOLD ENAMELLING	408	SAIL BYZANTIUM		28
WRITTEN IN GOLD UPON A PURPLE STAIN,	461	HARUN RASHID		10
IS BUT A HEAVY, GOLD EMBROIDERED BANNER,	469	HARUN RASHID	V	188
NOT BLIND WITH GOLD, NOR DAZZLED BY THE GOLD	470	HARUN RASHID	V	191
NOT BLIND WITH GOLD, NOR DAZZLED BY THE GOLD	470	HARUN RASHID	V	191
IN TOMBS OF GOLD AND LAPIS LAZULI	483	OIL AND BLOOD		1
IN TOMBS OF GOLD AND LAPIS-LAZULI	483	OIL AND BLOOD	V	1
GET ALL THE GOLD AND SILVER THAT YOU CAN,	500	VACILLATION		19
THREE KEGS OF GOLD.	596	COLONEL MARTIN		49
CARRY THE GOLD ABOUT THE TOWN,	596	COLONEL MARTIN		52
"AND DID YOU KEEP NO GOLD, TOM?	596	COLONEL MARTIN		64
WHO SITS IN LONELY SPLENDOUR, MAIL'D IN GOLD,	651	ISLE STAT I 1		163
THE EVENING GLEAMS ARE GREEN AND GOLD AND RED	656	ISLE STAT I 3		22

PAGE   TITLE   LINE

GOLD (CONTINUED)
THE MOBS OF STARS IN GOLD AND GREEN AND BLUE, ... 663 ISLE STAT II 2   43
HE TURNS WHERE, HUNG LIKE DROPS OF DRIPPING GOLD, . . . 710 FERENCZ RENYI   18
HE TURNS WHERE, HUNG LIKE DROPS OF LIQUID GOLD, ... 710 FERENCZ RENYI V   18
AMONG THE GOLD, THE AMBER, AND THE RED." . . . . 712 FERENCZ RENYI   76
HIGHER AND HIGHER GOLD WITH EVENING LIGHT: . . . . 714 FERENCZ RENYI   113
GOLD UNTO GOLD, A GLEAM IN ITS LONG HAIR, ... 720 WITCH VIVIEN   3
GOLD UNTO GOLD, A GLEAM IN ITS LONG HAIR, ... 720 WITCH VIVIEN   3
WE WILL BRING A CROWN OF GOLD, ... 726 LOVERS QUARREL   13
WITH SHIELD AND ARMOUR WROUGHT WITH GOLD, ... 741 EARL PAUL   37
HAD I NOT GOLD AND SILVER, AND ENOUGH . . . . 748 SHADOW WATER A   32
ARMLETS OF GOLD OR SHIELDS WITH GOLDEN NAILS . . . . . . 749 SHADOW WATER A   43
BELIEVE THAT GOLD AND WOMEN TAKEN IN WAR . . . . 754 SHADOW WATER A   159
MADE OF DIM GOLD, RAVE OUT IN SECRET TOMBS, ... 765 SHADOW WATER A   345
GOLD-EMBROIDERED
BEAR THE GOLD-EMBROIDERED DRESS-- . . . . 124 CATHLEEN PARA V   6
WHERE GOLD-EMBROIDERED BANNERS OF THE CALIF'S . . . . . 461 HARUN RASHID   V   6
GOLDEN
A GOLDEN CRESCENT LIT THE PLAIN, ...   2 OISIN 1   V   7BB
TO THE MUSIC OF THE GOLDEN RHYME . . . . 14 OISIN 1   V   176
UNDER THE GOLDEN EVENING LIGHT. . . . . 25 OISIN 1   385
GOLDEN THE NAILS OF HIS BIRD-CLAWS, ... 50 OISIN 3   45
ON THE FAR GOLDEN PEAK: ENORMOUS SHAPES, ... 74 ANASHU VIJAYA   68
WHEN SUMMER GLUTS THE GOLDEN BEES, ... 84 MAD KING GOLL   38
WHERE SUMMER GLUTS THE GOLDEN BEES, ... 84 MAD KING GOLL V   38
UNDER THE GOLDEN OR THE SILVER SKIES: . . . . 127 DREAM OF FAERY   21
THE GOLDEN APPLES OF THE SUN. . . . . 150 WANDER AENGUS   24
FASTEN YOUR HAIR WITH A GOLDEN PIN, ... 157 BELOVED RHYMES   1
IS IT THESE THAT WITH GOLDEN THURIBLES . . . . 167 BLESSED   23
IS IT THOSE THAT WITH GOLDEN THURIBLES . . . . 167 BLESSED   V   23
OR AS THE CHANGING SPEARS FLUNG BY THE GOLDEN STARS . . . 175 ELEMENT POWERS V   15
ENWROUGHT WITH GOLDEN AND SILVER LIGHT, ... 176 CLOTHS HEAVEN   2
COUPLED WITH GOLDEN CHAINS, AND SING AS THEY FLY. . . . . 204 WITHER BOUGHS   18
TO FIND IT WHEN NIGHT FALLS LAID ON A GOLDEN BIER. . . . . 209 UNDER THE MOON   10
WHEN THE SUN LOOKED OUT OF HIS GOLDEN HOOD, ... 210 RAGGED WOOD   3
WHEN THE SUN LOOKED OUT OF HIS GOLDEN HOOD?-- . . . . . . 211 RAGGED WOOD   7
IN A GOLDEN AND SILVER WOOD: . . . . 214 HAPPY TOWNLAND   10
FROM GOLDEN AND SILVER BOUGHS: . . . . 215 HAPPY TOWNLAND   24
FROM THE GOLDEN AND SILVER BOUGHS. . . . . 215 HAPPY TOWNLAND V   24
OF THE GREAT GOLDEN NET THAT IS ABOUT US. . . . . 238 SHADOW WATER B   352
YOU CANNOT LEAP OUT OF THE GOLDEN NET. . . . . 238 SHADOW WATER B   360
I'LL GIVE A GOLDEN GALLEY FULL OF FRUIT, ... 240 SHADOW WATER B   373
AND BEAT THE GOLDEN HELMET WITH THEIR SWORDS? . . . . . . 243 SHADOW WATER B   425
HAVE BURIED NOTHING BUT MY GOLDEN ARMS. . . . . 243 SHADOW WATER B   431
AND STRIKE THE GOLDEN PILLARS WITH MY HANDS. . . . . . . 246 SHADOW WATER B   502
AND MADE A GOLDEN CRADLE . . . . 308 PLAYER QUEEN   3
AND MADE A GOLDEN GOWN, ... 308 PLAYER QUEEN   10
THE GOLDEN TOP OF CARE? . . . . 309 PLAYER QUEEN   20
OF GOLDEN KING AND SILVER LADY, ... 331 ROUND TOWER   13
THAT GOLDEN KING AND THAT WILD LADY . . . . 332 ROUND TOWER   19
THAT LADY AND THAT GOLDEN KING . . . . 332 ROUND TOWER   23
OR SET UPON A GOLDEN BOUGH TO SING . . . . 408 SAIL BYZANTIUM   30
AND ALL THE GOLDEN GRASSHOPPERS AND BEES. . . . . 428 NINETEEN 19   8
AND ALL HIS GOLDEN GRASSHOPPERS AND BEES. . . . . 428 NINETEEN 19   V   8
WORLD-FAMOUS GOLDEN THIGHED PYTHAGORAS . . . . 445 SCHOOL CHILDR V   45
WHERE GOLDEN CROCUS AND NARCISSUS BLOOM, ... 447 COLONUS PRAISE   18
MIRACLE, BIRD OR GOLDEN HANDIWORK, ... 497 BYZANTIUM   17
PLANTED ON THE STAR-LIT GOLDEN BOUGH, ... 497 BYZANTIUM   19
MIRACLE, BIRD OR GOLDEN HANDY-WORK . . . . 497 BYZANTIUM   V   17
PLANTED ON THE STARLIT GOLDEN BOUGH, ... 497 BYZANTIUM   V   19
THE GOLDEN SMITHIES OF THE EMPEROR! . . . . 498 BYZANTIUM   35
SLEEP UPON A GOLDEN BED . . . . 522 LULLABY   5
I CARRY THE SUN IN A GOLDEN CUP, ... 525 DANCING DAYS   7
I CARRY THE SUN IN A GOLDEN CUP, ... 525 DANCING DAYS   15
I CARRY THE SUN IN A GOLDEN CUP, ... 525 DANCING DAYS   23
BUT THE GOLDEN RACE LOOKS DIM, ... 530 DELPHIC ORACLE   4
SAID THE MAN IN THE GOLDEN BREASTPLATE . . . . 598 STONE CROSS   7
SAID THE MAN IN THE GOLDEN BREASTPLATE . . . . 599 STONE CROSS   15
SAID THE MAN IN THE GOLDEN BREASTPLATE . . . . 599 STONE CROSS   23
SAID THE OLD MAN IN THE GOLDEN BREASTPLATE . . . . 599 STONE CROSS   V   23
THE GOLDEN PLOUGH AND HARROW AND SPOKE ALOUD . . . . . . 609 IN TARAS HALLS   12
THERE ALL THE GOLDEN CODGERS LAY, ... 611 NEWS ORACLE   1
HERE WHERE LABURNUM HANGS HER GOLDEN FLEECE: . . . . . . 670 ISLE STAT II 3   102
AS SLOWLY AUTUMN CLIMBED THE GOLDEN THRONE . . . . 690 MOSADA 1   V   1A
SAVE, WITH THE LITTLE GOLDEN GREEDY CARP, ... 720 WITCH VIVIEN   2
NAY, RISE AND FLATTER HER WITH GOLDEN RHYME, ... 724 KANVA ON SELF   19
THE SUNFLOWERS WEAVE A GOLDEN CLIME, ... 736 SUMMER EVENING   9
ARMLETS OF GOLD OR SHIELDS WITH GOLDEN NAILS . . . . . . 749 SHADOW WATER A   43
TILL HIS EDAINE, NO LONGER A GOLDEN FLY . . . . 757 SHADOW WATER A   210
I FOUGHT TWELVE BATTLES DRESSED IN GOLDEN ARMOUR. . . . . 761 SHADOW WATER A   271
OF GOLDEN ARMED AOLAN AND THE QUEEN . . . . 766 SHADOW WATER A V   375
OF THE GOLDEN APPLE TREE: . . . . 771 SPINNING SONG   9
GOLDEN-ARMED
IT WAS GOLDEN-ARMED IOLLAN, AND HE DIED . . . . 242 SHADOW WATER B   406
FOR GOLDEN-ARMED IOLLAN HAS BEEN KILLED. . . . . 242 SHADOW WATER B   410
FOR GOLDEN-ARMED IOLLAN THAT I LOVED. . . . . 242 SHADOW WATER B   421
O! O! O! O! FOR GOLDEN-ARMED IOLLAN. . . . . 243 SHADOW WATER B   428
I NEVER HAVE BEEN GOLDEN-ARMED IOLLAN. . . . . 244 SHADOW WATER B   464
OF GOLDEN-ARMED IOLAN AND THE QUEEN . . . . 766 SHADOW WATER A   375
GOLDEN-CRESTED
WHO GIVETH TO THE GOLDEN-CRESTED WREN . . . . 698 MOSADA 2   51

331

		PAGE	TITLE		LINE
GOLDEN-THIGHED					
	WORLD-FAMOUS GOLDEN-THIGHED PYTHAGORAS • • • • • • •	445	SCHOOL CHILDR		45
GOLDFISH					
	ONE HAND AMID THE GOLDFISH IN THE POOL: • • • • • • •	463	HARUN RASHID		44
GOLD-FISH					
	IT SEEMED A GOLD-FISH SWIMMING IN A BOWL. • • • • • •	472	ALL SOUL NIGHT		40
GOLDS					
	HER GOLDS, HER AMBERS, AND HER BLUES, • • • • • •	13	OISIN 1		163
	HER GOLDS, HER AZURES, AND HER BLUES, • • • • • •	13	OISIN 1	V	163
GOLD-SEWN					
	GOLD-SEWN SILK ON THE SWORD-BLADE, • • • • • • • •	484	SYMBOLS		5
GOLD-SHOD					
	SCARCE WORTHY OF A HOOF GOLD-SHOD. • • • • • • • •	2	OISIN 1	V	7Y
GOLDSMITH					
	THAT GOLDSMITH AND THE DEAN. • • • • • • • • •	481	BLOOD AND MOON		18
	GOLDSMITH DELIBERATELY SIPPING AT THE HONEY-POT OF HIS MIND,	481	BLOOD AND MOON		21
	GOLDSMITH DELIBERATELY SIPPING AT THE HONEY POT OF HIS MIND:	481	BLOOD AND MOON	V	21
	A POT-HOUSE BENCH WITH OLIVER GOLDSMITH ONCE. • • • •	486	SEVEN SAGES		3
	GOLDSMITH AND BURKE, SWIFT AND THE BISHOP OF CLOYNE • • •	486	SEVEN SAGES		9
	OLIVER GOLDSMITH SANG WHAT HE HAD SEEN, • • • • • •	487	SEVEN SAGES		17
GOLDSMITHS					
	BUT SUCH A FORM AS GRECIAN GOLDSMITHS MAKE • • • • •	408	SAIL BYZANTIUM		27
GOLD-SOWN					
	GOLD-SOWN SILK ON THE SWORD BLADE: • • • • • • • •	484	SYMBOLS	V	5
GOLL					
	THE MADNESS OF KING GOLL • • • • • • • • • • •	81	MAD KING GOLL		T
GOMEZ					
	FEET OF DARK GOMEZ, WHERE NOW WANDER YE? • • • • •	690	MOSADA 1		11
	WHEN MY LOST LOVER LEFT THESE ARMS. MY GOMEZ • • • •	701	MOSADA 3		51
	LOOK UP, LOOK UP, THY GOMEZ IS BY THEE. • • • • •	701	MOSADA 3		68
	GRIEVE NOT, FOR GOMEZ KNEELS BESIDE THEE—GOMEZ, • • •	702	MOSADA 3		90
	GRIEVE NOT, FOR GOMEZ KNEELS BESIDE THEE—GOMEZ, • • •	702	MOSADA 3		90
	SAFE ON THE BREAST OF GOMEZ LIES THY HEAD, • • • • •	703	MOSADA 3		101
	GIVE TO THY GOMEZ. GOMEZ—HE HAS GONE • • • • •	703	MOSADA 3		110
	GIVE TO THY GOMEZ. GOMEZ—HE HAS GONE • • • • •	703	MOSADA 3		110
	SAFE ON THE BREAST OF GOMEZ IS THY HEAD, • • • • • •	703	MOSADA 3	V	101
GONE					
	IS THY COMPANION GONE FROM THEE?" • • • • • • • •	6	OISIN 1	V	52
	OR THE SOFTNESS OF YOUTH BE GONE FROM OUR FACES, • • •	27	OISIN 1		410
	WILL THE SOFTNESS OF YOUTH BE GONE FROM OUR FACES, • • •	27	OISIN 1	V	410
	OR THE SOFTNESS OF YOUTH BE GONE FROM OUR FACES, • • •	27	OISIN 1	V	419C
	OR THE SOFTNESS OF YOUTH BE GONE FROM OUR FACES, • • •	28	OISIN 1	V	426
	THE ISLE WAS OVER NOW AND GONE: • • • • • • • •	28	OISIN 1	V	427B
	HE HAD GONE WHISPERING FORTH WITH CUMBERED HEART, • • •	37	OISIN 2	V	111
	BUT SHE WHOSE HOURS OF TENDERNESS WERE GONE • • • •	38	OISIN 2		138
	REMEMBERING HOW I PACED IN DAYS GONE O'ER, • • • • •	44	OISIN 2	V	227
	THE MOIL OF MY CENTURIES FILLED ME: AND GONE LIKE A SEA-COVERED STONE	51	OISIN 3		70
	AND THE HORSE WAS GONE IN THE DISTANCE, • • • • • •	52	OISIN 3		75
	OF TWILIGHT AND SLUMBER WERE GONE, AND THAT HOOFS IMPATIENTLY STEPT.	54	OISIN 3		112
	AND THE DREAMS OF THE ISLANDS WERE GONE, • • • • • •	59	OISIN 3		175
	I MUST BE GONE: THERE IS A GRAVE • • • • • • • •	67	HAPPY SHEPHERD		45
	FAREWELL: I MUST BE GONE I-WIS, • • • • • • • •	67	HAPPY SHEPHERD	V	46D
	THE SAD, SAD THOUGHT HAS GONE FROM ME NOW WHOLLY: • •	72	ANASHU VIJAYA		19
	AND NOW THE OLD MAN'S DREAMS ARE GONE, • • • • • •	98	FOXHUNTER		19
	THEY HAVE GONE DOWN UNDER THE SAME WHITE STARS, • • •	115	ROSE OF BATTLE		34
	CABINS GONE NOW, OLD WELL-SIDES, OLD DEAR PLACES, • • •	130	BOOK STORIES	V	23
	AS IN THE OLD DAYS LONG GONE BY, • • • • • • • •	131	OLD PENSIONER	V	15
	THE WELL-KNOWN FACES ARE ALL GONE, • • • • • • •	132	OLD PENSIONER	V	17
	"WHEN YOU WERE GONE, HE TURNED AND DIED • • • • •	133	FR GILLIGAN		37
	WERE GONE LIKE A DRIFTING SMOKE: • • • • • • • •	145	HOST OF AIR		40
	BUT THE OLD MEN AND DANCERS WERE GONE, • • • • • •	145	HOST OF AIR	V	39
	I WILL FIND OUT WHERE SHE HAS GONE, • • • • • • •	150	WANDER AENGUS		19
	I WILL FIND OUT WHERE SHE IS GONE • • • • • • • •	150	WANDER AENGUS	V	19
	SHE HAS GONE WEEPING AWAY. • • • • • • • • •	152	LOSS OF LOVE		7
	TO THE CAVE, WHERE DATHI THE BLESSED HAD GONE, • • • •	166	BLESSED	V	3
	AND WHEN IT IS GONE WE ARE DEAD: • • • • • • • •	168	BLESSED		30
	AND WHEN IT IS GONE WE DIE: • • • • • • • • •	168	BLESSED	V	30
	WHERE HAS MAID QUIET GONE TO, • • • • • • • • •	171	MAID QUIET		1
	THAT'S ALL BUT GONE: FOR THE PROUD HEART IS GONE, • • •	181	QUEEN MAEVE		20
	THAT'S ALL BUT GONE: FOR THE PROUD HEART IS GONE, • • •	181	QUEEN MAEVE		20
	KINGS OF THE GREAT PLAIN HAVE COME AND GONE • • • •	183	QUEEN MAEVE	V	81
	WITH WISDOM, THEY WANDER TILL ALL THE YEARS HAVE GONE BY:	204	WITHER BOUGHS		45
	YOU DO NOT SEE MY PURPOSE. I SHALL HAVE GONE • • • •	238	SHADOW WATER B		357
	YOU DID NOT SEE MY PURPOSE. I SHALL HAVE GONE • • • •	238	SHADOW WATER B	V	357
	FOR EVERYTHING IS GONE. COME HITHER, AIBRIC, • • • •	241	SHADOW WATER B		402
	BUT, DEAR, CLING CLOSE TO ME: SINCE YOU WERE GONE, • • •	257	RECONCILIATION		11
	BUT THERE IT'S GONE: I WILL NOT TAKE • • • • • •	274	GREY ROCK		92
	BUT WHEN NINE DAYS HAD GONE I STOOD AGAIN • • • • •	282	TWO KINGS		131
	ROMANTIC IRELAND'S DEAD AND GONE, • • • • • • •	289	SEPTEMBER 1913		7
	THEY HAVE GONE ABOUT THE WORLD LIKE WIND, • • • • •	289	SEPTEMBER 1913		11
	ROMANTIC IRELAND'S DEAD AND GONE, • • • • • • •	289	SEPTEMBER 1913		15
	ROMANTIC IRELAND'S DEAD AND GONE, • • • • • • •	290	SEPTEMBER 1913		23
	BUT LET THEM BE, THEY'RE DEAD AND GONE, • • • • • •	290	SEPTEMBER 1913		31
	LET THESE CONTENT YOU AND BE GONE AGAIN: • • • • •	292	TO A SHADE		8
	AND TILL ANOTHER NIGHT HAD GONE, • • • • • • • •	297	THREE BEGGARS		51
	"I'LL SLEEP UNTIL THE WINTER'S GONE, • • • • • • •	305	HOUR DAWN		57
	"I'D LIKE TO SLEEP TILL WINTER'S GONE • • • • • • •	305	HOUR DAWN		60

		PAGE	TITLE		LINE

GONE (CONTINUED)

	PAGE	TITLE		LINE
THAT HAD GONE	309	REALISTS		7
BABBLING OF FALLEN MAJESTY, RECORDS WHAT'S GONE.	314	FALLEN MAJESTY		4
THESE, THESE REMAIN, BUT I RECORD WHAT'S GONE. A CROWD	315	FALLEN MAJESTY		6
ALL TILL MY YOUTH WAS GONE	315	FRIENDS		18
THE BARE CHIMNEY IS GONE BLACK OUT	327	ROBERT GREGORY		84
WHERE MANY A KING HAS GONE	330	BONE OF A HARE		2
WE HAVE GONE ROUND AND ROUND	332	SOLOMON SHEBA		6
APPEARS, BUT WHEN WE HAVE GONE IS GONE AGAIN,	334	LIVING BEAUTY		6
APPEARS, BUT WHEN WE HAVE GONE IS GONE AGAIN,	334	LIVING BEAUTY		6
APPEARS, AND WHEN WE HAVE GONE IS GONE AGAIN,	334	LIVING BEAUTY	V	6
APPEARS, AND WHEN WE HAVE GONE IS GONE AGAIN,	334	LIVING BEAUTY	V	6
YET PRAISE THE WINTERS GONE!	336	YOUNG BEAUTY		15
THE SHEEP HAD GONE FROM THEIRS. I KNOW RIGHT WELL	339	SHEP GOATHERD		15
TILL WINTER BLASTS WERE GONE, BUT SPEAK OF HER	340	SHEP GOATHERD		33
NO SETTLED MAN. AND NOW THAT HE IS GONE	341	SHEP GOATHERD		55
THEIR ANGRY TEARS, ARE GONE.	344	DEJECTION		6
THE SCULLION GONE WILD."	349	HAWK		6
I HAVE GONE ABOUT THE HOUSE, GONE UP AND DOWN	350	HER PRAISE		2
I HAVE GONE ABOUT THE HOUSE, GONE UP AND DOWN	350	HER PRAISE		2
AND ALL THE SHAPELY BODY NO TITTLE GONE ASTRAY.	354	HIS PHOENIX		30
FIVE-AND-TWENTY YEARS HAVE GONE	360	ALF POLLEXFEN		1
FIVE AND TWENTY YEARS HAVE GONE	360	ALF POLLEXFEN	V	1
THE COMFORT THAT YOU MADE? ALTHOUGH MY WITS HAVE GONE	391	UNDER SATURN		5
YOUR COMING BROUGHT, THOUGH I ACKNOWLEDGE I HAVE GONE	391	UNDER SATURN	V	5
THAT ARE IMPATIENT TO BE GONE!	413	TOWER		102
NOR HATE OF WHAT'S TO COME, NOR PITY FOR WHAT'S GONE,	427	PHANTOM HATRED		30
MANY INGENIOUS LOVELY THINGS ARE GONE	428	NINETEEN 19		1
AND GONE ARE PHIDIAS' FAMOUS IVORIES	428	NINETEEN 19		7
MANY INGENUOUS LOVELY THINGS ARE GONE	428	NINETEEN 19	V	1
AND GONE ARE PHIDIAS' CARVEN IVORIES	428	NINETEEN 19	V	7
BEFORE THAT BRIEF GLEAM OF ITS LIFE BE GONE,	430	NINETEEN 19		63
AND MY SLEEP IS GONE.	454	EMPTY CUP		10
OF ALL THAT ARE GONE,	458	SECRETS OF OLD		14
OF FRIENDS THAT ARE GONE,	458	SECRETS OF OLD	V	14
ARE GONE AWAY, AND SOME THAT STAY	458	HIS WILDNESS		5
WHEN ALL THOSE ROOMS AND PASSAGES ARE GONE,	489	COOLE PARK 29		26
AND IN THE MORNING'S GONE, NO MAN KNOWS WHY;	490	COOLE BALLYLEE		20
MY FIFTIETH YEAR HAD COME AND GONE,	501	VACILLATION		35
SO GET YOU GONE, VON HUEGEL, THOUGH WITH BLESSINGS ON YOUR HEAD.	503	VACILLATION		89
WHERE HAD HER SWEETNESS GONE?	503	QUARREL IN AGE		1
IF TIME WERE BUT GONE."	510	JANE JUDGMENT		19
THE SOONER LOVE IS GONE,	511	JANE AND JACK		4
"MY FRIENDS ARE GONE, BUT THAT'S A TRUTH	513	JANE TALK BISH		9
THOSE DANCING DAYS ARE GONE	524	DANCING DAYS		T
THOSE DANCING DAYS ARE GONE,	524	DANCING DAYS		2
DEAR, I MUST BE GONE	535	PARTING		1
WHAT MATTER FOR THE SCENE, THE SCENE ONCE GONE!	542	PARN FUNERAL 1		19
THINGS UNBORN, THINGS THAT ARE GONE,	562	NEEDLES EYE		3
HIS GLORY AND HIS MONUMENTS ARE GONE.	563	MERU		14
A GREATER, A MORE GRACIOUS TIME HAS GONE!	564	GYRES		12
AND IF YOUR LOVE WERE GONE	569	THREE BUSHES		4
ALL NEIGHBOURLY CONTENT AND EASY TALK ARE GONE,	580	CURSE CROMWELL		9
JOHN BULL HAS GONE TO INDIA	583	GHOST ROG CASE		21
HE'D GONE TO GREAT EXPENSE	585	ORAHILLY		13
THE WISDOM OF THE PEOPLE'S GONE,	607	SONGS BURDEN 2		16
BUT HAD GONE OUT TO DIE	608	SONGS BURDEN 3		20
THAT KNOWING BETTER TALK HAD GONE	627	STATES HOLIDAY		7
BUT WHERE ARE THEY GONE?	628	JANE MOUNTAIN		8
WHO KEEPS THE TILL. NOW THAT MY LADDER'S GONE,	630	CIRCUS ANIMALS		38
BUT BODY GONE HE SLEEPS NO MORE,	633	MAN AND ECHO		29
EYES STARED OUT OF THE BRANCHES AND WERE GONE.	634	CUCHULAIN COMF		3
CAME AND WERE GONE. HE LEANT UPON A TREE	634	CUCHULAIN COMF		5
THEIR MONEY SPENT, THEIR WINE GONE SOUR,	635	BLACK TOWER		3
WHEN THAT GREATER DREAM HAD GONE	639	BEN BULBEN		63
FLY! FLY! SO THESE BRAVE SHEPHERDS BOTH ARE GONE!	649	ISLE STAT I 1		112
MY PRETTY CHILD, SINCE HE HAS GONE, OH SAY	658	ISLE STAT II 1		3
YOU MUST BE GONE! THE ROLLING GRAINS OF SAND	663	ISLE STAT II 2		34
I WOULD HAVE GONE ALSO! BUT FAR AWAY	663	ISLE STAT II 2		37
NASCHINA'S GONE, DRAWN BY A THIRST OF LOVE,	664	ISLE STAT II 2		59
WE ARE GONE!	669	ISLE STAT II 3		82
NAY, HE IS GONE. WAKE! WAKE! AS A BEE SIPS	678	ISLE STAT II 3		305
GIVE TO THY GOMEZ. GOMEZ--HE HAS GONE	703	MOSADA 3		110
GIVE TO THY VALLENCE. VALLENCE--HE HAS GONE	703	MOSADA 3	V	110
STILL WANDER THROUGH THE WORLD. HE'S GONE, HE'S GONE.	703	MOSADA 3		121
STILL WANDER THROUGH THE WORLD. HE'S GONE, HE'S GONE.	703	MOSADA 3		121
HAS FLICKERED AND GONE OUT. I AM NOT WELL.	704	MOSADA 3		129
GONE THE STARS AND GONE THE WHITE MOON	718	PHANTOM SHIP		3
GONE THE STARS AND GONE THE WHITE MOON,	718	PHANTOM SHIP		3
. . . GONE AND PUFFED AWAY AND DEAD.	718	PHANTOM SHIP		3
THE MAN IS GONE WHO GUIDED YE, UNWEARY,	738	MOURN THEN ON		3
THE MAN IS GONE WHO FROM HIS LONELY STATION	738	MOURN THEN ON		7
AND NOW THEY ARE ALL GONE, I FOLLOW STILL.	749	SHADOW WATER A		37
THE YEARS THAT HAVE GONE OVER HER FROM THE HOUR	760	SHADOW WATER A		256
I WILL DRINK OUT OF THE STREAM. THE STREAM IS GONE!	761	SHADOW WATER A		273
THERE! THERE! THEY HAVE GONE QUICKLY, FOR ALREADY	764	SHADOW WATER A		326
THAT HAVE GONE THITHER TO LOOK FOR THE LOUD STREAMS,	765	SHADOW WATER A		348
HAVE FALLEN AND MY SUN AND MOON GONE OUT.	767	SHADOW WATER A	V	405
THEY ARE GONE, THEY ARE GONE. THE PROUD MAY LIE BY THE PROUD.	777	SONG DEIRDRE 3		1

GONE   (CONTINUED)
    THEY ARE GONE, THEY ARE GONE. THE PROUD MAY LIE BY THE   777 SONG DEIRDRE 3   1
      PROUD.
    THEY ARE GONE, THEY ARE GONE. WHISPERING WERE ENOUGH. . .   778 SONG DEIRDRE 3   3
    THEY ARE GONE, THEY ARE GONE. WHISPERING WERE ENOUGH. . .   778 SONG DEIRDRE 3   3
    EAGLES HAVE GONE INTO THEIR CLOUDY BED. . . . .   778 SONG DEIRDRE 3   6
    BUT NOW THE NIGHT IS GONE. . . . .   783 GREY ROUND   24
    WHAT THOUGH THEY DANCED! THOSE DAYS ARE GONE, ...   788 HAWTHORN TREE   5
GONG
    GOES TO THE BARBAROUS CLANGOUR OF A GONG. . . . . . .   430 NINETEEN 19   58
    GOES TO THE BARBAROUS CLANGOUR OF GONG. . . . .   430 NINETEEN 19   V   58
    AFTER GREAT CATHEDRAL GONG! . . . .   497 BYZANTIUM   4
    WHEN GONG AND CONCH DECLARE THE HOUR TO BLESS . . . . .   611 STATUES   23
GONG-TORMENTED
    THAT DOLPHIN-TORN, THAT GONG-TORMENTED SEA. . . . . .   498 BYZANTIUM   40
GONNE
    THE BLINDS DRAWN UP"! MAUD GONNE AT HOWTH STATION WAITING   578 LOFTY THINGS   10
      A TRAIN,
GOOD
    "GOOD REASON HAVE I FOR MY LOVE," . . . .   7 OISIN 1   V   62
    EQUAL TO GOOD OR GRIEVOUS CHANCE . . . .   24 OISIN 1   372
    EQUAL TO GOOD OR EVIL CHANCE . . . .   24 OISIN 1   V   371
    A GOOD NAME IS GOODLY TO HEAR OF, AND A GOOD NAME SURELY   51 OISIN 3   V   63
      IS THINE.
    A GOOD NAME IS GOODLY TO HEAR OF, AND A GOOD NAME SURELY   51 OISIN 3   V   63
      IS THINE.
    WORDS ALONE ARE CERTAIN GOOD. . . . .   65 HAPPY SHEPHERD   10
    FOR WORDS ALONE ARE CERTAIN GOOD! . . . .   66 HAPPY SHEPHERD   43
    AND WORDS ALONE ARE CERTAIN GOOD, ...   66 HAPPY SHEPHERD V   43
    GOOD FATHER JOHN O'HART . . . .   91 FATHER OHART   1
    I SAW A NEIGHBOUR GOOD. . . . .   95 MOLL MAGEE   V   36
    TO SEE YOU SO GOOD! . . . .   118 CRADLE SONG   6
    SPINNING AT ALL TIMES ERI'S GOOD TO-MORROW, ...   129 BOOK STORIES   V   10
    UNDER THE FRUIT OF EVIL AND OF GOOD! . . . .   137 TO SOME I TALK   9
    AND BLOWING US EVIL AND GOOD; . . . .   158 TO HIS HEART   V   4A
    "WHERE ALL ARE COMELY AND GOOD? . . . .   167 BLESSED   22
    FOR THE GOOD ARE ALWAYS THE MERRY, ...   178 FIDDLER DOONEY   13
    MORE STILL THAN THEY HAD BEEN FOR A GOOD MONTH, . . .   182 QUEEN MAEVE   54
    OUR GIVER OF GOOD COUNSEL AND GOOD LUCK." . . . . .   185 QUEEN MAEVE   102
    OUR GIVER OF GOOD COUNSEL AND GOOD LUCK." . . . . .   185 QUEEN MAEVE   102
    BECAUSE THEY HAVE MADE SO GOOD A FRIEND. . . . . . .   195 BAILE AILLINN   159
    AND BEING IN GOOD HEART, BECAUSE . . . .   197 BAILE AILLINN   191
    A GOOD ROUND SUM UPON THIS CRUISE, AND TURN-- . . .   222 SHADOW WATER B   5
    WHAT GOOD IS THERE IN THIS HARD WAY OF LIVING, . . .   225 SHADOW WATER B   69
    YOU'LL BE AS GOOD A LEADER. BE OF YOUR TROOP! . . .   225 SHADOW WATER B   73
    COULD NOT AMEND. I HAVE GOOD SPIRITS ENOUGH. . . .   227 SHADOW WATER B   116
    I HAVE GOOD REASON FOR THAT THOUGHT. AND NOW . . .   238 SHADOW WATER B   354
    WE'LL FIND SO GOOD A THING AS THAT WE HAVE LOST? . .   258 KING NO KING   13
    WE, TOO, HAD GOOD ATTENDANCE ONCE, ...   266 GALWAY RACES   5
    IS NOT THAT HOW GOOD STORIES RUN?-- . . . .   271 GREY ROCK   13
    BEFORE THAT ROOMFUL OR AS GOOD. . . . .   273 GREY ROCK   52
    AND I AM IN NO GOOD REPUTE . . . .   276 GREY ROCK   127
    KNOWING THAT SILENCE BRINGS NO GOOD TO KINGS, ...   279 TWO KINGS   57
    WHAT THE EXULTANT HEART CALLS GOOD . . . .   288 TO WEALTHY MAN   33
    IF A GOOD EASTER WIND WERE BLOWING, ...   306 HOUR DAWN   86
    I COUNT MY GOOD AND BAD, ...   316 FRIENDS   22
    THE COMMON GOOD OF LIFE, ...   317 NIGHT COME   5
    OF SUN AND MOON THAT A GOOD HOUR . . . .   331 ROUND TOWER   11
    WHAT TURNED SO GOOD A SHEPHERD FROM HIS CHARGE. . . .   339 SHEP GOATHERD   16
    HAPPIER DAYS THOUGHT GOOD; . . . .   365 HER RACE   4
    WHAT'S GOOD OR BAD, OR WHAT IT IS TO TRIUMPH . . . .   376 PHASES OF MOON   108
    KNOWING NOT EVIL AND GOOD; . . . .   382 VISION ROBART   12
    IN IGNORANT GOOD WILL, ...   392 EASTER 1916   V   18
    HAD IGNORANT GOOD WILL! . . . .   392 EASTER 1916   V   19
    BARTER THAT HORN AND EVERY GOOD . . . .   405 FOR DAUGHTER   62
    GOOD FELLOWS SHUFFLED CARDS IN AN OLD BAWN! . . . .   411 TOWER   65
    COME LET US MOCK AT THE GOOD . . . .   432 NINETEEN 19   103
    TO HELP GOOD, WISE OR GREAT . . . .   432 NINETEEN 19   110
    AND AFTER THAT THERE'S NOTHING GOOD . . . .   434 WHEEL   5
    NOW THE GOOD CALIPH'S LEARNED TREASURER, ...   461 HARUN RASHID   3
    AND WHAT'S THE GOOD OF AN ESCAPE . . . .   479 SELF AND SOUL   55
    OF ALL GOOD MEN AND WOMEN, ...   531 FATHER CHILD   3
    "BODES ME LITTLE GOOD." . . . .   539 MEETING   6
    MONEY IS GOOD AND A GIRL MIGHT BE BETTER, ...   544 TO SAME TUNE 1   3
    BUT GOOD STRONG BLOWS ARE DELIGHTS TO THE MIND." . .   544 TO SAME TUNE 1   4
    BUT A GOOD STRONG CAUSE AND BLOWS ARE DELIGHT." . .   545 TO SAME TUNE 1   14
    "MONEY IS GOOD AND A GIRL MIGHT BE BETTER, ...   545 TO SAME TUNE 1   21
    BUT A GOOD STRONG CAUSE"--THE ROPE GAVE A JERK THERE, . .   545 TO SAME TUNE 1   23
    BUT A GOOD STRONG CAUSE AND THE BLOWS ARE DELIGHT." . .   545 TO SAME TUNE 1 V   14
    TIME FOR US ALL TO PICK OUT A GOOD TUNE, ...   548 TO SAME TUNE 3   13
    WHAT IS THE GOOD OF A MAN AND HE . . . .   551 SONGS REWRIT 1   7
    WHAT IS THE GOOD OF A MAN IF HE . . . .   551 SONGS REWRIT 1 V   7
    AND O HE WAS A GOOD MAN . . . .   571 THREE BUSHES   68
    BUT THERE'S NO GOOD COMPLAINING, FOR MONEY'S RANT IS ON.   580 CURSE CROMWELL   10
    AND BLACKENED HIS GOOD NAME. . . . .   582 ROGER CASEMENT   8
    ESTABLISHED IT FOR GOOD! . . . .   584 ORAHILLY   6
    WHATEVER GOOD A FARMER'S GOT . . . .   586 PARNELLITES   13
    AND WHAT'S THE GOOD OF WOMEN, FOR ALL THAT THEY CAN SAY   592 PILGRIM   4
    PROCLAIMED BOTH GOOD AND GREAT! . . . .   597 MODEL LAUREATE   4
    A GOOD MAN ON A HORSE, ...   604 YOU CONTENT   12
    IN SOME GOOD COMPANY, ...   605 YOU CONTENT   18

		PAGE	TITLE		LINE

GOOD (CONTINUED)
A ROOF, GOOD CLOTHES, PASSION, LOVE PERHAPS, ... 609 IN TARAS HALLS 8
MONEY IS GOOD AND A GIRL MIGHT BE BETTER, ... 616 MARCH SONGS 3 3
BUT GOOD STRONG BLOWS ARE DELIGHTS TO THE MIND." . . . 616 MARCH SONGS 3 4
BUT A GOOD STRONG CAUSE AND BLOWS ARE DELIGHT." . . . . 616 MARCH SONGS 3 14
"MONEY IS GOOD AND A GIRL MIGHT BE BETTER, ... 616 MARCH SONGS 3 21
BUT A GOOD STRONG CAUSE"--THE ROPE GAVE A JERK THERE, . 616 MARCH SONGS 3 23
I HAVE FOUND NOTHING HALF SO GOOD . . . . 624 APPARITIONS 9
SHOULD STARVE GOOD MEN AND BAD ADVANCE, ... 626 OLD MEN BE MAD 10
THE BLESSED GOD WAS GOOD TO SEND US SUCH, ... 683 SEEKER 40
SHOULD I BE GOOD? BUT YOU ARE BEAUTIFUL. . . . . . . 692 MOSADA 1 62
NOT GOOD! BUT YOU ARE LIKE THE BUTTERFLIES. . . . . . 693 MOSADA 1 65
THE WAGES OF SIN IS DEATH. NO USE. NO GOOD. . . . . . 697 MOSADA 2 42
THOUGH YOUNGEST OF ALL IN OUR GOOD BAND, ... 707 FAIRY PEDANT 11
THOUGH YOUNGEST OF ALL IN OUR GOOD BAND, ... 708 FAIRY PEDANT 39
THY NAME IS?" "RENYI." "OF?" "THIS VILLAGE." "GOOD! 709 FERENCZ RENYI 13
THY NAME IS?" "FERENCZ RENYI." "OF?" "THIS VILLAGE." 709 FERENCZ RENYI V 13
   "GOOD!
SEARCHED THE UNSEARCHABLE--WHY GOOD MEN WEEP! . . . . . 710 FERENCZ RENYI 32
WHY THOSE WHO DO GOOD OFTEN BE NOT GOOD, ... 710 FERENCZ RENYI 33
WHY THOSE WHO DO GOOD OFTEN BE NOT GOOD, ... 710 FERENCZ RENYI 33
THIS SULLEN PEASANT SPOILS THE GOOD SUNSHINE, ... 711 FERENCZ RENYI 42
THIS SULLEN PEASANT SPOILS THE GOOD RED WINE. . . . . . 711 FERENCZ RENYI 43
THIS SULLEN PEASANT CHILLS THE GOOD SUNSHINE. . . . . . 711 FERENCZ RENYI V 42
THIS SULLEN PEASANT SOURS THE GOOD RED WINE. . . . . . 711 FERENCZ RENYI V 43
I HOLD HIM DEARER THAN THE GOOD, ... 723 GIRLS SONG A 7
ARE PRAYERS OF PATIENT MEN AND GOOD." . . . . 725 LEGEND 6
AND WILL FIND HER GOOD AT HEART, ... 726 LOVERS QUARREL 10
HOW "THE ONLY GOOD IS MUSING MILD, ... 728 PRIEST FAIRY 13
FOR ALL GOOD MEN NOW FALLEN ILL, ... 736 IN CHURCH 5
I HAVE GOOD PILOTS, AIBRIC. WHEN MEN DIE . . . . . . 750 SHADOW WATER A 81
BUT HER GOOD MAN ANSWERED HER . . . . 772 SONG DEIRDRE 1 V 9
WE CALLED IT A GOOD DEATH. TODAY . . . . 791 REPRISALS 3
GOOD-BYE
EGYPT AND GREECE, GOOD-BYE, AND GOOD-BYE, ROME! . . . . 563 MERU 8
EGYPT AND GREECE, GOOD-BYE, AND GOOD-BYE, ROME! . . . . 563 MERU 8
"GOOD-BYE, GOOD-BYE, MY HUSBAND," . . . . 779 GOING THE ROAD 9
"GOOD-BYE, GOOD-BYE, MY HUSBAND," . . . . 779 GOING THE ROAD 9
GOODLY
AND TELL OF YOUR GOODLY HOUSEHOLD AND THE GOODLY WORKS 51 OISIN 3 62
   OF YOUR HANDS,
AND TELL OF YOUR GOODLY HOUSEHOLD AND THE GOODLY WORKS 51 OISIN 3 62
   OF YOUR HANDS,
A GOOD NAME IS GOODLY TO HEAR OF, AND A GOOD NAME SURELY 51 OISIN 3 V 63
   IS THINE.
WAS CARRIED TO THE GOODLY HOUSE . . . . 192 BAILE AILLINN 72
GOODMAN
BUT HER GOODMAN ANSWERED HER! . . . . 772 SONG DEIRDRE 1 9
GOODNESS
THAT FANCIED GOODNESS MIGHT BE GAY, ... 432 NINETEEN 19 104
GOODNIGHT
THE SECOND BEST'S A GAY GOODNIGHT AND QUICKLY TURN AWAY. 459 FROM OEDIPUS 12
GOODS
AND HIM WHO SOLD TILLAGE, AND HOUSE, AND GOODS, ... 170 SECRET ROSE 22
GOOD-WILL
IN IGNORANT GOOD-WILL, ... 392 EASTER 1916 18
GOOSE
WHEN NIGHT WAS AT ITS DEEPEST, A WILD GOOSE . . . . . 181 QUEEN MAEVE 36
WRINKLED LIKE THE FOOT OF A GOOSE, ... 508 JANE BISHOP 16
"THEY KILLED MY GOOSE AND A CAT. . . . . 546 TO SAME TUNE 2 8
"THEY KILLED MY GOOSE AND A CAT. . . . . 546 TO SAME TUNE 2 18
"THEY KILLED MY GOOSE AND A CAT. . . . . 547 TO SAME TUNE 2 28
ALL METAPHOR, MALACHI, STILTS AND ALL. A BARNACLE GOOSE 623 HIGH TALK 11
GORE-BOOTH
IN MEMORY OF EVA GORE-BOOTH AND CON MARKIEWICZ . . . . 475 EVA GORE-BOOTH T
GORIAS
THE TOWERY GATES OF GORIAS, ... 196 BAILE AILLINN 161
GORSE
BY THE GORSE ON THE HIGH LAND, ... 726 LOVERS QUARREL 4
GORT
MUTTERED THE OLD CRANE OF GORT. . . . . 295 THREE BEGGARS 6
AND SMITHY WORK FROM THE GORT FORGE, ... 406 CARVED STONE 3
GOSPELLER
BY SOME PEASANT GOSPELLER! . . . . 440 WISDOM 5
WHEN SOME PEASANT GOSPELLER . . . . 440 WISDOM V 5
GOSPELLERS'
THROUGH THE PEASANT GOSPELLERS' . . . . 440 WISDOM V 5
GOT
O'DRISCOLL GOT UP FROM THE GRASS, ... 145 HOST OF AIR V 37
AND WHEN I HAD GOT MY WILL AND DRAWN YOU HERE, ... 284 TWO KINGS 158
"OH GOD IF HE GOT LOOSE!" AND THEN . . . . 307 HOUR DAWN V 118
"WHEN SHE WAS GOT," MY MOTHER SANG, ... 308 PLAYER QUEEN 13
THAT THOSE THAT WE HAVE LOVED GOT THEIR LONG FINGERS . 375 PHASES OF MOON 66
ALL THAT SHE GOT SHE SPENT, ... 392 EASTER 1916 V 20
WHERE GOT I THAT TRUTH? . . . . 439 FRAGMENTS 5
KING ABUNDANCE GOT HIM ON . . . . 440 WISDOM 16
AND THEN THE SPEAKERS GOT IT . . . . 582 ROGER CASEMENT 15
WHATEVER GOOD A FARMER'S GOT . . . . 586 PARNELLITES 13
THE PRIESTS HAVE GOT A BOOK THAT SAYS . . . . . . 621 JOHN KINSELLA 25
HE HAD DREAMED THE COW HAD GOT WITHIN . . . . . . 729 PRIEST FAIRY 33

335

GOVERN
    THE GIFTS THAT GOVERN MEN, AND AFTER THESE . . . . . . 264 HOUSE SHAKEN   10
    WHERE ARE THE CAPTAINS THAT GOVERN MANKIND? . . . . . 548 TO SAME TUNE 3   22
    WHERE ARE THE CAPTAINS THAT GOVERN MANKIND? . . . . . 615 MARCH SONGS 2   22
GOVERNED
    GIRLS THAT HAVE GOVERNED CITIES, ... 789 SINGING HEAD   15
GOVERNMENT
    ON A RECENT GOVERNMENT APPOINTMENT IN IRELAND . . . . . 317 APPOINTMENT   V   T
    BEING OUT OF HEART WITH GOVERNMENT . . . . 317 APPOINTMENT   1
    BEING OUT OF HEART AT GOVERNMENT . . . . 317 APPOINTMENT   V   1
    NO GOVERNMENT APPOINTED HIM. . . . . 318 APPOINTMENT   12
    PLANNED IN A GOVERNMENT OFFICE, SHORTEN HIS LIFE, . . . 372 ON GOING HOUSE   15
    OR LACKING THAT, GOVERNMENT IN SUCH HANDS, ... 543 PARN FUNERAL 2   7
GOWN   SEE NIGHT-GOWN
    AND HE WORE LARGE HOLES IN HIS GOWN. . . . . 92 FATHER OHART   12
    SHE ROSE IN HER PALE NIGHT GOWN, ... 159 CAP AND BELLS V 10
    ONE GATHERS UP HIS PURPLE GOWN; . . . . 212 BLESS PSALTER   9
    AND MADE A GOLDEN GOWN, ... 308 PLAYER QUEEN   10
    OR A YOUNG GIRL DRESSED OUT IN HER NEW GOWN, ... 350 HER PRAISE   4
GRACE
    HOW MANY LOVED YOUR MOMENTS OF GLAD GRACE, ... 121 YOU ARE OLD   5
    FULL OF EARTH'S OLD TIMID GRACE. . . . . 124 CATHLEEN PARA   12
    WITH THE OLD KINDNESS, THE OLD DISTINGUISHED GRACE, . . . 362 HER COURTESY   1
    GIVE HER A LITTLE GRACE, ... 367 HER CHRIS TREE   9
GRACIOUS
    A GRACIOUS, GENTLE, KINGLY BOY. . . . . 82 MAD KING GOLL V 8
    A GREATER, A MORE GRACIOUS TIME HAS GONE; . . . . . . 564 GYRES   12
    BEAUTIFUL, GRACIOUS, IN HER VENETIAN WAY, ... 602 GALLERY REVIS V 14
    HERE, WHERE MEN KNOW THE GRACIOUS WOODLAND JOYS, ... 651 ISLE STAT I 1 154
    OH! GRACIOUS PAN, TAKE NOW THY SERVANT'S PART. . . . . 657 ISLE STAT I 3 77
GRADUAL
    TO GRADUAL TIME'S LAST GIFT, A WRITTEN SPEECH . . . . . 264 HOUSE SHAKEN   11
GRAIN
    I HAVE NOT A CRUMB OF COMFORT, NOT A GRAIN. . . . . . 200 FOLLY COMFORT   7
    BUT HEART THERE IS NO COMFORT, NOT A GRAIN; . . . . . 200 FOLLY COMFORT V 7
    IN THE MAD ABSTRACT DARK AND GROUND IT GRAIN BY GRAIN . . 442 BLACK CENTAUR   8
    IN THE MAD ABSTRACT DARK AND GROUND IT GRAIN BY GRAIN . . 442 BLACK CENTAUR   8
GRAINS
    YOU MUST BE GONE: THE ROLLING GRAINS OF SAND . . . . . 663 ISLE STAT II 2 34
    THE PASSING OF THOSE LITTLE GRAINS IS SNOW . . . . . . 722 WITCH VIVIEN   48
GRAMMAR
    THAT GRAMMAR SCHOOL OF COURTESIES . . . . 288 TO WEALTHY MAN 15
    THE MALL AND EADES'S GRAMMAR SCHOOL, ... 360 ALF POLLEXFEN 15
GRANARY
    SLEEK AS ANY GRANARY MOUSE . . . . 2 OISIN 1   V 7M
    MORE SLEEK THAN ANY GRANARY MOUSE, ... 4 OISIN 1   36
    SLEEK AS ANY GRANARY MOUSE, ... 4 OISIN 1   V 37
    THE HARVEST'S IN: THE GRANARY DOORS ARE SHUT: . . . . . 755 SHADOW WATER A 177
GRAND
    JEWELRY SO GRAND." . . . . 595 COLONEL MARTIN 33
GRANDAM
    WHEN WERE YOU BORN? BEFORE YOUR GRANDAM EVE. . . . . . 721 WITCH VIVIEN   32
GRANDCHILDREN   SEE GREAT-GRANDCHILDREN
    WHERE HER GRANDCHILDREN SLEPT, AND CRIED ALOUD, ... 185 QUEEN MAEVE   109
    AMONG HIS CHILDREN, GRANDCHILDREN AND GREAT-GRANDCHILDREN: 790 DEDICATION   6
GRAND-CHILDREN
    WHERE HER GRAND-CHILDREN SLEPT, AND CRIED ALOUD . . . . 185 QUEEN MAEVE V 109
GRAND-DAD
    AND WANT HE DID; FOR MY OWN GRAND-DAD . . . . 596 COLONEL MARTIN 68
    AND WANT HE DID FOR MY GRAND-DAD SAW . . . . 596 COLONEL MARTIN V 68
GRANDDAD   SEE GREAT-GRANDDAD
GRANDDAUGHTER
    THE DAUGHTER AND THE GRANDDAUGHTER OF KINGS . . . . . 237 SHADOW WATER B 334
    THE DAUGHTER AND GRANDDAUGHTER OF KINGS . . . . 237 SHADOW WATER B V 334
GRANDEST
    AND BOUGHT THE GRANDEST JEWELRY . . . . 595 COLONEL MARTIN 21
GRANDFATHER   SEE GREAT-GRANDFATHER
    GRANDFATHER SANG IT UNDER THE GALLOWS: . . . . 544 TO SAME TUNE 1   1
    GRANDFATHER SAID IN THE GREAT REBELLION: . . . . . . 544 TO SAME TUNE 1 V 1
    GRANDFATHER SANG IT UNDER THE GALLOWS: . . . . 615 MARCH SONGS 3   1
GRANDFATHER'S   SEE GREAT-GRANDFATHER'S
    ON GREAT GRANDFATHER'S BATTERED TOMB." . . . . 332 ROUND TOWER V 30
GRANDFATHERS   SEE GREAT-GRANDFATHERS
    OLD FATHERS, GREAT GRANDFATHERS, ... 518 LOVES LONENESS V 1
GRANDSON   SEE GREAT-GRANDSON
    BUT FOR HER GRANDSON NOW: THERE IS NO CHANGE . . . . . 340 SHEP GOATHERD 39
    GRANDSON, OR GREAT-GRANDSON, ... 604 YOU CONTENT   2
GRANIA
    AND GRANIA, WALKING AND SMILING, SEWED WITH HER NEEDLE   53 OISIN 3   94
        OF BONE.
GRANIA'S
    AMID THAT FIRST ASTONISHMENT, WITH GRANIA'S SHADE, . . . 366 HER COURAGE   4
    WHILE WONDERING STILL TO BE A SHADE, WITH GRANIA'S SHADE, 366 HER COURAGE V 4
GRANT
    GOD GRANT ME--NO, NOT HERE, ... 346 ON WOMAN   25
    GOD GRANT A BLESSING ON THIS TOWER AND COTTAGE . . . . 371 ON GOING HOUSE   1
    FOR SHEPHERD LADS IN GALILEE: AND GRANT . . . . 371 ON GOING HOUSE   4
    FOR WHAT MERE BOOK CAN GRANT A KNOWLEDGE . . . . . . 386 ROBARTES DANCE 20
    GRANT ME AN OLD MAN'S FRENZY, ... 576 ACRE OF GRASS   13
GRANTED
    MAY SHE BE GRANTED BEAUTY AND YET NOT . . . . 403 FOR DAUGHTER   17

GRAPE-CLUSTER
    HANG ON THE SIDE OF THE ROUND GRAPE-CLUSTER; • • • • •   646 ISLE STAT I 1   45
GRAPES
    THE HEAVY CLUSTERS OF THE GRAPES WERE FULL, • • • • •   690 MOSADA 1   13
GRASP
    TO GRASP THE WOMAN. YOU HAVE DARED TO TOUCH HER? • • •   223 SHADOW WATER B   39
    WAS MOVING. BLEEDING NOW, HIS GRASP UNLOCKS, • • • • •   688 TWO TITANS   42
GRASS   SEE KNOT-GRASS SPEAR-GRASS
    THE HARE LEAPED IN THE GRASS. YOUNG NIAMH CAME • • • •   44 OISIN 2   V 229
    A VALLEY FLOWED DOWN FROM HIS HOOFS, AND THERE IN THE LONG   48 OISIN 3   26
        GRASS LAY,
    WHEN A GLOW-WORM WAS GREEN ON A GRASS LEAF, • • • •   53 OISIN 3   V 99
    • • • AND GAZED ON THE GRASS WITH A SIGH. • • • • • •   54 OISIN 3   100
    • • • THE FLESH OF HIS FACE AS DRIED GRASS, • • • • • •   59 OISIN 3   173
    • • • AND MARCH ON AS OXEN MOVE OVER YOUNG GRASS; • • • •   62 OISIN 3   211
    AS A GRASS SEED CRUSHED BY A PEBBLE, AS A WOLF SUCKED UNDER   63 OISIN 3   V 220
        A WEIR.
    WHO MADE THE GRASS AND MADE THE WORMS AND MADE MY FEATHERS   77 INDIAN ON GOD   18
        GAY,
    ALONG THE GRASS, ALONG THE SANDS, • • • • • • • •   78 INDIAN TO LOVE   9
    SHE BID ME TAKE LIFE EASY, AS THE GRASS GROWS ON THE WEIRS;   90 SALLEY GARDENS   7
    "PUT THE CHAIR UPON THE GRASS; • • • • • • • • •   97 FOXHUNTER   9
    "NOW LEAVE THE CHAIR DOWN ON THE GRASS, • • • • • • •   97 FOXHUNTER   V 9
    "NOW LEAVE THE CHAIR UPON THE GRASS, • • • • • • •   97 FOXHUNTER   V 9
    ON THE SUN-SMITTEN GRASS; • • • • • • • • • •   99 FOXHUNTER   42
    THE FIELD-MOUSE RUNNING BY ME IN THE GRASS, • • • • •   101 ROSE UPON ROOD   17
    THE FIELD MOUSE RUNNING BY ME IN THE GRASS, • • • • •   101 ROSE UPON ROOD V 17
    AND WHERE HER SON, FINMOLE, ON THE SMOOTH GRASS • • •   106 CUCHULAIN SEA V 18
    UNDERNEATH THE GRASS AND CLOVER, • • • • • • • •   124 CATHLEEN PARA   3
    ON MUNSTER GRASS AND CONNEMARA SKIES. • • • • • •   130 BOOK STORIES   24
    ON MUNSTER GRASS, OR CONNEMARA SKIES. • • • • • •   130 BOOK STORIES   V 24
    O'DRISCOLL GOT UP FROM THE GRASS, • • • • • • • •   145 HOST OF AIR   V 37
    AND WALK AMONG LONG DAPPLED GRASS, • • • • • • •   150 WANDER AENGUS   21
    AND WALK AND WALK THROUGH SUMMER GRASS, • • • • • •   150 WANDER AENGUS V 21
    AND WHEN THE UPROAR RAN ALONG THE GRASS • • • • • •   186 QUEEN MAEVE   127
    ALIGHTED ON THE WINDY GRASS. • • • • • • • • •   195 BAILE AILLINN   138
    BUT A WILD APPLE HID THE GRASS • • • • • • • •   197 BAILE AILLINN   189
    OR AVALLON THE GRASS GREEN HOLLOW, OR JOYOUS ISLE • •   209 UNDER THE MOON V   2
    WHERE MY GOATS BROWSE ON THE SCARCE GRASS OR LEAP • •   339 SHEP GOATHERD   8
    OR ON THE CLOSE-CROPPED GRASS • • • • • • • • •   343 SHEP GOATHERD   103
    THEY SAY HE COUNTED GRASS, • • • • • • • • • •   345 ON WOMAN   14
    BECAUSE THE MOUNTAIN GRASS • • • • • • • • • •   350 MEMORY   4
    AMONG THE COARSE GRASS AND THE CAMEL-DUNG. • • • • •   369 EGO DOMINUS   31
    AMONG THE COARSE GRASS AND THE CAMEL DUNG. • • • • •   369 EGO DOMINUS   V 31
    MINNALOUSHE RUNS IN THE GRASS • • • • • • • •   378 CAT AND MOON   9
    MINNALOUSHE CREEPS THROUGH THE GRASS • • • • • • •   378 CAT AND MOON   17
    MINNALOUSHE CREEPS THROUGH THE GRASS • • • • • • •   379 CAT AND MOON   25
    BUT THE CRUSHED GRASS WHERE WE HAVE LAIN; • • • • •   389 SOLOMON WITCH   42
    UPON A BLADE OF GRASS. • • • • • • • • • • •   505 GRAT INSTRUCT   4
    THE GRASS MY BED; • • • • • • • • • • • •   510 JANE JUDGMENT   12
    SCATTERED ON THE LEVEL GRASS • • • • • • • • •   530 DELPHIC ORACLE   6
    LIES IN A CIRCLE ON THE GRASS; THEREIN • • • • • •   555 RIBH AT TOMB   26
    GRASS PLOT OF THE GARDEN; • • • • • • • • •   568 SWEET DANCER   3
    AN ACRE OF GRASS • • • • • • • • • • • •   575 ACRE OF GRASS   T
    AN ACRE OF GREEN GRASS • • • • • • • • • •   575 ACRE OF GRASS   2
    BY OISIN ON THE GRASS; • • • • • • • • • •   611 NEWS ORACLE   6
    AND NO MAN KNOWS WHAT TREADS THE GRASS. • • • • •   614 MARCH SONGS 2   10
    AND NO MAN KNOWS WHAT TREADS THE GRASS. • • • • •   615 MARCH SONGS 2   20
    AND NO MAN KNOWS WHAT TREADS THE GRASS. • • • • •   615 MARCH SONGS 2   30
    TALL DAMES GO WALKING IN GRASS GREEN AVALON. • • • • •   627 STATES HOLIDAY V REF
    FLOWERS AND GRASS AND CLOUDLESS SKY. • • • • • •   639 BEN BULBEN   57
    YON WIND GOES SADLY, AND THE GRASS AND TREES • • • •   652 ISLE STAT I 2   10
    O'ER THE GRASS LIGHT-ENDAPPLED • • • • • • • •   654 ISLE STAT I 2   63
    SAVING A GREEN FROG DEAD UPON THE GRASS. • • • • •   676 ISLE STAT II 3   269
    THE CHILD PURSUING LIZARDS IN THE GRASS, • • • • •   686 LIFE   1
    BRIGHT ON A GRASS BLADE'S UNDER SIDE, MIGHT HEAR, • • •   689 NETTLESHIP   10
    OF HIS SAD GOD; AND DOWN AMONG THE GRASS • • • • •   690 MOSADA 1   16
    AROUND MY HEAD AND DANCED AMONG THE GRASS; • • • • •   690 MOSADA 1   19
    ON THEIR SWAYING BLADES OF GRASS, • • • • • • •   705 DAWN-SONG   14
    MY MOTHER DREW FORTH FROM THE LONG GRASS • • • • •   708 FAIRY PEDANT   23
    IN THE LONG GRASS--FOUR EYES DROOP LOW--A SEAT • • • •   716 DWELT SYCAMORE   11
    FEED A FIRE WITH STEMS OF GRASS; • • • • • • • •   727 LOVERS QUARREL   42
    THE CHILD WHO CHASES LIZARDS IN THE GRASS, • • • • •   734 QUATRAIN APHOR   1
    THE CHILD PURSUING LIZARDS IN THE GRASS, • • • • •   734 QUATRAIN APHOR V   1
    I AWAIT YOUR WORDS AS THE BLIND GRASS AWAITS • • • •   756 SHADOW WATER A 181
    THE GRASS AND THE BLUE SHADOW ON THE STREAM • • • • •   761 SHADOW WATER A 280
    WHO CAN HAVE TROD IN THE GRASS? • • • • • • • •   781 MY HEART BEAT   4
GRASS-BARNACLE
    FROM THE GREAT GRASS-BARNACLE CALLING, • • • • • • •   57 OISIN 3   156
GRASS-BLADES
    WHILE O'ER THE BUDS, AND O'ER THE GRASS-BLADES, BRIGHT • •   704 REMEMBRANCE   3
GRASS-BLADES'
    UPON THE GRASS-BLADES' BENDING TIPS, • • • • • • •   3 OISIN 1   V 7II
GRASS-COLOURED
    HE HAD RAGGED LONG GRASS-COLOURED HAIR; • • • • • •   190 BAILE AILLINN   26
GRASSES
    AMONG THE WOODLAND GRASSES SWEET, • • • • • • • •   15 OISIN 1   V 199
    AND THE LONG GREY GRASSES, WHOSE TENDEREST TOUCHES • • •   27 OISIN 1   V 415B
    GREY SAND ON THE GREEN OF THE GRASSES AND OVER THE DRIPPING   48 OISIN 3   14
        TREES,

		PAGE	TITLE	LINE

GRASSES   (CONTINUED)
GREY SANDS ON THE GREEN OF THE GRASSES AND OVER THE   48 OISIN 3   V 14
  DRIPPING TREES,
FROM HIS HOOVES IN THE HEAVY GRASSES, WITH MONSTROUS   48 OISIN 3   V 27
  SLUMBERING FOLK,
AND, SHAKING THE PLUMES OF THE GRASSES . . . .   49 OISIN 3   35
. . . THERE CAMPING IN GRASSES DEEP, ...   50 OISIN 3   54
IN THE ROOTS OF THE GRASSES, THE SORRELS, I LAID MY BODY   52 OISIN 3   73
  AS LOW;
GREY SAND ON THE GREEN OF THE GRASSES AND OVER THE DRIPPING   57 OISIN 3   142
  TREES,
GREY SANDS ON THE GREEN OF THE GRASSES AND OVER THE   57 OISIN 3   V 142
  DRIPPING TREES,
WHERE LONG GREY GRASSES BOW AND BEND, ...   736 SUMMER EVENING   6
GRASS-GREEN
NOR AVALON THE GRASS-GREEN HOLLOW, NOR JOYOUS ISLE, ...   209 UNDER THE MOON   2
TALL DAMES GO WALKING IN GRASS-GREEN AVALON. .   .   .   .   .   627 STATES HOLIDAY   13
TALL DAMES GO WALKING IN GRASS-GREEN AVALON. .   .   .   .   .   627 STATES HOLIDAY   26
TALL DAMES GO WALKING IN GRASS-GREEN AVALON. .   .   .   .   .   627 STATES HOLIDAY   39
MOURN YE ON GRASS-GREEN PLAINS OF ERI FATED, ...   738 MOURN THEN ON   9
GRASSHOPPER
THE HEART IN ME LONGING TO LEAP LIKE A GRASSHOPPER INTO   60 OISIN 3   182
  HER HEART;
A LONG, BROWN GRASSHOPPER OF MAIDS! PEACE, SIR! .   .   .   .   661 ISLE STAT II 1   69
BUT LOUD THE GRASSHOPPER THAT SITS BENEATH. .   .   .   .   .   662 ISLE STAT II 2   8
GRASSHOPPERS
AND ALL THE GOLDEN GRASSHOPPERS AND BEES. .   .   .   .   .   .   428 NINETEEN 19   8
AND ALL HIS GOLDEN GRASSHOPPERS AND BEES. .   .   .   .   .   .   428 NINETEEN 19   V   8
OR TRAFFIC IN THE GRASSHOPPERS OR BEES. . .   .   .   430 NINETEEN 19   48
OR TRAFFIC IN THE GRASSHOPPERS AND BEES? .   .   .   .   .   .   430 NINETEEN 19   V 48
GRASS-LEAF
WHEN A GLOW-WORM WAS GREEN ON A GRASS-LEAF, ...   53 OISIN 3   99
GRASSY
CAME TO THE CAIRN-HEAPED GRASSY HILL . . .   .   3 OISIN 1   17
"BUT WE ARE APART IN THE GRASSY PLACES, ...   27 OISIN 1   408
ALL DRIPPING ON A GRASSY SLOPE, AND SAW THEM CEASE TO CHASE   76 INDIAN ON GOD   4
HE MADE THE WORLD TO BE A GRASSY ROAD .   .   .   .   112 ROSE OF WORLD   14
ON GRASSY MATTRESS I HAD LAID ME, ...   387 SOLOMON WITCH   3
UPON EUROTAS' GRASSY BANK .   .   .   .   522 LULLABY   14
OF SOLDIERS RANKED IS ON A GRASSY SPOT, ...   712 FERENCZ RENYI   64
OF SOLDIERS DRAWN IS ON A GRASSY SPOT, ...   712 FERENCZ RENYI V 64
GRASS-YELLOW
HE HAD RAGGED, LONG GRASS-YELLOW HAIR; .   .   .   .   190 BAILE AILLINN V 26
GRATED
THE BOAT'S PROW GRATED ON THE SHALLOW SAND, ...   659 ISLE STAT II 1   11
GRATITUDE
AND BLESSED, I GIVE MY GRATITUDE, ...   380 SAINT HUNCH   14
HER CHILDISH GRATITUDE FOR LOVE AND MATCH YOUR FIFTY YEARS?   450 OWEN AHERNE   23
OF CHILDREN'S GRATITUDE OR WOMAN'S LOVE. . .   .   .   .   .   500 VACILLATION   26
GRATITUDE TO THE UNKNOWN INSTRUCTORS .   .   .   .   505 GRAT INSTRUCT   T
GRATITUDE TO THE UNKNOWN POWERS .   .   .   .   505 GRAT INSTRUCT V   T
GRATTAN
THE PEOPLE OF BURKE AND OF GRATTAN .   .   .   .   414 TOWER   132
GRATTAN'S
IN GRATTAN'S HOUSE. MY GREAT-GRANDFATHER SHARED . . .   .   .   486 SEVEN SAGES   2
GRAVE
I MUST BE GONE! THERE IS A GRAVE .   .   .   .   67 HAPPY SHEPHERD   45
BEFORE THEY HEAPED HIS GRAVE UNDER THE HILL; .   .   .   .   .   127 DREAM OF FAERY   16
THE MAN HAS FOUND NO COMFORT IN THE GRAVE. . .   .   .   .   .   128 DREAM OF FAERY   48
AND OVER THE GRAVE OF CLOOTH-NA-BARE; .   .   .   .   140 HOSTING SIDHE   2
THEY HAVE HEAPED THE STONES ABOVE HIS GRAVE .   .   .   .   .   193 BAILE AILLINN   115
THIS SWORD IS TO LIE BESIDE HIM IN THE GRAVE. .   .   .   .   .   242 SHADOW WATER B 412
THAT IN THE BLINDING LIGHT BEYOND THE GRAVE .   .   .   .   .   258 KING NO KING   12
HE HAD BETRAYED ME TO HIS GRAVE, ...   275 GREY ROCK   96
IT'S WITH O'LEARY IN THE GRAVE. .   .   .   .   289 SEPTEMBER 1913   8
IT'S WITH O'LEARY IN THE GRAVE. .   .   .   .   289 SEPTEMBER 1913   16
IT'S WITH O'LEARY IN THE GRAVE. .   .   .   .   290 SEPTEMBER 1913   24
THEY'RE WITH O'LEARY IN THE GRAVE. .   .   .   .   290 SEPTEMBER 1913   32
SICK OF HIS GRAVE HAS WAKENED ME? .   .   .   .   303 HOUR DAWN   37
BUT LET HIM KEEP HIS GRAVE FOR ONCE .   .   .   .   303 HOUR DAWN   38
BUT LITTLE NEED THE GRAVE DISTRESS. . .   .   .   338 TOM OROUGHLEY   10
I'D DANCE A MEASURE ON HIS GRAVE." .   .   .   .   338 TOM OROUGHLEY   16
AND LITTLE NEED THE GRAVE DISTRESS. . .   .   .   338 TOM OROUGHLEY V 10
BUT IN THE GRAVE ALL, ALL, SHALL BE RENEWED. . .   .   .   .   356 BROKEN DREAMS   21
FOR CERTAINLY HE SANK INTO HIS GRAVE .   .   .   .   370 EGO DOMINUS   57
ALL THAT YOU HAVE DISCOVERED IN THE GRAVE, ...   413 TOWER   107
FROM CRADLE RUN TO GRAVE .   .   .   .   449 HERO GIRL FOOL   19
FROM GRAVE TO CRADLE RUN INSTEAD; .   .   .   .   449 HERO GIRL FOOL   20
AND I CALL UP MACGREGOR FROM THE GRAVE, ...   473 ALL SOUL NIGHT   61
I CALL MACGREGOR MATHERS FROM HIS GRAVE, ...   473 ALL SOUL NIGHT V 61
GRAVE IS HEAPED ON GRAVE .   .   .   .   496 MOHINI CHATTER   19
GRAVE IS HEAPED ON GRAVE .   .   .   .   496 MOHINI CHATTER   19
NOR GRAVE NOR BED DENIED, ...   513 JANE TALK BISH   10
OUT OF THE GRAVE. SADDLE AND RIDE .   .   .   .   549 SEVERED HEAD   V   4
AND SET A ROSE-TREE ON HER GRAVE, ...   571 THREE BUSHES   73
A DEAD MAN IN HIS GRAVE. .   .   .   .   592 DRUNK SOBRIETY   12
"FORGETTING HUMAN WORDS," A GRAVE DEEP FACE. . .   .   .   .   603 GALLERY REVIS   49
DIGGERS AND CARPENTERS MAKE GRAVE AND COFFIN; .   .   .   .   609 IN TARAS HALLS   17
SAW THAT THE GRAVE WAS DEEP, THE COFFIN SOUND, ...   609 IN TARAS HALLS   18
GRAVE-DIGGERS
THAT THE GRAVE-DIGGERS IN A DREAMY FRENZY .   .   .   .   .   243 SHADOW WATER B 430

```
                                                          PAGE     TITLE       LINE
GRAVE-DIGGERS'
    THOUGH GRAVE-DIGGERS' TOIL IS LONG,  . . . . . . . .   637 BEN BULBEN          21
GRAVE-EYED
    WITH PURPLE SANDALS SWEEP THE GRAVE-EYED HOURS-- . . . .  705 REMEMBRANCE        5
GRAVEL
    OUR SHADOWS ROVE THE GARDEN GRAVEL STILL, . . . . . .   435 NEW FACES           7
GRAVELLED
    O WHAT IF LEVELLED LAWNS AND GRAVELLED WAYS  . . . . .  418 ANCEST HOUSES      29
GRAVES
    BUT NEVER, NEVER ON OUR GRAVES,  . . . . . . . . . .     21 OISIN 1            313
    NEVER, NEVER ON OUR GRAVES, . . . . . . . . . . . .      21 OISIN 1         V  313
    AND HEAR THE NARROW GRAVES CALLING MY CHILD AND ME. . .  147 UNAPPEAS HOST       6
    THEIR GRAVES INTO HER CHARGE, . . . . . . . . . . .     571 THREE BUSHES       58
    CAST ON THE SOUND, ON, ON. THIS NIGHT OF GRAVES,  . . .  665 ISLE STAT II 2     71
GRAVITY
    WITH AN IMPASSIONED GRAVITY . . . . . . . . . . . .     386 ROBARTES DANCE     21
GRAY
    THE FAERY THING FLEW WITH HER O'ER THE GRAY  . . . . .  663 ISLE STAT II 2     38
    AND ONE IN THE OLD GRAY HOUSE . . . . . . . . . . .     771 SPINNING SONG       4
GRAZE
    OF FLIGHT ARE DONE. MOST FAIR OF ALL WHO GRAZE  . . . .  649 ISLE STAT I 1     118
    NASCHINA, HAIL! MOST FAIR OF ALL WHO GRAZE . . . . . .  649 ISLE STAT I 1     120
GRAZED
    WHOSE HOOVES THE TOPS OF THE SURGES GRAZED,  . . . . .   12 OISIN 1         V 142A
GRAZING
    THAT FOUND WHEN I HAD NEITHER GOAT NOR GRAZING  . . . .  340 SHEP GOATHERD      31
    OR ELSE AT MEADOW OR AT GRAZING OVERLOOKS . . . . . .   340 SHEP GOATHERD      37
GREASE
    THAT IS MADE OUT OF THE GREASE . . . . . . . . . . .    776 AGAINST WITCH      24
GREASY
    BUT FUMBLE IN A GREASY TILL . . . . . . . . . . . .     289 SEPTEMBER 1913      2
GREAT
    "NOT SO, GREAT KING! FOR I HAVE NE'ER  . . . . . . .      6 OISIN 1         V   55
    OF THE GREAT ROUND SUN, FROM HIS CENTRAL FIRES. . . . .   13 OISIN 1         V  168
    AS THEY GAZE AT EACH OTHER, "OH, WHERE IS THAT GREAT ONE?"  28 OISIN 1       V 423H
    BURST FROM A GREAT DOOR MARRED BY MANY A BLOW . . . .    31 OISIN 2            29
    BURIED AND MIGHTY. WHEN THROUGH THE GREAT DOOR  . . . .   39 OISIN 2           151
    OF A GREAT EEL; IT CHANGED, AND I BUT SMOTE . . . . .    40 OISIN 2           176
    FOR GREAT OUR ERROR, GREAT OUR GUILT." . . . . . . .     43 OISIN 2         V 208H
    FOR GREAT OUR ERROR, GREAT OUR GUILT." . . . . . . .     43 OISIN 2         V 208H
    FROM THE GREAT GRASS-BARNACLE CALLING . . . . . . . .    57 OISIN 3           156
    WHO STILL WERE OLD WHEN THE GREAT SEA WAS YOUNG; . . .    74 ANASHU VIJAYA      69
    AND GREAT BOUGHS DROP TRANQUILLITY; . . . . . . . .      77 INDIAN TO LOVE      2
    THE GREAT BOUGHS, AND THE BURNISHED DOVE  . . . . . .    78 INDIAN TO LOVE V   16
    AND GREAT BOUGHS, AND THE BURNISHED DOVE  . . . . . .    78 INDIAN TO LOVE V   16
    AND THEY INHERIT THE GREAT SLEEP. . . . . . . . . .      83 MAD KING GOLL  V   22
    AND ALL THESE THINGS WERE WONDERFUL AND GREAT; . . . .  104 FERGUS DRUID       37
    AH! DRUID, DRUID, HOW GREAT WEBS OF SORROW . . . . . .  104 FERGUS DRUID       39
    HAS SLAIN SO MIGHTY ARMIES, SO GREAT KINGS,  . . . . .  106 CUCHULAIN SEA  V  10A
    "THE RED BRANCH CAMP IN A GREAT COMPANY . . . . . . .   108 CUCHULAIN SEA      33
    "THE RED BRANCH GATHER A GREAT COMPANY . . . . . . .    108 CUCHULAIN SEA  V   33
    WOULD COME AT LAST TO GOD'S GREAT TOWN, . . . . . . .   113 ROSE OF PEACE      11
    SENT ONE OF HIS GREAT ANGELS DOWN . . . . . . . . .     134 FR GILLIGAN        43
    IN THOSE GREAT IGNORANT LEAFY WAYS; . . . . . . . .     135 TWO TREES          16
    THE WRONG OF UNSHAPELY THINGS IS A WRONG TOO GREAT TO BE  143 ROSE IN HEART      5
        TOLD;
    THE WRONG OF THE THINGS MISSHAPEN IS WRONG TOO GREAT TO   143 ROSE IN HEART  V   5
        BE TOLD;
    AND DREAM ABOUT THE GREAT AND THEIR PRIDE; . . . . .    166 EVIL OF BELOV       2
    BUT WEIGH THIS SONG WITH THE GREAT AND THEIR PRIDE; . .  166 EVIL OF BELOV       4
    MEN HAVE NAMED BEAUTY. THY GREAT LEAVES ENFOLD . . . .  169 SECRET ROSE         7
    MEN HAVE NAMED BEAUTY. YOUR GREAT LEAVES ENFOLD. . . .  169 SECRET ROSE    V    7
    THE HOUR OF THY GREAT WIND OF LOVE AND HATE. . . . .    170 SECRET ROSE        28
    SURELY THINE HOUR HAS COME, THY GREAT WIND BLOWS,  . .  170 SECRET ROSE        31
    BEND DOWN AND PRAY FOR THE GREAT SIN I WOVE IN SONG, .  173 SPEAKS HEARERS V    5
    GREAT POWERS OF FALLING WAVE AND WIND AND WINDY FIRE, .  174 ELEMENT POWERS      7
    YOU GREAT ANGELIC POWERS OF WIND, AND WAVE, AND FIRE, .  174 ELEMENT POWERS V    7
    GREAT ELEMENTAL POWERS OF WIND, AND WAVE, AND FIRE, . .  174 ELEMENT POWERS V    7
    GREAT RULERS OF THE STILLNESS, LET HER NO LONGER BE . .  175 ELEMENT POWERS V   13
    GREAT RULERS OF STILLNESS, LET HER NO LONGER BE . . .   175 ELEMENT POWERS V   13
    MAEVE THE GREAT QUEEN WAS PACING TO AND FRO, . . . .    180 QUEEN MAEVE         9
    BUT THAT QUEEN, WHO MORE THAN HALF THE NIGHT . . . .    180 QUEEN MAEVE        16
    HAVE I NOT BID YOU TELL OF THAT GREAT QUEEN . . . . .   181 QUEEN MAEVE        34
    AND YET HAD BEEN GREAT BODIED AND GREAT LIMBED, . . .   181 QUEEN MAEVE        25
    AND YET HAD BEEN GREAT BODIED AND GREAT LIMBED, . . .   181 QUEEN MAEVE    V   25
    IT WAS BEFORE THE TIME OF THE GREAT WAR . . . . . . .   182 QUEEN MAEVE        57
    MAEVE WALKED THROUGH THAT GREAT HALL, AND WITH A SIGH .  182 QUEEN MAEVE        62
    A KING OF THE GREAT PLAIN WOULD SPEAK WITH YOU." . . .  183 QUEEN MAEVE        78
    KINGS OF THE GREAT PLAIN HAVE COME AND GONE . . . . .   183 QUEEN MAEVE    V   81
    AND I WOULD HAVE YOUR HELP IN MY GREAT NEED, . . . .    184 QUEEN MAEVE        98
    AS MIDDLE NIGHT GREAT CATS WITH SILVER CLAWS, . . . .   185 QUEEN MAEVE       115
    OUTRUN THE MEASURE. I'D TELL OF THAT GREAT QUEEN . . .  187 QUEEN MAEVE       141
    WHO WAS IT PUT SO GREAT A SCORN . . . . . . . . . .     190 BAILE AILLINN      41
    WHERE WILD BEES HIVE ON THE GREAT PLAIN. . . . . . .    194 BAILE AILLINN     123
    THOUGH NOTHING TROUBLES THE GREAT STREAMS . . . . . .   196 BAILE AILLINN     172
    AMONG PIGEONS AND BEES, WHILE THAT GREAT ARCHER, . . .  198 SEVEN WOODS        12
    BECAUSE OF THAT GREAT NOBLENESS OF HERS . . . . . . .   200 FOLLY COMFORT       9
    INTO THEIR SHINING LIMBS--I'VE HAD GREAT TEACHERS. . .  231 SHADOW WATER B    195
    OF THE GREAT GOLDEN NET THAT IS ABOUT US. . . . . . .   238 SHADOW WATER B    352
    BUT I HAVE DONE SO GREAT A WRONG AGAINST YOU, . . . .   245 SHADOW WATER B    483
    HOW GREAT A WRONG IT IS TO LET ONE'S THOUGHT . . . .    246 SHADOW WATER B    514
```

339

GREAT   (CONTINUED)

	PAGE	TITLE	LINE
FOR WE HAVE FOUND A TREASURE THAT'S SO GREAT	248	SHADOW WATER B	540
OR HURLED THE LITTLE STREETS UPON THE GREAT,	256	NO SECOND TROY	4
AND THEREFORE, FRIEND, IF YOUR GREAT RACE WERE RUN	265	THESE CLOUDS	7
IN THEIR GREAT HOUSE AT SLIEVENAMON,	271	GREY ROCK	15
OF THE GREAT DOOR; BUT THOUGH THE HANGING LAMPS	279	TWO KINGS	49
AND SAW WHERE IN THE MIDST OF THE GREAT HALL	279	TWO KINGS	60
THE SPEAKING OF IT COULD BE NO GREAT WRONG,	281	TWO KINGS	104
LIKE THE EYES OF SOME GREAT KITE SCOURING THE WOODS,	283	TWO KINGS	150
PRAISED THEIR GREAT VICTORIES AND GAVE THEM JOY	286	TWO KINGS	V 218B
UPON GREAT JUAN RIDING BY!	294	HATED PLAYBOY	4
AT GREAT JUAN RIDING BY!	294	HATED PLAYBOY	V 4
WHILE THAT GREAT JUAN GALLOPED BY!	294	HATED PLAYBOY	V 4
A GREAT LAD WITH A BEERY FACE	303	HOUR DAWN	27
HE GAVE HIM A GREAT PUMMELLING,	307	HOUR DAWN	113
THAT HAS MADE A GREAT PEACOCK	310	PEACOCK	2
SO GREAT A SWEETNESS FLOWS	316	FRIENDS	27
AND SCATTER WHEELING IN GREAT BROKEN RINGS	322	SWANS AT COOLE	11
WE DREAMED THAT A GREAT PAINTER HAD BEEN BORN	326	ROBERT GREGORY	65
ON GREAT GRANDFATHER'S BATTERED TOMB."	332	ROUND TOWER	V 30
AND DIED IN THE GREAT WAR BEYOND THE SEA.	339	SHEP GOATHERD	22
AND GREAT ART BEATEN DOWN.	348	FISHERMAN	24
AND YOU KNOW WELL HOW GREAT THE LONGING HAS BEEN,	352	PEOPLE	7
IN THEIR GREAT WINDOW LOOKING AT THE DAWN!	352	PEOPLE	15
TO GREAT SHAPELY KNEES	355	PROPERTIUS	2
SO GREAT HER PORTION IN THAT PEACE YOU MAKE	356	BROKEN DREAMS	12
MY GREAT WOOD LECTERN AND THE FIRE	358	PRESENCES	10
A NOBODY IN A GREAT THRONG,	361	ALF POLLEXFEN	29
PARDON, GREAT ENEMY,	366	HER CHRIS TREE	1
AND BY THE IMITATION OF GREAT MASTERS.	370	EGO DOMINUS	66
BUT WHAT THE GREAT AND PASSIONATE HAVE USED	371	ON GOING HOUSE	7
A MAN THAT FINDS GREAT BITTERNESS	379	SAINT HUNCH	2
THAT GREAT ROGUE ALCIBIADES.	379	SAINT HUNCH	12
MY GREAT RESPONSIBILITIES?	380	SONGS FOOL 1	18
THIS GREAT PURPLE BUTTERFLY,	381	SONG OF FOOL	1
OF HIS GREAT BIRCH AND HIS GREAT BOOK.	381	SONG OF FOOL	8
OF HIS GREAT BIRCH AND HIS GREAT BOOK.	381	SONG OF FOOL	8
THERE IS GREAT DANGER IN THE BODY.	386	ROBARTES DANCE	38
WITHIN MY ARMS GREAT SOLOMON,	387	SOLOMON WITCH	4
BECAUSE OF THE GREAT GLOOM THAT IS IN MY MIND.	403	FOR DAUGHTER	8
WHILE THAT GREAT QUEEN, THAT ROSE OUT OF THE SPRAY,	404	FOR DAUGHTER	27
SO GREAT A GLORY DID THE SONG CONFER.	410	TOWER	40
AND ONE WAS DROWNED IN THE GREAT BOG OF CLOONE.	411	TOWER	48
WHOSE IMAGES, IN THE GREAT MEMORY STORED,	412	TOWER	85
WHILE THEIR GREAT WOODEN DICE BEAT ON THE BOARD.	412	TOWER	88
FROM A GREAT LABYRINTH OUT OF PRIDE,	413	TOWER	116
FROM SOME GREAT LABYRINTH OUT OF PRIDE,	413	TOWER	V 116
AMID GREAT CHAMBERS AND LONG GALLERIES, LINED	418	ANCEST HOUSES	36
AND A GREAT ARMY BUT A SHOWY THING!	429	NINETEEN 19	18
COME LET US MOCK AT THE GREAT	432	NINETEEN 19	93
TO HELP GOOD, WISE OR GREAT	432	NINETEEN 19	110
THERE LURCHES PAST, HIS GREAT EYES WITHOUT THOUGHT	433	NINETEEN 19	126
A SUDDEN BLOW! THE GREAT WINGS BEATING STILL	441	LEDA AND SWAN	1
O CHESTNUT TREE, GREAT ROOTED BLOSSOMER,	446	SCHOOL CHILDR	V 61
THE GREAT GREY-EYED ATHENE STARES THEREON.	447	COLONUS PRAISE	16
WHERE THE GREAT MOTHER, MOURNING FOR HER DAUGHTER	447	COLONUS PRAISE	19
SHE WHO HAD BROUGHT GREAT HECTOR DOWN	455	HIS MEMORIES	15
AND PETER THAT HAD GREAT AFFAIRS	456	FRIENDS YOUTH	13
FOR THE GREAT CALIF'S TREASURER AND MY FRIEND,	460	HARUN RASHID	V 2
THROUGH THE GREAT GALLERY OF THE TREASURE HOUSE	461	HARUN RASHID	5
AT THE GREAT BOOK OF SAPPHO'S SONG! BUT NO,	461	HARUN RASHID	12
SO GREAT ITS FAME. WHEN FITTING TIME HAS PASSED	461	HARUN RASHID	19
TAKE THIS LIGHT PARCHMENT, PASS THROUGH THE GREAT CHAMBER	461	HARUN RASHID	V 5
WHAT GREAT HARUN AL-RASHID, OCCUPIED	462	HARUN RASHID	24
WITH THE GREAT TOIL AND CEREMONY OF STATE,	462	HARUN RASHID	V 25
THAT YEAR WHEN GREAT HAROUN EL RASHID KILLED	462	HARUN RASHID	V 31
TO SHOW HOW VIOLENT GREAT HEARTS CAN LOSE	463	HARUN RASHID	47
THAT IT WAS MADE IN YOUR GREAT FATHER'S REIGN."	464	HARUN RASHID	72
"GREAT PRINCE, FORGIVE THE FREEDOM OF MY SPEECH!	464	HARUN RASHID	74
OR WAS IT SHE THAT SPOKE OR SOME GREAT DJINN?	467	HARUN RASHID	135
FROM THE GREAT TREATISE OF PARMENIDES!	469	HARUN RASHID	183
MIDNIGHT HAS COME, AND THE GREAT CHRIST CHURCH BELL	470	ALL SOUL NIGHT	1
IT IS ALL SOULS' NIGHT AND THE GREAT CHRIST CHURCH BELL	470	ALL SOUL NIGHT	V 1
GREAT WINDOWS OPEN TO THE SOUTH,	475	EVA GORE-BOOTH	2
WE THE GREAT GAZEBO BUILT,	476	EVA GORE-BOOTH	30
A GREAT MAN IN HIS PRIDE	476	DEATH	7
SO GREAT A SWEETNESS FLOWS INTO THE BREAST	479	SELF AND SOUL	69
THOUGH THE GREAT SONG RETURN NO MORE	485	NINETEENTH CEN	1
FROM FOUR GREAT MINDS THAT HATED WHIGGERY.	486	SEVEN SAGES	7
HARRIED, AND BURKE'S GREAT MELODY AGAINST IT.	487	SEVEN SAGES	16
GREAT WORKS CONSTRUCTED THERE IN NATURE'S SPITE	488	COOLE PARK 29	5
GREAT ROOMS WHERE TRAVELLED MEN AND CHILDREN FOUND	491	COOLE BALLYLEE	29
WE SHIFT ABOUT—ALL THAT GREAT GLORY SPENT—	491	COOLE BALLYLEE	39
MAN SHIFTS ABOUT—ALL THAT GREAT GLORY SPENT—	491	COOLE BALLYLEE	V 39
BY THOSE GREAT HONEY-COLOURED	492	ANNE GREGORY	3
MUCH ON THE GREAT QUESTIONER!	494	AT ALGECIRAS	16
OR, AS GREAT SAGES SAY,	496	MOHINI CHATTER	27
AFTER GREAT CATHEDRAL GONG!	497	BYZANTIUM	4
IT SEEMED, SO GREAT MY HAPPINESS,	501	VACILLATION	43
IN HIS NOSTRILS, THE GREAT LORD OF CHOU	502	VACILLATION	59
GREAT HATRED, LITTLE ROOM,	506	REMORSE SPEECH	12

340

		PAGE	TITLE	LINE
GREAT (CONTINUED)				
GREAT EUROPA PLAYED THE FOOL		509	JANE REPROVED	5.
WHERE THE GREAT BATTLE WAS		512	JANE ON GOD	10
OLD FATHERS, GREAT GRANDFATHERS,		518	LOVES LONENESS V	1
IN A GREAT TUMULT OF THE AIR,		519	HER DREAM	6
BEHOLD THAT GREAT PLOTINUS SWIM,		530	DELPHIC ORACLE	1
BUT HAD GREAT PLEASURE WITH A LAD		538	LAST CONFESS	5
BY THAT GREAT GLORY DRIVEN WILD.		540	FROM ANTIGONE	13
UNDER THE GREAT COMEDIAN'S TOMB THE CROWD,		541	PARN FUNERAL 1	1
THAT WOMAN, THE GREAT MOTHER IMAGING,		541	PARN FUNERAL 1	13
GRANDFATHER SAID IN THE GREAT REBELLION:		544	TO SAME TUNE 1 V	1
ALL THAT GREAT PAST TO A TROUBLE OF FOOLS:		546	TO SAME TUNE 2	22
GREAT NATIONS BLOSSOM ABOVE:		547	TO SAME TUNE 3	5
. . . "THE KING OF THE GREAT CLOCK TOWER"		549	SEVERED HEAD	T
WHAT SAYS THE CLOCK IN THE GREAT CLOCK TOWER?		549	SEVERED HEAD	3
WHAT SAYS THE CLOCK IN THE GREAT CLOCK TOWER?		550	SEVERED HEAD	10
WHAT SAYS THE CLOCK IN THE GREAT CLOCK TOWER?		550	SEVERED HEAD	17
FOR THINGS BELOW ARE COPIES, THE GREAT SMARAGDINE TABLET SAID.		556	RIBH PATRICK	6
I STUDY HATRED WITH GREAT DILIGENCE,		558	RIBH CHRISTIAN	3
THE GREAT STAGE CURTAIN ABOUT TO DROP,		565	LAPIS LAZULI	13
AUGUSTA GREGORY SEATED AT HER GREAT ORMOLU TABLE,		577	LOFTY THINGS	7
BUT A GREAT DANE THAT CANNOT BAY THE MOON		579	DOR WELLESLEY	10
NOR SATISFIED CONSCIENCE, BUT THAT GREAT FAMILY		579	DOR WELLESLEY	14
I CAME ON A GREAT HOUSE IN THE MIDDLE OF THE NIGHT,		581	CURSE CROMWELL	25
HE'D GONE TO GREAT EXPENSE		585	ORAHILLY	13
THE GREAT DAY		590	GREAT DAY	T
FRAGMENTS THE GREAT DAY		590	GREAT DAY V	T
A GREAT BLACK RAGGED BIRD APPEARED WHEN I WAS IN THE BOAT:		593	PILGRIM	16
WITH FLOPPING AND WITH FLAPPING IT MADE A GREAT DISPLAY,		593	PILGRIM	18
A GREAT BLACK BIRD APPEARED WHEN I WAS IN THE BOAT,		593	PILGRIM V	16
WITH THEIR FLOPPING AND THEIR FLAPPING IT MADE A GREAT DISPLAY		593	PILGRIM V	18
PROCLAIMED BOTH GOOD AND GREAT:		597	MODEL LAUREATE	4
A GREAT EBULLIENT GREAT PORTRAIT CERTAINLY:		602	GALLERY REVIS	27
AN EBULLIENT GREAT PORTRAIT CERTAINLY:		602	GALLERY REVIS V	27
AND THE GREAT WATER SIGHED FOR LOVE,		611	NEWS ORACLE	3
ALL THAT GREAT PAST TO A TROUBLE OF FOOLS:		614	MARCH SONGS 1	22
GREAT NATIONS BLOSSOM ABOVE:		614	MARCH SONGS 2	5
ITS GREAT BATTLE LOST,		617	LONG-LEG FLY	2
WHAT GREAT TOMB-HAUNTER SWEEPS THE DISTANT SKY		618	BRONZE HEAD	4
ON GANGLING STOCKS GROWN GREAT, GREAT STOCKS RUN DRY,		619	BRONZE HEAD	25
ON GANGLING STOCKS GROWN GREAT, GREAT STOCKS RUN DRY,		619	BRONZE HEAD	25
THOSE GREAT SEA-HORSES BARE THEIR TEETH AND LAUGH AT THE DAWN.		623	HIGH TALK	14
I LIVED AMONG GREAT HOUSES,		626	STATES HOLIDAY	1
AM I A GREAT LORD CHANCELLOR		627	STATES HOLIDAY	14
WITH A GREAT COCK'S FEATHER,		627	STATES HOLIDAY	37
GREAT BLADDERED EMER SAT,		628	JANE MOUNTAIN V	15
DID WORDS OF MINE PUT TOO GREAT STRAIN		632	MAN AND ECHO	13
THE SPIRITUAL INTELLECT'S GREAT WORK,		632	MAN AND ECHO	20
NOR CAN THERE BE WORK SO GREAT		632	MAN AND ECHO	23
NOR CAN THERE BE A WORK SO GREAT		632	MAN AND ECHO V	23
SHALL WE IN THAT GREAT NIGHT REJOICE?		633	MAN AND ECHO	38
SWEARS THAT HE HEARS THE KING'S GREAT HORN.		636	BLACK TOWER	24
WHAT HIS GREAT FOREFATHERS DID,		638	BEN BULBEN	39
AND THE GREAT GREY LYNX'S SKIN: IN SOOTH, METHINKS		650	ISLE STAT I 1	151
THAT I MYSELF COULD SHOOT A GREAT GREY LYNX,		650	ISLE STAT I 1	152
FOR THERE THE GREAT ENCHANTRESS LIVES. AND THERE		653	ISLE STAT I 2	38
WILL HE HAVE HAPPINESS? GREAT SOBS HER BEING SHAKE.		676	ISLE STAT II 3	247
THE LION, THE WORLD'S GREAT SOLITARY, BENDS		689	NETTLESHIP	5
WHY THESE NEW FEARS? THE GREAT MONK EBREMAR,		692	MOSADA 1	46
SHE WAS A GREAT ENCHANTRESS ONCE OF YORE,		693	MOSADA 1	78
NO MORE: TAKE ME INSTEAD OF HER, GREAT SIRS.		695	MOSADA 1	114
FROM THE GREAT PAINTED WINDOW WRAPS HIS BROW,		697	MOSADA 2	37
OF THE GREAT WARRIORS WHOSE NAMES HAVE SUNG		698	MOSADA 2	60
SOME GREAT ONE. NO: I HEAR THE WAVERING STEPS		720	WITCH VIVIEN	12
I DREAMT SOME GREAT ONE. AH, MY BEAUTIFUL,		720	WITCH VIVIEN	14
AND THEN THE GREAT ONES COME, AND LAST THE KING.		722	WITCH VIVIEN	54
NOW THY GREAT WHITE DOLL TO HOLD--		726	LOVERS QUARREL	15
"OF OUR GREAT QUEEN IS EVER HEARD		729	PRIEST FAIRY	41
"SHIELD BREAKER, GREAT SHIELD BREAKER,"		740	EARL PAUL	25
FOR HIS GREAT HARDIHOOD.		741	EARL PAUL	56
SHE OFFERS GREAT REWARDS IF WE TURN EAST		755	SHADOW WATER A	169
WE BRING YOU THIS GREAT QUEEN.		755	SHADOW WATER A	166
AMONG GREAT TREES, AND IN THE WINGS OF OWLS,		762	SHADOW WATER A	285
RUIN ON A GREAT KING'S HOUSE		775	AGAINST WITCH	3
OR BURNED GREAT CITIES DOWN,		789	SINGING HEAD	16
GREAT-AUNTS				
ON UNCLES, AUNTS, GREAT-UNCLES OR GREAT-AUNTS,		604	YOU CONTENT	3
GREAT-BLADDERED				
GREAT-BLADDERED EMER SAT,		628	JANE MOUNTAIN	15
GREAT-BODIED				
AND YET HAD BEEN GREAT-BODIED AND GREAT-LIMBED,		181	QUEEN MAEVE	25
GREATER				
AND HAD THE GREATER JOY IN PRAISING HER,		410	TOWER	37
GREATER GLORY IN THE SUN,		494	AT ALGECIRAS	13
A GREATER WITH A LESSER PANG ASSUAGE		537	HER VISION	5
THE GREATER GROWS MY LIGHT		559	HE AND SHE	9
A GREATER, A MORE GRACIOUS TIME HAS GONE:		564	GYRES	12
THAT IRELAND'S MIND BE GREATER,		608	SONGS BURDEN 3	21

341

<pre>
                                                              PAGE   TITLE   LINE

GREATER   (CONTINUED)
      NO! GREATER THAN PYTHAGORAS, FOR THE MEN   . . . . . .   610 STATUES   9
      WHEN THAT GREATER DREAM HAD GONE   . . . .   639 BEN BULBEN   63
      BENEATH THE WEIGHT OF GREATER GRIEF THAN I! . . . . .   661 ISLE STAT II 1   63
GREATEST
      WHAT IF THOSE THINGS THE GREATEST OF MANKIND   . . . . . 418 ANCEST HOUSES   38
      WHEN THE FULL MOON SWAM TO ITS GREATEST HEIGHT   . . . . 468 HARUN RASHID   151
      "GREATEST SINCE REMBRANDT," ACCORDING TO JOHN SYNGE! . . 602 GALLERY REVIS   26
GREAT-GRANDCHILDREN
      AMONG HIS CHILDREN, GRANDCHILDREN AND GREAT-GRANDCHILDREN! 790 DEDICATION   6
GREAT-GRANDDAD
      WHAT IF MY GREAT-GRANDDAD HAD A PAIR THAT WERE TWENTY FOOT 622 HIGH TALK   2
        HIGH,
GREAT-GRANDFATHER
      MY GREAT-GRANDFATHER SPOKE TO EDMUND BURKE . . . . . .   486 SEVEN SAGES   1
      IN GRATTAN'S HOUSE. MY GREAT-GRANDFATHER SHARED . . . . 486 SEVEN SAGES   2
GREAT-GRANDFATHER'S
      ON GREAT-GRANDFATHER'S BATTERED TOMB." . . . .   331 ROUND TOWER   6
      ON GREAT-GRANDFATHER'S BATTERED TOMB." . . . .   332 ROUND TOWER   30
      MY GREAT-GRANDFATHER'S FATHER TALKED OF MUSIC, ...   486 SEVEN SAGES   4
      MY GREAT-GRANDFATHER'S FATHER TALKED OF MUSIC AND PAINTING, 486 SEVEN SAGES   V   4
GREAT-GRANDFATHERS
      OLD FATHERS, GREAT-GRANDFATHERS, ...   518 LOVES LONENESS   1
GREAT-GRANDSON
      AND MAYBE THE GREAT-GRANDSON OF THAT HOUSE, ...   418 ANCEST HOUSES   23
      GRANDSON, OR GREAT-GRANDSON, ...   604 YOU CONTENT   2
GREAT-LIMBED
      AND YET HAD BEEN GREAT-BODIED AND GREAT-LIMBED, ... 181 QUEEN MAEVE   25
GREATNESS
      AND SEEMED THE GREATNESS OF THE WORLD IN TEARS, ... 120 SORROW OF LOVE   6
      HE THINKS OF HIS PAST GREATNESS . . . .   177 PAST GREATNESS   T
      MONGAN THINKS OF HIS PAST GREATNESS . . . .   177 PAST GREATNESS V   T
      HAVE ALL THAT GREATNESS, AND NOT HERS ALONE, ...   186 QUEEN MAEVE   133
      HAVE YOU MADE GREATNESS YOUR COMPANION, ...   265 THESE CLOUDS   9
      BUT TAKE OUR GREATNESS WITH OUR VIOLENCE? . . . . . .   418 ANCEST HOUSES   32
      BUT TAKE OUR GREATNESS WITH OUR BITTERNESS? . . . . .   418 ANCEST HOUSES   40
      THE GREATNESS OF MY LOVE. DID I NOT RULE . . . . . .   748 SHADOW WATER A V   32
GREAT-ROOTED
      O CHESTNUT-TREE, GREAT-ROOTED BLOSSOMER, ...   446 SCHOOL CHILDR   61
GREAT-UNCLES
      ON UNCLES, AUNTS, GREAT-UNCLES OR GREAT-AUNTS, ...   604 YOU CONTENT   3
GRECIAN
      BUT SUCH A FORM AS GRECIAN GOLDSMITHS MAKE . . . . .   408 SAIL BYZANTIUM   27
      WITH PERSIAN EMBASSY OR GRECIAN WAR, ...   462 HARUN RASHID   25
GREECE
      BY SUCKING AT THE DUGS OF GREECE. . . . .   288 TO WEALTHY MAN   28
      AMONG THE KINGS OF GREECE AND FRANCE." . . . . . .   296 THREE BEGGARS V   32A
      AND THE PROUD STONES OF GREECE, ...   415 TOWER   159
      EGYPT AND GREECE, GOOD-BYE, AND GOOD-BYE, ROME! . . .   563 MERU   8
      OR THE KING OF GREECE. . . . .   627 STATES HOLIDAY   19
GREEDY
      SAVE, WITH THE LITTLE GOLDEN GREEDY CARP, ...   720 WITCH VIVIEN   2
GREEK
      TILL ALL HIS GREEK AND LATIN LEARNING SEEMED . . . . .   324 ROBERT GREGORY   21
      GREEK ALEXANDER FROM MY FLESH, ...   379 SAINT HUNCH   10
      WITH PERSIAN WARS OR GREEK AMBASSADORS . . . . . .   462 HARUN RASHID   V   25
      AN ABSTRACT GREEK ABSURDITY HAS CRAZED THE MAN-- . . .   556 RIBH PATRICK   1
      ABSTRACTIONS OF THE GREEK PHILOSOPHY HAVE CRAZED THE MAN, 556 RIBH PATRICK   V   1
GREEKS
      GREEKS WERE BUT LOVERS! ALL THAT COUNTRY ROUND . . .   430 NINETEEN 19   V   43
GREEN   SEE SEA-GREEN BLUE-GREEN GRASS-GREEN GREY-GREEN
      FOR OUR BEST WERE DEAD ON GAVRA'S GREEN. . . . . . .   2 OISIN 1   V   71
      THAT SLOPING GREEN DE DANAAN SOD . . . .   20 OISIN 1   299
      THE SEAWEED-COVERED PILLARS! AND THE GREEN . . . . .   31 OISIN 2   32
      TWO WALLS, A ROOF, A FLOOD! THERE TREMBLING GREEN . . .   31 OISIN 2   V   32
      THAT WAS MOST DISTANT FROM THE DOOR! GREEN SLIME . . . . 37 OISIN 2   113
      WHILE HIGH FRAIL CLOUDLETS, FED WITH A GREEN LIGHT, . . . 40 OISIN 2   165
      DAWN PASSIONED! FED WITH A FAINT GREEN LIGHT, ...   40 OISIN 2   V   165
      GREY SAND ON THE GREEN OF THE GRASSES AND OVER THE DRIPPING 48 OISIN 3   14
        TREES,
      GREY SANDS ON THE GREEN OF THE GRASSES AND OVER THE   48 OISIN 3   V   14
        DRIPPING TREES,
      WHEN A GLOW-WORM WAS GREEN ON A GRASS-LEAF, ...   53 OISIN 3   99
      WHEN A GLOW-WORM WAS GREEN ON A GRASS LEAF, ...   53 OISIN 3   V   99
      GREY SAND ON THE GREEN OF THE GRASSES AND OVER THE DRIPPING 57 OISIN 3   142
        TREES,
      GREY SANDS ON THE GREEN OF THE GRASSES AND OVER THE   57 OISIN 3   V   142
        DRIPPING TREES,
      ONE STAR SHONE FAINT AND GREEN, ...   95 MOLL MAGEE   30
      A GREEN DROP IN THE SURGE, A GLEAM OF LIGHT . . . . .   104 FERGUS DRUID   33
      GO THERE AND DWELL ON THE GREEN FOREST RIM, ...   108 CUCHULAIN SEA V   35
      UPON A DIM, GREEN, WELL-BELOVED ISLE, ...   126 DREAM OF FAERY V   8
      THERE WAS A GREEN BRANCH HUNG WITH MANY A BELL . . . .   129 BOOK STORIES   1
      I TORE IT FROM GREEN BOUGHS WINDS TORE AND TOSSED . . . 130 BOOK STORIES   13
      I TORE IT FROM GREEN BOUGHS WINDS TOSSED AND HURLED, . . 130 BOOK STORIES   V   13
      GREEN BOUGHS OF TOSSING ALWAYS, WEARY, WEARY, ...   130 BOOK STORIES   V   14
      I TORE IT FROM THE GREEN BOUGHS OF OLD ERI, ...   130 BOOK STORIES   V   15
      GREEN OAK AND POPLAR TREE! . . . .   132 OLD PENSIONER V   16
      OR UNDER GREEN SODS LAY. . . . .   132 FR GILLIGAN   4
      I HUNGER TO BUILD THEM ANEW AND SIT ON A GREEN KNOLL APART, 143 ROSE IN HEART   6
      AND HE, BEING LAID UPON GREEN BOUGHS, ...   192 BAILE AILLINN   71
</pre>

```
                                                            PAGE    TITLE          LINE
GREEN  (CONTINUED)
    O TUFTED REEDS, BEND LOW AND LOW IN POOLS ON THE GREEN   206 HANRAHANS SONG V    1
         LAND,
    OR AVALLON THE GRASS GREEN HOLLOW, OR JOYOUS ISLE   . . . 209 UNDER THE MOON V   2
    AS THOUGH THEY HAD BEEN HIDDEN BY GREEN BOUGHS  . . . . . 217 WOODS OF COOLE     6
    THEIR SUDDEN FRAGRANCES ON THE GREEN AIR; . . . . . . . . 217 WOODS OF COOLE    10
    AND THE GREEN QUIET, HAVE UPLIFTED THE HEART? . . . . . . 219 WOODS OF COOLE    40
    AND WHERE BEECH-TREES HAD MIXED A PALE GREEN LIGHT  . . . 277 TWO KINGS          5
    BETWEEN THE PALE GREEN LIGHT OF THE BEECH LEAVES . . . . 277 TWO KINGS       V  5
    WHERE CERTAIN BEECHES MIXED A PALE GREEN LIGHT . . . . . 277 TWO KINGS       V  5
    AND WHERE BEECH TREES HAD MIXED A PALE GREEN LIGHT . . . 277 TWO KINGS       V  5
    WANDERED BETWEEN THE BLUE AND THE GREEN LEAF . . . . . . 278 TWO KINGS         41
    THE ROUND GREEN EYES AND THE LONG WAVERING BODIES  . . . 343 DEJECTION          2
    IN THE GREEN SHADOW OF FERRARA WALL; . . . . . . . . . . 352 PEOPLE             9
    IN THE GREEN SHADOW ON FERRARA WALL; . . . . . . . . . . 352 PEOPLE          V  9
    AND THAT HE WILL TURN GREEN WITH RAGE  . . . . . . . . . 385 ROBARTES DANCE    16
    WHEREVER GREEN IS WORN, . . . . . . . . . . . . . . . . 394 EASTER 1916       78
    "TO MAKE THE GREEN COME OUT AGAIN . . . . . . . . . . . 396 ROSE TREE          9
    O MAY SHE LIVE LIKE SOME GREEN LAUREL . . . . . . . . . 405 FOR DAUGHTER      47
    EVEN WHERE HORRIBLE GREEN PARROTS CALL AND SWING. . . . 442 BLACK CENTAUR      2
    BECAUSE OF SOME GREEN WING, GATHERED OLD MUMMY WHEAT . . 442 BLACK CENTAUR      7
    UNWEARIED EYES UPON THOSE HORRIBLE GREEN BIRDS. . . . . 442 BLACK CENTAUR     16
    EVEN WHERE THE HORRIBLE GREEN PARROTS CALL AND SWING. . 442 BLACK CENTAUR   V  2
    IS HALF ALL GLITTERING FLAME AND HALF ALL GREEN . . . . 500 VACILLATION       12
    IS HALF ALL GLITTERING FLAME AND HALF A GREEN . . . . . 500 VACILLATION     V 12
    AN ACRE OF GREEN GRASS . . . . . . . . . . . . . . . . 575 ACRE OF GRASS      2
    ON A STORM-BITTEN GREEN. . . . . . . . . . . . . . . . 606 SONGS BURDEN 2     4
    ON THE GREEN LANDS I WALK . . . . . . . . . . . . . . 607 SONGS BURDEN 2    20
    TALL DAMES GO WALKING IN GRASS GREEN AVALON. . . . . . 627 STATES HOLIDAY V REF
    UPON HIS WINGS. THRO' YONDER GREEN ABYSS . . . . . . . 649 ISLE STAT I 1    114
    OF GREEN ARCADIA DO NOT HIDE, I TROW, . . . . . . . . 651 ISLE STAT I 1    166
    OF YONDER LAKE, FROM WHOSE GREEN BANKS ALWAY . . . . . 653 ISLE STAT I 2     33
    AND NOD TO ONE ANOTHER, LIES A GREEN. . . . . . . . . 653 ISLE STAT I 2     35
    O'ER THE GREEN EDEN-SOD; . . . . . . . . . . . . . . 654 ISLE STAT I 2     65
    AWAY IN THE GREEN PARADISE, . . . . . . . . . . . . . 654 ISLE STAT I 2     70
    O'ER THE GREEN EDEN-SOD, . . . . . . . . . . . . . . 654 ISLE STAT I 2     75
    FROM THE GREEN SHADED HOLLOW . . . . . . . . . . . . 655 ISLE STAT I 2     82
    ACORNS GREEN, WITH EYES AWAKE. . . . . . . . . . . . 655 ISLE STAT I 3      5
    I FOLLOWED HIM FROM MY GREEN LAIR, . . . . . . . . . 655 ISLE STAT I 3      6
    THE EVENING GLEAMS ARE GREEN AND GOLD AND RED . . . . 656 ISLE STAT I 3     22
    THE MOBS OF STARS IN GOLD AND GREEN AND BLUE, . . . . 663 ISLE STAT II 2    43
    FROM WHOSE GREEN BANKS NO LIVING THING MAY ROVE, . . . 664 ISLE STAT II 2    57
    O, LADY, THOU WHOSE VESTITURE OF GREEN . . . . . . . 667 ISLE STAT II 3    34
    I PLUCKED HER BACKWARDS BY HER DRESS OF GREEN. . . . 676 ISLE STAT II 3   264
    SAVING A GREEN FROG DEAD UPON THE GRASS. . . . . . . 676 ISLE STAT II 3   269
    AND THROB WITHIN THE CIRCLES OF GREEN DAWN. . . . . . 701 MOSADA 3          54
    AYE AND SHAKES IN SEA GREEN WAVERINGS, ALONG THE FISHERS' 718 PHANTOM SHIP  V  2
         STREET.
    IN THE GREEN HILL'S INMOST PART. . . . . . . . . . . 726 LOVERS QUARREL    12
    WAKE THE LARKS UPON THE GREEN. . . . . . . . . . . . 727 LOVERS QUARREL    46
    BENEATH A POINTED CAP OF GREEN; . . . . . . . . . . 728 PRIEST FAIRY      22
    TO THE GREEN ISLE OF WIGHT . . . . . . . . . . . . . 740 EARL PAUL         10
GREENISH
    GREENISH AND SLIPPERY. TIME AFTER TIME . . . . . . .  37 OISIN 2        V 114
GREENNESS
    AND FROM ITS MURMURING GREENNESS, CALM OF FAERY, . . . 129 BOOK STORIES      3
    AND THERE'S BUT COMMON GREENNESS AFTER THAT. . . . . 422 MY DESCENDANS      8
    VAST GREENNESS, WHERE ETERNAL RUMOUR DWELLS, . . . . 657 ISLE STAT I 3     45
GREEN-PATED
    PORTLY GREEN-PATED BIRD . . . . . . . . . . . . . . 400 DEMON BEAST       28
GREET
    GREET HIM COURTEOUS, GREET HIM KIND, . . . . . . . . 717 FAIRY DOCTOR   V 21
    GREET HIM COURTEOUS, GREET HIM KIND, . . . . . . . . 717 FAIRY DOCTOR   V 21
    FIRST I GREET MACCARTAN, REVOLUTIONARY LEADER. . . . 790 DEDICATION        1
GREGORY
    IN MEMORY OF MAJOR ROBERT GREGORY . . . . . . . . . 323 ROBERT GREGORY    T
    IN MEMORY OF ROBERT GREGORY . . . . . . . . . . . . 323 ROBERT GREGORY V  T
    FOR ANNE GREGORY . . . . . . . . . . . . . . . . . 492 ANNE GREGORY      T
    ANNE GREGORY . . . . . . . . . . . . . . . . . . . 492 ANNE GREGORY   V  T
    AUGUSTA GREGORY SEATED AT HER GREAT ORMOLU TABLE, . . 577 LOFTY THINGS      7
    MANCINI'S PORTRAIT OF AUGUSTA GREGORY, . . . . . . . 602 GALLERY REVIS    25
    JOHN SYNGE, I AND AUGUSTA GREGORY, THOUGHT . . . . . 603 GALLERY REVIS    41
GREGORY'S
    BUT GREGORY'S WOOD AND ONE BARE HILL . . . . . . . . 403 FOR DAUGHTER      4
    BUT GREGORY'S WOODS AND ONE BARE HILL . . . . . . . 403 FOR DAUGHTER   V  4
    AUGUSTA GREGORY'S SON; HER SISTER'S SON, . . . . . . 602 GALLERY REVIS    21
GREW
    THAT I WOULD GO WITH HER, THEY GREW . . . . . . . .  10 OISIN 1        V 111A
    AND EVER NEARER, NEARER GREW; . . . . . . . . . . .  15 OISIN 1          200
    UNTIL THE TOSSING ARMS GREW STILL . . . . . . . . .  21 OISIN 1          322
    THE FLOWERS STILL GREW THERE; FAR ON THE SEA'S WASTE  39 OISIN 2          163
    TILL THE FAR DOORWAY GREW A BURNING BLOT . . . . . .  39 OISIN 2        V 152
    THE FLOWERS STILL GREW THERE. MOVED BEYOND HIM THE SEA'S 39 OISIN 2      V 163
         WASTE;
    KINGFISHER COLOUR GREW WITH RAGE. HE ROSE . . . . .  40 OISIN 2        V 169
    THE DRUID SWORD OF MANANAN, HE GREW . . . . . . . .  40 OISIN 2        V 174
    THE DEAD GOD'S SWORD, TO MANY FORMS HE GREW, . . . .  40 OISIN 2        V 175
    HORROR FROM HORROR GREW; BUT WHEN THE WEST . . . . .  41 OISIN 2          180
    A BEECH-BOUGH TO ME, AND MY HEART GREW SORE, . . . .  44 OISIN 2          226
    A BEECH BOUGH TO ME, AND MY HEART GREW SORE, . . . .  44 OISIN 2        V 226
    BUT THE TREES GREW TALLER AND CLOSER, . . . . . . .  48 OISIN 3           17

                                   343
```

```
                                            PAGE    TITLE         LINE
GREW   (CONTINUED)
   BUT TALLER THE TREES GREW AND CLOSER, . . .   . . . . .   . .   48 OISIN 3      V   17
   THE WAILING GREW DISTANT: I RODE BY THE WOODS OF          56 OISIN 3        137
      THE WRINKLING BARK,
   THE FIELDS GREW FATTER DAY BY DAY, . . . . . . . . .      82 MAD KING GOLL      7
   IN MY MOST SECRET SPIRIT GREW . . . . . . . . . .         83 MAD KING GOLL     27
   WHEN THE MORN GREW FROSTY AND CLEAR. . . . . . . .        95 MOLL MAGEE        20
   MY MAN GREW RED AND PALE, . . . . . . . . . . .           95 MOLL MAGEE        22
   AND ALL GREW FRIENDLY FOR A LITTLE WHILE. . . . . .      129 BOOK STORIES       8
   AND ALL WHO HEARD GREW FRIENDLY FOR A WHILE. . . . .     129 BOOK STORIES    V  8
   THEY SLOWLY INTO MILLIONS GREW, . . . . . . . . .        133 FR GILLIGAN       17
   WHILE THE NIGHT GREW, ABOVE THE FADING COALS, . . . .    136 TO SOME I TALK V   3
   AND HE SAW HOW THE REEDS GREW DARK . . . . . . . .       144 HOST OF AIR        5
   AND ONCE, WHEN THE OWLS GREW STILL, . . . . . . . .      159 CAP AND BELLS  V   2
   IT TALKED, ERE THE MORN GREW WHITE. . . . . . . . .      159 CAP AND BELLS  V   6
   TILL STARS GREW OUT OF THE AIR. . . . . . . . . .        160 CAP AND BELLS     28
   THE STARS GREW OUT OF THE AIR. . . . . . . . . .         160 CAP AND BELLS  V  28
   WHILE BIRDS GREW SILENT ONE BY ONE. . . . . . . . .      176 BELOVED DEAD   V  13
   AND WHEN I'VE HEARD HOW THEY GREW OLD AND DIED, . .      186 QUEEN MAEVE      136
   OF THIS OR THAT THING, NOR GREW COLD . . . . . . .       189 BAILE AILLINN      9
   OF THIS OR THAT THING, OR GREW COLD . . . . . . .        189 BAILE AILLINN  V   9
   AND WHEN NO FACE GREW PITEOUS . . . . . . . . . .        191 BAILE AILLINN     62
   THAT OLD MAN CLIMBED: THE DAY GREW DIM; . . . . . .      194 BAILE AILLINN    134
   AND GREW TO BE OUT OF FASHION . . . . . . . . .          211 O DO NOT LOVE      3
   AND I GREW WEARY OF THE SUN . . . . . . . . . .          256 WORDS              5
   THOUGH ALWAYS AT MY WORDS HIS TROUBLE GREW; . . . .      281 TWO KINGS         91
   ALL SHOUTED TILL THEIR ANGER GREW . . . . . . . .        297 THREE BEGGARS     46
   AND THEREUPON THEIR ANGER GREW . . . . . . . . .         297 THREE BEGGARS  V  46
   AND EVEN OLD MEN'S EYES GREW DIM, THIS HAND ALONE, . .   314 FALLEN MAJESTY     2
   THAT SOLOMON GREW WISE . . . . . . . . . . .             345 ON WOMAN          11
   UNTIL HER VOICE GREW SHRILL. . . . . . . . . .           392 EASTER 1916       20
   COLD STONE AND WATER. I GREW WILD, . . . . . . . .       399 BREAK OF DAY      14
   FOR ALL MEN'S THOUGHTS GREW CLEAR . . . . . . . .        400 DEMON BEAST       19
   FOR ALL MEN'S THOUGHT GREW CLEAR . . . . . . . .         400 DEMON BEAST    V  19
   MUST DRIVE THE ARABIAN HOST. THE VOICE GREW STILL, . .   467 HARUN RASHID     145
   MADE DRIVE THE ARABIAN HOST. THE VOICE GREW STILL, . .   467 HARUN RASHID   V 145
   GROUNDS WHERE PLUM AND CABBAGE GREW. . . . . . . .       577 WHAT THEN         13
   CONTACT EVERYTHING ANTAEUS-LIKE GREW STRONG. . . . .     603 GALLERY REVIS     44
   CONTACT ALL THINGS ANTAEUS-LIKE GREW STRONG; . . . .     603 GALLERY REVIS  V  44
   UNDER THE TROPIC SHADE, GREW ROUND AND SLOW, . . .       610 STATUES           18
   GREW IN PURE MIND, BUT OUT OF WHAT BEGAN? . . . . .      630 CIRCUS ANIMALS    34
   ALONG THE SEA: AND MANY A MAN GREW HUSHED . . . . .      693 MOSADA 1          86
   SO LITTLE. AS THE MONTHS PASSED BY WE GREW . . . .       713 FERENCZ RENYI     93
   AND THEN HIS HEART GREW WELL-NIGH DEAD . . . . . .       730 PRIEST FAIRY      59
   THEY GREW SO VERY STILL, I WIS . . . . . . . .           730 PRIEST FAIRY      66
   AND THEREON GREW A TENDER ROOT, . . . . . . . .          743 DANAAN QUICK      13
   AND THEREON GREW A TENDER STEM, . . . . . . . .          743 DANAAN QUICK      14
   AND THEREON GREW THE RUDDY FRUIT . . . . . . . .         743 DANAAN QUICK      15
   BUT YOU GREW WEARY OF HER. WHEN I HOLD . . . . .         749 SHADOW WATER A    53
   I GREW AS OLD AS TIME, AND SHE GROWS YOUNG . . . .       761 SHADOW WATER A   259
GREY   SEE STONE-GREY DOVE-GREY MOUSE-GREY ASH-GREY
   OR THE GREY WANDERING OSPREY SORROW." . . . . . .         20 OISIN 1          303
   OR THE WILD GREY OSPREY SORROW." . . . . . . . .          20 OISIN 1        V 303
   NOR THE GREY WANDERING OSPREY SORROW." . . . . . .        21 OISIN 1          319
   OR THE WILD GREY OSPREY SORROW." . . . . . . . .          21 OISIN 1        V 319
   NOR THE GREY WANDERING OSPREY SORROW." . . . . . .        23 OISIN 1          342
   OR FEAR THE WILD GREY OSPREY SORROW." . . . . . .         23 OISIN 1        V 342
   AND THE LONG GREY GRASSES, WHOSE TENDEREST TOUCHES  . . . 27 OISIN 1        V 415B
   SCARCE LEFT A WHITENING FEATHER, GREY AND SERE; . . . .   34 OISIN 2        V  76A
   GREY IN THE MIDST LIKE A SMALL RIVULET'S FLOW, . . . .    37 OISIN 2        V 117
   IT DIED AFAR. GREY SLEET THOSE TOWERS HID . . . . .       46 OISIN 2        V 245
   . . . THE SEA'S EDGE BARREN AND GREY, . . . . . .         48 OISIN 3           13
   GREY SAND ON THE GREEN OF THE GRASSES AND OVER THE DRIPPING  48 OISIN 3        14
      TREES,
   GREY SANDS ON THE GREEN OF THE GRASSES AND OVER THE      48 OISIN 3        V  14
      DRIPPING TREES,
   . . . WHERE ALL IS BARREN AND GREY, . . . . . . .        56 OISIN 3          141
   GREY SAND ON THE GREEN OF THE GRASSES AND OVER THE DRIPPING  57 OISIN 3       142
      TREES,
   GREY SANDS ON THE GREEN OF THE GRASSES AND OVER THE      57 OISIN 3        V 142
      DRIPPING TREES,
   GREY TRUTH IS NOW HER PAINTED TOY; . . . . . . .          65 HAPPY SHEPHERD     4
   THE SUN HAS LAID HIS CHIN ON THE GREY WOOD, . . . .       72 ANASHU VIJAYA     24
   THE SUN HATH LAID HIS CHIN ON THE GREY WOOD, . . . .      72 ANASHU VIJAYA  V  24
   THE DAUGHTER OF THE GREY OLD WOOD-CUTTER, . . . . .       74 ANASHU VIJAYA  V  63
   THE GREY WOLF KNOWS ME: ONE EAR . . . . . . . .           84 MAD KING GOLL     45
   THE DIM GREY SANDS WITH LIGHT, . . . . . . . .            87 STOLEN CHILD      14
   THE DRUID, GREY, WOOD-NURTURED, QUIET-EYED, . . . .      101 ROSE UPON ROOD     4
   THE DRUID, GREY, WOOD NURTURED, QUIET EYED, . . . .      101 ROSE UPON ROOD V   4
   A THIN GREY MAN HALF LOST IN GATHERING NIGHT. . . . .    102 FERGUS DRUID       7
   A THIN, GREY MAN, HALF-LOST IN GATHERING NIGHT. . . . .  102 FERGUS DRUID   V   7
   LOOK ON MY THIN GREY HAIR AND HOLLOW CHEEKS . . . .      103 FERGUS DRUID      23
   AND THE GREY TIDE, THE RED BRANCH MULTITUDE . . . .      108 CUCHULAIN SEA  V  38B
   AND SHE, TO WIN HIM, HIS GREY HAIR CARESSED; . . . .     110 CUCHULAIN SEA     73
   AND WAGE GOD'S BATTLES IN THE LONG GREY SHIPS. . . .     114 ROSE OF BATTLE    20
   "FROM THE GREY SHIPS AND BATTLES NEVER WON. . . . .      114 ROSE OF BATTLE V   8
   MADE YOU OF US, AND OF THE DIM GREY SEA. . . . . .       115 ROSE OF BATTLE    30
   WHILE I STAND ON THE ROADWAY, OR ON THE PAVEMENTS GREY,  117 ISLE INNISFREE    11
   WHILE I STAND ON THE ROADWAY, OR ON THE PAVEMENT GREY, . 117 ISLE INNISFREE V  11
   WHEN YOU ARE OLD AND GREY AND FULL OF SLEEP, . . . .     120 YOU ARE OLD        1
   A LUG-WORM WITH ITS GREY AND MUDDY MOUTH . . . . .       127 DREAM OF FAERY    18
```

344

		PAGE	TITLE	LINE
GREY	(CONTINUED)			
LAUGH, HEART, AGAIN IN THE GREY TWILIGHT,		147	INTO TWILIGHT	3
DEW EVER SHINING AND TWILIGHT GREY;		148	INTO TWILIGHT	6
AND LOVE IS LESS KIND THAN THE GREY TWILIGHT,		148	INTO TWILIGHT	15
WHERE SUCH GREY CLOUDS OF INCENSE ROSE		156	FORGOT BEAUTY	13
THE GREY CAIRN ON THE HILL, WHEN DAY SINKS DROWNED IN DEW,		161	BLACK PIG	6
BY A GREY SHORE WHERE THE WIND NEVER BLEW,		170	SECRET ROSE	14
NOR THE GREY RUSH WHEN THE WIND IS HIGH,		189	BAILE AILLINN	2
NOR THE GREY RUSH WHEN WIND IS HIGH		189	BAILE AILLINN V	2
IN THE GREY REEDS THAT NIGHT AND MORN		190	BAILE AILLINN	42
BUT THE GREY RUSH UNDER THE WIND		192	BAILE AILLINN	88
AND THE GREY BIRD WITH CROOKED BILL		192	BAILE AILLINN	89
"YOUR WELL-BELOVED'S HAIR HAS THREADS OF GREY,		199	FOLLY COMFORT	2
"YOUR WELL-BELOVED'S HAIR HAS A THREAD OF GREY,		199	FOLLY COMFORT V	2
"YOUR WELL BELOVED'S HAIR HAS THREADS OF GREY,		199	FOLLY COMFORT V	2
FOR THE GREY WINDS ARE BLOWING UP, OUT OF THE CLINGING SEAS!		207	HANRAHANS SONG V	12
LIKE A GREY GULL UPON THE BREAST OF EACH.		223	SHADOW WATER B	24
AND THOUGH THEY'RE BUT THE COLOUR OF GREY ASH,		247	SHADOW WATER B	528
TO CRY ALOUD TO THE GREY BIRDS, AND DREAMS,		252	SHADOW WATER B	618
AND NOW, BEING GREY,		255	WOMAN HOMER	9
THE GREY ROCK		270	GREY ROCK	T
THE GREY ROCK AND THE WINDY LIGHT?		275	GREY ROCK	111
THE GREY WING UPON EVERY TIDE!		290	SEPTEMBER 1913	18
WHEN GREY GULLS FLIT ABOUT INSTEAD OF MEN,		292	TO A SHADE	6
WHEN GREY GULLS FLY ABOUT INSTEAD OF MEN,		292	TO A SHADE V	6
OF GREY STONES AND A ROCKY LEDGE		302	HOUR DAWN	12
WHAT MADE US DREAM THAT HE COULD COMB GREY HAIR?		327	ROBERT GREGORY	88
UPON A GREY OLD BATTERED TOMBSTONE		331	ROUND TOWER	7
UPON THE GREY OLD BATTERED TOMBSTONE		331	ROUND TOWER V	7
TO A GREY PLACE ON A HILL		347	FISHERMAN	3
IN GREY CONNEMARA CLOTHES		347	FISHERMAN	4
AND GREY CONNEMARA CLOTH,		348	FISHERMAN	30
THERE IS GREY IN YOUR HAIR.		355	BROKEN DREAMS	1
IN THE GREY STONE TOMB HE MADE.		360	ALF POLLEXFEN	5
ON THE GREY SAND BESIDE THE SHALLOW STREAM		367	EGO DOMINUS	1
ON THE GREY ROCK OF CASHEL THE MIND'S EYE		382	VISION ROBART	1
ON THE GREY ROCK OF CASHEL I SUDDENLY SAW		383	VISION ROBART	17
FROM COUNTER OR DESK AMONG GREY		392	EASTER 1916	3
A GREY GULL LOST ITS FEAR AND FLEW		397	POLIT PRISONER	3
WHILE ON THAT OLD GREY STONE I SAT		406	IN TIME OF WAR	2
A GREY STONE FIREPLACE WITH AN OPEN HEARTH,		419	MY HOUSE	12
A GREY STONE FIRE-PLACE WITH AN OPEN HEARTH,		419	MY HOUSE V	12
AND THE GREAT GREY LYNX'S SKIN! IN SOOTH, METHINKS		650	ISLE STAT I 1	151
THAT I MYSELF COULD SHOOT A GREAT GREY LYNX.		650	ISLE STAT I 1	152
THE POPLARS GAZE ACROSS THE WATERS GREY,		653	ISLE STAT I 2	34
I COULD GAZE, GAZE UPON THINE EYES' CLEAR GREY!		671	ISLE STAT II 3	147
I COULD GAZE, GAZE UPON THINE EYES OF GREY!		671	ISLE STAT II 3 V	147
BUT ART THOU HAPPY? THOSE GREY EYES OF THINE.		672	ISLE STAT II 3	151
AND WHEREFORE, THEN, SHOULD THY GREY EYES		686	LIFE	7
IN HIS OWN HOUSE OR 'MONG THE MERCHANTS GREY,		693	MOSADA 1	87
STANDS EACH GREY AND SILENT PHANTOM ON THE SAME REGARDLESS SPOT--		719	PHANTOM SHIP	25
JOYS AND FEARS IN THEIR GREY FACES THAT THE LIVE EARTH - KNOWETH NOT!		719	PHANTOM SHIP	26
GREY HAIRS AND CRUTCHES, CRUTCHES AND GREY HAIRS,		721	WITCH VIVIEN	20
GREY HAIRS AND CRUTCHES, CRUTCHES AND GREY HAIRS,		721	WITCH VIVIEN	20
A GREY PROFESSOR PASSING CRIED,		725	LEGEND	9
FLED FROM HIS BROW WHERE THE HAIR WAS GREY!		728	PRIEST FAIRY	10
HE THOUGHT WISE THINGS AS HIS GREY HEAD NODDED.		728	PRIEST FAIRY	12
HE DREW FROM HIS CAP A FEATHER GREY,		729	PRIEST FAIRY	29
WHERE LONG GREY GRASSES BOW AND BEND,		736	SUMMER EVENING	6
LIKE A GREY OWL MEN HARRY OUT		740	EARL PAUL	23
AND MURMURED: "O LONG GREY CLOAK,		744	GLOVE CLOAK	11
THEY ARE CHANGED AND AS GREY BIRDS FLY OUT TO SEA,		750	SHADOW WATER A	82
OR BE HIS FOOD, I FOLLOW THE GREY WINGS,		751	SHADOW WATER A	101
A GREY BIRD HAS FLOWN BY. HE HAS FLOWN UPWARD.		753	SHADOW WATER A	134
THAT FORGAEL HAS FOLLOWED THE GREY BIRDS ALONE,		767	SHADOW WATER A	402
A HIGH, GREY CAIRN. WHAT MORE IS TO BE SAID?		778	SONG DEIRDRE 3	5
AT THE GREY ROUND OF THE HILL		782	GREY ROUND	1
GREY-EYED				
THE GREAT GREY-EYED ATHENE STARES THEREON.		447	COLONUS PRAISE	16
GREY-GREEN				
A GREY-GREEN CUP OF JADE,		781	MY HEART BEAT	15
GREY-HAIRED				
A GREY-HAIRED YOUTH, WHOSE CHEEKS HAD NEVER FOUND,		687	TWO TITANS	7
GREY-LEAVED				
EVEN THE GREY-LEAVED OLIVE-TREE		446	COLONUS PRAISE	12
EVEN THE GREY-LEAVED OLIVE TREE		446	COLONUS PRAISE V	12
GLITTERING AMONG GREY-LEAVED OLIVE-TREES,		447	COLONUS PRAISE	21
GLITTERING AMONG GREY-LEAVED OLIVE TREES,		447	COLONUS PRAISE V	21
GREYNESS				
AND DRIFTING GREYNESS, WHILE THIS MONOTONE,		45	OISIN 2	232
AND DRIFTING GREYNESS. CAME THIS MONOTONE		45	OISIN 2 V	232
GRIDDLE				
IS DEAD. THE BOY THAT BRINGS MY GRIDDLE CAKE		339	SHEP GOATHERD V	20
GRIDDLE-CAKE				
IS DEAD. THE BOY THAT BRINGS MY GRIDDLE-CAKE		339	SHEP GOATHERD	20
GRIEF				
IN GRIEF SWAYED TO AND FRO.		133	FR GILLIGAN	36
THAT I WOULD LOOK UPON FOR EVER? MY GRIEF!		244	SHADOW WATER B	462

```
                                                               PAGE      TITLE            LINE
GRIEF   (CONTINUED)
    HOW DOES SHE BEAR HER GRIEF?  THERE IS NOT A SHEPHERD  .  .   340 SHEP GOATHERD         28
    SOME MEDICABLE HERB TO MAKE OUR GRIEF  .  .  .  .  .  .  .    342 SHEP GOATHERD         86
    AND THINKING OF THAT FIT OF GRIEF OR RAGE  .  .  .  .  .  .   443 SCHOOL CHILDR         17
    MAY KNOW NOT WHAT HE KNOWS, BUT KNOWS NOT GRIEF.  .  .  .  .  500 VACILLATION          18
    WITH LOOSENED HAIR OR FOREHEADS GRIEF DISTRAUGHT,  .  .  .    537 HER VISION       V   18
    NAY, GRIEF IN FEEDING ON OLD GRIEF GROWS LESS.  .  .  .  .    659 ISLE STAT II 1       19
    NAY, GRIEF IN FEEDING ON OLD GRIEF GROWS LESS.  .  .  .  .    659 ISLE STAT II 1       19
    GRIEF NEEDS MUCH FEEDING THEN.  OF HIM I SWEAR  .  .  .  .    659 ISLE STAT II 1       20
    OLD MISER HOARDS OF GRIEF TO TELL AND TELL!  .  .  .  .  .    661 ISLE STAT II 1       55
    THOU HAST AN OVER-NIMBLE TONGUE.  THY GRIEF,  .  .  .  .  .   661 ISLE STAT II 1       59
    MORE GRIEF IS MINE.  NO MAN SHALL EVER STOOP  .  .  .  .  .   661 ISLE STAT II 1       62
    BENEATH THE WEIGHT OF GREATER GRIEF THAN I)  .  .  .  .  .    661 ISLE STAT II 1       63
    O'ER GRIEF.  THE WORLD DRINKS SORROW FROM THE BEAMS  .  .     664 ISLE STAT II 2       46
    OF GRIEF.  AND IF THEY SAY, "ANTONIO LAUGHED,"  .  .  .  .    664 ISLE STAT II 2       51
    AND NEVER HEARD OF GRIEF OR CARE  .  .  .  .  .  .  .  .  .   667 ISLE STAT II 3       21
    AH! YOU ARE WEEPING! HERE SHOULD ALL GRIEF CEASE.  .  .  .    672 ISLE STAT II 3      149
    IN LIST'NING SILENCE GAZING ON OUR GRIEF.  .  .  .  .  .  .   702 MOSADA 3             87
GRIEF-DISTRAUGHT
    WITH LOOSENED HAIR OR FOREHEADS GRIEF-DISTRAUGHT,  .  .  .    537 HER VISION           18
GRIEF'S
    TILL SUDDENLY IN GRIEF'S CONTAGION CAUGHT,  .  .  .  .  .  .  537 HER VISION           22
    SAY THEN,--"A POPINJAY BEFORE GRIEF'S SHAFT  .  .  .  .  .    664 ISLE STAT II 2       52
GRIEFS
    FOR LONG THE BURTHEN OF THEIR TALKING GRIEFS.  .  .  .  .  .  693 MOSADA 1             71
    SHE SMILES--IS HAPPY WITH HER WANDERING GRIEFS.  .  .  .  .   702 MOSADA 3             95
GRIEVE
    AND HE BEGAN TO GRIEVE.  .  .  .  .  .  .  .  .  .  .  .  .   132 FR GILLIGAN           8
    TO KNOW THE MOUNTAIN AND THE VALLEY GRIEVE  .  .  .  .  .  .  343 SHEP GOATHERD    V  117
    AND HEAVEN, AND HOLINESS.  LET'S TALK AND GRIEVE,  .  .  .    702 MOSADA 3             84
    GRIEVE NOT, FOR GOMEZ KNEELS BESIDE THEE--GOMEZ,  .  .  .  .  702 MOSADA 3             90
    GRIEVE NOT, FOR VALLENCE KNEELS BESIDE THEE--VALLENCE,  .  .  702 MOSADA 3         V   90
GRIEVED
    TO KNOW THE MOUNTAIN AND THE VALLEY HAVE GRIEVED  .  .  .  .  343 SHEP GOATHERD       117
GRIEVES
    DRIVEN BY A STORM THAT EVER GRIEVES.  .  .  .  .  .  .  .  .  135 TWO TREES        V   28
GRIEVING
    A QUENCHLESS GRIEVING OF LOVE MELODY.  .  .  .  .  .  .  .    645 ISLE STAT I 1        21
GRIEVOUS
    OF GRIEVOUS TIME ON HIS OLD CRUTCHES,  .  .  .  .  .  .  .  .  23 OISIN 1         V 341B
    EQUAL TO GOOD OR GRIEVOUS CHANCE!  .  .  .  .  .  .  .  .  .   24 OISIN 1             372
GRIFFITH
    GUARDED! GRIFFITH STARING IN HYSTERICAL PRIDE!  .  .  .  .    601 GALLERY REVIS         4
GRIMALKIN
    GRIMALKIN CRAWLS TO BUDDHA'S EMPTINESS.  .  .  .  .  .  .  .   611 STATUES              24
GRINDING
    AN OLD SLAVE GRINDING AT A HEAVY QUERN,  .  .  .  .  .  .  .   104 FERGUS DRUID         35
GRIP
    NOTHING BUT GRIP OF CLAW, AND THE EYE'S COMPLACENCY,  .  .    427 PHANTOM HATRED       31
GRIPPED
    HER HANDS ON EITHER SIDE HAD GRIPPED THE BENCH,  .  .  .  .   279 TWO KINGS            63
    HANDS GRIPPED IN HANDS, TOES CLOSE TOGETHER,  .  .  .  .  .   332 ROUND TOWER          21
GRIPS
    WHO GRIPS HIS LONG SPEAR SO TO PUSH  .  .  .  .  .  .  .  .    385 ROBARTES DANCE        3
GRISLY
    .  .  WHEN, ROLLED IN A GRISLY PEACE,  .  .  .  .  .  .  .     47 OISIN 3               9
GROAN
    AND WITH A GROAN, AS IF THE MORTAL BREATH  .  .  .  .  .  .   185 QUEEN MAEVE         103
    HEARING HIM GROAN AND STRETCH  .  .  .  .  .  .  .  .  .  .    319 DOLLS                13
    TO SHUFFLE, GRUNT AND GROAN,  .  .  .  .  .  .  .  .  .  .     599 STONE CROSS          20
GROANED
    HEARING THE FAR-OFF SINGING GUILE, AND GROANED,  .  .  .  .   693 MOSADA 1             88
    HEARING THE FAR OFF SINGING GUILE AND GROANED,  .  .  .  .    693 MOSADA 1         V   88
GROOM       SEE BRIDE-GROOM
GROOMED     SEE WELL-GROOMED
GROPE
    WE GROPE, AND GROPE IN VAIN,  .  .  .  .  .  .  .  .  .  .     487 CRAZED MOON           5
    WE GROPE, AND GROPE IN VAIN,  .  .  .  .  .  .  .  .  .  .     487 CRAZED MOON           5
    OR GROPE WITH A DIRTY HAND.  .  .  .  .  .  .  .  .  .  .  .   599 SPIRIT MEDIUM         8
    OR GROPE WITH A DIRTY HAND.  .  .  .  .  .  .  .  .  .  .  .   600 SPIRIT MEDIUM        16
    OR GROPE WITH A DIRTY HAND.  .  .  .  .  .  .  .  .  .  .  .   600 SPIRIT MEDIUM        24
GROPED
    I GROPED MY WAY FROM BEECH TO HAZEL WOOD,  .  .  .  .  .  .   283 TWO KINGS           139
    I GROPED MY WAY THROUGH BOUGHS, AND OVER ROOTS,  .  .  .  .   283 TWO KINGS        V  139
GROSS
    WHILE OUR GROSS PALATES DRINK FROM THE WHOLE WINE,  .  .  .   471 ALL SOUL NIGHT       10
GROUND
    THE FENIANS ON THE HUMAN GROUND  .  .  .  .  .  .  .  .  .     10 OISIN 1         V 114C
    LONG SIGHS AROSE IN OUR SPIRITS, BENEATH US BUBBLED THE       48 OISIN 3              20
        GROUND.
    .  .  .  FLUNG LOOSELY ALONG THE DIM GROUND)  .  .  .  .  .    50 OISIN 3              45
    IN A REVERIE FORGETFUL OF ALL THINGS, OVER THE BUBBLING       56 OISIN 3             140
        GROUND.
    IN REVERIE FORGETFUL OF ALL THINGS, OVER THE BUBBLING         56 OISIN 3         V  140
        GROUND.
    BURIED UNDER THE SLEEPY GROUND,  .  .  .  .  .  .  .  .  .     67 HAPPY SHEPHERD       48
    (WHO'S BURIED IN THE SLEEPY GROUND),  .  .  .  .  .  .  .  .   67 HAPPY SHEPHERD V     48
    OR DO YOU LONG FOR THE DIM SLEEPY GROUND,  .  .  .  .  .  .   109 CUCHULAIN SEA        60
    UNDER THE DOCK-LEAVES IN THE GROUND,  .  .  .  .  .  .  .  .   176 BELOVED DEAD         12
    THAT HAVE ONE SHADOW ON THE GROUND!  .  .  .  .  .  .  .  .    195 BAILE AILLINN       154
    WHO'S BURROWING SOMEWHERE IN THE GROUND,  .  .  .  .  .  .     272 GREY ROCK            33
```

PAGE   TITLE   LINE

GROUND (CONTINUED)
  THAT HAD MADE PRINTS UPON THE GROUND, 274 GREY ROCK   79
  SHE CAST HERSELF UPON THE GROUND 275 GREY ROCK   107
  TO WHERE SHE MOANED UPON THE GROUND, 275 GREY ROCK   119
  THEREON SHE CAST HERSELF UPON THE GROUND, 275 GREY ROCK   V 107
  AND THE GROUND IVY'S BLUER LIGHT, A STAG 277 TWO KINGS   V 6
  I CHOSE THIS BURROW UNDER GROUND. 305 HOUR DAWN   73
  THE WATER-HEN MUST CHANGE HER GROUND; 326 ROBERT GREGORY 55
  THE WATERHEN MUST CHANGE HER GROUND; 326 ROBERT GREGORY V 55
  OUR SHADOWS ON THE GROUND 333 SOLOMON SHEBA 14
  UNLESS A PETAL HIT THE GROUND, 389 SOLOMON WITCH 40
  AN ACRE OF STONY GROUND, 419 MY HOUSE   3
  IN THE MAD ABSTRACT DARK AND GROUND IT GRAIN BY GRAIN 442 BLACK CENTAUR 8
  IMMORTAL LADIES TREAD THE GROUND 446 COLONUS PRAISE 6
  THERE, ON BLOOD-SATURATED GROUND, HAVE STOOD 482 BLOOD AND MOON 35
  THERE, ON BLOOD SATURATED GROUND, HAVE STOOD 482 BLOOD AND MOON V 35
  AND DEDICATE--EYES BENT UPON THE GROUND, 489 COOLE PARK 29 29
  I--LOVE'S SKEIN UPON THE GROUND, 511 JANE AND JACK 9
  ALL HAPPINESS IN ITS OWN CAUSE OR GROUND. 557 RIBH ECSTASY 4
  NO PROUDER TROD THE GROUND, 587 PARNELLITES 22
  AND WERE THE LAST TO CHOOSE THE SETTLED GROUND, 621 HOUND VOICE 2
  TO DIE FOR HER IN AIR OR GROUND. 668 ISLE STAT II 3 52
  BEHOLD, I BEND BEFORE THEE TO THE GROUND 683 SEEKER   43
  BEHOLD, I BEND BEFORE THEE TO THE GROUND; 684 SEEKER   61
  BEHOLD, I BEND BEFORE THEE TO THE GROUND! 684 SEEKER   67
  BEHOLD I BOW BEFORE THEE TO THE GROUND! 684 SEEKER   V 67
  ONE WHOSE FOOTFALL SHAKES THE GROUND. 727 LOVERS QUARREL 32
GROUND-IVY'S
  WITH THE GROUND-IVY'S BLUE, HE SAW A STAG 277 TWO KINGS   6
GROUNDS
  GROUNDS WHERE PLUM AND CABBAGE GREW, 577 WHAT THEN   13
GROUSE
  I GAZED AT HIM LIKE GROUSE UPON A KITE; 283 TWO KINGS   152
GROVE
  AND THE SHADOWY HAZEL GROVE 119 PITY OF LOVE   6
  IN THE FORBIDDEN SACRED GROVE 389 SOLOMON WITCH 39
  OR WINDING THROUGH THE GROVE 530 DELPHIC ORACLE 7
  THROUGH JONATHAN SWIFT'S DARK GROVE HE PASSED, AND THERE 543 PARN FUNERAL 2 11
GROW
  AFORETIME, AND SHALL NOT GROW SAD 22 OISIN 1   V 340E
  I HEARD ONE SAY, "HIS EYES GROW DIM 25 OISIN 1   380
  O HAD YOU SEEN BEAUTIFUL NIAMH GROW WHITE AS THE WATERS 54 OISIN 3   109
    ARE WHITE,
  SHE BID ME TAKE LOVE EASY, AS THE LEAVES GROW ON THE TREE; 90 SALLEY GARDENS 3
  SHE BID ME TAKE LOVE EASY, AS THE LEAVES GROW ON THE TREES; 90 SALLEY GARDENS V 3
  THE SUN UPON ALL THINGS THAT GROW 98 FOXHUNTER   15
  GROW SWEET WITH HIS MOOD. 118 CRADLE SONG V 8
  GROW GAY WITH HIS MOOD. 118 CRADLE SONG V 8
  THINE EYES GROW FULL OF TENDER CARE; 135 TWO TREES   19
  THY TENDER EYES GROW ALL UNKIND; 136 TWO TREES   39
  "SHE WILL GROW OLD AND DIE, AND SHE HAS WEPT!" 186 QUEEN MAEVE 138
  O WHEN WILL YOU GROW WEARY?" THEY HAD VANISHED; 187 QUEEN MAEVE 152
  GROW GENTLE WITHOUT SORROWING, 193 BAILE AILLINN 110
  GROW GENTLE WITHOUT SORROWINGS; 193 BAILE AILLINN V 110
  OR YOU WILL GROW OUT OF FASHION 212 O DO NOT LOVE 11
  I WOULD GROW JEALOUS OF THE IVORY ROOF, 246 SHADOW WATER B 501
  AND KNITTED MESH TO MESH, WE GROW IMMORTAL; 252 SHADOW WATER B 616
  AND KNITTING MESH TO MESH, WE GROW IMMORTAL; 252 SHADOW WATER B V 616
  BEFORE WE GROW OLD AND DIE. 261 DRINKING SONG 4
  AND THE SWEET LAUGHING EAGLE THOUGHTS THAT GROW 264 HOUSE SHAKEN 5
  "AND THERE I'LL GROW RESPECTED AT MY EASE, 300 BEGGAR CRIED 17
  TOIL AND GROW RICH, 310 WITCH   1
  TILL PRIDE HAD MADE HER EYES GROW BRIGHT, 314 MEMORY YOUTH 10
  AND PLEASURE MADE HER CHEEKS GROW RED, 314 MEMORY YOUTH 11
  BUT I GROW OLD AMONG DREAMS, 329 MEN IMPROVE 16
  THAT SAW THE WICKS GROW YELLOW IN THE DAWN; 352 PEOPLE   18
  OR WHEN I GROW EXCITED WITH WINE, 357 DEEP-SWORN VOW 5
  GROW RICH, POPULAR AND FULL OF INFLUENCE, 369 EGO DOMINUS 43
  AND YET, TWICE BORN, TWICE BURIED, GROW HE MUST, 374 PHASES OF MOON 48
  AND ON THE INSTANT WOULD GROW WISE. 385 ROBARTES DANCE 12
  BUT WHY SHOULD YOU GROW SUDDENLY AFRAID 390 IMAGE PAST   29
  . . . ALL ENTANGLEMENTS OF MANKIND GROW, 459 FROM OEDIPUS 5
  AND IF HER EYE SHOULD NOT GROW BRIGHT FOR MINE 464 HARUN RASHID 81
  AND I GROW HALF CONTENTED TO BE BLIND; 473 ALL SOUL NIGHT 70
  MAKE HUMAN INTERCOURSE GROW LESS AND LESS; 473 ALL SOUL NIGHT 75
  HISTORIC NATIONS GROW 547 TO SAME TUNE 3 V 5
  MIND'S BREAD GROW SWEET. 554 CHURCH STATE 6
  CONDUCT AND WORK GROW COARSE, AND COARSE THE SOUL, 564 GYRES   17
  IT CANNOT GROW BY AN INCH OR AN OUNCE. 566 LAPIS LAZULI 24
  HE MUST GROW A FAMOUS MAN; 576 WHAT THEN   2
  "YOUR LIFE CAN GROW MUCH SWEETER IF YOU WILL 634 CUCHULAIN COMF 12
  HEAR ME, AND, SHEPHERD, HEARING ME, GROW DUMB. 646 ISLE STAT I 1 31
  HERE GROW THAT SHY, RETIRING SISTERHOOD, 651 ISLE STAT I 2 4
  SHALL GROW THY BEAUTY AND THY DREAMLESS TRUTH, 674 ISLE STAT II 3 207
  THE WARMTH OF LIFE IS CHILLING, AND THE SHADOWS GROW 675 ISLE STAT II 3 232
  QUITE SOON THE CORNFIELD, WHERE THE POPPIES GROW 699 MOSADA 3   7
  ALONG THE CORNFIELD, WHERE THE POPPIES GROW, 699 MOSADA 3 V 7
  SO SMALL MAKES ONE GROW WEAK AND TOTTERING! 700 MOSADA 3   35
  THEN THE STARS GROW OUT OF HEAVEN WITH THEIR COUNTENANCES 719 PHANTOM SHIP 30
    FAIR.
  HAS BLOSSOMED, AND I GROW AS OLD AS TIME. 756 SHADOW WATER A 179

		PAGE	TITLE	LINE

GROW (CONTINUED)
OR GROW KIND, FOR THEY ANOINT . . . . 776 AGAINST WITCH   21
GROWETH
GROWETH THE GOBLIN FLOWER OF JOY, HER CARE, ... 653 ISLE STAT I 2   39
GROWING
THE HARES RUN BY ME GROWING BOLD. . . . . 84 MAD KING GOLL   47
THE HARE RUNS BY ME GROWING BOLD-- . . . . 84 MAD KING GOLL V   47
AND HARES RUN NEAR ME GROWING BOLD. . . . . 84 MAD KING GOLL V   47
BUT ONE SMALL KNOT-GRASS GROWING BY THE POOL . . . . . 127 DREAM OF FAERY   29
BUT ONE SMALL KNOT-GRASS GROWING BY THE RIM . . . . . 127 DREAM OF FAERY   29
AH, WORLD-WIDE NATION, ALWAYS GROWING SORROW, ... 130 BOOK STORIES V   11
AH, WORLDWIDE NATION, ALWAYS GROWING SORROW! . . . . 130 BOOK STORIES V   11
THE HOLY TREE IS GROWING THERE; . . . . 134 TWO TREES   2
ITS TERROR GROWING WILDER AT EVERY FOOT-FALL, ... 279 TWO KINGS   V 45D
ITS TERROR GROWING WILDER AT EVERY FOOTFALL . . . . . 279 TWO KINGS   V 45D
NOW I AM GROWING OLD, ... 346 ON WOMAN   28
AND THAT MERE GROWING OLD, THAT BRINGS . . . . 401 DEMON BEAST   38
SUFFICE THE AGEING MAN AS ONCE THE GROWING BOY. . . . 427 PHANTOM HATRED   40
AND WHEN WE TALKED OF GROWING UP . . . . 456 SUMMER SPRING   5
ENDURE THAT TOIL OF GROWING UP! . . . . 478 SELF AND SOUL   44
SCORN THE SORT NOW GROWING UP . . . . 639 BEN BULBEN   70
THE DOVES WHOSE GROWING FORMS HE'D WATCHED. NOT THESE . . 710 FERENCZ RENYI   21
THE DOVES WHOSE GROWING FORM HE'D WATCHED. NOT THESE . . 710 FERENCZ RENYI V   21
AND JOY, IN GROWING DEEPER AND MORE DEEP, ... 735 QUATRAIN APHOR   27
GROWN
AND THINGS THAT HAVE GROWN SAD ARE WICKED, ... 20 OISIN 1   301
GROWN DESOLATE, WHISPER AND SIGH TO EACH OTHER! . . . 26 OISIN 1   403
GROWN DESOLATE, WHISPER AND SIGH TO EACH OTHER. . . . 27 OISIN 1   V 407
. . . LONG WARLESS, GROWN WHITER THAN CURDS. . . . . 49 OISIN 3   36
. . . LONG-WARLESS, GROWN WHITER THAN CURDS. . . . . 49 OISIN 3   V   36
I SAW HOW THOSE SLUMBERERS, GROWN WEARY, ... 50 OISIN 3   54
. . . GROWN MILD WITH MYSTERIOUS THOUGHT, ... 55 OISIN 3   121
AND THINE OWN SADNESS, WHEREOF STARS, GROWN OLD . . . 101 ROSE UPON ROOD   6
BUT NOW I HAVE GROWN NOTHING, KNOWING ALL. . . . . . 104 FERGUS DRUID   38
BUT NOW I HAVE GROWN NOTHING, BEING ALL! . . . . . . 104 FERGUS DRUID   38
"BUT YOU HAVE GROWN TO BE THE TALLER MAN." . . . . . 107 CUCHULAIN SEA   27
BEAUTY GROWN SAD WITH ITS ETERNITY . . . . 115 ROSE OF BATTLE   29
WHEN YOU HAVE GROWN, ... 118 CRADLE SONG   12
MY DEAR, WHEN YOU'RE GROWN! . . . . 118 CRADLE SONG   V   12
WHEN, DEAR, YOU HAVE GROWN. . . . . 118 CRADLE SONG   V   12
UNTIL THE SAP OF SUMMER HAD GROWN WEARY! . . . . . . 130 BOOK STORIES   14
IT HAD GROWN WISE-TONGUED BY THINKING . . . . 159 CAP AND BELLS   7
IT HAD GROWN MOST WISE WITH THINKING . . . . 159 CAP AND BELLS   V   7
AND IT HAD GROWN WISE BY THINKING . . . . 159 CAP AND BELLS   V   7
IT HAD GROWN SWEET-TONGUED BY DREAMING . . . . 160 CAP AND BELLS   17
BECAUSE THEIR BODIES HAD GROWN OLD. . . . . 189 BAILE AILLINN   10
AS WHEN NEWLY GROWN TO BE A WOMAN, ... 199 ARROW   4
WE SAT GROWN QUIET AT THE NAME OF LOVE; . . . . 205 ADAMS CURSE   28
THAT IT HAD ALL SEEMED HAPPY, AND YET WE'D GROWN . . 206 ADAMS CURSE   37
AND YOU HAVE GROWN TO BE A BURNING SOD . . . . 245 SHADOW WATER B   487
THAT HAS GROWN WEARY OF THE WANDERING DANCE, ... 285 TWO KINGS   183
THAT HAS GROWN WEARY OF THE WHIRLING DANCE, ... 285 TWO KINGS   V 183
POOR MEN HAVE GROWN TO BE RICH MEN, ... 301 RUN PARADISE   15
AND RICH MEN GROWN TO BE POOR AGAIN, ... 301 RUN PARADISE   16
AND MANY A DARLING WIT'S GROWN DULL . . . . 301 RUN PARADISE   18
THAT'S GROWN UNEASY NEAR THE DAWN . . . . 303 HOUR DAWN   V   33
GROWN TIRED OF HIS OWN COMPANY? . . . . 303 HOUR DAWN   V   37
AND THEN, GROWN WEARY, PRAYED AND CURSED . . . . . . 307 HOUR DAWN   117
THEIR HEARTS HAVE NOT GROWN OLD; . . . . 323 SWANS AT COOLE   22
HAVING GROWN SLUGGISH AND CONTEMPLATIVE. . . . . . . 325 ROBERT GREGORY   40
TILL THE YELLOW EYE HAS GROWN MILD, ... 349 HAWK   3
SHE HAS NOT GROWN UNCIVIL. . . . . 365 HER RACE   1
DO NOT BECAUSE THIS DAY I HAVE GROWN SATURNINE . . . 390 UNDER SATURN   1
SHE SEEMED TO HAVE GROWN CLEAN AND SWEET . . . . . . 397 POLIT PRISONER   17
A FIGURE THAT HAS GROWN SO FABULOUS . . . . 412 TOWER   77
THE HEART'S GROWN BRUTAL FROM THE FARE; . . . . 425 STARES NEST   17
GROWN TIRED OF THEIR SOLITUDE, ... 432 NINETEEN 19   V 105
IF YOU, THAT HAVE GROWN OLD, WERE THE FIRST DEAD, . . 435 NEW FACES   1
SEEMED FOR A WHILE TO HAVE GROWN YOUNG AGAIN; . . . . 462 HARUN RASHID   36
AND MAY HAVE GROWN MORE ARROGANT BEING A GHOST, . . . 473 ALL SOUL NIGHT   80
SO THAT HIS ELEMENTS HAVE GROWN SO FINE . . . . 473 ALL SOUL NIGHT   82
CRAZY JANE GROWN OLD LOOKS AT THE DANCERS . . . . . . 514 JANE GROWN OLD   T
THAT WHEN THEY HAD GROWN LARGE . . . . 571 THREE BUSHES   60
"THE WORK IS DONE," GROWN OLD HE THOUGHT, ... 577 WHAT THEN   16
ALL THAT IS NOT ITSELF! I HAD GROWN WILD . . . . . . 619 BRONZE HEAD   20
ON GANGLING STOCKS GROWN GREAT, GREAT STOCKS RUN DRY, . 619 BRONZE HEAD   25
ALMINTOR, THOU HAST GROWN SO FULL OF RUTH, ... 652 ISLE STAT I 2   26
AND STONY-HEARTED; NOW THOU HAST GROWN KIND, ... 670 ISLE STAT II 3   91
BUT, FOR A BOY, HOW LONG THINE HAIR HAS GROWN! . . . 670 ISLE STAT II 3   104
WILD CRIES, GROWN SWEET WITH LULLS AND LINGERINGS LONG. 674 ISLE STAT II 3   222
THREE TIMES THE ROSES HAVE GROWN LESS AND LESS, . . . 690 MOSADA 1   1
AND YON FEW STARS GROWN DIM, LIKE EYES OF LOVERS . . 700 MOSADA 3   33
'TIS THOU, FOR THEY'VE GROWN BLUE AROUND THE NAILS. . 700 MOSADA 3   46
LIKE HAPPY THOUGHTS GROWN SAD IN EVIL DAYS. . . . . . 703 MOSADA 3   116
THE SPIRIT OF YOUNG RENYI HAS GROWN OLD. . . . . . . 710 FERENCZ RENYI   17
SHE BIDS US FOLLOW HER. I HAVE GROWN WEARY . . . . . 758 SHADOW WATER A   218
IT MAY BE, AND HAVE GROWN WEARY OF LOVE. . . . . . . 767 SHADOW WATER A   390
GROWS
THEN SHE SIGHED GENTLY, "IT GROWS LATE. . . . . 9 OISIN 1   102
THE RED SUN FALLS AND THE WORLD GROWS DIM." . . . . . 9 OISIN 1   105
THE HARE GROWS OLD AS SHE PLAYS IN THE SUN . . . . . 27 OISIN 1   412

348

			PAGE	TITLE	LINE
GROWS	(CONTINUED)				
"OLD GROWS THE HARE AS SHE PLAYS IN THE SUN, • • • • •			28	OISIN 1	V 420
WHILE OUR LOVE GROWS AN INDIAN STAR, • • • • • • • •			78	INDIAN TO LOVE	13
WHILE GROWS OUR LOVE AN INDIAN STAR, • • • • • • • •			78	INDIAN TO LOVE	V 13
SHE BID ME TAKE LIFE EASY, AS THE GRASS GROWS ON THE WEIRS!			90	SALLEY GARDENS	7
FOR THERE A FATAL IMAGE GROWS • • • • • • • • •			135	TWO TREES	25
WIND AND UNWIND THEIR DANCES WHEN THE LIGHT GROWS COOL • •			203	WITHER BOUGHS	13
WIND AND UNWIND DANCING WHEN THE LIGHT GROWS COOL • • •			203	WITHER BOUGHS	V 13
WHERE PASSION GROWS TO BE A CHANGELESS THING, • • • • •			231	SHADOW WATER B	213
"NIGHT GROWS UNEASY NEAR THE DAWN • • • • • • • • •			303	HOUR DAWN	33
THAT THE HEART GROWS OLD? • • • • • • • • • • • •			334	SONG	6
THAT THE HEART GROWS OLD? • • • • • • • • • • • •			335	SONG	12
THAT THE HEART GROWS OLD? • • • • • • • • • • • •			335	SONG	18
BUT GROWS MORE GENTLE WHEN HE SPEAKS HER NAME, • • • • •			340	SHEP GOATHERD	29
"HE GROWS YOUNGER EVERY SECOND • • • • • • • • • •			342	SHEP GOATHERD	89
GROWS COMELIER. ELEVEN PASS, AND THEN • • • • • • •			374	PHASES OF MOON	44
THE HEART GROWS BRUTAL FROM THE FARE, • • • • • • • •			425	STARES NEST	V 17
"AND THE NIGHT GROWS ROUGH." • • • • • • • • • •			526	AM OF IRELAND	13
THE GREATER GROWS MY LIGHT • • • • • • • • • • •			559	HE AND SHE	9
WHEN AN OLD MAN'S BLOOD GROWS COLD? • • • • • • • •			588	OLD WICKED MAN	13
NO MAN GROWS OLD, NO GIRL GROWS COLD, • • • • • • • •			621	JOHN KINSELLA	31
NO MAN GROWS OLD, NO GIRL GROWS COLD, • • • • • • • •			621	JOHN KINSELLA	31
WHEN A MAN GROWS OLD HIS JOY • • • • • • • • • •			624	APPARITIONS	17
GROWS MORE DEEP DAY AFTER DAY, • • • • • • • • • •			624	APPARITIONS	18
AND TILL HIS INTELLECT GROWS SURE • • • • • • • • •			633	MAN AND ECHO	30
THERE IN THE TOMB THE DARK GROWS BLACKER, • • • • • •			636	BLACK TOWER	27
EVEN THE WISEST MAN GROWS TENSE • • • • • • • • •			638	BEN BULBEN	33
NAY, GRIEF IN FEEDING ON OLD GRIEF GROWS LESS. • • • •			659	ISLE STAT II 1	19
I, AS MUSIC THAT GROWS MUTE, • • • • • • • • • •			668	ISLE STAT II 3	65
THE FOOT-WORN WAY IS LONG, AND IT GROWS DARK. • • • • •			702	MOSADA 3	92
THE FOOTWORN WAY IS LONG, AND IT GROWS DARK. • • • • •			702	MOSADA 3	V 92
THE WORLD GROWS OLD AND PLAYS THE FOOL." • • • • • •			725	LEGEND	12
I GREW AS OLD AS TIME, AND SHE GROWS YOUNG • • • • •			761	SHADOW WATER A	259
GROWS YOUNG AND A MAN'S HEART GROWS OLD IN A TWINKLING.			761	SHADOW WATER A	263
GROWS YOUNG AND A MAN'S HEART GROWS OLD IN A TWINKLING.			761	SHADOW WATER A	263
IS THIS POOR BODY THAT REDDENS AND GROWS PALE. • • • •			764	SHADOW WATER A	341
GRUBS					
THE MOTHER BIRDS BRING GRUBS AND FLIES. • • • • • • •			424	STARES NEST	3
GRUMBLE					
WHEN IT IS OVER, NOR ONE TO GRUMBLE AT US. • • • • • •			225	SHADOW WATER B	67
GRUNT					
TO SHUFFLE, GRUNT AND GROAN, • • • • • • • • • •			599	STONE CROSS	20
GRUNTING					
AND LAY IN THE DARKNESS, GRUNTING, AND TURNING TO HIS REST.			153	CHANGE BELOVED	12
GUAIRE					
KING GUAIRE WALKED AMID HIS COURT • • • • • • • •			295	THREE BEGGARS	8
BUT GUAIRE LAUGHED WITH SECRET THOUGHT, • • • • • • •			295	THREE BEGGARS	19
WITH HIS OLD THOUGHTS, KING GUAIRE WENT • • • • • • •			296	THREE BEGGARS	26
AND WHEN OLD GUAIRE CAME AND STOOD • • • • • • • •			297	THREE BEGGARS	54
GUARD					
PRAYERS FOR THE LAND. O BRAHMA, GUARD IN SLEEP • • • •			75	ANASHU VIJAYA	85
AND THROUGH THAT NEW BLADE'S GUARD THE OLD BLADE BROKE,			110	CUCHULAIN SEA	66
THOSE THAT I GUARD I DO NOT LOVE! • • • • • • • • •			328	IRISH AIRMAN	4
GOD GUARD ME FROM THOSE THOUGHTS MEN THINK • • • • • •			553	PRAYER OLD AGE	1
STAND WE ON GUARD OATH-BOUND! • • • • • • • • • •			636	BLACK TOWER	26
GUARDED	SEE DRAGON-GUARDED				
GUARDED! GRIFFITH STARING IN HYSTERICAL PRIDE! • • • •			601	GALLERY REVIS	4
BEFORE HIM ONE WELL GUARDED, WITH BOUND HANDS! • • • •			709	FERENCZ RENYI	10
GUARD-HOUSE					
AND HURRIED TO THE GUARD-HOUSE DOOR. • • • • • • • •			725	LEGEND	16
GUARDIAN					
THEY ARE THE FLOWERS' GUARDIAN SPRIGHTS! • • • • • •			666	ISLE STAT II 3	18
GUARDLESS					
• • • AND GUARDLESS THE SACRED CAIRN AND THE RATH, • • •			58	OISIN 3	163
GUARDS					
GO TO THE GUARDS OF THE HEAVENLY FOLD • • • • • • •			141	EVERLAST VOICE	2
GUARDSMEN'S					
THE GUARDSMEN'S DROWSY CHARGERS WOULD NOT PRANCE. • • •			429	NINETEEN 19	24
GUARIMOND					
IT IS THE SHEPHERD GUARIMOND, WHO LOVETH WELL • • • • •			661	ISLE STAT II 1	53
YOUNG GUARIMOND HE TELLS THEM O'ER AND O'ER, • • • • •			661	ISLE STAT II 1	56
GUERDON					
A GUERDON OF DEEP-ROOTED PAIN, • • • • • • • • • •			668	ISLE STAT II 3	59
SORROW THAT GIVES FOR GUERDON LIBERTY, • • • • • • •			686	DRAWING-ROOM	6
SORROW, THAT GIVES FOR GUERDON LIBERTY, • • • • • • •			734	QUATRAIN APHOR	6
GUESS					
OR ARCHIMEDES' GUESS, • • • • • • • • • • • •			784	WOMANS BEAUTY	12
GUEST					
• • • WHEN THERE ENTERS THE STRONGLY ARMED GUEST! • • •			62	OISIN 3	210
IT SPEEDS THE PARTING GUEST. • • • • • • • • • •			434	YOUTH AND AGE	4
GUIDE					
UPON THE WIND, AND GUIDE MINE ARROW'S COURSE. • • • • •			657	ISLE STAT I 3	62
GUIDED					
THE MAN IS GONE WHO GUIDED YE, UNWEARY, • • • • • •			738	MOURN THEN ON	3
GUIDES					
AND HER GUIDES ARE ANGELS SEVEN, • • • • • • • • •			125	CATHLEEN PARA	V 15
THE MOOR-HEN GUIDES UPON THE STREAM, • • • • • • • •			424	ROAD AT DOOR	12
HE GUIDES YE FROM THE TOMB! • • • • • • • • • •			738	MOURN THEN ON	14
GUIDING	SEE SHEEP-GUIDING				
ALL CHOICE, AND GIVE TO CHANCE FOR GUIDING CHANCE • • •			656	ISLE STAT I 3	39
FOR GUIDING OF THE GODS. THE SACRED BLOOM • • • • •			656	ISLE STAT I 3	41

		PAGE	TITLE	LINE

GUIDING   (CONTINUED)
FICKLE THE GUIDING HIS ARROW SHALL FIND!   . . . . . .   657 ISLE STAT I 3   66
GUIDO
THE MAN THAT LAPO AND THAT GUIDO KNEW?   . . . . . .   368 EGO DOMINUS   26
BEING MOCKED BY GUIDO FOR HIS LECHEROUS LIFE, ...   369 EGO DOMINUS   33
GUIDOBALDO
AND GUIDOBALDO, WHEN HE MADE   . . . .   287 TO WEALTHY MAN   14
GUILE
REWORDING IN MELODIOUS GUILE   . . . .   66 HAPPY SHEPHERD   39
REWORDING IN MELODIOUS GUILE   . . . .   66 HAPPY SHEPHERD V   39
IT CHARMED AWAY THE MERCHANT FROM HIS GUILE, ...   129 BOOK STORIES   5
THE DEMONS, WITH THEIR SUBTLE GUILE, ...   135 TWO TREES   22
I WILL DISSOLVE AWAY THE FAERIES' GUILE;   . . . . .   677 ISLE STAT II 3   282
HEARING THE FAR-OFF SINGING GUILE, AND GROANED, ...   693 MOSADA 1   88
HEARING THE FAR OFF SINGING GUILE AND GROANED, ...   693 MOSADA 1 V   88
GUILT
FOR GREAT OUR ERROR, GREAT OUR GUILT."   . . . . . .   43 OISIN 2   V 208H
BECAUSE THAT WERE A GUILT AGAINST HER KING, ...   280 TWO KINGS   V 74A
THEY CONVICTED US OF GUILT!   . . . .   476 EVA GORE-BOOTH   31
NONE SHARED OUR GUILT! NOR DID WE PLAY A PART   . . . .   542 PARN FUNERAL 1   22
GUILTY
TILL JUDGMENT HAS BEEN GIVEN, AND IF GUILTY, ...   280 TWO KINGS   74
GUINEAS
BEFORE YOU'LL PUT YOUR GUINEAS DOWN, ...   287 TO WEALTHY MAN   5
BEFORE YOU'VE PUT YOUR GUINEAS DOWN, ...   287 TO WEALTHY MAN V   5
GUINEVERE
THEREIN ARE MANY QUEENS LIKE BRANWEN AND GUINEVERE;   . . .   209 UNDER THE MOON   11
GULL
LIKE A GREY GULL UPON THE BREAST OF EACH.   . . . . .   223 SHADOW WATER B   24
THERE! THERE THEY COME! GULL, GANNET, OR DIVER, ...   233 SHADOW WATER B   244
A GREY GULL LOST ITS FEAR AND FLEW   . . . . . .   397 POLIT PRISONER   3
TO WATCH A WHITE GULL TAKE   . . . .   400 DEMON BEAST   24
GULLEON'S
FROM GULLEON'S PLACE OF PRIDE, ...   171 MAID QUIET   V 4B
GULLS
WHEN GREY GULLS FLIT ABOUT INSTEAD OF MEN, ...   292 TO A SHADE   6
WHEN GREY GULLS FLY ABOUT INSTEAD OF MEN, ...   292 TO A SHADE   V   6
GULPH
INTO A DESPERATE GULPH OF LOVE!   . . . .   7 OISIN 1   73
AND HURLED THEM IN THE GULPH OF SLEEP!   . . . . . .   83 MAD KING GOLL   22
GUN
AND THOUGH HE KEEP A DOG AND A GUN, ...   301 RUN PARADISE   12
AS THOUGH I'D A GUN   . . . .   359 TO A SQUIRREL   4
GUNNEL
AND DROP HIM FROM THE GUNNEL. I DARE NOT DO IT.   . . . .   222 SHADOW WATER B   15
GUNSHOT
AS THOUGH TO DIE BY GUNSHOT WERE   . . . .   424 ROAD AT DOOR   4
GUNSHOT OR A NOOSE, ...   620 JOHN KINSELLA   2
GUSHES
WHERE THE WANDERING WATER GUSHES   . . . .   88 STOLEN CHILD   28
GUSHING
ALL FLAME-LIKE GUSHING FROM THE HOLLOW STONES, ...   650 ISLE STAT I 1   129
GUST
I SHALL BE CARRIED IN THE GUST, COMMAND, ...   281 TWO KINGS   101
GUTTER
THE ABOUNDING GUTTER HAD BEEN HELICON   . . . . . .   398 LEADERS CROWD   6
GUTTERS
"HOW MAY A MORTAL WHOSE LIFE GUTTERS OUT   . . . . .   184 QUEEN MAEVE   85
GYMNASTS'
AND YONDER IN THE GYMNASTS' GARDEN THRIVES   . . . . .   446 COLONUS PRAISE   9
GYPSY
LIKE SOME LAST COURTIER AT A GYPSY CAMPING-PLACE   . . . .   314 FALLEN MAJESTY   3
LIKE SOME LAST COURTIER AT A GYPSY CAMPING PLACE   . . . .   314 FALLEN MAJESTY V   3
GYRE
THOUGH I HAD LONG PERNED IN THE GYRE, ...   400 DEMON BEAST   5
TURNING AND TURNING IN THE WIDENING GYRE   . . . . .   401 SECOND COMING   1
COME FROM THE HOLY FIRE, PERNE IN A GYRE, ...   408 SAIL BYZANTIUM   19
ON THAT UNFASHIONABLE GYRE AGAIN.   . . . .   565 GYRES   24
GYRES
ALL, ALL THOSE GYRES AND CUBES AND MIDNIGHT THINGS   . . .   469 HARUN RASHID   184
THOSE CONES AND CUBES AND GYRES, THOSE MIDNIGHT THINGS,   . .   469 HARUN RASHID   V 184
THERE ALL THE GYRES CONVERGE IN ONE, ...   557 THERE   3
THE GYRES .   . . .   564 GYRES   T
THE GYRES! THE GYRES! OLD ROCKY FACE, LOOK FORTH!   . . .   564 GYRES   1
THE GYRES! THE GYRES! OLD ROCKY FACE, LOOK FORTH!   . . .   564 GYRES   1
THAT HEAVENS HAD OPENED. GYRES RUN ON!   . . . . . .   639 BEN BULBEN   62
GYRING
GYRING, SPIRING TO AND FRO   . . . .   135 TWO TREES   15
NOW GYRING DOWN AND PERNING THERE   . . . .   400 DEMON BEAST   26
THIS WINDING, GYRING, SPIRING TREADMILL OF A STAIR   . . .   480 BLOOD AND MOON   17
HA
THE PHANTOMS COME! HA! HA! THEY COME, THEY COME!   . . .   694 MOSADA 1   97
THE PHANTOMS COME! HA! HA! THEY COME, THEY COME!   . . .   694 MOSADA 1   97
WHAT ROSEATE FINGERS! HA, HA! HA, HA, HA!   . . . .   720 WITCH VIVIEN   15
WHAT ROSEATE FINGERS! HA, HA! HA, HA, HA!   . . . .   720 WITCH VIVIEN   15
WHAT ROSEATE FINGERS! HA, HA! HA, HA, HA !   . . . .   720 WITCH VIVIEN   15
WHAT ROSEATE FINGERS! HA, HA! HA, HA, HA!   . . . .   720 WITCH VIVIEN   15
WHAT ROSEATE FINGERS! HA, HA! HA, HA, HA!   . . . .   720 WITCH VIVIEN   15
FIVE=SIX. HA, TIME!   . . . .   721 WITCH VIVIEN   42
HABILIMENT
THIS BEGGARLY HABILIMENT--   . . . .   539 MEETING   17

	PAGE	TITLE	LINE

HABIT
    THE ANCIENT HABIT STICKS, ...   431 NINETEEN 19   74
    LIKE MEN WHO LIVE BY HABIT. EVERY DAY . . . .   463 HARUN RASHID   56
    NO PLEASING HABIT ENDS, ...   621 JOHN KINSELLA   30
    PIERCED THROUGH, CHATTERING FROM HABIT IN THE SUN, . . .   664 ISLE STAT II 2   53
HABITS
    TO BRIBE OR THREAT; HABITS THAT MADE OLD WRONG . . .   428 NINETEEN 19   11
HABITUAL
    THE HABITUAL CONTENT OF EACH WITH EACH . . . .   258 KING NO KING   15
HACK
    BASALTIC PILLARS MARRED WITH HEW AND HACK . . . . .   31 OISIN 2   V   30
HADES
    CAN LIKE THE COCKS OF HADES CROW, ...   498 BYZANTIUM   20
HADES'
    FOR HADES' BOBBIN BOUND IN MUMMY-CLOTH . . . .   497 BYZANTIUM   11
    FOR HADES' BOBBIN BOUND IN MUMMY CLOTH . . . .   497 BYZANTIUM   V   11
HAG
    WHETHER TO MAID OR HAG! . . . .   525 DANCING DAYS   22
HAIL
    HAIL! HAIL, MY ANASHUYA. NO! BE STILL. . . . .   71 ANASHU VIJAYA   11
    HAIL! HAIL, MY ANASHUYA. NO! BE STILL. . . . .   71 ANASHU VIJAYA   11
    HAIL! HAIL, MY ANASHUYA. NAY; BE STILL. . . . . . .   71 ANASHU VIJAYA   V   11
    HAIL! HAIL, MY ANASHUYA. NAY; BE STILL. . . . . . .   71 ANASHU VIJAYA   V   11
    MIRRORED IN STREAMS THAT NEITHER HAIL NOR RAIN . . .   184 QUEEN MAEVE   89
    BY RIVERS WHERE NOR RAIN NOR HAIL HAS DIMMED . . . .   184 QUEEN MAEVE   V   87
    MIRRORED IN WATERS THAT NOR HAIL NOR RAIN . . . . .   184 QUEEN MAEVE   V   89
    AND PINCHES AMONG HAIL AND SNOW? . . . .   191 BAILE AILLINN   46
    OF THE FOUL WEATHER, HAIL AND RAIN, ...   424 ROAD AT DOOR   9
    I HAIL THE SUPERHUMAN! . . . .   497 BYZANTIUM   15
    THEIR SHEEP IN ARCADY, NASCHINA, HAIL! . . . .   649 ISLE STAT I 1   119
    NASCHINA, HAIL! MOST FAIR OF ALL WHO GRAZE . . . . .   649 ISLE STAT I 1   120
    THEIR SHEEP IN ARCADY, NASCHINA, HAIL! . . . .   649 ISLE STAT I 1   121
    NASCHINA, HAIL! I'D DRIVE THY WOOLLY SHEEP, ...   649 ISLE STAT I 1   122
HAILED
    SHOUTED, AND HAILED HIM! HE HUNG THERE A STAR, . . .   36 OISIN 2   107
    SHOUTED AND HAILED HIM. STILL HE HUNG CONTENT, . . .   36 OISIN 2   V   107
HAIR   SEE HORSE-HAIR
    THE HORSEMEN WITH THEIR FLOATING HAIR, ...   2 OISIN 1   7
    WERE LOLLING THEIR TONGUES, AND THE SILKEN HAIR . . .   2 OISIN 1   V   7S
    A CITRON COLOUR GLOOMED IN HER HAIR, ...   3 OISIN 1   24
    AND PEARLY WHITE HIS WELL-GROOMED HAIR. . . . . . .   3 OISIN 1   V   7CC
    HER HAIR WAS OF A CITRON TINCTURE. . . . .   3 OISIN 1   V   24
    WHERE ARE YOU WITH YOUR LONG ROUGH HAIR? . . . . . .   11 OISIN 1   126
    WHERE ARE YE WITH YOUR LONG ROUGH HAIR? . . . . . .   11 OISIN 1   V   126
    WITH QUENCHLESS GAZE AND FLUTTERING HAIR. . . . . .   12 OISIN 1   145
    AND WITH QUENCHLESS EYES AND FLUTTERING HAIR . . . .   12 OISIN 1   V   144
    WOVEN INTO HER HAIR, BEFORE DARK TOWERS . . . . . .   30 OISIN 2   22
    IN NIAM'S HAIR--WHEN ROSE A WORLD OF TOWERS . . . .   30 OISIN 2   V   22
    WOVE IN HER FLOWER-LIKE HAIR, BEFORE DARK TOWERS . .   30 OISIN 2   V   22
    AND IN THE SHADOW OF MY HAIR LIE HID, ...   33 OISIN 2   66
    SHOUTED. WITH FIRE OF HAIR ABOUT HER SWIRLED, . . .   38 OISIN 2   V   134
    AND HUNG WITH SLIME, AND WHISPERING IN HIS HAIR, . . .   43 OISIN 2   216
    HUNG ROUND WITH SLIME, AND WHISPERING IN HIS HAIR, . . .   43 OISIN 2   V   216
    CAME NOW THE SLIDING OF TEARS AND SWEEPING OF MIST-COLD HAIR,   47 OISIN 3   7
    CAME NOW THE SLIDING OF TEARS AND SWEEPING OF MIST COLD HAIR,   47 OISIN 3   V   7
    AND WRAPPING MY FACE IN MY HAIR, ...   59 OISIN 3   177
    WITH MINGLING HAIR, AND PLAY UPON ONE LUTE. . . . .   71 ANASHU VIJAYA   10
    WITH ALL YOUR WHIRLING HAIR, AND DROP MANY AN AZURE TEAR.   73 ANASHU VIJAYA   46
    WITH ALL YOUR WHIRLING HAIR, AND DROP THROUGH SPACE AN AZURE TEAR.   73 ANASHU VIJAYA   V   46
    WITH ALL YOUR WHIRLING HAIR, AND DROP TEAR UPON AZURE TEAR.   73 ANASHU VIJAYA   V   46
    WITH ALL OUR WHIRLING HAIR, AND DROP MANY AN AZURE TEAR.   73 ANASHU VIJAYA   V   46
    THEIR HAIR ALONG THE MOUNTAINS ROLLED AND FILLED . . .   74 ANASHU VIJAYA   71
    IN BOSOM AND HAIR. "AH, DO NOT MOURN," HE SAID, . .   80 EPHEMERA   20
    IN BOSOM AND HAIR. THEN HE: "LET US NOT MOURN . . .   80 EPHEMERA   V   20
    ORCHIL SHAKES OUT HER LONG DARK HAIR . . . .   85 MAD KING GOLL   62
    WHOM THE DEVILS HAVE BY THE HAIR. . . . .   92 FATHER OHART   14
    LOOK ON MY THIN GREY HAIR AND HOLLOW CHEEKS . . . .   103 FERGUS DRUID   23
    AND SAID, CASTING ASIDE HIS DRAGGLED HAIR, ...   105 CUCHULAIN SEA   V   3
    AND SHE, TO WIN HIM, HIS GREY HAIR CARESSED! . . . .   110 CUCHULAIN SEA   73
    WITH BLOWN, SPRAY-DABBLED HAIR GATHER AT HAND. . . .   114 ROSE OF BATTLE   6
    THE THRONGS WITH BLOWN WET HAIR ARE GATHERING NEAR. .   114 ROSE OF BATTLE   V   6
    THE LONG HAIR IS ON HER FACE! . . . .   124 CATHLEEN PARA   V   10
    THE LONG HAIR SHADOWS HER FACE! . . . .   124 CATHLEEN PARA   10
    REMEMBERING ALL THAT SHAKEN HAIR . . . .   135 TWO TREES   17
    WHEN LOOKING ON THEIR SHAKEN HAIR, ...   135 TWO TREES   V   17
    CAOILTE TOSSING HIS BURNING HAIR, ...   140 HOSTING SIDHE   3
    OUR CHEEKS ARE PALE, OUR HAIR IS UNBOUND, ...   140 HOSTING SIDHE   7
    CAOILTE TOSSING HIS BURNING HAIR, ...   141 HOSTING SIDHE   15
    AND DREAMED OF THE LONG DIM HAIR . . . .   144 HOST OF AIR   7
    OF HER LONG DIM HAIR. . . . .   145 HOST OF AIR   28
    WERE DROWNED IN HER LONG DIM HAIR. . . . .   145 HOST OF AIR   36
    WITH APPLE BLOSSOM IN HER HAIR . . . .   150 WANDER AENGUS   14
    WITH APPLE-BLOSSOM IN HER HAIR . . . .   150 WANDER AENGUS   V   14
    WITH APPLE BLOSSOMS IN HER HAIR, ...   150 WANDER AENGUS   V   14
    THE SHADOWY BLOSSOM OF MY HAIR . . . .   152 HEART OF WOMAN   7
    O HIDING HAIR AND DEWY EYES, ...   152 HEART OF WOMAN   9
    PALE BROWS, STILL HANDS AND DIM HAIR, ...   152 LOSS OF LOVE   1
    PALE BROW, STILL HANDS, AND DIM HAIR, ...   152 LOSS OF LOVE   V   1

351

HAIR (CONTINUED)

OVER MY HEART, AND YOUR HAIR FALL OVER MY BREAST, . . . 154 BELOVED PEACE   10
OVER MY HEART, AND YOUR HAIR FALL ABOUT MY BREAST . . . 154 BELOVED PEACE   V   10
PASSION-DIMMED EYES AND LONG HEAVY HAIR . . . . 155 REPROVE CURLEW   4
WOVEN BY LADIES IN THEIR HAIR, ... 156 FORGOT BEAUTY   10
FASTEN YOUR HAIR WITH A GOLDEN PIN, ... 157 BELOVED RHYMES   1
AND BIND UP YOUR LONG HAIR AND SIGH; . . . . 158 BELOVED RHYMES   8
OF A FLUTTER OF FLOWER-LIKE HAIR; . . . . 160 CAP AND BELLS   18
UNDER A CLOUD OF HER HAIR, ... 160 CAP AND BELLS   26
ON A FLUTTER OF FLOWER-LIKE HAIR; . . . . 160 CAP AND BELLS   V   18
AND HER HAIR WAS A FOLDED FLOWER . . . . 161 CAP AND BELLS   35
CRUMPLE THE ROSE IN YOUR HAIR; . . . . 162 ASKS FORGIVE   4
CRUSH THE ROSE IN YOUR HAIR, ... 162 ASKS FORGIVE   V   4
WITH YOUR DIM HEAVY HAIR, ... 163 ASKS FORGIVE   22
WITH YOUR DIM SHADOWY HAIR, ... 163 ASKS FORGIVE   V   22
THEIR HEADS ON YOUR KNEES, AND DROWN THEIR EYES WITH YOUR   163 VALLEY LOVERS   6
    HAIR,
HALF CLOSE YOUR EYELIDS, LOOSEN YOUR HAIR, ... 166 EVIL OF BELOV   1
WE WILL BEND DOWN AND LOOSEN OUR HAIR OVER YOU, ... 172 TRAV PASSION   6
BUT KNOW YOUR HAIR WAS BOUND AND WOUND . . . . 176 BELOVED DEAD   9
BUT KNOW YOUR HAIR WAS BOUND AND BOUND . . . . 176 BELOVED DEAD   V   9
MAY NOT LIE ON THE BREAST NOR HIS LIPS ON THE HAIR . . . 177 PAST GREATNESS   9
WOULD NOT LIE ON THE BREAST, OR HIS LIPS ON THE HAIR, . . 177 PAST GREATNESS V   9
HE HAD RAGGED LONG GRASS-COLOURED HAIR; . . . . 190 BAILE AILLINN   26
HE HAD RAGGED, LONG GRASS-YELLOW HAIR; . . . . 190 BAILE AILLINN   V   26
TO STIR THEIR COVERLET AND THEIR HAIR, ... 197 BAILE AILLINN   186
"YOUR WELL-BELOVED'S HAIR HAS THREADS OF GREY, ... 199 FOLLY COMFORT   2
"YOUR WELL-BELOVED'S HAIR HAS A THREAD OF GREY, ... 199 FOLLY COMFORT   V   2
"YOUR WELL BELOVED'S HAIR HAS THREADS OF GREY, ... 199 FOLLY COMFORT   V   2
O MY SHARE OF THE WORLD, O YELLOW HAIR; . . . . 211 RAGGED WOOD   11
SWEET WITH ALL MUSIC, OUT OF HIS LONG HAIR, ... 219 HARP OF AENGUS   8
IT WAS IN ALL HIS BATTLES, I WILL SPREAD MY HAIR, . . . 242 SHADOW WATER B   413
BEND LOWER, THAT I MAY COVER YOU WITH MY HAIR, ... 251 SHADOW WATER B   613
I AM LOOPED IN THE LOOPS OF HER HAIR, ... 268 BROWN PENNY   8
YOU'D CRY, "SOME WOMAN'S YELLOW HAIR . . . . 290 SEPTEMBER 1913   28
WHILE HE'D RUMMAGED RAGS AND HAIR, ... 299 THREE HERMITS   29
THE GOLD INTO MY HAIR, ... 309 PLAYER QUEEN   18
THE GOLD UPON MY HAIR, ... 309 PLAYER QUEEN   V   18
AND TUMBLE OUT YOUR HAIR . . . . 312 CHILD DANCING   4
WHAT MADE US DREAM THAT HE COULD COMB GREY HAIR? . . . 327 ROBERT GREGORY   88
HAIR SPREAD ON THE WIND THEY MADE; . . . . 332 ROUND TOWER   22
THERE IS GREY IN YOUR HAIR. . . . . 355 BROKEN DREAMS   1
AS IF THE HAIR STOOD UP ON MY HEAD. . . . . 358 PRESENCES   2
SHE LIES, HER LOVELY PITEOUS HEAD AMID DULL RED HAIR . . 362 HER COURTESY   2
OF DULL RED HAIR WAS FLOWING . . . . 363 DOLLS DRAWINGS   6
ATHENE TAKES ACHILLES BY THE HAIR, ... 374 PHASES OF MOON   45
GO PLUCK ATHENE BY THE HAIR! . . . . 386 ROBARTES DANCE   19
AMONG THE STARRY EDDIES OF HER HAIR . . . . 390 IMAGE PAST   27
THAT HER HAIR STREAMS UPON THE WIND, ... 390 IMAGE PAST   40
AND HAD THAT COLOUR UPON CHEEK OR HAIR, ... 444 SCHOOL CHILDR   22
THE HEAVENLY CIRCUIT! BERENICE'S HAIR; . . . . 483 VERONIC NAPKIN   1
AND NOT YOUR YELLOW HAIR." . . . . 492 ANNE GREGORY   6
AND NOT MY YELLOW HAIR." . . . . 492 ANNE GREGORY   12
AND NOT YOUR YELLOW HAIR." . . . . 492 ANNE GREGORY   18
AND BIDS MY HAIR STAND UP? . . . . 499 MOTHER OF GOD   15
AND MAKES MY HAIR STAND UP? . . . . 499 MOTHER OF GOD   V   15
BUT WHEN HE WOUND HER COAL-BLACK HAIR . . . . 514 JANE GROWN OLD   3
BERENICE'S BURNING HAIR, ... 519 HER DREAM   8
A BARGAIN WITH THAT HAIR. . . . . 520 HIS BARGAIN   11
THAT HIS HAIR IS BEAUTIFUL, ... 531 FATHER CHILD   7
ENTANGLED IN MY HAIR . . . . 532 FIRST CONFESS   2
WITH LOOSENED HAIR OR FOREHEADS GRIEF-DISTRAUGHT, . . . 537 HER VISION   18
WITH LOOSENED HAIR OR FOREHEADS GRIEF DISTRAUGHT, . . . 537 HER VISION   V   18
BECAUSE HE HAD FEATHERS INSTEAD OF HAIR. . . . . . . 550 SEVERED HEAD   20
OH, MORE DARK THY GLEAMING HAIR IS . . . . 647 ISLE STAT I 1   51
WITH STREAMING HAIR AS WANDERING LIGHTS . . . . 667 ISLE STAT II 3   19
E'EN THEN, BEFORE HER SHEPHERD HAIR . . . . 668 ISLE STAT II 3   54
BUT, FOR A BOY, HOW LONG THINE HAIR HAS GROWN! . . . . 670 ISLE STAT II 3   104
OVER HER SPOTTED FLESH AND FLYING HAIR . . . . 687 TWO TITANS   15
STREWING UPON THE ROCKS THEIR STEEL-BLUE HAIR, ... 687 TWO TITANS   30
HER HEAD CAST BACKWARD IN HER UNLOOSED HAIR. . . . . . 701 MOSADA 3   67
GOLD UNTO GOLD, A GLEAM IN ITS LONG HAIR, ... 720 WITCH VIVIEN   3
MY FINGERS FEEL HIS AMBER HAIR. . . . . 723 GIRLS SONG A   8
FLED FROM HIS BROW WHERE THE HAIR WAS GREY; . . . . . 728 PRIEST FAIRY   10
AND HIS HAIR WAS AS YELLOW AS WAVING WHEAT. . . . . . 729 PRIEST FAIRY   26
BRUSHING BACK HIS YELLOW HAIR; . . . . 729 PRIEST FAIRY   38
AND HIS HAIR WAS AS DARK AS A PLOVER'S EYE. . . . . . 729 PRIEST FAIRY   46
BOWS THE BEDOUIN'S WHITENING HAIR-- . . . . 733 STREET DANCERS   45
THEIR HAIR MINGLES ON SOME STRINGED INSTRUMENT, ... 752 SHADOW WATER A   123
AND A COLD WIND IS BLOWING IN MY HAIR. . . . . 761 SHADOW WATER A   277
I HAVE WET THIS BRAID OF HAIR WITH TEARS WHILE ASLEEP. . 762 SHADOW WATER A   294
SWEET WITH ALL MUSIC, OUT OF HIS LONG HAIR, ... 762 SHADOW WATER A   303
COVER THEIR FACES WITH THEIR HAIR AND WEEP. . . . . . 764 SHADOW WATER A   333
THAT I WOULD MIX WITH YOURS, AND IN THIS HAIR . . . . 765 SHADOW WATER A   351
AND MINGLING HAIR FALL FROM THE FIERY BOUGHS, ... 765 SHADOW WATER A   368
LOOK ON THIS BODY AND THIS HEAVY HAIR; . . . . 767 SHADOW WATER A   397
MY LOVE SHAKES OUT HER HAIR UPON THE STREAMS . . . . 768 SHADOW WATER A   416
BEND LOWER, THAT I MAY COVER YOU WITH MY HAIR, ... 769 SHADOW WATER A   429
I HIDE YOU WITH MY HAIR, THAT WE MAY GAZE . . . . . . 769 SHADOW WATER A V   429

HAIR-DYE

"BUT I CAN GET A HAIR-DYE . . . . 492 ANNE GREGORY   7

```
                                        PAGE    TITLE            LINE
HAIRED    SEE RED-HAIRED FLOATING-HAIRED WHITE-HAIRED LONG-HAIRED FAIR-HAIRED GREY-HAIRED
HAIRS
     HAIRS SPREAD ON THE WIND THEY MADE:  . . . . . .   332 ROUND TOWER      V   22
     GREY HAIRS AND CRUTCHES, CRUTCHES AND GREY HAIRS,  . . .  721 WITCH VIVIEN        20
     GREY HAIRS AND CRUTCHES, CRUTCHES AND GREY HAIRS,  . . .  721 WITCH VIVIEN        20
HALCYON'S
     YON ARCHER, HE WHO HATH THE HALCYON'S WING . . . . . .  679 ISLE STAT II 3     316
     AMONG THE BOUGHS, BLUE AS THE HALCYON'S WING, . . . . .  683 SEEKER             38
     WITHIN THE WOODWAYS, BLUE AS THE HALCYON'S WING, . . . .  683 SEEKER          V   38
HALE
     TO THE HORN, AND HE BE HALE AND HEARTY. . . . . . .   243 SHADOW WATER B     447
     WHEN WE HALE MEN LIE STRETCHED IN SLUMBER . . . . .   636 BLACK TOWER         23
HALF
     OISIN, THOU ART HALF HEATHEN STILL: . . . . . .      4 OISIN 1         V   31
     WAS SLUMBERING HALF IN THE SEA-WAYS: . . . . . . .   26 OISIN 1            395
     HALF SLUMBERED WITH HIS SAFFRON BLAZE: . . . . . .   26 OISIN 1            395
     WAS SLUMBERING HALF IN THE SEA WAYS: . . . . . . .   26 OISIN 1         V  395
     ERE HALF THE SWIFT THINGS THAT SHE DREAMT ON WERE DONE,  28 OISIN 1         V  422
     HALF LOST IN VAPOUR, SHADOWS CALLED OUR NAMES, . . .   29 OISIN 2         V    3
     FLOATED IN ALL HER SINGING. HALF ENTRANCED . . . . .   30 OISIN 2         V   19
     HALF IN THE UNVESSELLED SEA, WE CLIMBED THE STAIR . . .   32 OISIN 2            47
     HALF IN THE UNVESSELLED SEA. WE'D MOUNTED FAR! . . .   32 OISIN 2         V   47
     HALF IN THE UNVESSELLED SEA, WE CLIMBED THE STAIRS . . .   32 OISIN 2         V   47
     HALF OPEN HIS EYES WERE, AND HELD ME, . . . . .      51 OISIN 3            65
     HALF WAKENING, WE LIFTED OUR EYELIDS, . . . . . .   54 OISIN 3           100
     LATER A SOUND CAME, HALF LOST IN THE SOUND OF A SHORE FAR  57 OISIN 3           155
        AWAY,
     LIE NOW HALF HIDDEN UNDER PENDULOUS LIDS, . . . . .   79 EPHEMERA        V    2
     A THIN GREY MAN HALF LOST IN GATHERING NIGHT. . . . .  102 FERGUS DRUID        7
     FOR HALF HIS FLOCK WERE IN THEIR BEDS, . . . . .     132 FR GILLIGAN         3
     FOR HALF HIS FLOCK LAY IN THEIR BEDS . . . . . .     132 FR GILLIGAN     V    3
     ROOTS HALF HIDDEN UNDER SNOWS, . . . . . . . .       135 TWO TREES          27
     AND ROOTS HALF HIDDEN UNDER SNOWS . . . . . . .      135 TWO TREES       V   27
     AND CLAP THEIR HANDS TOGETHER, AND HALF CLOSE THEIR EYES,  146 UNAPPEAS HOST       2
     BELOVED, LET YOUR EYES HALF CLOSE, AND YOUR HEART BEAT .  154 BELOVED PEACE       9
     THRONE OVER THRONE WHERE IN HALF SLEEP, . . . . .   156 FORGOT BEAUTY      22
     WITH HER CLOUD-PALE EYELIDS HALF COVERING HER DIM EYES:  163 VALLEY LOVERS   V    4
     HALF CLOSE YOUR EYELIDS, LOOSEN YOUR HAIR, . . . . .  166 EVIL OF BELOV       1
     TO GATHER THE HALF OF YOUR BLESSEDNESS . . . . . .  167 BLESSED             7
     "WITH THE SECRETS OF GOD HALF BLIND, . . . . . .    168 BLESSED            26
     OF NIGHT AND LIGHT AND THE HALF LIGHT, . . . . .    176 CLOTHS HEAVEN   V    4
     FLICKERING ''ITH ASH AND HAZEL, BUT HALF SHOWED . . .  180 QUEEN MAEVE        12
     BUT THAT GREAT QUEEN, WHO MORE THAN HALF THE NIGHT . . .  180 QUEEN MAEVE        16
     HALF CRAZY WITH THE THOUGHT, SHE TOO HAS WEPT! . . .  186 QUEEN MAEVE       140
     HE HAD HALF A CLOAK TO KEEP HIM DRY, . . . . . .    190 BAILE AILLINN      29
     IF ANYBODY HALF AS FAIR . . . . . . . . . .         191 BAILE AILLINN      53
     IS BUT HALF YOURS: HE KNEADED IN THE DOUGH . . . .   201 OLD MEMORY          6
     HEAVY LIKE STONE, THEIR WISDOM BEING HALF SILENCE. . .  218 WOODS OF COOLE     26
     OF THE EVER-LIVING HALF SO DANGEROUS . . . . . .    224 SHADOW WATER B     46
     MORE MIGHTY THAN THE STARS HALF TROUBLED ME, . . . .  237 SHADOW WATER B    332
     AND I'VE BUT HALF? O NO! AND IF THERE IS, . . . .   245 SHADOW WATER B    475
     IF THERE BE HALF A HUNDRED MORE, WHAT MATTER? . . . .  245 SHADOW WATER B    476
     NO, NO, NOR HALF A THOUGHT: BUT DO NOT SPEAK. . . .   245 SHADOW WATER B    478
     I HALF REMEMBER. IT HAS BEEN IN MY DREAMS. . . . .   251 SHADOW WATER B    606
     HALF LION, HALF CHILD, IS AT PEACE. . . . . . .     260 UNWORTH PRAISE     20
     HALF LION, HALF CHILD, IS AT PEACE. . . . . . .     260 UNWORTH PRAISE     20
     AND HALF THE KINGS, BEFORE SUNDOWN . . . . . .      273 GREY ROCK          69
     AND HALF HIS KINGS, BEFORE SUNDOWN . . . . . .      273 GREY ROCK       V   69
     IN THE HALF LIGHT, AND RUNS TO ITS OWN DOOR . . . .  279 TWO KINGS       V  45C
     BUT IF NOT LIVING, HALF THE WORLD IS LOST." . . . .  280 TWO KINGS       V   86
     HAD HALF AWAKENED SOME OLD MEMORY-- . . . . . .     284 TWO KINGS         172
     HAD HALF WAKENED SOME OLD MEMORY, . . . . . . .     284 TWO KINGS       V  172
     SO SLEPT FOR HALF A YEAR OR SO: . . . . . . .       305 HOUR DAWN          67
     AND SLEPT FOR HALF A YEAR OR SO! . . . . . . .      305 HOUR DAWN       V   67
     EVEN A HALF HOUR'S NOTHINGNESS, . . . . . . .       305 HOUR DAWN       V   70
     SO PERILOUS THAT HALF THE ASTONISHED MEET . . . . .  326 ROBERT GREGORY     61
     THERE'S NOTHING OF HIM LEFT BUT HALF A SCORE . . . .  341 SHEP GOATHERD      56
     A MAN CONFUSEDLY IN A HALF DREAM . . . . . . .      351 HER PRAISE          8
     THOUGH PLAY IS BUT HALF DONE-- . . . . . . .        364 END OF DAY          7
     WE ARE BUT CRITICS, OR BUT HALF CREATE, . . . . .   368 EGO DOMINUS        15
     FROM DOORED AND WINDOWED CLIFF, OR HALF UPTURNED . . .  368 EGO DOMINUS        30
     FROM THE FIRST CRESCENT TO THE HALF, THE DREAM . . .  373 PHASES OF MOON     36
     BECAUSE YOU ARE FORGOTTEN: HALF OUT OF LIFE, . . . .  376 PHASES OF MOON     96
     TO MAKE IT LINGER HALF A DAY. . . . . . . .         401 DEMON BEAST        42
     ONCE MORE THE STORM IS HOWLING, AND HALF HID . . . .  403 FOR DAUGHTER        1
     HALF DRESSED IN NATIONAL UNIFORM, . . . . . . .     424 ROAD AT DOOR        7
     THE HALF READ WISDOM OF DAEMONIC IMAGES, . . . . .  427 PHANTOM HATRED V   39
     THE WINGS HALF SPREAD FOR FLIGHT, . . . . . . .     430 NINETEEN 19        65
     THE HALF IMAGINED, THE HALF WRITTEN PAGE. . . . . .  431 NINETEEN 19     V   83
     THE HALF IMAGINED, THE HALF WRITTEN PAGE. . . . . .  431 NINETEEN 19     V   83
     AND THAT ALONE, YET I, BEING DRIVEN HALF INSANE . . .  442 BLACK CENTAUR       6
     HALF RUNNING, DROPPED AT THE FIRST RIDGE OF THE DESERT  468 HARUN RASHID      155
     I THOUGHT HIM HALF A LUNATIC, HALF KNAVE, . . . . .  473 ALL SOUL NIGHT     64
     I THOUGHT HIM HALF A LUNATIC, HALF KNAVE, . . . . .  473 ALL SOUL NIGHT     64
     AND I GROW HALF CONTENTED TO BE BLIND! . . . . .    473 ALL SOUL NIGHT     70
     HALF DEAD AT THE TOP. . . . . . . . . . .           480 BLOOD AND MOON     12
     HALF DEAD AT THE TOP? NO MATTER WHAT I SAID, . . . .  482 BLOOD AND MOON     48
     AND HALF A DOZEN IN FORMATION THERE, . . . . . .    489 COOLE PARK 29      20
     IS HALF ALL GLITTERING FLAME AND HALF ALL GREEN . . .  500 VACILLATION        12
     IS HALF ALL GLITTERING FLAME AND HALF ALL GREEN . . .  500 VACILLATION        12
```

353

	PAGE	TITLE		LINE

HALF   (CONTINUED)
```
    AND HALF IS HALF AND YET IS ALL THE SCENE:  . . . . . .    500 VACILLATION          14
    AND HALF IS HALF AND YET IS ALL THE SCENE:  . . . . . .    500 VACILLATION          14
    AND HALF AND HALF CONSUME WHAT THEY RENEW,  . . . . . .    500 VACILLATION          15
    AND HALF AND HALF CONSUME WHAT THEY RENEW,  . . . . . .    500 VACILLATION          15
    IS HALF ALL GLITTERING FLAME AND HALF A GREEN  . . . . .   500 VACILLATION      V   12
    IS HALF ALL GLITTERING FLAME AND HALF A GREEN  . . . . .   500 VACILLATION      V   12
    HALF TURNED AND FIXED A GLAZING EYE ON MINE,  . . . . .    537 HER VISION           26
    LOOKED HALF ASLEEP ALL DAY.  . . . . . . . .    570 THREE BUSHES         34
    HAD TRAVELLED HALF THE NIGHT.  . . . . . . . .    585 ORAHILLY             17
    CASEMENT UPON TRIAL, HALF HIDDEN BY THE BARS,  . . . . .   601 GALLERY REVIS         3
    HALF LEGENDARY MEN.  . . . . . . . . . . .    605 YOU CONTENT          16
    SO WHEN I TAKE ON HALF A SCORE .  . . . . . .    605 SONGS BURDEN 1        7
    SOME FEW HALF WAKE AND HALF RENEW THEIR CHOICE,  . . . .   622 HOUND VOICE           6
    SOME FEW HALF WAKE AND HALF RENEW THEIR CHOICE,  . . . .   622 HOUND VOICE           6
    I HAVE FOUND NOTHING HALF SO GOOD .  . . . . . .    624 APPARITIONS           9
    AS MY LONG-PLANNED HALF SOLITUDE, .  . . . . . .    624 APPARITIONS          10
    WHERE I CAN SIT UP HALF THE NIGHT .  . . . . . .    624 APPARITIONS          11
    AS MY LONG PLANNED HALF SOLITUDE, .  . . . . . .    624 APPARITIONS      V   10
    HALF LIT, SO FLAPT THE WINGS ACROSS THE LAKE--  . . . .    659 ISLE STAT II 1       17
    A STAR-LIT RAPIER, HALF BLOOD-DARK, .  . . . . .    671 ISLE STAT II 3      125
    THEY SAY THE WISH ITSELF IS HALF THE SIN:  . . . . .    692 MOSADA 1             48
    HALF ASLEEP THE OLD COW CROPS, . . . . . . .    706 DAWN-SONG            20
    HALF HID.  HE BRINGS THE PEASANT'S ONLY KIN, . . . . .    711 FERENCZ RENYI        50
    HALF DIZZY WITH THE LIGHTNING THERE RUNS A GATHERING BAND--  718 PHANTOM SHIP          9
    NOW HALF DIZZY WITH THE LIGHTNING THERE RUNS A GATHERING     718 PHANTOM SHIP     V    9
      BAND:
    "AND HALF FORGET THIS BED OF STRAW  . . . . . .    739 EARL PAUL             5
    IF WHEN THE BATTLE IS HALF WON,  . . . . . . .    743 DANAAN QUICK         19
    WHEN SOMETHING, HALF A LAMB AND HALF A GOAT,  . . . . .    747 SHADOW WATER A V     11
    WHEN SOMETHING, HALF A LAMB AND HALF A GOAT,  . . . . .    747 SHADOW WATER A V     11
    I SPARED HER HANDMAID, TOO: BUT HALF WAY HITHER  . . . .   755 SHADOW WATER A V    167
    I AM HALF BLINDED.  I AM HALF BLINDED, TOO.  . . . . .    759 SHADOW WATER A V    235
    I AM HALF BLINDED.  I AM HALF BLINDED, TOO.  . . . . .    759 SHADOW WATER A V    235
    WERE HE ANYTHING BY HALF, .  . . . . . . . .    772 SONG DEIRDRE 1       13
HALF-AWAKENED
    WHERE BUT HALF-AWAKENED ADAM  . . . . . . . .    638 BEN BULBEN           47
HALF-CLOSED
    PACING WITH HALF-CLOSED EYELIDS IN A SUNNY SPOT  . . . .   366 HER COURAGE           7
    THE QUIVERING HALF-CLOSED EYELIDS, THE RAGS OF CLOUD OR     427 PHANTOM HATRED       26
      OF LACE,
HALF-DEAD
    THE HALF-DEAD DRAGON WAS HER THOUGHT, . . . . . . .    385 ROBARTES DANCE        6
HALF-DECEIT
    INTO THE HALF-DECEIT OF SOME INTOXICANT . . . . . . .    429 NINETEEN 19          34
HALF-DONE
    THOUGH PLAY IS BUT HALF-DONE--  . . . . . . . .    364 END OF DAY       V    7
HALF-DRUNK
    HALF-DRUNK OR WHOLE-MAD SOLDIERY  . . . . . . .    791 REPRISALS            15
HALF-FLIES
    AND RUNS OR A WHILE HALF-FLIES .  . . . . . .    341 SHEP GOATHERD        64
    AND RUNS FOR A WHILE OR A WHILE HALF-FLIES . . . . . .    341 SHEP GOATHERD    V   64
HALF-FORGOTTEN
    OF HALF-FORGOTTEN INNOCENT OLD PLACES:  . . . . .    130 BOOK STORIES         22
    HELMETS, AND SWORDS, AND HALF-FORGOTTEN THINGS  . . . .    257 RECONCILIATION        6
HALF-HOUR'S
    EVEN A HALF-HOUR'S NOTHINGNESS, .  . . . . . .    305 HOUR DAWN            70
HALF-IMAGINED
    THE HALF-IMAGINED, THE HALF-WRITTEN PAGE:  . . . . .    431 NINETEEN 19          83
HALF-LEGENDARY
    HALF-LEGENDARY MEN.  . . . . . . . . . . .    605 YOU CONTENT      V   16
HALF-LEGGED
    TO VALUE BEER: NO HALF-LEGGED FOOL  . . . . . .    304 HOUR DAWN            52
HALF-LIGHT
    OF NIGHT AND LIGHT AND THE HALF-LIGHT, . . . . . . .    176 CLOTHS HEAVEN         4
HALF-LOST
    A THIN, GREY MAN, HALF-LOST IN GATHERING NIGHT. . . . .    102 FERGUS DRUID     V    7
HALF-LYING
    AND THEN, HALF-LYING ON THE CHAIR, .  . . . . .    132 FR GILLIGAN      V   13
HALF-MOUNTED
    COME OLD, NECESSITOUS, HALF-MOUNTED MAN:  . . . . .    412 TOWER                90
HALFPENCE
    AND ADD THE HALFPENCE TO THE PENCE  . . . . . .    289 SEPTEMBER 1913        3
HALFPENNIES
    BY BIDDY'S HALFPENNIES HAVE LAIN .  . . . . . .    287 TO WEALTHY MAN        3
    WHO QUARRELS OVER HALFPENNIES . . . . . . . .    621 JOHN KINSELLA        33
HALF-PENNIES
    BY BIDDY'S HALF-PENNIES HAVE LAIN . . . . . . .    287 TO WEALTHY MAN   V    3
    WHO QUARRELS OVER HALF-PENNIES .  . . . . . .    621 JOHN KINSELLA    V   33
HALFPENNY
    THEY THREW A HALFPENNY INTO MY CAP, . . . . . . .    300 RUN PARADISE          2
HALF-READ
    THE HALF-READ WISDOM OF DAEMONIC IMAGES, . . . . . .    427 PHANTOM HATRED       39
    THE HALF-READ WISDOM OF DEMONIC IMAGES, . . . . . .    427 PHANTOM HATRED V     39
HALF-WAKENING
    HALF-WAKENING, WE LIFTED OUR EYELIDS, . . . . . .     54 OISIN 3          V  100
HALFWAY
    SWEETEN THE LITTLE HALFWAY HOUSE  . . . . . . .    567 LAPIS LAZULI     V   48
HALF-WAY
    SWEETENS THE LITTLE HALF-WAY HOUSE  . . . . . . .    567 LAPIS LAZULI         48
```

354

PAGE   TITLE   LINE

HALF-WRITTEN
    THE HALF-IMAGINED, THE HALF-WRITTEN PAGE: . . . . . .   431 NINETEEN 19   83
HALL
    THAN DOVES THAT MOANED ROUND EMAN'S HALL . . . . . .   3 OISIN 1   V 7EE
    AND PRAISE THEE IN MY WESTERN HALL." . . . .   8 OISIN 1   V   79
    THE FLOOR OF ALMHUIN'S HOSTING HALL . . . .   13 OISIN 1   156
    THE FLOOR OF EMAN'S DANCING HALL . . . .   13 OISIN 1   156
    THE FLOOR OF EMEN'S HOISTING HALL . . . .   13 OISIN 1   156
    THE FLOOR OF ALLEN'S HOSTING HALL . . . .   13 OISIN 1   V 156
    SHE BADE THEM BRING US TO THE HALL-- . . . .   16 OISIN 1   217
    WENT WE TO FIND THEIR PRINCE'S HALL-- . . . .   16 OISIN 1   V 217
    AND SWEPT OUT OF THE WATTLED HALL . . . .   20 OISIN 1   292
    NOT EVEN YOUR GOD COULD HAVE THROWN DOWN THAT HALL: . .   36 OISIN 2   109
    AND STOOD WITHIN THE HALL. A MISTY RAY . . . . . .   36 OISIN 2   V 104
    NOT E'EN THY GOD COULD HAVE THROWN DOWN THAT HALL: . .   36 OISIN 2   V 109
    UNDER THE DEEPEST SHADOWS OF THE HALL . . . . . .   37 OISIN 2   119
    OUT OF THE SEVENFOLD SEAS, BUILT THE DARK HALL . . . .   38 OISIN 2   131
    OUT OF THE SEVEN-FOLD SEAS, BUILT THE DARK HALL . . .   38 OISIN 2   V 131
    WITH A PALE LIGHT, I JOURNEYED ROUND THE HALL . . . .   39 OISIN 2   153
    OF MISTY DAWN: WHEN, CIRCLING ROUND THE HALL, . . .   39 OISIN 2   V 153
    THEN IN THAT HALL, LIT BY THE DIM SEA-SHINE, ...   41 OISIN 2   187
    THEN IN THAT HALL, LIT BY THE DIM SEA SHINE, ...   41 OISIN 2   V 187
    LIKE ROTTED FLESH, AND STONE BY STONE MY HALL . . . .   45 OISIN 2   V 236
    MINE WAS THE THRONE IN EMAN'S HALL, ...   81 MAD KING GOLL V   2
    MAEVE WALKED THROUGH THAT GREAT HALL, AND WITH A SIGH . 182 QUEEN MAEVE   62
    AND SAW WHERE IN THE MIDST OF THE GREAT HALL . . . . 279 TWO KINGS   60
    STAND UNDER THE ROUGH ROOF-TIMBERS OF THE HALL . . . 377 PHASES OF MOON   125
    OR ROUND THE CITY HALL, ... 608 SONGS BURDEN 3   6
    CLOSE TO THE CITY HALL HE DIED: . . . . 608 SONGS BURDEN 3   12
    HIS TEMPLE AND HIS BANQUET HALL: . . . . 671 ISLE STAT II 3   134
    THAT WITH THEIR FIERY RUIN FILL THE HALL, ... 683 SEEKER   45
HALLOWED
    THIS BOOK OR THAT, COME TO THIS HALLOWED PLACE . . . . 604 GALLERY REVIS   51
HALLS
    AMONG THE RINGING HALLS A SHOUT . . . .   20 OISIN 1   V 288
    IN TARA'S HALLS . . . . 609 IN TARAS HALLS   T
    A MAN I PRAISE THAT ONCE IN TARA'S HALLS . . . . . . 609 IN TARAS HALLS   1
    AND AS A SLAVE BEEN WAKEFUL IN THE HALLS . . . . . . 724 KANVA ON SELF   5
HALT
    UNDER BROKEN STONE I HALT . . . . 632 MAN AND ECHO   2
HALVE
    DREAMED, OR DID WE HALVE A DREAM . . . . 398 BREAK OF DAY   3
HALVED
    KNEW THAT WE'D HALVED A SOUL . . . . 457 SUMMER SPRING   6
HAMLET
    THERE STRUTS HAMLET, THERE IS LEAR, ... 565 LAPIS LAZULI   10
    THEY KNOW THAT HAMLET AND LEAR ARE GAY: . . . . . . 565 LAPIS LAZULI   16
    THOUGH HAMLET RAMBLES AND LEAR RAGES, ... 566 LAPIS LAZULI   21
    NO HAMLET THIN FROM EATING FLIES, A FAT . . . . . . 610 STATUES   19
HAMMER
    AND THE NAME OF THE DEMON WHOSE HAMMER . . . .   52 OISIN 3   80
    DOWN, DOWN, HAMMER THEM DOWN, ... 544 TO SAME TUNE 1   9
    DOWN, DOWN, HAMMER THEM DOWN, ... 545 TO SAME TUNE 1   19
    DOWN, DOWN, HAMMER THEM DOWN, ... 545 TO SAME TUNE 1   29
    DOWN, DOWN, HAMMER THEM DOWN, ... 546 TO SAME TUNE 2 V REF
    DOWN, DOWN, HAMMER THEM DOWN, ... 548 TO SAME TUNE 3 V REF
HAMMERED
    OF HAMMERED SILVER, AND DRINK . . . . 215 HAPPY TOWNLAND   50
    ON METAL GOBAN'D HAMMERED AT, ... 271 GREY ROCK   19
    HAD HAMMERED OUT ON MOUNTAIN TOP . . . . 271 GREY ROCK   23
    OLD GOBAN HAMMERED THEM AND WROUGHT THEM, ... 271 GREY ROCK   V 23
    OF HAMMERED GOLD AND GOLD ENAMELLING . . . . 408 SAIL BYZANTIUM   28
HAMMERS
    HOW THE HAMMERS SPRING ON THE ANVIL, ON THE SPEARHEAD'S   52 OISIN 3   83
      BURNING SPOT:
    AND THE NAMES OF THE DEMONS WHOSE HAMMERS . . . . . .   52 OISIN 3   V 80
    BEAT ON IT WITH THEIR HAMMERS DAY AND NIGHT. . . . . . 687 TWO TITANS   4
HAND
    WITH AN APPLE OF GOLD IN HER TOSSING HAND: . . . . .   12 OISIN 1   143
    AN APPLE OF GOLD IN HER TOSSING HAND: . . . .   12 OISIN 1   V 143
    OF MEN AND LADIES, HAND IN HAND, ...   15 OISIN 1   202
    OF MEN AND LADIES, HAND IN HAND, ...   15 OISIN 1   202
    OF YOUTHS AND MAIDENS HAND IN HAND, ...   15 OISIN 1   V 202
    OF YOUTHS AND MAIDENS HAND IN HAND, ...   15 OISIN 1   V 202
    OF MEN AND MAIDENS, HAND IN HAND, ...   15 OISIN 1   V 202
    OF MEN AND MAIDENS, HAND IN HAND, ...   15 OISIN 1   V 202
    HER PEARL-PALE HAND AND THE HEM OF HER DRESS. . . . .   16 OISIN 1   216
    ONE HAND UPHELD HIS BEARDLESS CHIN, ...   17 OISIN 1   250
    ONE HAND BENEATH HIS BEARDLESS CHIN, ...   17 OISIN 1   V 251
    WITHIN HIS OTHER HAND WERE FLITTING . . . .   18 OISIN 1   V 253
    WE FLUNG ON HIGH EACH WAVING HAND, ...   22 OISIN 1   325
    FLUNG ON HIGH EACH WAVING HAND, ...   22 OISIN 1   V 325
    SOME WANDERED EVER HAND IN HAND: . . . .   25 OISIN 1   389
    SOME WANDERED EVER HAND IN HAND: . . . .   25 OISIN 1   389
    HIS HAND ALONG THE RUNNEL'S SIDE, AS THOUGH . . . . .   39 OISIN 2   162
    OF RAVENING SORROW, OR THE HAND OF WRATH? . . . . .   42 OISIN 2   199
    . . . I FLUNG IT FIVE YARDS WITH MY HAND, ...   60 OISIN 3   187
    AND FEEL THE SOFTNESS OF EACH OTHER'S HAND, ...   74 ANASHU VIJAYA   57
    WHILE SLOWLY HE WHOSE HAND HELD HERS REPLIED: . . . .   80 EPHEMERA   11
    WHILE SLOWLY ANSWERED HE WHOSE HAND HELD HERS-- . . .   80 EPHEMERA   V   11
    WHEN MY HAND PASSED FROM WIRE TO WIRE . . . .   86 MAD KING GOLL   65

355

		PAGE	TITLE	LINE

HAND   (CONTINUED)

	PAGE	TITLE	LINE
WITH A FAERY, HAND IN HAND,	87	STOLEN CHILD	11
WITH A FAERY, HAND IN HAND,	87	STOLEN CHILD	11
WITH A FAERY, HAND IN HAND,	87	STOLEN CHILD	26
WITH A FAERY, HAND IN HAND,	87	STOLEN CHILD	26
WITH A FAERY, HAND IN HAND,	88	STOLEN CHILD	40
WITH A FAERY, HAND IN HAND,	88	STOLEN CHILD	40
WITH A FAERY, HAND IN HAND,	89	STOLEN CHILD	52
WITH A FAERY, HAND IN HAND,	89	STOLEN CHILD	52
WITH A FAERY, HAND AND HAND,	89	STOLEN CHILD V	52
WITH A FAERY, HAND AND HAND,	89	STOLEN CHILD V	52
AND ON MY LEANING SHOULDER SHE LAID HER SNOW-WHITE HAND.	90	SALLEY GARDENS	6
WITH BLOWN, SPRAY-DABBLED HAIR GATHER AT HAND.	114	ROSE OF BATTLE	6
NEAR NO ACCUSTOMED HAND!	123	DREAM OF DEATH	2
WE COME BETWEEN HIM AND THE DEED OF HIS HAND,	141	HOSTING SIDHE	11
AND KISS HER LIPS AND TAKE HER HAND,	150	WANDER AENGUS V	20
FOR THAT PALE BREAST AND LINGERING HAND	156	FORGOT BEAUTY	15
FOR THAT DIM BROW AND LINGERING HAND	156	FORGOT BEAUTY V	15
YOU NEED BUT LIFT A PEARL-PALE HAND,	158	BELOVED RHYMES	7
TO HER RIGHT HAND CAME THE RED ONE,	160	CAP AND BELLS	31
TO HER LEFT HAND CAME THE BLUE.	160	CAP AND BELLS	32
WITH BEAUTY HAND IN HAND?	174	ELEMENT POWERS V	6
WITH BEAUTY HAND IN HAND?	174	ELEMENT POWERS V	6
SHE LAID A HAND ON EITHER OF HIS SHOULDERS,	182	QUEEN MAEVE	49
HELP THEM THAT WANDER WITH HAND CLASPING HAND,	184	QUEEN MAEVE	86
HELP THEM THAT WANDER WITH HAND CLASPING HAND,	184	QUEEN MAEVE	86
HELP THEM THAT PACE, HAND IN UNWITHERING HAND,	184	QUEEN MAEVE	86
HELP THEM THAT PACE, HAND IN UNWITHERING HAND,	184	QUEEN MAEVE V	86
A YOUNG MAN CRIED AND KISSED HER HAND,	191	BAILE AILLINN	60
UNDER A BITTER BLACK WIND THAT BLOWS FROM THE LEFT HAND!	206	HANRAHANS SONG	2
UNDER THE BITTER BLACK WINDS BLOWING OUT OF THE LEFT HAND!	206	HANRAHANS SONG V	2
THAT MAKES ME FEAR TO RAISE A HAND AGAINST HIM,	222	SHADOW WATER B V	16A
THAT I WILL NEVER LIFT A HAND AGAINST YOU.	227	SHADOW WATER B	108
TOO MANY YEARS TO LIFT A HAND AGAINST YOU.	227	SHADOW WATER B	111
BELIEVED THERE WAS SOME OTHER NEAR AT HAND.	229	SHADOW WATER B	154
THAN A STRONG BODY AND A READY HAND.	232	SHADOW WATER B	236
BEFORE A HAND CAN TOUCH ME. MY HANDS ARE STILL!	238	SHADOW WATER B	358
WHERE IS MY SWORD THAT FELL OUT OF MY HAND	241	SHADOW WATER B	397
THE WEAK LAY HAND ON WHAT THE STRONG HAS DONE,	265	THESE CLOUDS	3
NOW NOTHING BUT COMES READIER TO THE HAND	267	ALL TEMPT ME	4
STOOD ON MY PATH. TREMBLING FROM HAND TO FOOT	283	TWO KINGS V 151	
GIVING HIS HAND TO THAT MAN AND TO THIS,	286	TWO KINGS V 218A	
YOUR OPEN HAND BUT SHOWS OUR LOSS,	288	TO WEALTHY MAN	29
AND SOMEBODY PUTS HIS HAND IN THE DISH	301	RUN PARADISE	5
WHEN CLOSE TO HIS RIGHT HAND A HEAP	302	HOUR DAWN	11
WENT DOWN UPON A HAND AND KNEE	304	HOUR DAWN V	45
BUT THE OTHER PUSHED HIS HAND ASIDE,	304	HOUR DAWN V	48
AND EVEN OLD MEN'S EYES GREW DIM, THIS HAND ALONE,	314	FALLEN MAJESTY	2
AND ONE BECAUSE HER HAND	315	FRIENDS	10
AND LOST THE OLD NONCHALANCE OF THE HAND;	368	EGO DOMINUS	13
STAND UP AND LIFT YOUR HAND AND BLESS	379	SAINT HUNCH	1
A BUDDHA, HAND AT REST,	383	VISION ROBART	19
HAND LIFTED UP THAT BLEST!	383	VISION ROBART	20
SURELY SOME REVELATION IS AT HAND!	402	SECOND COMING	9
SURELY THE SECOND COMING IS AT HAND.	402	SECOND COMING	10
ON MASTER-WORK OF INTELLECT OR HAND,	429	NINETEEN 19	37
ON MASTER WORK OF INTELLECT OR HAND,	429	NINETEEN 19 V	37
THAT WOULD NOT LIFT A HAND MAYBE	432	NINETEEN 19	109
THAT WOULD NOT LIFT A HAND MAY BE	432	NINETEEN 19 V	109
AND SHOULD SOME CRAZY HAND DARE TOUCH A DAUGHTER	433	NINETEEN 19	122
BID THE GHOST HAVE SWORD IN HAND!	435	FOR MY SON V	9
AND LAY THE HEART UPON HER HAND	437	SONGS PLAY 1	4
BUT SINCE I LAID A HAND THEREON	451	FIRST LOVE	7
FOR EVERY HAND IS LUNATIC	451	FIRST LOVE	11
A STUMPIER ON EITHER HAND!	460	THREE MONUMENT	4
ONE HAND AMID THE GOLDFISH IN THE POOL!	463	HARUN RASHID	44
THE EXTRAVAGANCE OF SPRING! OR MOVE A HAND	466	HARUN RASHID	125
ROMANTIC FISH SWAM IN NETS COMING TO THE HAND!	485	THREE MOVEMENT	2
THE HAND AND LASH THAT BEAT DOWN FRIGID ROME?	560	WHENCE COME	10
YOU, SHOULD HAND EXPLORE A THIGH,	573	LADYS 3RD SONG	11
AS THOUGH THAT HAND COULD REACH TO WHERE THEY STAND,	579	DOR WELLESLEY	2
DELIGHTFUL TO THE TOUCH! TIGHTEN THAT HAND	579	DOR WELLESLEY	4
HIS STOUT STICK UNDER HIS HAND,	588	OLD WICKED MAN	20
BOUND A THONG ABOUT HIS HAND,	595	COLONEL MARTIN	25
AND HE LAID THEM ON HER HAND.	595	COLONEL MARTIN	35
OR GROPE WITH A DIRTY HAND.	599	SPIRIT MEDIUM	8
OR GROPE WITH A DIRTY HAND.	600	SPIRIT MEDIUM	16
OR GROPE WITH A DIRTY HAND.	600	SPIRIT MEDIUM	24
AN ABBOT OR ARCHBISHOP WITH AN UPRAISED HAND	601	GALLERY REVIS	9
A HAND UNDER HIS HEAD.	617	LONG-LEG FLY	8
HIS HAND MOVES TO AND FRO.	618	LONG-LEG FLY	28
THE WAVES IN YONDER LAKE WHERE POINTS MY HAND	652	ISLE STAT I 2	13
AND PONDER IT IF THEY WILL)! THEN NEAR AT HAND	659	ISLE STAT II 1	10
ONE HAND BROW-SHADING, FAR ACROSS THE NIGHT,	663	ISLE STAT II 2	27
ALL SWIM WITH TEARS. THE FAERY BOAT'S AT HAND!	663	ISLE STAT II 2	33
WAS BROKEN IN HIS QUIVERING HAND.	671	ISLE STAT II 3	126
THY FLICKERING HAND? WHAT MEAN THE LIGHTS THAT RISE	674	ISLE STAT II 3	198
HAYNAU, THE MAN OF SYSTEM, LIFTS HIS HAND	712	FERENCZ RENYI	62
I'M WEAK, AND BY THE HAND SHALL HOLD EACH ONE	712	FERENCZ RENYI V	57
AND BE SO HAPPY." TO HIS HAND SHE CLINGS,	714	FERENCZ RENYI V	100

HAND (CONTINUED)
"WATCHER, WHEREFORE HAVE YE CALLED US?" EYES GO AFTER   718 PHANTOM SHIP   10
    HIS LEAN HAND,
    WE WILL LEAD YOU HAND IN HAND . . . .   726 LOVERS QUARREL   2
    WE WILL LEAD YOU HAND IN HAND . . . .   726 LOVERS QUARREL   2
    SITTING ON MY RIGHT HAND." . . . .   741 EARL PAUL   60
    AND WERE ALL DREAMS, IT WOULD NOT WEIGH IN THE HAND. . . 750 SHADOW WATER A 77
    THIS BLADE OUT OF MY HAND AND DIED OF A SUDDEN. . . . .   755 SHADOW WATER A 168
    THE HAND THAT WOUNDS HIM, BECAUSE THE GODS ARE HIS FRIENDS. 758 SHADOW WATER A 232
    THE HAND THAT WOUNDS. A WHITE BIRD BEATS HIS WINGS . . . 758 SHADOW WATER A V 232
    WHERE A HAND ON THE BELL . . . .   780 WELL AND TREE   4
HANDIWORK
    SHALL MAKE HER LOOK UPON HER HANDIWORK, ...   282 TWO KINGS   115
    MIRACLE, BIRD OR GOLDEN HANDIWORK, ...   497 BYZANTIUM   17
    MORE MIRACLE THAN BIRD OR HANDIWORK, ...   497 BYZANTIUM   18
    NO HANDIWORK OF CALLIMACHUS, ...   566 LAPIS LAZULI   29
HANDLE
    MAY HANDLE NOTHING AND SET EYES ON NOTHING . . . . .   371 ON GOING HOUSE   6
HANDLED
    THAT I HAVE HANDLED LEAST, LEAST LOOKED UPON. . . . .   367 EGO DOMINUS   9
    WHO HANDLED MARBLE AS IF IT WERE BRONZE, ...   566 LAPIS LAZULI   30
HANDLES
    NINE SWORDS WITH HANDLES OF RHINOCEROS HORN . . . . .   239 SHADOW WATER B   368
HANDMAID
    I WOULD HAVE SPARED HER HANDMAID, BUT SHE CAUGHT . . .   755 SHADOW WATER A   167
    I SPARED HER HANDMAID, TOO; BUT HALF WAY HITHER . . .   755 SHADOW WATER A V 167
HANDMAIDS
    THE HANDMAIDS LAUGH AND WHISPER IN THE DOOR. . . . .   759 SHADOW WATER A   242
HAND'S
    THAT NEVER DID A HAND'S TURN? AIBRIC! AIBRIC! . . . .   228 SHADOW WATER B   130
HANDS
    OF BATTLES BROKEN BY HIS HANDS, ...   7 OISIN 1   67
    ALL MEN, AND STRONGER OF HIS HANDS, ...   7 OISIN 1   V   63
    AND WEPT, AND RAISED THEIR LAMENTING HANDS, ...   10 OISIN 1   112
    THEY WEPT, AND RAISED LAMENTING HANDS. . . . . . .   10 OISIN 1   V   112
    A HARP OF SILVER IN MY HANDS, ...   16 OISIN 1   V   232
    NOR HAVE HANDS HELD A WEARY TOOL; . . . .   19 OISIN 1   283
    AND HANDS THAT HOLD NO WEARISOME TOOL, ...   22 OISIN 1   340
    OUR HANDS HAVE KNOWN NO WEARYING TOOL, ...   22 OISIN 1   V   339
    THESE NOW OUTWORN AND WITHERED HANDS . . . . . .   23 OISIN 1   349
    THESE NOW O'ERWORN AND WITHERED HANDS, ...   23 OISIN 1   V   348
    I TURNED IT IN MY HANDS; THE STAINS . . . .   24 OISIN 1   368
    AND CAUGHT MY HANDS, BUT SPAKE NO WORD . . . . . .   25 OISIN 1   374
    AND CAUGHT MY HANDS AND SPAKE NO WORD . . . . . .   25 OISIN 1   V   374
    AND BLOWS ON HIS HANDS IN THE FIRE'S WARM BLAZE; . . . 26 OISIN 1   404
    TAKING THE MORTAL WARRIORS BY THE HANDS; . . . . .   29 OISIN 2   V   10B
    BUT NIAM WITH HER HANDS CARESSED HIS EARS, ...   30 OISIN 2   V   26
    YOUNG WARRIOR." "NAY," I ANSWERED; "MY HANDS BURN . .   35 OISIN 2   V   89B
    GOD SHAKES THE WORLD WITH RESTLESS HANDS. MORE NEAR .   43 OISIN 2   V   208
    CEASED ON OUR HANDS AND OUR FACES, ON HAZEL AND OAK LEAF, 48 OISIN 3   23
        THE LIGHT,
    . . . THEIR HANDS WERE THE CLAWS OF BIRDS, ...   49 OISIN 3   34
    LAID HANDS ON THE BELL-BRANCH AND SWAYED IT, ...   51 OISIN 3   56
    AND TELL OF YOUR GOODLY HOUSEHOLD AND THE GOODLY WORKS   51 OISIN 3   62
        OF YOUR HANDS,
    AND EVEN THE NAMES OF HIS FATHERS, AND EVEN THE WORKS OF   51 OISIN 3   V   62
        HIS HANDS?
    LORD OF THE CROZIERS, YOU EVEN HAD LIFTED YOUR HANDS AND   54 OISIN 3   110
        WEPT;
    LORD OF THE CROZIERS, THOU EVEN HADST LIFTED THY HANDS   54 OISIN 3   V   110
        AND WEPT;
    MUCH WONDERING TO SEE UPON ALL HANDS, OF WATTLES   58 OISIN 3   162
        AND WOODWORK MADE,
    MUCH WONDERING TO SEE UPON ALL HANDS, OF WATTLES   58 OISIN 3   V   162
        AND WOOD-WORK MADE,
    PUT THE STAFF IN MY HANDS; . . . .   61 OISIN 3   201
    AND LAID YOU ON THE GATES OF EVENING WITH HIS QUIET HANDS. 72 ANASHU VIJAYA   22
    AND LAID YE ON THE GATES OF EVENING WITH HIS QUIET HANDS.   72 ANASHU VIJAYA V 22
    SING, TILL YOU RAISE YOUR HANDS AND SIGH, ...   73 ANASHU VIJAYA   45
    SING, TILL YE RAISE YOUR HANDS AND SIGH, ...   73 ANASHU VIJAYA V   45
    AND FEEL THE SOFTNESS OF EACH OTHER'S HANDS, ...   74 ANASHU VIJAYA V   57
    A LONELY LAUGHTER, AND MAY KISS HIS HANDS TO ME IN SLEEP.   75 ANASHU VIJAYA   82
    AN INNER LAUGHTER, AND MAY KISS HIS HANDS TO ME IN SLEEP.   75 ANASHU VIJAYA V 82
    A LONELY LAUGHTER, THAT HE MAY KISS HANDS TO ME IN SLEEP.   75 ANASHU VIJAYA   82
    AND WANDER EVER WITH WOVEN HANDS, ...   78 INDIAN TO LOVE   7
    THESE HANDS WON MANY A TORQUE OF GOLD. . . . . . .   83 MAD KING GOLL   23
    THESE HANDS SLEW MANY WARRIORS BOLD-- . . . . . .   83 MAD KING GOLL V   23
    THESE HANDS SLEW MANY ROBBERS BOLD-- . . . . . .   83 MAD KING GOLL V   23
    THESE HANDS SLEW MANY A SEAMAN BOLD. . . . . . .   83 MAD KING GOLL V   23
    I WANDER ON, AND WAVE MY HANDS, ...   84 MAD KING GOLL   43
    AND CRUMPLED IN MY HANDS THE STAFF . . . .   84 MAD KING GOLL   33
    AND BROKE BETWEEN MY HANDS THE STAFF . . . . . .   84 MAD KING GOLL V   33
    MINGLING HANDS AND MINGLING GLANCES . . . . . .   87 STOLEN CHILD   18
    UPON HIS WASTED HANDS, ...   98 FOXHUNTER   22
    UPON HIS WASTED HANDS. . . . .   98 FOXHUNTER   V   24
    AND ON THESE HANDS THAT MAY NOT LIFT THE SWORD . . .   103 FERGUS DRUID   24
    "AND BREAKS THE RIDGE OF BATTLE WITH HIS HANDS." . . . 107 CUCHULAIN SEA V   26
    THE DRUIDS CHANTED, SWAYING IN THEIR HANDS . . . .   111 CUCHULAIN SEA V   82
    THE DRUIDS CHAUNTED, SWAYING IN THEIR HANDS . . . .   111 CUCHULAIN SEA V   82
    OF HOW GOD LEANS HIS HANDS OUT OF THE SKY, ...   128 DREAM OF FAERY V   43
    THAT GOD HAD LEANED HIS HANDS OUT OF THE SKY, . . .   128 DREAM OF FAERY V   43

		PAGE	TITLE	LINE
HANDS (CONTINUED)				
THAT GOD HAD LEANT HIS HANDS OUT OF THE SKY,	• • • • •	128	DREAM OF FAERY V	43
THE SAD BELLS BOW THE FOREHEAD ON THE HANDS.	• • • • •	130	BOOK STORIES V	20
WITH A TWINKLING OF ANCIENT HANDS.	• • • • • •	144	HOST OF AIR	24
AND CLAP THEIR HANDS TOGETHER, AND HALF CLOSE THEIR EYES,		146	UNAPPEAS HOST	2
AND KISS HER LIPS AND TAKE HER HANDS;	• • • • • •	150	WANDER AENGUS	20
PALE BROWS, STILL HANDS AND DIM HAIR,	• • • • •	152	LOSS OF LOVE	1
PALE BROW, STILL HANDS, AND DIM HAIR,	• • • • •	152	LOSS OF LOVE V	1
I BRING YOU WITH REVERENT HANDS	• • • • •	157	POET BELOVED	1
QUEENS WROUGHT WITH GLIMMERING HANDS;	• • • • •	162	ASKS FORGIVE	12
AND HANDS HURL IN THE DEEP	• • • •	165	CRY OF SEDGE	6
BUT DATHI FOLDED HIS HANDS AND SMILED	• • • •	167	BLESSED	11
SAW THE PIERCED HANDS AND ROOD OF ELDER RISE	• • • • •	169	SECRET ROSE	10
THE KNOTTED SCOURGE, THE NAIL-PIERCED HANDS, THE WOUNDED SIDE,		172	TRAV PASSION V	4
THAT WORK TOO DIFFICULT FOR MORTAL HANDS	• • • • •	182	QUEEN MAEVE	67
DREAMED OF THE HANDS THAT WOULD UNLACE	• • • •	193	BAILE AILLINN	104
THEY HAD HANDS LIKE CLAWS, AND THEIR KNEES	• • • • •	208	OLD MEN ADMIRE	4
HURRY TO BLESS THE HANDS THAT PLAY,	• • • • • •	212	BLESS PSALTER	1
O KINSMEN, BLESS THE HANDS THAT PLAY.	• • • • •	213	BLESS PSALTER	15
OUR HANDS, OUR HANDS MUST EBB AWAY.	• • • • •	213	BLESS PSALTER	18
OUR HANDS, OUR HANDS MUST EBB AWAY.	• • • • •	213	BLESS PSALTER	18
BUT BLESS OUR HANDS THAT EBB AWAY.	• • • • •	213	BLESS PSALTER	20
BECAUSE HER HANDS HAD BEEN MADE WILD BY LOVE.	• • • •	219	HARP OF AENGUS	9
HE COULD NOT SEE THEM, BUT I HELD OUT MY HANDS	• • • •	223	SHADOW WATER B	38
AND THEN SMOOTH OUT WITH IVORY HANDS AND SIGH,	• • • •	228	SHADOW WATER B	133
WHO HAVE SLAIN MY HUSBAND AND LAID HANDS UPON ME.	• • •	235	SHADOW WATER B	282
LET GO MY HANDS! WHY DO YOU CAST A SHADOW?	• • • •	235	SHADOW WATER B	283
THAT RAISED THEIR HANDS AGAINST HIM. THERE ARE SOME	•	235	SHADOW WATER B	291
IT WAS THEIR HANDS THAT PLUCKED THE WINDS AWAKE	• • •	237	SHADOW WATER B	324
BEFORE A HAND CAN TOUCH ME. MY HANDS ARE STILL;	• • •	238	SHADOW WATER B	358
AND WRING MY HANDS, AND WAIL HIM BITTERLY,	• • • •	242	SHADOW WATER B	414
BETTER THAN MY OWN HANDS. I HAVE DECEIVED YOU	• • •	244	SHADOW WATER B	466
AND STRIKE THE GOLDEN PILLARS WITH MY HANDS.	• • • •	246	SHADOW WATER B	502
O SILVER FISH THAT MY TWO HANDS HAVE TAKEN	• • • •	251	SHADOW WATER B	609
BY THE ANCIENT HOLY HANDS THAT BROUGHT THEM	• • •	271	GREY ROCK V	21
MORE HANDS IN HEIGHT THAN ANY STAG IN THE WORLD	• • •	277	TWO KINGS	9
KING EOCHAID SEIZED THE HORNS IN HIS STRONG HANDS	• •	278	TWO KINGS	24
THE HANDS THAT GATHERED UP THE MIGHT OF THE WORLD,	• •	278	TWO KINGS	29
EOCHAID SEIZED BOTH THE HORNS IN HIS STRONG HANDS	• •	278	TWO KINGS V	24
HER HANDS ON EITHER SIDE HAD GRIPPED THE BENCH,	• • •	279	TWO KINGS	63
AND CARRIED HIM HIS FOOD WITH MY OWN HANDS,	• • • •	280	TWO KINGS	88
AND FOR NINE DAYS HE HAD FOOD FROM OTHER HANDS	• • •	282	TWO KINGS	126
THRUST HIM AWAY WITH BOTH MY HANDS AND CRIED,	• • •	285	TWO KINGS	202
MY HANDS WERE PRESSED TO VANISHED SUDDENLY,	• • • •	286	TWO KINGS	208
IN HIS FULL HANDS WHAT, HAD THEY ONLY KNOWN,	• • • •	292	TO A SHADE	11
HANDS GRIPPED IN HANDS, TOES CLOSE TOGETHER,	• • • •	332	ROUND TOWER	21
HANDS GRIPPED IN HANDS, TOES CLOSE TOGETHER,	• • • •	332	ROUND TOWER	21
YOUR SMALL HANDS WERE NOT BEAUTIFUL,	• • • • • •	356	BROKEN DREAMS	29
THE HANDS THAT I HAVE KISSED,	• • • • • •	357	BROKEN DREAMS	35
HANDS, DO WHAT YOU'RE BID;	• • • • •	358	BALLOON MIND	1
OR FROM SOME BLOODY WHIP IN THEIR OWN HANDS.	• • •	375	PHASES OF MOON	68
IN THE PRISON OF MY HANDS,	• • • • •	381	SONG OF FOOL	2
WHY HAVE YOU LAID YOUR HANDS UPON MY EYES?	• • • •	389	IMAGE PAST	15
SOUL CLAP ITS HANDS AND SING, AND LOUDER SING	• • •	407	SAIL BYZANTIUM	11
LOVE-LORN, INDIFFERENT HANDS MIGHT COME UPON IT	• •	461	HARUN RASHID	14
A BOY'S LOVELORN INDIFFERENT HANDS MIGHT FIND	• •	461	HARUN RASHID V	14
HANDS UPON EITHER SHOULDER MADE HER MOVE,	• • • •	466	HARUN RASHID V 125B
OUR HANDS ARE BLENCHED, OUR FINGERS SEEM	• • • •	488	CRAZED MOON	14
BELOVED BOOKS THAT FAMOUS HANDS HAVE BOUND,	• • •	491	COOLE BALLYLEE	27
AND EVERYTHING THAT YOUR OWN HANDS HAVE WROUGHT,	• •	501	VACILLATION	31
HEALING FROM ITS LETTERED SLAB. THOSE SELF-SAME HANDS PERCHANCE		503	VACILLATION	82
OR LACKING THAT, GOVERNMENT IN SUCH HANDS,	• • • •	543	PARN FUNERAL 2	7
THOSE HANDS TO CLOSE THESE EYES,	• • • • • •	587	OLD WICKED MAN	6
HANDS THAT ARE BUSY WITH HIS BEADS	• • • • •	588	OLD WICKED MAN	25
OF THE PIED PANTHER-KITTENS FROM MY HANDS	• • • •	674	ISLE STAT II 3	219
A LOTUS IN THEIR HANDS--YOUNG MOORISH GIRL	• • • •	694	MOSADA 1	103
NO NEED TO BIND MY HANDS. WHERE ARE YE, SIRS?	• • •	695	MOSADA 1	110
THE BURTHEN OF THY TRUTH. REACH DOWN THY HANDS	• •	698	MOSADA 2	53
BEFORE HIM ONE WELL GUARDED, WITH BOUND HANDS;	• • •	709	FERENCZ RENYI	10
I'M WEAK, AND BY THE HANDS SHALL HOLD EACH ONE	• • •	712	FERENCZ RENYI	57
AND BE SO HAPPY." TO HIS HANDS SHE CLINGS,	• • • •	714	FERENCZ RENYI	100
AWAY HER CLINGING HANDS, AND TURNS. SHE THROWS	• • •	714	FERENCZ RENYI	102
YON BAUBLE OF THE HEAVENS, HE LIFTS HIS HANDS,	• • •	715	FERENCZ RENYI	119
ON THE DROWNED MEN'S HANDS AND FACES, ON THE SPARS AND ON THE SAILS.		719	PHANTOM SHIP	22
AND THEN SMOOTH OUT WITH IVORY HANDS AND SIGH.	• • • •	750	SHADOW WATER A	70
A BOY AND GIRL HOLD ONE ANOTHER'S HANDS;	• • • • •	752	SHADOW WATER A	122
BECAUSE HER HANDS HAD BEEN MADE WILD BY LOVE;	• • • •	762	SHADOW WATER A	304
I KNOW YOU NOW, BESEECHING HANDS AND EYES.	• • • •	763	SHADOW WATER A	312
BESEECHING HANDS AND MORE BESEECHING EYES?	• • • •	763	SHADOW WATER A V	312
THE LOVE I KNOW IS HIDDEN IN THESE HANDS	• • • •	765	SHADOW WATER A	350
AND LANGUORS THAT AWAKE IN MINGLING HANDS	• • • •	765	SHADOW WATER A	367
O SILVER FISH THAT MY TWO HANDS HAVE TAKEN	• • • •	769	SHADOW WATER A	425
THOSE WILD HANDS THAT HAVE EMBRACED	• • • • •	776	AGAINST WITCH	32
HANDSOME				
IN REALMS WHERE THE HANDSOME WERE MANY,	• • • •	50	OISIN 3	50
IN A REALM WHERE THE HANDSOME ARE MANY,	• • • •	50	OISIN 3	50
IN REALMS WHERE THE HANDSOME ARE MANY,	• • •	50	OISIN 3 V	50
SOME FEW HAVE HANDSOME RIDERS, ARE GARLANDED	• • • •	432	NINETEEN 19	114

		PAGE	TITLE	LINE

HANDSOMEST
    THE HANDSOMEST YOUNG MAN THERE, ... 145 HOST OF AIR 34
HANDY-WORK
    MIRACLE, BIRD OR GOLDEN HANDY-WORK . . . . 497 BYZANTIUM V 17
    MORE MIRACLE THAN BIRD OR HANDY-WORK . . . . . 497 BYZANTIUM V 18
HANG
    LIKE CRIMSON METEORS HANG IN THE GLOOM, ... 21 OISIN 1 306
    AND WHEN THE DEW-DROWNED STARS HANG IN THE AIR . . . . 32 OISIN 2 54
    WHERE BANNERS OF THE CALIPHS HANG, NIGHT-COLOURED . . . 461 HARUN RASHID 6
    ALL THINGS HANG LIKE A DROP OF DEW . . . . 505 GRAT INSTRUCT 3
    SO NEVER HANG YOUR HEART UPON . . . . 509 JANE REPROVED 12
    THAT ALL MUST HANG THEIR TRUST . . . . 583 GHOST ROG CASE 16
    WHERE MY FRIENDS' PORTRAITS HANG AND LOOK THEREON; . . . 604 GALLERY REVIS 52
    HANG ON THE SIDE OF THE ROUND GRAPE-CLUSTER; . . . . . 646 ISLE STAT I 1 45
    LONG CITRON COILS THAT HANG AROUND THEE, BLOWN . . . . 670 ISLE STAT II 3 105
    OF OUR NATIVITY HANG SIDE BY SIDE, ... 701 MOSADA 3 53
    WHY DO YOU HANG SO HEAVY IN MY ARMS? . . . . . . 703 MOSADA 3 108
    AND HANG O'ER THE HISTORIED STONE! . . . . 707 FAIRY PEDANT 6
    HANG THE MIST-THREADS FOR A LITTLE WHILE LIKE COBWEBS IN 719 PHANTOM SHIP 29
        THE AIR;
    HANG THE MIST THREADS FOR A LITTLE WHILE LIKE COBWEBS IN 719 PHANTOM SHIP V 29
        THE AIR;
HANGER   SEE COAT-HANGER
HANGETH
    WHO MADE THE WORLD AND RULETH IT, HE HANGETH ON A STALK, . 76 INDIAN ON GOD 10
    BECAUSE ST. JOSEPH'S IMAGE HANGETH HERE . . . . . . 676 ISLE STAT II 3 266
HANGING
    HER EYES WERE SOFT AS DEWDROPS HANGING . . . . . . 3 OISIN 1 V 7HH
    AND HANGING ITS PAPER FLOWERS FROM POST TO POST, . . . 198 SEVEN WOODS 8
    OF THE GREAT DOOR; BUT THOUGH THE HANGING LAMPS . . . 279 TWO KINGS 49
    OF SILVER HANGING ROUND LAME COLA'S NECK-- . . . . 691 MOSADA 1 V 35
    HER HANGING MANSION. GIVE TO ME, I PRAY, ... 698 MOSADA 2 52
    AND HANGING O'ER THE HUSH OF WILLOW BOWERS, ... 705 REMEMBRANCE 8
HANGMAN'S
    FOR WHOM THE HANGMAN'S ROPE WAS SPUN, ... 289 SEPTEMBER 1913 13
HANGS
    THE DARKNESS COMES. A CLOUD HANGS OVERHEAD-- . . . . 43 OISIN 2 V 208A
    A HUSH! AH, ME! IT HANGS TO STRIKE US DEAD. . . . . 43 OISIN 2 V 208B
    WHO BUT AWAITS HIS HOUR TO SHOOT, STILL HANGS . . . . 198 SEVEN WOODS 13
    AND HE THAT ATTIS' IMAGE HANGS BETWEEN . . . . . . 500 VACILLATION 16
    WHEN DARK HANGS UPON THE WATER . . . . 589 OLD WICKED MAN 34
    WITHIN THE DROWSY BLOSSOM HANGS THE BEE; . . . . . 645 ISLE STAT I 1 2
    HERE WHERE LABURNUM HANGS HER GOLDEN FLEECE; . . . . 670 ISLE STAT II 3 102
    HANGS ON MY BREAST! LISTEN, WE SHALL BE SAFE. . . . 701 MOSADA 3 73
    HANGS O'ER ALL THE WOODED EARTH. . . . . 731 STREET DANCERS 8
HANRAHAN
    HANRAHAN REPROVES THE CURLEW . . . . 155 REPROVE CURLEW V T
    HANRAHAN LAMENTS BECAUSE OF HIS WANDERINGS . . . . 171 MAID QUIET V T
    HANRAHAN SPEAKS TO THE LOVERS OF HIS SONGS IN COMING DAYS 173 SPEAKS HEARERS V T
    THE SONG OF RED HANRAHAN . . . . 206 HANRAHANS SONG V T
    AND I MYSELF CREATED HANRAHAN . . . . 411 TOWER 57
    HANRAHAN ROSE IN FRENZY THERE . . . . 412 TOWER 71
    GO THEREFORE! BUT LEAVE HANRAHAN, ... 413 TOWER 103
    ALEEL, HIS COUNTESS; HANRAHAN . . . . 550 SEVERED HEAD 15
HANRAHAN'S
    RED HANRAHAN'S SONG ABOUT IRELAND . . . . 206 HANRAHANS SONG T
HAPLESS
    AND I WOULD PLEASE THE HAPLESS FAUN, ... 67 HAPPY SHEPHERD 47
    THAT I MAY SOOTHE THAT HAPLESS FAUN . . . . . . 67 HAPPY SHEPHERD V 47
    BEHOLD THE HAPLESS SLEEPERS STANDING BY. . . . . . 677 ISLE STAT II 3 281
HAPPEN
    THAT SOMETHING IS ABOUT TO HAPPEN, I THINK . . . . . 609 IN TARAS HALLS 4
HAPPENED
    OF WONDERS THAT HAVE HAPPENED . . . . 215 HAPPY TOWNLAND 47
HAPPENS
    NO MATTER WHAT HAPPENS AND WHO TAKES THE FALL, . . . 545 TO SAME TUNE 1 22
    NO MATTER WHAT HAPPENS OR WHO TAKES THE FALL, . . . 545 TO SAME TUNE 1 V 22
    WHAT HAPPENS A TREE THAT HAS NOTHING WITHIN IT? . . . 548 TO SAME TUNE 3 23
    WHAT HAPPENS TO A TREE THAT HAS NOTHING WITHIN IT? . . . 548 TO SAME TUNE 3 V 23
    NO MATTER WHAT HAPPENS AND WHO TAKES THE FALL, . . . 616 MARCH SONGS 3 22
HAPPIER
    THAT HAPPIER BREATH HAD MOVED, HER HUSBAND TURNED . . . 185 QUEEN MAEVE 105
    YET DREAMED THAT BEINGS HAPPIER THAN MEN . . . . . 218 WOODS OF COOLE 18
    AND WHEN WE HAVE IT WE ARE NO HAPPIER, ... 228 SHADOW WATER B 126
    OR HAPPIER THOUGHTED WHEN THE DAY IS SPENT . . . . 292 TO A SHADE V 4
    OR LEAVE THEM HAPPIER THAN BEFORE. . . . . 328 IRISH AIRMAN 8
    HAPPIER DAYS THOUGHT GOOD! . . . . 365 HER RACE 4
    IT MADE HIM HAPPIER TO KNOW . . . . 400 DEMON BEAST 14
    ALL HIS HAPPIER DREAMS CAME TRUE-- . . . . 577 WHAT THEN 11
    FOR HAPPIER LOVE BUT FINDS UNHAPPINESS, ... 750 SHADOW WATER A 67
HAPPIER-THOUGHTED
    OR HAPPIER-THOUGHTED WHEN THE DAY IS SPENT . . . . 292 TO A SHADE 4
HAPPIEST
    THAT WOULD BE HAPPIEST. HE IS A KING . . . . . 768 SHADOW WATER A 410
    THAT WOULD BE HAPPIEST, FOR THERE IS NONE . . . . 768 SHADOW WATER A V 410
HAPPILY
    THAT ALL THINGS FELL OUT HAPPILY, ... 189 BAILE AILLINN 22
HAPPINESS
    HAVE HAPPINESS WITHOUT AN END, ... 195 BAILE AILLINN 158
    I HAVE NO HAPPINESS IN DREAMING OF BRYCELINDE, . . . 209 UNDER THE MOON 1
    I FIND NO HAPPINESS IN SHADY BRYCELINDE . . . . . 209 UNDER THE MOON V 1

PAGE TITLE LINE

HAPPINESS (CONTINUED)
    I'D NEVER COME UPON THE HAPPINESS . . . . 226 SHADOW WATER B 87
    TO HURRY TO THEIR HIDDEN HAPPINESS . . . . 234 SHADOW WATER B 268
    TO UNIMAGINABLE HAPPINESS. . . . . 247 SHADOW WATER B 524
    AN UNIMAGINABLE HAPPINESS. . . . . 248 SHADOW WATER B 553
    AND IF THAT HAPPINESS BE MORE THAN DREAMS, ... 248 SHADOW WATER B 554
    HAPPINESS TO CHILDREN AND TO MEN." . . . . 282 TWO KINGS 121
    AND WITH HIM HAVE FOUND EVERY HAPPINESS . . . . . . 284 TWO KINGS 174
    UNDER A BOW, HE CRIED, "WHAT HAPPINESS . . . . . . 284 TWO KINGS 177
    CAN LOVERS HAVE THAT KNOW THEIR HAPPINESS . . . . . 284 TWO KINGS 178
    ALONE WITH ALL THIS USELESS HAPPINESS?" . . . . . . 285 TWO KINGS 200
    IMPULSIVE MEN THAT LOOK FOR HAPPINESS . . . . 369 EGO DOMINUS 40
    REMEMBER HIS DELIBERATE HAPPINESS. . . . . 370 EGO DOMINUS 53
    FORGOT IN CRUEL HAPPINESS . . . . 453 MERMAID 5
    AND SHE AND I, BEING SUNK IN HAPPINESS, ... 463 HARUN RASHID 51
    HAPPINESS . . . . 499 VACILLATION V T
    IT SEEMED, SO GREAT MY HAPPINESS, ... 501 VACILLATION 43
    ALL HAPPINESS IN ITS OWN CAUSE OR GROUND. . . . . . 557 RIBH ECSTASY 4
    WILL HE HAVE HAPPINESS? GREAT SOBS HER BEING SHAKE. . . 676 ISLE STAT II 3 247
    THE GODS HATE HAPPINESS, AND WEAVE THEIR NETS . . . 767 SHADOW WATER A 399
HAPPY
    HAPPY AS CHILDREN WITH UNWITHERING LIPS, ... 30 OISIN 2 V 14B
    THE SONG OF THE HAPPY SHEPHERD . . . . 64 HAPPY SHEPHERD T
    FOR HAPPY LOVERS PASSED TWO BY TWO WHERE I STOOD; . . . 163 VALLEY LOVERS 2
    BECAUSE IT IS ALONE OF ALL THINGS HAPPY. . . . . . 198 SEVEN WOODS 9
    HAS MADE THEM SO HAPPY AND HOPELESS, SO DEAF AND SO BLIND 204 WITHER BOUGHS 20
    THAT IT HAD ALL SEEMED HAPPY, AND YET WE'D GROWN . . 206 ADAMS CURSE 37
    THE HAPPY TOWNLAND . . . . 213 HAPPY TOWNLAND T
    WHERE MANY HUNDRED SQUIRRELS ARE AS HAPPY . . . . . 217 WOODS OF COOLE 5
    ARE YOU NOT HAPPY WINGED BODIES NOW? . . . . 234 SHADOW WATER B 273
    NOW THAT YOU HAVE HAPPY WINGED BODIES? . . . . . . 234 SHADOW WATER B V 273
    IN HAPPY DANCES UNDER A WINDY MOON, ... 245 SHADOW WATER B 470
    "AND CANNOT HAVE A HUMOROUS HAPPY SPEECH." . . . . 300 BEGGAR CRIED 16
    AND SHE SEEMED HAPPY AS A KING, ... 313 MEMORY YOUTH V 6
    HIS ART IS HAPPY, BUT WHO KNOWS HIS MIND? . . . . . 370 EGO DOMINUS 54
    IS ALWAYS HAPPY LIKE A BIRD OR A BEAST; . . . . . . 373 PHASES OF MOON 38
    A STUPID HAPPY CREATURE . . . . 400 DEMON BEAST 31
    OR EVERY BELLOWS BURST, BE HAPPY STILL. . . . . . . 405 FOR DAUGHTER 72
    UPON SOME BRAND-NEW HAPPY DAY; . . . . 432 NINETEEN 19 V 106
    THAT SHE IS HAPPY BEING CRAZY; . . . . 568 SWEET DANCER 10
    NO MAN CAN KNOW A HAPPY MAN . . . . 598 STONE CROSS 11
    OF AN UNBROKEN HAPPY MIND, ... 626 OLD MEN BE MAD 14
    AND SEE AGAIN THE HAPPY WOODLAND LIGHT, ... 664 ISLE STAT II 2 58
    OF THE HAPPY FLOWER MINIONS. . . . . 667 ISLE STAT II 3 29
    AND THE HAPPY WINGED DAY, ... 668 ISLE STAT II 3 64
    BUT ART THOU HAPPY? LET ME GAZE ON THEE . . . . . . 671 ISLE STAT II 3 144
    BUT ART THOU HAPPY? YOUTH, I AM AT PEACE. . . . . . 672 ISLE STAT II 3 150
    BUT ART THOU HAPPY? THOSE GREY EYES OF THINE . . . 672 ISLE STAT II 3 151
    THOU SHALT OUTLIVE THINE AMOROUS HAPPY TIME, . . . 674 ISLE STAT II 3 203
    SHE SMILES--IS HAPPY WITH HER WANDERING GRIEFS. . . 702 MOSADA 3 95
    LIKE HAPPY THOUGHTS GROWN SAD IN EVIL DAYS. . . . . 703 MOSADA 3 116
    AND BE SO HAPPY." TO HIS HANDS SHE CLINGS, ... 714 FERENCZ RENYI 100
    AND BE SO HAPPY." TO HIS HAND SHE CLINGS, ... 714 FERENCZ RENYI V 100
    OH, SO HAPPY WOULD WE BE! . . . . 726 LOVERS QUARREL 16
    IN HAPPY DANCES, UNDER A WINDY MOON; . . . . 763 SHADOW WATER A 318
    FOR LOVE IS KIND AND HAPPY. O COME WITH ME! . . . 767 SHADOW WATER A 396
HARBOUR
    AND THE FISHER MEN AND WOMEN FROM THE DRIPPING HARBOUR WALL 718 PHANTOM SHIP 11
    . . . SEE, SHE ROUNDS THE HARBOUR CLEAR. . . . . . 718 PHANTOM SHIP 13
HARBOURING   SEE ECHO-HARBOURING
HARD
    CAME AFTER THE HARD GAZE OF YOUTH, OR AN OLD MAN LIFTED 59 OISIN 3 170
       HIS HEAD!
    A WEARY WOMAN SLEEPS SO HARD! . . . . 95 MOLL MAGEE 21
    AND THINK THAT YOU WERE HARD AND UNKIND, ... 146 FISH 7
    THOUGH NOW IT'S HARD, TILL TROUBLE IS AT AN END; . . 200 FOLLY COMFORT V 5
    WHAT GOOD IS THERE IN THIS HARD WAY OF LIVING, . . 225 SHADOW WATER B 69
    WOMEN ARE HARD AND PROUD AND STUBBORN-HEARTED, . . 245 SHADOW WATER B 479
    HOW HARD A LIFE HER SERVANT LIVES. . . . . 336 YOUNG BEAUTY 14
    AND THEN HE LAUGHED TO THINK THAT WHAT SEEMED HARD . . 377 PHASES OF MOON 136
    AND TOILED SO HARD AND LATE . . . . 432 NINETEEN 19 95
    FOR IN MY FIRST HARD SPRINGTIME WE WERE FRIENDS, . . 473 ALL SOUL NIGHT 62
    FOR IN MY FIRST HARD SPRING-TIME WE WERE FRIENDS, . . 473 ALL SOUL NIGHT V 62
    SO HARD I STRUCK. . . . . 518 HIS CONFIDENCE 8
    REMOTE FROM ALL THE HARD EARTH TROUBLES, ... 731 PRIEST FAIRY 80
    HAS MOULDED THE HARD YEARS. . . . . 738 MOURN THEN ON 8
    AND THIS HARD FLAG OF STONE, ... 739 EARL PAUL 6
HARDER
    IS TO WORK HARDER THAN ALL THESE, AND YET . . . . . 205 ADAMS CURSE 11
    BRED TO A HARDER THING . . . . 291 TO A FRIEND 9
    BLINDER SORROWS, HARDER WAGE-- . . . . 733 STREET DANCERS 58
HARDEST
    HE SET HIS CHISEL TO THE HARDEST STONE. . . . . . . 369 EGO DOMINUS 32
HARDIHOOD
    FOR HIS GREAT HARDIHOOD. . . . . 741 EARL PAUL 56
HARD-LIVING
    HARD-LIVING MEN AND MEN OF THOUGHT . . . . 787 HUDDON DUDDON 13
HARDLY
    I HARDLY HEAR THE CURLEW CRY, ... 189 BAILE AILLINN 1
    WILL HARDLY SEEM WORTH THINKING OF . . . . 202 NEVER GIVE ALL 2
    THE SECOND COMING! HARDLY ARE THOSE WORDS OUT . . . 402 SECOND COMING 11

360

HARDLY   (CONTINUED)
      HARDLY DARED TO WET HIS MOUTH . . . .   454 EMPTY CUP   3
      WHILE THE WIND IS LIGHT. THE OAR CAN HARDLY MOVE HER, . . .   754 SHADOW WATER A   157
HARD-RIDING
      HARD-RIDING COUNTRY GENTLEMEN, ...   639 BEN BULBEN   75
HARE
      THE HARE GROWS OLD AS SHE PLAYS IN THE SUN . . . .   27 OISIN 1   412
      "OLD GROWS THE HARE AS SHE PLAYS IN THE SUN, ... 28 OISIN 1   V   420
      THE HARE LEAPED IN THE GRASS. YOUNG NIAMH CAME . . .   44 OISIN 2   229
      THE HARE RUNS BY ME GROWING BOLD-- . . . .   84 MAD KING GOLL   V   47
      THE COLLAR-BONE OF A HARE . . . .   330 BONE OF A HARE   T
      THE COLLAR-BONE OF A HARE . . . .   330 BONE OF A HARE   10
      THROUGH THE WHITE THIN BONE OF A HARE. . . . . . .   330 BONE OF A HARE   16
      WHERE THE MOUNTAIN HARE HAS LAIN. . . . .   350 MEMORY   6
      A SPECKLED CAT AND A TAME HARE . . . .   380 SONGS FOOL 1   1
      THE HARE MAY RUN TILL IT'S FOUND . . . .   380 SONGS FOOL 1   11
      WHERE THE BROWN HARE MIGHT BE, ...   381 SONGS FOOL 2   4
      AND THAT HE CHANGED INTO A HARE. . . . .   412 TOWER   70
      THE DEATH OF THE HARE . . . .   453 DEATH OF HARE   T
      THE HARE LEAP TO THE WOOD, ...   453 DEATH OF HARE   2
      AT THE DEATH OF THE HARE. . . . .   453 DEATH OF HARE   12
      AS THE MOORFOWL AND THE HARE, ...   706 DAWN-SONG   28
      THE HARE HATH LAID ASLEEP HER FROLIC WITS, ...   712 FERENCZ RENYI   72
HARE'S
      A PEERING HARE'S:" AND YET I MURMURED NOT, ...   684 SEEKER   56
HARES
      OF PLANETS WATCHING, WATCHING THE RACE OF HARES . . . .   44 OISIN 2   V 228B
      THE HARES RUN BY ME GROWING BOLD. . . . .   84 MAD KING GOLL   47
      AND YOUNG HARES BROOK MY HARMLESS HOLD-- . . . . .   84 MAD KING GOLL   V   47
      AND HARES RUN NEAR ME GROWING BOLD. . . . .   84 MAD KING GOLL   V   47
      FROM HUMAN THOUGHT, AS HARES AND MICE AND CONEYS . . .   218 WOODS OF COOLE   31
HARK
      HARK! HE'S DEAD--MY DROWSY BROTHER, ...   656 ISLE STAT I 3   18
      AND ONE ALONE OF ALL WOULD HARK, ...   671 ISLE STAT II 3   123
HARLOT
      ONE IS A HARLOT, AND ONE A CHILD . . . .   358 PRESENCES   12
      THE HARLOT AND THE CHILD. . . . .   601 THOSE IMAGES   12
HARM
      OUT OF ALL HARM, ...   574 MAIDS 1ST SONG   8
HARMLESS
      AND YOUNG HARES BROOK MY HARMLESS HOLD-- . . . . . .   84 MAD KING GOLL   V   47
HARMONIC
      WITH THAT SONG LEADING WHERE HARMONIC WOODS . . . . .   657 ISLE STAT I 3   43
HARMONIOUS
      WITH YOUR HARMONIOUS CHOIR . . . .   174 ELEMENT POWERS   8
      WITH YOUR HARMONIOUS QUIRE . . . .   174 ELEMENT POWERS V   8
      DIZZY WITH HARMONIOUS SOUND, ...   446 COLONUS PRAISE   7
HARMONY
      AND ALL THAT FAMOUS HARMONY OF LEAVES, ...   120 SORROW OF LOVE   3
HARNESS
      "HARNESS AN ASS AND CART, ...   596 COLONEL MARTIN   51
HAROUN
      BELOVED HAROUN EL RASHID, OCCUPIED . . . .   462 HARUN RASHID   V   24
      THAT YEAR WHEN GREAT HAROUN EL RASHID KILLED . . . . .   462 HARUN RASHID   V   31
HARP
      GAVE ME A HARP, AND BID ME SING, ...   16 OISIN 1   232
      A HARP OF SILVER IN MY HANDS, ...   16 OISIN 1   V   232
      GAVE ME A HARP, AND BADE ME SING, ...   16 OISIN 1   V   232
      AND CAUGHT THE SILVER HARP AWAY, ...   17 OISIN 1   240
      "O SADDEST HARP IN ALL THE WORLD, ...   17 OISIN 1   245
      THE HARP AWAY. A DOLOROUS POOL . . . .   17 OISIN 1   V   240
      THEREIN THE SILVER HARP HE HURLED, ...   17 OISIN 1   244
      "THE SADDEST HARP IN ALL THE WORLD!" . . . .   17 OISIN 1   246
      I SAW THIS HARP ALL SONGLESS LIE, ...   85 MAD KING GOLL   V   55
      AND ALL AROUND THE HARP STRING TOLD HIS PRAISE, ...   109 CUCHULAIN SEA   V   44
      AWOKE THE HARP STRINGS LONG AGO. . . . .   190 BAILE AILLINN   V   37
      WERE HOVERING OVER THE HARP STRINGS . . . . . .   195 BAILE AILLINN   V 141
      I HEAR THE HARP STRINGS PRAISE THEM, OR HEAR THEIR MOURNFUL   210 UNDER THE MOON V   16
            TALK.
      I HEAR THE HARP STRING PRAISE THEM OR HEAR THEIR MOURNFUL   210 UNDER THE MOON V   16
            TALK.
      AS MEN IN THE OLD TIMES, BEFORE THE HARP BEGAN, ...   219 WOODS OF COOLE V   43
      THE HARP OF AENGUS . . . .   219 HARP OF AENGUS   T
      HE MADE A HARP WITH DRUID APPLE-WOOD . . . . . .   220 HARP OF AENGUS   11
      HE MADE A HARP WITH DRUID APPLE WOOD . . . . . .   220 HARP OF AENGUS   V   11
      WERE'T NOT THAT THERE IS MAGIC IN HIS HARP, ...   222 SHADOW WATER B   16
      THAT THERE IS MAGIC IN THAT HARP OF HIS, ...   222 SHADOW WATER B   V   16
      AND FOR THIS END THEY GAVE ME MY OLD HARP . . . .   237 SHADOW WATER B   327
      YOUR RAVING OF A MESSAGE AND A HARP . . . . . .   237 SHADOW WATER B   331
      THEY GAVE ME THAT OLD HARP OF THE NINE SPELLS . . . .   237 SHADOW WATER B   V 327
      HAS COME INTO THE JEWELS OF THE HARP . . . . . .   239 SHADOW WATER B   V 371A
      AND THAT OLD HARP AWAKENS OF ITSELF . . . . . .   252 SHADOW WATER B   617
      PLAYED ON HIS HARP. AND I WOULD BE AS SAD . . . .   747 SHADOW WATER A   3
      GAVE HIM HIS HARP. NOW THAT HE IS ASLEEP, ...   748 SHADOW WATER A   18
      TAUGHT ME WISE MUSIC, AND GAVE ME THIS OLD HARP, ...   750 SHADOW WATER A   76
      BUT WOMEN AND JUGGLERS AND PLAYERS ON THE HARP, ...   752 SHADOW WATER A   115
      I AM AFRAID OF THE HARP. O! WINGS ON WINGS! . . . .   759 SHADOW WATER A   236
      I AM AFRAID OF HIS LOW-LAUGHING HARP. . . . . . .   759 SHADOW WATER A   239
      I AM AFRAID OF HIS LOW LAUGHING HARP. . . . . . .   759 SHADOW WATER A   V 239
      AND LEAN YOUR LIPS DEVOUTLY TO THIS HARP, ...   762 SHADOW WATER A   287
      FOR HE WHO GAVE IT CALLED IT AENGUS' HARP . . . . .   762 SHADOW WATER A   288

```
                                                         PAGE     TITLE            LINE
HARP   (CONTINUED)
        HE MADE A HARP WITH DRUID APPLE WOOD . . . . . . . .   763  SHADOW WATER A     306
        HE MADE A HARP WITH DRUID APPLE-WOOD . . . . . . .     763  SHADOW WATER A V   306
        UPON THIS WORLD NO LONGER. THE HARP CRIES OUT. . . . . 769  SHADOW WATER A V   430
HARPER
        IT WAS THAT HARPER PUT IT IN MY THOUGHTS, . . . . . .  243  SHADOW WATER B     423
HARPER'S
        OF THE HARPER'S DAUGHTER AND HER FRIEND. . . . . . .   192  BAILE AILLINN       76
        WHERE THAT WISE HARPER'S FINGER RAN. . . . . . . . .   195  BAILE AILLINN      156
        WHERE THAT WISE HARPER'S FINGERS RAN. . . . . . . .    195  BAILE AILLINN V    156
        OF THE HARPER'S DAUGHTER IF THEY WILL, . . . . . . .   197  BAILE AILLINN      199
HARPERS
        OF HARPERS AND YOUNG MEN! AND THEY . . . . . . . .     189  BAILE AILLINN       19
        AND HARPERS, PACING WITH HIGH HEAD . . . . . . . .     193  BAILE AILLINN      107
        AND HARPERS PONDERING WITH BOWED HEAD . . . . . . .    193  BAILE AILLINN V    107
        HEARING THE HARPERS PLAY, THE PINE-WOOD CRACKLE, . . . 759  SHADOW WATER A     241
        HEARING THE HARPERS PLAY, THE PINE WOOD CRACKLE, . . . 759  SHADOW WATER A V   241
HARPING
        NINE MOONS. AND FROM THE HARPING OF THE FOOL? . . . .  747  SHADOW WATER A      14
HARPS
        AS MEN IN THE OLD TIMES, BEFORE THE HARPS BEGAN, . . . 219  WOODS OF COOLE      43
HARPSTRING
        AND ALL AROUND THE HARPSTRING TOLD HIS PRAISE, . . . . 109  CUCHULAIN SEA V     44
        I HEAR THE HARPSTRING PRAISE THEM OR HEAR THEIR MOURNFUL 210 UNDER THE MOON V   16
            TALK.
HARP-STRING
        AND ALL AROUND THE HARP-STRING TOLD HIS PRAISE, . . . . 109 CUCHULAIN SEA       44
        I HEAR THE HARP-STRING PRAISE THEM, OR HEAR THEIR MOURNFUL 210 UNDER THE MOON   16
            TALK.
HARP-STRINGS
        AWOKE THE HARP-STRINGS LONG AGO. . . . . . . . . . .   190  BAILE AILLINN       37
        WERE HOVERING OVER THE HARP-STRINGS . . . . . . . .    195  BAILE AILLINN      141
        THE HARP-STRINGS HAVE BEGUN TO CRY OUT TO THE EAGLES. . 769 SHADOW WATER A     431
HARRIED
        SUDDENLY, AND RAN AT THEM AND HARRIED THEM. . . . . .  185  QUEEN MAEVE        119
        COULD, HE WAS SO HARRIED, CHEER! . . . . . . . . .     412  TOWER               76
        COULD, SO HE WAS HARRIED, CHEER! . . . . . . . . .     412  TOWER          V    76
        HARRIED, AND BURKE'S GREAT MELODY AGAINST IT. . . . .  487  SEVEN SAGES         16
        AND HARRIED ALBAN TOWNS, AND OVERTHREW . . . . . . .   749  SHADOW WATER A      40
HARRIERS
        SHE RODE TO HARRIERS? . . . . . . . . . . . . .       392  EASTER 1916         23
HARROW
        THE GOLDEN PLOUGH AND HARROW AND SPOKE ALOUD . . . . . 609  IN TARAS HALLS      12
HARRY
        BUT HARRY US WITH HOPES THAT COME TO NOTHING, . . . .  250  SHADOW WATER B     579
        THAT WE MAY HARRY HIM." THEREON . . . . . . . . .      275  GREY ROCK          106
        LIKE A GREY OWL MEN HARRY OUT . . . . . . . . . .      740  EARL PAUL           23
HARSH
        THAT WOULD BE HARSH FOR CHILDREN THAT HAVE STRAYED. . . 201 OLD MEMORY          12
        THAT HAD BEEN HARSH FOR CHILDREN THAT HAVE STRAYED. . . 201 OLD MEMORY     V    12
        AND WOULD BE NO HARSH FRIEND. WHEN NIGHT HAD DEEPENED, 283  TWO KINGS          138
        AND I HAVE NOTHING BUT HARSH SUN! . . . . . . . . .    344  DEJECTION      V     8
        SWEET AND HARSH, HARSH AND SWEET, . . . . . . . . .    382  SONG OF FOOL        10
        SWEET AND HARSH, HARSH AND SWEET, . . . . . . . . .    382  SONG OF FOOL        10
        TOLD OF A HARSH REPROOF, OR TRIVIAL EVENT . . . . . .  443  SCHOOL CHILDR       11
HARSHNESS
        HARSHNESS OF THEIR DESIRE . . . . . . . . . . . .      345  ON WOMAN            20
HART
        OF THE DREAR HART LAKE. . . . . . . . . . . . .       143  HOST OF AIR          4
HARUN
        THE GIFT OF HARUN AL-RASHID . . . . . . . . . . .      460  HARUN RASHID         T
        DESERT GEOMETRY OR THE GIFT OF HARUN AL-RASCHID . . .  460  HARUN RASHID   V     T
        WHAT GREAT HARUN AL-RASHID, OCCUPIED . . . . . . . .   462  HARUN RASHID        24
HARVEST
        THAT SLUMBERED IN THE HARVEST MOON, . . . . . . . .     85  MAD KING GOLL       50
        THAT SLUMBERED 'NEATH THE HARVEST MOON, . . . . . .     85  MAD KING GOLL  V    50
HARVESTERS
        MARINERS, ROUGH HARVESTERS! . . . . . . . . . . .      540  FROM ANTIGONE        5
        MARINERS, WILD HARVESTERS! . . . . . . . . . . .      540  FROM ANTIGONE  V     5
HARVEST'S
        THE HARVEST'S IN! THE GRANARY DOORS ARE SHUT! . . . .  755  SHADOW WATER A     177
HARVEST-TIME
        WATCHING OUR SHEPHERD SPORTS AT HARVEST-TIME . . . . . 340  SHEP GOATHERD       41
HASSAN
        AND HASSAN WILL BE WITH THEM--HE WAS SO SMALL, . . . . 699  MOSADA 3            13
        HASSAN IS WITH THEM TOO--HE WAS SO SMALL, . . . . .    699  MOSADA 3       V    13
HASTE
        SIGHING REPLIED: "WHAT NEED HAVE WE FOR HASTE . . . .  276  TWO KINGS      V     C
        DID I ON QUIVERING PINIONS HASTE, . . . . . . . .     670  ISLE STAT II 3     111
HASTEN
        DRIPPING AND DOUBLING LANDWARD, AS THOUGH THEY WOULD HASTEN  48 OISIN 3         15
            AWAY,
        DRIPPING AND DOUBLING LANDWARD, AS THOUGH THEY WOULD HASTEN  57 OISIN 3        143
            AWAY,
        NOR WOULD YOU RISE AND HASTEN AWAY, . . . . . . . .    176  BELOVED DEAD         7
HASTY
        MOST COURTEOUS TO SLOW AGE AND HASTY YOUTH, . . . . .  339  SHEP GOATHERD       19
HAT
        AFTER A RAGGED HAT IN BISCAY BAY! . . . . . . . . .    270  PARDON FATHERS      14
        WITH A HAT OUT OF FASHION, . . . . . . . . . . .      627  STATES HOLIDAY      29
```

```
                                                      PAGE    TITLE           LINE
HATCHES
    THE HOLD IS FULL OF TREASURE.  FULL TO THE HATCHES. . . .   247 SHADOW WATER B     532
HATE
    BY KNOWING NOR TUMULT NOR HATE NOR STRIFE, . . . . . . .      9 OISIN 1            95
    THE THINGS THAT MOST OF ALL I HATE! . . . . . . . . .        24 OISIN 1           359
    TWO THINGS THAT 'FORE ALL ELSE I HATE, . . . . . . . .       24 OISIN 1       V   359
    AND I MUST NEEDS ENDURE AND HATE AND WEEP, . . . . . .       35 OISIN 2            85
    HATE ON AND LOVE THROUGH UNREPINING HOURS. . . . . . .       80 EPHEMERA           22
    I FIND UNDER THE BOUGHS OF LOVE AND HATE, . . . . . .       101 ROSE UPON ROOD     10
    THE HOUR OF THY GREAT WIND OF LOVE AND HATE. . . . . .      170 SECRET ROSE        28
    HE DOES NOT HATE SEAFARERS AS HE HATES . . . . . . .        224 SHADOW WATER B     53
    AND SHOOK WITH HATE AND FEAR. . . . . . . . . . . .         254 WOMAN HOMER         4
    THOSE THAT I FIGHT I DO NOT HATE, . . . . . . . . .         328 IRISH AIRMAN        3
    THE LIVING MEN THAT I HATE, . . . . . . . . . . .           347 FISHERMAN          13
    YET KNOWS THAT TO BE CHOKED WITH HATE . . . . . .           405 FOR DAUGHTER       52
    NOR HATE OF WHAT'S TO COME, NOR PITY FOR WHAT'S GONE, . .   427 PHANTOM HATRED     30
    THEY HAD ALL THAT HAD THEIR HATE; . . . . . . . . .         514 JANE GROWN OLD     13
    SAY THAT OF LIVING MEN I HATE . . . . . . . . . .           539 MEETING            11
    WHY DO I HATE MAN, WOMAN OR EVENT? . . . . . . . .          558 RIBH CHRISTIAN      7
    SO DID FANATICISM AND HATE ENSLAVE IT, . . . . . . .        630 CIRCUS ANIMALS     22
    AND PLAY WITH HIS IMMORTAL HATE. . . . . . . . . .          736 SUMMER EVENING     12
    BECAUSE THE UNAMBITIOUS THAT HATE THE GODS . . . . . .      754 SHADOW WATER A V  158
    THE GODS HATE HAPPINESS, AND WEAVE THEIR NETS . . . . .     767 SHADOW WATER A    399
    TILL THE SIDE OF HATE COMES UP. . . . . . . . . .           776 AGAINST WITCH      35
HATED      SEE GOD-HATED
    HAS HATED EVERY MAN THAT'S NOT IN LOVE, . . . . . .         224 SHADOW WATER B     51
    ON THOSE THAT HATED "THE PLAYBOY . . . . . . . .            294 HATED PLAYBOY       T
    ON THOSE THAT HATED "THE PLAY-BOY . . . . . . . .           294 HATED PLAYBOY   V   T
    FROM FOUR GREAT MINDS THAT HATED WHIGGERY. . . . . .        486 SEVEN SAGES         7
    ALL HATED WHIGGERY! BUT WHAT IS WHIGGERY? . . . . . .       486 SEVEN SAGES        10
    I WHO HAVE ALWAYS HATED WORK, . . . . . . . . .             605 YOU CONTENT        19
    IS HE WHO LABOURED ON, DERIDED, HATED, . . . . . .          738 MOURN THEN ON      11
HATER
    I BECAME A MAN, A HATER OF THE WIND, . . . . . . .          177 PAST GREATNESS      7
HATES
    HE DOES NOT HATE SEAFARERS AS HE HATES . . . . . . .        224 SHADOW WATER B     53
    CRAMM'D ALL HER YOUTH; AND HATES HAVE BOUGHT AND SOLD . .   687 TWO TITANS         13
HATING
    EACH HATING WHAT THE OTHER LOVED, . . . . . . . .           539 MEETING             3
    IN HATING GOD SHE MAY CREEP CLOSE TO GOD. . . . . .         558 RIBH CHRISTIAN V   18
HATRED
    FOR SOMEBODY HID HATRED AND HOPE AND DESIRE AND FEAR . . .  153 CHANGE BELOVED      4
    AND I HAVE HATRED AND HOPE AND DESIRE AND FEAR . . .        153 CHANGE BELOVED V    4
    FOR LOVE IS WAR, AND THERE IS HATRED IN IT; . . . .         244 SHADOW WATER B    459
    BETWEEN MY HATRED AND DESIRE, . . . . . . . . .             400 DEMON BEAST         6
    IF THERE'S NO HATRED IN A MIND . . . . . . . . .            405 FOR DAUGHTER       54
    AN INTELLECTUAL HATRED IS THE WORST, . . . . . .            405 FOR DAUGHTER       57
    CONSIDERING THAT, ALL HATRED DRIVEN HENCE, . . . . .        405 FOR DAUGHTER       65
    FOR ARROGANCE AND HATRED ARE THE WARES . . . . . .          406 FOR DAUGHTER       75
    I SEE PHANTOMS OF HATRED AND OF THE HEART'S . . .           425 PHANTOM HATRED      T
    AND WOULD THROUGH HATRED OF THE BAYS . . . . . . .          436 FOR MY SON         15
    OR OUT OF ABSTRACT HATRED, AND SHED BLOOD, . . . .          482 BLOOD AND MOON     38
    TURN HATRED INTO SPORT. . . . . . . . . . . .               506 REMORSE SPEECH      8
    GREAT HATRED, LITTLE ROOM, . . . . . . . . . .              506 REMORSE SPEECH     12
    I STUDY HATRED WITH GREAT DILIGENCE, . . . . . .            558 RIBH CHRISTIAN      3
    A DARKER KNOWLEDGE AND IN HATRED TURN . . . . . .           558 RIBH CHRISTIAN     14
    HATRED OF GOD MAY BRING THE SOUL TO GOD. . . . . .          558 RIBH CHRISTIAN     18
    OUT OF THEIR HATRED. MY BELOVED, FAREWELL. . . . .          767 SHADOW WATER A    400
    HATRED MAY BE SWEET TO THE TASTE." . . . . . . .            776 AGAINST WITCH      31
    HATRED MAY BE SWEET IN THE TASTE." . . . . . . .            776 AGAINST WITCH V    31
HATS
    NINE BOOKS OR NINE HATS . . . . . . . . . . .               628 JANE MOUNTAIN       3
HAUGHTIER
    BUT HERE'S A HAUGHTIER TEXT, . . . . . . . . .              259 UNWORTH PRAISE     12
    AND BUILDINGS THAT A HAUGHTIER AGE DESIGNED, . . . .        418 ANCEST HOUSES      34
    AND HAUGHTIER HEADED BURKE THAT PROVED THE STATE A TREE     481 BLOOD AND MOON     22
HAUGHTIER-HEADED
    AND HAUGHTIER-HEADED BURKE THAT PROVED THE STATE A TREE,    481 BLOOD AND MOON     22
HAUGHTY
    THEREON DID SHE LOOK HAUGHTY AND SWEET! . . . . . .           6 OISIN 1            54
    SHE'LL NOT ASK A HAUGHTY DRESS; . . . . . . . . .           124 CATHLEEN PARA       6
    THEIR HAUGHTY IMAGES THAT CANNOT WITHER, . . . . .          184 QUEEN MAEVE        87
    THEIR HAUGHTY IMAGES THAT CANNOT FADE, . . . . . .          184 QUEEN MAEVE    V   88
    THE HAUGHTY IMAGES, THAT CANNOT PERISH . . . . . .          184 QUEEN MAEVE    V   88
    OF SOME MOST HAUGHTY DEED OR THOUGHT . . . . . . .          436 FOR MY SON         13
HAUNTED      SEE FAIRY-HAUNTED
    I AM HAUNTED BY NUMBERLESS ISLANDS, AND MANY A DANAAN       122 WHITE BIRDS         9
        SHORE.
HAUNTER      SEE TOMB-HAUNTER
HAUNTS
    AMONG THE HAUNTS OF BEE AND BIRD. . . . . . . .             729 PRIEST FAIRY       42
HAVING
    AND HAVING SUCH WIDE-OPEN, SHINING EYES. . . . . .          231 SHADOW WATER B    200
    HAVING THEIR LIFE IN HIM. THOUGH IT BE THE MOON . . .       240 SHADOW WATER B    377
    BROKEN-HEARTED, HAVING LOST HIS QUEEN . . . . . .           242 SHADOW WATER B    407
    BROKENHEARTED, HAVING LOST HIS QUEEN . . . . . .            242 SHADOW WATER B V  407
    AND HAVING LIT UPON THIS WOMAN THERE, . . . . . .           248 SHADOW WATER B    542
    AND HAVING LIT UPON THIS WOMAN HERE, . . . . . .            248 SHADOW WATER B V  542
    IN HAVING ONE ANOTHER? HOW COULD I REST . . . . .           249 SHADOW WATER B    571
    BELOVED, HAVING DRAGGED THE NET ABOUT US, . . . .           252 SHADOW WATER B    615
    AND SLEEPY HAVING HAD THEIR MEAL! . . . . . . .             271 GREY ROCK      V   17
```

363

		PAGE	TITLE		LINE
HAVING	(CONTINUED)				
	AND HAVING SAID IT, BURST IN TEARS.	273	GREY ROCK		48
	HAVING NO THOUGHT BUT FOR HIS QUEEN EDAIN,	276	TWO KINGS	V	I
	HAVING LOVED GOD ONCE, BUT MAYBE	299	THREE HERMITS		26
	AND HAVING TALKED TO SOME LATE HOUR	324	ROBERT GREGORY		4
	HAVING GROWN SLUGGISH AND CONTEMPLATIVE.	325	ROBERT GREGORY		40
	AND HAVING NO DESIRE THEY CANNOT TELL	376	PHASES OF MOON		107
	BUT HAVING NO DESIRE THEY CANNOT TELL	376	PHASES OF MOON	V	107
	HAVING INHERITED A VIGOROUS MIND	422	MY DESCENDANTS		1
	AND HAVING STRETCHED AND YAWNED AWHILE	612	NEWS ORACLE		11
	WHERE DWELL THE MINDS OF OLD MEN HAVING PEACE,	721	WITCH VIVIEN		22
HAWK					
	AND THE WOOD-WOMAN, WHOSE LOVER WAS CHANGED TO A BLUE-EYED HAWK:	209	UNDER THE MOON		13
	AND THE WOOD WOMAN, WHOSE LOVER WAS CHANGED TO A BLUE-EYED HAWK:	209	UNDER THE MOON	V	13
	THE HAWK	349	HAWK		T
	"CALL DOWN THE HAWK FROM THE AIR:	349	HAWK		1
	YELLOW-EYED HAWK OF THE MIND,	349	HAWK		14
	PULL DOWN ESTABLISHED HONOUR: HAWK FOR NEWS	398	LEADERS CROWD		3
	WITH AN EYE LIKE A HAWK,	627	STATES HOLIDAY		32
	UP THERE SOME HAWK OR OWL HAS STRUCK,	633	MAN AND ECHO		43
HAWKING	SEE A-HAWKING				
HAWKS					
	TO BRAZEN HAWKS. NOR SELF-DELIGHTING REVERIE,	427	PHANTOM HATRED		29
HAWTHORN					
	THE FALLING HAWTHORN BLOOM. BY MERE AND BROOK	677	ISLE STAT II 3	279
	THE WICKED HAWTHORN TREE.	788	HAWTHORN TREE	V	T
	SAID THE WICKED, CROOKED, HAWTHORN TREE:	788	HAWTHORN TREE		6
	SAID THE WICKED, CROOKED, HAWTHORN TREE.	788	HAWTHORN TREE		14
HAY					
	BRUSH LIGHTLY AS HAY MOUSE EARTH'S PEBBLES,	56	OISIN 3	V	128
	TILL, FATTENING THE WINDS OF THE MORNING, AN ODOUR OF NEW-MOWN HAY	57	OISIN 3		153
	AN ODOUR OF THE NEW-MOWN HAY	502	VACILLATION		58
HAY-COCK					
	AS A HAY-COCK OUT ON THE FLOOD, OR A WOLF SUCKED UNDER A WEIR.	63	OISIN 3		220
HAYMOUSE					
	BRUSH LIGHTLY AS HAYMOUSE EARTH'S PEBBLES,	56	OISIN 3		128
HAYNAU					
	THE AUSTRIAN HAYNAU HE, IN MANY LANDS	709	FERENCZ RENYI		8
	THE SOLDIER THUS, AND HAYNAU—"PEASANT, SPEAK	711	FERENCZ RENYI		54
	HAYNAU, THE MAN OF SYSTEM, LIFTS HIS HAND	712	FERENCZ RENYI		62
	HAYNAU, THINE HOUR HAS COME, THY FOLLOWERS FAR	715	FERENCZ RENYI		117
HAYNAU'S					
	"CHOOSE!" RESTLESS HAYNAU'S FINGERS TAPPING GO.	711	FERENCZ RENYI		41
	FROM HAYNAU'S LIFTED FINGERS—TWO DRAW NIGH	714	FERENCZ RENYI		104
HAYSTACK					
	WHEREBY THE HAYSTACK- AND ROOF-LEVELLING WIND,	403	FOR DAUGHTER		5
HAZEL					
	THAT SPRANG UNDER THE SEVEN HAZEL TREES,	35	OISIN 2		84
	AN ISLE LAY LEVEL BEFORE US, WITH DRIPPING HAZEL AND OAK?	47	OISIN 3		10
	AN ISLE LAY LEVEL BEFORE US, DRIPPING WITH HAZEL AND OAK?	47	OISIN 3	V	10
	CEASED ON OUR HANDS AND OUR FACES, ON HAZEL AND OAK LEAF, THE LIGHT,	48	OISIN 3		23
	. . . FOR, CUMBROUS WITH STEMS OF THE HAZEL AND OAK,	48	OISIN 3		25
	. . . FAR FROM THE HAZEL AND OAK,	57	OISIN 3		146
	AND THE SHADOWY HAZEL GROVE	119	PITY OF LOVE		6
	I WENT OUT TO THE HAZEL WOOD,	149	WANDER AENGUS		1
	AND CUT AND PEELED A HAZEL WAND:	149	WANDER AENGUS		3
	AND CUT AND PEELED A HAZEL ROD .	149	WANDER AENGUS	V	3
	A MAN WITH A HAZEL WAND CAME WITHOUT SOUND:	153	CHANGE BELOVED		6
	A MAN WITH A WAND OF HAZEL CAME WITHOUT SOUND:	153	CHANGE BELOVED	V	6
	I HAVE BEEN A HAZEL TREE, AND THEY HUNG	177	PAST GREATNESS	V	3
	FLICKERING WITH ASH AND HAZEL, BUT HALF SHOWED	180	QUEEN MAEVE		12
	WHERE HAZEL AND ASH AND PRIVET BLIND THE PATHS:	217	WOODS OF COOLE		8
	I GROPED MY WAY FROM BEECH TO HAZEL WOOD,	283	TWO KINGS		139
	WESTWARD OF TARA, AMONG THE HAZEL TREES—	283	TWO KINGS	V	135
	TILL OAK AND HAZEL CEASED AND BEECH BEGAN,	283	TWO KINGS	V	139A
	HAZEL LAVERY LIVING AND DYING, THAT TALE	602	GALLERY REVIS		23
	"WE BURIED LATE IN A HAZEL DELL	729	PRIEST FAIRY		43
HAZELS					
	OF HOLLIES, AND HAZELS, AND OAK TREES, A VALLEY WAS SLOPING AWAY	48	OISIN 3	V	26
	SHOULD BE SO SIMPLE—A BAT ROSE FROM THE HAZELS	377	PHASES OF MOON		137
HAZEL-TREE					
	I HAVE BEEN A HAZEL-TREE, AND THEY HUNG	177	PAST GREATNESS		3
HAZEL-TREES					
	WESTWARD OF TARA, AMONG THE HAZEL-TREES—	283	TWO KINGS		135
HEAD	SEE RED-HEAD MAST-HEAD GOAT-HEAD				
	"AND EVERY HERO DROOP HIS HEAD?	4	OISIN 1		33
	"WHY, AS YE RIDE, DROOPS LOW EACH HEAD?	4	OISIN 1	V	32
	THERE WAS, OH PATRICK, BY THY HEAD,	7	OISIN 1	V	71
	BOAST NOT, NOR MOURN WITH DROOPING HEAD	11	OISIN 1		129
	AND SIGHING BOWED HER GENTLE HEAD,	12	OISIN 1		149
	AS WE KISSED EACH ROSE'S HEAD:	21	OISIN 1	V	307
	AND KISSED MY EYES, AND, SWAYING HER BRIGHT HEAD	29	OISIN 2		6
	AND NOW SANG NIAM, SWAYING HER BRIGHT HEAD	29	OISIN 2	V	6
	SO SANG YOUNG NIAM, SWAYING HER BRIGHT HEAD,	30	OISIN 2	V	15
	HE SHIVERING PAUSED, AND RAISED HIS HEAD AND SCREAMED.	30	OISIN 2	V	25

		PAGE	TITLE		LINE

HEAD (CONTINUED)

	PAGE	TITLE		LINE
IT BRINGS NO SHAME UPON A HUMAN HEAD	35	OISIN 2	V	90A
WITH BOWED HEAD, TREMBLING WHEN THE WHITE BLADE SHONE, . .	38	OISIN 2		137
AND ON MY BOSOM LAID HER WEEPING HEAD.	46	OISIN 2		250
DARK BALOR, AS OLD AS A FOREST, CAR-BORNE, HIS MIGHTY HEAD SUNK	53	OISIN 3		91
CAME BALOR, AS OLD AS A FOREST, CAR BORNE, HIS MIGHTY HEAD SUNK	53	OISIN 3	V	91
NOT COUGHING, MY HEAD ON MY KNEES, ...	58	OISIN 3		159
I WOULD LEAVE NO SAINT'S HEAD ON HIS BODY	58	OISIN 3		160
CAME AFTER THE HARD GAZE OF YOUTH, OR AN OLD MAN LIFTED HIS HEAD!	59	OISIN 3		170
. . . OR WAS LIFTED AN OLD MAN'S MILD HEAD.	59	OISIN 3	V	170
YET STILL SHE TURNS HER RESTLESS HEAD!	65	HAPPY SHEPHERD		5
WHILE HE BENT DOWN HIS FADING HEAD, ...	82	MAD KING GOLL		10
BENDING LOW HIS PIOUS HEAD, ...	82	MAD KING GOLL	V	10
BENDING LOW HIS FADING HEAD, ...	82	MAD KING GOLL	V	10
HIS EYELIDS DROOP, HIS HEAD FALLS LOW, ...	98	FOXHUNTER		13
HIS EYELIDS CLOSE, HIS HEAD DROOPS LOW, ...	98	FOXHUNTER	V	13
LIFTS SLOW HIS WINTRY HEAD!	99	FOXHUNTER		46
UPON HIS HEAD TO CAST AWAY MY SORROW.	102	FERGUS DRUID		14
UPON HIS HEAD TO CAST AWAY MY CARE.	102	FERGUS DRUID	V	14
AND STILL I FEEL THE CROWN UPON MY HEAD.	103	FERGUS DRUID		20
BUT STILL I FEEL THE CROWN UPON MY HEAD.	103	FERGUS DRUID	V	20
THE SORROWS OF THE WORLD BOW DOWN MY HEAD, ...	104	FERGUS DRUID	V	38A
"YOUR HEAD A WHILE SEEMED LIKE A WOMAN'S HEAD	110	CUCHULAIN SEA		63
"YOUR HEAD A WHILE SEEMED LIKE A WOMAN'S HEAD	110	CUCHULAIN SEA		63
WITH HEAD BOWED ON HIS KNEES CUCHULAIN STAYED!	110	CUCHULAIN SEA		71
WITH HEAD BOWED ON HIS KNEES, CUCHULLIN STAID, ...	110	CUCHULAIN SEA	V	71
A CHAPLET FOR YOUR HEAD.	113	ROSE OF PEACE		8
THREATEN THE HEAD THAT I LOVE.	119	PITY OF LOVE		8
ALL THREATEN THE HEAD THAT I LOVE.	119	PITY OF LOVE	V	8
THE SHAKING OF ITS LEAFY HEAD	134	TWO TREES		9
BECAUSE A FIRE WAS IN MY HEAD, ...	149	WANDER AENGUS		2
OF THE MATCHING OF RIBBONS FOR BOSOM AND HEAD, ...	151	OLD MOTHER		6
AND WRAPPED THE FLAMES ABOVE HIS HOLY HEAD!	162	ASKS FORGIVE		17
AND GATHERED THE FLAMES ABOVE HIS HOLY HEAD.	162	ASKS FORGIVE	V	17
CUMHAL CALLED OUT, BENDING HIS HEAD, ...	166	BLESSED		1
CUMHAL CALLED OUT, BOWING HIS HEAD, ...	167	BLESSED	V	4A
AND HE NODS A DRUNKEN HEAD.	168	BLESSED		32
YOU WOULD COME HITHER, AND BEND YOUR HEAD, ...	175	BELOVED DEAD		3
AND I WOULD LAY MY HEAD ON YOUR BREAST!	175	BELOVED DEAD		4
KNOWING ONE, OUT OF ALL THINGS, ALONE, THAT HIS HEAD . .	177	PAST GREATNESS		8
A WALL BEHIND HIS BACK, OVER HIS HEAD	180	QUEEN MAEVE		5
BUT OUT OF THE DARK AIR OVER HER HEAD THERE CAME	187	QUEEN MAEVE		153
AN OLD MAN CAUGHT THE HORSE'S HEAD	191	BAILE AILLINN		57
AND HARPERS, PACING WITH HIGH HEAD	193	BAILE AILLINN		107
AND HARPERS PONDERING WITH BOWED HEAD	193	BAILE AILLINN	V	107
O HEART! O HEART! IF SHE'D BUT TURN HER HEAD, ...	200	FOLLY COMFORT		13
BUT WITH A MAN'S HEAD, OR A FAIR WOMAN'S, ...	233	SHADOW WATER B		245
AND NOW A LAGGARD WITH A WOMAN'S HEAD	234	SHADOW WATER B		260
THAT I MIGHT LAY IT ON YOUR HEAD AS A CROWN.	246	SHADOW WATER B		511
"SUCH A DELICATE HIGH HEAD, ...	259	PEACE		7
BEFORE HIS CHAIR AND BENDING DOWN MY HEAD	282	TWO KINGS		132
STOOD ON MY PATH. TREMBLING FROM HEAD TO FOOT	283	TWO KINGS		151
CROW UPON TARA." KING EOCHAID BOWED HIS HEAD	286	TWO KINGS		211
ABOUT YOUR HEAD TILL THE DUST STOPS YOUR EAR, ...	293	TO A SHADE		20
CAN RAVEL OUT WHAT'S IN MY HEAD.	295	THREE BEGGARS		12
I SHAKE FROM HEAD TO FOOT.	316	FRIENDS		28
HEAD UPON SHOULDER LEANT!	319	DOLLS		18
THE BELL-BEAT OF THEIR WINGS ABOVE MY HEAD, ...	323	SWANS AT COOLE		17
AND QUARRELS ARE BLOWN UP UPON THAT HEAD!	324	ROBERT GREGORY		13
PITY, AN ACHING HEAD, ...	346	ON WOMAN		38
AS THOUGH SOME OTHER NAME RAN IN HIS HEAD.	351	HER PRAISE		9
OF SOME STRANGE WOMAN'S NAME THAT RAN IN HIS HEAD. . . .	351	HER PRAISE	V	9
AFTER NINE YEARS, I SINK MY HEAD ABASHED.	353	PEOPLE		37
IF HEAD AND LIMB HAVE BEAUTY AND THE INSTEP'S HIGH AND LIGHT	354	HIS PHOENIX		21
SHE MIGHT, SO NOBLE FROM HEAD	355	PROPERTIUS		1
AS IF THE HAIR STOOD UP ON MY HEAD.	358	PRESENCES		2
IS TO SCRATCH YOUR HEAD	359	TO A SQUIRREL		7
SHE LIES, HER LOVELY PITEOUS HEAD AMID DULL RED HAIR . .	362	HER COURTESY		2
PLEASE A FANTASTIC HEAD.	366	HER CHRIS TREE		8
WITH MOTIONLESS HEAD ERECT.	383	VISION ROBART		32
NOW SHE HAS THROWN HER ARMS ABOVE HER HEAD!	390	IMAGE PAST		36
I HAVE PASSED WITH A NOD OF THE HEAD	392	EASTER 1916		5
THE GLITTERING EYES IN A DEATH'S HEAD	400	DEMON BEAST		9
A SHAPE WITH LION BODY AND THE HEAD OF A MAN, ...	402	SECOND COMING		14
ALL BREAK AND VANISH, AND EVIL GATHERS HEAD!	433	NINETEEN 19		117
BID A STRONG GHOST STAND AT THE HEAD	435	FOR MY SON		1
WITH SIXTY OR MORE WINTERS ON ITS HEAD, ...	444	SCHOOL CHILDR		38
FIRST TROD ON THE MOUNTAIN'S HEAD	488	CRAZED MOON		9
A MOMENT'S MEMORY TO THAT LAURELLED HEAD.	489	COOLE ARK 29		32
SO GET YOU GONE, VON HUEGEL, THOUGH WITH BLESSINGS ON YOUR HEAD.	503	VACILLATION		89
MAY CALL DOWN CURSES ON HIS HEAD	508	JANE BISHOP		4
WHEN HE TURNED HIS HEAD	511	JANE AND JACK		16
WHEN YOU TURNED YOUR HEAD	511	JANE AND JACK	V	16
HAD TURNED HIS STATELY HEAD.	526	AM OF IRELAND		10
AND LAY DOWN THAT HEAD	534	CONSOLATION		4
ALTERNATIVE SONG FOR THE SEVERED HEAD IN	549	SEVERED HEAD		T

```
                                                    PAGE    TITLE            LINE
HEAD   (CONTINUED)
    WITHOUT A THING IN HIS HEAD . . . . . . . . . . . .   552 SONGS REWRIT 2      10
    ALONE WITH A CRAZY HEAD. . . . . . . . . . . . . .    552 SONGS REWRIT 2 V    12
    TO THOSE THAT NEVER SAW THIS TONSURED HEAD . . . .    555 RIBH AT TOMB         4
    BLACK OUT! HEAVEN BLAZING INTO THE HEAD! . . . . .    566 LAPIS LAZULI        19
    HE DROPPED UPON HIS HEAD AND DIED. . . . . . . . .    571 THREE BUSHES        52
    HIS ROD AND ITS BUTTING HEAD . . . . . . . . . . .    575 MAIDS 2ND SONG       3
    BEAUTIFUL LOFTY THINGS! O'LEARY'S NOBLE HEAD! . . .   577 LOFTY THINGS         1
    "OF PLASTER SAINTS"! HIS BEAUTIFUL MISCHIEVOUS HEAD THROWN  577 LOFTY THINGS   4
      BACK.
    PALLAS ATHENE IN THAT STRAIGHT BACK AND ARROGANT HEAD! . . .  578 LOFTY THINGS  11
    THE DOOR ABOVE HIS HEAD . . . . . . . . . . . . .    585 ORAHILLY            33
    A HAND UNDER HIS HEAD. . . . . . . . . . . . . . .    617 LONG-LEG FLY         8
    A BRONZE HEAD  . . . . . . . . . . . . . . . . . .    618 BRONZE HEAD          T
    HERE AT RIGHT OF THE ENTRANCE THIS BRONZE HEAD, . .   618 BRONZE HEAD          1
    THEN CERTAIN SHROUDS THAT MUTTERED HEAD TO HEAD . .   634 CUCHULAIN COMF       4
    THEN CERTAIN SHROUDS THAT MUTTERED HEAD TO HEAD . .   634 CUCHULAIN COMF       4
    UNDER BARE BEN BULBEN'S HEAD . . . . . . . . . . .    640 BEN BULBEN          84
    OF SWORD-BLUE WAVES OF CALM; WHILE O'ER HEAD BLINK . . .  663 ISLE STAT II 2   42
    A BEARDED WITCH, HER SLUGGISH HEAD LOW BENT  . . .    685 SEEKER              72
    OF FAILURE, AND TO CROWN HER CROWNLESS HEAD, . . .    688 TWO TITANS          48
    LOWLY THE HEAD OF HIS MAGNIFICENCE . . . . . . . .    689 NETTLESHIP           6
    DOWN LOW THE HEAD OF HIS MAGNIFICENCE  . . . . . .    689 NETTLESHIP       V   6
    AROUND MY HEAD AND DANCED AMONG THE GRASS! . . . .    690 MOSADA 1            19
    POURS UP AND FLOATS IN FRAGRANCE ROUND MY HEAD . .    691 MOSADA 1            40
    POURS UP AND FLOATS IN FRAGRANCE O'ER MY HEAD . . .   691 MOSADA 1         V  40
    AND IN HER SINGING WOVE AROUND HER HEAD  . . . . .    693 MOSADA 1            84
    HER HEAD CAST BACKWARD IN HER UNLOOSED HAIR. . . .    701 MOSADA 3            67
    UPON THY FACE?  HOW HEAVILY THY HEAD . . . . . . .    701 MOSADA 3            72
    SAFE ON THE BREAST OF GOMEZ LIES THY HEAD, . . . .    703 MOSADA 3           101
    SAFE ON THE BREAST OF VALLENCE IS THY HEAD . . . .    703 MOSADA 3         V 101
    SAFE ON THE BREAST OF GOMEZ IS THY HEAD, . . . . .    703 MOSADA 3         V 101
    AH! WOE FOR YOUR WINGS AND YOUR HEAD-- . . . . . .    708 FAIRY PEDANT        34
    BUT THIS ONE--THIS ONE.  NOW HIS HEAD DROPS LOW, .    711 FERENCZ RENYI       39
    "A LITTLE WILL I LAY MY WEARY HEAD, . . . . . . .     712 FERENCZ RENYI       75
    HE THOUGHT WISE THINGS AS HIS GREY HEAD NODDED. . .   728 PRIEST FAIRY        12
    AND KEEP A COVERED HEAD." . . . . . . . . . . . .     742 EARL PAUL           64
    AND UNDER LOVERS' EYELIDS.  BEND YOUR HEAD . . . .    762 SHADOW WATER A     286
    IN THE TOWER OVER HEAD, . . . . . . . . . . . . .     772 SONG DEIRDRE 1 V     3
    TO THE TOWER OVER HEAD, . . . . . . . . . . . . .     772 SONG DEIRDRE 1 V     3
    MY HEAD IS IN A CLOUD! . . . . . . . . . . . . . .    782 HEART FRIGHT         8
    THE SINGING HEAD AND THE LADY  . . . . . . . . . .    789 SINGING HEAD    V    T
    HIS HEAD FROM OFF HIS BODY  . . . . . . . . . . . .   789 SINGING HEAD         5
    I BADE THEM FETCH HIS HEAD. . . . . . . . . . . .     789 SINGING HEAD        12
HEADED     SEE MAN-HEADED SLEEPY-HEADED CAT-HEADED MANY-HEADED HAUGHTIER-HEADED
    AND HAUGHTIER HEADED BURKE THAT PROVED THE STATE A TREE  481 BLOOD AND MOON V  22
HEADLONG
    AND FOLLOWING HER AT A HEADLONG SPEED  . . . . . .     12 OISIN 1         V 144
    WHEN THE HEADLONG LIGHT IS LOOSE, . . . . . . . .     414 TOWER              135
HEAD'S     SEE SPEAR-HEAD'S
HEADS      SEE HILL-HEADS
    THAT RAISE THEIR HEADS AND WANDER SINGING, . . . .     27 OISIN 1            419
    . . . AND O'ER YOUR CAR HEADS PEER . . . . . . . .     73 ANASHU VIJAYA   V  45
    OF HOW I HEAR ON HILL HEADS HIGH . . . . . . . . .     85 MAD KING GOLL   V  53
    IT SEEMED THEY RAISED THEIR LITTLE SILVER HEADS, . .   126 DREAM OF FAERY     6
    THEIR HEADS ON YOUR KNEES, AND DROWN THEIR EYES WITH YOUR  163 VALLEY LOVERS   6
      HAIR,
    YOU PUT SUCH FOLLY IN OUR HEADS  . . . . . . . . .    190 BAILE AILLINN      32
    THEIR HEADS BEING TURNED WITH PRAISE AND FLATTERY! . .  245 SHADOW WATER B  480
    THEY HAVE BEEN CIRCLING OVER OUR HEADS IN THE AIR, . .  247 SHADOW WATER B  525
    BALD HEADS FORGETFUL OF THEIR SINS . . . . . . . .    337 SCHOLARS             1
    OLD, LEARNED, RESPECTABLE BALD HEADS . . . . . . .    337 SCHOLARS             2
    OLD MARBLE HEADS, OLD PICTURES EVERYWHERE! . . . .    491 COOLE BALLYLEE      28
    A MYRIAD HEADS HAVE LAIN." " . . . . . . . . . . .    496 MOHINI CHATTER      11
    WHAT HEADS SHAKE OR NOD? . . . . . . . . . . . . .    505 RESULT THOUGHT      18
    I KNOCK THEIR HEADS ABOUT. . . . . . . . . . . . .    605 SONGS BURDEN 1       8
    THEIR UNREMEMBERING HEARTS AND HEADS . . . . . . .    639 BEN BULBEN          72
    GO UP AND DOWN, AND RAISE THEIR HEADS AND SING . .    682 SEEKER              30
    WHILE WE SHAKE OUR HEADS AND SCOLD . . . . . . . .    727 LOVERS QUARREL      54
    AND PLUMED HEADS ABOUT HIM, . . . . . . . . . . .     740 EARL PAUL           31
    WHERE NIAM HEADS THE REVELRY. . . . . . . . . . .     743 DANAAN QUICK        29
HEADY
    THAT HAS THE HEADY FLAVOUR OF NEW WINE, . . . . .     240 SHADOW WATER B     374
    BEING TOO HIGH, THEIR HEADY PROPHECIES . . . . . .    250 SHADOW WATER B     578
HEALED     SEE NEW-HEALED
    AND HEALED MY WOUNDS WITH UNGUENTS OUT OF FLOWERS  . .   41 OISIN 2          185
    THEY HEALED MY WOUNDS! AND ON THE SKIN SUPINE . . .     41 OISIN 2        V 187
    HIS HEALED SHAPE! AND FOR A HUNDRED YEARS  . . . .     44 OISIN 2        V 221
    HIS NEW HEALED SHAPE!  AND FOR A HUNDRED YEARS . .      44 OISIN 2        V 221
HEALING
    HEALING FROM ITS LETTERED SLAB.  THOSE SELF-SAME HANDS   503 VACILLATION     82
      PERCHANCE
    OTHERS KNOW THE HEALING EARTH, . . . . . . . . . .    733 STREET DANCERS      53
    ALL THE HEALING EARTH MAY-TREASURE, . . . . . . .     733 STREET DANCERS      63
    ALL THE HEALING EARTH MAY TREASURE, . . . . . . .     733 STREET DANCERS  V   63
HEALTH
    AND FIND MY HEALTH AGAIN IN THE SEA AIR," . . . .     299 BEGGAR CRIED         2
    WHETHER HEALTH, WEALTH OR PEACE OF MIND WERE SPENT . .  429 NINETEEN 19      36
    IS DRINKING HER HEALTH WHEN LONE, ALONE-- . . . .     551 SONGS REWRIT 1 V     4
    MY MEDIAEVAL KNEES LACK HEALTH UNTIL THEY BEND, . .   603 GALLERY REVIS       33
    HONOUR HAD LIVED SO LONG, THEIR HEALTH I FOUND. . .   603 GALLERY REVIS   V   35
```

366

HEALTHY
   "HE LIVES?" "HE LIVES AND IS A HEALTHY MAN." . . . . .   280 TWO KINGS   84
   I HAVE AS HEALTHY FLESH AND BLOOD AS ANY RHYMER'S HAD, . . 450 OWEN AHERNE   10
HEAP
   AND SHOULD HE DIE TO HEAP HIS BURIAL-MOUND . . . .   280 TWO KINGS   82
   AND SHOULD HE DIE TO HEAP HIS BURIAL MOUND . . . . 280 TWO KINGS   V   82
   AND THEY WERE WHIRLING IN A HEAP. . . . .   297 THREE BEGGARS   47
   TILL THEY WERE WHIRLING IN A HEAP. . . . .   297 THREE BEGGARS   V   47
   WHEN CLOSE TO HIS RIGHT HAND A HEAP . . . .   302 HOUR DAWN   11
HEAPED   SEE WEB-HEAPED CAIRN-HEAPED
   WHERE MEN HAVE HEAPED NO BURIAL-MOUNDS, ...   8 OISIN 1   82
   WHERE MEN HAVE HEAPED NO BURIAL MOUNDS, ...   8 OISIN 1   V   82
   HEAPED BESIDE THE GLIMMERING WAVES, ...   21 OISIN 1   314
   MY SOUL, MY PREY, AND THIS MY HEAPED PILE. . . . . . .   45 OISIN 2   V 239B
   THEIR NAKED AND GLEAMING BODIES POURED OUT AND HEAPED IN   48 OISIN 3   28
     THE WAY.
   . . . HEAPED LOOSE WHERE THEY LAY. . . . .   48 OISIN 3   V   28
   BEFORE THEY HEAPED HIS GRAVE UNDER THE HILL; . . . . .   127 DREAM OF FAERY   16
   COME, HEART, WHERE HILL IS HEAPED UPON HILL: . . . . .   148 INTO TWILIGHT   9
   FOR WHOM THE CAIRN'S BUT HEAPED ANEW. . . . .   192 BAILE AILLINN   84
   THEY HAVE HEAPED THE STONES ABOVE HIS GRAVE . . . . . .   193 BAILE AILLINN   115
   AND INSULT HEAPED UPON HIM FOR HIS PAINS. . . . .   292 TO A SHADE   15
   AND HEAPED UP STONE ON STONE, ...   307 HOUR DAWN   116
   AND HEAPED UP STONE ON STONE AGAIN, ...   307 HOUR DAWN   118
   AND AFTER HEAPED THE STONES AGAIN . . . .   307 HOUR DAWN   V   116
   GRAVE IS HEAPED ON GRAVE . . . .   496 MOHINI CHATTER   19
   BIRTH IS HEAPED ON BIRTH . . . .   496 MOHINI CHATTER   23
HEAPED-UP
   AND THEN ON HEAPED-UP SKINS OF OTTERS SLEPT. . . . . .   41 OISIN 2   191
HEAR
   AND LIGHTNING FLASH FOR EVER? CEASE AND HEAR. . . . .   42 OISIN 2   V 207
   SAINT, DO YOU WEEP? I HEAR AMID THE THUNDER . . . . .   43 OISIN 2   209
   SAINT, DOST THOU WEEP? I HEAR AMID THE THUNDER . . . .   43 OISIN 2   V 209
   "I HEAR MY SOUL DROP DOWN INTO DECAY, ...   45 OISIN 2   235
   A GOOD NAME IS GOODLY TO HEAR OF, AND A GOOD NAME SURELY   51 OISIN 3   V   63
     IS THINE.
   CRIED OUT, DIM SEA, HEAR MY MOST PITEOUS STORY! . . . .   68 SAD SHEPHERD   9
   "OH SEA, OLD SEA, HEAR THOU MY PITEOUS STORY!" . . . .   68 SAD SHEPHERD   V   9
   NO OTHER.--HEAR, AND MAY THE INDOLENT FLOCKS . . . . .   71 ANASHU VIJAYA   4
   MAY PANTHERS END HIM.--HEAR, AND LOAD OUR KING . . . .   71 ANASHU VIJAYA   6
   WHO NEVER HEAR THE UNFORGIVING HOUND. . . . .   75 ANASHU VIJAYA   75
   OF HOW I HEAR ON HILL-HEADS HIGH . . . .   85 MAD KING GOLL   V   53
   OF HOW I HEAR ON HILL HEADS HIGH . . . .   85 MAD KING GOLL   V   53
   WITH EYES OF SADNESS CAME TO HEAR . . . .   85 MAD KING GOLL   V   62
   WITH EYES OF SADNESS ROSE TO HEAR, ...   85 MAD KING GOLL   V   62
   IN SOLEMN REVERIE ROSE TO HEAR . . . .   85 MAD KING GOLL   V   62
   HE'LL HEAR NO MORE THE LOWING . . . .   88 STOLEN CHILD   44
   THEY HEAR HIM FEEBLY SAY, ...   99 FOXHUNTER   32
   LEST I NO MORE HEAR COMMON THINGS THAT CRAVE: . . . . .   101 ROSE UPON ROOD   15
   BUT SEEK ALONE TO HEAR THE STRANGE THINGS SAID . . . .   101 ROSE UPON ROOD   19
   I OFTEN HEAR HIM SINGING TO AND FRO, ...   109 CUCHULAIN SEA   V   49
   I OFTEN HEAR THE SWEET SOUND OF HIS BOW. . . . .   109 CUCHULAIN SEA   V   50
   WE SHALL NO LONGER HEAR THE LITTLE CRY . . . .   115 ROSE OF BATTLE   35
   I HEAR LAKE WATER LAPPING WITH LOW SOUNDS BY THE SHORE!   117 ISLE INNISFREE   10
   I HEAR IT IN THE DEEP HEART'S CORE. . . . .   117 ISLE INNISFREE   12
   I HEAR LAKE WATER LAPPING WITH LOW SOUNDS ON THE SHORE!   117 ISLE INNISFREE   V   10
   AND HEAR THE NARROW GRAVES CALLING MY CHILD AND ME. . .   147 UNAPPEAS HOST   6
   AND HEAR THE WINDS HAVE SHAKEN, THE UNAPPEASABLE HOST .   147 UNAPPEAS HOST   V   11
   DO YOU NOT HEAR ME CALLING, WHITE DEER WITH NO HORNS?   153 CHANGE BELOVED   1
   I HEAR THE SHADOWY HORSES, THEIR LONG MANES A-SHAKE,   154 BELOVED PEACE   1
   I HEAR WHITE BEAUTY SIGHING, TOO, ...   156 FORGOT BEAUTY   19
   I HEAR PALE BEAUTY SIGHING TOO, ...   156 FORGOT BEAUTY   V   19
   I HARDLY HEAR THE CURLEW CRY, ...   189 BAILE AILLINN   1
   OUR HEARTS CAN HEAR THE VOICES CHIDE. . . . .   192 BAILE AILLINN   94
   OUR HEART CAN HEAR THE VOICES CHIDE. . . . .   192 BAILE AILLINN   V   94
   I HEAR THE HARP-STRING PRAISE THEM, OR HEAR THEIR MOURNFUL 210 UNDER THE MOON   16
     TALK.
   I HEAR THE HARP-STRING PRAISE THEM, OR HEAR THEIR MOURNFUL 210 UNDER THE MOON   16
     TALK.
   I HEAR THE HARP STRINGS PRAISE THEM, OR HEAR THEIR MOURNFUL 210 UNDER THE MOON V   16
     TALK.
   I HEAR THE HARP STRINGS PRAISE THEM, OR HEAR THEIR MOURNFUL 210 UNDER THE MOON V   16
     TALK.
   I HEAR THE HARPSTRING PRAISE THEM OR HEAR THEIR MOURNFUL   210 UNDER THE MOON   16
     TALK.
   I HEAR THE HARPSTRING PRAISE THEM OR HEAR THEIR MOURNFUL   210 UNDER THE MOON V   16
     TALK.
   I HEAR THE HARP STRING PRAISE THEM OR HEAR THEIR MOURNFUL   210 UNDER THE MOON V   16
     TALK.
   I HEAR THE HARP STRING PRAISE THEM OR HEAR THEIR MOURNFUL   210 UNDER THE MOON V   16
     TALK.
   HAVE THE BIRDS PASSED US? I COULD HEAR YOUR VOICE, . .   226 SHADOW WATER B   81
   AND IF SHE HEAR HIM MUTTER OF WILD RIDERS, ...   230 SHADOW WATER B   175
   SPEAK LOWER, OR THEY'LL HEAR. THEY CANNOT HEAR: . . .   232 SHADOW WATER B   228
   SPEAK LOWER, OR THEY'LL HEAR. THEY CANNOT HEAR! . . .   232 SHADOW WATER B   228
   AND I WILL HEAR THEM TALKING IN A MINUTE. . . . . . .   233 SHADOW WATER B   250
   NOW I CAN HEAR. THERE'S ONE OF THEM THAT SAYS, . . .   233 SHADOW WATER B   252
   THEY CANNOT HEAR MY VOICE: BUT WHAT'S THE MEANING? . .   234 SHADOW WATER B   275
   YOU'LL HEAR THEM CALLING OUT TO ONE ANOTHER . . . . .   247 SHADOW WATER B   521
   WITH HUMAN VOICES. O I CAN HEAR THEM NOW. . . . . . .   247 SHADOW WATER B   522
   THEY'RE CRYING OUT, COULD YOU BUT HEAR THEIR WORDS, . .   247 SHADOW WATER B   529

PAGE TITLE LINE

HEAR (CONTINUED)

	PAGE	TITLE		LINE
THAT YOU MAY NEVER HEAR THE CRY OF THE BIRDS,	250	SHADOW WATER B		575
AND WHISPERING THAT NONE BUT HE SHOULD HEAR,	281	TWO KINGS		110
AND CLINGING TO IT I COULD HEAR THE COCKS	286	TWO KINGS		210
AND HEAR AMID THE GARDEN'S NIGHTLY PEACE,"	300	BEGGAR CRIED		18
SHE IS FOREMOST OF THOSE THAT I WOULD HEAR PRAISED.	350	HER PRAISE		1
SHE IS FOREMOST OF THOSE THAT I WOULD HEAR PRAISED.	351	HER PRAISE		10
TILL I COULD HEAR THEIR HEARTS BEATING,	358	PRESENCES		11
THE FALCON CANNOT HEAR THE FALCONER,	401	SECOND COMING		2
THE FALCON CAN NOT HEAR THE FALCONER,	401	SECOND COMING	V	2
SHOULD HEAR MY LIVING FEET, NOR WOULD I TREAD	435	NEW FACES		3
TO HEAR A JACKASS BRAY,	455	HIS MEMORIES		10
WERE I BUT THERE AND NONE TO HEAR	458	HIS WILDNESS		7
CAN HEAR THE ARMED MAN SPEAK.	470	HARUN RASHID		193
THAT STORMS ARE SHAKING, HEAR THE ARMED MAN SPEAK.	470	HARUN RASHID	V	193
IT MAY BE ALL THAT HEAR	471	ALL SOUL NIGHT		19
FOR MAYBE ALL THAT HEAR	474	ALL SOUL NIGHT		89
SAVING THE RHYME RATS HEAR BEFORE THEY DIE.	542	PARN FUNERAL 1		28
"HEAR, GENTLEMEN, LADIES, AND ALL MANKIND,	544	TO SAME TUNE 1		2
DID EVER MEN HEAR SUCH A SONG?	570	THREE BUSHES		45
THAT I MAY HEAR IF WE SHOULD KISS	573	LADYS 3RD SONG		9
CAN PAY THE POET FOR A VERSE AND HEAR THE FIDDLE SOUND,	581	CURSE CROMWELL		21
I COME TO HEAR IT STRIKE."	585	ORAHILLY		26
THAT ALL ATTENDANTS AND THE CASUAL CROWD MIGHT HEAR.	609	IN TARAS HALLS		13
"HEAR, GENTLEMEN, LADIES, AND ALL MANKIND,	615	MARCH SONGS 3		2
HEAR ME, AND, SHEPHERD, HEARING ME, GROW DUMB.	646	ISLE STAT I 1		31
WITHIN THE FOLD TO HEAR THE CREAKING GATE--	646	ISLE STAT I 1		41
I HEAR THE WHOLE SKY'S SORROW IN ONE VOICE.	652	ISLE STAT I 2		22
AND WHEREFORE HAVE WE COME? A SONG TO HEAR.	652	ISLE STAT I 2		27
THEY HEAR THE STORY OF THE WIND,	655	ISLE STAT I 3		11
PEACE, PEACE, THE EARTH'S A-QUAKE. I HEAR .	656	ISLE STAT I 3		20
AND HEAR, AND JUDGE. MY POPINJAY, WHAT NOW?	660	ISLE STAT II 1		40
BUT WHY ART THOU SO SILENT? DID'ST THOU HEAR	670	ISLE STAT II 3		96
HOW SPED THY QUEST? THIS PRELUDE WE'LL NOT HEAR IT.	673	ISLE STAT II 3		174
IN THY WAN FACE? HEAR THOU, O DAUGHTER OF THE DAYS,	674	ISLE STAT II 3		200
SHALL FEED. I SHALL NOT IN THE EVENINGS HEAR	674	ISLE STAT II 3		220
IN THY WAN FACE? HEAR, DAUGHTER OF THE DAYS.	674	ISLE STAT II 3	V	200
BRIGHT ON A GRASS BLADE'S UNDER SIDE, MIGHT HEAR,	689	NETTLESHIP		10
WILL YOU NOT HEAR MY LAST NEW SONG? HUSH, HUSH!	695	MOSADA 2		1
YOU'RE FULL OF WORDINESS. COME, HEAR MY SONG.	696	MOSADA 2		8
BE STILL, I HEAR THE STEP OF EBREMAR.	697	MOSADA 2		34
I WILL NOT HEAR, THE MOORISH GIRL MUST DIE.	697	MOSADA 2		39
NO USE. AWAY, HEAR, THOU ENDURING GOD,	698	MOSADA 2		50
NO USE. AWAY, HEAR OH! THOU ENDURING GOD,	698	MOSADA 2	V	50
I HEAR THE MURMUR AS THEY RAISE THE BEAMS	699	MOSADA 3		17
MY LOVE, WE WILL HEAR, I AND YOU, WE WILL HEAR,	717	LOVE SONG		4
MY LOVE, WE WILL HEAR, I AND YOU, WE WILL HEAR,	717	LOVE SONG		4
. . . AH! WHAT BELL-NOTES DO THEY HEAR?	718	PHANTOM SHIP		14
SOME GREAT ONE. NO, I HEAR THE WAVERING STEPS	720	WITCH VIVIEN		12
HOW STILL IT IS! I HEAR THE CARP GO SPLASH,	722	WITCH VIVIEN		62
AND NOW AND THEN A BUBBLE RISE. I HEAR	722	WITCH VIVIEN		63
BELOVED, HEAR MY BITTER TALE!--	742	DANAAN QUICK		1
FOR WHILE I BLAMED THEM I COULD HEAR	743	DANAAN QUICK		27
NOW FOUR TOGETHER! I SHALL HEAR THEIR WORDS	753	SHADOW WATER A		139

HEARD

	PAGE	TITLE		LINE
AND HEARD THE FOEMEN'S BUCKLERS RATTLE,	10	OISIN 1		123
AND HEARD THE FOEMAN'S BUCKLERS RATTLE,	10	OISIN 1	V	123
AND WHEN THEY HEARD HER VOICE THEY RAN	15	OISIN 1		213
I HEARD ONE SAY, "HIS EYES GROW DIM	25	OISIN 1		380
I HEARD ONE SAY, "WITHIN HIS EYES	25	OISIN 1	V	380
IT PASSETH AWAY, AND IS HEARD OF NO LONGER.	26	OISIN 1	V	399B
FOR GOD HAS HEARD, AND SPEAKS HIS ANGRY MIND,	42	OISIN 2		206
UNDER A BEECH AT ALMHUIN AND HEARD THE THIN	44	OISIN 2		228
THE REST YOU HAVE HEARD OF, O CROZIERED MAN!	60	OISIN 3		189
THE REST THOU HAST HEARD OF, THOU CROSIERED ONE--	60	OISIN 3	V	189
IN CLANGING SPACE A MOMENT HEARD,	65	HAPPY SHEPHERD		20
'MID CLANGING SPACE A MOMENT HEARD	65	HAPPY SHEPHERD	V	20
BUT NAUGHT THEY HEARD, FOR THEY ARE ALWAYS LISTENING,	68	SAD SHEPHERD		15
BUT NAUGHT THEY HEARD, FOR THEY ARE EVER LISTENING,	68	SAD SHEPHERD	V	15
MAYBE YOU HAVE NOT HEARD OF US, YOU HAVE COME FORTH SO NEWLY,	75	ANASHU VIJAYA		78
WHO NEVER HEARD THE UNFORGIVING HOUND.	75	ANASHU VIJAYA	V	75
EACH OTHER ROUND IN CIRCLES, AND HEARD THE ELDEST SPEAK!	76	INDIAN ON GOD		5
I PASSED A LITTLE FURTHER ON AND HEARD A LOTUS TALK!	76	INDIAN ON GOD		9
EACH OTHER ROUND IN CIRCLES, AND I HEARD THE ELDEST SPEAK!--	76	INDIAN ON GOD	V	5
I PACED A LITTLE FURTHER ON AND HEARD A LOTUS TALK!--	76	INDIAN ON GOD	V	9
I PASSED A LITTLE FURTHER ON AND HEARD A PEACOCK SAY!	77	INDIAN ON GOD		17
I PACED A LITTLE FURTHER AND I HEARD A PEACOCK SAY!--	77	INDIAN ON GOD	V	17
I PASSED A LITTLE FURTHER AND I HEARD A PEACOCK SAY!--	77	INDIAN ON GOD	V	17
IS HEARD ON THE WATER, AS THEY WERE, THE PROUD AND APART,	91	OLD FISHERMAN		10
I HAVE OFTEN HEARD HIM SINGING TO AND FRO,	109	CUCHULAIN SEA		49
I HAVE OFTEN HEARD THE SWEET SOUND OF HIS BOW.	109	CUCHULAIN SEA		50
STARED ON THE HORSES OF THE SEA, AND HEARD	111	CUCHULAIN SEA		84
UPON THE WHARVES OF SORROW, AND HEARD RING	115	ROSE OF BATTLE		27
AND HEARD THE MOURNFUL BREEZE.	123	DREAM OF DEATH	V	12
FOR ALL WHO HEARD IT DREAMED A LITTLE WHILE.	129	BOOK STORIES	V	8
AND ALL WHO HEARD GREW FRIENDLY FOR A WHILE.	129	BOOK STORIES	V	8
WHEN THEY ARE HEARD UPON THE WIND,	136	TWO TREES	V	37
HAVE YOU NOT HEARD THAT OUR HEARTS ARE OLD,	141	EVERLAST VOICE		5
HE HEARD WHILE HE SANG AND DREAMED	144	HOST OF AIR		9

HEARD (CONTINUED)
BUT HE HEARD HIGH UP IN THE AIR . . . . . . 145 HOST OF AIR   41
AND WHEN I'VE HEARD HOW THEY GREW OLD AND DIED, ... 186 QUEEN MAEVE   136
I HAVE HEARD THE PIGEONS OF THE SEVEN WOODS . . . . 198 SEVEN WOODS   1
ALTHOUGH WE NEVER HEARD OF IT AT SCHOOL . . . . . 205 ADAMS CURSE V   19
I HEARD THE OLD, OLD MEN SAY, ... 208 OLD MEN ADMIRE   1
I HEARD THE OLD, OLD MEN SAY, ... 208 OLD MEN ADMIRE   7
BECAUSE OF SOMETHING I HEARD OF UNDER THE THIN HORN . 210 UNDER THE MOON V 17
BECAUSE OF A STORY I HEARD UNDER THE THIN HORN . . . 210 UNDER THE MOON V 17
BECAUSE OF A STORY I HEARD UNDER A THIN HORN . . . 210 UNDER THE MOON V 17
I HEARD UNDER A RAGGED HOLLOW WOOD, ... 210 RAGGED WOOD V   1
OR HAVE YOU HEARD THAT SLIDING SILVER-SHOED . . . 211 RAGGED WOOD   5
LIKE PLOVERS THAT HAVE HEARD THE CALL. . . . . 213 BLESS PSALTER   13
I'VE HEARD A RUSTLING OVERHEAD IN THE WIND. . . . 223 SHADOW WATER B 28
AND HAS BEEN DANGEROUS TO HIM. I HAVE HEARD . . . 224 SHADOW WATER B 52
YOU SAY THAT ALSO? YOU HAVE HEARD THE VOICES, . . 228 SHADOW WATER B 136
MUST BE SUBSTANTIAL SOMEWHERE. I HAVE HEARD THE DRUIDS 229 SHADOW WATER B 162
WHEN I FIRST HEARD THE NEWS? AH, THERE IT IS! . . . 241 SHADOW WATER B 398
FOR I HAVE HEARD THAT HE WAS PROUD AND LAUGHING, . . 242 SHADOW WATER B 415
I KNEW HIM WELL, AND WHILE I HEARD HIM LAUGHING . . 242 SHADOW WATER B 419
BECAUSE HE HAD NOT HEARD OF ANYTHING . . . . . 258 KING NO KING   3
HE'D HEARD THAT DIN ON THE HORIZON'S EDGE . . . . 286 TWO KINGS   V 217A
"I HEARD A SEA-MEW CRY, ... 308 PLAYER QUEEN   14
"I HEARD A SEAMEW CRY, ... 308 PLAYER QUEEN V 14
HER HUSBAND HAS HEARD THE WRETCH, ... 319 DOLLS   15
I HEARD HIM FIRST, BUT MAN IS A FOOL." . . . . 341 SHEP GOATHERD V 74
AND BIRTHDAYS AND HOLIDAYS SUCH PRAISES CAN BE HEARD . 353 HIS PHOENIX   2
AT ALL THESE DEATH-BEDS WOMEN HEARD . . . . . 361 ALF POLLEXFEN   36
AT ALL THESE DEATHBEDS WOMEN HEARD . . . . . 361 ALF POLLEXFEN V 36
AND CALLED HER NAME, SHE HAD HEARD, ... 381 SONGS FOOL 2   11
YET BE BUT SINEW. I HAVE HEARD SAID . . . . 386 ROBARTES DANCE   37
AND OF A MIDDLETON, WHOSE NAME YOU NEVER HEARD, . . 391 UNDER SATURN   8
YOU HEARD THAT LABOURING MAN WHO HAD SERVED MY PEOPLE. 391 UNDER SATURN   11
  HE SAID
AND HEARD THE SEA-WIND SCREAM UPON THE TOWER, . . . 403 FOR DAUGHTER   10
WHAT A STAR SANG AND CARELESS MUSES HEARD! . . . 445 SCHOOL CHILDR   47
AND NEEDS NO CRUELTY. I HAVE HEARD ONE SAY . . 448 HERO GIRL FOOL   13
WHAT NO DECEPTION WON. I HAVE HEARD THEM SAY . . 448 HERO GIRL FOOL V 13
HAD HEARD IMPOSSIBLE HISTORY OF MY PAST! . . . . 466 HARUN RASHID   108
I HEARD HER VOICE, "TURN THAT I MAY EXPOUND . . . 467 HARUN RASHID   132
HEARD ALL THE ANXIETY OF MY PASSIONATE YOUTH, . . 468 HARUN RASHID   168
MIMICKING WHAT THEY HEARD, AS CHILDREN MIMIC! . . 487 SEVEN SAGES   25
"I HEARD AN OLD RELIGIOUS MAN . . . . . . 492 ANNE GREGORY   13
NOR SAW MY BODY FALL NOR HEARD IT SHRIEK, . . . 537 HER VISION   29
SADDLE AND RIDE, I HEARD A MAN SAY, ... 549 SEVERED HEAD   1
IMAGES RIDE, I HEARD A MAN SAY, ... 549 SEVERED HEAD V   1
NOR HEARD THIS VOICE THAT NINETY YEARS HAVE CRACKED. . 555 RIBH AT TOMB   5
SURMOUNT THEIR BONES! BUT SPEAK WHAT NONE HAVE HEARD. 555 RIBH AT TOMB   9
SURMOUNTS THEIR BONES! BUT SPEAK WHAT NONE HAVE HEARD. 555 RIBH AT TOMB V   9
DOUBTLESS I SPOKE OR SANG WHAT I HAD HEARD . . . 557 RIBH ECSTASY   2
I HAVE HEARD THAT HYSTERICAL WOMEN SAY . . . . 565 LAPIS LAZULI   1
HAD HEARD I HAD NOT HEARD?" . . . . . . 585 ORAHILLY   22
HAD HEARD I HAD NOT HEARD?" . . . . . . 585 ORAHILLY   22
WHEN HE HEARD THAT STORY TOLD, ... 596 COLONEL MARTIN 47
AND ALL MEN HEARD THEM SWEAR . . . . . . 596 COLONEL MARTIN 60
WHEN HE HAD HEARD THAT STORY TOLD . . . . . 596 COLONEL MARTIN V 47
YOU THAT MITCHEL'S PRAYER HAVE HEARD, ... 638 BEN BULBEN   25
AND HAS NOT HEARD ABSOLVO TE. . . . . . 656 ISLE STAT I 3   19
AND HEARD EACH UNSEEN ECHO ON HER THRONE, . . . 657 ISLE STAT I 3   48
HE SAT, AND THEN I HEARD THE WHITE LAKE SING, . . 659 ISLE STAT II 1 15
MY SINKING BRAIN!--CEASE!--CEASE! HEARD YE YON SOUND? . 665 ISLE STAT II 2 73
AND NEVER HEARD OF GRIEF OR CARE . . . . . 667 ISLE STAT II 3 21
FORTH! FORTH! O SPIRITS, YE HAVE HEARD YOUR TASK! . . 669 ISLE STAT II 3 81
OR AUGHT REMOTE! OR HAST THOU NEVER HEARD . . . 672 ISLE STAT II 3 153
I HEARD THE DEATHFUL MONOTONE, ... 673 ISLE STAT II 3 183
THIS HEARD I WHERE AMONG THE APPLE TREES, . . . 686 LIFE   19
HEARD YOU? YOUR LUTE HUNG IN THE WINDOW SOUNDED! . 694 MOSADA 1   95
HEARD YOU? YOUR LUTE UPON THE WALL HAS SOUNDED! . 694 MOSADA 1 V   95
"OF OUR GREAT QUEEN IS EVER HEARD . . . . . 729 PRIEST FAIRY   41
AND WHEN THEY HEARD THAT TALE OF HIS . . . . 730 PRIEST FAIRY   65
WERE YOU A FAIRY YOU'D HAVE HEARD . . . . . 730 PRIEST FAIRY   67
HEARD THE VOICE OF THEIR DISMAY, ... 730 PRIEST FAIRY   74
THIS HEARD I WHERE, AMID THE APPLE TREES, . . . 735 QUATRAIN APHOR 17
THIS HEARD I WHERE AMONG THE APPLE TREES, . . . 735 QUATRAIN APHOR V 19
AND HEARD THE MUSIC IN THE WIND, AND SAW . . . 747 SHADOW WATER A   5
AND SPOKEN IN THE COUNCIL, AND HEARD TALES . . . 748 SHADOW WATER A 28
AND I HAVE HEARD THEM CALL FROM WIND TO WIND . . 750 SHADOW WATER A 83
HE HAS HEARD ME AND NOT YOU. NINE DAYS AGO . . 752 SHADOW WATER A 113
HE HAS HEARD ME BECAUSE I PROMISED ALL. . . . 752 SHADOW WATER A 116
WHERE I HAD HEARD NO FEET BUT THE GODS' CAME. . . 756 SHADOW WATER A V 191B
I HAVE HEARD IN THE NIGHT AIR . . . . . . 783 GREY ROUND   6
MY HEART RAN WILD WHEN IT HEARD . . . . . 783 GREY ROUND   21
I HAVE HEARD FROM FAR BELOW . . . . . . 783 GREY ROUND   25
AND HEARD THE DEAD LIPS SING. . . . . . 790 SINGING HEAD   24
HEARD'ST
FOR SO SHE WILLED--THOU HEARD'ST? UPON THE BREAST . . 653 ISLE STAT I 2   32
HEARERS
A DRUID KINDNESS, ON ALL HEARERS FELL. . . . . 129 BOOK STORIES   4
THE LOVER SPEAKS TO THE HEARERS OF HIS SONGS IN COMING DAYS 173 SPEAKS HEARERS T
A LOVER SPEAKS TO THE HEARERS OF HIS SONGS IN COMING DAYS 173 SPEAKS HEARERS V T
HEARERS AND HEARTENERS OF THE WORK! . . . . . 266 GALWAY RACES   6

HEARERS   (CONTINUED)

	PAGE	TITLE	LINE
HEARERS, HEARTENERS OF THE WORK, ...	266	GALWAY RACES	V	6

HEARING
HEARING AEDH TOUCH THE MOURNFUL STRINGS OF GOLD." . . .	35	OISIN 2	87
HEARING THE SHAKING OF SHIELDS	62	OISIN 3	207
HEARING HELL LOUD WITH A MURMUR, AS SHOUTING AND MOCKING WE SWEEP,	62	OISIN 3	208
THEIR HEARING, AND SOME COMFORT GIVE, BUT THEY	68	SAD SHEPHERD	V	6
IF IT BE NOT THAT HEARING MESSAGES	236	SHADOW WATER B	319
ON HEARING THAT THE STUDENTS OF OUR NEW UNIVERSITY . .	262	STUDENTS AGIT	T
HEARING THE WHOLE EARTH CHANGE ITS TUNE, ...	266	GALWAY RACES	12
SOME PASSION HAD MADE HER STONE. HEARING A FOOT . . .	279	TWO KINGS	65
HEARING HIM GROAN AND STRETCH	319	DOLLS	13
ALL'S CHANGED SINCE I, HEARING AT TWILIGHT, ...	322	SWANS AT COOLE	15
HEARING IT NOW HAVE SIGHED FOR THAT YOUNG MAN	342	SHEP GOATHERD	77
HEAR ME, AND, SHEPHERD, HEARING ME, GROW DUMB.	646	ISLE STAT I 1	31
HEARING THE FAR-OFF SINGING GUILE, AND GROANED, . . .	693	MOSADA 1	88
HEARING THE FAR OFF SINGING GUILE, AND GROANED, . . .	693	MOSADA 1	V	88
HEARING THE HARPERS PLAY, THE PINE-WOOD CRACKLE, . . .	759	SHADOW WATER A	241
HEARING THE HARPERS PLAY, THE PINE WOOD CRACKLE, . . .	759	SHADOW WATER A	V	241
BEYOND HEARING OR SEEING, ...	784	WOMANS BEAUTY	11

HEARKEN
HEARKEN, YE SWALLOWS!--I HAVE HOARDED UP	699	MOSADA 3	23

HEARS
HE HEARS THE STORM IN THE CHIMNEY ABOVE, ...	26	OISIN 1	404
FOR HIM WHO HEARS LOVE SING AND NEVER CEASE, ...	114	ROSE OF BATTLE	10
HE HEARS THE CRY OF THE SEDGE	165	CRY OF SEDGE	T
AEDH HEARS THE CRY OF THE SEDGE	165	CRY OF SEDGE	V	T
ONE HEARS THE RUMBLE OF IT FAR BELOW	420	MY HOUSE	V	20B
SHE HEARS ME STRIKE THE BOARD AND SAY	531	FATHER CHILD	1
SWEARS THAT HE HEARS THE KING'S GREAT HORN.	636	BLACK TOWER	24
AND HEARS THE ROAR OF THE STREAMS WHERE, DRUIDS SAY, .	749	SHADOW WATER A	46

HEART   SEE HONEY-HEART
WITH A HEAVY HEART AND A WANDERING MIND, ...	2	OISIN 1	2
OF THE THINGS THAT HIS HEART STILL KNOWS WERE SWEET-- . .	26	OISIN 1	V	402
WHILE HIS HEART STILL DREAMS OF BATTLE AND LOVE . . .	27	OISIN 1	406
AS THOUGH HE TOLD HIS NEVER-SLUMBERING HEART	32	OISIN 2	44
AS THOUGH UNTO HIS NEVER SLUMBERING HEART	32	OISIN 2	V	44
AS THOUGH HE TOLD HIS NEVER SLUMBERING HEART	32	OISIN 2	V	44
HE HAD SAT DOWN AND SIGHED WITH CUMBERED HEART, . . .	37	OISIN 2	111
HE HAD GONE WHISPERING FORTH WITH CUMBERED HEART, . .	37	OISIN 2	V	111
THROUGH HEART AND SPINE, AND CAST HIM IN THE WAVE . .	41	OISIN 2	182
THROUGH HEART AND DEMON SPINE, AND IN THE WAVE . . .	41	OISIN 2	V	182
A BEECH-BOUGH TO ME, AND MY HEART GREW SORE, ...	44	OISIN 2	226
A BEECH BOUGH TO ME, AND MY HEART GREW SORE, ...	44	OISIN 2	V	226
. . . KEENED IN THE GATES OF MY HEART.	57	OISIN 3	152
THE HEART IN ME LONGING TO LEAP LIKE A GRASSHOPPER INTO HER HEART,	60	OISIN 3	182
THE HEART IN ME LONGING TO LEAP LIKE A GRASSHOPPER INTO HER HEART,	60	OISIN 3	182
SAVING IN THINE OWN HEART. SEEK, THEN, ...	66	HAPPY SHEPHERD	27
THEIR SADNESS THROUGH A HOLLOW, PEARLY HEART, ...	68	SAD SHEPHERD	21
THEIR SADNESS THROUGH THE HOLLOWS OF ITS HEART. . . .	68	SAD SHEPHERD	V	21
A METEOR OF THE BURNING HEART, ...	78	INDIAN TO LOVE	14
IS OUR FIRST KISS, AND AH, HOW OLD MY HEART!"	80	EPHEMERA	9
SHY ONE OF MY HEART, ...	89	ISLE IN WATER	2
WHEN I WAS A BOY WITH NEVER A CRACK IN MY HEART. . . .	91	OLD FISHERMAN	4
WHEN I WAS A BOY WITH NEVER A CRACK IN MY HEART. . . .	91	OLD FISHERMAN	8
WHEN I WAS A BOY WITH NEVER A CRACK IN MY HEART. . . .	91	OLD FISHERMAN	12
HE HOLDS DEEP COMMUNE WITH HIS HEART:	99	FOXHUNTER	43
AND THE WHOLE WORLD WEIGHS DOWN UPON MY HEART-- . . .	104	FERGUS DRUID	V	38A
AND IN MY HEART THE DAEMONS AND THE GODS	104	FERGUS DRUID	V	38B
IS HID IN THE HEART OF LOVE!	119	PITY OF LOVE	2
HIS HEART HUNG ALL UPON A SILKEN DRESS, ...	126	DREAM OF FAERY	2
BELOVED, GAZE IN THINE OWN HEART, ...	134	TWO TREES	1
BELOVED, GAZE IN THINE OWN HEART.	135	TWO TREES	20
MY HEART WOULD BRIM WITH DREAMS ABOUT THE TIMES . . .	136	TO SOME I TALK	2
MADE IRELAND'S HEART BEGIN TO BEAT!	138	TO IRELAND	12
I CAST MY HEART INTO MY RHYMES, ...	139	TO IRELAND	45
MAY KNOW HOW MY HEART WENT WITH THEM	139	TO IRELAND	47
EMPTY YOUR HEART OF ITS MORTAL DREAM.	140	HOSTING SIDHE	5
FILLING THY HEART WITH A MORTAL DREAM, ...	140	HOSTING SIDHE	V	6
WE COME BETWEEN HIM AND THE HOPE OF HIS HEART.	141	HOSTING SIDHE	12
THE LOVER TELLS OF THE ROSE IN HIS HEART	142	ROSE IN HEART	T
THE ROSE IN MY HEART	142	ROSE IN HEART	V	T
AEDH TELLS OF THE ROSE IN HIS HEART	142	ROSE IN HEART	V	T
. . . IN THE DEEPS OF MY HEART.	143	ROSE IN HEART	4
. . . IN THE DEEPS OF MY HEART.	143	ROSE IN HEART	8
AND HIS HEART WAS BLACKENED BY DREAD, ...	145	HOST OF AIR	V	40B
WITH HEAVY WHITENING WINGS, AND A HEART FALLEN COLD! .	147	UNAPPEAS HOST	4
O HEART THE WINDS HAVE SHAKEN, THE UNAPPEASABLE HOST .	147	UNAPPEAS HOST	11
AND HEART THE WINDS HAVE SHAKEN, THE UNAPPEASABLE HOST .	147	UNAPPEAS HOST	V	11
OUT-WORN HEART, IN A TIME OUT-WORN, ...	147	INTO TWILIGHT	1
LAUGH, HEART, AGAIN IN THE GREY TWILIGHT, ...	147	INTO TWILIGHT	3
SIGH, HEART, AGAIN IN THE DEW OF THE MORN.	147	INTO TWILIGHT	4
OUTWORN HEART IN A TIME OUTWORN, ...	147	INTO TWILIGHT	V	1
COME, HEART, WHERE HILL IS HEAPED UPON HILL!	148	INTO TWILIGHT	9
THE HEART OF THE WOMAN	151	HEART OF WOMAN	T
MY HEART UPON HIS WARM HEART LIES, ...	152	HEART OF WOMAN	11
MY HEART UPON HIS WARM HEART LIES, ...	152	HEART OF WOMAN	11
SHE LOOKED IN MY HEART ONE DAY	152	LOSS OF LOVE	5

HEART   (CONTINUED)

	PAGE	TITLE		LINE
BELOVED, LET YOUR EYES HALF CLOSE, AND YOUR HEART BEAT	154	BELOVED PEACE		9
OVER MY HEART, AND YOUR HAIR FALL OVER MY BREAST,	154	BELOVED PEACE		10
OVER MY HEART, AND YOUR HAIR FALL ABOUT MY BREAST	154	BELOVED PEACE	V	10
MY HEART UPON THE LOVELINESS	155	FORGOT BEAUTY		2
AND WITH HEART MORE OLD THAN THE HORN	157	POET BELOVED		5
AND WITH THE HEART MORE OLD THAN THE HORN	157	POET BELOVED	V	5
I BADE MY HEART BUILD THESE POOR RHYMES!	158	BELOVED RHYMES		3
TO HIS HEART, BIDDING IT HAVE NO FEAR	158	TO HIS HEART		T
TO MY HEART, BIDDING IT HAVE NO FEAR	158	TO HIS HEART	V	T
BE YOU STILL, BE YOU STILL, TREMBLING HEART!	158	TO HIS HEART		1
HE BADE HIS HEART GO TO HER,	159	CAP AND BELLS		13
AND THE HEART AND THE SOUL CAME THROUGH,	160	CAP AND BELLS		30
IN HER HEART SHE FOUND A TUNE,	160	CAP AND BELLS	V	26
THE HEART AND THE SOUL CAME THROUGH!	160	CAP AND BELLS	V	30
IF THIS IMPORTUNATE HEART TROUBLE YOUR PEACE	162	ASKS FORGIVE		1
AND THEREFORE MY HEART WILL BOW, WHEN DEW	164	PERFECT BEAUTY		6
AND THEREFORE MY HEART BOWS DOWN ANEW,	164	PERFECT BEAUTY	V	6
TO FILL YOUR HEART WITH CONTENT."	167	BLESSED		20
AND WHITHER THE WISE HEART KNOWS!	168	BLESSED		34
ARE HURTLING THROUGH MY HEART.	171	MAID QUIET		8
ARE CALLING THROUGH MY HEART.	171	MAID QUIET	V	8
AND SMOKE FROM THIS DEAD HEART DRIFTS THROUGH THE VIOLET AIR	173	SPEAKS HEARERS		3
TILL MAURYA OF THE WOUNDED HEART CRY A SWEET CRY,	173	SPEAKS HEARERS	V	6
THAT'S ALL BUT GONE! FOR THE PROUD HEART IS GONE,	181	QUEEN MAEVE		20
AND THE FOOL HEART OF THE COUNTING-HOUSE FEARS ALL	181	QUEEN MAEVE		21
AND SHE'D HAD LUCKY EYES AND A HIGH HEART,	181	QUEEN MAEVE		27
SUDDEN AND LAUGHING. O UNQUIET HEART,	181	QUEEN MAEVE		30
WITH SPEEDY FEET AND A MOST THANKFUL HEART!	185	QUEEN MAEVE		100
WITH HOLY SHADOWS." HER HIGH HEART WAS GLAD,	186	QUEEN MAEVE		126
FOR YOU, ALTHOUGH YOU'VE NOT HER WANDERING HEART,	186	QUEEN MAEVE		132
BAILE'S HEART WAS BROKEN IN TWO!	192	BAILE AILLINN		70
OUR HEART CAN HEAR THE VOICES CHIDE.	192	BAILE AILLINN	V	94
AH! WISE, MY HEART KNOWS WELL HOW WISE.	193	BAILE AILLINN		99
TO MAKE THE SAVAGE HEART OF LOVE	193	BAILE AILLINN		109
BEFORE HER LOVE-WORN HEART HAD BROKE,	194	BAILE AILLINN		127
QUIET'S WILD HEART, LIKE DAILY MEAT!	196	BAILE AILLINN		178
AND BEING IN GOOD HEART, BECAUSE	197	BAILE AILLINN		191
AND YOU ARE MORE HIGH OF HEART THAN SHE,	197	BAILE AILLINN		202
THAT EMPTY THE HEART. I HAVE FORGOT AWHILE	198	SEVEN WOODS		5
WANDERS LAUGHING AND EATING HER WILD HEART	198	SEVEN WOODS		11
ALL THAT YOU NEED IS PATIENCE." HEART CRIES, "NO,	200	FOLLY COMFORT		6
O HEART! O HEART! IF SHE'D BUT TURN HER HEAD,	200	FOLLY COMFORT		13
O HEART! O HEART! IF SHE'D BUT TURN HER HEAD,	200	FOLLY COMFORT		13
BUT HEART THERE IS NO COMFORT, NOT A GRAIN!	200	FOLLY COMFORT	V	7
NEVER GIVE ALL THE HEART	202	NEVER GIVE ALL		T
NEVER GIVE ALL THE HEART, FOR LOVE	202	NEVER GIVE ALL		1
O NEVER GIVE THE HEART OUTRIGHT,	202	NEVER GIVE ALL		8
FOR HE GAVE ALL HIS HEART AND LOST.	202	NEVER GIVE ALL		14
NOR LANDS THAT SEEM TOO DIM TO BE BURDENS ON THE HEART!	209	UNDER THE MOON		5
OR LANDS THAT SEEMED TOO OLD TO BE BURDENS ON THE HEART,	209	UNDER THE MOON	V	5
WHOSE HEART WOULD BREAK IN TWO,	213	HAPPY TOWNLAND		2
AND THE GREEN QUIET, HAVE UPLIFTED THE HEART?	219	WOODS OF COOLE		40
I COULD GIVE ALL MY HEART TO THAT RED MOLL	222	SHADOW WATER B		9
THAT THE HEART LONGS FOR. WHAT IS LOVE ITSELF,	230	SHADOW WATER B		183
O HEART, BE AT PEACE, BECAUSE	259	UNWORTH PRAISE		1
OUT OF MY HEART. THERE'S SOMETHING AILS OUR COLT	260	FASC DIFFICULT		4
AND AFTER SET YOUR HEART TO BEAT,	263	MASK		9
WHAT DOES HE CARE IF MY HEART BREAK?	275	GREY ROCK		104
WHY SHOULD THE FAITHFULLEST HEART MOST LOVE	275	GREY ROCK		112
BETWEEN THE PILLARS WITH A BEATING HEART	279	TWO KINGS		59
THAT MAKE THE HEART AKIN TO THE DUMB STONE."	281	TWO KINGS		94
SHE'LL NOT BE PROUD, KNOWING WITHIN HER HEART	282	TWO KINGS		118
WHAT THE EXULTANT HEART CALLS GOOD	288	TO WEALTHY MAN		33
THE LINEAMENTS, A HEART THAT LAUGHTER HAS MADE SWEET,	315	FALLEN MAJESTY		5
THE LINEAMENTS, THE HEART THAT LAUGHTER HAS MADE SWEET,	315	FALLEN MAJESTY	V	5
HEART AND DELIGHTED HEART!	315	FRIENDS	V	9
HEART AND DELIGHTED HEART!	315	FRIENDS	V	9
AND THEREUPON IMAGINATION AND HEART WERE DRIVEN	316	COLD HEAVEN		3
BEING OUT OF HEART WITH GOVERNMENT	317	APPOINTMENT		1
BEING OUT OF HEART AT GOVERNMENT	317	APPOINTMENT	V	1
AND NOW MY HEART IS SORE.	322	SWANS AT COOLE		14
IN THE AFFECTIONS OF OUR HEART,	324	ROBERT GREGORY		12
PASSIONATE AND SIMPLE LIKE HIS HEART.	325	ROBERT GREGORY		32
WHEREIN THE GAZING HEART DOUBLES HER MIGHT.	326	ROBERT GREGORY		69
OF THAT LATE DEATH TOOK ALL MY HEART FOR SPEECH.	328	ROBERT GREGORY		96
MY DISCONTENTED HEART TO DRAW CONTENT	334	LIVING BEAUTY		3
THAN 'TWERE AN APPARITION. O HEART, WE ARE OLD!	334	LIVING BEAUTY		8
THAT THE HEART GROWS OLD?	334	SONG		6
THAT THE HEART GROWS OLD?	335	SONG		12
BUT THE HEART THAT I HAD!	335	SONG		14
THAT THE HEART GROWS OLD?	335	SONG		18
WHAT MAKES YOUR HEART BEAT SO!	336	YOUNG GIRL		3
WHO BROKE MY HEART FOR HER	336	YOUNG GIRL		6
OR PUT HIS HEART INTO SOME GAME	343	SHEP GOATHERD		105
AND YET, BECAUSE MY HEART LEAPED AT HER WORDS,	353	PEOPLE		35
WHO IS MY BEAUTY'S EQUAL, THOUGH THAT MY HEART DENIES,	354	HIS PHOENIX		27
AND HOW SHOULD HER HEART FAIL HER	365	HER RACE		9
HIS SENSES AND HIS HEART UNSATISFIED,	370	EGO DOMINUS		58
OF BODY AND SOUL. THE LOVER'S HEART KNOWS THAT.	375	PHASES OF MOON		71

371

	PAGE	TITLE	LINE

HEART   (CONTINUED)

AN IMAGE OF MY HEART THAT IS SMITTEN THROUGH	389	IMAGE PAST	8
TO SOME WHO ARE NEAR MY HEART,	393	EASTER 1916	34
CAN MAKE A STONE OF THE HEART.	394	EASTER 1916	58
CONSUME MY HEART AWAY; SICK WITH DESIRE	408	SAIL BYZANTIUM	21
O HEART, O TROUBLED HEART--THIS CARICATURE,	409	TOWER	2
O HEART, O TROUBLED HEART--THIS CARICATURE,	409	TOWER	2
NO MOON; ONLY AN ACHING HEART	421	MY TABLE	13
HAD SUCH AN ACHING HEART	422	MY TABLE	28
WE HAD FED THE HEART ON FANTASIES,	425	STARES NEST	16
WE HAVE FED THE HEART ON FANTASIES,	425	STARES NEST V	16
THE HEART GROWS BRUTAL FROM THE FARE,	425	STARES NEST V	17
BUT O! AMBITIOUS HEART, HAD SUCH A PROOF DRAWN FORTH	427	PHANTOM HATRED	36
AND TEAR THE HEART OUT OF HIS SIDE,	437	SONGS PLAY 1	3
AND LAY THE HEART UPON HER HAND	437	SONGS PLAY 1	4
AND BEAR THAT BEATING HEART AWAY;	437	SONGS PLAY 1	5
MAN'S OWN RESINOUS HEART HAS FED.	438	SONGS PLAY 2	16
BUT FEEL THE STRANGE HEART BEATING WHERE IT LIES?	441	LEDA AND SWAN	8
AND FEELS THE STRANGE HEART BEATING WHERE IT LIES;	441	LEDA AND SWAN V	8
AND THEREUPON MY HEART IS DRIVEN WILD:	444	SCHOOL CHILDR	23
FOR THE HEART CRIES THAT WHAT DECEPTION WINS	448	HERO GIRL FOOL	6
THE HEART REPLIES	449	OWEN AHERNE V	T
A STRANGE THING SURELY THAT MY HEART, WHEN LOVE HAD COME UNSOUGHT	449	OWEN AHERNE	1
BUT O! MY HEART COULD BEAR NO MORE WHEN THE UPLAND CAUGHT THE WIND;	450	OWEN AHERNE	11
I RAN, I RAN, FROM MY LOVE'S SIDE BECAUSE MY HEART WENT MAD.	450	OWEN AHERNE	12
THE HEART BEHIND ITS RIB LAUGHED OUT.	450	OWEN AHERNE	13
O BUT HER HEART WOULD BREAK TO LEARN MY THOUGHTS ARE FAR AWAY."	450	OWEN AHERNE	20
"SPEAK ALL YOUR MIND," MY HEART SANG OUT,	450	OWEN AHERNE	21
A HEART OF FLESH AND BLOOD.	451	FIRST LOVE	6
AND FOUND A HEART OF STONE	451	FIRST LOVE	8
THEN SUDDENLY MY HEART IS WRUNG	453	DEATH OF HARE	7
AND HIS BEATING HEART WOULD BURST.	454	EMPTY CUP	6
AND THE HEART THUMPS AT MY SIDE,	456	FRIENDS YOUTH	18
THE HEART NEED SUFFER NO DEFEAT; BUT I	464	HARUN RASHID	77
MY HEART COULD NEVER TURN FROM DAILY RUIN,	464	HARUN RASHID	83
MY HEART MUST LOOK UPON A DAILY RUIN	464	HARUN RASHID V	83
BECAUSE THE HEART IN HIS BLOOD-SODDEN BREAST	481	BLOOD AND MOON	20
FOR ALL HIS TIMID HEART, THERE THAT SLOW MAN,	489	COOLE PARK 29	12
THE HEART REMORSE.	500	VACILLATION	8
FROM MAN'S BLOOD-SODDEN HEART ARE SPRUNG	502	VACILLATION	67
HAD SCOOPED OUT PHARAOH'S MUMMY. I--THOUGH HEART MIGHT FIND RELIEF	503	VACILLATION	84
HOMER IS MY EXAMPLE AND HIS UNCHRISTENED HEART.	503	VACILLATION	87
MY FANATIC HEART.	506	REMORSE SPEECH	5
MY FANATIC HEART.	506	REMORSE SPEECH	10
A FANATIC HEART.	506	REMORSE SPEECH	15
AND ALL MY HEART SEEMED GAY:	507	STREAM AND SUN	3
REPENTANCE KEEPS MY HEART IMPURE;	507	STREAM AND SUN	6
SO NEVER HANG YOUR HEART UPON	509	JANE REPROVED	12
THE HEART IN MY SIDE,	516	MANS SONG	3
FOR THE HEART CANNOT LIE,	516	MANS SONG	14
TO MY OFFENDED HEART	516	MANS SONG	17
I BROKE MY HEART IN TWO	518	HIS CONFIDENCE	7
AND MY HEART UNMOVED?	532	BEFORE WORLD	12
WHERE HIS HEART MY HEART DID SEEM	535	CHOSEN	15
WHERE HIS HEART MY HEART DID SEEM	535	CHOSEN	15
CUT OUT HIS HEART. SOME MASTER OF DESIGN	541	PARN FUNERAL 1	14
UPON A PAINTED STAGE WHEN WE DEVOURED HIS HEART.	542	PARN FUNERAL 1	23
HAD DE VALERA EATEN PARNELL'S HEART	542	PARN FUNERAL 2	2
HAD COSGRAVE EATEN PARNELL'S HEART, THE LAND'S	543	PARN FUNERAL 2	5
HE SANG IT FROM HIS HEART.	544	TO SAME TUNE	6
FOR ALL MY HEART HAS HAD FOR ITS HIRE	551	SONGS REWRIT 1	3
FOR ALL THAT MY HEART HAS HAD FOR ITS HIRE	551	SONGS REWRIT 1 V	3
THEN HE STRUGGLED WITH THE HEART;	561	FOUR AGES MAN	3
HIS PROUD HEART HE LEFT BEHIND.	561	FOUR AGES MAN	6
BUT THERE'S ANOTHER KNOWLEDGE THAT MY HEART DESTROYS,	580	CURSE CROMWELL	17
WORDS I HAVE THAT CAN PIERCE THE HEART,	588	OLD WICKED MAN	16
MY HEART RECOVERING WITH COVERED EYES;	602	GALLERY REVIS	18
HEART SMITTEN WITH EMOTION, I SINK DOWN,	602	GALLERY REVIS V	17
HER HEART MOUNT UP ON HIGH!	608	SONGS BURDEN 3	22
HE SANG IT FROM HIS HEART.	616	MARCH SONGS 3	6
HIS EMPTY HEART IS FULL AT LENGTH,	624	APPARITIONS	19
I MUST BE SATISFIED WITH MY HEART, ALTHOUGH	629	CIRCUS ANIMALS	4
THEMES OF THE EMBITTERED HEART, OR SO IT SEEMS,	629	CIRCUS ANIMALS	13
IN THE FOUL RAG-AND-BONE SHOP OF THE HEART.	630	CIRCUS ANIMALS	40
HEART MYSTERIES THERE, AND YET WHEN ALL IS SAID	630	CIRCUS ANIMALS V	27
IN THE FOUL RAG AND BONE SHOP OF THE HEART.	630	CIRCUS ANIMALS V	40
LAUGHS ALOUD, HIS HEART AT PEACE.	638	BEN BULBEN	32
THOUGH MY LOVE-SICK HEART IS RENDING,	646	ISLE STAT I 1	38
IN THE HEART OF THE DAWN THE RIVERS ARE SINGING,	648	ISLE STAT I 1	91
AND THERE TO ITS OWN HEART FOR EVER MOANS.	650	ISLE STAT I 1	131
WITHIN MINE HEART; AND NAUGHT BUT SORROW NOW	659	ISLE STAT II 1	26
OH, HEART! HER DIRGE! WITH RUSHING ARMS THE WAVES	665	ISLE STAT II 2	70
LEST ON THINE HEART THE STONY SEAL	667	ISLE STAT II 3	41
O LET ME PASS! THE SPELLS FROM OFF THE HEART	668	ISLE STAT II 3	44
THE WORLD, WITHIN HIS FOLDED HEART,	671	ISLE STAT II 3	133
THE WATER-SERPENT SINGS HIS HEART	673	ISLE STAT II 3	184

HEART   (CONTINUED)
  SO BE THOU STILL, DEAR HEART, A LITTLE WHILE! . . . . 677 ISLE STAT II 3   283
  HAVE I SLEPT LONG? LONG YEARS, WITH HUNGRY HEART . . . 677 ISLE STAT II 3   286
  MY ECHOING HEART. NOW RAISE THY VOICE AND SPEAK! . . . 683 SEEKER   47
  "BEHOLD THE KNIGHT OF THE WATERFALL, WHOSE HEART . . . . 684 SEEKER   54
  THAT FILL THE BLAZING HOLLOWS OF MY HEART. . . . . . . 684 SEEKER   V 69D
  THE ORB OF THE MOST INNER LIVING HEART . . . . . . 689 NETTLESHIP   15
  HE LOVES OUR BROTHER PETER IN HIS HEART. . . . . . 696 MOSADA 2   16
  DEAR HEART, THERE IS A SECRET WAY THAT LEADS . . . . . 702 MOSADA 3   75
  THE HEART OF THE PITILESS PLACE . . . . . . 708 FAIRY PEDANT   V 30
  AND THEN HIS HEART FILLS FULL OF LOVE, ... 716 FAIRY DOCTOR   11
  AND THEN HIS HEART IS FULL OF LOVE, ... 716 FAIRY DOCTOR   V 11
  CLOSE AND MORE CLOSE--I FEEL HIM IN MY HEART-- . . . . 720 WITCH VIVIEN   11
  AND WILL FIND HER GOOD AT HEART, ... 726 LOVERS QUARREL   10
  UNTO THE HEART OF THE WOODLAND STRAYING, ... 728 PRIEST FAIRY   1
  WITH OPEN MOUTH AND BEATING HEART. . . . . . . 729 PRIEST FAIRY   32
  AND THEN HIS HEART GREW WELL-NIGH DEAD . . . . . . 730 PRIEST FAIRY   59
  AWAY IN THE HEART OF THE ANTIQUE WOOD! . . . . . 730 PRIEST FAIRY   64
  THE BEATING OF A LEV'RET'S HEART! . . . . . . 730 PRIEST FAIRY   69
  SORROWS SAPPING BRAIN AND HEART. . . . . . . 733 STREET DANCERS   60
  THE SOUL UPON THE ASHES OF THE HEART." . . . . 735 QUATRAIN APHOR   16
  THE HEART OF NOON FOLDS SILENCE AND FOLDS SLEEP, ... 735 QUATRAIN APHOR   25
  WANDERS AND WAILS BEFORE MY HEART MOST TRUE . . . . 738 YOU ARE SAD   8
  TILL THEY COME WHERE YOUR SAD, SAD HEART IS, ... 739 WHERE BOOKS GO   5
  WHEN FLYING TO THE HEART OF LIGHT . . . . . . 742 DANAAN QUICK   8
  AND THOUGHT THAT SHE HAD NO HEART." . . . . . 744 GLOVE CLOAK   4
  KEEP HIDDEN AND COVERED HER HEART!" . . . . . 744 GLOVE CLOAK   12
  FOR LOVE IS A-WEAVING WHEN A WOMAN'S HEART . . . . . 761 SHADOW WATER A   262
  GROWS YOUNG AND A MAN'S HEART GROWS OLD IN A TWINKLING. 761 SHADOW WATER A   263
  AH, THEY HAVE PIERCED HIS HEART! I HAVE SLEPT LONG! 761 SHADOW WATER A   270
  OF VOICES AND OF DREAMS. O HEART, BE STILL! . . . . 765 SHADOW WATER A   362
  HEART ON HEART, OR MOUTH ON MOUTH, ... 777 SONG DEIRDRE 2   9
  HEART ON HEART, OR MOUTH ON MOUTH, ... 777 SONG DEIRDRE 2   9
  WHY DOES MY HEART BEAT SO? . . . . 781 MY HEART BEAT   1
  WHY SHOULD THE HEART TAKE FRIGHT? . . . . . . 781 HEART FRIGHT   1
  MY RASCAL HEART IS PROUD . . . . 782 HEART FRIGHT   10
  MY HEART RAN WILD WHEN IT HEARD . . . . . . 783 GREY ROUND   21
  WHY DOES YOUR HEART BEAT THUS? . . . . . . 785 YOUR HEART   1
  ITS STRANGE HEART BEATING FAST . . . . . . 785 YOUR HEART   6
  O STILL THAT HEART AT LAST. . . . . . . 785 YOUR HEART   8
  WHAT MAKES HER HEART BEAT THUS, ... 785 YOUR HEART   V   1
  WHAT MAKES YOUR HEART SO BEAT? . . . . 786 YOUR HEART   27
  THE HEART WELL WORN UPON THE SLEEVE MAY BE THE BEST OF 790 HEART SLEEVE   1
    SIGHTS,
HEARTACHE
  THERE'S MANY A ONE SHALL FIND OUT ALL HEARTACHE . . . . 205 ADAMS CURSE   16
HEART-BREAK
  SHE FELL AND DIED OF THE HEART-BREAK." . . . . . . 191 BAILE AILLINN   64
HEARTBURN
  I'VE NOTHING TO COMPLAIN OF BUT HEARTBURN, ... 227 SHADOW WATER B V 116A
HEARTED   SEE BROKEN-HEARTED WEARY-HEARTED STUBBORN-HEARTED STONY-HEARTED HONEY-HEARTED
             EASTERN-HEARTED
  AS WEARY HEARTED AS THAT HOLLOW MOON. . . . . . . 206 ADAMS CURSE   V 38
HEARTENERS
  HEARERS AND HEARTENERS OF THE WORK! . . . . . 266 GALWAY RACES   6
  AND WE FIND HEARTENERS AMONG MEN . . . . . . 266 GALWAY RACES   15
  HEARERS, HEARTENERS OF THE WORK, ... 266 GALWAY RACES   V   6
  AND FIND HEARTENERS AMONG MEN . . . . . . 266 GALWAY RACES   V 15
HEARTH
  BESIDE HER CLEAN-SWEPT HEARTH, HER QUIET SHADE! . . . . 114 ROSE OF BATTLE   11
  BESIDES HER CLEAN SWEPT HEARTH, HER QUIET SHADE! . . . . 114 ROSE OF BATTLE V 11
  I HAD A CHAIR AT EVERY HEARTH, ... 131 OLD PENSIONER V   1
  IN HER HIGH HOUSE AT CRUACHAN! THE LONG HEARTH, ... 180 QUEEN MAEVE   11
  A GREY STONE FIREPLACE WITH AN OPEN HEARTH, ... 419 MY HOUSE   12
  A GREY STONE FIRE-PLACE WITH AN OPEN HEARTH, ... 419 MY HOUSE   V 12
  BY AN OLD HEARTH, AND HE . . . . 780 WELL AND TREE   12
HEARTHSTONE
  EAT AT MY HEARTHSTONE. . . . . 380 SONGS FOOL 1   2
  THE THRESHOLD AND THE HEARTHSTONE, ... 775 AGAINST WITCH   6
  BUT THE THRESHOLD AND HEARTHSTONE. . . . . . . 776 AGAINST WITCH   40
HEARTIER
  AND HEARTIER LOVES! THAT LAMP IS FROM THE TOMB. . . . . 398 LEADERS CROWD   12
HEARTIEST
  HE MIGHT HAVE BEEN YOUR HEARTIEST WELCOMER. . . . . . 326 ROBERT GREGORY   56
HEART-MYSTERIES
  HEART-MYSTERIES THERE, AND YET WHEN ALL IS SAID . . . . 630 CIRCUS ANIMALS   27
HEART-REVEALING
  THE HEART-REVEALING INTIMACY . . . . 404 FOR DAUGHTER   23
HEART'S
  I HEAR IT IN THE DEEP HEART'S CORE. . . . . . . 117 ISLE INNISFREE   12
  BECAUSE A LOVER'S HEART'S WORN OUT, ... 191 BAILE AILLINN   65
  OUR HEART'S DESIRE NOW THAT WE ARE SO LIGHT." . . . . 233 SHADOW WATER B   255
  WHILE UP FROM MY HEART'S ROOT . . . . . . 316 FRIENDS   26
  FOR YOUR SOLE SAKE--THAT ALL HEART'S ACHE HAVE KNOWN, 355 BROKEN DREAMS   7
  AND GIVEN TO OTHERS ALL HEART'S ACHE, ... 355 BROKEN DREAMS   8
  BUT FOR YOUR SAKE--THAT ALL HEART'S ACHE HAVE KNOWN, 355 BROKEN DREAMS V   7
  THE HEART'S GROWN BRUTAL FROM THE FARE! . . . . 425 STARES NEST   17
  I SEE PHANTOMS OF HATRED AND OF THE HEART'S . . . . 425 PHANTOM HATRED   T
  MY HEART'S AGONY . . . . 452 HUMAN DIGNITY   10
  HEART'S PURPLE--AND ALL THESE I SET . . . . . . 478 SELF AND SOUL   28
  THIS LOVE THAT MAKES MY HEART'S BLOOD STOP . . . . 499 MOTHER OF GOD   13

```
                                                     PAGE      TITLE          LINE
HEART'S    (CONTINUED)
      AND IN THE HEART'S PRIDE.  .  .  .  .  .  .  .  .    513  JANE TALK BISH       12
      I SAID THAT SHE HAD DANCED HEART'S TRUTH,  .  .  .  .  .  .    514  JANE GROWN OLD        9
      BUT MY HEART'S VICTIM AND ITS TORTURER.  .  .  .  .  .  .    537  HER VISION           32
      MY PRETTY PAISTIN IS MY HEART'S DESIRE,  .  .  .  .  .  .    550  SONGS REWRIT 1 V      1
      THAT BLONDE GIRL THERE IS MY HEART'S DESIRE,  .  .  .  .  .    550  SONGS REWRIT 1 V      1
      O BUT HEART'S WINE SHALL RUN PURE,  .  .  .  .  .  .  .  .    554  CHURCH STATE          5
      HIS HEART'S DESIRE WHERE THE WORLD DWINDLES OUT?  .  .  .  .    747  SHADOW WATER A       13
      FORGAEL MAY FIND HIS HEART'S DESIRE ON BOARD  .  .  .  .  .    751  SHADOW WATER A      107
      YOUR HEART'S DESIRE AND THE END OF ALL OUR TROUBLE!  .  .  .    755  SHADOW WATER A      175
      AND NONE KNOWS WHEREFORE! BUT THE HEART'S DESIRE  .  .  .  .    764  SHADOW WATER A      340
HEARTS
      A RUMOUR OF DELIGHTED HEARTS.  .  .  .  .  .  .  .  .  .     16  OISIN 1             230
      "MEN'S HEARTS OF OLD WERE DROPS OF FLAME  .  .  .  .  .  .     19  OISIN 1             276
      BUT NOW HEARTS CRY THAT HEARTS ARE SLAVES,  .  .  .  .  .  .     19  OISIN 1             280
      BUT NOW HEARTS CRY THAT HEARTS ARE SLAVES,  .  .  .  .  .  .     19  OISIN 1             280
      WITH HEARTS THAT KNOW NOR LAW NOR RULE,  .  .  .  .  .  .     22  OISIN 1             339
      HAS CLOVEN AND RENT THEIR HEARTS IN TWAIN,  .  .  .  .  .  .     66  HAPPY SHEPHERD       33
      HAS TORN AND RENT THEIR HEARTS IN TWAIN,  .  .  .  .  .  .     66  HAPPY SHEPHERD V     33
      "PASSION HAS OFTEN WORN OUR WANDERING HEARTS."  .  .  .  .     80  EPHEMERA             12
      "OFTEN HAS PASSION WORN OUR WANDERING HEARTS,  .  .  .  .  .     80  EPHEMERA        V    12
      THE HEARTS OF THE WORLD-TROUBLING SEAMEN,  .  .  .  .  .  .     82  MAD KING GOLL         4
      BY GOD TO THE BRIGHT HEARTS OF THOSE LONG DEAD,  .  .  .  .    101  ROSE UPON ROOD       20
      BEFORE YOU WERE, OR ANY HEARTS TO BEAT,  .  .  .  .  .  .    112  ROSE OF WORLD        12
      BEFORE YE WERE, OR ANY HEARTS TO BEAT,  .  .  .  .  .  .    112  ROSE OF WORLD   V    12
      OF THEIR SAD HEARTS, THAT MAY NOT LIVE NOR DIE.  .  .  .  .    114  ROSE OF BATTLE       24
      OF OUR SAD HEARTS, THAT MAY NOT LIVE NOR DIE.  .  .  .  .    115  ROSE OF BATTLE       36
      HAS AWAKED IN OUR HEARTS, MY BELOVED, A SADNESS THAT MAY     122  WHITE BIRDS           4
         NOT DIE.
      HAS AWAKED IN OUR HEARTS, MY BELOVED, A SADNESS THAT NEVER   122  WHITE BIRDS     V     4
         MAY DIE.
      HAVE YOU NOT HEARD THAT OUR HEARTS ARE OLD,  .  .  .  .  .    141  EVERLAST VOICE        5
      AND ALL MEN'S HEARTS MUST BURN AND BEAT!  .  .  .  .  .  .    158  BELOVED RHYMES        9
      "O HEARTS OF WIND-BLOWN FLAME!  .  .  .  .  .  .  .  .    162  ASKS FORGIVE          6
      O PITEOUS HEARTS, CHANGING TILL CHANGE BE DEAD  .  .  .  .    163  ASKS FORGIVE         19
      AND TROUBLE WITH SIGHS FOR ALL HEARTS WITHOUT REST  .  .  .    163  ASKS FORGIVE    V    23
      OUR HEARTS ENDURE THE SCOURGE, THE PLAITED THORNS, THE WAY    172  TRAV PASSION          3
      OUR HEARTS ENDURE THE PLAITED THORN, THE CROWDED WAY,  .  .    172  TRAV PASSION    V     3
      OUR HEARTS CAN HEAR THE VOICES CHIDE.  .  .  .  .  .  .  .    192  BAILE AILLINN        94
      HAVE GIVEN THEIR HEARTS UP TO THE PLAY.  .  .  .  .  .  .    202  NEVER GIVE ALL       10
      BUT WE HAVE HIDDEN IN OUR HEARTS THE FLAME OUT OF THE EYES  .  .    207  HANRAHANS SONG        4
      ANGERS THAT ARE LIKE NOISY CLOUDS HAVE SET OUR HEARTS        207  HANRAHANS SONG        8
         ABEAT!
      LIKE TATTERED CLOUDS OF THE WORLD, PASSIONS CALL AND OUR     207  HANRAHANS SONG V      8
         HEARTS BEAT!
      ANGERS THAT ARE LIKE BUNDLED CLOUDS HAVE SET OUR HEARTS      207  HANRAHANS SONG V      8
         ABEAT!
      BUT OUR HEARTS ARE LIGHTED FROM THE FLAME IN THE EYES  .  .    207  HANRAHANS SONG V      9
      WHEN THEIR HEARTS ARE SO HIGH  .  .  .  .  .  .  .  .  .    214  HAPPY TOWNLAND       21
      THEIR HEARTS WOULD BE LIKE A CUP  .  .  .  .  .  .  .  .    215  HAPPY TOWNLAND       31
      FOR THEIR HEARTS WOULD BE LIKE A CUP  .  .  .  .  .  .  .    215  HAPPY TOWNLAND V     31
      TO FIND IF HEARTS BE WILD AND WISE,  .  .  .  .  .  .  .    263  MASK                  4
      THEIR HEARTS HAVE NOT GROWN OLD!  .  .  .  .  .  .  .  .    323  SWANS AT COOLE       22
      BE BUT THE BREAKERS OF MEN'S HEARTS OR ENGINES OF DELIGHT!    354  HIS PHOENIX          23
      TILL I COULD HEAR THEIR HEARTS BEATING!  .  .  .  .  .  .    358  PRESENCES            11
      OWN NOTHING BUT THEIR BLIND, STUPEFIED HEARTS.  .  .  .  .    370  EGO DOMINUS          69
      HEARTS WITH ONE PURPOSE ALONE  .  .  .  .  .  .  .  .  .    393  EASTER 1916          41
      HEARTS ARE NOT HAD AS A GIFT BUT HEARTS ARE EARNED  .  .  .    404  FOR DAUGHTER         34
      HEARTS ARE NOT HAD AS A GIFT BUT HEARTS ARE EARNED  .  .  .    404  FOR DAUGHTER         34
      AND HELEN HAS ALL LIVING HEARTS BETRAYED.  .  .  .  .  .  .    411  TOWER                53
      NOTHING BUT STILLNESS CAN REMAIN WHEN HEARTS ARE FULL  .  .    426  PHANTOM HATRED       23
      AND YET THEY TOO BREAK HEARTS—O PRESENCES  .  .  .  .  .    445  SCHOOL CHILDR        53
      TO SHOW HOW VIOLENT GREAT HEARTS CAN LOSE  .  .  .  .  .  .    463  HARUN RASHID         47
      TO WHERE THE DAMNED HAVE HOWLED AWAY THEIR HEARTS,  .  .  .    474  ALL SOUL NIGHT       95
      AND OUR HEARTS ARE TORN.  .  .  .  .  .  .  .  .  .  .  .    519  LOVES LONENESS       12
      THEIR UNREMEMBERING HEARTS AND HEADS  .  .  .  .  .  .  .    639  BEN BULBEN           72
      SUCH MEN, SUCH HEARTS.  BUT, UNCOUTH HUNTER, THOU  .  .  .    651  ISLE STAT I 1       167
      AS ON THOSE OTHER HEARTS WERE LAID.  .  .  .  .  .  .  .    667  ISLE STAT II 3       42
      IT IS THE VOICE OF ALL OUR HEARTS THAT LAUGH.  .  .  .  .    681  SEEKER                7
      I'D GLAD FOLKS' HEARTS WITH BLITHER SONG."  .  .  .  .  .    731  PRIEST FAIRY         82
      THESE ARE THEIR LURES, BUT THEY HAVE SET THEIR HEARTS  .  .    757  SHADOW WATER A      206
      FOLDING THEIR HEARTS' DESIRE TO THEIR GLAD HEARTS.  .  .  .    765  SHADOW WATER A      349
      THE NETS THE GODS HAVE WOVEN AND OUR OWN HEARTS,  .  .  .  .    766  SHADOW WATER A      383
HEARTS'
      OUR HEARTS' DESIRE NOW THAT WE ARE SO LIGHT."  .  .  .  .    753  SHADOW WATER A      145
      FOLDING THEIR HEARTS' DESIRE TO THEIR GLAD HEARTS.  .  .  .    765  SHADOW WATER A      349
HEART-SMITTEN
      HEART-SMITTEN WITH EMOTION I SINK DOWN,  .  .  .  .  .  .  .    602  GALLERY REVIS        17
HEART-STRINGS
      MINE HEART-STRINGS ARE ALL BROKEN SAVING ONE,  .  .  .  .  .    684  SEEKER          V   69B
HEARTY
      TO THE HORN, AND HE BE HALE AND HEARTY.  .  .  .  .  .  .  .    243  SHADOW WATER B      447
HEAT
      THROUGH SUMMER'S HEAT AND WINTER'S COLD.  .  .  .  .  .  .     86  MAD KING GOLL        71
      "FROM HEAT AND COLD AND WIND AND WAVE!  .  .  .  .  .  .  .    193  BAILE AILLINN       114
      TILL HER BOWELS ARE IN HEAT,  .  .  .  .  .  .  .  .  .    638  BEN BULBEN           49
HEATH
      O'ER HILL AND HEATH AND SPONGY FEN,  .  .  .  .  .  .  .  .     83  MAD KING GOLL V      32
      OVER THE HEATH AND SPONGY FEN,  .  .  .  .  .  .  .  .  .     83  MAD KING GOLL V      32
      BY HEATH OR HOLLOW OR RUSHY MERE,  .  .  .  .  .  .  .  .    716  FAIRY DOCTOR         10
```

374

		PAGE	TITLE		LINE

HEATHEN
YOU ARE STILL WRECKED AMONG HEATHEN DREAMS, ... 4 OISIN 1 31
OISIN, THOU ART HALF HEATHEN STILL! . . . . 4 OISIN 1 V 31
TELL ON, NOR BOW THY HEATHEN CREST . . . . 11 OISIN 1 V 131A
THIS HEATHEN HORDE AWAY. YOU NEED NOT HOPE! . . . . . 696 MOSADA 2 5
THE HEATHEN. YEA, AND SHAKE THE SULLEN KINGS . . . . 698 MOSADA 2 55
HEATHER
WE RODE BEYOND THE FURZE AND HEATHER, ... 9 OISIN 1 V 101A
AMID WET ROCKS AND HEATHER, ... 311 PEACOCK 8
BETWEEN ROCK AND WET HEATHER, ... 311 PEACOCK V 8
OUT OF A NEIGHBOURING BUNCH OF HEATHER! . . . . . 728 PRIEST FAIRY 20
HEAVE
WHAT MATTER? HEAVE NO SIGH, LET NO TEAR DROP, ... 564 GYRES 11
HEAVED
HEAVED BESIDE THE GLIMMERING WAVES, ... 21 OISIN 1 V 314
WHAT SACRED DRAMA THROUGH HER BODY HEAVED . . . . . 560 WHENCE COME 11
BUT HEAVED A SIGH IF THE CHAMBERMAID . . . . . . 570 THREE BUSHES 33
HEAVEN
AND EARTH AND HEAVEN AND HELL WOULD DIE, ... 19 OISIN 1 271
DARKEN! HEAVEN IS ANGRY. CEASE! UNTO MY MIND, . . . 42 OISIN 2 V 205
WHEN HEAVEN AND HELL ARE MET, ... 112 ROSE OF PEACE 2
A PEACE OF HEAVEN WITH HELL, ... 113 ROSE OF PEACE 16
GOD'S LAUGHING IN HEAVEN . . . . 118 CRADLE SONG 5
GOD SMILES IN HIGH HEAVEN . . . . 118 CRADLE SONG V 5
ALL THE HEAVENS BOW DOWN TO HEAVEN, ... 125 CATHLEEN PARA 15
SHE GOES DOWN THE FLOOR OF HEAVEN, ... 125 CATHLEEN PARA V 13
AND ABOVE THE DEEP OF HEAVEN, ... 125 CATHLEEN PARA V 15
DESOLATE WINDS THAT BEAT THE DOORS OF HEAVEN, AND BEAT . . 147 UNAPPEAS HOST 9
HE WISHES FOR THE CLOTHS OF HEAVEN . . . . . . 176 CLOTHS HEAVEN T
AEDH WISHES FOR THE CLOTHS OF HEAVEN . . . . . . 176 CLOTHS HEAVEN V T
. . . WHEN A PART OF THE CONSTELLATIONS OF HEAVEN . . 177 PAST GREATNESS T
HEAVEN KNOWS WHAT CALAMITY! . . . . 193 BAILE AILLINN 112
THE COLD HEAVEN . . . . 316 COLD HEAVEN T
SUDDENLY I SAW THE COLD AND ROOK-DELIGHTING HEAVEN . . 316 COLD HEAVEN 1
SUDDENLY I SAW THE COLD AND ROOK DELIGHTING HEAVEN . . 316 COLD HEAVEN V 1
HEAVEN HAS PUT AWAY THE STROKE OF HER DOOM, ... 356 BROKEN DREAMS 11
WHEN ALL IS FED WITH LIGHT AND HEAVEN IS BARE. . . . 375 PHASES OF MOON 74
EVEN ACCUSING HEAVEN BECAUSE . . . . 399 BREAK OF DAY 15
THE SWAN HAS LEAPED INTO THE DESOLATE HEAVEN! . . . . 431 NINETEEN 19 79
THAT IS TO SAY, ASCENDS TO HEAVEN! . . . . . . 478 SELF AND SOUL 38
HOW IN THE NAME OF HEAVEN CAN HE ESCAPE . . . . . 479 SELF AND SOUL 50
CAN BUT SHOW THAT HEAVEN YAWNS! . . . . 509 JANE REPROVED 4
MADE THE JOINTS OF HEAVEN CRACK! . . . . 509 JANE REPROVED 11
PRAY THAT HEAVEN PROTECT US . . . . 518 LOVES LONENESS 5
HEAVEN AND EARTH OUT OF THEIR PLACES, ... 540 FROM ANTIGONE 8
BLACK OUT! HEAVEN BLAZING INTO THE HEAD! . . . . . 566 LAPIS LAZULI 19
BUT MASTERFUL HEAVEN HAD INTERVENED TO SAVE IT, . . . 630 CIRCUS ANIMALS 20
A MAN HAS THE FIELDS OF HEAVEN, ... 643 SONG FAERIES 1
A MAN HAS A HOPE FOR HEAVEN, ... 643 SONG FAERIES V 1
LOVE FROM HEAVEN CAME OF YORE . . . . 648 ISLE STAT I 1 77
A MAN HAS A HOPE FOR HEAVEN, ... 676 ISLE STAT II 3 248
AND HEAVEN, AND HOLINESS. LET'S TALK AND GRIEVE, . . . 702 MOSADA 3 84
THEN THE STARS GROW OUT OF HEAVEN WITH THEIR COUNTENANCES . 719 PHANTOM SHIP 30
FAIR.
WHEN EARTH AND HEAVEN HAVE BEEN FOLDED UP! . . . . 765 SHADOW WATER A 366
THAT BLOW WHEN HEAVEN AND EARTH ARE WITHERING, . . . 767 SHADOW WATER A 395
HEAVENLY
GO TO THE GUARDS OF THE HEAVENLY FOLD . . . . . 141 EVERLAST VOICE 2
AND THAT ALL HEAVENLY GLORY SYMBOLISE-- . . . . . 445 SCHOOL CHILDR 55
THAN THE HEAVENLY CIRCUIT OF ITS STARS . . . . . 451 FIRST LOVE 17
THAN HEAVENLY CIRCUIT OF ITS STARS . . . . . . 451 FIRST LOVE V 17
THE HEAVENLY CIRCUIT! BERENICE'S HAIR! . . . . . 483 VERONIC NAPKIN 1
A HEAVENLY MANSION, RAGING IN THE DARK. . . . . . 491 COOLE BALLYLEE V 40D
A HEAVENLY MANSION, RAGING IN THE DARK, ... 495 CHOICE 4
LIVE IN A HEAVENLY MANSION, ... 513 JANE TALK BISH 5
AND HEAVENLY MUSIC IF THEY GAVE IT WIT! . . . . . 533 HER TRIUMPH 6
HEAVEN'S
LOOSED LONG AGO FROM HEAVEN'S GATE, ... 24 OISIN 1 362
LOOKED DOWN ON YOU FROM HEAVEN'S DOOR-POST . . . . 112 ROSE OF PEACE 3
LOOKED DOWN ON YOU FROM HEAVEN'S DOOR-POSTS, . . . 112 ROSE OF PEACE V 3
AND BY THE HEAVEN'S ALL-LABOURING BROODS! . . . . 164 PERFECT BEAUTY V 5
AND BY THE HEAVEN'S UN-LABOURING BROODS! . . . . 164 PERFECT BEAUTY V 5
HAD I THE HEAVEN'S EMBROIDERED CLOTHS, ... 176 CLOTHS HEAVEN V 1
THAT IS HEAVEN'S PART, OUR PART . . . . 394 EASTER 1916 60
AND THAT ITS OWN SWEET WILL IS HEAVEN'S WILL! . . . 405 FOR DAUGHTER 69
KNOWING THAT NONE COULD PASS HEAVEN'S DOOR . . . . 422 MY TABLE 26
KNOWING THAT NONE WHO PASS HEAVEN'S DOOR . . . . 422 MY TABLE V 26
KNOWING THAT NONE CAN PASS HEAVEN'S DOOR . . . . 422 MY TABLE V 26
RUN FOR A MILE UNDIMMED IN HEAVEN'S FACE . . . . 490 COOLE BALLYLEE 3
ALL HEAVEN'S FLOOR, WITH VAPOURS BEDDED-- . . . . 705 DAWN-SONG 11
AND HEAVEN'S A CLOUDY BLOT. . . . . 782 HEART FRIGHT 17
HEAVENS
ALL THE HEAVENS BOW DOWN TO HEAVEN, ... 125 CATHLEEN PARA 15
THE MIST HAS COVERED THE HEAVENS, AND YOU AND I . . . 251 SHADOW WATER B 604
TREMBLING IN THE BLUE HEAVENS LIKE A WHITE FAWN . . . 251 SHADOW WATER B 611
AN IMAGE OF THE MOVING HEAVENS, ... 480 BLOOD AND MOON 14
THE HEAVENS IN MY WOMB. . . . . 499 MOTHER OF GOD 5
ALL THE LABOURING HEAVENS SIGH. . . . . 573 LADYS 3RD SONG 12
THAT HEAVENS HAD OPENED. GYRES RUN ON! . . . . . 639 BEN BULBEN 62
WHERE ALL NIGHT LONG THE HEAVENS WEEP AND WEEP, . . . 649 ISLE STAT I 1 124
THE HEAVENS ALL STAR-THROBBING ARE A-LIT. . . . . 671 ISLE STAT II 3 143

```
                                                          PAGE      TITLE          LINE
HEAVENS   (CONTINUED)
     THE HEAVENS ALL STAR-THROBBING ARE ALIT. . . . . . .  671 ISLE STAT II 3 V   143
     YON BAUBLE OF THE HEAVENS, HE LIFTS HIS HANDS, . . . . 715 FERENCZ RENYI      119
     A QUARTER OF THE HEAVENS FROM OUR RIGHT WAY. . . . . . 754 SHADOW WATER A     155
     TREMBLING IN THE BLUE HEAVENS LIKE A WHITE FAWN . . . . 769 SHADOW WATER A    427
HEAVENS'
     HAD I THE HEAVENS' EMBROIDERED CLOTHS, . . . . . . . . 176 CLOTHS HEAVEN        1
     CREEPING ALONG THE HEAVENS' PURPLE CUP, . . . . . . . 714 FERENCZ RENYI      112
HEAVES
     I WAVE THEM HITHER, MY BREAST HEAVES WITH JOY. . . . . 694 MOSADA 1            98
HEAVIER
     THAT YOU MIGHT HAVE A HEAVIER PURSE, . . . . . . . . . 273 GREY ROCK           56
HEAVIEST
     YOU HAVE THE HEAVIEST ARM UNDER THE SKY." . . . . . . 107 CUCHULAIN SEA        24
HEAVILY
     A HEAVILY BUILT FALSTAFFAN MAN, . . . . . . . . . . . 423 ROAD AT DOOR   V     2
     UPON THY FACE? HOW HEAVILY THY HEAD . . . . . . . . . 701 MOSADA 3            72
HEAVILY-BUILT
     A HEAVILY-BUILT FALSTAFFIAN MAN, . . . . . . . . . . . 423 ROAD AT DOOR        2
HEAVINESS
     THE HEAVINESS OF DESIRE, . . . . . . . . . . . . . . . 168 BLESSED        V    38
     HAD FILLED THE HOUSE WITH DRUID HEAVINESS; . . . . . . 181 QUEEN MAEVE         40
HEAVING
     AND BROKE THE HEAVING RANKS OF BATTLE! . . . . . . . .  10 OISIN 1            124
     . . . AND HEAVING THE PILLAR OF HIS THROAT, . . . . . .  51 OISIN 3            59
     OUR BREASTS ARE HEAVING, OUR EYES ARE AGLEAM, . . . . . 140 HOSTING SIDHE       8
     FOR BREASTS ARE HEAVING AND EYES A-GLEAM, . . . . . . 140 HOSTING SIDHE  V     7
     OUR BREASTS ARE HEAVING, OUR EYES ARE A-GLEAM, . . . . 140 HOSTING SIDHE  V     8
     BY THE SLOW HEAVING OCEAN--MUMBLING MOTHER OF THE DEAD. 719 PHANTOM SHIP       34
HEAVY       SEE VINEGAR-HEAVY DREAM-HEAVY HISSOP-HEAVY ROSE-HEAVY
     WITH A HEAVY HEART AND A WANDERING MIND, . . . . . . .   2 OISIN 1             2
     FROM HIS HOOVES IN THE HEAVY GRASSES, WITH MONSTROUS    48 OISIN 3        V   27
        SLUMBERING FOLK,
     AND THOUGHT, I WILL MY HEAVY STORY TELL . . . . . . .  68 SAD SHEPHERD        19
     AND LO--MY HEAVY BURTHEN MAY DEPART;" . . . . . . . .  69 SAD SHEPHERD   V    24
     THE HEAVY BOUGHS, THE BURNISHED DOVE . . . . . . . . .  78 INDIAN TO LOVE     16
     OF PURPLE AND OF HEAVY GOLD; . . . . . . . . . . . . .  81 MAD KING GOLL  V    3
     AND SING, AND SHAKE MY HEAVY LOCKS. . . . . . . . . .  84 MAD KING GOLL       44
     THE LINES ARE NOT HEAVY, NOR HEAVY THE LONG NETS BROWN--  91 OLD FISHERMAN V    5
     THE LINES ARE NOT HEAVY, NOR HEAVY THE LONG NETS BROWN--  91 OLD FISHERMAN V    5
     CAME FLYING, HEAVY AND SAD; . . . . . . . . . . . . .  93 FATHER OHART       34
     AND HEAVY MORTAL HOPES THAT TOIL AND PASS; . . . . . . 101 ROSE UPON ROOD     18
     AN OLD SLAVE GRINDING AT A HEAVY QUERN, . . . . . . . 104 FERGUS DRUID       35
     ALL THE HEAVY DAYS ARE OVER; . . . . . . . . . . . . . 124 CATHLEEN PARA       1
     THE HEAVY STEPS OF THE PLOUGHMAN, SPLASHING THE WINTRY  143 ROSE IN HEART      3
        MOULD,
     THE HEAVY STEPS OF THE PLOUGHMAN SPLASHING THE WINTER   143 ROSE IN HEART V    3
        MOULD,
     WITH HEAVY WHITENING WINGS, AND A HEART FALLEN COLD; . . . 147 UNAPPEAS HOST   4
     THEIR HOOFS HEAVY WITH TUMULT, THEIR EYES GLIMMERING WHITE! 154 BELOVED PEACE  2
     THE HORSES OF DISASTER PLUNGE IN THE HEAVY CLAY; . . . 154 BELOVED PEACE       8
     PASSION-DIMMED EYES AND LONG HEAVY HAIR . . . . . . . 155 REPROVE CURLEW      4
     SHE DREW IN THE HEAVY CASEMENT . . . . . . . . . . . . 159 CAP AND BELLS      11
     WITH YOUR DIM HEAVY HAIR, . . . . . . . . . . . . . . 163 ASKS FORGIVE       22
     AMONG PALE EYELIDS, HEAVY WITH THE SLEEP . . . . . . . 169 SECRET ROSE         6
     MEN HAVE NAMED BEAUTY.  YOUR HEAVY LEAVES ENFOLD . . . 169 SECRET ROSE    V    7
     THAT IT MAY DROP FAINT PERFUME, AND BE HEAVY WITH DEW, . 172 TRAV PASSION      7
     HIS HEAVY RINGS UNCOILED FROM GLIMMERING DEEP TO DEEP; . 174 ELEMENT POWERS    5
     WAS THAT, THE AIR BEING HEAVY AND THE DOGS . . . . . . 182 QUEEN MAEVE        53
     O HEAVY SWOLLEN WATERS, BRIM THE FALL OF THE OAK TREES, 207 HANRAHANS SONG V  11
     LIKE HEAVY FLOODED WATERS OUR BODIES AND OUR BLOOD; . . 208 HANRAHANS SONG    13
     LIKE HEAVY SWOLLEN WATERS ARE OUR BODIES AND OUR BLOOD; 208 HANRAHANS SONG V  13
     WHEN ALL THIS HEAVY HISTORY'S DONE; . . . . . . . . . 213 BLESS PSALTER      17
     THEY UNHOOK THEIR HEAVY SWORDS . . . . . . . . . . . . 215 HAPPY TOWNLAND     23
     HEAVY LIKE STONE, THEIR WISDOM BEING HALF SILENCE. . . 218 WOODS OF COOLE     26
     BUT THE STAG STOOPED ITS HEAVY BRANCHING HORNS, . . . 277 TWO KINGS      V   12
     NOR HEAVY KNITTING OF THE BROW . . . . . . . . . . . . 318 APPOINTMENT         9
     TWO HEAVY TRESTLES, AND A BOARD . . . . . . . . . . . 421 MY TABLE            1
     I WRAPPED HER IN A HEAVY HOODED CLOAK, . . . . . . . . 468 HARUN RASHID   V  154
     I WRAPPED HER IN A HEAVY HOODED CLOAK, AND SHE . . . . 468 HARUN RASHID   V  154
     IS BUT A HEAVY, GOLD EMBROIDERED BANNER, . . . . . . . 469 HARUN RASHID   V  188
     BUT UNDER HEAVY LOADS OF TRAMPLED CLAY . . . . . . . . 483 OIL AND BLOOD       4
     BUT HEAVY FRUIT.  HOW SWIFT THE ARGUMENT . . . . . . . 665 ISLE STAT II 2     66
     HEAVY WITH WOOL THE SHEEP ARE GATHERED IN, . . . . . . 681 SEEKER              1
     THE HEAVY CLUSTERS OF THE GRAPES WERE FULL, . . . . . 690 MOSADA 1           13
     THIS DEATH IS HEAVY IN MY VEINS LIKE SLEEP. . . . . . 701 MOSADA 3           57
     WHY DO YOU HANG SO HEAVY IN MY ARMS? . . . . . . . . . 703 MOSADA 3          108
     WHERE THE ROSES IN SCARLET ARE HEAVY . . . . . . . . . 707 FAIRY PEDANT        3
     WITH CREATURES OF OUR HEAVY NIGHT, . . . . . . . . . . 743 DANAAN QUICK       10
     LOOK ON THIS BODY AND THIS HEAVY HAIR; . . . . . . . . 767 SHADOW WATER A    397
HEBER'S
     THERE WAS NO MIGHTIER SOUL OF HEBER'S LINE; . . . . .  36 OISIN 2            95
HEBRIDES
     AND PASSED THE OUTER HEBRIDES, AND TOOK . . . . . . . 749 SHADOW WATER A     42
     AND PASSED THE NORTHERN HEBRIDES, AND TOOK . . . . . . 749 SHADOW WATER A V   42
     AMONG THE HEBRIDES.  WHEN SHE AWAKENS. . . . . . . . . 760 SHADOW WATER A V  255
HECTOR
     HECTOR IS IN THE DUST, NIETZSCHE IS BORN, . . . . . . 374 PHASES OF MOON     46
     TO THINK OF BURIED HECTOR . . . . . . . . . . . . . . 455 HIS MEMORIES        5
     SHE WHO HAD BROUGHT GREAT HECTOR DOWN . . . . . . . . 455 HIS MEMORIES       15
     HECTOR IS DEAD AND THERE'S A LIGHT IN TROY; . . . . . 564 GYRES               7
```

HEDGES
  AND WHEN ABOUNDING HEDGES RING . . . . 434 WHEEL   3
  AND WHEN ABOUNDING HEDGES SING . . . . 434 WHEEL   V   3
HEED
  AND ALL MUST PAY HIM HEED, ... YOU HEED ME NOT!   583 GHOST ROG CASE   22
  THE BOAT DRAWS NEAR AND NEAR. YOU HEED ME NOT! . . . . . 663 ISLE STAT II 2   23
  CEASE! THERNOT'S WOUNDED, CEASE! THEY WILL NOT HEED. . . . 665 ISLE STAT II 2   64
  NOR LAW NOR PARLIAMENT TAKE HEED. . . . . 791 REPRISALS   22
HEEDS
  NOR HEEDS THE OLD, DIM PROTEST AND THE CRY . . . . . . 689 NETTLESHIP   14
HEEL
  . . . AT THE HEEL OF A CENTURY FELL, ... 54 OISIN 3   102
  THAT TOSSED A BARE HEEL WHEN AT SCHOOL, ... 301 RUN PARADISE   19
  FROM HEEL TO THROAT! . . . . 320 COAT   4
  HEEL UP AND WEIGHT ON TOE, MUST FACE THE WALL . . . . . 363 DOLLS FACES   3
  TO DRUM WITH HER HEEL AND TO LEAP? . . . . 381 SONGS FOOL 2   9
  A SORT OF BATTERED KETTLE AT THE HEEL. . . . . 409 TOWER   16
HEELS
  THEY SAT UPON THEIR HEELS TO RAIL, ... 297 THREE BEGGARS   53
  OR SAT UPON THEIR HEELS TO RAIL . . . . 297 THREE BEGGARS V   53
  THAT PATCHING OLD HEELS THEY MAY SHRIEK, I TAKE TO CHISEL   623 HIGH TALK   8
    AND PLANE.
HEIGHT
  OF THE FLOOD AND FLAME, OF THE HEIGHT AND WOOD, ... 148 INTO TWILIGHT V   11
  MORE HANDS IN HEIGHT THAN ANY STAG IN THE WORLD . . . . 277 TWO KINGS   9
  THAT ON THE LONELY HEIGHT WHERE ALL ARE IN GOD'S EYE, . . 291 PAUDEEN   6
  WHEN THE FULL MOON SWAM TO ITS GREATEST HEIGHT . . . . 468 HARUN RASHID   151
HEIGHTS
  WHEN I CLAMBER TO THE HEIGHTS OF SLEEP, ... 357 DEEP-SWORN VOW   4
HEIR
  ON THE HEIR OF ULADH, BUAN'S SON, ... 189 BAILE AILLINN   4
  AILLINN, WHO WAS KING LUGAIDH'S HEIR. . . . . 189 BAILE AILLINN   7
HEIRS
  AND ON MY HEIRS, IF ALL REMAIN UNSPOILED, ... 371 ON GOING HOUSE   2
  MY BODILY HEIRS MAY FIND, ... 420 MY HOUSE   28
HELD
  AS THOUGH HE HELD AN EARTHLY MEAD . . . . 2 OISIN 1   V   7X
  HE HELD THAT FLASHING SCEPTRE UP. . . . . 18 OISIN 1   260
  NOR HAVE HANDS HELD A WEARY TOOL, ... 19 OISIN 1   283
  BENEATH HAD PACED CONTENT! WE HELD OUR WAY . . . . . . 36 OISIN 2   103
  BASALTIC, MIGHT HAVE PACED. WE HELD OUR WAY . . . . . 36 OISIN 2   V   103
  LAID IT AND SIGHED! I HELD A SWORD WHOSE SHINE . . . . 37 OISIN 2   126
  ONCE HELD BETWEEN MY ARMS, WITH LIVID CHOP . . . . . . 40 OISIN 2   V   178
  I HELD A DRIPPING CORPSE, WITH LIVID CHOP . . . . . . 40 OISIN 2   V   178
  AND I BUT HELD A CORPSE, WITH LIVID CHOP . . . . . . 40 OISIN 2   V   178
  HELD TO THE TOWERS WITH BOASTING SONGS AND GAY. . . . . 41 OISIN 2   V 184C
  HALF OPEN HIS EYES WERE, AND HELD ME, ... 51 OISIN 3   65
  WHILE SLOWLY HE WHOSE HAND HELD HERS REPLIED! . . . . . 80 EPHEMERA   11
  WHILE SLOWLY ANSWERED HE WHOSE HAND HELD HERS-- . . . . 80 EPHEMERA   V   11
  A THOUSAND YEARS AGO YOU HELD HIGH TALK . . . . 187 QUEEN MAEVE   150
  THAT HELD THE LAND TOGETHER THERE, ... 194 BAILE AILLINN   132
  HE COULD NOT SEE THEM, BUT I HELD OUT MY HANDS . . . . 223 SHADOW WATER B   38
  DRAGON THAT LOVED THE WORLD AND HELD US TO IT, ... 251 SHADOW WATER B   598
  I HELD A PAINTED STEERING OAR, ... 253 HIS DREAM   V   2
  WHO SAID, "BECAUSE SHE HELD ME IN . . . . 274 GREY ROCK   86
  A ROMAN CAESAR IS HELD DOWN . . . . 379 SAINT HUNCH   4
  "A MAN IF I BUT HELD HIM SO . . . . 521 THREE THINGS   9
  AND AFTER THAT I HELD MY FINGERS UP, ... 537 HER VISION   9
  OF ALL THAT SCHOLARLY GENERATIONS HAD HELD DEAR! . . . . 603 GALLERY REVIS V 37A
  A MOUTHFUL HELD THE EXTREME OF LIFE AND DEATH. . . . . 619 BRONZE HEAD   14
  AND HELD HER IN MY ARMS! . . . . 631 POLITICS   12
  A KID, HELD BY ONE SOFT WHITE EAR FOR TETHER, ... 715 DWELT SYCAMORE   3
  I HAVE CUT THE CORDS THAT HELD THIS GALLEY TO OURS. . . 768 SHADOW WATER A V 421
HELEN
  WHEN HELEN LIVED . . . . 293 HELEN LIVED   T
  WHERE HELEN WALKED WITH HER BOY, ... 293 HELEN LIVED   9
  HELEN BEING CHOSEN FOUND LIFE FLAT AND DULL . . . . . 404 FOR DAUGHTER   25
  AND HELEN HAS ALL LIVING HEARTS BETRAYED. . . . . . . 411 TOWER   53
  FROM THE LIMBS OF HELEN SANK . . . . 522 LULLABY   V   17
  TROY BACKED ITS HELEN! TROY DIED AND ADORED; . . . . . 547 TO SAME TUNE 3   4
  TROY LOOKED ON HELEN, IT DIED AND ADORED; . . . . . . 547 TO SAME TUNE 3 V   4
  TROY BACKED ITS HELEN! TROY DIED AND ADORED; . . . . . 614 MARCH SONGS 2   4
  A HELEN OF SOCIAL WELFARE DREAM, ... 626 OLD MEN BE MAD   7
HELEN'S
  THAT FIRST DAWN IN HELEN'S ARMS? . . . . 522 LULLABY   6
  THAT FIRST NIGHT IN HELEN'S ARMS. . . . . 522 LULLABY   V   6
HELICON
  THE ABOUNDING GUTTER HAD BEEN HELICON . . . . 398 LEADERS CROWD   6
HELL
  AND EARTH AND HEAVEN AND HELL WOULD DIE, ... 19 OISIN 1   271
  . . . ON THE BURNING STONES OF WIDE HELL, ... 61 OISIN 3   198
  HEARING HELL LOUD WITH A MURMUR, AS SHOUTING AND MOCKING   62 OISIN 3   208
    WE SWEEP.
  NONE WAR ON THE MASTERS OF HELL, ... 62 OISIN 3   214
  WHEN HEAVEN AND HELL ARE MET, ... 112 ROSE OF PEACE   2
  A PEACE OF HEAVEN WITH HELL. . . . . 113 ROSE OF PEACE   16
  THE DOORS OF HELL AND BLOW THERE MANY A WHIMPERING GHOST!   147 UNAPPEAS HOST   10
  EUNUCHS RAN THROUGH HELL AND MET . . . . 294 HATED PLAYBOY   2
  HELL MOUTH LAY OPEN NEAR THAT PLACE, ... 303 HOUR DAWN   25
  BUT THE HELL MOUTH AT CRUACHAN . . . . 303 HOUR DAWN   V   24
  FROM THE HELL MOUTH AT CRUACHAN . . . . 307 HOUR DAWN   V 120

	PAGE	TITLE	LINE

HELL   (CONTINUED)
THEY SAID I'D BURN IN HELL UNLESS I TOLD. . . . .   694 MOSADA 1   108
"NO, THY HOME IS DEEPEST HELL, ...   697 MOSADA 2   26
HER SOUL FROM SEAS OF ENDLESS FLAME IN HELL. . . . . .   698 MOSADA 2   47
SO THEY ESCAPE FROM HELL. BUT, PARDON ME, ...   704 MOSADA 3   132
HELL'S
ROUND ABOUT HELL'S GATE TO STARE . . . .   294 HATED PLAYBOY V   3
HELM
AND FLY AMONG THE FOAM. THRUST DOWN THE HELM, ...   750 SHADOW WATER A   88
GIVE ME THE HELM! CALL HITHER THOSE WHO LIE . . . .   751 SHADOW WATER A   91
NODS BY THE HELM, AND NEARER TO THE SAIL . . . . .   752 SHADOW WATER A   119
HELMET
AND BEAT THE GOLDEN HELMET WITH THEIR SWORDS? . . . . .   243 SHADOW WATER B   425
HELMETS
HELMETS, AND SWORDS, AND HALF-FORGOTTEN THINGS . . . .   257 RECONCILIATION   6
HURL HELMETS, CROWNS, AND SWORDS INTO THE PIT. . . .   257 RECONCILIATION   10
HELMS
THE ANCIENT BEARDS, THE HELMS OF RUBY AND GOLD . . .   169 SECRET ROSE   8
AND ALL THEIR HELMS OF SILVER HOVERING SIDE BY SIDE, . .   318 MAGI   5
HELMSMAN'S
A TRADING GALLEY IN HER HELMSMAN'S EYES. . . . . . .   751 SHADOW WATER A   95
HELP
HELP! HELP! AND HURL HIM FROM OUR COAST . . . . . .   83 MAD KING GOLL V 17
HELP! HELP! AND HURL HIM FROM OUR COAST . . . . . .   83 MAD KING GOLL V 17
NO WOMAN'S LOVED ME, NO MAN SOUGHT MY HELP. . . . . .   103 FERGUS DRUID   26
NO MAIDEN LOVES ME, NO MAN SEEKS MY HELP, ...   103 FERGUS DRUID   26
NO WOMAN LOVES ME, NO MAN SEEKS MY HELP, ...   103 FERGUS DRUID V 26
TO HELP ME IN MY NEED. . . . .   134 FR GILLIGAN   44
TO HELP HER LIGHT FOOT HERE AND THERE, ...   138 TO IRELAND   V 14
ABOUT MY THRESHOLD TO COUNSEL AND TO HELP?" . . . .   183 QUEEN MAEVE   82
THE PARTED LIPS REPLIED, "I SEEK YOUR HELP, ...   183 QUEEN MAEVE   83
ABOUT MY DOOR TO COUNSEL AND TO HELP." . . . . . .   183 QUEEN MAEVE   V 82
HELP THEM THAT WANDER WITH HAND CLASPING HAND, ...   184 QUEEN MAEVE   86
AND I WOULD HAVE YOUR HELP IN MY GREAT NEED, ...   184 QUEEN MAEVE   98
HELP THEM THAT PACE, HAND IN UNWITHERING HAND, ...   184 QUEEN MAEVE   V 86
NO MORTAL CAN. YES! IF THEY GIVE US HELP. . . . . .   229 SHADOW WATER B   165
AND THERE'S NO HELP IN WORDS. TO THE OTHER SHIP, . .   250 SHADOW WATER B   585
AND WHAT, GOD HELP US, COULD THEY SAVE? . . . . .   289 SEPTEMBER 1913   14
HOW THEREFORE COULD SHE HELP BUT BRAID . . . . . .   309 PLAYER QUEEN   17
MAGICAL SHAPES. BY THE HELP OF AN IMAGE . . . . .   367 EGO DOMINUS   7
TO HELP GOOD, WISE OR GREAT . . . .   432 NINETEEN 19   110
IN THIS MY CHOICE. SOME GOD MIGHT HELP! IF SO . . .   656 ISLE STAT I 3   37
THAT MURMURS WITH HOLY WOODS, AND WIN THEIR HELP . . . .   757 SHADOW WATER A   199
HELPED
I HELPED YOUR FATHERS WHEN THEY BUILT THESE WALLS, . . .   184 QUEEN MAEVE   97
"BECAUSE I HELPED TO WIND THE CLOCK . . . .   585 ORAHILLY   25
HELPER
THIS OTHER HIS HELPER AND FRIEND . . . .   392 EASTER 1916   26
HELPFUL
HELPFUL AND SHY. . . . .   89 ISLE IN WATER   14
HELPLESS
HELPLESS, MEN LIFTING THE LIDS OF HIS WEARY   53 OISIN 3   92
AND DEATH-MAKING EYE.
HELPLESS, MEN LIFTING THE LIDS OF HIS WEARY   53 OISIN 3   V 92
AND DEATH-POURING EYE.
BEFORE THE FULL MOON, HELPLESS AS A WORM. . . . . .   374 PHASES OF MOON   49
HE HOLDS HER HELPLESS BREAST UPON HIS BREAST. . . . .   441 LEDA AND SWAN   4
HAS LAID HER HELPLESS FACE UPON HER BREAST. . . . .   441 LEDA AND SWAN V   4
HEM
HER PEARL-PALE HAND AND THE HEM OF HER DRESS. . . . .   16 OISIN 1   216
HER FINGERS AND HER GARMENTS' HEM. . . . . . .   16 OISIN 1   V 216
AND SHAKE THEIR COVERLET'S HEM. . . . .   33 OISIN 2   V 62
BECAUSE THE RED-ROSE-BORDERED HEM . . . .   137 TO IRELAND   6
BECAUSE THE RED ROSE BORDERED HEM . . . .   137 TO IRELAND   V   6
AFTER THE RED-ROSE-BORDERED HEM. . . . .   139 TO IRELAND   30
AFTER THE RED-ROSE-BORDERED HEM. . . . .   139 TO IRELAND   48
AFTER THE RED ROSE BORDERED HEM. . . . .   139 TO IRELAND   V 30
AFTER THE RED ROSE BORDERED HEM. . . . .   139 TO IRELAND   V 48
FOUGHT ONCE FOR SELF-SAME REASON ON THE HEM . . . .   660 ISLE STAT II 1   32
THY GARMENTS' HEM, THOU VISIONARY ONE! . . . . . .   684 SEEKER   71
THY GARMENT'S HEM, THOU VISIONARY ONE! . . . . . .   684 SEEKER   V 71
HEN   SEE MOOR-HEN WATER-HEN
MARE OR STALLION, COCK OR HEN, ...   529 TOM LUNATIC   15
OF HEN WIVES AND OF QUEER OLD MEN . . . .   607 SONGS BURDEN 2 V 23
HENCE
O WOMEN, KNEELING BY YOUR ALTAR-RAILS LONG HENCE, . .   173 SPEAKS HEARERS   1
O COLLEENS, KNEELING BY YOUR ALTAR RAILS LONG HENCE, . .   173 SPEAKS HEARERS V 1
O, WOMEN, KNEELING BY YOUR ALTAR RAILS LONG HENCE, . .   173 SPEAKS HEARERS V 1
CONSIDERING THAT, ALL HATRED DRIVEN HENCE, ...   405 FOR DAUGHTER   65
MEETING LONG HENCE THE PHANTOM HERDSMAN, KING . . . .   675 ISLE STAT II 3 242
HENRY
SOMEWHERE OFF HENRY STREET! . . . .   585 ORAHILLY   31
MY NAME IS HENRY MIDDLETON, ...   606 SONGS BURDEN 2   1
HENS   SEE MOOR-HENS PEA-HENS
AND HENS TO MOOR-COCKS CALL! . . . .   393 EASTER 1916   54
OTTERS BELOW AND MOOR HENS ON THE TOP, ...   490 COOLE BALLYLEE V 2
HENWIVES
OF HENWIVES AND OF QUEER OLD MEN . . . .   607 SONGS BURDEN 2   23
HERALD
THERE CRIED A HERALD, "TO OUR VALLEYS . . . . . .   82 MAD KING GOLL V 14
CRIED A HERALD, "PEACE WITH THINE! . . . . . .   82 MAD KING GOLL V 14

		PAGE	TITLE		LINE

HERALD   (CONTINUED)
CRIED A HERALD, "TO OUR VALLEYS   . . .   82 MAD KING GOLL   V   14
AFAR, CLEAR-SHINING ON THE HERALD HILLS, ...   645 ISLE STAT I 1   14
THE FAIRIES' HERALD SPAKE ONCE MORE!   . . . .   730 PRIEST FAIRY   53
HERALD'S
THE HERALD'S CRY, THE SOLDIER'S TREAD   . . . .   438 SONGS PLAY 2   13
HERB
SOME MEDICABLE HERB TO MAKE OUR GRIEF   . . . .   342 SHEP GOATHERD   86
BY WATER, HERB AND SOLITARY PRAYER   . . . .   555 RIBH AT TOMB   23
AND MANY A HERB AND MANY A SPELL   . . . .   717 FAIRY DOCTOR   17
HERBLESS
DUSKY AND HERBLESS, WHERE A BUBBLING STRAIN   . . . . .   39 OISIN 2   V   156
BARKING. ALONG THE HERBLESS PLAIN, WITH BLOWS   . . . .   40 OISIN 2   V   170
HERBS
THUS DO I BURN THESE PRECIOUS HERBS, WHOSE SMOKE   . . . .   691 MOSADA 1   39
AND MANY HERBS AND MANY A SPELL   . . . .   717 FAIRY DOCTOR   17
HERD
TO IDLE LIFE AWAY, A COMMON HERD."   . . . .   107 CUCHULAIN SEA   21
OF A MOROCCAN FLOCK OR HERD, ...   493 AT ALGECIRAS   V   3
HERDED
HERDED THE CATTLE CAME WITH STUMBLING FEET, ...   106 CUCHULAIN SEA   19
HERDING
HERDING THE PACK. UNQUIET WANDERER   . . . .   292 TO A SHADE   V   18
HERDS
HAVE A SPEED LIKE THE SPEED OF THE SALMON HERDS,   . . .   9 OISIN 1   98
AND SWIFTER THAN THE SALMON HERDS!   . . . .   9 OISIN 1   V   96
THAT YOU STAY IDLING HERE WITH FLOCKS AND HERDS."   . .   107 CUCHULAIN SEA   V   21
THAT YOU STAY IDLING HERE WITH FLOCK AND HERDS."   . .   107 CUCHULAIN SEA   V   21
TO IDLE LIFE AWAY WITH FLOCKS AND HERDS."   . . . .   107 CUCHULAIN SEA   V   21
ARE TRODDEN AND BROKEN BY THE HERDS, ...   190 BAILE AILLINN   43
ON THE HORIZON EDGE BELLOWED THE HERDS.   . . . . .   279 TWO KINGS   56
THEREON THE BELLOWING OF THE EMPOUNDED HERDS   . . . .   286 TWO KINGS   214
OF THE MOROCCAN FLOCKS AND HERDS   . . . .   493 AT ALGECIRAS   3
ROUND US HERDS OF SHADOWS STEAL--   . . . .   737 IN FIRELIGHT   6
WHO MIGHT HAVE FLOCKS AND HERDS AND MANY THRALLS,   . .   757 SHADOW WATER A   216
O, AENGUS OF THE HERDS, WATCH OVER ME!   . . . . . .   762 SHADOW WATER A   291
HERDSMAN
A HERDSMAN CAME FROM INLAND VALLEYS, ...   82 MAD KING GOLL   14
THE CRAZY HERDSMAN THAT WILL TELL HIS FELLOWS   . . . .   229 SHADOW WATER B   167
MEETING LONG HENCE THE PHANTOM HERDSMAN, KING   . . . .   675 ISLE STAT II 3   242
HERDSMEN
TO THAT HIGH HILL THE HERDSMEN NAME   . . . .   194 BAILE AILLINN   129
HERESIES
THAT SHE FORSWEAR HER HERESIES AND SAVE   . . . . .   698 MOSADA 2   46
CAST OFF THY HERESIES, AND SAVE THY SOUL   . . . . .   701 MOSADA 3   64
HERESY
I WILL BURN HERESY FROM THIS MAD EARTH, ...   697 MOSADA 2   40
HERITAGE
SOMETHING OF EVERY PADDLER'S HERITAGE--   . . . . . .   444 SCHOOL CHILDR   21
LONDON STREETS HAVE HERITAGE, ...   733 STREET DANCERS   57
HERMIT
A BLIND HERMIT RINGS THE HOUR.   . . . .   484 SYMBOLS   2
HERMITS
THE THREE HERMITS   . . . .   298 THREE HERMITS   T
THREE OLD HERMITS TOOK THE AIR   . . . .   298 THREE HERMITS   1
HERMITS UPON MOUNT MERU OR EVEREST, ...   563 MERU   9
HERO
"AND EVERY HERO DROOP HIS HEAD?   . . . .   4 OISIN 1   33
THE HERO, THE GIRL, AND THE FOOL   . . . .   447 HERO GIRL FOOL   T
HERODIAS'
HERODIAS' DAUGHTERS HAVE RETURNED AGAIN, ...   433 NINETEEN 19   118
HEROES
THE HUNTING OF HEROES SHOULD BE GLAD."   . . . . . .   4 OISIN 1   39
"THE HUNTING OF HEROES SHOULD BE GLAD!   . . . . . .   4 OISIN 1   V   32
"FOR HUNTING HEROES SHOULD BE GLAD.   . . . . . .   4 OISIN 1   V   34
AND ON THE HEROES LYING SLAIN   . . . .   5 OISIN 1   42
HEROES'
BECAUSE THE HEROES' CRESCENT IS THE TWELFTH.   . . . . .   374 PHASES OF MOON V   47
HEROIC
BUT AN HEROIC DREAM.   . . . .   255 WOMAN HOMER   21
BANISHED HEROIC MOTHER MOON AND VANISHED, ...   344 DEJECTION   9
HEROIC MOTHER MOON HAS VANISHED, ...   344 DEJECTION   V   9
WHAT BUT HEROIC WANTONNESS?   . . . .   550 SEVERED HEAD   13
HEROIC REVERIE MOCKED BY CLOWN AND KNAVE, ...   619 BRONZE HEAD   27
THROUGH SEVEN HEROIC CENTURIES;   . . . . . .   640 BEN BULBEN   80
HEROICALLY
HEROICALLY LOST, HEROICALLY FOUND.   . . . . . .   578 CRAZED GIRL   8
HEROICALLY LOST, HEROICALLY FOUND.   . . . . . .   578 CRAZED GIRL   8
HERON
THEN, MOUNTED ON A HERON, O'ER THE DEEP   . . . . .   33 OISIN 2   V   64
AND HERON OUT OF THE SKIES."   . . . .   167 BLESSED   10
AND FAR AWAY THE HERON SAILS, I WIS.   . . . . . .   649 ISLE STAT I 1   116
WAKE! THE HERON, RISING, HATH   . . . .   705 DAWN-SONG   17
STRAYING AS THE HERON STRAYETH, ...   706 DAWN-SONG   27
HERON-BILLED
THE HERON-BILLED PALE CATTLE-BIRDS   . . . .   493 AT ALGECIRAS   1
THE HERON-BILLED PALE CATTLE BIRD, ...   493 AT ALGECIRAS   V   1
THE HERON-BILLED PALE CATTLE BIRDS, ...   493 AT ALGECIRAS   V   1
HERON'S
HOW THE FALCONER FOLLOWS THE FALCON IN THE WEEDS OF THE   52 OISIN 3   79
HERON'S PLOT,

379

```
                                                    PAGE    TITLE             LINE

HERON'S   (CONTINUED)
     THE HERON'S HUNCH UPON HIS BACK,  . . . . . . . . .   508 JANE BISHOP          19
     AY, BOY. LET'S SEE IF THAT SAME HERON'S DEAD.  . . . .  651 ISLE STAT I 1      169
HERONS
     WHERE FLAPPING HERONS WAKE  . . . . . . . . . . .      86 STOLEN CHILD          4
     AND THE JOY OF THE STREAMS WHERE LONG-LIMBED HERONS WADE:  674 ISLE STAT II 3  217
HERO'S
     BRED TO BE A HERO'S WAGE. . . . . . . . . . . . . .    258 PEACE                3
     BECAUSE THE HERO'S CRESCENT IS THE TWELFTH. . . . . .  374 PHASES OF MOON      47
HERRING
     THE HERRING ARE NOT IN THE TIDES AS THEY WERE OF OLD:  . .  91 OLD FISHERMAN    5
HERRINGS
     MY WORK WAS SALTIN' HERRINGS  . . . . . . . . . . .    94 MOLL MAGEE            7
     FLASHES AS IF IT WERE A NET OF HERRINGS. . . . . . .   248 SHADOW WATER B     536
HESITATE
     HESITATE OR STAY? . . . . . . . . . . . . . . .       505 RESULT THOUGHT      17
HEW
     BASALTIC PILLARS MARRED WITH HEW AND HACK  . . . . .    31 OISIN 2          V  30
     EVADING, TURNING: ONCE DID I HEW AND HEW  . . . . .     40 OISIN 2          V 176
     EVADING, TURNING: ONCE DID I HEW AND HEW  . . . . .     40 OISIN 2          V 176
HIBERNIAN
     ON MR. NETTLESHIP'S PICTURE AT THE ROYAL HIBERNIAN ACADEMY.  688 NETTLESHIP      T
HIBERNIANS
     . . . HAVE JOINED THE ANCIENT ORDER OF HIBERNIANS AND THE  262 STUDENTS AGIT  V  T
     . . .
HID        SEE LEAF-HID VAPOUR-HID
     AND IN THE SHADOW OF MY HAIR LIE HID,  . . . . . .     33 OISIN 2             66
     IT DIED AFAR.  GREY SLEET THOSE TOWERS HID  . . . .    46 OISIN 2          V 245
     HID UNDER QUIET BOUGHS APART, . . . . . . . . . .      78 INDIAN TO LOVE      12
     HID IN THE EARTH'S MOST HIDDEN PART, . . . . . . .     78 INDIAN TO LOVE V    12
     HID UNDER QUIET BOWS APART, . . . . . . . . . .        78 INDIAN TO LOVE V    12
     THERE WE'VE HID OUR FAERY VATS, . . . . . . . . .      87 STOLEN CHILD         6
     GO DWELL UPON THE SEA CLIFFS, VAPOUR HID, . . . . .   105 CUCHULAIN SEA   V    4
     IS HID IN THE HEART OF LOVE: . . . . . . . . . .      119 PITY OF LOVE         2
     HAD HID AWAY EARTH'S OLD AND WEARY CRY. . . . . . .   120 SORROW OF LOVE  V    4
     AND HID HIS FACE AMID A CROWD OF STARS. . . . . . .   121 YOU ARE OLD         12
     FOR SOMEBODY HID HATRED AND HOPE AND DESIRE AND FEAR  . 153 CHANGE BELOVED     4
     IN THE HID PLACE, BEING CRAZED BY LOVE. . . . . . .   195 BAILE AILLINN      143
     BUT A WILD APPLE HID THE GRASS. . . . . . . . . .     197 BAILE AILLINN      189
     AT THE MOTH HOUR AND HID IT IN HER BOSOM. . . . . .   199 ARROW           V    6
     WHERE ONE FOUND LANCELOT CRAZED AND HID HIM FOR A WHILE:  209 UNDER THE MOON   3
     WHERE ONE FOUND LANCELOT CRAZED, AND HID HIM FOR AWHILE.  209 UNDER THE MOON   3
     AND HID HER AMONG FRUITS OF JEWEL-STONE . . . . . .   224 SHADOW WATER B      49
     "ALTHOUGH THE THING THAT YOU HAVE HID WERE EVIL, . . . 281 TWO KINGS         103
     SUDDENLY HID LOVE'S MOON AWAY. . . . . . . . . .      313 MEMORY YOUTH         7
     ONCE MORE THE STORM IS HOWLING, AND HALF HID  . . .   403 FOR DAUGHTER         1
     UNFRIENDLY LAMPLIGHT HID UNDER ITS SHADE, . . . . .   523 LONG SILENCE         3
     THINGS HID IN THEIR MARROW-BONES  . . . . . . . .     589 OLD WICKED MAN      41
     HID FROM ALL THOSE WARTY LADS . . . . . . . . .       589 OLD WICKED MAN      43
     OR CHILD HID IN THE WOMB. . . . . . . . . . . .       589 OLD WICKED MAN      53
     THINGS HID IN THEIR MARROWBONES . . . . . . . . .     589 OLD WICKED MAN  V   41
     THINGS HID IN THEIR MARROW BONES  . . . . . . . .     589 OLD WICKED MAN  V   41
     FOR YE ARE HID WITH VAPOUR.  ROUND THE STAKE  . . .   695 MOSADA 1           111
     FOR YE ARE HID WITH VAPOURS?  ROUND THE STAKE  . .    695 MOSADA 1        V  111
     HALF HID.  HE BRINGS THE PEASANT'S ONLY KIN, . . .    711 FERENCZ RENYI       50
     YET ONE JOY HAVE I, HID CLOSE, . . . . . . . . .      744 ROSY CROSS           8
     FOR I HAVE SEEN A SHIP HID IN THE FOG. . . . . . .    751 SHADOW WATER A      89
     OR A GOD HID THEM UNDER THE SHADOW OF WINGS. . . . .  752 SHADOW WATER A     125
HIDDEN
     HID IN THE EARTH'S MOST HIDDEN PART, . . . . . . .     78 INDIAN TO LOVE V    12
     LIE NOW HALF HIDDEN UNDER PENDULOUS LIDS, . . . . .    79 EPHEMERA        V    2
     LAY HIDDEN IN THE SMALL SLATE-COLOURED THING: . . .   104 FERGUS DRUID        40
     LAY HIDDEN IN THE SMALL SLATE-COLOURED BAG: . . . .   104 FERGUS DRUID    V   40
     "THE DOOMS OF MEN ARE IN GOD'S HIDDEN PLACE." . . .   110 CUCHULAIN SEA       62
     "THE DOOMS OF MEN ARE IN GOD'S HIDDEN HOARD." . . .   110 CUCHULAIN SEA   V   62
     THE SURETY OF ITS HIDDEN ROOT . . . . . . . . .       134 TWO TREES            7
     ROOTS HALF HIDDEN UNDER SNOWS, . . . . . . . . .      135 TWO TREES           27
     AND ROOTS HALF HIDDEN UNDER SNOWS . . . . . . . .     135 TWO TREES       V   27
     THE EAST HER HIDDEN JOY BEFORE THE MORNING BREAK, . .  154 BELOVED PEACE      4
     AND LINGERED IN THE HIDDEN DESOLATE PLACE . . . . .   162 ASKS FORGIVE        15
     BUT WE HAVE HIDDEN IN OUR HEARTS THE FLAME OUT OF THE EYES  207 HANRAHANS SONG  4
     AS THOUGH THEY HAD BEEN HIDDEN BY GREEN BOUGHS  . . .  217 WOODS OF COOLE     6
     TO HURRY TO THEIR HIDDEN HAPPINESS  . . . . . . .     234 SHADOW WATER B     268
     TO AN OLD EMPTY WOODMAN'S HOUSE THAT'S HIDDEN . . .   282 TWO KINGS          134
     OBEDIENT TO SOME HIDDEN MAGICAL BREATH. . . . . . .   382 VISION ROBART       13
     MAY SHE BECOME A FLOURISHING HIDDEN TREE  . . . . .   404 FOR DAUGHTER        41
     WE SHOULD BE HIDDEN FROM THEIR EYES, . . . . . . .    454 HIS MEMORIES         1
     HIDDEN FROM EYESIGHT TO THE UNNOTICED END. . . . . .  472 ALL SOUL NIGHT      50
     UPON THE STAR THAT MARKS THE HIDDEN POLE: . . . . .   477 SELF AND SOUL        5
     NAKED AND HIDDEN AWAY, . . . . . . . . . . . .        510 JANE JUDGMENT       13
     HIDDEN BY OLD AGE AWHILE . . . . . . . . . . .        539 MEETING              1
     GOD'S LOVE HAS HIDDEN HIM . . . . . . . . . . .       574 MAIDS 1ST SONG       7
     CASEMENT UPON TRIAL, HALF HIDDEN BY THE BARS, . . .   601 GALLERY REVIS        3
     GIVE TONGUE, PROCLAIM THEIR HIDDEN NAME--"HOUND VOICE."  622 HOUND VOICE       7
     KEEP HIDDEN AND COVERED HER HEART!" . . . . . . .     744 GLOVE CLOAK         12
     THE LOVE I KNOW IS HIDDEN IN THESE HANDS  . . . . .   765 SHADOW WATER A     350
HIDE
     HAD NEITHER HOPE NOR FEAR.  I BADE THEM HIDE  . . . .   38 OISIN 2           139
     . . . THE SHIELD OUT OF OSIER AND HIDE: . . . . . .    52 OISIN 3            82
     TO THOSE ABOUT, "BEAT HIM WITH THONGS OF HIDE . . . .  106 CUCHULAIN SEA  V  17A
     ALTHOUGH YOU HIDE IN THE EBB AND FLOW . . . . . . .   146 FISH                 1

                                 380
```

```
                                              PAGE    TITLE          LINE
HIDE    (CONTINUED)
     WILL HIDE US FROM THE BITTER STORM. . . . . . . . .   152 HEART OF WOMAN        8
     SHALL HIDE US FROM THE BITTER STORM. . . . . . . .    152 HEART OF WOMAN   V    8
     AND HIDE THEIR TOSSING MANES AND THEIR TUMULTUOUS FEET. 154 BELOVED PEACE   V   12
     COVER OVER AND HIDE, FOR HE HAS NO PART . . . . . .   158 TO HIS HEART         6
     TO HIDE FROM THE TROUBLED DAY . . . . . . . . . .     166 BLESSED         V    4
     WHEN SONGS I WOVE FOR MY BELOVED HIDE THE PRAYER, . .  173 SPEAKS HEARERS       2
     IS EDEN FAR AWAY, OR DO YOU HIDE . . . . . . . .      218 WOODS OF COOLE      30
     WHY DO YOU TURN AWAY AND HIDE YOUR FACE, . . . . . .  244 SHADOW WATER B     461
     THEN I.REPLIED, "ALTHOUGH YOU HIDE A SECRET, . . . .  281 TWO KINGS           95
     AND HIDE IT THERE, FOR CALIPHS TO WORLD'S END . . . . 461 HARUN RASHID        17
     IF YOU SHOULD HIDE MY PARCHMENT IN THAT BOOK . . . .  461 HARUN RASHID    V   13
     MUST NEEDS NEGLECT, I CANNOT HIDE THE TRUTH . . . .   462 HARUN RASHID        26
     MUST NEEDS NEGLECT, BUT CANNOT HIDE THE TRUTH, . . .  462 HARUN RASHID    V   26
     NOR CAN HE HIDE IN HOLY BLACK . . . . . . . . . .     508 JANE BISHOP         18
     THAT CANNOT IN THAT TRASH AND TINSEL HIDE! . . . . .  558 RIBH CHRISTIAN      17
     A GENTLE QUESTIONING LOOK THAT CANNOT HIDE . . . . .  601 GALLERY REVIS        6
     DISTRACTED GENTLENESS THAT CANNOT HIDE . . . . . .    601 GALLERY REVIS   V    6
     OF GREEN ARCADIA DO NOT HIDE, I TROW, . . . . . . .   651 ISLE STAT I 1      166
     THE PANTHER WITH HER YELLOW HIDE, . . . . . . . . .   658 ISLE STAT I 3       83
     DOWN THE VAPOURS FALL AND HIDE THEM FROM THE CHILDREN OF 719 PHANTOM SHIP     27
        A DAY,
     HIDE WHERE HE WILL, IN WAVE OR WRINKLED MOON, . . . .  720 WITCH VIVIEN        8
     AND BID THEM HIDE IN SHADOW OF THE SAIL. . . . . .    751 SHADOW WATER A      93
     I HIDE YOU WITH MY HAIR, THAT WE MAY GAZE . . . . .   769 SHADOW WATER A  V  429
HIDES
     THAT HIDES US FROM ALL HUMAN SPYING, . . . . . . .     22 OISIN 1        V 338A
     THAT HIDES AWAY THE DYING SUN . . . . . . . . . .      85 MAD KING GOLL       63
     WHEN SONG I WOVE FOR MY BELOVED HIDES THE PRAYER, . .  173 SPEAKS HEARERS  V    2
     DIM INCHY WOOD, THAT HIDES BADGER AND FOX . . . . .   218 WOODS OF COOLE      13
     DEARER THAN ANY THAT THE DUMB STONE HIDES, . . . . .  281 TWO KINGS       V   96
     AND THE NEW STILL HIDES HER HORN. . . . . . . . .     382 VISION ROBART        4
     IN THE DEEP ALCOVES DIMNESS SMILES AND HIDES. . . . . 685 DRAWING-ROOM         4
     NOW STEPS DRAW CLOSE, HE HIDES BENEATH A DRUM. . . .  713 FERENCZ RENYI       78
     IN THE DEEP ALCOVE'S DIMNESS SMILES AND HIDES." . . . 735 QUATRAIN APHOR      24
     IN THE DEEP ALCOVES DIMNESS SMILES AND HIDES. . . . . 735 QUATRAIN APHOR  V   24
     HE CANNOT WAKE THE GOD THAT HIDES IN IT. . . . . . .  748 SHADOW WATER A      19
HIDING
     THE WEAK WORM HIDING DOWN IN ITS SMALL CAVE, . . . .  101 ROSE UPON ROOD      16
     O HIDING HAIR AND DEWY EYES, . . . . . . . . . .      152 HEART OF WOMAN       9
     AND HIDING THEIR TOSSING MANES AND THEIR TUMULTUOUS FEET. 154 BELOVED PEACE   12
     HIDING AMID THE CARGO OF A STEAMSHIP, . . . . . . .   578 CRAZED GIRL          5
     HIDING AWAY THE OCEAN'S YELPING FLOCKS. . . . . . .   688 TWO TITANS          38
     HIDING MY FACE, I CRIED LONG, BITTERLY. . . . . . .   690 MOSADA 1            17
     HIDING THE REBELS WORM IN YONDER WOOD . . . . . . .   709 FERENCZ RENYI       14
     HIDING THE REBELS SWARM IN YONDER WOOD . . . . . . .  709 FERENCZ RENYI   V   14
     HIDING THE REBEL WORMS IN YONDER WOOD, . . . . . . .  709 FERENCZ RENYI   V   14
HIERARCHY
     THE FATHER AND HIS ANGELIC HIERARCHY . . . . . . .    483 VERONIC NAPKIN       4
HIGH      SEE SHOULDER-HIGH
     AND MANY PRINCES OF HIGH NAME. . . . . . . . . . .      7 OISIN 1        V   68
     WE FLUNG ON HIGH EACH WAVING HAND, . . . . . . . .     22 OISIN 1            325
     FLUNG ON HIGH EACH WAVING HAND, . . . . . . . . .      22 OISIN 1        V  325
     FROM HIGH ABOVE, LIKE FEATHERS OF YOUNG BIRDS . . . .  32 OISIN 2        V   50
     NOR THE HIGH GODS WHO NEVER LIVED, MAY FIGHT . . . .   34 OISIN 2             80
     AND THEN WE CLIMBED THE STAIR TO A HIGH DOOR! . . . .  36 OISIN 2            101
     AND UP THE STAIR WE TOILED TO A HIGH DOOR, . . . . .   36 OISIN 2        V  101
     DRIFTING ON HIGH, AND WITH A STRAINING THROAT . . . .  36 OISIN 2        V  106
     I WAITED HOUR BY HOUR, AND THE HIGH DOME, . . . . .    39 OISIN 2            147
     WHILE HIGH FRAIL CLOUDLETS, FED WITH A GREEN LIGHT, . .  40 OISIN 2           165
     GAVE TO HIGH NOON AND NOON TO NIGHT GAVE WAY! . . . .   40 OISIN 2           172
     HIGH AS THE SADDLE-GIRTH, COVERING AWAY FROM OUR GLANCES 47 OISIN 3            2
        THE TIDE!
     HIGH AS THE SADDLE GIRTH, COVERING AWAY FROM OUR GLANCES 47 OISIN 3       V    2
        THE TIDE!
     OF THE HIGH PEOPLE OF SORACA NOR IN GLAMOUR BY DEMONS   50 OISIN 3       V   50
        FLUNG,
     I RODE AWAY ON THE SURGES, WHERE, HIGH AS THE SADDLE-BOW, 57 OISIN 3         147
     I RODE AWAY ON THE SURGES, WHERE HIGH AS THE SADDLE BOW  57 OISIN 3       V  147
     I RODE AWAY ON THE SURGES, WHERE, HIGH AS THE SADDLEBOW, 57 OISIN 3       V  147
     AND HE, OF HIS HIGH COMRADE SORROW DREAMING, . . . . . 67 SAD SHEPHERD        2
     AND HE, OF HIS HIGH KINSMAN SORROW DREAMING, . . . . . 67 SAD SHEPHERD   V    2
     AND STARLIGHT GLEAMED, AND CLOUDS FLEW HIGH, . . . .   84 MAD KING GOLL      34
     OF HOW I HEAR ON HILL-HEADS HIGH . . . . . . . . .     85 MAD KING GOLL  V   53
     OF HOW I HEAR ON HILL HEADS HIGH . . . . . . . . .     85 MAD KING GOLL  V   53
     SING IN THEIR HIGH AND LONELY MELODY. . . . . . . .   101 ROSE UPON ROOD       8
     TROY PASSED AWAY IN ONE HIGH FUNERAL GLEAM, . . . .   111 ROSE OF WORLD        4
     GOD SMILES IN HIGH HEAVEN . . . . . . . . . . .       118 CRADLE SONG     V    5
     BUT HE HEARD HIGH UP IN THE AIR . . . . . . . . .     145 HOST OF AIR         41
     BROOD HER HIGH LONELY MYSTERIES. . . . . . . . . .    156 FORGOT BEAUTY       24
     AND YOUR HIGH BEAUTY FALL AND BE LOST . . . . . . .   173 PLEADS FRIEND   V    7
     IN HER HIGH HOUSE AT CRUACHAN! THE LONG HEARTH, . . .  180 QUEEN MAEVE        11
     AND SHE'D HAD LUCKY EYES AND A HIGH HEART, . . . . .  181 QUEEN MAEVE         27
     HE SAID, "HIGH QUEEN OF CRUACHAN AND MAGH AI, . . . .  183 QUEEN MAEVE        77
     QUEEN OF HIGH CRUACHAN." "I OBEY YOUR WILL . . . . .  184 QUEEN MAEVE         99
     WITH HOLY SHADOWS." HER HIGH HEART WAS GLAD, . . . .  186 QUEEN MAEVE        126
     FOR THERE IS NO HIGH STORY ABOUT QUEENS . . . . . .   186 QUEEN MAEVE        134
     A THOUSAND YEARS AGO YOU HELD HIGH TALK . . . . . .   187 QUEEN MAEVE        150
     NOR THE GREY RUSH WHEN THE WIND IS HIGH, . . . . . .  189 BAILE AILLINN       2
     NOR THE GREY RUSH WHEN WIND IS HIGH . . . . . . . .   189 BAILE AILLINN   V    2
     AND HARPERS, PACING WITH HIGH HEAD . . . . . . . .    193 BAILE AILLINN     107
```

	PAGE	TITLE	LINE

HIGH (CONTINUED)

TO THAT HIGH HILL THE HERDSMEN NAME . . . .   194 BAILE AILLINN   129
AND YOU ARE MORE HIGH OF HEART THAN SHE, ...   197 BAILE AILLINN   202
SO MUCH COMPOUNDED OF HIGH COURTESY . . . .   205 ADAMS CURSE   24
TO LOVE YOU IN THE OLD HIGH WAY OF LOVE: . . . . . .   206 ADAMS CURSE   36
THE OLD BROWN THORN-TREES BREAK IN TWO HIGH OVER CUMMEN   206 HANRAHANS SONG   1
    STRAND,
THE OLD BROWN THORN TREES BREAK IN TWO HIGH OVER CUMANN'S   206 HANRAHANS SONG V   1
    STRAND,
THE WIND HAS BUNDLED UP THE CLOUDS HIGH OVER KNOCKNAREA,   207 HANRAHANS SONG   6
THE YELLOW POOL HAS OVERFLOWED HIGH UP ON CLOOTH-NA-BARE,   207 HANRAHANS SONG   11
O TATTERED CLOUDS OF THE WORLD, CALL FROM THE HIGH CAIRN   207 HANRAHANS SONG V   6
    OF MAIVE,
THE WINDS HAVE BUNDLED UP THE CLOUDS HIGH OVER KNOCKNAREA   207 HANRAHANS SONG V   6
THE YELLOW POOL HAS OVERFLOWED HIGH UPON CLOOTH-NA-BARE,   207 HANRAHANS SONG V   11
WHEN THEIR HEARTS ARE SO HIGH . . . .   214 HAPPY TOWNLAND   21
IN THE HIGH HOLLOW TOWNLAND . . . .   214 HAPPY TOWNLAND V   3
POURED OUT WINE FOR THE HIGH INVISIBLE ONES. . . . .   219 WOODS OF COOLE   44
AND THE HIGH FAME THAT COME TO THEM IN MARRIAGE, . .   232 SHADOW WATER B   235
IN THE WASTE OF THE HIGH AIR, THAT WE MAY WANDER . .   234 SHADOW WATER B   263
BEING TOO BUSY IN THE AIR AND THE HIGH AIR, ...   234 SHADOW WATER B   274
I'D DO YOUR WILL, BUT THEY ARE TOO HIGH--TOO HIGH. .   250 SHADOW WATER B   577
I'D DO YOUR WILL, BUT THEY ARE TOO HIGH--TOO HIGH. .   250 SHADOW WATER B   577
BEING TOO HIGH, THEIR HEADY PROPHECIES . . . . . .   250 SHADOW WATER B   578
THERE ON THE HIGH AND PAINTED STERN . . . .   253 HIS DREAM V   1
BEING HIGH AND SOLITARY AND MOST STERN? . . . . . .   257 NO SECOND TROY   10
"SUCH A DELICATE HIGH HEAD, ...   259 PEACE   7
HOW SHOULD THEIR LUCK RUN HIGH ENOUGH TO REACH . . .   264 HOUSE SHAKEN   9
WROUGHT OF HIGH LAUGHTER, LOVELINESS AND EASE? . . .   264 HOUSE SHAKEN   12
WHEN WE ARE HIGH AND AIRY HUNDREDS SAY . . . . . .   265 ABBEY THEATRE   2
TILL THAT BE TUMBLED THAT WAS LIFTED HIGH . . . . .   265 THESE CLOUDS   4
AND CHILDREN WHEN THEY SPRING UP SHOULDER HIGH. . . .   343 SHEP GOATHERD V   119
IF HEAD AND LIMB HAVE BEAUTY AND THE INSTEP'S HIGH AND   354 HIS PHOENIX   21
    LIGHT
AND MOUNTS MORE DIZZY HIGH THE MORE IT RAINS . . . .   417 ANCEST HOUSES   5
BUT ALL IS CHANGED, THAT HIGH HORSE RIDERLESS, . . .   492 COOLE BALLYLEE   46
SPEAKING TO A DRUNKEN AUDIENCE HIGH NONSENSICAL WORDS: 577 LOFTY THINGS   6
THE PROUD FURIES EACH WITH HER TORCH ON HIGH. . . .   579 DOR WELLESLEY   16
HER HEART MOUNT UP ON HIGH: . . . .   608 SONGS BURDEN 3   22
HIGH TALK . . . .   622 HIGH TALK   T
PROCESSIONS THAT LACK HIGH STILTS HAVE NOTHING THAT CATCHES   622 HIGH TALK   1
    THE EYE.
WHAT IF MY GREAT-GRANDDAD HAD A PAIR THAT WERE TWENTY FOOT   622 HIGH TALK   2
    HIGH,
BLENCHING ON HIGH THE DULL STARS SICKEN . . . . . .   646 ISLE STAT I 1   46
WITH ROLLING FIRE, BEYOND THE HIGH TREES TURBANED . .   656 ISLE STAT I 3   32
TO BUILD THE CIRCLING SEATS, WHERE HIGH IN AIR . . .   699 MOSADA 3   18
OF CEASELESS LONELINESS AND HIGH REGRET . . . . . .   705 REMEMBRANCE   9
HIVES, CURRANT BUSHES. THERE HIS KIN ARE. HIGH . . .   710 FERENCZ RENYI   25
THERE LIVE HIS SISTER AND HIS MOTHER. HIGH . . . .   710 FERENCZ RENYI V   25
HIVES, CURRANT-BUSHES. THERE HIS KIN ARE. HIGH . . .   710 FERENCZ RENYI V   25
I AM TO BE YOUR WIFE. A VILLAGE HIGH . . . . . .   713 FERENCZ RENYI   97
I WAS TO BE YOUR WIFE. A VILLAGE HIGH . . . . . .   713 FERENCZ RENYI V   97
SAY WHAT RINGER RINGS AT MIDNIGHT: FOR, IN THE BELFRY HIGH,   718 PHANTOM SHIP   15
BY THE GORSE ON THE HIGH LAND, ...   726 LOVERS QUARREL   4
THREE SPANS HIGH AS HE ROSE TO HIS FEET, ...   729 PRIEST FAIRY   25
WHO IS SIX FEET HIGH IN HIS SOCKS AT LEAST? . . . .   729 PRIEST FAIRY   28
YE ON THE BROAD HIGH MOUNTAINS OF OLD ERI, ...   737 MOURN THEN ON   1
HITHER AND THITHER AND SAY AT THE HIGH NOON . . . .   767 SHADOW WATER A   404
AMONG HIGH MOUNTAINS, AND THE MOUNTAIN ROBBERS . . .   768 SHADOW WATER A   411
A HIGH, GREY CAIRN. WHAT MORE IS TO BE SAID? . . .   778 SONG DEIRDRE 3   5

HIGH-BORN
A PEARL-PALE, HIGH-BORN LADY, WHO RODE . . . . . .   3 OISIN 1   20
SELF-BORN, HIGH-BORN, AND SOLITARY TRUTHS, ...   467 HARUN RASHID   141
BEGOT: SELF-BORN, HIGH-BORN, AND SOLITARY. . . . .   467 HARUN RASHID V   141

HIGHER
TO THE OTHER SIDE, AND HIGHER IN THE AIR. . . . . .   234 SHADOW WATER B   259
AND MINE WERE BUT FIFTEEN FOOT, NO MODERN STALKS . .   623 HIGH TALK   3
    UPON HIGHER,
HIGHER AND HIGHER GOLD WITH EVENING LIGHT: . . . . .   714 FERENCZ RENYI   113
HIGHER AND HIGHER GOLD WITH EVENING LIGHT: . . . . .   714 FERENCZ RENYI   113
TO THE OTHER SIDE AND HIGHER IN THE AIR. . . . . .   753 SHADOW WATER A   149

HIGHEST
WHY THEY WHO WILL THE HIGHEST SOMETIMES BROOD, . . .   711 FERENCZ RENYI   34

HIGH-HORSE
BUT FASHION'S CHANGED, THAT HIGH-HORSE RIDERLESS . .   492 COOLE BALLYLEE V   46

HIGHLAND
WHERE DIPS THE ROCKY HIGHLAND . . . .   86 STOLEN CHILD   1

HIGH-PITCHED
AND THEREUPON WITH AGED, HIGH-PITCHED VOICE . . . .   375 PHASES OF MOON   84

HIGHWAY
TO LOVE YOU IN THE OLD HIGHWAY OF LOVE: . . . . . .   206 ADAMS CURSE V   36

HILL
CAME TO THE CAIRN-HEAPED GRASSY HILL . . . .   3 OISIN 1   17
UPON THE WOODY CENTRAL HILL: . . . .   22 OISIN 1   323
TILL ON THE CENTRAL HILL WE HUSHED . . . .   22 OISIN 1 V   323
ROLLING ALONG IN DREAMS FROM HILL TO HILL. . . . .   68 SAD SHEPHERD   11
ROLLING ALONG IN DREAMS FROM HILL TO HILL. . . . .   68 SAD SHEPHERD   11
O'ER HILL AND HEATH AND SPONGY FEN, ...   83 MAD KING GOLL V   32
OF HOW I HEAR ON HILL HEADS HIGH . . . .   85 MAD KING GOLL V   53
AND I MUST WANDER WOOD AND HILL . . . .   86 MAD KING GOLL   70

HILL   (CONTINUED)
        OF THE CALVES ON THE WARM HILL SIDE, ...   88 STOLEN CHILD   V   45
        I FEAST AMID MY PEOPLE ON THE HILL, ...   103 FERGUS DRUID   17
        UPON A SWORD, A FIR-TREE ON A HILL, ...   104 FERGUS DRUID   34
        UPON A SWORD, A FIR TREE ON A HILL, ...   104 FERGUS DRUID   34
        BEFORE THEY HEAPED HIS GRAVE UNDER THE HILL; . . . .   127 DREAM OF FAERY   16
        HE SLEPT UNDER THE HILL OF LUGNAGALL; . . . .   128 DREAM OF FAERY   37
        THAT YOU CALL IN BIRDS, IN WIND ON THE HILL, ...   141 EVERLAST VOICE   6
        COME, HEART, WHERE HILL IS HEAPED UPON HILL; . . . .   148 INTO TWILIGHT   9
        COME, HEART, WHERE HILL IS HEAPED UPON HILL; . . . .   148 INTO TWILIGHT   9
        THE GREY CAIRN ON THE HILL, WHEN DAY SINKS DROWNED IN DEW, 161 BLACK PIG   6
        AND SET THEM DIGGING UNDER BUAL'S HILL. . . . . . .   184 QUEEN MAEVE   93
        AND SET THEM DIGGING INTO ANBUAL'S HILL. . . . . . .   184 QUEEN MAEVE   V   93
        AND SET THEM DIGGING IN THE WEST OF THE HILL. . . . .   184 QUEEN MAEVE   V   93
        TO MIDDLE NIGHT, THEY DUG INTO THE HILL. . . . . . .   185 QUEEN MAEVE   114
        TO THAT HIGH HILL THE HERDSMEN NAME . . . .   194 BAILE AILLINN   129
        THE HILL SEAT OF LAIGHEN, BECAUSE . . . .   194 BAILE AILLINN   130
        THE HONEY-PALE MOON LAY LOW ON THE SLEEPY HILL, . .   203 WITHER BOUGHS   5
        THE HONEY PALE MOON HUNG LOW ON THE SLEEPY HILL, . .   203 WITHER BOUGHS   V   5
        EDAIN CAME OUT OF MIDHIR'S HILL, AND LAY . . . . . .   219 HARP OF AENGUS   1
        SOMEWHERE WITHIN SOME HOLLOW HILL, ...   271 GREY ROCK   V   14
        UPON URBINO'S WINDY HILL, ...   288 TO WEALTHY MAN   17
        SOON TOPPLES DOWN THE HILL. . . . .   335 YOUNG BEAUTY   6
        TO A GREY PLACE ON A HILL . . . .   347 FISHERMAN   3
        BUT GREGORY'S WOOD AND ONE BARE HILL . . . .   403 FOR DAUGHTER   4
        BUT GREGORY'S WOODS AND ONE BARE HILL . . . .   403 FOR DAUGHTER   V   4
        OF HILL TWO SHEPHERDS COME. FAREWELL! I'LL DON . .   659 ISLE STAT II 1   28
        THE VIOLETS ARE THAT ON THE WOODED HILL . . . . . .   713 FERENCZ RENYI   95
        EDAINE CAME OUT OF MIDHER'S HILL, AND LAY . . . . .   762 SHADOW WATER A   296
        BEYOND A HILL AND A HILL. . . . .   774 COME RIDE   4
        BEYOND A HILL AND A HILL. . . . .   774 COME RIDE   4
        BEYOND A HILL AND A HILL THERE . . . .   774 COME RIDE   16
        BEYOND A HILL AND A HILL THERE . . . .   774 COME RIDE   16
        AT THE GREY ROUND OF THE HILL . . . .   782 GREY ROUND   1
HILL-HEADS
        OF HOW I HEAR ON HILL-HEADS HIGH . . . .   85 MAD KING GOLL   V   53
HILL'S
        IN THE GREEN HILL'S INMOST PART. . . . .   726 LOVERS QUARREL   12
HILLS
        AND THE CRY OF THE HOUNDS ON THE HILLS OF OLD. . . .   27 OISIN 1   407
        FROM THE HILLS ABOVE GLEN-CAR, ...   88 STOLEN CHILD   29
        MAKE THE HILLS REPLY." . . . .   98 FOXHUNTER   26
        AND MAKE THE HILLS REPLY." . . . .   98 FOXHUNTER   V   26
        MAKE THE HILLS REPLY." . . . .   99 FOXHUNTER   34
        AND MAKE THE HILLS REPLY." . . . .   99 FOXHUNTER   V   34
        IN BARREN HILLS AND MARSHY LAND, ...   150 WANDER AENGUS   V   18
        THAT HE HAS BEEN ALL NIGHT UPON THE HILLS, ...   229 SHADOW WATER B   168
        HE HAD OFTEN PLAYED HIS PIPES AMONG MY HILLS, . . .   339 SHEP GOATHERD   23
        THE HOLY CENTAURS OF THE HILLS ARE VANISHED; . . .   344 DEJECTION   7
        THE HOLY CENTAURS OF THE HILLS ARE BANISHED; . . .   344 DEJECTION   V   7
        ARE MET ON THE WASTE HILLS BY COUNTRYMEN . . . . .   375 PHASES OF MOON   76
        ARE MET ON THE WASTE HILLS BY COUNTRY MEN . . . . .   375 PHASES OF MOON V   76
        AMID THE RUSTLE OF HIS PLANTED HILLS, ...   417 ANCEST HOUSES   2
        I WILL FIND OUT SOME CAVERN IN THE HILLS . . . . .   448 HERO GIRL FOOL V   11
        I AM MAD ABOUT THE HILLS," . . . .   587 OLD WICKED MAN   2
        BECAUSE WE LOVE BARE HILLS AND STUNTED TREES . . .   621 HOUND VOICE   1
        AFAR, CLEAR-SHINING ON THE HERALD HILLS, ...   645 ISLE STAT I 1   14
        BETWEEN THE HORNED HILLS--SHEPHERDS, FAREWELL! . . .   682 SEEKER   27
        SINCE 'MONG MY PEOPLE, TENTED ON THE HILLS, ...   690 MOSADA 1   4
        BUT NO, IN THIS WARM WEATHER, 'MONG THE HILLS, . . .   699 MOSADA 3   9
        DAY'S DEAD, ALL FLAME-BEWILDERED, AND THE HILLS . .   702 MOSADA 3   86
        'TIS LATE, WAIT ONE MORE DAY; BELOW THE HILLS . . .   702 MOSADA 3   91
        FROM THE HILLS OF EARTH HAVE PEALED . . . . . .   705 DAWN-SONG   5
        AND LOST AND FAR IN YONDER HILLS I KNOW; . . . . .   713 FERENCZ RENYI   98
        WHERE IN THE WOODS OR HILLS THE REBELS BE?" . . . .   713 FERENCZ RENYI   V   83A
        OF PASTURE-LAND AND PLOUGH-LAND AMONG THE HILLS? . .   748 SHADOW WATER A   33
        A FRUITFUL LAND UNDER THE AIBHLIN HILLS? . . . . .   748 SHADOW WATER A   33
        THEY OVERFLOW THE HILLS, ...   781 MY HEART BEAT   12
HILLSIDE
        OF THE CALVES ON THE WARM HILLSIDE . . . .   88 STOLEN CHILD   45
HILL-SIDE
        OF THE CALVES ON THE WARM HILL-SIDE. . . . .   88 STOLEN CHILD   V   45
HILLY
        OF HOLLOW WOOD AND THE HILLY WOOD . . . .   148 INTO TWILIGHT   V   11
        THROUGH HOLLOW LANDS AND HILLY LANDS, ...   150 WANDER AENGUS   18
        THROUGH HILLY LANDS AND HOLLOW LANDS, ...   150 WANDER AENGUS   V   18
        WHEN THE WIND COMES BLOWING ACROSS THE HILLY LAND; .   207 HANRAHANS SONG V   7
        FROM HILLY LOCHLANN; BUT OUR SAIL HAS PASSED . . . .   749 SHADOW WATER A   44
HIMALAY
        DREAD OATH, WHO DWELL ON SACRED HIMALAY, ...   74 ANASHU VIJAYA   67
HIRE
        AND HAD BUT BROKEN KNEES FOR HIRE . . . .   411 TOWER   62
        SAEVA INDIGNATIO AND THE LABOURER'S HIRE, ...   481 BLOOD AND MOON   28
        FOR ALL MY HEART HAS HAD FOR ITS HIRE . . . . . .   551 SONGS REWRIT 1   3
        FOR ALL MY TOIL HAS HAD FOR ITS HIRE . . . . . .   551 SONGS REWRIT 1 V   3
        FOR ALL THAT MY HEART HAS HAD FOR ITS HIRE . . . .   551 SONGS REWRIT 1 V   3
HISS
        A CONTRAPUNTAL SERPENT HISS, ...   573 LADYS 3RD SONG   10
HISSING
        HE TOLD OF EVERY FROTH-DROP HISSING, FLYING. . . . .   32 OISIN 2   V   45

383

```
                                                             PAGE      TITLE          LINE
HISSOP-HEAVY
    THE HISSOP-HEAVY SPONGE, THE FLOWERS BY KIDRON STREAM; . .   172  TRAV PASSION  V    5
HISTORIANS
    ALL THOSE LEARNED HISTORIANS, . . . . . . . . . . . .        584  ORAHILLY           5
HISTORIC
    HISTORIC NATIONS GROW . . . . . . . . . . . . . .            547  TO SAME TUNE 3 V   5
HISTORIED
    AND HANG O'ER THE HISTORIED STONE; . . . . . . . .           707  FAIRY PEDANT       6
HISTORIES
    TO STUDY READING BOOKS AND HISTORIES, . . . . . . .          443  SCHOOL CHILDR  V   4
    FOR HISTORIES ARE THERE TO PROVE . . . . . . . .             583  GHOST ROG CASE    23
    SAD HISTORIES ARE LETTERED ON THY CHEEK. . . . . . .         660  ISLE STAT II 1    52
    AND LET THEM TELL SAD HISTORIES, TILL THEIR EYES . . . .     663  ISLE STAT II 2    32
HISTORY
    OF HER, WHOSE HISTORY BEGAN . . . . . . . . .               137  TO IRELAND         7
    BECAUSE AN ANCIENT HISTORY SAID , . . . . . . . .           303  HOUR DAWN         24
    TO STUDY READING-BOOKS AND HISTORY . . . . . . .            443  SCHOOL CHILDR      4
    TO STUDY READING BOOKS AND HISTORY . . . . . . .            443  SCHOOL CHILDR  V   4
    HAD HEARD IMPOSSIBLE HISTORY OF MY PAST; . . . . . .        466  HARUN RASHID     108
    IMAGINED SOME IMPOSSIBLE HISTORY . . . . . . . .            466  HARUN RASHID     109
    FAIL, AND THAT HISTORY TURNS INTO RUBBISH, . . . . .        546  TO SAME TUNE 2    21
    IRELAND'S HISTORY IN THEIR LINEAMENTS TRACE; . . . .        604  GALLERY REVIS     53
    FAIL, AND THAT HISTORY TURNS INTO RUBBISH, . . . . .        614  MARCH SONGS 1     21
    THE HISTORY HERE IN THE STONE NOW; . . . . . . .            707  FAIRY PEDANT      15
    THE HISTORY HERE IN THE STONE-- . . . . . . . .            707  FAIRY PEDANT   V  15
HISTORY'S
    WHEN ALL THIS HEAVY HISTORY'S DONE; . . . . . . .          213  BLESS PSALTER     17
HIT
    WHATEVER WOMAN'S LOVER HAD HIT HER FANCY, . . . . .        181  QUEEN MAEVE       24
    THE ONLY RICHES THAT HAVE HIT MY FANCY. . . . . . .        226  SHADOW WATER B    96
    UNLESS A PETAL HIT THE GROUND, . . . . . . . .            389  SOLOMON WITCH     40
    TIME FOR US ALL BOYS, TO HIT ON A TUNE BOYS, . . . .      548  TO SAME TUNE 3 V  13
HITCHED
    HITCHED IT ON HIS BACK. . . . . . . . . . . .            595  COLONEL MARTIN    26
HITHER
    YOU WOULD COME HITHER, AND BEND YOUR HEAD, . . . . .      175  BELOVED DEAD       3
    AND BLEW ME HITHER TO MY LASTING SORROW, . . . . .       235  SHADOW WATER B   288
    AND BLEW YOU HITHER; AND THEIR MOUTHS HAVE PROMISED . .  237  SHADOW WATER B   325
    FOR EVERYTHING IS GONE.  COME HITHER, AIBRIC, . . . .    241  SHADOW WATER B   402
    HITHER AND THITHER TO AND FRO THEY TROD . . . . .       278  TWO KINGS         26
    HITHER, TO OUR DISGRACE, . . . . . . . . . .           319  DOLLS             11
    FAIR SHEPHERD, AS WE WANDERED HITHER, . . . . .        669  ISLE STAT II 3    83
    BUT NOW I WAVE HER HITHER TO MY SIDE. . . . . .        694  MOSADA 1          91
    I WAVE THEM HITHER, MY BREAST HEAVES WITH JOY. . . .   694  MOSADA 1          98
    GIVE ME THE HELM: CALL HITHER THOSE WHO LIE . . . .    751  SHADOW WATER A    91
    I SPARED HER HANDMAID, TOO; BUT HALF WAY HITHER . .    755  SHADOW WATER A   167
    AND EVIL FORTUNE HAVE OVERTHROWN SAILED HITHER . . .   757  SHADOW WATER A   196
    ON TEARS AND LAUGHTER; THEY HAVE LURED YOU HITHER . .  757  SHADOW WATER A   207
    AND LURED ME HITHER, THAT YOU MIGHT BE MY LOVE. . .    757  SHADOW WATER A   208
    I HAVE COME HITHER BECAUSE I HOPED TO COME . . . .     757  SHADOW WATER A   197
    AND I SHALL LAUGH WITH JOY.  COME HITHER, AIBRIC, . .  760  SHADOW WATER A   249
    HITHER AND THITHER AND SAY AT THE HIGH NOON . . . .    767  SHADOW WATER A   404
HIVE
    AND CHASE THE WILD BEE HOMEWARD TO HIS HIVE . . . .     32  OISIN 2        V 50D
    NINE BEAN-ROWS WILL I HAVE THERE, A HIVE FOR THE HONEY-BEE, 117 ISLE INNISFREE     3
    NINE BEAN ROWS WILL I HAVE THERE, A HIVE FOR THE HONEY BEE, 117 ISLE INNISFREE V   3
    WHERE WILD BEES HIVE ON THE GREAT PLAIN. . . . . .     194  BAILE AILLINN    123
HIVES
    HIVES, CURRANT BUSHES.  THERE HIS KIN ARE.  HIGH . . . . 710  FERENCZ RENYI    25
    HIVES, CURRANT-BUSHES.  THERE HIS KIN ARE.  HIGH . . . . 710  FERENCZ RENYI  V 25
HO
    HO! HO! HO! THE MERRY BLADE!-- . . . . . . . . .       727  LOVERS QUARREL    26
    HO! HO! HO! THE MERRY BLADE!-- . . . . . . . . .       727  LOVERS QUARREL    26
    HO! HO! HO! THE MERRY BLADE!-- . . . . . . . . .       727  LOVERS QUARREL    26
HOARD
    "THE DOOMS OF MEN ARE IN GOD'S HIDDEN HOARD." . . . .  110  CUCHULAIN SEA  V  62
    AMONG THE GIANT KINGS WHOSE HOARD, . . . . . . .      196  BAILE AILLINN    164
HOARDED
    STITCHING AT A PURPLE HOARDED . . . . . . . .         440  WISDOM            12
    HEARKEN, YE SWALLOWS!--I HAVE HOARDED UP . . . . .    699  MOSADA 3          23
HOARDS
    OLD MISER HOARDS OF GRIEF TO TELL AND TELL! . . . .   661  ISLE STAT II 1    55
HOARIEST
    BENT LOW WITH TOIL AND HOARIEST YEARS.  THE OTHER . . . 711  FERENCZ RENYI    52
HOARSER
    CAME KEENERS HOARSER THAN ROOKS, . . . . . . . . .     92  FATHER OHART      22
HOARY
    WHY THOU OUTLIVEST, BLIND AND HOARY, . . . . . . .      2  OISIN 1        V   2
    WHERE ARE NOW THE OLD KINGS HOARY? . . . . . . .       65  HAPPY SHEPHERD V  13
    A HOARY HUNTER LEANING ON HIS BOW, . . . . . . .      672  ISLE STAT II 3   157
HOB
    OR THE KETTLE ON THE HOB . . . . . . . . . . .         88  STOLEN CHILD      46
HOISTING
    THE FLOOR OF EMEN'S HOISTING HALL . . . . . . . .      13  OISIN 1        V 156
HOLD
    BID THEM AWAY AND HOLD THEIR PEACE; . . . . . . .      15  OISIN 1          212
    AND HANDS THAT HOLD NO WEARISOME TOOL, . . . . .       22  OISIN 1          340
    OR HOURS PASSED BY, YET HOLD THE MORNING RAYS . . . .  30  OISIN 2           20
    WHOM BRAHMA, TOUCHING WITH HIS FINGER, PRAISES, FOR YOU 73  ANASHU VIJAYA     42
        HOLD
    WHOM BRAHMA, TOUCHING WITH HIS FINGER, PRAISES, FOR YE HOLD  73  ANASHU VIJAYA V 42
```

384

HOLD   (CONTINUED)
   AND YOUNG HARES BROOK MY HARMLESS HOLD--   • • • • •   84 MAD KING GOLL V   47
   IN THE DIM GLASS THE DEMONS HOLD, • • • • • • • 135 TWO TREES   30
   OR, REMEMBERING HERS, THEY WILL HOLD NO OTHER FACE FAIR   163 VALLEY LOVERS V   7
   WE HOLD, BECAUSE OUR MEMORY IS • • • • • • • • 192 BAILE AILLINN   85
   THE EVER-LIVING HOLD US. DO WHAT YOU WILL, • • • • 238 SHADOW WATER B   359
   THE HOLD IS FULL OF TREASURE. FULL TO THE HATCHES. • • 247 SHADOW WATER B   532
   THAT IF WE HOLD THAT FLIGHT THEY'LL LEAVE THE PLACE, • • 265 ABBEY THEATRE   3
   TO HOLD THE SACRED STUFF HE BREWS • • • • • • 272 GREY ROCK   24
   TO HOLD THE WINE THEY BUY OF HIM. • • • • • • 272 GREY ROCK V 25
   THEN DREW HIS SWORD TO HOLD ITS LEVELLED POINT • • • 277 TWO KINGS   14
   THAT GIRL MY UNREMEMBERING NIGHTS HOLD FAST • • • 384 VISION ROBART   50
   THINGS FALL APART; THE CENTRE CANNOT HOLD; • • • • 402 SECOND COMING   3
   THINGS FALL APART; THE CENTRE CAN NOT HOLD, • • • 402 SECOND COMING V 3
   THEY HOLD THEIR PUBLIC MEETINGS WHERE • • • • • 460 THREE MONUMENT   1
   SUCH THOUGHT--SUCH THOUGHT HAVE I THAT HOLD IT TIGHT • • 474 ALL SOUL NIGHT   91
   TO HOLD HIMSELF UPRIGHT: • • • • • • • • • 515 GIRLS SONG B   7
   A MOUTHFUL HOLD THE EXTREME OF LIFE AND DEATH. • • • 619 BRONZE HEAD V 14
   THE AGELESS SENTINELS WHO HOLD THEIR WATCH • • • 664 ISLE STAT II 2   45
   AND EVEN SHE SHALL NEVER HOLD • • • • • • • 668 ISLE STAT II 3   50
   HOLD FESTIVAL ACROSS THE LAND, • • • • • • 671 ISLE STAT II 3 128
   STAY, STAY, OR I WILL HOLD YOUR WHITE ARMS DOWN. • • 694 MOSADA 1   92
   I'M WEAK, AND BY THE HANDS SHALL HOLD EACH ONE • • 712 FERENCZ RENYI   57
   I'M WEAK, AND BY THE HAND SHALL HOLD EACH ONE • • 712 FERENCZ RENYI V 57
   I HOLD HIM DEARER THAN THE GLAD, • • • • • • 723 GIRLS SONG A   3
   I HOLD HIM DEARER THAN THE GOOD, • • • • • • 723 GIRLS SONG A   7
   I HOLD HIM DEARER THAN THE WISE, • • • • • • 723 GIRLS SONG A   11
   NOW THY GREAT WHITE DOLL TO HOLD-- • • • • • 726 LOVERS QUARREL   15
   BUT YOU GREW WEARY OF HER. WHEN I HOLD • • • 749 SHADOW WATER A   53
   A BOY AND GIRL HOLD ONE ANOTHER'S HANDS; • • • 752 SHADOW WATER A 122
   BUT WILL IT HOLD WHILE WE ARE EMPTYING HER? • • 754 SHADOW WATER A 156
   THE GODS HOLD WATCH ABOUT THE WORDS OF A QUEEN. • • 756 SHADOW WATER A 191
   ALTHOUGH WIDE WORLD HOLD NOT • • • • • • • 786 YOUR HEART   16
HOLDING
   AND CAME AGAIN, HOLDING A SECOND LIGHT • • • • 37 OISIN 2   124
   HOLDING THAT HORSE, AND SADLY CALLED MY NAME; • • • 44 OISIN 2   230
   HOLDING THAT HORSE LONG SEEN NOT, NIAM STOOD. • • 44 OISIN 2 V 230
   THAT HE IS HOLDING UP BETWEEN US THERE, • • • • 240 SHADOW WATER B   378
   AND SILENCE HOLDING REVELRY AND FEAST; • • • • • 705 REMEMBRANCE   12
HOLDS
   HE HOLDS YOU WITH AN IRON BOND, • • • • • • 22 OISIN 1   333
   WHO HOLDS THE WORLD BETWEEN HIS BILL AND MADE US STRONG   76 INDIAN ON GOD   6
     OR WEAK
   WHO HOLDS THE WORLD BETWEEN HIS BILL AND MAKES US STRONG   76 INDIAN ON GOD V 6
     OR WEAK
   HE HOLDS DEEP COMMUNE WITH HIS HEART; • • • • 99 FOXHUNTER   43
   DANGER NO REFUGE HOLDS, AND WAR NO PEACE, • • • 114 ROSE OF BATTLE   9
   I THOUGHT, "HE HOLDS HER DEAR," • • • • • • 254 WOMAN HOMER   3
   HE HOLDS HER HELPLESS BREAST UPON HIS BREAST. • • • 441 LEDA AND SWAN   4
   HE HOLDS HIM FROM DESIRE, ALL BUT STOPS HIS BREATHING LEST   559 MAGIC DRUM   1
   WHAT MATTER? THOSE THAT ROCKY FACE HOLDS DEAR, • • • • 564 GYRES   18
HOLE   SEE RABBIT-HOLE
   CAME UP OUT OF THE HOLE, AND RED-EARED HOUNDS • • • 185 QUEEN MAEVE   117
   A DARK DEEP HOLE IN THE ROCK'S FACE, • • • • • 303 HOUR DAWN V 21
   MERELY FOR STUMBLING ON THIS HOLE • • • • • • 304 HOUR DAWN   54
   TO MAKE A CLATTER IN THE HOLE • • • • • • • 304 HOUR DAWN V 54
   BECAUSE HE HAS STUMBLED ON THIS HOLE • • • • 304 HOUR DAWN V 54
   UPON HIS HUNKERS IN THE HOLE, • • • • • • 306 HOUR DAWN   81
   UNDER ITS ROCKY HOLE. • • • • • • • • 420 MY HOUSE V 20C
   WHO ARE BUT WEASELS FIGHTING IN A HOLE. • • • 429 NINETEEN 19   32
   SPREAD TO A LAKE AND DROP INTO A HOLE. • • • • 490 COOLE BALLYLEE   7
   SPREAD TO A LAKE AND RUN INTO A HOLE. • • • • 490 COOLE BALLYLEE V 7
   IN CAVERN, CREVICE, HOLE, • • • • • • • 546 TO SAME TUNE 2   5
   IN CAVERN, CREVICE OR HOLE, • • • • • • 546 TO SAME TUNE 2 V 5
   INTO A RABBIT HOLE • • • • • • • • 571 THREE BUSHES V 51
   IN CAVERN, CREVICE, OR HOLE, • • • • • • 613 MARCH SONGS 1   5
HOLES
   AND HE WORE SMALL HOLES IN HIS SHOES, • • • • • 92 FATHER OHART   11
   AND HE WORE LARGE HOLES IN HIS GOWN. • • • • • 92 FATHER OHART   12
HOLIDAY
   MIGHT PROCLAIM A HOLIDAY; • • • • • • • 432 NINETEEN 19   106
   THE STATESMAN'S HOLIDAY • • • • • • • 626 STATES HOLIDAY   T
HOLIDAYS
   AND BIRTHDAYS AND HOLIDAYS SUCH PRAISES CAN BE HEARD • • 353 HIS PHOENIX   2
HOLIEST
   FOR HOLIEST TEACHERS OF HIS WILL, • • • • • • 736 IN CHURCH   7
   HOLIEST, HOLIEST SEVEN, • • • • • • • 771 SPINNING SONG   11
   HOLIEST, HOLIEST SEVEN, • • • • • • • 771 SPINNING SONG   11
HOLINESS
   THAT MEN HAVE REVERENCE FOR THEIR HOLINESS • • • 448 HERO GIRL FOOL   14
   THE HOLINESS OF MONKS, AND AFTER • • • • • 640 BEN BULBEN   76
   THE HOLINESS OF THE MONKS, AND AFTER • • • • 640 BEN BULBEN V 76
   AND HEAVEN, AND HOLINESS. LET'S TALK AND GRIEVE, • • • 702 MOSADA 3   84
HOLLIES
   OF HOLLIES, AND HAZELS, AND OAK TREES, A VALLEY WAS SLOPING   48 OISIN 3 V 26
     AWAY
HOLLO
   I'LL HOLLO ALL THOSE LOVERS OUT AND CRY-- • • • • • 211 RAGGED WOOD V 10
   HOLLO HIM ON WITH HORSE AND HOUND, • • • • • 272 GREY ROCK   35
HOLLOW
   IT DOWN IN A LEAF-HID, HOLLOW PLACE • • • • • • 17 OISIN 1   242

HOLLOW   (CONTINUED)
LAY 'NEATH US: OF ITS HOLLOW COOL . . . .   17 OISIN 1   V 241
AND THE EARS OF THE HORSE WENT SINKING AWAY IN THE HOLLOW   48 OISIN 3   21
  NIGHT,
AND DEW-BLANCHED HORNS, IN WHOSE HOLLOW A CHILD OF THREE   49 OISIN 3   30
  YEARS OLD
THEIR SADNESS THROUGH A HOLLOW, PEARLY HEART: . . . . . .   68 SAD SHEPHERD   21
TO FILL THEIR DARK-BEAKED HOLLOW GALLEYS. . . . . . .   82 MAD KING GOLL   16
THAT HE MAY FILL HIS HOLLOW GALLEYS. . . . .   82 MAD KING GOLL   V 16
TO FILL WITH COWS HIS HOLLOW GALLEYS." . . . .   82 MAD KING GOLL   V 16
LOOK ON MY THIN GREY HAIR AND HOLLOW CHEEKS . . . . .   103 FERGUS DRUID   23
OF SUN AND MOON AND HOLLOW AND WOOD . . . .   148 INTO TWILIGHT   11
OF HOLLOW WOOD AND THE HILLY WOOD . . . .   148 INTO TWILIGHT   V 11
THROUGH HOLLOW LANDS AND HILLY LANDS, ...   150 WANDER AENGUS   18
THROUGH HILLY LANDS AND HOLLOW LANDS, ...   150 WANDER AENGUS   V 18
FOR ALL THEIR BEAUTY'S LIKE A HOLLOW DREAM, ...   184 QUEEN MAEVE   88
FOR ALL THEIR BEAUTY, LIKE A HOLLOW DREAM?" . . . . .   184 QUEEN MAEVE   V 89
ALTHOUGH THEIR BEAUTY'S LIKE A HOLLOW DREAM" . . . .   184 QUEEN MAEVE   V 89
AS WEARY-HEARTED AS THAT HOLLOW MOON. . . . .   206 ADAMS CURSE   38
AS WEARY HEARTED AS THAT HOLLOW MOON. . . . .   206 ADAMS CURSE   V 38
NOR AVALON THE GRASS-GREEN HOLLOW, NOR JOYOUS ISLE, . .   209 UNDER THE MOON   2
OR AVALLON THE GRASS GREEN HOLLOW, OR JOYOUS ISLE . .   209 UNDER THE MOON   V 2
THE HOLLOW WOOD . . . .   210 RAGGED WOOD   V T
I HEARD UNDER A RAGGED HOLLOW WOOD, ...   210 RAGGED WOOD   V 1
O HURRY TO THE HOLLOW WOOD, FOR THERE . . . .   211 RAGGED WOOD   V 9
IN THE HIGH HOLLOW TOWNLAND . . . .   214 HAPPY TOWNLAND   V 3
SOMEWHERE WITHIN SOME HOLLOW HILL, ...   271 GREY ROCK   V 14
A DARK DEEP HOLLOW IN THE ROCK. . . . .   303 HOUR DAWN   21
THAT HE HAS MADE THAT HOLLOW FACE OF HIS . . . . . .   368 EGO DOMINUS   20
OR WAS THE HUNGER THAT HAD MADE IT HOLLOW . . . . .   368 EGO DOMINUS   23
ON THEIR HOLLOW TOP, ...   415 TOWER   171
HOLLOW OF CHEEK AS THOUGH IT DRANK THE WIND . . . . .   444 SCHOOL CHILDR   27
THROUGH THE HOLLOW OF AN EAR: . . . .   499 MOTHER OF GOD   2
ALL FLAME-LIKE GUSHING FROM THE HOLLOW STONES, ...   650 ISLE STAT I 1   129
FROM THE SHADOWY HOLLOW . . . .   654 ISLE STAT I 2   56
ARISE FROM THE HOLLOW, ...   654 ISLE STAT I 2   68
FROM THE SHADOWY HOLLOW . . . .   654 ISLE STAT I 2   78
FROM THE GREEN SHADED HOLLOW . . . .   655 ISLE STAT I 2   82
FORTH FROM THE HOLLOW ALDER TRUNK . . . .   670 ISLE STAT II 3   120
AND HOLLOW LULLING THE YOUNG WINDS WITH SONG. . . . .   675 ISLE STAT II 3   226
BY HEATH OR HOLLOW OR RUSHY MERE, ...   716 FAIRY DOCTOR   10
THE HOLLOW WOODLANDS FEEL HIM THERE, ...   737 SUMMER EVENING   17
HOLLOW-CHEEKED
YONDER HE COMES: BRIGHT-EYED, AND HOLLOW-CHEEKED . . . .   697 MOSADA 2   35
HOLLOWS
AND DEW-BLANCHED HORNS, IN WHOSE HOLLOWS A CHILD OF THREE   49 OISIN 3   V 31
  YEARS OLD
THEIR SADNESS THROUGH THE HOLLOWS OF ITS HEART, ...   68 SAD SHEPHERD   V 21
CRIED OUT THE HOLLOWS OF THE SEA. . . . .   397 POLIT PRISONER   24
THAT FILL THE BLAZING HOLLOWS OF MY HEART. . . . . .   684 SEEKER   V 69D
HOLY
THE HOLY TREE IS GROWING THERE: . . . .   134 TWO TREES   2
FROM JOY THE HOLY BRANCHES START, ...   134 TWO TREES   3
UPON HER HOLY QUIETUDE. . . . .   138 TO IRELAND   V 16
AND WRAPPED THE FLAMES ABOVE HIS HOLY HEAD: . . . . .   162 ASKS FORGIVE   17
AND GATHERED THE FLAMES ABOVE HIS HOLY HEAD, ...   162 ASKS FORGIVE   V 17
WHO SOUGHT THEE IN THE HOLY SEPULCHRE, ...   169 SECRET ROSE   3
WHO SOUGHT THEE AT THE HOLY SEPULCHRE. . . . . . .   169 SECRET ROSE   V 3
WITH HOLY SHADOWS." HER HIGH HEART WAS GLAD, ...   186 QUEEN MAEVE   126
FROM THE HOLY ORCHARDS, WHERE THERE IS NONE . . . . .   196 BAILE AILLINN   174
BUT PURER THAN A TALL CANDLE BEFORE THE HOLY ROOD . . .   208 HANRAHANS SONG   14
AND CARRIES IT BETWEEN US. HOLY FIRE . . . .   239 SHADOW WATER B   371
THAT MUST, AS IF IT HAD NOT HOLY BLOOD . . . . . .   260 FASC DIFFICULT   5
BY THE ANCIENT HOLY HANDS THAT BROUGHT THEM . . . . .   271 GREY ROCK   V 21
IS FROM THE HOLY SHADES THAT ROVE . . . .   275 GREY ROCK   110
THAT THE SHADES OF HOLY MEN . . . .   298 THREE HERMITS   17
THE HOLY CENTAURS OF THE HILLS ARE VANISHED: . . . . .   344 DEJECTION   7
THE HOLY CENTAURS OF THE HILLS ARE BANISHED: . . . . .   344 DEJECTION   V 7
THROUGH THE HOLY IMAGES . . . .   355 PROPERTIUS   5
WHERE THOSE THAT HAVE OBEYED THE HOLY LAW . . . . .   356 BROKEN DREAMS   33
TO THE HOLY CITY OF BYZANTIUM . . . .   408 SAIL BYZANTIUM   16
O SAGES STANDING IN GOD'S HOLY FIRE . . . .   408 SAIL BYZANTIUM   17
COME FROM THE HOLY FIRE, PERNE IN A GYRE, ...   408 SAIL BYZANTIUM   19
UNLESS THE HOLY WRITINGS LIE, ...   436 FOR MY SON   28
WHERE HOLY DIONYSUS DIED, ...   437 SONGS PLAY 1   2
AND LIVE AMONG THE ANCIENT HOLY MEN, ...   448 HERO GIRL FOOL   V 11A
BEING BUT HOLY SHOWS . . . .   454 HIS MEMORIES   2
BODIES OF HOLY MEN AND WOMEN EXUDE . . . .   483 OIL AND BLOOD   2
NOR CAN HE HIDE IN HOLY BLACK . . . .   508 JANE BISHOP   18
WHEN THE HOLY BIRD, THAT THERE . . . .   522 LULLABY   15
AND THE HOLY LAND OF IRELAND, ...   526 AM OF IRELAND   2
AND THE HOLY LAND OF IRELAND, ...   526 AM OF IRELAND   15
AND THE HOLY LAND OF IRELAND, ...   527 AM OF IRELAND   28
HOLY JOE, THE BEGGAR-MAN, ...   529 TOM LUNATIC   8
I TURN THE PAGES OF MY HOLY BOOK. . . . .   555 RIBH AT TOMB   27
ROUND LOUGH DERG'S HOLY ISLAND I WENT UPON THE STONES, .   593 PILGRIM   6
OF HOLY PETER OF THE BURNING GATE: . . . .   696 MOSADA 2   V 20
HE'D FIND FOR THIS SOME HOLY TEXT. . . . .   728 PRIEST FAIRY   16
IN THE HOLY CHURCH OF GOD. . . . .   735 IN CHURCH   4
IN THE HOLY CHURCH OF GOD. . . . .   736 IN CHURCH   16
THAT MURMURS WITH HOLY WOODS, AND WIN THEIR HELP . . .   757 SHADOW WATER A   199

<table>
<tr><td></td><td></td><td>PAGE</td><td>TITLE</td><td>LINE</td></tr>
</table>

HOLY   (CONTINUED)

	PAGE	TITLE	LINE
WHERE TRUE-LOVE WANDERS AMONG THE HOLY WOODS.	764	SHADOW WATER A	337
WHERE TRUE LOVE WANDERS AMONG THE HOLY WOODS.	764	SHADOW WATER A V	337
WHERE ARE THESE BOUGHS? WHERE ARE THE HOLY WOODS	765	SHADOW WATER A	359
SIX HOLY CREATURES,	770	BLOOD BOND	14
O SHUFFLING OF HOLY SHOES!	774	COME RIDE	15

HOME

	PAGE	TITLE	LINE
MY HOME IS FAR FROM WHERE THE TIDE	5	OISIN 1 V	46
TO JOIN HIS BROTHERS IN THE HOME OF YEARS	30	OISIN 2 V	17
AND HOME TO ME AGAIN,	33	OISIN 2	65
WINDOWLESS, PILLARLESS, MULTITUDINOUS HOME	39	OISIN 2	148
HOME IN THE BLESSED MOONLIGHT	94	MOLL MAGEE V	11
AND FETCH ME HOME AGIN!	96	MOLL MAGEE	42
"BUT IF YOUR MASTER COMES HOME TRIUMPHING	106	CUCHULAIN SEA	12
THE HOME WHERE I WAS SAFE AND WARM?	151	HEART OF WOMAN V	6
WITH! "YOU MUST HOME AGAIN, AND WED	191	BAILE AILLINN	58
THAT I MAY DROWN MYSELF? BETTER STEER HOME,	222	SHADOW WATER B	12
IT WOULD BE BETTER TO TURN HOME AGAIN,	222	SHADOW WATER B V	12
AND YOU HAD SPREAD A SAIL FOR HOME, A WIND	236	SHADOW WATER B	309
AND MEASURE OUT A COURSE AND BRING US HOME,	238	SHADOW WATER B	362
LET'S HOME! I'D GIVE SOME RUBIES TO A WOMAN.	248	SHADOW WATER B	537
TO FANCY THAT SHE'D BRING YOU HOME AGAIN.	248	SHADOW WATER B	549
LET'S HOME AND SPEND IT IN OUR VILLAGES.	248	SHADOW WATER B V	538A
FOR HE WILL SHELTER YOU AND BRING YOU HOME."	250	SHADOW WATER B	590
"WE RIDE BUT SLOWLY THOUGH SO NEAR OUR HOME,"	276	TWO KINGS V	A
A STERNER CONSCIENCE AND A FRIENDLIER HOME,	321	REED WHISPERER	8
I CANNOT FIND THE PEACE OF HOME	332	ROUND TOWER	29
DECIDED HE WOULD JOURNEY HOME,	361	ALF POLLEXFEN	30
DECIDED HE MUST JOURNEY HOME,	361	ALF POLLEXFEN V	30
NEVER TO LEAVE THAT VALLEY HIS FATHERS CALLED THEIR HOME.	391	UNDER SATURN	16
WITH HER WHITE FINGER. I LED HER HOME ASLEEP	468	HARUN RASHID	158
WHAT BROUGHT THEM THERE SO FAR FROM THEIR HOME,	549	SEVERED HEAD	8
"NOT TO DIE ON THE STRAW AT HOME,	587	OLD WICKED MAN	5
AND HE CAME SAILING HOME.	594	COLONEL MARTIN	6
SO STAY AT HOME AND DRINK YOUR BEER	598	STONE CROSS	5
CALL THE MUSES HOME.	600	THOSE IMAGES	8
"OR DRIVEN FROM HOME AND LEFT TO DIE IN FEAR."	635	CUCHULAIN COMF	22
AND HATH HER HOME BY MANY-FOLDED DELLS.	657	ISLE STAT I 3	46
THE TALKING WINDS HAVE FOUND THEIR HOME,	686	LIFE	9
"NO, THY HOME IS DEEPEST HELL,	697	MOSADA 2	26
THEY WILL LEAD HER HOME AGAIN	727	LOVERS QUARREL	49
HE CAME TO THE HOME OF THE FOREST PEOPLE	728	PRIEST FAIRY	5
AND THOU CANST DWELL IN THINE OWN HOME,	739	EARL PAUL	3
ANOTHER LEADER, AND TURN HOME AGAIN.	748	SHADOW WATER A	16
BUT WOULD TURN HOME AGAIN. NO MAN HAD DOUBTS	749	SHADOW WATER A	38
AND TURN HIS GALLEY ABOUT AND BRING ME HOME.	751	SHADOW WATER A	108
I SHALL BE HOME NOW IN A LITTLE WHILE,	759	SHADOW WATER A	240
THE WINDS AND WATERS TO BE YOUR HOME FOR EVER!	762	SHADOW WATER A	282
THE WINDS AND WATERS TO BE YOUR HOME FOREVER!	762	SHADOW WATER A V	282
AND WE GO HOME. COME, AIBRIC! END YOUR TALE	766	SHADOW WATER A	374

HOMEBREW

	PAGE	TITLE	LINE
OF THE HOMEBREW THERE, UNTIL	776	AGAINST WITCH V	38

HOME-BREW

	PAGE	TITLE	LINE
OF THE HOME-BREW THERE, UNTIL	776	AGAINST WITCH	38

HOMER

	PAGE	TITLE	LINE
A WOMAN HOMER SUNG	254	WOMAN HOMER	T
A WOMAN HOMER SUNG,	255	WOMAN HOMER	19
WITH HOMER THAT WAS A BLIND MAN,	411	TOWER	52
MERE DREAMS, MERE DREAMS! YET HOMER HAD NOT SUNG	417	ANCEST HOUSES	9
THOUGH MOUNTED IN THAT SADDLE HOMER RODE	492	COOLE BALLYLEE	47
WHAT THEME HAD HOMER BUT ORIGINAL SIN?	502	VACILLATION	77
HOMER IS MY EXAMPLE AND HIS UNCHRISTENED HEART.	503	VACILLATION	87
HORACE THERE BY HOMER STANDS,	524	MAD AS MIST	7
AND MANY-MINDED HOMER WERE	524	MAD AS MIST	17

HOMER'S

	PAGE	TITLE	LINE
THAT COULD SHOW WHAT HOMER'S AGE	258	PEACE	2
BY HOMER'S PARAGON	384	VISION ROBART	56

HOMES

	PAGE	TITLE	LINE
WHERE HOMES ONCE WHITENED VALE AND MOUNTAIN CREST!	709	FERENCZ RENYI	3

HOMESTEAD

	PAGE	TITLE	LINE
IN HIS DIVINE HOMESTEAD,	113	ROSE OF PEACE	6

HOMESTEADS

	PAGE	TITLE	LINE
THEY LEFT THEIR HOMESTEADS TO FATTEN THE FOXES,	546	TO SAME TUNE 2	3
THEY LEFT THEIR HOMESTEADS TO SHELTER THE FOXES,	546	TO SAME TUNE 2 V	3
THEY LEFT THEIR HOMESTEADS TO FATTEN THE FOXES,	613	MARCH SONGS 1	3

HOMEWARD

	PAGE	TITLE	LINE
AND CHASE THE WILD BEE HOMEWARD TO HIS HIVE	32	OISIN 2 V	50D
ALONG THE LAKE. THE CRANE HAS HOMEWARD FLED.	656	ISLE STAT I 3	23
WITH BERRIES. PLACID AS A HOMEWARD BEE,	710	FERENCZ RENYI	29
A WOODMAN ON HIS HOMEWARD WAY	730	PRIEST FAIRY	73
AND, HURRYING HOMEWARD, FALL UPON SOME LAND	767	SHADOW WATER A	384

HOMEWARDS

	PAGE	TITLE	LINE
I HAVE TURNED HOMEWARDS. IN THE EYES OF THE GODS,	757	SHADOW WATER A	202

HONEST

	PAGE	TITLE	LINE
DUTIFUL HUSBAND, HONEST WIFE BY TURN,	376	PHASES OF MOON	99

HONESTY

	PAGE	TITLE	LINE
IF IT LACK HONESTY.	584	GHOST ROG CASE	28

HONEY

	PAGE	TITLE	LINE
AND BOWLS OF BARLEY, HONEY, AND WINE,	3	OISIN 1	8
AND DROPS OF HONEY ARE HIS WORDS,	7	OISIN 1 V	64
AND OIL AND WINE AND HONEY AND MILK,	8	OISIN 1	92

HONEY   (CONTINUED)
  AND HONEY, AND OIL, AND WINE, AND MILK, ...   8 OISIN 1   V 92
  FROM BEES AMONG THEIR HONEY MARTS, ...   16 OISIN 1   V 229
  WITH BOOM OF BEES IN HONEY MARTS, ...   16 OISIN 1   V 229
  LIKE DROPS OF HONEY CAME THEIR WORDS, ...   26 OISIN 1   398
  NINE BEAN ROWS WILL I HAVE THERE, A HIVE FOR THE HONEY BEE,   117 ISLE INNISFREE V   3
  TO BLESS THAT ISLE WITH HONEY IN HIS TONES, ...   128 DREAM OF FAERY V 44
  BAILE, WHO HAD THE HONEY MOUTH; . . . .   189 BAILE AILLINN   V   5
  YOUNG BAILE HONEY MOUTH, WHOM SOME . . . .   189 BAILE AILLINN   V 16
  I RUN TO BAILE HONEY MOUTH . . . .   191 BAILE AILLINN   V 48
  AND NOW THAT HONEY MOUTH IS LAID . . . .   192 BAILE AILLINN   V 80
  THE HONEY PALE MOON HUNG LOW ON THE SLEEPY HILL, ...   203 WITHER BOUGHS   V   5
  MY WALL IS LOOSENING, HONEY BEES . . . .   424 STARES NEST   V   4
  HONEY OF GENERATION HAD BETRAYED, ...   444 SCHOOL CHILDR   34
  GOLDSMITH DELIBERATELY SIPPING AT THE HONEY POT OF HIS   481 BLOOD AND MOON V 21
    MIND;
  I NEVER KNEW A NIGHT SO HONEY SWEET. . . . .   702 MOSADA 3   V 99
  WILD BEES' HONEY LAID FOR THEE." . . . .   730 PRIEST FAIRY   56
HONEY-BEE
  NINE BEAN-ROWS WILL I HAVE THERE, A HIVE FOR THE HONEY-BEE,   117 ISLE INNISFREE   3
HONEY-BEES
  MY WALL IS LOOSENING; HONEY-BEES, ...   424 STARES NEST   4
  THAN IN OUR LOVE; O HONEY-BEES, ...   425 STARES NEST   19
  THAN IN OUR LOVES; OH, HONEY-BEES . . . .   425 STARES NEST   V 19
HONEY-COLOURED
  BY THOSE GREAT HONEY-COLOURED . . . .   492 ANNE GREGORY   3
HONEYCOMB
  THEIR BITTERNESS AND FIND THE HONEYCOMB. . . . . . .   463 HARUN RASHID   48
  THE LION AND THE HONEYCOMB, WHAT HAS SCRIPTURE SAID? . .   503 VACILLATION   88
HONEY-COMB
  THE LION AND THE HONEY-COMB, WHAT HAS SCRIPTURE SAID? . .   503 VACILLATION   V 88
HONEYED
  BRINGING ME HONEYED, WANDERING THOUGHT . . . .   7 OISIN 1   V 65
HONEY-HEART
  NOR FAERIES IN THE HONEY-HEART OF JUNE ASTIR. . . . . .   661 ISLE STAT II 1   73
HONEY-HEARTED
  THE HONEY-HEARTED LEISURE OF THE LIGHT, ...   705 REMEMBRANCE   7
HONEY-MARTS
  WITH BOOM OF BEES IN HONEY-MARTS, ...   16 OISIN 1   229
HONEY-MOUTH
  YOUNG BAILE HONEY-MOUTH, WHOM SOME . . . .   189 BAILE AILLINN   16
  I RUN TO BAILE HONEY-MOUTH, ...   191 BAILE AILLINN   48
  AND NOW THAT HONEY-MOUTH IS LAID . . . .   192 BAILE AILLINN   80
HONEY-PALE
  THE HONEY-PALE MOON LAY LOW ON THE SLEEPY HILL, ...   203 WITHER BOUGHS   5
HONEY-POT
  GOLDSMITH DELIBERATELY SIPPING AT THE HONEY-POT OF HIS   481 BLOOD AND MOON   21
    MIND,
HONEY-SWEET
  I NEVER KNEW A NIGHT SO HONEY-SWEET. . . . .   702 MOSADA 3   99
HONEY-THICKENED
  IN ALL ITS HONEY-THICKENED TUNE . . . .   736 SUMMER EVENING   7
HONIED
  A HONIED RINGING; UNDER THE NEW SKIES . . . .   130 BOOK STORIES   V 21
HONOUR
  IN HONOUR SOON BY HIS MASTER'S SIDE . . . .   26 OISIN 1   V 399C
  BEING HONOUR BRED, WITH ONE . . . .   291 TO A FRIEND   5
  PULL DOWN ESTABLISHED HONOUR; HAWK FOR NEWS . . . . .   398 LEADERS CROWD   3
  NO HONOUR LEAVE ITS MIGHTY MONUMENT, ...   429 NINETEEN 19   38
  TALKED OF HONOUR AND OF TRUTH, ...   431 NINETEEN 19   90
  IF HONOUR FIND HIM IN THE WINTRY BLAST? . . . .   479 SELF AND SOUL   56
  ACCEPT THE MIRACLES OF THE SAINTS AND HONOUR SANCTITY? . .   503 VACILLATION   79
  BUT IN HONOUR SPLIT HIS LOVE . . . .   573 LADYS 3RD SONG   7
  HONOUR HAD LIVED SO LONG, ALL LACKING FOUND. . . . . .   603 GALLERY REVIS   35
  HONOUR HAD LIVED SO LONG, THEIR HEALTH I FOUND. . . . .   603 GALLERY REVIS   V 35
HONOURED
  HONOURED BY ALL IN THEIR DEGREES, ...   380 SAINT HUNCH   15
HOOD   SEE CRADLE-HOOD MONK'S-HOOD
  NODDING HER RUSSET HOOD? . . . .   171 MAID QUIET   2
  NODDING HER PURPLE HOOD? . . . .   171 MAID QUIET   V   2
  UNDER HER PURPLE HOOD. . . . .   171 MAID QUIET   V   8
  WHEN THE SUN LOOKED OUT OF HIS GOLDEN HOOD, ...   210 RAGGED WOOD   V   3
  WHEN THE SUN LOOKED OUT OF HIS GOLDEN HOOD?-- . . . . .   211 RAGGED WOOD   7
  "I WILL NOT BE CLAPPED IN A HOOD, ...   349 HAWK   7
  A KIND OLD NUN IN A WHITE HOOD REPLIES; . . . . . .   443 SCHOOL CHILDR   2
  IN MASKER'S CLOAK AND HOOD. . . . .   539 MEETING   2
  YOUR HOOD IS THREADBARE--SEE THAT IT BE CHANGED . . . .   704 MOSADA 3   133
HOODED
  LET HIM BE HOODED OR CAGED . . . .   349 HAWK   2
  I WRAPPED HER IN A HOODED CLOAK, AND SHE, ...   468 HARUN RASHID   154
  I WRAPPED HER IN A HEAVY HOODED CLOAK, ...   468 HARUN RASHID   V 154
  I WRAPPED HER IN A HEAVY HOODED CLOAK, AND SHE . . . .   468 HARUN RASHID   V 154
HOOD'S   SEE MONK'S-HOOD'S
HOOF   SEE HORSE-HOOF
  SCARCE WORTHY OF A HOOF GOLD-SHOD. . . . .   2 OISIN 1   V 7Y
  MY DREAMS WERE LIVING. NOW THE HOOF . . . .   25 OISIN 1   V 382
  AND HOOF AND HORN THAT HAD SUCKED IN THEIR SPEED . . . .   278 TWO KINGS   30
  BEYOND THE FLING OF THE DULL ASS'S HOOF . . . .   321 REED WHISPERER   5
  BUT WHEN HIS HORSE HAD PUT ITS HOOF . . . .   571 THREE BUSHES   50
HOOFS
  WITH HOOFS OF THE PALE FINDRINNY . . . .   25 OISIN 1   383

			PAGE	TITLE		LINE

HOOFS   (CONTINUED)
    WITH HOOFS OF THE RUDDY FINDRINNY . . . .   25 OISIN 1   V   383
    A VALLEY FLOWED DOWN FROM HIS HOOFS, AND THERE IN THE LONG   48 OISIN 3   26
        GRASS LAY,
    OF TWILIGHT AND SLUMBER WERE GONE, AND THAT HOOFS   54 OISIN 3   112
        IMPATIENTLY STEPT.
    . . . THE STRONG HOOFS CRUSHING THE SAND AND THE SHELLS,   58 OISIN 3   157
    . . . THE STRONG HOOFS CRUSHING THE SANDS AND THE SHELLS   58 OISIN 3   V   157
    THEIR HOOFS HEAVY WITH TUMULT, THEIR EYES GLIMMERING WHITE; 154 BELOVED PEACE   2
    AND UNDER HER HOOFS THE MARIGOLDS BEATEN. . . . . . .   729 PRIEST FAIRY   36
HOOK   SEE REAPING-HOOK
    THAT RUN BEFORE THE REAPING HOOK AND LIE . . . . . .   218 WOODS OF COOLE V 32
    AND THOUGH I HAVE TURNED THE TALK BY HOOK OR CROOK . . .   350 HER PRAISE   5
HOOKED
    BENT DOWN ABOVE EACH HOOKED KNEE, ...   26 OISIN 1   392
    BENT LOW ABOVE EACH HOOKED KNEE, ...   26 OISIN 1   V   392
    AND HOOKED A BERRY TO A THREAD; . . . .   149 WANDER AENGUS   4
    AND HOOKED A LITTLE SILVER TROUT. . . . .   149 WANDER AENGUS V   8
HOOKS
    SHOOK THE ALE-HORNS AND SHIELDS UPON THEIR HOOKS; . . .   181 QUEEN MAEVE   38
    SHOOK THE ALE HORNS AND SHIELDS UPON THEIR HOOKS; . . .   181 QUEEN MAEVE   V   38
HOOLIHAN   SEE KATHLEEN-NY-HOOLIHAN
HOOPED
    CIVILIZATION IS HOOPED TOGETHER, BROUGHT . . . . . .   563 MERU   1
NO MAIN ITEM   SEE BARREL-HOOPS
HOOTED
    HAD HOOTED FOR AN HUNDRED YEARS, ...   670 ISLE STAT II 3   116
    UP-RAISED HIS VOICE, AND HOOTED ME. . . . .   670 ISLE STAT II 3   117
    HE HOOTED AS I WANDERED BY. . . . .   670 ISLE STAT II 3   121
    UPRAISED HIS VOICE, AND HOOTED ME. . . . .   670 ISLE STAT II 3 V 117
HOOVES
    FOR GOLD HIS HOOVES AND SILK HIS REIN, ...   2 OISIN 1   V   7Z
    FOR THE SPARKLING HOOVES THEY SANK NOT IN; . . . . . .   10 OISIN 1   V 114A
    WHOSE HOOVES THE TOPS OF THE SURGES GRAZED, ...   12 OISIN 1   V 142A
    I LAY, AS OVER SEA THE LIGHT HOOVES GLANCED . . . . . .   30 OISIN 2   V 19A
    OF DANAAN HOOVES WE URGED OUR WAY BETWEEN . . . .   31 OISIN 2   V   31
    FROM HIS HOOVES IN THE HEAVY GRASSES, WITH MONSTROUS   48 OISIN 3   V   27
        SLUMBERING FOLK,
    . . . BENEATH ME THE HOOVES IMPATIENTLY STEPT. . . . .   54 OISIN 3   V 112
    . . . THE GOLD HOOVES CRUSHING THE SANDS AND THE SHELLS   58 OISIN 3   V 157
    YOUR HOOVES HAVE STAMPED AT THE BLACK MARGIN OF THE WOOD, 442 BLACK CENTAUR   1
HOPE
    MY ENEMY AND HOPE; DEMONS FOR FRIGHT . . . .   34 OISIN 2   81
    WITH HOPE, MINE ENEMY. AS HE BY NIGHT . . . .   34 OISIN 2   V   81
    HAD NEITHER HOPE NOR FEAR. I BADE THEM HIDE . . . . .   38 OISIN 2   139
    LEST NIAMH SHUDDER. FULL OF HOPE AND DREAD . . . . .   41 OISIN 2   183
    WHILE HUSHED FROM FEAR, OR LOUD WITH HOPE, A BAND . . .   114 ROSE OF BATTLE   5
    WE COME BETWEEN HIM AND THE HOPE OF HIS HEART. . . . .   141 HOSTING SIDHE   12
    AND WHERE IS THERE HOPE OR DEED AS FAIR? . . . . . .   141 HOSTING SIDHE   14
    THOUGH HOPE FALL FROM YOU AND LOVE DECAY, ...   148 INTO TWILIGHT   7
    AND HOPE IS LESS DEAR THAN THE DEW OF THE MORN. . . . .   148 INTO TWILIGHT   16
    THOUGH HOPE FALL FROM THEE OR LOVE DECAY . . . . . .   148 INTO TWILIGHT V   7
    FOR SOMEBODY HID HATRED AND HOPE AND DESIRE AND FEAR . .   153 CHANGE BELOVED   4
    AND I HAVE HATRED AND HOPE AND DESIRE AND FEAR . . . .   153 CHANGE BELOVED V   4
    O VANITY OF SLEEP, HOPE, DREAM, ENDLESS DESIRE, ...   154 BELOVED PEACE   7
    LILIES OF DEATH-PALE HOPE, ROSES OF PASSIONATE DREAM. . .   172 TRAV PASSION   8
    MIRACLE, ECSTASY, THE IMPOSSIBLE HOPE, ...   227 SHADOW WATER B   102
    LOVES IN BRIEF LONGING AND DECEIVING HOPE . . . . . .   228 SHADOW WATER B   146
    TO GO--FOR HOPE WOULD GIVE HIS LIMBS THE POWER-- . . .   282 TWO KINGS   V 133A
    FOR HOPE WOULD GIVE HIS LIMBS THE POWER--AND AWAIT . .   283 TWO KINGS   136
    THE BEGGAR DEAF TO ALL BUT HOPE . . . .   304 HOUR DAWN   V   44
    HOPE THAT YOU MAY UNDERSTAND! . . . .   309 REALISTS   1
    DO, BUT AWAKE A HOPE TO LIVE . . . .   309 REALISTS   6
    DO BUT WAKE THE HOPE TO LIVE . . . .   309 REALISTS   V   6
    TO HOPE A THING SO DEAR . . . .   346 ON WOMAN   27
    THAT IS OUR MODERN HOPE, AND BY ITS LIGHT . . . . . .   368 EGO DOMINICUS   11
    THEY HAVE LOUD MUSIC, HOPE EVERY DAY RENEWED . . . . .   398 LEADERS CROWD   11
    ONE DEAR HOPE HAD HE; . . . .   471 ALL SOUL NIGHT   28
    NOR DREAD NOR HOPE ATTEND . . . .   476 DEATH   1
    A VAIN HOPE . . . .   553 CHURCH STATE   V   T
    IF YOU ARE WORTH MY HOPE! NEITHER CONTENT . . . . . .   579 DOR WELLESLEY   13
    A MAN HAS A HOPE FOR HEAVEN, ...   643 SONG FAERIES   V   1
    A MAN HAS A HOPE FOR HEAVEN, ...   676 ISLE STAT II 3   248
    THIS HEATHEN HORDE AWAY. YOU NEED NOT HOPE; . . . . .   696 MOSADA 2   5
    CAST OUT ALL HOPE, CAST OUT ALL FEAR, ...   743 DANAAN QUICK   25
    AND TURN BRIEF LONGING AND DECEIVING HOPE . . . . . .   750 SHADOW WATER A   59
    THAN IN BRIEF LONGING AND DECEIVING HOPE . . . . . .   750 SHADOW WATER A   65
    WHEN ONE HAS LEAPT ON BOARD. NO, FOR I HAVE HOPE . . .   751 SHADOW WATER A   106
    HAVE BID ME HOPE, SAIL TO THE LOCHLANN SHORE . . . . .   756 SHADOW WATER A V 184
    IS BUT BRIEF LONGING, AND DECEIVING HOPE, ...   765 SHADOW WATER A   354
HOPED
    MORE RICHES THAN THEY EVER HOPED TO FIND? . . . . . .   226 SHADOW WATER B   94
    WHAT I HAD HOPED 'TWOULD BE . . . .   347 FISHERMAN   10
    BECAUSE I HAD HOPED TO COME, AS DREAMS FORETOLD, . . .   757 SHADOW WATER A   197
    I HAVE COME HITHER BECAUSE I HOPED TO COME . . . . . .   757 SHADOW WATER A V 197
HOPELESS
    HOPELESS FOR EVER; ANCIENT OISIN KNOWS, ...   42 OISIN 2   202
    HOPELESS FOR EVER, THEY ALONE SHALL SEEK . . . . . .   42 OISIN 2   V 200
    HAS MADE THEM SO HAPPY AND HOPELESS, SO DEAF AND SO BLIND 204 WITHER BOUGHS   20
    HOPELESS AND DEAR, OR TERRIBLE TO THINK ON, ...   281 TWO KINGS   96
    TO SEEK NOT HOPELESS HAVE I CROSSED THE GLOOM, ...   656 ISLE STAT I 3   42

	PAGE	TITLE		LINE
HOPELESS (CONTINUED)				
SHALL NOT SO HOPELESS PROVE! SOME GOD MAY REST • • • •	657	ISLE STAT I 3		61
HOPES				
AND HEAVY MORTAL HOPES THAT TOIL AND PASS! • • • • • •	101	ROSE UPON ROOD		18
AND BROOD ON HOPES AND FEAR NO MORE. • • • • • • •	125	GOES FERGUS		6
AND BROOD ON HOPES AND FEARS NO MORE. • • • • • •	125	GOES FERGUS	V	6
OR HOPES THAT IN MERE HOPING FLICKER AND CEASE! • • •	162	ASKS FORGIVE		3
AND HOPES THAT IN MERE HOPING FLICKER AND CEASE! • • •	162	ASKS FORGIVE	V	3
BUT HARRY US WITH HOPES THAT COME TO NOTHING, • • • • •	250	SHADOW WATER B		579
HOPING				
HOPING AND FEARING, BROUGHT ME WINE AND BREAD. • • • •	41	OISIN 2	V 184A	
OR HOPES THAT IN MERE HOPING FLICKER AND CEASE! • • •	162	ASKS FORGIVE		3
AND HOPES THAT IN MERE HOPING FLICKER AND CEASE! • • •	162	ASKS FORGIVE	V	3
AND ALL THEIR EYES STILL FIXED, HOPING TO FIND ONCE MORE,	318	MAGI		6
DREADING AND HOPING ALL! • • • • • • • • • • • •	476	DEATH		4
HOPING MORE SUBSTANTIAL JOY • • • • • • • • • •	494	AT ALGECIRAS		9
HOPING A MORE SUBSTANTIAL JOY • • • • • • • • • •	494	AT ALGECIRAS	V	9
HORACE				
HORACE THERE BY HOMER STANDS, • • • • • • • • • •.	524	MAD AS MIST		7
HORDE				
THIS HEATHEN HORDE AWAY. YOU NEED NOT HOPE! • • • • •	696	MOSADA 2		5
HORIZON				
ON THE HORIZON EDGE BELLOWED THE HERDS. • • • • • • •	279	TWO KINGS		56
WHEN THE HORIZON FADES, • • • • • • • • • • • •	416	TOWER		193
HORIZON'S				
HE'D HEARD THAT DIN ON THE HORIZON'S EDGE • • • • • •	286	TWO KINGS	V 217A	
(FOR SINCE THE HORIZON'S BOUGHT STRANGE DOGS ARE STILL)	579	DOR WELLESLEY		7
HORN				
"WHY DO YOU WIND NO HORN?" SHE SAID, • • • • • • • •	4	OISIN 1		32
WHY DO YE SOUND NO HORN?" SHE SAID. • • • • • • • •	4	OISIN 1	V	33
WHY DO YOU WIND NO HORN?" SHE SAID. • • • • • • • •	4	OISIN 1	V	33
SHALL FOLLOW YOUR HORN AND OBEY YOUR WHIM, • • • • • •	9	OISIN 1		99
AND STIRS THE YOUNG KID'S BUDDING HORN • • • • • • •	18	OISIN 1		264
A-MURMUR LIKE YOUNG PARTRIDGE! WITH LOUD HORN • • • • •	32	OISIN 2		52
WHEN THEY AWAKE UPSPRINGING! WITH LOUD HORN • • • • •	32	OISIN 2	V	52
CEASE, CEASE, O MOURNFUL, LAUGHING FENIAN HORN! • • • •	43	OISIN 2		213
AH, CEASE, THOU MOURNFUL, LAUGHING FENIAN HORN! • • • •	43	OISIN 2	V	213
AH, CEASE, YOU MOURNFUL, LAUGHING FENIAN HORN! • • • • •	43	OISIN 2	V	213
SNATCHING THE HORN OF NIAMH! I BLEW A LONG LINGERING NOTE.	51	OISIN 3		57
SNATCHING THE HORN OF NIAM, I BLEW FORTH A LINGERING NOTE!	51	OISIN 3	V	57
SNATCHING THE HORN OF NIAM, I BLEW A LINGERING NOTE! • •	51	OISIN 3	V	57
"HUNTSMAN RODY, BLOW THE HORN, • • • • • • • • • •	98	FOXHUNTER		25
"NOW HUNTSMAN RODY, BLOW THY HORN, • • • • • • • • •	98	FOXHUNTER	V REF	
"MY HUNTSMAN RODY, BLOW THE HORN, • • • • • • • • •	98	FOXHUNTER	V REF	
"HUNTSMAN RODY, BLOW THE HORN, • • • • • • • • • •	99	FOXHUNTER		33
"I CANNOT BLOW UPON MY HORN, • • • • • • • • • • •	99	FOXHUNTER		35
AND GOD STANDS WINDING HIS LONELY HORN, • • • • • • •	148	INTO TWILIGHT		13
AND WITH HEART MORE OLD THAN THE HORN • • • • • • •	157	POET BELOVED		5
AND WITH THE HEART MORE OLD THAN THE HORN • • • • • •	157	POET BELOVED	V	5
WHEN THE LONG WARS FOR THE WHITE HORN • • • • • • •	189	BAILE AILLINN		14
BECAUSE OF SOMETHING TOLD UNDER THE FAMISHED HORN • • •	210	UNDER THE MOON		17
BECAUSE OF SOMETHING I HEARD OF UNDER THE THIN HORN • • •	210	UNDER THE MOON	V	17
BECAUSE OF A STORY I HEARD UNDER THE THIN HORN • • • •	210	UNDER THE MOON		17
BECAUSE OF A STORY I HEARD UNDER A THIN HORN • • • • •	210	UNDER THE MOON	V	17
AND LIFT UP AN OLD HORN • • • • • • • • • • • •	215	HAPPY TOWNLAND		49
NINE SWORDS WITH HANDLES OF RHINOCEROS HORN • • • • • •	239	SHADOW WATER B		368
TO THE HORN, AND HE BE HALE AND HEARTY. • • • • • • •	243	SHADOW WATER B		447
AGAINST THE STAG. WHEN HORN AND STEEL WERE MET • • • •	277	TWO KINGS		15
THE HORN RESOUNDED AS THOUGH IT HAD BEEN SILVER, • • • •	277	TWO KINGS		16
HORN LOCKED IN SWORD, THEY TUGGED AND STRUGGLED THERE • •	277	TWO KINGS		18
TO STAY THE STAG'S NEXT RUSH. WHEN SWORD MET HORN • • •	277	TWO KINGS	V	15
AND HOOF AND HORN THAT HAD SUCKED IN THEIR SPEED • • • •	278	TWO KINGS		30
UNTIL AT LAST THE UNLOCKED HORN HAD TORN • • • • • • •	278	TWO KINGS	V	21
A LONG BLAST UPON THE HORN THAT BROUGHT • • • • • • •	324	ROBERT GREGORY		22
AND THE NEW STILL HIDES HER HORN. • • • • • • • • •	382	VISION ROBART		4
WHEREBY THE HORN OF PLENTY IS UNDONE. • • • • • • • •	404	FOR DAUGHTER		32
OUT OF THE MOUTH OF PLENTY'S HORN, • • • • • • • • •	405	FOR DAUGHTER		60
BARTER THAT HORN AND EVERY GOOD • • • • • • • • • •	405	FOR DAUGHTER		62
CEREMONY'S A NAME FOR THE RICH HORN, • • • • • • • •	406	FOR DAUGHTER		79
OR THAT OF THE FABULOUS HORN, • • • • • • • • • • •	414	TOWER		136
THIN IS THE MOON'S HORN! • • • • • • • • • • • •	519	LOVES LONENESS		8
SWEARS THAT HE HEARS THE KING'S GREAT HORN. • • • • • •	636	BLACK TOWER		24
A HORN! SOME TROOP OF ROBBERS WINDING GOES • • • • •	649	ISLE STAT I 1		110
HORNED SEE WHITE-HORNED				
BETWEEN THE HORNED HILLS--SHEPHERDS, FAREWELL! • • • •	682	SEEKER		27
HORNLESS				
THAN THE HORNLESS DEER WE CHASED THAT MORN, • • • • • •	2	OISIN 1	V	7P
THE HORNLESS DEER IS NOT MORE SAD • • • • • • • • •	4	OISIN 1		34
WE GALLOPED! NOW A HORNLESS DEER • • • • • • • • •	11	OISIN 1		139
ON, ON! AND NOW A HORNLESS DEER • • • • • • • • • •	11	OISIN 1	V	139
A RED-EARED HOUND FOLLOWS A HORNLESS DEER. • • • • • •	764	SHADOW WATER A		325
HORN'S				
THE HORN'S SWEET NOTE AND THE TOOTH OF THE HOUND. • • •	380	SONGS FOOL 1		12
THE HORN'S SWEET NOTE AND THE TOOTH OF THE HOUND. • • •	381	SONGS FOOL 2		14
HORNS SEE ALE-HORNS				
AND DEW-BLANCHED HORNS, IN WHOSE HOLLOW A CHILD OF THREE YEARS OLD	49	OISIN 3		30
AND DEW-BLANCHED HORNS, IN WHOSE HOLLOWS A CHILD OF THREE YEARS OLD	49	OISIN 3	V	31
THE HORNS AND SHIELDS AND WILD SWAN'S PINIONS! • • • •	82	MAD KING GOLL	V	5
DO YOU NOT HEAR ME CALLING, WHITE DEER WITH NO HORNS? • •	153	CHANGE BELOVED		1

HORNS   (CONTINUED)
   SHOOK THE ALE HORNS AND SHIELDS UPON THEIR HOOKS; • • • 181 QUEEN MAEVE   V   38
   BUT THE STAG STOOPED ITS HEAVY BRANCHING HORNS, • • • 277 TWO KINGS   V   12
   UNTIL AT LAST THE DOUBLE HORNS, DRAWN BACKWARD, • • • 278 TWO KINGS   21
   KING EOCHAID SEIZED THE HORNS IN HIS STRONG HANDS • • 278 TWO KINGS   24
   EOCHAID SEIZED BOTH THE HORNS IN HIS STRONG HANDS • 278 TWO KINGS   V   24
   ASIDE!--THE WILD HORNS TOLD ALMINTOR'S END, • • • 665 ISLE STAT II 2   68
HORRIBLE
   AND HORRIBLE SPLENDOUR OF DESIRE; • • • • • • 411 TOWER   63
   EVEN WHERE HORRIBLE GREEN PARROTS CALL AND SWING. • 442 BLACK CENTAUR   2
   UNWEARIED EYES UPON THOSE HORRIBLE GREEN BIRDS. • • 442 BLACK CENTAUR   16
   EVEN WHERE THE HORRIBLE GREEN PARROTS CALL AND SWING. • 442 BLACK CENTAUR V   2
   YOU THINK IT HORRIBLE THAT LUST AND RAGE • • • • 591 SPUR   1
   OH DEATH IS HORRIBLE! AND FOUL, FOUL, FOUL! • • • 675 ISLE STAT II 3 238
HORROR
   HORROR FROM HORROR GREW; BUT WHEN THE WEST • • • • 41 OISIN 2   180
   HORROR FROM HORROR GREW; BUT WHEN THE WEST • • • • 41 OISIN 2   180
   • • • DEEP HORROR OF EYES AND OF WINGS, • • • • • 62 OISIN 3   205
   DROVE HORROR FROM HIS MOTHER'S BREAST. • • • • 440 WISDOM   20
   I STRUGGLED WITH THE HORROR OF DAYBREAK, • • • 535 CHOSEN   10
   A CREEPING HORROR IS ALL OVER ME. • • • • • 681 SEEKER   12
HORSE   SEE CART-HORSE HIGH-HORSE
   ON A HORSE WITH BRIDLE OF FINDRINNY; • • • • • 3 OISIN 1   21
   BUT WHEN THE HORSE HAD FELT MY WEIGHT, • • • • 9 OISIN 1   109
   THE HORSE TOWARDS THE MUSIC RACED, • • • • • 13 OISIN 1   169
   WE TIED THE HORSE IN A LEAFY CLUMP, • • • • • 14 OISIN 1   194
   AND FOUND THE HORSE AND BRIDLED HIM, • • • • • 25 OISIN 1   378
   ON HORSE AND SEA AND SADDLE SHONE. • • • • • 28 OISIN 1   V 427D
   ABOUT THEM; AND THE HORSE OF FAERY SCREAMED • • • 30 OISIN 2   24
   TYING THE HORSE TO HIS VAST FOOT THAT LAY • • • 32 OISIN 2   46
   HOLDING THAT HORSE, AND SADLY CALLED MY NAME; • • 44 OISIN 2   230
   HOLDING THAT HORSE LONG SEEN NOT, NIAM STOOD. • • 44 OISIN 2   V 230
   AND THE EARS OF THE HORSE WENT SINKING AWAY IN THE HOLLOW 48 OISIN 3   21
      NIGHT,
   TILL THE HORSE GAVE A WHINNY; • • • • • • • 48 OISIN 3   25
   AND THE HORSE WAS GONE IN THE DISTANCE, • • • • 52 OISIN 3   75
   I AWOKE: THE STRANGE HORSE WITHOUT SUMMONS OUT OF • 54 OISIN 3   105
      THE DISTANCE RAN,
   AND THEIR HOUND, AND THEIR HORSE, AND THEIR LOVE, • • • 59 OISIN 3   176
   I FELL ON THE PATH, AND THE HORSE WENT AWAY LIKE A SUMMER 60 OISIN 3   190
      FLY;
   HE ROUSED HIS HORSE OUT OF ITS SLEEP, • • • • • 133 FR GILLIGAN   27
   OLD BUTLERS WHEN YOU TOOK TO HORSE AND STOOD • • 270 PARDON FATHERS V   10
   HOLLO HIM ON WITH HORSE AND HOUND, • • • • • 272 GREY ROCK   35
   I CALL FOR SPADE AND HORSE AND HOUND. • • • • 275 GREY ROCK   105
   UPON HIS TREMBLING HORSE, THEN DROVE THE SPUR, • • 277 TWO KINGS   11
   HE THOUGHT TO HAVE GIVEN HIS HORSE THE SPUR, BUT SAW 277 TWO KINGS   V   48
   HE SAT WITH TIGHTENED REIN AMAZED, HIS HORSE • • 277 TWO KINGS   V   10
   THE ENTRAILS OF THE HORSE. DROPPING HIS SWORD • • 278 TWO KINGS   23
   THE DISEMBOWELLED HORSE. KING EOCHAID RAN • • • 278 TWO KINGS   45
   THROUGH THE ENTRAILS OF THE HORSE. DROPPING HIS SWORD • 278 TWO KINGS   V   23
   THE DISEMBOWELLED HORSE. KING EOCHAID GAZED, • • 278 TWO KINGS   V   45
   AND LAY IT ALL UPON A HORSE"; • • • • • • • 296 THREE BEGGARS   35
   LIKE AN OLD HORSE IN A POUND." • • • • • • 333 SOLOMON SHEBA   8
   AND RODE OUR WINGED HORSE; • • • • • • • 392 EASTER 1916   25
   AND OUR WINGED METTLESOME HORSE. • • • • • 392 EASTER 1916   V   25
   THE HORSE THAT COMES FROM THE ROAD, • • • • 393 EASTER 1916   45
   AND A HORSE PLASHES WITHIN IT; • • • • • • 393 EASTER 1916   52
   GATHERED A SCORE OF HORSE AND SPENT HIS DAYS • • 420 MY HOUSE   22
   I KNEW THAT HORSE PLAY, KNEW IT FOR A MURDEROUS THING. 442 BLACK CENTAUR V   4
   BUT ALL IS CHANGED, THAT HIGH HORSE RIDERLESS, • 492 COOLE BALLYLEE 46
   BUT WHEN HIS HORSE HAD PUT ITS HOOF • • • • • 571 THREE BUSHES   50
   A GOOD MAN ON A HORSE, • • • • • • • • 604 YOU CONTENT   12
   AN OLD HORSE LOOKED ACROSS A FENCE, • • • • • 725 LEGEND   27
HORSEBACK
   ON FOOT, ON HORSEBACK OR IN BATTLE-CARS." • • • 107 CUCHULAIN SEA   30
   HORSEMAN ERECT UPON HORSEBACK • • • • • • 589 OLD WICKED MAN 52
   A BEGGAR UPON HORSEBACK LASHES A BEGGAR ON FOOT. • • 590 GREAT DAY   2
   A BEGGAR UPON HORSEBACK LASHES A BEGGAR UPON FOOT; • • 590 GREAT DAY   V   2
HORSE-BACK
   CAMEL-BACK, HORSE-BACK, ASS-BACK, MULE-BACK, • • • 566 LAPIS LAZULI   26
HORSE-BOYS
   WHERE THE TIRED HORSE-BOYS LAY UPON THE RUSHES, • • 180 QUEEN MAEVE   13
   BUT THE HORSE-BOYS SLEPT ON, AS THOUGH SOME POWER • 181 QUEEN MAEVE   39
HORSED   SEE TWO-HORSED
   THERE IN A TWO HORSED CARRIAGE • • • • • • 628 JANE MOUNTAIN V   13
HORSEHAIR
   "EACH ONE A HORSEHAIR SHIRT HATH ON, • • • • • 43 OISIN 2   V 208C
HORSE-HAIR
   STARING UPON A BEDOUIN'S HORSE-HAIR ROOF • • • • 368 EGO DOMINUS   29
HORSE-HOOF
   A HORSE-HOOF SLIDES ON THE BRIM, • • • • • • 393 EASTER 1916   51
HORSEMAN
   SOLDIER, SCHOLAR, HORSEMAN, HE, • • • • • • • 327 ROBERT GREGORY 70
   SOLDIER, SCHOLAR, HORSEMAN, HE, • • • • • • • 327 ROBERT GREGORY 78
   SOLDIER, SCHOLAR, HORSEMAN, HE, • • • • • • • 327 ROBERT GREGORY 86
   HORSEMAN ERECT UPON HORSEBACK • • • • • • 589 OLD WICKED MAN 52
   HORSEMAN, PASS BY! • • • • • • • • • 640 BEN BULBEN   94
HORSEMANSHIP
   FOR HORSEMANSHIP AT MEETS OR AT RACECOURSES, • • • 325 ROBERT GREGORY 35
   WELL KNOWN FOR HORSEMANSHIP TO CONNACHT MEN • • • 325 ROBERT GREGORY V 34

```
                                                              PAGE    TITLE          LINE
HORSEMANSHIP   (CONTINUED)
   FOR HORSEMANSHIP AT MEETS OR AT RACE-COURSES, . . . . .    325 ROBERT GREGORY V   35
HORSEMEN
   THE HORSEMEN WITH THEIR FLOATING HAIR, . . . . . . . .       2 OISIN 1            7
   A HUNDRED HORSEMEN ON THE BASALT FLOOR . . . . . . . .      36 OISIN 2          102
   WHERETHROUGH A HUNDRED HORSEMEN ON THE FLOOR . . . . .      36 OISIN 2        V 102
   WITH HORSEMEN HURRYING NEAR AND FAR, . . . . . . . .        83 MAD KING GOLL  V  18
   AND THEN THE CLASH OF FALLEN HORSEMEN AND THE CRIES . . .  161 BLACK PIG          3
   AYE, HORSEMEN FOR COMPANIONS, . . . . . . . . . . .        266 GALWAY RACES        7
   AND THE TALL MEN AND THE SWORDSMEN AND THE HORSEMEN, WHERE 580 CURSE CROMWELL      4
      ARE THEY?
   FROM MOUNTAIN TO MOUNTAIN RIDE THE FIERCE HORSEMEN. . . .  605 SONGS BURDEN 1      9
   FROM MOUNTAIN TO MOUNTAIN RIDE THE FIERCE HORSEMEN. . . .  606 SONGS BURDEN 1     18
   FROM MOUNTAIN TO MOUNTAIN RIDE THE FIERCE HORSEMEN. . . .  606 SONGS BURDEN 1     27
   FROM MOUNTAIN TO MOUNTAIN RIDE THE FIERCE HORSEMEN. . . .  607 SONGS BURDEN 2      9
   FROM MOUNTAIN TO MOUNTAIN RIDE THE FIERCE HORSEMEN. . . .  607 SONGS BURDEN 2     18
   FROM MOUNTAIN TO MOUNTAIN RIDE THE FIERCE HORSEMEN. . . .  607 SONGS BURDEN 2     27
   FROM MOUNTAIN TO MOUNTAIN RIDE THE FIERCE HORSEMEN. . . .  608 SONGS BURDEN 3      9
   FROM MOUNTAIN TO MOUNTAIN RIDE THE FIERCE HORSEMEN. . . .  608 SONGS BURDEN 3     18
   FROM MOUNTAIN TO MOUNTAIN RIDE THE FIERCE HORSEMEN. . . .  608 SONGS BURDEN 3     27
   SWEAR BY THOSE HORSEMEN, BY THOSE WOMEN . . . . . . .      637 BEN BULBEN          5
HORSE-PLAY
   I KNEW THAT HORSE-PLAY, KNEW IT FOR A MURDEROUS THING. . . 442 BLACK CENTAUR       4
HORSE'S
   AN OLD MAN CAUGHT THE HORSE'S HEAD . . . . . . . .         191 BAILE AILLINN      57
   RENDING THE HORSE'S FLANK.  KING EOCHAID REELED, . . . .   277 TWO KINGS          13
   RIPPED THROUGH THE HORSE'S FLANKS.  KING EOCHAID REELED,   277 TWO KINGS       V  13
   ON A FANTASTIC RIDE, MY HORSE'S FLANKS ARE SPURRED . . .   391 UNDER SATURN        6
   ON A FANTASTIC RIDE I SWEAR MY HORSE'S FLANKS WERE SPURRED 391 UNDER SATURN    V   6
HORSES    SEE SEA-HORSES
   THE FENIAN HORSES; ARMOUR TORN ASUNDER; . . . . . . .      43 OISIN 2           210
   THE HORSES OF THE FENIANS--TEARING ASUNDER . . . . . .      43 OISIN 2         V 210
   BETWEEN WOOD'S RIM AND THE HORSES OF THE SEA. . . . . .    108 CUCHULAIN SEA      34
   BETWEEN THE GAME AND THE HORSES OF THE SEA. . . . . . .    108 CUCHULAIN SEA   V  34
   THAT HE MAY FIGHT THE HORSES OF THE SEA." . . . . . .      111 CUCHULAIN SEA      81
   STARED ON THE HORSES OF THE SEA, AND HEARD . . . . . .     111 CUCHULAIN SEA      84
   TWO LOVE POEMS   THE SHADOWY HORSES . . . . . . . .        154 BELOVED PEACE   V   T
   I HEAR THE SHADOWY HORSES, THEIR LONG MANES A-SHAKE, . .   154 BELOVED PEACE       1
   THE HORSES OF DISASTER PLUNGE IN THE HEAVY CLAY, . . .     154 BELOVED PEACE       8
   THE HORSES OF DISASTER PLUNGE IN THE DESOLATE CLAY. . .    154 BELOVED PEACE   V   8
   I BECAME A RUSH THAT HORSES TREAD; . . . . . . . . .       177 PAST GREATNESS      6
   THE RIDERS UPON THE GALLOPING HORSES, . . . . . . .        266 GALWAY RACES        3
   THAT RIDE UPON HORSES. . . . . . . . . . . . . . .         266 GALWAY RACES       16
   THE RIDERS UPON THE SWIFT HORSES . . . . . . . . . .       266 GALWAY RACES    V   3
   RIDERS UPON THE SWIFT HORSES, . . . . . . . . . . .        266 GALWAY RACES    V   3
   THE RIDERS AND THE GALLOPING HORSES, . . . . . . . .       266 GALWAY RACES    V   3
   THAT COULD HAVE SHOWN HOW PURE-BRED HORSES . . . . . .     325 ROBERT GREGORY     36
   THAT COULD HAVE SHOWN HOW PUREBRED HORSES . . . . . .      325 ROBERT GREGORY V   36
   ABOVE THE CLOUDY SHOULDERS OF THE HORSES; . . . . . .      344 DAWN               12
   VIOLENCE UPON THE ROADS; VIOLENCE OF HORSES; . . . . .     432 NINETEEN 19       113
   COME PRAISE COLONUS' HORSES, AND COME PRAISE . . . . .     446 COLONUS PRAISE      1
   OF HORSES AND HORSES OF THE SEA, WHITE HORSES. . . . .     447 COLONUS PRAISE     32
   OF HORSES AND HORSES OF THE SEA, WHITE HORSES. . . . .     447 COLONUS PRAISE     32
   OF HORSES AND HORSES OF THE SEA, WHITE HORSES. . . . .     447 COLONUS PRAISE     32
   ARMOURED HORSES NEIGH . . . . . . . . . . . . . .          512 JANE ON GOD         9
   LOVERS OF HORSES AND OF WOMEN, SHALL, . . . . . . .        564 GYRES              19
   AMONG THE DOGS AND HORSES THAT UNDERSTAND MY TALK. . .     581 CURSE CROMWELL     30
HORSES'
   AND YET HIS MIND OUTRAN THE HORSES' FEET. . . . . . .      326 ROBERT GREGORY     64
HORTON'S
   HORTON'S THE FIRST I CALL.  HE LOVED STRANGE THOUGHT . .   471 ALL SOUL NIGHT     21
HOSE
   HE HAD KNEES THAT STUCK OUT OF HIS HOSE; . . . . . .       190 BAILE AILLINN      27
HOST    SEE BATTLE-HOST
   ERE FALL OF EVENING, MY MAILED HOST, . . . . . . . .        83 MAD KING GOLL  V   19
   OF ALL THIS HOST SO BOUND FROM CHILDHOOD ON." . . . . .    109 CUCHULAIN SEA      56
   IF MICHAEL, LEADER OF GOD'S HOST . . . . . . . . . .       112 ROSE OF PEACE       1
   THE FAERY HOST . . . . . . . . . . . . . . . . .           140 HOSTING SIDHE   V   T
   THE HOST . . . . . . . . . . . . . . . . . . .             140 HOSTING SIDHE   V   T
   THE HOST IS RIDING FROM KNOCKNAREA . . . . . . . . .       140 HOSTING SIDHE       1
   THE HOST IS RUSHING 'TWIXT NIGHT AND DAY, . . . . . .      141 HOSTING SIDHE      13
   THE HOST OF THE AIR . . . . . . . . . . . . . . .          143 HOST OF AIR         T
   FOR THESE WERE THE HOST OF THE AIR; . . . . . . . .        144 HOST OF AIR        26
   THE UNAPPEASABLE HOST . . . . . . . . . . . . . .          146 UNAPPEAS HOST       T
   O HEART THE WINDS HAVE SHAKEN, THE UNAPPEASABLE HOST . .   147 UNAPPEAS HOST      11
   AND HEART THE WINDS HAVE SHAKEN, THE UNAPPEASABLE HOST .   147 UNAPPEAS HOST      11
   AND HEAR THE WINDS HAVE SHAKEN, THE UNAPPEASABLE HOST .    147 UNAPPEAS HOST   V  11
   WITH THE LOUD HOST BEFORE THE SEA, . . . . . . . .         276 GREY ROCK         128
   MUST DRIVE THE ARABIAN HOST.  THE VOICE GREW STILL, . .    467 HARUN RASHID      145
   MADE DRIVE THE ARABIAN HOST.  THE VOICE GREW STILL, . .    467 HARUN RASHID    V 145
   BUT HE'D OBJECT TO THE HOST, . . . . . . . . . . .         473 ALL SOUL NIGHT     77
HOSTED
   "I ONLY OF THE RED BRANCH HOSTED NOW," . . . . . . .       109 CUCHULAIN SEA   V  55
HOSTING
   THE FLOOR OF ALMHUIN'S HOSTING HALL . . . . . . . .         13 OISIN 1           156
   THE FLOOR OF ALLEN'S HOSTING HALL . . . . . . . . .         13 OISIN 1         V 156
   THE HOSTING OF THE SIDHE . . . . . . . . . . . .           140 HOSTING SIDHE       T
   HE SEES THE FAIRY HOSTING MOVE . . . . . . . . . .         716 FAIRY DOCTOR        9
HOSTS
   IF MICHAEL, LEADER OF GOD'S HOSTS . . . . . . . . .        112 ROSE OF PEACE   V   1
```

```
                                                        PAGE    TITLE            LINE
HOT
    AND KISSED THE SCEPTRE WITH HOT LIPS, . . . . . . . . .   18  OISIN 1        V  258
    WITH THE HOT BLOOD OF YOUTH, OF LOVE CROSSED LONG AGO; . .  316  COLD HEAVEN       6
    IS HOT TO SHOW WHATEVER IT HAS FOUND, . . . . . . . .   340  SHEP GOATHERD      44
HOULIHAN
    OF CATHLEEN, THE DAUGHTER OF HOULIHAN. . . . . . . . .   207  HANRAHANS SONG      5
    OF CATHLEEN, THE DAUGHTER OF HOULIHAN. . . . . . . . .   207  HANRAHANS SONG     10
    IS CATHLEEN, THE DAUGHTER OF HOULIHAN. . . . . . . . .   208  HANRAHANS SONG     15
HOUND
    PASSED BY US, CHASED BY A PHANTOM HOUND . . . . . . . .    11  OISIN 1          140
    PASSED BY US, CHASED OF A PHANTOM HOUND . . . . . . . .    11  OISIN 1        V  140
    HIS TOOTHLESS HOUND AT HIS NERVELESS FEET, . . . . . .    26  OISIN 1        V  400
    THE YOUTH AND LADY AND THE DEER AND HOUND; . . . . . .    29  OISIN 2            4
    ONCE MORE--THE YOUTH AND LADY, DEER AND HOUND; . . . .    29  OISIN 2        V    2
    THE DEER AND THE HOUND, AND THE LADY AND YOUTH, . . . .    47  OISIN 3        V    3
    AND THEIR HOUND, AND THEIR HORSE, AND THEIR LOVE, . . .    59  OISIN 3          176
    WHO NEVER HEAR THE UNFORGIVING HOUND. . . . . . . . .    75  ANASHU VIJAYA     75
    WHO NEVER HEARD THE UNFORGIVING HOUND. . . . . . . . .    75  ANASHU VIJAYA  V  75
    BRING HOUND AND HUNTSMAN HERE, . . . . . . . . . . .    97  FOXHUNTER      V  10
    ONE BLIND HOUND ONLY LIES APART . . . . . . . . . . .    99  FOXHUNTER         41
    THE BLIND HOUND WITH A MOURNFUL DIN . . . . . . . . .    99  FOXHUNTER         45
    THE OLDEST HOUND WITH MOURNFUL DIN, . . . . . . . . .    99  FOXHUNTER      V  45
    I HAVE BEEN CHANGED TO A HOUND WITH ONE RED EAR; . . .   153  CHANGE BELOVED     2
    AND NOW MY CALLING IS BUT THE CALLING OF A HOUND; . . .   153  CHANGE BELOVED     8
    OF THE CROWNED MAGI; AND THE HOUND OF CU . . . . . . .   169  SECRET ROSE    V   9
    WHERE THE HOUND OF ULADH SAT BEFORE . . . . . . . . .   192  BAILE AILLINN     73
    HOLLO HIM ON WITH HORSE AND HOUND, . . . . . . . . .   272  GREY ROCK         35
    I CALL FOR SPADE AND HORSE AND HOUND. . . . . . . . .   275  GREY ROCK        105
    THE HORN'S SWEET NOTE AND THE TOOTH OF THE HOUND. . . .   380  SONGS FOOL 1      12
    THE HORN'S SWEET NOTE AND THE TOOTH OF THE HOUND. . . .   381  SONGS FOOL 2      14
    HOUND VOICE . . . . . . . . . . . . . . . . . . .   621  HOUND VOICE        T
    SO MANY YEARS COMPANIONED BY A HOUND, . . . . . . . .   621  HOUND VOICE        4
    GIVE TONGUE, PROCLAIM THEIR HIDDEN NAME--"HOUND VOICE." .   622  HOUND VOICE        7
    AND YET GAVE TONGUE. "HOUND VOICES" WERE THEY ALL. . . .   622  HOUND VOICE        9
    BUT HE'S A LYING HOUND! . . . . . . . . . . . . . .   636  BLACK TOWER       25
    A SIBYL, WITH FIERCE FACE AS OF A HOUND . . . . . . .   687  TWO TITANS         9
    A RED HOUND RUNNING FROM A SILVER ARROW. . . . . . . .   747  SHADOW WATER A     6
    I HAVE FORGOTTEN WHEREFORE. THE RED HOUND . . . . . .   747  SHADOW WATER A     8
    WERE THEY BUT LIFTED UP. THE RED HOUND IS FLED. . . . .   761  SHADOW WATER A   266
    A HOUND THAT HAD LAIN IN THE RED RUSHES . . . . . . .   761  SHADOW WATER A   278
    A RED-EARED HOUND FOLLOWS A HORNLESS DEER. . . . . . .   764  SHADOW WATER A   325
    THE PALE HOUND AND THE DEER WANDER FOR EVER . . . . .   764  SHADOW WATER A   330
    THE PALE HOUND AND THE DEER WANDER FOREVER . . . . . .   764  SHADOW WATER A V 330
HOUNDS    SEE DEER-HOUNDS SLEUTH-HOUNDS
    WE RODE IN SORROW, WITH STRONG HOUNDS THREE, . . . . .     2  OISIN 1        V  7C
    WHEN WE FOLLOWED A DEER WITH OUR BAYING HOUNDS, . . . .     3  OISIN 1           14
    AND THERE I WILL GIVE YOU A HUNDRED HOUNDS; . . . . .     8  OISIN 1           86
    THERE SHALT THOU HAVE, AND A HUNDRED HOUNDS . . . . .     8  OISIN 1        V  86
    I CHASED WITH HOUNDS THE FLYING DEER. . . . . . . . .    10  OISIN 1        V 121
    AND HOUNDS FOR CENTURIES DUST AND AIR. . . . . . . .    11  OISIN 1          131
    AND THE CRY OF THE HOUNDS ON THE HILLS OF OLD. . . . .    27  OISIN 1          407
    AND THEIR HOUNDS, AND THEIR STEEDS, AND THEIR LOVES, . .    59  OISIN 3        V 176
    BRING RODY AND HIS HOUNDS, . . . . . . . . . . . .    97  FOXHUNTER         10
    FOR LEADING AGED HOUNDS AND YOUNG . . . . . . . . .    98  FOXHUNTER         23
    AND NOW WITH AGED HOUNDS AND YOUNG . . . . . . . . .    98  FOXHUNTER      V  21
    HOUNDS ARE GAZING ON HIS FACE, . . . . . . . . . . .    99  FOXHUNTER         39
    AGED HOUNDS AND YOUNG. . . . . . . . . . . . . . .    99  FOXHUNTER         40
    THE HOUNDS WAIL FOR THE DEAD. . . . . . . . . . . .    99  FOXHUNTER         48
    THE HOUNDS ARE GAZING ON HIS FACE, . . . . . . . . .    99  FOXHUNTER      V  39
    AND HOUNDS ARE GAZING ON HIS FACE, . . . . . . . . .    99  FOXHUNTER      V  39
    THE OLD HOUNDS AND THE YOUNG. . . . . . . . . . . .    99  FOXHUNTER      V  40
    BOTH AGED HOUNDS AND YOUNG. . . . . . . . . . . . .    99  FOXHUNTER      V  40
    ARE OLD AND PUPPY HOUNDS; . . . . . . . . . . . . .    99  FOXHUNTER      V  44
    THE HOUNDS KEEN FOR THE DEAD. . . . . . . . . . . .    99  FOXHUNTER      V  48
    CAME UP OUT OF THE HOLE, AND RED-EARED HOUNDS . . . .   185  QUEEN MAEVE      117
    SHE HAD RIDDEN WELL TO HOUNDS. . . . . . . . . . . .   392  EASTER 1916    V  23
    A PACK OF HOUNDS AND NOT A PACK OF CARDS, . . . . . .   411  TOWER             69
    AND FIND OUR ANCIENT HOUNDS BEFORE THE DOOR, . . . . .   622  HOUND VOICE       16
    AND CHANTS OF VICTORY AMID THE ENCIRCLING HOUNDS. . . .   622  HOUND VOICE       21
    THAT LIVES AMONG THE WOODS OF THE DARK HOUNDS. . . . .   766  SHADOW WATER A   376
    WHEN THE DARK HOUNDS WERE LOOSED. COME TO THE ALE. . . .   766  SHADOW WATER A   379
    THEY WOULD CHANGE THEM INTO HOUNDS . . . . . . . . .   775  AGAINST WITCH     15
HOUR    SEE MOTH-HOUR DEATH-HOUR BIRTH-HOUR
    AND TANGLED CREEPERS EVERY HOUR . . . . . . . . . .    16  OISIN 1          223
    WHERE TANGLING CREEPERS EVERY HOUR . . . . . . . . .    16  OISIN 1        V 223
    AS THOUGH HIS HOUR WERE COME. WE SOUGHT THE PART . . .    37  OISIN 2          112
    AS THOUGH HIS HOUR WERE ON HIM. TO THE PART . . . . .    37  OISIN 2        V 112
    I WAITED HOUR BY HOUR, AND THE HIGH DOME . . . . . .    39  OISIN 2          147
    I WAITED HOUR BY HOUR, AND THE HIGH DOME . . . . . .    39  OISIN 2          147
    HOUR AFTER HOUR I WAITED, AND THE DOME . . . . . . .    39  OISIN 2        V 147
    HOUR AFTER HOUR I WAITED, AND THE DOME . . . . . . .    39  OISIN 2        V 147
    WITH WISDOM HOUR BY HOUR.--MAY WE TWO STAND, . . . . .    71  ANASHU VIJAYA      7
    WITH WISDOM HOUR BY HOUR.--MAY WE TWO STAND, . . . . .    71  ANASHU VIJAYA      7
    WITH WISDOM HOUR BY HOUR.--MAY WE TOO STAND, . . . . .    71  ANASHU VIJAYA  V   7
    WITH WISDOM HOUR BY HOUR.--MAY WE TOO STAND, . . . . .    71  ANASHU VIJAYA  V   7
    THE HOUR WHEN KAMA, FULL OF SLEEPY LAUGHTER, . . . . .    72  ANASHU VIJAYA     26
    THE HOUR WHEN KAMA, WITH A SUMPTUOUS SMILE, . . . . .    72  ANASHU VIJAYA  V  26
    HE IS A FAMOUS FISHER; HOUR BY HOUR . . . . . . . .    73  ANASHU VIJAYA     36
    HE IS A FAMOUS FISHER; HOUR BY HOUR . . . . . . . .    73  ANASHU VIJAYA     36
    THE HOUR OF THE WANING OF LOVE HAS BESET US, . . . . .    79  FALLING LEAVES     5
    TOGETHER IN THAT HOUR OF GENTLENESS . . . . . . . .    80  EPHEMERA           6
```

HOUR   (CONTINUED)
    FOR MY REMEMBERING HOUR IS DONE: . . . .   86 MAD KING GOLL   V   69
    "HE DIED AN HOUR AGO." . . . .   133 FR GILLIGAN   34
    DROWNING LOVE'S LONELY HOUR IN DEEP TWILIGHT OF REST, . . . 154 BELOVED PEACE   11
    A MORE DREAM-HEAVY HOUR THAN THIS: . . . .   156 FORGOT BEAUTY   17
    ENFOLD ME IN MY HOUR OF HOURS: WHERE THOSE . . . . .   169 SECRET ROSE   2
    THE HOUR OF THY GREAT WIND OF LOVE AND HATE. . . . .   170 SECRET ROSE   28
    SURELY THINE HOUR HAS COME, THY GREAT WIND BLOWS, . . .   170 SECRET ROSE   31
    WHO BUT AWAITS HIS HOUR TO SHOOT, STILL HANGS . . . .   198 SEVEN WOODS   13
    AT THE MOTH HOUR AND HID IT IN HER BOSOM. . . . . .   199 ARROW   V   6
    AND FROM THAT HOUR HE HAS WATCHED OVER NONE . . . .   220 HARP OF AENGUS   13
    TOWARDS THE HOUR FOR SPEAKING OF THE DEAD? . . . . .   276 TWO KINGS   V   D
    THE HOUR BEFORE DAWN . . . .   302 HOUR DAWN   T
    IN THE BAD HOUR BEFORE THE DAWN." . . . .   304 HOUR DAWN   55
    BUT THE HOUR WHEN YOU SHALL PASS AWAY . . . . . .   306 HOUR DAWN   96
    AND HAVING TALKED TO SOME LATE HOUR . . . .   324 ROBERT GREGORY   4
    OF SUN AND MOON THAT A GOOD HOUR . . . .   331 ROUND TOWER   11
    IS MEMORY OR FOREKNOWLEDGE OF THE HOUR . . . . . .   375 PHASES OF MOON   73
    AND WHAT ROUGH BEAST, ITS HOUR COME ROUND AT LAST, . .   402 SECOND COMING   21
    AND FOR AN HOUR I HAVE WALKED AND PRAYED . . . . .   403 FOR DAUGHTER   7
    I HAVE WALKED AND PRAYED FOR THIS YOUNG CHILD AN HOUR .   403 FOR DAUGHTER   9
    OR THAT OF THE HOUR . . . .   414 TOWER   139
    THROUGH TOO MUCH BUSINESS WITH THE PASSING HOUR, . . .   423 MY DESCENDANTS   11
    AWAIT THE HOUR OF WAR, ENTER THE SMALL, ...   461 HARUN RASHID   V   8
    I SAY THAT A DJINN SPOKE. A LIVELONG HOUR . . . .   467 HARUN RASHID   136
    I SAY THAT A DJIN SPOKE. A LIVE LONG HOUR . . . .   467 HARUN RASHID   V 136
    I SAY THAT A JINN SPOKE. A LIVE-LONG HOUR . . . .   467 HARUN RASHID   V 136
    SHOULD LAUGH AND WEEP AN HOUR UPON THE CLOCK. . . .   471 ALL SOUL NIGHT   20
    SHOULD LAUGH AND WEEP AN HOUR UPON THE CLOCK. . . .   474 ALL SOUL NIGHT   90
    SHOULD WEEP AND LAUGH AN HOUR UPON THE CLOCK. . . .   474 ALL SOUL NIGHT V 90
    A BLIND HERMIT RINGS THE HOUR. . . . .   484 SYMBOLS   2
    AND SCOLD FOR AN HOUR." . . . .   510 JANE JUDGMENT   9
    WHEN GONG AND CONCH DECLARE THE HOUR TO BLESS . . .   611 STATUES   23
    WHAT HOUR OF TERROR COMES TO TEST THE SOUL, ...   622 HOUND VOICE   11
    THE PREACHER WATCHING FOR THE EVIL HOUR TO PASS, . . .   686 LIFE   3
    THE HOUR OF INCANTATION COMES A-TIPTOE, ...   691 MOSADA 1   37
    YOUNG MOORISH GIRL, THY FINAL HOUR IS HERE: . . . .   701 MOSADA 3   63
    HAYNAU, THINE HOUR HAS COME, THY FOLLOWERS FAR . . .   715 FERENCZ RENYI 117
    THE MAN WHOSE HOUR OF DEATH DRAWS NIGH, ...   716 FAIRY DOCTOR   6
    "WAKEN, WAKEN, SLEEPY FISHERS: NO HOUR IS THIS FOR SLEEP,"   718 PHANTOM SHIP   7
    A FULL HOUR LONG, WHEN ROSE A FEATHER . . . . . .   728 PRIEST FAIRY   19
    THE PREACHER WATCHING FOR THE ILL HOUR TO PASS-- . . .   734 QUATRAIN APHOR   3
    THE PREACHER WATCHING FOR THE EVIL HOUR TO PASS, . . .   734 QUATRAIN APHOR V 3
    WEIGH THEM IN AN HOUR OF DREAMING, ...   737 IN FIRELIGHT   11
    THE YEARS THAT HAVE GONE OVER HER FROM THE HOUR . . .   760 SHADOW WATER A 256
    AND FROM THAT HOUR HE HAS WATCHED OVER NONE . . . .   763 SHADOW WATER A 308
    THAT COMES WITH LOVE, COMES MURMURING OF AN HOUR . . .   765 SHADOW WATER A 365
    "TILL THE SUN GOES DOWN AND AN HOUR OF THE CLOCK" . . .   779 GOING THE ROAD   7
HOURED   SEE TWELVE-HOURED
HOUR-GLASS
    I'LL PLAY YOU FOR YOUR OLD HOUR-GLASS. YOU SEE . . .   721 WITCH VIVIEN   36
HOURLY
    THE HOURLY KINDNESS, THE DAY'S COMMON SPEECH, ...   258 KING NO KING   14
HOUR'S   SEE HALF-HOUR'S
    EVEN A HALF HOUR'S NOTHINGNESS, ...   305 HOUR DAWN   V   70
HOURS
    AND LOVE, IN THE HOURS WHEN YOUTH HAS CEASED: . . . .   2 OISIN 1   V   7A
    I KNOW NOT IF DAYS PASSED OR HOURS, ...   11 OISIN 1   133
    I KNEW NOT IF DAYS PASSED OR HOURS, ...   11 OISIN 1   V 133
    AND, NOW OUR WANDERING HOURS WERE DONE, ...   14 OISIN 1   177
    AND ALL LISTLESS HOURS FEAR US, ...   21 OISIN 1   317
    OR HOURS PASSED BY, YET HOLD THE MORNING RAYS . . .   30 OISIN 2   20
    FLASHING--I KNOW NOT WERE IT HOURS OR DAYS, ...   30 OISIN 2   V 19B
    BUT SHE WHOSE HOURS OF TENDERNESS WERE GONE . . . .   38 OISIN 2   138
    THAT LACKEY THE WORN MOON IN MIDNIGHT HOURS, ...   41 OISIN 2   V 185A
    WERE WE DAYS LONG OR HOURS LONG IN RIDING, ...   47 OISIN 3   9
    ALL EMPTIED OF PURPLE HOURS AS A BEGGAR'S CLOAK IN THE   63 OISIN 3   219
        RAIN,
    HATE ON AND LOVE THROUGH UNREPINING HOURS. . . . .   80 EPHEMERA   22
    ABOVE THE TIDE OF HOURS, TROUBLE THE AIR, ...   114 ROSE OF BATTLE   3
    ABOVE THE TIDE OF HOURS, RISE ON THE AIR, ...   114 ROSE OF BATTLE V 3
    AND THE LONG DEW-DROPPING HOURS OF THE NIGHT, . . .   116 FAERY SONG   7
    FOR HOURS WHEN ALL MUST FADE LIKE DEW, ...   156 FORGOT BEAUTY   20
    ENFOLD ME IN MY HOUR OF HOURS: WHERE THOSE . . . . .   169 SECRET ROSE   2
    I SAID: "A LINE WILL TAKE US HOURS MAYBE: . . . . .   204 ADAMS CURSE   4
    HE DREADS THE WEIGHT OF MORTAL HOURS. . . . . . .   212 BLESS PSALTER   11
    AND FOR A DOZEN HOURS HAVE BEEN A PART . . . . .   230 SHADOW WATER B 171
    HE GAVE THE HOURS THEY HAD SET FREE . . . . . .   288 TO WEALTHY MAN   22
    FROM BITTEREST HOURS: . . . .   293 HELEN LIVED   6
    WITH PURPLE SANDALS SWEEP THE GRAVE-EYED HOURS-- . . .   705 REMEMBRANCE   5
    AND NUMBER THEIR DAYS AND THEIR HOURS-- . . . . .   707 FAIRY PEDANT   19
    TALKING HOURS SWIFTLY PASS: . . . .   727 LOVERS QUARREL   44
    HOW MANY HOURS TO DAYBREAK, BECAUSE LOVE . . . . .   767 SHADOW WATER A 405
HOUSE   SEE FARM-HOUSE COUNTING-HOUSE GUARD-HOUSE PUBLIC-HOUSE POT-HOUSE
    IN HIS OWN LEAFY FOREST HOUSE, ...   2 OISIN 1   V   7L
    IN HIS OWN LEAFY FOREST HOUSE . . . .   4 OISIN 1   37
    IN THE POPPY-HUNG HOUSE OF THE TWILIGHT FLUTED: . . .   8 OISIN 1   V 83
    A HOUSE OF WATTLES, CLAY, AND SKIN: . . . .   17 OISIN 1   249
    A FIRWOOD HOUSE, ALL COVERED OVER . . . .   17 OISIN 1   V 248
    IN THE HOUSE OF A CHILD, OF A FRIEND, OF A BROTHER. . .   26 OISIN 1   401
    IN THE HOUSE OF HIS FRIEND, OF HIS KIN, OF HIS BROTHER,   26 OISIN 1   V 405

	PAGE	TITLE		LINE
HOUSE (CONTINUED)				
AND THE ROOF FALLS IN OF HIS TUNNELLED HOUSE. • • • • •	27	OISIN 1	V	419
AND THE ROOF FALLS IN OF HIS TUNNELLED HOUSE. • • • • •	28	OISIN 1		423
• • • NO. NEITHER IN HOUSE OF A CANN • • • • • • • • •	50	OISIN 3	V	49
AND DWELL IN THE HOUSE OF THE FENIANS, BE THEY IN FLAMES OR AT FEAST.	63	OISIN 3		224
I WILL GO TO THE HOUSE OF THE FENIANS, BE THEY IN FLAMES OR AT FEAST.	63	OISIN 3	V	223
BUT TELL ALONE YOUR NAME AND HOUSE TO HIM • • • • • •	108	CUCHULAIN SEA	V	36
AND HE RAN TO THE DOOR OF HIS HOUSE: • • • • • • • •	145	HOST OF AIR	V	40C
THE HOUSE WHERE I WAS SAFE AND WARM: • • • • • • • •	151	HEART OF WOMAN		6
AND HIM WHO SOLD TILLAGE, AND HOUSE, AND GOODS, • • • •	170	SECRET ROSE		22
IN HER HIGH HOUSE AT CRUACHAN: THE LONG HEARTH, • • •	180	QUEEN MAEVE		11
HAD FILLED THE HOUSE WITH DRUID HEAVINESS: • • • • •	181	QUEEN MAEVE		40
WE SHADOWS, WHILE THEY UPROOT HIS EARTHY HOUSE, • • •	184	QUEEN MAEVE		94
WE SHADOWS, WHILE THEY UPROOT THE EARTHY HOUSE • • • •	184	QUEEN MAEVE	V	94
CAME TO THE THRESHOLD OF THE PAINTED HOUSE • • • • •	185	QUEEN MAEVE		108
WAS CARRIED TO THE GOODLY HOUSE • • • • • • • • •	192	BAILE AILLINN		72
OR THE DOOR-PILLARS OF ONE HOUSE, • • • • • • • • •	195	BAILE AILLINN		152
OR THE DOOR PILLARS OF ONE HOUSE. • • • • • • • • •	195	BAILE AILLINN	V	152
HE CARRIED EDAIN OFF FROM A KING'S HOUSE, • • • • • •	224	SHADOW WATER B		48
OR FUMBLING IN A DREAM ABOUT THE HOUSE? • • • • • •	230	SHADOW WATER B		174
UPON A HOUSE SHAKEN BY THE LAND AGITATION • • • • •	264	HOUSE SHAKEN		T
TO A CERTAIN COUNTRY HOUSE IN TIME OF CHANGE • • • •	264	HOUSE SHAKEN	V	T
UPON A THREATENED HOUSE • • • • • • • • • • • •	264	HOUSE SHAKEN		T
HOW SHOULD THE WORLD BE LUCKIER IF THIS HOUSE, • • • •	264	HOUSE SHAKEN		1
IN THEIR GREAT HOUSE AT SLIEVENAMON. • • • • • • •	271	GREY ROCK		15
HE RAN TOWARDS THE HOUSE HIS FATHERS BUILT • • • • •	279	TWO KINGS	V	45E
THE FIGHTING-MEN AND SERVANTS OF THIS HOUSE, • • • •	280	TWO KINGS		70
THE FIGHTING MEN AND SERVANTS OF THIS HOUSE, • • • •	280	TWO KINGS	V	70
TO AN OLD EMPTY WOODMAN'S HOUSE THAT'S HIDDEN • • • •	282	TWO KINGS		134
FOUND THAT OLD HOUSE, A SPUTTERING TORCH WITHIN, • • •	283	TWO KINGS		140
AND FOUND THE HOUSE, A SPUTTERING TORCH WITHIN, • • •	283	TWO KINGS	V	140
OF THEIR RETURN TO THAT ANCESTRAL HOUSE. • • • • •	286	TWO KINGS	V	218C
"AND GET A COMFORTABLE WIFE AND HOUSE • • • • • •	299	BEGGAR CRIED		5
AND NOT A HOUSE TO THE PLAIN'S EDGE, • • • • • • •	302	HOUR DAWN		10
A DOLL IN THE DOLL-MAKER'S HOUSE • • • • • • • • •	319	DOLLS		1
NOW THAT WE'RE ALMOST SETTLED IN OUR HOUSE • • • • •	323	ROBERT GREGORY		1
NOW THAT WE'VE ALMOST SETTLED IN OUR HOUSE • • • • •	323	ROBERT GREGORY	V	1
IN ALL LOVELY INTRICACIES OF A HOUSE • • • • • • •	327	ROBERT GREGORY		74
SHE GOES ABOUT HER HOUSE ERECT AND CALM • • • • • •	340	SHEP GOATHERD		35
BUT LEFT THE HOUSE AS IN HIS FATHER'S TIME • • • • •	341	SHEP GOATHERD		53
I HAVE GONE ABOUT THE HOUSE, GONE UP AND DOWN • • • •	350	HER PRAISE		2
WILL COME FROM THE HOUSE, AND SAY— • • • • • • •	364	END OF DAY		6
A PRAYER ON GOING INTO MY HOUSE • • • • • • • • •	371	ON GOING HOUSE		T
OR, THE HOUSE DOOR LEFT UNSHUT, • • • • • • • • •	380	SONGS FOOL 1		10
IN CORMAC'S RUINED HOUSE. • • • • • • • • • • •	384	VISION ROBART		68
AND MAY HER BRIDEGROOM BRING HER TO A HOUSE • • • •	405	FOR DAUGHTER		73
AND MAY HER BRIDE-GROOM BRING HER TO A HOUSE • • • •	405	FOR DAUGHTER	V	73
ON THE FOUNDATIONS OF A HOUSE, OR WHERE • • • • • •	409	TOWER		18
AN ANCIENT BANKRUPT MASTER OF THIS HOUSE. • • • • •	412	TOWER		80
AND MAYBE THE GREAT-GRANDSON OF THAT HOUSE, • • • •	418	ANCEST HOUSES		23
MY HOUSE • • • • • • • • • • • • • • • • •	419	MY HOUSE		T
WHEN IT WAS FORGED. IN SATO'S HOUSE, • • • • • • •	421	MY TABLE		9
FOR AN OLD NEIGHBOUR'S FRIENDSHIP CHOSE THE HOUSE • •	423	MY DESCENDANTS		21
COME BUILD IN THE EMPTY HOUSE OF THE STARE. • • • •	424	STARES NEST		5
A MAN IS KILLED, OR A HOUSE BURNED. • • • • • • •	425	STARES NEST		8
COME BUILD IN THE EMPTY HOUSE OF THE STARE. • • • •	425	STARES NEST		10
COME BUILD IN THE EMPTY HOUSE OF THE STARE. • • • •	425	STARES NEST		15
COME BUILD IN THE EMPTY HOUSE OF THE STARE. • • • •	425	STARES NEST		20
THROUGH THE GREAT GALLERY OF THE TREASURE HOUSE • • •	461	HARUN RASHID		5
"I HAVE BROUGHT A SLENDER BRIDE INTO THE HOUSE: • • •	463	HARUN RASHID		49
PERCHED IN SOME WINDOW OF HER MOTHER'S HOUSE • • • •	466	HARUN RASHID		106
AND SWEPT THE HOUSE AND SANG ABOUT HER WORK • • • •	468	HARUN RASHID		148
WALKED THROUGH THE HOUSE. UNNOTICED AND UNFELT • • •	468	HARUN RASHID		153
AND ONCE AGAIN SHE ROSE AND SWEPT THE HOUSE • • • •	468	HARUN RASHID		159
IMMENSE MIRACULOUS HOUSE • • • • • • • • • • •	472	ALL SOUL NIGHT		38
IN GRATTAN'S HOUSE. MY GREAT-GRANDFATHER SHARED • •	486	SEVEN SAGES		2
UPON AN AGED WOMAN AND HER HOUSE, • • • • • • • •	488	COOLE PARK 29		2
BEFORE THEIR EYES A HOUSE • • • • • • • • • • •	512	JANE ON GOD		13
SWEETENS THE LITTLE HALF-WAY HOUSE • • • • • • •	567	LAPIS LAZULI		48
SWEETEN THE LITTLE HALFWAY HOUSE • • • • • • • •	567	LAPIS LAZULI	V	48
IF STRANGE MEN COME FROM THE HOUSE • • • • • • •	568	SWEET DANCER		8
MIDNIGHT, AN OLD HOUSE • • • • • • • • • • • •	575	ACRE OF GRASS		5
A SMALL OLD HOUSE, WIFE, DAUGHTER, SON, • • • • • •	577	WHAT THEN		12
NOTHING BUT CROMWELL'S HOUSE AND CROMWELL'S MURDEROUS CREW.	580	CURSE CROMWELL		2
I CAME ON A GREAT HOUSE IN THE MIDDLE OF THE NIGHT, • • •	581	CURSE CROMWELL		25
AND THERE'S NO LUCK ABOUT A HOUSE • • • • • • • •	584	GHOST ROG CASE		27
NOW I AM IN THE PUBLIC HOUSE AND LEAN UPON THE WALL, • •	593	PILGRIM	V	21
A SMALL FORGOTTEN HOUSE THAT'S SET • • • • • • •	606	SONGS BURDEN 2		3
WENT TO THE SACRED HOUSE AND STOOD BETWEEN • • • • •	609	IN TARAS HALLS		11
SUMMONED THE GENERATIONS OF HIS HOUSE, • • • • • •	609	IN TARAS HALLS		19
THAT WHEREBY A HOUSE LAY WRECKED? • • • • • • • •	632	MAN AND ECHO		16
THAT WHEREBY A HOUSE WAS WRECKED? • • • • • • • •	632	MAN AND ECHO	V	16
EVEN FROM BOYHOOD, IN MY FATHER'S HOUSE, • • • • • •	683	SEEKER		48
IN HIS OWN HOUSE OR 'MONG THE MERCHANTS GREY, • • • •	693	MOSADA		87
RINGED ROUND AND FONDLED, A BROWN FARM HOUSE SEES. • •	710	FERENCZ RENYI	V	23
TO HIS OWN HOUSE DID HIM BETAKE, • • • • • • • •	725	LEGEND		30
AT THE HOUSE OF WEARY MEN • • • • • • • • • • •	727	LOVERS QUARREL		51
AND CAME AND DWELT IN HIS OWN HOUSE, • • • • • • •	742	EARL PAUL		67
GIVE ME A HUNDRED SHEEP. GIVE ME A HOUSE • • • • • •	758	SHADOW WATER A		220

395

	PAGE	TITLE		LINE
HOUSE (CONTINUED)				
AND ONE IN THE OLD GRAY HOUSE . . .	771	SPINNING SONG		4
ONE LIVES IN THE HOUSE OF THE SUN, ...	771	SPINNING SONG		6
AND ONE IN THE HOUSE OF THE MOON, ...	771	SPINNING SONG		7
I HAVE SPUN IN THE HOUSE THIS NIGHT!	771	SPINNING SONG		13
RUIN ON A GREAT KING'S HOUSE	775	AGAINST WITCH		3
TO THE COMFORTABLE DOOR OF HIS HOUSE.	780	WELL AND TREE		6
I HAVE MET IN A MAN'S HOUSE	785	YOUR HEART		3
A HOUSE, A SWORD, A SHIP, A MASK.	788	BRAVEST ASK		2
HOUSEHOLD				
THEN MUSE THEY ON THE HOUSEHOLD WOOL INTENT, ...	32	OISIN 2	V	55
. . . NO, NEITHER IN HOUSEHOLD OF CAN, ...	50	OISIN 3	V	49
AND TELL OF YOUR GOODLY HOUSEHOLD AND THE GOODLY WORKS OF YOUR HANDS,	51	OISIN 3		62
TO MAEVE AND TO MAEVE'S HOUSEHOLD, OWING ALL	187	QUEEN MAEVE		147
I BADE HIM GO WHEN ALL HIS HOUSEHOLD SLEPT	282	TWO KINGS		133
THE WOMEN OF HIS HOUSEHOLD WERE ASLEEP, ...	282	TWO KINGS	V	133
OF THE HOUSEHOLD SPIES!	536	PARTING		3
BUT IN THAT WOMAN, IN THAT HOUSEHOLD WHERE	603	GALLERY REVIS		34
HOUSES				
AND THE GAUNT HOUSES PUT ON MAJESTY!	292	TO A SHADE		7
EIGHTEENTH-CENTURY HOUSES.	392	EASTER 1916		4
ANCESTRAL HOUSES	417	ANCEST HOUSES		T
MEDITATIONS IN TIME OF CIVIL WAR ANCESTRAL HOUSES . .	417	ANCEST HOUSES	V	T
I LIVED AMONG GREAT HOUSES, ...	626	STATES HOLIDAY		1
SCARCE THE OLD AND WIZEN HOUSES HAD THEIR DOORS AND WINDOWS SHUT.	718	PHANTOM SHIP		5
SCARCE THE OLD AND WIZENED HOUSES HAD THEIR DOORS AND WINDOWS SHUT.	718	PHANTOM SHIP	V	5
HOVER				
DESOLATE WINDS THAT HOVER IN THE FLAMING WEST!	147	UNAPPEAS HOST		8
THAT SAW YOUNG NIAMH HOVER WITH LOVE-LORN FACE	162	ASKS FORGIVE		13
THEY HOVER OVER THE MASTHEAD AWHILE	233	SHADOW WATER B		246
TWO HOVER THERE TOGETHER, AND ONE SAYS, ...	753	SHADOW WATER A		142
HOVERING				
AMID THE HOVERING, PITEOUS, PENITENTIAL THRONG." . . .	173	SPEAKS HEARERS		8
WERE HOVERING OVER THE HARP-STRINGS	195	BAILE AILLINN		141
WERE HOVERING OVER THE HARP STRINGS	195	BAILE AILLINN	V	141
AND ALL THEIR HELMS OF SILVER HOVERING SIDE BY SIDE, . .	318	MAGI		5
HOVERING OVER THE WOOD	349	HAWK		10
OF THE HOVERING THING NIGHT BROUGHT ME.	390	IMAGE PAST		42
A RUSH, A SUDDEN WHEEL, AND HOVERING STILL	441	LEDA AND SWAN	V	1
HOVERS				
HE HOVERS ABOVE THE MAST AND WAITS HIS KIND!	753	SHADOW WATER A		135
HOWEVER				
HOWEVER THEY MAY TAKE IT, ...	520	HIS BARGAIN		7
HOWL				
BETWEEN THEM A GATEWAY OF BRASS, AND THE HOWL OF THE ANGELS WHO FELL.	61	OISIN 3		200
AND EVERY WINDY QUARTER HOWL	405	FOR DAUGHTER		71
HOWLED				
HOWLED, MIAU-D, BARKED, BRAYED, BELLED, YELLED, CRIED, CROWED,	387	SOLOMON WITCH		8
TO WHERE THE DAMNED HAVE HOWLED AWAY THEIR HEARTS, . . .	474	ALL SOUL NIGHT		95
BUT I WOKE IN AN OLD RUIN THAT THE WINDS HOWLED THROUGH!	581	CURSE CROMWELL		28
HOWLING				
ONCE MORE THE STORM IS HOWLING, AND HALF HID	403	FOR DAUGHTER		1
HOWLS				
ARE THE MOB THAT HOWLS AT THE DOOR!	554	CHURCH STATE		10
HOWTH				
THE BLINDS DRAWN UP"! MAUD GONNE AT HOWTH STATION WAITING A TRAIN,	578	LOFTY THINGS		10
HUCKSTER'S				
THAT HAS NOT PASSED THROUGH ANY HUCKSTER'S LOIN, ...	269	PARDON FATHERS		8
HUDDLE				
THEY HUDDLE FROM MAN'S PONDERING MIND, ...	138	TO IRELAND	V	26
HUDDLING				
AND YONDER HUDDLING BLACKNESS DRAWETH NIGH--	663	ISLE STAT II 2		15
HUDDON				
"HUDDON AND DUDDON AND DANIEL O'LEARY, ...	529	TOM LUNATIC		7
HUDDON, DUDDON AND DANIEL O'LEARY	787	HUDDON DUDDON		1
HUDDON, DUDDON AND DANIEL O'LEARY	787	HUDDON DUDDON		6
HUDDON, DUDDON AND DANIEL O'LEARY	787	HUDDON DUDDON		11
HUEGEL				
VON HUEGEL	499	VACILLATION	V	T
MUST WE PART, VON HUEGEL, THOUGH MUCH ALIKE, FOR WE . . .	503	VACILLATION		78
SO GET YOU GONE, VON HUEGEL, THOUGH WITH BLESSINGS ON YOUR HEAD.	503	VACILLATION		89
HUES				
DREAMING OF HER OWN MELTING HUES, ...	13	OISIN 1		162
AND DREAMS OF HER OWN MELTING HUES, ...	13	OISIN 1	V	162
HUGE				
HUGE FORMS OF STONE! BETWEEN THE LIDS OF ONE	31	OISIN 2	V	37
SAID NIAM. "AY, AND HUGE. WHEN YE HAVE LED	35	OISIN 2	V	89
BREWED BY THE SEA-GODS, FROM HUGE CUPS THAT LAY	41	OISIN 2		189
BREWED OF THE SEA-GODS, FROM HUGE CUPS THAT LAY	41	OISIN 2	V	189
BREWED BY THE SEA GODS, FROM HUGE CUPS THAT LAY	41	OISIN 2	V	189
AND EACH OF THE HUGE WHITE CREATURES WAS HUGER THAN FOURSCORE MEN!	49	OISIN 3		33
AND EACH OF THE HUGE WHITE CREATURES WAS HUGER THAN FOUR-SCORE MEN!	49	OISIN 3	V	33

```
                                                          PAGE     TITLE          LINE
HUGE   (CONTINUED)
      AND THE CHIEF OF THE HUGE WHITE CREATURES, . . . . . . .      50 OISIN 3            43
      AND BEFORE I WENT BY THEM SO HUGE AND SO SPEEDY WITH EYES      59 OISIN 3        V  169
         SO BRIGHT,
      THEY COME WHERE SOME HUGE WATCHER IS, . . . . . . . .         196 BAILE AILLINN     168
      WOULD RISE OF A SUDDEN, OR A WAVE SO HUGE . . . . . .         236 SHADOW WATER B    310
HUGER
      AND EACH OF THE HUGE WHITE CREATURES WAS HUGER THAN            49 OISIN 3            33
         FOURSCORE MEN,
      AND EACH OF THE HUGE WHITE CREATURES WAS HUGER THAN            49 OISIN 3        V   33
         FOUR-SCORE MEN,
HUGH
      AND BECAUSE I WENT BY THEM SO HUGH AND SO SPEEDY WITH EYES     59 OISIN 3           169
         SO BRIGHT,
      IMPETUOUS MEN, SHAWE-TAYLOR AND HUGH LANE, . . . . . .        489 COOLE PARK 29      14
      HUGH LANE, "ONLIE BEGETTER" OF ALL THESE, . . . . . .         602 GALLERY REVIS      22
HUGS
      WHAT WOMAN HUGS HER INFANT THERE? . . . . . . . . . .         625 NATIVITY            1
      HUGS AND PETS AND PATS YON NEWT, . . . . . . . . . .          727 LOVERS QUARREL     27
HULL
      CEASE THE SAILS THEIR FLAPPING UPROAR, AND THE HULL NO        719 PHANTOM SHIP       18
         LONGER ROLLS.
      CEASE THE SAILS, THEIR FLAPPING UPROAR TO THE HULL           719 PHANTOM SHIP    V  18
         NO LONGER ROLLS.
HUM
      HUM IN THE LIME-TREE FLOWERS; AND PUT AWAY . . . . . .        198 SEVEN WOODS         3
      HUM IN THE LIME TREE FLOWERS; AND PUT AWAY . . . . . .        198 SEVEN WOODS     V   3
HUMAN      SEE SUPER-HUMAN
      BUT WE RODE OUT FROM THE HUMAN LANDS. . . . . . . . .          10 OISIN 1           114
      THE FENIANS ON THE HUMAN GROUND . . . . . . . . . . .          10 OISIN 1        V 114C
      MY HUMAN SORROW HER WHITE ARMS WOUND. . . . . . . . .          11 OISIN 1           138
      MY HUMAN SADNESS FAY ARMS WOUND. . . . . . . . . . .           11 OISIN 1        V 138
      BUT WHEN I SANG OF HUMAN JOY . . . . . . . . . . . .           17 OISIN 1           234
      THAN THIS STRANGE HUMAN BARD," HE CRIED, . . . . . . .         17 OISIN 1           239
      AND WHEN I SANG OF HUMAN JOY . . . . . . . . . . . .           17 OISIN 1        V 234
      THAT HIDES US FROM ALL HUMAN SPYING, . . . . . . . .           22 OISIN 1        V 338A
      THE HUMAN SADNESS DAWNS ONCE MORE!" . . . . . . . . .          25 OISIN 1        V 381
      ON THE OLD SORROWS OF HIS HUMAN DAYS. . . . . . . . .          29 OISIN 2        V  12
      IT BRINGS NO SHAME UPON A HUMAN HEAD . . . . . . . .           35 OISIN 2        V 90A
      AND DEAD IS ALL THEIR HUMAN TRUTH. . . . . . . . . .           66 HAPPY SHEPHERD     34
      COME AWAY, O HUMAN CHILD! . . . . . . . . . . . . .            87 STOLEN CHILD        9
      COME AWAY, O HUMAN CHILD! . . . . . . . . . . . . .            87 STOLEN CHILD       24
      COME AWAY, O HUMAN CHILD! . . . . . . . . . . . . .            88 STOLEN CHILD       38
      FOR HE COMES, THE HUMAN CHILD, . . . . . . . . . . .           88 STOLEN CHILD       50
      COME, O HUMAN CHILD! . . . . . . . . . . . . . . .             88 STOLEN CHILD    V  38
      THERE WAS NO HUMAN KEENING, . . . . . . . . . . . .            93 FATHER OHART       29
      AND NOW AT LAST YOU WEAR A HUMAN SHAPE, . . . . . . .         102 FERGUS DRUID        6
      AND NOW AT LAST YOU TAKE ON HUMAN SHAPE—— . . . . . .         102 FERGUS DRUID    V   6
      AT HUMAN TYRANNY, . . . . . . . . . . . . . . . . .           131 OLD PENSIONER      10
      FROM HUMAN THOUGHT, AS HARES AND MICE AND CONEYS . . .        218 WOODS OF COOLE     31
      WITH HUMAN VOICES. O I CAN HEAR THEM NOW. . . . . . .         247 SHADOW WATER B    522
      THIS HUMAN LIFE BLOTTED FROM MEMORY, . . . . . . . .          285 TWO KINGS         198
      FOR THERE'S NO HUMAN LIFE AT THE FULL OR THE DARK. . .        373 PHASES OF MOON     35
      NOR ANY HUMAN SIGHT WITHIN IT . . . . . . . . . . .           389 SOLOMON WITCH      41
      WITH HUMAN LOVE. . . . . . . . . . . . . . . . . .            436 FOR MY SON         32
      HUMAN DIGNITY . . . . . . . . . . . . . . . . . .             452 HUMAN DIGNITY       T
      FROM HUMAN DIGNITY. . . . . . . . . . . . . . . . .           452 HUMAN DIGNITY      12
      MAKE HUMAN INTERCOURSE GROW LESS AND LESS, . . . . . .        473 ALL SOUL NIGHT     75
      SERVED HUMAN LIBERTY. . . . . . . . . . . . . . . .           493 SWIFTS EPITAPH      6
      THE FURY AND THE MIRE OF HUMAN VEINS. . . . . . . . .         497 BYZANTIUM           8
      IT IS OF GOD AND PASSES HUMAN WIT. . . . . . . . . .          558 RIBH CHRISTIAN      2
      THEY SAY IT IS MORE HUMAN . . . . . . . . . . . . .           599 STONE CROSS        19
      "FORGETTING HUMAN WORDS," A GRAVE DEEP FACE. . . . . .        603 GALLERY REVIS      49
      HUMAN, SUPERHUMAN, A BIRD'S ROUND EYE, . . . . . . .          618 BRONZE HEAD         2
      HUMAN, SUPER-HUMAN, A BIRD'S ROUND EYE, . . . . . . .         618 BRONZE HEAD     V   2
      THEY SANG, BUT HAD NOR HUMAN TUNES NOR WORDS, . . . . .       635 CUCHULAIN COMF     23
      BACK IN THE HUMAN MIND AGAIN. . . . . . . . . . . .           637 BEN BULBEN         24
      OF HUMAN SORROW LET THEM MORALIZE; . . . . . . . . .          663 ISLE STAT II 2     31
      UNTOUCHED OF HUMAN JOY OR HUMAN LOVE? . . . . . . . .         684 SEEKER             65
      UNTOUCHED OF HUMAN JOY OR HUMAN LOVE? . . . . . . . .         684 SEEKER             65
      THE WRINKLED SQUANDERER OF HUMAN WEALTH. . . . . . .          720 WITCH VIVIEN       16
      HIS TOO HUMAN BREAST. . . . . . . . . . . . . . . .           786 YOUR HEART         21
HUMBLER
      OR THE HUMBLER WORM, I CLIMBED BEN BULBEN'S BACK . . . .      409 TOWER               9
HUMBLY
      THAT ALL MEN EVERMORE MAY HUMBLY BOW . . . . . . . .          688 TWO TITANS         49
      BENDING HUMBLY EVERY KNEE, . . . . . . . . . . . . .          726 LOVERS QUARREL     14
HUMID
      I PASSED ALONG THE WATER'S EDGE BELOW THE HUMID TREES, . .     76 INDIAN ON GOD       1
HUMILITY
      FOUND PRIDE ESTABLISHED IN HUMILITY, . . . . . . . .          489 COOLE PARK 29      15
      OF ALL THAT PRIDE AND THAT HUMILITY? . . . . . . . .          602 GALLERY REVIS      29
HUMMING
      GO GATHER BY THE HUMMING SEA . . . . . . . . . . . .          66 HAPPY SHEPHERD     35
      AND HUMMING SANDS, WHERE WINDY SURGES WEND, . . . . .         68 SAD SHEPHERD        4
HUMMING-SEA
      GO GATHER BY THE HUMMING-SEA . . . . . . . . . . . .          66 HAPPY SHEPHERD V   35
HUMOROUS
      "AND CANNOT HAVE A HUMOROUS HAPPY SPEECH." . . . . . .        300 BEGGAR CRIED       16
      A HUMOROUS, UNAMBITIOUS MAN, . . . . . . . . . . . .          361 ALF POLLEXFEN      25
```

HUMP
    UNDER THIS HUMP, GOD TRIES EACH MAN . . . . 379 SAINT HUNCH   5
HUNCH
    THE HERON'S HUNCH UPON HIS BACK, ... 508 JANE BISHOP   19
HUNCHBACK
    HUNCHBACK AND SAINT AND FOOL ARE THE LAST CRESCENTS. . . . 377 PHASES OF MOON   118
    "HUNCHBACK AND SAINT AND FOOL," AND THAT THEY CAME . . . 377 PHASES OF MOON   132
    THE SAINT AND THE HUNCHBACK . . . . 379 SAINT HUNCH   T
HUNDRED
    AND THERE I WILL GIVE YOU A HUNDRED HOUNDS: . . . . . . 8 OISIN 1   86
    AND A HUNDRED ROBES OF MURMURING SILK, ... 8 OISIN 1   88
    AND A HUNDRED CALVES AND A HUNDRED SHEEP . . . . . . 8 OISIN 1   89
    AND A HUNDRED CALVES AND A HUNDRED SHEEP . . . . . . 8 OISIN 1   89
    AND A HUNDRED SPEARS AND A HUNDRED BOWS, ... 8 OISIN 1   91
    AND A HUNDRED SPEARS AND A HUNDRED BOWS, ... 8 OISIN 1   91
    WHILE A HUNDRED YOUTHS, MIGHTY OF LIMB, ... 8 OISIN 1   94
    AND A HUNDRED STEEDS, TUMULTUOUS-FOOTED, ... 8 OISIN 1   V 85A
    THERE SHALT THOU HAVE, AND A HUNDRED HOUNDS . . . . . 8 OISIN 1   V 86
    AND A HUNDRED ROBES OF THE SOFTEST SILK . . . . . . 8 OISIN 1   V 88
    AND A HUNDRED SWORDS AND A HUNDRED BOWS: . . . . . . 8 OISIN 1   V 91
    AND A HUNDRED SWORDS AND A HUNDRED BOWS: . . . . . . 8 OISIN 1   V 91
    AND A HUNDRED MAIDENS WISE AND YOUNG, ... 8 OISIN 1   V 94
    AND A HUNDRED LADIES, MERRY AS BIRDS, ... 9 OISIN 1   96
    AND A HUNDRED MAIDENS, MERRY AS BIRDS, ... 9 OISIN 1   V 96
    AND A HUNDRED YOUTHS, WHOSE LIMBS ARE STRUNG . . . . 9 OISIN 1   V 97
    O PATRICK! FOR A HUNDRED YEARS . . . . 23 OISIN 1   343
    O PATRICK! FOR A HUNDRED YEARS . . . . 23 OISIN 1   346
    O PATRICK! FOR A HUNDRED YEARS . . . . 23 OISIN 1   351
    O PATRICK! FOR A HUNDRED YEARS . . . . 23 OISIN 1   356
    A HUNDRED YEARS I CHASED THE BOAR, ... 23 OISIN 1   V 344
    OH, PATRICK, THERE A HUNDRED SEASONS . . . . 23 OISIN 1   V 345B
    AND TWICE A HUNDRED WERE THE VASSALS . . . . 23 OISIN 1   V 345E
    OH, PATRICK, THERE A HUNDRED YEARS, ... 23 OISIN 1   V 346
    WITH ME IN HER WHITE ARMS A HUNDRED YEARS . . . . . 30 OISIN 2   17
    A HUNDRED SEASONS: FOR A SOUND OF TEARS . . . . . . 30 OISIN 2   V 18
    THAT OLD, SEA-WEEDY, SQUARED, THREE HUNDRED FEET . . . 31 OISIN 2   V 30C
    A HUNDRED HORSEMEN ON THE BASALT FLOOR . . . . . . 36 OISIN 2   102
    WHERETHROUGH A HUNDRED HORSEMEN ON THE FLOOR . . . . 36 OISIN 2   V 102
    HIS NEW-HEALED SHAPE: AND FOR A HUNDRED YEARS . . . . 44 OISIN 2   221
    AN ENDLESS WAR. THE HUNDRED YEARS HAD CEASED: . . . 44 OISIN 2   224
    HIS HEALED SHAPE: AND FOR A HUNDRED YEARS . . . . . 44 OISIN 2   V 221
    HIS NEW HEALED SHAPE: AND FOR A HUNDRED YEARS . . . 44 OISIN 2   V 221
    AND MY YEARS THREE HUNDRED FELL ON ME, ... 60 OISIN 3   191
    THAT MOANS AND SIGHS A HUNDRED DAYS: . . . . 78 INDIAN TO LOVE   17
    AND TILL A HUNDRED MORNS HAD FLOWERED RED . . . . . 170 SECRET ROSE   17
    WHERE MANY HUNDRED SQUIRRELS ARE AS HAPPY . . . . . 217 WOODS OF COOLE   5
    NO, NOR WITH A HUNDRED MEN LIKE YOU . . . . 225 SHADOW WATER B V 74
    IF THERE BE HALF A HUNDRED MORE, WHAT MATTER? . . . . 245 SHADOW WATER B   476
    I'D PROMISED HIM TWO HUNDRED YEARS, ... 275 GREY ROCK   98
    FROM NINETEEN HUNDRED NINE OR TEN, PAVLOVA'S HAD THE CRY, 354 HIS PHOENIX   11
    THREE HUNDRED YEARS BEFORE THE FALL, ... 388 SOLOMON WITCH   11
    SCARED BY THE SPLASHING OF A HUNDRED COWS. . . . . . 419 MY HOUSE   V 10
    IT LAY FIVE HUNDRED YEARS. . . . . 421 MY TABLE   11
    NINETEEN HUNDRED AND NINETEEN . . . . 428 NINETEEN 19   T
    FIVE HUNDRED YEARS AGO, ABOUT IT LIE . . . . 478 SELF AND SOUL   26
    UPON A HUNDRED THOUSAND STAGES, ... 566 LAPIS LAZULI   23
    HE BADE, HIS HUNDRED AND FIRST YEAR AT END, ... 609 IN TARAS HALLS   19
    HAD HOOTED FOR AN HUNDRED YEARS, ... 670 ISLE STAT II 3   116
    AND TO GIVE YOU BESIDES A HUNDRED SHIELDS, ... 756 SHADOW WATER A   185
    A HUNDRED SWORDS, A HUNDRED DRINKING-BOWLS. . . . . . 756 SHADOW WATER A   186
    A HUNDRED SWORDS, A HUNDRED DRINKING-BOWLS. . . . . . 756 SHADOW WATER A   186
    BY SUN AND MOON AND A HUNDRED GODS AS WELL, ... 756 SHADOW WATER A   189
    I PROMISE YOU A HUNDRED DRINKING BOWLS, ... 756 SHADOW WATER A V 187
    A HUNDRED SHIELDS OF BRASS, A HUNDRED SWORDS, ... 756 SHADOW WATER A V 188
    A HUNDRED SHIELDS OF BRASS, A HUNDRED SWORDS, ... 756 SHADOW WATER A V 188
    A HUNDRED OXEN AND A HUNDRED SHEEP, ... 756 SHADOW WATER A V 189
    A HUNDRED OXEN AND A HUNDRED SHEEP, ... 756 SHADOW WATER A V 189
    GIVE ME A HUNDRED SHEEP. GIVE ME A HOUSE . . . . . 758 SHADOW WATER A   220
HUNDREDS
    WHEN WE ARE HIGH AND AIRY HUNDREDS SAY . . . . . . 265 ABBEY THEATRE   2
    WHILE THOSE SAME HUNDREDS MOCK ANOTHER DAY . . . . . 265 ABBEY THEATRE   4
    WHEN HUNDREDS STOOD ABOUT TO SEE . . . . 740 EARL PAUL   27
HUNDREDTH
    CHAINED WAS SHE. ON THEIR WINGS THE HUNDREDTH YEAR . . . 34 OISIN 2   V 76
    AN ENDLESS WAR. THE HUNDREDTH YEAR HAD CEASED. . . . 44 OISIN 2   V 224
    GIDDY WITH HIS HUNDREDTH YEAR, ... 298 THREE HERMITS   6
    GIDDY WITH HIS HUNDREDTH YEAR, ... 299 THREE HERMITS   31
    MY HUNDREDTH YEAR IS AT AN END. I THINK . . . . . . 609 IN TARAS HALLS   3
HUNDRED-THROATED
    HUNDRED-THROATED MORN IS SINGING, ... 647 ISLE STAT I 1   70
HUNDRED-YEAR-OLD
    A HUNDRED-YEAR-OLD MEMORY TO THE POOR: . . . . . . 269 PARDON FATHERS   6
HUNG   SEE POPPY-HUNG
    THE MIST-DROPS HUNG ON THE FRAGRANT TREES, ... 2 OISIN 1   V 7F
    AND IN THE BLOSSOMS HUNG THE BEES. . . . . 2 OISIN 1   V 7G
    HUNG, LIKE METEORS OF RED LIGHT, ... 21 OISIN 1   V 306
    HUNG FROM THE MORNING STAR: WHEN THESE MILD WORDS . . . 32 OISIN 2   49
    SHOUTED, AND HAILED HIM: HE HUNG THERE A STAR, . . . 36 OISIN 2   107
    SHOUTED AND HAILED HIM. STILL HE HUNG CONTENT, . . . 36 OISIN 2   V 107
    THAT WOMAN FOUND 'A RING HUNG ON THE WALL, ... 37 OISIN 2   120
    THAT MAIDEN FOUND A RING HUNG ON THE WALL, ... 37 OISIN 2   V 120

HUNG   (CONTINUED)
  HUNG IN THE PASSIONATE DAWN. HE SLOWLY TURNED! . . . . 40 OISIN 2   167
  HUNG THE FRAIL LOFTIER CLOUDLETS. TURNED HE SLOW-- . . . 40 OISIN 2   V 167
  AND HUNG WITH SLIME, AND WHISPERING IN HIS HAIR, ... 43 OISIN 2   216
  HUNG ROUND WITH SLIME, AND WHISPERING IN HIS HAIR, . . . 43 OISIN 2   V 216
  . . . HUNG LOW ON THE RIM OF THE SKY, ... 122 WHITE BIRDS   3
  . . . HUNG LOW IN THE FALL OF THE DEW! . . . . 122 WHITE BIRDS   7
  HIS HEART HUNG ALL UPON A SILKEN DRESS, ... 126 DREAM OF FAERY   2
  THERE WAS A GREEN BRANCH HUNG WITH MANY A BELL . . . . 129 BOOK STORIES   1
  I HAVE BEEN A HAZEL-TREE, AND THEY HUNG . . . . 177 PAST GREATNESS   3
  I HAVE BEEN A HAZEL TREE, AND THEY HUNG . . . . 177 PAST GREATNESS V   3
  THE HONEY PALE MOON HUNG LOW ON THE SLEEPY HILL, . . . 203 WITHER BOUGHS V   5
  OR ULADH WHEN NAISI HAD HUNG A SAIL UPON THE WIND! . . 209 UNDER THE MOON V   4
  OF THE HUNTER'S MOON, THAT HUNG BETWEEN THE NIGHT AND THE 210 UNDER THE MOON   18
   DAY,
  OF THE THIRD MOON, THAT HUNG BETWEEN THE NIGHT AND THE DAY, 210 UNDER THE MOON V   18
  OF OLD STRINGED INSTRUMENTS, HUNG THERE . . . . 271 GREY ROCK   V   20
  OF FIDDLES AND OF FLUTES HUNG THERE . . . . 271 GREY ROCK   V   20
  A DIAGRAM HUNG THERE INSTEAD, ... 485 STATISTICS   3
  WHERE THE GAUDY MOON IS HUNG. . . . . 502 VACILLATION   69
  LOW, LONG AND MUSICAL. A DEW-DROP HUNG . . . . 689 NETTLESHIP   9
  HUNG ON HIS DOUBLET--DEAR AND MOURNFUL CHILD, ... 691 MOSADA 1   35
  HEARD YOU? YOUR LUTE HUNG IN THE WINDOW SOUNDED! . . . 694 MOSADA 1   95
  HE TURNS WHERE, HUNG LIKE DROPS OF DRIPPING GOLD, . . . 710 FERENCZ RENYI   18
  HE TURNS WHERE, HUNG LIKE DROPS OF LIQUID GOLD, ... 710 FERENCZ RENYI V   18
HUNGARY
  LIBATIONS, FROM THE HUNGARY OF THE WEST. . . . . . . 709 FERENCZ RENYI   5
HUNGER
  TO HUNGER FIERCELY AFTER TRUTH. . . . . 66 HAPPY SHEPHERD   24
  I HUNGER TO BUILD THEM ANEW AND SIT ON A GREEN KNOLL APART, 143 ROSE IN HEART   6
  THAT WERE A DOUBLE HUNGER IN MY LIPS . . . . 285 TWO KINGS   206
  THAT WERE A DOUBLE HUNGER IN MY LIPS . . . . 285 TWO KINGS   V 206
  OR WAS THE HUNGER THAT HAD MADE IT HOLLOW . . . . . . 368 EGO DOMINUS   23
  A HUNGER FOR THE APPLE ON THE BOUGH . . . . 368 EGO DOMINUS   24
HUNGRY   SEE RAGE-HUNGRY
  THAT IF A DANCER STAYED HIS HUNGRY FOOT . . . . 127 DREAM OF FAERY   22
  CRUEL CLAW AND HUNGRY THROAT, ... 136 TWO TREES   36
  THE RAGE DRIVEN, RAGE TORMENTED, AND RAGE HUNGRY TROOP, 426 PHANTOM HATRED V   11
  BUT SANG, "O SEA-STARVED, HUNGRY SEA." . . . . 578 CRAZED GIRL   14
  "O SEA--STARVED, HUNGRY SEA." . . . . 578 CRAZED GIRL   V 14
  HAVE I SLEPT LONG? LONG YEARS. WITH HUNGRY HEART . . . 677 ISLE STAT II 3   286
HUNKERS
  UPON HIS HUNKERS IN THE HOLE, ... 306 HOUR DAWN   81
HUNT   SEE FOX-HUNTER
  . . . "THE FENIANS HUNT WOLVES IN THE NIGHT, ... 59 OISIN 3   171
  AND WIDE AWAKE KNOW THAT THE HUNT IS ON! . . . . . . 622 HOUND VOICE   17
  NOW THE HUNT BEGINS ANEW? . . . . 773 SONG DEIRDRE 1   18
HUNTER   SEE FOX-HUNTER
  YOU HUNTER OF THE FIELDS AFAR! . . . . 75 ANASHU VIJAYA   79
  BRING MY BROWN HUNTER NEAR, ... 97 FOXHUNTER   V   6
  AND SO A HUNTER CARRIES IN THE EYE . . . . 463 HARUN RASHID   61
  BY AN OLD HUNTER TALKING WITH GODS: . . . . 605 YOU CONTENT   23
  SUCH MEN, SUCH HEARTS. BUT, UNCOUTH HUNTER, THOU . . . 651 ISLE STAT I 1   167
  KNOW'ST NAUGHT OF THIS. AND, UNCOUTH HUNTER, NOW-- . . 651 ISLE STAT I 1   168
  AND WHITHER, UNCOUTH HUNTER? WHY SO FAST? . . . . . . 651 ISLE STAT I 2   1
  A HOARY HUNTER LEANING ON HIS BOW, ... 672 ISLE STAT II 3   157
HUNTER-FRIEND
  OF MY SAD HUNTER-FRIEND WILL ALL DEPART . . . . 668 ISLE STAT II 3   45
HUNTER-LOVER
  SHALL BE THE HUNTER-LOVER OF THY YOUTH. . . . . 674 ISLE STAT II 3   205
HUNTER'S
  AH, YOU WILL KNOW MY LOVED ONE BY HIS HUNTER'S ARROWS 75 ANASHU VIJAYA   80
   TRULY,
  OF THE HUNTER'S MOON, THAT HUNG BETWEEN THE NIGHT AND THE 210 UNDER THE MOON   18
   DAY,
  I WEARY OF YOUR SONGS AND HUNTER'S TOYS. . . . . . . 651 ISLE STAT I 1   157
  YON IS THE HUNTER'S, SIR ALMINTOR'S, PAGE! . . . . . . 660 ISLE STAT II 1   35
HUNTING
  THE HUNTING OF HEROES SHOULD BE GLAD." . . . . 4 OISIN 1   39
  "THE HUNTING OF HEROES SHOULD BE GLAD! . . . . 4 OISIN 1   V 32
  "FOR HUNTING HEROES SHOULD BE GLAD. . . . . 4 OISIN 1   V 34
  BESIDE THE PILED-UP HUNTING SPEARS, ... 23 OISIN 1   348
  OF WAR, AND THE CHASE, AND HUNTING, AND PLEASURE! . . . 26 OISIN 1   V 403
  AN ASHEN HUNTING SPEAR. . . . . 32 OISIN 2   56
  A LARCH-WOOD HUNTING SPEAR. . . . . 32 OISIN 2   V 56
  AN ASH-WOOD HUNTING SPEAR. . . . . 32 OISIN 2   V 56
HUNTING-CALL
  THAT FOLLOWED MY KEEN HUNTING-CALL-- . . . . 23 OISIN 1   V 345F
HUNTING-SPEAR
  AND FLUNG THE JOYOUS HUNTING-SPEAR! . . . . 23 OISIN 1   V 345A
HUNTING-SPEARS
  BESIDE THE PILED-UP HUNTING-SPEARS, ... 23 OISIN 1   V 349
HUNTSMAN
  BRING HOUND AND HUNTSMAN HERE, ... 97 FOXHUNTER   V 10
  THE HUNTSMAN NEAR HIM STANDS. . . . . 98 FOXHUNTER   24
  "HUNTSMAN RODY, BLOW THE HORN, ... 98 FOXHUNTER   25
  THE HUNTSMAN LOOSENS ON THE MORN . . . . 98 FOXHUNTER   27
  THE HUNTSMAN NEAR HIM STANDS. . . . . 98 FOXHUNTER   V 22
  "NOW HUNTSMAN RODY, BLOW THY HORN, ... 98 FOXHUNTER   V REF
  "MY HUNTSMAN RODY, BLOW THE HORN, ... 98 FOXHUNTER   V REF
  "HUNTSMAN RODY, BLOW THE HORN, ... 99 FOXHUNTER   33

		PAGE	TITLE		LINE
HURL					
HELP! HELP! AND HURL HIM FROM OUR COAST		83	MAD KING GOLL	V	17
AND HANDS HURL IN THE DEEP		165	CRY OF SEDGE		6
HURL HELMETS, CROWNS, AND SWORDS INTO THE PIT.		257	RECONCILIATION		10
OVERCOME THE EMPYREAN! HURL		540	FROM ANTIGONE		7
I HURL AWAY THESE ALL UNFAERY FEARS.		675	ISLE STAT II 3		228
THE STARS WOULD HURL THEIR CROWNS AMONG THE FOAM		761	SHADOW WATER A		265
OR THEY'D HURL A SPELL AT HIM,		775	AGAINST WITCH		18
HURLED					
WITH WHOM I HURLED THE HURRYING SPEAR,		10	OISIN 1		122
AND, WEEPING OVER THE WHITE STRINGS, HURLED		17	OISIN 1		241
THEREIN THE SILVER HARP HE HURLED,		17	OISIN 1	V	244
AND HURLED THEM IN THE GULPH OF SLEEP!		83	MAD KING GOLL		22
YOU, TOO, HAVE COME WHERE THE DIM TIDES ARE HURLED		115	ROSE OF BATTLE		26
I TORE IT FROM GREEN BOUGHS WINDS TOSSED AND HURLED,		130	BOOK STORIES	V	13
THE JEWELLED CROWNS THAT KINGS HAVE HURLED		155	FORGOT BEAUTY		4
AND HURLED IT FROM ITS PLACE BEFORE HIS FOOTSTOOL WHITE,		174	ELEMENT POWERS	V	3
AND HURLED IT FROM ITS PLACE AMID THE PEARLY LIGHT		174	ELEMENT POWERS	V	3
OR HURLED THE LITTLE STREETS UPON THE GREAT,		256	NO SECOND TROY		4
HURLEY					
RIDING TO HURLEY, OR IN THE BATTLE-HOST		229	SHADOW WATER B		169
FROM PLAYING HURLEY IN THE WOOD		743	DANAAN QUICK		9
HURLS					
HURLS THEIR SWOONING LUSTRE UP.		647	ISLE STAT I 1		49
HURRAH					
(HURRAH FOR THE FLOWERS OF SPRING,		567	FROM JAPANESE		3
HURRAH FOR REVOLUTION AND MORE CANNON-SHOT!		590	GREAT DAY		1
HURRAH FOR REVOLUTION AND CANNON COME AGAIN!		590	GREAT DAY		3
HURRAH FOR REVOLUTION AND MORE CANNON SHOT!		590	GREAT DAY	V	1
HURRIED					
HURRIED AWAY, AND OVER HER RAISED		12	OISIN 1	V	142B
I LAUGHED ALOUD AND HURRIED ON		83	MAD KING GOLL		31
"ANOTHER'S HURRIED OFF," CRIED HE,		193	BAILE AILLINN		113
OR HURRIED THEM OFF ON ITS OWN FURIOUS PATH!		430	NINETEEN 19		53
HURRIED THROUGH THE SMOOTH AND ROUGH		436	FOR MY SON		29
AND HURRIED TO THE GUARD-HOUSE DOOR,		725	LEGEND		16
I HURRIED FROM THE WOODY SHORE,		742	DANAAN QUICK		4
HURRIEDLY					
WHILE I WAS LOOKING THEY ROSE HURRIEDLY,		223	SHADOW WATER B		25
HURRIES					
WHAT HURRIES OUT THE KNAVE AND DOLT?		625	NATIVITY		9
HURRY					
THAT HURRY FROM UNMEASURED MIND		138	TO IRELAND		25
THAT PUT THIS HURRY IN MY SHOES."		194	BAILE AILLINN		125
O HURRY WHERE BY WATER AMONG THE TREES		210	RAGGED WOOD		1
O HURRY TO THE WATER AMID THE TREES,		210	RAGGED WOOD	V	1
O HURRY WHERE BY WATER AMONG TREES,		210	RAGGED WOOD	V	1
O HURRY TO THE RAGGED WOOD, FOR THERE		211	RAGGED WOOD		9
O HURRY TO THE WATER AMID THE TREES,		211	RAGGED WOOD	V	5
O HURRY TO THE HOLLOW WOOD, FOR THERE		211	RAGGED WOOD	V	9
HURRY TO BLESS THE HANDS THAT PLAY,		212	BLESS PSALTER		1
O NO, O NO! THEY HURRY DOWN		213	BLESS PSALTER		12
BUT DREAMS THAT HURRY FROM BEYOND THE WORLD		230	SHADOW WATER B		185
TO HURRY TO THEIR HIDDEN HAPPINESS		234	SHADOW WATER B		268
THE THIRD: "I'LL HURRY TO THE COURSE		296	THREE BEGGARS		33
WHILE I MUST HURRY UPON MY WAY,		301	RUN PARADISE		23
WHO SHUDDER AND HURRY BY: BODY AND SOUL		375	PHASES OF MOON		77
HURRY INTO EACH OTHER'S ARMS! THESE EYES,		555	RIBH AT TOMB		22
HURRY, HURRY, HURRY,		774	COME RIDE	V	REF
HURRY, HURRY, HURRY,		774	COME RIDE	V	REF
HURRY, HURRY, HURRY,		774	COME RIDE	V	REF
HURRYING					
WITH WHOM I HURLED THE HURRYING SPEAR,		10	OISIN 1		122
WITH HORSEMEN HURRYING NEAR AND FAR,		83	MAD KING GOLL	V	18
AND TIME AND BIRTH AND CHANGE ARE HURRYING BY.		153	CHANGE BELOVED		9
AND HURRYING TO THE SOUTH HE CAME		194	BAILE AILLINN	V	128
WESTWARD OF TARA. HURRYING TO HIS QUEEN		276	TWO KINGS		2
AND, HURRYING HOMEWARD, FALL UPON SOME LAND		767	SHADOW WATER A		384
HURT					
NO MAN SHOULD SEE TO DO ME HURT:		274	GREY ROCK		91
I HAD BEEN HURT"! AND TOPPLING BROUGHT		302	HOUR DAWN		19
I HAD BEEN HURT," THE OLD BEGGAR THOUGHT		302	HOUR DAWN	V	19
AND WE ARE HURT IF EITHER FRIEND SEEM COLD,		324	ROBERT GREGORY		10
IT FEARED TO GIVE ITS LOVE A HURT WITH ALL THE TEMPEST THERE:		450	OWEN AHERNE		7
IT FEARED THE HURT THAT SHE COULD GIVE AND THEREFORE IT WENT MAD.		450	OWEN AHERNE		8
AS AN HURT LEOPARD FILLS WITH CEASELESS MOAN,		674	ISLE STAT II 3		208
AS A HURT LEOPARD FILLS WITH CEASELESS MOAN		674	ISLE STAT II 3	V	208
HURTING					
A HURTING BEAM OF LIGHT,		741	EARL PAUL		38
A HURTING GLEAM OF LIGHT,		741	EARL PAUL	V	38
HURTLE					
SUDDENLY HURTLE BEFORE MY DREAM-AWAKENED EYES,		161	BLACK PIG		2
HURTLING					
ARE HURTLING THROUGH MY HEART.		171	MAID QUIET		8
HURTS					
WHAT HURTS THE SOUL		572	LADYS 1ST SONG		9
FOR HURTS AND AILS AND LOVER'S MOAN—		717	FAIRY DOCTOR		18
HUSBAND					
MY HUSBAND WAS A FISHER POOR		94	MOLL MAGEE	V	5

		PAGE	TITLE		LINE

HUSBAND   (CONTINUED)

MY HUSBAND STOOD UP PALE, ... 95 MOLL MAGEE V 22
SHE SAYS MY HUSBAND SURE WILL COME . . . . 96 MOLL MAGEE V 41
SHE SAW HER HUSBAND AILELL SLEEPING THERE, ... 183 QUEEN MAEVE 69
AND OF THAT FAMOUS FERGUS, NESSA'S HUSBAND, ... 183 QUEEN MAEVE 71
THAT HAPPIER BREATH HAD MOVED, HER HUSBAND TURNED . . . 185 QUEEN MAEVE 105
HAD CHOSEN A HUSBAND ANYWHERE . . . . 191 BAILE AILLINN 54
WHO HAVE SLAIN MY HUSBAND AND LAID HANDS UPON ME. . . . 235 SHADOW WATER B 282
MY HUSBAND AND MY KING DIED AT MY FEET, ... 237 SHADOW WATER B 337
AND KILLED A LOVER OR HUSBAND AT MY FEET-- . . . . . 246 SHADOW WATER B 491
I WAS YOUR HUSBAND WHEN YOU RODE THE AIR, ... 284 TWO KINGS 166
AND SHOWN MY HUSBAND SLEEPING THERE, I HAVE SIGHED, . . . 285 TWO KINGS 188
HER HUSBAND HAS HEARD THE WRETCH, ... 319 DOLLS 15
DUTIFUL HUSBAND, HONEST WIFE BY TURN, ... 376 PHASES OF MOON 99
A HUSBAND THAT HAD SOLD HIS WIFE . . . . 587 PARNELLITES 27
A HUSBAND WHO HAD SOLD HIS WIFE . . . . 587 PARNELLITES V 27
"GOOD-BYE, GOOD-BYE, MY HUSBAND," . . . . 779 GOING THE ROAD 9

HUSH

A HUSH! AH, ME! IT HANGS TO STRIKE US DEAD. . . . . . 43 OISIN 2 V 208B
MY SPIRIT ROCKED IN EVENING'S HUSH, THE RUSHES ROUND MY 76 INDIAN ON GOD V 2
  KNEES,
THEY WILL NOT HUSH, THE LEAVES A-FLUTTER ROUND ME, . . . 82 MAD KING GOLL 12
(THEY WILL NOT HUSH, THE LEAVES THAT ROUND ME FLUTTER-- 82 MAD KING GOLL V REF
  . . .
THEY WILL NOT HUSH, THE LEAVES A-FLUTTER ROUND ME, . . . 83 MAD KING GOLL 24
THEY WILL NOT HUSH, THE LEAVES A-FLUTTER ROUND ME, . . . 84 MAD KING GOLL 36
THEY WILL NOT HUSH, THE LEAVES A-FLUTTER ROUND ME, . . . 84 MAD KING GOLL 48
THEY WILL NOT HUSH, THE LEAVES A-FLUTTER ROUND ME, . . . 85 MAD KING GOLL 60
THEY WILL NOT HUSH, THE LEAVES A-FLUTTER ROUND ME, . . . 86 MAD KING GOLL 72
AND THE WHITE HUSH END ALL BUT THE LOUD BEAT . . . . . 137 TO SOME I TALK 15
AND THE WHITE HUSH END ALL THINGS BUT THE BEAT . . . . 137 TO SOME I TALK V 15
AT HUSH OF EVENING TILL GOD BURNS TIME . . . . . . 164 PERFECT BEAUTY V 7
AT HUSH OF EVENING TILL GOD BURN TIME . . . . 164 PERFECT BEAUTY V 7
WITH SINGING HUSH AND HUSH-A-BYE; . . . . 456 FRIENDS YOUTH 9
BUT HUSH, FOR I HAVE LOST THE THEME, ... 633 MAN AND ECHO 41
WILL YOU NOT HEAR MY LAST NEW SONG? HUSH, HUSH! . . . 695 MOSADA 2 1
WILL YOU NOT HEAR MY LAST NEW SONG? HUSH, HUSH! . . . 695 MOSADA 2 1
OH, HUSH THE WANDERING MUSIC OF THY MIND. . . . . . 703 MOSADA 3 106
AND HANGING O'ER THE HUSH OF WILLOW BOWERS, ... 705 REMEMBRANCE 8
HUSH! HUSH! HUSH! ON EVERY LIP . . . . 732 STREET DANCERS 18
HUSH! HUSH! HUSH! ON EVERY LIP . . . . 732 STREET DANCERS 18
HUSH! HUSH! HUSH! ON EVERY LIP . . . . 732 STREET DANCERS 18
HUSH! HUSH! HUSH! THEY PAUSE AND POINT . . . . . . 732 STREET DANCERS 31
HUSH! HUSH! HUSH! THEY PAUSE AND POINT . . . . . . 732 STREET DANCERS 31
HUSH! HUSH! HUSH! THEY PAUSE AND POINT . . . . . . 732 STREET DANCERS 31
HUSH! HUSH! HUSH! THEY PAUSE THEM WHERE . . . . . . 733 STREET DANCERS 44
HUSH! HUSH! HUSH! THEY PAUSE THEM WHERE . . . . . . 733 STREET DANCERS 44
HUSH! HUSH! HUSH! THEY PAUSE THEM WHERE . . . . . . 733 STREET DANCERS 44

HUSH-A-BYE

WITH SINGING HUSH AND HUSH-A-BYE; . . . . 456 FRIENDS YOUTH 9

HUSH'D

HUSH'D THE FISHERS, TILL A MOTHER CALLS BY NAME HER DROWNED 719 PHANTOM SHIP 23
  SON;

HUSHED

THEY HUSHED THEM, EVERY MAN AND MAID. . . . . 17 OISIN 1 V 235
AND THERE WE HUSHED THE REVELRY; . . . . 20 OISIN 1 V 295
BESIDE THE SEA, WHERE, HUSHED AND SLOW, ... 20 OISIN 1 V 292
WE HUSHED THE SINGING AND THE ROMP, ... 20 OISIN 1 V 296
TILL ON THE CENTRAL HILL WE HUSHED . . . . 22 OISIN 1 V 323
A WHITEBEARD STOOD HUSHED ON THE PATHWAY, ... 59 OISIN 3 173
WHEN EVE HAS HUSHED THE FEATHERED WAYS, ... 78 INDIAN TO LOVE 19
WHERE EVE HAS HUSHED THE FEATHERED WAYS, ... 78 INDIAN TO LOVE V 19
WHILE HUSHED FROM FEAR, OR LOUD WITH HOPE, A BAND . . . 114 ROSE OF BATTLE 5
AND HUSHED IN SLEEP THE ROARING RANKS OF BATTLE! . . . 129 BOOK STORIES 7
ON A FOOT-FALL HUSHED AND LIGHT, ... 159 CAP AND BELLS V 8
OF A FOOTFALL HUSHED AND LIGHT . . . . 159 CAP AND BELLS V 8
AND THOUGH I WOULD HAVE HUSHED THE CROWD, ... 253 HIS DREAM 5
THE SQUIRREL YONDER, HUSHED AND WISE, ... 686 LIFE 5
ALONG THE SEA; AND MANY A MAN GREW HUSHED . . . . . . 693 MOSADA 1 86

HUSKY

A HUSKY DEMON, DRY AS A WITHERED SEDGE . . . . . . 39 OISIN 2 V 158

HYDE

THERE HYDE BEFORE HE HAD BEATEN INTO PROSE . . . . . 489 COOLE PARK 29 9

HYMNS

THAT TREMBLES AND RESOUNDS WITH HYMNS TO THEE, ... 684 SEEKER V 69C

HYSTERICA

HYSTERICA PASSIO DRAGGED THIS QUARRY DOWN. . . . . . 542 PARN FUNERAL 1 21
HYSTERICA PASSIO OF ITS OWN EMPTINESS? . . . . . . 618 BRONZE HEAD 7

HYSTERICAL

I HAVE HEARD THAT HYSTERICAL WOMEN SAY . . . . . . 565 LAPIS LAZULI 1
GUARDED; GRIFFITH STARING IN HYSTERICAL PRIDE; . . . . 601 GALLERY REVIS 4

HYSTERICO-PASSIO

HYSTERICO-PASSIO OF ITS OWN EMPTINESS? . . . . . . 618 BRONZE HEAD V 7

ICE

TO HIS OWN ICE!" I GATHERED ROUND ME, ... 83 MAD KING GOLL V 18
QUEENS, THEIR EYES BLUE LIKE THE ICE, ... 214 HAPPY TOWNLAND 11
THAT SEEMED AS THOUGH ICE BURNED AND WAS BUT THE MORE ICE, 316 COLD HEAVEN 2
THAT SEEMED AS THOUGH ICE BURNED AND WAS BUT THE MORE ICE, 316 COLD HEAVEN 2

ICICLES

THE ICICLES THAT FAMISH ALL THE NORTH, ... 73 ANASHU VIJAYA 50

401

```
                                                         PAGE       TITLE          LINE
IDA'S
    AS FAIR AS ANY THAT ON IDA'S MOUNT  . . . . . . . .  650 ISLE STAT I 1          134
IDIOT
    WHO BUT AN IDIOT WOULD PRAISE  . . . . . . . . . .   780 WELL AND TREE            7
    WHO BUT AN IDIOT WOULD PRAISE  . . . . . . . . . .   780 WELL AND TREE           15
IDLE
    AN IDLE WORD IS NOW THEIR GLORY, . . . . . . . . .    65 HAPPY SHEPHERD          14
    TO IDLE LIFE AWAY, A COMMON HERD." . . . . . . . .   107 CUCHULAIN SEA           21
    TO IDLE LIFE AWAY WITH FLOCKS AND HERDS." . . . .    107 CUCHULAIN SEA   V       21
    YET NOW IT SEEMS AN IDLE TRADE ENOUGH." . . . . .    205 ADAMS CURSE             27
    "SOME POLITICIANS IDLE WORDS  . . . . . . . . . .    396 ROSE TREE       V        3
    ALL WOMEN DOTE UPON AN IDLE MAN  . . . . . . . .     500 VACILLATION             23
    BUT YONDER THING, YON IDLE NOISE, YON CROW,  . . .   648 ISLE STAT I 1          104
    DEAFENING US WITH IDLE SOUND-- . . . . . . . . . .   727 LOVERS QUARREL          30
IDLENESS
    AND THEIR DAY GOES OVER IN IDLENESS, . . . . . . .   151 OLD MOTHER               7
    THAT IDLENESS HAD BORNE TO PRIDE, . . . . . . . .    296 THREE BEGGARS           40
IDLER
    BE THOUGHT AN IDLER BY THE NOISY SET . . . . . . .   205 ADAMS CURSE             12
IDLING
    THAT YOU STAY IDLING HERE WITH FLOCKS AND HERDS." .  107 CUCHULAIN SEA   V       21
    THAT YOU STAY IDLING HERE WITH FLOCK AND HERDS." .   107 CUCHULAIN SEA   V       21
IGNOBLE
    IGNOBLE JOY, AND MORE IGNOBLE PAIN  . . . . . . .    687 TWO TITANS              12
    IGNOBLE JOY, AND MORE IGNOBLE PAIN  . . . . . . .    687 TWO TITANS              12
IGNOMINY
    ALL OF THAT WORST IGNOMINY . . . . . . . . . . .     436 FOR MY SON              23
    THE IGNOMINY OF BOYHOOD; THE DISTRESS  . . . . . .   478 SELF AND SOUL           45
IGNORANCE
    OF SWEETER IGNORANCE." . . . . . . . . . . . . .     343 SHEP GOATHERD          112
    IN CHILDISH IGNORANCE OF ALL THAT PASSED. . . . .    468 HARUN RASHID           149
    IN CHILDISH IGNORANCE OF ALL THAT PASSED. . . . .    468 HARUN RASHID           160
    SHE KEEPS THAT IGNORANCE, NOR HAS SHE NOW  . . . .   468 HARUN RASHID           164
    WHAT IF SHE LOSE HER IGNORANCE AND SO  . . . . . .   468 HARUN RASHID           170
IGNORANT
    IN THOSE GREAT IGNORANT LEAFY WAYS; . . . . . . .    135 TWO TREES               16
    HAVE TAUGHT TO IGNORANT MEN MOST VIOLENT WAYS,  . .  256 NO SECOND TROY           3
    AND BADE ALL WELCOME, BEING IGNORANT. . . . . . .    286 TWO KINGS              218
    AND RIDDEN TOWARDS IT, BEING IGNORANT. . . . . .     286 TWO KINGS       V      218
    ARE WHAT THE BLIND AND IGNORANT TOWN  . . . . . .    287 TO WEALTHY MAN           7
    TO FLATTER BEAUTY'S IGNORANT EAR. . . . . . . . .    337 SCHOLARS                 6
    I WOULD BE IGNORANT AS THE DAWN  . . . . . . . .     344 DAWN                     1
    I WOULD BE IGNORANT AS THE DAWN  . . . . . . . .     344 DAWN                    10
    IGNORANT AND WANTON AS THE DAWN. . . . . . . . .     344 DAWN                    14
    I WOULD BE AS IGNORANT AS THE DAWN,  . . . . . .     344 DAWN            V        1
    AND MADE--BEING POOR, AILING AND IGNORANT,  . . .    370 EGO DOMINUS             59
    SEEING THAT I, IGNORANT FOR SO LONG, . . . . . .     384 VISION ROBART           66
    IN IGNORANT GOOD-WILL, . . . . . . . . . . . . .     392 EASTER 1916             18
    IN IGNORANT GOOD WILL, . . . . . . . . . . . . .     392 EASTER 1916     V       18
    HAD IGNORANT GOOD WILL, . . . . . . . . . . . .      392 EASTER 1916     V       19
    CONSPIRING AMONG THE IGNORANT. . . . . . . . . .     475 EVA GORE-BOOTH           9
    WE LOVED EACH OTHER AND WERE IGNORANT. . . . . .     523 LONG SILENCE             8
    IGNORANT WHAT DRAMATIS PERSONAE SPAKE! . . . . .     560 WHENCE COME              4
    IGNORANT WHAT THAT DRAMATIST ENJOINS, . . . . . .    560 WHENCE COME              8
IL
    IL PENSEROSO'S PLATONIST TOILED ON . . . . . . .     419 MY HOUSE                14
ILL
    AND MAY SOME SUDDEN DREADFUL ILL BEFALL HER! . . .    74 ANASHU VIJAYA           59
    AND MAY SOME DREADFUL ILL BEFALL HER QUICK! . . .     74 ANASHU VIJAYA   V       59
    NOW THAT I AM OLD AND ILL, . . . . . . . . . . .     632 MAN AND ECHO             7
    ILL WORDS FOR ALL THINGS SOFT AND FAIR, . . . . .    723 GIRLS SONG A             6
    THE PREACHER WATCHING FOR THE ILL HOUR TO PASS-- .   734 QUATRAIN APHOR           3
    FOR ALL GOOD MEN NOW FALLEN ILL, . . . . . . . .     736 IN CHURCH                5
ILL-BRED
    THE ILL-BRED SON OF A LIVERY STABLE KEEPER-- . . .   370 EGO DOMINUS     V       61
    THE ILL-BRED SON OF A LIVERY STABLE-KEEPER-- . . .   370 EGO DOMINUS     V       61
ILLNESS
    A FRIEND'S ILLNESS . . . . . . . . . . . . . . .     267 FRIEND ILLNESS           T
    THROUGH THAT STRANGE ILLNESS THAT HAD FIXED HIM THERE, . . 280 TWO KINGS         81
ILLUSION
    BY MANIFOLD ILLUSION; BUT MAN'S LIFE IS THOUGHT, . . . 563 MERU                   3
ILLUSIONS
    THAT I HAVE THE BEST OF PILOTS. SHADOWS, ILLUSIONS, . . 249 SHADOW WATER B      565
IMAGE
    FOR I AM IN HIS IMAGE MADE, AND ALL THIS TINKLING TIDE . . 76 INDIAN ON GOD       11
    RAGING AT HIS OWN IMAGE IN THE ENAMELLED SEA. . . .    77 INDIAN TO LOVE           5
    RAGES AT HIS OWN IMAGE IN THE ENAMELLED SEA  . . .     77 INDIAN TO LOVE  V        5
    RAGING AT HIS OWN IMAGE IN THE DIM ENAMELLED SEA . .   77 INDIAN TO LOVE  V        5
    HAD BLOTTED OUT MAN'S IMAGE AND HIS CRY. . . . .      120 SORROW OF LOVE           4
    COULD BUT COMPOSE MAN'S IMAGE AND HIS CRY. . . .      120 SORROW OF LOVE          12
    FOR THERE A FATAL IMAGE GROWS  . . . . . . . . .      135 TWO TREES               25
    ARE WRONGING YOUR IMAGE THAT BLOSSOMS A ROSE . . .    143 ROSE IN HEART            4
    FOR MY DREAMS OF YOUR IMAGE THAT BLOSSOMS A ROSE . .  143 ROSE IN HEART            8
    AND SAW YOUR IMAGE WAS THERE! . . . . . . . . .       152 LOSS OF LOVE             6
    NOT IN ITS IMAGE ON THE MIRROR!  WHILE . . . . .      230 SHADOW WATER B         189
    WHEN WE HAVE PUT THEIR CHANGELESS IMAGE ON. . . .     250 SHADOW WATER B         582
    WHO HAS SEEN A GARDEN IMAGE OR TWISTED TREE  . . .    279 TWO KINGS       V      45B
    IN RAMBLING TALK WITH AN IMAGE OF AIR! . . . . .      357 BROKEN DREAMS           40
    MAGICAL SHAPES.  BY THE HELP OF AN IMAGE . . . .      367 EGO DOMINUS              7
    AND I WOULD FIND MYSELF AND NOT AN IMAGE. . . . .     367 EGO DOMINUS             10
    MOST OUT OF REACH?  AND IS THAT SPECTRAL IMAGE . .    368 EGO DOMINUS             25
```

		PAGE	TITLE	LINE
IMAGE (CONTINUED)				
AN IMAGE THAT MIGHT HAVE BEEN A STONY FACE	• • • • • •	368	EGO DOMINUS	28
BECAUSE I SEEK AN IMAGE, NOT A BOOK,	• • • • • •	370	EGO DOMINUS	67
OR IMAGE, FROM BEYOND THE LOADSTONE MOUNTAIN,	• • • •	371	ON GOING HOUSE	11
AN IMAGE OF MYSTERIOUS WISDOM WON BY TOIL;	• • • • •	373	PHASES OF MOON	18
ALL THOUGHT BECOMES AN IMAGE AND THE SOUL	• • • • •	374	PHASES OF MOON	58
FOR EACH AN IMAGINED IMAGE BRINGS	• • • • • • •	388	SOLOMON WITCH	26
AND FINDS A REAL IMAGE THERE;	• • • • • • •	388	SOLOMON WITCH	27
MAYBE AN IMAGE IS TOO STRONG	• • • • • •	388	SOLOMON WITCH	36
AN IMAGE FROM A PAST LIFE	• • • • • • •	389	IMAGE PAST	T
IMAGE OF POIGNANT RECOLLECTION.	• • • • • •	389	IMAGE PAST	7
AN IMAGE OF MY HEART THAT IS SMITTEN THROUGH	• • • •	389	IMAGE PAST	8
AN IMAGE UP, OR ANYTHING	• • • • • • •	390	IMAGE PAST	33
WHEN A VAST IMAGE OUT OF SPIRITUS MUNDI	• • • • •	402	SECOND COMING	12
AN ANCIENT IMAGE MADE OF OLIVE WOOD--	• • • •	428	NINETEEN 19	6
AN IMAGE OF ITS STATE;	• • • • • • •	430	NINETEEN 19	64
THAT IMAGE CAN BRING WILDNESS, BRING A RAGE	• • • •	431	NINETEEN 19	80
HER PRESENT IMAGE FLOATS INTO THE MIND--	• • • •	444	SCHOOL CHILDR	25
I RAGE AT MY OWN IMAGE IN THE GLASS	• • • • •	447	HERO GIRL FOOL	1
AT MY OWN IMAGE IN THE LOOKING-GLASS	• • • • •	447	HERO GIRL FOOL V	1
IF YOU HAVE SEEN THAT IMAGE AND NOT THE WOMAN.	• • •	448	HERO GIRL FOOL	8
IF YOU HAVE SEEN THAT IMAGE AND NOT MY WORTH.	• • •	448	HERO GIRL FOOL V	8
WHEN UPWARD TURNED, ON ONE SOLE IMAGE FELL;	• • • •	471	ALL SOUL NIGHT	34
WHEN UPWARD TURNED ON ONE SOUL IMAGE FELL,	• • • •	471	ALL SOUL NIGHT V	34
AN IMAGE OF SUCH POLITICS.	• • • • • • •	475	EVA GORE-BOOTH	13
AN IMAGE OF THE MOVING HEAVENS,	• • • • • •	480	BLOOD AND MOON	14
BEFORE ME FLOATS AN IMAGE, MAN OR SHADE,	• • • •	497	BYZANTIUM	9
SHADE MORE THAN MAN, MORE IMAGE THAN A SHADE;	• • •	497	BYZANTIUM	10
AND HE THAT ATTIS' IMAGE HANGS BETWEEN	• • • •	500	VACILLATION	16
I FOUND THAT IVORY IMAGE THERE	• • • • • •	514	JANE GROWN OLD	1
STRUGGLING FOR AN IMAGE ON THE TRACK	• • • • •	534	CHOSEN	2
A THOUGHTLESS IMAGE OF MANTEGNA'S THOUGHT--	• • •	537	HER VISION	20
A PIERCED BOY, IMAGE OF A STAR LAID LOW.	• • • •	541	PARN FUNERAL 1	12
(AN IMAGE OUT OF SPENSER AND THE COMMON TONGUE).	• •	603	GALLERY REVIS	40
ONE IMAGE CROSSED THE MANY-HEADED, SAT	• • • •	610	STATUES	17
BECAUSE ST. JOSEPH'S IMAGE HANGETH HERE	• • • •	676	ISLE STAT II 3	266
MY IMAGE YONDER? AH, MY BEAUTIFUL,	• • • • •	720	WITCH VIVIEN	4
TO DROWN IN ITS OWN IMAGE? EVEN THAT SLEEP	• • • •	765	SHADOW WATER A	364
IMAGED				
THE IMAGED METEORS HAD FLASHED AND RUN	• • • • •	31	OISIN 2	38
THE IMAGED METEORS HAD SHONE AND RUN,	• • • • •	31	OISIN 2 V	38
IMAGES				
THEIR HAUGHTY IMAGES THAT CANNOT WITHER,	• • • • •	184	QUEEN MAEVE	87
THEIR HAUGHTY IMAGES THAT CANNOT FADE,	• • • • •	184	QUEEN MAEVE V	88
THE HAUGHTY IMAGES, THAT CANNOT PERISH	• • • • •	184	QUEEN MAEVE V	88
WHEN THEY HAVE BUT LOOKED UPON THEIR IMAGES--	• • •	210	RAGGED WOOD	3
WHEN THEY HAVE BUT LOOKED UPON THEIR IMAGES,	• • •	211	RAGGED WOOD V	7
AND THE IMAGES I HAVE WOVEN IN THIS STORY	• • • •	218	WOODS OF COOLE	21
AND ALL THAT PROPHESYING IMAGES	• • • • • •	235	SHADOW WATER B	294
IVORY IMAGES WITH AMETHYST EYES.	• • • • • •	248	SHADOW WATER B	534
MAYBE YOUR IMAGES HAVE STOOD,	• • • • • •	273	GREY ROCK	50
OR CLIMBED AMONG THE IMAGES OF THE PAST--	• • • •	352	PEOPLE	10
THE UNPERTURBED AND COURTLY IMAGES--	• • • •	352	PEOPLE	11
THROUGH THE HOLY IMAGES	• • • • • • •	355	PROPERTIUS	5
MERE IMAGES; CHOSEN THIS PLACE TO LIVE IN	• • • •	373	PHASES OF MOON	13
FIXED UPON IMAGES THAT ONCE WERE THOUGHT;	• • • •	375	PHASES OF MOON	80
IMAGES CAN BREAK THE SOLITUDE	• • • • • •	375	PHASES OF MOON	82
THE COMMONNESS OF THOUGHT AND IMAGES	• • • • •	384	VISION ROBART	61
BUT IMAGES TO MAKE ME FONDER?	• • • • • •	390	IMAGE PAST	35
IMAGES AND MEMORIES	• • • • • • •	410	TOWER	22
WHOSE IMAGES, IN THE GREAT MEMORY STORED,	• • • •	412	TOWER	85
MONSTROUS FAMILIAR IMAGES SWIM TO THE MIND'S EYE.	• •	426	PHANTOM HATRED	8
THE HALF-READ WISDOM OF DAEMONIC IMAGES,	• • • •	427	PHANTOM HATRED	39
THE HALF-READ WISDOM OF DEMONIC IMAGES,	• • • •	427	PHANTOM HATRED	39
THE HALF READ WISDOM OF DEMONIC IMAGES,	• • • •	427	PHANTOM HATRED V	39
THUNDER OF FEET, TUMULT OF IMAGES,	• • • • •	433	NINETEEN 19	120
BOTH NUNS AND MOTHERS WORSHIP IMAGES,	• • • •	445	SCHOOL CHILDR	49
UPON THE GHOSTLY IMAGES OF THINGS	• • • • •	445	SCHOOL CHILDR V	42
THE UNPURGED IMAGES OF DAY RECEDE;	• • • • •	497	BYZANTIUM	1
THOSE IMAGES THAT YET	• • • • • • •	498	BYZANTIUM	38
FRESH IMAGES BEGET,	• • • • • • •	498	BYZANTIUM	39
WHAT IMAGES ARE THESE,	• • • • • • •	505	RESULT THOUGHT	13
IMAGES RIDE, I HEARD A MAN SAY,	• • • • • •	549	SEVERED HEAD V	1
THOSE IMAGES	• • • • • • •	600	THOSE IMAGES	T
SEEK THOSE IMAGES	• • • • • • •	601	THOSE IMAGES	9
AROUND ME THE IMAGES OF THIRTY YEARS;	• • • •	601	GALLERY REVIS	1
MY PERMANENT OR IMPERMANENT IMAGES	• • • • •	602	GALLERY REVIS	20
THOSE IMAGES THAT WAKEN IN THE BLOOD.	• • • •	622	HOUND VOICE	14
THOSE MASTERFUL IMAGES BECAUSE COMPLETE	• • . •	630	CIRCUS ANIMALS	33
AND ALL THE WISDOM THAT OLD IMAGES	• • • • •	764	SHADOW WATER A	344
AND ALL THAT PROPHESYING IMAGES	• • • • •	764	SHADOW WATER A V	344
WITH LIGHT IMAGES OF CLAY	• • • • • • •	775	AGAINST WITCH	12
IMAGINABLE				
AND PROVE OF ALL IMAGINABLE THINGS	• • • • •	371	EGO DOMINUS	73
AND PROVE IF ALL IMAGINABLE THINGS	• • • • •	371	EGO DOMINUS V	73
IMAGINATION				
THE BED OF LOVE, THAT IN THE IMAGINATION	• • • •	228	SHADOW WATER B	148
IN THE IMAGINATION AND INTELLECT?	• • • • • •	245	SHADOW WATER B	488
IMAGINATION CANNOT RECKON IT.	• • • • • •	248	SHADOW WATER B	541
AND THEREUPON IMAGINATION AND HEART WERE DRIVEN	• •	316	COLD HEAVEN	3
UNTIL IMAGINATION BROUGHT	• • • • • • •	328	ROBERT GREGORY	94

<pre>
                                                   PAGE   TITLE   LINE
IMAGINATION   (CONTINUED)
    THE CHIEF IMAGINATION OF CHRISTENDOM, ...   368 EGO DOMINUS   18
    IMAGINATION, NOR AN EAR AND EYE . . . .   409 TOWER   6
    UNTIL IMAGINATION, EAR AND EYE, ...   409 TOWER   13
    AND SEND IMAGINATION FORTH . . . .   410 TOWER   20
    DOES THE IMAGINATION DWELL THE MOST . . . .   413 TOWER   113
    WHY SHOULD THE IMAGINATION OF A MAN . . . .   477 SELF AND SOUL   17
    IF BUT IMAGINATION SCORN THE EARTH . . . .   478 SELF AND SOUL   21
    BID IMAGINATION RUN . . . .   494 AT ALGECIRAS   15
    IMAGINATION HAD BEEN SATISFIED, ...   543 PARN FUNERAL 2   6
    NEITHER LOOSE IMAGINATION, ...   575 ACRE OF GRASS   9
    IMAGINATION TO THAT PITCH WHERE IT CASTS OUT . . . . .   619 BRONZE HEAD   19
IMAGINATIONS
    IMAGINATIONS OF THEIR EYES, ...   272 GREY ROCK   28
IMAGINE
    IMAGINE THAT LOST LOVE, INSEPARABLE FROM MY THOUGHT . . . 390 UNDER SATURN   2
    IMAGINE THAT SOME LOST LOVE, UNASSAILABLE . . . . . .   390 UNDER SATURN   V   2
    "YOU BUT IMAGINE LIES ALL DAY, O MURDERER," I REPLIED. . 450 OWEN AHERNE   17
    DELIGHT TO IMAGINE THEM SEATED THERE: . . . .   567 LAPIS LAZULI   50
IMAGINED   SEE HALF-IMAGINED
    IMAGINED, AS THEY STRUCK THE WAY . . . .   189 BAILE AILLINN   20
    THE QUEENS THAT WERE IMAGINED LONG AGO, ...   201 OLD MEMORY   5
    IMAGINED BODIES ALL THEIR DAYS . . . .   386 ROBARTES DANCE   28
    FOR EACH AN IMAGINED IMAGE BRINGS . . . .   388 SOLOMON WITCH   26
    IMAGINED EVERYTHING. . . . .   419 MY HOUSE   17
    WHAT MY LABORIOUS LIFE IMAGINED, EVEN . . . .   431 NINETEEN 19   82
    THE HALF IMAGINED, THE HALF WRITTEN PAGE. . . . . .   431 NINETEEN 19   V   83
    IMAGINED HIM UPON THE FLOOR . . . .   440 WISDOM   V   6
    IMAGINED SOME IMPOSSIBLE HISTORY . . . .   466 HARUN RASHID   109
    THE POETS HAVE IMAGINED, TERRIBLE AND GAY." . . . . .   602 GALLERY REVIS   12
    BUT BOYS AND GIRLS, PALE FROM THE IMAGINED LOVE . . .   610 STATUES   4
    BEING IMAGINED WITHIN . . . .   785 WOMANS BEAUTY   23
    IMAGINED SUCH A FINE AFFAIR: . . . .   791 REPRISALS   14
IMAGINES
    IMAGINES BEST TO MAKE IT THRIVE. . . . .   287 TO WEALTHY MAN   8
IMAGING
    THE RIVER IMAGING THE FLASHING SKIES, ...   390 IMAGE PAST   20
    THAT WOMAN, THE GREAT MOTHER IMAGING, ...   541 PARN FUNERAL 1   13
IMAGINING
    BY ITS OWN BLIND IMAGINING, ...   191 BAILE AILLINN   67
    IMAGINING AND PONDERING . . . .   193 BAILE AILLINN   111
    IMAGINING 'TWOULD BETTER PLEASE . . . .   271 GREY ROCK   4
    IMAGINING A MAN, ...   348 FISHERMAN   28
    IMAGINING . . . .   390 IMAGE PAST   31
    IMAGINING IN EXCITED REVERIE . . . .   403 FOR DAUGHTER   13
    IMAGINING, MOON-ACCURSED, ...   454 EMPTY CUP   4
    IMAGINING MOON ACCURSED, ...   454 EMPTY CUP   V   4
    IMAGINING MEN. IMAGINING THAT I COULD . . . . . .   537 HER VISION   4
    IMAGINING MEN. IMAGINING THAT I COULD . . . . . .   537 HER VISION   4
IMAGININGS
    POET'S IMAGININGS . . . .   415 TOWER   160
IMITATE
    IMITATE HIM IF YOU DARE, ...   493 SWIFTS EPITAPH   4
IMITATED
    IMITATED FROM THE JAPANESE . . . .   567 FROM JAPANESE   T
IMITATION
    AND BY THE IMITATION OF GREAT MASTERS. . . . .   370 EGO DOMINUS   66
IMITATORS
    . . . CERTAIN BAD POETS, IMITATORS OF HIS AND MINE . . . 262 TO A POET   T
    . . . CERTAIN BAD POETS, IMITATORS OF HIS AND OF MINE . . 262 TO A POET   V   T
IMMEDIATE
    IMMEDIATE, MOURNFUL, WHITE WITH SUDDEN CARES, ...   44 OISIN 2   V 229A
IMMEDICABLE
    THAT THE IMMEDICABLE MOUND'S BEYOND . . . .   282 TWO KINGS   129
    THAT THE IMMEDICABLE WOUND'S BEYOND . . . .   282 TWO KINGS   V   129
IMMENSE
    . . . IMMENSE IN THEIR WRINKLING BARK: . . . .   48 OISIN 3   17
    IMMENSE MIRACULOUS HOUSE . . . .   472 ALL SOUL NIGHT   38
IMMENSITIES
    ALL ASIATIC VAGUE IMMENSITIES, ...   610 STATUES   12
IMMODERATE
    BORN OUT OF IMMODERATE THOUGHT: . . . .   772 SONG DEIRDRE 1   12
    LOVE IS AN IMMODERATE THING . . . .   777 SONG DEIRDRE 2   1
IMMORAL
    . . . HAVE JOINED THE AGITATION AGAINST IMMORAL LITERATURE 262 STUDENTS AGIT   T
    . . . AGITATION AGAINST IMMORAL LITERATURE . . . . . .   262 STUDENTS AGIT   V   T
IMMORTAL
    THAT IN IMMORTAL SILENCE SLEEPS . . . .   13 OISIN 1   161
    THE IMMORTAL DESIRE OF IMMORTALS WE SAW IN THEIR FACES,   47 OISIN 3   4
        AND SIGHED.
    WHEN AN IMMORTAL PASSION BREATHES IN MORTAL CLAY: . . . 172 TRAV PASSION   2
    HAVE PULLED THE IMMORTAL ROSE: . . . .   174 ELEMENT POWERS   2
    THEY BLOSSOMED TO IMMORTAL MIRTH. . . . .   189 BAILE AILLINN   12
    HAVE SEEN IMMORTAL, MILD, PROUD SHADOWS WALK: . . . . . 217 WOODS OF COOLE   12
    HOW SHALL I NAME YOU, IMMORTAL, MILD, PROUD SHADOWS? . . 218 WOODS OF COOLE   27
    I SHALL HAVE LOVE IN THEIR IMMORTAL FASHION: . . . . . 237 SHADOW WATER B   326
    THE IMMORTAL MOCKERS HAVE CAST INTO HIS MIND, ... 249 SHADOW WATER B   567
    AND KNITTED MESH TO MESH, WE GROW IMMORTAL: . . . . .   252 SHADOW WATER B   616
    AND KNITTING MESH TO MESH, WE GROW IMMORTAL: . . . . . 252 SHADOW WATER B V   616
    AND THESE IMMORTAL EYES SHED TEARS-- . . . .   275 GREY ROCK   100
    IMMORTAL LADIES TREAD THE GROUND . . . .   446 COLONUS PRAISE   6
</pre>

404

```
                                                      PAGE      TITLE            LINE
IMMORTAL  (CONTINUED)
      WELL NIGH IMMORTAL IN THIS CHARMED CLIME,  . . . . . .   674 ISLE STAT II 3      202
      WELL-NIGH IMMORTAL IN THIS CHARMED CLIME:  . . . . . .   674 ISLE STAT II 3  V   202
      AND PLAY WITH HIS IMMORTAL HATE. . . . . . . . . . .     736 SUMMER EVENING       12
      FOR AN IMMORTAL WOMAN, AS I THINK. . . . . . . . .       755 SHADOW WATER A      173
IMMORTALITY
      THAT AIR IN IMMORTALITY  . . . . . . . . . . . .         637 BEN BULBEN            8
      THAT AIRS IN IMMORTALITY . . . . . . . . . . . .         637 BEN BULBEN       V    8
      THAT AIRS AN IMMORTALITY . . . . . . . . . . . .         637 BEN BULBEN       V    8
IMMORTALS
      THE IMMORTALS MOVED AMONG THE FOUNTAINS . . . . . . .     25 OISIN 1            386
      THE IMMORTAL DESIRE OF IMMORTALS WE SAW IN THEIR FACES,   47 OISIN 3              4
            AND SIGHED.
      AND THAT I WOULD LEAVE THE IMMORTALS, . . . . . . .       54 OISIN 3            108
IMMORTALS'
      AND THOU SHALT KNOW THE IMMORTALS' LEISURE, . . . . .      9 OISIN 1         V  100
IMMOVABLE
      LIKE DRIFTS OF LEAVES, IMMOVABLE AND BRIGHT, . . . . .    40 OISIN 2            166
      LIKE DRIFTS OF LAUREL LEAVES, IMMOVABLE AND BRIGHT  . .   40 OISIN 2         V  166
      FOR SEPARATE, PERFECT, AND IMMOVABLE . . . . . . . .     375 PHASES OF MOON       81
      FOR PERFECTED, COMPLETED, AND IMMOVABLE . . . . . . .    375 PHASES OF MOON V     81
IMPART
      AND KNOW THEM TO THE BONE: IMPART TO US-- . . . . . .    265 ABBEY THEATRE         9
IMPASSIONED
      WITH AN IMPASSIONED GRAVITY . . . . . . . . . . . .      386 ROBARTES DANCE       21
IMPATIENT
      THAT ARE IMPATIENT TO BE GONE: . . . . . . . . . .       413 TOWER               102
IMPATIENTLY
      OF TWILIGHT AND SLUMBER WERE GONE, AND THAT HOOFS         54 OISIN 3            112
            IMPATIENTLY STEPT.
      . . . BENEATH ME THE HOOVES IMPATIENTLY STEPT. . . . .    54 OISIN 3         V  112
IMPERIOUS
      WITH ALL A WOMAN'S PASSION, A CHILD'S IMPERIOUS WAY,  . . 354 HIS PHOENIX          14
IMPERISHABLE
      BECAUSE WE ARE NOT PROUD, IMPERISHABLE, . . . . . . .    250 SHADOW WATER B      580
      IMPERISHABLE FIRE UNDER THE BOUGHS  . . . . . . . .      765 SHADOW WATER A      356
      THAT CAN CHANGE LOVE TO IMPERISHABLE FIRE? . . . . .     765 SHADOW WATER A      360
IMPERMANENT
      MY PERMANENT OR IMPERMANENT IMAGES: . . . . . . . .      602 GALLERY REVIS        20
IMPETUOUS
      A WHISPER OF IMPETUOUS FEET, . . . . . . . . . . .        15 OISIN 1            199
      IMPETUOUS MEN, SHAWE-TAYLOR AND HUGH LANE, . . . . . .   489 COOLE PARK 29        14
      ENAMOURED OF THE WAVES' IMPETUOUS LIPS. . . . . . .      677 ISLE STAT II 3      289
IMPLACABLE
      THOSE TERRIBLE IMPLACABLE STRAIGHT LINES  . . . . . .    467 HARUN RASHID        142
IMPORTANT
      ALONE: IMPORTANT AND WISE, . . . . . . . . . . .         379 CAT AND MOON         26
IMPORTUNATE
      IF THIS IMPORTUNATE HEART TROUBLE YOUR PEACE . . . . .   162 ASKS FORGIVE          1
IMPORTUNE
      AND IMPORTUNE WITH WEIGHTY WORDS THIS MOOR, . . . . .    698 MOSADA 2             45
      AND IMPORTUNE THEIR SOULS TO PENITENCE, . . . . . .      704 MOSADA 3            131
IMPOSSIBLE
      THOUGH NOW IT SEEM IMPOSSIBLE, AND SO  . . . . . .       200 FOLLY COMFORT         5
      THOUGH NOW IT SEEMS IMPOSSIBLE, AND SO  . . . . . .      200 FOLLY COMFORT V       5
      MIRACLE, ECSTASY, THE IMPOSSIBLE HOPE, . . . . . .       227 SHADOW WATER B      102
      WE'RE IN THE BODY THAT'S IMPOSSIBLE. . . . . . . .       230 SHADOW WATER B      190
      AMONG WHIMS NOT IMPOSSIBLE, AND THOUGH SCARRED, . . . .  374 PHASES OF MOON       41
      AMONG TASKS NOT IMPOSSIBLE, IT TAKES . . . . . .         376 PHASES OF MOON       92
      COULD THE IMPOSSIBLE COME TO PASS . . . . . . . .        385 ROBARTES DANCE        9
      THAT MORE EXPECTED THE IMPOSSIBLE-- . . . . . . .        409 TOWER                 7
      HAD HEARD IMPOSSIBLE HISTORY OF MY PAST: . . . . . .     466 HARUN RASHID        108
      IMAGINED SOME IMPOSSIBLE HISTORY . . . . . . . .         466 HARUN RASHID        109
IMPRISONED
      REPLY LIKE MOANING OF IMPRISONED ELF: . . . . . . .      652 ISLE STAT I 2        11
IMPROVE
      MEN IMPROVE WITH THE YEARS . . . . . . . . . . .         329 MEN IMPROVE           T
      FOR MEN IMPROVE WITH THE YEARS: . . . . . . . . .        329 MEN IMPROVE          11
IMPROVISATION
      IMPROVISATION, OR A SETTLED GAME . . . . . . . .         533 HER TRIUMPH           3
IMPROVISING
      THAT CRAZED GIRL IMPROVISING HER MUSIC, . . . . . . .    578 CRAZED GIRL           1
IMPULSE
      A LONELY IMPULSE OF DELIGHT . . . . . . . . . .          328 IRISH AIRMAN         11
IMPULSIVE
      IMPULSIVE MEN THAT LOOK FOR HAPPINESS  . . . . . . .     369 EGO DOMINUS          40
IMPURE
      WHAT MATTER IF THE DITCHES ARE IMPURE? . . . . . . .     478 SELF AND SOUL        42
      REPENTANCE KEEPS MY HEART IMPURE: . . . . . . . .        507 STREAM AND SUN        6
IMPURITIES
      DISCOVER IMPURITIES, CAN SHOW AT LAST  . . . . . . .     558 RIBH CHRISTIAN       10
IMPURITY
      AND PRIDE BRING IN IMPURITY: . . . . . . . . . .         460 THREE MONUMENT       11
INANIMATE
      MANKIND INANIMATE PHANTASY. . . . . . . . . . . .        406 IN TIME OF WAR        5
      MANKIND INANIMATE FANTASY. . . . . . . . . . . .         406 IN TIME OF WAR V      5
INARTICULATE
      CHANGED ALL HE SANG TO INARTICULATE MOAN . . . . . .      69 SAD SHEPHERD         27
      CHANGED ALL HIS WORDS TO INARTICULATE MOAN . . . . .      69 SAD SHEPHERD    V    27
INCANTATION
      THE HOUR OF INCANTATION COMES A-TIPTOE, . . . . . . .    691 MOSADA 1             37
```

	PAGE	TITLE	LINE

INCAPABLE
    A SOUL INCAPABLE OF REMORSE OR REST; • • • • • • • • •   601 GALLERY REVIS   7
INCENDIARY
    INCENDIARY OR BIGOT COULD BE FOUND • • • • • • • •   430 NINETEEN 19   45
INCENSE
    WHERE SUCH GREY CLOUDS OF INCENSE ROSE • • • • • •   156 FORGOT BEAUTY   13
    WHERE A SO SLEEPY INCENSE ROSE • • • • • • • •   156 FORGOT BEAUTY V 13
    A STICK OF INCENSE • • • • • • • • • • • •   619 STICK INCENSE   T
INCH
    IT CANNOT GROW BY AN INCH OR AN OUNCE. • • • • •   566 LAPIS LAZULI   24
INCHY
    DIM INCHY WOOD, THAT HIDES BADGER AND FOX • • •   218 WOODS OF COOLE   13
INCIDENT
    FANTASY OR INCIDENT • • • • • • • • • • •   504 QUARREL IN AGE   4
INCLEMENCY
    THE INCLEMENCY • • • • • • • • • • • • •   471 ALL SOUL NIGHT   29
INCLINE
    BUT AS THE OUTRAGEOUS STARS INCLINE • • • • • •   325 ROBERT GREGORY   38
INCOMPATIBLE
    A SOMETHING INCOMPATIBLE WITH LIFE; AND POWER, • •   482 BLOOD AND MOON   50
INCORRUPTIBLE
    THE INCORRUPTIBLE ROSE, • • • • • • • • •   168 BLESSED   36
INCREASE
    YET ALL MUST COPY COPIES, ALL INCREASE THEIR KIND; • • •   556 RIBH PATRICK   7
INCREASED
    THE WILD FOWL OF THE AIR INCREASED; • • • • • • •   82 MAD KING GOLL   8
INCREASES
    THAT KNOWLEDGE INCREASES UNREALITY, THAT • • • •   610 STATUES   21
INCREASING
    BECAUSE OF THE INCREASING NIGHT • • • • • • • •   624 APPARITIONS   21
IND
    WANDERING IN SULTRY PALACES OF IND, • • • • • • •   694 MOSADA 1   102
INDEED
    THAT YOU HAVE TALKED WITH APPARITIONS. INDEED • • •   342 SHEP GOATHERD   82
    AND LOOK MOST LIKE ME, BEING INDEED MY DOUBLE, • • •   371 EGO DOMINUS   72
    FRIENDS THAT HAVE BEEN FRIENDS INDEED; • • • • •   577 WHAT THEN   9
    I SHALL BE OLD INDEED." THEREON THE MAN • • • •   609 IN TARAS HALLS   10
INDIA
    AMERICAN COLONIES, IRELAND, FRANCE AND INDIA • • • •   487 SEVEN SAGES   15
    JOHN BULL HAS GONE TO INDIA • • • • • • • • •   583 GHOST ROG CASE   21
INDIAN
    THE INDIAN UPON GOD • • • • • • • • • • •   76 INDIAN ON GOD   T
    FROM THE BOOK OF KAURI THE INDIAN-- SECTION V. ON THE   76 INDIAN ON GOD V T
        NATURE OF GOD
    KANVA, THE INDIAN, ON GOD • • • • • • • • • •   76 INDIAN ON GOD V T
    THE INDIAN TO HIS LOVE • • • • • • • • • •   77 INDIAN TO LOVE   T
    AN INDIAN SONG • • • • • • • • • • • •   77 INDIAN TO LOVE V T
    WHILE OUR LOVE GROWS AN INDIAN STAR, • • • • • •   78 INDIAN TO LOVE   13
    WHILE GROWS OUR LOVE AN INDIAN STAR, • • • • • •   78 INDIAN TO LOVE V 13
    BY SOME LEARNED INDIAN • • • • • • • • •   472 ALL SOUL NIGHT   53
INDIANS
    WHERE THE INDIANS TRADE OR JAPANESE? • • • • • • •   361 ALF POLLEXFEN   20
INDIA'S
    OF INDIA'S RIVERS, ROLLING ON IN LIGHT. • • • • • •   682 SEEKER   V 20
INDIFFERENT
    AND LEFT HER TO THE INDIFFERENT STARS ABOVE • • • •   123 DREAM OF DEATH   9
    WITH AN INDIFFERENT EYE. • • • • • • • • • •   255 WOMAN HOMER   7
    INDIFFERENT HOW THE RANCOUR RAN, • • • • • • •   288 TO WEALTHY MAN   21
    BEING MORE INDIFFERENT TO OUR SOLITUDE • • • • •   334 LIVING BEAUTY   7
    OF LOVELY, SATISFIED, INDIFFERENT EYES. • • • • •   375 PHASES OF MOON   83
    BEFORE THE INDIFFERENT GARDEN DEITIES; • • • • •   418 ANCEST HOUSES   28
    GIVE PLACE TO AN INDIFFERENT MULTITUDE, GIVE PLACE • • •   427 PHANTOM HATRED   28
    A LAW INDIFFERENT TO BLAME OR PRAISE, • • • • • •   428 NINETEEN 19   10
    BEFORE THE INDIFFERENT BEAK COULD LET HER DROP? • • •   441 LEDA AND SWAN   14
    LOVE-LORN, INDIFFERENT HANDS MIGHT COME UPON IT • • •   461 HARUN RASHID   14
    A BOY'S LOVELORN INDIFFERENT HANDS MIGHT FIND • • • •   461 HARUN RASHID V 14
INDIGNANT
    INDIGNANT AT THE FUMBLING WITS, THE OBSCURE SPITE • •   291 PAUDEEN   1
    REEL SHADOWS OF THE INDIGNANT DESERT BIRDS. • • • •   402 SECOND COMING   17
    WIND SHADOWS OF THE INDIGNANT DESERT BIRDS. • • • •   402 SECOND COMING V 17
INDIGNATIO
    SAEVA INDIGNATIO AND THE LABOURER'S HIRE, • • • • •   481 BLOOD AND MOON   28
INDIGNATION
    SAVAGE INDIGNATION THERE • • • • • • • • • •   493 SWIFTS EPITAPH   2
INDIVIDUAL
    ARE NOT INDIVIDUAL, • • • • • • • • • • • •   600 SPIRIT MEDIUM   12
INDOLENCE
    A YOUNG GIRL IN THE INDOLENCE OF HER YOUTH, • • • •   359 WAR POEM   5
    WILD INDOLENCE AND MUSIC HAVE NO DATE. • • • • •   686 LIFE   20
    WILD INDOLENCE AND MUSIC HAVE NO DATE, • • • • •   735 QUATRAIN APHOR   18
INDOLENT
    NO OTHER.--HEAR, AND MAY THE INDOLENT FLOCKS • • • •   71 ANASHU VIJAYA   4
    BUT SOFT BEAUTY AND INDOLENT DESIRE. • • • • • •   181 QUEEN MAEVE   22
INDOMITABLE
    STILL THE INDOMITABLE IRISHRY. • • • • • • • •   640 BEN BULBEN   83
INDUSTRY
    HE HAD MUCH INDUSTRY AT SETTING OUT, • • • • • •   473 ALL SOUL NIGHT   71
INEFFABLE
    AND, LIKE A STORM, CRY THE INEFFABLE NAME, • • • •   137 TO SOME I TALK   12
INEXTRICABLE
    ONE INEXTRICABLE BEAM, • • • • • • • • • • •   411 TOWER   55

	PAGE	TITLE		LINE

INFAMY
I SOUGHT THEE NOT. MEN CALL ME INFAMY. . . . . 685 SEEKER 75
INFANCY
CONSIDERING WHAT WILD INFANCY . . . . 440 WISDOM 19
THE WORLD TO ITS FIERCE INFANCY AGAIN. . . . . 698 MOSADA 2 61
INFANT
AND MAKES THE INFANT FERNS UNWRAP . . . . 18 OISIN 1 265
WHAT WOMAN HUGS HER INFANT THERE? . . . . 625 NATIVITY 1
INFANTINE
WITH INFANTINE FINGERS . . . . 672 ISLE STAT II 3 168
INFERIOR
THAT LOVED INFERIOR ART, ... 422 MY TABLE 27
HAVE LOVED INFERIOR ART, ... 422 MY TABLE V 27
INFIDEL
WITH CHRISTIAN AND WITH INFIDEL, ... 594 COLONEL MARTIN 3
INFINITE
BENEATH THE BURTHEN OF THE INFINITE, ... 674 ISLE STAT II 3 212
BENEATH THE BURDEN OF THE INFINITE, ... 674 ISLE STAT II 3 V 212
INFIRM
INFIRM AND AGED I MIGHT STAY . . . . 605 YOU CONTENT 17
INFLUENCE
GROW RICH, POPULAR AND FULL OF INFLUENCE, ... 369 EGO DOMINUS 43
INGENIOUS
MANY INGENIOUS LOVELY THINGS ARE GONE . . . . 428 NINETEEN 19 1
INGENUOUS
MANY INGENUOUS LOVELY THINGS ARE GONE . . . . 428 NINETEEN 19 V 1
INGRATITUDE
EARNED SLANDER, INGRATITUDE, ... 260 UNWORTH PRAISE 16
INHABITANT
INHABITANT OF THE SOFT CHEEK OF A GIRL-- . . . . . . 540 FROM ANTIGONE 2
INHERIT
AND THEY INHERIT THE GREAT SLEEP. . . . . 83 MAD KING GOLL V 22
THEY SHALL INHERIT MY PRIDE, ... 414 TOWER 127
INHERITANCE
HAS HAD A LIKE INHERITANCE, ... 584 GHOST ROG CASE 25
INHERITED
SHADOWS THE INHERITED GLORY OF THE RICH. . . . . . . 418 ANCEST HOUSES 16
HAVING INHERITED A VIGOROUS MIND . . . . 422 MY DESCENDANTS 1
INHERITOR
FOR THE MOST RICH INHERITOR, ... 422 MY TABLE 25
CONTENT OR JOY; A LAST INHERITOR . . . . 491 COOLE BALLYLEE 30
INHUMAN
OF SOME INHUMAN MISERY . . . . 85 MAD KING GOLL 58
ALL, ALL, BY THAT INHUMAN . . . . 504 RESULT THOUGHT 5
INISHMURRAY
KEENING FROM INISHMURRAY, ... 93 FATHER OHART 37
INJURE
DID NOT INJURE ME; . . . . 532 FIRST CONFESS 3
INJUSTICE
BY THE INJUSTICE OF THE SKIES FOR PUNISHMENT? . . . . . 316 COLD HEAVEN 12
INK
ALL SHUFFLE THERE; ALL COUGH IN INK; . . . . 337 SCHOLARS 7
THEY'LL COUGH IN THE INK TO THE WORLD'S END; . . . . . 337 SCHOLARS V 7
IT CAN BE MURDERED WITH A SPOT OF INK. . . . . 491 COOLE BALLYLEE 24
INLAID
COULD SLEEP ON A COUCH OF RUSHES, AND ALL INWROUGHT AND 49 OISIN 3 31
  INLAID,
MORE COMELY THAN MAN MAY MAKE THEM, INLAID WITH SILVER 49 OISIN 3 V 29
  AND GOLD,
COULD SLEEP ON A BED OF RUSHES, AND ALL INWROUGHT 49 OISIN 3 V 31
  AND INLAID,
INLAND
A HERDSMAN CAME FROM INLAND VALLEYS, ... 82 MAD KING GOLL 14
INMOST
IN THE GREEN HILL'S INMOST PART. . . . . 726 LOVERS QUARREL 12
INN
BETWEEN TWO BARRELS AT THE INN. . . . . 551 SONGS REWRIT 1 10
INNER
AN INNER LAUGHTER, AND MAY KISS HIS HANDS TO ME IN SLEEP. 75 ANASHU VIJAYA V 82
THE ORB OF THE MOST INNER LIVING HEART . . . . 689 NETTLESHIP 15
INNISFREE
THE LAKE ISLE OF INNISFREE . . . . 117 ISLE INNISFREE T
I WILL ARISE AND GO NOW, AND GO TO INNISFREE, ... 117 ISLE INNISFREE 1
AND PLUCKED SMALL FRUITS ON INNISFREE. . . . . 742 DANAAN QUICK 5
INNKEEPER'S
O WHAT INNKEEPER'S DAUGHTER . . . . 789 SINGING HEAD 13
INNOCENCE
THE CEREMONY OF INNOCENCE IS DROWNED; . . . . 402 SECOND COMING 6
OUT OF THE MURDEROUS INNOCENCE OF THE SEA. . . . . . . 403 FOR DAUGHTER 16
THE SOUL RECOVERS RADICAL INNOCENCE . . . . 405 FOR DAUGHTER 66
ARE INNOCENCE AND BEAUTY BORN? . . . . 406 FOR DAUGHTER 78
INNOCENCE; AND WISDOM HE. . . . . 440 WISDOM 17
THE BLOOD OF INNOCENCE HAS LEFT NO STAIN. . . . . . . 482 BLOOD AND MOON 34
INNOCENCE AND PEACE DEPART. . . . . 561 FOUR AGES MAN 4
THE LOFTY INNOCENCE THAT IT HAS SLAIN, ... 614 MARCH SONGS 2 12
INNOCENT
OF HALF-FORGOTTEN INNOCENT OLD PLACES; . . . . 130 BOOK STORIES 22
WHO IS SELF-ACCUSED. IF SHE BE INNOCENT . . . . . . 280 TWO KINGS 72
THE INNOCENT AND THE BEAUTIFUL . . . . 476 EVA GORE-BOOTH 24
YOURSELF. NONE BUT THE INNOCENT CAN SEE. . . . . . . 692 MOSADA 1 59
TOUCH NOT THIS BOY, FOR HE IS INNOCENT. . . . . . . 694 MOSADA 1 106

407

		PAGE	TITLE		LINE

INNOCENTS
    THOSE INNOCENTS RE-LIVE THEIR DEATH, ... 612 NEWS ORACLE   15
    THESE INNOCENTS RELIVE THEIR DEATH, ... 612 NEWS ORACLE   V 15
INNUMERABLE
    THE SWIFT INNUMERABLE SPEARS, ... 2 OISIN 1   6
    INNUMERABLE, SINGING, EXULTANT; THE CLAY UNDERNEATH THEM 61 OISIN 3   203
        SHALL PANT,
    AND WHISPER, "THE INNUMERABLE REEDS . . . . 81 EPHEMERA   V 24E
    OLD RAGGED ELMS, OLD THORNS INNUMERABLE, ... 419 MY HOUSE   5
    THE INNUMERABLE CLANGING WINGS THAT HAVE PUT OUT THE MOON. 427 PHANTOM HATRED 32
    WHERE TO THEMSELVES INNUMERABLE BIRDS . . . . 682 SEEKER   25
INNUMEROUS
    NOW WHEREFORE HAST THOU TEARS INNUMEROUS? . . . . 723 KANVA ON SELF 1
INO   SEE KYLE-NA-INO
INSANE
    AND THAT ALONE; YET I, BEING DRIVEN HALF INSANE . . . . 442 BLACK CENTAUR 6
INSATIABLE
    THE SAD, THE LONELY, THE INSATIABLE, ... 114 ROSE OF BATTLE 21
INSEPARABLE
    IMAGINE THAT LOST LOVE, INSEPARABLE FROM MY THOUGHT . . . 390 UNDER SATURN 2
INSEPARABLY
    SURLY AND DISTANT, MIXED INSEPARABLY . . . . 45 OISIN 2   233
    RISING AND FALLING, MIXED INSEPARABLY, ... 45 OISIN 2   V 233
INSIDE
    AND YET STOOD STILL, BECAUSE INSIDE . . . . 303 HOUR DAWN   26
    A LITTLE BOY INSIDE THE SYCAMORE WOOD . . . . 715 DWELT SYCAMORE 5
INSIPID
    INSIPID AS THE DOUGH BEFORE IT IS BAKED, ... 376 PHASES OF MOON 112
INSOLENT
    OR NOISY, INSOLENT SPORT, ... 293 HELEN LIVED   4
    THE INSOLENT UNREPROVED, ... 347 FISHERMAN   16
    CLIPPED AN INSOLENT FARMER'S EARS . . . . 410 TOWER   31
    THAT INSOLENT FIEND ROBERT ARTISSON . . . . 433 NINETEEN 19   128
    WHOSE INSOLENT EYES UNUSED TO TEARS WOULD WEEP. . . . . 678 ISLE STAT II 3 302
INSPIRED
    OR INSPIRED BY FRENZY . . . . 576 ACRE OF GRASS 21
INSTANT
    AROSE, AND ON THE INSTANT CLAMOROUS EAVES, ... 120 SORROW OF LOVE 9
    I WILL END ALL YOUR MAGIC ON THE INSTANT. . . . . . . 242 SHADOW WATER B 411
    AND KNELT ABOVE IT WITH DRAWN KNIFE. ON THE INSTANT . . 278 TWO KINGS   37
    AND ON THE INSTANT WOULD GROW WISE. . . . . 385 ROBARTES DANCE 12
    MUST VANISH ON THE INSTANT IF THE MIND BUT CHANGE . . . 481 BLOOD AND MOON 27
        ITS THEME;
    FOR AN INSTANT STANDS AT EASE, ... 638 BEN BULBEN   31
INSTEAD
    WHEN GREY GULLS FLIT ABOUT INSTEAD OF MEN, ... 292 TO A SHADE   6
    WHEN GREY GULLS FLY ABOUT INSTEAD OF MEN, ... 292 TO A SHADE   V 6
    WHIRLS IN THE OLD INSTEAD, ... 430 NINETEEN 19   56
    FROM GRAVE TO CRADLE RUN INSTEAD; . . . . 449 HERO GIRL FOOL 20
    A DIAGRAM HUNG THERE INSTEAD, ... 485 STATISTICS   3
    BECAUSE HE HAD FEATHERS INSTEAD OF HAIR. . . . . . . 550 SEVERED HEAD   20
    INSTEAD OF THREAD AND NEEDLE . . . . 595 COLONEL MARTIN 23
    NO MORE; TAKE ME INSTEAD OF HER, GREAT SIRS. . . . . . 695 MOSADA 1   114
    AND THE PALE BLOSSOM; BUT I WOKE INSTEAD . . . . . . 761 SHADOW WATER A 281
INSTEP'S
    IF HEAD AND LIMB HAVE BEAUTY AND THE INSTEP'S HIGH AND 354 HIS PHOENIX   21
        LIGHT
INSTRUCTORS
    GRATITUDE TO THE UNKNOWN INSTRUCTORS . . . . 505 GRAT INSTRUCT T
INSTRUMENT
    TO SOME STRINGED INSTRUMENT NONE THERE HAD SEEN, ... 180 QUEEN MAEVE   4
    CARRIES A MUSICAL INSTRUMENT. . . . . 566 LAPIS LAZULI   42
    THEIR HAIR MINGLES ON SOME STRINGED INSTRUMENT, ... 752 SHADOW WATER A 123
INSTRUMENTS
    OF OLD STRINGED INSTRUMENTS, HUNG THERE . . . . 271 GREY ROCK   V 20
INSUFFICIENT
    RIBH CONSIDERS CHRISTIAN LOVE INSUFFICIENT . . . . . . 558 RIBH CHRISTIAN T
INSULT
    AND INSULT HEAPED UPON HIM FOR HIS PAINS, ... 292 TO A SHADE   15
    "THAT IS AN INSULT TO US." . . . . 319 DOLLS   3
INTELLECT
    IN THE IMAGINATION AND INTELLECT? . . . . 245 SHADOW WATER B 486
    OR BOYISH INTELLECT APPROVED, ... 328 ROBERT GREGORY 92
    IN TRIUMPH OF INTELLECT . . . . 383 VISION ROBART 31
    MONUMENTS OF UNAGEING INTELLECT. . . . . 407 SAIL BYZANTIUM 8
    ON MASTER-WORK OF INTELLECT OR HAND, ... 429 NINETEEN 19   37
    ON MASTER WORK OF INTELLECT OR HAND, ... 429 NINETEEN 19 V 37
    ATHENIAN INTELLECT ITS MASTERY . . . . 446 COLONUS PRAISE 11
    FOR INTELLECT WOULD MAKE US PROUD . . . . 460 THREE MONUMENT 10
    AND INTELLECT ITS WANDERING . . . . 478 SELF AND SOUL   22
    FOR INTELLECT NO LONGER KNOWS . . . . 478 SELF AND SOUL   36
    THE INTELLECT OF MAN IS FORCED TO CHOOSE . . . . . . 491 COOLE BALLYLEE V 40A
    THE INTELLECT OF MAN IS FORCED TO CHOOSE . . . . . . 495 CHOICE   1
    TEST EVERY WORK OF INTELLECT OR FAITH, ... 501 VACILLATION   30
    WHAT STALKED THROUGH THE POST OFFICE? WHAT INTELLECT, . . 611 STATUES   26
    AND TILL HIS INTELLECT GROWS SURE . . . . 633 MAN AND ECHO   30
    OUT OF INTELLECT AND SIGHT . . . . 633 MAN AND ECHO   35
INTELLECT'S
    THE SPIRITUAL INTELLECT'S GREAT WORK, ... 632 MAN AND ECHO   20
INTELLECTUAL
    AN INTELLECTUAL HATRED IS THE WORST, ... 405 FOR DAUGHTER   57

```
                                                            PAGE    TITLE            LINE
INTELLECTUAL   (CONTINUED)
     EVERYTHING THAT IS NOT GOD CONSUMED WITH INTELLECTUAL FIRE.   481 BLOOD AND MOON     30
     THE INTELLECTUAL SWEETNESS OF THOSE LINES  . . . . . . .     489 COOLE PARK 29      23
     AN INTELLECTUAL TUNE, . . . . . . . . . . . . . . . .        743 WISDOM DREAMS       2
INTELLIGIBLE
     NO COMMON INTELLIGIBLE SOUND   . . . . . . . . . .           578 CRAZED GIRL         13
INTEMPERANCE
     "HOW FEW THE MIND'S INTEMPERANCE RULE!  . . . . . . .        725 LEGEND              10
INTEMPERATE
     REMORSE FOR INTEMPERATE SPEECH . . . . . . . . . . .         506 REMORSE SPEECH       T
INTENSITY
     AND YET HE HAD THE INTENSITY . . . . . . . . . . .           327 ROBERT GREGORY      71
     ARE FULL OF PASSIONATE INTENSITY. . . . . . . . . . .        402 SECOND COMING        8
INTENT
     THEN MUSE THEY ON THE HOUSEHOLD WOOL INTENT, . . . . .        32 OISIN 2        V    55
     ALL THAT ARE DIFFERENT OF A BASE INTENT!  . . . . . .        398 LEADERS CROWD        2
     COULD KEEP A SWALLOW TO ITS FIRST INTENT!  . . . . . .       489 COOLE PARK 29       19
     WHEN ON LOVE INTENT! . . . . . . . . . . . . . . .           513 JANE TALK BISH      14
     A LIZARD CRAWLS--THE TWO MEN GAZE INTENT, . . . . . .        711 FERENCZ RENYI       47
INTERCOURSE
     MAKE HUMAN INTERCOURSE GROW LESS AND LESS! . . . . . .       473 ALL SOUL NIGHT      75
     FOR THE INTERCOURSE OF ANGELS IS A LIGHT . . . . . .         555 RIBH AT TOMB        15
INTEREST
     THAT FIRST UNNATURAL INTEREST IN MY BOOKS. . . . . . .       468 HARUN RASHID       165
     THAT FIRST STRANGE INTEREST IN MY BOOKS AND STUDIES.  . .    468 HARUN RASHID   V   165
INTERMINABLE
     CRAZED WITH ITS OWN INTERMINABLE SOUND, . . . . . . .         30 OISIN 2        V   23A
INTERVENED
     BUT MASTERFUL HEAVEN HAD INTERVENED TO SAVE IT. . . . .      630 CIRCUS ANIMALS      20
INTIMACY
     THE HEART-REVEALING INTIMACY   . . . . . . . . . .           404 FOR DAUGHTER        23
INTOLERABLE
     INTOLERABLE MUSIC FALLS. . . . . . . . . . . . . .           612 NEWS ORACLE         32
INTOXICANT
     INTO THE HALF-DECEIT OF SOME INTOXICANT . . . . . . .        429 NINETEEN 19         34
INTRICACIES
     IN ALL LOVELY INTRICACIES OF A HOUSE . . . . . . . .         327 ROBERT GREGORY      74
     THE WINE-DARK OF THE WOOD'S INTRICACIES, . . . . . .         446 COLONUS PRAISE       2
     THE WINE DARK OF THE WOOD'S INTRICACIES, . . . . . .         446 COLONUS PRAISE V     2
INTRICACY
     IN STORM-SCATTERED INTRICACY, . . . . . . . . . . .          501 VACILLATION         48
INTRICATE
     THROUGH INTRICATE MOTIONS RAN  . . . . . . . . . .           506 STREAM AND SUN       1
INTRIGUE
     WHO HAD SEEMED TO GLIDE TO SOME INTRIGUE IN HER RED SHOES,   363 DOLLS FACES          6
INTRODUCTION
     INTRODUCTION TO A DRAMATIC POEM  . . . . . . . . .           217 WOODS OF COOLE V     T
INTRODUCTORY
     INTRODUCTORY RHYMES  . . . . . . . . . . . . . .             217 WOODS OF COOLE V     T
     INTRODUCTORY LINES . . . . . . . . . . . . . . .             217 WOODS OF COOLE V     T
     INTRODUCTORY RHYMES  . . . . . . . . . . . . . .             269 PARDON FATHERS V     T
     INTRODUCTORY RHYME . . . . . . . . . . . . . .                269 PARDON FATHERS V     T
INVENT
     WHATEVER THEIR LOOSE FANTASY INVENT . . . . . . . .          398 LEADERS CROWD        4
     WHATEVER THEIR LOOSE PHANTASY INVENT . . . . . . . .         398 LEADERS CROWD  V     4
     WHAT FANATICS INVENT . . . . . . . . . . . . . .             503 QUARREL IN AGE       2
INVER
     AND SHOOK AT INVER AMERGIN . . . . . . . . . . .              81 MAD KING GOLL        3
INVIOLATE
     FAR-OFF, MOST SECRET, AND INVIOLATE ROSE, . . . . . .        169 SECRET ROSE          1
     FAR OFF, MOST SECRET, AND INVIOLATE ROSE, . . . . . .        169 SECRET ROSE    V     1
     FAR-OFF, MOST SECRET, AND INVIOLATE ROSE? . . . . . .        170 SECRET ROSE         32
     FAR OFF, MOST SECRET, AND INVIOLATE ROSE? . . . . . .        170 SECRET ROSE    V    32
INVISIBLE
     POURED OUT WINE FOR THE HIGH INVISIBLE ONES. . . . . .       219 WOODS OF COOLE      44
     FROM TERRIFIED, INVISIBLE BEAST OR BIRD! . . . . . .         389 IMAGE PAST           6
INVULNERABLE
     AND FOUGHT WITH THE INVULNERABLE TIDE. . . . . . . .         111 CUCHULAIN SEA       86
INWARDLY
     BUT INWARDLY, SURMISE COMPANIONS . . . . . . . . .           320 REED WHISPERER       4
INWROUGHT
     COULD SLEEP ON A COUCH OF RUSHES, AND ALL INWROUGHT AND       49 OISIN 3             31
          INLAID,
     COULD SLEEP ON A BED OF RUSHES, AND ALL INWROUGHT             49 OISIN 3        V    31
          AND INLAID,
IOLAN
     OF GOLDEN-ARMED IOLAN AND THE QUEEN . . . . . . . .          766 SHADOW WATER A     375
IOLLAN
     IT WAS GOLDEN-ARMED IOLLAN, AND HE DIED . . . . . .          242 SHADOW WATER B     406
     FOR GOLDEN-ARMED IOLLAN HAS BEEN KILLED. . . . . . .         242 SHADOW WATER B     410
     FOR GOLDEN-ARMED IOLLAN THAT I LOVED. . . . . . . .          242 SHADOW WATER B     421
     O! O! O! O! FOR GOLDEN-ARMED IOLLAN. . . . . . . .           243 SHADOW WATER B     428
     I NEVER HAVE BEEN GOLDEN-ARMED IOLLAN. . . . . . . .         244 SHADOW WATER B     464
IRELAND
     TO IRELAND IN THE COMING TIMES . . . . . . . . . .           137 TO IRELAND           T
     APOLOGIA ADDRESSED TO IRELAND IN THE COMING DAYS . . . .     137 TO IRELAND     V     T
     AND MAY THE THOUGHTS OF IRELAND BROOD . . . . . . .          138 TO IRELAND          15
     AND STILL THE THOUGHTS OF IRELAND BROOD, . . . . . .         138 TO IRELAND     V    15
     RED HANRAHAN'S SONG ABOUT IRELAND . . . . . . . . .          206 HANRAHANS SONG       T
     ROMANCE IN IRELAND . . . . . . . . . . . . . . .             289 SEPTEMBER 1913 V     T
     ROMANTIC IRELAND . . . . . . . . . . . . . . .               289 SEPTEMBER 1913 V     T
```

	PAGE	TITLE		LINE
IRELAND (CONTINUED)				
ON A RECENT GOVERNMENT APPOINTMENT IN IRELAND	317	APPOINTMENT	V	T
AMERICAN COLONIES, IRELAND, FRANCE AND INDIA	487	SEVEN SAGES		15
OUT OF IRELAND HAVE WE COME.	506	REMORSE SPEECH		11
"I AM OF IRELAND"	526	AM OF IRELAND		T
"I AM OF IRELAND"	526	AM OF IRELAND		1
AND THE HOLY LAND OF IRELAND,	526	AM OF IRELAND		2
COME DANCE WITH ME IN IRELAND."	526	AM OF IRELAND		5
"I AM OF IRELAND,	526	AM OF IRELAND		14
AND THE HOLY LAND OF IRELAND,	526	AM OF IRELAND		15
AND DANCE WITH ME IN IRELAND."	527	AM OF IRELAND		18
"I AM OF IRELAND,	527	AM OF IRELAND		27
AND THE HOLY LAND OF IRELAND,	527	AM OF IRELAND		28
AND DANCE WITH ME IN IRELAND."	527	AM OF IRELAND		31
ALL THAT WAS SAID IN IRELAND IS A LIE	542	PARN FUNERAL 1		26
"IRELAND SHALL GET HER FREEDOM AND YOU STILL BREAK STONE."	590	PARNELL		2
"THE DEAD IRELAND OF MY YOUTH, BUT AN IRELAND	602	GALLERY REVIS		11
"THE DEAD IRELAND OF MY YOUTH, BUT AN IRELAND	602	GALLERY REVIS		11
IRELAND AFTER THE REVOLUTION IV	628	JANE MOUNTAIN	V	T
AND ANCIENT IRELAND KNEW IT ALL.	637	BEN BULBEN		16
IRELAND'S				
THAT SANG, TO SWEETEN IRELAND'S WRONG,	137	TO IRELAND		3
WHO SANG TO SWEETEN IRELAND'S WRONG,	137	TO IRELAND	V	3
MADE IRELAND'S HEART BEGIN TO BEAT!	138	TO IRELAND		12
ALTHOUGH THE KING OF IRELAND'S DEAD	273	GREY ROCK		68
MURROUGH, THE KING OF IRELAND'S SON,	274	GREY ROCK		71
ROMANTIC IRELAND'S DEAD AND GONE,	289	SEPTEMBER 1913		7
ROMANTIC IRELAND'S DEAD AND GONE,	289	SEPTEMBER 1913		15
ROMANTIC IRELAND'S DEAD AND GONE,	290	SEPTEMBER 1913		23
DEFENDING IRELAND'S SOUL	546	TO SAME TUNE 2		6
IRELAND'S HISTORY IN THEIR LINEAMENTS TRACE!	604	GALLERY REVIS		53
THAT IRELAND'S MIND BE GREATER,	608	SONGS BURDEN 3		21
MUST IRELAND'S BLOOD BE SHED.	608	SONGS BURDEN 3		26
DEFENDING IRELAND'S SOUL.	613	MARCH SONGS 1		6
IRISH				
THE DEDICATION TO A BOOK OF STORIES SELECTED FROM THE IRISH NOVELISTS	129	BOOK STORIES		T
DEDICATION OF "IRISH TALES"	129	BOOK STORIES	V	T
JAMES AND HIS IRISH WHEN THE DUTCHMAN CROSSED!	270	PARDON FATHERS		12
AN IRISH AIRMAN FORESEES HIS DEATH	328	IRISH AIRMAN		T
AND SAVED THE IRISH POOR,	586	PARNELLITES		12
WE IRISH, BORN INTO THAT ANCIENT SECT	611	STATUES		28
IRISH POETS, LEARN YOUR TRADE,	639	BEN BULBEN		68
THAT SONG I'VE MADE. 'TIS OF AN IRISH TALE.	696	MOSADA 2		19
IRISHRY				
STILL THE INDOMITABLE IRISHRY.	640	BEN BULBEN		83
IRON				
HE RULES YOU WITH AN IRON ROD,	22	OISIN 1		332
HE HOLDS YOU WITH AN IRON BOND,	22	OISIN 1		333
IN A LONG IRON SLEEP, AS A FISH IN THE WATER GOES DUMB AS A STONE.	53	OISIN 3		96
THEIR SWORDS UPON THEIR IRON KNEES,	156	FORGOT BEAUTY		23
A SWORD UPON HIS IRON KNEES,	156	FORGOT BEAUTY	V	23
WHEN SHE THE IRON WROUGHT, OR	345	ON WOMAN		17
OR SHOD IN IRON, CLIMBED THE NARROW STAIRS,	412	TOWER		83
A SLOW LOW NOTE AND AN IRON BELL.	549	SEVERED HEAD		7
A SLOW LOW NOTE AND AN IRON BELL.	550	SEVERED HEAD		14
A SLOW LOW NOTE AND AN IRON BELL.	550	SEVERED HEAD		21
NOR EVER MADE AN IRON RED	606	SONGS BURDEN 1		14
OLD IRON, OLD BONES, OLD RAGS, THAT RAVING SLUT	630	CIRCUS ANIMALS		37
NOD TO THE IRON SHOES OF TIME,	736	SUMMER EVENING		11
IRRATIONAL				
IRRATIONAL STREAMS OF BLOOD ARE STAINING EARTH!	564	GYRES		5
IRREGULAR				
AN AFFABLE IRREGULAR,	423	ROAD AT DOOR		1
IRVING				
IRVING AND HIS PLUME OF PRIDE.	625	NATIVITY		8
ISAIAH'S				
ISAIAH'S COAL, WHAT MORE CAN MAN DESIRE?	502	VACILLATION		74
ISLAND				
THE ISLAND OF THE LIVING	1	OISIN 1	V	T
WRESTLED AMONG THE ISLAND BANDS.	23	OISIN 1		350
THE ISLAND OF VICTORIES	29	OISIN 2	V	T
TO THE ISLAND OF FORGETFULNESS, FOR LO!	46	OISIN 2		246
IS THE ISLAND OF CONTENT?" "NONE KNOW," SHE SAID!	46	OISIN 2		249
THE ISLAND OF FORGETFULNESS	47	OISIN 3	V	T
AN EPILOGUE TO "THE ISLAND OF STATUES" AND "THE SEEKER"	64	HAPPY SHEPHERD	V	T
THE ISLAND DREAMS UNDER THE DAWN	77	INDIAN TO LOVE		1
THERE LIES A LEAFY ISLAND	86	STOLEN CHILD		3
O DAUGHTER OF THE ISLAND OF WOODS!	164	PERFECT BEAUTY	V	1
ON THE ISLAND LAWNS, THEIR FEET WHERE THE PALE FOAM GLEAMS.	203	WITHER BOUGHS		14
BUT IN SOME ISLAND WHERE THE LIFE OF THE WORLD	249	SHADOW WATER B		559
ROUND LOUGH DERG'S HOLY ISLAND I WENT UPON THE STONES,	593	PILGRIM		6
THE ISLAND OF STATUES.	644	ISLE STAT I 1		T
LYRICS FROM "THE ISLAND OF STATUES"	646	ISLE STAT I 1	V	T
SMALL ISLAND, WHERE THE FULL SOFT SHEEN	653	ISLE STAT I 2		36
SOME SAY THAT ALL WHO TOUCH THE ISLAND LONE	653	ISLE STAT I 2		42
ISLAND OF STATUES A FRAGMENT	666	ISLE STAT II 3	V	T
HAD FELT THE ISLAND BREEZE, MY LORE	668	ISLE STAT II 3		55
FROM MY WIZARD ISLAND LAIR,	668	ISLE STAT II 3		63
HAD LEFT THE ISLAND BREEZE, MY LORE	668	ISLE STAT II 3	V	55

	PAGE	TITLE	LINE

ISLAND (CONTINUED)

WILT ROAM AWAY FROM THIS RICH ISLAND REST? • • • • • •	669	ISLE STAT II 3	88
WHO, SWIMMING, SOUGHT THE ISLAND LONE; • • • • • • •	673	ISLE STAT II 3	181
IN A FAR STILLNESS OF THE ISLAND DIE. • • • • • • •	675	ISLE STAT II 3 V	246
WHOSE DWELLING WAS A TREE-WRAPT ISLAND, LULLED • • • • •	693	MOSADA 1	79
OUT OF THAT ISLAND WHERE THE FOOL OF THE WOOD • • • • •	747	SHADOW WATER A	2

ISLANDS

THEY LOVE AND KISS IN ISLANDS FAR AWAY, • • • • • • •	29	OISIN 2 V	13
THE ISLANDS OF DANCING AND OF VICTORIES • • • • • • •	46	OISIN 2	247
AND THE DREAMS OF THE ISLANDS WERE GONE, • • • • • • •	59	OISIN 3	175
AND THE DREAMS OF THE ISLANDS WENT OUT OF ME, • • • • •	59	OISIN 3 V	175
I AM HAUNTED BY NUMBERLESS ISLANDS, AND MANY A DANAAN SHORE,	122	WHITE BIRDS	9
AND SOUGHT THROUGH LANDS AND ISLANDS NUMBERLESS YEARS, • •	170	SECRET ROSE	23
AND OF APPLE ISLANDS WHERE THE DANAAN KIND • • • • •	203	WITHER BOUGHS V	12
IN ISLANDS WHERE THE CHILDREN OF AENGUS WIND • • • • •	245	SHADOW WATER B	469
THROUGH THREE ENCHANTED ISLANDS, ALLEGORICAL DREAMS, • •	629	CIRCUS ANIMALS	11
EVEN THE WANDERING ISLANDS OF THE GODS, • • • • • • •	749	SHADOW WATER A	45

ISLE

THE ISLE LOOMED LARGELY IN THE LIGHT • • • • • • • •	25	OISIN 1 V	385
THE ISLE WAS OVER NOW AND GONE; • • • • • • • • •	28	OISIN 1 V	427B
AND SHIVERED, KNOWING THE ISLE OF MANY FEARS, • • • • •	30	OISIN 2	25
COME FROM THE ISLE OF THE LIVING." "THEN GET YE • • • •	34	OISIN 2 V	79
AND TRAMPLE MY DARK ISLE. • • • • • • • • • • • •	45	OISIN 2 V	239E
WHICH IS THE ISLE OF YOUTH?" "NONE KNOW," SHE SAID, • •	46	OISIN 2 V	249
AN ISLE LAY LEVEL BEFORE US, WITH DRIPPING HAZEL AND OAK,	47	OISIN 3	10
AN ISLE LAY LEVEL BEFORE US, DRIPPING WITH HAZEL AND OAK?	47	OISIN 3 V	10
"LIKE ME WERE SOME GALLEY FORSAKEN FAR OFF IN MERIDIAN ISLE.	55	OISIN 3	117
OUR ISLE AWAITS US, ON EACH LEA • • • • • • • • •	77	INDIAN TO LOVE V	2
TO AN ISLE IN THE WATER • • • • • • • • • • • •	89	ISLE IN WATER	T
TO AN ISLE IN THE WATER • • • • • • • • • • • •	89	ISLE IN WATER	7
TO AN ISLE IN THE WATER • • • • • • • • • • • •	89	ISLE IN WATER	15
THE LAKE ISLE OF INNISFREE • • • • • • • • • • •	117	ISLE INNISFREE	T
UPON A WOVEN WORLD-FORGOTTEN ISLE • • • • • • • •	126	DREAM OF FAERY	8
UPON A DIM, GREEN, WELL-BELOVED ISLE, • • • • • • •	126	DREAM OF FAERY V	8
TO BLESS THAT ISLE WITH HONEY IN HIS TONES, • • • • •	128	DREAM OF FAERY V	44
NOR AVALON THE GRASS-GREEN HOLLOW, NOR JOYOUS ISLE, • •	209	UNDER THE MOON	2
OR AVALLON THE GRASS GREEN HOLLOW, OR JOYOUS ISLE • •	209	UNDER THE MOON V	2
WITH SINGING SWEET AS E'ER ROUND LAKE-LULLED ISLE • • •	649	ISLE STAT I 1	106
THE LAKE-EMBOSOMED ISLE. NAY, THIS MY QUEST • • • • •	657	ISLE STAT I 3	60
YONDER'S THE ISLE IN SEARCH WHEREOF WE CAME; • • • • •	662	ISLE STAT II 2	13
TO YONDER ISLE, WHERE NEVER SAIL WAS FURLED, • • • • •	664	ISLE STAT II 2	56
AND CROUCH IN SOME FAR STILLNESS OF THE ISLE, AND DIE. • •	675	ISLE STAT II 3	246
OF THIS LAKE-NURTURED ISLE! LET THY KING BE • • • • •	679	ISLE STAT II 3	315
IN THE FAR ISLE SHE SANG HERSELF ASLEEP, • • • • • •	694	MOSADA 1	90
MAYBE IN SOME ISLE OF ISLES, • • • • • • • • • •	732	STREET DANCERS	27
TO THE GREEN ISLE OF WIGHT • • • • • • • • • • •	740	EARL PAUL	10

ISLE'S

"BUT NEVER THE YEARS IN THE ISLE'S SOFT PLACES • • • •	27	OISIN 1 V	419A
"BUT NEVER THE YEARS IN OUR ISLE'S SOFT PLACES • • • •	28	OISIN 1 V	424

ISLES   SEE SPICE-ISLES

ISLES OF THE LIVING AND OF VICTORIES • • • • • • • •	46	OISIN 2 V	247
"IN THE ISLES OF THE FARTHEST SEAS WHERE ONLY THE SPIRITS COME.	56	OISIN 3	133
AND I KNOW OF THE ISLES WHERE THE DANAAN KIND • • • • •	203	WITHER BOUGHS V	12
MAYBE IN SOME ISLE OF ISLES, • • • • • • • • • •	732	STREET DANCERS	27

ISOLATED

CHARACTER ISOLATED BY A DEED • • • • • • • • • •	630	CIRCUS ANIMALS	29

ISSUE

SHOULD KNOW WHAT ISSUE IS AT STAKE; • • • • • • • •	778	FRIENDS WRONG	3

ISSUED

HE WALKED THAT ROOM AND ISSUED THENCE • • • • • • •	438	SONGS PLAY 2	2

ITALIAN

FOR THE ITALIAN COMEDIES? • • • • • • • • • • •	287	TO WEALTHY MAN	13
WITH LEARNED ITALIAN THINGS. • • • • • • • • • •	415	TOWER	158
YET RISE FROM YOUR ITALIAN TOMB, • • • • • • • • •	791	REPRISALS	10

ITALY

WHENCE TURBULENT ITALY SHOULD DRAW • • • • • • • •	288	TO WEALTHY MAN	25

ITCH

ARE DRIVEN BY WEALTH AS BEGGARS BY THE ITCH," • • • • •	300	BEGGAR CRIED	14

ITERATION

AND BIRDLY ITERATION IS • • • • • • • • • • • •	67	HAPPY SHEPHERD V	46B

ITH

MY WORD WAS LAW FROM ITH TO EMAIN, • • • • • • • •	81	MAD KING GOLL	2

IVIED

THROUGH BUSH THEY PLUNGED AND OVER IVIED ROOT, • • • •	278	TWO KINGS	32

IVORIES

AND GONE ARE PHIDIAS' FAMOUS IVORIES • • • • • • •	428	NINETEEN 19	7
AND GONE ARE PHIDIAS' CARVEN IVORIES • • • • • • •	428	NINETEEN 19 V	7
OR BREAK IN BITS THE FAMOUS IVORIES • • • • • • •	430	NINETEEN 19	47

IVORY

AND THEN SMOOTH OUT WITH IVORY HANDS AND SIGH, • • • •	228	SHADOW WATER B	133
AND NOT A ROOF OF IVORY AND GOLD. • • • • • • • •	246	SHADOW WATER B	500
I WOULD GROW JEALOUS OF THE IVORY ROOF, • • • • • •	246	SHADOW WATER B	501
IVORY IMAGES WITH AMETHYST EYES. • • • • • • • •	248	SHADOW WATER B	534
I FOUND THAT IVORY IMAGE THERE • • • • • • • • •	514	JANE GROWN OLD	1
AND THEN SMOOTH OUT WITH IVORY HANDS AND SIGH. • • • •	750	SHADOW WATER A	70

IVY

SQUARE LEAVES OF THE IVY MOVED OVER US, BINDING US DOWN TO OUR REST.	52	OISIN 3	76

411

IVY   (CONTINUED)
   FROM WHERE THE OLD IVY CRAWLS ROUND THE OLD STEEPLE, . . 728 PRIEST FAIRY   6
IVY-COVERED
   WENT OUT. AMONG THE IVY-COVERED ROCKS, ... 283 TWO KINGS   147
IVY'S   SEE GROUND-IVY'S
   AND THE GROUND IVY'S BLUER LIGHT, A STAG . . . . . . 277 TWO KINGS   V   6
I-WIS
   FAREWELL! I MUST BE GONE I-WIS, ... 67 HAPPY SHEPHERD V 46D
JABBER
   JABBER AND SCREAM ABOUT HIM IN THE NIGHT! . . . . . 34 OISIN 2   82
   JABBER AND SCREAM. YET HE, FOR ALL HIS BOLD . . . . 34 OISIN 2   V 82
JACK   SEE STILT-JACK
   WITH EVERY JACK AND JILL? . . . . 335 YOUNG BEAUTY   3
   BECAUSE OF MY DEAR JACK THAT'S DEAD. . . . . . . 508 JANE BISHOP   5
   BANISHED JACK THE JOURNEYMAN, ... 508 JANE BISHOP   9
   BUT A BIRCH-TREE STOOD MY JACK! . . . . 508 JANE BISHOP   20
   JACK HAD MY VIRGINITY, ... 508 JANE BISHOP   22
   BUT A BIRCH TREE STOOD MY JACK! . . . . . . 508 JANE BISHOP V 20
   CRAZY JANE AND JACK THE JOURNEYMAN . . . . . 511 JANE AND JACK   T
   I HAD WILD JACK FOR A LOVER! . . . . 512 JANE ON GOD   19
JACKASS
   TO HEAR A JACKASS BRAY! . . . . 455 HIS MEMORIES   10
JACQUES
   "VENGEANCE FOR JACQUES MOLAY." IN CLOUD-PALE RAGS, OR 426 PHANTOM HATRED   10
     IN LACE,
   FOR VENGEANCE ON THE MURDERERS OF JACQUES MOLAY. . . . 426 PHANTOM HATRED   16
   "VENGENCE FOR JACQUES MOLAY." IN CLOUD PALE RAGS, OR IN 426 PHANTOM HATRED V 10
     LACE,
JADE
   A GREY-GREEN CUP OF JADE, ... 781 MY HEART BEAT   15
JAFFER
   HIS VIZIR JAFFER FOR AN UNKNOWN REASON! . . . . . . 462 HARUN RASHID   32
JAFFER'S
   SEEMED SO ON PURPOSE, MUTTERED JAFFER'S FRIENDS, . . . 462 HARUN RASHID   37
JAGS
   A DOME MADE OUT OF ENDLESS CARVEN JAGS, ... 38 OISIN 2   144
   WAITED. ABOVE, IN ENDLESS CARVEN JAGS, ... 38 OISIN 2   V 144
JAILBIRD
   THAT RAMBLING JAILBIRD BILLY SAID! . . . . 332 ROUND TOWER   26
JAILOR
   THUS SPAKE THE TOWN JAILOR . . . . 740 EARL PAUL   13
JAMES
   JAMES AND HIS IRISH WHEN THE DUTCHMAN CROSSED! . . . 270 PARDON FATHERS 12
   JAMES CONNOLLY REPLIED, ... 396 ROSE TREE   8
JAMMED
   ANOINTING, TORCH JAMMED DOWN BETWEEN THE FLAGS, . . . 38 OISIN 2   V 143
JANE
   CRAZY JANE AND THE BISHOP . . . . 507 JANE BISHOP   T
   EIGHT POEMS CRAZY JANE AND THE BISHOP . . . . . 507 JANE BISHOP V   T
   CRAZY JANE REPROVED . . . . 509 JANE REPROVED   T
   CRAZY JANE ON THE DAY OF JUDGMENT . . . . . . 510 JANE JUDGMENT   T
   AND THAT IS WHAT JANE SAID. . . . . 510 JANE JUDGMENT   5
   AND THAT IS WHAT JANE SAID. . . . . 510 JANE JUDGMENT 15
   CRAZY JANE AND JACK THE JOURNEYMAN . . . . . 511 JANE AND JACK   T
   CRAZY JANE ON GOD . . . . 512 JANE ON GOD   T
   CRAZY JANE TALKS WITH THE BISHOP . . . . . . 513 JANE TALK BISH T
   CRAZY JANE GROWN OLD LOOKS AT THE DANCERS . . . 514 JANE GROWN OLD T
   CRAZY JANE AND THE DANCERS . . . . 514 JANE GROWN OLD V T
   COULD CRAZY JANE PUT OFF OLD AGE . . . . . . 606 SONGS BURDEN 1 19
   CRAZY JANE ON THE MOUNTAIN . . . . 628 JANE MOUNTAIN   T
   (SAID CRAZY JANE) . . . . 628 JANE MOUNTAIN   2
   (SAID CRAZY JANE) . . . . 628 JANE MOUNTAIN 12
JAPANESE
   WHERE THE INDIANS TRADE OR JAPANESE? . . . . . . 361 ALF POLLEXFEN 20
   THEY HAD A PRIEST SAY MASS, AND EVEN THE JAPANESE, . . . 363 DOLLS FACES   2
   IMITATED FROM THE JAPANESE . . . . 567 FROM JAPANESE   T
JASMINE
   WHEN EVENING STIRS THE JASMINE BOUGH, AND YET . . . . 463 HARUN RASHID   53
   WHEN EVENING STIRS THE JASMINE, AND YET . . . . . 463 HARUN RASHID V 53
   "AND YET THE JASMINE SEASON WARMS OUR BLOOD." . . . . 464 HARUN RASHID   73
JAUNTING
   JAUNTING, JOURNEYING . . . . 342 SHEP GOATHERD   95
JAWS
   BY THESE WIRE-JOINTED JAWS AND LIMBS OF WOOD, ... 382 VISION ROBART   10
   ABOVE, SALIVA DRIPPING FROM HIS JAWS, ... 689 NETTLESHIP   4
JAY'S
   THE JAY'S NEST BY MY WINDOW . . . . 424 STARES NEST   V T
JEALOUS
   I WOULD GROW JEALOUS OF THE IVORY ROOF, ... 246 SHADOW WATER B 501
   I AM JEALOUS OF THE LOOK MEN TURN ON YOU . . . . 447 HERO GIRL FOOL V A
   THAT IS A LIGHT MY JEALOUS SOUL HAS SENT. . . . . 558 RIBH CHRISTIAN 8
JEALOUSY
   JEALOUSY . . . . 70 ANASHU VIJAYA V T
   ALL THEIR JEALOUSY DISPLAY, ... 726 LOVERS QUARREL 22
JENNY   SEE SPINNING-JENNY
JERK
   BUT A GOOD STRONG CAUSE"--THE ROPE GAVE A JERK THERE, . . 545 TO SAME TUNE 1 23
   BUT A GOOD STRONG CAUSE"--THE ROPE GAVE A JERK THERE, . . 616 MARCH SONGS 3 23
JERRY
   DAN AND JERRY LOUT . . . . 520 HIS BARGAIN   5
   DAN AND JERRY TOUT, ... 520 HIS BARGAIN V 5

                                         PAGE   TITLE   LINE
JESSAMINE
    HIS GARDEN RINGED WITH JESSAMINE, ...   729 PRIEST FAIRY   34
JEST
    A WORD AND A JEST. . . . .   293 HELEN LIVED   12
JESTER
    THE JESTER WALKED IN THE GARDEN: . . . .   159 CAP AND BELLS   1
    A QUEEN WAS LOVED BY A JESTER, ...   159 CAP AND BELLS   V   1
    A QUEEN WAS BELOVED BY A JESTER, ...   159 CAP AND BELLS   V   1
JET
    AND HAD DISPORTED IN THE STILLY JET, ...   31 OISIN 2   39
    AND HAD DISPORTED IN THE EYES STILL JET . . . . . .   31 OISIN 2   V   39
    THE ABOUNDING GLITTERING JET: THOUGH NOW IT SEEMS . . 417 ANCEST HOUSES   12
    LIKE THIS PURE JET, NOW LOST AMID BLUE SKY, ...   464 HARUN RASHID   64
    BUT COULD NOT CAST A SINGLE JET THEREON. . . . . .   482 BLOOD AND MOON   39
    A CLOVEN, DANCING JET, ...   680 LOVE AND DEATH   2
JEW
    HE SPOKE WITH TURK AND JEW, ...   594 COLONEL MARTIN   2
    LIKE AN OLD JEW MAN, ...   620 JOHN KINSELLA   14
JEWEL
    SOBRIETY IS A JEWEL . . . .   592 DRUNK SOBRIETY   5
JEWELLED
    THE JEWELLED CROWNS THAT KINGS HAVE HURLED . . . . .   155 FORGOT BEAUTY   4
JEWELRY
    AND BOUGHT THE GRANDEST JEWELRY . . . .   595 COLONEL MARTIN   21
    PUT JEWELRY IN THE PACK, ...   595 COLONEL MARTIN   24
    JEWELRY SO GRAND." . . . .   595 COLONEL MARTIN   33
JEWELS
    HAS COME INTO THE JEWELS OF THE HARP . . . .   239 SHADOW WATER B V 371A
JEWEL-STONE
    AND HID HER AMONG FRUITS OF JEWEL-STONE . . . . . .   224 SHADOW WATER B   49
JIG
    SO WE DANCE A FAIRY JIG . . . .   726 LOVERS QUARREL   19
JILL
    WITH EVERY JACK AND JILL? . . . .   335 YOUNG BEAUTY   3
JINN
    I SAY THAT A JINN SPOKE. A LIVE-LONG HOUR . . . . .   467 HARUN RASHID   V 136
JOAN
    DARK JOAN CALL THE BERRIES SWEET, ...   743 DANAAN QUICK   28
JOE
    HOLY JOE, THE BEGGAR-MAN, ...   529 TOM LUNATIC   8
JOHN
    GOOD FATHER JOHN O'HART . . . .   91 FATHER OHART   1
    BUT FATHER JOHN WENT UP, ...   92 FATHER OHART   9
    AND FATHER JOHN WENT DOWN: . . . .   92 FATHER OHART   10
    AND THESE WERE THE WORKS OF JOHN, ...   93 FATHER OHART   25
    AND THAT ENQUIRING MAN JOHN SYNGE COMES NEXT, . . .   324 ROBERT GREGORY   25
    BUT WHERE IS LAID THE SAILOR JOHN . . . .   360 ALF POLLEXFEN   17
    WHERE HAVE THEY LAID THE SAILOR JOHN? . . . . . .   361 ALF POLLEXFEN   23
    THAT MEDITATIVE MAN, JOHN SYNGE, AND THOSE . . . .   489 COOLE PARK 29   13
    JOHN BULL AND THE SEA ARE FRIENDS: . . . .   583 GHOST ROG CASE   4
    JOHN BULL HAS STOOD FOR PARLIAMENT, ...   583 GHOST ROG CASE   11
    JOHN BULL HAS GONE TO INDIA . . . .   583 GHOST ROG CASE   21
    "GREATEST SINCE REMBRANDT," ACCORDING TO JOHN SYNGE: . . 602 GALLERY REVIS   26
    JOHN SYNGE, I AND AUGUSTA GREGORY, THOUGHT . . . .   603 GALLERY REVIS   41
    AND HERE'S JOHN SYNGE HIMSELF, THAT ROOTED MAN, . .   603 GALLERY REVIS   48
    AND HERE'S JOHN SYNGE, A MEDITATIVE MAN, ...   603 GALLERY REVIS   V   48
    JOHN KINSELLA'S LAMENT FOR MRS. MARY MOORE . . . .   620 JOHN KINSELLA   T
    AND JOHN WILL PARDON THEE, ...   739 EARL PAUL   2
    AND JOHN ROSE UP AND STOOD, ...   741 EARL PAUL   54
JOHN'S
    IN TRUST TOOK HE JOHN'S LANDS: . . . .   92 FATHER OHART   5
JOHNSON
    DOWSON AND JOHNSON MOST I PRAISE-- . . . .   273 GREY ROCK   62
    LIONEL JOHNSON COMES THE FIRST TO MIND, ...   324 ROBERT GREGORY   17
JOIN
    TO JOIN HIS BROTHERS IN THE HOME OF YEARS . . . . .   30 OISIN 2   V   17
    BEEN BONE AND SINEW: WHEN SUCH BODIES JOIN . . . .   555 RIBH AT TOMB   12
    THEY SEEM TO JOIN HER PRAYER-- . . . .   736 IN CHURCH   12
JOINED
    BY ROOTS THAT JOINED ABOVE OUR PLUMES-- . . . . .   16 OISIN 1   V 224C
    WE JOINED HIM FOR HIS PAY, BUT HAVE HAD NONE . . .   225 SHADOW WATER B V 68A
    DO YOU, TOO, DOUBT ME? HAVE YOU JOINED THEIR PLOT? . . . 227 SHADOW WATER B   106
    . . . HAVE JOINED THE AGITATION AGAINST IMMORAL LITERATURE 262 STUDENTS AGIT   T
    . . . HAVE JOINED THE ANCIENT ORDER OF HIBERNIANS AND THE 262 STUDENTS AGIT   V   T
    NOR STRAINING JOY, BUT WHOLE IS JOINED TO WHOLE: . . .   555 RIBH AT TOMB   14
JOINT
    IF TIME WERE SUPPLER IN THE JOINT, ...   306 HOUR DAWN   94
    ALL THEIR BODIES, JOINT BY JOINT, ...   776 AGAINST WITCH   22
    ALL THEIR BODIES, JOINT BY JOINT, ...   776 AGAINST WITCH   22
JOINTED   SEE WIRE-JOINTED
JOINTS
    WITH QUAKING JOINTS AND TERROR-STRICKEN FACES, . . .   185 QUEEN MAEVE   121
    WITH QUAKING JOINTS AND TERROR STRUCKEN FACES, . . .   185 QUEEN MAEVE   V 121
    WITH QUAKING JOINTS AND TERROR-STRUCKEN FACES, . . .   185 QUEEN MAEVE   V 121
    MADE THE JOINTS OF HEAVEN CRACK: . . . .   509 JANE REPROVED   11
JOKE
    THE WITTY MAN AND HIS JOKE . . . .   347 FISHERMAN   19
JOKES
    COMES CRACKING JOKES OF CIVIL WAR . . . .   423 ROAD AT DOOR   3

413

```
                                                          PAGE    TITLE           LINE

JOLLY
    HE HAD SEEN A RED-HAIRED JOLLY LAD  . . . . . . . .   303 HOUR DAWN      V   27
JOLT
    SHIVER UNDER THE LASH, STRAIN, SWEAT AND JOLT . . . . .  260 FASC DIFFICULT     7
JONATHAN
    "JONATHAN SWIFT'S AT REST! . . . . . . . . . . . .   493 SWIFTS EPITAPH V   1
    THROUGH JONATHAN SWIFT'S DARK GROVE HE PASSED, AND THERE  543 PARN FUNERAL 2   11
JONSON'S
    --BEN JONSON'S PHRASE--AND FIND WHEN JUNE IS COME  . . .  321 REED WHISPERER     6
    BEN JONSON'S PHRASE--AND STILL MAY TURN MY FEET . . . .  321 REED WHISPERER V   6
JOSEPH
    SAINT JOSEPH THOUGHT THE WORLD WOULD MELT . . . . . .  619 STICK INCENSE      3
JOSEPH'S
    BECAUSE ST. JOSEPH'S IMAGE HANGETH HERE . . . . . . .  676 ISLE STAT II 3   266
JOSTLED
    JOSTLED AND SHOUTED THOSE WAR-WASTED MEN, . . . . . . .  286 TWO KINGS        216
    FARMERS JOSTLED AT THE FAIR . . . . . . . . . . . .   410 TOWER             39
    CROWDS JOSTLED AT THE FAIR  . . . . . . . . . . . .   410 TOWER          V   39
JOT
    MY ANGRY KING-REMEMBERING SOUL ONE JOT. . . . . . . .   36 OISIN 2           94
    THEY STIRRED MY SPACIOUS SOUL IN ME NO JOT-- . . . . .   36 OISIN 2       V   94
    NOR SHOOK MY FIRM AND SPACIOUS SOUL ONE JOT! . . . . .   36 OISIN 2       V   94
    MY ANGRY, KING REMEMBERING SOUL ONE JOT! . . . . . . .   36 OISIN 2       V   94
JOURNALIST
    A JOURNALIST MAKES UP HIS LIES . . . . . . . . . .   598 STONE CROSS        3
    TURN TO A DRUNKEN JOURNALIST! . . . . . . . . . . .   626 OLD MEN BE MAD     4
JOURNEY
    SPLASHED ALL WITH CLAY AND JOURNEY DULL, . . . . . . .   82 MAD KING GOLL V   13
    "I ONLY ASK WHAT WAY MY JOURNEY LIES, . . . . . . . .  108 CUCHULAIN SEA     31
    THE CLOUDS ON THEIR JOURNEY ABOVE, . . . . . . . . .  119 PITY OF LOVE       4
    AND YOU HAVE TOLD ME THAT THEIR JOURNEY LIES . . . . .  231 SHADOW WATER B   205
    DECIDED HE WOULD JOURNEY HOME, . . . . . . . . . . .  361 ALF POLLEXFEN     30
    DECIDED HE MUST JOURNEY HOME, . . . . . . . . . . .  361 ALF POLLEXFEN V   30
    ON THE SOUL'S JOURNEY. HOW IT IS WHIRLED ABOUT, . . .  472 ALL SOUL NIGHT    54
    . . . A LOG-BOOK OF THE SUN'S JOURNEY AND THE MOON'S!  480 BLOOD AND MOON    14
    . . . A LOG BOOK OF THE SUN'S JOURNEY AND THE MOON'S, . 480 BLOOD AND MOON V  14
JOURNEY-DULL
    WITH ALL HIS COLOURS JOURNEY-DULL, . . . . . . . . .   82 MAD KING GOLL V   13
JOURNEYED
    WITH A PALE LIGHT, I JOURNEYED ROUND THE HALL . . . . .   39 OISIN 2          153
    BURIED AND MIGHTY. THENCE I JOURNEYED NOT . . . . . .   39 OISIN 2       V  151
JOURNEYING
    JAUNTING, JOURNEYING . . . . . . . . . . . . . . .   342 SHEP GOATHERD     95
JOURNEYMAN
    BANISHED JACK THE JOURNEYMAN, . . . . . . . . . . .   508 JANE BISHOP        9
    A ROARING, RANTING JOURNEYMAN. . . . . . . . . . . .  509 JANE REPROVED     13
    CRAZY JANE AND JACK THE JOURNEYMAN  . . . . . . . . .  511 JANE AND JACK      T
JOURNEY-MAN
    A ROARING RANTING JOURNEY-MAN. . . . . . . . . . . .  509 JANE REPROVED V   13
JOURNEY'S
    AND I MAY DINE AT JOURNEY'S END  . . . . . . . . . .  336 YOUNG BEAUTY      17
    THAT I MAY DINE AT JOURNEY'S END . . . . . . . . . .  336 YOUNG BEAUTY  V   17
JOURNEYS
    THE CAPTIVE'S JOURNEYS TO AND FRO WERE WRIT . . . . .   37 OISIN 2          116
    THE CAPTIVES' JOURNEYS TO AND FRO WERE WRIT . . . . .   37 OISIN 2       V  116
    MAN EVER JOURNEYS ON WITH THEM . . . . . . . . . . .  139 TO IRELAND        29
JOVIAL
    I SAW HIS JOVIAL MOOD BRING ONCE A SMILE  . . . . . .  696 MOSADA 2          14
JOY
    BUT WHEN I SANG OF HUMAN JOY  . . . . . . . . . . .    17 OISIN 1          234
    AND WHEN I SANG OF HUMAN JOY  . . . . . . . . . . .    17 OISIN 1       V  234
    "JOY DROWNS THE TWILIGHT IN THE DEW, . . . . . . . .    18 OISIN 1          261
    AND IF JOY WERE NOT ON THE EARTH, . . . . . . . . .    18 OISIN 1          269
    "'TIS JOY MAKES SWIM THE SAPPY TIDE, . . . . . . . .    18 OISIN 1       V  261
    FOR JOY THE LITTLE PLANETS RUN . . . . . . . . . . .    18 OISIN 1       V  267
    IF JOY WERE NOWHERE ON THE EARTH . . . . . . . . . .    18 OISIN 1       V  269
    OR DROPS OF SILVER JOY THAT FELL . . . . . . . . . .    19 OISIN 1          278
    FOR JOY IS GOD AND GOD IS JOY." . . . . . . . . . .    19 OISIN 1          286
    FOR JOY IS GOD AND GOD IS JOY." . . . . . . . . . .    19 OISIN 1          286
    "THE SOUL IS A DROP OF JOY AFAR. . . . . . . . . . .    19 OISIN 1       V  276
    SANG, "GOD IS JOY AND JOY IS GOD, . . . . . . . . .    20 OISIN 1          300
    SANG, "GOD IS JOY AND JOY IS GOD, . . . . . . . . .    20 OISIN 1          300
    AND OVER IS THEIR ANTIQUE JOY . . . . . . . . . . .    64 HAPPY SHEPHERD     2
    FOR RUTH AND JOY HAVE BROTHERHOOD, . . . . . . . . .    66 HAPPY SHEPHERD V  42
    AND SLEEK YOUNG JOY IS NO MORE FICKLE, . . . . . . .    77 INDIAN TO LOVE    5C
    FIELDS FATTENING SLOW, MEN WISE IN JOY, . . . . . . .    82 MAD KING GOLL V   6
    "I HAVE NO REST, NOR JOY, NOR PEACE, . . . . . . . .   132 FR GILLIGAN        9
    FROM JOY THE HOLY BRANCHES START, . . . . . . . . .   134 TWO TREES          3
    THE EAST HER HIDDEN JOY BEFORE THE MORNING BREAK, . .  154 BELOVED PEACE      4
    THE EAST TELLS ALL HER SECRET JOY BEFORE DAYBREAK, . .  154 BELOVED PEACE  V   4
    AND ALL THAT TOSSING OF YOUR WINGS IS JOY, . . . . .  244 SHADOW WATER B   451
    SPONTANEOUS JOY AND NATURAL CONTENT . . . . . . . .   260 FASC DIFFICULT     3
    PRAISED THEIR GREAT VICTORIES AND GAVE THEM JOY  . .  286 TWO KINGS     V 218B
    WHAT JOY IS IN MY DAYS! . . . . . . . . . . . . .    315 FRIENDS            3
    AN AIMLESS JOY IS A PURE JOY," . . . . . . . . . .   338 TOM OROUGHLEY      4
    AN AIMLESS JOY IS A PURE JOY," . . . . . . . . . .   338 TOM OROUGHLEY      4
    OF ALL 'TWAS PAIN OR JOY TO LEARN, . . . . . . . . .  342 SHEP GOATHERD     98
    WHO HAVE LIVED IN JOY AND LAUGHED INTO THE FACE OF DEATH.  366 HER COURAGE   10
    WHO LIVED IN SHAMELESS JOY AND LAUGHED INTO THE FACE OF  366 HER COURAGE  V  10
        DEATH.
    THAT LIVED IN JOY AND LAUGHED INTO THE FACE OF DEATH. . .  366 HER COURAGE V  10
```

```
                                                              PAGE     TITLE            LINE
JOY   (CONTINUED)
    WHO HAVE LIVED IN JOY AND LAUGHED IN THE FACE OF DEATH.    366 HER COURAGE      V    10
    FOR AIMLESS JOY HAD MADE ME STOP  . . . . . . . . . .      400 DEMON BEAST           22
    AND HAD THE GREATER JOY IN PRAISING HER, . . . . . . .     410 TOWER                 37
    IT HAD BUT MADE US PINE THE MORE.  THE ABSTRACT JOY, . .   427 PHANTOM HATRED        38
    AND THAT WAS THE BEGINNING OF A JOY  . . . . . . . . .     465 HARUN RASHID     V   103
    CONTENT OR JOY; A LAST INHERITOR  . . . . . . . . . . .    491 COOLE BALLYLEE        30
    HOPING MORE SUBSTANTIAL JOY . . . . . . . . . . . . .      494 AT ALGECIRAS           9
    HOPING A MORE SUBSTANTIAL JOY  . . . . . . . . . . . .     494 AT ALGECIRAS     V     9
    WHAT IS JOY  . . . . . . . . . . . . . . . . . . . .       499 VACILLATION      V     T
    WHAT IS JOY?  . . . . . . . . . . . . . . . . . . . .      500 VACILLATION           10
    NOR STRAINING JOY, BUT WHOLE IS JOINED TO WHOLE; . . .     555 RIBH AT TOMB          14
    DRINKING JOY AS IT WERE MILK UPON HIS BREAST. . . . .      559 MAGIC DRUM             3
    CRY AT THE ONSET OF THEIR SEXUAL JOY  . . . . . . . .      560 WHENCE COME            2
    CRY AT THE ONSET OF THE SEXUAL JOY  . . . . . . . . .      560 WHENCE COME      V     2
    WE THAT LOOK ON BUT LAUGH IN TRAGIC JOY. . . . . . .       564 GYRES                  8
    AND NEVER HAVE I DANCED FOR JOY. . . . . . . . . . .       567 FROM JAPANESE          9
    WHEN A MAN GROWS OLD HIS JOY  . . . . . . . . . . . .      624 APPARITIONS           17
    ITS JOY OR NIGHT SEEM BUT A DREAM; . . . . . . . . .       633 MAN AND ECHO          42
    ITS JOY OR NIGHT SEEMS BUT A DREAM. . . . . . . . . .      633 MAN AND ECHO     V    42
    JOY AND LOVE ARE ONE EXISTENCE. . . . . . . . . . . .      647 ISLE STAT I 1         71
    SADNESS, SOUL OF JOY MOST DEEP, . . . . . . . . . . .      647 ISLE STAT I 1         74
    GROWETH THE GOBLIN FLOWER OF JOY, HER CARE, . . . . .      653 ISLE STAT I 2         39
    AND THE JOY OF THE STREAMS WHERE LONG-LIMBED HERONS WADE;  674 ISLE STAT II 3       217
    UNTOUCHED OF HUMAN JOY OR HUMAN LOVE?  . . . . . . . .     684 SEEKER                65
    FOR ALL MY JOY--AH, WOE; . . . . . . . . . . . . . .       685 SEEKER                79
    AND JOY, THE TOUCHING OF WHOSE FINGER LENDS  . . . . .     686 DRAWING-ROOM           7
    IGNOBLE JOY, AND MORE IGNOBLE PAIN  . . . . . . . . .      687 TWO TITANS            12
    WITH LITTLE CRIES OF JOY HE KISSED THE RAIN  . . . . .     688 TWO TITANS            33
    I WAVE THEM HITHER, MY BREAST HEAVES WITH JOY. . . . .     694 MOSADA 1              98
    THOUGHTLESS JOY AND SORROW SAGE. . . . . . . . . . .       733 STREET DANCERS        47
    AND JOY, THE TOUCHING OF WHOSE FINGER LENDS  . . . . .     734 QUATRAIN APHOR         7
    AND JOY, IN GROWING DEEPER AND MORE DEEP, . . . . . .      735 QUATRAIN APHOR        27
    YET ONE JOY HAVE I, HID CLOSE, . . . . . . . . . . .       744 ROSY CROSS             8
    AND I SHALL LAUGH WITH JOY.  COME HITHER, AIBRIC, . .      760 SHADOW WATER A       249
    THOUGH BATTLE JOY MAY BE SO DEAR  . . . . . . . . . .      791 REPRISALS              7
JOYOUS
    AND FLUNG THE JOYOUS HUNTING-SPEAR; . . . . . . . . .       23 OISIN 1          V 345A
    THE JOYOUS FLOCKS OF DEER AND ANTELOPE, . . . . . . .       75 ANASHU VIJAYA         74
    THE JOYOUS FLOCKS OF DEER AND ANTELOPES, . . . . . .        75 ANASHU VIJAYA    V    74
    NOR AVALON THE GRASS-GREEN HOLLOW, NOR JOYOUS ISLE, . .    209 UNDER THE MOON         2
    OR AVALLON THE GRASS GREEN HOLLOW, OR JOYOUS ISLE  . .     209 UNDER THE MOON   V     2
    IS NOT MORE FAIR AND JOYOUS THAN SHE IS  . . . . . . .     661 ISLE STAT II 1        71
JOY'S
    JOY'S BROTHER, FEAR, DWELLS EVER IN EACH BREAST--  . . .   651 ISLE STAT I 1        155
    JOY'S BROTHER, FEAR, LURKS IN EACH LEAFY WAY. . . . .      651 ISLE STAT I 1        156
JOYS
    HERE, WHERE MEN KNOW THE GRACIOUS WOODLAND JOYS, . . .     651 ISLE STAT I 1        154
    TO JOYS UNHUMAN, AND TO THEE--SPEAK! SPEAK! . . . . .      684 SEEKER                60
    JOYS AND FEARS IN THEIR GREY FACES THAT THE LIVE EARTH     719 PHANTOM SHIP          26
        KNOWETH NOT;
    THOUGHTLESS JOYS AND SORROWS SAGE. . . . . . . . . .       733 STREET DANCERS   V   47
JUAN
    UPON GREAT JUAN RIDING BY; . . . . . . . . . . . . .       294 HATED PLAYBOY          4
    AT GREAT JUAN RIDING BY; . . . . . . . . . . . . . .       294 HATED PLAYBOY    V     4
    WHILE THAT GREAT JUAN GALLOPED BY; . . . . . . . . .       294 HATED PLAYBOY    V     4
JUBILANT
    A JUBILANT LIFE AMONG THE LEAVES, RETURN, . . . . . .       35 OISIN 2          V  89A
JUDGE
    JUDGE OF THE STARS, AND FIND A COURSE FOR US? . . . .      224 SHADOW WATER B        61
    FOR HE CAN JUDGE THE STARS AS WELL AS FORGAEL. . . . .     225 SHADOW WATER B        63
    TO JUDGE IF A LIGHT SLEEPING FOOL . . . . . . . . . .      304 HOUR DAWN        V    52
    TO THIS BARE SOUL, LET ALL MEN JUDGE THAT CAN  . . . .     542 PARN FUNERAL 1        30
    THE JUDGE AT THE ASSIZE COURT, . . . . . . . . . . .       596 COLONEL MARTIN        46
    YOU THAT WOULD JUDGE ME, DO NOT JUDGE ALONE  . . . . .     603 GALLERY REVIS         50
    YOU THAT WOULD JUDGE ME, DO NOT JUDGE ALONE  . . . . .     603 GALLERY REVIS         50
    TO JUDGE WHAT I HAVE DONE. . . . . . . . . . . . . .       604 YOU CONTENT            4
    EYES SPIRITUALISED BY DEATH CAN JUDGE, . . . . . . .       604 YOU CONTENT            7
    LET HIM BETWEEN US JUDGE, FOR HE CAN GAUGE  . . . . .      660 ISLE STAT II 1        36
    AND HEAR, AND JUDGE. MY POPINJAY, WHAT NOW? . . . . .      660 ISLE STAT II 1        40
    THIS THING WE ASK; MUST WE TWO FIGHT?--JUDGE THOU. . .     660 ISLE STAT II 1        41
    BEING ALMINTOR'S PAGE.  NOW JUDGE YOU HERE. . . . . .      660 ISLE STAT II 1        47
    NOW, JUDGE, MUST SHEPHERD THERNOT THERE AND I . . . .      661 ISLE STAT II 1        65
JUDGMENT
    WHEN I GAVE JUDGMENT, AND HIS WORDS WERE WISE, . . . .     102 FERGUS DRUID          11
    FOR I WOULD HAVE YOUR JUDGMENT UPON ONE . . . . . . .      280 TWO KINGS             71
    TILL JUDGMENT HAS BEEN GIVEN, AND IF GUILTY, . . . . .     280 TWO KINGS             74
    CRAZY JANE ON THE DAY OF JUDGMENT . . . . . . . . . .      510 JANE JUDGMENT          T
    THEN STANDS IN JUDGMENT ON HIS SOUL, . . . . . . . .       633 MAN AND ECHO          33
JUGGLER
    THE RED MAN THE JUGGLER SENT . . . . . . . . . . . .       412 TOWER                 92
JUGGLERIES
    AND THERE, IN JUGGLERIES OF SIGHT AND SENSE, . . . . .     231 SHADOW WATER B       216
    CAUGHT BY AN OLD MAN'S JUGGLERIES . . . . . . . . . .      411 TOWER                 60
JUGGLERS
    BUT WOMEN AND JUGGLERS AND PLAYERS ON THE HARP. . . .      752 SHADOW WATER A       115
JUGGLING
    FROM MAEVE AND ALL THAT JUGGLING PLAIN, . . . . . . .      307 HOUR DAWN            120
    THAT JUGGLING NATURE MOUNTS, HER COIL IN THEIR EMBRACES    556 RIBH PATRICK           9
        TWINED.
```

		PAGE	TITLE		LINE

JUICE
    NOW FROM THAT JUICE THAT MADE THEM WISE • • • • • • • •   272 GREY ROCK   26
    BUT FROM THE JUICE THAT MADE THEM WISE • • • • • • • •   272 GREY ROCK   V   26
    A CRAZY JUICE THAT MAKES THE PULSES BEAT • • • • • •   384 VISION ROBART   54
    WITH A MIRACLE-WORKING JUICE • • • • • • • • •   776 AGAINST WITCH   23
JULIET
    AND FLINGS HERSELF OUT OF THE ROOM WHEN JULIET WOULD BE   354 HIS PHOENIX   13
      BRIDE
    AND FLINGS HERSELF OUT OF THE ROOM WHEN JULIET WOULD BE   354 HIS PHOENIX   V   13
      A BRIDE
JUNCTURE
    WHAT JUNCTURE OF THE APPLE AND THE YEW, • • • • • • •   555 RIBH AT TOMB   8
JUNE
    THE NIGHT SMELLED RICH WITH JUNE. • • • • • • •   160 CAP AND BELLS   V   28
    --BEN JONSON'S PHRASE--AND FIND WHEN JUNE IS COME • •   321 REED WHISPERER   6
    NOR FAERIES IN THE HONEY-HEART OF JUNE ASTIR. • • • •   661 ISLE STAT II 1   73
    BY BOSKY JUNE I SWEAR, AND BY THE BEE, HER MINISTER. • •   661 ISLE STAT II 1   74
JUNES
    IN THE JUNES THAT WERE WARMER THAN THESE ARE, • • • • •   91 OLD FISHERMAN   3
JUNO
    OR ELSE ALL JUNO FROM AN URN DISPLAYS • • • • • • •   418 ANCEST HOUSES   27
JUNO'S
    JUNO'S PEACOCK SCREAMED. • • • • • • • • • • •   422 MY TABLE   32
JUPITER
    IF JUPITER AND SATURN MEET, • • • • • • • • • •   562 CONJUNCTIONS   1
JUST
    AND MY BABY WAS JUST BORN! • • • • • • • •   94 MOLL MAGEE   14
    JUST TRUTH ENOUGH TO SHOW THAT HIS WHOLE LIFE • • • •   373 PHASES OF MOON   22
    JUST NOW MY SOUL ROSE UP AND TOUCHED IT, FAR • • • •   705 REMEMBRANCE   13
JUSTICE
    HE FOUND THE UNPERSUADABLE JUSTICE, HE FOUND • • • •   369 EGO DOMINUS   36
JUSTIFY
    JUSTIFY ALL THOSE RENOWNED GENERATIONS! • • • • • • •   545 TO SAME TUNE 2   1
    JUSTIFY ALL THOSE RENOWNED GENERATIONS, • • • • • • •   546 TO SAME TUNE 2   11
    JUSTIFY ALL THAT HAVE SUNK IN THEIR BLOOD, • • • • •   546 TO SAME TUNE 2   12
    JUSTIFY ALL THAT HAVE DIED ON THE SCAFFOLD, • • • • •   546 TO SAME TUNE 2   13
    JUSTIFY ALL THAT HAVE FLED, THAT HAVE STOOD, • • • •   546 TO SAME TUNE 2   14
    JUSTIFY ALL THAT HAVE FLED OR HAVE STOOD, • • • • •   546 TO SAME TUNE 2   V   14
KAMA
    THE HOUR WHEN KAMA, FULL OF SLEEPY LAUGHTER, • • • •   72 ANASHU VIJAYA   26
    THE HOUR WHEN KAMA, WITH A SUMPTUOUS SMILE, • • • •   72 ANASHU VIJAYA   V   26
KANVA
    KANVA, THE INDIAN, ON GOD • • • • • • • • • • •   76 INDIAN ON GOD   V   T
    KANVA ON HIMSELF. • • • • • • • • • • • •   723 KANVA ON SELF   T
KATE
    AND OUR POOR KATE OR NAN IS LESS • • • • • • •   190 BAILE AILLINN   35
    AND WHEN WE WALK WITH KATE OR NAN • • • • • • •   192 BAILE AILLINN   92
KATHLEEN
    KATHLEEN • • • • • • • • • • • • • •   124 CATHLEEN PARA   V   T
KATHLEEN-NY-HOOLIHAN
    OF KATHLEEN-NY-HOOLIHAN. • • • • • • • • •   207 HANRAHANS SONG V   REF
    OUR KATHLEEN-NY-HOOLIHAN. • • • • • • • • •   208 HANRAHANS SONG V   15
KAURI
    FROM THE BOOK OF KAURI THE INDIAN--   SECTION V.   ON THE   76 INDIAN ON GOD   V   T
      NATURE OF GOD
KEATS
    NO ONE DENIES TO KEATS LOVE OF THE WORLD! • • • • •   370 EGO DOMINUS   52
KEDRON
    THE VINEGAR-HEAVY SPONGE, THE FLOWERS BY KEDRON STREAM!   172 TRAV PASSION   5
KEEN   SEE RAZOR-KEEN
    THAT FOLLOWED MY KEEN HUNTING-CALL-- • • • • • •   23 OISIN 1   V 345F
    I STOOD! KEEN STARS ABOVE ME SHONE, • • • • • •   83 MAD KING GOLL   29
    AROUND ME SHONE KEEN EYES OF MEN! • • • • • • •   83 MAD KING GOLL   30
    THE HOUNDS KEEN FOR THE DEAD. • • • • • • • •   99 FOXHUNTER   V   48
    HOW CAN WE RAISE THE KEEN THAT DO NOT KNOW • • • •   240 SHADOW WATER B   389
    THAT I SHOULD KEEN HIM FROM THE FULL OF THE MOON • •   243 SHADOW WATER B   446
    THERE'S KEEN DELIGHT IN WHAT WE HAVE! • • • • • •   485 NINETEENTH CEN   2
    AND EYES THAT HAD SO KEEN A SIGHT? • • • • • •   529 TOM LUNATIC   4
    SHOWERED AWAY THE KEEN DEW DROPS! • • • • • • •   705 DAWN-SONG   18
KEENED
    • • • KEENED IN THE GATES OF MY HEART. • • • • • •   57 OISIN 3   152
KEENERS
    CAME KEENERS HOARSER THAN ROOKS, • • • • • • •   92 FATHER OHART   22
KEENIN'
    AND KEENIN' TO MYSEL'. • • • • • • • • • •   96 MOLL MAGEE   48
KEENING
    HE BADE THEM GIVE OVER THEIR KEENING! • • • • •   93 FATHER OHART   23
    THERE WAS NO HUMAN KEENING! • • • • • • • •   93 FATHER OHART   29
    CAME KEENING IN THAT DAY. • • • • • • • • •   93 FATHER OHART   32
    KEENING IN FROM TIRARAGH! • • • • • • • • •   93 FATHER OHART   35
    KEENING FROM BALLINAFAD! • • • • • • • • •   93 FATHER OHART   36
    KEENING FROM INISHMURRAY! • • • • • • • • •   93 FATHER OHART   37
    OLD WOMEN WERE KEENING THE DEAD! • • • • • • •   145 HOST OF AIR   V   40D
KEEP
    SHOOT ON HIM SHAFTS OF QUIETNESS, THAT HE MAY EVER KEEP   75 ANASHU VIJAYA   81
    SHOOT ON HIM SHAFTS OF QUIETNESS, AND ORDER HIM TO KEEP   75 ANASHU VIJAYA   V   81
    "THE RED BRANCH KINGS A TIRELESS BANQUET KEEP, • • • •   108 CUCHULAIN SEA   V   33
    CUCHULAIN CRIED, "HAVE MADE AND KEEP THAT VOW." • •   109 CUCHULAIN SEA   V   56
    THE ROAD-SIDE TREES KEEP MURMURING-- • • • • • •   131 OLD PENSIONER   V   13
    HE HAD HALF A CLOAK TO KEEP HIM DRY, • • • • • •   190 BAILE AILLINN   29
    AND KEEP TO THE ONE WEARY MARRIAGE-BED. • • • • •   224 SHADOW WATER B   55

		PAGE	TITLE	LINE

KEEP (CONTINUED)

	PAGE	TITLE	LINE
AND KEEP TO THE ONE WEARY MARRIAGE BED.	224	SHADOW WATER B V	55
WHY DO YOU NEED A SWORD? BUT YOU MAY KEEP IT. . .	241	SHADOW WATER B	400
WE'LL KEEP THE SECRET--A NEW TRICK TO PLEASE. . . .	265	ABBEY THEATRE	10
THAN MOUND AND STONE THAT KEEP ALL VIRTUE IN, . . .	281	TWO KINGS	106
TO KEEP HIS FELLOWS FROM THEIR SLEEP;	297	THREE BEGGARS	45
AND THOUGH HE KEEP A DOG AND A GUN, ...	301	RUN PARADISE	12
TO KEEP HIM UPRIGHT WHILE HE CURSED.	302	HOUR DAWN	6
BUT LET HIM KEEP HIS GRAVE FOR ONCE	303	HOUR DAWN	38
BUT I ALONE BEING BLESSED KEEP	307	HOUR DAWN	104
TO KEEP THE BODY YOUNG.	334	SONG	4
WHO WERE NOT BORN TO KEEP IN TRIM	336	YOUNG BEAUTY	10
WHAT ELSE HE GIVE OR KEEP	346	ON WOMAN	24
CANNOT BUT KEEP THE FORM	350	MEMORY	5
THE EYE OF THE MIND NOR KEEP MY TONGUE FROM SPEECH."	353	PEOPLE	34
OTHERS BECAUSE YOU DID NOT KEEP	357	DEEP-SWORN VOW	1
WE POETS KEEP OUR MOUTHS SHUT, FOR IN TRUTH . . .	359	WAR POEM V	2
A POET KEEP HIS MOUTH SHUT, FOR IN TRUTH	359	WAR POEM V	2
OR KEEP US ALL AWAKE WITH BAYING AT THE MOON, . . .	364	DOLLS FACES	11
FOR ENGLAND MAY KEEP FAITH	394	EASTER 1916	68
THEY MUST TO KEEP THEIR CERTAINTY ACCUSE	398	LEADERS CROWD	1
TO KEEP A DROWSY EMPEROR AWAKE;	408	SAIL BYZANTIUM	29
AND MAY DEPARTING TWILIGHT KEEP	435	FOR MY SON	5
AND THERE IS NONE SO FIT TO KEEP A WATCH AND KEEP .	442	BLACK CENTAUR	15
AND THERE IS NONE SO FIT TO KEEP A WATCH AND KEEP .	442	BLACK CENTAUR	15
BUT KEEP A MARBLE OR A BRONZE REPOSE.	445	SCHOOL CHILDR	52
CRUELTY MUST KEEP; THEREFORE BE WARNED AND GO . . .	448	HERO GIRL FOOL	7
MY CRUELTY MUST KEEP; AND SO BEGONE	448	HERO GIRL FOOL V	7
AND HAVE NO NEED OF CRUELTY TO KEEP	448	HERO GIRL FOOL V	12A
MUST KEEP THAT PERFECT, AS THEY KEEP HER SONG, . .	461	HARUN RASHID	18
MUST KEEP THAT PERFECT, AS THEY KEEP HER SONG, . .	461	HARUN RASHID	18
COULD KEEP A SWALLOW TO ITS FIRST INTENT;	489	COOLE PARK 29	19
YET KEEP HIS SUBSTANCE WHOLE.	573	LADYS 2ND SONG	13
THAT THE SWORDSMEN AND THE LADIES CAN STILL KEEP COMPANY,	581	CURSE CROMWELL	20
AND KEEP ME DANCING STILL	591	DRUNK SOBRIETY	2
AND THEREFORE KEEP ME DANCING	592	DRUNK SOBRIETY	7
KEEP DANCING LIKE A WAVE, ...	592	DRUNK SOBRIETY	10
"AND DID YOU KEEP NO GOLD, TOM?	596	COLONEL MARTIN	64
SHOULD KEEP THEIR LOVERS WAITING, ...	597	MODEL LAUREATE	7
KEEP THEIR LOVERS WAITING?	597	MODEL LAUREATE	8
AND KEEP THEIR LOVERS WAITING, ...	597	MODEL LAUREATE	15
KEEP THEIR LOVERS WAITING.	597	MODEL LAUREATE	16
WOULD KEEP HIS LOVER WAITING, ...	598	MODEL LAUREATE	23
KEEP HIS LOVER WAITING?	598	MODEL LAUREATE	24
KEEP THOSE CHILDREN OUT.	618	LONG-LEG FLY	24
FOR DEATH WHO TAKES WHAT MAN WOULD KEEP, ...	620	JOHN KINSELLA	3
TO KEEP THE SOUL OF MAN ALIVE, ...	620	JOHN KINSELLA	19
WHILE MAN CAN STILL HIS BODY KEEP	633	MAN AND ECHO	25
MAIDEN, COME FORTH! THE WOODS KEEP WATCH FOR THEE; .	645	ISLE STAT I 1	1
AND THY MEMORY I KEEP, ...	647	ISLE STAT I 1	59
I KEEP SUCH THINGS ABOUT ME; THEY ARE FOOD	721	WITCH VIVIEN	37
AND KEEP A COVERED HEAD."	742	EARL PAUL	64
KEEP HIDDEN AND COVERED HER HEART!"	744	GLOVE CLOAK	12
SHE WOULD WEAVE A NET TO TAKE US. SHE MIGHT KEEP FAITH;	756	SHADOW WATER A	190
THAT DESPAIR AND KEEP THE PACE	787	HUDDON DUDDON	9

KEEPER SEE STABLE-KEEPER

	PAGE	TITLE	LINE
THE COARSE-BRED SON OF A LIVERY-STABLE KEEPER-- . . .	370	EGO DOMINUS	61
THE ILL-BRED SON OF A LIVERY STABLE KEEPER-- . . .	370	EGO DOMINUS V	61

KEEPING

	PAGE	TITLE	LINE
A REASON FOR KEEPING SILENT	359	WAR POEM V	T
KEEPING ALL THE KERRY MEN	585	ORAHILLY	14
I THERE HAD BEEN KEEPING	672	ISLE STAT II 3	171

KEEPS

	PAGE	TITLE	LINE
THAT KEEPS THE STARS IN THEIR ROUND, ...	165	CRY OF SEDGE	5
SHE KEEPS THAT IGNORANCE, NOR HAS SHE NOW	468	HARUN RASHID	164
REPENTANCE KEEPS MY HEART IMPURE;	507	STREAM AND SUN	6
KEEPS PARNELL IN HIS MIND.	586	PARNELLITES	20
WHO KEEPS THE TILL. NOW THAT MY LADDER'S GONE, . .	630	CIRCUS ANIMALS	38

KEGS

	PAGE	TITLE	LINE
CARE MORE ABOUT THE KEGS OF SILVER AND GOLD	232	SHADOW WATER B	234
THREE KEGS OF GOLD.	596	COLONEL MARTIN	49
YOU HAD THREE KEGS" SAID HE.	596	COLONEL MARTIN	65

KENNEL

	PAGE	TITLE	LINE
"TO STABLE AND TO KENNEL GO;	97	FOXHUNTER	5

KEPT

	PAGE	TITLE	LINE
THAT KEPT DIM WATERS FROM THE SKY;	17	OISIN 1	243
KEPT TIME WITH THEIR BRIGHT WINGS AND FEET; . . .	26	OISIN 1	397
THE EVER-LIVING HAVE KEPT MY BARGAIN FOR ME, . . .	232	SHADOW WATER B	223
YOU KEPT THE MUSES' STERNER LAWS, ...	273	GREY ROCK	59
I HAVE KEPT MY FAITH, THOUGH FAITH WAS TRIED, . . .	276	GREY ROCK	124
IN DAYS YOU HAVE NOT KEPT IN MEMORY, ...	284	TWO KINGS	168
WHO HAD SEEN, BEING KEPT FOR SHOW, ...	319	DOLLS	5
OR ESSERKELLY PLAIN, FEW KEPT HIS PACE;	326	ROBERT GREGORY	59
AND ESERKELLY PLAINS, FEW KEPT HIS PACE;	326	ROBERT GREGORY V	59
OR ESERKELLY PLAINS, FEW KEPT HIS PACE;	326	ROBERT GREGORY V	59
THEY HAD KEPT A STEADY PACE AS THOUGH THEIR BEDS, .	372	PHASES OF MOON	5
THIS MAN HAD KEPT A SCHOOL	392	EASTER 1916	24
AND AFTER KEPT IT FROM DECAY;	460	THREE MONUMENT	7
"I KEPT HER MUCH IN THE COUNTRY	594	COLONEL MARTIN	10
HOW FERENCZ RENYI KEPT SILENT.	709	FERENCZ RENYI	T

KERCHIEF
    THAT FOLLOWED IF I LET THE KERCHIEF FALL! • • • • • •   533 HER TRIUMPH   4
KERRY
    KEEPING ALL THE KERRY MEN • • • • • • • • • •   585 ORAHILLY   14
KESTREL
    LIES TORN AND ROTTING. THE FIERCE KESTREL BIRDS • • •   675 ISLE STAT II 3   234
KETTLE
    OR THE KETTLE ON THE HOB • • • • • • • • • •   88 STOLEN CHILD   46
    A SORT OF BATTERED KETTLE AT THE HEEL. • • • • • •   409 TOWER   16
    THE DRUMS AND THE KETTLE DRUMS • • • • • • •   527 AM OF IRELAND V 21
KETTLEDRUM
    TRUMPET AND KETTLEDRUM, • • • • • • • • •   317 NIGHT COME   9
KETTLEDRUMS
    THE DRUMS AND THE KETTLEDRUMS • • • • • • •   527 AM OF IRELAND   21
KETTLES
    OLD KETTLES, OLD BOTTLES, AND A BROKEN CAN, • • •   630 CIRCUS ANIMALS   36
KEVIN
    KEVIN O'HIGGINS' COUNTENANCE THAT WEARS • • • •   601 GALLERY REVIS   5
    KEVIN O'HIGGINS, AND THAT LOOK HE WEARS, • • •   601 GALLERY REVIS V 5
KEY   SEE LIFE-KEY
    WE ARE CLOSED IN, AND THE KEY IS TURNED • • • •   425 STARES NEST   6
    WE ARE CLOSED IN, AND THE KEY TURNED • • • • •   425 STARES NEST V 6
KEYS
    HAVE KEYS TO MY OLD GATE. • • • • • • • •   607 SONGS BURDEN 2   8
KHAKI
    THE KHAKI FROM HIS BACK? • • • • • • • •   627 STATES HOLIDAY   17
KICKED
    BUT HE KICKED BEFORE HE DIED, • • • • • • •   545 TO SAME TUNE 1   25
    BUT HE KICKED BEFORE HE DIED, • • • • • • •   616 MARCH SONGS 3   25
KID
    A KID, HELD BY ONE SOFT WHITE EAR FOR TETHER, • •   715 DWELT SYCAMORE   3
KIDRON
    THE HISSOP-HEAVY SPONGE, THE FLOWERS BY KIDRON STREAM! • •   172 TRAV PASSION V 5
KID'S
    AND STIRS THE YOUNG KID'S BUDDING HORN, • • • • •   18 OISIN 1   264
KILBARNET
    MY BROTHER IS PRIEST OF KILBARNET, • • • • • •   178 FIDDLER DOONEY V   3
KILL
    I'D KILL HIM WHILE WE HAVE THE CHANCE TO DO IT. • •   224 SHADOW WATER B V 58
    AND FORGAEL IN THE OTHER SCALE! KILL FORGAEL, • • •   225 SHADOW WATER B   76
    THEN STUMBLING TO THE KILL BESIDE THE SHORE; • • •   622 HOUND VOICE   19
    THAT STUMBLING TO THE KILL BESIDE THE SHORE; • • •   622 HOUND VOICE V 19
    I'D KILL HER IF SHE WERE. NAY, DO NOT FEAR! • • •   669 ISLE STAT II 3   69
    THREE MOONS. IT WERE BEST TO KILL HIM, AND CHOOSE OUT •   748 SHADOW WATER A   15
    AND NO MAN KILL ME! FOR SOME WIND HAS BLOWN • • •   751 SHADOW WATER A   97
    BUT NOW I WILL KILL HER. ALL COMES TO AN END. • • •   755 SHADOW WATER A   176
KILLED
    BUT ALL THAT ARE KILLED IN BATTLE • • • • • • •   215 HAPPY TOWNLAND   25
    FOR HE WAS KILLED. O! O! O! O! O! O! • • • • •   242 SHADOW WATER B   409
    FOR GOLDEN-ARMED IOLLAN HAS BEEN KILLED. • • • •   242 SHADOW WATER B   410
    THEY KILLED HIM AT MY FEET. O! O! O! O! • • • •   242 SHADOW WATER B   420
    AND KILLED A LOVER OR HUSBAND AT MY FEET-- • • •   246 SHADOW WATER B   491
    A MAN IS KILLED, OR A HOUSE BURNED, • • • • • •   425 STARES NEST   8
    THAT YEAR WHEN GREAT HAROUN EL RASHID KILLED • • •   462 HARUN RASHID V 31
    "THEY KILLED MY GOOSE AND A CAT. • • • • • •   546 TO SAME TUNE 2   8
    "THEY KILLED MY GOOSE AND A CAT. • • • • • •   546 TO SAME TUNE 2   18
    "THEY KILLED MY GOOSE AND A CAT. • • • • • •   547 TO SAME TUNE 2   28
    WAS FORGAEL'S COURAGE THAT THE MUSIC KILLED. • • •   747 SHADOW WATER A   9
    I HAD KILLED HIM LONG AGO, BUT THAT THE FOOL • • •   748 SHADOW WATER A   17
    SO THESE WOULD HAVE KILLED FORGAEL WHILE ASLEEP • •   748 SHADOW WATER A   25
    WITH ONE YOU HAVE KILLED AND DIE! FOR WHEN I LEFT •   758 SHADOW WATER A   226
    WITH SOME YOU HAVE KILLED AND DIE! FOR WHEN I LEFT • •   758 SHADOW WATER A V 226
KILLS
    AND WOOD-OF-WONDERS, WHERE ONE KILLS AN OX AT DAWN, • • •   209 UNDER THE MOON   9
KILTARTAN
    MY COUNTRY IS KILTARTAN CROSS, • • • • • • • •   328 IRISH AIRMAN   5
    FLIT TO KILTARTAN CROSS AND STAY • • • • • • •   791 REPRISALS   11
KILTARTAN'S
    MY COUNTRYMEN KILTARTAN'S POOR, • • • • • • • •   328 IRISH AIRMAN   6
KILVARNET
    MY COUSIN IS PRIEST IN KILVARNET, • • • • • •   178 FIDDLER DOONEY   3
    MY BROTHER IS PRIEST IN KILVARNET, • • • • • •   178 FIDDLER DOONEY V   3
KIMONOS
    TWO GIRLS IN SILK KIMONOS, BOTH • • • • • • •   475 EVA GORE-BOOTH   3
    TWO GIRLS IN SILK KIMONOS, BOTH • • • • • • •   475 EVA GORE-BOOTH   19
KIN
    BUT WHERE ARE YOUR NOBLE KITH AND KIN, • • • • • •   5 OISIN 1   44
    THY NAME, THY KIN, AND THY COUNTRY," • • • • • •   5 OISIN 1 V 44
    IN THE HOUSE OF HIS FRIEND, OF HIS KIN, OF HIS BROTHER, •   26 OISIN 1 V 405
    RODE FROM THE COUNTRY OF HER KIN, • • • • • •   191 BAILE AILLINN   50
    AND THE NEAREST KIN OF THE MOON, • • • • • • •   378 CAT AND MOON   3
    "FAIR AND FOUL ARE NEAR OF KIN, • • • • • • •   513 JANE TALK BISH   7
    HIVES, CURRANT BUSHES. THERE HIS KIN ARE. HIGH • •   710 FERENCZ RENYI   25
    HIVES, CURRANT-BUSHES. THERE HIS KIN ARE. HIGH • •   710 FERENCZ RENYI V 25
    HALF HID. HE BRINGS THE PEASANT'S ONLY KIN, • • •   711 FERENCZ RENYI   50
    "NOW HATH HE KITH OR KIN, OR ANY FRIEND?" • • • •   712 FERENCZ RENYI   66
KIND   SEE WOMAN-KIND MAN-KIND GOD-KIND
    BUT ONLY KIND AND MERRY BREATH, • • • • • •   19 OISIN 1   285
    O SIGH, O FLUTTERING SIGH, BE KIND TO ME! • • • •   33 OISIN 2   57
    FOR THE KIND WIRES ARE TORN AND STILL, • • • • •   86 MAD KING GOLL   69
    WEARY AND KIND ONE LINGERED BY HIS SEAT; • • • •   112 ROSE OF WORLD   13

```
                                                               PAGE    TITLE         LINE
KIND   (CONTINUED)
     WEARY AND KIND ONE STOOD BESIDE HIS SEAT!  . . . . .  .    112 ROSE OF WORLD  V   13
     AND LOVE IS LESS KIND THAN THE GREY TWILIGHT, . . . . .    148 INTO TWILIGHT      15
     THE POWERS, NOT KIND LIKE YOU, CAME WHERE GOD'S GARDEN     174 ELEMENT POWERS V    1
          BLOWS,
     ONE THAT IS EVER KIND SAID YESTERDAY!  . . . . .  . .      199 FOLLY COMFORT       1
     "YOUR STRENGTH, THAT IS SO LOFTY AND FIERCE AND KIND,  . . 201 OLD MEMORY          3
     BUT A BRIEF, DREAMY, KIND DELIGHT. . . . . . . . .  . .    202 NEVER GIVE ALL      7
     I KNOW WHERE A DIM MOON DRIFTS, WHERE THE DANAAN KIND . .  203 WITHER BOUGHS      12
     AND I KNOW OF THE ISLES WHERE THE DANAAN KIND . . . . .    203 WITHER BOUGHS  V   12
     AND OF APPLE ISLANDS WHERE THE DANAAN KIND . . . . . .     203 WITHER BOUGHS  V   12
     BUT OF A BEAUTIFUL, UNHEARD-OF KIND . . . . . . . .  .     228 SHADOW WATER B    142
     WITH BEAUTY LIKE A TIGHTENED BOW, A KIND . . . . . .  .    256 NO SECOND TROY      8
     YET OLD ROMANCE BEING KIND, LET HIM PREVAIL . . . . .      258 KING NO KING        5
     A KIND MILD WOMAN HAD SHE BEEN, WHO POURED . . . . .  .    279 TWO KINGS      V  62A
     BUT NOW SHE HAD NO MILD AND NO KIND LOOK! . . . . .  .     279 TWO KINGS      V  62D
     YET THEY WERE OF A DIFFERENT KIND,  . . . . . . . .  .     289 SEPTEMBER 1913      9
     OF YOUR OWN PASSIONATE SERVING KIND WHO HAD BROUGHT . . .  292 TO A SHADE         10
     OF YOUR OWN PASSIONATE SERVING KIND WHO HAS BROUGHT . . .  292 TO A SHADE         10
     KIND EYES SHOULD BE MORE LEARN'D? . . . . . . . .  . .     312 TWO YEAR LATER      2
     A FRIENDSHIP OF HER KIND . . . . . . . . . . . .  .  .     345 ON WOMAN            4
     HE HAS FOUND, AFTER THE MANNER OF HIS KIND, . . . . .      373 PHASES OF MOON     12
     A KIND OLD NUN IN A WHITE HOOD REPLIES! . . . . . .  .     443 SCHOOL CHILDR       2
     AND I THOUGH NEVER OF LEDAEAN KIND . . . . . . . .  . .    444 SCHOOL CHILDR      29
     THERE IS A COMFORTABLE KIND OF OLD SCARECROW. . . . .  .   444 SCHOOL CHILDR      32
     YET ALL MUST COPY COPIES, ALL INCREASE THEIR KIND! . . .   556 RIBH PATRICK        7
     HE WAS OF SUCH A KIND . . . . . . . . . . . . .  . .       586 PARNELLITES        18
     "KIND ARE ALL YOUR WORDS, MY DEAR, . . . . . . . .  . .    588 OLD WICKED MAN     10
     AND STONY-HEARTED; NOW THOU HAST GROWN KIND, . . . . .     670 ISLE STAT II 3     91
     NOW BE COURTEOUS, NOW BE KIND, . . . . . . . . .  . .      717 FAIRY DOCTOR       21
     GREET HIM COURTEOUS, GREET HIM KIND, . . . . . . .  . .    717 FAIRY DOCTOR   V   21
     HE HOVERS ABOVE THE MAST AND WAITS HIS KIND! . . . . .     753 SHADOW WATER A    135
     FOR LOVE IS KIND AND HAPPY. O COME WITH ME! . . . . .      767 SHADOW WATER A    396
     OR GROW KIND, FOR THEY ANOINT . . . . . . . .  .  . .      776 AGAINST WITCH      21
     AND LETS THE KIND WORM TAKE THE LOT! . . . . . . . .  .    779 ACCURSED WHO        4
KINDER
     THIS BEAUTY'S KINDER, YET FOR A REASON . . . . . .  . .    199 ARROW               7
KINDLING
     MAKING WAY FROM THE KINDLING SURGES, I RODE ON A           58 OISIN 3            161
          BRIDLE-PATH
KINDLY
     AND LOVE IS KINDLY AND DECEITLESS, . . . . . . . .  . .    77 INDIAN TO LOVE  V   5D
     I SAW A KINDLY NEIGHBOUR . . . . . . . . . . . .  . .      95 MOLL MAGEE         35
     BUT, KINDLY OLD ROUT . . . . . . . . . . . . .  .  . .    142 MOODS          V    5
KINDNESS
     A DRUID KINDNESS, ON ALL HEARERS FELL. . . . . .  . .      129 BOOK STORIES        4
     THE HOURLY KINDNESS, THE DAY'S COMMON SPEECH, . . .  . .   258 KING NO KING       14
     AND THANKED HER FOR HER KINDNESS TO HIS BROTHER, . . . .   286 TWO KINGS         212
     "I THANK YOU FOR YOUR KINDNESS TO MY BROTHER, . . . .  .   286 TWO KINGS      V  212
     REMEMBERING KINDNESS DONE, AND HOW CAN I, . . . . .  .     340 SHEP GOATHERD      30
     WITH THE OLD KINDNESS, THE OLD DISTINGUISHED GRACE, . . .  362 HER COURTESY        1
     LOSE NATURAL KINDNESS AND MAYBE . . . . . . . . .  . .     404 FOR DAUGHTER       22
     FROM A GLAD KINDNESS CANNOT TAKE HIS EYES. . . . . .  .    404 FOR DAUGHTER       40
     LIKE THE MOON HER KINDNESS IS, . . . . . . . . .  . .      452 HUMAN DIGNITY       1
     IF KINDNESS I MAY CALL . . . . . . . . . . . .  .  . .     452 HUMAN DIGNITY       2
KINDRED
     WHEN TWO CLOSE KINDRED MEET, . . . . . . . . .  . .  .     378 CAT AND MOON       12
     A PROUD WOMAN NOT KINDRED OF HIS SOUL. . . . . . .  . .    479 SELF AND SOUL      64
     RISE AS KINDRED SHOULD. . . . . . . . . . . .  .  . .      518 LOVES LONENESS      2
     CONVICTED COWARDS ALL, BY KINDRED SLAIN . . . . . .  .     634 CUCHULAIN COMF     21
KINDRED'S
     AND TELL ME HOW MY KINDRED'S TEARS ARE WELLING, . . .  .    33 OISIN 2        V   66
KINDS
     LIKE AN OLD PAUPER, IN ALL KINDS OF WEATHER! . . . .  .    205 ADAMS CURSE         9
KINE
     THE MERRY LAMBS AND THE COMPLACENT KINE, . . . . .  . .     75 ANASHU VIJAYA      86
     THE MERRY LAMBS AND ALL THE KINE COMPLACENT, . . . .  .     75 ANASHU VIJAYA      86
     HAVE THEY NE'ER SEEN THE EYES OF LYNX OR KINE, . . . .     672 ISLE STAT II 3    152
KING   SEE SEA-KING
     IS NIAM, DAUGHTER OF THE KING . . . . . . . . .  . .        5 OISIN 1        V   49
     "I HAVE NOT YET, WAR-WEARY KING, . . . . . . . .  . .        6 OISIN 1        V   55
     "NOT SO, GREAT KING! FOR I HAVE NE'ER . . . . . .  . .        6 OISIN 1        V   55
     MY ANGRY, KING REMEMBERING SOUL ONE JOT! . . . . .  . .     36 OISIN 2        V   94
     I CRIED, "COME OUT OF THE SHADOW, KING OF THE NAILS OF      51 OISIN 3           61
          GOLD!
     MAY PANTHERS END HIM.--HEAR, AND LOAD OUR KING . . .  .     71 ANASHU VIJAYA       6
     THE MADNESS OF KING GOLL . . . . . . . . . . .  .  . .      81 MAD KING GOLL       T
     I WAS A WISE YOUNG KING OF OLD! . . . . . . . . .  . .      81 MAD KING GOLL  V    1
     WHAT WOULD YOU, KING OF THE PROUD RED BRANCH KINGS? . . .  102 FERGUS DRUID        8
     WHAT WOULD YOU, KING OF THE PROUD RED BRANCH KINGS? . . .  102 FERGUS DRUID       15
     A KING AND PROUD! AND THAT IS MY DESPAIR. . . . . .  .     103 FERGUS DRUID       16
     WHAT WOULD YOU, FERGUS? BE NO MORE A KING, . . . . .       103 FERGUS DRUID       21
     A KING IS BUT A FOOLISH LABOURER . . . . . . . .  . .      103 FERGUS DRUID       27
     WHAT WOULD YOU? I WOULD BE NO MORE A KING, . . . . .       103 FERGUS DRUID   V   21
     WHAT WOULD YOU, KING OF THE PROUD RED BRANCH KINGS? . . .  103 FERGUS DRUID   V   21
     I'D PUT AWAY THE FOOLISH MIGHT OF A KING, . . . . .  .     103 FERGUS DRUID   V  21A
     A WILD AND FOOLISH LABOURER IS A KING . . . . . .  . .     103 FERGUS DRUID   V   27
     A KING SITTING UPON A CHAIR OF GOLD-- . . . . . .  . .     104 FERGUS DRUID       36
     AND CONCHUBAR, THE RED BRANCH KING OF KINGS, . . . .  .    109 CUCHULAIN SEA      45
     CUMHAL THE KING, BEING ANGRY AND SAD, . . . . . .  . .     166 BLESSED        V    1
     OF THE CROWNED MAGI! AND THE KING WHOSE EYES . . . .  .    169 SECRET ROSE         9
```

419

PAGE   TITLE   LINE

KING   (CONTINUED)
    AND THE PROUD DREAMING KING WHO FLUNG THE CROWN . . . . . 170 SECRET ROSE   19
    A KING OF THE GREAT PLAIN WOULD SPEAK WITH YOU." . . . . 183 QUEEN MAEVE   78
    AND WITH GLAD VOICE MAEVE ANSWERED HIM, "WHAT KING . . . 183 QUEEN MAEVE   79
    AILLINN, WHO WAS KING LUGAIDH'S HEIR. . . . . 189 BAILE AILLINN   7
    SOME GOD OR KING HAD MADE THE LAWS . . . . 194 BAILE AILLINN   131
    A KING AND A QUEEN ARE WANDERING THERE, AND THE SOUND . . 204 WITHER BOUGHS   19
    THERE IS A KING AND QUEEN UPON HER DECK, ... 232 SHADOW WATER B   226
    MY HUSBAND AND MY KING DIED AT MY FEET, ... 237 SHADOW WATER B   337
    WHAT NAME HAD THAT DEAD KING? ARTHUR OF BRITAIN? . . . 242 SHADOW WATER B   404
    BEND LOWER, O KING, THAT I MAY CROWN YOU WITH IT. . . . 251 SHADOW WATER B   607
    KING AND NO KING . . . . 258 KING NO KING   T
    KING AND NO KING . . . . 258 KING NO KING   T
    THE NO KING CRIED WHO AFTER THAT WAS KING, ... 258 KING NO KING   2
    THE NO KING CRIED WHO AFTER THAT WAS KING, ... 258 KING NO KING   2
    ALTHOUGH THE KING OF IRELAND'S DEAD . . . . 273 GREY ROCK   68
    MURROUGH, THE KING OF IRELAND'S SON, ... 274 GREY ROCK   71
    KING EOCHAID CAME AT SUNDOWN TO A WOOD . . . . . . 276 TWO KINGS   1
    KING EOCHAID SAID, AND HE THAT BORE HIS SHIELD . . . . 276 TWO KINGS   V   8
    RENDING THE HORSE'S FLANK. KING EOCHAID REELED, . . . 277 TWO KINGS   13
    RIPPED THROUGH THE HORSE'S FLANKS. KING EOCHAID REELED, 277 TWO KINGS   V   13
    KING EOCHAID SEIZED THE HORNS IN HIS STRONG HANDS . . . 278 TWO KINGS   24
    THE DISEMBOWELLED HORSE. KING EOCHAID RAN . . . . . 278 TWO KINGS   45
    THE DISEMBOWELLED HORSE. KING EOCHAID GAZED, ... 278 TWO KINGS   V   45
    BECAUSE THAT WERE A GUILT AGAINST HER KING, ... 280 TWO KINGS   V   74A
    AND RAISE HIS PILLAR STONE." KING EOCHAID SAID, . . . 280 TWO KINGS   V   83
    YET ANSWERED HIM, "I AM KING EOCHAID'S WIFE . . . . 284 TWO KINGS   173
    CROW UPON TARA." KING EOCHAID BOWED HIS HEAD . . . . 286 TWO KINGS   211
    AND IN THE MIDST KING EOCHAID'S BROTHER STOOD, . . . 286 TWO KINGS   217
    UPON KING EOCHAID'S FACE, WHO LOWERED HIS FACE . . . 286 TWO KINGS   V 211A
    AND FOR THE LOVE THAT YOU HAVE SHOWN YOUR KING, . . . 286 TWO KINGS   V 212A
    KING GUAIRE WALKED AMID HIS COURT . . . . 295 THREE BEGGARS   8
    WITH HIS OLD THOUGHTS, KING GUAIRE WENT . . . . . 296 THREE BEGGARS   26
    TO A POET OR A KING . . . . 299 THREE HERMITS   27
    AND THERE THE KING IS BUT AS THE BEGGAR. . . . . . 301 RUN PARADISE   7
    AND THERE THE KING IS BUT AS THE BEGGAR. . . . . . 301 RUN PARADISE   14
    AND THERE THE KING IS BUT AS THE BEGGAR. . . . . . 301 RUN PARADISE   21
    AND THERE THE KING IS BUT AS THE BEGGAR. . . . . . 301 RUN PARADISE   28
    AND SHE SEEMED HAPPY AS A KING, ... 313 MEMORY YOUTH   V   6
    BUT LIVED AS 'TWERE A KING . . . . 317 NIGHT COME   6
    WHERE MANY A KING HAS GONE . . . . 330 BONE OF A HARE   2
    OF GOLDEN KING AND SILVER LADY, ... 331 ROUND TOWER   13
    THAT GOLDEN KING AND THAT WILD LADY . . . . . 332 ROUND TOWER   19
    THAT LADY AND THAT GOLDEN KING . . . . . . 332 ROUND TOWER   23
    INTO A PLOUGHSHARE? PARLIAMENT AND KING . . . . 429 NINETEEN 19   20
    KING ABUNDANCE GOT HIM ON . . . . 440 WISDOM   16
    UPON THE BOTTOM OF A KING OF KINGS; . . . . . 445 SCHOOL CHILDR   44
    SHRIEKS, "I AM KING OF THE PEACOCKS," . . . . . 456 FRIENDS YOUTH   15
    "I HAVE BEEN A KING, ... 495 MOHINI CHATTER   5
    . . . "THE KING OF THE GREAT CLOCK TOWER" . . . 549 SEVERED HEAD   T
    THE KING THAT COULD MAKE HIS PEOPLE STARE, . . . 550 SEVERED HEAD   19
    PITCH LIKE KING BILLY BOMB-BALLS IN . . . . . 565 LAPIS LAZULI   7
    MY KING A LOST KING, AND LOST SOLDIERS MY MEN; . . 591 WHAT WAS LOST   3
    MY KING A LOST KING, AND LOST SOLDIERS MY MEN; . . 591 WHAT WAS LOST   3
    OR THE KING OF GREECE, ... 627 STATES HOLIDAY   19
    A KING HAD SOME BEAUTIFUL COUSINS. . . . . . 628 JANE MOUNTAIN   7
    CARES WHAT KING SETS UP HIS RULE. . . . . . 635 BLACK TOWER   14
    MEETING LONG HENCE THE PHANTOM HERDSMAN, KING . . 675 ISLE STAT II 3   242
    YOUTH, HERE WILL WE ABIDE, AND BE THOU KING . . . 679 ISLE STAT II 3   314
    OF THIS LAKE-NURTURED ISLE! LET THY KING BE . . . 679 ISLE STAT II 3   315
    CLEAR-BROWED ARCADIAN, THOU SHALT BE OUR KING! . . 679 ISLE STAT II 3   318
    CLEAR-BROWED ARCADIAN, THOU SHALT BE OUR KING! . . 679 ISLE STAT II 3   321
    AND THEN THE GREAT ONES COME, AND LAST THE KING. . . 722 WITCH VIVIEN   54
    EARL PAUL CAME WHERE THE KING SAT, ... 740 EARL PAUL   29
    AND YOU, MY AIBRIC, WHO HAVE BEEN A KING . . . 748 SHADOW WATER A   27
    ENDS ALL THINGS. I HAVE SLAIN THE LOCHLANN KING. . 754 SHADOW WATER A   163
    I AND THAT MIGHTY KING A SUDDEN BLOW . . . . 757 SHADOW WATER A   195
    OF THE TWELVE KINGS OF THE WORLD TO BE MY KING, . 757 SHADOW WATER A   214
    THAT WOULD BE HAPPIEST. HE IS A KING . . . . 768 SHADOW WATER A   410
    I CROWN YOU WITH THIS CROWN. BEND LOWER, O KING, . 768 SHADOW WATER A   423
    WHETHER A KING OR CLOWN; . . . . 789 SINGING HEAD   18
    FOR PRAISE OF CLOWN OR KING, ... 789 SINGING HEAD   20
    THEN FARRELL, STEEL KING, MASTER OF MEN, . . . 790 DEDICATION   5
KINGDOM
    TO MY OWN KINGDOM IN THE SEA-- . . . . . . 8 OISIN 1   V   80A
    IN WHAT FAR KINGDOM DO YOU GO, ... 10 OISIN 1   115
    IN WHAT FAR KINGDOM DO YE GO, ... 10 OISIN 1   V   115
    AND BRING HER TO HER KINGDOM AND HER PEOPLE. . . 755 SHADOW WATER A   170
    MUSIC OF A LOST KINGDOM . . . . 782 GREY ROUND   2
    MUSIC OF A LOST KINGDOM? . . . . 783 GREY ROUND   12
KINGDOMS
    COME AND DREAM OF KINGS AND KINGDOMS, ... 737 IN FIRELIGHT   1
    KINGDOMS RISING, KINGDOMS FALLING, ... 737 IN FIRELIGHT   9
    KINGDOMS RISING, KINGDOMS FALLING, ... 737 IN FIRELIGHT   9
KINGFISHER
    AND THE KINGFISHER TURNS TO A BALL OF DUST, . . . 27 OISIN 1   V   418
    AND THE KINGFISHER TURNS TO A BALL OF DUST, . . . 28 OISIN 1   422
    KINGFISHER COLOUR GREW WITH RAGE. HE ROSE . . . 40 OISIN 2   V   169
    BEFORE I DROPPED ASLEEP, A KINGFISHER . . . . 761 SHADOW WATER A   274
KINGFISHERS
    LIKE WINGS OF KINGFISHERS; AND HE AROSE . . . . . 40 OISIN 2   169

420

KINGLY
    A GENTLE YET A KINGLY CHILD! . . . .   82 MAD KING GOLL   V   8
    A GRACIOUS, GENTLE, KINGLY BOY. . . . .   82 MAD KING GOLL   V   8
    PEACE-MAKING, MILD, A KINGLY BOY. . . . .   82 MAD KING GOLL   V   8
KING-REMEMBERING
    MY ANGRY KING-REMEMBERING SOUL ONE JOT. . . . . . .   36 OISIN 2   94
KING'S
    HE CARRIED EDAIN OFF FROM A KING'S HOUSE, ...   224 SHADOW WATER B   48
    SEEING, KING'S SON, WHAT WOUNDS YOU HAVE." . . . .   275 GREY ROCK   94
    FOR HE AND THE KING'S SON WERE DEAD. . . . .   275 GREY ROCK   97
    AND MANY A KING'S DAUGHTER, ...   330 BONE OF A HARE   3
    WHO, WHEN HIS OWN RIGHT KING'S FORGOTTEN, ...   635 BLACK TOWER   13
    SWEARS THAT HE HEARS THE KING'S GREAT HORN. . . .   636 BLACK TOWER   24
    THEN TURNED HE FROM THE KING'S COURT, ...   742 EARL PAUL   65
    RUIN ON A GREAT KING'S HOUSE . . . .   775 AGAINST WITCH   3
KINGS   SEE BEGGAR-KINGS
    "I LOVED NO MAN, THOUGH KINGS BESOUGHT, ...   7 OISIN 1   62
    FULL MANY BOWING KINGS BESOUGHT ME, ...   7 OISIN 1   V   67
    WARS SHADOWY, VAST, EXULTANT! FAIRY KINGS . . . .   29 OISIN 2   V   9
    CAME BY ME THE KINGS OF THE RED BRANCH, ...   53 OISIN 3   87
    WHERE ARE NOW THE WARRING KINGS, ...   65 HAPPY SHEPHERD   11
    WHERE ARE NOW THE WARRING KINGS? . . . .   65 HAPPY SHEPHERD   13
    THE KINGS OF THE OLD TIME ARE DEAD! . . . .   65 HAPPY SHEPHERD   17
    WHERE ARE NOW THE OLD KINGS HOARY? . . . .   65 HAPPY SHEPHERD   V   13
    THE KINGS OF THE OLD TIME ARE FLED. . . . .   65 HAPPY SHEPHERD   V   17
    WHAT WOULD YOU, KING OF THE PROUD RED BRANCH KINGS? . 102 FERGUS DRUID   8
    WHAT WOULD YOU, KING OF THE PROUD RED BRANCH KINGS? . 102 FERGUS DRUID   15
    WHAT WOULD YOU, KING OF THE PROUD RED BRANCH KINGS? . 103 FERGUS DRUID   V   21
    HAS SLAIN SO MIGHTY ARMIES, SO GREAT KINGS, ...   106 CUCHULAIN SEA   V   10A
    "THE RED BRANCH KINGS A TIRELESS BANQUET KEEP, . .   108 CUCHULAIN SEA   V   33
    AMONG THOSE FEASTING KINGS CUCHULAIN DWELT, . . .   108 CUCHULAIN SEA   V   39
    AND CONCHUBAR, THE RED BRANCH KING OF KINGS, . . .   109 CUCHULAIN SEA   V   45
    THE JEWELLED CROWNS THAT KINGS HAVE HURLED . . . .   155 FORGOT BEAUTY   4
    OF THE CROWNED MAGI, AND THE KINGS WHOSE EYES . . .   169 SECRET ROSE   V   9
    KINGS OF THE GREAT PLAIN HAVE COME AND GONE . . .   183 QUEEN MAEVE   V   81
    WITH THE FIRST KINGS OF MANY-PILLARED CRUACHAN. . .   187 QUEEN MAEVE   151
    WITH THE FIRST KINGS OF MANY PILLARED CRUACHAN . . . 187 QUEEN MAEVE   V   151
    AMONG THE GIANT KINGS WHOSE HOARD, ...   196 BAILE AILLINN   164
    OR ON THE UNPEOPLED WAVES WITH KINGS TO PULL AT THE OAR, 210 UNDER THE MOON   15
    THEY HAVE IT THAT THE PLANS OF KINGS AND QUEENS . . . 235 SHADOW WATER B   296
    THE DAUGHTER AND THE GRANDDAUGHTER OF KINGS . . .   237 SHADOW WATER B   334
    THE DAUGHTER AND GRANDDAUGHTER OF KINGS . . . . .   237 SHADOW WATER B   V   334
    NOTHING TO MAKE A SONG ABOUT BUT KINGS, ...   257 RECONCILIATION   5
    AND HALF THE KINGS, BEFORE SUNDOWN . . . .   273 GREY ROCK   69
    AND HALF HIS KINGS, BEFORE SUNDOWN . . . .   273 GREY ROCK   V   69
    THE TWO KINGS . . . .   276 TWO KINGS   T
    KNOWING THAT SILENCE BRINGS NO GOOD TO KINGS, . . .   279 TWO KINGS   57
    AMONG THE KINGS OF GREECE AND FRANCE." . . . . .   296 THREE BEGGARS   V   32A
    UPON THE BOTTOM OF A KING OF KINGS! . . . .   445 SCHOOL CHILDR   44
    ALL SORTS OF KINGS HAVE SAT . . . .   597 MODEL LAUREATE   2
    SOME BOAST OF BEGGAR-KINGS AND KINGS . . . . . .   597 MODEL LAUREATE   9
    THE HEATHEN. YEA, AND SHAKE THE SULLEN KINGS . . .   698 MOSADA 2   55
    COME AND DREAM OF KINGS AND KINGDOMS, ...   737 IN FIRELIGHT   1
    TOWARDS A COUNTRY WHERE THERE ARE NO KINGS. . . .   755 SHADOW WATER A   165
    OF THE TWELVE KINGS OF THE WORLD TO BE MY KING, . .   757 SHADOW WATER A   214
    AND HAVE BEEN WOOED BY THE TWELVE KINGS OF THE EARTH, 757 SHADOW WATER A   V   214
KINSALE
    TO MY OWN PLACE, KINSALE. . . . . ,   95 MOLL MAGEE   24
    TO THE EARL OF KINSALE, ...   740 EARL PAUL   14
    THE CAPTIVE FROM KINSALE. . . . .   740 EARL PAUL   28
    THE EARL OF KINSALE SAID, ...   742 EARL PAUL   62
    ON THE CLIFF OF KINSALE. . . . .   742 EARL PAUL   68
KINSELLA'S
    JOHN KINSELLA'S LAMENT FOR MRS. MARY MOORE . . . .   620 JOHN KINSELLA   T
KINSMAN
    AND HE, OF HIS HIGH KINSMAN SORROW DREAMING, ...   67 SAD SHEPHERD   V   2
KINSMEN
    O KINSMEN OF THE THREE IN ONE, ...   213 BLESS PSALTER   14
    O KINSMEN, BLESS THE HANDS THAT PLAY. . . . . . .   213 BLESS PSALTER   15
KISS
    THAT I MIGHT HAVE YOUR SON TO KISS." . . . .   6 OISIN 1   59
    YET LOVE AND KISS ON DIM SHORES FAR AWAY . . . . .   29 OISIN 2   13
    THEY LOVE AND KISS IN ISLANDS FAR AWAY, ...   29 OISIN 2   13
    BUT LOVE AND KISS ON DIM SHORES FAR AWAY . . . .   29 OISIN 2   V   13
    NOW CUFF HIM OFF. HE'S OFF! A KISS FOR YOU, ...   73 ANASHU VIJAYA   39
    A LONELY LAUGHTER, AND MAY KISS HIS HANDS TO ME IN SLEEP. 75 ANASHU VIJAYA   82
    AN INNER LAUGHTER, AND MAY KISS HIS HANDS TO ME IN SLEEP. 75 ANASHU VIJAYA V   82
    A LONELY LAUGHTER, THAT HE MAY KISS HANDS TO ME IN SLEEP. 75 ANASHU VIJAYA V   82
    WITH A KISS AND A TEAR ON THY DROOPING BROW. . . . .   79 FALLING LEAVES   8
    IS OUR FIRST KISS, AND AH, HOW OLD MY HEART!" . . .   80 EPHEMERA   9
    I SIGH THAT KISS YOU, ...   118 CRADLE SONG   9
    I KISS YOU AND KISS YOU, ...   118 CRADLE SONG   9
    I KISS YOU AND KISS YOU, ...   118 CRADLE SONG   V   9
    DID THE KISS OF MOTHER MARY . . . .   124 CATHLEEN PARA   9
    HERS THE KISS OF MOTHER MARY, ...   124 CATHLEEN PARA   V   9
    DREAM, UNTIL GOD BURN NATURE WITH A KISS? . . . .   128 DREAM OF FAERY   47
    UNTIL HE BURN UP NATURE WITH A KISS!-- . . . . .   128 DREAM OF FAERY   V   47
    I KISS MY WAILING CHILD AND PRESS IT TO MY BREAST, . 147 UNAPPEAS HOST   5
    AND KISS HER LIPS AND TAKE HER HANDS! . . . . . .   150 WANDER AENGUS   20
    AND KISS HER LIPS AND TAKE HER HAND, ...   150 WANDER AENGUS   V   20
    AND WHEN YOU SIGH FROM KISS TO KISS . . . .   156 FORGOT BEAUTY   18

KISS (CONTINUED)
AND WHEN YOU SIGH FROM KISS TO KISS . . . .   156 FORGOT BEAUTY   18
AND LOST THE WORLD AND EMER FOR A KISS; . . . .   170 SECRET ROSE   15
A CHILD'S LAUGHTER, A WOMAN'S KISS. . . . .   190 BAILE AILLINN   40
AND TREMBLE WITH THEIR LOVE AND KISS. . . . .   196 BAILE AILLINN   169
THAT IT FADES OUT FROM KISS TO KISS; . . . .   202 NEVER GIVE ALL   5
THAT IT FADES OUT FROM KISS TO KISS; . . . .   202 NEVER GIVE ALL   5
BUT WE BEND TOGETHER AND KISS THE QUIET FEET . . . . . 207 HANRAHANS SONG V   4
AND KISS MORE LIPS THAN LASTING PEACEABLE MEN . . . . . 225 SHADOW WATER B   71
A LUCKY BATTLE, OR A WOMAN'S KISS . . . .   227 SHADOW WATER B   115
THEY TAKE A KISS FOR WHAT A KISS IS WORTH, ...   229 SHADOW WATER B   157
THEY TAKE A KISS FOR WHAT A KISS IS WORTH, ...   229 SHADOW WATER B   157
HAVE CALLED ME THEIR BELOVED, I'LL NOT KISS THEM. . . . 237 SHADOW WATER B   336
UNTIL MY BODY GIVE YOU KISS FOR KISS. . . . .   238 SHADOW WATER B   345
UNTIL MY BODY GIVE YOU KISS FOR KISS. . . . .   238 SHADOW WATER B   345
YOUR SOUL SHALL GIVE THE KISS. I AM NOT AFRAID, . . .   238 SHADOW WATER B   346
OR I HAD NO WOMAN THERE TO KISS; . . . .   305 HOUR DAWN   66
AND PAY BUT A KISS FOR A KISS. . . . .   330 BONE OF A HARE   8
AND PAY BUT A KISS FOR A KISS. . . . .   330 BONE OF A HARE   8
I CELEBRATE THE SILENT KISS THAT ENDS SHORT LIFE OR LONG. 459 FROM OEDIPUS   9
THAT I MAY HEAR IF WE SHOULD KISS . . . .   573 LADYS 3RD SONG   9
AND SHALL BE DONE, IF YOU WILL DEIGN TO KISS . . . . . 669 ISLE STAT II 3   79
AH, LET US KISS EACH OTHER'S EYES, ...   686 LIFE   15
TO PLACE A KISS OF FIRE ON THE DIM BROW . . . . . .   688 TWO TITANS   47
SO YOU MUST GO; KISS ME BEFORE YOU GO. . . . .   702 MOSADA 3   96
THE WOMEN NONE CAN KISS AND THRIVE, ...   775 AGAINST WITCH   8
WOMEN, THAT NONE CAN KISS AND THRIVE, ...   775 AGAINST WITCH V   8
THEY WILL GIVE HIM KISS FOR KISS . . . .   776 AGAINST WITCH   29
THEY WILL GIVE HIM KISS FOR KISS . . . .   776 AGAINST WITCH   29
KISSED
HAD KISSED MY FATHER, LONG-ARMED FIN, ...   10 OISIN 1   V 112B
AND KISSED, AS THEY WOULD NEVER CEASE, ...   16 OISIN 1   215
AND KISSED THE SCEPTRE WITH RED LIPS, ...   18 OISIN 1   258
AND KISSED THE SCEPTRE WITH HOT LIPS, ...   18 OISIN 1   V 258
AS WE KISSED EACH ROSE'S HEAD; . . . .   21 OISIN 1   V 307
AND KISSED MY EYES, AND, SWAYING HER BRIGHT HEAD . . . . 29 OISIN 2   6
A YOUNG MAN CRIED AND KISSED HER HAND, ...   191 BAILE AILLINN   60
BUT WE HAVE ALL BENT LOW AND LOW AND KISSED THE QUIET FEET 207 HANRAHANS SONG   9
YET NEVER HAVE TWO LOVERS KISSED BUT THEY . . . . . .   229 SHADOW WATER B   153
HE HAS STOOPED DOWN AND KISSED HER ON THE LIPS. . . . . 232 SHADOW WATER B   230
AND KISSED HER DUSKY FACE, ...   332 SOLOMON SHEBA   2
AND KISSED HER ARAB EYES, ...   333 SOLOMON SHEBA   18
THE HANDS THAT I HAVE KISSED, ...   357 BROKEN DREAMS   35
AND AFTER KISSED A STONE, ...   384 VISION ROBART   64
I KISSED A STONE; . . . .   628 JANE MOUNTAIN   20
WITH LITTLE CRIES OF JOY HE KISSED THE RAIN . . . . .   688 TWO TITANS   33
AND KNOW YOU NOT SHE KISSED THAT PIOUS CHILD . . . . . 696 MOSADA 2   6
KISSES
OH, CAN MY KISSES BRING A FLUSH NO MORE . . . . . .   701 MOSADA 3   71
KISSING
NOR MOUTH FROM KISSING, NOR FROM WINE UNWET; . . . .   311 MOUNTAIN TOMB   7
NOR MOUTH WITH KISSING NOR WITH WINE UNWET. . . . . .   311 MOUNTAIN TOMB V   7
NOR MOUTH WITH KISSING NOR WITH THE WINE UNWET. . . . . 311 MOUNTAIN TOMB V   7
KITCHEN
AND SCRUB A KITCHEN PAVEMENT, OR BREAK STONES . . . .   204 ADAMS CURSE   8
KITE
LIKE THE EYES OF SOME GREAT KITE SCOURING THE WOODS, . . 283 TWO KINGS   150
I GAZED AT HIM LIKE GROUSE UPON A KITE; . . . .   283 TWO KINGS   152
KITH
BUT WHERE ARE YOUR NOBLE KITH AND KIN, ...   5 OISIN 1   44
"NOW HATH HE KITH OR KIN, OR ANY FRIEND?" . . . . . .   712 FERENCZ RENYI   66
KITTENS   SEE PANTHER-KITTENS
KNAVE
NOR KNAVE NOR DOLT CAN BREAK . . . .   259 UNWORTH PRAISE   2
FROM SELF-SAME DOLT AND KNAVE; . . . .   260 UNWORTH PRAISE   17
ON THE DAY'S WAR WITH EVERY KNAVE AND DOLT, ...   260 FASC DIFFICULT   10
AND NO KNAVE BROUGHT TO BOOK . . . .   347 FISHERMAN   17
DUMBFOUNDED BEFORE A KNAVE, ...   349 HAWK   16
I THOUGHT HIM HALF A LUNATIC, HALF KNAVE, ...   473 ALL SOUL NIGHT   64
FOOL, RASCAL, KNAVE, ...   496 MOHINI CHATTER   8
I RANTED TO THE KNAVE AND FOOL, ...   506 REMORSE SPEECH   1
WHAT MATTER IF THE KNAVE . . . .   525 DANCING DAYS   10
HEROIC REVERIE MOCKED BY CLOWN AND KNAVE, ...   619 BRONZE HEAD   27
WHAT HURRIES OUT THE KNAVE AND DOLT? . . . .   625 NATIVITY   9
KNEAD
LONGING TO KNEAD AND PULL IT INTO SHAPE . . . . . .   246 SHADOW WATER B   510
THITHER THY DUST, AND KNEAD IT WITH A CRY, ...   688 TWO TITANS   52
KNEADED
IS BUT HALF YOURS; HE KNEADED IN THE DOUGH . . . . .   201 OLD MEMORY   6
WHEN ALL THE DOUGH HAS BEEN SO KNEADED UP . . . . .   377 PHASES OF MOON   114
KNEE
BENT DOWN ABOVE EACH HOOKED KNEE, ...   26 OISIN 1   392
BENT LOW ABOVE EACH HOOKED KNEE, ...   26 OISIN 1   V 392
WENT DOWN UPON A HAND AND KNEE . . . .   304 HOUR DAWN   V 45
THE SPECKLED CAT SLEPT ON MY KNEE; . . . .   381 SONGS FOOL 2   2
WAILING UPON A WOMAN'S KNEE, ...   436 FOR MY SON   22
AND ALL SHALL BEND THE KNEE . . . .   516 MANS SONG   16
THE DEVOTEE PROFFERS A KNEE TO HIS LORD, ...   547 TO SAME TUNE 3   2
I WOULD THAT I DRANK WITH MY LOVE ON MY KNEE, ...   551 SONGS REWRIT 1   9
COULD I BUT DRINK, MY LOVE ON MY KNEE . . . . . .   551 SONGS REWRIT 1 V   9
O COULD I DRINK, MY LOVE ON MY KNEE, ...   551 SONGS REWRIT 1 V   9

		PAGE	TITLE		LINE

KNEE (CONTINUED)
    HER KNEE CAP BROKEN; THAT GIRL I DECLARE . . . .   578 CRAZED GIRL   V   6
    NO BOOKS UPON THE KNEE, AND NO ONE THERE . . . .   579 DOR WELLESLEY   9
    THE DEVOTEE PROFFERS A KNEE TO HIS LORD, ...   614 MARCH SONGS 2   2
    BENDING HUMBLY EVERY KNEE, ...   726 LOVERS QUARREL   14
    AND COME KNEELING ON ONE KNEE, ...   727 LOVERS QUARREL   53
KNEE-CAP
    HER KNEE-CAP BROKEN, THAT GIRL I DECLARE . . . . . .   578 CRAZED GIRL   6
KNEEL
    BEFORE THY FEET SHALL KNEEL DOWN ALL . . . .   7 OISIN 1   V   77
    SHALL KNEEL AND PRAISE YOU, ONE BY ONE, ...   8 OISIN 1   78
    BUT KNEEL AND WEAR OUT THE FLAGS AND PRAY FOR YOUR SOUL   63 OISIN 3   215
        THAT IS LOST
    BUT WEEP YOU AND KNEEL; WEAR OUT THE FLAGS; . . . . .   63 OISIN 3   V 215
    KNEEL, USHEEN, WEAR OUT THE FLAGS AND PRAY FOR YOUR SOUL   63 OISIN 3   V 215
        THAT IS LOST
    I RISE IN THE DAWN, AND I KNEEL AND BLOW . . . . . .   150 OLD MOTHER   1
    I RISE AT THE DAWN, AND I KNEEL AND BLOW . . . . . .   150 OLD MOTHER   V   1
    I KNEEL BY THEE--NO PARTING NOW--LOOK UP. . . . . . .   702 MOSADA 3   94
KNEELING
    O WOMEN, KNEELING BY YOUR ALTAR-RAILS LONG HENCE, . .   173 SPEAKS HEARERS   1
    O COLLEENS, KNEELING BY YOUR ALTAR RAILS LONG HENCE, .   173 SPEAKS HEARERS V   1
    O, WOMEN, KNEELING BY YOUR ALTAR RAILS LONG HENCE, . .   173 SPEAKS HEARERS V   1
    A REVOLUTIONARY SOLDIER KNEELING TO BE BLESSED; . . .   601 GALLERY REVIS   8
    AND COME KNEELING ON ONE KNEE, ...   727 LOVERS QUARREL   53
KNEELS
    GRIEVE NOT, FOR GOMEZ KNEELS BESIDE THEE--GOMEZ, . . .   702 MOSADA 3   90
    GRIEVE NOT, FOR VALLENCE KNEELS BESIDE THEE--VALLENCE, . 702 MOSADA 3   V   90
KNEES
    . . . HIS KNEES IN THE SOFT STAR-FLAME, ...   50 OISIN 3   43
    NOT COUGHING, MY HEAD ON MY KNEES, ...   58 OISIN 3   159
    BUT WEEP THOU, AND WEAR THOU THE FLAGS WITH THY KNEES,   63 OISIN 3   V 215
        . . .
    BUT WEEP YOU, AND WEAR YOU THE FLAGS WITH YOUR KNEES, . . 63 OISIN 3   V 215
    MY SPIRIT ROCKED IN EVENING LIGHT, THE RUSHES ROUND MY   76 INDIAN ON GOD   2
        KNEES,
    MY SPIRIT ROCKED IN EVENING'S HUSH, THE RUSHES ROUND MY   76 INDIAN ON GOD V   2
        KNEES,
    UPON HIS KNEES BY MY FOOTSTOOL . . . .   82 MAD KING GOLL   V   13
    WITH HEAD BOWED ON HIS KNEES CUCHULAIN STAYED; . . .   110 CUCHULAIN SEA   71
    WITH HEAD BOWED ON HIS KNEES, CUCHULLIN STAID, . . .   110 CUCHULAIN SEA   V   71
    THEIR SWORDS UPON THEIR IRON KNEES, ...   156 FORGOT BEAUTY   23
    A SWORD UPON HIS IRON KNEES, ...   156 FORGOT BEAUTY   V   23
    THEIR HEADS ON YOUR KNEES, AND DROWN THEIR EYES WITH YOUR 163 VALLEY LOVERS   6
        HAIR,
    AND CUMHAL SAID, BENDING HIS KNEES, ...   167 BLESSED   5
    HE HAD KNEES THAT STUCK OUT OF HIS HOSE; . . . . . .   190 BAILE AILLINN   27
    THEY HAD HANDS LIKE CLAWS, AND THEIR KNEES . . . . .   208 OLD MEN ADMIRE   4
    PLANTED ON HIS KNEES, ...   333 SOLOMON SHEBA   10
    TO GREAT SHAPELY KNEES . . . .   355 PROPERTIUS   2
    AND HAD BUT BROKEN KNEES FOR HIRE . . . .   411 TOWER   62
    ROUGH MEN-AT-ARMS, CROSS-GARTERED TO THE KNEES . . .   412 TOWER   82
    ROUGH MEN AT ARMS, CROSS-GARTERED TO THE KNEES . . .   412 TOWER   V   82
    BEFORE SHE HAD SPREAD A BOOK UPON HER KNEES . . . . .   466 HARUN RASHID   120
    THE CONSECRATED BLADE UPON MY KNEES . . . .   477 SELF AND SOUL   9
    THE CONSECRATED SWORD UPON MY KNEES . . . .   477 SELF AND SOUL   V   9
    STRAIGHTEN AGED KNEES, ...   505 RESULT THOUGHT   16
    MY MEDIAEVAL KNEES LACK HEALTH UNTIL THEY BEND, . . .   603 GALLERY REVIS   33
    SAID TO THE WOMAN ON HIS KNEES, "LIE STILL. . . . .   609 IN TARAS HALLS   2
    PROPPED UPON MY TWO KNEES, ...   628 JANE MOUNTAIN   19
    UPON MY KNEES I PRAY YOU, LET IT SLEEP, ...   693 MOSADA 1   72
    AND THOU SHALT BEND, ENDURING GOD, THE KNEES . . . .   698 MOSADA 2   59
    AND THOU SHALL BEND, ENDURING GOD, THE KNEES . . . .   698 MOSADA 2   V   59
    HAST THOU NOT SAT OF YORE UPON THE KNEES . . . . . .   724 KANVA ON SELF   9
KNELT
    AND KNELT THERE, EVERY GIRL AND MAN, ...   15 OISIN 1   214
    AND KNELT THEM, EVERY MAID AND MAN, ...   15 OISIN 1   V 214
    AND MEN AND LADIES KNELT THEM THERE . . . .   18 OISIN 1   255
    AND MEN AND MAIDENS KNELT THEM THERE . . . .   18 OISIN 1   V 255
    AND HIS YOUNG SWEETHEART CLOSE BESIDE HIM KNELT, . . .   108 CUCHULAIN SEA   40
    AND HIS YOUNG DEAR ONE CLOSE BESIDE HIM KNELT, . . .   108 CUCHULAIN SEA   V   40
    HE KNELT, AND LEANING ON THE CHAIR . . . .   132 FR GILLIGAN   13
    HE KNELT, PRAYED, FELL ASLEEP; . . . .   132 FR GILLIGAN   V   14
    HE KNELT HIM AT THAT WORD. . . . .   133 FR GILLIGAN   40
    AND KNELT ABOVE IT WITH DRAWN KNIFE. ON THE INSTANT   278 TWO KINGS   37
    I KNELT IN THE DIRT. . . . .   516 MANS SONG   15
KNEW
    NEAR BY, THE FENIANS SAW, AND KNEW . . . .   10 OISIN 1   V 111
    I KNEW NOT IF DAYS PASSED OR HOURS, ...   11 OISIN 1   V 133
    WE CANTERED TO THE SHORE, AND KNEW . . . .   14 OISIN 1   178
    FOR WE KNEW WELL THE OLD WAS OVER, ...   25 OISIN 1   379
    FOR WELL WE KNEW THE OLD WAS OVER, ...   25 OISIN 1   V 379
    AND WHEN HE KNEW THE SWORD OF MANANNAN . . . .   40 OISIN 2   173
    WE TRAMPLED TO AND FRO. WHEN HIS MIND KNEW . . . .   40 OISIN 2   V 173
    BUT WHEN AT WITHERING OF THE SUN HE KNEW . . . . .   40 OISIN 2   V 173
    AND WHEN AT WITHERING OF THE SUN HE KNEW . . . . .   40 OISIN 2   V 173
    THRUSTING HIS NOSE TO MY SHOULDER; HE KNEW IN HIS BOSOM   54 OISIN 3   106
        DEEP
    SNATCHING THE BIRD IN SECRET; NOR KNEW I, EMBOSOMED APART, 57 OISIN 3   150
    . . . AND I KNEW HOW MEN SORROW AND PASS, ...   59 OISIN 3   175
    . . . AND I KNEW HOW MEN PASS, ...   59 OISIN 3   V 175

PAGE   TITLE   LINE

KNEW   (CONTINUED)
THE LOVE I LIVED, THE DREAM I KNEW.   139 TO IRELAND   34
HE KNEW NOW THE FOLK OF THE AIR,   145 HOST OF AIR   V   40A
THEY KNEW HIM! HIS CHANGED BODY WAS   195 BAILE AILLINN   139
ALL THE LOVE STORIES THAT THEY KNEW.   197 BAILE AILLINN   197
I KNEW HIM WELL, AND WHILE I HEARD HIM LAUGHING   242 SHADOW WATER B   419
I KNEW A WOMAN NONE COULD PLEASE,   272 GREY ROCK   41
SHE STARTED AND THEN KNEW WHOSE FOOT IT WAS!   280 TWO KINGS   66
FOR HE KNEW BETTER HOW TO LIVE.   288 TO WEALTHY MAN   30
FOR ALL THE SLEEPER KNEW OR CARED!   307 HOUR DAWN   115
WE KNEW, THOUGH SHE'D NOT SAID A WORD,   314 MEMORY YOUTH   16
AND KNEW, THOUGH SHE'D NOT SAID A WORD,   314 MEMORY YOUTH   V   16
AS THOUGH HE KNEW HIMSELF, AS IT WERE, A CUCKOO,   341 SHEP GOATHERD   54
I KNEW A PHOENIX IN MY YOUTH, SO LET THEM HAVE THEIR DAY.   353 HIS PHOENIX   8
I KNEW A PHOENIX IN MY YOUTH, SO LET THEM HAVE THEIR DAY.   354 HIS PHOENIX   16
I KNEW A PHOENIX IN MY YOUTH, SO LET THEM HAVE THEIR DAY.   354 HIS PHOENIX   24
I KNEW A PHOENIX IN MY YOUTH, SO LET THEM HAVE THEIR DAY.   354 HIS PHOENIX   32
THE MAN THAT LAPO AND THAT GUIDO KNEW?   368 EGO DOMINUS   26
I KNEW THAT I HAD SEEN, HAD SEEN AT LAST   384 VISION ROBART   49
NOT HIS, NOT MINE." AND HE THAT KNEW   387 SOLOMON WITCH   V   6
SHE THAT BUT LITTLE PATIENCE KNEW,   397 POLIT PRISONER   1
BUT KNEW MY FINGER COULD BUT HAVE TOUCHED   399 BREAK OF DAY   13
BUT KNEW MY FINGER WOULD HAVE TOUCHED   399 BREAK OF DAY   V   13
I KNEW THAT ONE IS ANIMATE,   406 IN TIME OF WAR   4
I KNEW THAT HORSE-PLAY, KNEW IT FOR A MURDEROUS THING.   442 BLACK CENTAUR   4
I KNEW THAT HORSE-PLAY, KNEW IT FOR A MURDEROUS THING.   442 BLACK CENTAUR   4
WHERE SEVEN EPHESIAN TOPERS SLEPT AND NEVER KNEW   442 BLACK CENTAUR   11
I KNEW THAT HORSE PLAY, KNEW IT FOR A MURDEROUS THING.   442 BLACK CENTAUR   V   4
I KNEW THAT HORSE PLAY, KNEW IT FOR A MURDEROUS THING.   442 BLACK CENTAUR   V   4
KNEW THAT WE'D HALVED A SOUL   457 SUMMER SPRING   6
"IF BUT THE SHIRT UPON MY BODY KNEW IT   462 HARUN RASHID   33
THAT SPEECH WAS ALL THAT THE TOWN KNEW, BUT HE   462 HARUN RASHID   35
THAT NEVER KNEW THAT STRAIN WOULD SCARCE SEEM BRIGHT,   465 HARUN RASHID   88
THAN ALL MY BURSTING SPRINGTIME KNEW. A GIRL   466 HARUN RASHID   105
AND KNEW THAT SWEET EXTREMITY OF PRIDE   471 ALL SOUL NIGHT   22
BURKE WAS A WHIG. WHETHER THEY KNEW OR NOT,   486 SEVEN SAGES   8
NOR KNEW, DRUNKEN WITH SINGING AS WITH WINE,   537 HER VISION   30
A MIND MICHAEL ANGELO KNEW   576 ACRE OF GRASS   19
CLIMBING, FALLING SHE KNEW NOT WHERE,   578 CRAZED GIRL   4
FOR ALL TONGUES HE KNEW.   594 COLONEL MARTIN   4
OF SOLITARY BEDS, KNEW WHAT THEY WERE,   610 STATUES   5
DREAMER OF THE MIDDLE AGES. EMPTY EYEBALLS KNEW   610 STATUES   20
DREAMER OF THE MIDDLE-AGES. EMPTY EYE-BALLS KNEW   610 STATUES   V   20
WE PICKED EACH OTHER FROM AFAR AND KNEW   622 HOUND VOICE   10
A GIRL THAT KNEW ALL DANTE ONCE   626 OLD MEN BE MAD   5
SOME KNEW WHAT AILED THE WORLD   627 STATES HOLIDAY   9
THAT THE WITCH OF ATLAS KNEW,   637 BEN BULBEN   3
AND ANCIENT IRELAND KNEW IT ALL.   637 BEN BULBEN   16
I NEVER KNEW AN EVE SO MARVELLOUS STILL.   702 MOSADA 3   88
IT IS THE DARKEST EVE I EVER KNEW.   702 MOSADA 3   93
I NEVER KNEW A NIGHT SO HONEY-SWEET.   702 MOSADA 3   99
I NEVER KNEW A NIGHT SO HONEY SWEET.   702 MOSADA 3   V   99
I NEVER KNEW A NIGHT SO DEW-BEDROWNED.   703 MOSADA 3   105
I NEVER KNEW A NIGHT SO BITTER COLD.   704 MOSADA 3   124
I SAT ME DOWN BESIDE THEE, AND I KNEW   713 FERENCZ RENYI   92
THEIR BRIEF LIVES I NEVER KNEW.   787 HUDDON DUDDON   5

KNIFE
AND KNELT ABOVE IT WITH DRAWN KNIFE. ON THE INSTANT   278 TWO KINGS   37
DREW A KNIFE TO STRIKE HIM DEAD,   514 JANE GROWN OLD   10

KNIGHT
IN THIS ALTAR-PIECE THE KNIGHT,   385 ROBARTES DANCE   2
TO PROVE HIS LOVE A KNIGHT WITH LANCE IN REST   651 ISLE STAT I 1   158
"BEHOLD THE KNIGHT OF THE WATERFALL, WHOSE HEART   684 SEEKER   54
FOR A KNIGHT, COME FROM NORMANDY   740 EARL PAUL   7
TO THROW THE NORMAN KNIGHT." "   740 EARL PAUL   12
STOOD THERE THE NORMAN KNIGHT.   741 EARL PAUL   40

KNIGHTLY
YEA, NOBLE AND MOST KNIGHTLY HATH IT BEEN.   679 ISLE STAT II 3   320

KNIGHTS
HAS TWELVE KNIGHTS OVERTHROWN!   740 EARL PAUL   8
FOR HE HAD OVERTHROWN TWELVE KNIGHTS   741 EARL PAUL   43

KNIT
THAT COMES OF THE BEST KNIT TO THE BEST? ALTHOUGH   264 HOUSE SHAKEN   7
THERE ALL THE BARREL-HOOPS ARE KNIT,   557 THERE   1

KNITTED
OF KNITTED MUSIC. OFT THE FOND REPINING   33 OISIN 2   V   68C
AND KNITTED MESH TO MESH, WE GROW IMMORTAL!   252 SHADOW WATER B   616
THOUGHTS LONG KNITTED INTO A SINGLE THOUGHT,   488 COOLE PARK 29   7

KNITTING
WORTH KNITTING TO A MEASURE OF SWEET SOUND?   181 QUEEN MAEVE   33
AND KNITTING MESH TO MESH! WE GROW IMMORTAL!   252 SHADOW WATER B   V   616
NOR HEAVY KNITTING OF THE BROW   318 APPOINTMENT   9

KNOCK
I KNOCK THEIR HEADS ABOUT.   605 SONGS BURDEN 1   8
AND KNOCK THE OTHERS DOWN.   606 SONGS BURDEN 1   26
OR THE RIFLE KNOCK HIM DEAD,   637 BEN BULBEN   V   18

KNOCKED
THE COLONEL KNOCKED ON THE RICH MAN'S DOOR,   595 COLONEL MARTIN   28
THE COLONEL KNOCKED ON A RICH MAN'S DOOR,   595 COLONEL MARTIN   V   28

KNOCKFEFIN
ON CREVROE OR BROAD KNOCKFEFIN, WITH MANY OF OLD THEY FEAST   59 OISIN 3   179

424

KNOCKFEFIN   (CONTINUED)
   ON CREVROE OR ON BROAD KNOCKFEFIN, WITH MANY OF OLD THEY   59 OISIN 3   V 179
      FAST
KNOCKNAREA
   THE BIRDS FROM KNOCKNAREA . . . .   93 FATHER OHART   30
   THE HOST IS RIDING FROM KNOCKNAREA . . . .   140 HOSTING SIDHE   1
   VEERING, FLEETING, FICKLE, THE WINDS OF KNOCKNAREA, . . .   206 HANRAHANS SONG V 1
   THE WIND HAS BUNDLED UP THE CLOUDS HIGH OVER KNOCKNAREA,   207 HANRAHANS SONG   6
   THE WINDS HAVE BUNDLED UP THE CLOUDS HIGH OVER KNOCKNAREA   207 HANRAHANS SONG V 6
   OUT OF BEN BULBEN AND KNOCKNAREA, ...   549 SEVERED HEAD   2
KNOCKNASHEE
   AND THE WORLD ROUND KNOCKNASHEE . . . .   93 FATHER OHART   31
KNOCKS
   OR THE RIFLE KNOCKS HIM DEAD, ...   637 BEN BULBEN   18
KNOLL
   I HUNGER TO BUILD THEM ANEW AND SIT ON A GREEN KNOLL APART, 143 ROSE IN HEART   6
KNOT-GRASS
   BUT ONE SMALL KNOT-GRASS GROWING BY THE POOL . . . . .   127 DREAM OF FAERY   29
   BUT ONE SMALL KNOT-GRASS GROWING BY THE RIM . . . . .   127 DREAM OF FAERY V 29
KNOTTED
   THE KNOTTED SCOURGE, THE NAIL-PIERCED HANDS, THE WOUNDED   172 TRAV PASSION   V   4
      SIDE,
   THE LIGHT IS DANCING O'ER THE KNOTTED TREES, ...   662 ISLE STAT II 2   2
KNOW
   AND YOU SHALL KNOW THE DANAAN LEISURE! . . . .   9 OISIN 1   100
   AND THOU SHALT KNOW THE IMMORTALS' LEISURE, ...   9 OISIN 1   V 100
   I KNOW NOT IF DAYS PASSED OR HOURS, ...   11 OISIN 1   133
   WITH HEARTS THAT KNOW NOR LAW NOR RULE, ...   22 OISIN 1   339
   AND PEAK AND PINE WE KNOW NOT WHY, ...   22 OISIN 1   V 340C
   WE ONLY KNOW THAT WE WERE GLAD, ...   22 OISIN 1   V 340D
   TROUBLED HER SONG. I DO NOT KNOW IF DAYS . . . . . .   30 OISIN 2   19
   FLASHING--I KNOW NOT WERE IT HOURS OR DAYS, ...   30 OISIN 2   V 19B
   IS THE ISLAND OF CONTENT?" "NONE KNOW," SHE SAID! . . .   46 OISIN 2   249
   WHICH IS THE ISLE OF YOUTH?" "NONE KNOW," SHE SAID, . .   46 OISIN 2   V 249
   WHAT KNOW THE PILOTS OF THE STARS OF TEARS? . . . . .   73 ANASHU VIJAYA   47
   AH, YOU WILL KNOW MY LOVED ONE BY HIS HUNTER'S ARROWS   75 ANASHU VIJAYA   80
      TRULY,
   I KNOW THE WORD THEY CRY, "ETERNITY!" . . . .   81 EPHEMERA   V 24F
   AND AH, THEY KNOW NOT, AS THEY PINE AND CEASE, ...   81 EPHEMERA   V 24I
   AND LEARN TO CHAUNT A TONGUE MEN DO NOT KNOW. . . . . .   101 ROSE UPON ROOD   21
   AND LEARN TO CHANT A TONGUE MEN DO NOT KNOW. . . . . .   101 ROSE UPON ROOD V 21
   "HE BADE ME LET ALL KNOW HE GIVES HIS NAME . . . . . .   109 CUCHULAIN SEA   52
   KNOW, THAT I WOULD ACCOUNTED BE . . . .   137 TO IRELAND   1
   MAY KNOW HOW MY HEART WENT WITH THEM . . . .   139 TO IRELAND   47
   THE PEOPLE OF COMING DAYS WILL KNOW . . . .   146 FISH   3
   BUT KNOW YOUR HAIR WAS BOUND AND WOUND . . . .   176 BELOVED DEAD   9
   BUT KNOW YOUR HAIR WAS BOUND AND BOUND . . . .   176 BELOVED DEAD V 9
   AND WEEP BECAUSE I KNOW ALL THINGS NOW! . . . .   177 PAST GREATNESS   2
   YET THEY THAT KNOW ALL THINGS BUT KNOW . . . .   190 BAILE AILLINN   38
   YET THEY THAT KNOW ALL THINGS BUT KNOW . . . .   190 BAILE AILLINN   38
   WHO KNOW THE WAY THAT NAOISE WENT? . . . .   193 BAILE AILLINN   96
   THEY KNOW ALL WONDERS, FOR THEY PASS . . . .   196 BAILE AILLINN   160
   THEY KNOW UNDYING THINGS, FOR THEY . . . .   196 BAILE AILLINN   170
   I AM CONTENTED, FOR I KNOW THAT QUIET . . . .   198 SEVEN WOODS   10
   YOU'D KNOW THE FOLLY OF BEING COMFORTED. . . . . . .   200 FOLLY COMFORT   14
   I KNOW OF THE LEAFY PATHS THAT THE WITCHES TAKE . . . .   203 WITHER BOUGHS   9
   I KNOW WHERE A DIM MOON DRIFTS, WHERE THE DANAAN KIND . .   203 WITHER BOUGHS   12
   I KNOW OF THE LEAFY PATH THAT THE WITCHES TAKE, ...   203 WITHER BOUGHS V 9
   AND I KNOW OF THE ISLES WHERE THE DANAAN KIND . . . .   203 WITHER BOUGHS V 12
   I KNOW OF THE SLEEPY COUNTRY, WHERE SWANS FLY ROUND . .   204 WITHER BOUGHS   17
   I KNOW, AND THE CURLEW AND PEEWIT ON ECHTGE OF STREAMS.   204 WITHER BOUGHS   22
   AND THE CURLEW AND PEEWIT KNOW ON ECHTGE OF STREAMS. . .   204 WITHER BOUGHS V 22
   REPLIED! "TO BE BORN WOMAN IS TO KNOW-- . . . . . .   205 ADAMS CURSE   18
   "THERE IS ONE THING THAT ALL WE WOMEN KNOW . . . . . .   205 ADAMS CURSE   V 18
   I ONLY KNOW THAT ALL WE KNOW COMES FROM YOU, ...   218 WOODS OF COOLE   28
   I ONLY KNOW THAT ALL WE KNOW COMES FROM YOU, ...   218 WOODS OF COOLE   28
   THAT SHE AMONG HER WINDS MIGHT KNOW HE WEPT! . . . . .   220 HARP OF AENGUS   12
   THAT SHE AMONG HER WOODS MIGHT KNOW HE WEPT! . . . . .   220 HARP OF AENGUS V 12
   NO, NO, DO NOT SAY THAT. YOU KNOW RIGHT WELL . . . . .   227 SHADOW WATER B   107
   IT MAY BE THAT THE EVER-LIVING KNOW IT-- . . . . . .   229 SHADOW WATER B   164
   CAN KNOW THAT ECSTASY. FORGAEL! FORGAEL! . . . . . .   231 SHADOW WATER B   203
   AND I WOULD KNOW IF YOU WILL GIVE ME VENGEANCE. . . . .   235 SHADOW WATER B   301
   AND KNOW THAT IT IS FEARLESS. DO WHAT YOU WILL, ...   238 SHADOW WATER B   350
   YOU DID NOT KNOW WHAT BROUGHT HIM TO HIS END, ...   240 SHADOW WATER B   382
   HOW CAN WE RAISE THE KEEN THAT DO NOT KNOW . . . . .   240 SHADOW WATER B   389
   I KNOW THAT HE DIED A THOUSAND YEARS AGO, ...   241 SHADOW WATER B   392
   DO YOU NOT KNOW ME, LADY? I AM HE . . . .   243 SHADOW WATER B   426
   YOU KNOW THE COUNSELS OF THE EVER-LIVING, ...   244 SHADOW WATER B   450
   I DO NOT UNDERSTAND. I KNOW YOUR FACE . . . .   244 SHADOW WATER B   465
   YOU KNOW THE COUNCILS OF THE EVER-LIVING, ...   244 SHADOW WATER B V 450
   I WOULD NOT LET YOU SPEAK, FOR I WOULD KNOW . . . . .   246 SHADOW WATER B   492
   FOR YOU ARE LOOKING AT THE SEA. DO YOU NOT KNOW . . . .   246 SHADOW WATER B   513
   'TWAS YOU THAT EGGED HIM TO IT, FOR YOU KNOW . . . . .   248 SHADOW WATER B   550
   I DO NOT KNOW FOR CERTAIN, BUT I KNOW . . . .   249 SHADOW WATER B   564
   I DO NOT KNOW FOR CERTAIN, BUT I KNOW . . . .   249 SHADOW WATER B   564
   AND I THAT HAVE NOT YOUR FAITH, HOW SHALL I KNOW . . . .   258 KING NO KING   11
   THAT'S ALL WE SHALL KNOW FOR TRUTH . . . .   261 DRINKING SONG   3
   AND KNOW THEM TO THE BONE! IMPART TO US-- . . . . . .   265 ABBEY THEATRE   9
   I KNOW A WOMAN NONE COULD PLEASE, ...   272 GREY ROCK   V 41
   CAN LOVERS HAVE THAT KNOW THEIR HAPPINESS . . . . . .   284 TWO KINGS   178
   WHAT CAN THEY KNOW OF LOVE THAT DO NOT KNOW . . . . .   285 TWO KINGS   193

WHAT CAN THEY KNOW OF LOVE THAT DO NOT KNOW . . . . . .   285 TWO KINGS   193
AND DO NOT KNOW THAT YOU WOULD BRING, ...   306 HOUR DAWN   93
TO KNOW WHEN MICHAEL'S TRUMPET CRIES . . . .   307 HOUR DAWN   100
WILL GATHER, AND NOT KNOW IT WALKS THE VERY STREET . . .   315 FALLEN MAJESTY   7
WILL GATHER AND NOT KNOW THAT THROUGH ITS VERY STREET . . 315 FALLEN MAJESTY V   7
I KNOW THAT I SHALL MEET MY FATE . . . .   328 IRISH AIRMAN   1
I KNOW WHAT WAGES BEAUTY GIVES, ...   336 YOUNG BEAUTY   13
MY DEAR, MY DEAR, I KNOW . . . .   336 YOUNG GIRL   1
CAN KNOW IT AS I KNOW, ...   336 YOUNG GIRL   5
CAN KNOW IT AS I KNOW, ...   336 YOUNG GIRL   5
ALL KNOW THE MAN THEIR NEIGHBOUR KNOWS. . . . .   337 SCHOLARS   10
THE SHEEP HAD GONE FROM THEIRS. I KNOW RIGHT WELL . . .   339 SHEP GOATHERD   15
TO KNOW THE MOUNTAIN AND THE VALLEY HAVE GRIEVED . . . .   343 SHEP GOATHERD   117
TO KNOW THE MOUNTAIN AND THE VALLEY GRIEVE . . . . .   343 SHEP GOATHERD   V   117
AND KNOW WHAT ONCE I HAVE KNOWN, ...   346 ON WOMAN   34
IF THERE BE RAGS ENOUGH HE WILL KNOW HER NAME . . . .   351 HER PRAISE   15
AND YOU KNOW WELL HOW GREAT THE LONGING HAS BEEN, . .   352 PEOPLE   7
WHO KNOW IT ALL RING AT HIS DOOR, AND SPEAK . . . .   373 PHASES OF MOON   21
HE WOULD NEVER KNOW ME AFTER ALL THESE YEARS . . . .   377 PHASES OF MOON   129
DOES MINNALOUSHE KNOW THAT HIS PUPILS . . . . . .   379 CAT AND MOON   21
I DO NOT KNOW, THAT KNOW I AM AFRAID . . . .   390 IMAGE PAST   41
I DO NOT KNOW, THAT KNOW I AM AFRAID . . . .   390 IMAGE PAST   41
WE KNOW THEIR DREAM! ENOUGH . . . .   394 EASTER 1916   70
TO KNOW THEY DREAMED AND ARE DEAD! . . . .   394 EASTER 1916   71
OR CALUMNY A SONG. HOW CAN THEY KNOW . . . . .   398 LEADERS CROWD   7
IT MADE HIM HAPPIER TO KNOW . . . .   400 DEMON BEAST   14
THE DARKNESS DROPS AGAIN! BUT NOW I KNOW . . . . .   402 SECOND COMING   18
AND KNOW WHATEVER FLOURISH AND DECLINE . . . . . .   423 MY DESCENDANTS   23
NOR KNOW THAT WHAT DISTURBS OUR BLOOD . . . . . .   434 WHEEL   7
WHO HAVE PLANNED HIS MURDER, FOR THEY KNOW . . . . .   436 FOR MY SON   12
TO TELL YOUR SIMPLEST WANT, AND KNOW, ...   436 FOR MY SON   V   21
HOW CAN WE KNOW THE DANCER FROM THE DANCE? . . . . .   446 SCHOOL CHILDR   64
CAN KNOW THE STORIES THAT WE KNOW . . . .   458 SECRETS OF OLD   11
CAN KNOW THE STORIES THAT WE KNOW . . . .   458 SECRETS OF OLD   11
AS THAT OLD WANDERING BEGGAR AND THESE GOD-HATED CHILDREN 459 FROM OEDIPUS   6
    KNOW.
THAT NONE MIGHT KNOW THAT HE WAS CONSCIENCE-STRUCK-- . .   462 HARUN RASHID   38
THAT SPEECH WAS ALL THAT THE COURT KNOW, BUT HE . .   462 HARUN RASHID   V   35
THAT NONE MIGHT KNOW THAT HE WAS CONSCIENCE STRUCK, . .   462 HARUN RASHID   V   38
YOU KNOW THE SAYING, "CHANGE THE BRIDE WITH SPRING," . .   463 HARUN RASHID   50
I KNOW NOT WHAT THE YOUNGER DREAMS-- . . . . . .   475 EVA GORE-BOOTH   10
DEAR SHADOWS, NOW YOU KNOW IT ALL, ...   476 EVA GORE-BOOTH   21
RUN TILL ALL THE SAGES KNOW . . . .   476 EVA GORE-BOOTH   29
FLOWERS FROM I KNOW NOT WHAT EMBROIDERY-- . . . . .   478 SELF AND SOUL   27
MAY KNOW NOT WHAT HE KNOWS, BUT KNOWS NOT GRIEF. . . .   500 VACILLATION   18
I KNOW, ALTHOUGH WHEN LOOKS MEET . . . .   511 JANE AND JACK   1
AND YOU KNOW WHO. . . . .   515 GIRLS SONG B   4
WHAT MATTER? FOR I KNOW . . . .   518 HIS CONFIDENCE   9
"THREE DEAR THINGS THAT WOMEN KNOW," . . . .   521 THREE THINGS   7
AS DID THAT WILD TRISTRAM KNOW . . . .   522 LULLABY   8
AND I SEEM TO KNOW . . . .   523 MAD AS MIST   4
ALL KNOW THEIR TALE, ALL KNOW WHAT LEAF AND TWIG, . . .   555 RIBH AT TOMB   7
ALL KNOW THEIR TALE, ALL KNOW WHAT LEAF AND TWIG, . . .   555 RIBH AT TOMB   7
WHAT CAN SHE KNOW UNTIL HE BID HER KNOW! . . . . .   558 RIBH CHRISTIAN   23
WHAT CAN SHE KNOW UNTIL HE BID HER KNOW! . . . . .   558 RIBH CHRISTIAN   23
BEAT DOWN UPON THEIR NAKED BODIES, KNOW . . . . .   563 MERU   12
FOR EVERYBODY KNOWS OR ELSE SHOULD KNOW . . . . .   565 LAPIS LAZULI   4
THEY KNOW THAT HAMLET AND LEAR ARE GAY! . . . . .   565 LAPIS LAZULI   16
"I KNOW THAT I MUST DROP DOWN DEAD . . . . . .   569 THREE BUSHES   17
KNOW WHERE ITS ROOTS BEGAN. . . . .   571 THREE BUSHES   76
NEITHER KNOW WHAT I AM . . . .   572 LADYS 1ST SONG   3
KNOW WORSE EVIL OF THE BODY! . . . .   573 LADYS 3RD SONG   6
THOUGHT FOR I KNOW NOT WHERE, ...   574 LOVERS SONG   2
WHAT CAN THEY KNOW THAT WE KNOW THAT KNOW THE TIME TO DIE? 580 CURSE CROMWELL   14
WHAT CAN THEY KNOW THAT WE KNOW THAT KNOW THE TIME TO DIE? 580 CURSE CROMWELL   14
WHAT CAN THEY KNOW THAT WE KNOW THAT KNOW THE TIME TO DIE? 580 CURSE CROMWELL   14
WHO CAN KNOW THE YEAR, MY DEAR, ...   588 OLD WICKED MAN   12
I KNOW AS FEW CAN KNOW, ...   589 OLD WICKED MAN   47
I KNOW AS FEW CAN KNOW, ...   589 OLD WICKED MAN   47
ALL KNOW THAT ALL THE DEAD IN THE WORLD ABOUT THAT PLACE   593 PILGRIM   11
    ARE STUCK,
NO MAN CAN KNOW A HAPPY MAN . . . .   598 STONE CROSS   11
I KNOW WHAT DEVIL'S TRADE THEY LEARN . . . . . .   607 SONGS BURDEN 2   12
WE KNOW WHAT RASCAL MIGHT HAS DEFILED, ...   614 MARCH SONGS 2   11
AND WIDE AWAKE KNOW THAT THE HUNT IS ON! . . . . .   622 HOUND VOICE   17
YOUNG MEN KNOW NOTHING OF THIS SORT . . . . . .   626 OLD MEN BE MAD   16
OBSERVANT OLD MEN KNOW IT WELL! . . . .   626 OLD MEN BE MAD   17
AND WHEN THEY KNOW WHAT OLD BOOKS TELL, ...   626 OLD MEN BE MAD   18
KNOW WHY AN OLD MAN SHOULD BE MAD. . . . . . .   626 OLD MEN BE MAD   20
WHAT DO WE KNOW BUT THAT WE FACE . . . .   633 MAN AND ECHO   39
MAINLY BECAUSE OF WHAT WE ONLY KNOW . . . . . .   634 CUCHULAIN COMF   14
KNOW THAT WHEN ALL WORDS ARE SAID . . . .   638 BEN BULBEN   27
KNOW HIS WORK OR CHOOSE HIS MATE. . . . .   638 BEN BULBEN   36
HERE, WHERE MEN KNOW THE GRACIOUS WOODLAND JOYS, . . .   651 ISLE STAT I 1   154
AND NOT TOO CLEAR, HOW WILL THE NEW GOD KNOW . . . .   658 ISLE STAT I 3   79
I LIKE YOU, AND, IN SOOTH I KNOW NOT WHY. . . . .   661 ISLE STAT II 1   64
NASCHINA. OH, I KNOW HER WELL—A LAME, ...   661 ISLE STAT II 1   67
TO WATCH THEE PASS? YET DEEPER THAN MEN KNOW . . . .   672 ISLE STAT II 3   158
I KNOW NOT OF THE THINGS YOU SPEAK. BUT WHAT . . . .   675 ISLE STAT II 3   239
BY THEE SPELL-BOUND? THOU SHALT KNOW MORE! . . . .   675 ISLE STAT II 3   241

```
                                                PAGE   TITLE            LINE

KNOW   (CONTINUED)
    BUT NOW MY WANDERING SHALL BE DONE, I KNOW.  . . . . .    682 SEEKER              21
    BUT SOON MY WANDERING SHALL BE DONE I KNOW.  . . . . .    682 SEEKER          V   21
    I KNOW NOT WHAT I AM.  I SOUGHT THEE NOT. .  . . . . .    685 SEEKER              76
    SHE WAS MY ONLY FRIEND! I'M LAME, YOU KNOW-- . . . . .    695 MOSADA 1          115
    AND KNOW YOU NOT SHE KISSED THAT PIOUS CHILD . . . . .    696 MOSADA 2            6
    ONCE IN THY NATION NONE SHALL KNOW THAT I  . . . . . .    702 MOSADA 3           82
    AMONG THY NATION NONE SHALL KNOW THAT I .  . . . . . .    702 MOSADA 3       V   82
    I AM SO YOUNG.  DOST THOU NO LONGER KNOW,  . . . . . .    713 FERENCZ RENYI      88
    AND LOST AND FAR IN YONDER HILLS I KNOW!  . . . . . .     713 FERENCZ RENYI      98
    COME I KNOW WHERE, FAR AWAY . . . . . . . . . . . .      727 LOVERS QUARREL     34
    "MAN OF WISDOM, DOST THOU KNOW . . . . . . . . . . .     729 PRIEST FAIRY       47
    IF THESE MERRY ONES SHOULD KNOW, . . . . . . . . . .     731 STREET DANCERS      9
    IF THESE MERRY ONES SHOULD KNOW, . . . . . . . . . .     732 STREET DANCERS     22
    IF THESE MERRY ONES SHOULD KNOW, . . . . . . . . . .     732 STREET DANCERS     35
    IF THESE MERRY ONES SHOULD KNOW. . . . . . . . . . .     733 STREET DANCERS     48
    OTHERS KNOW THE HEALING EARTH, . . . . . . . . . . .     733 STREET DANCERS     53
    OTHERS KNOW THE STARRY MIRTH! . . . . . . . . . . .      733 STREET DANCERS     54
    IF THESE MERRY ONES SHOULD KNOW, . . . . . . . . . .     733 STREET DANCERS     61
    AND I AM OLD AS TIME, BECAUSE I KNOW . . . . . . .       756 SHADOW WATER A V  179
    GATHER ABOUT HIM, THAT THE GODS MAY NOT KNOW . . . .     758 SHADOW WATER A    231
    AND GATHER ROUND HIM, THAT NO GOD MAY KNOW . . . . .     758 SHADOW WATER A V  231
    THAT SHE AMONG HER WINDS MIGHT KNOW HE WEPT! . . . .     763 SHADOW WATER A    307
    I KNOW YOU NOW, BESEECHING HANDS AND EYES. . . . . .     763 SHADOW WATER A    312
    THE LOVE I KNOW IS HIDDEN IN THESE HANDS . . . . . .     765 SHADOW WATER A    350
    ALL THAT KNOW LOVE AMONG THE WINDS OF THE WORLD . .      767 SHADOW WATER A    386
    I KNOW HE WILL OBEY YOU! AND IF YOUR EYES . . . . .      768 SHADOW WATER A    408
    SHOULD KNOW WHAT ISSUE IS AT STAKE! . . . . . . . .      778 FRIENDS WRONG       3
    GAVE ALL THE LOVE THAT WOMEN KNOW! . . . . . . . .       789 SINGING HEAD       21
KNOWER
    IS FROM THE OUGHT, OR KNOWER FROM THE KNOWN-- . . . .    478 SELF AND SOUL      37
KNOWEST
    THOU KNOWEST THIS, AND HOW FROM 'MID THE DANCE . . . .   683 SEEKER             51
KNOWETH
    JOYS AND FEARS IN THEIR GREY FACES THAT THE LIVE EARTH   719 PHANTOM SHIP       26
        KNOWETH NOT!
KNOWING
    BY KNOWING NOR TUMULT NOR HATE NOR STRIFE, . . . . . .     9 OISIN 1           95
    AND SHIVERED, KNOWING THE ISLE OF MANY FEARS, . . . .     30 OISIN 2           25
    BUT NOW I HAVE GROWN NOTHING, KNOWING ALL. . . . . .     104 FERGUS DRUID       38
    KNOWING ONE, OUT OF ALL THINGS, ALONE, THAT HIS HEAD    177 PAST GREATNESS      8
    KNOWING IT FOR THE WORLD'S END?  WHERE THE WORLD ENDS   226 SHADOW WATER B    100
    KNOWING THAT SILENCE BRINGS NO GOOD TO KINGS, . . . .    279 TWO KINGS          57
    KNOWING THAT HE SHOULD FIND UPON HER LIPS  . . . . .     280 TWO KINGS          77
    SHE'LL NOT BE PROUD, KNOWING WITHIN HER HEART . . . .    282 TWO KINGS         118
    KNOWING NOT EVIL AND GOOD! . . . . . . . . . . . . .     382 VISION ROBART      12
    KNOWING THAT NONE COULD PASS HEAVEN'S DOOR . . . . .     422 MY TABLE           26
    KNOWING THAT NONE WHO PASS HEAVEN'S DOOR . . . . . .     422 MY TABLE       V   26
    KNOWING THAT NONE CAN PASS HEAVEN'S DOOR . . . . . .     422 MY TABLE       V   26
    AND KNOWING THAT THE FUTURE WOULD BE VEXED . . . . .     472 ALL SOUL NIGHT     44
    NOT KNOWING WHAT UNEARTHLY STUFF . . . . . . . . . .     599 STONE CROSS        21
    THAT KNOWING BETTER TALK HAD GONE . . . . . . . . .      627 STATES HOLIDAY      7
    KNOWING THAT THOU HADST SINGLED ME WITH WORD . . . .     684 SEEKER             57
KNOWLEDGE
    KNOWLEDGE HE SHALL UNWIND . . . . . . . . . . . .        343 SHEP GOATHERD     107
    ALL KNOWLEDGE LOST IN TRANCE . . . . . . . . . . .       343 SHEP GOATHERD    -111
    I WOULD BE--FOR NO KNOWLEDGE IS WORTH A STRAW-- . . .    344 DAWN               13
    FOR WHAT MERE BOOK CAN GRANT A KNOWLEDGE . . . . . .     386 ROBARTES DANCE     20
    DID SHE PUT ON HIS KNOWLEDGE WITH HIS POWER  . . . .     441 LEDA AND SWAN      13
    IT SEEMS I MUST BUY KNOWLEDGE WITH MY PEACE. . . . .     468 HARUN RASHID      169
    WHAT KNOWLEDGE OR ITS LACK HAD SET AWRY. . . . . . .     490 COOLE BALLYLEE     22
    WHAT KNOWLEDGE OR ITS LACK HAS SET AWRY. . . . . . .     490 COOLE BALLYLEE V   22
    A DARKER KNOWLEDGE AND IN HATRED TURN . . . . . . .      558 RIBH CHRISTIAN     14
    BUT THERE'S ANOTHER KNOWLEDGE THAT MY HEART DESTROYS,    580 CURSE CROMWELL     17
    THAT KNOWLEDGE INCREASES UNREALITY, THAT . . . . . .     610 STATUES            21
KNOWN      SEE WELL-KNOWN
    HAVE KNOWN THREE CENTURIES, POETS SING, . . . . . .        2 OISIN 1            3
    WHERE BROKEN FAITH HAS NEVER BEEN KNOWN, . . . . . .       8 OISIN 1           84
    TO SHORES WHERE DYING HAS NEVER BEEN KNOWN, . . . . .      8 OISIN 1        V   84
    OUR HANDS HAVE KNOWN NO WEARYING TOOL. . . . . . . .      22 OISIN 1        V  339
    OUR LIVES HAVE KNOWN NO LAW NOR RULE! . . . . . . . .     22 OISIN 1        V  340
    HAVE FACES ALIVE WITH SUCH BEAUTY BEEN KNOWN TO THE SALT  50 OISIN 3           51
        EYE OF MAN,
    ARE FACES ALIVE WITH SUCH BEAUTY MADE KNOWN TO THE SALT   50 OISIN 3        V   51
        EYE OF MAN,
    ARE FACES ALIVE WITH SUCH BEAUTY MADE KNOWN TO THE SOFT   50 OISIN 3        V   51
        EYE OF MAN,
    AND HE HAD KNOWN AT LAST SOME TENDERNESS . . . . . .     126 DREAM OF FAERY      3
    AND HE HAD KNOWN AT LAST SOME PRUDENT YEARS . . . . .    127 DREAM OF FAERY     15
    AND MIGHT HAVE KNOWN AT LAST UNHAUNTED SLEEP . . . . .   128 DREAM OF FAERY     38
    NEITHER COULD HAVE KNOWN . . . . . . . . . . . . .       211 O DO NOT LOVE       6
    IS NOT KNOWN AMONG MEN, . . . . . . . . . . . . .        215 HAPPY TOWNLAND     28
    YOU'VE NEVER KNOWN, I'D LAY A WAGER ON IT, . . . . .     227 SHADOW WATER B    113
    AS THEY HAVE KNOWN IT.  NOW THE SECRET'S OUT! . . . .    228 SHADOW WATER B    140
    AS THOSE THAT CAN OUTLIVE THE MOON HAVE KNOWN IT, . .    230 SHADOW WATER B    193
    AND WE ARE ALMOST ON HER!  WE HAD NOT KNOWN . . . . .    232 SHADOW WATER B    220
    BUT HAVE YOU KNOWN A DOG TO PRAISE HIS FLEAS? . . . .    262 TO A POET      V    4
    SHE WOULD NOT LOOK IN ANY KNOWN MAN'S FACE . . . . .     280 TWO KINGS          73
    WOULD NEVER LOOK AGAIN ON KNOWN MAN'S FACE." . . . .     280 TWO KINGS          75
    WILL NEVER LOOK AGAIN ON KNOWN MAN'S FACE." . . . . .    280 TWO KINGS      V   75
    BECAUSE OF ALL THINGS KNOWN . . . . . . . . . . . .      291 TO A FRIEND        15
```

427

KNOWN   (CONTINUED)
    IN HIS FULL HANDS WHAT, HAD THEY ONLY KNOWN, ...   292 TO A SHADE   11
    BEING YOUNG YOU HAVE NOT KNOWN . . . .   312 CHILD DANCING   6
    IN MUSCULAR YOUTH WELL KNOWN TO MAYO MEN   . . . . . .   325 ROBERT GREGORY   34
    WELL KNOWN FOR HORSEMANSHIP TO CONNACHT MEN   . . . . .   325 ROBERT GREGORY V   34
    AND KNOW WHAT ONCE I HAVE KNOWN, ...   346 ON WOMAN   34
    FOR YOUR SOLE SAKE--THAT ALL HEART'S ACHE HAVE KNOWN,   . .   355 BROKEN DREAMS   7
    BUT FOR YOUR SAKE--THAT ALL HEART'S ACHE HAVE KNOWN,   . .   355 BROKEN DREAMS V   7
    THAT SO MANY LANDS HAD KNOWN, ...   360 ALF POLLEXFEN   18
    HAVE YOU NOT ALWAYS KNOWN IT? THE SONG WILL HAVE IT   . .   374 PHASES OF MOON   65
    GAZED UPON ALL THINGS KNOWN, ALL THINGS UNKNOWN, ...   383 VISION ROBART   30
    THE GENTLENESS NONE THERE HAD EVER KNOWN! . . . . . .   418 ANCEST HOUSES   21
    TO TELL YOUR SIMPLEST WANT, AND KNOWN, ...   436 FOR MY SON   21
    IS FROM THE OUGHT, OR KNOWER FROM THE KNOWN-- . . . . .   478 SELF AND SOUL   37
    ALL COULD BE KNOWN OR SHOWN . . . .   510 JANE JUDGMENT   18
    CAN MAKE THE TRUTH KNOWN. . . . .   575 ACRE OF GRASS   12
    ALL THE OLYMPIANS! A THING NEVER KNOWN AGAIN. . . . . .   578 LOFTY THINGS   12
    SOME HAVE KNOWN A LIKELY LAD . . . .   625 OLD MEN BE MAD   2
    HAST THOU NOT KNOWN ALL SORROW AND DELIGHT . . . . . .   723 KANVA ON SELF   2
    HAST THOU NOT KNOWN A RAJA'S DREAMLESS SLUMBER? . . . .   724 KANVA ON SELF   8
    THAT HAVE KNOWN LOVE AMONG THE WINDS OF THE WORLD   . . .   767 SHADOW WATER A   392
    NAMES WHEREBY A MAN HAS KNOWN . . . .   775 AGAINST WITCH   5
KNOWS
    OF THE THINGS THAT HIS HEART STILL KNOWS WERE SWEET-- . .   26 OISIN 1   V 402
    HOPELESS FOR EVER! ANCIENT OISIN KNOWS, ...   42 OISIN 2   202
    AY, OISIN KNOWS, FOR HE IS OF THE WEAK, ...   42 OISIN 2   V 202
    THE GREY WOLF KNOWS ME! BY ONE EAR . . . .   84 MAD KING GOLL   45
    THE WILD BOAR KNOWS ME, BY ONE EAR . . . .   84 MAD KING GOLL   V 45
    AND SOMETIMES I AM SURE SHE KNOWS . . . .   96 MOLL MAGEE   49
    AND WHITHER THE WISE HEART KNOWS! . . . .   168 BLESSED   34
    THE POWERS WHOSE NAME AND SHAPE NO LIVING CREATURE KNOWS   174 ELEMENT POWERS   1
    AH! WISE, MY HEART KNOWS WELL HOW WISE. . . . .   193 BAILE AILLINN   99
    HEAVEN KNOWS WHAT CALAMITY! . . . .   193 BAILE AILLINN   112
    HE THAT MADE THIS KNOWS ALL THE COST, ...   202 NEVER GIVE ALL   13
    THE ROOTS OF THE WORLD. WHO KNOWS THAT SHADOWS . . .   227 SHADOW WATER B V 104
    OF THAT MORE POWERFUL LIFE? HIS WIFE KNOWS BETTER. . . .   230 SHADOW WATER B   172
    SHE KNOWS THAT IT WAS BUT THE CART-HORSE COUGHING . . .   230 SHADOW WATER B   176
    WHEN SHE KNOWS THAT. WHAT IS IT THAT YOU ARE MUTTERING--   236 SHADOW WATER B   303
    HE KNOWS THAT HE IS TAKING YOU TO DEATH! . . . . . .   249 SHADOW WATER B   562
    ALL KNOW THE MAN THEIR NEIGHBOUR KNOWS. . . . .   337 SCHOLARS   10
    IF THEY HAVE SINNED NOBODY KNOWS! . . . .   337 SCHOLARS   V 10
    SHE KNOWS HERSELF A WOMAN, ...   365 HER RACE   5
    HIS ART IS HAPPY, BUT WHO KNOWS HIS MIND? . . . . . .   370 EGO DOMINUS   54
    OF BODY AND SOUL. THE LOVER'S HEART KNOWS THAT. . . . .   375 PHASES OF MOON   71
    WHO KNOWS HOW SHE DRANK THE WIND . . . .   381 SONGS FOOL 2   6
    YET KNOWS THAT TO BE CHOKED WITH HATE . . . .   405 FOR DAUGHTER   52
    IT KNOWS NOT WHAT IT IS! AND GATHER ME . . . .   408 SAIL BYZANTIUM   23
    IT KNOWS NOT WHAT IT IS! GATHER ME . . . .   408 SAIL BYZANTIUM V 23
    FROM SHALLOW WITS! WHO KNOWS NO WORK CAN STAND, ...   429 NINETEEN 19   35
    THAT PASSION, PIETY OR AFFECTION KNOWS. . . . .   445 SCHOOL CHILDR   54
    AND THAT NONE LIVING KNOWS. . . . .   455 HIS MEMORIES   6
    HE KNOWS DEATH TO THE BONE-- . . . .   476 DEATH   11
    FOR INTELLECT NO LONGER KNOWS . . . .   478 SELF AND SOUL   36
    AND IN THE MORNING'S GONE, NO MAN KNOWS WHY! . . . . .   490 COOLE BALLYLEE   20
    EVERY COMMON WOMAN KNOWS. . . . .   499 MOTHER OF GOD   7
    MAY KNOW NOT WHAT HE KNOWS, BUT KNOWS NOT GRIEF. . . . .   500 VACILLATION   18
    MAY KNOW NOT WHAT HE KNOWS, BUT KNOWS NOT GRIEF. . . . .   500 VACILLATION   18
    THE BISHOP HAS A SKIN, GOD KNOWS, ...   508 JANE BISHOP   15
    WHAT NONE OTHER KNOWS, ...   538 LAST CONFESS   18
    AND ALL IT KNOWS IS THAT ONE WORD "REJOICE!" . . . . .   564 GYRES   16
    FOR EVERYBODY KNOWS OR ELSE SHOULD KNOW . . . .   565 LAPIS LAZULI   4
    FOR HE KNOWS HOW TO SAY, ...   583 GHOST ROG CASE   14
    NO MAN KNOWS WHICH IS WHICH, ...   599 STONE CROSS   14
    KNOWS I HAVE LIVED SO LONG. . . . .   607 SONGS BURDEN 2   26
    AND YET WHO KNOWS WHAT'S YET TO COME? . . . .   608 SONGS BURDEN 3   23
    AND NO MAN KNOWS WHAT TREADS THE GRASS. . . . .   614 MARCH SONGS 2   10
    AND NO MAN KNOWS WHAT TREADS THE GRASS. . . . .   615 MARCH SONGS 2   20
    AND NO MAN KNOWS WHAT TREADS THE GRASS. . . . .   615 MARCH SONGS 2   30
    NONE OTHER KNOWS WHAT PLEASURES MAN . . . .   620 JOHN KINSELLA   9
    LION AND WOMAN AND THE LORD KNOWS WHAT. . . . .   629 CIRCUS ANIMALS   8
    YET HERE'S A TRAVELLED MAN THAT KNOWS . . . .   631 POLITICS   5
    AND COLA, SEEING, KNOWS THE SIGN AND COMES. . . . . .   691 MOSADA 1   38
    AND COLA, SEEING, KNOWS THE SIGN AND RISES. . . . . .   691 MOSADA 1   V 38
    IF PETER WOULD BUT ASK HER LIFE--WHO KNOWS? . . . . .   696 MOSADA 2   17
    HE KNOWS BY SIGNS OF SECRET WIT . . . .   716 FAIRY DOCTOR   5
    AMONG THE WATERS THAT NO PILOT KNOWS. . . . .   750 SHADOW WATER A   80
    ALL THAT TIME KNOWS. SPEAK TO ME, QUEEN. O SPEAK! . .   756 SHADOW WATER A V 180
    AND NONE KNOWS WHEREFORE! BUT THE HEART'S DESIRE . . .   764 SHADOW WATER A   340
    IN THE LAND THAT NO ONE KNOWS. . . . .   774 COME RIDE   17
    IN THE LAND THAT NO-ONE KNOWS. . . . .   774 COME RIDE   V 17
    NOBODY KNOWS WHAT MAY BEFALL, ...   788 HAWTHORN TREE   13
KNOW'ST
    KNOW'ST NAUGHT OF THIS. AND, UNCOUTH HUNTER, NOW-- . . .   651 ISLE STAT I 1   168
KUSTA
    KUSTA BEN LUKA IS MY NAME, I WRITE   . . . .   460 HARUN RASHID   1
KYLE-DORTHA
    SHADY KYLE-DORTHA! SUNNIER KYLE-NA-NO, ...   217 WOODS OF COOLE   4
KYLE-NA-INO
    TO KYLE-NA-INO AND TO THAT ANCIENT ROOF . . . .   321 REED WHISPERER V   7
KYLE-NA-NO
    SHADY KYLE-DORTHA! SUNNIER KYLE-NA-NO, ...   217 WOODS OF COOLE   4

		PAGE	TITLE	LINE

KYLE-NA-NO   (CONTINUED)
AT KYLE-NA-NO UNDER THAT ANCIENT ROOF . . . .   321 REED WHISPERER   7
TO A SQUIRREL AT KYLE-NA-NO . . . .   359 TO A SQUIRREL   T

KYTELER
TO WHOM THE LOVE-LORN LADY KYTELER BROUGHT . . . .   433 NINETEEN 19   129

LABAN
AND NIAMH AND LABAN AND FAND, WHO COULD CHANGE TO AN OTTER   209 UNDER THE MOON   12
   OR FAWN,
AND FAND, AND NIAM, AND LABAN, WHO COULD CHANGE TO AN OTTER   209 UNDER THE MOON V   12
   OR FAWN,

LABORIOUS
HIS SLEEPLESS CANDLE AND LABORIOUS PEN. . . . .   375 PHASES OF MOON   86
MAY THIS LABORIOUS STAIR AND THIS STARK TOWER . . . . .   423 MY DESCENDANTS   13
WHAT MY LABORIOUS LIFE IMAGINED, EVEN . . . .   431 NINETEEN 19   82

LABOUR
THE PAIN OF WOUNDS, THE LABOUR OF THE SPEAR, ...   104 FERGUS DRUID   V   38D
WE WHO STILL LABOUR BY THE CROMLECH ON THE SHORE, . . .   161 BLACK PIG   5
WE POETS LABOUR ALL OUR DAYS, ...   164 PERFECT BEAUTY V   2
THAT WE MUST LABOUR TO BE BEAUTIFUL." . . . .   205 ADAMS CURSE   20
LABOUR IS BLOSSOMING OR DANCING WHERE . . . .   445 SCHOOL CHILDR   57

LABOURED
IS HE WHO LABOURED ON, DERIDED, HATED, ...   738 MOURN THEN ON   11

LABOURER
A KING IS BUT A FOOLISH LABOURER . . . .   103 FERGUS DRUID   27
A WILD AND FOOLISH LABOURER IS A KING . . . .   103 FERGUS DRUID   V   27
THEN FEARING THAT SOME LABOURER, ON HIS WAY . . . . .   283 TWO KINGS   145
NOR THE BEST LABOURER DEAD . . . .   312 CHILD DANCING   9

LABOURER'S
SAEVA INDIGNATIO AND THE LABOURER'S HIRE, ...   481 BLOOD AND MOON   28

LABOURING   SEE UN-LABOURING ALL-LABOURING
WE AND THE LABOURING WORLD ARE PASSING BY! . . . . .   112 ROSE OF WORLD   6
DOOMED LIKE ODYSSEUS AND THE LABOURING SHIPS . . . .   120 SORROW OF LOVE   7
AND ALL THE SORROWS OF HER LABOURING SHIPS, ...   120 SORROW OF LOVE V   7
AND ALL THE TROUBLE OF HER LABOURING SHIPS, ...   120 SORROW OF LOVE V   7
WE, WHO ARE LABOURING BY THE CROMLECH ON THE SHORE, . .   161 BLACK PIG   V   5
THE POETS LABOURING ALL THEIR DAYS . . . .   164 PERFECT BEAUTY   2
SINCE ADAM'S FALL BUT NEEDS MUCH LABOURING. . . . . .   205 ADAMS CURSE   22
LABOURING IN ECSTASY. . . . .   315 FRIENDS   16
HER LABOURING MEN, AS THOUGH HER DARLING LIVED, . . .   340 SHEP GOATHERD   38
YOU HEARD THAT LABOURING MAN WHO HAD SERVED MY PEOPLE.   391 UNDER SATURN   11
   HE SAID
A SUFFERING PASSION AND A LABOURING THOUGHT? . . . .   420 MY HOUSE   V   20J
ALL THE LABOURING HEAVENS SIGH. . . . .   573 LADYS 3RD SONG   12

LABOURS
AND ALL THE EXULTANT LABOURS OF THE STRONG. . . . .   42 OISIN 2   195
OF ANCIENT WARRIORS, THE LABOURS OF THE STRONG. . . .   42 OISIN 2   V   195

LABURNUM
HERE WHERE LABURNUM HANGS HER GOLDEN FLEECE! . . . .   670 ISLE STAT II 3   102

LABYRINTH
THE LABYRINTH OF HER DAYS . . . .   260 UNWORTH PRAISE   13
TO DIE INTO THE LABYRINTH OF ITSELF! . . . .   374 PHASES OF MOON   55
INTO THE LABYRINTH OF ANOTHER'S BEING! . . . . . .   413 TOWER   112
FROM A GREAT LABYRINTH OUT OF PRIDE, ...   413 TOWER   116
FROM SOME GREAT LABYRINTH OUT OF PRIDE, ...   413 TOWER   V   116
IS LOST AMID THE LABYRINTH THAT HE HAS MADE . . . .   431 NINETEEN 19   70
THEIR PURPOSE IN THE LABYRINTH OF THE WIND! . . . .   433 NINETEEN 19   121
THAT THIS UNCONQUERABLE LABYRINTH OF THE BIRDS, . . .   481 BLOOD AND MOON   23
THE LABYRINTH OF THE MIND, ...   785 WOMANS BEAUTY   24

LACE
IN RUSTLE OF LACE OR SILKEN STUFF, ...   358 PRESENCES   5
"VENGEANCE FOR JACQUES MOLAY." IN CLOUD-PALE RAGS, OR   426 PHANTOM HATRED   10
   IN LACE,
"VENGENCE FOR JACQUES MOLAY." IN CLOUD PALE RAGS, OR IN   426 PHANTOM HATRED V   10
   LACE,
THE QUIVERING HALF-CLOSED EYELIDS, THE RAGS OF CLOUD OR   427 PHANTOM HATRED   26
   OF LACE,

LACERATE
CANNOT LACERATE HIS BREAST. . . . .   493 SWIFTS EPITAPH   3

LACK
I AM ACCUSTOMED TO THEIR LACK OF BREATH, ...   325 ROBERT GREGORY   45
THE BEST LACK ALL CONVICTION, WHILE THE WORST . . . .   402 SECOND COMING   7
THE BEST LACK CONVICTION, WHILE THE WORST . . . . .   402 SECOND COMING V   7
AND YET IT LACK ALL GLORY! AND PERCHANCE . . . . .   429 NINETEEN 19   23
THAT HIS MOTHER MAY NOT LACK . . . .   435 FOR MY SON   7
WHAT KNOWLEDGE OR ITS LACK HAD SET AWRY, ...   490 COOLE BALLYLEE   22
WHAT KNOWLEDGE OR ITS LACK HAS SET AWRY, ...   490 COOLE BALLYLEE V   22
WHAT, BE A SINGER BORN AND LACK A THEME? . . . . .   502 VACILLATION   73
"A CHILD FOUND ALL A CHILD CAN LACK, ...   521 THREE THINGS   3
IF IT LACK HONESTY. . . . .   584 GHOST ROG CASE   28
MY MEDIAEVAL KNEES LACK HEALTH UNTIL THEY BEND, . . .   603 GALLERY REVIS   33
PROCESSIONS THAT LACK HIGH STILTS HAVE NOTHING THAT CATCHES   622 HIGH TALK   1
   THE EYE.
LACK NOTHING THAT A SOLDIER NEEDS, ...   635 BLACK TOWER   4

LACKED
YOU HAVE LACKED ARTICULATE SPEECH . . . .   436 FOR MY SON   20
WHERE NONE HAS REIGNED THAT LACKED A NAME AND FAME . . .   491 COOLE BALLYLEE   31
HE LACKED THOSE YEARS THAT GO WITH SKILL, ...   608 SONGS BURDEN 3   14
IN MARBLE OR IN BRONZE, LACKED CHARACTER. . . . . .   610 STATUES   3

LACKEY
THAT LACKEY THE WORN MOON IN MIDNIGHT HOURS, ...   41 OISIN 2   V 185A

429

LACKING
    LACKING THE COUNTENANCE OF OUR FRIENDS. AND YET . . . . . 368 EGO DOMINUS   17
    OR LACKING THAT, GOVERNMENT IN SUCH HANDS, ... 543 PARN FUNERAL 2   7
    BUT ACTORS LACKING MUSIC . . . . 599 STONE CROSS   17
    HONOUR HAD LIVED SO LONG, ALL LACKING FOUND. . . . . . 603 GALLERY REVIS   35
LACKS
    A SINGLE SOUL THAT LACKS A SWEET CRYSTALLINE CRY. . . . . 291 PAUDEEN   8
    A LOVE THAT LACKS ITS PROPER FOOD; . . . . 569 THREE BUSHES   3
LAD
    A GREAT LAD WITH A BEERY FACE . . . . 303 HOUR DAWN   27
    HE HAD SEEN A RED-HAIRED JOLLY LAD . . . . 303 HOUR DAWN   V 27
    SEMELE'S LAD A GAY COMPANION. . . . . 446 COLONUS PRAISE   8
    EVERY COLONUS LAD OR LASS DISCOURSES . . . . 447 COLONUS PRAISE   29
    A MERMAID FOUND A SWIMMING LAD, ... 452 MERMAID   1
    WHAT LIVELY LAD MOST PLEASURED ME . . . . 538 LAST CONFESS   1
    BUT HAD GREAT PLEASURE WITH A LAD . . . . 538 LAST CONFESS   5
    NIAMH THAT RODE ON IT; LAD AND LASS . . . . 550 SEVERED HEAD   11
    SOME HAVE KNOWN A LIKELY LAD . . . . 625 OLD MEN BE MAD   2
LADDER'S
    WHO KEEPS THE TILL. NOW THAT MY LADDER'S GONE, ... 630 CIRCUS ANIMALS   38
LADDERS
    I MUST LIE DOWN WHERE ALL THE LADDERS START, ... 630 CIRCUS ANIMALS   39
LADEN   SEE STAR-LADEN ODOUR-LADEN WAR-LADEN
    WAR LADEN GALLEYS, AND ARMIES ON WHITE ROADS, ... 757 SHADOW WATER A V 203
LADIES   SEE COURT-LADIES'
    AND A HUNDRED LADIES, MERRY AS BIRDS, ... 9 OISIN 1   96
    OF MEN AND LADIES, HAND IN HAND, ... 15 OISIN 1   202
    AND MEN AND LADIES KNELT THEM THERE . . . . 18 OISIN 1   255
    BY DREAMING LADIES UPON CLOTH . . . . 156 FORGOT BEAUTY   7
    WOVEN BY LADIES IN THEIR HAIR, ... 156 FORGOT BEAUTY   10
    THE DEW-COLD LILIES LADIES BORE . . . . 156 FORGOT BEAUTY   11
    ALL THE WILD WITCHES, THOSE MOST NOBLE LADIES, ... 343 DEJECTION   4
    TO LORDS AND LADIES OF BYZANTIUM . . . . 408 SAIL BYZANTIUM   31
    MAGICAL UNICORNS BEAR LADIES ON THEIR BACKS. . . . . . 426 PHANTOM HATRED   18
    THE LADIES CLOSE THEIR MUSING EYES. NO PROPHECIES, . . 426 PHANTOM HATRED   19
    IMMORTAL LADIES TREAD THE GROUND . . . . . ., . . . 446 COLONUS PRAISE   6
    "HEAR, GENTLEMEN, LADIES, AND ALL MANKIND; . . . . . . 544 TO SAME TUNE 1   2
    THAT THE SWORDSMEN AND THE LADIES CAN STILL KEEP COMPANY, 581 CURSE CROMWELL   20
    "HEAR, GENTLEMEN, LADIES, AND ALL MANKIND! . . . . . . 615 MARCH SONGS 3   2
    SING THE LORDS AND LADIES GAY . . . . 640 BEN BULBEN   78
    LOVELY LADIES DANCING IN IT. . . . . 788 HAWTHORN TREE   4
LADIES'
    HAVE CLOSED THE LADIES' EYES, THEIR MINDS ARE BUT A POOL 426 PHANTOM HATRED   21
LADLE
    A LADLE AND A TUB OF BEER, ... 303 HOUR DAWN   29
    HAD DIPPED THE WOODEN LADLE DEEP . . . . 304 HOUR DAWN   46
    SHALL DIP HIS NOSE INTO MY LADLE . . . . 304 HOUR DAWN   53
    AND TOOK THE WOODEN LADLE UP . . . . 304 HOUR DAWN   V 46
    WOULD HAVE HIS FILL OUT OF MY LADLE . . . . 304 HOUR DAWN   V 53
    DIPPING HIS NOSE INTO MY LADLE . . . . 304 HOUR DAWN   V 53
    HE DIPPED HIS LADLE IN THE TUB . . .. 307 HOUR DAWN   107
LADS   SEE FISHER-LADS
    THOUGH LADS ARE MAKING PIKES AGAIN . . . . 131 OLD PENSIONER   7
    OR RUN WHERE LADS REFORM OUR DAYTIME . . . . 343 SHEP GOATHERD V 105
    FOR SHEPHERD LADS IN GALILEE; AND GRANT . . . . 371 ON GOING HOUSE   4
    WERE YOU AND I UNLETTERED LADS . . . . 524 MAD AS MIST   11
    HID FROM ALL THOSE WARTY LADS . . . . 589 OLD WICKED MAN   43
    A DANCE FOR THE FISHER LADS; . . . . 589 OLD WICKED MAN V 33
    LADS AND LASSES, TWO AND TWO, ... 705 DAWN-SONG   15
LADY
    A PEARL-PALE, HIGH-BORN LADY, WHO RODE . . . . 3 OISIN 1   20
    AND NOW A LADY RODE LIKE THE WIND . . . . 12 OISIN 1   142
    AND ONCE A LADY BY MY SIDE . . . . 16 OISIN 1   231
    THE YOUTH AND LADY AND THE DEER AND HOUND; . . . . . . 29 OISIN 2   4
    ONCE MORE—THE YOUTH AND LADY, DEER AND HOUND; . . . . 29 OISIN 2   V 2
    A LADY WITH SOFT EYES LIKE FUNERAL TAPERS, ... 33 OISIN 2   69
    THE DEER AND THE HOUND, AND THE LADY AND YOUTH, ... 47 OISIN 3   V 3
    THIS LADY BY THE TREES"; . . . . 123 DREAM OF DEATH V 10
    "O LADY, WED WITH ONE OF US"; . . . . 191 BAILE AILLINN   61
    THE DELICATE-STEPPING STAG AND HIS LADY SIGH, ... 210 RAGGED WOOD   2
    THE DELICATE STEPPING STAG AND HIS LADY SIGH . . . . . 210 RAGGED WOOD   V 2
    DO YOU NOT KNOW ME, LADY? I AM HE . . . . 243 SHADOW WATER B   426
    IF THE LADY BE YOUNG AND FAIR." . . . . 268 BROWN PENNY   6
    OR A WITTY LOVELY LADY." . . . . 299 THREE HERMITS   28
    OF GOLDEN KING AND SILVER LADY, ... 331 ROUND TOWER   13
    THAT GOLDEN KING AND THAT WILD LADY . . . . 332 ROUND TOWER   19
    THAT LADY AND THAT GOLDEN KING . . . . 332 ROUND TOWER   23
    WILL SAY TO AN OLD MAN, "TELL ME OF THAT LADY . . . . . 356 BROKEN DREAMS   17
    THE CERTAINTY THAT I SHALL SEE THAT LADY . . . . . . 356 BROKEN DREAMS   22
    SEVEN POEMS I UPON A DYING LADY . . . . 362 HER COURTESY V T
    VEHEMENT AND WITTY SHE HAD SEEMED—; THE VENETIAN LADY . . 363 DOLLS FACES   5
    THE MOST EXALTED LADY LOVED BY A MAN. . . . . 369 EGO DOMINUS   37
    LOVED THE LADY; AND IT'S PLAIN . . . . 385 ROBARTES DANCE   5
    AND THUS DECLARED THAT ARAB LADY; . . . . 387 SOLOMON WITCH   1
    TO WHOM THE LOVE-LORN LADY KYTELER BROUGHT . . . . . . 433 NINETEEN 19   129
    NOTHING COULD BRING HIM, WHEN HIS LADY DIED, ... 471 ALL SOUL NIGHT   25
    FOR HE CANNOT SEE MY LADY . . . . 552 SONGS REWRIT 2   3
    BUT RHYMES FOR A BEAUTIFUL LADY, ... 552 SONGS REWRIT 2   11
    SAID LADY ONCE TO LOVER, ... 569 THREE BUSHES   1
    THAT LOVELY LADY SAID, ... 569 THREE BUSHES   9
    "BECAUSE MY LADY CAME . . . . 570 THREE BUSHES   37

430

	PAGE	TITLE	LINE
LADY (CONTINUED)			
HIS LADY SAW IT ALL	571	THREE BUSHES	53
FOR I THAT AM HIS DAYLIGHT LADY	573	LADYS 3RD SONG	5
SHE ALONE, MY LADY, LINGERETH	646	ISLE STAT I 1	28
SAD LADY OF THE DEEP, POURS DOWN HER LIGHT!	650	ISLE STAT I 1	127
O, LADY, THOU WHOSE VESTITURE OF GREEN	667	ISLE STAT II 3	34
SAD LADY, CEASE!	672	ISLE STAT II 3	160
NAMES AFTER ME. LADY--I COME. FORGIVE,	695	MOSADA 1	117
"I AM LONE LADY QUIETNESS, MY SWEET"	716	DWELT SYCAMORE	13
COME, FATHER. LADY, I NOR REST NOR SIT.	720	WITCH VIVIEN	18
LOVELY LADY OR GALLANT MAN	788	HAWTHORN TREE	7
LOVELY LADY AND GALLANT MAN	788	HAWTHORN TREE V	7
THE SINGING HEAD AND THE LADY	789	SINGING HEAD V	T
LADY'S SEE COURT-LADY'S			
UPON THIS LADY'S BEAUTY	329	MEN IMPROVE	5
THAT MOST RESPECTED LADY'S EVERY WISH,	410	TOWER	29
BESIDE HER LADY'S MAN,	571	THREE BUSHES	72
THE LADY'S FIRST SONG	572	LADYS 1ST SONG	T
THE LADY'S SECOND SONG	572	LADYS 2ND SONG	T
THE LADY'S THIRD SONG	573	LADYS 3RD SONG	T
LAEN			
WE RODE IN SADNESS ABOVE LOUGH LAEN,	2	OISIN 1 V	7H
LAGGARD			
AND NOW A LAGGARD WITH A WOMAN'S HEAD	234	SHADOW WATER B	260
THEY ARE STILL WAITING! AND NOW THE LAGGARD COMES,	754	SHADOW WATER A	150
THEY ARE STILL WAITING! AND A LAGGARD COMES,	754	SHADOW WATER A V	150
LAGOON			
BY THE LAGOON YOU LOVE SO MUCH,	386	ROBARTES DANCE	29
LAID			
AND SIGHING LAID THE PEARLY TIP	12	OISIN 1	150
SAID NIAM, AS SHE LAID THE TIP.	12	OISIN 1 V	150
AND WHILE THEY SANG, A SINGER LAID	16	OISIN 1 V	231
LAID IT AND SIGHED! I HELD A SWORD WHOSE SHINE	37	OISIN 2	126
LAID IT AND SIGHED--A SWORD WHOSE WIZARD SHINE	37	OISIN 2 V	126
AND ON MY BOSOM LAID HER WEEPING HEAD.	46	OISIN 2	250
COULD SLEEP ON A COUCH OF RUSHES--ROUND AND ABOUT THEM LAID.	49	OISIN 3 V	32
LAID HANDS ON THE BELL-BRANCH AND SWAYED IT,	51	OISIN 3	56
IN THE ROOTS OF THE GRASSES, THE SORRELS, I LAID MY BODY AS LOW:	52	OISIN 3	73
SAD NIAM CAME NEAR ME, AND LAID HER BROWS ON THE MIDST OF MY BREAST	52	OISIN 3 V	74
AFRAID, THEIR EARS ON THE EARTH LAID,	62	OISIN 3	206
AND LAID YOU ON THE GATES OF EVENING WITH HIS QUIET HANDS.	72	ANASHU VIJAYA	22
THE SUN HAS LAID HIS CHIN ON THE GREY WOOD,	72	ANASHU VIJAYA	24
AND LAID YE ON THE GATES OF EVENING WITH HIS QUIET HANDS.	72	ANASHU VIJAYA V	22
THE SUN HATH LAID HIS CHIN ON THE GREY WOOD,	72	ANASHU VIJAYA V	24
AND ON MY LEANING SHOULDER SHE LAID HER SNOW-WHITE HAND.	90	SALLEY GARDENS	6
TO HIM SEEMED EASY, SO I LAID THE CROWN	102	FERGUS DRUID	13
WITH THE FEET LAID SIDE BY SIDE.	124	CATHLEEN PARA	4
THAT GOD HAS LAID HIS FINGERS ON THE SKY,	128	DREAM OF FAERY	43
WHERE ONLY BODY'S LAID ASLEEP.	138	TO IRELAND	22
WHEN I HAD LAID IT ON THE FLOOR	149	WANDER AENGUS	9
WHEN I HAD LAID IT ON A STOOL	149	WANDER AENGUS V	9
AND MY WHITE BREAST ON HIS HE LAID.	151	HEART OF WOMAN	4
SHE LAID THEM UPON HER BOSOM,	160	CAP AND BELLS	25
SHE LAID A HAND ON EITHER OF HIS SHOULDERS,	182	QUEEN MAEVE	49
AND HE, BEING LAID UPON GREEN BOUGHS,	192	BAILE AILLINN	71
AND NOW THAT HONEY-MOUTH IS LAID	192	BAILE AILLINN	80
AND NOW THAT HONEY MOUTH IS LAID	192	BAILE AILLINN V	80
TO FIND IT WHEN NIGHT FALLS LAID ON A GOLDEN BIER.	209	UNDER THE MOON	10
WHO HAVE SLAIN MY HUSBAND AND LAID HANDS UPON ME.	235	SHADOW WATER B	282
LAID ON THE DEATH-BED,	335	SONG	16
LAID ON THE DEATH BED.	335	SONG V	16
LAID HIS STRONG BONES DOWN IN DEATH	360	ALF POLLEXFEN	3
AND AFTER TWENTY YEARS THEY LAID	360	ALF POLLEXFEN	6
BUT WHERE IS LAID THE SAILOR JOHN	360	ALF POLLEXFEN	17
LAID HIS STRONG BONES IN DEATH	360	ALF POLLEXFEN V	3
WHERE HAVE THEY LAID THE SAILOR JOHN?	361	ALF POLLEXFEN	23
ON GRASSY MATTRESS I HAD LAID ME,	387	SOLOMON WITCH	3
WHY HAVE YOU LAID YOUR HANDS UPON MY EYES?	389	IMAGE PAST	15
AND HOW CAN BODY, LAID IN THAT WHITE RUSH,	441	LEDA AND SWAN	7
HAS LAID HER HELPLESS FACE UPON HIS BREAST.	441	LEDA AND SWAN V	4
ALL THE STRETCHED BODY'S LAID ON THE WHITE RUSH	441	LEDA AND SWAN V	7
BUT SINCE I LAID A HAND THEREON	451	FIRST LOVE	7
BEAUTY AND FOOL TOGETHER LAID.	484	SYMBOLS	6
AND LAID THEM ON LOVE'S LETTERED TOMB!	519	HER DREAM	4
A PIERCED BOY, IMAGE OF A STAR LAID LOW.	541	PARN FUNERAL 1	12
THAT IS IN QUICKLIME LAID.	582	ROGER CASEMENT	24
THAT IS IN THE QUICK-LIME LAID.	582	ROGER CASEMENT V	24
FOR SOON WE LIE WHERE HE IS LAID,	586	PARNELLITES	5
AND HE LAID THEM ON HER HAND.	595	COLONEL MARTIN	35
IN DRUMCLIFF CHURCHYARD YEATS IS LAID.	640	BEN BULBEN	85
AS ON THOSE OTHER HEARTS WERE LAID.	667	ISLE STAT II 3	42
IF ON HIS LIPS THE ENCHANTED FLOWER BE LAID!	668	ISLE STAT II 3	46
THE HARE HATH LAID ASLEEP HER FROLIC WITS,	712	FERENCZ RENYI	72
WILD BEES' HONEY LAID FOR THEE."	730	PRIEST FAIRY	56
LAIGHEN			
THE HILL SEAT OF LAIGHEN, BECAUSE	194	BAILE AILLINN	130
LAIN			
WHEN I HAD LAIN IT ON A STOOL,	149	WANDER AENGUS V	9

431

			PAGE	TITLE		LINE
LAIN	(CONTINUED)					
	BY BIDDY'S HALFPENNIES HAVE LAIN		287	TO WEALTHY MAN		3
	BY BIDDY'S HALF-PENNIES HAVE LAIN		287	TO WEALTHY MAN	V	3
	WHERE THE MOUNTAIN HARE HAS LAIN.		350	MEMORY		6
	BUT THE CRUSHED GRASS WHERE WE HAVE LAIN; . . .		389	SOLOMON WITCH		42
	A MYRIAD HEADS HAVE LAIN." "		496	MOHINI CHATTER		11
	THAT SO STILL HAD LAIN.		516	MANS SONG		4
	A HOUND THAT HAD LAIN IN THE RED RUSHES		761	SHADOW WATER A		278
LAIR						
	. . . LURED FROM HIS LAIR IN THE MOULD;		53	OISIN 3		99
	NO FOX CAN FOUL THE LAIR THE BADGER SWEPT-- . .		603	GALLERY REVIS		39
	I FOLLOWED HIM FROM MY GREEN LAIR, ...		655	ISLE STAT I 3		6
	FROM MY WIZARD ISLAND LAIR, ...		668	ISLE STAT II 3		63
	WE WILL FIND HER FAVOURITE LAIR, ...		706	DAWN-SONG		26
LAKE						
	BY THE LONE BORDER OF THE LAKE ONCE MORE, . . .		79	EPHEMERA		5
	STAND BY THE BORDER OF THE LAKE ONCE MORE, . . .		79	EPHEMERA	V	5
	ON THE LONE BORDER OF THE LAKE ONCE MORE! . . .		80	EPHEMERA		17
	ON THE LONE BORDER OF THE SULLEN LAKE.		80	EPHEMERA	V	17
	OF SLEUTH WOOD IN THE LAKE, ...		86	STOLEN CHILD		2
	THE LAKE ISLE OF INNISFREE		117	ISLE INNISFREE		T
	I HEAR LAKE WATER LAPPING WITH LOW SOUNDS BY THE SHORE;		117	ISLE INNISFREE		10
	I HEAR LAKE WATER LAPPING WITH LOW SOUNDS ON THE SHORE;		117	ISLE INNISFREE	V	10
	OF THE DREAR HART LAKE.		143	HOST OF AIR		4
	OF THIS DESOLATE LAKE		165	CRY OF SEDGE		2
	AND THEIR SECRET SMILE, OUT OF THE DEPTHS OF THE LAKE;		203	WITHER BOUGHS		11
	AND THEIR SECRET SMILE, OUT OF THE DEEPS OF THE LAKE;		203	WITHER BOUGHS	V	11
	IN THAT MYSTERIOUS, ALWAYS BRIMMING LAKE . . .		356	BROKEN DREAMS		32
	BESIDE THE LITTLE LAKE		400	DEMON BEAST		23
	SPREAD TO A LAKE AND DROP INTO A HOLE.		490	COOLE BALLYLEE		7
	THE GLITTERING REACHES OF THE FLOODED LAKE. . .		490	COOLE BALLYLEE		16
	SPREAD TO A LAKE AND RUN INTO A HOLE.		490	COOLE BALLYLEE	V	7
	ROUND THE MAREOTIC LAKE		636	BEN BULBEN		2
	OVER THE LAKE THE WATER-FLOWERS		647	ISLE STAT I 1		66
	THE WAVES IN YONDER LAKE WHERE POINTS MY HAND .		652	ISLE STAT I 2		13
	OF YONDER LAKE, FROM WHOSE GREEN BANKS ALWAY .		653	ISLE STAT I 2		33
	UNTO THE DOLOROUS BORDER OF THE FAIRY LAKE. . .		655	ISLE STAT I 2		85
	NODDING BY THE FLICKERING LAKE, ...		655	ISLE STAT I 3		3
	O'ER THE LAKE THIS VERY DAY.		656	ISLE STAT I 3		17
	ALONG THE LAKE. THE CRANE HAS HOMEWARD FLED. .		656	ISLE STAT I 3		23
	BEYOND THE LAKE, WHOSE SMALLEST WAVE WAS BURDENED		656	ISLE STAT I 3		31
	FROM YONDER PINNACLE ABOVE THE LAKE		657	ISLE STAT I 3		63
	HE PASSED ACROSS THE LAKE. WHEN WE TWO CAME .		658	ISLE STAT II 1		5
	WE SAW THE DOLOROUS LAKE; AND THEN THY NAME .		659	ISLE STAT II 1		7
	HE SAT, AND THEN I HEARD THE WHITE LAKE SING, .		659	ISLE STAT II 1		15
	HALF LIT, SO FLAPT THE WINGS ACROSS THE LAKE--		659	ISLE STAT II 1		17
	IN BUSY FLAKES; RE-SHINING FROM THE LAKE, . .		662	ISLE STAT II 2		3
	HERE, FACING TO THE LAKE, AND NO NAME GILD; . .		663	ISLE STAT II 2		20
	SWIFT LAKE. A VERY LITTLE THING THAT IS, . .		669	ISLE STAT II 3		78
	A WRIGGLING THING ON THE WHITE LAKE MOVED, . .		673	ISLE STAT II 3		176
	A-FLUTTERING THE PAINTED POPULACE OF LAKE . . .		675	ISLE STAT II 3		224
	FIERCE MORTAL, AND CROUCHED LOW BESIDE THE LAKE		675	ISLE STAT II 3	V	245A
	ABOVE THE FARM-HOUSE BY THE LITTLE LAKE		699	MOSADA 3		3
	AND NOW THAT CITY IS A LAKE.		725	LEGEND		32
	COME, BESIDE A SANDY LANE, ...		727	LOVERS QUARREL		41
	TO MIND HIS COWS AND SWINE BY THE RED LAKE. . .		752	SHADOW WATER A		112
LAKE-EMBOSOMED						
	THE LAKE-EMBOSOMED ISLE. NAY, THIS MY QUEST . .		657	ISLE STAT I 3		60
LAKE-LULLED						
	WITH SINGING SWEET AS E'ER ROUND LAKE-LULLED ISLE . .		649	ISLE STAT I 1		106
LAKE-NURTURED						
	OF THIS LAKE-NURTURED ISLE! LET THY KING BE . .		679	ISLE STAT II 3		315
LAKE'S						
	BY WHAT LAKE'S EDGE OR POOL		323	SWANS AT COOLE		28
	UPON THE BORDER OF THAT LAKE'S A WOOD		490	COOLE BALLYLEE		9
	CARVED; HERE, BEYOND THE LAKE'S SLOW-MUFFLED TREAD, . .		662	ISLE STAT II 2		11
LAKES						
	BY LAKES AND MEADOW LANDS AND LAWNS AFAR, . . .		32	OISIN 2	V	50F
LAMB						
	WHEN SOMETHING, HALF A LAMB AND HALF A GOAT, . .		747	SHADOW WATER A	V	11
LAMB'S						
	BUT FAINTER THAN A YOUNG LAMB'S BLEAT.		26	OISIN 1		399
	AND FAINTER THAN A YOUNG LAMB'S BLEAT.		26	OISIN 1	V	399
LAMBS						
	THE MERRY LAMBS AND THE COMPLACENT KINE, . . .		75	ANASHU VIJAYA		86
	THE MERRY LAMBS AND ALL THE KINE COMPLACENT, .		75	ANASHU VIJAYA	V	86
	BY THE PASTURE WHERE THE LAMBS		726	LOVERS QUARREL		5
LAME						
	A RABBIT OLD AND LAME LIMPED DOWN THE PATH; . .		80	EPHEMERA		15
	NASCHINA. OH, I KNOW HER WELL--A LAME, . . .		661	ISLE STAT II 1		67
	AMONG THE FRUIT! BUT THERE, LAME COLA CROUCHES		691	MOSADA 1		32
	AMONG THE FRUIT. BUT YON, LAME COLA CROUCHES .		691	MOSADA 1	V	32
	OF SILVER HANGING ROUND LAME COLA'S NECK-- . .		691	MOSADA 1	V	35
	SHE WAS MY ONLY FRIEND! I'M LAME, YOU KNOW-- .		695	MOSADA 1		115
LAME-FOOTED						
	THEY SAY I AM ALL UGLINESS; LAME-FOOTED . . .		692	MOSADA 1		60
LAMENT						
	JOHN KINSELLA'S LAMENT FOR MRS. MARY MOORE . .		620	JOHN KINSELLA		T
LAMENTATION						
	AND ALL THAT LAMENTATION OF THE LEAVES, . . .		120	SORROW OF LOVE		11
	THE LAMENTATION OF THE OLD PENSIONER		131	OLD PENSIONER		T

		PAGE	TITLE		LINE
LAMENTING					
	AND WEPT, AND RAISED THEIR LAMENTING HANDS,	10	OISIN 1		112
	THEY WEPT, AND RAISED LAMENTING HANDS.	10	OISIN 1	V	112
	LAMENTING THAT A MAN SHOULD DIE:	361	ALF POLLEXFEN		38
	BEAT OUT THEIR LIVES LAMENTING O'ER THE SAND:	652	ISLE STAT I 2		14
LAMENTS					
	AEDH LAMENTS THE LOSS OF LOVE	152	LOSS OF LOVE	V	T
	MONGAN LAMENTS THE CHANGE THAT HAS COME UPON HIM AND HIS BELOVED	153	CHANGE BELOVED	V	T
	HANRAHAN LAMENTS BECAUSE OF HIS WANDERINGS	171	MAID QUIET	V	T
LAMP					
	AS A LAMP SHADOW--NO--NO LAMP, THE SUN.	229	SHADOW WATER B		160
	AS A LAMP SHADOW--NO--NO LAMP, THE SUN.	229	SHADOW WATER B		160
	A LAMP BURNS ON BESIDE THE OPEN BOOK	367	EGO DOMINUS		3
	A LAMP BURNS ON ABOVE THE OPEN BOOK	367	EGO DOMINUS	V	3
	LUXURIANT SONG. WHY SHOULD YOU LEAVE THE LAMP	370	EGO DOMINUS		62
	TRUTH FLOURISHES WHERE THE STUDENT'S LAMP HAS SHONE,	398	LEADERS CROWD		8
	AND HEARTIER LOVES: THAT LAMP IS FROM THE TOMB.	398	LEADERS CROWD		12
	HIS LONG LAMP CHIMNEY SHAPED LIKE THE STEM	566	LAPIS LAZULI	V	33
LAMP-CHIMNEY					
	HIS LONG LAMP-CHIMNEY SHAPED LIKE THE STEM	566	LAPIS LAZULI		33
LAMPLIGHT					
	UNFRIENDLY LAMPLIGHT HID UNDER ITS SHADE,	523	LONG SILENCE		3
LAMPS					
	OF THE GREAT DOOR: BUT THOUGH THE HANGING LAMPS	279	TWO KINGS		49
LANCE					
	FROM SOME DEAD WARRIOR'S BROKEN LANCE:	24	OISIN 1		367
	IT WAS OF SOME DEAD WARRIOR'S LANCE.	24	OISIN 1	V	367
	SHINING BRIGHT AS A NEW LANCE:	125	CATHLEEN PARA	V	14
	SO LET US DANCE WHERE THE YELLOW LANCE	643	SONG FAERIES		7
	TO PROVE HIS LOVE A KNIGHT WITH LANCE IN REST	651	ISLE STAT I 1		158
	SO LET US DANCE WHERE THE YELLOW LANCE	676	ISLE STAT II 3		254
LANCELOT					
	WHERE ONE FOUND LANCELOT CRAZED AND HID HIM FOR A WHILE:	209	UNDER THE MOON		3
	WHERE ONE FOUND LANCELOT CRAZED, AND HID HIM FOR AWHILE,	209	UNDER THE MOON	V	3
LAND	SEE PLOUGH-LAND PASTURE-LAND LITTLE-LAND				
	IS NIAMH, AND MY LAND WHERE TIDE	5	OISIN 1	V	48
	"WERE THESE TWO BORN IN THE DANAAN LAND,	12	OISIN 1		146
	WAS A BEAUTIFUL YOUTH FROM AN UNKNOWN LAND.	12	OISIN 1	V	145
	BUT NOW A WANDERING LAND BREEZE CAME	13	OISIN 1		165
	OVER THE BARE AND WOODY LAND,	15	OISIN 1		198
	BUT WE IN A LONELY LAND ABIDE	22	OISIN 1		337
	IN WHAT LAND DO THE POWERLESS TURN THE BEAK	42	OISIN 2		198
	PRAYERS FOR THE LAND. I WILL WAIT HERE, AMRITA.	71	ANASHU VIJAYA		13
	PRAYERS FOR THE LAND. PRAY ON, AND I WILL WAIT YOU,	71	ANASHU VIJAYA	V	13
	PRAYERS FOR THE LAND. O BRAHMA, GUARD IN SLEEP	75	ANASHU VIJAYA		85
	THE PEASANTS OF THAT LAND,	123	DREAM OF DEATH		4
	A DRUID LAND, A DRUID TUNE:	139	TO IRELAND		32
	IN BARREN HILLS AND MARSHY LAND,	150	WANDER AENGUS		18
	COME FROM A MORE DREAM-HEAVY LAND,	156	FORGOT BEAUTY		16
	O, WHEN SHALL SORROW WANDER NO MORE IN THE LAND	174	ELEMENT POWERS	V	5
	CALLED RATHER BAILE LITTLE LAND,	189	BAILE AILLINN	V	17
	WITH SOMEBODY IN YOUR OWN LAND."	191	BAILE AILLINN		59
	THAT HELD THE LAND TOGETHER THERE,	194	BAILE AILLINN		132
	O TUFTED REEDS, BEND LOW AND LOW IN POOLS ON THE GREEN LAND,	206	HANRAHANS SONG	V	1
	WHEN THE WIND COMES BLOWING ACROSS THE HILLY LAND:	207	HANRAHANS SONG	V	7
	LAND OF THE TOWER, WHEN AENGUS HAS THROWN THE GATES APART,	209	UNDER THE MOON	V	8
	LAND FOR YOUR CHILDREN OR MONEY IN A POT."	228	SHADOW WATER B		125
	IN THIS BLIND BITTER LAND."	256	WORDS		4
	UPON A HOUSE SHAKEN BY THE LAND AGITATION	264	HOUSE SHAKEN		T
	THE SEEMING NEEDS OF MY FOOL-DRIVEN LAND:	267	ALL TEMPT ME		3
	FROM WELL SIDE OR FROM PLOUGH LAND, WAS THEIR NOISE:	279	TWO KINGS	V	53
	TO PLOUGH OR PASTURE LAND, MIGHT SEE ME THERE	283	TWO KINGS	V	146
	IN A DRAGON-GUARDED LAND,	309	REALISTS		3
	YOU SAY THAT WE SHOULD STILL THE LAND	395	SIXTEEN DEAD		7
	SHAKESPEAREAN FISH SWAM THE SEA, FAR AWAY FROM LAND:	485	THREE MOVEMENT		1
	AND THE HOLY LAND OF IRELAND,	526	AM OF IRELAND		2
	AND THE HOLY LAND OF IRELAND,	526	AM OF IRELAND		15
	AND THE HOLY LAND OF IRELAND,	527	AM OF IRELAND		28
	NO CIVIL RANCOUR TORN THE LAND APART.	542	PARN FUNERAL 2		4
	"THIS LAND OF SAINTS," AND THEN AS THE APPLAUSE DIED OUT,	577	LOFTY THINGS		3
	THE WINGED WONDER OF ALL FAERY LAND.	657	ISLE STAT I 3		57
	HOLD FESTIVAL ACROSS THE LAND,	671	ISLE STAT II 3		128
	SHEPHERDS, I CAME THIS MORNING TO YOUR LAND	682	SEEKER		15
	A VOICE CAME CALLING ME TO THIS YOUR LAND,	682	SEEKER		22
	A VOICE HAS TOLD ME HOW WITHIN THIS LAND	682	SEEKER	V	22
	I CANNOT GO INTO THE BLOODLESS LAND	722	WITCH VIVIEN		67
	BY THE GORSE ON THE HIGH LAND,	726	LOVERS QUARREL		4
	THEN GO TO HIS OWN LAND,	741	EARL PAUL		58
	A FRUITFUL LAND UNDER THE AIBHLIN HILLS?	748	SHADOW WATER A	V	33
	AND, HURRYING HOMEWARD, FALL UPON SOME LAND	767	SHADOW WATER A		384
	IN THE LAND THAT NO ONE KNOWS.	774	COME RIDE		17
	IN THE LAND THAT NO-ONE KNOWS.	774	COME RIDE	V	17
	BETWEEN TWO FURROWS UPON THE PLOUGHED LAND	784	WOMANS BEAUTY		4
	BETWEEN DARK FURROWS UPON THE PLOUGHED LAND.	784	WOMANS BEAUTY		6
LAND-OF-THE-TOWER					
	LAND-OF-THE-TOWER, WHERE AENGUS HAS THROWN THE GATES APART,	209	UNDER THE MOON		8
LANDOR					
	WITH LANDOR AND WITH DONNE.	336	YOUNG BEAUTY		18

433

	PAGE	TITLE	LINE

LANDOR'S
LANDOR'S TARPAULIN ON THE ROOF. . . . .   625 NATIVITY   6
LAND'S
HAD COSGRAVE EATEN PARNELL'S HEART, THE LAND'S . . . .   543 PARN FUNERAL 2   5
LANDS
AT EVENING IN THEIR RAINLESS LANDS." . . . .   7 OISIN 1   70
AT EVENING IN THEIR RAINLESS LANDS. . . . .   7 OISIN 1   V 66
BUT WE RODE OUT FROM THE HUMAN LANDS. . . . .   10 OISIN 1   114
AND BADE ME SING OF EARTHLY LANDS: . . . .   17 OISIN 1   V 233
WEDDING THE QUEENS OF EARTHLY LANDS WITH RINGS . . . .   29 OISIN 2   V 10
OF SEA-SPRUNG PEARL, AND QUEENS OF FAIRY LANDS . . . .   29 OISIN 2   V 10A
BY LAKES AND MEADOW LANDS AND LAWNS AFAR, ...   32 OISIN 2   V 50F
YOUR QUESTIONER, OISIN, IS WORTHY, HE COMES FROM THE FENIAN   51 OISIN 3   64
   LANDS."
WORTHY'S THY QUESTIONER, OISIN, HE FROM THE FENIAN LANDS."   51 OISIN 3   V 64
"THEN GO THROUGH THE LANDS IN THE SADDLE AND SEE WHAT THE   55 OISIN 3   125
   MORTALS DO,
. . . THOUGH SPACIOUS HIS LANDS WERE AND STRONG. . . . .   58 OISIN 3   160
SEND PEACE ON ALL THE LANDS AND FLICKERING CORN.-- . . .   71 ANASHU VIJAYA   1
MURMURING HOW FAR AWAY ARE THE UNQUIET LANDS: . . . . .   78 INDIAN TO LOVE   10
MURMURING HOW FAR AWAY ARE ALL EARTH'S FEVERISH LANDS. . .   78 INDIAN TO LOVE V 10
MURMURING GENTLY HOW FAR OFF ARE THE UNQUIET LANDS! . . .   78 INDIAN TO LOVE V 10
TO A SHONEEN WHO HAD FREE LANDS . . . .   92 FATHER OHART   3
IN TRUST TOOK HE JOHN'S LANDS: . . . .   92 FATHER OHART   5
AH, EXILES WANDERING OVER LANDS AND SEAS, ...   129 BOOK STORIES   9
AH, EXILES, WANDERING OVER MANY LANDS, ...   130 BOOK STORIES   V 17
THROUGH HOLLOW LANDS AND HILLY LANDS, ...   150 WANDER AENGUS   18
THROUGH HOLLOW LANDS AND HILLY LANDS, ...   150 WANDER AENGUS   18
THROUGH HILLY LANDS AND HOLLOW LANDS, ...   150 WANDER AENGUS V 18
THROUGH HILLY LANDS AND HOLLOW LANDS, ...   150 WANDER AENGUS V 18
IN DOVE-GREY FAERY LANDS: . . . .   162 ASKS FORGIVE   10
AND SOUGHT THROUGH LANDS AND ISLANDS NUMBERLESS YEARS, . .   170 SECRET ROSE   23
NOR LANDS THAT SEEM TOO DIM TO BE BURDENS ON THE HEART: 209 UNDER THE MOON   5
OR LANDS THAT SEEMED TOO OLD TO BE BURDENS ON THE HEART,   209 UNDER THE MOON V 5
THAT SO MANY LANDS HAD KNOWN, ...   360 ALF POLLEXFEN   18
QUIET LANDS OR UNQUIET SEAS . . . .   360 ALF POLLEXFEN   19
ON THE GREEN LANDS I WALK . . . .   607 SONGS BURDEN 2   20
THE AUSTRIAN HAYNAU HE, IN MANY LANDS . . . .   709 FERENCZ RENYI   8
AND OVER TILLAGE FIELDS AND PASTURE LANDS . . . . . .   715 FERENCZ RENYI   120
AND FOLLOWING O'ER THE FIELDS AND PASTURE LANDS, ...   715 FERENCZ RENYI V 120
LANDSMAN
MANY A LANDSMAN, MANY A SEAMAN. . . . .   82 MAD KING GOLL V 4
HE, THOUGH BUT A LANDSMAN, WENT TO THE MAST-HEAD: . . .   790 DEDICATION   4
LANDSMEN
MOVED ROUND ME, OF SEAMEN OR LANDSMEN, ALL WHO ARE WINTER   53 OISIN 3   86
   TALES:
LAND-UNDER-WAVE
LAND-UNDER-WAVE, WHERE OUT OF THE MOON'S LIGHT AND THE   209 UNDER THE MOON   6
   SUN'S
LANDWARD
DRIPPING AND DOUBLING LANDWARD, AS THOUGH THEY WOULD HASTEN   48 OISIN 3   15
   AWAY,
DRIPPING AND DOUBLING LANDWARD, AS THOUGH THEY WOULD HASTEN   57 OISIN 3   143
   AWAY,
LANE
BY ROCKY LANE AND FEN: . . . .   133 FR GILLIGAN   30
GATHERED A CROWD IN SOME BYZANTINE LANE, ...   180 QUEEN MAEVE   2
FOR THAT OLD MADGE COMES DOWN THE LANE, ...   456 FRIENDS YOUTH   5
IMPETUOUS MEN, SHAWE-TAYLOR AND HUGH LANE, ...   489 COOLE PARK 29   14
HUGH LANE, "ONLIE BEGETTER" OF ALL THESE: . . . . . .   602 GALLERY REVIS   22
MAYBE NOW IN SOME FAR LANE, ...   731 STREET DANCERS   14
WAS CRIED IN STREET AND LANE . . . .   740 EARL PAUL   26
LANGUAGE
MY LANGUAGE BEATEN . . . .   572 LADYS 1ST SONG   5
LANGUID
OF LANGUID EVENING THAT ENTWINED US. . . . .   25 OISIN 1   V 385A
GOES DROPPING FROM HIS EYES A LANGUID LIGHT, ...   34 OISIN 1   V 81A
HIS LANGUID TAIL ABOVE US, LIT WITH MYRIAD SPOTS OF LIGHT.   77 INDIAN ON GOD   20
AND IN THE SIBYL'S EYES A LANGUID FLAME . . . . . .   688 TWO TITANS   41
STAGGERING WITH LANGUID EYE. . . . .   717 FAIRY DOCTOR   V 16
LANGUOR
NOR LANGUOR NOR FATIGUE: AN ENDLESS FEAST, ...   44 OISIN 2   223
NO LANGUOR, NO FATIGUE: AN ENDLESS FEAST, ...   44 OISIN 2   V 223
NOR LANGUOR NOR FATIGUE: AND ENDLESS FEAST, ...   44 OISIN 2   V 223
FROM DEATH'S LATE LANGUOR AS THESE LINES I READ . . . .   734 QUATRAIN APHOR   14
LANGUORS
AND LANGUORS THAT AWAKE IN MINGLING HANDS . . . . . .   765 SHADOW WATER A   367
LANTERN
MY LANTERN IS TOO LOYAL NOT TO SHOW . . . .   464 HARUN RASHID   71
LANTHORN
LEAPS AND TIME'S OLD LANTHORN DIMS. . . . .   777 SONG DEIRDRE 2   5
LAP
WHAT YOUTHFUL MOTHER, A SHAPE UPON HER LAP . . . . .   444 SCHOOL CHILDR   33
LAPIS
IN TOMBS OF GOLD AND LAPIS LAZULI . . . .   483 OIL AND BLOOD   1
LAPIS LAZULI . . . .   565 LAPIS LAZULI   T
ARE CARVED IN LAPIS LAZULI, ...   566 LAPIS LAZULI   38
LAPIS-LAZULI
IN TOMBS OF GOLD AND LAPIS-LAZULI . . . .   483 OIL AND BLOOD V 1
LAPO
THE MAN THAT LAPO AND THAT GUIDO KNEW? . . . . . .   368 EGO DOMINUS   26

434

		PAGE	TITLE	LINE

LAPPED
    "ALTHOUGH I'D LIE LAPPED UP IN LINEN . . . .   331 ROUND TOWER   1
    LAPPED IN THE LEMON DAFFODILS; A BEE . . . .   716 DWELT SYCAMORE   10
LAPPING
    I HEAR LAKE WATER LAPPING WITH LOW SOUNDS BY THE SHORE;   117 ISLE INNISFREE   10
    I HEAR LAKE WATER LAPPING WITH LOW SOUNDS ON THE SHORE;   117 ISLE INNISFREE V   10
    WORN THIN BY THE LAPPING OF WATER, ...   330 BONE OF A HARE   11
    OF SAD QUEEN DIDO SHONE THE LAPPING FIRE . . . . . .   645 ISLE STAT I 1   9
LAPWING
    THE LAPWING AT THEIR FOOLISH CRIES . . . .   306 HOUR DAWN   77
LAPWINGS
    A PAIR OF LAPWINGS, ONE OLD SHEEP, ...   302 HOUR DAWN   9
LARCH-WOOD
    A LARCH-WOOD HUNTING SPEAR. . . . .   32 OISIN 2   V   56
LARDER
    FOR LARDER AND SPIT ARE BARE, ...   349 HAWK   4
LARGE
    AND MY TEARS WERE LARGE LIKE TO BERRIES, AND I MURMURED,   59 OISIN 3   V 178
    . . .
    AND HE WORE LARGE HOLES IN HIS GOWN. . . . .   92 FATHER OHART   12
    O BUT WE TALKED AT LARGE BEFORE . . . .   395 SIXTEEN DEAD   1
    THAT WHEN THEY HAD GROWN LARGE . . . .   571 THREE BUSHES   60
    AH! HOW LARGE MICE USED TO BE . . . .   727 LOVERS QUARREL   39
LARGELY
    THE ISLE LOOMED LARGELY IN THE LIGHT . . . .   25 OISIN 1   V 385
LARGER
    AND MY TEARS WERE LARGER THAN BERRIES, AND I MURMURED,   59 OISIN 3   178
    . . .
    LARGER SPARROWS OF THE TOWN, ...   731 STREET DANCERS   5
LARK
    YON EAGER LARK, THAT FILLS WITH SONG THE WHOLE . . . .   652 ISLE STAT I 2   18
LARKS
    WAKE THE LARKS UPON THE GREEN. . . . .   727 LOVERS QUARREL   46
LASH
    SHIVER UNDER THE LASH, STRAIN, SWEAT AND JOLT . . . . .   260 FASC DIFFICULT   7
    WHAT MASTER MADE THE LASH. WHENCE HAD THEY COME, . . .   560 WHENCE COME   9
    THE HAND AND LASH THAT BEAT DOWN FRIGID ROME? . . . .   560 WHENCE COME   10
    THE BEGGARS HAVE CHANGED PLACES, BUT THE LASH GOES ON. .   590 GREAT DAY   4
    WHEN YOU ARE ABOARD THE LOCHLANN GALLEY, LASH . . . . .   752 SHADOW WATER A   128
LASHED
    ONE LASHED HER TAIL; HER EYES LIT BY THE MOON . . . . .   383 VISION ROBART   29
LASHES
    IF I MAKE THE LASHES DARK . . . .   531 BEFORE WORLD   1
    THE FLAGELLANT LASHES THOSE SUBMISSIVE LOINS . . . . .   560 WHENCE COME   7
    A BEGGAR UPON HORSEBACK LASHES A BEGGAR ON FOOT. . . .   590 GREAT DAY   2
    A BEGGAR UPON HORSEBACK LASHES A BEGGAR UPON FOOT; . .   590 GREAT DAY   V   2
LASS
    "AND THOUGH I'D MARRY WITH A COMELY LASS, ...   300 BEGGAR CRIED   9
    COURT HIS SHEPHERD LASS, ...   343 SHEP GOATHERD   104
    WHEN SHEBA WAS HIS LASS, ...   345 ON WOMAN   16
    EVERY COLONUS LAD OR LASS DISCOURSES . . . .   447 COLONUS PRAISE   29
    NIAMH THAT RODE ON IT; LAD AND LASS . . . .   550 SEVERED HEAD   11
    THAT PARNELL LOVED A LASS. . . . .   586 PARNELLITES   16
    AND PARNELL LOVED HIS LASS. . . . .   587 PARNELLITES   32
    AND PARNELL LOVED A LASS. . . . .   587 PARNELLITES   V   32
LASSES
    LADS AND LASSES, TWO AND TWO, ...   705 DAWN-SONG   15
LAST
    FOR HIS LAST DAYS TO LIE IN WAIT. . . . .   24 OISIN 1   363
    MUST MURMUR AT LAST, "UNJUST, UNJUST"! . . . .   28 OISIN 1   420
    AT LAST THE MOON AND STARS SHONE, AND A FLIGHT . . . .   31 OISIN 2   V   34
    AND CLIMBED SO LONG, I THOUGHT THE LAST STEPS WERE . .   32 OISIN 2   48
    AND WHERE OUR FOOTFALL 'LIGHTED LAST THERE CAME . . .   37 OISIN 2   V 119
    "LAST OF MY RACE, THREE THINGS I RULE ALONE-- . . . . .   45 OISIN 2   V 239A
    SONG OF THE LAST ARCADIAN . . . .   64 HAPPY SHEPHERD V   T
    AND NOW AT LAST YOU WEAR A HUMAN SHAPE, ...   102 FERGUS DRUID   6
    AND NOW AT LAST YOU TAKE ON HUMAN SHAPE— . . . . . .   102 FERGUS DRUID   V   6
    AT LAST CUCHULAIN SPAKE, "SOME MAN HAS MADE . . . . .   109 CUCHULAIN SEA   47
    AT LAST CUCHULAIN SPAKE, "A YOUNG MAN STRAYS . . . . .   109 CUCHULAIN SEA V   47
    WOULD COME AT LAST TO GOD'S GREAT TOWN, ...   113 ROSE OF PEACE   11
    AND WHEN AT LAST, DEFEATED IN HIS WARS, ...   115 ROSE OF BATTLE   33
    AND HE HAD KNOWN AT LAST SOME TENDERNESS, ...   126 DREAM OF FAERY   3
    AND HE HAD KNOWN AT LAST SOME PRUDENT YEARS . . . . .   127 DREAM OF FAERY   15
    AND MIGHT HAVE KNOWN AT LAST UNHAUNTED SLEEP . . . . .   128 DREAM OF FAERY   38
    WHERE THE LAST PHOENIX DIED, ...   162 ASKS FORGIVE   16
    WE SAW THE LAST EMBERS OF DAYLIGHT DIE, ...   205 ADAMS CURSE   29
    IN THE LAST RIDGE OF THE BARLEY? DO OUR WOODS . . . .   218 WOODS OF COOLE   33
    TO GRADUAL TIME'S LAST GIFT, A WRITTEN SPEECH . . . .   264 HOUSE SHAKEN   11
    UNTIL AT LAST THE DOUBLE HORNS, DRAWN BACKWARD, . . .   278 TWO KINGS   21
    BUT WHEN AT LAST HE FORCED THOSE SINEWY FLANKS . . . .   278 TWO KINGS   35
    UNTIL AT LAST THE UNLOCKED HORN HAD TORN . . . . . .   278 TWO KINGS   V   21
    AND THEN AT LAST BEING WIDE AWAKE . . . .   304 HOUR DAWN   V   40
    FOR ALL LIFE LONGS FOR THE LAST DAY . . . .   306 HOUR DAWN   98
    LIKE SOME LAST COURTIER AT A GYPSY CAMPING—PLACE . . .   314 FALLEN MAJESTY   3
    LIKE SOME LAST COURTIER AT A GYPSY CAMPING PLACE . . .   314 FALLEN MAJESTY V   3
    WHEN HAVE I LAST LOOKED ON . . . .   343 DEJECTION   1
    LAST EVENING? THAT I, WHO HAD SAT . . . .   349 HAWK   15
    THE LAST STROKE OF MIDNIGHT DIES. . . . .   357 BROKEN DREAMS   37
    THEY RAN FROM CRADLE TO CRADLE TILL AT LAST . . . . .   375 PHASES OF MOON   69
    THAT THE LAST SERVILE CRESCENT HAS SET FREE? . . . . .   376 PHASES OF MOON   103
    HUNCHBACK AND SAINT AND FOOL ARE THE LAST CRESCENTS. . .   377 PHASES OF MOON   118

LAST (CONTINUED)

	PAGE	TITLE		LINE
UNDER THE THREE LAST CRESCENTS OF THE MOON,	377	PHASES OF MOON		133
I KNEW THAT I HAD SEEN, HAD SEEN AT LAST	384	VISION ROBART		49
"LAST NIGHT, WHERE UNDER THE WILD MOON	387	SOLOMON WITCH		2
CHANCE BEING AT ONE WITH CHOICE AT LAST,	388	SOLOMON WITCH		14
AND THIS FOUL WORLD WERE DEAD AT LAST.	388	SOLOMON WITCH		16
AND WHEN AT LAST THAT MURDER'S OVER	388	SOLOMON WITCH		24
THEREFORE A BLESSED MOON LAST NIGHT	388	SOLOMON WITCH		31
AND WHEN AT LAST,	389	IMAGE PAST		10
WHEN SLEEP AT LAST HAS COME	394	EASTER 1916		63
AND WHAT ROUGH BEAST, ITS HOUR COME ROUND AT LAST,	402	SECOND COMING		21
AND LEARNS AT LAST THAT IT IS SELF-DELIGHTING,	405	FOR DAUGHTER		67
LAST REACH OF GLITTERING STREAM	414	TOWER		143
AND THERE SING HIS LAST SONG.	414	TOWER		144
LAST NIGHT THEY TRUNDLED DOWN THE ROAD	425	STARES NEST		13
AND I MERE SHADE AT LAST	449	HERO GIRL FOOL		25
OCTOBER LAST I FOUND IT TOO	454	EMPTY CUP		7
AND PAUSE AT LAST, I WAS ABOUT TO SAY,	461	HARUN RASHID		11
AND SINK INTO ITS OWN DELIGHT AT LAST.	473	ALL SOUL NIGHT		60
CASTS UPON HIS EYES UNTIL AT LAST	479	SELF AND SOUL		53
CONTENT OR JOY; A LAST INHERITOR	491	COOLE BALLYLEE		30
WE WERE THE LAST ROMANTICS--CHOSE FOR THEME	491	COOLE BALLYLEE		41
WHEN THE LAST THREAD HAS RUN,	520	HIS BARGAIN		10
A LAST CONFESSION	538	LAST CONFESS		T
DISCOVER IMPURITIES, CAN SHOW AT LAST	558	RIBH CHRISTIAN		10
YET THEY, SHOULD THE LAST SCENE BE THERE,	565	LAPIS LAZULI		12
AND WERE THE LAST TO CHOOSE THE SETTLED GROUND,	621	HOUND VOICE		2
LAST NIGHT I LAY ON THE MOUNTAIN,	628	JANE MOUNTAIN		11
MAYBE AT LAST, BEING BUT A BROKEN MAN,	629	CIRCUS ANIMALS		3
AND SINKS AT LAST INTO THE NIGHT.	633	MAN AND ECHO		36
SO! MID THE WILLOW-GLADE YOU PAUSE AT LAST.	651	ISLE STAT I 2		2
TILL HIS LAST WRETCHEDNESS WAS O'ER AND DONE."	664	ISLE STAT II 2		54
SINKS DOWN AT LAST WITH YONDER MINARET,	691	MOSADA 1	V	36
AT LAST. BUT NOW I WAVE HER TO MY SIDE.	694	MOSADA 1	V	91
WILL YOU NOT HEAR MY LAST NEW SONG? HUSH, HUSH!	695	MOSADA 2		1
A WEAK, THIN CHILD, WHEN LAST I SAW HIM THERE.	699	MOSADA 3		14
A WEIGHTY QUESTION, FOR IT IS THE LAST.	700	MOSADA 3		37
WE MEET AT LAST, THE MINISTERING STARS	701	MOSADA 3		52
HIS BONDS AWAY, SORE STRUGGLING. NOW AT LAST	714	FERENCZ RENYI		116
YOUNG FERENCZ RENYI BURSTS HIS BONDS--AT LAST,	714	FERENCZ RENYI	V	116
WHY DO YOU LAUGH? I LAUGH THE LAST ALWAYS.	721	WITCH VIVIEN		25
AND THEN THE GREAT ONES COME, AND LAST THE KING.	722	WITCH VIVIEN		54
O STILL THAT HEART AT LAST.	785	YOUR HEART		8
ALTHOUGH YOUR LAST EXCITING YEAR	791	REPRISALS		5

LASTING

AND KISS MORE LIPS THAN LASTING PEACEABLE MEN	225	SHADOW WATER B		71
AND BLEW ME HITHER TO MY LASTING SORROW,	235	SHADOW WATER B		288
FROM LASTING WATCHERS, THAT OUTLIVE THE MOON,	236	SHADOW WATER B		320
WHY MUST THE LASTING LOVE WHAT PASSES,	275	GREY ROCK		114
HE THAT SINGS A LASTING SONG	553	PRAYER OLD AGE		3

LATCH

| HE ROSE THE LATCH AND WENT UPSTAIRS | 594 | COLONEL MARTIN | | 7 |

LATCHES

| AND PUSHED THE LATCHES DOWN. | 159 | CAP AND BELLS | | 12 |

LATE

THEN SHE SIGHED GENTLY, "IT GROWS LATE.	9	OISIN 1		102
THEN SIGHED SHE SOFTLY, "LATE! 'TIS LATE!	9	OISIN 1	V	102
THEN SIGHED SHE SOFTLY, "LATE! 'TIS LATE!	9	OISIN 1	V	102
WITH MISERY, OR THAT SHE WOULD OF LATE	256	NO SECOND TROY		2
AND HAVING TALKED TO SOME LATE HOUR	324	ROBERT GREGORY		4
OF THAT LATE DEATH TOOK ALL MY HEART FOR SPEECH.	328	ROBERT GREGORY		96
DESPITE A DWINDLING AND LATE RISEN MOON,	372	PHASES OF MOON	V	6
SAT LATE, OR SHELLEY'S VISIONARY PRINCE:	373	PHASES OF MOON		16
PROSPER BUT LITTLE, HAS DRIED UP OF LATE,	405	FOR DAUGHTER		51
AND TOILED SO HARD AND LATE	432	NINETEEN 19		95
ALTHOUGH OF LATE ESTRANGED.	473	ALL SOUL NIGHT		63
NO OTHER BIRD MAY ENTER IN. WELL? LATE--	659	ISLE STAT II 1		24
TOO LATE, TOO LATE, FOR I AM NEAR TO DEATH.	701	MOSADA 3		55
TOO LATE, TOO LATE, FOR I AM NEAR TO DEATH.	701	MOSADA 3		55
'TIS LATE, WAIT ONE MORE DAY; BELOW THE HILLS	702	MOSADA 3		91
"WE BURIED LATE IN A HAZEL DELL	729	PRIEST FAIRY		43
FROM DEATH'S LATE LANGUOR AS THESE LINES I READ	734	QUATRAIN APHOR		14

LATE-LOST

| AND THUS, MY LATE-LOST NIAM, DIDST THOU SAY: | 34 | OISIN 2 | V | 78 |

LATELY

WHERE IS THE OWL THAT LATELY FLEW	646	ISLE STAT I 1		32
AYE, VERY LATELY, SORROW CAME TO WEEP	659	ISLE STAT II 1		25

LATER

LATER A SOUND CAME, HALF LOST IN THE SOUND OF A SHORE FAR AWAY,	57	OISIN 3		155
. . . AND LATER THE SHORE-WEEDS BROWN.	57	OISIN 3		156
TWO YEARS LATER	312	TWO YEAR LATER		T
AND LATER HAD MUCH TROUBLE FROM A FOOL,	404	FOR DAUGHTER		26
FORTY YEARS LATER	542	PARN FUNERAL 2	V	T
BUT LATER MIGHT HAVE BEEN	608	SONGS BURDEN 3		15
THAT WILL BE LATER, DAY IS SCARCELY DAWNING.	699	MOSADA 3		12
THAT WILL BE LATER, DAY IS DAWNING.	699	MOSADA 3	V	12

LATE-RISEN

| DESPITE A DWINDLING AND LATE-RISEN MOON, | 372 | PHASES OF MOON | | 6 |

LATEST

| TO MICHELOZZO'S LATEST PLAN | 288 | TO WEALTHY MAN | | 23 |

436

```
                                                      PAGE    TITLE          LINE
LATEST   (CONTINUED)
    WHO HAD MURMURED OF GIORGIONE AT HIS LATEST BREATH--  . .   366 HER COURAGE      8
LATIN
    TILL ALL HIS GREEK AND LATIN LEARNING SEEMED . . . . .    324 ROBERT GREGORY    21
    IT FOLLOWS FROM THIS LATIN TEXT  . . . . . . . . .        386 ROBARTES DANCE    43
LATTICE
    TENDING THE ROSES ROUND HIS LATTICE DOOR. . . . . . .     692 MOSADA 1          53
LATTICED
    A LATTICED WINDOW. HIS GLANCE WENT UP AT TIMES . . . .    180 QUEEN MAEVE        6
LAUGH
    AMONG THEMSELVES LAUGH ON AND SING ALWAY; . . . . . .      68 SAD SHEPHERD       7
    ONE WITH THE WAVES THAT SOFTLY ROUND US LAUGH AND DART.    78 INDIAN TO LOVE V  15
    OF MY LONG SPEAR, WITH SCREAM AND LAUGH, . . . . . .       84 MAD KING GOLL  V  34
    OF MY LONG SPEAR WITH SONG AND LAUGH . . . . . . . .       84 MAD KING GOLL  V  34
    THE DANAAN CHILDREN LAUGH, IN CRADLES OF WROUGHT GOLD, .  146 UNAPPEAS HOST      1
    THE FAERY CHILDREN LAUGH IN CRADLES OF WROUGHT GOLD,   .  146 UNAPPEAS HOST  V   1
    LAUGH, HEART, AGAIN IN THE GREY TWILIGHT, . . . . . .     147 INTO TWILIGHT      3
    AND LAUGH OUT THEIR WHIMSEY AND WORK OUT THEIR WILL. .    148 INTO TWILIGHT  V  12
    LAUGH OUT THEIR WHIMSEY AND WORK OUT THEIR WILL. . . .    148 INTO TWILIGHT  V  12
    WE ARE ALONE FOR EVER, AND I LAUGH, . . . . . . . .       251 SHADOW WATER B   602
    SO WITH A LAUGH AT HIS OWN FEAR . . . . . . . . .         303 HOUR DAWN         31
    AND THREW HIM UP TO LAUGH ON THE BOUGH; . . . . . .       318 APPOINTMENT       11
    AND LAUGH OVER THE UNTROUBLED WATER . . . . . . . .       330 BONE OF A HARE    14
    AND ALL LAUGH IN THE SUN. . . . . . . . . . . .           400 DEMON BEAST        8
    AND THEN I LAUGH TILL TEARS RUN DOWN . . . . . . .        456 FRIENDS YOUTH     17
    THE THREE OLD RASCALS LAUGH ALOUD. . . . . . . . .        460 THREE MONUMENT    12
    SHOULD LAUGH AND WEEP AN HOUR UPON THE CLOCK. . . . .     471 ALL SOUL NIGHT    20
    SHOULD LAUGH AND WEEP AN HOUR UPON THE CLOCK. . . . .     474 ALL SOUL NIGHT V  90
    SHOULD WEEP AND LAUGH AN HOUR UPON THE CLOCK. . . . .     474 ALL SOUL NIGHT V  90
    WE MUST LAUGH AND WE MUST SING, . . . . . . . . .         479 SELF AND SOUL     70
    WE THAT LOOK ON BUT LAUGH IN TRAGIC JOY. . . . . . .      564 GYRES              8
    THAT CAN MAKE A CAT LAUGH, OR . . . . . . . . . .         589 OLD WICKED MAN    39
    THE ECSTATIC WATERS LAUGH BECAUSE . . . . . . . . .       612 NEWS ORACLE       17
    THOSE GREAT SEA-HORSES BARE THEIR TEETH AND LAUGH AT THE  623 HIGH TALK         14
       DAWN.
    TILL I LAUGH WHEN OTHERS WEEP, . . . . . . . . . .        647 ISLE STAT I 1     61
    WEEPING WHEN ALL OTHERS LAUGH. . . . . . . . . . .        647 ISLE STAT I 1     62
    IT IS THE VOICE OF ALL OUR HEARTS THAT LAUGH. . . . .     681 SEEKER             7
    A TOSSING LAUGH BETWEEN THEIR REDNESS 'BIDES-- . . .      685 DRAWING-ROOM       2
    AND LAUGH OUR LOVE AWAY. . . . . . . . . . . . .          686 LIFE              16
    AND LOSS OF YOUR LAUGH AND ITS LIGHTNESS-- . . . . .      708 FAIRY PEDANT      33
    HE RUSHES, ROLLING FROM HIS LIPS A MADMAN'S LAUGH. . .    715 FERENCZ RENYI    122
    WHY DO YOU LAUGH?  I LAUGH THE LAST ALWAYS. . . . . .     721 WITCH VIVIEN      25
    WHY DO YOU LAUGH?  I LAUGH THE LAST ALWAYS. . . . . .     721 WITCH VIVIEN      25
    A TOSSING LAUGH BETWEEN THEIR RED ABIDES; . . . . . .     735 QUATRAIN APHOR    22
    A TOSSING LAUGH BETWEEN THEIR REDNESS 'BIDES-- . . .      735 QUATRAIN APHOR  V 22
    THE HANDMAIDS LAUGH AND WHISPER IN THE DOOR. . . . .      759 SHADOW WATER A   242
    AND I SHALL LAUGH WITH JOY.  COME HITHER, AIBRIC, . .     760 SHADOW WATER A   249
    LOVERS, IF THEY MAY NOT LAUGH, . . . . . . . . .          772 SONG DEIRDRE 1    15
LAUGH'D
    AND LAUGH'D, SO, SO ALONG THE BUBBLING RILLS . . . .      645 ISLE STAT I 1     18
LAUGHED
    AND LAUGHED LIKE MURMURS OF THE SEA; . . . . . . .         15 OISIN 1          210
    I LAUGHED AT TIMES UNNUMBERED TREASONS, . . . . . .        23 OISIN 1        V 345D
    I LAUGHED ALOUD AND HURRIED ON . . . . . . . . . .         83 MAD KING GOLL     31
    I LAUGHED BECAUSE BIRDS FLUTTERED BY, . . . . . . .        84 MAD KING GOLL     33
    WHERE I HAVE LAUGHED AND SPUN AND PLAYED? . . . . . .     151 HEART OF WOMAN V   2
    HE RAN AND LAUGHED UNTIL HE CAME . . . . . . . . .        194 BAILE AILLINN    128
    BUT GUAIRE LAUGHED WITH SECRET THOUGHT, . . . . . . .     295 THREE BEGGARS     19
    WHO HAVE LIVED IN JOY AND LAUGHED INTO THE FACE OF DEATH. 366 HER COURAGE       10
    WHO LIVED IN SHAMELESS JOY AND LAUGHED INTO THE FACE OF   366 HER COURAGE    V  10
       DEATH.
    THAT LIVED IN JOY AND LAUGHED INTO THE FACE OF DEATH. . . 366 HER COURAGE    V  10
    WHO HAVE LIVED IN JOY AND LAUGHED IN THE FACE OF DEATH. . 366 HER COURAGE    V  10
    AHERNE LAUGHED, THINKING OF THE MAN WITHIN, . . . . .     375 PHASES OF MOON    85
    AND THEN HE LAUGHED TO THINK THAT WHAT SEEMED HARD . .    377 PHASES OF MOON   136
    THE HEART BEHIND ITS RIB LAUGHED OUT. . . . . . . .       450 OWEN AHERNE       13
    LAUGHED; AND PLUNGING DOWN . . . . . . . . . . .          453 MERMAID            4
    FLINGING FROM HIS ARMS I LAUGHED . . . . . . . . .        538 LAST CONFESS       7
    AND LAUGHED UPON HIS BREAST TO THINK . . . . . . .        538 LAST CONFESS      11
    HER BARGAIN STRUCK WE LAUGHED AND TALKED . . . . . .      620 JOHN KINSELLA     15
    'TIS HERE THE ARROW.FELL! THE BREEZES LAUGHED . . . .     657 ISLE STAT I 3     70
    OF GRIEF.  AND IF THEY SAY, "ANTONIO LAUGHED," . . .      664 ISLE STAT II 2    51
    I LAUGHED?  AND WHY IS THAT A THING SO DEAR? . . . .      670 ISLE STAT II 3    97
    "I LAUGHED UPON THE LIPS OF SOPHOCLES, . . . . . .        686 LIFE              17
    IN CREVICED ROCKS, AND LAUGHED TO THE OLD SEA, . . . .    688 TWO TITANS        34
    "I LAUGHED UPON THE LIPS OF SOPHOCLES. . . . . . .        735 QUATRAIN APHOR    19
    THEY DREAM THAT LAUGHED IN THE SUN. . . . . . . .         783 GREY ROUND        13
    THEY DREAMED THAT LAUGHED IN THE SUN. . . . . . .         783 GREY ROUND     V  13
    DANCED, LAUGHED, LOVED, FOUGHT THROUGH . . . . . . .      787 HUDDON DUDDON      4
LAUGHING   SEE LOW-LAUGHING EVER-LAUGHING
    TO THAT LOW LAUGHING WOODLAND RHYME. . . . . . . .         14 OISIN 1          176
    AND TOUCH THE LAUGHING SILVER STRING; . . . . . . .        17 OISIN 1          233
    CEASE, CEASE, O MOURNFUL, LAUGHING FENIAN HORN! . . .      43 OISIN 2          213
    AH, CEASE, THOU MOURNFUL, LAUGHING FENIAN HORN! . . .      43 OISIN 2          213
    AH, CEASE, YOU MOURNFUL, LAUGHING FENIAN HORN! . . .       43 OISIN 2        V 213
    GOD'S LAUGHING IN HEAVEN . . . . . . . . . . . .          118 CRADLE SONG        5
    IT HAD BECOME A LAUGHING GIRL, . . . . . . . . .          149 WANDER AENGUS  V  13
    SUDDEN AND LAUGHING, O UNQUIET HEART, . . . . . .         181 QUEEN MAEVE       30
    AND WITH LOW MURMURING LAUGHING SPEECH . . . . . .        195 BAILE AILLINN    137
    WANDERS LAUGHING AND EATING HER WILD HEART . . . . .      198 SEVEN WOODS       11
```

437

		PAGE	TITLE	LINE

LAUGHING   (CONTINUED)
```
    THE SUN WAS LAUGHING SWEETLY,  . . . . . . . . . .    214 HAPPY TOWNLAND       15
    THE SUN WAS LAUGHING SWEETLY,  . . . . . . . . . .    215 HAPPY TOWNLAND       35
    THE SUN WAS LAUGHING SWEETLY,  . . . . . . . . . .    216 HAPPY TOWNLAND       55
    ONE OF THE LAUGHING PEOPLE--AND SHE AND I . . . .     231 SHADOW WATER B      211
    FOR I HAVE HEARD THAT HE WAS PROUD AND LAUGHING, . .  242 SHADOW WATER B      415
    I KNEW HIM WELL, AND WHILE I HEARD HIM LAUGHING . .   242 SHADOW WATER B      419
    AND WHILE WE'RE IN OUR LAUGHING, WEEPING FIT, . . .   257 RECONCILIATION        9
    AND THE SWEET LAUGHING EAGLE THOUGHTS THAT GROW . .   264 HOUSE SHAKEN          5
    STARED AT THE GODS WITH LAUGHING LIP. . . . . . .     276 GREY ROCK           123
    AND LIKE A LAUGHING STRING . . . . . . . . . . .      291 TO A FRIEND          11
    THE YOUNG MEN EVERY NIGHT APPLAUD THEIR GABY'S LAUGHING  353 HIS PHOENIX         9
       EYE,
    THAT WOMEN LAUGHING, OR TIMID OR WILD, . . . . . .    358 PRESENCES             4
    WHAT IF A LAUGHING EYE . . . . . . . . . . . .        367 HER CHRIS TREE       10
    I GET A LAUGHING FIT, . . . . . . . . . . . . .       455 FRIENDS YOUTH         4
    IN THE LONG ECHOING STREET THE LAUGHING DANCERS THRONG,  459 FROM OEDIPUS         7
    IN THE LONG ECHOING STREETS THE LAUGHING DANCERS THRONG,  459 FROM OEDIPUS   V    7
    PROUD, OPEN-EYED AND LAUGHING TO THE TOMB. . . .      501 VACILLATION          34
    "A LAUGHING, CRYING, SACRED SONG, . . . . . . . .     570 THREE BUSHES         43
    THOU'LT TEACH ME LAUGHING, AND I'LL TEACH THEE PEACE, .  670 ISLE STAT II 3   101
    LAUGHING GOES IN WILDEST MOOD, . . . . . . . . .      732 STREET DANCERS       41
    I AM AFRAID OF HIS LOW LAUGHING HARP. . . . . . .     759 SHADOW WATER A V    239
    IS LAUGHING THROUGH A MORTAL'S EYES. O LOOK! . . .    763 SHADOW WATER A      324
    WHERE SOME LAUGHING ELEMENT . . . . . . . . . .       777 SONG DEIRDRE 2        4
LAUGHS
    LAUGHS ALOUD, HIS HEART AT PEACE. . . . . . . . .     638 BEN BULBEN           32
    LAUGHS NOT. IT DWELLS ALONE ON MORTAL LIPS! . . . .   670 ISLE STAT II 3      100
LAUGHTER
    WITH LAUGHTER LOW, AND TENDER, AND SWEET! . . . .       6 OISIN 1         V   54
    SHE SAID, WITH LAUGHTER TENDER AND SWEET! . . . .       6 OISIN 1         V   54
    OF PENSIVE LAUGHTER, UNHUMAN SOUND, . . . . . . .      11 OISIN 1            136
    AND ONCE A SUDDEN LAUGHTER SPRANG . . . . . . .        16 OISIN 1            225
    LAUGHTER AND CRIES. THE ARMIES CLASH AND SHOCK, . .    43 OISIN 2            211
    OF ARMOUR--LAUGHTER AND CRIES--THE ARMIES' SHOCK. . .  43 OISIN 2         V  211
    . . . WITH ROARING OF LAUGHTER AND SONGS. . . .        53 OISIN 3             87
    WENT THE LAUGHTER OF SCORN FROM MY MOUTH . . . . .     58 OISIN 3            168
    WITHOUT LAUGHTER, A SHOW UNTO CHILDREN, . . . . .      63 OISIN 3            218
    WITHOUT LAUGHTER, A COUGHING, ALONE WITH REMEMBRANCE AND  63 OISIN 3      V  218
       FEAR!
    THE HOUR WHEN KAMA, FULL OF SLEEPY LAUGHTER, . . .     72 ANASHU VIJAYA       26
    A LONELY LAUGHTER, AND MAY KISS HIS HANDS TO ME IN SLEEP.  75 ANASHU VIJAYA   82
    AN INNER LAUGHTER, AND MAY KISS HIS HANDS TO ME IN SLEEP.  75 ANASHU VIJAYA V  82
    A LONELY LAUGHTER, THAT HE MAY KISS HANDS TO ME IN SLEEP.  75 ANASHU VIJAYA V  82
    OR FLING MY LAUGHTER TO THE SUN . . . . . . . .        86 MAD KING GOLL   V   69
    AND FLING MY LAUGHTER TO THE SUN . . . . . . . .       86 MAD KING GOLL   V   69
    OR COMES IN LAUGHTER FROM THE SEA'S SAD LIPS, . . .   114 ROSE OF BATTLE       19
    THAT HE'S A LOVELESS MAN! GAY BELLS BRING LAUGHTER . . 130 BOOK STORIES         18
    MY BELL BRANCH MURMURS! THE GAY BELLS BRING LAUGHTER, . 130 BOOK STORIES   V   18
    UNTIL HE FOUND, WITH LAUGHTER AND WITH TEARS, . . .   170 SECRET ROSE          24
    A CHILD'S LAUGHTER, A WOMAN'S KISS. . . . . . . .     190 BAILE AILLINN        40
    AND FIND THEIR LAUGHTER SWEETER TO THE TASTE . . .    228 SHADOW WATER B      134
    TO MAKE LOW LAUGHTER MORE THAN MEAT AND DRINK, . .    230 SHADOW WATER B      186
    BUT LAUGHTER AND TEARS--LAUGHTER, LAUGHTER, AND TEARS! . 235 SHADOW WATER B    298
    BUT LAUGHTER AND TEARS--LAUGHTER, LAUGHTER, AND TEARS! . 235 SHADOW WATER B    298
    BUT LAUGHTER AND TEARS--LAUGHTER, LAUGHTER, AND TEARS! . 235 SHADOW WATER B    298
    WROUGHT OF HIGH LAUGHTER, LOVELINESS AND EASE? . . .  264 HOUSE SHAKEN         12
    THE LINEAMENTS, A HEART THAT LAUGHTER HAS MADE SWEET, . 315 FALLEN MAJESTY       5
    THE LINEAMENTS, THE HEART THAT LAUGHTER HAS MADE SWEET, 315 FALLEN MAJESTY V   5
    THAT IS LIKE LAUGHTER, SPRANG AGAIN . . . . . . .     318 APPOINTMENT           6
    AND WHEN SHE MEETS OUR GAZE HER EYES ARE LAUGHTER LIT . 362 HER COURTESY   V    5
    LAUGHTER NOT TIME DESTROYED MY VOICE . . . . . . .    455 FRIENDS YOUTH         1
    PORTER-DRINKERS' RANDY LAUGHTER! . . . . . . . .      640 BEN BULBEN           77
    AND OUR LAUGHTER OVER AND DONE! . . . . . . . .       643 SONG FAERIES          6
    MOCKING WITH PATIENT LAUGHTER ALL THE NIGHT . . .     657 ISLE STAT I 3        52
    FOR PEACE AND LAUGHTER HAVE BEEN SELDOM FRIENDS. . .  670 ISLE STAT II 3      103
    AGAIN THE WOODLAND LAUGHTER, AND THE CLEAR . . .      674 ISLE STAT II 3      221
    AND OUR LAUGHTER OVER AND DONE! . . . . . . . .       676 ISLE STAT II 3      253
    A TITAN, WITH LOUD LAUGHTER, . . . . . . . . . .      680 LOVE AND DEATH       11
    FROM ITS FIRST SIGHS AND LAUGHTER, BEFORE THE SLEEP,  754 SHADOW WATER A      161
    ON TEARS AND LAUGHTER! THEY HAVE LURED YOU HITHER . . 757 SHADOW WATER A      207
LAUGHTER-LIPPED
    LAUGHTER-LIPPED, BUT FOR HER BRAIN . . . . . . .      668 ISLE STAT II 3       58
LAUGHTER-LIT
    AND WHEN SHE MEETS OUR GAZE HER EYES ARE LAUGHTER-LIT, .  362 HER COURTESY       5
LAUNCH
    BUT, THE BIRD IN MY FINGERS, I MOUNTED, MINDFUL ONLY TO   54 OISIN 3       V  111
       LAUNCH
LAUREATE
    A MODEL FOR THE LAUREATE . . . . . . . . . . .        597 MODEL LAUREATE        T
LAUREL
    AMONG THE LEAVES OF THE LAUREL WALL, . . . . . . .      3 OISIN 1         V  7FF
    LIKE DRIFTS OF LAUREL LEAVES, IMMOVABLE AND BRIGHT . .  40 OISIN 2         V  166
    O MAY SHE LIVE LIKE SOME GREEN LAUREL . . . . . .     405 FOR DAUGHTER         47
    AND CUSTOM FOR THE SPREADING LAUREL TREE. . . . .     406 FOR DAUGHTER         80
    PROFFERING ITS SACRED LAUREL CROWNS, . . . . . . .    612 NEWS ORACLE          23
LAURELLED
    A MOMENT'S MEMORY TO THAT LAURELLED HEAD. . . . .     489 COOLE PARK 29        32
LAVELL
    O'SULLIVAN RUA TO MARY LAVELL . . . . . . . . .       155 FORGOT BEAUTY   V     T
    O'SULLIVAN THE RED TO MARY LAVELL. . . . . . . .      157 POET BELOVED    V     T
```

438

		PAGE	TITLE		LINE

LAVELL   (CONTINUED)
    TWO POEMS BY O'SULLIVAN THE RED CONCERNING MARY LAVELL.   157 POET BELOVED   V   T
LAVERY
    HAZEL LAVERY LIVING AND DYING, THAT TALE   . . . . . .   602 GALLERY REVIS   23
LAVISH
    BETWEEN THE LAVISH SHELTER OF A WOOD . . . .   108 CUCHULAIN SEA   V 38A
LAW
    BUT HERE THERE IS NOR LAW NOR RULE, ...   19 OISIN 1   282
    BUT, WARRIOR, HERE THERE IS NO LAW;   . . . .   19 OISIN 1   V   283
    WITH HEARTS THAT KNOW NOR LAW NOR RULE, ...   22 OISIN 1   339
    OUR LIVES HAVE KNOWN NO LAW NOR RULE: . . . .   22 OISIN 1   V   340
    MY WORD WAS LAW FROM ITH TO EMAIN.   . . . .   81 MAD KING GOLL   2
    IN LOGIC AND IN NATURAL LAW . . . .   288 TO WEALTHY MAN   27
    NOR LAW, NOR DUTY BADE ME FIGHT, ...   328 IRISH AIRMAN   9
    WHERE THOSE THAT HAVE OBEYED THE HOLY LAW   . . . . . .   356 BROKEN DREAMS   33
    A LAW INDIFFERENT TO BLAME OR PRAISE, ...   428 NINETEEN 19   10
    OR THOSE WHO NEED HIS BOUNTY OR HIS LAW, ...   462 HARUN RASHID   V 25A
    THE FLAMING CIRCLE OF THE OUTER LAW, ...   689 NETTLESHIP   13
    NOR LAW NOR PARLIAMENT TAKE HEED.   . . . .   791 REPRISALS   22
LAWN
    AND STILL I DREAM HE TREADS THE LAWN, ...   67 HAPPY SHEPHERD   51
    THE PEAHENS DANCE ON A SMOOTH LAWN, ...   77 INDIAN TO LOVE   3
    BROWN LOLLARD TREADS UPON THE LAWN, ...   98 FOXHUNTER   17
    HIS LOLLARD LEAD THEY ROUND THE LAWN, ...   98 FOXHUNTER   V   17
    BROWN DERMOT TREADS UPON THE LAWN, ...   98 FOXHUNTER   V   17
    AND ALIGHT AT THE COMELY TREES AND THE LAWN, ...   330 BONE OF A HARE   4
    AFAR FROM OUR LAWN AND OUR LEVEE, ...   706 FAIRY PEDANT   1
LAWNS
    WE PASSED BY WOODS, AND LAWNS OF CLOVER, ...   25 OISIN 1   377
    BY WOODS OF MOSS, BY LAWNS OF CLOVER, ...   25 OISIN 1   V   377
    BY LAKES AND MEADOW LANDS AND LAWNS AFAR, ...   32 OISIN 2   V 50F
    ON THE ISLAND LAWNS, THEIR FEET WHERE THE PALE FOAM GLEAMS.   203 WITHER BOUGHS   14
    SURELY AMONG A RICH MAN'S FLOWERING LAWNS, ...   417 ANCEST HOUSES   1
    O WHAT IF LEVELLED LAWNS AND GRAVELLED WAYS   . . . . .   418 ANCEST HOUSES   29
LAWS
    SOME GOD OR KING HAD MADE THE LAWS   . . . .   194 BAILE AILLINN   131
    YOU KEPT THE MUSES' STERNER LAWS, ...   273 GREY ROCK   59
    IT HAD SET DOWN AMONG ITS LAWS: . . . .   399 BREAK OF DAY   16
LAY
    AND THE WHITE BODY THAT LAY BY MINE;   . . . .   3 OISIN 1   10
    LAY 'NEATH US: OF ITS HOLLOW COOL   . . . .   17 OISIN 1   V   241
    I LAY, AS OVER SEA THE LIGHT HOOVES GLANCED   . . . . .   30 OISIN 2   19A
    TYING THE HORSE TO HIS VAST FOOT THAT LAY   . . . . . .   32 OISIN 2   46
    MOST DISTANT STRODE WE. ON THE FLOOR LAY SLIME, . . .   37 OISIN 2   V   113
    WE LAY ON SKINS OF OTTERS, AND DRANK WINE, ...   41 OISIN 2   188
    BREWED BY THE SEA-GODS, FROM HUGE CUPS THAT LAY . . .   41 OISIN 2   189
    BREWED OF THE SEA-GODS, FROM HUGE CUPS THAT LAY . . .   41 OISIN 2   V   189
    BREWED BY THE SEA GODS, FROM HUGE CUPS THAT LAY . . .   41 OISIN 2   V   189
    AN ISLE LAY LEVEL BEFORE US, WITH DRIPPING HAZEL AND OAK?   47 OISIN 3   10
    AN ISLE LAY LEVEL BEFORE US, DRIPPING WITH HAZEL AND OAK?   47 OISIN 3   V   10
    A VALLEY FLOWED DOWN FROM HIS HOOFS, AND THERE IN THE LONG   48 OISIN 3   26
        GRASS LAY,
    . . . HEAPED LOOSE WHERE THEY LAY.   . . . .   48 OISIN 3   V   28
    LAY LOOSE IN A PLACE OF SHADOW; WE DREW THE REINS BY HIS   50 OISIN 3   44
        SIDE.
    AND THE PEARL-PALE NIAMH LAY BY ME, ...   52 OISIN 3   74
    AND PEARL-PALE NEAVE LAY BY ME, HER BROW ON THE MIDST OF   52 OISIN 3   V   74
        MY BREAST;
    . . . THEY LAY 'NEATH THE SAND-SACK AT LENGTH   . . . .   60 OISIN 3   V   186
    AND SAW WHERE THIS OLD TYMPAN LAY   . . . .   85 MAD KING GOLL   55
    I LAY UPON MY BABY;   . . . .   95 MOLL MAGEE   17
    "LAY ME IN A CUSHIONED CHAIR;   . . . .   97 FOXHUNTER   1
    "NOW LAY ME IN A CUSHIONED CHAIR, ...   97 FOXHUNTER   V   1
    LAY HIDDEN IN THE SMALL SLATE-COLOURED THING!   . . . .   104 FERGUS DRUID   40
    LAY HIDDEN IN THE SMALL SLATE-COLOURED BAG! . . . . .   104 FERGUS DRUID   V   40
    WONDERING TO LAY HER IN THAT SOLITUDE, ...   123 DREAM OF DEATH   5
    OR UNDER GREEN SODS LAY.   . . . .   132 FR GILLIGAN   4
    FOR HALF HIS FLOCK LAY IN THEIR BEDS   . . . .   132 FR GILLIGAN   V   3
    AND LAY IN THE DARKNESS, GRUNTING, AND TURNING TO HIS REST.   153 CHANGE BELOVED   12
    I CRIED IN MY DREAM, O WOMEN, BID THE YOUNG MEN LAY . .   163 VALLEY LOVERS   5
    AND I CRIED IN MY DREAM "O WOMEN, BID THE YOUNG MEN LAY   163 VALLEY LOVERS   V   5
    AND I WOULD LAY MY HEAD ON YOUR BREAST! . . . .   175 BELOVED DEAD   4
    O WOULD, BELOVED, THAT YOU LAY   . . . .   176 BELOVED DEAD   11
    WHERE THE TIRED HORSE-BOYS LAY UPON THE RUSHES, . . .   180 QUEEN MAEVE   13
    A YEW-TREE WHERE HIS BODY LAY;   . . . .   197 BAILE AILLINN   188
    A YEW TREE WHERE HIS BODY LAY;   . . . .   197 BAILE AILLINN   V   188
    THE HONEY-PALE MOON LAY LOW ON THE SLEEPY HILL, . . .   203 WITHER BOUGHS   5
    O! LAY THE SHRILLY TRUMPET DOWN, ...   212 BLESS PSALTER   4
    EDAIN CAME OUT OF MIDHIR'S HILL, AND LAY   . . . . . .   219 HARP OF AENGUS   1
    YOU'VE NEVER KNOWN, I'D LAY A WAGER ON IT, ...   227 SHADOW WATER B   113
    THAT I MIGHT LAY IT ON YOUR HEAD AS A CROWN. . . . . .   246 SHADOW WATER B   511
    THE WEAK LAY HAND ON WHAT THE STRONG HAS DONE,   . . .   265 THESE CLOUDS   3
    AND LAY IT ALL UPON A HORSE"!   . . . .   296 THREE BEGGARS   35
    HELL MOUTH LAY OPEN NEAR THAT PLACE, ...   303 HOUR DAWN   25
    I LAY ABOUT ME WITH THE TAWS   . . . .   379 SAINT HUNCH   8
    THE WOMAN THAT BY ME LAY   . . . .   398 BREAK OF DAY   2
    BUT SHE THAT BESIDE ME LAY . . . .   399 BREAK OF DAY   21
    IT LAY FIVE HUNDRED YEARS. . . . .   421 MY TABLE   11
    AND LAY THE HEART UPON HER HAND . . . .   437 SONGS PLAY 1   4
    OUT OF DARK NIGHT WHERE LAY   . . . .   439 FRAGMENTS   9
    AND YET THERE BEAUTY LAY;   . . . .   455 HIS MEMORIES   12

439

LAY   (CONTINUED)

		PAGE	TITLE	LINE
THE FIRST OF ALL THE TRIBE LAY THERE		455	HIS MEMORIES	13
AND SHE LAY DOWN UPON HER BED AND SLEPT,		467	HARUN RASHID	146
"NAKED I LAY,		510	JANE JUDGMENT	11
I DREAMED AS IN MY BED I LAY,		519	HER DREAM	1
AND LAY DOWN THAT HEAD		534	CONSOLATION	4
AND SEEMED TO STAND ALTHOUGH IN BED I LAY.		535	CHOSEN	9
OF ALL THAT WITH ME LAY?		538	LAST CONFESS	2
ALONE AND ALONE NINE NIGHTS I LAY		551	SONGS REWRIT 1	13
NINE NIGHTS I LAY IN LONGING SORE		551	SONGS REWRIT 1 V	13
NINE NIGHTS I LAY IN AND IN LONGING SORE		551	SONGS REWRIT 1 V	13
BUT THERE I LAY AND I WHISTLED IN VAIN.		551	SONGS REWRIT 1 V	16
WHERE THE BALES AND THE BASKETS LAY		578	CRAZED GIRL	12
THAT BY THEIR BODIES LAY.		589	OLD WICKED MAN	44
HE NEVER LAY BEHIND FOUR WALLS		606	SONGS BURDEN 1	12
AND OUT AND LAY OUR LEADERSHIP		606	SONGS BURDEN 1	23
LAY IN THE COFFIN, STOPPED HIS BREATH AND DIED.		609	IN TARAS HALLS	20
THERE ALL THE GOLDEN CODGERS LAY,		611	NEWS ORACLE	1
LAY SIGHING LIKE THE REST.		612	NEWS ORACLE	12
LAST NIGHT I LAY ON THE MOUNTAIN,		628	JANE MOUNTAIN	11
I LAY STRETCHED OUT IN THE DIRT		628	JANE MOUNTAIN	21
THAT WHEREBY A HOUSE LAY WRECKED?		632	MAN AND ECHO	16
THE OTTERS DREAMING LAY. AYE!		677	ISLE STAT II 3	280
THE OTTERS DREAMING LAY. NASCHINA! AY!		677	ISLE STAT II 3 V	280
O BROTHER, LAY THY FLUTE UPON THY LIPS:		681	SEEKER	6
WHERE SHALL I LAY ME DOWN? THAT QUESTION IS		700	MOSADA 3	36
NAY HERE, I'LL LAY ME DOWN WHERE I CAN WATCH		700	MOSADA 3	39
"A LITTLE WILL I LAY MY WEARY HEAD,		712	FERENCZ RENYI	75
WHERE WORM THE REBELS, OR MY BULLETS LAY		713	FERENCZ RENYI	83
LAY DOWN THE BURDEN OF THY RACE,		736	SUMMER EVENING	14
EDAINE CAME OUT OF MIDHER'S HILL, AND LAY		762	SHADOW WATER A	296

LAYER

| AND DROP TWIGS LAYER UPON LAYER. | | 415 | TOWER | 168 |
| AND DROP TWIGS LAYER UPON LAYER. | | 415 | TOWER | 168 |

LAYS

| AND LAYS THEM IN A ROW. | | 89 | ISLE IN WATER | 6 |

LAZULI   SEE LAPIS-LAZULI

IN TOMBS OF GOLD AND LAPIS LAZULI		483	OIL AND BLOOD	1
LAPIS LAZULI		565	LAPIS LAZULI	T
ARE CARVED IN LAPIS LAZULI,		566	LAPIS LAZULI	38

LAZY

| WHEN THE LAZY THREAD HAS RUN-- | | 520 | HIS BARGAIN V | 10 |

LEA

| OUR ISLE AWAITS US, ON EACH LEA | | 77 | INDIAN TO LOVE V | 2 |

LEAD

THEY LEAD US BY LONG AND SHADOWY WAYS		16	OISIN 1 V	221
I LEAD ALONG THE WOODLAND DEER:		84	MAD KING GOLL	46
LEAD MY LOLLARD TO AND FRO,		97	FOXHUNTER	7
AND LEAD HIM SLOWLY TO AND FRO,		97	FOXHUNTER	7
AND LEAD HIM GENTLY IN A RING,		97	FOXHUNTER V	7
HIS LOLLARD LEAD THEY ROUND THE LAWN,		98	FOXHUNTER	17
AND LEAD US TO THE LIKE--IF THEY		387	ROBARTES DANCE	47
TO LEAD HER AWAY, DO NOT SAY		568	SWEET DANCER	9
LEAD THEM GENTLY ASTRAY:		568	SWEET DANCER	11
LEAD ME, I PRAY THEE, TO THE STATUED PLACE!		667	ISLE STAT II 3	37
WE WILL LEAD YOU HAND IN HAND		726	LOVERS QUARREL	2
LEAD THEY ONE WITH FOOLISH CARE,		727	LOVERS QUARREL	29
THEY WILL LEAD HER HOME AGAIN		727	LOVERS QUARREL	49
TO LEAD US TO THE STREAMS WHERE THE WORLD ENDS.		765	SHADOW WATER A	369

LEADER

IF MICHAEL, LEADER OF GOD'S HOST		112	ROSE OF PEACE	1
IF MICHAEL, LEADER OF GOD'S HOSTS		112	ROSE OF PEACE V	1
YOU'LL BE AS GOOD A LEADER. BE OF YOUR TROOP!		225	SHADOW WATER B V	73
BLIND AND LEADER OF THE BLIND		397	POLIT PRISONER	11
ANOTHER LEADER, AND TURN HOME AGAIN.		748	SHADOW WATER A	16
AND WHOM WILL YOU MAKE LEADER? WHO WILL MAKE		748	SHADOW WATER A	20
FIRST I GREET MACCARTAN, REVOLUTIONARY LEADER.		790	DEDICATION	1

LEADERS

| THE LEADERS OF THE CROWD | | 398 | LEADERS CROWD | T |

LEADERSHIP

| AND OUT AND LAY OUR LEADERSHIP | | 606 | SONGS BURDEN 1 | 23 |

LEADING

FOR LEADING AGED HOUNDS AND YOUNG		98	FOXHUNTER	23
AND YET I CANNOT THINK THEY'RE LEADING ME		230	SHADOW WATER B	191
IT'S CERTAIN THEY ARE LEADING YOU TO DEATH.		231	SHADOW WATER B	201
WITH THAT SONG LEADING WHERE HARMONIC WOODS		657	ISLE STAT I 3	43

LEADS

| DEAR HEART, THERE IS A SECRET WAY THAT LEADS | | 702 | MOSADA 3 | 75 |

LEAF   SEE GRASS-LEAF

CEASED ON OUR HANDS AND OUR FACES, ON HAZEL AND OAK LEAF, THE LIGHT,		48	OISIN 3	23
WHEN A GLOW-WORM WAS GREEN ON A GRASS LEAF,		53	OISIN 3 V	99
"I WOULD DIE LIKE A SMALL WITHERED LEAF IN THE AUTUMN,		56	OISIN 3	131
BY A BROAD WATER-LILY LEAF:		195	BAILE AILLINN	146
WANDERED BETWEEN THE BLUE AND THE GREEN LEAF		278	TWO KINGS	41
CAN NEVER TEAR THE LINNET FROM THE LEAF.		405	FOR DAUGHTER	56
ARE YOU THE LEAF, THE BLOSSOM OR THE BOLE?		446	SCHOOL CHILDR	62
NOW BATHING LILY LEAF AND FISH'S SCALE,		464	HARUN RASHID	65
NOW BATHING LILY LEAF AND FISHES' SCALE,		464	HARUN RASHID V	65
THE AVENGING LEAF THOSE FIELDS RAISED UP AGAINST IT.		487	SEVEN SAGES	20

LEAF   (CONTINUED)

	PAGE	TITLE	LINE
THAT STARING FURY AND THE BLIND LUSH LEAF	500	VACILLATION	17
ALL KNOW THEIR TALE, ALL KNOW WHAT LEAF AND TWIG,	555	RIBH AT TOMB	7
AS A LEAF THAT IS OLD, AND WITHERED, AND COLD,	643	SONG FAERIES	3
AS A LEAF THAT IS OLD, AND WITHERED, AND COLD,	644	SONG FAERIES	15
THE AIR IS STILL ABOVE, AND STILL EACH LEAF,	662	ISLE STAT II 2	7
AS A LEAF THAT IS OLD, AND WITHERED, AND COLD,	676	ISLE STAT II 3	250
AS A LEAF THAT IS OLD, AND WITHERED, AND COLD,	676	ISLE STAT II 3	262
AND ALL WAS DIMNESS, TILL A DYING LEAF	690	MOSADA 1	20
YONDER A LEAF	700	MOSADA 3	41
WHERE THE SHAKING LEAF WITH THE BEAM WAS PLAYING,	728	PRIEST FAIRY	2

LEAFAGE

AND CHAPLET THEIR CALM BROWS WITH LEAFAGE DIM,	127	DREAM OF FAERY V	32
AND CHAPLET THEIR CALM BROWS WITH LEAFAGE COOL:	127	DREAM OF FAERY V	32
CLOUDY LEAFAGE OF THE SKY,	501	VACILLATION	46

LEAF-CROWNED

| AND NO ONE ANY LEAF-CROWNED DANCER MISS | 128 | DREAM OF FAERY V | 46 |

LEAF-HID

| IT DOWN IN A LEAF-HID, HOLLOW PLACE | 17 | OISIN 1 | 242 |

LEAFLESS

A FIR-TREE ROARING IN ITS LEAFLESS TOP:	40	OISIN 2	177
A FIR TREE ROARING IN ITS LEAFLESS TOP,	40	OISIN 2 V	177
CRIES OUT THE LEAFLESS TREE,	780	WELL AND TREE	10

LEAF-SOWN

| ON THE LEAF-SOWN, NEW-MOWN, SMOOTH | 568 | SWEET DANCER | 2 |
| ON THE LEAF-SOWN, NEW MOWN, SMOOTH | 568 | SWEET DANCER V | 2 |

LEAFY

IN HIS OWN LEAFY FOREST HOUSE,	2	OISIN 1 V	7L
IN HIS OWN LEAFY FOREST HOUSE	4	OISIN 1	37
WE TIED THE HORSE IN A LEAFY CLUMP,	14	OISIN 1	194
THERE LIES A LEAFY ISLAND	86	STOLEN CHILD	3
HIS EVENING FIRE AMID THE LEAFY SHADE.	109	CUCHULAIN SEA	48
AFTER SHORT FIGHTING IN THE LEAFY SHADE,	109	CUCHULAIN SEA	57
AND AS IT FALLS AWAKENS LEAFY TUNES:--	127	DREAM OF FAERY V	23
THE SHAKING OF ITS LEAFY HEAD	134	TWO TREES	9
IN THOSE GREAT IGNORANT LEAFY WAYS:	135	TWO TREES	16
WHO AMID LEAFY LIGHTS AND SHADES	193	BAILE AILLINN	103
AND AMID LEAFY LIGHT HE CRIED,	193	BAILE AILLINN V	113
I KNOW OF THE LEAFY PATHS THAT THE WITCHES TAKE	203	WITHER BOUGHS	9
I KNOW OF THE LEAFY PATH THAT THE WITCHES TAKE,	203	WITHER BOUGHS V	9
POOR RACE OF LEAFY ARCADY, YOUR LOVE	650	ISLE STAT I 1	145
JOY'S BROTHER, FEAR, LURKS IN EACH LEAFY WAY.	651	ISLE STAT I 1	156
EVE-SOOTHED IN SOME FAR LEAFY REST,	686	LIFE	10
OF A WIDE WOOD'S LEAFY LEISURE,	731	STREET DANCERS	11

LEAGUES

| THOUSANDS OF LEAGUES OVERSEA, | 341 | SHEP GOATHERD | 63 |

LEAN

IN THE FENIANS' DWELLINGS OF WATTLE LEAN ON THE CHESSBOARDS AND PLAY,	55	OISIN 3	115
I CLIMB TO THE TOWER-TOP AND LEAN UPON BROKEN STONE,	425	PHANTOM HATRED	1
I CLIMB TO THE TOWER TOP AND LEAN UPON BROKEN STONE,	425	PHANTOM HATRED V	1
OR EYES THAT RAGE HAS BRIGHTENED, ARMS IT HAS MADE LEAN,	427	PHANTOM HATRED	27
OF EYES THAT RAGE HAS BRIGHTENED, ARMS IT HAS MADE LEAN,	427	PHANTOM HATRED V	27
NOW I AM IN THE PUBLIC-HOUSE AND LEAN UPON THE WALL,	593	PILGRIM	21
NOW I AM IN THE TAVERN AND LEAN AGAINST THE WALL,	593	PILGRIM V	21
NOW I AM IN THE PUBLIC HOUSE AND LEAN UPON THE WALL,	593	PILGRIM V	21
"WATCHER, WHEREFORE HAVE YE CALLED US?" EYES GO AFTER HIS LEAN HAND,	718	PHANTOM SHIP	10
AND LEAN YOUR LIPS DEVOUTLY TO THIS HARP,	762	SHADOW WATER A	287

LEANED

| THAT GOD HAD LEANED HIS HANDS OUT OF THE SKY, | 128 | DREAM OF FAERY V | 43 |

LEANING

LEANING DOWN FROM THE GEM-STUDDED SADDLE,	60	OISIN 3	187
LEANING FORTH FROM THE GEM-STUDDED SADDLE,	60	OISIN 3 V	187
LEANING SOFTLY OUT	88	STOLEN CHILD	35
AND ON MY LEANING SHOULDER SHE LAID HER SNOW-WHITE HAND.	90	SALLEY GARDENS	6
HE KNELT, AND LEANING ON THE CHAIR	132	FR GILLIGAN	13
LEANING OR STANDING OR WALKING	356	BROKEN DREAMS	23
A HOARY HUNTER LEANING ON HIS BOW,	672	ISLE STAT II 3	157
THE MAYOR CAME, LEANING HIS DEAF EAR--	725	LEGEND	13

LEANNESS

| FOR REMEMBRANCE, LIFTING HER LEANNESS, | 57 | OISIN 3 | 152 |

LEANS

OF HOW GOD LEANS HIS HANDS OUT OF THE SKY,	128	DREAM OF FAERY V	43
ONE LEANS AND MUTTERS BY THE WALL--	212	BLESS PSALTER	10
WHO LEANS UPON A STICK,	525	DANCING DAYS	20
LEANS ON HIS ELBOWS, GAZING AT THE SEA.	752	SHADOW WATER A	127

LEANT

WHEN THE EARLIEST DEW-WASHED STAR FROM EVE HATH LEANT,	32	OISIN 2 V	54
THAT GOD HAD LEANT HIS HANDS OUT OF THE SKY,	128	DREAM OF FAERY V	43
HEAD UPON SHOULDER LEANT	319	DOLLS	18
MAN-PICKER NIAMH LEANT AND SIGHED	611	NEWS ORACLE	5
CAME AND WERE GONE. HE LEANT UPON A TREE	634	CUCHULAIN COMF	5

LEAP

LEAP IN THE MEADOW. ON THE MISTY STAIRS	44	OISIN 2 V	229
THE HEART IN ME LONGING TO LEAP LIKE A GRASSHOPPER INTO HER HEART:	60	OISIN 3	182
TO AND FRO WE LEAP	87	STOLEN CHILD	20
YOU CANNOT LEAP OUT OF THE GOLDEN NET.	238	SHADOW WATER B	360
WHERE MY GOATS BROWSE ON THE SCARCE GRASS OR LEAP	339	SHEP GOATHERD	8
TO DRUM WITH HER HEEL AND TO LEAP?	381	SONGS FOOL 2	9

LEAP   (CONTINUED)
```
    THAT LOFTY WHITE STAG, LEAP . . . . . . . . . .   399  BREAK OF DAY         24
    THE FOUNTAIN LEAP, AND AT DAWN . . . . . . . . .  414  TOWER               124
    THE HARE LEAP TO THE WOOD, . . . . . . . . . . .  453  DEATH OF HARE         2
    SHALL LEAP INTO THE LIGHT LOST . . . . . . . . .  511  JANE AND JACK        11
    ROE COULD RUN OR DOE COULD LEAP . . . . . . . .   522  LULLABY              10
    ROE COULD LEAP OR DOE COULD RUN! . . . . . . . .  522  LULLABY              12
    STAG COULD RUN AND ROE LEAP . . . . . . . . . .   522  LULLABY          V   10
    STAG COULD LEAP AND ROE COULD RUN. . . . . . . .  522  LULLABY          V   12
    ALL THAT COULD RUN OR LEAP OR SWIM . . . . . . .  528  DANCER CRUACH         6
    ALL THAT RUN OR LEAP OR SWIM . . . . . . . . . .  528  DANCER CRUACH    V    6
    OENONE SAW THE FIRES OF TROIA LEAP, . . . . . .   645  ISLE STAT I 1        17
LEAPED
    THE HARE LEAPED IN THE GRASS.  YOUNG NIAMH CAME . . . .  44  OISIN 2      V  229
    AND HOW YOU HAVE LEAPED TIMES OUT OF MIND . . . .  146  FISH                 5
    NOR ON OLYMPUS LEAPED FROM CLOUD TO CLOUD, . . .   260  FASC DIFFICULT       6
    NOR ON AN OLYMPUS LEAPED FROM CLOUD TO CLOUD, . .  260  FASC DIFFICULT   V   6
    OLD MERCHANT SKIPPER THAT LEAPED OVERBOARD . . .   270  PARDON FATHERS      13
    YOU MERCHANT SKIPPER THAT LEAPED OVERBOARD . . .   270  PARDON FATHERS   V  13
    AND MERCHANT SKIPPER THAT LEAPED OVERBOARD . . .   270  PARDON FATHERS   V  13
    AT MOONEEN HE HAD LEAPED A PLACE . . . . . . . .   326  ROBERT GREGORY      60
    AND YET, BECAUSE MY HEART LEAPED AT HER WORDS, . . 353  PEOPLE              35
    THE SWAN HAS LEAPED INTO THE DESOLATE HEAVEN! . .  431  NINETEEN 19         79
    LEAPED UP INTO THE AIR. . . . . . . . . . . . .    741  EARL PAUL           36
LEAPING
    OF DANCERS LEAPING IN THE AIR! . . . . . . . . .    18  OISIN 1            254
    LEAPING TO SHAKE A COBWEB FROM THE RAFTER! . . .   130  BOOK STORIES     V  19
    AND THE WAVES ARE LEAPING WHITE, . . . . . . . .   646  ISLE STAT I 1       27
    AND, LEAPING TO THEIR FEET, FAR ECHOES CRIED, . .  659  ISLE STAT II 1      13
LEAPS
    LEAPS UPWARD, AS IF ALL THE STREAMS O' THE WORLD . . .  249  SHADOW WATER B  560
    LOVE LEAPS UPON ITS COURSE. . . . . . . . . . .    518  HIS CONFIDENCE      12
    LEAPS AND TIME'S OLD LANTHORN DIMS. . . . . . . .  777  SONG DEIRDRE 2       5
LEAPT
    WHEN ONE HAS LEAPT ON BOARD.  NO, FOR I HAVE HOPE . . .  751  SHADOW WATER A  106
LEAR
    THERE STRUTS HAMLET, THERE IS LEAR, . . . . . .    565  LAPIS LAZULI        10
    THEY KNOW THAT HAMLET AND LEAR ARE GAY! . . . .    565  LAPIS LAZULI        16
    THOUGH HAMLET RAMBLES AND LEAR RAGES, . . . . .    566  LAPIS LAZULI        21
    TILL I AM TIMON AND LEAR . . . . . . . . . . . .   576  ACRE OF GRASS       15
LEARN
    AND LEARN TO CHAUNT A TONGUE MEN DO NOT KNOW. . .  101  ROSE UPON ROOD      21
    AND LEARN TO CHANT A TONGUE MEN DO NOT KNOW. . .   101  ROSE UPON ROOD   V  21
    BUT LEARN THE DREAMING WISDOM THAT IS YOURS. . .   103  FERGUS DRUID        22
    AND LEARN TO PRAY WHEN YOU PRAY, . . . . . . . .   167  BLESSED              8
    AND LEARN THE PRAYERS THAT YOU SAY. . . . . . . .  167  BLESSED          V   8
    WE'LL LEARN THAT SLEEPING IS NOT DEATH, . . . .    266  GALWAY RACES        11
    THAT HE MIGHT LEARN THE SHEPHERDS' WILL. . . . .   288  TO WEALTHY MAN      19
    THE SECOND! "I SHALL LEARN A TRADE"! . . . . . .   296  THREE BEGGARS       32
    AND LEARN THAT THE BEST THING IS . . . . . . . .   330  BONE OF A HARE       6
    OF ALL 'TWAS PAIN OR JOY TO LEARN, . . . . . . .   342  SHEP GOATHERD       98
    MAYBE THE MOON MAY LEARN, . . . . . . . . . . .    378  CAT AND MOON        14
    LEARN THAT WE WERE CRACK-PATED WHEN WE DREAMED. .  431  NINETEEN 19         88
    THE CHILDREN LEARN TO CIPHER AND TO SING, . . .    443  SCHOOL CHILDR        3
    O BUT HER HEART WOULD BREAK TO LEARN MY THOUGHTS ARE FAR  450  OWEN AHERNE     20
      AWAY."
    BOOK II  WHAT THE CALIPH REFUSED TO LEARN . . .    460  HARUN RASHID     V   T
    THEN MY DELIVERED SOUL HERSELF SHALL LEARN . . .   558  RIBH CHRISTIAN      13
    SOUL MUST LEARN A LOVE THAT IS . . . . . . . . .   573  LADYS 2ND SONG      15
    CHILDLESS, I THOUGHT. "MY CHILDREN MAY LEARN HERE . . .  603  GALLERY REVIS  V  36
    I KNOW WHAT DEVIL'S TRADE THEY LEARN . . . . . .   607  SONGS BURDEN 2      12
    IRISH POETS, LEARN YOUR TRADE, . . . . . . . . .   639  BEN BULBEN          68
LEARN'D
    KIND EYES SHOULD BE MORE LEARN'D? . . . . . . .    312  TWO YEAR LATER       2
LEARNED
    THAT THEY WOULD SIGH AND QUOTE WITH LEARNED LOOKS . . .  205  ADAMS CURSE     25
    POETS WITH WHOM I LEARNED MY TRADE, . . . . . .    270  GREY ROCK            1
    WHERE WIT AND BEAUTY LEARNED THEIR TRADE . . . .   288  TO WEALTHY MAN      16
    THAT MIGHT THE LEARNED PLEASE, . . . . . . . . .   333  SOLOMON SHEBA       12
    OLD, LEARNED, RESPECTABLE BALD HEADS . . . . . .   337  SCHOLARS             2
    ARE LEARNED IN WAITING.  YOU CANNOT BUT HAVE SEEN . . .  340  SHEP GOATHERD   48
    --PEDANT IN PASSION, LEARNED IN OLD COURTESIES, .  363  DOLLS FACES          4
    BOOK I  WHAT THE CALIPH PARTLY LEARNED . . . . .   372  PHASES OF MOON   V   T
    REFORMER, MERCHANT, STATESMAN, LEARNED MAN, . .    376  PHASES OF MOON      98
    LEARNED LIKE A MAN?  PAUL VERONESE . . . . . . .   386  ROBARTES DANCE      26
    IT HAD NOT LEARNED ITS LESSON. . . . . . . . . .   389  IMAGE PAST          14
    IN COURTESY I'D HAVE HER CHIEFLY LEARNED! . . .    404  FOR DAUGHTER        33
    WITH LEARNED ITALIAN THINGS . . . . . . . . . .    415  TOWER              158
    IN A LEARNED SCHOOL . . . . . . . . . . . . . .    416  TOWER              183
    OUR LEARNED MEN HAVE URGED . . . . . . . . . . .   421  MY TABLE            15
    NOW THE GOOD CALIPH'S LEARNED TREASURER, . . . .   461  HARUN RASHID         3
    THE PARCHMENT WILL DISCLOSE TO SOME LEARNED MAN .  461  HARUN RASHID        20
    THOUGH BUT A FEW LEARNED MEN SHALL LOOK WITHIN, .  461  HARUN RASHID     V  18A
    ON OLD DRY WRITING IN A LEARNED TONGUE, . . . .    466  HARUN RASHID       123
    SHE SEEMED THE LEARNED MAN AND I THE CHILD! . .    467  HARUN RASHID       137
    BY SOME LEARNED INDIAN . . . . . . . . . . . . .   472  ALL SOUL NIGHT      53
    LEARNED IN BODILY LOWLINESS . . . . . . . . . .    513  JANE TALK BISH      11
    WHERE--WROTE A LEARNED ASTROLOGER-- . . . . . .    535  CHOSEN              17
    ALL THOSE LEARNED HISTORIANS, . . . . . . . . .    584  ORAHILLY             5
    AND COME WITH LEARNED LOVERS OR WITH WHAT MEN YOU MAY, . . 593  PILGRIM      23
    AND COME WITH LEARNED LOVERS OR WITH WHAT MAN YOU MAY, . . 593  PILGRIM    V  23
```

LEARNED   (CONTINUED)
   MALACHI STILT-JACK AM I, WHATEVER I LEARNED HAS RUN WILD,   623 HIGH TALK   9
   OH, LEARNED IS EACH MONK'S-HOOD'S MIND, ... 655 ISLE STAT I 3   8
   SIR PAGE, ALMINTOR'S FRIEND, AND THEREFORE LEARNED . . . 660 ISLE STAT II 1   38
   HE WAS A MAN MOST LEARNED AND MOST MILD, ... 692 MOSADA 1   51
LEARNING
   NO LEARNING FROM THE STARRY MEN, ... 66 HAPPY SHEPHERD   28
   THAT LOVED HIS LEARNING BETTER THAN MANKIND, ... 324 ROBERT GREGORY   18
   TILL ALL HIS GREEK AND LATIN LEARNING SEEMED . . . . 324 ROBERT GREGORY   21
   DARE MATCH IN LEARNING WITH US TWO, ... 333 SOLOMON SHEBA   21
   FOR LEARNING AND DEFENCE. . . . . 380 SONGS FOOL 1   5
   HAS A LEARNING IN HIS EYE . . . . 381 SONG OF FOOL   3
   PASS BOOKS OF LEARNING FROM BYZANTIUM . . . . . 461 HARUN RASHID   9
LEARNS
   AND LEARNS AT LAST THAT IT IS SELF-DELIGHTING, ... 405 FOR DAUGHTER   67
LEARNT
   NOW I HAVE LEARNT TO BE PROUD . . . . 349 HAWK   9
   HE HAD LEARNT FROM PATER, AND TO ROUND HIS TALE . . 373 PHASES OF MOON   27
   THAT IS HOW HE LEARNT SO WELL . . . . . . 382 SONG OF FOOL   11
   THE LOT OF LOVE IS CHOSEN. I LEARNT THAT MUCH . . . 534 CHOSEN   1
LEAST
   WHERE CARE CANNOT TROUBLE THE LEAST OF OUR DAYS, . . . 27 OISIN 1   409
   WILL SCATTER IN RUIN THE LEAST OF OUR DAYS, ... 27 OISIN 1   V 419B
   THE LEAST OF DOORS: BEYOND ON A DIM PLAIN, ... 39 OISIN 2   155
   THE LEAST OF DOORS: BEYOND THE DOOR A PLAIN, ... 39 OISIN 2   V 155
   HAD PITY ON THE LEAST OF THINGS . . . . . . 134 FR GILLIGAN   47
   DO MEN WHO LEAST DESIRE GET MOST, ... 295 THREE BEGGARS   13
   THAT I HAVE HANDLED LEAST, LEAST LOOKED UPON. . . . 367 EGO DOMINUS   9
   THAT I HAVE HANDLED LEAST, LEAST LOOKED UPON. . . . 367 EGO DOMINUS   9
   FOR CERTAIN MINUTES AT THE LEAST . . . . . . 399 DEMON BEAST   1
   A NUN AT LEAST HAS ALL MEN'S REVERENCE . . . . 448 HERO GIRL FOOL   12
   FOR THEY AT LEAST HAVE ALL MEN'S REVERENCE . . . . 448 HERO GIRL FOOL V   12
   CAME TO THE LEAST CONSIDERED OF HIS COURTIERS: . . 462 HARUN RASHID   42
   COXCOMB WAS THE LEAST HE SAID: . . . . . 508 JANE BISHOP   6
   THERE STOOD A MAN, OF MEN THE LEAST-- . . . . 729 PRIEST FAIRY   24
   WHO IS SIX FEET HIGH IN HIS SOCKS AT LEAST? . . . . 729 PRIEST FAIRY   28
LEATHER
   WITH THONGS OF LEATHER." AS SHE SPAKE IT WAS: . . . 106 CUCHULAIN SEA V 17B
LEATHER-COATED
   AND LEATHER-COATED MEN WITH SLINGS . . . . 193 BAILE AILLINN V 111
LEATHERN
   AND CAPTIVES BOUND WITH LEATHERN THONGS . . . . . 7 OISIN 1   77
   MY CAPTIVES, BOUND IN LEATHERN THONGS, ... 8 OISIN 1   V 78
LEAVE
   AND THAT I WOULD LEAVE THE IMMORTALS, ... 54 OISIN 3   108
   I WOULD LEAVE NO SAINT'S HEAD ON HIS BODY . . . . 58 OISIN 3   160
   "NOW LEAVE THE CHAIR DOWN ON THE GRASS, . . . 97 FOXHUNTER   V   9
   "NOW LEAVE THE CHAIR UPON THE GRASS, ... 97 FOXHUNTER   V   9
   COME NEAR, COME NEAR, COME NEAR--AH, LEAVE ME STILL . . 101 ROSE UPON ROOD   13
   LEAVE THE BODY'S COLOURED PRIDE . . . . . . 124 CATHLEEN PARA   2
   THAT IF WE HOLD THAT FLIGHT THEY'LL LEAVE THE PLACE, . . 265 ABBEY THEATRE   3
   LEAVE PAUDEENS TO THEIR PITCH AND TOSS: . . . . 288 TO WEALTHY MAN V   31
   AND LEAVE NO SMOKING WICK BEHIND, ... 306 HOUR DAWN   97
   OR LEAVE THEM HAPPIER THAN BEFORE. . . . . . 328 IRISH AIRMAN   8
   BUT PUT NO NAME AND LEAVE THEM AT HER DOOR. . . . 343 SHEP GOATHERD   116
   YOUR BEAUTY CAN BUT LEAVE AMONG US . . . . . 356 BROKEN DREAMS   14
   PADDLE AND ARE PERFECT. LEAVE UNCHANGED . . . 357 BROKEN DREAMS   34
   "COME IN AND LEAVE THE PLAY." . . . . . . 364 END OF DAY   8
   LUXURIANT SONG. WHY SHOULD YOU LEAVE THE LAMP . . 370 EGO DOMINUS   62
   NEVER TO LEAVE THAT VALLEY HIS FATHERS CALLED THEIR HOME. 391 UNDER SATURN   16
   GO THEREFORE: BUT LEAVE HANRAHAN, ... 413 TOWER   103
   I LEAVE BOTH FAITH AND PRIDE . . . . . . 416 TOWER   173
   AND LEAVE A WOMAN AND A MAN BEHIND . . . . . 422 MY DESCENDANTS   3
   TO LEAVE A WOMAN AND A MAN BEHIND . . . . . 422 MY DESCENDANTS V   3
   CAN LEAVE THE MOTHER, MURDERED AT HER DOOR, . . . 429 NINETEEN 19   27
   NO HONOUR LEAVE ITS MIGHTY MONUMENT, ... 429 NINETEEN 19   38
   TO LEAVE SOME MONUMENT BEHIND, ... 432 NINETEEN 19   96
   THEY'D SOONER LEAVE THEIR COSSETING . . . . . 455 HIS MEMORIES   9
   FOR SHOULD YOU LEAVE MY LETTER THERE, A BOY'S . . . 461 HARUN RASHID   13
   AND ALL COMPLEXITIES OF FURY LEAVE, ... 498 BYZANTIUM   29
   SEEK OUT REALITY, LEAVE THINGS THAT SEEM. . . . 502 VACILLATION   72
   THE MORE I LEAVE THE DOOR UNLATCHED . . . . . 511 JANE AND JACK   3
   I COULD BUT LEAVE HIM TO HIS FATE: . . . . . 514 JANE GROWN OLD   11
   LEAVE NOTHING BUT THE NOTHINGS THAT BELONG . . . 542 PARN FUNERAL 1   29
   WHAT IF I BADE YOU LEAVE . . . . 600 THOSE IMAGES   1
   TO PASS AND LEAVE THEM THERE . . . . . . 680 LOVE AND DEATH   1
   THERE IS NO LEAVE TAKING. I GO NO MORE. . . . . 702 MOSADA 3   V 100
   AH: CRUEL ONES, LEAVE ME ALONE NOW . . . . . 707 FAIRY PEDANT   13
   AH: CRUEL ONES, LEAVE ME ALONE. . . . . . 707 FAIRY PEDANT   V   13
   AH: LEAVE ME, I PRAY YOU AND BEG. . . . . . 708 FAIRY PEDANT   22
   OR LEAVE SOME SERVICE ALL UNDONE, ... 743 DANAAN QUICK   21
   UPON CLEAR NIGHTS THEY LEAVE THE UPPER AIR . . . . 750 SHADOW WATER A   87
   AND LEAVE HER DREAMING. WHEN I LOOKED ON HER, . . 761 SHADOW WATER A V   258
   BUT NEVER, NEVER DANGLING LEAVE THE LIVER AND THE LIGHTS. 790 HEART SLEEVE   2
LEAVED   SEE GREY-LEAVED
LEAVES   SEE BEECH-LEAVES DOCK-LEAVES
   AMONG THE LEAVES OF THE LAUREL WALL, ... 3 OISIN 1   V 7FF
   FALL THE LEAVES OF OTHER ROSES, ... 21 OISIN 1   311
   SHALL FALL THE LEAVES OF DAMASK ROSES. . . . . 21 OISIN 1   315
   A JUBILANT LIFE AMONG THE LEAVES, RETURN, ... 35 OISIN 2   V 89A
   LIKE DRIFTS OF LEAVES, IMMOVABLE AND BRIGHT, . . . 40 OISIN 2   166

443

	PAGE	TITLE		LINE

LEAVES   (CONTINUED)
    LIKE DRIFTS OF LAUREL LEAVES, IMMOVABLE AND BRIGHT . . .   40 OISIN 2 V 166
    . . . AND THE LEAVES OF THE MURAL GLEN, ...   49 OISIN 3   35
    COULD FONDLE THE LEAVES WITH HIS FINGERS, ...   49 OISIN 3   38
    SQUARE LEAVES OF THE IVY MOVED OVER US, BINDING US DOWN   52 OISIN 3   76
        TO OUR REST.
    THE FLIES BELOW THE LEAVES, AND THE YOUNG MICE . . . .   75 ANASHU VIJAYA   87
    ONE WITH THE LEAVES, ONE WITH THE DOVE . . . .   78 INDIAN TO LOVE V 16
    THE FALLING OF THE LEAVES . . . .   79 FALLING LEAVES   T
    FALLING OF THE LEAVES . . . .   79 FALLING LEAVES V   T
    AUTUMN IS OVER THE LONG LEAVES THAT LOVE US, ...   79 FALLING LEAVES   1
    YELLOW THE LEAVES OF THE ROWAN ABOVE US, ...   79 FALLING LEAVES   3
    AND YELLOW THE WET WILD-STRAWBERRY LEAVES. . . . . . .   79 FALLING LEAVES   4
    PENSIVE THEY PACED ALONG THE FADED LEAVES, ...   80 EPHEMERA   10
    THE WOODS WERE ROUND THEM, AND THE YELLOW LEAVES . . .   80 EPHEMERA   13
    TURNING, HE SAW THAT SHE HAD THRUST DEAD LEAVES . . .   80 EPHEMERA   18
    THEY WILL NOT HUSH, THE LEAVES A-FLUTTER ROUND ME, . .   82 MAD KING GOLL   12
    . . . THE BEECH LEAVES OLD. . . . .   82 MAD KING GOLL   12
    (THEY WILL NOT HUSH, THE LEAVES THAT ROUND ME FLUTTER--   82 MAD KING GOLL V REF
    . . .
    THEY WILL NOT HUSH, THE LEAVES A-FLUTTER ROUND ME, . .   83 MAD KING GOLL   24
    . . . THE BEECH LEAVES OLD. . . . .   83 MAD KING GOLL   24
    THEY WILL NOT HUSH, THE LEAVES A-FLUTTER ROUND ME, . .   84 MAD KING GOLL   36
    . . . THE BEECH LEAVES OLD. . . . .   84 MAD KING GOLL   36
    THEY WILL NOT HUSH, THE LEAVES A-FLUTTER ROUND ME, . .   84 MAD KING GOLL   48
    . . . THE BEECH LEAVES OLD. . . . .   84 MAD KING GOLL   48
    THEY WILL NOT HUSH, THE LEAVES A-FLUTTER ROUND ME, . .   85 MAD KING GOLL   60
    . . . THE BEECH LEAVES OLD. . . . .   85 MAD KING GOLL   60
    --FROM POOLS AND ROTTING LEAVES--ME SING . . . .   85 MAD KING GOLL V 63
    THEY WILL NOT HUSH, THE LEAVES A-FLUTTER ROUND ME, . .   86 MAD KING GOLL   72
    . . . THE BEECH LEAVES OLD. . . . .   86 MAD KING GOLL   72
    SHE BID ME TAKE LOVE EASY, AS THE LEAVES GROW ON THE TREE;   90 SALLEY GARDENS   3
    SHE BID ME TAKE LOVE EASY, AS THE LEAVES GROW ON THE TREES;   90 SALLEY GARDENS V 3
    AND ALL THAT FAMOUS HARMONY OF LEAVES, ... 120 SORROW OF LOVE   3
    AND ALL THAT LAMENTATION OF THE LEAVES, ... 120 SORROW OF LOVE   11
    AND THE LOUD SONG OF THE EVER-SINGING LEAVES . . . . . 120 SORROW OF LOVE V 3
    AND THE LOUD CHANTING OF THE UNQUIET LEAVES, ... 120 SORROW OF LOVE V 11
    AND THE LOUD CHAUNTING OF THE UNQUIET LEAVES, ... 120 SORROW OF LOVE V 11
    AND LEAVES SHOOK IN THE WIND; . . . . 133 FR GILLIGAN   18
    BROKEN BOUGHS AND BLACKENED LEAVES. . . . . 135 TWO TREES   28
    WITH BROKEN BOUGHS AND BLACKENED LEAVES . . . . 135 TWO TREES V 26
    THE WINDS AWAKEN, THE LEAVES WHIRL ROUND, ... 140 HOSTING SIDHE   6
    "THAT DROWSILY DROPS FAINT LEAVES ON HIM . . . . 168 BLESSED   37
    "THE ROSE THAT MUST DROP, OUT OF SWEET LEAVES, ... 168 BLESSED V 37
    MEN HAVE NAMED BEAUTY. THY GREAT LEAVES ENFOLD . . . . 169 SECRET ROSE   7
    MEN HAVE NAMED BEAUTY. YOUR HEAVY LEAVES ENFOLD . . . 169 SECRET ROSE V 7
    MEN HAVE NAMED BEAUTY. YOUR GREAT LEAVES ENFOLD . . . 169 SECRET ROSE V 7
    AMONG MY LEAVES IN TIMES OUT OF MIND; . . . . 177 PAST GREATNESS   5
    SHINING ON WATER AND FALLEN AMONG LEAVES, ... 218 WOODS OF COOLE   38
    O FLOWER OF THE BRANCH, O BIRD AMONG THE LEAVES, . . . 251 SHADOW WATER B 608
    THOUGH LEAVES ARE MANY, THE ROOT IS ONE; . . . . 261 COMING WISDOM   1
    I SWAYED MY LEAVES AND FLOWERS IN THE SUN; . . . . . . 261 COMING WISDOM   3
    BETWEEN THE PALE GREEN LIGHT OF THE BEECH LEAVES . . . 277 TWO KINGS V 5
    AND WHERE THE STONE STRUCK FIRE, WHILE IN THE LEAVES   278 TWO KINGS   33
    CAST BUT DEAD LEAVES TO MATHEMATICAL EQUALITY; . . . . 481 BLOOD AND MOON   24
    CASTS BUT DEAD LEAVES TO MATHEMATICAL EQUALITY; . . . 481 BLOOD AND MOON V 24
    AND DEAFENING MUSIC SHOOK THE LEAVES; A TROOP . . . . 537 HER VISION   13
    THOUGH SOMEWHAT BROKEN BY THE LEAVES, THAT LIGHT . . . 555 RIBH AT TOMB   25
    LEAVES WHAT MAN WOULD LOSE. . . . . 620 JOHN KINSELLA   4
    AS THE LEAVES IN AUTUMN SCATTER. . . . . 648 ISLE STAT I 1   90
    THE BIRDS THAT NESTLE IN THE LEAVES ARE SAD, ... 652 ISLE STAT I 2   15
    MID BUBBLING LEAVES A WANDERING SONG-RAPT BIRD . . . . 672 ISLE STAT II 3 154
    MID BABBLING LEAVES A WANDERING SONG-RAPT BIRD . . . . 672 ISLE STAT II 3 V 154
    UNTIL MY BEARD IS IN THE TWISTED LEAVES . . . . 683 SEEKER   44
    LIE STREWN THE YELLOW LEAVES--THE CLOTTED LEAVES. . . 684 SEEKER   69
    LIE STREWN THE YELLOW LEAVES--THE CLOTTED LEAVES. . . 684 SEEKER   69
    LIE STREWN THE CLOTTED LEAVES--THE DEAD OLD LEAVES. . . 684 SEEKER V 69
    LIE STREWN THE CLOTTED LEAVES--THE DEAD OLD LEAVES. . . 684 SEEKER V 69
    THE PATH O'ER-MUFFLED WITH THE LEAVES--DEAD LEAVES, . . 703 MOSADA 3 115
    THE PATH O'ER-MUFFLED WITH THE LEAVES--DEAD LEAVES, . . 703 MOSADA 3 115
    THE PATH O'ER MUFFLED WITH THE LEAVES--DEAD LEAVES, . . 703 MOSADA 3 V 115
    THE PATH O'ER MUFFLED WITH THE LEAVES--DEAD LEAVES, . . 703 MOSADA 3 V 115
    O FLOWER OF THE BRANCH, O BIRD AMONG THE LEAVES, . . . 769 SHADOW WATER A 424
LEAVE-TAKING
    THERE IS NO LEAVE-TAKING. I GO NO MORE. . . . . 702 MOSADA 3 100
LEBEEN-LONE
    AM I TO LIVE ON LEBEEN-LONE?" . . . . 295 THREE BEGGARS   5
    "FOR ALL MY PAINS ON LEBEEN-LONE?" . . . . 295 THREE BEGGARS   7
LECHER
    OLD LECHER WITH A LOVE ON EVERY WIND, ... 413 TOWER 105
    AN ANCIENT LECHER TOOK TO GEESE . . . . 792 GEORGE MOORE   3
LECHEROUS
    I AM SO LECHEROUS WITH ABSTINENCE . . . . 222 SHADOW WATER B V 8
    BEING MOCKED BY GUIDO FOR HIS LECHEROUS LIFE, ... 369 EGO DOMINUS   33
LECHING
    A LECHING SONG," THEY SAID. . . . . 570 THREE BUSHES   44
LECTERN
    MY GREAT WOOD LECTERN AND THE FIRE . . . . 358 PRESENCES   10
LED   SEE DREAM-LED
    THEY LED US BY LONG AND SHADOWY WAYS . . . . 16 OISIN 1 221
    SAID NIAM. "AY, AND HUGE. WHEN YE HAVE LED . . . . . 35 OISIN 2 V 89

LED   (CONTINUED)
    HOW THE MEN OF THE SAND-SACK LED ME TO SHAUL, • • • • • •   61 OISIN 3   V 193
    LED ON BY GENTLE WAYS! • • • • • • • • • • • • • •   113 ROSE OF PEACE   12
    HAS HE NOT LED US INTO THESE WASTE SEAS • • • • • • •   221 SHADOW WATER B   1
    LED BY A FOOTSOLE DIPPED IN BLOOD • • • • • • • • • •   274 GREY ROCK   78
    LED BY A FOOT-SOLE DIPPED IN BLOOD • • • • • • • • •   274 GREY ROCK   V 78
    THAT SHEBA LED A DANCE. • • • • • • • • • • • • • •   346 ON WOMAN   43
    WITH HER WHITE FINGER. I LED HER HOME ASLEEP • • • • •   468 HARUN RASHID   158
    WHAT MANHOOD LED THE DANCE! • • • • • • • • • • • •   488 CRAZED MOON   12
    BECAUSE PIEBALD PONIES, LED BEARS, CAGED LIONS, MAKE BUT   623 HIGH TALK   5
        POOR SHOWS,
    FIRST THAT SEA-RIDER OISIN LED BY THE NOSE • • • • • •   629 CIRCUS ANIMALS   10
    I'VE LED THEE HERE, AND AS A WHEEL • • • • • • • • •   667 ISLE STAT II 3   39
    SERENE. THEY'RE LED AWAY, AND WHERE A BAND • • • • •   712 FERENCZ RENYI   63
LEDA
    LEDA AND THE SWAN • • • • • • • • • • • • • • • •   441 LEDA AND SWAN   T
    BOOK III DOVE OR SWAN I. LEDA • • • • • • • • • •   441 LEDA AND SWAN   V T
    BOOK V! DOVE OR SWAN I LEDA • • • • • • • • • • •   441 LEDA AND SWAN   V T
    FROM THE LIMBS OF LEDA SANK • • • • • • • • • • • •   522 LULLABY   17
LEDAEAN
    I DREAM OF A LEDAEAN BODY, BENT • • • • • • • • • •   443 SCHOOL CHILDR   9
    AND I THOUGH NEVER OF LEDAEAN KIND • • • • • • • • •   444 SCHOOL CHILDR   29
LEDGE   SEE WINDOW-LEDGE
    SHE BUILDS HER NEST UPON A NARROW LEDGE • • • • • • •   285 TWO KINGS   194
    OF GREY STONES AND A ROCKY LEDGE • • • • • • • • • •   302 HOUR DAWN   12
LEE   SEE PAIRC-NA-LEE
LEFT
    OF MOONLIT STEPS GLIMMERED! AND LEFT AND RIGHT • • • •   31 OISIN 2   35
    SCARCE LEFT A WHITENING FEATHER, GREY AND SERE! • • • •   34 OISIN 2   V 76A
    FOR ALL YOUR CROZIERS, THEY HAVE LEFT THE PATH • • • •   42 OISIN 2   200
    AND LEFT HER TO THE INDIFFERENT STARS ABOVE • • • • •   123 DREAM OF DEATH   9
    WE AND OUR BITTERNESS HAVE LEFT NO TRACES • • • • • •   130 BOOK STORIES   23
    HE LEFT THEM WHERE SHE WENT BY. • • • • • • • • • •   160 CAP AND BELLS   24
    TO HER LEFT HAND CAME THE BLUE. • • • • • • • • • •   160 CAP AND BELLS   32
    UNDER A BITTER BLACK WIND THAT BLOWS FROM THE LEFT HAND!   206 HANRAHANS SONG   2
    UNDER THE BITTER BLACK WINDS BLOWING OUT OF THE LEFT HAND!   206 HANRAHANS SONG V   2
    AND I AM LEFT ALONE WITH MY BELOVED, • • • • • • • •   251 SHADOW WATER B   600
    MERCHANT AND SCHOLAR WHO HAVE LEFT ME BLOOD • • • • •   269 PARDON FATHERS   7
    TRADERS OR SOLDIERS WHO HAVE LEFT ME BLOOD • • • • • •   269 PARDON FATHERS V   7
    AND LEFT MERE SLEEP. HE'LL WAKE WHEN THE SUN WAKES, • •   284 TWO KINGS   161
    AND LEFT THEM TO THEIR ARGUMENT. • • • • • • • • • •   296 THREE BEGGARS   28
    AND THERE BE NOTHING BUT GOD LEFT! • • • • • • • • •   307 HOUR DAWN   103
    VANISHED, AND LEFT BUT MEMORIES, THAT SHOULD BE OUT OF   316 COLD HEAVEN   5
        SEASON
    BUT LEFT THE HOUSE AS IN HIS FATHER'S TIME • • • • • •   341 SHEP GOATHERD   53
    THERE'S NOTHING OF HIM LEFT BUT HALF A SCORE • • • • •   341 SHEP GOATHERD   56
    THAT MICHAEL ROBARTES LEFT, YOU WALK IN THE MOON, • • •   367 EGO DOMINUS   4
    OR, THE HOUSE DOOR LEFT UNSHUT, • • • • • • • • • •   380 SONGS FOOL 1   10
    THERE'S NOT A NEIGHBOUR LEFT TO SAY • • • • • • • • •   412 TOWER   78
    HAS BUT ONE COMFORT LEFT! ALL TRIUMPH WOULD • • • • •   429 NINETEEN 19   39
    AND LEFT ME BUT A LOUT. • • • • • • • • • • • • •   451 FIRST LOVE   14
    AND I LEFT SHIVERING. THE VOICE HAS DRAWN • • • • • •   469 HARUN RASHID   179
    THE BLOOD OF INNOCENCE HAS LEFT NO STAIN. • • • • • •   482 BLOOD AND MOON   34
    IN LUCK OR OUT THE TOIL HAS LEFT ITS MARK! • • • • •   491 COOLE BALLYLEE V   40F
    IN LUCK OR OUT THE TOIL HAS LEFT ITS MARK! • • • • •   495 CHOICE   6
    BUT WERE I LEFT TO LIE ALONE • • • • • • • • • • •   511 JANE AND JACK   13
    THEY LEFT THEIR BODIES TO FATTEN THE WOLVES, • • • • •   545 TO SAME TUNE 2   2
    THEY LEFT THEIR HOMESTEADS TO FATTEN THE FOXES, • • • •   546 TO SAME TUNE 2   3
    THEY LEFT THEIR HOMESTEADS TO SHELTER THE FOXES, • • • •   546 TO SAME TUNE 2 V   3
    HIS PROUD HEART HE LEFT BEHIND. • • • • • • • • • •   561 FOUR AGES MAN   6
    WHAT'S LEFT TO SIGH FOR? • • • • • • • • • • • • •   574 MAIDS 1ST SONG   5
    WHAT IS THERE LEFT TO SAY? • • • • • • • • • • • •   580 CURSE CROMWELL   8
    WHAT IS THERE LEFT TO SAY? • • • • • • • • • • • •   580 CURSE CROMWELL   16
    WHAT IS THERE LEFT TO SAY? • • • • • • • • • • • •   581 CURSE CROMWELL   24
    WHAT IS THERE LEFT TO SAY? • • • • • • • • • • • •   581 CURSE CROMWELL   32
    THEY LEFT THEIR BODIES TO FATTEN THE WOLVES, • • • • •   613 MARCH SONGS 1   2
    THEY LEFT THEIR HOMESTEADS TO FATTEN THE FOXES, • • • •   613 MARCH SONGS 1   3
    AND WONDERED WHAT WAS LEFT FOR MASSACRE TO SAVE. • • • •   619 BRONZE HEAD   28
    "OR DRIVEN FROM HOME AND LEFT TO DIE IN FEAR." • • • •   635 CUCHULAIN COMF   22
    MICHAEL ANGELO LEFT A PROOF • • • • • • • • • • • •   638 BEN BULBEN   45
    MICHAELANGELO LEFT A PROOF • • • • • • • • • • • • •   638 BEN BULBEN   V 45
    LONG ERE AN ARROW WHIZZED OR SWORD LEFT SHEATH • • • •   650 ISLE STAT I 1   135
    HAD LEFT THE ISLAND BREEZE, MY LORE • • • • • • • •   668 ISLE STAT II 3 V   55
    WHEN MY LOST LOVER LEFT THESE ARMS. MY GOMEZ. • • • •   701 MOSADA 3   51
    WHEN MY LOST LOVER LEFT THESE ARMS. MY VALLENCE, • • •   701 MOSADA 3   V 51
    THE PRIEST LOOKED NEITHER TO RIGHT NOR LEFT, • • • • •   730 PRIEST FAIRY   49
    I LEFT HER LIVING, THINKING THAT I HAD FOUND • • • • •   755 SHADOW WATER A   174
    WITH ONE YOU HAVE KILLED AND DIE! FOR WHEN I LEFT • • •   758 SHADOW WATER A   226
    WITH SOME YOU HAVE KILLED AND DIE! FOR WHEN I LEFT • • •   758 SHADOW WATER A V   226
LEG
    AS THE ONE STURDY LEG COULD DO • • • • • • • • • • •   302 HOUR DAWN   5
LEGEND
    A LEGEND OF THE PHANTOM SHIP. • • • • • • • • • • •   718 PHANTOM SHIP   V T
    A LEGEND. •   724 LEGEND   T
LEGENDARY   SEE HALF-LEGENDARY
    HALF LEGENDARY MEN. • • • • • • • • • • • • • • • •   605 YOU CONTENT   16
LEGGED   SEE BANDY-LEGGED LONG-LEGGED THREE-LEGGED HALF-LEGGED ONE-LEGGED BOW-LEGGED
LEGS   SEE DADDY-LONG-LEGS
    UPON ITS BANDY LEGS. RUN AT THEM NOW, • • • • • • •   233 SHADOW WATER B   239
    ON HIS YELLOW LEGS THROUGH OUR MEADOWS, • • • • • • •   341 SHEP GOATHERD   65

<pre>
                                                     PAGE   TITLE   LINE
LEGS   (CONTINUED)
      UPON HIS YELLOW LEGS THROUGH OUR MEADOWS, ...   341 SHEP GOATHERD   V   65
      STRETCHED UP ON TWO LEGS FROM THE MAT, ...   381 SONGS FOOL 2   7
      THEIR LEGS LONG, DELICATE AND SLENDER, AQUAMARINE THEIR   426 PHANTOM HATRED   17
        EYES,
      STAND UPRIGHT ON YOUR LEGS AWHILE, ...   586 PARNELLITES   3
LEISURE
      AND YOU SHALL KNOW THE DANAAN LEISURE! . . . .   9 OISIN 1   100
      AND THOU SHALT KNOW THE IMMORTALS' LEISURE, ...   9 OISIN 1   V 100
      THE WARRIOR DREAMS IN AN AGED LEISURE . . . .   26 OISIN 1   V 401
      A DEMON'S LEISURE! EYES, FIRST WHITE, NOW BURNED . . . .   40 OISIN 2   168
      A DEMON'S LEISURE. EYES FIRST WHITE AS SNOW, ...   40 OISIN 2   V 168
      THE HONEY-HEARTED LEISURE OF THE LIGHT, ...   705 REMEMBRANCE   7
      OF A WIDE WOOD'S LEAFY LEISURE, ...   731 STREET DANCERS   11
LEISURED
      OF FACES, WAITED! AND THE LEISURED GAZE . . . .   39 OISIN 2   149
      OF FACES, WATCHED ME, AND THE LEISURED GAZE . . . . .   39 OISIN 2   V 149
LEMAN
      FOR THERE THE TALL DEER AND HIS LEMAN SIGH . . . . . .   210 RAGGED WOOD   V   2
      FOR THERE THE TALL DEER AND HIS LEMAN CRY . . . . . .   211 RAGGED WOOD   V   6
      BECOME A STRANGER'S LEMAN! AND THAT YOU, ...   757 SHADOW WATER A   215
LEMON
      UNDER A LEMON TREE BESIDE YOUR DOOR! . . . .   693 MOSADA 1   68
      LAPPED IN THE LEMON DAFFODILS! A BEE . . . .   716 DWELT SYCAMORE   10
LEMON-TINTED
      IN LEMON-TINTED LINES, SO BLAZE THE DAFFODILS. . . . .   645 ISLE STAT I 1   19
LEND
      HE CALLED ALOUD TO ALL THE STARS TO LEND . . . . . .   68 SAD SHEPHERD   V   5
LENDS
      AND JOY, THE TOUCHING OF WHOSE FINGER LENDS . . . . .   686 DRAWING-ROOM   7
      AND JOY, THE TOUCHING OF WHOSE FINGER LENDS . . . . .   734 QUATRAIN APHOR   7
LENGTH
      DEEP SUNKEN ON THE BLADE'S LENGTH, "MANANAN!" . . . . .   38 OISIN 2   V 128
      . . . BUT FELL WITH THEIR BURDEN AT LENGTH. . . . . .   60 OISIN 3   186
      . . . THEY LAY 'NEATH THE SAND-SACK AT LENGTH . . . .   60 OISIN 3   V 186
      THAT EVERY YEAR I HAVE CRIED, "AT LENGTH . . . . . .   256 WORDS   9
      AH, BUT PEACE THAT COMES AT LENGTH, ...   259 PEACE   10
      AND DRINK, AND YOU WILL SLEEP THAT LENGTH." . . . . .   305 HOUR DAWN   59
      YOU WILL SLEEP THAT LENGTH; AND AT THE FIRST . . . . .   305 HOUR DAWN   V   59
      I TOILED LONG YEARS AND AT LENGTH . . . .   505 RESULT THOUGHT   9
      TOILED LONG YEARS AND AT LENGTH . . . .   505 RESULT THOUGHT V   9
      HIS EMPTY HEART IS FULL AT LENGTH, ...   624 APPARITIONS   19
      AT ARM'S LENGTH, THUS TILL DUMB ETERNITY . . . . .   671 ISLE STAT II 3   145
      ITS PAVEN LENGTH TOWARDS THE RIVER'S MARGE . . . . .   702 MOSADA 3   76
LENGTHEN
      AND THERE IS SALT TO LENGTHEN OUT THE SMART . . . . .   324 ROBERT GREGORY   11
LENGTHENING
      TO HIS SHAPE IN THE LENGTHENING SHADOWS, ...   341 SHEP GOATHERD   V   70
LEOPARD
      AS AN HURT LEOPARD FILLS WITH CEASELESS MOAN, ...   674 ISLE STAT II 3   208
      AS A HURT LEOPARD FILLS WITH CEASELESS MOAN . . . .   674 ISLE STAT II 3 V   208
LEOPARD-COLOURED
      ARISE THE LEOPARD-COLOURED TREES! . . . .   84 MAD KING GOLL   40
LEOPARDS
      OF THE DARK LEOPARDS OF THE MOON? . . . .   343 DEJECTION   3
LESS
      WERE THE WINDS LESS SOFT THAN THE BREATH OF A PIGEON . .   56 OISIN 3   134
      NOR BE I ANY LESS OF THEM, ...   137 TO IRELAND   5
      NOR MAY I LESS BE COUNTED ONE . . . .   138 TO IRELAND   17
      AND LOVE IS LESS KIND THAN THE GREY TWILIGHT, ...   148 INTO TWILIGHT   15
      AND HOPE IS LESS DEAR THAN THE DEW OF THE MORN. . . .   148 INTO TWILIGHT   16
      AND OUR POOR KATE OR NAN IS LESS . . . .   190 BAILE AILLINN   35
      THAT HAS LESS UPS AND DOWNS THAN ROBBERY. . . . . .   222 SHADOW WATER B   7
      BUT YEAR BY YEAR I FOUND THAT LESS . . . .   305 HOUR DAWN   68
      LESS BITTER. THEY HAVE BROUGHT ME FROM THAT RIDGE . .   342 SHEP GOATHERD   87
      MAKE HUMAN INTERCOURSE GROW LESS AND LESS! . . . . .   473 ALL SOUL NIGHT   75
      MAKE HUMAN INTERCOURSE GROW LESS AND LESS! . . . . .   473 ALL SOUL NIGHT   75
      AND TWENTY MINUTES MORE OR LESS . . . .   501 VACILLATION   42
      AND FINDS THERE NOTHING TO MAKE ITS TERROR LESS . . .   618 BRONZE HEAD   6
      NAY, GRIEF IN FEEDING ON OLD GRIEF GROWS LESS. . . . .   659 ISLE STAT II 1   19
      THREE TIMES THE ROSES HAVE GROWN LESS AND LESS, . . .   690 MOSADA 1   1
      THREE TIMES THE ROSES HAVE GROWN LESS AND LESS, . . .   690 MOSADA 1   1
LESSER
      AND MANY A LESSER BELL SOUND THROUGH THE ROOM! . . . .   470 ALL SOUL NIGHT   2
      INTO SOME LESSER THING. . . . .   517 HER ANXIETY   5
      A GREATER WITH A LESSER PANG ASSUAGE . . . .   537 HER VISION   5
      FIRST DREAMS, AND GOBLINS, AND THE LESSER SPRITES, . .   722 WITCH VIVIEN   56
LESSON
      IT HAD NOT LEARNED ITS LESSON. . . . .   389 IMAGE PAST   14
LEST
      LEST THEY SHOULD LOOK UPON SOME DREADFUL SIGHT! . . .   38 OISIN 2   142
      STOOD TIMIDLY. LEST THEY SHOULD SEE SOME SIGHT . . .   38 OISIN 2   V 141
      LEST NIAMH SHUDDER. FULL OF HOPE AND DREAD . . . .   41 OISIN 2   183
      CAST THE LOOSE BULK, LEST NIAM FEAR HIM DEAD! . . . .   41 OISIN 2   V 183
      LEST ALL THY TOILING ONLY BREEDS . . . .   66 HAPPY SHEPHERD   25
      LEST I NO MORE HEAR COMMON THINGS THAT CRAVE! . . . .   101 ROSE UPON ROOD   15
      "BUT LEST YOU ARE MY ENEMY, ...   263 MASK   11
      HE HOLDS HIM FROM DESIRE, ALL BUT STOPS HIS BREATHING LEST 559 MAGIC DRUM   1
      AS I MY WATCHING LEST YOU WAKE, ...   658 ISLE STAT I 3   95
      LEST ON THINE HEART THE STONY SEAL . . . .   667 ISLE STAT II 3   41
      LEST HE MAY SOME GLAMOUR FOLD . . . .   717 FAIRY DOCTOR   22
</pre>

LEST   (CONTINUED)

		PAGE	TITLE		LINE
LEST SOME GLAMOUR HE MAY FOLD		717	FAIRY DOCTOR	V	22
WHISPER LEST WE TOO MAY SADDEN,		737	IN FIRELIGHT		5
BEND LOWER LEST YOUR BATTLE-AXES GLIMMER.		752	SHADOW WATER A		117
BEND LOWER LEST YOUR BATTLE AXES GLIMMER.		752	SHADOW WATER A	V	117

LET

		PAGE	TITLE		LINE
NOR THY COMPANIONS. LET THEM REST,		11	OISIN 1	V	130
THE FENIANS. LET THEIR DEER-HOUNDS SLEEP.		11	OISIN 1	V	131
LET US PART, ERE THE SEASON OF PASSION FORGET US,		79	FALLING LEAVES		7
"ALTHOUGH OUR LOVE IS WANING, LET US STAND		79	EPHEMERA		4
"THOUGH OUR SAD LOVE IS FADING, LET US YET		79	EPHEMERA	V	4
IN BOSOM AND HAIR. THEN HE: "LET US NOT MOURN		80	EPHEMERA	V	20
"HE BADE ME LET ALL KNOW HE GIVES HIS NAME		109	CUCHULAIN SEA		52
BELOVED, LET YOUR EYES HALF CLOSE, AND YOUR HEART BEAT		154	BELOVED PEACE		9
LET THE STARRY WINDS AND THE FLAME AND THE FLOOD		158	TO HIS HEART		5
DIM POWERS OF DROWSY THOUGHT, LET HER NO LONGER BE		175	ELEMENT POWERS		13
BUT LET A GENTLE SILENCE WROUGHT WITH MUSIC FLOW		175	ELEMENT POWERS		17
GREAT RULERS OF THE STILLNESS, LET HER NO LONGER BE		175	ELEMENT POWERS	V	13
GREAT RULERS OF STILLNESS, LET HER NO LONGER BE		175	ELEMENT POWERS	V	13
BUT LET A GENTLE SILENCE ENWROUGHT WITH MUSIC FLOW		175	ELEMENT POWERS	V	17
OR LET ITS MEANING MIX INTO THE STRINGS.		180	QUEEN MAEVE		8
LET RUSH AND BIRD CRY OUT THEIR FILL		197	BAILE AILLINN		198
"LET PEEWIT CALL AND CURLEW CRY WHERE THEY WILL,		203	WITHER BOUGHS		2
THAT WOULD LET THE SPADE LIE,		215	HAPPY TOWNLAND		30
AND LET THE DREAM GO BY. IT'S NOT A DREAM,		229	SHADOW WATER B		158
LET GO MY HANDS! WHY DO YOU CAST A SHADOW?		235	SHADOW WATER B		283
WHEN SHE FINDS OUT I WILL NOT LET HER GO--		236	SHADOW WATER B		302
THAT YOU'LL NOT LET ME GO? I AM A QUEEN.		236	SHADOW WATER B		304
I WOULD NOT LET YOU SPEAK, FOR I WOULD KNOW		246	SHADOW WATER B		492
HOW GREAT A WRONG IT IS TO LET ONE'S THOUGHT		246	SHADOW WATER B		514
LET THE BIRDS SCATTER, FOR THE TREE IS BROKEN,		250	SHADOW WATER B		584
YET OLD ROMANCE BEING KIND, LET HIM PREVAIL		258	KING NO KING		5
"O NO, MY DEAR, LET ALL THAT BE:		263	MASK		13
BUT LET THAT BE--THE GODS WERE STILL		271	GREY ROCK	V	16
THAN LOVER'S MUSIC--LET THAT BE,		276	GREY ROCK		130
LET PAUDEENS PLAY AT PITCH AND TOSS,		288	TO WEALTHY MAN		31
BUT LET THEM BE, THEY'RE DEAD AND GONE,		290	SEPTEMBER 1913		31
LET THESE CONTENT YOU AND BE GONE AGAIN:		292	TO A SHADE		8
SHE NEED NOT BE TOO COMELY--LET IT PASS,"		300	BEGGAR CRIED		10
BUT LET HIM KEEP HIS GRAVE FOR ONCE		303	HOUR DAWN		38
LET THERE BE NO FOOT SILENT IN THE ROOM,		311	MOUNTAIN TOMB	V	6
SONG, LET THEM TAKE IT,		320	COAT		8
LET THE YOUNG WISH. BUT WHAT HAS BROUGHT YOU HERE?		339	SHEP GOATHERD		6
I LET THEM STRAY. I THOUGHT OF RHYME ALONE,		339	SHEP GOATHERD		11
LET HIM BE HOODED OR CAGED		349	HAWK		2
I KNEW A PHOENIX IN MY YOUTH, SO LET THEM HAVE THEIR DAY.		353	HIS PHOENIX		8
I KNEW A PHOENIX IN MY YOUTH, SO LET THEM HAVE THEIR DAY.		354	HIS PHOENIX		16
I KNEW A PHOENIX IN MY YOUTH, SO LET THEM HAVE THEIR DAY.		354	HIS PHOENIX		24
I KNEW A PHOENIX IN MY YOUTH, SO LET THEM HAVE THEIR DAY.		354	HIS PHOENIX		32
AND LET YOU GO.		359	TO A SQUIRREL		8
AMID THE DREAMS OF YOUTH) LET HER COME FACE TO FACE,		366	HER COURAGE		3
O! SOLOMON! LET US TRY AGAIN."		389	SOLOMON WITCH		44
SO LET HER THINK OPINIONS ARE ACCURSED.		405	FOR DAUGHTER		58
COME LET US MOCK AT THE GREAT		432	NINETEEN 19		93
COME LET US MOCK AT THE WISE:		432	NINETEEN 19		98
COME LET US MOCK AT THE GOOD		432	NINETEEN 19		103
LET THE NEW FACES PLAY WHAT TRICKS THEY WILL		435	NEW FACES		5
BEFORE THE INDIFFERENT BEAK COULD LET HER DROP?		441	LEDA AND SWAN		14
LET THE CAGE BIRD AND THE CAGE BIRD MATE		450	OWEN AHERNE		16
O LET HER CHOOSE A YOUNG MAN NOW AND ALL FOR HIS WILD SAKE."		450	OWEN AHERNE		24
AND LET ALL BASE AMBITION BE,		460	THREE MONUMENT		9
AND LET IT FALL UNNOTICED TO THE FLOOR.		461	HARUN RASHID		15
"LET ALL THINGS PASS AWAY."		502	VACILLATION		61
"LET ALL THINGS PASS AWAY."		502	VACILLATION		66
"LET ALL THINGS PASS AWAY."		502	VACILLATION		71
COME, LET ME SING INTO YOUR EAR:		524	DANCING DAYS		1
THAT FOLLOWED IF I LET THE KERCHIEF FALL!		533	HER TRIUMPH		4
THAT BIRD . . . LET HIM SING ON,		536	PARTING		12
"LET OTHERS BOAST THEIR FILL," SAID I,		539	MEETING		7
TO THIS BARE SOUL, LET ALL MEN JUDGE THAT CAN		542	PARN FUNERAL 1		30
WHAT MATTER? HEAVE NO SIGH, LET NO TEAR DROP,		564	GYRES		11
LET HER FINISH HER DANCE,		568	SWEET DANCER		12
LET HER FINISH HER DANCE,		568	SWEET DANCER		13
AND LET HIM THINK ME THERE,		570	THREE BUSHES		23
LET THE FOOLS RAGE, I SWERVED IN NAUGHT,		577	WHAT THEN		18
AND LET THE NEIGHBOURS VOTE,		598	STONE CROSS		6
ALL THAT IS FINISHED, LET IT FADE.		613	MARCH SONGS 1		10
AND ALL THAT'S FINISHED, LET IT FADE.		613	MARCH SONGS 1		20
AND ALL THAT'S FINISHED, LET IT FADE.		614	MARCH SONGS 1		30
AMONG THOSE BIRD-LIKE THINGS CAME, AND LET FALL		634	CUCHULAIN COMF		8
NOR LET THE MODISH PAINTER SHIRK		638	BEN BULBEN		38
SO LET US DANCE WHERE THE YELLOW LANCE		643	SONG FAERIES		7
SO LET US DANCE ON FRINGED WAVES,		644	SONG FAERIES		9
SOME CAST OF DIE, OR LET SOME ARROW GLANCE		656	ISLE STAT I 3		40
LET HIM BETWEEN US JUDGE, FOR HE CAN GAUGE		660	ISLE STAT II 1		36
IN ALL SUCH THINGS, PRAY LET THINE EARS BE TURNED,		660	ISLE STAT II 1		39
HERE WHERE THE ROUND WAVES COME, HERE LET THEM BUILD,		663	ISLE STAT II 2		19
A WHITE, DUMB THING OF TEARS, HERE LET IT STAND,		663	ISLE STAT II 2		21
AND ONCE A-YEAR LET THE ARCADIANS COME,		663	ISLE STAT II 2		29
OF HUMAN SORROW LET THEM MORALIZE:		663	ISLE STAT II 2		31

<pre>
                                                      PAGE   TITLE   LINE
LET   (CONTINUED)
      AND LET THEM TELL SAD HISTORIES, TILL THEIR EYES . . . .   663 ISLE STAT II 2   32
      AND LET THE TALE BE MOURNFUL EACH ONE TELLS. . . . . .   663 ISLE STAT II 2   36
      O LET ME PASS! THE SPELLS FROM OFF THE HEART . . . . .   668 ISLE STAT II 3   44
      O LET ME PASS! THAT FLOWER NONE . . . .   668 ISLE STAT II 3   47
      FOR SUCH A CALL. LET THE WILD WORD BE CRIED . . . . .   669 ISLE STAT II 3   76
      BUT ART THOU HAPPY? LET ME GAZE ON THEE . . . . . .   671 ISLE STAT II 3   144
      BEFORE I AM TOO WEAK, FIERCE MORTAL, LET ME FLY, ...   675 ISLE STAT II 3   245
      BEFORE I AM TOO WEAK, OH LET ME FLY, ...   675 ISLE STAT II 3 V 245
      SO LET US DANCE WHERE THE YELLOW LANCE . . . . . .   676 ISLE STAT II 3   254
      SO LET US DANCE ON THE FRINGED WAVES, ...   676 ISLE STAT II 3   256
      OF THIS LAKE-NURTURED ISLE! LET THY KING BE . . . . .   679 ISLE STAT II 3   315
      THEN LET ME SEE THY FACE BEFORE I DIE. . . . . . .   684 SEEKER   66
      AH, LET US KISS EACH OTHER'S EYES, ...   686 LIFE   15
      UPON MY KNEES I PRAY YOU, LET IT SLEEP, ...   693 MOSADA 1   72
      THEM ALL, AND LET THEM FIND YOU IN THE VAPOUR. . . . .   694 MOSADA 1   V 108A
      WE GATHERED. FERENCZ, DO NOT LET ME DIE. . . . . . .   713 FERENCZ RENYI V   96
      I SWEAR IT. LET EVERY MAN DRAW OUT HIS SWORD. . . . .   758 SHADOW WATER A   230
      LET HIM WHO BREAKS IT . . . .   770 BLOOD BOND   4
      LET THE SEA BEAR WITNESS, ...   770 BLOOD BOND   7
      LET THE WIND BEAR WITNESS, ...   770 BLOOD BOND   8
      LET THE EARTH BEAR WITNESS, ...   770 BLOOD BOND   9
      LET THE FIRE BEAR WITNESS, ...   770 BLOOD BOND   10
      LET THE DEW BEAR WITNESS, ...   770 BLOOD BOND   11
      LET THE STARS BEAR WITNESS! . . . .   770 BLOOD BOND   12
      I'D LET THE WHOLE WORLD GO; . . . .   782 HEART FRIGHT   9
LETHEAN
      NO LONGER IN LETHEAN FOLIAGE CAUGHT . . . .   500 VACILLATION   27
LET'S
      LET'S HOME; I'D GIVE SOME RUBIES TO A WOMAN. . . . . .   248 SHADOW WATER B   537
      LET'S HOME AND SPEND IT IN OUR VILLAGES. . . . . . .   248 SHADOW WATER B V 538A
      AY, BOY. LET'S SEE IF THAT SAME HERON'S DEAD. . . . .   651 ISLE STAT I 1   169
      I COULD NOT GO. LET'S TALK, AND LET'S BE SAD, ...   651 ISLE STAT I 2   7
      I COULD NOT GO. LET'S TALK, AND LET'S BE SAD, ...   651 ISLE STAT I 2   7
      AND HEAVEN, AND HOLINESS. LET'S TALK AND GRIEVE, . . .   702 MOSADA 3   84
LETS
      THERE DREAMY TIME LETS FALL HIS SICKLE . . . .   77 INDIAN TO LOVE V   5A
      AND LETS THE KIND WORM TAKE THE LOT! . . . .   779 ACCURSED WHO   4
LET'ST
      "ASSASSIN, MY ASSASSIN! THOU WHO LET'ST ME DIE, ...   714 FERENCZ RENYI   106
LETTER
      AND FOR NO EAR BUT HIS. CARRY THIS LETTER . . . . . .   461 HARUN RASHID   4
      FOR SHOULD YOU LEAVE MY LETTER THERE, A BOY'S . . . .   461 HARUN RASHID   13
      AT THE BOTTOM OF A LETTER, FIFTY MEN. . . . .   790 DEDICATION   10
LETTERED
      HEALING FROM ITS LETTERED SLAB. THOSE SELF-SAME HANDS   503 VACILLATION   82
          PERCHANCE
      AND LAID THEM ON LOVE'S LETTERED TOMB! . . . .   519 HER DREAM   4
      SAD HISTORIES ARE LETTERED ON THY CHEEK. . . . . . .   660 ISLE STAT II 1   52
LETTERS
      THEREON IN OGHAM LETTERS, "MANANNAN"! . . . .   38 OISIN 1   128
      IN CHANGELESS OGHAM LETTERS WRIT-- . . . .   194 BAILE AILLINN   117
      THAT LIFE AND LETTERS SEEM . . . .   255 WOMAN HOMER   20
LEVEE
      AFAR FROM OUR LAWN AND OUR LEVEE, ...   706 FAIRY PEDANT   1
LEVEL
      WAS NOT MORE LEVEL THAN THE SEA, ...   13 OISIN 1   157
      AN ISLE LAY LEVEL BEFORE US, WITH DRIPPING HAZEL AND OAK?   47 OISIN 3   10
      AN ISLE LAY LEVEL BEFORE US, DRIPPING WITH HAZEL AND OAK?   47 OISIN 3   V   10
      AND DANCE UPON THE LEVEL SHORE? . . . .   125 GOES FERGUS   3
      WHO DANCED ON A LEVEL PLACE. . . . .   144 HOST OF AIR   14
      AND ALL THINGS AT ONE COMMON LEVEL LIE. . . . . . .   265 THESE CLOUDS   6
      BUT ACTUAL SHELLS OF ROSSES' LEVEL SHORE. . . . . . .   494 AT ALGECIRAS   12
      SCATTERED ON THE LEVEL GRASS . . . .   530 DELPHIC ORACLE   6
LEVELLED
      THEN DREW HIS SWORD TO HOLD ITS LEVELLED POINT . . . .   277 TWO KINGS   14
      BUT DREW HIS SWORD, AND THOUGHT WITH LEVELLED POINT . . .   277 TWO KINGS   V   14
      O WHAT IF LEVELLED LAWNS AND GRAVELLED WAYS . . . . .   418 ANCEST HOUSES   29
LEVELLING
      NOR THOUGHT OF THE LEVELLING WIND. . . . .   432 NINETEEN 19   97
      A LEVELLING, RANCOROUS, RATIONAL SORT OF MIND . . . . .   486 SEVEN SAGES   11
LEV'RET'S
      THE BEATING OF A LEV'RET'S HEART; . . . .   730 PRIEST FAIRY   69
LIAR
      LIAR AND FLATTERER OF THE WEAK, IN WHAT STRANGE CLIME . .   42 OISIN 2   V 198
LIBATIONS
      LIBATIONS, FROM THE HUNGARY OF THE WEST. . . . . . .   709 FERENCZ RENYI   5
LIBERAL
      FINE MANNERS, LIBERAL SPEECH, ...   506 REMORSE SPEECH   7
LIBERTY
      SERVED HUMAN LIBERTY. . . . .   493 SWIFTS EPITAPH   6
      SORROW THAT GIVES FOR GUERDON LIBERTY, ...   686 DRAWING-ROOM   6
      SORROW, THAT GIVES FOR GUERDON LIBERTY, ...   734 QUATRAIN APHOR   6
LIBRARY
      FOR THE SAN MARCO LIBRARY, ...   288 TO WEALTHY MAN   24
LICE
      THEY WERE COMMINGLING LICE AND BLOOD. . . . .   297 THREE BEGGARS   56
LICKED
      WHAT FROM THE FOREST CAME? WHAT BEAST HAS LICKED   560 MAGIC DRUM   6
          ITS YOUNG?
</pre>

448

	PAGE	TITLE		LINE
LICKS				
BUT HERE THE LIONESS LICKS HER SOFT CUB • • • • • • •	688	NETTLESHIP		2
LIDLESS				
TO BREED THE LIDLESS EYE THAT LOVES THE SUN? • • • • •	264	HOUSE SHAKEN		4
LIDS				
UPON DARK THRONES. BETWEEN THE LIDS OF ONE • • • • •	31	OISIN 2		37
HUGE FORMS OF STONE: BETWEEN THE LIDS OF ONE • • • • •	31	OISIN 2	V	37
HELPLESS, MEN LIFTING THE LIDS OF HIS WEARY	53	OISIN 3		92
AND DEATH—MAKING EYE.				
HELPLESS, MEN LIFTING THE LIDS OF HIS WEARY	53	OISIN 3	V	92
AND DEATH—POURING EYE.				
ARE BOWED IN SORROW UNDER PENDULOUS LIDS, • • • • • •	79	EPHEMERA		2
LIE NOW HALF HIDDEN UNDER PENDULOUS LIDS, • • • • • •	79	EPHEMERA	V	2
ARE BOWED IN SORROW UNDER THEIR TREMBLING LIDS, • • • •	79	EPHEMERA	V	2
LIE				
AND IN SOME GLOOMY BARROW LIE • • • • • • • • • •	19	OISIN 1		272
AND IN SOME URN FUNEREAL LIE • • • • • • • • • •	19	OISIN 1	V	272
FOR HIS LAST DAYS TO LIE IN WAIT. • • • • • • • •	24	OISIN 1		363
AND IN THE SHADOW OF MY HAIR LIE HID, • • • • • • •	33	OISIN 2		66
TO LIE UNTIL THE FOURTH MORN SAW EMERGE • • • • • • •	44	OISIN 2		220
TO LIE THERE 'TILL THE FOURTH DAY SAW EMERGE • • • • •	44	OISIN 2	V	220
TO LIE UNTIL THE FOURTH SUN SAW EMERGE • • • • • • •	44	OISIN 2	V	220
• • • "WHEN THE FALLEN ON FALLEN LIE ROLLED: • • • • •	52	OISIN 3		78
• • • "WHERE WHITE CLOUDS LIE SPREAD • • • • • • •	59	OISIN 3		178
WHERE MEN LIE FROZEN IN THE GLIMMERING SNOW: • • • • •	73	ANASHU VIJAYA		51
LIE NOW HALF HIDDEN UNDER PENDULOUS LIDS, • • • • • •	79	EPHEMERA	V	2
I SAW THIS HARP ALL SONGLESS LIE, • • • • • • • •	85	MAD KING GOLL	V	55
AND THE YOUNG LIE LONG AND DREAM IN THEIR BED • • • • •	150	OLD MOTHER		5
WHILE THE YOUNG LIE LONG AND DREAM IN THEIR BED • • • • •	150	OLD MOTHER	V	5
BUT THE YOUNG LIE LONG AND DREAM IN THEIR BED • • • • •	150	OLD MOTHER	V	5
YOUR BREAST WILL NOT LIE BY THE BREAST • • • • • • •	165	CRY OF SEDGE		9
YOUR BREAST WILL NOT LIE ON THE BREAST • • • • • • •	165	CRY OF SEDGE	V	9
BY A SPILLED WINE-CUP LIE. • • • • • • • • • •	168	BLESSED	V	32
MAY NOT LIE ON THE BREAST NOR HIS LIPS ON THE HAIR, • •	177	PAST GREATNESS		9
WOULD NOT LIE ON THE BREAST, OR HIS LIPS ON THE HAIR, • •	177	PAST GREATNESS	V	9.
THAT WOULD LET THE SPADE LIE, • • • • • • • • • •	215	HAPPY TOWNLAND		30
THAT RUN BEFORE THE REAPING-HOOK AND LIE • • • • • •	218	WOODS OF COOLE		32
THAT RUN BEFORE THE REAPING HOOK AND LIE • • • • • •	218	WOODS OF COOLE	V	32
THIS SWORD IS TO LIE BESIDE HIM IN THE GRAVE. • • • • •	242	SHADOW WATER B		412
AND ALL THINGS AT ONE COMMON LEVEL LIE. • • • • • •	265	THESE CLOUDS		6
WHAT'S THAT BUT TO LIE • • • • • • • • • • •	310	WITCH		2
"ALTHOUGH I'D LIE LAPPED UP IN LINEN • • • • • • •	331	ROUND TOWER		1
TOO PERFECT AT THE FULL TO LIE IN A CRADLE, • • • • •	374	PHASES OF MOON		60
DRINKING THE FOUL DITCH WHERE THEY LIE? • • • • • •	397	POLIT PRISONER		12
UNLESS THE HOLY WRITINGS LIE, • • • • • • • • •	436	FOR MY SON		28
SO LIKE A BIT OF STONE I LIE • • • • • • • • • •	452	HUMAN DIGNITY		7
FIVE HUNDRED YEARS AGO, ABOUT IT LIE • • • • • • •	478	SELF AND SOUL		26
LIE BODIES OF THE VAMPIRES FULL OF BLOOD: • • • • • •	483	OIL AND BLOOD		5
WHAT ARE ALL THOSE FISH THAT LIE GASPING ON THE STRAND? • •	485	THREE MOVEMENT		3
BUT WERE I LEFT TO LIE ALONE • • • • • • • • • •	511	JANE AND JACK		13
FOR THE HEART CANNOT LIE • • • • • • • • • •	516	MANS SONG		14
PROVE THAT I LIE. • • • • • • • • • • • •	517	HER ANXIETY		6
PROVE THAT I LIE. • • • • • • • • • • • •	517	HER ANXIETY		12
ALL THAT WAS SAID IN IRELAND IS A LIE • • • • • • •	542	PARN FUNERAL 1		26
UNTIL THE TOWN LIE BEATEN FLAT. • • • • • • • • •	565	LAPIS LAZULI		8
"SO YOU MUST LIE BESIDE HIM • • • • • • • • • •	570	THREE BUSHES		22
AND I MUST LIE BETWEEN THE SHEETS • • • • • • • •	570	THREE BUSHES		40
TO LIE BETWEEN YOUR FEET? • • • • • • • • • •	572	LADYS 2ND SONG		2
FOR SOON WE LIE WHERE HE IS LAID, • • • • • • • •	586	PARNELLITES		5
THOUGH DRUNKARDS LIE AND SNORE. • • • • • • • •	592	DRUNK SOBRIETY		8
SAID TO THE WOMAN ON HIS KNEES, "LIE STILL. • • • • •	609	IN TARAS HALLS		2
TO MANY WOMEN I HAVE SAID, "LIE STILL," • • • • • •	609	IN TARAS HALLS		6
I MUST LIE DOWN WHERE ALL THE LADDERS START, • • • • •	630	CIRCUS ANIMALS		39
I LIE AWAKE NIGHT AFTER NIGHT • • • • • • • • •	632	MAN AND ECHO		9
SLEEPLESS WOULD LIE DOWN AND DIE. • • • • • • • •	632	MAN AND ECHO		18
LIE DOWN AND DIE. THAT WERE TO SHIRK • • • • • • •	632	MAN AND ECHO		19
WHEN WE HALE MEN LIE STRETCHED IN SLUMBER • • • • • •	636	BLACK TOWER		23
LIE STREWN THE YELLOW LEAVES—THE CLOTTED LEAVES. • • • •	684	SEEKER		69
LIE STREWN THE CLOTTED LEAVES—THE DEAD OLD LEAVES. • • • •	684	SEEKER	V	69
THOU'RT WELCOME. LIE THERE CLOSE AGAINST MY FINGERS. • •	700	MOSADA 3		44
THAT SICKENING NEAR THEIR MOTHERS LIE: • • • • • •	717	FAIRY DOCTOR		16
GIVE ME THE HELM! CALL HITHER THOSE WHO LIE • • • • •	751	SHADOW WATER A		91
I SWEAR IT, THOUGH I GLADLY WOULD LIE DOWN • • • • • •	758	SHADOW WATER A		225
THEY ARE GONE, THEY ARE GONE. THE PROUD MAY LIE BY THE	777	SONG DEIRDRE 3		1
PROUD.				
AND ALL MEN LIE THAT SAY THAT I • • • • • • • • •	789	SINGING HEAD		3
THEY LIE THAT SAY, IN MOCKERY • • • • • • • • •	789	SINGING HEAD		9
THEN CLOSE YOUR EARS WITH DUST AND LIE • • • • • • •	791	REPRISALS		23
LIED				
THEIR CHILDREN'S CHILDREN SHALL SAY THEY HAVE LIED. • • • •	166	EVIL OF BELOV		6
LIES				
LIES FAR." I MOUNTED, AND SHE BOUND ME • • • • • •	9	OISIN 1	V	106
FOR HE IS WEAK AND POOR AND BLIND, AND LIES • • • • •	42	OISIN 2		203
BLIND AND NIGH DEAF, WITH WITHERED ARMS HE LIES • • • • •	42	OISIN 2	V	203
TILL I SAW WHERE MAEVE LIES SLEEPING • • • • • • •	60	OISIN 3		184
BEFORE US LIES ETERNITY: OUR SOULS • • • • • • • •	81	EPHEMERA		23
THERE LIES A LEAFY ISLAND • • • • • • • • • •	86	STOLEN CHILD		3
ONE BLIND HOUND ONLY LIES APART • • • • • • • •	99	FOXHUNTER		41
"I ONLY ASK WHAT WAY MY JOURNEY LIES, • • • • • • •	108	CUCHULAIN SEA		31
"GOD ONLY SEES WHAT DOOM FOR ME LIES STORED." • • • • •	110	CUCHULAIN SEA	V	62
BUT NOW LIES UNDER BOARDS. • • • • • • • • • •	123	DREAM OF DEATH		12

449

		PAGE	TITLE	LINE

LIES   (CONTINUED)
AND THE FRET LIES ON ME. . . . . 131 OLD PENSIONER V 6
AND THE FRET LIES ON ME. . . . . 132 OLD PENSIONER V 18
AND MY BREAST LIES UPON HIS BREAST. . . . . 151 HEART OF WOMAN 4
MY HEART UPON HIS WARM HEART LIES, ... 152 HEART OF WOMAN 11
AND YOU HAVE TOLD ME THAT THEIR JOURNEY LIES . . . . . 231 SHADOW WATER B 205
WHO, WERE IT PROVED HE LIES. . . . . 291 TO A FRIEND 6
LIES ONE LONG SOUGHT . . . . 310 WITCH 7
MANY A SON AND DAUGHTER LIES . . . . 360 ALF POLLEXFEN 13
SHE LIES, HER LOVELY PITEOUS HEAD AMID DULL RED HAIR . 362 HER COURTESY 2
BRING WHERE OUR BEAUTY LIES . . . . 362 DOLLS DRAWINGS 1
BY PEN AND PAPER LIES, ... 421 MY TABLE 3
BUT FEEL THE STRANGE HEART BEATING WHERE IT LIES? . . . 441 LEDA AND SWAN 8
AND FEELS THE STRANGE HEART BEATING WHERE IT LIES; . . 441 LEDA AND SWAN V 8
"YOU BUT IMAGINE LIES ALL DAY, O MURDERER," I REPLIED. . 450 OWEN AHERNE 17
"AND ALL THOSE LIES HAVE BUT ONE END, POOR WRETCHES TO
     BETRAY; . . . . 450 OWEN AHERNE 18
AND SPEAK BUT LIES. CALL UP TO MEMORY . . . . 462 HARUN RASHID V 30
THE BODY OF SAINT TERESA LIES UNDECAYED IN TOMB, . . . 503 VACILLATION 80
LIES IN A CIRCLE ON THE GRASS; THEREIN . . . . 555 RIBH AT TOMB 26
AND NOW LIES SUNK IN SLEEP. WHAT CLIMBS THE STAIR? . . 579 DOR WELLESLEY 11
BUT NOW LIES SUNK IN SLEEP. WHAT CLIMBS THE STAIR? . . 579 DOR WELLESLEY V 11
HE TELLS HIS LIES BY ROTE; . . . . 598 STONE CROSS 2
A JOURNALIST MAKES UP HIS LIES . . . . 598 STONE CROSS 3
AS LIES DARK WATER IN A MURMUROUS GLADE, ... 650 ISLE STAT I 1 138
AND NOD TO ONE ANOTHER, LIES A GREEN, ... 653 ISLE STAT I 2 35
WHEN SHE IN A CAVERN LIES, ... 658 ISLE STAT I 3 86
LIES TORN AND ROTTING. THE FIERCE KESTREL BIRDS . . . 675 ISLE STAT II 3 234
THE FAERY FLOWER LIES UPON THY LIPS. . . . . 677 ISLE STAT II 3 277
THE FAERY BLOSSOM LIES UPON THY LIPS. . . . . 677 ISLE STAT II 3 285
THE FAERY BLOSSOM LIES UPON THY LIPS; . . . . 678 ISLE STAT II 3 291
WHERE LIES THE LONG-LOST FOREST OF THE SPRITE, ... 682 SEEKER 23
THERE LIES THE LONG-LOST FOREST OF THE SPRITE, ... 682 SEEKER V 23
ABOUT THE SEA. BEFORE HER LIES THAT YOUTH, ... 687 TWO TITANS 22
WHERE LIES A SHALLOP IN THE YELLOW REEDS, ... 702 MOSADA 3 77
SAFE ON THE BREAST OF GOMEZ LIES THY HEAD, ... 703 MOSADA 3 101
AND SEE HOW THICK THE DEW LIES ON MY FACE. . . . . . . 703 MOSADA 3 104
WHERE LIES THE COW AT PEACE BESIDE HER CALF, ... 715 FERENCZ RENYI 121
LIES A CHILLY FINGER TIP, ... 732 STREET DANCERS 19
LIES A CHUBBY FINGER-TIP, ... 732 STREET DANCERS V 19
LOOK! THERE SHE LIES UNDER A FLAPPING SAIL. . . . . . . 751 SHADOW WATER A 90
A WOMAN LIES AMONG EMBROIDERIES. . . . . 752 SHADOW WATER A 120
LIETH
THE GOBLIN FLOWER LIETH ON THY LIPS. . . . . 678 ISLE STAT II 3 298
LIEUTENANT
A BROWN LIEUTENANT AND HIS MEN, ... 424 ROAD AT DOOR 6
LIFE   SEE DEATH-IN-LIFE
BUT NOW TWO THINGS DEVOUR MY LIFE; . . . . 24 OISIN 1 358
AND NOW HAVE FALLEN ON MY LIFE . . . . 24 OISIN 1 V 358
UPON THE LIFE THAT FADES AND FLICKERS AND DIES, ... 29 OISIN 2 12
A JUBILANT LIFE AMONG THE LEAVES, RETURN, ... 35 OISIN 2 V 89A
. . . WHEN LIFE IN MY BODY HAS CEASED, ... 63 OISIN 3 222
AND LIFE THE SANDALS OF HER FLEETNESS. . . . . 77 INDIAN TO LOVE V 5B
AND LIFE IS OVER SAVE THE MURMUR AND THE SWEETNESS. . . 77 INDIAN TO LOVE V 5E
I RULED AND RULED MY LIFE WITHIN-- . . . . 82 MAD KING GOLL V 7
SHE BID ME TAKE LIFE EASY, AS THE GRASS GROWS ON THE WEIRS; 90 SALLEY GARDENS 7
I SEE MY LIFE GO DRIFTING LIKE A RIVER . . . . 104 FERGUS DRUID 31
I SEE MY LIFE GO DRIPPING LIKE A STREAM . . . . 104 FERGUS DRUID V 31
TO IDLE LIFE AWAY, A COMMON HERD." . . . . 107 CUCHULAIN SEA 21
TO IDLE LIFE AWAY WITH FLOCKS AND HERDS." . . . . 107 CUCHULAIN SEA V 21
THE FLAMING CIRCLE OF OUR LIFE. . . . . 135 TWO TREES V 16
I AM NO MORE WITH LIFE AND DEATH, ... 152 HEART OF WOMAN 10
WHO HAD BEEN THE LOVER OF HER MIDDLE LIFE. . . . . . . 183 QUEEN MAEVE 72
"HOW MAY A MORTAL WHOSE LIFE GUTTERS OUT . . . . 184 QUEEN MAEVE 85
THAT ALL THIS LIFE CAN GIVE US IS . . . . 190 BAILE AILLINN 39
THAT ALL LIFE HAS TO GIVE US IS . . . . 190 BAILE AILLINN V 39
THAT ALL LIFE HAD TO GIVE US IS . . . . 190 BAILE AILLINN V 39
AWAKEN TO LIFE AGAIN. . . . . 215 HAPPY TOWNLAND 26
FOR I AM GETTING ON IN LIFE--TO SOMETHING . . . . 222 SHADOW WATER B 6
WHERE I AM RID OF LIFE--THE EVENTS OF THE WORLD-- . . . 227 SHADOW WATER B 121
WHEN THEY HAVE TWENTY YEARS; IN MIDDLE LIFE . . . . . . 229 SHADOW WATER B 156
OF THAT MORE POWERFUL LIFE? HIS WIFE KNOWS BETTER. . . 230 SHADOW WATER B 172
HAD THE WORLD'S TOTAL LIFE GATHERED UP, IT SEEMED, . . 231 SHADOW WATER B 194
YOU'D NEVER DOUBT THAT IT WAS LIFE THEY PROMISED . . . 231 SHADOW WATER B 197
THEY THAT HAVE ALL THE WISDOM THAT'S IN LIFE, ... 235 SHADOW WATER B 293
HAVING THEIR LIFE IN HIM. THOUGH IT BE THE MOON . . . 240 SHADOW WATER B 377
BUT IN SOME ISLAND WHERE THE LIFE OF THE WORLD . . . . 249 SHADOW WATER B 559
HAVE WE NOT EVERYTHING THAT LIFE CAN GIVE . . . . 249 SHADOW WATER B 570
THAT LIFE AND LETTERS SEEM . . . . 255 WOMAN HOMER 20
"WERE NOT ALL HER LIFE BUT STORM, ... 259 PEACE 4
THAT HAS MORE LIFE IN IT THAN DEATH, ... 271 GREY ROCK 8
I'D SAVED HIS LIFE, YET FOR THE SAKE . . . . 275 GREY ROCK 102
I'D SAVE HIS LIFE, YET FOR THE SAKE . . . . 275 GREY ROCK V 102
AND LOOSEN ON US DREAMS THAT WASTE OUR LIFE, ... 281 TWO KINGS 107
THIS HUMAN LIFE BLOTTED FROM MEMORY, ... 285 TWO KINGS 198
CAN BLOT OUT OF MY MEMORY THIS LIFE . . . . 285 TWO KINGS 204
A POOR LIFE, DO WHAT HE CAN, ... 301 RUN PARADISE 11
I'D HAVE A MERRY LIFE ENOUGH . . . . 306 HOUR DAWN 85
FOR ALL LIFE LONGS FOR THE LAST DAY . . . . 306 HOUR DAWN 98
MY LIFE OF EVERY PLEASANT THOUGHT . . . . 307 HOUR DAWN 110
THE COMMON GOOD OF LIFE, ... 317 NIGHT COME 5

PAGE   TITLE   LINE

LIFE   (CONTINUED)
```
A PORTION OF MY MIND AND LIFE, AS IT WERE,                325 ROBERT GREGORY     42
IN BALANCE WITH THIS LIFE, THIS DEATH.                    328 IRISH AIRMAN       16
HOW HARD A LIFE HER SERVANT LIVES,                        336 YOUNG BEAUTY       14
YOU SING AS ALWAYS OF THE NATURAL LIFE,                   342 SHEP GOATHERD      75
AND, THOUGH YOU HAVE PASSED THE BEST OF LIFE, STILL TRACE, 367 EGO DOMINUS        5
BEING MOCKED BY GUIDO FOR HIS LECHEROUS LIFE,            369 EGO DOMINUS        33
OUT OF NO TRAGIC WAR, LOVERS OF LIFE,                    369 EGO DOMINUS        39
PLANNED IN A GOVERNMENT OFFICE, SHORTEN HIS LIFE,        372 ON GOING HOUSE     15
JUST TRUTH ENOUGH TO SHOW THAT HIS WHOLE LIFE            373 PHASES OF MOON     22
FOR THERE'S NO HUMAN LIFE AT THE FULL OR THE DARK.       373 PHASES OF MOON     35
BECAUSE YOU ARE FORGOTTEN, HALF OUT OF LIFE,            376 PHASES OF MOON     96
O NOT SINCE LIFE BEGAN.                                 382 VISION ROBART       8
THAT, IT MAY BE, HAD DANCED HER LIFE AWAY,             383 VISION ROBART      22
THAT IT MAYBE HAD DANCED HER LIFE AWAY,               383 VISION ROBART  V   22
AN IMAGE FROM A PAST LIFE                              389 IMAGE PAST          T
A SWEETHEART FROM ANOTHER LIFE FLOATS THERE           390 IMAGE PAST         22
HELEN BEING CHOSEN FOUND LIFE FLAT AND DULL           404 FOR DAUGHTER       25
DEATH AND LIFE WERE NOT                               415 TOWER             148
LIFE OVERFLOWS WITHOUT AMBITIOUS PAINS!               417 ANCEST HOUSES       3
AND RAINS DOWN LIFE UNTIL THE BASIN SPILLS,           417 ANCEST HOUSES       4
LIFE SCARCE CAN CAST A FRAGRANCE ON THE WIND,         422 MY DESCENDANTS      5
BEFORE THAT BRIEF GLEAM OF ITS LIFE BE GONE,          430 NINETEEN 19        63
WHAT MY LABORIOUS LIFE IMAGINED, EVEN                 431 NINETEEN 19        82
ENDURE WHAT LIFE GOD GIVES AND ASK NO LONGER SPAN!    459 FROM OEDIPUS        1
I CELEBRATE THE SILENT KISS THAT ENDS SHORT LIFE OR LONG. 459 FROM OEDIPUS     9
NEVER TO HAVE DRAWN THE BREATH OF LIFE,               459 FROM OEDIPUS       11
NEVER TO HAVE DRUNK THE BREATH OF LIFE,               459 FROM OEDIPUS   V   11
SO STRAINS TO LOOK BEYOND OUR LIFE, AN EYE            465 HARUN RASHID       87
BEING ALL BRIMMED WITH LIFE?"  "WERE IT BUT TRUE      465 HARUN RASHID       90
I WOULD HAVE FOUND THE BEST THAT LIFE CAN GIVE,       465 HARUN RASHID       91
MUST NEEDS BE IN THIS LIFE AND IN WHAT FOLLOWS        465 HARUN RASHID       95
SO LONGS TO LOOK BEYOND OUR LIFE, AN EYE              465 HARUN RASHID   V   87
BEING SO BRIMMED WITH LIFE.  "IF THAT COULD BE        465 HARUN RASHID   V   90
AND YET AGAIN, IF IT BE LIFE TO PITCH                 479 SELF AND SOUL      58
A SOMETHING INCOMPATIBLE WITH LIFE! AND POWER,        482 BLOOD AND MOON     50
SEEMED ONCE MORE DEAR THAN LIFE! ANCESTRAL TREES,     491 COOLE BALLYLEE     34
PERFECTION OF THE LIFE, OR OF THE WORK,               491 COOLE BALLYLEE V  40B
PERFECTION OF THE LIFE, OR OF THE WORK,               495 CHOICE              2
FOUND ALL THE PLEASURE THAT LIFE GAVE"!               521 THREE THINGS       11
BY MANIFOLD ILLUSION! BUT MAN'S LIFE IS THOUGHT,      563 MERU                3
HER EIGHTIETH WINTER APPROACHING!  "YESTERDAY HE THREATENED 578 LOFTY THINGS    8
  MY LIFE.
OR DEMONSTRATE IN MY OWN LIFE                         605 YOU CONTENT        21
MORE DREAD THE LIFE THAT WE LIVE,                     615 MARCH SONGS 2      15
A MOUTHFUL HELD THE EXTREME OF LIFE AND DEATH.        619 BRONZE HEAD        14
A MOUTHFUL HOLD THE EXTREME OF LIFE AND DEATH.        619 BRONZE HEAD    V   14
"YOUR LIFE CAN GROW MUCH SWEETER IF YOU WILL          634 CUCHULAIN COMF     12
ON LIFE, ON DEATH.                                    640 BEN BULBEN         93
THE WARMTH OF LIFE IS CHILLING, AND THE SHADOWS GROW  675 ISLE STAT II 3    232
LIFE.                                                 686 LIFE                T
OF OCEAN FAN THEE INTO LIFE, AND FOLD                 688 TWO TITANS         56
WILL HE NOT SPARE HER LIFE?  HOW WOULD ONE MATTER     696 MOSADA 2            3
IF PETER WOULD BUT ASK HER LIFE--WHO KNOWS?           696 MOSADA 2           17
"NOW ANSWER, IF THIS LIFE BE DEAR TO THEE,            713 FERENCZ RENYI  V   83
SO MEN IN LIFE AND I IN MAGIC PLAY!                   722 WITCH VIVIEN       55
LIFE                                                  734 QUATRAIN APHOR V    T
AND NEED NO MORE OF LIFE TILL THE WHITE WINGS         751 SHADOW WATER A    102
WOULD END THIS PEACEFUL LIFE THAT ROTS THE BONES,     752 SHADOW WATER A    110
AND WHILE SHE FADES AND LIFE WITHERS AWAY,            768 SHADOW WATER A    422
HAD WOVEN HER OF WIND.  LIFE WITHERS OUT              768 SHADOW WATER A V  423
O, WHAT IS LIFE BUT A MOUTHFUL OF AIR?                788 HAWTHORN TREE       9
```
LIFE-IN-DEATH
```
I CALL IT DEATH-IN-LIFE AND LIFE-IN-DEATH.            497 BYZANTIUM          16
```
LIFE-KEY
```
OR DEATH THAT COMETH WITH THE NEXT LIFE-KEY?          724 KANVA ON SELF      18
```
LIFELESS
```
NEIGHING ALONG THE LIFELESS WASTE!                    13 OISIN 1           170
```
LIFE'S
```
WHOSE LIPS HAD LIFE'S MOST PROSPEROUS GLOW?           10 OISIN 1           118
AS 'TWERE ALL LIFE'S EPITOME.                        327 ROBERT GREGORY     87
THAT OUT OF LIFE'S OWN SELF-DELIGHT HAD SPRUNG       417 ANCEST HOUSES      11
THAT OUT OF LIFE'S OWN SELF DELIGHT HAD SPRUNG       417 ANCEST HOUSES  V   11
HERE AT LIFE'S END                                   575 ACRE OF GRASS       8
NOR, GAZING FORTH WHERE LIFE'S SAD SICKLES REAP,     710 FERENCZ RENYI      31
```
LIFETIME
```
THE REPUTATION OF HIS LIFETIME LOST                  351 PEOPLE              5
```
LIFT
```
BUT LIFT A MOURNFUL ULALU,                            86 MAD KING GOLL      68
AND LIFT AN ULULU FORLORN,                            86 MAD KING GOLL  V   68
AND ON THESE HANDS THAT MAY NOT LIFT THE SWORD,      103 FERGUS DRUID       24
YOUNG MAN, LIFT UP YOUR RUSSET BROW,                 125 GOES FERGUS         4
AND LIFT YOUR TENDER EYELIDS, MAID,                  125 GOES FERGUS         5
LIFT UP BEFORE US WHEN THEY PASS,                    135 TWO TREES          23
LIFT UP BEFORE US AS THEY PASS,                      135 TWO TREES      V   23
AND THEY SIGH IF THE WIND BUT LIFT A TRESS!          151 OLD MOTHER          8
AND THEY SIGH IF THE WIND BUT LIFT UP A TRESS!       151 OLD MOTHER     V    8
YOU NEED BUT LIFT A PEARL-PALE HAND,                 158 BELOVED RHYMES      7
AND LIFT UP AN OLD HORN                              215 HAPPY TOWNLAND     49
THAT I WILL NEVER LIFT A HAND AGAINST YOU.           227 SHADOW WATER B    108
TOO MANY YEARS TO LIFT A HAND AGAINST YOU.           227 SHADOW WATER B    111
```

451

LIFT   (CONTINUED)

    THAT LIFT US TO THE FLOWING, CHANGING WORLD . . . . . . 230 SHADOW WATER B   182
    O WHY DO YOU NOT LIFT YOUR EYES TO MINE? . . . . 246 SHADOW WATER B   498
    I LIFT THE GLASS TO MY MOUTH, ... 261 DRINKING SONG   5
    STAND UP AND LIFT YOUR HAND AND BLESS . . . . 379 SAINT HUNCH   1
    THAT WOULD NOT LIFT A HAND MAYBE . . . . 432 NINETEEN 19   109
    THAT WOULD NOT LIFT A HAND MAY BE . . . . 432 NINETEEN 19   V   109
    LIFT, EVERY MOTHER'S SON, ... 548 TO SAME TUNE 3 V   15
    LIFT, LIFT, LIFT UP THE TUNE. . . . . 548 TO SAME TUNE 3 V   16
    LIFT, LIFT, LIFT UP THE TUNE. . . . . 548 TO SAME TUNE 3 V   16
    LIFT, LIFT, LIFT UP THE TUNE. . . . . 548 TO SAME TUNE 3 V   16
    MARCH, MARCH, LIFT UP THE SONG: . . . . 549 TO SAME TUNE 3 V   26
    LIFT, LIFT, LIFT UP THE SONG. . . . . 549 TO SAME TUNE 3 V   26
    LIFT, LIFT, LIFT UP THE SONG. . . . . 549 TO SAME TUNE 3 V   26
    LIFT, LIFT, LIFT UP THE SONG. . . . . 549 TO SAME TUNE 3 V   26
    LIFT MY SOUL FROM RAYLESS NIGHT-- . . . . 648 ISLE STAT I 1   95
    I TRY TO LIFT MINE ARMS--THEY FALL AGAIN. . . . . . . 701 MOSADA 3   56
    LIFT THEIR CHINS AND TOSS THEIR CURLS, ... 726 LOVERS QUARREL   23
    LIFT THEIR CHINS AND TURN AWAY. . . . . 726 LOVERS QUARREL   24

LIFTED

    LIFTED THE DOME, WHERE FACE IN CARVEN FACE . . . . . . 39 OISIN 2   V   145
    HALF WAKENING, WE LIFTED OUR EYELIDS. . . . . 54 OISIN 3   100
    LORD OF THE CROZIERS, YOU EVEN HAD LIFTED YOUR HANDS AND 54 OISIN 3   110
        WEPT:
    HALF-WAKENING, WE LIFTED OUR EYELIDS, ... 54 OISIN 3   V   100
    LORD OF THE CROSIERS, THOU EVEN HADST LIFTED THY HANDS 54 OISIN 3   V   110
        AND WEPT:
    CAME AFTER THE HARD GAZE OF YOUTH, OR AN OLD MAN LIFTED 59 OISIN 3   170
        HIS HEAD:
    . . . OR WAS LIFTED AN OLD MAN'S MILD HEAD. . . . . . 59 OISIN 3   V   170
    . . . THEY LIFTED AND SHOULDERED A SACK FULL OF SAND, 60 OISIN 3   V   185
    LIFTED THE CURTAIN OF HER SLEEPING-ROOM, ... 182 QUEEN MAEVE   63
    LIFTED THE CURTAIN OF HER SLEEPING ROOM, ... 182 QUEEN MAEVE   V   63
    TILL THAT BE TUMBLED THAT WAS LIFTED HIGH . . . . . . 265 THESE CLOUDS   4
    ALL THOSE HAD LIFTED UP THE DIM . . . . 272 GREY ROCK   27
    HAND LIFTED UP THAT BLEST: . . . . 383 VISION ROBART   20
    FROM HAYNAU'S LIFTED FINGERS--TWO DRAW NIGH . . . . . 714 FERENCZ RENYI   104
    WERE THEY BUT LIFTED UP.   THE RED HOUND IS FLED. . . . 761 SHADOW WATER A   266

LIFTING   SEE NEVER-LIFTING

    HELPLESS, MEN LIFTING THE LIDS OF HIS WEARY . . . . . 53 OISIN 3   92
        AND DEATH-MAKING EYE.
    HELPLESS, MEN LIFTING THE LIDS OF HIS WEARY . . . . . 53 OISIN 3   V   92
        AND DEATH-POURING EYE.
    FOR REMEMBRANCE, LIFTING HER LEANNESS, ... 57 OISIN 3   152
    LIFTING HIS DELICATE FEET. . . . . 378 CAT AND MOON   10

LIFTS

    LIFTS SLOW HIS WINTRY HEAD: . . . . 99 FOXHUNTER   46
    AND LIFTS HIS DELICATE FEET. . . . . 378 CAT AND MOON   V   10
    AND LIFTS TO THE CHANGING MOON . . . . 379 CAT AND MOON   27
    A NEIGHBOURING CRICKET LIFTS HIS SHRILLY SHOUT . . . . 711 FERENCZ RENYI   45
    HAYNAU, THE MAN OF SYSTEM, LIFTS HIS HAND . . . . . . 712 FERENCZ RENYI   62
    YON BAUBLE OF THE HEAVENS, HE LIFTS HIS HANDS, ... 715 FERENCZ RENYI   119

LIGHT   SEE STAR-LIGHT TORCH-LIGHT CANDLE-LIGHT HALF-LIGHT

    PIERCED WITH SOFT LIGHT THE SHALLOWING DEEPS. . . . . 13 OISIN 1   164
    LIKE DROPS OF FROZEN RAINBOW LIGHT, ... 14 OISIN 1   183
    HUNG, LIKE METEORS OF RED LIGHT, ... 21 OISIN 1   V   306
    UNDER THE GOLDEN EVENING LIGHT, ... 25 OISIN 1   385
    THE ISLE LOOMED LARGELY IN THE LIGHT . . . . 25 OISIN 1   V   385
    THE ODOROUS WEIGHT OF HIS CURLS OF LIGHT, ... 28 OISIN 1   V 423D
    THE MIST CLOSED ROUND US: PEARLY LIGHT . . . . 28 OISIN 1   V 427C
    I LAY, AS OVER SEA THE LIGHT HOOVES GLANCED . . . . . 30 OISIN 2   V 19A
    AND SURGING PHOSPHORUS ALONE GAVE LIGHT. . . . . 31 OISIN 2   33
    OF SURGING PHOSPHORUS ALONE GAVE LIGHT. . . . . 31 OISIN 2   V   33
    AND THROUGH THEIR EYES NO LIGHT OF MOON OR DAY . . . . 34 OISIN 2   77
    GOES DROPPING FROM HIS EYES A LANGUID LIGHT, ... 34 OISIN 2   V 81A
    AND CAME AGAIN, HOLDING A SECOND LIGHT . . . . 37 OISIN 2   124
    AWHILE, AND CAME AGAIN, A SECOND LIGHT . . . . 37 OISIN 2   V   124
    WITH A PALE LIGHT, I JOURNEYED ROUND THE HALL . . . . 39 OISIN 2   153
    WHILE HIGH FRAIL CLOUDLETS, FED WITH A GREEN LIGHT, . . 40 OISIN 2   165
    DAWN PASSIONED, FED WITH A FAINT GREEN LIGHT, ... 40 OISIN 2   V   165
    LIGHT IS MAN'S LOVE, AND LIGHTER IS MAN'S RAGE: . . . 45 OISIN 2   243
    CEASED ON OUR HANDS AND OUR FACES, ON HAZEL AND OAK LEAF, 48 OISIN 3   23
        THE LIGHT,
    SOUNDLESS SHALL BE THE FOOTFALL LIGHT . . . . 70 CLOAK BOAT   13
    SUDDEN AND LIGHT." . . . . 70 CLOAK BOAT   15
    MY SPIRIT ROCKED IN EVENING LIGHT, THE RUSHES ROUND MY 76 INDIAN ON GOD   2
        KNEES,
    HIS LANGUID TAIL ABOVE US, LIT WITH MYRIAD SPOTS OF LIGHT. 77 INDIAN ON GOD   20
    THE DIM GREY SANDS WITH LIGHT, ... 87 STOLEN CHILD   14
    A GREEN DROP IN THE SURGE, A GLEAM OF LIGHT . . . . . 104 FERGUS DRUID   33
    GO THERE, AND LIGHT A CAMP-FIRE AT WOOD'S RIM! . . . . 108 CUCHULAIN SEA   35
    GO THERE, AND LIGHT A CAMP FIRE AT WOOD'S RIM! . . . . 108 CUCHULAIN SEA V   35
    HAVE DOWERED THE STARS WITH MERRY LIGHT! . . . . 134 TWO TREES   6
    TO LIGHT A MEASURE HERE AND THERE: . . . . 138 TO IRELAND   14
    THE LIGHT FALL OF HER FLYING FEET . . . . 138 TO IRELAND   V   11
    TO HELP HER LIGHT FOOT HERE AND THERE, ... 138 TO IRELAND   V   14
    LIVE BUT TO LIGHT YOUR PASSING FEET. . . . . 158 BELOVED RHYMES   12
    OF A QUIET AND LIGHT FOOTFALL: . . . . 159 CAP AND BELLS   8
    ON A FOOT-FALL HUSHED AND LIGHT, ... 159 CAP AND BELLS V   8
    OF A FOOTFALL HUSHED AND LIGHT . . . . 159 CAP AND BELLS V   8
    OF A QUIET AND LIGHT FOOT-FALL: . . . . 159 CAP AND BELLS V   8

		PAGE	TITLE		LINE
LIGHT (CONTINUED)					
AND THE GIRDLE OF LIGHT IS UNBOUND,		165	CRY OF SEDGE		8
AND HURLED IT FROM ITS PLACE AMID THE PEARLY LIGHT		174	ELEMENT POWERS	V	3
AS THE LIGHT ON THE SEA,		175	ELEMENT POWERS	V	14
AND LIGHT WERE PALING OUT OF THE WEST,		175	BELOVED DEAD	V	2
ENWROUGHT WITH GOLDEN AND SILVER LIGHT,		176	CLOTHS HEAVEN		2
OF NIGHT AND LIGHT AND THE HALF-LIGHT,		176	CLOTHS HEAVEN		4
OF NIGHT AND LIGHT AND THE HALF LIGHT,		176	CLOTHS HEAVEN	V	4
OF NIGHT AND LIGHT AND THE HALF LIGHT,		176	CLOTHS HEAVEN	V	4
SHE FOLLOWED WITH LIGHT FOOTFALL IN THE MIDST,		186	QUEEN MAEVE		128
AND IN THE LIGHT BODIES OF BIRDS		190	BAILE AILLINN		44
AND AMID LEAFY LIGHT HE CRIED,		193	BAILE AILLINN	V	113
TALL, PROUD AND RUDDY, AND LIGHT WINGS		195	BAILE AILLINN		140
SCALE RUBBING SCALE WHERE LIGHT IS DIM		195	BAILE AILLINN		145
OF MORNING LIGHT IN A DIM SKY!		195	BAILE AILLINN		150
BUT LIGHT FROM THE PALE STARS, AND GLEAMS		196	BAILE AILLINN		173
AWAKEN WANDERINGS OF LIGHT AIR		197	BAILE AILLINN		185
WIND AND UNWIND THEIR DANCES WHEN THE LIGHT GROWS COOL		203	WITHER BOUGHS		13
WIND AND UNWIND DANCING WHEN THE LIGHT GROWS COOL		203	WITHER BOUGHS	V	13
LAND-UNDER-WAVE, WHERE OUT OF THE MOON'S LIGHT AND THE SUN'S		209	UNDER THE MOON		6
AND DO YOU GATHER ABOUT US WHEN PALE LIGHT		218	WOODS OF COOLE		37
EVEN THOUGH IT BE THE LIGHTEST OF LIGHT LOVE,		230	SHADOW WATER B		184
SHALL LIGHT UPON A PLACE IN THE WORLD'S CORE,		231	SHADOW WATER B		212
"HOW LIGHT WE ARE, NOW WE ARE CHANGED TO BIRDS!"		233	SHADOW WATER B		253
OUR HEART'S DESIRE NOW THAT WE ARE SO LIGHT."		233	SHADOW WATER B		255
THAT IN THE BLINDING LIGHT BEYOND THE GRAVE		258	KING NO KING		12
THE GREY ROCK AND THE WINDY LIGHT		275	GREY ROCK		111
AND WHERE BEECH-TREES HAD MIXED A PALE GREEN LIGHT		277	TWO KINGS		5
BETWEEN THE PALE GREEN LIGHT OF THE BEECH LEAVES		277	TWO KINGS	V	5
WHERE CERTAIN BEECHES MIXED A PALE GREEN LIGHT		277	TWO KINGS	V	5
AND WHERE BEECH TREES HAD MIXED A PALE GREEN LIGHT		277	TWO KINGS	V	5
AND THE GROUND IVY'S BLUER LIGHT, A STAG		277	TWO KINGS	V	6
SHOWED THEIR FAINT LIGHT THROUGH THE UNSHUTTERED WINDOWS,		279	TWO KINGS		50
IN THE HALF LIGHT, AND RUNS TO ITS OWN DOOR		279	TWO KINGS	V	45C
AS ON THE BLUE LIGHT OF A SWORD, A MAN		283	TWO KINGS		148
AMONG THE STONES AND THORN-TREES, UNDER MORNING LIGHT!		291	PAUDEEN		3
AMONG THE STONES AND THORN TREES, UNDER MORNING LIGHT,		291	PAUDEEN	V	3
TILL EVEN I SLEEP LIGHT! BUT WHO		303	HOUR DAWN		34
SO THAT IT SEEMS EVEN I SLEEP LIGHT!		303	HOUR DAWN	V	34
TO JUDGE IF A LIGHT SLEEPING FOOL		304	HOUR DAWN	V	52
AND VANITY HER FOOTFALL LIGHT,		314	MEMORY YOUTH		12
RIDDLED WITH LIGHT. AH! WHEN THE GHOST BEGINS TO QUICKEN,		316	COLD HEAVEN		9
IF HEAD AND LIMB HAVE BEAUTY AND THE INSTEP'S HIGH AND LIGHT		354	HIS PHOENIX		21
THAT IS OUR MODERN HOPE, AND BY ITS LIGHT		368	EGO DOMINUS		11
AND THE LIGHT PROVES THAT HE IS READING STILL.		373	PHASES OF MOON		11
THE LONELY LIGHT THAT SAMUEL PALMER ENGRAVED,		373	PHASES OF MOON		17
BECAUSE, IT MAY BE, OF THE CANDLE LIGHT		373	PHASES OF MOON	V	14
WHEN ALL IS FED WITH LIGHT AND HEAVEN IS BARE.		375	PHASES OF MOON		74
BECAUSE ALL DARK, LIKE THOSE THAT ARE ALL LIGHT,		376	PHASES OF MOON		104
THE LIGHT IN THE TOWER WINDOW WAS PUT OUT.		377	PHASES OF MOON		139
THE PURE COLD LIGHT IN THE SKY		378	CAT AND MOON		7
I SAW BY THE MOON'S LIGHT		383	VISION ROBART		27
THAT DRAGON THROUGH THE FADING LIGHT,		385	ROBARTES DANCE		4
THOUGH SEVERAL, ARE A SINGLE LIGHT,		388	SOLOMON WITCH		29
FOR THE PROSAIC LIGHT OF DAY—		411	TOWER		46
WHEN THE HEADLONG LIGHT IS LOOSE,		414	TOWER		135
VALLEY, RIVER, AND ELMS, UNDER THE LIGHT OF A MOON		426	PHANTOM HATRED		3
VALLEY, RIVER, ELMS, UNDER THE LIGHT OF A MOON		426	PHANTOM HATRED	V	3
BUT THOSE THE CANDLES LIGHT ARE NOT AS THOSE		445	SCHOOL CHILDR		50
SINCE FIRST WE SAW THE LIGHT,		456	SUMMER SPRING		4
TAKE THIS LIGHT PARCHMENT, PASS THROUGH THE GREAT CHAMBER		461	HARUN RASHID	V	5
PICK OUT MY FEATURES IN SUCH LIGHT AND SHADE		466	HARUN RASHID	V	116
OR DID THE TORCH LIGHT OF THAT MYSTERY		466	HARUN RASHID	V	115
AND FEARING THAT MY LIGHT DISTURBED HER SLEEP		467	HARUN RASHID	V	130
AND WROTE BY CANDLE LIGHT! BUT HER FORM MOVED		467	HARUN RASHID	V	129
THE LIGHT OF EVENING, LISSADELL,		475	EVA GORE-BOOTH		1
CROSS THE NARROW STRAITS TO LIGHT		494	AT ALGECIRAS		4
CROSSES THE NARROW STRAITS TO LIGHT		494	AT ALGECIRAS	V	4
CROSS THOSE NARROW STRAITS TO LIGHT		494	AT ALGECIRAS	V	4
SHALL LEAP INTO THE LIGHT LOST		511	JANE AND JACK		11
WENT IN THE DAWNING LIGHT		512	JANE ON GOD		3
NATURE'S PURE UNCHANGING LIGHT?		529	TOM LUNATIC		6
THAT LIGHT IS FROM THE MOON.		536	PARTING		11
FOR THE INTERCOURSE OF ANGELS IS A LIGHT		555	RIBH AT TOMB		15
MADE AQUILINE, ARE OPEN TO THAT LIGHT.		555	RIBH AT TOMB		24
THOUGH SOMEWHAT BROKEN BY THE LEAVES, THAT LIGHT		555	RIBH AT TOMB		25
THAT IS A LIGHT MY JEALOUS SOUL HAS SENT.		558	RIBH CHRISTIAN		8
"HIS LIGHT HAD STRUCK ME BLIND		559	HE AND SHE		5
THE GREATER GROWS MY LIGHT		559	HE AND SHE		9
HECTOR IS DEAD AND THERE'S A LIGHT IN TROY!		564	GYRES		7
BUT A WILD OLD MAN IN THE LIGHT,		589	OLD WICKED MAN		38
AS THOUGH WITH MAGNANIMITY OF LIGHT,		618	BRONZE HEAD		9
I, THROUGH THE TERRIBLE NOVELTY OF LIGHT, STALK ON, STALK ON!		623	HIGH TALK		13
WHILE THE WORLD IS ROLL'D IN LIGHT.		646	ISLE STAT I 1		29
PASSETH THE MOON WITH HER SICKLE OF LIGHT,		648	ISLE STAT I 1		82
MUSIC OF MY SOUL AND LIGHT—		648	ISLE STAT I 1		97
SAD LADY OF THE DEEP, POURS DOWN HER LIGHT!		650	ISLE STAT I 1		127
GOES FLICKERING IN REVERBERATED LIGHT.		653	ISLE STAT I 2		53

		PAGE	TITLE	LINE

LIGHT   (CONTINUED)
```
   THE LIGHT IS DANCING O'ER THE KNOTTED TREES,  . . . . .     662 ISLE STAT II 2        2
   AND SEE AGAIN THE HAPPY WOODLAND LIGHT,  . . . . . . .      664 ISLE STAT II 2       58
   SOUNDLESS SHALL BE THE FOOTFALL LIGHT  . . . . . .         666 ISLE STAT II 3       13
   SUDDEN AND LIGHT. . . . . . . . . . . . . .               666 ISLE STAT II 3       15
   AS LIGHT OF TRIUMPH IN THY GOBLIN EYES--  . . . . .        674 ISLE STAT II 3      199
   THOSE TWAIN ARE DUST. WAKE!  LIGHT AS A BEE SIPS          678 ISLE STAT II 3      290
   OF ASIAN RIVERS, ROLLING ON IN LIGHT.  . . . . .          682 SEEKER               20
   OF INDIA'S RIVERS, ROLLING ON IN LIGHT.  . . . . . .      682 SEEKER           V   20
   TO LIGHTEST OF LIGHT THINGS ALL SANCTITY.  . . . . .      686 DRAWING-ROOM          8
   BRUISING THE DARKNESS WITH THEIR CRACKLING LIGHT!         687 TWO TITANS            2
   FROM FASTING--SEE, THE RED LIGHT SLANTING DOWN  . . .     697 MOSADA 2             36
   THE HONEY-HEARTED LEISURE OF THE LIGHT,  . . . . .        705 REMEMBRANCE           7
   OF HER HE LOVED FIXED ON HIM FULL OF LIGHT,  . . . .      710 FERENCZ RENYI        27
   HIGHER AND HIGHER GOLD WITH EVENING LIGHT!  . . . .       714 FERENCZ RENYI       113
   WITHOUT THERE OF A LITTLE, LIGHT OLD MAN!  . . . . .      720 WITCH VIVIEN         13
   THAT WATCH ME WITH THEIR SUPPLIANT LIGHT--  . . . .       723 GIRLS SONG A         10
   BY A WINDOW'S FEEBLE LIGHT  . . . . . . . . .            731 STREET DANCERS        3
   SINGING TO THEIR LIGHT FOOTFALL.  . . . . . . .          732 STREET DANCERS       30
   DROPPING LIQUID RAINBOW LIGHT,  . . . . . . . .          732 STREET DANCERS       33
   TO LIGHTEST OF ALL LIGHT THINGS SANCTITY.  . . . .       734 QUATRAIN APHOR        8
   TO LIGHTEST OF LIGHT THINGS ALL SANCTITY.  . . . .       734 QUATRAIN APHOR   V    8
   A HURTING BEAM OF LIGHT,  . . . . . . . . .             741 EARL PAUL            38
   A HURTING GLEAM OF LIGHT,  . . . . . . . .              741 EARL PAUL        V   38
   WHEN FLYING TO THE HEART OF LIGHT  . . . . . .           742 DANAAN QUICK          8
   "HOW LIGHT WE ARE NOW WE ARE CHANGED TO BIRDS!"          753 SHADOW WATER A      143
   OUR HEARTS' DESIRE NOW THAT WE ARE SO LIGHT."  .         753 SHADOW WATER A      145
   WHILE THE WIND IS LIGHT.  THE OAR CAN HARDLY MOVE HER,   754 SHADOW WATER A      157
   WHERE THE MOON MAKES A CLOUDY LIGHT IN THE MIST.  .      764 SHADOW WATER A      329
   THE LOVE OF ALL UNDER THE LIGHT OF THE SUN  . . .        765 SHADOW WATER A      353
   WITH LIGHT IMAGES OF CLAY  . . . . . . . .              775 AGAINST WITCH        12
   ACCURSED WHO BRINGS TO LIGHT OF DAY  . . . . .           779 ACCURSED WHO          1
   DIMMED AT THREE-QUARTER LIGHT,  . . . . . . .            786 YOUR HEART           32
   DIMMED AT THREE QUARTER LIGHT  . . . . . . .             786 YOUR HEART       V   32
```
LIGHTED
```
   BUT OUR HEARTS ARE LIGHTED FROM THE FLAME IN THE EYES . .  207 HANRAHANS SONG V      9
   ITS OPEN LIGHTED DOORWAY AND ITS WINDOWS ALL ALIGHT,  . .  581 CURSE CROMWELL       26
   AS THOUGH UPON A LIGHTED SCREEN.  . . . . . . . .         626 OLD MEN BE MAD       12
```
'LIGHTED
```
   AND WHERE OUR FOOTFALL 'LIGHTED LAST THERE CAME  . . . .    37 OISIN 2         V  119
```
LIGHT-ENDAPPLED
```
   O'ER THE GRASS LIGHT-ENDAPPLED. . . . . . . . . .         654 ISLE STAT I 2        63
```
LIGHTENED
```
   AT TIMES OUR SLUMBER WAS LIGHTENED. . . . . . . . .        53 OISIN 3              97
```
LIGHTER
```
   BUT THE TALE, THOUGH WORDS BE LIGHTER THAN AIR,  . . .      3 OISIN 1              11
   LIGHT IS MAN'S LOVE, AND LIGHTER IS MAN'S RAGE!  . . .     45 OISIN 2             243
   WITH WORDS LIGHTER THAN AIR,  . . . . . . . . .          162 ASKS FORGIVE          2
   TROD WITH A LIGHTER TREAD. . . . . . . . . . .           323 SWANS AT COOLE       18
```
LIGHTEST
```
   EVEN THOUGH IT BE THE LIGHTEST OF LIGHT LOVE,  . . . .     230 SHADOW WATER B      184
   TO LIGHTEST OF LIGHT THINGS ALL SANCTITY.  . . . . .      686 DRAWING-ROOM          8
   TO LIGHTEST OF ALL LIGHT THINGS SANCTITY.  . . . . .      734 QUATRAIN APHOR        8
   TO LIGHTEST OF LIGHT THINGS ALL SANCTITY.  . . . . .      734 QUATRAIN APHOR   V    8
```
'LIGHTING
```
   AMONG THEM 'LIGHTING FROM OUR STEED,  . . . . . . .        14 OISIN 1         V  193
```
LIGHTLESS
```
   AND IN HER EYES A LIGHTLESS STARE,  . . . . . . .         668 ISLE STAT II 3       60
```
LIGHTLY
```
   AND SANG WE LIGHTLY TO EACH BLOOM  . . . . . . .          21 OISIN 1         V 306B
   BRUSH LIGHTLY AS HAYMOUSE EARTH'S PEBBLES,  . . . . .      56 OISIN 3             128
   BRUSH LIGHTLY AS HAY MOUSE EARTH'S PEBBLES,  . . . .       56 OISIN 3         V  128
   THEY WEIGHED SO LIGHTLY WHAT THEY GAVE. . . . . .         290 SEPTEMBER 1913       30
   "O WORDS ARE LIGHTLY SPOKEN,"  . . . . . . . .           396 ROSE TREE             1
   WITH THEIR MUSHROOMS LIGHTLY THREADED  . . . . .          705 DAWN-SONG            13
   O SHINING ONES, LIGHTLY WITH SONG PASS,  . . . . .        708 FAIRY PEDANT         21
```
LIGHTNESS
```
   AND LOSS OF YOUR LAUGH AND ITS LIGHTNESS--  . . . . .     708 FAIRY PEDANT         33
```
LIGHTNING
```
   ARE CHOKED WITH THUNDER, LIGHTNING, AND FIERCE WIND,  . .   42 OISIN 2             205
   AND LIGHTNING FLASH FOR EVER? CEASE AND HEAR. . . . .      42 OISIN 2         V  207
   NOW WORDS THAT CALLED UP THE LIGHTNING  . . . . . .       171 MAID QUIET            7
   FOR THE WORDS THAT CALLED UP THE LIGHTNING  . . . . .     171 MAID QUIET       V    7
   WITH LIGHTNING, YOU WENT FROM ME, AND I COULD FIND  . .   257 RECONCILIATION        4
   "THAT SOME STREAM OF LIGHTNING  . . . . . . . .          589 OLD WICKED MAN       55
   AN OLD GHOST'S THOUGHTS ARE LIGHTNING,  . . . . . .       600 SPIRIT MEDIUM        17
   AND WHEN ONCE MORE THE LIGHTNING GENII PASSED,  . . .     687 TWO TITANS           29
   WHEN FLASH ON FLASH ONCE MORE THE LIGHTNING CAME,  . .  . 688 TWO TITANS           39
   FLAMES THE SHUTTLE OF THE LIGHTNING ACROSS THE DRIVING    718 PHANTOM SHIP          1
      SLEET,
   HALF DIZZY WITH THE LIGHTNING THERE RUNS A GATHERING BAND-- 718 PHANTOM SHIP         9
   NOW HALF DIZZY WITH THE LIGHTNING THERE RUNS A GATHERING  718 PHANTOM SHIP     V    9
      BAND!
```
LIGHTNINGS
```
   STABLING HIS UNLOOSED LIGHTNINGS IN THEIR STALL,  . . . .   36 OISIN 2             110
   THE VISION OF A ROCK WHERE LIGHTNINGS WHIRL'D  . . . .     687 TWO TITANS            1
   THE LIGHTNINGS PULSE--BEHOLD HER, AYE BEHOLD--  . . . .    687 TWO TITANS           11
```
LIGHT-OBLITERATING
```
   THROUGH LIGHT-OBLITERATING GARDEN FOLIAGE WHAT MAGIC DRUM?  560 MAGIC DRUM           4
```
LIGHTS
```
   AROUND A SCEPTRE OF ALL LIGHTS,  . . . . . . . .          18 OISIN 1         V  254
```

	PAGE	TITLE	LINE

LIGHTS   (CONTINUED)
AND LIGHTS THE CURTAINED ROOM, ...   89 ISLE IN WATER   10
GOD LIGHTS THE STARS, HIS CANDLES, ...   96 MOLL MAGEE   51
AND THOUGH THE SEVEN LIGHTS BOWED IN THEIR DANCE AND WEPT,   174 ELEMENT POWERS   3
AND LIGHTS WERE PALING OUT OF THE WEST, ...   175 BELOVED DEAD   2
WHILE LIGHTS WERE PALING ONE BY ONE. . . . .   176 BELOVED DEAD   13
WHO AMID LEAFY LIGHTS AND SHADES . . . .   193 BAILE AILLINN   103
THE EVERLASTING TAPER LIGHTS THE GLOOM: . . . . . .   311 MOUNTAIN TOMB   10
O'ER HER NEST THE LIGHTS ARE BLENDING: . . . . . .   646 ISLE STAT I 1   36
SUCH MAY I LOVE. THE SHUDDERING FOREST LIGHTS . .   651 ISLE STAT I 1   165
WITH STREAMING HAIR AS WANDERING LIGHTS . . . . . .   667 ISLE STAT II 3   19
THY FLICKERING HAND? WHAT MEAN THE LIGHTS THAT RISE .   674 ISLE STAT II 3   198
BUT NEVER, NEVER DANGLING LEAVE THE LIVER AND THE LIGHTS.   790 HEART SLEEVE   2
LIKE   SEE FLOWER-LIKE MOUSE-LIKE CANDLE-LIKE MOTH-LIKE BIRD-LIKE ANTAEUS-LIKE
            DANCE-LIKE
MUST LIVE TO BE OLD LIKE THE WANDERING MOON. . . . . .   3 OISIN 1   12
AND LIKE A SUNSET WERE HER LIPS, ...   3 OISIN 1   22
THAT WAVERED LIKE THE SUMMER STREAMS, ...   4 OISIN 1   29
AND WAVERED LIKE A SUMMER RILL, ...   4 OISIN 1   V   29
THAT ARE LIKE COLOURED ASIAN BIRDS . . . .   7 OISIN 1   69
AND THE DAYS PASS BY LIKE A WAYWARD TUNE, ...   8 OISIN 1   83
HAVE A SPEED LIKE THE SPEED OF THE SALMON HERDS, . .   9 OISIN 1   98
AND NOW A LADY RODE LIKE THE WIND . . . .   12 OISIN 1   142
BUT NOW THE MOON LIKE A WHITE ROSE SHONE . . . . .   12 OISIN 1   152
AND NOW A MAIDEN RODE LIKE THE WIND . . . .   12 OISIN 1   V 142
LIKE SOOTY FINGERS, MANY A TREE . . . .   13 OISIN 1   171
OR CLUNG THEREON LIKE SWARMING BEES: . . . .   14 OISIN 1   181
LIKE DROPS OF FROZEN RAINBOW LIGHT, ...   14 OISIN 1   183
AND LAUGHED LIKE MURMURS OF THE SEA: . . . .   15 OISIN 1   210
LIKE TO A MERRY WANDERING ROUT . . . .   18 OISIN 1   253
FOLDED LIKE A FROZEN FLY! . . . .   19 OISIN 1   273
LIKE CRIMSON METEORS HANG IN THE GLOOM, ...   21 OISIN 1   306
HUNG, LIKE METEORS OF RED LIGHT, ...   21 OISIN 1   V 306
LIKE BUBBLES IN A FROZEN POND: . . . .   22 OISIN 1   336
IN MURMURS, LIKE A FRIGHTED BIRD. . . . .   25 OISIN 1   376
SOME DANCED LIKE SHADOWS ON THE MOUNTAINS, ...   25 OISIN 1   388
EACH FOREHEAD LIKE AN OBSCURE STAR . . . .   26 OISIN 1   391
LIKE DROPS OF HONEY CAME THEIR WORDS, ...   26 OISIN 1   398
LIKE TULIPS IN THE AIR A-WINGING, ...   27 OISIN 1   417
AND THE MOON LIKE A PALE ROSE WITHER AWAY." . . . .   28 OISIN 1   427
LIKE A BRIDE BENDING OVER HER MIRROR ADORNING, . .   28 OISIN 1   V 423E
AND THEN AWAY, AWAY, LIKE WHIRLING FLAMES: . . . .   29 OISIN 2   2
AND THEN AWAY, AWAY, LIKE SPIRAL FLAMES: . . . . .   29 OISIN 2   V   2
YET SANG NO MORE AS WHEN, LIKE A BROWN BEE . . . .   30 OISIN 2   15
BUT SANG NO MORE, AS WHEN, LIKE A BROWN BEE . . . .   30 OISIN 2   V   15
FANNED THE DELIGHTED AIR LIKE WINGS OF BIRDS: . . .   32 OISIN 2   50
A-MURMUR LIKE YOUNG PARTRIDGE: WITH LOUD HORN . . .   32 OISIN 2   52
FROM HIGH ABOVE, LIKE FEATHERS OF YOUNG BIRDS . . .   32 OISIN 2   V   50
"THEY MURMUR LIKE YOUNG PARTRIDGE IN THE MORN, . .   32 OISIN 2   V   51
A LADY WITH SOFT EYES LIKE FUNERAL TAPERS, ...   33 OISIN 2   69
DOWN ON US WITH HER EYES LIKE FUNERAL TAPERS. . . .   33 OISIN 2   V   69
A MAIDEN WITH SOFT EYES LIKE FUNERAL TAPERS, . . .   33 OISIN 2   V   69
AS LIKE A RUDDY MOTH THEY WAVED AND FLUTTERED. . .   34 OISIN 2   V   72
LIKE A SMALL RIVER, AND WHERE FEET TOUCHED CAME . .   37 OISIN 2   117
GREY IN THE MIDST LIKE A SMALL RIVULET'S FLOW, . .   37 OISIN 2   V 117
SCARED OF ITS GLITTERING LIKE A METEOR STAR, . . .   38 OISIN 2   V 137
LIKE DRIFTS OF LEAVES, IMMOVABLE AND BRIGHT, . . .   40 OISIN 2   166
LIKE WINGS OF KINGFISHERS! AND HE AROSE . . . . . .   40 OISIN 2   169
LIKE DRIFTS OF LAUREL LEAVES, IMMOVABLE AND BRIGHT . .   40 OISIN 2   V 166
LIKE ROTTED FLESH, AND STONE BY STONE MY HALL . . .   45 OISIN 2   V 236
LIKE AN ARMY OF OLD MEN LONGING FOR REST FROM THE MOAN   48 OISIN 3   16
    OF THE SEAS.
. . . A SOUND LIKE THE STIRRING OF FLIES. . . . . . .   51 OISIN 3   58
SOFTER THAN SNOW-FLAKES IN APRIL AND PIERCING THE MARROW   51 OISIN 3   68
    LIKE FLAME.
THE MOIL OF MY CENTURIES FILLED ME: AND GONE LIKE   51 OISIN 3   70
    A SEA-COVERED STONE
SOFTER THAN SNOWFLAKES IN APRIL, AND PIERCING THE MARROW   51 OISIN 3   V   68
    LIKE FLAME.
A STARLING LIKE THEM THAT FORGATHERED 'NEATH A MOON . . .   54 OISIN 3   103
"LIKE ME WERE SOME GALLEY FORSAKEN FAR OFF IN MERIDIAN   55 OISIN 3   117
    ISLE,
"I WOULD DIE LIKE A SMALL WITHERED LEAF IN THE AUTUMN,   56 OISIN 3   131
    . . .
LIKE AN ARMY OF OLD MEN LONGING FOR REST FROM THE MOAN   57 OISIN 3   144
    OF THE SEAS.
WHEN THEY FROZE THE CLOTH ON MY BODY LIKE ARMOUR RIVETED   57 OISIN 3   151
    FAST,
CAME, AND MY FOREHEAD FELL LOW, AND MY TEARS LIKE BERRIES   57 OISIN 3   154
    FELL DOWN:
LIKE AN ARMY OF OLD MEN LOUNGING FOR REST FROM THE FOAM   57 OISIN 3   V 144
    OF THE SEAS.
. . . LIKE THE ROARING OF WIND IN A WOOD. . . . . . .   58 OISIN 3   168
COMING FORTH FROM THE SEA LIKE THE MORNING . . . . . .   58 OISIN 3   V 158
. . . AND THEIR EYES THAT GLIMMER LIKE SILK. . . . . .   59 OISIN 3   176
AND MY TEARS WERE LARGE LIKE TO BERRIES, AND I MURMURED,   59 OISIN 3   V 178
    . . .
THE HEART IN ME LONGING TO LEAP LIKE A GRASSHOPPER INTO   60 OISIN 3   182
    HER HEART:
I FELL ON THE PATH, AND THE HORSE WENT AWAY LIKE A SUMMER   60 OISIN 3   190
    FLY:

```
                                                      PAGE    TITLE           LINE
LIKE  (CONTINUED)
     CONCEIVE A THING SO SAD AND SOFT, A GENTLE THING LIKE ME?    77 INDIAN ON GOD       16
     LIKE SWARMING BEES, ONE WITH THE DOVE . . . . . . . .        78 INDIAN TO LOVE  V   16
     FELL LIKE FAINT METEORS IN THE GLOOM, AND ONCE  . . . .      80 EPHEMERA           14
     IT QUENCHED, WITH SOUND LIKE FALLING DEW, . . . . . .        86 MAD KING GOLL      66
     YOU WAVES, THOUGH YOU DANCE BY MY FEET LIKE CHILDREN AT      90 OLD FISHERMAN       1
       PLAY,
     YE WAVES, THOUGH YE DANCE 'FORE MY FEET LIKE CHILDREN AT     90 OLD FISHERMAN  V    1
       PLAY,
     THIS BODY TREMBLING LIKE A WIND-BLOWN REED,                 103 FERGUS DRUID       25
     I SEE MY LIFE GO DRIFTING LIKE A RIVER . . . . . . .        104 FERGUS DRUID       31
     I SEE MY LIFE GO DRIPPING LIKE A STREAM . . . . . . .       104 FERGUS DRUID   V   31
     "WITH HIM IS ONE SWEET-THROATED LIKE A BIRD." . . . .       106 CUCHULAIN SEA      16
     "WITH HIM IS ONE SWEET THROATED LIKE A BIRD,                106 CUCHULAIN SEA  V   16
     WHO HAS A LIKE VOW FROM THEIR TRIPLE DUN." . . . . .        108 CUCHULAIN SEA      38
     STARED LIKE THE SPRING UPON THE ANCIENT SKIES, . . .        108 CUCHULAIN SEA      41
     WHO HAD A LIKE VOW FROM OUR TRIPLE DUN,                     109 CUCHULAIN SEA  V   54
     "YOUR HEAD A WHILE SEEMED LIKE A WOMAN'S HEAD . . . .       110 CUCHULAIN SEA  V   63
     WHO DREAMED THAT BEAUTY PASSES LIKE A DREAM? . . . .        111 ROSE OF WORLD       1
     LIKE THE PALE WATERS IN THEIR WINTRY RACE, . . . . .        112 ROSE OF WORLD       8
     DOOMED LIKE ODYSSEUS AND THE LABOURING SHIPS . . . .        120 SORROW OF LOVE      7
     AND MIDNIGHT THERE ENFOLD THEM LIKE A FLEECE . . . .        128 DREAM OF FAERY     34
     A GENTLE FEELING WRAPS THEM LIKE A FLEECE, . . . .          128 DREAM OF FAERY V   34
     OF PASSIONATE MEN, LIKE BATS IN THE DEAD TREES: . . .       136 TO SOME I TALK      5
     AND, LIKE A STORM, CRY THE INEFFABLE NAME, . . . .          137 TO SOME I TALK     12
     LIKE A CANDLE BURNT OUT, . . . . . . . . . . .              142 MOODS               2
     . . . REMADE, LIKE A CASKET OF GOLD . . . . . .             143 ROSE IN HEART       7
     . . . RE-MADE LIKE A CASKET OF GOLD . . . . . .             143 ROSE IN HEART  V    7
     WERE GONE LIKE A DRIFTING SMOKE: . . . . . . . .            145 HOST OF AIR        40
     AND STARS LIKE MOTHS WERE SHINING OUT, . . . . .            149 WANDER AENGUS  V    6
     FOR HOURS WHEN ALL MUST FADE LIKE DEW, . . . . .            156 FORGOT BEAUTY      20
     THEY SET UP A NOISE LIKE CRICKETS, . . . . . . .            161 CAP AND BELLS      33
     AND CUMHAL SAW LIKE A DRIFTING SMOKE . . . . . .            167 BLESSED            13
     LIKE THE SPARKS BLOWN OUT OF A SMITHY, AND DIE? . . .       170 SECRET ROSE        30
     THE POWERS, NOT KIND LIKE YOU, CAME WHERE GOD'S GARDEN      174 ELEMENT POWERS V    1
       BLOWS,
     LIKE THE PALE CUP OF THE SEA, . . . . . . . . .             175 ELEMENT POWERS     14
     FOLK DANCE LIKE A WAVE OF THE SEA: . . . . . . .            178 FIDDLER DOONEY      2
     AND DANCE LIKE A WAVE OF THE SEA. . . . . . . .             179 FIDDLER DOONEY     20
     AND WISDOM THAT CAUGHT FIRE LIKE THE DRIED FLAX, . . .      181 QUEEN MAEVE        28
     FOR ALL THEIR BEAUTY'S LIKE A HOLLOW DREAM. . . .           184 QUEEN MAEVE        88
     FOR ALL THEIR BEAUTY, LIKE A HOLLOW DREAM?" . . .           184 QUEEN MAEVE    V   89
     ALTHOUGH THEIR BEAUTY'S LIKE A HOLLOW DREAM" . . .          184 QUEEN MAEVE    V   89
     BODIES OF SHADOW AND BLIND EYES LIKE PEARLS, . . .          185 QUEEN MAEVE       116
     QUIET'S WILD HEART, LIKE DAILY MEAT: . . . . . .            196 BAILE AILLINN     178
     LIKE THEM THAT ARE NO MORE ALIVE. . . . . . . .             197 BAILE AILLINN     207
     LIKE AN OLD PAUPER, IN ALL KINDS OF WEATHER: . . .          205 ADAMS CURSE         9
     OUR COURAGE BREAKS LIKE AN OLD TREE IN A BLACK WIND AND     207 HANRAHANS SONG      3
       DIES,
     ANGERS THAT ARE LIKE NOISY CLOUDS HAVE SET OUR HEARTS       207 HANRAHANS SONG      8
       ABEAT:
     LIKE TUFTED REEDS OUR COURAGE DROOPS IN A BLACK WIND AND    207 HANRAHANS SONG V    3
       DIES:
     LIKE TATTERED CLOUDS OF THE WORLD, PASSIONS CALL AND OUR    207 HANRAHANS SONG V    8
       HEARTS BEAT:
     ANGERS THAT ARE LIKE BUNDLED CLOUDS HAVE SET OUR HEARTS     207 HANRAHANS SONG V    8
       ABEAT:
     LIKE HEAVY FLOODED WATERS OUR BODIES AND OUR BLOOD: . .     208 HANRAHANS SONG     13
     LIKE HEAVY SWOLLEN WATERS ARE OUR BODIES AND OUR BLOOD:     208 HANRAHANS SONG V   13
     THEY HAD HANDS LIKE CLAWS, AND THEIR KNEES . . . .          208 OLD MEN ADMIRE      4
     WERE TWISTED LIKE THE OLD THORN-TREES . . . . .             208 OLD MEN ADMIRE      5
     LIKE THE WATERS." . . . . . . . . . . . .                   208 OLD MEN ADMIRE      9
     WERE TWISTED LIKE THE OLD THORN TREES . . . . .             208 OLD MEN ADMIRE V    5
     THEREIN ARE MANY QUEENS LIKE BRANWEN AND GUINEVERE: . .     209 UNDER THE MOON     11
     LIKE AN OLD SONG. . . . . . . . . . . . .                   211 O DO NOT LOVE       4
     LIKE AN OLD SONG. . . . . . . . . . . . .                   212 O DO NOT LOVE      12
     LIKE PLOVERS THAT HAVE HEARD THE CALL. . . . . .            213 BLESS PSALTER      13
     QUEENS, THEIR EYES BLUE LIKE THE ICE, . . . . .             214 HAPPY TOWNLAND     11
     THEIR HEARTS WOULD BE LIKE A CUP . . . . . . .              215 HAPPY TOWNLAND     31
     FOR THEIR HEARTS WOULD BE LIKE A CUP . . . . .              215 HAPPY TOWNLAND V   31
     I HAD NOT EYES LIKE THOSE ENCHANTED EYES, . . . .           218 WOODS OF COOLE     17
     HEAVY LIKE STONE, THEIR WISDOM BEING HALF SILENCE. . .      218 WOODS OF COOLE     26
     LIKE A GREY GULL UPON THE BREAST OF EACH. . . . .           223 SHADOW WATER B     24
     NO, NOR WITH A HUNDRED MEN LIKE YOU . . . . . .             225 SHADOW WATER B     74
     HAS SHE NOT SEEN HIM LYING LIKE A LOG, . . . . .            230 SHADOW WATER B    173
     LIKE CHARMED APPLES MADE OF CHRYSOPRASE, . . . .            231 SHADOW WATER B    214
     SHE WILL BE LIKE A WILD CAT: FOR THESE QUEENS . . .         232 SHADOW WATER B    233
     ALONE AND WINGED. OUR LOVE SHALL BE LIKE THEIRS . .         250 SHADOW WATER B    581
     TREMBLING IN THE BLUE HEAVENS LIKE A WHITE FAWN . .         251 SHADOW WATER B    611
     WITH BEAUTY LIKE A TIGHTENED BOW, A KIND . . . .            256 NO SECOND TROY     8
     THAT IS NOT NATURAL IN AN AGE LIKE THIS, . . . .            257 NO SECOND TROY     9
     THAT WERE LIKE MEMORIES OF YOU—BUT NOW . . . .              257 RECONCILIATION     7
     TILL THEY HAD CHANGED US TO LIKE STRENGTH?" . . .           259 PEACE          V    9
     'TWERE POLITIC TO DO THE LIKE BY THESE: . . . .             262 TO A POET           3
     THAT TURNS AND CHANGES LIKE HIS DRAUGHTY SEAS? . .          265 ABBEY THEATRE      12
     FOR ONE THAT WAS LIKE WOMAN MADE . . . . . . .              272 GREY ROCK          29
     OF MEN AND WOMEN MADE LIKE THESE: . . . . . .               272 GREY ROCK          43
     IT VANISHED LIKE A SHADOW, AND A CRY . . . . .              278 TWO KINGS          38
     LIKE THE EYES OF SOME GREAT KITE SCOURING THE WOODS, . .    283 TWO KINGS         150
     I GAZED AT HIM LIKE GROUSE UPON A KITE: . . . .             283 TWO KINGS         152
     THEY HAVE GONE ABOUT THE WORLD LIKE WIND, . . . .           289 SEPTEMBER 1913     11
```

LIKE (CONTINUED)

	PAGE	TITLE	LINE
AND LIKE A LAUGHING STRING	291	TO A FRIEND	11
LIKE GENTLE BLOOD, HAS BEEN DRIVEN FROM THE PLACE, . . .	292	TO A SHADE	14
EVEN LIKE THESE TO RAIL AND SWEAT	294	HATED PLAYBOY	5
AND LIKE THESE TO RAIL AND SWEAT	294	HATED PLAYBOY V	5
SANG UNNOTICED LIKE A BIRD, ...	298	THREE HERMITS	7
SANG UNNOTICED LIKE A BIRD.	299	THREE HERMITS	32
TO TAKE MY FANCY LIKE THE WIND	301	RUN PARADISE	26
"I'D LIKE TO SLEEP TILL WINTER'S GONE	305	HOUR DAWN	60
LIKE SOME OLD RABBIT TO MY CLEFT	307	HOUR DAWN	105
LIKE SOME LAST COURTIER AT A GYPSY CAMPING—PLACE	314	FALLEN MAJESTY	3
LIKE SOME LAST COURTIER AT A GYPSY CAMPING PLACE	314	FALLEN MAJESTY V	3
THAT IS LIKE LAUGHTER, SPRANG AGAIN	318	APPOINTMENT	6
WITH ALL THEIR ANCIENT FACES LIKE RAIN-BEATEN STONES, . .	318	MAGI	4
PASSIONATE AND SIMPLE LIKE HIS HEART.	325	ROBERT GREGORY	32
COULD LIKE A BRACE OF BLACKBIRDS SING.	332	ROUND TOWER	24
LIKE AN OLD HORSE IN A POUND."	333	SOLOMON SHEBA	8
"LIKE THE SPECKLED BIRD THAT STEERS	341	SHEP GOATHERD	62
AND I THAT MADE LIKE MUSIC IN MY YOUTH	342	SHEP GOATHERD	76
AND LIVE LIKE SOLOMON	346	ON WOMAN	42
COURTESY AND PASSION INTO ONE LIKE THOSE	352	PEOPLE	17
HAS SET ME MUTTERING LIKE A FOOL.	356	BROKEN DREAMS	26
I THINK IT BETTER THAT IN TIMES LIKE THESE	359	WAR POEM	1
I THINK IT BETTER THAT AT TIMES LIKE THESE	359	WAR POEM V	1
OR, IT MAY BE, LIKE A BOY'S.	363	DOLLS DRAWINGS	9
BECAUSE THE PRIEST MUST HAVE LIKE EVERY DOG HIS DAY . . .	364	DOLLS FACES	10
SHE IS PLAYING LIKE A CHILD	364	END OF DAY	1
AND LOOK MOST LIKE ME, BEING INDEED MY DOUBLE, ...	371	EGO DOMINUS	72
IS ALWAYS HAPPY LIKE A BIRD OR A BEAST, ...	373	PHASES OF MOON	38
BECAUSE ALL DARK, LIKE THOSE THAT ARE ALL LIGHT, ...	376	PHASES OF MOON	104
CRYING TO ONE ANOTHER LIKE THE BATS, ...	376	PHASES OF MOON	106
AND THE MOON SPUN ROUND LIKE A TOP, ...	378	CAT AND MOON	2
LIKE THE CLANGOUR OF A BELL, ...	382	SONG OF FOOL	9
LEARNED LIKE A MAN? PAUL VERONESE	386	ROBARTES DANCE	26
AND LEAD US TO THE LIKE—IF THEY	387	ROBARTES DANCE	47
BEFORE MY TIME, SEEM LIKE A VIVID MEMORY.	391	UNDER SATURN	10
LIKE ANY ROCK-BRED, SEA-BORNE BIRD, ...	397	POLIT PRISONER	18
I WOULD HAVE TOUCHED IT LIKE A CHILD	399	BREAK OF DAY	12
THAT ALL HER THOUGHTS MAY LIKE THE LINNET BE, ...	404	FOR DAUGHTER	42
O MAY SHE LIVE LIKE SOME GREEN LAUREL	405	FOR DAUGHTER	47
TREE, LIKE A SOOTY FINGER, STARTS FROM THE EARTH, . . .	410	TOWER	19
PRIDE, LIKE THAT OF THE MORN, ...	414	TOWER	134
IN SOME LIKE CHAMBER, SHADOWING FORTH	419	MY HOUSE	15
CURVED LIKE NEW MOON, MOON-LUMINOUS, ...	421	MY TABLE	10
AND SEEMED UNCHANGING LIKE THE SWORD.	421	MY TABLE	21
CURVED LIKE NEW MOON, MOON LUMINOUS, ...	421	MY TABLE V	10
A MIST THAT IS LIKE BLOWN SNOW IS SWEEPING OVER ALL, . .	425	PHANTOM HATRED	2
TRANSPARENT LIKE THE WIND, ...	449	HERO GIRL FOOL	27
THOUGH NURTURED LIKE THE SAILING MOON	451	FIRST LOVE	1
LIKE THE MOON HER KINDNESS IS, ...	452	HUMAN DIGNITY	1
SO LIKE A BIT OF STONE I LIE	452	HUMAN DIGNITY	7
AND BODIES BROKEN LIKE A THORN	454	HIS MEMORIES	3
MY ARMS ARE LIKE THE TWISTED THORN	455	HIS MEMORIES	11
SOUNDS LIKE AN OLD SONG.	457	SECRETS OF OLD	6
THOUGH MARGERY IS LIKE A FISH	457	SECRETS OF OLD V	7
LIKE MEN WHO LIVE BY HABIT, EVERY DAY	463	HARUN RASHID	56
LIKE THIS PURE JET, NOW LOST AMID BLUE SKY, ...	464	HARUN RASHID	64
LIKE PASSION STIRS THE PEACOCK AND HIS MATE, ...	465	HARUN RASHID	100
STILL RAZOR-KEEN, STILL LIKE A LOOKING-GLASS	477	SELF AND SOUL	11
STILL RAZOR-KEEN, STILL LIKE A LOOKING GLASS	477	SELF AND SOUL V	11
ROSE LIKE THESE WALLS FROM THESE	480	BLOOD AND MOON	6
IS EVERY MODERN NATION LIKE THE TOWER, ...	482	BLOOD AND MOON	47
LIKE EVERYTHING THAT HAS THE STAIN OF BLOOD, ...	482	BLOOD AND MOON	51
IS EVERY NATION LIKE THE TOWER	482	BLOOD AND MOON V	47
LIKE MILK SPILT ON A STONE, ...	484	SPILT MILK	4
THEY CAME LIKE SWALLOWS AND LIKE SWALLOWS WENT, ...	489	COOLE PARK 29	17
THEY CAME LIKE SWALLOWS AND LIKE SWALLOWS WENT.	489	COOLE PARK 29	17
AND, LIKE THE SOUL, IT SAILS INTO THE SIGHT	490	COOLE BALLYLEE	19
LIKE SOME POOR ARAB TRIBESMAN AND HIS TENT.	491	COOLE BALLYLEE	40
SPOKE THESE, OR WORDS LIKE THESE.	496	MOHINI CHATTER	15
CAN LIKE THE COCKS OF HADES CROW, ...	498	BYZANTIUM	20
TARGETED, TROD LIKE SPRING.	504	QUARREL IN AGE	16
ALL THINGS HANG LIKE A DROP OF DEW	505	GRAT INSTRUCT	3
WHAT MADE ME LIVE LIKE THESE THAT SEEM	507	STREAM AND SUN	14
WHAT BIDS ME LIVE LIKE THESE THAT SEEM	507	STREAM AND SUN V	14
CRIED THAT WE LIVED LIKE BEAST AND BEAST, ...	508	JANE BISHOP	13
WRINKLED LIKE THE FOOT OF A GOOSE, ...	508	JANE BISHOP	16
THOUGH LIKE A ROAD	512	JANE ON GOD	20
LOVE IS LIKE THE LION'S TOOTH.	514	JANE GROWN OLD	7
LOVE IS LIKE THE LION'S TOOTH.	514	JANE GROWN OLD	14
LOVE IS LIKE THE LION'S TOOTH.	515	JANE GROWN OLD	21
ARE SOMEWHERE SLEEPING LIKE A TOP	525	DANCING DAYS	13
WE LIVED LIKE MEN THAT WATCH A PAINTED STAGE.	542	PARN FUNERAL 1	18
PITCH LIKE KING BILLY BOMB-BALLS IN	565	LAPIS LAZULI	7
HIS LONG LAMP-CHIMNEY SHAPED LIKE THE STEM	566	LAPIS LAZULI	33
HIS LONG LAMP CHIMNEY SHAPED LIKE THE STEM	566	LAPIS LAZULI V	33
LIKE A DUMB BEAST IN A SHOW, ...	572	LADYS 1ST SONG	2
HAS HAD A LIKE INHERITANCE, ...	584	GHOST ROG CASE	25
KEEP DANCING LIKE A WAVE, ...	592	DRUNK SOBRIETY	10
FOR THINGS LIKE THESE WHAT DECENT MAN	598	MODEL LAUREATE	22
THE ROARING TINKER IF YOU LIKE, ...	605	SONGS BURDEN 1	1

457

		PAGE	TITLE	LINE
LIKE (CONTINUED)				
LAY SIGHING LIKE THE REST.		612	NEWS ORACLE	12
STOOD, TOOK DEATH LIKE A TUNE		613	MARCH SONGS 1	15
LIKE A LONG-LEGGED FLY UPON THE STREAM		617	LONG-LEG FLY	9
LIKE A LONG-LEGGED FLY UPON THE STREAM		617	LONG-LEG FLY	19
LIKE A LONG-LEGGED FLY UPON THE STREAM		618	LONG-LEG FLY	29
LIKE AN OLD JEW MAN,		620	JOHN KINSELLA	14
WITH AN EYE LIKE A HAWK.		627	STATES HOLIDAY	32
'TIS MORN! LIKE OLD MEN'S EYES THE STARS ARE PALE,		645	ISLE STAT I 1	4
DRIFT AND FLOAT LIKE SILVER SHIPS!		647	ISLE STAT I 1	67
REPLY LIKE MOANING OF IMPRISONED ELF!		652	ISLE STAT I 2	11
THE SKIES MORE DIM, THOUGH BURNING LIKE A SHIELD,		656	ISLE STAT I 3	26
AND THE WAVES BOWED BEFORE IT LIKE MOWN CORN,		657	ISLE STAT I 3	56
FROM THE WOOD'S WAYS, THEN, LIKE A SILVER FLAME,		658	ISLE STAT II 1	6
I LIKE YOU, AND, IN SOOTH I KNOW NOT WHY.		661	ISLE STAT II 1	64
BEHOLD, HOW LIKE A SWARM OF FIERY BEES		662	ISLE STAT II 2	1
DEEP IN HIS SOUL, LIKE RAIN UPON A SOIL		692	MOSADA 1	56
NOT GOOD; BUT YOU ARE LIKE THE BUTTERFLIES.		693	MOSADA 1	65
I HAD A SISTER LIKE HER ONCE, MY FRIEND.		696	MOSADA 2	11
AND YON FEW STARS GROWN DIM, LIKE EYES OF LOVERS		700	MOSADA 3	33
THIS DEATH IS HEAVY IN MY VEINS LIKE SLEEP.		701	MOSADA 3	57
LIKE HAPPY THOUGHTS GROWN SAD IN EVIL DAYS.		703	MOSADA 3	116
HE TURNS WHERE, HUNG LIKE DROPS OF DRIPPING GOLD,		710	FERENCZ RENYI	18
HE TURNS WHERE, HUNG LIKE DROPS OF LIQUID GOLD,		710	FERENCZ RENYI V	18
LIKE SMALL BROWN MOTHS, A-TREMBLE. "RENYI SAY		713	FERENCZ RENYI	82
LIKE SMALL BROWN MOTHS, A-TREMBLE CEASELESSLY.		713	FERENCZ RENYI V	82
HANG THE MIST-THREADS FOR A LITTLE WHILE LIKE COBWEBS IN THE AIR!		719	PHANTOM SHIP	29
HANG THE MIST THREADS FOR A LITTLE WHILE LIKE COBWEBS IN THE AIR,		719	PHANTOM SHIP V	29
PUFFED LIKE PUFF-BALLS ON A TREE,		727	LOVERS QUARREL	37
WHERE THE MOSS WAS SPREAD LIKE HIS OWN DOORMAT.		728	PRIEST FAIRY	8
AND LIKE A SILVER TRUMPET RING.		736	SUMMER EVENING	4
AND LIKE A SILVER TRUMPET RING.		737	SUMMER EVENING	20
LIKE A GREY OWL MEN HARRY OUT		740	EARL PAUL	23
WHEN SOMETHING THAT WAS BEARDED LIKE A GOAT		747	SHADOW WATER A	11
ARE DOUBTFUL LIKE THESE PULLERS OF THE OAR!		748	SHADOW WATER A	30
SHE WILL ANSWER NOW LIKE ANY WAITING WOMAN		757	SHADOW WATER A	193
THAT I WOULD SHED LIKE TWILIGHT OVER YOU.		765	SHADOW WATER A	352
HAVE FOUND IT LIKE THE FROTH UPON THE ALE.		767	SHADOW WATER A	387
TREMBLING IN THE BLUE HEAVENS LIKE A WHITE FAWN		769	SHADOW WATER A	427
LIKE BROTHER TO BROTHER,		769	BLOOD BOND	2
LIKE SON TO FATHER.		769	BLOOD BOND V	2
LIKE SON TO FATHER.		770	BLOOD BOND	3
COME RIDE LIKE THE MARCH WIND!		774	COME RIDE	6
RUN LIKE THE MARCH WIND!		774	COME RIDE V	6
LIKE WINE THAT FILLS TO THE TOP		781	MY HEART BEAT	14
A WOMAN'S BEAUTY IS LIKE A WHITE		784	WOMANS BEAUTY	1
FRAIL BIRD, LIKE A WHITE SEA-BIRD ALONE		784	WOMANS BEAUTY	2
LIKED				
BUT LIKED THE WAY HIS FINGER SMELT.		619	STICK INCENSE	4
LIKELIHOOD				
OUT OF ALL LIKELIHOOD, OR REASON,		389	IMAGE PAST	9
LIKELY				
NO LIKELY END COULD BRING THEM LOSS		328	IRISH AIRMAN	7
THROW LIKELY COUPLES INTO BED		606	SONGS BURDEN 1	25
SOME HAVE KNOWN A LIKELY LAD		625	OLD MEN BE MAD	2
LIKENESS				
BUT NOT THE EXACT LIKENESS, THE SIMPLICITY OF A CHILD,		354	HIS PHOENIX	28
LILAC				
OF LILAC O'ER THE PULSING WATER GLEAMS,		664	ISLE STAT II 2	48
LILIES				
THE DEW-COLD LILIES LADIES BORE		156	FORGOT BEAUTY	11
LILIES OF DEATH-PALE HOPE, ROSES OF PASSIONATE DREAM.		172	TRAV PASSION	8
WHITE LILIES, AND HER SONG FLEW FORTH AFAR		693	MOSADA 1	85
LILY SEE WATER-LILY				
WHERE DAFFODIL AND LILY WAVE,		67	HAPPY SHEPHERD	46
. . . DEW-DABBLED, THE LILY AND ROSE!		122	WHITE BIRDS	5
SOON FAR FROM THE ROSE AND THE LILY . . .		122	WHITE BIRDS	11
. . . DEW DABBLED, THE LILY AND ROSE!		122	WHITE BIRDS V	5
NOW BATHING LILY LEAF AND FISH'S SCALE,		464	HARUN RASHID	65
NOW BATHING LILY LEAF AND FISHES' SCALE,		464	HARUN RASHID V	65
AND THY NECK'S A POISED LILY!		647	ISLE STAT I 1	55
THE LONG LILY BLOWS,		672	ISLE STAT II 3	165
A LILY BLANCHED PLACE, SHE SAT AND SANG,		693	MOSADA 1 V	83
LILY-BLANCHED				
A LILY-BLANCHED PLACE, SHE SAT AND SANG,		693	MOSADA 1	83
LIMB				
THERE WAS NO LIMB OF MINE BUT FELL		7	OISIN 1	72
NO LIMB OF ME THAT WAS NOT FALLEN		7	OISIN 1 V	72
WHILE A HUNDRED YOUTHS, MIGHTY OF LIMB,		8	OISIN 1	94
--IT HAD SUCH DIGNITY OF LIMB—		254	HIS DREAM	11
BRED THAT FIERCE TOOTH AND CLEANLY LIMB		318	APPOINTMENT	10
IF HEAD AND LIMB HAVE BEAUTY AND THE INSTEP'S HIGH AND LIGHT		354	HIS PHOENIX	21
THAT DREAM IS A NORM! AND SHOULD SOME LIMB OF THE DEVIL		372	ON GOING HOUSE	12
DOWN LIMB AND BREAST OR DOWN THAT GLIMMERING BELLY		560	MAGIC DRUM	5
LIMBED SEE GREAT-LIMBED LONG-LIMBED				
AND YET HAD BEEN GREAT BODIED AND GREAT LIMBED,		181	QUEEN MAEVE V	25
LIMBS				
AND A HUNDRED YOUTHS, WHOSE LIMBS ARE STRUNG		9	OISIN 1 V	97

```
                                                           PAGE     TITLE              LINE
LIMBS   (CONTINUED)
     AND OVER THE LIMBS AND THE VALLEY THE SLOW OWLS WANDERED    49 OISIN 3              41
        AND CAME,
     . . . THE LIMBS OF THE FENIANS ARE TOST!  . . . . . .       62 OISIN 3             213
     WITH STILL AND STONY LIMBS AND OPEN EYES. . . . . . .      182 QUEEN MAEVE          46
     INTO THEIR SHINING LIMBS--I'VE HAD GREAT TEACHERS. . . .   231 SHADOW WATER B      195
     TO GO--FOR HOPE WOULD GIVE HIS LIMBS THE POWER-- . . . .   282 TWO KINGS         V 133A
     FOR HOPE WOULD GIVE HIS LIMBS THE POWER--AND AWAIT . . .   283 TWO KINGS           136
     PUSH OUT HIS VIGOROUS LIMBS AND RUB HIS EYES, . . . . .    284 TWO KINGS           162
     BY THESE WIRE-JOINTED JAWS AND LIMBS OF WOOD, . . . . .    382 VISION ROBART        10
     ON LIMBS THAT HAD RUN WILD. . . . . . . . . . . . . .      394 EASTER 1916          64
     STRETCH OUT YOUR LIMBS AND SLEEP A LONG SATURNIAN SLEEP!   442 BLACK CENTAUR        13
     SHE MOVED HER LIMBS CONFUSEDLY AS THOUGH . . . . . .       466 HARUN RASHID      V 125A
     SO THAT I HAD THE LIMBS TO TRY . . . . . . . . . . .       515 JANE GROWN OLD       19
     FROM THE LIMBS OF LEDA SANK . . . . . . . . . . . . .      522 LULLABY              17
     FROM THE LIMBS OF HELEN SANK . . . . . . . . . . . . .     522 LULLABY           V  17
     PRIMORDIAL MOTHERHOOD FORSAKE HIS LIMBS, THE CHILD         559 MAGIC DRUM            2
        NO LONGER REST.
     LIMBS A LOVE IN COMMON . . . . . . . . . . . . . . .       573 LADYS 2ND SONG       17
     HER LIMBS ARE DELICATE AS AN EYELID, . . . . . . . .       612 NEWS ORACLE          27
     AND HER GIGANTIC LIMBS.  THE WEARY THIRST . . . . . .      687 TWO TITANS           16
     HAD NOT ALL HIS LIMBS A STIR . . . . . . . . . . . .       772 SONG DEIRDRE 1       11
     IN THE TUMULT OF THE LIMBS . . . . . . . . . . . . .       777 SONG DEIRDRE 2        7
LIME    SEE QUICK-LIME
     HUM IN THE LIME TREE FLOWERS! AND PUT AWAY . . . . . .     198 SEVEN WOODS       V   3
     NEITHER CATALPA-TREE NOR SCENTED LIME  . . . . . . .       435 NEW FACES             2
     NEITHER CATALPA TREE NOR SCENTED LIME  . . . . . . .       435 NEW FACES         V   2
     A SYCAMORE AND LIME TREE LOST IN NIGHT . . . . . . .       488 COOLE PARK 29     V   3
LIMESTONE
     ON LIMESTONE QUARRIED NEAR THE SPOT . . . . . . . .        640 BEN BULBEN           90
LIME-TREE
     HUM IN THE LIME-TREE FLOWERS! AND PUT AWAY . . . . . .     198 SEVEN WOODS           3
     A SYCAMORE AND LIME-TREE LOST IN NIGHT . . . . . . .       488 COOLE PARK 29         3
LIMP
     LIMP AS A WORM, . . . . . . . . . . . . . . . . . .        575 MAIDS 2ND SONG        4
LIMPED
     A RABBIT OLD AND LAME LIMPED DOWN THE PATH!  . . . . .      80 EPHEMERA             15
LIMPS
     SHE LIMPS ALONG IN AN AGED WHITENESS!  . . . . . . .        27 OISIN 1             415
     SHE LIMPS ALONG IN AN AGED WHITENESS.  . . . . . . .        28 OISIN 1           V 423
LINE
     BEFORE GOD WAS OR MY OLD LINE BEGAN! . . . . . . . .        29 OISIN 2               8
     THINGS DONE ERE GOD FIRST WAS OR MY OLD LINE BEGAN! . . .   29 OISIN 2           V   8
     THERE WAS NO MIGHTIER SOUL OF HEBER'S LINE! . . . . .       36 OISIN 2              95
     MY SOUL, ONCE GLORY OF ITS ANCIENT LINE, . . . . . .        36 OISIN 2           V  95
     I CRIED, "THOU ART SURELY A WARRIOR, FORGETTING HIS FAMOUS  51 OISIN 3           V  61
        LINE,
     I SAID! "A LINE WILL TAKE US HOURS MAYBE! . . . . . .      204 ADAMS CURSE           4
     TO THAT STERN COLOUR AND THAT DELICATE LINE . . . . .      326 ROBERT GREGORY       67
     THE LONG FLOWING LINE, . . . . . . . . . . . . . .         355 PROPERTIUS            3
LINEAGE
     BUT TELL YOUR NAME AND LINEAGE TO HIM  . . . . . . .       108 CUCHULAIN SEA        36
     ANOTHER LINEAGE FEED THE CROW, . . . . . . . . . . .       437 SONGS PLAY 1         10
LINEAMENTS
     THE LINEAMENTS, A HEART THAT LAUGHTER HAS MADE SWEET, . .  315 FALLEN MAJESTY        5
     THE LINEAMENTS, THE HEART THAT LAUGHTER HAS MADE SWEET,    315 FALLEN MAJESTY V      5
     OF HER UNBLEMISHED LINEAMENTS, A WHITENESS WITH NO STAIN,  353 HIS PHOENIX           3
     THE LINEAMENTS THAT PLEASE THEIR VIEW . . . . . . .        387 ROBARTES DANCE       49
     SHOWS THROUGH OUR LINEAMENTS.  MY CANDLE'S BRIGHT, . . .   464 HARUN RASHID         70
     AND ANCIENT LINEAMENTS ARE BLOTTED OUT. . . . . . .        564 GYRES                 4
     IRELAND'S HISTORY IN THEIR LINEAMENTS TRACE! . . . . .     604 GALLERY REVIS        53
     THE LINEAMENTS OF A PLUMMET-MEASURED FACE. . . . . .       611 STATUES              32
LINED
     AMID GREAT CHAMBERS AND LONG GALLERIES, LINED . . . . .    418 ANCEST HOUSES        36
LINEN
     "ALTHOUGH I'D LIE LAPPED UP IN LINEN . . . . . . . .       331 ROUND TOWER           1
     BETWEEN THE PANTRY AND THE LINEN CHEST, . . . . . . .      340 SHEP GOATHERD     V  36
     A BUNDLE OF LINEN.  SHROUDS BY TWO AND THREE . . . . .     634 CUCHULAIN COMF        9
LINEN-CARRIER
     AND THEREUPON THAT LINEN-CARRIER SAID! . . . . . . .       634 CUCHULAIN COMF       11
LINEN-CHEST
     BETWEEN THE PANTRY AND THE LINEN-CHEST, . . . . . . .      340 SHEP GOATHERD        36
LINES    SEE FISHING-LINES
     THE LINES ARE NOT HEAVY, NOR HEAVY THE LONG NETS BROWN--    91 OLD FISHERMAN V       5
     WITH SHORE LINES IN THE SAY! . . . . . . . . . . . .        94 MOLL MAGEE            6
     INTRODUCTORY LINES . . . . . . . . . . . . . . . . .       217 WOODS OF COOLE V      T
     OF SUCH NOBLE LINES," I SAID, . . . . . . . . . . .        259 PEACE                 6
     EDIT AND ANNOTATE THE LINES . . . . . . . . . . . .        337 SCHOLARS              3
     LINES WRITTEN IN DEJECTION . . . . . . . . . . . . .       343 DEJECTION             T
     THOSE TERRIBLE IMPLACABLE STRAIGHT LINES  . . . . . .      467 HARUN RASHID        142
     THE INTELLECTUAL SWEETNESS OF THOSE LINES . . . . . .      489 COOLE PARK 29        23
     DO NOT BREAK UP THEIR LINES TO WEEP. . . . . . . .         565 LAPIS LAZULI         15
     IN LEMON-TINTED LINES, SO BLAZE THE DAFFODILLS. . . . .    645 ISLE STAT I 1        19
     FROM DEATH'S LATE LANGUOR AS THESE LINES I READ . . .      734 QUATRAIN APHOR       14
LINGER
     MAYBE THEY LINGER BY THE WAY. . . . . . . . . . . .        212 BLESS PSALTER         8
     IS SHADOW, AND NOT LINGER WRETCHEDLY . . . . . . . .       230 SHADOW WATER B      180
     BUT WHAT'S THE MEANING?  WHY DO YOU LINGER THERE? . . .    234 SHADOW WATER B      271
     WHY LINGER?  RUN TO YOUR DESIRE, . . . . . . . . . .       234 SHADOW WATER B      272
     AS THOUGH SHE HAD BEEN FORCED TO LINGER . . . . . .        390 IMAGE PAST           23
     TO MAKE IT LINGER HALF A DAY. . . . . . . . . . . .        401 DEMON BEAST          42
```

459

		PAGE	TITLE	LINE

LINGER   (CONTINUED)
```
    (SOMETHING MAY LINGER THERE THOUGH ALL ELSE DIE!)  . . .   618 BRONZE HEAD          5
    IN TROUBLE IS, THE DOE WILL LINGER NEAR. . . . . . .   713 FERENCZ RENYI       80
    I LINGER WHILE THE BIRDS ARE ON THE WING, . . . . . .   754 SHADOW WATER A V   157
LINGERED    SEE OVER-LINGERED
    HE HATH OVER LINGERED HIS WELCOME! THE DAYS, . . . . .    27 OISIN 1         V 406
    SCARCELY A FEATHER LINGERED, THEN YOU SEEMED . . . . .   102 FERGUS DRUID        4
    WEARY AND KIND ONE LINGERED BY HIS SEAT! . . . . . . .   112 ROSE OF WORLD      13
    AND LINGERED IN THE HIDDEN DESOLATE PLACE . . . . . .   162 ASKS FORGIVE       15
    OR HAVE LINGERED AWHILE AND SAID . . . . . . . . . .   392 EASTER 1916         7
LINGERETH
    SHE ALONE, MY LADY, LINGERETH . . . . . . . . . . .   646 ISLE STAT I 1      28
LINGERING
    SNATCHING THE HORN OF NIAMH, I BLEW A LONG LINGERING NOTE.    51 OISIN 3          57
    SNATCHING THE HORN OF NIAM, I BLEW FORTH A LINGERING NOTE!    51 OISIN 3          57
    SNATCHING THE HORN OF NIAM, I BLEW A LINGERING NOTE!  . .    51 OISIN 3       V  57
    AND PRESSING ON, OR LINGERING SLOW WITH FEAR, . . . . .   114 ROSE OF BATTLE V   5
    FOR THAT PALE BREAST AND LINGERING HAND . . . . . . .   156 FORGOT BEAUTY      15
    FOR THAT DIM BROW AND LINGERING HAND . . . . . . . .   156 FORGOT BEAUTY  V   15
LINGERINGS
    WILD CRIES, GROWN SWEET WITH LULLS AND LINGERINGS LONG.   674 ISLE STAT II 3    222
LINGERS
    OR THE FLAME OF THE BLUE STAR THAT LINGERS . . . . . .   122 WHITE BIRDS         7
    AND THE WAN WAVE THAT LINGERS . . . . . . . . . . .   672 ISLE STAT II 3    166
LINK
    IF FOLLY LINK WITH ELEGANCE . . . . . . . . . . . .   598 STONE CROSS        13
LINKED
    SWEPT ON THE DANCE'S LINKED FLOW, . . . . . . . . . .    20 OISIN 1        V 291
    ONCE MORE THE DANCE'S LINKED FLOW, . . . . . . . . .    22 OISIN 1        V 323A
    LINKED BY A GOLD CHAIN EACH TO EACH, . . . . . . . .   194 BAILE AILLINN     136
LINKS
    IF FOLLY LINKS WITH ELEGANCE   . . . . . . . . . . .   598 STONE CROSS    V  13
LINNET
    THAT ALL HER THOUGHTS MAY LIKE THE LINNET BE, . . . .   404 FOR DAUGHTER       42
    CAN NEVER TEAR THE LINNET FROM THE LEAF. . . . . . .   405 FOR DAUGHTER       56
LINNET'S
    AND EVENING FULL OF THE LINNET'S WINGS. . . . . . . .   117 ISLE INNISFREE      8
LINNETS'
    AND EVENING FULL OF THE LINNETS' WINGS. . . . . . . .   117 ISLE INNISFREE V   8
LION
    "O FLAMING LION OF THE WORLD, O WHEN WILL YOU TURN TO YOUR    56 OISIN 3         129
       REST?"
    O FLAMING LION OF THE WORLD, O WHEN WILL YOU TURN TO YOUR    56 OISIN 3         136
       REST?"
    "OH, FLAMING LION OF THE WORLD, OH, WHEN WILT THOU TURN    56 OISIN 3       V 129
       TO THY REST?"
    AND IN THE FLAMING FORESTS COWER THE LION . . . . . .    73 ANASHU VIJAYA     52
    THEY SEE IN FLAMING FORESTS COWER THE LION . . . . . .    73 ANASHU VIJAYA V   52
    A DREAM THAT A LION HAD DREAMED  . . . . . . . . .   259 UNWORTH PRAISE      7
    HALF LION, HALF CHILD, IS AT PEACE. . . . . . . . .   260 UNWORTH PRAISE     20
    A SPHINX WITH WOMAN BREAST AND LION PAW, . . . . . .   383 VISION ROBART      18
    A SHAPE WITH LION BODY AND THE HEAD OF A MAN, . . . .   402 SECOND COMING      14
    THE LION AND THE HONEYCOMB, WHAT HAS SCRIPTURE SAID?  . .   503 VACILLATION        88
    THE LION AND THE HONEY-COMB, WHAT HAS SCRIPTURE SAID?  . .   503 VACILLATION    V  88
    THE LION AND THE VIRGIN, . . . . . . . . . . . .   601 THOSE IMAGES       11
    LION AND WOMAN AND THE LORD KNOWS WHAT. . . . . . .   629 CIRCUS ANIMALS      8
    THE LION, THE WORLD'S GREAT SOLITARY, BENDS . . . . .   689 NETTLESHIP          5
LIONEL
    LIONEL JOHNSON COMES THE FIRST TO MIND, . . . . . . .   324 ROBERT GREGORY     17
LIONESS
    AND LIONESS, WITH ALL THEIR WHIMPERING CUBS! . . . . .    73 ANASHU VIJAYA     53
    BUT HERE THE LIONESS LICKS HER SOFT CUB . . . . . .   688 NETTLESHIP          2
LION'S
    LOVE IS LIKE THE LION'S TOOTH. . . . . . . . . . .   514 JANE GROWN OLD      7
    LOVE IS LIKE THE LION'S TOOTH. . . . . . . . . . .   514 JANE GROWN OLD     14
    LOVE IS LIKE THE LION'S TOOTH. . . . . . . . . . .   515 JANE GROWN OLD     21
    HE'LL SNAP HIS SWORD. RAISED IS THE LION'S PAW. . . .   664 ISLE STAT II 2  ' 63
LIONS
    BECAUSE PIEBALD PONIES, LED BEARS, CAGED LIONS, MAKE BUT   623 HIGH TALK           5
       POOR SHOWS,
    BRAVED LIONS FOR MY SAKE, . . . . . . . . . . . .   789 SINGING HEAD        2
LIP
    OF ONE LONG FINGER ON MY LIP. . . . . . . . . . . .    12 OISIN 1          151
    MURMURING SOFTLY LIP TO LIP, . . . . . . . . . . .    78 INDIAN TO LOVE      8
    MURMURING SOFTLY LIP TO LIP, . . . . . . . . . . .    78 INDIAN TO LOVE      8
    THOUGH I'D MY FINGER ON MY LIP, . . . . . . . . . .   254 HIS DREAM          13
    STARED AT THE GODS WITH LAUGHING LIP. . . . . . . .   276 GREY ROCK         123
    WHATEVER COULD RECALL THE LIP OF LOVER. . . . . . . .   537 HER VISION          8
    HUSH! HUSH! HUSH! ON EVERY LIP . . . . . . . . . .   732 STREET DANCERS     18
LIPPED    SEE LAUGHTER-LIPPED LOOSE-LIPPED
    NO LOOSE LIPPED DEMAGOGUE HAD WON THE DAY, . . . . . .   542 PARN FUNERAL 2 V   3
LIPS    SEE FROTH-LIPS
    AND LIKE A SUNSET WERE HER LIPS, . . . . . . . . .     3 OISIN 1           22
    WHOSE LIPS HAD LIFE'S MOST PROSPEROUS GLOW? . . . . .    10 OISIN 1          118
    FROM ALL THEIR LIPS, AND ONCE THEY SANG . . . . . .    16 OISIN 1          226
    AND KISSED THE SCEPTRE WITH RED LIPS, . . . . . . .    18 OISIN 1          258
    AND KISSED THE SCEPTRE WITH HOT LIPS, . . . . . . .    18 OISIN 1        V 258
    HAPPY AS CHILDREN WITH UNWITHERING LIPS, . . . . . .    30 OISIN 2        V 14B
    THE STREAM CHURNED, CHURNED, AND CHURNED--HIS LIPS APART,    31 OISIN 2           43
    . . . AND CHURNED. HIS LIPS WERE ROLLED APART, . . .    31 OISIN 2        V  43
    FLUTTER ALONG THE FROTH LIPS OF THE SEA, . . . . . .    33 OISIN 2           58
```

		PAGE	TITLE		LINE
LIPS	(CONTINUED)				
AND SHORES THE FROTH LIPS WET!	• • • • • • •	33	OISIN 2		59
FLUTTER ALONG THE FROTH LIPS OF THE SEA	• • • • • •	33	OISIN 2		64
SO PALE! AND SOUNDS OF WONDER HER LIPS UTTERED,	• • • •	34	OISIN 2	V	71
UPON THE LIPS OF SEA-GODS IN THEIR DAY!	• • • • •	41	OISIN 2		190
AND NOW THE WARMTH OF SIGHS, AND AFTER THE QUIVER OF LIPS.		47	OISIN 3		8
HE, SHAKING THE FOLD OF HIS LIPS,	• • • • • • • •	51	OISIN 3		59
HIS LIPS MOVED SLOWLY IN ANSWER, NO ANSWER OUT OF THEM CAME!		51	OISIN 3		66
HE, SHAKING THE FOLDS OF HIS LIPS	• • • • • • • •	51	OISIN 3	V	59
COMING OUT OF THE SEA AS THE DAWN COMES, A CHAUNT OF LOVE ON MY LIPS,		58	OISIN 3		158
• • • WITH RED LIPS MURMURING A SONG,	• • • • • •	58	OISIN 3	V	158
AND TO ITS LIPS THY STORY TELL,	• • • • • •	66	HAPPY SHEPHERD		37
HE SPAKE ONCE MORE AND FONDLED WITH HIS LIPS	• • • •	81	EPHEMERA	V	24A
GLIMMERING IN HER DROOPED EYES, SAW HER LIPS MOVE	• • •	81	EPHEMERA	V	24D
PARTED HER LIPS WITH A LOUD SUDDEN CRY!	• • • • •	105	CUCHULAIN SEA		8
FOR THESE RED LIPS, WITH ALL THEIR MOURNFUL PRIDE,	• • •	111	ROSE OF WORLD		2
OR COMES IN LAUGHTER FROM THE SEA'S SAD LIPS,	• • • • •	114	ROSE OF BATTLE		19
A GIRL AROSE THAT HAD RED MOURNFUL LIPS	• • • • •	120	SORROW OF LOVE		5
AND THEN YOU CAME WITH THOSE RED MOURNFUL LIPS,	• • • •	120	SORROW OF LOVE	V	5
AND MADE MY LIPS AND MUSIC WED,	• • • • • • •	134	TWO TREES		11
OUR ARMS ARE WAVING, OUR LIPS ARE APART!	• • • • •	140	HOSTING SIDHE		9
"ARMS ARE A-WAVING AND LIPS APART	• • • • • • •	140	HOSTING SIDHE	V	9
OUR ARMS ARE WEAVING, OUR LIPS ARE APART!	• • • • •	140	HOSTING SIDHE	V	9
AND KISS HER LIPS AND TAKE HER HANDS!	• • • • • •	150	WANDER AENGUS		20
AND KISS HER LIPS AND TAKE HER HAND,	• • • • • •	150	WANDER AENGUS	V	20
AND HER RED LIPS SANG THEM A LOVE-SONG	• • • • • •	160	CAP AND BELLS		27
HER RED LIPS SANG THEM A LOVE-SONG,	• • • • • •	160	CAP AND BELLS		27
AND HER RED LIPS SANG THEM A LOVE SONG.	• • • • • •	160	CAP AND BELLS	V	27
AND COVER YOUR LIPS WITH ODOROUS TWILIGHT AND SAY,	• • •	162	ASKS FORGIVE		5
COVER YOUR LIPS WITH ROSE-HEAVY TWILIGHT, AND SAY!	• • •	162	ASKS FORGIVE	V	5
MAY NOT LIE ON THE BREAST NOR HIS LIPS ON THE HAIR,	• • •	177	PAST GREATNESS		9
WOULD NOT LIE ON THE BREAST, OR HIS LIPS ON THE HAIR,	• •	177	PAST GREATNESS	V	9
BROKE FROM HIS PARTED LIPS AND BROKE AGAIN,	• • • • •	182	QUEEN MAEVE		48
THE PARTED LIPS REPLIED, "I SEEK YOUR HELP,	• • • •	183	QUEEN MAEVE		83
COULD BUT AWAKEN SADLY UPON LIPS	• • • • • •	185	QUEEN MAEVE		104
A MURMUR OF SOFT WORDS AND MEETING LIPS.	• • • • •	187	QUEEN MAEVE		154
FOR THEY, FOR ALL SMOOTH LIPS CAN SAY.	• • • • •	202	NEVER GIVE ALL		9
AND KISS MORE LIPS THAN LASTING PEACEABLE MEN	• • • •	225	SHADOW WATER B		71
WHAT THE WORLD'S MILLION LIPS ARE THIRSTING FOR	• • • •	229	SHADOW WATER B		161
WITH SO RED LIPS, AND RUNNING ON SUCH FEET,	• • • • •	231	SHADOW WATER B		199
HE HAS STOOPED DOWN AND KISSED HER ON THE LIPS.	• • •	232	SHADOW WATER B		230
TO BE HIS BEDFELLOW? UNTIL YOUR LIPS	• • • • •	237	SHADOW WATER B		335
ALL THAT IS NOT THE MEETING OF OUR LIPS.	• • • • •	246	SHADOW WATER B		506
MY FANCY, AND SET MY BOYISH LIPS TO SAY,	• • • • •	270	PARDON FATHERS		17
HER EYES WERE COLD AND STEADY, HER LIPS TIGHT.	• • •	279	TWO KINGS		64
KNOWING THAT HE SHOULD FIND UPON HER LIPS	• • • •	280	TWO KINGS		77
"SPEAKING OF LOVE THROUGH OTHER LIPS AND LOOKING	• • •	283	TWO KINGS		155
THAT WERE A DOUBLE HUNGER IN MY LIPS	• • • • •	285	TWO KINGS		206
THAT WERE A DOUBLE HUNGER ON MY LIPS	• • • • •	285	TWO KINGS	V	206
AND TOUCHED HER FOREHEAD WITH HIS LIPS AND SAID!	• • •	286	TWO KINGS	V	211B
UPON THE LIPS OF COMMON MEN	• • • • • • • •	361	ALF POLLEXFEN		33
THEIR SHROUDS ARE BLOODY AND THEIR LIPS ARE WET.	• • •	483	OIL AND BLOOD		6
AND THE LIPS MORE SCARLET,	• • • • • • • •	532	BEFORE WORLD		3
LIVE LIPS UPON A PLUMMET-MEASURED FACE.	• • • • •	610	STATUES		8
BLOSSOMS OPEN DEWY LIPS!	• • • • • • •	647	ISLE STAT I 1		65
IF ON HIS LIPS THE ENCHANTED FLOWER BE LAID!	• • • •	668	ISLE STAT II 3		46
MY LIPS, FAIR YOUTH. IT SHALL BE AS YOU ASK.	• • •	669	ISLE STAT II 3		80
LAUGHS NOT. IT DWELLS ALONE ON MORTAL LIPS!	• • •	670	ISLE STAT II 3		100
IS IN THY FACE, AND LIPS TOGETHER PRESSED!	• • • •	671	ISLE STAT II 3		139
THE FAERY FLOWER LIES UPON THY LIPS.	• • • • •	677	ISLE STAT II 3		277
THE FAERY BLOSSOM LIES UPON THY LIPS.	• • • • •	677	ISLE STAT II 3		285
ENAMOURED OF THE WAVES' IMPETUOUS LIPS.	• • • • •	677	ISLE STAT II 3		289
THE FAERY BLOSSOM LIES UPON THY LIPS!	• • • • •	678	ISLE STAT II 3		291
THE GOBLIN FLOWER LIETH ON THY LIPS.	• • • • •	678	ISLE STAT II 3		298
THE FAERY BLOSSOM BROODS UPON THY LIPS.	• • • •	678	ISLE STAT II 3		306
O BROTHER, LAY THY FLUTE UPON THY LIPS!	• • • • •	681	SEEKER		6
TO DEATH. HIS LIPS ARE GLUED, WITH QUIVERING TOUCH,	• •	684	SEEKER	V	63
WHAT, LOVER, DIE BEFORE OUR LIPS HAVE MET?	• • • •	685	SEEKER		80
AROUND THE TWITTER OF THE LIPS OF DUST	• • • • •	685	DRAWING-ROOM		1
"I LAUGHED UPON THE LIPS OF SOPHOCLES,	• • • • •	686	LIFE		17
GATHERED ON HER OWN LIPS, OH YOUTH, AND FLING	• • •	688	TWO TITANS		53
SLID CIRCLING DOWN AND SOFTLY TOUCHED MY LIPS	• • • •	690	MOSADA 1		21
WITH POISONOUS LIPS, AND HE IS PINING SINCE?	• • • •	696	MOSADA 2		7
YOU'RE PALE, MY LORD. HIS LIPS ARE QUIVERING!	• • •	704	MOSADA 2		127
HE RUSHES, ROLLING FROM HIS LIPS A MADMAN'S LAUGH.	• • •	715	FERENCZ RENYI		122
THE GHOSTS WENT BY ME WITH THEIR LIPS APART	• • • •	734	QUATRAIN APHOR		13
"I LAUGHED UPON THE LIPS OF SOPHOCLES,	• • • • •	735	QUATRAIN APHOR		19
"AROUND, THE TWITTER OF THE LIPS OF DUST	• • • • •	735	QUATRAIN APHOR		21
AND LEAN YOUR LIPS DEVOUTLY TO THIS HARP,	• • • • •	762	SHADOW WATER A		287
AND HEARD THE DEAD LIPS SING.	• • • • • • •	790	SINGING HEAD		24
LIQUID					
OUR TREAD, AS ROSE AND FELL THE LIQUID TONES	• • • •	33	OISIN 2	V	68B
HE TURNS WHERE, HUNG LIKE DROPS OF LIQUID GOLD,	• • •	710	FERENCZ RENYI	V	18
DROPPING LIQUID RAINBOW LIGHT,	• • • • • • •	732	STREET DANCERS		33
LIQUORICE					
AND THAT IS CURED BY A BOILED LIQUORICE ROOT.	• • • •	227	SHADOW WATER B	V	116B
LISADILL					
AS HE WENT BY THE SANDS OF LISADILL	• • • • • •	127	DREAM OF FAERY	V	13

461

LISS
    AND HIM WHO DROVE THE GODS OUT OF THEIR LISS, ...   170 SECRET ROSE   16
LISSADELL
    HE WANDERED BY THE SANDS OF LISSADELL, ...   127 DREAM OF FAERY   13
    THE LIGHT OF EVENING, LISSADELL, ...   475 EVA GORE-BOOTH   1
LISTEN
    . . . SHALL LISTEN AND RISE UP AND WEEP! . . . .   62 OISIN 3   206
    BUT THE YOUNG QUEEN WOULD NOT LISTEN! . . . .   159 CAP AND BELLS   9
    AND LISTEN TO ME FOR A WHILE. THE SAILORS . . . . .   226 SHADOW WATER B   92
    AND LISTEN TO ME FOR AWHILE. THE SAILORS . . . . . .   226 SHADOW WATER B V   92
    LISTEN TO THAT LOW-LAUGHING STRING OF THE MOON . . . .   243 SHADOW WATER B   432
    THAT FLY INTO THE WEST? BUT LISTEN, LISTEN! . . . . .   247 SHADOW WATER B   518
    THAT FLY INTO THE WEST? BUT LISTEN, LISTEN! . . . . .   247 SHADOW WATER B   518
    IF YOU'LL BUT LISTEN CLOSELY TO THAT CRYING . . . . .   247 SHADOW WATER B   520
    AND LISTEN AT THE CORNERS HAS NOT COME! . . . .   293 TO A SHADE   22
    HOW COULD YOU DREAM THEY'D LISTEN . . . .   395 SIXTEEN DEAD   13
    WILL WONDERING LISTEN, AND THIS TALE SHALL EASE . . . .   693 MOSADA 1   70
    HANGS ON MY BREAST! LISTEN, WE SHALL BE SAFE. . . . .   701 MOSADA 3   73
LISTENED
    AS THOUGH ONE LISTENED THERE, AND HIS VOICE SANK . . . .   180 QUEEN MAEVE   7
    FOR YOU HAVE LISTENED TO ME PLAYING IT . . . .   243 SHADOW WATER B   434
LISTENING
    BUT NAUGHT THEY HEARD, FOR THEY ARE ALWAYS LISTENING, . .   68 SAD SHEPHERD   15
    BUT NAUGHT THEY HEARD, FOR THEY ARE EVER LISTENING, . . .   68 SAD SHEPHERD V   15
    AND THEY WERE LISTENING THERE BEYOND THE SAIL. . . . .   223 SHADOW WATER B   37
    AND LISTENING TO THE CRY OF WIND AND WAVE . . . . . .   236 SHADOW WATER B   315
    AND LISTENING TO THE CRY OF THE WIND AND WAVE . . . . .   236 SHADOW WATER B V   315
    AN OATEN PIPE UNTO A LISTENING FAWN, ...   678 ISLE STAT II 3   301
    AN OATEN PIPE UNTO A LISTENING FAUN, ...   678 ISLE STAT II 3 V   301
    LISTENING, UPON THEIR SHADOWS STOOD. . . . .   725 LEGEND   8
LISTENS
    BUT THETIS' BELLY LISTENS. . . . .   612 NEWS ORACLE   29
LISTLESS
    AND ALL LISTLESS HOURS FEAR US, ...   21 OISIN 1   317
LIST'NING
    IN LIST'NING SILENCE GAZING ON OUR GRIEF. . . . .   702 MOSADA 3   87
LIT   SEE LAUGHTER-LIT A-LIT STAR-LIT
    A GOLDEN CRESCENT LIT THE PLAIN, ...   2 OISIN 1   V 78B
    THEN IN THAT HALL, LIT BY THE DIM SEA-SHINE, ...   41 OISIN 2   187
    THEN IN THAT HALL, LIT BY THE DIM SEA SHINE, ...   41 OISIN 2   V 187
    HIS LANGUID TAIL ABOVE US, LIT WITH MYRIAD SPOTS OF LIGHT.   77 INDIAN ON GOD   20
    WHAT MEASURER TIME HAS LIT ABOVE, ...   139 TO IRELAND   38
    AND HAVING LIT UPON THIS WOMAN THERE, ...   248 SHADOW WATER B   542
    AND HAVING LIT UPON THIS WOMAN HERE, ...   248 SHADOW WATER B V   542
    TO HAVE LIT UPON AS CLEAN AND SWEET A TALE . . . . . .   258 KING NO KING   8
    "WERE IT NOT THAT WHEN THE DAWN HAS LIT MY BED . . . . .   285 TWO KINGS   187
    YET NEVER HAVE I LIT ON A FRIEND . . . .   301 RUN PARADISE   25
    WHERE EVERY DAY MY FOOTFALL SHOULD HAVE LIT . . . . . .   352 PEOPLE   8
    AND WHEN SHE MEETS OUR GAZE HER EYES ARE LAUGHTER LIT . .   362 HER COURTESY V   5
    WE HAVE LIT UPON THE GENTLE, SENSITIVE MIND . . . . . .   368 EGO DOMINUS   12
    ONE LASHED HER TAIL! HER EYES LIT BY THE MOON . . . . .   383 VISION ROBART   29
    LIT UP THE DARK MAHOGANY AND THE WINE, ...   410 TOWER   27
    HAVE LIT UPON A WOMAN WHO SO SHARES . . . .   465 HARUN RASHID   85
    HAD SO LIT UP THE WHOLE . . . .   472 ALL SOUL NIGHT   37
    FLAMES THAT NO FAGGOT FEEDS, NOR STEEL HAS LIT, ...   498 BYZANTIUM   26
    SUDDENLY LIT UP . . . .   512 JANE ON GOD   16
    "HAVE NO LIT CANDLES IN YOUR ROOM," . . . .   569 THREE BUSHES   8
    WHERE NO LIT CANDLES ARE, ...   570 THREE BUSHES V   25
    THAT BROAD NOON HAS NEVER LIT, ...   632 MAN AND ECHO   4
    HALF LIT, SO FLAPT THE WINGS ACROSS THE LAKE— . . . . .   659 ISLE STAT II 1   17
    I LIT BY THE THING, 'TWAS A SHEPHERD-BOY, ...   673 ISLE STAT II 3   180
    HAVE LIT LONE TAPERS. NOW THE NIGHT WAS CAST, ...   687 TWO TITANS   27
    CASTLE DARGAN'S RUIN ALL LIT, ...   788 HAWTHORN TREE   3
LITERATURE
    . . . HAVE JOINED THE AGITATION AGAINST IMMORAL LITERATURE   262 STUDENTS AGIT   T
    . . . AGITATION AGAINST IMMORAL LITERATURE . . . . . .   262 STUDENTS AGIT V   T
LITTER
    SHOULDERED A LITTER WITH A WOUNDED MAN, ...   537 HER VISION   14
LITTLE
    MAID NIAM FROM A LITTLE TRUMP . . . .   14 OISIN 1   V 194
    OUT OF A LITTLE SILVER TRUMP! . . . .   15 OISIN 1   196
    AND MAKES THE LITTLE PLANETS RUN! . . . .   18 OISIN 1   268
    FOR JOY THE LITTLE PLANETS RUN . . . .   18 OISIN 1   V 267
    AND STAY A LITTLE WHILE, AND BID THEM WEEP! . . . . . .   33 OISIN 2   60
    A LITTLE RUNNEL MADE A BUBBLING STRAIN, ...   39 OISIN 2   156
    ROSE FROM A LITTLE RUNNEL ON WHOSE EDGE . . . .   39 OISIN 2   V 157
    THY FRETFUL WORDS A LITTLE WHILE, ...   66 HAPPY SHEPHERD   40
    A LITTLE FROM THE OTHER SHADES APART, ...   71 ANASHU VIJAYA   9
    SIGH, O YOU LITTLE STARS! O SIGH AND SHAKE YOUR   72 ANASHU VIJAYA   18
      BLUE APPAREL!
    SING, O YOU LITTLE STARS! O SING AND RAISE YOUR RAPTUROUS   72 ANASHU VIJAYA   20
      CAROL
    SIGH, OH YE LITTLE STARS! OH, SIGH AND SHAKE YOUR BLUE   72 ANASHU VIJAYA V   18
      APPAREL!
    SING, OH YE LITTLE STARS! OH, SING, AND RAISE YOUR   72 ANASHU VIJAYA V   20
      RAPTUROUS CAROL
    I PASSED A LITTLE FURTHER ON AND HEARD A LOTUS TALK! . .   76 INDIAN ON GOD   9
    A LITTLE WAY WITHIN THE GLOOM A ROEBUCK RAISED HIS EYES .   76 INDIAN ON GOD   13
    I PACED A LITTLE FURTHER ON AND HEARD A LOTUS TALK!— . .   76 INDIAN ON GOD V   9
    I PASSED A LITTLE FURTHER ON AND HEARD A PEACOCK SAY! . .   77 INDIAN ON GOD   17
    I PACED A LITTLE FURTHER AND I HEARD A PEACOCK SAY!— . .   77 INDIAN ON GOD V   17

LITTLE   (CONTINUED)
    I PASSED A LITTLE FURTHER AND I HEARD A PEACOCK SAY:-- . .   77 INDIAN ON GOD   V   17
    THE LITTLE WAVES THAT WALKED IN EVENING WHITENESS, . . .   81 EPHEMERA   V   24C
    I CAME UPON A LITTLE TOWN . . . .   85 MAD KING GOLL   49
    AS ONCE WITHIN A LITTLE TOWN . . . .   85 MAD KING GOLL   V   49
    TIME WAS, AS IN A LITTLE TOWN, ...   85 MAD KING GOLL   V   49
    ONCE, WHILE WITHIN A LITTLE TOWN . . . .   85 MAD KING GOLL   V   49
    SHE PASSED THE SALLEY GARDENS WITH LITTLE SNOW-WHITE FEET.   90 SALLEY GARDENS   2
    COME ROUND ME, LITTLE CHILDER: . . . .   94 MOLL MAGEE   1
    YE LITTLE CHILDER DEAR, ...   95 MOLL MAGEE   18
    THE LITTLE STRAWS WERE TURNIN' ROUND . . . . . .   95 MOLL MAGEE   31
    SO NOW, YE LITTLE CHILDER, ...   96 MOLL MAGEE   53
    A LITTLE SPACE FOR THE ROSE-BREATH TO FILL! . . .   101 ROSE UPON ROOD   14
    TAKE, IF YOU MUST, THIS LITTLE BAG OF DREAMS: . .   104 FERGUS DRUID   29
    GOD'S BELL HAS CLAIMED THEM BY THE LITTLE CRY . .   114 ROSE OF BATTLE   23
    WE SHALL NO LONGER HEAR THE LITTLE CRY . . . . .   115 ROSE OF BATTLE   35
    MURMUR, A LITTLE SADLY, HOW LOVE FLED . . . . .   121 YOU ARE OLD   10
    MURMUR, A LITTLE SAD, "FROM US FLED LOVE, . . .   121 YOU ARE OLD   V   10
    IT SEEMED THEY RAISED THEIR LITTLE SILVER HEADS,   126 DREAM OF FAERY   6
    TOLD WHERE--AH, LITTLE, ALL-UNNEEDED VOICE!-- .   127 DREAM OF FAERY V   30
    AND ALL GREW FRIENDLY FOR A LITTLE WHILE. . . .   129 BOOK STORIES   8
    FOR ALL WHO HEARD IT DREAMED A LITTLE WHILE. . .   129 BOOK STORIES   V   8
    AND RODE WITH LITTLE CARE, ...   133 FR GILLIGAN   28
    OR ONLY GAZE A LITTLE WHILE: . . . .   135 TWO TREES   24
    OVER THE LITTLE SILVER CORDS, ...   146 FISH   6
    AND CAUGHT A LITTLE SILVER TROUT. . . . .   149 WANDER AENGUS   8
    AND HOOKED A LITTLE SILVER TROUT. . . . .   149 WANDER AENGUS   V   8
    O WHAT TO ME THE LITTLE ROOM . . . .   151 HEART OF WOMAN   1
    A LITTLE STOLEN TRESS. I, TOO, AWAIT . . . . .   170 SECRET ROSE   27
    CALLED RATHER BAILE LITTLE LAND. . . . .   189 BAILE AILLINN V   17
    WHEN THEY HAD RIDDEN A LITTLE WAY . . . .   191 BAILE AILLINN   56
    THEREFORE IT IS BUT LITTLE NEWS . . . .   194 BAILE AILLINN   124
    AND LITTLE SHADOWS COME ABOUT HER EYES: . . . .   199 FOLLY COMFORT   3
    AND THERE ARE LITTLE CREASES ABOUT HER EYES: . .   199 FOLLY COMFORT V   3
    THE LITTLE FOX HE MURMURED, ...   214 HAPPY TOWNLAND   13
    BUT THE LITTLE RED FOX MURMURED, ...   214 HAPPY TOWNLAND   17
    THE LITTLE FOX HE MURMURED, ...   215 HAPPY TOWNLAND   33
    BUT THE LITTLE RED FOX MURMURED, ...   215 HAPPY TOWNLAND   37
    AND BLOW A LITTLE NOISE . . . .   215 HAPPY TOWNLAND   43
    THE LITTLE FOX HE MURMURED, ...   216 HAPPY TOWNLAND   53
    BUT THE LITTLE RED FOX MURMURED, ...   216 HAPPY TOWNLAND   57
    OR HURLED THE LITTLE STREETS UPON THE GREAT, . .   256 NO SECOND TROY   4
    "WHILE I HAVE HIM AND YOU IT MATTERS LITTLE . .   280 TWO KINGS   85
    BUT LITTLE TIME HAD THEY TO PRAY . . . .   289 SEPTEMBER 1913   12
    OF A MOST RIDICULOUS LITTLE BIRD . . . .   314 MEMORY YOUTH   20
    A LITTLE NEARER TO HIS THOUGHT . . . .   324 ROBERT GREGORY   23
    A DEAL I'D SWEAT AND LITTLE EARN . . . .   331 ROUND TOWER   2
    "IF LITTLE PLANNED IS LITTLE SINNED . . . . . .   338 TOM OROUGHLEY   9
    "IF LITTLE PLANNED IS LITTLE SINNED . . . . . .   338 TOM OROUGHLEY   9
    BUT LITTLE NEED THE GRAVE DISTRESS. . . . . . .   338 TOM OROUGHLEY   10
    "OH, LITTLE PLANNED IS LITTLE SINNED . . . . . .   338 TOM OROUGHLEY V   9
    "OH, LITTLE PLANNED IS LITTLE SINNED . . . . . .   338 TOM OROUGHLEY V   9
    AND LITTLE NEED THE GRAVE DISTRESS. . . . . . .   338 TOM OROUGHLEY V   10
    AND WHEN 'TWAS DONE SO LITTLE HAD I DONE . . . .   341 SHEP GOATHERD   59
    GIVE HER A LITTLE GRACE, ...   367 HER CHRIS TREE   9
    YET LITTLE PEACE HE HAD, ...   383 VISION ROBART   35
    O LITTLE DID THEY CARE WHO DANCED BETWEEN, . . .   383 VISION ROBART   37
    AND LITTLE SHE BY WHOM HER DANCE WAS SEEN . . .   383 VISION ROBART   38
    SHE THAT BUT LITTLE PATIENCE KNEW, ...   397 POLIT PRISONER   1
    BESIDE THE LITTLE LAKE . . . .   400 DEMON BEAST   23
    PROSPER BUT LITTLE, HAS DRIED UP OF LATE. . . .   405 FOR DAUGHTER   51
    AND BROUGHT THEM IN A LITTLE COVERED DISH. . . .   410 TOWER   32
    THOUGHT THAT UNLESS A LITTLE POWDER BURNED . . .   429 NINETEEN 19   21
    THE WOMEN TAKE SO LITTLE STOCK . . . .   455 HIS MEMORIES   7
    AND WAIT WAR'S MUSIC: PASS THE LITTLE GALLERY: 461 HARUN RASHID   8
    GREAT HATRED, LITTLE ROOM, ...   506 REMORSE SPEECH   12
    "BODES ME LITTLE GOOD." . . . .   539 MEETING   6
    SWEETENS THE LITTLE HALF-WAY HOUSE . . . .   567 LAPIS LAZULI   48
    SWEETEN THE LITTLE HALFWAY HOUSE . . . .   567 LAPIS LAZULI   V   48
    THAT HAD SUCH LITTLE SENSE . . . .   585 ORAHILLY   11
    AND THAT SHOULD MOTHER SEEK HER SON SHE'D HAVE BUT LITTLE   593 PILGRIM   12
       LUCK
    OR SAD SEA-SHELLS WHERE LITTLE ECHOES SIT? . . .   650 ISLE STAT I 1   149
    SUCH QUESTS AS THESE, I TROW, NEED LITTLE WIT. .   650 ISLE STAT I 1   150
    THERE'S LITTLE I'D REFUSE THEE, DEAREST YOUTH. .   669 ISLE STAT II 3   71
    SWIFT LAKE. A VERY LITTLE THING THAT IS, . . .   669 ISLE STAT II 3   78
    SO BE THOU STILL, DEAR HEART, A LITTLE WHILE: .   677 ISLE STAT II 3   283
    THE PLAIN, A LITTLE FAIR-HAIRED MAID I LOVE. .   679 ISLE STAT II 3   312
    THERE DWELLS A LITTLE FAIR-HAIRED MAID I LOVE. .   679 ISLE STAT II 3 V 312
    WITH LITTLE VOICES SONGS OF FEARFUL THINGS. . .   682 SEEKER   31
    A LITTLE WHILE AND--RED EVE DIES-- . . . . . .   686 LIFE   13
    WITH LITTLE CRIES OF JOY HE KISSED THE RAIN . .   688 TWO TITANS   33
    AND FLOWERS AND LITTLE CHILDREN. SUDDENLY . . .   688 TWO TITANS   36
    SINKS, SHINING ON THE LITTLE CRUCIFIX . . . . .   691 MOSADA 1   34
    A-SHINING ON THE LITTLE CRUCIFIX . . . .   691 MOSADA 1   V   34
    A LITTLE MOORISH GIRL? SMALL WORTH. MY SONG--   696 MOSADA 2   10
    AS QUIET AS THE LITTLE RIVULETS . . . .   698 MOSADA 2   57
    ABOVE THE FARM-HOUSE BY THE LITTLE LAKE . . . .   699 MOSADA 3   3
    A LITTLE NEARER THOSE BRIGHT STARS. TELL ME, .   701 MOSADA 3   59
    YOU ARE WASTING AWAY, LITTLE FAIRY. . . . . . .   707 FAIRY PEDANT   12
    WHILE I MURMUR A LITTLE AND PONDER . . . .   707 FAIRY PEDANT   14

LITTLE   (CONTINUED)
      YOU ARE WASTING AWAY, LITTLE FAIRY. . . . .   707 FAIRY PEDANT   20
      YOU ARE WASTING AWAY, LITTLE FAIRY. . . . .   708 FAIRY PEDANT   28
      SHE IS WASTING AWAY, LITTLE FAIRY. . . . .   708 FAIRY PEDANT   40
      ABOLISHED BY A MIRE OF LITTLE THINGS, ...   711 FERENCZ RENYI   36
      "A LITTLE WILL I LAY MY WEARY HEAD, ...   712 FERENCZ RENYI   75
      BELOVED, HOW TWO LITTLE YEARS AGO . . . .   713 FERENCZ RENYI   89
      SO LITTLE. AS THE MONTHS PASSED BY WE GREW . . . . .   713 FERENCZ RENYI   93
      A LITTLE BOY OUTSIDE THE SYCAMORE WOOD . . . . . .   715 DWELT SYCAMORE   1
      A LITTLE BOY INSIDE THE SYCAMORE WOOD . . . .   715 DWELT SYCAMORE   5
      A LITTLE WITHERED MAN, AND OLD. . . . .   716 FAIRY DOCTOR   4
      THE LITTLE WITHERED MAN, AND OLD. . . . .   717 FAIRY DOCTOR   24
      HANG THE MIST-THREADS FOR A LITTLE WHILE LIKE COBWEBS IN   719 PHANTOM SHIP   29
         THE AIR;
      HANG THE MIST THREADS FOR A LITTLE WHILE LIKE COBWEBS IN   719 PHANTOM SHIP   V   29
         THE AIR,
      SAVE, WITH THE LITTLE GOLDEN GREEDY CARP, ...   720 WITCH VIVIEN   2
      WITHOUT THERE OF A LITTLE, LIGHT OLD MAN; . . . . .   720 WITCH VIVIEN   13
      THE PASSING OF THOSE LITTLE GRAINS IS SNOW . . . . .   722 WITCH VIVIEN   48
      AND LITTLE BOYS PLAYED PITCH AND TOSS. . . . . . .   725 LEGEND   4
      "IF I WERE FREE TO DO AS LITTLE . . . .   731 PRIEST FAIRY   77
      THE LITTLE OLD GLOVE OF A CHILD: . . . .   744 GLOVE CLOAK   9
      AND WHEN YOU CAME TO SCORN OUR LITTLE WARS . . . . .   749 SHADOW WATER A V   34
      I SHALL BE HOME NOW IN A LITTLE WHILE, ...   759 SHADOW WATER A   240
      SHE WILL SAY SOMETHING IN A LITTLE WHILE, ...   760 SHADOW WATER A   248
      HOW LITTLE AND REEDY A SOUND AWAKES A GOD . . . . .   760 SHADOW WATER A   252
LITTLE-LAND
      CALLED RATHER BAILE LITTLE-LAND, ...   189 BAILE AILLINN   17
LIVE   SEE RE-LIVE
      MUST LIVE TO BE OLD LIKE THE WANDERING MOON. . . . . .   3 OISIN 1   12
      "MY BROTHERS AND MY SISTERS LIVE AND THRIVE, ...   32 OISIN 2   V   50C
      FORMS WITHOUT NUMBER! WHEN THE LIVE WEST FLASHED . .   41 OISIN 2   V   180
      FOR NO LIVE CREATURES LIVED THERE, NO WEASELS MOVED IN   48 OISIN 3   19
         THE DARK:
      FOR NO LIVE CREATURES LIVE THERE, NO WEASELS MOVE IN THE   56 OISIN 3   139
         DARK:
      FOR NO LIVE CREATURES LIVE THERE, NO WEASELS MOVE IN THE   56 OISIN 3   139
         DARK:
      NO LIVE MAN GOES THITHER, ...   62 OISIN 3   V   214
      YOU LIVE, AND ON THE VILLAGE BORDER SHE, ...   74 ANASHU VIJAYA   62
      YOU LIVE, AND ON THE BORDER OF THE VILLAGE SHE, . . .   74 ANASHU VIJAYA V   62
      IN ALL POOR FOOLISH THINGS THAT LIVE A DAY, ...   101 ROSE UPON ROOD   11
      OF THEIR SAD HEARTS, THAT MAY NOT LIVE NOR DIE. . . .   114 ROSE OF BATTLE   24
      OF OUR SAD HEARTS, THAT MAY NOT LIVE NOR DIE. . . . .   115 ROSE OF BATTLE   36
      AND LIVE ALONE IN THE BEE-LOUD GLADE. . . . . . .   117 ISLE INNISFREE   4
      AND TALKED OF THE DARK FOLK WHO LIVE IN SOULS . . . .   136 TO SOME I TALK   4
      FOR THERE LIVE THE MYSTIC BROTHERHOOD . . . . . .   148 INTO TWILIGHT V   10
      LIVE BUT TO LIGHT YOUR PASSING FEET. . . . .   158 BELOVED RHYMES   12
      BUT WITH THE BURNING, LIVE, UNSHAKEN VOICE . . . . .   183 QUEEN MAEVE   75
      THE NOTES THEY WAKEN SHALL LIVE ON . . . .   213 BLESS PSALTER   16
      THE PROUD AND CARELESS NOTES LIVE ON, ...   213 BLESS PSALTER   19
      THAT HAVE HAD DREAMS FOR FATHER, LIVE IN US. . . . .   252 SHADOW WATER B   619
      AND BEEN CONTENT TO LIVE. . . . .   256 WORDS   16
      WHY MUST I LIVE SOME THIRTY, FORTY YEARS, ...   285 TWO KINGS   199
      FOR HE KNEW BETTER HOW TO LIVE. . . . .   288 TO WEALTHY MAN   30
      AM I TO LIVE ON LEBEEN-LONE?" . . . .   295 THREE BEGGARS   5
      DO, BUT AWAKE A HOPE TO LIVE . . . .   309 REALISTS   6
      DO BUT WAKE THE HOPE TO LIVE . . . .   309 REALISTS   V   6
      LIVE HE OR DIE . . . .   310 PEACOCK   7
      SO CHANGED ME THAT I LIVE . . . .   315 FRIENDS   15
      AND SOLID MEN, FOR ALL THEIR PASSION, LIVE . . . . .   325 ROBERT GREGORY   37
      IF I SHOULD LIVE AS LIVE THE NEIGHBOURS," . . . . .   331 ROUND TOWER   3
      IF I SHOULD LIVE AS LIVE THE NEIGHBOURS;" . . . . .   331 ROUND TOWER   3
      IF I SHOULD LIVE AS LIVES THE NEIGHBOURS" . . . . .   331 ROUND TOWER   V   3
      AND LIVE LIKE SOLOMON . . . .   346 ON WOMAN   42
      A DAPHNE AND A MARY WHO LIVE IN PRIVACY: . . . . .   354 HIS PHOENIX   18
      MERE IMAGES: CHOSEN THIS PLACE TO LIVE IN . . . . .   373 PHASES OF MOON   13
      LIVE IN UNCOMPOSITE BLESSEDNESS, ...   387 ROBARTES DANCE   46
      MINUTE BY MINUTE THEY LIVE: . . . .   393 EASTER 1916   55
      O MAY SHE LIVE LIKE SOME GREEN LAUREL . . . . . .   405 FOR DAUGHTER   47
      AND LIVE AMONG THE ANCIENT HOLY MEN, ...   448 HERO GIRL FOOL V   11A
      LIKE MEN WHO LIVE BY HABIT. EVERY DAY . . . . . .   463 HARUN RASHID   56
      I SAY THAT A DJIN SPOKE. A LIVE LONG HOUR . . . . .   467 HARUN RASHID   V   136
      WHAT MATTER IF I LIVE IT ALL ONCE MORE? . . . . . .   478 SELF AND SOUL   43
      I AM CONTENT TO LIVE IT ALL AGAIN . . . .   479 SELF AND SOUL   57
      WHAT MADE ME LIVE LIKE THESE THAT SEEM . . . . . .   507 STREAM AND SUN   14
      WHAT BIDS ME LIVE LIKE THESE THAT SEEM . . . . . .   507 STREAM AND SUN V   14
      LIVE IN A HEAVENLY MANSION, ...   513 JANE TALK BISH   5
      IN THAT FAITH I LIVE OR DIE." . . . .   529 TOM LUNATIC   18
      LIVE LONE, ALONE WITH A SPECKLED SHIN? . . . . . .   551 SONGS REWRIT 1 V   8
      HOW CAN SHE LIVE TILL IN HER BLOOD HE LIVE: . . . .   558 RIBH CHRISTIAN   24
      HOW CAN SHE LIVE TILL IN HER BLOOD HE LIVE: . . . .   558 RIBH CHRISTIAN   24
      BUT STORIES THAT LIVE LONGEST . . . .   587 PARNELLITES   29
      "ALL MEN LIVE IN SUFFERING, ...   589 OLD WICKED MAN   46
      AND DRUNK OR SOBER LIVE AT EASE . . . .   597 MODEL LAUREATE   13
      FROM THOSE THEY LIVE AMONG, ...   607 SONGS BURDEN 2   13
      LIVE LIPS UPON A PLUMMET-MEASURED FACE. . . . . . .   610 STATUES   8
      MORE DREAD THE LIFE THAT WE LIVE, ...   615 MARCH SONGS 2   15
      A VISION OF TERROR THAT IT MUST LIVE THROUGH . . . .   619 BRONZE HEAD   17
      LIVE TO BEAR CHILDREN TO A DUNCE! . . . .   626 OLD MEN BE MAD   6
      THERE LIVE HIS SISTER AND HIS MOTHER. HIGH . . . . .   710 FERENCZ RENYI V   25

LIVE   (CONTINUED)
   JOYS AND FEARS IN THEIR GREY FACES THAT THE LIVE EARTH   719 PHANTOM SHIP   26
     KNOWETH NOT,
   LIVE, FOR I SAW THEM DANCING THERE. . . . .   788 HAWTHORN TREE   12
LIVED   SEE LONG-LIVED
   NOR THE HIGH GODS WHO NEVER LIVED, MAY FIGHT . . . . .   34 OISIN 2   80
   FOR NO LIVE CREATURES LIVED THERE, NO WEASELS MOVED IN   48 OISIN 3   19
     THE DARK.
   SO LIVED I AND LIVED NOT, SO WROUGHT I AND WROUGHT NOT,   53 OISIN 3   95
   . . .
   SO LIVED I AND LIVED NOT, SO WROUGHT I AND WROUGHT NOT,   53 OISIN 3   95
   . . .
   THE LOVE I LIVED, THE DREAM I KNEW. . . . .   139 TO IRELAND   34
   HAS LOVER LIVED, BUT LONGED TO WIVE . . . .   197 BAILE AILLINN   206
   SEVEN OLD SISTERS WIND THE THREADS OF THE LONG LIVED ONES, 209 UNDER THE MOON V   7
   NONE BUT THE DEAD, OR THOSE THAT NEVER LIVED, ...   231 SHADOW WATER B   202
   WHEN HELEN LIVED . . . .   293 HELEN LIVED   T
   SHE LIVED IN STORM AND STRIFE, ...   317 NIGHT COME   1
   BUT LIVED AS 'TWERE A KING . . . .   317 NIGHT COME   6
   HER LABOURING MEN, AS THOUGH HER DARLING LIVED, ...   340 SHEP GOATHERD   38
   BETWEEN THE NIGHT AND MORNING. I MIGHT HAVE LIVED, . . .   351 PEOPLE   6
   WAS, "YOU, THAT HAVE NOT LIVED IN THOUGHT BUT DEED, . . .   353 PEOPLE   30
   WHO HAVE LIVED IN JOY AND LAUGHED INTO THE FACE OF DEATH.   366 HER COURAGE   10
   WHO LIVED IN SHAMELESS JOY AND LAUGHED INTO THE FACE OF   366 HER COURAGE   V   10
     DEATH.
   THAT LIVED IN JOY AND LAUGHED INTO THE FACE OF DEATH. . .   366 HER COURAGE   V   10
   WHO HAVE LIVED IN JOY AND LAUGHED IN THE FACE OF DEATH.   366 HER COURAGE   V   10
   ONCE HE LIVED A SCHOOLMASTER . . . .   381 SONG OF FOOL   5
   BUT LIVED WHERE MOTLEY IS WORN, ...   392 EASTER 1916   14
   BEYOND THAT RIDGE LIVED MRS. FRENCH, AND ONCE . . . . .   410 TOWER   25
   WHO'D LIVED SOMEWHERE UPON THAT ROCKY PLACE. . . . . .   410 TOWER   35
   NEVER TO HAVE LIVED IS BEST, ANCIENT WRITERS SAY, . . .   459 FROM OEDIPUS   10
   LIVED AT MY SIDE, THOUGHT TIME'S DISFIGURING TOUCH . . .   466 HARUN RASHID   110
   LIVED AT MY SIDE, THAT TIME'S DISFIGURING TOUCH . . . .   466 HARUN RASHID   V 110
   A SPOT WHEREON THE FOUNDERS LIVED AND DIED . . . . . .   491 COOLE BALLYLEE   33
   NO MAN HAS EVER LIVED THAT HAD ENOUGH . . . .   500 VACILLATION   25
   ALL LIVES THAT HAS LIVED, ...   504 QUARREL IN AGE   9
   EVERY THING THAT HAS LIVED . . . .   504 QUARREL IN AGE V   9
   CRIED THAT WE LIVED LIKE BEAST AND BEAST, ...   508 JANE BISHOP   13
   WE LIVED LIKE MEN THAT WATCH A PAINTED STAGE. . . . .   542 PARN FUNERAL 1   18
   SEVENTY YEARS HAVE I LIVED, ...   567 FROM JAPANESE   2
   SEVENTY YEARS HAVE I LIVED . . . .   567 FROM JAPANESE   5
   SEVENTY YEARS HAVE I LIVED, ...   567 FROM JAPANESE   7
   THE CHAMBERMAID LIVED LONG, AND TOOK . . . .   571 THREE BUSHES   57
   HE THOUGHT THE SAME AND LIVED BY RULE, ...   576 WHAT THEN   3
   HONOUR HAD LIVED SO LONG, ALL LACKING FOUND. . . . .   603 GALLERY REVIS   35
   HONOUR HAD LIVED SO LONG, THEIR HEALTH I FOUND. . . .   603 GALLERY REVIS V   35
   KNOWS I HAVE LIVED SO LONG. . . . .   607 SONGS BURDEN 2   26
   I LIVED AMONG GREAT HOUSES. . . . .   626 STATES HOLIDAY   1
   WHO, DREAMING TO A WONDROUS AGE, LIVED ON, ...   692 MOSADA 1   52
   ANY THAT LIVED, AND I HAVE BROUGHT MY GALLEY . . . .   756 SHADOW WATER A V 191A
LIVELONG
   AND HAD THE LIVELONG SUMMER DAY TO SPEND. . . . . .   409 TOWER   10
   I SAY THAT A DJINN SPOKE. A LIVELONG HOUR . . . . .   467 HARUN RASHID   136
LIVE-LONG
   I SAY THAT A JINN SPOKE. A LIVE-LONG HOUR . . . . .   467 HARUN RASHID   V 136
   DREAMING THE LIVE-LONG SUMMER IN THE SHADE, ...   650 ISLE STAT I 1   139
LIVELY
   WHAT LIVELY LAD MOST PLEASURED ME . . . .   538 LAST CONFESS   1
LIVER
   BUT NEVER, NEVER DANGLING LEAVE THE LIVER AND THE LIGHTS.   790 HEART SLEEVE   2
LIVERPOOL
   IN LONDON OR IN LIVERPOOL, ...   360 ALF POLLEXFEN   16
LIVERY
   THE ILL-BRED SON OF A LIVERY STABLE KEEPER— . . . . .   370 EGO DOMINUS   V   61
   THE ILL-BRED SON OF A LIVERY STABLE-KEEPER— . . . . .   370 EGO DOMINUS   V   61
LIVERY-STABLE
   THE COARSE-BRED SON OF A LIVERY-STABLE KEEPER— . . . .   370 EGO DOMINUS   61
LIVES
   OUR LIVES HAVE KNOWN NO LAW NOR RULE, ...   22 OISIN 1   V 340
   IS AN UNDYING MOORFOWL, AND HE LIVES BEYOND THE SKY. . .   76 INDIAN ON GOD   7
   SHALL WARM THEIR LIVES AT MANY A RUSTLING FLAME." . .   80 EPHEMERA   V 12B
   LIVES ON THIS LONELY FACE. . . . .   112 ROSE OF WORLD   10
   IN THEIR LONG LIVES? WILL YOU BE OF OUR TROOP . . .   225 SHADOW WATER B   72
   IN THEIR LONG LIVES? IF YOU'LL BE OF OUR TROOP . . .   225 SHADOW WATER B V   72
   WE'LL OUT, FOR THE WORLD LIVES AS LONG AGO, ...   257 RECONCILIATION   8
   ALL THEIR LIVES THROUGH INTO SOME DRIFT OF WINGS. . .   265 ABBEY THEATRE   7
   "HE LIVES?" "HE LIVES AND IS A HEALTHY MAN." . . . .   280 TWO KINGS   84
   "HE LIVES?" "HE LIVES AND IS A HEALTHY MAN." . . . .   280 TWO KINGS   84
   IF I SHOULD LIVE AS LIVES THE NEIGHBOURS" . . . . .   331 ROUND TOWER   V   3
   HOW HARD A LIFE HER SERVANT LIVES. . . . .   336 YOUNG BEAUTY   14
   THAT LIVES IN MEMORY. . . . .   459 HIS WILDNESS   10
   ALL LIVES THAT HAS LIVED, ...   504 QUARREL IN AGE   9
   LIVES THAT LONELY THING . . . .   504 QUARREL IN AGE   14
   LIVES, THAT MUCH IS CERTAIN, ...   504 QUARREL IN AGE V   10
   IT HAD NOT TOUCHED OUR LIVES. BUT POPULAR RAGE, . . .   542 PARN FUNERAL 1   20
   MANY TIMES MAN LIVES AND DIES . . . .   637 BEN BULBEN   13
   BEAT OUT THEIR LIVES LAMENTING O'ER THE SAND, ...   652 ISLE STAT I 2   14
   FOR THERE THE GREAT ENCHANTRESS LIVES. AND THERE . . .   653 ISLE STAT I 2   38
   FOR, AH, OUR LIVES WERE BUT TWO STARRY WORDS . . . .   675 ISLE STAT II 3   236
   UPON THEIR THRONES. THE LIVES OF MEN SHALL FLOW . . .   698 MOSADA 2   56

```
                                                          PAGE     TITLE          LINE
LIVES   (CONTINUED)
    IN OTHER LIVES?  HAST THOU NOT QUAFFED OLD WINE  . . . .    724 KANVA ON SELF       12
    I THINK HE LIVES IN LOCHLANN.  NO, NOT THERE:  . . . .      760 SHADOW WATER A  V 254A
    THAT LIVES AMONG THE WOODS OF THE DARK HOUNDS.  . . . .     766 SHADOW WATER A     376
    ONE LIVES UNDER THE WAVES,  . . . . . . . . . .            770 SPINNING SONG        2
    ONE LIVES IN THE HOUSE OF THE SUN,  . . . . . . .          771 SPINNING SONG        6
    AND ONE LIVES UNDER THE BOUGHS  . . . . . . . .            771 SPINNING SONG        8
    "LIVES ALL HIS DAYS  . . . . . . . . . . . . .            780 WELL AND TREE        3
    THEIR BRIEF LIVES I NEVER KNEW.  . . . . . . . .          787 HUDDON DUDDON        5
LIVID
    AND THEREUPON I DREW THE LIVID CHOP  . . . . . . .         40 OISIN 2            178
    ONCE HELD BETWEEN MY ARMS, WITH LIVID CHOP  . . . .        40 OISIN 2          V 178
    I HELD A DRIPPING CORPSE, WITH LIVID CHOP  . . . . .       40 OISIN 2          V 178
    AND I BUT HELD A CORPSE, WITH LIVID CHOP  . . . . .        40 OISIN 2          V 178
LIVING   SEE EVER-LIVING HARD-LIVING OUT-LIVING
    THE ISLAND OF THE LIVING  . . . . . . . . . . .            1 OISIN 1          V   T
    MY DREAMS WERE LIVING.  NOW THE HOOF  . . . . . .          25 OISIN 1          V 382
    "NEITHER THE LIVING, NOR THE UNLABOURING DEAD,  . . .      34 OISIN 2            79
    COME FROM THE ISLE OF THE LIVING."  "THEN GET YE  . . .    34 OISIN 2          V  79
    ISLES OF THE LIVING AND OF VICTORIES  . . . . . .          46 OISIN 2          V 247
    THIS WOULD I SAY, MOST WISE OF LIVING SOULS:  . . .       102 FERGUS DRUID         9
    THE POWERS WHOSE NAME AND SHAPE NO LIVING CREATURE KNOWS  174 ELEMENT POWERS       1
    IN COMFORTABLE SLEEP: ALL LIVING SLEPT  . . . . . .      180 QUEEN MAEVE         15
    WHAT GOOD IS THERE IN THIS HARD WAY OF LIVING,  . . .    225 SHADOW WATER B      69
    FOR NEITHER I NOR ANY LIVING MAN  . . . . . . . .        250 SHADOW WATER B     588
    NOR HAD THERE BEEN THE NOISE OF LIVING THING  . . . .    279 TWO KINGS           54
    AND THERE HAD BEEN NO SOUND OF LIVING THING  . . . .    279 TWO KINGS         V  54
    "IF HE BE LIVING STILL THE WHOLE WORLD'S MINE,  . . .   280 TWO KINGS         V  85
    BUT IF NOT LIVING, HALF THE WORLD IS LOST."  . . . .    280 TWO KINGS         V  86
    THAT DYING CHOSE THE LIVING WORLD FOR TEXT  . . . .     324 ROBERT GREGORY      26
    THE LIVING BEAUTY  . . . . . . . . . . . . . .         333 LIVING BEAUTY        T
    THE LIVING BEAUTY IS FOR YOUNGER MEN:  . . . . . .     334 LIVING BEAUTY        9
    THE LIVING MEN THAT I HATE  . . . . . . . . . .        347 FISHERMAN           13
    TO TROUBLE THE LIVING STREAM.  . . . . . . . . .       393 EASTER 1916         44
    AND HELEN HAS ALL LIVING HEARTS BETRAYED.  . . . .     411 TOWER               53
    SHOULD HEAR MY LIVING FEET, NOR WOULD I TREAD  . . .   435 NEW FACES            3
    THE LIVING SEEM MORE SHADOWY THAN THEY.  . . . . .     435 NEW FACES            8
    SHE STANDS BEFORE ME AS A LIVING CHILD.  . . . . .    444 SCHOOL CHILDR       24
    MIRACLE-BRED OUT OF THE LIVING STONE:  . . . . . .    446 COLONUS PRAISE      13
    AND THAT NONE LIVING KNOWS.  . . . . . . . . .        455 HIS MEMORIES         6
    FARISTAH, AND NO LIVING EAR BUT HIS.  . . . . . .     461 HARUN RASHID      V  4
    NONE BUT THE LIVING MOCK,  . . . . . . . . . .        471 ALL SOUL NIGHT      17
    NO LIVING MAN CAN DRINK FROM THE WHOLE WINE.  . . .    474 ALL SOUL NIGHT      85
    WHEREAT THE LIVING MOCK,  . . . . . . . . . .         474 ALL SOUL NIGHT      87
    A LIVING MAN IS BLIND AND DRINKS HIS DROP.  . . . .    478 SELF AND SOUL       41
    A PROPERTY OF THE LIVING: BUT NO STAIN  . . . . .      482 BLOOD AND MOON      52
    SAY THAT OF LIVING MEN I HATE  . . . . . . . . .       539 MEETING             11
    AND NOW NONE LIVING CAN,  . . . . . . . . . .         571 THREE BUSHES        74
    AND TOM MAKE OUT A LIVING  . . . . . . . . . .        597 COLONEL MARTIN      70
    WHEN TOM MADE OUT A LIVING  . . . . . . . . .         597 COLONEL MARTIN   V  70
    HAZEL LAVERY LIVING AND DYING, THAT TALE  . . . .     602 GALLERY REVIS       23
    LIVING, WIDE WINGED, ON THE WATERS FLOAT.  . . . .    657 ISLE STAT I 3       54
    AND LOUDLY TWICE THE LIVING WINGS FLAPT WIDE,  . . .   659 ISLE STAT II 1      12
    FROM WHOSE GREEN BANKS NO LIVING THING MAY ROVE,  . .  664 ISLE STAT II 2      57
    THE ORB OF THE MOST INNER LIVING HEART  . . . . .     689 NETTLESHIP          15
    THE LIVING WOODS FOREGO THEIR CARE,  . . . . . .      736 SUMMER EVENING       1
    I LEFT HER LIVING, THINKING THAT I HAD FOUND  . . .    755 SHADOW WATER A     174
    THE FALLING BLOSSOMS, AND THE DEAD THE LIVING.  . . .  756 SHADOW WATER A     182
    I WAIT YOUR WORDS AS THE DEAD WAIT THE LIVING.  . . .  756 SHADOW WATER A  V 182
    LIVING OR DYING.  BID AIBRIC TO YOUR COUNTRY,  . . .   768 SHADOW WATER A     413
LIZARD
    A LIZARD CRAWLS--THE TWO MEN GAZE INTENT,  . . . . .    711 FERENCZ RENYI       47
LIZARDS
    THE CHILD PURSUING LIZARDS IN THE GRASS,  . . . . .    686 LIFE                 1
    THE CHILD WHO CHASES LIZARDS IN THE GRASS,  . . . .    734 QUATRAIN APHOR       1
    THE CHILD PURSUING LIZARDS IN THE GRASS,  . . . . .    734 QUATRAIN APHOR   V   1
LO
    TO THE ISLAND OF FORGETFULNESS, FOR LO:  . . . . .     46 OISIN 2            246
    AND LO: MY ANCIENT BURDEN MAY DEPART.  . . . . . .     69 SAD SHEPHERD        24
    AND LO--MY HEAVY BURTHEN MAY DEPART:"  . . . . . .     69 SAD SHEPHERD     V  24
LOAD
    MAY PANTHERS END HIM.--HEAR, AND LOAD OUR KING  . . .    71 ANASHU VIJAYA       6
    YOUTH'S DREAMY LOAD, TILL SHE  . . . . . . . .        315 FRIENDS             14
    OR SHIFT TIME'S FILTHY LOAD,  . . . . . . . . .       505 RESULT THOUGHT      15
LOADED
    NOT LOADED CENTURIES MIGHT VAPOUR.  RAN  . . . . .      38 OISIN 2          V 127
    WAS LOADED WITH THE MEMORY OF DAYS  . . . . . . .      39 OISIN 2            150
    HE UNPACKS THE LOADED PERN  . . . . . . . . . .       342 SHEP GOATHERD       97
    I LOSE:  THEY'RE LOADED DICE.  TIME ALWAYS PLAYS  . .   721 WITCH VIVIEN        44
    WITH LOADED DICE.  ANOTHER CHANCE:  COME, FATHER:  . .  721 WITCH VIVIEN        45
LOADS
    BUT UNDER HEAVY LOADS OF TRAMPLED CLAY  . . . . .      483 OIL AND BLOOD        4
LOADSTONE
    OR IMAGE, FROM BEYOND THE LOADSTONE MOUNTAIN,  . . .   371 ON GOING HOUSE      11
LOAM
    OUT OF THE FOREST LOAM,  . . . . . . . . . . .        439 FRAGMENTS            8
LOCHLANN
    FROM HILLY LOCHLANN: BUT OUR SAIL HAS PASSED  . . .    749 SHADOW WATER A      44
    A GALLEY FROM THE LOCHLANN SEAS: HER FLAG  . . . .     751 SHADOW WATER A      98
    WHEN YOU ARE ABOARD THE LOCHLANN GALLEY, LASH  . . .   752 SHADOW WATER A     128
    ENDS ALL THINGS.  I HAVE SLAIN THE LOCHLANN KING.  . .  754 SHADOW WATER A     163
```

	PAGE	TITLE		LINE

LOCHLANN   (CONTINUED)
    BESIDE A LOCHLANN WHARF, AND THOUGH SHE HAD SWORN   • • •   756 SHADOW WATER A   188
    HAVE BID ME HOPE, SAIL TO THE LOCHLANN SHORE   • • • • •   756 SHADOW WATER A V 184
    IN SOUTHERN LOCHLANN. I WOULD NOT OBEY • • • • • • •   756 SHADOW WATER A V 191
    I THINK HE LIVES IN LOCHLANN. NO, NOT THERE! • • • •   760 SHADOW WATER A V 254A
    SEEK AIBRIC ON THE LOCHLANN GALLEY, AND TELL HIM   • • •   767 SHADOW WATER A   401
LOCK
    MADE LOCK, STOCK AND BARREL • • • • • • • • • • •   415 TOWER   150
LOCKE
    LOCKE SANK INTO A SWOON! • • • • • • • • • • • •   439 FRAGMENTS   1
LOCKED
    HORN LOCKED IN SWORD, THEY TUGGED AND STRUGGLED THERE   • •   277 TWO KINGS   18
    THOUGH I HAVE LOCKED MY GATE ON THEM,   • • • • • • •   607 SONGS BURDEN 2   10
LOCKS
    • • • THE OWLS HAD BUILDED THEIR NESTS IN THEIR LOCKS, • •   49 OISIN 3   39
    AND SING, AND SHAKE MY HEAVY LOCKS• • • • • • • • •   84 MAD KING GOLL   44
    UNDER THE SHADOW OF STUPID STRAW-PALE LOCKS, • • • • •   433 NINETEEN 19   127
    THAT I HAD SHORN MY LOCKS AWAY • • • • • • • • • •   519 HER DREAM   3
LODGE
    CRIED FROM THE PORTER'S LODGE, AND WITH LONG CLAMOUR   • •   181 QUEEN MAEVE   37
LOFTIER
    HUNG THE FRAIL LOFTIER CLOUDLETS. TURNED HE SLOW-- • • •   40 OISIN 2   V 167
    HAD GIVEN THEIR CHILDREN'S CHILDREN LOFTIER THOUGHT, • •   292 TO A SHADE   12
LOFTY
    AND MANY A PRINCE OF LOFTY NAME, • • • • • • • • •   7 OISIN 1   V 63
    AND MANY A MAN OF LOFTY NAME, • • • • • • • • • •   7 OISIN 1   V 63
    "YOUR STRENGTH, THAT IS SO LOFTY AND FIERCE AND KIND, • •   201 OLD MEMORY   3
    ON NO LONG BENCH NOR LOFTY MILKING-SHED • • • • • • •   341 SHEP GOATHERD   51
    OF SORROWFUL, AUSTERE, SWEET, LOFTY PIPE TUNES. • • • •   341 SHEP GOATHERD   57
    ON NO LONG BENCH NOR LOFTY MILKING SHED • • • • • • •   341 SHEP GOATHERD   V 51
    UPON SOME LOFTY ROCK TO STARE • • • • • • • • • •   397 POLIT PRISONER   21
    THAT LOFTY WHITE STAG, LEAP • • • • • • • • • • •   399 BREAK OF DAY   24
    OR LOFTY SLOPE WHERE IT STILL SNOWS • • • • • • • •   567 LAPIS LAZULI   46
    BEAUTIFUL LOFTY THINGS • • • • • • • • • • • •   577 LOFTY THINGS   T
    BEAUTIFUL LOFTY THINGS! O'LEARY'S NOBLE HEAD! • • • •   577 LOFTY THINGS   1
    A BEAUTIFUL LOFTY THING, OR A THING • • • • • • • •   578 CRAZED GIRL   7
    THE LOFTY INNOCENCE THAT IT HAS SLAIN, • • • • • • •   614 MARCH SONGS 2   12
LOG
    HAS SHE NOT SEEN HIM LYING LIKE A LOG, • • • • • • •   230 SHADOW WATER B   173
    • • • A LOG BOOK OF THE SUN'S JOURNEY AND THE MOON'S, • •   480 BLOOD AND MOON   V 14
LOG-BOOK
    • • • A LOG-BOOK OF THE SUN'S JOURNEY AND THE MOON'S! • •   480 BLOOD AND MOON   14
LOGIC
    IN LOGIC AND IN NATURAL LAW • • • • • • • • • •   288 TO WEALTHY MAN   27
    "THOUGH LOGIC CHOPPERS RULE THE TOWN, • • • • • • •   337 TOM OROUGHLEY   V   1
    AND IS THEIR LOGIC TO OUTWEIGH • • • • • • • • • •   395 SIXTEEN DEAD   11
LOGIC-CHOPPERS
    "THOUGH LOGIC-CHOPPERS RULE THE TOWN, • • • • • • •   337 TOM OROUGHLEY   1
LOIE
    WHEN LOIE FULLER'S CHINESE DANCERS ENWOUND • • • • • •   430 NINETEEN 19   49
LOIN
    THAT HAS NOT PASSED THROUGH ANY HUCKSTER'S LOIN, • • • •   269 PARDON FATHERS   8
LOINS
    A SHUDDER IN THE LOINS ENGENDERS THERE • • • • • •   441 LEDA AND SWAN   9
    THE FLAGELLANT LASHES THOSE SUBMISSIVE LOINS • • • • •   560 WHENCE COME   7
    SPOILT WHAT OLD LOINS HAVE SENT? • • • • • • • • •   604 YOU CONTENT   6
LOITERING
    WHILE THOSE DEAD MEN ARE LOITERING THERE • • • • • •   395 SIXTEEN DEAD   5
LOLLARD
    LEAD MY LOLLARD TO AND FRO, • • • • • • • • • •   97 FOXHUNTER   7
    MY LOLLARD OLD AND DEAR.• • • • • • • • • • • •   97 FOXHUNTER   V   8
    BROWN LOLLARD TREADS UPON THE LAWN, • • • • • • • •   98 FOXHUNTER   17
    HIS LOLLARD LEAD THEY ROUND THE LAWN, • • • • • • •   98 FOXHUNTER   V 17
LOLLING
    WERE LOLLING THEIR TONGUES, AND THE SILKEN HAIR • • • •   2 OISIN 1   V 7S
LOMAIR
    BRAN, SGEOLAN, AND LOMAIR, • • • • • • • • • •   2 OISIN 1   V 7D
    AND BRAN, SGEOLAN, AND LOMAIR • • • • • • • • • •   2 OISIN 1   V 7R
    WITH BRAN, SCEOLAN, AND LOMAIR, • • • • • • • • •   3 OISIN 1   15
    AND BRAN, SCEOLAN, AND LOMAIR, • • • • • • • • •   11 OISIN 1   125
    I MUSED ON THE CHASE WITH THE FENIANS, AND BRAN, SCEOLAN,   47 OISIN 3   5
        LOMAIR,
    WHEN THE FENIANS MADE FORAY AT MORNING WITH BRAN, SCEOLAN,   54 OISIN 3   104
        LOMAIR.
    WHAT PLACE HAVE CAOILTE AND CONAN, AND BRAN, SCEOLAN,   61 OISIN 3   195
        LOMAIR?
    WHAT PLACE HAVE CAOLTE AND FIN, AND BRAN, SGEOLAN, LOMAIR?   61 OISIN 3   V 195
    I WILL GO TO CAOILTE, AND CONAN, AND BRAN, SCEOLAN, LOMAIR,   63 OISIN 3   223
    TO FIN, CAOLTE, AND CONAN, AND BRAN, SGEOLAN, LOMAIR. • •   63 OISIN 3   V 224
LONDON
    IN LONDON OR IN LIVERPOOL! • • • • • • • • • •   360 ALF POLLEXFEN   16
    IN A CROWDED LONDON SHOP, • • • • • • • • • •   501 VACILLATION   37
    SINGING IN THIS LONDON STREET, • • • • • • • • •   731 STREET DANCERS   1
    LONDON STREETS HAVE HERITAGE, • • • • • • • • •   733 STREET DANCERS   57
LONE   SEE LEBEEN-LONE
    I MOUNTED, AND WE PASSED OVER THE LONE • • • • • •   45 OISIN 2   231
    I MOUNTED, AND WE RODE ACROSS THE LONE • • • • • •   45 OISIN 2   V 231
    WE SHALL MINGLE NO MORE, NOR OUR GAZES EMPTY THEIR   56 OISIN 3   132
        SWEETNESS LONE
    BUT THE SAD DWELLER BY THE SEA-WAYS LONE • • • • • •   69 SAD SHEPHERD   26
    BUT THE SAD DWELLER BY THE SEAWAYS LONE • • • • • • •   69 SAD SHEPHERD   V 26

467

LONE (CONTINUED)

BY THE LONE BORDER OF THE LAKE ONCE MORE, ...	79	EPHEMERA	5
ON THE LONE BORDER OF THE LAKE ONCE MORE!	80	EPHEMERA	17
ON THE LONE BORDER OF THE SULLEN LAKE.	80	EPHEMERA V	17
DID SHE IN TOUCHING THAT LONE WING	397	POLIT PRISONER	7
IS DRINKING HER HEALTH WHEN LONE, ALONE--	551	SONGS REWRIT 1 V	4
LIVE LONE, ALONE WITH A SPECKLED SHIN?	551	SONGS REWRIT 1 V	8
LONE, AND WANTING THEE, I WEEP;	647	ISLE STAT I 1	72
SOME SAY THAT ALL WHO TOUCH THE ISLAND LONE	653	ISLE STAT I 2	42
LONE REGENT OF THE WOODS, DEEP MUTTERING.	657	ISLE STAT I 3	49
WHO, SWIMMING, SOUGHT THE ISLAND LONE!	673	ISLE STAT II 3	181
BEHOLD THE LOVING LOVELESS FLOWER OF LONE WAYS, . . .	674	ISLE STAT II 3	201
AND AIMLESS WANDERINGS THE WOODLANDS LONE, ...	674	ISLE STAT II 3	209
HAVE LIT LONE TAPERS. NOW THE NIGHT WAS CAST, . . .	687	TWO TITANS	27
"I AM LONE LADY QUIETNESS, MY SWEET, ...	716	DWELT SYCAMORE	13
CLAMOUR OF THE LONE NIGHTJAR.	732	STREET DANCERS	21

LONELINESS

IN ALL THEIR LONELINESS AND PAIN.	290	SEPTEMBER 1913	27
AND WHEN HE PLAYED IT WAS THEIR LONELINESS	339	SHEP GOATHERD	24
THEIR BEAUTY DROPPED OUT OF THE LONELINESS	375	PHASES OF MOON	70
THE SOUL REMEMBERING ITS LONELINESS	375	PHASES OF MOON	88
MUCH BOISTEROUS COURAGE, BEFORE LONELINESS	473	ALL SOUL NIGHT	72
LOVE'S LONELINESS	518	LOVES LONENESS	T
IF EVER LOVER'S LONELINESS	518	LOVES LONENESS	3
OF CEASELESS LONELINESS AND HIGH REGRET	705	REMEMBRANCE	9

LONELY

BUT WE IN A LONELY LAND ABIDE	22	OISIN 1	337
STOOD LONELY, WITH DIM EYEBALLS ON EACH SIDE, ...	34	OISIN 2 V	74
AND LONELY AND LONGING FOR NIAMH, I SHIVERED AND TURNED ME ABOUT,	60	OISIN 3	181
AND SHIVERING AND LONELY, AND LONGING FOR NIAM, I TURNED ME ABOUT:	60	OISIN 3 V	181
FOR LONELY TO MOVE 'MONG THE SOFT EYES	63	OISIN 3 V	222
A LONELY LAUGHTER, AND MAY KISS HIS HANDS TO ME IN SLEEP.	75	ANASHU VIJAYA	82
A LONELY LAUGHTER, THAT HE MAY KISS HIS HANDS TO ME IN SLEEP.	75	ANASHU VIJAYA V	82
HERE WE WILL MOOR OUR LONELY SHIP	78	INDIAN TO LOVE	6
THERE WE WILL MOOR OUR LONELY SHIP	78	INDIAN TO LOVE V	6
SING IN THEIR HIGH AND LONELY MELODY.	101	ROSE UPON ROOD	8
LIVES ON THIS LONELY FACE.	112	ROSE OF WORLD	10
THE SAD, THE LONELY, THE INSATIABLE, ...	114	ROSE OF BATTLE	21
OLD SILENCE BIDS A LONELY FOLK REJOICE, ...	127	DREAM OF FAERY V	31
AND GOD STANDS WINDING HIS LONELY HORN, ...	148	INTO TWILIGHT	13
DROWNING LOVE'S LONELY HOUR IN DEEP TWILIGHT OF REST, . .	154	BELOVED PEACE	11
BROOD HER HIGH LONELY MYSTERIES.	156	FORGOT BEAUTY	24
ON HER MOST LONELY MYSTERIES.	156	FORGOT BEAUTY V	24
WITH THE LONELY, MAJESTICAL MULTITUDE.	158	TO HIS HEART	7
WITH THE LONELY, PROUD, WINGED MULTITUDE.	158	TO HIS HEART V	7
AND I FELL ASLEEP UPON LONELY ECHTGE OF STREAMS. . . .	203	WITHER BOUGHS	6
THAT ON THE LONELY HEIGHT WHERE ALL ARE IN GOD'S EYE, . .	291	PAUDEEN	6
A LONELY IMPULSE OF DELIGHT	328	IRISH AIRMAN	11
I MOURN FOR THAT MOST LONELY THING; AND YET GOD'S WILL BE DONE!	354	HIS PHOENIX	31
THE LONELY LIGHT THAT SAMUEL PALMER ENGRAVED, ...	373	PHASES OF MOON	17
TOO LONELY FOR THE TRAFFIC OF THE WORLD!	374	PHASES OF MOON	61
WITH ALL YOUTH'S LONELY WILDNESS STIRRED, ...	397	POLIT PRISONER	16
TO EXALT A LONELY MIND, ...	420	MY HOUSE	29
PARDONED, DRAGS OUT LONELY YEARS	475	EVA GORE-BOOTH	8
LIVES THAT LONELY THING	504	QUARREL IN AGE	14
A LONELY GHOST THE GHOST IS	511	JANE AND JACK	7
IN THIS LONELY PLACE.	617	LONG-LEG FLY	14
WHERE ALL NIGHT LONG THE LONELY MOON, THE WHITE . . .	650	ISLE STAT I 1	126
BY DAY AND NIGHT A LONELY FOUNTAIN SINGS, ...	650	ISLE STAT I 1	130
WHO SITS IN LONELY SPLENDOUR, MAIL'D IN GOLD, ...	651	ISLE STAT I 1	163
DID HER LONELY WATCHING TAKE	658	ISLE STAT I 3	94
OF BEAMS A-FLICKER ON YON LONELY FIR.	661	ISLE STAT II 1	72
BETWEEN THE LONELY FOREST AND THE SAND.	663	ISLE STAT II 2	22
TWO LONELY SPIRITS WAIT.	680	LOVE AND DEATH	18
SHALL AWAKE WITH LONELY BLEAT, ...	726	LOVERS QUARREL	6
THE MAN IS GONE WHO FROM HIS LONELY STATION	738	MOURN THEN ON	7
HAS MADE IT BUT A LONELY THING.	781	HEART FRIGHT	4

LONG   SEE DAY-LONG LIVE-LONG DADDY-LONG-LEGS

WHOSE LONG WOOL WHITER THAN SEA-FROTH FLOWS, ...	8	OISIN 1	90
WHOSE LONG WOOL WHITER THAN SEA FROTH FLOWS, ...	8	OISIN 1 V	90
WHERE ARE YOU WITH YOUR LONG ROUGH HAIR?	11	OISIN 1	126
COMPANIONS LONG ACCURST AND DEAD, ...	11	OISIN 1	130
WHERE ARE YE WITH YOUR LONG ROUGH HAIR?	11	OISIN 1 V	126
OF ONE LONG FINGER ON MY LIP.	12	OISIN 1	151
BLEW ONE LONG NOTE. FROM OVER REED	14	OISIN 1 V	195
ERE LONG AN ANSWERING WHISPER FLEW, ...	15	OISIN 1 V	197
THEY LED US BY LONG AND SHADOWY WAYS	16	OISIN 1	221
THEY LEAD US BY LONG AND SHADOWY WAYS	16	OISIN 1 V	221
AND EACH ONE SAID, WITH A LONG, LONG SIGH, ...	17	OISIN 1	244
AND EACH ONE SAID, WITH A LONG, LONG SIGH, ...	17	OISIN 1	244
WITH ONE LONG GLANCE FOR GIRL AND BOY	19	OISIN 1	287
WITH ONE LONG GLANCE ON MAID AND BOY	19	OISIN 1 V	287
IN A LONG AND SHADOWY ROW, ...	20	OISIN 1 V	295
WE WENT A-FISHING IN LONG BOATS	23	OISIN 1	352
I LOVED AND SANG, AND IN LONG WASSAILS	23	OISIN 1 V	345C
LOOSED LONG AGO FROM HEAVEN'S GATE, ...	24	OISIN 1	362
AND THE LONG GREY GRASSES, WHOSE TENDEREST TOUCHES . .	27	OISIN 1	V 415B
FROM MACE AND SWORD AND POLE-AXE, LONG AGO	31	OISIN 2	30

LONG (CONTINUED)

	PAGE	TITLE		LINE
STRETCHED HIS LONG ARM TO WHERE, A MISTY SMOTHER,	31	OISIN 2		42
AND CLIMBED SO LONG, I THOUGHT THE LAST STEPS WERE	32	OISIN 2		48
LOOK TO LONG FISHING-LINES, OR POINT AND PARE	32	OISIN 2		55
LONG WHILE, ARE WHIPS OF STEEL." "IS HE SO DREAD?"	35	OISIN 2	V	88
HOLDING THAT HORSE LONG SEEN NOT, NIAM STOOD.	44	OISIN 2	V	230
WERE WE DAYS LONG OR HOURS LONG IN RIDING,	47	OISIN 3		9
WERE WE DAYS LONG OR HOURS LONG IN RIDING,	47	OISIN 3		9
LONG SIGHS AROSE IN OUR SPIRITS, BENEATH US BUBBLED THE GROUND.	48	OISIN 3		20
A VALLEY FLOWED DOWN FROM HIS HOOFS, AND THERE IN THE LONG GRASS LAY,	48	OISIN 3		26
. . . LONG WARLESS, GROWN WHITER THAN CURDS.	49	OISIN 3		36
SO LONG WERE THEY SLEEPING,	49	OISIN 3		39
FILLING THE FIBROUS DIMNESS WITH LONG GENERATIONS OF EYES.	49	OISIN 3		40
SNATCHING THE HORN OF NIAMH, I BLEW A LONG LINGERING NOTE.	51	OISIN 3		57
IN A LONG IRON SLEEP, AS A FISH IN THE WATER GOES DUMB AS A STONE.	53	OISIN 3		96
NO MORE TO CRAWL ON THE SEAS WITH LONG OARS MILE AFTER MILE,	55	OISIN 3		119
LONG FLED THE FOAM-FLAKES AROUND ME, THE WINDS FLED OUT OF THE VAST,	57	OISIN 3		149
. . . "THE FENIANS A LONG TIME ARE DEAD."	59	OISIN 3		172
. . . HE CRIED, "NO, THE GODS A LONG TIME ARE DEAD."	59	OISIN 3		180
. . . HE CRIED, "NAY, THE GODS A LONG TIME ARE DEAD."	59	OISIN 3	V	180
AUTUMN IS OVER THE LONG LEAVES THAT LOVE US,	79	FALLING LEAVES		1
OF MY LONG SPEAR, WITH SCREAM AND LAUGH,	84	MAD KING GOLL	V	34
OF MY LONG SPEAR WITH SONG AND LAUGH	84	MAD KING GOLL	V	34
ORCHIL SHAKES OUT HER LONG DARK HAIR .	85	MAD KING GOLL		62
THE LINES ARE NOT HEAVY, NOR HEAVY THE LONG NETS BROWN—	91	OLD FISHERMAN	V	5
THE WHOLE OF THE LONG DAY.	94	MOLL MAGEE		8
HE SMOOTHS THE LONG BROWN NOSE.	98	FOXHUNTER		20
BY GOD TO THE BRIGHT HEARTS OF THOSE LONG DEAD,	101	ROSE UPON ROOD		20
"I HAVE WAITED, MOTHER, FOR THAT WORD!	107	CUCHULAIN SEA		22
"LONG HAVE I WAITED, MOTHER, FOR THOSE WORDS!	107	CUCHULAIN SEA	V	22
"I HAVE LONG WAITED, MOTHER, FOR THOSE WORDS!	107	CUCHULAIN SEA	V	22
OR DO YOU LONG FOR THE DIM SLEEPY GROUND,	109	CUCHULAIN SEA		60
AND THROUGH THE OTHER'S SHIELD HIS LONG BLADE BROKE,	110	CUCHULAIN SEA	V	66
AND WENT DOWN TO THE LONG SANDS ALONE,	111	CUCHULAIN SEA		84
AND HE WENT DOWN TO THE LONG SANDS ALONE,	111	CUCHULAIN SEA	V	84
STOOD UP, AND CAME TO THE LONG SANDS ALONE!	111	CUCHULAIN SEA	V	84
AND WAGE GOD'S BATTLES IN THE LONG GREY SHIPS.	114	ROSE OF BATTLE		20
OUR LONG SHIPS LOOSE THOUGHT-WOVEN SAILS AND WAIT,	115	ROSE OF BATTLE		31
AND THE LONG DEW-DROPPING HOURS OF THE NIGHT,	116	FAERY SONG		7
THE LONG HAIR IS ON HER FACE!	124	CATHLEEN PARA	V	10
THE LONG HAIR SHADOWS HER FACE!	124	CATHLEEN PARA		10
AS IN THE OLD DAYS LONG GONE BY,	131	OLD PENSIONER	V	15
OF THEIR LONG WINGS, THE FLASH OF THEIR WHITE FEET.	137	TO SOME I TALK		16
OF THEIR LONG WINGS, THE FLASH OF THEIR SWIFT FEET.	137	TO SOME I TALK	V	16
AND DREAMED OF THE LONG DIM HAIR	144	HOST OF AIR		7
OF HER LONG DIM HAIR.	145	HOST OF AIR		28
WERE DROWNED IN HER LONG DIM HAIR.	145	HOST OF AIR		36
AND WALK AMONG LONG DAPPLED GRASS,	150	WANDER AENGUS		21
AND THE YOUNG LIE LONG AND DREAM IN THEIR BED	150	OLD MOTHER		5
WHILE THE YOUNG LIE LONG AND DREAM IN THEIR BED	150	OLD MOTHER	V	5
BUT THE YOUNG LIE LONG AND DREAM IN THEIR BED	150	OLD MOTHER	V	5
I HEAR THE SHADOWY HORSES, THEIR LONG MANES A-SHAKE,	154	BELOVED PEACE		1
PASSION-DIMMED EYES AND LONG HEAVY HAIR	155	REPROVE CURLEW		4
THAT HAS LONG FADED FROM THE WORLD!	155	FORGOT BEAUTY		3
THAT HAS LONG FADED IN THE WORLD!	155	FORGOT BEAUTY	V	3
AND BIND UP YOUR LONG HAIR AND SIGH!	158	BELOVED RHYMES		8
IN A LONG AND STRAIGHT BLUE GARMENT	159	CAP AND BELLS	V	5
AND STILL MURMUR AND LONG!	163	ASKS FORGIVE		18
O WOMEN, KNEELING BY YOUR ALTAR-RAILS LONG HENCE,	173	SPEAKS HEARERS		1
O COLLEENS, KNEELING BY YOUR ALTAR RAILS LONG HENCE,	173	SPEAKS HEARERS	V	1
O, WOMEN, KNEELING BY YOUR ALTAR RAILS LONG HENCE,	173	SPEAKS HEARERS	V	1
IN HER HIGH HOUSE AT CRUACHAN, THE LONG HEARTH,	180	QUEEN MAEVE		11
CRIED FROM THE PORTER'S LODGE, AND WITH LONG CLAMOUR	181	QUEEN MAEVE		37
ONE THAT THE GENERATIONS HAD LONG WAITED	182	QUEEN MAEVE		66
WITH LONG WHITE BODIES CAME OUT OF THE AIR	185	QUEEN MAEVE		118
WHEN THE LONG WARS FOR THE WHITE HORN	189	BAILE AILLINN		14
HE HAD RAGGED LONG GRASS-COLOURED HAIR!	190	BAILE AILLINN		26
AWOKE THE HARP-STRINGS LONG AGO.	190	BAILE AILLINN		37
HE HAD RAGGED, LONG GRASS-YELLOW HAIR!	190	BAILE AILLINN	V	26
AWOKE THE HARP STRINGS LONG AGO.	190	BAILE AILLINN	V	37
HAVE SUCH LONG MEMORIES THAT THEY STILL	192	BAILE AILLINN		90
BUT THE GODS LONG AGO DECREED	194	BAILE AILLINN		119
AND THAT LONG FIGHTING AT THE FORD,	197	BAILE AILLINN		194
THE QUEENS THAT WERE IMAGINED LONG AGO,	201	OLD MEMORY		5
THROUGH THE LONG YEARS OF YOUTH, AND WHO WOULD HAVE THOUGHT	201	OLD MEMORY		7
THROUGH THE LONG DAYS OF YOUTH, AND WHO WOULD HAVE THOUGHT	201	OLD MEMORY	V	7
I LONG FOR YOUR MERRY AND TENDER AND PITIFUL WORDS,	203	WITHER BOUGHS		3
SEVEN OLD SISTERS WIND THE THREADS OF THE LONG LIVED ONES,	209	UNDER THE MOON	V	7
O DO NOT LOVE TOO LONG	211	O DO NOT LOVE		T
DO NOT LOVE TOO LONG	211	O DO NOT LOVE	V	T
SWEETHEART, DO NOT LOVE TOO LONG!	211	O DO NOT LOVE		1
I LOVED LONG AND LONG,	211	O DO NOT LOVE		2
I LOVED LONG AND LONG,	211	O DO NOT LOVE		2
O DO NOT LOVE TOO LONG,	212	O DO NOT LOVE		10
SWEET WITH ALL MUSIC, OUT OF HIS LONG HAIR,	219	HARP OF AENGUS		8
FOR LONG ENOUGH? AYE, LONG AND LONG ENOUGH.	221	SHADOW WATER B		2

		PAGE	TITLE		LINE
LONG (CONTINUED)					
FOR LONG ENOUGH? AYE, LONG AND LONG ENOUGH.		221	SHADOW WATER B		2
FOR LONG ENOUGH? AYE, LONG AND LONG ENOUGH.		221	SHADOW WATER B		2
AS THAT WILD AENGUS. LONG BEFORE HER DAY		224	SHADOW WATER B		47
IN THEIR LONG LIVES? WILL YOU BE OF OUR TROOP		225	SHADOW WATER B		72
THIS LONG WHILE NOW! WE HAD NOT TURNED AGAINST HIM		225	SHADOW WATER B	V	68B
IN THEIR LONG LIVES? IF YOU'LL BE OF OUR TROOP		225	SHADOW WATER B	V	72
I ALMOST LONG THAT IT WERE POSSIBLE!		236	SHADOW WATER B		306
CRIED OUT THE WHOLE NIGHT LONG.		254	HIS DREAM		16
WE'LL OUT, FOR THE WORLD LIVES AS LONG AGO!		257	RECONCILIATION		8
IN MOMENTARY ANGER LONG AGO!		258	KING NO KING		10
THAT LONG TO GIVE THEMSELVES FOR WAGE,		262	STUDENTS AGIT		2
"ALTHOUGH THE EVENT WAS LONG IN DOUBT,		273	GREY ROCK		67
"A WEARY WOOING AND A LONG," HE SAID,		283	TWO KINGS		154
HE HAD COUNTED, WHERE LONG YEARS AGO		302	HOUR DAWN		7
HE COUNTED, WHERE LONG YEARS AGO		302	HOUR DAWN	V	7
BUT THE OTHER CRIED, "YOU LONG FOR SPRING		306	HOUR DAWN	V	91
LIES ONE LONG SOUGHT		310	WITCH		7
WITH THE HOT BLOOD OF YOUTH, OF LOVE CROSSED LONG AGO!		316	COLD HEAVEN		6
--SEEING THAT FAME HAS PERISHED THIS LONG WHILE,		321	REED WHISPERER		11
A LONG BLAST UPON THE HORN THAT BROUGHT		324	ROBERT GREGORY		22
BUT THAT, LONG TRAVELLING, HE HAD COME		325	ROBERT GREGORY		28
AND ALL DAY LONG I LOOK		329	MEN IMPROVE		4
"ALL DAY LONG FROM MID-DAY		332	SOLOMON SHEBA		3
ALL DAY LONG FROM SHADOWLESS NOON		332	SOLOMON SHEBA		5
"ALL DAY LONG FROM MIDDAY		332	SOLOMON SHEBA	V	3
AND ALL DAY LONG WE HAVE FOUND		333	SOLOMON SHEBA		22
ON NO LONG BENCH NOR LOFTY MILKING-SHED		341	SHEP GOATHERD		51
ON NO LONG BENCH NOR LOFTY MILKING SHED		341	SHEP GOATHERD	V	51
TILL THAT IS THEIR LONG SHOUTING PLAYTIME!		343	SHEP GOATHERD	V	106
THE ROUND GREEN EYES AND THE LONG WAVERING BODIES		343	DEJECTION		2
IT'S LONG SINCE I BEGAN		347	FISHERMAN		6
I WILL TALK NO MORE OF BOOKS OR THE LONG WAR		351	HER PRAISE		11
THE LONG FLOWING LINE,		355	PROPERTIUS		3
SINCE HE WHO HAD BEEN CONTENTED LONG,		361	ALF POLLEXFEN		28
THAT THOSE THAT WE HAVE LOVED GOT THEIR LONG FINGERS		375	PHASES OF MOON		66
SEEING THAT I, IGNORANT FOR SO LONG,		384	VISION ROBART		66
WHO GRIPS HIS LONG SPEAR SO TO PUSH		385	ROBARTES DANCE		3
WHEN THE LONG LOOKING-GLASS IS FULL,		387	ROBARTES DANCE		50
TOO LONG A SACRIFICE		394	EASTER 1916		57
WHEN LONG AGO I SAW HER RIDE		397	POLIT PRISONER		13
THOUGH I HAD LONG PERNED IN THE GYRE,		400	DEMON BEAST		5
FISH, FLESH, OR FOWL, COMMEND ALL SUMMER LONG		407	SAIL BYZANTIUM		5
FLOAT OUT UPON A LONG		414	TOWER		142
AMID GREAT CHAMBERS AND LONG GALLERIES, LINED		418	ANCEST HOUSES		36
WHERE THROUGH LONG WARS AND SUDDEN NIGHT ALARMS		420	MY HOUSE		24
WHERE THROUGH LONG WARS AND SUDDEN NIGHT ALARMS		420	MY HOUSE	V	24
THEIR LEGS LONG, DELICATE AND SLENDER, AQUAMARINE THEIR EYES,		426	PHANTOM HATRED		17
PUBLIC OPINION RIPENING FOR SO LONG		428	NINETEEN 19		13
STRETCH OUT YOUR LIMBS AND SLEEP A LONG SATURNIAN SLEEP!		442	BLACK CENTAUR		13
I WALK THROUGH THE LONG SCHOOLROOM QUESTIONING!		443	SCHOOL CHILDR		1
BUT WHAT CARE I THAT LONG FOR A MAN'S LOVE?		448	HERO GIRL FOOL		17
IN THE LONG ECHOING STREET THE LAUGHING DANCERS THRONG,		459	FROM OEDIPUS		7
I CELEBRATE THE SILENT KISS THAT ENDS SHORT LIFE OR LONG.		459	FROM OEDIPUS		9
IN THE LONG ECHOING STREETS THE LAUGHING DANCERS THRONG,		459	FROM OEDIPUS	V	7
I SAY THAT A DJIN SPOKE. A LIVE LONG HOUR		467	HARUN RASHID	V	136
AND TWO LONG GLASSES BRIMMED WITH MUSCATEL		470	ALL SOUL NIGHT		4
LONG PAST HIS PRIME REMEMBER THINGS THAT ARE		477	SELF AND SOUL		18
THOUGHTS LONG KNITTED INTO A SINGLE THOUGHT,		488	COOLE PARK 29		7
THINGS SAID OR DONE LONG YEARS AGO,		501	VACILLATION		51
I TOILED LONG YEARS AND AT LENGTH		505	RESULT THOUGHT		9
TOILED LONG YEARS AND AT LENGTH		505	RESULT THOUGHT	V	9
AFTER LONG SILENCE.		523	LONG SILENCE		T
SPEECH AFTER LONG SILENCE! IT IS RIGHT,		523	LONG SILENCE		1
"THAT IS A LONG WAY OFF,		526	AM OF IRELAND		11
I LONG FOR TRUTH, AND YET		533	FIRST CONFESS		7
STOOD OR HAVE MARCHED THE NIGHT LONG		546	TO SAME TUNE 2		15
OR HAVE MARCHED THE NIGHT LONG,		546	TO SAME TUNE 2	V	15
CUCHULAIN THAT FOUGHT NIGHT LONG WITH THE FOAM,		549	SEVERED HEAD		9
THINGS THOUGHT TOO LONG CAN BE NO LONGER THOUGHT,		564	GYRES		2
HIS LONG LAMP-CHIMNEY SHAPED LIKE THE STEM		566	LAPIS LAZULI		33
HIS LONG LAMP CHIMNEY SHAPED LIKE THE STEM		566	LAPIS LAZULI	V	33
THE CHAMBERMAID LIVED LONG, AND TOOK		571	THREE BUSHES		57
LONG LOOKED HE IN HER FACE,		571	THREE BUSHES		67
FROM TIME LONG PASSED AWAY.		589	OLD WICKED MAN		42
HONOUR HAD LIVED SO LONG, ALL LACKING FOUND.		603	GALLERY REVIS		35
HONOUR HAD LIVED SO LONG, THEIR HEALTH I FOUND.		603	GALLERY REVIS	V	35
KNOWS I HAVE LIVED SO LONG.		607	SONGS BURDEN 2		26
AS MY LONG PLANNED HALF SOLITUDE,		624	APPARITIONS	V	10
IF HE DIED LONG AGO		635	BLACK TOWER		15
THOUGH GRAVE-DIGGERS' TOIL IS LONG,		637	BEN BULBEN		21
THAT PALE, LONG VISAGED COMPANY		637	BEN BULBEN	V	7
SOMETHING DROPS FROM EYES LONG BLIND,		638	BEN BULBEN		29
LONG YEARS AGO, A CHURCH STANDS NEAR,		640	BEN BULBEN		87
WHERE ALL NIGHT LONG THE HEAVENS WEEP AND WEEP,		649	ISLE STAT I 1		124
WHERE ALL NIGHT LONG THE LONELY MOON, THE WHITE		650	ISLE STAT I 1		126
LONG ERE AN ARROW WHIZZED OR SWORD LEFT SHEATH		650	ISLE STAT I 1		135
AND ELVISH WISDOM, AND LONG YEARS OF YOUTH		653	ISLE STAT I 2		47
LONG YEARS AGO, AND UNTO STONE CONGEALED.		656	ISLE STAT I 3		28
UNTO HER DOOR! FOR THIS, WHERE NOD THE LONG		660	ISLE STAT II 1		43

470

LONG   (CONTINUED)
A LONG, BROWN GRASSHOPPER OF MAIDS! PEACE, SIR! . . . . 661 ISLE STAT II 1   69
A SHEPHERDESS LONG YEARS FORETOLD! . . . . 668 ISLE STAT II 3   49
BUT, FOR A BOY, HOW LONG THINE HAIR HAS GROWN! . . . . 670 ISLE STAT II 3   104
LONG CITRON COILS THAT HANG AROUND THEE, BLOWN . . . . 670 ISLE STAT II 3   105
THE LONG LILY BLOWS. . . . . 672 ISLE STAT II 3   165
WILD CRIES, GROWN SWEET WITH LULLS AND LINGERINGS LONG. . 674 ISLE STAT II 3   222
MEETING LONG HENCE THE PHANTOM HERDSMAN, KING . . . . 675 ISLE STAT II 3   242
HAVE I SLEPT LONG? LONG YEARS. WITH HUNGRY HEART . . 677 ISLE STAT II 3   286
HAVE I SLEPT LONG? LONG YEARS. WITH HUNGRY HEART . . 677 ISLE STAT II 3   286
SEAFARER, WAKE! WAS MY SLEEP LONG? LONG YEARS. . . . 678 ISLE STAT II 3   292
SEAFARER, WAKE! WAS MY SLEEP LONG? LONG YEARS. . . . 678 ISLE STAT II 3   292
HE IS LONG DEAD. WAKE! SOFT AS A BEE SIPS . . . . . 678 ISLE STAT II 3   297
WAS MY SLEEP LONG, OH, YOUTH? LONG, LONG AND DEEP. . . 678 ISLE STAT II 3   299
WAS MY SLEEP LONG, OH, YOUTH? LONG, LONG AND DEEP. . . 678 ISLE STAT II 3   299
WAS MY SLEEP LONG, OH, YOUTH? LONG, LONG AND DEEP. . . 678 ISLE STAT II 3   299
SLEEPER, AWAKE! HOW LONG MY SLEEP? UNNUMBERED . . . 678 ISLE STAT II 3   307
SHE IS LONG AGES DUST. AH, WOE IS ME! . . . . . . 679 ISLE STAT II 3   313
OR LONG ERE THIS HAD LOST THEIR RUDDY STAIN! . . . . 687 TWO TITANS   8
WORN WITH LONG STRUGGLES! AND THE WAVES HAVE SUNG . . 687 TWO TITANS   23
LOW, LONG AND MUSICAL. A DEW-DROP HUNG . . . . . . 689 NETTLESHIP   9
HIDING MY FACE, I CRIED LONG, BITTERLY. . . . . . . 690 MOSADA 1   17
DOWN THE LONG VALLEYS FROM MY PEOPLE'S TENTS. . . . . 691 MOSADA 1   30
FOR LONG THE BURTHEN OF THEIR TALKING GRIEFS. . . . . 693 MOSADA 1   71
HE WILL BE TALLER NOW--'TWAS LONG AGO. . . . . . . 699 MOSADA 3   15
ERE LONG SHALL FALTER THROUGH THE NOISY SQUARE, . . . 699 MOSADA 3   21
SOFT AS A LONG DEAD FOOTSTEP WHISPERING THROUGH . . . 699 MOSADA 3   V   5
THE FOOT-WORN WAY IS LONG, AND IT GROWS DARK. . . . 702 MOSADA 3   V 92
THE FOOTWORN WAY IS LONG, AND IT GROWS DARK. . . . . 702 MOSADA 3   V 92
MY MOTHER DREW FORTH FROM THE LONG GRASS . . . . . 708 FAIRY PEDANT   23
BUT SPEECHLESS, AND THE MAIDEN WITH LONG WAIL . . . . 713 FERENCZ RENYI   85
IN THE LONG GRASS--FOUR EYES DROOP LOW--A SEAT . . . 716 DWELT SYCAMORE   11
ALL THOSE LONG FORGOTTEN FISHERS, TILL IN THE EASTERN SKIES 719 PHANTOM SHIP V 32
GOLD UNTO GOLD, A GLEAM IN ITS LONG HAIR, ... 720 WITCH VIVIEN   3
LONG BEFORE THE MORNING FIRE . . . . 727 LOVERS QUARREL   45
A FULL HOUR LONG, WHEN ROSE A FEATHER . . . . . . 728 PRIEST FAIRY   19
"AND CUT NO WOOD THE WHOLE DAY LONG, ... 731 PRIEST FAIRY   81
LONG THOU FOR NOTHING, NEITHER SAD NOR GAY! . . . . 734 QUATRAIN APHOR   9
LONG THOU FOR NOTHING, NEITHER NIGHT NOR DAY! . . . . 734 QUATRAIN APHOR 10
NOT EVEN "I LONG TO SEE THY LONGING OVER," . . . . 734 QUATRAIN APHOR 11
WHERE LONG GREY GRASSES BOW AND BEND, ... 736 SUMMER EVENING   6
THROUGH THE LONG BITTER WAY. . . . . 738 MOURN THEN ON   4
GOD PLANTED HIM LONG AGO. . . . . 743 WISDOM DREAMS   8
AND MURMURED: "O LONG GREY CLOAK, ... 744 GLOVE CLOAK   11
I HAD KILLED HIM LONG AGO, BUT THAT THE FOOL . . . . 748 SHADOW WATER A   17
AH, THEY HAVE PIERCED HIS HEART! I HAVE SLEPT LONG! . . 761 SHADOW WATER A 270
SWEET WITH ALL MUSIC, OUT OF HIS LONG HAIR, ... 762 SHADOW WATER A 303
I HAVE STOOD SO LONG BY A GAP IN THE WALL . . . . . 788 HAWTHORN TREE   15
I HAVE STOPPED SO LONG A GAP IN THE WALL . . . . . 788 HAWTHORN TREE V 15
LONG-ARMED
HAD KISSED MY FATHER, LONG-ARMED FIN, ...   10 OISIN 1   V 112B
LONGED
HAS LOVER LIVED, BUT LONGED TO WIVE . . . . 197 BAILE AILLINN 206
SO BITTERLY, YOU'D DREAM THEY LONGED TO LOOK . . . . 265 ABBEY THEATRE   6
THE SWEETNESS THAT ALL LONGED FOR NIGHT AND DAY, . . . 418 ANCEST HOUSES 20
WHOSE FOOTFALL I HAVE LONGED FOR, THREE SAD SUMMERS. . . 692 MOSADA 1   45
LONGER
"VEX THEM NO LONGER," NIAMH SAID, ...   12 OISIN 1   148
IT PASSETH AWAY, AND IS HEARD OF NO LONGER. . . . .   26 OISIN 1   V 399B
NO LONGER GLAD AS ON THAT MORNING, SPED . . . . .   30 OISIN 2   V 16
WE SHALL NO LONGER HEAR THE LITTLE CRY . . . . . 115 ROSE OF BATTLE   35
AND CALL TO MY BELOVED AND ME: "NO LONGER FLY . . . 173 SPEAKS HEARERS   7
DIM POWERS OF DROWSY THOUGHT, LET HER NO LONGER BE . . 175 ELEMENT POWERS 13
GREAT RULERS OF THE STILLNESS, LET HER NO LONGER BE . . 175 ELEMENT POWERS V 13
GREAT RULERS OF STILLNESS, LET HER NO LONGER BE . . . 175 ELEMENT POWERS V 13
FOR WE WILL GAZE UPON THIS WORLD NO LONGER. . . . . 251 SHADOW WATER B 614
FOR HE WILL GAZE UPON THIS WORLD NO LONGER. . . . . 251 SHADOW WATER B V 614
FOR WE WILL GAZE UPON THE WORLD NO LONGER. . . . . 251 SHADOW WATER B V 614
I WAS NO LONGER TERRIFIED--HIS VOICE . . . . . . 284 TWO KINGS   171
I AM NO LONGER FAINT . . . . 335 SONG   9
YOUNG MEN NO LONGER SUDDENLY CATCH THEIR BREATH . . . 355 BROKEN DREAMS   2
ENDURE WHAT LIFE GOD GIVES AND ASK NO LONGER SPAN! . . 459 FROM OEDIPUS   1
FOR INTELLECT NO LONGER KNOWS . . . . 478 SELF AND SOUL 36
NO LONGER IN LETHEAN FOLIAGE CAUGHT . . . . 500 VACILLATION 27
PRIMORDIAL MOTHERHOOD FORSAKE HIS LIMBS, THE CHILD
NO LONGER REST, ... 559 MAGIC DRUM   2
THINGS THOUGHT TOO LONG CAN BE NO LONGER THOUGHT, . . . 564 GYRES   2
I'LL SEE HIM LONGER IF I STAND OUT HERE . . . . . 703 MOSADA 3   113
I AM SO YOUNG. DOST THOU NO LONGER KNOW, ... 713 FERENCZ RENYI   88
CEASE THE SAILS THEIR FLAPPING UPROAR, AND THE HULL NO 719 PHANTOM SHIP   18
LONGER ROLLS.
CEASE THE SAILS, THEIR FLAPPING UPROAR TO THE HULL 719 PHANTOM SHIP V 18
NO LONGER ROLLS.
TILL HIS EDAINE, NO LONGER A GOLDEN FLY . . . . . . 757 SHADOW WATER A 210
AND SHE, NO LONGER BLOWN AMONG THE WINDS, ... 763 SHADOW WATER A 323
FOR WE WILL GAZE UPON THIS WORLD NO LONGER. . . . . 769 SHADOW WATER A 430
UPON THIS WORLD NO LONGER. THE HARP CRIES OUT. . . . 769 SHADOW WATER A V 430
LONGEST
BUT STORIES THAT LIVE LONGEST . . . . 587 PARNELLITES   29
LONGEVITY
A SYMBOL OF LONGEVITY! . . . . 566 LAPIS LAZULI   40

		PAGE	TITLE		LINE

LONG-FORGOTTEN
THOSE WARRIORS OF A LONG-FORGOTTEN DAY, ... 30 OISIN 2 V 14A
AND LONG-FORGOTTEN MURIAS, ... 196 BAILE AILLINN 163
LONG-HAIRED
THE LONG-HAIRED WARRIORS, THE SPREAD FEAST; . . . . . 2 OISIN 1 V 7
LONGHI
HER DOMINO, HER PANNIERED SKIRT COPIED FROM LONGHI; . . . 363 DOLLS FACES 7
LONGING SEE DEATH-LONGING EVER-LONGING LOVE-LONGING
LIKE AN ARMY OF OLD MEN LONGING FOR REST FROM THE MOAN 48 OISIN 3 16
OF THE SEAS,
LIKE AN ARMY OF OLD MEN LONGING FOR REST FROM THE MOAN 57 OISIN 3 144
OF THE SEAS,
AND LONELY AND LONGING FOR NIAMH, I SHIVERED AND TURNED 60 OISIN 3 181
ME ABOUT,
THE HEART IN ME LONGING TO LEAP LIKE A GRASSHOPPER INTO 60 OISIN 3 182
HER HEART;
AND SHIVERING AND LONELY, AND LONGING FOR NIAM, I TURNED 60 OISIN 3 V 181
ME ABOUT,
THAT MURMURING AND LONGING CAME . . . . 162 ASKS FORGIVE 8
THAT LONGING AND MURMURING CAME . . . . 162 ASKS FORGIVE V 8
AND TROUBLE WITH A SIGH FOR ALL THINGS LONGING FOR REST 163 ASKS FORGIVE 23
LOVES IN BRIEF LONGING AND DECEIVING HOPE . . . . . . 228 SHADOW WATER B 146
LONGING TO KNEAD AND PULL IT INTO SHAPE . . . . . . 246 SHADOW WATER B 510
AND YOU KNOW WELL HOW GREAT THE LONGING HAS BEEN, . . . 352 PEOPLE 7
WHERE EVEN LONGING DROWNS UNDER ITS OWN EXCESS; . . . . 426 PHANTOM HATRED 22
IS BUT ITS LONGING FOR THE TOMB. . . . . 434 WHEEL 8
THE SOUTH WIND BROUGHT IT LONGING, AND THE EAST WIND 449 OWEN AHERNE 5
DESPAIR,
THE SOUTH WIND BROUGHT IT LONGING, AND THE EAST BROUGHT 449 OWEN AHERNE V 5
IN DESPAIR,
THE SOUTH WIND BROUGHT IT LONGING, AND THE EAST BROUGHT 449 OWEN AHERNE V 5
IT DESPAIR,
DELIGHT BECOMES DEATH-LONGING IF ALL LONGING ELSE BE VAIN. 459 FROM OEDIPUS 3
DREAD HAS FOLLOWED LONGING, ... 519 LOVES LONENESS 11
NINE NIGHTS I LAY IN LONGING SORE . . . . 551 SONGS REWRIT 1 V 13
NINE NIGHTS I LAY AND IN LONGING SORE . . . . 551 SONGS REWRIT 1 13
NOT EVEN "I LONG TO SEE THY LONGING OVER," . . . . . . 734 QUATRAIN APHOR 11
AND TURN BRIEF LONGING AND DECEIVING HOPE . . . . . . 750 SHADOW WATER A 59
THAN IN BRIEF LONGING AND DECEIVING HOPE . . . . . . 750 SHADOW WATER A 65
IS BUT BRIEF LONGING, AND DECEIVING HOPE, ... 765 SHADOW WATER A 354
WHEN LOVE LONGING IS BUT DROUGHT . . . . 777 SONG DEIRDRE 2 V 11
LONGINGS
OF BIRDS EVEN, LONGINGS FOR AERY . . . . 708 FAIRY PEDANT 26
LONG-LEGGED
THE LONG-LEGGED MOOR-HENS DIVE, ... 393 EASTER 1916 53
WHERE LONG-LEGGED MOOR-HENS DIVE, ... 393 EASTER 1916 V 53
OVER THEM FLIES A LONG-LEGGED BIRD, ... 566 LAPIS LAZULI 39
LONG-LEGGED FLY . . . . 617 LONG-LEG FLY T
LIKE A LONG-LEGGED FLY UPON THE STREAM . . . . 617 LONG-LEG FLY 9
LIKE A LONG-LEGGED FLY UPON THE STREAM . . . . 617 LONG-LEG FLY 19
LIKE A LONG-LEGGED FLY UPON THE STREAM . . . . 618 LONG-LEG FLY 29
LONG-LIMBED
AND THE JOY OF THE STREAMS WHERE LONG-LIMBED HERONS WADE; 674 ISLE STAT II 3 217
LONG-LIVED
SEVEN OLD SISTERS WIND THE THREADS OF THE LONG-LIVED ONES, 209 UNDER THE MOON 7
LONG-LOST
WHERE LIES THE LONG-LOST FOREST OF THE SPRITE, ... 682 SEEKER 23
THERE LIES THE LONG-LOST FOREST OF THE SPRITE, ... 682 SEEKER V 23
SOFT AS THE WHISPERING OF A LONG-LOST FOOTSTEP . . . . 699 MOSADA 3 5
LONG-OARED
REMEMBERING ITS LONG-OARED COMPANIONS, ... 55 OISIN 3 118
LONG-PLANNED
AS MY LONG-PLANNED HALF SOLITUDE, ... 624 APPARITIONS 10
LONGS
. . . AND HIS BELOVED, AND LONGS FOR THE END OF THE WORLD 153 CHANGE BELOVED T
THAT THE HEART LONGS FOR. WHAT IS LOVE ITSELF, ... 230 SHADOW WATER B 183
FOR ALL LIFE LONGS FOR THE LAST DAY . . . . 306 HOUR DAWN 98
SO LONGS TO LOOK BEYOND OUR LIFE, AN EYE . . . . . . 465 HARUN RASHID V 87
AND BODILY TENDERNESS; AND HE WHO LONGS . . . . 750 SHADOW WATER A 66
O! WHY IS LOVE SO CRAZY THAT IT LONGS . . . . 765 SHADOW WATER A 363
LONG-VISAGED
THAT PALE, LONG-VISAGED COMPANY . . . . 637 BEN BULBEN 7
LONG-WARLESS
. . . LONG-WARLESS, GROWN WHITER THAN CURDS. . . . . . 49 OISIN 3 V 36
LOOK
THEREON DID SHE LOOK HAUGHTY AND SWEET; . . . . . . 6 OISIN 1 54
LOOK TO LONG FISHING-LINES, OR POINT AND PARE . . . . 32 OISIN 2 55
LEST THEY SHOULD LOOK UPON SOME DREADFUL SIGHT; . . . . 38 OISIN 2 142
LOOK ON MY THIN GREY HAIR AND HOLLOW CHEEKS . . . . . 103 FERGUS DRUID 23
AND SLOWLY READ, AND DREAM OF THE SOFT LOOK . . . . . 121 YOU ARE OLD 3
WITH "LOOK AT THAT OLD FELLOW THERE; . . . . 131 OLD PENSIONER V 3
THERE'S NO MAN MAY LOOK UPON HER, NO MAN, ... 199 ARROW 3
IN A WHITE BREAKING WAVE; THEY HAD THE LOOK . . . . . 223 SHADOW WATER B 34
LOOK THERE! THERE IN THE MIST! A SHIP OF SPICE! . . . 232 SHADOW WATER B 219
THEY ARE TOO BUSY WITH EACH OTHER. LOOK! . . . . . 232 SHADOW WATER B 229
AND I WOULD HAVE YOU LOOK INTO MY FACE . . . . 238 SHADOW WATER B 349
THAT I WOULD LOOK UPON FOR EVER? MY GRIEF! . . . . . 244 SHADOW WATER B 462
WHY ARE YOU LOOKING AT THE SEA? LOOK THERE! . . . . 246 SHADOW WATER B 516
I TOO, I TOO. WHY DO YOU LOOK AWAY? . . . . 246 SHADOW WATER B V 507
WHAT MORE HAVE YOU TO LOOK FOR ON THE SEAS? . . . . . 248 SHADOW WATER B 543
OR LOOK UPON THEM. WERE THEY BUT LOWLIER . . . . . 250 SHADOW WATER B 576

		PAGE	TITLE	LINE
LOOK (CONTINUED)				
WILL LOOK UPON HIS FACE AGAIN. GO WITH HIM,		250	SHADOW WATER B	589
I LOOK AT YOU, AND I SIGH.		261	DRINKING SONG	6
DEAR CRAOIBHIN AOIBHIN, LOOK INTO OUR CASE.		264	ABBEY THEATRE	1
SO BITTERLY, YOU'D DREAM THEY LONGED TO LOOK		265	ABBEY THEATRE	6
BUT NOW SHE HAD NO MILD AND NO KIND LOOK:		279	TWO KINGS V	62D
SHE WOULD NOT LOOK IN ANY KNOWN MAN'S FACE		280	TWO KINGS	73
WOULD NEVER LOOK AGAIN ON KNOWN MAN'S FACE."		280	TWO KINGS	75
WILL NEVER LOOK AGAIN ON KNOWN MAN'S FACE."		280	TWO KINGS V	75
SHALL MAKE HER LOOK UPON HER HANDIWORK,		282	TWO KINGS	115
LOOK UP IN THE SUN'S EYE AND GIVE		288	TO WEALTHY MAN	32
WHETHER TO LOOK UPON YOUR MONUMENT		292	TO A SHADE	2
AND SNORED, NO PHANTOM BY HIS LOOK.		303	HOUR DAWN	30
PLAINLY NO PHANTOM BY HIS LOOK:		303	HOUR DAWN V	30
WITH SCARCE A PITYING LOOK?		315	FRIENDS	19
WHAT EAGLE LOOK STILL SHOWS,		316	FRIENDS	25
AND NOW THEIR BREATHLESS FACES SEEM TO LOOK		325	ROBERT GREGORY	43
AND THEIR BREATHLESS FACES SEEM TO LOOK		325	ROBERT GREGORY V	43
AND ALL DAY LONG I LOOK		329	MEN IMPROVE	4
YET DID BUT LOOK, ROCKING THE GLITTERING COACH		344	DAWN V	11
AND THAT PROUD LOOK AS THOUGH SHE HAD GAZED INTO THE BURNING SUN,		354	HIS PHOENIX	29
YET ALWAYS WHEN I LOOK DEATH IN THE FACE,		357	DEEP-SWORN VOW	3
AND SHE MAY LOOK FROM THE BED		366	HER CHRIS TREE	6
IMPULSIVE MEN THAT LOOK FOR HAPPINESS		369	EGO DOMINUS	40
AND LOOK MOST LIKE ME, BEING INDEED MY DOUBLE,		371	EGO DOMINUS	72
AND BOTH LOOK UP TO ME ALONE		380	SONGS FOOL 1	4
AS I LOOK UP TO PROVIDENCE.		380	SONGS FOOL 1	6
WITH A STARK, DENYING LOOK:		381	SONG OF FOOL	6
THE SOUL'S UNCHANGING LOOK:		422	MY TABLE	24
I LOOK UPON ONE CHILD OR T'OTHER THERE		443	SCHOOL CHILDR	18
I AM JEALOUS OF THE LOOK MEN TURN ON YOU		447	HERO GIRL FOOL V	A
THEN PETER HAD A MURDERING LOOK,		457	SUMMER SPRING	9
THOUGH BUT A FEW LEARNED MEN SHALL LOOK WITHIN,		461	HARUN RASHID V	18A
MY HEART MUST LOOK UPON A DAILY RUIN		464	HARUN RASHID	83
SO STRAINS TO LOOK BEYOND OUR LIFE, AN EYE		465	HARUN RASHID	87
SO LONGS TO LOOK BEYOND OUR LIFE, AN EYE		465	HARUN RASHID V	87
EVERYTHING WE LOOK UPON IS BLEST.		479	SELF AND SOUL	72
I CANNOT LOOK THEREON,		501	VACILLATION	49
LOOK ON THAT FIRE, SALVATION WALKS WITHIN.		502	VACILLATION	76
WHAT IF I LOOK UPON A MAN		532	BEFORE WORLD	9
WHERE CAN SHE LOOK UNTIL HE MAKE THE SHOW!		558	RIBH CHRISTIAN	22
THE GYRES! THE GYRES! OLD ROCKY FACE, LOOK FORTH;		564	GYRES	1
WE THAT LOOK ON BUT LAUGH IN TRAGIC JOY.		564	GYRES	8
IF SOUL MAY LOOK AND BODY TOUCH,		573	LADYS 2ND SONG	19
HE FIXED A BITTER LOOK:		585	ORAHILLY	24
A GENTLE QUESTIONING LOOK THAT CANNOT HIDE		601	GALLERY REVIS	6
KEVIN O'HIGGINS, AND THAT LOOK HE WEARS,		601	GALLERY REVIS V	5
WHERE MY FRIENDS' PORTRAITS HANG AND LOOK THEREON;		604	GALLERY REVIS	52
CALCULATIONS THAT LOOK BUT CASUAL FLESH, PUT DOWN		610	STATUES	11
CAN THERE BE MERCY IN THAT LOOK?		625	NATIVITY	12
FOR, LOOK YOU, SAD'S THE MURMUR OF THE BEES,		652	ISLE STAT I 2	9
YOUR WEEPING FITS! LOOK YOU, SO VERY STRAIT		659	ISLE STAT II 1	22
LOOK UP, LOOK UP, THY GOMEZ IS BY THEE.		701	MOSADA 3	68
LOOK UP, LOOK UP, THY GOMEZ IS BY THEE.		701	MOSADA 3	68
LOOK UP, LOOK UP, THY VALLENCE IS BY THEE.		701	MOSADA 3 V	68
LOOK UP, LOOK UP, THY VALLENCE IS BY THEE.		701	MOSADA 3 V	68
I KNEEL BY THEE--NO PARTING NOW--LOOK UP,		702	MOSADA 3	94
FOR NIGHT COMES FAST. LOOK DOWN ON ME, MY LOVE,		703	MOSADA 3	103
LOOK ON ME ONCE. WHY SINK YOUR EYELIDS THUS?		703	MOSADA 3	107
LOVE, WILL YOU DIE WHEN WE HAVE MET? ONE LOOK.		703	MOSADA 3	109
LOOK ON ME ONCE. WHY SINK YOUR EYELIDS SO?		703	MOSADA 3 V	107
LOOK! THERE SHE LIES UNDER A FLAPPING SAIL.		751	SHADOW WATER A	90
AENGUS LOOKS ON YOU WHEN I LOOK! HE AWAITS		757	SHADOW WATER A	209
AENGUS LOOKS ON YOU WHEN I LOOK! HE WAITS		757	SHADOW WATER A V	209
I AM CAUGHT IN WOVEN NETS OF ENCHANTMENT. LOOK!		762	SHADOW WATER A	293
IS LAUGHING THROUGH A MORTAL'S EYES. O LOOK!		763	SHADOW WATER A	324
THAT HAVE GONE THITHER TO LOOK FOR THE LOUD STREAMS,		765	SHADOW WATER A	348
LOOK ON THIS BODY AND THIS HEAVY HAIR!		767	SHADOW WATER A	397
SHOULD LOOK UPON HIS EYES WITH LOVE, IN THE END		768	SHADOW WATER A	409
SHOULD LOOK UPON HIS EYES WITH LOVE UNTO THE END		768	SHADOW WATER A V	409
LOOKED				
AS ANY RUDDY MOTH, LOOKED DOWN ON US;		34	OISIN 2	72
LOOKED DOWN ON ME; AND IN THE SELF-SAME PLACE		39	OISIN 2	146
I LOOKED ON MY COLD BABY		95	MOLL MAGEE	19
LOOKED DOWN ON YOU FROM HEAVEN'S DOOR-POST		112	ROSE OF PEACE	3
LOOKED DOWN ON YOU FROM HEAVEN'S DOOR-POSTS,		112	ROSE OF PEACE V	3
SHE LOOKED IN MY HEART ONE DAY		152	LOSS OF LOVE	5
WHEN THEY HAVE BUT LOOKED UPON THEIR IMAGES--		210	RAGGED WOOD	3
WHEN THE SUN LOOKED OUT OF HIS GOLDEN HOOD,		210	RAGGED WOOD V	3
WHEN THE SUN LOOKED OUT OF HIS GOLDEN HOOD?--		211	RAGGED WOOD	7
WHEN THEY HAVE BUT LOOKED UPON THEIR IMAGES,		211	RAGGED WOOD V	7
UNTIL THE MOON HAD SET; AND WHEN I LOOKED		223	SHADOW WATER B	22
HAD YOU LOOKED ON THEM FACE TO FACE AS I DID,		231	SHADOW WATER B	198
FOOL, FOOL! ALTHOUGH YOU HAVE LOOKED INTO MY FACE		238	SHADOW WATER B	356
MY ENEMY. I LOOKED UPON THE MOON,		246	SHADOW WATER B	509
I HAVE LOOKED UPON THOSE BRILLIANT CREATURES,		322	SWANS AT COOLE	13
I HAVE LOOKED UPON THESE BRILLIANT CREATURES		322	SWANS AT COOLE V	13
WHEN HAVE I LAST LOOKED ON		343	DEJECTION	1
THAT HAS LOOKED DOWN		344	DAWN	2
ALL DAY I'D LOOKED IN THE FACE		347	FISHERMAN	9

473

LOOKED   (CONTINUED)
    THAT NEVER LOOKED UPON MAN WITH DESIRE, ...   358 PRESENCES   13
    HAVE LOOKED INTO YOUR FACE? . . . .   367 HER CHRIS TREE   11
    THAT I HAVE HANDLED LEAST, LEAST LOOKED UPON. . . . .   367 EGO DOMINUS   9
    THE CREEPING CAT, LOOKED UP. . . . .   378 CAT AND MOON   4
    . . . NEVER TO HAVE LOOKED INTO THE EYE OF DAY; . . .   459 FROM OEDIPUS   11
    . . . AT ALL NOR LOOKED INTO THE EYE OF DAY. . . . .   459 FROM OEDIPUS   V 11
    WHEN IT HAS LOOKED IN GLORY FROM A CLOUD. . . . . . .   482 BLOOD AND MOON   54
    THAT NEVER LOOKED OUT OF THE EYE OF A SAINT . . . . .   486 SEVEN SAGES   12
    I TURNED ABOUT AND LOOKED WHERE BRANCHES BREAK . . .   490 COOLE BALLYLEE   15
    I TURNED ABOUT AND LOOKED WHERE BRANCHES BROKE . . .   490 COOLE BALLYLEE   V 15
    TROY LOOKED ON HELEN, IT DIED AND ADORED; . . . . .   547 TO SAME TUNE 3   V 4
    MY LOVER LOOKED SO GAY" . . . .   570 THREE BUSHES   32
    LOOKED HALF ASLEEP ALL DAY. . . . .   570 THREE BUSHES   34
    LONG LOOKED HE IN HER FACE, ...   571 THREE BUSHES   67
    AND NEVER HAVE I LOOKED UPON . . . .   595 COLONEL MARTIN   32
    WHEREVER I HAD LOOKED I HAD LOOKED UPON . . . .   602 GALLERY REVIS   19
    WHEREVER I HAD LOOKED I HAD LOOKED UPON . . . .   602 GALLERY REVIS   19
    PLOTINUS CAME AND LOOKED ABOUT. . . . .   611 NEWS ORACLE   9
    AS THOUGH A STERNER EYE LOOKED THROUGH HER EYE . . .   619 BRONZE HEAD   23
    AN OLD HORSE LOOKED ACROSS A FENCE, ...   725 LEGEND   27
    THE PRIEST LOOKED NEITHER TO RIGHT NOR LEFT, ...   730 PRIEST FAIRY   49
    AND LOOKED ON NO ONE THERE . . . .   741 EARL PAUL   34
    AND LEAVE HER DREAMING. WHEN I LOOKED ON HER, . . .   761 SHADOW WATER A   V 258
    THE MOMENT HE HAS LOOKED AT YOU, ...   786 YOUR HEART   18
LOOKING
    LOOKING ON HER, ALEEL, THE SWINEHERD, SAID; . . . .   106 CUCHULAIN SEA   V 9
    WHEN LOOKING ON THEIR SHAKEN HAIR, ...   135 TWO TREES   V 17
    HE CHANGED ME SUDDENLY; I WAS LOOKING ANOTHER WAY; .   153 CHANGE BELOVED   7
    WHILE I WAS LOOKING THEY ROSE HURRIEDLY, ...   223 SHADOW WATER B   25
    FOR YOU ARE LOOKING AT THE SEA. DO YOU NOT KNOW . .   246 SHADOW WATER B   513
    WHY ARE YOU LOOKING AT THE SEA? LOOK THERE! . . . .   246 SHADOW WATER B   516
    "SPEAKING OF LOVE THROUGH OTHER LIPS AND LOOKING . .   283 TWO KINGS   155
    FROM STONE TO STONE. I AM LOOKING FOR STRAYED SHEEP;   339 SHEP GOATHERD   9
    IN THEIR GREAT WINDOW LOOKING AT THE DAWN! . . . . .   352 PEOPLE   15
    STILL RAZOR-KEEN, STILL LIKE A LOOKING GLASS . . . .   477 SELF AND SOUL   V 11
    I'M LOOKING FOR THE FACE I HAD . . . .   532 BEFORE WORLD   7
    GAVE WOMEN DREAMS AND DREAMS THEIR LOOKING GLASS. . .   610 STATUES   V 16
LOOKING-GLASS
    "BUT THERE'S A DEVIL IN A LOOKING-GLASS." . . . . .   300 BEGGAR CRIED   12
    IS WHAT YOUR LOOKING-GLASS CAN SHOW, ...   385 ROBARTES DANCE   15
    WHEN THE LONG LOOKING-GLASS IS FULL, ...   387 ROBARTES DANCE   50
    OR HERS BEFORE A LOOKING-GLASS, FOR SUCH, ...   403 FOR DAUGHTER   19
    AT MY OWN IMAGE IN THE LOOKING-GLASS . . . .   447 HERO GIRL FOOL   V 1
    STILL RAZOR-KEEN, STILL LIKE A LOOKING-GLASS . . . .   477 SELF AND SOUL   11
    GAVE WOMEN DREAMS AND DREAMS THEIR LOOKING-GLASS. . .   610 STATUES   16
LOOKS
    AND LOOKS UPON THE POOR. . . . .   96 MOLL MAGEE   52
    BUT GATHER WITH YOUR SHININ' LOOKS . . . .   96 MOLL MAGEE   55
    THAT THEY WOULD SIGH AND QUOTE WITH LEARNED LOOKS . .   205 ADAMS CURSE   25
    LOOKS AT THE CRADLE AND BAWLS, ...   319 DOLLS   2
    AND OF A RED-HAIRED YEATS WHOSE LOOKS, ALTHOUGH HE DIED 391 UNDER SATURN   9
    I KNOW, ALTHOUGH WHEN LOOKS MEET . . . .   511 JANE AND JACK   1
    CRAZY JANE GROWN OLD LOOKS AT THE DANCERS . . . . .   514 JANE GROWN OLD   T
    BUT THE GOLDEN RACE LOOKS DIM, ...   530 DELPHIC ORACLE   4
    MY LOVER LOOKS SO GAY." . . . .   570 THREE BUSHES   V 32
    THAT NOBODY LOOKS; HER FEET . . . .   617 LONG-LEG FLY   16
    NOT TO ALLOW HIS LOOKS TO TELL . . . .   624 APPARITIONS   13
    AENGUS LOOKS ON YOU WHEN I LOOK! HE AWAITS . . . . .   757 SHADOW WATER A   209
    AMONG THE WINDS, LOOKS UNDER YOUR PALE EYELIDS. . . .   757 SHADOW WATER A   211
    AENGUS LOOKS ON YOU WHEN I LOOK! HE WAITS . . . . .   757 SHADOW WATER A   V 209
LOOM
    OR WEAVER BENT AT HIS LOOM, ...   589 OLD WICKED MAN   51
    AND ON THIS LOOM I WEAVE THY DESTINY." . . . .   716 DWELT SYCAMORE   14
LOOMED
    THE ISLE LOOMED LARGELY IN THE LIGHT . . . .   25 OISIN 1   V 385
LOONY'D
    "A LOONY'D BOAST OF SUCH A LOVE," . . . .   539 MEETING   13
LOOPED
    I AM LOOPED IN THE LOOPS OF HER HAIR. . . . .   268 BROWN PENNY   8
LOOPHOLE
    AS AT THE LOOPHOLE THERE . . . .   415 TOWER   166
    AND AT THE LOOPHOLE THERE, ...   415 TOWER   V 166
LOOPS
    I AM LOOPED IN THE LOOPS OF HER HAIR. . . . .   268 BROWN PENNY   8
LOOSE
    SHAKE THE LOOSE REINS! YOU SLAVES OF GOD, ...   22 OISIN 1   331
    SHAKE THE LOOSE REINS! YE SLAVES OF GOD, ...   22 OISIN 1   V 331
    AND HIS LOOSE BULK BE THROWN IN THE LOUD TIDE." . .   35 OISIN 2   91
    CAST THE LOOSE BULK, LEST NIAM FEAR HIM DEAD! . . .   41 OISIN 2   V 183
    . . . HEAPED LOOSE WHERE THEY LAY. . . . .   48 OISIN 3   V 28
    LAY LOOSE IN A PLACE OF SHADOW! WE DREW THE REINS BY HIS 50 OISIN 3   44
        SIDE.
    OUR LONG SHIPS LOOSE THOUGHT-WOVEN SAILS AND WAIT, . .   115 ROSE OF BATTLE   31
    "OH GOD IF HE GOT LOOSE!" AND THEN . . . .   307 HOUR DAWN   V 118
    WHATEVER THEIR LOOSE FANTASY INVENT . . . .   398 LEADERS CROWD   4
    WHATEVER THEIR LOOSE PHANTASY INVENT . . . .   398 LEADERS CROWD   V 4
    WHEN THE HEADLONG LIGHT IS LOOSE, ...   414 TOWER   135
    ARE BUT LOOSE THREAD, ARE BUT LOOSE THREAD; . . . .   449 HERO GIRL FOOL   23
    ARE BUT LOOSE THREAD, ARE BUT LOOSE THREAD; . . . .   449 HERO GIRL FOOL   23
    NO LOOSE LIPPED DEMAGOGUE HAD WON THE DAY, ...   542 PARN FUNERAL 2   V 3

		PAGE	TITLE	LINE

LOOSE   (CONTINUED)
```
    NEITHER LOOSE IMAGINATION,  . . . . . . . . .       575 ACRE OF GRASS       9
    . . . NIGHT SPLITS AND THE DAWN BREAKS LOOSE;  . . . . .   623 HIGH TALK        12
    NOW FLINGING LOOSE THE SLANTING SAIL,  . . . . . . .    742 DANAAN QUICK      3
LOOSED
    LOOSED LONG AGO FROM HEAVEN'S GATE,  . . . . . . . .     24 OISIN 1         362
    MERE ANARCHY IS LOOSED UPON THE WORLD,  . . . . . .    402 SECOND COMING     4
    THE BLOOD-DIMMED TIDE IS LOOSED, AND EVERYWHERE  . . . .   402 SECOND COMING     5
    WHEN THE DARK HOUNDS WERE LOOSED.  COME TO THE ALE. . . .   766 SHADOW WATER A  379
LOOSE-LIPPED
    NO LOOSE-LIPPED DEMAGOGUE HAD WON THE DAY,  . . . . . .   542 PARN FUNERAL 2    3
LOOSELY
    . . . FLUNG LOOSELY ALONG THE DIM GROUND;  . . . . . .    50 OISIN 3          45
LOOSEN
    HALF CLOSE YOUR EYELIDS, LOOSEN YOUR HAIR,  . . . . . .   166 EVIL OF BELOV     1
    WE WILL BEND DOWN AND LOOSEN OUR HAIR OVER YOU,  . . . .   172 TRAV PASSION      6
    AND LOOSEN ON US DREAMS THAT WASTE OUR LIFE,  . . . . .   281 TWO KINGS       107
    MERELY TO LOOSEN OUT A TRESS  . . . . . . . . .        390 IMAGE PAST       26
LOOSENED
    HE SAT WITH TIGHTENED REIN AND LOOSENED MOUTH  . . . .    277 TWO KINGS        10
    OR IT MAY BE LOOSENED IN REPOSE,  . . . . . . . .       386 ROBARTES DANCE    35
    WITH LOOSENED HAIR OR FOREHEADS GRIEF-DISTRAUGHT,  . . .   537 HER VISION       18
    WITH LOOSENED HAIR OR FOREHEADS GRIEF DISTRAUGHT,  . . .   537 HER VISION    V  18
LOOSENING
    OF LOOSENING MASONRY, AND THERE  . . . . . . . .        424 STARES NEST       2
    MY WALL IS LOOSENING; HONEY-BEES,  . . . . . . . .      424 STARES NEST       4
    MY WALL IS LOOSENING, HONEY BEES,  . . . . . . . .      424 STARES NEST    V  4
    THE FEATHERED GLORY FROM HER LOOSENING THIGHS?  . . . .   441 LEDA AND SWAN     6
LOOSENS
    THE HUNTSMAN LOOSENS ON THE MORN  . . . . . . . . .      98 FOXHUNTER        27
LORD
    LORD OF THE CROZIERS, YOU EVEN HAD LIFTED YOUR HANDS AND    54 OISIN 3         110
        WEPT .
    LORD OF THE CROSIERS, THOU EVEN HADST LIFTED THY HANDS     54 OISIN 3      V  110
        AND WEPT;
    LORD, WHAT WOULD THEY SAY  . . . . . . . . . .         337 SCHOLARS         11
    LORD EDWARD AND WOLFE TONE,  . . . . . . . . .         395 SIXTEEN DEAD      16
    IN HIS NOSTRILS, THE GREAT LORD OF CHOU  . . . . . .      502 VACILLATION      59
    THE DEVOTEE PROFFERS A KNEE TO HIS LORD,  . . . . . .     547 TO SAME TUNE 3    2
    THE LORD HAVE MERCY UPON US.  . . . . . . . . .        572 LADYS 2ND SONG    7
    THE LORD HAVE MERCY UPON US.  . . . . . . . . .        573 LADYS 2ND SONG   14
    THE LORD HAVE MERCY UPON US.  . . . . . . . . .        573 LADYS 2ND SONG   21
    THE DEVOTEE PROFFERS A KNEE TO HIS LORD,  . . . . . .     614 MARCH SONGS 2     2
    AM I A GREAT LORD CHANCELLOR  . . . . . . . . .        627 STATES HOLIDAY   14
    LION AND WOMAN AND THE LORD KNOWS WHAT. . . . . . .      629 CIRCUS ANIMALS    8
    WAKING HE THANKS THE LORD THAT HE  . . . . . . . .      633 MAN AND ECHO     27
    "SEND WAR IN OUR TIME, O LORD!"  . . . . . . . .        638 BEN BULBEN       26
    SLEEPING LORD OF ARCHERY,  . . . . . . . . . .         658 ISLE STAT I 3    81
    SLEEPING LORD OF ARCHERY.  . . . . . . . . . .         658 ISLE STAT I 3    96
    WHY THESE NEW FEARS?  THE SERVANT OF THE LORD,  . . . .   692 MOSADA 1      V  46
    MY LORD, IF IT MUST BE, I PRAY DESCEND  . . . . . .      697 MOSADA 2         43
    MY LORD, YOU CALLED?  NOT I.  THIS MAID IS DEAD. . . .    704 MOSADA 3        125
    YOU'RE PALE, MY LORD.  HIS LIPS ARE QUIVERING;  . . .     704 MOSADA 3        127
LORD'S
    THE FLAGRANT SIGNAL OF HER LORD'S RETURN,  . . . . . .    645 ISLE STAT I 1    13
LORDS
    TO LORDS AND LADIES OF BYZANTIUM  . . . . . . . .       408 SAIL BYZANTIUM   31
    SING THE LORDS AND LADIES GAY  . . . . . . . . .        640 BEN BULBEN       78
LORE
    HAD FELT THE ISLAND BREEZE, MY LORE  . . . . . . .       668 ISLE STAT II 3   55
    HAD LEFT THE ISLAND BREEZE, MY LORE  . . . . . . .       668 ISLE STAT II 3 V 55
LORN.    SEE LOVE-LORN
LOSE
    LOSE NATURAL KINDNESS AND MAYBE  . . . . . . . .        404 FOR DAUGHTER     22
    AND WHAT IF MY DESCENDANTS LOSE THE FLOWER  . . . . .     423 MY DESCENDANTS    9
    TO SHOW HOW VIOLENT GREAT HEARTS CAN LOSE  . . . . .      463 HARUN RASHID     47
    WHAT IF SHE LOSE HER IGNORANCE AND SO  . . . . . .       468 HARUN RASHID    170
    WERE SHE TO LOSE HER LOVE, BECAUSE SHE HAD LOST  . . .    469 HARUN RASHID    175
    HER CONFIDENCE IN MINE, OR EVEN LOSE  . . . . . .        469 HARUN RASHID    176
    LEAVES WHAT MAN WOULD LOSE.  . . . . . . . . .         620 JOHN KINSELLA     4
    I LOSE!  THEY'RE LOADED DICE.  TIME ALWAYS PLAYS  . . .   721 WITCH VIVIEN     44
    AND I MUST LOSE MORE TIME BECAUSE THESE FOOLS  . . . .    754 SHADOW WATER A  158
LOSS
    BUT HAVE NO SHARE IN LOSS OR VICTORY.  . . . . . .       104 FERGUS DRUID  V 38E
    THE LOVER MOURNS FOR THE LOSS OF LOVE  . . . . . .       152 LOSS OF LOVE      T
    AEDH LAMENTS THE LOSS OF LOVE  . . . . . . . . .        152 LOSS OF LOVE   V  T
    YOUR OPEN HAND BUT SHOWS OUR LOSS,  . . . . . . .       288 TO WEALTHY MAN   29
    NO LIKELY END COULD BRING THEM LOSS  . . . . . . .       328 IRISH AIRMAN      7
    HAS PLUCKED A FLOWER AND SUNG HER LOSS;  . . . . . .     447 COLONUS PRAISE   22
    AH! WOE FOR THE LOSS OF YOUR FACE,  . . . . . . .       708 FAIRY PEDANT     32
    AND LOSS OF YOUR LAUGH AND ITS LIGHTNESS—  . . . . .     708 FAIRY PEDANT     33
    HE WHO MEASURES GAIN AND LOSS,  . . . . . . . .        744 ROSY CROSS        1
    HE WHO MEASURES GAIN AND LOSS,  . . . . . . . .        744 ROSY CROSS        9
LOST      SEE LATE-LOST HALF-LOST LONG-LOST
    HALF LOST IN VAPOUR, SHADOWS CALLED OUR NAMES,  . . .     29 OISIN 2       V  3
    AND THEN LOST NIAMH MURMURED, "LOVE, WE GO  . . . .      46 OISIN 2         245
    LOST NIAM MOURN AND SAY, "AH, LOVE, WE GO  . . . . .      46 OISIN 2       V 245B
    NOR LOST IN THE STAR-FIRES AND ODOURS . . . . . .        56 OISIN 3         135
    LATER A SOUND CAME, HALF LOST IN THE SOUND OF A SHORE FAR   57 OISIN 3         155
        AWAY,
```

475

	PAGE	TITLE		LINE

LOST   (CONTINUED)
BUT KNEEL AND WEAR OUT THE FLAGS AND PRAY FOR YOUR SOUL ... 63 OISIN 3 ... 215
   THAT IS LOST
   . . . FOR THY SOUL THAT IS LOST, ... 63 OISIN 3 V 215
KNEEL, USHEEN, WEAR OUT THE FLAGS AND PRAY FOR YOUR SOUL ... 63 OISIN 3 V 215
   THAT IS LOST
A THIN GREY MAN HALF LOST IN GATHERING NIGHT. . . . . . 102 FERGUS DRUID 7
AND I DREAMED MY LOST LOVE CAME STEALTHILY OUT OF THE WOOD 163 VALLEY LOVERS 3
AND LOST THE WORLD AND EMER FOR A KISS! . . . . . . 170 SECRET ROSE 15
YOUR BEAUTY PERISH AND BE LOST . . . . 173 PLEADS FRIEND 7
AND YOUR HIGH BEAUTY FALL AND BE LOST . . . . 173 PLEADS FRIEND V 7
TILL THE ATTORNEY FOR LOST SOULS CRY HER SWEET CRY, . . 173 SPEAKS HEARERS 6
OR BIRDS LOST IN THE ONE CLEAR SPACE . . . . . . 195 BAILE AILLINN 149
OR BIRDS LOST IN ONE CLEAR SPACE . . . . 195 BAILE AILLINN V 149
FOR HE GAVE ALL HIS HEART AND LOST. . . . . 202 NEVER GIVE ALL 14
WE'D BETTER GO, FOR WE HAVE LOST THIS CHANCE. . . . 226 SHADOW WATER B 80
FOR THEY'RE MY ONLY PILOTS. IF I LOST THEM . . . 226 SHADOW WATER B 85
BROKEN-HEARTED, HAVING LOST HIS QUEEN . . . . . . 242 SHADOW WATER B 407
BROKENHEARTED, HAVING LOST HIS QUEEN . . . . 242 SHADOW WATER B V 407
WE'LL FIND SO GOOD A THING AS THAT WE HAVE LOST? . . . 258 KING NO KING 13
TILL YOUR BAD MASTER BLENCHED AND ALL WAS LOST! . . . 270 PARDON FATHERS V 12
WHO HAD LOST SOME UNIMAGINABLE TREASURE . . . . . . 278 TWO KINGS 40
WHAT MAN YOU HAVE LOST, WHAT EVIL YOU HAVE FOUND." . . 280 TWO KINGS 86
BUT IF NOT LIVING, HALF THE WORLD IS LOST." . . . . 280 TWO KINGS V 86
THAT I MAY FIND THE SLEEP I HAVE LOST." . . . . . . 303 HOUR DAWN 39
I HAVE TO FIND THE SLEEP I HAVE LOST." . . . . . . 303 HOUR DAWN V 39
LOVE LOST AS SOON AS WON, ... 312 CHILD DANCING 8
I HAVE NOT LOST DESIRE . . . . 335 SONG 13
AND CERTAIN LOST COMPANIONS OF MY OWN, ... 342 SHEP GOATHERD 78
ALL KNOWLEDGE LOST IN TRANCE . . . . 343 SHEP GOATHERD 111
THE REPUTATION OF HIS LIFETIME LOST . . . . 351 PEOPLE 5
AND LOST THE OLD NONCHALANCE OF THE HAND! . . . . . 368 EGO DOMINUS 13
IN THINKING OF HIS LOST RENOWN. . . . . 379 SAINT HUNCH 3
IMAGINE THAT LOST LOVE, INSEPARABLE FROM MY THOUGHT . . 390 UNDER SATURN 2
IMAGINE THAT SOME LOST LOVE, UNASSAILABLE . . . . . 390 UNDER SATURN V 2
A GREY GULL LOST ITS FEAR AND FLEW . . . . 397 POLIT PRISONER 3
UPON A WOMAN WON OR WOMAN LOST? . . . . 413 TOWER 114
IF ON THE LOST, ADMIT YOU TURNED ASIDE . . . . . . 413 TOWER 115
IS LOST AMID THE LABYRINTH THAT HE HAS MADE . . . . 431 NINETEEN 19 70
AND I REMEMBER WILDNESS LOST . . . . 453 DEATH OF HARE 9
LIKE THIS PURE JET, NOW LOST AMID BLUE SKY, ... 464 HARUN RASHID 64
WERE SHE TO LOSE HER LOVE, BECAUSE SHE HAD LOST . . . 469 HARUN RASHID 175
NOR DAZZLED BY THE EMBROIDERY, NOR LOST . . . . . . 470 HARUN RASHID 191
A SYCAMORE AND LIME-TREE LOST IN NIGHT . . . . . . 488 COOLE PARK 29 3
A SYCAMORE AND LIME TREE LOST IN NIGHT . . . . . . 488 COOLE PARK 29 V 3
SHALL LEAP INTO THE LIGHT LOST . . . . 511 JANE AND JACK 11
WHERE FOR ITS MOMENT BOTH SEEM LOST, CONSUMED. . . . 555 RIBH AT TOMB 16
ALL MEN HAVE AIMED AT, FOUND AND LOST! . . . . . . 566 LAPIS LAZULI 18
IF I LOST MY CHASTITY? . . . . 570 THREE BUSHES 20
HEROICALLY LOST, HEROICALLY FOUND. . . . . 578 CRAZED GIRL 8
WHAT WAS LOST . . . . 591 WHAT WAS LOST T
I SING WHAT WAS LOST AND DREAD WHAT WAS WON, ... 591 WHAT WAS LOST 1
MY KING A LOST KING, AND LOST SOLDIERS MY MEN! . . . 591 WHAT WAS LOST 3
MY KING A LOST KING, AND LOST SOLDIERS MY MEN! . . . 591 WHAT WAS LOST 3
ITS GREAT BATTLE LOST. . . . . 617 LONG-LEG FLY 2
BUT HUSH, FOR I HAVE LOST THE THEME, ... 633 MAN AND ECHO 41
WHAT IS IT, FRIEND? HE LOST I! THE WOODS THE CHIEF . . 661 ISLE STAT II 1 60
THY PEACE. AH, NOW I'LL WAKE THESE SLEEPERS, LOST . . 677 ISLE STAT II 3 274
OR LONG ERE THIS HAD LOST THEIR RUDDY STAIN! . . . 687 TWO TITANS 8
SOFT AS THE WHISPERING OF A LOST FOOTSTEP . . . . . 699 MOSADA 3 V 5
WHEN MY LOST LOVER LEFT THESE ARMS, MY GOMEZ . . . 701 MOSADA 3 51
WHEN MY LOST LOVER LEFT THESE ARMS, MY VALLENCE, . . 701 MOSADA 3 V 51
AND LOST AND FAR IN YONDER HILLS I KNOW! . . . . . 713 FERENCZ RENYI 98
FOR OTHER STAKES WE PLAY. YOU LOST THE GLASS. . . . 722 WITCH VIVIEN 50
I AM DULL TO-DAY, OR YOU WERE NOW ALL LOST. . . . . 722 WITCH VIVIEN 59
"THEY ARE LOST, THEY ARE LOST, EACH ONE," CRIED HE. . . 730 PRIEST FAIRY 58
"THEY ARE LOST, THEY ARE LOST, EACH ONE," CRIED HE. . . 730 PRIEST FAIRY 58
I SHALL FIND OUT IF I HAVE LOST MY WAY . . . . . . 753 SHADOW WATER A 137
I SHALL FIND OUT IF I HAVE LOST THE WAY . . . . . 753 SHADOW WATER A V 137
AND ONE SPINNER IS LOST. . . . . 771 SPINNING SONG 10
EMPTIED, RUINED, WRACKED, AND LOST, ... 776 AGAINST WITCH 27
MUSIC OF A LOST KINGDOM . . . . 782 GREY ROUND 2
A MAN IS LOST OF A SUDDEN, ... 783 GREY ROUND 9
MUSIC OF A LOST KINGDOM? . . . . 783 GREY ROUND 12

LOT
MEASURE THE LOT! FORGIVE MYSELF THE LOT! . . . . . 479 SELF AND SOUL 67
MEASURE THE LOT! FORGIVE MYSELF THE LOT! . . . . . 479 SELF AND SOUL 67
BLACKENS ALL OUR LOT? . . . . 534 CONSOLATION 10
THE LOT OF LOVE IS CHOSEN. I LEARNT THAT MUCH . . . 534 CHOSEN 1
I CHOSE IT FOR MY LOT! IF QUESTIONED ON . . . . . 535 CHOSEN 11
FOR I CAN PUT THE WHOLE LOT DOWN, AND ALL I HAVE TO SAY 593 PILGRIM 24
AND LETS THE KIND WORM TAKE THE LOT! . . . . . . 779 ACCURSED WHO 4

LOTUS
I PASSED A LITTLE FURTHER ON AND HEARD A LOTUS TALK! . . 76 INDIAN ON GOD 9
I PACED A LITTLE FURTHER ON AND HEARD A LOTUS TALK!— . . 76 INDIAN ON GOD V 9
A LOTUS IN THEIR HANDS—YOUNG MOORISH GIRL . . . . . 694 MOSADA 1 103

LOUD   SEE BEE-LOUD
A—MURMUR LIKE YOUNG PARTRIDGE! WITH LOUD HORN . . . . 32 OISIN 2 52
WHEN THEY AWAKE UPSPRINGING! WITH LOUD HORN . . . . 32 OISIN 2 V 52
AND HIS LOOSE BULK BE THROWN IN THE LOUD TIDE." . . . 35 OISIN 2 91
OF THE LOUD CRASHING AND EARTH SHAKING FIGHT . . . . 38 OISIN 2 141

476

PAGE   TITLE   LINE

LOUD   (CONTINUED)
AND BY ME, IN SOFT RED RAIMENT, THE FENIANS MOVED IN LOUD   53 OISIN 3   93
    STREAMS,
HEARING HELL LOUD WITH A MURMUR, AS SHOUTING AND MOCKING   62 OISIN 3   208
    WE SWEEP.
AND MY LOUD BRAZEN BATTLE-CARS . . . .   83 MAD KING GOLL   18
AND WITH LOUD SINGING I RUSHED ON . . . .   83 MAD KING GOLL   V   31
PARTED HER LIPS WITH A LOUD SUDDEN CRY. . . . . . .   105 CUCHULAIN SEA   8
THAT HE MAY FIGHT THE WAVES OF THE LOUD SEA." . . . .   111 CUCHULAIN SEA   V   81
THAT HE MIGHT FIGHT THE WAVES OF THE LOUD SEA." . . . .   111 CUCHULAIN SEA   V   81
WHILE HUSHED FROM FEAR, OR LOUD WITH HOPE, A BAND . . .   114 ROSE OF BATTLE   5
AND THE LOUD SONG OF THE EVER-SINGING LEAVES . . . . .   120 SORROW OF LOVE   V   3
AND THE LOUD CHANTING OF THE UNQUIET LEAVES, ...   120 SORROW OF LOVE   V   11
AND THE LOUD CHAUNTING OF THE UNQUIET LEAVES, ...   120 SORROW OF LOVE   V   11
AND THE WHITE HUSH END ALL BUT THE LOUD BEAT . . . . .   137 TO SOME I TALK   15
FROM MARBLE CITIES LOUD WITH TABORS OF OLD . . . . .   162 ASKS FORGIVE   9
NOR GAVE LOUD SERVICE TO A CAUSE . . . .   273 GREY ROCK   57
WITH THE LOUD HOST BEFORE THE SEA, ...   276 GREY ROCK   128
THEY HAVE LOUD MUSIC, HOPE EVERY DAY RENEWED . . . . .   398 LEADERS CROWD   11
THAT CRAFTY DEMON AND THAT LOUD BEAST . . . .   399 DEMON BEAST   2
NOW THAT THE LOUD BEAST RAN . . . .   400 DEMON BEAST   16
COME WITH LOUD CRY AND PANTING BREAST . . . .   412 TOWER   86
UPON CROAGH PATRICK SANG IT LOUD: . . . .   528 DANCER CRUACH   V   5
WHILE HIS LOUD SONG REPROVES . . . .   536 PARTING   7
I'LL QUENCH HIS SINGING WITH LOUD SONG-- . . . . . .   647 ISLE STAT I 1   63
LOUD FOR THEE THE MORNING CRIETH, ...   648 ISLE STAT I 1   86
OH, CEASE YOUR SINGING! WILD AND SHRILL AND LOUD, . . .   648 ISLE STAT I 1   99
BUT LOUD THE GRASSHOPPER THAT SITS BENEATH. . . . . .   662 ISLE STAT II 2   8
A TITAN, WITH LOUD LAUGHTER, ...   680 LOVE AND DEATH   11
THAT HAVE GONE THITHER TO LOOK FOR THE LOUD STREAMS, . .   765 SHADOW WATER A   348
THOUGH WE WERE BIDDEN TO SING, CRY NOTHING LOUD. . . . .   778 SONG DEIRDRE 3   2
TO THE LOUD SANDS BEFORE DAY HAS BROKEN. . . . . . .   784 WOMANS BEAUTY   18
LOUD-CRASHING
OF THE LOUD-CRASHING AND EARTH-SHAKING FIGHT, ...   38 OISIN 2   141
LOUDER
SOUL CLAP ITS HANDS AND SING, AND LOUDER SING . . . . .   407 SAIL BYZANTIUM   11
BUT LOUDER SANG THAT GHOST, "WHAT THEN?" . . . . . .   577 WHAT THEN   20
LOUDLY
AND HE CALLED LOUDLY TO THE STARS TO BEND . . . . . .   68 SAD SHEPHERD   5
AND LOUDLY TWICE THE LIVING WINGS FLAPT WIDE, ...   659 ISLE STAT II 1   12
LOUGH
WE RODE IN SADNESS ABOVE LOUGH LAEN, ...   2 OISIN 1   V   7H
ROUND LOUGH DERG'S HOLY ISLAND I WENT UPON THE STONES, . .   593 PILGRIM   6
LOUGHLAN
AND THOUGH THEY HAVE TO CROSS THE LOUGHLAN WATERS . . .   282 TWO KINGS   113
AND THOUGH THEY HAVE TO CROSS THE LOUGHLAN SEAS . . . .   282 TWO KINGS   V   113
LOUNGING
LIKE AN ARMY OF OLD MEN LOUNGING FOR REST FROM THE FOAM   57 OISIN 3   V   144
    OF THE SEAS.
LOUR
I CAN SCOFF AND LOUR . . . .   510 JANE JUDGMENT   8
LOUT
I NEEDS MUST MARRY SOME POOR LOUT," . . . .   273 GREY ROCK   47
I NEED MUST MARRY SOME POOR LOUT," . . . .   273 GREY ROCK   V   47
WITH SKELPING HIS BIG BRAWLING LOUT, ...   301 RUN PARADISE   9
A DRUNKEN, VAINGLORIOUS LOUT. . . . .   393 EASTER 1916   32
A DRUNKEN, VAIN-GLORIOUS LOUT. . . . .   393 EASTER 1916   V   32
AND LEFT ME BUT A LOUT, ...   451 FIRST LOVE   14
DAN AND JERRY LOUT . . . .   520 HIS BARGAIN   5
A LOUT BEGETS A LOUT, ...   605 SONGS BURDEN 1   6
A LOUT BEGETS A LOUT, ...   605 SONGS BURDEN 1   6
LOVE   SEE TRUE-LOVE
AND LOVE, IN THE HOURS WHEN YOUTH HAS CEASED: . . . . .   2 OISIN 1   V   7A
FOR LOVE OF USHEEN MY FEET RAN . . . .   6 OISIN 1   V   57
FOR LOVE OF OISIN FOAM WET FEET . . . .   6 OISIN 1   V   57
FOR LOVE OF OISIN FOAM-WET FEET . . . .   6 OISIN 1   V   57
INTO A DESPERATE GULPH OF LOVE! . . . .   7 OISIN 1   73
"GOOD REASON HAVE I FOR MY LOVE." . . . .   7 OISIN 1   V   62
LOVE, TILL THE DANAAN POETS BROUGHT . . . .   7 OISIN 1   V   63
IN LOVE. I CRIED, "THEE WILL I WED, ...   7 OISIN 1   V   74
AND THE BLUSHES OF FIRST LOVE NEVER HAVE FLOWN: . . . .   8 OISIN 1   85
AND THE FLUSHES OF FIRST LOVE NEVER HAVE FLOWN: . . . .   8 OISIN 1   V   85
MUSIC AND LOVE AND SLEEP AWAIT. . . . .   9 OISIN 1   103
FOLDED IN LOVE THAT FEARS NO MORROW, ...   23 OISIN 1   341
FOR LOVE THEY FOLLOWED ONE AND ALL! . . . .   23 OISIN 1   V 345G
WHILE HIS HEART STILL DREAMS OF BATTLE AND LOVE . . . .   27 OISIN 1   406
YET LOVE AND KISS ON DIM SHORES FAR AWAY . . . . .   29 OISIN 2   13
THEY LOVE AND KISS IN ISLANDS FAR AWAY, ...   29 OISIN 2   V   13
BUT LOVE AND KISS ON DIM SHORES FAR AWAY . . . . .   29 OISIN 2   V   13
LIGHT IS MAN'S LOVE, AND LIGHTER IS MAN'S RAGE: . . . .   45 OISIN 2   243
AND THEN LOST NIAMH MURMURED, "LOVE, WE GO . . . . .   46 OISIN 2   245
LOST NIAM MOURN AND SAY, "AH, LOVE, WE GO . . . . .   46 OISIN 2   V 245B
. . . IN THE DIMNESS THEY LOVE GOING BY: . . . . . .   53 OISIN 3   98
COMING OUT OF THE SEA AS THE DAWN COMES, A CHAUNT OF LOVE   58 OISIN 3   158
    ON MY LIPS,
AND THEIR HOUND, AND THEIR HORSE, AND THEIR LOVE, . . .   59 OISIN 3   176
THROUGH THE DEMON LOVE OF ITS YOUTH . . . .   63 OISIN 3   216
WHEN WANDERING IN THE FOREST, IF HE LOVE . . . . . .   71 ANASHU VIJAYA   3
BE PLENTIFUL.--AND IF HE LOVE ANOTHER, ...   71 ANASHU VIJAYA   5
AS IN THE WOODS HE WANDERS, IF HE LOVE . . . . . .   71 ANASHU VIJAYA   V   3
BE PLENTY.--IF HE GIVES ANOTHER LOVE, ...   71 ANASHU VIJAYA   V   5

LOVE   (CONTINUED)

	PAGE	TITLE	LINE
AMRITA, WHILE--AH ME! YOU LOVE ANOTHER,	74	ANASHU VIJAYA	58
I LOVED ANOTHER! NOW I LOVE NO OTHER.	74	ANASHU VIJAYA	60
VIJAYA, SWEAR TO HER LOVE NEVER MORE.	74	ANASHU VIJAYA	65
OF RED FLAMINGOES! AND MY LOVE, VIJAYA!	75	ANASHU VIJAYA	89
OF RED FLAMINGO! AND MY LOVE, VIJAYA,	75	ANASHU VIJAYA V	89
THE INDIAN TO HIS LOVE	77	INDIAN TO LOVE	T
AND LOVE IS KINDLY AND DECEITLESS,	77	INDIAN TO LOVE V	5D
WHILE OUR LOVE GROWS AN INDIAN STAR,	78	INDIAN TO LOVE	13
WHILE GROWS OUR LOVE AN INDIAN STAR.	78	INDIAN TO LOVE V	13
AUTUMN IS OVER THE LONG LEAVES THAT LOVE US,	79	FALLING LEAVES	1
THE HOUR OF THE WANING OF LOVE HAS BESET US,	79	FALLING LEAVES	5
BECAUSE OUR LOVE IS WANING." AND THEN SHE!	79	EPHEMERA	3
"ALTHOUGH OUR LOVE IS WANING, LET US STAND	79	EPHEMERA	4
VEILED IN A DREAMY SORROW FOR THEIR LOVE	79	EPHEMERA V	2A
"THOUGH OUR SAD LOVE IS FADING, LET US YET	79	EPHEMERA V	4
HATE ON AND LOVE THROUGH UNREPINING HOURS,	80	EPHEMERA	22
ARE LOVE, AND A CONTINUAL FAREWELL."	81	EPHEMERA	24
DOWN BY THE SALLEY GARDENS MY LOVE AND I DID MEET!	90	SALLEY GARDENS	1
SHE BID ME TAKE LOVE EASY, AS THE LEAVES GROW ON THE TREE!	90	SALLEY GARDENS	3
IN A FIELD BY THE RIVER MY LOVE AND I DID STAND,	90	SALLEY GARDENS	5
SHE BID ME TAKE LOVE EASY, AS THE LEAVES GROW ON THE TREES!	90	SALLEY GARDENS V	3
I FIND UNDER THE BOUGHS OF LOVE AND HATE,	101	ROSE UPON ROOD	10
FOR HIM WHO HEARS LOVE SING AND NEVER CEASE,	114	ROSE OF BATTLE	10
BUT GATHER ALL FOR WHOM NO LOVE HATH MADE	114	ROSE OF BATTLE	12
SILENCE AND LOVE!	116	FAERY SONG	6
THE PITY OF LOVE	119	PITY OF LOVE	T
IS HID IN THE HEART OF LOVE!	119	PITY OF LOVE	2
THREATEN THE HEAD THAT I LOVE.	119	PITY OF LOVE	8
ALL THREATEN THE HEAD THAT I LOVE.	119	PITY OF LOVE V	8
THE SORROW OF LOVE	119	SORROW OF LOVE	T
AND LOVED YOUR BEAUTY WITH LOVE FALSE OR TRUE,	121	YOU ARE OLD	6
MURMUR, A LITTLE SADLY, HOW LOVE FLED	121	YOU ARE OLD	10
AND LOVED YOUR BEAUTY WILL LOVE FALSE OR TRUE!	121	YOU ARE OLD V	6
MURMUR, A LITTLE SAD, "FROM US FLED LOVE.	121	YOU ARE OLD V	10
SHE WAS MORE BEAUTIFUL THAN THY FIRST LOVE,	123	DREAM OF DEATH	11
WHERE PEOPLE LOVE BESIDE THE RAVELLED SEAS!	126	DREAM OF FAERY	9
WHERE PEOPLE LOVE BESIDE STAR-LADEN SEAS!	126	DREAM OF FAERY V	9
THAT TALKED OF LOVE OR POLITICS,	131	OLD PENSIONER	5
THE LOVE I LIVED, THE DREAM I KNEW,	139	TO IRELAND	34
AND WE, OUR SINGING AND OUR LOVE,	139	TO IRELAND	37
NO PLACE FOR LOVE AND DREAM AT ALL!	139	TO IRELAND	43
THOUGH HOPE FALL FROM YOU AND LOVE DECAY,	148	INTO TWILIGHT	7
AND LOVE IS LESS KIND THAN THE GREY TWILIGHT,	148	INTO TWILIGHT	15
THOUGH HOPE FALL FROM THEE OR LOVE DECAY	148	INTO TWILIGHT V	7
THE LOVER MOURNS FOR THE LOSS OF LOVE	152	LOSS OF LOVE	T
AEDH LAMENTS THE LOSS OF LOVE	152	LOSS OF LOVE V	T
WOULD END IN LOVE IN THE END!	152	LOSS OF LOVE	4
MIGHT FADE IN LOVE IN THE END!	152	LOSS OF LOVE V	4
TWO LOVE POEMS THE SHADOWY HORSES	154	BELOVED PEACE V	T
AND HER RED LIPS SANG THEM A LOVE SONG.	160	CAP AND BELLS V	27
AND THE QUIET OF LOVE IN HER FEET.	161	CAP AND BELLS	36
AND I DREAMED MY LOST LOVE CAME STEALTHILY OUT OF THE WOOD	163	VALLEY LOVERS	3
THE HOUR OF THY GREAT WIND OF LOVE AND HATE.	170	SECRET ROSE	28
ENCIRCLE HER I LOVE AND SING HER INTO PEACE,	174	ELEMENT POWERS	9
CRY OF HIS LOVE WITH THEIR PITIFUL CRIES.	177	PAST GREATNESS V	12
AND THE MERRY LOVE THE FIDDLE,	179	FIDDLER DOONEY	15
AND THE MERRY LOVE TO DANCE.	179	FIDDLER DOONEY	16
FOR I AM AENGUS, AND I AM CROSSED IN LOVE."	183	QUEEN MAEVE	84
CAER, HIS BLUE-EYED DAUGHTER THAT I LOVE.	184	QUEEN MAEVE	96
CAER, HIS BLUE EYED DAUGHTER THAT I LOVE.	184	QUEEN MAEVE V	96
THEIR LOVE WAS NEVER DROWNED IN CARE	189	BAILE AILLINN	8
NO COMMON LOVE IS TO OUR MIND,	190	BAILE AILLINN	34
TO MAKE THE SAVAGE HEART OF LOVE	193	BAILE AILLINN	109
OF THE EBB OF ALL THINGS TO MAKE LOVE	193	BAILE AILLINN V	109
IN THE HID PLACE, BEING CRAZED BY LOVE.	195	BAILE AILLINN	143
AND TREMBLE WITH THEIR LOVE AND KISS.	196	BAILE AILLINN	169
ALL THE LOVE STORIES THAT THEY KNEW.	197	BAILE AILLINN	197
FOR WHEN WE HAVE BLAMED THE WIND WE CAN BLAME LOVE!	201	OLD MEMORY	10
NEVER GIVE ALL THE HEART, FOR LOVE	202	NEVER GIVE ALL	1
IF DEAF AND DUMB AND BLIND WITH LOVE?	202	NEVER GIVE ALL	12
THERE HAVE BEEN LOVERS WHO THOUGHT LOVE SHOULD BE	205	ADAMS CURSE	23
WE SAT GROWN QUIET AT THE NAME OF LOVE!	205	ADAMS CURSE	28
TO LOVE YOU IN THE OLD HIGH WAY OF LOVE!	206	ADAMS CURSE	36
TO LOVE YOU IN THE OLD HIGH WAY OF LOVE!	206	ADAMS CURSE	36
TO LOVE YOU IN THE OLD HIGHWAY OF LOVE!	206	ADAMS CURSE V	36
TO LOVE YOU IN THE OLD HIGHWAY OF LOVE!	206	ADAMS CURSE V	36
O DO NOT LOVE TOO LONG	211	O DO NOT LOVE	T
DO NOT LOVE TOO LONG	211	O DO NOT LOVE V	T
SWEETHEART, DO NOT LOVE TOO LONG!	211	O DO NOT LOVE	1
O DO NOT LOVE TOO LONG,	212	O DO NOT LOVE	10
BECAUSE HER HANDS HAD BEEN MADE WILD BY LOVE.	219	HARP OF AENGUS	9
HAS HATED EVERY MAN THAT'S NOT IN LOVE,	224	SHADOW WATER B	51
AND ALL THE OTHERS! BUT IT MUST BE LOVE	228	SHADOW WATER B	139
FOR IT IS LOVE THAT I AM SEEKING FOR,	228	SHADOW WATER B	141
BUT HE THAT GETS THEIR LOVE AFTER THE FASHION	228	SHADOW WATER B	145
THE BED OF LOVE, THAT IN THE IMAGINATION	228	SHADOW WATER B	148
THAT THE HEART LONGS FOR. WHAT IS LOVE ITSELF,	230	SHADOW WATER B	183
EVEN THOUGH IT BE THE LIGHTEST OF LIGHT LOVE,	230	SHADOW WATER B	184
TO DEATH! FOR THEY THAT PROMISED TO ME LOVE	230	SHADOW WATER B	192
OR SOMEWHERE, I SHALL FIND THE LOVE THEY HAVE PROMISED.	231	SHADOW WATER B	208

478

LOVE (CONTINUED)

	PAGE	TITLE		LINE
I SHALL HAVE LOVE IN THEIR IMMORTAL FASHION:	237	SHADOW WATER B		326
AND YET YOU TALK OF LOVE. THE MOVEMENT OF TIME	237	SHADOW WATER B		338
BECAUSE I HAVE AWAKENED HER TO LOVE	243	SHADOW WATER B		439
THERE IS NOT ONE AMONG YOU THAT MADE LOVE	244	SHADOW WATER B		454
FOR LOVE IS WAR, AND THERE IS HATRED IN IT:	244	SHADOW WATER B		459
IS IT THAT THOUGH YOUR EYES ARE FULL OF LOVE	245	SHADOW WATER B		473
WANDER A MOMENT WHEN ONE IS IN LOVE?	246	SHADOW WATER B		515
ALONE AND WINGED. OUR LOVE SHALL BE LIKE THEIRS	250	SHADOW WATER B		581
AND LOVE COMES IN AT THE EYE:	261	DRINKING SONG		2
LOVE OR DECEIT."	263	MASK		7
TO FIND OUT IF I MIGHT LOVE.	268	BROWN PENNY		4
"GO AND LOVE, GO AND LOVE, YOUNG MAN,	268	BROWN PENNY		5
"GO AND LOVE, GO AND LOVE, YOUNG MAN,	268	BROWN PENNY		5
O LOVE IS THE CROOKED THING,	268	BROWN PENNY		9
FOR HE WOULD BE THINKING OF LOVE	268	BROWN PENNY		12
HER LOVE, AND WOULD NOT HAVE ME DIE,	274	GREY ROCK		87
WHY SHOULD THE FAITHFULLEST HEART MOST LOVE	275	GREY ROCK		112
WHY MUST THE LASTING LOVE WHAT PASSES,	275	GREY ROCK		114
"SPEAKING OF LOVE THROUGH OTHER LIPS AND LOOKING	283	TWO KINGS		155
YOUR EMPTY BED." "HOW SHOULD I LOVE," I ANSWERED,	285	TWO KINGS		186
OR HOW SHOULD LOVE BE WORTH ITS PAINS WERE IT NOT	285	TWO KINGS		190
BEING WEARIED OUT, I LOVE IN MAN THE CHILD?	285	TWO KINGS		192
WHAT CAN THEY KNOW OF LOVE THAT DO NOT KNOW	285	TWO KINGS		193
AND FOR THE LOVE THAT YOU HAVE SHOWN YOUR KING,	286	TWO KINGS	V	212A
TO MOCK AT EVERYTHING I LOVE	306	HOUR DAWN		83
LOVE LOST AS SOON AS WON,	312	CHILD DANCING		8
LOVE AND THE BIRD	313	MEMORY YOUTH	V	T
I HAD THE WISDOM LOVE BRINGS FORTH:	313	MEMORY YOUTH		2
I HAD THE WISDOM LOVE CAN BRING,	313	MEMORY YOUTH	V	2
THAT EVEN THE BEST OF LOVE MUST DIE,	314	MEMORY YOUTH		17
WERE IT NOT THAT LOVE UPON THE CRY	314	MEMORY YOUTH		19
WITH THE HOT BLOOD OF YOUTH, OF LOVE CROSSED LONG AGO:	316	COLD HEAVEN		6
THOSE THAT I GUARD I DO NOT LOVE:	328	IRISH AIRMAN		4
IN THE NARROW THEME OF LOVE	333	SOLOMON SHEBA		7
THERE'S NOT A THING BUT LOVE CAN MAKE	333	SOLOMON SHEBA		23
IN THE ONE NARROW THEME OF LOVE	333	SOLOMON SHEBA	V	7
RETURNED AND YET UNREQUITED LOVE.	358	PRESENCES		8
FOR THOSE THAT LOVE THE WORLD SERVE IT IN ACTION,	369	EGO DOMINUS		42
NO ONE DENIES TO KEATS LOVE OF THE WORLD:	370	EGO DOMINUS		52
FOR THOSE THAT LOVE ARE SAD.	383	VISION ROBART		36
BY THE LAGOON YOU LOVE SO MUCH,	386	ROBARTES DANCE		29
FOR THOUGH LOVE HAS A SPIDER'S EYE	388	SOLOMON WITCH		19
IMAGINE THAT LOST LOVE, INSEPARABLE FROM MY THOUGHT	390	UNDER SATURN		2
IMAGINE THAT SOME LOST LOVE, UNASSAILABLE	390	UNDER SATURN	V	2
AND WHAT IF EXCESS OF LOVE	394	EASTER 1916		72
NOTHING THAT WE LOVE OVER-MUCH	399	BREAK OF DAY		17
I MUST RECALL A MAN THAT NEITHER LOVE	412	TOWER		74
OLD LECHER WITH A LOVE ON EVERY WIND,	413	TOWER		105
AND MEMORIES OF LOVE,	415	TOWER		161
SEEING THAT LOVE AND FRIENDSHIP ARE ENOUGH,	423	MY DESCENDANTS		20
AND DECKED AND ALTERED IT FOR A GIRL'S LOVE,	423	MY DESCENDANTS		22
THAN IN OUR LOVE: O HONEY-BEES,	425	STARES NEST		19
MAN IS IN LOVE AND LOVES WHAT VANISHES,	429	NINETEEN 19		42
TO BE IN LOVE AND LOVE WHAT VANISHES.	429	NINETEEN 19	V	42
TO BE IN LOVE AND LOVE WHAT VANISHES.	429	NINETEEN 19	V	42
WITH HUMAN LOVE.	436	FOR MY SON		32
LOVE'S PLEASURE DRIVES HIS LOVE AWAY,	438	SONGS PLAY 2		11
FOR ALL MEN LOVE YOUR WORTH: AND I MUST RAGE	447	HERO GIRL FOOL	V	8
BUT WHAT CARE I THAT LONG FOR A MAN'S LOVE?	448	HERO GIRL FOOL		17
A FAITHFUL LOVE, A FAITHFUL LOVE.	449	HERO GIRL FOOL		29
A FAITHFUL LOVE, A FAITHFUL LOVE.	449	HERO GIRL FOOL		29
A STRANGE THING SURELY THAT MY HEART, WHEN LOVE HAD COME UNSOUGHT	449	OWEN AHERNE		1
IT FEARED TO GIVE ITS LOVE A HURT WITH ALL THE TEMPEST THERE:	450	OWEN AHERNE		7
HER CHILDISH GRATITUDE FOR LOVE AND MATCH YOUR FIFTY YEARS?	450	OWEN AHERNE		23
FIRST LOVE	451	FIRST LOVE		T
A MAN YOUNG AND OLD FIRST LOVE	451	FIRST LOVE	V	T
REMEMBERING THAT HER SHRIEK WAS LOVE	456	FRIENDS YOUTH		19
FOR PEG AND MEG AND PARIS' LOVE	458	HIS WILDNESS		3
YOU THINK THAT LOVE HAS SEASONS, AND YOU THINK	464	HARUN RASHID		75
ITSELF AND NOT SOME OTHER SOUL." "THAT LOVE	465	HARUN RASHID		94
EVERY PHILOSOPHER SHOULD PRAISE THAT LOVE.	465	HARUN RASHID		97
ITSELF AND NOT SOME OTHER SOUL. "SUCH LOVE	465	HARUN RASHID	V	94
PHILOSOPHERS SHOULD PRAISE THE LOVE THE MOST,	465	HARUN RASHID	V	97
YET WAS IT LOVE OF ME, OR WAS IT LOVE	466	HARUN RASHID		112
YET WAS IT LOVE OF ME, OR WAS IT LOVE	466	HARUN RASHID		112
DREAM THAT I LOVE HER ONLY FOR THE VOICE,	469	HARUN RASHID		171
WERE SHE TO LOSE HER LOVE, BECAUSE SHE HAD LOST	469	HARUN RASHID		175
ITS FIRST SIMPLICITY, LOVE, VOICE AND ALL,	469	HARUN RASHID		177
DREAM THAT I LOVE HER ONLY FOR THAT VOICE,	469	HARUN RASHID	V	171
ITS FIRST SIMPLICITY, LOVE AND ALL,	469	HARUN RASHID	V	177
FOR EVERY SEPARATE QUALITY OF LOVE:	469	HARUN RASHID	V	189A
THAT'S CALLED PLATONIC LOVE	471	ALL SOUL NIGHT		23
ANODYNE FOR HIS LOVE.	471	ALL SOUL NIGHT		26
EMBLEMATICAL OF LOVE AND WAR?	477	SELF AND SOUL		19
LOVE YOU FOR YOURSELF ALONE	492	ANNE GREGORY		5
MAY LOVE ME FOR MYSELF ALONE	492	ANNE GREGORY		11
COULD LOVE YOU FOR YOURSELF ALONE	492	ANNE GREGORY		17
THE THREEFOLD TERROR OF LOVE: A FALLEN FLARE	499	MOTHER OF GOD		1

479

	PAGE	TITLE	LINE

LOVE   (CONTINUED)

	PAGE	TITLE		LINE
THIS LOVE THAT MAKES MY HEART'S BLOOD STOP	499	MOTHER OF GOD		13
THE THREE-FOLD TERROR OF LOVE! A FALLEN FLARE	499	MOTHER OF GOD	V	1
OF CHILDREN'S GRATITUDE OR WOMAN'S LOVE.	500	VACILLATION		26
"LOVE IS ALL	510	JANE JUDGMENT		1
WHAT TRUE LOVE BE?	510	JANE JUDGMENT		17
THE SOONER LOVE IS GONE.	511	JANE AND JACK		4
FOR LOVE IS BUT A SKEIN UNWOUND	511	JANE AND JACK		5
WHEN ON LOVE INTENT!	513	JANE TALK BISH		14
BUT LOVE HAS PITCHED HIS MANSION IN	513	JANE TALK BISH		15
LOVE IS LIKE THE LION'S TOOTH.	514	JANE GROWN OLD		7
LOVE IS LIKE THE LION'S TOOTH.	514	JANE GROWN OLD		14
LOVE IS LIKE THE LION'S TOOTH.	515	JANE GROWN OLD		21
ALL TRUE LOVE MUST DIE,	517	HER ANXIETY		3
LOVE IS NEARER DEATH.	517	HER ANXIETY		11
UNDYING LOVE TO BUY	517	HIS CONFIDENCE		1
FOR UNDYING LOVE?	518	HIS CONFIDENCE		6
LOVE LEAPS UPON ITS COURSE.	518	HIS CONFIDENCE		12
AND ALL THE CHOIR OF LOVE.	531	DELPHIC ORACLE		10
I'D HAVE HIM LOVE THE THING THAT WAS	532	BEFORE WORLD		15
BECAUSE I HAD FANCIED LOVE A CASUAL	533	HER TRIUMPH		2
THE LOT OF LOVE IS CHOSEN. I LEARNT THAT MUCH	534	CHOSEN		1
TOO OLD FOR A MAN'S LOVE I STOOD IN RAGE	536	HER VISION		3
TOO OLD FOR A MAN'S LOVE I STOOD AND RAGED	536	HER VISION	V	1
"A LOONY'D BOAST OF SUCH A LOVE,"	539	MEETING		13
I WOULD THAT I DRANK WITH MY LOVE ON MY KNEE,	551	SONGS REWRIT 1		9
COULD I BUT DRINK, MY LOVE ON MY KNEE	551	SONGS REWRIT 1	V	9
O COULD I DRINK, MY LOVE ON MY KNEE,	551	SONGS REWRIT 1	V	9
THINKING TO MEET MY LOVE ONCE MORE	551	SONGS REWRIT 1	V	15
AND COULD BEGET OR BEAR THEMSELVES COULD THEY BUT LOVE AS HE.	556	RIBH PATRICK		12
RIBH CONSIDERS CHRISTIAN LOVE INSUFFICIENT	558	RIBH CHRISTIAN		T
WHY SHOULD I SEEK FOR LOVE OR STUDY IT?	558	RIBH CHRISTIAN		1
A LOVE THAT LACKS ITS PROPER FOOD!	569	THREE BUSHES		3
AND IF YOUR LOVE WERE GONE	569	THREE BUSHES		4
HOW COULD YOU SING THOSE SONGS OF LOVE?	569	THREE BUSHES		5
"I LOVE A MAN IN SECRET,	569	THREE BUSHES		15
I AM IN LOVE	572	LADYS 1ST SONG		7
HE SHALL LOVE MY SOUL AS THOUGH	572	LADYS 2ND SONG		8
HE SHALL LOVE YOUR BODY	572	LADYS 2ND SONG		10
LOVE CRAM LOVE'S TWO DIVISIONS	573	LADYS 2ND SONG		12
SOUL MUST LEARN A LOVE THAT IS	573	LADYS 2ND SONG		15
LIMBS A LOVE IN COMMON	573	LADYS 2ND SONG		17
BUT IN HONOUR SPLIT HIS LOVE	573	LADYS 3RD SONG		7
GOD'S LOVE HAS HIDDEN HIM	574	MAIDS 1ST SONG		7
"LOVE TO GIVE OR TO WITHHOLD	588	OLD WICKED MAN		21
A ROOF, GOOD CLOTHES, PASSION, LOVE PERHAPS,	609	IN TARAS HALLS		8
BUT NEVER ASKED FOR LOVE! SHOULD I ASK THAT,	609	IN TARAS HALLS		9
BUT BOYS AND GIRLS, PALE FROM THE IMAGINED LOVE	610	STATUES		4
AND THE GREAT WATER SIGHED FOR LOVE,	611	NEWS ORACLE		3
THERE SIGHED AMID HIS CHOIR OF LOVE	611	NEWS ORACLE		7
WHERE WADES THE CHOIR OF LOVE	612	NEWS ORACLE		22
LOVE HAS BLINDED HIM WITH TEARS!	612	NEWS ORACLE		28
WHERE WADE THE CHOIR OF LOVE	612	NEWS ORACLE	V	22
BECAUSE WE LOVE BARE HILLS AND STUNTED TREES	621	HOUND VOICE		1
THIS DREAM ITSELF HAD ALL MY THOUGHT AND LOVE.	630	CIRCUS ANIMALS		24
PLAYERS AND PAINTED STAGE TOOK ALL MY LOVE,	630	CIRCUS ANIMALS		31
WINE OR LOVE DRUG HIM TO SLEEP,	633	MAN AND ECHO		26
WINE OR LOVE DRUGS HIM TO SLEEP,	633	MAN AND ECHO	V	26
A QUENCHLESS GRIEVING OF LOVE MELODY.	645	ISLE STAT I 1		21
JOY AND LOVE ARE ONE EXISTENCE.	647	ISLE STAT I 1		71
LOVE AND SORROW, ONE EXISTENCE,	647	ISLE STAT I 1		73
LOVE FROM HEAVEN CAME OF YORE	648	ISLE STAT I 1		77
POOR RACE OF LEAFY ARCADY, YOUR LOVE	650	ISLE STAT I 1		145
TO PROVE HIS LOVE A KNIGHT WITH LANCE IN REST	651	ISLE STAT I 1		158
SUCH MAY I LOVE. THE SHUDDERING FOREST LIGHTS	651	ISLE STAT I 1		165
HER LOVE! TO HER WHO WEARS THAT BLOOM COMES TRUTH.	653	ISLE STAT I 2		46
TWO MEN WHO LOVE ONE MAID HAVE AMPLE CAUSE	659	ISLE STAT II 1		30
WE LOVE NASCHINA BOTH. WHOM LOVES SHE BEST?	660	ISLE STAT II 1		48
ALMINTOR WITH HER LOVE. WHO ART THOU?--SPEAK.	660	ISLE STAT II 1		50
FOR THIS THING FIGHT--WE LOVE ONE MAID? HER NAME?	661	ISLE STAT II 1		66
IF HER YE LOVE. AYE, COLIN, WE MUST FIGHT.	662	ISLE STAT II 1		76
NASCHINA'S GONE, DRAWN BY A THIRST OF LOVE,	664	ISLE STAT II 2		59
THE DIRGE OF HER YE LOVE. CEASE!--CEASE!	665	ISLE STAT II 2		74
LOVE STORM! AND STAINED WITH MIST THE NEW MOONS FLARE.	678	ISLE STAT II 3	V	294
LOVE STORM AND STAINED WITH MIST THE NEW MOON'S FLARE.	678	ISLE STAT II 3	V	294
THE PLAIN, A LITTLE FAIR-HAIRED MAID I LOVE.	679	ISLE STAT II 3		312
THERE DWELLS A LITTLE FAIR-HAIRED MAID I LOVE.	679	ISLE STAT II 3	V	312
LOVE AND DEATH.	680	LOVE AND DEATH		T
AND THEY'LL ANSWER DEATH AND LOVE.	680	LOVE AND DEATH		16
ARE THE SPIRITS LOVE AND DEATH.	680	LOVE AND DEATH		32
OF LOVE FROM OUT A DREAMLESS RACE FOR STRIFE,	684	SEEKER		58
UNTOUCHED OF HUMAN JOY OR HUMAN LOVE?	684	SEEKER		65
OUR LOVE SHALL BE OF YESTERDAY,	686	LIFE		14
AND LAUGH OUR LOVE AWAY.	686	LIFE		16
AND, NODDING TO AND FRO, SANG SONGS OF LOVE,	688	TWO TITANS		35
THE SHADOWS PASS! BUT NOW, I LOVE MY RING,	700	MOSADA 3		27
AND OUT-SPREAD ARMS. BE NOT SO PALE, DEAR LOVE.	701	MOSADA 3		70
FOR NIGHT COMES FAST. LOOK DOWN ON ME, MY LOVE,	703	MOSADA 3		103
LOVE, WILL YOU DIE WHEN WE HAVE MET? ONE LOOK	703	MOSADA 3		109
POOR LOVE AND SORROW, WITH THEIR ARMS THROWN ROUND	703	MOSADA 3		119

```
                                                    PAGE    TITLE         LINE
LOVE  (CONTINUED)
    SPEAK, FERENCZ, SPEAK.  WE LOVE EACH OTHER.  SEE,  .  .  .  .    713  FERENCZ RENYI      87
    TO LOVE EACH OTHER.  IN MY PRAYER-BOOK STILL  .  .  .  .  .      713  FERENCZ RENYI      94
    TO LOVE EACH OTHER.  IN MY PRAYER BOOK STILL  .  .  .  .  .      713  FERENCZ RENYI   V  94
    AND THEN HIS HEART FILLS FULL OF LOVE,  .  .  .  .  .  .  .      716  FAIRY DOCTOR       11
    AND THEN HIS HEART IS FULL OF LOVE,  .  .  .  .  .  .  .  .      716  FAIRY DOCTOR    V  11
    LOVE SONG  .  .  .  .  .  .  .  .  .  .  .  .  .  .  .  .  .     717  LOVE SONG           T
    MY LOVE, WE WILL GO, WE WILL GO, I AND YOU,  .  .  .  .  .      717  LOVE SONG           1
    MY LOVE, WE WILL HEAR, I AND YOU, WE WILL HEAR,  .  .  .  .     717  LOVE SONG           4
    SUCH WAR PLOTS, PEACE PLOTS, LOVE PLOTS--EVERY SIDE!  .  .      722  WITCH VIVIEN       66
    FULL MOODY IS MY LOVE AND SAD,  .  .  .  .  .  .  .  .  .  .     723  GIRLS SONG A        1
    MY LOVE HATH MANY AN EVIL MOOD,  .  .  .  .  .  .  .  .  .  .    723  GIRLS SONG A        5
    MY LOVE HATH MANY A RUTHLESS MOOD,  .  .  .  .  .  .  .  .       723  GIRLS SONG A    V   5
    SINGING A LOVE RHYME TO HIMSELF.  .  .  .  .  .  .  .  .  .      741  EARL PAUL          41
    I DOUBT YOUR WISDOM, BUT DO NOT DOUBT MY LOVE.  .  .  .  .      748  SHADOW WATER A     31
    THE GREATNESS OF MY LOVE.  DID I NOT RULE  .  .  .  .  .  .      748  SHADOW WATER A  V  32
    I THOUGHT SHE LOVED YOU, AND I THOUGHT HER LOVE  .  .  .  .     749  SHADOW WATER A     51
    AND YET, THERE IS A LOVE THAT THE GODS GIVE,  .  .  .  .  .      749  SHADOW WATER A     56
    THE FOOL FORETOLD ME I WOULD FIND THIS LOVE  .  .  .  .  .      750  SHADOW WATER A     62
    FOR HAPPIER LOVE BUT FINDS UNHAPPINESS.  .  .  .  .  .  .  .     750  SHADOW WATER A     67
    ARE BETTER THAN THE WOODS WHERE NO LOVE FADES  .  .  .  .       754  SHADOW WATER A    160
    WHOSE SHADOW IS THE SLEEP THAT COMES WITH LOVE,  .  .  .  .     754  SHADOW WATER A    162
    AND LURED ME HITHER, THAT YOU MIGHT BE MY LOVE.  .  .  .  .     757  SHADOW WATER A    208
    WHEN SHE DREAMT FIRST OF LOVE, SHALL FLICKER OUT  .  .  .  .    760  SHADOW WATER A    257
    AND TELL ME A LOVE STORY WHILE I DRINK.  .  .  .  .  .  .  .     760  SHADOW WATER A  V 250
    WHEN SHE DREAMED FIRST OF LOVE, SHALL FLICKER OUT  .  .  .      760  SHADOW WATER A  V 257
    FOR LOVE IS A-WEAVING WHEN A WOMAN'S HEART  .  .  .  .  .  .    761  SHADOW WATER A    262
    BECAUSE HER HANDS HAD BEEN MADE WILD BY LOVE!  .  .  .  .       762  SHADOW WATER A    304
    THAT MY TRUE LOVE WOULD COME IN A SHIP OF PEARL  .  .  .  .     763  SHADOW WATER A  V 315
    WHERE TRUE LOVE WANDERS AMONG THE HOLY WOODS.  .  .  .  .       764  SHADOW WATER A  V 337
    WHAT WERE TRUE LOVE AMONG THE RUSH OF HIS STREAMS?  .  .  .     764  SHADOW WATER A  V 338
    THE LOVE I KNOW IS HIDDEN IN THESE HANDS  .  .  .  .  .  .      765  SHADOW WATER A    350
    THE LOVE OF ALL UNDER THE LIGHT OF THE SUN  .  .  .  .  .  .    765  SHADOW WATER A    353
    AND BODILY TENDERNESS; BUT LOVE IS MADE  .  .  .  .  .  .  .     765  SHADOW WATER A    355
    THAT CAN CHANGE LOVE TO IMPERISHABLE FIRE?  .  .  .  .  .  .    765  SHADOW WATER A    360
    O! WHY IS LOVE SO CRAZY THAT IT LONGS  .  .  .  .  .  .  .      765  SHADOW WATER A    363
    THAT COMES WITH LOVE, COMES MURMURING OF AN HOUR  .  .  .  .    765  SHADOW WATER A    365
    ALL THAT KNOW LOVE AMONG THE WINDS OF THE WORLD  .  .  .  .     767  SHADOW WATER A    386
    IT MAY BE, AND HAVE GROWN WEARY OF LOVE.  .  .  .  .  .  .  .    767  SHADOW WATER A    390
    BUT I AM NEW TO LOVE.  GO AMONG THESE  .  .  .  .  .  .  .      767  SHADOW WATER A    391
    THAT HAVE KNOWN LOVE AMONG THE WINDS OF THE WORLD  .  .  .      767  SHADOW WATER A    392
    LOVE WAS NOT MADE FOR DARKNESS AND THE WINDS  .  .  .  .  .      767  SHADOW WATER A    394
    FOR LOVE IS KIND AND HAPPY.  O COME WITH ME!  .  .  .  .  .      767  SHADOW WATER A    396
    HOW MANY HOURS TO DAYBREAK, BECAUSE LOVE  .  .  .  .  .  .      767  SHADOW WATER A    405
    I THINK THAT THERE IS LOVE IN AIBRIC'S EYES.  .  .  .  .  .      768  SHADOW WATER A    407
    SHOULD LOOK UPON HIS EYES WITH LOVE, IN THE END  .  .  .  .     768  SHADOW WATER A    409
    MY LOVE SHAKES OUT HER HAIR UPON THE STREAMS  .  .  .  .  .      768  SHADOW WATER A    416
    WHY HAVE YOU CLOVEN ME WITH A MORTAL LOVE?  .  .  .  .  .  .    768  SHADOW WATER A    419
    SHOULD LOOK UPON HIS EYES WITH LOVE UNTO THE END  .  .  .  .    768  SHADOW WATER A  V 409
    "LOVE WOULD BE A THING OF NAUGHT  .  .  .  .  .  .  .  .  .      772  SONG DEIRDRE 1     10
    AT THE BURNING WHEEL OF LOVE  .  .  .  .  .  .  .  .  .  .  .    776  AGAINST WITCH      34
    LOVE IS AN IMMODERATE THING  .  .  .  .  .  .  .  .  .  .  .     777  SONG DEIRDRE 2      1
    WHAT'S THE MERIT IN LOVE PLAY,  .  .  .  .  .  .  .  .  .  .     777  SONG DEIRDRE 2  V   6
    WHEN LOVE LONGING IS BUT DROUGHT  .  .  .  .  .  .  .  .  .      777  SONG DEIRDRE 2  V  11
    INTO THE SECRET WILDERNESS OF THEIR LOVE.  .  .  .  .  .  .      778  SONG DEIRDRE 3      4
    A MAN BUT WILL GIVE YOU HIS LOVE  .  .  .  .  .  .  .  .  .      786  YOUR HEART         17
    AND LOVE WENCH WISDOM'S CRUEL FACE.  .  .  .  .  .  .  .  .      787  HUDDON DUDDON      10
    AND LOVE WENCH—WISDOM'S CRUEL FACE.  .  .  .  .  .  .  .  .      787  HUDDON DUDDON   V  10
    GAVE ALL THE LOVE THAT WOMEN KNOW!  .  .  .  .  .  .  .  .       789  SINGING HEAD       21
LOVED
    "I LOVED NO MAN, THOUGH KINGS BESOUGHT,  .  .  .  .  .  .  .      7  OISIN 1            62
    "I LOVED NO MAN, THOUGH CANNS BESOUGHT,  .  .  .  .  .  .  .      7  OISIN 1         V  62
    I NE'ER LOVED ANY TILL SONG BROUGHT ME  .  .  .  .  .  .  .      7  OISIN 1         V  69
    I LOVED AND SANG, AND IN LONG WASSAILS  .  .  .  .  .  .  .     23  OISIN 1         V 345C
    IT WERE SAD TO GAZE ON THE BLESSED AND NO MAN I LOVED OF       63  OISIN 3           221
        OLD THERE!
    IT WAS SAD TO GAZE ON THE BLESSED AND NO MAN I LOVED OF        63  OISIN 3         V 221
        OLD THERE!
    I LOVED ANOTHER! NOW I LOVE NO OTHER.  .  .  .  .  .  .  .      74  ANASHU VIJAYA      60
    AH, YOU WILL KNOW MY LOVED ONE BY HIS HUNTER'S ARROWS          75  ANASHU VIJAYA      80
        TRULY,
    ALL LOVED HIM, ONLY THE SHONEEN,  .  .  .  .  .  .  .  .  .     92  FATHER OHART       13
    NO WOMAN'S LOVED ME, NO MAN SOUGHT MY HELP.  .  .  .  .  .      103  FERGUS DRUID       26
    THAT I LOVED ONCE."  AGAIN THE FIGHTING SPED,  .  .  .  .  .     110  CUCHULAIN SEA      64
    HOW MANY LOVED YOUR MOMENTS OF GLAD GRACE,  .  .  .  .  .  .    121  YOU ARE OLD         5
    AND LOVED YOUR BEAUTY WITH LOVE FALSE OR TRUE,  .  .  .  .      121  YOU ARE OLD         6
    BUT ONE MAN LOVED THE PILGRIM SOUL IN YOU,  .  .  .  .  .  .    121  YOU ARE OLD         7
    AND LOVED THE SORROWS OF YOUR CHANGING FACE;  .  .  .  .  .      121  YOU ARE OLD         8
    AND LOVED YOUR BEAUTY WILL LOVE FALSE OR TRUE!  .  .  .  .      121  YOU ARE OLD     V   6
    AND MEN WHO LOVED THE CAUSE THAT NEVER DIES.  .  .  .  .  .      130  BOOK STORIES    V  24
    AND YET THE BEAUTIES THAT I LOVED  .  .  .  .  .  .  .  .  .     131  OLD PENSIONER      15
    A QUEEN WAS LOVED BY A JESTER.  .  .  .  .  .  .  .  .  .  .     159  CAP AND BELLS   V   1
    WOULD NONE HAD EVER LOVED BUT YOU AND I!  .  .  .  .  .  .      210  RAGGED WOOD         4
    O THAT NONE EVER LOVED BUT YOU AND I!  .  .  .  .  .  .  .      210  RAGGED WOOD     V   4
    O THAT NONE EVER LOVED BUT YOU AND I!  .  .  .  .  .  .  .      211  RAGGED WOOD         8
    NO ONE HAS EVER LOVED BUT YOU AND I.  .  .  .  .  .  .  .  .     211  RAGGED WOOD        12
    I LOVED LONG AND LONG,  .  .  .  .  .  .  .  .  .  .  .  .  .    211  O DO NOT LOVE       2
    FOR THAT BRIEF SIGHING.  IF YOU HAD LOVED SOME WOMAN--  .  .    228  SHADOW WATER B    135
    AND AS SOON FINISHED.  ALL THAT EVER LOVED  .  .  .  .  .  .    229  SHADOW WATER B    151
    HAVE LOVED THAT WAY--THERE IS NO OTHER WAY.  .  .  .  .  .      229  SHADOW WATER B    152
    FOR GOLDEN-ARMED IOLLAN THAT I LOVED.  .  .  .  .  .  .  .      242  SHADOW WATER B    421

                                    481
```

		PAGE	TITLE	LINE
LOVED	(CONTINUED)			
BUT WHAT IS IT THAT MADE ME SAY I LOVED HIM?		242	SHADOW WATER B	422
HAVE I NOT LOVED YOU FOR A THOUSAND YEARS?		244	SHADOW WATER B	463
I LOVED HIM; I WOULD COVER UP MY EARS,		246	SHADOW WATER B	494
DRAGON THAT LOVED THE WORLD AND HELD US TO IT,		251	SHADOW WATER B	598
HAVING LOVED GOD ONCE, BUT MAYBE		299	THREE HERMITS	26
THAT LOVED HIS LEARNING BETTER THAN MANKIND,		324	ROBERT GREGORY	18
WERE LOVED BY HIM; THE OLD STORM-BROKEN TREES		326	ROBERT GREGORY	50
ALL THOSE THAT MANHOOD TRIED, OR CHILDHOOD LOVED		327	ROBERT GREGORY	91
THE DEAD MAN THAT I LOVED,		347	FISHERMAN	14
THE MOST EXALTED LADY LOVED BY A MAN.		369	EGO DOMINUS	37
THAT THOSE THAT WE HAVE LOVED GOT THEIR LONG FINGERS		375	PHASES OF MOON	66
BEING FIXED ON ALL THINGS LOVED, ALL THINGS UNLOVED,		383	VISION ROBART	34
LOVED THE LADY; AND IT'S PLAIN		385	ROBARTES DANCE	5
LOVED AND THOUGHT HIMSELF BELOVED,		404	FOR DAUGHTER	39
MY MIND, BECAUSE THE MINDS THAT I HAVE LOVED,		405	FOR DAUGHTER	49
THAT LOVED INFERIOR ART,		422	MY TABLE	27
HAVE LOVED INFERIOR ART,		422	MY TABLE	V 27
I HAVE LOVED YOU BETTER THAN MY SOUL FOR ALL MY WORDS,		442	BLACK CENTAUR	14
I HAVE RAGED AT MY OWN STRENGTH BECAUSE YOU HAVE LOVED IT.		448	HERO GIRL FOOL	9
THAT ONLY GOD HAS LOVED US FOR OURSELVES,		448	HERO GIRL FOOL	16
HOW SUCH A PAIR LOVED MANY YEARS		458	SECRETS OF OLD	15
HORTON'S THE FIRST I CALL. HE LOVED STRANGE THOUGHT		471	ALL SOUL NIGHT	21
WE LOVED EACH OTHER AND WERE IGNORANT.		523	LONG SILENCE	8
AND LOVED IN MISERY,		538	LAST CONFESS	4
THAT I LOVED BODILY,		538	LAST CONFESS	6
AND THOUGH IT LOVED IN MISERY		538	LAST CONFESS	21
EACH HATING WHAT THE OTHER LOVED,		539	MEETING	3
LOVED HIM WITH HER SOUL.		571	THREE BUSHES	55
THAT PARNELL LOVED A LASS.		586	PARNELLITES	16
AND PARNELL LOVED HIS COUNTRY,		587	PARNELLITES	31
AND PARNELL LOVED HIS LASS.		587	PARNELLITES	32
AND PARNELL LOVED A LASS.		587	PARNELLITES	V 32
POETRY, MUSIC, I HAVE LOVED, AND YET		599	SPIRIT MEDIUM	1
"GOD I HAVE LOVED, BUT SHOULD I ASK RETURN		609	IN TARAS HALLS	14
AND ONLY SHEEP HE LOVED OF ALL THE TROOP,		661	ISLE STAT II	61
OF HER HE LOVED FIXED ON HIM FULL OF LIGHT,		710	FERENCZ RENYI	27
A FAIRY WHOM WE LOVED FULL WELL;		729	PRIEST FAIRY	44
AND, THOUGH YOU LOVED HER, GAVE HER UP TO ME?		749	SHADOW WATER A	50
I THOUGHT SHE LOVED YOU, AND I THOUGHT HER LOVE		749	SHADOW WATER A	51
NO MAN NOR WOMAN HAS LOVED OTHERWISE		750	SHADOW WATER A	64
NO MAN OR WOMAN HAS LOVED OTHERWISE		750	SHADOW WATER A V	64
TO WANDER IN; YOU HAVE LOVED MANY WOMEN,		767	SHADOW WATER A	389
HE THAT HAS LOVED THE BEST		786	YOUR HEART	19
DANCED, LAUGHED, LOVED, FOUGHT THROUGH		787	HUDDON DUDDON	4
LOVE-DEW				
BUT THE LOVE-DEW DIMS OUR EYES TILL THE DAY		28	OISIN 1	424
LOVE-DREAMS				
AND THRO' THE ODOROUS AIR LOVE-DREAMS ARE WINGING--		645	ISLE STAT I 1	5
LOVELESS				
THAT HE'S A LOVELESS MAN; GAY BELLS BRING LAUGHTER		130	BOOK STORIES	18
DESCENDS INTO THE LOVELESS DUST.		540	FROM ANTIGONE	16
BEHOLD THE LOVING LOVELESS FLOWER OF LONE WAYS,		674	ISLE STAT II 3	201
LOVELIER				
AND LOVELIER THAN THE MOON UPON THE SEA;		106	CUCHULAIN SEA V	16A
SHE IS NOT WISER NOR LOVELIER,		197	BAILE AILLINN	201
LOVELIEST				
HAVE I NOT SEEN THE LOVELIEST WOMAN BORN		405	FOR DAUGHTER	59
HAS FOUND THE LOVELIEST SPECTACLE THERE IS.		447	COLONUS PRAISE	24
LOVELINESS				
MY HEART UPON THE LOVELINESS		155	FORGOT BEAUTY	2
BUILDING A SORROWFUL LOVELINESS		158	BELOVED RHYMES	5
A WOMAN OF SO SHINING LOVELINESS		170	SECRET ROSE	25
WROUGHT OF HIGH LAUGHTER, LOVELINESS AND EASE?		264	HOUSE SHAKEN	12
IN THE FIRST LOVELINESS OF WOMANHOOD,		356	BROKEN DREAMS	24
OR ARROGANT LOVELINESS.		390	IMAGE PAST	25
OF THEIR OWN SWEETNESS, BODIES OF THEIR LOVELINESS.		426	PHANTOM HATRED	24
TRADITIONAL SANCTITY AND LOVELINESS;		491	COOLE BALLYLEE	42
THAT LOVELINESS?		784	WOMANS BEAUTY	14
THIS LOVELINESS?		785	WOMANS BEAUTY	28
LOVE-LONGING				
WHEN LOVE-LONGING IS BUT DROUTH		777	SONG DEIRDRE 2	11
LOVELORN				
A BOY'S LOVELORN INDIFFERENT HANDS MIGHT FIND		461	HARUN RASHID V	14
LOVE-LORN				
THAT SAW YOUNG NIAMH HOVER WITH LOVE-LORN FACE		162	ASKS FORGIVE	13
TO WHOM THE LOVE-LORN LADY KYTELER BROUGHT		433	NINETEEN 19	129
LOVE-LORN, INDIFFERENT HANDS MIGHT COME UPON IT		461	HARUN RASHID	14
LOVELY				
O LOVELY TO SEE IN ALL MEN'S SIGHT		69	CLOAK BOAT	3
WHO BEING LOVELY WAS SO WISE--		193	BAILE AILLINN	98
FOR EVERYTHING THAT'S LOVELY IS		202	NEVER GIVE ALL	6
OR A WITTY LOVELY LADY."		299	THREE HERMITS	28
IN ALL LOVELY INTRICACIES OF A HOUSE		327	ROBERT GREGORY	74
ONE HAD A LOVELY FACE,		350	MEMORY	1
SHE LIES, HER LOVELY PITEOUS HEAD AMID DULL RED HAIR		362	HER COURTESY	2
OF LOVELY, SATISFIED, INDIFFERENT EYES.		375	PHASES OF MOON	83
AMID MOST LOVELY PLACES; SMITTEN AS THOUGH		389	IMAGE PAST	13
MANY INGENIOUS LOVELY THINGS ARE GONE		428	NINETEEN 19	1
MANY INGENUOUS LOVELY THINGS ARE GONE		428	NINETEEN 19 V	1
AND IS SO LOVELY THAT IT SETS TO RIGHT		490	COOLE BALLYLEE	21

482

	PAGE	TITLE	LINE
LOVELY (CONTINUED)			
THAT LOVELY LADY SAID,	569	THREE BUSHES	9
AND A PROUD MAN'S A LOVELY MAN,	587	PARNELLITES	23
OH, LOVELY TO SEE IN ALL MEN'S SIGHT	666	ISLE STAT II 3	3
WITH MANY A LOVELY FACE	740	EARL PAUL	30
LOVELY LADIES DANCING IN IT.	788	HAWTHORN TREE	4
LOVELY LADY OR GALLANT MAN	788	HAWTHORN TREE	7
YET ALL THE LOVELY THINGS THAT WERE	788	HAWTHORN TREE	11
LOVELY LADY AND GALLANT MAN	788	HAWTHORN TREE V	7
LOVE-MAKING			
. . . LOVE-MAKING OR PIERCING THE TEMPEST WITH SAILS.	53	OISIN 3	88
LOVE-PLAY			
WHAT'S THE MERIT IN LOVE-PLAY,	777	SONG DEIRDRE 2	6
LOVER SEE HUNTER-LOVER GHOST-LOVER			
AND LOVER THERE BY LOVER BE AT PEACE.	128	DREAM OF FAERY	35
AND LOVER THERE BY LOVER BE AT PEACE.	128	DREAM OF FAERY	35
THE LOVER TELLS OF THE ROSE IN HIS HEART	142	ROSE IN HEART	T
THE LOVER MOURNS FOR THE LOSS OF LOVE	152	LOSS OF LOVE	T
THE LOVER ASKS FORGIVENESS BECAUSE OF HIS MANY MOODS	162	ASKS FORGIVE	T
THE LOVER MOURNS BECAUSE OF HIS WANDERINGS	171	MAID QUIET V	T
THE LOVER PLEADS WITH HIS FRIEND FOR OLD FRIENDS	172	PLEADS FRIEND	T
THE LOVER SPEAKS TO THE HEARERS OF HIS SONGS IN COMING DAYS	173	SPEAKS HEARERS	T
A LOVER SPEAKS TO THE HEARERS OF HIS SONGS IN COMING DAYS	173	SPEAKS HEARERS V	T
WHATEVER WOMAN'S LOVER HAD HIT HER FANCY,	181	QUEEN MAEVE	24
WHO HAD BEEN THE LOVER OF HER MIDDLE LIFE.	183	QUEEN MAEVE	72
HAS LOVER LIVED, BUT LONGED TO WIVE	197	BAILE AILLINN	206
AND THE WOOD-WOMAN, WHOSE LOVER WAS CHANGED TO A BLUE-EYED HAWK!	209	UNDER THE MOON	13
AND THE WOOD WOMAN, WHOSE LOVER WAS CHANGED TO A BLUE-EYED HAWK!	209	UNDER THE MOON V	13
AND KILLED A LOVER OR HUSBAND AT MY FEET--	246	SHADOW WATER B	491
UNWEARIED STILL, LOVER BY LOVER,	323	SWANS AT COOLE	19
UNWEARIED STILL, LOVER BY LOVER,	323	SWANS AT COOLE	19
HER LOVER THOUGHT, UPON THE GLASS .	385	ROBARTES DANCE	11
FOR EVERY NERVE, AND TESTS A LOVER	388	SOLOMON WITCH	22
A LOVER WITH A SPIDER'S EYE	388	SOLOMON WITCH V	19
FOR EVERY NERVE! LOVER TESTS LOVER	388	SOLOMON WITCH V	22
FOR EVERY NERVE! LOVER TESTS LOVER	388	SOLOMON WITCH V	22
THE LOVER SPEAKS .	449	OWEN AHERNE V	T
REJOICE AS LOVER SHOULD .	453	DEATH OF HARE	4
AND WHAT HAD DROWNED A LOVER ONCE .	457	SECRETS OF OLD	5
THAT CHANGED A LOVER FOR A BULL.	509	JANE REPROVED	6
THAT LOVER OF A NIGHT .	512	JANE ON GOD	1
I HAD WILD JACK FOR A LOVER!	512	JANE ON GOD	19
WHATEVER COULD RECALL THE LIP OF LOVER.	537	HER VISION	8
FOR LOVER IN THE PAST!	539	MEETING	10
SAID LADY ONCE TO LOVER,	569	THREE BUSHES	1
MY LOVER LOOKED SO GAY"!	570	THREE BUSHES	32
MY LOVER LOOKS SO GAY."	570	THREE BUSHES V	32
WHEN YOU AND MY TRUE LOVER MEET	573	LADYS 3RD SONG	1
WOULD KEEP HIS LOVER WAITING,	598	MODEL LAUREATE	23
KEEP HIS LOVER WAITING?	598	MODEL LAUREATE	24
LOVER, THE VOICE THAT SUMMONED THEE WAS MINE.	685	SEEKER	77
WHAT, LOVER, DIE BEFORE OUR LIPS HAVE MET?	685	SEEKER	80
WHEN MY LOST LOVER LEFT THESE ARMS. MY GOMEZ	701	MOSADA 3	51
WHEN MY LOST LOVER LEFT THESE ARMS. MY VALLENCE,	701	MOSADA 3 V	51
LOVER'S			
THAT TIME CAN NEVER MAR A LOVER'S VOWS	126	DREAM OF FAERY	10
BECAUSE A LOVER'S HEART'S WORN OUT,	191	BAILE AILLINN	65
THAN LOVER'S MUSIC--LET THAT BE,	276	GREY ROCK	130
OF BODY AND SOUL. THE LOVER'S HEART KNOWS THAT.	375	PHASES OF MOON	71
BUT BEAR IN MIND YOUR LOVER'S WAGE	385	ROBARTES DANCE	14
IF EVER LOVER'S LONELINESS	518	LOVES LONENESS	3
THE LOVER'S SONG	574	LOVERS SONG	T
IN TERROR FLINGS HER AT HER LOVER'S FEET.	713	FERENCZ RENYI V	85
FOR HURTS AND AILS AND LOVER'S MOAN--	717	FAIRY DOCTOR	18
A LOVER'S QUARREL AMONG THE FAIRIES.	726	LOVERS QUARREL	T
LOVERS			
AND HOW THOSE LOVERS NEVER TURN THEIR EYES	29	OISIN 2	11
WHY SHOULD THOSE LOVERS THAT NO LOVERS MISS	128	DREAM OF FAERY	46
WHY SHOULD THOSE LOVERS THAT NO LOVERS MISS	128	DREAM OF FAERY	46
HE TELLS OF A VALLEY FULL OF LOVERS	163	VALLEY LOVERS	T
THE VALLEY OF LOVERS	163	VALLEY LOVERS V	T
AEDH TELLS OF A VALLEY FULL OF LOVERS	163	VALLEY LOVERS V	T
FOR HAPPY LOVERS PASSED TWO BY TWO WHERE I STOOD!	163	VALLEY LOVERS	2
HANRAHAN SPEAKS TO THE LOVERS OF HIS SONGS IN COMING DAYS	173	SPEAKS HEARERS V	T
UNTIL TWO LOVERS CAME OUT OF THE AIR	187	QUEEN MAEVE	143
THEN MAEVE! "O AENGUS, MASTER OF ALL LOVERS,	187	QUEEN MAEVE	149
THERE HAVE BEEN LOVERS WHO THOUGHT LOVE SHOULD BE	205	ADAMS CURSE	23
I WILL DRIVE ALL THOSE LOVERS OUT AND CRY--	211	RAGGED WOOD	10
I'LL HOLLO ALL THOSE LOVERS OUT AND CRY--	211	RAGGED WOOD V	10
BUT FAITHFUL LOVERS.	220	HARP OF AENGUS	14
'TWAS AENGUS AND EDAIN, THE WANDERING LOVERS,	224	SHADOW WATER B	42
TO WHOM ALL LOVERS PRAY, BUT WHAT OF THAT?	224	SHADOW WATER B	43
YET NEVER HAVE TWO LOVERS KISSED BUT THEY	229	SHADOW WATER B	153
AND THAT IS WHY THEIR LOVERS ARE AFRAID	245	SHADOW WATER B	481
CAN LOVERS HAVE THAT KNOW THEIR HAPPINESS	284	TWO KINGS	178
ONE'S HAD HER FILL OF LOVERS, ANOTHER'S HAD BUT ONE,	354	HIS PHOENIX	19
OUT OF NO TRAGIC WAR, LOVERS OF LIFE,	369	EGO DOMINUS	39
GREEKS WERE BUT LOVERS! ALL THAT COUNTRY ROUND	430	NINETEEN 19 V	43
THAT EVEN LOVERS DROWN.	453	MERMAID	6

483

```
                                                        PAGE     TITLE          LINE
LOVERS    (CONTINUED)
    OF ALL ARABIA'S LOVERS I ALONE--  . . . . . . . .    470 HARUN RASHID        190
    "OLD LOVERS YET MAY HAVE . . . . . . . . . . . . .    496 MOHINI CHATTER       17
    OLD LOVERS YET SHALL HAVE  . . . . . . . . . . . .    496 MOHINI CHATTER V     17
    SUCH BODY LOVERS HAVE,  . . . . . . . . . . . . . .   517 HER ANXIETY           7
    ALL OTHER LOVERS BEING ESTRANGED OR DEAD, . . . . .   523 LONG SILENCE          2
    BIDS ALL TRUE LOVERS REST,  . . . . . . . . . . . .   536 PARTING               6
    THOSE LOVERS, PURIFIED BY TRAGEDY,  . . . . . . . .   555 RIBH AT TOMB         21
    LOVERS OF HORSES AND OF WOMEN, SHALL, . . . . . . .   564 GYRES                19
    THE LOVERS AND THE DANCERS ARE BEATEN INTO THE CLAY,  580 CURSE CROMWELL        3
    AND COME WITH LEARNED LOVERS OR WITH WHAT MEN YOU MAY, 593 PILGRIM             23
    AND COME WITH LEARNED LOVERS OR WITH WHAT MAN YOU MAY, 593 PILGRIM           V 23
    SHOULD KEEP THEIR LOVERS WAITING, . . . . . . . . .   597 MODEL LAUREATE        7
    KEEP THEIR LOVERS WAITING?  . . . . . . . . . . . .   597 MODEL LAUREATE        8
    AND KEEP THEIR LOVERS WAITING,  . . . . . . . . . .   597 MODEL LAUREATE       15
    KEEP THEIR LOVERS WAITING.  . . . . . . . . . . . .   597 MODEL LAUREATE       16
    AND DEAD AS ARE THE LOVERS OF OLD RIME  . . . . . .   674 ISLE STAT II 3      204
    AND DEAD AS ARE THE LOVERS OF OLD RHYME . . . . . .   674 ISLE STAT II 3 V    204
    I'LL SING THE SONGS THE DUSKY LOVERS SING,  . . . .   694 MOSADA 1            101
    AND YON FEW STARS GROWN DIM, LIKE EYES OF LOVERS  .   700 MOSADA 3             33
    HE WATCHES OVER NONE BUT FAITHFUL LOVERS. . . . . .   762 SHADOW WATER A      295
    BUT FAITHFUL LOVERS.  SOMETHING GLITTERS THERE--  .   763 SHADOW WATER A      309
    BUT FAITHFUL LOVERS.  WHITHER HAVE YOU COME,  . . .   763 SHADOW WATER A V    309
    TO SNATCH ALIVE OUT OF THE STREAMS ALL LOVERS . . .   765 SHADOW WATER A      347
    LOVERS, IF THEY MAY NOT LAUGH,  . . . . . . . . . .   772 SONG DEIRDRE 1       15
    OF ALL THAT LOVERS SAID,  . . . . . . . . . . . . .   789 SINGING HEAD         10
LOVERS'
    BEFORE THEY DROWNED THEIR LOVERS' EYES  . . . . . .   156 FORGOT BEAUTY V     10A
    AND UNDER LOVERS' EYELIDS.  BEND YOUR HEAD  . . . .   762 SHADOW WATER A      286
LOVE'S
    OR LOVE'S FIRST TENDERNESS DIE IN OUR GAZE. . . . .    27 OISIN 1            411
    OR LOVE'S FIRST TENDERNESS DIE IN OUR GAZE. . . . .    27 OISIN 1         V 419D
    OR LOVE'S FIRST TENDERNESS DIE IN OUR GAZE." . . . .   28 OISIN 1         V  427
    UPON LOVE'S BITTER MYSTERY: . . . . . . . . . . . .   125 GOES FERGUS          8
    DROWNING LOVE'S LONELY HOUR IN DEEP TWILIGHT OF REST,  154 BELOVED PEACE       11
    WHERE LOVE'S TO GIVE AND TO SPARE:  . . . . . . . .   214 HAPPY TOWNLAND V     4
    SUDDENLY HID LOVE'S MOON AWAY.  . . . . . . . . . .   313 MEMORY YOUTH         7
    LOVE'S MOON WAS WITHERING AWAY. . . . . . . . . . .   313 MEMORY YOUTH   V     7
    RHYMED OUT IN LOVE'S DESPAIR  . . . . . . . . . . .   337 SCHOLARS             5
    LOVE'S PLEASURE DRIVES HIS LOVE AWAY, . . . . . . .   438 SONGS PLAY 2        11
    I RAN, I RAN, FROM MY LOVE'S SIDE BECAUSE MY HEART WENT 450 OWEN AHERNE        12
      MAD.
    A QUALITY OF WISDOM FROM HER LOVE'S . . . . . . . .   469 HARUN RASHID       180
    QUALITY OF WISDOM FROM LOVE'S QUALITY,  . . . . . .   469 HARUN RASHID   V   180
    I--LOVE'S SKEIN UPON THE GROUND,  . . . . . . . . .   511 JANE AND JACK        9
    LOVE'S LONELINESS . . . . . . . . . . . . . . . . .   518 LOVES LONENESS       T
    AND LAID THEM ON LOVE'S LETTERED TOMB:  . . . . . .   519 HER DREAM            4
    NO, NIGHT'S BIRD AND LOVE'S  . . . . . . . . . . .    536 PARTING              5
    I OFFER TO LOVE'S PLAY  . . . . . . . . . . . . . .   536 PARTING             13
    AND, THOUGH LOVE'S BITTER-SWEET HAD ALL COME BACK,    537 HER VISION          27
    LOVE CRAM LOVE'S TWO DIVISIONS  . . . . . . . . . .   573 LADYS 2ND SONG      12
LOVES
    WE SANG THE LOVES AND ANGERS WITHOUT SLEEP, . . . .    42 OISIN 2            194
    THE SPACIOUS LOVES, THE ANGER WITHOUT SLEEP . . . .    42 OISIN 2         V  194
    AND THEIR HOUNDS, AND THEIR STEEDS, AND THEIR LOVES,   59 OISIN 3         V  176
    "THAT WE ARE TIRED, FOR OTHER LOVES AWAIT US: . . .    80 EPHEMERA            21
    NO MAIDEN LOVES ME, NO MAN SEEKS MY HELP, . . . . .   103 FERGUS DRUID   V    26
    NO WOMAN LOVES ME, NO MAN SEEKS MY HELP,  . . . . .   103 FERGUS DRUID   V    26
    WHO LOVES YOU, NO WHITE ARMS TO WRAP YOU ROUND, . .   109 CUCHULAIN SEA       59
    THERE THE LOVES A CIRCLE GO,  . . . . . . . . . . .   135 TWO TREES           13
    WINGED LOVES BORNE ON IN GENTLE STRIFE, . . . . . .   135 TWO TREES      V    14
    OF THE WOMAN THAT HE LOVES, UNTIL HE DIES.  . . . .   177 PAST GREATNESS      10
    VEERING, FLEETING, FICKLE, OUR LOVES AND ANGERS MEET: 207 HANRAHANS SONG V     3
    LOVES IN BRIEF LONGING AND DECEIVING HOPE . . . . .   228 SHADOW WATER B     146
    TO BREED THE LIDLESS EYE THAT LOVES THE SUN?  . . .   264 HOUSE SHAKEN         4
    TO CHANGE MY LOVES WHILE DANCING  . . . . . . . . .   330 BONE OF A HARE       7
    AND HEARTIER LOVES: THAT LAMP IS FROM THE TOMB. . .   398 LEADERS CROWD       12
    THAN IN OUR LOVES: OH, HONEY-BEES,  . . . . . . . .   425 STARES NEST    V    19
    MAN IS IN LOVE AND LOVES WHAT VANISHES, . . . . . .   429 NINETEEN 19         42
    AND NOT THEIR WORTH.  GOD LOVES US FOR OUR WORTH:     448 HERO GIRL FOOL V    15
    CHANGE THEIR LOVES ABOUT. . . . . . . . . . . . . .   520 HIS BARGAIN          6
    BECAUSE HE LOVES TOO MUCH.  . . . . . . . . . . . .   588 OLD WICKED MAN      15
    WE LOVE NASCHINA BOTH.  WHOM LOVES SHE BEST? . . .    660 ISLE STAT II 1      48
    MY WORDS WERE ALL: "HERE NO LOVES WANE AND WITHER,    669 ISLE STAT II 3      84
    HE LOVES OUR BROTHER PETER IN HIS HEART.  . . . . .   696 MOSADA 2            16
LOVE-SICK
    THOUGH MY LOVE-SICK HEART IS RENDING, . . . . . . .   646 ISLE STAT I 1       38
LOVE-SONG
    AND HER RED LIPS SANG THEM A LOVE-SONG  . . . . . .   160 CAP AND BELLS       27
    HER RED LIPS SANG THEM A LOVE-SONG, . . . . . . . .   160 CAP AND BELLS  V    27
LOVE-STORY
    AND TELL ME A LOVE-STORY WHILE I DRINK. . . . . . .   760 SHADOW WATER A     250
LOVE-TALES
    THE LOVE-TALES WROUGHT WITH SILKEN THREAD . . . . .   155 FORGOT BEAUTY        6
    THE LOVE-TALES WOVE WITH SILKEN THREAD  . . . . . .   155 FORGOT BEAUTY  V     6
LOVETH
    IT IS THE SHEPHERD GUARIMOND, WHO LOVETH WELL . . .   661 ISLE STAT II 1      53
LOVE-WORN
    BEFORE HER LOVE-WORN HEART HAD BROKE, . . . . . . .   194 BAILE AILLINN      127
LOVING
    AS, FULL OF LOVING FANTASY, . . . . . . . . . . . .    13 OISIN 1            158
```

```
                                                         PAGE    TITLE             LINE
LOVING  (CONTINUED)
      IF HE STOP LOVING ME, . . . . . . . . . . . . .    569 THREE BUSHES            18
      BEHOLD THE LOVING LOVELESS FLOWER OF LONE WAYS, . . . .  674 ISLE STAT II 3   201
LOW
      "WHY, AS YE RIDE, DROOPS LOW EACH HEAD? . . . . . . .      4 OISIN 1      V    32
      AND THOSE ON GAVRA LYING LOW, . . . . . . .               5 OISIN 1      V    41
      WITH LAUGHTER LOW, AND TENDER, AND SWEET! . . . . . .     6 OISIN 1      V    54
      AND WITH LOW MURMURS, WE RODE ON, . . . . . . .          13 OISIN 1          159
      TO THAT LOW LAUGHING WOODLAND RHYME. . . . . . . .       14 OISIN 1          176
      AND WITH LOW MURMURS PRAYED TO HIM, . . . . . . .        18 OISIN 1          257
      BENT LOW ABOVE EACH HOOKED KNEE, . . . . . . . .         26 OISIN 1      V   392
      IN THE ROOTS OF THE GRASSES, THE SORRELS, I LAID MY BODY  52 OISIN 3         73
          AS LOW!
      HOW THE SLOW, BLUE-EYED OXEN OF FINN LOW SADLY AT EVENING  52 OISIN 3        84
          TIDE,
      CAME, AND MY FOREHEAD FELL LOW, AND MY TEARS LIKE BERRIES  57 OISIN 3       154
          FELL DOWN!
      BENDING LOW HIS PIOUS HEAD, . . . . . . . .              82 MAD KING GOLL V  10
      BENDING LOW HIS FADING HEAD, . . . . . . . .            82 MAD KING GOLL V  10
      HIS EYELIDS DROOP, HIS HEAD FALLS LOW, . . . . . .       98 FOXHUNTER         13
      HIS EYELIDS CLOSE, HIS HEAD DROOPS LOW, . . . . . .      98 FOXHUNTER     V   13
      I HEAR LAKE WATER LAPPING WITH LOW SOUNDS BY THE SHORE!  117 ISLE INNISFREE   10
      I HEAR LAKE WATER LAPPING WITH LOW SOUNDS ON THE SHORE!  117 ISLE INNISFREE V 10
      . . . HUNG LOW ON THE RIM OF THE SKY, . . . . . .       122 WHITE BIRDS        3
      . . . HUNG LOW IN THE FALL OF THE DEW! . . . . . .      122 WHITE BIRDS        7
      A-TELLING WITH THEIR LOW AND REEDY CRY . . . . . .      128 DREAM OF FAERY V  42
      PROCLAIMING WITH A LOW AND REEDY CRY, . . . . . .       128 DREAM OF FAERY V  42
      IN TWILIGHT SHAKEN WITH LOW SIGHS! . . . . . . .        156 FORGOT BEAUTY V  10B
      HIS FACE BOWED LOW TO WEEP THE END . . . . . .          192 BAILE AILLINN     75
      AND WITH LOW MURMURING LAUGHING SPEECH . . . . . .      195 BAILE AILLINN    137
      THE HONEY-PALE MOON LAY LOW ON THE SLEEPY HILL, . . . .  203 WITHER BOUGHS     5
      THE HONEY PALE MOON HUNG LOW ON THE SLEEPY HILL, . . . .  203 WITHER BOUGHS V   5
      ON FINDING THAT HER VOICE IS SWEET AND LOW . . . . .    205 ADAMS CURSE       17
      IN FINDING THAT IT'S YOUNG AND MILD AND LOW. . . . . .   205 ADAMS CURSE   V  17
      O TUFTED REEDS, BEND LOW AND LOW IN POOLS ON THE GREEN  206 HANRAHANS SONG V   1
          LAND,
      O TUFTED REEDS, BEND LOW AND LOW IN POOLS ON THE GREEN  206 HANRAHANS SONG     1
          LAND,
      BUT WE HAVE ALL BENT LOW AND LOW AND KISSED THE QUIET FEET  207 HANRAHANS SONG   9
      BUT WE HAVE ALL BENT LOW AND LOW AND KISSED THE QUIET FEET  207 HANRAHANS SONG   9
      TO MAKE LOW LAUGHTER MORE THAN MEAT AND DRINK, . . . .   230 SHADOW WATER B  186
      AND HE, WITH THAT LOW WHINNYING SOUND . . . . . .       318 APPOINTMENT        5
      A PIERCED BOY, IMAGE OF A STAR LAID LOW. . . . . .      541 PARN FUNERAL 1    12
      A SLOW LOW NOTE AND AN IRON BELL. . . . . .             549 SEVERED HEAD       7
      A SLOW LOW NOTE AND AN IRON BELL! . . . . . .           550 SEVERED HEAD      14
      A SLOW LOW NOTE AND AN IRON BELL! . . . . . .           550 SEVERED HEAD      21
      OR STAY CONTENT ON THE LOW, . . . . . . . .             589 OLD WICKED MAN    49
      THE WOMEN THAT I PICKED SPOKE SWEET AND LOW . . . . .    622 HOUND VOICE       8
      WHEN LOW THE SUN SANK DOWN IN CLOTTED FLAME . . . . .    656 ISLE STAT I 3     30
      HE WAS OUR ANCIENT GOD. IF I SPEAK LOW, . . . . .       658 ISLE STAT I 3     78
      LOW BOWED AND DUMB UPON THE SAND, . . . . . .           671 ISLE STAT II 3   130
      FIERCE MORTAL, AND CROUCHED LOW BESIDE THE LAKE . . . .  675 ISLE STAT II 3 V 245A
      A BEARDED WITCH, HER SLUGGISH HEAD LOW BENT . . . . .    685 SEEKER           72
      LOW, LONG AND MUSICAL. A DEW-DROP HUNG . . . . .        689 NETTLESHIP         9
      DOWN LOW THE HEAD OF HIS MAGNIFICENCE . . . . .         689 NETTLESHIP    V    6
      BUT THIS ONE--THIS ONE. NOW HIS HEAD DROPS LOW, . . . .  711 FERENCZ RENYI    39
      BENT LOW WITH TOIL AND HOARIEST YEARS. THE OTHER . . . .  711 FERENCZ RENYI   52
      DROOPETH NOW HIS FOREHEAD LOW . . . . . .               711 FERENCZ RENYI V  39
      IN THE LONG GRASS--FOUR EYES DROOP LOW--A SEAT . . . .   716 DWELT SYCAMORE   11
      HIS MOODS BOW LOW HIS SOMBRE CREST, . . . . .          723 GIRLS SONG A       2
      I AM AFRAID OF HIS LOW LAUGHING HARP. . . . . .         759 SHADOW WATER A V 239
LOWER
      AND, AS THE SUN SANK EVER LOWER, . . . . . .            13 OISIN 1       V 170A
      SPEAK LOWER, OR THEY'LL HEAR. THEY CANNOT HEAR! . . . .   232 SHADOW WATER B  228
      BEND LOWER, O KING, THAT I MAY CROWN YOU WITH IT. . . . .  251 SHADOW WATER B 607
      BEND LOWER, THAT I MAY COVER YOU WITH MY HAIR, . . . .   251 SHADOW WATER B  613
      BEND LOWER LEST YOUR BATTLE-AXES GLIMMER. . . . . .     752 SHADOW WATER A   117
      BEND LOWER LEST YOUR BATTLE AXES GLIMMER. . . . . .     752 SHADOW WATER A V 117
      I CROWN YOU WITH THIS CROWN. BEND LOWER, O KING, . . . .  768 SHADOW WATER A  423
      BEND LOWER, THAT I MAY COVER YOU WITH MY HAIR, . . . .   769 SHADOW WATER A  429
LOWERED
      UPON KING EOCHAID'S FACE, WHO LOWERED HIS FACE . . . .   286 TWO KINGS     V 211A
LOWING
      HE'LL HEAR NO MORE THE LOWING . . . . . . .             88 STOLEN CHILD      44
LOW-LAUGHING
      LISTEN TO THAT LOW-LAUGHING STRING OF THE MOON . . . .   243 SHADOW WATER B  432
      I AM AFRAID OF HIS LOW-LAUGHING HARP. . . . . .         759 SHADOW WATER A  239
LOWLIER
      OR LOOK UPON THEM. WERE THEY BUT LOWLIER . . . . .      250 SHADOW WATER B  576
LOWLINESS
      LEARNED IN BODILY LOWLINESS . . . . . . .              513 JANE TALK BISH    11
LOWLY
      LOWLY THE HEAD OF HIS MAGNIFICENCE . . . . .           689 NETTLESHIP·        6
LOYAL
      MY LANTERN IS TOO LOYAL NOT TO SHOW . . . . . .        464 HARUN RASHID      71
LUCK
      OUR GIVER OF GOOD COUNSEL AND GOOD LUCK." . . . . .     185 QUEEN MAEVE      102
      HOW SHOULD THEIR LUCK RUN HIGH ENOUGH TO REACH . . . .   264 HOUSE SHAKEN     9
      THOSE WINE-DRENCHED EYES, AND CURSE OUR LUCK . . . . .   272 GREY ROCK       39
      AND THOSE FIERCE EYES, AND CURSE OUR LUCK . . . . .     272 GREY ROCK     V  39
      "IT'S CERTAIN THAT MY LUCK IS BROKEN," . . . . .       332 ROUND TOWER      25
```

485

	PAGE	TITLE		LINE
LUCK (CONTINUED)				
WHEN MY LUCK CHANGED AND THEY DARED MEET MY FACE, . . .	352	PEOPLE		25
WHEN MY LUCK CHANGED AND THEY DARED TO MEET MY FACE, . . .	352	PEOPLE	V	25
AND RUTH ST. DENIS HAD MORE CHARM ALTHOUGH SHE HAD POOR LUCK:	353	HIS PHOENIX		10
IN LUCK OR OUT THE TOIL HAS LEFT ITS MARK:	491	COOLE BALLYLEE V		40F
IN LUCK OR OUT THE TOIL HAS LEFT ITS MARK:	495	CHOICE		6
AND THERE'S NO LUCK ABOUT A HOUSE	584	GHOST ROG CASE		27
AND THAT SHOULD MOTHER SEEK HER SON SHE'D HAVE BUT LITTLE LUCK	593	PILGRIM		12
OUR LUCK IS WITHERED AWAY, ...	783	GREY ROUND		18
LUCKIER				
HOW SHOULD THE WORLD BE LUCKIER IF THIS HOUSE, ...	264	HOUSE SHAKEN		1
LUCKY				
AND SHE'D HAD LUCKY EYES AND A HIGH HEART, ...	181	QUEEN MAEVE		27
IT IS LUCKY THAT THEIR STORY	215	HAPPY TOWNLAND		27
A LUCKY BATTLE, OR A WOMAN'S KISS	227	SHADOW WATER B		115
"MAYBE I SHALL BE LUCKY YET, ...	297	THREE BEGGARS		61
I HAVE A LUCKY WOODEN SHIN	302	HOUR DAWN		18
THAT WERE A LUCKY DEATH, ...	431	NINETEEN 19		77
"THAT WAS A LUCKY THOUGHT OF MINE, ...	570	THREE BUSHES		31
LUGAIDH'S				
AILLINN, WHO WAS KING LUGAIDH'S HEIR.	189	BAILE AILLINN		7
LUGNAGALL				
HE SLEPT UNDER THE HILL OF LUGNAGALL:	128	DREAM OF FAERY		37
LUG-WORM				
A LUG-WORM WITH ITS GREY AND MUDDY MOUTH	127	DREAM OF FAERY		18
LUKA				
KUSTA BEN LUKA IS MY NAME, I WRITE	460	HARUN RASHID		1
LUKE				
OF OLD LUKE WADDING'S PORTRAIT SAID	400	DEMON BEAST		10
LULLABULLOO				
LULLABULLOO, BULOO, BULOO, LULLABULLOO, BULLO.	594	COLONEL MARTIN V		REF
LULLABULLOO, BULOO, BULOO, LULLABULLOO, BULLO.	594	COLONEL MARTIN V		REF
LULLABY				
AND SING IT LULLABY.	459	HIS WILDNESS		12
LULLABY	522	LULLABY		T
LULLED SEE LAKE-LULLED				
LULLED WEARINESS, AND SOFTLY ROUND	11	OISIN 1		137
LULLED WEARINESS: AND CLOSELY ROUND	11	OISIN 1	V	137
WHOSE DWELLING WAS A TREE-WRAPT ISLAND, LULLED	693	MOSADA 1		79
LULLING				
AND HOLLOW LULLING THE YOUNG WINDS WITH SONG.	675	ISLE STAT II 3		226
LULLS				
WILD CRIES, GROWN SWEET WITH LULLS AND LINGERINGS LONG.	674	ISLE STAT II 3		222
LULLY				
RAYMOND LULLY AND HIS WIFE PERNELLA	253	HIS DREAM	V	T
LUMBERING				
THE CRY OF A CHILD BY THE ROADWAY, THE CREAK OF A LUMBERING CART,	142	ROSE IN HEART		2
LUMINOUS SEE MOON-LUMINOUS				
UNTIL A CURLEW CRIED AND IN THE LUMINOUS WIND	291	PAUDEEN		4
CURVED LIKE NEW MOON, MOON LUMINOUS	421	MY TABLE	V	10
ALTHOUGH THAT WESTERN CLOUD IS LUMINOUS, ...	488	COOLE PARK 29		4
LUNATIC				
FOR EVERY HAND IS LUNATIC	451	FIRST LOVE		11
I THOUGHT HIM HALF A LUNATIC, HALF KNAVE, ...	473	ALL SOUL NIGHT		64
TOM THE LUNATIC	528	TOM LUNATIC		T
SANG OLD TOM THE LUNATIC	528	TOM LUNATIC		1
LUNGED				
THROUGH MANY SHAPES: I LUNGED AT THE SMOOTH THROAT . . .	40	OISIN 2		175
TO MANY SHAPES: I LUNGED AT THE SMOOTH THROAT	40	OISIN 2	V	175
SURGED UP IN PLUMY FIRE, I LUNGED AND DRAVE	41	OISIN 2		181
LUNGING				
WITH SURGE OF PLUMY FIRE, LUNGING I DRAVE	41	OISIN 2	V	181
LURCHES				
THERE LURCHES PAST, HIS GREAT EYES WITHOUT THOUGHT . . .	433	NINETEEN 19		126
LURE				
OUT OF MERE WANTONNESS TO LURE A SAIL	750	SHADOW WATER A		79
THEY LURE US TO THE STREAMS WHERE THE WORLD ENDS. . . .	764	SHADOW WATER A		334
THESE MESSENGERS TO LURE MEN TO HIS PEACE, ...	764	SHADOW WATER A		336
LURED				
. . LURED FROM HIS LAIR IN THE MOULD:	53	OISIN 3		99
PLUNGE, LURED BY A SOFTENING EYE, ...	413	TOWER		110
ON TEARS AND LAUGHTER: THEY HAVE LURED YOU HITHER . . .	757	SHADOW WATER A		207
AND LURED ME HITHER, THAT YOU MIGHT BE MY LOVE.	757	SHADOW WATER A		208
LURES				
THESE ARE THEIR LURES, BUT THEY HAVE SET THEIR HEARTS . . .	757	SHADOW WATER A		206
LURID				
FROM THE DEEP EARTH UNTO THE LURID SKY	662	ISLE STAT II 2		5
LURKS				
JOY'S BROTHER, FEAR, LURKS IN EACH LEAFY WAY.	651	ISLE STAT I 1		156
LUSH				
THAT STARING FURY AND THE BLIND LUSH LEAF	500	VACILLATION		17
LUST				
YOU THINK IT HORRIBLE THAT LUST AND RAGE	591	SPUR		1
LUSTRE				
AWAKEN, AWAKEN TO NEW-BORN LUSTRE:	646	ISLE STAT I 1		43
HURLS THEIR SWOONING LUSTRE UP.	647	ISLE STAT I 1		49
LUTE				
WITH MINGLING HAIR, AND PLAY UPON ONE LUTE.	71	ANASHU VIJAYA		10

LUTE   (CONTINUED)
    HERE'S A MONTENEGRIN LUTE, ...   627 STATES HOLIDAY   22
    ON A GIRL'S FORGOTTEN LUTE, ...   668 ISLE STAT II 3   66
    HEARD YOU? YOUR LUTE HUNG IN THE WINDOW SOUNDED! . . . 694 MOSADA 1   95
    HEARD YOU? YOUR LUTE UPON THE WALL HAS SOUNDED! . . . . 694 MOSADA 1   V 95
LUTE-THRONGED
    WHEN THE FLAMING LUTE-THRONGED ANGELIC DOOR IS WIDE! . . 172 TRAV PASSION   1
LUXURIANT
    LUXURIANT SONG. WHY SHOULD YOU LEAVE THE LAMP . . . .   370 EGO DOMINUS   62
LUXURY
    SHUT OUT FROM ALL THE LUXURY OF THE WORLD, ...   370 EGO DOMINUS   60
LYING   SEE HALF-LYING
    AND ON THE HEROES LYING SLAIN . . . .   5 OISIN 1   42
    AND THOSE ON GAVRA LYING LOW, ...   5 OISIN 1   V 41
    TO ONE VAST FOOT, FROTH-SPLASHED, WITH CURVED TOES LYING   32 OISIN 2   V 46A
    BUT NOW THE LYING CLERICS MURDER SONG . . . .   42 OISIN 2   196
    WERE YOU BUT LYING COLD AND DEAD, ...   175 BELOVED DEAD   1
    HAS SHE NOT SEEN HIM LYING LIKE A LOG, ...   230 SHADOW WATER B 173
    THROUGH ALL THE LYING DAYS OF MY YOUTH . . . .   261 COMING WISDOM   2
    SHE WOULD NOT HAVE US SAD BECAUSE SHE IS LYING THERE, . . 362 HER COURTESY   4
    LYING ALONE ON A BED . . . .   552 SONGS REWRIT 2 V 10
    BUT HE'S A LYING HOUND! . . . .   636 BLACK TOWER   25
LYNX
    THAT I MYSELF COULD SHOOT A GREAT GREY LYNX, ...   650 ISLE STAT I 1   152
    HAVE THEY NE'ER SEEN THE EYES OF LYNX OR KINE, ...   672 ISLE STAT II 3 152
LYNX'S
    AND THE GREAT GREY LYNX'S SKIN! IN SOOTH, METHINKS . .   650 ISLE STAT I 1   151
LYRIC
    A LYRIC FROM AN UNPUBLISHED PLAY . . . .   263 MASK   V   T
LYRICS
    LYRICS FROM "THE ISLAND OF STATUES" . . . .   646 ISLE STAT I 1 V   T
MA
    WAKE, MA CUSHLA, SLEEPY-HEADED! . . . .   705 DAWN-SONG   9
MAC
    CAME BLANAID, MAC NESSA, TALL FERGUS WHO FEASTWARD OF OLD   53 OISIN 3   89
        TIME SLUNK,
    CAME BLANID, MAC NESSA, CUCHULIN! . . . .   53 OISIN 3   V 89
    CAME BLANID, MAC NESSA, AND FERGUS WHO FEASTWARD OF OLD   53 OISIN 3   V 89
        TIME SLUNK,
MACBRIDE
    MACDONAGH AND MACBRIDE . . . .   394 EASTER 1916   75
MACCARTAN
    FIRST I GREET MACCARTAN, REVOLUTIONARY LEADER. . . . .   790 DEDICATION   1
MACDONAGH
    MACDONAGH AND MACBRIDE . . . .   394 EASTER 1916   75
MACDONAGH'S
    MACDONAGH'S BONY THUMB? . . . .   395 SIXTEEN DEAD   12
MACE
    FROM MACE AND SWORD AND POLE-AXE, LONG AGO . . . . . .   31 OISIN 2   30
    BY MACE AND SPEAR AND SWORD OF SEA-GODS, NAILS . . . .   31 OISIN 2   V 30A
MACGREGOR
    AND I CALL UP MACGREGOR FROM THE GRAVE, ...   473 ALL SOUL NIGHT   61
    I CALL MACGREGOR MATHERS FROM HIS GRAVE, ...   473 ALL SOUL NIGHT V 61
MACKEREL-CROWDED
    THE SALMON-FALLS, THE MACKEREL-CROWDED SEAS, ...   407 SAIL BYZANTIUM   4
    THE SALMON-FALLS, THE MACKEREL-CROWDED SEAS, ...   407 SAIL BYZANTIUM V 4
MAD   SEE WHOLE-MAD
    A MAD SONG . . . .   149 WANDER AENGUS V   T
    HAVE DRIVEN TRAVELLERS MAD FOR THEIR OWN SPORT. . . . .   227 SHADOW WATER B 105
    MAY NOT HAVE DRIVEN YOU MAD FOR THEIR OWN SPORT? . . . . 227 SHADOW WATER B V 105
    BRING MADNESS? QUEEN, I AM NOT MAD. YET SAY . . . .   236 SHADOW WATER B 316
    WOULD RISE AGAINST ME. NO, I AM NOT MAD-- . . . . .   236 SHADOW WATER B 318
    THE EVER-LIVING HAVE MADE YOU MAD! BUT NO, ...   248 SHADOW WATER B 546
    WHEREON MAD FINGERS PLAY . . . .   291 TO A FRIEND   12
    UNTIL I AM DRIVEN MAD, ...   346 ON WOMAN   35
    EVEN TO EYES THAT BEAUTY HAD DRIVEN MAD, ...   390 IMAGE PAST   34
    FOR IF I TRIUMPH I MUST MAKE MEN MAD— . . . .   411 TOWER   56
    IN THE MAD ABSTRACT DARK AND GROUND IT GRAIN BY GRAIN . . 442 BLACK CENTAUR   8
    IT COULD NOT BEAR THAT BURDEN AND THEREFORE IT WENT MAD.   449 OWEN AHERNE   4
    IT FEARED THE HURT THAT SHE COULD GIVE AND THEREFORE IT   450 OWEN AHERNE   8
        WENT MAD.
    I RAN, I RAN, FROM MY LOVE'S SIDE BECAUSE MY HEART WENT   450 OWEN AHERNE   12
        MAD.
    . . . "YOU HAVE CALLED ME MAD," IT SAID, ...   450 OWEN AHERNE   13
    MAD AS THE MIST AND SNOW . . . .   523 MAD AS MIST   T
    MAD AS THE MIST AND SNOW. . . . .   523 MAD AS MIST   6
    MAD AS THE MIST AND SNOW? . . . .   524 MAD AS MIST   12
    MAD AS THE MIST AND SNOW. . . . .   524 MAD AS MIST   18
    "BECAUSE I AM MAD ABOUT WOMEN . . . .   587 OLD WICKED MAN   1
    I AM MAD ABOUT THE HILLS," . . . .   587 OLD WICKED MAN   2
    WHY SHOULD NOT OLD MEN BE MAD? . . . .   625 OLD MEN BE MAD   T
    WHY SHOULD NOT OLD MEN BE MAD? . . . .   625 OLD MEN BE MAD   1
    KNOW WHY AN OLD MAN SHOULD BE MAD. . . . .   626 OLD MEN BE MAD   20
    AND A MAN IS FIGHTING MAD, ...   638 BEN BULBEN   28
    I BID THEE STAY, RENOUNCING THY MAD QUEST." . . . . .   669 ISLE STAT II 3   89
    AND ROARS, MAD WITH THE TOUCH OF THE UNKNOWN, ... 689 NETTLESHIP   7
    I WILL BURN HERESY FROM THIS MAD EARTH, ...   697 MOSADA 2   40
    GOD! THEY'RE MAD TO FLY SUCH CANVAS!" . . . . . .   718 PHANTOM SHIP   14
    AND ALL HER STARLIGHT IS WITH SORROW MAD, ...   738 YOU ARE SAD   3
MADAM
    CAN DISTURB GLOBE-TROTTING MADAM . . . .   638 BEN BULBEN   48

	PAGE	TITLE		LINE
MADDENED				
HAS MADDENED EVERY MOTHER'S SON":	290	SEPTEMBER 1913		29
MADDENED BY THAT SINEWY THIGH.	294	HATED PLAYBOY	V	6
AND CERTAIN MEN, BEING MADDENED BY THOSE RHYMES, ...	410	TOWER		41
MADE SEE RE-MADE				
THEIR CLOAKS MADE OUT OF YELLOW SILK, ...	15	OISIN 1		205
THEIR BRATTAS MADE OUT OF YELLOW SILK, ...	15	OISIN 1	V	205
AND MADE IN ALL THEIR DISTANT PARTS, ...	16	OISIN 1		228
WHERE TREES MADE SUDDEN CAVERN-GLOOMS	16	OISIN 1	V	224B
SINCE GOD MADE TIME AND DEATH AND SLEEP: THE OTHER . . .	31	OISIN 2		41
AND A SAD MOUTH, THAT FEAR MADE TREMULOUS	34	OISIN 2		71
MADE THE WAY SLIPPERY, AND TIME ON TIME	37	OISIN 2		114
A DOME MADE OUT OF ENDLESS CARVEN JAGS, ...	38	OISIN 2		144
A LITTLE RUNNEL MADE A BUBBLING STRAIN.	39	OISIN 2		156
WHILE THE WOOD-PECKER MADE A MERRY DIN.	44	OISIN 2	V	228
ARE FACES ALIVE WITH SUCH BEAUTY MADE KNOWN TO THE SALT EYE OF MAN,	50	OISIN 3	V	51
ARE FACES ALIVE WITH SUCH BEAUTY MADE KNOWN TO THE SOFT EYE OF MAN,	50	OISIN 3	V	51
. . . MADE CONCHUBAR'S SWORD-BLADE OF OLD.	52	OISIN 3		80
THAT THE SPEAR-SHAFT IS MADE OUT OF ASHWOOD, ...	52	OISIN 3		82
. . . MADE ARMOUR FOR CONOR THE OLD.	52	OISIN 3	V	80
. . . MADE ARMOUR FOR CONHOR OF OLD.	52	OISIN 3	V	80
. . . MADE ARMOUR FOR MIDHIR OF OLD	52	OISIN 3	V	80
THAT THE SPEARSHAFT IS MADE OUT OF ASHWOOD.	52	OISIN 3	V	82
WHEN THE FENIANS MADE FORAY AT MORNING WITH BRAN, SCEOLAN, LOMAIR.	54	OISIN 3		104
I SAW FROM A DISTANT SADDLE: FROM THE EARTH SHE MADE HER MOAN:	56	OISIN 3		130
AND THE WINDS MADE THE SANDS ON THE SEA'S EDGE	57	OISIN 3		145
AS MY MIND MADE THE NAMES OF THE FENIANS.	57	OISIN 3		146
MUCH WONDERING TO SEE UPON ALL HANDS, OF WATTLES AND WOODWORK MADE,	58	OISIN 3		162
MUCH WONDERING TO SEE UPON ALL HANDS, OF WATTLES AND WOOD-WORK MADE,	58	OISIN 3	V	162
TO MIGHTY BRAHMA, HE WHO MADE YOU MANY AS THE SANDS, . .	72	ANASHU VIJAYA		21
WITHIN THE TEMPLE, DEVIOUS WALKING, MADE	72	ANASHU VIJAYA		32
TO MIGHTY BRAHMA--HE WHO MADE YE MANY AS THE SANDS, . . .	72	ANASHU VIJAYA	V	21
TO MIGHTY BRAHMA, WHO HAS MADE YOU MANY AS THE SANDS, . .	72	ANASHU VIJAYA	V	21
WHO HOLDS THE WORLD BETWEEN HIS BILL AND MADE US STRONG OR WEAK	76	INDIAN ON GOD		6
WHO MADE THE WORLD AND RULETH IT, HE HANGETH ON A STALK,	76	INDIAN ON GOD		10
FOR I AM IN HIS IMAGE MADE, AND ALL THIS TINKLING TIDE . .	76	INDIAN ON GOD		11
WHO MADE THE GRASS AND MADE THE WORMS AND MADE MY FEATHERS GAY,	77	INDIAN ON GOD		18
WHO MADE THE GRASS AND MADE THE WORMS AND MADE MY FEATHERS GAY,	77	INDIAN ON GOD		18
WHO MADE THE GRASS AND MADE THE WORMS AND MADE MY FEATHERS GAY,	77	INDIAN ON GOD		18
HE MADE FOR HER AN ARMY CEASE TO BE."	106	CUCHULAIN SEA	V	16B
"MY FATHER," MADE HE, SMILING, ANSWER THEN, ...	107	CUCHULAIN SEA		25
FOR HE WHO MADE YOU BITTER MADE YOU WISE."	108	CUCHULAIN SEA		32
FOR HE WHO MADE YOU BITTER MADE YOU WISE."	108	CUCHULAIN SEA		32
FOR GOD WHO MADE YOU BITTER MADE YOU WISE."	108	CUCHULAIN SEA	V	32
FOR GOD WHO MADE YOU BITTER MADE YOU WISE."	108	CUCHULAIN SEA	V	32
AT LAST CUCHULAIN SPAKE, "SOME MAN HAS MADE	109	CUCHULAIN SEA		47
CUCHULAIN CRIED, "HAVE MADE AND KEEP THAT VOW."	109	CUCHULAIN SEA	V	56
HE MADE THE WORLD TO BE A GRASSY ROAD	112	ROSE OF WORLD		14
BUT GATHER ALL FOR WHOM NO LOVE HATH MADE	114	ROSE OF BATTLE		12
MADE YOU OF US, AND OF THE DIM GREY SEA.	115	ROSE OF BATTLE		30
AND A SMALL CABIN BUILD THERE, OF CLAY AND WATTLES MADE:	117	ISLE INNISFREE		2
AND A SMALL CABIN BUILT THERE, OF CLAY AND WATTLES MADE:	117	ISLE INNISFREE	V	2
A CROSS THEY HAD MADE OUT OF TWO BITS OF WOOD, ...	123	DREAM OF DEATH		7
BEFORE EARTH MADE OF HIM HER SLEEPY CARE:	126	DREAM OF FAERY	V	4
"HE WHO HATH MADE THE NIGHT OF STARS	134	FR GILLIGAN		41
AND MADE MY LIPS AND MUSIC WED, ...	134	TWO TREES		11
MADE WHEN GOD SLEPT IN TIMES OF OLD.	135	TWO TREES		32
BEFORE GOD MADE THE ANGELIC CLAN, ...	138	TO IRELAND		8
MADE IRELAND'S HEART BEGIN TO BEAT:	138	TO IRELAND		12
THAT HAS MADE FAT THE MURDEROUS MOTH:	156	FORGOT BEAUTY		8
HE MADE HIS SOUL GO UPWARD	159	CAP AND BELLS	V	3
I MADE IT OUT OF A MOUTHFUL OF AIR, ...	166	EVIL OF BELOV		5
AT NEED, AND MADE HER BEAUTIFUL AND FIERCE, ...	181	QUEEN MAEVE		29
WITH BODIES MADE OUT OF SOFT FIRE. THE ONE, ...	187	QUEEN MAEVE		144
SOME GOD OR KING HAD MADE THE LAWS	194	BAILE AILLINN		131
OR THE TWO STRINGS THAT MADE ONE SOUND	195	BAILE AILLINN		155
BECAUSE THEY HAVE MADE SO GOOD A FRIEND.	195	BAILE AILLINN		159
MADE OF THE APPLE AND THE YEW, ...	197	BAILE AILLINN		196
MADE OUT OF A WILD THOUGHT, IS IN MY MARROW.	199	ARROW		2
HE THAT MADE THIS KNOWS ALL THE COST, ...	202	NEVER GIVE ALL		13
HAS MADE THEM SO HAPPY AND HOPELESS, SO DEAF AND SO BLIND	204	WITHER BOUGHS		20
I HAVE MADE THIS POEM FOR YOU, THAT MEN MAY READ IT . .	219	WOODS OF COOLE		41
AND SLEEPY BOUGHS, AND BOUGHS WHERE APPLES MADE	219	HARP OF AENGUS		5
BECAUSE HER HANDS HAD BEEN MADE WILD BY LOVE.	219	HARP OF AENGUS		9
HE MADE A HARP WITH DRUID APPLE-WOOD	220	HARP OF AENGUS		11
HE MADE A HARP WITH DRUID APPLE WOOD	220	HARP OF AENGUS	V	11
YOU HAVE TAKEN PAY AND MADE YOUR BARGAIN FOR IT.	225	SHADOW WATER B		68
THE MIND IS MADE UNCHANGING, FOR IT FINDS	227	SHADOW WATER B		101
I'LL SHOW YOU THAT I AM MADE DIFFERENTLY.	227	SHADOW WATER B		119
THEY HAVE MADE YOU FOLLOW THE MAN-HEADED BIRDS, ...	231	SHADOW WATER B		204
LIKE CHARMED APPLES MADE OF CHRYSOPRASE, ...	231	SHADOW WATER B		214

488

MADE (CONTINUED)

	PAGE	TITLE		LINE
MADE OF DIM GOLD RAVE OUT IN SECRET TOMBS:	235	SHADOW WATER B		295
BUT WHAT IS IT THAT MADE ME SAY I LOVED HIM?	242	SHADOW WATER B		422
THERE IS NOT ONE AMONG YOU THAT MADE LOVE	244	SHADOW WATER B		454
THE EVER-LIVING HAVE MADE YOU MAD: BUT NO,	248	SHADOW WATER B		546
WHAT COULD HAVE MADE HER PEACEFUL WITH A MIND	256	NO SECOND TROY		6
THAT NOBLENESS MADE SIMPLE AS A FIRE,	256	NO SECOND TROY		7
BECAUSE WE HAVE MADE OUR ART OF COMMON THINGS,	265	ABBEY THEATRE		5
HAVE YOU MADE GREATNESS YOUR COMPANION,	265	THESE CLOUDS		9
THE SMOKY TORCHES MADE A GLARE	271	GREY ROCK		18
AND SMOKY TORCHES MADE A GLARE	271	GREY ROCK	V	18
NOW FROM THAT JUICE THAT MADE THEM WISE	272	GREY ROCK		26
FOR ONE THAT WAS LIKE WOMAN MADE	272	GREY ROCK		29
OF MEN AND WOMEN MADE LIKE THESE:	272	GREY ROCK		43
BUT FROM THE JUICE THAT MADE THEM WISE	272	GREY ROCK	V	26
BUT NEVER MADE A POORER SONG	273	GREY ROCK		55
THAT HAD MADE PRINTS UPON THE GROUND,	274	GREY ROCK		79
AND RENT HER CLOTHES AND MADE HER MOAN:	275	GREY ROCK		108
A CLUMP OF BEECH TREES MADE AN EMPTY SPACE	277	TWO KINGS	V	4A
NOR DOOR, NOR MOUTH, NOR SLIPPER MADE A NOISE,	279	TWO KINGS		51
SOME PASSION HAD MADE HER STONE. HEARING A FOOT	279	TWO KINGS		65
THAT MADE THE BODY SEEM AS IT WERE A STRING	284	TWO KINGS		176
AND GUIDOBALDO, WHEN HE MADE	287	TO WEALTHY MAN		14
UNLESS DESIRE HAD MADE THEM SO."	295	THREE BEGGARS		18
OR IF THEY MADE A MOMENT'S STAY	297	THREE BEGGARS		52
I'VE STOOD AS I WERE MADE OF STONE	297	THREE BEGGARS		64
AND MADE A GOLDEN CRADLE	308	PLAYER QUEEN		3
AND MADE A GOLDEN GOWN,	308	PLAYER QUEEN		10
THAT HAS MADE A GREAT PEACOCK	310	PEACOCK		2
TILL PRIDE HAD MADE HER EYES GROW BRIGHT,	314	MEMORY YOUTH		10
AND PLEASURE MADE HER CHEEKS GROW RED,	314	MEMORY YOUTH		11
THE LINEAMENTS, A HEART THAT LAUGHTER HAS MADE SWEET,	315	FALLEN MAJESTY		5
THE LINEAMENTS, THE HEART THAT LAUGHTER HAS MADE SWEET,	315	FALLEN MAJESTY	V	5
I MADE MY SONG A COAT	320	COAT		1
THOSE UNDREAMT ACCIDENTS THAT HAVE MADE ME	321	REED WHISPERER		10
SINCE I FIRST MADE MY COUNT:	322	SWANS AT COOLE		8
WHAT MADE US DREAM THAT HE COULD COMB GREY HAIR?	327	ROBERT GREGORY		88
HAIR SPREAD ON THE WIND THEY MADE:	332	ROUND TOWER		22
HAIRS SPREAD ON THE WIND THEY MADE,	332	ROUND TOWER	V	22
AND I THAT MADE LIKE MUSIC IN MY YOUTH	342	SHEP GOATHERD		76
OF ALL THAT HE HAD MADE.	342	SHEP GOATHERD		99
AND TOOK THEIR TABLETS AND MADE SUMS--	344	DAWN	V	9
THAT MADE THEM STRETCH AND YAWN,	345	ON WOMAN		21
SHUDDER THAT MADE THEM ONE.	346	ON WOMAN		23
IN THE GREY STONE TOMB HE MADE.	360	ALF POLLEXFEN		5
(I HAVE NO SPEECH BUT SYMBOL, THE PAGAN SPEECH I MADE	365	HER COURAGE		2
THAT MADE HER DIARMUID DEAR, AND SOME OLD CARDINAL	366	HER COURAGE		6
AND THAT MADE HER DERMUID DEAR, AND SOME OLD CARDINAL	366	HER COURAGE	V	6
THAT HE HAS MADE THAT HOLLOW FACE OF HIS	368	EGO DOMINUS		20
OR WAS THE HUNGER THAT HAD MADE IT HOLLOW	368	EGO DOMINUS		23
YET SURELY THERE ARE MEN WHO HAVE MADE THEIR ART	369	EGO DOMINUS		38
AND MADE--BEING POOR, AILING AND IGNORANT,	370	EGO DOMINUS		59
WHAT MADE THAT SOUND? A RAT OR WATER-HEN	372	PHASES OF MOON		8
THEREON I MADE MY MOAN,	384	VISION ROBART		63
THE COMFORT THAT YOU MADE? ALTHOUGH MY WITS HAVE GONE	391	UNDER SATURN		5
IT MADE HIM HAPPIER TO KNOW	400	DEMON BEAST		14
FOR AIMLESS JOY HAD MADE ME STOP	400	DEMON BEAST		22
BEING MADE BEAUTIFUL OVERMUCH,	403	FOR DAUGHTER		20
FOR BEAUTY'S VERY SELF, HAS CHARM MADE WISE,	404	FOR DAUGHTER		37
STRANGE, BUT THE MAN WHO MADE THE SONG WAS BLIND:	411	TOWER		49
TILL MAN MADE UP THE WHOLE,	415	TOWER		149
MADE LOCK, STOCK AND BARREL	415	TOWER		150
BEING OF THAT METAL MADE	416	TOWER		178
THAT MADE A CATCH IN THE BREATH--	416	TOWER		191
HAS MADE THE VERY OWLS IN CIRCLES MOVE:	423	MY DESCENDANTS		18
OR EYES THAT RAGE HAS BRIGHTENED, ARMS IT HAS MADE LEAN,	427	PHANTOM HATRED		27
IT MADE BUT MADE US PINE THE MORE. THE ABSTRACT JOY,	427	PHANTOM HATRED		38
OF EYES THAT RAGE HAS BRIGHTENED, ARMS IT HAS MADE LEAN,	427	PHANTOM HATRED	V	27
AN ANCIENT IMAGE MADE OF OLIVE WOOD--	428	NINETEEN 19		6
TO BRIBE OR THREAT: HABITS THAT MADE OLD WRONG	428	NINETEEN 19		11
IS LOST AMID THE LABYRINTH THAT HE HAS MADE	431	NINETEEN 19		70
MADE ALL PLATONIC TOLERANCE VAIN	438	SONGS PLAY 2		7
MADE PLATO'S TOLERANCE IN VAIN,	438	SONGS PLAY 2	V	7
THE WEST WIND MADE IT PITIFUL, AND THE NORTH WIND AFRAID.	449	OWEN AHERNE		6
"BECAUSE I MADE YOU TURN AWAY AND RUN FROM THAT YOUNG CHILD:	450	OWEN AHERNE		14
THAT IT WAS MADE IN YOUR GREAT FATHER'S REIGN."	464	HARUN RASHID		72
HANDS UPON EITHER SHOULDER MADE HER MOVE,	466	HARUN RASHID	V	125B
WHAT'S BOWED YOUR SHOULDER AND MADE PALE YOUR CHEEK":	467	HARUN RASHID		133
MADE DRIVE THE ARABIAN HOST. THE VOICE GREW STILL,	467	HARUN RASHID	V	145
THAT MADE THE MAGNITUDE AND GLORY THERE	483	VERONIC NAPKIN		5
MADE MY ATTENTION STRAY.	507	STREAM AND SUN		5
WHAT MADE ME LIVE LIKE THESE THAT SEEM	507	STREAM AND SUN		14
MADE THE JOINTS OF HEAVEN CRACK:	509	JANE REPROVED		11
BEFORE THE WORLD WAS MADE.	516	MANS SONG		12
I MADE, AND MAY NOT BREAK IT	520	HIS BARGAIN		9
SOMETHING MADE THESE EYEBALLS WEARY	529	TOM LUNATIC		11
BEFORE THE WORLD WAS MADE.	531	BEFORE WORLD		T
BEFORE THE WORLD WAS MADE.	532	BEFORE WORLD		8
BEFORE THE WORLD WAS MADE.	532	BEFORE WORLD		16
WHAT MADE THEM MOUNT AND WHAT MADE THEM COME,	549	SEVERED HEAD	V	8

	PAGE	TITLE		LINE

MADE   (CONTINUED)

WHAT MADE THEM MOUNT AND WHAT MADE THEM COME, ... 549 SEVERED HEAD   V   8
MADE AQUILINE, ARE OPEN TO THAT LIGHT. . . . . . . 555 RIBH AT TOMB   24
WHAT MASTER MADE THE LASH. WHENCE HAD THEY COME, . . . 560 WHENCE COME   9
MADE DRAPERIES THAT SEEMED TO RISE . . . . 566 LAPIS LAZULI   31
SHE MADE A FULL CONFESSION. . . . . 571 THREE BUSHES   66
PLEASURE HAS MADE HIM . . . . 574 MAIDS 1ST SONG   9
WOUND, WOUND, AND SHE MADE IN HER TRIUMPH . . . . . 578 CRAZED GIRL   11
AND ALL MY FRIENDS WERE THERE AND MADE ME WELCOME TOO, . . 581 CURSE CROMWELL   27
THAT SOME AMENDS BE MADE . . . . 582 ROGER CASEMENT   22
O WHAT HAS MADE THAT SUDDEN NOISE? . . . . 583 GHOST ROG CASE   1
THAT TRAGIC STORY MADE. . . . . 587 PARNELLITES   26
WITH FLOPPING AND WITH FLAPPING IT MADE A GREAT DISPLAY, . 593 PILGRIM   18
WITH THEIR FLOPPING AND THEIR FLAPPING IT MADE A GREAT   593 PILGRIM   V 18
    DISPLAY

WHEN TOM MADE OUT A LIVING . . . . 597 COLONEL MARTIN V 70
NOR EVER MADE AN IRON RED . . . . 606 SONGS BURDEN 1   14
WHAT MADE THE DRAPERY GLISTEN SO? . . . . 625 NATIVITY   3
WHAT MADE THE CEILING WATERPROOF? . . . . 625 NATIVITY   5
OR THE MAN THAT MADE THE MOTORS? . . . . 627 STATES HOLIDAY   20
SING WHATEVER IS WELL MADE, ... 639 BEN BULBEN   69
THE SHEPHERD PARIS FOR OENONE MADE, ... 650 ISLE STAT I 1   136
MADE THEM OF FIRE AND CLAY. . . . . 680 LOVE AND DEATH   12
WORN BY THE SOLSTICE FIERCE, AND MADE IT PURE. . . . . 692 MOSADA 1   57
THAT SONG I'VE MADE. 'TIS OF AN IRISH TALE. . . . . 696 MOSADA 2   19
THAT SONG I'VE MADE--IS OF A RUSSIAN TALE . . . . . 696 MOSADA 2   V 19
IN SPACE, MADE EQUAL WITH A SIGH, WE MET. . . . . . 705 REMEMBRANCE   14
ON THE NOSE OF THE SLEEPER HE MADE IT PLAY, ... 729 PRIEST FAIRY   30
AND MADE THE TYRANT BOW. . . . . 738 MOURN THEN ON   12
AND MADE THEIR GLORY NAUGHT. . . . . 741 EARL PAUL   44
AND MADE THE BRIGHT SPEAR BEND, ... 741 EARL PAUL   46
BECAUSE A GOD HAS MADE HIM WISE WITH DREAMS, ... 748 SHADOW WATER A   26
AND SLEEPY BOUGHS, AND BOUGHS WHERE APPLES MADE . . . . 762 SHADOW WATER A   300
BECAUSE HER HANDS HAD BEEN MADE WILD BY LOVE, ... 762 SHADOW WATER A   304
HE MADE A HARP WITH DRUID APPLE WOOD . . . . . . 763 SHADOW WATER A   306
HE MADE A HARP WITH DRUID APPLE-WOOD . . . . 763 SHADOW WATER A V 306
ALL DIES AMONG THOSE STREAMS. THE FOOL HAS MADE . . . . 764 SHADOW WATER A   335
THE FOOL, WHO HAS MADE THE WISDOM THAT MEN WRITE . . . 764 SHADOW WATER A   342
MADE OF DIM GOLD, RAVE OUT IN SECRET TOMBS, ... 765 SHADOW WATER A   345
AND BODILY TENDERNESS, BUT LOVE IS MADE . . . . . . 765 SHADOW WATER A   355
LOVE WAS NOT MADE FOR DARKNESS AND THE WINDS . . . . . 767 SHADOW WATER A   394
HAS MADE MY FEET UNSTEADY, AND BLINDED ME. . . . . 767 SHADOW WATER A   406
WHERE THE DEW IS MADE BEFORE DAWN, ... 771 SPINNING SONG   5
THAT IS MADE OUT OF THE GREASE. . . . . 776 AGAINST WITCH   24
HAS MADE IT BUT A LONELY THING. . . . . 781 HEART FRIGHT   4

MADEST

THOU CALLED'ST ME FORTH. AND HOW THOU MADEST ME . . . . 683 SEEKER   52

MADGE

FOR THAT OLD MADGE COMES DOWN THE LANE, ... 456 FRIENDS YOUTH   5
MADGE TELLS ME WHAT I DARED NOT THINK . . . . . . 457 SECRETS OF OLD   3

MADGE'S

IF THROWN IN MADGE'S WAY, ... 457 SECRETS OF OLD   8

MADMAN'S

HE RUSHES, ROLLING FROM HIS LIPS A MADMAN'S LAUGH. . . . 715 FERENCZ RENYI   122

MADNESS

THE MADNESS OF KING GOLL . . . . 81 MAD KING GOLL   T
BRING MADNESS? QUEEN, I AM NOT MAD. YET SAY . . . . . 236 SHADOW WATER B   316

MADONNA

MADONNA FROM MY BREAST? . . . . 686 LIFE   12

MAEVE

WHERE PASSIONATE MAEVE IS STONY-STILL, ... 3 OISIN 1   18
TILL I SAW WHERE MAEVE LIES SLEEPING . . . . 60 OISIN 3   184
THE OLD AGE OF QUEEN MAEVE . . . . 180 QUEEN MAEVE   T
MAEVE THE GREAT QUEEN WAS PACING TO AND FRO, ... 180 QUEEN MAEVE   9
MAEVE WALKED, YET WITH SLOW FOOTFALL, BEING OLD, ... 181 QUEEN MAEVE   43
MAEVE WAITED, AND WHEN THAT EAR-PIERCING NOISE . . . . 182 QUEEN MAEVE   47
MAEVE WALKED THROUGH THAT GREAT HALL, AND WITH A SIGH . . 182 QUEEN MAEVE   62
AND WITH GLAD VOICE MAEVE ANSWERED HIM, "WHAT KING . . . 183 QUEEN MAEVE   79
AND WITH GLAD VOICE MAEVE ANSWERED "MANY A TIME . . . . 183 QUEEN MAEVE   V 79
BUT MAEVE, AND NOT WITH A SLOW FEEBLE FOOT, ... 185 QUEEN MAEVE   107
TILL MAEVE CALLED OUT, "THESE ARE BUT COMMON MEN. . . . 186 QUEEN MAEVE   122
TO MAEVE AND TO MAEVE'S HOUSEHOLD, OWING ALL . . . . . 187 QUEEN MAEVE   147
THEN MAEVE, "O AENGUS, MASTER OF ALL LOVERS, ... 187 QUEEN MAEVE   149
AND THROWN THE THUNDER ON THE STONES FOR ALL THAT MAEVE 207 HANRAHANS SONG   7
    CAN SAY.
FROM MAEVE AND ALL THAT JUGGLING PLAIN, ... 307 HOUR DAWN   120

MAEVE'S

TO MAEVE AND TO MAEVE'S HOUSEHOLD, OWING ALL . . . . . 187 QUEEN MAEVE   147
QUEEN MAEVE'S NINE MAINES HAD BEEN NURSED, ... 302 HOUR DAWN   8
WHAT ONE OF MAEVE'S NINE BRAWLING SONS . . . . . . 303 HOUR DAWN   36
HAS ONE OF MAEVE'S NINE BRAWLING SONS . . . . . . 303 HOUR DAWN   V 36

MAGAI

BETWEEN THE WOOD OF DURAS AND MAGAI . . . . 276 TWO KINGS   V   G

MAGEE

THE BALLAD OF MOLL MAGEE . . . . 94 MOLL MAGEE   T
BUT PITY MOLL MAGEE. . . . . 94 MOLL MAGEE   4
AND PITY MOLL MAGEE. . . . . 96 MOLL MAGEE   56

MAGH

HE SAID, "HIGH QUEEN OF CRUACHAN AND MAGH AI, ... 183 QUEEN MAEVE   77

MAGI

OF THE CROWNED MAGI, AND THE KING WHOSE EYES . . . . . 169 SECRET ROSE   9

490

MAGI   (CONTINUED)
    OF THE CROWNED MAGI: AND THE HOUND OF CU . . . . . .   169 SECRET ROSE   V   9
    OF THE CROWNED MAGI: AND THE KINGS WHOSE EYES . . . . . 169 SECRET ROSE   V   9
    THE MAGI . . . .   318 MAGI   T
MAGIC
    WERE'T NOT THAT THERE IS MAGIC IN HIS HARP, ... 222 SHADOW WATER B   16
    THAT THERE IS MAGIC IN THAT HARP OF HIS, ... 222 SHADOW WATER B   V   16
    A MAGIC THAT CAN CALL A DEMON UP, ... 238 SHADOW WATER B   344
    I WILL END ALL YOUR MAGIC ON THE INSTANT. . . . . 242 SHADOW WATER B   411
    BY MAGIC STRINGS, I'LL MAKE THIS ANSWER TO IT: . . . . 243 SHADOW WATER B   440
    MY MAGIC STRINGS, I'LL MAKE THIS ANSWER TO IT: . . . . 243 SHADOW WATER B   V 440
    IF YOU HAD TAKEN ME BY MAGIC SPELLS, ... 245 SHADOW WATER B   490
    WHAT MAGIC DRUM? . . . . 559 MAGIC DRUM   T
    THROUGH LIGHT-OBLITERATING GARDEN FOLIAGE WHAT MAGIC DRUM? 560 MAGIC DRUM   4
    TAKEN IN MAGIC, IN THE CHURCH'S NAME . . . . 694 MOSADA 1   104
    WITH PITILESS MAGIC HAS BOUND YOU-- . . . . 708 FAIRY PEDANT   31
    SO MEN IN LIFE AND I IN MAGIC PLAY: . . . . 722 WITCH VIVIEN   55
MAGICAL
    CHAUNT IN HIS EAR DELUSIONS MAGICAL, ... 111 CUCHULAIN SEA   80
    GO, CAST ON HIM DELUSIONS MAGICAL, ... 111 CUCHULAIN SEA   V   80
    THE MAGICAL POWERS TO AND FRO. . . . . 138 TO IRELAND   V   24
    MAGICAL SHAPES. BY THE HELP OF AN IMAGE . . . . 367 EGO DOMINUS   7
    OBEDIENT TO SOME HIDDEN MAGICAL BREATH. . . . . 382 VISION ROBART   13
    MAGICAL UNICORNS BEAR LADIES ON THEIR BACKS. . . . . . 426 PHANTOM HATRED   18
MAGICIAN
    OBEYS. SOME FIERCE MAGICIAN FLIES OR WALKS . . . . . 720 WITCH VIVIEN   9
MAGNANIMITIES
    THEIR MAGNANIMITIES OF SOUND, ... 404 FOR DAUGHTER   44
MAGNANIMITY
    THE STRENGTH THAT GIVES OUR BLOOD AND STATE MAGNANIMITY 481 BLOOD AND MOON   29
      . . .
    AS THOUGH WITH MAGNANIMITY OF LIGHT, ... 618 BRONZE HEAD   9
MAGNIFICENCE
    MONUMENTS OF ITS OWN MAGNIFICENCE: . . . . 407 SAIL BYZANTIUM   14
    LOWLY THE HEAD OF HIS MAGNIFICENCE . . . . 689 NETTLESHIP   6
    DOWN LOW THE HEAD OF HIS MAGNIFICENCE . . . . 689 NETTLESHIP   V   6
MAGNIFIED
    MY MEMORIES HAD MAGNIFIED . . . . 399 BREAK OF DAY   10
MAGNIFY
    CONSIDER MOST TO MAGNIFY, OR TO BLESS, ... 418 ANCEST HOUSES   39
MAGNITUDE
    THAT MADE THE MAGNITUDE AND GLORY THERE . . . . 483 VERONIC NAPKIN   5
MAGNUS
    OF MAGNUS ANNUS AT THE SPRING, ... 437 SONGS PLAY 1   7
MAHOGANY
    LIT UP THE DARK MAHOGANY AND THE WINE, ... 410 TOWER   27
MAHRAJAS
    OF RAJAS AND MAHRAJAS BEYOND NUMBER? . . . . 724 KANVA ON SELF   6
MAID   SEE WAITING-MAID SERVING-MAID
    AND NOW A MAID, ON A SWIFT BROWN STEED . . . .   12 OISIN 1   V 142
    MAID NIAM FROM A LITTLE TRUMP . . . . 14 OISIN 1   V 194
    AND KNELT THEM, EVERY MAID AND MAN, ... 15 OISIN 1   V 214
    THEY HUSHED THEM, EVERY MAN AND MAID. . . . . 17 OISIN 1   V 235
    WITH ONE LONG GLANCE ON MAID AND BOY . . . .   19 OISIN 1   V 287
    AROSE FROM EVERY MAID AND BOY, ...   20 OISIN 1   V 289
    HE SPAKE TO THE YOUNG MAN, "IS THERE NO MAID . . . . . 109 CUCHULAIN SEA   58
    THEN CONCHUBAR SENT THAT SWEET-THROATED MAID, ... 110 CUCHULAIN SEA   72
    THEN CONCOBAR SENT THAT SWEET THROATED MAID . . . . . . 110 CUCHULAIN SEA   V   72
    AND LIFT YOUR TENDER EYELIDS, MAID, ... 125 GOES FERGUS   5
    MAID QUIET . . . . 171 MAID QUIET   T
    WHERE HAS MAID QUIET GONE TO, ... 171 MAID QUIET   1
    I NEVER HAVE SEEN MAID QUIET . . . . 171 MAID QUIET   V   1
    NO WAITING MAID SHOULD EVER SPREAD . . . . 194 BAILE AILLINN   V 120
    A SERVING MAID AND A SERVING MAN, ... 301 RUN PARADISE   V   13
    AND EVERY MAN AND MAID AND BOY . . . . 337 TOM OROUGHLEY   2
    WHETHER TO MAID OR HAG: . . . . 525 DANCING DAYS   22
    "I AM SORRY," SAID THE MAID. . . . . 595 COLONEL MARTIN   29
    TWO MEN WHO LOVE ONE MAID HAVE AMPLE CAUSE . . . . . . 659 ISLE STAT II 1   30
    FOR THIS THING FIGHT--WE LOVE ONE MAID? HER NAME? . . . 661 ISLE STAT II 1   66
    THE PLAIN, A LITTLE FAIR-HAIRED MAID I LOVE. . . . . . 679 ISLE STAT II 3   312
    THERE DWELLS A LITTLE FAIR-HAIRED MAID I LOVE. . . . . 679 ISLE STAT II 3   V 312
    MY LORD, YOU CALLED? NOT I. THIS MAID IS DEAD. . . . . 704 MOSADA 3   125
    THEN EACH WIFE AND MAID AND MOTHER CALLS BY NAME   719 PHANTOM SHIP   24
      SOME DROWNED ONE.
    DO NOT FEAR US, EARTHLY MAID! . . . . 726 LOVERS QUARREL   1
    TEASING EVERY WILFUL MAID. . . . . 727 LOVERS QUARREL   28
MAIDEN
    A MAIDEN, ON A SLENDER STEED, ...   2 OISIN 1   V 7V
    "O PLEASANT MAIDEN," ANSWERED FINN. . . . .   5 OISIN 1   V   40
    NOW, PLEASANT MAIDEN, TELL TO ME . . . .   5 OISIN 1   V   43
    OF THE YOUNG. "YOUNG MAIDEN, WHAT MAY BRING . . . . .   5 OISIN 1   V   50
    AND NOW A MAIDEN RODE LIKE THE WIND . . . . 12 OISIN 1   V 142
    AND ONCE A MAIDEN BY MY SIDE . . . .   16 OISIN 1   V 231
    FULL MANY MORE, WHEN PEERED A MAIDEN SWEET . . . . . .   33 OISIN 2   V 68F
    A MAIDEN WITH SOFT EYES LIKE FUNERAL TAPERS, ...   33 OISIN 2   V   69
    OH MAIDEN." "ARE YE SPIRITS OF THE SEA, ...   34 OISIN 2   V 78B
    THAT MAIDEN FOUND A RING HUNG ON THE WALL, ...   37 OISIN 2   V 120
    AND AH, YOU PROUD MAIDEN, YOU ARE NOT SO FAIR WHEN HIS OAR 91 OLD FISHERMAN   9
    PROUD MAIDEN, YE ARE NOT SO FAIR, WHEN HIS OAR . . . .   91 OLD FISHERMAN   V   9
    NO MAIDEN LOVES ME, NO MAN SEEKS MY HELP, ...   103 FERGUS DRUID   V   26
    MAIDEN, COME FORTH: THE WOODS KEEP WATCH FOR THEE: . . 645 ISLE STAT I 1   1

491

	PAGE	TITLE		LINE
MAIDEN (CONTINUED)				
SLOW WATERS, AND THE BOAT AND MAIDEN SINK	663	ISLE STAT II 2		39
THAT MAIDEN BRING THEY. WHEN THE TALL RED DEER	713	FERENCZ RENYI		79
BUT SPEECHLESS, AND THE MAIDEN WITH LONG WAIL	713	FERENCZ RENYI		85
WHITE, RENYI SILENT STANDS; THAT MAIDEN SWEET	713	FERENCZ RENYI	V	84
OF MOSS, A MAIDEN WEAVING. SINGETH SHE!	716	DWELT SYCAMORE		12
AND, MAIDEN, BE THOU MIRTHFUL TOO, ...	736	SUMMER EVENING		13
MAIDEN'S				
AS SOME DEAD MAIDEN'S SINGING IN A DREAM.	654	ISLE STAT I 2		59
MAIDENS				
AND FEET OF MAIDENS DANCING IN TUNE, ...	3	OISIN 1	V	9
AND A HUNDRED MAIDENS WISE AND YOUNG, ...	8	OISIN 1	V	94
AND A HUNDRED MAIDENS, MERRY AS BIRDS, ...	9	OISIN 1	V	96
OF YOUTHS AND MAIDENS HAND IN HAND, ...	15	OISIN 1	V	202
OF MEN AND MAIDENS, HAND IN HAND, ...	15	OISIN 1	V	202
AND MEN AND MAIDENS KNELT THEM THERE	18	OISIN 1	V	255
AND, AH, YE PROUD MAIDENS, YE ARE NOT SO FAIR, WHEN HIS OAR	91	OLD FISHERMAN	V	9
MAIDS SEE WAITING-MAIDS				
WHERE AILLINN RODE WITH WAITING MAIDS	193	BAILE AILLINN	V	102
A LONG, BROWN GRASSHOPPER OF MAIDS! PEACE, SIR!	661	ISLE STAT II 1		69
A FASHION WITH US MOORISH MAIDS, BEGOT	700	MOSADA 3		25
MAIL				
OR CARRY THE RINGED MAIL UPON MY BACK, ...	463	HARUN RASHID		58
A COAT OF GILDED MAIL.	740	EARL PAUL		16
WITH A CLANG OF HIS DIM MAIL, ...	742	EARL PAUL		66
MAIL'D				
WHO SITS IN LONELY SPLENDOUR, MAIL'D IN GOLD, ...	651	ISLE STAT I 1		163
MAILED				
ERE FALL OF EVENING, MY MAILED HOST, ...	83	MAD KING GOLL	V	19
I DREW AT EVENING MY MAILED MEN, ...	83	MAD KING GOLL	V	19
MAIMED				
MAIMED US AT THE START.	506	REMORSE SPEECH		13
MAINE				
NOT I, NOR MAINE THERE, NOR DUACH'S SON.	748	SHADOW WATER A		22
EOCHA AND MAINE ARE ALWAYS QUARRELLING.	766	SHADOW WATER A		371
MAINES				
THE CHILDREN OF THE MAINES OUT OF SLEEP.	184	QUEEN MAEVE		92
QUEEN MAEVE'S NINE MAINES HAD BEEN NURSED, ...	302	HOUR DAWN		8
MAINES'				
THE MAINES' CHILDREN DROPPED THEIR SPADES, AND STOOD . .	185	QUEEN MAEVE		120
THE MAINES' CHILDREN HAVE NOT DROPPED THEIR SPADES . . .	186	QUEEN MAEVE		123
MAINLY				
MAINLY BECAUSE OF WHAT WE ONLY KNOW	634	CUCHULAIN COMF		14
MAIVE				
WHERE PASSIONATE MAIVE IS STONY STILL!	3	OISIN 1	V	18
O TATTERED CLOUDS OF THE WORLD, CALL FROM THE HIGH CAIRN	207	HANRAHANS SONG	V	6
OF MAIVE,				
MAJESTIC				
HIS MAJESTIC MOTHER SAT	440	WISDOM		11
MAJESTICAL				
WITH THE LONELY, MAJESTICAL MULTITUDE.	158	TO HIS HEART		7
WITH THE PROUD, MAJESTICAL MULTITUDE.	158	TO HIS HEART	V	7
WHERE RISE THE WALLS MAJESTICAL ABOVE	679	ISLE STAT II 3		311
MAJESTY				
THE MAJESTY THAT SHUTS HIS BURNING EYE!	265	THESE CLOUDS		2
THE MAJESTY THAT SHUTS HIS BURNING EYE.	265	THESE CLOUDS		12
WHO HAD UNNATURAL MAJESTY, AND EYES	283	TWO KINGS		149
AND THE GAUNT HOUSES PUT ON MAJESTY!	292	TO A SHADE		7
FALLEN MAJESTY	314	FALLEN MAJESTY		T
BABBLING OF FALLEN MAJESTY, RECORDS WHAT'S GONE.	314	FALLEN MAJESTY		4
MAJOR				
IN MEMORY OF MAJOR ROBERT GREGORY	323	ROBERT GREGORY		T
MAKE				
YET WILL I MAKE ALL PLAIN FOR THEE.	2	OISIN 1	V	7B
"AND I WILL MAKE A THOUSAND SONGS, ...	7	OISIN 1		75
I BELLOW TO THE WINDS WHEN STORMS MAKE MOAN, ...	45	OISIN 2	V	239D
AND MORE COMELY THAN MAN CAN MAKE THEM	49	OISIN 3		32
MORE COMELY THAN MAN MAY MAKE THEM, INLAID WITH SILVER .	49	OISIN 3	V	29
AND GOLD,				
MAKE CLEAN AS A BROOM CLEANS, ...	62	OISIN 3		211
"WHAT DO YOU MAKE SO FAIR AND BRIGHT?"	69	CLOAK BOAT		1
"I MAKE THE CLOAK OF SORROW!	69	CLOAK BOAT		2
MAKE THE HILLS REPLY."	98	FOXHUNTER		26
AND MAKE THE HILLS REPLY."	98	FOXHUNTER	V	26
MAKE THE HILLS REPLY."	99	FOXHUNTER		34
AND MAKE THE HILLS REPLY."	99	FOXHUNTER	V	34
AND SOFTLY MAKE A ROSY PEACE, ...	113	ROSE OF PEACE		15
AND WITH THE CLASHING OF THEIR SWORD-BLADES MAKE . . .	137	TO SOME I TALK		13
AND WITH THE CLANGING OF THEIR SWORD-BLADES MAKE . . .	137	TO SOME I TALK	V	13
AND WITH THE CLASHING OF THEIR SWORD BLADES MAKE . . .	137	TO SOME I TALK	V	13
IN DRUID VAPOUR AND MAKE THE TORCHES DIM!	169	SECRET ROSE		11
TO MAKE THE SAVAGE HEART OF LOVE	193	BAILE AILLINN		109
OF THE EBB OF ALL THINGS TO MAKE LOVE	193	BAILE AILLINN	V	109
MAKE THEIR FAINT THUNDER, AND THE GARDEN BEES	198	SEVEN WOODS		2
TIME CAN BUT MAKE IT EASIER TO BE WISE	200	FOLLY COMFORT		4
TIME CAN BUT MAKE HER BEAUTY OVER AGAIN!	200	FOLLY COMFORT		8
THE WATERS OF SLEEP CAN MAKE A CHATTERING TONGUE	218	WOODS OF COOLE		25
THESE DOZEN WEEKS. AND I HAD THOUGHT TO MAKE	222	SHADOW WATER B		4
TO MAKE AN END WHILE HE IS SLEEPING THERE.	222	SHADOW WATER B	V	14
TO MAKE AN END OF FORGAEL WHILE HE SLEEPS.	225	SHADOW WATER B		65
TO MAKE LOW LAUGHTER MORE THAN MEAT AND DRINK, ...	230	SHADOW WATER B		186

492

		PAGE	TITLE		LINE
MAKE	(CONTINUED)				
TO MAKE HER FAST WHILE WE ARE PLUNDERING HER.		232	SHADOW WATER B		225
BY MAGIC STRINGS, I'LL MAKE THIS ANSWER TO IT!		243	SHADOW WATER B		440
AND YET YOU MAKE A CLAMOUR OF REPROACH.		243	SHADOW WATER B		444
MY MAGIC STRINGS, I'LL MAKE THIS ANSWER TO IT!		243	SHADOW WATER B	V	440
WAS DONE TO MAKE IT PLAIN!		256	WORDS		8
NOTHING TO MAKE A SONG ABOUT BUT KINGS,		257	RECONCILIATION		5
"O NO, MY DEAR, YOU MAKE SO BOLD		263	MASK		3
"I BID THEM MAKE HIS BED UNDER THIS ROOF		280	TWO KINGS		87
THAT MAKE THE HEART AKIN TO THE DUMB STONE."		281	TWO KINGS		94
SHALL MAKE HER LOOK UPON HER HANDIWORK,		282	TWO KINGS		115
IMAGINES BEST TO MAKE IT THRIVE.		287	TO WEALTHY MAN		8
AND WHAT COULD MAKE THEIR MUSCLES TAUT		295	THREE BEGGARS		17
"AND MAKE MY SOUL BEFORE MY PATE IS BARE."		299	BEGGAR CRIED		4
REMINDED HIM THAT HE COULD MAKE,		302	HOUR DAWN		13
TO MAKE A CLATTER IN THE HOLE		304	HOUR DAWN	V	54
THE FORD WHERE DRINKING CATTLE MAKE A STIR		326	ROBERT GREGORY		53
THERE'S NOT A THING BUT LOVE CAN MAKE		333	SOLOMON SHEBA		23
COULD MAKE ME WISH FOR ANYTHING THIS DAY,		338	SHEP GOATHERD		3
AND MAKE THE DAYLIGHT SWEET ONCE MORE! BUT WHEN		339	SHEP GOATHERD		13
SOME MEDICABLE HERB TO MAKE OUR GRIEF		342	SHEP GOATHERD		86
OR WHO HAVE FOUND A PAINTER TO MAKE THEM SO FOR PAY		353	HIS PHOENIX		6
THERE'LL BE THAT CROWD TO MAKE MEN WILD THROUGH ALL THE CENTURIES,		354	HIS PHOENIX	V	25
AND MAY BE THERE'LL BE SOME YOUNG BELLE WALK OUT TO MAKE MEN WILD		354	HIS PHOENIX	V	26
AND MAYBE THERE'LL BE SOME YOUNG BELLE WALK OUT TO MAKE MEN WILD		354	HIS PHOENIX	V	26
SO GREAT HER PORTION IN THAT PEACE YOU MAKE		356	BROKEN DREAMS		12
BUT IMAGES TO MAKE ME FONDER?		390	IMAGE PAST		35
BECAUSE I HAVE NO OTHER YOUTH, CAN MAKE ME PINE!		391	UNDER SATURN		3
BEING A PORTION OF MY YOUTH, CAN MAKE ME PINE		391	UNDER SATURN	V	3
CAN MAKE A STONE OF THE HEART.		394	EASTER 1916		58
"TO MAKE THE GREEN COME OUT AGAIN		396	ROSE TREE		9
CAN MAKE A RIGHT ROSE TREE."		396	ROSE TREE		18
TO MAKE IT LINGER HALF A DAY.		401	DEMON BEAST		42
BEAUTY TO MAKE A STRANGER'S EYE DISTRAUGHT,		403	FOR DAUGHTER		18
BUT SUCH A FORM AS GRECIAN GOLDSMITHS MAKE		408	SAIL BYZANTIUM		27
FOR IF I TRIUMPH I MUST MAKE MEN MAD.		411	TOWER		56
NOW SHALL I MAKE MY SOUL,		416	TOWER		181
THAT WE MIGHT MAKE IT WHOLE!		457	SUMMER SPRING		8
WE THREE MAKE UP A SOLITUDE!		457	SECRETS OF OLD		9
FOR INTELLECT WOULD MAKE US PROUD		460	THREE MONUMENT		10
THAT MAKE A MAN'S SOUL OR A WOMAN'S SOUL		465	HARUN RASHID		93
MAKE HUMAN INTERCOURSE GROW LESS AND LESS!		473	ALL SOUL NIGHT		75
IF I MAKE THE LASHES DARK		531	BEFORE WORLD		1
THE KING THAT COULD MAKE HIS PEOPLE STARE,		550	SEVERED HEAD		19
WHERE CAN SHE LOOK UNTIL HE MAKE THE SHOW!		558	RIBH CHRISTIAN		22
WASH! MAKE YOUR BODY SWEET!		572	LADYS 2ND SONG		4
CAN MAKE THE TRUTH KNOWN,		575	ACRE OF GRASS		12
THAT CAN MAKE A CAT LAUGH, OR		589	OLD WICKED MAN		39
AND TOM MAKE OUT A LIVING		597	COLONEL MARTIN		70
THAT MAKE THE MUSES SING.		601	THOSE IMAGES		16
I SCRUB ITS FLOORS AND MAKE MY BED,		607	SONGS BURDEN 2		5
BRACE ME AND MAKE ME STRONG!		607	SONGS BURDEN 2		24
DIGGERS AND CARPENTERS MAKE GRAVE AND COFFIN!		609	IN TARAS HALLS		17
WITH NO MORE SOUND THAN THE MICE MAKE		618	LONG-LEG FLY		27
AND FINDS THERE NOTHING TO MAKE ITS TERROR LESS		618	BRONZE HEAD		6
BECAUSE PIEBALD PONIES, LED BEARS, CAGED LIONS, MAKE BUT POOR SHOWS,		623	HIGH TALK		5
WOULD NOT MAKE HIM A MAN.		628	JANE MOUNTAIN		4
"OBEY OUR ANCIENT RULE AND MAKE A SHROUD!		634	CUCHULAIN COMF		13
MAKE HIM FILL THE CRADLES RIGHT.		638	BEN BULBEN		41
ALAS! I MAKE YOU SADDER, SHEPHERDESS.		659	ISLE STAT II 1		18
MAKE MOAN AND CRY. WITHIN YON SUNLESS VALLEY,		682	SEEKER		26
TO MAKE US GLAD WITH WONDER AS WE SAT		683	SEEKER		41
AND FOR HIM MAKE ME WISE AND BRIGHT.		723	GIRLS SONG A		12
AND WHOM WILL YOU MAKE LEADER? WHO WILL MAKE		748	SHADOW WATER A		20
AND WHOM WILL YOU MAKE LEADER? WHO WILL MAKE		748	SHADOW WATER A		20
MAKE GALLEYS OUT OF WIND THAT CHANGE TO WIND		751	SHADOW WATER A		105
BECAUSE THESE WATERS MAKE ALL WOMEN ONE.		757	SHADOW WATER B		194
THEY WOULD MAKE A PRINCE DECAY		775	AGAINST WITCH		11
MAKER					
THE MAKER OF THE STARS AND WORLDS		724	LEGEND		1
THE MAKER OF THE STARS AND WORLDS		725	LEGEND		29
MAKER'S	SEE DOLL-MAKER'S				
MAKES					
AND MAKES THE INFANT FERNS UNWRAP,		18	OISIN 1		265
AND MAKES THE LITTLE PLANETS RUN!		18	OISIN 1		268
"'TIS JOY MAKES SWIM THE SAPPY TIDE,		18	OISIN 1	V	261
WHO HOLDS THE WORLD BETWEEN HIS BILL AND MAKES US STRONG OR WEAK		76	INDIAN ON GOD	V	6
A DANAAN FRUITAGE MAKES A SHOWER OF MOONS,		127	DREAM OF FAERY	V	22
THAT MAKES ME FEAR TO RAISE A HAND AGAINST HIM,		222	SHADOW WATER B	V	16A
BUT THE REALITY THAT MAKES OUR PASSION		229	SHADOW WATER B		159
DELIGHT MAKES ALL OF THE ONE MIND,		266	GALWAY RACES		2
WHAT MAKES YOUR HEART BEAT SO!		336	YOUNG GIRL		3
A CRAZY JUICE THAT MAKES THE PULSES BEAT		384	VISION ROBART		54
MAN MAKES A SUPERHUMAN		415	TOWER		164
MAN MAKES A SUPERMAN,		415	TOWER	V	164
IT MAKES MY PASSION STRONGER BUT TO THINK		465	HARUN RASHID		99

493

MAKES   (CONTINUED)
   THIS LOVE THAT MAKES MY HEART'S BLOOD STOP . . . . . .   499 MOTHER OF GOD   13
   AND MAKES MY HAIR STAND UP? . . . .   499 MOTHER OF GOD   V   15
   MY BODY MAKES NO MOAN . . . .   512 JANE ON GOD   22
   YOU ASK WHAT MAKES ME SIGH, OLD FRIEND, ...   524 MAD AS MIST   13
   WHAT MAKES ME SHUDDER SO? . . . .   524 MAD AS MIST   14
   FROM ALL THAT MAKES A WISE OLD MAN . . . .   553 PRAYER OLD AGE   5
   A JOURNALIST MAKES UP HIS LIES . . . .   598 STONE CROSS   3
   MAKES NO DEMAND. . . . .   600 SPIRIT MEDIUM   22
   MAKES ME SWEET MUSIC . . . .   627 STATES HOLIDAY   24
   THE RATTLE OF THOSE ARMS MAKES US AFRAID. . . . . .   634 CUCHULAIN COMF   15
   SO SMALL MAKES ONE GROW WEAK AND TOTTERING! . . . .   700 MOSADA 3   35
   OWLS THERE BE WHOM AGE MAKES NUMB; . . . .   727 LOVERS QUARREL   35
   THAT THE RED RUST MAKES DIM." . . . .   740 EARL PAUL   20
   THE WHITE FOOL MAKES AT MORNING OUT OF FOAM; . . . .   761 SHADOW WATER A   261
   WHERE THE MOON MAKES A CLOUDY LIGHT IN THE MIST. . . .   764 SHADOW WATER A   329
   WHAT MAKES HER HEART BEAT THUS, ...   785 YOUR HEART   V   1
   WHAT MAKES YOUR HEART SO BEAT? . . . .   786 YOUR HEART   27
MAKE-UP
   FOR PAINTED FORMS OR BOXES OF MAKE-UP . . . .   564 GYRES   13
MAKING   SEE LOVE-MAKING DEATH-MAKING PEACE-MAKING
   MAKING A WORLD ABOUT HER IN THE AIR, ...   37 OISIN 2   122
   MAKING A WORLD ABOUT HER, PASSED FROM SIGHT . . . . .   37 OISIN 2   V   123
   MAKING WAY FROM THE KINDLING SURGES, I RODE ON A   58 OISIN 3   161
     BRIDLE-PATH
   . . . THEY WILL RISE, MAKING CLOUDS WITH THEIR BREATH, . .   61 OISIN 3   202
   THEN FEAST, MAKING CONVERSE OF WARS, ...   62 OISIN 3   212
   THEN FEAST, MAKING CONVERSE OF EIRE, OF WARS, ...   62 OISIN 3   V   212
   THOUGH LADS ARE MAKING PIKES AGAIN . . . .   131 OLD PENSIONER   7
   MAKING ALL ONE O'ER ROCK AND SEA AND SKIES! . . . . .   687 TWO TITANS   28
   NOW MAKING BUSY WITH THE OAR, ...   742 DANAAN QUICK   2
MALACHI
   MALACHI STILT-JACK AM I, WHATEVER I LEARNED HAS RUN WILD,   623 HIGH TALK   9
   ALL METAPHOR, MALACHI, STILTS AND ALL. A BARNACLE GOOSE   623 HIGH TALK   11
MALEDICTION
   AND SANG MY MALEDICTION WITH THE REST. . . . . . .   537 HER VISION   24
MALICIOUS
   THERE ARE MALICIOUS THINGS, ALTHOUGH . . . .   435 FOR MY SON   V   10
   THE MIRROR OF MALICIOUS EYES . . . .   479 SELF AND SOUL   52
   BLENCHED BY THAT MALICIOUS DREAM . . . .   488 CRAZED MOON   16
   AND COCKED A MALICIOUS EYE, ...   527 AM OF IRELAND   25
MALIGN
   OF HIS DEATH AND CHANGE MALIGN. . . . .   648 ISLE STAT I 1   80
MALL
   THE MALL AND EADES'S GRAMMAR SCHOOL, ...   360 ALF POLLEXFEN   15
MALLET
   THAT WITH A MALLET OR A CHISEL MODELLED THESE . . . . .   610 STATUES   10
MAN   SEE SERVING-MAN TRAVELLING-MAN FANCY-MAN JOURNEY-MAN BEGGAR-MAN
   BEEN SPOKEN OF WITH ANY MAN! . . . .   6 OISIN 1   56
   OF OISIN, THE YOUNG MAN, MY SON? . . . .   6 OISIN 1   V   60
   BY THIS YOUNG MAN, USHEEN MY SON?" . . . .   6 OISIN 1   V   60
   PRINCESS, BY THIS YOUNG MAN, MY SON?" . . . .   6 OISIN 1   V   61
   ON THIS YOUNG MAN, OISIN, MY SON? . . . .   6 OISIN 1   V   61
   "I LOVED NO MAN, THOUGH KINGS BESOUGHT, ...   7 OISIN 1   62
   "I LOVED NO MAN, THOUGH CANNS BESOUGHT, ...   7 OISIN 1   V   62
   AND MANY A MAN OF LOFTY NAME, ...   7 OISIN 1   63
   AND A BEAUTIFUL YOUNG MAN FOLLOWED BEHIND . . . . . .   12 OISIN 1   144
   A BEAUTIFUL YOUNG MAN FOLLOWED BEHIND. . . . .   12 OISIN 1   V   145
   AND KNELT THERE, EVERY GIRL AND MAN, ...   15 OISIN 1   214
   AND KNELT THEM, EVERY MAID AND MAN, ...   15 OISIN 1   V   214
   A BEAUTIFUL YOUNG MAN DREAMED WITHIN . . . .   17 OISIN 1   248
   THEY HUSHED THEM, EVERY MAN AND MAID. . . . .   17 OISIN 1   V   235
   THERE WAS A WONDROUS YOUNG MAN SITTING. . . . . . .   18 OISIN 1   V   252
   WITH A CLEAR VOICE THE YOUNG MAN CRIED, ...   18 OISIN 1   V   260
   "AN OLD MAN STIRS THE FIRE TO A BLAZE, ...   26 OISIN 1   400
   NOW, MAN OF CROZIERS, SHADOWS CALLED OUR NAMES . . . .   29 OISIN 2   1
   AND HER BRIGHT BODY, SANG OF FAERY AND MAN . . . . .   29 OISIN 2   7
   NOW, MAN OF CROSIERS, PHANTOMS DREW AROUND . . . . .   29 OISIN 2   V   1
   AND HER BRIGHT BODY—NOW OF FAY AND MAN! . . . . . .   29 OISIN 2   V   7
   AND TELL ME THAT YOU FOUND A MAN UNBID, ...   33 OISIN 2   67
   AND MORE COMELY THAN MAN CAN MAKE THEM . . . . . .   49 OISIN 3   32
   MORE COMELY THAN MAN MAY MAKE THEM, INLAID WITH SILVER   49 OISIN 3   V   29
     AND GOLD,
   HAVE FACES ALIVE WITH SUCH BEAUTY BEEN KNOWN TO THE SALT   50 OISIN 3   51
     EYE OF MAN,
   ARE FACES ALIVE WITH SUCH BEAUTY MADE KNOWN TO THE SALT   50 OISIN 3   V   51
     EYE OF MAN,
   ARE FACES ALIVE WITH SUCH BEAUTY MADE KNOWN TO THE SOFT   50 OISIN 3   V   51
     EYE OF MAN,
   AND, MAN OF THE MANY WHITE CROZIERS, A CENTURY THERE I   52 OISIN 3   77
     FORGOT
   AND, MAN OF THE MANY WHITE CROZIERS, A CENTURY THERE I   52 OISIN 3   81
     FORGOT
  -BUT IN DREAMS, MILD MAN OF THE CROZIERS, ...   53 OISIN 3   85
   SO WATCHED I WHEN, MAN OF THE CROZIERS, ...   54 OISIN 3   101
   THAT ONCE MORE MOVED IN MY BOSOM THE ANCIENT SADNESS OF   54 OISIN 3   107
     MAN,
   CAME AFTER THE HARD GAZE OF YOUTH, OR AN OLD MAN LIFTED   59 OISIN 3   170
     HIS HEAD!
   THE REST YOU HAVE HEARD OF, O CROZIERED MAN! . . . . .   60 OISIN 3   189
   A CREEPING OLD MAN, FULL OF SLEEP, ...   60 OISIN 3   192

		PAGE	TITLE		LINE
MAN	(CONTINUED)				
. . . AN OLD MAN SURROUNDED WITH DREAMS.		61	OISIN 3		196
NO LIVE MAN GOES THITHER,		62	OISIN 3	V	214
. . . AND NO MAN MAY WAR WITH THE STRONG SPIRITS WAGE:		62	OISIN 3	V	214
IT WERE SAD TO GAZE ON THE BLESSED AND NO MAN I LOVED OF OLD THERE:		63	OISIN 3		221
IT WAS SAD TO GAZE ON THE BLESSED AND NO MAN I LOVED OF OLD THERE:		63	OISIN 3	V	221
THERE WAS A MAN WHOM SORROW NAMED HIS FRIEND,		67	SAD SHEPHERD		1
AND THEN THE MAN WHOM SORROW NAMED HIS FRIEND		68	SAD SHEPHERD		8
AND THEN THE MAN WHOM SORROW NAMED HIS FRIEND		68	SAD SHEPHERD		17
THEN CRIED THE MAN WHOM SORROW NAMED HIS FRIEND:		68	SAD SHEPHERD	V	8
FROM GIRL AND BOY AND MAN AND BEAST:		82	MAD KING GOLL	V	6
AND EVERY MUMBLING OLD MAN SAID,		82	MAD KING GOLL	V	9
AND EVERY WHISPERING OLD MAN SAID,		82	MAD KING GOLL	V	9
"THIS YOUNG MAN BRINGS THE AGE OF GOLD."		82	MAD KING GOLL	V	11
FOR HE WAS A MAN OF BOOKS.		93	FATHER OHART		24
MY MAN WAS A POOR FISHER		94	MOLL MAGEE		5
MY MAN GREW RED AND PALE,		95	MOLL MAGEE		22
SHE SAYS MY MAN WILL SURELY COME,		96	MOLL MAGEE		41
A THIN GREY MAN HALF LOST IN GATHERING NIGHT.		102	FERGUS DRUID		7
A THIN, GREY MAN, HALF-LOST IN GATHERING NIGHT.		102	FERGUS DRUID	V	7
NO WOMAN'S LOVED ME, NO MAN SOUGHT MY HELP.		103	FERGUS DRUID		26
NO MAIDEN LOVES ME, NO MAN SEEKS MY HELP,		103	FERGUS DRUID	V	26
NO WOMAN LOVES ME, NO MAN SEEKS MY HELP,		103	FERGUS DRUID	V	26
A MAN CAME SLOWLY FROM THE SETTING SUN,		105	CUCHULAIN SEA		1
"NO MAN ALIVE, NO MAN AMONG THE DEAD,		106	CUCHULAIN SEA		10
"NO MAN ALIVE, NO MAN AMONG THE DEAD,		106	CUCHULAIN SEA		10
BUT WHEREFORE NOW?" "THERE IS A MAN TO DIE:		107	CUCHULAIN SEA		23
"BUT YOU HAVE GROWN TO BE THE TALLER MAN."		107	CUCHULAIN SEA		27
"HE IS THE MIGHTIEST MAN IN SHIP OR DUN."		107	CUCHULAIN SEA	V	28
SOME FEASTING MAN THAT THE SAME OATH HAS BOUND."		108	CUCHULAIN SEA		38
SOME FEATING MAN THAT THE SAME OATH HAS BOUND."		108	CUCHULAIN SEA	V	38
AT LAST CUCHULAIN SPAKE, "SOME MAN HAS MADE		109	CUCHULAIN SEA		47
SEEK OUT WHAT MAN HE IS." ONE WENT AND CAME.		109	CUCHULAIN SEA		51
SOME FEASTING MAN THAT THE SAME OATH HAS BOUND."		109	CUCHULAIN SEA		54
CUCHULAIN CRIED, "I AM THE ONLY MAN		109	CUCHULAIN SEA		55
HE SPAKE TO THE YOUNG MAN, "IS THERE NO MAID		109	CUCHULAIN SEA		58
AT LAST CUCHULAIN SPAKE, "A YOUNG MAN STRAYS		109	CUCHULAIN SEA	V	47
"SOME FEATING MAN THAT THE SAME OATH HAS BOUND."		109	CUCHULAIN SEA	V	54
BUT ONE MAN LOVED THE PILGRIM SOUL IN YOU,		121	YOU ARE OLD		7
MAN HAD NO MORE TO DO—		123	DREAM OF DEATH	V	8
YOUNG MAN, LIFT UP YOUR RUSSET BROW,		125	GOES FERGUS		4
THE MAN WHO DREAMED OF FAERYLAND		126	DREAM OF FAERY		T
A MAN WHO DREAMED OF FAIRYLAND		126	DREAM OF FAERY	V	T
BUT WHEN A MAN POURED FISH INTO A PILE,		126	DREAM OF FAERY		5
NOW THAT THE EARTH HAD TAKEN MAN AND ALL:		128	DREAM OF FAERY		40
THE MAN HAS FOUND NO COMFORT IN THE GRAVE.		128	DREAM OF FAERY		48
NOW THAT OLD EARTH HAD TAKEN MAN AND ALL:		128	DREAM OF FAERY	V	40
THAT COUNTRY WHERE A MAN CAN BE SO CROSSED:		130	BOOK STORIES		16
THAT HE'S A LOVELESS MAN: GAY BELLS BRING LAUGHTER		130	BOOK STORIES		18
ANOTHER POOR MAN SENT FOR HIM,		132	FR GILLIGAN		7
"MAVRONE, MAVRONE: THE MAN HAS DIED		133	FR GILLIGAN		25
"AND IS THE POOR MAN DEAD?" HE CRIED.		133	FR GILLIGAN		33
"OCHONE, OCHONE: THE MAN HAS DIED,		133	FR GILLIGAN	V	25
THAT GOD GIVES UNTO MAN IN SLEEP.		138	TO IRELAND	V	22
MAN EVER JOURNEYS ON WITH THEM		139	TO IRELAND		29
AND A YOUNG MAN BROUGHT HIM RED WINE		144	HOST OF AIR		19
THE HANDSOMEST YOUNG MAN THERE,		145	HOST OF AIR		34
THE DESIRE OF MAN AND OF WOMAN.		153	CHANGE BELOVED	V	T
A MAN WITH A HAZEL WAND CAME WITHOUT SOUND:		153	CHANGE BELOVED	V	6
A MAN WITH A WAND OF HAZEL CAME WITHOUT SOUND:		153	CHANGE BELOVED	V	6
I BECAME A MAN, A HATER OF THE WIND,		177	PAST GREATNESS		7
THEY FOUND AN OLD MAN RUNNING THERE:		190	BAILE AILLINN		25
AN OLD MAN CAUGHT THE HORSE'S HEAD		191	BAILE AILLINN		57
A YOUNG MAN CRIED AND KISSED HER HAND,		191	BAILE AILLINN		60
REMEMBER DEIRDRE AND HER MAN:		192	BAILE AILLINN		91
THAT OLD MAN CLIMBED: THE DAY GREW DIM:		194	BAILE AILLINN		134
FOR THIS YOUNG GIRL AND THIS YOUNG MAN		195	BAILE AILLINN		157
THERE'S NO MAN MAY LOOK UPON HER, NO MAN,		199	ARROW		3
THERE'S NO MAN MAY LOOK UPON HER, NO MAN,		199	ARROW		3
AN OLD MAN PLAYS THE BAGPIPES		214	HAPPY TOWNLAND		9
A BEAUTIFUL YOUNG MAN AND GIRL CAME UP		223	SHADOW WATER B		33
HAS HATED EVERY MAN THAT'S NOT IN LOVE,		224	SHADOW WATER B		51
THERE'S NOT A MAN BUT WILL BE GLAD OF IT		225	SHADOW WATER B		66
HAS BEAUTIFUL WOMEN TO PLEASE EVERY MAN.		228	SHADOW WATER B		144
THAT EVERY MAN SHOULD CARRY HIS OWN SOUL		235	SHADOW WATER B		299
WE'LL PUT THIS MAN TO DEATH. I PROMISE IT.		238	SHADOW WATER B		363
WHEN I HAVE SAID FAREWELL TO THIS MAN HERE,		250	SHADOW WATER B		587
FOR NEITHER I NOR ANY LIVING MAN		250	SHADOW WATER B		588
IF ANY MAN DREW NEAR		254	WOMAN HOMER		1
"GO AND LOVE, GO AND LOVE, YOUNG MAN,		268	BROWN PENNY		5
YOU MOST OF ALL, SILENT AND FIERCE OLD MAN,		270	PARDON FATHERS		15
"COME OUT AND DIG FOR A DEAD MAN,		272	GREY ROCK		32
THE SHOUTING OF AN UNSEEN MAN:		274	GREY ROCK		76
WHERE BY OLD THORN-TREES THAT MAN STOOD:		274	GREY ROCK		80
THEREON A YOUNG MAN MET HIS EYE,		274	GREY ROCK		85
NO MAN SHOULD SEE TO DO ME HURT:		274	GREY ROCK		91
WHERE BY OLD THORN TREES THAT MAN STOOD:		274	GREY ROCK	V	80
"HE LIVES?" "HE LIVES AND IS A HEALTHY MAN."		280	TWO KINGS		84
WHAT MAN YOU HAVE LOST, WHAT EVIL YOU HAVE FOUND."		280	TWO KINGS		86

MAN   (CONTINUED)

	PAGE	TITLE	LINE
AS ON THE BLUE LIGHT OF A SWORD, A MAN	283	TWO KINGS	148
BEING WEARIED OUT, I LOVE IN MAN THE CHILD?	285	TWO KINGS	192
GIVING HIS HAND TO THAT MAN AND TO THIS,	286	TWO KINGS V	218A
TO A WEALTHY MAN WHO PROMISED A SECOND SUBSCRIPTION	287	TO WEALTHY MAN	T
FOR THEY ARE AT THEIR OLD TRICKS YET. A MAN	292	TO A SHADE	9
WHOM MAN OR DEVIL CANNOT TIRE,	295	THREE BEGGARS	16
ONE OF YOU THREE IS A RICH MAN,	295	THREE BEGGARS	21
A SERVING MAID AND A SERVING MAN,	301	RUN PARADISE V	13
A ONE-LEGGED, ONE-ARMED, ONE-EYED MAN	302	HOUR DAWN	1
BUT I'LL HAVE NO MAN CALL ME GHOST."	304	HOUR DAWN	41
"IT'S PLAIN THAT YOU ARE NO RIGHT MAN	306	HOUR DAWN	82
AND THERE'S NO MAN BUT COCKS HIS EAR	306	HOUR DAWN	99
THERE'S NOT A MAN CAN REPORT	319	DOLLS	8
THE MAN AND THE WOMAN BRING	319	DOLLS	10
AND THAT ENQUIRING MAN JOHN SYNGE COMES NEXT,	324	ROBERT GREGORY	25
OUR SIDNEY AND OUR PERFECT MAN,	325	ROBERT GREGORY	47
NOR PUBLIC MAN, NOR ANGRY CROWDS,	328	IRISH AIRMAN	10
NOR PUBLIC MAN, NOR CHEERING CROWDS,	328	IRISH AIRMAN V	10
"THERE'S NOT A MAN OR WOMAN	333	SOLOMON SHEBA	19
ALL KNOW THE MAN THEIR NEIGHBOUR KNOWS.	337	SCHOLARS	10
AND EVERY MAN AND MAID AND BOY	337	TOM OROUGHLEY	2
NO SETTLED MAN. AND NOW THAT HE IS GONE	341	SHEP GOATHERD	55
HE CAME, BUT MAN IS A FOOL."	341	SHEP GOATHERD	74
I HEARD HIM FIRST, BUT MAN IS A FOOL."	341	SHEP GOATHERD V	74
HEARING IT NOW HAVE SIGHED FOR THAT YOUNG MAN	342	SHEP GOATHERD	77
A MAN MAY FIND IN NO MAN	345	ON WOMAN	3
A MAN MAY FIND IN NO MAN	345	ON WOMAN	3
THE FRECKLED MAN WHO GOES	347	FISHERMAN	2
THIS WISE AND SIMPLE MAN.	347	FISHERMAN	8
THE DEAD MAN THAT I LOVED,	347	FISHERMAN	14
THE CRAVEN MAN IN HIS SEAT,	347	FISHERMAN	15
THE WITTY MAN AND HIS JOKE	347	FISHERMAN	19
THE CLEVER MAN WHO CRIES	347	FISHERMAN	21
IMAGINING A MAN,	348	FISHERMAN	28
A MAN WHO DOES NOT EXIST,	348	FISHERMAN	35
A MAN WHO IS BUT A DREAM;	348	FISHERMAN	36
AS A MAN DOES WHO HAS PUBLISHED A NEW BOOK,	350	HER PRAISE	3
A MAN CONFUSEDLY IN A HALF DREAM	351	HER PRAISE	8
A MAN--SO VAGUELY THAT HE SEEMED TO DREAM--	351	HER PRAISE V	8
A YOUNG MAN WHEN THE OLD MEN ARE DONE TALKING	356	BROKEN DREAMS	16
WILL SAY TO AN OLD MAN, "TELL ME OF THAT LADY	356	BROKEN DREAMS	17
THAT NEVER LOOKED UPON MAN WITH DESIRE,	358	PRESENCES	13
OR AN OLD MAN UPON A WINTER'S NIGHT.	359	WAR POEM	6
UPON A MELANCHOLY MAN	360	ALF POLLEXFEN	11
A HUMOROUS, UNAMBITIOUS MAN,	361	ALF POLLEXFEN	25
LAMENTING THAT A MAN SHOULD DIE;	361	ALF POLLEXFEN	38
THE MAN THAT LAPO AND THAT GUIDO KNEW?	368	EGO DOMINUS	26
THE MOST EXALTED LADY LOVED BY A MAN.	369	EGO DOMINUS	37
AN OLD MAN COCKED HIS EAR UPON A BRIDGE;	372	PHASES OF MOON	1
WERE DISTANT STILL. AN OLD MAN COCKED HIS EAR.	372	PHASES OF MOON	7
WERE DISTANT. AN OLD MAN COCKED HIS EAR.	372	PHASES OF MOON V	7
THE CRADLES THAT A MAN MUST NEEDS BE ROCKED IN;	373	PHASES OF MOON	34
BUT SUMMONS TO ADVENTURE AND THE MAN	373	PHASES OF MOON	37
AHERNE LAUGHED, THINKING OF THE MAN WITHIN,	375	PHASES OF MOON	85
REFORMER, MERCHANT, STATESMAN, LEARNED MAN,	376	PHASES OF MOON	98
BUT TAKE ME FOR SOME DRUNKEN COUNTRY MAN;	377	PHASES OF MOON V	130
A MAN THAT FINDS GREAT BITTERNESS	379	SAINT HUNCH	2
UNDER THIS HUMP. GOD TRIES EACH MAN	379	SAINT HUNCH	5
THE PARTICULAR IS POUNDED TILL IT IS MAN.	382	VISION ROBART	6
LEARNED LIKE A MAN? PAUL VERONESE	386	ROBARTES DANCE	26
GIVE MAN HIS THOUGHT OR HIS MERE BODY?	386	ROBARTES DANCE	40
YOU HEARD THAT LABOURING MAN WHO HAD SERVED MY PEOPLE. HE SAID	391	UNDER SATURN	11
THIS MAN HAD KEPT A SCHOOL	392	EASTER 1916	24
THIS MAN HAD MANAGED A SCHOOL	392	EASTER 1916 V	24
THIS OTHER MAN I HAD DREAMED	393	EASTER 1916	31
A SHAPE WITH LION BODY AND THE HEAD OF A MAN,	402	SECOND COMING	14
YET CHOSE A BANDY-LEGGED SMITH FOR MAN.	404	FOR DAUGHTER	29
AND MANY A POOR MAN THAT HAS ROVED,	404	FOR DAUGHTER	38
AN AGED MAN IS BUT A PALTRY THING,	407	SAIL BYZANTIUM	9
A SERVING MAN THAT COULD DIVINE	410	TOWER V	28
STRANGE, BUT THE MAN WHO MADE THE SONG WAS BLIND;	411	TOWER	49
WITH HOMER THAT WAS A BLIND MAN,	411	TOWER	52
I MUST RECALL A MAN THAT NEITHER LOVE	412	TOWER	74
COME OLD, NECESSITOUS, HALF-MOUNTED MAN;	412	TOWER	90
THE RED MAN THE JUGGLER SENT	412	TOWER	92
THE MAN DROWNED IN A BOG'S MIRE,	413	TOWER	95
TILL MAN MADE UP THE WHOLE,	415	TOWER	149
MAN MAKES A SUPERHUMAN	415	TOWER	164
MAN MAKES A SUPERMAN;	415	TOWER V	164
SOME VIOLENT BITTER MAN, SOME POWERFUL MAN	418	ANCEST HOUSES	17
SOME VIOLENT BITTER MAN, SOME POWERFUL MAN	418	ANCEST HOUSES	17
AND LEAVE A WOMAN AND A MAN BEHIND	422	MY DESCENDANTS	3
TO LEAVE A WOMAN AND A MAN BEHIND	422	MY DESCENDANTS V	3
A HEAVILY-BUILT FALSTAFFIAN MAN,	423	ROAD AT DOOR	2
A HEAVILY BUILT FALSTAFFIAN MAN,	423	ROAD AT DOOR V	2
A MAN IS KILLED, OR A HOUSE BURNED,	425	STARES NEST	8
SUFFICE THE AGEING MAN AS ONCE THE GROWING BOY.	427	PHANTOM HATRED	40
MAN IS IN LOVE AND LOVES WHAT VANISHES,	429	NINETEEN 19	42
A MAN IN HIS OWN SECRET MEDITATION	431	NINETEEN 19	69

MAN   (CONTINUED)

		PAGE	TITLE		LINE
A WOMAN AND A MAN,		436	FOR MY SON		27
EVERYTHING THAT MAN ESTEEMS		438	SONGS PLAY 2		9
A SIXTY-YEAR-OLD SMILING PUBLIC MAN.		443	SCHOOL CHILDR		8
A SIXTY YEAR OLD SMILING PUBLIC MAN.		443	SCHOOL CHILDR	V	8
O LET HER CHOOSE A YOUNG MAN NOW AND ALL FOR HIS		450	OWEN AHERNE		24
WILD SAKE."					
A MAN YOUNG AND OLD FIRST LOVE		451	FIRST LOVE	V	T
A CRAZY MAN THAT FOUND A CUP,		454	EMPTY CUP		1
AND WAS A PUSHING MAN		456	FRIENDS YOUTH		14
HOW SUCH A MAN PLEASED WOMEN MOST		458	SECRETS OF OLD		13
HOW SUCH A MAN HAD PLEASURED MOST		458	SECRETS OF OLD	V	13
FOR THAT IS NATURAL TO A MAN		459	HIS WILDNESS		9
CEASE TO REMEMBER THE DELIGHTS OF YOUTH, TRAVEL-WEARIED		459	FROM OEDIPUS		2
AGED MAN:					
THE PARCHMENT WILL DISCLOSE TO SOME LEARNED MAN		461	HARUN RASHID		20
SHE SEEMED THE LEARNED MAN AND I THE CHILD:		467	HARUN RASHID		137
CAN HEAR THE ARMED MAN SPEAK.		470	HARUN RASHID		193
THAT STORMS ARE SHAKING, HEAR THE ARMED MAN SPEAK.		470	HARUN RASHID	V	193
NO LIVING MAN CAN DRINK FROM THE WHOLE WINE.		474	ALL SOUL NIGHT		85
A MAN AWAITS HIS END		476	DEATH		3
A GREAT MAN IN HIS PRIDE		476	DEATH		7
MAN HAS CREATED DEATH.		476	DEATH		12
WHY SHOULD THE IMAGINATION OF A MAN		477	SELF AND SOUL		17
THAT MAN IS STRICKEN DEAF AND DUMB AND BLIND,		478	SELF AND SOUL		35
A LIVING MAN IS BLIND AND DRINKS HIS DROP.		478	SELF AND SOUL		41
THAT MAN IS DEAF AND DRUNK AND BLIND		478	SELF AND SOUL	V	35
WHAT MATTER IF A BLIND MAN DRINK HIS DROP?		478	SELF AND SOUL	V	41
OF BOYHOOD CHANGING INTO MAN:		479	SELF AND SOUL		46
THE UNFINISHED MAN AND HIS PAIN		479	SELF AND SOUL		47
THE FINISHED MAN AMONG HIS ENEMIES?--		479	SELF AND SOUL		49
A BLIND MAN BATTERING BLIND MEN:		479	SELF AND SOUL		60
THE FOLLY THAT MAN DOES		479	SELF AND SOUL		62
FOR ALL HIS TIMID HEART, THERE THAT SLOW MAN		489	COOLE PARK 29		12
THAT MEDITATIVE MAN, JOHN SYNGE, AND THOSE		489	COOLE PARK 29		13
AND IN THE MORNING'S GONE, NO MAN KNOWS WHY:		490	COOLE BALLYLEE		20
MAN SHIFTS ABOUT--ALL THAT GREAT GLORY SPENT--		491	COOLE BALLYLEE	V	39
THE INTELLECT OF MAN IS FORCED TO CHOOSE		491	COOLE BALLYLEE	V	40A
THE MIND OF MAN OR ELEVATE A RHYME:		492	COOLE BALLYLEE		45
"NEVER SHALL A YOUNG MAN,		492	ANNE GREGORY		1
"I HEARD AN OLD RELIGIOUS MAN		492	ANNE GREGORY		13
THE INTELLECT OF MAN IS FORCED TO CHOOSE		495	CHOICE		1
ALL THAT MAN IS,		497	BYZANTIUM		6
BEFORE ME FLOATS AN IMAGE, MAN OR SHADE,		497	BYZANTIUM		9
SHADE MORE THAN MAN, MORE IMAGE THAN A SHADE:		497	BYZANTIUM		10
MAN RUNS HIS COURSE:		499	VACILLATION		2
ALL WOMEN DOTE UPON AN IDLE MAN		500	VACILLATION		23
NO MAN HAS EVER LIVED THAT HAD ENOUGH		500	VACILLATION		25
I SAT, A SOLITARY MAN,		501	VACILLATION		36
ISAIAH'S COAL, WHAT MORE CAN MAN DESIRE?		502	VACILLATION		74
EZEKIEL'S COAL, WHAT MORE CAN MAN DESIRE?		502	VACILLATION	V	74
DID I BECOME A CHRISTIAN MAN AND CHOOSE FOR MY BELIEF		503	VACILLATION		85
SENSE THAN A COMMON MAN?		507	STREAM AND SUN		10
THE SOLID MAN AND THE COXCOMB.		508	JANE BISHOP		7
THE SOLID MAN AND THE COXCOMB.		508	JANE BISHOP		14
THE SOLID MAN AND THE COXCOMB.		508	JANE BISHOP		21
THE SOLID MAN AND THE COXCOMB.		509	JANE BISHOP		28
MY FANCY ON A MAN,		515	GIRLS SONG B		3
SAW I AN OLD MAN YOUNG		515	GIRLS SONG B		11
OR YOUNG MAN OLD?		515	GIRLS SONG B		12
OR A YOUNG MAN OLD?		515	GIRLS SONG B	V	12
"A MAN IF I BUT HELD HIM SO		521	THREE THINGS		9
FACE TO FACE MY RIGHTFUL MAN		521	THREE THINGS		16
A MAN MAY PUT PRETENCE AWAY		525	DANCING DAYS		19
ONE MAN, ONE MAN ALONE		526	AM OF IRELAND		6
ONE MAN, ONE MAN ALONE		526	AM OF IRELAND		6
ONE SOLITARY MAN		526	AM OF IRELAND		8
ONE MAN, AND ONE MAN ALONE		526	AM OF IRELAND	V	6
ONE MAN, AND ONE MAN ALONE		526	AM OF IRELAND	V	6
BIRD, BEAST, FISH OR MAN,		529	TOM LUNATIC		14
BEING MENTIONED WITH A MAN		531	FATHER CHILD		4
WHAT IF I LOOK UPON A MAN		532	BEFORE WORLD		9
WHERE MAN IS COMFORTED.		534	CONSOLATION		6
MY UTMOST PLEASURE WITH A MAN		535	CHOSEN		12
SHOULDERED A LITTER WITH A WOUNDED MAN,		537	HER VISION		14
THAT SUCH AS I HAD SUCH A MAN		539	MEETING		9
SUCH A MAN THE MOST."		539	MEETING		12
THE RICH MAN AND HIS AFFAIRS,		540	FROM ANTIGONE		3
WHETHER IT BE AN ANIMAL OR A MAN.		542	PARN FUNERAL 1		31
"ON, ON, MY DARLING MAN".		545	TO SAME TUNE 1		16
"WHO'D CARE TO DIG 'EM," SAID THE OLD, OLD MAN,		548	TO SAME TUNE 3		7
TIME I WERE BURIED." SAID THE OLD, OLD MAN.		548	TO SAME TUNE 3		10
"WHO'D CARE TO DIG 'EM," SAID THE OLD, OLD MAN,		548	TO SAME TUNE 3		17
TIME I WERE BURIED," SAID THE OLD, OLD MAN.		548	TO SAME TUNE 3		20
"WHO'D CARE TO DIG 'EM," SAID THE OLD, OLD MAN,		549	TO SAME TUNE 3		27
TIME I WERE BURIED," SAID THE OLD, OLD MAN.		549	TO SAME TUNE 3		30
SADDLE AND RIDE, I HEARD A MAN SAY,		549	SEVERED HEAD		1
IMAGES RIDE, I HEARD A MAN SAY,		549	SEVERED HEAD	V	1
THAT SEEMED BUT A WILD WENCHING MAN:		550	SEVERED HEAD		16
WHAT IS THE GOOD OF A MAN AND HE		551	SONGS REWRIT 1		7
WHAT IS THE GOOD OF A MAN IF HE		551	SONGS REWRIT 1	V	7

497

OR ANYTHING ELSE BUT A MAN	552 SONGS REWRIT 2 V	9
FROM ALL THAT MAKES A WISE OLD MAN	553 PRAYER OLD AGE	5
A FOOLISH, PASSIONATE MAN.	553 PRAYER OLD AGE	12
AN ABSTRACT GREEK ABSURDITY HAS CRAZED THE MAN--	556 RIBH PATRICK	1
. . . MAN, WOMAN, CHILD (A DAUGHTER OR A SON),	556 RIBH PATRICK	2
AS MAN, AS BEAST, AS AN EPHEMERAL FLY BEGETS, GODHEAD BEGETS GODHEAD,	556 RIBH PATRICK	5
ABSTRACTIONS OF THE GREEK PHILOSOPHY HAVE CRAZED THE MAN,	556 RIBH PATRICK V	1
WHY DO I HATE MAN, WOMAN OR EVENT?	558 RIBH CHRISTIAN	7
A PASSION-DRIVEN EXULTANT MAN SINGS OUT	560 WHENCE COME	5
THE FOUR AGES OF MAN	561 FOUR AGES MAN	T
SEVENTY YEARS MAN AND BOY,	567 FROM JAPANESE	8
NO RAGGED BEGGAR MAN,	567 FROM JAPANESE V	6
I SHOULD BE BLAMED, YOUNG MAN.	569 THREE BUSHES	6
"I LOVE A MAN IN SECRET,	569 THREE BUSHES	15
DID EVER MAN RIDE SUCH A RACE?	570 THREE BUSHES	47
AND O HE WAS A GOOD MAN	571 THREE BUSHES	68
BESIDE HER LADY'S MAN,	571 THREE BUSHES	72
WHAT SORT OF MAN IS COMING	572 LADYS 2ND SONG	1
HE MUST GROW A FAMOUS MAN!	576 WHAT THEN	2
AND WHETHER A MAN BE RICH OR POOR	582 ROGER CASEMENT V	19
FOUND MANY A FAMOUS MAN THERE!	584 GHOST ROG CASE	35
BUT FOR WHAT SOME TRAVELLING MAN	585 ORAHILLY	21
AND PRAISE OUR CHOSEN MAN!	586 PARNELLITES	2
EVERY MAN THAT SINGS A SONG	586 PARNELLITES	19
FOR PARNELL WAS A PROUD MAN,	587 PARNELLITES	21
AND A PROUD MAN'S A LOVELY MAN,	587 PARNELLITES	23
THE WILD OLD WICKED MAN	587 OLD WICKED MAN	T
SAID THAT WILD OLD WICKED MAN	587 OLD WICKED MAN	3
FROM THE OLD MAN IN THE SKIES.	588 OLD WICKED MAN	8
I HAVE WHAT NO YOUNG MAN CAN HAVE	588 OLD WICKED MAN	14
THEN SAID SHE TO THAT WILD OLD MAN,	588 OLD WICKED MAN	19
I GAVE IT ALL TO AN OLDER MAN!	588 OLD WICKED MAN	23
THAT OLD MAN IN THE SKIES.	588 OLD WICKED MAN	24
"A YOUNG MAN IN THE DARK AM I,	589 OLD WICKED MAN	37
BUT A WILD OLD MAN IN THE LIGHT,	589 OLD WICKED MAN	38
FROM THE OLD MAN IN THE SKIES	589 OLD WICKED MAN	56
NO RIGHT-TAUGHT MAN DENIES.	590 OLD WICKED MAN	58
BUT A COARSE OLD MAN AM I,	590 OLD WICKED MAN	59
NO RIGHT TAUGHT MAN DENIES.	590 OLD WICKED MAN V	58
PARNELL CAME DOWN THE ROAD, HE SAID TO A CHEERING MAN!	590 PARNELL	1
THAT I MAY STAY A SOBER MAN	591 DRUNK SOBRIETY	3
A DEAD MAN IN HIS GRAVE.	592 DRUNK SOBRIETY	12
A DRUNKARD IS A DEAD MAN,	592 DRUNK SOBRIETY	15
AND THERE I FOUND AN OLD MAN, AND THOUGH I PRAYED ALL DAY	593 PILGRIM	8
AND THAT OLD MAN BESIDE ME: NOTHING WOULD HE SAY	593 PILGRIM	9
AND COME WITH LEARNED LOVERS OR WITH WHAT MAN YOU MAY,	593 PILGRIM V	23
"O WHAT'S A WIFELESS MAN?" SAID HE,	594 COLONEL MARTIN	5
AND O HE WAS A CLEVER MAN,	595 COLONEL MARTIN	39
HIS WIFE HE FOUND AND THE RICH MAN	595 COLONEL MARTIN	43
THE COLONEL SAID TO TOM HIS MAN,	596 COLONEL MARTIN	50
A MAN WITH A PISTOL STOOD.	596 COLONEL MARTIN	56
AND THE RICH MAN HAD PAID THEM WELL	596 COLONEL MARTIN	57
THAT THEY COULD NEVER SHOOT A MAN	596 COLONEL MARTIN	61
FOR THINGS LIKE THESE WHAT DECENT MAN	598 MODEL LAUREATE	22
A STATESMAN IS AN EASY MAN,	598 STONE CROSS	1
SAID THE MAN IN THE GOLDEN BREASTPLATE	598 STONE CROSS	7
NO MAN CAN KNOW A HAPPY MAN	598 STONE CROSS	11
NO MAN CAN KNOW A HAPPY MAN	598 STONE CROSS	11
NO MAN KNOWS WHICH IS WHICH,	598 STONE CROSS	14
SAID THE MAN IN THE GOLDEN BREASTPLATE	599 STONE CROSS	15
SAID THE MAN IN THE GOLDEN BREASTPLATE	599 STONE CROSS	23
SAID THE OLD MAN IN THE GOLDEN BREASTPLATE	599 STONE CROSS V	23
AND HERE'S JOHN SYNGE HIMSELF, THAT ROOTED MAN,	603 GALLERY REVIS	48
AND HERE'S JOHN SYNGE, A MEDITATIVE MAN,	603 GALLERY REVIS V	48
A GOOD MAN ON A HORSE,	604 YOU CONTENT	12
SANDYMOUNT CORBETS, THAT NOTABLE MAN	604 YOU CONTENT	13
BEST PLEASE A WANDERING MAN.	606 SONGS BURDEN 1	17
PRAISE EVERY MAN THAT CAME AGAIN,	608 SONGS BURDEN 3	7
PRAISE EVERY MAN THAT FELL.	608 SONGS BURDEN 3	8
WHO WAS THE FIRST MAN SHOT THAT DAY?	608 SONGS BURDEN 3	10
A MAN I PRAISE THAT ONCE IN TARA'S HALLS	609 IN TARAS HALLS	1
I SHALL BE OLD INDEED." THEREON THE MAN	609 IN TARAS HALLS	10
AND NO MAN KNOWS WHAT TREADS THE GRASS.	614 MARCH SONGS 2	10
AND NO MAN KNOWS WHAT TREADS THE GRASS.	615 MARCH SONGS 2	20
AND NO MAN KNOWS WHAT TREADS THE GRASS.	615 MARCH SONGS 2	30
"ON, ON, MY DARLING MAN."	616 MARCH SONGS 3	16
"OH, ON, MY DARLING MAN."	616 MARCH SONGS 3 V	16
FOR DEATH WHO TAKES WHAT MAN WOULD KEEP,	620 JOHN KINSELLA	3
LEAVES WHAT MAN WOULD LOSE.	620 JOHN KINSELLA	4
NONE OTHER KNOWS WHAT PLEASURES MAN	620 JOHN KINSELLA	9
LIKE AN OLD JEW MAN,	620 JOHN KINSELLA	14
TO KEEP THE SOUL OF MAN ALIVE,	620 JOHN KINSELLA	19
NO MAN GROWS OLD, NO GIRL GROWS COLD,	621 JOHN KINSELLA	31
OR SEEM PLAUSIBLE TO A MAN OF SENSE,	624 APPARITIONS	4
WHEN A MAN GROWS OLD HIS JOY	624 APPARITIONS	17
NOT A MAN BUT DELACROIX.	625 NATIVITY	4
KNOW WHY AN OLD MAN SHOULD BE MAD.	626 OLD MEN BE MAD	20
OR THE MAN THAT MADE THE MOTORS?	627 STATES HOLIDAY	20
WOULD NOT MAKE HIM A MAN.	628 JANE MOUNTAIN	4

```
                                                      PAGE   TITLE           LINE
MAN   (CONTINUED)
      HER VIOLENT MAN . . . . . . . . . . . . . .     628 JANE MOUNTAIN        16
      MAYBE AT LAST, BEING BUT A BROKEN MAN, . . . .   629 CIRCUS ANIMALS        3
      AND WHEN THE FOOL AND BLIND MAN STOLE THE BREAD  630 CIRCUS ANIMALS       25
      YET HERE'S A TRAVELLED MAN THAT KNOWS . . . .    631 POLITICS              5
      THE MAN AND THE ECHO . . . . . . . . . . .       632 MAN AND ECHO          T
      MAN AND THE ECHO . . . . . . . . . . . .         632 MAN AND ECHO      V   T
      WHILE MAN CAN STILL HIS BODY KEEP . . . . .      633 MAN AND ECHO         25
      A MAN THAT HAD SIX MORTAL WOUNDS, A MAN . . .    634 CUCHULAIN COMF        1
      A MAN THAT HAD SIX MORTAL WOUNDS, A MAN . . .    634 CUCHULAIN COMF        1
      CAME CREEPING UP BECAUSE THE MAN WAS STILL. . .  634 CUCHULAIN COMF       10
      ALL MUST TOGETHER DO." THAT DONE, THE MAN . .    634 CUCHULAIN COMF       17
      MANY TIMES MAN LIVES AND DIES . . . . . . .      637 BEN BULBEN           13
      WHETHER MAN DIE IN HIS BED . . . . . . . .       637 BEN BULBEN           17
      IS THE WORST MAN HAS TO FEAR. . . . . . . .      637 BEN BULBEN           20
      AND A MAN IS FIGHTING MAD, . . . . . . . .       638 BEN BULBEN           28
      EVEN THE WISEST MAN GROWS TENSE . . . . . .      638 BEN BULBEN           33
      BRING THE SOUL OF MAN TO GOD, . . . . . . .      638 BEN BULBEN           40
      A MAN HAS THE FIELDS OF HEAVEN, . . . . . .      643 SONG FAERIES          1
      A MAN HAS A HOPE FOR HEAVEN, . . . . . . .       643 SONG FAERIES      V   1
      MORE GRIEF IS MINE. NO MAN SHALL EVER STOOP      661 ISLE STAT II 1       62
      A MAN WHO BY A DEAD MAN STOOD. . . . . . . .     671 ISLE STAT II 3      124
      A MAN WHO BY A DEAD MAN STOOD. . . . . . . .     671 ISLE STAT II 3      124
      A MAN HAS A HOPE FOR HEAVEN, . . . . . . .       676 ISLE STAT II 3      248
      DOTH STILL THE MAN WHOM EACH STERN ROVER FEARS,  678 ISLE STAT II 3      295
      TWO SPIRIT THINGS A MAN HATH FOR HIS FRIENDS,    686 DRAWING-ROOM          5
      THE DARK STILL MAN, HAS COME AND SAYS 'TIS SIN,  692 MOSADA 1             47
      HE WAS A MAN MOST LEARNED AND MOST MILD, . .     692 MOSADA 1             51
      ALONG THE SEA, AND MANY A MAN GREW HUSHED . .    693 MOSADA 1             86
      FAMOUS, A MAN OF RULES, A VICTOR.  STANDS . .    709 FERENCZ RENYI         9
      HAYNAU, THE MAN OF SYSTEM, LIFTS HIS HAND . .    712 FERENCZ RENYI        62
      A LITTLE WITHERED MAN, AND OLD. . . . . . .      716 FAIRY DOCTOR          4
      THE MAN WHOSE HOUR OF DEATH DRAWS NIGH, . . .    716 FAIRY DOCTOR          6
      THE LITTLE WITHERED MAN, AND OLD. . . . . .      717 FAIRY DOCTOR         24
      WITHOUT THERE OF A LITTLE, LIGHT OLD MAN, . .    720 WITCH VIVIEN         13
      THERE STOOD A MAN, OF MEN THE LEAST-- . . .      729 PRIEST FAIRY         24
      "MAN OF WISDOM, FROM THY SLEEPING . . . . .      729 PRIEST FAIRY         39
      "MAN OF WISDOM, DOST THOU KNOW . . . . . .       729 PRIEST FAIRY         47
      TWO SPIRIT-THINGS A MAN HATH FOR HIS FRIENDS--   734 QUATRAIN APHOR        5
      TWO SPIRIT THINGS A MAN HATH FOR HIS FRIENDS,    734 QUATRAIN APHOR V      5
      THE MAN IS GONE WHO GUIDED YE, UNWEARY, . . .    738 MOURN THEN ON         3
      THE MAN IS GONE WHO FROM HIS LONELY STATION .    738 MOURN THEN ON         7
      AND HER DIM WAVE BIDS MAN BE NO MORE GLAD, . .   738 YOU ARE SAD          11
      BUT WOULD TURN HOME AGAIN. NO MAN HAD DOUBTS .   749 SHADOW WATER A       38
      NO MAN NOR WOMAN HAS LOVED OTHERWISE . . . .     750 SHADOW WATER A       64
      NO MAN OR WOMAN HAS LOVED OTHERWISE . . . .      750 SHADOW WATER A V     64
      AND NO MAN KILL ME, FOR SOME WIND HAS BLOWN .    751 SHADOW WATER A       97
      THE TIDE NARROWS BETWEEN, AND ONE OLD MAN . .    752 SHADOW WATER A      118
      BEYOND THE SAIL A MAN WITH A RED CROWN . . .     752 SHADOW WATER A      126
      I SWEAR IT. LET EVERY MAN DRAW OUT HIS SWORD.    758 SHADOW WATER A      230
      TO CRY HIS FOLDING CRY. THERE IS SOME MAN . .    760 SHADOW WATER A V    253
      BUT HER GOOD MAN ANSWERED HER . . . . . . .      772 SONG DEIRDRE 1 V      9
      NAMES WHEREBY A MAN HAS KNOWN . . . . . . .      775 AGAINST WITCH         5
      BUT THE MAN IS THRICE FORLORN, . . . . . .       776 AGAINST WITCH        26
      BUT THE MAN IS TWICE FORLORN, . . . . . . .      776 AGAINST WITCH  V     26
      AND I MET WITH A MAN THAT WAS NO RIGHT MAN . .   779 GOING THE ROAD        3
      AND I MET WITH A MAN THAT WAS NO RIGHT MAN . .   779 GOING THE ROAD        3
      "THE MAN THAT I PRAISE," . . . . . . . . .       780 WELL AND TREE         1
      "THE MAN THAT I PRAISE," . . . . . . . . .       780 WELL AND TREE         9
      A MAN IS LOST OF A SUDDEN, . . . . . . . .       783 GREY ROUND            9
      WHAT BONDS NO MAN COULD UNBIND, . . . . . .      785 WOMANS BEAUTY        22
      A MAN BUT WILL GIVE YOU HIS LOVE . . . . . .     786 YOUR HEART           17
      WHAT MAN IS AT YOUR SIDE? . . . . . . . .        786 YOUR HEART           28
      IS THERE NO MAN AT YOUR SIDE? . . . . . . .      786 YOUR HEART     V     28
      LOVELY LADY OR GALLANT MAN . . . . . . . .       788 HAWTHORN TREE         7
      LOVELY LADY AND GALLANT MAN . . . . . . . .      788 HAWTHORN TREE  V      7
      NOW A NOTABLE MAN ON STAGE AND ON SCREEN, . .    790 DEDICATION            8
      CAN GHOST OR MAN BE SATISFIED? . . . . . . .     791 REPRISALS             4
MANACLE
      MANACLE HIS SOUL UPON THE RED SEA BOTTOM. . . .  372 ON GOING HOUSE       16
MANAGE
      MANAGE THE TALK UNTIL HER NAME COME ROUND. . . . 351 HER PRAISE           14
      MANAGE TO TALK UNTIL HER NAME COME ROUND. . . .  351 HER PRAISE     V     14
MANAGED
      THIS MAN HAD MANAGED A SCHOOL . . . . . . .      392 EASTER 1916    V     24
MANAGEMENT
      THEATRE BUSINESS, MANAGEMENT OF MEN. . . . . .   260 FASC DIFFICULT       11
MANANAN
      DEEP SUNKEN ON THE BLADE'S LENGTH, "MANANAN!"     38 OISIN 2        V    128
      THE DRUID SWORD OF MANANAN, HE GREW . . . . .     40 OISIN 2        V    174
      AND TELL HOW MANANAN SACKED MURIAS . . . . .     766 SHADOW WATER A      377
MANANAN'S
      AND MANANAN'S DARK TOWER, STONE BY STONE, . . .   45 OISIN 2        V    236
MANANNAN
      THEREON IN OGHAM LETTERS, "MANANNAN", . . . .     38 OISIN 2             128
      AND WHEN HE KNEW THE SWORD OF MANANNAN . . . .    40 OISIN 2             173
      ALL MANNIONS COME FROM MANANNAN, . . . . . .     606 SONGS BURDEN 1       10
MANANNAN'S
      AND MANANNAN'S DARK TOWER, STONE AFTER STONE, .   45 OISIN 2             236
MAN-AT-ARMS
      TWO MEN HAVE FOUNDED HERE. A MAN-AT-ARMS . . .   420 MY HOUSE             21
```

499

```
                                                        PAGE     TITLE        LINE
MAN-AT-ARMS   (CONTINUED)
   TWO MEN HAVE FOUND IT HERE.  A MAN-AT-ARMS . . . . . .   420 MY HOUSE      V   21
MANCINI'S
   MANCINI'S PORTRAIT OF AUGUSTA GREGORY, . . . . . . . .   602 GALLERY REVIS     25
MANE
   AND 'TWEEN HIS EARS, ABOVE HIS MANE, . . . . . . . . .     2 OISIN 1       V  7AA
   ON DELICATE SENSITIVE EAR OR TOSSING MANE, . . . . . .   433 NINETEEN 19      115
MANES
   I HEAR THE SHADOWY HORSES, THEIR LONG MANES A-SHAKE, .   154 BELOVED PEACE      1
   AND HIDING THEIR TOSSING MANES AND THEIR TUMULTUOUS FEET.  154 BELOVED PEACE     12
   AND HIDE THEIR TOSSING MANES AND THEIR TUMULTUOUS FEET.  154 BELOVED PEACE  V   12
MANGAN
   WITH DAVIS, MANGAN, FERGUSON, . . . . . . . . . . . .   138 TO IRELAND        18
MAN-HEADED
   HAS EVER COME BUT THOSE MAN-HEADED BIRDS, . . . . . .   226 SHADOW WATER B    99
   THEY HAVE MADE YOU FOLLOW THE MAN-HEADED BIRDS, . . . .  231 SHADOW WATER B   204
   THEY HAVE BADE YOU FOLLOW THE MAN-HEADED BIRDS, . . . .  231 SHADOW WATER B V 204
MANHOOD
   POUR WINE AND DANCE IF MANHOOD STILL HAVE PRIDE, . . .   311 MOUNTAIN TOMB      1
   ALL THOSE THAT MANHOOD TRIED, OR CHILDHOOD LOVED . . .   327 ROBERT GREGORY    91
   WHAT MANHOOD LED THE DANCE! . . . . . . . . . . . .     488 CRAZED MOON       12
MANIFOLD
   BY MANIFOLD ILLUSION! BUT MAN'S LIFE IS THOUGHT, . . .   563 MERU               3
MANKIND
   AND WHISPERED TO MANKIND. . . . . . . . . . . . . .     133 FR GILLIGAN       20
   POUR WINE AND DANCE, IF MANKIND STILL HAVE PRIDE, . .   311 MOUNTAIN TOMB  V   1
   THAT LOVED HIS LEARNING BETTER THAN MANKIND, . . . . .   324 ROBERT GREGORY    18
   WITH THE MINUTE PARTICULARS OF MANKIND? . . . . . . .   384 VISION ROBART     42
   MANKIND INANIMATE PHANTASY. . . . . . . . . . . . .     406 IN TIME OF WAR     5
   MANKIND INANIMATE FANTASY. . . . . . . . . . . . . .    406 IN TIME OF WAR V   5
   WHAT IF THOSE THINGS THE GREATEST OF MANKIND . . . . .  418 ANCEST HOUSES     38
   TO AFFLICT MANKIND, BUT NOW . . . . . . . . . . . .     431 NINETEEN 19       86
   AND SO REMEMBERS THAT WHEN ALL MANKIND . . . . . . .    447 COLONUS PRAISE    26
   . . . ALL ENTANGLEMENTS OF MANKIND GROW, . . . . . .    459 FROM OEDIPUS       5
   . . . HAD DRAGGED HIM DOWN INTO MANKIND, . . . . . .    481 BLOOD AND MOON    20
   "HEAR, GENTLEMEN, LADIES, AND ALL MANKIND! . . . . .    544 TO SAME TUNE 1     2
   WHERE ARE THE CAPTAINS THAT GOVERN MANKIND? . . . . .   548 TO SAME TUNE 3    22
   FROM EVERY THOUGHT OF GOD MANKIND HAS HAD. . . . . .    558 RIBH CHRISTIAN    15
   FORGOTTEN ELSE BY MANKIND, . . . . . . . . . . . .     576 ACRE OF GRASS     23
   WHERE ARE THE CAPTAINS THAT GOVERN MANKIND? . . . . .   615 MARCH SONGS 2     22
   "HEAR, GENTLEMEN, LADIES, AND ALL MANKIND! . . . . .    615 MARCH SONGS 3      2
   PROFANE PERFECTION OF MANKIND. . . . . . . . . . .     639 BEN BULBEN        52
   AT CHANCES AND AT MOMENTS WITH MANKIND. . . . . . .    721 WITCH VIVIEN      35
MAN-KIND
   OF GOD-KIND AND MAN-KIND. . . . . . . . . . . . . .    770 BLOOD BOND         6
MANLY
   THERE ONE THAT RUFFLED IN A MANLY POSE . . . . . . .    489 COOLE PARK 29     11
MANNA
   AND--MERCY IS THE MANNA OF THE WORLD. . . . . . . .    697 MOSADA 2          41
MANNED
   AND MANNED AN ARGOSY AND SAILING DIED. . . . . . . .    693 MOSADA 1          89
MANNER
   ALL MANNER OF BLESSED SOULS, . . . . . . . . . . .     167 BLESSED           14
   ALL MANNER OF BLESSEDEST SOULS, . . . . . . . . .      167 BLESSED        V  14
   HE HAS FOUND, AFTER THE MANNER OF HIS KIND, . . . .    373 PHASES OF MOON    12
MANNERS
   FINE MANNERS, LIBERAL SPEECH, . . . . . . . . . .      506 REMORSE SPEECH     7
MANNION
   BUT MANNION IS MY NAME, . . . . . . . . . . . . .      605 SONGS BURDEN 1     2
MANNIONS
   ALL MANNIONS COME FROM MANANNAN, . . . . . . . . .     606 SONGS BURDEN 1    10
MAN-PICKER
   MAN-PICKER NIAMH LEANT AND SIGHED . . . . . . . . .    611 NEWS ORACLE        5
MAN'S
   FOR NO MAN'S CRY SHALL EVER MOUNT SO FAR! . . . . .     36 OISIN 2          108
   NOR NO MAN'S CRY SHALL EVER MOUNT SO FAR! . . . . .     36 OISIN 2       V  108
   LIGHT IS MAN'S LOVE, AND LIGHTER IS MAN'S RAGE! . .     45 OISIN 2          243
   LIGHT IS MAN'S LOVE, AND LIGHTER IS MAN'S RAGE! . .     45 OISIN 2          243
   IN MIDST OF AN OLD MAN'S BOSOM! OWLS RUFFLING AND PACING 50 OISIN 3          47
      AROUND
   IN THE MIDST OF AN OLD MAN'S BOSOM! OWLS RUFFLING        50 OISIN 3       V  47
      AND PACING AROUND
   . . . OR WAS LIFTED AN OLD MAN'S MILD HEAD. . . . .     59 OISIN 3       V 170
   IN EACH MAN'S EARS OF SORROW-- . . . . . . . . . .     70 CLOAK BOAT     V  14
   AND NOW THE OLD MAN'S DREAMS ARE GONE, . . . . . .     98 FOXHUNTER        19
   FIRE IS IN THE OLD MAN'S EYES, . . . . . . . . . .     98 FOXHUNTER        29
   A FIRE IS IN THE OLD MAN'S EYES, . . . . . . . . .     98 FOXHUNTER        29
   COME NEAR, THAT NO MORE BLINDED BY MAN'S FATE, . .    101 ROSE UPON ROOD     9
   AND GOD WOULD BID MAN'S WARFARE CEASE, . . . . . .    113 ROSE OF PEACE  V  13
   HAD BLOTTED OUT MAN'S IMAGE AND HIS CRY. . . . . .    120 SORROW OF LOVE     4
   COULD BUT COMPOSE MAN'S IMAGE AND HIS CRY. . . . .    120 SORROW OF LOVE    12
   THE SICK MAN'S WIFE OPENED THE DOOR! . . . . . . .    133 FR GILLIGAN       31
   THEY HUDDLE FROM MAN'S PONDERING MIND, . . . . . .    138 TO IRELAND     V  26
   AND NOT WITH HIS OWN VOICE OR A MAN'S VOICE, . . .    183 QUEEN MAEVE       74
   BUT WITH A MAN'S HEAD, OR A FAIR WOMAN'S, . . . . .    233 SHADOW WATER B   245
   THE YOUNG MAN'S SONG . . . . . . . . . . . . . .      268 BROWN PENNY    V   T
   SHE WOULD NOT LOOK IN ANY KNOWN MAN'S FACE . . . .    280 TWO KINGS         73
   WOULD NEVER LOOK AGAIN ON KNOWN MAN'S FACE. . . .     280 TWO KINGS         75
   WILL NEVER LOOK AGAIN ON KNOWN MAN'S FACE." . . .     280 TWO KINGS      V  75
   END IN A BEAUTIFUL MAN'S OR WOMAN'S BODY. . . . .     374 PHASES OF MOON    64
   CAUGHT BY AN OLD MAN'S JUGGLERIES . . . . . . . .     411 TOWER             60
```

		PAGE	TITLE	LINE

MAN'S   (CONTINUED)
SURELY AMONG A RICH MAN'S FLOWERING LAWNS,		417	ANCEST HOUSES	1
IN PITY FOR MAN'S DARKENING THOUGHT		438	SONGS PLAY 2	1
MAN'S OWN RESINOUS HEART HAS FED.		438	SONGS PLAY 2	16
O SELF-BORN MOCKERS OF MAN'S ENTERPRISE!		445	SCHOOL CHILDR	56
BUT WHAT CARE I THAT LONG FOR A MAN'S LOVE?		448	HERO GIRL FOOL	17
THAT MAKE A MAN'S SOUL OR A WOMAN'S SOUL		465	HARUN RASHID	93
IS A MAN'S MOCKERY OF THE CHANGELESS SOUL."		465	HARUN RASHID	102
INTO THE FROG-SPAWN OF A BLIND MAN'S DITCH,		479	SELF AND SOUL	59
FROM MAN'S BLOOD-SODDEN HEART ARE SPRUNG		502	VACILLATION	67
YOUNG MAN'S SONG		516	MANS SONG	T
FOR A MAN'S ATTENTION		533	FIRST CONFESS	10
TOO OLD FOR A MAN'S LOVE I STOOD IN RAGE		536	HER VISION	3
TOO OLD FOR A MAN'S LOVE I STOOD AND RAGED		536	HER VISION V	1
BY MANIFOLD ILLUSION! BUT MAN'S LIFE IS THOUGHT,		563	MERU	3
GRANT ME AN OLD MAN'S FRENZY,		576	ACRE OF GRASS	13
AN OLD MAN'S EAGLE MIND.		576	ACRE OF GRASS	24
AND A PROUD MAN'S A LOVELY MAN,		587	PARNELLITES	23
WHEN AN OLD MAN'S BLOOD GROWS COLD?		588	OLD WICKED MAN	13
A DRUNKEN MAN'S PRAISE OF SOBRIETY		591	DRUNK SOBRIETY	T
IN A YOUNG MAN'S BED."		594	COLONEL MARTIN	17
THE COLONEL KNOCKED ON THE RICH MAN'S DOOR,		595	COLONEL MARTIN	28
THE COLONEL KNOCKED ON A RICH MAN'S DOOR.		595	COLONEL MARTIN V	28
THINK WHERE MAN'S GLORY MOST BEGINS AND ENDS,		604	GALLERY REVIS	54
AS THAT WHICH CLEANS MAN'S DIRTY SLATE.		633	MAN AND ECHO	24
OR WHISPER THAT A MAN'S A FOOL		635	BLACK TOWER	12
IN EACH MAN'S EARS OF SORROW,		666	ISLE STAT II 3	14
THERE WAS SOME TALKING OF MAN'S GOD,		725	LEGEND	19
GROWS YOUNG AND A MAN'S HEART GROWS OLD IN A TWINKLING.		761	SHADOW WATER A	263
I HAVE MET IN A MAN'S HOUSE .		785	YOUR HEART	3

MANSION
OF THAT OLD GEORGIAN MANSION, MIX		475	EVA GORE-BOOTH	16
A HEAVENLY MANSION, RAGING IN THE DARK,		491	COOLE BALLYLEE V	40D
A HEAVENLY MANSION, RAGING IN THE DARK.		495	CHOICE	4
LIVE IN A HEAVENLY MANSION,		513	JANE TALK BISH	5
BUT LOVE HAS PITCHED HIS MANSION IN		513	JANE TALK BISH	15
THE BARRED WOODPECKER'S MANSION IS AND DEEP,		659	ISLE STAT II 1	23
AND WHO WILL THROW HIS MANSION DOWN		671	ISLE STAT II 3	135
AND THROUGH THE MANSION OF THE SPIRIT ROVE		681	SEEKER	2
HER HANGING MANSION. GIVE TO ME, I PRAY,		698	MOSADA 2	52

MANSIONS
| MANSIONS OF MEMORIES AND MELLOW THOUGHTS | | 721 | WITCH VIVIEN | 21 |

MANTEGNA'S
| A THOUGHTLESS IMAGE OF MANTEGNA'S THOUGHT— | | 537 | HER VISION | 20 |

MANTLING
| AT THE MANTLING OF THE BLOOD. | | 453 | DEATH OF HARE | 6 |
| OR MANTLING OF THE BLOOD. | | 453 | DEATH OF HARE V | 6 |

MANUSCRIPT
| AND NOW HE SEEKS IN BOOK OR MANUSCRIPT | | 373 | PHASES OF MOON | 19 |

MANY
OF MANY A FIGURED EMBROIDERY!		4	OISIN 1	27
THAT MANY A PEACEFUL MOMENT HAD,		4	OISIN 1	35
OF MANY A FIGURED CREATURE STRANGE,		4	OISIN 1 V	27
OF PRINCES THERE IS MANY A ONE."		6	OISIN 1 V	61
AND MANY A PRINCE OF LOFTY NAME,		7	OISIN 1 V	63
AND MANY A MAN OF LOFTY NAME.		7	OISIN 1 V	63
FULL MANY BOWING KINGS BESOUGHT ME,		7	OISIN 1 V	67
AND MANY PRINCES OF HIGH NAME.		7	OISIN 1 V	68
AND MANY A MILE IS THE FAERY STATE,		9	OISIN 1 V	103
AND BID ME STAY, WITH MANY A TEAR!		10	OISIN 1	113
WHERE MANY A TRUMPET-TWISTED SHELL		13	OISIN 1	160
LIKE SOOTY FINGERS, MANY A TREE		13	OISIN 1	171
WE RODE ON MURMURING. MANY A SHELL		13	OISIN 1 V	159
AND ON THE SHORES WERE MANY BOATS		14	OISIN 1	188
AND TRIMMED WITH MANY A CRIMSON FEATHER!		15	OISIN 1	206
TRIMMED ROUND WITH MANY A CRIMSON FEATHER!		15	OISIN 1 V	206
OF MANY A SLAUGHTERED FOREST ROVER.		17	OISIN 1	V 249A
SAVE ONLY MANY TIMES MY NAME.		25	OISIN 1	375
SHONE MANY TIMES AMONG THE GLIMMERING FLOWERS		30	OISIN 2	21
AND SHIVERED, KNOWING THE ISLE OF MANY FEARS,		30	OISIN 2	25
BURST FROM A GREAT DOOR MARRED BY MANY A BLOW		31	OISIN 2	29
OF MANY THOUSAND STEPS. SAT EITHER SIDE,		31	OISIN 2 V	35
FULL MANY MORE, WHEN PEERED A MAIDEN SWEET		33	OISIN 2	V 68F
THROUGH MANY SHAPES! I LUNGED AT THE SMOOTH THROAT		40	OISIN 2	175
THE DEAD GOD'S SWORD, TO MANY FORMS HE GREW,		40	OISIN 2 V	175
TO MANY SHAPES! I LUNGED AT THE SMOOTH THROAT		40	OISIN 2 V	175
AND MANY PATER NOSTERS SAID SINCE DAWN.		43	OISIN 2	V 208D
FIN, CONAN, OSCAR, MANY MORE, THE TIDE		44	OISIN 2	V 228A
IN ONE WAS A BRANCH SOFT-SHINING WITH BELLS MORE MANY THAN SIGHS		50	OISIN 3	46
IN REALMS WHERE THE HANDSOME WERE MANY,		50	OISIN 3	50
IN A REALM WHERE THE HANDSOME ARE MANY,		50	OISIN 3	50
IN REALMS WHERE THE HANDSOME ARE MANY,		50	OISIN 3 V	50
AND, MAN OF THE MANY WHITE CROZIERS, A CENTURY THERE I FORGOT		52	OISIN 3	77
AND, MAN OF THE MANY WHITE CROZIERS, A CENTURY THERE I FORGOT		52	OISIN 3	81
ON CREVROE OR BROAD KNOCKFEFIN, WITH MANY OF OLD THEY FEAST		59	OISIN 3	179
ON CREVROE OR ON BROAD KNOCKFEFIN, WITH MANY OF OLD THEY FAST		59	OISIN 3 V	179
OF ALL THE MANY CHANGING THINGS		65	HAPPY SHEPHERD	7

MANY   (CONTINUED)

		PAGE	TITLE		LINE
TO MIGHTY BRAHMA, HE WHO MADE YOU MANY AS THE SANDS,	. .	72	ANASHU VIJAYA		21
TO MIGHTY BRAHMA——HE WHO MADE YE MANY AS THE SANDS,	. . .	72	ANASHU VIJAYA	V	21
TO MIGHTY BRAHMA, WHO HAS MADE YOU MANY AS THE SANDS,	. .	72	ANASHU VIJAYA	V	21
WITH ALL YOUR WHIRLING HAIR, AND DROP MANY AN AZURE TEAR,	.	73	ANASHU VIJAYA		46
WITH ALL OUR WHIRLING HAIR, AND DROP MANY AN AZURE TEAR.	.	73	ANASHU VIJAYA	V	46
SHALL WARM THEIR LIVES AT MANY A RUSTLING FLAME."	. . .	80	EPHEMERA		128
MANY A LANDSMAN, MANY A SEAMAN.	. . . .	82	MAD KING GOLL	V	4
MANY A LANDSMAN, MANY A SEAMAN.	. . . .	82	MAD KING GOLL	V	4
THESE HANDS WON MANY A TORQUE OF GOLD.	. . . . . .	83	MAD KING GOLL		23
THESE HANDS SLEW MANY WARRIORS BOLD——	. . . . . .	83	MAD KING GOLL	V	23
THESE HANDS SLEW MANY ROBBERS BOLD——	. . . . . .	83	MAD KING GOLL	V	23
THESE HANDS SLEW MANY A SEAMAN BOLD.	. . . . . .	83	MAD KING GOLL	V	23
MY SORROW! FOR MANY A CREAK GAVE THE CREEL IN THE CART	.	91	OLD FISHERMAN		6
AH WOE! FULL MANY A CREAK GAVE THE CREEL IN THE CART	.	91	OLD FISHERMAN	V	6
AH ME! FULL MANY A CREAK GAVE THE CREEL IN THE CART	.	91	OLD FISHERMAN	V	6
AND NOW MOVES MANY A PLEASANT TONGUE .	. . . . . .	98	FOXHUNTER		21
AND MOVES THERE MANY A PLEASANT TONGUE,	. . . . . .	98	FOXHUNTER	V	23
FROM CHANGE TO CHANGE! I HAVE BEEN MANY THINGS——	. . .	104	FERGUS DRUID		32
"NAY, HE IS OLD AND SAD WITH MANY WARS,	. . . . .	107	CUCHULAIN SEA	V	29
"BUT HE IS OLD AND SAD WITH MANY WARS."	. . . . . .	107	CUCHULAIN SEA	V	30
HOW MANY LOVED YOUR MOMENTS OF GLAD GRACE,	. . . . .	121	YOU ARE OLD		5
I AM HAUNTED BY NUMBERLESS ISLANDS, AND MANY A DANAAN SHORE,		122	WHITE BIRDS		9
THERE WAS A GREEN BRANCH HUNG WITH MANY A BELL	. . . .	129	BOOK STORIES		1
AH, EXILES, WANDERING OVER MANY SEAS,	. . . . .	129	BOOK STORIES	V	9
AH, EXILES, WANDERING OVER MANY LANDS,	. . . . . .	130	BOOK STORIES	V	17
TO THOSE WITH WHOM I HAVE TALKED MANY TIMES,	. . . .	136	TO SOME I TALK	V	2
AND MANY A SWEET THING SAID,	. . . .	144	HOST OF AIR		18
AND BLAME YOU WITH MANY BITTER WORDS.	. . . . . .	146	FISH		8
THE DOORS OF HELL AND BLOW THERE MANY A WHIMPERING GHOST!		147	UNAPPEAS HOST		10
THROUGH MANY A SACRED CORRIDOR	. . . .	156	FORGOT BEAUTY		12
THE LOVER ASKS FORGIVENESS BECAUSE OF HIS MANY MOODS	. .	162	ASKS FORGIVE		T
MICHAEL ROBARTES ASKS FORGIVENESS BECAUSE OF HIS MANY MOODS		162	ASKS FORGIVE	V	T
AND WONDERING WHO OF THE MANY CHANGING SIDHE	. . . .	181	QUEEN MAEVE		41
TO MANY THOUSAND EYES, AND TO HER OWN	. . . . .	182	QUEEN MAEVE		65
AND WITH GLAD VOICE MAEVE ANSWERED "MANY A TIME	. . .	183	QUEEN MAEVE	V	79
FRIEND OF THESE MANY YEARS, YOU TOO HAD STOOD	. . . .	186	QUEEN MAEVE		130
FRIEND OF THESE MANY YEARS, YOU TO HAVE STOOD	. . . .	186	QUEEN MAEVE	V	130
WITH THE FIRST KINGS OF MANY PILLARED CRUACHAN	. . . .	187	QUEEN MAEVE	V	151
TO MANY PASTURED MUIRTHEMNE,	. . . .	189	BAILE AILLINN	V	21
AFTER THE DEATHS OF MANY MEN,	. . . .	197	BAILE AILLINN		193
THERE'S MANY A ONE SHALL FIND OUT ALL HEARTACHE	. . .	205	ADAMS CURSE		16
THEREIN ARE MANY QUEENS LIKE BRANWEN AND GUINEVERE!	. .	209	UNDER THE MOON		11
THERE'S MANY A STRONG FARMER	. . . .	213	HAPPY TOWNLAND		1
WHERE MANY HUNDRED SQUIRRELS ARE AS HAPPY	. . . . .	217	WOODS OF COOLE		5
FLEW WESTWARD! AND MANY A TIME SINCE THEN	. . . .	223	SHADOW WATER B		27
THESE MANY DAYS! AND YET THERE MUST BE MANY	. . . .	226	SHADOW WATER B		89
THESE MANY DAYS! AND YET THERE MUST BE MANY	. . . .	226	SHADOW WATER B		89
TOO MANY YEARS TO LIFT A HAND AGAINST YOU.	. . . . .	227	SHADOW WATER B		111
THOUGH LEAVES ARE MANY, THE ROOT IS ONE!	. . . . .	261	COMING WISDOM		1
WEARY OF MANY QUESTIONS! "THERE ARE THINGS	. . . .	281	TWO KINGS		93
AND MANY A DARLING WIT'S GROWN DULL	. . . . . .	301	RUN PARADISE		18
MANY TIMES TROUBLED YEARS,	. . . .	315	FRIENDS	V	7
THEY WERE MY CLOSE COMPANIONS MANY A YEAR,	. . . .	325	ROBERT GREGORY		41
WHERE MANY A KING HAS GONE	. . . .	330	BONE OF A HARE		2
AND MANY A KING'S DAUGHTER,	. . . .	330	BONE OF A HARE		3
THOUGH I HAVE MANY WORDS,	. . . .	334	SONG		7
MANY A SON AND DAUGHTER LIES	. . . .	360	ALF POLLEXFEN		13
THAT SO MANY LANDS HAD KNOWN,	. . . .	360	ALF POLLEXFEN		18
THROUGHOUT SO MANY VARYING CENTURIES	. . . . . .	371	ON GOING HOUSE		8
SHUDDERS IN MANY CRADLES! ALL IS CHANGED,	. . . . .	375	PHASES OF MOON		89
SO MANY TIMES CHILDISH DELIGHT,	. . . .	399	BREAK OF DAY		11
YET MANY, THAT HAVE PLAYED THE FOOL	. . . . . .	404	FOR DAUGHTER		36
AND MANY A POOR MAN THAT HAS ROVED	. . . .	404	FOR DAUGHTER		38
WONDER HOW MANY TIMES I COULD HAVE PROVED MY WORTH	. . .	427	PHANTOM HATRED		34
MANY INGENIOUS LOVELY THINGS ARE GONE	. . . . .	428	NINETEEN 19		1
WE TOO HAD MANY PRETTY TOYS WHEN YOUNG!	. . . . .	428	NINETEEN 19		9
MANY INGENUOUS LOVELY THINGS ARE GONE	. . . . . .	428	NINETEEN 19	V	1
I HAVE ATTEMPTED MANY THINGS	. . . .	451	FIRST LOVE		9
HOW SUCH A PAIR LOVED MANY YEARS	. . . .	458	SECRETS OF OLD		15
AND MANY A LESSER BELL SOUND THROUGH THE ROOM!	. . . .	470	ALL SOUL NIGHT		2
MANY A TIME I THINK TO SEEK	. . . .	475	EVA GORE-BOOTH		14
MANY TIMES HE DIED,	. . . .	476	DEATH		5
MANY TIMES ROSE AGAIN.	. . . .	476	DEATH		6
HOW MANY YEARS AGO .	. . . .	524	MAD AS MIST		10
THEIR EYES MID MANY WRINKLES, THEIR EYES,	. . . . .	567	LAPIS LAZULI		55
FOUND MANY A FAMOUS MAN THERE!	. . . .	584	GHOST ROG CASE		35
AND I HAVE MANY MORE,	. . . .	586	PARNELLITES		10
TO MANY WOMEN I HAVE SAID, "LIE STILL!"	. . . . .	609	IN TARAS HALLS		6
AND EMPTIED MANY A CAN!	. . . .	620	JOHN KINSELLA		16
SO MANY YEARS COMPANIONED BY A HOUND,	. . . . . .	621	HOUND VOICE		4
MANY TIMES MAN LIVES AND DIES	. . . .	637	BEN BULBEN		13
BY MANY SOUGHT, AND 'TIS A FOREST TALE,	. . . . .	653	ISLE STAT I 2		40
I PASSED BY MANY CAVES OF DRIPPING STONE,	. . . . .	657	ISLE STAT I 3		47
TWO CAME, HIS NAME AND MINE ON MANY A TREE	. . . .	662	ISLE STAT II 2		10
AND THAT WAS STRANGE! BUT THIS IS MANY A WORLD	. . .	664	ISLE STAT II 3		60
AND WHEN THOU HAST THESE THINGS FOR MANY AGES FELT,	. . .	674	ISLE STAT II 3		214
THOUGH SAD IS MANY A SPIRIT .	. . . .	680	LOVE AND DEATH		23
THE SULLEN WOOD. BUT MANY WOODS I SEE	. . . . . .	682	SEEKER		24
THEN HAS THIS ONE BEEN SINNED FULL MANY TIMES.	. . . .	692	MOSADA 1		49

MANY   (CONTINUED)
    ALONG THE SEA: AND MANY A MAN GREW HUSHED . . . . . . 693 MOSADA 1   86
    WHEN THERE ARE MANY? EBREMAR WILL STAMP . . . . . . 696 MOSADA 2   4
    THE AUSTRIAN HAYNAU HE, IN MANY LANDS . . . . . . 709 FERENCZ RENYI   8
    AND MANY A HERB AND MANY A SPELL . . . . 717 FAIRY DOCTOR   17
    AND MANY A HERB AND MANY A SPELL . . . . 717 FAIRY DOCTOR   17
    AND MANY HERBS AND MANY A SPELL . . . . 717 FAIRY DOCTOR   V 17
    AND MANY HERBS AND MANY A SPELL . . . . 717 FAIRY DOCTOR   V 17
    THEN GIVE ME TRIUMPH IN MY MANY PLOTS. . . . . . . 722 WITCH VIVIEN   51
    MY LOVE HATH MANY AN EVIL MOOD, ... 723 GIRLS SONG A   5
    MY LOVE HATH MANY A RUTHLESS MOOD, ... 723 GIRLS SONG A   V 5
    AND MANY A PURPLE GILLYFLOWER EATEN, ... 729 PRIEST FAIRY   35
    WITH MANY A LOVELY FACE . . . . 740 EARL PAUL   30
    HOW MANY MOONS HAVE DIED FROM THE FULL MOON . . . . 747 SHADOW WATER A   10
    WHO MIGHT HAVE FLOCKS AND HERDS AND MANY THRALLS, . . 757 SHADOW WATER A   216
    TO WANDER IN: YOU HAVE LOVED MANY WOMEN, ... 767 SHADOW WATER A   389
    HOW MANY HOURS TO DAYBREAK, BECAUSE LOVE . . . . . 767 SHADOW WATER A   405
    OR, FOR MANY SHAPES THEY HAVE, ... 775 AGAINST WITCH   14
    AND MANY A NIGHT IT SEEMS . . . . 781 MY HEART BEAT   9
    HOW MANY CENTURIES SPENT . . . . 784 WOMANS BEAUTY   7
    OF MANY A TRAGIC TOMB: . . . . 785 YOUR HEART   10
    OF MANY A TRAGIC TOMB: . . . . 786 YOUR HEART   23
    OF MANY A TRAGIC TOMB: . . . . 786 YOUR HEART   36
MANY-CHANGING
    AND WONDERING WHO OF THE MANY-CHANGING SIDHE . . . . 181 QUEEN MAEVE   41
    WHO OF THE WANDERING MANY-CHANGING ONES . . . . . 182 QUEEN MAEVE   51
    SHE TOLD THEM OF THE MANY-CHANGING ONES: . . . . . 185 QUEEN MAEVE   112
MANY-COLOURED
    THE MANY-COLOURED DANCERS RUSHED, ...   21 OISIN 1   V 322
MANY-FOLDED
    AND HATH HER HOME BY MANY-FOLDED DELLS. . . . . . 657 ISLE STAT I 3   46
MANY-HEADED
    THE MANY-HEADED FOAM AT SALAMIS. . . . . 610 STATUES   14
    ONE IMAGE CROSSED THE MANY-HEADED, SAT . . . . . 610 STATUES   17
MANY-MINDED
    AND MANY-MINDED HOMER WERE . . . . 524 MAD AS MIST   17
MANY-PASTURED
    TO MANY-PASTURED MUIRTHEMNE, ... 189 BAILE AILLINN   21
MANY-PILLARED
    WITH THE FIRST KINGS OF MANY-PILLARED CRUACHAN. . . . 187 QUEEN MAEVE   151
MANY-SORROWED
    THE WILLOW OF THE MANY-SORROWED WORLD. . . . . . 130 BOOK STORIES V 16
MANY-TIMES-TROUBLED
    MANY-TIMES-TROUBLED YEARS, ... 315 FRIENDS   7
MAPS
    WHERE THE MAPS ARE SPREAD, ... 617 LONG-LEG FLY   6
MAR
    THAT TIME CAN NEVER MAR A LOVER'S VOWS . . . . . 126 DREAM OF FAERY   10
    HOW TIME MAY NEVER MAR THEIR FAERY VOWS . . . . . 126 DREAM OF FAERY V 10
    FOR TRIUMPH CAN BUT MAR OUR SOLITUDE. . . . . . 431 NINETEEN 19   78
    SHEPHERD, TO MAR THE MORNING HAST THOU COME? . . . . 646 ISLE STAT I 1   30
MARBLE
    PAINTING WITH SHADOW ALL THE MARBLE STEPS: . . . .   72 ANASHU VIJAYA   30
    FROM MARBLE CITIES LOUD WITH TABORS OF OLD . . . . 162 ASKS FORGIVE   9
    A WEATHER-WORN, MARBLE TRITON . . . . 329 MEN IMPROVE   2
    A WEATHER-WORN, MARBLE TRITON . . . . 329 MEN IMPROVE   17
    IN BRONZE, OR THAT IN DAZZLING MARBLE APPEARS, . . . 334 LIVING BEAUTY   5
    FOR ALL ITS BRONZE AND MARBLE, 'S BUT A MOUSE. . . 418 ANCEST HOUSES   24
    BUT KEEP A MARBLE OR A BRONZE REPOSE. . . . . . 445 SCHOOL CHILDR   52
    SAT DOWN UPON THE FOUNTAIN'S MARBLE EDGE, ... 463 HARUN RASHID   43
    OLD MARBLE HEADS, OLD PICTURES EVERYWHERE: . . . . 491 COOLE BALLYLEE   28
    ON THE MARBLE TABLE-TOP. . . . . 501 VACILLATION   39
    UNDER A MARBLE FLAG? . . . . 525 DANCING DAYS   14.
    FROM MARBLE OF A BROKEN SEPULCHRE, ... 565 GYRES   20
    WHO HANDLED MARBLE AS IF IT WERE BRONZE, ... 566 LAPIS LAZULI   30
    IN MARBLE OR IN BRONZE, LACKED CHARACTER. . . . . 610 STATUES   3
    NO MARBLE, NO CONVENTIONAL PHRASE: . . . . . . 640 BEN BULBEN   89
    AND ONE ARM POINTING THUS, IN MARBLE WHITE. . . . 663 ISLE STAT II 2   28
    THAT FROM THE MILK-WHITE MARBLE . . . . . . 680 LOVE AND DEATH   3
MARBLES
    MARBLES OF THE DANCING FLOOR . . . . 498 BYZANTIUM   36
MARCH
    . . . AND MARCH ON AS OXEN MOVE OVER YOUNG GRASS: . .   62 OISIN 3   211
    COLD AS THE MARCH WIND HIS EYES, ... 531 FATHER CHILD   8
    COME MARCH, SINGING THIS SONG, ... 544 TO SAME TUNE 1 V REF
    MARCH, MARCH——HOW DOES IT RUN?—— . . . . . . 548 TO SAME TUNE 3   15
    MARCH, MARCH——HOW DOES IT RUN?—— . . . . . . 548 TO SAME TUNE 3   15
    MARCH, MARCH, LIFT UP THE SONG: . . . . 549 TO SAME TUNE 3   26
    MARCH, MARCH, LIFT UP THE SONG: . . . . 549 TO SAME TUNE 3   26
    MARCH WIND, AND ANY OLD TUNE, ... 615 MARCH SONGS 2   25
    MARCH, MARCH, AND HOW DOES IT RUN? . . . . . . 615 MARCH SONGS 2   26
    MARCH, MARCH, AND HOW DOES IT RUN? . . . . . . 615 MARCH SONGS 2   26
    AS BLOSSOMS, WHEN THE WINDS OF MARCH . . . . . 671 ISLE STAT II 3 127
    COME RIDE LIKE THE MARCH WIND: . . . . 774 COME RIDE   6
    RUN LIKE THE MARCH WIND: . . . . 774 COME RIDE   V   6
    RED BIRD OF MARCH, BEGIN TO CROW: . . . . . . 782 HEART FRIGHT   5
    RED BIRD OF MARCH, BEGIN TO CROW: . . . . . . 782 HEART FRIGHT   12
    RED BIRD OF MARCH, BEGIN TO CROW: . . . . . . 782 HEART FRIGHT   19
    THE STRONG MARCH BIRDS A-CROW. . . . . 783 GREY ROUND   26
MARCHED
    STOOD OR HAVE MARCHED THE NIGHT LONG . . . . . . 546 TO SAME TUNE 2   15

	PAGE	TITLE	LINE

MARCHED   (CONTINUED)
OR HAVE MARCHED THE NIGHT LONG, ...   546 TO SAME TUNE 2 V   15
MARCHES
WHAT MARCHES THROUGH THE MOUNTAIN PASS?   . . . .   614 MARCH SONGS 2   7
WHAT MARCHES DOWN THE MOUNTAIN PASS?   . . . .   615 MARCH SONGS 2   17
WHAT MARCHES DOWN THE MOUNTAIN PASS?   . . . .   615 MARCH SONGS 2   27
MARCHING
TAKE TO THE ROADS AND GO MARCHING ALONG.   . . . . .   548 TO SAME TUNE 3   14
O MARCHING WIND, O A BLAST OF THE WIND, ...   548 TO SAME TUNE 3   24
MARCHING, MARCHING ALONG.   . . . .   549 TO SAME TUNE 3   25
MARCHING, MARCHING ALONG.   . . . .   549 TO SAME TUNE 3   25
THREE MARCHING SONGS   . . . .   613 MARCH SONGS 1   T
A BLAST OF THE WIND, O A MARCHING WIND, ...   615 MARCH SONGS 2   24
A BLAST OF WIND, O A MARCHING WIND, ...   615 MARCH SONGS 2 V   24
MARCO
FOR THE SAN MARCO LIBRARY, ...   288 TO WEALTHY MAN   24
MARE
MARE OR STALLION, COCK OR HEN, ...   529 TOM LUNATIC   15
MOUNTED THE MARE OF TIME, ...   529 TOM CRUACHAN   5
SOME BACK A MARE THROWN FROM A THOROUGHBRED, ...   547 TO SAME TUNE 3   3
SOME BACK A MARE THROWN FROM A THOROUGH-BRED, ...   547 TO SAME TUNE 3 V   3
SOME BACK A MARE THROWN FROM A THOROUGHBRED, ...   614 MARCH SONGS 2   3
MAREOTIC
OR BY THE MAREOTIC SEA   . . . .   401 DEMON BEAST   45
ROUND THE MAREOTIC LAKE   . . . .   636 BEN BULBEN   2
MARGARET
THERE'S MARGARET AND MARJORIE AND DOROTHY AND NAN,   . . .   354 HIS PHOENIX   17
MARGE
IN ENDLESS DARK, AND BY THE WEEDY MARGE   . . . . . .   682 SEEKER   19
ITS PAVEN LENGTH TOWARDS THE RIVER'S MARGE   . . . . . .   702 MOSADA 3   76
MARGERY
THOUGH MARGERY IS STRICKEN DUMB   . . . .   457 SECRETS OF OLD   7
THOUGH MARGERY IS LIKE A FISH   . . . .   457 SECRETS OF OLD V   7
MARGIN
YOUR HOOVES HAVE STAMPED AT THE BLACK MARGIN OF THE WOOD,   442 BLACK CENTAUR   1
MARIE
"AVE MARIE," MUTTERED HE   . . . .   730 PRIEST FAIRY   51
MARIGOLDS
AND UNDER HER HOOFS THE MARIGOLDS BEATEN.   . . . . . .   729 PRIEST FAIRY   36
MARINERS
THE MARINERS OF NIGHT ABOVE, ...   139 TO IRELAND   V   38
MARINERS, ROUGH HARVESTERS!   . . . .   540 FROM ANTIGONE   5
MARINERS, WILD HARVESTERS!   . . . .   540 FROM ANTIGONE V   5
MARJORIE
THERE'S MARGARET AND MARJORIE AND DOROTHY AND NAN,   . . .   354 HIS PHOENIX   17
MARK
IN LUCK OR OUT THE TOIL HAS LEFT ITS MARK!   . . . . .   491 COOLE BALLYLEE V   40F
IN LUCK OR OUT THE TOIL HAS LEFT ITS MARK!   . . . . .   495 CHOICE   6
MARK AND DIGEST MY TALE, CARRY IT AFAR   . . . . . .   554 RIBH AT TOMB   3
I CHOOSE ANOTHER MARK.   . . . .   588 OLD WICKED MAN   29
MARKED
HAS MARKED A DISTANT OBJECT DOWN, ...   337 TOM OROUGHLEY   3
AND THERE MARKED OUT THOSE EMBLEMS ON THE SAND   . . . .   468 HARUN RASHID   156
AND THERE MARKED OUT EMBLEMS ON THE SAND   . . . . . .   468 HARUN RASHID   V 156
BEFORE I HAD MARKED HIM ON HIS NORTHERN WAY, ...   535 CHOSEN   8
"THOSE SIX FEET MARKED IN CHALK?   . . . .   548 TO SAME TUNE 3   8
"THOSE SIX FEET MARKED IN CHALK?   . . . .   548 TO SAME TUNE 3   18
"THOSE SIX FEET MARKED IN CHALK?   . . . .   549 TO SAME TUNE 3   28
MARKET
HIS MUMMERS TO THE MARKET PLACE, ...   287 TO WEALTHY MAN V   10
SAT UNDERNEATH THE MARKET CROSS, ...   724 LEGEND   2
MARKET-PLACE
HIS MUMMERS TO THE MARKET-PLACE, ...   287 TO WEALTHY MAN   10
MARKETS
FROM MARKETS AND FROM FAIRS   . . . .   420 MY HOUSE   19
MARKIEWICZ
IN MEMORY OF EVA GORE-BOOTH AND CON MARKIEWICZ   . . . .   475 EVA GORE-BOOTH   T
MARKS
THE NETTED MARKS OF CRAWLING SCALES SEA-SPRUNG   . . . .   37 OISIN 2   V 115
UPON THE STAR THAT MARKS THE HIDDEN POLE!   . . . . .   477 SELF AND SOUL   5
MARMALADE
THE STRUGGLE OF THE FLY IN MARMALADE.   . . . .   369 EGO DOMINUS   45
MARRED
BURST FROM A GREAT DOOR MARRED BY MANY A BLOW   . . . . .   31 OISIN 2   29
BASALTIC PILLARS MARRED WITH HEW AND HACK   . . . . . .   31 OISIN 2   V   30
MARRIAGE
WHEN THEY HAD COME TO THE MARRIAGE BED!   . . . . . .   193 BAILE AILLINN V   106
BAILE AND AILLINN'S MARRIAGE BED, ...   194 BAILE AILLINN   V 121
AND KEEP TO THE ONE WEARY MARRIAGE BED.   . . . . . .   224 SHADOW WATER B V   55
AND THE HIGH FAME THAT COME TO THEM IN MARRIAGE,   . . .   232 SHADOW WATER B   235
AND ALL THAT MURMURING IS BUT A MARRIAGE SONG!   . . . .   244 SHADOW WATER B V   452
THAT PACKED HIS MARRIAGE DAY   . . . .   317 NIGHT COME   7
THROUGH TOO MUCH PLAY, OR MARRIAGE WITH A FOOL?   . . . .   423 MY DESCENDANTS   12
MARRIAGE-BED
WHEN THEY HAD COME TO THE MARRIAGE-BED!   . . . . . .   193 BAILE AILLINN   106
BAILE AND AILLINN'S MARRIAGE-BED, ...   194 BAILE AILLINN   121
AND KEEP TO THE ONE WEARY MARRIAGE-BED.   . . . . . .   224 SHADOW WATER B   55
MARRIAGE-DAY
THAT PACKED HIS MARRIAGE-DAY   . . . .   317 NIGHT COME   V   7
MARRIAGES
MARRIAGES, ALLIANCES AND FAMILIES, ...   491 COOLE BALLYLEE   36

MARRIAGE-SONG
    AND ALL THAT MURMURING'S BUT A MARRIAGE-SONG; • • • • •   244 SHADOW WATER B   452
MARRIED   SEE NEW-MARRIED
    OUR MARRIED VOICES WILDLY TROLLED. • • • • • • • •   85 MAD KING GOLL   59
    OUR MARRIED VOICE WILDLY TROLLED. • • • • • • • •   85 MAD KING GOLL   V 59
    AND THEY MARRIED BEYOND THEIR PLACE. • • • • • • •   92 FATHER OHART   8
    MY MARRIED SISTER PUT INTO MY CARE • • • • • • •   276 TWO KINGS   V E
    THAT SHE MIGHT BE THAT SPRIGHTLY GIRL WHO HAD MARRIED WITH   353 HIS PHOENIX   V 4
        A BIRD;
    BY SOME NEW MARRIED BRIDE I TAKE • • • • • • • •   535 CHOSEN   V 13
    "HAS MARRIED AND STAYS • • • • • • • •   780 WELL AND TREE   11
MARROW
    SOFTER THAN SNOW-FLAKES IN APRIL AND PIERCING THE MARROW   51 OISIN 3   68
        LIKE FLAME.
    SOFTER THAN SNOWFLAKES IN APRIL, AND PIERCING THE MARROW   51 OISIN 3   V 68
        LIKE FLAME.
    MADE OUT OF A WILD THOUGHT, IS IN MY MARROW. • • • •   199 ARROW   2
    BETTER GO DOWN UPON YOUR MARROW BONES • • • • • •   204 ADAMS CURSE   V 7
    TO BURN US TO THE MARROW IF WE STRIKE. • • • • •   239 SHADOW WATER B   372
    YOU HAVE DRIED THE MARROW FROM THE BONE? • • • •   289 SEPTEMBER 1913   5
    THINKS IN A MARROW BONE; • • • • • • • •   553 PRAYER OLD AGE   V 4
    THINGS HID IN THEIR MARROW BONES • • • • • •   589 OLD WICKED MAN   V 41
    I PRAYED AT ALL THE STATIONS UPON MY MARROW BONES, • • •   593 PILGRIM   V 7
MARROW-BONE
    THINKS IN A MARROW-BONE; • • • • • • • •   553 PRAYER OLD AGE   4
MARROWBONES
    THINGS HID IN THEIR MARROWBONES • • • • • • •   589 OLD WICKED MAN   V 41
MARROW-BONES
    BETTER GO DOWN UPON YOUR MARROW-BONES • • • •   204 ADAMS CURSE   7
    THINGS HID IN THEIR MARROW-BONES • • • • •   589 OLD WICKED MAN   41
    I PRAYED AT ALL THE STATIONS UPON MY MARROW-BONES, • •   593 PILGRIM   7
MARRY
    BEING FORBID TO MARRY ON EARTH, • • • • • • •   189 BAILE AILLINN   11
    I NEEDS MUST MARRY SOME POOR LOUT," • • • • • •   273 GREY ROCK   47
    I NEED MUST MARRY SOME POOR LOUT," • • • • • •   273 GREY ROCK   V 47
    "AND THOUGH I'D MARRY WITH A COMELY LASS, • • • •   300 BEGGAR CRIED   9
    AT THE OLD BITTER WORLD WHERE THEY MARRY IN CHURCHES, • •   330 BONE OF A HARE   13
    AT ALL WHO MARRY IN CHURCHES, • • • • • •   330 BONE OF A HARE   15
MARS
    ON BREAST OF MARS THE GODDESS SIGHED. • • • • • •   562 CONJUNCTIONS   4
MARSH
    WITH HIS SNIPE MARSH AND HIS TROUT. • • • • •   92 FATHER OHART   V 4
    CLOGGED IN A MARSH WHERE THE SLOW MARSH CLAY CLINGS, • •   711 FERENCZ RENYI   35
    CLOGGED IN A MARSH WHERE THE SLOW MARSH CLAY CLINGS, • •   711 FERENCZ RENYI   35
MARSHY
    IN BARREN HILLS AND MARSHY LAND, • • • • • •   150 WANDER AENGUS   V 18
MART
    SORDID SORROWS OF THE MART. • • • • • • •   733 STREET DANCERS   59
MARTEN-CAT
    AND MARTEN-CAT, AND BORDERS THAT OLD WOOD • • • •   218 WOODS OF COOLE   14
MARTIN
    AND MARTIN CAT, AND BORDERS THAT OLD WOOD • • • •   218 WOODS OF COOLE   V 14
    COLONEL MARTIN • • • • • • • •   594 COLONEL MARTIN   T
MARTIN'S
    BEYOND OLD MARTIN'S BYRE. • • • • • • •   95 MOLL MAGEE   34
    BEYOND OLD MARTIN'S WOOD, • • • • • • •   95 MOLL MAGEE   34
MARTS   SEE HONEY-MARTS
    FROM BEES AMONG THEIR HONEY MARTS, • • • • •   16 OISIN 1   V 229
    WITH BOOM OF BEES IN HONEY MARTS, • • • • •   16 OISIN 1   V 229
MARTYRS
    THE MARTYRS CALL THE WORLD." AND THEREUPON • • • •   205 ADAMS CURSE   14
    THE MARTYRS CALL THE WORLD." THAT WOMAN THEN • • • •   205 ADAMS CURSE   V 14
MARVEL
    SHALL WITHER THAT OLD MARVEL, FOR • • • • • •   447 COLONUS PRAISE   15
    THAT DAY BY DAY I STUDY AND MARVEL AT, • • • •   468 HARUN RASHID   157
MARVELLOUS
    TORE FROM THE CLOUDS HIS MARVELLOUS MOON. • • • •   314 MEMORY YOUTH   21
    THREW UP IN THE AIR HIS MARVELLOUS MOON. • • • •   314 MEMORY YOUTH   V 21
    THE MARVELLOUS STAG OF ARTHUR, • • • • • •   399 BREAK OF DAY   23
    AS IF SOME MARVELLOUS EMPTY SEA-SHELL FLUNG • •   417 ANCEST HOUSES   13
    A MARVELLOUS ACCOMPLISHMENT, • • • • • •   421 MY TABLE   17
    BECAUSE I HAVE A MARVELLOUS THING TO SAY, • • •   471 ALL SOUL NIGHT   15
    A CERTAIN MARVELLOUS THING • • • • • •   471 ALL SOUL NIGHT   16
    I NEVER KNEW AN EVE SO MARVELLOUS STILL. • • • •   702 MOSADA 3   88
MARY
    DID THE KISS OF MOTHER MARY • • • • • •   124 CATHLEEN PARA   9
    HERS THE KISS OF MOTHER MARY, • • • • • •   124 CATHLEEN PARA   V 9
    O'SULLIVAN RUA TO MARY LAVELL • • • • • •   155 FORGOT BEAUTY   V T
    O'SULLIVAN THE RED TO MARY LAVELL. • • • • •   157 POET BELOVED   V T
    TWO POEMS BY O'SULLIVAN THE RED CONCERNING MARY LAVELL.   157 POET BELOVED   V T
    A DAPHNE AND A MARY WHO LIVE IN PRIVACY; • • • •   354 HIS PHOENIX   18
    FOUR POEMS CRACKED MARY AND THE BISHOP • • •   507 JANE BISHOP   V T
    CRACKED MARY REPROVED • • • • • • •   509 JANE REPROVED   V T
    CRACKED MARY AND THE DANCERS • • • • • •   514 JANE GROWN OLD   V T
    JOHN KINSELLA'S LAMENT FOR MRS. MARY MOORE • • •   620 JOHN KINSELLA   T
    BUT MY DEAR MARY MOORE • • • • • • •   620 JOHN KINSELLA   8
MARY'S
    IS COMELIER THAN CANDLES AT MOTHER MARY'S FEET. • • •   147 UNAPPEAS HOST   12
    BY THE DOOR OF MARY'S GARDEN • • • • • •   680 LOVE AND DEATH   31
MASCULINE
    RECALL THAT MASCULINE TRINITY. • • • • • • •   556 RIBH PATRICK   2

```
                                                      PAGE      TITLE              LINE
MASK
    THE MASK . . . . . . . .  . . . . . . . .  . .    263 MASK                        T
    "PUT OFF THAT MASK OF BURNING GOLD    . . . . . . 263 MASK                        1
    "IT WAS THE MASK ENGAGED YOUR MIND,  . . . . . .  263 MASK                        8
    A HOUSE, A SWORD, A SHIP, A MASK. . . . . . . .   788 BRAVEST ASK                 2
MASKER'S
    IN MASKER'S CLOAK AND HOOD, . . . . . . . . .     539 MEETING                     2
MASONRY
    MAY BUILD IN THE CRACKED MASONRY AND CRY . . . .  423 MY DESCENDANTS             15
    OF LOOSENING MASONRY, AND THERE  . . . . . . .    424 STARES NEST                 2
MASONS
    AND MASONS DROVE FROM MILES AWAY . . . . . . .    360 ALF POLLEXFEN               9
MASS
    THEY HAD A PRIEST SAY MASS, AND EVEN THE JAPANESE, . . .  363 DOLLS FACES         2
    AND TOOK A MASS OF SHADOWS FOR ITS MEAT, . . . .  444 SCHOOL CHILDR   V          28
MASSACRE
    AND WONDERED WHAT WAS LEFT FOR MASSACRE TO SAVE. . . . .  619 BRONZE HEAD        28
MASSED
    BUT WE OLD MEN ARE MASSED AGAINST THE WORLD. . . . .  486 SEVEN SAGES            14
MAST
    WHAT ARE YOU CALLING OUT ABOVE THE MAST? . . . . 243 SHADOW WATER B            437
    HE HOVERS ABOVE THE MAST AND WAITS HIS KIND! . . 753 SHADOW WATER A            135
    HE, DISGUISED AS A SAILOR BEFORE THE MAST, . . . 790 DEDICATION                 2
MASTER
    "BUT IF YOUR MASTER COMES HOME TRIUMPHING  . . . 106 CUCHULAIN SEA             12
    MASTER OF THE STILL STARS AND OF THE FLAMING DOOR. . . . 161 BLACK PIG          8
    THEN MAEVE: "O AENGUS, MASTER OF ALL LOVERS, . . 187 QUEEN MAEVE              149
    AND HE MY MASTER FROM MY CHILDHOOD UP! . . . . . 225 SHADOW WATER B            77
    EVEN IF FORGAEL HAD NOT BEEN MY MASTER  . . . .  225 SHADOW WATER B  V         76
    BEING AS DOUBTFUL? I HAVE CALLED YOU MASTER . .  227 SHADOW WATER B           110
    TILL YOUR BAD MASTER BLENCHED AND ALL WAS LOST!  270 PARDON FATHERS  V         12
    AN ANCIENT BANKRUPT MASTER OF THIS HOUSE. . . .  412 TOWER                     80
    ON MASTER WORK OF INTELLECT OR HAND. . . . . .   429 NINETEEN 19     V         37
    TILL MEDITATION MASTER ALL ITS PARTS, . . . . .  474 ALL SOUL NIGHT           92
    CUT OUT HIS HEART. SOME MASTER OF DESIGN . . .   541 PARN FUNERAL 1           14
    THEIR SCHOOL A CROWD, HIS MASTER SOLITUDE! . .   543 PARN FUNERAL 2           10
    THEIR SCHOOL THE CROWD, HIS MASTER SOLITUDE, . . 543 PARN FUNERAL 2  V         10
    WHAT CAN SHE TAKE UNTIL HER MASTER GIVE! . . .   558 RIBH CHRISTIAN           21
    WHAT MASTER MADE THE LASH. WHENCE HAD THEY COME, 560 WHENCE COME               9
    OUR MASTER CAESAR IS IN THE TENT . . . . . .     617 LONG-LEG FLY              5
    THEY WILL HAVE FOR MASTER NONE . . . . . . .     776 AGAINST WITCH   V         39
    THEN FARRELL, STEEL KING, MASTER OF MEN, . . .   790 DEDICATION                5
MASTERED
    TILL TOES MASTERED A SWEET MEASURE, . . . . . .  331 ROUND TOWER              15
    MOUTH MASTERED A SWEET SOUND, . . . . . . . .    331 ROUND TOWER              16
    SO MASTERED BY THE BRUTE BLOOD OF THE AIR, . .   441 LEDA AND SWAN            12
    I MOCKED, BEING CRAZY, BUT YOU MASTERED IT . .   533 HER TRIUMPH               8
MASTERFUL
    HATH COME A SEA-KING MASTERFUL, . . . . . . .    82 MAD KING GOLL    V        15
    SOUTHWARD A SEA-KING MASTERFUL . . . . . . . .   82 MAD KING GOLL    V        15
    COMES A SEA-KING MASTERFUL . . . . . . . . .     82 MAD KING GOLL    V        15
    WOMEN CAN FIND." WITH A MOST MASTERFUL VOICE, .  284 TWO KINGS               175
    BUT MASTERFUL HEAVEN HAD INTERVENED TO SAVE IT.  630 CIRCUS ANIMALS           20
    THOSE MASTERFUL IMAGES BECAUSE COMPLETE . . .    630 CIRCUS ANIMALS           33
MASTERING
    UTTERING, MASTERING IT, . . . . . . . . . .      480 BLOOD AND MOON            5
MASTER'S
    IN HONOUR SOON BY HIS MASTER'S SIDE . . . . .    26 OISIN 1          V 399C
    BUT WHEN THE MASTER'S BURIED MICE CAN PLAY, . .  418 ANCEST HOUSES            22
    THEIR SCHOOL A CROWD, HIS MASTER'S SOLITUDE! . . 543 PARN FUNERAL 2  V         10
MASTERS        SEE SINGING-MASTERS
    THE MIGHTIER MASTERS OF A MIGHTIER RACE: . . .   38 OISIN 2                  133
    ROOTED IN FOAM AND CLOUDS. THERE MIGHTIER MASTERS MET .  38 OISIN 2     V    132
    NONE WAR ON THE MASTERS OF HELL, . . . . . . .   62 OISIN 3                  214
    A MYSTICAL PRAYER TO THE MASTERS OF THE ELEMENTS, . . .  174 ELEMENT POWERS V  T
    O MASTERS OF THE GLITTERING TOWN! . . . . . .    212 BLESS PSALTER             3
    AND BY THE IMITATION OF GREAT MASTERS. . . . .   370 EGO DOMINUS              66
    AND BE THE SINGING MASTERS OF MY SOUL. . . . .   408 SAIL BYZANTIUM  V         20
    AND EDDY TO EDDY. MASTERS OF OUR DREAMS, . . .   768 SHADOW WATER A           418
    THEY WILL HAVE FOR MASTERS NONE . . . . . . .    776 AGAINST WITCH            39
MASTER-WORK
    ON MASTER-WORK OF INTELLECT OR HAND, . . . . .   429 NINETEEN 19              37
MASTERY
    RIGHT MASTERY OF NATURAL THINGS, . . . . . . .   401 DEMON BEAST              37
    ATHENIAN INTELLECT ITS MASTERY, . . . . . . .    446 COLONUS PRAISE           11
MASTHEAD
    THEY HOVER OVER THE MASTHEAD AWHILE . . . . .    233 SHADOW WATER B           246
    CIRCLING AND CIRCLING OVER THE MASTHEAD? . . .   234 SHADOW WATER B           266
MAST-HEAD
    HE, THOUGH BUT A LANDSMAN, WENT TO THE MAST-HEAD! . . .  790 DEDICATION        4
MAT
    STRETCHED UP ON TWO LEGS FROM THE MAT, . . . .   381 SONGS FOOL 2              7
    SITTING ON A WARM SMOOTH MAT . . . . . . . .     726 LOVERS QUARREL           11
MATCH
    DARE MATCH IN LEARNING WITH US TWO, . . . . .    333 SOLOMON SHEBA            21
    HER CHILDISH GRATITUDE FOR LOVE AND MATCH YOUR FIFTY YEARS? 450 OWEN AHERNE   23
    ARISE AND BID ME STRIKE A MATCH . . . . . . .    476 EVA GORE-BOOTH           26
    BID ME STRIKE A MATCH AND BLOW. . . . . . . .    476 EVA GORE-BOOTH           32
MATCHING
    OF THE MATCHING OF RIBBONS FOR BOSOM AND HEAD, .  151 OLD MOTHER               6
    OF THE MATCHING OF RIBBONS THE BLUE AND THE RED, . . .  151 OLD MOTHER   V     6
```

MATCHING   (CONTINUED)
   MATCHING OUR BROKEN-HEARTED WIT AGAINST HER WIT, ... 362 HER COURTESY   7
MATE
   HOW COULD SHE MATE WITH FIFTY YEARS THAT WAS SO WILDLY   450 OWEN AHERNE   15
     BRED?
   LET THE CAGE BIRD AND THE CAGE BIRD MATE . . . . . . 450 OWEN AHERNE   16
   . . . AND THE WILD BIRD MATE IN THE WILD." . . . . 450 OWEN AHERNE   16
   LIKE PASSION STIRS THE PEACOCK AND HIS MATE, ... 465 HARUN RASHID   100
   KNOW HIS WORK OR CHOOSE HIS MATE . . . . 638 BEN BULBEN   36
   AMONG THE WHIMPERING GHOSTS. MATE THUS. ALREADY? . . 722 WITCH VIVIEN   68
MATERNAL
   ON THE MATERNAL MIDNIGHT OF MY BREAST . . . . . . 535 CHOSEN   7
MATHEMATICAL
   CAST BUT DEAD LEAVES TO MATHEMATICAL EQUALITY! . . . 481 BLOOD AND MOON   24
   CASTS BUT DEAD LEAVES TO MATHEMATICAL EQUALITY! . . . 481 BLOOD AND MOON V   24
MATHERS
   I CALL MACGREGOR MATHERS FROM HIS GRAVE, ... 473 ALL SOUL NIGHT V   61
MATTER
   TOWARDS THE COUNTRY OF THE DEAD. WHAT MATTER . . . . 231 SHADOW WATER B 206
   IF THERE BE HALF A HUNDRED MORE, WHAT MATTER? . . . . 245 SHADOW WATER B 476
   WHAT MATTER, SO THERE IS BUT FIRE . . . . . . 263 MASK   14
   "IF YOU HAD BROACHED A MATTER . . . . 333 SOLOMON SHEBA   11
   AND THERE ARE--BUT NO MATTER IF THERE ARE SCORES BESIDE! 354 HIS PHOENIX   15
   WHAT MATTER THAT NO CANNON HAD BEEN TURNED . . . . 429 NINETEEN 19   19
   BE MIMICRY?" "WHAT MATTER IF OUR SOULS . . . . . 464 HARUN RASHID   66
   BUT NAMES ARE NOTHING. WHAT MATTER WHO IT BE, . . 473 ALL SOUL NIGHT   81
   WHAT MATTER IF THE DITCHES ARE IMPURE? . . . . . 478 SELF AND SOUL   42
   WHAT MATTER IF I LIVE IT ALL ONCE MORE? . . . . 478 SELF AND SOUL   43
   WHAT MATTER IF A BLIND MAN DRINK HIS DROP? . . . 478 SELF AND SOUL V   41
   HALF DEAD AT THE TOP? NO MATTER WHAT I SAID, . . . 482 BLOOD AND MOON   48
   FOR NO MATTER WHAT IS SAID . . . . 514 JANE GROWN OLD   12
   WHAT MATTER? FOR I KNOW . . . . 518 HIS CONFIDENCE   9
   WHAT MATTER IF THE KNAVE . . . . 525 DANCING DAYS   10
   WHAT MATTER FOR THE SCENE, THE SCENE ONCE GONE! . . 542 PARN FUNERAL 1   19
   NO MATTER WHAT HAPPENS AND WHO TAKES THE FALL, . . 545 TO SAME TUNE 1   22
   NO MATTER WHAT HAPPENS OR WHO TAKES THE FALL, . . . 545 TO SAME TUNE 1 V   22
   HERE IS FRESH MATTER, POET, ... 553 CHURCH STATE   1
   MATTER FOR OLD AGE MEET! . . . . 553 CHURCH STATE   2
   WHAT MATTER THAT YOU UNDERSTOOD NO WORD! . . . . 557 RIBH ECSTASY   1
   WHAT MATTER THOUGH NUMB NIGHTMARE RIDE ON TOP, . . 564 GYRES   9
   WHAT MATTER? HEAVE NO SIGH, LET NO TEAR DROP, . . . 564 GYRES   11
   WHAT MATTER? OUT OF CAVERN COMES A VOICE, . . . 564 GYRES   15
   WHAT MATTER? THOSE THAT ROCKY FACE HOLDS DEAR, . . 564 GYRES   18
   WHAT MATTER? OUT OF CAVERN COME A VOICE . . . . 564 GYRES   V   15
   WHAT MATTER, WE ARE BUT WOMEN. . . . . . . 572 LADYS 2ND SONG   3
   NO MATTER WHAT DISASTER OCCURRED . . . . . . 578 CRAZED GIRL   9
   NO MATTER WHAT THE NAMES THEY WEAR! . . . . . 582 ROGER CASEMENT V   17
   NO MATTER WHAT HAPPENS AND WHO TAKES THE FALL, . . 616 MARCH SONGS 3   22
   SOME THINK IT A MATTER OF COURSE THAT CHANCE . . . 626 OLD MEN BE MAD   9
   SOME THINK IT MATTER OF COURSE THAT CHANCE . . . . 626 OLD MEN BE MAD V   9
   WILL HE NOT SPARE HER LIFE? HOW WOULD ONE MATTER . . 696 MOSADA 2   3
MATTERS
   WHAT MATTERS WERE AFOOT AMONG THE SIDHE, ... 182 QUEEN MAEVE   61
   ARE DUST ON THE MOTH'S WING! THAT NOTHING MATTERS . . 235 SHADOW WATER B 297
   "WHILE I HAVE HIM AND YOU IT MATTERS LITTLE . . . . 280 TWO KINGS   85
MATTOCK
   AND A SMALL AND A FEEBLE POPULACE STOOPING WITH MATTOCK   58 OISIN 3   164
     AND SPADE,
   AND A SMALL AND A FEEBLE RACE STOOPING WITH MATTOCK AND   58 OISIN 3   V 164
     SPADE.
   AND A SMALL AND FEEBLE RACE STOOPING WITH MATTOCK   58 OISIN 3   V 164
     AND SPADE.
MATTRESS
   ON GRASSY MATTRESS I HAD LAID ME, ... 387 SOLOMON WITCH   3
MAUD
   THE BLINDS DRAWN UP"! MAUD GONNE AT HOWTH STATION WAITING 578 LOFTY THINGS   10
     A TRAIN,
MAULED
   THEY MAULED AND BIT THE WHOLE NIGHT THROUGH! . . . . 297 THREE BEGGARS   48
   THEY MAULED AND BIT TILL THE DAY SHONE! . . . . . 297 THREE BEGGARS   49
   THEY MAULED AND BIT THROUGH ALL THAT DAY . . . . 297 THREE BEGGARS   50
   THEY'D MAULED AND BITTEN THE NIGHT THROUGH, ... 297 THREE BEGGARS V   48
MAUNDERING
   MAUNDERING HERE, AND MAUNDERING THERE, ... 451 FIRST LOVE   15
   MAUNDERING HERE, AND MAUNDERING THERE, ... 451 FIRST LOVE   15
MAURYA
   TILL MAURYA OF THE WOUNDED HEART CRY A SWEET CRY, . . 173 SPEAKS HEARERS V   6
MAURYA'S
   IS COMELIER THAN CANDLES BEFORE MAURYA'S FEET. . . . 147 UNAPPEAS HOST V   12
MAVRONE
   "MAVRONE, MAVRONE! THE MAN HAS DIED . . . . . . 133 FR GILLIGAN   25
   "MAVRONE, MAVRONE! THE MAN HAS DIED . . . . . . 133 FR GILLIGAN   25
MAXIMS
   AND YET UPON THESE MAXIMS MEDITATE! . . . . . . 500 VACILLATION   22
MAYBE
   MAYBE YOU HAVE NOT HEARD OF US, YOU HAVE COME FORTH SO   75 ANASHU VIJAYA   78
     NEWLY,
   I SAID! "A LINE WILL TAKE US HOURS MAYBE! . . . . 204 ADAMS CURSE   4
   MAYBE THEY LINGER BY THE WAY. . . . . 212 BLESS PSALTER   8
   MAYBE IT IS BUT NATURAL TO DOUBT ME. . . . . . 227 SHADOW WATER B 112
   ANOTHER ANSWERS, "MAYBE WE SHALL FIND . . . . . 233 SHADOW WATER B 254

MAYBE   (CONTINUED)
      MAYBE YOUR IMAGES HAVE STOOD, ...   273 GREY ROCK   50
      "MAYBE I SHALL BE LUCKY YET, ...   297 THREE BEGGARS   61
      AND MAYBE I SHALL TAKE A TROUT . . . .   297 THREE BEGGARS   67
      HAVING LOVED GOD ONCE, BUT MAYBE . . . .   299 THREE HERMITS   26
      OR MAYBE TO MIDSUMMER DAY," . . . .   305 HOUR DAWN   58
      MAYBE THE WEATHER WAS ACCURSED . . . .   305 HOUR DAWN   65
      I'LL SAY AND MAYBE DREAM I HAVE DRAWN CONTENT, . .   333 LIVING BEAUTY   V   1
      THAT MAYBE "I AM SORRY" IN PLAIN PROSE . . . . . .   341 SHEP GOATHERD   60
      MAYBE A TWELVEMONTH SINCE . . . .   348 FISHERMAN   25
      POEM MAYBE AS COLD . . . .   348 FISHERMAN   39
      MAYBE A TWELVE-MONTH SINCE . . . .   348 FISHERMAN   V   25
      THERE IS A QUEEN IN CHINA, OR MAYBE IT'S IN SPAIN, . . 353 HIS PHOENIX   1
      AND MAYBE THERE'LL BE SOME YOUNG BELLE WALK OUT TO MAKE 354 HIS PHOENIX   V   26
         MEN WILD
      BUT MAYBE SOME OLD GAFFER MUTTERS A BLESSING . . . .   355 BROKEN DREAMS   4
      FEATURES, OR MAYBE SHOWING . . . .   363 DOLLS DRAWINGS   4
      MAYBE THE MOON MAY LEARN, ...   378 CAT AND MOON   14
      THAT IT MAYBE HAD DANCED HER LIFE AWAY, ...   383 VISION ROBART   V   22
      MAYBE THE BRIDE-BED BRINGS DESPAIR, ...   388 SOLOMON WITCH   25
      MAYBE AN IMAGE IS TOO STRONG . . . .   388 SOLOMON WITCH   36
      OR MAYBE IS NOT STRONG ENOUGH." . . . .   388 SOLOMON WITCH   37
      "MAYBE A BREATH OF POLITIC WORDS . . . .   396 ROSE TREE   3
      OR MAYBE BUT A WIND THAT BLOWS . . . .   396 ROSE TREE   5
      LOSE NATURAL KINDNESS AND MAYBE . . . .   404 FOR DAUGHTER   22
      AND MAYBE THE GREAT-GRANDSON OF THAT HOUSE, ...   418 ANCEST HOUSES   23
      THAT WOULD NOT LIFT A HAND MAYBE . . . .   432 NINETEEN 19   109
      WHEN MAYBE THRICE IN EVERY MOON HER MOUTH . . . . .   468 HARUN RASHID   162
      FOR MAYBE ALL THAT HEAR . . . .   474 ALL SOUL NIGHT   89
      AND MAYBE WE ARE ALL THE SAME . . . .   570 THREE BUSHES   24
      AND MAYBE WE ARE ALL THE SAME . . . .   570 THREE BUSHES   26
      OR MAYBE SUBSTANCE CAN BE COMPOSITE, ...   619 BRONZE HEAD   12
      MAYBE AT LAST, BEING BUT A BROKEN MAN, ...   629 CIRCUS ANIMALS   3
      AND MAYBE WHAT THEY SAY IS TRUE . . . .   631 POLITICS   9
      SOME DAY YOU'LL BUY THEM, MAYBE. NEVER! NEVER? . . . 721 WITCH VIVIEN   24
      MAYBE NOW IN SOME FAR LANE, ...   731 STREET DANCERS   14
      MAYBE IN SOME ISLE OF ISLES, ...   732 STREET DANCERS   27
      MAYBE NOW A BEDOUIN'S BROOD, ...   732 STREET DANCERS   40
      AND THE OTHER ANSWERS, "MAYBE WE SHALL FIND . . . .   753 SHADOW WATER A   144
      OR MAYBE AN AGATE CUP. . . . .   781 MY HEART BEAT   16
      MAYBE I SHALL NOT DIE AT ALL. . . . .   788 HAWTHORN TREE   16
MAYHAP
      MAYHAP 'TWERE BETTER THAT ASIDE I THROW . . . . . .   656 ISLE STAT I 3   38
      ONCE MORE THOSE SHEPHERDS COME. MAYHAP SOME MIRTH . . 664 ISLE STAT II 2   49
MAYO
      IN MUSCULAR YOUTH WELL KNOWN TO MAYO MEN . . . . .   325 ROBERT GREGORY   34
      IN MUSCULAR YOUTH WELLKNOWN TO MAYO MEN . . . . .   325 ROBERT GREGORY V   34
MAYOR
      THE MAYOR CAME, LEANING HIS DEAF EAR— . . . . . .   725 LEGEND   13
MAY-TREASURE
      ALL THE HEALING EARTH MAY-TREASURE, ...   733 STREET DANCERS   63
MCTAGGART
      PROFOUND MCTAGGART THOUGHT SO, AND IN A BREATH . . . 619 BRONZE HEAD   13
MEAD
      AS THOUGH HE HELD AN EARTHLY MEAD . . . .   2 OISIN 1   V   7X
      WE PASSED IN SILENCE O'ER THE MEAD, ...   25 OISIN 1   V 376A
MEADOW
      BY LAKES AND MEADOW LANDS AND LAWNS AFAR, ...   32 OISIN 2   V 50F
      LEAP IN THE MEADOW. ON THE MISTY STAIRS . . . . .   44 OISIN 2   V 229
      WEAK, IN THE MIDST OF THE MEADOW. . . . .   54 OISIN 3   102
      OR ELSE AT MEADOW OR AT GRAZING OVERLOOKS . . . . .   340 SHEP GOATHERD   37
MEADOW-MICE
      AND GAZE ON THE MEADOW-MICE WARY, ...   707 FAIRY PEDANT   18
MEADOWS
      AMONG THE WINDY MEADOWS OF THE DAWN." . . . . . .   234 SHADOW WATER B   264
      ON HIS YELLOW LEGS THROUGH OUR MEADOWS, ...   341 SHEP GOATHERD   65
      UPON HIS YELLOW LEGS THROUGH OUR MEADOWS, ...   341 SHEP GOATHERD V   65
      THROUGH GOD-FORSAKEN MEADOWS! MRS. FRENCH, ...   412 TOWER   93
      AMONG THE WINDY MEADOWS OF THE DAWN." . . . . . .   754 SHADOW WATER A   153
      WE WILL FIND OUT VALLEYS AND WOODS AND MEADOWS . . . 767 SHADOW WATER A   388
      OR AMONG WINDS THAT MOVE IN THE MEADOWS AND WOODS. . . 768 SHADOW WATER A V   413
MEADOW-SAFFRONS
      WHERE THE MEADOW-SAFFRONS BLOW, ...   680 LOVE AND DEATH   6
MEAGRE
      FROM MEAGRE GIRLHOOD'S PUTTING ON . . . .   356 BROKEN DREAMS   9
MEAL
      AND SLEEPY HAVING HAD THEIR MEAL! . . . .   271 GREY ROCK   V   17
      TILL HIS MORNING MEAL COME ROUND: . . . .   435 FOR MY SON   4
MEAN
      MEAN ROOF-TREES WERE THE STURDIER FOR ITS FALL, . . . 264 HOUSE SHAKEN   8
      YOU MEAN THEY ARGUED. PUT IT SO! . . . .   385 ROBARTES DANCE   13
      HERE'S THE GIST OF WHAT THEY MEAN. . . . .   637 BEN BULBEN   12
      THY FLICKERING HAND? WHAT MEAN THE LIGHTS THAT RISE . 674 ISLE STAT II 3   198
MEANING
      OR LET ITS MEANING MIX INTO THE STRINGS. . . . . .   180 QUEEN MAEVE   8
      A MEANING IN THAT CIRCLING OVERHEAD? . . . .   234 SHADOW WATER B   270
      BUT WHAT'S THE MEANING? WHY DO YOU LINGER THERE? . . 234 SHADOW WATER B   271
      THEY CANNOT HEAR MY VOICE! BUT WHAT'S THE MEANING? . . 234 SHADOW WATER B   275
      THAT CANNOT BE THE MEANING OF THE BIRDS. . . . . .   235 SHADOW WATER B   278
      THE MEANING OF THAT MONSTROUS DAY. THEN SHE! . . . . 280 TWO KINGS   78
      DAY AFTER DAY, YET NEVER FIND THE MEANING. . . . . .   377 PHASES OF MOON   135

			PAGE	TITLE	LINE

MEANING   (CONTINUED)
WHAT'S THE MEANING OF ALL SONG? . . . .   502 VACILLATION   70
MEANINGLESS
OR POLITE MEANINGLESS WORDS, ...   392 EASTER 1916   6
POLITE MEANINGLESS WORDS, ...   392 EASTER 1916   8
MEANS
BY ANY OTHER MEANS. YOU CALL IT PASSION, ...   244 SHADOW WATER B   455
IT'S PLAIN THE BIBLE MEANS . . . .   345 ON WOMAN   10
MEANT
AND THAT DEAR WORDS MEANT NOTHING?" BUT ENOUGH, . . .   201 OLD MEMORY   9
THAT THINK SWORD-STROKES WERE BETTER MEANT . . . . .   276 GREY ROCK   129
THAT THINK SWORD STROKES WERE BETTER MEANT . . . . .   276 GREY ROCK   V 129
WHAT ROBERT BROWNING MEANT . . . .   605 YOU CONTENT   22
MEASURE
WHO WHEN THEY DANCE TO A FITFUL MEASURE . . . . . .   9 OISIN 1   97
IN A VIGOUR MORE THAN MORTAL MEASURE, ...   9 OISIN 1   V   98
THE MEASURE OF HER FLYING FEET . . . .   138 TO IRELAND   11
TO LIGHT A MEASURE HERE AND THERE; . . . .   138 TO IRELAND   14
WORTH KNITTING TO A MEASURE OF SWEET SOUND? . . . .   181 QUEEN MAEVE   33
OUTRUN THE MEASURE. I'D TELL OF THAT GREAT QUEEN . . .   187 QUEEN MAEVE   141
THAT WEIGH AND MEASURE ALL IN THESE WASTE SEAS-- . .   235 SHADOW WATER B   292
AND MEASURE OUT A COURSE AND BRING US HOME, ...   238 SHADOW WATER B   362
THERE IS NO MEASURE THAT IT WOULD NOT BURST. . . . .   245 SHADOW WATER B   484
HAVE BEEN THE MEASURE OF THAT CARE." BUT EOCHAID, . .   276 TWO KINGS   V   H
TILL TOES MASTERED A SWEET MEASURE, ...   331 ROUND TOWER   15
I'D DANCE A MEASURE ON HIS GRAVE." . . . .   338 TOM OROUGHLEY   16
FOR RHYME CAN BEAT A MEASURE OUT OF TROUBLE . . . .   339 SHEP GOATHERD   12
MEASURE THE LOT; FORGIVE MYSELF THE LOT; . . . . .   479 SELF AND SOUL   67
AND MEASURE OUT THE WAYS OF CHIVALRY. . . . . . .   660 ISLE STAT II 1   37
NAY, GIVE IT ME, AND I WILL SOUND A MEASURE; . . .   681 SEEKER   9
AND MEASURE THE MINDS OF THE FLOWERS, ...   707 FAIRY PEDANT   17
AS THOUGH THEY'D VOWED TO MEASURE ALL ITS WAYS, . .   711 FERENCZ RENYI   48
WOULD THEY FOOT SO FLEET A MEASURE? . . . .   731 STREET DANCERS   12
WOULD THEY FOOT SO FLEET A MEASURE? . . . .   732 STREET DANCERS   25
WOULD THEY FOOT SO FLEET A MEASURE? . . . .   732 STREET DANCERS   38
WOULD THEY FOOT SO FLEET A MEASURE? . . . .   733 STREET DANCERS   51
WOULD THEY FOOT SO FLEET A MEASURE? . . . .   733 STREET DANCERS   64
WERE HIS MEASURE RUNNING DRY. . . . .   772 SONG DEIRDRE 1   14
MEASURED   SEE PLUMMET-MEASURED
UPON A MEASURED QUIETUDE. . . . .   138 TO IRELAND   16
YET HE WHO TREADS IN MEASURED WAYS . . . .   138 TO IRELAND   27
YOU HAVE MEASURED OUT THE ROAD THAT THE SOUL TREADS . .   342 SHEP GOATHERD   80
MEASURELESS
A MEASURELESS CONSUMMATION THAT HE DREAMED. . . . .   324 ROBERT GREGORY   24
MEASUREMENT
WHAT CALCULATION, NUMBER, MEASUREMENT, REPLIED? . .   611 STATUES   27
MEASUREMENT BEGAN OUR MIGHT; . . . .   638 BEN BULBEN   42
IN TOILS OF MEASUREMENT . . . .   784 WOMANS BEAUTY   9
IN TOIL OF MEASUREMENT . . . .   784 WOMANS BEAUTY   V   9
MEASURER
WHAT MEASURER TIME HAS LIT ABOVE, ...   139 TO IRELAND   38
MEASURES
HE WHO MEASURES GAIN AND LOSS, ...   744 ROSY CROSS   1
HE WHO MEASURES GAIN AND LOSS, ...   744 ROSY CROSS   9
WERE HIS MEASURES RUNNING DRY. . . . .   772 SONG DEIRDRE 1 V   14
MEASURING
ON THAT OLD QUEEN MEASURING A TOWN . . . .   344 DAWN   3
ON THE OLD QUEEN MEASURING A TOWN . . . .   344 DAWN   V   3
MEAT
THOSE TWO CAME CARRYING WINE AND MEAT AND BREAD, . . .   41 OISIN 2   184
QUIET'S WILD HEART, LIKE DAILY MEAT; . . . . . .   196 BAILE AILLINN   178
TO MAKE LOW LAUGHTER MORE THAN MEAT AND DRINK, . . .   230 SHADOW WATER B   186
FOR ALL WERE FULL OF WINE AND MEAT. . . . . . .   271 GREY ROCK   17
TO TAKE THE ROSES FOR HIS MEAT. . . . .   382 SONG OF FOOL   12
AND YET IN FLYING FLING INTO MY MEAT . . . . . .   384 VISION ROBART   53
A CRAZY SALAD WITH THEIR MEAT . . . .   404 FOR DAUGHTER   31
AND TOOK A MESS OF SHADOWS FOR ITS MEAT? . . . .   444 SCHOOL CHILDR   28
AND TOOK A MASS OF SHADOWS FOR ITS MEAT, ...   444 SCHOOL CHILDR V   28
AND MEAT TO THE ASLAUGA SHEE . . . .   743 DANAAN QUICK   17
AND TASTE WITH ME THE FAERIES' MEAT, ...   743 DANAAN QUICK   26
MECHANICAL
AND NEVER STOOP TO A MECHANICAL . . . .   417 ANCEST HOUSES   7
MEDDLE
OR MEDDLE WITH OUR GIVE AND TAKE . . . .   395 SIXTEEN DEAD   17
MEDDLING
HE HAS HAD ENOUGH OF MEDDLING WHO CAN PLEASE . . .   359 WAR POEM   4
MEDIAEVAL
MY MEDIAEVAL KNEES LACK HEALTH UNTIL THEY BEND, . . .   603 GALLERY REVIS   33
MEDIAN
WHAT MEDIAN, PERSIAN, BABYLONIAN, ...   420 MY HOUSE   V 20D
MEDIATION
A MEDIATION IN TIME OF WAR . . . .   406 IN TIME OF WAR V   T
MEDICABLE
SOME MEDICABLE HERB TO MAKE OUR GRIEF . . . . .   342 SHEP GOATHERD   86
MEDICINE
FOR MEDICINE." THEREON HE CRIED ALOUD, ...   281 TWO KINGS   98
MEDITATE
I MEDITATE UPON A SWALLOW'S FLIGHT, ...   488 COOLE PARK 29   1
AND YET UPON THESE MAXIMS MEDITATE; . . . . . .   500 VACILLATION   22
TO MEDITATE ON. . . . .   628 JANE MOUNTAIN   6
AS THOUGH TO MEDITATE ON WOUNDS AND BLOOD. . . .   634 CUCHULAIN COMF   6

509

		PAGE	TITLE	LINE
MEDITATION				
THE MEDITATION OF THE OLD FISHERMAN		90	OLD FISHERMAN	T
A MEDITATION IN TIME OF WAR		406	IN TIME OF WAR	T
A MAN IN HIS OWN SECRET MEDITATION		431	NINETEEN 19	69
TILL MEDITATION MASTER ALL ITS PARTS,		474	ALL SOUL NIGHT	92
AT ALGECIRAS--A MEDITATION UPON DEATH		493	AT ALGECIRAS	T
A MEDITATION WRITTEN DURING SICKNESS AT ALGECIRAS		493	AT ALGECIRAS	V T
FOR ANTIQUARIAN MEDITATION. AY,		721	WITCH VIVIEN	38
MEDITATIONS				
MEDITATIONS IN TIME OF CIVIL WAR ANCESTRAL HOUSES		417	ANCEST HOUSES	V T
FOR MEDITATIONS UPON UNKNOWN THOUGHT		473	ALL·SOUL NIGHT	74
MEDITATIONS UPON DEATH		493	AT ALGECIRAS	V T
MEDITATIVE				
THE MEDITATIVE CRITIC: ALL ARE ON THEIR TOES,		363	DOLLS FACES	8
THAT MEDITATIVE MAN, JOHN SYNGE, AND THOSE		489	COOLE PARK 29	13
AND HERE'S JOHN SYNGE, A MEDITATIVE MAN,		603	GALLERY REVIS	V 48
MEDIUM				
THE SPIRIT MEDIUM		599	SPIRIT MEDIUM	T
MEDIUM'S				
OUT OF A MEDIUM'S MOUTH,		439	FRAGMENTS	6
MEEK				
OR HAST THOU NEVER SEEN, WITH VISAGE MEEK,		672	ISLE STAT II 3	156
MEET				
AND WHERE THE WOOD AND WATERS MEET		14	OISIN 1	193
AND WHERE THE WOODS AND WATERS MEET		14	OISIN 1	V 193
DOWN BY THE SALLEY GARDENS MY LOVE AND I DID MEET:		90	SALLEY GARDENS	1
AND CRIED WITH ANGRY VOICE, "IT IS NOT MEET		107	CUCHULAIN SEA	20
AND CRIED OUT TO HIM, "SON IT IS NOT MEET		107	CUCHULAIN SEA	V 20
AND CALLED OUT TO HIM, "SON IT IS NOT MEET		107	CUCHULAIN SEA	V 20
THAT YOU COME HERE TO MEET THIS ANCIENT SWORD?"		109	CUCHULAIN SEA	V 61
MAY SURELY MEET THEIR ANCIENT GAZE,		139	TO IRELAND	V 28
VEERING, FLEETING, FICKLE, OUR LOVES AND ANGERS MEET:		207	HANRAHANS SONG	V 3
BY THE WOOD'S EDGE WHERE ONLY EQUALS MEET,		321	REED WHISPERER	V 8
ALWAYS WE'D HAVE THE NEW FRIEND MEET THE OLD		324	ROBERT GREGORY	9
SO PERILOUS THAT HALF THE ASTONISHED MEET		326	ROBERT GREGORY	61
I KNOW THAT I SHALL MEET MY FATE		328	IRISH AIRMAN	1
WHEN MY LUCK CHANGED AND THEY DARED MEET MY FACE,		352	PEOPLE	25
WHEN MY LUCK CHANGED AND THEY DARED TO MEET MY FACE,		352	PEOPLE	V 25
SUDDENLY I MEET YOUR FACE.		357	DEEP-SWORN VOW	6
WHEN TWO CLOSE KINDRED MEET,		378	CAT AND MOON	12
UNDER BEN BULBEN TO THE MEET,		397	POLIT PRISONER	14
BIRTH-HOUR AND DEATH-HOUR MEET,		496	MOHINI CHATTER	26
I KNOW, ALTHOUGH WHEN LOOKS MEET		511	JANE AND JACK	1
THINKING TO MEET MY LOVE ONCE MORE		551	SONGS REWRIT 1	V 15
MATTER FOR OLD AGE MEET:		553	CHURCH STATE	2
IF JUPITER AND SATURN MEET		562	CONJUNCTIONS	1
WHEN YOU AND MY TRUE LOVER-MEET		573	LADYS 3RD SONG	1
NOW HER SHEEP ALL BROWSING MEET		646	ISLE STAT I 1	22
BENDING HER FACE O'ER HIS, SHE WATCHES MEET		688	TWO TITANS	45
YET SOMEWHERE IN THE FOOTSORE WORLD WE MEET,		691	MOSADA 1	23
WE MEET--WE TWO. HOW MERRY ALL THESE ARE		691	MOSADA 1	31
WE MEET AT LAST, THE MINISTERING STARS		701	MOSADA 3	52
MEETING				
A MURMUR OF SOFT WORDS AND MEETING LIPS.		187	QUEEN MAEVE	154
ALL THAT IS NOT THE MEETING OF OUR LIPS.		246	SHADOW WATER B	506
MEETING		539	MEETING	T
MEETING LONG HENCE THE PHANTOM HERDSMAN, KING		675	ISLE STAT II 3	242
MEETINGS				
THEY HOLD THEIR PUBLIC MEETINGS WHERE		460	THREE MONUMENT	1
MEET'S				
THE MEET'S UPON THE MOUNTAIN-SIDE.		549	SEVERED HEAD	6
THE MEET'S UPON THE MOUNTAIN SIDE.		549	SEVERED HEAD	V 6
MEETS				
FOR HORSEMANSHIP AT MEETS OR AT RACECOURSES,		325	ROBERT GREGORY	35
IN MUSCULAR YOUTH, AT MEETS OR AT RACECOURSES,		325	ROBERT GREGORY	35
FOR HORSEMANSHIP AT MEETS OR AT RACE-COURSES,		325	ROBERT GREGORY	V 35
AND WHEN SHE MEETS OUR GAZE HER EYES ARE LAUGHTER-LIT,		362	HER COURTESY	5
AND WHEN SHE MEETS OUR GAZE HER EYES ARE LAUGHTER LIT		362	HER COURTESY	V 5
WHERE EVERYTHING THAT MEETS THE EYE,		639	BEN BULBEN	56
MEG				
FOR PEG AND MEG AND PARIS' LOVE		458	HIS WILDNESS	3
MELANCHOLY				
TO WANDER BY THEIR MELANCHOLY MINDS.		72	ANASHU VIJAYA	33
A MELANCHOLY THAT A CUP OF WINE,		227	SHADOW WATER B	114
UPON A MELANCHOLY MAN		360	ALF POLLEXFEN	11
BUT A SUDDEN MELANCHOLY		667	ISLE STAT II 3	30
MELLOW				
MANSIONS OF MEMORIES AND MELLOW THOUGHTS		721	WITCH VIVIEN	21
TO THOSE YOUR "MELLOW" WARES HAVE WEARIED OUT.		721	WITCH VIVIEN	27
MELODIES				
ONE ASKS FOR MOURNFUL MELODIES:		567	LAPIS LAZULI	53
MELODIOUS				
REWORDING IN MELODIOUS GUILE		66	HAPPY SHEPHERD	39
REWARDING IN MELODIOUS GUILE		66	HAPPY SHEPHERD	V 39
MELODY				
SING IN THEIR HIGH AND LONELY MELODY.		101	ROSE UPON ROOD	8
HAS GIVEN THE WAVES THEIR MELODY,		134	TWO TREES	10
HARRIED, AND BURKE'S GREAT MELODY AGAINST IT.		487	SEVEN SAGES	16
A QUENCHLESS GRIEVING OF LOVE MELODY.		645	ISLE STAT I 1	21
MELT				
MELT DOWN, AS IT WERE WAX IN THE SUN'S RAYS:		428	NINETEEN 19	12

510

MELT   (CONTINUED)
    SAINT JOSEPH THOUGHT THE WORLD WOULD MELT • • • • • •   619 STICK INCENSE   3
MELTED
    THE SINGING MELTED IN THE NIGHT; • • • • • • • •   28 OISIN 1   V 427A
    MELTED AND FLOWED, AND IN THE SELF-SAME PLACE • • • •   39 OISIN 2   146
MELTING
    DREAMING OF HER OWN MELTING HUES, • • • • • • • •   13 OISIN 1   162
    AND DREAMS OF HER OWN MELTING HUES, • • • • • • •   13 OISIN 1   V 162
MEMORIAM
    IN MEMORIAM • • • • • • • • • • • • •   737 MOURN THEN ON   V   T
MEMORIES
    WERE THE MEMORIES OF THE WHOLE OF MY SORROW • • •   52 OISIN 3   71
    • • • AND THE MEMORIES OF THE WHOLE OF MY MIRTH, • • • •   52 OISIN 3   71
    SPEAK, YOU TOO ARE OLD WITH YOUR MEMORIES, • • • • •   61 OISIN 3   196
    SPEAK, THOU TOO ART OLD WITH THY MEMORIES, • • • • •   61 OISIN 3   V 196
    GAY BELLS OR SAD, THEY BRING YOU MEMORIES • • • •   130 BOOK STORIES   21
    THEY BRING YOU MEMORIES OF OLD VILLAGE FACES, • •   130 BOOK STORIES   V 22
    HAVE SUCH LONG MEMORIES THAT THEY STILL • • • • • •   192 BAILE AILLINN   90
    THAT WERE LIKE MEMORIES OF YOU--BUT NOW • • • • •   257 RECONCILIATION   7
    VANISHED, AND LEFT BUT MEMORIES, THAT SHOULD BE OUT OF   316 COLD HEAVEN   5
        SEASON
    VAGUE MEMORIES, NOTHING BUT MEMORIES. • • • • •   356 BROKEN DREAMS   15
    VAGUE MEMORIES, NOTHING BUT MEMORIES, • • • • •   356 BROKEN DREAMS   V 15
    VAGUE MEMORIES, NOTHING BUT MEMORIES, • • • • •   356 BROKEN DREAMS   20
    VAGUE MEMORIES, NOTHING BUT MEMORIES, • • • • •   356 BROKEN DREAMS   V 20
    VAGUE MEMORIES, NOTHING BUT MEMORIES. • • • • •   357 BROKEN DREAMS   41
    VAGUE MEMORIES, NOTHING BUT MEMORIES. • • • • •   357 BROKEN DREAMS   V 41
    BY CHILDISH MEMORIES OF AN OLD CROSS POLLEXFEN, • • • •   391 UNDER SATURN   7
    MY MEMORIES HAD MAGNIFIED • • • • • • • • •   399 BREAK OF DAY   10
    IMAGES AND MEMORIES • • • • • • • • • • •   410 TOWER   22
    FOR I NEED ALL HIS MIGHTY MEMORIES. • • • • • •   413 TOWER   104
    AND MEMORIES OF LOVE, • • • • • • • • • •   415 TOWER   161
    MEMORIES OF THE WORDS OF WOMEN, • • • • • • •   415 TOWER   162
    HIS MEMORIES • • • • • • • • • • • • •   454 HIS MEMORIES   T
    MEMORIES OF THE TALK • • • • • • • • • •   607 SONGS BURDEN 2   22
    MANSIONS OF MEMORIES AND MELLOW THOUGHTS • • • • •   721 WITCH VIVIEN   21
MEMORY
    IN BROODING MEMORY, NOR WEEP. • • • • • • •   11 OISIN 1   V 131B
    IN SOME DIM MEMORY OR ANCIENT MOOD, • • • • •   36 OISIN 2   99
    WRAPT ROUND IN SOME DIM MEMORY, IT SEEMED--   36 OISIN 2   V 99
    WAS LOADED WITH THE MEMORY OF DAYS • • • • •   39 OISIN 2   150
    'TIS OVER; FAR WITH MEMORY I SWAY AND ROCK. • •   43 OISIN 2   V 212
    AND TURNED THE FARMER'S MEMORY FROM HIS CATTLE.   129 BOOK STORIES   6
    ARE IN MY MEMORY; • • • • • • • • • •   132 OLD PENSIONER   16
    WE HOLD, BECAUSE OUR MEMORY IS • • • • • • •   192 BAILE AILLINN   85
    OLD MEMORY • • • • • • • • • • • • •   201 OLD MEMORY   T
    AWAKENS AN OLD MEMORY, AND SAY, • • • • • •   201 OLD MEMORY   2
    WHERE WINGS HAVE MEMORY OF WINGS, AND ALL • •   264 HOUSE SHAKEN   6
    A HUNDRED-YEAR-OLD MEMORY TO THE POOR; • • • •   269 PARDON FATHERS   6
    IN DAYS YOU HAVE NOT KEPT IN MEMORY, • • • •   284 TWO KINGS   168
    HAD HALF AWAKENED SOME OLD MEMORY-- • • • •   284 TWO KINGS   172
    HAD HALF WAKENED SOME OLD MEMORY, • • • • •   284 TWO KINGS   V 172
    THIS HUMAN LIFE BLOTTED FROM MEMORY, • • • •   285 TWO KINGS   198
    CAN BLOT OUT OF MY MEMORY THIS LIFE • • • •   285 TWO KINGS   204
    A MEMORY OF YOUTH • • • • • • • • • •   313 MEMORY YOUTH   T
    IN MEMORY OF MAJOR ROBERT GREGORY • • • • •   323 ROBERT GREGORY   T
    IN MEMORY OF ROBERT GREGORY • • • • • • •   323 ROBERT GREGORY V   T
    MEMORY • • • • • • • • • • • • • •   350 MEMORY   T
    IN MEMORY OF ALFRED POLLEXFEN • • • • • • •   360 ALF POLLEXFEN   T
    IN MEMORY • • • • • • • • • • • • •   360 ALF POLLEXFEN   V   T
    WHO CARRIED IN THEIR MEMORY • • • • • • •   361 ALF POLLEXFEN   34
    IS MEMORY OR FOREKNOWLEDGE OF THE HOUR • • •   375 PHASES OF MOON   73
    BEFORE MY TIME, SEEM LIKE A VIVID MEMORY. • •   391 UNDER SATURN   10
    WHOSE IMAGES, IN THE GREAT MEMORY STORED, • •   412 TOWER   85
    AND THAT IF MEMORY RECUR, THE SUN'S • • • •   414 TOWER   119
    THAT LIVES IN MEMORY, • • • • • • • • •   459 HIS WILDNESS   10
    EVEN FROM THAT DELIGHT MEMORY TREASURES SO, • •   459 FROM OEDIPUS   4
    AND SPEAK BUT LIES. CALL UP TO MEMORY • • •   462 HARUN RASHID   V   30
    IN MEMORY OF EVA GORE-BOOTH AND CON MARKIEWICZ   475 EVA GORE-BOOTH   T
    A MOMENT'S MEMORY TO THAT LAURELLED HEAD. • •   489 COOLE PARK 29   32
    OR GARDENS RICH IN MEMORY GLORIFIED • • • •   491 COOLE BALLYLEE   35
    MOCK AT THE MEMORY OF BOTH O'NEILLS, • • • •   546 TO SAME TUNE 2   24
    MOCK AT THE MEMORY OF BOTH O'NEILLS, • • • •   614 MARCH SONGS 1   24
    TO ENGROSS THE PRESENT AND DOMINATE MEMORY. • •   630 CIRCUS ANIMALS   30
    AND THY MEMORY I KEEP, • • • • • • • •   647 ISLE STAT I 1   59
    HIS MEMORY NOW IS A TALL PILLAR, BURNING • •   738 MOURN THEN ON   15
    OUT OF MEMORY AND MIND. • • • • • • • •   775 AGAINST WITCH   10
    A MEMORY, EVEN TO THE DEAD, • • • • • • •   791 REPRISALS   8
MEN   SEE FIGHTING-MEN
    THE BAD OLD DAYS. THOU WERT, MEN SING, • • •   2 OISIN 1   V   3
    CRIED FIN; AND CRIED SHE, "MEN OF FAME, • • •   5 OISIN 1   V 45
    ALL MEN, AND STRONGER OF HIS HANDS, • • • •   7 OISIN 1   V 63
    WHERE MEN HAVE HEAPED NO BURIAL-MOUNDS, • • •   8 OISIN 1   82
    WHERE MEN HAVE HEAPED NO BURIAL MOUNDS, • • •   8 OISIN 1   V 82
    OF MEN AND LADIES, HAND IN HAND, • • • • •   15 OISIN 1   202
    OF MEN AND MAIDENS, HAND IN HAND, • • • • •   15 OISIN 1   V 202
    AND MEN AND LADIES KNELT THEM THERE • • • •   18 OISIN 1   255
    AND MEN AND MAIDENS KNELT THEM THERE • • • •   18 OISIN 1   V 255
    O'ER MEN WHO SLEEP, AND WAKE, AND DIE, • • •   22 OISIN 1   V 340B
    WITH ALL THE ANCIENT SORROW OF MEN"; • • • •   25 OISIN 1   381
    WHO WEDDED MEN WITH RINGS OF DRUID GOLD; • • •   29 OISIN 2   10

```
                                                        PAGE      TITLE            LINE
MEN    (CONTINUED)
    THE SADDEST OF ALL MEN."  . . . . . . . . .          33 OISIN 2               68
    "FOR ALL MEN FLEE THE DEMONS"! BUT MOVED NOT  . . . .  36 OISIN 2             93
    TO RULE MORE MIGHTY MEN, AND TO THE WORLD  . . . . .  38 OISIN 2           V 133
    WAR ON THE MIGHTIEST MEN UNDER THE SKIES, . . . . . .  45 OISIN 2             241
    LIKE AN ARMY OF OLD MEN LONGING FOR REST FROM THE MOAN 48 OISIN 3             16
        OF THE SEAS.
    AND EACH OF THE HUGE WHITE CREATURES WAS HUGER THAN    49 OISIN 3             33
        FOURSCORE MEN!
    AND EACH OF THE HUGE WHITE CREATURES WAS HUGER THAN    49 OISIN 3           V 33
        FOUR-SCORE MEN;
    HELPLESS, MEN LIFTING THE LIDS OF HIS WEARY            53 OISIN 3             92
        AND DEATH-MAKING EYE.
    HELPLESS, MEN LIFTING THE LIDS OF HIS WEARY            53 OISIN 3           V 92
        AND DEATH-POURING EYE.
    . . . AND MOVE WHERE THE OLD MEN AND YOUNG  . . . . .  55 OISIN 3             114
    . . . AND SEE WHAT THE MORTAL MEN DO, . . . . . . . .  55 OISIN 3           V 125
    LIKE AN ARMY OF OLD MEN LONGING FOR REST FROM THE MOAN 57 OISIN 3             144
        OF THE SEAS.
    LIKE AN ARMY OF OLD MEN LOUNGING FOR REST FROM THE FOAM 57 OISIN 3          V 144
        OF THE SEAS.
    . . . AND I KNEW HOW MEN SORROW AND PASS, . . . . . .  59 OISIN 3             175
    . . . AND I KNEW HOW MEN PASS, . . . . . . . . . . .   59 OISIN 3           V 175
    WITH A SOB FOR MEN WAXING SO WEAKLY, . . . . . . . .   60 OISIN 3             188
    HOW THE MEN OF THE SAND-SACK SHOWED ME A CHURCH . . .  61 OISIN 3             193
    HOW THE MEN OF THE SAND-SACK LED ME TO SHAUL . . . .   61 OISIN 3           V 193
    NO LEARNING FROM THE STARRY MEN, . . . . . . . . . .   66 HAPPY SHEPHERD      28
    WHERE MEN LIE FROZEN IN THE GLIMMERING SNOW! . . . .   73 ANASHU VIJAYA       51
    FIELDS FATTENING SLOW, MEN WISE IN JOY, . . . . . .    82 MAD KING GOLL     V 6
    I CALLED MY BATTLE-BREAKING MEN . . . . . . . . . .    83 MAD KING GOLL       17
    AROUND ME SHONE KEEN EYES OF MEN! . . . . . . . . .    83 MAD KING GOLL       30
    I DREW AT EVENING MY MAILED MEN, . . . . . . . . .     83 MAD KING GOLL     V 19
    AND SHONE AROUND THE EYES OF MEN! . . . . . . . . .    83 MAD KING GOLL     V 30
    AND LEARN TO CHAUNT A TONGUE MEN DO NOT KNOW . . . .  101 ROSE UPON ROOD      21
    AND LEARN TO CHANT A TONGUE MEN DO NOT KNOW. . . . .  101 ROSE UPON ROOD    V 21
    "STILL TREADS THE WORLD AMID HIS ARMED MEN."  . . .   107 CUCHULAIN SEA     V 26
    AMONG THOSE FEASTING MEN CUCHULAIN DWELT, . . . . .   108 CUCHULAIN SEA       39
    "THE DOOMS OF MEN ARE IN GOD'S HIDDEN PLACE." . . .   110 CUCHULAIN SEA       62
    THEN CONCHUBAR, THE SUBTLEST OF ALL MEN, . . . . .    110 CUCHULAIN SEA       75
    "THE DOOMS OF MEN ARE IN GOD'S HIDDEN HOARD." . . .   110 CUCHULAIN SEA     V 62
    REST FAR FROM MEN. . . . . . . . . . . . . . . . .    116 FAERY SONG          10
    AND MEN WHO LOVED THE CAUSE THAT NEVER DIES. . . .    130 BOOK STORIES      V 24
    OF PASSIONATE MEN, LIKE BATS IN THE DEAD TREES! . .   136 TO SOME I TALK      5
    AND HE SAW YOUNG MEN AND YOUNG GIRLS . . . . . . .    144 HOST OF AIR         13
    TO OLD MEN PLAYING AT CARDS . . . . . . . . . . .     144 HOST OF AIR         23
    HE PLAYED WITH THE MERRY OLD MEN . . . . . . . . .    145 HOST OF AIR         29
    OLD MEN AND YOUNG MEN AND YOUNG GIRLS . . . . . .     145 HOST OF AIR         39
    OLD MEN AND YOUNG MEN AND YOUNG GIRLS . . . . . .     145 HOST OF AIR         39
    BUT THE OLD MEN AND DANCERS WERE GONE, . . . . . .    145 HOST OF AIR       V 39
    I CRIED IN MY DREAM, O WOMEN, BID THE YOUNG MEN LAY   163 VALLEY LOVERS       5
    AND I CRIED IN MY DREAM "O WOMEN, BID THE YOUNG MEN LAY 163 VALLEY LOVERS   V 5
    WOMEN AND CHILDREN, YOUNG MEN WITH BOOKS, . . . . .   167 BLESSED             15
    AND OLD MEN WITH CROZIERS AND STOLES. . . . . . . .   167 BLESSED             16
    CHILDREN AND WOMEN AND TONSURED YOUNG MEN, . . . .    167 BLESSED           V 15
    MEN HAVE NAMED BEAUTY. THY GREAT LEAVES ENFOLD . .    169 SECRET ROSE         7
    MEN HAVE NAMED BEAUTY. YOUR HEAVY LEAVES ENFOLD . .   169 SECRET ROSE       V 7
    MEN HAVE NAMED BEAUTY. YOUR GREAT LEAVES ENFOLD . .   169 SECRET ROSE       V 7
    THAT MEN THRESHED CORN AT MIDNIGHT BY A TRESS, . .    170 SECRET ROSE         26
    TILL MAEVE CALLED OUT, "THESE ARE BUT COMMON MEN. .   186 QUEEN MAEVE         122
    OF HARPERS AND YOUNG MEN! AND THEY . . . . . . . .    189 BAILE AILLINN       19
    AND OLD AND YOUNG MEN RODE WITH HER! . . . . . . .    191 BAILE AILLINN       51
    AND LEATHER-COATED MEN WITH SLINGS . . . . . . . .    193 BAILE AILLINN     V 111
    AFTER THE DEATHS OF MANY MEN, . . . . . . . . . .     197 BAILE AILLINN       193
    THE OLD MEN ADMIRING THEMSELVES IN THE WATER . . .    208 OLD MEN ADMIRE      T
    I HEARD THE OLD, OLD MEN SAY, . . . . . . . . . .     208 OLD MEN ADMIRE      1
    I HEARD THE OLD, OLD MEN SAY, . . . . . . . . . .     208 OLD MEN ADMIRE      7
    IS NOT KNOWN AMONG MEN, . . . . . . . . . . . . .     215 HAPPY TOWNLAND      28
    ON WET ROADS WHERE MEN WALK, . . . . . . . . . . .    215 HAPPY TOWNLAND      48
    YET DREAMED THAT BEINGS HAPPIER THAN MEN . . . . .    218 WOODS OF COOLE      18
    I HAVE MADE THIS POEM FOR YOU, THAT MEN MAY READ IT . 219 WOODS OF COOLE      41
    AS MEN IN THE OLD TIMES, BEFORE THE HARPS BEGAN, . .  219 WOODS OF COOLE      43
    AS MEN IN THE OLD TIMES, BEFORE THE HARP BEGAN, . .   219 WOODS OF COOLE    V 43
    PEACEABLE MEN THAT SHUT THE WIND AWAY, . . . . . .    224 SHADOW WATER B      54
    AND KISS MORE LIPS THAN LASTING PEACEABLE MEN . . .   225 SHADOW WATER B      71
    NO, NOR WITH A HUNDRED MEN LIKE YOU . . . . . . . .   225 SHADOW WATER B    V 74
    WHEN SHE FINDS OUT WE HAVE BETTER MEN ABOARD . . .    232 SHADOW WATER B      231
    ARMED MEN HAVE COME UPON US! O I AM SLAIN! . . . .    233 SHADOW WATER B      241
    ARMED MEN HAVE COME UPON US! O I AM SLAIN! . . . .    233 SHADOW WATER B      243
    MEN RAN UPON THE SHORE. . . . . . . . . . . . . .     253 HIS DREAM         V 4
    HAVE TAUGHT TO IGNORANT MEN MOST VIOLENT WAYS, . .    256 NO SECOND TROY      3
    THEATRE BUSINESS, MANAGEMENT OF MEN. . . . . . . .    260 FASC DIFFICULT      11
    THE GIFTS THAT GOVERN MEN, AND AFTER THESE . . . .    264 HOUSE SHAKEN        10
    OR IS THERE NONE, MOST POPULAR OF MEN, . . . . . .    265 ABBEY THEATRE       13
    AND WE FIND HEARTENERS AMONG MEN . . . . . . . . .    266 GALWAY RACES        15
    AND FIND HEARTENERS AMONG MEN . . . . . . . . . .     266 GALWAY RACES      V 15
    FOR HE IS THE WORST OF ALL DEAD MEN." . . . . . . .   272 GREY ROCK           36
    OF MEN AND WOMEN MADE LIKE THESE! . . . . . . . .     272 GREY ROCK           43
    WHY ARE THE GODS BY MEN BETRAYED?" . . . . . . . .    275 GREY ROCK           115
    HE HAD OUTRIDDEN HIS WAR-WASTED MEN . . . . . . . .   277 TWO KINGS           3
    HE HAD OUT-RIDDEN HIS WAR-WASTED MEN . . . . . . .    277 TWO KINGS         V 3
    THE FIGHTING MEN AND SERVANTS OF THIS HOUSE, . . .    280 TWO KINGS         V 70
```

		PAGE	TITLE		LINE
MEN (CONTINUED)

MY MEN, WHETHER IT PLEASE HER OR DISPLEASE, ... 281 TWO KINGS 112
AND TAKE HER IN THE MIDDLE OF ARMED MEN, ... 282 TWO KINGS 114
HAPPINESS TO CHILDREN AND TO MEN." . . . . 282 TWO KINGS 121
JOSTLED AND SHOUTED THOSE WAR-WASTED MEN, ... 286 TWO KINGS 216
FOR MEN WERE BORN TO PRAY AND SAVE: . . . . 289 SEPTEMBER 1913 6
WHEN GREY GULLS FLIT ABOUT INSTEAD OF MEN, ... 292 TO A SHADE 6
WHEN GREY GULLS FLY ABOUT INSTEAD OF MEN, ... 292 TO A SHADE V 6
THAT MEN DESERT, ... 293 HELEN LIVED 2
OF THE MEN AND WOMEN OF TROY, ... 293 HELEN LIVED 11
DO MEN WHO LEAST DESIRE GET MOST, ... 295 THREE BEGGARS 13
THAT THE SHADES OF HOLY MEN . . . . 298 THREE HERMITS 17
POOR MEN HAVE GROWN TO BE RICH MEN, ... 301 RUN PARADISE 15
POOR MEN HAVE GROWN TO BE RICH MEN, ... 301 RUN PARADISE 15
AND RICH MEN GROWN TO BE POOR AGAIN, ... 301 RUN PARADISE 16
WHAT CAN BOOKS OF MEN THAT WIVE . . . . 309 REALISTS 2
IN MUSCULAR YOUTH WELL KNOWN TO MAYO MEN . . . . . . 325 ROBERT GREGORY 34
IN MUSCULAR YOUTH WELLKNOWN TO MAYO MEN . . . . 325 ROBERT GREGORY V 34
AND SOLID MEN, FOR ALL THEIR PASSION, LIVE . . . . . 325 ROBERT GREGORY 37
WELL KNOWN FOR HORSEMANSHIP TO CONNACHT MEN . . . . . 325 ROBERT GREGORY V 34
NOR PUBLIC MEN, NOR CHEERING CROWDS, ... 328 IRISH AIRMAN 10
MEN IMPROVE WITH THE YEARS . . . . 329 MEN IMPROVE T
FOR MEN IMPROVE WITH THE YEARS! . . . . 329 MEN IMPROVE 11
THE LIVING BEAUTY IS FOR YOUNGER MEN: . . . . 334 LIVING BEAUTY 9
THAT YOUNG MEN, TOSSING ON THEIR BEDS, ... 337 SCHOLARS 4
HER LABOURING MEN, AS THOUGH HER DARLING LIVED, . . . 340 SHEP GOATHERD 38
OR ON THE WITHERED MEN THAT SAW . . . . 344 DAWN 5
THE LIVING MEN THAT I HATE, ... 347 FISHERMAN 13
THE YOUNG MEN EVERY NIGHT APPLAUD THEIR GABY'S LAUGHING 353 HIS PHOENIX 9
    EYE,
AND WHO CAN SAY BUT SOME YOUNG BELLE MAY WALK AND TALK 354 HIS PHOENIX 26
    MEN WILD
THERE'LL BE THAT CROWD TO MAKE MEN WILD THROUGH ALL THE 354 HIS PHOENIX V 25
    CENTURIES,
AND MAY BE THERE'LL BE SOME YOUNG BELLE WALK OUT TO MAKE 354 HIS PHOENIX V 26
    MEN WILD
AND MAYBE THERE'LL BE SOME YOUNG BELLE WALK OUT TO MAKE 354 HIS PHOENIX V 26
    MEN WILD
YOUNG MEN NO LONGER SUDDENLY CATCH THEIR BREATH . . . 355 BROKEN DREAMS 2
A YOUNG MAN WHEN THE OLD MEN ARE DONE TALKING . . . . 356 BROKEN DREAMS 16
UPON THE LIPS OF COMMON MEN . . . . 361 ALF POLLEXFEN 33
YET SURELY THERE ARE MEN WHO HAVE MADE THEIR ART . . 369 EGO DOMINUS 38
IMPULSIVE MEN THAT LOOK FOR HAPPINESS . . . . 369 EGO DOMINUS 40
THOSE MEN THAT IN THEIR WRITINGS ARE MOST WISE . . . 370 EGO DOMINUS 68
WOULD CARRY IT AWAY TO BLASPHEMOUS MEN. . . . . 371 EGO DOMINUS 79
ARE MET ON THE WASTE HILLS BY COUNTRY MEN . . . . . . 375 PHASES OF MOON V 76
MEN THAT DO ALL BY RULE. . . . . 380 SONGS FOOL 1 14
SIXTEEN DEAD MEN . . . . 395 SIXTEEN DEAD T
THE SIXTEEN MEN WERE SHOT, ... 395 SIXTEEN DEAD 2
WHILE THOSE DEAD MEN ARE LOITERING THERE . . . . . . 395 SIXTEEN DEAD 5
THAT IS NO COUNTRY FOR OLD MEN. THE YOUNG . . . . . . 407 SAIL BYZANTIUM 1
AND CERTAIN MEN, BEING MADDENED BY THOSE RHYMES, . . 410 TOWER 41
FOR IF I TRIUMPH I MUST MAKE MEN MAD. . . . . 411 TOWER 56
ROUGH MEN AT ARMS, CROSS-GARTERED TO THE KNEES . . . 412 TOWER V 82
AND CERTAIN MEN AT ARMS THERE WERE . . . . 412 TOWER V 84
DID ALL OLD MEN AND WOMEN, RICH AND POOR, ... 413 TOWER 97
I CHOOSE UPSTANDING MEN . . . . 414 TOWER 122
TO YOUNG UPSTANDING MEN . . . . 416 TOWER 174
BITTER AND VIOLENT MEN, MIGHT REAR IN STONE . . . . . 418 ANCEST HOUSES 19
TWO MEN HAVE FOUNDED HERE. A MAN-AT-ARMS . . . . . . 420 MY HOUSE 21
TWO MEN HAVE FOUND IT HERE. A MAN-AT-ARMS . . . . . . 420 MY HOUSE V 21
OUR LEARNED MEN HAVE URGED . . . . 421 MY TABLE 15
MEN AND THEIR BUSINESS TOOK . . . . 421 MY TABLE 23
A BROWN LIEUTENANT AND HIS MEN, ... 424 ROAD AT DOOR 6
ALL MEN ARE DANCERS AND THEIR TREAD . . . . 430 NINETEEN 19 57
I AM JEALOUS OF THE LOOK MEN TURN ON YOU . . . . . . 447 HERO GIRL FOOL V A
FOR ALL MEN LOVE YOUR WORTH! AND I MUST RAGE . . . . 447 HERO GIRL FOOL B
THAT MEN HAVE REVERENCE FOR THEIR HOLINESS . . . . . 448 HERO GIRL FOOL 14
ALL MEN HAVE PRAISED MY STRENGTH BUT NOT MY WORTH. . 448 HERO GIRL FOOL V 9
AND LIVE AMONG THE ANCIENT HOLY MEN, ... 448 HERO GIRL FOOL V 11A
THOUGH BUT A FEW LEARNED MEN SHALL LOOK WITHIN, . . . 461 HARUN RASHID V 18A
LIKE MEN WHO LIVE BY HABIT. EVERY DAY . . . . 463 HARUN RASHID 56
CONFRONTING MURDEROUS MEN . . . . 476 DEATH 8
A BLIND MAN BATTERING BLIND MEN: . . . . 479 SELF AND SOUL 60
BODIES OF HOLY MEN AND WOMEN EXUDE . . . . 483 OIL AND BLOOD 2
MORE WOMEN BORN THAN MEN." . . . . 485 STATISTICS 2
BUT WE OLD MEN ARE MASSED AGAINST THE WORLD. . . . . 486 SEVEN SAGES 14
BUT WE OLD MEN ARE OUT AGAINST THE WORLD. . . . . . . 486 SEVEN SAGES V 14
IMPETUOUS MEN, SHAWE-TAYLOR AND HUGH LANE, ... 489 COOLE PARK 29 14
GREAT ROOMS WHERE TRAVELLED MEN AND CHILDREN FOUND . 491 COOLE BALLYLEE 29
THAT YOUNG MEN IN DESPAIR . . . . 492 ANNE GREGORY 10
MEN DANCE ON DEATHLESS FEET." . . . . 496 MOHINI CHATTER 28
THAT ARE NOT SUITED FOR SUCH MEN AS COME . . . . . . 501 VACILLATION 33
AND CRIED TO BATTLE-WEARY MEN, ... 502 VACILLATION 65
MEN COME, MEN GO, ... 512 JANE ON GOD 5
MEN COME, MEN GO, ... 512 JANE ON GOD 5
THAT MEN PASS OVER . . . . 512 JANE ON GOD 21
MEN HAVE PASSED OVER . . . . 512 JANE ON GOD V 21
AMONG BIRDS OR BEASTS OR MEN . . . . 528 DANCER CRUACH 2
THOUGH FANTASTIC MEN SUPPOSE . . . . 530 OLD TOM AGAIN 4
OF ALL GOOD MEN AND WOMEN, ... 531 FATHER CHILD 3

513

MEN   (CONTINUED)

	PAGE	TITLE	LINE
IMAGINING MEN. IMAGINING THAT I COULD	537	HER VISION	4
SAY THAT OF LIVING MEN I HATE	539	MEETING	11
WE LIVED LIKE MEN THAT WATCH A PAINTED STAGE.	542	PARN FUNERAL 1	18
TO THIS BARE SOUL, LET ALL MEN JUDGE THAT CAN	542	PARN FUNERAL 1	30
GOD GUARD ME FROM THOSE THOUGHTS MEN THINK	553	PRAYER OLD AGE	1
ALL MEN HAVE AIMED AT, FOUND AND LOST!	566	LAPIS LAZULI	18
IF STRANGE MEN COME FROM THE HOUSE	568	SWEET DANCER	8
DID EVER MEN HEAR SUCH A SONG?	570	THREE BUSHES	45
AND THE TALL MEN AND THE SWORDSMEN AND THE HORSEMEN, WHERE ARE THEY?	580	CURSE CROMWELL	4
DRAW ROUND, BELOVED AND BITTER MEN,	584	GHOST ROG CASE	37
KEEPING ALL THE KERRY MEN	585	ORAHILLY	14
"ALL MEN LIVE IN SUFFERING,	589	OLD WICKED MAN	46
MY KING A LOST KING, AND LOST SOLDIERS MY MEN!	591	WHAT WAS LOST	3
AND ALL DEAD MEN ARE DRUNK.	592	DRUNK SOBRIETY	16
AND COME WITH LEARNED LOVERS OR WITH WHAT MEN YOU MAY,	593	PILGRIM	23
AND ALL MEN HEARD THEM SWEAR	596	COLONEL MARTIN	60
THAT MEN AND WOMEN OF ALL SORTS	597	MODEL LAUREATE	3
PUTS ALL MEN IN A FRIGHT.	597	MODEL LAUREATE	12
THE MUSE IS MUTE WHEN PUBLIC MEN	597	MODEL LAUREATE	17
APPROVED PATTERNS OF WOMEN OR OF MEN	602	GALLERY REVIS	31
HALF LEGENDARY MEN.	605	YOU CONTENT	16
HALF-LEGENDARY MEN.	605	YOU CONTENT V	16
OF HENWIVES AND OF QUEER OLD MEN	607	SONGS BURDEN 2	23
OF HEN WIVES AND OF QUEER OLD MEN	607	SONGS BURDEN 2 V	23
NO! GREATER THAN PYTHAGORAS, FOR THE MEN	610	STATUES	9
WHERE MEN FORGIVE IF THE BELLY GAIN?	615	MARCH SONGS 2	14
AND MEN RECALL THAT FACE,	617	LONG-LEG FLY	12
WHY SHOULD NOT OLD MEN BE MAD?	625	OLD MEN BE MAD	T
WHY SHOULD NOT OLD MEN BE MAD?	625	OLD MEN BE MAD	1
SHOULD STARVE GOOD MEN AND BAD ADVANCE,	626	OLD MEN BE MAD	10
YOUNG MEN KNOW NOTHING OF THIS SORT,	626	OLD MEN BE MAD	16
OBSERVANT OLD MEN KNOW IT WELL.	626	OLD MEN BE MAD	17
CERTAIN MEN THE ENGLISH SHOT?	632	MAN AND ECHO	12
SAY THAT THE MEN OF THE OLD BLACK TOWER,	635	BLACK TOWER	1
THAT ALL ARE OATH-BOUND MEN!	635	BLACK TOWER	5
WHEN WE HALE MEN LIE STRETCHED IN SLUMBER	636	BLACK TOWER	23
THEY BUT THRUST THEIR BURIED MEN	637	BEN BULBEN	23
WHOM MEN HAVE NAMED ARCADIA'S SWEETEST TONGUE.	649	ISLE STAT I 1	109
HERE, WHERE MEN KNOW THE GRACIOUS WOODLAND JOYS,	651	ISLE STAT I 1	154
SUCH MEN, SUCH HEARTS. BUT, UNCOUTH HUNTER, THOU	651	ISLE STAT I 1	167
ABOVE THESE MEN WHOSE MOUTHS WERE SEALED	656	ISLE STAT I 3	27
TWO MEN WHO LOVE ONE MAID HAVE AMPLE CAUSE	659	ISLE STAT II 1	30
NO, NO! WHEN THAT SHALL BE, THEN MEN MAY CALL	662	ISLE STAT II 1	79
TO WATCH THEE PASS? YET DEEPER THAN MEN KNOW	672	ISLE STAT II 3	158
A COWARD IN THE FIELD! AND ALL MEN CRIED!	684	SEEKER	53
I SOUGHT THEE NOT. MEN CALL ME INFAMY.	685	SEEKER	75
THAT ALL MEN EVERMORE MAY HUMBLY BOW	688	TWO TITANS	49
AND DYING MEN--AND YET--BUT NO, FAREWELL	698	MOSADA 2	49
UPON THEIR THRONES. THE LIVES OF MEN SHALL FLOW	698	MOSADA 2	56
THE MEN ARE BUSY IN THE GLIMMERING SQUARE.	699	MOSADA 3	16
SEARCHED THE UNSEARCHABLE--WHY GOOD MEN WEEP!	710	FERENCZ RENYI	32
A LIZARD CRAWLS--THE TWO MEN GAZE INTENT,	711	FERENCZ RENYI	47
AND THE FISHER MEN AND WOMEN FROM THE DRIPPING HARBOUR WALL	718	PHANTOM SHIP	11
WHERE DWELL THE MINDS OF OLD MEN HAVING PEACE,	721	WITCH VIVIEN	22
SO MEN IN LIFE AND I IN MAGIC PLAY!	722	WITCH VIVIEN	55
AND THE OLD MEN WERE WALKING, WALKING,	725	LEGEND	3
ARE PRAYERS OF PATIENT MEN AND GOOD."	725	LEGEND	6
THE BOYS, THE WOMEN, AND OLD MEN,	725	LEGEND	7
AND SENT THE OLD MEN ON THEIR WAY,	725	LEGEND	23
AT THE HOUSE OF WEARY MEN	727	LOVERS QUARREL	51
THERE STOOD A MAN, OF MEN THE LEAST--	729	PRIEST FAIRY	24
FOR ALL GOOD MEN NOW FALLEN ILL,	736	IN CHURCH	5
FOR MERRY MEN THAT WEEP,	736	IN CHURCH	6
AND COMMON MEN THAT SLEEP.	736	IN CHURCH	8
MEN CRY "BRING PAUL, SHIELD BREAKER,	740	EARL PAUL	11
LIKE A GREY OWL MEN HARRY OUT	740	EARL PAUL	23
MEN CRY! "BRING PAUL, SHIELD-BREAKER,	740	EARL PAUL V	11
THAT ARE A POISON TO ALL MEN	743	DANAAN QUICK	16
FORGAEL, SEEK OUT CONTENT, WHERE OTHER MEN	750	SHADOW WATER A	71
I HAVE GOOD PILOTS, AIBRIC. WHEN MEN DIE	750	SHADOW WATER A	81
BEST PLEASES YOU. ARMED MEN HAVE COME UPON US.	752	SHADOW WATER A	131
ARMED MEN HAVE COME UPON US. O! I AM SLAIN!	753	SHADOW WATER A	133
THESE MESSENGERS TO LURE MEN TO HIS PEACE,	764	SHADOW WATER A	336
THE FOOL, WHO HAS MADE THE WISDOM THAT MEN WRITE	764	SHADOW WATER A	342
I HAVE COMMANDED MEN IN DREAMS. BELOVED,	766	SHADOW WATER A	381
SO WORTHY AMONG MEN. I FOLLOW YOU,	768	SHADOW WATER A V	412
HARD-LIVING MEN AND MEN OF THOUGHT	787	HUDDON DUDDON	13
HARD-LIVING MEN AND MEN OF THOUGHT	787	HUDDON DUDDON	13
AND ALL MEN LIE THAT SAY THAT I	789	SINGING HEAD	3
THEN FARRELL, STEEL KING, MASTER OF MEN,	790	DEDICATION	5
AT THE BOTTOM OF A LETTER, FIFTY MEN.	790	DEDICATION	10
MEN THAT REVERE YOUR FATHER YET	791	REPRISALS	17
AND SUCKLE CHILDREN NOW? ARMED MEN	791	REPRISALS	20

MEN-AT-ARMS

	PAGE	TITLE	LINE
ROUGH MEN-AT-ARMS, CROSS-GARTERED TO THE KNEES	412	TOWER	82
AND CERTAIN MEN-AT-ARMS THERE WERE	412	TOWER	84
MEN-AT-ARMS TREAD!	512	JANE ON GOD	8

MEND

	PAGE	TITLE	LINE
AND THEN I MUST MEND AND BAKE AND SWEEP	150	OLD MOTHER V	3

MEND   (CONTINUED)
    O BUT WE DREAMED TO MEND . . . .   431 NINETEEN 19   84
MEN'S
    "MEN'S HEARTS OF OLD WERE DROPS OF FLAME   . . . .   19 OISIN 1   276
    O LOVELY TO SEE IN ALL MEN'S SIGHT   . . . .   69 CLOAK BOAT   3
    IN ALL MEN'S SIGHT." . . . .   69 CLOAK BOAT   5
    IN ALL MEN'S EARS OF SORROW, ...   70 CLOAK BOAT   14
    AMID MEN'S SOULS, THAT WAVER AND GIVE PLACE   . . . . . . 112 ROSE OF WORLD   7
    AMID MEN'S SOULS THAT DAY BY DAY GIVE PLACE, ... 112 ROSE OF WORLD   V 7
    TO SEE MEN'S SOULS BARTERED AND BOUGHT. . . . . 136 TWO TREES   V 36
    AND ALL MEN'S HEARTS MUST BURN AND BEAT; . . . . 158 BELOVED RHYMES   9
    AND EVEN OLD MEN'S EYES GREW DIM, THIS HAND ALONE, . . . 314 FALLEN MAJESTY   2
    DELIGHT MEN'S EYES WHEN I AWAKE SOME DAY . . . . 323 SWANS AT COOLE   29
    THOUGH SHE HAD YOUNG MEN'S PRAISE AND OLD MEN'S BLAME, . . 351 HER PRAISE   17
    THOUGH SHE HAD YOUNG MEN'S PRAISE AND OLD MEN'S BLAME, . . 351 HER PRAISE   17
    BE BUT THE BREAKERS OF MEN'S HEARTS OR ENGINES OF DELIGHT; 354 HIS PHOENIX   23
    FOR ALL MEN'S THOUGHTS GREW CLEAR . . . . 400 DEMON BEAST   19
    FOR ALL MEN'S THOUGHT GREW CLEAR . . . . 400 DEMON BEAST   V 19
    A NUN AT LEAST HAS ALL MEN'S REVERENCE . . . . 448 HERO GIRL FOOL   12
    FOR THEY AT LEAST HAVE ALL MEN'S REVERENCE . . . . 448 HERO GIRL FOOL V 12
    'TIS MORN; LIKE OLD MEN'S EYES THE STARS ARE PALE, . . . 645 ISLE STAT I 1   4
    OH, LOVELY TO SEE IN ALL MEN'S SIGHT . . . . 666 ISLE STAT II 3   3
    IN ALL MEN'S SIGHT. 666 ISLE STAT II 3   5
    A ROVER I, WHO COME FROM WHERE MEN'S EARS . . . . 678 ISLE STAT II 3   293
    ON THE DROWNED MEN'S HANDS AND FACES, ON THE SPARS AND   719 PHANTOM SHIP   22
        ON THE SAILS.
    THAN OLD MEN'S ANY DAY, AS MERLIN FOUND. . . . . 721 WITCH VIVIEN   47
MENTAL
    A BODILY OR MENTAL FURNITURE. . . . . 558 RIBH CHRISTIAN   20
MENTIONED
    BEING MENTIONED WITH A MAN . . . . 531 FATHER CHILD   4
MERCHANT
    IT CHARMED AWAY THE MERCHANT FROM HIS GUILE, ... 129 BOOK STORIES   5
    BEFORE THE MERCHANT AND THE CLERK . . . . 266 GALWAY RACES   8
    OLD DUBLIN MERCHANT "FREE OF TEN AND FOUR" . . . . 269 PARDON FATHERS   3
    MERCHANT AND SCHOLAR WHO HAVE LEFT ME BLOOD . . . . 269 PARDON FATHERS   7
    OLD DUBLIN MERCHANT "FREE OF THE TEN AND FOUR" . . . . . 269 PARDON FATHERS   V 3
    OLD MERCHANT SKIPPER THAT LEAPED OVERBOARD . . . . 270 PARDON FATHERS   13
    YOU MERCHANT SKIPPER THAT LEAPED OVERBOARD . . . . 270 PARDON FATHERS   13
    AND MERCHANT SKIPPER THAT LEAPED OVERBOARD . . . . 270 PARDON FATHERS   V 13
    REFORMER, MERCHANT, STATESMAN, LEARNED MAN, ... 376 PHASES OF MOON   98
MERCHANTS
    IN HIS OWN HOUSE OR 'MONG THE MERCHANTS GREY, ... 693 MOSADA 1   87
MERCY
    THE LORD HAVE MERCY UPON US. . . . . 572 LADYS 2ND SONG   7
    THE LORD HAVE MERCY UPON US. . . . . 573 LADYS 2ND SONG   14
    THE LORD HAVE MERCY UPON US. . . . . 573 LADYS 2ND SONG   21
    CAN THERE BE MERCY IN THAT LOOK? . . . . 625 NATIVITY   12
    AND——MERCY IS THE MANNA OF THE WORLD. . . . . 697 MOSADA 2   41
MERE
    OR HOPES THAT IN MERE HOPING FLICKER AND CEASE; . . . . . 162 ASKS FORGIVE   3
    AND HOPES THAT IN MERE HOPING FLICKER AND CEASE; . . . . 162 ASKS FORGIVE   V 3
    MERE BONE AND MUSCLE THROWN ASIDE, ... 273 GREY ROCK   51
    AND LEFT MERE SLEEP. HE'LL WAKE WHEN THE SUN WAKES, . . . 284 TWO KINGS   161
    OR MERE COMPANIONS OF MY YOUTH, ... 324 ROBERT GREGORY   7
    MERE IMAGES; CHOSEN THIS PLACE TO LIVE IN . . . . 373 PHASES OF MOON   13
    FOR WHAT MERE BOOK CAN GRANT A KNOWLEDGE . . . . 386 ROBARTES DANCE   20
    GIVE MAN HIS THOUGHT OR HIS MERE BODY? . . . . 386 ROBARTES DANCE   40
    AND THAT MERE GROWING OLD, THAT BRINGS . . . . 401 DEMON BEAST   38
    MERE ANARCHY IS LOOSED UPON THE WORLD, ... 402 SECOND COMING   4
    MERE DREAMS, MERE DREAMS! YET HOMER HAD NOT SUNG . . . . 417 ANCEST HOUSES   9
    MERE DREAMS, MERE DREAMS! YET HOMER HAD NOT SUNG . . . . 417 ANCEST HOUSES   9
    MOCKED ME WITH PRAISE OF MY MERE OPPOSITE; . . . . 448 HERO GIRL FOOL   4
    MOCK ME WITH PRAISE OF MY MERE OPPOSITE; . . . . 448 HERO GIRL FOOL   V 4
    AND I MERE SHADE AT LAST . . . . 449 HERO GIRL FOOL   25
    WHERE FASHION OR MERE FANTASY DECREES . . . . 491 COOLE BALLYLEE   38
    ALL MERE COMPLEXITIES, ... 497 BYZANTIUM   7
    THE FALLING HAWTHORN BLOOM. BY MERE AND BROOK . . . . . . 677 ISLE STAT II 3   279
    BY HEATH OR HOLLOW OR RUSHY MERE, ... 716 FAIRY DOCTOR   10
    OUT OF MERE WANTONNESS TO LURE A SAIL . . . . 750 SHADOW WATER A   79
    OR IN MERE WOMAN'S CRUELTY . . . . 789 SINGING HEAD   11
MERELY
    "WOULD IT WERE ANYTHING BUT MERELY VOICE!" . . . . 258 KING NO KING   1
    MERELY FOR STUMBLING ON THIS HOLE . . . . 304 HOUR DAWN   54
    THAT MERELY STOOD, ROCKING THE GLITTERING COACH . . . . . 344 DAWN   11
    BY MERELY WALKING IN A ROOM. . . . . 356 BROKEN DREAMS   13
    MERELY TO LOOSEN OUT A TRESS . . . . 390 IMAGE PAST   26
MERGE
    SO DID THEIR ROSES MERGE. . . . . 571 THREE BUSHES   62
MERIDIAN
    "LIKE ME WERE SOME GALLEY FORSAKEN FAR OFF IN MERIDIAN   55 OISIN 3   117
        ISLE,
MERIT
    WHAT'S THE MERIT IN LOVE-PLAY, ... 777 SONG DEIRDRE 2   6
    WHAT'S THE MERIT IN LOVE PLAY, ... 777 SONG DEIRDRE 2   V 6
MERLIN
    YET WHITER BEARD HAVE YOU THAN MERLIN HAD. . . . . 721 WITCH VIVIEN   30
    THAN OLD MEN'S ANY DAY, AS MERLIN FOUND. . . . . 721 WITCH VIVIEN   47
MERMAID
    THE MERMAID . . . . 452 MERMAID   T
    A MERMAID FOUND A SWIMMING LAD, ... 452 MERMAID   1

MERMAID   (CONTINUED)
    A MERMAID, NOT A PUNK! . . . .   592 DRUNK SOBRIETY   14
MERRIMENT
    NOR BUT IN MERRIMENT BEGIN A CHASE, ...   405 FOR DAUGHTER   45
    NOR BUT IN MERRIMENT A QUARREL. . . . .   405 FOR DAUGHTER   46
MERRY
    THOSE MERRY COUPLES DANCING IN TUNE, ...   3 OISIN 1   9
    AND A HUNDRED LADIES, MERRY AS BIRDS, ...   9 OISIN 1   96
    AND A HUNDRED MAIDENS, MERRY AS BIRDS, ...   9 OISIN 1   V 96
    AND NIAMH BLEW THREE MERRY NOTES . . . .   14 OISIN 1   195
    A SORROW WRAPPED EACH MERRY FACE, ...   17 OISIN 1   235
    LIKE TO A MERRY WANDERING ROUT . . . .   18 OISIN 1   253
    BUT ONLY KIND AND MERRY BREATH, ...   19 OISIN 1   285
    WHILE THE WOOD-PECKER MADE A MERRY DIN, ...   44 OISIN 2   V 228
    THE MERRY LAMBS AND THE COMPLACENT KINE, ...   75 ANASHU VIJAYA   86
    THE MERRY LAMBS AND ALL THE KINE COMPLACENT, ...   75 ANASHU VIJAYA   V 86
    AS MERRY AS A BIRD." . . . .   133 FR GILLIGAN   38
    HAVE DOWERED THE STARS WITH MERRY LIGHT! . . . .   134 TWO TREES   6
    AWAY FROM THE MERRY BANDS, ...   144 HOST OF AIR   22
    HE PLAYED WITH THE MERRY OLD MEN . . . .   145 HOST OF AIR   29
    AWAY FROM THE MERRY DANCE. . . . .   145 HOST OF AIR   32
    FOR THE GOOD ARE ALWAYS THE MERRY, ...   178 FIDDLER DOONEY   13
    AND THE MERRY LOVE THE FIDDLE, ...   179 FIDDLER DOONEY   15
    AND THE MERRY LOVE TO DANCE! . . . .   179 FIDDLER DOONEY   16
    I LONG FOR YOUR MERRY AND TENDER AND PITIFUL WORDS, ...   203 WITHER BOUGHS   3
    HOW HAVE I WRONGED HER NOW THAT SHE IS MERRY? . . . . . .   244 SHADOW WATER B   448
    AND THEREON, MERRY AS A BIRD . . . .   296 THREE BEGGARS   25
    A CURSING ROGUE WITH A MERRY FACE, ...   302 HOUR DAWN   1
    I'D HAVE A MERRY LIFE ENOUGH . . . .   306 HOUR DAWN   85
    WE MEET--WE TWO. HOW MERRY ALL THESE ARE . . . . . .   691 MOSADA 1   31
    HO! HO! HO! THE MERRY BLADE!-- . . . .   727 LOVERS QUARREL   26
    IF THESE MERRY ONES SHOULD KNOW, ...   731 STREET DANCERS   9
    IF THESE MERRY ONES SHOULD KNOW, ...   732 STREET DANCERS   22
    IF THESE MERRY ONES SHOULD KNOW, ...   732 STREET DANCERS   35
    IF THESE MERRY ONES SHOULD KNOW, ...   733 STREET DANCERS   48
    IF THESE MERRY ONES SHOULD KNOW, ...   733 STREET DANCERS   61
    FOR MERRY MEN THAT WEEP, ...   736 IN CHURCH   6
MERU
    MERU . . . .   563 MERU   T
    HERMITS UPON MOUNT MERU OR EVEREST, ...   563 MERU   9
MESH
    FOR NEITHER I NOR YOU CAN BREAK A MESH . . . . . .   238 SHADOW WATER B   351
    AND KNITTED MESH TO MESH, WE GROW IMMORTAL! . . . . .   252 SHADOW WATER B   616
    AND KNITTED MESH TO MESH, WE GROW IMMORTAL! . . . . .   252 SHADOW WATER B   616
    AND KNITTING MESH TO MESH, WE GROW IMMORTAL! . . . . .   252 SHADOW WATER B V 616
    AND KNITTING MESH TO MESH, WE GROW IMMORTAL! . . . . .   252 SHADOW WATER B V 616
MESS
    AND TOOK A MESS OF SHADOWS FOR ITS MEAT? . . . . . .   444 SCHOOL CHILDR   28
MESSAGE
    YOUR RAVING OF A MESSAGE AND A HARP . . . . . .   237 SHADOW WATER B   331
    IS IT YOUR MESSAGE, STARS, THAT WHEN DEATH COMES . . . .   701 MOSADA 3   60
MESSAGES
    IF IT BE NOT THAT HEARING MESSAGES . . . . . .   236 SHADOW WATER B   319
    THAT WERE CLEAR MESSAGES FROM THE EVER-LIVING, ...   243 SHADOW WATER B   442
MESSENGER
    HE STOOD A MESSENGER. IN APRIL'S PRIME . . . . . .   690 MOSADA 1   6
MESSENGERS
    IF I REFUSED THE MESSENGERS AND PILOTS . . . . . .   249 SHADOW WATER B   572
    THESE MESSENGERS TO LURE MEN TO HIS PEACE, ...   764 SHADOW WATER A   336
MET
    WHEN AMBLING DOWN THE VALE WE MET . . . .   2 OISIN 1   V 7U
    ROOTED IN FOAM AND CLOUDS. THERE MIGHTIER MASTERS MET . .   38 OISIN 2   V 132
    WHEN HEAVEN AND HELL ARE MET, ...   112 ROSE OF PEACE   2
    WHEN THEY FOR WAR ARE MET, ...   112 ROSE OF PEACE   V 2
    WHO MET FAND WALKING AMONG FLAMING DEW . . . . . .   169 SECRET ROSE   13
    THEREON A YOUNG MAN MET HIS EYE, ...   274 GREY ROCK   85
    AGAINST THE STAG. WHEN HORN AND STEEL WERE MET . . . .   277 TWO KINGS   15
    AS THOUGH A STAG AND UNICORN WERE MET . . . . . .   277 TWO KINGS   19
    TO STAY THE STAG'S NEXT RUSH. WHEN SWORD MET HORN . . . .   277 TWO KINGS   V 15
    THE STRONG THIGH AND THE AGILE THIGH WERE MET, ...   278 TWO KINGS   28
    EUNUCHS RAN THROUGH HELL AND MET . . . .   294 HATED PLAYBOY   2
    O WOULD THAT WE HAD MET . . . .   329 MEN IMPROVE   14
    NEVER UNTIL THIS MOMENT HAVE WE MET . . . . . .   339 SHEP GOATHERD   7
    ARE MET ON THE WASTE HILLS BY COUNTRYMEN . . . . . .   375 PHASES OF MOON   76
    ARE MET ON THE WASTE HILLS BY COUNTRY MEN . . . . . .   375 PHASES OF MOON V   76
    I HAVE MET THEM AT CLOSE OF DAY . . . .   391 EASTER 1916   1
    I MET THE BISHOP ON THE ROAD . . . .   513 JANE TALK BISH   1
    "IS THAT MORNING WHEN I MET . . . .   521 THREE THINGS   15
    "THAT I HAVE MET WITH SUCH," SAID HE, ...   539 MEETING   5
    BUT OF THE DEATH HE MET . . . .   585 ORAHILLY   29
    THE COLONEL MET A PEDLAR, ...   595 COLONEL MARTIN   19
    I MET HER ALL BUT FIFTY YEARS AGO . . . .   602 GALLERY REVIS   15
    WHAT, LOVER, DIE BEFORE OUR LIPS HAVE MET? . . . . . .   685 SEEKER   80
    LOVE, WILL YOU DIE WHEN WE HAVE MET? ONE LOOK . . . .   703 MOSADA 3   109
    IN SPACE, MADE EQUAL WITH A SIGH, WE MET. . . . . . .   705 REMEMBRANCE   14
    THE DIM SPEAR MET THE BRIGHT SPEAR, ...   741 EARL PAUL   45
    THE DIM SPEAR MET THE BRIGHT SPEAR . . . .   741 EARL PAUL   V 49
    AND I MET WITH A MAN THAT WAS NO RIGHT MAN . . . . .   779 GOING THE ROAD   3
    I HAVE MET IN A MAN'S HOUSE . . . .   785 YOUR HEART   3
METAL   SEE ROAD-METAL
    AS THOUGH IT DRAGGED ROAD METAL. MY CURSE ON PLAYS . . .   260 FASC DIFFICULT V   8

		PAGE	TITLE		LINE

METAL   (CONTINUED)
    ON METAL GOBAN'D HAMMERED AT, ... 271 GREY ROCK   19
    ALL WORK IN METAL OR IN WOOD, ... 327 ROBERT GREGORY   76
    BEING OF THAT METAL MADE . . . . 416 TOWER   178
    IN GLORY OF CHANGELESS METAL . . . . 498 BYZANTIUM   22
METAPHOR
    NOT SUCH AS ARE IN NEWTON'S METAPHOR, ... 494 AT ALGECIRAS   11
    ALL METAPHOR, MALACHI, STILTS AND ALL. A BARNACLE GOOSE 623 HIGH TALK   11
METEOR
    SCARED OF ITS GLITTERING LIKE A METEOR STAR, ... 38 OISIN 2   V 137
    A METEOR OF THE BURNING HEART, ... 78 INDIAN TO LOVE   14
    WE TIRE OF THE FLAME OF THE METEOR, BEFORE IT CAN FADE   122 WHITE BIRDS   2
      AND FLEE,
    AH, DREAM NOT OF THEM, MY BELOVED, THE FLAME OF THE METEOR 122 WHITE BIRDS   6
      THAT GOES,
    FOR WE TIRE OF THE FLAME OF THE METEOR BEFORE IT CAN PASS 122 WHITE BIRDS   V 2
      BY AND FLEE
    WE TIRE OF THE FLAME OF THE METEOR, BEFORE IT CAN PASS   122 WHITE BIRDS   V 2
      BY AND FLEE,
METEORS
    LIKE CRIMSON METEORS HANG IN THE GLOOM, ... 21 OISIN 1   306
    HUNG, LIKE METEORS OF RED LIGHT, ... 21 OISIN 1   V 306
    THE IMAGED METEORS HAD FLASHED AND RUN . . . . 31 OISIN 2   38
    THE IMAGED METEORS HAD SHONE AND RUN, ... 31 OISIN 2   38
    FELL LIKE FAINT METEORS IN THE GLOOM, AND ONCE . . . . 80 EPHEMERA   14
METHINKS
    AND THE GREAT GREY LYNX'S SKIN! IN SOOTH, METHINKS . . . 650 ISLE STAT I 1   151
METTLESOME
    AND OUR WINGED METTLESOME HORSE. . . . . 392 EASTER 1916   V 25
MEW   SEE SEA-MEW
MIAU-D
    HOWLED, MIAU-D, BARKED, BRAYED, BELLED, YELLED, CRIED,   387 SOLOMON WITCH   8
      CROWED,
MICE   SEE MEADOW-MICE
    THE FLIES BELOW THE LEAVES, AND THE YOUNG MICE . . . . 75 ANASHU VIJAYA   87
    AND OVER THE MICE IN THE BARLEY SHEAVES! . . . . 79 FALLING LEAVES   2
    OR SEE THE BROWN MICE BOB . . . . 88 STOLEN CHILD   48
    OR MICE IN THE ONE WHEATEN SHEAF . . . . 195 BAILE AILLINN   147
    FROM HUMAN THOUGHT, AS HARES AND MICE AND CONEYS . . . . 218 WOODS OF COOLE   31
    BUT WHEN THE MASTER'S BURIED MICE CAN PLAY, ... 418 ANCEST HOUSES   22
    WITH NO MORE SOUND THAN THE MICE MAKE . . . . 618 LONG-LEG FLY   27
    AH! HOW LARGE MICE USED TO BE . . . . 727 LOVERS QUARREL   39
MICHAEL
    IF MICHAEL, LEADER OF GOD'S HOST . . . . 112 ROSE OF PEACE   1
    IF MICHAEL, LEADER OF GOD'S HOSTS . . . . 112 ROSE OF PEACE   V 1
    MICHAEL ROBARTES BIDS HIS BELOVED BE AT PEACE . . . . . 154 BELOVED PEACE   V T
    MICHAEL ROBARTES REMEMBERS FORGOTTEN BEAUTY . . . . . . 155 FORGOT BEAUTY   V T
    MICHAEL ROBARTES ASKS FORGIVENESS BECAUSE OF HIS MANY MOODS 162 ASKS FORGIVE   V T
    . . . MICHAEL, GABRIEL, AND RAPHAEL . . . . 174 ELEMENT POWERS   V T
    MICHAEL WILL UNHOOK HIS TRUMPET . . . . 215 HAPPY TOWNLAND   41
    COULD TRUMPETER MICHAEL BE SO BRAVE?" . . . . 338 TOM OROUGHLEY   13
    THAT MICHAEL ROBARTES LEFT, YOU WALK IN THE MOON, . . . 367 EGO DOMINUS   4
    THE DOUBLE VISION OF MICHAEL ROBARTES . . . . 382 VISION ROBART   T
    MICHAEL ROBARTES AND THE DANCER . . . . 385 ROBARTES DANCE   T
    WHILE MICHAEL ANGELO'S SISTINE ROOF, ... 386 ROBARTES DANCE   32
    THAT MY MICHAEL MAY SLEEP SOUND, ... 435 FOR MY SON   2
    A MIND MICHAEL ANGELO KNEW . . . . 576 ACRE OF GRASS   19
    MICHAEL ANGELO. . . . . 618 LONG-LEG FLY   26
    MICHAEL ANGELO LEFT A PROOF . . . . 638 BEN BULBEN   45
MICHAELANGELO
    MICHAELANGELO LEFT A PROOF . . . . 638 BEN BULBEN   V 45
MICHAEL'S
    TO KNOW WHEN MICHAEL'S TRUMPET CRIES . . . . 307 HOUR DAWN   100
MICHELOZZO'S
    TO MICHELOZZO'S LATEST PLAN . . . . 288 TO WEALTHY MAN   23
MID
    THEIR EYES MID MANY WRINKLES, THEIR EYES, ... 567 LAPIS LAZULI   55
    SO! MID THE WILLOW-GLADE YOU PAUSE AT LAST. . . . . . . 651 ISLE STAT I 2   2
    MID BUBBLING LEAVES A WANDERING SONG-RAPT BIRD . . . . . 672 ISLE STAT II 3   154
    MID BABBLING LEAVES A WANDERING SONG-RAPT BIRD . . . . . 672 ISLE STAT II 3 V 154
'MID
    BUT TO BE 'MID THE SHOOTING OF FLIES . . . . 55 OISIN 3   V 120
    'MID CLANGING SPACE A MOMENT HEARD . . . . 65 HAPPY SHEPHERD V 20
    AND THEY WILL WAR, 'MID WONDROUS ELFIN-SIGHTS! . . . . . 651 ISLE STAT I 1   164
    THOU KNOWEST THIS, AND HOW FROM 'MID THE DANCE . . . . . 683 SEEKER   51
MIDDAY
    "ALL DAY LONG FROM MIDDAY . . . . 332 SOLOMON SHEBA   V 3
MID-DAY
    "ALL DAY LONG FROM MID-DAY . . . . 332 SOLOMON SHEBA   3
MIDDLE
    WITH CHAIN SEA-ROTTED, ROUND HER MIDDLE TIED, ... 34 OISIN 2   V 75
    WHO HAD BEEN THE LOVER OF HER MIDDLE LIFE. . . . . . . 183 QUEEN MAEVE   72
    TO MIDDLE NIGHT, THEY DUG INTO THE HILL. . . . . 185 QUEEN MAEVE   114
    AS MIDDLE NIGHT GREAT CATS WITH SILVER CLAWS, ... 185 QUEEN MAEVE   115
    WHEN THEY HAVE TWENTY YEARS! IN MIDDLE LIFE . . . . . . 229 SHADOW WATER B   156
    WESTWARD OF TARA. WHERE IN THE MIDDLE WOOD . . . . . . 277 TWO KINGS   V   4
    AND TAKE HER IN THE MIDDLE OF ARMED MEN, ... 282 TWO KINGS   114
    I CAME ON A GREAT HOUSE IN THE MIDDLE OF THE NIGHT, . . . 581 CURSE CROMWELL   25
    FIND IN MIDDLE AIR . . . . 601 THOSE IMAGES   13
    DREAMER OF THE MIDDLE AGES. EMPTY EYEBALLS KNEW . . . . 610 STATUES   20
    OF MIDDLE AGE. "HIS SISTER HERE AND MOTHER." . . . . . 711 FERENCZ RENYI   53

```
                                                    PAGE    TITLE          LINE
MIDDLE-AGE
  RESTRAINING RECKLESS MIDDLE-AGE?  • • • • • • • •   262 STUDENTS AGIT        4
MIDDLE-AGES
  DREAMER OF THE MIDDLE-AGES.  EMPTY EYE-BALLS KNEW  • • •  610 STATUES     V  20
MIDDLETON
  AND OF A MIDDLETON, WHOSE NAME YOU NEVER HEARD, • • • •   391 UNDER SATURN       8
  THE SMUGGLER MIDDLETON, BUTLERS FAR BACK, • • • • • •     605 YOU CONTENT       15
  MY NAME IS HENRY MIDDLETON, • • • • • • • • •            606 SONGS BURDEN 2       1
MIDHER'S
  EDAINE CAME OUT OF MIDHER'S HILL, AND LAY • • • • • •     762 SHADOW WATER A     296
  WHEN MIDHER'S WIFE HAD CHANGED HER TO A FLY • • • • •     763 SHADOW WATER A     305
MIDHIR
  • • • MADE ARMOUR FOR MIDHIR OF OLD • • • • • • • •        52 OISIN 3       V  80
MIDHIR'S
  THAT EDAIN, MIDHIR'S WIFE, HAD WOVE • • • • • • •        195 BAILE AILLINN     142
  EDAIN CAME OUT OF MIDHIR'S HILL, AND LAY • • • • • •     219 HARP OF AENGUS       1
  WHEN MIDHIR'S WIFE HAD CHANGED HER TO A FLY, • • • •     220 HARP OF AENGUS      10
MIDNIGHT
  THAT LACKEY THE WORN MOON IN MIDNIGHT HOURS, • • • • •    41 OISIN 2      V 185A
  FOR HE HAS WROUGHT MIDNIGHT AND DAWN AND DAY• • • • •     43 OISIN 2          208
  • • • TILL STARLIGHT AND MIDNIGHT PART• • • • • • •       60 OISIN 3          184
  AND MIDNIGHT THERE ENFOLD THEM LIKE A FLEECE • • • • •   128 DREAM OF FAERY      34
  THAT MEN THRESHED CORN AT MIDNIGHT BY A TRESS, • • • •   170 SECRET ROSE        26
  AT THE MOST QUIET MIDNIGHT IS TO BE STRICKEN• • • • •    236 SHADOW WATER B     321
  ONCE, WHEN MIDNIGHT SMOTE THE AIR, • • • • • • •         294 HATED PLAYBOY        1
  THE STATELY MIDNIGHT THROUGH UNTIL THEY STOOD • • • •    352 PEOPLE            14
  THE LAST STROKE OF MIDNIGHT DIES• • • • • • •            357 BROKEN DREAMS      37
  HAVE SEEN HIS MIDNIGHT CANDLE GLIMMERING• • • • • •      420 MY HOUSE           20
  HAD SEEN HIS MIDNIGHT CANDLE GLIMMERING • • • • • •      420 MY HOUSE       V   20
  NOR BLEAR-EYED WISDOM OUT OF MIDNIGHT OIL• • • • • •     446 SCHOOL CHILDR      60
  IS BUT A PAYMENT FOR THAT MIDNIGHT VOICE • • • • • •     469 HARUN RASHID      173
  ALL, ALL THOSE GYRES AND CUBES AND MIDNIGHT THINGS •     469 HARUN RASHID      184
  THOSE CONES AND CUBES AND GYRES, THOSE MIDNIGHT THINGS,  469 HARUN RASHID   V  184
  MIDNIGHT HAS COME, AND THE GREAT CHRIST CHURCH BELL • •  470 ALL SOUL NIGHT       1
  FOR IT IS NOW MIDNIGHT: • • • • • • • • • •             470 ALL SOUL NIGHT  V   3
  IN THE RICH MIDNIGHT OF THE GARDEN TREES • • • • • •     494 AT ALGECIRAS        5
  IN THE RICH MIDNIGHT OF THE GARDEN TREE • • • • • •      494 AT ALGECIRAS   V    5
  AT MIDNIGHT ON THE EMPEROR'S PAVEMENT FLIT • • • • •     498 BYZANTIUM          25
  THAT I, MIDNIGHT UPON THE STROKE• • • • • • •            507 JANE BISHOP         2
  ON THE MATERNAL MIDNIGHT OF MY BREAST • • • • • •        535 CHOSEN              7
  AT WINE-DARK MIDNIGHT IN THE SACRED WOOD, • • • • •      536 HER VISION          2
  AT STROKE OF MIDNIGHT SOUL CANNOT ENDURE • • • • • •     558 RIBH CHRISTIAN     19
  AT STROKE OF MIDNIGHT GOD SHALL WIN• • • • • • •         561 FOUR AGES MAN       8
  "THAT I AT MIDNIGHT BY THE CLOCK • • • • • • •           569 THREE BUSHES       10
  AT MIDNIGHT TO MY ROOM, • • • • • • • • •                570 THREE BUSHES       39
  MIDNIGHT, AN OLD HOUSE • • • • • • • • • •               575 ACRE OF GRASS       5
  STRETCH TOWARDS THE MOONLESS MIDNIGHT OF THE TREES, • •  579 DOR WELLESLEY       1
  AND PRESSED AT MIDNIGHT IN SOME PUBLIC PLACE • • • •     610 STATUES             7
  CRIES A VOICE AT ROARING MIDNIGHT BESIDE THE MOONLESS DEEP, 718 PHANTOM SHIP      8
  SAY WHAT RINGER RINGS AT MIDNIGHT: FOR, IN THE BELFRY HIGH, 718 PHANTOM SHIP     15
  FOR NOON AND MIDNIGHT FROM EACH OTHER BORROW, • • • • •  735 QUATRAIN APHOR     26
MIDNIGHT'S
  THERE MIDNIGHT'S ALL A GLIMMER, AND NOON A PURPLE GLOW,  117 ISLE INNISFREE      7
MIDNIGHTS
  BUT NO DOGS BARKED, AND MIDNIGHTS CHIMED, • • • • • •    570 THREE BUSHES       29
  AND NO DOGS BARKED THROUGH MIDNIGHTS CHIMED • • • •      570 THREE BUSHES   V   29
MIDST
  GREY IN THE MIDST LIKE A SMALL RIVULET'S FLOW, • • • •    37 OISIN 2       V  117
  IN MIDST OF AN OLD MAN'S BOSOM: OWLS RUFFLING AND PACING  50 OISIN 3           47
    AROUND
  IN THE MIDST OF AN OLD MAN'S BOSOM: OWLS RUFFLING         50 OISIN 3       V   47
    AND PACING AROUND
  • • • HER BROW ON THE MIDST OF MY BREAST: • • • • • •     52 OISIN 3           74
  SAD NIAM CAME NEAR ME, AND LAID HER BROWS ON THE MIDST    52 OISIN 3       V   74
    OF MY BREAST
  AND PEARL-PALE NEAVE LAY BY ME, HER BROW ON THE MIDST OF  52 OISIN 3       V   74
    MY BREAST:
  WEAK, IN THE MIDST OF THE MEADOW, • • • • • • • •         54 OISIN 3          102
  • • • FROM HIS MILES IN THE MIDST OF THE AIR, • • • •     54 OISIN 3          103
  SHE FOLLOWED WITH LIGHT FOOTFALL IN THE MIDST, • • • •   186 QUEEN MAEVE       128
  AND SAW WHERE IN THE MIDST OF THE GREAT HALL • • • •     279 TWO KINGS          60
  AND IN THE MIDST KING EOCHAID'S BROTHER STOOD, • • • •   286 TWO KINGS         217
  THE STONE'S IN THE MIDST OF ALL• • • • • • • •           393 EASTER 1916        56
MIDSUMMER
  OR MAYBE TO MIDSUMMER DAY," • • • • • • • • •            305 HOUR DAWN          58
MIEN
  (HOW GLAD WAS HER MIEN!), • • • • • • • • • •            654 ISLE STAT I 2      72
MIGHT
  I'D PUT AWAY THE FOOLISH MIGHT OF A KING, • • • • •      103 FERGUS DRUID   V  21A
  ONE MOMENT HAS NO MIGHT UPON THE MOMENT • • • • • •      237 SHADOW WATER B    340
  "WHY ARE THEY FAITHLESS WHEN THEIR MIGHT • • • • •       275 GREY ROCK         109
  THE HANDS THAT GATHERED UP THE MIGHT OF THE WORLD, • •   278 TWO KINGS          29
  WHEREIN THE GAZING HEART DOUBLES HER MIGHT• • • • •      326 ROBERT GREGORY     69
  EXHAUST HIS GLORY AND HIS MIGHT: • • • • • • •           438 SONGS PLAY 2       14
  MIGHT OF THE CHURCH AND THE STATE, • • • • • • •         554 CHURCH STATE        3
  HE FOUGHT THE MIGHT OF ENGLAND • • • • • • • •           586 PARNELLITES        11
  WE KNOW WHAT RASCAL MIGHT HAS DEFILED, • • • • • •       614 MARCH SONGS 2      11
  MEASUREMENT BEGAN OUR MIGHT: • • • • • • • •             638 BEN BULBEN         42
  SUSTAINS HIS SOUL IN COURAGE OR IN MIGHT• • • • • •      650 ISLE STAT I 1     144
  WHERE THEIR SINEWY MIGHT IS STRUNG • • • • • • •         658 ISLE STAT I 3      88
```

518

		PAGE	TITLE		LINE
MIGHTIER					
NO MIGHTIER CREATURES BAY AT THE MOON;	• • • • • • •	8	OISIN 1		87
THERE WAS NO MIGHTIER SOUL OF HEBER'S LINE;	• • • • •	36	OISIN 2		95
THE MIGHTIER MASTERS OF A MIGHTIER RACE;	• • • • •	38	OISIN 2		133
THE MIGHTIER MASTERS OF A MIGHTIER RACE;	• • • • •	38	OISIN 2		133
ROOTED IN FOAM AND CLOUDS. THERE MIGHTIER MASTERS MET	• •	38	OISIN 2	V	132
FOR I AM MIGHTIER NOW BY FAR THAN THEE,	• • • • •	673	ISLE STAT II 3		193
AND SAID IT WAS MIGHTIER THAN THE SUN AND MOON,	• • • •	762	SHADOW WATER A		289
MIGHTIEST					
WAR ON THE MIGHTIEST MEN UNDER THE SKIES,	• • • • • •	45	OISIN 2		241
"HE IS THE MIGHTIEST MAN IN SHIP OR DUN."	• • • • •	107	CUCHULAIN SEA	V	28
THE MIGHTIEST OF THE PRINCES OF THE WORLD	• • • • •	462	HARUN RASHID		41
AMONG THE QUEENS, AND CHOSE THE MIGHTIEST	• • • • •	757	SHADOW WATER A		213
MIGHTY					
"I AM NEAVE, A CHILD OF THE MIGHTY SHEE,	• • • • • •	5	OISIN 1	V	48
WHILE A HUNDRED YOUTHS, MIGHTY OF LIMB,	• • • • •	8	OISIN 1		94
CAME SWIMMING SADLY DOWN THE MIGHTY STAIR.	• • • •	32	OISIN 2	V	50B
TO RULE MORE MIGHTY MEN, AND TO THE WORLD	• • • • •	38	OISIN 2	V	133
BURIED AND MIGHTY. WHEN THROUGH THE GREAT DOOR	• • •	39	OISIN 2		151
BURIED AND MIGHTY. THENCE I JOURNEYED NOT	• • • • •	39	OISIN 2	V	151
THEIR MIGHTY AND NAKED AND GLEAMING BODIES	• • • • •	48	OISIN 3	V	28
DARK BALOR, AS OLD AS A FOREST, CAR-BORNE, HIS MIGHTY HEAD SUNK		53	OISIN 3		91
CAME BALOR, AS OLD AS A FOREST, CAR BORNE, HIS MIGHTY HEAD SUNK		53	OISIN 3	V	91
BY MIGHTY BRAHMA'S EVER-RUSTLING ROBE,	• • • • • •	71	ANASHU VIJAYA		14
BY MIGHTY BRAHMA'S EVER-RUSTLING ROBE,	• • • • • •	71	ANASHU VIJAYA	V	14
TO MIGHTY BRAHMA, HE WHO MADE YOU MANY AS THE SANDS,	• •	72	ANASHU VIJAYA		21
TO MIGHTY BRAHMA——HE WHO MADE YE MANY AS THE SANDS,	• •	72	ANASHU VIJAYA	V	21
TO MIGHTY BRAHMA, WHO HAS MADE YOU MANY AS THE SANDS,	• •	72	ANASHU VIJAYA	V	21
HAS SLAIN SO MIGHTY ARMIES, SO GREAT KINGS,	• •	106	CUCHULAIN SEA	V	10A
"CUCHULAIN I, MIGHTY CUCHULAIN'S SON."	• • • • • •	110	CUCHULAIN SEA		68
"I AM FINMOLE, MIGHTY CUCHULAIN'S SON."	• • • • •	110	CUCHULAIN SEA	V	68
WHAT POWER THAT IS MORE MIGHTY THAN DESIRE,	• • • •	234	SHADOW WATER B		267
THAT IS MORE MIGHTY THAN THE SUN AND MOON,	• • • •	237	SHADOW WATER B		328
MORE MIGHTY THAN THE STARS HALF TROUBLED ME,	• • •	237	SHADOW WATER B		332
FOR I NEED ALL HIS MIGHTY MEMORIES,	• • • • • •	413	TOWER		104
NO HONOUR LEAVE ITS MIGHTY MONUMENT,	• • • • •	429	NINETEEN 19		38
TO MIGHTY PARIS WHEN HE FOUND	• • • • • • •	522	LULLABY		4
ROUNDS A MIGHTY SCENE,	• • • • • • •	599	STONE CROSS		22
I AND THAT MIGHTY KING A SUDDEN BLOW	• • • • •	757	SHADOW WATER A		195
HAVE CALLED HIM MIGHTY. I WILL FOLLOW YOU	• • • •	768	SHADOW WATER A		412
MILCH					
CAN CALL THE MILCH COWS	• • • • • • • • •	780	WELL AND TREE		5
MILCH-COWS					
CAN CALL THE MILCH-COWS	• • • • • • • •	780	WELL AND TREE	V	5
MILD					
ON A MORNING MISTY AND MILD AND FAIR.	• • • • •	2	OISIN 1	V	7E
HIS MISTRESS WAS MORE MILD AND FAIR	• • • • •	3	OISIN 1	V	7DD
HUNG FROM THE MORNING STAR; WHEN THESE MILD WORDS	• •	32	OISIN 2		49
BUT IN DREAMS, MILD MAN OF THE CROZIERS,	• • • •	53	OISIN 3		85
• • • GROWN MILD WITH MYSTERIOUS THOUGHT,	• • • •	55	OISIN 3		121
• • • OR WAS LIFTED AN OLD MAN'S MILD HEAD.	• • • •	59	OISIN 3	V	170
AND WITH A RULE SERENE AND MILD	• • • • • •	82	MAD KING GOLL	V	6
PEACE-MAKING, MILD, A KINGLY BOY.	• • • • • •	82	MAD KING GOLL	V	8
AND THAT MILD WOMAN OF THE SOUTH,	• • • • • •	189	BAILE AILLINN		6
THAT BEAUTIFUL MILD WOMAN, YOUR CLOSE FRIEND,	• • •	204	ADAMS CURSE		2
THAT BEAUTIFUL MILD WOMAN FOR WHOSE SAKE	• • • •	205	ADAMS CURSE		15
MURMURED WITH HER YOUNG VOICE FOR WHOSE MILD SAKE	• •	205	ADAMS CURSE	V	15
IN FINDING THAT IT'S YOUNG AND MILD AND LOW,	• • •	205	ADAMS CURSE	V	17
HAVE SEEN IMMORTAL, MILD, PROUD SHADOWS WALK;	• • • •	217	WOODS OF COOLE		12
HOW SHALL I NAME YOU, IMMORTAL, MILD, PROUD SHADOWS?	• •	218	WOODS OF COOLE		27
A KIND MILD WOMAN HAD SHE BEEN, WHO POURED	• • • •	279	TWO KINGS	V	62A
BUT NOW SHE HAD NO MILD AND NO KIND LOOK;	• • • •	279	TWO KINGS	V	62D
TILL THE YELLOW EYE HAS GROWN MILD,	• • • • •	349	HAWK		3
HE WAS A MAN MOST LEARNED AND MOST MILD,	• • • •	692	MOSADA 1		51
ABOVE, THE WOODS WHERE WITH THE SOFT MILD EYE	• • •	710	FERENCZ RENYI		26
HOW "THE ONLY GOOD IS MUSING MILD,	• • • • • •	728	PRIEST FAIRY		13
OF SOME MILD WOMAN, OR IN CHILDREN'S WAYS.	• • • •	750	SHADOW WATER A		74
MILE					
AND MANY A MILE IS THE FAERY STATE,	• • • • •	9	OISIN 1	V	103
NO MORE TO CRAWL ON THE SEAS WITH LONG OARS MILE AFTER MILE,		55	OISIN 3		119
NO MORE TO CRAWL ON THE SEAS WITH LONG OARS MILE AFTER MILE,		55	OISIN 3		119
RUN FOR A MILE UNDIMMED IN HEAVEN'S FACE	• • • •	490	COOLE BALLYLEE		3
AND FOUND. 'TIS WELL!——ANOTHER MILE OF WAY	• • • •	651	ISLE STAT I 2		6
MILES					
• • • FROM HIS MILES IN THE MIDST OF THE AIR,	• • • •	54	OISIN 3		103
AND MASONS DROVE FROM MILES AWAY	• • • • • •	360	ALF POLLEXFEN		9
IN THE SOUTH SEA'S AZURE MILES,	• • • • • • •	732	STREET DANCERS		28
IN THE SOUTH SEAS' AZURE MILES,	• • • • • • •	732	STREET DANCERS	V	28
MILK					
AND OIL AND WINE AND HONEY AND MILK,	• • • • •	8	OISIN 1		92
AND HONEY, AND OIL, AND WINE, AND MILK,	• • • • •	8	OISIN 1	V	92
THEIR BROWS WERE WHITE AS FRAGRANT MILK,	• • • •	15	OISIN 1		204
THEIR BROWS WERE WHITE AS THE FRAGRANT MILK	• • • •	15	OISIN 1	V	204
• • • HE SAD AS A CHILD WITHOUT MILK;	• • • • •	59	OISIN 3		174
THAT IS TO AGE WHAT MILK IS TO A CHILD?	• • • • •	469	HARUN RASHID		174
SPILT MILK	• • • • • • • • • • •	484	SPILT MILK		T
LIKE MILK SPILT ON A STONE.	• • • • • • • •	484	SPILT MILK		4

519

```
                                                     PAGE      TITLE          LINE
MILK   (CONTINUED)
      THIS FALLEN STAR MY MILK SUSTAINS,  . . . . . .    499 MOTHER OF GOD         12
      DRINKING JOY AS IT WERE MILK UPON HIS BREAST. . . . . .   559 MAGIC DRUM      3
      OR SUCKED SUCH MILK AS HE, . . . . . . . . . .   584 GHOST ROG CASE         26
MILKING
      ON NO LONG BENCH NOR LOFTY MILKING SHED . . . . . . .   341 SHEP GOATHERD V    51
MILKING-PLACE
      THE MILKING-PLACE, THE SHELTERED FARM? . . . . . . .   151 HEART OF WOMAN V    6
MILKING-SHED
      ON NO LONG BENCH NOR LOFTY MILKING-SHED . . . . . . .   341 SHEP GOATHERD      51
MILK-PALE
      AND AT HIS CRY THERE CAME NO MILK-PALE FACE . . . . .    38 OISIN 2          134
MILK-WHITE
      WHEELS BY MILK-WHITE ASSES DRAWN  . . . . . . .   502 VACILLATION           62
      AS THE CANKER-WORM ON A MILK-WHITE ROSE: . . . . . .   673 ISLE STAT II 3    177
      THAT FROM THE MILK-WHITE MARBLE  . . . . . . . . .   680 LOVE AND DEATH      3
MILKY
      OF MILKY BRIGHTNESS TO AND FRO . . . . . . . . .    22 OISIN 1            328
      FLED FOAM UNDERNEATH US, AND ROUND US, A WANDERING AND    47 OISIN 3          1
         MILKY SMOKE,
      FLED FOAM UNDERNEATH US, AND ROUND US, A WANDERING AND    47 OISIN 3         12
         MILKY SMOKE.
      FLED FOAM UNDERNEATH US, AND AROUND US, A WANDERING AND   47 OISIN 3      V   1
         MILKY SMOKE.
      FLED FOAM UNDERNEATH ME, AND ROUND ME, A WANDERING AND    57 OISIN 3        148
         MILKY SMOKE.
      THE BRILLIANT MOON AND ALL THE MILKY SKY, . . . . . .   119 SORROW OF LOVE     2
MILL
      WITH OLD MILL BOARDS AND SEA-GREEN SLATES, . . . . .   406 CARVED STONE       2
      NOR THE MILL OF THE MIND . . . . . . . . . .   575 ACRE OF GRASS         10
MILLION
      WHILE ROUND THE SHORE A MILLION STOOD  . . . . . .    14 OISIN 1          182
      WHAT THE WORLD'S MILLION LIPS ARE THIRSTING FOR  . . . .   229 SHADOW WATER B   161
MILLION-FOOTED
      FAR FLEETER THAN THE MILLION-FOOTED SEA. . . . . . .   670 ISLE STAT II 3    108
MILLIONS
      WHERE WHITE DEWDROPS IN MILLIONS FALL: . . . . . .    16 OISIN 1        V  222
      THEY SLOWLY INTO MILLIONS GREW,  . . . . . . .   133 FR GILLIGAN         17
MILTON'S
      FROM THE FAR TOWER WHERE MILTON'S PLATONIST . . . . .   373 PHASES OF MOON     15
MIMIC
      MIMICKING WHAT THEY HEARD, AS CHILDREN MIMIC: . . . . .   487 SEVEN SAGES       25
MIMICKING
      MIMICKING WHAT THEY HEARD, AS CHILDREN MIMIC: . . . . .   487 SEVEN SAGES       25
MIMICRY
      A MIMICRY OF YOUTH. CAN POET'S THOUGHT . . . . .   463 HARUN RASHID       62
      A MIMICRY OF YOUTH. AN ARTIST'S THOUGHT, . . . . .   463 HARUN RASHID V     62
      BE MIMICRY?" "WHAT MATTER IF OUR SOULS . . . . . .   464 HARUN RASHID       66
      CAN BE NO MIMICRY. "WHAT IF OUR SOULS . . . . . .   464 HARUN RASHID V     66
MINARET
      SINKS DOWN AT LAST WITH YONDER MINARET, . . . . . . .   691 MOSADA 1     V    36
MIND
      WITH A HEAVY HEART AND A WANDERING MIND, . . . . .     2 OISIN 1            2
      "HOW COMES IT, PRINCESS, THAT YOUR MIND . . . . . .     6 OISIN 1      V  59A
      WRAPPED IN THE THINGS OF THE UNHUMAN MIND, . . . . .    36 OISIN 2           98
      ROLLED IN THE THINGS OF THE UNHUMAN MIND, . . . . .    36 OISIN 2      V   98
      WE TRAMPLED TO AND FRO. WHEN HIS MIND KNEW . . . .    40 OISIN 2      V  173
      FOR GOD HAS HEARD, AND SPEAKS HIS ANGRY MIND: . . . .    42 OISIN 2          206
      DARKEN: HEAVEN IS ANGRY. CEASE! UNTO MY MIND, . . . .    42 OISIN 2      V  205
      AS MY MIND MADE THE NAMES OF THE FENIANS. . . .    57 OISIN 3          146
      ANOTHER FILLS YOUR MIND. MY MOTHER'S NAME. . . . .    71 ANASHU VIJAYA     16
      SOME OTHER FILLS YOUR MIND. MY MOTHER'S NAME. . . . .    71 ANASHU VIJAYA V   16
      HIS MIND RAN ALL ON MONEY CARES AND FEARS, . . . . .   127 DREAM OF FAERY     14
      THAT HURRY FROM UNMEASURED MIND . . . . . . .   138 TO IRELAND         25
      THEY HUDDLE FROM MAN'S PONDERING MIND, . . . . . .   138 TO IRELAND    V   26
      AND HOW YOU HAVE LEAPED TIMES OUT OF MIND . . . .   146 FISH                5
      BECAUSE YOUR CRYING BRINGS TO MY MIND . . . . . .   155 REPROVE CURLEW      3
      AMONG MY LEAVES IN TIMES OUT OF MIND: . . . . . .   177 PAST GREATNESS      5
      NO COMMON LOVE IS TO OUR MIND, . . . . . . . .   190 BAILE AILLINN      34
      THAT OUT OF SIGHT IS OUT OF MIND. . . . . . . .   192 BAILE AILLINN      87
      IT MIGHT CALL UP A NEW AGE, CALLING TO MIND . . . .   201 OLD MEMORY          4
      FOR THE ROADS ARE UNENDING, AND THERE IS NO PLACE TO MY   203 WITHER BOUGHS      4
         MIND."
      I WOULD BE OF YOUR MIND: BUT WHEN HE PLAYS IT . . . .   222 SHADOW WATER B     17
      IF WE WERE OF ONE MIND I'D DO IT. WERE'T NOT . . . .   222 SHADOW WATER B V   15
      THE MIND IS MADE UNCHANGING, FOR IT FINDS . . . .   227 SHADOW WATER B    101
      IF YOU WILL GIVE ME ALL YOUR MIND AWHILE-- . . . .   227 SHADOW WATER B    117
      THE IMMORTAL MOCKERS HAVE CAST INTO HIS MIND, . . . .   249 SHADOW WATER B    567
      WHAT COULD HAVE MADE HER PEACEFUL WITH A MIND . . . .   256 NO SECOND TROY     6
      "IT WAS THE MASK ENGAGED YOUR MIND, . . . . . .   263 MASK                8
      TIME OUT OF MIND, BECAME TOO RUINOUS . . . . . .   264 HOUSE SHAKEN        3
      DELIGHT MAKES ALL OF THE ONE MIND, . . . . . .   266 GALWAY RACES        2
      AND FOR NINE DAYS MY MIND WENT WHIRLING ROUND . . . .   282 TWO KINGS         127
      I PRAISED HER BODY AND HER MIND . . . . . . .   314 MEMORY YOUTH        9
      MIND AND DELIGHTED MIND: . . . . . . . . .   315 FRIENDS             9
      MIND AND DELIGHTED MIND: . . . . . . . . .   315 FRIENDS             9
      FOR ALL THAT COME INTO MY MIND ARE DEAD. . . . . .   324 ROBERT GREGORY     16
      LIONEL JOHNSON COMES THE FIRST TO MIND, . . . . .   324 ROBERT GREGORY     17
      A PORTION OF MY MIND AND LIFE, AS IT WERE . . . . .   325 ROBERT GREGORY     42
      AND YET HIS MIND OUTRAN THE HORSES' FEET. . . . . .   326 ROBERT GREGORY     64
      THAT SHAKES THE SHUTTER, TO HAVE BROUGHT TO MIND . . .   327 ROBERT GREGORY     90
```

MIND   (CONTINUED)

	PAGE	TITLE		LINE
I BALANCED ALL, BROUGHT ALL TO MIND,	328	IRISH AIRMAN		13
THROUGH VICTORIES OF THE MIND,	343	SHEP GOATHERD		108
THAT GIVES UP ALL HER MIND,	345	ON WOMAN		2
YELLOW-EYED HAWK OF THE MIND,	349	HAWK		14
OF THE ANALYTIC MIND, CAN NEITHER CLOSE	353	PEOPLE		33
THE EYE OF THE MIND NOR KEEP MY TONGUE FROM SPEECH."	353	PEOPLE		34
I WAS ABASHED, AND NOW THEY COME TO MIND	353	PEOPLE		36
AND SMOOTH OUT STAIN AND BLEMISH WITH THE ELEGANCE OF HIS MIND:	353	HIS PHOENIX		7
THE BALLOON OF THE MIND	358	BALLOON MIND		T
BRING THE BALLOON OF THE MIND	358	BALLOON MIND		2
WE HAVE LIT UPON THE GENTLE, SENSITIVE MIND	368	EGO DOMINUS		12
HIS ART IS HAPPY, BUT WHO KNOWS HIS MIND?	370	EGO DOMINUS		54
AS WITH THE CAT-O'-NINE-TAILS OF THE MIND,	374	PHASES OF MOON		42
AND YET THEY SPEAK WHAT'S BLOWN INTO THE MIND:	376	PHASES OF MOON		110
DEFORMITY OF BODY AND OF MIND.	377	PHASES OF MOON		123
BEFORE SHE HAD SETTLED HER MIND	381	SONGS FOOL 2		8
FOR WHAT BUT EYE AND EAR SILENCE THE MIND	384	VISION ROBART		41
MIND MOVED YET SEEMED TO STOP	384	VISION ROBART		43
BUT BEAR IN MIND YOUR LOVER'S WAGE	385	ROBARTES DANCE		14
RECALL THE YEARS BEFORE HER MIND	397	POLIT PRISONER		8
BECAUSE OF THE GREAT GLOOM THAT IS IN MY MIND.	403	FOR DAUGHTER		8
MY MIND, BECAUSE THE MINDS THAT I HAVE LOVED,	405	FOR DAUGHTER		49
IF THERE'S NO HATRED IN A MIND	405	FOR DAUGHTER		54
BECAUSE OF HER OPINIONATED MIND	405	FOR DAUGHTER		61
BRING UP OUT OF THAT DEEP CONSIDERING MIND	413	TOWER		106
TO EXALT A LONELY MIND,	420	MY HOUSE		29
MIND FROM MIND HAS CAUGHT:	420	MY HOUSE	V	20G
MIND FROM MIND HAS CAUGHT:	420	MY HOUSE	V	20G
HAVING INHERITED A VIGOROUS MIND	422	MY DESCENDANTS		1
AS VIGOROUS OF MIND, AND YET IT SEEMS	422	MY DESCENDANTS		4
FRENZIES BEWILDER, REVERIES PERTURB THE MIND	426	PHANTOM HATRED		7
WHETHER HEALTH, WEALTH OR PEACE OF MIND WERE SPENT	429	NINETEEN 19		36
THAT HAD SUCH BURDENS ON THE MIND	432	NINETEEN 19		94
HER PRESENT IMAGE FLOATS INTO THE MIND--	444	SCHOOL CHILDR		25
BECAUSE THIS COUNTRY HAS A PIOUS MIND	447	COLONUS PRAISE		25
I CAN EXCHANGE OPINION WITH ANY NEIGHBOURING MIND,	450	OWEN AHERNE		9
"SPEAK ALL YOUR MIND," MY HEART SANG OUT,	450	OWEN AHERNE		21
. . . "SPEAK ALL YOUR MIND: WHO CARES,	450	OWEN AHERNE		21
NOR THOUGHT OUT OF HER MIND OR MINE BEGOT,	467	HARUN RASHID		140
NOR THOUGHT OUT OF HER MIND OR OUT OF MINE	467	HARUN RASHID	V	140
THE BEAUTY OF A WOMAN'S MIND OR BODY	469	HARUN RASHID	V	187
I NEED SOME MIND THAT, IF THE CANNON SOUND	471	ALL SOUL NIGHT		11
AND WHAT IF MIND SEEM CHANGED,	473	ALL SOUL NIGHT		66
AND IT SEEM CHANGED WITH THE MIND,	473	ALL SOUL NIGHT		67
AND WHAT IF MIND SEEMED CHANGE	473	ALL SOUL NIGHT	V	66
AND IT SEEMED CHANGED WITH THE MIND,	473	ALL SOUL NIGHT	V	67
PICTURES OF THE MIND, RECALL	475	EVA GORE-BOOTH		17
SET ALL YOUR MIND UPON THE STEEP ASCENT,	477	SELF AND SOUL		2
AND FALLS INTO THE BASIN OF THE MIND	478	SELF AND SOUL		34
GOLDSMITH DELIBERATELY SIPPING AT THE HONEY-POT OF HIS MIND,	481	BLOOD AND MOON		21
MUST VANISH ON THE INSTANT IF THE MIND BUT CHANGE ITS THEME:	481	BLOOD AND MOON		27
GOLDSMITH DELIBERATELY SIPPING AT THE HONEY POT OF HIS MIND:	481	BLOOD AND MOON	V	21
A LEVELLING, RANCOROUS, RATIONAL SORT OF MIND	486	SEVEN SAGES		11
THE MIND OF MAN OR ELEVATE A RHYME:	492	COOLE BALLYLEE		45
DID AN OLDER MIND COMMEND--	494	AT ALGECIRAS		10
BUT GOOD STRONG BLOWS ARE DELIGHTS TO THE MIND."	544	TO SAME TUNE 1		4
IN THE MIND ALONE:	553	PRAYER OLD AGE		2
. . . DAMPED BY THE BODY OR THE MIND,	556	RIBH PATRICK		8
OF EVERYTHING THAT IS NOT MIND OR SENSE.	558	RIBH CHRISTIAN		6
THEN HE STRUGGLED WITH THE MIND:	561	FOUR AGES MAN		5
ON MIND, ON NEST.	574	LOVERS SONG		5
NOR THE MILL OF THE MIND	575	ACRE OF GRASS		10
A MIND MICHAEL ANGELO KNEW	576	ACRE OF GRASS		19
AN OLD MAN'S EAGLE MIND.	576	ACRE OF GRASS		24
KEEPS PARNELL IN HIS MIND.	586	PARNELLITES		20
O MIND YOUR FEET, O MIND YOUR FEET,	592	DRUNK SOBRIETY		9
O MIND YOUR FEET, O MIND YOUR FEET,	592	DRUNK SOBRIETY		9
THE CAVERN OF THE MIND?	600	THOSE IMAGES		2
THAT IRELAND'S MIND BE GREATER,	608	SONGS BURDEN 3		21
HOW CAN THE MIND FORGIVE?	615	MARCH SONGS 2		16
BUT GOOD STRONG BLOWS ARE DELIGHTS TO THE MIND."	616	MARCH SONGS 3		4
HIS MIND MOVES UPON SILENCE.	617	LONG-LEG FLY		10
HER MIND MOVES UPON SILENCE.	617	LONG-LEG FLY		20
HIS MIND MOVES UPON SILENCE.	618	LONG-LEG FLY		30
OF AN UNBROKEN HAPPY MIND,	626	OLD MEN BE MAD		14
AND MIND AND BODY SHRANK.	626	STATES HOLIDAY		4
GREW IN PURE MIND, BUT OUT OF WHAT BEGAN?	630	CIRCUS ANIMALS		34
BACK IN THE HUMAN MIND AGAIN.	637	BEN BULBEN		24
HE COMPLETES HIS PARTIAL MIND,	638	BEN BULBEN		30
BEFORE THE SECRET WORKING MIND:	639	BEN BULBEN		51
CAST YOUR MIND ON OTHER DAYS	640	BEN BULBEN		81
OH, LEARNED IS EACH MONK'S-HOOD'S MIND,	655	ISLE STAT I 3		8
IN THE FAR WORLD WILL VANISH FROM THY MIND,	670	ISLE STAT II 3		93
HE DIGS HIS CABBAGES. HE BRINGS TO MIND	696	MOSADA 2		18
OH, HUSH THE WANDERING MUSIC OF THY MIND.	703	MOSADA 3		106
CLOSELY ROUND US, BODY AND MIND--	717	FAIRY DOCTOR		23

MIND   (CONTINUED)
        TO MIND HIS COWS AND SWINE BY THE RED LAKE. . . . . . .   752 SHADOW WATER A   112
        AND STABLING TO YOUR MIND. . . . .   774 COME RIDE   8
        OUT OF MEMORY AND MIND. . . . .   775 AGAINST WITCH   10
        THE LABYRINTH OF THE MIND. . . . .   785 WOMANS BEAUTY   24
MINDED   SEE MANY-MINDED
        A NEIGHBOUR MINDED HER BY DAY. . . . .   94 MOLL MAGEE   15
        I MINDED HER TILL MORN. . . . .   94 MOLL MAGEE   16
MINDFUL
        BUT, THE BIRD IN MY FINGERS, I MOUNTED, MINDFUL ONLY TO   54 OISIN 3   V 111
            LAUNCH
MIND'S
        NOW AS AT ALL TIMES I CAN SEE IN THE MIND'S EYE, ...   318 MAGI   1
        MORE PLAIN TO THE MIND'S EYE THAN ANY FACE . . . . . .   368 EGO DOMINUS   21
        CAUGHT UP IN CONTEMPLATION, THE MIND'S EYE . . . . . .   375 PHASES OF MOON   79
        ON THE GREY ROCK OF CASHEL THE MIND'S EYE . . . . . .   382 VISION ROBART   1
        ALTHOUGH I SAW IT ALL IN THE MIND'S EYE . . . .   383 VISION ROBART   25
        MONSTROUS FAMILIAR IMAGES SWIM TO THE MIND'S EYE. . . .   426 PHANTOM HATRED   8
        WOUND IN MIND'S PONDERING . . . .   471 ALL SOUL NIGHT   13
        BUT THINK THAT HIS MIND'S EYE, ...   471 ALL SOUL NIGHT   33
        WOUND IN MIND'S WANDERING . . . .   474 ALL SOUL NIGHT   99
        MIND'S BREAD GROW SWEET. . . . .   554 CHURCH STATE   6
        "HOW FEW THE MIND'S INTEMPERANCE RULE! . . . .   725 LEGEND   10
MINDS
        FOR THEIR DIM MINDS WERE WITH THE ANCIENT THINGS. . . .   34 OISIN 2   77
        TO WANDER BY THEIR MELANCHOLY MINDS. . . . .   72 ANASHU VIJAYA   33
        MY MIND, BECAUSE THE MINDS THAT I HAVE LOVED, ...   405 FOR DAUGHTER   49
        HAVE CLOSED THE LADIES' EYES, THEIR MINDS ARE BUT A POOL   426 PHANTOM HATRED   21
        THAT SEEMS UNNATURAL TO ARABIAN MINDS, ...   464 HARUN RASHID   79
        FROM FOUR GREAT MINDS THAT HATED WHIGGERY. . . . . . .   486 SEVEN SAGES   7
        OUR MINDS ARE AT THEIR BEST THIS NIGHT, ...   523 MAD AS MIST   3
        AND MEASURE THE MINDS OF THE FLOWERS, ...   707 FAIRY PEDANT   17
        WHERE DWELL THE MINDS OF OLD MEN HAVING PEACE, ...   721 WITCH VIVIEN   22
MINE
        AND THE WHITE BODY THAT LAY BY MINE; . . . .   3 OISIN 1   10
        THERE WAS NO LIMB OF MINE BUT FELL . . . .   7 OISIN 1   72
        WITH HOPE, MINE ENEMY. AS HE BY NIGHT . . . .   34 OISIN 2   V   81
        BURNING BETWEEN HER FINGERS, AND IN MINE . . . .   37 OISIN 2   125
        AND MINE OWN WORDS RE-ECHOING SHALL SEND . . . . . .   68 SAD SHEPHERD   V   20
        AND MINE OWN TALE AGAIN FOR ME SHALL SING, ...   68 SAD SHEPHERD   V   22
        AND MINE OWN WHISPERING WORDS BE COMFORTING, ...   68 SAD SHEPHERD   V   23
        "YOUR EYES THAT ONCE WERE NEVER WEARY OF MINE . . . . .   79 EPHEMERA   1
        MINE WAS A CHAIR OF SKINS AND GOLD, ...   81 MAD KING GOLL V   1
        MINE WAS THE THRONE IN EMAN'S HALL, ...   81 MAD KING GOLL V   2
        MINE WERE CLAN MORNA'S TRIBES UNTOLD, ...   81 MAD KING GOLL V   3
        AND MINE WAS EVERY TROPHIED WALL, ...   82 MAD KING GOLL V   4
        OF ONE WHO IS NO FRIEND TO ME OR TO MINE, ...   184 QUEEN MAEVE   V 94A
        AND BEAT THE BULWARK OF YOUR SHIP ON MINE, ...   236 SHADOW WATER B   312
        O WHY DO YOU NOT LIFT YOUR EYES TO MINE? . . . . . .   246 SHADOW WATER B   498
        . . . CERTAIN BAD POETS, IMITATORS OF HIS AND MINE . . . 262 TO A POET   T
        . . . CERTAIN BAD POETS, IMITATORS OF HIS AND OF MINE .   262 TO A POET   V   T
        NOTHING BUT THAT TO PROVE YOUR BLOOD AND MINE. . . . .   270 PARDON FATHERS   22
        THE MORAL'S YOURS BECAUSE IT'S MINE. . . . .   271 GREY ROCK   11
        "IF HE BE LIVING STILL THE WHOLE WORLD'S MINE, ...   280 TWO KINGS   V   85
        NOR AN UNLAUGHING MOUTH, BUT MINE THAT MOURNS, ...   285 TWO KINGS   184
        THAT DEEP-SWORN VOW HAVE BEEN FRIENDS OF MINE; . . . .   357 DEEP-SWORN VOW   2
        THAT DEEP SWORN VOW, HAVE BEEN FRIENDS OF MINE, ...   357 DEEP-SWORN VOW V   2
        TRUE SONG, THOUGH SPEECH, "MINE AUTHOR SUNG IT ME." . .   373 PHASES OF MOON   30
        NOT HIS, NOT MINE." WHO UNDERSTOOD . . . .   387 SOLOMON WITCH   6
        NOT HIS, NOT MINE." AND HE THAT KNEW . . . .   387 SOLOMON WITCH V   6
        BEING DEAR AS MINE ARE DEAR. . . . .   400 DEMON BEAST   20
        THESE STONES REMAIN THEIR MONUMENT AND MINE. . . . . .   423 MY DESCENDANTS   24
        AND IF HER EYE SHOULD NOT GROW BRIGHT FOR MINE . . . .   464 HARUN RASHID   81
        NOR THOUGHT OUT OF HER MIND OR MINE BEGOT, ...   467 HARUN RASHID   140
        NOR THOUGHT OUT OF HER MIND OR OUT OF MINE . . . . . .   467 HARUN RASHID   V 140
        HER CONFIDENCE IN MINE, OR EVEN LOSE . . . .   469 HARUN RASHID   176
        BUT MINE SAW STELLA ONCE. WHENCE CAME OUR THOUGHT? . .   486 SEVEN SAGES   6
        MINE SAW STELLA ONCE. WHENCE CAME OUR THOUGHT? . . . .   486 SEVEN SAGES   V   6
        MINE SAW STELLA ONCE. WHEN CAME OUR THOUGHT? . . . . .   486 SEVEN SAGES   V   6
        MINE MUST WALK WHEN DEAD. . . . .   511 JANE AND JACK   18
        MINE WOULD WALK, BEING DEAD. . . . .   511 JANE AND JACK V   18
        HALF TURNED AND FIXED A GLAZING EYE ON MINE, ...   537 HER VISION   26
        "THAT WAS A LUCKY THOUGHT OF MINE, ...   570 THREE BUSHES   31
        AND MINE WERE BUT FIFTEEN FOOT, NO MODERN STALKS . . .   623 HIGH TALK   3
            UPON HIGHER,
        DID THAT PLAY OF MINE SEND OUT . . . .   632 MAN AND ECHO   11
        DID WORDS OF MINE PUT TOO GREAT STRAIN . . . .   632 MAN AND ECHO   13
        UPON THE WIND, AND GUIDE MINE ARROW'S COURSE. . . . .   657 ISLE STAT I 3   62
        I'LL SEND MINE ARROW, NOW MY ONE RESOURCE; . . . . . .   657 ISLE STAT I 3   64
        WITHIN MINE HEART; AND NAUGHT BUT SORROW NOW . . . . .   659 ISLE STAT II 1   26
        MORE GRIEF IS MINE. NO MAN SHALL EVER STOOP . . . . .   661 ISLE STAT II 1   62
        TWO CAME, HIS NAME AND MINE ON MANY A TREE . . . . .   662 ISLE STAT II 2   10
        IN SAND HIS NAME AND MINE I'VE ALSO READ. . . . . .   662 ISLE STAT II 2   12
        TO MINE, AND HE IS SLOWLY SUCKING FORTH . . . . . .   684 SEEKER   V 63A
        MINE HEART-STRINGS ARE ALL BROKEN SAVING ONE, ...   684 SEEKER   V 69B
        LOVER, THE VOICE THAT SUMMONED THEE WAS MINE. . . . .   685 SEEKER   77
        WANDER AWAY FROM MINE? . . . .   686 LIFE   8
        I TRY TO LIFT MINE ARMS--THEY FALL AGAIN. . . . . .   701 MOSADA 3   56
        MINE WHERE WATERS BROOD AND TOSS! . . . .   744 ROSY CROSS   7
        AGAINST MY FACE AND EYES. MINE TOO ARE BEATEN. . . . .   759 SHADOW WATER A V 233

		PAGE	TITLE	LINE

MINGLE
    WE SHALL MINGLE NO MORE, NOR OUR GAZES EMPTY THEIR   56 OISIN 3   132
        SWEETNESS LONE
MINGLED
    WHO SIGH WITH MINGLED SORROW AND CONTENT, ... 136 TO SOME I TALK   7
    TILL THE DAWN BREAK UPON THOSE MINGLED SEAS. . . . . . 494 AT ALGECIRAS   6
MINGLES
    THEIR HAIR MINGLES ON SOME STRINGED INSTRUMENT, ... 752 SHADOW WATER A   123
MINGLING
    MINGLING OF SWORD AND WAR-AXE, WHILE THE DAY . . . . . 40 OISIN 2   V   171
    WITH MINGLING HAIR, AND PLAY UPON ONE LUTE. . . . . . 71 ANASHU VIJAYA   10
    MINGLING HANDS AND MINGLING GLANCES . . . . 87 STOLEN CHILD   18
    MINGLING HANDS AND MINGLING GLANCES . . . . 87 STOLEN CHILD   18
    AND LANGUORS THAT AWAKE IN MINGLING HANDS . . . . . . 765 SHADOW WATER A   367
    AND MINGLING HAIR FALL FROM THE FIERY BOUGHS, ... 765 SHADOW WATER A   368
    ALL THAT MINGLING OF OUR BREATH, ... 777 SONG DEIRDRE 2   10
MINION
    OH FAMOUS DYING MINION OF THE SUN, ... 673 ISLE STAT II 3   197
MINIONS
    OF THE HAPPY FLOWER MINIONS. . . . . 667 ISLE STAT II 3   29
'MINISHED
    WITH 'MINISHED BEAUTY, MULTIPLIED COMMONPLACE, ... 472 ALL SOUL NIGHT   45
MINISTER
    BY BOSKY JUNE I SWEAR, AND BY THE BEE, HER MINISTER. . . 661 ISLE STAT II 1   74
MINISTERING
    WE MEET AT LAST, THE MINISTERING STARS . . . . 701 MOSADA 3   52
MINNALOUSHE
    BLACK MINNALOUSHE STARED AT THE MOON, ... 378 CAT AND MOON   5
    MINNALOUSHE RUNS IN THE GRASS . . . . 378 CAT AND MOON   9
    DO YOU DANCE, MINNALOUSHE, DO YOU DANCE? . . . . . . 378 CAT AND MOON   11
    MINNALOUSHE CREEPS THROUGH THE GRASS . . . . 378 CAT AND MOON   17
    DOES MINNALOUSHE KNOW THAT HIS PUPILS . . . . 379 CAT AND MOON   21
    MINNALOUSHE CREEPS THROUGH THE GRASS . . . . 379 CAT AND MOON   25
MINNOWED
    HE RUFFLES WITH HIS BILL THE MINNOWED STREAMS. . . . . 73 ANASHU VIJAYA   37
MINOS
    PLATO THERE AND MINOS PASS, ... 531 DELPHIC ORACLE   8
MINSTREL-WORD
    AS FLAMING MINSTREL-WORD UPON HIS CREST. . . . . . . 679 ISLE STAT II 3   317
MINUTE
    BUT O, IN A MINUTE SHE CHANGED— . . . . 212 O DO NOT LOVE   9
    AND I WILL HEAR THEM TALKING IN A MINUTE. . . . . . . 233 SHADOW WATER B   250
    HIS NAME WILL COME INTO OUR THOUGHTS IN A MINUTE. . . . 241 SHADOW WATER B   391
    I HAD NOT WAKED A SINGLE MINUTE, ... 305 HOUR DAWN   72
    WITH THE MINUTE PARTICULARS OF MANKIND? . . . . . . 384 VISION ROBART   42
    AND THE MOON IS WILDER EVERY MINUTE. . . . . 389 SOLOMON WITCH   43
    MINUTE BY MINUTE THEY CHANGE: . . . . 393 EASTER 1916   48
    MINUTE BY MINUTE THEY CHANGE: . . . . 393 EASTER 1916   48
    CHANGES MINUTE BY MINUTE: . . . . 393 EASTER 1916   50
    CHANGES MINUTE BY MINUTE: . . . . 393 EASTER 1916   50
    MINUTE BY MINUTE THEY LIVE: . . . . 393 EASTER 1916   55
    MINUTE BY MINUTE THEY LIVE: . . . . 393 EASTER 1916   55
    MINUTE BY MINUTE CHANGE. . . . . 393 EASTER 1916   V   48
    MINUTE BY MINUTE CHANGE. . . . . 393 EASTER 1916   V   48
    THOSE DEEDS WERE BEST THAT GAVE THE MINUTE WINGS . . . . 533 HER TRIUMPH   5
MINUTES
    FOR CERTAIN MINUTES AT THE LEAST . . . . 399 DEMON BEAST   1
    AND TWENTY MINUTES MORE OR LESS . . . . 501 VACILLATION   42
    FOR TWENTY MINUTES IN SOME STUDIO. . . . . 602 GALLERY REVIS   16
    OH, WOULD THE BUSY MINUTES MIGHT FOLD UP . . . . . . 702 MOSADA 3   97
MIRACLE
    MIRACLE, ECSTASY, THE IMPOSSIBLE HOPE, ... 227 SHADOW WATER B   102
    THAT SEEMED SHEER MIRACLE TO THE MULTITUDE, ... 428 NINETEEN 19   2
    MIRACLE HAD ITS PLAYTIME WHERE . . . . 440 WISDOM   8
    MIRACLE, BIRD OR GOLDEN HANDIWORK, ... 497 BYZANTIUM   17
    MORE MIRACLE THAN BIRD OR HANDIWORK, ... 497 BYZANTIUM   18
    MIRACLE, BIRD OR GOLDEN HANDY-WORK . . . . 497 BYZANTIUM   V   17
    MORE MIRACLE THAN BIRD OR HANDY-WORK . . . . 497 BYZANTIUM   V   18
    THE MIRACLE THAT GAVE THEM SUCH A DEATH . . . . . . 555 RIBH AT TOMB   10
MIRACLE-BRED
    MIRACLE-BRED OUT OF THE LIVING STONE: . . . . 446 COLONUS PRAISE   13
MIRACLES
    ACCEPT THE MIRACLES OF THE SAINTS AND HONOUR SANCTITY? . . 503 VACILLATION   79
    COURAGEOUS MIRACLES! THE SUNLIGHT SHONE . . . . . . 649 ISLE STAT I 1   113
MIRACLE-WORKING
    WITH A MIRACLE-WORKING JUICE . . . . 776 AGAINST WITCH   23
MIRACULOUS
    A SWEET, MIRACULOUS, TERRIFYING SOUND. . . . . 277 TWO KINGS   17
    IMMENSE MIRACULOUS HOUSE . . . . 472 ALL SOUL NIGHT   38
    MIRACULOUS OIL, ODOUR OF VIOLET. . . . . 483 OIL AND BLOOD   3
    BATHED IN MIRACULOUS OIL, SWEET ODOURS FROM IT COME, . . 503 VACILLATION   81
    AND A MIRACULOUS STRANGE BIRD SHRIEKS AT US. . . . . . 534 HER TRIUMPH   12
    AND BOTH ADRIFT ON THE MIRACULOUS STREAM . . . . . . 535 CHOSEN   16
MIRE
    WAS DIM WITH MIRE OF A MORTAL SHORE, ... 15 OISIN 1   208
    WAS DIM WITH THE MIRE OF A MORTAL SHORE, ... 15 OISIN 1   V   208
    AND TRAMPLED IN THE BUBBLING MIRE, ... 83 MAD KING GOLL   26
    AND TRAMPLED ON THE BUBBLING MIRE, ... 83 MAD KING GOLL V   26
    TOILED WITH EMPOUNDED CATTLE THROUGH THE MIRE, ... 276 TWO KINGS   V   2
    THAT WITH EMPOUNDED CATTLE TROD THE MIRE, ... 277 TWO KINGS   4
    TILL ALL THE PLACE WAS BEATEN INTO MIRE. . . . . . . 278 TWO KINGS   27

```
                                                              PAGE    TITLE            LINE
MIRE   (CONTINUED)
     BUT FOR THE TRODDEN MIRE, THE POOL OF BLOOD,  . . . . .  278 TWO KINGS            44
     THE MAN DROWNED IN A BOG'S MIRE,  . . . . . . . . . .    413 TOWER                95
     THE FURY AND THE MIRE OF HUMAN VEINS.  . . . . . . . .    497 BYZANTIUM             8
     AND ALL COMPLEXITIES OF MIRE OR BLOOD.  . . . . . . .     498 BYZANTIUM            24
     ASTRADDLE ON THE DOLPHIN'S MIRE AND BLOOD,  . . . . .     498 BYZANTIUM            33
     A STRADDLE ON THE DOLPHIN'S MIRE AND BLOOD  . . . . .     498 BYZANTIUM       V    33
     THAT THING ALL BLOOD AND MIRE, THAT BEAST-TORN WRECK,  .  537 HER VISION           25
     AND BLOOD AND MIRE THE SENSITIVE BODY STAIN?  . . . .     564 GYRES                10
     ABOLISHED BY A MIRE OF LITTLE THINGS.  . . . . . . .      711 FERENCZ RENYI        36
MIRROR
     LIKE A BRIDE BENDING OVER HER MIRROR ADORNING,  . . . .    28 OISIN 1         V 423E
     BREATHE ON THE BURNISHED MIRROR OF THE WORLD  . . . . .   228 SHADOW WATER B      132
     NOT IN ITS IMAGE ON THE MIRROR!  WHILE  . . . . . . .     230 SHADOW WATER B      189
     YOU MAY, THAT MIRROR FOR A SCHOOL,  . . . . . . . .       335 YOUNG BEAUTY          7
     MIRROR RESEMBLING DREAMS.  . . . . . . . . . . . .        415 TOWER           V   165
     SATISFIED IF A TROUBLED MIRROR SHOW IT,  . . . . . . .    430 NINETEEN 19          62
     CONTENTED THAT A TROUBLED MIRROR SHOW IT,  . . . . . .    430 NINETEEN 19     V    62
     THE MIRROR OF MALICIOUS EYES  . . . . . . . . . .        479 SELF AND SOUL        52
     AND ALL THE RANT'S A MIRROR OF MY MOOD!  . . . . . .     490 COOLE BALLYLEE       13
     AND ALL THE RANT A MIRROR OF MY MOOD!  . . . . . . .     490 COOLE BALLYLEE  V    13
     FROM MIRROR AFTER MIRROR,  . . . . . . . . . . . .       532 BEFORE WORLD          5
     FROM MIRROR AFTER MIRROR.  . . . . . . . . . . . .       532 BEFORE WORLD          5
     THE MIRROR SCALED SERPENT IS MULTIPLICITY,  . . . . .    556 RIBH PATRICK    V    10
     MIRROR ON MIRROR MIRRORED IS ALL THE SHOW.  . . . . .    610 STATUES              22
     MIRROR ON MIRROR MIRRORED IS ALL THE SHOW.  . . . . .    610 STATUES              22
     BREATHE ON THE BURNISHED MIRROR OF THE WORLD  . . . . .   750 SHADOW WATER A       69
MIRRORED
     MIRRORED IN STREAMS THAT NEITHER HAIL NOR RAIN  . . . .   184 QUEEN MAEVE          89
     MIRRORED IN WATERS THAT NOR HAIL NOR RAIN  . . . . . .    184 QUEEN MAEVE     V    89
     MIRROR ON MIRROR MIRRORED IS ALL THE SHOW.  . . . . .    610 STATUES              22
     AS FIGURES MOVING MIRRORED IN A GLASS,  . . . . . . .    676 ISLE STAT II 3      270
MIRROR-RESEMBLING
     MIRROR-RESEMBLING DREAM.  . . . . . . . . . . . .        415 TOWER               165
MIRRORS
     MIRRORS A STILL SKY!  . . . . . . . . . . . . . .        322 SWANS AT COOLE        4
MIRROR-SCALED
     THE MIRROR-SCALED SERPENT IS MULTIPLICITY,  . . . . .    556 RIBH PATRICK         10
MIRTH
     . . . AND THE MEMORIES OF THE WHOLE OF MY MIRTH,  . . .    52 OISIN 3              71
     HIS SHOUTING DAYS WITH MIRTH WERE CROWNED!  . . . . .     67 HAPPY SHEPHERD       50
     OR SIGHS AMID THE WANDERING, STARRY MIRTH,  . . . . .    114 ROSE OF BATTLE       18
     ONE WITH HER ARE MIRTH AND DUTY!  . . . . . . . . .      124 CATHLEEN PARA   V     5
     THEY BLOSSOMED TO IMMORTAL MIRTH.  . . . . . . . . .     189 BAILE AILLINN        12
     ONCE MORE THOSE SHEPHERDS COME.  MAYHAP SOME MIRTH  . .   664 ISLE STAT II 2       49
     IN THEIR DAYS OF YOUTHFUL MIRTH!  . . . . . . . . .      727 LOVERS QUARREL       40
     FAR AWAY THE STARRY MIRTH  . . . . . . . . . . . .       731 STREET DANCERS        7
     OTHER PEOPLE'S MIRTH AND PLEASURE,  . . . . . . . .      732 STREET DANCERS       24
     OTHER PEOPLE'S MIRTH AND PLEASURE,  . . . . . . . .      732 STREET DANCERS       37
     OTHER'S PEOPLE'S MIRTH AND PLEASURE.  . . . . . . .      733 STREET DANCERS       50
     OTHERS KNOW THE STARRY MIRTH!  . . . . . . . . . .       733 STREET DANCERS       54
     AND HER OLD WIND THAT NO MIRTH EVER HAD,  . . . . . .    738 YOU ARE SAD           7
MIRTHFUL
     WITH MIRTHFUL SONGS BEFORE THE DAWN.  . . . . . . .       67 HAPPY SHEPHERD       49
     WITH MIRTHFUL SONGS TILL RISE THE DAWN.  . . . . . .      67 HAPPY SHEPHERD  V    49
     AND, MAIDEN, BE THOU MIRTHFUL TOO.  . . . . . . . .      736 SUMMER EVENING       13
     AND PIERCED THE MIRTHFUL BREAST,  . . . . . . . . .      741 EARL PAUL            50
MISCALCULATE
     I TRAP YOU.  CHECK.  I DO MISCALCULATE.  . . . . . .     722 WITCH VIVIEN         58
MISCHIEF
     WHATEVER MISCHIEF SEEMED  . . . . . . . . . . . .        431 NINETEEN 19          85
     WHAT EVER MISCHIEF SEEMED  . . . . . . . . . . . .       431 NINETEEN 19     V    85
MISCHIEVOUS
     "OF PLASTER SAINTS"! HIS BEAUTIFUL MISCHIEVOUS HEAD THROWN  577 LOFTY THINGS       4
           BACK.
MISER
     SOME OLD MISER TELLS HIS STORE!  . . . . . . . . .      647 ISLE STAT I 1        58
     OLD MISER HOARDS OF GRIEF TO TELL AND TELL!  . . . .     661 ISLE STAT II 1       55
MISERABLE
     ONCE MORE HOW ON THAT MISERABLE DAY  . . . . . . . .     658 ISLE STAT II 1        4
MISERIES
     THROUGH MISERIES UNHUMAN EVER ON  . . . . . . . . .      684 SEEKER               59
     TILL THEIR FIERCE MISERIES WITHIN HIS EYES  . . . . .    687 TWO TITANS           26
MISERRIMUS
     MISERRIMUS  . . . . . . . . . . . . . . . . . .           67 SAD SHEPHERD    V     T
MISERY
     OF SOME INHUMAN MISERY  . . . . . . . . . . . . .         85 MAD KING GOLL        58
     OF SOME UNHUMAN MISERY  . . . . . . . . . . . . .         85 MAD KING GOLL   V    58
     WITH MISERY, OR THAT SHE WOULD OF LATE  . . . . . . .    256 NO SECOND TROY        2
     CONTENT TO TRACE THAT MISERY TO ITS SOURCE,  . . . . .   479 SELF AND SOUL   V    65
     AND LOVED IN MISERY,  . . . . . . . . . . . . . .       538 LAST CONFESS          4
     AND THOUGH IT LOVED IN MISERY  . . . . . . . . . .       538 LAST CONFESS         21
MISREPRESENT
     SOME ANCIENT FAMOUS AUTHORS MISREPRESENT,  . . . . .     579 DOR WELLESLEY        15
MISS
     THAT I SHALL MISS YOU  . . . . . . . . . . . . . .      118 CRADLE SONG          11
     AH! HOW I SHALL MISS YOU,  . . . . . . . . . . . .      118 CRADLE SONG     V    11
     AH, HOW SHALL I MISS YOU,  . . . . . . . . . . . .      118 CRADLE SONG     V    11
     WHY SHOULD THOSE LOVERS THAT NO LOVERS MISS  . . . .     128 DREAM OF FAERY       46
     AND NO ONE ANY LEAF-CROWNED DANCER MISS  . . . . . .     128 DREAM OF FAERY  V    46
     I SENT AN ARROW.  AND I SAW YOU MISS!  . . . . . . .     649 ISLE STAT I 1       115
```

		PAGE	TITLE	LINE

MISS'D
NAY, NAY, I MISS'D HIM NOT; HIS DAYS . . . . 649 ISLE STAT I 1   117
MISSHAPEN
THE WRONG OF THE THINGS MISSHAPEN IS WRONG TOO GREAT TO   143 ROSE IN HEART   V   5
    BE TOLD;
MIST
THE MIST CLOSED ROUND US; PEARLY LIGHT . . . .   28 OISIN 1   V 427C
CAME NOW THE SLIDING OF TEARS AND SWEEPING OF MIST COLD   47 OISIN 3   V   7
    HAIR,
THE PHANTOM, BEAUTY, IN A MIST OF TEARS; . . . .   73 ANASHU VIJAYA   55
LOOK THERE! THERE IN THE MIST! A SHIP OF SPICE! . . . .   232 SHADOW WATER B   219
THE MIST HAS COVERED THE HEAVENS, AND YOU AND I . . .   251 SHADOW WATER B   604
IN THE BROKEN MIST . . . .   349 HAWK   11
A MIST THAT IS LIKE BLOWN SNOW IS SWEEPING OVER ALL, . .   425 PHANTOM HATRED   2
AND THOSE WHITE GLIMMERING FRAGMENTS OF THE MIST SWEEP BY.   426 PHANTOM HATRED   6
MAD AS THE MIST AND SNOW . . . .   523 MAD AS MIST   T
MAD AS THE MIST AND SNOW. . . . .   523 MAD AS MIST   6
MAD AS THE MIST AND SNOW? . . . .   524 MAD AS MIST   12
MAD AS THE MIST AND SNOW. . . . .   524 MAD AS MIST   18
WITH CLINGING MIST, EACH STAR-FOUGHT WANDERER CAME . .   656 ISLE STAT I 3   33
LOVE STORM; AND STAINED WITH MIST THE NEW MOONS FLARE. .   678 ISLE STAT II 3   294
LOVE STORM AND STAINED WITH MIST THE NEW MOON'S FLARE .   678 ISLE STAT II 3 V 294
HANG THE MIST THREADS FOR A LITTLE WHILE LIKE COBWEBS IN   719 PHANTOM SHIP   V 29
    THE AIR,
WHERE THE MOON MAKES A CLOUDY LIGHT IN THE MIST. . . .   764 SHADOW WATER A   329
MISTAKE
NOW THAT YOUR TONGUE CANNOT PERSUADE THE CHILD TILL SHE   450 OWEN AHERNE   22
    MISTAKE
MIST-COLD
CAME NOW THE SLIDING OF TEARS AND SWEEPING OF MIST-COLD   47 OISIN 3   7
    HAIR,
CAME NOW THE SLIDING OF TEARS AND SWEEPING OF MIST-COLD   47 OISIN 3   V 7
    AIR,
MIST-COVERED
AND NOW FLED BY, MIST-COVERED, WITHOUT SOUND, ...   29 OISIN 2   3
MIST-DROPS
THE MIST-DROPS HUNG ON THE FRAGRANT TREES, ...   2 OISIN 1   V 7F
MISTOOK
BUT THEY MISTOOK THE BRIGHTNESS OF THE MOON . . . . .   411 TOWER   45
MISTRESS
HIS MISTRESS WAS MORE MILD AND FAIR . . . .   3 OISIN 1   V 7DD
"MY MISTRESS CANNOT SEE THESE THINGS, ...   595 COLONEL MARTIN   30
"TAKE ALL TO YOUR MISTRESS," . . . .   595 COLONEL MARTIN   34
MISTS
AWAY FROM ME WHERE MISTS OF EVENING DRINK . . . . . .   663 ISLE STAT II 2   40
HE FADES AMONG THE MISTS; HOW FAST THEY COME, ...   703 MOSADA 3   117
MIST-THREADS
HANG THE MIST-THREADS FOR A LITTLE WHILE LIKE COBWEBS IN   719 PHANTOM SHIP   29
    THE AIR;
MISTY
ON A MORNING MISTY AND MILD AND FAIR. . . . .   2 OISIN 1   V 7E
CLOSED IN THE MISTY AIR PROFOUND. . . . .   10 OISIN 1   V 114D
THAT HAS DRUNK FULL, SHE CROSSED THE MISTY SEA . . . .   30 OISIN 2   16
STRETCHED HIS LONG ARM TO WHERE, A MISTY SMOTHER, . . .   31 OISIN 2   42
OF EVERY FOAMDROP ON ITS MISTY WAY. . . . .   32 OISIN 2   45
AND STOOD WITHIN; CLOTHED IN A MISTY RAY . . . .   36 OISIN 2   104
AND STOOD WITHIN THE HALL. A MISTY RAY . . . .   36 OISIN 2   V 104
FEEBLER AND FEEBLER SHONE THE MISTY GLARE. . . . . . .   37 OISIN 2   V 121
OF MISTY DAWN; WHEN, CIRCLING ROUND THE HALL, ...   39 OISIN 2   V 153
LEAP IN THE MEADOW. ON THE MISTY STAIRS . . . .   44 OISIN 2   229
I PACE REMEMBERING. FROM MY MISTY THRONE . . . .   45 OISIN 2   V 239C
UPON THE MISTY BORDER OF THE WOOD, ...   251 SHADOW WATER B   612
AMONG THESE MISTY WATERS. TWO! NOW FOUR! . . . . . .   753 SHADOW WATER A   138
UPON THE MISTY BORDER OF THE WOOD,— . . . .   769 SHADOW WATER A   428
MITCHEL'S
YOU THAT MITCHEL'S PRAYER HAVE HEARD, ...   638 BEN BULBEN   25
MIX
OR LET ITS MEANING MIX INTO THE STRINGS. . . . . . .   180 QUEEN MAEVE   8
COULD WE BUT MIX OURSELVES INTO A DREAM, ...   230 SHADOW WATER B   188
I MIGHT HAVE HAD NO FRIEND THAT COULD NOT MIX . . . .   352 PEOPLE   16
OF THAT OLD GEORGIAN MANSION, MIX . . . .   475 EVA GORE-BOOTH   16
THAT I WOULD MIX WITH YOURS, AND IN THIS HAIR . . . .   765 SHADOW WATER A   351
MIXED   SEE UN-MIXED
SURLY AND DISTANT, MIXED INSEPARABLY . . . .   45 OISIN 2   233
RISING AND FALLING, MIXED INSEPARABLY, ...   45 OISIN 2   V 233
AND MIXED WITH THE SOUND OF THAT ROARER . . . .   60 OISIN 3   V 184
MY BREATH IS MIXED INTO HIS BREATH. . . . .   152 HEART OF WOMAN   12
AND WHERE BEECH-TREES HAD MIXED A PALE GREEN LIGHT . .   277 TWO KINGS   5
WHERE CERTAIN BEECHES MIXED A PALE GREEN LIGHT . . . .   277 TWO KINGS   V 5
AND WHERE BEECH TREES HAD MIXED A PALE GREEN LIGHT . .   277 TWO KINGS   V 5
TWO THOUGHTS WERE SO MIXED UP I COULD NOT TELL . . . .   471 ALL SOUL NIGHT   31
MOAN
I BELLOW TO THE WINDS WHEN STORMS MAKE MOAN, ...   45 OISIN 2   V 239D
LIKE AN ARMY OF OLD MEN LONGING FOR REST FROM THE MOAN   48 OISIN 3   16
    OF THE SEAS.
I SAW FROM A DISTANT SADDLE; FROM THE EARTH SHE MADE HER   56 OISIN 3   130
    MOAN;
LIKE AN ARMY OF OLD MEN LONGING FOR REST FROM THE MOAN   57 OISIN 3   144
    OF THE SEAS.
CHANGED ALL HE SANG TO INARTICULATE MOAN . . . . . .   69 SAD SHEPHERD   27
CHANGED ALL HIS WORDS TO INARTICULATE MOAN . . . . . .   69 SAD SHEPHERD   V 27

		PAGE	TITLE	LINE

MOAN (CONTINUED)

IN THREE DAYS' TIME HE STOOD UP WITH A MOAN, ... 111 CUCHULAIN SEA V 83
IN THREE DAYS' TIME, CUCHULAIN WITH A MOAN . . . . 111 CUCHULAIN SEA V 83
AND RENT HER CLOTHES AND MADE HER MOAN: . . . . . . 275 GREY ROCK 108
BUT THE SECOND MOCKED HIS MOAN: . . . . 299 THREE HERMITS 24
THEREON I MADE MY MOAN, ... 384 VISION ROBART 63
MY BODY MAKES NO MOAN . . . . 512 JANE ON GOD 22
AS AN HURT LEOPARD FILLS WITH CEASELESS MOAN, ... 674 ISLE STAT II 3 208
AS A HURT LEOPARD FILLS WITH CEASELESS MOAN . . . . . . 674 ISLE STAT II 3 V 208
MAKE MOAN AND CRY. WITHIN YON SUNLESS VALLEY, ... 682 SEEKER 26
AND WHO WILL MOAN IN THE UNDER PIT, ... 716 FAIRY DOCTOR 7
FOR HURTS AND AILS AND LOVER'S MOAN-- . . . . . . 717 FAIRY DOCTOR 18

MOANED

THAN DOVES THAT MOANED ROUND EMAN'S HALL . . . . . . 3 OISIN 1 V 7EE
TO WHERE SHE MOANED UPON THE GROUND, ... 275 GREY ROCK 119
MOANED THE OTHER, "THEY ARE THROWN . . . . 299 THREE HERMITS 22
MY BODY HAS NOT MOANED . . . . 512 JANE ON GOD V 22

MOANING

REPLY LIKE MOANING OF IMPRISONED ELF: . . . . 652 ISLE STAT I 2 11

MOANS

THAT MOANS AND SIGHS A HUNDRED DAYS: . . . . 78 INDIAN TO LOVE 17
AND THERE TO ITS OWN HEART FOR EVER MOANS. . . . . . 650 ISLE STAT I 1 131

MOB

ARE THE MOB THAT HOWLS AT THE DOOR: . . . . 554 CHURCH STATE 10

MOBILE

THE PRIMUM MOBILE THAT FASHIONED US . . . . 423 MY DESCENDANTS 17

MOBS

THEIR MOBS PUT UNDER THEIR FEET. . . . . 554 CHURCH STATE 4
THE MOBS OF STARS IN GOLD AND GREEN AND BLUE, ... 663 ISLE STAT II 2 43

MOCHARABUIEE

MY BROTHER IN MOCHARABUIEE. . . . . 178 FIDDLER DOONEY 4

MOCK

THEN MOCK AT DEATH AND TIME WITH GLANCES . . . . . 19 OISIN 1 274
WHILE THOSE SAME HUNDREDS MOCK ANOTHER DAY . . . . . 265 ABBEY THEATRE 4
BUT WHEN THEY MOCK US, THAT WE MOCK AGAIN? . . . . . 265 ABBEY THEATRE 14
BUT WHEN THEY MOCK US, THAT WE MOCK AGAIN? . . . . . 265 ABBEY THEATRE 14
AND MOCK HIM TO HIS FACE AND THEN . . . . 272 GREY ROCK 34
TO MOCK AT EVERYTHING I LOVE . . . . 306 HOUR DAWN 83
I MOCK PLOTINUS' THOUGHT . . . . 415 TOWER 146
COME LET US MOCK AT THE GREAT . . . . 432 NINETEEN 19 93
COME LET US MOCK AT THE WISE: . . . . 432 NINETEEN 19 98
COME LET US MOCK AT THE GOOD . . . . 432 NINETEEN 19 103
MOCK MOCKERS AFTER THAT . . . . 432 NINETEEN 19 108
MOCK ME WITH PRAISE OF MY MERE OPPOSITE: . . . . . 448 HERO GIRL FOOL V 4
NONE BUT THE LIVING MOCK, ... 471 ALL SOUL NIGHT 17
WHEREAT THE LIVING MOCK, ... 474 ALL SOUL NIGHT 87
THOSE THAT COME AFTER SHALL MOCK AT O'DONNELL, . . . 546 TO SAME TUNE 2 23
MOCK AT THE MEMORY OF BOTH O'NEILLS, ... 546 TO SAME TUNE 2 24
THOSE THAT COME AFTER SHALL MOCK O'DONNELL, ... 546 TO SAME TUNE 2 V 23
MOCK EMMET, MOCK PARNELL: . . . . 547 TO SAME TUNE 2 25
MOCK EMMET, MOCK PARNELL: . . . . 547 TO SAME TUNE 2 25
THOSE THAT COME AFTER SHALL MOCK AT O'DONNELL, . . . 614 MARCH SONGS 1 23
MOCK AT THE MEMORY OF BOTH O'NEILLS, ... 614 MARCH SONGS 1 24
MOCK EMMET, MOCK PARNELL, ... 614 MARCH SONGS 1 25
MOCK EMMET, MOCK PARNELL, ... 614 MARCH SONGS 1 25
I MOCK AT ALL SO BURNING OUT. . . . . 787 HUDDON DUDDON 15
BUT HOW THEY MOCK US BURNING OUT. . . . . . . 787 HUDDON DUDDON V 15

MOCKED

WE MOCKED AT TIME AND FATE AND CHANCE . . . . . . 20 OISIN 1 291
BUT THE SECOND MOCKED HIS MOAN: . . . . 299 THREE HERMITS 24
BEING MOCKED BY GUIDO FOR HIS LECHEROUS LIFE, ... 369 EGO DOMINUS 33
MOCKED ME WITH PRAISE OF MY MERE OPPOSITE: . . . . . 448 HERO GIRL FOOL 4
I MOCKED, BEING CRAZY, BUT YOU MASTERED IT . . . . . 533 HER TRIUMPH 8
HEROIC REVERIE MOCKED BY CLOWN AND KNAVE, ... 619 BRONZE HEAD 27

MOCKERS   SEE BE-MOCKERS

HE MUSED UPON HIS MOCKERS' WITHOUT FAIL . . . . . 127 DREAM OF FAERY 26
THE IMMORTAL MOCKERS HAVE CAST INTO HIS MIND, ... 249 SHADOW WATER B 567
MOCK MOCKERS AFTER THAT . . . . 432 NINETEEN 19 108
O SELF-BORN MOCKERS OF MAN'S ENTERPRISE: . . . . . 445 SCHOOL CHILDR 56

MOCKERY

IF RAILING AND REPROACH AND MOCKERY . . . . . . 243 SHADOW WATER B 438
TRAFFIC IN MOCKERY. . . . . 432 NINETEEN 19 112
IS A MAN'S MOCKERY OF THE CHANGELESS SOUL." . . . . 465 HARUN RASHID 102
IN MOCKERY I HAVE SET . . . . 480 BLOOD AND MOON 8
IN MOCKERY OF A TIME . . . . 480 BLOOD AND MOON 11
WHAT GAVE THAT ROAR OF MOCKERY, ... 583 GHOST ROG CASE 7
THEY LIE THAT SAY, IN MOCKERY . . . . 789 SINGING HEAD 9

MOCKING

HEARING HELL LOUD WITH A MURMUR, AS SHOUTING AND MOCKING 62 OISIN 3 208
   WE SWEEP.
OF A MOCKING TALE OR A GIBE . . . . 392 EASTER 1916 10
WHEN MOCKING MUSES CHOSE THE COUNTRY WENCH. . . . . 413 TOWER 96
MOCKING WITH PATIENT LAUGHTER ALL THE NIGHT . . . . 657 ISLE STAT I 3 52

MOCKS

AND MOCKS RETURNING VICTORY, HE PASSED . . . . . . 279 TWO KINGS 58

MODEL

A MODEL FOR THE LAUREATE . . . . 597 MODEL LAUREATE T

MODELLED

A NEW MODELLED DOLL, OR DRAWING, ... 362 DOLLS DRAWINGS 2
THAT WITH A MALLET OR A CHISEL MODELLED THESE . . . . 610 STATUES 10

	PAGE	TITLE	LINE

MODERN
    THAT IS OUR MODERN HOPE, AND BY ITS LIGHT   • • • • •   368 EGO DOMINUS   11
    IN THE BEST MODERN WAY—THE CHILDREN'S EYES   • • • • •   443 SCHOOL CHILDR   6
    IS EVERY MODERN NATION LIKE THE TOWER,   • • • • • •   482 BLOOD AND MOON   47
    ETERNALISED THE BODY OF A MODERN SAINT THAT ONCE • • • •   503 VACILLATION   83
    APPLAUD A MODERN THRONE!   • • • • • • • • • •   597 MODEL LAUREATE   18
    WE THREE ALONE IN MODERN TIMES HAD BROUGHT • • • • •   603 GALLERY REVIS   45
    BUT THROWN UPON THIS FILTHY MODERN TIDE • • • • • •   611 STATUES   29
    AND MINE WERE BUT FIFTEEN FOOT, NO MODERN STALKS   623 HIGH TALK   3
       UPON HIGHER,
    SCOFF THEY AT THE MODERN EARTH—   • • • • • • • •   727 LOVERS QUARREL   38
MODISH
    NOR LET THE MODISH PAINTER SHIRK   • • • • • • • • •   638 BEN BULBEN   38
MOHINI
    MOHINI CHATTERJEE   • • • • • • • • • • • • •   495 MOHINI CHATTER   T
    MOHINI CHATTERJEE   • • • • • • • • • • • • •   496 MOHINI CHATTER   14
MOIDERED
    AND MOIDERED IN THAT SNARE   • • • • • • • • •   783 GREY ROUND   8
MOIL
    THE MOIL OF MY CENTURIES FILLED ME! AND GONE LIKE   51 OISIN 3   70
       A SEA-COVERED STONE
MOIST
    DROPS ON HIS BOSOM, SOMBRE, MOIST AND SLOW.   • • • •   711 FERENCZ RENYI   40
    UPON HIS BOSOM, SOMBRE, MOIST AND SLOW. • • • • • •   711 FERENCZ RENYI   V   40
MOISTENED
    ABOUNDING FOLIAGE MOISTENED WITH THE DEW!   • • • • •   500 VACILLATION   13
MOISTURE
    A MOUTH THAT HAS NO MOISTURE AND NO BREATH • • • • •   497 BYZANTIUM   13
MOLAY
    "VENGEANCE FOR JACQUES MOLAY." IN CLOUD-PALE RAGS, OR   426 PHANTOM HATRED   10
       IN LACE,
    FOR VENGEANCE ON THE MURDERERS OF JACQUES MOLAY • • • •   426 PHANTOM HATRED   16
    "VENGENCE FOR JACQUES MOLAY." IN CLOUD PALE RAGS, OR IN   426 PHANTOM HATRED V   10
       LACE,
MOLE
    BEYOND EAGLE OR MOLE,   • • • • • • • • • • •   784 WOMANS BEAUTY   10
MOLL
    THE BALLAD OF MOLL MAGEE   • • • • • • • • • •   94 MOLL MAGEE   T
    BUT PITY MOLL MAGEE.   • • • • • • • • • • • •   94 MOLL MAGEE   4
    AND PITY MOLL MAGEE.   • • • • • • • • • • • •   96 MOLL MAGEE   56
    I COULD GIVE ALL MY HEART TO THAT RED MOLL   • • • •   222 SHADOW WATER B   9
    FOR THAT RED MOLL THAT HAD BUT THE ONE EYE.   • • • •   222 SHADOW WATER B V   10
MOMENT
    THAT MANY A PEACEFUL MOMENT HAD,   • • • • • • •   4 OISIN 1   35
    IN CLANGING SPACE A MOMENT HEARD,   • • • • • • •   65 HAPPY SHEPHERD   20
    'MID CLANGING SPACE A MOMENT HEARD   • • • • • •   65 HAPPY SHEPHERD   20
    DYING AT EVERY MOMENT IN THE WORLD,   • • • • • •   226 SHADOW WATER B   90
    THAT NONE MIGHT TAKE YOU FROM ME. FOR A MOMENT   • • •   237 SHADOW WATER B   330
    ONE MOMENT HAS NO MIGHT UPON THE MOMENT   • • • • •   237 SHADOW WATER B   340
    ONE MOMENT HAS NO MIGHT UPON THE MOMENT   • • • • •   237 SHADOW WATER B   340
    WANDER A MOMENT WHEN ONE IS IN LOVE?   • • • • • •   246 SHADOW WATER B   515
    NEVER UNTIL THIS MOMENT HAVE WE MET   • • • • • •   339 SHEP GOATHERD   7
    UPON A MOMENT, AND SO STRETCHED IT OUT   • • • • •   384 VISION ROBART   46
    ALL THAT TO THIS MOMENT CHARMED YOU?   • • • • • •   390 IMAGE PAST   21
    ENDURES A MOMENT OR A DAY.   • • • • • • • • •   438 SONGS PLAY 2   10
    WHERE FOR ITS MOMENT BOTH SEEM LOST, CONSUMED.   • • •   555 RIBH AT TOMB   16
    SHOUTED A MOMENT 'TWEEN THE EARTH AND SKY.   • • • •   675 ISLE STAT II 3   237
    I HAVE BEEN WAITING YOU. A MOMENT SINCE   • • • •   763 SHADOW WATER A   313
    IT PASSED BUT A MOMENT AGO.   • • • • • • • • •   781 MY HEART BEAT   3
    IT PASSED BY A MOMENT AGO.   • • • • • • • • •   781 MY HEART BEAT   V   3
    THE MOMENT HE HAS LOOKED AT YOU,   • • • • • • •   786 YOUR HEART   18
MOMENTARY
    A MOMENTARY GLEAM OF PHOSPHORUS FLAME.   • • • • • •   37 OISIN 2   118
    A MOMENTARY GLIMMER OF VAGUE PHOSPHORUS FLAME.   • • • •   37 OISIN 2   V   120
    IN MOMENTARY ANGER LONG AGO!   • • • • • • • •   258 KING NO KING   10
    MOMENTARY THOUGHTS   • • • • • • • • • • •   260 FASC DIFFICULT V   T
    THEIR MOMENTARY CRIES BEFORE IT IS DAWN,   • • • • •   371 EGO DOMINUS   78
    IN MOMENTARY WONDER STARE UPON .   • • • • • • •   443 SCHOOL CHILDR   7
    NOISE! AND A FLASH, A MOMENTARY BLOT.   • • • • •   714 FERENCZ RENYI   110
    NOISE! UPROAR! AND A MOMENTARY BLOT.   • • • • • •   714 FERENCZ RENYI   V   110
MOMENT'S
    YET IF IT DOES NOT SEEM A MOMENT'S THOUGHT,   • • • •   204 ADAMS CURSE   5
    OR IF THEY MADE A MOMENT'S STAY   • • • • • • •   297 THREE BEGGARS   52
    A MOMENT'S MEMORY TO THAT LAURELLED HEAD.   • • • • •   489 COOLE PARK 29   32
MOMENTS
    THE MOMENTS PASS AND PASS!   • • • • • • • •   99 FOXHUNTER   44
    HOW MANY LOVED YOUR MOMENTS OF GLAD GRACE,   • • • •   121 YOU ARE OLD   5
    THE MOMENTS PASSED AS AT A PLAY!   • • • • • • •   313 MEMORY YOUTH   1
    AT CHANCES AND AT MOMENTS WITH MANKIND. • • • • •   721 WITCH VIVIEN   35
MONEY
    AND GAVE ME MONEY, AND BADE ME GO .   • • • • •   95 MOLL MAGEE   23
    HIS MIND RAN ALL ON MONEY CARES AND FEARS,   • • • •   127 DREAM OF FAERY   14
    LAND FOR YOUR CHILDREN OR MONEY IN A POT."   • • • •   228 SHADOW WATER B   125
    MONEY IS GOOD AND A GIRL MIGHT BE BETTER,   • • • •   544 TO SAME TUNE 1   3
    MONEY I HAD, AND IT WENT IN THE NIGHT,   • • • • •   544 TO SAME TUNE 1   12
    "MONEY IS GOOD AND A GIRL MIGHT BE BETTER,   • • • •   545 TO SAME TUNE 1   21
    SUFFICIENT MONEY FOR HIS NEED,   • • • • • • •   577 WHAT THEN   8
    MONEY IS GOOD AND A GIRL MIGHT BE BETTER,   • • • •   616 MARCH SONGS 3   3
    MONEY I HAD, AND IT WENT IN THE NIGHT,   • • • • •   616 MARCH SONGS 3   12
    "MONEY IS GOOD AND A GIRL MIGHT BE BETTER,   • • • •   616 MARCH SONGS 3   21
    THEIR MONEY SPENT, THEIR WINE GONE SOUR,   • • • • •   635 BLACK TOWER   3

	PAGE	TITLE		LINE

MONEY'S
    MY MONEY'S ALL USED UP, ...   96 MOLL MAGEE   38
    BUT THERE'S NO GOOD COMPLAINING, FOR MONEY'S RANT IS ON.   580 CURSE CROMWELL   10
'MONG
    FOR LONELY TO MOVE 'MONG THE SOFT EYES . . . .   63 OISIN 3   V 222
    WALKING GHOSTLY 'MONG THE DEW, ...   67 HAPPY SHEPHERD V   52
    'MONG THE FEET OF ANGELS SEVEN, ...   125 CATHLEEN PARA   13
    AND 'MONG THE STUNTED ASH-TREES' DROOPING RINGS, . .   650 ISLE STAT I 1   128
    FORSWEARS HIS WANDERING 'MONG THE PINE, ...   686 LIFE   6
    SINCE 'MONG MY PEOPLE, TENTED ON THE HILLS, ...   690 MOSADA 1   4
    IN HIS OWN HOUSE OR 'MONG THE MERCHANTS GREY, . . .   693 MOSADA 1   87
    BUT NO, IN THIS WARM WEATHER, 'MONG THE HILLS, . . .   699 MOSADA 3   9
    NESTED 'MONG THE VAPOURS BROWN. . . . .   731 STREET DANCERS   6
MONGAN
    MONGAN LAMENTS THE CHANGE THAT HAS COME UPON HIM AND HIS   153 CHANGE BELOVED V   T
        BELOVED
    SONG OF MONGAN . . . .   177 PAST GREATNESS V   T
    MONGAN THINKS OF HIS PAST GREATNESS . . . .   177 PAST GREATNESS V   T
MONK
    WHY THESE NEW FEARS? THE GREAT MONK EBREMAR, ...   692 MOSADA 1   46
MONKEY
    WITH A MONKEY ON A CHAIN, ...   627 STATES HOLIDAY   36
MONK'S-HOOD
    OF THE MONK'S-HOOD HOW THEY SHAKE, ...   655 ISLE STAT I 3   2
MONK'S-HOOD'S
    OH, LEARNED IS EACH MONK'S-HOOD'S MIND, ...   655 ISLE STAT I 3   8
MONKS
    THE HOLINESS OF MONKS, AND AFTER . . . .   640 BEN BULBEN   76
    THE HOLINESS OF THE MONKS, AND AFTER . . . .   640 BEN BULBEN   V 76
MONOTONE
    AND DRIFTING GREYNESS, WHILE THIS MONOTONE, ...   45 OISIN 2   232
    AND DRIFTING GREYNESS. CAME THIS MONOTONE . . . .   45 OISIN 2   V 232
    I HEARD THE DEATHFUL MONOTONE, ...   673 ISLE STAT II 3   183
MONSTROUS
    UNDER THE STARLIGHT AND SHADOW, A MONSTROUS SLUMBERING   48 OISIN 3   27
        FOLK,
    FROM HIS HOOVES IN THE HEAVY GRASSES, WITH MONSTROUS   48 OISIN 3   V 27
        SLUMBERING FOLK,
    CAME SOUND FROM THOSE MONSTROUS SLEEPERS, ...   51 OISIN 3   58
    HE IS A MONSTROUS PEACOCK, AND HE WAVETH ALL THE NIGHT . .   77 INDIAN ON GOD   19
    THE MEANING OF THAT MONSTROUS DAY. THEN SHE' . . . .   280 TWO KINGS   78
    THE MONSTROUS CRYING OF WIND? . . . .   312 CHILD DANCING   12
    ALL I HAD RHYMED OF THAT MONSTROUS THING . . . . .   358 PRESENCES   7
    ALL I HAVE RHYMED OF THAT MONSTROUS THING . . . . .   358 PRESENCES   V 7
    MONSTROUS FAMILIAR IMAGES SWIM TO THE MIND'S EYE. . . .   426 PHANTOM HATRED   8
MONTASHIGI
    MONTASHIGI, THIRD OF HIS FAMILY, FASHIONED IT . . . .   478 SELF AND SOUL   25
    MONTASHIGI OF OSAFUME FASHIONED IT . . . .   478 SELF AND SOUL V   25
MONTENEGRIN
    HERE'S A MONTENEGRIN LUTE, ...   627 STATES HOLIDAY   22
MONTH   SEE TWELVE-MONTH
    MORE STILL THAN THEY HAD BEEN FOR A GOOD MONTH, ...   182 QUEEN MAEVE   54
MONTHS
    AND WONDER WHAT HAS AILED HIM THESE TWELVE MONTHS." . . .   284 TWO KINGS   163
    SO LITTLE. AS THE MONTHS PASSED BY WE GREW   713 FERENCZ RENYI   93
MONTHS'
    OUTRODE HIS TROOP THAT AFTER TWELVE MONTHS' WAR . . . .   276 TWO KINGS   V 1
MONUMENT
    WHETHER TO LOOK UPON YOUR MONUMENT . . . .   292 TO A SHADE   2
    THESE STONES REMAIN THEIR MONUMENT AND MINE. . . . .   423 MY DESCENDANTS   24
    NO HONOUR LEAVE ITS MIGHTY MONUMENT, ...   429 NINETEEN 19   38
    TO LEAVE SOME MONUMENT BEHIND, ...   432 NINETEEN 19   96
MONUMENTS
    MONUMENTS OF UNAGEING INTELLECT. . . . .   407 SAIL BYZANTIUM   8
    MONUMENTS OF ITS OWN MAGNIFICENCE! . . . .   407 SAIL BYZANTIUM   14
    THE THREE MONUMENTS . . . .   460 THREE MONUMENT   T
    HIS GLORY AND HIS MONUMENTS ARE GONE. . . . . . .   563 MERU   14
MOOD
    AND PONDERED IN A SOFT VAIN MOOD . . . .   14 OISIN 1   184
    IN SOME DIM MEMORY OR ANCIENT MOOD, ...   36 OISIN 2   99
    WITH NO RETURNING GLANCE, IN WORDLESS MOOD . . . . .   44 OISIN 2   V 230A
    THEY WERE OF NO WORDY MOOD! . . . .   65 HAPPY SHEPHERD V 13A
    ARE GAY WITH HIS MOOD. . . . .   118 CRADLE SONG   8
    GROW SWEET WITH HIS MOOD. . . . .   118 CRADLE SONG   V 8
    GROW GAY WITH HIS MOOD. . . . .   118 CRADLE SONG   V 8
    THE TALE DROVE HIS FINE ANGRY MOOD AWAY. . . . . .   128 DREAM OF FAERY   36
    AND ALL THE RANT'S A MIRROR OF MY MOOD! . . . . .   490 COOLE BALLYLEE   13
    AND ALL THE RANT A MIRROR OF MY MOOD! . . . . . .   490 COOLE BALLYLEE V   13
    I SAW HIS JOVIAL MOOD BRING ONCE A SMILE . . . . .   696 MOSADA 2   14
    AND FREE—'TWILL THIEVE AWAY WITH SLEEPY MOOD . . . .   700 MOSADA 3   30
    TROTTED BESIDE HIM IN A PLAYFUL MOOD. . . . . . .   715 DWELT SYCAMORE   4
    AND THE CUCKOO UNSEEN IN HIS FESTIVAL MOOD; . . . . .   717 LOVE SONG   7
    MY LOVE HATH MANY AN EVIL MOOD, ...   723 GIRLS SONG A   5
    MY LOVE HATH MANY A RUTHLESS MOOD, ...   723 GIRLS SONG A V 5
    LAUGHING GOES IN WILDEST MOOD, ...   732 STREET DANCERS   41
MOODS
    THE MOODS . . . .   142 MOODS   T
    OF THE FIRE-BORN MOODS . . . .   142 MOODS   6
    THE LOVER ASKS FORGIVENESS BECAUSE OF HIS MANY MOODS . .   162 ASKS FORGIVE   T
    MICHAEL ROBARTES ASKS FORGIVENESS BECAUSE OF HIS MANY MOODS   162 ASKS FORGIVE V T
    HIS MOODS BOW LOW HIS SOMBRE CREST, ...   723 GIRLS SONG A   2

MOODY
    FULL MOODY IS MY LOVE AND SAD, ...   723 GIRLS SONG A   1
MOON
    MUST LIVE TO BE OLD LIKE THE WANDERING MOON. . . . .   3 OISIN 1   12
    AND SLEEP DROWN SUN AND MOON AND STAR." . . . . . .   5 OISIN 1   V   49
    NO MIGHTIER CREATURES BAY AT THE MOON; . . . .   8 OISIN 1   87
    WHERE I WOULD BE WHEN THE WHITE MOON CLIMBS, ...   9 OISIN 1   104
    BUT NOW THE MOON LIKE A WHITE ROSE SHONE . . . . . .   12 OISIN 1   152
    SLEEP THERE TILL THE MOON AND THE STARS DIE!" . . . .   17 OISIN 1   246
    IT FELL, OR FROM THE TWISTED MOON . . . .   19 OISIN 1   V 278
    AND THE PALE BLOSSOM OF THE MOON, ...   20 OISIN 1   288
    AND THE THIN CRESCENT OF THE MOON, ...   20 OISIN 1   288
    AND THE MOON LIKE A PALE ROSE WITHER AWAY." . . . . .   28 OISIN 1   427
    AT LAST THE MOON AND STARS SHONE, AND A FLIGHT . . .   31 OISIN 2   V   34
    AND THROUGH THEIR EYES NO LIGHT OF MOON OR DAY . . .   34 OISIN 2   77
    THAT LACKEY THE WORN MOON IN MIDNIGHT HOURS, ...   41 OISIN 2   V 185A
    AND THE MOON GOAD THE WATERS NIGHT AND DAY, ...   45 OISIN 2   238
    "BUT TILL THE MOON HAS TAKEN ALL, I WAGE . . . . .   45 OISIN 2   240
    A STARLING LIKE THEM THAT FORGATHERED 'NEATH A MOON . . .   54 OISIN 3   103
    THAT SLUMBERED IN THE HARVEST MOON, ...   85 MAD KING GOLL   50
    THAT SLUMBERED 'NEATH THE HARVEST MOON, ...   85 MAD KING GOLL V   50
    TILL THE MOON HAS TAKEN FLIGHT; . . . .   87 STOLEN CHILD   19
    AND LOVELIER THAN THE MOON UPON THE SEA; . . . . .   106 CUCHULAIN SEA V 16A
    OR IN THE SUN AND MOON, OR ON THE EARTH, ...   114 ROSE OF BATTLE   17
    THE BRILLIANT MOON AND ALL THE MILKY SKY, ...   119 SORROW OF LOVE   2
    THE FULL ROUND MOON AND THE STAR-LADEN SKY, ...   119 SORROW OF LOVE V   2
    A CLIMBING MOON UPON AN EMPTY SKY, ...   120 SORROW OF LOVE   10
    THE CRUMBLING MOON, THE WHITE STARS IN THE SKY, . . .   120 SORROW OF LOVE V   10
    THE CURD-PALE MOON, THE WHITE STARS IN THE SKY, . . .   120 SORROW OF LOVE V   10
    IT SEEMED THE SUN AND MOON WERE IN THE FRUIT! . . . .   127 DREAM OF FAERY   23
    AH, FAERIES, DANCING UNDER THE MOON, ...   139 TO IRELAND   31
    OF THE PALE TIDE WHEN THE MOON HAS SET, ...   146 FISH   2
    OF SUN AND MOON AND HOLLOW AND WOOD, ...   148 INTO TWILIGHT   11
    AND THE CHANGING MOON WORK OUT THEIR WILL. . . . . .   148 INTO TWILIGHT V   12
    THE SILVER APPLES OF THE MOON, ...   150 WANDER AENGUS   23
    AND HAD ROOTED THE SUN AND MOON AND STARS OUT OF THE SKY   153 CHANGE BELOVED   11
    AND ROOTED THE SUN AND MOON AND STARS OUT OF THE SKY, . .   153 CHANGE BELOVED V   11
    WHEN WINDS HAVE GATHERED AND SUN AND MOON BURNED DIM   175 ELEMENT POWERS   15
    ABOUT THE STARS AND MOON AND SUN! . . . .   176 BELOVED DEAD   10
    ABOVE THE STARS AND MOON AND SUN! . . . .   176 BELOVED DEAD V   10
    OR APPLES OF THE SUN AND MOON. . . . .   196 BAILE AILLINN   176
    I CRIED WHEN THE MOON WAS MURMURING TO THE BIRDS! . .   203 WITHER BOUGHS   1
    THE HONEY-PALE MOON LAY LOW ON THE SLEEPY HILL, . . .   203 WITHER BOUGHS   5
    I KNOW WHERE A DIM MOON DRIFTS, WHERE THE DANAAN KIND . .   203 WITHER BOUGHS   12
    THE HONEY PALE MOON HUNG LOW ON THE SLEEPY HILL, . . .   203 WITHER BOUGHS V   5
    A MOON, WORN AS IF IT HAD BEEN A SHELL . . . . . .   206 ADAMS CURSE   31
    AS WEARY-HEARTED AS THAT HOLLOW MOON. . . . .   206 ADAMS CURSE   38
    A MOON--MOON WORN AS IF IT HAD BEEN A SHELL . . . .   206 ADAMS CURSE   31
    A MOON--MOON WORN AS IF IT HAD BEEN A SHELL . . . .   206 ADAMS CURSE V   31
    AS WEARY HEARTED AS THAT HOLLOW MOON. . . . .   206 ADAMS CURSE V   38
    UNDER THE MOON . . . .   209 UNDER THE MOON   T
    OF THE HUNTER'S MOON, THAT HUNG BETWEEN THE NIGHT AND THE   210 UNDER THE MOON   18
    DAY,
    OF THE THIRD MOON, THAT HUNG BETWEEN THE NIGHT AND THE DAY,   210 UNDER THE MOON V   18
    I WILL DRIVE OUT THE DEER AND MOON AND CRY-- . . . .   211 RAGGED WOOD V   10
    THE MOON PLUCKED AT MY REIN; . . . .   214 HAPPY TOWNLAND   16
    THE MOON PLUCKED AT MY REIN; . . . .   215 HAPPY TOWNLAND   36
    THE MOON PLUCKED AT MY REIN; . . . .   216 HAPPY TOWNLAND   56
    AND ALL THE ALE RAN OUT AT THE NEW MOON; . . . . .   222 SHADOW WATER B V   11
    AT THE FULL MOON? HE PLAYED ALL THROUGH THE NIGHT. . .   223 SHADOW WATER B   21
    UNTIL THE MOON HAD SET; AND WHEN I LOOKED . . . . .   223 SHADOW WATER B   22
    AS THOSE THAT CAN OUTLIVE THE MOON HAVE KNOWN IT, . .   230 SHADOW WATER B   193
    AS THOSE THAT CAN OUTLIVE THE MOON HAVE SHOWN IT, . .   230 SHADOW WATER B V 193
    UNTIL THE OVERBURTHENED MOON IS DEAD. . . . .   231 SHADOW WATER B   218
    FROM LASTING WATCHERS, THAT OUTLIVE THE MOON, ...   236 SHADOW WATER B   320
    THAT IS MORE MIGHTY THAN THE SUN AND MOON, ...   237 SHADOW WATER B   328
    HE HAS PUT A SUDDEN DARKNESS OVER THE MOON. . . . . .   239 SHADOW WATER B   367
    HE HAS CAUGHT THE CRESCENT MOON OUT OF THE SKY, . . .   239 SHADOW WATER B   370
    HAVING THEIR LIFE IN HIM. THOUGH IT BE THE MOON . . .   240 SHADOW WATER B   377
    LISTEN TO THAT LOW-LAUGHING STRING OF THE MOON . . .   243 SHADOW WATER B   432
    THAT I SHOULD KEEN HIM FROM THE FULL OF THE MOON . . .   243 SHADOW WATER B   446
    IN HAPPY DANCES UNDER A WINDY MOON, ...   245 SHADOW WATER B   470
    AM I TO FEAR THE WAVES, OR IS THE MOON . . . . . .   246 SHADOW WATER B   508
    MY ENEMY? I LOOKED UPON THE MOON, ...   246 SHADOW WATER B   509
    WHERE NO CHILD'S BORN BUT TO OUTLIVE THE MOON." . . .   247 SHADOW WATER B   531
    SING ON! SOMEWHERE AT SOME NEW MOON, ...   266 GALWAY RACES   10
    BUT SOME DAY AND AT SOME NEW MOON . . . .   266 GALWAY RACES V   10
    SING ON! SOMETIME, AND AT SOME NEW MOON . . . . . .   266 GALWAY RACES V   10
    AND THE SHADOWS EATEN THE MOON. . . . .   268 BROWN PENNY   14
    AMONG THE AFRICAN MOUNTAINS OF THE MOON, ...   277 TWO KINGS   20
    IN AFRICA ON MOUNTAIN OF THE MOON, ...   277 TWO KINGS V   20
    THE FRENZY OF THE BEGGARS' MOON . . . .   296 THREE BEGGARS   43
    THE FRENZY OF THE BEGGAR'S MOON . . . .   296 THREE BEGGARS V   43
    SUDDENLY HID LOVE'S MOON AWAY. . . . .   313 MEMORY YOUTH   7
    LOVE'S MOON WAS WITHERING AWAY. . . . .   313 MEMORY YOUTH V   7
    TORE FROM THE CLOUDS HIS MARVELLOUS MOON. . . . . . .   314 MEMORY YOUTH   21
    THREW UP IN THE AIR HIS MARVELLOUS MOON. . . . . . .   314 MEMORY YOUTH V   21
    OF SUN AND MOON THAT A GOOD HOUR . . . .   331 ROUND TOWER   11
    OF THE DARK LEOPARDS OF THE MOON? . . . .   343 DEJECTION   3
    BANISHED HEROIC MOTHER MOON AND VANISHED; . . . . . .   344 DEJECTION   9
    HEROIC MOTHER MOON HAS VANISHED, ...   344 DEJECTION V   9

MOON   (CONTINUED)

THE STARS FADE OUT WHERE THE MOON COMES,   344 DAWN   8
THE PESTLE OF THE MOON   346 ON WOMAN   30
OR KEEP US ALL AWAKE WITH BAYING AT THE MOON,   364 DOLLS FACES   11
THAT MICHAEL ROBARTES LEFT, YOU WALK IN THE MOON,   367 EGO DOMINUS   4
THE PHASES OF THE MOON   372 PHASES OF MOON   T
. . . I.   THE WHEEL AND THE PHASES OF THE MOON   372 PHASES OF MOON V   T
DESPITE A DWINDLING AND LATE-RISEN MOON,   372 PHASES OF MOON   6
DESPITE A DWINDLING AND LATE RISEN MOON,   372 PHASES OF MOON V   6
SING ME THE CHANGES OF THE MOON ONCE MORE!   373 PHASES OF MOON   29
TWENTY-AND-EIGHT THE PHASES OF THE MOON,   373 PHASES OF MOON   31
BUT WHILE THE MOON IS ROUNDING TOWARDS THE FULL   373 PHASES OF MOON   39
BEFORE THE FULL MOON, HELPLESS AS A WORM.   374 PHASES OF MOON   49
THE THIRTEENTH MOON BUT SETS THE SOUL AT WAR   374 PHASES OF MOON   50
UNDER THE FRENZY OF THE FOURTEENTH MOON,   374 PHASES OF MOON   53
AND AFTER THAT THE CRUMBLING OF THE MOON.   375 PHASES OF MOON   87
UNDER THE THREE LAST CRESCENTS OF THE MOON,   377 PHASES OF MOON   133
THE CAT AND THE MOON   378 CAT AND MOON   T
AND THE MOON SPUN ROUND LIKE A TOP,   378 CAT AND MOON   2
AND THE NEAREST KIN OF THE MOON,   378 CAT AND MOON   3
BLACK MINNALOUSHE STARED AT THE MOON,   378 CAT AND MOON   5
MAYBE THE MOON MAY LEARN,   378 CAT AND MOON   14
THE SACRED MOON OVERHEAD   379 CAT AND MOON   19
AND LIFTS TO THE CHANGING MOON   379 CAT AND MOON   27
WHEN THE OLD MOON IS VANISHED FROM THE SKY   382 VISION ROBART   3
WHEN THE OLD MOON IS VANISHING FROM THE SKY   382 VISION ROBART V   3
ONE LASHED HER TAIL, HER EYES LIT BY THE MOON   383 VISION ROBART   29
OF THE DARK MOON AND THE FULL,   384 VISION ROBART   60
"LAST NIGHT, WHERE UNDER THE WILD MOON   387 SOLOMON WITCH   2
THEREFORE A BLESSED MOON LAST NIGHT   388 SOLOMON WITCH   31
AND THE MOON IS WILDER EVERY MINUTE.   389 SOLOMON WITCH   43
BUT THEY MISTOOK THE BRIGHTNESS OF THE MOON   411 TOWER   45
O MAY THE MOON AND SUNLIGHT SEEM   411 TOWER   54
AYE, SUN AND MOON AND STAR, ALL,   415 TOWER   152
CURVED LIKE NEW MOON, MOON-LUMINOUS,   421 MY TABLE   10
NO MOON! ONLY AN ACHING HEART   421 MY TABLE   13
CURVED LIKE NEW MOON, MOON LUMINOUS,   421 MY TABLE V   10
CURVED LIKE NEW MOON, MOON LUMINOUS,   421 MY TABLE V   10
VALLEY, RIVER, AND ELMS, UNDER THE LIGHT OF A MOON   426 PHANTOM HATRED   3
VALLEY, RIVER, ELMS, UNDER THE LIGHT OF A MOON   426 PHANTOM HATRED V   3
THE INNUMERABLE CLANGING WINGS THAT HAVE PUT OUT THE MOON.   427 PHANTOM HATRED   32
PROTECTED FROM THE CIRCLE OF THE MOON   428 NINETEEN 19   3
ABOVE THE MURDEROUS TREACHERY OF THE MOON,   428 NINETEEN 19 V   3
THOUGH NURTURED LIKE THE SAILING MOON   451 FIRST LOVE   1
THAT TRAVELS ON THE MOON.   451 FIRST LOVE   12
WHEN THE MOON SAILS OUT.   451 FIRST LOVE   18
LIKE THE MOON HER KINDNESS IS,   452 HUMAN DIGNITY   1
IMAGINING MOON ACCURSED,   454 EMPTY CUP V   4
WHEN THE FULL MOON SWAM TO ITS GREATEST HEIGHT   468 HARUN RASHID   151
WHEN MAYBE THRICE IN EVERY MOON HER MOUTH   468 HARUN RASHID   162
WHEREVER THE ORBIT OF THE MOON CAN REACH,   472 ALL SOUL NIGHT   55
BLOOD AND THE MOON.   480 BLOOD AND MOON   T
THE PURITY OF THE UNCLOUDED MOON   482 BLOOD AND MOON   31
AND CLAMOUR IN DRUNKEN FRENZY FOR THE MOON.   482 BLOOD AND MOON   42
CAN COME UPON THE VISAGE OF THE MOON   482 BLOOD AND MOON   53
THE CRAZED MOON   487 CRAZED MOON   T
THE MOON IS STAGGERING IN THE SKY!   487 CRAZED MOON   2
FLY-CATCHERS OF THE MOON,   488 CRAZED MOON   13
OR, BY THE MOON EMBITTERED, SCORN ALOUD   498 BYZANTIUM   21
WHERE THE GAUDY MOON IS HUNG.   502 VACILLATION   69
THE MOON IN A SILVER BAG.   525 DANCING DAYS   8
THE MOON IN A SILVER BAG.   525 DANCING DAYS   16
THE MOON IN A SILVER BAG.   525 DANCING DAYS   24
THAT LIGHT IS FROM THE MOON.   536 PARTING   11
AS THE MOON SIDLES UP   559 HE AND SHE   1
AS TRIPS THE SCARED MOON   559 HE AND SHE   3
SHE SINGS AS THE MOON SINGS!   559 HE AND SHE   7
AS TRIPS THE SACRED MOON   559 HE AND SHE V   3
BUT A GREAT DANE THAT CANNOT BAY THE MOON   579 DOR WELLESLEY   10
BUT HE TOOK DOWN THE MOON   616 MARCH SONGS 3   8
BUT HE TOOK DOWN THE MOON   616 MARCH SONGS 3   18
BUT HE TOOK DOWN THE MOON   616 MARCH SONGS 3   28
PASSETH THE MOON WITH HER SICKLE OF LIGHT,   648 ISLE STAT I 1   82
WHERE ALL NIGHT LONG THE LONELY MOON, THE WHITE   650 ISLE STAT I 1   126
YONDER THE SICKLE OF THE MOON SAILS ON,   688 NETTLESHIP   1
GONE THE STARS AND GONE THE WHITE MOON,   718 PHANTOM SHIP   3
HIDE WHERE HE WILL, IN WAVE OR WRINKLED MOON,   720 WITCH VIVIEN   8
FROM THE DISTAFF OF THE MOON.   743 WISDOM DREAMS   4
HOW MANY MOONS HAVE DIED FROM THE FULL MOON   747 SHADOW WATER A   10
BE PATIENT YET A WHILE! FOR THIS NINTH MOON,   748 SHADOW WATER A   23
BEING THE MOON OF BIRTH, MAY END OUR DOUBT.   748 SHADOW WATER A   24
BE PATIENT YET AWHILE! FOR THIS NINTH MOON,   748 SHADOW WATER A V   23
I WILL SWEAR BY SUN AND MOON TO PARDON ALL   756 SHADOW WATER A   183
BY SUN AND MOON AND A HUNDRED GODS AS WELL,   756 SHADOW WATER A   189
AND WILL YOU SWEAR IT BY THE SUN AND MOON?   758 SHADOW WATER A   229
AND SAID IT WAS MIGHTIER THAN THE SUN AND MOON,   762 SHADOW WATER A   289
IN HAPPY DANCES, UNDER A WINDY MOON!   763 SHADOW WATER A   318
WHERE THE MOON MAKES A CLOUDY LIGHT IN THE MIST.   764 SHADOW WATER A   329
HAVE FALLEN AND MY SUN AND MOON GONE OUT,   767 SHADOW WATER A V   405
AND ONE IN THE HOUSE OF THE MOON,   771 SPINNING SONG   7

	PAGE	TITLE	LINE
MOON-ACCURSED			
IMAGINING, MOON-ACCURSED, ...	454 EMPTY CUP	4
MOONBEAMS			
THE RAINS ARE FROM HIS DRIPPING WING, THE MOONBEAMS FROM	76 INDIAN ON GOD	8
HIS EYE.			
MOONEEN			
AT MOONEEN HE HAD LEAPED A PLACE	326 ROBERT GREGORY	60
MOONLESS			
FROM MOONLESS PLACE TO PLACE.	379 CAT AND MOON V	18
WERE SOME DEAR CHEEK. UPON A MOONLESS NIGHT	466 HARUN RASHID	127
WERE SOME DEAR FACE. UPON A MOONLESS NIGHT	466 HARUN RASHID V	127
STRETCH TOWARDS THE MOONLESS MIDNIGHT OF THE TREES, . . .	579 DOR WELLESLEY	1
CRIES A VOICE AT ROARING MIDNIGHT BESIDE THE MOONLESS DEEP.	718 PHANTOM SHIP	8
MOONLIGHT			
WHERE THE WAVE OF MOONLIGHT GLOSSES	87 STOLEN CHILD	13
UNDER THE BLESSED MOONLIGHT, ...	94 MOLL MAGEE	11
HOME IN THE BLESSED MOONLIGHT	94 MOLL MAGEE V	11
FROM MOONLIGHT PLACE TO PLACE, ...	379 CAT AND MOON V	18
OR WINTRY MOONLIGHT SINK THE FIELD	501 VACILLATION	47
THERE IN THE TOMB DROPS THE FAINT MOONLIGHT, ...	636 BLACK TOWER	17
WHOSE BEARD A MOONLIGHT RIVER IS, WHOSE BROW	657 ISLE STAT I 3	73
MOONLIT			
OF MOONLIT STEPS GLIMMERED: AND LEFT AND RIGHT	31 OISIN 2	35
AND FACE THAT SEEMED WROUGHT OUT OF MOONLIT VAPOURS, . .	33 OISIN 2	70
HER FACE SEEMED FASHIONED ALL OF MOONLIT VAPOURS, . . .	33 OISIN 2 V	70
FROM MOONLIT PLACE TO PLACE.	379 CAT AND MOON	18
THAT OTHER'S MOONLIT EYEBALLS NEVER MOVED, ...	383 VISION ROBART	33
AND SEEM TO CLING UPON THE MOONLIT SKIES	482 BLOOD AND MOON	44
A STARLIT OR A MOONLIT DOME DISDAINS	497 BYZANTIUM	5
A STARLIGHT OR A MOONLIT DOME DISTAINS	497 BYZANTIUM V	5
MOON-LUMINOUS			
CURVED LIKE NEW MOON, MOON-LUMINOUS, ...	421 MY TABLE	10
MOON'S			
OUT OF THE MOON'S PALE TWISTED SHELL:	19 OISIN 1	279
LAND-UNDER-WAVE, WHERE OUT OF THE MOON'S LIGHT AND THE	209 UNDER THE MOON	6
SUN'S			
THE FULL AND THE MOON'S DARK AND ALL THE CRESCENTS, . .	373 PHASES OF MOON	32
WHEN THE MOON'S FULL THOSE CREATURES OF THE FULL . . .	375 PHASES OF MOON	75
I SAW BY THE MOON'S LIGHT	383 VISION ROBART	27
AND WHEN THE MOON'S POT-BELLIED	455 FRIENDS YOUTH	3
. . . A LOG-BOOK OF THE SUN'S JOURNEY AND THE MOON'S:	480 BLOOD AND MOON	14
. . . A LOG BOOK OF THE SUN'S JOURNEY AND THE MOON'S,	480 BLOOD AND MOON V	14
THIN IS THE MOON'S HORN:	519 LOVES LONENESS	8
LOVE STORM AND STAINED WITH MIST THE NEW MOON'S FLARE	678 ISLE STAT II 3 V	294
COME AWAY WHILE THE MOON'S IN THE WOODLAND, ...	707 FAIRY PEDANT	9
COME AWAY WHILE THE MOON'S IN THE WOODLAND, ...	708 FAIRY PEDANT	37
DANCING ON THE MOON'S BROAD STAIN, ...	731 STREET DANCERS	15
WHEN MOON'S ROUND IS FINISHED	786 YOUR HEART	33
MOONS			
A DANAAN FRUITAGE MAKES A SHOWER OF MOONS, ...	127 DREAM OF FAERY V	22
AND DRUID MOONS, AND MURMURING OF BOUGHS, ...	219 HARP OF AENGUS	4
LOVE STORM: AND STAINED WITH MIST THE NEW MOONS FLARE. .	678 ISLE STAT II 3	294
HOW MANY MOONS HAVE DIED FROM THE FULL MOON	747 SHADOW WATER A	10
NINE MOONS. AND FROM THE HARPING OF THE FOOL?	747 SHADOW WATER A	14
THREE MOONS. IT WERE BEST TO KILL HIM, AND CHOOSE OUT .	748 SHADOW WATER A	15
AND DRUID MOONS, AND MURMURING OF BOUGHS, ...	762 SHADOW WATER A	299
MOONSHINE			
FLICKERING UNDER THE WHITE MOONSHINE?	646 ISLE STAT I 1	33
MOON-STRUCK			
MOON-STRUCK BY THE DESPAIRING	487 CRAZED MOON	3
MOON-WHITE			
ARE CHANGED FOR EVER INTO MOON-WHITE STONE.	653 ISLE STAT I 2	43
MOONY			
DANCING IN SOME MOONY PLACE, ...	647 ISLE STAT I 1	54
AND CALM, ROBED ALL IN RAIMENT MOONY WHITE.	693 MOSADA 1	77
MOOR			
HERE WE WILL MOOR OUR LONELY SHIP	78 INDIAN TO LOVE	6
THERE WE WILL MOOR OUR LONELY SHIP	78 INDIAN TO LOVE V	6
OTTERS BELOW AND MOOR HENS ON THE TOP, ...	490 COOLE BALLYLEE V	2
THE STAR-TAUGHT MOOR, SAID THUS IT WAS DECREED	691 MOSADA 1	25
AND IMPORTUNE WITH WEIGHTY WORDS THIS MOOR, ...	698 MOSADA 2	45
MOOR-COCKS			
AND HENS TO MOOR-COCKS CALL:	393 EASTER 1916	54
MOORE			
JOHN KINSELLA'S LAMENT FOR MRS. MARY MOORE	620 JOHN KINSELLA	T
BUT MY DEAR MARY MOORE, ...	620 JOHN KINSELLA	8
ON GEORGE MOORE:	792 GEORGE MOORE	T
MOORE ONCE HAD VISITS FROM THE MUSE	792 GEORGE MOORE	1
MOORED			
COVER YOUR EARS: FOR ONCE WE HAD MOORED OUR GALLEY . . .	756 SHADOW WATER A	187
MOORFOWL			
MY SPIRIT ROCKED IN SLEEP AND SIGHS: AND SAW THE MOORFOWL	76 INDIAN ON GOD	3
PACE			
IS AN UNDYING MOORFOWL, AND HE LIVES BEYOND THE SKY. . .	76 INDIAN ON GOD	7
AS THE MOORFOWL AND THE HARE, ...	706 DAWN-SONG	28
MOOR-HEN			
THE MOOR-HEN GUIDES UPON THE STREAM, ...	424 ROAD AT DOOR	12
MOOR-HENS			
THE LONG-LEGGED MOOR-HENS DIVE, ...	393 EASTER 1916	53
WHERE LONG-LEGGED MOOR-HENS DIVE, ...	393 EASTER 1916 V	53
OTTERS BELOW AND MOOR-HENS ON THE TOP, ...	490 COOLE BALLYLEE	2

531

		PAGE	TITLE	LINE

MOORISH

A LOTUS IN THEIR HANDS--YOUNG MOORISH GIRL . . . . . . 694 MOSADA 1 — 103
A LITTLE MOORISH GIRL? SMALL WORTH. MY SONG-- . . . . 696 MOSADA 2 — 10
I WILL NOT HEAR! THE MOORISH GIRL MUST DIE. . . . . . 697 MOSADA 2 — 39
A FASHION WITH US MOORISH MAIDS, BEGOT . . . . . . 700 MOSADA 3 — 25
YOUNG MOORISH GIRL, THY FINAL HOUR IS HERE! . . . . . 701 MOSADA 3 — 63

MOORS

FROM POISON! FOR YOU CANNOT TRUST THESE MOORS. . . . . 704 MOSADA 3 — 126
I ALWAYS SAID YOU COULD NOT TRUST THESE MOORS. . . . . 704 MOSADA 3 — V 134A

MOPING

MOPING FOR ONE VOYAGE MORE. . . . . 361 ALF POLLEXFEN — 22

MORALISE

THAT IT MAY MORALISE . . . . 421 MY TABLE — 4

MORALIST

SOME MORALIST OR MYTHOLOGICAL POET . . . . 430 NINETEEN 19 — 59

MORALIZE

OF HUMAN SORROW LET THEM MORALIZE! . . . . 663 ISLE STAT II 2 — 31

MORAL'S

THE MORAL'S YOURS BECAUSE IT'S MINE. . . . . . . 271 GREY ROCK — 11

MORE

THE STAG WE CHASED WAS NOT MORE SAD, ... 2 OISIN 1 — V 7J
HIS MISTRESS WAS MORE MILD AND FAIR . . . . . . 3 OISIN 1 — V 7DD
THE HORNLESS DEER IS NOT MORE SAD . . . . 4 OISIN 1 — 34
MORE SLEEK THAN ANY GRANARY MOUSE, ... 4 OISIN 1 — 36
THE STAG YE CHASE IS NOT MORE SAD, ... 4 OISIN 1 — V 35
IN A VIGOUR MORE THAN MORTAL MEASURE, ... 9 OISIN 1 — V 98
WAS NOT MORE LEVEL THAN THE SEA, ... 13 OISIN 1 — 157
ONCE MORE THE DANCE'S LINKED FLOW, ... 22 OISIN 1 — V 323A
AND ONCE MORE SADDLED THE WHITE STEED, ... 25 OISIN 1 — V 378
THE HUMAN SADNESS DAWNS ONCE MORE!" . . . . 25 OISIN 1 — V 381
"GAZE NO MORE ON THE PHANTOMS," NIAMH SAID, ... 29 OISIN 2 — 5
ONCE MORE--THE YOUTH AND LADY, DEER AND HOUND! . . . . 29 OISIN 2 — V 2
YET SANG NO MORE AS WHEN, LIKE A BROWN BEE . . . . . 30 OISIN 2 — 15
BUT SANG NO MORE, AS WHEN, LIKE A BROWN BEE . . . . . 30 OISIN 2 — V 15
FULL MANY MORE, WHEN PEERED A MAIDEN SWEET . . . . . 33 OISIN 2 — V 68F
ONCE MORE UNTO YOUR FLOWERS, FOR NONE MAY FIGHT, ... 34 OISIN 2 — V 80
TO RULE MORE MIGHTY MEN, AND TO THE WORLD . . . . . 38 OISIN 2 — V 133
AND WHEN THE SUN ONCE MORE IN SAFFRON STEPT, ... 41 OISIN 2 — 192
BUT WHEN THE SUN ONCE MORE IN SAFFRON STEPT, ... 41 OISIN 2 — V 192
AND ONCE MORE TO A DAY-LONG BATTLE FELL, ... 43 OISIN 2 — 218
GOD SHAKES THE WORLD WITH RESTLESS HANDS. MORE NEAR . . 43 OISIN 2 — V 208
AND WE ONCE MORE UNTO OUR FIGHTING FELL. . . . . . 43 OISIN 2 — V 218
FIN, CONAN, OSCAR, MANY MORE, THE TIDE . . . . . . 44 OISIN 2 — V 228A
AND MORE COMELY THAN MAN CAN MAKE THEM . . . . . . 49 OISIN 3 — 32
MORE COMELY THAN MAN MAY MAKE THEM, INLAID WITH SILVER . 49 OISIN 3 — V 29
 AND GOLD,
IN ONE WAS A BRANCH SOFT-SHINING WITH BELLS MORE MANY THAN 50 OISIN 3 — 46
 SIGHS
WRAPT IN THE WAVE OF THAT MUSIC, WITH WEARINESS MORE THAN 51 OISIN 3 — 69
 OF EARTH,
THAT ONCE MORE MOVED IN MY BOSOM THE ANCIENT SADNESS OF . 54 OISIN 3 — 107
 MAN,
NO MORE TO CRAWL ON THE SEAS WITH LONG OARS MILE AFTER . 55 OISIN 3 — 119
 MILE,
. . . YOU WILL COME NO MORE TO MY SIDE. . . . . . . 56 OISIN 3 — 128
WE SHALL MINGLE NO MORE, NOR OUR GAZES EMPTY THEIR . . 56 OISIN 3 — 132
 SWEETNESS LONE
. . . NO MORE SHALT THOU BE BY MY SIDE. . . . . . 56 OISIN 3 — V 128
I WILL PRAY NO MORE WITH THE SMOOTH STONES! . . . . . 63 OISIN 3 — V 221
VIJAYA, SWEAR TO HER LOVE NEVER MORE. . . . . . . 74 ANASHU VIJAYA — 65
AND SLEEK YOUNG JOY IS NO MORE FICKLE, ... 77 INDIAN TO LOVE — V 5C
BY THE LONE BORDER OF THE LAKE ONCE MORE, ... 79 EPHEMERA — 5
STAND BY THE BORDER OF THE LAKE ONCE MORE, ... 79 EPHEMERA — V 5
ON THE LONE BORDER OF THE LAKE ONCE MORE! . . . . . 80 EPHEMERA — 17
HE SPAKE ONCE MORE AND FONDLED WITH HIS LIPS . . . . . 81 EPHEMERA — V 24A
FOR THE WORLD'S MORE FULL OF WEEPING THAN YOU CAN . . 87 STOLEN CHILD — 12
 UNDERSTAND.
FOR THE WORLD'S MORE FULL OF WEEPING THAN YOU CAN . . 87 STOLEN CHILD — 27
 UNDERSTAND.
FOR THE WORLD'S MORE FULL OF WEEPING THAN YOU CAN . . 88 STOLEN CHILD — 41
 UNDERSTAND.
HE'LL HEAR NO MORE THE LOWING . . . . 88 STOLEN CHILD — 44
FROM A WORLD MORE FULL OF WEEPING THAN HE CAN UNDERSTAND. 89 STOLEN CHILD — 53
FOR THE WORLD'S MORE FULL OF WEEPING THAN HE CAN UNDERSTAND 89 STOLEN CHILD — V 53
. . . THE WAVES WERE MORE GAY, ... 91 OLD FISHERMAN — 3
TO SEE THE WORLD ONCE MORE. . . . . 97 FOXHUNTER — 4
COME NEAR, THAT NO MORE BLINDED BY MAN'S FATE, ... 101 ROSE UPON ROOD — 9
LEST I NO MORE HEAR COMMON THINGS THAT CRAVE! . . . . 101 ROSE UPON ROOD — 15
WHAT WOULD YOU, FERGUS? BE NO MORE A KING, ... 103 FERGUS DRUID — 21
WHAT WOULD YOU? I WOULD BE NO MORE A KING, ... 103 FERGUS DRUID — V 21
BUT NOW I HAVE NO NEED TO WATCH IT MORE." . . . . . 105 CUCHULAIN SEA — 5
BUT NOW MY YEARS OF WATCHING ARE NO MORE." . . . . . 105 CUCHULAIN SEA — V 5
THEREON HE SHOOK THE MORE AND CAST HIM DOWN . . . . . 106 CUCHULAIN SEA — 14
MORE MOURNFUL THAN THE DEPTH OF STARRY SKIES, ... 108 CUCHULAIN SEA — V 42
"I PUT YOU FROM YOUR PAIN. I CAN NO MORE." . . . . . 110 CUCHULAIN SEA — 69
FOR THREE DAYS MORE IN DREADFUL QUIETUDE, ... 110 CUCHULAIN SEA — 78
MORE FLEETING THAN THE SEA'S FOAM-FICKLE FACE, ... 112 ROSE OF WORLD — V 8
MORE FLEETING THAN THE SEA'S FOAM FICKLE FACE, ... 112 ROSE OF WORLD — V 8
BROODING NO MORE UPON GOD'S WARS . . . . 113 ROSE OF PEACE — 5
WHO HAVE SOUGHT MORE THAN IS IN RAIN OR DEW . . . . . 114 ROSE OF BATTLE — 16

532

	PAGE	TITLE		LINE
MORE (CONTINUED)				
WHERE TIME WOULD SURELY FORGET US, AND SORROW COME NEAR US NO MORE:	122	WHITE BIRDS		10
WHERE SURELY TIME WOULD FORGET US AND SORROW COME NEAR US NO MORE:	122	WHITE BIRDS	V	10
SHE WAS MORE BEAUTIFUL THAN THY FIRST LOVE,	123	DREAM OF DEATH		11
MAN HAD NO MORE TO DO—	123	DREAM OF DEATH	V	8
AND BROOD ON HOPES AND FEAR NO MORE.	125	GOES FERGUS		6
AND NO MORE TURN ASIDE AND BROOD	125	GOES FERGUS		7
AND BROOD ON HOPES AND FEARS NO MORE.	125	GOES FERGUS	V	6
AND AT THAT SINGING HE WAS NO MORE WISE.	127	DREAM OF FAERY		24
WHEN THE MOTHS CAME ONCE MORE,	133	FR GILLIGAN		22
WHEN MOTHS CAME ONCE MORE,	133	FR GILLIGAN	V	22
GAZE NO MORE IN THE BITTER GLASS	135	TWO TREES		21
GAZE NO MORE IN THE BITTER GLASS.	136	TWO TREES		40
MY RHYMES MORE THAN THEIR RHYMING TELL	138	TO IRELAND		20
"AND BROOD NO MORE WHERE THE FIRE IS BRIGHT	140	HOSTING SIDHE	V	5
FLAME UNDER FLAME, TILL TIME BE NO MORE:	141	EVERLAST VOICE		4
I AM NO MORE WITH LIFE AND DEATH,	152	HEART OF WOMAN		10
O CURLEW, CRY NO MORE IN THE AIR,	155	REPROVE CURLEW		1
COME FROM A MORE DREAM-HEAVY LAND,	156	FORGOT BEAUTY		16
A MORE DREAM-HEAVY HOUR THAN THIS:	156	FORGOT BEAUTY		17
AND WITH HEART MORE OLD THAN THE HORN	157	POET BELOVED		5
AND WITH THE HEART MORE OLD THAN THE HORN	157	POET BELOVED	V	5
WHEN THE OWLS CALLED OUT NO MORE:	159	CAP AND BELLS		14
WHEN THE BATS CRIED OUT NO MORE:	159	CAP AND BELLS	V	14
O, WHEN SHALL SORROW WANDER NO MORE IN THE LAND	174	ELEMENT POWERS	V	5
BUT THAT GREAT QUEEN, WHO MORE THAN HALF THE NIGHT	180	QUEEN MAEVE		16
MORE STILL THAN THEY HAD BEEN FOR A GOOD MONTH,	182	QUEEN MAEVE		54
AND YOU ARE MORE HIGH OF HEART THAN SHE,	197	BAILE AILLINN		202
LIKE THEM THAT ARE NO MORE ALIVE.	197	BAILE AILLINN		207
BURNS BUT MORE CLEARLY. O SHE HAD NOT THESE WAYS	200	FOLLY COMFORT		11
IT ALL, AND MORE THAN IT ALL, WOULD COME TO NAUGHT,	201	OLD MEMORY		8
OR, IF THERE NEEDS BE MORE, BE NOTHING SAID	201	OLD MEMORY		11
IT ALL, MORE THAN IT ALL, WOULD COME TO NAUGHT,	201	OLD MEMORY	V	8
AND MORE I MAY NOT WRITE OF, FOR THEY THAT CLEAVE	218	WOODS OF COOLE		24
AND WINDS AND PONDS COVER MORE QUIET WOODS,	218	WOODS OF COOLE		34
MORE SHINING WINDS, MORE STAR-GLIMMERING PONDS?	218	WOODS OF COOLE		35
MORE SHINING WINDS, MORE STAR-GLIMMERING PONDS?	218	WOODS OF COOLE		35
AND MORE I MAY NOT WRITE OF, FOR THEM THAT CLEAVE	218	WOODS OF COOLE	V	24
UNLESS WE DRAIN MORE FLAGONS IN A YEAR	225	SHADOW WATER B		70
AND KISS MORE LIPS THAN LASTING PEACEABLE MEN	225	SHADOW WATER B		71
MORE RICHES THAN THEY EVER HOPED TO FIND?	226	SHADOW WATER B		94
WHY SHOULD YOU BE MORE FAITHFUL THAN THE REST,	227	SHADOW WATER B		109
IS NO MORE THAN A WINE-CUP IN THE TASTING,	229	SHADOW WATER B		150
IS NO MORE THAN A WINE CUP IN THE TASTING,	229	SHADOW WATER B	V	150
OF THAT MORE POWERFUL LIFE? HIS WIFE KNOWS BETTER.	230	SHADOW WATER B		172
TO MAKE LOW LAUGHTER MORE THAN MEAT AND DRINK,	230	SHADOW WATER B		186
CARE MORE ABOUT THE KEGS OF SILVER AND GOLD	232	SHADOW WATER B		234
WHAT POWER THAT IS MORE MIGHTY THAN DESIRE	234	SHADOW WATER B		267
ALTHOUGH YOU ARE MORE BEAUTIFUL THAN ANY,	236	SHADOW WATER B		305
THAT IS MORE MIGHTY THAN THE SUN AND MOON,	237	SHADOW WATER B		328
MORE MIGHTY THAN THE STARS HALF TROUBLED ME,	237	SHADOW WATER B		332
IF THERE BE HALF A HUNDRED MORE, WHAT MATTER?	245	SHADOW WATER B		476
WHAT MORE HAVE YOU TO LOOK FOR ON THE SEAS?	248	SHADOW WATER B		543
AND IF THAT HAPPINESS BE MORE THAN DREAMS,	248	SHADOW WATER B		554
MORE THAN THE FROTH, THE FEATHER, THE DUST-WHIRL,	248	SHADOW WATER B		555
MORE THAN THE FROTH, THE FEATHER, THE DUSTWHIRL,	248	SHADOW WATER B	V	555
THAT BALANCED WITH A WORD IS MORE THAN NOISE:	258	KING NO KING		4
AND THESE THINGS CAME, SO MUCH THE MORE THEREBY	265	THESE CLOUDS		8
THAT HAS MORE LIFE IN IT THAN DEATH,	271	GREY ROCK		8
NO MORE REMEMBERING WHAT HAD BEEN,	276	GREY ROCK		122
MORE HANDS IN HEIGHT THAN ANY STAG IN THE WORLD	277	TWO KINGS		9
AND I BUT ASKED THE MORE, TILL HE CRIED OUT,	281	TWO KINGS		92
BUT ASKED THE MORE UNTIL HE SPOKE THESE WORDS,	281	TWO KINGS	V	92A
A FARMER HAS MORE DIGNITY."	296	THREE BEGGARS		37
KIND EYES SHOULD BE MORE LEARN'D?	312	TWO YEAR LATER		2
THAT SEEMED AS THOUGH ICE BURNED AND WAS BUT THE MORE ICE,	316	COLD HEAVEN		2
AND ALL THEIR EYES STILL FIXED, HOPING TO FIND ONCE MORE,	318	MAGI		6
FOR THERE'S MORE ENTERPRISE	320	COAT		9
BEING MORE INDIFFERENT TO OUR SOLITUDE	334	LIVING BEAUTY		7
I THOUGHT NO MORE WAS NEEDED	334	SONG		1
MORE THAN ANOTHER	336	YOUNG GIRL		2
AND MAKE THE DAYLIGHT SWEET BUT WHEN	339	SHEP GOATHERD		13
BUT GROWS MORE GENTLE WHEN HE SPEAKS HER NAME,	340	SHEP GOATHERD		29
I WILL TALK NO MORE OF BOOKS OR THE LONG WAR	351	HER PRAISE		11
AND RUTH ST. DENIS HAD MORE CHARM ALTHOUGH SHE HAD POOR LUCK:	353	HIS PHOENIX		10
YOU ARE MORE BEAUTIFUL THAN ANY ONE,	356	BROKEN DREAMS		27
YOU WERE MORE BEAUTIFUL THAN ANY ONE,	356	BROKEN DREAMS	V	27
YOU ARE MORE BEAUTIFUL THAN ANYONE	356	BROKEN DREAMS	V	27
MOPING FOR ONE VOYAGE MORE.	361	ALF POLLEXFEN		22
MORE PLAIN TO THE MIND'S EYE THAN ANY FACE	368	EGO DOMINUS		21
SING ME THE CHANGES OF THE MOON ONCE MORE:	373	PHASES OF MOON		29
THE FIRST THIN CRESCENT IS WHEELED ROUND ONCE MORE.	377	PHASES OF MOON		116
WHAT VOICE MORE SWEET THAN HERS	392	EASTER 1916		21
BEING NO MORE DEMONIAC	400	DEMON BEAST		30
AND TWICE A THOUSAND MORE	401	DEMON BEAST		47
ONCE MORE THE STORM IS HOWLING, AND HALF HID	403	FOR DAUGHTER		1
AS TO A DOG'S TAIL? NEVER HAD I MORE	409	TOWER		4
THAT MORE EXPECTED THE IMPOSSIBLE—	409	TOWER		7

<pre>
                                                    PAGE   TITLE   LINE
MORE   (CONTINUED)
    AS UPON A DOG'S TAIL. NEVER HAD I MORE . . . . .   409 TOWER   V   4
    AND MOUNTS MORE DIZZY HIGH THE MORE IT RAINS . . . .   417 ANCEST HOUSES   5
    AND MOUNTS MORE DIZZY HIGH THE MORE IT RAINS . . . .   417 ANCEST HOUSES   5
    BUT THAT HE FOUND MORE SUBSTANCE THERE THAN DREAMS. . . .   417 ANCEST HOUSES V   10
    AN ANCIENT BRIDGE, AND A MORE ANCIENT TOWER, ...   419 MY HOUSE   1
    MORE SUBSTANCE IN OUR ENMITIES . . . .   425 STARES NEST   18
    IT HAD BUT MADE US PINE THE MORE. THE ABSTRACT JOY. . .   427 PHANTOM HATRED   38
    WHAT MORE IS THERE TO SAY? THAT COUNTRY ROUND . . .   430 NINETEEN 19   43
    THE LIVING SEEM MORE SHADOWY THAN THEY. . . . . .   435 NEW FACES   8
    WITH SIXTY OR MORE WINTERS ON ITS HEAD, ...   444 SCHOOL CHILDR   38
    IF YOU ARE NO MORE STRENGTH THAN I AM BEAUTY . . . . .   448 HERO GIRL FOOL   10
    BUT O! MY HEART COULD BEAR NO MORE WHEN THE UPLAND CAUGHT   450 OWEN AHERNE   11
        THE WIND!
    MORE SONGS OF AN OLD COUNTRYMAN . . . .   454 HIS MEMORIES V   T
    CAN SHAKE MORE BLOSSOM FROM AUTUMNAL CHILL . . . . .   465 HARUN RASHID V 104
    THAT BRINGS MORE BLOSSOM TO AUTUMNAL CHILL . . . .   465 HARUN RASHID V 104
    GAVE BUT MORE REASON FOR A WOMAN'S CARE. . . . .   466 HARUN RASHID   111
    AND MAY HAVE GROWN MORE ARROGANT BEING A GHOST. . . .   473 ALL SOUL NIGHT   80
    A CHARTER TO COMMIT THE CRIME ONCE MORE. . . . . .   478 SELF AND SOUL   32
    WHAT MATTER IF I LIVE IT ALL ONCE MORE? . . . . .   478 SELF AND SOUL   43
    MORE BLESSED STILL THIS TOWER! . . . .   480 BLOOD AND MOON   2
    THOUGH THE GREAT SONG RETURN NO MORE . . . . . .   485 NINETEENTH CEN   1
    MORE WOMEN BORN THAN MEN." . . . .   485 STATISTICS   4
    SEEMED ONCE MORE DEAR THAN LIFE! ANCESTRAL TREES, . . .   491 COOLE BALLYLEE   34
    HOPING MORE SUBSTANTIAL JOY . . . .   494 AT ALGECIRAS   9
    HOPING A MORE SUBSTANTIAL JOY . . . .   494 AT ALGECIRAS V   9
    SHADE MORE THAN MAN, MORE IMAGE THAN A SHADE! . . . .   497 BYZANTIUM   10
    SHADE MORE THAN MAN, MORE IMAGE THAN A SHADE! . . . .   497 BYZANTIUM   10
    MORE MIRACLE THAN BIRD OR HANDIWORK, ...   497 BYZANTIUM   18
    MORE MIRACLE THAN BIRD OR HANDY-WORK, ...   497 BYZANTIUM   V   18
    AND TWENTY MINUTES MORE OR LESS . . . .   501 VACILLATION   42
    ISAIAH'S COAL, WHAT MORE CAN MAN DESIRE? . . . .   502 VACILLATION   74
    EZEKIEL'S COAL, WHAT MORE CAN MAN DESIRE? . . . .   502 VACILLATION   V   74
    BETTER CONDUCT MYSELF OR HAVE MORE . . . .   507 STREAM AND SUN   9
    THE MORE I LEAVE THE DOOR UNLATCHED . . . . . .   511 JANE AND JACK   3
    AND THE EYES MORE BRIGHT . . . .   531 BEFORE WORLD   2
    AND THE LIPS MORE SCARLET. . . . .   532 BEFORE WORLD   3
    HAD EVEN O'DUFFY--BUT I NAME NO MORE-- . . . . .   543 PARN FUNERAL 2   9
    NO MORE SANG HE, FOR HIS THROAT WAS TOO SMALL! . . .   545 TO SAME TUNE 1   24
    HE SAID NO MORE FOR HIS THROAT WAS TOO SMALL. . . .   545 TO SAME TUNE 1 V 24
    MUCH I TALK, MORE I WALK! . . . .   548 TO SAME TUNE 3   9
    MUCH I TALK, MORE I WALK! . . . .   548 TO SAME TUNE 3   19
    MUCH I TALK, MORE I WALK! . . . .   549 TO SAME TUNE 3   29
    THINKING TO MEET MY LOVE ONCE MORE . . . .   551 SONGS REWRIT 1 V 15
    WANDER IN DREAMS NO MORE! . . . .   554 CHURCH STATE   8
    A GREATER, A MORE GRACIOUS TIME HAS GONE! . . . .   564 GYRES   12
    WHICH IS THE MORE BLEST? . . . .   573 LADYS 2ND SONG   20
    AND I HAVE MANY MORE! . . . .   586 PARNELLITES   10
    HURRAH FOR REVOLUTION AND MORE CANNON-SHOT! . . . .   590 GREAT DAY   1
    HURRAH FOR REVOLUTION AND MORE CANNON SHOT! . . . .   590 GREAT DAY   V   1
    THEY SAY IT IS MORE HUMAN . . . .   599 STONE CROSS   19
    MORE DREAD THE LIFE THAT WE LIVE. . . . .   615 MARCH SONGS 2   15
    NO MORE SANG HE, FOR HIS THROAT WAS TOO SMALL! . . .   616 MARCH SONGS 3   24
    WITH NO MORE SOUND THAN THE MICE MAKE . . . . .   618 LONG-LEG FLY   27
    STUMBLING UPON THE BLOOD-DARK TRACK ONCE MORE, . . .   622 HOUND VOICE   18
    GROWS MORE DEEP DAY AFTER DAY. . . . .   624 APPARITIONS   18
    BUT BODY GONE HE SLEEPS NO MORE, ...   633 MAN AND ECHO   29
    OH, MORE DARK THY GLEAMING HAIR IS . . . . . .   647 ISLE STAT I 1   51
    AND THINE EYES MORE BRIGHT THAN FAERY'S, ...   647 ISLE STAT I 1   53
    THE SKIES MORE DIM, THOUGH BURNING LIKE A SHIELD, . .   656 ISLE STAT I 3   26
    NO MORE A-ROVING SHALT THOU SEE . . . .   658 ISLE STAT I 3   82
    ONCE MORE HOW ON THAT MISERABLE DAY . . . . . .   658 ISLE STAT II 1   4
    WE'VE TALKED AND TALKED, AND NOT A WHIT MORE RARE . .   659 ISLE STAT II 1   21
    WITH THEIR UNHUMAN SORROWS. CEASE! NO MORE! . . . .   661 ISLE STAT II 1   58
    MORE GRIEF IS MINE. NO MAN SHALL EVER STOOP . . .   661 ISLE STAT II 1   62
    IS NOT MORE FAIR AND JOYOUS THAN SHE IS . . . . .   661 ISLE STAT II 1   71
    ANTONIO, IF I RETURN NO MORE, ...   663 ISLE STAT II 2   17
    ONCE MORE THOSE SHEPHERDS COME. MAYHAP SOME MIRTH .   664 ISLE STAT II 2   49
    MORE WONDERFUL! AND WE HAVE SWORDS. O NIGHT . . .   664 ISLE STAT II 2   61
    HAD DRIVEN HER FORTH, FOR EVER MORE . . . . . .   668 ISLE STAT II 3   56
    YET EVER MORE, THROUGH ALL THY DAYS OF RUTH, . . .   674 ISLE STAT II 3   206
    AND NEVER ANY MORE THE WIDE-EYED BANDS . . . . .   674 ISLE STAT II 3   218
    MORE DARK BENEATH THE POPLARS, WHERE YON OWL . . .   675 ISLE STAT II 3   233
    BY THEE SPELL-BOUND? THOU SHALT KNOW MORE! . . . .   675 ISLE STAT II 3   241
    IGNOBLE JOY, AND MORE IGNOBLE PAIN . . . .   687 TWO TITANS   12
    AND WHEN ONCE MORE THE LIGHTNING GENII PASSED, . . .   687 TWO TITANS   29
    WHEN FLASH ON FLASH ONCE MORE THE LIGHTNING CAME, . .   688 TWO TITANS   39
    NO MORE! TAKE ME INSTEAD OF HER, GREAT SIRS! . . .   695 MOSADA 1   114
    EVER MORE TO SPEAK A WORD . . . .   697 MOSADA 2   32
    OH, CAN MY KISSES BRING A FLUSH NO MORE . . . . .   701 MOSADA 3   71
    'TIS LATE, WAIT ONE MORE DAY! BELOW THE HILLS . . .   702 MOSADA 3   91
    THERE IS NO LEAVE-TAKING. I GO NO MORE. . . . .   702 MOSADA 3   100
    THERE IS NO LEAVE TAKING. I GO NO MORE. . . . .   702 MOSADA 3   V 100
    OF TRAITOR EVER MORE IS ON OUR NAME." . . . . .   712 FERENCZ RENYI V   61
    CLOSE AND MORE CLOSE--I FEEL HIM IN MY HEART-- . . .   720 WITCH VIVIEN   11
    A BIRD WALK ON THE DOORSTEP. CHECK ONCE MORE. . . .   722 WITCH VIVIEN   64
    THE FAIRIES' HERALD SPAKE ONCE MORE. . . . . .   730 PRIEST FAIRY   53
    AND JOY, IN GROWING DEEPER AND MORE DEEP, ...   735 QUATRAIN APHOR   27
    AND DREAD NO MORE FOUL AUTUMN'S WING, ...   737 SUMMER EVENING   18
    AND HER DIM WAVE BIDS MAN BE NO MORE GLAD, ...   738 YOU ARE SAD   11
</pre>

534

MORE   (CONTINUED)
    AND SAID: "I WILL SEE HER NO MORE," . . . .   744 GLOVE CLOAK   6
    AND NEED NO MORE OF LIFE TILL THE WHITE WINGS . . . . .   751 SHADOW WATER A   102
    AND I MUST LOSE MORE TIME BECAUSE THESE FOOLS . . . . .   754 SHADOW WATER A   158
    AND MORE, IF YOU WILL WAR AGAINST THE DANES . . . . .   756 SHADOW WATER A V   190
    TILL HIS EDAINE, NO MORE A SILVER FLY . . . .   757 SHADOW WATER A V   210
    BESEECHING HANDS AND MORE BESEECHING EYES? . . . . . .   763 SHADOW WATER A V   312
    A HIGH, GREY CAIRN. WHAT MORE IS TO BE SAID? . . . . .   778 SONG DEIRDRE 3   5
MORN
    THAN THE HORNLESS DEER WE CHASED THAT MORN, ...   2 OISIN 1   V   7P
    I CHASED AT MORN THE FLYING DEER, ...   10 OISIN 1   121
    AND "WAKEN, COURTIERS OF THE MORN!" . . . .   18 OISIN 1   V   262
    "MY BROTHERS SPRING OUT OF THEIR BEDS AT MORN, ...   32 OISIN 2   51
    "THEY MURMUR LIKE YOUNG PARTRIDGE IN THE MORN, ...   32 OISIN 2   V   51
    WE FEASTED FOR THREE DAYS. ON THE FOURTH MORN . . . . .   43 OISIN 2   214
    THREE DAYS WE FEASTED, WHEN ON THE FOURTH MORN . . . .   43 OISIN 2   V   214
    TO LIE UNTIL THE FOURTH MORN SAW EMERGE . . . .   44 OISIN 2   220
    TO LIE UNTIL THE FOURTH MORN SUN EMERGE . . . .   44 OISIN 2   V   220
    I MINDED HER TILL MORN. . . . .   94 MOLL MAGEE   16
    WHEN THE MORN GREW FROSTY AND CLEAR. . . . .   95 MOLL MAGEE   20
    THE HUNTSMAN LOOSENS ON THE MORN . . . .   98 FOXHUNTER   27
    SIGH, HEART, AGAIN IN THE DEW OF THE MORN. . . . . . .   147 INTO TWILIGHT   4
    AND HOPE IS LESS DEAR THAN THE DEW OF THE MORN. . . . .   148 INTO TWILIGHT   16
    IT TALKED, ERE THE MORN GREW WHITE. . . . .   159 CAP AND BELLS V   6
    IT TALKED BEFORE MORN WAS WHITE, ...   159 CAP AND BELLS V   6
    AND AS SOON AS THE MORN HAD WHITENED, ...   160 CAP AND BELLS V   23
    IN THE GREY REEDS THAT NIGHT AND MORN . . . .   190 BAILE AILLINN   42
    EVENING AND MORN, THE STEEP STREET OF URBINO . . . . .   352 PEOPLE   V   12
    PRIDE, LIKE THAT OF THE MORN, ...   414 TOWER   134
    AND WHEN I WAKE TOWARDS MORN I DREAD MYSELF, ...   448 HERO GIRL FOOL   5
    CATCHING SMALL BIRDS IN THE DEW OF THE MORN . . . . .   636 BLACK TOWER   22
    'TIS MORN: THY SHEEP ARE WANDERING DOWN THE VALE— . . .   645 ISLE STAT I 1   3
    'TIS MORN: LIKE OLD MEN'S EYES THE STARS ARE PALE, . .   645 ISLE STAT I 1   4
    'TIS MORN, AND FROM THE DEW-DRENCH'D WOOD I'VE SPED . .   645 ISLE STAT I 1   6
    COME FORTH: THE MORN IS FAIR: AS FROM THE PYRE . . . .   645 ISLE STAT I 1   8
    HUNDRED-THROATED MORN IS SINGING, ...   647 ISLE STAT I 1   70
    FROM MORN THE TWAIN UNTIL THE EVENING PALES . . . . .   651 ISLE STAT I 1   161
    EACH CAME ONE MORN, WITH WELCOMING OF SONG, ...   660 ISLE STAT II 1   42
    UNTIL THIS MORN. AS ADDER'S BACK . . . .   667 ISLE STAT II 3   22
    UNTIL THIS MORN. THE SKY WITH WRACK . . . .   667 ISLE STAT II 3 V 22
    AT MORN, AND WITH HER FEET EACH COBWEB RENDS, ...   670 ISLE STAT II 3   99
MORNA'S
    MINE WERE CLAN MORNA'S TRIBES UNTOLD, ...   81 MAD KING GOLL V   3
MORN-BEWILDERED
    MORN-BEWILDERED, AND THE CUP . . . .   646 ISLE STAT I 1   47
MORNIN'
    BLOWIN' HER MORNIN' FIRE. . . . .   95 MOLL MAGEE   36
    IN THE FROSTY MORNIN' CLEAR. . . . .   95 MOLL MAGEE   V   20
    A-BLOWIN' OF HER MORNIN' FIRE, ...   95 MOLL MAGEE   V   35
MORNING
    ON A MORNING MISTY AND MILD AND FAIR. . . . .   2 OISIN 1   V   7E
    THAT FROM THE SAFFRON MORNING CAME, ...   19 OISIN 1   277
    AND THE STARS SHALL ARISE AND SAY IN THE MORNING, . . .   28 OISIN 1   V 423G
    OR HOURS PASSED BY, YET HOLD THE MORNING RAYS . . . . .   30 OISIN 2   20
    NO LONGER GLAD AS ON THAT MORNING, SPED . . . .   30 OISIN 2   V   16
    YET DIMLY DEEM I THAT THE MORNING RAYS . . . .   30 OISIN 2   V   20
    HUNG FROM THE MORNING STAR: WHEN THESE MILD WORDS . .   32 OISIN 2   49
    WHEN THE FENIANS MADE FORAY AT MORNING WITH BRAN, SCEOLAN,   54 OISIN 3   104
      LOMAIR.
    TILL, FATTENING THE WINDS OF THE MORNING, AN ODOUR   57 OISIN 3   153
      OF NEW-MOWN HAY
    COMING FORTH FROM THE SEA LIKE THE MORNING . . . . . .   58 OISIN 3   V 158
    AND UNDER THE BLINK O' THE MORNING STAR, ...   83 MAD KING GOLL V   20
    DROPPING FROM THE VEILS OF THE MORNING TO WHERE THE CRICKET 117 ISLE INNISFREE   6
      SINGS:
    AND SANG WHAT GOLD MORNING OR EVENING SHEDS . . . . .   126 DREAM OF FAERY   7
    A RAPTUROUS MUSIC, TILL THE MORNING BREAK . . . . . .   137 TO SOME I TALK 14
    CONTINUAL MUSIC TILL THE MORNING BREAK, ...   137 TO SOME I TALK 14
    THE EAST HER HIDDEN JOY BEFORE THE MORNING BREAK, . . .   154 BELOVED PEACE   4
    AND WHEN THE MORNING WHITENED . . . .   160 CAP AND BELLS   23
    OF MORNING LIGHT IN A DIM SKY: . . . .   195 BAILE AILLINN   150
    OUT OF THE RUNNING STREAM, O MORNING STAR. . . . . . .   251 SHADOW WATER B 610
    AMONG THE STONES AND THORN-TREES, UNDER MORNING LIGHT: . . 291 PAUDEEN   3
    AMONG THE STONES AND THORN TREES, UNDER MORNING LIGHT, . . 291 PAUDEEN   V   3
    BETWEEN THE NIGHT AND MORNING. I MIGHT HAVE LIVED, . .   351 PEOPLE   6
    EVENING AND MORNING, THE STEEP STREET OF URBINO . . . .   352 PEOPLE   12
    THAT NIGHT AND MORNING I MAY THRASH . . . .   379 SAINT HUNCH   9
    THAT EVERY MORNING ROSE AGAIN . . . .   385 ROBARTES DANCE 7
    HIS "MORNING" AND HIS "NIGHT" DISCLOSE . . . .   386 ROBARTES DANCE 33
    SCARCE SPREAD A GLORY TO THE MORNING BEAMS, ...   422 MY DESCENDANTS   6
    TILL HIS MORNING MEAL COME ROUND: . . . .   435 FOR MY SON   4
    THE MORNING STARS TO SING, ...   436 FOR MY SON   19
    UNTIL THE MORNING BREAK AS ON A DARK BREAST. . . . . .   494 AT ALGECIRAS V   6
    "IS THAT MORNING WHEN I MET . . . .   521 THREE THINGS   15
    AND NIGHT AND MORNING SING: . . . .   627 STATES HOLIDAY 12
    SHEPHERD, TO MAR THE MORNING HAST THOU COME? . . . . .   646 ISLE STAT I 1   30
    LOUD FOR THEE THE MORNING CRIETH. . . . .   648 ISLE STAT I 1   86
    FAR THE MORNING VAPOURS SHATTER, ...   648 ISLE STAT I 1   89
    SHEPHERDS, I CAME THIS MORNING TO YOUR LAND . . . . .   682 SEEKER   15
    WE'LL FLY FROM THIS BEFORE THE MORNING STAR. . . . . .   702 MOSADA 3   74
    FOR YOUR FEET THE MORNING PRAYETH: . . . .   706 DAWN-SONG   25

	PAGE	TITLE		LINE

MORNING   (CONTINUED)
```
    WHILE THE MORNING STAR DECAYETH  . . . . .        706 DAWN-SONG             29
    CAME OLIVE FIRES OF MORNING AND ON THE DARKNESS FED, . .  719 PHANTOM SHIP          33
    CAME THE OLIVE FIRE OF MORNING, AND ON THE DARKNESS FED,  719 PHANTOM SHIP    V     33
    LONG BEFORE THE MORNING FIRE  . . . . . .          727 LOVERS QUARREL        45
    THE WHITE FOOL MAKES AT MORNING OUT OF FOAM! . . . .  761 SHADOW WATER A       261
    OUT OF A RUNNING STREAM, O MORNING STAR . . . . . .  769 SHADOW WATER A       426
MORNING'S
    ALL DREAD AFAR TILL MORNING'S BACK, . . . . .      435 FOR MY SON             6
    AND IN THE MORNING'S GONE, NO MAN KNOWS WHY! . . . . .  490 COOLE BALLYLEE        20
    AND TROUBLED EYES CAME MORNING'S FIRST-BORN GLOW!   648 ISLE STAT I 1        103
MORNINGS
    BUT FOR THOSE MORNINGS WHEN I FIND  . . . . .      306 HOUR DAWN             76
    I FADE, AND SHALL NOT SEE THE MORNINGS WAKE, . . . .  674 ISLE STAT II 3       223
MORNS
    AND TILL A HUNDRED MORNS HAD FLOWERED RED . . . . .  170 SECRET ROSE           17
MOROCCAN
    OF THE MOROCCAN FLOCKS AND HERDS . . . . . .       493 AT ALGECIRAS           3
    OF A MOROCCAN FLOCK OR HERD, . . . . . .           493 AT ALGECIRAS    V      3
MORROW      SEE TO-MORROW
    AND THINGS THAT FEAR THE DAWN OF THE MORROW  . . . .  20 OISIN 1             302
    AND WE FEAR NO DAWNING MORROW, . . . . . .          21 OISIN 1             318
    AND WE NEVER FEAR THE MORROW . . . . . .            21 OISIN 1      V       318
    FOLDED IN LOVE THAT FEARS NO MORROW, . . . . .      23 OISIN 1             341
    OR TIRED ON ANY DAWNING MORROW, . . . . . .         23 OISIN 1      V       341
    AND PLANNING, PLOTTING ALWAYS THAT SOME MORROW . . .  129 BOOK STORIES         10
MORTAL
    YOUR MORTAL SHORES TILL TIME IS DONE!"  . . . . .    6 OISIN 1      V        59
    IN A VIGOUR MORE THAN MORTAL MEASURE,  . . . . .     9 OISIN 1      V        98
    OR HAVE THEY BREATHED THE MORTAL AIR?" . . . . .     12 OISIN 1             147
    WAS DIM WITH MIRE OF A MORTAL SHORE,  . . . . .      15 OISIN 1             208
    WAS DIM WITH THE MIRE OF A MORTAL SHORE, . . . .     15 OISIN 1      V      208
    TAKING THE MORTAL WARRIORS BY THE HANDS!  . . . .    29 OISIN 2      V      10B
    FOR NEVER MORTAL CRY SO FAR HATH SENT. . . . .       36 OISIN 2             108
    . . . AND SEE WHAT THE MORTAL MEN DO, . . . . .      55 OISIN 3      V      125
    AND HEAVY MORTAL HOPES THAT TOIL AND PASS! . . . .  101 ROSE UPON ROOD        18
    "NOT ANY GOD ALIVE NOR MORTAL DEAD, . . . . .      106 CUCHULAIN SEA   V     10
    EMPTY YOUR HEART OF ITS MORTAL DREAM. . . . . .    140 HOSTING SIDHE          5
    FILLING THY HEART WITH A MORTAL DREAM, . . . . .   140 HOSTING SIDHE   V      6
    WHEN AN IMMORTAL PASSION BREATHES IN MORTAL CLAY!  172 TRAV PASSION           2
    THAT WORK TOO DIFFICULT FOR MORTAL HANDS  . . . .  182 QUEEN MAEVE           67
    "HOW MAY A MORTAL WHOSE LIFE GUTTERS OUT  . . . .  184 QUEEN MAEVE           85
    AND WITH A GROAN, AS IF THE MORTAL BREATH  . . . .  185 QUEEN MAEVE          103
    HE DREADS THE WEIGHT OF MORTAL HOURS. . . . . .    212 BLESS PSALTER         11
    NO MORTAL CAN.  YES! IF THEY GIVE US HELP. . . . .  229 SHADOW WATER B       165
    FOR EVERY TATTER IN ITS MORTAL DRESS, . . . . .    407 SAIL BYZANTIUM        12
    A MAN THAT HAD SIX MORTAL WOUNDS, A MAN . . . .    634 CUCHULAIN COMF         1
    LAUGHS NOT.  IT DWELLS ALONE ON MORTAL LIPS!  . .  670 ISLE STAT II 3       100
    BEFORE I AM TOO WEAK, FIERCE MORTAL, LET ME FLY, . .  675 ISLE STAT II 3       245
    FIERCE MORTAL, AND CROUCHED LOW BESIDE THE LAKE  . .  675 ISLE STAT II 3 V 245A
    THEIR DREAD OF AUTUMN'S MORTAL WING. . . . . .     736 SUMMER EVENING
    WHY HAVE YOU CLOVEN ME WITH A MORTAL LOVE? . . . .  768 SHADOW WATER A       419
MORTAL'S
    BEYOND A MORTAL'S YEARS.  I WAIT THE SONG  . . . .  653 ISLE STAT I 2         48
    HIS WELL-BELOVED THROUGH A MORTAL'S EYES!  . . . .  763 SHADOW WATER A       322
    IS LAUGHING THROUGH A MORTAL'S EYES.  O LOOK!  . .  763 SHADOW WATER A       324
MORTALS
    "THEN GO THROUGH THE LANDS IN THE SADDLE AND SEE WHAT THE   55 OISIN 3           125
        MORTALS DO,
    HOW WE ALONE OF MORTALS ARE . . . . . . .          78 INDIAN TO LOVE        11
MOSADA
    MOSADA. . . . . . . . . .                         689 MOSADA 1               T
    MOSADA, IT IS THEN SO MUCH THE WORSE! . . . .      692 MOSADA 1        V    41A
    FROM THE UNDYING WORM.  SHE SLEEPS--MOSADA--  . . .  701 MOSADA 3            65
    FROM DATELESS PAIN.  SHE SLEEPS--MOSADA--THOU--  . .  701 MOSADA 3       V    65
    MOSADA!  OH, MOSADA! . . . . . . .                704 MOSADA 3           124A
    MOSADA!  OH, MOSADA! . . . . . . .                704 MOSADA 3       V   124A
MOSAIC      SEE GLASS-MOSAIC
    AS IN THE GOLD MOSAIC OF A WALL, . . . . . .      408 SAIL BYZANTIUM        18
MOSCOW
    TO MOSCOW OR TO ROME. . . . . . . . .            600 THOSE IMAGES           6
MOSS
    BY WOODS OF MOSS, BY LAWNS OF CLOVER, . . . .      25 OISIN 1      V      377
    OF MOSS, A MAIDEN WEAVING, SINGETH SHE! . . . .   716 DWELT SYCAMORE        12
    WHERE THE MOSS WAS SPREAD LIKE HIS OWN DOORMAT. . .  728 PRIEST FAIRY           8
    IN A WOOD OF DEW AND MOSS, . . . . . .            744 ROSY CROSS             5
MOSSY
    TO PRISONS GO, AND MOSSY RUIN REST  . . . . .     709 FERENCZ RENYI          2
    TO PRISON GO, AND MOSSY RUIN REST  . . . . .      709 FERENCZ RENYI   V      2
MOST
    WHOSE LIPS HAD LIFE'S MOST PROSPEROUS GLOW? . . .   10 OISIN 1             118
    THE THINGS THAT MOST OF ALL I HATE! . . . .        24 OISIN 1             359
    THAT WAS MOST DISTANT FROM THE DOOR; GREEN SLIME, .  37 OISIN 2             113
    MOST DISTANT STRODE WE.  ON THE FLOOR LAY SLIME, .  37 OISIN 2      V      113
    CRIED OUT, DIM SEA, HEAR MY MOST PITEOUS STORY! . .  68 SAD SHEPHERD           9
    HID IN THE EARTH'S MOST HIDDEN PART, . . . . .     78 INDIAN TO LOVE V      12
    IN MY MOST SECRET SPIRIT GREW . . . . . .          83 MAD KING GOLL         27
    THIS WOULD I SAY, MOST WISE OF LIVING SOULS! . . .  102 FERGUS DRUID           9
    ON HER MOST LONELY MYSTERIES. . . . . .           156 FORGOT BEAUTY   V     24
    IT HAD GROWN MOST WISE WITH THINKING . . . .      159 CAP AND BELLS   V      7
    FAR-OFF, MOST SECRET, AND INVIOLATE ROSE, . . . .  169 SECRET ROSE           1
```

MOST   (CONTINUED)

	PAGE	TITLE		LINE
FAR OFF, MOST SECRET, AND INVIOLATE ROSE,	169	SECRET ROSE	V	1
FAR-OFF, MOST SECRET, AND INVIOLATE ROSE?	170	SECRET ROSE		32
FAR OFF, MOST SECRET, AND INVIOLATE ROSE?	170	SECRET ROSE	V	32
BUT THINK ABOUT OLD FRIENDS THE MOST:	173	PLEADS FRIEND		5
BUT THINK OF YOUR OLD FRIENDS THE MOST:	173	PLEADS FRIEND	V	5
WITH SPEEDY FEET AND A MOST THANKFUL HEART!	185	QUEEN MAEVE		100
AT THE MOST QUIET MIDNIGHT IS TO BE STRICKEN.	236	SHADOW WATER B		321
IF SOMETHING THAT'S MOST FABULOUS WERE TRUE--	245	SHADOW WATER B		489
HAVE TAUGHT TO IGNORANT MEN MOST VIOLENT WAYS,	256	NO SECOND TROY		3
BEING HIGH AND SOLITARY AND MOST STERN?	257	NO SECOND TROY		10
OR IS THERE NONE, MOST POPULAR OF MEN,	265	ABBEY THEATRE		13
YOU MOST OF ALL, SILENT AND FIERCE OLD MAN,	270	PARDON FATHERS		15
DOWSON AND JOHNSON MOST I PRAISE--	273	GREY ROCK		62
HE CLAIMED HIS COUNTRY'S NEED WAS MOST,	275	GREY ROCK		101
WHY SHOULD THE FAITHFULLEST HEART MOST LOVE	275	GREY ROCK		112
WOMEN CAN FIND." WITH A MOST MASTERFUL VOICE,	284	TWO KINGS		175
WOMEN CAN FIND." WITH A MOST BURNING VOICE	284	TWO KINGS	V	175
THAT IS MOST DIFFICULT.	291	TO A FRIEND		16
DO MEN WHO LEAST DESIRE GET MOST,	295	THREE BEGGARS		13
OR GET THE MOST WHO MOST DESIRE?"	295	THREE BEGGARS		14
OR GET THE MOST WHO MOST DESIRE?"	295	THREE BEGGARS		14
A BEGGAR SAID, "THEY GET THE MOST	295	THREE BEGGARS		15
INTO SOME MOST FEARFUL SHAPE."	299	THREE HERMITS		23
OF A MOST RIDICULOUS LITTLE BIRD	314	MEMORY YOUTH		20
IN A MOST DESOLATE STONY PLACE,	325	ROBERT GREGORY		30
MOST COURTEOUS TO SLOW AGE AND HASTY YOUTH,	339	SHEP GOATHERD		19
ALL THE WILD WITCHES, THOSE MOST NOBLE LADIES,	343	DEJECTION		4
WHERE WHO HAS SERVED THE MOST IS MOST DEFAMED,	351	PEOPLE		4
WHERE WHO HAS SERVED THE MOST IS MOST DEFAMED,	351	PEOPLE		4
I MOURN FOR THAT MOST LONELY THING: AND YET GOD'S WILL BE DONE!	354	HIS PHOENIX		31
MOST OUT OF REACH? AND IS THAT SPECTRAL IMAGE	368	EGO DOMINUS		25
THE MOST EXALTED LADY LOVED BY A MAN.	369	EGO DOMINUS		37
THOSE MEN THAT IN THEIR WRITINGS ARE MOST WISE	370	EGO DOMINUS		68
AND LOOK MOST LIKE ME, BEING INDEED MY DOUBLE,	371	EGO DOMINUS		72
THE MOST UNLIKE, BEING MY ANTI-SELF,	371	EGO DOMINUS		74
HE FOLLOWS WHATEVER WHIM'S MOST DIFFICULT	374	PHASES OF MOON		40
CHOOSING WHATEVER TASK'S MOST DIFFICULT	376	PHASES OF MOON		91
BUT MOST TO ALCIBIADES.	380	SAINT HUNCH		16
AMID MOST LOVELY PLACES: SMITTEN AS THOUGH	389	IMAGE PAST		13
HE HAD DONE MOST BITTER WRONG	393	EASTER 1916		33
THAT MOST RESPECTED LADY'S EVERY WISH,	410	TOWER		29
DOES THE IMAGINATION DWELL THE MOST	413	TOWER		113
CONSIDER MOST TO MAGNIFY, OR TO BLESS,	418	ANCEST HOUSES		39
SOUL'S BEAUTY BEING MOST ADORED,	421	MY TABLE		22
FOR THE MOST RICH INHERITOR,	422	MY TABLE		25
AND I, THAT COUNT MYSELF MOST PROSPEROUS,	423	MY DESCENDANTS		19
OF SOME MOST HAUGHTY DEED OR THOUGHT	436	FOR MY SON		13
HOW SUCH A MAN PLEASED WOMEN MOST	458	SECRETS OF OLD		13
HOW SUCH A MAN HAD PLEASURED MOST	458	SECRETS OF OLD	V	13
OUR MOST RENOWNED PATRIOTS STAND,	460	THREE MONUMENT		2
PHILOSOPHERS SHOULD PRAISE THAT LOVE THE MOST,	465	HARUN RASHID	V	97
OLD FELLOW-STUDENT, WHOSE MOST PATIENT EAR	468	HARUN RASHID		167
OLD FELLOW STUDENT, WHOSE MOST PATIENT EAR	468	HARUN RASHID	V	167
WHETHER OF HER OR GOD HE THOUGHT THE MOST,	471	ALL SOUL NIGHT		32
OR INTO THAT MOST FECUND DITCH OF ALL,	479	SELF AND SOUL		61
THE BOOK OF THE PEOPLE: WHATEVER MOST CAN BLESS	492	COOLE BALLYLEE		44
WHAT SEEMS MOST WELCOME IN THE TOMB--PLAY A PREDESTINED PART.	503	VACILLATION		86
THAT THE MOST COULD PLEASURE YOU,	525	DANCING DAYS		11
WHAT MOST COULD SHAKE HIS SOUL!	529	TOM CRUACHAN		3
WHAT MOST CAN SHAKE HIS SOUL!	529	TOM CRUACHAN	V	3
WHAT LIVELY LAD MOST PLEASURED ME	538	LAST CONFESS		1
SUCH A MAN THE MOST."	539	MEETING		12
A MOST ASTONISHING THING--	567	FROM JAPANESE		1
OF THAT MOST SENSUOUS SILENCE OF THE NIGHT	579	DOR WELLESLEY		6
TO THIS MOST GALLANT GENTLEMAN	582	ROGER CASEMENT		23
DO MOST EXCITE MY SPLEEN,	599	STONE CROSS		18
THINK WHERE MAN'S GLORY MOST BEGINS AND ENDS,	604	GALLERY REVIS		54
MOVE MOST GENTLY IF MOVE YOU MUST	617	LONG-LEG FLY		13
YET A MOST GENTLE WOMAN: WHO CAN TELL	618	BRONZE HEAD		10
SADNESS, SOUL OF JOY MOST DEEP,	647	ISLE STAT I 1		74
OF FLIGHT ARE DONE. MOST FAIR OF ALL WHO GRAZE	649	ISLE STAT I 1		118
NASCHINA, HAIL! MOST FAIR OF ALL WHO GRAZE	649	ISLE STAT I 1		120
OR SOME SMALL BEAST MOST WONDERFULLY FURR'D,	650	ISLE STAT I 1		148
OH, BOY, I'M BOUND ON A MOST FEARFUL QUEST:	653	ISLE STAT I 2		31
THIS BLOSSOM IS MOST NEAR. STATUE! OH, THOU	657	ISLE STAT I 3		72
YEA, NOBLE AND MOST KNIGHTLY HATH IT BEEN.	679	ISLE STAT II 3		320
THE ORB OF THE MOST INNER LIVING HEART	689	NETTLESHIP		15
HE WAS A MAN MOST LEARNED AND MOST MILD,	692	MOSADA 1		51
HE WAS A MAN MOST LEARNED AND MOST MILD,	692	MOSADA 1		51
THE PROUDEST OR MOST COY OF SPIRIT THINGS,	720	WITCH VIVIEN		7
WANDERS AND WAILS BEFORE MY HEART MOST TRUE	738	YOU ARE SAD		8
THAT THEY FOLLOW, FOR AT MOST	776	AGAINST WITCH		28

MOTH

	PAGE	TITLE		LINE
AS ANY RUDDY MOTH, LOOKED DOWN ON US:	34	OISIN 2		72
AS LIKE A RUDDY MOTH THEY WAVED AND FLUTTERED.	34	OISIN 2	V	72
THAT HAS MADE FAT THE MURDEROUS MOTH:	156	FORGOT BEAUTY		8
AT THE MOTH HOUR AND HID IT IN HER BOSOM.	199	ARROW	V	6
WHAT BRUSHES FLY AND MOTH ASIDE?	625	NATIVITY		7

537

```
                                                       PAGE      TITLE       LINE
MOTHER      SEE FOSTER-MOTHER
    "MY FATHER AND MY MOTHER ARE  . . . . . . . . . .      5 OISIN 1           46
    "I HAVE LONG WAITED, MOTHER, FOR THAT WORD!  . . .    107 CUCHULAIN SEA    22
    "LONG HAVE I WAITED, MOTHER, FOR THOSE WORDS, . . .   107 CUCHULAIN SEA  V 22
    "I HAVE LONG WAITED, MOTHER, FOR THOSE WORDS! . . .   107 CUCHULAIN SEA  V 22
    DID THE KISS OF MOTHER MARY  . . . . . . . . . .      124 CATHLEEN PARA     9
    HERS THE KISS OF MOTHER MARY, . . . . . . . . . .     124 CATHLEEN PARA     9
    IS COMELIER THAN CANDLES AT MOTHER MARY'S FEET.  . .  147 UNAPPEAS HOST    12
    YOUR MOTHER EIRE IS ALWAYS YOUNG, . . . . . . . .     148 INTO TWILIGHT     5
    THY MOTHER ERI IS ALWAYS YOUNG,  . . . . . . . .      148 INTO TWILIGHT  V  5
    THE SONG OF THE OLD MOTHER  . . . . . . . . . .       150 OLD MOTHER        T
    "PRAISE GOD AND GOD'S MOTHER," DATHI SAID,  . . .     167 BLESSED          17
    "FOR GOD AND GOD'S MOTHER HAVE SENT  . . . . . .      167 BLESSED          18
    O WHERE IS OUR MOTHER OF PEACE . . . . . . . . .      171 MAID QUIET     V  1
    AND OUR MOTHER OF PEACE HAS FORGOT ME  . . . . .      171 MAID QUIET     V  7
    FASHIONED TO BE THE MOTHER OF STRONG CHILDREN!  . .   181 QUEEN MAEVE      26
    THE ALE CUP IS MY FATHER AND MY MOTHER. . . . . .     222 SHADOW WATER B V 11B
    MY MOTHER TOLD ME THAT THERE IS NOT ONE  . . . .      224 SHADOW WATER B   45
    MY MOTHER DANDLED ME AND SANG. . . . . . . . . .      308 PLAYER QUEEN      1
    "HE WENT AWAY," MY MOTHER SANG, . . . . . . . .       308 PLAYER QUEEN      5
    "WHEN SHE WAS GOT," MY MOTHER SANG, . . . . . .       308 PLAYER QUEEN     13
    SUFFER AS YOUR MOTHER SUFFERED, . . . . . . . .       313 TWO YEAR LATER    9
    I HAD MY SHARE OF MOTHER WIT! . . . . . . . . .       313 MEMORY YOUTH   V  3
    NOT EVEN YOUR OWN MOTHER . . . . . . . . . . .        336 YOUNG GIRL        4
    UNDER HIS FINGERS.  I HAD IT FROM HIS MOTHER, . .     339 SHEP GOATHERD    26
    MAY BE A QUIET THOUGHT TO WIFE AND MOTHER, . . .      343 SHEP GOATHERD   118
    BANISHED HEROIC MOTHER MOON AND VANISHED, . . . .     344 DEJECTION         9
    HEROIC MOTHER MOON HAS VANISHED, . . . . . . . .      344 DEJECTION      V  9
    AS A MOTHER NAMES HER CHILD . . . . . . . . . .       394 EASTER 1916      62
    THE MOTHER BIRD WILL REST . . . . . . . . . . .       415 TOWER           170
    THE MOTHER BIRDS BRING GRUBS AND FLIES. . . . . .     424 STARES NEST       3
    CAN LEAVE THE MOTHER, MURDERED AT HER DOOR, . . .     429 NINETEEN 19      27
    THAT HIS MOTHER MAY NOT LACK . . . . . . . . .        435 FOR MY SON        7
    HIS MAJESTIC MOTHER SAT . . . . . . . . . . .         440 WISDOM           11
    WHAT YOUTHFUL MOTHER, A SHAPE UPON HER LAP . . .      444 SCHOOL CHILDR    33
    WHERE THE GREAT MOTHER, MOURNING FOR HER DAUGHTER . . 447 COLONUS PRAISE   19
    THE MOTHER OF GOD . . . . . . . . . . . . . .         499 MOTHER OF GOD     T
    THAT WOMAN, THE GREAT MOTHER IMAGING, . . . . . .     541 PARN FUNERAL 1   13
    RECALL HIS TRINITY.  A FATHER, MOTHER, CHILD (A DAUGHTER   556 RIBH PATRICK V   2
        OR A SON),
    CAN TOUCH BY MOTHER WIT . . . . . . . . . . .         589 OLD WICKED MAN   40
    AND THAT SHOULD MOTHER SEEK HER SON SHE'D HAVE BUT LITTLE  593 PILGRIM      12
        LUCK
    FOR MOTHER EVE'S WINNING . . . . . . . . . . .        654 ISLE STAT I 2    61
    BUT A MOTHER PANTHER NEVER . . . . . . . . . .        658 ISLE STAT I 3    92
    DOWN TO THE MOTHER OF THE FOILED AND DEAD. . . . .    688 TWO TITANS       50
    MY MOTHER DREW FORTH FROM THE LONG GRASS  . . . .     708 FAIRY PEDANT     23
    THERE LIVE HIS SISTER AND HIS MOTHER.  HIGH . . . .   710 FERENCZ RENYI  V 25
    OF MIDDLE AGE.  "HIS SISTER HERE AND MOTHER." . . .   711 FERENCZ RENYI    53
    THAT ANCIENT MOTHER CRIES, "SPEAK NOT, MY SON. . .    711 FERENCZ RENYI    56
    HUSH'D THE FISHERS, TILL A MOTHER CALLS BY NAME HER DROWNED  719 PHANTOM SHIP  23
        SON!
    THEN EACH WIFE AND MAID AND MOTHER CALLS BY NAME      719 PHANTOM SHIP     24
        SOME DROWNED ONE.
    BY THE SLOW HEAVING OCEAN--MUMBLING MOTHER OF THE DEAD.  719 PHANTOM SHIP   34
    PRAYED BESIDE THE OCEAN, THE OLD MUMBLING MOTHER OF THE   719 PHANTOM SHIP V 34
        DEAD.
    SHE PRAYS FOR FATHER, MOTHER DEAR, . . . . . . .      735 IN CHURCH         1
    HER PRAYER FOR FATHER, MOTHER DEAR, . . . . . .       736 IN CHURCH        13
    THE MOTHER OF THE STARS WEEPS TOO, . . . . . . .      738 YOU ARE SAD       2
    THE MOTHER OF THE WIND MOURNS TOO, . . . . . . .      738 YOU ARE SAD       6
    THE MOTHER OF THE WAVE SIGHS TOO, . . . . . . .       738 YOU ARE SAD      10
    I SAT BESIDE MY FOSTER MOTHER, AND NOW . . . . .      762 SHADOW WATER A V 292
    MY FOSTER MOTHER SANG IN AN OLD RHYME . . . . . .     763 SHADOW WATER A V 314
MOTHERHOOD
    PRIMORDIAL MOTHERHOOD FORSAKE HIS LIMBS, THE CHILD    559 MAGIC DRUM        2
        NO LONGER REST,
MOTHER-OF-PEARL
    WITH THE DELICATE MOTHER-OF-PEARL, . . . . . . .      509 JANE REPROVED    10
MOTHER'S     SEE FOSTER-MOTHER'S
    ANOTHER FILLS YOUR MIND.  MY MOTHER'S NAME. . . .      71 ANASHU VIJAYA    16
    SOME OTHER FILLS YOUR MIND.  MY MOTHER'S NAME. . .     71 ANASHU VIJAYA  V 16
    O WHAT TO ME MY MOTHER'S CARE, . . . . . . . .        151 HEART OF WOMAN    5
    THERE WAS NO MOTHER'S SON BUT SAID, . . . . . .       253 HIS DREAM         6
    HAS MADDENED EVERY MOTHER'S SON"! . . . . . . .       290 SEPTEMBER 1913   29
    HE DREAMS HIMSELF HIS MOTHER'S PRIDE, . . . . . .     343 SHEP GOATHERD   110
    DROVE HORROR FROM HIS MOTHER'S BREAST. . . . . .      440 WISDOM           20
    THAT ANIMATE A MOTHER'S REVERIES, . . . . . . .       445 SCHOOL CHILDR    51
    PERCHED IN SOME WINDOW OF HER MOTHER'S HOUSE . . .    466 HARUN RASHID    106
    I CARRY FROM MY MOTHER'S WOMB . . . . . . . .         506 REMORSE SPEECH   14
    IN MY MOTHER'S WOMB. . . . . . . . . . . . .          511 JANE AND JACK    12
    LIFT, EVERY MOTHER'S SON, . . . . . . . . . .         548 TO SAME TUNE 3 V 15
    MY FOSTER MOTHER'S GARDEN IN THE SOUTH . . . . .      758 SHADOW WATER A V 227
MOTHERS
    BOTH NUNS AND MOTHERS WORSHIP IMAGES, . . . . .       445 SCHOOL CHILDR    49
    THAT SICKENING NEAR THEIR MOTHERS LIE! . . . . .      717 FAIRY DOCTOR     16
MOTHER-WIT
    I HAD MY SHARE OF MOTHER-WIT, . . . . . . . .         313 MEMORY YOUTH      3
MOTH-HOUR
    AT THE MOTH-HOUR OF EVE, . . . . . . . . . . .        132 FR GILLIGAN       6
    AND THE MOTH-HOUR WENT FROM THE FIELDS, . . . . .     133 FR GILLIGAN      15
```

	PAGE	TITLE	LINE

MOTH-LIKE
AND MOTH-LIKE STARS WERE FLICKERING OUT, ...   149 WANDER AENGUS   6
GENTLY SHOOK THEIR MOTH-LIKE WINGS; . . . .   667 ISLE STAT II 3   26
MOTH'S
ARE DUST ON THE MOTH'S WING: THAT NOTHING MATTERS . . .   235 SHADOW WATER B   297
THAT HAVE BUILT ALL ARE DUST ON A MOTH'S WING. . . . .   757 SHADOW WATER A   205
MOTHS   SEE NIGHT-MOTHS
THAT FEED WHITE MOTHS BY SOME DE DANAAN SHRINE; . . . .   41 OISIN 2   186
FEEDING WHITE MOTHS AROUND SOME EASTERN SHRINE, ...   41 OISIN 2   V 186
WHEN THE MOTHS CAME ONCE MORE; . . . .   133 FR GILLIGAN   22
WHEN MOTHS CAME ONCE MORE, ...   133 FR GILLIGAN   V 22
AND WHEN WHITE MOTHS WERE ON THE WING, ...   149 WANDER AENGUS   5
AND STARS LIKE MOTHS WERE SHINING OUT, ...   149 WANDER AENGUS   V   6
THE MOTHS ARE WHEN THEY ARE BURNED? . . . .   313 TWO YEAR LATER   4
A COUPLE OF NIGHT MOTHS ARE ON THE WING, ...   482 BLOOD AND MOON   46
AS MOTHS WITH BROKEN WINGS, AND AS WE SIT . . . . . .   671 ISLE STAT II 3   142
LIKE SMALL BROWN MOTHS, A-TREMBLE. "RENYI SAY . . . .   713 FERENCZ RENYI   82
LIKE SMALL BROWN MOTHS, A-TREMBLE CEASELESSLY. . . . .   713 FERENCZ RENYI   V 82
MOTION
WHAT MOTION OF THE SUN OR STREAM . . . .   507 STREAM AND SUN   11
MOTIONED
SHE MOTIONED HIM AFAR, AND ROSE AND SPOKE: . . . . . .   280 TWO KINGS   68
MOTIONLESS
THEIR MOTIONLESS EYEBALLS OF SPIRITS . . . .   55 OISIN 3   121
WITH MOTIONLESS HEAD ERECT. . . . .   383 VISION ROBART   32
MOTIONS
THROUGH INTRICATE MOTIONS RAN . . . .   506 STREAM AND SUN   1
MOTLEY
BUT LIVED WHERE MOTLEY IS WORN: . . . .   392 EASTER 1916   14
MOTORS
OR THE MAN THAT MADE THE MOTORS? . . . .   627 STATES HOLIDAY   20
MOULD
. . . LURED FROM HIS LAIR IN THE MOULD: . . . . . .   53 OISIN 3   99
THE HEAVY STEPS OF THE PLOUGHMAN, SPLASHING THE WINTRY   143 ROSE IN HEART   3
  MOULD,
THE HEAVY STEPS OF THE PLOUGHMAN SPLASHING THE WINTER   143 ROSE IN HEART V   3
  MOULD,
FROM BEAUTY THAT IS CAST OUT OF A MOULD . . . . . .   334 LIVING BEAUTY   4
FAILURE FOR GLORY DOWN ON THEE, AND MOULD . . . . . .   688 TWO TITANS   54
MOULDED
IN MOULDED PLASTER OR IN CARVEN STONE? . . . .   327 ROBERT GREGORY   77
HIS BODY MOULDED FROM WITHIN HIS BODY . . . .   374 PHASES OF MOON   43
HAS MOULDED THE HARD YEARS. . . . .   738 MOURN THEN ON   8
MOULDERING
AMONG THE MOULDERING OF ANCIENT WOODS . . . .   74 ANASHU VIJAYA   61
THAT SHAKES A MOULDERING COBWEB FROM THE RAFTER: . . . .   130 BOOK STORIES   19
AND SHAKE A MOULDERING COBWEB FROM THE RAFTER, ...   130 BOOK STORIES   V 19
MOULDING
MOULDING IT OF DUST OR SAND, ...   600 SPIRIT MEDIUM   14
MOUND   SEE BURIAL-MOUND
AND RAISED ABOVE HER MOUND . . . .   123 DREAM OF DEATH   6
A BOY OF TWENTY YEARS:--A MOUND AND STONE . . . . . .   276 TWO KINGS   V   F
AND SHOULD HE DIE TO HEAP HIS BURIAL MOUND . . . . . .   280 TWO KINGS   V 82
THAN MOUND AND STONE THAT KEEP ALL VIRTUE IN, ...   281 TWO KINGS   106
WHEN NETTLES WAVE UPON A SHAPELESS MOUND . . . . . .   489 COOLE PARK 29   27
A MOUND OF REFUSE OR THE SWEEPINGS OF A STREET, ...   630 CIRCUS ANIMALS   35
A MOUND OF REFUSE OR THE SWEEPINGS OF THE STREET, . . .   630 CIRCUS ANIMALS V 35
MOUND'S
THAT THE IMMEDICABLE MOUND'S BEYOND . . . .   282 TWO KINGS   129
MOUNDS   SEE BURIAL-MOUNDS
AND PASSING THE FIRBOLGS' BURIAL MOUNDS, ...   3 OISIN 1   V 16
WHERE MEN HAVE HEAPED NO BURIAL MOUNDS, ...   8 OISIN 1   V 82
MOUNT
"O OISIN, MOUNT BY ME AND RIDE . . . .   8 OISIN 1   80
MOUNT MY WHITE STEED, FOR THE FAIRY STATE . . . . . .   9 OISIN 1   V 103
FOR NO MAN'S CRY SHALL EVER MOUNT SO FAR: . . . . . .   36 OISIN 2   108
NOR NO MAN'S CRY SHALL EVER MOUNT SO FAR: . . . . . .   36 OISIN 2   V 108
ALL SUDDENLY MOUNT . . . .   322 SWANS AT COOLE   10
O BID ME MOUNT AND SAIL UP THERE . . . .   458 HIS WILDNESS   1
WHAT MADE THEM MOUNT AND WHAT MADE THEM COME, ...   549 SEVERED HEAD   V   8
HERMITS UPON MOUNT MERU OR EVEREST, ...   563 MERU   9
HE THAT'S MOUNTING UP MUST ON HIS NEIGHBOUR MOUNT, . . .   580 CURSE CROMWELL   11
HER HEART MOUNT UP ON HIGH: . . . .   608 SONGS BURDEN 3   22
AS FAIR AS ANY THAT ON IDA'S MOUNT . . . .   650 ISLE STAT I 1   134
MOUNTAIN
AND THERE AT THE FOOT OF THE MOUNTAIN, ...   60 OISIN 3   185
A MURMURING A MOUNTAIN TUNE, ...   85 MAD KING GOLL V 52
MURMURING A MOUNTAIN TUNE, ...   85 MAD KING GOLL V 52
HAD COME THROUGH THE MOUNTAIN SIDE, ...   171 MAID QUIET   V 4B
AND TRAMPLED THE MOUNTAIN AWAY, ...   171 MAID QUIET   V 4C
HAD HAMMERED OUT ON MOUNTAIN TOP . . . .   271 GREY ROCK   23
IN AFRICA ON MOUNTAIN OF THE MOON, ...   277 TWO KINGS   V 20
THE MOUNTAIN TOMB . . . .   311 MOUNTAIN TOMB   T
THE CATARACT SMOKES UPON THE MOUNTAIN SIDE, ...   311 MOUNTAIN TOMB   3
THE CATARACT SMOKES ON THE MOUNTAIN SIDE. . . . . . .   311 MOUNTAIN TOMB   3
HAD SOUNDED BETTER TO YOUR MOUNTAIN FANCY. . . . . .   341 SHEP GOATHERD   61
THEY SAY THAT ON YOUR BARREN MOUNTAIN RIDGE . . . . .   342 SHEP GOATHERD   79
TO KNOW THE MOUNTAIN AND THE VALLEY HAVE GRIEVED . . . .   343 SHEP GOATHERD   117
TO KNOW THE MOUNTAIN AND THE VALLEY GRIEVE . . . . .   343 SHEP GOATHERD V 117
BECAUSE THE MOUNTAIN GRASS . . . .   350 MEMORY   4
WHERE THE MOUNTAIN HARE HAS LAIN. . . . .   350 MEMORY   6

		PAGE	TITLE		LINE

MOUNTAIN   (CONTINUED)

	PAGE	TITLE		LINE
OR IMAGE, FROM BEYOND THE LOADSTONE MOUNTAIN,	371	ON GOING HOUSE		11
FROM MOUNTAIN STEEP TO STEEP.	399	BREAK OF DAY		25
THAT CLIMB THE MOUNTAIN SIDE,	416	TOWER	V	175
CRIED, CASTING OFF THE MOUNTAIN SNOW,	502	VACILLATION		60
THE MOUNTAIN THROWS A SHADOW,	519	LOVES LONENESS		7
FROM MOUNTAIN CREST TO CREST.	536	PARTING		10
THE MEET'S UPON THE MOUNTAIN SIDE.	549	SEVERED HEAD	V	6
THERE, ON THE MOUNTAIN AND THE SKY,	567	LAPIS LAZULI		51
FROM MOUNTAIN TO MOUNTAIN RIDE THE FIERCE HORSEMEN.	605	SONGS BURDEN 1		9
FROM MOUNTAIN TO MOUNTAIN RIDE THE FIERCE HORSEMEN.	605	SONGS BURDEN 1		9
FROM MOUNTAIN TO MOUNTAIN RIDE THE FIERCE HORSEMEN.	606	SONGS BURDEN 1		18
FROM MOUNTAIN TO MOUNTAIN RIDE THE FIERCE HORSEMEN.	606	SONGS BURDEN 1		18
FROM MOUNTAIN TO MOUNTAIN RIDE THE FIERCE HORSEMEN.	606	SONGS BURDEN 1		27
FROM MOUNTAIN TO MOUNTAIN RIDE THE FIERCE HORSEMEN.	606	SONGS BURDEN 1		27
FROM MOUNTAIN TO MOUNTAIN RIDE THE FIERCE HORSEMEN.	607	SONGS BURDEN 2		9
FROM MOUNTAIN TO MOUNTAIN RIDE THE FIERCE HORSEMEN.	607	SONGS BURDEN 2		9
FROM MOUNTAIN TO MOUNTAIN RIDE THE FIERCE HORSEMEN.	607	SONGS BURDEN 2		18
FROM MOUNTAIN TO MOUNTAIN RIDE THE FIERCE HORSEMEN.	607	SONGS BURDEN 2		18
FROM MOUNTAIN TO MOUNTAIN RIDE THE FIERCE HORSEMEN.	607	SONGS BURDEN 2		27
FROM MOUNTAIN TO MOUNTAIN RIDE THE FIERCE HORSEMEN.	607	SONGS BURDEN 2		27
FROM MOUNTAIN TO MOUNTAIN RIDE THE FIERCE HORSEMEN.	608	SONGS BURDEN 3		9
FROM MOUNTAIN TO MOUNTAIN RIDE THE FIERCE HORSEMEN.	608	SONGS BURDEN 3		9
FROM MOUNTAIN TO MOUNTAIN RIDE THE FIERCE HORSEMEN.	608	SONGS BURDEN 3		18
FROM MOUNTAIN TO MOUNTAIN RIDE THE FIERCE HORSEMEN.	608	SONGS BURDEN 3		18
FROM MOUNTAIN TO MOUNTAIN RIDE THE FIERCE HORSEMEN.	608	SONGS BURDEN 3		27
FROM MOUNTAIN TO MOUNTAIN RIDE THE FIERCE HORSEMEN.	608	SONGS BURDEN 3		27
DOWN THE MOUNTAIN WALLS	612	NEWS ORACLE		30
WHAT MARCHES THROUGH THE MOUNTAIN PASS?	614	MARCH SONGS 2		7
WHAT MARCHES DOWN THE MOUNTAIN PASS?	615	MARCH SONGS 2		17
WHAT MARCHES DOWN THE MOUNTAIN PASS?	615	MARCH SONGS 2		27
CRAZY JANE ON THE MOUNTAIN	628	JANE MOUNTAIN		T
LAST NIGHT I LAY ON THE MOUNTAIN,	628	JANE MOUNTAIN		11
OLD BONES UPON THE MOUNTAIN SHAKE.	635	BLACK TOWER		10
OLD BONES UPON THE MOUNTAIN SHAKE.	636	BLACK TOWER		20
OLD BONES UPON THE MOUNTAIN SHAKE.	636	BLACK TOWER		30
IN AUTUMN, WHEN FAR DOWN THE MOUNTAIN SLOPES	690	MOSADA 1		12
WHERE HOMES ONCE WHITENED VALE AND MOUNTAIN CREST:	709	FERENCZ RENYI		3
OR YONDER MOUNTAIN. WHERE? THOU SHALT BE FREE--	710	FERENCZ RENYI	V	15
THE MOUNTAIN OF THE GODS, THE UNAPPEASABLE GODS	764	SHADOW WATER A		332
AMONG HIGH MOUNTAINS, AND THE MOUNTAIN ROBBERS	768	SHADOW WATER A		411
OR GO BESIDE HIM TO HIS MOUNTAIN WARS.	768	SHADOW WATER A		414

MOUNTAINOUS

	PAGE	TITLE		LINE
WHERE GODS ARE BROODING IN A MOUNTAINOUS PLACE	757	SHADOW WATER A		198

MOUNTAIN'S

	PAGE	TITLE		LINE
FIRST TROD ON THE MOUNTAIN'S HEAD	488	CRAZED MOON		9
UPON THE MOUNTAIN'S BROW. YONDER HE TREADS	703	MOSADA 3		114

MOUNTAINS

	PAGE	TITLE		LINE
SOME DANCED LIKE SHADOWS ON THE MOUNTAINS,	25	OISIN 1		388
THEIR HAIR ALONG THE MOUNTAINS ROLLED AND FILLED	74	ANASHU VIJAYA		71
WOLF-BREEDING MOUNTAINS, GALLERIED EMAN,	81	MAD KING GOLL	V	2
AND PACED UPON THE MOUNTAINS OVERHEAD	121	YOU ARE OLD		11
HE PACED UPON THE MOUNTAINS FAR ABOVE,	121	YOU ARE OLD	V	11
AND THE MOUNTAINS AND WOODS	142	MOODS		3
THE MOUNTAINS AND WOODS	142	MOODS	V	3
AND TRAMPLED THE MOUNTAINS AWAY,	171	MAID QUIET	V	4C
AMONG THE AFRICAN MOUNTAINS OF THE MOON,	277	TWO KINGS		20
AND ALONG THE MOUNTAINS PASS,	705	DAWN-SONG		12
OR YONDER MOUNTAINS. WHERE? THOU SHALT BE FREE--	710	FERENCZ RENYI		15
YE ON THE BROAD HIGH MOUNTAINS OF OLD ERI,	737	MOURN THEN ON		1
AMONG HIGH MOUNTAINS, AND THE MOUNTAIN ROBBERS	768	SHADOW WATER A		411

MOUNTAIN-SIDE

	PAGE	TITLE		LINE
CLIMBING THE MOUNTAIN-SIDE,	416	TOWER		175
THE MEET'S UPON THE MOUNTAIN-SIDE.	549	SEVERED HEAD		6

MOUNTAIN-TOP

	PAGE	TITLE		LINE
I DRAGGED FROM GOBAN'S MOUNTAIN-TOP	304	HOUR DAWN		50

MOUNTED   SEE HALF-MOUNTED BELL-MOUNTED

	PAGE	TITLE		LINE
AND THEN I MOUNTED AND SHE BOUND ME	9	OISIN 1		106
LIES FAR." I MOUNTED, AND SHE BOUND ME	9	OISIN 1	V	106
WE MOUNTED ON THE STAIR, THE WHITE STEED TYING,	32	OISIN 2	V	46
HALF IN THE UNVESSELLED SEA. WE'D MOUNTED FAR:	32	OISIN 2	V	47
THEN, MOUNTED ON A HERON, O'ER THE DEEP	33	OISIN 2	V	64
SOBBED INTO SILENCE. WE HAD MOUNTED FEET	33	OISIN 2	V	68E
I MOUNTED, AND WE PASSED OVER THE LONE	45	OISIN 2		231
I MOUNTED, AND WE RODE ACROSS THE LONE	45	OISIN 2	V	231
BUT, THE BIRD IN MY FINGERS, I MOUNTED,	54	OISIN 3		111
BUT, THE BIRD IN MY FINGERS, I MOUNTED, MINDFUL ONLY TO LAUNCH	54	OISIN 3	V	111
WHEN THEY HAVE MOUNTED UP,	415	TOWER		169
THOUGH MOUNTED IN THAT SADDLE HOMER RODE	492	COOLE BALLYLEE		47
MOUNTED THE MARE OF TIME,	529	TOM CRUACHAN		5

MOUNTING

	PAGE	TITLE		LINE
AT SUDDEN THUNDER OF THE MOUNTING SWAN	490	COOLE BALLYLEE		14
HE THAT'S MOUNTING UP MUST ON HIS NEIGHBOUR MOUNT,	580	CURSE CROMWELL		11

MOUNTS

	PAGE	TITLE		LINE
AND MOUNTS MORE DIZZY HIGH THE MORE IT RAINS	417	ANCEST HOUSES		5
THAT JUGGLING NATURE MOUNTS, HER COIL IN THEIR EMBRACES TWINED.	556	RIBH PATRICK		9

MOURN

	PAGE	TITLE		LINE
BOAST NOT, NOR MOURN WITH DROOPING HEAD	11	OISIN 1		129
LOST NIAM MOURN AND SAY, "AH, LOVE, WE GO	46	OISIN 2	V	245B

```
                                                        PAGE      TITLE          LINE
MOURN   (CONTINUED)
     IN BOSOM AND HAIR.  "AH, DO NOT MOURN," HE SAID,  . . . .    80 EPHEMERA           20
     IN BOSOM AND HAIR.  THEN HE: "LET US NOT MOURN  . . . .      80 EPHEMERA        V  20
     I MOURN FOR THAT MOST LONELY THING: AND YET GOD'S WILL      354 HIS PHOENIX         31
          BE DONE!
     MOURN--AND THEN ONWARD!  . . . . . . . . . . .             737 MOURN THEN ON        T
     MOURN ALL THE NIGHT AND DAY,  . . . . . . . . .            737 MOURN THEN ON        2
     MOURN YE ON GRASS-GREEN PLAINS OF ERI FATED,  . . . .      738 MOURN THEN ON        9
     MOURN--AND THEN ONWARD, THERE IS NO RETURNING  . . . .     738 MOURN THEN ON       13
MOURNFUL
     MOURNFUL, AND GATHERED ON THE SANDS:  . . . . . . .         10 OISIN 1         V 111B
     HEARING AEDH TOUCH THE MOURNFUL STRINGS OF GOLD."  . . .    35 OISIN 2            87
     BACCHANT AND MOURNFUL, PASSING TO AND FRO  . . . . .        39 OISIN 2           161
     CEASE, CEASE, O MOURNFUL, LAUGHING FENIAN HORN!  . . . .    43 OISIN 2           213
     AH, CEASE, THOU MOURNFUL, LAUGHING FENIAN HORN!  . . . .    43 OISIN 2         V 213
     AH, CEASE, YOU MOURNFUL, LAUGHING FENIAN HORN!  . . . .     43 OISIN 2         V 213
     IMMEDIATE, MOURNFUL, WHITE WITH SUDDEN CARES,  . . . .      44 OISIN 2         V 229A
     WATCHED ME WITH MOURNFUL WONDER OUT OF THE WELLS OF HIS     51 OISIN 3            60
          EYES.
     BUT LIFT A MOURNFUL ULALU,  . . . . . . . . . . .           86 MAD KING GOLL       68
     THE BLIND HOUND WITH MOURNFUL DIN  . . . . . . . .          99 FOXHUNTER           45
     THE OLDEST HOUND WITH MOURNFUL DIN,  . . . . . . .          99 FOXHUNTER       V   45
     STARED ON THE MOURNFUL WONDER OF HIS EYES,  . . . . .      108 CUCHULAIN SEA       41
     MORE MOURNFUL THAN THE DEPTH OF STARRY SKIES,  . . . .     108 CUCHULAIN SEA   V   42
     UPON THE MOURNFUL WONDER OF HIS EYES,  . . . . . .         108 CUCHULAIN SEA   V   42
     FOR THESE RED LIPS, WITH ALL THEIR MOURNFUL PRIDE,  . .    111 ROSE OF WORLD        2
     MOURNFUL THAT NO NEW WONDER MAY BETIDE,  . . . . .         111 ROSE OF WORLD        3
     A GIRL AROSE THAT HAD RED MOURNFUL LIPS  . . . . .         120 SORROW OF LOVE       5
     AND THEN YOU CAME WITH THOSE RED MOURNFUL LIPS,  . . .     120 SORROW OF LOVE  V    5
     AND GAZED UPON THE MOURNFUL STARS ABOVE,  . . . . .        123 DREAM OF DEATH      11
     AND HEARD THE MOURNFUL BREEZE.  . . . . . . . . .          123 DREAM OF DEATH      12
     CARRY ALL THAT MOURNFUL BEAUTY  . . . . . . . . .          124 CATHLEEN PARA        7
     I HEAR THE HARP-STRING PRAISE THEM, OR HEAR THEIR MOURNFUL 210 UNDER THE MOON      16
          TALK.
     I HEAR THE HARP STRINGS PRAISE THEM, OR HEAR THEIR MOURNFUL 210 UNDER THE MOON V   16
          TALK.
     I HEAR THE HARPSTRING PRAISE THEM OR HEAR THEIR MOURNFUL    210 UNDER THE MOON V   16
          TALK.
     I HEAR THE HARP STRING PRAISE THEM OR HEAR THEIR MOURNFUL   210 UNDER THE MOON V   16
          TALK.
     SO MOURNFUL THAT IT SEEMED THE CRY OF ONE  . . . . .       278 TWO KINGS           39
     ONE ASKS FOR MOURNFUL MELODIES:  . . . . . . . .           567 LAPIS LAZULI        53
     AND LET THE TALE BE MOURNFUL EACH ONE TELLS.  . . . .      663 ISLE STAT II 2      36
     NOW THEIR SONGS ARE MOURNFUL WHOLLY  . . . . . . .         667 ISLE STAT II 3      32
     HUNG ON HIS DOUBLET--DEAR AND MOURNFUL CHILD,  . . . .     691 MOSADA 1            35
     TO THE EVER-LONGING AND MOURNFUL SPIRIT SAY.  . . . .      734 QUATRAIN APHOR      12
     MOURNFUL UNDER MOURNFUL STARS.  . . . . . . . . .          737 IN FIRELIGHT         4
     MOURNFUL UNDER MOURNFUL STARS.  . . . . . . . . .          737 IN FIRELIGHT         4
     (AH, MOURNFUL DANAAN QUICKEN TREE!)  . . . . . . .         742 DANAAN QUICK         6
     (AH, MOURNFUL DANAAN QUICKEN TREE!)  . . . . . . .         743 DANAAN QUICK        12
     (AH, MOURNFUL DANAAN QUICKEN TREE!)  . . . . . . .         743 DANAAN QUICK        18
     (AH, MOURNFUL DANAAN QUICKEN TREE!)  . . . . . . .         743 DANAAN QUICK        24
     (AH, MOURNFUL DANAAN QUICKEN TREE!)  . . . . . . .         743 DANAAN QUICK        30
MOURNING
     WHERE THE GREAT MOTHER, MOURNING FOR HER DAUGHTER  . .     447 COLONUS PRAISE      19
MOURNS
     THE LOVER MOURNS FOR THE LOSS OF LOVE  . . . . . .         152 LOSS OF LOVE         T
     HE MOURNS FOR THE CHANGE THAT HAS COME UPON HIM . . .      153 CHANGE BELOVED       T
     THE LOVER MOURNS BECAUSE OF HIS WANDERINGS  . . . .        171 MAID QUIET      V    T
     NOR AN UNLAUGHING MOUTH, BUT MINE THAT MOURNS,  . . .      285 TWO KINGS          184
     THE MOTHER OF THE WIND MOURNS TOO,  . . . . . . .          738 YOU ARE SAD          6
MOURTEEN
     MY BROTHER MOURTEEN IS WORN OUT  . . . . . . . . .         301 RUN PARADISE         8
MOUSE     SEE FIELD-MOUSE
     SLEEK AS ANY GRANARY MOUSE  . . . . . . . . . .              2 OISIN 1         V  7M
     MORE SLEEK THAN ANY GRANARY MOUSE,  . . . . . . .            4 OISIN 1            36
     SLEEK AS ANY GRANARY MOUSE,  . . . . . . . . . .             4 OISIN 1         V  37
     AND "A WEARINESS SOON IS MY SPEED," SAYS THE MOUSE,  . .    27 OISIN 1         V 417
     AND "MY SPEED IS A WEARINESS," FALTERS THE MOUSE,  . .      28 OISIN 1           421
     BRUSH LIGHTLY AS HAY MOUSE EARTH'S PEBBLES,  . . . .        56 OISIN 3         V 128
     THE FIELD MOUSE RUNNING BY ME IN THE GRASS,  . . . .       101 ROSE UPON ROOD  V  17
     FOR ALL ITS BRONZE AND MARBLE, 'S BUT A MOUSE.  . . .      418 ANCEST HOUSES       24
     WHERE NOTHING STIRS BUT A MOUSE.  . . . . . . . .          575 ACRE OF GRASS        6
     A MOUSE FROM HIS SLEEPING,  . . . . . . . . . .            672 ISLE STAT II 3     172
MOUSE-GREY
     WHERE MOUSE-GREY WATERS ARE FLOWING,  . . . . . . .        119 PITY OF LOVE         7
     THE MOUSE-GREY WATERS ON FLOWING.  . . . . . . . .         119 PITY OF LOVE    V    5
MOUSELIKE
     NOW OLD AND MOUSELIKE.  FOR AN ANSWERING SIGN  . . . .      36 OISIN 2         V  96
MOUSE-LIKE
     NOW IT IS OLD AND MOUSE-LIKE.  FOR A SIGN  . . . . .        36 OISIN 2            96
MOUSETAIL
     COME YOU, COLTSFOOT, MOUSETAIL, COME!  . . . . . .         727 LOVERS QUARREL      33
MOUTH     SEE HONEY-MOUTH CAVE-MOUTH
     AND A SAD MOUTH, THAT FEAR MADE TREMULOUS  . . . .          34 OISIN 2            71
     WENT THE LAUGHTER OF SCORN FROM MY MOUTH . . .              58 OISIN 3           168
     AND IN FOLDS ROUND HIS EYES AND HIS MOUTH,  . . . .         59 OISIN 3           174
     A LUG-WORM WITH ITS GREY AND MUDDY MOUTH  . . . . .        127 DREAM OF FAERY      18
     WITH A BLINK IN HIS EYES AT THE CAVE MOUTH,  . . . .       166 BLESSED         V    3
     BAILE, WHO HAD THE HONEY MOUTH:  . . . . . . . .           189 BAILE AILLINN        5
     YOUNG BAILE HONEY MOUTH, WHOM SOME  . . . . . . .          189 BAILE AILLINN   V   16
```

	PAGE	TITLE		LINE

MOUTH   (CONTINUED)

		PAGE	TITLE		LINE
I RUN TO BAILE HONEY MOUTH		191	BAILE AILLINN	V	48
AND NOW THAT HONEY MOUTH IS LAID		192	BAILE AILLINN	V	80
WINE COMES IN AT THE MOUTH		261	DRINKING SONG		1
I LIFT THE GLASS TO MY MOUTH,		261	DRINKING SONG		5
HE SAT WITH TIGHTENED REIN AND LOOSENED MOUTH		277	TWO KINGS		10
NOR DOOR, NOR MOUTH, NOR SLIPPER MADE A NOISE,		279	TWO KINGS		51
NOR AN UNLAUGHING MOUTH, BUT MINE THAT MOURNS,		285	TWO KINGS		184
YOUR ENEMY, AN OLD FOUL MOUTH, HAD SET		292	TO A SHADE		17
AN OLD FOUL MOUTH THAT ONCE CRIED OUT ON YOU		292	TO A SHADE	V	17
AN OLD FOUL MOUTH THAT SLANDERED YOU HAD SET		292	TO A SHADE	V	17
HELL MOUTH LAY OPEN NEAR THAT PLACE,		303	HOUR DAWN		25
BUT THE HELL MOUTH AT CRUACHAN		303	HOUR DAWN	V	24
I SHOULD NOT BE TOO DOWN IN THE MOUTH		306	HOUR DAWN		88
FROM THE HELL MOUTH AT CRUACHAN		307	HOUR DAWN	V	120
NOR MOUTH FROM KISSING, NOR FROM WINE UNWET,		311	MOUNTAIN TOMB		7
NOR MOUTH WITH KISSING NOR WITH WINE UNWET,		311	MOUNTAIN TOMB	V	7
NOR MOUTH WITH KISSING NOR WITH THE WINE UNWET,		311	MOUNTAIN TOMB	V	7
MOUTH MASTERED A SWEET SOUND,		331	ROUND TOWER		16
A POET'S MOUTH BE SILENT, FOR IN TRUTH		359	WAR POEM		2
A POET KEEP HIS MOUTH SHUT, FOR IN TRUTH		359	WAR POEM	V	2
OUT OF THE MOUTH OF PLENTY'S HORN,		405	FOR DAUGHTER		60
OUT OF A MEDIUM'S MOUTH,		439	FRAGMENTS		6
HARDLY DARED TO WET HIS MOUTH		454	EMPTY CUP		3
THE WILD STAG AND THE DOE, THAT MOUTH TO MOUTH		465	HARUN RASHID		101
THE WILD STAG AND THE DOE, THAT MOUTH TO MOUTH		465	HARUN RASHID		101
WHEN MAYBE THRICE IN EVERY MOON HER MOUTH		468	HARUN RASHID		162
A MOUTH THAT HAS NO MOISTURE AND NO BREATH		497	BYZANTIUM		13
. . . MOVE HIS MOUTH AND SINEWY TONGUE,		560	MAGIC DRUM		5
AND PART HIS FOAMING MOUTH WITH EAGER EYE--		688	TWO TITANS		46
WITH OPEN MOUTH AND BEATING HEART,		729	PRIEST FAIRY		32
HEART ON HEART, OR MOUTH ON MOUTH,		777	SONG DEIRDRE 2		9
HEART ON HEART, OR MOUTH ON MOUTH,		777	SONG DEIRDRE 2		9

MOUTHFUL

		PAGE	TITLE		LINE
I MADE IT OUT OF A MOUTHFUL OF AIR,		166	EVIL OF BELOV		5
THAT ANOTHER MOUTHFUL		454	EMPTY CUP		5
A MOUTHFUL HELD THE EXTREME OF LIFE AND DEATH,		619	BRONZE HEAD		14
A MOUTHFUL HOLD THE EXTREME OF LIFE AND DEATH.		619	BRONZE HEAD	V	14
O, WHAT IS LIFE BUT A MOUTHFUL OF AIR?		788	HAWTHORN TREE		9

MOUTHS

		PAGE	TITLE		LINE
THE MOUTHS THAT SPEAK, THE NOTES AND STRINGS,		212	BLESS PSALTER		2
AND BLEW YOU HITHER; AND THEIR MOUTHS HAVE PROMISED		237	SHADOW WATER B		325
AMONG THOSE MOUTHS THAT SING THEIR SWEETHEARTS' PRAISE,		285	TWO KINGS		185
WE POETS KEEP OUR MOUTHS SHUT, FOR IN TRUTH		359	WAR POEM	V	2
BREATHLESS MOUTHS MAY SUMMON;		497	BYZANTIUM		14
ABOVE THESE MEN WHOSE MOUTHS WERE SEALED		656	ISLE STAT I 3		27

MOVE

		PAGE	TITLE		LINE
. . . AND MOVE WHERE THE OLD MEN AND YOUNG		55	OISIN 3		114
FOR NO LIVE CREATURES LIVE THERE, NO WEASELS MOVE IN THE DARK;		56	OISIN 3		139
WATCHING THE BLESSED ONES MOVE FAR OFF, AND THE SMILE ON GOD'S FACE,		61	OISIN 3		199
. . . AND MARCH ON AS OXEN MOVE OVER YOUNG GRASS;		62	OISIN 3		211
FOR LONELY TO MOVE 'MONG THE SOFT EYES		63	OISIN 3	V	222
GLIMMERING IN HER DROOPED EYES, SAW HER LIPS MOVE		81	EPHEMERA	V	24D
HIS FINGERS MOVE AND SWAY,		98	FOXHUNTER		30
THE STARS OF GOD WHERE THEY MOVE		119	PITY OF LOVE	V	4
THE VERSES THAT COULD MOVE THEM ON THE DAY		257	RECONCILIATION		2
HAS MADE THE VERY OWLS IN CIRCLES MOVE;		423	MY DESCENDANTS		18
THE EXTRAVAGANCE OF SPRING; OR MOVE A HAND		466	HARUN RASHID		125
HANDS UPON EITHER SHOULDER MADE HER MOVE,		466	HARUN RASHID	V	125B
. . . MOVE HIS MOUTH AND SINEWY TONGUE,		560	MAGIC DRUM		5
HIS NUMBERS, THOUGH THEY MOVED OR SEEMED TO MOVE		610	STATUES		2
MOVE MOST GENTLY IF MOVE YOU MUST		617	LONG-LEG FLY		13
MOVE MOST GENTLY IF MOVE YOU MUST		617	LONG-LEG FLY		13
WILL MOVE THE FAINT FAR THUNDER-SOUND, AS THOUGH		699	MOSADA 3	V	10
YOU MOVE IN ANOTHER DOMINION		707	FAIRY PEDANT		5
HE SEES THE FAIRY HOSTING MOVE		716	FAIRY DOCTOR		9
WHILE THE WIND IS LIGHT. THE OAR CAN HARDLY MOVE HER,		754	SHADOW WATER A		157
OR AMONG WINDS THAT MOVE IN THE MEADOWS AND WOODS.		768	SHADOW WATER A	V	413

MOVED

		PAGE	TITLE		LINE
THE IMMORTALS MOVED AMONG THE FOUNTAINS		25	OISIN 1		386
THE FAIRIES MOVED AMONG THE FOUNTAINS,		25	OISIN 1	V	386
"FOR ALL MEN FLEE THE DEMONS"; BUT MOVED NOT		36	OISIN 2		93
THE FLOWERS STILL GREW THERE. MOVED BEYOND HIM THE SEA'S WASTE;		39	OISIN 2	V	163
FOR NO LIVE CREATURES LIVED THERE, NO WEASELS MOVED IN THE DARK;		48	OISIN 3		19
HIS LIPS MOVED SLOWLY IN ANSWER, NO ANSWER OUT OF THEM CAME;		51	OISIN 3		66
SQUARE LEAVES OF THE IVY MOVED OVER US, BINDING US DOWN TO OUR REST,		52	OISIN 3		76
MOVED ROUND ME, OF SEAMEN OR LANDSMEN, ALL WHO ARE WINTER TALES;		53	OISIN 3		86
OR MOVED AS THEY MOVED ONCE,		53	OISIN 3		88
OR MOVED AS THEY MOVED ONCE,		53	OISIN 3		88
AND BY ME, IN SOFT RED RAIMENT, THE FENIANS MOVED IN LOUD STREAMS,		53	OISIN 3		93
THAT ONCE MORE MOVED IN MY BOSOM THE ANCIENT SADNESS OF MAN,		54	OISIN 3		107
THAT HAPPIER BREATH HAD MOVED, HER HUSBAND TURNED		185	QUEEN MAEVE		105

MOVED   (CONTINUED)
    MOVED ROUND ME IN THE SHADOWS, AND AT NIGHT   • • • •   218 WOODS OF COOLE   19
    MOVED ROUND ME IN THE VOICES AND THE FIRES, • • • •   218 WOODS OF COOLE   23
    THAT OTHER'S MOONLIT EYEBALLS NEVER MOVED, • • • •   383 VISION ROBART   33
    MIND MOVED YET SEEMED TO STOP • • • • • •   384 VISION ROBART   43
    SHE MOVED HER LIMBS CONFUSEDLY AS THOUGH • • •   466 HARUN RASHID   V 125A
    AND WROTE BY CANDLE-LIGHT; BUT HER FORM MOVED, • • •   467 HARUN RASHID   129
    AND WROTE BY CANDLE LIGHT; BUT HER FORM MOVED • • •   467 HARUN RASHID   V 129
    HIS NUMBERS, THOUGH THEY MOVED OR SEEMED TO MOVE • • •   610 STATUES   2
    A WRIGGLING THING ON THE WHITE LAKE MOVED, • • • •   673 ISLE STAT II 3 176
MOVEMENT
    BECOME ONE MOVEMENT, ENERGY, DELIGHT, • • •   231 SHADOW WATER B 217
    AND YET YOU TALK OF LOVE. THE MOVEMENT OF TIME • • •   237 SHADOW WATER B 338
    OR BODILY MOVEMENT DID I DARE, • • • • • •   514 JANE GROWN OLD   5
MOVEMENTS
    THREE MOVEMENTS • • • • • • • • • • •   485 THREE MOVEMENT   T
MOVES
    FOR THERE MOVES ALIVE IN YOUR FINGERS • • •   55 OISIN 3   124
    SHE MOVES IN THE FIRELIGHT • • • • • •   89 ISLE IN WATER   3
    AND NOW MOVES MANY A PLEASANT TONGUE • • • •   98 FOXHUNTER   21
    AND MOVES THERE MANY A PLEASANT TONGUE, • • • •   98 FOXHUNTER   V 23
    HIS MIND MOVES UPON SILENCE. • • • • •   617 LONG-LEG FLY   10
    HER MIND MOVES UPON SILENCE. • • • • •   617 LONG-LEG FLY   20
    HIS HAND MOVES TO AND FRO. • • • • • •   618 LONG-LEG FLY   28
    HIS MIND MOVES UPON SILENCE. • • • • •   618 LONG-LEG FLY   30
    HER SPIRIT. AS SHE MOVES, THE FOAM-GLOBES BURST • •   687 TWO TITANS   14
    RE-SHINING IN HIS EYES. SO EVER MOVES • • •   689 NETTLESHIP   12
    WHERE MOVES THERE ANY BEAUTIFUL AS I, • • •   720 WITCH VIVIEN   1
    CHECK. AH! HOW BRIGHT YOUR EYES. HOW SWIFT YOUR MOVES.   722 WITCH VIVIEN   61
MOVETH
    FOR MOVETH ALIVE IN THY FINGERS THE FLUTTERING SADNESS   55 OISIN 3   V 124
       OF EARTH.
    THAT DREAMS. SHE MOVETH, FEELING IN HER BRAIN • • •   687 TWO TITANS   10
MOVIN'
    BUT ALWAYS, AS I'M MOVIN' ROUND, • • • • • •   96 MOLL MAGEE   43
MOVING   SEE EVER-MOVING
    A WEASEL MOVING ON FROM STONE TO STONE, • • •   102 FERGUS DRUID   5
    IS MOVING ITS SLOW THIGHS, WHILE ALL ABOUT IT • • •   402 SECOND COMING   16
    AN IMAGE OF THE MOVING HEAVENS. • • • • •   480 BLOOD AND MOON   14
    ALL STATELY WOMEN MOVING TO A SONG • • • •   537 HER VISION   17
    THAT OF OLD WERT MOVING EVER, • • • • •   658 ISLE STAT I 3   91
    AS FIGURES MOVING MIRRORED IN A GLASS, • • •   676 ISLE STAT II 3 270
    WAS MOVING. BLEEDING NOW, HIS GRASP UNLOCKS, • •   688 TWO TITANS   42
    BEYOND WHERE THE WATERS ARE MOVING, • • • •   739 WHERE BOOKS GO   7
    MOVING THERE AND WALKING; • • • • •   785 YOUR HEART   5
MOWN   SEE NEW-MOWN
    ON THE LEAF-SOWN, NEW MOWN, SMOOTH • • • •   568 SWEET DANCER   V 2
    AND THE WAVES BOWED BEFORE IT LIKE MOWN CORN, • •   657 ISLE STAT I 3   56
MR
    AND "MR. ALFRED" BE AGAIN • • • • • • •   361 ALF POLLEXFEN   32
    ON MR. NETTLESHIP'S PICTURE AT THE ROYAL HIBERNIAN ACADEMY.   688 NETTLESHIP   T
MRS
    BEYOND THAT RIDGE LIVED MRS. FRENCH, AND ONCE • • •   410 TOWER   25
    THROUGH GOD-FORSAKEN MEADOWS; MRS. FRENCH, • • •   412 TOWER   93
    JOHN KINSELLA'S LAMENT FOR MRS. MARY MOORE • • •   620 JOHN KINSELLA   T
MUCH   SEE OVER-MUCH
    AND YET, OF YORE, MUCH PEACE HE HAD • • • •   2 OISIN 1   V 7K
    AND YET, OF YORE, MUCH PEACE HE HAD, • • • •   4 OISIN 1   V 36
    SO MUCH REMAINED THAT ON THE EVENING STAR • • •   32 OISIN 2   V 48
    MUCH WONDERING TO SEE UPON ALL HANDS, OF WATTLES   58 OISIN 3   162
       AND WOODWORK MADE,
    MUCH WONDERING TO SEE UPON ALL HANDS, OF WATTLES   58 OISIN 3   V 162
       AND WOOD-WORK MADE,
    SINCE ADAM'S FALL BUT NEEDS MUCH LABOURING. • • •   205 ADAMS CURSE   22
    SO MUCH COMPOUNDED OF HIGH COURTESY • • • •   205 ADAMS CURSE   24
    WE WERE SO MUCH AT ONE. • • • • • • •   212 O DO NOT LOVE   8
    THAT MUCH IS CERTAIN. I SHALL FIND A WOMAN, • •   231 SHADOW WATER B 209
    SO MUCH STERNNESS AND SUCH CHARM." • • • •   259 PEACE   V 8
    AND THESE THINGS CAME, SO MUCH THE MORE THEREBY •   265 THESE CLOUDS   8
    CALLED CRUACHAN, AND IT WAS AS MUCH • • • •   302 HOUR DAWN   4
    CURSING THE WIND. IT WAS AS MUCH • • • •   302 HOUR DAWN   V 4
    THOUGH COURTEOUS TO THE WORST; MUCH FALLING HE • •   324 ROBERT GREGORY 19
    MUCH TOO SOLEMN SEEMED; • • • • • •   342 SHEP GOATHERD 91
    MUCH TOO SOLEMN AND RESERVED. • • • • •   342 SHEP GOATHERD 94
    BY THE LAGOON YOU LOVE SO MUCH, • • • •   386 ROBARTES DANCE 29
    FROM CHILDHOOD ON, HAD NOW SO MUCH • • • •   397 POLIT PRISONER   2
    AND LATER HAD MUCH TROUBLE FROM A FOOL, • • •   404 FOR DAUGHTER   26
    THROUGH TOO MUCH BUSINESS WITH THE PASSING HOUR, • •   423 MY DESCENDANTS 11
    THROUGH TOO MUCH PLAY, OR MARRIAGE WITH A FOOL? • •   423 MY DESCENDANTS 12
    MUCH DID I RAGE WHEN YOUNG, • • • • •   434 YOUTH AND AGE   1
    IN AFTER TIME THEY WILL SPEAK MUCH OF ME • • •   462 HARUN RASHID   29
    BEFORE THAT END MUCH HAD SHE RAVELLED OUT • • •   472 ALL SOUL NIGHT 51
    HE HAD MUCH INDUSTRY AT SETTING OUT, • • • •   473 ALL SOUL NIGHT 71
    MUCH BOISTEROUS COURAGE, BEFORE LONELINESS • •   473 ALL SOUL NIGHT 72
    CRAZED THROUGH MUCH CHILD-BEARING • • • •   487 CRAZED MOON   1
    MUCH ON THE GREAT QUESTIONER; • • • • •   494 AT ALGECIRAS   16
    MUST WE PART, VON HUEGEL, THOUGH MUCH ALIKE, FOR WE • •   503 VACILLATION   78
    SO MUCH IS CERTAIN; • • • • • • •   504 QUARREL IN AGE 10
    LIVES; THAT MUCH IS CERTAIN; • • • • •   504 QUARREL IN AGE V 10
    NOR SO MUCH AS PARISH PRIEST, • • • • •   508 JANE BISHOP   11
    AND MUCH SAID HE AND I. • • • • • •   513 JANE TALK BISH   2

<pre>
                                                       PAGE   TITLE   LINE
MUCH   (CONTINUED)
       THE LOT OF LOVE IS CHOSEN. I LEARNT THAT MUCH . . . . 534 CHOSEN   1
       BEAST GAVE BEAST AS MUCH. . . . .   538 LAST CONFESS   12
       MUCH I TALK, MORE I WALK; . . . .   548 TO SAME TUNE 3   9
       MUCH I TALK, MORE I WALK; . . . .   548 TO SAME TUNE 3   19
       MUCH I TALK, MORE I WALK; . . . .   549 TO SAME TUNE 3   29
       BECAUSE HE LOVES TOO MUCH. . . . .   588 OLD WICKED MAN   15
       THAT I DO MUCH ADORE; . . . .   592 DRUNK SOBRIETY   6
       "I KEPT HER MUCH IN THE COUNTRY . . . .   594 COLONEL MARTIN   10
       AND SHE WAS MUCH ALONE, ...   594 COLONEL MARTIN   11
       "YOUR LIFE CAN GROW MUCH SWEETER IF YOU WILL . . .   634 CUCHULAIN COMF   12
       O'ER MUCH I'VE TALKED; I SHALL BE SILENT SOON, . .   657 ISLE STAT I 3   75
       GRIEF NEEDS MUCH FEEDING THEN. OF HIM I SWEAR . .   659 ISLE STAT II 1   20
       MOSADA, IT IS THEN SO MUCH THE WORSE; . . . . . .   692 MOSADA 1   V 41A
       THE VAPOUR IS MUCH THICKER. GOD! THE STAKE! . . .   695 MOSADA 1   112
       A SAINT OF MUNSTER, WHEN MUCH FASTING, SAW . . . .   696 MOSADA 2   20
       SO MUCH OF WEALTH AS MAY BEFIT THEIR RANK! . . . .   756 SHADOW WATER A V 186
       AND A STRONG GALLEY. I GIVE YOU ALL AS MUCH. . . .   758 SHADOW WATER A   222
       THERE'S SO MUCH TO THINK ABOUT . . . .   772 SONG DEIRDRE 1   7
MUCH-TOIL
       OR WEEDING OR PLOUGHING WITH FACES A-SHINING WITH MUCH-TOIL 58 OISIN 3   165
          WET;
MUCK
       WHAT'S EQUALITY?--MUCK IN THE YARD! . . . .   547 TO SAME TUNE 3 V   4
MUD
       MY WORKS ARE ALL STAMPED DOWN INTO THE SULTRY MUD. . . 442 BLACK CENTAUR   3
MUDDY
       A LUG-WORM WITH ITS GREY AND MUDDY MOUTH . . . . .   127 DREAM OF FAERY   18
MUFFLED   SEE SLOW-MUFFLED CLOUD-O'ER-MUFFLED O'ER-MUFFLED
       THE PATH O'ER MUFFLED WITH THE LEAVES--DEAD LEAVES, . . 703 MOSADA 3   V 115
MUIRTHEMNE
       TO MANY-PASTURED MUIRTHEMNE, ...   189 BAILE AILLINN   21
       TO MANY PASTURED MUIRTHEMNE, ...   189 BAILE AILLINN V   21
       IN MUIRTHEMNE, AND OVER IT . . . .   194 BAILE AILLINN   116
MULE-BACK
       CAMEL-BACK, HORSE-BACK, ASS-BACK, MULE-BACK, ...   566 LAPIS LAZULI   26
MULTIPLICITY
       THE MIRROR-SCALED SERPENT IS MULTIPLICITY, ...   556 RIBH PATRICK   10
       THE MIRROR SCALED SERPENT IS MULTIPLICITY, ...   556 RIBH PATRICK V   10
MULTIPLIED
       WITH 'MINISHED BEAUTY, MULTIPLIED COMMONPLACE, . . .   472 ALL SOUL NIGHT   45
       DIMINISHED BEAUTY, MULTIPLIED COMMONPLACE; . . . .   472 ALL SOUL NIGHT V 45
MULTITUDE
       AND THE GREY TIDE, THE RED BRANCH MULTITUDE . . . .   108 CUCHULAIN SEA V 38B
       AND OF THE EMBATTLED FLAMING MULTITUDE . . . . .   137 TO SOME I TALK   10
       AND OF THE PROUD EMBATTLED MULTITUDE . . . . . .   137 TO SOME I TALK V 10
       WITH THE LONELY, MAJESTICAL MULTITUDE. . . . . .   158 TO HIS HEART   7
       WITH THE LONELY, PROUD, WINGED MULTITUDE. . . . .   158 TO HIS HEART   V   7
       WITH THE PROUD, MAJESTICAL MULTITUDE. . . . . . .   158 TO HIS HEART   V   7
       GIVE PLACE TO AN INDIFFERENT MULTITUDE, GIVE PLACE . . 427 PHANTOM HATRED   28
       THAT SEEMED SHEER MIRACLE TO THE MULTITUDE, ...   428 NINETEEN 19   2
       A MURMURING FAERY MULTITUDE, ...   742 DANAAN QUICK   7
MULTITUDINOUS
       WINDOWLESS, PILLARLESS, MULTITUDINOUS HOME . . . . .   39 OISIN 2   148
MUMBLING
       AND EVERY MUMBLING OLD MAN SAID, ...   82 MAD KING GOLL V   9
       AND TRAILING CRIMSON VANS, A MUMBLING BROOD, . . .   687 TWO TITANS   20
       BY THE SLOW HEAVING OCEAN--MUMBLING MOTHER OF THE DEAD. 719 PHANTOM SHIP   34
       PRAYED BESIDE THE OCEAN, THE OLD MUMBLING MOTHER OF THE 719 PHANTOM SHIP   V 34
          DEAD.
MUMMERS
       HIS MUMMERS TO THE MARKET-PLACE, ...   287 TO WEALTHY MAN   10
       HIS MUMMERS TO THE MARKET PLACE, ...   287 TO WEALTHY MAN V 10
MUMMIES
       AS MUMMIES IN THE MUMMY-CLOTH ARE WOUND; . . . .   471 ALL SOUL NIGHT   14
       AS MUMMIES IN THE MUMMY CLOTH ARE WOUND; . . . .   471 ALL SOUL NIGHT V 14
       AS MUMMIES IN THE MUMMY-CLOTH ARE WOUND. . . . .   474 ALL SOUL NIGHT   100
       AS MUMMIES IN THE MUMMY CLOTH ARE WOUND. . . . .   474 ALL SOUL NIGHT V 100
MUMMY
       BECAUSE OF SOME GREEN WING, GATHERED OLD MUMMY WHEAT . . 442 BLACK CENTAUR   7
       AS MUMMIES IN THE MUMMY CLOTH ARE WOUND; . . . .   471 ALL SOUL NIGHT V 14
       I HAVE MUMMY TRUTHS TO TELL . . . .   474 ALL SOUL NIGHT   86
       AS MUMMIES IN THE MUMMY CLOTH ARE WOUND. . . . .   474 ALL SOUL NIGHT V 100
       FOR HADES' BOBBIN BOUND IN MUMMY CLOTH . . . . .   497 BYZANTIUM   V 11
       HAD SCOOPED OUT PHARAOH'S MUMMY. I--THOUGH HEART MIGHT 503 VACILLATION   84
          FIND RELIEF
       WHAT A CROP OF MUMMY WHEAT! . . . .   562 CONJUNCTIONS   2
MUMMY-CLOTH
       AS MUMMIES IN THE MUMMY-CLOTH ARE WOUND; . . . .   471 ALL SOUL NIGHT   14
       AS MUMMIES IN THE MUMMY-CLOTH ARE WOUND. . . . .   474 ALL SOUL NIGHT   100
       FOR HADES' BOBBIN BOUND IN MUMMY-CLOTH . . . . .   497 BYZANTIUM   11
MUMMY-DEAD
       EVERYTHING ELSE WITHERED AND MUMMY-DEAD. . . . . .   618 BRONZE HEAD   3
MUNDI
       ROSA MUNDI . . . .   111 ROSE OF WORLD V   T
       WHEN A VAST IMAGE OUT OF SPIRITUS MUNDI . . . . .   402 SECOND COMING   12
MUNICIPAL
       . . . TO THE DUBLIN MUNICIPAL GALLERY IF IT WERE PROVED 287 TO WEALTHY MAN   T
       THE MUNICIPAL GALLERY REVISITED . . . .   601 GALLERY REVIS   T
       THE MUNICIPAL GALLERY RE-VISITED . . . .   601 GALLERY REVIS V   T
</pre>

		PAGE	TITLE	LINE
MUNSTER				
ON MUNSTER GRASS AND CONNEMARA SKIES.		130	BOOK STORIES	24
ON MUNSTER GRASS, OR CONNEMARA SKIES.		130	BOOK STORIES V	24
A SAINT OF MUNSTER, WHEN MUCH FASTING, SAW		696	MOSADA 2	20
MURAL				
. . . AND THE LEAVES OF THE MURAL GLEN,		49	OISIN 3	35
WATCHED HER THOSE SEAMLESS FACES FROM THE VALLEY'S MURAL GIRTH		55	OISIN 3 V	122
MURDER				
BUT NOW THE LYING CLERICS MURDER SONG		42	OISIN 2	196
WHO HAVE PLANNED HIS MURDER, FOR THEY KNOW		436	FOR MY SON	12
MAY MURDER THEM IN PASSING BY		791	REPRISALS	21
MURDERED				
AND PROUD AS PRIAM MURDERED WITH HIS PEERS;		120	SORROW OF LOVE	8
CAN LEAVE THE MOTHER, MURDERED AT HER DOOR,		429	NINETEEN 19	27
IT CAN BE MURDERED WITH A SPOT OF INK.		491	COOLE BALLYLEE	24
WHEN STRANGERS MURDERED EMMET, FITZGERALD, TONE,		541	PARN FUNERAL 1	17
MURDERER				
"YOU BUT IMAGINE LIES ALL DAY, O MURDERER," I REPLIED.		450	OWEN AHERNE	17
MURDERERS				
"VENGEANCE UPON THE MURDERERS," THE CRY GOES UP,		426	PHANTOM HATRED	9
FOR VENGEANCE ON THE MURDERERS OF JACQUES MOLAY.		426	PHANTOM HATRED	16
MURDERING				
THEN PETER HAD A MURDERING LOOK,		457	SUMMER SPRING	9
ARE MURDERING YOUR TENANTS THERE.		791	REPRISALS	16
MURDEROUS				
THAT HAS MADE FAT THE MURDEROUS MOTH;		156	FORGOT BEAUTY	8
OUT OF THE MURDEROUS INNOCENCE OF THE SEA.		403	FOR DAUGHTER	16
ABOVE THE MURDEROUS TREACHERY OF THE MOON,		428	NINETEEN 19 V	3
I KNEW THAT HORSE-PLAY, KNEW IT FOR A MURDEROUS THING.		442	BLACK CENTAUR	4
I KNEW THAT HORSE PLAY, KNEW IT FOR A MURDEROUS THING.		442	BLACK CENTAUR V	4
IN BEAUTY'S MURDEROUS BROOD,		451	FIRST LOVE	2
CONFRONTING MURDEROUS MEN		476	DEATH	8
THE MURDEROUS STEALTH OF DAY.		536	PARTING	8
NOTHING BUT CROMWELL'S HOUSE AND CROMWELL'S MURDEROUS CREW,		580	CURSE CROMWELL	2
MURDER'S				
AND WHEN AT LAST THAT MURDER'S OVER		388	SOLOMON WITCH	24
MURIAS				
AND LONG-FORGOTTEN MURIAS,		196	BAILE AILLINN	163
FROM MURMURING MURIAS; ON CUPS--		271	GREY ROCK V	22
AND TELL HOW MANANAN SACKED MURIAS		766	SHADOW WATER A	377
MURMUR SEE A-MURMUR				
MUST MURMUR AT LAST, "UNJUST, UNJUST!"		28	OISIN 1	420
"THEY MURMUR LIKE YOUNG PARTRIDGE IN THE MORN,		32	OISIN 2 V	51
FROM SLEEPER UNTO SLEEPER MURMUR YOU,		33	OISIN 2 V	60
HEARING HELL LOUD WITH A MURMUR, AS SHOUTING AND MOCKING WE SWEEP,		62	OISIN 3	208
AND LIFE IS OVER SAVE THE MURMUR AND THE SWEETNESS.		77	INDIAN TO LOVE V	5E
AND ALL IS OVER SAVE THE MURMUR AND THE SWEETNESS.		77	INDIAN TO LOVE V	5E
MURMUR, A LITTLE SADLY, HOW LOVE FLED		121	YOU ARE OLD	10
MURMUR, A LITTLE SAD, "FROM US FLED LOVE.		121	YOU ARE OLD V	10
AH, WHEREFORE MURMUR YE		131	OLD PENSIONER V	14
AND STILL MURMUR AND LONG!		163	ASKS FORGIVE	18
AND YOU WOULD MURMUR TENDER WORDS,		175	BELOVED DEAD	5
A MURMUR OF SOFT WORDS AND MEETING LIPS.		187	QUEEN MAEVE	154
TO MURMUR NAME UPON NAME,		394	EASTER 1916	61
AND MURMUR IT WITH BATED BREATH, AS THOUGH		298	LEADERS CROWD	5
FOR, LOOK YOU, SAD'S THE MURMUR OF THE BEES,		652	ISLE STAT I 2	9
I HEAR THE MURMUR AS THEY RAISE THE BEAMS		699	MOSADA 3	17
WHILE I MURMUR A LITTLE AND PONDER		707	FAIRY PEDANT	14
WHILE THEY MURMUR, "AFTER THIS		776	AGAINST WITCH	30
MURMURED				
AND MURMURED SNATCHES OF DELIGHT;		14	OISIN 1	187
AND THEN LOST NIAMH MURMURED, "LOVE, WE GO		46	OISIN 2	245
AS SHE MURMURED, "O WANDERING OISIN,		55	OISIN 3	123
. . . I MURMURED, "IN OLD AGE THEY CEASED";		59	OISIN 3	177
AND MY TEARS WERE LARGER THAN BERRIES, AND I MURMURED,		59	OISIN 3	178
AND MY TEARS WERE LARGE LIKE TO BERRIES, AND I MURMURED,		59	OISIN 3 V	178
MURMURED WITH HER YOUNG VOICE FOR WHOSE MILD SAKE		205	ADAMS CURSE V	15
THE LITTLE FOX HE MURMURED,		214	HAPPY TOWNLAND	13
BUT THE LITTLE RED FOX MURMURED,		214	HAPPY TOWNLAND	17
THE LITTLE FOX HE MURMURED,		215	HAPPY TOWNLAND	33
BUT THE LITTLE RED FOX MURMURED,		215	HAPPY TOWNLAND	37
THE LITTLE FOX HE MURMURED,		216	HAPPY TOWNLAND	53
BUT THE LITTLE RED FOX MURMURED,		216	HAPPY TOWNLAND	57
AND MURMURED "MAY GOD CURSE THE NIGHT		303	HOUR DAWN V	32B
WHO HAD MURMURED OF GIORGIONE AT HIS LATEST BREATH--		366	HER COURAGE	8
MURMURED THE WISDOM OF THE DESERT DJINNS,		468	HARUN RASHID	163
HAS MURMURED WISDOM OF THE DESERT DJINNS,		468	HARUN RASHID V	163
A PEERING HARE'S!" AND YET I MURMURED NOT,		684	SEEKER	56
THE BISHOP MURMURED, "ATHEIST!		725	LEGEND	21
AND MURMURED: "O LONG GREY CLOAK,		744	GLOVE CLOAK	11
MURMURING				
AND A HUNDRED ROBES OF MURMURING SILK,		8	OISIN 1	88
WE RODE ON MURMURING. MANY A SHELL		13	OISIN 1 V	159
THE MURMURING BIRDS IN SOLEMN POMP		20	OISIN 1 V	293
OF MURMURING OCEAN, AND BEHIND US		25	OISIN 1 V	384
. . . WITH RED LIPS MURMURING A SONG,		58	OISIN 3 V	158
PIERCING THE TWILIGHT WITH THEIR MURMURING BARBS.		72	ANASHU VIJAYA	28

		PAGE	TITLE		LINE
MURMURING	**(CONTINUED)**				
MURMURING SOFTLY LIP TO LIP,		78	INDIAN TO LOVE		8
MURMURING HOW FAR AWAY ARE THE UNQUIET LANDS!		78	INDIAN TO LOVE		10
MURMURING HOW FAR AWAY ARE ALL EARTH'S FEVERISH LANDS.		78	INDIAN TO LOVE	V	10
MURMURING GENTLY HOW FAR OFF ARE THE UNQUIET LANDS!		78	INDIAN TO LOVE	V	10
MURMURING, TO A FITFUL TUNE,		85	MAD KING GOLL		52
A MURMURING A MOUNTAIN TUNE,		85	MAD KING GOLL	V	52
MURMURING A MOUNTAIN TUNE,		85	MAD KING GOLL	V	52
IN THE WHITE BORDER OF THE MURMURING SEA!		103	FERGUS DRUID		19
AND FROM ITS MURMURING GREENNESS, CALM OF FAERY,		129	BOOK STORIES		3
THE ROAD-SIDE TREES KEEP MURMURING--		131	OLD PENSIONER	V	13
MURMURING A WIZARD SONG FOR THEE.		134	TWO TREES		12
THAT MURMURING AND LONGING CAME		162	ASKS FORGIVE		8
THAT LONGING AND MURMURING CAME		162	ASKS FORGIVE	V	8
AND DRUNK UP THE MURMURING TIDE!		171	MAID QUIET	V	4D
AND WITH LOW MURMURING LAUGHING SPEECH		195	BAILE AILLINN		137
I CRIED WHEN THE MOON WAS MURMURING TO THE BIRDS!		203	WITHER BOUGHS		1
AND DRUID MOONS, AND MURMURING OF BOUGHS,		219	HARP OF AENGUS		4
AND ALL THAT MURMURING IS BUT A MARRIAGE SONG!		244	SHADOW WATER B	V	452
FROM MURMURING MURIAS! ON CUPS--		271	GREY ROCK	V	22
AND WANDERED MURMURING EVERYWHERE, "MY CHILD, MY CHILD!"		619	BRONZE HEAD		21
A MURMURING FAERY MULTITUDE,		742	DANAAN QUICK		7
AND DRUID MOONS, AND MURMURING OF BOUGHS,		762	SHADOW WATER A		299
THAT COMES WITH LOVE, COMES MURMURING OF AN HOUR		765	SHADOW WATER A		365
MURMURING'S					
AND ALL THAT MURMURING'S BUT A MARRIAGE-SONG!		244	SHADOW WATER B		452
MURMUROUS					
DROPPING! A MURMUROUS DROPPING! OLD SILENCE AND THAT ONE SOUND!		48	OISIN 3		18
WHERE EVER IS MURMUROUS DROPPING, OLD SILENCE AND THAT ONE SOUND!		56	OISIN 3		138
AS LIES DARK WATER IN A MURMUROUS GLADE,		650	ISLE STAT I 1		138
MURMURS					
AND WITH LOW MURMURS, WE RODE ON,		13	OISIN 1		159
AND LAUGHED LIKE MURMURS OF THE SEA!		15	OISIN 1		210
AND WITH LOW MURMURS PRAYED TO HIM,		18	OISIN 1		257
IN MURMURS, LIKE A FRIGHTED BIRD.		25	OISIN 1		376
MY BELL BRANCH MURMURS! THE GAY BELLS BRING LAUGHTER,		130	BOOK STORIES	V	18
SEVEN ODOURS, SEVEN MURMURS, SEVEN WOODS.		218	WOODS OF COOLE		16
SHE MURMURS INTO HIS EAR,		319	DOLLS		17
AND THEN NEW MURMURS CAME NEW UTTERING		657	ISLE STAT I 3		50
ALONE AMONG THE MURMURS OF THE DAWN.		702	MOSADA 3		81
MURMURS OF HER CHILDREN TALKING--		705	DAWN-SONG		6
WITH CRIES AND MURMURS. SUDDENLY HE FLINGS		714	FERENCZ RENYI		101
AMONG THE MURMURS OF THE BEES,		728	PRIEST FAIRY		18
AND A STRING MURMURS AS THOUGH TIME WERE DEAD		752	SHADOW WATER A		124
THAT MURMURS WITH HOLY WOODS, AND WIN THEIR HELP		757	SHADOW WATER A		199
MURROUGH					
MURROUGH, THE KING OF IRELAND'S SON,		274	GREY ROCK		71
AND BEING THANKFUL MURROUGH FOUND,		274	GREY ROCK		77
MUSCATEL					
AND TWO LONG GLASSES BRIMMED WITH MUSCATEL		470	ALL SOUL NIGHT		4
THE FUME OF MUSCATEL		473	ALL SOUL NIGHT		83
MUSCLE					
MERE BONE AND MUSCLE THROWN ASIDE,		273	GREY ROCK		51
THERE IS NO MUSCLE IN THE ARM! AND AFTER,		374	PHASES OF MOON		52
SHARP THEIR SPADES, THEIR MUSCLE STRONG,		637	BEN BULBEN	V	22
MUSCLES					
AND WHAT COULD MAKE THEIR MUSCLES TAUT		295	THREE BEGGARS		17
SHARP THEIR SPADES, THEIR MUSCLES STRONG,		637	BEN BULBEN		22
MUSCULAR					
IN MUSCULAR YOUTH WELL KNOWN TO MAYO MEN		325	ROBERT GREGORY		34
IN MUSCULAR YOUTH WELLKNOWN TO MAYO MEN		325	ROBERT GREGORY	V	34
IN MUSCULAR YOUTH, AT MEETS OR AT RACECOURSES,		325	ROBERT GREGORY	V	35
MUSE					
THEN MUSE THEY ON THE HOUSEHOLD WOOL INTENT,		32	OISIN 2	V	55
THAT WE MAY MUSE IN THE STARLIGHT AND TALK OF THE BATTLES OF OLD!		51	OISIN 3		63
IT SEEMS THAT I MUST BID THE MUSE GO PACK,		409	TOWER		11
THE MUSE IS MUTE WHEN PUBLIC MEN		597	MODEL LAUREATE		17
GHOSTS OF HER VANISHED GLORIES, MUSE AND STALK		687	TWO TITANS		21
REMEMBERING THEE, I MUSE, WHILE FADES IN FLIGHT		705	REMEMBRANCE		6
MOORE ONCE HAD VISITS FROM THE MUSE		792	GEORGE MOORE		1
MUSED					
I MUSED ON THE CHASE WITH THE FENIANS, AND BRAN, SCEOLAN, LOMAIR,		47	OISIN 3		5
I SAT AND MUSED AND DRANK SWEET WINE!		82	MAD KING GOLL		13
HE MUSED BESIDE THE WELL OF SCANAVIN.		127	DREAM OF FAERY		25
HE MUSED UPON HIS MOCKERS! WITHOUT FAIL		127	DREAM OF FAERY		26
MUSES					
WHEN MOCKING MUSES CHOSE THE COUNTRY WENCH.		413	TOWER		96
AND THEN DID ALL THE MUSES SING		437	SONGS PLAY 1		6
WHAT A STAR SANG AND CARELESS MUSES HEARD!		445	SCHOOL CHILDR		47
THAT NOBLE BLADE THE MUSES BUCKLED ON,		489	COOLE PARK 29		10
AND WE AND ALL THE MUSES ARE THINGS OF NO ACCOUNT.		580	CURSE CROMWELL		12
CALL THE MUSES HOME.		600	THOSE IMAGES		8
THAT MAKE THE MUSES SING.		601	THOSE IMAGES		16
MUSES'					
YOU KEPT THE MUSES' STERNER LAWS,		273	GREY ROCK		59
MUSHROOMS					
GATHERING MUSHROOMS IN THE DEW.		705	DAWN-SONG		8

		PAGE	TITLE	LINE
MUSHROOMS (CONTINUED)				
WITH THEIR MUSHROOMS LIGHTLY THREADED	• • • • • •	705	DAWN-SONG	13
GATHERING MUSHROOMS IN THE DEW.	• • • • • • • • •	705	DAWN-SONG	16
GATHERING MUSHROOMS IN THE DEW.	• • • • • • • • •	706	DAWN-SONG	24
GATHERING MUSHROOMS IN THE DEW.	• • • • • • • • •	706	DAWN-SONG	32
MUSIC				
MUSIC AND LOVE AND SLEEP AWAIT,	• • • • • • • • •	9	OISIN 1	103
THE HORSE TOWARDS THE MUSIC RACED,	• • • • • • • •	13	OISIN 1	169
THE STEED TOWARDS THE MUSIC RACED,	• • • • • • • •	13	OISIN 1 V	169
TO THE MUSIC OF THE GOLDEN RHYME	• • • • • • •	14	OISIN 1 V	176
ROLLED ROUND WITH MUSIC OF THE SIGHING SPRAY: • • • • •	30	OISIN 2	14
OF KNITTED MUSIC. OFT THE FOND REPINING	• • • • • •	33	OISIN 2 V	68C
AND NEVER FIND, THOUGH YE IN MUSIC SPEAK. • • • • • •	42	OISIN 2 V	201
WRAPT IN THE WAVE OF THAT MUSIC, WITH WEARINESS MORE THAN OF EARTH,	51	OISIN 3	69
AND WHEN THE WANDERING MUSIC DIES • • • • • • • •	99	FOXHUNTER	31
PUT THAT MUSIC IN HER FACE? • • • • • • • • • •	124	CATHLEEN PARA	10
AND MADE MY LIPS AND MUSIC WED, • • • • • • • • •	134	TWO TREES	11
A RAPTUROUS MUSIC, TILL THE MORNING BREAK • • • • • •	137	TO SOME I TALK	14
CONTINUAL MUSIC TILL THE MORNING BREAK, • • • • • •	137	TO SOME I TALK V	14
BUT LET A GENTLE SILENCE WROUGHT WITH MUSIC FLOW • • •	175	ELEMENT POWERS	17
BUT LET A GENTLE SILENCE ENWROUGHT WITH MUSIC FLOW • • •	175	ELEMENT POWERS V	17
AS THOUGH THEIR MUSIC WERE ENOUGH • • • • • • • •	193	BAILE AILLINN	108
A MUSIC THAT HAD THOUGHT ENOUGH • • • • • • • •	193	BAILE AILLINN V	108
SWEET WITH ALL MUSIC, OUT OF HIS LONG HAIR, • • • • •	219	HARP OF AENGUS	8
THAN LOVER'S MUSIC--LET THAT BE, • • • • • • • •	276	GREY ROCK	130
BUT WITH A VOICE THAT HAD UNNATURAL MUSIC, • • • • • •	283	TWO KINGS	153
AND I THAT MADE LIKE MUSIC IN MY YOUTH • • • • • •	342	SHEP GOATHERD	76
THEY HAVE LOUD MUSIC, HOPE EVERY DAY RENEWED • • • • •	398	LEADERS CROWD	11
CAUGHT IN THAT SENSUAL MUSIC ALL NEGLECT • • • • • •	407	SAIL BYZANTIUM	7
MUSIC HAD DRIVEN THEIR WITS ASTRAY-- • • • • • • • •	411	TOWER	47
NOR MUSIC NOR AN ENEMY'S CLIPPED EAR • • • • • • •	412	TOWER	75
O BODY SWAYED TO MUSIC, O BRIGHTENING GLANCE, • • • • •	446	SCHOOL CHILDR	63
O BODY SWAYED TO MUSIC BRIGHTENING GLANCE • • • • • •	446	SCHOOL CHILDR V	63
AND WAIT WAR'S MUSIC: PASS THE LITTLE GALLERY: • • • •	461	HARUN RASHID	8
MY GREAT-GRANDFATHER'S FATHER TALKED OF MUSIC, • • • •	486	SEVEN SAGES	4
MY GREAT-GRANDFATHER'S FATHER TALKED OF MUSIC AND PAINTING,	486	SEVEN SAGES V	4
WORDS FOR MUSIC PERHAPS • • • • • • • • • • •	507	JANE BISHOP V	T
A SONG FOR MUSIC • • • • • • • • • • • • •	524	DANCING DAYS V	T
AND HEAVENLY MUSIC IF THEY GAVE IT WIT: • • • • • •	533	HER TRIUMPH	6
AND DEAFENING MUSIC SHOOK THE LEAVES: A TROOP • • • •	537	HER VISION	13
THAT CRAZED GIRL IMPROVISING HER MUSIC, • • • • • • •	578	CRAZED GIRL	1
SHE STOOD IN DESPERATE MUSIC WOUND, • • • • • • •	578	CRAZED GIRL	10
BUT ACTORS LACKING MUSIC • • • • • • • • • •	599	STONE CROSS	17
POETRY, MUSIC, I HAVE LOVED, AND YET • • • • • • •	599	SPIRIT MEDIUM	1
POETRY AND MUSIC I HAVE BANISHED, • • • • • • • •	600	SPIRIT MEDIUM	19
INTOLERABLE MUSIC FALLS. • • • • • • • • • • •	612	NEWS ORACLE	32
MAKES ME SWEET MUSIC • • • • • • • • • • •	627	STATES HOLIDAY	24
COME FORTH, COME FORTH, MY MUSIC FLOWS FOR THEE, • • • •	645	ISLE STAT I 1	20
MUSIC OF MY SOUL AND LIGHT-- • • • • • • • • •	648	ISLE STAT I 1	97
I, AS MUSIC THAT GROWS MUTE, • • • • • • • • •	668	ISLE STAT II 3	65
WILD INDOLENCE AND MUSIC HAVE NO DATE. • • • • • •	686	LIFE	20
FOR THAT'S THE SWEETEST MUSIC FOR SAD SOULS. • • • • •	702	MOSADA 3	85
OH, HUSH THE WANDERING MUSIC OF THY MIND. • • • • • •	703	MOSADA 3	106
WILD INDOLENCE AND MUSIC HAVE NO DATE, • • • • • •	735	QUATRAIN APHOR	18
AND HEARD THE MUSIC IN THE WIND, AND SAW • • • • • •	747	SHADOW WATER A	5
WAS FORGAEL'S COURAGE THAT THE MUSIC KILLED. • • • • •	747	SHADOW WATER A	9
TAUGHT ME WISE MUSIC, AND GAVE ME THIS OLD HARP: • • •	750	SHADOW WATER A	76
SWEET WITH ALL MUSIC, OUT OF HIS LONG HAIR, • • • • •	762	SHADOW WATER A	303
MUSIC OF A LOST KINGDOM • • • • • • • • • •	782	GREY ROUND	2
A WANDERING AIRY MUSIC: • • • • • • • • • •	783	GREY ROUND	7
MUSIC OF A LOST KINGDOM? • • • • • • • • • •	783	GREY ROUND	12
A WANDERING AIRY MUSIC: • • • • • • • • • •	783	GREY ROUND	17
MUSICAL				
SHALL BLOW INTO RUIN OUR MUSICAL DAYS, • • • • • • •	28	OISIN 1 V	425
CARRIES A MUSICAL INSTRUMENT. • • • • • • • • •	566	LAPIS LAZULI	42
LOW, LONG AND MUSICAL. A DEW-DROP HUNG • • • • • •	689	NETTLESHIP	9
MUSING				
THE LADIES CLOSE THEIR MUSING EYES. NO PROPHECIES, • • •	426	PHANTOM HATRED	19
HOW "THE ONLY GOOD IS MUSING MILD, • • • • • • •	728	PRIEST FAIRY	13
MUSINGLY				
MUSINGLY WANDERED THE VILLAGE PRIEST. • • • • • • •	728	PRIEST FAIRY	3
MUTE				
THE MUSE IS MUTE WHEN PUBLIC MEN • • • • • • • •	597	MODEL LAUREATE	17
I, AS MUSIC THAT GROWS MUTE, • • • • • • • • •	668	ISLE STAT II 3	65
MUTTER				
BECAUSE I MUTTER AS I GO: • • • • • • • • •	94	MOLL MAGEE	3
WHEN IN RAGGED VAPOUR THEY MUTTER NIGHT AND DAY, • • •	206	HANRAHANS SONG V	2
MUTTER SUCH THINGS AS THEY AWAKE FROM TRANCE. • • • •	229	SHADOW WATER B	163
AND IF SHE HEAR HIM MUTTER OF WILD RIDERS, • • • • •	230	SHADOW WATER B	175
I'D STAND AND MUTTER THERE UNTIL HE CAUGHT • • • • •	377	PHASES OF MOON	131
MUTTERED				
MUTTERED THE OLD CRANE OF GORT. • • • • • • • •	295	THREE BEGGARS	6
SEEMED SO ON PURPOSE, MUTTERED JAFFER'S FRIENDS, • • • •	462	HARUN RASHID	37
THEN CERTAIN SHROUDS THAT MUTTERED HEAD TO HEAD • • • •	634	CUCHULAIN COMF	4
"AVE MARIE," MUTTERED HE • • • • • • • • • •	730	PRIEST FAIRY	51
MUTTERING				
WHEN SHE KNOWS THAT. WHAT IS IT THAT YOU ARE MUTTERING--	236	SHADOW WATER B	303
THE ONE DISASTROUS ZODIAC, MUTTERING, • • • • • • •	282	TWO KINGS	128
FIRST WAS MUTTERING A PRAYER, • • • • • • • • •	298	THREE HERMITS	3
HAS SET ME MUTTERING LIKE A FOOL. • • • • • • • •	356	BROKEN DREAMS	26

547

MUTTERING   (CONTINUED)
```
     LONE REGENT OF THE WOODS, DEEP MUTTERING, . . . . . .   657 ISLE STAT I 3      49
MUTTERS
     ONE LEANS AND MUTTERS BY THE WALL-- . . . . . . . . .   212 BLESS PSALTER      10
     BUT MAYBE SOME OLD GAFFER MUTTERS A BLESSING . . . . .   355 BROKEN DREAMS       4
MYRIAD
     HIS LANGUID TAIL ABOVE US, LIT WITH MYRIAD SPOTS OF LIGHT.   77 INDIAN ON GOD    20
     AND ALL THE BURDEN OF HER MYRIAD YEARS. . . . . . . .   120 SORROW OF LOVE V     8
     AND ALL THE TROUBLE OF HER MYRIAD YEARS. . . . . . .   120 SORROW OF LOVE V     8
     A MYRIAD HEADS HAVE LAIN." " . . . . . . . . . . . .   496 MOHINI CHATTER     11
     HAVE NOT A MYRIAD SWAYED BELOW STRANGE TREES . . . . .   724 KANVA ON SELF      11
MYRIADS
     WHERE DROPS OF DEW IN MYRIADS FALL, . . . . . . . . .    16 OISIN 1           222
     OF MYRIADS OF BELOVEDS, AND ON THINE . . . . . . . .   724 KANVA ON SELF      10
MYRRH
     AND COVERS AWAY THE SMOKE OF MYRRH AND FRANKINCENSE; . .   173 SPEAKS HEARERS     4
MYSTERIES     SEE HEART-MYSTERIES
     BROOD HER HIGH LONELY MYSTERIES. . . . . . . . . . .   156 FORGOT BEAUTY      24
     ON HER MOST LONELY MYSTERIES. . . . . . . . . . . .   156 FORGOT BEAUTY V    24
     YOUR THIRST FOR THOSE OLD CRABBED MYSTERIES, . . . . .   465 HARUN RASHID      86
     HEART MYSTERIES THERE, AND YET WHEN ALL IS SAID . . .   630 CIRCUS ANIMALS V   27
MYSTERIOUS
     . . . GROWN MILD WITH MYSTERIOUS THOUGHT, . . . . . .    55 OISIN 3          121
     MYSTERIOUS, BEAUTIFUL; . . . . . . . . . . . . . .   323 SWANS AT COOLE     26
     IN THAT MYSTERIOUS, ALWAYS BRIMMING LAKE . . . . . .   356 BROKEN DREAMS      32
     I CALL TO THE MYSTERIOUS ONE WHO YET . . . . . . . .   371 EGO DOMINUS        70
     AN IMAGE OF MYSTERIOUS WISDOM WON BY TOIL; . . . . .   373 PHASES OF MOON     18
     COMPANIONSHIP IN THOSE MYSTERIOUS THINGS . . . . . .   465 HARUN RASHID      92
MYSTERY
     ON THEIR VAST FACES MYSTERY AND DREAMS; . . . . . . .    74 ANASHU VIJAYA     70
     THE DRUIDS TOOK THEM TO THEIR MYSTERY, . . . . . . .   111 CUCHULAIN SEA     82
     TO THESE OLD NIGHT SHALL ALL HER MYSTERY TELL; . . .   114 ROSE OF BATTLE    22
     UPON LOVE'S BITTER MYSTERY; . . . . . . . . . . . .   125 GOES FERGUS        8
     THE UNCONTROLLABLE MYSTERY ON THE BESTIAL FLOOR. . . .   318 MAGI               8
     A MYSTERY THAT ELSE HAD FOUND NO CHRONICLER . . . . .   461 HARUN RASHID      21
     OF THE STARK MYSTERY THAT HAS DAZED MY SIGHT, . . . .   466 HARUN RASHID     113
     OR DID THE TORCHLIGHT OF THAT MYSTERY . . . . . . .   466 HARUN RASHID     115
     OF THAT STARK MYSTERY WHERE I AM PLUNGED . . . . . .   466 HARUN RASHID   V 113
     OR DID THE TORCH LIGHT OF THAT MYSTERY . . . . . . .   466 HARUN RASHID   V 115
     OR DID THE TORCH-LIGHT OF THAT MYSTERY . . . . . . .   466 HARUN RASHID   V 115
     AND NOW MY UTMOST MYSTERY IS OUT. . . . . . . . . .   469 HARUN RASHID     187
     THAT OPENS HER MYSTERY AND FRIGHT. . . . . . . . . .   624 APPARITIONS       22
     GLAD, SIMPLE--NAY, HE SOUGHT NOT MYSTERY, . . . . . .   710 FERENCZ RENYI     30
MYSTIC
     FOR THERE LIVE THE MYSTIC BROTHERHOOD . . . . . . .   148 INTO TWILIGHT  V  10
MYSTICAL
     FOR THERE THE MYSTICAL BROTHERHOOD . . . . . . . . .   148 INTO TWILIGHT     10
     A MYSTICAL PRAYER TO THE MASTERS OF THE ELEMENTS, . . .   174 ELEMENT POWERS V   T
MYTHOLOGICAL
     SOME MORALIST OR MYTHOLOGICAL POET . . . . . . . . .   430 NINETEEN 19       59
MYTHOLOGIES
     OUT OF OLD MYTHOLOGIES . . . . . . . . . . . . . .   320 COAT               3
NA        SEE KYLE-NA-INO KYLE-NA-NO PAIRC-NA-LEE CLOOTH-NA-BARE PAIRC-NA-TARAV
          PAIRC-NA-CARRAIG
NAIL
     AND PAID YOU ON THE NAIL. TAKE UP THAT ROPE . . . . .   232 SHADOW WATER B   224
     STARED AT THE WINE-DARK NAIL, OR DARK THAT RAN . . .   537 HER VISION        10
NAILED
     AND THEY HAD NAILED THE BOARDS ABOVE HER FACE, . . . .   123 DREAM OF DEATH     3
     AND AFTER NAILED UPON THE NIGHT . . . . . . . . . .   519 HER DREAM          7
NAIL-PIERCED
     THE KNOTTED SCOURGE, THE NAIL-PIERCED HANDS, THE WOUNDED   172 TRAV PASSION   V   4
        SIDE,
NAILS
     BY MACE AND SPEAR AND SWORD OF SEA-GODS, NAILS . . . .    31 OISIN 2        V 30A
     GOLDEN THE NAILS OF HIS BIRD-CLAWS, . . . . . . . .    50 OISIN 3           45
     I CRIED, "COME OUT OF THE SHADOW, KING OF THE NAILS OF    51 OISIN 3           61
        GOLD;
     I CRIED, "COME OUT OF THE SHADOW, CANN OF THE NAILS OF    51 OISIN 3        V  61
        GOLD;
     AND DIRTY NAILS OF CARPENTERS. . . . . . . . . . .   440 WISDOM         V   7
     'TIS THOU, FOR THEY'VE GROWN BLUE AROUND THE NAILS. . .   700 MOSADA 3          46
     ARMLETS OF GOLD OR SHIELDS WITH GOLDEN NAILS . . . .   749 SHADOW WATER A    43
NAISI
     OR ULADH WHEN NAISI HAD HUNG A SAIL UPON THE WIND; . .   209 UNDER THE MOON V   4
NAKED
     THEIR NAKED AND GLEAMING BODIES POURED OUT AND HEAPED IN    48 OISIN 3           28
        THE WAY.
     THEIR MIGHTY AND NAKED AND GLEAMING BODIES . . . . .    48 OISIN 3        V  28
     OUT NAKED ON THE ROADS, AS THE BOOKS SAY, AND STRICKEN . .   316 COLD HEAVEN     11
     IN WALKING NAKED. . . . . . . . . . . . . . . . .   320 COAT              10
     "NAKED I LAY, . . . . . . . . . . . . . . . . . .   510 JANE JUDGMENT     11
     NAKED AND HIDDEN AWAY, . . . . . . . . . . . . . .   510 JANE JUDGMENT     13
     NAKED TO NAKED GOES, . . . . . . . . . . . . . . .   538 LAST CONFESS      16
     NAKED TO NAKED GOES, . . . . . . . . . . . . . . .   538 LAST CONFESS      16
     BEAT DOWN UPON THEIR NAKED BODIES, KNOW . . . . . .   563 MERU              12
NAME
     AENGUS AND EDAIN, MY OWN NAME . . . . . . . . . . .     5 OISIN 1           47
     THY NAME, THY KIN, AND THY COUNTRY," . . . . . . . .     5 OISIN 1        V  44
     AENGUS AND EDAIN, AND MY NAME . . . . . . . . . . .     5 OISIN 1        V  47
```

		PAGE	TITLE		LINE
NAME (CONTINUED)					
YE WORN DEED-DOERS, AND MY NAME		5	OISIN 1	V	48
RHYME THAT RHYMED UPON OISIN'S NAME, ...		7	OISIN 1		64
AND SET YOUR NAME ALL NAMES ABOVE, ...		7	OISIN 1		76
AND MANY A PRINCE OF LOFTY NAME, ...		7	OISIN 1	V	63
AND MANY A MAN OF LOFTY NAME, ...		7	OISIN 1		63
"RHYME, THAT RHYMED TO USHEEN'S NAME, ...		7	OISIN 1	V	64
AND MANY PRINCES OF HIGH NAME.		7	OISIN 1	V	68
SAVE ONLY MANY TIMES MY NAME, ...		25	OISIN 1		375
THAT SEA-GOD'S NAME, WHO IN A DEEP CONTENT		38	OISIN 2		129
THAT SEA GOD'S NAME, WHO IN A DEEP CONTENT		38	OISIN 2	V	129
HOLDING THAT HORSE, AND SADLY CALLED MY NAME, . . .		44	OISIN 2		230
A GOOD NAME IS GOODLY TO HEAR OF, AND A GOOD NAME SURELY IS THINE.		51	OISIN 3		63
A GOOD NAME IS GOODLY TO HEAR OF, AND A GOOD NAME SURELY IS THINE.		51	OISIN 3	V	63
AND THE NAME OF THE DEMON WHOSE HAMMER		52	OISIN 3		80
ANOTHER FILLS YOUR MIND. MY MOTHER'S NAME.		71	ANASHU VIJAYA		16
SOME OTHER FILLS YOUR MIND. MY MOTHER'S NAME. . . .		71	ANASHU VIJAYA	V	16
BUT TELL YOUR NAME AND LINEAGE TO HIM		108	CUCHULAIN SEA		36
BUT TELL ALONE YOUR NAME AND HOUSE TO HIM		108	CUCHULAIN SEA	V	36
"HE BADE ME LET ALL KNOW HE GIVES HIS NAME		109	CUCHULAIN SEA		52
THE CARS OF BATTLE AND HIS OWN NAME CRIED, ...		111	CUCHULAIN SEA		85
AND, LIKE A STORM, CRY THE INEFFABLE NAME, ...		137	TO SOME I TALK		12
AND SOME ONE CALLED ME BY MY NAME, ...		149	WANDER AENGUS		12
AND SOMEONE CALLED ME BY MY NAME.		149	WANDER AENGUS	V	12
WHO CALLED ME BY MY NAME AND RAN		150	WANDER AENGUS		15
THAT CALLED ME BY MY NAME AND RAN		150	WANDER AENGUS	V	15
THE POWERS WHOSE NAME AND SHAPE NO LIVING CREATURE KNOWS		174	ELEMENT POWERS		1
TO THAT HIGH HILL THE HERDSMEN NAME		194	BAILE AILLINN		129
WE SAT GROWN QUIET AT THE NAME OF LOVE, ...		205	ADAMS CURSE		28
HOW SHALL I NAME YOU, IMMORTAL, MILD, PROUD SHADOWS? . .		218	WOODS OF COOLE		27
WHAT NAME TO CALL HIM BY? COME TO HIS SHIP. . . .		240	SHADOW WATER B		390
HIS NAME WILL COME INTO OUR THOUGHTS IN A MINUTE. . .		241	SHADOW WATER B		391
WHAT NAME HAD THAT DEAD KING? ARTHUR OF BRITAIN? .		242	SHADOW WATER B		404
BY THE SWEET NAME OF DEATH.		254	HIS DREAM		12
BY THE SWEET NAME OF DEATH.		254	HIS DREAM		20
AND CARVE HIS NAME IN OGHAM." EOCHAID SAID, . . .		280	TWO KINGS		83
I'LL NAME THE FRIENDS THAT CANNOT SUP WITH US . . .		323	ROBERT GREGORY		2
BUT GROWS MORE GENTLE WHEN HE SPEAKS HER NAME, . .		340	SHEP GOATHERD		29
BUT PUT NO NAME AND LEAVE THEM AT HER DOOR.		343	SHEP GOATHERD		116
AS THOUGH SOME OTHER NAME RAN IN HIS HEAD.		351	HER PRAISE		9
MANAGE THE TALK UNTIL HER NAME COME ROUND.		351	HER PRAISE		14
IF THERE BE RAGS ENOUGH HE WILL KNOW HER NAME . . .		351	HER PRAISE		15
OF SOME STRANGE WOMAN'S NAME THAT RAN IN HIS HEAD. .		351	HER PRAISE	V	9
MANAGE TO TALK UNTIL HER NAME COME ROUND.		351	HER PRAISE	V	14
AND CALLED HER NAME, SHE HAD HEARD, ...		381	SONGS FOOL 2		11
AND OF A MIDDLETON, WHOSE NAME YOU NEVER HEARD, . .		391	UNDER SATURN		8
TO MURMUR NAME UPON NAME, ...		394	EASTER 1916		61
TO MURMUR NAME UPON NAME, ...		394	EASTER 1916		61
CEREMONY'S A NAME FOR THE RICH HORN, ...		406	FOR DAUGHTER		79
KUSTA BEN LUKA IS MY NAME, I WRITE		460	HARUN RASHID		1
HOW IN THE NAME OF HEAVEN CAN HE ESCAPE		479	SELF AND SOUL		50
WHERE NONE HAS REIGNED THAT LACKED A NAME AND FAME .		491	COOLE BALLYLEE		31
WHATEVER'S WRITTEN IN WHAT POETS NAME		492	COOLE BALLYLEE		43
ALL THAT IS WRITTEN IN WHAT POETS NAME		492	COOLE BALLYLEE	V	43
HAD EVEN O'DUFFY--BUT I NAME NO MORE--		543	PARN FUNERAL 2		9
INTO ONE NAME, ...		572	LADYS 1ST SONG		6
AND BLACKENED HIS GOOD NAME.		582	ROGER CASEMENT		8
SING A "THE" BEFORE HIS NAME, ...		584	ORAHILLY		3
BUT MANNION IS MY NAME, ...		605	SONGS BURDEN 1		2
MY NAME IS HENRY MIDDLETON, ...		606	SONGS BURDEN 2		1
GIVE TONGUE, PROCLAIM THEIR HIDDEN NAME--"HOUND VOICE."		622	HOUND VOICE		7
AND IN THAT TERROR'S NAME OBEYED THE CALL, ...		622	HOUND VOICE		12
THE COUNTESS CATHLEEN WAS THE NAME I GAVE IT, . . .		629	CIRCUS ANIMALS		18
WE SAW THE DOLOROUS LAKE, AND THEN THY NAME		659	ISLE STAT II 1		7
FOR THIS THING FIGHT--WE LOVE ONE MAID? HER NAME? .		661	ISLE STAT II 1		66
TWO CAME, HIS NAME AND MINE ON MANY A TREE		662	ISLE STAT II 2		10
IN SAND HIS NAME AND MINE I'VE ALSO READ.		662	ISLE STAT II 2		12
HERE, FACING TO THE LAKE, AND NO NAME GILD, ...		663	ISLE STAT II 2		20
TAKEN IN MAGIC, IN THE CHURCH'S NAME		694	MOSADA 1		104
THY NAME IS?" "RENYI." "OF?" "THIS VILLAGE." "GOOD!		709	FERENCZ RENYI		13
THY NAME IS?" "FERENCZ RENYI." "OF?" "THIS VILLAGE." "GOOD!		709	FERENCZ RENYI	V	13
OF TRAITOR EVERMORE IS ON OUR NAME."		712	FERENCZ RENYI		61
OF' TRAITOR EVER MORE IS ON OUR NAME."		712	FERENCZ RENYI	V	61
HUSH'D THE FISHERS, TILL A MOTHER CALLS BY NAME HER DROWNED SON,		719	PHANTOM SHIP		23
THEN EACH WIFE AND MAID AND MOTHER CALLS BY NAME SOME DROWNED ONE.		719	PHANTOM SHIP		24
NAMED					
AND NAMED HIM BY SWEET NAMES. A FOAMING TIDE . . .		30	OISIN 2		27
THERE WAS A MAN WHOM SORROW NAMED HIS FRIEND, . . .		67	SAD SHEPHERD		1
AND THEN THE MAN WHOM SORROW NAMED HIS FRIEND . . .		68	SAD SHEPHERD		8
AND THEN THE MAN WHOM SORROW NAMED HIS FRIEND . . .		68	SAD SHEPHERD		17
THEN CRIED THE MAN WHOM SORROW NAMED HIS FRIEND, . .		68	SAD SHEPHERD	V	8
FAR, FAR AWAY. I NAMED HIM AFTER YOU.		72	ANASHU VIJAYA		35
FAR, FAR AWAY. I'VE NAMED HIM AFTER YOU.		72	ANASHU VIJAYA	V	35
MEN HAVE NAMED BEAUTY. THY GREAT LEAVES ENFOLD . .		169	SECRET ROSE		7
MEN HAVE NAMED BEAUTY. YOUR HEAVY LEAVES ENFOLD . .		169	SECRET ROSE	V	7
MEN HAVE NAMED BEAUTY. YOUR GREAT LEAVES ENFOLD . .		169	SECRET ROSE	V	7

NAMED   (CONTINUED)
    IF THESE HAVE NAMED IT RIGHT . . . .   500 VACILLATION   V   9
    WHOM MEN HAVE NAMED ARCADIA'S SWEETEST TONGUE. . . . .   649 ISLE STAT I 1   109
NAMES
    AND SET YOUR NAME ALL NAMES ABOVE, ...   7 OISIN 1   76
    NOW, MAN OF CROZIERS, SHADOWS CALLED OUR NAMES . . . .   29 OISIN 2   1
    HALF LOST IN VAPOUR, SHADOWS CALLED OUR NAMES, . . .   29 OISIN 2   V   3
    AND NAMED HIM BY SWEET NAMES. A FOAMING TIDE . . . .   30 OISIN 2   27
    AND CALLED HIM SWEETEST NAMES AND SOOTHED HIS FEARS. . .   30 OISIN 2   V   27
    AND EVEN THE NAMES OF HIS FATHERS, AND EVEN THE WORKS OF   51 OISIN 3   V   62
        HIS HANDS?
    AND THE NAMES OF THE DEMONS WHOSE HAMMERS . . . . . .   52 OISIN 3   V   80
    AS MY MIND MADE THE NAMES OF THE FENIANS. . . . . .   57 OISIN 3   146
    THE NAMES THAT STILLED YOUR CHILDISH PLAY, ...   289 SEPTEMBER 1913   10
    AS A MOTHER NAMES HER CHILD . . . .   394 EASTER 1916   62
    BUT NAMES ARE NOTHING. WHAT MATTER WHO IT BE, ...   473 ALL SOUL NIGHT   81
    BUT NAMES ARE NOTHING. I CARE NOT WHO IT BE. . . . .   473 ALL SOUL NIGHT V   81
    THAT HAS THE WORST OF ALL BAD NAMES! . . . .   531 FATHER CHILD   5
    NO MATTER WHAT THE NAMES THEY WEAR! . . . .   582 ROGER CASEMENT V   17
    NAMES AFTER ME. LADY--I COME. FORGIVE, ...   695 MOSADA 1   117
    OF THE GREAT WARRIORS WHOSE NAMES HAVE SUNG . . . . .   698 MOSADA 2   60
    AND UNFORGOTTEN NAMES, AND THE COLD STARS . . . . .   757 SHADOW WATER A   204
    NAMES WHEREBY A MAN HAS KNOWN . . . .   775 AGAINST WITCH   5
    THEN THOSE OTHERS THAT ARE BUT NAMES OR NAMES . . . .   790 DEDICATION   9
    THEN THOSE OTHERS THAT ARE BUT NAMES OR NAMES . . . .   790 DEDICATION   9
NAMING
    NAMING IT WITH ECSTATIC BREATH, ...   254 HIS DREAM   18
NAN
    AND OUR POOR KATE OR NAN IS LESS . . . .   190 BAILE AILLINN   35
    AND WHEN WE WALK WITH KATE OR NAN . . . .   192 BAILE AILLINN   92
    THERE'S MARGARET AND MARJORIE AND DOROTHY AND NAN, . . .   354 HIS PHOENIX   17
NAOISE
    WHO KNOW THE WAY THAT NAOISE WENT? . . . .   193 BAILE AILLINN   96
    NOR ULADH, WHEN NAOISE HAD THROWN A SAIL UPON THE WIND!   209 UNDER THE MOON   4
NAPE
    BY THE DARK WEBS, HER NAPE CAUGHT IN HIS BILL, ...   441 LEDA AND SWAN   3
NAPKIN
    VERONICA'S NAPKIN . . . .   483 VERONIC NAPKIN   T
    A PATTERN ON A NAPKIN DIPPED IN BLOOD. . . . .   483 VERONIC NAPKIN   8
NAPS
    IN THEIR DOWNY CAPS, AND STARTLE THE NAPS . . . . .   644 SONG FAERIES   11
    IN THEIR DOWNY CAPS, AND STARTLE THE NAPS . . . . .   676 ISLE STAT II 3   258
NARCISSUS
    WHERE GOLDEN CROCUS AND NARCISSUS BLOOM, ...   447 COLONUS PRAISE   18
NARROW
    AND TOSS AND TURN IN NARROW CAVES! . . . .   19 OISIN 1   281
    AND HEAR THE NARROW GRAVES CALLING MY CHILD AND ME. . .   147 UNAPPEAS HOST   6
    SHE BUILDS HER NEST UPON A NARROW LEDGE . . . . . .   285 TWO KINGS   194
    CLIMB UP THE NARROW WINDING STAIR TO BED! . . . . .   324 ROBERT GREGORY   5
    IN THE NARROW THEME OF LOVE . . . .   333 SOLOMON SHEBA   7
    ARE BUT A NARROW POUND." . . . .   333 SOLOMON SHEBA   16
    THE WORLD A NARROW POUND." . . . .   333 SOLOMON SHEBA   24
    IN THE ONE NARROW THEME OF LOVE . . . .   333 SOLOMON SHEBA V   7
    INTO ITS NARROW SHED. . . . .   358 BALLOON MIND   4
    AS NARROW NATURES WOULD . . . .   365 HER RACE   2
    OR SHOD IN IRON, CLIMBED THE NARROW STAIRS, ...   412 TOWER   83
    CROSS THE NARROW STRAITS TO LIGHT . . . .   494 AT ALGECIRAS   4
    CROSSES THE NARROW STRAITS TO LIGHT . . . .   494 AT ALGECIRAS V   4
    CROSS THOSE NARROW STRAITS TO LIGHT . . . .   494 AT ALGECIRAS V   4
    IN THE NARROW PASS! . . . .   512 JANE ON GOD   11
    THE WOMEN-SLINGERS ON THE NARROW BRIDGE, ...   749 SHADOW WATER A   41
    A CAPTIVE WOMAN FROM THE NARROW BRIDGE, ...   749 SHADOW WATER A   49
    THE WOMEN SLINGERS ON THE NARROW BRIDGE, ...   749 SHADOW WATER A V   41
NARROWS
    THE TIDE NARROWS BETWEEN, AND ONE OLD MAN . . . . .   752 SHADOW WATER A   118
NASCHINA
    TO WELCOME THEE, NASCHINA, WITH SWEET SINGING. . . . .   645 ISLE STAT I 1   7
    THEIR SHEEP IN ARCADY, NASCHINA, HAIL! . . . . .   649 ISLE STAT I 1   119
    NASCHINA, HAIL! MOST FAIR OF ALL WHO GRAZE . . . .   649 ISLE STAT I 1   120
    THEIR SHEEP IN ARCADY, NASCHINA, HAIL! . . . . .   649 ISLE STAT I 1   121
    NASCHINA, HAIL! I'D DRIVE THY WOOLLY SHEEP, ...   649 ISLE STAT I 1   122
    NASCHINA, WHEREFORE ARE YOUR EYES SO BRIGHT . . . .   650 ISLE STAT I 1   141
    OH STAY, NASCHINA, STAY! . . . .   650 ISLE STAT I 1   153
    WE LOVE NASCHINA BOTH. WHOM LOVES SHE BEST? . . . .   660 ISLE STAT II 1   48
    NASCHINA. OH, I KNOW HER WELL--A LAME, ...   661 ISLE STAT II 1   67
    THE OTTERS DREAMING LAY. NASCHINA! AY! . . . .   677 ISLE STAT II 3 V   280
NASCHINA'S
    NASCHINA'S GONE, DRAWN BY A THIRST OF LOVE, ...   664 ISLE STAT II 2   59
    AND OF NASCHINA'S NOW THEY TELL--REND! REND! . . .   665 ISLE STAT II 2   69
NATION
    AH, WORLD-WIDE NATION, ALWAYS GROWING SORROW, . . .   130 BOOK STORIES V   11
    AH, WORLDWIDE NATION, ALWAYS GROWING SORROW! . . .   130 BOOK STORIES V   11
    IS EVERY MODERN NATION LIKE THE TOWER, ...   482 BLOOD AND MOON   47
    IS EVERY NATION LIKE THE TOWER . . . .   482 BLOOD AND MOON V   47
    'TWAS EVENING, AND THE CRICKET NATION SANG . . . .   690 MOSADA 1   18
    ONCE IN THY NATION NONE SHALL KNOW THAT I . . . .   702 MOSADA 3   82
    AMONG THY NATION NONE SHALL KNOW THAT I . . . . .   702 MOSADA 3 V   82
    THEREFORE, O NATION OF THE BLEEDING BREAST, ...   709 FERENCZ RENYI   4
    YE BY THE WAVES THAT CLOSE IN OUR SAD NATION, . . .   738 MOURN THEN ON   5
NATIONAL
    HALF DRESSED IN NATIONAL UNIFORM, ...   424 ROAD AT DOOR   7

550

		PAGE	TITLE		LINE
NATIONS					
	AND DROWNED THE TREASURES OF NINE CONQUERED NATIONS,	235	SHADOW WATER B		287
	GREAT NATIONS BLOSSOM ABOVE!	547	TO SAME TUNE 3		5
	HISTORIC NATIONS GROW	547	TO SAME TUNE 3	V	5
	WHEN NATIONS ARE EMPTY UP THERE AT THE TOP,	548	TO SAME TUNE 3		11
	GREAT NATIONS BLOSSOM ABOVE!	614	MARCH SONGS 2		5
	BOWING NATIONS, PLUMED WARS--	737	IN FIRELIGHT		10
NATIVITY					
	A NATIVITY	625	NATIVITY		T
	THAT WHEN THE STARS OF OUR NATIVITY	691	MOSADA 1		28
	OF OUR NATIVITY HANG SIDE BY SIDE,	701	MOSADA 3		53
NATURAL					
	MAYBE IT IS BUT NATURAL TO DOUBT ME.	227	SHADOW WATER B		112
	THERE'S NOBODY IS NATURAL BUT A ROBBER,	233	SHADOW WATER B		237
	THAT IS NOT NATURAL IN AN AGE LIKE THIS,	257	NO SECOND TROY		9
	SPONTANEOUS JOY AND NATURAL CONTENT	260	FASC DIFFICULT		3
	IN LOGIC AND IN NATURAL LAW	288	TO WEALTHY MAN		27
	YOU SING AS ALWAYS OF THE NATURAL LIFE,	342	SHEP GOATHERD		75
	WHEN IT HAS VANISHED FROM OUR NATURAL EYES!	342	SHEP GOATHERD		81
	CAN HAVE THE PURITY OF A NATURAL FORCE,	353	PEOPLE		31
	THAT EVERY NATURAL VICTORY	401	DEMON BEAST		34
	RIGHT MASTERY OF NATURAL THINGS,	401	DEMON BEAST		37
	LOSE NATURAL KINDNESS AND MAYBE	404	FOR DAUGHTER		22
	MY BODILY FORM FROM ANY NATURAL THING,	408	SAIL BYZANTIUM		26
	THROUGH NATURAL DECLENSION OF THE SOUL,	423	MY DESCENDANTS		10
	FOR THAT IS NATURAL TO A MAN	459	HIS WILDNESS		9
	A DOZEN NIGHTS OF NATURAL SLEEP, AND THEN	468	HARUN RASHID		150
	THAT'S HOW ALL NATURAL OR SUPERNATURAL STORIES RUN.	556	RIBH PATRICK		3
	NATURAL AND SUPERNATURAL WITH THE SELF-SAME RING ARE WED.	556	RIBH PATRICK		4
NATURE					
	FROM THE BOOK OF KAURI THE INDIAN-- SECTION V. ON THE	76	INDIAN ON GOD	V	T
	NATURE OF GOD				
	DREAM, UNTIL GOD BURN NATURE WITH A KISS?	128	DREAM OF FAERY		47
	UNTIL HE BURN UP NATURE WITH A KISS!--	128	DREAM OF FAERY	V	47
	THAT IT CAN TAKE WHAT FORM COOK NATURE FANCIES	377	PHASES OF MOON		115
	THAT IT CAN TAKE WHAT FORM COOK NATURE FANCY	377	PHASES OF MOON	V	115
	SO SENSITIVE HIS NATURE SEEMED,	392	EASTER 1916		29
	COULD ROUSE MY WHOLE NATURE.	400	DEMON BEAST		32
	ONCE OUT OF NATURE I SHALL NEVER TAKE	408	SAIL BYZANTIUM		25
	PLATO THOUGHT NATURE BUT A SPUME THAT PLAYS	445	SCHOOL CHILDR		41
	THAT JUGGLING NATURE MOUNTS, HER COIL IN THEIR EMBRACES	556	RIBH PATRICK		9
	TWINED.				
	THE SAGE, WHO DEEP IN CENTRAL NATURE DELVES,	686	LIFE		2
	THE SAGE WHO DEEP IN CENTRAL NATURE DELVES,	734	QUATRAIN APHOR		2
NATURE'D					
	FOR NATURE'D PULLED HER TRAGIC BUSKIN ON	490	COOLE BALLYLEE	V	12
NATURE'S					
	GREAT WORKS CONSTRUCTED THERE IN NATURE'S SPITE	488	COOLE PARK 29		5
	FOR NATURE'S PULLED HER TRAGIC BUSKIN ON	490	COOLE BALLYLEE		12
	FOR NATURE'S PULLED HER TRAGIC BUCKSKIN ON	490	COOLE BALLYLEE	V	12
	NATURE'S PURE UNCHANGING LIGHT?	529	TOM LUNATIC		6
NATURES					
	AS NARROW NATURES WOULD	365	HER RACE		2
	BY QUIET NATURES UNDERSTOOD	405	FOR DAUGHTER		63
	TOLD, AND IT SEEMED THAT OUR TWO NATURES BLENT	443	SCHOOL CHILDR		13
NAUGHT					
	. . . THE STRENGTH OF THE BELL-BRANCH IS NAUGHT,	55	OISIN 3		123
	BUT NAUGHT THEY HEARD, FOR THEY ARE ALWAYS LISTENING,	68	SAD SHEPHERD		15
	BUT NAUGHT THEY HEARD, FOR THEY ARE EVER LISTENING,	68	SAD SHEPHERD	V	15
	TILL THERE BE NAUGHT BUT THRONE ON THRONE	156	FORGOT BEAUTY	V	21
	IT ALL, AND MORE THAN IT ALL, WOULD COME TO NAUGHT,	201	OLD MEMORY		8
	IT ALL, MORE THAN IT ALL, WOULD COME TO NAUGHT,	201	OLD MEMORY	V	8
	OUR STITCHING AND UNSTITCHING HAS BEEN NAUGHT.	204	ADAMS CURSE		6
	THEY CLOSED THEIR BLOOD-SHOT EYES FOR NAUGHT.	296	THREE BEGGARS	V	44
	WE HAVE NAUGHT FOR DEATH BUT TOYS,	363	DOLLS DRAWINGS		11
	LET THE FOOLS RAGE, I SWERVED IN NAUGHT,	577	WHAT THEN		18
	KNOW'ST NAUGHT OF THIS. AND, UNCOUTH HUNTER, NOW--	651	ISLE STAT I 1		168
	WITHIN MINE HEART! AND NAUGHT BUT SORROW NOW	659	ISLE STAT II 1		26
	AND MADE THEIR GLORY NAUGHT.	741	EARL PAUL		44
	"LOVE WOULD BE A THING OF NAUGHT	772	SONG DEIRDRE 1		10
	ON NAUGHT HAS SET STORE	780	WELL AND TREE		13
NAY					
	YOUNG WARRIOR." "NAY," I ANSWERED; "MY HANDS BURN	35	OISIN 2	V	89B
	. . . HE CRIED, "NAY, THE GODS A LONG TIME ARE DEAD."	59	OISIN 3	V	180
	AND ENTER, AND NONE SAYETH "NAY"	62	OISIN 3	V	210
	HAIL! HAIL, MY ANASHUYA. NAY! BE STILL.	71	ANASHU VIJAYA	V	11
	FAREWELL, VIJAYA. NAY, NO WORD, NO WORD!	75	ANASHU VIJAYA		83
	"NAY, YOU ARE TALLER THAN CUCHULAIN, SON."	107	CUCHULAIN SEA	V	27
	"NAY, HE IS OLD AND SAD WITH MANY WARS,	107	CUCHULAIN SEA	V	29
	NAY, NAY, I MISS'D HIM NOT! HIS DAYS	649	ISLE STAT I 1		117
	NAY, NAY, I MISS'D HIM NOT! HIS DAYS	649	ISLE STAT I 1		117
	NAY, NAY, ALMINTOR, YONDER SONG IS GLAD.	652	ISLE STAT I 2		23
	NAY, NAY, ALMINTOR, YONDER SONG IS GLAD.	652	ISLE STAT I 2		23
	THE LAKE-EMBOSOMED ISLE. NAY, THIS MY QUEST	657	ISLE STAT I 3		60
	NAY, GRIEF IN FEEDING ON OLD GRIEF GROWS LESS.	659	ISLE STAT II 1		19
	I'D KILL HER IF SHE WERE. NAY, DO NOT FEAR!	669	ISLE STAT II 3		69
	NAY, HE IS GONE. WAKE! WAKE! AS A BEE SIPS	678	ISLE STAT II 3		305
	NAY, GIVE IT ME, AND I WILL SOUND A MEASURE!	681	SEEKER		9
	NAY HERE, I'LL LAY ME DOWN WHERE I CAN WATCH	700	MOSADA 3		39
	GLAD, SIMPLE--NAY, HE SOUGHT NOT MYSTERY,	710	FERENCZ RENYI		30
	WE GATHERED. FERENCZ, NAY, I MUST NOT DIE!	713	FERENCZ RENYI		96

NAY (CONTINUED)

BESIDE THE WILLOW. NAY, TO YONDER STAR,	715 FERENCZ RENYI		118
BENEATH THE WILLOW--NAY, TO YONDER STAR,	715 FERENCZ RENYI	V	118
NAY, RISE AND FLATTER HER WITH GOLDEN RHYME,	724 KANVA ON SELF		19

NEAR

CAOILTE, CONAN, AND FINN CAME NEAR,	10 OISIN 1		111
NEAR BY, THE FENIANS SAW, AND KNEW	10 OISIN 1	V	111
FOR NEITHER DEATH NOR CHANGE COMES NEAR US,	21 OISIN 1		316
FOR CHANGE AND DEATH THEY COME NOT NEAR US,	21 OISIN 1	V	316
GOD SHAKES THE WORLD WITH RESTLESS HANDS. MORE NEAR	43 OISIN 2	V	208
SAD NIAM CAME NEAR ME, AND LAID HER BROWS ON THE MIDST OF MY BREAST	52 OISIN 3	V	74
AMRITA. DRAW YOU NEAR, AND 'NEATH YON PILLAR	71 ANASHU VIJAYA	V	13A
WITH HORSEMEN HURRYING NEAR AND FAR,	83 MAD KING GOLL	V	18
AND HARES RUN NEAR ME GROWING BOLD.	84 MAD KING GOLL	V	47
BRING MY BROWN HUNTER NEAR,	97 FOXHUNTER	V	6
THE HUNTSMAN NEAR HIM STANDS.	98 FOXHUNTER		24
THE HUNTSMAN NEAR HIM STANDS,	98 FOXHUNTER	V	22
COME NEAR ME, WHILE I SING THE ANCIENT WAYS!	100 ROSE UPON ROOD		2
COME NEAR, THAT NO MORE BLINDED BY MAN'S FATE,	101 ROSE UPON ROOD		9
COME NEAR, COME NEAR, COME NEAR--AH, LEAVE ME STILL	101 ROSE UPON ROOD		13
COME NEAR, COME NEAR, COME NEAR--AH, LEAVE ME STILL	101 ROSE UPON ROOD		13
COME NEAR, COME NEAR, COME NEAR, LEAVE ME STILL	101 ROSE UPON ROOD		13
COME NEAR! I WOULD, BEFORE MY TIME TO GO,	101 ROSE UPON ROOD		22
NEAR TO CUCHULLIN, ROUND A QUICKEN TREE,	111 CUCHULAIN SEA	V	81A
THE THRONGS WITH BLOWN WET HAIR ARE GATHERING NEAR.	114 ROSE OF BATTLE	V	6
WHERE TIME WOULD SURELY FORGET US, AND SORROW COME NEAR US NO MORE!	122 WHITE BIRDS		10
WHERE SURELY TIME WOULD FORGET US AND SORROW COME NEAR US NO MORE!	122 WHITE BIRDS	V	10
NEAR NO ACCUSTOMED HAND!	123 DREAM OF DEATH		2
BELIEVED THERE WAS SOME OTHER NEAR AT HAND,	229 SHADOW WATER B		154
IF ANY MAN DREW NEAR	254 WOMAN HOMER		1
"WE RIDE BUT SLOWLY THOUGH SO NEAR OUR HOME,"	276 TWO KINGS	V	A
"THOUGH THE DOOR OF DEATH IS NEAR	298 THREE HERMITS		8
HELL MOUTH LAY OPEN NEAR THAT PLACE,	303 HOUR DAWN		25
"NIGHT GROWS UNEASY NEAR THE DAWN	303 HOUR DAWN		33
THAT'S GROWN UNEASY NEAR THE DAWN	303 HOUR DAWN	V	33
WAS BURIED NEAR THE ASTROLOGER,	361 ALF POLLEXFEN		26
UPON THE OPEN ROAD, NEAR TO THE SLIGO QUAY--	391 UNDER SATURN		12
TO SOME WHO ARE NEAR MY HEART,	393 EASTER 1916		34
"FAIR AND FOUL ARE NEAR OF KIN,	513 JANE TALK BISH		7
LONG YEARS AGO, A CHURCH STANDS NEAR,	640 BEN BULBEN		87
ON LIMESTONE QUARRIED NEAR THE SPOT	640 BEN BULBEN		90
SOME BARBAROUS, UN-FAERY THING DRAW NEAR.	656 ISLE STAT I 3		21
THIS BLOSSOM IS MOST NEAR. STATUE! OH, THOU	657 ISLE STAT I 3		72
AND PONDER IT IF THEY WILL)! THEN NEAR AT HAND	659 ISLE STAT II 1		10
THE BOAT DRAWS NEAR AND NEAR. YOU HEED ME NOT!	663 ISLE STAT II 2		23
THE BOAT DRAWS NEAR AND NEAR. YOU HEED ME NOT!	663 ISLE STAT II 2		23
AND ALL HIS VEINS HAD NEAR RUN DRY,	670 ISLE STAT II 3		119
THOU WILT NOT SPEAK, AND I WITH AGE AM NEAR	684 SEEKER		62
TOO LATE, TOO LATE, FOR I AM NEAR TO DEATH.	701 MOSADA 3		55
I SAW A GIRL AFRAID TO BE TOO NEAR,	712 FERENCZ RENYI		68
IN TROUBLE IS, THE DOE WILL LINGER NEAR.	713 FERENCZ RENYI		80
THAT SICKENING NEAR THEIR MOTHERS LIE!	717 FAIRY DOCTOR		16
AND DEATH, OH MY FAIR ONE, WILL NEVER COME NEAR	717 LOVE SONG		8
NEAR BY, BUT IN THE SHADOW OF THE SAIL,	752 SHADOW WATER A		121

NEARER

AND EVER NEARER, NEARER GREW!	15 OISIN 1		200
AND EVER NEARER, NEARER GREW!	15 OISIN 1		200
NEARER THE CASTLE CAME WE. A VAST TIDE,	31 OISIN 2	V	27A
A LITTLE NEARER TO HIS THOUGHT	324 ROBERT GREGORY		23
ARE NEARER TO THE SURFACE OF THE BODY	464 HARUN RASHID		67
LOVE IS NEARER DEATH.	517 HER ANXIETY		11
A LITTLE NEARER THOSE BRIGHT STARS. TELL ME,	701 MOSADA 3		59
NODS BY THE HELM, AND NEARER TO THE SAIL	752 SHADOW WATER A		119
IF I GO NEARER TO THE WINDWARD SIDE,	753 SHADOW WATER A		140

NEAREST

MY CHAIR WAS NEAREST TO THE FIRE	131 OLD PENSIONER		3
AND THE NEAREST KIN OF THE MOON,	378 CAT AND MOON		3
TOOK UP THE NEAREST AND BEGAN TO SEW.	634 CUCHULAIN COMF		18

NEARLY

THEY HAVE FLOWN AWAY TOGETHER. WE ARE NEARLY	754 SHADOW WATER A		154

NEAT

TO CUT AND SEW, BE NEAT IN EVERYTHING	443 SCHOOL CHILDR		5

'NEATH

LAY 'NEATH US! OF ITS HOLLOW COOL	17 OISIN 1	V	241
I SAW NOT WHO! 'NEATH OTHER SKIES	25 OISIN 1	V	381A
AT EMAN, 'NEATH THE BEECH TREES, ON EACH SIDE,	44 OISIN 2	V	228
A STARLING LIKE THEM THAT FORGATHERED 'NEATH A MOON	54 OISIN 3		103
. . . THEY LAY 'NEATH THE SAND-SACK AT LENGTH	60 OISIN 3	V	186
AMRITA. DRAW YOU NEAR, AND 'NEATH YON PILLAR	71 ANASHU VIJAYA	V	13A
THAT SLUMBERED 'NEATH THE HARVEST MOON,	85 MAD KING GOLL	V	50
AND 'NEATH IT SIT, AND OF THE WOVEN SUM	663 ISLE STAT II 2		30
ARE 'NEATH ITS PROW, AND CRUSHING SHELLS.	663 ISLE STAT II 2		35
TRAILING AND SHINING 'NEATH THE FLICKERING GLARE.	688 TWO TITANS		32
YOURSELF INTO THE DUNGEON 'NEATH OUR FEET	697 MOSADA 2		44
A SCORE OF YARDS OFF 'NEATH A WILLOW, SHOT.	712 FERENCZ RENYI		65
NO TASTE HAVE I FOR SLUMBER 'NEATH AN OAK.	721 WITCH VIVIEN		31

NEAVE

"I AM NEAVE, A CHILD OF THE MIGHTY SHEE,	5 OISIN 1	V	48

NEAVE   (CONTINUED)
    FOR NEAVE SANG CONTINUALLY . . . .   11 OISIN 1   V   134
    AND PEARL-PALE NEAVE LAY BY ME, HER BROW ON THE MIDST OF   52 OISIN 3   V   74
       MY BREAST:
    O, HAD YOU SEEN BEAUTIFUL NEAVE WAIL TO HERSELF AND BLANCH,   54 OISIN 3   V   109
NECESSITOUS
    COME OLD, NECESSITOUS, HALF-MOUNTED MAN! . . . . . .   412 TOWER   90
NECK
    AND HIS NECK AND HIS BREAST AND HIS ARMS . . . . .   145 HOST OF AIR   35
    OF SILVER HANGING ROUND LAME COLA'S NECK-- . . . . . .   691 MOSADA 1   V   35
    UP WITH THE NECK AND CLAP THE WING, ...   782 HEART FRIGHT   6
    UP WITH THE NECK AND CLAP THE WING, ...   782 HEART FRIGHT   13
    UP WITH THE NECK AND CLAP THE WING, ...   782 HEART FRIGHT   20
    STRETCH NECK AND CLAP THE WING, ...   783 GREY ROUND   27
NECKLACE
    UPON MY NECKLACE. BUT THE GOBLIN QUEEN . . . .   676 ISLE STAT II 3   267
NECK'S
    AND THY NECK'S A POISED LILY! . . . .   647 ISLE STAT I 1   55
NECKS
    EACH OTHER'S NECKS, AND WHISPERING AS THEY GO, ...   703 MOSADA 3   120
NEED
    BUT NOW I HAVE NO NEED TO WATCH IT MORE." . . . . . .   105 CUCHULAIN SEA   5
    TO HELP ME IN MY NEED. . . . .   134 FR GILLIGAN   44
    YOU NEED BUT LIFT A PEARL-PALE HAND, ...   158 BELOVED RHYMES   7
    AT NEED, AND MADE HER BEAUTIFUL AND FIERCE, ...   181 QUEEN MAEVE   29
    AND I WOULD HAVE YOUR HELP IN MY GREAT NEED, ...   184 QUEEN MAEVE   98
    ALL THAT YOU NEED IS PATIENCE." HEART CRIES, "NO, . . .   200 FOLLY COMFORT   6
    PATIENCE IS ALL THAT YOU HAVE NEED OF." NO, . . .   200 FOLLY COMFORT   V   6
    NO NEED TO DROWN, FOR, IF YOU WILL PARDON US . . . . .   238 SHADOW WATER B   361
    QUEEN, GIVE IT ME. NO, I HAVE NEED OF IT. . . . .   241 SHADOW WATER B   399
    WHY DO YOU NEED A SWORD? BUT YOU MAY KEEP IT. . . . .   241 SHADOW WATER B   400
    NOW THAT HE'S DEAD I HAVE NO NEED OF IT, ...   241 SHADOW WATER B   401
    I NEED MUST MARRY SOME POOR LOUT," . . . .   273 GREY ROCK   V   47
    HE CLAIMED HIS COUNTRY'S NEED WAS MOST, ...   275 GREY ROCK   101
    SIGHING REPLIED: "WHAT NEED HAVE WE FOR HASTE . . . .   276 TWO KINGS   V   C
    WHAT NEED YOU, BEING COME TO SENSE, ...   289 SEPTEMBER 1913   1
    SHE NEED NOT BE TOO COMELY--LET IT PASS," . . . . .   300 BEGGAR CRIED   10
    AND ALL THAT I NEED DO IS TO WISH . . . .   300 RUN PARADISE   4
    WHAT NEED HAVE YOU TO CARE . . . .   312 CHILD DANCING   2
    WHAT NEED HAVE YOU TO DREAD . . . .   312 CHILD DANCING   11
    WHAT NEED THAT YOU SHOULD DREAD . . . .   312 CHILD DANCING   11
    WHO COMES AT NEED, ALTHOUGH NOT NOW AS ONCE . . . . .   320 REED WHISPERER   2
    BUT LITTLE NEED THE GRAVE DISTRESS. . . . .   338 TOM OROUGHLEY   10
    AND LITTLE NEED THE GRAVE DISTRESS. . . . .   338 TOM OROUGHLEY   V   10
    FOR I NEED ALL HIS MIGHTY MEMORIES. . . . .   413 TOWER   104
    AND HAVE NO NEED OF CRUELTY TO KEEP . . . .   448 HERO GIRL FOOL V   12A
    OR THOSE WHO NEED HIS BOUNTY OR HIS LAW, ...   462 HARUN RASHID   V   25A
    THE HEART NEED SUFFER NO DEFEAT: BUT I . . . .   464 HARUN RASHID   77
    I NEED SOME MIND THAT, IF THE CANNON SOUND . . . . .   471 ALL SOUL NIGHT   11
    I NEED NO OTHER THING, ...   474 ALL SOUL NIGHT   98
    ALTHOUGH THEIR CHILDREN NEED A RICH ESTATE: . . . . .   500 VACILLATION   24
    OF BAILE AND AILLINN YOU NEED NOT SPEAK, ...   555 RIBH AT TOMB   6
    SUFFICIENT MONEY FOR HIS NEED, ...   577 WHAT THEN   8
    BUT HE HAS NEED OF ALL THAT STRENGTH . . . .   624 APPARITIONS   20
    SUCH QUESTS AS THESE! I TROW, NEED LITTLE WIT. . . . .   650 ISLE STAT I 1   150
    NO NEED TO BIND MY HANDS. WHERE ARE YE, SIRS? . . . .   695 MOSADA 1   110
    THIS HEATHEN HORDE AWAY. YOU NEED NOT HOPE! . . . .   696 MOSADA 2   5
    I DO NOT NEED YOUR SCYTHE. MAY THAT BRING PEACE . . .   721 WITCH VIVIEN   26
    AND NEED NO MORE OF LIFE TILL THE WHITE WINGS . . . .   751 SHADOW WATER A   102
NEEDED
    I THOUGHT NO MORE WAS NEEDED . . . .   334 SONG   1
NEEDLE
    AND GRANIA, WALKING AND SMILING, SEWED WITH HER NEEDLE   53 OISIN 3   94
       OF BONE.
    AND ALL THE WHILE HER NEEDLE PULLED . . . .   308 PLAYER QUEEN   7
    INSTEAD OF THREAD AND NEEDLE . . . .   595 COLONEL MARTIN   23
NEEDLE'S
    STOOD IN THE CIRCUIT OF A NEEDLE'S EYE. . . . . . .   483 VERONIC NAPKIN   6
    A NEEDLE'S EYE . . . .   562 NEEDLES EYE   T
    CAME OUT OF A NEEDLE'S EYE! . . . .   562 NEEDLES EYE   2
    FROM NEEDLE'S EYE STILL GOAD IT ON. . . . .   562 NEEDLES EYE   4
NEEDLES
    BUT SLENDER NEEDLES OF BONE! . . . .   488 CRAZED MOON   15
NEEDLES'
    "WE THREAD THE NEEDLES' EYES, AND ALL WE DO . . . . .   634 CUCHULAIN COMF   16
NEEDLESS
    WAS IT NEEDLESS DEATH AFTER ALL? . . . .   394 EASTER 1916   67
NEEDS
    AND I MUST NEEDS ENDURE AND HATE AND WEEP, ...   35 OISIN 2   85
    FOR SHE NEEDS NOT HER SAD BEAUTY-- . . . . . .   124 CATHLEEN PARA V   7
    OR, IF THERE NEEDS BE MORE, BE NOTHING SAID . . . . .   201 OLD MEMORY   11
    SINCE ADAM'S FALL BUT NEEDS MUCH LABOURING. . . . . .   205 ADAMS CURSE   22
    THE SEEMING NEEDS OF MY FOOL-DRIVEN LAND! . . . . . .   267 ALL TEMPT ME   3
    I NEEDS MUST MARRY SOME POOR LOUT," . . . .   273 GREY ROCK   47
    THE CRADLES THAT A MAN MUST NEEDS BE ROCKED IN! . . . .   373 PHASES OF MOON   34
    "IT NEEDS TO BE BUT WATERED!" . . . .   396 ROSE TREE   7
    AND NEEDS NO CRUELTY. I HAVE HEARD ONE SAY . . . . .   448 HERO GIRL FOOL   13
    MUST NEEDS NEGLECT, I CANNOT HIDE THE TRUTH . . . . .   462 HARUN RASHID   26
    MUST NEEDS NEGLECT, BUT CANNOT HIDE THE TRUTH, ...   462 HARUN RASHID   V   26
    MUST NEEDS BE IN THIS LIFE AND IN WHAT FOLLOWS . . . .   465 HARUN RASHID   95

NEEDS (CONTINUED)
   AND FAIR NEEDS FOUL," I CRIED. • • • • • • • • • • 513 JANE TALK BISH   8
   AND GIVEN EVERYTHING A WOMAN NEEDS, • • • • • • • 609 IN TARAS HALLS   7
   LACK NOTHING THAT A SOLDIER NEEDS, • • • • • • • • 635 BLACK TOWER   4
   GRIEF NEEDS MUCH FEEDING THEN. OF HIM I SWEAR • • • • 659 ISLE STAT II 1 20
NE'ER
   "NOT SO, GREAT KING; FOR I HAVE NE'ER • • • • • • • 6 OISIN 1   V 55
   I NE'ER LOVED ANY TILL SONG BROUGHT ME • • • • • • 7 OISIN 1   V 69
   HAVE THEY NE'ER SEEN THE EYES OF LYNX OR KINE, • • • 672 ISLE STAT II 3 152
NEGLECT
   CAUGHT IN THAT SENSUAL MUSIC ALL NEGLECT • • • • • 407 SAIL BYZANTIUM   7
   MUST NEEDS NEGLECT, I CANNOT HIDE THE TRUTH • • • • 462 HARUN RASHID   26
   MUST NEEDS NEGLECT, BUT CANNOT HIDE THE TRUTH, • • • 462 HARUN RASHID V 26
NEIGH
   ARMOURED HORSES NEIGH • • • • • • • • • • • • • • 512 JANE ON GOD   9
NEIGHBOUR
   A NEIGHBOUR MINDED HER BY DAY, • • • • • • • • • • 94 MOLL MAGEE   15
   NO NEIGHBOUR COULD I SEE. • • • • • • • • • • • • 95 MOLL MAGEE   28
   I SAW A KINDLY NEIGHBOUR • • • • • • • • • • • • • 95 MOLL MAGEE   35
   I SAW A NEIGHBOUR GOOD. • • • • • • • • • • • • • 95 MOLL MAGEE   V 36
   ALL KNOW THE MAN THEIR NEIGHBOUR KNOWS. • • • • • • 337 SCHOLARS   10
   THERE'S NOT A NEIGHBOUR LEFT TO SAY • • • • • • • • 412 TOWER   78
   AWAY FROM NEIGHBOUR OR FRIEND, • • • • • • • • • • 472 ALL SOUL NIGHT 47
   HE THAT'S MOUNTING UP MUST ON HIS NEIGHBOUR MOUNT, • • • 580 CURSE CROMWELL 11
NEIGHBOURING
   FROM SOMEWHERE IN THE NEIGHBOURING COTTAGES. • • • • 411 TOWER   59
   I CAN EXCHANGE OPINION WITH ANY NEIGHBOURING MIND, • • • 450 OWEN AHERNE   9
   A NEIGHBOURING CRICKET LIFTS HIS SHRILLY SHOUT • • • • 711 FERENCZ RENYI   45
   OUT OF A NEIGHBOURING BUNCH OF HEATHER; • • • • • • 728 PRIEST FAIRY   20
NEIGHBOURLY
   ALL NEIGHBOURLY CONTENT AND EASY TALK ARE GONE, • • • • 580 CURSE CROMWELL 9
NEIGHBOUR'S
   FOR AN OLD NEIGHBOUR'S FRIENDSHIP CHOSE THE HOUSE • • • 423 MY DESCENDANTS 21
NEIGHBOURS
   IF I SHOULD LIVE AS LIVE THE NEIGHBOURS," • • • • • • 331 ROUND TOWER   3
   IF I SHOULD LIVE AS LIVES THE NEIGHBOURS" • • • • • • 331 ROUND TOWER   V 3
   THE RHETORICIAN WOULD DECEIVE HIS NEIGHBOURS, • • • • • 369 EGO DOMINUS   46
   AND LET THE NEIGHBOURS VOTE, • • • • • • • • • • • 598 STONE CROSS   6
   THAT IF THEIR NEIGHBOURS FIGURED PLAIN, • • • • • • 626 OLD MEN BE MAD 11
NEIGHBOURS'
   NOR IN HIS NEIGHBOURS' EYES? • • • • • • • • • • • 291 TO A FRIEND   8
NEIGHED
   HE SHOOK HIMSELF AND NEIGHED THREE TIMES; • • • • • • 10 OISIN 1   110
   AND NEIGHED THREE TIMES. WHEN, WONDERING • • • • • • 10 OISIN 1   V 110A
NEIGHING
   NEIGHING ALONG THE LIFELESS WASTE; • • • • • • • • • 13 OISIN 1   170
NERVE
   FOR EVERY NERVE, AND TESTS A LOVER • • • • • • • • 388 SOLOMON WITCH   22
   FOR EVERY NERVE; LOVER TESTS LOVER • • • • • • • • 388 SOLOMON WITCH V 22
NERVELESS
   HIS TOOTHLESS HOUND AT HIS NERVELESS FEET, • • • • • • 26 OISIN 1   V 400
   I BURST THE CHAIN; STILL EARLESS, NERVELESS, BLIND, • • • 36 OISIN 2   97
   STILL EARLESS, NERVELESS, BLIND, THE EAGLES STOOD. • • • 36 OISIN 2   100
   STILL EARLESS, NERVELESS, BLIND, THE EAGLES DREAMED. • • • 36 OISIN 2   V 100
NESSA
   CAME BLANAID, MAC NESSA, TALL FERGUS WHO FEASTWARD OF OLD • • 53 OISIN 3   89
     TIME SLUNK,
   CAME BLANID, MAC NESSA, CUCHULIN; • • • • • • • • • 53 OISIN 3   V 89
   CAME BLANID, MAC NESSA, AND FERGUS WHO FEASTWARD OF OLD • • 53 OISIN 3   V 89
     TIME SLUNK,
NESSA'S
   AND OF THAT FAMOUS FERGUS, NESSA'S HUSBAND, • • • • • • 183 QUEEN MAEVE   71
NEST
   • • • WHO SLEEPS ON HER NEST, • • • • • • • • • • • 56 OISIN 3   134
   SHE BUILDS HER NEST UPON A NARROW LEDGE • • • • • • • 285 TWO KINGS   194
   BUT THE RIGHT TWIGS FOR AN EAGLE'S NEST; • • • • • • 288 TO WEALTHY MAN 36
   WHEN FIRST IT SPRANG OUT OF THE NEST • • • • • • • • 397 POLIT PRISONER 20
   AND SO WARM HER WILD NEST. • • • • • • • • • • • • 415 TOWER   172
   THE STARE'S NEST BY MY WINDOW • • • • • • • • • • • 424 STARES NEST   T
   THE JAY'S NEST BY MY WINDOW • • • • • • • • • • • • 424 STARES NEST   V T
   ON MIND, ON NEST, • • • • • • • • • • • • • • • • 574 LOVERS SONG   5
   O'ER HER NEST THE LIGHTS ARE BLENDING; • • • • • • • 646 ISLE STAT I 1   36
   AS ALIEN AS A CUCKOO IN A ROBIN'S NEST, • • • • • • 671 ISLE STAT II 3 138
   ALIEN AS CUCKOO IN A ROBIN'S NEST, • • • • • • • • 671 ISLE STAT II 3 V 138
NESTED
   NESTED 'MONG THE VAPOURS BROWN. • • • • • • • • • • 731 STREET DANCERS 6
NESTLE
   THE BIRDS THAT NESTLE IN THE LEAVES ARE SAD, • • • • • 652 ISLE STAT I 2   15
   WHERE SPICE-ISLES NESTLE ON THE STAR-TROD SEAS, • • • • 682 SEEKER   17
NESTLES
   THAT NESTLES ALONE IN THE WHISTLING WIND, • • • • • • 657 ISLE STAT I 3   68
NESTS
   • • • THE OWLS HAD BUILDED THEIR NESTS IN THEIR LOCKS, • • • 49 OISIN 3   39
   FROM YEAR TO YEAR BY THE UNNUMBERED NESTS • • • • • • 74 ANASHU VIJAYA   72
NET
   • • • CROZIERED ONE, CAUGHT IN YOUR NET; • • • • • • • 58 OISIN 3   167
   • • • CROZIERED ONE, CAUGHT IN THY NET— • • • • • • • 58 OISIN 3   V 167
   • • • CROZIERED ONE, CAUGHT IN THEIR NET; • • • • • • 58 OISIN 3   V 167
   ABOUT THE CASTING OUT OF MY NET, • • • • • • • • • 146 FISH   4
   I THINK THAT HE HAS FORGAEL IN HIS NET, • • • • • • • 224 SHADOW WATER B 56
   AND DRAGS HIM THROUGH THE SEA. WELL, NET OR NONE, • • • 224 SHADOW WATER B 57

			PAGE	TITLE		LINE

NET   (CONTINUED)
```
    BOTH YOU AND I ARE TAKEN IN THE NET.  . . . . . . . . .    237 SHADOW WATER B      323
    OF THE GREAT GOLDEN NET THAT IS ABOUT US.  . . . . . .     238 SHADOW WATER B      352
    YOU CANNOT LEAP OUT OF THE GOLDEN NET.  . . . . . . .      238 SHADOW WATER B      360
    FLASHES AS IF IT WERE A NET OF HERRINGS.  . . . . . .      248 SHADOW WATER B      536
    BELOVED, HAVING DRAGGED THE NET ABOUT US,  . . . . . .     252 SHADOW WATER B      615
    SHE WOULD WEAVE A NET TO TAKE US.  SHE MIGHT KEEP FAITH!   756 SHADOW WATER A      190
    OR THAN THE SHIVERING CASTING NET OF THE STARS.  . . .     762 SHADOW WATER A  V   290
    O! I WOULD BREAK THIS NET THE GODS HAVE WOVEN  . . . .     765 SHADOW WATER A      361
```
NETS
```
    WHO PACED IN THE EVE BY THE NETS ON THE PEBBLY SHORE,  .    91 OLD FISHERMAN        11
    THE LINES ARE NOT HEAVY, NOR HEAVY THE LONG NETS BROWN--    91 OLD FISHERMAN    V    5
    COME CLEAR OF THE NETS OF WRONG AND RIGHT;  . . . . .      147 INTO TWILIGHT         2
    COME CLEAR OFF THE NETS OF WRONG AND RIGHT!  . . . . .     147 INTO TWILIGHT    V    2
    THE NETS OF DAY AND NIGHT.  . . . . . . . . . . . .        175 ELEMENT POWERS       12
    ROMANTIC FISH SWAM IN NETS COMING TO THE HAND;  . . .      485 THREE MOVEMENT        2
    I AM CAUGHT IN WOVEN NETS OF ENCHANTMENT.  LOOK!  . .      762 SHADOW WATER A      293
    THE GODS WEAVE NETS, AND TAKE US IN THEIR NETS,  . . .     764 SHADOW WATER A      339
    THE GODS WEAVE NETS, AND TAKE US IN THEIR NETS,  . . .     764 SHADOW WATER A      339
    THE NETS THE GODS HAVE WOVEN AND OUR OWN HEARTS,  . . .    766 SHADOW WATER A      383
    THE GODS HATE HAPPINESS, AND WEAVE THEIR NETS .  . . .     767 SHADOW WATER A      399
```
NETTED
```
    THE NETTED MARKS OF CRAWLING SCALES SEA-SPRUNG  . . .       37 OISIN 2         V  115
```
NETTLES
```
    WHEN NETTLES WAVE UPON A SHAPELESS MOUND  . . . . . .      489 COOLE PARK 29        27
```
NETTLESHIP'S
```
    ON MR. NETTLESHIP'S PICTURE AT THE ROYAL HIBERNIAN ACADEMY.  688 NETTLESHIP         T
```
NEVER
```
    A SWIFTER CREATURE NEVER WAS BORN,  . . . . . . . . .        2 OISIN 1         V   70
    WHERE BROKEN FAITH HAS NEVER BEEN KNOWN,  . . . . . .        8 OISIN 1             84
    AND THE BLUSHES OF FIRST LOVE NEVER HAVE FLOWN!  . . .       8 OISIN 1             85
    TO SHORES WHERE DYING HAS NEVER BEEN KNOWN,  . . . . .       8 OISIN 1         V   84
    AND THE FLUSHES OF FIRST LOVE NEVER HAVE FLOWN!  . . .       8 OISIN 1         V   85
    AND KISSED, AS THEY WOULD NEVER CEASE,  . . . . . . .       16 OISIN 1            215
    "A SADDER CREATURE NEVER STEPT . . . . . . . . . . .        17 OISIN 1            238
    BUT NEVER, NEVER ON OUR GRAVES,  . . . . . . . . . .        21 OISIN 1            313
    BUT NEVER, NEVER ON OUR GRAVES,  . . . . . . . . . .        21 OISIN 1            313
    NEVER, NEVER ON OUR GRAVES, . . . . . . . . . . . .         21 OISIN 1            313
    NEVER, NEVER ON OUR GRAVES, . . . . . . . . . . . .         21 OISIN 1            313
    AND WE NEVER FEAR THE MORROW  . . . . . . . . . . .         21 OISIN 1            318
    "BUT NEVER WITH US WHERE THE WILD FOWL CHASES  . . . .      27 OISIN 1            408
    "BUT NEVER THE YEARS IN THE ISLE'S SOFT PLACES  . . .       27 OISIN 1         V 419A
    "BUT NEVER THE YEARS IN OUR ISLE'S SOFT PLACES  . . .       28 OISIN 1         V  424
    AND HOW THOSE LOVERS NEVER TURN THEIR EYES .  . . . .       29 OISIN 2             11
    HOW SUCH A WARRIOR NEVER TURNED HIS GAZE  . . . . . .       29 OISIN 2             11
    AS THOUGH UNTO HIS NEVER SLUMBERING HEART  . . . . .        32 OISIN 2         V   44
    AS THOUGH HE TOLD HIS NEVER SLUMBERING HEART  . . . .       32 OISIN 2         V   44
    NOR THE HIGH GODS WHO NEVER LIVED, MAY FIGHT  . . . .       34 OISIN 2             80
    FOR NEVER MORTAL CRY SO FAR HATH SENT,  . . . . . . .       36 OISIN 2         V  108
    AND NEVER FIND, THOUGH YE IN MUSIC SPEAK.  . . . . .        42 OISIN 2         V  201
    AND NEVER A SONG SANG NIAMH, AND OVER MY FINGER-TIPS  .     47 OISIN 3              6
    . . . THE SPITTLE ON HIS BEARD NEVER DRY,  . . . . .        53 OISIN 3             90
    . . . WITH THE SPITTLE ON HIS BEARD NEVER DRY.  . . .       60 OISIN 3            192
    VIJAYA, SWEAR TO HER LOVE NEVER MORE.  . . . . . . .        74 ANASHU VIJAYA       65
    WHO NEVER HEAR THE UNFORGIVING HOUND.  . . . . . . .        75 ANASHU VIJAYA       75
    WHO NEVER HEARD THE UNFORGIVING HOUND.  . . . . . . .       75 ANASHU VIJAYA   V   75
    MAY NEVER RESTLESS FAY WITH FIDGET FINGER  . . . . .        75 ANASHU VIJAYA   V   90
    "YOUR EYES THAT ONCE WERE NEVER WEARY OF MINE .  . . .      79 EPHEMERA             1
    WHEN I WAS A BOY WITH NEVER A CRACK IN MY HEART.  . .       91 OLD FISHERMAN        4
    WHEN I WAS A BOY WITH NEVER A CRACK IN MY HEART.  . .       91 OLD FISHERMAN        8
    WHEN I WAS A BOY WITH NEVER A CRACK IN MY HEART.  . .       91 OLD FISHERMAN       12
    TO DO. AND DO AND DO AND NEVER DREAM.  . . . . . . .       103 FERGUS DRUID    V   28
    TURN IF YOU MAY FROM BATTLES NEVER DONE,  . . . . . .      114 ROSE OF BATTLE       7
    FOR HIM WHO HEARS LOVE SING AND NEVER CEASE,  . . . .      114 ROSE OF BATTLE      10
    "FROM THE GREY SHIPS AND BATTLES NEVER WON.  . . . .       114 ROSE OF BATTLE  V    8
    HAS AWAKED IN OUR HEARTS, MY BELOVED, A SADNESS THAT NEVER 122 WHITE BIRDS     V    4
       MAY DIE.
    THAT TIME CAN NEVER MAR A LOVER'S VOWS  . . . . . . .      126 DREAM OF FAERY      10
    HOW TIME MAY NEVER MAR THEIR LOVER'S VOWS  . . . . .       126 DREAM OF FAERY  V   10
    AND MEN WHO LOVED THE CAUSE THAT NEVER DIES.  . . . .      130 BOOK STORIES    V   24
    HE RODE NOW AS HE NEVER RODE,  . . . . . . . . . . .       133 FR GILLIGAN         29
    BECAUSE THE BLOSSOMING DREAMS HAVE NEVER BENT  . . . .     136 TO SOME I TALK       8
    AND NEVER WAS PIPING SO SAD,  . . . . . . . . . . .        144 HOST OF AIR         11
    AND NEVER WAS PIPING SO GAY,  . . . . . . . . . . .        144 HOST OF AIR         12
    AND NEVER WAS PIPING SO SAD,  . . . . . . . . . . .        145 HOST OF AIR         43
    AND NEVER WAS PIPING SO GAY,  . . . . . . . . . . .        145 HOST OF AIR         44
    BY A GREY SHORE WHERE THE WIND NEVER BLEW,  . . . . .      170 SECRET ROSE         14
    I NEVER HAVE SEEN MAID QUIET  . . . . . . . . . . .        171 MAID QUIET      V    1
    OF THOSE THAT, IT MAY BE, CAN NEVER AGE.  . . . . . .      183 QUEEN MAEVE         76
    OF THOSE THAT IT MAY BE SHALL NEVER FADE.  . . . . .       183 QUEEN MAEVE     V   76
    BY RIVERS WHERE THE RAIN HAS NEVER DIMMED  . . . . .       184 QUEEN MAEVE     V   87
    THEIR LOVE WAS NEVER DROWNED IN CARE  . . . . . . . .      189 BAILE AILLINN        8
    THOSE OTHER TWO! FOR NEVER YET  . . . . . . . . . .        197 BAILE AILLINN      205
    NEVER GIVE ALL THE HEART  . . . . . . . . . . . . .        202 NEVER GIVE ALL       T
    NEVER GIVE ALL THE HEART, FOR LOVE  . . . . . . . .        202 NEVER GIVE ALL       1
    CERTAIN, AND THEY NEVER DREAM  . . . . . . . . . . .       202 NEVER GIVE ALL       4
    O NEVER GIVE THE HEART OUTRIGHT,  . . . . . . . . .        202 NEVER GIVE ALL       8
    ALTHOUGH WE NEVER HEARD OF IT AT SCHOOL  . . . . . .       205 ADAMS CURSE     V   19
    WILL NEVER FIND US THERE . . . . . . . . . . . . .        213 HAPPY TOWNLAND  V    2
    YOU'RE CERTAIN OF IT? I NEVER WAKE FROM SLEEP  . . .       226 SHADOW WATER B      83
    I'D NEVER COME UPON THE HAPPINESS  . . . . . . . . .       226 SHADOW WATER B      87
    THAT I WILL NEVER LIFT A HAND AGAINST YOU.  . . . . .      227 SHADOW WATER B     108
```

555

NEVER   (CONTINUED)

YOU'VE NEVER KNOWN, I'D LAY A WAGER ON IT, ...   227 SHADOW WATER B   113
THAT NEVER DID A HAND'S TURN? AIBRIC! AIBRIC! . . . . .   228 SHADOW WATER B   130
YET NEVER HAVE TWO LOVERS KISSED BUT THEY . . . . .   229 SHADOW WATER B   153
YOU'D NEVER DOUBT THAT IT WAS LIFE THEY PROMISED . . . .   231 SHADOW WATER B   197
NONE BUT THE DEAD, OR THOSE THAT NEVER LIVED, ...   231 SHADOW WATER B   202
I NEVER HAVE BEEN GOLDEN-ARMED IOLLAN. . . . . . .   244 SHADOW WATER B   464
I'LL NEVER GIVE ANOTHER THOUGHT TO IT! . . . . . .   245 SHADOW WATER B   477
THAT YOU MAY NEVER HEAR THE CRY OF THE BIRDS, ...   250 SHADOW WATER B   575
BUT NEVER MADE A POORER SONG . . . .   273 GREY ROCK   55
WOULD NEVER LOOK AGAIN ON KNOWN MAN'S FACE." . . . .   280 TWO KINGS   75
WILL NEVER LOOK AGAIN ON KNOWN MAN'S FACE." . . . .   280 TWO KINGS   V   75
"NEVER WILL I BELIEVE THERE IS ANY CHANGE . . . .   285 TWO KINGS   203
YET NEVER HAVE I LIT ON A FRIEND . . . .   301 RUN PARADISE   25
AND NEVER COULD HAVE RESTED IN THE TOMB . . . . .   325 ROBERT GREGORY   27
NEVER UNTIL THIS MOMENT HAVE WE MET . . . . . .   339 SHEP GOATHERD   7
YET NEVER COULD, ALTHOUGH . . . .   345 ON WOMAN   13
YET NEVER HAVE I, NOW NOR ANY TIME, ...   352 PEOPLE   28
THAT NEVER LOOKED UPON MAN WITH DESIRE, ...   358 PRESENCES   13
HE NEVER FOUND HIS REST ASHORE, ...   361 ALF POLLEXFEN   21
WHAT HE SHALL NEVER FIND. WHY SHOULD NOT YOU . . . .   373 PHASES OF MOON   20
AND NEVER WROTE A BOOK, YOUR THOUGHT IS CLEAR. . . . .   376 PHASES OF MOON   97
THAT HE WILL NEVER FIND! I'D PLAY A PART! . . . . .   377 PHASES OF MOON   128
HE WOULD NEVER KNOW ME AFTER ALL THESE YEARS . . . .   377 PHASES OF MOON   129
DAY AFTER DAY, YET NEVER FIND THE MEANING. . . . . .   377 PHASES OF MOON   135
WE NEVER THOUGHT TO ENQUIRE . . . .   381 SONGS FOOL 2   3
UNDER BLANK EYES AND FINGERS NEVER STILL . . . . .   382 VISION ROBART   5
THAT OTHER'S MOONLIT EYEBALLS NEVER MOVED, ...   383 VISION ROBART   33
WHO NEVER GAVE THE BURNING TOWN A THOUGHT! . . . . .   384 VISION ROBART   57
AND NEVER CREW AGAIN TILL NOW. . . . .   388 SOLOMON WITCH   12
NEVER UNTIL THIS NIGHT HAVE I BEEN STIRRED. . . . . .   389 IMAGE PAST   1
MY EYES SHOULD NEVER REST? . . . .   389 IMAGE PAST   18
AND OF A MIDDLETON, WHOSE NAME YOU NEVER HEARD, ...   391 UNDER SATURN   8
NEVER TO LEAVE THAT VALLEY HIS FATHERS CALLED THEIR HOME. .   391 UNDER SATURN   16
THAT NEVER YET HAD FREEMAN . . . .   401 DEMON BEAST   36
THAT CHOOSES RIGHT, AND NEVER FIND A FRIEND. . . . . .   404 FOR DAUGHTER   24
CAN NEVER TEAR THE LINNET FROM THE LEAF. . . . . .   405 FOR DAUGHTER   56
ONCE OUT OF NATURE I SHALL NEVER TAKE . . . . .   408 SAIL BYZANTIUM   25
AS TO A DOG'S TAIL? NEVER HAD I MORE . . . . .   409 TOWER   4
AS UPON A DOG'S TAIL. NEVER HAD I MORE . . . . .   409 TOWER   V   4
AND NEVER STOOP TO A MECHANICAL . . . . . .   417 ANCEST HOUSES   7
THEY NEVER SAW HOW SEASONS RUN, ...   432 NINETEEN 19   101
NOAH'S FRESHET NEVER REACHED. . . . .   440 WISDOM   15
WHERE SEVEN EPHESIAN TOPERS SLEPT AND NEVER KNEW . . .   442 BLACK CENTAUR   11
AND I THOUGH NEVER OF LEDAEAN KIND . . . . . .   444 SCHOOL CHILDR   29
NEVER TO HAVE LIVED IS BEST, ANCIENT WRITERS SAY! . . . .   459 FROM OEDIPUS   10
NEVER TO HAVE DRAWN THE BREATH OF LIFE, ...   459 FROM OEDIPUS   11
. . . . NEVER TO HAVE LOOKED INTO THE EYE OF DAY! . . . .   459 FROM OEDIPUS   11
NEVER TO HAVE DRUNK THE BREATH OF LIFE, ...   459 FROM OEDIPUS   V   11
MY HEART COULD NEVER TURN FROM DAILY RUIN. . . . . .   464 HARUN RASHID   83
THAT NEVER KNEW THAT STRAIN WOULD SCARCE SEEM BRIGHT, . .   465 HARUN RASHID   88
ON OLD DRY FAGGOTS THAT COULD NEVER PLEASE . . . . .   466 HARUN RASHID   124
AND TOLD HIM SO, BUT FRIENDSHIP NEVER ENDS! . . . . .   473 ALL SOUL NIGHT   65
THAT NEVER LOOKED OUT OF THE EYE OF A SAINT . . . .   486 SEVEN SAGES   12
BUT NEVER SAW THE TREFOIL STAINED WITH BLOOD, ...   487 SEVEN SAGES   19
"NEVER SHALL A YOUNG MAN, ...   492 ANNE GREGORY   1
SO NEVER HANG YOUR HEART UPON . . . .   509 JANE REPROVED   12
HAD I NEVER THOUGHT . . . .   534 CONSOLATION   8
"BUT NEVER DARE TO BOAST . . . .   539 MEETING   8
TO THOSE THAT NEVER SAW THIS TONSURED HEAD . . . . .   555 RIBH AT TOMB   4
SENTENCES THAT HE HAS NEVER THOUGHT! . . . . . .   560 WHENCE COME   6
AND NEVER HAVE I DANCED FOR JOY. . . . . . .   567 FROM JAPANESE   9
ALL THE OLYMPIANS; A THING NEVER KNOWN AGAIN. . . . .   578 LOFTY THINGS   12
IT NEVER CROSSED THE SEA BECAUSE . . . . . .   583 GHOST ROG CASE   3
CAN NEVER CLOSE THOSE EYES." . . . .   588 OLD WICKED MAN   26
BUT I NEVER STOPPED TO QUESTION, WHAT COULD THE BOATMAN SAY   593 PILGRIM   19
AND NEVER HAVE I LOOKED UPON . . . .   595 COLONEL MARTIN   32
THAT THEY COULD NEVER SHOOT A MAN . . . . . .   596 COLONEL MARTIN   61
"I NEVER THOUGHT OF THAT, SIR." . . . .   596 COLONEL MARTIN   66
I NEVER BADE YOU GO . . . .   600 THOSE IMAGES   5
DEEP-ROOTED THINGS," BUT NEVER FORESAW ITS END, ...   603 GALLERY REVIS   37
WHAT DEEP ROOTS ARE," AND NEVER FORESAW THE END . .   603 GALLERY REVIS   V   37
HE NEVER LAY BEHIND FOUR WALLS . . . .   606 SONGS BURDEN 1   12
BUT NEVER ASKED FOR LOVE! SHOULD I ASK THAT, ...   609 IN TARAS HALLS   9
BUT NEVER SAID A THING. . . . .   627 STATES HOLIDAY   10
THAT BROAD NOON HAS NEVER LIT, ...   632 MAN AND ECHO   4
AND NEVER GET THE ANSWERS RIGHT. . . . . . .   632 MAN AND ECHO   10
OF THE SONGS THAT NEVER SLEEP. . . . .   647 ISLE STAT I 1   76
THAT FLOWER I SEEK. THOU NEVER WILT RETURN. . . . .   653 ISLE STAT I 2   44
BUT A MOTHER PANTHER NEVER . . . .   658 ISLE STAT I 3   92
TO YONDER ISLE, WHERE NEVER SAIL WAS FURLED, ...   664 ISLE STAT II 2   63
AND NEVER HEARD OF GRIEF OR CARE . . . . . .   667 ISLE STAT II 3   21
AND EVEN SHE SHALL NEVER HOLD . . . .   668 ISLE STAT II 3   50
OR AUGHT REMOTE! OR HAST THOU NEVER HEARD . . . .   672 ISLE STAT II 3   153
OR HAST THOU NEVER SEEN, WITH VISAGE MEEK, ...   672 ISLE STAT II 3   156
AND NEVER ANY MORE THE WIDE-EYED BANDS . . . . .   674 ISLE STAT II 3   218
A GREY-HAIRED YOUTH, WHOSE CHEEKS HAD NEVER FOUND, . . .   687 TWO TITANS   7
WITH WONDERFUL WHITE SANDS, WHERE NEVER YET . . . .   693 MOSADA 1   81
WITH WONDERFUL WHITE SAND, WHERE NEVER YET . . . .   693 MOSADA 1   V   81
I NEVER KNEW AN EVE SO MARVELLOUS STILL. . . . . .   702 MOSADA 3   88
THEIR THIEVING WINGS THAT WE MIGHT NEVER PART. . . . .   702 MOSADA 3   98

		PAGE	TITLE		LINE

NEVER (CONTINUED)

I NEVER KNEW A NIGHT SO HONEY-SWEET. . . . . 702 MOSADA 3 99
I NEVER KNEW A NIGHT SO HONEY SWEET. . . . . 702 MOSADA 3 V 99
I NEVER KNEW A NIGHT SO DEW-BEDROWNED. . . . . 703 MOSADA 3 105
I NEVER KNEW A NIGHT SO BITTER COLD. . . . . 704 MOSADA 3 124
AND DEATH, OH MY FAIR ONE, WILL NEVER COME NEAR . . . . 717 LOVE SONG 8
NEVER STORM AROSE SO SWIFTLY; SCARCE THE CHILDREN WERE 718 PHANTOM SHIP 4
    IN BED,
SOME DAY YOU'LL BUY THEM, MAYBE. NEVER! NEVER? . . . . 721 WITCH VIVIEN 24
SOME DAY YOU'LL BUY THEM, MAYBE. NEVER! NEVER? . . . . 721 WITCH VIVIEN 24
AND NEVER REST IN THEIR FLIGHT. . . . . 739 WHERE BOOKS GO 4
HIS FACE HAS NEVER GLADDENED SINCE HE CAME . . . . . . 747 SHADOW WATER A 1
AND WILL YOU SWEAR NEVER TO BE AVENGED . . . . 758 SHADOW WATER A 223
BODIES THAT CAN NEVER TIRE . . . . 776 AGAINST WITCH 20
AND CAN NEVER BE CONTENT . . . . 777 SONG DEIRDRE 2 2
THEIR BRIEF LIVES I NEVER KNEW. . . . . 787 HUDDON DUDDON 5
BUT NEVER STOOD BEFORE A STAKE . . . . 790 SINGING HEAD 23
BUT NEVER, NEVER DANGLING LEAVE THE LIVER AND THE LIGHTS. 790 HEART SLEEVE 2
BUT NEVER, NEVER DANGLING LEAVE THE LIVER AND THE LIGHTS. 790 HEART SLEEVE 2
NEVER-ANXIOUS
AND ALWAYS NEVER-ANXIOUS SLEEP; . . . . 8 OISIN 1 93
NEVER-LIFTING
IN THE NEVER-LIFTING DARK. . . . . 658 ISLE STAT I 3 89
NEVER-SLUMBERING
AS THOUGH HE TOLD HIS NEVER-SLUMBERING HEART . . . . . 32 OISIN 2 44
NEW   SEE BRAND-NEW
BLOSSOM IN SOME NEW CRIMSON FLOWER. . . . . 16 OISIN 1 224
WE SAW, SOME NEW, SOME PRINTED WHEN THE PLACE WAS YOUNG, 37 OISIN 2 V 116
HIS NEW HEALED SHAPE! AND FOR A HUNDRED YEARS . . . . 44 OISIN 2 V 221
NEW DREAMS, NEW DREAMS! THERE IS NO TRUTH . . . . . . 66 HAPPY SHEPHERD 26
NEW DREAMS, NEW DREAMS! THERE IS NO TRUTH . . . . . . 66 HAPPY SHEPHERD 26
I HAVE FORGIVEN, O NEW STAR! . . . . 75 ANASHU VIJAYA 77
ARE WITH NEW SORROW WRUNG! . . . . 99 FOXHUNTER 38
AND THROUGH THAT NEW BLADE'S GUARD THE OLD BLADE BROKE, 110 CUCHULAIN SEA 66
MOURNFUL THAT NO NEW WONDER MAY BETIDE, ... 111 ROSE OF WORLD 3
GIVE TO THESE CHILDREN, NEW FROM THE WORLD, ... 116 FAERY SONG 5
GIVE TO THESE CHILDREN, NEW FROM THE WORLD, ... 116 FAERY SONG 9
SHINING BRIGHT AS A NEW LANCE! . . . . 125 CATHLEEN PARA V 14
THE SINGING SHOOK HIM OUT OF HIS NEW EASE. . . . . . . 126 DREAM OF FAERY 12
A HONIED RINGING! UNDER THE NEW SKIES . . . . 130 BOOK STORIES V 21
AND NEW FRIENDS BUSY WITH YOUR PRAISE, ... 173 PLEADS FRIEND 3
AND OF NEW FRIENDS ARE GLAD WITH YOUR PRAISE, ... 173 PLEADS FRIEND V 3
TARA UPROOTED, AND NEW COMMONNESS . . . . 198 SEVEN WOODS 6
IT MIGHT CALL UP A NEW AGE, CALLING TO MIND . . . . . 201 OLD MEMORY 4
AND ALL THE ALE RAN OUT AT THE NEW MOON; . . . . . . 222 SHADOW WATER B V 11
THAT HAS THE HEADY FLAVOUR OF NEW WINE, ... 240 SHADOW WATER B 374
ON HEARING THAT THE STUDENTS OF OUR NEW UNIVERSITY . . . 262 STUDENTS AGIT T
WE'LL KEEP THE SECRET--A NEW TRICK TO PLEASE. . . . . 265 ABBEY THEATRE 10
SING ON! SOMEWHERE AT SOME NEW MOON. . . . . 266 GALWAY RACES 10
BUT SOME DAY AND AT SOME NEW MOON . . . . 266 GALWAY RACES V 10
SING ON! SOMETIME, AND AT SOME NEW MOON . . . . 266 GALWAY RACES V 10
OF A NEW FRIEND HE HAS TURNED A GHOST. . . . . 275 GREY ROCK 103
THAT SOME NEW DAY MAY BREED THE BEST . . . . 288 TO WEALTHY MAN 34
ALWAYS WE'D HAVE THE NEW FRIEND MEET THE OLD . . . . . 324 ROBERT GREGORY 9
NEW WELCOME AND OLD WISDOM AT HER FIRE . . . . 340 SHEP GOATHERD 32
AS A MAN DOES WHO HAS PUBLISHED A NEW BOOK, ... 350 HER PRAISE 3
OR A YOUNG GIRL DRESSED OUT IN HER NEW GOWN, ... 350 HER PRAISE 4
A WOMAN SPOKE OF SOME NEW TALE SHE HAD READ, ... 350 HER PRAISE 7
A NEW MODELLED DOLL, OR DRAWING, ... 362 DOLLS DRAWINGS 2
A NEW DANCE TURN. . . . . 378 CAT AND MOON 16
A NEW DANCE TUNE. . . . . 378 CAT AND MOON V 16
AND NEW DANCE TURN. . . . . 378 CAT AND MOON V 16
HAS TAKEN A NEW PHASE. . . . . 379 CAT AND MOON 20
AND THE NEW STILL HIDES HER HORN. . . . . 382 VISION ROBART 4
FOR THOSE NEW COMRADES THEY HAVE FOUND, ... 395 SIXTEEN DEAD 15
CURVED LIKE NEW MOON, MOON-LUMINOUS, ... 421 MY TABLE 10
CURVED LIKE NEW MOON, MOON LUMINOUS, ... 421 MY TABLE V 10
WHIRLS OUT NEW RIGHT AND WRONG, ... 430 NINETEEN 19 55
THE NEW FACES . . . . 435 NEW FACES T
LET THE NEW FACES PLAY WHAT TRICKS THEY WILL . . . . . 435 NEW FACES 5
ARE BUT A NEW EXPRESSION OF HER BODY . . . . 469 HARUN RASHID 185
BY SOME NEW MARRIED BRIDE I TAKE . . . . 535 CHOSEN V 13
ON THE LEAF-SOWN, NEW MOWN, SMOOTH . . . . 568 SWEET DANCER V 2
BUT THAT IS NOTHING NEW. . . . . 581 ROGER CASEMENT 4
AND THAT IS SOMETHING NEW! . . . . 582 ROGER CASEMENT 12
BECAUSE OF THOSE NEW DEAD . . . . 599 SPIRIT MEDIUM 2
BUT EVEN AT THE STARTING-POST, ALL SLEEK AND NEW, . . . 619 BRONZE HEAD 15
A NEW DAY'S TROOP OF WASP AND BEE . . . . 646 ISLE STAT I 1 44
AND THEN NEW MURMURS CAME NEW UTTERING . . . . 657 ISLE STAT I 3 50
AND THEN NEW MURMURS CAME NEW UTTERING . . . . 657 ISLE STAT I 3 50
AND NOT TOO CLEAR, HOW WILL THE NEW GOD KNOW . . . . . 658 ISLE STAT I 3 79
LOVE STORM; AND STAINED WITH MIST THE NEW MOONS FLARE. . 678 ISLE STAT II 3 294
LOVE STORM AND STAINED WITH MIST THE NEW MOON'S FLARE . 678 ISLE STAT II 3 V 294
WHY THESE NEW FEARS? THE GREAT MONK EBREMAR, ... 692 MOSADA 1 46
WHY THESE NEW FEARS? THE SERVANT OF THE LORD, ... 692 MOSADA 1 V 46
WILL YOU NOT HEAR MY LAST NEW SONG? HUSH, HUSH! . . . 695 MOSADA 2 1
A STRANGER NEW ARISEN WAIT . . . . 696 MOSADA 2 V 22
FLOATING FROM YON BARRED WINDOW. NEW COMER, ... 700 MOSADA 3 43
BUT I AM NEW TO LOVE. GO AMONG THESE . . . . 767 SHADOW WATER A 391
NEW-BORN
AWAKEN, AWAKEN TO NEW-BORN LUSTRE; . . . . 646 ISLE STAT I 1 43

557

	PAGE	TITLE	LINE

NEW-COMER
    FLOATING FROM YON BARRED WINDOW. SMALL NEW-COMER, . . .   700 MOSADA 3   43
NEW-FANGLED
    OF THEIR TALL, NEW-FANGLED QUEEN. . . . .   727 LOVERS QUARREL   48
NEW-HEALED
    HIS NEW-HEALED SHAPE; AND FOR A HUNDRED YEARS . . . . .   44 OISIN 2   221
NEWLY
    MAYBE YOU HAVE NOT HEARD OF US, YOU HAVE COME FORTH SO   75 ANASHU VIJAYA   78
        NEWLY,
    AS WHEN NEWLY GROWN TO BE A WOMAN, ...   199 ARROW   4
NEW-MARRIED
    BY SOME NEW-MARRIED BRIDE, I TAKE . . . .   535 CHOSEN   13
    WHERE MAY NEW-MARRIED WOMEN SIT . . . .   791 REPRISALS   19
NEW-MOWN
    TILL, FATTENING THE WINDS OF THE MORNING, AN ODOUR   57 OISIN 3   153
        OF NEW-MOWN HAY
    AN ODOUR OF THE NEW-MOWN HAY . . . .   502 VACILLATION   58
    ON THE LEAF-SOWN, NEW-MOWN, SMOOTH . . . .   568 SWEET DANCER   2
NEWS
    AND THEY HAVE NEWS OF DEIRDRE'S EYES, ...   193 BAILE AILLINN   97
    THEREFORE IT IS BUT LITTLE NEWS . . . .   194 BAILE AILLINN   124
    WHEN I FIRST HEARD THE NEWS? AH, THERE IT IS! . . .   241 SHADOW WATER B 398
    BROUGHT THE BARE NEWS. HE HAD THROWN THE CROOK AWAY . .   339 SHEP GOATHERD   21
    PULL DOWN ESTABLISHED HONOUR; HAWK FOR NEWS . . . .   398 LEADERS CROWD   3
    AND WHEN THE STORY'S FINISHED, WHAT'S THE NEWS? . . .   491 COOLE BALLYLEE V 40E
    WHEN ALL THAT STORY'S FINISHED, WHAT'S THE NEWS? . .   495 CHOICE   5
    NEWS FOR THE DELPHIC ORACLE . . . .   611 NEWS ORACLE   T
NEWT
    HUGS AND PETS AND PATS YON NEWT, ...   727 LOVERS QUARREL   27
NEWTON'S
    NOT SUCH AS ARE IN NEWTON'S METAPHOR, ...   494 AT ALGECIRAS   11
NEW-TORN
    CUT OUT OUR RHYMES ON STRIPS OF NEW-TORN BARK . . . .   343 SHEP GOATHERD   115
NEW-WASHED
    . . . FOR WHITER THAN NEW-WASHED FLEECE . . . . . .   47 OISIN 3   11
NEXT
    AND ALL THAT NIGHT, AND ALL THROUGH THE NEXT DAY . . .   185 QUEEN MAEVE   113
    TO STAY THE STAG'S NEXT RUSH. WHEN SWORD MET HORN . .   277 TWO KINGS   V 15
    AND THAT ENQUIRING MAN JOHN SYNGE COMES NEXT, . . .   324 ROBERT GREGORY   25
    OF THAT OR THE NEXT WINTER WOULD BE DEATH. . . . . .   471 ALL SOUL NIGHT   30
    ON FLORENCE EMERY I CALL THE NEXT, ...   472 ALL SOUL NIGHT   41
    BECAUSE THIS AGE AND THE NEXT AGE . . . .   598 STONE CROSS   9
    OR DEATH THAT COMETH WITH THE NEXT LIFE-KEY? . . . .   724 KANVA ON SELF   18
NIAM
    IS NIAM, DAUGHTER OF THE KING . . . .   5 OISIN 1   V 49
    YOUNG NIAM, AND THOU SHALT BE CALLEN . . . . . .   7 OISIN 1   V 75
    SANG NIAM, AND THEIR DEWY SHOWERS . . . .   11 OISIN 1   V 135
    SAID NIAM, AS SHE LAID THE TIP . . . .   12 OISIN 1   V 150
    MAID NIAM FROM A LITTLE TRUMP . . . .   14 OISIN 1   V 194
    BUT NIAM, WITH A SAD DISTRESS, ...   15 OISIN 1   V 211
    THEN SOFTLY TO ME NIAM CAME, ...   25 OISIN 1   V 373
    AND NOW SANG NIAM, SWAYING HER BRIGHT HEAD . . . .   29 OISIN 2   V 6
    SO SANG YOUNG NIAM, SWAYING HER BRIGHT HEAD, . . .   30 OISIN 2   V 15
    BUT NIAM WITH HER HANDS CARESSED HIS EARS, ...   30 OISIN 2   V 26
    AND THUS, MY LATE-LOST NIAM, DIDST THOU SAY: . . .   34 OISIN 2   V 78
    SAID NIAM. "AY, AND HUGE. WHEN YE HAVE LED . . .   35 OISIN 2   V 89
    TO FLY A SPIRIT," NIAM WEEPING SAID. . . . . . .   35 OISIN 2   V 92
    THE STRANGER WATCHED THE SWORD; BUT NIAM FAR, . . .   38 OISIN 2   V 136
    CAST THE LOOSE BULK, LEST NIAM FEAR HIM DEAD; . . .   41 OISIN 2   V 183
    HOLDING THAT HORSE LONG SEEN NOT, NIAM STOOD. . . .   44 OISIN 2   V 230
    LOST NIAM MOURN AND SAY, "AH, LOVE, WE GO . . . .   46 OISIN 2   V 245B
    YE HAVE NO POWER." "AND, NIAM, SAY, OF THESE . . .   46 OISIN 2   V 248
    SNATCHING THE HORN OF NIAM, I BLEW FORTH A LINGERING NOTE!   51 OISIN 3   V 57
    SNATCHING THE HORN OF NIAM, I BLEW A LINGERING NOTE! . .   51 OISIN 3   V 57
    SAD NIAM CAME NEAR ME, AND LAID HER BROWS ON THE MIDST   52 OISIN 3   V 74
        OF MY BREAST
    OH, HADST THOU SEEN BEAUTIFUL NIAM WAIL TO HERSELF AND   54 OISIN 3   V 109
        BLANCH,
    AND SOFTLY COME TO THY NIAM OVER THE TOPS OF THE TIDE;   52 OISIN 3   V 126
    BUT WEEP FOR THY NIAM, OH OISIN, WEEP; FOR IF ONLY THY SHOE   55 OISIN 3   V 127
    AND SHIVERING AND LONELY, AND LONGING FOR NIAM, I TURNED   60 OISIN 3   V 181
        ME ABOUT,
    AND FAND, AND NIAM, AND LABAN, WHO COULD CHANGE TO AN OTTER   209 UNDER THE MOON V 12
        OR FAWN,
    WHERE NIAM HEADS THE REVELRY. . . . .   743 DANAAN QUICK   29
NIAMH
    NIAMH, AND MY COUNTRY FAR . . . .   5 OISIN 1   48
    IS NIAMH, AND MY LAND WHERE TIDE . . . .   5 OISIN 1   V 48
    AND NIAMH BE WITH YOU FOR A WIFE." . . . . . .   9 OISIN 1   101
    AND NIAMH SANG CONTINUALLY . . . .   11 OISIN 1   134
    "VEX THEM NO LONGER," NIAMH SAID, ...   12 OISIN 1   148
    AND NIAMH BLEW THREE MERRY NOTES . . . .   14 OISIN 1   195
    BUT NIAMH WITH A SWIFT DISTRESS . . . .   15 OISIN 1   211
    THE GENTLE NIAMH WAS MY WIFE; . . . .   24 OISIN 1   357
    THEREON YOUNG NIAMH SOFTLY CAME . . . .   25 OISIN 1   373
    "GAZE NO MORE ON THE PHANTOMS," NIAMH SAID, . . .   29 OISIN 2   5
    NOR CEASED UNTIL WHITE NIAMH STROKED HIS EARS . . .   30 OISIN 2   26
    "I BRING DELIVERANCE," PEARL-PALE NIAMH SAID. . . .   34 OISIN 2   78
    "FLEE FROM HIM," PEARL-PALE NIAMH WEEPING CRIED; . . .   35 OISIN 2   92
    BUT ONLY EXULTANT FACES. NIAMH STOOD . . . . .   38 OISIN 2   136
    LEST NIAMH SHUDDER. FULL OF HOPE AND DREAD . . .   41 OISIN 2   183

			PAGE	TITLE		LINE

NIAMH   (CONTINUED)
```
      OUTCRY OF BATS.   AND THEN YOUNG NIAMH CAME . . . . . .     44 OISIN 2          229
      THE HARE LEAPED IN THE GRASS.  YOUNG NIAMH CAME . . . .     44 OISIN 2       V  229
      AND THEN LOST NIAMH MURMURED, "LOVE, WE GO . . . . . .      46 OISIN 2          245
      AND NEVER A SONG SANG NIAMH, AND OVER MY FINGER-TIPS . .    47 OISIN 3            6
      SNATCHING THE HORN OF NIAMH, I BLEW A LONG LINGERING NOTE.  51 OISIN 3           57
      AND THE PEARL-PALE NIAMH LAY BY ME, . . . . . . . . .       52 OISIN 3           74
      O HAD YOU SEEN BEAUTIFUL NIAMH GROW WHITE AS THE WATERS     54 OISIN 3          109
        ARE WHITE,
      I CRIED, "O NIAMH!  O WHITE ONE! IF ONLY A TWELVE-HOURED    55 OISIN 3          113
        DAY,
      AND SOFTLY COME TO YOUR NIAMH OVER THE TOPS OF THE TIDE!    55 OISIN 3          126
      BUT WEEP FOR YOUR NIAMH, O OISIN, WEEP! FOR IF ONLY YOUR    55 OISIN 3          127
        SHOE
      AND LONELY AND LONGING FOR NIAMH, I SHIVERED AND TURNED     60 OISIN 3          181
        ME ABOUT.
      AND NIAMH CALLING AWAY, COME AWAY!  . . . . . . .          140 HOSTING SIDHE      4
      AND NIAMH CALLING AWAY, COME AWAY. . . . . . . . .         141 HOSTING SIDHE     16
      THAT SAW YOUNG NIAMH HOVER WITH LOVE-LORN FACE . . . .     162 ASKS FORGIVE      13
      AND NIAMH AND LABAN AND FAND, WHO COULD CHANGE TO AN OTTER 209 UNDER THE MOON    12
        OR FAWN.
      NIAMH THAT RODE ON IT! LAD AND LASS . . . . . . . .        550 SEVERED HEAD      11
      MAN-PICKER NIAMH LEANT AND SIGHED . . . . . . . . .        611 NEWS ORACLE        5
NIAM'S
      IN NIAM'S HAIR--WHEN ROSE A WORLD OF TOWERS  . . . . .      30 OISIN 2       V   22
NIETZSCHE
      HECTOR IS IN THE DUST, NIETZSCHE IS BORN, . . . . . .      374 PHASES OF MOON    46
NIGH      SEE WELL-NIGH
      AND NOW STILL SAD OUR TROOP DREW NIGH . . . . . .           17 OISIN 1       V  247
      AND NIGH UNTO HIM EACH ONE DREW, . . . . . . . .            18 OISIN 1       V  257
      BLIND AND NIGH DEAF, WITH WITHERED ARMS HE LIES . . . .     42 OISIN 2       V  203
      THEN HE SANG SOFTLY NIGH THE PEARLY RIM!  . . . . .         69 SAD SHEPHERD      25
      THEN SANG HE SOFTLY NIGH THE PEARLY RIM!  . . . . .         69 SAD SHEPHERD   V  25
      AND SHOREWARD WAVES, WE NIGH HAVE FOUGHT! WAVES BRING      660 ISLE STAT II      44
      AND YONDER HUDDLING BLACKNESS DRAWETH NIGH-- . . . .       663 ISLE STAT II 2    15
      WELL NIGH IMMORTAL IN THIS CHARMED CLIME, . . . . .        674 ISLE STAT II 3   202
      WHY NOT?  HE IS HER OWN! AND CROUCHING NIGH . . . . .      688 TWO TITANS        44
      WHERE IS OUR BROTHER PETER?  WHEN YOU'RE NIGH, . . . .     696 MOSADA 2          12
      FROM HAYNAU'S LIFTED FINGERS--TWO DRAW NIGH . . . .        714 FERENCZ RENYI    104
      THE MAN WHOSE HOUR OF DEATH DRAWS NIGH, . . . . . .        716 FAIRY DOCTOR       6
      NIGH OF HIS WITS BY FEAR BEREFT. . . . . . . . . .         730 PRIEST FAIRY      50
NIGHEST
      THE NIGHEST BLOSSOM WHERE IT FALLS I'LL TAKE. . . . .      657 ISLE STAT I 3     65
NIGHT     SEE TO-NIGHT
      DAMASK ROSES IN THE NIGHT, . . . . . . . . . .             21 OISIN 1       V 306A
      BY RIVERS AND THE WOODS' OLD NIGHT! . . . . . . .          25 OISIN 1          387
      THE RIVERS, AND THE WOOD'S OLD NIGHT. . . . . . .          25 OISIN 1       V  387
      THAT SCARES WITH HIS BUSTLE THE DELICATE NIGHT, . . . .    28 OISIN 1       V 423B
      THE SINGING MELTED IN THE NIGHT! . . . . . . . .           28 OISIN 1       V 427A
      JABBER AND SCREAM ABOUT HIM IN THE NIGHT! . . . . .        34 OISIN 2           82
      WITH HOPE, MINE ENEMY.  AS HE BY NIGHT . . . . . .         34 OISIN 2       V   81
      GAVE TO HIGH NOON AND NOON TO NIGHT GAVE WAY! . . . .      40 OISIN 2          172
      AMID THE SHADES OF NIGHT, HE CHANGED AND RAN . . . .       40 OISIN 2          174
      AND THE MOON GOAD THE WATERS NIGHT AND DAY, . . . . .      45 OISIN 2          238
      AND THE EARS OF THE HORSE WENT SINKING AWAY IN THE HOLLOW  48 OISIN 3           21
        NIGHT,
      . . . "THE FENIANS HUNT WOLVES IN THE NIGHT, . . . . .     59 OISIN 3          171
      O SWIFT ON THE SEAS ALL DAY AND NIGHT  . . . . . .         70 CLOAK BOAT         8
      ALL DAY AND NIGHT." . . . . . . . . . . . .                70 CLOAK BOAT        10
      HE IS A MONSTROUS PEACOCK, AND HE WAVETH ALL THE NIGHT .   77 INDIAN ON GOD     19
      HOW I HAVE FOLLOWED, NIGHT AND DAY, . . . . . . .          85 MAD KING GOLL     53
      WE FOOT IT ALL THE NIGHT, . . . . . . . . . . .            87 STOLEN CHILD      16
      A THIN GREY MAN HALF LOST IN GATHERING NIGHT. . . . .     102 FERGUS DRUID       7
      A THIN, GREY MAN, HALF-LOST IN GATHERING NIGHT. . . .     102 FERGUS DRUID   V   7
      TO THESE OLD NIGHT SHALL ALL HER MYSTERY TELL! . . . .    114 ROSE OF BATTLE    22
      AND THE LONG DEW-DROPPING HOURS OF THE NIGHT, . . . .     116 FAERY SONG         7
      I WILL ARISE AND GO NOW, FOR ALWAYS NIGHT AND DAY . . .   117 ISLE INNISFREE     9
      WHEN EARTHY NIGHT HAD DRUNK HIS BODY IN! . . . . .        127 DREAM OF FAERY    28
      WAS WEARY NIGHT AND DAY! . . . . . . . . . .              132 FR GILLIGAN        2
      "HE WHO HATH MADE THE NIGHT OF STARS . . . . . .          134 FR GILLIGAN       41
      HAS PLANTED QUIET IN THE NIGHT! . . . . . . . .           134 TWO TREES          8
      THAT THE STORMY NIGHT RECEIVES, . . . . . . . .           135 TWO TREES         26
      WHILE THE NIGHT GREW, ABOVE THE FADING COALS, . . . .     136 TO SOME I TALK V   3
      THE MARINERS OF NIGHT ABOVE, . . . . . . . . .            139 TO IRELAND     V  38
      THE HOST IS RUSHING 'TWIXT NIGHT AND DAY, . . . . .       141 HOSTING SIDHE     13
      AT THE COMING OF NIGHT TIDE, . . . . . . . . .            144 HOST OF AIR    V   6
      UNDER MY FEET THAT THEY FOLLOW YOU NIGHT AND DAY. . . .   153 CHANGE BELOVED     5
      UNDER MY FEET, THAT I FOLLOW YOU, NIGHT AND DAY, . . .    153 CHANGE BELOVED V   5
      THE NORTH UNFOLDS ABOVE THEM CLINGING, CREEPING NIGHT, .  154 BELOVED PEACE      3
      THE NORTH UNROLLS ABOVE THEM CLINGING, CREEPING NIGHT, .  154 BELOVED PEACE  V   3
      SHE ROSE IN HER PALE NIGHT GOWN, . . . . . . . .          159 CAP AND BELLS  V  10
      THE NIGHT SMELLED RICH WITH JUNE. . . . . . . .           160 CAP AND BELLS  V  28
      O WINDS, OLDER THAN CHANGING OF NIGHT AND DAY, . . . .    162 ASKS FORGIVE       7
      O WINDS, ELDER THAN CHANGING OF NIGHT AND DAY, . . . .    162 ASKS FORGIVE   V   7
      "O BLESSEDNESS COMES IN THE NIGHT AND THE DAY . . . .     168 BLESSED           33
      INTO THE BLINDING NIGHT.-- . . . . . . . . . .            174 ELEMENT POWERS V   4
      THE NETS OF DAY AND NIGHT. . . . . . . . . . .            175 ELEMENT POWERS    12
      OF NIGHT AND LIGHT AND THE HALF-LIGHT, . . . . .          176 CLOTHS HEAVEN      4
      OF NIGHT AND LIGHT AND THE HALF LIGHT, . . . . .          176 CLOTHS HEAVEN  V   4
      BUT THAT GREAT QUEEN, WHO MORE THAN HALF THE NIGHT . . .  180 QUEEN MAEVE       16
      WHEN NIGHT WAS AT ITS DEEPEST, A WILD GOOSE . . . . .     181 QUEEN MAEVE       36
```

559

NIGHT   (CONTINUED)

AND ALL THAT NIGHT, AND ALL THROUGH THE NEXT DAY . . . . .   185 QUEEN MAEVE   113
TO MIDDLE NIGHT, THEY DUG INTO THE HILL. . . . .   185 QUEEN MAEVE   114
AS MIDDLE NIGHT GREAT CATS WITH SILVER CLAWS, ...   185 QUEEN MAEVE   115
IN THE GREY REEDS THAT NIGHT AND MORN . . . .   190 BAILE AILLINN   42
WHO WHEN NIGHT THICKENS ARE AFLOAT . . . .   196 BAILE AILLINN   179
WHEN IN RAGGED VAPOUR THEY MUTTER NIGHT AND DAY, ...   206 HANRAHANS SONG V   2
TO FIND IT WHEN NIGHT FALLS LAID ON A GOLDEN BIER. . . . .   209 UNDER THE MOON   10
OF THE HUNTER'S MOON, THAT HUNG BETWEEN THE NIGHT AND THE   210 UNDER THE MOON   18
    DAY,
OF THE THIRD MOON, THAT HUNG BETWEEN THE NIGHT AND THE DAY, 210 UNDER THE MOON V   18
MOVED ROUND ME IN THE SHADOWS, AND AT NIGHT . . . . . .   218 WOODS OF COOLE   19
AT THE FULL MOON? HE PLAYED ALL THROUGH THE NIGHT. . . .   223 SHADOW WATER B   21
I SAW THEM ON THAT NIGHT AS WELL AS YOU. . . . .   223 SHADOW WATER B   29
THE OTHER NIGHT, WHILE HE WAS PLAYING IT, ...   223 SHADOW WATER B   32
I SAW THEM, TOO, ONE NIGHT. FORGAEL WAS PLAYING, ...   223 SHADOW WATER B   36
THAT HE HAS BEEN ALL NIGHT UPON THE HILLS, ...   229 SHADOW WATER B   168
BUT MY BELOVED--THAT NIGHT AND DAY HAD PERISHED, ...   246 SHADOW WATER B   504
CRIED OUT THE WHOLE NIGHT LONG, ...   254 HIS DREAM   16
'TWAS ROUNDLY SPOKE, BUT WHEN NIGHT CAME . . . .   275 GREY ROCK   95
AND WOULD BE NO HARSH FRIEND. WHEN NIGHT HAD DEEPENED,   283 TWO KINGS   138
I WAITED TILL THE NIGHT WAS ON THE TURN, ...   283 TWO KINGS   144
THEY MAULED AND BIT THE WHOLE NIGHT THROUGH; . . . . . .   297 THREE BEGGARS   48
AND TILL ANOTHER NIGHT HAD GONE, ...   297 THREE BEGGARS   51
THEY'D MAULED AND BITTEN THE NIGHT THROUGH, ...   297 THREE BEGGARS V   48
"NIGHT GROWS UNEASY NEAR THE DAWN . . . .   303 HOUR DAWN   33
AND MURMURED "MAY GOD CURSE THE NIGHT . . . .   303 HOUR DAWN   V   32B
THAT THE NIGHT COME . . . .   317 NIGHT COME   T
THAT THE NIGHT COME. . . . .   317 NIGHT COME   12
THIS NIGHT CAN SET US QUARRELLING, ...   324 ROBERT GREGORY   15
BETWEEN THE NIGHT AND MORNING. I MIGHT HAVE LIVED, . . .   351 PEOPLE   6
THE YOUNG MEN EVERY NIGHT APPLAUD THEIR GABY'S LAUGHING   353 HIS PHOENIX   9
    EYE,
THIS NIGHT HAS BEEN SO STRANGE THAT IT SEEMED . . . . .   358 PRESENCES   1
OR AN OLD MAN UPON A WINTER'S NIGHT. . . . .   359 WAR POEM   6
THAT NIGHT AND MORNING I MAY THRASH . . . .   379 SAINT HUNCH   9
NOW AT ITS FIFTEENTH NIGHT. . . . .   383 VISION ROBART   28
HIS "MORNING" AND HIS "NIGHT" DISCLOSE . . . .   386 ROBARTES DANCE   33
"LAST NIGHT, WHERE UNDER THE WILD MOON . . . .   387 SOLOMON WITCH   2
THEREFORE A BLESSED MOON LAST NIGHT . . . .   388 SOLOMON WITCH   31
"THE NIGHT HAS FALLEN; NOT A SOUND . . . .   389 SOLOMON WITCH   38
NEVER UNTIL THIS NIGHT HAVE I BEEN STIRRED. . . . . . .   389 IMAGE PAST   1
THAT ANY NIGHT COULD BRING . . . .   390 IMAGE PAST   32
OF THE HOVERING THING NIGHT BROUGHT ME. . . . .   390 IMAGE PAST   42
NO, NO, NOT NIGHT BUT DEATH; . . . .   394 EASTER 1916   66
THAT PLAGUE ME DAY AND NIGHT; . . . .   399 DEMON BEAST   3
THE SWEETNESS THAT ALL LONGED FOR NIGHT AND DAY, ...   418 ANCEST HOUSES   20
WHERE THROUGH LONG WARS AND SUDDEN NIGHT ALARMS . . . .   420 MY HOUSE   24
WHERE THROUGH LONG WARS AND SUDDEN NIGHT ALARUMS . . . .   420 MY HOUSE   V   24
LAST NIGHT THEY TRUNDLED DOWN THE ROAD . . . .   425 STARES NEST   13
THE NIGHT CAN SWEAT WITH TERROR AS BEFORE . . . .   429 NINETEEN 19   29
THOSE WINDS THAT CLAMOUR OF APPROACHING NIGHT. . . . . .   431 NINETEEN 19   68
IN THE OLD ROOMS; NIGHT CAN OUTBALANCE DAY, ...   435 NEW FACES   6
WHATEVER FLAMES UPON THE NIGHT . . . .   438 SONGS PLAY 2   15
OUT OF DARK NIGHT WHERE LAY . . . .   439 FRAGMENTS   9
SUMMER AND WINTER, DAY AND NIGHT, ...   447 COLONUS PRAISE   31
AND TALKED AWAY THE NIGHT, ...   456 SUMMER SPRING   2
WERE SOME DEAR CHEEK. UPON A MOONLESS NIGHT . . . . . .   466 HARUN RASHID   127
WERE SOME DEAR FACE. UPON A MOONLESS NIGHT . . . . . .   466 HARUN RASHID   V   127
ALL SOULS' NIGHT . . . .   470 ALL SOULS NIGHT   T
AND IT IS ALL SOULS' NIGHT. . . . .   470 ALL SOUL NIGHT   3
IT IS ALL SOULS' NIGHT AND THE GREAT CHRIST CHURCH BELL   470 ALL SOUL NIGHT V   1
THINK OF ANCESTRAL NIGHT THAT CAN, ...   478 SELF AND SOUL   20
EMBLEMATICAL OF THE NIGHT, ...   478 SELF AND SOUL   30
A COUPLE OF NIGHT MOTHS ARE ON THE WING, ...   482 BLOOD AND MOON V   46
A SYCAMORE AND LIME-TREE LOST IN NIGHT . . . .   488 COOLE PARK 29   3
A SYCAMORE AND LIME TREE LOST IN NIGHT . . . .   488 COOLE PARK 29 V   3
EVERY NIGHT IN BED, ...   495 MOHINI CHATTER   4
NIGHT RESONANCE RECEDES, NIGHT-WALKERS' SONG . . . . . .   497 BYZANTIUM   3
OF DAY AND NIGHT; . . . .   500 VACILLATION   6
THOSE BRANCHES OF THE NIGHT AND DAY . . . .   502 VACILLATION   68
WANDERS OUT INTO THE NIGHT . . . .   508 JANE BISHOP   25
PASSING ON THE ROAD THAT NIGHT, ...   511 JANE AND JACK   17
THAT LOVER OF A NIGHT . . . .   512 JANE ON GOD   1
AND AFTER NAILED UPON THE NIGHT . . . .   519 HER DREAM   7
THAT FIRST NIGHT IN HELEN'S ARMS. . . . .   522 LULLABY   V   6
THE CURTAINS DRAWN UPON UNFRIENDLY NIGHT, ...   523 LONG SILENCE   4
OUR MINDS ARE AT THEIR BEST THIS NIGHT, ...   523 MAD AS MIST   3
"AND THE NIGHT GROWS ROUGH." . . . .   526 AM OF IRELAND   13
IF EMPTY NIGHT REPLIES? . . . .   533 FIRST CONFESS   18
WHILE NIGHT SHUTS THE EYES . . . .   535 PARTING   2
MONEY I HAD, AND IT WENT IN THE NIGHT, ...   544 TO SAME TUNE 1   12
STOOD OR HAVE MARCHED THE NIGHT LONG . . . .   546 TO SAME TUNE 2   15
OR HAVE MARCHED THE NIGHT LONG, ...   546 TO SAME TUNE 2 V   15
CUCHULAIN THAT FOUGHT NIGHT LONG WITH THE FOAM, ...   549 SEVERED HEAD   9
TO-MORROW NIGHT I WILL BREAK DOWN THE DOOR. . . . . . .   551 SONGS REWRIT 1   6
TO-MORROW NIGHT I WILL BREAK DOWN THE DOOR. . . . . . .   551 SONGS REWRIT 1   12
TO-MORROW NIGHT I WILL BREAK DOWN THE DOOR. . . . . . .   551 SONGS REWRIT 1   18
TOMORROW NIGHT I WILL BREAK DOWN THE DOOR. . . . .   551 SONGS REWRIT 1 V   REF
TO-MORROW NIGHT I WILL BREAK IN THE DOOR. . . . .   551 SONGS REWRIT 1 V   REF
BECAUSE YOU HAVE FOUND ME IN THE PITCH-DARK NIGHT . . .   554 RIBH AT TOMB   1

```
                                                    PAGE     TITLE         LINE

NIGHT   (CONTINUED)
     BECAUSE YOU HAVE IT IN THE PITCH DARK NIGHT    . . .      554 RIBH AT TOMB      V     1
     BECAUSE YOU HAVE FOUND ME. IN THE PITCH DARK NIGHT  . . .  554 RIBH AT TOMB     V     1
     CAVERNED IN NIGHT UNDER THE DRIFTED SNOW, . . . . .        563 MERU                  10
     THAT DAY BRINGS ROUND THE NIGHT, THAT BEFORE DAWN  . . .   563 MERU                  13
     AND AT NIGHT TIME WOULD SHE SAY, . . . . . . . .           570 THREE BUSHES     V    30
     STRANGE NIGHT HAS COME! . . . . . . . . . . .             574 MAIDS 1ST SONG        6
     OF THAT MOST SENSUOUS SILENCE OF THE NIGHT . . . . .       579 DOR WELLESLEY         6
     I CAME ON A GREAT HOUSE IN THE MIDDLE OF THE NIGHT, . . .  581 CURSE CROMWELL       25
     HAD TRAVELLED HALF THE NIGHT. . . . . . . . . .           585 ORAHILLY             17
     THEIR ROBBERY BY NIGHT! . . . . . . . . . .              607 SONGS BURDEN 2       15
     MONEY I HAD, AND IT WENT IN THE NIGHT, . . . . .          616 MARCH SONGS 3        12
     FAR UP IN THE STRETCHES OF NIGHT! . . . . . . .           623 HIGH TALK            12
     . . . NIGHT SPLITS AND THE DAWN BREAKS LOOSE! . . . .      623 HIGH TALK            12
     WHERE I CAN SIT UP HALF THE NIGHT . . . . . . .           624 APPARITIONS          11
     BECAUSE OF THE INCREASING NIGHT . . . . . . .            624 APPARITIONS          21
     AND NIGHT AND MORNING SING! . . . . . . . .             627 STATES HOLIDAY       12
     LAST NIGHT I LAY ON THE MOUNTAIN, . . . . . . .           628 JANE MOUNTAIN        11
     I LIE AWAKE NIGHT AFTER NIGHT . . . . . . . .            632 MAN AND ECHO          9
     I LIE AWAKE NIGHT AFTER NIGHT . . . . . . . .            632 MAN AND ECHO          9
     AND SINKS AT LAST INTO THE NIGHT. . . . . . .            633 MAN AND ECHO         36
     INTO THE NIGHT. O ROCKY VOICE, . . . . . . .            633 MAN AND ECHO         37
     SHALL WE IN THAT GREAT NIGHT REJOICE? . . . . . .         633 MAN AND ECHO         38
     ITS JOY OR NIGHT SEEM BUT A DREAM! . . . . . .           633 MAN AND ECHO         42
     ITS JOY OR NIGHT SEEMS BUT A DREAM. . . . . .            633 MAN AND ECHO     V   42
     WEARY OF REAPING THE BARREN NIGHT . . . . . .           648 ISLE STAT I 1        84
     LIFT MY SOUL FROM RAYLESS NIGHT-- . . . . . .            648 ISLE STAT I 1        95
     STRICKEN ALL THE NIGHT IS PAST-- . . . . . .            648 ISLE STAT I 1        96
     WHERE ALL NIGHT LONG THE HEAVENS WEEP AND WEEP, . . .     649 ISLE STAT I 1       124
     WHERE ALL NIGHT LONG THE LONELY MOON, THE WHITE . . .     650 ISLE STAT I 1       126
     BY DAY AND NIGHT A LONELY FOUNTAIN SINGS, . . . .         650 ISLE STAT I 1       130
     THERE! THERE! DOST THOU NOT SEE?  I SEE THE NIGHT, . .    653 ISLE STAT I 2        54
     MOCKING WITH PATIENT LAUGHTER ALL THE NIGHT . . . .      657 ISLE STAT I 3        52
     ONE HAND BROW-SHADING, FAR ACROSS THE NIGHT, . . . .     663 ISLE STAT II 2       27
     MORE WONDERFUL!  AND WE HAVE SWORDS. O NIGHT . . .       664 ISLE STAT II 2       61
     CAST ON THE SOUND, ON, ON. THIS NIGHT OF GRAVES, . .     665 ISLE STAT II 2       71
     O SWIFT ON THE SEAS ALL DAY AND NIGHT . . . . .         666 ISLE STAT II 3        8
     ALL DAY AND NIGHT. . . . . . . . . . .                666 ISLE STAT II 3       10
     IT IS, YET SHALL IT FAIL THEE DAY AND NIGHT . . .        674 ISLE STAT II 3      211
     WEARY OF WATCHING ROUND THE FIRE AT NIGHT. . . .         683 SEEKER               42
     BEAT ON IT WITH THEIR HAMMERS DAY AND NIGHT. . . .       687 TWO TITANS            4
     HAVE LIT LONE TAPERS. NOW THE NIGHT WAS CAST, . . .      687 TWO TITANS           27
     THIS EVE, TO-MORROW, OR TO-MORROW NIGHT. . . .          699 MOSADA 3              2
     THE BURGHERS OF THE NIGHT FADE ONE BY ONE. . . .         700 MOSADA 3             40
     OH, ALLAH! IT WAS THUS THEY SHONE THAT NIGHT . . .       701 MOSADA 3             50
     I NEVER KNEW A NIGHT SO HONEY-SWEET. . . . .            702 MOSADA 3             99
     I NEVER KNEW A NIGHT SO HONEY SWEET. . . . .            702 MOSADA 3         V   99
     FOR NIGHT COMES FAST.  LOOK DOWN ON ME, MY LOVE, . .     703 MOSADA 3            103
     I NEVER KNEW A NIGHT SO DEW-BEDROWNED. . . . .           703 MOSADA 3            105
     I NEVER KNEW A NIGHT SO BITTER COLD. . . . .            704 MOSADA 3            124
     OF RHYME! REMEMBERING THEE, THIS CRESCENT NIGHT, . . .   704 REMEMBRANCE           2
     BENEATH THE FLAMING EYEBALLS OF THE NIGHT, . . . .       723 KANVA ON SELF         4
     LONG THOU FOR NOTHING, NEITHER NIGHT NOR DAY! . . .      734 QUATRAIN APHOR       10
     MOURN ALL THE NIGHT AND DAY, . . . . . . .              737 MOURN THEN ON         2
     AND SING TO YOU IN THE NIGHT, . . . . . . .             739 WHERE BOOKS GO        6
     TILL DAY AND NIGHT TIME END. . . . . . . .             741 EARL PAUL            48
     WITH CREATURES OF OUR HEAVY NIGHT, . . . . .            743 DANAAN QUICK         10
     I HAVE SPUN IN THE HOUSE THIS NIGHT! . . . . .           771 SPINNING SONG        13
     AND MANY IT SEEMS . . . . . . . . . . .                781 MY HEART BEAT         9
     THE BITTER SWEETNESS OF THE NIGHT . . . . . .           781 HEART FRIGHT          3
     BECAUSE THE NIGHT WINDS BLOW . . . . . . .             782 HEART FRIGHT         16
     I HAVE HEARD IN THE NIGHT AIR . . . . . . .             783 GREY ROUND            6
     BUT NOW THE NIGHT IS GONE. . . . . . . . .             783 GREY ROUND           24
     AT DAYBREAK AFTER STORMY NIGHT . . . . . . .            784 WOMANS BEAUTY         3
NIGHT-COLOURED
     WHERE BANNERS OF THE CALIPHS HANG, NIGHT-COLOURED  . . .  461 HARUN RASHID          6
NIGHT-DARK
     IN THE CONFUSION OF ITS NIGHT-DARK FOLDS, . . . . .       470 HARUN RASHID        192
NIGHTFALL
     TOWARDS NIGHTFALL UPON CERTAIN SET APART . . . .         325 ROBERT GREGORY       29
     TOWARDS NIGHTFALL UPON A RACE . . . . . . .             325 ROBERT GREGORY       31
     TOWARDS NIGHTFALL UPON A PLACE . . . . . . .            325 ROBERT GREGORY V     31
     "BEFORE NIGHTFALL I'LL PICK A POCKET . . . . .           332 ROUND TOWER          27
     WHAT IS IT BUT NIGHTFALL? . . . . . . . .              394 EASTER 1916          65
NIGHT-GOWN
     SHE ROSE IN HER PALE NIGHT-GOWN! . . . . . .            159 CAP AND BELLS        10
NIGHTINGALE
     THE NIGHTINGALE THAT DEAFENS DAYLIGHT THERE, . . . .     446 COLONUS PRAISE        3
NIGHTINGALE'S
     A PIECE OF A NIGHTINGALE'S EGG, . . . . . . .           708 FAIRY PEDANT         24
NIGHTJAR
     CLAMOUR OF THE LONE NIGHTJAR. . . . . . . .            732 STREET DANCERS       21
NIGHTLY
     AND HEAR AMID THE GARDEN'S NIGHTLY PEACE," . . . .       300 BEGGAR CRIED         18
     NIGHTLY, AND STARTLED BY THAT SOUND . . . . .            326 ROBERT GREGORY       54
     I TOLD HIM THAT NIGHTLY FROM SIX TO SEVEN I SAT AT THIS   578 LOFTY THINGS          9
       TABLE,
NIGHTMARE
     WERE VEXED TO NIGHTMARE BY A ROCKING CRADLE, . . . .     402 SECOND COMING        20
     NOW DAYS ARE DRAGON-RIDDEN, THE NIGHTMARE . . . .        429 NINETEEN 19          25
     NOW DAYS ARE DRAGON RIDDEN, THE NIGHTMARE . . . .        429 NINETEEN 19      V   25
```

```
                                                                PAGE      TITLE          LINE
NIGHTMARE   (CONTINUED)
      WHAT MATTER THOUGH NUMB NIGHTMARE RIDE ON TOP,  .  .  .  .  .   564 GYRES              9
NIGHT-MOTHS
      A COUPLE OF NIGHT-MOTHS ARE ON THE WING.  .  .  .  .  .  .  .   482 BLOOD AND MOON    46
NIGHT'S
      AND FILLS WITH STARS NIGHT'S PURPLE CUP,  .  .  .  .  .  .  .    18 OISIN 1          262
      I WEEP--I WEEP BECAUSE BARE NIGHT'S ABOVE,  .  .  .  .  .  .   246 SHADOW WATER B   499
      BUT BRILLIANT AS THE NIGHT'S EMBROIDERY,  .  .  .  .  .  .  .   461 HARUN RASHID       7
      OR THE DAY'S VANITY, THE NIGHT'S REMORSE.  .  .  .  .  .  .   491 COOLE BALLYLEE V  40H
      OR THE DAY'S VANITY, THE NIGHT'S REMORSE.  .  .  .  .  .  .   495 CHOICE             8
      NIGHT'S RESONANCE RECEDES, NIGHT-WALKERS SONG  .  .  .  .  .   497 BYZANTIUM      V   3
      ALL NIGHT'S FATHOMLESS WISDOM COME,  .  .  .  .  .  .  .  .   519 HER DREAM          2
      NO, NIGHT'S BIRD AND LOVE'S  .  .  .  .  .  .  .  .  .  .  .   536 PARTING            5
NIGHTS
      IT'S CERTAIN I'D SLEEP EASIER O' NIGHTS  .  .  .  .  .  .  .   224 SHADOW WATER B    59
      THAT GIRL MY UNREMEMBERING NIGHTS HOLD FAST  .  .  .  .  .  .   384 VISION ROBART    50
      HER NIGHTS IN ARGUMENT  .  .  .  .  .  .  .  .  .  .  .  .  .   392 EASTER 1916       19
      A DOZEN NIGHTS OF NATURAL SLEEP, AND THEN  .  .  .  .  .  .   468 HARUN RASHID     150
      ALONE AND ALONE NINE NIGHTS I LAY  .  .  .  .  .  .  .  .  .   551 SONGS REWRIT 1    13
      NINE NIGHTS I LAY IN LONGING SORE  .  .  .  .  .  .  .  .  .   551 SONGS REWRIT 1 V  13
      NINE NIGHTS I LAY AND IN LONGING SORE  .  .  .  .  .  .  .  .   551 SONGS REWRIT 1 V  13
      UPON CLEAR NIGHTS THEY LEAVE THE UPPER AIR  .  .  .  .  .  .   750 SHADOW WATER A    87
NIGHT-TIDE
      AT THE COMING OF NIGHT-TIDE,  .  .  .  .  .  .  .  .  .  .  .   144 HOST OF AIR        6
NIGHT-VESTED
      THROUGH THIS NIGHT-VESTED PLACE THE RED BEAMS BREAK.  .  .   662 ISLE STAT II 2     4
NIGHT-WALKERS
      NIGHT'S RESONANCE RECEDES, NIGHT-WALKERS SONG  .  .  .  .  .   497 BYZANTIUM      V   3
NIGHT-WALKERS'
      NIGHT RESONANCE RECEDES, NIGHT-WALKERS' SONG  .  .  .  .  .   497 BYZANTIUM          3
NIGHT-WANDERING
      WHAT ROGUE IS NIGHT-WANDERING?  .  .  .  .  .  .  .  .  .  .   781 MY HEART BEAT      5
NIMBLE        SEE OVER-NIMBLE
NINE       SEE FORTY-NINE NINETEEN-TWENTY-NINE CAT-O'-NINE-TAILS
      AND SUNKEN SHAPE, A NINE DAYS' CORPSE SEA-DASHED--  .  .  .    40 OISIN 2        V 179
      NINE BEAN-ROWS WILL I HAVE THERE, A HIVE FOR THE HONEY-BEE,   117 ISLE INNISFREE     3
      NINE BEAN ROWS WILL I HAVE THERE, A HIVE FOR THE HONEY BEE,   117 ISLE INNISFREE V   3
      I'D GIVE THE PROFIT OF NINE VOYAGES  .  .  .  .  .  .  .  .   222 SHADOW WATER B V   9
      AND DROWNED THE TREASURES OF NINE CONQUERED NATIONS,  .  .   235 SHADOW WATER B   287
      THEY GAVE ME THAT OLD HARP OF THE NINE SPELLS  .  .  .  .   237 SHADOW WATER B V 327
      NINE SWORDS WITH HANDLES OF RHINOCEROS HORN  .  .  .  .  .   239 SHADOW WATER B   368
      AND FOR NINE DAYS HE HAD FOOD FROM OTHER HANDS,  .  .  .  .   282 TWO KINGS        126
      AND FOR NINE DAYS MY MIND WENT WHIRLING ROUND  .  .  .  .  .   282 TWO KINGS        127
      BUT WHEN NINE DAYS HAD GONE I STOOD AGAIN  .  .  .  .  .  .   282 TWO KINGS        131
      QUEEN MAEVE'S NINE MAINES HAD BEEN NURSED,  .  .  .  .  .  .   302 HOUR DAWN          8
      WHAT ONE OF MAEVE'S NINE BRAWLING SONS  .  .  .  .  .  .  .   303 HOUR DAWN         36
      HAS ONE OF MAEVE'S NINE BRAWLING SONS  .  .  .  .  .  .  .   303 HOUR DAWN      V  36
      MY SLEEP WERE NOW NINE CENTURIES  .  .  .  .  .  .  .  .  .   306 HOUR DAWN         75
      ARE NINE AND FIFTY SWANS  .  .  .  .  .  .  .  .  .  .  .  .   322 SWANS AT COOLE V   6
      AFTER NINE YEARS, I SINK MY HEAD ABASHED.  .  .  .  .  .  .   353 PEOPLE            37
      FROM NINETEEN HUNDRED NINE OR TEN, PAVLOVA'S HAD THE CRY,    354 HIS PHOENIX       11
      ALONE AND ALONE NINE NIGHTS I LAY  .  .  .  .  .  .  .  .  .   551 SONGS REWRIT 1    13
      NINE NIGHTS I LAY IN LONGING SORE  .  .  .  .  .  .  .  .  .   551 SONGS REWRIT 1 V  13
      NINE NIGHTS I LAY AND IN LONGING SORE  .  .  .  .  .  .  .  .   551 SONGS REWRIT 1 V  13
      NINE BOOKS OR NINE HATS  .  .  .  .  .  .  .  .  .  .  .  .   628 JANE MOUNTAIN      3
      NINE BOOKS OR NINE HATS  .  .  .  .  .  .  .  .  .  .  .  .   628 JANE MOUNTAIN      3
      NINE MOONS.  AND FROM THE HARPING OF THE FOOL?  .  .  .  .   747 SHADOW WATER A    14
      HE HAS HEARD ME AND NOT YOU.  NINE DAYS AGO  .  .  .  .  .   752 SHADOW WATER A   113
      FOR THESE NINE YEARS? O ARROW UPON ARROW!  .  .  .  .  .  .   761 SHADOW WATER A   268
NINE-AND-FIFTY
      ARE NINE-AND-FIFTY SWANS.  .  .  .  .  .  .  .  .  .  .  .  .   322 SWANS AT COOLE     6
NINETEEN
      FROM NINETEEN HUNDRED NINE OR TEN, PAVLOVA'S HAD THE CRY,    354 HIS PHOENIX       11
      NINETEEN HUNDRED AND NINETEEN  .  .  .  .  .  .  .  .  .  .   428 NINETEEN 19        T
      NINETEEN HUNDRED AND NINETEEN  .  .  .  .  .  .  .  .  .  .   428 NINETEEN 19        T
      COME PRAISE NINETEEN SIXTEEN,  .  .  .  .  .  .  .  .  .  .   608 SONGS BURDEN 3 V   2
      SOME NINETEEN GERMAN PLANES, THEY SAY,  .  .  .  .  .  .  .   791 REPRISALS          1
NINETEEN-SEVEN
      .  .  OF THE WESTERN WORLD", [NINETEEN-SEVEN]  .  .  .  .  .   294 HATED PLAYBOY      T
NINETEEN-SIXTEEN
      EASTER [NINETEEN-SIXTEEN]  .  .  .  .  .  .  .  .  .  .  .  .   391 EASTER 1916        T
      COME PRAISE NINETEEN-SIXTEEN,  .  .  .  .  .  .  .  .  .  .   608 SONGS BURDEN 3     2
NINETEENTH
      THE NINETEENTH AUTUMN HAS COME UPON ME  .  .  .  .  .  .  .   322 SWANS AT COOLE     7
      THE NINETEENTH CENTURY AND AFTER  .  .  .  .  .  .  .  .  .   485 NINETEENTH CEN     T
NINETEEN-THIRTEEN
      SEPTEMBER [NINETEEN-THIRTEEN]  .  .  .  .  .  .  .  .  .  .   289 SEPTEMBER 1913     T
NINETEEN-THIRTY-ONE
      COOLE PARK AND BALLYLEE, [NINETEEN-THIRTY-ONE]  .  .  .  .   490 COOLE BALLYLEE     T
      COOLE AND BALLYLEE, [NINETEEN-THIRTY-ONE ]  .  .  .  .  .   490 COOLE BALLYLEE V   T
NINETEEN-THIRTY-TWO
      COOLE PARK AND BALLYLEE [NINETEEN-THIRTY-TWO]  .  .  .  .   490 COOLE BALLYLEE V   T
NINETEEN-TWENTY-NINE
      COOLE PARK, [NINETEEN-TWENTY-NINE ]  .  .  .  .  .  .  .  .   488 COOLE PARK 29      T
NINETY
      NOR HEARD THIS VOICE THAT NINETY YEARS HAVE CRACKED.  .  .   555 RIBH AT TOMB       5
NINETY-FOUR
      FOR HE'D DIED AT NINETY-FOUR.  .  .  .  .  .  .  .  .  .  .    93 FATHER OHART      28
NINEVEH
      THE CROWNS OF NINEVEH.  .  .  .  .  .  .  .  .  .  .  .  .  .   439 FRAGMENTS         10
      WHERE BABYLON OR NINEVEH  .  .  .  .  .  .  .  .  .  .  .  .   502 VACILLATION       63
```

                                562

NINTH
    BE PATIENT YET A WHILE: FOR THIS NINTH MOON, ... 748 SHADOW WATER A   23
    BE PATIENT YET AWHILE: FOR THIS NINTH MOON, ... 748 SHADOW WATER A V 23
NOAH'S
    NOAH'S FRESHET NEVER REACHED. . . . . 440 WISDOM   15
NOBLE
    BUT WHERE ARE YOUR NOBLE KITH AND KIN, ... 5 OISIN 1   44
    OF NOBLE OISIN AND HIS FAME, ... 7 OISIN 1 V 66
    IN WAR, THE NOBLE FENIANS STEPT. . . . . 24 OISIN 1 V 372
    TALL AND NOBLE BUT WITH FACE AND BOSOM . . . . . . 199 ARROW   5
    OF SUCH NOBLE LINES," I SAID, ... 259 PEACE   6
    ALL THE WILD WITCHES, THOSE MOST NOBLE LADIES, . . . 343 DEJECTION   4
    SHE MIGHT, SO NOBLE FROM HEAD . . . . 355 PROPERTIUS   1
    THAT NOBLE BLADE THE MUSES BUCKLED ON, ... 489 COOLE PARK 29   10
    IN NOBLE RAGE REPLIED. . . . . 516 MANS SONG   5
    THE WORKMAN, NOBLE AND SAINT, AND ALL THINGS RUN . . 565 GYRES   23
    WITH EVERY NOBLE BEAST. . . . . 573 LADYS 2ND SONG   18
    WITH EVERY NOBLE BREAST. . . . . 573 LADYS 2ND SONG V 18
    BEAUTIFUL LOFTY THINGS: O'LEARY'S NOBLE HEAD: . . . 577 LOFTY THINGS   1
    DREAM OF THE NOBLE AND THE BEGGAR-MAN. . . . . . . 603 GALLERY REVIS   47
    DREAM OF THE NOBLE AND THE BEGGARMAN. . . . . . . 603 GALLERY REVIS V 47
    O, MY ALMINTOR, NOBLE WAS THY QUEST: . . . . 679 ISLE STAT II 3   319
    YEA, NOBLE AND MOST KNIGHTLY HATH IT BEEN. . . . . . 679 ISLE STAT II 3   320
NOBLENESS
    BECAUSE OF THAT GREAT NOBLENESS OF HERS, ... 200 FOLLY COMFORT   9
    THAT NOBLENESS MADE SIMPLE AS A FIRE, ... 256 NO SECOND TROY   7
    "YOUR STRENGTH AND NOBLENESS WILL PASS AWAY"? . . . . 285 TWO KINGS   189
NOBLY
    THAT HE MIGHT BE NOBLY BREECHED . . . . 440 WISDOM   13
NOBODY
    THERE'S NOBODY IS NATURAL BUT A ROBBER, ... 233 SHADOW WATER B   237
    THERE IS NOBODY WISE ENOUGH . . . . 268 BROWN PENNY   10
    THAT NOBODY CAN BUY OR BIND: . . . . 301 RUN PARADISE   27
    IF THEY HAVE SINNED NOBODY KNOWS: . . . . 337 SCHOLARS V 10
    A NOBODY IN A GREAT THRONG, ... 361 ALF POLLEXFEN   29
    THAT NOBODY LOOKS: HER FEET, ... 617 LONG-LEG FLY   16
    NOBODY KNOWS WHAT MAY BEFALL. . . . . 788 HAWTHORN TREE   13
NOD
    I HAVE PASSED WITH A NOD OF THE HEAD . . . . 392 EASTER 1916   5
    WHAT HEADS SHAKE OR NOD? . . . . 505 RESULT THOUGHT   18
    AND NOD TO ONE ANOTHER, LIES A GREEN, ... 653 ISLE STAT I 2   35
    UNTO HER DOOR: FOR THIS, WHERE NOD THE LONG . . . . 660 ISLE STAT II 1   43
    SOON WILL THE CHURCHMEN NOD ABOVE THE CROWD. . . . . 699 MOSADA 3   19
    NOD TO THE IRON SHOES OF TIME, ... 736 SUMMER EVENING   11
NODDED
    ONCE, WHILE HE NODDED ON A CHAIR, ... 132 FR GILLIGAN   5
    NODDED UPON THE WALL, ... 400 DEMON BEAST   12
    HE THOUGHT WISE THINGS AS HIS GREY HEAD NODDED. . . . 728 PRIEST FAIRY   12
NODDING
    AND NODDING BY THE FIRE, TAKE DOWN THIS BOOK, ... 120 YOU ARE OLD   2
    NODDING HER RUSSET HOOD? . . . . 171 MAID QUIET   2
    NODDING HER PURPLE HOOD? . . . . 171 MAID QUIET V 2
    NODDING ALONE AND APART, ... 171 MAID QUIET V 6
    NODDING BY THE FLICKERING LAKE, ... 655 ISLE STAT I 3   3
    AND, NODDING TO AND FRO, SANG SONGS OF LOVE, ... 688 TWO TITANS   35
NODS
    AND HE NODS A DRUNKEN HEAD. . . . . 168 BLESSED   32
    NODS BY THE HELM, AND NEARER TO THE SAIL . . . . . 752 SHADOW WATER A   119
NOISE
    THEY SET UP A NOISE LIKE CRICKETS, ... 161 CAP AND BELLS   33
    MAEVE WAITED, AND WHEN THAT EAR-PIERCING NOISE . . . 182 QUEEN MAEVE   47
    AND BLOW A LITTLE NOISE . . . . 215 HAPPY TOWNLAND   43
    THAT BALANCED WITH A WORD IS MORE THAN NOISE: . . . . 258 KING NO KING   4
    NOR DOOR, NOR MOUTH, NOR SLIPPER MADE A NOISE, . . . 279 TWO KINGS   51
    FROM WELL-SIDE OR FROM PLOUGH-LAND, WAS THERE NOISE: . 279 TWO KINGS   53
    NOR HAD THERE BEEN THE NOISE OF LIVING THING . . . . 279 TWO KINGS   54
    FROM WELL SIDE OR FROM PLOUGH LAND, WAS THEIR NOISE: . 279 TWO KINGS V 53
    FROM WELLSIDE OR FROM PLOUGHLAND, WAS THERE NOISE: . . 279 TWO KINGS V 53
    O WHAT HAS MADE THAT SUDDEN NOISE? . . . . 583 GHOST ROG CASE   1
    BUT YONDER THING, YON IDLE NOISE, YON CROW, ... 648 ISLE STAT I 1   104
    NOISE: AND A FLASH, A MOMENTARY BLOT. . . . . . . 714 FERENCZ RENYI   110
    NOISE: UPROAR! AND A MOMENTARY BLOT. . . . . . . 714 FERENCZ RENYI V 110
NOISY
    BE THOUGHT AN IDLER BY THE NOISY SET . . . . . . 205 ADAMS CURSE   12
    ANGERS THAT ARE LIKE NOISY CLOUDS HAVE SET OUR HEARTS 207 HANRAHANS SONG   8
        ABEAT,
    OR NOISY, INSOLENT SPORT, ... 293 HELEN LIVED   4
    A NOISY AND FILTHY THING." . . . . 319 DOLLS   12
    ERE LONG SHALL FALTER THROUGH THE NOISY SQUARE, . . . 699 MOSADA 3   21
    THE NOISY WORLD DIVIDES. HOW SOON A DEED . . . . . 700 MOSADA 3   34
NONCHALANCE
    AND LOST THE OLD NONCHALANCE OF THE HAND: . . . . . 368 EGO DOMINUS   13
NONE
    OF SOME FORGOTTEN FIEND. NOW NONE ASSAILS . . . . . 31 OISIN 2 V 30B
    ONCE MORE UNTO YOUR FLOWERS, FOR NONE MAY FIGHT, . . . 34 OISIN 2 V 80
    NONE MAY BEGUILE HIM, AND HIS PASSIONS COLD . . . . 35 OISIN 2 V 83A
    IS THE ISLAND OF CONTENT?" "NONE KNOW," SHE SAID: . 46 OISIN 2   249
    WHICH IS THE ISLE OF YOUTH?" "NONE KNOW," SHE SAID, . 46 OISIN 2 V 249
    AND ENTER, AND NONE SAYETH "NO" . . . . 62 OISIN 3   210
    NONE WAR ON THE MASTERS OF HELL! . . . . 62 OISIN 3   214
    AND ENTER, AND NONE SAYETH "NAY" . . . . 62 OISIN 3 V 210

NONE   (CONTINUED)   PAGE   TITLE   LINE

        THAT NONE MAY FEEL THE POWER OF SQUALL AND WAVE, ...   128 DREAM OF FAERY V   45
        TO SOME STRINGED INSTRUMENT NONE THERE HAD SEEN, ...   180 QUEEN MAEVE   4
        BEFORE HIS EYES, HE HAS TEARS FOR NONE, ...   192 BAILE AILLINN   82
        FROM THE HOLY ORCHARDS, WHERE THERE IS NONE . . . . . .   196 BAILE AILLINN   174
        WOULD NONE HAD EVER LOVED BUT YOU AND I! . . . .   210 RAGGED WOOD   4
        O THAT NONE EVER LOVED BUT YOU AND I! . . . .   210 RAGGED WOOD   V   4
        O THAT NONE EVER LOVED BUT YOU AND I! . . . .   211 RAGGED WOOD   8
        AND FROM THAT HOUR HE HAS WATCHED OVER NONE . . . . .   220 HARP OF AENGUS   13
        AND DRAGS HIM THROUGH THE SEA. WELL, NET OR NONE, . . .   224 SHADOW WATER B   57
        WE JOINED HIM FOR HIS PAY, BUT HAVE HAD NONE . . . . .   225 SHADOW WATER B V   68A
        NONE BUT THE DEAD, OR THOSE THAT NEVER LIVED, ...   231 SHADOW WATER B   202
        THAT NONE MIGHT TAKE YOU FROM ME. FOR A MOMENT . . .   237 SHADOW WATER B   330
        THERE IS NONE TO TAKE HIS SIDE. I AM ON HIS SIDE. . . .   239 SHADOW WATER B   364
        OR IS THERE NONE, MOST POPULAR OF MEN, ...   265 ABBEY THEATRE   13
        I KNEW A WOMAN NONE COULD PLEASE, ...   272 GREY ROCK   41
        I KNOW A WOMAN NONE COULD PLEASE, ...   272 GREY ROCK   V   41
        AND WHISPERING THAT NONE BUT HE SHOULD HEAR, ...   281 TWO KINGS   110
        NONE CLOSED HIS BLOOD-SHOT EYES BUT SOUGHT . . . . .   296 THREE BEGGARS   44
        WHAT NONE CAN UNDERSTAND, ...   315 FRIENDS   12
        WHAT NONE CAN HAVE AND THRIVE, ...   315 FRIENDS   13
        THE GENTLENESS NONE THERE HAD EVER KNOWN! . . . . .   418 ANCEST HOUSES   21
        KNOWING THAT NONE COULD PASS HEAVEN'S DOOR . . . . .   422 MY TABLE   26
        KNOWING THAT NONE WHO PASS HEAVEN'S DOOR . . . . . .   422 MY TABLE   V   26
        KNOWING THAT NONE CAN PASS HEAVEN'S DOOR . . . . . .   422 MY TABLE   V   26
        NONE DARED ADMIT, IF SUCH A THOUGHT WERE HIS, ...   430 NINETEEN 19   44
        AND THERE IS NONE SO FIT TO KEEP A WATCH AND KEEP . .   442 BLACK CENTAUR   15
        AND THAT NONE LIVING KNOWS. . . . .   455 HIS MEMORIES   6
        FOR NONE ALIVE TO-DAY . . . .   458 SECRETS OF OLD   10
        FOR NONE ALIVE TODAY . . . .   458 SECRETS OF OLD V   10
        WERE I BUT THERE AND NONE TO HEAR . . . .   458 HIS WILDNESS   7
        THAT NONE MIGHT KNOW THAT HE WAS CONSCIENCE-STRUCK-- .   462 HARUN RASHID   38
        THAT NONE MIGHT KNOW THAT HE WAS CONSCIENCE STRUCK, .   462 HARUN RASHID V   38
        BUT I BEING NONE CAN PRAISE ITS OPPOSITE. . . . . .   465 HARUN RASHID   98
        NONE BUT THE LIVING MOCK. . . . .   471 ALL SOUL NIGHT   17
        AND WE THAT HAVE SHED NONE MUST GATHER THERE . . . .   482 BLOOD AND MOON   41
        WHERE NONE HAS REIGNED THAT LACKED A NAME AND FAME . . .   491 COOLE BALLYLEE   31
        NONE SO OLD AS HE AND I! . . . .   508 JANE BISHOP   V   6
        WHAT NONE OTHER KNOWS, ...   538 LAST CONFESS   18
        NONE SHARED OUR GUILT! NOR DID WE PLAY A PART . . . .   542 PARN FUNERAL 1   22
        SURMOUNT THEIR BONES! BUT SPEAK WHAT NONE HAVE HEARD. .   555 RIBH AT TOMB   9
        SURMOUNTS THEIR BONES! BUT SPEAK WHAT NONE HAVE HEARD. .   555 RIBH AT TOMB V   9
        "NONE CAN RELY UPON . . . .   569 THREE BUSHES   2
        AND NOW NONE LIVING CAN, ...   571 THREE BUSHES   74
        THAT NONE OF ANOTHER BREED . . . .   583 GHOST ROG CASE   24
        WHERE NONE GAINSAY THEIR RIGHT, ...   597 MODEL LAUREATE   14
        NONE OTHER KNOWS WHAT PLEASURES MAN . . . . . .   620 JOHN KINSELLA   9
        AND UNDERSTOOD, WHAT NONE HAVE UNDERSTOOD, ...   622 HOUND VOICE   13
        WITH TEARS? I WEARY OF YE. THERE IS NONE . . . .   650 ISLE STAT I 1   142
        O LET ME PASS! THAT FLOWER NONE . . . .   668 ISLE STAT II 3   47
        AND NONE THERE IS, IF SUCH THERE WERE, ...   668 ISLE STAT II 3   53
        YOURSELF. NONE BUT THE INNOCENT CAN SEE. . . . .   692 MOSADA 1   59
        ONCE IN THY NATION NONE SHALL KNOW THAT I . . . .   702 MOSADA 3   82
        AMONG THY NATION NONE SHALL KNOW THAT I . . . . .   702 MOSADA 3   V   82
        AND--NO! I'LL NONE OF THESE, OLD FATHER WRINKLES, .   721 WITCH VIVIEN
        NONE SHOULD ESCAPE MY SWORD! I WOULD SEND ALL . . .   752 SHADOW WATER A   111
        I PROMISED HIM THAT NONE SHOULD ESCAPE MY SWORD . .   752 SHADOW WATER A   114
        HE WATCHES OVER NONE BUT FAITHFUL LOVERS. . . . .   762 SHADOW WATER A   295
        AND FROM THAT HOUR HE HAS WATCHED OVER NONE . . .   763 SHADOW WATER A   308
        AND NONE KNOWS WHEREFORE! BUT THE HEART'S DESIRE . .   764 SHADOW WATER A   340
        I WILL FOLLOW YOU. I WILL HAVE NONE OF YOU. . . .   768 SHADOW WATER A   415
        THAT WOULD BE HAPPIEST, FOR THERE IS NONE . . . .   768 SHADOW WATER A V   410
        THE WOMEN NONE CAN KISS AND THRIVE, ...   775 AGAINST WITCH   8
        WOMEN, THAT NONE CAN KISS AND THRIVE, ...   775 AGAINST WITCH V   8
        THEY WILL HAVE FOR MASTERS NONE . . . .   776 AGAINST WITCH   39
        THEY WILL HAVE FOR MASTER NONE . . . .   776 AGAINST WITCH V   39
NONSENSICAL
        SPEAKING TO A DRUNKEN AUDIENCE HIGH NONSENSICAL WORDS! . .   577 LOFTY THINGS   6
NOOK
        HE CRAWLED INTO THAT PLEASANT NOOK. . . . .   303 HOUR DAWN   32
NOON
        SAVE DEER TOWARDS NOON THAT WATER SOUGHT. . . . . .   17 OISIN 1   V   243
        THEY CHASE AT NOON THE DEER. . . . .   32 OISIN 2   V   53
        GAVE TO HIGH NOON AND NOON TO NIGHT GAVE WAY! . . . .   40 OISIN 2   172
        GAVE TO HIGH NOON AND NOON TO NIGHT GAVE WAY! . . . .   40 OISIN 2   172
        GAVE TO THE NOON, AND NOON TO EVE GAVE WAY, ...   40 OISIN 2   172
        GAVE TO THE NOON, AND NOON TO EVE GAVE WAY, ...   40 OISIN 2   V   172
        GAVE TO THE NOON, AND NOON TO EVE GAVE WAY, ...   40 OISIN 2   V   172
        THERE MIDNIGHT'S ALL A GLIMMER, AND NOON A PURPLE GLOW, .   117 ISLE INNISFREE   7
        SLEEP BEFORE THE THIRD NOON SOUNDS." . . . .   295 THREE BEGGARS   24
        SANG THROUGH THEIR TEETH FROM NOON TO NOON! . . . .   296 THREE BEGGARS   41
        SANG THROUGH THEIR TEETH FROM NOON TO NOON! . . . .   296 THREE BEGGARS   41
        ALL DAY LONG FROM SHADOWLESS NOON . . . .   332 SOLOMON SHEBA   5
        NOON UPON THE CLOCK, ...   525 DANCING DAYS   18
        THAT BROAD NOON HAS NEVER LIT, ...   632 MAN AND ECHO   4
        NOON WRAPT THE TREES IN VEILS OF VIOLET WEATHER, . . .   715 DWELT SYCAMORE   7
        NOON WRAPPED THE WOODS IN VEILS OF VIOLET WEATHER! . .   715 DWELT SYCAMORE V   7
        THE HEART OF NOON FOLDS SILENCE AND FOLDS SLEEP, . . .   735 QUATRAIN APHOR   25
        FOR NOON AND MIDNIGHT FROM EACH OTHER BORROW, ...   735 QUATRAIN APHOR   26
        HITHER AND THITHER AND SAY AT THE HIGH NOON . . . .   767 SHADOW WATER A   404
NO-ONE
        IN THE LAND THAT NO-ONE KNOWS. . . . .   774 COME RIDE   V   17

PAGE   TITLE   LINE

NOONTIDE
    THEY CHASE THE NOONTIDE DEER! • • • • • • • • •   32 OISIN 2   53
NOON-TIDE
    THEY CHASE THE NOON-TIDE DEER! • • • • • • • •   32 OISIN 2   V 53
NOOSE
    WHILE THERE'S A ROPE TO RUN INTO A NOOSE • • • • • •   238 SHADOW WATER B   347
    GUNSHOT OR A NOOSE, • • • • • • • • • • • • •   620 JOHN KINSELLA   2
NORM
    WE TAKE IT FOR THE NORM! YET SHOULD I DREAM • • •   371 ON GOING HOUSE   9
    THAT DREAM IS A NORM! AND SHOULD SOME LIMB OF THE DEVIL   372 ON GOING HOUSE   12
NORMAN
    UPON THE NORMAN UPLAND OR IN THAT POPLAR SHADE, • • • •   449 OWEN AHERNE   2
    TO THROW THE NORMAN KNIGHT." " • • • • • • • •   740 EARL PAUL   12
    STOOD THERE THE NORMAN KNIGHT. • • • • • • • •   741 EARL PAUL   40
NORMANDY
    FOR A KNIGHT, COME FROM NORMANDY • • • • • • • • •   740 EARL PAUL   7
NORTH
    THE ICICLES THAT FAMISH ALL THE NORTH, • • • • • •   73 ANASHU VIJAYA   50
    SANG THAT SOMEWHERE TO NORTH OR WEST OR SOUTH • • • • •   127 DREAM OF FAERY   19
    SANG HOW SOMEWHERE TO NORTH OR EAST OR SOUTH • • • • •   127 DREAM OF FAERY V   19
    SANG HOW SOMEWHERE TO NORTH OR WEST OR SOUTH • • • • •   127 DREAM OF FAERY V   19
    FOR THEY WILL RIDE THE NORTH WHEN THE GER-EAGLE FLIES, • •   146 UNAPPEAS HOST   3
    THE NORTH UNFOLDS ABOVE THEM CLINGING, CREEPING NIGHT, • •   154 BELOVED PEACE   3
    THE NORTH UNROLLS ABOVE THEM CLINGING, CREEPING NIGHT, • •   154 BELOVED PEACE V   3
    NOR THE COLD NORTH HAS TROUBLED?" HE REPLIED, • • • •   184 QUEEN MAEVE   90
    THE NORTH WIND TUMBLES TO AND FRO • • • • • • • •   191 BAILE AILLINN   45
    THAT NORTH WIND TUMBLES TO AND FRO • • • • • • •   191 BAILE AILLINN V   45
    THE RIDER FROM THE NORTH • • • • • • • • • •   213 HAPPY TOWNLAND V   T
    STRAYING TOO FAR INTO THE NORTH OR SOUTH, • • • • •   226 SHADOW WATER B   86
    A CLOUD BLOWN FROM THE CUT-THROAT NORTH • • • • • •   313 MEMORY YOUTH   6
    THE WEST WIND MADE IT PITIFUL, AND THE NORTH WIND AFRAID.   449 OWEN AHERNE   6
    WHEREON THE BLEAK NORTH BLOWS. • • • • • • • •   454 HIS MEMORIES   4
    AND WHEN YOU CAME, THE NORTH UNDER YOUR SAILS, • • • •   749 SHADOW WATER A   34
    WHEN WE ROWED NORTH, SINGING ABOVE THE OARS, • • • •   749 SHADOW WATER A   39
    TO CONQUER AMONG THE COUNTRIES OF THE NORTH. • • • • •   757 SHADOW WATER A   200
NORTHERN
    "HE DRIVES AWAY THE NORTHERN COLD." • • • • • • •   82 MAD KING GOLL   11
    UPON THE NORTHERN UPLAND OR IN THAT POPLAR SHADE, • • •   449 OWEN AHERNE   V 2
    BEFORE I HAD MARKED HIM ON HIS NORTHERN WAY, • • • • •   535 CHOSEN   8
    AND PASSED THE NORTHERN HEBRIDES, AND TOOK • • • • •   749 SHADOW WATER A V   42
NORTHUMBERLAND
    "AND ALL DOWN FROM NORTHUMBERLAND • • • • • • • • •   740 EARL PAUL   9
NOSE
    THRUSTING HIS NOSE TO MY SHOULDER! HE KNEW IN HIS BOSOM   54 OISIN 3   106
    DEEP
    HE SMOOTHS THE LONG BROWN NOSE. • • • • • • • •   98 FOXHUNTER   20
    SHALL DIP HIS NOSE INTO MY LADLE • • • • • • • •   304 HOUR DAWN   53
    DIPPING HIS NOSE INTO MY LADLE • • • • • • • • •   304 HOUR DAWN   V 53
    WITH FACE AND NOSE PRESSED TO A SWEET-SHOP WINDOW, • • •   370 EGO DOMINUS   56
    WITH FACE AND NOSE PRESSED TO A SWEETSHOP WINDOW. • • • •   370 EGO DOMINUS   V 56
    FIRST THAT SEA-RIDER OISIN LED BY THE NOSE • • • • •   629 CIRCUS ANIMALS   10
    AND RUBBED ALONG THE RAIL HIS NOSE. • • • • • • •   725 LEGEND   28
    ON THE NOSE OF THE SLEEPER HE MADE IT PLAY! • • • • •   729 PRIEST FAIRY   30
NOSTERS
    AND MANY PATER NOSTERS SAID SINCE DAWN. • • • • • •   43 OISIN 2   V 208D
NOSTRIL
    THE COLD BLOWN SPRAY IN MY NOSTRIL. • • • • • • •   399 BREAK OF DAY   20
NOSTRILS
    IN HIS NOSTRILS, THE GREAT LORD OF CHOU • • • • • •   502 VACILLATION   59
NOTABLE
    SANDYMOUNT CORBETS, THAT NOTABLE MAN • • • • • • •   604 YOU CONTENT   13
    NOW A NOTABLE MAN ON STAGE AND ON SCREEN! • • • • • •   790 DEDICATION   8
NOTE
    BLEW ONE LONG NOTE. FROM OVER REED • • • • • •   14 OISIN 1   V 195
    SNATCHING THE HORN OF NIAMH, I BLEW A LONG LINGERING NOTE.   51 OISIN 3   57
    SNATCHING THE HORN OF NIAM, I BLEW FORTH A LINGERING NOTE!   51 OISIN 3   V 57
    SNATCHING THE HORN OF NIAM, I BLEW A LINGERING NOTE! • •   51 OISIN 3   V 57
    THE HORN'S SWEET NOTE AND THE TOOTH OF THE HOUND. • •   380 SONGS FOOL 1   12
    THE HORN'S SWEET NOTE AND THE TOOTH OF THE HOUND. • •   381 SONGS FOOL 2   14
    A SLOW LOW NOTE AND AN IRON BELL. • • • • • • •   549 SEVERED HEAD   7
    A SLOW LOW NOTE AND AN IRON BELL. • • • • • • •   550 SEVERED HEAD   14
    A SLOW LOW NOTE AND AN IRON BELL. • • • • • • •   550 SEVERED HEAD   21
    NOT A SAD NOTE WILL I SING. • • • • • • • • •   646 ISLE STAT I 1   39
NOTES   SEE BELL-NOTES
    AND NIAMH BLEW THREE MERRY NOTES • • • • • • •   14 OISIN 1   195
    THE MOUTHS THAT SPEAK, THE NOTES AND STRINGS, • • • •   212 BLESS PSALTER   2
    THE NOTES THEY WAKEN SHALL LIVE ON • • • • • •   213 BLESS PSALTER   16
    THE PROUD AND CARELESS NOTES LIVE ON, • • • • • •   213 BLESS PSALTER   19
NOTHING
    BUT NOW I HAVE GROWN NOTHING, KNOWING ALL. • • • • •   104 FERGUS DRUID   38
    BUT NOW I HAVE GROWN NOTHING, BEING ALL! • • • • •   104 FERGUS DRUID   V 38
    HE HAD FALLEN ASLEEP, AND, THOUGH HE HAD DREAMED NOTHING,   182 QUEEN MAEVE   55
    THOUGH NOTHING TROUBLES THE GREAT STREAMS • • • • •   196 BAILE AILLINN   172
    AND THAT DEAR WORDS MEANT NOTHING?" BUT ENOUGH, • • •   201 OLD MEMORY   9
    OR, IF THERE NEEDS BE MORE, BE NOTHING SAID • • • •   201 OLD MEMORY   11
    OR CRY ABOUT ONE'S EARS. NOTHING TO FEAR. • • • •   222 SHADOW WATER B   19
    BUT THERE WERE OTHERS. I HAVE SEEN NOTHING PASS. • •   226 SHADOW WATER B   82
    WHERE NO SHIP SAILS, WHERE NOTHING THAT'S ALIVE • •   226 SHADOW WATER B   98
    THAT NOTHING CAN AMEND IT BUT THESE WATERS • • • •   227 SHADOW WATER B   120
    I'VE NOTHING TO COMPLAIN OF BUT HEARTBURN, • • • •   227 SHADOW WATER B V 116A
    ARE DUST ON THE MOTH'S WING! THAT NOTHING MATTERS • • •   235 SHADOW WATER B   297

565

		PAGE	TITLE		LINE

NOTHING   (CONTINUED)

	PAGE	TITLE		LINE
UPON HIS SHOULDERS. YOU'VE NOTHING BUT WILD WORDS,	235	SHADOW WATER B		300
THERE'S NOTHING IN THE WORLD THAT'S WORTH A FEAR.	238	SHADOW WATER B		353
HAVE BURIED NOTHING BUT MY GOLDEN ARMS.	243	SHADOW WATER B		431
I WEEP BECAUSE I'VE NOTHING FOR YOUR EYES	246	SHADOW WATER B		496
I WOULD THAT THERE WAS NOTHING IN THE WORLD	246	SHADOW WATER B		503
THE CRAZY NOTHING THAT I THINK IT IS,	248	SHADOW WATER B		556
BUT HARRY US WITH HOPES THAT COME TO NOTHING,	250	SHADOW WATER B		579
NOTHING TO MAKE A SONG ABOUT BUT KINGS,	257	RECONCILIATION		5
NOW NOTHING BUT COMES READIER TO THE HAND	267	ALL TEMPT ME		4
I HAVE NO CHILD, I HAVE NOTHING BUT A BOOK,	270	PARDON FATHERS		21
NOTHING BUT THAT TO PROVE YOUR BLOOD AND MINE.	270	PARDON FATHERS		22
"WHAT IS THIS TROUBLE?" HE WOULD ANSWER NOTHING,	281	TWO KINGS		90
TO A FRIEND WHOSE WORK HAS COME TO NOTHING	290	TO A FRIEND		T
AND THERE BE NOTHING BUT GOD LEFT;	307	HOUR DAWN		103
NOTHING BUT DARKNESS OVERHEAD.	314	MEMORY YOUTH		14
THERE'S NOTHING OF HIM LEFT BUT HALF A SCORE	341	SHEP GOATHERD		56
I HAVE NOTHING BUT THE EMBITTERED SUN;	344	DEJECTION		8
AND I HAVE NOTHING BUT HARSH SUN;	344	DEJECTION	V	8
VAGUE MEMORIES, NOTHING BUT MEMORIES.	356	BROKEN DREAMS		15
VAGUE MEMORIES, NOTHING BUT MEMORIES,	356	BROKEN DREAMS		20
VAGUE MEMORIES, NOTHING BUT MEMORIES.	357	BROKEN DREAMS		41
OWN NOTHING BUT THEIR BLIND, STUPEFIED HEARTS.	370	EGO DOMINUS		69
MAY HANDLE NOTHING AND SET EYES ON NOTHING	371	ON GOING HOUSE		6
MAY HANDLE NOTHING AND SET EYES ON NOTHING	371	ON GOING HOUSE		6
THERE CAN BE NOTHING SOLIDER TILL I DIE;	383	VISION ROBART		26
THERE'S NOTHING BUT OUR OWN RED BLOOD	396	ROSE TREE		17
NOTHING THAT WE LOVE OVER-MUCH	399	BREAK OF DAY		17
THAT NOTHING STRANGE; THE TRAGEDY BEGAN	411	TOWER		51
PLUNGES TOWARDS NOTHING, ARMS AND FINGERS SPREADING WIDE	426	PHANTOM HATRED		13
FOR THE EMBRACE OF NOTHING; AND I, MY WITS ASTRAY	426	PHANTOM HATRED		14
NOTHING BUT STILLNESS CAN REMAIN WHEN HEARTS ARE FULL	426	PHANTOM HATRED		23
NOTHING BUT GRIP OF CLAW, AND THE EYE'S COMPLACENCY,	427	PHANTOM HATRED		31
AND AFTER THAT THERE'S NOTHING GOOD	434	WHEEL		5
FROM NOTHING EVERY DAY, AND TEACH	436	FOR MY SON		18
OUT OF NOTHING IT CAME,	439	FRAGMENTS		7
NOTHING COULD BRING HIM, WHEN HIS LADY DIED,	471	ALL SOUL NIGHT		25
BUT NAMES ARE NOTHING. WHAT MATTER WHO IT BE,	473	ALL SOUL NIGHT		81
BUT NAMES ARE NOTHING. I CARE NOT WHO IT BE.	473	ALL SOUL NIGHT	V	81
NOTHING CAN STAY MY GLANCE	474	ALL SOUL NIGHT		93
"PRAY FOR NOTHING, SAY	495	MOHINI CHATTER		3
NOTHING SAID OR DONE CAN REACH	506	REMORSE SPEECH		9
FOR NOTHING CAN BE SOLE OR WHOLE	513	JANE TALK BISH		17
NOTHING BUT DISSEMBLING,	532	FIRST CONFESS		5
NOTHING BUT COQUETRY.	532	FIRST CONFESS		6
LEAVE NOTHING BUT THE NOTHINGS THAT BELONG	542	PARN FUNERAL 1		29
WHAT HAPPENS A TREE THAT HAS NOTHING WITHIN IT?	548	TO SAME TUNE 3		23
WHAT HAPPENS TO A TREE THAT HAS NOTHING WITHIN IT?	548	TO SAME TUNE 3	V	23
OR ANY RICH, DARK NOTHING DISINTER	565	GYRES		22
THAT IF NOTHING DRASTIC IS DONE	565	LAPIS LAZULI		5
THAT IF NOTHING DRASTIC CAN BE DONE	565	LAPIS LAZULI	V	5
WHERE NOTHING STIRS BUT A MOUSE.	575	ACRE OF GRASS		6
NOTHING THAT COMMON WOMEN PONDER ON	579	DOR WELLESLEY		12
NOTHING BUT CROMWELL'S HOUSE AND CROMWELL'S MURDEROUS CREW,	580	CURSE CROMWELL		2
BUT THAT IS NOTHING NEW.	581	ROGER CASEMENT		4
AND THAT OLD MAN BESIDE ME, NOTHING WOULD HE SAY	593	PILGRIM		9
WHAT IF THERE'S NOTHING UP THERE AT THE TOP?	615	MARCH SONGS 2		21
WHAT TEARS DOWN A TREE THAT HAS NOTHING WITHIN IT?	615	MARCH SONGS 2		23
WHAT TEARS DOWN A TREE HAS NOTHING WITHIN IT?	615	MARCH SONGS 2	V	23
HIS EYES FIXED UPON NOTHING,	617	LONG-LEG FLY		7
AND FINDS THERE NOTHING TO MAKE ITS TERROR LESS	618	BRONZE HEAD		6
BUT NOTHING SATISFIED THE FOOL	620	JOHN KINSELLA		7
PROCESSIONS THAT LACK HIGH STILTS HAVE NOTHING THAT CATCHES THE EYE.	622	HIGH TALK		1
I HAVE FOUND NOTHING HALF SO GOOD	624	APPARITIONS		9
YOUNG MEN KNOW NOTHING OF THIS SORT,	626	OLD MEN BE MAD		16
LACK NOTHING THAT A SOLDIER NEEDS,	635	BLACK TOWER		4
FADED AND VANISHED, NOTHING NOW IS SEEN,	676	ISLE STAT II 3		268
LONG THOU FOR NOTHING, NEITHER SAD NOR GAY;	734	QUATRAIN APHOR		9
LONG THOU FOR NOTHING, NEITHER NIGHT NOR DAY;	734	QUATRAIN APHOR		10
I HAVE FOUND NOTHING BUT THESE EMPTY WATERS;	757	SHADOW WATER A		201
THOUGH WE WERE BIDDEN TO SING, CRY NOTHING LOUD.	778	SONG DEIRDRE 3		2

NOTHINGNESS

	PAGE	TITLE		LINE
EVEN A HALF-HOUR'S NOTHINGNESS,	305	HOUR DAWN		70
EVEN A HALF HOUR'S NOTHINGNESS,	305	HOUR DAWN	V	70

NOTHINGS

	PAGE	TITLE		LINE
LEAVE NOTHING BUT THE NOTHINGS THAT BELONG	542	PARN FUNERAL 1		29

NOTORIETY

	PAGE	TITLE		LINE
NOTORIETY.	320	REED WHISPERER	V	T

NOTORIOUS

	PAGE	TITLE		LINE
NOTORIOUS, TILL ALL MY PRICELESS THINGS	321	REED WHISPERER		13

NOUGHT

	PAGE	TITLE		LINE
BRING THAT TO NOUGHT.	436	FOR MY SON		16
BURN THEIR BODIES UP FOR NOUGHT,	787	HUDDON DUDDON		14

NOURISH

	PAGE	TITLE		LINE
WOULD NOURISH HIS WHIM.	310	PEACOCK		6
FROM MY OLD FATHERS, I MUST NOURISH DREAMS	422	MY DESCENDANTS		2
NOURISH THE PANTHERS IN DIM SOLITUDES;	657	ISLE STAT I 3		44

NOVELIST

	PAGE	TITLE		LINE
THE DEDICATION TO A BOOK OF STORIES SELECTED FROM THE IRISH NOVELISTS	129	BOOK STORIES		T

		PAGE	TITLE	LINE

NOVELS
HE NOW GETS NOVELS AT HIS EASE. . . . . 792 GEORGE MOORE 4
NOVELTY
I, THROUGH THE TERRIBLE NOVELTY OF LIGHT, STALK ON, STALK 623 HIGH TALK 13
ON!
NOWHERE
IF JOY WERE NOWHERE ON THE EARTH . . . . 18 OISIN 1 V 269
. . . FOR NOWHERE IN ANY CLANN . . . . 50 OISIN 3 V 49
NOWISE
THEN NOWISE WORSHIP DUSTY DEEDS, ... 65 HAPPY SHEPHERD 22
NOYES
COME ALFRED NOYES AND ALL THE TROUP . . . . 582 ROGER CASEMENT V 17
NUMB
WHAT MATTER THOUGH NUMB NIGHTMARE RIDE ON TOP, ... 564 GYRES 9
OWLS THERE BE WHOM AGE MAKES NUMB! . . . . 727 LOVERS QUARREL 35
NUMBER
FORMS WITHOUT NUMBER! WHEN THE LIVE WEST FLASHED . . . 41 OISIN 2 V 180
YET I NUMBER HIM IN THE SONG! . . . . 393 EASTER 1916 35
WHAT CALCULATION, NUMBER, MEASUREMENT, REPLIED? . . . . 611 STATUES 27
AND NUMBER THEIR DAYS AND THEIR HOURS-- . . . . 707 FAIRY PEDANT 19
OF RAJAS AND MAHRAJAS BEYOND NUMBER? . . . . 724 KANVA ON SELF 6
NUMBERLESS
I DREW OUT OF THE NUMBERLESS . . . . 24 OISIN 1 V 365
I AM HAUNTED BY NUMBERLESS ISLANDS, AND MANY A DANAAN 122 WHITE BIRDS 9
SHORE,
THE BOOKS OF MY NUMBERLESS DREAMS, ... 157 POET BELOVED 2
WHITE WOMAN WITH NUMBERLESS DREAMS, ... 157 POET BELOVED 7
AND SOUGHT THROUGH LANDS AND ISLANDS NUMBERLESS YEARS, . . 170 SECRET ROSE 23
NUMBERS
HIS NUMBERS, THOUGH THEY MOVED OR SEEMED TO MOVE . . . 610 STATUES 2
HE NUMBERS. HE A BROWN FARM-HOUSE SEES, ... 710 FERENCZ RENYI 22
HE NUMBERS. HE, WITH FLOWERING CURRANT TREES, . . . 710 FERENCZ RENYI V 22
NUN
A KIND OLD NUN IN A WHITE HOOD REPLIES! . . . . 443 SCHOOL CHILDR 2
I HAD BETTER FIND A CONVENT AND TURN NUN! . . . . . 448 HERO GIRL FOOL 11
A NUN AT LEAST HAS ALL MEN'S REVERENCE . . . . . . 448 HERO GIRL FOOL 12
NUNS
BOTH NUNS AND MOTHERS WORSHIP IMAGES, ... 445 SCHOOL CHILDR 49
NURSE
BEING ALL ALONE I'D NURSE A STONE . . . . 459 HIS WILDNESS 11
NURSED
QUEEN MAEVE'S NINE MAINES HAD BEEN NURSED, ... 302 HOUR DAWN 8
NURTURED   SEE WOOD-NURTURED ROCK-NURTURED LAKE-NURTURED
THE DRUID, GREY, WOOD NURTURED, QUIET EYED, ... 101 ROSE UPON ROOD V 4
THOUGH NURTURED LIKE THE SAILING MOON . . . . 451 FIRST LOVE 1
NUT
AH! IT DWELT WITHIN THE TWILIGHT AS THE WORM WITHIN THE 718 PHANTOM SHIP 6
NUT.
NY   SEE KATHLEEN-NY-HOOLIHAN
NYMPH
SLIM ADOLESCENCE THAT A NYMPH HAS STRIPPED, ... 612 NEWS ORACLE 25
NYMPHS   SEE SEA-NYMPHS
SEA NYMPHS IN THEIR PEARLY WAGGONS, ... 309 REALISTS V 5
FLASH FISHLIKE; NYMPHS AND SATYRS . . . . 612 NEWS ORACLE 35
OAK
AN ISLE LAY LEVEL BEFORE US, WITH DRIPPING HAZEL AND OAK? 47 OISIN 3 10
AN ISLE LAY LEVEL BEFORE US, DRIPPING WITH HAZEL AND OAK? 47 OISIN 3 V 10
CEASED ON OUR HANDS AND OUR FACES, ON HAZEL AND OAK LEAF, 48 OISIN 3 23
THE LIGHT,
. . . FOR, CUMBROUS WITH STEMS OF THE HAZEL AND OAK, . . 48 OISIN 3 25
OF HOLLIES, AND HAZELS, AND OAK TREES, A VALLEY WAS SLOPING 48 OISIN 3 V 26
AWAY
. . . FAR FROM THE HAZEL AND OAK, ... 57 OISIN 3 146
GREEN OAK AND POPLAR TREE! . . . . 132 OLD PENSIONER V 16
O HEAVY SWOLLEN WATERS, BRIM THE FALL OF THE OAK TREES, 207 HANRAHANS SONG V 11
TILL OAK AND HAZEL CEASED AND BEECH BEGAN, ... 283 TWO KINGS V 139A
BRING ME TO THE BLASTED OAK . . . . 507 JANE BISHOP 1
AND BIDS ME TO THE OAK, FOR HE . . . . 508 JANE BISHOP 23
SET ME BY THAT OAK, FOR HE . . . . 508 JANE BISHOP V 22
AND BIDS ME TO THAT OAK, FOR HE, ... 508 JANE BISHOP V 23
UNDER OAK AND BEECHEN BOUGH, ... 522 LULLABY 11
UNDER OAK AND BEECHES BOUGH, ... 522 LULLABY V 11
NO TASTE HAVE I FOR SLUMBER 'NEATH AN OAK. . . . . . 721 WITCH VIVIEN 31
OAKEN
TO THE SCENTED OAKEN PRESS. . . . . 124 CATHLEEN PARA 8
THOU HAST FORGOTTEN. ON THE OAKEN STOOL . . . . . . 713 FERENCZ RENYI 91
OAK-TREE
AND UNDER A SHADY OAK-TREE SAT, ... 728 PRIEST FAIRY 7
OAR   SEE STEERING-OAR
AND AH, YOU PROUD MAIDEN, YOU ARE NOT SO FAIR WHEN HIS OAR 91 OLD FISHERMAN 9
PROUD MAIDEN, YE ARE NOT SO FAIR, WHEN HIS OAR . . . 91 OLD FISHERMAN V 9
AND, AH, YE PROUD MAIDENS, YE ARE NOT SO FAIR, WHEN HIS OAR 91 OLD FISHERMAN V 9
OR ON THE UNPEOPLED WAVES WITH KINGS TO PULL AT THE OAR, 210 UNDER THE MOON 15
I HELD A PAINTED STEERING OAR, ... 253 HIS DREAM V 2
THE BUTT END OF A STEERING OAR, ... 253 HIS DREAM V 2
POSEIDON GAVE IT BIT AND OAR, ... 447 COLONUS PRAISE 28
OF THAT OAR AND OF THAT BIT! . . . . 447 COLONUS PRAISE 30
NOW MAKING BUSY WITH THE OAR, ... 742 DANAAN QUICK 2
ARE DOUBTFUL LIKE THESE PULLERS OF THE OAR! . . . . . 748 SHADOW WATER A 30
WHILE THE WIND IS LIGHT. THE OAR CAN HARDLY MOVE HER, . . 754 SHADOW WATER A 157
BE PULLERS OF THE OAR UNTIL YOU DIE? . . . . 757 SHADOW WATER A 217

567

```
                                                              PAGE      TITLE           LINE
OAR   (CONTINUED)
    THERE--THERE--BY THE OAR.  THE CROWN OF A FAR COUNTRY. . .   763  SHADOW WATER A      310
OARED       SEE LONG-OARED
OARING
    THEY WALK ON SHORES UNSEEN OF OARING GALLEYS, . . . . .       30  OISIN 2          V  14D
OARS
    NO MORE TO CRAWL ON THE SEAS WITH LONG OARS MILE AFTER        55  OISIN 3             119
        MILE,
    AND NOT THE BANKS OF OARS THAT SWAM UPON . . . . . .         610  STATUES              13
    WHEN WE ROWED NORTH, SINGING ABOVE THE OARS, . . . . .       749  SHADOW WATER A       39
    HAVE FOUND DELIGHT, IN THE RESOUNDING OARS, . . . . .        750  SHADOW WATER A       72
OATEN
    AN OATEN PIPE UNTO A LISTENING FAWN, . . . . . . . .         678  ISLE STAT II 3      301
    AN OATEN PIPE UNTO A LISTENING FAUN, . . . . . . . .         678  ISLE STAT II 3   V  301
OATH
    DREAD OATH, WHO DWELL ON SACRED HIMALAY, . . . . . .          74  ANASHU VIJAYA        67
    SOME FEASTING MAN THAT THE SAME OATH HAS BOUND." . . . .     108  CUCHULAIN SEA        38
    SOME FEATING MAN THAT THE SAME OATH HAS BOUND." . . . .      108  CUCHULAIN SEA    V   38
    SOME FEASTING MAN THAT THE SAME OATH HAS BOUND." . . . .     109  CUCHULAIN SEA        54
    "SOME FEATING MAN THAT THE SAME OATH HAS BOUND." . . . .     109  CUCHULAIN SEA    V   54
OATH-BOUND
    THAT ALL ARE OATH-BOUND MEN! . . . . . . . . . . .           635  BLACK TOWER           5
    STAND WE ON GUARD OATH-BOUND! . . . . . . . . . .            636  BLACK TOWER          26
OATMEAL
    ROUND AND ROUND THE OATMEAL CHEST. . . . . . . . .            88  STOLEN CHILD     V   49
OATMEAL-CHEST
    ROUND AND ROUND THE OATMEAL-CHEST. . . . . . . . .            88  STOLEN CHILD         49
OBEDIENCE
    AT THE PERFECTION OF ONE'S OWN OBEDIENCE! . . . . . .        376  PHASES OF MOON      109
OBEDIENT
    THEMSELVES OBEDIENT, . . . . . . . . . . . . .              382  VISION ROBART        11
    OBEDIENT TO SOME HIDDEN MAGICAL BREATH. . . . . . .         382  VISION ROBART        13
OBEY
    SHALL FOLLOW YOUR HORN AND OBEY YOUR WHIM, . . . . .           9  OISIN 1             99
    QUEEN OF HIGH CRUACHAN."  "I OBEY YOUR WILL . . . . .        184  QUEEN MAEVE          99
    I HAVE DONE RIGHT.  WHAT COULD I BUT OBEY? . . . . .         243  SHADOW WATER B      443
    AND WORDS OBEY MY CALL"; . . . . . . . . . . .              256  WORDS                12
    TRIUMPH THAT WE OBEY. . . . . . . . . . . . .               382  VISION ROBART        16
    "OBEY OUR ANCIENT RULE AND MAKE A SHROUD! . . . . . .       634  CUCHULAIN COMF       13
    IN SOUTHERN LOCHLANN.  I WOULD NOT OBEY . . . . . .          756  SHADOW WATER A   V  191
    I KNOW HE WILL OBEY YOU! AND IF YOUR EYES . . . . .          768  SHADOW WATER A      408
OBEYED
    WHERE THOSE THAT HAVE OBEYED THE HOLY LAW . . . . .          356  BROKEN DREAMS        33
    WHERE EVERY FOOT OBEYED HER GLANCE! . . . . . . .            488  CRAZED MOON          11
    WHERE VERY FOOT OBEYED HER GLANCE! . . . . . . .             488  CRAZED MOON      V   11
    TILL TRUTH OBEYED HIS CALL! . . . . . . . . . .             576  ACRE OF GRASS        18
    AND IN THAT TERROR'S NAME OBEYED THE CALL, . . . . .        622  HOUND VOICE          12
OBEYING
    AND BID THEM WANDER OBEYING YOUR WILL, . . . . . . .        141  EVERLAST VOICE        3
OBEYS
    OBEYS.  SOME FIERCE MAGICIAN FLIES OR WALKS . . . . .        720  WITCH VIVIEN          9
OBJECT
    HAS MARKED A DISTANT OBJECT DOWN, . . . . . . . .            337  TOM OROUGHLEY         3
    BUT HE'D OBJECT TO THE HOST, . . . . . . . . .              473  ALL SOUL NIGHT       77
OBLITERATING       SEE LIGHT-OBLITERATING
OBSCURE
    EACH FOREHEAD LIKE AN OBSCURE STAR . . . . . . . .           26  OISIN 1             391
    INDIGNANT AT THE FUMBLING WITS, THE OBSCURE SPITE . . .     291  PAUDEEN               1
    OUT OF THE OBSCURE DARK OF THE RICH STREAMS, . . . . .      417  ANCEST HOUSES        14
OBSCURITY
    CRAWLED FROM OBSCURITY, AND SET UPON ME . . . . . .          352  PEOPLE               26
OBSERVANT
    OBSERVANT OLD MEN KNOW IT WELL! . . . . . . . . .            626  OLD MEN BE MAD       17
OBSTACLE
    MY CHILD SLEEPS ON.  THERE IS NO OBSTACLE . . . . .          403  FOR DAUGHTER          3
O'BYRNES
    WHERE THE O'BYRNES AND BYRNES ARE BURIED, . . . . .          331  ROUND TOWER           9
OCCUPIED
    WHAT GREAT HARUN AL-RASHID, OCCUPIED . . . . . . .           462  HARUN RASHID         24
    BELOVED HAROUN EL RASHID, OCCUPIED . . . . . . .            462  HARUN RASHID     V   24
OCCURRED
    NO MATTER WHAT DISASTER OCCURRED . . . . . . . .            578  CRAZED GIRL           9
OCEAN
    OF MURMURING OCEAN, AND BEHIND US . . . . . . .              25  OISIN 1          V  384
    OF OCEAN FAN THEE INTO LIFE, AND FOLD . . . . . .           688  TWO TITANS           56
    BY THE SLOW HEAVING OCEAN--MUMBLING MOTHER OF THE DEAD.     719  PHANTOM SHIP         34
    PRAYED BESIDE THE OCEAN, THE OLD MUMBLING MOTHER OF THE     719  PHANTOM SHIP     V   34
        DEAD.
OCEAN'S
    A VAPOURY FOOTFALL ON THE OCEAN'S SLEEPY BLAZE. . . . .      78  INDIAN TO LOVE   V   20
    HIDING AWAY THE OCEAN'S YELPING FLOCKS. . . . . . .         688  TWO TITANS           38
OCHONE
    "OCHONE, OCHONE! THE MAN HAS DIED, . . . . . . .            133  FR GILLIGAN      V   25
    "OCHONE, OCHONE! THE MAN HAS DIED, . . . . . . .            133  FR GILLIGAN      V   25
OCTOBER
    UNDER THE OCTOBER TWILIGHT THE WATER . . . . . . .          322  SWANS AT COOLE        3
    OCTOBER LAST I FOUND IT TOO . . . . . . . . . .            454  EMPTY CUP             7
ODDS
    AND WHAT'S THE ODDS IF SUCH AS THESE . . . . . . .          597  MODEL LAUREATE        5
    TALKED OF ODDS AND ENDS. . . . . . . . . . .               627  STATES HOLIDAY        8
```

O'DONNELL
    DOWN TO THE TUNE OF O'DONNELL ABU. . . . . 544 TO SAME TUNE 1   10
    DOWN TO THE TUNE OF O'DONNELL ABU. . . . . 545 TO SAME TUNE 1   20
    DOWN TO THE TUNE OF O'DONNELL ABU. . . . . 545 TO SAME TUNE 1   30
    THOSE THAT COME AFTER SHALL MOCK AT O'DONNELL, ... 546 TO SAME TUNE 2   23
    DOWN TO THE TUNE OF O'DONNELL ABU. . . . . 546 TO SAME TUNE 2 V REF
    THOSE THAT COME AFTER SHALL MOCK O'DONNELL, ... 546 TO SAME TUNE 2 V 23
    DOWN TO THE TUNE OF O'DONNELL ABU. . . . . 548 TO SAME TUNE 3 V REF
    THOSE THAT COME AFTER SHALL MOCK AT O'DONNELL, . . . 614 MARCH SONGS 1   23
ODOROUS
    THE ODOROUS WEIGHT OF HIS CURLS OF LIGHT, ... 28 OISIN 1   V 423D
    AND COVER YOUR LIPS WITH ODOROUS TWILIGHT AND SAY, . . 162 ASKS FORGIVE   5
    THE ODOROUS TWILIGHT THERE. . . . . 163 ASKS FORGIVE   24
    AND THRO' THE ODOROUS AIR LOVE-DREAMS ARE WINGING-- . 645 ISLE STAT I 1   5
    AND CLINGING WITH THE DEW OF ODOROUS SHOWERS, ... 704 REMEMBRANCE   4
ODOUR
    TILL, FATTENING THE WINDS OF THE MORNING, AN ODOUR   57 OISIN 3   153
        OF NEW-MOWN HAY
    AND SHEDS FAINT ODOUR THROUGH THE AIR; . . . . 85 MAD KING GOLL V   64
    ODOUR OF BLOOD WHEN CHRIST WAS SLAIN . . . . 438 SONGS PLAY 2   6
    ODOUR OF BLOOD ON THE ANCESTRAL STAIR! . . . . 482 BLOOD AND MOON   40
    MIRACULOUS OIL, ODOUR OF VIOLET, ... 483 OIL AND BLOOD   3
    AN ODOUR OF THE NEW-MOWN HAY . . . . 502 VACILLATION   58
ODOUR-LADEN
    WHERE TIME IS DROWNED IN ODOUR-LADEN WINDS . . . . . 219 HARP OF AENGUS   3
    DREAMING IN THEIR SOFT ODOUR-LADEN SLEEP; . . . . . . 650 ISLE STAT I 1   125
    WHERE TIME IS DROWNED IN ODOUR-LADEN WINDS . . . . . 762 SHADOW WATER A   298
ODOURS
    NOR LOST IN THE STAR-FIRES AND ODOURS . . . . 56 OISIN 3   135
    AND SHEDS FAINT ODOURS THROUGH THE AIR! . . . . . . 85 MAD KING GOLL   64
    SEVEN ODOURS, SEVEN MURMURS, SEVEN WOODS. . . . . . 218 WOODS OF COOLE   16
    BATHED IN MIRACULOUS OIL, SWEET ODOURS FROM IT COME, . 503 VACILLATION   81
O'DRISCOLL
    O'DRISCOLL DROVE WITH A SONG . . . . 143 HOST OF AIR   1
    O'DRISCOLL SCATTERED THE CARDS . . . . 145 HOST OF AIR   37
    O'DRISCOLL GOT UP FROM THE GRASS, ... 145 HOST OF AIR   V 37
O'DUFFY
    HAD EVEN O'DUFFY--BUT I NAME NO MORE-- . . . . . . 543 PARN FUNERAL 2   9
ODYSSEUS
    DOOMED LIKE ODYSSEUS AND THE LABOURING SHIPS . . . 120 SORROW OF LOVE   7
OEDIPUS
    FROM "OEDIPUS AT COLONUS" . . . . 459 FROM OEDIPUS   T
OEDIPUS'
    AND YET I WEEP--OEDIPUS' CHILD . . . . 540 FROM ANTIGONE   15
OENONE
    OENONE SAW THE FIRES OF TROIA LEAP, ... 645 ISLE STAT I 1   17
    THE SHEPHERD PARIS FOR OENONE MADE. . . . . 650 ISLE STAT I 1   136
O'ER   SEE CLOUD-O'ER-MUFFLED
    A STORMY SUNSET O'ER DOOMED SHIPS. . . . . 3 OISIN 1   V 23
    TO PEAK AND PINE O'ER OISIN'S FAME." . . . . . . 7 OISIN 1   V 70
    ON, ON, WE GALLOPED O'ER THE SEA. . . . . 11 OISIN 1   V 132
    O'ER MEN WHO SLEEP, AND WAKE, AND DIE, ... 22 OISIN 1   V 340B
    WE PASSED IN SILENCE O'ER THE MEAD, ... 25 OISIN 1   V 376A
    AND SHAKES O'ER THE WIDTH OF THE SEA-WORLD BORDER . 28 OISIN 1   V 423C
    THEN, MOUNTED ON A HERON, O'ER THE DEEP . . . . . 33 OISIN 2   V 64
    REMEMBERING HOW I PACED IN DAYS GONE O'ER, ... 44 OISIN 2   V 227
    . . . AND O'ER YOUR CAR HEADS PEER . . . . 73 ANASHU VIJAYA V   45
    I RULED O'ER ALL MY FAIR DOMINIONS, ... 82 MAD KING GOLL V   7
    O'ER HILL AND HEATH AND SPONGY FEN, ... 83 MAD KING GOLL V   32
    O'ER HER NEST THE LIGHTS ARE BLENDING! . . . . . 646 ISLE STAT I 1   36
    SEE, I TELL THY BEAUTIES O'ER, ... 647 ISLE STAT I 1   56
    SINGING O'ER AND O'ER AND O'ER . . . . 648 ISLE STAT I 1   79
    SINGING O'ER AND O'ER AND O'ER . . . . 648 ISLE STAT I 1   79
    SINGING O'ER AND O'ER AND O'ER . . . . 648 ISLE STAT I 1   79
    TO WELCOME THEE, WHEN O'ER THE OWLET'S WINGS . . . 648 ISLE STAT I 1   102
    BEAT OUT THEIR LIVES LAMENTING O'ER THE SAND; . . 652 ISLE STAT I 2   14
    O'ER THE GRASS LIGHT-ENDAPPLED . . . . 654 ISLE STAT I 2   63
    O'ER THE GREEN EDEN-SOD; . . . . 654 ISLE STAT I 2   65
    O'ER THE GREEN EDEN-SOD, ... 654 ISLE STAT I 2   75
    O'ER THE LAKE THIS VERY DAY. . . . . 656 ISLE STAT I 3   17
    O'ER MUCH I'VE TALKED! I SHALL BE SILENT SOON, . . 657 ISLE STAT I 3   75
    WATCHING O'ER HER AWFUL YOUNG, ... 658 ISLE STAT I 3   87
    O'ER HER YOUNG SO EAGERLY . . . . 658 ISLE STAT I 3   93
    YOUNG GUARIMOND HE TELLS THEM O'ER AND O'ER, . . . 661 ISLE STAT II 1   56
    YOUNG GUARIMOND HE TELLS THEM O'ER AND O'ER, . . . 661 ISLE STAT II 1   56
    THE LIGHT IS DANCING O'ER THE KNOTTED TREES, . . . 662 ISLE STAT II 2   2
    THE FAERY THING FLEW WITH HER O'ER THE GRAY . . . 663 ISLE STAT II 2   38
    OF SWORD-BLUE WAVES OF CALM; WHILE O'ER HEAD BLINK . 663 ISLE STAT II 2   42
    O'ER GRIEF. THE WORLD DRINKS SORROW FROM THE BEAMS . 664 ISLE STAT II 2   46
    OF LILAC O'ER THE PULSING WATER GLEAMS, ... 664 ISLE STAT II 2   48
    TILL HIS LAST WRETCHEDNESS WAS O'ER AND DONE." . . 664 ISLE STAT II 2   54
    THE SKY WAS BANDED O'ER WITH WRACK. . . . . 667 ISLE STAT II 3   23
    BEFORE A DEATH. O'ER WAVE AND BANK . . . . 673 ISLE STAT II 3   185
    MY DREAMS O'ER THOUGHTS OF PLENTY, AS THE RED- . . 681 SEEKER   V 3
    MAKING ALL ONE O'ER ROCK AND SEA AND SKIES; . . . 687 TWO TITANS   28
    BENDING HER FACE O'ER HIS, SHE WATCHES MEET . . . 688 TWO TITANS   45
    POURS UP AND FLOATS IN FRAGRANCE O'ER MY HEAD . . . 691 MOSADA 1   V 40
    THE PATH O'ER MUFFLED WITH THE LEAVES--DEAD LEAVES, . 703 MOSADA 3   V 115
    WHILE O'ER THE BUDS, AND O'ER THE GRASS-BLADES, BRIGHT . 704 REMEMBRANCE   3
    WHILE O'ER THE BUDS, AND O'ER THE GRASS-BLADES, BRIGHT . 704 REMEMBRANCE   3

		PAGE	TITLE	LINE

O'ER   (CONTINUED)
    AND HANGING O'ER THE HUSH OF WILLOW BOWERS, ... 705 REMEMBRANCE   8
    AND HANG O'ER THE HISTORIED STONE, ... 707 FAIRY PEDANT   6
    AND FOLLOWING O'ER THE FIELDS AND PASTURE LANDS, ... 715 FERENCZ RENYI   V 120
    HANGS O'ER ALL THE WOODED EARTH. . . . . 731 STREET DANCERS   8
O'ER-APPLED
    WHEN THE TREE WAS O'ER-APPLED . . . . 654 ISLE STAT I 2   60
O'ER-MUFFLED
    THE PATH O'ER-MUFFLED WITH THE LEAVES--DEAD LEAVES, . . . 703 MOSADA 3   115
O'ERWORN
    THESE NOW O'ERWORN AND WITHERED HANDS, ... 23 OISIN 1   V 348
OFF   SEE FAR-OFF
    "LIKE ME WERE SOME GALLEY FORSAKEN FAR OFF IN MERIDIAN   55 OISIN 3   117
      ISLE,
    WATCHING THE BLESSED ONES MOVE FAR OFF, AND THE SMILE ON   61 OISIN 3   199
      GOD'S FACE,
    NOW CUFF HIM OFF. HE'S OFF! A KISS FOR YOU, ... 73 ANASHU VIJAYA   39
    NOW CUFF HIM OFF. HE'S OFF! A KISS FOR YOU, ... 73 ANASHU VIJAYA   39
    MURMURING GENTLY HOW FAR OFF ARE THE UNQUIET LANDS! . . . 78 INDIAN TO LOVE   V 10
    FAR OFF BY FURTHEST ROSSES . . . . 87 STOLEN CHILD   15
    DIE OFF THE FEEBLE SOUNDS! . . . . 99 FOXHUNTER   V 42
    COME CLEAR OFF THE NETS OF WRONG AND RIGHT! . . . . . 147 INTO TWILIGHT   V   2
    AND WAVED IT OFF ON THE AIR. . . . . 160 CAP AND BELLS   20
    FAR OFF, MOST SECRET, AND INVIOLATE ROSE, ... 169 SECRET ROSE   V   1
    FAR OFF, MOST SECRET, AND INVIOLATE ROSE? . . . . . 170 SECRET ROSE   V 32
    WILL OVERTHROW HIS SHADOWS AND CARRY OFF . . . . . 184 QUEEN MAEVE   95
    "ANOTHER'S HURRIED OFF," CRIED HE, ... 193 BAILE AILLINN   113
    HE CARRIED EDAIN OFF FROM A KING'S HOUSE, ... 224 SHADOW WATER B   48
    HOW ARE WE BETTER OFF THAN SEAGHAN THE FOOL, ... 228 SHADOW WATER B   129
    WE HAVE BEEN NO BETTER OFF THAN SEAGHAN THE FOOL, . . . 228 SHADOW WATER B V 129
    "PUT OFF THAT MASK OF BURNING GOLD . . . . 263 MASK   1
    BEFORE HIM OR BEHIND, BUT THAT FAR OFF . . . . . . 279 TWO KINGS   55
    "TIME TO PUT OFF THE WORLD AND GO SOMEWHERE . . . . . 299 BEGGAR CRIED   1
    WERE NOT OUR BEDS FAR OFF I'D RING THE BELL, ... 377 PHASES OF MOON   124
    SHOOK OFF THE WATER FROM HIS BACK! . . . . 400 DEMON BEAST   29
    OR HURRIED THEM OFF ON ITS OWN FURIOUS PATH! . . . . 430 NINETEEN 19   53
    WHERE WE SHOULD CAST OFF BODY AND TRADE . . . . . . 431 NINETEEN 19   73
    I'D TEAR IT OFF AND THROW IT IN THE FIRE." . . . . . 462 HARUN RASHID   34
    THAT IF THE SPRING BEAR OFF WHAT THE SPRING GAVE . . . . 464 HARUN RASHID   76
    CRIED, CASTING OFF THE MOUNTAIN SNOW, ... 502 VACILLATION   60
    "THAT IS A LONG WAY OFF, ... 526 AM OF IRELAND   11
    BUT WHEN THIS SOUL, ITS BODY OFF, ... 538 LAST CONFESS   15
    SOMEWHERE OFF HENRY STREET! . . . . 585 ORAHILLY   31
    COULD CRAZY JANE PUT OFF OLD AGE . . . . 606 SONGS BURDEN 1   19
    EUROPE PUT OFF THAT FOAM WHEN PHIDIAS . . . . . . 610 STATUES   15
    THEY PITCH THEIR BURDENS OFF. . . . . 612 NEWS ORACLE   13
    O LET ME PASS! THE SPELLS FROM OFF THE HEART . . . . 668 ISLE STAT II 3   44
    FAR OFF IN DROWSY VALLEYS . . . . 680 LOVE AND DEATH   5
    HEARING THE FAR OFF SINGING GUILE AND GROANED, ... 693 MOSADA 1   V 88
    CAST OFF THY HERESIES, AND SAVE THY SOUL . . . . . 701 MOSADA 3   64
    WAVES OFF THE FLIES, AND WARMS HIM IN THE SHINE. . . . 709 FERENCZ RENYI   7
    A SCORE OF YARDS OFF 'NEATH A WILLOW, SHOT. . . . . 712 FERENCZ RENYI   65
    HER OFF AND TURNS AWAY. SHE THROWS . . . . . . 714 FERENCZ RENYI   V 102
    AND DROVE THE BOYS AND WOMEN OFF. . . . . 725 LEGEND   24
    HIS HEAD FROM OFF HIS BODY . . . . 789 SINGING HEAD   5
OFFENDED
    TO MY OFFENDED HEART . . . . 516 MANS SONG   17
OFFER
    I, PRIESTESS OF THIS TEMPLE, OFFER UP . . . . . 71 ANASHU VIJAYA   12
    I, PRIESTESS OF THIS TEMPLE, OFFER UP . . . . . 75 ANASHU VIJAYA   84
    I OFFER TO LOVE'S PLAY . . . . 536 PARTING   13
OFFERED
    O YOU WILL TAKE WHATEVER'S OFFERED . . . . 313 TWO YEAR LATER   7
OFFERS
    SHE OFFERS GREAT REWARDS IF WE TURN EAST . . . . . 755 SHADOW WATER A   169
OFFICE
    PLANNED IN A GOVERNMENT OFFICE, SHORTEN HIS LIFE, . . . 372 ON GOING HOUSE   15
    THAT OFFICE FOOLS HAVE RUN, ... 598 MODEL LAUREATE   20
    THAT FOUGHT IN THE POST OFFICE . . . . 608 SONGS BURDEN 3   5
    WHAT STALKED THROUGH THE POST OFFICE? WHAT INTELLECT, . . 611 STATUES   26
OFFICER
    COMMANDING OFFICER THAT TORE . . . . 627 STATES HOLIDAY   16
OFT
    OF KNITTED MUSIC. OFT THE FOND REPINING . . . . . 33 OISIN 2   V 68C
    FLOWED ON ANEW, AND OFT, ANEW DECLINING, ... 33 OISIN 2   V 68D
OFTEN
    "PASSION HAS OFTEN WORN OUR WANDERING HEARTS." . . . . 80 EPHEMERA   12
    "OFTEN HAS PASSION WORN OUR WANDERING HEARTS, ... 80 EPHEMERA   V 12
    I HAVE OFTEN HEARD HIM SINGING TO AND FRO, ... 109 CUCHULAIN SEA   49
    I HAVE OFTEN HEARD THE SWEET SOUND OF HIS BOW. . . . . 109 CUCHULAIN SEA   50
    I OFTEN HEAR HIM SINGING TO AND FRO, ... 109 CUCHULAIN SEA   V 49
    I OFTEN HEAR THE SWEET SOUND OF HIS BOW. . . . . . 109 CUCHULAIN SEA   V 50
    YOU SAY, AS I HAVE OFTEN GIVEN TONGUE . . . . . . 262 TO A POET   1
    HE HAD OFTEN PLAYED HIS PIPES AMONG MY HILLS, ... 339 SHEP GOATHERD   23
    AND OFTEN THOSE FIRST DAYS I SAW HER STARE . . . . . 466 HARUN RASHID   122
    OFTEN AT EVENING WHEN A BOY . . . . 494 AT ALGECIRAS   7
    OFTEN HE HAD BENT DOWN SOME BOUGH ALL BRIGHT . . . . 710 FERENCZ RENYI   28
    WHY THOSE WHO DO GOOD OFTEN BE NOT GOOD, ... 710 FERENCZ RENYI   33
    OFTEN HE HAD BENT DOWN SOME BOUGH ALL BRIGHT WITH BERRIES! 710 FERENCZ RENYI   V 28
OGHAM
    THEREON IN OGHAM LETTERS, "MANANNAN"! . . . . . . 38 OISIN 2   128

```
                                                         PAGE    TITLE          LINE

OGHAM   (CONTINUED)
      IN CHANGELESS OGHAM LETTERS WRIT--  . . . . . . . .    194 BAILE AILLINN     117
      AND CARVE HIS NAME IN OGHAM." EOCHAID SAID, . . . .    280 TWO KINGS          83
O'GRADY
      STANDISH O'GRADY SUPPORTING HIMSELF BETWEEN THE TABLES . .  577 LOFTY THINGS   5
O'HART
      THE BALLAD OF FATHER O'HART . . . . . . . . . . .      91 FATHER OHART         T
      FATHER O'HART  . . . . . . . . . . . . . . . .        91 FATHER OHART    V    T
      GOOD FATHER JOHN O'HART  . . . . . . . . . . . .      91 FATHER OHART         1
O'HIGGINS
      O'HIGGINS ITS SOLE STATESMAN HAD NOT DIED. . . . .     543 PARN FUNERAL 2      8
      KEVIN O'HIGGINS, AND THAT LOOK HE WEARS,  . . . . .    601 GALLERY REVIS  V    5
O'HIGGINS'
      KEVIN O'HIGGINS' COUNTENANCE THAT WEARS  . . . . . .   601 GALLERY REVIS       5
OHONE
      AND HAS NOT YET BEEN WAKED. OHONE! O! O! O!  . . . .   241 SHADOW WATER B    393
OIL
      AND OIL AND WINE AND HONEY AND MILK,  . . . . . . .      8 OISIN 1            92
      AND HONEY, AND OIL, AND WINE, AND MILK,  . . . . . .     8 OISIN 1       V    92
      I BADE, BECAUSE THE WICK AND OIL ARE SPENT  . . . . .  333 LIVING BEAUTY       1
      THE WICK OF YOUTH BEING BURNED AND THE OIL SPENT, . .  334 LIVING BEAUTY  V    3
      WHEN OIL AND WICK ARE BURNED IN ONE;  . . . . . . .    388 SOLOMON WITCH      30
      NOR BLEAR-EYED WISDOM OUT OF MIDNIGHT OIL. . . . . .   446 SCHOOL CHILDR      60
      OIL AND BLOOD  . . . . . . . . . . . . . . . .        483 OIL AND BLOOD       T
      MIRACULOUS OIL, ODOUR OF VIOLET. . . . . . . . . .     483 OIL AND BLOOD       3
      BATHED IN MIRACULOUS OIL, SWEET ODOURS FROM IT COME, . .  503 VACILLATION     81
OILY
      WE RODE ACROSS THE OILY SEA,  . . . . . . . . . .      10 OISIN 1       V   114
OISIN
      THE WANDERINGS OF OISIN  . . . . . . . . . . . .        1 OISIN 1             T
      THE WANDERINGS OF OISIN AND HOW A DEMON TRAPPED HIM . .  1 OISIN 1       V    T
      OISIN, TELL ME THE FAMOUS STORY  . . . . . . . . .      2 OISIN 1       V    1
      OISIN, THOU ART HALF HEATHEN STILL!  . . . . . . .      4 OISIN 1       V   31
      FOR LOVE OF OISIN FOAM WET FEET  . . . . . . . . .      6 OISIN 1       V   57
      FOR LOVE OF OISIN FOAM-WET FEET  . . . . . . . . .      6 OISIN 1       V   57
      OF OISIN, THE YOUNG MAN, MY SON?  . . . . . . . .       6 OISIN 1       V   60
      ON THIS YOUNG MAN, OISIN, MY SON?"  . . . . . . . .     6 OISIN 1       V   61
      OF NOBLE OISIN AND HIS FAME,  . . . . . . . . . .       7 OISIN 1       V   66
      "O OISIN, MOUNT BY ME AND RIDE  . . . . . . . . .       8 OISIN 1            80
      "OISIN, THOU MUST AWAY WITH ME  . . . . . . . . .       8 OISIN 1       V   80
      BARD OISIN, BOAST NOT OF THY DEEDS  . . . . . . .      11 OISIN 1       V  129
      HOPELESS FOR EVER! ANCIENT OISIN KNOWS,  . . . . . .   42 OISIN 2           202
      AY, OISIN KNOWS, FOR HE IS OF THE WEAK,  . . . . . .   42 OISIN 2       V  202
      YOUR QUESTIONER, OISIN, IS WORTHY, HE COMES FROM THE FENIAN  51 OISIN 3      64
          LANDS."
      WORTHY'S THY QUESTIONER, OISIN, HE FROM THE FENIAN LANDS."  51 OISIN 3   V   64
      AS SHE MURMURED, "O WANDERING OISIN,  . . . . . . .    55 OISIN 3           123
      BUT WEEP FOR YOUR NIAMH, O OISIN, WEEP! FOR IF ONLY YOUR  55 OISIN 3        127
          SHOE
      BUT WEEP FOR THY NIAM, OH OISIN, WEEP! FOR IF ONLY THY SHOE  55 OISIN 3 V  127
      BY OISIN ON THE GRASS!  . . . . . . . . . . . . .     611 NEWS ORACLE         6
      FIRST THAT SEA-RIDER OISIN LED BY THE NOSE  . . . . .  629 CIRCUS ANIMALS     10
OISIN'S
      RHYME THAT RHYMED UPON OISIN'S NAME,  . . . . . . .     7 OISIN 1            64
      TO PEAK AND PINE O'ER OISIN'S FAME."  . . . . . . .     7 OISIN 1       V   70
      FOR THESE WERE ANCIENT OISIN'S FATE  . . . . . . .     24 OISIN 1           361
OLD       SEE SIXTY-YEAR-OLD HUNDRED-YEAR-OLD WORLD-OLD
      THE BAD OLD DAYS. THOU WERT, MEN SING,  . . . . .       2 OISIN 1       V    3
      MUST LIVE TO BE OLD LIKE THE WANDERING MOON. . . . .    3 OISIN 1           12
      "MEN'S HEARTS OF OLD WERE DROPS OF FLAME  . . . . .    19 OISIN 1          276
      IN OTHER YEARS FROM SOME OLD STAR,  . . . . . . . .    19 OISIN 1       V  277
      OF GRIEVOUS TIME ON HIS OLD CRUTCHES,  . . . . . . .   23 OISIN 1       V 341B
      FOR WE KNEW WELL THE OLD WAS OVER.  . . . . . . . .    25 OISIN 1          379
      BY RIVERS AND THE WOODS' OLD NIGHT;  . . . . . . . .   25 OISIN 1          387
      FOR WELL WE KNEW THE OLD WAS OVER,  . . . . . . . .    25 OISIN 1       V  379
      THE RIVERS, AND THE WOOD'S OLD NIGHT.  . . . . . . .   25 OISIN 1       V  387
      "AN OLD MAN STIRS THE FIRE TO A BLAZE,  . . . . . .    26 OISIN 1          400
      WATCHED THE OLD SUN THAT IN SEA-WAYS  . . . . . . .    26 OISIN 1       V  394
      AND THE CRY OF THE HOUNDS ON THE HILLS OF OLD. . . .   27 OISIN 1          407
      THE HARE GROWS OLD AS SHE PLAYS IN THE SUN  . . . .    27 OISIN 1          412
      "OLD GROWS THE HARE AS SHE PLAYS IN THE SUN,  . . .    28 OISIN 1       V  420
      BEFORE GOD WAS OR MY OLD LINE BEGAN;  . . . . . . .    29 OISIN 2            8
      WARS SHADOWY, VAST, EXULTANT; FAERIES OF OLD  . . .    29 OISIN 2            9
      THINGS DONE ERE GOD FIRST WAS OR MY OLD LINE BEGAN; .  29 OISIN 2       V    8
      ON THE OLD SORROWS OF HIS HUMAN DAYS.  . . . . . . .   29 OISIN 2       V   12
      THAT OLD, SEA-WEEDY, SQUARED, THREE HUNDRED FEET  . .  31 OISIN 2       V  30C
      TO TWO OLD EAGLES, FULL OF ANCIENT PRIDE,  . . . . .   34 OISIN 2           74
      NOW IT IS OLD AND MOUSE-LIKE. FOR A SIGN  . . . . .    36 OISIN 2           96
      NOW OLD AND MOUSELIKE. FOR AN ANSWERING SIGN  . . .    36 OISIN 2       V   96
      PATRICK, BEFORE THY CRAFT DIES EACH OLD SONG. . . . .  42 OISIN 2       V  196
      OLD AND REMEMBERING, WHAT AVAILS THE WIND  . . . . .   42 OISIN 2       V  206
      LIKE AN ARMY OF OLD MEN LONGING FOR REST FROM THE MOAN  48 OISIN 3        16
          OF THE SEAS.
      DROPPING; A MURMUROUS DROPPING; OLD SILENCE AND THAT ONE  48 OISIN 3       18
          SOUND;
      AND DEW-BLANCHED HORNS, IN WHOSE HOLLOW A CHILD OF THREE  49 OISIN 3       30
          YEARS OLD
      AND DEW-BLANCHED HORNS, IN WHOSE HOLLOWS A CHILD OF THREE  49 OISIN 3   V  31
          YEARS OLD
      IN MIDST OF AN OLD MAN'S BOSOM; OWLS RUFFLING AND PACING  50 OISIN 3       47
          AROUND
```

		PAGE	TITLE		LINE

OLD   (CONTINUED)

	PAGE	TITLE		LINE
IN THE MIDST OF AN OLD MAN'S BOSOM; OWLS RUFFLING AND PACING AROUND	50	OISIN 3	V	47
THAT WE MAY MUSE IN THE STARLIGHT AND TALK OF THE BATTLES OF OLD;	51	OISIN 3		63
. . . MADE CONCHUBAR'S SWORD-BLADE OF OLD.	52	OISIN 3		80
. . . MADE ARMOUR FOR CONOR THE OLD.	52	OISIN 3	V	80
. . . MADE ARMOUR FOR CONHOR OF OLD.	52	OISIN 3	V	80
. . . MADE ARMOUR FOR MIDHIR OF OLD	52	OISIN 3	V	80
CAME BLANAID, MAC NESSA, TALL FERGUS WHO FEASTWARD OF OLD TIME SLUNK,	53	OISIN 3		89
DARK BALOR, AS OLD AS A FOREST, CAR-BORNE, HIS MIGHTY HEAD SUNK	53	OISIN 3		91
CAME BLANID, MAC NESSA, AND FERGUS WHO FEASTWARD OF OLD TIME SLUNK,	53	OISIN 3	V	89
CAME CAR-BORNE BALOR, AS OLD AS A FOREST, HIS VAST FACE SUNK	53	OISIN 3	V	91
CAME BALOR, AS OLD AS A FOREST, CAR BORNE, HIS MIGHTY HEAD SUNK	53	OISIN 3	V	91
. . . AND MOVE WHERE THE OLD MEN AND YOUNG	55	OISIN 3		114
WHERE EVER IS MURMUROUS DROPPING, OLD SILENCE AND THAT ONE SOUND;	56	OISIN 3		138
LIKE AN ARMY OF OLD MEN LONGING FOR REST FROM THE MOAN OF THE SEAS.	57	OISIN 3		144
LIKE AN ARMY OF OLD MEN LOUNGING FOR REST FROM THE FOAM OF THE SEAS.	57	OISIN 3	V	144
CAME AFTER THE HARD GAZE OF YOUTH, OR AN OLD MAN LIFTED HIS HEAD!	59	OISIN 3		170
. . . I MURMURED, "IN OLD AGE THEY CEASED";	59	OISIN 3		177
ON CREVROE OR BROAD KNOCKFEFIN, WITH MANY OF OLD THEY FEAST	59	OISIN 3		179
. . . OR WAS LIFTED AN OLD MAN'S MILD HEAD.	59	OISIN 3	V	170
ON CREVROE OR ON BROAD KNOCKFEFIN, WITH MANY OF OLD THEY FAST	59	OISIN 3	V	179
I TURNED AND RODE TO THE WESTWARD, AND FOLLOWED THE SEA'S OLD SHOUT	60	OISIN 3		183
. . . A SOB FOR THE FENIANS' OLD STRENGTH.	60	OISIN 3		188
A CREEPING OLD MAN, FULL OF SLEEP, ...	60	OISIN 3		192
AND RODE ON TILL OVER THE WORLD'S RIM FLOATED THE SEA'S OLD SHOUT,	60	OISIN 3	V	183
SPEAK, YOU TOO ARE OLD WITH YOUR MEMORIES, ...	61	OISIN 3		196
. . . AN OLD MAN SURROUNDED WITH DREAMS.	61	OISIN 3		196
THE WAR-SONGS THAT ROUSED THEM OF OLD;	61	OISIN 3		202
SPEAK, THOU TOO ART OLD WITH THY MEMORIES, ...	61	OISIN 3	V	196
. . . AND OF OLD WOUNDS, AND TURN TO OUR REST.	62	OISIN 3		212
. . . AND OF OLD WOUNDS AND REST.	62	OISIN 3	V	212
AH ME! TO BE SHAKEN WITH COUGHING AND BROKEN WITH OLD AGE AND PAIN,	63	OISIN 3		217
IT WERE SAD TO GAZE ON THE BLESSED AND NO MAN I LOVED OF OLD THERE!	63	OISIN 3		221
AH ME! TO BE OLD WITHOUT SUCCOUR, A SHOW UNTO CHILDREN, A STAIN,	63	OISIN 3	V	217
IT WAS SAD TO GAZE ON THE BLESSED AND NO MAN I LOVED OF OLD THERE!	63	OISIN 3	V	221
OF OLD THE WORLD ON DREAMING FED;	64	HAPPY SHEPHERD		3
THE KINGS OF THE OLD TIME ARE DEAD;	65	HAPPY SHEPHERD		17
TO THE OLD CRACKED TUNE THAT CHRONOS SINGS, ...	65	HAPPY SHEPHERD	V	9
WHERE ARE NOW THE OLD KINGS HOARY?	65	HAPPY SHEPHERD	V	13
THE KINGS OF THE OLD TIME ARE FLED;	65	HAPPY SHEPHERD	V	17
MY SONGS OF OLD EARTH'S DREAMY YOUTH!	67	HAPPY SHEPHERD		54
THE SEA SWEPT ON AND CRIED HER OLD CRY STILL, ...	68	SAD SHEPHERD		10
"OH SEA, OLD SEA, HEAR THOU MY PITEOUS STORY!"	68	SAD SHEPHERD	V	9
SEE HOW THE SACRED OLD FLAMINGOES COME, ...	72	ANASHU VIJAYA		29
THE VAN OF WANDERING QUIET; ERE YOU BE TOO CALM AND OLD,	73	ANASHU VIJAYA		43
THE VAN OF WANDERING QUIET; ERE YE BE TOO CALM AND OLD,	73	ANASHU VIJAYA	V	43
WITH HER OLD FATHER THE BLIND WOOD-CUTTER;	74	ANASHU VIJAYA		63
WHO STILL WERE OLD WHEN THE GREAT SEA WAS YOUNG;	74	ANASHU VIJAYA		69
THE DAUGHTER OF THE GREY OLD WOOD-CUTTER.	74	ANASHU VIJAYA	V	63
IS OUR FIRST KISS, AND AH, HOW OLD MY HEART!"	80	EPHEMERA		9
A RABBIT OLD AND LAME LIMPED DOWN THE PATH;	80	EPHEMERA		15
I WAS A WISE YOUNG KING OF THE	81	MAD KING GOLL	V	1
. . . THE BEECH LEAVES OLD.	82	MAD KING GOLL		12
AND EVERY MUMBLING OLD MAN SAID;	82	MAD KING GOLL	V	9
AND EVERY WHISPERING OLD MAN SAID, ...	82	MAD KING GOLL	V	9
. . . THE BEECH-LEAVES OLD.	82	MAD KING GOLL	V	REF
. . . THE BEECH LEAVES OLD.	83	MAD KING GOLL		24
. . . THE BEECH LEAVES OLD.	84	MAD KING GOLL		36
. . . THE BEECH LEAVES OLD.	84	MAD KING GOLL		48
AND SAW WHERE THIS OLD TYMPAN LAY	85	MAD KING GOLL		55
. . . THE BEECH LEAVES OLD.	85	MAD KING GOLL		60
. . . THE BEECH LEAVES OLD.	86	MAD KING GOLL		72
AN OLD SONG RE-SUNG	90	SALLEY GARDENS	V	T
THE MEDITATION OF THE OLD FISHERMAN	90	OLD FISHERMAN		T
THE HERRING ARE NOT IN THE TIDES AS THEY WERE OF OLD; . .	91	OLD FISHERMAN		5
THE YOUNG BIRDS AND OLD BIRDS	93	FATHER OHART		33
WHO DIG OLD CUSTOMS UP.	93	FATHER OHART		40
BEYOND OLD MARTIN'S BYRE	95	MOLL MAGEE		34
BEYOND OLD MARTIN'S WOOD, ...	95	MOLL MAGEE	V	34
THE BALLAD OF THE OLD FOX-HUNTER	97	FOXHUNTER	V	T
THE BALLAD OF THE OLD FOXHUNTER	97	FOXHUNTER	V	T
MY LOLLARD OLD AND DEAR.	97	FOXHUNTER	V	8
HIS OLD EYES CLOUD WITH DREAMS;	98	FOXHUNTER		14

OLD (CONTINUED)

	PAGE	TITLE		LINE
AND NOW THE OLD MAN'S DREAMS ARE GONE,	98	FOXHUNTER		19
FIRE IS IN THE OLD MAN'S EYES,	98	FOXHUNTER		29
A FIRE IS IN THE OLD MAN'S EYES,	98	FOXHUNTER	V	29
THE OLD HOUNDS AND THE YOUNG,	99	FOXHUNTER		40
ARE OLD AND PUPPY HOUNDS;	99	FOXHUNTER		44
AND THINE OWN SADNESS, WHEREOF STARS, GROWN OLD	101	ROSE UPON ROOD		6
SING OF OLD EIRE AND THE ANCIENT WAYS;	101	ROSE UPON ROOD		23
AN OLD SLAVE GRINDING AT A HEAVY QUERN,	104	FERGUS DRUID		35
"NAY, HE IS OLD AND SAD WITH MANY WARS,	107	CUCHULAIN SEA	V	29
"BUT HE IS OLD AND SAD WITH MANY WARS."	107	CUCHULAIN SEA	V	30
FEASTED, AND WITH THEM OLD CUCHULAIN DWELT,	108	CUCHULAIN SEA	V	39
AND THROUGH THAT NEW BLADE'S GUARD THE OLD BLADE BROKE,	110	CUCHULAIN SEA		66
TO THESE OLD NIGHT SHALL ALL HER MYSTERY TELL;	114	ROSE OF BATTLE		22
WE WHO ARE OLD, OLD AND GAY,	116	FAERY SONG		1
WE WHO ARE OLD, OLD AND GAY,	116	FAERY SONG		1
O SO OLD!	116	FAERY SONG		2
US WHO ARE OLD, OLD AND GAY,	116	FAERY SONG		13
US WHO ARE OLD, OLD AND GAY,	116	FAERY SONG		13
O SO OLD!	116	FAERY SONG		14
AND THE OLD PLANETS SEVEN	118	CRADLE SONG	V	7
THE OLD PLANETS SEVEN	118	CRADLE SONG		7
HAD HID AWAY EARTH'S OLD AND WEARY CRY.	120	SORROW OF LOVE	V	4
ARE SHAKEN WITH EARTH'S OLD AND WEARY CRY.	120	SORROW OF LOVE	V	12
WHEN YOU ARE OLD	120	YOU ARE OLD		T
WHEN YOU ARE OLD AND GREY AND FULL OF SLEEP,	120	YOU ARE OLD		1
FULL OF EARTH'S OLD TIMID GRACE.	124	CATHLEEN PARA		12
OLD SILENCE BIDS ITS CHOSEN RACE REJOICE,	127	DREAM OF FAERY		31
OLD SILENCE BIDS A LONELY FOLK REJOICE,	127	DREAM OF FAERY	V	31
NOW THAT OLD EARTH HAD TAKEN MAN AND ALL!	128	DREAM OF FAERY	V	40
AN OLD POEM RE-WRITTEN	129	BOOK STORIES	V	T
OF HALF-FORGOTTEN INNOCENT OLD PLACES:	130	BOOK STORIES		22
I TORE IT FROM THE GREEN BOUGHS OF OLD ERI,	130	BOOK STORIES	V	15
THEY BRING YOU MEMORIES OF OLD VILLAGE FACES,	130	BOOK STORIES		22
CABINS GONE NOW, OLD WELL-SIDES, OLD DEAR PLACES,	130	BOOK STORIES	V	23
CABINS GONE NOW, OLD WELL-SIDES, OLD DEAR PLACES,	130	BOOK STORIES	V	23
THE LAMENTATION OF THE OLD PENSIONER	131	OLD PENSIONER		T
THE OLD PENSIONER	131	OLD PENSIONER	V	T
WITH "LOOK AT THAT OLD FELLOW THERE;	131	OLD PENSIONER	V	3
AS IN THE OLD DAYS LONG GONE BY,	131	OLD PENSIONER	V	15
THE OLD PRIEST PETER GILLIGAN	132	FR GILLIGAN		1
THE OLD PRIEST PETER GILLIGAN	133	FR GILLIGAN		23
THE OLD PRIEST PETER GILLIGAN	133	FR GILLIGAN		35
THE OLD PRIEST PETER GILLIGAN	133	FR GILLIGAN		39
MADE WHEN GOD SLEPT IN TIMES OF OLD.	135	TWO TREES		32
OF THE DIM WISDOMS OLD AND DEEP,	138	TO IRELAND	V	21
HAVE YOU NOT HEARD THAT OUR HEARTS ARE OLD,	141	EVERLAST VOICE		5
BUT, KINDLY OLD ROUT	142	MOODS	V	5
ALL THINGS UNCOMELY AND BROKEN, ALL THINGS WORN OUT AND OLD,	142	ROSE IN HEART		1
ALL THINGS UNCOMELY AND BROKEN, ALL THINGS WORN AND OLD,	142	ROSE IN HEART	V	1
TO OLD MEN PLAYING AT CARDS	144	HOST OF AIR		23
HE PLAYED WITH THE MERRY OLD MEN	145	HOST OF AIR		29
OLD MEN AND YOUNG MEN AND YOUNG GIRLS	145	HOST OF AIR		39
BUT THE OLD MEN AND DANCERS WERE GONE,	145	HOST OF AIR	V	39
OLD WOMEN WERE KEENING THE DEAD!	145	HOST OF AIR	V	40D
THOUGH I AM OLD WITH WANDERING	150	WANDER AENGUS		17
THE SONG OF THE OLD MOTHER	150	OLD MOTHER		T
WHILE I MUST WORK BECAUSE I AM OLD,	151	OLD MOTHER		9
AND I MUST WORK BECAUSE I AM OLD.	151	OLD MOTHER	V	10
AND DREAMED THAT THE OLD DESPAIR	152	LOSS OF LOVE		3
THE ROSES THAT OF OLD TIME WERE	156	FORGOT BEAUTY		9
AND WITH HEART MORE OLD THAN THE HORN	157	POET BELOVED		5
AND WITH THE HEART MORE OLD THAN THE HORN	157	POET BELOVED	V	5
OUT OF THE BATTLES OF OLD TIMES.	158	BELOVED RHYMES		6
OUT OF THE OLD DAYS	158	TO HIS HEART	V	T
REMEMBER THE WISDOM OUT OF THE OLD DAYS!	158	TO HIS HEART		2
FROM MARBLE CITIES LOUD WITH TABORS OF OLD	162	ASKS FORGIVE		9
AND OLD MEN WITH CROZIERS AND STOLES.	167	BLESSED		16
THE LOVER PLEADS WITH HIS FRIEND FOR OLD FRIENDS	172	PLEADS FRIEND		T
THE POET PLEADS WITH HIS FRIEND FOR OLD FRIENDS	172	PLEADS FRIEND	V	T
BUT THINK ABOUT OLD FRIENDS THE MOST!	173	PLEADS FRIEND		5
BUT THINK OF YOUR OLD FRIENDS THE MOST!	173	PLEADS FRIEND	V	5
THAT MY OLD CARE MAY CEASE;	174	ELEMENT POWERS		10
HE WILL SMILE ON THE THREE OLD SPIRITS,	178	FIDDLER DOONEY		11
THE OLD AGE OF QUEEN MAEVE	180	QUEEN MAEVE		T
THOUGH NOW IN HER OLD AGE, IN HER YOUNG AGE	180	QUEEN MAEVE		18
SHE HAD BEEN BEAUTIFUL IN THAT OLD WAY	180	QUEEN MAEVE		19
HAD COME AS IN THE OLD TIMES TO COUNSEL HER,	181	QUEEN MAEVE		42
MAEVE WALKED, YET WITH SLOW FOOTFALL, BEING OLD,	181	QUEEN MAEVE		43
HAD COME, AS IN OLD TIMES, TO COUNSEL HER,	181	QUEEN MAEVE	V	42
AS IN THE OLD DAYS WHEN THEY WOULD COME AND GO	183	QUEEN MAEVE		81
TILL IT DIED OUT WHERE AN OLD THORN-TREE STOOD.	186	QUEEN MAEVE		129
AND WHEN I'VE HEARD HOW THEY GREW OLD AND DIED,	186	QUEEN MAEVE		136
"SHE WILL GROW OLD AND DIE, AND SHE HAS WEPT!"	186	QUEEN MAEVE		138
TILL IT DIED OUT WHERE AN OLD THORN TREE STOOD.	186	QUEEN MAEVE	V	129
BECAUSE THEIR BODIES HAD GROWN OLD.	189	BAILE AILLINN		10
THEY FOUND AN OLD MAN RUNNING THERE!	190	BAILE AILLINN		25
AND OLD AND YOUNG MEN RODE WITH HER!	191	BAILE AILLINN		51
AN OLD MAN CAUGHT THE HORSE'S HEAD	191	BAILE AILLINN		57
NOW HAD THAT OLD GAUNT CRAFTY ONE,	193	BAILE AILLINN		100

OLD   (CONTINUED)

	PAGE	TITLE		LINE
IN OLD TIMES AMONG THE CLOUDS OF THE AIR.	194	BAILE AILLINN		133
THAT OLD MAN CLIMBED; THE DAY GREW DIM;	194	BAILE AILLINN		134
AND POETS FOUND, OLD WRITERS SAY,	197	BAILE AILLINN		187
THE UNAVAILING OUTCRIES AND THE OLD BITTERNESS	198	SEVEN WOODS		4
I COULD WEEP THAT THE OLD IS OUT OF SEASON.	199	ARROW		8
OLD MEMORY	201	OLD MEMORY		T
AWAKENS AN OLD MEMORY, AND SAY,	201	OLD MEMORY		2
LIKE AN OLD PAUPER, IN ALL KINDS OF WEATHER;	205	ADAMS CURSE		9
PRECEDENTS OUT OF BEAUTIFUL OLD BOOKS;	205	ADAMS CURSE		26
TO LOVE YOU IN THE OLD HIGH WAY OF LOVE;	206	ADAMS CURSE		36
TO LOVE YOU IN THE OLD HIGHWAY OF LOVE;	206	ADAMS CURSE	V	36
THE OLD BROWN THORN-TREES BREAK IN TWO HIGH OVER CUMMEN STRAND,	206	HANRAHANS SONG		1
THE OLD BROWN THORN TREES BREAK IN TWO HIGH OVER CUMANN'S STRAND,	206	HANRAHANS SONG	V	1
OUR COURAGE BREAKS LIKE AN OLD TREE IN A BLACK WIND AND DIES,	207	HANRAHANS SONG		3
THE OLD MEN ADMIRING THEMSELVES IN THE WATER	208	OLD MEN ADMIRE		T
I HEARD THE OLD, OLD MEN SAY,	208	OLD MEN ADMIRE		1
I HEARD THE OLD, OLD MEN SAY,	208	OLD MEN ADMIRE		1
WERE TWISTED LIKE THE OLD THORN-TREES	208	OLD MEN ADMIRE		5
I HEARD THE OLD, OLD MEN SAY,	208	OLD MEN ADMIRE	V	7
I HEARD THE OLD, OLD MEN SAY,	208	OLD MEN ADMIRE		7
WERE TWISTED LIKE THE OLD THORN TREES	208	OLD MEN ADMIRE	V	5
SEVEN OLD SISTERS WIND THE THREADS OF THE LONG-LIVED ONES,	209	UNDER THE MOON		7
OR LANDS THAT SEEMED TOO OLD TO BE BURDENS ON THE HEART,	209	UNDER THE MOON	V	5
SEVEN OLD SISTERS WIND THE THREADS OF THE LONG LIVED ONES,	209	UNDER THE MOON	V	7
EVEN IN AN OLD STORY, IS A BURDEN NOT TO BE BORNE.	210	UNDER THE MOON		20
LIKE AN OLD SONG.	211	O DO NOT LOVE		4
LIKE AN OLD SONG.	212	O DO NOT LOVE		12
O DEATH'S OLD BONY FINGER	213	HAPPY TOWNLAND	V	1
AN OLD MAN PLAYS THE BAGPIPES	214	HAPPY TOWNLAND		9
AND LIFT UP AN OLD HORN	215	HAPPY TOWNLAND		49
WHERE OLD AGE CANNOT FIND THEM; PAIRC-NA-LEE,	217	WOODS OF COOLE		7
AND MARTEN-CAT, AND BORDERS THAT OLD WOOD	218	WOODS OF COOLE		14
AND MARTIN CAT, AND BORDERS THAT OLD WOOD	218	WOODS OF COOLE	V	14
AS MEN IN THE OLD TIMES, BEFORE THE HARPS BEGAN,	219	WOODS OF COOLE		43
AS MEN IN THE OLD TIMES, BEFORE THE HARP BEGAN,	219	WOODS OF COOLE	V	43
WHAT DO YOU CALL IT?--THAT OLD PROMISE-BREAKER,	228	SHADOW WATER B		122
BECAUSE OF THAT OLD DRAUGHT UNDER THE DOOR,	228	SHADOW WATER B		127
AND FOR THIS END THEY GAVE ME MY OLD HARP,	237	SHADOW WATER B		327
THEY GAVE ME THAT OLD HARP OF THE NINE SPELLS	237	SHADOW WATER B	V	327
AND THAT OLD HARP AWAKENS OF ITSELF	252	SHADOW WATER B		617
YET OLD ROMANCE BEING KIND, LET HIM PREVAIL	258	KING NO KING		5
BEFORE WE GROW OLD AND DIE.	261	DRINKING SONG		4
AND THEN, "I AM OLD ENOUGH";	268	BROWN PENNY		2
PARDON, OLD FATHERS, IF YOU STILL REMAIN	269	PARDON FATHERS		1
OLD DUBLIN MERCHANT "FREE OF TEN AND FOUR"	269	PARDON FATHERS		3
OLD COUNTRY SCHOLAR, ROBERT EMMET'S FRIEND,	269	PARDON FATHERS		5
OLD DUBLIN MERCHANT "FREE OF THE TEN AND FOUR"	269	PARDON FATHERS	V	3
OLD MERCHANT SKIPPER THAT LEAPED OVERBOARD	270	PARDON FATHERS		13
YOU MOST OF ALL, SILENT AND FIERCE OLD MAN,	270	PARDON FATHERS		15
OLD BUTLERS WHEN YOU TOOK TO HORSE AND STOOD	270	PARDON FATHERS	V	10
HERE'S AN OLD STORY I'VE REMADE,	270	GREY ROCK		3
HERE'S AN OLD STORY I'VE RE-MADE,	270	GREY ROCK	V	3
OLD WHOLESOME GOBAN HAD NO SAY;	271	GREY ROCK		10
ON OLD DEEP SILVER ROLLING THERE	271	GREY ROCK		20
OF OLD STRINGED INSTRUMENTS, HUNG THERE	271	GREY ROCK	V	20
OLD GOBAN HAMMERED THEM AND WROUGHT THEM,	271	GREY ROCK	V	23
WHERE BY OLD THORN-TREES THAT MAN STOOD;	274	GREY ROCK		80
WHERE BY OLD THORN TREES THAT MAN STOOD;	274	GREY ROCK	V	80
TO AN OLD EMPTY WOODMAN'S HOUSE THAT'S HIDDEN	282	TWO KINGS		134
FOUND THAT OLD HOUSE, A SPUTTERING TORCH WITHIN,	283	TWO KINGS		140
HAD HALF AWAKENED SOME OLD MEMORY--	284	TWO KINGS		172
HAD HALF WAKENED SOME OLD MEMORY,	284	TWO KINGS	V	172
OF OUR OLD PAUDEEN IN HIS SHOP, I STUMBLED BLIND	291	PAUDEEN		2
FOR THEY ARE AT THEIR OLD TRICKS YET. A MAN	292	TO A SHADE		9
YOUR ENEMY, AN OLD FOUL MOUTH, HAD SET	292	TO A SHADE		17
AN OLD FOUL MOUTH THAT ONCE CRIED OUT ON YOU	292	TO A SHADE	V	17
AN OLD FOUL MOUTH THAT SLANDERED YOU HAD SET	292	TO A SHADE	V	17
MUTTERED THE OLD CRANE OF GORT.	295	THREE BEGGARS		6
AND THERE TO THREE OLD BEGGARS SAID,	295	THREE BEGGARS		10
WITH HIS OLD THOUGHTS, KING GUAIRE WENT	296	THREE BEGGARS		26
"THOUGH I AM OLD I SHALL PERSUADE	296	THREE BEGGARS		30
AND WHEN OLD GUAIRE CAME AND STOOD	297	THREE BEGGARS		54
THREE OLD HERMITS TOOK THE AIR	298	THREE HERMITS		1
NOW IT HAS FILLED AN OLD SOCK FULL;	301	RUN PARADISE		20
THE WIND IS OLD AND STILL AT PLAY	301	RUN PARADISE		22
A PAIR OF LAPWINGS, ONE OLD SHEEP,	302	HOUR DAWN		9
I HAD BEEN HURT," THE OLD BEGGAR THOUGHT	302	HOUR DAWN		19
AND STUFFED WITH ALL THAT'S OLD AND BAD;	303	HOUR DAWN	V	25
THAT'S STUFFED WITH ALL THAT'S OLD AND BAD;	303	HOUR DAWN	V	25
LIKE SOME OLD RABBIT TO MY CLEFT	307	HOUR DAWN		105
BUT I AM OLD AND YOU ARE YOUNG,	313	TWO YEAR LATER		11
AND EVEN OLD MEN'S EYES GREW DIM, THIS HAND ALONE,	314	FALLEN MAJESTY		2
OUT OF OLD MYTHOLOGIES	320	COAT		3
THEIR HEARTS HAVE NOT GROWN OLD;	323	SWANS AT COOLE		22
ALWAYS WE'D HAVE THE NEW FRIEND MEET THE OLD	324	ROBERT GREGORY		9
AND THEN I THINK OF OLD GEORGE POLLEXFEN,	325	ROBERT GREGORY		33
OUT OF SOME OLD PICTURE-BOOK;	325	ROBERT GREGORY		44

OLD (CONTINUED)

	PAGE	TITLE	LINE
OUT OF SOME OLD PICTURE BOOK;	325	ROBERT GREGORY V	44
WERE LOVED BY HIM; THE OLD STORM-BROKEN TREES	326	ROBERT GREGORY	50
BUT I GROW OLD AMONG DREAMS,	329	MEN IMPROVE	16
AT THE OLD BITTER WORLD WHERE THEY MARRY IN CHURCHES,	330	BONE OF A HARE	13
UPON A GREY OLD BATTERED TOMBSTONE	331	ROUND TOWER	7
UPON THE GREY OLD BATTERED TOMBSTONE	331	ROUND TOWER V	7
LIKE AN OLD HORSE IN A POUND."	333	SOLOMON SHEBA	8
THAN 'TWERE AN APPARITION. O HEART, WE ARE OLD;	334	LIVING BEAUTY	8
THAT THE HEART GROWS OLD?	334	SONG	6
THAT THE HEART GROWS OLD?	335	SONG	12
THAT THE HEART GROWS OLD?	335	SONG	18
WITH OLD EZEKIEL'S CHERUBIM	336	YOUNG BEAUTY	11
OLD, LEARNED, RESPECTABLE BALD HEADS	337	SCHOLARS	2
BEING OLD, BUT THAT THE OLD ALONE MIGHT DIE,	339	SHEP GOATHERD	4
BEING OLD, BUT THAT THE OLD ALONE MIGHT DIE,	339	SHEP GOATHERD	4
NEW WELCOME AND OLD WISDOM AT HER FIRE	340	SHEP GOATHERD	32
OLD GOATHERDS AND OLD GOATS, IF IN ALL ELSE	340	SHEP GOATHERD	46
OLD GOATHERDS AND OLD GOATS, IF IN ALL ELSE	340	SHEP GOATHERD	46
AT SOME OLD WINDING WHITETHORN ROOT	342	SHEP GOATHERD	101
WHEN I HAVE SHUT THESE EWES AND THIS OLD RAM	343	SHEP GOATHERD	113
ON THAT OLD QUEEN MEASURING A TOWN	344	DAWN	3
ON THE OLD QUEEN MEASURING A TOWN	344	DAWN V	3
NOW I AM GROWING OLD,	346	ON WOMAN	28
AND CRIED, "BEFORE I AM OLD	348	FISHERMAN	37
THE OLD COOK ENRAGED,	349	HAWK	5
AND BE WELL PLEASED REMEMBERING IT, FOR IN THE OLD DAYS,	351	HER PRAISE	16
THOUGH SHE HAD YOUNG MEN'S PRAISE AND OLD MEN'S BLAME,	351	HER PRAISE	17
AMONG THE POOR BOTH OLD AND YOUNG GAVE HER PRAISE.	351	HER PRAISE	18
BUT MAYBE SOME OLD GAFFER MUTTERS A BLESSING	355	BROKEN DREAMS	4
A YOUNG MAN WHEN THE OLD MEN ARE DONE TALKING	356	BROKEN DREAMS	16
WILL SAY TO AN OLD MAN, "TELL ME OF THAT LADY	356	BROKEN DREAMS	17
FOR OLD SAKE'S SAKE.	357	BROKEN DREAMS	36
OR AN OLD MAN UPON A WINTER'S NIGHT.	359	WAR POEM	6
SINCE OLD WILLIAM POLLEXFEN	360	ALF POLLEXFEN	2
WITH THE OLD KINDNESS, THE OLD DISTINGUISHED GRACE,	362	HER COURTESY	1
WITH THE OLD KINDNESS, THE OLD DISTINGUISHED GRACE,	362	HER COURTESY	1
—PEDANT IN PASSION, LEARNED IN OLD COURTESIES,	363	DOLLS FACES	4
THAT MADE HER DIARMUID DEAR, AND SOME OLD CARDINAL	366	HER COURAGE	6
AND THAT MADE HER DERMUID DEAR, AND SOME OLD CARDINAL	366	HER COURAGE V	6
UNDER YOUR OLD WIND-BEATEN TOWER, WHERE STILL	367	EGO DOMINUS	2
AND LOST THE OLD NONCHALANCE OF THE HAND;	368	EGO DOMINUS	13
AN OLD MAN COCKED HIS EAR UPON A BRIDGE;	372	PHASES OF MOON	1
WERE DISTANT STILL. AN OLD MAN COCKED HIS EAR.	372	PHASES OF MOON	7
WERE DISTANT. AN OLD MAN COCKED HIS EAR.	372	PHASES OF MOON V	7
WHEN THE OLD MOON IS VANISHED FROM THE SKY	382	VISION ROBART	3
WHEN THE OLD MOON IS VANISHING FROM THE SKY	382	VISION ROBART V	3
BY CHILDISH MEMORIES OF AN OLD CROSS POLLEXFEN,	391	UNDER SATURN	7
OF OLD LUKE WADDING'S PORTRAIT SAID	400	DEMON BEAST	10
AND THAT MERE GROWING OLD, THAT BRINGS	401	DEMON BEAST	38
FOR AN OLD BELLOWS FULL OF ANGRY WIND?	405	FOR DAUGHTER	64
WHILE ON THAT OLD GREY STONE I SAT	406	IN TIME OF WAR	2
UNDER THE OLD WIND-BROKEN TREE,	406	IN TIME OF WAR	3
WITH OLD MILL BOARDS AND SEA-GREEN SLATES,	406	CARVED STONE	2
THAT IS NO COUNTRY FOR OLD MEN. THE YOUNG	407	SAIL BYZANTIUM	1
CAUGHT BY AN OLD MAN'S JUGGLERIES	411	TOWER	60
GOOD FELLOWS SHUFFLED CARDS IN AN OLD BAWN;	411	TOWER	65
COME OLD, NECESSITOUS, HALF-MOUNTED MAN;	412	TOWER	90
DID ALL OLD MEN AND WOMEN, RICH AND POOR,	413	TOWER	97
AS I DO NOW AGAINST OLD AGE?	413	TOWER	100
OLD LECHER WITH A LOVE ON EVERY WIND,	413	TOWER	105
WITH DELICATE FEET UPON OLD TERRACES,	418	ANCEST HOUSES	26
OLD RAGGED ELMS, OLD THORNS INNUMERABLE,	419	MY HOUSE	5
OLD RAGGED ELMS, OLD THORNS INNUMERABLE,	419	MY HOUSE	5
FROM MY OLD FATHERS, I MUST NOURISH DREAMS	422	MY DESCENDANTS	2
FOR AN OLD NEIGHBOUR'S FRIENDSHIP CHOSE THE HOUSE	423	MY DESCENDANTS	21
TO BRIBE OR THREAT; HABITS THAT MADE OLD WRONG	428	NINETEEN 19	11
WHIRLS IN THE OLD INSTEAD;	430	NINETEEN 19	56
THEY FIXED OLD ACHING EYES,	432	NINETEEN 19	100
IF YOU, THAT HAVE GROWN OLD, WERE THE FIRST DEAD,	435	NEW FACES	1
IN THE OLD ROOMS; NIGHT CAN OUTBALANCE DAY,	435	NEW FACES	6
BECAUSE OF SOME GREEN WING, GATHERED OLD MUMMY WHEAT	442	BLACK CENTAUR	7
A KIND OLD NUN IN A WHITE HOOD REPLIES;	443	SCHOOL CHILDR	2
A SIXTY YEAR OLD SMILING PUBLIC MAN;	443	SCHOOL CHILDR V	8
THERE IS A COMFORTABLE KIND OF OLD SCARECROW.	444	SCHOOL CHILDR	32
OLD CLOTHES UPON OLD STICKS TO SCARE A BIRD.	445	SCHOOL CHILDR	48
OLD CLOTHES UPON OLD STICKS TO SCARE A BIRD.	445	SCHOOL CHILDR	48
SHALL WITHER THAT OLD MARVEL, FOR	447	COLONUS PRAISE	15
A MAN YOUNG AND OLD FIRST LOVE	451	FIRST LOVE V	T
TWO SONGS FROM THE OLD COUNTRYMAN	454	EMPTY CUP V	T
THE OLD COUNTRYMAN	454	EMPTY CUP V	T
MORE SONGS OF AN OLD COUNTRYMAN	454	HIS MEMORIES V	T
FOR THAT OLD MADGE COMES DOWN THE LANE,	456	FRIENDS YOUTH	5
WE SAT UNDER AN OLD THORN-TREE,	456	SUMMER SPRING	1
THE SECRETS OF THE OLD	457	SECRETS OF OLD	T
I HAVE OLD WOMEN'S SECRETS NOW	457	SECRETS OF OLD	1
SOUNDS LIKE AN OLD SONG.	457	SECRETS OF OLD	6
AS THAT OLD WANDERING BEGGAR AND THESE GOD-HATED CHILDREN KNOW.	459	FROM OEDIPUS	6
THE THREE OLD RASCALS LAUGH ALOUD.	460	THREE MONUMENT	12
"BUT SUCH AS YOU AND I DO NOT SEEM OLD	463	HARUN RASHID	55

OLD   (CONTINUED)

	PAGE	TITLE	LINE
YOUR THIRST FOR THOSE OLD CRABBED MYSTERIES,	465	HARUN RASHID	86
ON OLD DRY WRITING IN A LEARNED TONGUE,	466	HARUN RASHID	123
ON OLD DRY FAGGOTS THAT COULD NEVER PLEASE	466	HARUN RASHID	124
OLD FELLOW-STUDENT, WHOSE MOST PATIENT EAR	468	HARUN RASHID	167
OLD FELLOW STUDENT, WHOSE MOST PATIENT EAR	468	HARUN RASHID V	167
WHEN WITHERED OLD AND SKELETON-GAUNT,	475	EVA GORE-BOOTH	12
OF THAT OLD GEORGIAN MANSION, MIX	475	EVA GORE-BOOTH	16
THAT FLOWERING, SILKEN, OLD EMBROIDERY, TORN	477	SELF AND SOUL	13
A STORM-BEATEN OLD WATCH-TOWER,	484	SYMBOLS	1
A STORM-BEATEN OLD WATCH TOWER,	484	SYMBOLS V	1
BUT WE OLD MEN ARE MASSED AGAINST THE WORLD.	486	SEVEN SAGES	14
BUT WE OLD MEN ARE OUT AGAINST THE WORLD.	486	SEVEN SAGES V	14
OLD MARBLE HEADS, OLD PICTURES EVERYWHERE!	491	COOLE BALLYLEE	28
OLD MARBLE HEADS, OLD PICTURES EVERYWHERE!	491	COOLE BALLYLEE	28
THAT OLD PERPLEXITY AN EMPTY PURSE,	491	COOLE BALLYLEE V	40G
"I HEARD AN OLD RELIGIOUS MAN	492	ANNE GREGORY	13
THAT OLD PERPLEXITY AN EMPTY PURSE,	495	CHOICE	7
"OLD LOVERS YET MAY HAVE	496	MOHINI CHATTER	17
THE OLD TROOPS PARADE,	496	MOHINI CHATTER	22
OLD LOVERS YET SHALL HAVE	496	MOHINI CHATTER V	17
QUARREL IN OLD AGE	503	QUARREL IN AGE	T
THAT HAD FORGIVEN OLD AGE.	504	QUARREL IN AGE	8
OLD SAGES WERE NOT DECEIVED!	504	QUARREL IN AGE	11
YET HE, AN OLD BOOK IN HIS FIST,	508	JANE BISHOP	12
NONE SO OLD AS HE AND I!	508	JANE BISHOP V	6
CRAZY JANE GROWN OLD LOOKS AT THE DANCERS	514	JANE GROWN OLD	T
SAW I AN OLD MAN YOUNG	515	GIRLS SONG B	11
OR YOUNG MAN OLD?	515	GIRLS SONG B	12
OR A YOUNG MAN OLD?	515	GIRLS SONG B V	12
OLD FATHERS, GREAT-GRANDFATHERS,	518	LOVES LONENESS	1
OLD FATHERS, GREAT GRANDFATHERS,	518	LOVES LONENESS V	1
YOU ASK WHAT MAKES ME SIGH, OLD FRIEND,	524	MAD AS MIST	13
SANG OLD TOM THE LUNATIC	528	TOM LUNATIC	1
OLD TOM AT CRUACHAN	529	TOM CRUACHAN V	T
OLD TOM AGAIN	530	OLD TOM AGAIN	T
A WOMAN YOUNG AND OLD I FATHER AND CHILD	531	FATHER CHILD V	T
TOO OLD FOR A MAN'S LOVE I STOOD IN RAGE	536	HER VISION	3
TOO OLD FOR A MAN'S LOVE I STOOD AND RAGED	536	HER VISION V	1
HIDDEN BY OLD AGE AWHILE	539	MEETING	1
"WHO'D CARE TO DIG 'EM," SAID THE OLD, OLD MAN,	548	TO SAME TUNE 3	7
"WHO'D CARE TO DIG 'EM," SAID THE OLD, OLD MAN,	548	TO SAME TUNE 3	7
TIME I WERE BURIED," SAID THE OLD, OLD MAN.	548	TO SAME TUNE 3	10
TIME I WERE BURIED," SAID THE OLD, OLD MAN.	548	TO SAME TUNE 3	10
O ANY OLD WORDS TO A TUNE.	548	TO SAME TUNE 3	16
"WHO'D CARE TO DIG 'EM," SAID THE OLD, OLD MAN,	548	TO SAME TUNE 3	17
"WHO'D CARE TO DIG 'EM," SAID THE OLD, OLD MAN,	548	TO SAME TUNE 3	17
TIME I WERE BURIED," SAID THE OLD, OLD MAN.	548	TO SAME TUNE 3	20
TIME I WERE BURIED," SAID THE OLD, OLD MAN.	548	TO SAME TUNE 3	20
"WHO'D CARE TO DIG 'EM," SAID THE OLD, OLD MAN,	549	TO SAME TUNE 3	27
"WHO'D CARE TO DIG 'EM," SAID THE OLD, OLD MAN,	549	TO SAME TUNE 3	27
TIME I WERE BURIED," SAID THE OLD, OLD MAN.	549	TO SAME TUNE 3	30
TIME I WERE BURIED," SAID THE OLD, OLD MAN.	549	TO SAME TUNE 3	30
I WOULD THAT I WERE AN OLD BEGGAR	552	SONGS REWRIT 2	1
O WOULD THAT I WERE AN OLD BEGGAR	552	SONGS REWRIT 2 V	1
A PRAYER FOR OLD AGE	553	PRAYER OLD AGE	T
OLD AGE	553	PRAYER OLD AGE V	T
FROM ALL THAT MAKES A WISE OLD MAN	553	PRAYER OLD AGE	5
THAT I MAY SEEM, THOUGH I DIE OLD,	553	PRAYER OLD AGE	11
MATTER FOR OLD AGE MEET!	553	CHURCH STATE	2
THE GYRES! THE GYRES! OLD ROCKY FACE, LOOK FORTH!	564	GYRES	1
OLD CIVILISATIONS PUT TO THE SWORD.	566	LAPIS LAZULI	27
WHEN SHE WAS OLD AND DYING,	571	THREE BUSHES	64
MIDNIGHT, AN OLD HOUSE	575	ACRE OF GRASS	5
GRANT ME AN OLD MAN'S FRENZY,	576	ACRE OF GRASS	13
AN OLD MAN'S EAGLE MIND.	576	ACRE OF GRASS	24
A SMALL OLD HOUSE, WIFE, DAUGHTER, SON,	577	WHAT THEN	12
"THE WORK IS DONE," GROWN OLD HE THOUGHT,	577	WHAT THEN	16
AND THEY BUT FAMOUS OLD UPHOLSTERIES	579	DOR WELLESLEY	3
AND THERE IS AN OLD BEGGAR WANDERING IN HIS PRIDE--	580	CURSE CROMWELL	5
AS THE FOX IN THE OLD FABLE DESTROYED THE SPARTAN BOY'S,	580	CURSE CROMWELL	18
BUT I WOKE IN AN OLD RUIN THAT THE WINDS HOWLED THROUGH!	581	CURSE CROMWELL	28
BUT THIS IS NOT THE OLD SEA	583	GHOST ROG CASE	5
NOR THIS THE OLD SEASHORE.	583	GHOST ROG CASE	6
THE WILD OLD WICKED MAN	587	OLD WICKED MAN	T
SAID THAT WILD OLD WICKED MAN	587	OLD WICKED MAN	3
FROM THE OLD MAN IN THE SKIES.	588	OLD WICKED MAN	8
WHEN AN OLD MAN'S BLOOD GROWS COLD?	588	OLD WICKED MAN	13
THEN SAID SHE TO THAT WILD OLD MAN,	588	OLD WICKED MAN	19
THAT OLD MAN IN THE SKIES.	588	OLD WICKED MAN	24
BUT A WILD OLD MAN IN THE LIGHT,	589	OLD WICKED MAN	38
FROM THE OLD MAN IN THE SKIES	589	OLD WICKED MAN	56
BUT A COARSE OLD MAN AM I,	590	OLD WICKED MAN	59
SHOULD DANCE ATTENTION UPON MY OLD AGE!	591	SPUR	2
SHOULD DANCE ATTENDANCE UPON MY OLD AGE!	591	SPUR V	2
AND THERE I FOUND AN OLD MAN, AND THOUGH I PRAYED ALL DAY	593	PILGRIM	8
AND THAT OLD MAN BESIDE ME, NOTHING WOULD HE SAY	593	PILGRIM	9
THE OLD STONE CROSS	598	STONE CROSS	T
UNDER THE OLD STONE CROSS.	598	STONE CROSS	8
UNDER THE OLD STONE CROSS.	599	STONE CROSS	16
UNDER THE OLD STONE CROSS.	599	STONE CROSS	24

OLD   (CONTINUED)

SAID THE OLD MAN IN THE GOLDEN BREASTPLATE . . . . . .   599 STONE CROSS   V   23
AN OLD GHOST'S THOUGHTS ARE LIGHTNING, ...   600 SPIRIT MEDIUM   17
SPOILT WHAT OLD LOINS HAVE SENT? . . . .   604 YOU CONTENT   6
SET UP THE OLD STONE CROSS, ...   604 YOU CONTENT   10
OLD WILLIAM POLLEXFEN, ...   604 YOU CONTENT   14
BY AN OLD HUNTER TALKING WITH GODS! . . . .   605 YOU CONTENT   23
COULD CRAZY JANE PUT OFF OLD AGE . . . .   606 SONGS BURDEN 1   19
COULD THAT OLD GOD RISE UP AGAIN . . . .   606 SONGS BURDEN 1   21
HAVE KEYS TO MY OLD GATE. . . . .   607 SONGS BURDEN 2   8
OF HENWIVES AND OF QUEER OLD MEN . . . .   607 SONGS BURDEN 2   23
OF HEN WIVES AND OF QUEER OLD MEN . . . .   607 SONGS BURDEN 2 V   23
THAT THE ADVENTURE OF OLD AGE BEGINS. . . . . . .   609 IN TARAS HALLS   5
I SHALL BE OLD INDEED." THEREON THE MAN . . . . .   609 IN TARAS HALLS   10
BUT TIME AMENDS OLD WRONG, ...   613 MARCH SONGS 1   9
ON AN OLD TAMBOURINE. . . . .   613 MARCH SONGS 1   16
BUT TIME AMENDS OLD WRONG, ...   613 MARCH SONGS 1   19
BUT TIME AMENDS OLD WRONG, ...   614 MARCH SONGS 1   29
MARCH WIND, AND ANY OLD TUNE, ...   615 MARCH SONGS 2   25
ROBBERS HAD TAKEN HIS OLD TAMBOURINE, ...   616 MARCH SONGS 3   7
ROBBERS HAD TAKEN HIS OLD TAMBOURINE. . . . .   616 MARCH SONGS 3   10
ROBBERS HAD TAKEN HIS OLD TAMBOURINE. . . . .   616 MARCH SONGS 3   17
ROBBERS HAD TAKEN HIS OLD TAMBOURINE. . . . .   616 MARCH SONGS 3   20
ROBBERS HAD TAKEN HIS OLD TAMBOURINE, ...   616 MARCH SONGS 3   27
ROBBERS HAD TAKEN HIS OLD TAMBOURINE, ...   616 MARCH SONGS 3   30
NOW MY OLD BAWD IS DEAD? . . . .   620 JOHN KINSELLA   12
LIKE AN OLD JEW MAN, ...   620 JOHN KINSELLA   14
AND BEING OLD SHE PUT A SKIN . . . .   621 JOHN KINSELLA   21
NOW MY OLD BAWD IS DEAD? . . . .   621 JOHN KINSELLA   24
NO MAN GROWS OLD, NO GIRL GROWS COLD, ...   621 JOHN KINSELLA   31
NOW MY OLD BAWD IS DEAD? . . . .   621 JOHN KINSELLA   36
THAT PATCHING OLD HEELS THEY MAY SHRIEK, I TAKE TO CHISEL   623 HIGH TALK   8
    AND PLANE.
WHEN A MAN GROWS OLD HIS JOY . . . .   624 APPARITIONS   17
WHY SHOULD NOT OLD MEN BE MAD? . . . .   625 OLD MEN BE MAD   T
WHY SHOULD NOT OLD MEN BE MAD? . . . .   625 OLD MEN BE MAD   1
OBSERVANT OLD MEN KNOW IT WELL! . . . .   626 OLD MEN BE MAD   17
AND WHEN THEY KNOW WHAT OLD BOOKS TELL, ...   626 OLD MEN BE MAD   18
KNOW WHY AN OLD MAN SHOULD BE MAD. . . . .   626 OLD MEN BE MAD   20
AND ITS OLD SOLE STRING . . . .   627 STATES HOLIDAY   23
WITH OLD PATCHED SHOES, ...   627 STATES HOLIDAY   30
WITH AN OLD FOUL TUNE. . . . .   627 STATES HOLIDAY   38
WINTER AND SUMMER TILL OLD AGE BEGAN . . . .   629 CIRCUS ANIMALS   5
WHAT CAN I BUT ENUMERATE OLD THEMES? . . . .   629 CIRCUS ANIMALS   9
THAT MIGHT ADORN OLD SONGS OR COURTLY SHOWS! . . . . .   629 CIRCUS ANIMALS   14
OLD KETTLES, OLD BOTTLES, AND A BROKEN CAN, ...   630 CIRCUS ANIMALS   36
OLD KETTLES, OLD BOTTLES, AND A BROKEN CAN, ...   630 CIRCUS ANIMALS   36
OLD IRON, OLD BONES, OLD RAGS, THAT RAVING SLUT . . . .   630 CIRCUS ANIMALS   37
OLD IRON, OLD BONES, OLD RAGS, THAT RAVING SLUT . . . .   630 CIRCUS ANIMALS   37
NOW THAT I AM OLD AND ILL, ...   632 MAN AND ECHO   7
SAY THAT THE MEN OF THE OLD BLACK TOWER, ...   635 BLACK TOWER   1
OLD BONES UPON THE MOUNTAIN SHAKE. . . . .   635 BLACK TOWER   10
OLD BONES UPON THE MOUNTAIN SHAKE. . . . .   636 BLACK TOWER   20
THE TOWER'S OLD COOK THAT MUST CLIMB AND CLAMBER . . . .   636 BLACK TOWER   21
OLD BONES UPON THE MOUNTAIN SHAKE. . . . .   636 BLACK TOWER   30
AS A LEAF THAT IS OLD, AND WITHERED, AND COLD, ...   643 SONG FAERIES   3
AS A LEAF THAT IS OLD, AND WITHERED, AND COLD, ...   644 SONG FAERIES   15
'TIS MORN! LIKE OLD MEN'S EYES THE STARS ARE PALE, . . .   645 ISLE STAT I 1   4
SOME OLD MISER TELLS HIS STORE! . . . .   647 ISLE STAT I 1   58
SINGING OF ARMS AND BATTLES SOME OLD STAVE, ...   650 ISLE STAT I 1   137
WILL STRUGGLE. OR HE'LL SEEK ENCHANTER OLD, ...   651 ISLE STAT I 1   162
IS STONE! OLD SLEEPER! THIS SAME AFTERNOON . . . . .   657 ISLE STAT I 3   74
THAT OF OLD WERT MOVING EVER, ...   658 ISLE STAT I 3   91
NAY, GRIEF IN FEEDING ON OLD GRIEF GROWS LESS. . . . .   659 ISLE STAT II 1   19
OLD MISER HOARDS OF GRIEF TO TELL AND TELL! . . . . .   661 ISLE STAT II 1   55
AND DEAD AS ARE THE LOVERS OF OLD RIME . . . .   674 ISLE STAT II 3   204
AND DEAD AS ARE THE LOVERS OF OLD RHYME . . . . . .   674 ISLE STAT II 3 V   204
AS A LEAF THAT IS OLD, AND WITHERED, AND COLD, ...   676 ISLE STAT II 3   250
AS A LEAF THAT IS OLD, AND WITHERED, AND COLD, ...   676 ISLE STAT II 3   262
OLD WARRIOR, WAKE! FOR SOFT AS A BEE SIPS, ...   677 ISLE STAT II 3   284
LIE STREWN THE CLOTTED LEAVES—THE DEAD OLD LEAVES. . . .   684 SEEKER   V   69
THROUGH HIS SAD SOUL FOR EVER OLD AND YOUNG, ...   687 TWO TITANS   25
IN CREVICED ROCKS, AND LAUGHED TO THE OLD SEA, ...   688 TWO TITANS   34
NOR HEEDS THE OLD, DIM PROTEST AND THE CRY . . . . .   689 NETTLESHIP   14
WHERE SAT OLD SUMMER FADING INTO SONG, ...   690 MOSADA 1   V   18
SHALL SEE A THING TO TALK ON WHEN YOU'RE OLD, ...   693 MOSADA 1   67
HER DREAMS ARE TALKING WITH OLD YEARS. AWAKE, ...   702 MOSADA 3   89
HALF ASLEEP THE OLD COW CROPS, ...   706 DAWN-SONG   20
THE SPIRIT OF YOUNG RENYI HAS GROWN OLD. . . . . . .   710 FERENCZ RENYI   17
IF THESE BE PRECIOUS." "I AM OLD AND WEAK," . . . . .   711 FERENCZ RENYI   55
FOR I AM OLD AND WEAK." AND AT HER SIDE . . . . .   712 FERENCZ RENYI   59
A LITTLE WITHERED MAN, AND OLD. . . . .   716 FAIRY DOCTOR   4
THE LITTLE WITHERED MAN, AND OLD. . . . .   717 FAIRY DOCTOR   24
SCARCE THE OLD AND WIZEN HOUSES HAD THEIR DOORS AND WINDOWS   718 PHANTOM SHIP   5
    SHUT.
SCARCE THE OLD AND WIZENED HOUSES HAD THEIR DOORS   718 PHANTOM SHIP   V   5
    AND WINDOWS SHUT.
PRAYED BESIDE THE OCEAN, THE OLD MUMBLING MOTHER OF THE   719 PHANTOM SHIP   V   34
    DEAD.
WITHOUT THERE OF A LITTLE, LIGHT OLD MAN! . . . . .   720 WITCH VIVIEN   13

OLD (CONTINUED)
    WHERE DWELL THE MINDS OF OLD MEN HAVING PEACE, ... 721 WITCH VIVIEN   22
    AND--NO! I'LL NONE OF THESE, OLD FATHER WRINKLES. . . . 721 WITCH VIVIEN   23
    I'LL PLAY YOU FOR YOUR OLD HOUR-GLASS. YOU SEE . . . . 721 WITCH VIVIEN   36
    THAN OLD MEN'S ANY DAY, AS MERLIN FOUND. . . . . . 721 WITCH VIVIEN   47
    UPON MY SOUL, OLD TIME. NO! THUS IT STANDS. . . . 722 WITCH VIVIEN   49
    CHANCE, AND NOT SKILL, HAS FAVOURED YOU, OLD FATHER! . 722 WITCH VIVIEN   60
    IN OTHER LIVES? HAST THOU NOT QUAFFED OLD WINE . . 724 KANVA ON SELF   12
    AND THE OLD MEN WERE WALKING, WALKING, ... 725 LEGEND   3
    THE BOYS, THE WOMEN, AND OLD MEN, ... 725 LEGEND   7
    THE WORLD GROWS OLD AND PLAYS THE FOOL." . . . . . 725 LEGEND   12
    AND SENT THE OLD MEN ON THEIR WAY, ... 725 LEGEND   23
    AN OLD HORSE LOOKED ACROSS A FENCE, ... 725 LEGEND   27
    AND OUR SLAVES BE AS OF OLD. . . . . 727 LOVERS QUARREL   56
    FROM WHERE THE OLD IVY CRAWLS ROUND THE OLD STEEPLE, . 728 PRIEST FAIRY   6
    FROM WHERE THE OLD IVY CRAWLS ROUND THE OLD STEEPLE, . 728 PRIEST FAIRY   6
    YE ON THE BROAD HIGH MOUNTAINS OF OLD ERI, . . . 737 MOURN THEN ON   1
    AND HER OLD WIND THAT NO MIRTH EVER HAD, ... 738 YOU ARE SAD   7
    "GO BRING ME MY OLD ARMOUR . . . . 740 EARL PAUL   19
    THE LITTLE OLD GLOVE OF A CHILD! . . . . . . 744 GLOVE CLOAK   9
    TAUGHT ME WISE MUSIC, AND GAVE ME THIS OLD HARP! . . 750 SHADOW WATER A   76
    THE TIDE NARROWS BETWEEN, AND ONE OLD MAN . . . 752 SHADOW WATER A   118
    HAS BLOSSOMED, AND I GROW AS OLD AS TIME. . . . . 756 SHADOW WATER A   179
    AND I AM OLD AS TIME, BECAUSE I KNOW . . . . . 756 SHADOW WATER A V   179
    I GREW AS OLD AS TIME, AND SHE GROWS YOUNG . . . 761 SHADOW WATER A   259
    GROWS YOUNG AND A MAN'S HEART GROWS OLD IN A TWINKLING. 761 SHADOW WATER A   263
    MY FOSTER-MOTHER SANG IN AN OLD RHYME . . . . . 763 SHADOW WATER A   314
    MY FOSTER MOTHER SANG IN AN OLD RHYME . . . . . 763 SHADOW WATER A V   314
    AND ALL THE WISDOM THAT OLD IMAGES, ... 764 SHADOW WATER A   344
    AND ONE IN THE OLD GRAY HOUSE . . . . 771 SPINNING SONG   4
    LEAPS AND TIME'S OLD LANTHORN DIMS. . . . . . . 777 SONG DEIRDRE 2   5
    BY AN OLD HEARTH, AND HE . . . . 780 WELL AND TREE   12
    HAVE NOT OLD WRITERS SAID . . . . 781 MY HEART BEAT   6
    THEN THAT OLD ABBEY ACTOR, DUDLEY DIGGES, ... 790 DEDICATION   7
OLDEN
    WEAVING OLDEN DANCES, ... 87 STOLEN CHILD   17
OLDER
    O WINDS, OLDER THAN CHANGING OF NIGHT AND DAY, . . . 162 ASKS FORGIVE   7
    THE OLDER IS CONDEMNED TO DEATH, ... 475 EVA GORE-BOOTH   7
    DID AN OLDER MIND COMMEND-- . . . . 494 AT ALGECIRAS   10
    RIBH PREFERS AN OLDER THEOLOGY . . . . 556 RIBH PATRICK   V   T
    I GAVE IT ALL TO AN OLDER MAN! . . . . 588 OLD WICKED MAN   23
OLDEST
    THE OLDEST HOUND WITH MOURNFUL DIN, ... 99 FOXHUNTER   V   45
    BUT THE OLDEST OF ALL THE DOLLS, ... 319 DOLLS   4
O'LEARY
    IT'S WITH O'LEARY IN THE GRAVE. . . . . 289 SEPTEMBER 1913   8
    IT'S WITH O'LEARY IN THE GRAVE. . . . . 289 SEPTEMBER 1913   16
    IT'S WITH O'LEARY IN THE GRAVE. . . . . 290 SEPTEMBER 1913   24
    THEY'RE WITH O'LEARY IN THE GRAVE. . . . . . . 290 SEPTEMBER 1913   32
    "HUDDON AND DUDDON AND DANIEL O'LEARY, ... 529 TOM LUNATIC   7
    HUDDON, DUDDON AND DANIEL O'LEARY . . . . . . 787 HUDDON DUDDON   1
    HUDDON, DUDDON AND DANIEL O'LEARY . . . . . . 787 HUDDON DUDDON   6
    HUDDON, DUDDON AND DANIEL O'LEARY . . . . . . 787 HUDDON DUDDON   11
O'LEARY'S
    BEAUTIFUL LOFTY THINGS: O'LEARY'S NOBLE HEAD; . . 577 LOFTY THINGS   1
OLIVE
    AN ANCIENT IMAGE MADE OF OLIVE WOOD-- . . . . . 428 NINETEEN 19   6
    EVEN THE GREY-LEAVED OLIVE TREE . . . . 446 COLONUS PRAISE V   12
    GLITTERING AMONG GREY-LEAVED OLIVE TREES, . . . 447 COLONUS PRAISE V   21
    CAME OLIVE FIRES OF MORNING AND ON THE DARKNESS FED, . 719 PHANTOM SHIP   33
    CAME THE OLIVE FIRE OF MORNING, AND ON THE DARKNESS FED, 719 PHANTOM SHIP   V   33
OLIVER
    A POT-HOUSE BENCH WITH OLIVER GOLDSMITH ONCE. . . . 486 SEVEN SAGES   3
    OLIVER GOLDSMITH SANG WHAT HE HAD SEEN, ... 487 SEVEN SAGES   17
OLIVE-TREE
    EVEN THE GREY-LEAVED OLIVE-TREE . . . . 446 COLONUS PRAISE   12
OLIVE-TREES
    GLITTERING AMONG GREY-LEAVED OLIVE-TREES, . . . 447 COLONUS PRAISE   21
OLLAVE
    AND EVERY ANCIENT OLLAVE SAID, ... 82 MAD KING GOLL   9
OLYMPIANS
    ALL THE OLYMPIANS: A THING NEVER KNOWN AGAIN. . . . 578 LOFTY THINGS   12
OLYMPUS
    NOR ON OLYMPUS LEAPED FROM CLOUD TO CLOUD, . . . 260 FASC DIFFICULT   6
    NOR ON AN OLYMPUS LEAPED FROM CLOUD TO CLOUD, . . 260 FASC DIFFICULT V   6
OMEN
    AN OMEN! AN OMEN! . . . . 681 SEEKER   11
    AN OMEN! AN OMEN! . . . . 681 SEEKER   11
ONCE
    AND ONCE A SUDDEN LAUGHTER SPRANG . . . . . . 16 OISIN 1   225
    FROM ALL THEIR LIPS, AND ONCE THEY SANG . . . . 16 OISIN 1   226
    AND ONCE A LADY BY MY SIDE . . . . 16 OISIN 1   231
    AND ONCE A MAIDEN BY MY SIDE . . . . 16 OISIN 1   V   231
    ONCE MORE THE DANCE'S LINKED FLOW, ... 22 OISIN 1   V 323A
    WHEN ONCE BESIDE THE SHORE I STOOD, ... 24 OISIN 1   V   364
    AND ONCE MORE SADDLED THE WHITE STEED, ... 25 OISIN 1   V   378
    THE HUMAN SADNESS DAWNS ONCE MORE! . . . . . 25 OISIN 1   V   381
    ONCE MORE--THE YOUTH AND LADY, DEER AND HOUND! . . 29 OISIN 2   V   2
    ONCE MORE UNTO YOUR FLOWERS, FOR NONE MAY FIGHT, . . . 34 OISIN 2   V   80

		PAGE	TITLE	LINE

ONCE   (CONTINUED)

MY SOUL, ONCE GLORY OF ITS ANCIENT LINE, ... 36 OISIN 2   V   95
SEA-GOD, THAT ONCE, TO GIVE HIS SLAVES CONTENT, ... 38 OISIN 2   V 129
EVADING, TURNING, ONCE DID I HEW AND HEW . . . . 40 OISIN 2   V 176
ONCE HELD BETWEEN MY ARMS, WITH LIVID CHOP . . . . 40 OISIN 2   178
AND WHEN THE SUN ONCE MORE IN SAFFRON STEPT, ... 41 OISIN 2   192
BUT WHEN THE SUN ONCE MORE IN SAFFRON STEPT, ... 41 OISIN 2   V 192
AND ONCE MORE TO A DAY-LONG BATTLE FELL, ... 43 OISIN 2   218
AND WE ONCE MORE UNTO OUR FIGHTING FELL. . . . . 43 OISIN 2   V 218
OR MOVED AS THEY MOVED ONCE, ... 53 OISIN 3   88
THAT ONCE MORE MOVED IN MY BOSOM THE ANCIENT SADNESS OF 54 OISIN 3   107
MAN,
IF I WERE AS I ONCE WAS, ... 58 OISIN 3   157
SOUGHT ONCE AGAIN THE SHORE, AND FOUND A SHELL, ... 68 SAD SHEPHERD   18
SOUGHT ONCE AGAIN THE SHORE, AND CHOSE A SHELL . . . . . 68 SAD SHEPHERD V 18
"YOUR EYES THAT ONCE WERE NEVER WEARY OF MINE . . . . . 79 EPHEMERA   1
BY THE LONE BORDER OF THE LAKE ONCE MORE, ... 79 EPHEMERA   5
STAND BY THE BORDER OF THE LAKE ONCE MORE, ... 79 EPHEMERA   V   5
FELL LIKE FAINT METEORS IN THE GLOOM, AND ONCE . . . . . 80 EPHEMERA   14
ON THE LONE BORDER OF THE LAKE ONCE MORE! . . . . . . 80 EPHEMERA   17
HE SPAKE ONCE MORE AND FONDLED WITH HIS LIPS . . . . . . 81 EPHEMERA   V 24A
AS ONCE WITHIN A LITTLE TOWN . . . . 85 MAD KING GOLL V 49
ONCE, WHILE WITHIN A LITTLE TOWN . . . . 85 MAD KING GOLL V 49
TO SEE THE WORLD ONCE MORE. . . . . 97 FOXHUNTER   4
THAT I LOVED ONCE." AGAIN THE FIGHTING SPED, ... 110 CUCHULAIN SEA   64
YOUR EYES HAD ONCE, AND OF THEIR SHADOWS DEEP; . . . . . 121 YOU ARE OLD   4
ONCE, WHILE HE NODDED ON A CHAIR, ... 132 FR GILLIGAN   5
WHEN THE MOTHS CAME ONCE MORE, ... 133 FR GILLIGAN   22
WHEN MOTHS CAME ONCE MORE, ... 133 FR GILLIGAN V 22
AND ONCE, WHEN THE OWLS GREW STILL, ... 159 CAP AND BELLS V 2
WE, TOO, HAD GOOD ATTENDANCE ONCE, ... 266 GALWAY RACES   5
AN OLD FOUL MOUTH THAT ONCE CRIED OUT ON YOU . . . . . 292 TO A SHADE   V 17
ONCE, WHEN MIDNIGHT SMOTE THE AIR, ... 294 HATED PLAYBOY   1
HAVING LOVED GOD ONCE, BUT MAYBE . . . . 299 THREE HERMITS   26
BUT LET HIM KEEP HIS GRAVE FOR ONCE . . . . 303 HOUR DAWN   38
ALTHOUGH CROWDS GATHERED ONCE IF SHE BUT SHOWED HER FACE, 314 FALLEN MAJESTY   1
WHEREON A THING ONCE WALKED THAT SEEMED A BURNING CLOUD. 315 FALLEN MAJESTY   8
ONCE WALKED A THING THAT SEEMED, AS IT WERE, A BURNING 315 FALLEN MAJESTY V 8
CLOUD.
AND ALL THEIR EYES STILL FIXED, HOPING TO FIND ONCE MORE, 318 MAGI   6
WHO COMES AT NEED, ALTHOUGH NOT NOW AS ONCE . . . . . 320 REED WHISPERER   2
AND MAKE THE DAYLIGHT SWEET ONCE MORE! BUT WHEN . . . . 339 SHEP GOATHERD   13
TO FIND WHAT ONCE I HAD . . . . 346 ON WOMAN   33
AND KNOW WHAT ONCE I HAVE KNOWN, ... 346 ON WOMAN   34
SING ME THE CHANGES OF THE MOON ONCE MORE! . . . . . . 373 PHASES OF MOON   29
FIXED UPON IMAGES THAT ONCE WERE THOUGHT! . . . . . . 375 PHASES OF MOON   80
THE FIRST THIN CRESCENT IS WHEELED ROUND ONCE MORE. . . . 377 PHASES OF MOON 116
THE BURNING BOW THAT ONCE COULD SHOOT AN ARROW . . . . 377 PHASES OF MOON 119
ONCE HE LIVED A SCHOOLMASTER . . . . 381 SONG OF FOOL   5
ONCE MORE THE STORM IS HOWLING, AND HALF HID . . . . . 403 FOR DAUGHTER   1
WHEN ALL IS RUIN ONCE AGAIN. . . . . 406 CARVED STONE   6
ONCE OUT OF NATURE I SHALL NEVER TAKE . . . . 408 SAIL BYZANTIUM   25
BEYOND THAT RIDGE LIVED MRS. FRENCH, AND ONCE . . . . . 410 TOWER   25
OR ANYTHING CALLED CONSCIENCE ONCE! . . . . 413 TOWER   118
SUFFICE THE AGEING MAN AS ONCE THE GROWING BOY. . . . . 427 PHANTOM HATRED   40
HAD PRETTY PLUMAGE ONCE--ENOUGH OF THAT, ... 444 SCHOOL CHILDR   30
AND WHAT HAD DROWNED A LOVER ONCE, ... 457 SECRETS OF OLD   5
TO ABD AL-RABBAN! FELLOW-ROYSTERER ONCE, ... 460 HARUN RASHID   2
TO ABD-AL-RABBAN! FELLOW ROYSTERER ONCE . . . . . . 460 HARUN RASHID V 2
AND ONCE AGAIN SHE ROSE AND SWEPT THE HOUSE . . . . . 468 HARUN RASHID   159
A CHARTER TO COMMIT THE CRIME ONCE MORE. . . . . . . 478 SELF AND SOUL   32
WHAT MATTER IF I LIVE IT ALL ONCE MORE? . . . . . . 478 SELF AND SOUL   43
. . . THOUGHT'S CROWNED POWERS HE CALLED THEM ONCE. . . . 480 BLOOD AND MOON   15
A POT-HOUSE BENCH WITH OLIVER GOLDSMITH ONCE. . . . . . 486 SEVEN SAGES   3
BUT MINE SAW STELLA ONCE. WHENCE CAME OUR THOUGHT? . . . 486 SEVEN SAGES   6
MINE SAW STELLA ONCE. WHENCE CAME OUR THOUGHT? . . . 486 SEVEN SAGES   V 6
MINE SAW STELLA ONCE. WHEN CAME OUR THOUGHT? . . . . 486 SEVEN SAGES   V 6
SEEMED ONCE MORE DEAR THAN LIFE! ANCESTRAL TREES, . . . 491 COOLE BALLYLEE   34
ETERNALISED THE BODY OF A MODERN SAINT THAT ONCE . . . . 503 VACILLATION   83
WHAT MATTER FOR THE SCENE, THE SCENE ONCE GONE! . . . . 542 PARN FUNERAL 1   19
THINKING TO MEET MY LOVE ONCE MORE . . . . 551 SONGS REWRIT 1 V 15
TRANSFIGURED TO PURE SUBSTANCE WHAT HAD ONCE . . . . . 555 RIBH AT TOMB   11
AND ALL THE DROP-SCENES DROP AT ONCE . . . . 566 LAPIS LAZULI   22
AND ALL THE DROP SCENES DROP AT ONCE . . . . 566 LAPIS LAZULI V 22
SAID LADY ONCE TO LOVER, ... 569 THREE BUSHES   1
A MAN I PRAISE THAT ONCE IN TARA'S HALLS . . . . . 609 IN TARAS HALLS   1
NO DARK TOMB-HAUNTER ONCE! HER FORM ALL FULL . . . . . 618 BRONZE HEAD   8
STUMBLING UPON THE BLOOD-DARK TRACK ONCE MORE, ... 622 HOUND VOICE   18
A GIRL THAT KNEW ALL DANTE ONCE . . . . 626 OLD MEN BE MAD   5
ONCE MORE HOW ON THAT MISERABLE DAY . . . . . . 658 ISLE STAT II 1   4
FOUGHT ONCE FOR SELF-SAME REASON ON THE HEM . . . . . 660 ISLE STAT II 1 32
AND ONCE A-YEAR LET THE ARCADIANS COME, ... 663 ISLE STAT II 2 29
ONCE MORE THOSE SHEPHERDS COME. MAYHAP SOME MIRTH . . . 664 ISLE STAT II 2 49
AND WHEN ONCE MORE THE LIGHTNING GENII PASSED, ... 687 TWO TITANS   29
WHEN FLASH ON FLASH ONCE MORE THE LIGHTNING CAME, . . . 688 TWO TITANS   39
SHE WAS A GREAT ENCHANTRESS ONCE OF YORE, ... 693 MOSADA 1   78
AH! NOW I'M EASTERN-HEARTED ONCE AGAIN, ... 694 MOSADA 1   99
I HAD A SISTER LIKE HER ONCE, MY FRIEND. . . . . . 696 MOSADA 2   11
I SAW HIS JOVIAL MOOD BRING ONCE A SMILE . . . . . 696 MOSADA 2   14
A POISON DROP. A TOY, A FANCY ONCE, ... 700 MOSADA 3   24

579

		PAGE	TITLE		LINE

ONCE   (CONTINUED)
```
        A POISON DROP.  THE TOY OF FANCY ONCE,  . . . . . . .     700 MOSADA 3        V   24
        ONCE IN THY NATION NONE SHALL KNOW THAT I  . . . . . .     702 MOSADA 3            82
        LOOK ON ME ONCE.  WHY SINK YOUR EYELIDS THUS? . . . . .    703 MOSADA 3           107
        LOOK ON ME ONCE.  WHY SINK YOUR EYELIDS SO?  . . . . .     703 MOSADA 3        V  107
        WHERE HOMES ONCE WHITENED VALE AND MOUNTAIN CREST;  . .    709 FERENCZ RENYI        3
        A BIRD WALK ON THE DOORSTEP.  CHECK ONCE MORE.  . . . .    722 WITCH VIVIEN        64
        THE FAIRIES' HERALD SPAKE ONCE MORE;  . . . . . . . .      730 PRIEST FAIRY        53
        COVER YOUR EARS! FOR ONCE WE HAD MOORED OUR GALLEY  . .    756 SHADOW WATER A     187
        MOORE ONCE HAD VISITS FROM THE MUSE  . . . . . . . .       792 GEORGE MOORE         1
ONE      SEE NO-ONE NINETEEN-THIRTY-ONE
        THEN DID YOU ANSWER, PEARL-PALE ONE,  . . . . . . . .        6 OISIN 1         V   53
        BEEN SPOKEN OF WITH ANY ONE;  . . . . . . . . . . .          6 OISIN 1         V   56
        OF PRINCES THERE IS MANY A ONE."  . . . . . . . . . .        6 OISIN 1         V   61
        SHALL KNEEL AND PRAISE YOU, ONE BY ONE,  . . . . . . .       8 OISIN 1             78
        SHALL KNEEL AND PRAISE YOU, ONE BY ONE,  . . . . . . .       8 OISIN 1             78
        ALL PEARLY WHITE, SAVE ONE RED EAR;  . . . . . . . .        12 OISIN 1            141
        OF ONE LONG FINGER ON MY LIP.  . . . . . . . . . . .        12 OISIN 1            151
        BLEW ONE LONG NOTE.  FROM OVER REED  . . . . . . . .        14 OISIN 1         V  195
        UNTIL ONE CAME, A TEARFUL BOY;  . . . . . . . . . . .       17 OISIN 1            237
        AND EACH ONE SAID, WITH A LONG, LONG SIGH,  . . . . .       17 OISIN 1            244
        ONE HAND UPHELD HIS BEARDLESS CHIN,  . . . . . . . .        17 OISIN 1            250
        AND ONE A SCEPTRE FLASHING OUT  . . . . . . . . . . .       17 OISIN 1            251
        AND ONE CAME CLOSE, A TEARFUL BOY.  . . . . . . . . .       17 OISIN 1         V  237
        ONE HAND BENEATH HIS BEARDLESS CHIN,  . . . . . . . .       17 OISIN 1         V  251
        AND NIGH UNTO HIM EACH ONE DREW;  . . . . . . . . . .       18 OISIN 1         V  257
        WITH ONE LONG GLANCE FOR GIRL AND BOY  . . . . . . .        19 OISIN 1            287
        WITH ONE LONG GLANCE ON MAID AND BOY  . . . . . . . .       19 OISIN 1         V  287
        EACH ONE WOVEN TO THE OTHER,  . . . . . . . . . . .         22 OISIN 1            334
        EACH ONE WOVEN TO HIS BROTHER  . . . . . . . . . . .        22 OISIN 1            335
        FOR LOVE THEY FOLLOWED ONE AND ALL!  . . . . . . . .        23 OISIN 1         V 345G
        WHEN ONE DAY BY THE TIDE I STOOD,  . . . . . . . . .        24 OISIN 1            364
        WHEN ONE DAY BY THE SHORE I STOOD,  . . . . . . . . .       24 OISIN 1            364
        I HEARD ONE SAY, "HIS EYES GROW DIM  . . . . . . . .        25 OISIN 1            380
        I HEARD ONE SAY, "WITHIN HIS EYES  . . . . . . . . .        25 OISIN 1            380
        AS THEY GAZE AT EACH OTHER, "OH, WHERE IS THAT GREAT ONE?"  28 OISIN 1         V 423H
        UPON DARK THRONES.  BETWEEN THE LIDS OF ONE  . . . . .      31 OISIN 2             37
        HUGE FORMS OF STONE; BETWEEN THE LIDS OF ONE  . . . .       31 OISIN 2         V   37
        TO ONE VAST FOOT, FROTH-SPLASHED, WITH CURVED TOES LYING    32 OISIN 2         V  46A
        AND ONE WHOM YOU WILL GO TO WITHOUT TELLING,  . . . .       33 OISIN 2         V   67
        AND TELL ME HOW YOU CAME TO ONE UNBID,  . . . . . . .       33 OISIN 2         V   67
        MY ANGRY KING-REMEMBERING SOUL ONE JOT.  . . . . . .        36 OISIN 2             94
        NOR SHOOK MY FIRM AND SPACIOUS SOUL ONE JOT;  . . . .       36 OISIN 2         V   94
        MY ANGRY, KING REMEMBERING SOUL ONE JOT;  . . . . . .       36 OISIN 2         V   94
        "EACH ONE A HORSEHAIR SHIRT HATH ON,  . . . . . . . .       43 OISIN 2         V 208C
        DROPPING; A MURMUROUS DROPPING; OLD SILENCE AND THAT ONE    48 OISIN 3             18
            SOUND;
        . . . AND THE WHOLE OF THE WORLD WAS ONE.  . . . . . .      48 OISIN 3             24
        IN ONE WAS A BRANCH SOFT-SHINING WITH BELLS MORE MANY THAN  50 OISIN 3             46
            SIGHS
        I CRIED, "O NIAMH! O WHITE ONE! IF ONLY A TWELVE-HOURED     55 OISIN 3            113
            DAY,
        WHERE EVER IS MURMUROUS DROPPING, OLD SILENCE AND THAT      56 OISIN 3            138
            ONE SOUND;
        . . . CROZIERED ONE, CAUGHT IN YOUR NET!  . . . . . .       58 OISIN 3            167
        . . . CROZIERED ONE, CAUGHT IN THY NET—  . . . . . .        58 OISIN 3         V  167
        . . . CROZIERED ONE, CAUGHT IN THEIR NET!  . . . . . .      58 OISIN 3         V  167
        THE REST THOU HAST HEARD OF, THOU CROZIERED ONE— . . .      60 OISIN 3         V  189
        WITH MINGLING HAIR, AND PLAY UPON ONE LUTE.  . . . . .      71 ANASHU VIJAYA       10
        YON TALL ONE EYES MY SUPPER; CHASE HIM AWAY,  . . . .       72 ANASHU VIJAYA       34
        YON TALL ONE EYES MY SUPPER; SWIFTLY CHASE HIM  . . .       72 ANASHU VIJAYA   V   34
        AH, YOU WILL KNOW MY LOVED ONE BY HIS HUNTER'S ARROWS       75 ANASHU VIJAYA       80
            TRULY,
        ONE WITH THE TIDE THAT GLEAMS, THE WINGS THAT GLEAM AND     78 INDIAN TO LOVE      15
            DART,
        ONE WITH THE WAVES THAT SOFTLY ROUND US LAUGH AND DART.     78 INDIAN TO LOVE  V   15
        ONE WITH THE GLIMMERING TIDE,  . . . . . . . . . . .        78 INDIAN TO LOVE  V   15
        LIKE SWARMING BEES, ONE WITH THE DOVE  . . . . . . .        78 INDIAN TO LOVE  V   16
        ONE WITH THE LEAVES; ONE WITH THE DOVE  . . . . . . .       78 INDIAN TO LOVE  V   16
        ONE WITH THE LEAVES; ONE WITH THE DOVE  . . . . . . .       78 INDIAN TO LOVE  V   16
        THE GREY WOLF KNOWS ME; BY ONE EAR  . . . . . . . .         84 MAD KING GOLL       45
        THE WILD BOAR KNOWS ME, BY ONE EAR  . . . . . . . .         84 MAD KING GOLL   V   45
        SHY ONE, SHY ONE,  . . . . . . . . . . . . . . .           89 ISLE IN WATER        1
        SHY ONE, SHY ONE,  . . . . . . . . . . . . . . .           89 ISLE IN WATER        1
        SHY ONE OF MY HEART,  . . . . . . . . . . . . . .          89 ISLE IN WATER        2
        BUT IF WHEN ANY ONE DIED,  . . . . . . . . . . . .         92 FATHER OHART    V   21
        ONE STAR SHONE FAINT AND GREEN,  . . . . . . . . . .       95 MOLL MAGEE          30
        "AND OF MY SERVANTS SOME ONE GO,  . . . . . . . . .        97 FOXHUNTER       V    5
        AND SOME ONE FROM THE STABLE BRING  . . . . . . . .        97 FOXHUNTER       V    5
        AND SOME ONE FROM THE STABLES BRING  . . . . . . . .       97 FOXHUNTER       V    5
        ONE BLIND HOUND ONLY LIES APART  . . . . . . . . . .       99 FOXHUNTER           41
        "WITH HIM IS ONE SWEET-THROATED LIKE A BIRD."  . . . .    106 CUCHULAIN SEA       16
        "WITH HIM IS ONE SWEET-THROATED LIKE A BIRD,  . . . .     106 CUCHULAIN SEA   V   16
        WHOSE BLADE COMPELS, AND BID THEM SEND YOU ONE  . . .     108 CUCHULAIN SEA       37
        AND HIS YOUNG DEAR ONE CLOSE BESIDE HIM KNELT,  . . .     108 CUCHULAIN SEA   V   40
        SEEK OUT WHAT MAN HE IS."  ONE WENT AND CAME.  . . . .    109 CUCHULAIN SEA       51
        AT THE SWORD POINT, AND BADE ME BRING HIM ONE  . . . .    109 CUCHULAIN SEA   V   53
        TROY PASSED AWAY IN ONE HIGH FUNERAL GLEAM,  . . . .      111 ROSE OF WORLD        4
        WEARY AND KIND ONE LINGERED BY HER SEAT!  . . . . .       112 ROSE OF WORLD       13
        WEARY AND KIND ONE STOOD BESIDE HER SEAT;  . . . . .      112 ROSE OF WORLD   V   13
        I CALL, AS THEY GO BY ME ONE BY ONE,  . . . . . . .       114 ROSE OF BATTLE       8
```

ONE   (CONTINUED)

	PAGE	TITLE		LINE
I CALL, AS THEY GO BY ME ONE BY ONE,	114	ROSE OF BATTLE		8
"TURN IF YE MAY," I CALL OUT TO EACH ONE,	114	ROSE OF BATTLE	V	7
BUT ONE MAN LOVED THE PILGRIM SOUL IN YOU,	121	YOU ARE OLD		7
I DREAMED THAT ONE HAD DIED IN A STRANGE PLACE	123	DREAM OF DEATH		1
ONE WITH HER ARE MIRTH AND DUTY!	124	CATHLEEN PARA	V	5
BUT ONE SMALL KNOT-GRASS GROWING BY THE POOL	127	DREAM OF FAERY		29
BUT ONE SMALL KNOT-GRASS GROWING BY THE RIM	127	DREAM OF FAERY		29
AND NO ONE ANY LEAF-CROWNED DANCER MISS	128	DREAM OF FAERY		46
WHEN NO ONE TURNED TO SEE	131	OLD PENSIONER	V	2
SENT ONE OF HIS GREAT ANGELS DOWN	134	FR GILLIGAN		43
NOR MAY I LESS BE COUNTED ONE	138	TO IRELAND		17
WHAT ONE IN THE ROUT	142	MOODS		5
UNTIL ONE BORE BRIDGET HIS BRIDE	145	HOST OF AIR		31
AND SOME ONE CALLED ME BY MY NAME!	149	WANDER AENGUS		12
SHE LOOKED IN MY HEART ONE DAY	152	LOSS OF LOVE		5
I HAVE BEEN CHANGED TO A HOUND WITH ONE RED EAR!	153	CHANGE BELOVED		2
TO HER RIGHT HAND CAME THE RED ONE,	160	CAP AND BELLS		31
AND ONE HAS SEEN IN THE REDNESS OF WINE	168	BLESSED		35
WHILE LIGHTS WERE PALING ONE BY ONE,	176	BELOVED DEAD		13
WHILE LIGHTS WERE PALING ONE BY ONE.	176	BELOVED DEAD		13
WHILE BIRDS GREW SILENT ONE BY ONE.	176	BELOVED DEAD	V	13
WHILE BIRDS GREW SILENT ONE BY ONE	176	BELOVED DEAD	V	13
KNOWING ONE, OUT OF ALL THINGS, ALONE, THAT HIS HEAD	177	PAST GREATNESS		8
AS THOUGH ONE LISTENED THERE, AND HIS VOICE SANK	180	QUEEN MAEVE		7
ONE THAT THE GENERATIONS HAD LONG WAITED	182	QUEEN MAEVE		66
OF ONE WHO IS NO FRIEND TO ME OR TO MINE,	184	QUEEN MAEVE	V	94A
WITH BODIES MADE OUT OF SOFT FIRE. THE ONE,	187	QUEEN MAEVE		144
"O LADY, WED WITH ONE OF US"!	191	BAILE AILLINN		61
NOW HAD THAT OLD GAUNT CRAFTY ONE,	193	BAILE AILLINN		100
OR MICE IN THE ONE WHEATEN SHEAF	195	BAILE AILLINN		147
OR BIRDS LOST IN THE ONE CLEAR SPACE	195	BAILE AILLINN		149
OR, IT MAY BE, THE EYELIDS OF ONE EYE,	195	BAILE AILLINN		151
OR THE DOOR-PILLARS OF ONE HOUSE,	195	BAILE AILLINN		152
THAT HAVE ONE SHADOW ON THE GROUND!	195	BAILE AILLINN		154
OR THE TWO STRINGS THAT MADE ONE SOUND	195	BAILE AILLINN		155
OR BIRDS LOST IN ONE CLEAR SPACE	195	BAILE AILLINN	V	149
OR THE DOOR PILLARS OF ONE HOUSE,	195	BAILE AILLINN	V	152
ONE IS EVER KIND SAID YESTERDAY!	199	FOLLY COMFORT		1
WE SAT TOGETHER AT ONE SUMMER'S END,	204	ADAMS CURSE		1
THERE'S MANY A ONE SHALL FIND OUT ALL HEARTACHE	205	ADAMS CURSE		16
"THERE IS ONE THING THAT ALL WE WOMEN KNOW	205	ADAMS CURSE	V	18
I HAD A THOUGHT FOR NO ONE BUT YOUR EARS!	206	ADAMS CURSE	V	34
AND ONE BY ONE WE DROP AWAY."	208	OLD MEN ADMIRE		3
AND ONE BY ONE WE DROP AWAY."	208	OLD MEN ADMIRE		3
WHERE ONE FOUND LANCELOT CRAZED AND HID HIM FOR A WHILE!	209	UNDER THE MOON		3
AND WOOD-OF-WONDERS, WHERE ONE KILLS AN OX AT DAWN,	209	UNDER THE MOON		9
WHERE ONE FOUND LANCELOT CRAZED, AND HID HIM FOR AWHILE,	209	UNDER THE MOON	V	3
NO ONE HAS EVER LOVED BUT YOU AND I.	211	RAGGED WOOD		12
WE WERE SO MUCH AT ONE.	212	O DO NOT LOVE		8
ONE GATHERS UP HIS PURPLE GOWN!	212	BLESS PSALTER		9
ONE LEANS AND MUTTERS BY THE WALL--	212	BLESS PSALTER		10
O KINSMEN OF THE THREE IN ONE,	213	BLESS PSALTER		14
AND WHEN ONE CHANGED HER TO A SILVER FLY,	220	HARP OF AENGUS		10
THAT HAD BUT THE ONE EYE. CAN NO BEWITCHMENT	222	SHADOW WATER B		10
FOR THAT RED MOLL THAT HAD BUT THE ONE EYE.	222	SHADOW WATER B	V	10
IF WE WERE OF ONE MIND I'D DO IT. WERE'T NOT	222	SHADOW WATER B	V	15
I SAW THEM, TOO, ONE NIGHT. FORGAEL WAS PLAYING,	223	SHADOW WATER B		36
MY MOTHER TOLD ME THAT THERE IS NOT ONE	224	SHADOW WATER B		45
AND KEEP TO THE ONE WEARY MARRIAGE-BED,	224	SHADOW WATER B		55
AND KEEP TO THE ONE WEARY MARRIAGE BED,	224	SHADOW WATER B	V	55
WHEN IT IS OVER, NOR ONE TO GRUMBLE AT US.	225	SHADOW WATER B		67
BE OF YOUR TROOP! AIBRIC BE ONE OF YOU	225	SHADOW WATER B		75
ONE OF THE EVER-LIVING, AS I THINK--	231	SHADOW WATER B		210
ONE OF THE LAUGHING PEOPLE--AND SHE AND I	231	SHADOW WATER B		211
BECOME ONE MOVEMENT, ENERGY, DELIGHT,	231	SHADOW WATER B		217
AND WHERE IS ONE WOMAN THERE'LL BE OTHERS.	232	SHADOW WATER B		227
ONE--AND ONE--A COUPLE--FIVE TOGETHER!	233	SHADOW WATER B		249
ONE--AND ONE--A COUPLE--FIVE TOGETHER!	233	SHADOW WATER B		249
NOW I CAN HEAR. THERE'S ONE OF THEM THAT SAYS,	233	SHADOW WATER B		252
AND THEN ONE ASKS ANOTHER HOW HE DIED,	234	SHADOW WATER B		256
THEY WOULD NOT SEND ME ONE THAT CASTS A SHADOW.	235	SHADOW WATER B		285
IS SHAKEN IN THESE SEAS, AND WHAT ONE DOES	237	SHADOW WATER B		339
ONE MOMENT HAS NO MIGHT UPON THE MOMENT	237	SHADOW WATER B		340
THERE IS NOT ONE AMONG YOU THAT MADE LOVE	244	SHADOW WATER B		454
WANDER A MOMENT WHEN ONE IS IN LOVE?	246	SHADOW WATER B		515
YOU'LL HEAR THEM CALLING OUT TO ONE ANOTHER	247	SHADOW WATER B		521
HAD RUN INTO ONE FOUNTAIN. SPEAK TO HIM.	249	SHADOW WATER B		561
IN HAVING ONE ANOTHER? HOW COULD I REST	249	SHADOW WATER B		571
THOUGH LEAVES ARE MANY, THE ROOT IS ONE!	261	COMING WISDOM		1
WHERE PASSION AND PRECISION HAVE BEEN ONE	264	HOUSE SHAKEN		2
AND ALL THINGS AT ONE COMMON LEVEL LIE.	265	THESE CLOUDS		6
DELIGHT MAKES ALL OF THE ONE MIND,	266	GALWAY RACES		2
ONE TIME IT WAS A WOMAN'S FACE, OR WORSE--	267	ALL TEMPT ME		2
THAT ONE BELIEVED HE HAD A SWORD UPSTAIRS!	267	ALL TEMPT ME		8
ONE CANNOT BEGIN IT TOO SOON.	268	BROWN PENNY		16
FOR ONE THAT WAS LIKE WOMAN MADE	272	GREY ROCK		29
SO MOURNFUL THAT IT SEEMED THE CRY OF ONE	278	TWO KINGS		39
FOR I WOULD HAVE YOUR JUDGMENT UPON ONE	280	TWO KINGS		71
ALWAYS IN HIS ONE SEAT, AND BID ME CARE HIM	280	TWO KINGS		80

PAGE   TITLE   LINE

1E (CONTINUED)

```
THE ONE DISASTROUS ZODIAC, MUTTERING . . . . . . . .    282  TWO KINGS            128
BEING HONOUR BRED, WITH ONE . . . . . . . . . . .       291  TO A FRIEND            5
ONE OF YOU THREE IS A RICH MAN, . . . . . . . .         295  THREE BEGGARS         21
"AND IF I WIN," ONE BEGGAR SAID. . . . . . . .          296  THREE BEGGARS         29
ONE TO ANOTHER SIGHED AND CRIED! . . . . . . .          296  THREE BEGGARS         38
ONE BEGGAR CRIED! "YOU'RE SHAMMING SLEEP," . . .        297  THREE BEGGARS    V    45
AS THE ONE STURDY LEG COULD DO . . . . . . . .          302  HOUR DAWN              5
A PAIR OF LAPWINGS, ONE OLD SHEEP, . . . . . . .        302  HOUR DAWN              9
WHAT ONE OF MAEVE'S NINE BRAWLING SONS . . . . .        303  HOUR DAWN             36
HAS ONE OF MAEVE'S NINE BRAWLING SONS . . . . .         303  HOUR DAWN        V    36
AND WHEN AT ONE YEAR'S END I FOUND . . . . . .          305  HOUR DAWN             71
LIES ONE LONG SOUGHT . . . . . . . . . . .              310  WITCH                  7
HAS NO ONE SAID THOSE DARING . . . . . . . . .          312  TWO YEAR LATER         1
ONE BECAUSE NO THOUGHT, . . . . . . . . . . .           315  FRIENDS                4
AND ONE BECAUSE HER HAND . . . . . . . . . . .          315  FRIENDS               10
ONE THAT NO PASSING THOUGHT, . . . . . . . . .          315  FRIENDS          V     4
HOW COULD I PRAISE THAT ONE? . . . . . . . . .          316  FRIENDS               20
HOW SHOULD I PRAISE THAT ONE? . . . . . . . .           316  FRIENDS          V    20
AS THOUGH HE HAD BUT THAT ONE TRADE ALONE. . . .        327  ROBERT GREGORY        80
THE ENTIRE COMBUSTIBLE WORLD IN ONE SMALL ROOM . .      327  ROBERT GREGORY        82
ALL THE COMBUSTIBLE WORLD IN ONE SMALL ROOM . . .       327  ROBERT GREGORY V      82
WE HAVE TALKED IN THE ONE PLACE, . . . . . . .          332  SOLOMON SHEBA          4
IN THE ONE NARROW THEME OF LOVE . . . . . . .           333  SOLOMON SHEBA    V     7
SHUDDER THAT MADE THEM ONE. . . . . . . . . . .         346  ON WOMAN              23
AND ALL BECAUSE OF SOME ONE . . . . . . . . . .         346  ON WOMAN              40
I SHALL HAVE WRITTEN HIM ONE . . . . . . . . .          348  FISHERMAN             38
ONE HAD A LOVELY FACE, . . . . . . . . . . .            350  MEMORY                 1
COURTESY AND PASSION INTO ONE LIKE THOSE . . . .        352  PEOPLE                17
I MIGHT HAVE USED THE ONE SUBSTANTIAL RIGHT . . .       352  PEOPLE                19
ONE'S HAD HER FILL OF LOVERS, ANOTHER'S HAD BUT ONE,    354  HIS PHOENIX           19
YOU ARE MORE BEAUTIFUL THAN ANY ONE, . . . . . .        356  BROKEN DREAMS         27
YOU WERE MORE BEAUTIFUL THAN ANY ONE, . . . . .         356  BROKEN DREAMS    V    27
ALL DAY IN THE ONE CHAIR . . . . . . . . . .            357  BROKEN DREAMS         38
ONE IS A HARLOT, AND ONE A CHILD . . . . . . .          358  PRESENCES             12
ONE IS A HARLOT, AND ONE A CHILD . . . . . . .          358  PRESENCES             12
AND ONE, IT MAY BE, A QUEEN. . . . . . . . . .          358  PRESENCES             14
MOPING FOR ONE VOYAGE MORE. . . . . . . . . . .         361  ALF POLLEXFEN         22
SHOWS HER THAT SOME ONE SOON . . . . . . . . .          364  END OF DAY             5
NO ONE DENIES TO KEATS LOVE OF THE WORLD! . . . .       370  EGO DOMINUS           52
I CALL TO THE MYSTERIOUS ONE WHO YET . . . . . .        371  EGO DOMINUS           70
CRYING TO ONE ANOTHER LIKE THE BATS! . . . . . .        376  PHASES OF MOON       106
ONE LASHED HER TAIL! HER EYES LIT BY THE MOON . .       383  VISION ROBART         29
CHANCE BEING AT ONE WITH CHOICE AT LAST, . . . .        388  SOLOMON WITCH         14
WHEN OIL AND WICK ARE BURNED IN ONE! . . . . . .        388  SOLOMON WITCH         30
HEARTS WITH ONE PURPOSE ALONE . . . . . . . . .         393  EASTER 1916           41
BUT GREGORY'S WOOD AND ONE BARE HILL . . . . . .        403  FOR DAUGHTER           4
BUT GREGORY'S WOODS AND ONE BARE HILL . . . . .         403  FOR DAUGHTER     V     4
ROOTED IN ONE DEAR PERPETUAL PLACE. . . . . . .         405  FOR DAUGHTER          48
FOR ONE THROB OF THE ARTERY, . . . . . . . . .          406  IN TIME OF WAR         1
I KNEW THAT ONE IS ANIMATE, . . . . . . . . .           406  IN TIME OF WAR         4
IN ONE ANOTHER'S ARMS, BIRDS IN THE TREES . . . .       407  SAIL BYZANTIUM         2
AND ONE WAS DROWNED IN THE GREAT BOG OF CLOONE. .       411  TOWER                 48
ONE INEXTRICABLE BEAM, . . . . . . . . . . .            411  TOWER                 55
THAT ALL BUT THE ONE CARD BECAME . . . . . . .          411  TOWER                 68
ONE HEARS THE RUMBLE OF IT FAR BELOW . . . . . .        420  MY HOUSE         V  20B
HAS BUT ONE COMFORT LEFT! ALL TRIUMPH WOULD . . .       429  NINETEEN 19           39
INTO THE YOLK AND WHITE OF THE ONE SHELL. . . . .       443  SCHOOL CHILDR         16
I LOOK UPON ONE CHILD OR T'OTHER THERE . . . . .        443  SCHOOL CHILDR         18
AND NEEDS NO CRUELTY. I HAVE HEARD ONE SAY . . .        448  HERO GIRL FOOL        13
"AND ALL THOSE LIES HAVE BUT ONE END, POOR WRETCHES TO  450  OWEN AHERNE           18
   BETRAY!
AND FELL THE ONE IN T'OTHER'S ARMS . . . . . .          457  SUMMER SPRING          7
AND SUCH A PAIR BUT ONE, . . . . . . . . . .            458  SECRETS OF OLD        16
ONE AMONG THE BIRDS OF THE AIR, . . . . . . . .         460  THREE MONUMENT         3
ONE HAND AMID THE GOLDFISH IN THE POOL! . . . . .       463  HARUN RASHID          44
TWO CONTEMPLATING PASSIONS CHOSE ONE THEME . . . .      466  HARUN RASHID         117
AND I ALONE, ONE IN TEN THOUSAND YEARS, . . . . .       470  HARUN RASHID     V   190
ONE DEAR HOPE HAD HE! . . . . . . . . . . .             471  ALL SOUL NIGHT        28
WHEN UPWARD TURNED, ON ONE SOLE IMAGE FELL! . . .       471  ALL SOUL NIGHT        34
WHEN UPWARD TURNED ON ONE SOUL IMAGE FELL, . . .        471  ALL SOUL NIGHT V      34
BEAUTIFUL, ONE A GAZELLE. . . . . . . . . . .           475  EVA GORE-BOOTH         4
ONE OR THE OTHER OUT AND SPEAK . . . . . . . .          475  EVA GORE-BOOTH        15
BEAUTIFUL, ONE A GAZELLE. . . . . . . . . . .           475  EVA GORE-BOOTH        20
THERE ONE THAT RUFFLED IN A MANLY POSE . . . . .        489  COOLE PARK 29         11
ONE DEAR BRILLIANT WOMAN! . . . . . . . . . .           504  RESULT THOUGHT         2
ERE THE ONE OR T'OTHER DIE, . . . . . . . . .           508  JANE BISHOP      V     5
ONE MAN, ONE MAN ALONE . . . . . . . . . . .            526  AM OF IRELAND          6
ONE MAN, ONE MAN ALONE . . . . . . . . . . .            526  AM OF IRELAND          6
ONE SOLITARY MAN . . . . . . . . . . . . .              526  AM OF IRELAND          8
ONE MAN, AND ONE MAN ALONE . . . . . . . . .            526  AM OF IRELAND    V     6
ONE MAN, AND ONE MAN ALONE . . . . . . . . .            526  AM OF IRELAND    V     6
ONE THAT IS PERFECT OR AT PEACE, . . . . . . .          528  DANCER CRUACH          3
THE REST I PASS, ONE SENTENCE I UNSAY. . . . . .        542  PARN FUNERAL 2         1
I PASS THE REST--ONE SENTENCE I UNSAY-- . . . . .       542  PARN FUNERAL 2 V       1
THERE ALL THE GYRES CONVERGE IN ONE, . . . . . .        557  THERE                  3
AND ALL IT KNOWS IS THAT ONE WORD "REJOICE!" . . .      564  GYRES                 16
ONE ASKS FOR MOURNFUL MELODIES! . . . . . . . .         567  LAPIS LAZULI          53
INTO ONE NAME! . . . . . . . . . . . . .                572  LADYS 1ST SONG         6
NO BOOKS UPON THE KNEE, AND NO ONE THERE . . . . .      579  DOR WELLESLEY          9
BUT COPY SOME ONE ACTION, . . . . . . . . . .           600  SPIRIT MEDIUM         13
```

		PAGE	TITLE	LINE
ONE	(CONTINUED)			
THREE SONGS TO THE ONE BURDEN		605	SONGS BURDEN 1	T
ONE IMAGE CROSSED THE MANY-HEADED, SAT		610	STATUES	17
THAT ALL'S ARRANGED IN ONE CLEAR VIEW,		633	MAN AND ECHO	31
ONE ANOTHER IN THIS PLACE?		633	MAN AND ECHO	40
JOY AND LOVE ARE ONE EXISTENCE.		647	ISLE STAT I 1	71
LOVE AND SORROW, ONE EXISTENCE.		647	ISLE STAT I 1	73
I HEAR THE WHOLE SKY'S SORROW IN ONE VOICE.		652	ISLE STAT I 2	22
AND NOD TO ONE ANOTHER, LIES A GREEN,		653	ISLE STAT I 2	35
I'LL SEND MINE ARROW, NOW MY ONE RESOURCE:		657	ISLE STAT I 3	64
TWO MEN WHO LOVE ONE MAID HAVE AMPLE CAUSE		659	ISLE STAT II 1	30
EACH CAME ONE MORN, WITH WELCOMING OF SONG,		660	ISLE STAT II 1	42
FOR THIS THING FIGHT--WE LOVE ONE MAID? HER NAME?		661	ISLE STAT II 1	66
EACH ONE AT GAZE FOR AYE UPON HIS WHIRLING THRONE.		662	ISLE STAT II 1	81
ONE HAND BROW-SHADING, FAR ACROSS THE NIGHT,		663	ISLE STAT II 2	27
AND ONE ARM POINTING THUS, IN MARBLE WHITE.		663	ISLE STAT II 2	28
AND LET THE TALE BE MOURNFUL EACH ONE TELLS.		663	ISLE STAT II 2	36
I'LL HAVE. OH, ABSENT ONE 'TIS NOT FOR DEARTH		664	ISLE STAT II 2	50
WHO SEEK MAY FIND, SAVE ONLY ONE,		668	ISLE STAT II 3	48
THAT ONE SHALL DIE, UNLESS ONE DIE FOR HER.		669	ISLE STAT II 3	74
THAT ONE SHALL DIE, UNLESS ONE DIE FOR HER.		669	ISLE STAT II 3	74
AND ONE ALONE OF ALL WOULD HARK,		671	ISLE STAT II 3	123
A SCARLET BLOOM. WHY RAISEST THOU, PALE ONE,		673	ISLE STAT II 3	196
IF ONE SHOULD RISE BESIDE THEE,		680	LOVE AND DEATH	27
THY GARMENTS' HEM, THOU VISIONARY ONE!		684	SEEKER	71
MINE HEART-STRINGS ARE ALL BROKEN SAVING ONE,		684	SEEKER	V 69B
THY GARMENT'S HEM, THOU VISIONARY ONE!		684	SEEKER	V 71
TO ONE ANOTHER WITH A COILING CHAIN:		687	TWO TITANS	6
MAKING ALL ONE O'ER ROCK AND SEA AND SKIES:		687	TWO TITANS	28
THEN HAS THIS ONE BEEN SINNED FULL MANY TIMES.		692	MOSADA 1	49
I AM: ONE SHOULDER TURNED AWRY--WHY THEN		692	MOSADA 1	61
ONE SHOULDER TWISTED, AND THE CHILDREN CRY		695	MOSADA 1	116
WILL HE NOT SPARE HER LIFE? HOW WOULD ONE MATTER		696	MOSADA 2	3
SO SMALL MAKES ONE GROW WEAK AND TOTTERING!		700	MOSADA 3	35
THE BURGHERS OF THE NIGHT FADE ONE BY ONE.		700	MOSADA 3	40
THE BURGHERS OF THE NIGHT FADE ONE BY ONE.		700	MOSADA 3	40
BE ONE? I THINK ALL'S FINISHED NOW AND SEALED.		701	MOSADA 3	62
'TIS LATE, WAIT ONE MORE DAY: BELOW THE HILLS		702	MOSADA 3	91
UNHAPPY ONE. GO NOT, GO NOT, GO NOT:		703	MOSADA 3	102
LOVE, WILL YOU DIE WHEN WE HAVE MET? ONE LOOK		703	MOSADA 3 .	109
BEFORE HIM ONE WELL GUARDED, WITH BOUND HANDS:		709	FERENCZ RENYI	10
UNTUNED BY THEIR OWN STRIVING. IF ONE SUCH		711	FERENCZ RENYI	37
BUT THIS ONE--THIS ONE. NOW HIS HEAD DROPS LOW,		711	FERENCZ RENYI	39
BUT THIS ONE--THIS ONE. NOW HIS HEAD DROPS LOW,		711	FERENCZ RENYI	39
TWO WOMEN, WITHERED ONE AND SMALL AND THIN,		711	FERENCZ RENYI	51
I'M WEAK, AND BY THE HANDS SHALL HOLD EACH ONE		712	FERENCZ RENYI	57
I'M WEAK, AND BY THE HAND SHALL HOLD EACH ONE .		712	FERENCZ RENYI	V 57
THE YOUNG ONE WITH THE OTHERS." RENYI'S PALE		713	FERENCZ RENYI	84
AND SOFT, ONE GLIMMERING STAR. RENYI HAS CAST		714	FERENCZ RENYI	115
AND SOFT, ONE GLIMMERING STAR--WITH POWER VAST:		714	FERENCZ RENYI	V 115
A KID, HELD BY ONE SOFT WHITE EAR FOR TETHER,		715	DWELT SYCAMORE	3
AND DEATH, OH MY FAIR ONE, WILL NEVER COME NEAR		717	LOVE SONG	8
THEN EACH WIFE AND MAID AND MOTHER CALLS BY NAME		719	PHANTOM SHIP	24
SOME DROWNED ONE.				
WHAT ROSEATE FINGERS! NO: NOR IS THERE ONE		720	WITCH VIVIEN	5
SOME GREAT ONE. NO: I HEAR THE WAVERING STEPS		720	WITCH VIVIEN	12
I DREAMT SOME GREAT ONE. AH, MY BEAUTIFUL		720	WITCH VIVIEN	14
LEAD THEY ONE WITH FOOLISH CARE,		727	LOVERS QUARREL	29
ONE WHOSE BREATHING SHAKES THE AIR,		727	LOVERS QUARREL	31
ONE WHOSE FOOTFALL SHAKES THE GROUND.		727	LOVERS QUARREL	32
AND COME KNEELING ON ONE KNEE,		727	LOVERS QUARREL	53
"THEY ARE LOST, THEY ARE LOST, EACH ONE," CRIED HE.		730	PRIEST FAIRY	58
AND LOOKED ON NO ONE THERE		741	EARL PAUL	34
WISDOM AND DREAMS ARE ONE,		743	WISDOM DREAMS	5
YET ONE JOY HAVE I, HID CLOSE,		744	ROSY CROSS	8
AND GAZE ON ONE ANOTHER THROUGH OUR EYES,		749	SHADOW WATER A	58
WHEN ONE HAS LEAPT ON BOARD. NO, FOR I HAVE HOPE		751	SHADOW WATER A	106
THE TIDE NARROWS BETWEEN, AND ONE OLD MAN		752	SHADOW WATER A	118
A BOY AND GIRL HOLD ONE ANOTHER'S HANDS:		752	SHADOW WATER A	122
TWO HOVER THERE TOGETHER, AND ONE SAYS,		753	SHADOW WATER A	142
AND THEN ONE ASKS ANOTHER HOW HE DIED,		753	SHADOW WATER A	146
BECAUSE THESE WATERS MAKE ALL WOMEN ONE.		757	SHADOW WATER A	194
WITH ONE YOU HAVE KILLED AND DIE: FOR WHEN I LEFT		758	SHADOW WATER A	226
IN ONE ANOTHER'S ARMS. AENGUS HAS SEEN		763	SHADOW WATER A	321
AND WHEN ONE CHANGED HER TO A SILVER FLY,		763	SHADOW WATER A V	305
ONE LIVES UNDER THE WAVES,		770	SPINNING SONG	2
AND ONE WHERE THE WINDS ARE WOVE,		771	SPINNING SONG	3
AND ONE IN THE OLD GRAY HOUSE		771	SPINNING SONG	4
ONE LIVES IN THE HOUSE OF THE SUN,		771	SPINNING SONG	6
AND ONE IN THE HOUSE OF THE MOON,		771	SPINNING SONG	7
AND ONE LIVES UNDER THE BOUGHS		771	SPINNING SONG	8
AND ONE SPINNER IS LOST.		771	SPINNING SONG	10
THAT HAVE ONE ANOTHER'S EYES?		773	SONG DEIRDRE 1	24
IN THE LAND THAT NO ONE KNOWS.		774	COME RIDE	17
I WAS GOING THE ROAD ONE DAY		779	GOING THE ROAD	1
SOME ONE SHOULD STAY AT HER SIDE.		786	YOUR HEART	V 28
ONE-ARMED				
A ONE-LEGGED, ONE-ARMED, ONE-EYED MAN		302	HOUR DAWN	V 1
ONE-EYED				
A ONE-LEGGED, ONE-ARMED, ONE-EYED MAN		302	HOUR DAWN	V 1

```
                                                      PAGE    TITLE            LINE
O'NEILLS
    MOCK AT THE MEMORY OF BOTH O'NEILLS, . . . . . . .  546 TO SAME TUNE 2       24
    MOCK AT THE MEMORY OF BOTH O'NEILLS, . . . . . . .  614 MARCH SONGS 1        24
ONE-LEGGED
    A ONE-LEGGED, ONE-ARMED, ONE-EYED MAN  . . . . . .  302 HOUR DAWN        V    1
ONE'S
    I HAD A THOUGHT FOR NO ONE'S BUT YOUR EARS: . . . .  206 ADAMS CURSE          34
    STRANGE CREATURES FLUTTER UP BEFORE ONE'S EYES, . .  222 SHADOW WATER B       18
    OR CRY ABOUT ONE'S EARS. NOTHING TO FEAR. . . . .    222 SHADOW WATER B       19
    HOW GREAT A WRONG IT IS TO LET ONE'S THOUGHT . . .   246 SHADOW WATER B      514
    ONE'S HAD HER FILL OF LOVERS, ANOTHER'S HAD BUT ONE, . 354 HIS PHOENIX        19
    AT THE PERFECTION OF ONE'S OWN OBEDIENCE: . . . .    376 PHASES OF MOON      109
    I, TOO, WILL FOLLOW FOR THIS EVIL-STARRED ONE'S SAKE . 655 ISLE STAT I 2      84
ONES
    "WHO ARE THE RIDING ONES?" I SAID. . . . . . . . .   12 OISIN 1          V  146
    WATCHING THE BLESSED ONES MOVE FAR OFF, AND THE SMILE ON 61 OISIN 3          199
        GOD'S FACE,
    . . . OF BEST ONES A SAD THING WERE-- . . . . . .    63 OISIN 3          V  222
    WHO OF THE WANDERING MANY-CHANGING ONES . . . . . .  182 QUEEN MAEVE          51
    SHE TOLD THEM OF THE MANY-CHANGING ONES: . . . . .   185 QUEEN MAEVE         112
    SEVEN OLD SISTERS WIND THE THREADS OF THE LONG-LIVED ONES, 209 UNDER THE MOON   7
    SEVEN OLD SISTERS WIND THE THREADS OF THE LONG LIVED ONES, 209 UNDER THE MOON V 7
    POURED OUT WINE FOR THE HIGH INVISIBLE ONES. . . .   219 WOODS OF COOLE       44
    WITHHOLDS THEM NOW? HAVE THE EVER-LIVING ONES . . .  234 SHADOW WATER B      269
    THAT THE SHAPE-CHANGERS, THE EVER-LAUGHING ONES, . . 249 SHADOW WATER B      566
    IN THEIR STIFF, PAINTED CLOTHES, THE PALE UNSATISFIED ONES 318 MAGI             2
    AH! CRUEL ONES, LEAVE ME ALONE NOW . . . . . . . .   707 FAIRY PEDANT         13
    AH! CRUEL ONES, LEAVE ME ALONE . . . . . . . . . .   707 FAIRY PEDANT     V   13
    O SHINING ONES, LIGHTLY WITH SONG PASS, . . . . .    708 FAIRY PEDANT         21
    AND THEN THE GREAT ONES COME, AND LAST THE KING. . . 722 WITCH VIVIEN         54
    YONDER FOOLISH ONES WILL TIRE . . . . . . . . . .    727 LOVERS QUARREL       47
    IF THESE MERRY ONES SHOULD KNOW, . . . . . . . . .   731 STREET DANCERS        9
    IF THESE MERRY ONES SHOULD KNOW, . . . . . . . . .   732 STREET DANCERS       22
    IF THESE MERRY ONES SHOULD KNOW, . . . . . . . . .   732 STREET DANCERS       35
    IF THESE MERRY ONES SHOULD KNOW, . . . . . . . . .   733 STREET DANCERS       48
    IF THESE MERRY ONES SHOULD KNOW, . . . . . . . . .   733 STREET DANCERS       61
ONION
    WHAT TH' ONION SELLERS THOUGHT OR DID . . . . . . .  287 TO WEALTHY MAN V     11
ONION-SELLERS
    WHAT TH' ONION-SELLERS THOUGHT OR DID . . . . . . .  287 TO WEALTHY MAN       11
ONLIE
    HUGH LANE, "ONLIE BEGETTER" OF ALL THESE: . . . . .  602 GALLERY REVIS        22
ONLY
    "YOU ONLY WILL I WED," I CRIED, . . . . . . . . .     7 OISIN 1              74
    BUT ONLY KIND AND MERRY BREATH, . . . . . . . . .    19 OISIN 1             285
    WE ONLY KNOW THAT WE WERE GLAD . . . . . . . . . .   22 OISIN 1          V 340D
    SAVE ONLY MANY TIMES MY NAME, . . . . . . . . . .    25 OISIN 1             375
    BUT ONLY EXULTANT FACES. NIAMH STOOD . . . . . . .   38 OISIN 2             136
    BUT, THE BIRD IN MY FINGERS, I MOUNTED, MINDFUL ONLY TO 54 OISIN 3         V  111
        LAUNCH
    I CRIED, "O NIAMH! O WHITE ONE! IF ONLY A TWELVE-HOURED 55 OISIN 3           113
        DAY,
    BUT WEEP FOR YOUR NIAMH, O OISIN, WEEP: FOR IF ONLY YOUR 55 OISIN 3          127
        SHOE
    BUT WEEP FOR THY NIAM, OH OISIN, WEEP: FOR IF ONLY THY SHOE 55 OISIN 3      V  127
    "IN THE ISLES OF THE FARTHEST SEAS WHERE ONLY THE SPIRITS 56 OISIN 3         133
        COME.
    ONLY A SUDDEN FLAMING WORD, . . . . . . . . . . .    65 HAPPY SHEPHERD       19
    LEST ALL THY TOILING ONLY BREEDS . . . . . . . . .   66 HAPPY SHEPHERD       25
    ALL LOVED HIM, ONLY THE SHONEEN, . . . . . . . . .   92 FATHER OHART         13
    ONE BLIND HOUND ONLY LIES APART . . . . . . . . .    99 FOXHUNTER            41
    "I ONLY ASK WHAT WAY MY JOURNEY LIES, . . . . . .    108 CUCHULAIN SEA        31
    CUCHULAIN CRIED, "I AM THE ONLY MAN . . . . . . .    109 CUCHULAIN SEA        55
    "I ONLY OF THE RED BRANCH HOSTED NOW," . . . . . .   109 CUCHULAIN SEA    V   55
    "GOD ONLY SEES WHAT DOOM FOR ME LIES STORED." . . .  110 CUCHULAIN SEA    V   62
    WERE WE ONLY WHITE BIRDS, MY BELOVED, . . . . . .    122 WHITE BIRDS          12
    OR ONLY GAZE A LITTLE WHILE: . . . . . . . . . . .   135 TWO TREES            24
    WHERE ONLY BODY'S LAID ASLEEP. . . . . . . . . . .   138 TO IRELAND           22
    OR ONLY TO THE WATER IN THE WEST: . . . . . . . .    155 REPROVE CURLEW        2
    OR ONLY TO WATERS IN THE WEST: . . . . . . . . . .   155 REPROVE CURLEW V      2
    OR ONLY TO THE WATERS IN THE WEST: . . . . . . . .   155 REPROVE CURLEW V      2
    THAT ONLY GOD'S EYES DID NOT CLOSE: . . . . . . .    156 FORGOT BEAUTY        14
    THAT ONLY THE GODS' EYES DID NOT CLOSE: . . . . . .  156 FORGOT BEAUTY    V   14
    BUT I, BEING POOR, HAVE ONLY MY DREAMS: . . . . . .  176 CLOTHS HEAVEN         6
    I ONLY KNOW THAT ALL WE KNOW COMES FROM YOU, . . .   218 WOODS OF COOLE       28
    FOR THEY'RE MY ONLY PILOTS. IF I LOST THEM . . . .   226 SHADOW WATER B       85
    THE ONLY RICHES THAT HAVE HIT MY FANCY. . . . . .    226 SHADOW WATER B       96
    "ONLY THE WASTEFUL VIRTUES EARN THE SUN": . . . . .  270 PARDON FATHERS       18
    THAT ONLY GODS MAY BUY OF HIM. . . . . . . . . . .   272 GREY ROCK            25
    IN HIS FULL HANDS WHAT, HAD THEY ONLY KNOWN, . . .   292 TO A SHADE           11
    FOR ONLY RUBBISH COMES MY WAY. . . . . . . . . .     295 THREE BEGGARS         4
    "WHY, BEER IS ONLY BEER." "BUT SAY . . . . . . .     305 HOUR DAWN            56
    BY THE WOOD'S EDGE WHERE ONLY EQUALS MEET, . . . .   321 REED WHISPERER V      8
    NO MOON: ONLY AN ACHING HEART . . . . . . . . . .    421 MY TABLE             13
    THAT ONLY GOD HAS LOVED US FOR OURSELVES, . . . . .  448 HERO GIRL FOOL       16
    OR BRIGHTEN ONLY FOR SOME YOUNGER EYE, . . . . . .   464 HARUN RASHID         82
    DREAM THAT I LOVE HER ONLY FOR THE VOICE, . . . . .  469 HARUN RASHID        171
    DREAM THAT I LOVE HER ONLY FOR THAT VOICE, . . . . . 469 HARUN RASHID     V  171
    ONLY THE DEAD CAN BE FORGIVEN: . . . . . . . . . .   478 SELF AND SOUL        39
    THAT ONLY GOD, MY DEAR, . . . . . . . . . . . . .    492 ANNE GREGORY         16
    MAINLY BECAUSE OF WHAT WE ONLY KNOW . . . . . . .    634 CUCHULAIN COMF       14
```

		PAGE	TITLE		LINE

ONLY (CONTINUED)
WITH ONLY BED AND BEDSTEAD THERE, ... 639 BEN BULBEN 61
WE MUST GET SWORDS. IS'T THE ONLY WAY? OH, SEE, . . . 660 ISLE STAT II 1 34
AND ONLY SHEEP HE LOVED OF ALL THE TROOP. . . . . . 661 ISLE STAT II 1 61
WHO SEEK MAY FIND, SAVE ONLY ONE, ... 668 ISLE STAT II 3 48
TILL THOU REMEMBEREST ONLY HOW THE SEA . . . . 670 ISLE STAT II 3 94
SHE WAS MY ONLY FRIEND: I'M LAME, YOU KNOW-- . . . . . 695 MOSADA 1 115
TWO ONLY NOW THEY ARE, TWO SIDE BY SIDE. . . . . . . 700 MOSADA 3 49
HALF HID. HE BRINGS THE PEASANT'S ONLY KIN, ... 711 FERENCZ RENYI 50
HOW "THE ONLY GOOD IS MUSING MILD, ... 728 PRIEST FAIRY 13
AND THAT DREAM ONLY SHINE BEFORE HER FEET. . . . . . 761 SHADOW WATER A 258
ONSET
CRY AT THE ONSET OF THEIR SEXUAL JOY . . . . 560 WHENCE COME 2
CRY AT THE ONSET OF THE SEXUAL JOY . . . . 560 WHENCE COME V 2
ONWARD
THEN ONWARD IN THE WINDING THICKET . . . . 20 OISIN 1 V 304
MOURN--AND THEN ONWARD! . . . . 737 MOURN THEN ON T
MOURN--AND THEN ONWARD, THERE IS NO RETURNING . . . . 738 MOURN THEN ON 13
ONYX
ALL WISDOM SHUT INTO HIS ONYX EYES, ... 311 MOUNTAIN TOMB 11
ALL WISDOM SHUT INTO ITS ONYX EYES. . . . . 311 MOUNTAIN TOMB V 11
OOZY   SEE FOAM-OOZY
WHERE CYPRESS IS AND OOZY PINE, ... 670 ISLE STAT II 3 110
OPAL
OF OPAL AND RUBY AND PALE CHRYSOLITE . . . . 219 HARP OF AENGUS 6
OF OPAL AND RUBY AND PALE CHRYSOLITE . . . . 762 SHADOW WATER A 301
OPEN   SEE WIDE-OPEN
HALF OPEN HIS EYES WERE, AND HELD ME, . . . 51 OISIN 3 65
WITH STILL AND STONY LIMBS AND OPEN EYES. . . . . . . 182 QUEEN MAEVE 46
YOUR OPEN HAND BUT SHOWS OUR LOSS, ... 288 TO WEALTHY MAN 29
HELL MOUTH LAY OPEN NEAR THAT PLACE, ... 303 HOUR DAWN 25
A LAMP BURNS ON BESIDE THE OPEN BOOK . . . . 367 EGO DOMINUS 3
A LAMP BURNS ON ABOVE THE OPEN BOOK . . . . 367 EGO DOMINUS V 3
BURNING ALONE BESIDE AN OPEN BOOK, ... 370 EGO DOMINUS 63
UPON THE OPEN ROAD, NEAR TO THE SLIGO QUAY-- . . . . 391 UNDER SATURN 12
A GREY STONE FIREPLACE WITH AN OPEN HEARTH, ... 419 MY HOUSE 12
A GREY STONE FIRE-PLACE WITH AN OPEN HEARTH, ... 419 MY HOUSE V 12
GREAT WINDOWS OPEN TO THE SOUTH, ... 475 EVA GORE-BOOTH 2
AN OPEN BOOK AND EMPTY CUP . . . . 501 VACILLATION 38
AND HERE IS TULLY'S OPEN PAGE. . . . . 524 MAD AS MIST 9
WITH OPEN BOOK YOU ASK ME WHAT I DO. . . . . 554 RIBH AT TOMB 2
MADE AQUILINE, ARE OPEN TO THAT LIGHT. . . . . 555 RIBH AT TOMB 24
ITS OPEN LIGHTED DOORWAY AND ITS WINDOWS ALL ALIGHT, . . 581 CURSE CROMWELL 26
THEIR WOUNDS OPEN AGAIN. . . . . 612 NEWS ORACLE 16
BLOSSOMS OPEN DEWY LIPS! . . . . 647 ISLE STAT I 1 65
THEN HE SHOUTED, "OPEN WIDE . . . . 697 MOSADA 2 24
AND HE SHOUTED OPEN WIDE . . . . 697 MOSADA 2 V 24
THE STRANGER SHOUTED, "OPEN WIDE . . . . 697 MOSADA 2 V 24
THE BISHOP CAME WITH OPEN BOOK, ... 725 LEGEND 17
WITH OPEN MOUTH AND BEATING HEART. . . . . 729 PRIEST FAIRY 32
ARE SHOT AT ON THE OPEN PLAIN. . . . . 791 REPRISALS 18
OPENED
THE BIRDS, FOR HE OPENED THEIR CAGES . . . . 92 FATHER OHART 17
THE SICK MAN'S WIFE OPENED THE DOOR: . . . . 133 FR GILLIGAN 31
SHE OPENED HER DOOR AND HER WINDOW, ... 160 CAP AND BELLS 29
THAT HEAVENS HAD OPENED. GYRES RUN ON: . . . . . . 639 BEN BULBEN 62
OPEN-EYED
PROUD, OPEN-EYED AND LAUGHING TO THE TOMB. . . . . . 501 VACILLATION 34
OPEN-HANDEDNESS
AND FOR HIS OPEN-HANDEDNESS, DISGRACE: . . . . . . 292 TO A SHADE 16
OPENIN'
WHEN, OPENIN' WIDE HIS DOOR, ... 96 MOLL MAGEE 50
OPENS
THAT OPENS HER MYSTERY AND FRIGHT. . . . . 624 APPARITIONS 22
OPHELIA
THAT'S OPHELIA, THAT CORDELIA: . . . . 565 LAPIS LAZULI 11
OPINION
OPINION IS NOT WORTH A RUSH: . . . . 385 ROBARTES DANCE 1
PUBLIC OPINION RIPENING FOR SO LONG . . . . 428 NINETEEN 19 13
I CAN EXCHANGE OPINION WITH ANY NEIGHBOURING MIND, . . 450 OWEN AHERNE 9
OPINIONATED
BECAUSE OF HER OPINIONATED MIND . . . . 405 FOR DAUGHTER 61
OPINIONS
SO LET HER THINK OPINIONS ARE ACCURSED. . . . . . . 405 FOR DAUGHTER 58
OPOPONAX
NO: BUT OPOPONAX AND CINNAMON. . . . . 232 SHADOW WATER B 222
OPPOSITE
I CALL TO MY OWN OPPOSITE, SUMMON ALL . . . . . . 367 EGO DOMINUS 8
I THINK HE FASHIONED FROM HIS OPPOSITE . . . . . . 368 EGO DOMINUS 27
MOCKED ME WITH PRAISE OF MY MERE OPPOSITE: . . . . . 448 HERO GIRL FOOL 4
MOCK ME WITH PRAISE OF MY MERE OPPOSITE: . . . . . . 448 HERO GIRL FOOL V 4
BUT I BEING NONE CAN PRAISE ITS OPPOSITE. . . . . . 465 HARUN RASHID 98
OPPOSITION
BY OPPOSITION, SQUARE AND TRINE: . . . . 325 ROBERT GREGORY 39
OPPRESSED
BEING BY THE WORLD OPPRESSED, ... 434 YOUTH AND AGE 2
OPTIC
WHO FOLLOW WITH THE OPTIC GLASS . . . . 66 HAPPY SHEPHERD 29
ORACLE
THE DELPHIC ORACLE UPON PLOTINUS . . . . 530 DELPHIC ORACLE T
NEWS FOR THE DELPHIC ORACLE . . . . 611 NEWS ORACLE T

585

PAGE   TITLE   LINE

O'RAHILLY
    THE O'RAHILLY . . . . 584 ORAHILLY   T
    SING OF THE O'RAHILLY, ... 584 ORAHILLY   1
    SING OF THE O'RAHILLY . . . . 585 ORAHILLY   10
    "HERE DIED THE O'RAHILLY. . . . . 585 ORAHILLY   34
ORB
    THE ORB OF THE MOST INNER LIVING HEART . . . . . . 689 NETTLESHIP   15
ORBIT
    WHEREVER THE ORBIT OF THE MOON CAN REACH, ... 472 ALL SOUL NIGHT 55
ORCHARD-CIRCLED
    TO THE ORCHARD-CIRCLED FARM; . . . . 727 LOVERS QUARREL 50
ORCHARDS
    FROM THE HOLY ORCHARDS, WHERE THERE IS NONE . . . . 196 BAILE AILLINN 174
ORCHIL
    ORCHIL SHAKES OUT HER LONG DARK HAIR . . . . . . 85 MAD KING GOLL   62
ORDER
    SHOOT ON HIM SHAFTS OF QUIETNESS, AND ORDER HIM TO KEEP 75 ANASHU VIJAYA V 81
    . . . HAVE JOINED THE ANCIENT ORDER OF HIBERNIANS AND THE 262 STUDENTS AGIT V T
    WHEN ORDER HAS WEAKENED OR FACTION IS STRONG, ... 548 TO SAME TUNE 3 12
ORIGINAL
    WHAT THEME HAD HOMER BUT ORIGINAL SIN? . . . . . . 502 VACILLATION   77
ORION
    TOLD HIM, THAT WHEN ORION ROSE, AND ALL . . . . . 282 TWO KINGS V 132A
ORMOLU
    AUGUSTA GREGORY SEATED AT HER GREAT ORMOLU TABLE, . . . 577 LOFTY THINGS   7
ORMONDES
    WELCOME, AND THE ORMONDES ALL . . . . 400 DEMON BEAST   11
ORNAMENTAL
    AMID THE ORNAMENTAL BRONZE AND STONE . . . . 428 NINETEEN 19   5
ORO
    ORO, ORO! . . . . 551 SONGS REWRIT 1 5
    ORO, ORO! . . . . 551 SONGS REWRIT 1 5
    ORO, ORO! . . . . 551 SONGS REWRIT 1 11
    ORO, ORO! . . . . 551 SONGS REWRIT 1 11
    ORO, ORO! . . . . 551 SONGS REWRIT 1 17
    ORO, ORO! . . . . 551 SONGS REWRIT 1 17
O'ROUGHLEY
    TOM O'ROUGHLEY . . . . 337 TOM OROUGHLEY   T
    OR SO DID TOM O'ROUGHLEY SAY . . . . 338 TOM OROUGHLEY   5
OSAFUME
    MONTASHIGI OF OSAFUME FASHIONED IT . . . . 478 SELF AND SOUL V 25
OSCAR
    FIN, CONAN, OSCAR, MANY MORE, THE TIDE . . . . . . 44 OISIN 2 V 228A
    NO OSCAR RULED THE TABLE, ... 626 STATES HOLIDAY 5
OSCAR'S
    WE THOUGHT ON OSCAR'S PENCILLED URN. . . . . . . 2 OISIN 1 V 70
    "WE THINK ON OSCAR'S PENCILLED URN, ... 5 OISIN 1   41
OSIER
    . . . THE SHIELD OUT OF OSIER AND HIDE; . . . . . 52 OISIN 3   82
OSPREY
    NOR SORROW WITH HER OSPREY CLAW. . . . . 19 OISIN 1 V 285
    OR THE GREY WANDERING OSPREY SORROW." . . . . . . 20 OISIN 1   303
    OR THE WILD GREY OSPREY SORROW," . . . . 20 OISIN 1 V 303
    NOR THE GREY WANDERING OSPREY SORROW." . . . . . . 21 OISIN 1   319
    OR THE WILD GREY OSPREY SORROW." . . . . 21 OISIN 1 V 319
    NOR THE GREY WANDERING OSPREY SORROW." . . . . . . 23 OISIN 1   342
    OR FEAR THE WILD GREY OSPREY SORROW." . . . . . . 23 OISIN 1 V 342
    THE OSPREY OF SORROW GOES AFTER AND CLUTCHES, ... 27 OISIN 1 V 415D
O'SULLIVAN
    WINDLE-STRAWS I. O'SULLIVAN RUA TO THE CURLEW . . . 155 REPROVE CURLEW T
    O'SULLIVAN RUA TO MARY LAVELL . . . . 155 FORGOT BEAUTY V T
    O'SULLIVAN THE RED TO MARY LAVELL. . . . . 157 POET BELOVED V T
    TWO POEMS BY O'SULLIVAN THE RED CONCERNING MARY LAVELL. . 157 POET BELOVED V T
    O'SULLIVAN RUA TO THE SECRET ROSE . . . . 169 SECRET ROSE V T
    O'SULLIVAN THE RED UPON HIS WANDERINGS . . . . . . 171 MAID QUIET V T
OTHERWISE
    NO MAN NOR WOMAN HAS LOVED OTHERWISE . . . . . . 750 SHADOW WATER A 64
    NO MAN OR WOMAN HAS LOVED OTHERWISE . . . . 750 SHADOW WATER A V 64
OTTER
    I SAT ON CUSHIONED OTTER SKIN; . . . . 81 MAD KING GOLL V 1
    CHAIRED IN THE CUSHIONED OTTER SKIN, ... 82 MAD KING GOLL V 5
    AND NIAMH AND LABAN AND FAND, WHO COULD CHANGE TO AN OTTER 209 UNDER THE MOON 12
    OR FAWN,
    AND FAND, AND NIAM, AND LABAN, WHO COULD CHANGE TO AN OTTER 209 UNDER THE MOON V 12
    OR FAWN,
    SPLASHED, OR AN OTTER SLID INTO THE STREAM. . . . . 372 PHASES OF MOON 9
OTTERS
    WE LAY ON SKINS OF OTTERS, AND DRANK WINE, ... 41 OISIN 2 188
    AND THEN ON HEAPED-UP SKINS OF OTTERS SLEPT. . . . . 41 OISIN 2 191
    OTTERS BELOW AND MOOR-HENS ON THE TOP, ... 490 COOLE BALLYLEE 2
    OTTERS BELOW AND MOOR HENS ON THE TOP, ... 490 COOLE BALLYLEE V 2
    THE OTTERS DREAMING LAY. AYE! . . . . 677 ISLE STAT II 3 280
    THE OTTERS DREAMING LAY. NASCHINA! AY! . . . . . 677 ISLE STAT II 3 V 280
OTTER-SKIN
    I SAT ON CUSHIONED OTTER-SKIN! . . . . 81 MAD KING GOLL   1
    CHAIRED IN A CUSHIONED OTTER-SKIN . . . . 82 MAD KING GOLL V 5
OUGHT
    IS FROM THE OUGHT, OR KNOWER FROM THE KNOWN-- . . . . 478 SELF AND SOUL 37
OUNCE
    IT CANNOT GROW BY AN INCH OR AN OUNCE. . . . . . . 566 LAPIS LAZULI   24

	PAGE	TITLE		LINE

OUSEL
AND THE SALMON BEHOLD, AND THE OUSEL TOO, ... 717 LOVE SONG 3

OUT
BUT WE RODE OUT FROM THE HUMAN LANDS. . . . . 10 OISIN 1 114
ROSE EVER OUT OF THE WARM SEA; . . . . 13 OISIN 1 172
OUT OF A LITTLE SILVER TRUMP; . . . . 15 OISIN 1 196
AND FROM THE WOODS RUSHED OUT A BAND . . . . 15 OISIN 1 201
THEIR CLOAKS MADE OUT OF YELLOW SILK, ... 15 OISIN 1 205
THEIR BRATTAS MADE OUT OF YELLOW SILK, ... 15 OISIN 1 V 205
AND ONE A SCEPTRE FLASHING OUT . . . . 17 OISIN 1 251
OUT OF THE MOON'S PALE TWISTED SHELL; . . . . . . 19 OISIN 1 279
AND SWEPT OUT OF THE WATTLED HALL . . . . 20 OISIN 1 292
I DREW OUT OF THE NUMBERLESS . . . . 24 OISIN 1 V 365
AND WRAPPED IN DREAMS RODE OUT AGAIN . . . . . . 25 OISIN 1 382
"MY BROTHERS SPRING OUT OF THEIR BEDS AT MORN, ... 32 OISIN 2 51
AND FACE THAT SEEMED WROUGHT OUT OF MOONLIT VAPOURS, . . 33 OISIN 2 70
PASSED UNDER THE DIM DOORWAY, OUT OF SIGHT, ... 37 OISIN 2 123
PASSED UNDER A DIM DOORWAY, OUT OF SIGHT, ... 37 OISIN 2 V 123
OUT OF THE SEVENFOLD SEAS, BUILT THE DARK HALL . . . . 38 OISIN 2 131
A DOME MADE OUT OF ENDLESS CARVEN JAGS, ... 38 OISIN 2 144
OUT OF THE SEVEN-FOLD SEAS, BUILT THE DARK HALL . . . 38 OISIN 2 V 131
AND HEALED MY WOUNDS WITH UNGUENTS OUT OF FLOWERS . . . 41 OISIN 2 185
ROLLING HIS FLAGRANT WHEEL OUT OF THE DEEP, ... 42 OISIN 2 193
THEIR NAKED AND GLEAMING BODIES POURED OUT AND HEAPED IN 48 OISIN 3 28
    THE WAY.
WATCHED ME WITH MOURNFUL WONDER OUT OF THE WELLS OF HIS 51 OISIN 3 60
    EYES.
I CRIED, "COME OUT OF THE SHADOW, KING OF THE NAILS OF 51 OISIN 3 61
    GOLD!
HIS LIPS MOVED SLOWLY IN ANSWER, NO ANSWER OUT OF THEM 51 OISIN 3 66
    CAME!
I CRIED, "COME OUT OF THE SHADOW, CANN OF THE NAILS OF 51 OISIN 3 V 61
    GOLD!
THAT THE SPEAR-SHAFT IS MADE OUT OF ASHWOOD, ... 52 OISIN 3 82
. . . THE SHIELD OUT OF OSIER AND HIDE! . . . . . . 52 OISIN 3 82
THAT THE SPEARSHAFT IS MADE OUT OF ASHWOOD, ... 52 OISIN 3 V 82
I AWOKE! THE STRANGE HORSE WITHOUT SUMMONS OUT OF 54 OISIN 3 105
    THE DISTANCE RAN,
LONG FLED THE FOAM-FLAKES AROUND ME, THE WINDS FLED OUT 57 OISIN 3 149
    OF THE VAST,
COMING OUT OF THE SEA AS THE DAWN COMES, A CHAUNT OF LOVE 58 OISIN 3 158
    ON MY LIPS,
AND I RODE AND I RODE, AND I CRIED OUT, ... 59 OISIN 3 171
AND THE DREAMS OF THE ISLANDS WENT OUT OF ME, ... 59 OISIN 3 V 175
WE WILL TEAR OUT THE FLAMING STONES, AND BATTER THE GATEWAY 62 OISIN 3 209
    OF BRASS
WE WILL TEAR OUT THE RED FLAMING STONES, ... 62 OISIN 3 V 209
WE WILL TEAR THE RED FLAMING STONES OUT, ... 62 OISIN 3 V 209
BUT KNEEL AND WEAR OUT THE FLAGS AND PRAY FOR YOUR SOUL 63 OISIN 3 215
    THAT IS LOST
AS A HAY-COCK OUT ON THE FLOOD, OR A WOLF SUCKED UNDER 63 OISIN 3 220
    A WEIR.
BUT WEEP YOU AND KNEEL! WEAR OUT THE FLAGS! . . . . . 63 OISIN 3 V 215
KNEEL, USHEEN, WEAR OUT THE FLAGS AND PRAY FOR YOUR SOUL 63 OISIN 3 V 215
    THAT IS LOST
CRIED OUT, DIM SEA, HEAR MY MOST PITEOUS STORY! . . . . 68 SAD SHEPHERD 9
THEY PINE AWAY AND YELLOW AND WEAR OUT, ... 81 EPHEMERA V 24H
ORCHIL SHAKES OUT HER LONG DARK HAIR . . . . . . 85 MAD KING GOLL 62
LEANING SOFTLY OUT . . . . 88 STOLEN CHILD 35
IN PENAL DAYS RODE OUT . . . . 91 FATHER OHART 2
HE DROVE ME OUT AND SHUT THE DOOR, ... 95 MOLL MAGEE 25
AND STRETCHING OUT HER ARMS, RED WITH THE DYE, . . . 105 CUCHULAIN SEA V 7
MY FATHER STANDS." "AGED, WORN OUT WITH WARS . . . 107 CUCHULAIN SEA 29
AND CRIED OUT TO HIM, "SON IT IS NOT MEET . . . . 107 CUCHULAIN SEA V 20
AND CALLED OUT TO HIM, "SON IT IS NOT MEET . . . . 107 CUCHULAIN SEA V 20
SEEK OUT WHAT MAN HE IS." ONE WENT AND CAME. . . . . 109 CUCHULAIN SEA 51
HE WOULD GO WEAVE OUT OF THE STARS . . . . 113 ROSE OF PEACE 7
"TURN IF YE MAY," I CALL OUT TO EACH ONE, ... 114 ROSE OF BATTLE V 7
HAD BLOTTED OUT MAN'S IMAGE AND HIS CRY. . . . . . 120 SORROW OF LOVE 4
. . . BUOYED OUT ON THE FOAM OF THE SEA! . . . . . 122 WHITE BIRDS 12
A CROSS THEY HAD MADE OUT OF TWO BITS OF WOOD, ... 123 DREAM OF DEATH 7
THE SINGING SHOOK HIM OUT OF HIS NEW EASE. . . . . . 126 DREAM OF FAERY 12
OF HOW GOD LEANS HIS HANDS OUT OF THE SKY, ... 128 DREAM OF FAERY V 43
THAT GOD HAD LEANED HIS HANDS OUT OF THE SKY, ... 128 DREAM OF FAERY V 43
THAT GOD HAD LEANT HIS HANDS OUT OF THE SKY, ... 128 DREAM OF FAERY V 43
HE ROUSED HIS HORSE OUT OF ITS SLEEP, ... 133 FR GILLIGAN 27
WHILE I WROUGHT OUT THESE FITFUL DANAAN RHYMES, . . . 136 TO SOME I TALK 1
WHILE STILL I MAY I WRITE OUT TRUE . . . . . . 139 TO IRELAND V 33
LIKE A CANDLE BURNT OUT, ... 142 MOODS 2
ALL THINGS UNCOMELY AND BROKEN, ALL THINGS WORN OUT AND 142 ROSE IN HEART 1
    OLD,
AND OUT OF HIS DREAM AWOKE! . . . . 145 HOST OF AIR 38
ABOUT THE CASTING OUT OF MY NET, ... 146 FISH 4
AND HOW YOU HAVE LEAPED TIMES OUT OF MIND . . . . . 146 FISH 5
AND RIVER AND STREAM WORK OUT THEIR WILL. . . . . . 148 INTO TWILIGHT 12
AND LAUGH OUT THEIR WHIMSEY AND WORK OUT THEIR WILL. . . 148 INTO TWILIGHT V 12
AND LAUGH OUT THEIR WHIMSEY AND WORK OUT THEIR WILL. . . 148 INTO TWILIGHT V 12
LAUGH OUT THEIR WHIMSEY AND WORK OUT THEIR WILL. . . . 148 INTO TWILIGHT V 12
LAUGH OUT THEIR WHIMSEY AND WORK OUT THEIR WILL. . . . 148 INTO TWILIGHT V 12
AND THE CHANGING MOON WORK OUT THEIR WILL. . . . . . 148 INTO TWILIGHT V 12
I WENT OUT TO THE HAZEL WOOD, ... 149 WANDER AENGUS 1
AND MOTH-LIKE STARS WERE FLICKERING OUT, ... 149 WANDER AENGUS 6

587

OUT   (CONTINUED)

AND STARS LIKE MOTHS WERE SHINING OUT, ... 149 WANDER AENGUS   V   6
I WILL FIND OUT WHERE SHE HAS GONE, ... 150 WANDER AENGUS   19
I WILL FIND OUT WHERE SHE IS GONE . . . . 150 WANDER AENGUS   V 19
HE BADE ME OUT INTO THE GLOOM, ... 151 HEART OF WOMAN   3
AND HAD ROOTED THE SUN AND MOON AND STARS OUT OF THE SKY 153 CHANGE BELOVED   11
AND ROOTED THE SUN AND MOON AND STARS OUT OF THE SKY, . 153 CHANGE BELOVED V 11
THAT WAS SHAKEN OUT OVER MY BREAST! . . . . 155 REPROVE CURLEW   5
IT WORKED AT THEM, DAY OUT, DAY IN, ... 158 BELOVED RHYMES   4
OUT OF THE BATTLES OF OLD TIMES. . . . . 158 BELOVED RHYMES   6
OUT OF THE OLD DAYS . . . . 158 TO HIS HEART   V   T
REMEMBER THE WISDOM OUT OF THE OLD DAYS! . . . . . . 158 TO HIS HEART   2
WHEN THE OWLS CALLED OUT NO MORE! . . . . 159 CAP AND BELLS   14
WHEN THE BATS CRIED OUT NO MORE! . . . . 159 CAP AND BELLS   V 14
TILL STARS GREW OUT OF THE AIR. . . . . 160 CAP AND BELLS   28
AND WAVED IT OUT ON THE AIR. . . . . 160 CAP AND BELLS   V 20
THE STARS GREW OUT OF THE AIR. . . . . 160 CAP AND BELLS   V 28
AND I DREAMED MY LOST LOVE CAME STEALTHILY OUT OF THE WOOD 163 VALLEY LOVERS   3
I MADE IT OUT OF A MOUTHFUL OF AIR. . . . . 166 EVIL OF BELOV   5
CUMHAL CALLED OUT, BENDING HIS HEAD, ... 166 BLESSED   1
"I CAN BRING YOU SALMON OUT OF THE STREAMS . . . . . 167 BLESSED   9
AND HERON OUT OF THE SKIES." . . . . 167 BLESSED   10
CUMHAL CALLED OUT, BOWING HIS HEAD, ... 167 BLESSED   V 4A
"THE ROSE THAT MUST DROP, OUT OF SWEET LEAVES, . . . 168 BLESSED   V 37
AND HIM WHO DROVE THE GODS OUT OF THEIR LISS, . . . 170 SECRET ROSE   16
LIKE THE SPARKS BLOWN OUT OF A SMITHY, AND DIE? . . 170 SECRET ROSE   30
UNFOLD YOUR FLAMING WINGS AND COVER OUT OF SIGHT . . 175 ELEMENT POWERS   11
OUT OF THEIR WHIRLING CARS, ... 175 ELEMENT POWERS V   16
AND LIGHTS WERE PALING OUT OF THE WEST, ... 175 BELOVED DEAD   2
AND LIGHT WERE PALING OUT OF THE WEST, ... 175 BELOVED DEAD   V   2
AMONG MY LEAVES IN TIMES OUT OF MIND! . . . . 177 PAST GREATNESS   5
KNOWING ONE, OUT OF ALL THINGS, ALONE, THAT HIS HEAD   177 PAST GREATNESS   8
SUDDENLY AILELL SPOKE OUT OF HIS SLEEP, ... 183 QUEEN MAEVE   73
"HOW MAY A MORTAL WHOSE LIFE GUTTERS OUT . . . . . . 184 QUEEN MAEVE   85
THE CHILDREN OF THE MAINES OUT OF SLEEP, ... 184 QUEEN MAEVE   92
CAME UP OUT OF THE HOLE, AND RED-EARED HOUNDS . . . 185 QUEEN MAEVE   117
WITH LONG WHITE BODIES CAME OUT OF THE AIR . . . . . 185 QUEEN MAEVE   118
TILL MAEVE CALLED OUT, "THESE ARE BUT COMMON MEN. . 186 QUEEN MAEVE   122
TILL IT DIED OUT WHERE AN OLD THORN-TREE STOOD. . . 186 QUEEN MAEVE   129
AND WHEN I'D WRITE IT OUT ANEW, THE WORDS, ... 186 QUEEN MAEVE   139
TILL IT DIED OUT WHERE AN OLD THORN TREE STOOD. . . 186 QUEEN MAEVE   V 129
UNTIL TWO LOVERS CAME OUT OF THE AIR . . . . 187 QUEEN MAEVE   143
WITH BODIES MADE OUT OF SOFT FIRE.   THE ONE, . . . 187 QUEEN MAEVE   144
BUT OUT OF THE DARK AIR OVER HER HEAD THERE CAME . . 187 QUEEN MAEVE   153
RODE OUT OF EMAIN WITH A BAND . . . . 189 BAILE AILLINN   18
THAT ALL THINGS FELL OUT HAPPILY, ... 189 BAILE AILLINN   22
HE HAD KNEES THAT STUCK OUT OF HIS HOSE! . . . . . . 190 BAILE AILLINN   27
BECAUSE A LOVER'S HEART'S WORN OUT, ... 191 BAILE AILLINN   65
THAT OUT OF SIGHT IS OUT OF MIND, ... 192 BAILE AILLINN   87
THAT OUT OF SIGHT IS OUT OF MIND. . . . . 192 BAILE AILLINN   87
"HE IS WELL OUT OF WIND AND WAVE, ... 193 BAILE AILLINN   V 114
FAR OUT UNDER A WINDLESS SKY! . . . . 197 BAILE AILLINN   181
LET RUSH AND BIRD CRY OUT THEIR FILL . . . . 197 BAILE AILLINN   198
MADE OUT OF A WILD THOUGHT, IS IN MY MARROW. . . . . 199 ARROW   2
I COULD WEEP THAT THE OLD IS OUT OF SEASON. . . . . 199 ARROW   8
THAT IT FADES OUT FROM KISS TO KISS! . . . . 202 NEVER GIVE ALL   5
AND THEIR SECRET SMILE, OUT OF THE DEPTHS OF THE LAKE! 203 WITHER BOUGHS   11
AND THEIR SECRET SMILE, OUT OF THE DEEPS OF THE LAKE. 203 WITHER BOUGHS   V 11
THERE'S MANY A ONE SHALL FIND OUT ALL HEARTACHE . . 205 ADAMS CURSE   16
PRECEDENTS OUT OF BEAUTIFUL OLD BOOKS! . . . . 205 ADAMS CURSE   26
UNDER THE BITTER BLACK WINDS BLOWING OUT OF THE LEFT HAND! 206 HANRAHANS SONG V 2
BUT WE HAVE HIDDEN IN OUR HEARTS THE FLAME OUT OF THE EYES 207 HANRAHANS SONG 4
FOR THE WET WINDS ARE BLOWING OUT OF THE CLINGING AIR! 207 HANRAHANS SONG   12
WHEN THE RAIN IS PELTING OUT OF THE WINTRY AIR! . . 207 HANRAHANS SONG V 12
FOR THE GREY WINDS ARE BLOWING UP, OUT OF THE CLINGING
  SEAS!   207 HANRAHANS SONG V 12
LAND-UNDER-WAVE, WHERE OUT OF THE MOON'S LIGHT AND THE
  SUN'S   209 UNDER THE MOON   6
A QUEEN-WOMAN DRESSED OUT IN SILVER, CRY . . . . . . 210 RAGGED WOOD   V   2
WHEN THE SUN LOOKED OUT OF HIS GOLDEN HOOD, ... 210 RAGGED WOOD   V   3
WHEN THE SUN LOOKED OUT OF HIS GOLDEN HOOD?-- . . . 211 RAGGED WOOD   7
I WILL DRIVE ALL THOSE LOVERS OUT AND CRY-- . . . . 211 RAGGED WOOD   10
I WILL DRIVE OUT THE DEER AND MOON AND CRY-- . . . . 211 RAGGED WOOD   V 10
I'LL HOLLO ALL THOSE LOVERS OUT AND CRY-- . . . . . 211 RAGGED WOOD   V 10
AND GREW TO BE OUT OF FASHION . . . . 211 O DO NOT LOVE   3
OR YOU WILL GROW OUT OF FASHION . . . . 212 O DO NOT LOVE   11
IS EDEN OUT OF TIME AND OUT OF SPACE? . . . . 218 WOODS OF COOLE   36
IS EDEN OUT OF TIME AND OUT OF SPACE? . . . . 218 WOODS OF COOLE   36
POURED OUT WINE FOR THE HIGH INVISIBLE ONES. . . . . 219 WOODS OF COOLE   44
EDAIN CAME OUT OF MIDHIR'S HILL, AND LAY . . . . . . 219 HARP OF AENGUS   1
SWEET WITH ALL MUSIC, OUT OF HIS LONG HAIR, ... 219 HARP OF AENGUS   8
AND ALL THE ALE RAN OUT AT THE NEW MOON! . . . . . . 222 SHADOW WATER B V 11
HE COULD NOT SEE THEM, BUT I HELD OUT MY HANDS . . . 223 SHADOW WATER B   38
IF YOU WILL DRAW THAT SWORD OUT OF ITS SCABBARD . . 225 SHADOW WATER B   78
AND THEN SMOOTH OUT WITH IVORY HANDS AND SIGH, . . . 228 SHADOW WATER B   133
AS THEY HAVE KNOWN IT. NOW THE SECRET'S OUT! . . . 228 SHADOW WATER B   140
AENGUS AND EDAIN RAN UP OUT OF THE WAVE-- . . . . . 231 SHADOW WATER B   196
WHEN SHE FINDS OUT WE HAVE BETTER MEN ABOARD . . . . 232 SHADOW WATER B   231
MADE OF DIM GOLD RAVE OUT IN SECRET TOMBS! . . . . . 235 SHADOW WATER B   295
WHEN SHE FINDS OUT I WILL NOT LET HER GO-- . . . . . 236 SHADOW WATER B   302
IT HAD WASHED AMONG THE STARS AND PUT THEM OUT, . . 236 SHADOW WATER B   311
YOU CANNOT LEAP OUT OF THE GOLDEN NET. . . . . 238 SHADOW WATER B   360

OUT (CONTINUED)

	PAGE	TITLE	LINE
AND MEASURE OUT A COURSE AND BRING US HOME,	238	SHADOW WATER B	362
HE HAS CAUGHT THE CRESCENT MOON OUT OF THE SKY,	239	SHADOW WATER B	370
WHERE IS MY SWORD THAT FELL OUT OF MY HAND	241	SHADOW WATER B	397
IT WAS SO GIVEN OUT, BUT I WILL PROVE	243	SHADOW WATER B	429
WHAT ARE YOU CALLING OUT ABOVE THE MAST?	243	SHADOW WATER B	437
WHY, IT'S A WONDER OUT OF RECKONING	243	SHADOW WATER B	445
OUT OF ALL RECKONING. IS IT NOT TRUE	244	SHADOW WATER B	467
YOU'LL HEAR THEM CALLING OUT TO ONE ANOTHER	247	SHADOW WATER B	521
THEY'RE CRYING OUT, COULD YOU BUT HEAR THEIR WORDS,	247	SHADOW WATER B	529
WITH ALL THOSE SIGHTS AND ALL THAT CRYING OUT?	249	SHADOW WATER B	573
OUT OF THE RUNNING STREAM, O MORNING STAR,	251	SHADOW WATER B	610
CRIED OUT UPON THAT THING BENEATH	254	HIS DREAM	10
CRIED OUT THE WHOLE NIGHT LONG,	254	HIS DREAM	16
WE'LL OUT, FOR THE WORLD LIVES AS LONG AGO;	257	RECONCILIATION	8
HAS DRIED THE SAP OUT OF MY VEINS, AND RENT	260	FASC DIFFICULT	2
OUT OF MY HEART. THERE'S SOMETHING AILS OUR COLT	260	FASC DIFFICULT	4
I'LL FIND THE STABLE AND PULL OUT THE BOLT.	260	FASC DIFFICULT	13
TIME OUT OF MIND, BECAME TOO RUINOUS	264	HOUSE SHAKEN	3
OUT YONDER, WHERE THE RACE COURSE IS,	266	GALWAY RACES	V	1
TO FIND OUT IF I MIGHT LOVE.	268	BROWN PENNY	4
TO FIND OUT ALL THAT IS IN IT,	268	BROWN PENNY	11
OR TRADING OUT OF GALWAY INTO SPAIN,	269	PARDON FATHERS	4
HAD HAMMERED OUT ON MOUNTAIN TOP	271	GREY ROCK	23
"COME OUT AND DIG FOR A DEAD MAN,	272	GREY ROCK	32
HAD RAVELLED HER OWN STORY OUT,	272	GREY ROCK	45
"THE DANISH TROOP WAS DRIVEN OUT	273	GREY ROCK	65
A SQUIRREL WHINNIED AND A BIRD SCREAMED OUT;	278	TWO KINGS	34
"I HAVE SENT OUT INTO THE FIELDS AND WOODS	280	TWO KINGS	V	69
AND I BUT ASKED THE MORE, TILL HE CRIED OUT,	281	TWO KINGS	92
AND I, THAT I MIGHT FIND AND STUB IT OUT,	281	TWO KINGS	V	92
AND AT THOSE WORDS I ROSE AND I WENT OUT	282	TWO KINGS	125
AND STRETCHED OUT SLEEPING ON A PILE OF SKINS	283	TWO KINGS	141
TO SHAKE HIM OUT OF SLEEP, I COULD NOT ROUSE HIM.	283	TWO KINGS	143
WENT OUT. AMONG THE IVY-COVERED ROCKS,	283	TWO KINGS	147
SUCKED UP THE PASSION OUT OF HIM AGAIN	284	TWO KINGS	160
PUSH HIS VIGOROUS LIMBS AND RUB HIS EYES,	284	TWO KINGS	162
BEING WEARIED OUT, I LOVE IN MAN THE CHILD?	285	TWO KINGS	192
CAN BLOT OUT OF MY MEMORY THIS LIFE	285	TWO KINGS	204
AND RIDDEN OUT TO WELCOME THEM, AND NOW,	286	TWO KINGS	V	218
AND WHEN THEY DROVE OUT COSIMO,	288	TO WEALTHY MAN	20
NOW ALL THE TRUTH IS OUT,	290	TO A FRIEND	1
TO DRINK OF THAT SALT BREATH OUT OF THE SEA	292	TO A SHADE	5
AN OLD FOUL MOUTH THAT ONCE CRIED OUT ON YOU	292	TO A SHADE	V	17
CAN RAVEL OUT WHAT'S IN MY HEAD.	295	THREE BEGGARS	12
MY BROTHER MOURTEEN IS WORN OUT	301	RUN PARADISE	8
WOULD HAVE HIS FILL OUT OF MY LADLE	304	HOUR DAWN	V	53
AND DRANK AND YAWNED AND STRETCHED HIM OUT,	307	HOUR DAWN	108
AND TUMBLE OUT YOUR HAIR	312	CHILD DANCING	4
I HAVE FOUND OUT HOW DESPAIRING	313	TWO YEAR LATER V	3
VANISHED, AND LEFT BUT MEMORIES, THAT SHOULD BE OUT OF SEASON	316	COLD HEAVEN	5
AND I TOOK ALL THE BLAME OUT OF ALL SENSE AND REASON,	316	COLD HEAVEN	7
OUT NAKED ON THE ROADS, AS THE BOOKS SAY, AND STRICKEN	316	COLD HEAVEN	11
BEING OUT OF HEART WITH GOVERNMENT	317	APPOINTMENT	1
BEING OUT OF HEART AT GOVERNMENT	317	APPOINTMENT	V	1
OUT OF OLD MYTHOLOGIES	320	COAT	3
AND THERE IS SALT TO LENGTHEN OUT THE SMART	324	ROBERT GREGORY	11
OUT OF SOME OLD PICTURE-BOOK;	325	ROBERT GREGORY	44
OUT OF SOME OLD PICTURE BOOK;	325	ROBERT GREGORY	V	44
THE BARE CHIMNEY IS GONE BLACK OUT	327	ROBERT GREGORY	84
I AM WORN OUT WITH DREAMS;	329	MEN IMPROVE	1
FROM BEAUTY THAT IS CAST OUT OF A MOULD	334	LIVING BEAUTY	4
RHYMED OUT IN LOVE'S DESPAIR	337	SCHOLARS	5
WEAR OUT THE CARPET WITH THEIR SHOES	337	SCHOLARS	V	8
FOR RHYME CAN BEAT A MEASURE OUT OF TROUBLE	339	SHEP GOATHERD	12
YOU HAVE MEASURED OUT THE ROAD THAT THE SOUL TREADS	342	SHEP GOATHERD	80
CUT OUT OUR RHYMES ON STRIPS OF NEW-TORN BARK	343	SHEP GOATHERD	115
THE STARS FADE OUT WHERE THE MOON COMES,	344	DAWN	8
OR A YOUNG GIRL DRESSED OUT IN HER NEW GOWN,	350	HER PRAISE	4
AND SMOOTH OUT STAIN AND BLEMISH WITH THE ELEGANCE OF HIS MIND;	353	HIS PHOENIX	7
AND FLINGS HERSELF OUT OF THE ROOM WHEN JULIET WOULD BE BRIDE	354	HIS PHOENIX	13
THEY CAN SPREAD OUT WHAT SAIL THEY PLEASE FOR ALL I HAVE TO SAY,	354	HIS PHOENIX	22
AND FLINGS HERSELF OUT OF THE ROOM WHEN JULIET WOULD BE A BRIDE	354	HIS PHOENIX	V	13
AND MAY BE THERE'LL BE SOME YOUNG BELLE WALK OUT TO MAKE MEN WILD	354	HIS PHOENIX	V	26
AND MAYBE THERE'LL BE SOME YOUNG BELLE WALK OUT TO MAKE MEN WILD	354	HIS PHOENIX	V	26
MOST OUT OF REACH? AND IS THAT SPECTRAL IMAGE	368	EGO DOMINUS	25
DERIDED AND DERIDING, DRIVEN OUT	369	EGO DOMINUS	34
OUT OF NO TRAGIC WAR, LOVERS OF LIFE,	369	EGO DOMINUS	39
SHUT OUT FROM ALL THE LUXURY OF THE WORLD,	370	EGO DOMINUS	60
THEIR CONNEMARA CLOTH WORN OUT OF SHAPE;	372	PHASES OF MOON	4
SING OUT THE SONG; SING TO THE END, AND SING	374	PHASES OF MOON	56
BODY AND SOUL CAST OUT AND CAST AWAY	374	PHASES OF MOON	62
THEIR BEAUTY DROPPED OUT OF THE LONELINESS	375	PHASES OF MOON	70
BECAUSE YOU ARE FORGOTTEN, HALF OUT OF LIFE,	376	PHASES OF MOON	96

OUT   (CONTINUED)
OUT OF THE UP AND DOWN, THE WAGON-WHEEL . . . .   377 PHASES OF MOON   120
OUT OF THAT RAVING TIDE--IS DRAWN BETWIXT . . . . . .   377 PHASES OF MOON   122
AUSTERITY, A PLACE SET OUT FOR WISDOM . . . .   377 PHASES OF MOON   127
AND THEN I'D STAGGER OUT. HE'D CRACK HIS WITS . . . .   377 PHASES OF MOON   134
THE LIGHT IN THE TOWER WINDOW WAS PUT OUT. . . . . . .   377 PHASES OF MOON   139
OUT OF THE UP AND DOWN, THE WAGON WHEEL . . . .   377 PHASES OF MOON V 120
I START OUT OF MY SLEEP TO THINK . . . .   380 SONGS FOOL 1   7
UPON A MOMENT, AND SO STRETCHED IT OUT . . . .   384 VISION ROBART   46
I SUDDENLY CRIED OUT IN A STRANGE TONGUE . . . .   387 SOLOMON WITCH   5
HE THAT CROWED OUT ETERNITY . . . .   388 SOLOMON WITCH   17
TO FIND OUT SOME APPROPRIATE PAIN-- . . . .   388 SOLOMON WITCH   20
WILL FIND OUT SOME APPROPRIATE PAIN, ...   388 SOLOMON WITCH V   20
OUT OF ALL LIKELIHOOD, OR REASON, ...   389 IMAGE PAST   9
MERELY TO LOOSEN OUT A TRESS . . . .   390 IMAGE PAST   26
NO, NO, NOT SAID, BUT CRIED IT OUT--"YOU HAVE COME AGAIN, 391 IMAGE PAST   13
I WRITE IT OUT IN A VERSE-- . . . .   394 EASTER 1916   74
"TO MAKE THE GREEN COME OUT AGAIN . . . .   396 ROSE TREE   9
WHEN FIRST IT SPRANG OUT OF THE NEST . . . .   397 POLIT PRISONER   20
CRIED OUT THE HOLLOWS OF THE SEA. . . . .   397 POLIT PRISONER   24
RAN OUT OF MY SIGHT; . . . .   399 DEMON BEAST   4
THAN THAT I MAY FIND OUT A WAY . . . .   401 DEMON BEAST   41
THE SECOND COMING! HARDLY ARE THOSE WORDS OUT . . . .   402 SECOND COMING   11
WHEN A VAST IMAGE OUT OF SPIRITUS MUNDI . . . .   402 SECOND COMING   12
OUT OF THE MURDEROUS INNOCENCE OF THE SEA. . . . . . .   403 FOR DAUGHTER   16
WHILE THAT GREAT QUEEN, THAT ROSE OUT OF THE SPRAY, . .   404 FOR DAUGHTER   27
OUT OF THE MOUTH OF PLENTY'S HORN, ...   405 FOR DAUGHTER   60
ONCE OUT OF NATURE I SHALL NEVER TAKE . . . .   408 SAIL BYZANTIUM   25
I THOUGHT IT ALL OUT TWENTY YEARS AGO; . . . .   411 TOWER   64
BRING UP OUT OF THAT DEEP CONSIDERING MIND . . . . . .   413 TOWER   106
FROM A GREAT LABYRINTH OUT OF PRIDE, ...   413 TOWER   116
FROM SOME GREAT LABYRINTH OUT OF PRIDE, ...   413 TOWER   116
FROM SOME GREAT LABYRINTH OUT OF PRIDE, ...   413 TOWER   V 116
UNDER ECLIPSE AND THE DAY BLOTTED OUT. . . . .   414 TOWER   120
FLOAT OUT UPON A LONG . . . .   414 TOWER   142
OUT OF HIS BITTER SOUL . . . .   415 TOWER   151
THAT OUT OF LIFE'S OWN SELF-DELIGHT HAD SPRUNG . . . .   417 ANCEST HOUSES   11
OUT OF THE OBSCURE DARK OF THE RICH STREAMS, ...   417 ANCEST HOUSES   14
THAT OUT OF LIFE'S OWN SELF DELIGHT HAD SPRUNG . . . .   417 ANCEST HOUSES V   11
MY DAYS OUT OF THEIR AIMLESSNESS. . . . .   421 MY TABLE   5
A GLITTERING SWORD OUT OF THE EAST. A PUFF OF WIND . .   426 PHANTOM HATRED   5
REMEMBERED OUT OF BABYLONIAN ALMANACS, ...   426 PHANTOM HATRED   20
THE INNUMERABLE CLANGING WINGS THAT HAVE PUT OUT THE MOON. 427 PHANTOM HATRED   32
THAT THE WORST ROGUES AND RASCALS HAD DIED OUT. . . .   428 NINETEEN 19   16
WHIRLS OUT NEW RIGHT AND WRONG, ...   430 NINETEEN 19   55
THE BREAST THRUST OUT IN PRIDE . . . .   430 NINETEEN 19   66
TO BAR THAT FOUL STORM OUT; FOR WE . . . .   432 NINETEEN 19   111
AND TEAR THE HEART OUT OF HIS SIDE, ...   437 SONGS PLAY 1   3
OUT OF THE FABULOUS DARKNESS CALLED. . . . .   437 SONGS PLAY 1   16
OUT OF HIS SIDE. . . . .   439 FRAGMENTS   4
OUT OF A MEDIUM'S MOUTH; . . . .   439 FRAGMENTS   6
OUT OF NOTHING IT CAME, ...   439 FRAGMENTS   7
OUT OF THE FOREST LOAM, ...   439 FRAGMENTS   8
OUT OF DARK NIGHT WHERE LAY . . . .   439 FRAGMENTS   9
I BRING FULL-FLAVOURED WINE OUT OF A BARREL FOUND . . .   442 BLACK CENTAUR   10
STRETCH OUT YOUR LIMBS AND SLEEP A LONG SATURNIAN SLEEP; 442 BLACK CENTAUR   13
I BRING FULL FLAVOURED WINE OUT OF A BARREL FOUND . . .   442 BLACK CENTAUR   V   10
NOR BEAUTY BORN OUT OF ITS OWN DESPAIR. . . . .   445 SCHOOL CHILDR   59
NOR BLEAR-EYED WISDOM OUT OF MIDNIGHT OIL. . . . . . .   446 SCHOOL CHILDR   60
MIRACLE-BRED OUT OF THE LIVING STONE; . . . .   446 COLONUS PRAISE   13
I WILL FIND OUT SOME CAVERN IN THE HILLS . . . .   448 HERO GIRL FOOL V   11
SHOULD FIND NO BURDEN BUT ITSELF AND YET SHOULD BE WORN   449 OWEN AHERNE   3
     OUT.
THE HEART BEHIND ITS RIB LAUGHED OUT. . . . .   450 OWEN AHERNE   13
"SPEAK ALL YOUR MIND," MY HEART SANG OUT, ...   450 OWEN AHERNE   21
WHEN THE MOON SAILS OUT. . . . .   451 FIRST LOVE   18
I HAVE POINTED OUT THE YELLING PACK, ...   453 DEATH OF HARE   1
O WHAT A BURSTING OUT THERE WAS, ...   457 SUMMER SPRING   13
PICK OUT MY FEATURES IN SUCH LIGHT AND SHADE . . . . .   466 HARUN RASHID   116
NOR THOUGHT OUT OF HER MIND OR MINE BEGOT, ...   467 HARUN RASHID   140
NOR THOUGHT OUT OF HER MIND OR OUT OF MINE . . . . . .   467 HARUN RASHID   V   140
NOR THOUGHT OUT OF HER MIND OR OUT OF MINE . . . . . .   467 HARUN RASHID   V   140
AND THERE MARKED OUT THOSE EMBLEMS ON THE SAND . . . .   468 HARUN RASHID   156
AND THERE MARKED OUT EMBLEMS ON THE SAND . . . .   468 HARUN RASHID   V   156
AND NOW MY UTMOST MYSTERY IS OUT. . . . .   469 HARUN RASHID   187
OUT OF TEN THOUSAND WINTERS, I ALONE-- . . . .   470 HARUN RASHID   V   190
BEFORE THAT END MUCH HAD SHE RAVELLED OUT . . . . . .   472 ALL SOUL NIGHT   51
HE HAD MUCH INDUSTRY AT SETTING OUT . . . .   473 ALL SOUL NIGHT   71
PARDONED, DRAGS OUT LONELY YEARS . . . .   475 EVA GORE-BOOTH   8
ONE OR THE OTHER OUT AND SPEAK . . . .   475 EVA GORE-BOOTH   15
WHEN SUCH AS I CAST OUT REMORSE . . . .   479 SELF AND SOUL   68
ROSE OUT OF THE RACE . . . .   480 BLOOD AND MOON   4
OR OUT OF ABSTRACT HATRED, AND SHED BLOOD, ...   482 BLOOD AND MOON   38
MUST RAMBLE, AND THIN OUT . . . .   484 SPILT MILK   3
THAT NEVER LOOKED OUT OF THE EYE OF A SAINT . . . . .   486 SEVEN SAGES   12
OR OUT OF DRUNKARD'S EYE. ALL'S WHIGGERY NOW, ...   486 SEVEN SAGES   13
OR OUT OF A DRUNKARD'S EYE. ALL'S WHIGGERY NOW, . . .   486 SEVEN SAGES   V   13
BUT WE OLD MEN ARE OUT AGAINST THE WORLD. . . . . . .   486 SEVEN SAGES   V   14
OR OUT OF FOLLY INTO FOLLY CAME. . . . .   491 COOLE BALLYLEE   32
IN LUCK OR OUT THE TOIL HAS LEFT ITS MARK; . . . . . .   491 COOLE BALLYLEE V   40F
IN LUCK OR OUT THE TOIL HAS LEFT ITS MARK; . . . . . .   495 CHOICE   6
A RIVERY FIELD SPREAD OUT BELOW, ...   502 VACILLATION   57

	PAGE	TITLE	LINE

OUT (CONTINUED)

SEEK OUT REALITY, LEAVE THINGS THAT SEEM. . . . . . . 502 VACILLATION 72
HAD SCOOPED OUT PHARAOH'S MUMMY. I--THOUGH HEART MIGHT 503 VACILLATION 84
    FIND RELIEF
BUT I HAVE STRAIGHTENED OUT . . . . 505 RESULT THOUGHT 7
OUT OF IRELAND HAVE WE COME. . . . . 506 REMORSE SPEECH 11
WANDERS OUT INTO THE NIGHT . . . . 508 JANE BISHOP 25
MAY CALL A CURSE OUT OF THE SKY . . . . 508 JANE BISHOP V 4
I WENT OUT ALONE . . . . 515 GIRLS SONG B 1
THAT OUT OF ROCK, ... 518 HIS CONFIDENCE 10
OUT OF A DESOLATE SOURCE, ... 518 HIS CONFIDENCE 11
BUT SOMETHING BORE THEM OUT OF SIGHT . . . . 519 HER DREAM 5
I THOUGHT IT OUT THIS VERY DAY, ... 525 DANCING DAYS 17
"COME OUT OF CHARITY, ... 526 AM OF IRELAND 4
"COME OUT OF CHARITY, ... 527 AM OF IRELAND 17
"COME OUT OF CHARITY, ... 527 AM OF IRELAND 30
THINGS OUT OF PERFECTION SAIL, ... 530 OLD TOM AGAIN 1
THAT STEPPED OUT OF THEIR CLOTHES, ... 538 LAST CONFESS 14
HEAVEN AND EARTH OUT OF THEIR PLACES, ... 540 FROM ANTIGONE 8
CUT OUT HIS HEART. SOME MASTER OF DESIGN . . . . . 541 PARN FUNERAL 1 14
BRED OUT OF THE CONTAGION OF THE THRONG, ... 542 PARN FUNERAL 1 27
HE DID IT OUT OF PRIDE. . . . . 545 TO SAME TUNE 1 26
TIME FOR US ALL TO PICK OUT A GOOD TUNE, ... 548 TO SAME TUNE 3 13
OUT OF BEN BULBEN AND KNOCKNAREA, ... 549 SEVERED HEAD 2
OUT OF THE GRAVE. SADDLE AND RIDE . . . . 549 SEVERED HEAD V 4
I HAD THOUGHT TO HAVE CALLED HER OUT TO THE DOOR, . . 551 SONGS REWRIT 1 V 15
I PRAY--FOR FASHION'S WORD IS OUT . . . . 553 PRAYER OLD AGE 9
THOSE AMOROUS CRIES THAT OUT OF QUIET COME . . . . . 557 RIBH ECSTASY 7
A PASSION-DRIVEN EXULTANT MAN SINGS OUT . . . . . . 560 WHENCE COME 5
CAME OUT OF A NEEDLE'S EYE. . . . . 562 NEEDLES EYE 2
AND ANCIENT LINEAMENTS ARE BLOTTED OUT. . . . . . . 564 GYRES 4
WHAT MATTER? OUT OF CAVERN COMES A VOICE, ... 564 GYRES 15
WHAT MATTER? OUT OF CAVERN COME A VOICE . . . . . 564 GYRES V 15
AEROPLANE AND ZEPPELIN WILL COME OUT, ... 565 LAPIS LAZULI 6
BLACK OUT! HEAVEN BLAZING INTO THE HEAD! . . . . . 566 LAPIS LAZULI 19
ESCAPED OUT OF HER CROWD, ... 568 SWEET DANCER 5
OR OUT OF HER BLACK CLOUD. . . . . 568 SWEET DANCER 6
OUT OF ALL HARM, ... 574 MAIDS 1ST SONG 8
"THIS LAND OF SAINTS," AND THEN AS THE APPLAUSE DIED OUT, 577 LOFTY THINGS 3
AND WHEN I PAY ATTENTION I MUST OUT AND WALK . . . . 581 CURSE CROMWELL 29
THEY GAVE IT OUT TO ALL THE WORLD, ... 582 ROGER CASEMENT 11
AND COPIED OUT WHAT I COULD READ . . . . 584 GHOST ROG CASE 33
HE WROTE OUT THAT WORD HIMSELF, ... 585 ORAHILLY 7
OUT OF THAT CRAZY FIGHT! . . . . 585 ORAHILLY 15
CAN BURN OUT THAT SUFFERING . . . . 589 OLD WICKED MAN 57
SOME TWENTY FEET FROM TIP TO TIP HAD IT STRETCHED RIGHTLY 593 PILGRIM 17
    OUT,
SOME TWENTY FEET FROM TIP TO TIP HAD ITS WINGS STRETCHED 593 PILGRIM V 17
    RIGHTLY OUT,
THE COLONEL WENT OUT SAILING, ... 594 COLONEL MARTIN 1
THE COLONEL WENT OUT SAILING. . . . . 594 COLONEL MARTIN 9
THE COLONEL WENT OUT SAILING. . . . . 594 COLONEL MARTIN 18
THE COLONEL WENT OUT SAILING. . . . . 595 COLONEL MARTIN 27
THE COLONEL WENT OUT SAILING. . . . . 595 COLONEL MARTIN 36
THE COLONEL WENT OUT SAILING. . . . . 596 COLONEL MARTIN 45
THE COLONEL WENT OUT SAILING. . . . . 596 COLONEL MARTIN 54
THE COLONEL WENT OUT SAILING. . . . . 596 COLONEL MARTIN 63
AND TOM MAKE OUT A LIVING . . . . 597 COLONEL MARTIN 70
THE COLONEL WENT OUT SAILING. . . . . 597 COLONEL MARTIN 72
WHEN TOM MADE OUT A LIVING . . . . 597 COLONEL MARTIN V 70
(AN IMAGE OUT OF SPENSER AND THE COMMON TONGUE). . . 603 GALLERY REVIS 40
AND OUT AND LAY OUR LEADERSHIP . . . . 606 SONGS BURDEN 1 23
BUT HAD GONE OUT TO DIE . . . . 608 SONGS BURDEN 3 20
AND RATTLED OUT A TUNE! . . . . 616 MARCH SONGS 3 9
AND RATTLED OUT A TUNE! . . . . 616 MARCH SONGS 3 19
HE DID IT OUT OF PRIDE. . . . . 616 MARCH SONGS 3 26
AND RATTLED OUT A TUNE! . . . . 616 MARCH SONGS 3 29
KEEP THOSE CHILDREN OUT. . . . . 618 LONG-LEG FLY 24
IMAGINATION TO THAT PITCH WHERE IT CASTS OUT . . . . 619 BRONZE HEAD 19
THEN CLEANING OUT AND BANDAGING OF WOUNDS, ... 622 HOUND VOICE 20
WHAT HURRIES OUT THE KNAVE AND DOLT? . . . . 625 NATIVITY 9
RICHES DROVE OUT RANK, ... 626 STATES HOLIDAY 2
BASE DROVE OUT THE BETTER BLOOD, ... 626 STATES HOLIDAY 3
WITH A HAT OUT OF FASHION, ... 627 STATES HOLIDAY 29
I LAY STRETCHED OUT IN THE DIRT . . . . 628 JANE MOUNTAIN 21
AND THEN A COUNTER-TRUTH FILLED OUT ITS PLAY, . . . 629 CIRCUS ANIMALS 17
GREW IN PURE MIND, BUT OUT OF WHAT BEGAN? . . . . . 630 CIRCUS ANIMALS 34
DID THAT PLAY OF MINE SEND OUT . . . . 632 MAN AND ECHO 11
OUT OF INTELLECT AND SIGHT . . . . 633 MAN AND ECHO 35
DROPPING OUT OF SKY OR ROCK, ... 633 MAN AND ECHO 44
A STRICKEN RABBIT IS CRYING OUT, ... 633 MAN AND ECHO 45
EYES STARED OUT OF THE BRANCHES AND WERE GONE. . . . 634 CUCHULAIN COMF 3
ALL OUT OF SHAPE FROM TOE TO TOP, ... 639 BEN BULBEN 71
BEAT OUT THEIR LIVES LAMENTING O'ER THE SAND! . . . 652 ISLE STAT I 2 14
OUT OF THE AIR. AND WHEN? WHEN THE SUN GOES DOWN . 652 ISLE STAT I 2 29
AND MEASURE OUT THE WAYS OF CHIVALRY. . . . . 660 ISLE STAT II 1 37
OF LOVE FROM OUT A DREAMLESS RACE FOR STRIFE, . . . 684 SEEKER 58
FAR OUT UPON THE WATER WORLD AND RINGED . . . . . . 693 MOSADA 1 80
I'LL SEE HIM LONGER IF I STAND OUT HERE . . . . . . 703 MOSADA 3 113
HAS FLICKERED AND GONE OUT. I AM NOT WELL. . . . . 704 MOSADA 3 129
REMEMBERING THEE, I SEARCH OUT THESE FAINT FLOWERS . 704 REMEMBRANCE 1

591

		PAGE	TITLE	LINE

OUT   (CONTINUED)

	PAGE	TITLE		LINE
HE WHISPERS TO A SOLDIER, WHO GOES OUT--	711	FERENCZ RENYI		44
THEN THE STARS GROW OUT OF HEAVEN WITH THEIR COUNTENANCES FAIR.	719	PHANTOM SHIP		30
TO THOSE YOUR "MELLOW" WARES HAVE WEARIED OUT.	721	WITCH VIVIEN		27
OUT OF A NEIGHBOURING BUNCH OF HEATHER;	728	PRIEST FAIRY		20
MUST SPREAD OUT THEIR WINGS UNTIRING,	739	WHERE BOOKS GO		3
LIKE A GREY OWL MEN HARRY OUT	740	EARL PAUL		23
CAST OUT ALL HOPE, CAST OUT ALL FEAR,	743	DANAAN QUICK		25
CAST OUT ALL HOPE, CAST OUT ALL FEAR,	743	DANAAN QUICK		25
BUT WEAVING IT OUT OF THREADS	743	WISDOM DREAMS		3
OUT OF THAT ISLAND WHERE THE FOOL OF THE WOOD	747	SHADOW WATER A		2
HIS HEART'S DESIRE WHERE THE WORLD DWINDLES OUT?	747	SHADOW WATER A		13
THREE MOONS. IT WERE BEST TO KILL HIM, AND CHOOSE OUT	748	SHADOW WATER A		15
TIME AND THE WORLD AND ALL THINGS DWINDLE OUT.	749	SHADOW WATER A		47
AND THEN SMOOTH OUT WITH IVORY HANDS AND SIGH.	750	SHADOW WATER A		70
FORGAEL, SEEK OUT CONTENT, WHERE OTHER MEN	750	SHADOW WATER A		71
THE FOOL THAT CAME OUT OF THE WINTRY WOOD	750	SHADOW WATER A		75
OUT OF MERE WANTONNESS TO LURE A SAIL	750	SHADOW WATER A		79
THEY ARE CHANGED AND AS GREY BIRDS FLY OUT TO SEA,	750	SHADOW WATER A		82
MAKE GALLEYS OUT OF WIND THAT CHANGE TO WIND	751	SHADOW WATER A		105
NOW RUSH UPON HER AND FIND OUT WHAT PREY	752	SHADOW WATER A		130
I SHALL FIND OUT IF I HAVE LOST MY WAY	753	SHADOW WATER A		137
I SHALL FIND OUT IF I HAVE LOST THE WAY	753	SHADOW WATER A	V	137
AND SHE CRIES OUT, "I HAVE FLED TO MY BELOVED	754	SHADOW WATER A		151
THIS BLADE OUT OF MY HAND AND DIED OF A SUDDEN.	755	SHADOW WATER A		168
SHE CAUGHT THIS BLADE OUT OF MY BELT AND DIED.	755	SHADOW WATER A	V	168
I SWEAR IT. LET EVERY MAN DRAW OUT HIS SWORD.	758	SHADOW WATER A		230
STRIKE QUICKLY; IT WILL FADE OUT WHEN YOU STRIKE.	759	SHADOW WATER A		238
WHEN SHE DREAMT FIRST OF LOVE, SHALL FLICKER OUT	760	SHADOW WATER A		257
WHEN SHE DREAMED FIRST OF LOVE, SHALL FLICKER OUT	760	SHADOW WATER A	V	257
THE WHITE FOOL MAKES AT MORNING OUT OF FOAM;	761	SHADOW WATER A		261
I WILL DRINK OUT OF THE STREAM. THE STREAM IS GONE;	761	SHADOW WATER A		273
BREATHED OUT A DRUID VAPOUR, AND CRUMBLED AWAY	761	SHADOW WATER A		279
EDAINE CAME OUT OF MIDHER'S HILL, AND LAY	762	SHADOW WATER A		296
SWEET WITH ALL MUSIC, OUT OF HIS LONG HAIR,	762	SHADOW WATER A		303
MADE OF DIM GOLD, RAVE OUT IN SECRET TOMBS,	765	SHADOW WATER A		345
TO SNATCH ALIVE OUT OF THE STREAMS ALL LOVERS	765	SHADOW WATER A		347
WE WILL FIND OUT VALLEYS AND WOODS AND MEADOWS	767	SHADOW WATER A		388
OUT OF THEIR HATRED. MY BELOVED, FAREWELL.	767	SHADOW WATER A		400
HAVE FALLEN AND MY SUN AND MOON GONE OUT.	767	SHADOW WATER A	V	405
MY LOVE SHAKES OUT HER HAIR UPON THE STREAMS	768	SHADOW WATER A		416
HAD WOVEN HER OF WIND. LIFE WITHERS OUT	768	SHADOW WATER A		423
OUT OF A RUNNING STREAM, O MORNING STAR	769	SHADOW WATER A		426
THE HARP-STRINGS HAVE BEGUN TO CRY OUT TO THE EAGLES.	769	SHADOW WATER A		431
UPON THIS WORLD NO LONGER. THE HARP CRIES OUT.	769	SHADOW WATER A	V	430
IT HAS BEGUN TO CRY OUT TO THE EAGLES.	769	SHADOW WATER A	V	431
OR THE GANNETS CALLING OUT	772	SONG DEIRDRE 1		5
BORN OUT OF IMMODERATE THOUGHT;	772	SONG DEIRDRE 1		12
MAY THIS FIRE HAVE DRIVEN OUT	775	AGAINST WITCH		1
OUT OF MEMORY AND MIND.	775	AGAINST WITCH		10
MAY THIS FLAME HAVE DRIVEN OUT	775	AGAINST WITCH	V	1
THAT IS MADE OUT OF THE GREASE.	776	AGAINST WITCH		24
THAT DIES OUT BEFORE 'TIS DAY,	777	SONG DEIRDRE 2		8
CRIES OUT THE EMPTY WELL,	780	WELL AND TREE		2
CRIES OUT THE LEAFLESS TREE,	780	WELL AND TREE		10
THE DREAMING BONES CRY OUT	782	HEART FRIGHT		15
THE WINDS OUT OF CLARE-GALWAY	783	GREY ROUND		4
THE STARS ARE OUT OF SIGHT.	786	YOUR HEART		34
I MOCK AT ALL SO BURNING OUT.	787	HUDDON DUDDON		15
BUT HOW THEY MOCK US BURNING OUT.	787	HUDDON DUDDON	V	15

OUTBALANCE

| IN THE OLD ROOMS; NIGHT CAN OUTBALANCE DAY, | 435 | NEW FACES | | 6 |

OUT-BURN

| AS ARGIVE CLYTEMNESTRA SAW OUT-BURN | 645 | ISLE STAT I 1 | | 12 |

OUTCRIES

| THE UNAVAILING OUTCRIES AND THE OLD BITTERNESS | 198 | SEVEN WOODS | | 4 |

OUTCRY

| OUTCRY OF BATS. AND THEN YOUNG NIAMH CAME | 44 | OISIN 2 | | 229 |

OUTDANCED

| SO SHE HAD OUTDANCED THOUGHT. | 383 | VISION ROBART | | 39 |

OUTER

THE GLASS OF OUTER WEARINESS,	135	TWO TREES		31
TO THAT SMALL CHAMBER BY THE OUTER GATE.	181	QUEEN MAEVE		44
THE FLAMING CIRCLE OF THE OUTER LAW,	689	NETTLESHIP		13
AND PASSED THE OUTER HEBRIDES, AND TOOK	749	SHADOW WATER A		42

OUTGREW

| BUT OUTGREW THAT SCHOOL, | 506 | REMORSE SPEECH | | 2 |

OUTLANDISH

A CERTAIN POET IN OUTLANDISH CLOTHES	180	QUEEN MAEVE		1
IN SOME OUTLANDISH COAT BESIDE	303	HOUR DAWN	V	28
IN THAT OUTLANDISH GEAR,	526	AM OF IRELAND		7

OUTLAWED

| AND TOADS AND EVERY OUTLAWED THING | 85 | MAD KING GOLL | V | 61 |

OUTLAWS

| THE SONG OF OUTLAWS AND THEIR FEAR; | 85 | MAD KING GOLL | V | 64 |

OUTLIVE

AS THOSE THAT CAN OUTLIVE THE MOON HAVE KNOWN IT,	230	SHADOW WATER B		193
AS THOSE THAT CAN OUTLIVE THE MOON HAVE SHOWN IT,	230	SHADOW WATER B	V	193
FROM LASTING WATCHERS, THAT OUTLIVE THE MOON,	236	SHADOW WATER B		320
WHERE NO CHILD'S BORN BUT TO OUTLIVE THE MOON."	247	SHADOW WATER B		531

592

OUTLIVE (CONTINUED)
    WE THOUGHT IT WOULD OUTLIVE ALL FUTURE DAYS. . . . . . 428 NINETEEN 19   14
    THOU SHALT OUTLIVE THINE AMOROUS HAPPY TIME, ... 674 ISLE STAT II 3   203
OUTLIVEST
    WHY THOU OUTLIVEST, BLIND AND HOARY, ...   2 OISIN 1   V   2
OUT-LIVING
    IN DAY OUT-LIVING BATTLE, ON THE BREAST . . . . 750 SHADOW WATER A   73
OUTRAGEOUS
    AND THE OUTRAGEOUS CANNON, ... 317 NIGHT COME   10
    BUT AS THE OUTRAGEOUS STARS INCLINE . . . . 325 ROBERT GREGORY   38
    THE OUTRAGEOUS WAR SHALL FADE: . . . . 342 SHEP GOATHERD   100
OUTRAN
    AND YET HIS MIND OUTRAN THE HORSES' FEET. . . . . . . 326 ROBERT GREGORY   64
OUTRIDDEN
    HE HAD OUTRIDDEN HIS WAR-WASTED MEN . . . . 277 TWO KINGS   3
OUT-RIDDEN
    HE HAD OUT-RIDDEN HIS WAR-WASTED MEN . . . . 277 TWO KINGS   V   3
OUTRIGHT
    O NEVER GIVE THE HEART OUTRIGHT, ... 202 NEVER GIVE ALL   8
OUTRODE
    OUTRODE HIS TROOP THAT AFTER TWELVE MONTHS' WAR . . . . 276 TWO KINGS   V   1
OUTRUN
    OUTRUN THE MEASURE. I'D TELL OF THAT GREAT QUEEN . . . 187 QUEEN MAEVE   141
OUT-SCREAMS
    OUT-SCREAMS THE WHOLE SHELF: "ALTHOUGH . . . . 319 DOLLS   7
OUTSIDE
    THAT EVERYTHING OUTSIDE US IS . . . . 523 MAD AS MIST   5
    A LITTLE BOY OUTSIDE THE SYCAMORE WOOD . . . . 715 DWELT SYCAMORE   1
OUT-SPREAD
    AND OUT-SPREAD ARMS. BE NOT SO PALE, DEAR LOVE. . . . . 701 MOSADA 3   70
OUTWEIGH
    AND IS THEIR LOGIC TO OUTWEIGH . . . . 395 SIXTEEN DEAD   11
OUTWEIGHED
    OUTWEIGHED ALL OTHER YEARS, YOU SAID, ... 791 REPRISALS   6
OUTWORN
    THESE NOW OUTWORN AND WITHERED HANDS . . . . 23 OISIN 1   349
    OUTWORN HEART IN A TIME OUTWORN, ... 147 INTO TWILIGHT V   1
    OUTWORN HEART IN A TIME OUTWORN, ... 147 INTO TWILIGHT V   1
OUT-WORN
    OUT-WORN HEART, IN A TIME OUT-WORN, ... 147 INTO TWILIGHT   1
    OUT-WORN HEART, IN A TIME OUT-WORN, ... 147 INTO TWILIGHT   1
OVEN
    AND AFTER BAKED IT SLOWLY IN AN OVEN: BUT NOW . . . . . 442 BLACK CENTAUR   9
OVER
    OVER THE GLOSSY SEA." "O, WILD . . . .   6 OISIN 1   V   58
    WE GALLOPED OVER THE GLOSSY SEA: . . . . 11 OISIN 1   132
    HURRIED AWAY, AND OVER HER RAISED . . . . 12 OISIN 1   V 142B
    BLEW ONE LONG NOTE. FROM OVER REED . . . . 14 OISIN 1   V 195
    OVER THE BARE AND WOODY LAND, ... 15 OISIN 1   198
    AND, WEEPING OVER THE WHITE STRINGS, HURLED . . . . . 17 OISIN 1   241
    A FIRWOOD HOUSE, ALL COVERED OVER . . . . 17 OISIN 1   V 248
    AND BENDING OVER THEM SOFTLY SAID, ... 21 OISIN 1   307
    BENDING OVER THEM IN THE DANCE, ... 21 OISIN 1   308
    FOR WE KNEW WELL THE OLD WAS OVER. . . . . 25 OISIN 1   379
    OVER THE GLIMMERING PURPLE SEA. . . . . 25 OISIN 1   384
    FOR WELL WE KNEW THE OLD WAS OVER, ... 25 OISIN 1   V 379
    HE HATH OVER LINGERED HIS WELCOME: THE DAYS, ... 27 OISIN 1   V 406
    LIKE A BRIDE BENDING OVER HER MIRROR ADORNING, ... 28 OISIN 1   V 423E
    THE ISLE WAS OVER NOW AND GONE: . . . . 28 OISIN 1   V 427B
    I LAY, AS OVER SEA THE LIGHT HOOVES GLANCED . . . . . 30 OISIN 2   V 19A
    DARK STATUES GLIMMERED OVER THE PALE TIDE . . . . . . 31 OISIN 2   36
    "IS HE SO DREADFUL?" "BE NOT OVER BOLD, ... 35 OISIN 2   V 88
    'TIS OVER: FAR WITH MEMORY I SWAY AND ROCK. . . . . 43 OISIN 2   V 212
    I MOUNTED, AND WE PASSED OVER THE LONE . . . . . . 45 OISIN 2   231
    AND NEVER A SONG SANG NIAMH, AND OVER MY FINGER-TIPS . . 47 OISIN 3   6
    GREY SAND ON THE GREEN OF THE GRASSES AND OVER THE DRIPPING 48 OISIN 3   14
        TREES,
    GREY SANDS ON THE GREEN OF THE GRASSES AND OVER THE   48 OISIN 3   V 14
        DRIPPING TREES,
    AND OVER THE LIMBS AND THE VALLEY THE SLOW OWLS WANDERED 49 OISIN 3   41
        AND CAME.
    SQUARE LEAVES OF THE IVY MOVED OVER US, BINDING US DOWN 52 OISIN 3   76
        TO OUR REST.
    AND SOFTLY COME TO YOUR NIAMH OVER THE TOPS OF THE TIDE: 55 OISIN 3   126
    AND SOFTLY COME TO THY NIAM OVER THE TOPS OF THE TIDE: . . 52 OISIN 3   V 126
    IN A REVERIE FORGETFUL OF ALL THINGS, OVER THE BUBBLING 56 OISIN 3   140
        GROUND.
    IN REVERIE FORGETFUL OF ALL THINGS, OVER THE BUBBLING   56 OISIN 3   V 140
        GROUND.
    GREY SAND ON THE GREEN OF THE GRASSES AND OVER THE DRIPPING 57 OISIN 3   142
        TREES,
    GREY SANDS ON THE GREEN OF THE GRASSES AND OVER THE   57 OISIN 3   V 142
        DRIPPING TREES,
    AND RODE ON TILL OVER THE WORLD'S RIM FLOATED THE SEA'S 60 OISIN 3   V 183
        OLD SHOUT.
    . . . AND MARCH ON AS OXEN MOVE OVER YOUNG GRASS: . . . 62 OISIN 3   211
    AND OVER IS THEIR ANTIQUE JOY: . . . . 64 HAPPY SHEPHERD   2
    AND LIFE IS OVER SAVE THE MURMUR AND THE SWEETNESS. . . . 77 INDIAN TO LOVE V   5E
    AND ALL IS OVER SAVE THE MURMUR AND THE SWEETNESS. . . . 77 INDIAN TO LOVE V   5E
    AUTUMN IS OVER THE LONG LEAVES THAT LOVE US, ... 79 FALLING LEAVES   1
    AND OVER THE MICE IN THE BARLEY SHEAVES: . . . . . . 79 FALLING LEAVES   2

PAGE   TITLE   LINE

OVER (CONTINUED)

AUTUMN WAS OVER HIM, AND NOW THEY STOOD	80	EPHEMERA	16
OVER THE HEATH AND SPONGY FEN,	83	MAD KING GOLL V	32
OVER THE YOUNG STREAMS.	88	STOLEN CHILD	37
HE BADE THEM GIVE OVER THEIR KEENING;	93	FATHER OHART	23
OVER THE DOOR-STEP INTO THE AIR,	97	FOXHUNTER V	3
ALL THE HEAVY DAYS ARE OVER;	124	CATHLEEN PARA	1
AH, EXILES WANDERING OVER LANDS AND SEAS,	129	BOOK STORIES	9
AH, EXILES, WANDERING OVER MANY SEAS,	129	BOOK STORIES V	9
AH, EXILES, WANDERING OVER MANY LANDS,	130	BOOK STORIES V	17
AND OVER THE GRAVE OF CLOOTH-NA-BARE;	140	HOSTING SIDHE	2
OVER THE LITTLE SILVER CORDS,	146	FISH	6
DESOLATE WINDS THAT CRY OVER THE WANDERING SEA;	147	UNAPPEAS HOST	7
AND THEIR DAY GOES OVER IN IDLENESS,	151	OLD MOTHER	7
OVER MY HEART, AND YOUR HAIR FALL OVER MY BREAST,	154	BELOVED PEACE	10
OVER MY HEART, AND YOUR HAIR FALL OVER MY BREAST,	154	BELOVED PEACE	10
OVER MY HEART, AND YOUR HAIR FALL ABOUT MY BREAST	154	BELOVED PEACE V	10
THAT WAS SHAKEN OUT OVER MY BREAST:	155	REPROVE CURLEW	5
THRONE OVER THRONE WHERE IN HALF SLEEP,	156	FORGOT BEAUTY	22
COVER OVER AND HIDE, FOR HE HAS NO PART	158	TO HIS HEART	6
WE WILL BEND DOWN AND LOOSEN OUR HAIR OVER YOU,	172	TRAV PASSION	6
A WALL BEHIND HIS BACK, OVER HIS HEAD	180	QUEEN MAEVE	5
SHE COULD HAVE CALLED OVER THE RIM OF THE WORLD	181	QUEEN MAEVE	23
OVER THE WHITE-HORNED BULL AND THE BROWN BULL,	182	QUEEN MAEVE	58
BUT OUT OF THE DARK AIR OVER HER HEAD THERE CAME	187	QUEEN MAEVE	153
IN MUIRTHEMNE, AND OVER IT	194	BAILE AILLINN	116
WERE HOVERING OVER THE HARP-STRINGS	195	BAILE AILLINN	141
WERE HOVERING OVER THE HARP STRINGS	195	BAILE AILLINN V	141
WHILE OVER THEM BIRDS OF AENGUS FLY,	197	BAILE AILLINN	182
AND OVER THE TILLER AND THE PROW,	197	BAILE AILLINN	183
A CLOUDY QUIVER OVER PAIRC-NA-LEE.	198	SEVEN WOODS	14
TIME CAN BUT MAKE HER BEAUTY OVER AGAIN:	200	FOLLY COMFORT	8
THE OLD BROWN THORN-TREES BREAK IN TWO HIGH OVER CUMMEN STRAND,	206	HANRAHANS SONG	1
THE OLD BROWN THORN TREES BREAK IN TWO HIGH OVER CUMANN'S STRAND,	206	HANRAHANS SONG V	1
THE WIND HAS BUNDLED UP THE CLOUDS HIGH OVER KNOCKNAREA,	207	HANRAHANS SONG	6
THE WINDS HAVE BUNDLED UP THE CLOUDS HIGH OVER KNOCKNAREA	207	HANRAHANS SONG V	6
OVER THE RAMPARTS AND THE TOWERS,	212	BLESS PSALTER	6
RIVERS ARE RUNNING OVER	214	HAPPY TOWNLAND	7
WHERE RIVERS ARE RUNNING OVER	214	HAPPY TOWNLAND V	7
AND FROM THAT HOUR HE HAS WATCHED OVER NONE	220	HARP OF AENGUS	13
WHEN IT IS OVER, NOR ONE TO GRUMBLE AT US.	225	SHADOW WATER B	67
THEY HOVER OVER THE MASTHEAD AWHILE	233	SHADOW WATER B	246
CIRCLING AND CIRCLING OVER THE MASTHEAD?	234	SHADOW WATER B	266
HE HAS PUT A SUDDEN DARKNESS OVER THE MOON.	239	SHADOW WATER B	367
THEY HAVE BEEN CIRCLING OVER OUR HEADS IN THE AIR,	247	SHADOW WATER B	525
THROUGH BUSH THEY PLUNGED AND OVER IVIED ROOT,	278	TWO KINGS	32
I GROPED MY WAY THROUGH BOUGHS, AND OVER ROOTS,	283	TWO KINGS V	139
AS I CAME OVER WINDY GAP	300	RUN PARADISE	1
THEY TOPPLED OVER; "WERE IT NOT	302	HOUR DAWN	17
CONFUSION OF THE DEATH-BED OVER, IS IT SENT	316	COLD HEAVEN	10
AND LAUGH OVER THE UNTROUBLED WATER	330	BONE OF A HARE	14
WHEN HER SON'S TURN WAS OVER. SING YOUR SONG.	340	SHEP GOATHERD	42
HOVERING OVER THE WOOD	349	HAWK	10
OVER SOME SILKEN DRESS	363	DOLLS DRAWINGS	7
AND WHEN AT LAST THAT MURDER'S OVER	388	SOLOMON WITCH	24
COWARDICE, OVER SOME SILLY SUBTLE THOUGHT	413	TOWER V	117
A MIST THAT IS LIKE BLOWN SNOW IS SWEEPING OVER ALL,	425	PHANTOM HATRED	2
OVER THE BLACKENED EARTH	496	MOHINI CHATTER	21
THAT MEN PASS OVER	512	JANE ON GOD	21
MEN HAVE PASSED OVER	512	JANE ON GOD V	21
OVER THEM FLIES A LONG-LEGGED BIRD,	566	LAPIS LAZULI	39
I WALK IN A BATTLE FOUGHT OVER AGAIN,	591	WHAT WAS LOST	2
WHO QUARRELS OVER HALFPENNIES	621	JOHN KINSELLA	33
WHO QUARRELS OVER HALF-PENNIES	621	JOHN KINSELLA V	33
AND OUR LAUGHTER OVER AND DONE:	643	SONG FAERIES	6
OVER THE LAKE THE WATER-FLOWERS	647	ISLE STAT I 1	66
OVER THEM CRIMSON VAPOURS WINGING.	648	ISLE STAT I 1	92
BUT WHENCE, AND WHEN? OVER THE WILLOWS SERE	652	ISLE STAT I 2	28
OVER THE CROWN OF THE WILLOWS BROWN.	653	ISLE STAT I 2	30
OVER THE CROWN OF THE WILLOWS BROWN.	653	ISLE STAT I 2	51
OF THINE CRY OVER WOLD AND WATER WHITE,	669	ISLE STAT II 3	73
AND OUR LAUGHTER OVER AND DONE!	676	ISLE STAT II 3	253
A CREEPING HORROR IS ALL OVER ME.	681	SEEKER	12
OVER HER SPOTTED FLESH AND FLYING HAIR	687	TWO TITANS	15
AND OVER TILLAGE FIELDS AND PASTURE LANDS	715	FERENCZ RENYI	120
OVER THE SORREL-COVERED WOLD--	716	FAIRY DOCTOR	2
OVER THE BEADS OF HIS ROSARY.	730	PRIEST FAIRY	52
NOT EVEN "I LONG TO SEE THY LONGING OVER,"	734	QUATRAIN APHOR	11
THE YEARS THAT HAVE GONE OVER HER FROM THE HOUR	760	SHADOW WATER A	256
SHOOK THE PALE APPLE-BLOSSOM OVER IT:	761	SHADOW WATER A	275
SHOOK THE PALE APPLE BLOSSOM OVER IT:	761	SHADOW WATER A V	275
O, AENGUS OF THE HERDS, WATCH OVER ME!	762	SHADOW WATER A	291
HE WATCHES OVER NONE BUT FAITHFUL LOVERS.	762	SHADOW WATER A	295
AND FROM THAT HOUR HE HAS WATCHED OVER NONE	763	SHADOW WATER A	308
THAT I WOULD SHED LIKE TWILIGHT OVER YOU.	765	SHADOW WATER A	352
AND TELL ITS STORY OVER THEIR BROWN ALE.	767	SHADOW WATER A	393
IN THE TOWER OVER HEAD,	772	SONG DEIRDRE 1	3
TO THE TOWER OVER HEAD,	772	SONG DEIRDRE 1 V	3

PAGE   TITLE   LINE

OVERBOARD
   OLD MERCHANT SKIPPER THAT LEAPED OVERBOARD . . . . . .   270 PARDON FATHERS   13
   YOU MERCHANT SKIPPER THAT LEAPED OVERBOARD . . . . . .   270 PARDON FATHERS V   13
   AND MERCHANT SKIPPER THAT LEAPED OVERBOARD . . . . . .   270 PARDON FATHERS V   13
OVER-BOLD
   "IS HE SO DREADFUL?" "BE NOT OVER-BOLD, ...   35 OISIN 2   88
OVERBURTHENED
   UNTIL THE OVERBURTHENED MOON IS DEAD. . . . .   231 SHADOW WATER B   218
OVERCOME
   TILL GERMANY'S OVERCOME: . . . .   395 SIXTEEN DEAD   8
   OVERCOME--O BITTER SWEETNESS, ...   540 FROM ANTIGONE   1
   OVERCOME GODS UPON PARNASSUS: . . . .   540 FROM ANTIGONE   6
   OVERCOME THE EMPYREAN: HURL. . . . .   540 FROM ANTIGONE   7
   WOULD OVERCOME YOUR SORROW AND YOUR DREAMS. . . . . .   749 SHADOW WATER A   52
OVERFLOW
   THEY OVERFLOW THE HILLS, ...   781 MY HEART BEAT   12
OVERFLOWED
   THE YELLOW POOL HAS OVERFLOWED HIGH UP ON CLOOTH-NA-BARE, 207 HANRAHANS SONG   11
   THE YELLOW POOL HAS OVERFLOWED HIGH UPON CLOOTH-NA-BARE,   207 HANRAHANS SONG V   11
OVERFLOWS
   LIFE OVERFLOWS WITHOUT AMBITIOUS PAINS: . . . . . .   417 ANCEST HOUSES   3
   SUCH FULLNESS IN THAT QUARTER OVERFLOWS . . . . . .   478 SELF AND SOUL   33
OVERHEAD
   THE DARKNESS COMES. A CLOUD HANGS OVERHEAD-- . . . . .   43 OISIN 2   V 208A
   AND PACED UPON THE MOUNTAINS OVERHEAD . . . .   121 YOU ARE OLD   11
   FROM A BOUGH OVERHEAD, ...   215 HAPPY TOWNLAND   42
   I'VE HEARD A RUSTLING OVERHEAD IN THE WIND. . . . . .   223 SHADOW WATER B   28
   A MEANING IN THAT CIRCLING OVERHEAD? . . . .   234 SHADOW WATER B   270
   NOR GAVE GOD THANKS TILL OVERHEAD . . . .   307 HOUR DAWN   121
   AND GAVE GOD THANKS THAT OVERHEAD . . . .   307 HOUR DAWN   V 121
   NOTHING BUT DARKNESS OVERHEAD. . . . .   314 MEMORY YOUTH   14
   THE SACRED MOON OVERHEAD . . . .   379 CAT AND MOON   19
   TO THE TOWER OVERHEAD, ...   772 SONG DEIRDRE 1   3
OVER-LINGERED
   HE HAS OVER-LINGERED HIS WELCOME: THE DAYS, ...   26 OISIN 1   402
OVERLOOKS
   OR ELSE AT MEADOW OR AT GRAZING OVERLOOKS . . . . . .   340 SHEP GOATHERD   37
OVERMUCH
   BEING MADE BEAUTIFUL OVERMUCH, ...   403 FOR DAUGHTER   20
OVER-MUCH
   NOTHING THAT WE LOVE OVER-MUCH . . . .   399 BREAK OF DAY   17
OVER-NIMBLE
   THOU HAST AN OVER-NIMBLE TONGUE. THY GRIEF, ...   661 ISLE STAT II 1   59
OVERPOWER
   AND OVERPOWER THE CREW WHILE YET ASLEEP: . . . . . .   233 SHADOW WATER B   240
OVERSEA
   THOUSANDS OF LEAGUES OVERSEA, ...   341 SHEP GOATHERD   63
OVER-SEA
   FOR ALL HER WANDERINGS OVER-SEA: . . . .   197 BAILE AILLINN   203
OVER-SUBTLE
   COWARDICE, SOME SILLY OVER-SUBTLE THOUGHT . . . . . .   413 TOWER   117
OVERTHREW
   WOULD THAT THE STORM THAT OVERTHREW MY SHIPS, ...   235 SHADOW WATER B   286
   AND HARRIED ALBAN TOWNS, AND OVERTHREW . . . . . .   749 SHADOW WATER A   40
OVERTHROW
   WILL OVERTHROW HIS SHADOWS AND CARRY OFF . . . . . .   184 QUEEN MAEVE   95
OVERTHROWN
   THAT ALL BE OVERTHROWN. . . . .   45 OISIN 2   239
   ARE OVERTHROWN BY A WOMAN'S GAZE . . . .   164 PERFECT BEAUTY   4
   STILL OVERTHROWN BY A WOMAN'S GAZE, ...   164 PERFECT BEAUTY V   4
   THAT THEY, TIME OVERTHROWN, ...   384 VISION ROBART   47
   HAS TWELVE KNIGHTS OVERTHROWN: . . . .   740 EARL PAUL   8
   FOR HE HAD OVERTHROWN TWELVE KNIGHTS . . . .   741 EARL PAUL   43
   AND EVIL FORTUNE HAVE OVERTHROWN SAILED HITHER . . . .   757 SHADOW WATER A   196
OVERTURNED
   AND OVERTURNED THE DEMON WITH A SOUND . . . .   762 SHADOW WATER A   283
OWEN
   OWEN AHERNE AND HIS DANCERS . . . .   449 OWEN AHERNE   T
OWING
   TO MAEVE AND TO MAEVE'S HOUSEHOLD, OWING ALL . . . . .   187 QUEEN MAEVE   147
   IN OWING THEM THE BRIDE-BED THAT GIVES PEACE." . . . .   187 QUEEN MAEVE   148
OWL
   BECOME A ROOFLESS RUIN THAT THE OWL . . . .   423 MY DESCENDANTS   14
   OR DARK BETWIXT THE POLECAT AND THE OWL, ...   565 GYRES   21
   UP THERE SOME HAWK OR OWL HAS STRUCK, ...   633 MAN AND ECHO   43
   WHERE IS THE OWL THAT LATELY FLEW . . . .   646 ISLE STAT I 1   32
   AN OWL, WHO IN AN ALDER TREE . . . .   670 ISLE STAT II 3   115
   MORE DARK BENEATH THE POPLARS, WHERE YON OWL . . . . .   675 ISLE STAT II 3   233
   LIKE A GREY OWL MEN HARRY OUT . . . .   740 EARL PAUL   23
OWLET'S
   TO WELCOME THEE, WHEN O'ER THE OWLET'S WINGS . . . . .   648 ISLE STAT I 1   102
OWLETS
   SHE SLEEPS WITH OWLETS TWO AND TWO, ...   646 ISLE STAT I 1   34
OWLS
   . . . THE OWLS HAD BUILT THEIR NESTS IN THEIR LOCKS, . .   49 OISIN 3   39
   AND OVER THE LIMBS AND THE VALLEY THE SLOW OWLS WANDERED   49 OISIN 3   41
      AND CAME,
   IN MIDST OF AN OLD MAN'S BOSOM: OWLS RUFFLING AND PACING   50 OISIN 3   47
      AROUND
   IN THE MIDST OF AN OLD MAN'S BOSOM: OWLS RUFFLING   50 OISIN 3   V 47
      AND PACING AROUND

		PAGE	TITLE		LINE
OWLS	(CONTINUED)				
WHEN BRUSHED WITH THE WINGS OF THE OWLS,		53	OISIN 3		98
WHEN OWLS BEGAN TO CALL,		159	CAP AND BELLS		6
WHEN THE OWLS CALLED OUT NO MORE;		159	CAP AND BELLS		14
AND ONCE, WHEN THE OWLS GREW STILL,		159	CAP AND BELLS	V	2
HAS MADE THE VERY OWLS IN CIRCLES MOVE;		423	MY DESCENDANTS		18
AND SHOUT AT THE WISEST OWLS		644	SONG FAERIES		10
HE WROTE IT ON THE SANDS (THE OWLS MAY READ		659	ISLE STAT II 1		9
AND SHOUT AT THE WISEST OWLS		676	ISLE STAT II 3		257
OWLS THERE BE WHOM AGE MAKES NUMB;		727	LOVERS QUARREL		35
AMONG GREAT TREES, AND IN THE WINGS OF OWLS,		762	SHADOW WATER A		285
OWN					
IN HIS OWN LEAFY FOREST HOUSE,		2	OISIN 1	V	7L
IN HIS OWN LEAFY FOREST HOUSE		4	OISIN 1		37
AENGUS AND EDAIN, MY OWN NAME		5	OISIN 1		47
TO MY OWN KINGDOM IN THE SEA—		8	OISIN 1	V	80A
DREAMING OF HER OWN MELTING HUES,		13	OISIN 1		162
AND DREAMS OF HER OWN MELTING HUES,		13	OISIN 1	V	162
ON THEIR OWN SELVES IN THE WATERS WHITE,		14	OISIN 1	V	185
CRAZED WITH ITS OWN INTERMINABLE SOUND,		30	OISIN 2	V	23A
SAVING IN THINE OWN HEART. SEEK, THEN,		66	HAPPY SHEPHERD		27
THE DEWDROPS, FOR THE SOUND OF THEIR OWN DROPPING.		68	SAD SHEPHERD		16
TILL MY OWN WORDS, RE-ECHOING, SHALL SEND		68	SAD SHEPHERD		20
AND MY OWN TALE AGAIN FOR ME SHALL SING,		68	SAD SHEPHERD		22
AND MY OWN WHISPERING WORDS BE COMFORTING,		68	SAD SHEPHERD		23
THE DEW DROPS, FOR THE SOUND OF THEIR OWN DROPPING—		68	SAD SHEPHERD	V	16
AND MINE OWN WORDS RE-ECHOING SHALL SEND		68	SAD SHEPHERD	V	20
AND MINE OWN TALE AGAIN FOR ME SHALL SING,		68	SAD SHEPHERD	V	22
AND MINE OWN WHISPERING WORDS BE COMFORTING,		68	SAD SHEPHERD	V	23
RAGING AT HIS OWN IMAGE IN THE ENAMELLED SEA.		77	INDIAN TO LOVE		5
RAGES AT HIS OWN IMAGE IN THE ENAMELLED SEA		77	INDIAN TO LOVE	V	5
RAGING AT HIS OWN IMAGE IN THE DIM ENAMELLED SEA		77	INDIAN TO LOVE	V	5
TO HIS OWN ICE!" I GATHERED ROUND ME,		83	MAD KING GOLL	V	18
AND HIS OWN SNIPE AND TROUT.		92	FATHER OHART		4
TO MY OWN PLACE, KINSALE.		95	MOLL MAGEE		24
AND THINE OWN SADNESS, WHEREOF STARS, GROWN OLD		101	ROSE UPON ROOD		6
WITH HIS OWN FINGERS TOUCHED THE BRAZEN STRINGS.		109	CUCHULAIN SEA		46
WITH HIS OWN FINGER TOUCHED THE BRAZEN STRINGS,		109	CUCHULAIN SEA		46
THE CARS OF BATTLE AND HIS OWN NAME CRIED;		111	CUCHULAIN SEA		85
FOR I MUST OWN		118	CRADLE SONG		10
MY ARMS ROUND MY OWN;		118	CRADLE SONG		10
WITH ARMS ROUND MY OWN,		118	CRADLE SONG	V	10
MY PIGEON, MY OWN;		118	CRADLE SONG	V	10
WHEN HER OWN PEOPLE RULED THIS TRAGIC EIRE;		129	BOOK STORIES		2
WHEN HER OWN PEOPLE RULED IN WAVE-WORN ERI,		129	BOOK STORIES	V	2
BELOVED, GAZE IN THINE OWN HEART,		134	TWO TREES		1
BELOVED, GAZE IN THINE OWN HEART.		135	TWO TREES		20
AS IF THERE WERE NO TALE BUT YOUR OWN TALE		181	QUEEN MAEVE		32
TO MANY THOUSAND EYES, AND TO HER OWN		182	QUEEN MAEVE		65
AND NOT WITH HIS OWN VOICE OR A MAN'S VOICE,		183	QUEEN MAEVE		74
WITH SOMEBODY IN YOUR OWN LAND."		191	BAILE AILLINN		59
BY ITS OWN BLIND IMAGINING,		191	BAILE AILLINN		67
THEIR OWN THOUGHT FROM THE OTHER'S,		212	O DO NOT LOVE		7
HAVE DRIVEN TRAVELLERS MAD FOR THEIR OWN SPORT.		227	SHADOW WATER B		105
MAY NOT HAVE DRIVEN YOU MAD FOR THEIR OWN SPORT?		227	SHADOW WATER B	V	105
THAT EVERY MAN SHOULD CARRY HIS OWN SOUL		235	SHADOW WATER B		299
TO WIN A WOMAN IN HER OWN DESPITE,		244	SHADOW WATER B		458
BETTER THAN MY OWN HANDS. I HAVE DECEIVED YOU		244	SHADOW WATER B		466
TO WIN A WOMAN IS IN HER OWN DESPITE,		244	SHADOW WATER B	V	458
WE WOULD RETURN TO OUR OWN COUNTRY, FORGAEL,		248	SHADOW WATER B		539
THAT HER OWN STRANGENESS PERPLEXED;		260	UNWORTH PRAISE		14
HAD RAVELLED HER OWN STORY OUT,		272	GREY ROCK		45
IN THE HALF LIGHT, AND RUNS TO ITS OWN DOOR		279	TWO KINGS	V	45C
AND CARRIED HIM HIS FOOD WITH MY OWN HANDS,		280	TWO KINGS		88
WERE NEITHER SHAMED IN HIS OWN		291	TO A FRIEND		7
OF YOUR OWN PASSIONATE SERVING KIND WHO HAD BROUGHT		292	TO A SHADE		10
OF YOUR OWN PASSIONATE SERVING KIND WHO HAS BROUGHT		292	TO A SHADE	V	10
SO WITH A LAUGH AT HIS OWN FEAR		303	HOUR DAWN		31
HAS TIRED OF HIS OWN COMPANY?		303	HOUR DAWN		35
GROWN TIRED OF HIS OWN COMPANY?		303	HOUR DAWN	V	37
NOT EVEN YOUR OWN MOTHER		336	YOUNG GIRL		4
AND HIS OWN FLOCK WAS BROWSING AT THE DOOR.		340	SHEP GOATHERD		27
AND CERTAIN LOST COMPANIONS OF MY OWN.		342	SHEP GOATHERD		78
TO HIS OWN DAYSPRING,		342	SHEP GOATHERD		96
BECAUSE IT IS NOT HER OWN.		345	ON WOMAN		8
TO WRITE FOR MY OWN RACE		347	FISHERMAN		11
"FOR ALL THAT I HAVE DONE AT MY OWN CHARGE?		351	PEOPLE		2
I CALL TO MY OWN OPPOSITE, SUMMON ALL		367	EGO DOMINUS		8
OWN NOTHING BUT THEIR BLIND, STUPEFIED HEARTS.		370	EGO DOMINUS		69
IN ITS OWN BEING, AND WHEN THAT WAR'S BEGUN		374	PHASES OF MOON		51
OR FROM SOME BLOODY WHIP IN THEIR OWN HANDS.		375	PHASES OF MOON		68
AT THE PERFECTION OF ONE'S OWN OBEDIENCE;		376	PHASES OF MOON		109
WHEN HAD I MY OWN WILL?		382	VISION ROBART		7
THERE'S NOTHING BUT OUR OWN RED BLOOD		396	ROSE TREE		17
AND THAT ITS OWN SWEET WILL IS HEAVEN'S WILL;		405	FOR DAUGHTER		69
MONUMENTS OF ITS OWN MAGNIFICENCE;		407	SAIL BYZANTIUM		14
THAT OUT OF LIFE'S OWN SELF-DELIGHT HAD SPRUNG		417	ANCEST HOUSES		11
THAT OUT OF LIFE'S OWN SELF DELIGHT HAD SPRUNG		417	ANCEST HOUSES	V	11
WHERE EVEN LONGING DROWNS UNDER ITS OWN EXCESS;		426	PHANTOM HATRED		22
OF THEIR OWN SWEETNESS, BODIES OF THEIR LOVELINESS.		426	PHANTOM HATRED		24
TO CRAWL IN HER OWN BLOOD, AND GO SCOT-FREE;		429	NINETEEN 19		28

		PAGE	TITLE		LINE
OWN (CONTINUED)					
OR HURRIED THEM OFF ON ITS OWN FURIOUS PATH;		430	NINETEEN 19		53
A MAN IN HIS OWN SECRET MEDITATION		431	NINETEEN 19		69
MAN'S OWN RESINOUS HEART HAS FED.		438	SONGS PLAY 2		16
NOR BEAUTY BORN OUT OF ITS OWN DESPAIR,		445	SCHOOL CHILDR		59
I RAGE AT MY OWN IMAGE IN THE GLASS		447	HERO GIRL FOOL		1
AT MY OWN IMAGE IN THE LOOKING-GLASS		447	HERO GIRL FOOL	V	1
I HAVE RAGED AT MY OWN STRENGTH BECAUSE YOU HAVE LOVED IT.		448	HERO GIRL FOOL		9
PICKED HIM FOR HER OWN,		452	MERMAID		2
THE SOUL'S OWN YOUTH AND NOT THE BODY'S YOUTH		464	HARUN RASHID		69
AND SINK INTO ITS OWN DELIGHT AT LAST,		473	ALL SOUL NIGHT		60
BROUGHT FACE TO FACE WITH HIS OWN CLUMSINESS;		479	SELF AND SOUL		48
. . . OF ITS OWN DESIRE;		481	BLOOD AND MOON		29
AND EVERYTHING THAT YOUR OWN HANDS HAVE WROUGHT,		501	VACILLATION		31
AND GIVE HIS OWN AND TAKE HIS OWN		538	LAST CONFESS		19
AND GIVE HIS OWN AND TAKE HIS OWN		538	LAST CONFESS		19
AND RULE IN HIS OWN RIGHT;		538	LAST CONFESS		20
ALL HAPPINESS IN ITS OWN CAUSE OR GROUND.		557	RIBH ECSTASY		4
FOR THAT'S A PASSION IN MY OWN CONTROL.		558	RIBH CHRISTIAN		4
ON THEIR OWN FEET THEY CAME, OR ON SHIPBOARD,		566	LAPIS LAZULI		25
THEY HAVE SCHOOLING OF THEIR OWN, BUT I PASS THEIR SCHOOLING BY,		580	CURSE CROMWELL		13
AND WANT HE DID; FOR MY OWN GRAND-DAD		596	COLONEL MARTIN		68
OR DEMONSTRATE IN MY OWN LIFE		605	YOU CONTENT		21
HYSTERICA PASSIO OF ITS OWN EMPTINESS?		618	BRONZE HEAD		7
HYSTERICO-PASSIO OF ITS OWN EMPTINESS?		618	BRONZE HEAD	V	7
I THOUGHT MY DEAR MUST HER OWN SOUL DESTROY,		630	CIRCUS ANIMALS		21
WHO, WHEN HIS OWN RIGHT KING'S FORGOTTEN,		635	BLACK TOWER		13
AND THERE TO ITS OWN HEART FOR EVER MOANS.		650	ISLE STAT I 1		131
WHY NOT? HE IS HER OWN; AND CROUCHING NIGH		688	TWO TITANS		44
GATHERED ON HER OWN LIPS, OH YOUTH, AND FLING		688	TWO TITANS		53
IN HIS OWN HOUSE OR 'MONG THE MERCHANTS GREY,		693	MOSADA 1		87
ALONE WITH OUR OWN WHISPERS AND REPLIES—		702	MOSADA 3		80
UNTUNED BY THEIR OWN STRIVING. IF ONE SUCH		711	FERENCZ RENYI		37
GLAMOURED BY FAIRIES FOR THEIR OWN.		717	FAIRY DOCTOR		20
TO HIS OWN HOUSE DID HIM BETAKE;		725	LEGEND		30
WHERE THE MOSS WAS SPREAD LIKE HIS OWN DOORMAT,		728	PRIEST FAIRY		8
AND THOU CANST DWELL IN THINE OWN HOME,		739	EARL PAUL		3
GO BRING ME MY OWN ARMOUR		740	EARL PAUL	V	19
THEN GO TO HIS OWN LAND,		741	EARL PAUL		58
AND CAME AND DWELT IN HIS OWN HOUSE,		742	EARL PAUL		67
TO DROWN IN ITS OWN IMAGE? EVEN THAT SLEEP		765	SHADOW WATER A		364
THE NETS THE GODS HAVE WOVEN AND OUR OWN HEARTS,		766	SHADOW WATER A		383
YOUR OWN THOUGHT WILL HAVE DIED		786	YOUR HEART		30
HER OWN THOUGHT WILL HAVE DIED		786	YOUR HEART	V	30
OX					
AND WOOD-OF-WONDERS, WHERE ONE KILLS AN OX AT DAWN,		209	UNDER THE MOON		9
OXEN					
HOW THE SLOW, BLUE-EYED OXEN OF FINN LOW SADLY AT EVENING TIDE.		52	OISIN 3		84
. . . AND MARCH ON AS OXEN MOVE OVER YOUNG GRASS;		62	OISIN 3		211
AND TO GIVE WEALTH OF OXEN AND SHEEP TO ALL;		756	SHADOW WATER A		184
A HUNDRED OXEN AND A HUNDRED SHEEP,		756	SHADOW WATER A	V	189
PACE					
I PACE REMEMBERING. FROM MY MISTY THRONE		45	OISIN 2	V	239C
MY SPIRIT ROCKED IN SLEEP AND SIGHS; AND SAW THE MOORFOWL PACE		76	INDIAN ON GOD		3
OR PACE AND WEEP IN WOODS FORLORN,		86	MAD KING GOLL	V	68
AND PACE THE WOODS, AND DRIVE MY CHARIOT-WHEELS		103	FERGUS DRUID		18
AND PACE THE WOODS, AND DRIVE MY CHARIOT WHEELS		103	FERGUS DRUID		18
HELP THEM THAT PACE, HAND IN UNWITHERING HAND,		184	QUEEN MAEVE	V	86
SO THAT HIS PLAUTUS SET THE PACE		287	TO WEALTHY MAN		12
SO THAT HIS PLUTARCH SET THE PACE		287	TO WEALTHY MAN	V	12
OR ESSERKELLY PLAIN, FEW KEPT HIS PACE;		326	ROBERT GREGORY		59
AND ESERKELLY PLAINS, FEW KEPT HIS PACE;		326	ROBERT GREGORY	V	59
OR ESERKELLY PLAINS, FEW KEPT HIS PACE;		326	ROBERT GREGORY	V	59
THEY HAD KEPT A STEADY PACE AS THOUGH THEIR BEDS,		372	PHASES OF MOON		5
I PACE UPON THE BATTLEMENTS AND STARE		409	TOWER		17
THAT DESPAIR AND KEEP THE PACE		787	HUDDON DUDDON		9
PACED					
BENEATH HAD PACED CONTENT; WE HELD OUR WAY		36	OISIN 2		103
BASALTIC, MIGHT HAVE PACED. WE HELD OUR WAY		36	OISIN 2	V	103
REMEMBERING HOW I PACED IN DAYS GONE O'ER,		44	OISIN 2	V	227
I PACED A LITTLE FURTHER ON AND HEARD A LOTUS TALK;—		76	INDIAN ON GOD	V	9
I PACED A LITTLE FURTHER AND I HEARD A PEACOCK SAY;—		77	INDIAN ON GOD	V	17
PENSIVE THEY PACED ALONG THE FADED LEAVES,		80	EPHEMERA		10
WHO PACED IN THE EVE BY THE NETS ON THE PEBBLY SHORE,		91	OLD FISHERMAN		11
AND PACED UPON THE MOUNTAINS OVERHEAD		121	YOU ARE OLD		11
HE PACED UPON THE MOUNTAINS FAR ABOVE,		121	YOU ARE OLD	V	11
HAD PACED FROM DOOR TO FIRE AND FIRE TO DOOR.		180	QUEEN MAEVE		17
THROUGH SHEER BEWILDERMENT? SHE HAD NOT PACED		466	HARUN RASHID		118
PACES					
THAT SPRING FIVE PACES IN THEIR BOUNDS,		8	OISIN 1	V	86A
PACING					
IN MIDST OF AN OLD MAN'S BOSOM; OWLS RUFFLING AND PACING AROUND		50	OISIN 3		47
. . . AND PACING THE SHORES OF THE WANDERING SEAS,		50	OISIN 3		55
IN THE MIDST OF AN OLD MAN'S BOSOM; OWLS RUFFLING AND PACING AROUND		50	OISIN 3	V	47
. . . AND PACING THE SHORES OF THE SEVEN SEAS,		50	OISIN 3	V	55
AND, EVER PACING ON THE VERGE OF THINGS,		73	ANASHU VIJAYA		54

597

```
                                                          PAGE    TITLE              LINE
PACING  (CONTINUED)
    MAEVE THE GREAT QUEEN WAS PACING TO AND FRO,  . . . . .    180 QUEEN MAEVE           9
    AND HARPERS, PACING WITH HIGH HEAD  . . . . . . .         193 BAILE AILLINN       107
    PACING WITH HALF-CLOSED EYELIDS IN A SUNNY SPOT  . . . .  366 HER COURAGE           7
    THE PACING TO AND FRO ON POLISHED FLOORS  . . . . . .     418 ANCEST HOUSES        35
PACK
    THE PACK UPON HIM. GO, UNQUIET WANDERER,  . . . . . . .   292 TO A SHADE           18
    HERDING THE PACK. UNQUIET WANDERER  . . . . . .           292 TO A SHADE        V  18
    IT SEEMS THAT I MUST BID THE MUSE GO PACK,  . . . . . .   409 TOWER                11
    A PACK OF HOUNDS AND NOT A PACK OF CARDS,  . . . . . .    411 TOWER                69
    A PACK OF HOUNDS AND NOT A PACK OF CARDS,  . . . . . .    411 TOWER                69
    I HAVE POINTED OUT THE YELLING PACK,  . . . . . . .       453 DEATH OF HARE         1
    PUT JEWELRY IN THE PACK.  . . . . . . . . . . .           595 COLONEL MARTIN       24
PACKED
    THAT PACKED HIS MARRIAGE DAY  . . . . . . . .             317 NIGHT COME            7
    THAT PACKED HIS MARRIAGE-DAY  . . . . . . . .             317 NIGHT COME        V   7
PADDLE
    THEY PADDLE IN THE COLD  . . . . . . . . . .              323 SWANS AT COOLE       20
    AND PADDLE TO THE WRIST  . . . . . . . . . .              356 BROKEN DREAMS        31
    PADDLE AND ARE PERFECT. LEAVE UNCHANGED  . . . . . .      357 BROKEN DREAMS        34
PADDLED
    BUT TROD THE ROAD, OR PADDLED BY THE SHORE,  . . . . . .  447 COLONUS PRAISE V     27
PADDLER'S
    SOMETHING OF EVERY PADDLER'S HERITAGE--  . . . . . . .    444 SCHOOL CHILDR        21
PAGAN
    (I HAVE NO SPEECH BUT SYMBOL, THE PAGAN SPEECH I MADE  . .  365 HER COURAGE         2
    SAINT GEORGE OR ELSE A PAGAN PERSEUS:  . . . . . . .      533 HER TRIUMPH          10
PAGE
    TRAILS ALL ABOUT THE WRITTEN PAGE.  . . . . . . . .       138 TO IRELAND            9
    A CANDLE AND WRITTEN PAGE.  . . . . . . . .               419 MY HOUSE             13
    THE HALF-IMAGINED, THE HALF-WRITTEN PAGE:  . . . . . .    431 NINETEEN 19          83
    THE HALF IMAGINED, THE HALF WRITTEN PAGE.  . . . . . .    431 NINETEEN 19       V  83
    AS IF THAT WRITING OR THE FIGURED PAGE  . . . . . .       466 HARUN RASHID        126
    AS THOUGH THE WRITTEN OR THE PICTURED PAGE  . . . . . .   466 HARUN RASHID      V 126
    AND HERE IS TULLY'S OPEN PAGE.  . . . . . . . .           524 MAD AS MIST           9
    YON IS THE HUNTER'S, SIR ALMINTOR'S, PAGE:  . . . . . .   660 ISLE STAT II 1       35
    SIR PAGE, ALMINTOR'S FRIEND, AND THEREFORE LEARNED  . . . 660 ISLE STAT II 1       38
    BEING ALMINTOR'S PAGE. NOW JUDGE YOU HERE.  . . . . .     660 ISLE STAT II 1       47
PAGES
    I TURN THE PAGES OF MY HOLY BOOK.  . . . . . . .          555 RIBH AT TOMB         27
PAID
    AND PAID YOU ON THE NAIL. TAKE UP THAT ROPE  . . . . .    232 SHADOW WATER B      224
    (I WONDER IF THE BUILDER HAS BEEN PAID)  . . . . . .      292 TO A SHADE            3
    THEY ARE NEITHER PAID NOR PRAISED.  . . . . . . . .       473 ALL SOUL NIGHT       76
    THEY ARE NEITHER PAID OR PRAISED.  . . . . . . . .        473 ALL SOUL NIGHT V     76
    AND THE RICH MAN HAD PAID THEM WELL  . . . . . . .        596 COLONEL MARTIN       57
PAIN
    AH ME! TO BE SHAKEN WITH COUGHING AND BROKEN WITH OLD AGE   63 OISIN 3            217
        AND PAIN,
    THE PAIN OF WOUNDS, THE LABOUR OF THE SPEAR,  . . . . .   104 FERGUS DRUID    V  38D
    "I PUT YOU FROM YOUR PAIN. I CAN NO MORE."  . . . . .     110 CUCHULAIN SEA        69
    IN ALL THEIR LONELINESS AND PAIN,  . . . . . . .          290 SEPTEMBER 1913       27
    OF ALL 'TWAS PAIN OR JOY TO LEARN,  . . . . . . .         342 SHEP GOATHERD        98
    TO FIND OUT SOME APPROPRIATE PAIN--  . . . . . . .        388 SOLOMON WITCH        20
    WILL FIND OUT SOME APPROPRIATE PAIN,  . . . . . .         388 SOLOMON WITCH   V    20
    THE UNFINISHED MAN AND HIS PAIN  . . . . . . . .          479 SELF AND SOUL        47
    FOR CHILDREN BORN OF HER PAIN.  . . . . . . . .           487 CRAZED MOON           6
    A GUERDON OF DEEP-ROOTED PAIN,  . . . . . . . .           668 ISLE STAT II 3       59
    IGNOBLE JOY, AND MORE IGNOBLE PAIN  . . . . . . .         687 TWO TITANS           12
    FROM DATELESS PAIN. SHE SLEEPS--MOSADA--THOU--  . . . .   701 MOSADA 3        V    65
PAINS
    OR HOW SHOULD LOVE BE WORTH ITS PAINS WERE IT NOT  . . .  285 TWO KINGS           190
    AND INSULT HEAPED UPON HIM FOR HIS PAINS,  . . . . . .    292 TO A SHADE           15
    "FOR ALL MY PAINS ON LEBEEN-LONE?"  . . . . . . .         295 THREE BEGGARS         7
    LIFE OVERFLOWS WITHOUT AMBITIOUS PAINS:  . . . . . .      417 ANCEST HOUSES         3
    WHAT IS THIS FLESH I PURCHASED WITH MY PAINS,  . . . . .  499 MOTHER OF GOD        11
PAINT
    WOULD NOT PAINTERS PAINT A FORM  . . . . . . . .          259 PEACE                 5
    AND SHOULD THEY PAINT OR WRITE, STILL IT IS ACTION:  . . .369 EGO DOMINUS          44
    AND SHOULD THEY PAINT OR WRITE STILL IS IT ACTION,  . . . 369 EGO DOMINUS     V    44
    QUATTROCENTO PUT IN PAINT  . . . . . . . . . .            639 BEN BULBEN           53
    QUATTRO-CENTO PUT IN PAINT  . . . . . . . . . .           639 BEN BULBEN      V    53
PAINTED
    AND, AS THEY SANG, THE PAINTED BIRDS  . . . . . . .        26 OISIN 1             396
    GREY TRUTH IS NOW THE PAINTED TOY?  . . . . . . .          65 HAPPY SHEPHERD        4
    CAME TO THE THRESHOLD OF THE PAINTED HOUSE  . . . . . .   185 QUEEN MAEVE         108
    THERE ON THE HIGH AND PAINTED STERN  . . . . . . .        253 HIS DREAM       V     1
    I HELD A PAINTED STEERING OAR,  . . . . . . . .           253 HIS DREAM       V     2
    UPON A PAINTED BED?"  . . . . . . . . . . .               253 HIS DREAM       V     8
    AND FISH AND CROWD AND PAINTED SHIP,  . . . . . . .       254 HIS DREAM       V    15
    ON PAINTED PILLARS, ON A DEAL  . . . . . . . .            271 GREY ROCK       V    19
    UNTIL HE CAME BEFORE THE PAINTED WALL,  . . . . . .       279 TWO KINGS            47
    IN THEIR STIFF, PAINTED CLOTHES, THE PALE UNSATISFIED ONES 318 MAGI                 2
    SINBAD THE SAILOR'S BROUGHT A PAINTED CHEST,  . . . . .   371 ON GOING HOUSE       10
    ANOTHER ARGO'S PAINTED PROW.  . . . . . . . .             437 SONGS PLAY 1         11
    WHEN PAINTED PANEL, STATUARY,  . . . . . . . .            440 WISDOM                2
    UPON A PAINTED WALL.  . . . . . . . . . .                 452 HUMAN DIGNITY         6
    WE LIVED LIKE MEN THAT WATCH A PAINTED STAGE.  . . . . .  542 PARN FUNERAL 1       18
    UPON A PAINTED STAGE WHEN WE DEVOURED HIS HEART.  . . . . 542 PARN FUNERAL 1       23
    FOR PAINTED FORMS OR BOXES OF MAKE-UP  . . . . . .        564 GYRES                13
    OR FROM THE PAINTED SCENE  . . . . . . . . . .            608 SONGS BURDEN 3        4
```

598

		PAGE	TITLE		LINE

PAINTED (CONTINUED)

BEFORE THE PAINTED SCENE. . . . . 608 SONGS BURDEN 3   17
PLAYERS AND PAINTED STAGE TOOK ALL MY LOVE, ... 630 CIRCUS ANIMALS   31
A-FLUTTERING THE PAINTED POPULACE OF LAKE . . . . 675 ISLE STAT II 3   224
FROM THE GREAT PAINTED WINDOW WRAPS HIS BROW, ... 697 MOSADA 2   37

PAINTER

WE DREAMED THAT A GREAT PAINTER HAD BEEN BORN . . . . . 326 ROBERT GREGORY   65
OR WHO HAVE FOUND A PAINTER TO MAKE THEM SO FOR PAY . . . 353 HIS PHOENIX   6
NOR LET THE MODISH PAINTER SHIRK . . . . 638 BEN BULBEN   38

PAINTER'S

THE PAINTER'S BRUSH CONSUMES HIS DREAMS: . . . . . . 438 SONGS PLAY 2   12
IT SEEMED A QUATTROCENTO PAINTER'S THRONG . . . . . . 537 HER VISION   19
IT SEEMED A QUATTRO-CENTO PAINTER'S THRONG . . . . . . 537 HER VISION V 19

PAINTERS

WOULD NOT PAINTERS PAINT A FORM . . . . 259 PEACE   5

PAINTING

PAINTING WITH SHADOW ALL THE MARBLE STEPS: . . . . . . 72 ANASHU VIJAYA   30
IN PAINTING OR IN POTTERY, WENT . . . . 421 MY TABLE   18
MY GREAT-GRANDFATHER'S FATHER TALKED OF MUSIC AND PAINTING, 486 SEVEN SAGES V   4

PAINTINGS

PAINTINGS OF THE DOLPHIN-DRAWN . . . . 309 REALISTS   4
PAINTINGS OF THE DOLPHIN DRAWN: . . . . 309 REALISTS V   4

PAINTS

AND FOR THE PEEWIT PAINTS HIS CAP, ... 18 OISIN 1   266

PAIR

A PAIR OF LAPWINGS, ONE OLD SHEEP, ... 302 HOUR DAWN   9
HOW SUCH A PAIR LOVED MANY YEARS . . . . 458 SECRETS OF OLD   15
AND SUCH A PAIR BUT ONE, ... 458 SECRETS OF OLD   16
WHAT IF MY GREAT-GRANDDAD HAD A PAIR THAT WERE TWENTY FOOT 622 HIGH TALK   2
  HIGH,
POOR EARTH-ENKINDLED PAIR, ... 680 LOVE AND DEATH   22

PAIRC-NA-CARRAIG

DIM PAIRC-NA-CARRAIG, WHERE THE WILD BEES FLING . . . . 217 WOODS OF COOLE   9

PAIRC-NA-LEE

A CLOUDY QUIVER OVER PAIRC-NA-LEE. . . . . 198 SEVEN WOODS   14
WHERE OLD AGE CANNOT FIND THEM: PAIRC-NA-LEE, ... 217 WOODS OF COOLE   7

PAIRC-NA-TARAV

DIM PAIRC-NA-TARAV, WHERE ENCHANTED EYES . . . . . . 217 WOODS OF COOLE   11

PAISTIN

MY PAISTIN FINN IS MY SOLE DESIRE, ... 550 SONGS REWRIT 1   1
MY PRETTY PAISTIN IS MY HEART'S DESIRE, ... 550 SONGS REWRIT 1 V   1

PALACES

OUR SUDDEN PALACES IN THE STILL AIR . . . . 284 TWO KINGS   180
WANDERING IN SULTRY PALACES OF IND, ... 694 MOSADA 1   102

PALACE-YARD

THE PALACE-YARD AND RIVER-SIDE . . . . 295 THREE BEGGARS   9
FROM RIVER-SIDE AND PALACE-YARD . . . . 296 THREE BEGGARS   27

PALATE

CAN GIVE HIS SHARPENED PALATE ECSTASY . . . . 474 ALL SOUL NIGHT   84
GIVE TO HIS SHARPENED PALATE ECSTACY . . . . 474 ALL SOUL NIGHT V 84

PALATES

WHILE OUR GROSS PALATES DRINK FROM THE WHOLE WINE, . . . 471 ALL SOUL NIGHT   10

PALE   SEE STRAW-PALE CLOUD-PALE FOAM-PALE PEARL-PALE CURD-PALE MILK-PALE DEATH-PALE
         HONEY-PALE

AND IT WAS BOUND WITH A PEARL PALE SHELL . . . . . . 4 OISIN 1 V 28
IN THE PALE WEST, AND THE SUN'S RIM SANK, ... 12 OISIN 1   153
OUT OF THE MOON'S PALE TWISTED SHELL: . . . . 19 OISIN 1   279
AND THE PALE BLOSSOM OF THE MOON, ... 20 OISIN 1   288
WITH HOOFS OF THE PALE FINDRINNY . . . . 25 OISIN 1   383
OR SAT IN DREAMS ON THE PALE STRAND, ... 25 OISIN 1   390
AND THE MOON LIKE A PALE ROSE WITHER AWAY." . . . . . 28 OISIN 1   427
DARK STATUES GLIMMERED OVER THE PALE TIDE . . . . . . 31 OISIN 2   36
SO PALE! AND SOUNDS OF WONDER HER LIPS UTTERED, ... 34 OISIN 2 V 71
WITH A PALE LIGHT, I JOURNEYED ROUND THE HALL . . . . . 39 OISIN 2   153
FROM THEIR PALE THRONES AND COMFORT HIM, BUT THEY . . . 68 SAD SHEPHERD   6
MY MAN GREW RED AND PALE, ... 95 MOLL MAGEE   22
MY HUSBAND STOOD UP PALE, ... 95 MOLL MAGEE   22
WHY ARE YOU PALE AND SHAKE FROM FOOT TO CROWN?" . . . . 106 CUCHULAIN SEA V 13
LIKE THE PALE WATERS IN THEIR WINTRY RACE, ... 112 ROSE OF WORLD   8
TO SMILE ON THE PALE DAWN: AND GATHER YOU . . . . . . 114 ROSE OF BATTLE   15
OUR CHEEKS ARE PALE, OUR HAIR IS UNBOUND, ... 140 HOSTING SIDHE   7
OF THE PALE TIDE WHEN THE MOON HAS SET, ... 146 FISH   2
PALE BROWS, STILL HANDS AND DIM HAIR, ... 152 LOSS OF LOVE   1
PALE BROW, STILL HANDS, AND DIM HAIR, ... 152 LOSS OF LOVE V   1
THE WEST WEEPS IN PALE DEW AND SIGHS PASSING AWAY, . . . 154 BELOVED PEACE   5
FOR THAT PALE BREAST AND LINGERING HAND . . . . 156 FORGOT BEAUTY   15
I HEAR PALE BEAUTY SIGHING TOO, ... 156 FORGOT BEAUTY V 19
THAT IS BRIMMED FROM THE PALE FIRE OF TIME! . . . . . . 157 POET BELOVED   6
SHE ROSE IN HER PALE NIGHT-GOWN: . . . . 159 CAP AND BELLS   10
SHE ROSE IN HER PALE NIGHT GOWN, ... 159 CAP AND BELLS V 10
AND COVER THE PALE BLOSSOMS OF YOUR BREAST . . . . . . 163 ASKS FORGIVE   21
THEN COVER THE PALE BLOSSOM OF YOUR BREAST . . . . . . 163 ASKS FORGIVE V 21
AMONG PALE EYELIDS, HEAVY WITH THE SLEEP . . . . . . 169 SECRET ROSE   6
I WOULD THE PALE DEER HAD COME . . . . 171 MAID QUIET V 4A
LIKE THE PALE CUP OF THE SEA, ... 175 ELEMENT POWERS   14
BUT LIGHT FROM THE PALE STARS, AND GLEAMS . . . . . . 196 BAILE AILLINN   173
BLOSSOM PALE, SHE PULLED DOWN THE PALE BLOSSOM . . . . 199 ARROW V   5
BLOSSOM PALE, SHE PULLED DOWN THE PALE BLOSSOM . . . . 199 ARROW V   5
ON THE ISLAND LAWNS, THEIR FEET WHERE THE PALE FOAM GLEAMS. 203 WITHER BOUGHS   14
THE HONEY PALE MOON HUNG LOW ON THE SLEEPY HILL, ... 203 WITHER BOUGHS V   5
PALE SILVER-PROUD QUEEN-WOMAN OF THE SKY, ... 211 RAGGED WOOD   6

```
                                                         PAGE     TITLE            LINE
PALE  (CONTINUED)
     AND DO YOU GATHER ABOUT US WHEN PALE LIGHT  . . .  .  .  .   218  WOODS OF COOLE     37
     OF OPAL AND RUBY AND PALE CHRYSOLITE  . . .  .  .  .  .  .   219  HARP OF AENGUS      6
     AND WHERE BEECH-TREES HAD MIXED A PALE GREEN LIGHT  .  .  .  277  TWO KINGS           5
     BETWEEN THE PALE GREEN LIGHT OF THE BEECH LEAVES  .  .  .  . 277  TWO KINGS      V    5
     WHERE CERTAIN BEECHES MIXED A PALE GREEN LIGHT  .  .  .  .   277  TWO KINGS      V    5
     AND WHERE BEECH TREES HAD MIXED A PALE GREEN LIGHT  .  .  .  277  TWO KINGS      V    5
     IN THEIR STIFF, PAINTED CLOTHES, THE PALE UNSATISFIED ONES   318  MAGI                2
     "VENGENCE FOR JACQUES MOLAY." IN CLOUD PALE RAGS, OR IN      426  PHANTOM HATRED V   10
          LACE,
     THE CLOUD PALE UNICORNS, THE EYES OF AQUAMARINE. .  .  .  .  427  PHANTOM HATRED V   25
     WHAT'S BOWED YOUR SHOULDER AND MADE PALE YOUR CHEEK"?  .  .  467  HARUN RASHID      133
     THE HERON-BILLED PALE CATTLE-BIRDS  . . .  .  .  .  .  .  .  493  AT ALGECIRAS        1
     THE HERON-BILLED PALE CATTLE BIRD,  .  .  .  .  .  .  .  .   493  AT ALGECIRAS   V    1
     THE HERON-BILLED PALE CATTLE BIRDS,  .  .  .  .  .  .  .  .  493  AT ALGECIRAS   V    1
     BUT BOYS AND GIRLS, PALE FROM THE IMAGINED LOVE  .  .  .  .  610  STATUES             4
     THAT PALE, LONG-VISAGED COMPANY  .  .  .  .  .  .  .  .  .   637  BEN BULBEN          7
     THAT PALE, LONG VISAGED COMPANY  .  .  .  .  .  .  .  .  .   637  BEN BULBEN     V    7
     'TIS MORN! LIKE OLD MEN'S EYES THE STARS ARE PALE,  .  .  .  645  ISLE STAT I 1       4
     I'D BE ALONE.  WE TWO, BY THAT PALE FOUNT,  .  .  .  .  .    650  ISLE STAT I 1     132
     THE PALE ANEMONES.  WE'VE SOUGHT ALL DAY,  .  .  .  .  .  .  651  ISLE STAT I 2       5
     A SCARLET BLOOM.  WHY RAISEST THOU, PALE ONE,  .  .  .  .    673  ISLE STAT II 3    196
     THE VISION.  YOU ARE PALE AND WEEPING.  CHILD,  .  .  .  .   693  MOSADA 1           73
     I'M NOT OF THAT PALE COMPANY WHOSE FEET  .  .  .  .  .  .    699  MOSADA 3           20
     AND OUT-SPREAD ARMS.  BE NOT SO PALE, DEAR LOVE. .  .  .  .  701  MOSADA 3           70
     YOU'RE PALE, MY LORD.  HIS LIPS ARE QUIVERING. .  .  .  .    704  MOSADA 3          127
     A PEASANT PALE AND PRETTY, HER EYES FOR FEAR,  .  .  .  .    713  FERENCZ RENYI      81
     THE YOUNG ONE WITH THE OTHERS."  RENYI'S PALE .  .  .  .  .  713  FERENCZ RENYI      84
     A PEASANT, PALE AND PRETTY, HER EYES FROM FEAR,  .  .  .  .  713  FERENCZ RENYI  V   81
     "PRAY FOR THE SOULS IN PURGATORY," THE PALE PRIEST          719  PHANTOM SHIP       31
          TREMBLING CRIES.
     AMONG THE WINDS, LOOKS UNDER YOUR PALE EYELIDS. .  .  .  .   757  SHADOW WATER A    211
     SHOOK THE PALE APPLE-BLOSSOM OVER IT:  .  .  .  .  .  .  .   761  SHADOW WATER A    275
     AND THE PALE BLOSSOM! BUT I WOKE INSTEAD  .  .  .  .  .  .   761  SHADOW WATER A    281
     SHOOK THE PALE APPLE BLOSSOM OVER IT:  .  .  .  .  .  .  .   761  SHADOW WATER A V  275
     OF OPAL AND RUBY AND PALE CHRYSOLITE  .  .  .  .  .  .  .    762  SHADOW WATER A    301
     THE PALE HOUND AND THE DEER WANDER FOR EVER  .  .  .  .  .   764  SHADOW WATER A    330
     IS THIS POOR BODY THAT REDDENS AND GROWS PALE. .  .  .  .    764  SHADOW WATER A    341
     THE PALE HOUND AND THE DEER WANDER FOREVER  .  .  .  .  .    764  SHADOW WATER A V  330
     A FRAGILE, EXQUISITE, PALE SHELL. .  .  .  .  .  .  .  .  .  784  WOMANS BEAUTY      16
PALED
     AND AT THESE WORDS HE PALED, AS SHE HAD PALED,  .  .  .  .   280  TWO KINGS          76
     AND AT THESE WORDS HE PALED, AS SHE HAD PALED,  .  .  .  .   280  TWO KINGS          76
PALE-FACED
     PALE-FACED, ALONE UPON A BENCH, EDAIN  .  .  .  .  .  .  .   279  TWO KINGS          61
     PALE-FACED, ALONE UPON A BENCH, HIS WIFE  .  .  .  .  .  .   279  TWO KINGS      V   61
PALENESS
     UPON THE PALENESS OF A FINGER. .  .  .  .  .  .  .  .  .  .  390  IMAGE PAST         28
     A FEARFUL PALENESS CREEPS ACROSS HER BREAST  .  .  .  .  .   701  MOSADA 3           69
PALES
     FROM MORN THE TWAIN UNTIL THE EVENING PALES  .  .  .  .  .   651  ISLE STAT I 1     161
PALETTE
     THEY ARE SICK OF THE PALETTE AND FIDDLE-BOW, .  .  .  .  .   565  LAPIS LAZULI        2
PALING
     AND LIGHTS WERE PALING OUT OF THE WEST, .  .  .  .  .  .  .  175  BELOVED DEAD        2
     AND LIGHT WERE PALING OUT OF THE WEST. .  .  .  .  .  .  .   175  BELOVED DEAD   V    2
     WHILE LIGHTS WERE PALING ONE BY ONE. .  .  .  .  .  .  .  .  176  BELOVED DEAD       13
PALLAS
     AT PALLAS ATHENE'S SIDE. .  .  .  .  .  .  .  .  .  .  .  .  355  PROPERTIUS          6
     PALLAS ATHENE IN THAT STRAIGHT BACK AND ARROGANT HEAD!  . .  578  LOFTY THINGS       11
PALLOR
     PROPPED UPON PILLOWS, ROUGE ON THE PALLOR OF HER FACE. .  .  362  HER COURTESY        3
PALM
     CROWDED WITH BITTER FACES, THE WOUNDS IN PALM AND SIDE,      172  TRAV PASSION        4
     OF A SLENDER PALM, STOOD BUT A DAY!  .  .  .  .  .  .  .  .  566  LAPIS LAZULI       34
     ERE YONDER PALM COMMENCED HIS THOUSAND YEARS?  .  .  .  .    724  KANVA ON SELF      14
PALMER
     THE LONELY LIGHT THAT SAMUEL PALMER ENGRAVED. .  .  .  .  .  373  PHASES OF MOON     17
PALMER'S
     PALMER'S PHRASE, BUT AFTER THAT  .  .  .  .  .  .  .  .  .   639  BEN BULBEN         66
PALM-STEMS
     PAST THE SPEARS AND PALM-STEMS DRY, .  .  .  .  .  .  .  .   733  STREET DANCERS     42
PALTRY
     AN AGED MAN IS BUT A PALTRY THING,  .  .  .  .  .  .  .  .   407  SAIL BYZANTIUM      9
PAN
     NOR SOLDERED POT OR PAN! .  .  .  .  .  .  .  .  .  .  .  .  606  SONGS BURDEN 1     15
     OH! GRACIOUS PAN, TAKE NOW THY SERVANT'S PART. .  .  .  .    657  ISLE STAT I 3      77
     AS HERE I CAME I SAW GOD PAN.  HE PLAYED  .  .  .  .  .  .   678  ISLE STAT II 3    300
PANE
     BECAUSE WOMEN IN THE UPPER STOREYS DEMAND A FACE AT THE      623  HIGH TALK           7
          PANE,
PANEL
     WHEN PAINTED PANEL, STATUARY, .  .  .  .  .  .  .  .  .  .   440  WISDOM              2
PANG
     A COMPENSATION FOR THE PANG OF HIS BIRTH, .  .  .  .  .  .   444  SCHOOL CHILDR      39
     A GREATER WITH A LESSER PANG ASSUAGE  .  .  .  .  .  .  .    537  HER VISION          5
PANIC
     STRICKEN WITH PANIC FROM THE ATTACK, .  .  .  .  .  .  .  .  274  GREY ROCK          75
     IN FURY AND IN PANIC FLED  .  .  .  .  .  .  .  .  .  .  .   307  HOUR DAWN      V  119
PANNIERED
     HER DOMINO, HER PANNIERED SKIRT COPIED FROM LONGHI! .  .  .  363  DOLLS FACES         7
```

		PAGE	TITLE		LINE
PAN'S					
FROM WHERE PAN'S CAVERN IS	• • • • • • • • • •	612	NEWS ORACLE		31
PANSY'S					
THAN THE PEEPING PANSY'S FACE,	• • • • • • • • •	647	ISLE STAT I 1		52
PANT					
INNUMERABLE, SINGING, EXULTANT; THE CLAY UNDERNEATH THEM SHALL PANT,		61	OISIN 3		203
PANTHER					
THE PANTHER WITH HER YELLOW HIDE,	• • • • • • • •	658	ISLE STAT I 3		83
BUT A MOTHER PANTHER NEVER	• • • • • • • • • •	658	ISLE STAT I 3		92
PANTHER-KITTENS					
OF THE PIED PANTHER-KITTENS FROM MY HANDS	• • • • •	674	ISLE STAT II 3		219
PANTHERS					
MAY PANTHERS END HIM.--HEAR, AND LOAD OUR KING	• • •	71	ANASHU VIJAYA		6
NOURISH THE PANTHERS IN DIM SOLITUDES;	• • • • •	657	ISLE STAT I 3		44
OF DESERT-CAVES THE RED-EYED PANTHERS ROVE	• • • •	681	SEEKER		4
EYED PANTHERS IN THEIR DESERT CAVERNS ROVE	• • • • •	681	SEEKER	V	4
PANTING					
AND, GATHERED IN A PANTING BAND,	• • • • • • •	22	OISIN 1		324
COME WITH LOUD CRY AND PANTING BREAST	• • • • • •	412	TOWER		86
PANTRY					
BETWEEN THE PANTRY AND THE LINEN-CHEST,	• • • • • •	340	SHEP GOATHERD		36
BETWEEN THE PANTRY AND THE LINEN CHEST,	• • • • • •	340	SHEP GOATHERD	V	36
PAPER					
AND HANGING ITS PAPER FLOWERS FROM POST TO POST,	• • • •	198	SEVEN WOODS		8
BY PEN AND PAPER LIES,	• • • • • • • • • • • •	421	MY TABLE		3
PARABLE					
OR ELSE, TO ALTER PLATO'S PARABLE,	• • • • • • • •	443	SCHOOL CHILDR		15
PARADE					
THE OLD TROOPS PARADE,	• • • • • • • • • • •	496	MOHINI CHATTER		22
PARADIGM					
UPON A GHOSTLY PARADIGM OF THINGS;	• • • • • • •	445	SCHOOL CHILDR		42
PARADISE					
THE COUNTESS CATHLEEN IN PARADISE	• • • • • • • •	124	CATHLEEN PARA		T
RUNNING TO PARADISE	• • • • • • • • • • • • • •	300	RUN PARADISE		T
FOR I AM RUNNING TO PARADISE;	• • • • • • • • •	300	RUN PARADISE		3
AND I AM RUNNING TO PARADISE;	• • • • • • • • •	301	RUN PARADISE		10
AND I AM RUNNING TO PARADISE;	• • • • • • • • •	301	RUN PARADISE		17
FOR I AM RUNNING TO PARADISE;	• • • • • • • • •	301	RUN PARADISE		24
WHILE I AM RUNNING TO PARADISE.	• • • • • • • •	301	RUN PARADISE	V	REF
TRANSLUNAR PARADISE.	• • • • • • • • • • •	415	TOWER		156
THE FINAL PARADISE.	• • • • • • • • • • • •	415	TOWER	V	156
AWAY IN THE GREEN PARADISE,	• • • • • • • • • •	654	ISLE STAT I 2		70
PARADISE'S					
'FORE PARADISE'S GATE.	• • • • • • • • • • •	680	LOVE AND DEATH		20
PARAGON					
BY HOMER'S PARAGON	• • • • • • • • • • • • •	384	VISION ROBART		56
PARASITE					
THAT FEED ON SOME FOUL PARASITE	• • • • • • • •	493	AT ALGECIRAS		2
THAT FEEDS ON SOME FOUL PARASITE	• • • • • • • •	493	AT ALGECIRAS	V	2
PARCHED					
"WHEN ALL THE WELLS ARE PARCHED AWAY?	• • • • • • •	396	ROSE TREE		15
PARCHMENT					
THE PARCHMENT WILL DISCLOSE TO SOME LEARNED MAN	• • • •	461	HARUN RASHID		20
TAKE THIS LIGHT PARCHMENT, PASS THROUGH THE GREAT CHAMBER		461	HARUN RASHID	V	5
IF YOU SHOULD HIDE MY PARCHMENT IN THAT BOOK	• • • • •	461	HARUN RASHID	V	13
PARDON					
NO NEED TO DROWN, FOR, IF YOU WILL PARDON US	• • • • •	238	SHADOW WATER B		361
PARDON, OLD FATHERS, IF YOU STILL REMAIN	• • • • •	269	PARDON FATHERS		1
PARDON, AND YOU THAT DID NOT WEIGH THE COST,	• • • •	269	PARDON FATHERS	V	9
PARDON THAT FOR A BARREN PASSION'S SAKE,	• • • • •	270	PARDON FATHERS		19
PARDON, GREAT ENEMY,	• • • • • • • • • •	366	HER CHRIS TREE		1
UNTIL IT PARDON ME.	• • • • • • • • • • •	516	MANS SONG		18
SO THEY ESCAPE FROM HELL. BUT, PARDON ME,	• • • • •	704	MOSADA 3		132
AND JOHN WILL PARDON THEE,	• • • • • • • • •	739	EARL PAUL		2
I WILL SWEAR BY SUN AND MOON TO PARDON ALL	• • • • •	756	SHADOW WATER A		183
PARDONED					
PARDONED, DRAGS OUT LONELY YEARS	• • • • • • • •	475	EVA GORE-BOOTH		8
SAYING "EARL PAUL IS PARDONED	• • • • • • • • •	741	EARL PAUL		55
PARE					
LOOK TO LONG FISHING-LINES, OR POINT AND PARE	• • • • •	32	OISIN 2		55
PARENTS					
AY, AY. SWEAR BY THE PARENTS OF THE GODS,	• • • • •	74	ANASHU VIJAYA		66
SWEAR! BY THE PARENTS OF THE GODS, I SWEAR.	• • • • •	75	ANASHU VIJAYA		76
PARIS					
TO MIGHTY PARIS WHEN HE FOUND	• • • • • • • • •	522	LULLABY		4
WHAT WERE THEY WHEN PARIS FOUND	• • • • • • • •	522	LULLABY	V	4
IN COUNTRY SHAWL OR PARIS CLOAK, HAD PUT MY WITS ASTRAY,		592	PILGRIM		3
THE SHEPHERD PARIS FOR OENONE MADE,	• • • • • • •	650	ISLE STAT I 1		136
PARIS'					
FOR PEG AND MEG AND PARIS' LOVE	• • • • • • • •	458	HIS WILDNESS		3
PARISH					
NOR SO MUCH AS PARISH PRIEST,	• • • • • • • • •	508	JANE BISHOP		11
PARK					
COOLE PARK, [NINETEEN-TWENTY-NINE]	• • • • • • •	488	COOLE PARK 29		T
COOLE PARK	• • • • • • • • • • • • • • • •	488	COOLE PARK 29	V	T
COOLE PARK AND BALLYLEE, [NINETEEN-THIRTY-ONE]	• • • •	490	COOLE BALLYLEE		T
COOLE PARK AND BALLYLEE [NINETEEN-THIRTY-TWO]	• • • •	490	COOLE BALLYLEE	V	T
PARLIAMENT					
INTO A PLOUGHSHARE? PARLIAMENT AND KING	• • • • • •	429	NINETEEN 19		20
JOHN BULL HAS STOOD FOR PARLIAMENT,	• • • • • • •	583	GHOST ROG CASE		11

601

		PAGE	TITLE	LINE

PARLIAMENT   (CONTINUED)
NOR LAW NOR PARLIAMENT TAKE HEED. • • • • • • • • •   791 REPRISALS   22
PARMENIDES
PAUSE AT THE TREATISE OF PARMENIDES • • • • • • • •   461 HARUN RASHID   16
FROM THE GREAT TREATISE OF PARMENIDES¦ • • • • • • •   469 HARUN RASHID   183
PARNASSUS
OVERCOME GODS UPON PARNASSUS¦ • • • • • • • • • • •   540 FROM ANTIGONE   6
PARNELL
MOCK EMMET, MOCK PARNELL¦ • • • • • • • • • • • •   547 TO SAME TUNE 2   25
THAT PARNELL LOVED A LASS. • • • • • • • • • • • •   586 PARNELLITES   16
KEEPS PARNELL IN HIS MIND. • • • • • • • • • • • •   586 PARNELLITES   20
FOR PARNELL WAS A PROUD MAN. • • • • • • • • • • •   587 PARNELLITES   21
AND PARNELL LOVED HIS COUNTRY, • • • • • • • • • •   587 PARNELLITES   31
AND PARNELL LOVED HIS LASS. • • • • • • • • • • •   587 PARNELLITES   32
AND PARNELL LOVED A LASS. • • • • • • • • • • • •   587 PARNELLITES   V   32
PARNELL • • • • • • • • • • • • • • • • • • •   590 PARNELL   T
PARNELL CAME DOWN THE ROAD, HE SAID TO A CHEERING MAN¦ • • •   590 PARNELL   1
MOCK EMMET, MOCK PARNELL, • • • • • • • • • • •   614 MARCH SONGS 1   25
PARNELLITE
A PARNELLITE AT PARNELL'S FUNERAL • • • • • • • • •   541 PARN FUNERAL 1 V   T
PARNELLITES
COME GATHER ROUND ME, PARNELLITES • • • • • • • • •   586 PARNELLITES   T
COME GATHER ROUND ME, PARNELLITES, • • • • • • • •   586 PARNELLITES   1
PARNELL'S
PARNELL'S FUNERAL • • • • • • • • • • • • • • •   541 PARN FUNERAL 1   T
A PARNELLITE AT PARNELL'S FUNERAL • • • • • • • • •   541 PARN FUNERAL 1 V   T
HAD DE VALERA EATEN PARNELL'S HEART • • • • • • • •   542 PARN FUNERAL 2   2
HAD COSGRAVE EATEN PARNELL'S HEART, THE LAND'S • • • •   543 PARN FUNERAL 2   5
PARROT
A PARROT SWAYS UPON A TREE. • • • • • • • • • •   77 INDIAN TO LOVE   4
A PARROT SWAYING ON A TREE • • • • • • • • • • •   77 INDIAN TO LOVE V   4
PARROTS
EVEN WHERE HORRIBLE GREEN PARROTS CALL AND SWING. • • •   442 BLACK CENTAUR   2
EVEN WHERE THE HORRIBLE GREEN PARROTS CALL AND SWING. • • •   442 BLACK CENTAUR V   2
PART
AS THOUGH HIS HOUR WERE COME. WE SOUGHT THE PART • • •   37 OISIN 2   112
AS THOUGH HIS HOUR WERE ON HIM. TO THE PART • • • •   37 OISIN 2   V   112
• • • TILL STARLIGHT AND MIDNIGHT PART. • • • • • •   60 OISIN 3   184
HID IN THE EARTH'S MOST HIDDEN PART, • • • • • • •   78 INDIAN TO LOVE V   12
LET US PART, ERE THE SEASON OF PASSION FORGET US, • • •   79 FALLING LEAVES   7
COVER OVER AND HIDE, FOR HE HAS NO PART • • • • • •   158 TO HIS HEART   6
• • • WHEN A PART OF THE CONSTELLATIONS OF HEAVEN • • •   177 PAST GREATNESS   T
AND FOR A DOZEN HOURS HAVE BEEN A PART • • • • • •   230 SHADOW WATER B   171
BEING BUT A PART OF ANCIENT CEREMONY-- • • • • • •   321 REED WHISPERER   12
THAT HE WILL NEVER FIND¦ I'D PLAY A PART¦ • • • • •   377 PHASES OF MOON   128
HE, TOO, HAS RESIGNED HIS PART • • • • • • • • •   393 EASTER 1916   36
THAT IS HEAVEN'S PART, OUR PART • • • • • • • • •   394 EASTER 1916   60
THAT IS HEAVEN'S PART, OUR PART • • • • • • • • •   394 EASTER 1916   60
MUST WE PART, VON HUEGEL, THOUGH MUCH ALIKE, FOR WE • •   503 VACILLATION   78
WHAT SEEMS MOST WELCOME IN THE TOMB--PLAY A PREDESTINED • •   503 VACILLATION   86
    PART.
WOULD TRANSFORM THE PART, • • • • • • • • • • •   506 REMORSE SPEECH   3
NONE SHARED OUR GUILT¦ NOR DID WE PLAY A PART • • • •   542 PARN FUNERAL 1   22
IF WORTHY THEIR PROMINENT PART IN THE PLAY, • • • •   565 LAPIS LAZULI   14
THROW IT IN EVERY PART." • • • • • • • • • • •   596 COLONEL MARTIN   53
SHE THINKS, PART WOMAN, THREE PARTS A CHILD, • • • •   617 LONG-LEG FLY   15
OH¦ GRACIOUS PAN, TAKE NOW THY SERVANT'S PART. • • • •   657 ISLE STAT I 3   77
AND PART HIS FOAMING MOUTH WITH EAGER EYE-- • • • •   688 TWO TITANS   46
THEIR THIEVING WINGS THAT WE MIGHT NEVER PART. • • • •   702 MOSADA 3   98
IN THE GREEN HILL'S INMOST PART. • • • • • • • •   726 LOVERS QUARREL   12
PARTED
PARTED HER LIPS WITH A LOUD SUDDEN CRY. • • • • • •   105 CUCHULAIN SEA   8
BROKE FROM HIS PARTED LIPS AND BROKE AGAIN. • • • •   182 QUEEN MAEVE   48
THE PARTED LIPS REPLIED, "I SEEK YOUR HELP, • • • •   183 QUEEN MAEVE   83
PARTIAL
HE COMPLETES HIS PARTIAL MIND, • • • • • • • • •   638 BEN BULBEN   30
PARTICULAR
THE PARTICULAR IS POUNDED TILL IT IS MAN. • • • • •   382 VISION ROBART   6
PARTICULAR QUALITY. THE SIGNS AND SHAPES¦ • • • • •   469 HARUN RASHID   181
PARTICULARS
WITH THE MINUTE PARTICULARS OF MANKIND? • • • • • •   384 VISION ROBART   42
PARTING
IT SPEEDS THE PARTING GUEST. • • • • • • • • • •   434 YOUTH AND AGE   4
PARTING • • • • • • • • • • • • • • • • • •   535 PARTING   T
A BRIEF PARTING FROM THOSE DEAR • • • • • • • • •   637 BEN BULBEN   19
I KNEEL BY THEE--NO PARTING NOW--LOOK UP. • • • • •   702 MOSADA 3   94
PARTLY
BOOK I WHAT THE CALIPH PARTLY LEARNED • • • • • • •   372 PHASES OF MOON V   T
PARTRIDGE
A--MURMUR LIKE YOUNG PARTRIDGE¦ WITH LOUD HORN • • • •   32 OISIN 2   52
"THEY MURMUR LIKE YOUNG PARTRIDGE IN THE MORN, • • • •   32 OISIN 2   V   51
PARTS
AND MADE IN ALL THEIR DISTANT PARTS, • • • • • • •   16 OISIN 1   228
AND ROSE FROM ALL THEIR DISTANT PARTS, • • • • • •   16 OISIN 1   V   228
TILL MEDITATION MASTER ALL ITS PARTS, • • • • • •   474 ALL SOUL NIGHT   92
SHE THINKS, PART WOMAN, THREE PARTS A CHILD, • • • •   617 LONG-LEG FLY   15
PARTY
THE BISHOPS AND THE PARTY • • • • • • • • • • •   587 PARNELLITES   25
PASS
AND THE DAYS PASS BY LIKE A WAYWARD TUNE, • • • • •   8 OISIN 1   83
• • • AND I KNEW HOW MEN SORROW AND PASS, • • • • •   59 OISIN 3   175

602

	PAGE	TITLE		LINE
PASS (CONTINUED)				
• • • AND I KNEW HOW MEN PASS, • • • • • • • • •	59	OISIN 3	V	175
THE WHIRLING WAYS OF STARS THAT PASS-- • • • • • • • •	66	HAPPY SHEPHERD		30
AMRITA. THIS SAME EVE SHE WATCHED ME PASS. • • • • •	74	ANASHU VIJAYA	V	64
THAT I MAY CONTENTED PASS • • • • • • • • • • • •	97	FOXHUNTER		11
AND I ON THIS STRANGE ROAD WILL PASS • • • • • • • •	97	FOXHUNTER	V	11
THE MOMENTS PASS AND PASS! • • • • • • • • • • • •	99	FOXHUNTER		44
THE MOMENTS PASS AND PASS! • • • • • • • • • • • •	99	FOXHUNTER		44
AND HEAVY MORTAL HOPES THAT TOIL AND PASS! • • • • • •	101	ROSE UPON ROOD		18
FOR WE TIRE OF THE FLAME OF THE METEOR BEFORE IT CAN PASS	122	WHITE BIRDS	V	2
BY AND FLEE				
WE TIRE OF THE FLAME OF THE METEOR, BEFORE IT CAN PASS	122	WHITE BIRDS		2
BY AND FLEE!				
LIFT UP BEFORE US WHEN THEY PASS, • • • • • • • • •	135	TWO TREES		23
LIFT UP BEFORE US AS THEY PASS, • • • • • • • • • •	135	TWO TREES	V	23
YOU PASS NOT AWAY. • • • • • • • • • • • • • • • •	142	MOODS	V	7
THEY KNOW ALL WONDERS, FOR THEY PASS • • • • • • • •	196	BAILE AILLINN		160
BUT THERE WERE OTHERS. I HAVE SEEN NOTHING PASS. • • •	226	SHADOW WATER B		82
IF HE COULD PASS HER BY • • • • • • • • • • • • •	255	WOMAN HOMER		6
"YOUR STRENGTH AND NOBLENESS WILL PASS AWAY"? • • • • •	285	TWO KINGS		189
PASS THE DOOR OF BIRTH AGAIN, • • • • • • • • • • •	298	THREE HERMITS		19
SHE NEED NOT BE TOO COMELY--LET IT PASS," • • • • • •	300	BEGGAR CRIED		10
BUT THE HOUR WHEN YOU SHALL PASS AWAY • • • • • • •	306	HOUR DAWN		96
GROWS COMELIER. ELEVEN PASS, AND THEN • • • • • • • •	374	PHASES OF MOON		44
WILL PASS FROM CHANGE TO CHANGE, • • • • • • r • • •	379	CAT AND MOON		22
COULD THE IMPOSSIBLE COME TO PASS • • • • • • • • •	385	ROBARTES DANCE		9
KNOWING THAT NONE COULD PASS HEAVEN'S DOOR • • • • • •	422	MY TABLE		26
KNOWING THAT NONE WHO PASS HEAVEN'S DOOR • • • • • • •	422	MY TABLE	V	26
KNOWING THAT NONE CAN PASS HEAVEN'S DOOR • • • • • • •	422	MY TABLE	V	26
AND WHEN I PASS A COMPLIMENT • • • • • • • • • • •	453	DEATH OF HARE		3
AND WAIT WAR'S MUSIC! PASS THE LITTLE GALLERY! • • • •	461	HARUN RASHID		8
PASS BOOKS OF LEARNING FROM BYZANTIUM • • • • • • • •	461	HARUN RASHID		9
TAKE THIS LIGHT PARCHMENT, PASS THROUGH THE GREAT CHAMBER	461	HARUN RASHID	V	5
"LET ALL THINGS PASS AWAY." • • • • • • • • • • • •	502	VACILLATION		61
"LET ALL THINGS PASS AWAY." • • • • • • • • • • • •	502	VACILLATION		66
"LET ALL THINGS PASS AWAY." • • • • • • • • • • • •	502	VACILLATION		71
THEY BROUGHT TO PASS! • • • • • • • • • • • • • •	505	GRAT INSTRUCT		2
IN THE NARROW PASS! • • • • • • • • • • • • • • •	512	JANE ON GOD		11
THAT MEN PASS OVER • • • • • • • • • • • • • • •	512	JANE ON GOD		21
PLATO THERE AND MINOS PASS, • • • • • • • • • • • •	531	DELPHIC ORACLE		8
THE REST I PASS, ONE SENTENCE I UNSAY. • • • • • • •	542	PARN FUNERAL 2		1
I PASS THE REST--ONE SENTENCE I UNSAY-- • • • • • • •	542	PARN FUNERAL 2	V	1
THEY HAVE SCHOOLING OF THEIR OWN, BUT I PASS THEIR	580	CURSE CROMWELL		13
SCHOOLING BY,				
AND PASS THE BOTTLE ROUND. • • • • • • • • • • • •	586	PARNELLITES		8
HE BROUGHT IT ALL TO PASS! • • • • • • • • • • • •	586	PARNELLITES		14
SO PASS THE BOTTLE ROUND. • • • • • • • • • • • • •	587	PARNELLITES		24
WHAT MARCHES THROUGH THE MOUNTAIN PASS? • • • • • • •	614	MARCH SONGS 2		7
WHAT MARCHES DOWN THE MOUNTAIN PASS? • • • • • • • •	615	MARCH SONGS 2		17
WHAT MARCHES DOWN THE MOUNTAIN PASS? • • • • • • • •	615	MARCH SONGS 2		27
HORSEMAN, PASS BY! • • • • • • • • • • • • • • •	640	BEN BULBEN		94
O LET ME PASS! THE SPELLS FROM OFF THE HEART • • • • •	668	ISLE STAT II 3		44
O LET ME PASS! THAT FLOWER NONE • • • • • • • • • •	668	ISLE STAT II 3		47
PASS AWAY-- • • • • • • • • • • • • • • • • • •	668	ISLE STAT II 3		67
TO WATCH THEE PASS? YET DEEPER THAN MEN KNOW • • • • •	672	ISLE STAT II 3		158
THEY MAY NOT PASS THE PORTAL, • • • • • • • • • • •	680	LOVE AND DEATH		21
TO PASS AND LEAVE THEM THERE • • • • • • • • • • •	680	LOVE AND DEATH		24
THE PREACHER WATCHING FOR THE EVIL HOUR TO PASS, • • •	686	LIFE		3
I SAW HIM SIGH AND TURN AND PASS AWAY! • • • • • • •	690	MOSADA 1		14
CIRCLING THE BRAIN? MY BROTHERS WILL PASS DOWN • • • •	699	MOSADA 3		6
CIRCLING THE BRAIN? MY BROTHERS NOW PASS DOWN • • • • •	699	MOSADA 3	·V	6
THE SHADOWS PASS! BUT NOW, I LOVE MY RING, • • • • •	700	MOSADA 3		27
'TWILL PASS. I'LL SEE THE OTHER PRISONERS NOW, • • • •	704	MOSADA 3		130
AND ALONG THE MOUNTAINS PASS, • • • • • • • • • • •	705	DAWN-SONG		12
O SHINING ONES, LIGHTLY WITH SONG PASS, • • • • • • •	708	FAIRY PEDANT		21
TALKING HOURS SWIFTLY PASS! • • • • • • • • • • •	727	LOVERS QUARREL		44
THE PREACHER WATCHING FOR THE ILL HOUR TO PASS-- • • •	734	QUATRAIN APHOR		3
THE PREACHER WATCHING FOR THE EVIL HOUR TO PASS, • • •	734	QUATRAIN APHOR	V	3
IT WERE BETTER TO PASS BY, BECAUSE THE GODS • • • • •	751	SHADOW WATER A		104
AMONG THE WINDS AND WATERS! AND WHEN THEY PASS • • • •	764	SHADOW WATER A		331
DID NOT A SHADOW PASS? • • • • • • • • • • • • •	781	MY HEART BEAT		2
PASSAGE				
HAD WATCHED MY DAILY PASSAGE TO AND FRO! • • • • • •	466	HARUN RASHID		107
PASSAGES				
WHEN ALL THOSE ROOMS AND PASSAGES ARE GONE, • • • • •	489	COOLE PARK 29		26
PASSED				
I KNOW NOT IF DAYS PASSED OR HOURS, • • • • • • • •	11	OISIN 1		133
PASSED BY US, CHASED BY A PHANTOM HOUND • • • • • • •	11	OISIN 1		140
I KNEW NOT IF DAYS PASSED OR HOURS, • • • • • • • •	11	OISIN 1	V	133
PASSED BY US, CHASED OF A PHANTOM HOUND • • • • • • •	11	OISIN 1	V	140
WE PASSED THE PORTALS, AND WITHIN, • • • • • • • • •	17	OISIN 1	V	250
PASSED A-TIPTOE UP AND DOWN • • • • • • • • • • •	20	OISIN 1	V	294
WE PASSED BY WOODS, AND LAWNS OF CLOVER, • • • • • •	25	OISIN 1		377
WE PASSED IN SILENCE O'ER THE MEAD, • • • • • • • •	25	OISIN 1	V	376A
OR HOURS PASSED BY, YET HOLD THE MORNING RAYS • • • •	30	OISIN 2		20
PASSED UNDER THE DIM DOORWAY, OUT OF SIGHT, • • • • •	37	OISIN 2		123
MAKING A WORLD ABOUT HER, PASSED FROM SIGHT • • • • •	37	OISIN 2	V	123
PASSED UNDER A DIM DOORWAY, OUT OF SIGHT, • • • • • •	37	OISIN 2	V	123
I MOUNTED, AND WE PASSED OVER THE LONE • • • • • • •	45	OISIN 2		231
I PASSED ALONG THE WATER'S EDGE BELOW THE HUMID TREES, • •	76	INDIAN ON GOD		1
I PASSED A LITTLE FURTHER ON AND HEARD A LOTUS TALK! • •	76	INDIAN ON GOD		9

PAGE TITLE LINE

PASSED (CONTINUED)
 I PASSED A LITTLE FURTHER ON AND HEARD A PEACOCK SAY: 77 INDIAN ON GOD 17
 I PASSED A LITTLE FURTHER AND I HEARD A PEACOCK SAY:-- 77 INDIAN ON GOD V 17
 AND PASSED A-TIPTOE UP AND DOWN, 85 MAD KING GOLL V 51
 I PASSED A TIP-TOE UP AND DOWN, 85 MAD KING GOLL V 51
 I PASSED A-TIPTOE UP AND DOWN, 85 MAD KING GOLL V 51
 WHEN MY HAND PASSED FROM WIRE TO WIRE 86 MAD KING GOLL 65
 SHE PASSED THE SALLEY GARDENS WITH LITTLE SNOW-WHITE FEET. 90 SALLEY GARDENS 2
 TROY PASSED AWAY IN ONE HIGH FUNERAL GLEAM, 111 ROSE OF WORLD 4
 A SONG INTO THE AIR, AND SINGING PASSED 114 ROSE OF BATTLE 14
 BUT WHILE HE PASSED BEFORE A PLASHY PLACE, 127 DREAM OF FAERY 17
 FOR HAPPY LOVERS PASSED TWO BY TWO WHERE I STOOD, 163 VALLEY LOVERS 2
 I PASSED MY BROTHER AND COUSIN: 178 FIDDLER DOONEY 5
 FOR ALTHOUGH YEARS HAD PASSED AWAY 192 BAILE AILLINN 77
 HAVE THE BIRDS PASSED US? I COULD HEAR YOUR VOICE, 226 SHADOW WATER B 81
 BUT THAT I AM AFRAID THEY MAY HAVE PASSED, 226 SHADOW WATER B 84
 THAT HAS NOT PASSED THROUGH ANY HUCKSTER'S LOIN, 269 PARDON FATHERS 8
 BUT THE STAG STOOPED AND RAN AT HIM, AND PASSED, 277 TWO KINGS 12
 AND RAN AT HIM, AND PASSED, AND AS IT PASSED 277 TWO KINGS V 12A
 AND RAN AT HIM, AND PASSED, AND AS IT PASSED 277 TWO KINGS V 12A
 AND MOCKS RETURNING VICTORY, HE PASSED 279 TWO KINGS 58
 AND SO THE WEEKS PASSED BY, BUT WHEN I SAID, 280 TWO KINGS 89
 THE MOMENTS PASSED AS AT A PLAY: 313 MEMORY YOUTH 1
 AND, THOUGH YOU HAVE PASSED THE BEST OF LIFE, STILL TRACE, 367 EGO DOMINUS 5
 I HAVE PASSED WITH A NOD OF THE HEAD 392 EASTER 1916 5
 WHO TROD UPON THESE ROCKS OR PASSED THIS DOOR, 413 TOWER 98
 WHEN ALEXANDER'S EMPIRE PASSED, THEY SLEPT SO SOUND. 442 BLACK CENTAUR 12
 SO GREAT ITS FAME. WHEN FITTING TIME HAS PASSED 461 HARUN RASHID 19
 IN CHILDISH IGNORANCE OF ALL THAT PASSED. 468 HARUN RASHID 149
 IN CHILDISH IGNORANCE OF ALL THAT PASSED. 468 HARUN RASHID 160
 SEVEN CENTURIES HAVE PASSED AND IT IS PURE, 482 BLOOD AND MOON 33
 MEN HAVE PASSED OVER 512 JANE ON GOD V 21
 THROUGH JONATHAN SWIFT'S DARK GROVE HE PASSED, AND THERE 543 PARN FUNERAL 2 11
 FROM TIME LONG PASSED AWAY, 589 OLD WICKED MAN 42
 I PASSED BY MANY CAVES OF DRIPPING STONE, 657 ISLE STAT I 3 47
 HE PASSED ACROSS THE LAKE. WHEN WE TWO CAME 658 ISLE STAT II 1 5
 THEY PASSED A-TIP-TOE EVERYWHERE, 667 ISLE STAT II 3 20
 THEY PASSED A-TIPTOE EVERYWHERE, 667 ISLE STAT II 3 V 20
 THE SINGING SHEPHERDS, TOO, HAVE PASSED AWAY. 676 ISLE STAT II 3 271
 AND WHEN ONCE MORE THE LIGHTNING GENII PASSED, 687 TWO TITANS 29
 DRAW STAR TO STAR, AS ON THAT EVE HE PASSED 691 MOSADA 1 29
 SO LITTLE. AS THE MONTHS PASSED BY WE GREW 713 FERENCZ RENYI 93
 DEEP IN THE WOODLAND PASSED THEY. THE SIX FEET 716 DWELT SYCAMORE V 9
 SLOW THE CHAPEL BELL IS TOLLING AS THOUGH THE DEAD PASSED 718 PHANTOM SHIP 16
 BY.
 AND PASSED THE OUTER HEBRIDES, AND TOOK 749 SHADOW WATER A 42
 FROM HILLY LOCHLANN: BUT OUR SAIL HAS PASSED 749 SHADOW WATER A 44
 AND PASSED THE NORTHERN HEBRIDES, AND TOOK 749 SHADOW WATER A V 42
 IT PASSED BUT A MOMENT AGO. 781 MY HEART BEAT 3
 IT PASSED BY A MOMENT AGO. 781 MY HEART BEAT 3
PASSES
 WHO DREAMED THAT BEAUTY PASSES LIKE A DREAM? 111 ROSE OF WORLD 1
 WHY MUST THE LASTING LOVE WHAT PASSES, 275 GREY ROCK 114
 IT IS OF GOD AND PASSES HUMAN WIT. 558 RIBH CHRISTIAN 2
PASSETH
 IT PASSETH AWAY, AND IS HEARD OF NO LONGER. 26 OISIN 1 V 399B
 PASSETH THE MOON WITH HER SICKLE OF LIGHT, 648 ISLE STAT I 1 82
PASSING
 AND PASSING THE FIRBOLGS' BURIAL-MOUNDS, 3 OISIN 1 16
 AND PASSING THE FIRBOLGS' BURIAL MOUNDS, 3 OISIN 1 V 16
 BACCHANT AND MOURNFUL, PASSING TO AND FRO 39 OISIN 2 161
 WE AND THE LABOURING WORLD ARE PASSING BY: 112 ROSE OF WORLD 6
 UNDER THE PASSING STARS, FOAM OF THE SKY, 112 ROSE OF WORLD 9
 ARE PASSING ON TO WHERE MAY BE, 139 TO IRELAND 41
 THE WEST WEEPS IN PALE DEW AND SIGHS PASSING AWAY, 154 BELOVED PEACE 5
 LIVE BUT TO LIGHT YOUR PASSING FEET. 158 BELOVED RHYMES 12
 ONE THAT NO PASSING THOUGHT, 315 FRIENDS V 4
 ARE BUT A POST THE PASSING DOGS DEFILE. 321 REED WHISPERER 14
 WHEN YOU ARE PASSING: 355 BROKEN DREAMS 3
 OF WHAT IS PAST, OR PASSING, OR TO COME. 408 SAIL BYZANTIUM 32
 THROUGH TOO MUCH BUSINESS WITH THE PASSING HOUR, 423 MY DESCENDANTS 11
 TO PASSING BIRD, BUT I AM DUMB 452 HUMAN DIGNITY 11
 PASSING ON THE ROAD THAT NIGHT, 511 JANE AND JACK 17
 FOR PASSING ROUND THE BOTTLE WITH GIRLS IN RAGS OR SILK, 592 PILGRIM 2
 FOR PASSING ROUND THE BOTTLE WITH GIRLS IN RAG OR SILK, 592 PILGRIM V 2
 FROM ANY PASSING WRETCH: 598 STONE CROSS 12
 THE BRAIN. MY BROTHERS WILL BE PASSING DOWN 699 MOSADA 3 V 6
 THE PASSING OF THOSE LITTLE GRAINS IS SNOW 722 WITCH VIVIEN 48
 A GREY PROFESSOR PASSING CRIED, 725 LEGEND 9
 A PASSING WORD. 786 YOUR HEART 13
 A PASSING WORD. 786 YOUR HEART 26
 A PASSING WORD. 786 YOUR HEART 39
 MAY MURDER THEM IN PASSING BY 791 REPRISALS 21
PASSIO SEE HYSTERICO-PASSIO
 HYSTERICA PASSIO DRAGGED THIS QUARRY DOWN. 542 PARN FUNERAL 1 21
 HYSTERICA PASSIO OF ITS OWN EMPTINESS? 618 BRONZE HEAD 7
PASSION
 LET US PART, ERE THE SEASON OF PASSION FORGET US, 79 FALLING LEAVES 7
 WHEN THE POOR TIRED CHILD, PASSION, FALLS ASLEEP. 80 EPHEMERA 7
 "PASSION HAS OFTEN WORN OUR WANDERING HEARTS." 80 EPHEMERA 12
 "OFTEN HAS PASSION WORN OUR WANDERING HEARTS, 80 EPHEMERA V 12

604

		PAGE	TITLE	LINE
PASSION	(CONTINUED)			
WHITE WOMAN THAT PASSION HAS WORN	• • • • • •	157	POET BELOVED	3
THE TRAVAIL OF PASSION	• • • • • •	172	TRAV PASSION	T
WHEN AN IMMORTAL PASSION BREATHES IN MORTAL CLAY;	• • • •	172	TRAV PASSION	2
BUT THE REALITY THAT MAKES OUR PASSION	• • • •	229	SHADOW WATER B	159
WHERE PASSION GROWS TO BE A CHANGELESS THING,	• • • • •	231	SHADOW WATER B	213
BY ANY OTHER MEANS. YOU CALL IT PASSION.	• • • • •	244	SHADOW WATER B	455
WHERE PASSION AND PRECISION HAVE BEEN ONE	• • • • •	264	HOUSE SHAKEN	2
PRETENDING THAT THERE CAN BE PASSION	• • • • •	271	GREY ROCK	7
AND TREMBLING WITH HER PASSION SAID,	• • • • • •	272	GREY ROCK	31
SOME PASSION HAD MADE HER STONE. HEARING A FOOT	• • •	279	TWO KINGS	65
THAT PUT A PASSION IN THE SLEEPER THERE,	• • • • • •	284	TWO KINGS	157
SUCKED UP THE PASSION OUT OF HIM AGAIN	• • • • •	284	TWO KINGS	160
THEY'VE THE PASSION TO ESCAPE."	• • • • • •	299	THREE HERMITS	21
PASSION OR CONQUEST, WANDER WHERE THEY WILL,	• • • •	323	SWANS AT COOLE	23
AND SOLID MEN, FOR ALL THEIR PASSION, LIVE	• • • •	325	ROBERT GREGORY	37
COURTESY AND PASSION INTO ONE LIKE THOSE	• • • •	352	PEOPLE	17
WITH ALL A WOMAN'S PASSION, A CHILD'S IMPERIOUS WAY,	• •	354	HIS PHOENIX	14
THE POET STUBBORN WITH HIS PASSION SANG US	• • • • •	356	BROKEN DREAMS	18
WE HAVE GIVEN THE WORLD OUR PASSION,	• • • • • •	363	DOLLS DRAWINGS	10
--PEDANT IN PASSION, LEARNED IN OLD COURTESIES,	• • • • •	363	DOLLS FACES	4
A SUFFERING PASSION AND A LABOURING THOUGHT?	• • • •	420	MY HOUSE	V 20J
THAT PASSION, PIETY OR AFFECTION KNOWS,	• • • • •	445	SCHOOL CHILDR	54
IT MAKES MY PASSION STRONGER BUT TO THINK	• • • • •	465	HARUN RASHID	99
LIKE PASSION STIRS THE PEACOCK AND HIS MATE,	• • • •	465	HARUN RASHID	100
AND THAT TO SUCH A PITCH OF PASSION WROUGHT	• • • •	471	ALL SOUL NIGHT	24
HOW COULD PASSION RUN SO DEEP	• • • • • •	534	CONSOLATION	7
TO THINK HIS PASSION SUCH	• • • • • •	538	LAST CONFESS	8
WHEN THE CONFLAGRATION OF THEIR PASSION SINKS,	• • •	556	RIBH PATRICK	8
FOR THAT'S A PASSION IN MY OWN CONTROL,	• • • • •	558	RIBH CHRISTIAN	4
ETERNITY IS PASSION, GIRL OR BOY	• • • • •	560	WHENCE COME	1
A ROOF, GOOD CLOTHES, PASSION, LOVE PERHAPS,	• • • •	609	IN TARAS HALLS	8
THAT PASSION COULD BRING CHARACTER ENOUGH,	• • • •	610	STATUES	6
WHERE DREAM-FED PASSION IS AND PEACE ENCLOSES,	• • •	669	ISLE STAT II 3	85
THEIR PASSION AND THEIR RESTLESSNESS AND RUTH	• • • •	687	TWO TITANS	24
PASSIONATE				
WHERE PASSIONATE MAEVE IS STONY-STILL;	• • • • •	3	OISIN 1	18
WHERE PASSIONATE MAIVE IS STONY STILL;	• • • • •	3	OISIN 1	V 18
HUNG IN THE PASSIONATE DAWN. HE SLOWLY TURNED;	• • •	40	OISIN 2	167
• • • AND ITS GODLESS AND PASSIONATE AGE.	• • •	63	OISIN 3	216
OF PASSIONATE MEN, LIKE BATS IN THE DEAD TREES;	• •	136	TO SOME I TALK	5
I BRING YOU MY PASSIONATE RHYME.	• • • • •	157	POET BELOVED	8
LILIES OF DEATH-PALE HOPE, ROSES OF PASSIONATE DREAM.	• •	172	TRAV PASSION	8
TO PASSIONATE WOMEN IF IT SEEM	• • • • •	202	NEVER GIVE ALL	3
AENGUS AND EDAIN, THOSE PASSIONATE WANDERERS,	• • •	228	SHADOW WATER B	138
OF YOUR OWN PASSIONATE SERVING KIND WHO HAD BROUGHT	• •	292	TO A SHADE	10
OF YOUR OWN PASSIONATE SERVING KIND WHO HAS BROUGHT	• •	292	TO A SHADE	V 10
PASSIONATE AND SIMPLE LIKE HIS HEART.	• • • • •	325	ROBERT GREGORY	32
BE PASSIONATE, NOT BOUNTIFUL	• • • • • •	335	YOUNG BEAUTY	8
AND PASSIONATE AS THE DAWN."	• • • • • •	348	FISHERMAN	40
BUT WHAT THE GREAT AND PASSIONATE HAVE USED	• • • •	371	ON GOING HOUSE	7
ARE FULL OF PASSIONATE INTENSITY.	• • • • •	402	SECOND COMING	8
EXCITED, PASSIONATE, FANTASTICAL	• • • • •	409	TOWER	5
HEARD ALL THE ANXIETY OF MY PASSIONATE YOUTH,	• • • •	468	HARUN RASHID	168
A FOOLISH, PASSIONATE MAN.	• • • • •	553	PRAYER OLD AGE	12
SO PASSIONATE IS A SHADE,	• • • • • •	781	MY HEART BEAT	13
PASSION-DIMMED				
PASSION-DIMMED EYES AND LONG HEAVY HAIR	• • • • •	155	REPROVE CURLEW	4
PASSION-DRIVEN				
A PASSION-DRIVEN EXULTANT MAN SINGS OUT	• • • • • •	560	WHENCE COME	5
PASSIONED				
DAWN PASSIONED; FED WITH A FAINT GREEN LIGHT,	• • • •	40	OISIN 2	V 165
PASSION'S				
PARDON THAT FOR A BARREN PASSION'S SAKE,	• • • • •	270	PARDON FATHERS	19
AYE, THOUGH ALL PASSION'S IN THE GLANCE--	• • • • •	388	SOLOMON WITCH	21
PASSIONS				
NONE MAY BEGUILE HIM, AND HIS PASSIONS COLD	• • • •	35	OISIN 2	V 83A
YET WEARY WITH PASSIONS THAT FADED	• • • • • •	50	OISIN 3	52
LIKE TATTERED CLOUDS OF THE WORLD, PASSIONS CALL AND OUR		207	HANRAHANS SONG	V 8
HEARTS BEAT;				
TWO CONTEMPLATING PASSIONS CHOSE ONE THEME	• • • • •	466	HARUN RASHID	117
COMPLETENESS OF THEIR PASSIONS WON;	• • • • • •	637	BEN BULBEN	9
OF ANCIENT PASSIONS AND OF ANCIENT FEARS?	• • • • •	724	KANVA ON SELF	16
PAST				
IN DREARY DANCING PAST US WHIRLED	• • • • •	65	HAPPY SHEPHERD	8
A SONG INTO THE AIR, AND SINGING PAST	• • • • •	114	ROSE OF BATTLE	V 14
HE THINKS OF HIS PAST GREATNESS	• • • • • •	177	PAST GREATNESS	T
MONGAN THINKS OF HIS PAST GREATNESS	• • • • •	177	PAST GREATNESS	V T
OR CLIMBED AMONG THE IMAGES OF THE PAST--	• • • • •	352	PEOPLE	10
AN IMAGE FROM A PAST LIFE	• • • • • •	389	IMAGE PAST	T
YOUTH'S BITTERNESS BEING PAST,	• • • • • •	389	IMAGE PAST	11
OF WHAT IS PAST, OR PASSING, OR TO COME.	• • • • •	408	SAIL BYZANTIUM	32
THERE LURCHES PAST, HIS GREAT EYES WITHOUT THOUGHT	• •	433	NINETEEN 19	126
PROTECTING, TILL THE DANGER PAST,	• • • • • •	436	FOR MY SON	31
WHEN ALEXANDER'S EMPIRE PAST, THEY SLEPT SO SOUND.	• • •	442	BLACK CENTAUR	V 12
WHEN CRADLE AND SPOOL ARE PAST,	• • • • • •	449	HERO GIRL FOOL	24
HAD HEARD IMPOSSIBLE HISTORY OF MY PAST;	• • • • •	466	HARUN RASHID	108
LONG PAST HIS PRIME REMEMBER THINGS THAT ARE	• • • •	477	SELF AND SOUL	18
FOR LOVER IN THE PAST;	• • • • • •	539	MEETING	10
ALL THAT GREAT PAST TO A TROUBLE OF FOOLS;	• • • • •	546	TO SAME TUNE 2	22

		PAGE	TITLE	LINE

PAST (CONTINUED)

HOW SOUL MAY WALK WHEN ALL SUCH THINGS ARE PAST, ... 558 RIBH CHRISTIAN 11
ALL THAT GREAT PAST TO A TROUBLE OF FOOLS; . . . . . . 614 MARCH SONGS 1 22
STRICKEN ALL THE NIGHT IS PAST-- . . . . 648 ISLE STAT I 1 96
PAST THE SPEARS AND PALM-STEMS DRY, ... 733 STREET DANCERS 42
PAST THE CAMEL'S DREAMING EYE. . . . . 733 STREET DANCERS 43

PASTERN

WHOSE CAREFUL PASTERN PRESSED THE SOD . . . . 2 OISIN 1 V 7W

PASTURE

TO PLOUGH OR PASTURE LAND, MIGHT SEE ME THERE . . . . 283 TWO KINGS V 146
AND OVER TILLAGE FIELDS AND PASTURE LANDS . . . . . . 715 FERENCZ RENYI 120
AND FOLLOWING O'ER THE FIELDS AND PASTURE LANDS, . . . 715 FERENCZ RENYI V 120
BY THE PASTURE WHERE THE LAMBS . . . . 726 LOVERS QUARREL 5

PASTURED   SEE MANY-PASTURED

TO MANY PASTURED MUIRTHEMNE, ... 189 BAILE AILLINN V 21

PASTURE-LAND

TO PLOUGH OR PASTURE-LAND, MIGHT SEE ME THERE, ... 283 TWO KINGS 146
OF PASTURE-LAND AND PLOUGH-LAND AMONG THE HILLS? . . . 748 SHADOW WATER A 33

PATCH

SOME ROGUE OF THE WORLD STOLE THEM TO PATCH UP A FENCE 623 HIGH TALK 4
OR A FIRE.
MY THOUGHTS, AND YONDER BRIGHTENING PATCH OF SKY . . . 700 MOSADA 3 31

PATCHED

WITH OLD PATCHED SHOES, ... 627 STATES HOLIDAY 30

PATCHING

THAT PATCHING OLD HEELS THEY MAY SHRIEK, I TAKE TO CHISEL 623 HIGH TALK 8
AND PLANE.

PATE

"AND MAKE MY SOUL BEFORE MY PATE IS BARE." . . . . . 299 BEGGAR CRIED 4

PATED   SEE GREEN-PATED CRACK-PATED

PATER

AND MANY PATER NOSTERS SAID SINCE DAWN. . . . . 43 OISIN 2 V 208D
HE HAD LEARNT FROM PATER, AND TO ROUND HIS TALE . . . 373 PHASES OF MOON 27

PATH   SEE BRIDLE-PATH

FOR ALL YOUR CROZIERS, THEY HAVE LEFT THE PATH . . . . 42 OISIN 2 200
I FELL ON THE PATH, AND THE HORSE WENT AWAY LIKE A SUMMER 60 OISIN 3 190
FLY;
A RABBIT OLD AND LAME LIMPED DOWN THE PATH; . . . . . 80 EPHEMERA 15
I HAVE BEEN IN THE PATH OF STONES AND THE WOOD OF THORNS, 153 CHANGE BELOVED 3
I KNOW OF THE LEAFY PATH THAT THE WITCHES TAKE, . . . 203 WITHER BOUGHS V 9
BECAUSE IT STOOD UPON HIS PATH AND SEEMED . . . . . . 277 TWO KINGS 8
STOOD ON MY PATH. TREMBLING FROM HEAD TO FOOT . . . . 283 TWO KINGS 151
STOOD ON MY PATH. TREMBLING FROM HAND TO FOOT . . . . 283 TWO KINGS V 151
HAVE FOUND THE PATH MY GOATS' FEET CANNOT FIND. . . . 342 SHEP GOATHERD 84
HAVE FOUND THE PATH MY GOAT'S FEET CANNOT FIND. . . . 342 SHEP GOATHERD V 84
OR HURRIED THEM OFF ON ITS OWN FURIOUS PATH; . . . . 430 NINETEEN 19 53
MAY UNWIND THE WINDING PATH; . . . . 497 BYZANTIUM 12
THE PATH O'ER-MUFFLED WITH THE LEAVES--DEAD LEAVES, . . 703 MOSADA 3 115
THE PATH O'ER MUFFLED WITH THE LEAVES--DEAD LEAVES, . . 703 MOSADA 3 V 115
WEASEL WARMS HIM ON THE PATH, ... 705 DAWN-SONG 19
WHISPERING ALONG THE SUNNY PATH; . . . . 725 LEGEND 18
A PATH AMONG THESE WAVES AND WEIGH THE WIND? . . . . 748 SHADOW WATER A 21

PATHS

I KNOW OF THE LEAFY PATHS THAT THE WITCHES TAKE . . . 203 WITHER BOUGHS 9
WHERE HAZEL AND ASH AND PRIVET BLIND THE PATHS; . . . 217 WOODS OF COOLE 8
NOR ON THE ANCIENT BEATEN PATHS, THAT WOUND . . . . . 279 TWO KINGS 52
THE WOODLAND PATHS ARE DRY, ... 322 SWANS AT COOLE 2
CANNOT ENDURE TO THINK YOU TREAD THESE PATHS, ... 463 HARUN RASHID 52
THE GARDEN PATHS, NOR COUNTED UP THE ROOMS, ... 466 HARUN RASHID 119

PATHWAY

ON OUR DARK PATHWAY, TILL A COUNTLESS FLIGHT . . . . 31 OISIN 2 34
A WHITEBEARD STOOD HUSHED ON THE PATHWAY, ... 59 OISIN 3 173
BUT PRONE ON THE PATHWAY, PRONE STRUGGLING, ... 60 OISIN 3 V 186
AND ON MY PATHWAY STOOD . . . . 451 FIRST LOVE 4
THERE THY WANDERING PATHWAY GOES, ... 744 ROSY CROSS 6

PATIENCE

AWAITING IN PATIENCE THE STRAW-DEATH, ... 58 OISIN 3 167
ALL THAT YOU NEED IS PATIENCE." HEART CRIES, "NO, . . 200 FOLLY COMFORT 6
PATIENCE IS ALL THAT YOU HAVE NEED OF." NO, ... 200 FOLLY COMFORT V 6
SHE THAT BUT LITTLE PATIENCE KNEW, ... 397 POLIT PRISONER 1

PATIENT

AND SO BE PATIENT; BE WISE AND PATIENT FRIEND." . . . 200 FOLLY COMFORT V 6
AND SO BE PATIENT; BE WISE AND PATIENT FRIEND." . . . 200 FOLLY COMFORT V 6
OLD FELLOW-STUDENT, WHOSE MOST PATIENT EAR . . . . . 468 HARUN RASHID 167
OLD FELLOW STUDENT, WHOSE MOST PATIENT EAR . . . . . 468 HARUN RASHID V 167
MOCKING WITH PATIENT LAUGHTER ALL THE NIGHT . . . . . 657 ISLE STAT I 3 52
WITH PATIENT BEAUTY YONDER ATTIC BUST . . . . 685 DRAWING-ROOM 3
THAT RUSTLES IN THE REEDS WITH PATIENT PUSHES, . . . 699 MOSADA 3 4
THAT'S RUSTLING IN THE REEDS WITH PATIENT PUSHES, . . 699 MOSADA 3 V 4
ARE PRAYERS OF PATIENT MEN AND GOOD." . . . . 725 LEGEND 6
WITH PATIENT BEAUTY YONDER ATTIC BUST . . . . 735 QUATRAIN APHOR 23
BE PATIENT YET A WHILE; FOR THIS NINTH MOON, ... 748 SHADOW WATER A 23
BE PATIENT YET AWHILE; FOR THIS NINTH MOON, ... 748 SHADOW WATER A V 23

PATRICK   SEE CRO-PATRICK

O PATRICK, BY YOUR BRAZEN BELL, ... 7 OISIN 1 71
THERE WAS, OH PATRICK, BY THY HEAD, ... 7 OISIN 1 V 71
AND, PATRICK! BY YOUR BEARD, THEY WEPT, ... 17 OISIN 1 236
OH, PATRICK, BY THY BEARD, THEY WEPT, ... 17 OISIN 1 V 236
O PATRICK! FOR A HUNDRED YEARS . . . . 23 OISIN 1 343
O PATRICK! FOR A HUNDRED YEARS . . . . 23 OISIN 1 346
O PATRICK! FOR A HUNDRED YEARS . . . . 23 OISIN 1 351

	PAGE	TITLE		LINE

PATRICK   (CONTINUED)
```
      O PATRICK! FOR A HUNDRED YEARS  . . . . . . . . .      23 OISIN 1                356
      OH, PATRICK, ON THAT WOODY SHORE  . . . . . . . .      23 OISIN 1            V   343
      OH, PATRICK, THERE A HUNDRED SEASONS  . . . . . .      23 OISIN 1            V  345B
      OH, PATRICK, THERE A HUNDRED YEARS,  . . . . . . .     23 OISIN 1            V   346
      PATRICK, BEFORE THY CRAFT DIES EACH OLD SONG. . . .    42 OISIN 2            V   196
      UPON CROAGH PATRICK SANG IT LOUD; . . . . . . . .     528 DANCER CRUACH  V     5
      RIBH DENOUNCES PATRICK  . . . . . . . . . . . .       556 RIBH PATRICK          T
      FOR PATRICK PEARSE HAD SAID . . . . . . . . . . .     608 SONGS BURDEN 3       24
PATRIOTS
      OUR MOST RENOWNED PATRIOTS STAND, . . . . . . . .     460 THREE MONUMENT        2
PATS
      HUGS AND PETS AND PATS YON NEWT, . . . . . . . . .    727 LOVERS QUARREL       27
PATTERN
      AND PUT HIS PATTERN ROUND THEIR TOPS . . . . . . .    272 GREY ROCK        V   24
      A PATTERN ON A NAPKIN DIPPED IN BLOOD. . . . . . .    483 VERONIC NAPKIN        8
PATTERNS
      APPROVED PATTERNS OF WOMEN OR OF MEN . . . . . . .    602 GALLERY REVIS        31
      THROUGH THEIR ANCESTRAL PATTERNS DANCE, . . . . . .   612 NEWS ORACLE          19
PAUDEEN
      PAUDEEN  . . . . . . . . . . . . . . . . . . .        291 PAUDEEN               T
      OF OUR OLD PAUDEEN IN HIS SHOP, I STUMBLED BLIND . . . 291 PAUDEEN              2
PAUDEEN'S
      UNTIL ENOUGH OF PAUDEEN'S PENCE  . . . . . . . . .    287 TO WEALTHY MAN        2
PAUDEENS
      LET PAUDEENS PLAY AT PITCH AND TOSS, . . . . . . .    288 TO WEALTHY MAN       31
      LEAVE PAUDEENS TO THEIR PITCH AND TOSS; . . . . . .   288 TO WEALTHY MAN V     31
PAUL
      LEARNED LIKE A MAN?  PAUL VERONESE  . . . . . . .     386 ROBARTES DANCE       26
      THE BALLAD OF EARL PAUL  . . . . . . . . . . .        739 EARL PAUL             T
      MEN CRY "BRING PAUL, SHIELD BREAKER, . . . . . . .    740 EARL PAUL            11
      EARL PAUL STOOD ON THE BED OF STRAW, . . . . . . .    740 EARL PAUL            17
      WHEN PAUL RODE FROM THE TOWN . . . . . . . . . .      740 EARL PAUL            21
      EARL PAUL CAME WHERE THE KING SAT, . . . . . . . .    740 EARL PAUL            29
      MEN CRY: "BRING PAUL, SHIELD-BREAKER, . . . . . . .   740 EARL PAUL        V   11
      SAYING "EARL PAUL IS PARDONED  . . . . . . . . .      741 EARL PAUL            55
PAUPER
      LIKE AN OLD PAUPER, IN ALL KINDS OF WEATHER; . . . .  205 ADAMS CURSE           9
PAUSE
      AND PAUSE AT LAST, I WAS ABOUT TO SAY, . . . . . .    461 HARUN RASHID         11
      PAUSE AT THE TREATISE OF PARMENIDES  . . . . . . .    461 HARUN RASHID         16
      SO! MID THE WILLOW-GLADE YOU PAUSE AT LAST. . . . .   651 ISLE STAT I 2         2
      OF WAR.  OF YORE, TWO SHEPHERDS, WHERE WE PAUSE, . .  659 ISLE STAT II 1       31
      HUSH! HUSH! THEY PAUSE AND POINT . . . . . . . .      732 STREET DANCERS       31
      HUSH! HUSH! HUSH! THEY PAUSE THEM WHERE . . . . . .   733 STREET DANCERS       44
PAUSED
      HE SHIVERING PAUSED, AND RAISED HIS HEAD AND SCREAMED. . .  30 OISIN 2     V   25
      I PAUSED--THE STARS ABOVE ME FLASHED, . . . . . . .   83 MAD KING GOLL   V   29
      I PAUSED--THE STARS ABOVE ME SHONE  . . . . . . .     83 MAD KING GOLL   V   29
      I PAUSED--AND FAR AWAY I DASHED  . . . . . . . .      83 MAD KING GOLL   V   31
      I PAUSED--AND FAR AWAY RUSHED ON, . . . . . . . .     83 MAD KING GOLL   V   31
      DEEP IN THE WOODLAND PAUSED THEY, THE SIX FEET . . .  716 DWELT SYCAMORE        9
PAVEMENT
      WHILE I STAND ON THE ROADWAY, OR ON THE PAVEMENT GREY, . .  117 ISLE INNISFREE V  11
      AND SCRUB A KITCHEN PAVEMENT, OR BREAK STONES . . . . 204 ADAMS CURSE           8
      AT MIDNIGHT ON THE EMPEROR'S PAVEMENT FLIT . . . . .  498 BYZANTIUM            25
PAVEMENTS
      WHILE I STAND ON THE ROADWAY, OR ON THE PAVEMENTS GREY,  117 ISLE INNISFREE    11
PAVEN
      ITS PAVEN LENGTH TOWARDS THE RIVER'S MARGE . . . . .  702 MOSADA 3             76
PAVLOVA'S
      FROM NINETEEN HUNDRED NINE OR TEN, PAVLOVA'S HAD THE CRY,  354 HIS PHOENIX     11
PAW
      A SPHINX WITH WOMAN BREAST AND LION PAW, . . . . . .  383 VISION ROBART        18
      HE'LL SNAP HIS SWORD.  RAISED IS THE LION'S PAW. . . . 664 ISLE STAT II 2      63
PAWNS
      THUS PLAY WE FIRST WITH PAWNS, POOR THINGS AND WEAK;  . .  722 WITCH VIVIEN    53
PAY
      YOU HAVE TAKEN PAY AND MADE YOUR BARGAIN FOR IT. . . . .   225 SHADOW WATER B  68
      SILENCE! FOR YOU HAVE TAKEN FORGAEL'S PAY. . . . . .  225 SHADOW WATER B V     68
      WE JOINED HIM FOR HIS PAY, BUT HAVE HAD NONE . . . .  225 SHADOW WATER B V    68A
      AND PAY BUT A KISS FOR A KISS. . . . . . . . . .      330 BONE OF A HARE        8
      WE CANNOT PAY ITS TRIBUTE OF WILD TEARS. . . . . . .  334 LIVING BEAUTY        10
      OR WHO HAVE FOUND A PAINTER TO MAKE THEM SO FOR PAY . .  353 HIS PHOENIX        6
      CAN PAY THE POET FOR A VERSE AND HEAR THE FIDDLE SOUND,  581 CURSE CROMWELL    21
      AND WHEN I PAY ATTENTION I MUST OUT AND WALK . . . .  581 CURSE CROMWELL       29
      HE TAKES THE DEVIL'S PAY. . . . . . . . . . . .       582 ROGER CASEMENT V     20
      AND ALL MUST PAY HIM HEED, . . . . . . . . . . .      583 GHOST ROG CASE       22
PAYMENT
      IS BUT A PAYMENT FOR THAT MIDNIGHT VOICE . . . . . .  469 HARUN RASHID        173
      WHAT PAYMENT WERE ENOUGH . . . . . . . . . . . .      518 HIS CONFIDENCE        5
PAYMENTS
      WHAT PAYMENTS WERE ENOUGH  . . . . . . . . . . .      518 HIS CONFIDENCE V      5
PEACE
      AND YET, OF YORE, MUCH PEACE HE HAD . . . . . . .       2 OISIN 1          V   7K
      AND YET, OF YORE, MUCH PEACE HE HAD, . . . . . . .      4 OISIN 1          V   36
      BID THEM AWAY AND HOLD THEIR PEACE; . . . . . . .      15 OISIN 1             212
      . . . WHEN, ROLLED IN A GRISLY PEACE, . . . . . . .    47 OISIN 3               9
      FOR THY YOUTH WITHOUT PEACE, AND THY YEARS WITH THE DEMONS,  63 OISIN 3    V  216
      SEND PEACE ON ALL THE LANDS AND FLICKERING CORN.-- . . .   71 ANASHU VIJAYA    1
```

	PAGE	TITLE	LINE

PEACE (CONTINUED)
THAT WORD OF THE SOUL'S PEACE--"ETERNITY."	81	EPHEMERA V	24B
CRIED A HERALD, "PEACE WITH THINE!	82	MAD KING GOLL V	14
SING PEACE INTO HIS BREAST,	88	STOLEN CHILD	47
AND HE SAID WITH A SMILE, "HAVE PEACE NOW"!	92	FATHER OHART	19
THE ROSE OF PEACE	112	ROSE OF PEACE	T
THE PEACE OF THE ROSE	112	ROSE OF PEACE V	T
AND SOFTLY MAKE A ROSY PEACE,	113	ROSE OF PEACE	15
A PEACE OF HEAVEN WITH HELL,	113	ROSE OF PEACE	16
DANGER NO REFUGE HOLDS, AND WAR NO PEACE,	114	ROSE OF BATTLE	9
AND I SHALL HAVE SOME PEACE THERE, FOR PEACE COMES DROPPING SLOW,	117	ISLE INNISFREE	5
AND I SHALL HAVE SOME PEACE THERE, FOR PEACE COMES DROPPING SLOW,	117	ISLE INNISFREE	5
AND LOVER THERE BY LOVER BE AT PEACE.	128	DREAM OF FAERY	35
AND ALL THEIR TROUBLE DIES INTO ITS PEACE!--	128	DREAM OF FAERY V	35
"I HAVE NO REST, NOR JOY, NOR PEACE,	132	FR GILLIGAN	9
HE BIDS HIS BELOVED BE AT PEACE	154	BELOVED PEACE	T
MICHAEL ROBARTES BIDS HIS BELOVED BE AT PEACE	154	BELOVED PEACE V	T
IF THIS IMPORTUNATE HEART TROUBLE YOUR PEACE	162	ASKS FORGIVE	1
O WHERE IS OUR MOTHER OF PEACE	171	MAID QUIET V	1
AND OUR MOTHER OF PEACE HAS FORGOT ME	171	MAID QUIET V	7
ENCIRCLE HER I LOVE AND SING HER INTO PEACE,	174	ELEMENT POWERS	9
IN OWING THEM THE BRIDE-BED THAT GIVES PEACE."	187	QUEEN MAEVE	148
AND FLYING TOWARDS THEIR PEACE. PUT BY THESE THOUGHTS,	226	SHADOW WATER B	91
HAD SEEMED TO BE THE GIVER OF ALL PEACE,	228	SHADOW WATER B	149
PEACE	258	PEACE	T
AH, BUT PEACE THAT COMES AT LENGTH,	259	PEACE	10
O HEART, BE AT PEACE, BECAUSE	259	UNWORTH PRAISE	1
HALF LION, HALF CHILD, IS AT PEACE.	260	UNWORTH PRAISE	20
DELIGHT IN ART WHOSE END IS PEACE,	288	TO WEALTHY MAN	26
AND HEAR AMID THE GARDEN'S NIGHTLY PEACE,"	300	BEGGAR CRIED	18
I CANNOT FIND THE PEACE OF HOME	332	ROUND TOWER	29
SO GREAT HER PORTION IN THAT PEACE YOU MAKE	356	BROKEN DREAMS	12
YET LITTLE PEACE HE HAD,	383	VISION ROBART	35
I HAVE PREPARED MY PEACE.	415	TOWER	157
WHETHER HEALTH, WEALTH OR PEACE OF MIND WERE SPENT	429	NINETEEN 19	36
IT DROPPED THE REINS OF PEACE AND WAR	437	SONGS PLAY 1	14
NOR ACCIDENT OF PEACE NOR WAR	446	COLONUS PRAISE	14
UNCHANGING AND AT PEACE, AND IT IS RIGHT	465	HARUN RASHID	96
IT SEEMS I MUST BUY KNOWLEDGE WITH MY PEACE.	468	HARUN RASHID	169
ONE THAT IS PERFECT OR AT PEACE,	528	DANCER CRUACH	3
INNOCENCE AND PEACE DEPART.	561	FOUR AGES MAN	4
UNDER A RULE, UNDER THE SEMBLANCE OF PEACE	563	MERU	2
LAUGHS ALOUD, HIS HEART AT PEACE.	638	BEN BULBEN	32
PEACE, PEACE, THE EARTH'S A-QUAKE. I HEAR	656	ISLE STAT I 3	20
PEACE, PEACE, THE EARTH'S A-QUAKE. I HEAR	656	ISLE STAT I 3	20
A LONG, BROWN GRASSHOPPER OF MAIDS! PEACE, SIR!	661	ISLE STAT II 1	69
WHERE DREAM-FED PASSION IS AND PEACE ENCLOSES,	669	ISLE STAT II 3	85
THOU'LT TEACH ME LAUGHING, AND I'LL TEACH THEE PEACE,	670	ISLE STAT II 3	101
FOR PEACE AND LAUGHTER HAVE BEEN SELDOM FRIENDS.	670	ISLE STAT II 3	103
BUT ART THOU HAPPY? YOUTH, I AM AT PEACE.	672	ISLE STAT II 3	150
THESE ARE AT PEACE.	672	ISLE STAT II 3	159
THY PEACE. AH, NOW I'LL WAKE THESE SLEEPERS, LOST	677	ISLE STAT II 3	274
AND PEACE BE WITH YOU, PEACE AND WEALTH OF DAYS.	682	SEEKER	28
AND PEACE BE WITH YOU, PEACE AND WEALTH OF DAYS.	682	SEEKER	28
WHERE LIES THE COW AT PEACE BESIDE HER CALF,	715	FERENCZ RENYI	121
WHERE DWELL THE MINDS OF OLD MEN HAVING PEACE,	721	WITCH VIVIEN	22
I DO NOT NEED YOUR SCYTHE. MAY THAT BRING PEACE	721	WITCH VIVIEN	26
SUCH WAR PLOTS, PEACE PLOTS, LOVE PLOTS--EVERY SIDE!	722	WITCH VIVIEN	66
PEACE OF YOUTH AND PEACE OF AGE,	733	STREET DANCERS	46
PEACE OF YOUTH AND PEACE OF AGE,	733	STREET DANCERS	46
ARE WISER WITCHCRAFT, FOR OUR PEACE AWAKES	763	SHADOW WATER A	320
THESE MESSENGERS TO LURE MEN TO HIS PEACE,	764	SHADOW WATER A	336

PEACEABLE
PEACEABLE MEN THAT SHUT THE WIND AWAY,	224	SHADOW WATER B	54
AND KISS MORE LIPS THAN LASTING PEACEABLE MEN	225	SHADOW WATER B	71

PEACEFUL
THAT MANY A PEACEFUL MOMENT HAD,	4	OISIN 1	35
"HE BRINGS THE PEACEFUL AGE OF GOLD"--	82	MAD KING GOLL V	11
WHAT COULD HAVE MADE HER PEACEFUL WITH A MIND	256	NO SECOND TROY	6
WOULD END THIS PEACEFUL LIFE THAT ROTS THE BONES,	752	SHADOW WATER A	110

PEACE-MAKING
PEACE-MAKING, MILD, A KINGLY BOY.	82	MAD KING GOLL V	8

PEACHES
AND THRICE THE PEACHES FLUSHED UPON THE WALLS,	690	MOSADA 1	2

PEACOCK
I PASSED A LITTLE FURTHER ON AND HEARD A PEACOCK SAY!	77	INDIAN ON GOD	17
HE IS A MONSTROUS PEACOCK, AND HE WAVETH ALL THE NIGHT	77	INDIAN ON GOD	19
I PACED A LITTLE FURTHER AND I HEARD A PEACOCK SAY!--	77	INDIAN ON GOD V	17
I PASSED A LITTLE FURTHER AND I HEARD A PEACOCK SAY!--	77	INDIAN ON GOD V	17
THE PEACOCK	310	PEACOCK	T
THAT HAS MADE A GREAT PEACOCK	310	PEACOCK	2
O WHAT IF GARDENS WHERE THE PEACOCK STRAYS	418	ANCEST HOUSES	25
JUNO'S PEACOCK SCREAMED.	422	MY TABLE	32
BRONZED PEACOCK FEATHERS, RED COMBS OF HER COCKS.	433	NINETEEN 19	130
I'D HAVE A PEACOCK CRY,	458	HIS WILDNESS	8
LIKE PASSION STIRS THE PEACOCK AND HIS MATE,	465	HARUN RASHID	100
TORTOISESHELL BUTTERFLIES, PEACOCK BUTTERFLIES,	482	BLOOD AND MOON	45

PEACOCKS
SHRIEKS, "I AM KING OF THE PEACOCKS,"	456	FRIENDS YOUTH	15

608

```
                                                          PAGE    TITLE            LINE

PEAHENS
    THE PEAHENS DANCE ON A SMOOTH LAWN,  . . . . . . . .    77  INDIAN TO LOVE        3
PEA-HENS
    THE PEA-HENS DANCE, IN CRIMSON FEATHER  . . . . . . .    77  INDIAN TO LOVE V      3
PEAK
    TO PEAK AND PINE O'ER OISIN'S FAME."  . . . . . . .      7  OISIN 1         V    70
    AND PEAK AND PINE WE KNOW NOT WHY,  . . . . . . . .     22  OISIN 1         V  340C
    ON THE FAR GOLDEN PEAK: ENORMOUS SHAPES,  . . . . . .   74  ANASHU VIJAYA       68
PEALED
    FROM THE HILLS OF EARTH HAVE PEALED  . . . . . . . .   705  DAWN-SONG            5
PEAR
    A PEAR TREE BROKEN BY THE STORM.  . . . . . . . . .    424  ROAD AT DOOR    V   10
PEARL      SEE MOTHER-OF-PEARL
    AND IT WAS BOUND WITH A PEARL PALE SHELL  . . . . . .    4  OISIN 1         V   28
    OF SEA-SPRUNG PEARL, AND QUEENS OF FAIRY LANDS  . . .   29  OISIN 2         V  10A
    WHO COME WITH THEIR CROWNS OF PEARL AND THEIR SPINDLES 203  WITHER BOUGHS       10
        OF WOOL,
    ROLLING A BLIND PEARL EYE,  . . . . . . . . . . . .    552  SONGS REWRIT 2       2
    THAT MY TRUE-LOVE WOULD COME IN A SHIP OF PEARL  . . . 763  SHADOW WATER A     315
    THAT MY TRUE LOVE WOULD COME IN A SHIP OF PEARL  . . . 763  SHADOW WATER A V   315
PEARL-PALE
    A PEARL-PALE, HIGH-BORN LADY, WHO RODE  . . . . . .      3  OISIN 1             20
    AND IT WAS BOUND WITH A PEARL-PALE SHELL  . . . . . .    4  OISIN 1             28
    THEN DID YOU ANSWER, PEARL-PALE ONE?  . . . . . . .      6  OISIN 1         V   53
    HER PEARL-PALE HAND AND THE HEM OF HER DRESS.  . . .    16  OISIN 1            216
    "I BRING DELIVERANCE," PEARL-PALE NIAMH SAID.  . . .    34  OISIN 2             78
    "FLEE FROM HIM," PEARL-PALE NIAMH WEEPING CRIED,  . .   35  OISIN 2             92
    AND THE PEARL-PALE NIAMH LAY BY ME,  . . . . . . . .    52  OISIN 3             74
    AND PEARL-PALE NEAVE LAY BY ME, HER BROW ON THE MIDST OF 52 OISIN 3         V   74
        MY BREAST:
    YOU NEED BUT LIFT A PEARL-PALE HAND,  . . . . . . .    158  BELOVED RHYMES       7
PEARLS
    BODIES OF SHADOW AND BLIND EYES LIKE PEARLS,  . . . .  185  QUEEN MAEVE        116
    ANCESTRAL PEARLS ALL PITCHED INTO A STY,  . . . . .    619  BRONZE HEAD         26
PEARLY
    AND PEARLY WHITE HIS WELL-GROOMED HAIR.  . . . . . .     3  OISIN 1         V  7CC
    ALL PEARLY WHITE, SAVE ONE RED EAR:  . . . . . . .      12  OISIN 1            141
    AND SIGHING LAID THE PEARLY TIP  . . . . . . . . .      12  OISIN 1            150
    THE MIST CLOSED ROUND US: PEARLY LIGHT  . . . . . .     28  OISIN 1         V 427C
    AND DIE A PEARLY BROTHERHOOD:  . . . . . . . . . .      66  HAPPY SHEPHERD      42
    THEIR SADNESS THROUGH A HOLLOW, PEARLY HEART:  . . .    68  SAD SHEPHERD        21
    THEN HE SANG SOFTLY NIGH THE PEARLY RIM:  . . . . .     69  SAD SHEPHERD        25
    THEN SANG HE SOFTLY NIGH THE PEARLY RIM:  . . . . .     69  SAD SHEPHERD    V   25
    AND HURLED IT FROM ITS PLACE AMID THE PEARLY LIGHT  . 174  ELEMENT POWERS V     3
    SEA-NYMPHS IN THEIR PEARLY WAGONS,  . . . . . . . .    309  REALISTS             5
    SEA NYMPHS IN THEIR PEARLY WAGGONS,  . . . . . . . .   309  REALISTS             5
PEARSE
    AND CONNOLLY AND PEARSE  . . . . . . . . . . . . .     394  EASTER 1916         76
    NOW PEARSE IS DEAF AND DUMB?  . . . . . . . . . . .    395  SIXTEEN DEAD        10
    SAID PEARSE TO CONNOLLY,  . . . . . . . . . . . . .    396  ROSE TREE            2
    SAID PEARSE TO CONNOLLY,  . . . . . . . . . . . . .    396  ROSE TREE           14
    HE TOLD PEARSE AND CONNOLLY  . . . . . . . . . . .     585  ORAHILLY            12
    THEN ON PEARSE AND CONNOLLY  . . . . . . . . . . .     585  ORAHILLY            23
    FOR PATRICK PEARSE HAD SAID  . . . . . . . . . . .     608  SONGS BURDEN 3      24
    WHEN PEARSE SUMMONED CUCHULAIN TO HIS SIDE,  . . . .   611  STATUES             25
PEAR-TREE
    A PEAR-TREE BROKEN BY THE STORM.  . . . . . . . . .    424  ROAD AT DOOR        10
PEASANT
    TWO POEMS CONCERNING PEASANT VISIONARIES  A CRADLE SONG 146 UNAPPEAS HOST  V    T
    A PEASANT GIRL COMMENDED BY A SONG,  . . . . . . . .   410  TOWER               34
    BY SOME PEASANT GOSPELLER:  . . . . . . . . . . . .    440  WISDOM               5
    THROUGH THE PEASANT GOSPELLERS'  . . . . . . . . . .   440  WISDOM          V    5
    WHEN SOME PEASANT GOSPELLER  . . . . . . . . . . .     440  WISDOM          V    5
    THIS SULLEN PEASANT SPOILS THE GOOD SUNSHINE,  . . .   711  FERENCZ RENYI       42
    THIS SULLEN PEASANT SPOILS THE GOOD RED WINE.  . . .   711  FERENCZ RENYI       43
    THE SOLDIER THUS, AND HAYNAU--"PEASANT, SPEAK .  . .   711  FERENCZ RENYI       54
    THIS SULLEN PEASANT CHILLS THE GOOD SUNSHINE.  . . .   711  FERENCZ RENYI   V   42
    THIS SULLEN PEASANT SOURS THE GOOD RED WINE.  . . .    711  FERENCZ RENYI   V   43
    A PEASANT PALE AND PRETTY, HER EYES FOR FEAR,  . . .   713  FERENCZ RENYI   V   81
    A PEASANT YOUNG AND FAIR, HER EYES FOR FEAR  . . . .   713  FERENCZ RENYI   V   81
    A PEASANT, PALE AND PRETTY, HER EYES FROM FEAR,  . .   713  FERENCZ RENYI   V   81
PEASANTRY
    SING THE PEASANTRY, AND THEN  . . . . . . . . . .     639  BEN BULBEN          74
PEASANT'S
    WERE WE NOT BORN IN THE PEASANT'S COT  . . . . . .     615  MARCH SONGS 2       13
    WE WERE NOT BORN IN THE PEASANT'S COT  . . . . . .     615  MARCH SONGS 2       13
    HALF HID.  HE BRINGS THE PEASANT'S ONLY KIN,  . . . .  711  FERENCZ RENYI       50
PEASANTS
    THE PEASANTS OF THAT LAND,  . . . . . . . . . . .     123  DREAM OF DEATH       4
PEBBLE
    AS A GRASS SEED CRUSHED BY A PEBBLE, AS A WOLF SUCKED UNDER 63 OISIN 3      V  220
        A WEIR.
PEBBLES
    BRUSH LIGHTLY AS HAYMOUSE EARTH'S PEBBLES,  . . . . .   56  OISIN 3            128
    BRUSH LIGHTLY AS HAY MOUSE EARTH'S PEBBLES,  . . . .    56  OISIN 3         V  128
    THE RATTLE OF PEBBLES ON THE SHORE  . . . . . . . .    485  NINETEENTH CEN       3
PEBBLY
    WHO PACED IN THE EVE BY THE NETS ON THE PEBBLY SHORE,  . 91  OLD FISHERMAN      11
    ALONG THE PEBBLY STREET.  . . . . . . . . . . . .      94  MOLL MAGEE          12
PECKER      SEE WOOD-PECKER
```

```
                                                        PAGE    TITLE              LINE

PEDANT
    --PEDANT IN PASSION, LEARNED IN OLD COURTESIES,  . . . .    363 DOLLS FACES         4
    THE FAIRY PEDANT.  . . . . . . . . . . . . . . . . . . .    706 FAIRY PEDANT        T
PEDANTIC
    FROM THEIR PEDANTIC BABYLON . . . . . . . . . . . . . .     344 DAWN                6
PEDANTRY
    THOUGH PEDANTRY DENIES.  . . . . . . . . . . . . . . . .    345 ON WOMAN            9
PEDDLED
    PEDDLED IN THE THOROUGHFARES.  . . . . . . . . . . . . .    406 FOR DAUGHTER       76
PEDESTALLED
    FOG-DRIPPING, PEDESTALLED ABOVE THE TIDE,  . . . . . . .     31 OISIN 2        V   36
PEDLAR
    THE COLONEL MET A PEDLAR,  . . . . . . . . . . . . . .      595 COLONEL MARTIN     19
PEELED
    AND CUT AND PEELED A HAZEL WAND,  . . . . . . . . . . .     149 WANDER AENGUS       3
    AND CUT AND PEELED A HAZEL ROD .  . . . . . . . . . . .     149 WANDER AENGUS  V    3
PEEP
    AND STARS BEGAN TO PEEP.  . . . . . . . . . . . . . . .     133 FR GILLIGAN        16
    TILL STARS ARE BEGINNING TO BLINK AND PEEP;  . . . . .      150 OLD MOTHER          4
PEEPING
    THAN THE PEEPING PANSY'S FACE,  . . . . . . . . . . . .     647 ISLE STAT I 1      52
PEER
    . . . AND FROM YOUR CARHEADS PEER,  . . . . . . . . .        73 ANASHU VIJAYA      45
    . . . AND O'ER YOUR CAR HEADS PEER  . . . . . . . . .        73 ANASHU VIJAYA  V   45
PEERED
    FULL MANY MORE, WHEN PEERED A MAIDEN SWEET . . . . . .       33 OISIN 2        V  68F
    WHO PEERED ABOUT ON EVERY SIDE;  . . . . . . . . . . .      193 BAILE AILLINN  V  112
PEERING
    PEERING AND FLYING TO AND FRO,  . . . . . . . . . . . .     136 TWO TREES      V   35
    A PEERING HARE'S;" AND YET I MURMURED NOT, . . . . . .      684 SEEKER             56
PEERS
    OR WRESTLE WITH THEIR PEERS IN DEWY VALLEYS.  . . . . .      30 OISIN 2        V  14E
    AND PROUD AS PRIAM MURDERED WITH HIS PEERS;  . . . . .      120 SORROW OF LOVE      8
PEEWIT
    AND FOR THE PEEWIT PAINTS HIS CAP,  . . . . . . . . .        18 OISIN 1           266
    "LET PEEWIT CALL AND CURLEW CRY WHERE THEY WILL,  . . .     203 WITHER BOUGHS       2
    I KNOW, AND THE CURLEW AND PEEWIT ON ECHTGE OF STREAMS.     204 WITHER BOUGHS      22
    AND THE CURLEW AND PEEWIT KNOW ON ECHTGE OF STREAMS.  .     204 WITHER BOUGHS  V   22
PEG
    FOR PEG AND MEG AND PARIS' LOVE  . . . . . . . . . . .      458 HIS WILDNESS        3
PELEUS
    PELEUS ON THETIS STARES.  . . . . . . . . . . . . . . .     612 NEWS ORACLE        26
PELTING
    WHEN THE RAIN IS PELTING OUT OF THE WINTRY AIR;  . . . .    207 HANRAHANS SONG V   12
PEN
    WHETHER WE HAVE CHOSEN CHISEL, PEN OR BRUSH,  . . . . .     368 EGO DOMINUS        14
    HIS SLEEPLESS CANDLE AND LABORIOUS PEN.  . . . . . . .      375 PHASES OF MOON     86
    BY PEN AND PAPER LIES,  . . . . . . . . . . . . . . . .     421 MY TABLE            3
PENAL
    IN PENAL DAYS RODE OUT  . . . . . . . . . . . . . . .        91 FATHER OHART        2
PENANCE
    AND PENANCE IS THE PLAY,  . . . . . . . . . . . . . .       364 END OF DAY          2
    OR SING A PENANCE ON THE ROAD;  . . . . . . . . . . .       529 TOM LUNATIC        10
PENCE
    UNTIL ENOUGH OF PAUDEEN'S PENCE  . . . . . . . . . . .      287 TO WEALTHY MAN      2
    AND ADD THE HALFPENCE TO THE PENCE  . . . . . . . . .       289 SEPTEMBER 1913      3
PENCILLED
    WE THOUGHT ON OSCAR'S PENCILLED URN.  . . . . . . . . .       2 OISIN 1        V   70
    "WE THINK ON OSCAR'S PENCILLED URN,  . . . . . . . . .        5 OISIN 1            41
PENDULOUS
    ARE BOWED IN SORROW UNDER PENDULOUS LIDS,  . . . . . .       79 EPHEMERA            2
    LIE NOW HALF HIDDEN UNDER PENDULOUS LIDS,  . . . . . .       79 EPHEMERA       V    2
PENETRATION
    AND PENETRATION OF THEIR EYES.  WHERE YONDER BLOTCH . . .   664 ISLE STAT II 2     47
PENITENCE
    AND IMPORTUNE THEIR SOULS TO PENITENCE,  . . . . . . .      704 MOSADA 3          131
PENITENTIAL
    AMID THE HOVERING, PITEOUS, PENITENTIAL THRONG."  . . . .   173 SPEAKS HEARERS      8
PENNIES        SEE HALF-PENNIES
    WITH A BAG FULL OF PENNIES,  . . . . . . . . . . . . .      627 STATES HOLIDAY     35
PENNON
    WITH BANNERET AND PENNON,  . . . . . . . . . . . . . .      317 NIGHT COME          8
PENNY
    I HAD NOT GIVEN A PENNY FOR A SONG  . . . . . . . . .       267 ALL TEMPT ME        6
    BROWN PENNY . . . . . . . . . . . . . . . . . . . . .      268 BROWN PENNY         T
    WHEREFORE I THREW A PENNY  . . . . . . . . . . . . . .      268 BROWN PENNY         3
    AH, PENNY, BROWN PENNY, BROWN PENNY,  . . . . . . . .       268 BROWN PENNY         7
    AH, PENNY, BROWN PENNY, BROWN PENNY,  . . . . . . . .       268 BROWN PENNY         7
    AH, PENNY, BROWN PENNY, BROWN PENNY,  . . . . . . . .       268 BROWN PENNY         7
    AH, PENNY, BROWN PENNY, BROWN PENNY,  . . . . . . . .       268 BROWN PENNY        15
    AH, PENNY, BROWN PENNY, BROWN PENNY,  . . . . . . . .       268 BROWN PENNY        15
    AH, PENNY, BROWN PENNY, BROWN PENNY,  . . . . . . . .       268 BROWN PENNY        15
PENSEROSO'S
    IL PENSEROSO'S PLATONIST TOILED ON  . . . . . . . . .       419 MY HOUSE           14
PENSIONER
    THE LAMENTATION OF THE OLD PENSIONER  . . . . . . . .       131 OLD PENSIONER       T
    THE OLD PENSIONER . . . . . . . . . . . . . . . . . .       131 OLD PENSIONER  V    T
PENSIVE
    OF PENSIVE LAUGHTER, UNHUMAN SOUND,  . . . . . . . . .       11 OISIN 1           136
    PENSIVE THEY PACED ALONG THE FADED LEAVES,  . . . . .        80 EPHEMERA           10
```

		PAGE	TITLE		LINE
PENSIVELY					
PENSIVELY APART.		89	ISLE IN WATER		4
PEOPLE					
AMONG UNDYING PEOPLE HAS RUN		6	OISIN 1	V	60
OF THE HIGH PEOPLE OF SORACA NOR IN GLAMOUR BY DEMONS FLUNG,		50	OISIN 3	V	50
PEOPLE CAME INTO COLOONEY:		93	FATHER OHART		27
I FEAST AMID MY PEOPLE ON THE HILL,		103	FERGUS DRUID		17
WHERE PEOPLE LOVE BESIDE THE RAVELLED SEAS:		126	DREAM OF FAERY		9
WHERE PEOPLE LOVE BESIDE STAR-LADEN SEAS:		126	DREAM OF FAERY	V	9
WHEN HER OWN PEOPLE RULED THIS TRAGIC EIRE:		129	BOOK STORIES		2
WHEN HER OWN PEOPLE RULED IN WAVE-WORN ERI,		129	BOOK STORIES	V	2
FOR PEOPLE DIE AND DIE",		132	FR GILLIGAN		10
THE PEOPLE OF COMING DAYS WILL KNOW		146	FISH		3
TALKED OF HIS COUNTRY AND ITS PEOPLE, SANG		180	QUEEN MAEVE		3
ONE OF THE LAUGHING PEOPLE--AND SHE AND I		231	SHADOW WATER B		211
PROTECT ME NOW, GODS THAT MY PEOPLE SWEAR BY.		241	SHADOW WATER B		396
. . . THE PEOPLE WANTED PICTURES		287	TO WEALTHY MAN		T
ALL THINK WHAT OTHER PEOPLE THINK:		337	SCHOLARS		9
THE PEOPLE		351	PEOPLE		T
TO WHERE THE DUCHESS AND HER PEOPLE TALKED		352	PEOPLE		13
COMPLAINED OF THE PEOPLE." ALL I COULD REPLY		352	PEOPLE		29
YOU HEARD THAT LABOURING MAN WHO HAD SERVED MY PEOPLE. HE SAID		391	UNDER SATURN		11
THE PRIDE OF PEOPLE THAT WERE		414	TOWER		128
THE PEOPLE OF BURKE AND OF GRATTAN		414	TOWER		132
THE BOOK OF THE PEOPLE: WHATEVER MOST CAN BLESS		492	COOLE BALLYLEE		44
THE KING THAT COULD MAKE HIS PEOPLE STARE.		550	SEVERED HEAD		19
PYTHAGORAS PLANNED IT. WHY DID THE PEOPLE STARE?		610	STATUES		1
PREPARED A REST FOR THE PEOPLE OF GOD,		639	BEN BULBEN		65
BY A PEOPLE SADLY GAY:		680	LOVE AND DEATH		10
SINCE 'MONG MY PEOPLE, TENTED ON THE HILLS,		690	MOSADA 1		4
FOR I AND ALL MY PEOPLE WERE ACCURST		690	MOSADA 1		15
THE PLACE WAS EMPTY NOW OF PEOPLE.		725	LEGEND		25
HE CAME TO THE HOME OF THE FOREST PEOPLE		728	PRIEST FAIRY		5
THE PEOPLE CRIED "SHIELD-BREAKER!"		741	EARL PAUL		53
AND BRING HER TO HER KINGDOM AND HER PEOPLE.		755	SHADOW WATER A		170
AND BRING ME TO MY PEOPLE. I PROMISED THESE		756	SHADOW WATER A	V	185
FOR THOSE AMONG YOUR PEOPLE THAT ARE DEAD?		758	SHADOW WATER A	V	224
THAT I WOULD BID MY PEOPLE PUT TO DEATH.		760	SHADOW WATER A	V	254
PEOPLED					
IF HE HAD BROUGHT US AMONG PEOPLED SEAS,		225	SHADOW WATER B	V	68C
TOWARD PEOPLED TARA, NOR STOOD TO DRAW HIS BREATH		279	TWO KINGS		46
ON PEOPLED TARA, NOR STOOD TO DRAW HIS BREATH		279	TWO KINGS	V	46
TOWARDS PEOPLED TARA, NOR STOOD TO DRAW HIS BREATH		279	TWO KINGS	V	46
PEOPLE'S					
THE WISDOM OF THE PEOPLE'S GONE,		607	SONGS BURDEN 2		16
DOWN THE LONG VALLEYS FROM MY PEOPLE'S TENTS,		691	MOSADA 1		30
OTHER PEOPLE'S MIRTH AND PLEASURE,		732	STREET DANCERS		24
OTHER PEOPLE'S MIRTH AND PLEASURE,		732	STREET DANCERS		37
OTHER'S PEOPLE'S MIRTH AND PLEASURE,		733	STREET DANCERS		50
PERCH					
THERE'S NOT A PILOT ON THE PERCH		607	SONGS BURDEN 2		25
PERCHANCE					
AND YET IT LACK ALL GLORY: AND PERCHANCE		429	NINETEEN 19		23
HEALING FROM ITS LETTERED SLAB. THOSE SELF-SAME HANDS PERCHANCE		503	VACILLATION		82
PERCHED					
PERCHED IN SOME WINDOW OF HER MOTHER'S HOUSE		466	HARUN RASHID		106
PERCHES					
AGED AND WISE, THEY SEEK THEIR WONTED PERCHES		72	ANASHU VIJAYA		31
AND PERCHES ON A STONE:		456	FRIENDS YOUTH		16
PERCHING					
OR PERCHING ON THE TENTS, A-WEARY STILL		690	MOSADA 1		8
PERFECT					
HE TELLS OF THE PERFECT BEAUTY		164	PERFECT BEAUTY		T
AEDH TELLS OF THE PERFECT BEAUTY		164	PERFECT BEAUTY	V	T
TO BUILD A PERFECT BEAUTY IN RHYME		164	PERFECT BEAUTY		3
TO BUILD THE PERFECT BEAUTY IN RHYME,		164	PERFECT BEAUTY	V	3
OUR SIDNEY AND OUR PERFECT MAN,		325	ROBERT GREGORY		47
PADDLE AND ARE PERFECT. LEAVE UNCHANGED		357	BROKEN DREAMS		34
TOO PERFECT AT THE FULL TO LIE IN A CRADLE,		374	PHASES OF MOON		60
FOR SEPARATE, PERFECT, AND IMMOVABLE		375	PHASES OF MOON		81
MUST KEEP THAT PERFECT, AS THEY KEEP HER SONG,		461	HARUN RASHID		18
ONE THAT IS PERFECT OR AT PEACE,		528	DANCER CRUACH		3
PERFECTED					
FOR PERFECTED, COMPLETED, AND IMMOVABLE		375	PHASES OF MOON	V	81
PERFECTION					
AT THE PERFECTION OF ONE'S OWN OBEDIENCE:		376	PHASES OF MOON		109
BODY PERFECTION BROUGHT,		383	VISION ROBART		40
PERFECTION OF THE LIFE, OR OF THE WORK,		491	COOLE BALLYLEE	V	406
PERFECTION OF THE LIFE, OR OF THE WORK,		495	CHOICE		2
THINGS OUT OF PERFECTION SAIL,		530	OLD TOM AGAIN		1
SOMETHING TO PERFECTION BROUGHT":		577	WHAT THEN		19
PROFANE PERFECTION OF MANKIND.		639	BEN BULBEN		52
PERFECTLY					
AND ALL HE DID DONE PERFECTLY		327	ROBERT GREGORY		79
PERFORM					
ALL PERFORM THEIR TRAGIC PLAY,		565	LAPIS LAZULI		9
PERFUME					
THAT IT MAY DROP FAINT PERFUME, AND BE HEAVY WITH DEW,		172	TRAV PASSION		7

		PAGE	TITLE		LINE
PERHAPS					
	WORDS FOR MUSIC PERHAPS	507	JANE BISHOP	V	T
	A ROOF, GOOD CLOTHES, PASSION, LOVE PERHAPS, ...	609	IN TARAS HALLS		8
PERILOUS					
	SO PERILOUS THAT HALF THE ASTONISHED MEET	326	ROBERT GREGORY		61
PERILS					
	ALL BUT THE PERILS OF THE WOODLAND FLIGHT FORGOT, . . .	366	HER COURAGE	V	5
PERISH					
	YOUR BEAUTY PERISH AND BE LOST	173	PLEADS FRIEND		7
	THE HAUGHTY IMAGES, THAT CANNOT PERISH	184	QUEEN MAEVE	V	88
PERISHED					
	BUT MY BELOVED--THAT NIGHT AND DAY HAD PERISHED, ...	246	SHADOW WATER B		504
	HAD PERISHED THERE, BUT THE DANES RAN, ...	274	GREY ROCK		74
	--SEEING THAT FAME HAS PERISHED THIS LONG WHILE, ...	321	REED WHISPERER		11
PERISHING					
	OF UNKNOWN PERISHING ARMIES BEAT ABOUT MY EARS.	161	BLACK PIG		4
PERJURER					
	A PERJURER STOOD READY	582	ROGER CASEMENT		9
PERJURER'S					
	DESERT THE PERJURER'S SIDE;	582	ROGER CASEMENT		20
PERMANENT					
	MY PERMANENT OR IMPERMANENT IMAGES;	602	GALLERY REVIS		20
PERMIT					
	PERMIT FOUL YEARS TO WEAR	472	ALL SOUL NIGHT		49
PERN					
	HE UNPACKS THE LOADED PERN	342	SHEP GOATHERD		97
PERNE					
	COME FROM THE HOLY FIRE, PERNE IN A GYRE, ...	408	SAIL BYZANTIUM		19
PERNED					
	THOUGH I HAD LONG PERNED IN THE GYRE, ...	400	DEMON BEAST		5
PERNELLA					
	RAYMOND LULLY AND HIS WIFE PERNELLA	253	HIS DREAM	V	T
PERNING					
	NOW GYRING DOWN AND PERNING THERE	400	DEMON BEAST		26
	PERNING IN A BAND, ...	599	SPIRIT MEDIUM		6
PERPETUAL					
	ROOTED IN ONE DEAR PERPETUAL PLACE.	405	FOR DAUGHTER		48
PERPLEXED					
	THAT HER OWN STRANGENESS PERPLEXED;	260	UNWORTH PRAISE		14
	MY WRETCHED DRAGON IS PERPLEXED.	386	ROBARTES DANCE		41
	PERPLEXED HER FANTASY AND PLANNED HER CARE?	466	HARUN RASHID		114
	PERPLEXED HER PHANTASY AND PLANNED HER CARE?	466	HARUN RASHID	V	114
PERPLEXITY					
	THAT OLD PERPLEXITY AN EMPTY PURSE, ...	491	COOLE BALLYLEE	V	40G
	THAT OLD PERPLEXITY AN EMPTY PURSE, ...	495	CHOICE		7
PERSECUTION					
	HE FLED THE PERSECUTION OF HER GLORY	68	SAD SHEPHERD		12
	AND FROM THE PERSECUTION OF HER GLORY	68	SAD SHEPHERD	V	12
PERSEUS					
	SAINT GEORGE OR ELSE A PAGAN PERSEUS;	533	HER TRIUMPH		10
PERSIAN					
	WHAT MEDIAN, PERSIAN, BABYLONIAN, ...	420	MY HOUSE	V	20D
	WITH PERSIAN EMBASSY OR GRECIAN WAR, ...	462	HARUN RASHID		25
	WITH PERSIAN WARS OR GREEK AMBASSADORS	462	HARUN RASHID	V	25
PERSISTENCE					
	WITH UNFALTERING PERSISTENCE, ...	647	ISLE STAT I 1		69
	IS THE BURTHEN AND PERSISTENCE	647	ISLE STAT I 1		75
PERSONAE					
	IGNORANT WHAT DRAMATIS PERSONAE SPAKE;	560	WHENCE COME		4
PERSONS					
	I PUT THREE PERSONS IN THEIR PLACE	787	HUDDON DUDDON		8
PERSUADE					
	"THOUGH I AM OLD I SHALL PERSUADE	296	THREE BEGGARS		30
	NOW THAT YOUR TONGUE CANNOT PERSUADE THE CHILD TILL SHE	450	OWEN AHERNE		22
	MISTAKE				
PERTURB					
	FRENZIES BEWILDER, REVERIES PERTURB THE MIND;	426	PHANTOM HATRED		7
PERU					
	ON THRONES FROM CHINA TO PERU	597	MODEL LAUREATE		1
PERVERSE					
	PERVERSE CREATURE OF CHANCE, ...	346	ON WOMAN		41
PESTLE					
	THE PESTLE OF THE MOON	346	ON WOMAN		30
PETAL					
	UNLESS A PETAL HIT THE GROUND, ...	389	SOLOMON WITCH		40
	COMMON BIRD OR PETAL	498	BYZANTIUM		23
PETALS					
	IS BUT A SLIDING DROP OF RAIN BETWEEN HIS PETALS WIDE. . .	76	INDIAN ON GOD		12
	IS BUT A SLIDING DROP OF RAIN WITHIN HIS PETALS WIDE." . .	76	INDIAN ON GOD	V	12
	BUT THE TORN PETALS STREW THE GARDEN PLOT;	422	MY DESCENDANTS		7
	WHEN THE TORN PETALS STREW THE GARDEN PLOT;	422	MY DESCENDANTS	V	7
PETER					
	THE OLD PRIEST PETER GILLIGAN	132	FR GILLIGAN		1
	THE OLD PRIEST PETER GILLIGAN	133	FR GILLIGAN		23
	THE OLD PRIEST PETER GILLIGAN	133	FR GILLIGAN		35
	THE OLD PRIEST PETER GILLIGAN	133	FR GILLIGAN		39
	TO PETER SITTING IN STATE, ...	178	FIDDLER DOONEY		10
	AND PETER THAT HAD GREAT AFFAIRS	456	FRIENDS YOUTH		13
	THEN PETER HAD A MURDERING LOOK, ...	457	SUMMER SPRING		9
	WHERE IS OUR BROTHER PETER? WHEN YOU'RE NIGH, ...	696	MOSADA 2		12
	HE LOVES OUR BROTHER PETER IN HIS HEART.	696	MOSADA 2		16

612

```
                                                             PAGE     TITLE            LINE
PETER   (CONTINUED)
      IF PETER WOULD BUT ASK HER LIFE--WHO KNOWS?            696 MOSADA 2               17
      THIS VISION OF PETER AND THE BURNING GATE.            696 MOSADA 2               21
      OF HOLY PETER OF THE BURNING GATE!                     696 MOSADA 2        V     20
      THY SACRED DOOR!" BUT PETER CRIED,                    697 MOSADA 2               25
      ANSWERED PETER! "ENTER IN,                            697 MOSADA 2               30
PETER'S
      BY THE DOOR OF PETER'S GATE,                          696 MOSADA 2               23
      BESIDE THE DOOR OF PETER'S GATE.                      696 MOSADA 2        V     23
PETRONIUS
      THINKING OF SAINTS AND OF PETRONIUS ARBITER.          362 HER COURTESY            8
PETS
      HUGS AND PETS AND PATS YON NEWT,                      727 LOVERS QUARREL        27
PEWS
      THE SUNLIGHT FLICKERING ON THE PEWS,                  736 IN CHURCH               9
PHANTASY
      WHATEVER THEIR LOOSE PHANTASY INVENT                  398 LEADERS CROWD    V      4
      MANKIND INANIMATE PHANTASY,                           406 IN TIME OF WAR          5
      AND SPEAK BUT PHANTASY.  RECALL THE YEAR              462 HARUN RASHID     V     30
      PERPLEXED HER PHANTASY AND PLANNED HER CARE?          466 HARUN RASHID     V    114
PHANTOM
      PASSED BY US, CHASED BY A PHANTOM HOUND                11 OISIN 1                140
      PASSED BY US, CHASED BY A PHANTOM HOUND                11 OISIN 1          V    140
      THE PHANTOM, BEAUTY, IN A MIST OF TEARS!               73 ANASHU VIJAYA          55
      AND SNORED, NO PHANTOM BY HIS LOOK.                   303 HOUR DAWN              30
      PLAINLY NO PHANTOM BY HIS LOOK!                       303 HOUR DAWN        V     30
      MEETING LONG HENCE THE PHANTOM HERDSMAN, KING         675 ISLE STAT II 3        242
      THUS BECKON TO OUR AID A PHANTOM FAIR                 693 MOSADA 1               76
      THE PHANTOM SHIP.                                     718 PHANTOM SHIP           T
      A LEGEND OF THE PHANTOM SHIP.                         718 PHANTOM SHIP     V      T
      STANDS EACH GREY AND SILENT PHANTOM ON THE SAME REGARDLESS  719 PHANTOM SHIP    25
            SPOT--
PHANTOMS
      OR ARE YOU PHANTOMS WHITE AS SNOW,                     10 OISIN 1                117
      OR ARE YE PHANTOMS WHITE AS SNOW,"                     10 OISIN 1          V    117
      "FRET NOT WITH SPEECH THE PHANTOMS DREAD,"             12 OISIN 1                148
      "GAZE NO MORE ON THE PHANTOMS," NIAMH SAID,            29 OISIN 2                 5
      NOW, MAN OF CROSIERS, PHANTOMS DREW AROUND             29 OISIN 2          V      1
      "THESE FORMS?" "VEX NOT WITH SPEECH THE PHANTOMS DREAD." 29 OISIN 2        V      5
      I SEE PHANTOMS OF HATRED AND OF THE HEART'S           425 PHANTOM HATRED          T
      THE PHANTOMS OF HER FADED PLEASURES WALK!             687 TWO TITANS             19
      THE PHANTOMS COME! HA! HA! THEY COME, THEY COME!      694 MOSADA 1               97
      THE PHANTOMS COME! THEY COME, THEY COME, THEY COME!   694 MOSADA 1        V      97
PHARAOH'S
      HAD SCOOPED OUT PHARAOH'S MUMMY.  I--THOUGH HEART MIGHT  503 VACILLATION         84
            FIND RELIEF
PHASE
      HAS TAKEN A NEW PHASE.                                379 CAT AND MOON           20
PHASES
      THE PHASES OF THE MOON                                372 PHASES OF MOON          T
      . . . I.  THE WHEEL AND THE PHASES OF THE MOON        372 PHASES OF MOON  V       T
      TWENTY-AND-EIGHT THE PHASES OF THE MOON,              373 PHASES OF MOON         31
PHIDIAS
      EUROPE PUT OFF THAT FOAM WHEN PHIDIAS                 610 STATUES                15
      FORMS THAT GENTLER PHIDIAS WROUGHT.                   638 BEN BULBEN             44
PHIDIAS'
      AND GONE ARE PHIDIAS' FAMOUS IVORIES                  428 NINETEEN 19             7
      AND GONE ARE PHIDIAS' CARVEN IVORIES                  428 NINETEEN 19     V       7
PHILOSOPHER
      EVERY PHILOSOPHER SHOULD PRAISE THAT LOVE.            465 HARUN RASHID           97
PHILOSOPHERS
      PHILOSOPHERS SHOULD PRAISE THAT LOVE THE MOST,        465 HARUN RASHID     V     97
PHILOSOPHY
      WE PIECED OUR THOUGHTS INTO PHILOSOPHY,               429 NINETEEN 19            30
      ABSTRACTIONS OF THE GREEK PHILOSOPHY HAVE CRAZED THE MAN, 556 RIBH PATRICK  V     1
PHOENIX
      WHERE THE LAST PHOENIX DIED,                          162 ASKS FORGIVE           16
      THE PHOENIX                                           351 PEOPLE           V       T
      THEREON MY PHOENIX ANSWERED IN REPROOF,               352 PEOPLE                 22
      HIS PHOENIX                                           353 HIS PHOENIX             T
      I KNEW A PHOENIX IN MY YOUTH, SO LET THEM HAVE THEIR DAY.  353 HIS PHOENIX        8
      I KNEW A PHOENIX IN MY YOUTH, SO LET THEM HAVE THEIR DAY.  354 HIS PHOENIX       16
      I KNEW A PHOENIX IN MY YOUTH, SO LET THEM HAVE THEIR DAY.  354 HIS PHOENIX       24
      I KNEW A PHOENIX IN MY YOUTH, SO LET THEM HAVE THEIR DAY.  354 HIS PHOENIX       32
PHOSPHORUS
      AND SURGING PHOSPHORUS ALONE GAVE LIGHT                31 OISIN 2                33
      OF SURGING PHOSPHORUS ALONE GAVE LIGHT.                31 OISIN 2          V     33
      A MOMENTARY GLEAM OF PHOSPHORUS FLAME.                 37 OISIN 2               118
      A MOMENTARY GLIMMER OF VAGUE PHOSPHORUS FLAME.         37 OISIN 2          V    120
PHRASE
      --BEN JONSON'S PHRASE--AND FIND WHEN JUNE IS COME     321 REED WHISPERER          6
      BEN JONSON'S PHRASE--AND STILL MAY TURN MY FEET       321 REED WHISPERER  V       6
      PALMER'S PHRASE, BUT AFTER THAT                       639 BEN BULBEN             66
      NO MARBLE, NO CONVENTIONAL PHRASE!                    640 BEN BULBEN             89
PHRASING
      HAVE DONE THIS PHRASING, AND SAY WHY, IN SOOTH,       652 ISLE STAT I 2          25
PICK
      "BEFORE NIGHTFALL I'LL PICK A POCKET                  332 ROUND TOWER            27
      ANOTHER BOASTS, "I PICK AND CHOOSE AND HAVE BUT TWO OR  354 HIS PHOENIX          20
            THREE."
      PICK OUT MY FEATURES IN SUCH LIGHT AND SHADE          466 HARUN RASHID          116
```

613

```
                                                      PAGE     TITLE           LINE
PICK   (CONTINUED)
    TIME FOR US ALL TO PICK OUT A GOOD TUNE,  . . . . .   548  TO SAME TUNE 3     13
PICKED
    PICKED HIM FOR HER OWN,  . . . . . . . . . . . .      452  MERMAID             2
    PICKED UP ON A STREET.  . . . . . . . . . . . .       617  LONG-LEG FLY       18
    PICKED UP ON THE STREET.  . . . . . . . . . . .       617  LONG-LEG FLY    V  18
    THE WOMEN THAT I PICKED SPOKE SWEET AND LOW  . . .    622  HOUND VOICE         8
    WE PICKED EACH OTHER FROM AFAR AND KNEW  . . . . .    622  HOUND VOICE        10
    SO I HAVE PICKED A BETTER TRADE  . . . . . . . .      627  STATES HOLIDAY     11
PICKER     SEE MAN-PICKER
PICTURE
    OUT OF SOME OLD PICTURE BOOK;  . . . . . . . . .      325  ROBERT GREGORY  V  44
    ON A PICTURE OF A BLACK CENTAUR BY EDMUND DULAC  . .  442  BLACK CENTAUR       T
    SUGGESTED BY A PICTURE OF A BLACK CENTAUR  . . . . .  442  BLACK CENTAUR   V   T
    THOSE BODIES FROM A PICTURE OR A COIN  . . . . . .    537  HER VISION         28
    PICTURE AND BOOK REMAIN,  . . . . . . . . . . .       575  ACRE OF GRASS       1
    ON MR. NETTLESHIP'S PICTURE AT THE ROYAL HIBERNIAN ACADEMY.  688  NETTLESHIP   T
PICTURE-BOOK
    OUT OF SOME OLD PICTURE-BOOK;  . . . . . . . . .      325  ROBERT GREGORY     44
PICTURED
    A PICTURED BEAUTY,  . . . . . . . . . . . . . .       329  MEN IMPROVE         7
    AT ALL THAT IS NOT PICTURED THERE.  . . . . . . .     385  ROBARTES DANCE     17
    AS THOUGH THE WRITTEN OR THE PICTURED PAGE  . . . .   466  HARUN RASHID    V 126
    PICTURED, WHERE WANDER THE BELOVED FEET  . . . . .    692  MOSADA 1           44
PICTURES
    . . . THE PEOPLE WANTED PICTURES  . . . . . . . .     287  TO WEALTHY MAN      T
    AND ASKED ABOUT THE PICTURES OR THE TEXT;  . . . .    466  HARUN RASHID      121
    AND ASKED ABOUT THESE PICTURES OR THOSE OTHERS;  . .  466  HARUN RASHID    V 121
    PICTURES OF THE MIND, RECALL  . . . . . . . . .       475  EVA GORE-BOOTH     17
    OLD MARBLE HEADS, OLD PICTURES EVERYWHERE;  . . . .   491  COOLE BALLYLEE     28
PIEBALD
    BECAUSE PIEBALD PONIES, LED BEARS, CAGED LIONS, MAKE BUT  623  HIGH TALK       5
        POOR SHOWS.
PIECE      SEE ALTAR-PIECE
    A PIECE OF A NIGHTINGALE'S EGG,  . . . . . . . .      708  FAIRY PEDANT       24
PIECED
    WE PIECED OUR THOUGHTS INTO PHILOSOPHY,  . . . . .    429  NINETEEN 19        30
PIECES
    AND DEMONS BE BROKEN IN PIECES, AND TRAMPLED BENEATH THEM  61  OISIN 3       204
        IN DEATH.
    AND DEMONS, ALL BROKEN IN PIECES, BE TRAMPLED BENEATH THEM  61  OISIN 3    V 204
        IN DEATH.
PIED
    OF THE PIED PANTHER-KITTENS FROM MY HANDS  . . . .    674  ISLE STAT II 3    219
PIERCE
    AND PIERCE THE DEEP WOOD'S WOVEN SHADE,  . . . . .    125  GOES FERGUS         2
    AND PIERCE IT THROUGH WITH A GIMLET, AND STARE  . .   330  BONE OF A HARE     12
    THAT CAN PIERCE THE CLOUDS,  . . . . . . . . . .      576  ACRE OF GRASS      20
    WORDS I HAVE THAT CAN PIERCE THE HEART,  . . . . .    588  OLD WICKED MAN     16
PIERCED     SEE NAIL-PIERCED
    PIERCED WITH SOFT LIGHT THE SHALLOWING DEEPS.  . . .   13  OISIN 1           164
    "THIS DEMON SHALL BE PIERCED AND DROP AND DIE,  . .    35  OISIN 2         V  90
    PIERCED BY MY GLAD SINGING THROUGH,  . . . . . .       67  HAPPY SHEPHERD     53
    AND PIERCED HIM. "SPEAK BEFORE YOUR BREATH IS DONE."  110  CUCHULAIN SEA      67
    SAW THE PIERCED HANDS AND ROOD OF ELDER RISE  . .     169  SECRET ROSE        10
    AND SAYS, "A SWORD-BLADE PIERCED ME IN MY SLEEP."  .  234  SHADOW WATER B    257
    AND SAYS: "A SWORD BLADE PIERCED ME IN MY SLEEP."  .  234  SHADOW WATER B  V 257
    BUTTED BELOW THE SINGLE AND SO PIERCED  . . . . .     278  TWO KINGS          22
    THAT PIERCED MY BODY THROUGH?  . . . . . . . .        507  STREAM AND SUN     13
    RECALL THE CRETAN BARB THAT PIERCED A STAR?  . . .    541  PARN FUNERAL 1      7
    A PIERCED BOY, IMAGE OF A STAR LAID LOW.  . . . .     541  PARN FUNERAL 1     12
    PIERCED THROUGH, CHATTERING FROM HABIT IN THE SUN,  . 664  ISLE STAT II 2     53
    AND PIERCED THE MIRTHFUL BREAST,  . . . . . . .       741  EARL PAUL          50
    AND SAYS, "A SWORD-BLADE PIERCED ME IN MY SLEEP."  .  753  SHADOW WATER A    147
    AND SAYS, "A SWORD BLADE PIERCED ME IN MY SLEEP."  .  753  SHADOW WATER A  V 147
    AH, THEY HAVE PIERCED HIS HEART! I HAVE SLEPT LONG;  . 761 SHADOW WATER A    270
PIERCING    SEE EAR-PIERCING
    SOFTER THAN SNOW-FLAKES IN APRIL AND PIERCING THE MARROW  51  OISIN 3        68
        LIKE FLAME.
    SOFTER THAN SNOWFLAKES IN APRIL, AND PIERCING THE MARROW  51  OISIN 3     V  68
        LIKE FLAME.
    . . . LOVE-MAKING OR PIERCING THE TEMPEST WITH SAILS.  . 53  OISIN 3          88
    FORTH, PIERCING THE DISTANCE--  . . . . . . . . .      54  OISIN 3         V 112
    PIERCING THE TWILIGHT WITH THEIR MURMURING BARBS.  .   72  ANASHU VIJAYA      28
    PIERCING THE QUIVERING WATERS THROUGH AND THROUGH,  . 664  ISLE STAT II 2     44
PIETY
    THAT PASSION, PIETY OR AFFECTION KNOWS,  . . . . .    445  SCHOOL CHILDR      54
PIG
    THE VALLEY OF THE BLACK PIG  . . . . . . . . .        161  BLACK PIG           T
    THAT THIS PRAGMATICAL, PREPOSTEROUS PIG OF A WORLD,  . 481 BLOOD AND MOON     26
PIGEON
    WERE THE WINDS LESS SOFT THAN THE BREATH OF A PIGEON  . 56  OISIN 3         134
    MY PIGEON, MY OWN;  . . . . . . . . . . . . .         118  CRADLE SONG     V  10
PIGEONS
    I HAVE HEARD THE PIGEONS OF THE SEVEN WOODS  . . .    198  SEVEN WOODS         1
    AMONG PIGEONS AND BEES, WHILE THAT GREAT ARCHER,  . . 198  SEVEN WOODS        12
PIKES
    THOUGH LADS ARE MAKING PIKES AGAIN  . . . . . . .     131  OLD PENSIONER       7
PILE
    MY SOUL, MY PREY, AND THIS MY HEAPED PILE.  . . . .    45  OISIN 2         V 239B
    BUT WHEN A MAN POURED FISH INTO A PILE,  . . . . .    126  DREAM OF FAERY      5
```

		PAGE	TITLE	LINE

PILE (CONTINUED)
AND STRETCHED OUT SLEEPING ON A PILE OF SKINS • • • • •   283 TWO KINGS   141
PILED   SEE CLAY-PILED
PILED-UP
BESIDE THE PILED-UP HUNTING SPEARS, • • • • • • • • •   23 OISIN 1   348
BESIDE THE PILED-UP HUNTING-SPEARS, • • • • • • • • •   23 OISIN 1   V 349
PILFERERS
"THE DRUNKARDS, PILFERERS OF PUBLIC FUNDS, • • • • • •   352 PEOPLE   23
PILGRIM
BUT ONE MAN LOVED THE PILGRIM SOUL IN YOU, • • • • • •   121 YOU ARE OLD   7
THE PILGRIM • • • • • • • • • • • • • • • • • •   592 PILGRIM   T
COMPANIONING THE RIVER'S PILGRIM TORCH. • • • • • • •   703 MOSADA 3   112
PILGRIMS
AN AMBUSH, PILGRIMS AT THE WATER-SIDE, • • • • • • •   601 GALLERY REVIS   2
AN AMBUSH, PILGRIMS AT THE WATER SIDE, • • • • • • •   601 GALLERY REVIS V 2
PILIN'   SEE A-PILIN'
PILIN' THE WOOD OR PILIN' THE TURF, • • • • • • • •   96 MOLL MAGEE   45
PILIN' THE WOOD OR PILIN' THE TURF, • • • • • • • •   96 MOLL MAGEE   45
A-PILIN' WOOD OR PILIN' TURF, • • • • • • • • • •   96 MOLL MAGEE   V 45
PILLAR
• • • AND HEAVING THE PILLAR OF HIS THROAT, • • • •   51 OISIN 3   59
AMRITA. DRAW YOU NEAR, AND 'NEATH YON PILLAR • • • •   71 ANASHU VIJAYA V 13A
AND RAISE HIS PILLAR STONE." KING EOCHAID SAID, • •   280 TWO KINGS   V 83
HIS MEMORY NOW IS A TALL PILLAR, BURNING • • • • • •   738 MOURN THEN ON   15
PILLARED   SEE MANY-PILLARED
UNTIL THE PILLARED DARK BEGAN TO STIR • • • • • •   185 QUEEN MAEVE   110
WITH THE FIRST KINGS OF MANY PILLARED CRUACHAN • • • •   187 QUEEN MAEVE   V 151
PILLARLESS
WINDOWLESS, PILLARLESS, MULTITUDINOUS HOME • • • • • •   39 OISIN 2   148
PILLARS   SEE DOOR-PILLARS
THE SEAWEED-COVERED PILLARS, AND THE GREEN • • • • •   31 OISIN 2   32
BASALTIC PILLARS MARRED WITH HEW AND HACK • • • • •   31 OISIN 2   V 30
MY PILLARS TOWARDS THEIR FALL. • • • • • • • • •   44 OISIN 2   V 239
THE BRAZEN PILLARS OF HIS DOOR, • • • • • • • • •   192 BAILE AILLINN   74
OR THE DOOR PILLARS OF ONE HOUSE, • • • • • • • •   195 BAILE AILLINN V 152
AND STRIKE THE GOLDEN PILLARS WITH MY HANDS. • • • •   246 SHADOW WATER B 502
ON PAINTED PILLARS, ON A DEAL • • • • • • • • •   271 GREY ROCK   V 19
BETWEEN THE PILLARS WITH A BEATING HEART • • • • •   279 TWO KINGS   59
PILLOWS
PROPPED UPON PILLOWS, ROUGE ON THE PALLOR OF HER FACE. • •   362 HER COURTESY   3
PILOT
THE PILOT STAR AND THE CROOKED PLOUGH • • • • • •   177 PAST GREATNESS   4
THERE'S NOT A PILOT ON THE PERCH • • • • • • • •   607 SONGS BURDEN 2   25
GO PILOT THE COURSE OF HIS ARROW'S DECEIT, • • • •   657 ISLE STAT I 3   69
AMONG THE WATERS THAT NO PILOT KNOWS. • • • • • •   750 SHADOW WATER A   80
PILOTS
WHAT KNOW THE PILOTS OF THE STARS OF TEARS? • • • •   73 ANASHU VIJAYA   47
FOR THEY'RE MY ONLY PILOTS. IF I LOST THEM • • • •   226 SHADOW WATER B   85
WE HAVE TO FOLLOW, FOR THEY ARE OUR PILOTS, • • • •   247 SHADOW WATER B 527
THAT I HAVE THE BEST OF PILOTS. SHADOWS, ILLUSIONS, • •   249 SHADOW WATER B 565
IF I REFUSED THE MESSENGERS AND PILOTS • • • • • •   249 SHADOW WATER B 572
I HAVE GOOD PILOTS, AIBRIC. WHEN MEN DIE • • • • •   750 SHADOW WATER A   81
PIN   SEE DOOR-PIN
FASTEN YOUR HAIR WITH A GOLDEN PIN, • • • • • • •   157 BELOVED RHYMES   1
ROCK-NURTURED AOIFE TOOK A PIN, • • • • • • • •   274 GREY ROCK   88
WITH THE PIN OF A BROOCH, • • • • • • • • • •   344 DAWN   4
PINCHES
AND PINCHES AMONG HAIL AND SNOW? • • • • • • • •   191 BAILE AILLINN   46
PINCHING
IN PINCHING WAYS I TOIL AND TURN." • • • • • • •   19 OISIN 1   V 282
PINE
TO PEAK AND PINE O'ER OISIN'S FAME." • • • • • •   7 OISIN 1   V 70
AND PEAK AND PINE WE KNOW NOT WHY, • • • • • • •   22 OISIN 1   V 340C
THEY PINE AWAY AND YELLOW AND WEAR OUT, • • • • •   81 EPHEMERA   V 24H
AND AH, THEY KNOW NOT, AS THEY PINE AND CEASE, • • •   81 EPHEMERA   V 24I
BECAUSE I HAVE NO OTHER YOUTH, CAN MAKE ME PINE, • • •   391 UNDER SATURN   3
BEING A PORTION OF MY YOUTH, CAN MAKE ME PINE • • •   391 UNDER SATURN   3
IT HAD BUT MADE US PINE THE MORE. THE ABSTRACT JOY, • •   427 PHANTOM HATRED   38
WHERE CYPRESS IS AND OOZY PINE, • • • • • • • •   670 ISLE STAT II 3 110
FORSWEARS HIS WANDERING 'MONG THE PINE, • • • • • •   686 LIFE   6
HEARING THE HARPERS PLAY, THE PINE WOOD CRACKLE, • • •   759 SHADOW WATER A V 241
PINE-WOOD
HEARING THE HARPERS PLAY, THE PINE-WOOD CRACKLE, • • • •   759 SHADOW WATER A 241
PINING
WITH POISONOUS LIPS, AND HE IS PINING SINCE? • • • •   696 MOSADA 2   7
FOR ALL SAVE HIM WHO PINING FELL, • • • • • • • •   717 FAIRY DOCTOR   19
FOR ALL SAVE HE WHO PINING FELL, • • • • • • • •   717 FAIRY DOCTOR V 19
PINION
UNPRUNED IS YOUR BEAUTIFUL PINION • • • • • • • •   707 FAIRY PEDANT   7
PINIONS
THE HORNS AND SHIELDS AND WILD SWAN'S PINIONS, • • • •   82 MAD KING GOLL V 5
FROM THE EVER-MOVING PINIONS • • • • • • • • •   667 ISLE STAT II 3   28
DID I ON QUIVERING PINIONS HASTE, • • • • • • • •   670 ISLE STAT II 3 111
PINNACLE
FROM YONDER PINNACLE ABOVE THE LAKE • • • • • • •   657 ISLE STAT I 3   63
PIN'S
PROMISED THAT FOR A PIN'S SAKE • • • • • • • • •   274 GREY ROCK   90
PIOUS
BENDING LOW HIS PIOUS HEAD, • • • • • • • • • •   82 MAD KING GOLL V 10
BECAUSE THIS COUNTRY HAS A PIOUS MIND • • • • • •   447 COLONUS PRAISE   25
AND KNOW YOU NOT SHE KISSED THAT PIOUS CHILD • • • •   696 MOSADA 2   6

PIPE
   OF SORROWFUL, AUSTERE, SWEET, LOFTY PIPE TUNES. . . . . . 341 SHEP GOATHERD 57
   AN OATEN PIPE UNTO A LISTENING FAWN, ... 678 ISLE STAT II 3 301
   AN OATEN PIPE UNTO A LISTENING FAUN, ... 678 ISLE STAT II 3 V 301
PIPER
   A PIPER PIPING AWAY, ... 144 HOST OF AIR 10
   A PIPER PIPING AWAY, ... 145 HOST OF AIR 42
PIPES
   THE PLAYING UPON PIPES AND THE DANCING, ... 330 BONE OF A HARE 5
   HE HAD OFTEN PLAYED HIS PIPES AMONG MY HILLS, ... 339 SHEP GOATHERD 23
PIPING
   A PIPER PIPING AWAY, ... 144 HOST OF AIR 10
   AND NEVER WAS PIPING SO SAD, ... 144 HOST OF AIR 11
   AND NEVER WAS PIPING SO GAY. . . . . 144 HOST OF AIR 12
   A PIPER PIPING AWAY, ... 145 HOST OF AIR 42
   AND NEVER WAS PIPING SO SAD, ... 145 HOST OF AIR 43
   AND NEVER WAS PIPING SO GAY. . . . . 145 HOST OF AIR 44
PIRATES
   CRYING, THE PIRATES DROVE HIS SWINE . . . . 82 MAD KING GOLL 15
   FELL ON THE PIRATES BY THE DEEP, ... 83 MAD KING GOLL 21
   FELL ON THE PIRATES OF THE DEEP, ... 83 MAD KING GOLL V 21
PISTOL
   A MAN WITH A PISTOL STOOD, ... 596 COLONEL MARTIN 56
PISTOLS
   BUT THEY THREW DOWN THEIR PISTOLS . . . . 596 COLONEL MARTIN 59
PIT
   HURL HELMETS, CROWNS, AND SWORDS INTO THE PIT. . . . . 257 RECONCILIATION 10
   THOSE FROM THE PIT AND GALLERY . . . . 608 SONGS BURDEN 3 3
   AT THE BOTTOM OF A PIT . . . . 632 MAN AND ECHO 3
   AND WHO WILL MOAN IN THE UNDER PIT, ... 716 FAIRY DOCTOR 7
PITCH
   TO SUCH A PITCH MY THOUGHT . . . . 255 WOMAN HOMER 11
   LET PAUDEENS PLAY AT PITCH AND TOSS, ... 288 TO WEALTHY MAN 31
   LEAVE PAUDEENS TO THEIR PITCH AND TOSS: . . . . 288 TO WEALTHY MAN V 31
   TO SUCH A PITCH OF FOLLY I AM BROUGHT, ... 384 VISION ROBART 58
   AND THAT TO SUCH A PITCH OF PASSION WROUGHT . . . . . 471 ALL SOUL NIGHT 24
   AND YET AGAIN, IF IT BE LIFE TO PITCH . . . . 479 SELF AND SOUL 58
   BECAUSE YOU HAVE IT IN THE PITCH DARK NIGHT . . . . . 554 RIBH AT TOMB V 1
   BECAUSE YOU HAVE FOUND ME IN THE PITCH DARK NIGHT . . . 554 RIBH AT TOMB V 1
   HERE IN THE PITCH DARK ATMOSPHERE ABOVE . . . . 555 RIBH AT TOMB V 17
   PITCH LIKE KING BILLY BOMB-BALLS IN . . . . 565 LAPIS LAZULI 7
   THEIR DRINK, THEIR PITCH AND TOSS BY DAY, ... 607 SONGS BURDEN 2 V 14
   THEY PITCH THEIR BURDENS OFF. . . . . 612 NEWS ORACLE 24
   IMAGINATION TO THAT PITCH WHERE IT CASTS OUT . . . . . 619 BRONZE HEAD 19
   AND LITTLE BOYS PLAYED PITCH AND TOSS. . . . . 725 LEGEND 4
PITCH-AND-TOSS
   THEIR DRINK, THEIR PITCH-AND-TOSS BY DAY, ... 607 SONGS BURDEN 2 14
PITCH-DARK
   BECAUSE YOU HAVE FOUND ME IN THE PITCH-DARK NIGHT . . . 554 RIBH AT TOMB 1
   HERE IN THE PITCH-DARK ATMOSPHERE ABOVE . . . . 555 RIBH AT TOMB 17
PITCHED   SEE HIGH-PITCHED
   BUT LOVE HAS PITCHED HIS MANSION IN . . . . 513 JANE TALK BISH 15
   ANCESTRAL PEARLS ALL PITCHED INTO A STY, ... 619 BRONZE HEAD 26
PITCHES
   THAT PITCHES COMMON THINGS ABOUT. THERE STOOD . . . . 428 NINETEEN 19 4
PITEOUS
   CRIED OUT, DIM SEA, HEAR MY MOST PITEOUS STORY! . . . . 68 SAD SHEPHERD 9
   "OH SEA, OLD SEA, HEAR THOU MY PITEOUS STORY!" . . . . 68 SAD SHEPHERD V 9
   O PITEOUS HEARTS, CHANGING TILL CHANGE BE DEAD . . . . 163 ASKS FORGIVE 19
   AMID THE HOVERING, PITEOUS, PENITENTIAL THRONG." . . . 173 SPEAKS HEARERS 8
   AND WHEN NO FACE GREW PITEOUS . . . . 191 BAILE AILLINN 62
   SHE LIES, HER LOVELY PITEOUS HEAD AMID DULL RED HAIR . . 362 HER COURTESY 2
PITIFUL
   CRY OF HIS LOVE WITH THEIR PITIFUL CRIES. . . . . . . 177 PAST GREATNESS V 12
   I LONG FOR YOUR MERRY AND TENDER AND PITIFUL WORDS, . . 203 WITHER BOUGHS 3
   THE WEST WIND MADE IT PITIFUL, AND THE NORTH WIND AFRAID. 449 OWEN AHERNE 6
PITILESS
   A GAZE BLANK AND PITILESS AS THE SUN, ... 402 SECOND COMING 15
   THY SOUL SHALL BE, THOUGH PITILESS AND BRIGHT . . . . . 674 ISLE STAT II 3 210
   THE SOUL OF THE PITILESS PLACE . . . . 708 FAIRY PEDANT 30
   WITH PITILESS MAGIC HAS BOUND YOU-- . . . . 708 FAIRY PEDANT 31
   THE HEART OF THE PITILESS PLACE . . . . 708 FAIRY PEDANT V 30
PITRI'S
   AND MAY NO RESTLESS PITRI'S FIDGET FINGER . . . . . . 75 ANASHU VIJAYA V 90
PITTANCE
   WHETHER FOR DAILY PITTANCE OR IN BLIND FEAR . . . . . 482 BLOOD AND MOON 37
PITY
   BUT PITY MOLL MAGEE. . . . . 94 MOLL MAGEE 4
   AND PITY MOLL MAGEE. . . . . 96 MOLL MAGEE 56
   THE PITY OF LOVE . . . . 119 PITY OF LOVE T
   A PITY BEYOND ALL TELLING . . . . 119 PITY OF LOVE 1
   HAD PITY ON THE LEAST OF THINGS . . . . 134 FR GILLIGAN 47
   OUR QUESTIONING, BEYOND OUR PITY EVEN. . . . . 282 TWO KINGS 130
   QUESTION OF OURS, BEYOND OUR PITY EVEN. . . . . 282 TWO KINGS V 130
   PITY, AN ACHING HEAD, ... 346 ON WOMAN 38
   NOR HATE OF WHAT'S TO COME, NOR PITY FOR WHAT'S GONE, . 427 PHANTOM HATRED 30
   IN PITY FOR MAN'S DARKENING THOUGHT . . . . 438 SONGS PLAY 2 1
   I PITY ALL THE YOUNG, ... 607 SONGS BURDEN 2 11
   PITY THESE WEEPING EYES! I WILL FOLLOW YOU. . . . . . 768 SHADOW WATER A 420
PITY-CRAZED
   SHE, PITY-CRAZED, HAD GIVEN HER SOUL AWAY, ... 629 CIRCUS ANIMALS 19

616

		PAGE	TITLE	LINE

PITYIN'
    AND STILL, WITH PITYIN', SCORNIN' EYE, • • • • • • • 96 MOLL MAGEE   39
PITYING
    WITH SCARCE A PITYING LOOK? • • • • • • • • • 315 FRIENDS   19
    UNLESS SOME PITYING GOD SHALL SUCCOUR ME • • • • 656 ISLE STAT I 3   36
PLACE   SEE DANCING-PLACE CAMPING-PLACE FIRE-PLACE SHADOW-PLACE THRESHING-PLACE
        MARKET-PLACE
    IT DOWN IN A LEAF-HID, HOLLOW PLACE • • • • • • • 17 OISIN 1   242
    WE SAW, SOME NEW, SOME PRINTED WHEN THE PLACE WAS YOUNG, 37 OISIN 2   V 116
    LOOKED DOWN ON ME; AND IN THE SELF-SAME PLACE • • • • • 39 OISIN 2   146
    MELTED AND FLOWED; AND IN THE SELF-SAME PLACE • • • • 39 OISIN 2   V 146
    AND THEY WHO TO A FAR-OFF PLACE HAD FLED, • • • • • 41 OISIN 2   V 184
    NOW IN A PLACE OF STAR-FIRE, AND NOW IN A SHADOW-PLACE 49 OISIN 3   42
      WIDE;
    NOW IN A PLACE OF STAR-FIRE, AND NOW IN A SHADOW PLACE 49 OISIN 3   V 42
      WIDE;
    NOW IN A PLACE OF STAR-FIRE, AND NOW IN A SHADOW PLACE 49 OISIN 3   V 42
      WIDE;
    LAY LOOSE IN A PLACE OF SHADOW; WE DREW THE REINS BY HIS 50 OISIN 3   44
      SIDE.
    WHILE IN THIS PLACE AND THAT PLACE, • • • • • • • • 58 OISIN 3   166
    WHILE IN THIS PLACE AND THAT PLACE, • • • • • • • • 58 OISIN 3   166
    AND IN THIS PLACE AND THAT PLACE, • • • • • • • • 58 OISIN 3   V 166
    AND IN THIS PLACE AND THAT PLACE, • • • • • • • • 58 OISIN 3   V 166
    SORRY PLACE, WHERE FOR SWING OF THE WAR-AXE IN MY DIM EYES 61 OISIN 3   194
    • • •
    WHAT PLACE HAVE CAOILTE AND CONAN, AND BRAN, SCEOLAN, 61 OISIN 3   195
      LOMAIR?
    • • • ON THE BURNING STONES IS THEIR PLACE; • • • • • 61 OISIN 3   197
    WHAT PLACE HAVE CAOLTE AND FIN, AND BRAN, SGEOLAN, LOMAIR? 61 OISIN 3   V 195
    AND THEY MARRIED BEYOND THEIR PLACE. • • • • • • • 92 FATHER OHART   8
    TO MY OWN PLACE, KINSALE. • • • • • • • • • • • 95 MOLL MAGEE   24
    SERVANTS ROUND HIS CUSHIONED PLACE • • • • • • • 99 FOXHUNTER   37
    THE SERVANTS ROUND HIS CUSHIONED PLACE • • • • • • 99 FOXHUNTER   V 37
    "THE DOOMS OF MEN ARE IN GOD'S HIDDEN PLACE." • • • • 110 CUCHULAIN SEA 62
    AMID MEN'S SOULS, THAT WAVER AND GIVE PLACE, • • • • 112 ROSE OF WORLD   7
    AMID MEN'S SOULS THAT DAY BY DAY GIVE PLACE, • • • • 112 ROSE OF WORLD V 7
    I DREAMED THAT ONE HAD DIED IN A STRANGE PLACE • • • • 123 DREAM OF DEATH 1
    BUT WHILE HE PASSED BEFORE A PLASHY PLACE, • • • • • 127 DREAM OF FAERY 17
    NO PLACE FOR LOVE AND DREAM AT ALL; • • • • • • • 139 TO IRELAND   43
    WHO DANCED ON A LEVEL PLACE, • • • • • • • • • • 144 HOST OF AIR   14
    AND LINGERED IN THE HIDDEN DESOLATE PLACE • • • • • 162 ASKS FORGIVE   15
    FROM GULLEON'S PLACE OF PRIDE, • • • • • • • • • 171 MAID QUIET   V 4B
    AND HURLED IT FROM ITS PLACE BEFORE HIS FOOTSTOOL WHITE, 174 ELEMENT POWERS V 3
    AND HURLED IT FROM ITS PLACE AMID THE PEARLY LIGHT • • • 174 ELEMENT POWERS V 3
    THEIR BODICES IN SOME DIM PLACE • • • • • • • • • 193 BAILE AILLINN 105
    IN THE HID PLACE, BEING CRAZED BY LOVE. • • • • • • 195 BAILE AILLINN 143
    FORGOTTEN AT THE THRESHING PLACE; • • • • • • • • 195 BAILE AILLINN V 148
    FOR THE ROADS ARE UNENDING, AND THERE IS NO PLACE TO MY 203 WITHER BOUGHS   4
      MIND."
    SHALL LIGHT UPON A PLACE IN THE WORLD'S CORE, • • • • • 231 SHADOW WATER B 212
    WHERE DO YOU COME FROM? WHO BROUGHT YOU TO THIS PLACE? 235 SHADOW WATER B 284
    TO SOME SURE COUNTRY, SOME FAMILIAR PLACE. • • • • • 249 SHADOW WATER B 569
    THAT IF WE HOLD THAT FLIGHT THEY'LL LEAVE THE PLACE, • • 265 ABBEY THEATRE   3
    TILL ALL THE PLACE WAS BEATEN INTO MIRE. • • • • • 278 TWO KINGS   27
    HIS MUMMERS TO THE MARKET PLACE, • • • • • • • • 287 TO WEALTHY MAN V 10
    AMID A PLACE OF STONE, • • • • • • • • • • • • 291 TO A FRIEND   13
    LIKE GENTLE BLOOD, HAS BEEN DRIVEN FROM THE PLACE, • • • 292 TO A SHADE   14
    STUMBLED UPON THAT WINDY PLACE • • • • • • • • • 302 HOUR DAWN   3
    HELL MOUTH LAY OPEN NEAR THAT PLACE, • • • • • • • 303 HOUR DAWN   25
    BEING CERTAIN IT WAS NO RIGHT PLACE • • • • • • • 303 HOUR DAWN   V 23
    LIKE SOME LAST COURTIER AT A GYPSY CAMPING PLACE • • • • 314 FALLEN MAJESTY V 3
    EVIL OF THIS PLACE, • • • • • • • • • • • • • 319 DOLLS   9
    IN A MOST DESOLATE STONY PLACE, • • • • • • • • • 325 ROBERT GREGORY 30
    TOWARDS NIGHTFALL UPON A PLACE • • • • • • • • • 325 ROBERT GREGORY V 31
    AT MOONEEN HE HAD LEAPED A PLACE • • • • • • • • 326 ROBERT GREGORY 60
    WE HAVE TALKED IN THE ONE PLACE. • • • • • • • • 332 SOLOMON SHEBA   4
    I HAD DRIVEN EVERY RHYME INTO ITS PLACE • • • • • • 339 SHEP GOATHERD 14
    TO A GREY ROCK ON A HILL • • • • • • • • • • • 347 FISHERMAN   3
    CLIMBING UP TO A PLACE • • • • • • • • • • • • 348 FISHERMAN   31
    MERE IMAGES; CHOSEN THIS PLACE TO LIVE IN • • • • • 373 PHASES OF MOON 13
    AUSTERITY, A PLACE SET OUT FOR WISDOM • • • • • • • 377 PHASES OF MOON 127
    FROM MOONLIT PLACE TO PLACE, • • • • • • • • • • 379 CAT AND MOON   18
    FROM MOONLIT PLACE TO PLACE, • • • • • • • • • • 379 CAT AND MOON   18
    FROM MOONLESS PLACE TO PLACE, • • • • • • • • • 379 CAT AND MOON V 18
    FROM MOONLESS PLACE TO PLACE, • • • • • • • • • 379 CAT AND MOON V 18
    FROM MOONLIGHT PLACE TO PLACE, • • • • • • • • • 379 CAT AND MOON V 18
    FROM MOONLIGHT PLACE TO PLACE, • • • • • • • • • 379 CAT AND MOON V 18
    ROOTED IN ONE DEAR PERPETUAL PLACE. • • • • • • • 405 FOR DAUGHTER   48
    WHO'D LIVED SOMEWHERE UPON THAT ROCKY PLACE, • • • • 410 TOWER   35
    GIVE PLACE TO AN INDIFFERENT MULTITUDE, GIVE PLACE • • • 427 PHANTOM HATRED 28
    GIVE PLACE TO AN INDIFFERENT MULTITUDE, GIVE PLACE • • • 427 PHANTOM HATRED 28
    AND THEREUPON A COLLOQUY TOOK PLACE • • • • • • • 463 HARUN RASHID   45
    THAT THEREUPON A COLLOQUY TOOK PLACE • • • • • • • 463 HARUN RASHID V 45
    BLESSED BE THIS PLACE, • • • • • • • • • • • • 480 BLOOD AND MOON 1
    RUN UNDERGROUND, RISE IN A ROCKY PLACE • • • • • • 490 COOLE BALLYLEE 5
    THE PLACE OF EXCREMENT; • • • • • • • • • • • 513 JANE TALK BISH 16
    ALL KNOW THAT ALL THE DEAD IN THE WORLD ABOUT THAT PLACE 593 PILGRIM   11
      ARE STUCK,
    THIS BOOK OR THAT, COME TO THIS HALLOWED PLACE • • • • 604 GALLERY REVIS   51
    AND PRESSED AT MIDNIGHT IN SOME PUBLIC PLACE • • • • • 610 STATUES   7

```
                                                          PAGE    TITLE         LINE
PLACE    (CONTINUED)
    IN THIS LONELY PLACE. . . . .  . . . . . . . .   617 LONG-LEG FLY        14
    ONE ANOTHER IN THIS PLACE?  . . . . . . . . . .   633 MAN AND ECHO        40
    DANCING IN SOME MOONY PLACE. . . . . . . . . .    647 ISLE STAT I 1       54
    HERE IS THE PLACE, THE CLIFF-ENCIRCLED WOOD!  . . .   651 ISLE STAT I 2    3
    THROUGH THIS NIGHT-VESTED PLACE THE RED BEAMS BREAK. . . .   662 ISLE STAT II 2   4
    LEAD ME, I PRAY THEE, TO THE STATUED PLACE!  . . . .   667 ISLE STAT II 3   37
    WE TURNED AROUND THE PLACE ALWAY, . . . . . . .   667 ISLE STAT II 3      40
    TO PLACE A KISS OF FIRE ON THE DIM BROW . . . . . .   688 TWO TITANS       47
    A LILY-BLANCHED PLACE, SHE SAT AND SANG, . . . . .   693 MOSADA 1          83
    A LILY BLANCHED PLACE, SHE SAT AND SANG, . . . . .   693 MOSADA 1       V  83
    THE SOUL OF THE PITILESS PLACE . . . . . . . .    708 FAIRY PEDANT        30
    THE HEART OF THE PITILESS PLACE  . . . . . . .    708 FAIRY PEDANT     V  30
    ENCLOSE A QUIET PLACE OF BEDS BOX-BORDERED, BEES, . . .   710 FERENCZ RENYI   24
    THE PLACE WAS EMPTY NOW OF PEOPLE. . . . . . . .   725 LEGEND              25
    AN EVENING PRESENCE FILLS THE PLACE. . . . . . .   736 SUMMER EVENING      16
    BEFORE A SANDED PLACE!  . . . . . . . . . . . .   740 EARL PAUL           32
    WHERE GODS ARE BROODING IN A MOUNTAINOUS PLACE  . . .   757 SHADOW WATER A  198
    I PUT THREE PERSONS IN THEIR PLACE . . . . . . .   787 HUDDON DUDDON        8
PLACES
    "BUT WE ARE APART IN THE GRASSY PLACES, . . . . . .    27 OISIN 1          408
    "BUT NEVER THE YEARS IN THE ISLE'S SOFT PLACES  . . .    27 OISIN 1       V 419A
    "BUT NEVER THE YEARS IN OUR ISLE'S SOFT PLACES  . . .    28 OISIN 1       V 424
    OF HALF-FORGOTTEN INNOCENT OLD PLACES!  . . . . .   130 BOOK STORIES        22
    CABINS GONE NOW, OLD WELL-SIDES, OLD DEAR PLACES, . . .   130 BOOK STORIES V 23
    AMID MOST LOVELY PLACES! SMITTEN AS THOUGH . . . . .   389 IMAGE PAST       13
    HEAVEN AND EARTH OUT OF THEIR PLACES,  . . . . . .   540 FROM ANTIGONE        8
    THE BEGGARS HAVE CHANGED PLACES, BUT THE LASH GOES ON. . . .   590 GREAT DAY    4
    IN WASTE PLACES OF THE SKY, . . . . . . . . . .   772 SONG DEIRDRE 1       6
PLACID
    WITH BERRIES.  PLACID AS A HOMEWARD BEE, . . . . .   710 FERENCZ RENYI       29
    WATCHED OF PLACID POPLAR-TREES . . . . . . . . .   732 STREET DANCERS      16
    WATCHED OF PLACID POPLAR TREES, . . . . . . . .   732 STREET DANCERS      16
    SORROW-WORN, YET PLACID BROWED. . . . . . . . .   733 STREET DANCERS V    56
PLACID-BROWED
    SORROW-WORN, YET PLACID-BROWED. . . . . . . . .   733 STREET DANCERS      56
PLAGUE
    THAT PLAGUE ME DAY AND NIGHT  . . . . . . . . .   399 DEMON BEAST          3
    THEY WERE NOT SUCH A PLAGUE WHEN I WAS YOUNG! . . . . .   591 SPUR             3
PLAGUED
    AND ARE PLAGUED BY CROWDS, UNTIL . . . . . . .    298 THREE HERMITS       20
PLAIN
    YET WILL I MAKE ALL PLAIN FOR THEE. . . . . . . .    2 OISIN 1         V  7B
    A GOLDEN CRESCENT LIT THE PLAIN! . . . . . . . .     2 OISIN 1         V  7BB
    ON GABHRA'S RAVEN-COVERED PLAIN! . . . . . . . .     5 OISIN 1            43
    STROKED THE YOUNG WINDS AS THEY ROLLED ON THE PLAIN, . . .    27 OISIN 1  V 415C
    THE LEAST OF DOORS! BEYOND ON A DIM PLAIN . . . . .    39 OISIN 2         155
    THE LEAST OF DOORS! BEYOND THE DOOR A PLAIN, . . . .    39 OISIN 2       V 155
    BARKING.  ALONG THE HERBLESS PLAIN, WITH BLOWS  . . .    40 OISIN 2       V 170
    A KING OF THE GREAT PLAIN WOULD SPEAK WITH YOU."  . . .   183 QUEEN MAEVE    78
    KINGS OF THE GREAT PLAIN HAVE COME AND GONE  . . . .   183 QUEEN MAEVE      81
    WHERE WILD BEES HIVE ON THE GREAT PLAIN. . . . . .   194 BAILE AILLINN      123
    TO TELL THEM A PLAIN STORY.  THAT'S NOT THE STORY! . . .   245 SHADOW WATER B 482
    WAS DONE TO MAKE IT PLAIN! . . . . . . . . . .    256 WORDS                8
    SO IT'S PLAIN TO BE DISCERNED . . . . . . . . .   298 THREE HERMITS       16
    "IT'S PLAIN THAT YOU ARE NO RIGHT MAN  . . . . . .   306 HOUR DAWN          82
    FROM MAEVE AND ALL THAT JUGGLING PLAIN, . . . . . .   307 HOUR DAWN        120
    OR ESSERKELLY PLAIN, FEW KEPT HIS PACE! . . . . . .   326 ROBERT GREGORY     59
    THAT MAYBE "I AM SORRY" IN PLAIN PROSE  . . . . . .   341 SHEP GOATHERD      60
    IT'S PLAIN THE BIBLE MEANS  . . . . . . . . . .   345 ON WOMAN             1
    MORE PLAIN TO THE MIND'S EYE THAN ANY FACE  . . . .   368 EGO DOMINUS        21
    LOVED THE LADY! AND IT'S PLAIN . . . . . . . . .   385 ROBARTES DANCE       5
    O PLAIN AS PLAIN CAN BE . . . . . . . . . . . .   396 ROSE TREE           16
    O PLAIN AS PLAIN CAN BE . . . . . . . . . . . .   396 ROSE TREE           16
    DANCED ON CRUACHAN'S WINDY PLAIN, . . . . . . . .   528 DANCER CRUACH        4
    DANCED IT ON CRUACHAN'S WINDY PLAIN, . . . . . . .   528 DANCER CRUACH  V    4
    ON CRUACHAN'S PLAIN SLEPT HE . . . . . . . . . .   529 TOM CRUACHAN         1
    THAT IF THEIR NEIGHBOURS FIGURED PLAIN, . . . . . .   626 OLD MEN BE MAD     11
    THE PLAIN, A LITTLE FAIR-HAIRED MAID I LOVE. . . . .   679 ISLE STAT I 3    312
    PLAIN TO BE UNDERSTOOD. . . . . . . . . . . . .   785 YOUR HEART           2
    ARE SHOT AT ON THE OPEN PLAIN. . . . . . . . . .   791 REPRISALS           18
'PLAINING
    CURES FOR CALVES WITH 'PLAINING THROAT, . . . . . .   717 FAIRY DOCTOR      15
    CURES FOR CALF WITH 'PLAINING THROAT, . . . . . . .   717 FAIRY DOCTOR  V   15
PLAINLY
    PLAINLY NO PHANTOM BY HIS LOOK! . . . . . . . .   303 HOUR DAWN        V  30
PLAIN'S
    AND NOT A HOUSE TO THE PLAIN'S EDGE, . . . . . . .   302 HOUR DAWN          10
PLAINS
    ALONG THE BLOOD-BEDABBLED PLAINS, . . . . . . . .    24 OISIN 1          371
    REMEMBERING HOW ALONG THE PLAINS, . . . . . . . .    24 OISIN 1       V  370
    AND WE RODE ON THE PLAINS OF THE SEA'S EDGE! . . . . .    48 OISIN 3        13
    AND I RODE BY THE PLAINS OF THE SEA'S EDGE, . . . . .    56 OISIN 3       141
    AND ESERKELLY PLAINS, FEW KEPT HIS PACE! . . . . . .   326 ROBERT GREGORY V  59
    OR ESERKELLY PLAINS, FEW KEPT HIS PACE! . . . . . .   326 ROBERT GREGORY V  59
    MOURN YE ON GRASS-GREEN PLAINS OF ERI FATED, . . . . .   738 MOURN THEN ON   9
PLAITED
    OUR HEARTS ENDURE THE SCOURGE, THE PLAITED THORNS, THE WAY   172 TRAV PASSION   3
    OUR HEARTS ENDURE THE PLAITED THORN, THE CROWDED WAY, . .   172 TRAV PASSION V  3
PLAN
    TO MICHELOZZO'S LATEST PLAN . . . . . . . . . .   288 TO WEALTHY MAN      23
```

```
                                                              PAGE      TITLE           LINE
PLAN   (CONTINUED)
     "I HAD NO BETTER PLAN AT FIRST.  . . . . . . . . .      305 HOUR DAWN          63
     ACCORDING TO A DIFFERENT PLAN. . . . . . . . . . .      379 SAINT HUNCH         6
     1 UNDERSTOOD HIS PLAN.  . . . . . . . . . . . . .       400 DEMON BEAST        15
     "ACCORDING TO MY BOYISH PLAN!  . . . . . . . . . .      577 WHAT THEN          17
PLANE
     THAT PATCHING OLD HEELS THEY MAY SHRIEK, I TAKE TO CHISEL    623 HIGH TALK       8
        AND PLANE.
PLANES
     SOME NINETEEN GERMAN PLANES, THEY SAY, . . . . . . .     791 REPRISALS          1
PLANETS
     AND MAKES THE LITTLE PLANETS RUN! . . . . . . . . .      18 OISIN 1          268
     FOR JOY THE LITTLE PLANETS RUN . . . . . . . . . .       18 OISIN 1      V   267
     OF PLANETS WATCHING, WATCHING THE RACE OF HARES . . .     44 OISIN 2      V 228B
     AND THE OLD PLANETS SEVEN  . . . . . . . . . . .        118 CRADLE SONG   V     7
     THE OLD PLANETS SEVEN  . . . . . . . . . . . . .        118 CRADLE SONG   V     7
     WITH PLANETS IN HIS CARE,  . . . . . . . . . . .        134 FR GILLIGAN       46
     THE CARELESS PLANETS IN THEIR COURSES,  . . . . . .      344 DAWN               7
     THERE ALL THE PLANETS DROP IN THE SUN. . . . . . . .     557 THERE              4
PLANNED       SEE LONG-PLANNED
     "IF LITTLE PLANNED IS LITTLE SINNED  . . . . . . .      338 TOM OROUGHLEY       9
     "OH, LITTLE PLANNED IS LITTLE SINNED . . . . . . .      338 TOM OROUGHLEY  V    9
     PLANNED IN A GOVERNMENT OFFICE, SHORTEN HIS LIFE,  . . . 372 ON GOING HOUSE    15
     AND PLANNED TO BRING THE WORLD UNDER A RULE, . . .      429 NINETEEN 19       31
     WHO HAVE PLANNED HIS MURDER, FOR THEY KNOW . . . . .     436 FOR MY SON        12
     PERPLEXED HER FANTASY AND PLANNED HER CARE? . . . .      466 HARUN RASHID     114
     PERPLEXED HER PHANTASY AND PLANNED HER CARE? . . . .     466 HARUN RASHID     114
     THAT STIRRED HER FANTASY AND PLANNED HER CARE, . . .     466 HARUN RASHID  V  114
     PYTHAGORAS PLANNED IT.  WHY DID THE PEOPLE STARE? . . .  610 STATUES            1
     AS MY LONG PLANNED HALF SOLITUDE, . . . . . . . . .      624 APPARITIONS   V   10
PLANNING
     AND PLANNING, PLOTTING ALWAYS THAT SOME MORROW  . . . .  129 BOOK STORIES      10
PLANS
     THEY HAVE IT THAT THE PLANS OF KINGS AND QUEENS . . . .  235 SHADOW WATER B   296
PLANTED
     AND PLANTED CYPRESS ROUND! . . . . . . . . . . .        123 DREAM OF DEATH     8
     AND WONDERING PLANTED BY HER SOLITUDE  . . . . . .      123 DREAM OF DEATH V   5
     HAS PLANTED QUIET IN THE NIGHT! . . . . . . . . .       134 TWO TREES          8
     PLANTED ON HIS KNEES, . . . . . . . . . . . . .         333 SOLOMON SHEBA     10
     AMID THE RUSTLE OF HIS PLANTED HILLS, . . . . . . .      417 ANCEST HOUSES      2
     PLANTED ON THE STAR-LIT GOLDEN BOUGH, . . . . . . .      497 BYZANTIUM         19
     PLANTED ON THE STARLIT GOLDEN BOUGH, . . . . . . .       497 BYZANTIUM     V   19
     AND THERE TWO BUSHES PLANTED  . . . . . . . . . .       571 THREE BUSHES      59
     GOD PLANTED HIM LONG AGO. . . . . . . . . . . .         743 WISDOM DREAMS      8
     PLANTED IN THE RUNNING WAVE! . . . . . . . . . .        775 AGAINST WITCH     13
PLANTS
     AMONG THE PLANTS! THE FLOWERY SILENCE FELL . . . . . .   692 MOSADA 1          55
PLASHES
     AND A HORSE PLASHES WITHIN IT! . . . . . . . . .        393 EASTER 1916       52
PLASHY
     BUT WHILE HE PASSED BEFORE A PLASHY PLACE, . . . . .     127 DREAM OF FAERY    17
PLASTER
     IN MOULDED PLASTER OR IN CARVEN STONE? . . . . . . .     327 ROBERT GREGORY    77
     "OF PLASTER SAINTS"! HIS BEAUTIFUL MISCHIEVOUS HEAD THROWN  577 LOFTY THINGS     4
        BACK.
PLATE
     I COOK AND CHANGE MY PLATE, . . . . . . . . . . .       607 SONGS BURDEN 2     6
PLATO
     CHOOSE PLATO AND PLOTINUS FOR A FRIEND . . . . . .      409 TOWER             12
     PLATO THOUGHT NATURE BUT A SPUME THAT PLAYS  . . . .     445 SCHOOL CHILDR     41
     PLATO STANDS BELOW, . . . . . . . . . . . . . .         524 MAD AS MIST        8
     PLATO THERE AND MINOS PASS, . . . . . . . . . . .       531 DELPHIC ORACLE     8
PLATONIC
     SO THE PLATONIC YEAR . . . . . . . . . . . . .          430 NINETEEN 19       54
     MADE ALL PLATONIC TOLERANCE VAIN . . . . . . . . .      438 SONGS PLAY 2       7
     THAT'S CALLED PLATONIC LOVE, . . . . . . . . . .        471 ALL SOUL NIGHT    23
PLATONIST
     FROM THE FAR TOWER WHERE MILTON'S PLATONIST  . . . .     373 PHASES OF MOON    15
     IL PENSEROSO'S PLATONIST TOILED ON . . . . . . . .      419 MY HOUSE          14
     SOME PLATONIST AFFIRMS THAT IN THE STATION . . . . .     431 NINETEEN 19       72
PLATONISTS
     "THOSE PLATONISTS ARE A CURSE," HE SAID, . . . . . .     485 STATISTICS         1
PLATO'S
     AND CRY IN PLATO'S TEETH, . . . . . . . . . . .         415 TOWER            147
     MADE PLATO'S TOLERANCE IN VAIN, . . . . . . . . .       438 SONGS PLAY 2  V    7
     OR ELSE, TO ALTER PLATO'S PARABLE, . . . . . . . .      443 SCHOOL CHILDR     15
     WHO TALKS OF PLATO'S SPINDLE, . . . . . . . . . .       520 HIS BARGAIN        1
     "WHAT THEN?"  SANG PLATO'S GHOST.  "WHAT THEN?" . . .    576 WHAT THEN          5
     "WHAT THEN?"  SANG PLATO'S GHOST.  "WHAT THEN?" . . .    577 WHAT THEN         10
     "WHAT THEN?"  SANG PLATO'S GHOST.  "WHAT THEN?" . . .    577 WHAT THEN         15
PLAUSIBLE
     OR SEEM PLAUSIBLE TO A MAN OF SENSE, . . . . . . .      624 APPARITIONS        4
PLAUTUS
     SO THAT HIS PLAUTUS SET THE PACE . . . . . . . .        287 TO WEALTHY MAN    12
PLAY       SEE HORSE-PLAY LOVE-PLAY
     IN THE FENIANS' DWELLINGS OF WATTLE LEAN ON THE CHESSBOARDS   55 OISIN 3      115
        AND PLAY,
     WITH MINGLING HAIR, AND PLAY UPON ONE LUTE. . . . . .     71 ANASHU VIJAYA    10
     YOU WAVES, THOUGH YOU DANCE BY MY FEET LIKE CHILDREN AT    90 OLD FISHERMAN     1
        PLAY,
```

PLAY   (CONTINUED)

YE WAVES, THOUGH YE DANCE 'FORE MY FEET LIKE CHILDREN AT PLAY,	90	OLD FISHERMAN V	1
WHEN I PLAY ON MY FIDDLE IN DOONEY,	178	FIDDLER DOONEY	1
HAVE GIVEN THEIR HEARTS UP TO THE PLAY,	202	NEVER GIVE ALL	10
AND WHO COULD PLAY IT WELL ENOUGH	202	NEVER GIVE ALL	11
AND WHO CAN PLAY IT WELL ENOUGH	202	NEVER GIVE ALL V	11
HURRY TO BLESS THE HANDS THAT PLAY,	212	BLESS PSALTER	1
O KINSMEN, BLESS THE HANDS THAT PLAY.	213	BLESS PSALTER	15
A LYRIC FROM AN UNPUBLISHED PLAY	263	MASK V	T
LET PAUDEENS PLAY AT PITCH AND TOSS,	288	TO WEALTHY MAN	31
THE NAMES THAT STILLED YOUR CHILDISH PLAY	289	SEPTEMBER 1913	10
WHEREON MAD FINGERS PLAY	291	TO A FRIEND	12
THE ATTACK ON THE "PLAY BOY"	294	HATED PLAYBOY V	T
THE WIND IS OLD AND STILL AT PLAY	301	RUN PARADISE	22
THE PLAYER QUEEN SONG FROM AN UNFINISHED PLAY	308	PLAYER QUEEN V	T
THE MOMENTS PASSED AS AT A PLAY;	313	MEMORY YOUTH	1
COME PLAY WITH ME;	359	TO A SQUIRREL	1
AND PENANCE IS THE PLAY,	364	END OF DAY	2
THOUGH PLAY IS BUT HALF DONE--	364	END OF DAY	7
"COME IN AND LEAVE THE PLAY,	364	END OF DAY	8
THOUGH PLAY IS BUT HALF-DONE--	364	END OF DAY V	7
THAT HE WILL NEVER FIND: I'D PLAY A PART;	377	PHASES OF MOON	128
AND RIGHT BETWEEN THESE TWO A GIRL AT PLAY	383	VISION ROBART	21
BUT WHEN THE MASTER'S BURIED MICE CAN PLAY,	418	ANCEST HOUSES	22
THROUGH TOO MUCH PLAY, OR MARRIAGE WITH A FOOL?	423	MY DESCENDANTS	12
THE FINEST PLAY UNDER THE SUN.	424	ROAD AT DOOR	5
WHETHER TO PLAY, OR TO RIDE	431	NINETEEN 19	67
LET THE NEW FACES PLAY WHAT TRICKS THEY WILL	435	NEW FACES	5
TWO SONGS FROM A PLAY	437	SONGS PLAY 1	T
AS THOUGH GOD'S DEATH WERE BUT A PLAY.	437	SONGS PLAY 1	8
I KNEW THAT HORSE PLAY, KNEW IT FOR A MURDEROUS THING.	442	BLACK CENTAUR V	4
WHAT SEEMS MOST WELCOME IN THE TOMB--PLAY A PREDESTINED PART.	503	VACILLATION	86
I OFFER TO LOVE'S PLAY	536	PARTING	13
NONE SHARED OUR GUILT; NOR DID WE PLAY A PART	542	PARN FUNERAL 1	22
ALL PERFORM THEIR TRAGIC PLAY,	565	LAPIS LAZULI	9
IF WORTHY THEIR PROMINENT PART IN THE PLAY,	565	LAPIS LAZULI	14
ACCOMPLISHED FINGERS BEGIN TO PLAY.	567	LAPIS LAZULI	54
AND THEN A COUNTER-TRUTH FILLED OUT ITS PLAY,	629	CIRCUS ANIMALS	17
DID THAT PLAY OF MINE SEND OUT	632	MAN AND ECHO	11
I'LL PLAY YOU FOR YOUR OLD HOUR-GLASS. YOU SEE	721	WITCH VIVIEN	36
FOR OTHER STAKES WE PLAY. YOU LOST THE GLASS.	722	WITCH VIVIEN	50
THUS PLAY WE FIRST WITH PAWNS, POOR THINGS AND WEAK;	722	WITCH VIVIEN	53
SO MEN IN LIFE AND I IN MAGIC PLAY;	722	WITCH VIVIEN	55
ON THE NOSE OF THE SLEEPER HE MADE IT PLAY;	729	PRIEST FAIRY	30
AND PLAY WITH HIS IMMORTAL HATE.	736	SUMMER EVENING	12
HEARING THE HARPERS PLAY, THE PINE-WOOD CRACKLE,	759	SHADOW WATER A	241
HEARING THE HARPERS PLAY, THE PINE WOOD CRACKLE,	759	SHADOW WATER A V	241
CHORUS FOR A PLAY	771	SONG DEIRDRE 1 V	T
WHAT'S THE MERIT IN LOVE PLAY,	777	SONG DEIRDRE 2 V	6
THOSE CRAZY FINGERS PLAY	783	GREY ROUND	16

PLAYBOY

ON THOSE THAT HATED "THE PLAYBOY	294	HATED PLAYBOY	T
ON THOSE WHO DISLIKE THE PLAYBOY	294	HATED PLAYBOY V	T
THE ATTACK ON "THE PLAYBOY OF THE WESTERN WORLD"	294	HATED PLAYBOY V	T

PLAY-BOY

ON THOSE THAT HATED "THE PLAY-BOY	294	HATED PLAYBOY V	T

PLAYED

HE SAT AND PLAYED IN A DREAM	145	HOST OF AIR	27
HE PLAYED WITH THE MERRY OLD MEN	145	HOST OF AIR	29
HE SAT DOWN AND PLAYED IN A DREAM	145	HOST OF AIR V	27
WHERE I HAVE LAUGHED AND SPUN AND PLAYED?	151	HEART OF WOMAN V	2
AT THE FULL MOON? HE PLAYED ALL THROUGH THE NIGHT.	223	SHADOW WATER B	21
AS WHEN I ALSO PLAYED THE FOOL."	306	HOUR DAWN	79
HE HAD OFTEN PLAYED HIS PIPES AMONG MY HILLS,	339	SHEP GOATHERD	23
AND WHEN HE PLAYED IT WAS THEIR LONELINESS,	339	SHEP GOATHERD	24
YET MANY, THAT HAVE PLAYED THE FOOL	404	FOR DAUGHTER	36
SOLIDER ARISTOTLE PLAYED THE TAWS	445	SCHOOL CHILDR	43
GREAT EUROPA PLAYED THE FOOL	509	JANE REPROVED	5
WHEN SHE, AND THOUGH SOME SAID SHE PLAYED	514	JANE GROWN OLD	8
THAT SAT SO STILL AND PLAYED AT THE CHESS?	550	SEVERED HEAD	12
AS HERE I CAME I SAW GOD PAN. HE PLAYED	678	ISLE STAT II 3	300
AND LITTLE BOYS PLAYED PITCH AND TOSS.	725	LEGEND	4
PLAYED ON HIS HARP. AND I WOULD BE AS SAD	747	SHADOW WATER A	3

PLAYER

A SONG FROM "THE PLAYER QUEEN"	308	PLAYER QUEEN	T
THE PLAYER QUEEN SONG FROM AN UNFINISHED PLAY	308	PLAYER QUEEN V	T
AND THERE'S A PLAYER IN THE STATES WHO GATHERS UP HER CLOAK	354	HIS PHOENIX	12
AND THERE'S THE PLAYER IN THE STATES WHO GATHERS UP HER CLOAK	354	HIS PHOENIX V	12
THE PLAYER CONNOLLY,	608	SONGS BURDEN 3	11
THEY SAY YOU ARE A GAMBLER AND A PLAYER	721	WITCH VIVIEN	34

PLAYERS

THE PLAYERS ASK FOR A BLESSING ON THE PSALTERIES AND ON THEMSELVES	212	BLESS PSALTER	T
THE PLAYERS ASK FOR A BLESSING ON THE PSALTERIES AND THEMSELVES	212	BLESS PSALTER V	T
COME GATHER ROUND ME, PLAYERS ALL:	608	SONGS BURDEN 3	1
PLAYERS AND PAINTED STAGE TOOK ALL MY LOVE,	630	CIRCUS ANIMALS	31
BUT WOMEN AND JUGGLERS AND PLAYERS ON THE HARP.	752	SHADOW WATER A	115

		PAGE	TITLE	LINE

PLAYFUL
    TROTTED BESIDE HIM IN A PLAYFUL MOOD. . . . .   715 DWELT SYCAMORE   4
PLAYING
    TO OLD MEN PLAYING AT CARDS . . . .   144 HOST OF AIR   23
    THE OTHER NIGHT, WHILE HE WAS PLAYING IT, ...   223 SHADOW WATER B   32
    I SAW THEM, TOO, ONE NIGHT. FORGAEL WAS PLAYING,   223 SHADOW WATER B   36
    FOR YOU HAVE LISTENED TO ME PLAYING IT . . . . . .   243 SHADOW WATER B   434
    THE PLAYING UPON PIPES AND THE DANCING, ...   330 BONE OF A HARE   5
    SHE IS PLAYING LIKE A CHILD . . . .   364 END OF DAY   1
    WHERE THE SHAKING LEAF WITH THE BEAM WAS PLAYING,   728 PRIEST FAIRY   2
    FROM PLAYING HURLEY IN THE WOOD . . . .   743 DANAAN QUICK   9
PLAYS
    THE HARE GROWS OLD AS SHE PLAYS IN THE SUN . . . .   27 OISIN 1   412
    "OLD GROWS THE HARE AS SHE PLAYS IN THE SUN, . . .   28 OISIN 1   V 420
    AN OLD MAN PLAYS THE BAGPIPES . . . .   214 HAPPY TOWNLAND   9
    I WOULD BE OF YOUR MIND; BUT WHEN HE PLAYS IT . .   222 SHADOW WATER B   17
    AS THOUGH IT DRAGGED ROAD-METAL. MY CURSE ON PLAYS   260 FASC DIFFICULT   8
    AS THOUGH IT DRAGGED ROAD METAL. MY CURSE ON PLAYS   260 FASC DIFFICULT V   8
    PLATO THOUGHT NATURE BUT A SPUME THAT PLAYS . . .   445 SCHOOL CHILDR   41
    AND HE PLAYS TUNES BETWEEN YOUR FEET, ...   573 LADYS 3RD SONG   2
    I LOSE! THEY'RE LOADED DICE. TIME ALWAYS PLAYS . .   721 WITCH VIVIEN   44
    THE WORLD GROWS OLD AND PLAYS THE FOOL." . . . .   725 LEGEND   12
PLAYTIME
    TILL DAYTIME, PLAYTIME SEEM THE SAME; . . . . . .   343 SHEP GOATHERD   106
    TILL THAT IS THEIR LONG SHOUTING PLAYTIME; . . . .   343 SHEP GOATHERD V 106
    MIRACLE HAD ITS PLAYTIME WHERE . . . .   440 WISDOM   8
PLEADS
    THE LOVER PLEADS WITH HIS FRIEND FOR OLD FRIENDS .   172 PLEADS FRIEND   T
    THE POET PLEADS WITH HIS FRIEND FOR OLD FRIENDS .   172 PLEADS FRIEND V   T
    THE POET PLEADS WITH HIS FRIEND WITH THE ELEMENTAL POWERS . . .   174 ELEMENT POWERS   T
    AODH PLEADS WITH THE ELEMENTAL POWERS . . . . . .   174 ELEMENT POWERS V   T
PLEASANT
    "O PLEASANT WOMAN," ANSWERED FINN, ...   5 OISIN 1   40
    "O PLEASANT MAIDEN," ANSWERED FINN, ...   5 OISIN 1   V 40
    NOW, PLEASANT MAIDEN, TELL TO ME . . . .   5 OISIN 1   V 43
    AND SWEETER OF VOICE THAN THE PLEASANT BIRDS, . .   9 OISIN 1   V 95
    AND NOW MOVES THERE MANY A PLEASANT TONGUE . . .   98 FOXHUNTER   21
    AND MOVES THERE MANY A PLEASANT TONGUE, ...   98 FOXHUNTER   V 23
    HE CRAWLED INTO THAT PLEASANT NOOK. . . . .   303 HOUR DAWN   32
    MY LIFE OF EVERY PLEASANT THOUGHT . . . .   307 HOUR DAWN   110
PLEASE
    AND I WOULD PLEASE THE HAPLESS FAUN, ...   67 HAPPY SHEPHERD   47
    HAS BEAUTIFUL WOMEN TO PLEASE EVERY MAN. . . . . .   228 SHADOW WATER B   144
    WE'LL KEEP THE SECRET—A NEW TRICK TO PLEASE. . . .   265 ABBEY THEATRE   10
    IMAGINING 'TWOULD BETTER PLEASE . . . .   271 GREY ROCK   4
    I KNEW A WOMAN NONE COULD PLEASE, ...   272 GREY ROCK   41
    I KNOW A WOMAN NONE COULD PLEASE, ...   272 GREY ROCK   V 41
    MY MEN, WHETHER IT PLEASE HER OR DISPLEASE, . . .   281 TWO KINGS   112
    "SAY WHAT YOU PLEASE, BUT FROM DAYBREAK . . . . .   304 HOUR DAWN   42
    "SAY WHAT YOU PLEASE, BUT FROM DAY-BREAK . . . . .   304 HOUR DAWN   V 42
    THAT MIGHT THE LEARNED PLEASE, ...   333 SOLOMON SHEBA   12
    THEY CAN SPREAD OUT WHAT SAIL THEY PLEASE FOR ALL I HAVE   354 HIS PHOENIX   22
        TO SAY,
    HE HAS HAD ENOUGH OF MEDDLING WHO CAN PLEASE . .   359 WAR POEM   4
    PLEASE A FANTASTIC HEAD. . . . .   366 HER CHRIS TREE   8
    THE LINEAMENTS THAT PLEASE THEIR VIEW . . . . . .   387 ROBARTES DANCE   49
    TO PLEASE A COMPANION . . . .   392 EASTER 1916   11
    ON OLD DRY FAGGOTS THAT COULD NEVER PLEASE . . .   466 HARUN RASHID   124
    BEST PLEASE A WANDERING MAN. . . . .   606 SONGS BURDEN 1   17
    ACH, CALL ME WHAT YOU PLEASE! . . . .   627 STATES HOLIDAY   21
PLEASED
    PLEASED TO HAVE FILLED THE EYES . . . .   329 MEN IMPROVE   8
    AND BE WELL PLEASED REMEMBERING IT, FOR IN THE OLD DAYS,   351 HER PRAISE   16
    AND CHOSEN WHAT SCENERY HAD PLEASED ME BEST." . . .   352 PEOPLE   21
    HOW SUCH A MAN PLEASED WOMEN MOST . . . .   458 SECRETS OF OLD   13
PLEASES
    BEST PLEASES YOU. ARMED MEN HAVE COME UPON US. . .   752 SHADOW WATER A   131
PLEASING
    NO PLEASING HABIT ENDS, ...   621 JOHN KINSELLA   30
PLEASURE
    OF WAR, AND THE CHASE, AND HUNTING, AND PLEASURE;   26 OISIN 1   V 403
    PLEASURE ITSELF CAN BRING NO WEARINESS, ...   284 TWO KINGS   181
    GAVE ME SUCH PLEASURE I'D FORGO . . . .   305 HOUR DAWN   69
    AND PLEASURE MADE HER CHEEKS GROW RED, ...   314 MEMORY YOUTH   11
    PLEASURE THAT COMES WITH SLEEP, ...   345 ON WOMAN   22
    SHRIEK WITH PLEASURE IF WE SHOW . . . .   431 NINETEEN 19   91
    LOVE'S PLEASURE DRIVES HIS LOVE AWAY, ...   438 SONGS PLAY 2   11
    THE BODY IS NOT BRUISED TO PLEASURE SOUL, ...   445 SCHOOL CHILDR   58
    AND DID SUCH PLEASURE TAKE— . . . .   455 HIS MEMORIES   14
    WHETHER OF PLEASURE OR OF REST, ...   521 THREE THINGS   4
    FOUND ALL THE PLEASURE THAT LIFE GAVE"! . . . . .   521 THREE THINGS   11
    THAT THE MOST COULD PLEASURE YOU, ...   525 DANCING DAYS   11
    MY UTMOST PLEASURE WITH A MAN . . . .   535 CHOSEN   12
    BUT HAD GREAT PLEASURE WITH A LAD . . . .   538 LAST CONFESS   5
    PLEASURE HAS MADE HIM . . . .   574 MAIDS 1ST SONG   9
    FROM PLEASURE OF THE BED, ...   575 MAIDS 2ND SONG   1
    OTHER PEOPLE'S MIRTH AND PLEASURE, ...   732 STREET DANCERS   24
    OTHER PEOPLE'S MIRTH AND PLEASURE, ...   732 STREET DANCERS   37
    OTHER'S PEOPLE'S MIRTH AND PLEASURE, ...   733 STREET DANCERS   50
PLEASURED
    HOW SUCH A MAN HAD PLEASURED MOST . . . .   458 SECRETS OF OLD V 13

621

PLEASURED   (CONTINUED)
    WHAT LIVELY LAD MOST PLEASURED ME • • • • • • • • •   538 LAST CONFESS   1
PLEASURES
    AND CALLED THE PLEASURES EVIL • • • • • • • • • • •   365 HER RACE   3
    NONE OTHER KNOWS WHAT PLEASURES MAN • • • • • • • •   620 JOHN KINSELLA   9
    THE PHANTOMS OF HER FADED PLEASURES WALK: • • • • •   687 TWO TITANS   19
PLEDGE
    HAVE BEEN DEFEATED BY THAT PLEDGE YOU GAVE • • • • •   258 KING NO KING   9
PLENTIFUL
    BE PLENTIFUL.--AND IF HE LOVE ANOTHER, • • • • • • •   71 ANASHU VIJAYA   5
PLENTY
    BE PLENTY.--IF HE GIVES ANOTHER LOVE, • • • • • • •   71 ANASHU VIJAYA V   5
    WHEREBY THE HORN OF PLENTY IS UNDONE. • • • • • • •   404 FOR DAUGHTER   32
    MY DREAMS ROUND THOUGHTS OF PLENTY, AS IN GLOOM • • •   681 SEEKER   3
    MY DREAMS O'ER THOUGHTS OF PLENTY, AS THE RED- • • •   681 SEEKER   V 3
PLENTY'S
    OUT OF THE MOUTH OF PLENTY'S HORN, • • • • • • • • •   405 FOR DAUGHTER   60
PLODDED
    AND AS THE TIME TO DARKNESS PLODDED • • • • • • • •   728 PRIEST FAIRY   11
PLOT   SEE DEWY-PLOT
    HOW THE FALCONER FOLLOWS THE FALCON IN THE WEEDS OF THE   52 OISIN 3   79
        HERON'S PLOT.
    DO YOU, TOO, DOUBT ME? HAVE YOU JOINED THEIR PLOT? • •   227 SHADOW WATER B 106
    BUT THE TORN PETALS STREW THE GARDEN PLOT: • • • • •   422 MY DESCENDANTS   7
    WHEN THE TORN PETALS STREW THE GARDEN PLOT: • • • • •   422 MY DESCENDANTS V 7
    GRASS PLOT OF THE GARDEN: • • • • • • • • • • • •   568 SWEET DANCER   3
    WITH QUIET SHADE ITS EVER DEWY PLOT. • • • • • • • •   714 FERENCZ RENYI V 109
PLOTINUS
    CHOOSE PLATO AND PLOTINUS FOR A FRIEND • • • • • • •   409 TOWER   12
    THE DELPHIC ORACLE UPON PLOTINUS • • • • • • • • • •   530 DELPHIC ORACLE   T
    BEHOLD THAT GREAT PLOTINUS SWIM, • • • • • • • • • •   530 DELPHIC ORACLE   1
    PLOTINUS CAME AND LOOKED ABOUT, • • • • • • • • • •   611 NEWS ORACLE   9
PLOTINUS'
    I MOCK PLOTINUS' THOUGHT • • • • • • • • • • • • •   415 TOWER   146
PLOTS
    THEN GIVE ME TRIUMPH IN MY MANY PLOTS. • • • • • • •   722 WITCH VIVIEN   51
    DEFEAT IS DEATH. SHOULD MY PLOTS FAIL I'D DIE. • • •   722 WITCH VIVIEN   52
    I MUST BE CAREFUL NOW. I HAVE SUCH PLOTS-- • • • •   722 WITCH VIVIEN   65
    SUCH WAR PLOTS, PEACE PLOTS, LOVE PLOTS--EVERY SIDE: • •   722 WITCH VIVIEN   66
    SUCH WAR PLOTS, PEACE PLOTS, LOVE PLOTS--EVERY SIDE: • •   722 WITCH VIVIEN   66
    SUCH WAR PLOTS, PEACE PLOTS, LOVE PLOTS--EVERY SIDE: • •   722 WITCH VIVIEN   66
PLOTTING
    AND PLANNING, PLOTTING ALWAYS THAT SOME MORROW • • •   129 BOOK STORIES   10
    ARE PLOTTING FOR YOUR DEATH. HAVE I NOT GIVEN • • •   226 SHADOW WATER B   93
PLOUGH
    THE PILOT STAR AND THE CROOKED PLOUGH • • • • • • •   177 PAST GREATNESS   4
    FROM WELL SIDE OR FROM PLOUGH LAND, WAS THEIR NOISE: • •   279 TWO KINGS   V 53
    TO PLOUGH OR PASTURE-LAND, MIGHT SEE ME THERE, • • •   283 TWO KINGS   146
    TO PLOUGH OR PASTURE LAND, MIGHT SEE ME THERE • • •   283 TWO KINGS   V 146
    THE GOLDEN PLOUGH AND HARROW AND SPOKE ALOUD • • • •   609 IN TARAS HALLS   12
PLOUGHED
    BETWEEN TWO FURROWS UPON THE PLOUGHED LAND: • • • •   784 WOMANS BEAUTY   4
    BETWEEN DARK FURROWS UPON THE PLOUGHED LAND. • • • •   784 WOMANS BEAUTY   6
PLOUGHING
    OR WEEDING OR PLOUGHING WITH FACES A-SHINING WITH MUCH-TOIL   58 OISIN 3   165
        WET:
PLOUGHLAND
    FROM WELLSIDE OR FROM PLOUGHLAND, WAS THERE NOISE: • • •   279 TWO KINGS   V 53
PLOUGH-LAND
    FROM WELL-SIDE OR FROM PLOUGH-LAND, WAS THERE NOISE: • •   279 TWO KINGS   53
    OF PASTURE-LAND AND PLOUGH-LAND AMONG THE HILLS? • • •   748 SHADOW WATER A   33
PLOUGHMAN
    THE HEAVY STEPS OF THE PLOUGHMAN, SPLASHING THE WINTRY   143 ROSE IN HEART   3
        MOULD:
    THE HEAVY STEPS OF THE PLOUGHMAN SPLASHING THE WINTER   143 ROSE IN HEART V   3
        MOULD,
PLOUGHSHARE
    INTO A PLOUGHSHARE? PARLIAMENT AND KING • • • • • •   429 NINETEEN 19   20
PLOVER'S
    AND HIS HAIR WAS AS DARK AS A PLOVER'S EYE. • • • • •   729 PRIEST FAIRY   46
PLOVERS
    LIKE PLOVERS THAT HAVE HEARD THE CALL. • • • • • • •   213 BLESS PSALTER   13
PLUCK
    SHALL THEY TURN WROTH OR PLUCK THE WINGS OF TIME? • • •   42 OISIN 2   V 199
    AND PLUCK TILL TIME AND TIMES ARE DONE • • • • • •   150 WANDER AENGUS   22
    "O DO NOT PLUCK AT HIS REIN, • • • • • • • • • • •   214 HAPPY TOWNLAND   18
    "O DO NOT PLUCK AT HIS REIN, • • • • • • • • • • •   215 HAPPY TOWNLAND   38
    "O DO NOT PLUCK AT HIS REIN, • • • • • • • • • • •   216 HAPPY TOWNLAND   58
    GO PLUCK ATHENE BY THE HAIR: • • • • • • • • • • •   386 ROBARTES DANCE   19
PLUCKED
    THE MOON PLUCKED AT MY REIN: • • • • • • • • • • •   214 HAPPY TOWNLAND   16
    THE MOON PLUCKED AT MY REIN: • • • • • • • • • • •   215 HAPPY TOWNLAND   36
    THE MOON PLUCKED AT MY REIN: • • • • • • • • • • •   216 HAPPY TOWNLAND   56
    IT WAS THEIR HANDS THAT PLUCKED THE WINDS AWAKE • • • •   237 SHADOW WATER B 324
    SING, FOR IT MAY BE THAT YOUR THOUGHTS HAVE PLUCKED • • •   342 SHEP GOATHERD   85
    HAS PLUCKED A FLOWER AND SUNG HER LOSS: • • • • • •   447 COLONUS PRAISE   22
    ALL MY FINE FEATHERS WOULD BE PLUCKED AWAY • • • • • •   469 HARUN RASHID   178
    PLUCKED BITTER WISDOM THAT ENRICHED HIS BLOOD. • • • •   543 PARN FUNERAL 2   12
    WHEN THEY HAVE PLUCKED A ROSE THERE, • • • • • • • •   571 THREE BUSHES   75
    I PLUCKED HER BACKWARDS BY HER DRESS OF GREEN. • • • •   676 ISLE STAT II 3 264
    AND PLUCKED SMALL FRUITS ON INNISFREE. • • • • • • •   742 DANAAN QUICK   5

		PAGE	TITLE	LINE

PLUCKS
THAT PLUCKS THE TREES FOR BREAD? • • • • • • • • • 621 JOHN KINSELLA 34
PLUM
THOUGH DOUBTLESS PLUM OR CHERRY-BRANCH • • • • • • 567 LAPIS LAZULI 47
GROUNDS WHERE PLUM AND CABBAGE GREW, • • • • • • • 577 WHAT THEN 13
PLUMAGE
HAD PRETTY PLUMAGE ONCE--ENOUGH OF THAT, • • • • • • 444 SCHOOL CHILDR 30
PLUME
IRVING AND HIS PLUME OF PRIDE. • • • • • • • • • • 625 NATIVITY 8
PLUMED
DREAMING OF FLASHING FLIGHT AND OF THE PLUMED WAVE. • • • 650 ISLE STAT I 1 140
BOWING NATIONS, PLUMED WARS-- • • • • • • • • • • 737 IN FIRELIGHT 10
AND PLUMED HEADS ABOUT HIM, • • • • • • • • • • • 740 EARL PAUL 31
PLUMELESS
E'EN THOUGH HIS WINGS WERE PLUMELESS STUMPS, • • • • • 670 ISLE STAT II 3 118
PLUMES
BY ROOTS THAT JOINED ABOVE OUR PLUMES-- • • • • • • 16 OISIN 1 V 224C
AND, SHAKING THE PLUMES OF THE GRASSES • • • • • • • 49 OISIN 3 35
PLUMMET-MEASURED
LIVE LIPS UPON A PLUMMET-MEASURED FACE. • • • • • • 610 STATUES 8
THE LINEAMENTS OF A PLUMMET-MEASURED FACE. • • • • • 611 STATUES 32
PLUMY
HAD SURGED UP IN A PLUMY FIRE, I DRAVE • • • • • • 41 OISIN 2 181
WITH SURGE OF PLUMY FIRE, LUNGING I DRAVE • • • • • • 41 OISIN 2 V 181
SURGED UP IN PLUMY FIRE, I LUNGED AND DRAVE • • • • 41 OISIN 2 V 181
PLUNDERING
TO MAKE HER FAST WHILE WE ARE PLUNDERING HER. • • • • • 232 SHADOW WATER B 225
PLUNGE
THE HORSES OF DISASTER PLUNGE IN THE HEAVY CLAY! • • • • 154 BELOVED PEACE 8
THE HORSES OF DISASTER PLUNGE IN THE DESOLATE CLAY. • • 154 BELOVED PEACE V 8
PLUNGE, LURED BY A SOFTENING EYE, • • • • • • • • • 413 TOWER 110
UNTIL IT PLUNGE INTO THE SUN! • • • • • • • • • • 472 ALL SOUL NIGHT 56
AND THE BRUTE DOLPHINS PLUNGE • • • • • • • • • • 612 NEWS ORACLE 20
PLUNGED
THROUGH BUSH THEY PLUNGED AND OVER IVIED ROOT, • • • • 278 TWO KINGS 32
THAT PLUNGED IN STREAM AGAIN • • • • • • • • • • 419 MY HOUSE V 9
OF THAT STARK MYSTERY WHERE I AM PLUNGED • • • • • • 466 HARUN RASHID V 113
UNTIL IT PLUNGED INTO THE SUN! • • • • • • • • • • 472 ALL SOUL NIGHT V 56
PLUNGES
PLUNGES TOWARDS NOTHING, ARMS AND FINGERS SPREADING WIDE 426 PHANTOM HATRED 13
PLUNGING
LAUGHED; AND PLUNGING DOWN • • • • • • • • • • • 453 MERMAID 4
PLUTARCH
SO THAT HIS PLUTARCH SET THE PACE • • • • • • • • • 287 TO WEALTHY MAN V 12
PLUTO
BOOK IV THE GATES OF PLUTO I. THE FOOL BY THE ROADSIDE 447 HERO GIRL FOOL V T
POCKET
"BEFORE NIGHTFALL I'LL PICK A POCKET • • • • • • • • 332 ROUND TOWER 27
PODS SEE SEED-PODS
SEED PODS AND FLOWERS THAT ARE NOT ALL WILD POPPY. • • • 342 SHEP GOATHERD V 88
POEM
AN OLD POEM RE-WRITTEN • • • • • • • • • • • • 129 BOOK STORIES V T
INTRODUCTION TO A DRAMATIC POEM • • • • • • • • • 217 WOODS OF COOLE V T
I HAVE MADE THIS POEM FOR YOU, THAT MEN MAY READ IT • • 219 WOODS OF COOLE 41
POEM MAYBE AS COLD • • • • • • • • • • • • • • 348 FISHERMAN 39
POEM MAY BE AS COLD • • • • • • • • • • • • • 348 FISHERMAN V 39
ON BEING ASKED FOR A WAR POEM • • • • • • • • • • 359 WAR POEM T
POEMS
TWO POEMS CONCERNING PEASANT VISIONARIES A CRADLE SONG 146 UNAPPEAS HOST V T
TWO LOVE POEMS THE SHADOWY HORSES • • • • • • • • 154 BELOVED PEACE V T
TWO POEMS BY O'SULLIVAN THE RED CONCERNING MARY LAVELL. 157 POET BELOVED V T
SEVEN POEMS I UPON A DYING LADY • • • • • • • • 362 HER COURTESY V T
FOUR POEMS CRACKED MARY AND THE BISHOP • • • • • • 507 JANE BISHOP V T
EIGHT POEMS CRAZY JANE AND THE BISHOP • • • • • • • 507 JANE BISHOP V T
SEVEN POEMS GIRL'S SONG • • • • • • • • • • • • 515 GIRLS SONG B V T
POET
A POET TO HIS BELOVED • • • • • • • • • • • • • 157 POET BELOVED T
THE POET PLEADS WITH HIS FRIEND FOR OLD FRIENDS • • • • 172 PLEADS FRIEND V T
THE POET PLEADS WITH THE ELEMENTAL POWERS • • • • • • 174 ELEMENT POWERS T
A CERTAIN POET IN OUTLANDISH CLOTHES • • • • • • • 180 QUEEN MAEVE 1
TO A POET, WHO WOULD HAVE ME PRAISE • • • • • • • • 262 TO A POET T
DID NOT THE POET SING IT WITH SUCH AIRS • • • • • • 267 ALL TEMPT ME 7
DID NOT THE POET CARRY HIM WITH AN AIR • • • • • • • 267 ALL TEMPT ME V 7
TO A POET OR A KING • • • • • • • • • • • • • 299 THREE HERMITS 27
THE POET STUBBORN WITH HIS PASSION SANG US • • • • • 356 BROKEN DREAMS 18
A POET KEEP HIS MOUTH SHUT, FOR IN TRUTH • • • • • • 359 WAR POEM V 2
I, THE POET WILLIAM YEATS, • • • • • • • • • • 406 CARVED STONE 1
SOME MORALIST OR MYTHOLOGICAL POET • • • • • • • • 430 NINETEEN 19 59
HERE, TRAVELLER, SCHOLAR, POET, TAKE YOUR STAND • • • 489 COOLE PARK 29 25
HERE IS FRESH MATTER, POET, • • • • • • • • • • 553 CHURCH STATE 1
CAN PAY THE POET FOR A VERSE AND HEAR THE FIDDLE SOUND, 581 CURSE CROMWELL 21
POET AND SCULPTOR, DO THE WORK, • • • • • • • • • 638 BEN BULBEN 37
POETRY
AND YOU AND I, AND TALKED OF POETRY. • • • • • • • 204 ADAMS CURSE 3
HER POETRY, DANCING UPON THE SHORE, • • • • • • • 578 CRAZED GIRL 2
POETRY, MUSIC, I HAVE LOVED, AND YET • • • • • • • 599 SPIRIT MEDIUM 1
POETRY AND MUSIC I HAVE BANISHED, • • • • • • • • 600 SPIRIT MEDIUM 19
POET'S
A POET'S MOUTH BE SILENT, FOR IN TRUTH • • • • • • 359 WAR POEM 2
POET'S IMAGININGS • • • • • • • • • • • • • • 415 TOWER 160
A MIMICRY OF YOUTH. CAN POET'S THOUGHT • • • • • • 463 HARUN RASHID 62

623

```
                                                      PAGE    TITLE            LINE
POETS
    HAVE KNOWN THREE CENTURIES, POETS SING, . . . . . . .     2  OISIN 1             3
    UNTIL THE DANAAN POETS BROUGHT  . . . . . . . . . .       7  OISIN 1            63
    LOVE, TILL THE DANAAN POETS BROUGHT  . . . . . . . .      7  OISIN 1         V  63
    UNTIL THE DANAAN POETS CAME,  . . . . . . . . . . .       7  OISIN 1         V  64
    THE POETS LABOURING ALL THEIR DAYS  . . . . . . . .     164  PERFECT BEAUTY      2
    WE POETS LABOUR ALL OUR DAYS,  . . . . . . . . . .      164  PERFECT BEAUTY  V   2
    AND POETS FOUND, OLD WRITERS SAY,  . . . . . . . .      197  BAILE AILLINN     187
    . . . CERTAIN BAD POETS, IMITATORS OF HIS AND MINE . .  262  TO A POET           T
    . . . CERTAIN BAD POETS, IMITATORS OF HIS AND OF MINE .  262  TO A POET       V   T
    POETS WITH WHOM I LEARNED MY TRADE, . . . . . . . .    270  GREY ROCK           1
    WE POETS KEEP OUR MOUTHS SHUT, FOR IN TRUTH . . . . .  359  WAR POEM            2
    FOR SCHOLARS AND FOR POETS AFTER US, . . . . . . . .   488  COOLE PARK 29       6
    WHATEVER'S WRITTEN IN WHAT POETS NAME . . . . . . . .  492  COOLE BALLYLEE     43
    ALL THAT IS WRITTEN IN WHAT POETS NAME  . . . . . . .  492  COOLE BALLYLEE  V  43
    OF POETS THAT ARE ALWAYS GAY, . . . . . . . . . . .    565  LAPIS LAZULI        3
    POETS AND WITS ABOUT HIM DREW; . . . . . . . . . . .   577  WHAT THEN          14
    THE POETS HAVE IMAGINED, TERRIBLE AND GAY."  . . . .   602  GALLERY REVIS      12
    IRISH POETS, LEARN YOUR TRADE, . . . . . . . . . . .   639  BEN BULBEN         68
POIGNANT
    IMAGE OF POIGNANT RECOLLECTION. . . . . . . . . . .    389  IMAGE PAST          7
POINT       SEE SWORD-POINT COMPASS-POINT
    LOOK TO LONG FISHING-LINES, OR POINT AND PARE . . . .   32  OISIN 2            55
    AT THE SWORD POINT, AND BADE ME BRING HIM ONE . . . .  109  CUCHULAIN SEA   V  53
    AT THE SWORD POINT, AND WAITS TILL WE HAVE FOUND  . .  109  CUCHULAIN SEA   V  53
    THEN DREW HIS SWORD TO HOLD ITS LEVELLED POINT  . . .  277  TWO KINGS          14
    BUT DREW HIS SWORD, AND THOUGHT WITH LEVELLED POINT .  277  TWO KINGS       V  14
    OR THAT THE WIND WOULD SHIFT A POINT, . . . . . . .    306  HOUR DAWN          92
    THAT SEEMED TO WHIRL UPON A COMPASS POINT, . . . . .   489  COOLE PARK 29   V  21
    HUSH! HUSH! HUSH! THEY PAUSE AND POINT . . . . . .     732  STREET DANCERS     31
POINTED
    I HAVE POINTED OUT THE YELLING PACK, . . . . . . . .   453  DEATH OF HARE       1
    AND THEN A POINTED FACE WAS SEEN  . . . . . . . . .    728  PRIEST FAIRY       21
    BENEATH A POINTED CAP OF GREEN; . . . . . . . . . .    728  PRIEST FAIRY       22
POINTING
    AND ONE ARM POINTING THUS, IN MARBLE WHITE. . . . .    663  ISLE STAT II 2     28
POINTS
    THE WAVES IN YONDER LAKE WHERE POINTS MY HAND . . . .  652  ISLE STAT I 2      13
POISED
    AND THY NECK'S A POISED LILY; . . . . . . . . . . .    647  ISLE STAT I 1      55
POISON
    A POISON DROP. A TOY, A FANCY ONCE, . . . . . . . .    700  MOSADA 3           24
    A POISON DROP. THE TOY OF FANCY ONCE, . . . . . . .    700  MOSADA 3        V  24
    FROM POISON: FOR YOU CANNOT TRUST THESE MOORS. . . .   704  MOSADA 3          126
    THAT ARE A POISON TO ALL MEN  . . . . . . . . . . .    743  DANAAN QUICK       16
POISONOUS
    WITH POISONOUS LIPS, AND HE IS PINING SINCE? . . . .   696  MOSADA 2            7
POKED
    I POKED ABOUT A VILLAGE CHURCH  . . . . . . . . . .    584  GHOST ROG CASE     31
POLAR
    THE POLAR DRAGON SLEPT, . . . . . . . . . . . . .     174  ELEMENT POWERS      4
    AND WHERE THE POLAR WINDS AND WATERS WRESTLE  . . . .  682  SEEKER             18
POLE        SEE TENT-POLE
    UPON THE STAR THAT MARKS THE HIDDEN POLE; . . . . .    477  SELF AND SOUL       5
    THE POLE-STAR AND THE SILENCE OF THE POLE. . . . . .   477  SELF AND SOUL   V   8
    SOME FOUND A DIFFERENT POLE, AND WHERE IT STOOD  . .   483  VERONIC NAPKIN      7
    TENT POLE OF EDEN; THE TENT'S DRAPERY; . . . . . .     483  VERONIC NAPKIN  V   2
POLE-AXE
    FROM MACE AND SWORD AND POLE-AXE, LONG AGO  . . . .     31  OISIN 2            30
POLECAT
    OR DARK BETWIXT THE POLECAT AND THE OWL, . . . . .     565  GYRES              21
POLES
    . . . CEASE THE WINDS, AND ON THEIR POLES . . . . .    719  PHANTOM SHIP       17
POLE-STAR
    THE POLE-STAR AND THE SILENCE OF THE POLE. . . . . .   477  SELF AND SOUL   V   8
POLISHED
    THE POSTS OF POLISHED YEW, CIRCLED WITH BRONZE, . .    279  TWO KINGS          48
    THE PACING TO AND FRO ON POLISHED FLOORS  . . . . .    418  ANCEST HOUSES      35
POLITE
    OR POLITE MEANINGLESS WORDS, . . . . . . . . . . .    392  EASTER 1916         6
    POLITE MEANINGLESS WORDS, . . . . . . . . . . . .     392  EASTER 1916         8
POLITIC
    'TWERE POLITIC TO DO THE LIKE BY THESE; . . . . . .    262  TO A POET           3
    "MAYBE A BREATH OF POLITIC WORDS  . . . . . . . . .    396  ROSE TREE           3
POLITICAL
    ON A POLITICAL PRISONER . . . . . . . . . . . . .     397  POLIT PRISONER      T
POLITICIAN
    AND THERE'S A POLITICIAN . . . . . . . . . . . . .    631  POLITICS            7
POLITICIANS
    "SOME POLITICIANS IDLE WORDS  . . . . . . . . . . .    396  ROSE TREE       V   3
POLITICS
    THAT TALKED OF LOVE OR POLITICS, . . . . . . . . .    131  OLD PENSIONER       5
    IN ART OR POLITICS; . . . . . . . . . . . . . . .     431  NINETEEN 19        71
    AN IMAGE OF SUCH POLITICS. . . . . . . . . . . . .    475  EVA GORE-BOOTH     13
    POLITICS . . . . . . . . . . . . . . . . . . . .      631  POLITICS            T
    OR ON SPANISH POLITICS? . . . . . . . . . . . . .     631  POLITICS            4
POLLEXFEN
    AND THEN I THINK OF OLD GEORGE POLLEXFEN, . . . . .    325  ROBERT GREGORY     33
    IN MEMORY OF ALFRED POLLEXFEN . . . . . . . . . . .    360  ALF POLLEXFEN       T
    SINCE OLD WILLIAM POLLEXFEN . . . . . . . . . . .     360  ALF POLLEXFEN       2
    BY CHILDISH MEMORIES OF AN OLD CROSS POLLEXFEN, . .    391  UNDER SATURN        7
```

624

POLLEXFEN (CONTINUED)
    OLD WILLIAM POLLEXFEN, ...   604 YOU CONTENT   14
POMP
    THE MURMURING BIRDS IN SOLEMN POMP . . . .   20 OISIN 1   V   293
POND
    LIKE BUBBLES IN A FROZEN POND; . . . .   22 OISIN 1   336
    FROM POND AND FALLEN TREE--ME SING . . . . . .   85 MAD KING GOLL V   63
    SHAN-WALLA, WHERE A WILLOW-BORDERED POND . . . .   217 WOODS OF COOLE   2
    SHANWALLA, WHERE A WILLOW BORDERED POND . . . . .   217 WOODS OF COOLE V   2
PONDER
    NOTHING THAT COMMON WOMEN PONDER ON . . . . . .   579 DOR WELLESLEY   12
    AND PONDER IT IF THEY WILL); THEN NEAR AT HAND .   659 ISLE STAT II 1   10
    WHILE I MURMUR A LITTLE AND PONDER . . . .   707 FAIRY PEDANT   14
PONDERABLE
    IS PONDERABLE TO OUR TOUCH. . . . .   399 BREAK OF DAY   18
PONDERED
    AND PONDERED IN A SOFT VAIN MOOD . . . .   14 OISIN 1   184
    AND PONDERED ON THE GLORY OF HIS DAYS; . . . . .   108 CUCHULAIN SEA   43
    AND PONDERED ON THE WONDER OF HIS DAYS. . . . . .   108 CUCHULAIN SEA V   43
    "I HAVE CAP AND BELLS," HE PONDERED, ...   160 CAP AND BELLS   21
    "I'VE CAP AND BELL," HE PONDERED, ...   160 CAP AND BELLS   21
PONDERING
    THEY HUDDLE FROM MAN'S PONDERING MIND, ...   138 TO IRELAND   V   26
    IMAGINING AND PONDERING . . . .   193 BAILE AILLINN   111
    AND HARPERS PONDERING WITH BOWED HEAD . . . . .   193 BAILE AILLINN V   107
    WOUND IN MIND'S PONDERING . . . .   471 ALL SOUL NIGHT   13
PONDERS
    BECAUSE, TO HIM WHO PONDERS WELL, ...   138 TO IRELAND   19
PONDS
    AND WINDS AND PONDS COVER MORE QUIET WOODS, . . .   218 WOODS OF COOLE   34
    MORE SHINING WINDS, MORE STAR-GLIMMERING PONDS? . . 218 WOODS OF COOLE   35
PONIES
    BECAUSE PIEBALD PONIES, LED BEARS, CAGED LIONS, MAKE BUT   623 HIGH TALK   5
        POOR SHOWS,
PONY
    QUIET THE DOG, TETHER THE PONY . . . .   617 LONG-LEG FLY   3
POOL   SEE RINSING-POOL
    THE HARP AWAY. A DOLOROUS POOL . . . .   17 OISIN 1   V   240
    BUT ONE SMALL KNOT-GRASS GROWING BY THE POOL . . .   127 DREAM OF FAERY   29
    THE YELLOW POOL HAS OVERFLOWED HIGH UP ON CLOOTH-NA-BARE,   207 HANRAHANS SONG   11
    THE YELLOW POOL HAS OVERFLOWED HIGH UPON CLOOTH-NA-BARE,   207 HANRAHANS SONG V 11
    BUT FOR THE TRODDEN MIRE, THE POOL OF BLOOD, . . . 278 TWO KINGS   44
    BY WHAT LAKE'S EDGE OR POOL . . . .   323 SWANS AT COOLE   28
    TO HIS SHAPE AT THE RINSING POOL . . . .   341 SHEP GOATHERD V   70
    WHERE THE SHEEP ARE THROWN IN THE POOL, ...   341 SHEP GOATHERD V   71
    HAVE CLOSED THE LADIES' EYES, THEIR MINDS ARE BUT A POOL   426 PHANTOM HATRED 21
    ONE HAND AMID THE GOLDFISH IN THE POOL; . . . . .   463 HARUN RASHID   44
    THEY WERE SITTING ROUND A POOL, ...   667 ISLE STAT II 3   24
    AND THEY WERE SITTING ROUND A POOL. . . . .   667 ISLE STAT II 3 V   24
    I DREW MY SWORD TO FLING IT IN A POOL,-- . . . .   747 SHADOW WATER A   7
POOLS
    --FROM POOLS AND ROTTING LEAVES--ME SING . . . .   85 MAD KING GOLL V   63
    IN POOLS AMONG THE RUSHES . . . .   88 STOLEN CHILD   30
    IN SHADOWY POOLS, WHEN ARMIES FLED; . . . .   155 FORGOT BEAUTY   5
    O TUFTED REEDS, BEND LOW AND LOW IN POOLS ON THE GREEN   206 HANRAHANS SONG V   1
        LAND,
    I HAD WOVEN OF THE SLEEP THAT IS IN POOLS . . . .   762 SHADOW WATER A   284
POOR
    FOR HE IS WEAK AND POOR AND BLIND, AND LIES . . .   42 OISIN 2   203
    WHEN THE POOR TIRED CHILD, PASSION, FALLS ASLEEP.   80 EPHEMERA   7
    MY MAN WAS A POOR FISHER . . . .   94 MOLL MAGEE   5
    MY HUSBAND WAS A FISHER POOR . . . .   94 MOLL MAGEE   V   5
    AND LOOKS UPON THE POOR. . . . .   96 MOLL MAGEE   52
    IN ALL POOR FOOLISH THINGS THAT LIVE A DAY, . . .   101 ROSE UPON ROOD   11
    ANOTHER POOR MAN SENT FOR HIM, ...   132 FR GILLIGAN   7
    "AND IS THE POOR MAN DEAD?" HE CRIED. . . . . . .   133 FR GILLIGAN   33
    I BADE MY HEART BUILD THESE POOR RHYMES; . . . .   158 BELOVED RHYMES   3
    BUT I, BEING POOR, HAVE ONLY MY DREAMS; . . . . .   176 CLOTHS HEAVEN   6
    AND OUR POOR KATE OR NAN IS LESS . . . .   190 BAILE AILLINN   35
    I MIGHT HAVE THROWN POOR WORDS AWAY . . . . . .   256 WORDS   15
    A HUNDRED-YEAR-OLD MEMORY TO THE POOR; . . . . .   269 PARDON FATHERS   6
    I NEEDS MUST MARRY SOME POOR LOUT; . . . .   273 GREY ROCK   47
    I NEED MUST MARRY SOME POOR LOUT," . . . .   273 GREY ROCK   V   47
    A POOR LIFE, DO WHAT HE CAN; . . . .   301 RUN PARADISE   11
    POOR MEN HAVE GROWN TO BE RICH MEN, ...   301 RUN PARADISE   15
    AND RICH MEN GROWN TO BE POOR AGAIN, ...   301 RUN PARADISE   16
    MY COUNTRYMEN KILTARTAN'S POOR, ...   328 IRISH AIRMAN   6
    AMONG THE POOR BOTH OLD AND YOUNG GAVE HER PRAISE.   351 HER PRAISE   18
    AND RUTH ST. DENIS HAD MORE CHARM ALTHOUGH SHE HAD POOR   353 HIS PHOENIX   10
        LUCK;
    AND MADE--BEING POOR, AILING AND IGNORANT, . . .   370 EGO DOMINUS   59
    NOT A POOR FOOL UNDERSTANDS. . . . .   381 SONG OF FOOL   4
    AND MANY A POOR MAN THAT HAS ROVED, ...   404 FOR DAUGHTER   38
    DID ALL OLD MEN AND WOMEN, RICH AND POOR, ...   413 TOWER   97
    "AND ALL THOSE LIES HAVE BUT ONE END, POOR WRETCHES TO   450 OWEN AHERNE   18
        BETRAY;
    LIKE SOME POOR ARAB TRIBESMAN AND HIS TENT. . . .   491 COOLE BALLYLEE   40
    AND WHETHER A MAN BE RICH OR POOR . . . .   582 ROGER CASEMENT V   19
    AND SAVED THE IRISH POOR, ...   586 PARNELLITES   12
    DID ALL THAT FOR THE POOR. . . . .   596 COLONEL MARTIN   62

625

		PAGE	TITLE	LINE

POOR   (CONTINUED)
BECAUSE PIEBALD PONIES, LED BEARS, CAGED LIONS, MAKE BUT   623 HIGH TALK   5
    POOR SHOWS,
ON MY POOR BRAIN YOUR BUSY TUMULTS CROWD.   648 ISLE STAT I 1   100
POOR RACE OF LEAFY ARCADY, YOUR LOVE   650 ISLE STAT I 1   145
POOR SAD WOOD-RHAPSODISTS. NOT SO! THEY'RE GLAD.   652 ISLE STAT I 2   16
SLEW THEE, POOR SIBYL! COMRADES THOU AND I!   675 ISLE STAT II 3   235
POOR EARTH-ENKINDLED PAIR,   680 LOVE AND DEATH   22
POOR LOVE AND SORROW, WITH THEIR ARMS THROWN ROUND   703 MOSADA 3   119
THUS PLAY WE FIRST WITH PAWNS, POOR THINGS AND WEAK!   722 WITCH VIVIEN   53
THERE WAS SOME TALKING OF THE POOR--   725 LEGEND   14
IS THIS POOR BODY THAT REDDENS AND GROWS PALE.   764 SHADOW WATER A   341
POORER
BUT NEVER MADE A POORER SONG   273 GREY ROCK   55
POPE'S
SHUT THE DOOR OF THE POPE'S CHAPEL,   618 LONG-LEG FLY   23
POPINJAY
AND HEAR, AND JUDGE. MY POPINJAY, WHAT NOW?   660 ISLE STAT II 1   40
SAY THEN,--"A POPINJAY BEFORE GRIEF'S SHAFT   664 ISLE STAT II 2   52
POPLAR
GREEN OAK AND POPLAR TREE!   132 OLD PENSIONER   V   16
UPON THE NORMAN UPLAND OR, IN THAT POPLAR SHADE,   449 OWEN AHERNE   2
UPON THE NORTHERN UPLAND OR IN THAT POPLAR SHADE,   449 OWEN AHERNE   V   2
WATCHED OF PLACID POPLAR TREES,   732 STREET DANCERS V   16
POPLARS
THE POPLARS GAZE ACROSS THE WATERS GREY,   653 ISLE STAT I 2   34
MORE DARK BENEATH THE POPLARS, WHERE YON OWL   675 ISLE STAT II 3   233
POPLAR-TREES
WATCHED OF PLACID POPLAR-TREES   732 STREET DANCERS   16
POPPIES
FOR FAIR ARE POPPIES ON THE BROW!   67 HAPPY SHEPHERD   56
WEARY, WITH ALL HIS POPPIES GATHERED ROUND HIM.   72 ANASHU VIJAYA   25
QUITE SOON THE CORNFIELD, WHERE THE POPPIES GROW,   699 MOSADA 3   7
ALONG THE CORNFIELD, WHERE THE POPPIES GROW,   699 MOSADA 3   V   7
GOES HIS POPPIES NOW A-HAWKING!   705 DAWN-SONG   4
POPPY
SEED-PODS AND FLOWERS THAT ARE NOT ALL WILD POPPY.   342 SHEP GOATHERD   88
SEED PODS AND FLOWERS THAT ARE NOT ALL WILD POPPY.   342 SHEP GOATHERD V   88
POPPY-HUNG
IN THE POPPY-HUNG HOUSE OF THE TWILIGHT FLUTED!   8 OISIN 1   V   83
POPULACE
AND A SMALL AND A FEEBLE POPULACE STOOPING WITH MATTOCK   58 OISIN 3   164
    AND SPADE,
A-FLUTTERING THE PAINTED POPULACE OF LAKE   675 ISLE STAT II 3   224
POPULAR
OR IS THERE NONE, MOST POPULAR OF MEN,   265 ABBEY THEATRE   13
GROW RICH, POPULAR AND FULL OF INFLUENCE,   369 EGO DOMINUS   43
HER THOUGHT SOME POPULAR ENMITY!   397 POLIT PRISONER   10
FOR THOUGHT SOME POPULAR ENMITY,   397 POLIT PRISONER V   10
AND ALL THE POPULAR STATESMEN SAY   460 THREE MONUMENT   5
IT HAD NOT TOUCHED OUR LIVES. BUT POPULAR RAGE,   542 PARN FUNERAL 1   20
DISTRUSTFUL OF THAT POPULAR EYE   624 APPARITIONS   5
POPULOUS
AND BRING US INTO POPULOUS SEAS AGAIN?   225 SHADOW WATER B   74
PORTAL
THEY MAY NOT PASS THE PORTAL,   680 LOVE AND DEATH   21
PORTALS
WE PASSED THE PORTALS, AND WITHIN,   17 OISIN 1   V   250
PORTER
THE PORTER SLEPT, ALTHOUGH HE SAT UPRIGHT   182 QUEEN MAEVE   45
PORTER-DRINKERS'
PORTER-DRINKERS' RANDY LAUGHTER!   640 BEN BULBEN   77
PORTER'S
CRIED FROM THE PORTER'S LODGE, AND WITH LONG CLAMOUR   181 QUEEN MAEVE   37
PORTION
THAT OUR SUFFICIENT PORTION OF THE WORLD   282 TWO KINGS   119
A PORTION OF MY MIND AND LIFE, AS IT WERE,   325 ROBERT GREGORY   42
SO GREAT HER PORTION IN THAT PEACE YOU MAKE   356 BROKEN DREAMS   12
WHAT PORTION IN THE WORLD CAN THE ARTIST HAVE   369 EGO DOMINUS   49
BEING A PORTION OF MY YOUTH, CAN MAKE ME PINE   391 UNDER SATURN   V   3
PORTIONING
DID GOD IN PORTIONING WINE AND BREAD   386 ROBARTES DANCE   39
PORTIONS
THAT I MYSELF FOR PORTIONS OF THE YEAR   371 ON GOING HOUSE   5
PORTLY
PORTLY GREEN-PATED BIRD   400 DEMON BEAST   28
PORTRAIT
OF OLD LUKE WADDING'S PORTRAIT SAID   400 DEMON BEAST   10
THERE WAS NO PORTRAIT IN THE GALLERY   400 DEMON BEAST   17
BEFORE A WOMAN'S PORTRAIT SUDDENLY I STAND,   602 GALLERY REVIS   13
MANCINI'S PORTRAIT OF AUGUSTA GREGORY,   602 GALLERY REVIS   25
A GREAT EBULLIENT PORTRAIT CERTAINLY!   602 GALLERY REVIS   27
AN EBULLIENT GREAT PORTRAIT CERTAINLY!   602 GALLERY REVIS V   27
PORTRAITS.
WITH FAMOUS PORTRAITS OF OUR ANCESTORS!   418 ANCEST HOUSES   37
WHERE MY FRIENDS' PORTRAITS HANG AND LOOK THEREON!   604 GALLERY REVIS   52
POSE
THERE ONE THAT RUFFLED IN A MANLY POSE   489 COOLE PARK 29   11
POSEIDON
POSEIDON GAVE IT BIT AND OAR,   447 COLONUS PRAISE   28

POSSESSED
     IT IS POSSESSED. A PROPHESYING VOICE. . . . .   681 SEEKER   8
POSSESSION
     AS OTHERS WILL, WHEN FIRST THEY TAKE POSSESSION, ... 341 SHEP GOATHERD   52
POSSIBLE
     I ALMOST LONG THAT IT WERE POSSIBLE: . . . .   236 SHADOW WATER B   306
POST   SEE DOOR-POST STARTING-POST
     AND HANGING ITS PAPER FLOWERS FROM POST TO POST, ... 198 SEVEN WOODS   8
     AND HANGING ITS PAPER FLOWERS FROM POST TO POST, ... 198 SEVEN WOODS   8
     ARE BUT A POST THE PASSING DOGS DEFILE. . . . . . .   321 REED WHISPERER   14
     THE POST AND GARDEN-BOY ALONE . . . .   607 SONGS BURDEN 2   7
     THAT FOUGHT IN THE POST OFFICE . . . .   608 SONGS BURDEN 3   5
     WHAT STALKED THROUGH THE POST OFFICE? WHAT INTELLECT, . . 611 STATUES   26
     TO A DISTANT POST: . . . .   617 LONG-LEG FLY   4
POSTS   SEE DOOR-POSTS
     THE POSTS OF POLISHED YEW, CIRCLED WITH BRONZE, ...   279 TWO KINGS   48
POT   SEE HONEY-POT
     LAND FOR YOUR CHILDREN OR MONEY IN A POT." . . . . .   228 SHADOW WATER B   125
     TO STIR THE BOILING POT? . . . .   395 SIXTEEN DEAD   6
     GOLDSMITH DELIBERATELY SIPPING AT THE HONEY POT OF HIS   481 BLOOD AND MOON V   21
          MIND:
     NOR SOLDERED POT OR PAN: . . . .   606 SONGS BURDEN 1   15
POT-BELLIED
     AND WHEN THE MOON'S POT-BELLIED . . . .   455 FRIENDS YOUTH   3
POT-HOUSE
     A POT-HOUSE BENCH WITH OLIVER GOLDSMITH ONCE. . . . . .   486 SEVEN SAGES   3
POTION'S
     WHEN, THE POTION'S WORK BEING DONE, ...   522 LULLABY   9
POTTERY
     IN PAINTING OR IN POTTERY, WENT . . . .   421 MY TABLE   18
POUND
     LIKE AN OLD HORSE IN A POUND." . . . .   333 SOLOMON SHEBA   8
     ARE BUT A NARROW POUND." . . . .   333 SOLOMON SHEBA   16
     THE WORLD A NARROW POUND." . . . .   333 SOLOMON SHEBA   24
POUNDED
     THE PARTICULAR IS POUNDED TILL IT IS MAN. . . . . . .   382 VISION ROBART   6
POUNDS
     FOR HE SHALL HAVE A THOUSAND POUNDS . . . .   295 THREE BEGGARS   22
     THAT POUNDS UP ALL ANEW . . . .   346 ON WOMAN   31
POUR
     HER BEAUTY AS THE CONSTELLATIONS POUR . . . .   279 TWO KINGS   V 62B
     POUR WINE AND DANCE IF MANHOOD STILL HAVE PRIDE, ... 311 MOUNTAIN TOMB   1
     POUR WINE AND DANCE, IF MANKIND STILL HAVE PRIDE, ... 311 MOUNTAIN TOMB   V 1
     AND POUR UPON THE WORLD! AH! WELL-A-DAY! . . . . . .   703 MOSADA 3   118
     AND POUR UPON THE WORLD! AH! WELL A DAY! . . . . . .   703 MOSADA 3   V 118
POURED
     THEIR NAKED AND GLEAMING BODIES POURED OUT AND HEAPED IN   48 OISIN 3   28
          THE WAY.
     BUT WHEN A MAN POURED FISH INTO A PILE, ...   126 DREAM OF FAERY   5
     POURED OUT WINE FOR THE HIGH INVISIBLE ONES. . . . . .   219 WOODS OF COOLE   44
     A KIND MILD WOMAN HAD SHE BEEN, WHO POURED . . . . .   279 TWO KINGS   V 62A
POURING   SEE DEATH-POURING
     THE SOUTH IS POURING DOWN ROSES OF CRIMSON FIRE! . . . . 154 BELOVED PEACE   6
     THAT FROM THE FIRE IS EVER POURING UP . . . .   683 SEEKER   37
POURS
     POURS ROUND HIS SLEEPY STREAMS. . . . .   98 FOXHUNTER   V 16
     POURS ROUND IN SLEEPY STREAMS. . . . .   98 FOXHUNTER   V 16
     SAD LADY OF THE DEEP, POURS DOWN HER LIGHT: . . . . .   650 ISLE STAT I 1   127
     POURS UP AND FLOATS IN FRAGRANCE ROUND MY HEAD . . . .   691 MOSADA 1   40
     POURS UP AND FLOATS IN FRAGRANCE O'ER MY HEAD . . . .   691 MOSADA 1   V 40
POWDER
     THOUGHT THAT UNLESS A LITTLE POWDER BURNED . . . . .   429 NINETEEN 19   21
POWER
     ARE EMPTY OF ALL POWER." "AND WHICH OF THESE . . . .   46 OISIN 2   248
     YE HAVE NO POWER." "AND, NIAM, SAY, OF THESE . . . .   46 OISIN 2   V 248
     THAT NONE MAY FEEL THE POWER OF SQUALL AND WAVE, ... 128 DREAM OF FAERY V   45
     BUT THE HORSE-BOYS SLEPT ON, AS THOUGH SOME POWER . . .   181 QUEEN MAEVE   39
     BECAUSE EARTH, CRAZY FOR ITS BROKEN POWER, ...   186 QUEEN MAEVE   124
     WHAT POWER THAT IS MORE MIGHTY THAN DESIRE . . . . .   234 SHADOW WATER B   267
     TO GO--FOR HOPE WOULD GIVE HIS LIMBS THE POWER-- . . .   282 TWO KINGS   V 133A
     FOR HOPE WOULD GIVE HIS LIMBS THE POWER--AND AWAIT . . . 283 TWO KINGS   136
     DID SHE PUT ON HIS KNOWLEDGE WITH HIS POWER . . . . .   441 LEDA AND SWAN   13
     A BLOODY, ARROGANT POWER . . . .   480 BLOOD AND MOON   3
     A SOMETHING INCOMPATIBLE WITH LIFE; AND POWER, ...   482 BLOOD AND MOON   50
     AND SOFT, ONE GLIMMERING STAR--WITH POWER VAST: . . . . 714 FERENCZ RENYI V   115
     OF EQUAL POWER IN SPELLS AND SECRET RITES. . . . . .   720 WITCH VIVIEN   6
     FOR GOD GIVES POWER TO THE SAD . . . .   741 EARL PAUL   47
     FOR GOD GIVES POWER TO THE SAD . . . .   741 EARL PAUL   51
     PUT ALL YOUR POWER ON THE THREAD . . . .   771 SPINNING SONG   12
POWERFUL   SEE ALL-POWERFUL
     OF THAT MORE POWERFUL LIFE? HIS WIFE KNOWS BETTER. . . . 230 SHADOW WATER B   172
     SOME VIOLENT BITTER MAN, SOME POWERFUL MAN . . . . .   418 ANCEST HOUSES   17
     BY THE WEBBED TOES, AND THAT ALL POWERFUL BILL . . . .   441 LEDA AND SWAN   V   3
     A POWERFUL EMBLEM UP, ...   480 BLOOD AND MOON   9
     AND YET A WOMAN'S POWERFUL CHARACTER . . . .   489 COOLE PARK 29   18
POWERLESS
     IN WHAT LAND DO THE POWERLESS TURN THE BEAK . . . . .   42 OISIN 2   198
POWERS
     THE MAGICAL POWERS TO AND FRO. . . . .   138 TO IRELAND   V 24
     THE POET PLEADS WITH THE ELEMENTAL POWERS . . . . . .   174 ELEMENT POWERS   T
     AODH PLEADS WITH THE ELEMENTAL POWERS . . . .   174 ELEMENT POWERS V   T

		PAGE	TITLE		LINE

POWERS   (CONTINUED)

THE POWERS WHOSE NAME AND SHAPE NO LIVING CREATURE KNOWS	174	ELEMENT POWERS		1
GREAT POWERS OF FALLING WAVE AND WIND AND WINDY FIRE,	174	ELEMENT POWERS		7
THE POWERS, NOT KIND LIKE YOU, CAME WHERE GOD'S GARDEN BLOWS,	174	ELEMENT POWERS	V	1
YOU GREAT ANGELIC POWERS OF WIND, AND WAVE, AND FIRE,	174	ELEMENT POWERS	V	7
GREAT ELEMENTAL POWERS OF WIND, AND WAVE, AND FIRE,	174	ELEMENT POWERS	V	7
DIM POWERS OF DROWSY THOUGHT, LET HER NO LONGER BE	175	ELEMENT POWERS		13
. . . THOUGHT'S CROWNED POWERS HE CALLED THEM ONCE.	480	BLOOD AND MOON		15
GRATITUDE TO THE UNKNOWN POWERS	505	GRAT INSTRUCT	V	T

PRACTICE

PRACTICE A TINKER SHUFFLE	617	LONG-LEG FLY		17

PRACTISE

HE'LL PRACTISE ON THE SHEPHERD'S FLUTE,	343	SHEP GOATHERD		102

PRACTISED

AS HE THAT PRACTISED OR THAT UNDERSTOOD	327	ROBERT GREGORY		75

PRAGMATICAL

THAT THIS PRAGMATICAL, PREPOSTEROUS PIG OF A WORLD,	481	BLOOD AND MOON		26

PRAISE

SHALL KNEEL AND PRAISE YOU, ONE BY ONE,	8	OISIN 1		78
AND PRAISE THEE IN MY WESTERN HALL."	8	OISIN 1	V	79
AND ALL AROUND THE HARP-STRING TOLD HIS PRAISE,	109	CUCHULAIN SEA		44
AND ALL AROUND THE HARPSTRING TOLD HIS PRAISE,	109	CUCHULAIN SEA	V	44
AND ALL AROUND THE HARP STRING TOLD HIS PRAISE,	109	CUCHULAIN SEA	V	44
AND WHITE STARS TELL YOUR PRAISE,	113	ROSE OF PEACE		10
"PRAISE GOD AND GOD'S MOTHER," DATHI SAID,	167	BLESSED		17
AND NEW FRIENDS BUSY WITH YOUR PRAISE,	173	PLEADS FRIEND		3
AND OF NEW FRIENDS ARE GLAD WITH YOUR PRAISE,	173	PLEADS FRIEND	V	3
WHY DO YOU PRAISE ANOTHER, PRAISING HER,	181	QUEEN MAEVE		31
WHAT WERE OUR PRAISE TO THEM? THEY EAT	196	BAILE AILLINN		177
I HEAR THE HARP-STRING PRAISE THEM, OR HEAR THEIR MOURNFUL TALK.	210	UNDER THE MOON		16
I HEAR THE HARP STRINGS PRAISE THEM, OR HEAR THEIR MOURNFUL TALK.	210	UNDER THE MOON	V	16
I HEAR THE HARPSTRING PRAISE THEM OR HEAR THEIR MOURNFUL TALK.	210	UNDER THE MOON	V	16
I HEAR THE HARP STRING PRAISE THEM OR HEAR THEIR MOURNFUL TALK.	210	UNDER THE MOON	V	16
THEIR HEADS BEING TURNED WITH PRAISE AND FLATTERY;	245	SHADOW WATER B		480
AGAINST UNWORTHY PRAISE	259	UNWORTH PRAISE		T
WHAT, STILL YOU WOULD HAVE THEIR PRAISE!	259	UNWORTH PRAISE		11
TO A POET, WHO WOULD HAVE ME PRAISE	262	TO A POET		T
IN PRAISE OF WHAT ANOTHER'S SAID OR SUNG,	262	TO A POET		2
BUT HAVE YOU KNOWN A DOG TO PRAISE HIS FLEAS?	262	TO A POET	V	4
DOWSON AND JOHNSON MOST I PRAISE--	273	GREY ROCK		62
AMONG THOSE MOUTHS THAT SING THEIR SWEETHEARTS' PRAISE,	285	TWO KINGS		185
AND THOUGH I HAD HER PRAISE FOR IT,	313	MEMORY YOUTH		5
YET WE, FOR ALL THAT PRAISE, COULD FIND	314	MEMORY YOUTH		13
NOW MUST I THESE THREE PRAISE--	315	FRIENDS		1
HOW COULD I PRAISE THAT ONE?	316	FRIENDS		20
HOW SHOULD I PRAISE THAT ONE?	316	FRIENDS	V	20
YET PRAISE THE WINTERS GONE!	336	YOUNG BEAUTY		15
HER PRAISE	350	HER PRAISE		T
UNTIL HER PRAISE SHOULD BE THE UPPERMOST THEME,	350	HER PRAISE		6
THOUGH SHE HAD YOUNG MEN'S PRAISE AND OLD MEN'S BLAME,	351	HER PRAISE		17
AMONG THE POOR BOTH OLD AND YOUNG GAVE HER PRAISE.	351	HER PRAISE		18
A LAW INDIFFERENT TO BLAME OR PRAISE,	428	NINETEEN 19		10
COLONUS' PRAISE	446	COLONUS PRAISE		T
COME PRAISE COLONUS' HORSES, AND COME PRAISE	446	COLONUS PRAISE		1
COME PRAISE COLONUS' HORSES, AND COME PRAISE	446	COLONUS PRAISE		1
THAT'S SO UNLIKE MYSELF THAT WHEN YOU PRAISE IT	447	HERO GIRL FOOL		2
MOCKED ME WITH PRAISE OF MY MERE OPPOSITE;	448	HERO GIRL FOOL		4
IT IS AS THOUGH YOU PRAISE ANOTHER, OR EVEN	448	HERO GIRL FOOL	V	3
MOCK ME WITH PRAISE OF MY MERE OPPOSITE;	448	HERO GIRL FOOL	V	4
EVERY PHILOSOPHER SHOULD PRAISE THAT LOVE.	465	HARUN RASHID		97
BUT I BEING NONE CAN PRAISE ITS OPPOSITE.	465	HARUN RASHID		98
PHILOSOPHERS SHOULD PRAISE THAT LOVE THE MOST,	465	HARUN RASHID	V	97
THAT EVERY GIFT AND EVERY WORD OF PRAISE	469	HARUN RASHID		172
AND PRAISE OUR CHOSEN MAN;	586	PARNELLITES		2
A DRUNKEN MAN'S PRAISE OF SOBRIETY	591	DRUNK SOBRIETY		T
COME PRAISE NINETEEN-SIXTEEN,	608	SONGS BURDEN 3		2
PRAISE EVERY MAN THAT CAME AGAIN,	608	SONGS BURDEN 3		7
PRAISE EVERY MAN THAT FELL.	608	SONGS BURDEN 3		8
COME PRAISE NINETEEN SIXTEEN,	608	SONGS BURDEN 3	V	2
A MAN I PRAISE THAT ONCE IN TARA'S HALLS	609	IN TARAS HALLS		1
AND PRAISE A WAR AMONG THE ENDLESS SEAS,	749	SHADOW WATER A	V	35
THE PRAISE OF DEIRDRE .	771	SONG DEIRDRE 1	V	T
PRAISE THE BEAUTIFUL AND STRONG;	773	SONG DEIRDRE 1		19
PRAISE THE REDNESS OF THE YEW;	773	SONG DEIRDRE 1		20
PRAISE THE BLOSSOMING APPLE-STEM.	773	SONG DEIRDRE 1		21
WHAT IS ALL OUR PRAISE TO THEM	773	SONG DEIRDRE 1		23
PRAISE THE BLOSSOMING APPLE STEM;	773	SONG DEIRDRE 1	V	21
"THE MAN THAT I PRAISE,"	780	WELL AND TREE		1
WHO BUT AN IDIOT WOULD PRAISE	780	WELL AND TREE		7
"THE MAN THAT I PRAISE," "	780	WELL AND TREE		9
WHO BUT AN IDIOT WOULD PRAISE	780	WELL AND TREE		15
FOR PRAISE OF CLOWN OR KING,	789	SINGING HEAD		20

PRAISED

BUT WAS THERE EVER DOG THAT PRAISED HIS FLEAS?	262	TO A POET		4
BUT WHERE'S THE WILD DOG THAT HAS PRAISED HIS FLEAS?	262	TO A POET	V	4
PRAISED THEIR GREAT VICTORIES AND GAVE THEM JOY	286	TWO KINGS	V	218B

PAGE   TITLE   LINE

PRAISED   (CONTINUED)
    I PRAISED HER BODY AND HER MIND . . . .   314 MEMORY YOUTH   9
    MAY GOD BE PRAISED FOR WOMAN . . . .   345 ON WOMAN   1
    SHE IS FOREMOST OF THOSE THAT I WOULD HEAR PRAISED. . . 350 HER PRAISE   1
    SHE IS FOREMOST OF THOSE THAT I WOULD HEAR PRAISED. . . 351 HER PRAISE   10
    AND PRAISED THE COLOUR OF HER FACE, ...   410 TOWER   36
    IT IS AS THOUGH YOU PRAISED ANOTHER, OR EVEN . . .   448 HERO GIRL FOOL   3
    ALL MEN HAVE PRAISED MY STRENGTH BUT NOT MY WORTH. .   448 HERO GIRL FOOL V   9
    THEY ARE NEITHER PAID NOR PRAISED. . . . .   473 ALL SOUL NIGHT   76
    THEY ARE NEITHER PAID OR PRAISED. . . . .   473 ALL SOUL NIGHT V 76
    THAT CAN BE PRAISED OF ALL, ...   553 PRAYER OLD AGE   6
    AND PRAISED YOUR WAR AMONG THE ENDLESS SEAS, ...   749 SHADOW WATER A   35
PRAISES
    WHOM BRAHMA, TOUCHING WITH HIS FINGER, PRAISES, FOR YOU   73 ANASHU VIJAYA   42
        HOLD
    WHOM BRAHMA, TOUCHING WITH HIS FINGER, PRAISES, FOR YE HOLD 73 ANASHU VIJAYA V 42
    COUNT ALL THE PRAISES DUE . . . .   345 ON WOMAN   15
    AND BIRTHDAYS AND HOLIDAYS SUCH PRAISES CAN BE HEARD . . 353 HIS PHOENIX   2
PRAISING
    WHY DO YOU PRAISE ANOTHER, PRAISING HER, ...   181 QUEEN MAEVE   31
    AND HAD THE GREATER JOY IN PRAISING HER, ...   410 TOWER   37
PRANCE
    THE GUARDSMEN'S DROWSY CHARGERS WOULD NOT PRANCE. . . . 429 NINETEEN 19   24
PRANCED
    BELLOWED AND PRANCED IN THE ROUND TOWER, ...   331 ROUND TOWER   12
    UNTIL THEY PRANCED UPON THE TOP. . . . .   331 ROUND TOWER   18
PRANCING
    PRANCING ROUND AND PRANCING UP . . . .   331 ROUND TOWER   17
    PRANCING ROUND AND PRANCING UP . . . .   331 ROUND TOWER   17
PRAY
    GO CAST YOUR BODY ON THE STONES AND PRAY, ...   42 OISIN 2   207
    BUT KNEEL AND WEAR OUT THE FLAGS AND PRAY FOR YOUR SOUL   63 OISIN 3   215
        THAT IS LOST
    KNEEL, USHEEN, WEAR OUT THE FLAGS AND PRAY FOR YOUR SOUL 63 OISIN 3   V 215
        THAT IS LOST
    I WILL PRAY NO MORE WITH THE SMOOTH STONES, ...   63 OISIN 3   V 221
    PRAYERS FOR THE LAND. PRAY ON, AND I WILL WAIT YOU, . . 71 ANASHU VIJAYA V 13
    HE IS A GENTLE ROEBUCK, FOR HOW ELSE, I PRAY, COULD HE . 76 INDIAN ON GOD   15
    AND LEARN TO PRAY WHEN YOU PRAY. . . . .   167 BLESSED   8
    AND LEARN TO PRAY WHEN YOU PRAY. . . . .   167 BLESSED   8
    BEND DOWN AND PRAY FOR ALL THAT SIN I WOVE IN SONG, . . 173 SPEAKS HEARERS   5
    BEND DOWN AND PRAY FOR THE GREAT SIN I WOVE IN SONG, . . 173 SPEAKS HEARERS V 5
    TO WHOM ALL LOVERS PRAY. BUT WHAT OF THAT? . . . .   224 SHADOW WATER B   43
    FOR MEN WERE BORN TO PRAY AND SAVE, ...   289 SEPTEMBER 1913   6
    BUT LITTLE TIME HAD THEY TO PRAY . . . .   289 SEPTEMBER 1913   12
    FALL ASLEEP WHEN I SHOULD PRAY." . . . .   298 THREE HERMITS   12
    BUT PRAY TO GOD THAT HE EASE . . . .   380 SONGS FOOL 1   17
    I ASKED IF I SHOULD PRAY. . . . .   495 MOHINI CHATTER   1
    "PRAY FOR NOTHING, SAY . . . .   495 MOHINI CHATTER   3
    PRAY THAT HEAVEN PROTECT US . . . .   518 LOVES LONENESS   5
    PRAY I WILL AND SING I MUST, ...   540 FROM ANTIGONE   14
    I PRAY--FOR FASHION'S WORD IS OUT . . . .   553 PRAYER OLD AGE   9
    IN ALL SUCH THINGS, PRAY LET THINE EARS BE TURNED, . . 660 ISLE STAT II 1   39
    LEAD ME, I PRAY THEE, TO THE STATUED PLACE, ...   667 ISLE STAT II 3   37
    UPON MY KNEES I PRAY YOU, LET IT SLEEP, ...   693 MOSADA 1   72
    MY LORD, IF IT MUST BE, I PRAY DESCEND . . . . . .   697 MOSADA 2   43
    HER HANGING MANSION. GIVE TO ME, I PRAY, ...   698 MOSADA 2   52
    AH! LEAVE ME, I PRAY YOU AND BEG. . . . .   708 FAIRY PEDANT   22
    "PRAY FOR THE SOULS IN PURGATORY," THE PALE PRIEST . . 719 PHANTOM SHIP   31
        TREMBLING CRIES.
    I PRAY THAT I EVER BE WEAVING . . . .   743 WISDOM DREAMS   1
PRAYED
    AND WITH LOW MURMURS PRAYED TO HIM, ...   18 OISIN 1   257
    HE PRAYED AND FELL ASLEEP, ...   132 FR GILLIGAN   14
    HE KNELT, PRAYED, FELL ASLEEP. . . . .   132 FR GILLIGAN   V 14
    AND THEN, GROWN WEARY, PRAYED AND CURSED . . . . .   307 HOUR DAWN   117
    AND PRAYED AND CURSED AND PRAYED AND FLED . . . . .   307 HOUR DAWN   119
    AND CURSED AND PRAYED, AND PRAYED AND CURSED . . . .   307 HOUR DAWN   V 117
    AND CURSED AND PRAYED, AND PRAYED AND CURSED . . . .   307 HOUR DAWN   V 117
    AND FOR AN HOUR I HAVE WALKED AND PRAYED . . . . . .   403 FOR DAUGHTER   7
    I HAVE WALKED AND PRAYED FOR THIS YOUNG CHILD AN HOUR . . 403 FOR DAUGHTER   9
    I PRAYED AT ALL THE STATIONS UPON MY MARROW-BONES, . . 593 PILGRIM   7
    AND THERE I FOUND AN OLD MAN, AND THOUGH I PRAYED ALL DAY 593 PILGRIM   8
    I PRAYED AT ALL THE STATIONS UPON MY MARROW BONES, . . 593 PILGRIM   V   7
    PRAYED THOSE FORGOTTEN FISHERS, TILL IN THE EASTERN SKIES 719 PHANTOM SHIP   32
    PRAYED BESIDE THE OCEAN, THE OLD MUMBLING MOTHER OF THE 719 PHANTOM SHIP V 34
        DEAD.
PRAYER
    THAT WAS BRIMMED UP WITH PRAYER AND REST, ...   151 HEART OF WOMAN   2
    WHEN SONGS I WOVE FOR MY BELOVED HIDE THE PRAYER, . . . 173 SPEAKS HEARERS   2
    WHEN SONG I WOVE FOR MY BELOVED HIDES THE PRAYER, . . . 173 SPEAKS HEARERS V 2
    A MYSTICAL PRAYER TO THE MASTERS OF THE ELEMENTS, . . . 174 ELEMENT POWERS V T
    THEY READ IN THEIR BOOKS OF PRAYER, ...   178 FIDDLER DOONEY   6
    THEY READ IN A BOOK OF PRAYER, ...   178 FIDDLER DOONEY V   6
    AND PRAYER TO SHIVERING PRAYER, UNTIL . . . .   289 SEPTEMBER 1913   4
    AND PRAYER TO SHIVERING PRAYER, UNTIL . . . .   289 SEPTEMBER 1913   4
    FIRST WAS MUTTERING A PRAYER, ...   298 THREE HERMITS   3
    BECAUSE IT WAS YOUR PRAYER . . . .   355 BROKEN DREAMS   5
    A PRAYER ON GOING INTO MY HOUSE . . . .   371 ON GOING HOUSE   T
    A PRAYER FOR MY DAUGHTER . . . .   403 FOR DAUGHTER   T
    A PRAYER FOR MY SON . . . .   435 FOR MY SON   T

629

```
                                                   PAGE    TITLE          LINE
PRAYER   (CONTINUED)
        A PRAYER FOR OLD AGE  . . . . . . . . . .   553 PRAYER OLD AGE      T
        AND PRAYER COMES ROUND AGAIN-- . . . . . .  553 PRAYER OLD AGE     10
        BY WATER, HERB AND SOLITARY PRAYER . . . .  555 RIBH AT TOMB       23
        YOU THAT MITCHEL'S PRAYER HAVE HEARD, . . . 638 BEN BULBEN         25
        TO LOVE EACH OTHER.  IN MY PRAYER BOOK STILL  . . .  713 FERENCZ RENYI V  94
        THEY SEEM TO JOIN HER PRAYER-- . . . . . .  736 IN CHURCH          12
        HER PRAYER FOR FATHER, MOTHER DEAR, . . . . 736 IN CHURCH          13
        A PRAYER FOR EVERY FALLING TEAR  . . . . .  736 IN CHURCH          15
PRAYER-BOOK
        TO LOVE EACH OTHER.  IN MY PRAYER-BOOK STILL     713 FERENCZ RENYI   94
PRAYERS
        FASTING AND PRAYERS.  TELL ON.  YES, YES,   24 OISIN 1            360
        FASTING AND PRAYERS.  TELL ON.  AY, AY!  .  24 OISIN 1         V  360
        PRAYERS FOR THE LAND.  I WILL WAIT HERE, AMRITA. . . .  71 ANASHU VIJAYA     13
        PRAYERS FOR THE LAND.  PRAY ON, AND I WILL WAIT YOU,  71 ANASHU VIJAYA V  13
        PRAYERS FOR THE LAND.  O BRAHMA, GUARD IN SLEEP . . .  75 ANASHU VIJAYA     85
        AND LEARN THE PRAYERS THAT YOU SAY.  . . .  167 BLESSED        V   8
        ARE PRAYERS OF PATIENT MEN AND GOOD."  . .  725 LEGEND             6
PRAYETH
        FOR YOUR FEET THE MORNING PRAYETH!  . . . . 706 DAWN-SONG         25
PRAYING
        . . . AND PRAYING, AND WROTH WITH THE BELLS,  . . . .   58 OISIN 3          159
PRAYS
        SHE PRAYS FOR FATHER, MOTHER DEAR,  . . . . 735 IN CHURCH          1
        SHE PRAYS FOR EVERY FALLING TEAR  . . . . . 735 IN CHURCH          3
PREACHER
        THE PREACHER WATCHING FOR THE EVIL HOUR TO PASS,  . . .  686 LIFE              3
        THE PREACHER WATCHING FOR THE ILL HOUR TO PASS--  . . .  734 QUATRAIN APHOR    3
        THE PREACHER WATCHING FOR THE EVIL HOUR TO PASS,  . . .  734 QUATRAIN APHOR V  3
PRECEDENTS
        PRECEDENTS OUT OF BEAUTIFUL OLD BOOKS!  . . . . . . .  205 ADAMS CURSE       26
PRECIOUS
        BUT FRUIT THAT IS OF PRECIOUS STONE.  . .   196 BAILE AILLINN     175
        TREASURE ON TREASURE.  BOXES OF PRECIOUS SPICE.  . . .  247 SHADOW WATER B    533
        TREASURE AND TREASURE.  BOXES OF PRECIOUS SPICE. . . .  247 SHADOW WATER B V  533
        THUS DO I BURN THESE PRECIOUS HERBS, WHOSE SMOKE  . . .  691 MOSADA 1         39
        IF THESE BE PRECIOUS."  "I AM OLD AND WEAK,"  . . . .  711 FERENCZ RENYI     55
PRECIPICE
        ABOVE A WINDY PRECIPICE?"  THEN HE!  . . .  285 TWO KINGS         195
PRECISION
        WHERE PASSION AND PRECISION HAVE BEEN ONE  . . . . .  264 HOUSE SHAKEN       2
PREDESTINED
        WHEN HER SOUL FLIES TO THE PREDESTINED DANCING-PLACE  . .  365 HER COURAGE       1
        WHAT SEEMS MOST WELCOME IN THE TOMB--PLAY A PREDESTINED   503 VACILLATION      86
          PART.
        ACCOMPLISHED HIS PREDESTINED WILL.  . . .   522 LULLABY           16
PREFERRED
        PREFERRED TO TEACH A SCHOOL . . . . . . .   472 ALL SOUL NIGHT    46
PREFERS
        RIBH PREFERS AN OLDER THEOLOGY  . . . . .   556 RIBH PATRICK   V   T
PRELUDE
        HOW SPED THY QUEST?  THIS PRELUDE WE'LL NOT HEAR IT. . .  673 ISLE STAT II 3    174
PREPARATION
        BEGIN THE PREPARATION FOR YOUR DEATH . . . . . .  500 VACILLATION       28
PREPARED
        I HAVE PREPARED MY PEACE . . . . . . . . .   415 TOWER            157
        PREPARED A REST FOR THE PEOPLE OF GOD, . .   639 BEN BULBEN        65
PREPOSTEROUS
        THAT THIS PRAGMATICAL, PREPOSTEROUS PIG OF A WORLD, . . .  481 BLOOD AND MOON    26
PRESENCE
        NOR HAD FORGOT THE STRANGENESS OF MY PRESENCE  . . . .  466 HARUN RASHID   V 119A
        AN EVENING PRESENCE FILLS THE PLACE. . . . .  736 SUMMER EVENING   16
PRESENCES
        PRESENCES . . . . . . . . . . . . . . .   358 PRESENCES          T
        AND YET THEY TOO BREAK HEARTS--O PRESENCES  . . . . .  445 SCHOOL CHILDR     53
PRESENT
        THOUGHTS UPON THE PRESENT STATE OF THE WORLD  . . . .  428 NINETEEN 19    V   T
        HER PRESENT IMAGE FLOATS INTO THE MIND--  . . . . .   444 SCHOOL CHILDR     25
        TO ENGROSS THE PRESENT AND DOMINATE MEMORY. . . . . .  630 CIRCUS ANIMALS    30
PRESS
        TO THE SCENTED OAKEN PRESS. . . . . . . . .   124 CATHLEEN PARA      8
        I KISS MY WAILING CHILD AND PRESS IT TO MY BREAST,  . .  147 UNAPPEAS HOST      5
        WHEN MY ARMS WRAP YOU ROUND I PRESS  . . . . .  155 FORGOT BEAUTY      1
        WORK AT THE CIDER PRESS. . . . . . . . . .   774 COME RIDE         12
        WHAT WOUNDS, WHAT BLOODY PRESS, . . . . . .   785 WOMANS BEAUTY     26
PRESSED
        WHOSE CAREFUL PASTERN PRESSED THE SOD  . . . .  2 OISIN 1        V  7W
        PRESSED ON THE EVER-TREMBLING ROOF  . . . .  25 OISIN 1        V 383
        MY HANDS WERE PRESSED TO VANISHED SUDDENLY. . . . .  286 TWO KINGS        208
        WITH FACE AND NOSE PRESSED TO A SWEET-SHOP WINDOW,  . .  370 EGO DOMINUS       56
        WITH FACE AND NOSE PRESSED TO A SWEETSHOP WINDOW. . . .  370 EGO DOMINUS    V  56
        THE BIRD DESCENDS, AND HER FRAIL THIGHS ARE PRESSED . .  441 LEDA AND SWAN V   2
        PRESSED HER BODY TO HIS BODY, . . . . . . .   453 MERMAID            3
        AND PRESSED AT MIDNIGHT IN SOME PUBLIC PLACE  . . . .  610 STATUES            7
        IS IN THY FACE, AND LIPS TOGETHER PRESSED!  . . . .  671 ISLE STAT II 3   139
PRESSING
        AND PRESSING ON, OR LINGERING SLOW WITH FEAR, . . . .  114 ROSE OF BATTLE V   5
PRETENCE
        A PRETENCE OF WIT."  . . . . . . . . . . .   349 HAWK              18
        A MAN MAY PUT PRETENCE AWAY  . . . . . . .   525 DANCING DAYS      19
```

		PAGE	TITLE	LINE

PRETENDING
PRETENDING THAT THERE CAN BE PASSION • • • • • • • • 271 GREY ROCK 7
PRETTY
A PRETTY GIRL TO SHARE MY BED": • • • • • • • • 296 THREE BEGGARS 31
ON PRETTY THINGS THAT MAY • • • • • • 366 HER CHRIS TREE 7
WE TOO HAD MANY PRETTY TOYS WHEN YOUNG: • • • • • 428 NINETEEN 19 9
HAD PRETTY PLUMAGE ONCE--ENOUGH OF THAT, • • • • • • 444 SCHOOL CHILDR 30
MY PRETTY PAISTIN IS MY HEART'S DESIRE, • • • • • 550 SONGS REWRIT 1 V 1
COME SWISH AROUND, MY PRETTY PUNK, • • • • • • 591 DRUNK SOBRIETY 1
NO UPS AND DOWNS, MY PRETTY, • • • • • • 592 DRUNK SOBRIETY 13
WHAT SHALL I DO FOR PRETTY GIRLS • • • • • 620 JOHN KINSELLA 11
WHAT SHALL I DO FOR PRETTY GIRLS • • • • • 621 JOHN KINSELLA 23
WHAT SHALL I DO FOR PRETTY GIRLS • • • • • 621 JOHN KINSELLA 35
MY PRETTY CHILD, SINCE HE HAS GONE, OH SAY • 658 ISLE STAT II 1 3
A PEASANT PALE AND PRETTY, HER EYES FOR FEAR, • • • • 713 FERENCZ RENYI 81
A PEASANT, PALE AND PRETTY, HER EYES FROM FEAR, • • • • 713 FERENCZ RENYI V 81
PREVAIL
YET OLD ROMANCE BEING KIND, LET HIM PREVAIL • • • • • 258 KING NO KING 5
PREY
MY SOUL, MY PREY, AND THIS MY HEAPED PILE• • • • • • 45 OISIN 2 V 239B
THE STRONGEST OF THE WORLD, TO SNATCH MY PREY, • • • • 45 OISIN 2 V 241
AND NOT A GLOOMY BIRD OF PREY, • • • • • 338 TOM OROUGHLEY 8
NOW RUSH UPON HER AND FIND OUT WHAT PREY • • • • • • 752 SHADOW WATER A 130
PRIAM
AND PROUD AS PRIAM MURDERED WITH HIS PEERS: • • • • • 120 SORROW OF LOVE 8
PRICELESS
NOTORIOUS, TILL ALL MY PRICELESS THINGS • • • • • • 321 REED WHISPERER 13
PRIDE
AND TOLD THE PURPLE DEEPS THEIR PRIDE, • • • • • • 14 OISIN 1 186
"SWIFT ARE THE YEARS OF A WARRIOR'S PRIDE: • • • • • 26 OISIN 1 V 399A
TO TWO OLD EAGLES, FULL OF ANCIENT PRIDE, • • • • • 34 OISIN 2 74
TO EAGLES TWAIN THAT, FULL OF ANCIENT PRIDE, • • • • 34 OISIN 2 V 73
FOR THESE RED LIPS, WITH ALL THEIR MOURNFUL PRIDE, • • • 111 ROSE OF WORLD 2
LEAVE THE BODY'S COLOURED PRIDE • • • • • • • 124 CATHLEEN PARA 2
AND DREAM ABOUT THE GREAT AND THEIR PRIDE: • • • • 166 EVIL OF BELOV 2
BUT WEIGH THIS SONG WITH THE GREAT AND THEIR PRIDE: • • 166 EVIL OF BELOV 4
FROM GULLEON'S PLACE OF PRIDE, • • • • • 171 MAID QUIET V 4B
WHERE, WHERE BUT HERE HAVE PRIDE AND TRUTH, • • • • 262 STUDENTS AGIT 1
THAT THINGS IT WERE A PRIDE TO GIVE • • • • • 287 TO WEALTHY MAN 6
THAT IDLENESS HAD BORNE TO PRIDE, • • • • • • • 296 THREE BEGGARS 40
WITH THE PRIDE OF HIS EYE? • • • • • • • 310 PEACOCK 3
FOR THE PRIDE OF HIS EYE. • • • • • • • 311 PEACOCK 11
POUR WINE AND DANCE IF MANHOOD STILL HAVE PRIDE, • • • 311 MOUNTAIN TOMB 1
POUR WINE AND DANCE, IF MANKIND STILL HAVE PRIDE, • • • 311 MOUNTAIN TOMB V 1
TILL PRIDE HAD MADE HER EYES GROW BRIGHT, • • • • • 314 MEMORY YOUTH 10
HE DREAMS HIMSELF HIS MOTHER'S PRIDE, • • • • • • 343 SHEP GOATHERD 110
TO BE THE GARDEN'S PRIDE." • • • • • • • 396 ROSE TREE 12
FROM A GREAT LABYRINTH OUT OF PRIDE, • • • • • • 413 TOWER 116
FROM SOME GREAT LABYRINTH OUT OF PRIDE, • • • • • • 413 TOWER V 116
THEY SHALL INHERIT MY PRIDE, • • • • • • 414 TOWER 127
THE PRIDE OF PEOPLE THAT WERE • • • • • • 414 TOWER 128
PRIDE, LIKE THAT OF THE MORN, • • • • • • 414 TOWER 134
I LEAVE BOTH FAITH AND PRIDE • • • • • • 416 TOWER 173
THE BREAST THRUST OUT IN PRIDE • • • • • • 430 NINETEEN 19 66
AND THAT HE SHRIEKS FROM PRIDE. • • • • • • 456 FRIENDS YOUTH 20
AND PRIDE BRING IN IMPURITY: • • • • • • 460 THREE MONUMENT 11
AND KNEW THAT SWEET EXTREMITY OF PRIDE • • • • • 471 ALL SOUL NIGHT 22
A GREAT MAN IN HIS PRIDE • • • • • • 476 DEATH 7
WHEN SHE IN ALL HER VIRGINAL PRIDE • • • • • 488 CRAZED MOON 8
FOUND PRIDE ESTABLISHED IN HUMILITY, • • • • • • 489 COOLE PARK 29 15
AND IN THE HEART'S PRIDE. • • • • • • 513 JANE TALK BISH 12
HE DID IT OUT OF PRIDE. • • • • • • 545 TO SAME TUNE 1 26
THE SOLDIER TAKES PRIDE • • • • • • 547 TO SAME TUNE 3 V T
THE SOLDIER TAKES PRIDE IN SALUTING HIS CAPTAIN, • • • 547 TO SAME TUNE 3 1
SOLDIERS TAKE PRIDE IN SALUTING THEIR CAPTAIN, • • • 547 TO SAME TUNE 3 V 1
SOLDIERS TAKE PRIDE IN SALUTING THEIR CAPTAIN, • • • 548 TO SAME TUNE 3 21
AND THERE IS AN OLD BEGGAR WANDERING IN HIS PRIDE-- • • 580 CURSE CROMWELL 5
GUARDED: GRIFFITH STARING IN HYSTERICAL PRIDE: • • • 601 GALLERY REVIS 4
OF ALL THAT PRIDE AND THAT HUMILITY? • • • • • 602 GALLERY REVIS 29
THE SOLDIER TAKES PRIDE IN SALUTING HIS CAPTAIN, • • 614 MARCH SONGS 2 1
HE DID IT OUT OF PRIDE. • • • • • • • 616 MARCH SONGS 3 26
IRVING AND HIS PLUME OF PRIDE• • • • • • • 625 NATIVITY 8
OF THE FORESTS ALL THE PRIDE, • • • • • • 658 ISLE STAT I 3 84
PRIEST
THE PRIEST OF COLOONY • • • • • • 91 FATHER OHART V T
THE OLD PRIEST PETER GILLIGAN • • • • • • 132 FR GILLIGAN 1
THE OLD PRIEST PETER GILLIGAN • • • • • • 133 FR GILLIGAN 23
THE OLD PRIEST PETER GILLIGAN • • • • • • 133 FR GILLIGAN 35
THE OLD PRIEST PETER GILLIGAN • • • • • • 133 FR GILLIGAN 39
MY COUSIN IS PRIEST IN KILVARNET, • • • • • 178 FIDDLER DOONEY 3
MY BROTHER IS PRIEST OF KILBARNET, • • • • • 178 FIDDLER DOONEY V 3
MY BROTHER IS PRIEST IN KILVARNET, • • • • • 178 FIDDLER DOONEY V 3
THEY HAD A PRIEST SAY MASS, AND EVEN THE JAPANESE, • • 363 DOLLS FACES 2
BECAUSE THE PRIEST MUST HAVE LIKE EVERY DOG HIS DAY • • 364 DOLLS FACES 10
NOR SO MUCH AS PARISH PRIEST, • • • • • • 508 JANE BISHOP 11
THE PRIEST CAME WHERE SHE WAS: • • • • • 571 THREE BUSHES 65
"PRAY FOR THE SOULS IN PURGATORY," THE PALE PRIEST 719 PHANTOM SHIP 31
TREMBLING CRIES.
THE PRIEST AND THE FAIRY. • • • • • • • 728 PRIEST FAIRY T
MUSINGLY WANDERED THE VILLAGE PRIEST. • • • • • • 728 PRIEST FAIRY 3
AND STRAIGHT BEFORE THE SLEEPING PRIEST • • • • • 729 PRIEST FAIRY 23

631

```
                                                           PAGE    TITLE             LINE
PRIEST   (CONTINUED)
    NOW, WHAT HAS A FAIRY TO DO WITH A PRIEST . . . . . .   729  PRIEST FAIRY          27
    THE PRIEST LOOKED NEITHER TO RIGHT NOR LEFT, . . . . .  730  PRIEST FAIRY          49
PRIESTESS
    I, PRIESTESS OF THIS TEMPLE, OFFER UP  . . . . . . .     71  ANASHU VIJAYA         12
    I, PRIESTESS OF THIS TEMPLE, OFFER UP  . . . . . . .     75  ANASHU VIJAYA         84
PRIEST'S
    THOUGH NOT FOR THE PRIEST'S EAR, . . . . . . . . . .    620  JOHN KINSELLA         18
PRIESTS
    THE PRIESTS HAVE GOT A BOOK THAT SAYS . . . . . . .     621  JOHN KINSELLA         25
PRIME
    LONG PAST HIS PRIME REMEMBER THINGS THAT ARE  . . . .   477  SELF AND SOUL         18
    HE STOOD A MESSENGER. IN APRIL'S PRIME . . . . . . .    690  MOSADA 1               6
PRIMORDIAL
    PRIMORDIAL MOTHERHOOD FORSAKE HIS LIMBS, THE CHILD      559  MAGIC DRUM             2
        NO LONGER REST,
PRIMUM
    THE PRIMUM MOBILE THAT FASHIONED US . . . . . . . .     423  MY DESCENDANTS        17
PRINCE
    AND MANY A PRINCE OF LOFTY NAME, . . . . . . . . . .      7  OISIN 1          V    63
    SAT LATE, OR SHELLEY'S VISIONARY PRINCE: . . . . . .    373  PHASES OF MOON        16
    "GREAT PRINCE, FORGIVE THE FREEDOM OF MY SPEECH! . . .  464  HARUN RASHID          74
    THEY WOULD MAKE A PRINCE DECAY . . . . . . . . . .      775  AGAINST WITCH         11
PRINCE'S
    WENT WE TO FIND THEIR PRINCE'S HALL-- . . . . . . .      16  OISIN 1          V   217
PRINCES
    OF PRINCES THERE IS MANY A ONE." . . . . . . . . .       6  OISIN 1          V    61
    AND MANY PRINCES OF HIGH NAME. . . . . . . . . . .       7  OISIN 1          V    68
    THE MIGHTIEST OF THE PRINCES OF THE WORLD . . . . . .   462  HARUN RASHID          41
PRINCESS
    YOUNG PRINCESS, WHY WERT THOU BEGUILED  . . . . . .       6  OISIN 1          V    59
    YOUNG PRINCESS, WHEN WERE YOU BEGUILED  . . . . . .       6  OISIN 1          V    59
    "HOW COMES IT, PRINCESS, THAT YOUR MIND . . . . . .      6  OISIN 1          V    59A
    PRINCESS, BY THIS YOUNG MAN, MY SON?" . . . . . . .      6  OISIN 1          V    61
PRINCIPLES
    I HAVE PRINCIPLES TO PROVE ME RIGHT. . . . . . . .      386  ROBARTES DANCE        42
PRINTED
    WE SAW, SOME NEW, SOME PRINTED WHEN THE PLACE WAS YOUNG, 37  OISIN 2          V   116
PRINTS
    SHOWED PRINTS OF SEA-BORN SCALES, WHILE DOWN THROUGH IT  37  OISIN 2              115
    THAT HAD MADE PRINTS UPON THE GROUND, . . . . . . .    274  GREY ROCK             79
PRISON
    IN THE PRISON OF MY HANDS, . . . . . . . . . . . .     381  SONG OF FOOL           2
    TO PRISON GO, AND MOSSY RUIN REST . . . . . . . . .    709  FERENCZ RENYI    V     2
PRISONER
    ON A POLITICAL PRISONER . . . . . . . . . . . . .     397  POLIT PRISONER         T
PRISONERS
    'TWILL PASS. I'LL SEE THE OTHER PRISONERS NOW, . . . .  704  MOSADA 3             130
PRISONS
    TO PRISONS GO, AND MOSSY RUIN REST  . . . . . . . .    709  FERENCZ RENYI          2
PRIVACY
    A DAPHNE AND A MARY WHO LIVE IN PRIVACY: . . . . . .    354  HIS PHOENIX           18
PRIVET
    WHERE HAZEL AND ASH AND PRIVET BLIND THE PATHS: . . . . 217  WOODS OF COOLE         8
PROCESSIONS
    PROCESSIONS THAT LACK HIGH STILTS HAVE NOTHING THAT CATCHES 622  HIGH TALK          1
        THE EYE.
PROCLAIM
    PROCLAIM WITH THAT UNWEARIED, REEDY CRY . . . . . . .   128  DREAM OF FAERY        42
    MIGHT PROCLAIM A HOLIDAY: . . . . . . . . . . . .      432  NINETEEN 19          106
    GIVE TONGUE, PROCLAIM THEIR HIDDEN NAME--"HOUND VOICE." 622  HOUND VOICE            7
PROCLAIMED
    I EVERYWHERE PROCLAIMED THERE IS . . . . . . . . .     528  DANCER CRUACH    V     1
    PROCLAIMED BOTH GOOD AND GREAT: . . . . . . . . . .    597  MODEL LAUREATE        4
PROCLAIMING
    PROCLAIMING WITH A LOW AND REEDY CRY, . . . . . . .    128  DREAM OF FAERY   V    42
    I, PROCLAIMING THAT THERE IS . . . . . . . . . . .     528  DANCER CRUACH         1
    ACCLAIMING, PROCLAIMING, DECLAIMING HIM. . . . . . .   528  DANCER CRUACH         8
PRODIGIES
    OF WONDERS! EVE OF PRODIGIES! DRAW! DRAW! . . . . . .   664  ISLE STAT II 2        62
PRODUCTS
    BASE-BORN PRODUCTS OF BASE BEDS. . . . . . . . . .     639  BEN BULBEN            73
PROFANE
    PROFANE PERFECTION OF MANKIND. . . . . . . . . . .     639  BEN BULBEN            52
PROFESSOR
    A GREY PROFESSOR PASSING CRIED, . . . . . . . . . .    725  LEGEND                 9
PROFFERING
    PROFFERING ITS SACRED LAUREL CROWNS, . . . . . . . .   612  NEWS ORACLE           23
PROFFERS
    THE DEVOTEE PROFFERS A KNEE TO HIS LORD, . . . . . .   547  TO SAME TUNE 3         2
    THE DEVOTEE PROFFERS A KNEE TO HIS LORD, . . . . . .   614  MARCH SONGS 2          2
PROFIT
    I'D GIVE THE PROFIT OF NINE VOYAGES . . . . . . . .    222  SHADOW WATER B   V     9
PROFOUND
    CLOSED IN THE MISTY AIR PROFOUND. . . . . . . . . .     10  OISIN 1          V  114D
    PROFOUND MCTAGGART THOUGHT SO, AND IN A BREATH  . . .  619  BRONZE HEAD           13
PROLONG
    YOUTH TO PROLONG  . . . . . . . . . . . . . . .       334  SONG                   2
PROMINENT
    IF WORTHY THEIR PROMINENT PART IN THE PLAY, . . . . .  565  LAPIS LAZULI          14
```

632

PROMISE
    WE'LL PUT THIS MAN TO DEATH. I PROMISE IT. • • • • • 238 SHADOW WATER B   363
    I PROMISE YOU A HUNDRED DRINKING BOWLS, • • • • • • • • 756 SHADOW WATER A V 187
PROMISE-BREAKER
    WHAT DO YOU CALL IT?——THAT OLD PROMISE-BREAKER, • • • • 228 SHADOW WATER B   122
PROMISED
    THAT HAS BEEN PROMISED ME. I HAVE NOT SEEN THEM • • • • 226 SHADOW WATER B   88
    TO DEATH: FOR THEY THAT PROMISED TO ME LOVE • • • • • 230 SHADOW WATER B   192
    YOU'D NEVER DOUBT THAT IT WAS LIFE THEY PROMISED • • • • 231 SHADOW WATER B   197
    OR SOMEWHERE, I SHALL FIND THE LOVE THEY HAVE PROMISED. 231 SHADOW WATER B   208
    AND BLEW YOU HITHER; AND THEIR MOUTHS HAVE PROMISED • • • 237 SHADOW WATER B   325
    THAT IS NOT TRUE, FOR HE HAS PROMISED ME • • • • • • • 248 SHADOW WATER B   552
    PROMISED THAT FOR A PIN'S SAKE • • • • • • • • • • 274 GREY ROCK   90
    I'D PROMISED HIM TWO HUNDRED YEARS, • • • • • • • • • 275 GREY ROCK   98
    FOR THAT SHE PROMISED, AND FOR THAT REFUSED. • • • • • 286 TWO KINGS   213
    FOR THAT YOU PROMISED, AND FOR THAT REFUSED." • • • • • 286 TWO KINGS   V 213
    TO A WEALTHY MAN WHO PROMISED A SECOND SUBSCRIPTION • • • 287 TO WEALTHY MAN   T
    THE BIBLE PROMISED US, • • • • • • • • • • • • • 472 ALL SOUL NIGHT   39
    I PROMISED HIM THAT NONE SHOULD ESCAPE MY SWORD • • • • 752 SHADOW WATER A   114
    HE HAS HEARD ME BECAUSE I PROMISED ALL. • • • • • • • 752 SHADOW WATER A   116
    AND BRING ME TO MY PEOPLE. I PROMISED THESE • • • • • 756 SHADOW WATER A V 185
PRONE
    BUT PRONE ON THE PATHWAY, PRONE STRUGGLING, • • • • • • 60 OISIN 3   V 186
    BUT PRONE ON THE PATHWAY, PRONE STRUGGLING, • • • • • • 60 OISIN 3   V 186
PROOF
    FOR PROUD, SOFT, CEREMONIOUS PROOF • • • • • • • • • 386 ROBARTES DANCE   30
    BUT O! AMBITIOUS HEART, HAD SUCH A PROOF DRAWN FORTH • • 427 PHANTOM HATRED   36
    MICHAEL ANGELO LEFT A PROOF • • • • • • • • • • • 638 BEN BULBEN   45
    MICHAELANGELO LEFT A PROOF • • • • • • • • • • • 638 BEN BULBEN   V 45
    PROOF THAT THERE'S A PURPOSE SET • • • • • • • • • • 639 BEN BULBEN   50
PROPER
    A LOVE THAT LACKS ITS PROPER FOOD! • • • • • • • • • 569 THREE BUSHES   3
    PROPER TO MY BREAST, • • • • • • • • • • • • • • 573 LADYS 2ND SONG   16
    CLIMB TO OUR PROPER DARK, THAT WE MAY TRACE • • • • • 611 STATUES   31
PROPERTIUS
    A THOUGHT FROM PROPERTIUS • • • • • • • • • • • 355 PROPERTIUS   T
PROPERTY
    FOR WISDOM IS THE PROPERTY OF THE DEAD, • • • • • • • 482 BLOOD AND MOON   49
    A PROPERTY OF THE LIVING! BUT NO STAIN • • • • • • • 482 BLOOD AND MOON   52
PROPHECIES
    BEING TOO HIGH, THEIR HEADY PROPHECIES • • • • • • • 250 SHADOW WATER B   578
    THE LADIES CLOSE THEIR MUSING EYES. NO PROPHECIES, • • • 426 PHANTOM HATRED   19
PROPHESYING
    AND ALL THAT PROPHESYING IMAGES • • • • • • • • • • 235 SHADOW WATER B   294
    IT IS POSSESSED. A PROPHESYING VOICE. • • • • • • • • 681 SEEKER   8
    AND ALL THAT PROPHESYING IMAGES • • • • • • • • • • 764 SHADOW WATER A V 344
PROPINQUITY
    HAD SHATTERED HER SOUL. PROPINQUITY HAD BROUGHT • • • • 619 BRONZE HEAD   18
PROPPED
    PROPPED UPON PILLOWS, ROUGE ON THE PALLOR OF HER FACE. • • 362 HER COURTESY   3
    PROPPED UPON MY TWO KNEES, • • • • • • • • • • • 628 JANE MOUNTAIN   19
PROPS
    "THE PROPS," SAID HE, "OF STARS AND WORLDS • • • • • • 725 LEGEND   5
PROSAIC
    FOR THE PROSAIC LIGHT OF DAY—— • • • • • • • • • • 411 TOWER   46
PROSE
    THAT MAYBE "I AM SORRY" IN PLAIN PROSE • • • • • • • 341 SHEP GOATHERD   60
    THERE HYDE BEFORE HE HAD BEATEN INTO PROSE • • • • • • 489 COOLE PARK 29   9
PROSPER
    PROSPER BUT LITTLE, HAS DRIED UP OF LATE, • • • • • • 405 FOR DAUGHTER   51
PROSPEROUS
    WHOSE LIPS HAD LIFE'S MOST PROSPEROUS GLOW? • • • • • 10 OISIN 1   118
    AND I, THAT COUNT MYSELF MOST PROSPEROUS, • • • • • • 423 MY DESCENDANTS   19
PROTECT
    PROTECT ME NOW, GODS THAT MY PEOPLE SWEAR BY. • • • • 241 SHADOW WATER B   396
    CAN, TATTERED, STILL PROTECT, FADED ADORN. • • • • • 477 SELF AND SOUL   16
    PRAY THAT HEAVEN PROTECT US • • • • • • • • • • • 518 LOVES LONENESS   5
    THAT PROTECT YOUR BLOOD. • • • • • • • • • • • • 518 LOVES LONENESS   6
PROTECTED
    PROTECTED FROM THE CIRCLE OF THE MOON • • • • • • • 428 NINETEEN 19   3
PROTECTING
    PROTECTING, TILL THE DANGER PAST, • • • • • • • • • 436 FOR MY SON   31
    BUT NOT FROM HER PROTECTING CARE. • • • • • • • • • 522 LULLABY   18
PROTEST
    NOR HEEDS THE OLD, DIM PROTEST AND THE CRY • • • • • • 689 NETTLESHIP   14
PROTEUS
    IS THERE A BRIDLE FOR THIS PROTEUS • • • • • • • • • 265 ABBEY THEATRE   11
PROUD   SEE SILVER-PROUD
    AND FLOATING-HAIRED AND PROUD IN STRIFE: • • • • • • 9 OISIN 1   V 99
    UNLANGUID AS THE BIRDS, IN PROUD COMPANIONSHIPS: • • • • 30 OISIN 2   V 14C
    AND AH, YOU PROUD MAIDEN, YOU ARE NOT SO FAIR WHEN HIS OAR 91 OLD FISHERMAN   9
    IS HEARD ON THE WATER, AS THEY WERE, THE PROUD AND APART, 91 OLD FISHERMAN   10
    PROUD MAIDEN, YE ARE NOT SO FAIR, WHEN HIS OAR • • • • 91 OLD FISHERMAN V 9
    AND, AH, YE PROUD MAIDENS, YE ARE NOT SO FAIR, WHEN HIS OAR 91 OLD FISHERMAN V 9
    RED ROSE, PROUD ROSE, SAD ROSE OF ALL MY DAYS! • • • • 100 ROSE UPON ROOD   1
    RED ROSE, PROUD ROSE, SAD ROSE OF ALL MY DAYS. • • • • 101 ROSE UPON ROOD   24
    WHAT WOULD YOU, KING OF THE PROUD RED BRANCH KINGS? • • • 102 FERGUS DRUID   8
    WHAT WOULD YOU, KING OF THE PROUD RED BRANCH KINGS? • • • 102 FERGUS DRUID   15
    A KING AND PROUD! AND THAT IS MY DESPAIR. • • • • • 103 FERGUS DRUID   16
    WHAT WOULD YOU, KING OF THE PROUD RED BRANCH KINGS? • • • 103 FERGUS DRUID   V 21
    AND PROUD AS PRIAM MURDERED WITH HIS PEERS: • • • • • 120 SORROW OF LOVE   8

                                                    PAGE   TITLE   LINE
PROUD   (CONTINUED)
    AND OF THE PROUD EMBATTLED MULTITUDE . . . .   137 TO SOME I TALK V   10
    WITH THE LONELY, PROUD, WINGED MULTITUDE. . . . . . . 158 TO HIS HEART   V   7
    WITH THE PROUD, MAJESTICAL MULTITUDE. . . . .   158 TO HIS HEART   V   7
    AND THE PROUD DREAMING KING WHO FLUNG THE CROWN . . . 170 SECRET ROSE   19
    BE NOT UNKIND OR PROUD, ...   173 PLEADS FRIEND   4
    THAT'S ALL BUT GONE; FOR THE PROUD HEART IS GONE, . . . 181 QUEEN MAEVE   20
    TALL, PROUD AND RUDDY, AND LIGHT WINGS . . . . . .   195 BAILE AILLINN   140
    THE PROUD AND CARELESS NOTES LIVE ON, ...   213 BLESS PSALTER   19
    HAVE SEEN IMMORTAL, MILD, PROUD SHADOWS WALK; . . . . 217 WOODS OF COOLE   12
    HOW SHALL I NAME YOU, IMMORTAL, MILD, PROUD SHADOWS? . . 218 WOODS OF COOLE   27
    FOR I HAVE HEARD THAT HE WAS PROUD AND LAUGHING, . . . 242 SHADOW WATER B   415
    WOMEN ARE HARD AND PROUD AND STUBBORN-HEARTED, . . .   245 SHADOW WATER B   479
    BECAUSE WE ARE NOT PROUD, IMPERISHABLE, ...   250 SHADOW WATER B   580
    AND TROD SO SWEETLY PROUD . . . .   255 WOMAN HOMER   17
    BETWEEN THE PROUD AND THE PROUD. . . . .   259 UNWORTH PRAISE   10
    BETWEEN THE PROUD AND THE PROUD. . . . .   259 UNWORTH PRAISE   10
    AND COPY THEIR PROUD STEADY GAZE. . . . .   273 GREY ROCK   64
    SHE'LL NOT BE PROUD, KNOWING WITHIN HER HEART . . . . 282 TWO KINGS   118
    FOR WHAT PROUD DEATH MAY BRING . . . .   317 NIGHT COME   3
    WHERE THE PROUD, WAYWARD SQUIRREL WENT, ...   317 APPOINTMENT   3
    NOW I HAVE LEARNT TO BE PROUD . . . .   349 HAWK   9
    AND THAT PROUD LOOK AS THOUGH SHE HAD GAZED INTO   354 HIS PHOENIX   29
        THE BURNING SUN,
    FOR PROUD, SOFT, CEREMONIOUS PROOF . . . .   386 ROBARTES DANCE   30
    AND THE PROUD STONES OF GREECE . . . .   415 TOWER   159
    FOR INTELLECT WOULD MAKE US PROUD . . . .   460 THREE MONUMENT   10
    A PROUD WOMAN NOT KINDRED OF HIS SOUL. . . . . . .   479 SELF AND SOUL   64
    PROUD, OPEN-EYED AND LAUGHING TO THE TOMB. . . . . .   501 VACILLATION   34
    "A WOMAN CAN BE PROUD AND STIFF . . . .   513 JANE TALK BISH   13
    HIS PROUD HEART HE LEFT BEHIND. . . . .   561 FOUR AGES MAN   6
    THE PROUD FURIES EACH WITH HER TORCH ON HIGH. . . . . 579 DOR WELLESLEY   16
    FOR PARNELL WAS A PROUD MAN, ...   587 PARNELLITES   21
    AND A PROUD MAN'S A LOVELY MAN, ...   587 PARNELLITES   23
    THEY ARE GONE, THEY ARE GONE. THE PROUD MAY LIE BY THE 777 SONG DEIRDRE 3   1
        PROUD.
    THEY ARE GONE, THEY ARE GONE. THE PROUD MAY LIE BY THE 777 SONG DEIRDRE 3   1
        PROUD.
    MY RASCAL HEART IS PROUD . . . .   782 HEART FRIGHT   10
PROUDER
    NO PROUDER TROD THE GROUND, ...   587 PARNELLITES   22
PROUDEST
    THE PROUDEST OR MOST COY OF SPIRIT THINGS, ...   720 WITCH VIVIEN   7
PROUDLY
    PROUDLY IN HIS SAFFRON WALKING; . . . .   705 DAWN-SONG   2
PROVE
    IT WAS SO GIVEN OUT, BUT I WILL PROVE . . . . . .   243 SHADOW WATER B   429
    NOTHING BUT THAT TO PROVE YOUR BLOOD AND MINE. . . .   270 PARDON FATHERS   22
    AND PROVE OF ALL IMAGINABLE THINGS . . . .   371 EGO DOMINUS   73
    AND PROVE IF ALL IMAGINABLE THINGS . . . .   371 EGO DOMINUS   V   73
    I HAVE PRINCIPLES TO PROVE ME RIGHT. . . . .   386 ROBARTES DANCE   42
    THAT HE HAD FOUND A TEXT TO PROVE . . . .   492 ANNE GREGORY   15
    PROVE THAT I LIE. . . . .   517 HER ANXIETY   6
    PROVE THAT I LIE. . . . .   517 HER ANXIETY   12
    TO PROVE THEIR FORGERY TRUE! . . . .   582 ROGER CASEMENT   10
    FOR HISTORIES ARE THERE TO PROVE . . . .   583 GHOST ROG CASE   23
    COMPLEXION AND FORM PROVE SUPERHUMAN. . . . .   637 BEN BULBEN   6
    TO PROVE WHAT CAN YE DO? WHAT THINGS ABOVE . . . .   650 ISLE STAT I 1   146
    TO PROVE HIS LOVE A KNIGHT WITH LANCE IN REST . . . . 651 ISLE STAT I 1   158
    SHALL NOT SO HOPELESS PROVE! SOME GOD MAY REST . . . . 657 ISLE STAT I 3   61
PROVED
    . . . TO THE DUBLIN MUNICIPAL GALLERY IF IT WERE PROVED 287 TO WEALTHY MAN   T
        . . .
    WHO, WERE IT PROVED HE LIES, ...   291 TO A FRIEND   6
    WONDER HOW MANY TIMES I COULD HAVE PROVED MY WORTH . . 427 PHANTOM HATRED   34
    AND HAUGHTIER-HEADED BURKE THAT PROVED THE STATE A TREE, 481 BLOOD AND MOON   22
    AND GOD-APPOINTED BERKELEY THAT PROVED ALL THINGS A DREAM, 481 BLOOD AND MOON 25
    AND HAUGHTIER HEADED BURKE THAT PROVED THE STATE A TREE 481 BLOOD AND MOON V 22
PROVES
    AND THE LIGHT PROVES THAT HE IS READING STILL. . . . . 373 PHASES OF MOON   11
    BECAUSE IT PROVES THAT THINGS BOTH CAN AND CANNOT BE; . . 580 CURSE CROMWELL 19
PROVIDENCE
    AND THAT WOULD BE AGAINST GOD'S PROVIDENCE. . . . . . 339 SHEP GOATHERD   5
    AS I LOOK UP TO PROVIDENCE. . . . .   380 SONGS FOOL 1   6
PROW
    AND OVER THE TILLER AND THE PROW, ...   197 BAILE AILLINN   183
    ANOTHER ARGO'S PAINTED PROW . . . .   437 SONGS PLAY 1   11
    THE BOAT'S PROW GRATED ON THE SHALLOW SAND, ... 659 ISLE STAT II 1   11
    CURVING BENEATH THE PROW; AS SOME WILD DRAKE . . . .   659 ISLE STAT II 1   16
    ARE 'NEATH ITS PROW, AND CRUSHING SHELLS. . . . . .   663 ISLE STAT II 2   35
PROWS
    AND CARVEN FIGURES ON THEIR PROWS . . . .   14 OISIN 1   190
    AND CARVEN FIGURES ON THEIR PROWS . . . .   23 OISIN 1   354
PRUDENT
    AND HE HAD KNOWN AT LAST SOME PRUDENT YEARS . . . . . 127 DREAM OF FAERY   15
PSALTERIES
    THE PLAYERS ASK FOR A BLESSING ON THE PSALTERIES AND ON 212 BLESS PSALTER   T
        THEMSELVES
    THE PLAYERS ASK FOR A BLESSING ON THE PSALTERIES   212 BLESS PSALTER V   T
        AND THEMSELVES

PUBERTY
    THAT GIRLS AT PUBERTY MAY FIND . . . . 617 LONG-LEG FLY   21
PUBLIC
    NOR PUBLIC MEN, NOR CHEERING CROWDS, ... 328 IRISH AIRMAN   10
    NOR PUBLIC MAN, NOR ANGRY CROWDS, ... 328 IRISH AIRMAN V   10
    NOR PUBLIC MAN, NOR CHEERING CROWDS, ... 328 IRISH AIRMAN V   10
    "THE DRUNKARDS, PILFERERS OF PUBLIC FUNDS, ... 352 PEOPLE   23
    WHETHER IN PUBLIC OR IN SECRET RAGE . . . . 413 TOWER   99
    PUBLIC OPINION RIPENING FOR SO LONG . . . . 428 NINETEEN 19   13
    A SIXTY-YEAR-OLD SMILING PUBLIC MAN. . . . . 443 SCHOOL CHILDR   8
    A SIXTY YEAR OLD SMILING PUBLIC MAN. . . . . 443 SCHOOL CHILDR V   8
    THEY HOLD THEIR PUBLIC MEETINGS WHERE . . . . . . 460 THREE MONUMENT   1
    COME SPEAK YOUR BIT IN PUBLIC . . . . 582 ROGER CASEMENT   21
    NOW I AM IN THE PUBLIC HOUSE AND LEAN UPON THE WALL, . . 593 PILGRIM V   21
    THE MUSE IS MUTE WHEN PUBLIC MEN . . . . 597 MODEL LAUREATE   17
    AND PRESSED AT MIDNIGHT IN SOME PUBLIC PLACE . . . . . 610 STATUES   7
PUBLIC-HOUSE
    NOW I AM IN THE PUBLIC-HOUSE AND LEAN UPON THE WALL, . . 593 PILGRIM   21
PUBLISHED
    TO HAVE PUBLISHED ALL TO BE A WORLD'S DELIGHT. . . . . 327 ROBERT GREGORY   72
    AS A MAN DOES WHO HAS PUBLISHED A NEW BOOK, ... 350 HER PRAISE   3
PUDDLE
    HE HAD PUDDLE WATER IN HIS SHOES: . . . . 190 BAILE AILLINN V   28
PUDDLE-WATER
    HE HAD PUDDLE-WATER IN HIS SHOES: . . . . 190 BAILE AILLINN   28
PUFF
    A GLITTERING SWORD OUT OF THE EAST. A PUFF OF WIND . . . 426 PHANTOM HATRED   5
PUFF-BALLS
    PUFFED LIKE PUFF-BALLS ON A TREE, ... 727 LOVERS QUARREL   37
PUFFED
    . . . GONE AND PUFFED AWAY AND DEAD. . . . . 718 PHANTOM SHIP   3
    PUFFED LIKE PUFF-BALLS ON A TREE, ... 727 LOVERS QUARREL   37
PULL
    OR ON THE UNPEOPLED WAVES WITH KINGS TO PULL AT THE OAR, 210 UNDER THE MOON   15
    LONGING TO KNEAD AND PULL IT INTO SHAPE . . . . . . 246 SHADOW WATER B   510
    I'LL FIND THE STABLE AND PULL OUT THE BOLT. . . . . . 260 FASC DIFFICULT   13
    PULL DOWN THE BLINDS, BRING FIDDLE AND CLARIONET . . . . 311 MOUNTAIN TOMB   5
    BEING CAUGHT BETWEEN THE PULL . . . . 384 VISION ROBART   59
    PULL DOWN ESTABLISHED HONOUR: HAWK FOR NEWS . . . . . 398 LEADERS CROWD   5
    BRIGHTNESS THAT I PULL BACK . . . . 533 FIRST CONFESS   13
    THERE ARE SEVEN THAT PULL THE THREAD. . . . . . . 770 SPINNING SONG   1
PULLED
    HAVE PULLED THE IMMORTAL ROSE: . . . . 174 ELEMENT POWERS   2
    BLOSSOM PALE, SHE PULLED DOWN THE PALE BLOSSOM . . . . 199 ARROW V   5
    AND ALL THE WHILE HER NEEDLE PULLED . . . . 308 PLAYER QUEEN   7
    SHE PULLED THE THREAD AND BIT THE THREAD . . . . . . 308 PLAYER QUEEN   9
    HOW SINEW THAT HAS BEEN PULLED TIGHT, ... 386 ROBARTES DANCE   34
    FOR NATURE'S PULLED HER TRAGIC BUSKIN ON . . . . . . 490 COOLE BALLYLEE   12
    FOR NATURE'S PULLED HER TRAGIC BUCKSKIN ON . . . . . 490 COOLE BALLYLEE V   12
    FOR NATURE'D PULLED HER TRAGIC BUSKIN ON . . . . . 490 COOLE BALLYLEE V   12
PULLERS
    ARE DOUBTFUL LIKE THESE PULLERS OF THE OAR: . . . . . 748 SHADOW WATER A   30
    BE PULLERS OF THE OAR UNTIL YOU DIE? . . . . 757 SHADOW WATER A   217
PULSE
    THE LIGHTNINGS PULSE--BEHOLD HER, AYE BEHOLD-- . . . . 687 TWO TITANS   11
PULSES
    THAT FAN THE PULSES OF DELIGHTED AIR, ... 32 OISIN 2 V   50A
    A CRAZY JUICE THAT MAKES THE PULSES BEAT . . . . . . 384 VISION ROBART   54
PULSING
    OF LILAC O'ER THE PULSING WATER GLEAMS, ... 664 ISLE STAT II 2   48
PUMMELLED
    BUT MIGHT HAVE PUMMELLED AT A STONE . . . . 307 HOUR DAWN   114
PUMMELLING
    HE GAVE HIM A GREAT PUMMELLING, ... 307 HOUR DAWN   113
PUNISHMENT
    I ASK A FITTING PUNISHMENT FOR ALL . . . . 235 SHADOW WATER B   290
    BY THE INJUSTICE OF THE SKIES FOR PUNISHMENT? . . . . . 316 COLD HEAVEN   12
PUNK
    COME SWISH AROUND, MY PRETTY PUNK, ... 591 DRUNK SOBRIETY   1
    A MERMAID, NOT A PUNK: . . . . 592 DRUNK SOBRIETY   14
PUNY
    WITH FIERY SONG I'LL DROWN YON PUNY VOICE. . . . . . 648 ISLE STAT I 1   81
PUPILS
    DOES MINNALOUSHE KNOW THAT HIS PUPILS . . . . 379 CAT AND MOON   21
PUPPY
    ARE OLD AND PUPPY HOUNDS: . . . . 99 FOXHUNTER V   44
PURCHASED
    WHAT IS THIS FLESH I PURCHASED WITH MY PAINS, ... 499 MOTHER OF GOD   11
PURE
    BUT PURE AS A TALL CANDLE BEFORE THE TRINITY . . . . 208 HANRAHANS SONG V   14
    AN AIMLESS JOY IS A PURE JOY," . . . . 338 TOM OROUGHLEY   4
    THE PURE COLD LIGHT IN THE SKY . . . . 378 CAT AND MOON   7
    LIKE THIS PURE JET, NOW LOST AMID BLUE SKY, ... 464 HARUN RASHID   64
    SEVEN CENTURIES HAVE PASSED AND IT IS PURE, ... 482 BLOOD AND MOON   33
    SO ARROGANTLY PURE, A CHILD MIGHT THINK . . . . . 491 COOLE BALLYLEE   23
    NATURE'S PURE UNCHANGING LIGHT? . . . . 529 TOM LUNATIC   6
    O BUT HEART'S WINE SHALL RUN PURE, ... 554 CHURCH STATE   5
    TRANSFIGURED TO PURE SUBSTANCE WHAT HAD ONCE . . . . 555 RIBH AT TOMB   11
    GREW IN PURE MIND, BUT OUT OF WHAT BEGAN? . . . . . 630 CIRCUS ANIMALS   34
    WORN BY THE SOLSTICE FIERCE, AND MADE IT PURE. . . . , 692 MOSADA 1   57

PUREBRED
    THAT COULD HAVE SHOWN HOW PUREBRED HORSES . . . . . .   325 ROBERT GREGORY V 36
PURE-BRED
    THAT COULD HAVE SHOWN HOW PURE-BRED HORSES . . . . . .   325 ROBERT GREGORY   36
PURER
    BUT PURER THAN A TALL CANDLE BEFORE THE HOLY ROOD . . . 208 HANRAHANS SONG   14
    BUT PURER THAN A TALL CANDLE BEFORE THE BLESSED ROOD . . 208 HANRAHANS SONG V 14
PURGATORY
    BECAUSE THE FIRES OF PURGATORY HAVE ATE THEIR SHAPES AWAY! 593 PILGRIM   13
    "PRAY FOR THE SOULS IN PURGATORY," THE PALE PRIEST   719 PHANTOM SHIP   31
        TREMBLING CRIES.
PURIFIED
    THOSE LOVERS, PURIFIED BY TRAGEDY, ...   555 RIBH AT TOMB   21
PURITY
    CAN HAVE THE PURITY OF A NATURAL FORCE, ...   353 PEOPLE   31
    THAT PURITY BUILT UP THE STATE . . . .   460 THREE MONUMENT   6
    THE PURITY OF THE UNCLOUDED MOON . . . .   482 BLOOD AND MOON   31
PURPLE
    AND TOLD THE PURPLE DEEPS THEIR PRIDE, ...   14 OISIN 1   186
    AND FILLS WITH STARS NIGHT'S PURPLE CUP, ...   18 OISIN 1   262
    OVER THE GLIMMERING PURPLE SEA. . . . .   25 OISIN 1   384
    ALL EMPTIED OF PURPLE HOURS AS A BEGGAR'S CLOAK IN THE   63 OISIN 3   219
        RAIN,
    OF PURPLE AND OF HEAVY GOLD! . . . .   81 MAD KING GOLL V   3
    THERE MIDNIGHT'S ALL A GLIMMER, AND NOON A PURPLE GLOW,   117 ISLE INNISFREE   7
    "HE WHO IS WRAPPED IN PURPLE ROBES, ...   134 FR GILLIGAN   45
    FROM BATTLE-BANNERS, FOLD UPON PURPLE FOLD, ...   162 ASKS FORGIVE   11
    FROM BATTLE BANNERS FOLD UPON PURPLE FOLD, ...   162 ASKS FORGIVE V   11
    NODDING HER PURPLE HOOD? . . . .   171 MAID QUIET   V   2
    UNDER HER PURPLE HOOD. . . . .   171 MAID QUIET   V   8
    ONE GATHERS UP HIS PURPLE GOWN! . . . .   212 BLESS PSALTER   9
    THIS GREAT PURPLE BUTTERFLY, ...   381 SONG OF FOOL   1
    STITCHING AT A PURPLE HOARDED . . . .   440 WISDOM   12
    WRITTEN IN GOLD UPON A PURPLE STAIN, ...   461 HARUN RASHID   10
    HEART'S PURPLE--AND ALL THESE I SET . . . .   478 SELF AND SOUL   28
    THY WITHERED FOE, AND WITH THE PURPLE WING . . . . . .   688 TWO TITANS   55
    WITH PURPLE SANDALS SWEEP THE GRAVE-EYED HOURS-- . . .   705 REMEMBRANCE   5
    CREEPING ALONG THE HEAVENS' PURPLE CUP . . . .   714 FERENCZ RENYI   112
    AND MANY A PURPLE GILLYFLOWER EATEN, ...   729 PRIEST FAIRY   35
PURPOSE
    HIS PURPOSE DRIFTS AND DIES." . . . .   45 OISIN 2   244
    HIS PURPOSE DRIFTS AWAY." . . . .   45 OISIN 2   V 244
    YOU DO NOT SEE MY PURPOSE. I SHALL HAVE GONE . . . . .   238 SHADOW WATER B   357
    YOU DID NOT SEE MY PURPOSE. I SHALL HAVE GONE . . . . .   238 SHADOW WATER B V 357
    HEARTS WITH ONE PURPOSE ALONE . . . .   393 EASTER 1916   41
    THEIR PURPOSE IN THE LABYRINTH OF THE WIND! . . . . .   433 NINETEEN 19   121
    SEEMED SO ON PURPOSE, MUTTERED JAFFER'S FRIENDS, ... 462 HARUN RASHID   37
    PROOF THAT THERE'S A PURPOSE SET . . . .   639 BEN BULBEN   50
PURR
    THOUGH YOU GLOW AND YOU GLANCE, THOUGH YOU PURR AND YOU   90 OLD FISHERMAN   2
        DART!
    THOUGH YE GLOW AND YE GLANCE, THOUGH YE PURR AND YE DART, 90 OLD FISHERMAN V   2
PURSE
    THAT YOU MIGHT HAVE A HEAVIER PURSE, ...   273 GREY ROCK   56
    THAT OLD PERPLEXITY AN EMPTY PURSE, ...   491 COOLE BALLYLEE V 40G
    THAT OLD PERPLEXITY AN EMPTY PURSE, ...   495 CHOICE   7
PURSES
    GAVE THEIR BODIES, EMPTIED PURSES . . . .   789 SINGING HEAD   19
PURSUE
    PURSUES THE THOUGHTS THAT I PURSUE, ...   633 MAN AND ECHO   32
PURSUES
    PURSUES THE THOUGHTS THAT I PURSUE, ...   633 MAN AND ECHO   32
PURSUING
    THE CHILD PURSUING LIZARDS IN THE GRASS, ...   686 LIFE   1
    THE CHILD PURSUING LIZARDS IN THE GRASS, ...   734 QUATRAIN APHOR V   1
    WHAT PURSUING OR FLEEING, ...   785 WOMANS BEAUTY   25
PUSH
    PUSH OUT HIS VIGOROUS LIMBS AND RUB HIS EYES, ...   284 TWO KINGS   162
    WHO GRIPS HIS LONG SPEAR SO TO PUSH . . . .   385 ROBARTES DANCE   3
    HOW CAN THOSE TERRIFIED VAGUE FINGERS PUSH . . . . . .   441 LEDA AND SWAN   5
PUSHED
    AND PUSHED THE LATCHES DOWN. . . . .   159 CAP AND BELLS   12
    AND PUSHED THE BRASS BOLT DOWN. . . . .   159 CAP AND BELLS V   12
    BUT THE OTHER PUSHED HIS HAND ASIDE, ...   304 HOUR DAWN   V   48
PUSHES
    THAT RUSTLES IN THE REEDS WITH PATIENT PUSHES, ...   699 MOSADA 3   4
    THAT'S RUSTLING IN THE REEDS WITH PATIENT PUSHES, . . .   699 MOSADA 3   V   4
PUSHING
    AND PUSHING IT INTO MY SHIRT, ...   274 GREY ROCK   89
    AND WAS A PUSHING MAN . . . .   456 FRIENDS YOUTH   14
PUT
    PUT THE STAFF IN MY HANDS! . . . .   61 OISIN 3   201
    "PUT THE CHAIR UPON THE GRASS! . . . .   97 FOXHUNTER   9
    I'D PUT AWAY THE FOOLISH MIGHT OF A KING, ...   103 FERGUS DRUID V 21A
    "I PUT YOU FROM YOUR PAIN. I CAN NO MORE." . . . . .   110 CUCHULAIN SEA   69
    PUT THAT MUSIC IN HER FACE? . . . .   124 CATHLEEN PARA   10
    AND PUT A BERRY ON A THREAD! . . . .   149 WANDER AENGUS V   4
    YOU PUT SUCH FOLLY IN OUR HEADS . . . .   190 BAILE AILLINN   32
    WHO WAS IT PUT SO GREAT A SCORN . . . .   190 BAILE AILLINN   41
    THAT PUT THIS HURRY IN MY SHOES." . . . .   194 BAILE AILLINN   125
    HUM IN THE LIME-TREE FLOWERS; AND PUT AWAY . . . . . .   198 SEVEN WOODS   3

PUT   (CONTINUED)
HUM IN THE LIME TREE FLOWERS: AND PUT AWAY . . . . .   198 SEVEN WOODS   V   3
AND FLYING TOWARDS THEIR PEACE. PUT BY THESE THOUGHTS,   226 SHADOW WATER B   91
BUT IF I WERE TO PUT YOU ON THAT SHIP, ...   236 SHADOW WATER B   307
IT HAD WASHED AMONG THE STARS AND PUT THEM OUT, . . .   236 SHADOW WATER B   311
I CAN PUT FEAR AWAY AS A QUEEN SHOULD. . . . .   238 SHADOW WATER B   355
WE'LL PUT THIS MAN TO DEATH. I PROMISE IT. . . . . .   238 SHADOW WATER B   363
HE HAS PUT A SUDDEN DARKNESS OVER THE MOON. . . . . .   239 SHADOW WATER B   367
IT WAS THAT HARPER PUT IT IN MY THOUGHTS, ...   243 SHADOW WATER B   423
WHEN WE HAVE PUT THEIR CHANGELESS IMAGE ON. . . . . .   250 SHADOW WATER B   582
WHO CANNOT PUT ME FROM HIS SIGHT FOR EVER. . . . . . .   251 SHADOW WATER B   601
FORGAEL, BECAUSE YOU CANNOT PUT ME FROM YOU. . . . .   251 SHADOW WATER B   603
"PUT OFF THAT MASK OF BURNING GOLD . . . .   263 MASK   1
AND PUT HIS PATTERN ROUND THEIR TOPS . . . .   272 GREY ROCK   V   24
MY MARRIED SISTER PUT INTO MY CARE . . . .   276 TWO KINGS   V   E
SAID, "IF A WOMAN HAS PUT THIS ON YOU, ...   281 TWO KINGS   111
THAT PUT A PASSION IN THE SLEEPER THERE, ...   284 TWO KINGS   157
BEFORE YOU'LL PUT YOUR GUINEAS DOWN, ...   287 TO WEALTHY MAN   5
BEFORE YOU'VE PUT YOUR GUINEAS DOWN, ...   287 TO WEALTHY MAN V   5
AND THE GAUNT HOUSES PUT ON MAJESTY: . . . .   292 TO A SHADE   7
"TIME TO PUT OFF THE WORLD AND GO SOMEWHERE . . . . .   299 BEGGAR CRIED   1
YOU HAVE PUT THE THOUGHT IN RHYME. I WORKED ALL DAY,   341 SHEP GOATHERD   58
OR PUT HIS HEART INTO SOME GAME . . . .   343 SHEP GOATHERD   105
BUT PUT NO NAME AND LEAVE THEM AT HER DOOR. . . . . .   343 SHEP GOATHERD   116
HEAVEN HAS PUT AWAY THE STROKE OF HER DOOM, ...   356 BROKEN DREAMS   11
THE LIGHT IN THE TOWER WINDOW WAS PUT OUT. . . . . .   377 PHASES OF MOON   139
YOU MEAN THEY ARGUED. PUT IT SO: . . . .   385 ROBARTES DANCE   13
MAY I NOT PUT MYSELF TO COLLEGE? . . . .   385 ROBARTES DANCE   18
THE INNUMERABLE CLANGING WINGS THAT HAVE PUT OUT THE MOON.   427 PHANTOM HATRED   32
DID SHE PUT ON HIS KNOWLEDGE WITH HIS POWER . . . . .   441 LEDA AND SWAN   13
AND PUT ALL TROY TO WRECK-- . . . .   455 HIS MEMORIES   16
AND PUT ALL TROY TO WRACK-- . . . .   455 HIS MEMORIES   V   16
AND PUT THAT CRACK IN IT, ...   455 FRIENDS YOUTH   2
WHEN OUR BELOVED CALIPH PUT TO DEATH . . . .   462 HARUN RASHID   31
PUT HER IN A RAGE. . . . .   504 QUARREL IN AGE   6
A MAN MAY PUT PRETENCE AWAY . . . .   525 DANCING DAYS   19
"WHAT CHANGE HAS PUT MY THOUGHTS ASTRAY . . . .   529 TOM LUNATIC   3
THEIR MOBS PUT UNDER THEIR FEET. . . . .   554 CHURCH STATE   4
OLD CIVILISATIONS PUT TO THE SWORD. . . . .   566 LAPIS LAZULI   27
BUT WHEN HIS HORSE HAD PUT ITS HOOF . . . .   571 THREE BUSHES   50
IN COUNTRY SHAWL OR PARIS CLOAK, HAD PUT MY WITS ASTRAY,   592 PILGRIM   3
FOR I CAN PUT THE WHOLE LOT DOWN, AND ALL I HAVE TO SAY   593 PILGRIM   24
PUT JEWELRY IN THE PACK, ...   595 COLONEL MARTIN   24
HAVE I, THAT PUT IT INTO WORDS, ...   604 YOU CONTENT   5
COULD CRAZY JANE PUT OFF OLD AGE . . . .   606 SONGS BURDEN 1   19
CALCULATIONS THAT LOOK BUT CASUAL FLESH, PUT DOWN . .   610 STATUES   11
EUROPE PUT OFF THAT FOAM WHEN PHIDIAS . . . .   610 STATUES   15
AND BEING OLD SHE PUT A SKIN . . . .   621 JOHN KINSELLA   21
DID WORDS OF MINE PUT TOO GREAT STRAIN . . . .   632 MAN AND ECHO   13
QUATTROCENTO PUT IN PAINT . . . .   639 BEN BULBEN   53
QUATTRO-CENTO PUT IN PAINT . . . .   639 BEN BULBEN   V   53
THAT I WOULD BID MY PEOPLE PUT TO DEATH. . . . . . .   760 SHADOW WATER A V   254
PUT ALL YOUR POWER ON THE THREAD . . . .   771 SPINNING SONG   12
THE SHAPE-CHANGERS THAT CAN PUT . . . .   775 AGAINST WITCH   2
THE SHAPE CHANGERS THAT CAN PUT . . . .   775 AGAINST WITCH   V   2
I PUT THREE PERSONS IN THEIR PLACE . . . .   787 HUDDON DUDDON   8
PUTS
AND NOW THAT TIME PUTS WATER IN MY BLOOD, ...   222 SHADOW WATER B V   11A
AND SOMEBODY PUTS HIS HAND IN THE DISH . . . .   301 RUN PARADISE   5
PUTS ALL MEN IN A FRIGHT, ...   597 MODEL LAUREATE   12
PUTTING
FROM MEAGRE GIRLHOOD'S PUTTING ON . . . .   356 BROKEN DREAMS   9
PYRE
COME FORTH: THE MORN IS FAIR: AS FROM THE PYRE . . .   645 ISLE STAT I 1   8
TENDER AND FEARLESS ON HER FUNERAL PYRE: . . . . . .   688 NETTLESHIP   3
PYTHAGORAS
WORLD-FAMOUS GOLDEN-THIGHED PYTHAGORAS . . . .   445 SCHOOL CHILDR   45
WORLD-FAMOUS GOLDEN THIGHED PYTHAGORAS . . . .   445 SCHOOL CHILDR   V   45
THERE STATELY PYTHAGORAS . . . .   531 DELPHIC ORACLE   9
PYTHAGORAS PLANNED IT. WHY DID THE PEOPLE STARE? . .   610 STATUES   1
NO: GREATER THAN PYTHAGORAS, FOR THE MEN . . . . . .   610 STATUES   9
TALL PYTHAGORAS. . . . .   611 NEWS ORACLE   8
QUAFFED
OF WOLVES, OF BOREAL BEARS, WE QUAFFED THE WINE . . .   41 OISIN 2   V   188
IN OTHER LIVES? HAST THOU NOT QUAFFED OLD WINE . . .   724 KANVA ON SELF   12
QUAKE   SEE A-QUAKE
QUAKING
WITH QUAKING JOINTS AND TERROR-STRICKEN.FACES, . . .   185 QUEEN MAEVE   121
WITH QUAKING JOINTS AND TERROR STRICKEN FACES, . . .   185 QUEEN MAEVE   V   121
WITH QUAKING JOINTS AND TERROR-STRUCKEN FACES, . . .   185 QUEEN MAEVE   V   121
QUALITY
A QUALITY OF WISDOM FROM HER LOVE'S . . . .   469 HARUN RASHID   180
PARTICULAR QUALITY. THE SIGNS AND SHAPES: . . . . .   469 HARUN RASHID   181
QUALITY OF WISDOM FROM LOVE'S QUALITY. . . . .   469 HARUN RASHID   V   180
QUALITY OF WISDOM FROM LOVE'S QUALITY, ...   469 HARUN RASHID   V   180
FOR EVERY SEPARATE QUALITY OF LOVE: . . . .   469 HARUN RASHID   V 189A
QUARREL
THE QUARREL OF THE SPARROWS IN THE EAVES, ...   119 SORROW OF LOVE V   1
NOR BUT IN MERRIMENT A QUARREL. . . . .   405 FOR DAUGHTER   46
QUARREL IN OLD AGE . . . .   503 QUARREL IN AGE   T
A LOVER'S QUARREL AMONG THE FAIRIES. . . . .   726 LOVERS QUARREL   T

637

		PAGE	TITLE		LINE
QUARREL	(CONTINUED)				
	WE WILL NOT QUARREL, NOW THAT ALL IS WELL,	766	SHADOW WATER A		373
QUARRELLING					
	THIS NIGHT CAN SET US QUARRELLING,	324	ROBERT GREGORY		15
	THEY ARE ALWAYS QUARRELLING. GIVE ME YOUR SWORDS.	766	SHADOW WATER A		370
	EOCHA AND MAINE ARE ALWAYS QUARRELLING.	766	SHADOW WATER A		371
	ALE SETS THEM QUARRELLING. GIVE ME YOUR SWORDS.	766	SHADOW WATER A		372
	GIVE ME YOUR SWORDS. THEY ARE ALWAYS QUARRELLING.	766	SHADOW WATER A	V	370
QUARRELS					
	AND QUARRELS ARE BLOWN UP UPON THAT HEAD;	324	ROBERT GREGORY		13
	NOR QUARRELS WITH A THOUGHT	345	ON WOMAN		7
	WHO QUARRELS OVER HALFPENNIES	621	JOHN KINSELLA		33
	WHO QUARRELS OVER HALF-PENNIES	621	JOHN KINSELLA	V	33
QUARRIED					
	ON LIMESTONE QUARRIED NEAR THE SPOT	640	BEN BULBEN		90
QUARRY					
	HYSTERICA PASSIO DRAGGED THIS QUARRY DOWN.	542	PARN FUNERAL 1		21
QUARTER	SEE THREE-QUARTER				
	AND EVERY WINDY QUARTER HOWL	405	FOR DAUGHTER		71
	FROM EVERY QUARTER OF THE WORLD, CAN STAY	471	ALL SOUL NIGHT		12
	THAT QUARTER WHERE ALL THOUGHT IS DONE:	477	SELF AND SOUL		7
	SUCH FULLNESS IN THAT QUARTER OVERFLOWS	478	SELF AND SOUL		33
	A QUARTER OF THE HEAVENS FROM OUR RIGHT WAY.	754	SHADOW WATER A		155
	DIMMED AT THREE QUARTER LIGHT	786	YOUR HEART	V	32
QUATRAINS					
	QUATRAINS AND APHORISMS.	734	QUATRAIN APHOR		T
QUATTROCENTO					
	DID QUATTROCENTO FINGER FASHION IT	444	SCHOOL CHILDR		26
	IT SEEMED A QUATTROCENTO PAINTER'S THRONG,	537	HER VISION		19
	QUATTROCENTO PUT IN PAINT	639	BEN BULBEN		53
QUATTRO-CENTO					
	IT SEEMED A QUATTRO-CENTO PAINTER'S THRONG	537	HER VISION	V	19
	QUATTRO-CENTO PUT IN PAINT	639	BEN BULBEN	V	53
QUAY					
	UPON THE OPEN ROAD, NEAR TO THE SLIGO QUAY—	391	UNDER SATURN		12
QUEEN					
	BUT THE YOUNG QUEEN WOULD NOT LISTEN;	159	CAP AND BELLS		9
	A QUEEN WAS LOVED BY A JESTER,	159	CAP AND BELLS	V	1
	A QUEEN WAS BELOVED BY A JESTER,	159	CAP AND BELLS	V	1
	THE OLD AGE OF QUEEN MAEVE	180	QUEEN MAEVE		T
	MAEVE THE GREAT QUEEN WAS PACING TO AND FRO,	180	QUEEN MAEVE		9
	BUT THAT GREAT QUEEN, WHO MORE THAN HALF THE NIGHT	180	QUEEN MAEVE		16
	HAVE I NOT BID YOU TELL OF THAT GREAT QUEEN	181	QUEEN MAEVE		34
	HE SAID, "HIGH QUEEN OF CRUACHAN AND MAGH AI;	183	QUEEN MAEVE		77
	HE SAID "QUEEN OF UNSHELTERED CRUACHAN,	183	QUEEN MAEVE	V	77
	QUEEN OF HIGH CRUACHAN." "I OBEY YOUR WILL	184	QUEEN MAEVE		99
	OUTRUN THE MEASURE. I'D TELL OF THAT GREAT QUEEN	187	QUEEN MAEVE		141
	A KING AND A QUEEN ARE WANDERING THERE, AND THE SOUND	204	WITHER BOUGHS		19
	THERE IS A KING AND QUEEN UPON HER DECK,	232	SHADOW WATER B		226
	BUT HAVE NOT BITTEN YET. I AM A QUEEN,	235	SHADOW WATER B		280
	THAT YOU'LL NOT LET ME GO? I AM A QUEEN.	236	SHADOW WATER B		304
	BRING MADNESS? QUEEN, I AM NOT MAD. YET SAY	236	SHADOW WATER B		316
	I CAN PUT FEAR AWAY AS A QUEEN SHOULD.	238	SHADOW WATER B		355
	QUEEN, GIVE IT ME. NO, I HAVE NEED OF IT.	241	SHADOW WATER B		399
	BROKEN-HEARTED, HAVING LOST HIS QUEEN	242	SHADOW WATER B		407
	BROKENHEARTED, HAVING LOST HIS QUEEN	242	SHADOW WATER B	V	407
	WESTWARD OF TARA. HURRYING TO HIS QUEEN	276	TWO KINGS		2
	HAVING NO THOUGHT BUT FOR HIS QUEEN EDAIN,	276	TWO KINGS	V	1
	QUEEN MAEVE'S NINE MAINES HAD BEEN NURSED,	302	HOUR DAWN		8
	A SONG FROM "THE PLAYER QUEEN"	308	PLAYER QUEEN		T
	THE PLAYER QUEEN SONG FROM AN UNFINISHED PLAY	308	PLAYER QUEEN	V	T
	ON THAT OLD QUEEN MEASURING A TOWN	344	DAWN		3
	ON THE OLD QUEEN MEASURING A TOWN	344	DAWN	V	3
	THERE IS A QUEEN IN CHINA	353	HIS PHOENIX	V	T
	THERE IS A QUEEN IN CHINA, OR MAYBE IT'S IN SPAIN,	353	HIS PHOENIX		1
	THERE IS A QUEEN IN CHINA, OR MAY BE IT'S IN SPAIN,	353	HIS PHOENIX	V	1
	AND ONE, IT MAY BE, A QUEEN.	358	PRESENCES		14
	WHILE THAT GREAT QUEEN, THAT ROSE OUT OF THE SPRAY,	404	FOR DAUGHTER		27
	OF SAD QUEEN DIDO SHONE THE LAPPING FIRE	645	ISLE STAT I 1		9
	IS WORN AS THOUGH WITH FIRE. OH, GOBLIN QUEEN,	667	ISLE STAT II 3		36
	UPON MY NECKLACE. BUT THE GOBLIN QUEEN	676	ISLE STAT II 3		267
	OF THESE STAR-SHUDDERING SKIES, YOU ARE THE QUEEN.	679	ISLE STAT II 3		323
	OF THEIR TALL, NEW-FANGLED QUEEN.	727	LOVERS QUARREL		48
	"OF OUR GREAT QUEEN IS EVER HEARD	729	PRIEST FAIRY		41
	AND THEN THE FAY QUEEN SOBBED APART,	730	PRIEST FAIRY		70
	I HAVE BROUGHT HIS CROWN. AND I HAVE BROUGHT HIS QUEEN.	755	SHADOW WATER A		166
	WE BRING YOU THIS GREAT QUEEN.	755	SHADOW WATER A	V	166
	THE GODS HOLD WATCH ABOUT THE WORDS OF A QUEEN.	756	SHADOW WATER A		191
	ALL THAT TIME KNOWS. SPEAK TO ME, QUEEN. O SPEAK!	756	SHADOW WATER A	V	180
	IS IT YOUR WILL THAT I, WHO AM A QUEEN	757	SHADOW WATER A		212
	I CEASED TO BE A WOMAN, BEING A QUEEN.	758	SHADOW WATER A		228
	OF GOLDEN-ARMED IOLAN AND THE QUEEN	766	SHADOW WATER A		375
	OF GOLDEN ARMED AOLAN AND THE QUEEN	766	SHADOW WATER A	V	375
	QUEEN EDAINE	771	SONG DEIRDRE 1	V	T
	"WHY IS IT," QUEEN EDAIN SAID,	771	SONG DEIRDRE 1		1
QUEENS					
	WEDDING THE QUEENS OF EARTHLY LANDS WITH RINGS	29	OISIN 2	V	10
	OF SEA-SPRUNG PEARL, AND QUEENS OF FAIRY LANDS	29	OISIN 2	V	10A
	QUEENS WROUGHT WITH GLIMMERING HANDS;	162	ASKS FORGIVE		12
	FOR THERE IS NO HIGH STORY ABOUT QUEENS	186	QUEEN MAEVE		134
	THE QUEENS THAT WERE IMAGINED LONG AGO,	201	OLD MEMORY		5

638

	PAGE	TITLE	LINE

QUEENS (CONTINUED)
    THEREIN ARE MANY QUEENS LIKE BRANWEN AND GUINEVERE: . . . 209 UNDER THE MOON 11
    QUEENS, THEIR EYES BLUE LIKE THE ICE, ... 214 HAPPY TOWNLAND 11
    SHE WILL BE LIKE A WILD CAT: FOR THESE QUEENS . . . . . 232 SHADOW WATER B 233
    THEY HAVE IT THAT THE PLANS OF KINGS AND QUEENS . . . . 235 SHADOW WATER B 296
    WHILE TALKING WITH HIS QUEENS, ... 345 ON WOMAN 12
    AMONG THE QUEENS, AND CHOSE THE MIGHTIEST . . . . . . 757 SHADOW WATER A 213
QUEEN-WOMAN
    A QUEEN-WOMAN DRESSED OUT IN SILVER, CRY . . . . . . 210 RAGGED WOOD V 2
    PALE SILVER-PROUD QUEEN-WOMAN OF THE SKY, ... 211 RAGGED WOOD 6
QUEER
    OF HENWIVES AND OF QUEER OLD MEN . . . . 607 SONGS BURDEN 2 23
    OF HEN WIVES AND OF QUEER OLD MEN . . . . 607 SONGS BURDEN 2 V 23
QUENCH
    THAT SHE MAY QUENCH THE RICK SHE HAS FIRED: AND THOUGH . . 282 TWO KINGS 116
    I'LL QUENCH HIS SINGING WITH LOUD SONG— . . . . . . 647 ISLE STAT I 1 63
QUENCHED
    IT QUENCHED, WITH SOUND LIKE FALLING DEW, ... 86 MAD KING GOLL 66
QUENCHLESS
    WITH QUENCHLESS GAZE AND FLUTTERING HAIR. . . . . . . 12 OISIN 1 145
    AND WITH QUENCHLESS EYES AND FLUTTERING HAIR . . . . . 12 OISIN 1 V 144
    A QUENCHLESS GRIEVING OF LOVE MELODY. . . . . 645 ISLE STAT I 1 21
QUERN
    AN OLD SLAVE GRINDING AT A HEAVY QUERN, ... 104 FERGUS DRUID 35
QUEST
    WILL CIRCLE ROUND THE WORLD UPON A QUEST, ... 651 ISLE STAT I 1 159
    OH, BOY, I'M BOUND ON A MOST FEARFUL QUEST: . . . . . 653 ISLE STAT I 2 31
    THE LAKE-EMBOSOMED ISLE. NAY, THIS MY QUEST . . . . . 657 ISLE STAT I 3 60
    I BID THEE STAY, RENOUNCING THY MAD QUEST." . . . . . 669 ISLE STAT II 3 89
    HOW SPED THY QUEST? THIS PRELUDE WE'LL NOT HEAR IT. . . 673 ISLE STAT II 3 174
    O, MY ALMINTOR, NOBLE WAS THY QUEST: . . . . 679 ISLE STAT II 3 319
QUESTION
    "DAY AFTER DAY YOU QUESTION ME, AND I, ... 281 TWO KINGS 99
    QUESTION OF OURS, BEYOND OUR PITY EVEN. . . . . 282 TWO KINGS V 130
    FOR I WOULD ASK A QUESTION OF THEM ALL. . . . . 410 TOWER 24
    AS I WOULD QUESTION ALL, COME ALL WHO CAN: . . . . . . 412 TOWER 89
    WHAT HE CAN QUESTION, WHAT IF QUESTIONED I . . . . . . 494 AT ALGECIRAS 17
    WHAT HE MAY QUESTION, WHAT IF QUESTIONED I . . . . . . 494 AT ALGECIRAS V 17
    BUT I NEVER STOPPED TO QUESTION, WHAT COULD THE BOATMAN SAY 593 PILGRIM 19
    TURNS INTO A QUESTION TILL . . . . 632 MAN AND ECHO 8
    TO QUESTION HER——OH NO, I DID NOT FEAR, ... 676 ISLE STAT II 3 265
    WHERE SHALL I LAY ME DOWN? THAT QUESTION IS . . . . . 700 MOSADA 3 36
    A WEIGHTY QUESTION, FOR IT IS THE LAST. . . . . 700 MOSADA 3 37
QUESTIONED
    WHAT HE CAN QUESTION, WHAT IF QUESTIONED I . . . . . . 494 AT ALGECIRAS 17
    WHAT HE MAY QUESTION, WHAT IF QUESTIONED I . . . . . . 494 AT ALGECIRAS V 17
    I CHOSE IT FOR MY LOT! IF QUESTIONED ON . . . . . . 535 CHOSEN 11
    I SWEAR TO GOD I QUESTIONED THEM, AND ALL THEY HAD TO SAY 593 PILGRIM 14
    I SWEAR TO GOD I QUESTIONED THEM ALL AND ALL THEY HAD TO 593 PILGRIM V 14
        SAY
QUESTIONER
    YOUR QUESTIONER, OISIN, IS WORTHY, HE COMES FROM THE FENIAN 51 OISIN 3 64
        LANDS."
    WORTHY'S THY QUESTIONER, OISIN, HE FROM THE FENIAN LANDS." 51 OISIN 3 V 64
    MUCH ON THE GREAT QUESTIONER: . . . . 494 AT ALGECIRAS 16
QUESTIONING
    OUR QUESTIONING, BEYOND OUR PITY EVEN. . . . . 282 TWO KINGS 130
    I WALK THROUGH THE LONG SCHOOLROOM QUESTIONING: . . . . 443 SCHOOL CHILDR 1
    WHY THOSE QUESTIONING EYES . . . . 533 FIRST CONFESS 15
    A GENTLE QUESTIONING LOOK THAT CANNOT HIDE . . . . . . 601 GALLERY REVIS 6
QUESTIONS
    WEARY OF MANY QUESTIONS: "THERE ARE THINGS . . . . . 281 TWO KINGS 93
QUESTS
    SUCH QUESTS AS THESE, I TROW, NEED LITTLE WIT. . . . . 650 ISLE STAT I 1 150
QUICK
    AND MAY SOME DREADFUL ILL BEFALL HER QUICK! . . . . . 74 ANASHU VIJAYA V 59
    BLUE-EYED, AND A QUICK RUNNER ON BARE FEET, ... 242 SHADOW WATER B 416
QUICKEN
    NEAR TO CUCHULLIN, ROUND A QUICKEN TREE, ... 111 CUCHULAIN SEA V 81A
    AND TEN BY TEN UNDER A QUICKEN TREE, ... 111 CUCHULAIN SEA V 81A
    TALL WANDS OF ALDER AND WHITE QUICKEN WANDS. . . . . . 111 CUCHULAIN SEA V 82A
    UNDER THE WOVEN ROOFS OF QUICKEN BOUGHS:— . . . . . 126 DREAM OF FAERY V 11
    RIDDLED WITH LIGHT. AH! WHEN THE GHOST BEGINS TO QUICKEN, 316 COLD HEAVEN 9
    OF THE TARN WHERE YOUNG WAVES QUICKEN . . . . 647 ISLE STAT I 1 48
    THE DANAAN QUICKEN TREE . . . . 742 DANAAN QUICK T
    (AH, MOURNFUL DANAAN QUICKEN TREE!) . . . . 742 DANAAN QUICK 6
    (AH, MOURNFUL DANAAN QUICKEN TREE!) . . . . 743 DANAAN QUICK 12
    (AH, MOURNFUL DANAAN QUICKEN TREE!) . . . . 743 DANAAN QUICK 18
    (AH, MOURNFUL DANAAN QUICKEN TREE!) . . . . 743 DANAAN QUICK 24
    (AH, MOURNFUL DANAAN QUICKEN TREE!) . . . . 743 DANAAN QUICK 30
QUICKLIME
    THAT IS IN QUICKLIME LAID. . . . . 582 ROGER CASEMENT 24
QUICK-LIME
    THAT IS IN THE QUICK-LIME LAID. . . . . 582 ROGER CASEMENT V 24
QUICKLY
    THE SECOND BEST'S A GAY GOODNIGHT AND QUICKLY TURN AWAY. 459 FROM OEDIPUS 12
    STRIKE QUICKLY: IT WILL FADE OUT WHEN YOU STRIKE. . . . 759 SHADOW WATER A 238
    THERE! THERE! THEY HAVE GONE QUICKLY, FOR ALREADY . . 764 SHADOW WATER A 326
QUIET
    AND LAID YOU ON THE GATES OF EVENING WITH HIS QUIET HANDS. 72 ANASHU VIJAYA 22
    AND LAID YE ON THE GATES OF EVENING WITH HIS QUIET HANDS. 72 ANASHU VIJAYA V 22

	PAGE	TITLE	LINE

QUIET (CONTINUED)
THE VAN OF WANDERING QUIET: ERE YOU BE TOO CALM AND OLD, ... 73 ANASHU VIJAYA   43
THE VAN OF WANDERING QUIET: ERE YE BE TOO CALM AND OLD, ... 73 ANASHU VIJAYA V 43
HID UNDER QUIET BOUGHS APART, ... 78 INDIAN TO LOVE   12
HID UNDER QUIET BOWS APART, ... 78 INDIAN TO LOVE V 12
THE DRUID, GREY, WOOD NURTURED, QUIET EYED, ... 101 ROSE UPON ROOD V   4
BESIDE HER CLEAN-SWEPT HEARTH, HER QUIET SHADE: . . . . . . 114 ROSE OF BATTLE   11
BESIDES HER CLEAN SWEPT HEARTH, HER QUIET SHADE: . . . . . 114 ROSE OF BATTLE V 11
HAS PLANTED QUIET IN THE NIGHT;   . . . . 134 TWO TREES   8
OF A QUIET AND LIGHT FOOTFALL;   . . . . 159 CAP AND BELLS   8
OF A QUIET AND LIGHT FOOT-FALL;   . . . . 159 CAP AND BELLS V   8
AND THE QUIET OF LOVE IN HER FEET.   . . . . 161 CAP AND BELLS   36
MAID QUIET   . . . . 171 MAID QUIET   T
WHERE HAS MAID QUIET GONE TO, ... 171 MAID QUIET   1
I NEVER HAVE SEEN MAID QUIET   . . . . 171 MAID QUIET V   1
I AM CONTENTED, FOR I KNOW THAT QUIET   . . . . 198 SEVEN WOODS   10
WE SAT GROWN QUIET AT THE NAME OF LOVE: . . . . 205 ADAMS CURSE   28
BUT WE HAVE ALL BENT LOW AND LOW AND KISSED THE QUIET FEET   . . . 207 HANRAHANS SONG   9
BUT WE BEND TOGETHER AND KISS THE QUIET FEET   . . . . . 207 HANRAHANS SONG V   4
AND WINDS AND PONDS COVER MORE QUIET WOODS   . . . . . 218 WOODS OF COOLE   34
AND THE GREEN QUIET, HAVE UPLIFTED THE HEART?   . . . . . 219 WOODS OF COOLE   40
AT THE MOST QUIET MIDNIGHT IS TO BE STRICKEN. . . . . . . 236 SHADOW WATER B   321
MAY BE A QUIET THOUGHT TO WIFE AND MOTHER, ... 343 SHEP GOATHERD   118
QUIET LANDS OR UNQUIET SEAS, ... 360 ALF POLLEXFEN   19
BY QUIET NATURES UNDERSTOOD   . . . . 405 FOR DAUGHTER   63
THOSE AMOROUS CRIES THAT OUT OF QUIET COME   . . . . . . 557 RIBH ECSTASY   7
MY TEMPTATION IS QUIET.   . . . . 575 ACRE OF GRASS   7
QUIET THE DOG, TETHER THE PONY   . . . . 617 LONG-LEG FLY   3
ALL THINGS ARE QUIET IN THE EVE'S WIDE EYE.   . . . . . . 662 ISLE STAT II 2   6
AND ALL WAS QUIET ROUND ME SPREAD, ... 670 ISLE STAT II 3   112
AS QUIET AS THE CLAY-COLD DEAD.   . . . . 670 ISLE STAT II 3   113
AS QUIET AS THE LITTLE RIVULETS.   . . . . 698 MOSADA 2   57
ENCLOSE A QUIET PLACE OF BEDS BOX-BORDERED, BEES, ... 710 FERENCZ RENYI   24
WITH QUIET SHADE ITS EVER DEWY-PLOT.   . . . . 714 FERENCZ RENYI   109
WITH QUIET SHADE ITS EVER DEWY SPOT.   . . . . 714 FERENCZ RENYI V 109
WITH QUIET SHADE ITS EVER DEWY PLOT.   . . . . 714 FERENCZ RENYI V 109
QUIET-EYED
THE DRUID, GREY, WOOD-NURTURED, QUIET-EYED, ... 101 ROSE UPON ROOD   4
QUIETNESS
SHOOT ON HIM SHAFTS OF QUIETNESS, THAT HE MAY EVER KEEP   . 75 ANASHU VIJAYA   81
SHOOT ON HIM SHAFTS OF QUIETNESS, AND ORDER HIM TO KEEP   . 75 ANASHU VIJAYA V 81
"I AM LONE LADY QUIETNESS, MY SWEET, ... 716 DWELT SYCAMORE   13
QUIET'S
QUIET'S WILD HEART, LIKE DAILY MEAT: . . . . 196 BAILE AILLINN   178
QUIETUDE
FOR THREE DAYS MORE IN DREADFUL QUIETUDE, ... 110 CUCHULAIN SEA   78
UPON A MEASURED QUIETUDE.   . . . . 138 TO IRELAND   16
UPON HER HOLY QUIETUDE.   . . . . 138 TO IRELAND V 16
QUINTO-CENTO
WHAT QUINTO-CENTO FINGER FASHIONED IT, ... 444 SCHOOL CHILDR V 26
QUIRE
WITH YOUR HARMONIOUS QUIRE, ... 174 ELEMENT POWERS V   8
QUIRES
AND A FAR SOUND OF FEATHERY QUIRES: . . . . 13 OISIN 1   166
QUITE
QUITE SOON THE CORNFIELD, WHERE THE POPPIES GROW,   . . . 699 MOSADA 3   7
QUIVER
AND NOW THE WARMTH OF SIGHS, AND AFTER THE QUIVER OF LIPS.   . 47 OISIN 3   8
. . . AND THE QUIVER OF STRETCHED BOWSTRINGS, ... 62 OISIN 3   207
A CLOUDY QUIVER OVER PAIRC-NA-LEE.   . . . . 198 SEVEN WOODS   14
QUIVERING
IN A RED AND QUIVERING GARMENT   . . . . 160 CAP AND BELLS   15
IN A GARMENT RED AND QUIVERING, ... 160 CAP AND BELLS V 15
THE QUIVERING HALF-CLOSED EYELIDS, THE RAGS OF CLOUD OR   . 427 PHANTOM HATRED   26
  OF LACE,
DOTH NOT YON BIRD, YON QUIVERING BIRD, REJOICE?   . . . . 652 ISLE STAT I 2   21
PIERCING THE QUIVERING WATERS THROUGH AND THROUGH,   . . 664 ISLE STAT II 2   44
DID I ON QUIVERING PINIONS HASTE, ... 670 ISLE STAT II 3   111
WAS BROKEN IN HIS QUIVERING HAND.   . . . . 671 ISLE STAT II 3   126
HIS BODY SHAKE? AY, QUIVERING AS YON SMOKE   . . . . . 683 SEEKER   36
TO DEATH. HIS LIPS ARE GLUED, WITH QUIVERING TOUCH,   . . . 684 SEEKER V 63
YOU'RE PALE, MY LORD. HIS LIPS ARE QUIVERING: . . . . 704 MOSADA 3   127
AND SEIZE HER, AND THUS FLOATS HER QUIVERING CRY: . . . 714 FERENCZ RENYI   105
QUOTE
THAT THEY WOULD SIGH AND QUOTE WITH LEARNED LOOKS   . . . 205 ADAMS CURSE   25
RABBAN   SEE ABD-AL-RABBAN AL-RABBAN
RABBIT
A RABBIT OLD AND LAME LIMPED DOWN THE PATH: . . . . . 80 EPHEMERA   15
AND SHY AS A RABBIT, ... 89 ISLE IN WATER   13
LIKE SOME OLD RABBIT TO MY CLEFT   . . . . 307 HOUR DAWN   105
INTO A RABBIT HOLE   . . . . 571 THREE BUSHES V 51
A STRICKEN RABBIT IS CRYING OUT, ... 633 MAN AND ECHO   45
RABBIT-HOLE
INTO A RABBIT-HOLE   . . . . 571 THREE BUSHES   51
RACE
THE MIGHTIER MASTERS OF A MIGHTIER RACE: . . . . . . 38 OISIN 2   133
OF PLANETS WATCHING, WATCHING THE RACE OF HARES   . . . . 44 OISIN 2 V 228B
"LAST OF MY RACE, THREE THINGS I RULE ALONE--   . . . . . 45 OISIN 2 V 239A
AND A SMALL AND A FEEBLE RACE STOOPING WITH MATTOCK AND   . 58 OISIN 3 V 164
  SPADE.

```
                                                      PAGE      TITLE           LINE
RACE   (CONTINUED)
      AND A SMALL AND FEEBLE RACE STOOPING WITH MATTOCK          58 OISIN 3       V  164
         AND SPADE.
      SLEIVEENS WERE ALL HIS RACE:  . . . . . . . . .            92 FATHER OHART      6
      LIKE THE PALE WATERS IN THEIR WINTRY RACE,  . . . .       112 ROSE OF WORLD     8
      THERE DWELT A GAY, EXULTING, GENTLE RACE  . . . . . .     127 DREAM OF FAERY   20
      OLD SILENCE BIDS ITS CHOSEN RACE REJOICE,  . . . . .      127 DREAM OF FAERY   31
      AND THEREFORE, FRIEND, IF YOUR GREAT RACE WERE RUN  . .   265 THESE CLOUDS      7
      OUT YONDER, WHERE THE RACE COURSE IS,  . . . . . . .      266 GALWAY RACES    V  1
      CRYING ALOUD AS THE RACE COURSE IS,  . . . . . . . .      266 GALWAY RACES      14
      TOWARDS NIGHTFALL UPON A RACE  . . . . . . . . . . .      325 ROBERT GREGORY   31
      HE RODE A RACE WITHOUT A BIT?  . . . . . . . . . .        326 ROBERT GREGORY   63
      TO WRITE FOR MY OWN RACE . . . . . . . . . . . . .        347 FISHERMAN        11
      HER RACE  . . . . . . . . . . . . . . . . . . .           365 HER RACE          T
      UNRECKONABLE RACE:  . . . . . . . . . . . . . . .         365 HER RACE          8
      ROSE OUT OF THE RACE  . . . . . . . . . . . . . .         480 BLOOD AND MOON    4
      UNDER MY WINDOW-LEDGE THE WATERS RACE,  . . . . . .       490 COOLE BALLYLEE    1
      BUT THE GOLDEN RACE LOOKS DIM,  . . . . . . . . . .       530 DELPHIC ORACLE    4
      DID EVER MAN RIDE SUCH A RACE?  . . . . . . . . . .       570 THREE BUSHES     47
      THAT OF RACE AND THAT OF SOUL,  . . . . . . . . . .       637 BEN BULBEN       15
      POOR RACE OF LEAFY ARCADY, YOUR LOVE . . . . . . .        650 ISLE STAT I 1   145
      OF LOVE FROM OUT A DREAMLESS RACE FOR STRIFE, . . . .     684 SEEKER           58
      IN TRUTH, AN EVIL RACE.  WHY STRIVE FOR HER, . . . .      696 MOSADA 2          9
      LAY DOWN THE BURDEN OF THY RACE;  . . . . . . . . .       736 SUMMER EVENING   14
      "I ASK THAT I AND ALL MY RACE,"  . . . . . . . . .        742 EARL PAUL        61
      "MAY STAND BEFORE THY RACE AND THEE  . . . . . . .        742 EARL PAUL        63
RACECOURSE
      CRYING ALOUD AS THE RACECOURSE IS,  . . . . . . . .       266 GALWAY RACES      14
      THERE WHERE THE RACECOURSE IS . . . . . . . . . .         266 GALWAY RACES    V  1
RACE-COURSE
      CRYING ALOUD AS THE RACE-COURSE IS,  . . . . . . .        266 GALWAY RACES    V  14
RACECOURSES
      FOR HORSEMANSHIP AT MEETS OR AT RACECOURSES, . . . .      325 ROBERT GREGORY   35
      IN MUSCULAR YOUTH, AT MEETS OR AT RACECOURSES,  . . .     325 ROBERT GREGORY V  35
RACE-COURSES
      FOR HORSEMANSHIP AT MEETS OR AT RACE-COURSES, . . . .     325 ROBERT GREGORY V  35
RACED
      THE HORSE TOWARDS THE MUSIC RACED,  . . . . . . .         13 OISIN 1            169
      THE STEED TOWARDS THE MUSIC RACED,  . . . . . . .         13 OISIN 1         V  169
RACES
      AT GALWAY RACES . . . . . . . . . . . . . . . .           266 GALWAY RACES      T
      GALWAY RACES  . . . . . . . . . . . . . . . . .           266 GALWAY RACES    V  T
RACHLIN
      . . . FROM RACHLIN TO BERA OF SHIPS. . . . . . .          58 OISIN 3           160
RACK
      THEN THEY AND THEIR WISDOM WENT TO RACK: . . . . . .      566 LAPIS LAZULI     28
RADDLED
      AND RAISING ARMS ALL RADDLED WITH THE DYE, . . . . .      105 CUCHULAIN SEA     7
      SHE SMOTE WITH RADDLED FIST, AND WHERE HER SON  . . .     106 CUCHULAIN SEA    18
RADDLING
      TO EMER, RADDLING RAIMENT IN HER DUN,  . . . . . . .      105 CUCHULAIN SEA     2
RADICAL
      THE SOUL RECOVERS RADICAL INNOCENCE  . . . . . . . .      405 FOR DAUGHTER     66
RAFTER
      THAT SHAKES A MOULDERING COBWEB FROM THE RAFTER: . . .    130 BOOK STORIES     19
      LEAPING TO SHAKE A COBWEB FROM THE RAFTER: . . . .        130 BOOK STORIES   V  19
      AND SHAKE A MOULDERING COBWEB FROM THE RAFTER, . . .      130 BOOK STORIES   V  19
RAFTERY'S
      THEN DARKENING THROUGH "DARK" RAFTERY'S "CELLAR" DROP, .  490 COOLE BALLYLEE    4
RAG
      IN AS FOUL A RAG: . . . . . . . . . . . . . . .           525 DANCING DAYS      6
      CONSUMING ITS RAG AND BONE,  . . . . . . . . . . .        575 ACRE OF GRASS    11
      FOR PASSING ROUND THE BOTTLE WITH GIRLS IN RAG OR SILK,   592 PILGRIM        V  2
      SO COME IN RAG OR COME IN SILK, IN CLOAK OR COUNTRY SHAWL, 593 PILGRIM       V  22
      IN THE FOUL RAG AND BONE SHOP OF THE HEART.  . . . . .    630 CIRCUS ANIMALS V  40
RAG-AND-BONE
      IN THE FOUL RAG-AND-BONE SHOP OF THE HEART.  . . . .      630 CIRCUS ANIMALS   40
RAGE        SEE WAR-RAGE
      KINGFISHER COLOUR GREW WITH RAGE.  HE ROSE . . . . .      40 OISIN 2         V  169
      LIGHT IS MAN'S LOVE, AND LIGHTER IS MAN'S RAGE:  . . .    45 OISIN 2            243
      . . . WHO COULD BREAK UP THE WORLD IN THEIR RAGE: . .     62 OISIN 3            214
      BUT NOW THE WAR RAGE IN CUCHULAIN WOKE, . . . . . .       110 CUCHULAIN SEA  V  65
      AND CRAZY RASCALS RAGE THEIR FILL  . . . . . . . .        131 OLD PENSIONER     9
      WHEN TIME BEGAN TO RANT AND RAGE  . . . . . . . .         138 TO IRELAND       10
      TO RANT AND RAGE IN FLOOD AND WIND:  . . . . . . .        138 TO IRELAND       26
      THE BEGGAR IN A RAGE BEGAN . . . . . . . . . . .          306 HOUR DAWN        80
      AND THAT HE WILL TURN GREEN WITH RAGE  . . . . . .        385 ROBARTES DANCE   16
      WHETHER IN PUBLIC OR IN SECRET RAGE  . . . . . . .        413 TOWER            99
      HOW THE DAEMONIC RAGE  . . . . . . . . . . . . .          419 MY HOUSE         16
      HOW THE DEMONIC RAGE . . . . . . . . . . . . . .          419 MY HOUSE       V  16
      THE RAGE DRIVEN, RAGE TORMENTED, AND RAGE HUNGRY TROOP,   426 PHANTOM HATRED V  11
      THE RAGE DRIVEN, RAGE TORMENTED, AND RAGE HUNGRY TROOP,   426 PHANTOM HATRED V  11
      THE RAGE DRIVEN, RAGE TORMENTED, AND RAGE HUNGRY TROOP,   426 PHANTOM HATRED V  11
      OR EYES THAT RAGE HAS BRIGHTENED, ARMS IT HAS MADE LEAN,  427 PHANTOM HATRED   27
      OF EYES THAT RAGE HAS BRIGHTENED, ARMS IT HAS MADE LEAN,  427 PHANTOM HATRED V  27
      THAT IMAGE CAN BRING WILDNESS, BRING A RAGE  . . . .      431 NINETEEN 19      80
      MUCH DID I RAGE WHEN YOUNG,  . . . . . . . . . .          434 YOUTH AND AGE     1
      AND THINKING OF THAT FIT OF GRIEF OR RAGE  . . . . .      443 SCHOOL CHILDR    17
      I RAGE AT MY OWN IMAGE IN THE GLASS  . . . . . . .        447 HERO GIRL FOOL    1
      FOR ALL MEN LOVE YOUR WORTH: AND I MUST RAGE . . . .      447 HERO GIRL FOOL V  B
      PUT HER IN A RAGE.  . . . . . . . . . . . . . .           504 QUARREL IN AGE    6
```

RAGE   (CONTINUED)
   IN NOBLE RAGE REPLIED . . . .   516 MANS SONG   5
   TOO OLD FOR A MAN'S LOVE I STOOD IN RAGE   . . . . .   536 HER VISION   3
   HE IN HIS RAGE DECLARED: . . . .   539 MEETING   14
   IT HAD NOT TOUCHED OUR LIVES. BUT POPULAR RAGE, ...   542 PARN FUNERAL 1   20
   LET THE FOOLS RAGE, I SWERVED IN NAUGHT, ...   577 WHAT THEN   18
   YOU THINK IT HORRIBLE THAT LUST AND RAGE   . . . . .   591 SPUR   1
   AND FILL ME WITH THY RAGE, THAT I MAY BRUISE . . . . .   698 MOSADA 2   54
RAGED
   I HAVE RAGED AT MY OWN STRENGTH BECAUSE YOU HAVE LOVED IT.   448 HERO GIRL FOOL   9
   TOO OLD FOR A MAN'S LOVE I STOOD AND RAGED . . . . . .   536 HER VISION   V   1
RAGE-DRIVEN
   THE RAGE-DRIVEN, RAGE-TORMENTED, AND RAGE-HUNGRY TROOP,   426 PHANTOM HATRED   11
RAGE-HUNGRY
   THE RAGE-DRIVEN, RAGE-TORMENTED, AND RAGE-HUNGRY TROOP,   426 PHANTOM HATRED   11
RAGES
   RAGES AT HIS OWN IMAGE IN THE ENAMELLED SEA . . . . .   77 INDIAN TO LOVE V   5
   THOUGH HAMLET RAMBLES AND LEAR RAGES, ...   566 LAPIS LAZULI   21
RAGE-TORMENTED
   THE RAGE-DRIVEN, RAGE-TORMENTED, AND RAGE-HUNGRY TROOP,   426 PHANTOM HATRED   11
RAGGED
   AND SHAKE THEIR RAGGED WINGS: ALAS! . . . .   136 TWO TREES   38
   HE HAD RAGGED LONG GRASS-COLOURED HAIR! . . . . . .   190 BAILE AILLINN   26
   HE HAD RAGGED, LONG GRASS-YELLOW HAIR! . . . . . .   190 BAILE AILLINN V   26
   WHEN IN RAGGED VAPOUR THEY MUTTER NIGHT AND DAY, ...   206 HANRAHANS SONG V   2
   THE RAGGED WOOD . . . .   210 RAGGED WOOD   T
   I HEARD UNDER A RAGGED HOLLOW WOOD, ...   210 RAGGED WOOD   V   1
   O HURRY TO THE RAGGED WOOD, FOR THERE . . . .   211 RAGGED WOOD   9
   AFTER A RAGGED HAT IN BISCAY BAY: . . . .   270 PARDON FATHERS   14
   OLD RAGGED ELMS, OLD THORNS INNUMERABLE, ...   419 MY HOUSE   5
   UNDER THE RAGGED THORN? . . . .   519 LOVES LONENESS   10
   NO RAGGED BEGGAR-MAN. . . . .   567 FROM JAPANESE   6
   NO RAGGED BEGGAR MAN, ...   567 FROM JAPANESE V   6
   A GREAT BLACK RAGGED BIRD APPEARED WHEN I WAS IN THE BOAT: 593 PILGRIM   16
   WITH A RAGGED BANDIT CLOAK, ...   627 STATES HOLIDAY   31
   GAZE ON TILL RAGGED TIME HIMSELF DECAY. . . . .   672 ISLE STAT II 3   148
   ARE TWO RAGGED CHILDREN BRIGHT— . . . .   731 STREET DANCERS   4
RAGING
   RAGING AT HIS OWN IMAGE IN THE ENAMELLED SEA. . . . .   77 INDIAN TO LOVE   5
   RAGING AT HIS OWN IMAGE IN THE DIM ENAMELLED SEA . . .   77 INDIAN TO LOVE V   5
   A HEAVENLY MANSION, RAGING IN THE DARK, ...   491 COOLE BALLYLEE V   40D
   A HEAVENLY MANSION, RAGING IN THE DARK. . . . . . .   495 CHOICE   4
   RAVENING, RAGING, AND UPROOTING THAT HE MAY COME . . . .   563 MERU   6
   MY FATHER UPON THE ABBEY STAGE, BEFORE HIM A RAGING CROWD!   577 LOFTY THINGS   2
RAGS
   . . . SAILS TURNING TO THREADBARE RAGS: . . . .   55 OISIN 3   118
   . . . SAILS TURNING TO THREAD-BARE RAGS: . . . .   55 OISIN 3   V   118
   WHILE HE'D RUMMAGED RAGS AND HAIR, ...   299 THREE HERMITS   29
   A BUNDLE OF RAGS UPON A CRUTCH, ...   302 HOUR DAWN   2
   IF THERE BE RAGS ENOUGH HE WILL KNOW HER NAME . . . . .   351 HER PRAISE   15
   "VENGEANCE FOR JACQUES MOLAY." IN CLOUD-PALE RAGS, OR   426 PHANTOM HATRED   10
     IN LACE,
   "VENGENCE FOR JACQUES MOLAY." IN CLOUD PALE RAGS, OR IN   426 PHANTOM HATRED V   10
     LACE,
   THE QUIVERING HALF-CLOSED EYELIDS, THE RAGS OF CLOUD OR   427 PHANTOM HATRED   26
     OF LACE,
   FOR PASSING ROUND THE BOTTLE WITH GIRLS IN RAGS OR SILK,   592 PILGRIM   2
   SO COME IN RAGS OR COME IN SILK, IN CLOAK OR COUNTRY SHAWL,   593 PILGRIM   22
   OLD IRON, OLD BONES, OLD RAGS, THAT RAVING SLUT . . . .   630 CIRCUS ANIMALS   37
RAIL
   EVEN LIKE THESE TO RAIL AND SWEAT . . . .   294 HATED PLAYBOY   5
   AND LIKE THESE TO RAIL AND SWEAT . . . .   294 HATED PLAYBOY V   5
   THEY SAT UPON THEIR HEELS TO RAIL, ...   297 THREE BEGGARS   53
   OR SAT UPON THEIR HEELS TO RAIL . . . .   297 THREE BEGGARS V   53
   AND RUBBED ALONG THE RAIL HIS NOSE. . . . .   725 LEGEND   28
RAILING
   IF RAILING AND REPROACH AND MOCKERY . . . .   243 SHADOW WATER B   438
RAILS   SEE ALTAR-RAILS
   O COLLEENS, KNEELING BY YOUR ALTAR RAILS LONG HENCE, . .   173 SPEAKS HEARERS V   1
   O, WOMEN, KNEELING BY YOUR ALTAR RAILS LONG HENCE, . . .   173 SPEAKS HEARERS V   1
   AND THE GHASTLY GHOST-FLAMES GLIMMER ALL ALONG THE TAFFRAIL   719 PHANTOM SHIP   21
     RAILS
   AND THE GHASTLY GHOST FLAMES GLIMMER ALONG THE TAFFREL   719 PHANTOM SHIP   V   21
     RAILS,
RAIMENT
   AND BY ME, IN SOFT RED RAIMENT, THE FENIANS MOVED IN LOUD   53 OISIN 3   93
     STREAMS,
   TO EMER, RADDLING RAIMENT IN HER DUN, ...   105 CUCHULAIN SEA   2
   AND CALM, ROBED ALL IN RAIMENT MOONY WHITE. . . . . .   693 MOSADA 1   77
RAIN
   ALL EMPTIED OF PURPLE HOURS AS A BEGGAR'S CLOAK IN THE   63 OISIN 3   219
     RAIN,
   IS BUT A SLIDING DROP OF RAIN BETWEEN HIS PETALS WIDE. . .   76 INDIAN ON GOD   12
   IS BUT A SLIDING DROP OF RAIN WITHIN HIS PETALS WIDE." . .   76 INDIAN ON GOD V   12
   WHO HAVE SOUGHT MORE THAN IS IN RAIN OR DEW . . . . .   114 ROSE OF BATTLE   16
   ALTHOUGH I SHELTER FROM THE RAIN . . . .   131 OLD PENSIONER   1
   MIRRORED IN STREAMS THAT NEITHER HAIL NOR RAIN . . . .   184 QUEEN MAEVE   89
   BY RIVERS WHERE THE RAIN HAS NEVER DIMMED . . . . .   184 QUEEN MAEVE   V   87
   BY RIVERS WHERE NOR RAIN NOR HAIL HAS DIMMED . . . .   184 QUEEN MAEVE   V   87
   MIRRORED IN WATERS THAT NOR HAIL NOR RAIN . . . . .   184 QUEEN MAEVE   V   89
   WHEN THE RAIN IS PELTING OUT OF THE WINTRY AIR! . . . .   207 HANRAHANS SONG V   12

	PAGE	TITLE		LINE

RAIN   (CONTINUED)
    THE SOUND OF THE RAIN OR SOUND . . . .   419 MY HOUSE   6
    OF THE FOUL WEATHER, HAIL AND RAIN, ... 424 ROAD AT DOOR   9
    BETWEEN TWO BUSHES UNDER THE RAIN; . . . .   551 SONGS REWRIT 1 14
    WITH LITTLE CRIES OF JOY HE KISSED THE RAIN . . . . . 688 TWO TITANS   33
    DEEP IN HIS SOUL, LIKE RAIN UPON A SOIL . . . . . .   692 MOSADA 1   56
RAIN-BEATEN
    WITH ALL THEIR ANCIENT FACES LIKE RAIN-BEATEN STONES, . . 318 MAGI   4
RAINBOW
    LIKE DROPS OF FROZEN RAINBOW LIGHT, ...   14 OISIN 1   183
    DROPPING LIQUID RAINBOW LIGHT, ...   732 STREET DANCERS 33
RAINLESS
    AT EVENING IN THEIR RAINLESS LANDS." . . . .   7 OISIN 1   70
    AT EVENING IN THEIR RAINLESS LANDS. . . . .   7 OISIN 1   V   66
RAINS
    THE RAINS ARE FROM HIS DRIPPING WING, THE MOONBEAMS FROM   76 INDIAN ON GOD   8
        HIS EYE.
    AND RAINS DOWN LIFE UNTIL THE BASIN SPILLS, ...   417 ANCEST HOUSES   4
    AND MOUNTS MORE DIZZY HIGH THE MORE IT RAINS . . . .   417 ANCEST HOUSES   5
RAISE
    THAT RAISE THEIR HEADS AND WANDER SINGING, ...   27 OISIN 1   419
    SING, O YOU LITTLE STARS! O SING AND RAISE YOUR RAPTUROUS   72 ANASHU VIJAYA 20
        CAROL
    SING, OH YE LITTLE STARS! OH, SING, AND RAISE YOUR   72 ANASHU VIJAYA V 20
        RAPTUROUS CAROL
    SING, TILL YOU RAISE YOUR HANDS AND SIGH, ...   73 ANASHU VIJAYA 45
    SING, TILL YE RAISE YOUR HANDS AND SIGH, ...   73 ANASHU VIJAYA V 45
    THAT MAKES ME FEAR TO RAISE A HAND AGAINST HIM, ... 222 SHADOW WATER B V 16A
    HOW CAN WE RAISE THE KEEN THAT DO NOT KNOW . . . . .   240 SHADOW WATER B 389
    AND RAISE HIS PILLAR STONE." KING EOCHAID SAID, . . . 280 TWO KINGS   V 83
    DRAW ROUND AND RAISE A SHOUT; . . . .   584 GHOST ROG CASE 38
    THEN BID THEM RAISE MY STATUE ON THE SHORE; . . . . . 663 ISLE STAT II 2 18
    GO UP AND DOWN, AND RAISE THEIR HEADS AND SING . . . . 682 SEEKER   30
    MY ECHOING HEART. NOW RAISE THY VOICE AND SPEAK! . . . 683 SEEKER   47
    I HEAR THE MURMUR AS THEY RAISE THE BEAMS . . . . . . 699 MOSADA 3   17
    RAISE THE DOOR-PIN WITH ALARM, ...   727 LOVERS QUARREL 52
    TO RAISE INTO BEING . . . .   784 WOMANS BEAUTY   13
RAISED   SEE UP-RAISED
    AND WEPT, AND RAISED THEIR LAMENTING HANDS. . . . . .   10 OISIN 1   112
    THEY WEPT, AND RAISED LAMENTING HANDS. . . . .   10 OISIN 1   V 112
    HURRIED AWAY, AND OVER HER RAISED . . . .   12 OISIN 1   V 142B
    IN OUR RAISED EYES THERE FLASHED A GLOW . . . . . .   22 OISIN 1   327
    HE SHIVERING PAUSED, AND RAISED HIS HEAD AND SCREAMED. .   30 OISIN 2   V 25
    A LITTLE WAY WITHIN THE GLOOM A ROEBUCK RAISED HIS EYES   76 INDIAN ON GOD 13
    AND RAISED ABOVE HER MOUND . . . .   123 DREAM OF DEATH   6
    IT SEEMED THEY RAISED THEIR LITTLE SILVER HEADS, . . . 126 DREAM OF FAERY   6
    THAT RAISED THEIR HANDS AGAINST HIM. THERE ARE SOME . . 235 SHADOW WATER B 291
    AND WITH THAT CRY I HAVE RAISED MY CRY. . . . . . . 361 ALF POLLEXFEN   39
    OR RANK, RAISED FROM A COMMON . . . .   365 HER RACE   7
    THE AVENGING LEAF THOSE FIELDS RAISED UP AGAINST IT. . . 487 SEVEN SAGES   20
    THE ARCADIANS BRING, AND BID THE STONE BE RAISED . . . 663 ISLE STAT II 2 25
    HE'LL SNAP HIS SWORD. RAISED IS THE LION'S PAW. . . . 664 ISLE STAT II 2 63
    THE SHEPHERD RAISED HIS ARMS AND SANK, ...   673 ISLE STAT II 3 187
RAISEST
    A SCARLET BLOOM. WHY RAISEST THOU, PALE ONE, ... 673 ISLE STAT II 3 196
RAISING
    AND RAISING ARMS ALL RADDLED WITH THE DYE, ... 105 CUCHULAIN SEA   7
RAJA'S
    HAST THOU NOT KNOWN A RAJA'S DREAMLESS SLUMBER? . . . . 724 KANVA ON SELF   8
RAJAS
    OF RAJAS AND MAHRAJAS BEYOND NUMBER? . . . .   724 KANVA ON SELF   6
RAM
    WHEN I HAVE SHUT THESE EWES AND THIS OLD RAM . . . .   343 SHEP GOATHERD   113
    THE TRIVIAL DAYS AND RAM THEM WITH THE SUN, ... 500 VACILLATION   21
RAMBLE
    MUST RAMBLE, AND THIN OUT . . . .   484 SPILT MILK   3
RAMBLED
    OF ALL THAT RAMBLED THERE . . . .   526 AM OF IRELAND   9
RAMBLES
    THOUGH HAMLET RAMBLES AND LEAR RAGES, ... 566 LAPIS LAZULI   21
RAMBLING
    THAT RAMBLING JAILBIRD BILLY SAID; . . . .   332 ROUND TOWER   26
    IN RAMBLING TALK WITH AN IMAGE OF AIR; . . . . . .   357 BROKEN DREAMS   40
    AND BRING BEAUTY'S BLIND RAMBLING CELEBRANT; . . . .   412 TOWER   91
    SAID THE RAMBLING, SHAMBLING TRAVELLING-MAN; . . . . . 788 HAWTHORN TREE   2
    SAID THE RAMBLING, SHAMBLING TRAVELLING-MAN; . . . . . 788 HAWTHORN TREE   10
RAMMED
    AS THOUGH TO DRAW THEM CLOSER YET. RAMMED FULL . . . . 579 DOR WELLESLEY   5
RAMPARTS
    OVER THE RAMPARTS AND THE TOWERS, ...   212 BLESS PSALTER   6
    RAMPARTS AT YOUR EAR, ...   492 ANNE GREGORY   4
RAN
    RAN THROUGH THE FOAM AND RAN TO THIS . . . .   6 OISIN 1   58
    RAN THROUGH THE FOAM AND RAN TO THIS . . . .   6 OISIN 1   58
    FOR LOVE OF USHEEN MY FEET RAN . . . .   6 OISIN 1   V   57
    AND WHEN THEY HEARD HER VOICE THEY RAN . . . . . .   15 OISIN 1   213
    NO CENTURIES COULD DIM, AND A WORD RAN . . . . . .   38 OISIN 2   127
    NOT LOADED CENTURIES MIGHT VAPOUR. RAN . . . . . .   38 OISIN 2   V 127
    AMID THE SHADES OF NIGHT, HE CHANGED AND RAN . . . .   40 OISIN 2   174
    I AWOKE! THE STRANGE HORSE WITHOUT SUMMONS OUT OF   54 OISIN 3   105
        THE DISTANCE RAN,

643

```
                                                      PAGE     TITLE           LINE
RAN   (CONTINUED)
    HIS MIND RAN ALL ON MONEY CARES AND FEARS, . . . .    127  DREAM OF FAERY        14
    AND HE RAN TO THE DOOR OF HIS HOUSE: . . . . . . .    145  HOST OF AIR     V   40C
    WHO CALLED ME BY MY NAME AND RAN . . . . . .         150  WANDER AENGUS         15
    THAT CALLED ME BY MY NAME AND RAN . . . . . .        150  WANDER AENGUS   V     15
    SUDDENLY, AND RAN AT THEM AND HARRIED THEM. . .      185  QUEEN MAEVE          119
    AND WHEN THE UPROAR RAN ALONG THE GRASS . . . . .    186  QUEEN MAEVE          127
    HE RAN AND LAUGHED UNTIL HE CAME . . . . . . . .     194  BAILE AILLINN        128
    WHERE THAT WISE HARPER'S FINGER RAN. . . . . . .     195  BAILE AILLINN        156
    WHERE THAT WISE HARPER'S FINGERS RAN. . . . . .      195  BAILE AILLINN   V    156
    AND ALL THE ALE RAN OUT AT THE NEW MOON: . . . .     222  SHADOW WATER B  V     11
    AENGUS AND EDAIN RAN UP OUT OF THE WAVE-- . . . .    231  SHADOW WATER B       196
    MEN RAN UPON THE SHORE. . . . . . . . . . . . .      253  HIS DREAM       V      4
    BEFORE THEIR SLEEPY EYELIDS RAN . . . . . . . .      272  GREY ROCK             30
    AND AFTER, WHEN HER BLOOD RAN WILD, . . . . . .      272  GREY ROCK             44
    HAD PERISHED THERE, BUT THE DANES RAN, . . . . .     274  GREY ROCK             74
    BUT THE STAG STOOPED AND RAN AT HIM, AND PASSED, . . 277  TWO KINGS             12
    AND RAN AT HIM, AND PASSED, AND AS IT PASSED . . .   277  TWO KINGS       V    12A
    THE DISEMBOWELLED HORSE.  KING EOCHAID RAN . . . .   278  TWO KINGS             45
    HE RAN TOWARDS THE HOUSE HIS FATHERS BUILT . . .     279  TWO KINGS       V    45E
    BUT THAT SWEET-SOUNDING VOICE RAN ON: "WOMAN, . . .  284  TWO KINGS            165
    INDIFFERENT HOW THE RANCOUR RAN, . . . . . . . .     288  TO WEALTHY MAN        21
    EUNUCHS RAN THROUGH HELL AND MET . . . . . . . .     294  HATED PLAYBOY          2
    AS THOUGH SOME OTHER NAME RAN IN HIS HEAD. . . . .   351  HER PRAISE             9
    OF SOME STRANGE WOMAN'S NAME THAT RAN IN HIS HEAD.   351  HER PRAISE      V      9
    THEY RAN FROM CRADLE TO CRADLE TILL AT LAST . . .    375  PHASES OF MOON        69
    RAN OUT OF MY SIGHT: . . . . . . . . . . .           399  DEMON BEAST            4
    NOW THAT THE LOUD BEAST RAN . . . . . . . . . .      400  DEMON BEAST           16
    RAN AND WITH THE GARDEN SHEARS . . . . . . . . .     410  TOWER                 30
    AND THROUGH THE CENTURIES RAN . . . . . . . . .      421  MY TABLE              20
    AND WHEN THROUGH ALL THE TOWN THERE RAN . . . . .    436  FOR MY SON            25
    I RAN, I RAN, FROM MY LOVE'S SIDE BECAUSE MY HEART WENT   450  OWEN AHERNE       12
       MAD.
    I RAN, I RAN, FROM MY LOVE'S SIDE BECAUSE MY HEART WENT   450  OWEN AHERNE       12
       MAD.
    WHAT STIR RAN THROUGH THE COUNTRYSIDE . . . . . .    488  CRAZED MOON           10
    THROUGH INTRICATE MOTIONS RAN . . . . . . . . .      506  STREAM AND SUN         1
    OR BUT TO FIND IF WITHERED VEIN RAN BLOOD, . . . .   537  HER VISION             6
    STARED AT THE WINE-DARK NAIL, OR DARK THAT RAN . .   537  HER VISION            10
    HE RAN ON AHEAD . . . . . . . . . . . . . .          595  COLONEL MARTIN        42
    THAT ON TWO WHEELS RAN . . . . . . . . . . .         628  JANE MOUNTAIN         14
    MY HEART RAN WILD WHEN IT HEARD . . . . . . . .      783  GREY ROUND            21
RANCOROUS
    A LEVELLING, RANCOROUS, RATIONAL SORT OF MIND . . . . . 486  SEVEN SAGES        11
RANCOUR
    INDIFFERENT HOW THE RANCOUR RAN, . . . . . . . .     288  TO WEALTHY MAN        21
    NO CIVIL RANCOUR TORN THE LAND APART. . . . . .      542  PARN FUNERAL 2         4
RANDY
    PORTER-DRINKERS' RANDY LAUGHTER: . . . . . . .       640  BEN BULBEN            77
RANG
    TOGETHER, WHILE THE DARK WOODS RANG, . . . . . .      16  OISIN 1              227
RANGE
    AND BIRDS THAT ON THE SEVEN SEAS RANGE. . . . . .      4  OISIN 1         V    27A
    FROM CRESCENT TO ROUND THEY RANGE? . . . . . . .     379  CAT AND MOON          24
    THE RIDER, THE BIRDS THAT RANGE . . . . . . . .      393  EASTER 1916           46
RANGED
    FROM DREAM TO DREAM AND RHYME TO RHYME I HAVE RANGED  . .  357  BROKEN DREAMS    39
RANGER
    HOW CAME THIS RANGER . . . . . . . . . . . .         574  MAIDS 1ST SONG         1
RANK
    AND CLOUDS ARRAYED THEIR RANK ON RANK . . . . . .     12  OISIN 1              154
    AND CLOUDS ARRAYED THEIR RANK ON RANK . . . . . .     12  OISIN 1              154
    THE CLOUDS ARRAYED THEM RANK ON RANK . . . . . .      12  OISIN 1         V    154
    THE CLOUDS ARRAYED THEM RANK ON RANK . . . . . .      12  OISIN 1         V    154
    OR RANK, RAISED FROM A COMMON . . . . . . . . .      365  HER RACE               7
    RICHES DROVE OUT RANK, . . . . . . . . . . .         626  STATES HOLIDAY         2
    SO MUCH OF WEALTH AS MAY BEFIT THEIR RANK: . . . .   756  SHADOW WATER A  V    186
RANKED
    OF SOLDIERS RANKED IS ON A GRASSY SPOT, . . . . .    712  FERENCZ RENYI         64
RANKING
    RANKING HIS DRUIDS ROUND HIM TEN BY TEN, . . . . .   110  CUCHULAIN SEA         76
RANKS
    AND BROKE THE HEAVING RANKS OF BATTLE: . . . . .      10  OISIN 1              124
    AND HUSHED IN SLEEP THE ROARING RANKS OF BATTLE: . .  129  BOOK STORIES          7
RANN
    BALLAD AND STORY, RANN AND SONG: . . . . . . .       137  TO IRELAND             4
RANT
    WHEN TIME BEGAN TO RANT AND RAGE . . . . . . .       138  TO IRELAND            10
    TO RANT AND RAGE IN FLOOD AND WIND: . . . . . .      138  TO IRELAND            26
    AND ALL THE RANT A MIRROR OF MY MOOD: . . . . . .    490  COOLE BALLYLEE  V     13
    BUT THERE'S NO GOOD COMPLAINING, FOR MONEY'S RANT IS ON.  580  CURSE CROMWELL    10
RANTED
    I RANTED TO THE KNAVE AND FOOL, . . . . . . .        506  REMORSE SPEECH         1
RANTING
    A ROARING, RANTING JOURNEYMAN. . . . . . . . .       509  JANE REPROVED         13
    A ROARING RANTING JOURNEY-MAN. . . . . . . . .       509  JANE REPROVED   V     13
    HIS ROARING AND HIS RANTING . . . . . . . . .        606  SONGS BURDEN 1        16
    AND RANTING TIME RENEW. . . . . . . . . . .          606  SONGS BURDEN 1        20
    BUT WHERE THAT ROARING, RANTING CREW . . . . . .     787  HUDDON DUDDON          3
RANT'S
    AND ALL THE RANT'S A MIRROR OF MY MOOD: . . . . .    490  COOLE BALLYLEE        13
```

		PAGE	TITLE	LINE

RAPHAEL
   . . . MICHAEL, GABRIEL, AND RAPHAEL . . . .   174 ELEMENT POWERS V   T
RAPIER
   A STAR-LIT RAPIER, HALF BLOOD-DARK, ...   671 ISLE STAT II 3   125
RAPT   SEE SONG-RAPT
RAPTUROUS
   SING, O YOU LITTLE STARS! O SING AND RAISE YOUR RAPTUROUS   72 ANASHU VIJAYA   20
     CAROL
   SING, OH YE LITTLE STARS! OH, SING, AND RAISE YOUR   72 ANASHU VIJAYA V   20
     RAPTUROUS CAROL
   A RAPTUROUS MUSIC, TILL THE MORNING BREAK . . . . . .   137 TO SOME I TALK   14
RARE
   CLEAR FLUTED THEN THAT GOBLIN RARE-- . . . .   6 OISIN 1   V   54
   WE'VE TALKED AND TALKED, AND NOT A WHIT MORE RARE . .   659 ISLE STAT II 1   21
   THEN 'GAN TO SPEAK THAT GOBLIN RARE, ...   729 PRIEST FAIRY   37
RASCAL
   TRANSFORM THESE RASCAL BILLOWS INTO WOMEN . . . . . .   222 SHADOW WATER B   11
   FOOL, RASCAL, KNAVE, ...   496 MOHINI CHATTER   8
   WE KNOW WHAT RASCAL MIGHT HAS DEFILED, ...   614 MARCH SONGS 2   11
   MY RASCAL HEART IS PROUD . . . .   782 HEART FRIGHT   10
RASCALLY
   BUT A THIEVING RASCALLY CUR-- . . . .   552 SONGS REWRIT 2   7
RASCALS
   AND CRAZY RASCALS RAGE THEIR FILL . . . .   131 OLD PENSIONER   9
   THAT THE WORST ROGUES AND RASCALS HAD DIED OUT. . . .   428 NINETEEN 19   16
   THE THREE OLD RASCALS LAUGH ALOUD. . . . .   460 THREE MONUMENT   12
   OF RASCALS BLACK AND WHITE . . . .   597 MODEL LAUREATE   10
RASCHID   SEE AL-RASCHID
RASHID   SEE AL-RASHID
   BELOVED HAROUN EL RASHID, OCCUPIED . . . .   462 HARUN RASHID   V   24
   THAT YEAR WHEN GREAT HAROUN EL RASHID KILLED . . . .   462 HARUN RASHID   V   31
RAT
   WHAT MADE THAT SOUND? A RAT OR WATER-HEN . . . . . .   372 PHASES OF MOON   8
RATH
   . . . AND GUARDLESS THE SACRED CAIRN AND THE RATH, . . .   58 OISIN 3   163
   IN THE FAIRY-HAUNTED RATH, ...   706 DAWN-SONG   21
RATHER
   CALLED RATHER BAILE LITTLE-LAND, ...   189 BAILE AILLINN   17
   CALLED RATHER BAILE LITTLE LAND, ...   189 BAILE AILLINN V   17
RATIONAL
   A LEVELLING, RANCOROUS, RATIONAL SORT OF MIND . . . . .   486 SEVEN SAGES   11
RATS   SEE WATER-RATS
   THE DROWSY WATER RATS! . . . .   87 STOLEN CHILD   V   5
   SAVING THE RHYME RATS HEAR BEFORE THEY DIE. . . . . .   542 PARN FUNERAL 1   28
RATTLE
   AND HEARD THE FOEMEN'S BUCKLERS RATTLE, ...   10 OISIN 1   123
   AND HEARD THE FOEMAN'S BUCKLERS RATTLE, ...   10 OISIN 1   V   123
   THE RATTLE OF PEBBLES ON THE SHORE . . . .   485 NINETEENTH CEN   3
   THE RATTLE OF THOSE ARMS MAKES US AFRAID. . . . . . .   634 CUCHULAIN COMF   15
RATTLED
   AND RATTLED OUT A TUNE! . . . .   616 MARCH SONGS 3   9
   AND RATTLED OUT A TUNE! . . . .   616 MARCH SONGS 3   19
   AND RATTLED OUT A TUNE! . . . .   616 MARCH SONGS 3   29
RAVE
   TRICKLING ALONG THE EARTH, I RAVE! . . . .   19 OISIN 1   V   281
   AND SHAKE DOWN THUNDER ON THE STONES BECAUSE THE RED WINDS   207 HANRAHANS SONG V   7
     RAVE!
   MADE OF DIM GOLD RAVE OUT IN SECRET TOMBS! . . . . . .   235 SHADOW WATER B   295
   MADE OF DIM GOLD, RAVE OUT IN SECRET TOMBS, ...   765 SHADOW WATER A   345
RAVEL
   CAN RAVEL OUT WHAT'S IN MY HEAD. . . . .   295 THREE BEGGARS   12
RAVELLED
   WHERE PEOPLE LOVE BESIDE THE RAVELLED SEAS! . . . . .   126 DREAM OF FAERY   9
   WHATEVER RAVELLED WATERS RISE AND FALL . . . .   127 DREAM OF FAERY   32
   HAD RAVELLED HER OWN STORY OUT, ...   272 GREY ROCK   45
   BEFORE THAT END MUCH HAD SHE RAVELLED OUT . . . . . .   472 ALL SOUL NIGHT   51
RAVEN
   FIRST AS A RAVEN ON WHOSE ANCIENT WINGS . . . .   102 FERGUS DRUID   3
   HER RAVEN FLUTTERS. ROB HIM OF HIS FOOD . . . . . .   751 SHADOW WATER A   100
RAVEN-COVERED
   ON GABHRA'S RAVEN-COVERED PLAIN! . . . .   5 OISIN 1   43
RAVENING
   OF RAVENING SORROW, OR THE HAND OF WRATH? . . . . . .   42 OISIN 2   199
   RAVENING THROUGH CENTURY AFTER CENTURY, ...   563 MERU   5
   RAVENING, RAGING, AND UPROOTING THAT HE MAY COME . . .   563 MERU   6
RAVENS
   WHERE ROUND AND ROUND THE RAVENS GO. . . . .   5 OISIN 1   V   42
   AND NOW THE DAYLIGHT-DARKENING RAVENS FLOCK. . . . . .   43 OISIN 2   212
   ALL IS DONE NOW--I SEE THE RAVENS FLOCK-- . . . . . .   43 OISIN 2   V   212
   THE RAVENS OF UNRESTING THOUGHT! . . . .   136 TWO TREES   34
RAVING
   AND THEN ARISE, AND RAVING SLAY US ALL. . . . .   110 CUCHULAIN SEA   79
   YOUR RAVING OF A MESSAGE AND A HARP . . . .   237 SHADOW WATER B   331
   BUT ALL THAT'S RAVING. WHO IS THERE CAN COMPEL . . .   237 SHADOW WATER B   333
   OUT OF THAT RAVING TIDE--IS DRAWN BETWIXT . . . . . .   377 PHASES OF MOON   122
   BUT A RAVING AUTUMN SHEARS . . . .   475 EVA GORE-BOOTH   5
   OLD IRON, OLD BONES, OLD RAGS, THAT RAVING SLUT . . .   630 CIRCUS ANIMALS   37
RAY
   AND STOOD WITHIN! CLOTHED IN A MISTY RAY . . . . . .   36 OISIN 2   104
   AND STOOD WITHIN THE HALL. A MISTY RAY . . . .   36 OISIN 2   V   104

PAGE   TITLE   LINE

RAYLESS
    LIFT MY SOUL FROM RAYLESS·NIGHT—— · · · · · · · · ·   648 ISLE STAT I 1   95
RAYMOND
    RAYMOND LULLY AND HIS WIFE PERNELLA   · · · · · · ·   253 HIS DREAM   V   T
RAYS
    OR HOURS PASSED BY, YET HOLD THE MORNING RAYS · · · ·   30 OISIN 2   20
    YET DIMLY DEEM I THAT THE MORNING RAYS · · · · · ·   30 OISIN 2   V   20
    MELT DOWN, AS IT WERE WAX IN THE SUN'S RAYS: · · · ·   428 NINETEEN 19   12
    RETURNS THAT SOLDIER IN THE EVENING RAYS · · · · ·   711 FERENCZ RENYI   49
RAZOR-KEEN
    STILL RAZOR-KEEN, STILL LIKE A LOOKING-GLASS · · · ·   477 SELF AND SOUL   11
    STILL RAZOR-KEEN, STILL LIKE A LOOKING GLASS · · · ·   477 SELF AND SOUL V   11
REACH
    HOW SHOULD THEIR LUCK RUN HIGH ENOUGH TO REACH · · ·   264 HOUSE SHAKEN   9
    MOST OUT OF REACH? AND IS THAT SPECTRAL IMAGE · · ·   368 EGO DOMINUS   25
    LAST REACH OF GLITTERING STREAM · · · · · · · · ·   414 TOWER   143
    WHEREVER THE ORBIT OF THE MOON CAN REACH, · · · · ·   472 ALL SOUL NIGHT   55
    MAY REND WHAT COMES IN REACH. · · · · · · · · · ·   488 CRAZED MOON   18
    NOTHING SAID OR DONE CAN REACH · · · · · · · · · ·   506 REMORSE SPEECH   9
    AS THOUGH THAT HAND COULD REACH TO WHERE THEY STAND,   579 DOR WELLESLEY   2
    AH ME! I CANNOT REACH THEM——HERE AND THERE · · · · ·   694 MOSADA 1   93
    THE BURTHEN OF THY TRUTH. REACH DOWN THY HANDS · · ·   698 MOSADA 2   53
REACHED
    NOAH'S FRESHET NEVER REACHED. · · · · · · · · · ·   440 WISDOM   15
REACHES
    THE GLITTERING REACHES OF THE FLOODED LAKE. · · · ·   490 COOLE BALLYLEE   16
READ   SEE HALF-READ
    AND SLOWLY READ, AND DREAM OF THE SOFT LOOK · · · ·   121 YOU ARE OLD   3
    THEY READ IN THEIR BOOKS OF PRAYER: · · · · · · · ·   178 FIDDLER DOONEY   6
    I READ IN MY BOOK OF SONGS · · · · · · · · · · ·   178 FIDDLER DOONEY   7
    THEY READ IN A BOOK OF PRAYER, · · · · · · · · · ·   178 FIDDLER DOONEY V   6
    I READ IN A BOOK OF SONGS · · · · · · · · · · ·   178 FIDDLER DOONEY V   7
    I HAVE MADE THIS POEM FOR YOU, THAT MEN MAY READ IT ·   219 WOODS OF COOLE   41
    BEFORE THEY READ OF FORGAEL AND DECTORA, · · · · ·   219 WOODS OF COOLE   42
    A WOMAN SPOKE OF SOME NEW TALE SHE HAD READ, · · · ·   350 HER PRAISE   7
    CLIMBED UP MY CREAKING STAIR. THEY HAD READ · · · ·   358 PRESENCES   6
    THE HALF READ WISDOM OF DAEMONIC IMAGES, · · · · ·   427 PHANTOM HATRED V   39
    HE WHO CAN READ THE SIGNS NOR SINK UNMANNED · · · ·   429 NINETEEN 19   33
    OF ALL THE UNCOUNTED BOOKS THAT I HAVE READ, · · · ·   467 HARUN RASHID   139
    EVERYTHING HE WROTE WAS READ, · · · · · · · · · ·   577 WHAT THEN   6
    AND COPIED OUT WHAT I COULD READ · · · · · · · ·   584 GHOST ROG CASE   33
    THAT HAS READ AND THOUGHT, · · · · · · · · · · ·   631 POLITICS   8
    THAT HAS BOTH READ AND THOUGHT, · · · · · · · · ·   631 POLITICS   V   8
    HE WROTE IT ON THE SANDS (THE OWLS MAY READ · · · ·   659 ISLE STAT II 1   9
    IN SAND HIS NAME AND MINE I'VE ALSO READ. · · · · ·   662 ISLE STAT II 2   12
    FROM DEATH'S LATE LANGUOR AS THESE LINES I READ · · ·   734 QUATRAIN APHOR   14
READIER
    NOW NOTHING BUT COMES READIER TO THE HAND · · · · · ·   267 ALL TEMPT ME   4
READING
    READING SOME ENTANGLED STORY: · · · · · · · · · ·   65 HAPPY SHEPHERD   16
    AND THE LIGHT PROVES THAT HE IS READING STILL. · · ·   373 PHASES OF MOON   11
    TO STUDY READING BOOKS AND HISTORY · · · · · · ·   443 SCHOOL CHILDR V   4
    TO STUDY READING BOOKS AND HISTORIES, · · · · · · ·   443 SCHOOL CHILDR V   4
READING-BOOKS
    TO STUDY READING-BOOKS AND HISTORY, · · · · · · · ·   443 SCHOOL CHILDR   4
READY
    THAN A STRONG BODY AND A READY HAND. · · · · · · ·   232 SHADOW WATER B   236
    A PERJURER STOOD READY · · · · · · · · · · · ·   582 ROGER CASEMENT   9
    IN COIL ON COIL OF AZURE. ALL IS READY. · · · · ·   691 MOSADA 1   41
REAL
    AND FINDS A REAL IMAGE THERE: · · · · · · · · · ·   388 SOLOMON WITCH   27
REALISTS
    THE REALISTS · · · · · · · · · · · · · · · ·   309 REALISTS   T
REALITY
    BUT THE REALITY THAT MAKES OUR PASSION · · · · · ·   229 SHADOW WATER B   159
    AND THE REALITY: · · · · · · · · · · · · · ·   347 FISHERMAN   12
    IS BUT A VISION OF REALITY. · · · · · · · · · · ·   369 EGO DOMINUS   48
    SEEK OUT REALITY, LEAVE THINGS THAT SEEM. · · · · ·   502 VACILLATION   72
    INTO THE DESOLATION OF REALITY: · · · · · · · · ·   563 MERU   7
REALM
    IN A REALM WHERE THE HANDSOME ARE MANY, · · · · · ·   50 OISIN 3   V   50
REALMS
    IN REALMS WHERE THE HANDSOME WERE MANY, · · · · · ·   50 OISIN 3   50
    IN REALMS WHERE THE HANDSOME ARE MANY, · · · · · ·   50 OISIN 3   V   50
REAP
    NOR, GAZING FORTH WHERE LIFE'S SAD SICKLES REAP, · · · ·   710 FERENCZ RENYI   31
REAPING
    THAT RUN BEFORE THE REAPING HOOK AND LIE · · · · · ·   218 WOODS OF COOLE V   32
    WEARY OF REAPING THE BARREN NIGHT · · · · · · · ·   648 ISLE STAT I 1   84
REAPING-HOOK
    THAT RUN BEFORE THE REAPING-HOOK AND LIE · · · · · ·   218 WOODS OF COOLE   32
REAR
    BITTER AND VIOLENT MEN, MIGHT REAR IN STONE · · · · ·   418 ANCEST HOUSES   19
    THE RED SQUIRREL SHALL REAR HER YOUNG WHERE THOU   674 ISLE STAT II 3   215
        HAST DWELT——
REASON
    "GOOD REASON HAVE I FOR MY LOVE," · · · · · · · ·   7 OISIN 1   V   62
    THE REASON OF THE TREMBLING TREES— · · · · · · · ·   14 OISIN 1   179
    THIS BEAUTY'S KINDER, YET FOR A REASON · · · · · ·   199 ARROW   7
    I HAVE GOOD REASON FOR THAT THOUGHT. AND NOW · · · ·   238 SHADOW WATER B   354
    AND I TOOK ALL THE BLAME OUT OF ALL SENSE AND REASON, · ·   316 COLD HEAVEN   7

REASON   (CONTINUED)
    A REASON FOR KEEPING SILENT . . . .   359 WAR POEM   V   T
    OUT OF ALL LIKELIHOOD, OR REASON, ...   389 IMAGE PAST   9
    AND FOR THAT REASON AM I CRAZED . . . .   454 EMPTY CUP   9
    HIS VIZIR JAFFER FOR AN UNKNOWN REASON! . . . .   462 HARUN RASHID   32
    GAVE BUT MORE REASON FOR A WOMAN'S CARE. . . . .   466 HARUN RASHID   111
    AND HERE'S A COGENT REASON, ...   586 PARNELLITES   9
    AND HERE'S ANOTHER REASON, ...   586 PARNELLITES   15
    AND HERE'S A FINAL REASON, ...   586 PARNELLITES   17
    FOR REASON OF THE STATE . . . .   597 MODEL LAUREATE   6
    FOUGHT ONCE FOR SELF-SAME REASON ON THE HEM . . . . .   660 ISLE STAT II 1   32
REBEL
    HIDING THE REBEL WORMS IN YONDER WOOD, ...   709 FERENCZ RENYI   V   14
REBELLION
    GRANDFATHER SAID IN THE GREAT REBELLION! . . . . . .   544 TO SAME TUNE 1 V   1
REBELS
    HIDING THE REBELS WORM IN YONDER WOOD . . . .   709 FERENCZ RENYI   14
    HIDING THE REBELS SWARM IN YONDER WOOD . . . . . .   709 FERENCZ RENYI   V   14
    WHERE WORM THE REBELS, OR MY BULLETS LAY . . . . . .   713 FERENCZ RENYI   83
    WHERE IN THE WOODS OR HILLS THE REBELS BE?" . . . . .   713 FERENCZ RENYI   V 83A
RECALL
    RECALL THE YEARS BEFORE HER MIND . . . .   397 POLIT PRISONER   8
    I MUST RECALL A MAN THAT NEITHER LOVE . . . .   412 TOWER   74
    AND SPEAK BUT FANTASY. RECALL THE YEAR . . . .   462 HARUN RASHID   30
    AND SPEAK BUT PHANTASY. RECALL THE YEAR . . . . . .   462 HARUN RASHID   V   30
    PICTURES OF THE MIND, RECALL . . . .   475 EVA GORE-BOOTH   17
    WHATEVER COULD RECALL THE LIP OF LOVER. . . . .   537 HER VISION   8
    RECALL THE CRETAN BARB THAT PIERCED A STAR? . . . . .   541 PARN FUNERAL 1   7
    RECALL THAT MASCULINE TRINITY. . . . .   556 RIBH PATRICK   2
    RECALL HIS TRINITY. A FATHER, MOTHER, CHILD (A DAUGHTER 556 RIBH PATRICK   V   2
       OR A SON),
    FOR I WOULD NOT RECALL . . . .   599 SPIRIT MEDIUM   10
    AND MEN RECALL THAT FACE, ...   617 LONG-LEG FLY   12
RECALLED
    BUT SOMETHING IS RECALLED, ...   501 VACILLATION   55
RECEDE
    THE UNPURGED IMAGES OF DAY RECEDE; . . . .   497 BYZANTIUM   1
RECEDES
    NIGHT RESONANCE RECEDES, NIGHT-WALKERS' SONG . . . .   497 BYZANTIUM   3
    NIGHT'S RESONANCE RECEDES, NIGHT-WALKERS SONG . . . .   497 BYZANTIUM   V   3
RECEDING
    UNDER THE RECEDING WAVE. . . . .   485 NINETEENTH CEN   4
RECEIVES
    THAT THE STORMY NIGHT RECEIVES, ...   135 TWO TREES   26
RECENT
    ON A RECENT GOVERNMENT APPOINTMENT IN IRELAND . . . .   317 APPOINTMENT   V   T
RECKLESS
    RESTRAINING RECKLESS MIDDLE-AGE? . . . .   262 STUDENTS AGIT   4
RECKON
    IMAGINATION CANNOT RECKON IT. . . . .   248 SHADOW WATER B   541
RECKONED
    WHEN ALL THOUGHTS AND DEEDS ARE RECKONED, ...   298 THREE HERMITS   15
    THAT WERE ALL HIS BIRTHDAYS RECKONED . . . .   342 SHEP GOATHERD   90
    RECKONED UP EVERY UNFOREKNOWN, UNSEEING . . . .   413 TOWER   109
RECKONING
    WHY, IT'S A WONDER OUT OF RECKONING . . . .   243 SHADOW WATER B   445
    OUT OF ALL RECKONING. IS IT NOT TRUE . . . .   244 SHADOW WATER B   467
RECLINES
    THERE ON THAT SCAFFOLDING RECLINES . . . .   618 LONG-LEG FLY   25
RECOGNIZE
    RECOGNIZE THE FIVE . . . .   601 THOSE IMAGES   15
RECOLLECT
    AND YOU WILL RECOLLECT MY FACE AND VOICE, ...   243 SHADOW WATER B   433
RECOLLECTION
    IMAGE OF POIGNANT RECOLLECTION. . . . .   389 IMAGE PAST   7
    AS RECOLLECTION OR THE DRUG DECIDE, ...   444 SCHOOL CHILDR   36
RECONCILIATION
    RECONCILIATION . . . .   257 RECONCILIATION   T
RECORD
    THESE, THESE REMAIN, BUT I RECORD WHAT'S GONE. A CROWD   315 FALLEN MAJESTY   6
RECORDS
    BABBLING OF FALLEN MAJESTY, RECORDS WHAT'S GONE. . . .   314 FALLEN MAJESTY   4
RECOVER
    I COULD RECOVER IF I SHRIEKED . . . .   452 HUMAN DIGNITY   9
    I COULD RECOVER IF I SHRIEK . . . .   452 HUMAN DIGNITY   V   9
RECOVERED
    RECOVERED HIM UPON THE BED OF DEATH. . . . .   355 BROKEN DREAMS   6
RECOVERING
    MY HEART RECOVERING WITH COVERED EYES! . . . .   602 GALLERY REVIS   18
RECOVERS
    THE SOUL RECOVERS RADICAL INNOCENCE . . . .   405 FOR DAUGHTER   66
RECTOR
    THAT RED-HEADED RECTOR IN COUNTY DOWN, ...   604 YOU CONTENT   11
    AN ANCESTOR WAS RECTOR THERE . . . .   640 BEN BULBEN   86
RECUR
    AND THAT IF MEMORY RECUR, THE SUN'S . . . .   414 TOWER   119
RED   SEE BLOOD-RED
    THE RED SUN FALLS AND THE WORLD GROWS DIM." . . . .   9 OISIN 1   105
    YOU GO NOT WHERE THE RED DEER FEEDS, ...   11 OISIN 1   127
    YE GO NOT WHERE THE RED DEER FEEDS, ...   11 OISIN 1   V   127
    ALL PEARLY WHITE, SAVE ONE RED EAR! . . . .   12 OISIN 1   141

```
                                                    PAGE      TITLE           LINE
RED    (CONTINUED)
       WILD FLAMES OF RED AND GOLD AND BLUE,    . . . . . . .   18  OISIN 1           252
       AND KISSED THE SCEPTRE WITH RED LIPS,    . . . . . . .   18  OISIN 1           258
       WILD FLAMES OF RED AND CREAMY WHITES,    . . . . . . .   18  OISIN 1       V   255
       HUNG, LIKE METEORS OF RED LIGHT,  . . . . . . . . . .    21  OISIN 1       V   306
       CAME BY ME THE KINGS OF THE RED BRANCH, . . . . . . . .  53  OISIN 3            87
       AND BY ME, IN SOFT RED RAIMENT, THE FENIANS MOVED IN LOUD 53 OISIN 3            93
          STREAMS,
       CAME BY ME THE CANNS OF THE RED BRANCH . . . . . . . .   53  OISIN 3       V    87
       . . . WITH RED LIPS MURMURING A SONG, . . . . . . . .    58  OISIN 3       V   158
       WE WILL TEAR OUT THE RED FLAMING STONES, . . .  . . .    62  OISIN 3       V   209
       WE WILL TEAR THE RED FLAMING STONES OUT, . . .  . . .    62  OISIN 3       V   209
       ON THE RED FLAMING STONES WITHOUT REFUGE . . .  . . .    62  OISIN 3       V   213
       OF RED FLAMINGOES; AND MY LOVE, VIJAYA; . . .  . . . .   75  ANASHU VIJAYA      89
       OF RED FLAMINGO; AND MY LOVE, VIJAYA, . . . .  . . . .   75  ANASHU VIJAYA V    89
       MY MAN GREW RED AND PALE, . . . . . . . . . . .  . . .   95  MOLL MAGEE         22
       RED ROSE, PROUD ROSE, SAD ROSE OF ALL MY DAYS!  . . .   100  ROSE UPON ROOD      1
       RED ROSE, PROUD ROSE, SAD ROSE OF ALL MY DAYS.  . . .   101  ROSE UPON ROOD     24
       WHAT WOULD YOU, KING OF THE PROUD RED BRANCH KINGS? . .  102  FERGUS DRUID        8
       WHAT WOULD YOU, KING OF THE PROUD RED BRANCH KINGS? . .  102  FERGUS DRUID       15
       WHAT WOULD YOU, KING OF THE PROUD RED BRANCH KINGS? . .  103  FERGUS DRUID   V   21
       AND STRETCHING OUT HER ARMS, RED WITH THE DYE, . . . .  105  CUCHULAIN SEA  V    7
       "THE RED BRANCH CAMP IN A GREAT COMPANY  . . . . . . .  108  CUCHULAIN SEA      33
       "THE RED BRANCH KINGS A TIRELESS BANQUET KEEP, . . . .  108  CUCHULAIN SEA      33
       "THE RED BRANCH GATHER A GREAT COMPANY  . . . . . . .   108  CUCHULAIN SEA  V   33
       AND THE GREY TIDE, THE RED BRANCH MULTITUDE . . . . .   108  CUCHULAIN SEA  V   38B
       AND CONCHUBAR, THE RED BRANCH KING OF KINGS, . . . . .  109  CUCHULAIN SEA      45
       "I ONLY OF THE RED BRANCH HOSTED NOW," . . . . . . . .  109  CUCHULAIN SEA  V   55
       FOR THESE RED LIPS, WITH ALL THEIR MOURNFUL PRIDE, . .  111  ROSE OF WORLD       2
       A GIRL AROSE THAT HAD RED MOURNFUL LIPS . . . . . . .   120  SORROW OF LOVE      5
       AND THEN YOU CAME WITH THOSE RED MOURNFUL LIPS, . . .   120  SORROW OF LOVE V    5
       BECAUSE THE RED ROSE BORDERED HEM . . . . . . . . . .   137  TO IRELAND     V
       AFTER THE RED ROSE BORDERED HEM. . . . . . . . . . .    139  TO IRELAND     V   30
       AFTER THE RED ROSE BORDERED HEM. . . . . . . . . . .    139  TO IRELAND     V   48
       AND A YOUNG MAN BROUGHT HIM RED WINE . . . . . . . . .  144  HOST OF AIR        19
       OF THE MATCHING OF RIBBONS THE BLUE AND THE RED, . . .  151  OLD MOTHER     V    6
       I HAVE BEEN CHANGED TO A HOUND WITH ONE RED EAR; . . .  153  CHANGE BELOVED      2
       O'SULLIVAN THE RED TO MARY LAVELL. . . . . . . . . . .  157  POET BELOVED   V   T
       TWO POEMS BY O'SULLIVAN THE RED CONCERNING MARY LAVELL. 157  POET BELOVED   V   T
       IN A RED AND QUIVERING GARMENT . . . . . . . . . . .    160  CAP AND BELLS      15
       AND HER RED LIPS SANG THEM A LOVE-SONG . . . . . . .    160  CAP AND BELLS      27
       TO HER RIGHT HAND CAME THE RED ONE, . . . . . . . . .   160  CAP AND BELLS      31
       IN A GARMENT RED AND QUIVERING, . . . . . . . . . . .   160  CAP AND BELLS  V   15
       HER RED LIPS SANG THEM A LOVE-SONG . . . . . . . . .    160  CAP AND BELLS  V   27
       AND HER RED LIPS SANG THEM A LOVE SONG. . . . . . . .   160  CAP AND BELLS  V   27
       AND TILL A HUNDRED MORNS HAD FLOWERED RED . . . . . .   170  SECRET ROSE        17
       O'SULLIVAN THE RED UPON HIS WANDERINGS . . . . . . .    171  MAID QUIET     V   T
       RED HANRAHAN'S SONG ABOUT IRELAND . . . . . . . . . .   206  HANRAHANS SONG     T
       THE SONG OF RED HANRAHAN . . . . . . . . . . . . . .    206  HANRAHANS SONG V   T
       AND SHAKE DOWN THUNDER ON THE STONES BECAUSE THE RED WINDS 207 HANRAHANS SONG V  7
          RAVE!
       WITH RED BEER AND BROWN BEER. . . . . . . . . . . .     214  HAPPY TOWNLAND      8
       BUT THE LITTLE RED FOX MURMURED, . . . . . . . . . .    214  HAPPY TOWNLAND     17
       BUT THE LITTLE RED FOX MURMURED, . . . . . . . . . .    215  HAPPY TOWNLAND     37
       BUT THE LITTLE RED FOX MURMURED, . . . . . . . . . .    216  HAPPY TOWNLAND     57
       I COULD GIVE ALL MY HEART TO THAT RED MOLL . . . . .    222  SHADOW WATER B      9
       FOR THAT RED MOLL THAT HAD BUT THE ONE EYE. . . . . .   222  SHADOW WATER B V   10
       WITH SO RED LIPS, AND RUNNING ON SUCH FEET, . . . . .   231  SHADOW WATER B    199
       AND PLEASURE MADE HER CHEEKS GROW RED, . . . . . . .    314  MEMORY YOUTH       11
       SHE LIES, HER LOVELY PITEOUS HEAD AMID DULL RED HAIR    362  HER COURTESY        2
       OF DULL RED HAIR WAS FLOWING . . . . . . . . . . . .    363  DOLLS DRAWINGS      6
       WHO HAD SEEMED TO GLIDE TO SOME INTRIGUE IN HER RED SHOES, 363 DOLLS FACES      6
       NO RED AND WHITE OF A FACE, . . . . . . . . . . . .     365  HER RACE            6
       MANACLE HIS SOUL UPON THE RED SEA BOTTOM. . . . . . .   372  ON GOING HOUSE     16
       THERE'S NOTHING BUT OUR OWN RED BLOOD  . . . . . . .    396  ROSE TREE          17
       THE RED MAN THE JUGGLER SENT . . . . . . . . . . . .    412  TOWER              92
       BRONZED PEACOCK FEATHERS, RED COMBS OF HER COCKS. . .   433  NINETEEN 19       130
       BUT THE DARK CHANGED TO RED, AND TORCHES SHONE, . . .   537  HER VISION         12
       NOR EVER MADE AN IRON RED . . . . . . . . . . . . .     606  SONGS BURDEN 1     14
       THE EVENING GLEAMS ARE GREEN AND GOLD AND RED . . .     656  ISLE STAT I 3      22
       DULL-WITTED THING, WITH FACE RED SQUIRREL-BROWN. . . .  661  ISLE STAT II 1     68
       THROUGH THIS NIGHT-VESTED PLACE THE RED BEAMS BREAK. .  662  ISLE STAT II 2      4
       THE RED SQUIRREL SHALL REAR HER YOUNG WHERE THOU        674  ISLE STAT II 3    215
          HAST DWELT--
       MY DREAMS O'ER THOUGHTS OF PLENTY, AS THE RED-   . . .  681  SEEKER         V    3
       A LITTLE WHILE AND--RED EVE DIES-- . . . . . . . .      686  LIFE               13
       FROM FASTING--SEE, THE RED LIGHT SLANTING DOWN . . .    697  MOSADA 2           36
       AH! WOE FOR YOUR SLIPPERS OF RED. . . . . . . . . .     708  FAIRY PEDANT       36
       THIS SULLEN PEASANT SPOILS THE GOOD RED WINE. . . . .   711  FERENCZ RENYI      43
       THIS SULLEN PEASANT SOURS THE GOOD RED WINE. . . . .    711  FERENCZ RENYI  V   43
       AMONG THE GOLD, THE AMBER, AND THE RED." . . . . . .    712  FERENCZ RENYI      76
       AMONG THE BLUE, THE AMBER AND THE RED." . . . . . . .   712  FERENCZ RENYI  V   76
       THAT MAIDEN BRING THEY. WHEN THE TALL RED DEER . . .    713  FERENCZ RENYI      79
       A TOSSING LAUGH BETWEEN THEIR RED ABIDES; . . . . . .   735  QUATRAIN APHOR     22
       THAT THE RED RUST MAKES DIM." . . . . . . . . . . .     740  EARL PAUL          20
       A RED HOUND RUNNING FROM A SILVER ARROW. . . . . . .    747  SHADOW WATER A      6
       I HAVE FORGOTTEN WHEREFORE. THE RED HOUND . . . . .     747  SHADOW WATER A      8
       I SWORE BUT YESTERDAY IF THE RED GOD . . . . . . . .    751  SHADOW WATER A    109
       TO MIND HIS COWS AND SWINE BY THE RED LAKE. . . . . .   752  SHADOW WATER A    112
       BEYOND THE SAIL A MAN WITH A RED CROWN . . . . . . .    752  SHADOW WATER A    126
       WERE THEY BUT LIFTED UP. THE RED HOUND IS FLED. . . .   761  SHADOW WATER A    266
```

	PAGE	TITLE	LINE

RED   (CONTINUED)
    A HOUND THAT HAD LAIN IN THE RED RUSHES . . . .   761 SHADOW WATER A   278
    RED BIRD OF MARCH, BEGIN TO CROW! . . . .   782 HEART FRIGHT   5
    RED COCK, AND CROW! . . . .   782 HEART FRIGHT   7
    RED BIRD OF MARCH, BEGIN TO CROW! . . . .   782 HEART FRIGHT   12
    RED COCK, AND CROW! . . . .   782 HEART FRIGHT   14
    RED BIRD OF MARCH, BEGIN TO CROW! . . . .   782 HEART FRIGHT   19
    RED COCK, AND CROW! . . . .   782 HEART FRIGHT   21
    RED COCKS, AND CROW! . . . .   783 GREY ROUND   28
REDDENS
    IS THIS POOR BODY THAT REDDENS AND GROWS PALE. . . . .   764 SHADOW WATER A   341
REDDEST
    AND OF REDDEST STOLEN CHERRIES. . . . .   87 STOLEN CHILD   8
RED-EARED
    CAME UP OUT OF THE HOLE, AND RED-EARED HOUNDS . . . . .   185 QUEEN MAEVE   117
    A RED-EARED HOUND FOLLOWS A HORNLESS DEER. . . . . . .   764 SHADOW WATER A   325
RED-EYED
    OF DESERT-CAVES THE RED-EYED PANTHERS ROVE . . . . . .   681 SEEKER   4
    EYED PANTHERS IN THEIR DESERT CAVERNS ROVE . . . . . .   681 SEEKER   V   4
RED-HAIRED
    HE HAD SEEN A RED-HAIRED JOLLY LAD . . . .   303 HOUR DAWN   V   27
    AND OF A RED-HAIRED YEATS WHOSE LOOKS, ALTHOUGH HE DIED   391 UNDER SATURN   9
RED-HEAD
    YOUNG RED-HEAD STRETCHED HIMSELF TO YAWN . . . .   303 HOUR DAWN   V   32A
RED-HEADED
    THAT RED-HEADED RECTOR IN COUNTY DOWN, ...   604 YOU CONTENT   11
REDNESS
    AND ONE HAS SEEN IN THE REDNESS OF WINE . . . .   168 BLESSED   35
    A TOSSING LAUGH BETWEEN THEIR REDNESS 'BIDES-- . . . .   685 DRAWING-ROOM   2
    A TOSSING LAUGH BETWEEN THEIR REDNESS 'BIDES-- . . . .   735 QUATRAIN APHOR V   22
    PRAISE THE REDNESS OF THE YEW! . . . .   773 SONG DEIRDRE 1   20
RED-ROSE-BORDERED
    BECAUSE THE RED-ROSE-BORDERED HEM . . . .   137 TO IRELAND   6
    AFTER THE RED-ROSE-BORDERED HEM. . . . .   139 TO IRELAND   30
    AFTER THE RED-ROSE-BORDERED HEM. . . . .   139 TO IRELAND   48
RE-ECHOING
    TILL MY OWN WORDS, RE-ECHOING, SHALL SEND . . . . . .   68 SAD SHEPHERD   20
    AND MINE OWN WORDS RE-ECHOING SHALL SEND . . . .   68 SAD SHEPHERD   V   20
REED
    BLEW ONE LONG NOTE. FROM OVER REED . . . .   14 OISIN 1   V   195
    THIS BODY TREMBLING LIKE A WIND-BLOWN REED. . . . . .   103 FERGUS DRUID   25
    SOFT AS THE RUSTLE OF A REED FROM CLOYNE . . . .   487 SEVEN SAGES   22
REEDS
    AND WHISPER, "THE INNUMERABLE REEDS . . . .   81 EPHEMERA   V 24E
    FROM THE TALL AND THE TUFTED REEDS . . . .   143 HOST OF AIR   3
    AND HE SAW HOW THE REEDS GREW DARK . . . .   144 HOST OF AIR   5
    IN THE GREY REEDS THAT NIGHT AND MORN . . . .   190 BAILE AILLINN   42
    O TUFTED REEDS, BEND LOW AND LOW IN POOLS ON THE GREEN   206 HANRAHANS SONG V   1
        LAND,
    LIKE TUFTED REEDS OUR COURAGE DROOPS IN A BLACK WIND AND   207 HANRAHANS SONG V   3
        DIES!
    THAT RUSTLES IN THE REEDS WITH PATIENT PUSHES, ...   699 MOSADA 3   4
    THAT'S RUSTLING IN THE REEDS WITH PATIENT PUSHES, . . .   699 MOSADA 3   V   4
    WHERE LIES A SHALLOP IN THE YELLOW REEDS. . . . . . .   702 MOSADA 3   77
REED-THROATED
    WHILE I, FROM THAT REED-THROATED WHISPERER . . . . . .   320 REED WHISPERER   1
REEDY
    PROCLAIM WITH THAT UNWEARIED, REEDY CRY . . . .   128 DREAM OF FAERY   42
    A-TELLING WITH THEIR LOW AND REEDY CRY . . . .   128 DREAM OF FAERY V   42
    PROCLAIMING WITH A LOW AND REEDY CRY, ...   128 DREAM OF FAERY V   42
    HOW LITTLE AND REEDY A SOUND AWAKES A GOD . . . . . .   760 SHADOW WATER A   252
REEL
    REEL SHADOWS OF THE INDIGNANT DESERT BIRDS. . . . . .   402 SECOND COMING   17
REELED
    RENDING THE HORSE'S FLANK. KING EOCHAID REELED, . . .   277 TWO KINGS   13
    RIPPED THROUGH THE HORSE'S FLANKS. KING EOCHAID REELED,   277 TWO KINGS   V   13
    FROM THE WAVES THE SUN HATH REELED, ...   705 DAWN-SONG   1
REELING
    ON THAT WOMAN'S REELING BRAIN? . . . .   632 MAN AND ECHO   14
REFLECTION
    THE ELABORATE STARLIGHT THROWS A REFLECTION . . . . .   389 IMAGE PAST   2
REFLECTIONS
    THE ELABORATE STAR-LIGHT HAS THROWN REFLECTIONS . . . .   389 IMAGE PAST   V   2
REFORM
    OR RUN WHERE LADS REFORM OUR DAYTIME . . . .   343 SHEP GOATHERD   V   105
REFORMER
    REFORMER, MERCHANT, STATESMAN, LEARNED MAN, ...   376 PHASES OF MOON   98
REFUGE
    ON THE FLAMING STONES, WITHOUT REFUGE, ...   62 OISIN 3   213
    ON THE RED FLAMING STONES WITHOUT REFUGE . . . .   62 OISIN 3   V   213
    DANGER NO REFUGE HOLDS, AND WAR NO PEACE, ...   114 ROSE OF BATTLE   9
REFUSE
    THAT GAVE, THOUGH FREE TO REFUSE-- . . . .   414 TOWER   133
    AND IF IT TAKE THE SECOND MUST REFUSE . . . .   491 COOLE BALLYLEE V   40C
    AND IF IT TAKE THE SECOND MUST REFUSE . . . .   495 CHOICE   3
    A MOUND OF REFUSE OR THE SWEEPINGS OF A STREET, ...   630 CIRCUS ANIMALS   35
    A MOUND OF REFUSE OR THE SWEEPINGS OF THE STREET, . . .   630 CIRCUS ANIMALS V   35
    THERE'S LITTLE I'D REFUSE THEE, DEAREST YOUTH. . . . .   669 ISLE STAT II 3   71
    BUT FEARING THAT SHE WOULD REFUSE . . . .   792 GEORGE MOORE   2
REFUSED
    IF I REFUSED THE MESSENGERS AND PILOTS . . . .   249 SHADOW WATER B   572

	PAGE	TITLE	LINE

REFUSED   (CONTINUED)
FOR THAT SHE PROMISED, AND FOR THAT REFUSED. • • • • •   286 TWO KINGS   213
FOR THAT YOU PROMISED, AND FOR THAT REFUSED." • • • • •   286 TWO KINGS   V 213
BOOK II WHAT THE CALIPH REFUSED TO LEARN • • • • •   460 HARUN RASHID   V   T

REGARDLESS
STANDS EACH GREY AND SILENT PHANTOM ON THE SAME REGARDLESS   719 PHANTOM SHIP   25
    SPOT--

REGENT
LONE REGENT OF THE WOODS, DEEP MUTTERING, • • • • •   657 ISLE STAT I 3   49

REGRET
OF CEASELESS LONELINESS AND HIGH REGRET • • • • • •   705 REMEMBRANCE   9

REIGN
THAT IT WAS MADE IN YOUR GREAT FATHER'S REIGN." • • • •   464 HARUN RASHID   72

REIGNED
WHERE NONE HAS REIGNED THAT LACKED A NAME AND FAME • • •   491 COOLE BALLYLEE   31

REIN
FOR GOLD HIS HOOVES AND SILK HIS REIN, • • • • • •   2 OISIN 1   V   72
THE MOON PLUCKED AT MY REIN! • • • • • • • •   214 HAPPY TOWNLAND   16
"O DO NOT PLUCK AT HIS REIN, • • • • • • • •   214 HAPPY TOWNLAND   18
THE MOON PLUCKED AT MY REIN! • • • • • • • •   215 HAPPY TOWNLAND   36
"O DO NOT PLUCK AT HIS REIN, • • • • • • • •   215 HAPPY TOWNLAND   38
THE MOON PLUCKED AT MY REIN! • • • • • • • •   216 HAPPY TOWNLAND   56
"O DO NOT PLUCK AT HIS REIN, • • • • • • • •   216 HAPPY TOWNLAND   58
HE SAT WITH TIGHTENED REIN AND LOOSENED MOUTH • • • •   277 TWO KINGS   10
HE SAT WITH TIGHTENED REIN AMAZED, HIS HORSE • • • •   277 TWO KINGS   V   10
ROSE! SOME CONQUEROR DREW REIN • • • • • • • •   502 VACILLATION   64

REINS
SHAKE THE LOOSE REINS! YOU SLAVES OF GOD, • • • • •   22 OISIN 1   331
SHAKE THE LOOSE REINS! YE SLAVES OF GOD, • • • • •   22 OISIN 1   V 331
LAY LOOSE IN A PLACE OF SHADOW! WE DREW THE REINS BY HIS   50 OISIN 3   44
    SIDE.
IT DROPPED THE REINS OF PEACE AND WAR • • • • • •   437 SONGS PLAY 1   14

REITERANT
REITERANT. A BIRD GOES BY THE TENT, • • • • • •   711 FERENCZ RENYI   46
REITERANT. A BOY GOES BY THE TENT, • • • • • •   711 FERENCZ RENYI   46

REJOICE
OLD SILENCE BIDS ITS CHOSEN RACE REJOICE, • • • • •   127 DREAM OF FAERY   31
OLD SILENCE BIDS A LONELY FOLK REJOICE, • • • • •   127 DREAM OF FAERY V   31
REJOICE AS LOVER SHOULD • • • • • • • • • •   453 DEATH OF HARE   4
AND ALL IT KNOWS IS THAT ONE WORD "REJOICE!" • • • •   564 GYRES   16
SHALL WE IN THAT GREAT NIGHT REJOICE? • • • • • •   633 MAN AND ECHO   38
DOTH NOT YON BIRD, YON QUIVERING BIRD, REJOICE? • • •   652 ISLE STAT I 2   21

RELEASE
AND SHIRK IT IN VAIN. THERE IS NO RELEASE • • • •   632 MAN AND ECHO   21

RELIED
THAT ON A STICK RELIED • • • • • • • • • •   515 GIRLS SONG B   6

RELIEF
HAD SCOOPED OUT PHARAOH'S MUMMY. I--THOUGH HEART MIGHT   503 VACILLATION   84
    FIND RELIEF

RELIGIOUS
BECAUSE TO-DAY IS SOME RELIGIOUS FESTIVAL • • • • •   363 DOLLS FACES   .1
"I HEARD AN OLD RELIGIOUS MAN • • • • • • • •   492 ANNE GREGORY   13
IN THAT RELIGIOUS GLOOM! • • • • • • • • •   584 GHOST ROG CASE   34

RELIVE
THESE INNOCENTS RELIVE THEIR DEATH, • • • • • • •   612 NEWS ORACLE   V   15

RE-LIVE
THOSE INNOCENTS RE-LIVE THEIR DEATH, • • • • • • •   612 NEWS ORACLE   15

RELY
"NONE CAN RELY UPON • • • • • • • • • • •   569 THREE BUSHES   2

REMADE
• • • REMADE, LIKE A CASKET OF GOLD • • • • • •   143 ROSE IN HEART   7
HERE'S AN OLD STORY I'VE REMADE, • • • • • • •   270 GREY ROCK   3

RE-MADE
• • • RE-MADE LIKE A CASKET OF GOLD • • • • • •   143 ROSE IN HEART   V   7
HERE'S AN OLD STORY I'VE RE-MADE, • • • • • • •   270 GREY ROCK   V   3

REMAIN
PARDON, OLD FATHERS, IF YOU STILL REMAIN • • • • •   269 PARDON FATHERS   1
THESE, THESE REMAIN, BUT I RECORD WHAT'S GONE. A CROWD   315 FALLEN MAJESTY   6
AND ON MY HEIRS, IF ALL REMAIN UNSPOILED, • • • • •   371 ON GOING HOUSE   2
AND MAY THESE CHARACTERS REMAIN • • • • • • •   406 CARVED STONE   5
THESE STONES REMAIN THEIR MONUMENT AND MINE. • • • •   423 MY DESCENDANTS   24
NOTHING BUT STILLNESS CAN REMAIN WHEN HEARTS ARE FULL • •   426 PHANTOM HATRED   23
ALL THINGS REMAIN IN GOD. • • • • • • • •   512 JANE ON GOD   6
ALL THINGS REMAIN IN GOD. • • • • • • • •   512 JANE ON GOD   12
ALL THINGS REMAIN IN GOD. • • • • • • • •   512 JANE ON GOD   18
ALL THINGS REMAIN IN GOD. • • • • • • • •   512 JANE ON GOD   24
WENCHING, DRINKING, STILL REMAIN • • • • • • •   529 TOM LUNATIC   9
PICTURE AND BOOK REMAIN, • • • • • • • • •   575 ACRE OF GRASS   1

REMAINED
SO MUCH REMAINED THAT ON THE EVENING STAR • • • • •   32 OISIN 2   V   48

REMAINS
BRIGHTNESS REMAINS! A BRIGHTER STAR SHOOTS DOWN! • • • •   541 PARN FUNERAL 1   4
WHAT REMAINS TO SING ABOUT • • • • • • • • •   585 ORAHILLY   28

REMAKE
MYSELF MUST I REMAKE • • • • • • • • • •   576 ACRE OF GRASS   14
MYSELF I MUST REMAKE • • • • • • • • • •   576 ACRE OF GRASS   V   14
WHEN EVER I REMAKE A SONG, • • • • • • • • •   778 FRIENDS WRONG   .2
IT IS MYSELF THAT I REMAKE. • • • • • • • •   778 FRIENDS WRONG   4

REMBRANDT
"GREATEST SINCE REMBRANDT," ACCORDING TO JOHN SYNGE! • •   602 GALLERY REVIS   26

```
                                                                PAGE    TITLE            LINE
REMEDY
    NOR FIND A REMEDY."  "BUT WHAT IF I  . . . . . . . . .      464 HARUN RASHID          84
    AND FIND NO REMEDY.  "BUT WHAT IF I  . . . . . . . . .      464 HARUN RASHID    V      84
REMEMBER
    SAD TO REMEMBER, SICK WITH YEARS, . . . . . . . . .           2 OISIN 1                5
    REMEMBER THE WISDOM OUT OF THE OLD DAYS!  . . . . . .       158 TO HIS HEART           2
    HE COULD REMEMBER WHEN HE HAD HAD FINE DREAMS. . . . .      182 QUEEN MAEVE           56
    REMEMBER DEIRDRE AND HER MAN! . . . . . . . . . . . .       192 BAILE AILLINN         91
    DO YOU REMEMBER WHEN WE SANK THAT GALLEY  . . . . . .       223 SHADOW WATER B        20
    NO, NO--NOT ARTHUR.  I REMEMBER NOW. . . . . . . . .        242 SHADOW WATER B       405
    I HALF REMEMBER.  IT HAS BEEN IN MY DREAMS. . . . . .       251 SHADOW WATER B       606
    REMEMBER HIS DELIBERATE HAPPINESS. . . . . . . . .          370 EGO DOMINUS           53
    AND I REMEMBER WILDNESS LOST . . . . . . . . . . . .        453 DEATH OF HARE          9
    CEASE TO REMEMBER THE DELIGHTS OF YOUTH, TRAVEL-WEARIED     459 FROM OEDIPUS           2
        AGED MAN!
    LONG PAST HIS PRIME REMEMBER THINGS THAT ARE  . . . . .     477 SELF AND SOUL         18
    WHAT DID WE REMEMBER . . . . . . . . . . . . . .           519 LOVES LONENESS         9
    REMEMBER ALL THOSE RENOWNED GENERATIONS,  . . . . . .       613 MARCH SONGS 1          1
    REMEMBER ALL THOSE RENOWNED GENERATIONS,  . . . . . .       613 MARCH SONGS 1         11
    REMEMBER ALL THAT HAVE SUNK IN THEIR BLOOD,  . . . . .      613 MARCH SONGS 1         12
    REMEMBER ALL THAT HAVE DIED ON THE SCAFFOLD, . . . . .      613 MARCH SONGS 1         13
    REMEMBER ALL THAT HAVE FLED, THAT HAVE STOOD, . . . .       613 MARCH SONGS 1         14
    REMEMBER ALL THESE RENOWNED GENERATIONS,  . . . . . .       613 MARCH SONGS 1   V     11
    DO YOU REMEMBER, AIBRIC, HOW YOU BORE . . . . . . .         749 SHADOW WATER A        48
REMEMBERED
    SOME FEW REMEMBERED STILL WHEN I WAS YOUNG  . . . . .       410 TOWER                 33
    REMEMBERED OUT OF BABYLONIAN ALMANACS, . . . . . . .        426 PHANTOM HATRED        20
REMEMBEREST
    TILL THOU REMEMBEREST ONLY HOW THE SEA  . . . . . . .       670 ISLE STAT II 3        94
REMEMBERING   SEE KING-REMEMBERING
    'TIS SAD REMEMBERING, SICK WITH YEARS, . . . . . . .          2 OISIN 1         V      5
    REMEMBERING HOW THE FENIANS STEPT . . . . . . . . .         24 OISIN 1              370
    REMEMBERING HOW ALONG THE PLAINS, . . . . . . . . .         24 OISIN 1         V    370
    SMOTE ON THEIR BRAINS THAT DWELT REMEMBERING AYE. . . .     34 OISIN 2         V    77A
    MY ANGRY, KING REMEMBERING SOUL ONE JOT! . . . . . .        36 OISIN 2         V     94
    OLD AND REMEMBERING, WHAT AVAILS THE WIND . . . . . .       42 OISIN 2         V    206
    REMEMBERING HOW I HAD STOOD BY WHITE-HAIRED FINN . . .      44 OISIN 2              227
    REMEMBERING HOW I PACED IN DAYS GONE O'ER, . . . . .        44 OISIN 2         V    227
    REMEMBERING HOW I STOOD BY WHITE-HAIRED FINN  . . . .       44 OISIN 2         V    227
    I PACE REMEMBERING.  FROM MY MISTY THRONE . . . . . .       45 OISIN 2         V 239C
    . . . REMEMBERING ALONE THAT DELIGHT  . . . . . . .         54 OISIN 3              111
    REMEMBERING ITS LONG-OARED COMPANIONS, . . . . . . .        55 OISIN 3              118
    FOR MY REMEMBERING HOUR IS DONE! . . . . . . . . .          86 MAD KING GOLL   V     69
    REMEMBERING ALL THAT SHAKEN HAIR  . . . . . . . . .        135 TWO TREES             17
    OR REMEMBERING HERS THEY WILL FIND NO OTHER FACE FAIR  .    163 VALLEY LOVERS          7
    OR, REMEMBERING HERS, THEY WILL HOLD NO OTHER FACE FAIR     163 VALLEY LOVERS   V      7
    REMEMBERING THAT SHE TOO HAD SEEMED DIVINE . . . . . .      182 QUEEN MAEVE           64
    REMEMBERING THAT THE BEST I HAVE DONE . . . . . . .        256 WORDS                  7
    NO MORE REMEMBERING WHAT HAD BEEN, . . . . . . . . .        276 GREY ROCK            122
    REMEMBERING WHAT SHE HAD, . . . . . . . . . . . .          316 FRIENDS               24
    REMEMBERING KINDNESS DONE, AND HOW CAN I  . . . . . .       340 SHEP GOATHERD         30
    AND BE WELL PLEASED REMEMBERING IT, FOR IN THE OLD DAYS,    351 HER PRAISE            16
    THE SOUL REMEMBERING ITS LONELINESS  . . . . . . . .        375 PHASES OF MOON        88
    REMEMBERING THAT, IF WALKED SHE THERE, . . . . . . .        410 TOWER                 38
    REMEMBERING THAT HER SHRIEK WAS LOVE . . . . . . . .        456 FRIENDS YOUTH         19
    REMEMBERING A WOMAN'S BEAUTY. . . . . . . . . . . .         552 SONGS REWRIT 2  V     11
    REMEMBERING THEE, I SEARCH OUT THESE FAINT FLOWERS  . . .   704 REMEMBRANCE            1
    OF RHYME! REMEMBERING THEE, THIS CRESCENT NIGHT,  . . .     704 REMEMBRANCE            2
    REMEMBERING THEE, I MUSE, WHILE FADES IN FLIGHT . . . .     705 REMEMBRANCE            6
    I HAVE BEGUN REMEMBERING MY DREAMS. . . . . . . . . .       766 SHADOW WATER A       380
    REMEMBERING AND REMEMBERING. . . . . . . . . . . .         782 HEART FRIGHT          11
    REMEMBERING AND REMEMBERING. . . . . . . . . . . .         782 HEART FRIGHT          11
REMEMBERS
    HE REMEMBERS FORGOTTEN BEAUTY . . . . . . . . . . .         155 FORGOT BEAUTY          T
    MICHAEL ROBARTES REMEMBERS FORGOTTEN BEAUTY . . . . .       155 FORGOT BEAUTY   V      T
    AND SO REMEMBERS THAT WHEN ALL MANKIND  . . . . . . .       447 COLONUS PRAISE        26
REMEMBRANCE
    FOR REMEMBRANCE, LIFTING HER LEANNESS, . . . . . . . . .     57 OISIN 3              152
    . . . ALONE WITH REMEMBRANCE AND FEAR! . . . . . . .        63 OISIN 3              218
    WITHOUT LAUGHTER, A COUGHING, ALONE WITH REMEMBRANCE AND    63 OISIN 3         V    218
        FEAR!
    REMEMBRANCE. . . . . . . . . . . . . . . . . . .          704 REMEMBRANCE            T
REMINDED
    REMINDED HIM THAT HE COULD MAKE, . . . . . . . . . .       302 HOUR DAWN             13
REMORSE
    WHEN SUCH AS I CAST OUT REMORSE  . . . . . . . . .         479 SELF AND SOUL         68
    OR THE DAY'S VANITY, THE NIGHT'S REMORSE. . . . . . .       491 COOLE BALLYLEE V     40H
    OR THE DAY'S VANITY, THE NIGHT'S REMORSE. . . . . . .       495 CHOICE                 8
    THE HEART REMORSE. . . . . . . . . . . . . . . . .         500 VACILLATION            8
    REMORSE FOR INTEMPERATE SPEECH . . . . . . . . . .         506 REMORSE SPEECH         T
    A SOUL INCAPABLE OF REMORSE OR REST! . . . . . . . .       601 GALLERY REVIS          7
REMOTE
    OR AUGHT REMOTE! OR HAST THOU NEVER HEARD . . . . . .       672 ISLE STAT II 3       153
    REMOTE FROM ALL THE HARD EARTH TROUBLES, . . . . . .       731 PRIEST FAIRY          80
REND
    MAY REND WHAT COMES IN REACH. . . . . . . . . . . .        488 CRAZED MOON           18
    AND OF NASCHINA'S NOW THEY TELL--REND! REND! . . . . .      665 ISLE STAT II 2        69
    AND OF NASCHINA'S NOW THEY TELL--REND! REND! . . . . .      665 ISLE STAT II 2        69
RENDING
    RENDING THE HORSE'S FLANK.  KING EOCHAID REELED, . . . .    277 TWO KINGS             13
    THOUGH MY LOVE-SICK HEART IS RENDING, . . . . . . .         646 ISLE STAT I 1         38
```

	PAGE	TITLE	LINE

RENDS
 AT MORN, AND WITH HER FEET EACH COBWEB RENDS, • • • • •   670 ISLE STAT II 3   99
RENEW
 SO DID SHE YOUR STRENGTH RENEW, • • • • • • • • • •   259 UNWORTH PRAISE   6
 AND HALF AND HALF CONSUME WHAT THEY RENEW, • • • • • •   500 VACILLATION   15
 AND RANTING TIME RENEW, • • • • • • • • • • • • •   606 SONGS BURDEN 1   20
 SOME FEW HALF WAKE AND HALF RENEW THEIR CHOICE, • • • •   622 HOUND VOICE   6
RENEWED
 BUT IN THE GRAVE ALL, ALL, SHALL BE RENEWED. • • • • •   356 BROKEN DREAMS   21
 THEY HAVE LOUD MUSIC, HOPE EVERY DAY RENEWED • • • • •   398 LEADERS CROWD   11
RENOUNCE
 RENOUNCE THAT DRUDGERY, • • • • • • • • • • • • • •   600 THOSE IMAGES   7
RENOUNCING
 I BID THEE STAY, RENOUNCING THY MAD QUEST." • • • • •   669 ISLE STAT II 3   89
RENOWN
 IN THINKING OF HIS LOST RENOWN. • • • • • • • • • •   379 SAINT HUNCH   3
 ALL THE RENOWN THAT FELL. • • • • • • • • • • • • •   547 TO SAME TUNE 2   26
 ALL THE RENOWN THAT FELL. • • • • • • • • • • • • •   614 MARCH SONGS 1   26
RENOWNED
 OUR MOST RENOWNED PATRIOTS STAND, • • • • • • • • •   460 THREE MONUMENT   2
 JUSTIFY ALL THOSE RENOWNED GENERATIONS: • • • • • • •   545 TO SAME TUNE 2   1
 JUSTIFY ALL THOSE RENOWNED GENERATIONS: • • • • • • •   546 TO SAME TUNE 2   11
 REMEMBER ALL THOSE RENOWNED GENERATIONS, • • • • • • •   613 MARCH SONGS 1   1
 REMEMBER ALL THOSE RENOWNED GENERATIONS, • • • • • • •   613 MARCH SONGS 1   11
 REMEMBER ALL THESE RENOWNED GENERATIONS, • • • • • • •   613 MARCH SONGS 1 V   11
RENT
 HAS CLOVEN AND RENT THEIR HEARTS IN TWAIN, • • • • • •   66 HAPPY SHEPHERD   33
 HAS TORN AND RENT THEIR HEARTS IN TWAIN, • • • • • •   66 HAPPY SHEPHERD V   33
 HAS DRIED THE SAP OUT OF MY VEINS, AND RENT • • • • •   260 FASC DIFFICULT   2
 AND RENT HER CLOTHES AND MADE HER MOAN: • • • • • • •   275 GREY ROCK   108
 THAT HAS NOT BEEN RENT." • • • • • • • • • • • • •   513 JANE TALK BISH   18
RENYI
 HOW FERENCZ RENYI KEPT SILENT. • • • • • • • • • •   709 FERENCZ RENYI   T
 THY NAME IS?" "RENYI." "OF?" "THIS VILLAGE." "GOOD: 709 FERENCZ RENYI   13
 THY NAME IS?" "FERENCZ RENYI." "OF?" "THIS VILLAGE."   709 FERENCZ RENYI V   13
  "GOOD:
 THE SPIRIT OF YOUNG RENYI HAS GROWN OLD. • • • • • •   710 FERENCZ RENYI   17
 LIKE SMALL BROWN MOTHS, A-TREMBLE. "RENYI SAY • • • •   713 FERENCZ RENYI   82
 WHITE, RENYI SILENT STANDS: THAT MAIDEN SWEET • • • •   713 FERENCZ RENYI V   84
 I CURSE THEE--CURSE THEE!" RENYI SILENT STANDS, • • •   714 FERENCZ RENYI   107
 AND SOFT, ONE GLIMMERING STAR. RENYI HAS CAST • • • •   714 FERENCZ RENYI   115
 YOUNG FERENCZ RENYI BURSTS HIS BONDS--AT LAST, • • • •   714 FERENCZ RENYI V   116
RENYI'S
 THE YOUNG ONE WITH THE OTHERS." RENYI'S PALE • • • • •   713 FERENCZ RENYI   84
REPENTANCE
 REPENTANCE KEEPS MY HEART IMPURE: • • • • • • • • •   507 STREAM AND SUN   6
REPINING
 OF KNITTED MUSIC. OFT THE FOND REPINING • • • • • •   33 OISIN 2   V 68C
REPLIED
 THAT WANES." "AH, WISTFUL VOICE," REPLIED THE OTHER, • •   79 EPHEMERA   V 3
 WHILE SLOWLY HE WHOSE HAND HELD HERS REPLIED: • • • • •   80 EPHEMERA   11
 THE PARTED LIPS REPLIED, "I SEEK YOUR HELP, • • • • • •   183 QUEEN MAEVE   83
 NOR THE COLD NORTH HAS TROUBLED?" HE REPLIED, • • • • •   184 QUEEN MAEVE   90
 REPLIED: "TO BE BORN WOMAN IS TO KNOW-- • • • • • •   205 ADAMS CURSE   18
 SIGHING REPLIED: "WHAT NEED HAVE WE FOR HASTE • • • •   276 TWO KINGS   V C
 THEN I REPLIED, "ALTHOUGH YOU HIDE A SECRET, • • • •   281 TWO KINGS   95
 THEREON REPLIED: "A COCKEREL • • • • • • • • • • •   387 SOLOMON WITCH   9
 JAMES CONNOLLY REPLIED, • • • • • • • • • • • • •   396 ROSE TREE   8
 "YOU BUT IMAGINE LIES ALL DAY, O MURDERER," I REPLIED. • •   450 OWEN AHERNE   17
 IN NOBLE RAGE REPLIED • • • • • • • • • • • • • •   516 MANS SONG   5
 WHAT CALCULATION, NUMBER, MEASUREMENT, REPLIED? • • • •   611 STATUES   27
REPLIES
 A KIND OLD NUN IN A WHITE HOOD REPLIES: • • • • • • •   443 SCHOOL CHILDR   2
 THE HEART REPLIES • • • • • • • • • • • • • • • •   449 OWEN AHERNE   V T
 AND THEREUPON REPLIES • • • • • • • • • • • • • •   531 FATHER CHILD   6
 IF EMPTY NIGHT REPLIES? • • • • • • • • • • • • •   533 FIRST CONFESS   18
 ALONE WITH OUR OWN WHISPERS AND REPLIES-- • • • • • •   702 MOSADA 3   80
REPLY
 MAKE THE HILLS REPLY." • • • • • • • • • • • • • •   98 FOXHUNTER   26
 AND MAKE THE HILLS REPLY." • • • • • • • • • • • •   98 FOXHUNTER   V 26
 MAKE THE HILLS REPLY." • • • • • • • • • • • • • •   99 FOXHUNTER   34
 AND MAKE THE HILLS REPLY." • • • • • • • • • • • •   99 FOXHUNTER   V 34
 COMPLAINED OF THE PEOPLE." ALL I COULD REPLY • • • • •   352 PEOPLE   29
 CAN WITH A FITTING CONFIDENCE REPLY. • • • • • • • •   494 AT ALGECIRAS   18
 REPLY LIKE MOANING OF IMPRISONED ELF: • • • • • • • •   652 ISLE STAT I 2   11
REPORT
 THERE'S NOT A MAN CAN REPORT • • • • • • • • • • •   319 DOLLS   8
 ABASHED BY THAT REPORT, • • • • • • • • • • • • •   516 MANS SONG   13
REPOSE
 OR IT MAY BE LOOSENED IN REPOSE, • • • • • • • • • •   386 ROBARTES DANCE   35
 BUT KEEP A MARBLE OR A BRONZE REPOSE. • • • • • • • •   445 SCHOOL CHILDR   52
 VAIN GAIETY, VAIN BATTLE, VAIN REPOSE, • • • • • • • •   629 CIRCUS ANIMALS   12
REPRISALS
 REPRISALS • • • • • • • • • • • • • • • • • • •   791 REPRISALS   T
REPROACH
 IF RAILING AND REPROACH AND MOCKERY • • • • • • • •   243 SHADOW WATER B   438
 AND YET YOU MAKE A CLAMOUR OF REPROACH. • • • • • • •   243 SHADOW WATER B   444
 BUT IF IT BE REPROACH, I ANSWER THIS: • • • • • • • •   244 SHADOW WATER B   453
REPROOF
 THEREON MY PHOENIX ANSWERED IN REPROOF, • • • • • • •   352 PEOPLE   22
 TOLD OF A HARSH REPROOF, OR TRIVIAL EVENT • • • • • •   443 SCHOOL CHILDR   11

REPROVED
    THIS WAY WERE ALL REPROVED . . . .   93 FATHER OHART   39
    CRAZY JANE REPROVED . . . .   509 JANE REPROVED   T
    CRACKED MARY REPROVED . . . .   509 JANE REPROVED   V   T
REPROVES
    HE REPROVES THE CURLEW . . . .   155 REPROVE CURLEW   T
    HANRAHAN REPROVES THE CURLEW . . . .   155 REPROVE CURLEW   V   T
    WHILE HIS LOUD SONG REPROVES . . . .   536 PARTING   7
REPUTATION
    THE REPUTATION OF HIS LIFETIME LOST . . . .   351 PEOPLE   5
REPUTE
    AND I AM IN NO GOOD REPUTE . . . .   276 GREY ROCK   127
RESEMBLE
    RESEMBLE FORMS THAT ARE OR SEEM . . . .   639 BEN BULBEN   58
RESEMBLING   SEE MIRROR-RESEMBLING
    MIRROR RESEMBLING DREAMS. . . . .   415 TOWER   V 165
RESERVED
    MUCH TOO SOLEMN AND RESERVED. . . . .   342 SHEP GOATHERD   94
RE-SHINING
    IN BUSY FLAKES, RE-SHINING FROM THE LAKE, ...   662 ISLE STAT II 2   3
    RE-SHINING IN HIS EYES. SO EVER MOVES . . . . . .   689 NETTLESHIP   12
RESIGNED
    HE, TOO, HAS RESIGNED HIS PART . . . .   393 EASTER 1916   36
RESINOUS
    MAN'S OWN RESINOUS HEART HAS FED. . . . .   438 SONGS PLAY 2   16
RESOLVED
    BECOME OUR CAPTAIN, AIBRIC. I AM RESOLVED . . . . .   225 SHADOW WATER B   64
    ANTONIO! WE HAVE RESOLVED TO FIGHT. . . . .   664 ISLE STAT II 2   55
RESONANCE
    NIGHT RESONANCE RECEDES, NIGHT-WALKERS' SONG . . . .   497 BYZANTIUM   3
    NIGHT'S RESONANCE RECEDES, NIGHT-WALKERS SONG . . . . 497 BYZANTIUM   V   3
RESOUNDED
    THE HORN RESOUNDED AS THOUGH IT HAD BEEN SILVER, . . . 277 TWO KINGS   16
RESOUNDING
    HAVE FOUND DELIGHT, IN THE RESOUNDING OARS, ...   750 SHADOW WATER A   72
RESOUNDS
    THAT TREMBLES AND RESOUNDS WITH HYMNS TO THEE, ... 684 SEEKER   V 69C
RESOURCE
    I'LL SEND MINE ARROW, NOW MY ONE RESOURCE! . . . . . . 657 ISLE STAT I 3   64
RESPECT
    EARNING RESPECT! HAVE NO STRANGE FRIEND! . . . . . .   337 SCHOLARS   V   9
RESPECTABLE
    OLD, LEARNED, RESPECTABLE BALD HEADS . . . .   337 SCHOLARS   2
RESPECTED
    "AND THERE I'LL GROW RESPECTED AT MY EASE, ...   300 BEGGAR CRIED   17
    THAT MOST RESPECTED LADY'S EVERY WISH, ...   410 TOWER   29
RESPONSIBILITIES
    MY GREAT RESPONSIBILITIES? . . . .   380 SONGS FOOL 1   18
RESPONSIBILITY
    RESPONSIBILITY SO WEIGHS ME DOWN. . . . .   501 VACILLATION   50
REST
    NOR THY COMPANIONS. LET THEM REST . . . .   11 OISIN 1   V 130
    LIKE AN ARMY OF OLD MEN LONGING FOR REST FROM THE MOAN 48 OISIN 3   16
       OF THE SEAS.
    SQUARE LEAVES OF THE IVY MOVED OVER US, BINDING US DOWN 52 OISIN 3   76
       TO OUR REST.
    "O FLAMING LION OF THE WORLD, O WHEN WILL YOU TURN TO YOUR 56 OISIN 3   129
       REST?"
    O FLAMING LION OF THE WORLD, O WHEN WILL YOU TURN TO YOUR   56 OISIN 3   136
       REST?"
    "OH, FLAMING LION OF THE WORLD, OH, WHEN WILT THOU TURN   56 OISIN 3   V 129
       TO THY REST?"
    LIKE AN ARMY OF OLD MEN LONGING FOR REST FROM THE MOAN 57 OISIN 3   144
       OF THE SEAS.
    LIKE AN ARMY OF OLD MEN LOUNGING FOR REST FROM THE FOAM 57 OISIN 3   V 144
       OF THE SEAS.
    THE REST YOU HAVE HEARD OF, O CROZIERED MAN! . . . . . 60 OISIN 3   189
    THE REST THOU HAST HEARD OF, THOU CROSIERED ONE-- . . . 60 OISIN 3   V 189
    . . . AND OF OLD WOUNDS, AND TURN TO OUR REST. . . . . 62 OISIN 3   212
    . . . AND OF OLD WOUNDS AND REST. . . . .   62 OISIN 3   V 212
    REST FAR FROM MEN. . . . .   116 FAERY SONG   10
    "I HAVE NO REST, NOR JOY, NOR PEACE, ...   132 FR GILLIGAN   9
    THAT WAS BRIMMED UP WITH PRAYER AND REST! . . . . . . 151 HEART OF WOMAN   2
    AND LAY IN THE DARKNESS, GRUNTING, AND TURNING TO HIS REST. 153 CHANGE BELOVED 12
    DROWNING LOVE'S LONELY HOUR IN DEEP TWILIGHT OF REST, . . 154 BELOVED PEACE 11
    AND TROUBLE WITH A SIGH FOR ALL THINGS LONGING FOR REST 163 ASKS FORGIVE   23
    AND TROUBLE WITH SIGHS FOR ALL HEARTS WITHOUT REST . . 163 ASKS FORGIVE   V   23
    WHY SHOULD YOU BE MORE FAITHFUL THAN THE REST, ... 227 SHADOW WATER B   109
    IN HAVING ONE ANOTHER? HOW COULD I REST . . . . . .   249 SHADOW WATER B   571
    HAD GIVEN BUT AS THE REST . . . .   293 HELEN LIVED   10
    WHO DRAWS A BUCKET WITH THE REST . . . .   335 YOUNG BEAUTY   5
    HE NEVER FOUND HIS REST ASHORE, ...   361 ALF POLLEXFEN   21
    A BUDDHA, HAND AT REST. . . . .   383 VISION ROBART   19
    AND MAY THE DEVIL TAKE THE REST. . . . .   386 ROBARTES DANCE   24
    MY EYES SHOULD NEVER REST? . . . .   389 IMAGE PAST   18
    TO BREAK UPON A SLEEPER'S REST . . . .   412 TOWER   87
    THE MOTHER BIRD WILL REST . . . .   415 TOWER   170
    AND SHE CAN GET NO REST . . . .   456 FRIENDS YOUTH   8
    SWIFT HAS SAILED INTO HIS REST! . . . .   493 SWIFTS EPITAPH   1
    "JONATHAN SWIFT'S AT REST! . . . .   493 SWIFTS EPITAPH V   1
    SWIFT HAD SAILED INTO HIS REST! . . . .   493 SWIFTS EPITAPH V   1

```
                                                           PAGE      TITLE          LINE
REST   (CONTINUED)
     IN ALGECIRAS GARDENS, AND THERE REST  . . . . . . .   494  AT ALGECIRAS    V    5
     THAT HE MIGHT SET AT REST  . . . . . . . . . . . .    496  MOHINI CHATTER      12
     THINKING TO SET AT REST  . . . . . . . . . . . . .    496  MOHINI CHATTER  V   12
     WHETHER OF PLEASURE OR OF REST,  . . . . . . . . .    521  THREE THINGS         4
     OR FOUND A SUBTERRANEAN REST . . . . . . . . . . .    535  CHOSEN               6
     BIDS ALL TRUE LOVERS REST, . . . . . . . . . . . .    536  PARTING              6
     AND SANG MY MALEDICTION WITH THE REST. . . . . . .    537  HER VISION          24
     THE REST I PASS, ONE SENTENCE I UNSAY. . . . . . .    542  PARN FUNERAL 2       1
     I PASS THE REST--ONE SENTENCE I UNSAY-- . . . . . .   542  PARN FUNERAL 2  V    1
     PRIMORDIAL MOTHERHOOD FORSAKE HIS LIMBS, THE CHILD
       NO LONGER REST,                                     559  MAGIC DRUM           2
     NOW SINKS THE SAME REST  . . . . . . . . . . . . .    574  LOVERS SONG          4
     NOW SUNK IN REST, . . . . . . . . . . . . . . . .     574  MAIDS 1ST SONG       2
     DO NOT THE REST WITHHOLD. . . . . . . . . . . . . .   588  OLD WICKED MAN      11
     A SOUL INCAPABLE OF REMORSE OR REST; . . . . . . .    601  GALLERY REVIS        7
     LAY SIGHING LIKE THE REST. . . . . . . . . . . . .    612  NEWS ORACLE         12
     PREPARED A REST FOR THE PEOPLE OF GOD, . . . . . .    639  BEN BULBEN          65
     TO PROVE HIS LOVE A KNIGHT WITH LANCE IN REST  . .    651  ISLE STAT I 1  158
     SHALL NOT SO HOPELESS PROVE! SOME GOD MAY REST . .    657  ISLE STAT I 3       61
     WILT ROAM AWAY FROM THIS RICH ISLAND REST? . . . .    669  ISLE STAT II 3      88
     EVE-SOOTHED IN SOME FAR LEAFY REST, . . . . . . .     686  LIFE                10
     TO PRISONS GO, AND MOSSY RUIN REST . . . . . . . .    709  FERENCZ RENYI        2
     TO PRISON GO, AND MOSSY RUIN REST  . . . . . . . .    709  FERENCZ RENYI  V     2
     COME, FATHER. LADY, I NOR REST NOR SIT. . . . . .     720  WITCH VIVIEN        18
     AND NEVER REST IN THEIR FLIGHT, . . . . . . . . .     739  WHERE BOOKS GO       4
     TILL ALL THINGS ARE AT REST. . . . . . . . . . . .    741  EARL PAUL           52
RESTED
     I THOUGHT THE END HAD RESTED, WHEN THESE WORDS  . .    32  OISIN 2        V    49
     AND NEVER COULD HAVE RESTED IN THE TOMB  . . . . .    325  ROBERT GREGORY      27
RESTLESS
     GOD SHAKES THE WORLD WITH RESTLESS HANDS. MORE NEAR . .  43  OISIN 2      V   208
     YET STILL SHE TURNS HER RESTLESS HEAD; . . . . . .     65  HAPPY SHEPHERD       5
     AND MAY NO RESTLESS FAY WITH FIDGET FINGER . . . .     75  ANASHU VIJAYA       90
     MAY NEVER RESTLESS FAY WITH FIDGET FINGER . . . . .    75  ANASHU VIJAYA  V    90
     AND MAY NO RESTLESS PITRI'S FIDGET FINGER  . . . .     75  ANASHU VIJAYA  V    90
     "CHOOSE!" RESTLESS HAYNAU'S FINGERS TAPPING GO. . .   711  FERENCZ RENYI       41
RESTLESS-FOOTED
     WHERE GOES TO GAZE THE RESTLESS-FOOTED STAR  . . .     32  OISIN 2        V   50G
RESTLESSNESS
     THEIR PASSION AND THEIR RESTLESSNESS AND RUTH . . .   687  TWO TITANS          24
RESTORED
     RESTORED THIS TOWER FOR MY WIFE GEORGE; . . . . . .   406  CARVED STONE         4
RESTRAINING
     RESTRAINING RECKLESS MIDDLE-AGE? . . . . . . . . .    262  STUDENTS AGIT        4
RESULTS
     THE RESULTS OF THOUGHT . . . . . . . . . . . . . .    504  RESULT THOUGHT       T
RESUME
     AND MUST THE COMMON ROUND OF DAY RESUME. . . . . .    557  RIBH ECSTASY         8
RE-SUNG
     AN OLD SONG RE-SUNG  . . . . . . . . . . . . . . .     90  SALLEY GARDENS V     T
RETIRING
     HERE GROW THAT SHY, RETIRING SISTERHOOD, . . . . .    651  ISLE STAT I 2        4
RETURN
     RETURN WHEN YOU ARE WEARY, . . . . . . . . . . . .     33  OISIN 2        V    65
     A JUBILANT LIFE AMONG THE LEAVES, RETURN, . . . . .    35  OISIN 2        V   89A
     WE WOULD RETURN TO OUR OWN COUNTRY, FORGAEL, . . .    248  SHADOW WATER B     539
     YOU MUST RETURN, WHETHER YOU WOULD OR NO, . . . .     285  TWO KINGS          197
     OF THEIR RETURN TO THAT ANCESTRAL HOUSE. . . . . .    286  TWO KINGS      V  218C
     THOUGH THE GREAT SONG RETURN NO MORE . . . . . . .    485  NINETEENTH CEN       1
     "GOD I HAVE LOVED, BUT SHOULD I ASK RETURN . . . .    609  IN TARAS HALLS      14
     THE FLAGRANT SIGNAL OF HER LORD'S RETURN, . . . .     645  ISLE STAT I 1       13
     THAT FLOWER I SEEK. THOU NEVER WILT RETURN. . . .     653  ISLE STAT I 2       44
     MY SHEPHERD GARMENTS, AND RETURN ANON. . . . . . .    659  ISLE STAT II 1      29
     ANTONIO, IF I RETURN NO MORE, . . . . . . . . . .     663  ISLE STAT II 2      17
RETURNED
     RETURNED AND YET UNREQUITED LOVE. . . . . . . . . .   358  PRESENCES            8
     HERODIAS' DAUGHTERS HAVE RETURNED AGAIN, . . . . .    433  NINETEEN 19        118
RETURNING
     WITH NO RETURNING GLANCE, IN WORDLESS MOOD . . . .     44  OISIN 2        V  230A
     AND MOCKS RETURNING VICTORY, HE PASSED . . . . . .    279  TWO KINGS           58
     AWAITS RETURNING SPRING. . . . . . . . . . . . . .    517  HER ANXIETY          2
     MOURN--AND THEN ONWARD, THERE IS NO RETURNING . . .   738  MOURN THEN ON       13
RETURNS
     RETURNS THAT SOLDIER IN THE EVENING RAYS . . . . .    711  FERENCZ RENYI       49
REVEALING        SEE HEART-REVEALING
REVEL
     WHERE REVEL OF FOX-GLOVE IS AND REVEL OF ROSES." .    669  ISLE STAT II 3      86
     WHERE REVEL OF FOX-GLOVE IS AND REVEL OF ROSES." .    669  ISLE STAT II 3      86
     WHERE REVEL OF FOXGLOVE IS AND REVEL OF ROSES." .     669  ISLE STAT II 3 V    86
     WHERE REVEL OF FOXGLOVE IS AND REVEL OF ROSES." .     669  ISLE STAT II 3 V    86
REVELATION
     SURELY SOME REVELATION IS AT HAND; . . . . . . . .    402  SECOND COMING        9
REVELRY
     AND THERE WE HUSHED THE REVELRY; . . . . . . . . .     20  OISIN 1            295
     IN A SAD REVELRY HE SANG AND SWUNG . . . . . . . .     39  OISIN 2            160
     AND SILENCE HOLDING REVELRY AND FEAST; . . . . . .    705  REMEMBRANCE         12
     WHERE NIAM HEADS THE REVELRY. . . . . . . . . . . .   743  DANAAN QUICK        29
REVERBERATED
     GOES FLICKERING IN REVERBERATED LIGHT. . . . . . .    653  ISLE STAT I 2       53
```

654

PAGE   TITLE   LINE

REVERE
    MEN THAT REVERE YOUR FATHER YET . . . .   791 REPRISALS   17
REVERENCE
    A NUN AT LEAST HAS ALL MEN'S REVERENCE . . . .   448 HERO GIRL FOOL   12
    THAT MEN HAVE REVERENCE FOR THEIR HOLINESS . . . . . .   448 HERO GIRL FOOL   14
    . FOR THEY AT LEAST HAVE ALL MEN'S REVERENCE . . . . .   448 HERO GIRL FOOL V   12
REVERENT
    I BRING YOU WITH REVERENT HANDS . . . .   157 POET BELOVED   1
REVERIE
    IN A REVERIE FORGETFUL OF ALL THINGS, OVER THE BUBBLING   56 OISIN 3   140
      GROUND.
    IN REVERIE FORGETFUL OF ALL THINGS, OVER THE BUBBLING   56 OISIN 3   V   140
      GROUND.
    TROUBLING THE ENDLESS REVERIE. . . . .   65 HAPPY SHEPHERD   21
    IN THE UNIVERSE'S REVERIE. . . . .   65 HAPPY SHEPHERD V   21
    IN SOLEMN REVERIE ROSE TO HEAR . . . .   85 MAD KING GOLL V   62
    IMAGINING IN EXCITED REVERIE . . . .   403 FOR DAUGHTER   13
    IN REVERIE, OR IN VISION, SAW . . . .   420 MY HOUSE   V   20E
    TO BRAZEN HAWKS. NOR SELF-DELIGHTING REVERIE, ...   427 PHANTOM HATRED   29
    HEROIC REVERIE MOCKED BY CLOWN AND KNAVE, ...   619 BRONZE HEAD   27
REVERIES
    I TOO HAVE RHYMED MY REVERIES, BUT YOUTH . . . . . .   340 SHEP GOATHERD   43
    FRENZIES BEWILDER, REVERIES PERTURB THE MIND; . . . .   426 PHANTOM HATRED   7
    THAT ANIMATE A MOTHER'S REVERIES. . . . .   445 SCHOOL CHILDR   51
REVERSAL
    AN AGE IS THE REVERSAL OF AN AGE: . . . .   541 PARN FUNERAL 1   16
REVISITED
    IF YOU HAVE REVISITED THE TOWN, THIN SHADE, ...   292 TO A SHADE   1
    THE MUNICIPAL GALLERY REVISITED . . . .   601 GALLERY REVIS   T
RE-VISITED
    THE MUNICIPAL GALLERY RE-VISITED . . . .   601 GALLERY REVIS V   T
REVOLUTION
    HURRAH FOR REVOLUTION AND MORE CANNON-SHOT! . . . . .   590 GREAT DAY   1
    HURRAH FOR REVOLUTION AND CANNON COME AGAIN! . . . . .   590 GREAT DAY   3
    HURRAH FOR REVOLUTION AND MORE CANNON SHOT! . . . . .   590 GREAT DAY   V   1
    IRELAND AFTER THE REVOLUTION IV . . . .   628 JANE MOUNTAIN V   T
REVOLUTIONARY
    A REVOLUTIONARY SOLDIER KNEELING TO BE BLESSED; . . .   601 GALLERY REVIS   8
    FIRST I GREET MACCARTAN, REVOLUTIONARY LEADER. . . . .   790 DEDICATION   1
REWARD
    THE STRANGE REWARD OF ALL THAT DISCIPLINE. . . . . . .   374 PHASES OF MOON   57
    O BITTER REWARD . . . .   785 YOUR HEART   9
    O BITTER REWARD . . . .   786 YOUR HEART   22
    O BITTER REWARD . . . .   786 YOUR HEART   35
REWARDED
    HAD BEEN REWARDED THUS . . . .   384 VISION ROBART   67
REWARDING
    REWARDING IN MELODIOUS GUILE . . . .   66 HAPPY SHEPHERD V   39
REWARDS
    SHE OFFERS GREAT REWARDS IF WE TURN EAST . . . . . .   755 SHADOW WATER A   169
REWORDING
    REWORDING IN MELODIOUS GUILE . . . .   66 HAPPY SHEPHERD   39
REWRITTEN
    TWO SONGS REWRITTEN FOR THE TUNE'S SAKE . . . . . .   550 SONGS REWRIT 1   T
RE-WRITTEN
    AN OLD POEM RE-WRITTEN . . . .   129 BOOK STORIES   V   T
RHADAMANTHUS
    BLAND RHADAMANTHUS BECKONS HIM, ...   530 DELPHIC ORACLE   3
RHAPSODISTS   SEE WOOD-RHAPSODISTS
RHAPSODY
    ALL RHAPSODY HATH SORROW FOR ITS SOUL. . . . .   652 ISLE STAT I 2   17
RHETORICIAN
    THE RHETORICIAN WOULD DECEIVE HIS NEIGHBOURS, ...   369 EGO DOMINUS   46
RHINOCEROS
    NINE SWORDS WITH HANDLES OF RHINOCEROS HORN . . . . .   239 SHADOW WATER B   368
RHYME
    RHYME THAT RHYMED UPON OISIN'S NAME, ...   7 OISIN 1   64
    "RHYME, THAT RHYMED TO USHEEN'S NAME, ...   7 OISIN 1   V   64
    TO THAT LOW LAUGHING WOODLAND RHYME. . . . .   14 OISIN 1   176
    TO THE MUSIC OF THE GOLDEN RHYME . . . .   14 OISIN 1   V   176
    I BRING YOU MY PASSIONATE RHYME. . . . .   157 POET BELOVED   8
    TO BUILD A PERFECT BEAUTY IN RHYME . . . .   164 PERFECT BEAUTY   3
    TO BUILD THE PERFECT BEAUTY IN RHYME, ...   164 PERFECT BEAUTY V   3
    INTRODUCTORY RHYME . . . .   269 PARDON FATHERS   V   T
    CLOSING RHYME . . . .   320 REED WHISPERER V   T
    I LET THEM STRAY. I THOUGHT OF RHYME ALONE, ...   339 SHEP GOATHERD   11
    FOR RHYME CAN BEAT A MEASURE OUT OF TROUBLE . . . . .   339 SHEP GOATHERD   12
    I HAD DRIVEN EVERY RHYME INTO ITS PLACE . . . .   339 SHEP GOATHERD   14
    YOU HAVE PUT THE THOUGHT IN RHYME. I WORKED ALL DAY,   341 SHEP GOATHERD   58
    FROM DREAM TO DREAM AND RHYME TO RHYME I HAVE RANGED   357 BROKEN DREAMS   39
    FROM DREAM TO DREAM AND RHYME TO RHYME I HAVE RANGED   357 BROKEN DREAMS   39
    THAN SOULS THAT START NO GAME AND TURN NO RHYME! . . .   464 HARUN RASHID   68
    AND SING IT RHYME UPON RHYME . . . .   480 BLOOD AND MOON   10
    AND SING IT RHYME UPON RHYME . . . .   480 BLOOD AND MOON   10
    THE MIND OF MAN OR ELEVATE A RHYME: . . . .   492 COOLE BALLYLEE   45
    THAT MUST SING IN A RHYME . . . .   529 TOM CRUACHAN   2
    SAVING THE RHYME RATS HEAR BEFORE THEY DIE. . . . . .   542 PARN FUNERAL 1   28
    AND DEAD AS ARE THE LOVERS OF OLD RHYME . . . .   674 ISLE STAT II 3 V   204
    OF RHYME: REMEMBERING THEE, THIS CRESCENT NIGHT, . . .   704 REMEMBRANCE   2
    NAY, RISE AND FLATTER HER WITH GOLDEN RHYME, ...   724 KANVA ON SELF   19
    SINGING A LOVE RHYME TO HIMSELF, ...   741 EARL PAUL   41

RHYME   (CONTINUED)
     THAT CROWN WAS IN MY DREAMS--NO, NO--IN A RHYME. . . . .   763 SHADOW WATER A   311
     MY FOSTER-MOTHER SANG IN AN OLD RHYME . . . .   763 SHADOW WATER A   314
     MY FOSTER MOTHER SANG IN AN OLD RHYME . . . .   763 SHADOW WATER A V 314
RHYMED
     RHYME THAT RHYMED UPON OISIN'S NAME, ...   7 OISIN 1   64
     "RHYME, THAT RHYMED TO USHEEN'S NAME, ...   7 OISIN 1   V   64
     RHYMED OUT IN LOVE'S DESPAIR. . . . .   337 SCHOLARS   5
     I TOO HAVE RHYMED MY REVERIES, BUT YOUTH . . . . . .   340 SHEP GOATHERD   43
     ALL I HAD RHYMED OF THAT MONSTROUS THING . . . . . .   358 PRESENCES   7
     ALL I HAVE RHYMED OF THAT MONSTROUS THING . . . . . .   358 PRESENCES   V   7
RHYMER
     OR ANYTHING ELSE BUT A RHYMER . . . .   552 SONGS REWRIT 2   9
RHYMER'S
     I HAVE AS HEALTHY FLESH AND BLOOD AS ANY RHYMER'S HAD, . .   450 OWEN AHERNE   10
RHYMES
     WHILE I WROUGHT OUT THESE FITFUL DANAAN RHYMES, ...   136 TO SOME I TALK   1
     I DEDICATE THESE FITFUL DANAAN RHYMES . . . .   136 TO SOME I TALK V   1
     MY RHYMES MORE THAN THEIR RHYMING TELL . . . .   138 TO IRELAND   20
     I CAST MY HEART INTO MY RHYMES, ...   139 TO IRELAND   45
     HE GIVES HIS BELOVED CERTAIN RHYMES . . . .   157 BELOVED RHYMES   T
     AEDH GIVES HIS BELOVED CERTAIN RHYMES . . . .   157 BELOVED RHYMES V   T
     I BADE MY HEART BUILD THESE POOR RHYMES! . . . . . .   158 BELOVED RHYMES   3
     INTRODUCTORY RHYMES . . . .   217 WOODS OF COOLE V   T
     INTRODUCTORY RHYMES . . . .   269 PARDON FATHERS V   T
     CLOSING RHYMES . . . .   320 REED WHISPERER V   T
     CUT OUT OUR RHYMES ON STRIPS OF NEW-TORN BARK . . . . .   343 SHEP GOATHERD   115
     AND CERTAIN MEN, BEING MADDENED BY THOSE RHYMES, ...   410 TOWER   41
     BUT RHYMES FOR A BEAUTIFUL LADY, ...   552 SONGS REWRIT 2   11
RHYMING
     MY RHYMES MORE THAN THEIR RHYMING TELL . . . .   138 TO IRELAND   20
     HE RHYMING ALONE IN HIS BED. . . . .   552 SONGS REWRIT 2   12
RHYTHM
     TO THE RHYTHM OF THEIR FEET, ...   731 STREET DANCERS   2
RIB
     THE HEART BEHIND ITS RIB LAUGHED OUT. . . .   450 OWEN AHERNE   13
RIBBON
     A SHINING WEB, A FLOATING RIBBON OF CLOTH, ...   430 NINETEEN 19   50
RIBBONS
     OF THE MATCHING OF RIBBONS FOR BOSOM AND HEAD, ...   151 OLD MOTHER   6
     OF THE MATCHING OF RIBBONS THE BLUE AND THE RED, ...   151 OLD MOTHER   V   6
RIBH
     RIBH AT THE TOMB OF BAILE AND AILLINN . . . .   554 RIBH AT TOMB   T
     RIBH DENOUNCES PATRICK . . . .   556 RIBH PATRICK   T
     RIBH PREFERS AN OLDER THEOLOGY . . . .   556 RIBH PATRICK   V   T
     RIBH IN ECSTASY . . . .   557 RIBH ECSTASY   T
     RIBH CONSIDERS CHRISTIAN LOVE INSUFFICIENT . . . . . .   558 RIBH CHRISTIAN   T
RICE
     VIJAYA, I HAVE BROUGHT MY EVENING RICE! . . . . . .   72 ANASHU VIJAYA   23
     AH! THERE HE SNAPS MY RICE. I TOLD YOU SO. . . . . .   73 ANASHU VIJAYA   38
     BECAUSE YOU SAVED MY RICE. HAVE YOU NO THANKS? . . .   73 ANASHU VIJAYA   40
     FOR SPRING RICE HAD TO WHISPER IT, ...   582 ROGER CASEMENT   13
RICH
     THE NIGHT SMELLED RICH WITH JUNE. . . . .   160 CAP AND BELLS V   28
     ONE OF YOU THREE IS A RICH MAN, ...   295 THREE BEGGARS   21
     "NOR SHOULD SHE BE TOO RICH, BECAUSE THE RICH . . . . .   300 BEGGAR CRIED   13
     "NOR SHOULD SHE BE TOO RICH, BECAUSE THE RICH . . . . .   300 BEGGAR CRIED   13
     POOR MEN HAVE GROWN TO BE RICH MEN, ...   301 RUN PARADISE   15
     AND RICH MEN GROWN TO BE POOR AGAIN, ...   301 RUN PARADISE   16
     TOIL AND GROW RICH, ...   310 WITCH   1
     GROW RICH, POPULAR AND FULL OF INFLUENCE, ...   369 EGO DOMINUS   43
     CEREMONY'S A NAME FOR THE RICH HORN, ...   406 FOR DAUGHTER   79
     DID ALL OLD MEN AND WOMEN, RICH AND POOR, ...   413 TOWER   97
     SURELY AMONG A RICH MAN'S FLOWERING LAWNS, ...   417 ANCEST HOUSES   1
     OUT OF THE OBSCURE DARK OF THE RICH STREAMS, ...   417 ANCEST HOUSES   14
     SHADOWS THE INHERITED GLORY OF THE RICH. . . . . . .   418 ANCEST HOUSES   16
     FOR THE MOST RICH INHERITOR, ...   422 MY TABLE   25
     OR GARDENS RICH IN MEMORY GLORIFIED . . . .   491 COOLE BALLYLEE   35
     IN THE RICH MIDNIGHT OF THE GARDEN TREES . . . . . .   494 AT ALGECIRAS   5
     IN THE RICH MIDNIGHT OF THE GARDEN TREE . . . . . .   494 AT ALGECIRAS   V   5
     ALTHOUGH THEIR CHILDREN NEED A RICH ESTATE! . . . . .   500 VACILLATION   24
     DRY TIMBER UNDER THAT RICH FOLIAGE, ...   536 HER VISION   1
     THE RICH MAN AND HIS AFFAIRS, ...   540 FROM ANTIGONE   3
     RICH FOLIAGE THAT THE STARLIGHT GLITTERED THROUGH, . . .   541 PARN FUNERAL 1   8
     OR ANY RICH, DARK NOTHING DISINTER . . . .   565 GYRES   22
     AND WHETHER A MAN BE RICH OR POOR . . . .   582 ROGER CASEMENT V   19
     THE COLONEL KNOCKED ON THE RICH MAN'S DOOR, ...   595 COLONEL MARTIN   28
     HIS WIFE HE FOUND AND THE RICH MAN . . . .   595 COLONEL MARTIN   43
     THE COLONEL KNOCKED ON A RICH MAN'S DOOR. . . . . . .   595 COLONEL MARTIN V   28
     AND THE RICH MAN HAD PAID THEM WELL . . . .   596 COLONEL MARTIN   57
     THOUGH RICH ON EVERY SHORE . . . .   606 SONGS BURDEN 1   11
     WILT ROAM AWAY FROM THIS RICH ISLAND REST? . . . . .   669 ISLE STAT II 3   88
RICHES
     MORE RICHES THAN THEY EVER HOPED TO FIND? . . . . . .   226 SHADOW WATER B   94
     THE ONLY RICHES THAT HAVE HIT MY FANCY. . . . . . .   226 SHADOW WATER B   96
     WHAT RICHES CAN YOU FIND IN THIS WASTE SEA . . . . .   226 SHADOW WATER B   97
     WHAT'S RICHES TO HIM . . . .   310 PEACOCK   1
     RICHES DROVE OUT RANK, ...   626 STATES HOLIDAY   2
RICHNESS
     THEIR RICHNESS THROUGH THE SUMMER AND THE SPRING! . . .   279 TWO KINGS   V 62C

RICK
    THAT SHE MAY QUENCH THE RICK SHE HAS FIRED, AND THOUGH . . 282 TWO KINGS 116
RID
    WHERE I AM RID OF LIFE--THE EVENTS OF THE WORLD-- . . . . 227 SHADOW WATER B 121
    TO RID ME OF THE DEVIL IN MY SHOES," . . . . 299 BEGGAR CRIED 6
RIDDEN   SEE DRAGON-RIDDEN OUT-RIDDEN
    WHEN THEY HAD RIDDEN A LITTLE WAY . . . . 191 BAILE AILLINN 56
    AND RIDDEN OUT TO WELCOME THEM, AND NOW, ... 286 TWO KINGS V 218
    AND RIDDEN TOWARDS IT, BEING IGNORANT. . . . . 286 TWO KINGS V 218
    SHE HAD RIDDEN WELL TO HOUNDS. . . . . 392 EASTER 1916 V 23
    NOW DAYS ARE DRAGON RIDDEN, THE NIGHTMARE . . . . . . 429 NINETEEN 19 V 25
RIDDLED
    RIDDLED WITH LIGHT. AH! WHEN THE GHOST BEGINS TO QUICKEN, 316 COLD HEAVEN 9
RIDE
    "WHY, AS YE RIDE, DROOPS LOW EACH HEAD? . . . . 4 OISIN 1 V 32
    AND FROM WHAT COUNTRY DO YOU RIDE?" . . . . 5 OISIN 1 45
    AND INTO WHAT COUNTRY DO YOU RIDE?" . . . . 5 OISIN 1 V 45
    "O OISIN, MOUNT BY ME AND RIDE . . . . 8 OISIN 1 80
    FOR THEY WILL RIDE THE NORTH WHEN THE GER-EAGLE FLIES, . 146 UNAPPEAS HOST 3
    FOR THEY WILL RIDE THE WINDS WHEN THE GIER-EAGLE FLIES . 146 UNAPPEAS HOST V 3
    THAT RIDE UPON HORSES. . . . . 266 GALWAY RACES 16
    "WE RIDE BUT SLOWLY THOUGH SO NEAR OUR HOME," . . . . 276 TWO KINGS V A
    WHEN WITH THE GALWAY FOXHOUNDS HE WOULD RIDE . . . . . 326 ROBERT GREGORY 57
    ON A FANTASTIC RIDE, MY HORSE'S FLANKS ARE SPURRED . . . 391 UNDER SATURN 6
    ON A FANTASTIC RIDE I SWEAR MY HORSE'S FLANKS WERE SPURRED 391 UNDER SATURN V 6
    WHEN LONG AGO I SAW HER RIDE . . . . 397 POLIT PRISONER 13
    WHETHER TO PLAY, OR TO RIDE . . . . 431 NINETEEN 19 67
    I RIDE WITH FALCON TO THE RIVER'S EDGE . . . . 463 HARUN RASHID 57
    I RIDE WITH FALCON TO THE WATER'S EDGE . . . . 463 HARUN RASHID V 57
    SADDLE AND RIDE, I HEARD A MAN SAY, ... 549 SEVERED HEAD 1
    ALL THOSE TRAGIC CHARACTERS RIDE . . . . 549 SEVERED HEAD 4
    IMAGES RIDE, I HEARD A MAN SAY, ... 549 SEVERED HEAD V 1
    OUT OF THE GRAVE. SADDLE AND RIDE . . . . 549 SEVERED HEAD V 4
    WHAT MATTER THOUGH NUMB NIGHTMARE RIDE ON TOP, ... 564 GYRES 9
    DID EVER MAN RIDE SUCH A RACE? . . . . 570 THREE BUSHES 47
    FROM MOUNTAIN TO MOUNTAIN RIDE THE FIERCE HORSEMEN. . . 605 SONGS BURDEN 1 9
    FROM MOUNTAIN TO MOUNTAIN RIDE THE FIERCE HORSEMEN. . . 606 SONGS BURDEN 1 18
    FROM MOUNTAIN TO MOUNTAIN RIDE THE FIERCE HORSEMEN. . . 606 SONGS BURDEN 1 27
    FROM MOUNTAIN TO MOUNTAIN RIDE THE FIERCE HORSEMEN. . . 607 SONGS BURDEN 2 9
    FROM MOUNTAIN TO MOUNTAIN RIDE THE FIERCE HORSEMEN. . . 607 SONGS BURDEN 2 18
    FROM MOUNTAIN TO MOUNTAIN RIDE THE FIERCE HORSEMEN. . . 607 SONGS BURDEN 2 27
    FROM MOUNTAIN TO MOUNTAIN RIDE THE FIERCE HORSEMEN. . . 608 SONGS BURDEN 3 9
    FROM MOUNTAIN TO MOUNTAIN RIDE THE FIERCE HORSEMEN. . . 608 SONGS BURDEN 3 18
    FROM MOUNTAIN TO MOUNTAIN RIDE THE FIERCE HORSEMEN. . . 608 SONGS BURDEN 3 27
    BUT WHAT CARED I THAT SET HIM ON TO RIDE, ... 629 CIRCUS ANIMALS 15
    NOW THEY RIDE THE WINTRY DAWN . . . . 637 BEN BULBEN 10
    COME RIDE AND RIDE TO THE GARDEN, ... 773 COME RIDE 1
    COME RIDE AND RIDE TO THE GARDEN, ... 773 COME RIDE 1
    COME RIDE AND RIDE WITH A WILL! . . . . 773 COME RIDE 2
    COME RIDE AND RIDE WITH A WILL! . . . . 773 COME RIDE 2
    COME RIDE AND RIDE TO THE GARDEN, ... 774 COME RIDE 5
    COME RIDE AND RIDE TO THE GARDEN, ... 774 COME RIDE 5
    COME RIDE LIKE THE MARCH WIND! . . . . 774 COME RIDE 6
    COME RIDE AND RIDE TO THE GARDEN, ... 774 COME RIDE 13
    COME RIDE AND RIDE TO THE GARDEN, ... 774 COME RIDE 13
    COME RIDE AND RIDE TO THE GARDEN, ... 774 COME RIDE 18
    COME RIDE AND RIDE TO THE GARDEN, ... 774 COME RIDE 18
RIDER   SEE SEA-RIDER
    THE RIDER FROM THE NORTH . . . . 213 HAPPY TOWNLAND V T
    THE RIDER, THE BIRDS THAT RANGE . . . . 393 EASTER 1916 46
RIDERLESS
    BUT ALL IS CHANGED, THAT HIGH HORSE RIDERLESS, ... 492 COOLE BALLYLEE 46
    BUT FASHION'S CHANGED, THAT HIGH-HORSE RIDERLESS . . . 492 COOLE BALLYLEE V 46
RIDERS
    AND IF SHE HEAR HIM MUTTER OF WILD RIDERS, ... 230 SHADOW WATER B 175
    THE RIDERS UPON THE GALLOPING HORSES, ... 266 GALWAY RACES 3
    THE RIDERS UPON THE SWIFT HORSES . . . . 266 GALWAY RACES V 3
    RIDERS UPON THE SWIFT HORSES, ... 266 GALWAY RACES V 3
    THE RIDERS AND THE GALLOPING HORSES, ... 266 GALWAY RACES V 3
    SOME FEW HAVE HANDSOME RIDERS, ARE GARLANDED . . . . . 432 NINETEEN 19 114
RIDES
    RIDES UPON SLEEP, A DRUNKEN SOLDIERY . . . . 429 NINETEEN 19 26
RIDGE
    "AND BREAKS THE RIDGE OF BATTLE WITH HIS HANDS." . . . 107 CUCHULAIN SEA V 26
    IN THE LAST RIDGE OF THE BARLEY? DO OUR WOODS . . . . 218 WOODS OF COOLE 33
    THEY SAY THAT ON YOUR BARREN MOUNTAIN RIDGE . . . . . 342 SHEP GOATHERD 79
    LESS BITTER. THEY HAVE BROUGHT ME FROM THAT RIDGE . . 342 SHEP GOATHERD 87
    BEYOND THAT RIDGE LIVED MRS. FRENCH, AND ONCE . . . . 410 TOWER 25
    HALF RUNNING, DROPPED AT THE FIRST RIDGE OF THE DESERT . 468 HARUN RASHID 155
RIDICULOUS
    OF A MOST RIDICULOUS LITTLE BIRD . . . . 314 MEMORY YOUTH 20
RIDING   SEE HARD-RIDING
    "WHO ARE THE RIDING ONES?" I SAID. . . . . 12 OISIN 1 V 146
    WERE WE DAYS LONG OR HOURS LONG IN RIDING, ... 47 OISIN 3 9
    THE HOST IS RIDING FROM KNOCKNAREA . . . . 140 HOSTING SIDHE 1
    THAT WE ARE RIDING TO, ... 214 HAPPY TOWNLAND 4
    HE IS RIDING TO THE TOWNLAND . . . . 214 HAPPY TOWNLAND 19
    THAT WE WERE RIDING TO, ... 214 HAPPY TOWNLAND V 4
    HE IS RIDING TO THE TOWNLAND . . . . 215 HAPPY TOWNLAND 39
    HE IS RIDING TO THE TOWNLAND . . . . 216 HAPPY TOWNLAND 59
    RIDING TO HURLEY, OR IN THE BATTLE-HOST . . . . . . 229 SHADOW WATER B 169

657

```
                                              PAGE      TITLE            LINE
RIDING  (CONTINUED)
     UPON GREAT JUAN RIDING BY,  . . . . . . . . . .   294 HATED PLAYBOY          4
     AT GREAT JUAN RIDING BY,  . . . . . . . . . . .   294 HATED PLAYBOY    V     4
     AND ALL ALONE COMES RIDING THERE  . . . . . . .   550 SEVERED HEAD         18
RIFLE
     OR THE RIFLE KNOCKS HIM DEAD,  . . . . . . . . .  637 BEN BULBEN           18
     OR THE RIFLE KNOCK HIM DEAD,  . . . . . . . . .   637 BEN BULBEN      V    18
RIGHT
     OF MOONLIT STEPS GLIMMERED; AND LEFT AND RIGHT     31 OISIN 2             35
     COME CLEAR OF THE NETS OF WRONG AND RIGHT,  . .   147 INTO TWILIGHT        2
     COME CLEAR OFF THE NETS OF WRONG AND RIGHT,  . .  147 INTO TWILIGHT   V     2
     TO HER RIGHT HAND CAME THE RED ONE,  . . . . . .  160 CAP AND BELLS       31
     NO, NO, DO NOT SAY THAT.  YOU KNOW RIGHT WELL  .  227 SHADOW WATER B     107
     BUT IT WAS SUDDEN.  YOU ARE IN THE RIGHT,  . . .  240 SHADOW WATER B     383
     I HAVE DONE RIGHT.  WHAT COULD I BUT OBEY?  . .   243 SHADOW WATER B     443
     AND THEREFORE EARNED THE RIGHT--AND YET .  . . .  273 GREY ROCK           61
     BUT THE RIGHT TWIGS FOR AN EAGLE'S NEST;  . . .   288 TO WEALTHY MAN      36
     WHEN CLOSE TO HIS RIGHT HAND A HEAP  . . . . . .  302 HOUR DAWN           11
     BEING CERTAIN IT WAS NO RIGHT ROCK  . . . . . .   303 HOUR DAWN           23
     BEING CERTAIN IT WAS NO RIGHT PLACE  . . . . . .  303 HOUR DAWN       V   23
     "IT'S PLAIN THAT YOU ARE NO RIGHT MAN  . . . . .  306 HOUR DAWN           82
     THE SHEEP HAD GONE FROM THEIRS.  I KNOW RIGHT WELL 339 SHEP GOATHERD      15
     I MIGHT HAVE USED THE ONE SUBSTANTIAL RIGHT  . .  352 PEOPLE              19
     WE HAVE NO GIFT TO SET A STATESMAN RIGHT;  . . .  359 WAR POEM             3
     AND RIGHT BETWEEN THESE TWO A GIRL AT PLAY  . .   383 VISION ROBART       21
     CAN RULE BY SUPERNATURAL RIGHT . . . . . . . . .  386 ROBARTES DANCE      36
     I HAVE PRINCIPLES TO PROVE ME RIGHT. . . . . . .  386 ROBARTES DANCE      42
     CAN MAKE A RIGHT ROSE TREE."  . . . . . . . . .   396 ROSE TREE           18
     RIGHT MASTERY OF NATURAL THINGS,  . . . . . . .   401 DEMON BEAST         37
     THAT CHOOSES RIGHT, AND NEVER FIND A FRIEND. . .  404 FOR DAUGHTER        24
     ROSE FROM THE TABLE AND DECLARED IT RIGHT  . . .  410 TOWER               43
     WHIRLS OUT NEW RIGHT AND WRONG,  . . . . . . . .  430 NINETEEN 19         55
     UNCHANGING AND AT PEACE, AND IT IS RIGHT  . . .   465 HARUN RASHID        96
     FOR IT IS A GHOST'S RIGHT,  . . . . . . . . . .   470 ALL SOUL NIGHT       6
     WITH A COMMON WRONG OR RIGHT.  . . . . . . . . .  476 EVA GORE-BOOTH      23
     AND CLAIM AS BY A SOLDIER'S RIGHT  . . . . . . .  478 SELF AND SOUL       31
     AND IS SO LOVELY THAT IT SETS TO RIGHT  . . . .   490 COOLE BALLYLEE      21
     BUT IF THESE BE RIGHT . . . . . . . . . . . . .   500 VACILLATION          9
     IF THESE HAVE NAMED IT RIGHT . . . . . . . . . .  500 VACILLATION     V    9
     SPEECH AFTER LONG SILENCE; IT IS RIGHT,  . . . .  523 LONG SILENCE         1
     OR ASK IF ALL BE RIGHT  . . . . . . . . . . . .   532 BEFORE WORLD         4
     AND RULE IN HIS OWN RIGHT;  . . . . . . . . . .   538 LAST CONFESS        20
     DO NOT DENY HIS RIGHT;  . . . . . . . . . . . .   584 ORAHILLY             2
     NO RIGHT TAUGHT MAN DENIES.  . . . . . . . . . .  590 OLD WICKED MAN  V   58
     THAT RULE BECAUSE A STRONG RIGHT ARM  . . . . .   597 MODEL LAUREATE      11
     WHERE NONE GAINSAY THEIR RIGHT,  . . . . . . . .  597 MODEL LAUREATE      14
     HERE AT RIGHT OF THE ENTRANCE THIS BRONZE HEAD,   618 BRONZE HEAD          1
     WHICH OF HER FORMS HAS SHOWN HER SUBSTANCE RIGHT? 618 BRONZE HEAD         11
     AND NEVER GET THE ANSWERS RIGHT.  . . . . . . .   632 MAN AND ECHO        10
     WHO, WHEN HIS OWN RIGHT KING'S FORGOTTEN,  . . .  635 BLACK TOWER         13
     MAKE HIM FILL THE CRADLES RIGHT.  . . . . . . .   638 BEN BULBEN          41
     THE PRIEST LOOKED NEITHER TO RIGHT NOR LEFT,  .   730 PRIEST FAIRY        49
     SITTING ON MY RIGHT HAND."  . . . . . . . . . .   741 EARL PAUL           60
     A QUARTER OF THE HEAVENS FROM OUR RIGHT WAY.  .   754 SHADOW WATER A     155
     AND I MET WITH A MAN THAT WAS NO RIGHT MAN  . .   779 GOING THE ROAD       3
RIGHTFUL
     FACE TO FACE MY RIGHTFUL MAN  . . . . . . . . .   521 THREE THINGS        16
RIGHTLY
     SOME TWENTY FEET FROM TIP TO TIP HAD IT STRETCHED RIGHTLY   593 PILGRIM            17
        OUT,
     SOME TWENTY FEET FROM TIP TO TIP HAD ITS WINGS STRETCHED    593 PILGRIM      V     17
        RIGHTLY OUT,
RIGHT-TAUGHT
     NO RIGHT-TAUGHT MAN DENIES. . . . . . . . . . .   590 OLD WICKED MAN      58
RILL
     AND WAVERED LIKE A SUMMER RILL,  . . . . . . . .    4 OISIN 1         V   29
RILLS
     AND LAUGH'D, SO, SO ALONG THE BUBBLING RILLS  .   645 ISLE STAT I 1       18
RIM
     IN THE PALE WEST, AND THE SUN'S RIM SANK,  . . .   12 OISIN 1            153
     NOW IN THE SEA THE SUN'S RIM SANK,  . . . . . .    12 OISIN 1         V  153
     AND RODE ON TILL OVER THE WORLD'S RIM FLOATED THE SEA'S  60 OISIN 3     V  183
        OLD SHOUT,
     THEN HE SANG SOFTLY NIGH THE PEARLY RIM;  . . .    69 SAD SHEPHERD        25
     THEN SANG HE SOFTLY NIGH THE PEARLY RIM;  . . .    69 SAD SHEPHERD    V   25
     BETWEEN WOOD'S RIM AND THE HORSES OF THE SEA. .   108 CUCHULAIN SEA       34
     GO THERE, AND LIGHT A CAMP-FIRE AT WOOD'S RIM;    108 CUCHULAIN SEA       35
     GO THERE AND DWELL ON THE GREEN FOREST RIM.  .    108 CUCHULAIN SEA   V   35
     GO THERE, AND CAMP UPON THE FOREST'S RIM;  . . .  108 CUCHULAIN SEA   V   35
     GO THERE, AND LIGHT A CAMP FIRE AT WOOD'S RIM;    108 CUCHULAIN SEA   V   35
     . . . HUNG LOW ON THE RIM OF THE SKY;  . . . . .  122 WHITE BIRDS          3
     BUT ONE SMALL KNOT-GRASS GROWING BY THE RIM  . .  127 DREAM OF FAERY  V   29
     ABOVE ITS CLOUDY RIM;  . . . . . . . . . . . . .  175 ELEMENT POWERS      16
     SHE COULD HAVE CALLED OVER THE RIM OF THE WORLD   181 QUEEN MAEVE         23
RIME
     AND DEAD AS ARE THE LOVERS OF OLD RIME  . . . .   674 ISLE STAT II 3     204
RING
     THAT WOMAN FOUND A RING HUNG ON THE WALL,  . . .   37 OISIN 2            120
     AND IN THE RING A TORCH, AND WITH ITS FLARE  . .   37 OISIN 2            121
     THAT MAIDEN FOUND A RING HUNG ON THE WALL,  . .    37 OISIN 2         V  120
     OR GENTLY IN A RING. . . . . . . . . . . . . . .   97 FOXHUNTER            8
```

RING   (CONTINUED)
    AND LEAD HIM GENTLY IN A RING, ...   97 FOXHUNTER   V   7
    UPON THE WHARVES OF SORROW, AND HEARD RING . . . . . 115 ROSE OF BATTLE   27
    WHO KNOW IT ALL RING AT HIS DOOR, AND SPEAK . . . .   373 PHASES OF MOON   21
    WERE NOT OUR BEDS FAR OFF I'D RING THE BELL, ... 377 PHASES OF MOON   124
    AND WHEN ABOUNDING HEDGES RING . . . .   434 WHEEL   3
    NATURAL AND SUPERNATURAL WITH THE SELF-SAME RING ARE WED. 556 RIBH PATRICK   4
    BINDS, AS WITHIN A GIRDLE OR A RING, ...   657 ISLE STAT I 3   59
    UNTIL WE DIE WITHIN THE CHARMED RING . . . .   679 ISLE STAT II 3   322
    AND NOT COME THENCE; FOR HERE IN THIS SMALL RING-- . 699 MOSADA 3   22
    THE SHADOWS PASS; BUT NOW, I LOVE MY RING, ...   700 MOSADA 3   27
    AND LIKE A SILVER TRUMPET RING. . . . .   736 SUMMER EVENING   4
    AND LIKE A SILVER TRUMPET RING. . . . .   737 SUMMER EVENING   20
RINGDOVE'S
    FOLLOWED A RINGDOVE'S ASH-GREY GLEAM OF FEATHER. . . 715 DWELT SYCAMORE   6
RING-DOVE'S
    FOLLOWED THE RING-DOVE'S ASH-GREY GLEAM OF FEATHER. . 715 DWELT SYCAMORE V   6
RINGED   SEE BRONZE-RINGED
    OR CARRY THE RINGED MAIL UPON MY BACK, ...   463 HARUN RASHID   58
    FAR OUT UPON THE WATER WORLD AND RINGED . . . . . .   693 MOSADA 1   80
    RINGED ROUND AND FONDLED, A BROWN FARM HOUSE SEES. . 710 FERENCZ RENYI V   23
    HIS GARDEN RINGED WITH JESSAMINE. . . . .   729 PRIEST FAIRY   34
RINGER
    SAY WHAT RINGER RINGS AT MIDNIGHT; FOR, IN THE BELFRY HIGH, 718 PHANTOM SHIP 15
RINGING
    AMONG THE RINGING HALLS A SHOUT . . . .   20 OISIN 1   V 288
    A HONIED RINGING! UNDER THE NEW SKIES . . . .   130 BOOK STORIES   V   21
    EVER RINGING, RINGING, RINGING, ...   647 ISLE STAT I 1   68
    EVER RINGING, RINGING, RINGING, ...   647 ISLE STAT I 1   68
    EVER RINGING, RINGING, RINGING, ...   647 ISLE STAT I 1   68
    ALL THE WORLD IS RINGING, RINGING; . . . .   648 ISLE STAT I 1   93
    ALL THE WORLD IS RINGING, RINGING; . . . .   648 ISLE STAT I 1   93
RINGS   SEE DRAGON-RINGS
    WHO WEDDED MEN WITH RINGS OF DRUID GOLD; . . . . .   29 OISIN 2   10
    WEDDING THE QUEENS OF EARTHLY LANDS WITH RINGS . . .   29 OISIN 2   V   10
    HIS HEAVY RINGS UNCOILED FROM GLIMMERING DEEP TO DEEP; . 174 ELEMENT POWERS   5
    AND SCATTER WHEELING IN GREAT BROKEN RINGS . . . . . 322 SWANS AT COOLE   11
    A BLIND HERMIT RINGS THE HOUR. . . . .   484 SYMBOLS   2
    AND THEN YOU STOOD AMONG THE DRAGON RINGS. . . . . . 533 HER TRIUMPH   V   7
    AND 'MONG THE STUNTED ASH-TREES' DROOPING RINGS, . . 650 ISLE STAT I 1   128
    AT THEIR FEET THE WAVES IN RINGS . . . .   667 ISLE STAT II 3   25
    SAY WHAT RINGER RINGS AT MIDNIGHT; FOR, IN THE BELFRY HIGH, 718 PHANTOM SHIP 15
RINSING
    TO HIS SHAPE AT THE RINSING POOL . . . .   341 SHEP GOATHERD V   70
RINSING-POOL
    TO HIS SHAPE AT THE RINSING-POOL . . . .   341 SHEP GOATHERD   70
R.I.P.
    R.I.P." WRIT IN BLOOD. . . . .   585 ORAHILLY   35
RIPENED
    WHAT WHOLESOME SUN HAS RIPENED IS WHOLESOME FOOD TO EAT, 442 BLACK CENTAUR   5
RIPENING
    PUBLIC OPINION RIPENING FOR SO LONG . . . .   428 NINETEEN 19   13
RIPPED
    RIPPED THROUGH THE HORSE'S FLANKS. KING EOCHAID REELED, 277 TWO KINGS   V   13
RISE
    . . . THEY WILL RISE, MAKING CLOUDS WITH THEIR BREATH, . . 61 OISIN 3   202
    . . . SHALL LISTEN AND RISE UP AND WEEP; . . . . .   62 OISIN 3   206
    WITH MIRTHFUL SONGS TILL RISE THE DAWN. . . . . .   67 HAPPY SHEPHERD V   49
    ABOVE THE TIDE OF HOURS, RISE ON THE AIR, ...   114 ROSE OF BATTLE V   3
    WHATEVER RAVELLED WATERS RISE AND FALL . . . . . .   127 DREAM OF FAERY   32
    WHO RISE, WING ABOVE WING, FLAME ABOVE FLAME, . . .   137 TO SOME I TALK   11
    I RISE IN THE DAWN, AND I KNEEL AND BLOW . . . . .   150 OLD MOTHER   1
    I RISE AT THE DAWN, AND I KNEEL AND BLOW . . . . .   150 OLD MOTHER   V   1
    HE BADE HIS SOUL RISE UPWARD . . . .   159 CAP AND BELLS   3
    SAW THE PIERCED HANDS AND ROOD OF ELDER RISE . . .   169 SECRET ROSE   10
    TIME'S BITTER FLOOD WILL RISE, ...   173 PLEADS FRIEND   6
    NOR WOULD YOU RISE AND HASTEN AWAY, ...   176 BELOVED DEAD   7
    WOULD RISE OF A SUDDEN, OR A WAVE SO HUGE . . . .   236 SHADOW WATER B   310
    WOULD RISE AGAINST ME. NO, I AM NOT MAD-- . . .   236 SHADOW WATER B   318
    THAT, BEING DEAD, WE RISE, ...   415 TOWER   154
    ANOTHER TROY MUST RISE AND SET, ...   437 SONGS PLAY 1   9
    WHEN THOUGHTS RISE UP UNBID . . . .   473 ALL SOUL NIGHT   68
    RUN UNDERGROUND, RISE IN A ROCKY PLACE . . . . .   490 COOLE BALLYLEE   5
    RISE AS KINDRED SHOULD. . . . .   518 LOVES LONENESS   2
    MADE DRAPERIES THAT SEEMED TO RISE . . . .   566 LAPIS LAZULI   31
    COULD THAT OLD GOD RISE UP AGAIN . . . .   606 SONGS BURDEN 1   21
    WHEN THE WINTRY VAPOURS RISE. . . . .   643 SONG FAERIES   4
    WHEN THE WINTRY VAPOURS RISE. . . . .   644 SONG FAERIES   16
    THY FLICKERING HAND? WHAT MEAN THE LIGHTS THAT RISE . . 674 ISLE STAT II 3 198
    WHEN THE WINTRY VAPOURS RISE. . . . .   676 ISLE STAT II 3   251
    WHEN THE WINTRY VAPOURS RISE. . . . .   676 ISLE STAT II 3   263
    WHERE RISE THE WALLS MAJESTICAL ABOVE . . . . . .   679 ISLE STAT II 3   311
    IF ONE SHOULD RISE BESIDE THEE, ...   680 LOVE AND DEATH   27
    AND NOW AND THEN A BUBBLE RISE. I HEAR . . . . .   722 WITCH VIVIEN   63
    NAY, RISE AND FLATTER HER WITH GOLDEN RHYME, . . .   724 KANVA ON SELF   19
    TO THE FIDDLE'S RISE AND FALL. . . . .   726 LOVERS QUARREL   20
    YET RISE FROM YOUR ITALIAN TOMB, ...   791 REPRISALS   10
RISEN   SEE LATE-RISEN
    DESPITE A DWINDLING AND LATE RISEN MOON, ...   372 PHASES OF MOON V   6
RISES
    RISES, AND SHOWERS ABROAD HIS FRAGRANT ARROWS, . . .   72 ANASHU VIJAYA   27

PAGE TITLE   LINE

RISES (CONTINUED)
 THE RIVER RISES, AND IT SINKS AGAIN; . . . . 420 MY HOUSE V 20A
 AND COLA, SEEING, KNOWS THE SIGN AND RISES. . . . . . . 691 MOSADA 1 V 38
RISING
 RISING AND FALLING, MIXED INSEPARABLY, ... 45 OISIN 2 V 233
 FEET TO THE RISING AND SETTING MAY RUN, ... 591 WHAT WAS LOST 4
 WAKE! THE HERON, RISING; HATH . . . . 705 DAWN-SONG 17
 KINGDOMS RISING, KINGDOMS FALLING, ... 737 IN FIRELIGHT 9
RITES
 OF EQUAL POWER IN SPELLS AND SECRET RITES. . . . . . . 720 WITCH VIVIEN 6
RIVER
 AND RIVER, FERN AND FLOWERY CLUMP, ... 15 OISIN 1 V 196
 LIKE A SMALL RIVER, AND WHERE FEET TOUCHED CAME . . . . 37 OISIN 2 117
 IN A FIELD BY THE RIVER MY LOVE AND I DID STAND, . . . 90 SALLEY GARDENS 5
 I SEE MY LIFE GO DRIFTING LIKE A RIVER . . . . 104 FERGUS DRUID 31
 AND RIVER AND STREAM WORK OUT THEIR WILL; . . . . 148 INTO TWILIGHT 12
 THE RIVER IMAGING THE FLASHING SKIES. . . . . 390 IMAGE PAST 20
 THE RIVER RISES, AND IT SINKS AGAIN; . . . . 420 MY HOUSE V 20A
 VALLEY, RIVER, AND ELMS, UNDER THE LIGHT OF A MOON . . 426 PHANTOM HATRED 3
 VALLEY, RIVER, ELMS, UNDER THE LIGHT OF A MOON . . . . 426 PHANTOM HATRED V 3
 ON THE RUDDY RIVER SEDGE, ... 646 ISLE STAT I 1 25
 WHOSE BEARD A MOONLIGHT RIVER IS, WHOSE BROW . . . . . 657 ISLE STAT I 3 73
RIVER'S
 I RIDE WITH FALCON TO THE RIVER'S EDGE . . . . 463 HARUN RASHID 57
 ITS PAVEN LENGTH TOWARDS THE RIVER'S MARGE . . . . . . 702 MOSADA 3 76
 AFAR ALONG THE FLEET WHITE RIVER'S FACE-- . . . . 702 MOSADA 3 79
 COMPANIONING THE RIVER'S PILGRIM TORCH. . . . . 703 MOSADA 3 112
RIVERS
 BY RIVERS AND THE WOODS' OLD NIGHT; . . . . 25 OISIN 1 387
 THE RIVERS, AND THE WOOD'S OLD NIGHT. . . . . 25 OISIN 1 V 387
 "I AM FROM THOSE RIVERS AND I BID YOU CALL . . . . . . 184 QUEEN MAEVE 91
 BY RIVERS WHERE THE RAIN HAS NEVER DIMMED . . . . 184 QUEEN MAEVE V 87
 BY RIVERS WHERE NOR RAIN NOR HAIL HAS DIMMED . . . . . 184 QUEEN MAEVE V 87
 "I COME FROM THE UNDIMMED RIVERS TO BID YOU CALL . . . 184 QUEEN MAEVE V 91
 "I AM FROM THE UNDIMMED RIVERS. I BID YOU CALL . . . . 184 QUEEN MAEVE V 91
 "I AM FROM THOSE RIVERS AND WOULD HAVE YOU CALL . . . . 184 QUEEN MAEVE V 91
 RIVERS ARE RUNNING OVER . . . . 214 HAPPY TOWNLAND 7
 WHERE RIVERS ARE RUNNING OVER . . . . 214 HAPPY TOWNLAND V 7
 IN THE HEART OF THE DAWN THE RIVERS ARE SINGING, . . . 648 ISLE STAT I 1 91
 OF ASIAN RIVERS, ROLLING ON IN LIGHT. . . . . 682 SEEKER 20
 OF INDIA'S RIVERS, ROLLING ON IN LIGHT. . . . . 682 SEEKER V 20
RIVER-SIDE
 THE PALACE-YARD AND RIVER-SIDE . . . . 295 THREE BEGGARS 9
 FROM RIVER-SIDE AND PALACE-YARD . . . . 296 THREE BEGGARS 27
RIVERY
 FROM ROLLING VALE AND RIVERY GLEN; . . . . 83 MAD KING GOLL 19
 FROM ROLLING VALLEY AND RIVERY GLEN, ... 83 MAD KING GOLL V 17
 A RIVERY FIELD SPREAD OUT BELOW, ... 502 VACILLATION 57
RIVETED
 WHEN. THEY FROZE THE CLOTH ON MY BODY LIKE ARMOUR RIVETED 57 OISIN 3 151
  FAST,
RIVULET'S
 GREY IN THE MIDST LIKE A SMALL RIVULET'S FLOW, ... 37 OISIN 2 V 117
RIVULETS
 AS QUIET AS THE LITTLE RIVULETS . . . . 698 MOSADA 2 57
ROAD
 AND I ON THIS STRANGE ROAD WILL PASS . . . . 97 FOXHUNTER V 11
 GO WATCH THE ROAD BETWEEN THE WOOD AND TIDE, ... 105 CUCHULAIN SEA 4
 HE MADE THE WORLD TO BE A GRASSY ROAD . . . . 112 ROSE OF WORLD 14
 BUT NOW THAT THEY HAVE TAKEN TO THE ROAD . . . . 247 SHADOW WATER B 526
 YET SHE, SINGING UPON HER ROAD, ... 260 UNWORTH PRAISE 19
 AS THOUGH IT DRAGGED ROAD METAL. MY CURSE ON PLAYS . . 260 FASC DIFFICULT V 8
 THAT CAST THEIR SHADOWS UPON ROAD AND BRIDGE; . . . . . 326 ROBERT GREGORY 51
 YOU HAVE MEASURED OUT THE ROAD THAT THE SOUL TREADS . . 342 SHEP GOATHERD 80
 THAT SHADES THE ROAD, OR SETTING UP A COTTAGE . . . . . 372 ON GOING HOUSE 14
 HAD TROD THE UNEVEN ROAD. THEIR BOOTS WERE SOILED, . . 372 PHASES OF MOON 3
 UPON THE OPEN ROAD, NEAR TO THE SLIGO QUAY-- . . . . . 391 UNDER SATURN 12
 THE HORSE THAT COMES FROM THE ROAD, ... 393 EASTER 1916 45
 THE ROAD AT MY DOOR . . . . 423 ROAD AT DOOR T
 LAST NIGHT THEY TRUNDLED DOWN THE ROAD . . . . 425 STARES NEST 13
 BUT TROD THE ROAD, OR SPLASHED ABOUT THE SHORE, ... 447 COLONUS PRAISE 27
 BUT TROD THE ROAD, OR PADDLED BY THE SHORE, ... 447 COLONUS PRAISE V 27
 PASSING ON THE ROAD THAT NIGHT, ... 511 JANE AND JACK 17
 THOUGH LIKE A ROAD . . . . 512 JANE ON GOD 20
 I MET THE BISHOP ON THE ROAD . . . . 513 JANE TALK BISH 1
 OR SING A PENANCE ON THE ROAD; . . . . 529 TOM LUNATIC 10
 WHETHER THEY TAKE THE UPPER ROAD . . . . 589 OLD WICKED MAN 48
 PARNELL CAME DOWN THE ROAD, HE SAID TO A CHEERING MAN; . 590 PARNELL 1
 BY THE ROAD AN ANCIENT CROSS. . . . . 640 BEN BULBEN 88
 I WAS GOING THE ROAD ONE DAY . . . . 779 GOING THE ROAD 1
ROAD-METAL
 AS THOUGH IT DRAGGED ROAD-METAL. MY CURSE ON PLAYS . . 260 FASC DIFFICULT 8
ROADS
 FOR THE ROADS ARE UNENDING, AND THERE IS NO PLACE TO MY 203 WITHER BOUGHS 4
  MIND."
 ON WET ROADS WHERE MEN WALK, ... 215 HAPPY TOWNLAND 48
 OUT NAKED ON THE ROADS, AS THE BOOKS SAY, AND STRICKEN . . 316 COLD HEAVEN 11
 AND WHEN YOU HAVE SPOKEN TAKE THE ROADS AGAIN? . . . . 373 PHASES OF MOON 25
 VIOLENCE UPON THE ROADS: VIOLENCE OF HORSES; . . . . . 432 NINETEEN 19 113
 ROADS FULL OF BEGGARS, CATTLE IN THE FIELDS, ... 487 SEVEN SAGES 18
 WHAT SCHOOLING HAD THESE FOUR? THEY WALKED THE ROADS . . 487 SEVEN SAGES 24

```
                                                          PAGE     TITLE              LINE
ROADS   (CONTINUED)
     TAKE TO THE ROADS AND GO MARCHING ALONG.  . . . . . . .  548 TO SAME TUNE 3        14
     ROUND US THE WHITE ROADS ARE ENDLESS,  . . . . . . . .   737 IN FIRELIGHT           3
     WAR-LADEN GALLEYS, AND ARMIES ON WHITE ROADS, . . . . .  757 SHADOW WATER A       203
     WAR LADEN GALLEYS, AND ARMIES ON WHITE ROADS, . . . . .  757 SHADOW WATER A  V    203
ROADSIDE
     BOOK IV   THE GATES OF PLUTO  I.  THE FOOL BY THE ROADSIDE   447 HERO GIRL FOOL V    T
ROAD-SIDE
     THE ROAD-SIDE TREES KEEP MURMURING-- . . . . . . . . .   131 OLD PENSIONER   V     13
ROADWAY
     WHILE I STAND ON THE ROADWAY, OR ON THE PAVEMENTS GREY,    117 ISLE INNISFREE        11
     WHILE I STAND ON THE ROADWAY, OR ON THE PAVEMENT GREY, .   117 ISLE INNISFREE  V     11
     THE CRY OF A CHILD BY THE ROADWAY, THE CREAK OF A LUMBERING  142 ROSE IN HEART        2
       CART,
ROAM
     WILT ROAM AWAY FROM THIS RICH ISLAND REST? . . . . . .   669 ISLE STAT II 3        88
     AND WHEREFORE SHOULD THY BRIGHT BROW ROAM . . . . . . .  686 LIFE                  11
ROAR
     FOR WIND OR WATER'S ROAR? . . . . . . . . . . . . . .    312 CHILD DANCING          3
     WHAT GAVE THAT ROAR OF MOCKERY, . . . . . . . . . . .    583 GHOST ROG CASE         7
     THAT ROAR IN THE SEA'S ROAR? . . . . . . . . . . . . .   583 GHOST ROG CASE         8
     THAT ROAR IN THE SEA'S ROAR? . . . . . . . . . . . . .   583 GHOST ROG CASE         8
     THEY SHAKE WHEN THE WINDS ROAR, . . . . . . . . . . .    635 BLACK TOWER            9
     THEY SHAKE WHEN THE WINDS ROAR, . . . . . . . . . . .    636 BLACK TOWER           19
     THEY SHAKE WHEN THE WINDS ROAR, . . . . . . . . . . .    636 BLACK TOWER           29
     AND HEARS THE ROAR OF THE STREAMS WHERE, DRUIDS SAY, . .  749 SHADOW WATER A        46
ROARER
     AND MIXED WITH THE SOUND OF THAT ROARER . . . . . . . .   60 OISIN 3          V   184
ROARING
     A FIR-TREE ROARING IN ITS LEAFLESS TOP; . . . . . . .     40 OISIN 2              177
     A FIR TREE ROARING IN ITS LEAFLESS TOP, . . . . . . .     40 OISIN 2          V   177
     . . . WITH ROARING OF LAUGHTER AND SONGS, . . . . . .     53 OISIN 3               87
     . . . LIKE THE ROARING OF WIND IN A WOOD. . . . . . .     58 OISIN 3              168
     AND HUSHED IN SLEEP THE ROARING RANKS OF BATTLE; . . .   129 BOOK STORIES           7
     A ROARING, RANTING JOURNEYMAN. . . . . . . . . . . . .   509 JANE REPROVED         13
     A ROARING RANTING JOURNEY-MAN. . . . . . . . . . . . .   509 JANE REPROVED   V     13
     ALL THE STREAM THAT'S ROARING BY . . . . . . . . . . .   562 NEEDLES EYE            1
     THE ROARING TINKER IF YOU LIKE, . . . . . . . . . . .    605 SONGS BURDEN 1         1
     HIS ROARING AND HIS RANTING . . . . . . . . . . . . .    606 SONGS BURDEN 1        16
     CRIES A VOICE AT ROARING MIDNIGHT BESIDE THE MOONLESS DEEP.  718 PHANTOM SHIP        8
     BUT WHERE THAT ROARING, RANTING CREW . . . . . . . . .   787 HUDDON DUDDON          3
ROARS
     AND ROARS, MAD WITH THE TOUCH OF THE UNKNOWN, . . . . .  689 NETTLESHIP             7
ROASTING
     ROASTING BERRIES STEAM AND SHAKE-- . . . . . . . . . .   727 LOVERS QUARREL        43
ROB
     THE OTHER SHOUTED, "YOU WOULD ROB . . . . . . . . . .    307 HOUR DAWN            109
     HER RAVEN FLUTTERS. ROB HIM OF HIS FOOD . . . . . . .    751 SHADOW WATER A       100
ROBARTES
     MICHAEL ROBARTES BIDS HIS BELOVED BE AT PEACE . . . . .  154 BELOVED PEACE   V     T
     MICHAEL ROBARTES REMEMBERS FORGOTTEN BEAUTY . . . . .    155 FORGOT BEAUTY   V     T
     MICHAEL ROBARTES ASKS FORGIVENESS BECAUSE OF HIS MANY MOODS  162 ASKS FORGIVE V     T
     THAT MICHAEL ROBARTES LEFT, YOU WALK IN THE MOON, . . .   367 EGO DOMINUS           4
     THE DOUBLE VISION OF MICHAEL ROBARTES . . . . . . . .    382 VISION ROBART         T
     MICHAEL ROBARTES AND THE DANCER  . . . . . . . . . .     385 ROBARTES DANCE        T
ROBBED
     WAS ROBBED BEFORE EARTH GAVE THE WHEAT; . . . . . . .    196 BAILE AILLINN        166
ROBBER
     THERE'S NOBODY IS NATURAL BUT A ROBBER, . . . . . . .    233 SHADOW WATER B       237
ROBBERS
     FELL ON THE ROBBERS BY THE DEEP, . . . . . . . . . . .    83 MAD KING GOLL   V     21
     THESE HANDS SLEW MANY ROBBERS BOLD-- . . . . . . . . .    83 MAD KING GOLL   V     23
     ROBBERS HAD TAKEN HIS OLD TAMBOURINE. . . . . . . . .    616 MARCH SONGS 3          7
     ROBBERS HAD TAKEN HIS OLD TAMBOURINE. . . . . . . . .    616 MARCH SONGS 3         10
     ROBBERS HAD TAKEN HIS OLD TAMBOURINE. . . . . . . . .    616 MARCH SONGS 3         17
     ROBBERS HAD TAKEN HIS OLD TAMBOURINE. . . . . . . . .    616 MARCH SONGS 3         20
     ROBBERS HAD TAKEN HIS OLD TAMBOURINE. . . . . . . . .    616 MARCH SONGS 3         27
     ROBBERS HAD TAKEN HIS OLD TAMBOURINE. . . . . . . . .    616 MARCH SONGS 3         30
     A HORN! SOME TROOP OF ROBBERS WINDING GOES . . . . . .   649 ISLE STAT I 1        110
     AMONG HIGH MOUNTAINS, AND THE MOUNTAIN ROBBERS . . . .   768 SHADOW WATER A       411
ROBBERY
     THAT HAS LESS UPS AND DOWNS THAN ROBBERY. . . . . . .    222 SHADOW WATER B         7
     THEIR ROBBERY BY NIGHT; . . . . . . . . . . . . . . .    607 SONGS BURDEN 2        15
ROBE
     BY MIGHTY BRAHMA'S EVER-RUSTLING ROBE, . . . . . . . .    71 ANASHU VIJAYA         14
     STAND YOU. BY BRAHMA'S EVER-RUSTLING ROBE, . . . . . .    71 ANASHU VIJAYA   V     14
     BY MIGHTY BRAHMA'S EVER RUSTLING ROBE, . . . . . . . .    71 ANASHU VIJAYA   V     14
ROBED
     AND CALM, ROBED ALL IN RAIMENT MOONY WHITE. . . . . .    693 MOSADA 1              77
ROBERT
     OLD COUNTRY SCHOLAR, ROBERT EMMET'S FRIEND, . . . . .    269 PARDON FATHERS         5
     AND COUNTRY SCHOLAR, ROBERT EMMET'S FRIEND, . . . . .    269 PARDON FATHERS  V      5
     AND ROBERT EMMET AND WOLFE TONE. . . . . . . . . . .     290 SEPTEMBER 1913        21
     IN MEMORY OF MAJOR ROBERT GREGORY . . . . . . . . . .    323 ROBERT GREGORY        T
     IN MEMORY OF ROBERT GREGORY . . . . . . . . . . . . .    323 ROBERT GREGORY  V     T
     THAT INSOLENT FIEND ROBERT ARTISSON . . . . . . . . .    433 NINETEEN 19          128
     WHAT ROBERT BROWNING MEANT . . . . . . . . . . . . .     605 YOU CONTENT          22
ROBES
     AND A HUNDRED ROBES OF MURMURING SILK, . . . . . . . .     8 OISIN 1               88
     AND A HUNDRED ROBES OF THE SOFTEST SILK, . . . . . . .     8 OISIN 1          V    88
     THEIR ROBES WERE ALL OF YELLOW SILK . . . . . . . . .     15 OISIN 1          V   205
```

661

ROBES   (CONTINUED)
    "HE WHO IS WRAPPED IN PURPLE ROBES, ...   134 FR GILLIGAN   45
ROBIN'S
    AS ALIEN AS A CUCKOO IN A ROBIN'S NEST, ...   671 ISLE STAT II 3   138
    ALIEN AS CUCKOO IN A ROBIN'S NEST, ...   671 ISLE STAT II 3 V   138
ROCK   SEE THREE-ROCK
    'TIS OVER: FAR WITH MEMORY I SWAY AND ROCK. . . . .   43 OISIN 2   V 212
    THE GREY ROCK . . . .   270 GREY ROCK   T
    THE GREY ROCK AND THE WINDY LIGHT? . . . .   275 GREY ROCK   111
    A DARK DEEP HOLLOW IN THE ROCK. . . . .   303 HOUR DAWN   21
    BEING CERTAIN IT WAS NO RIGHT ROCK . . . .   303 HOUR DAWN   23
    AND DESOLATE THREE ROCK . . . .   310 PEACOCK   5
    BETWEEN ROCK AND WET HEATHER, ...   311 PEACOCK   V 8
    TO COLD CLARE ROCK AND GALWAY ROCK AND THORN, . . .   326 ROBERT GREGORY   66
    TO COLD CLARE ROCK AND GALWAY ROCK AND THORN, . . .   326 ROBERT GREGORY   66
    ON THE GREY ROCK OF CASHEL THE MIND'S EYE . . . . .   382 VISION ROBART   1
    ON THE GREY ROCK OF CASHEL I SUDDENLY SAW . . . . .   383 VISION ROBART   17
    UPON SOME LOFTY ROCK TO STARE . . . .   397 POLIT PRISONER   21
    THAT OUT OF ROCK, ...   518 HIS CONFIDENCE   10
    DROPPING OUT OF SKY OR ROCK. . . . .   633 MAN AND ECHO   44
    I SEE WITHIN A CLOVEN ROCK DISPART . . . .   673 ISLE STAT II 3   195
    THE VISION OF A ROCK WHERE LIGHTNINGS WHIRL'D . . . .   687 TWO TITANS   1
    TWO FIGURES CROUCHING ON THE BLACK ROCK, BOUND . . . .   687 TWO TITANS   5
    MAKING ALL ONE O'ER ROCK AND SEA AND SKIES: . . . .   687 TWO TITANS   28
ROCK-BORN
    TO THAT ROCK-BORN, ROCK-WANDERING FOOT, ...   276 GREY ROCK   125
ROCK-BRED
    LIKE ANY ROCK-BRED, SEA-BORNE BIRD: . . . .   397 POLIT PRISONER   18
ROCKED
    MY SPIRIT ROCKED IN EVENING LIGHT, THE RUSHES ROUND MY   76 INDIAN ON GOD   2
        KNEES,
    MY SPIRIT ROCKED IN SLEEP AND SIGHS: AND SAW THE MOORFOWL 76 INDIAN ON GOD   3
        PACE
    MY SPIRIT ROCKED IN EVENING'S HUSH, THE RUSHES ROUND MY   76 INDIAN ON GOD   V 2
        KNEES,
    UNTIL I CRIED AND TREMBLED AND ROCKED TO AND FRO, . . . 316 COLD HEAVEN   8
    THE CRADLES THAT A MAN MUST NEEDS BE ROCKED IN: . . .   373 PHASES OF MOON   34
ROCKING
    THAT MERELY STOOD, ROCKING THE GLITTERING COACH . . .   344 DAWN   11
    YET DID BUT LOOK, ROCKING THE GLITTERING COACH . . .   344 DAWN   V 11
    WERE VEXED TO NIGHTMARE BY A ROCKING CRADLE, ...   402 SECOND COMING   20
ROCK-NURTURED
    ROCK-NURTURED AOIFE TOOK A PIN, ...   274 GREY ROCK   88
ROCK'S
    A DARK DEEP HOLE IN THE ROCK'S FACE, ...   303 HOUR DAWN   V 21
ROCKS
    THE CORMORANTS SHIVER ON THEIR ROCKS: . . . . . .   84 MAD KING GOLL   42
    THIS WHOLE DAY HAVE I FOLLOWED IN THE ROCKS, ...   102 FERGUS DRUID   1
    THE WHOLE DAY HAVE I FOLLOWED IN THE ROCKS, ...   102 FERGUS DRUID   V 1
    WENT OUT. AMONG THE IVY-COVERED ROCKS, ...   283 TWO KINGS   147
    AMID WET ROCKS AND HEATHER, ...   311 PEACOCK   8
    WHO TROD UPON THESE ROCKS OR PASSED THIS DOOR, . . .   413 TOWER   98
    STREWING UPON THE ROCKS THEIR STEEL-BLUE HAIR, . . .   687 TWO TITANS   30
    IN CREVICED ROCKS, AND LAUGHED TO THE OLD SEA, . . .   688 TWO TITANS   34
    THE YOUTH HAD FLUNG HIS ARMS AROUND THE ROCKS, . . .   688 TWO TITANS   40
ROCK-WANDERING
    TO THAT ROCK-BORN, ROCK-WANDERING FOOT, ...   276 GREY ROCK   125
ROCKY
    BY ROCKY SHORE AND RUSHY FEN: . . . .   83 MAD KING GOLL   32
    WHERE DIPS THE ROCKY HIGHLAND . . . .   86 STOLEN CHILD   1
    BY ROCKY LANE AND FEN: . . . .   133 FR GILLIGAN   30
    OF GREY STONES AND A ROCKY LEDGE . . . .   302 HOUR DAWN   12
    WHO'D LIVED SOMEWHERE UPON THAT ROCKY PLACE, ...   410 TOWER   35
    UNDER ITS ROCKY HOLE. . . . .   420 MY HOUSE   V 20C
    RUN UNDERGROUND, RISE IN A ROCKY PLACE . . . .   490 COOLE BALLYLEE   5
    OR ROCKY CISTERN WHERE WE TREAD THE CLOTHES . . . .   499 MOTHER OF GOD   9
    THE GYRES! THE GYRES! OLD ROCKY FACE, LOOK FORTH: . .   564 GYRES   1
    WHAT MATTER? THOSE THAT ROCKY FACE HOLDS DEAR, . . .   564 GYRES   18
    INTO THE NIGHT. O ROCKY VOICE, ...   633 MAN AND ECHO   37
ROD
    HE RULES YOU WITH AN IRON ROD, ...   22 OISIN 1   332
    AND CUT AND PEELED A HAZEL ROD . . . .   149 WANDER AENGUS   V 3
    NO, NOT IN BOYHOOD WHEN WITH ROD AND FLY, ...   409 TOWER   8
    HIS ROD AND ITS BUTTING HEAD . . . .   575 MAIDS 2ND SONG   3
RODE
    WE RODE IN SORROW, WITH STRONG HOUNDS THREE, ...   2 OISIN 1   V 7C
    WE RODE IN SADNESS ABOVE LOUGH LAEN, ...   2 OISIN 1   V 7H
    A PEARL-PALE, HIGH-BORN LADY, WHO RODE . . . . . .   3 OISIN 1   20
    WE RODE BEYOND THE FURZE AND HEATHER, ...   9 OISIN 1   V 101A
    BUT WE RODE OUT FROM THE HUMAN LANDS. . . . . . .   10 OISIN 1   114
    WE RODE ACROSS THE OILY SEA, ...   10 OISIN 1   V 114
    AND NOW A LADY RODE LIKE THE WIND . . . .   12 OISIN 1   142
    AND NOW A MAIDEN RODE LIKE THE WIND . . . .   12 OISIN 1   V 142
    AND WITH LOW MURMURS, WE RODE ON, ...   13 OISIN 1   159
    WE RODE ON MURMURING. MANY A SHELL . . . .   13 OISIN 1   V 159
    AND WRAPPED IN DREAMS RODE OUT AGAIN . . . .   25 OISIN 1   382
    AND RODE AND STOOD BESIDE THE SHORE. . . . . . .   25 OISIN 1   V 379A
    WHEN GODS AND GIANTS WARRED. WE RODE BETWEEN . . .   31 OISIN 2   31
    I MOUNTED, AND WE RODE ACROSS THE LONE . . . . . .   45 OISIN 2   V 231
    AND WE RODE ON THE PLAINS OF THE SEA'S EDGE: . . . .   48 OISIN 3   13

		PAGE	TITLE		LINE
RODE	(CONTINUED)				
	THE WAILING GREW DISTANT; I RODE BY THE WOODS OF THE WRINKLING BARK,	56	OISIN 3		137
	AND I RODE BY THE PLAINS OF THE SEA'S EDGE,	56	OISIN 3		141
	I RODE AWAY ON THE SURGES, WHERE, HIGH AS THE SADDLE-BOW,	57	OISIN 3		147
	I RODE AWAY ON THE SURGES, WHERE HIGH AS THE SADDLE BOW	57	OISIN 3	V	147
	I RODE AWAY ON THE SURGES, WHERE, HIGH AS THE SADDLEBOW,	57	OISIN 3	V	147
	MAKING WAY FROM THE KINDLING SURGES, I RODE ON A BRIDLE-PATH	58	OISIN 3		161
	AND I RODE AND I RODE, AND I CRIED OUT,	59	OISIN 3		171
	AND I RODE AND I RODE, AND I CRIED OUT,	59	OISIN 3		171
	I TURNED AND RODE TO THE WESTWARD, AND FOLLOWED THE SEA'S OLD SHOUT	60	OISIN 3		183
	AND RODE ON TILL OVER THE WORLD'S RIM FLOATED THE SEA'S OLD SHOUT,	60	OISIN 3	V	183
	IN PENAL DAYS RODE OUT	91	FATHER OHART		2
	AND RODE WITH LITTLE CARE.	133	FR GILLIGAN		28
	HE RODE NOW AS HE NEVER RODE,	133	FR GILLIGAN		29
	HE RODE NOW AS HE NEVER RODE,	133	FR GILLIGAN		29
	RODE OUT OF EMAIN WITH A BAND	189	BAILE AILLINN		18
	RODE FROM THE COUNTRY OF HER KIN,	191	BAILE AILLINN		50
	AND OLD AND YOUNG MEN RODE WITH HER;	191	BAILE AILLINN		51
	WHERE AILLINN RODE WITH WAITING-MAIDS,	193	BAILE AILLINN		102
	WHERE AILLINN RODE WITH WAITING MAIDS	193	BAILE AILLINN	V	102
	I WAS YOUR HUSBAND WHEN YOU RODE THE AIR,	284	TWO KINGS		166
	HE RODE A RACE WITHOUT A BIT?	326	ROBERT GREGORY		63
	SHE RODE TO HARRIERS?	392	EASTER 1916		23
	AND RODE OUR WINGED HORSE;	392	EASTER 1916		25
	THOUGH MOUNTED IN THAT SADDLE HOMER RODE	492	COOLE BALLYLEE		47
	NIAMH THAT RODE ON IT; LAD AND LASS	550	SEVERED HEAD		11
	NO, NOT UNTIL HE RODE.	571	THREE BUSHES		48
	WHEN PAUL RODE FROM THE TOWN	740	EARL PAUL		21
RODY					
	BRING RODY AND HIS HOUNDS,	97	FOXHUNTER		10
	"HUNTSMAN RODY, BLOW THE HORN,	98	FOXHUNTER		25
	"NOW HUNTSMAN RODY, BLOW THY HORN,	98	FOXHUNTER		REF
	"MY HUNTSMAN RODY, BLOW THE HORN,	98	FOXHUNTER	V	REF
	"HUNTSMAN RODY, BLOW THE HORN,	99	FOXHUNTER	V	33
ROE					
	ROE COULD RUN OR DOE COULD LEAP	522	LULLABY		10
	ROE COULD LEAP OR DOE COULD RUN;	522	LULLABY		12
	STAG COULD RUN AND ROE COULD LEAP	522	LULLABY	V	10
	STAG COULD LEAP AND ROE COULD RUN.	522	LULLABY	V	12
ROEBUCK					
	A LITTLE WAY WITHIN THE GLOOM A ROEBUCK RAISED HIS EYES	76	INDIAN ON GOD		13
	HE IS A GENTLE ROEBUCK; FOR HOW ELSE, I PRAY, COULD HE	76	INDIAN ON GOD		15
ROGER					
	ROGER CASEMENT	581	ROGER CASEMENT		T
	I SAY THAT ROGER CASEMENT	581	ROGER CASEMENT		1
	THE GHOST OF ROGER CASEMENT	583	GHOST ROG CASE		T
	THE GHOST OF ROGER CASEMENT	583	GHOST ROG CASE		9
	THE GHOST OF ROGER CASEMENT	583	GHOST ROG CASE		19
	THE GHOST OF ROGER CASEMENT	584	GHOST ROG CASE		29
	THE GHOST OF ROGER CASEMENT	584	GHOST ROG CASE		39
ROGUE					
	A CURSING ROGUE WITH A MERRY FACE,	302	HOUR DAWN		1
	THAT GREAT ROGUE ALCIBIADES.	379	SAINT HUNCH		12
	SOME ROGUE OF THE WORLD STOLE THEM TO PATCH UP A FENCE OR A FIRE.	623	HIGH TALK		4
	WHAT ROGUE IS NIGHT-WANDERING?	781	MY HEART BEAT		5
ROGUES					
	THAT THE WORST ROGUES AND RASCALS HAD DIED OUT.	428	NINETEEN 19		16
ROLL'D					
	WHILE THE WORLD IS ROLL'D IN LIGHT.	646	ISLE STAT I 1		29
ROLLED					
	STROKED THE YOUNG WINDS AS THEY ROLLED ON THE PLAIN,	27	OISIN 1	V	415C
	ROLLED ROUND WITH MUSIC OF THE SIGHING SPRAY;	30	OISIN 2		14
	AND BLACKNESS IN THE DARK. THE SEA ROLLED ROUND,	30	OISIN 2	V	23
	. . . AND CHURNED. HIS LIPS WERE ROLLED APART,	31	OISIN 2	V	43
	ROLLED IN THE THINGS OF THE UNHUMAN MIND,	36	OISIN 2	V	98
	. . . WHEN, ROLLED IN A GRISLY PEACE,	47	OISIN 3		9
	. . . WHEN THE FALLEN ON FALLEN LIE ROLLED;	52	OISIN 3		78
	THEIR HAIR ALONG THE MOUNTAINS ROLLED AND FILLED	74	ANASHU VIJAYA		71
	AND RUSHES WAVED AND WATERS ROLLED.	84	MAD KING GOLL		35
	AND SONG THAT DOWN THE VALLEYS ROLLED--	84	MAD KING GOLL	V	35
	AND SONG THAT DOWN THE VALLEY ROLLED--	84	MAD KING GOLL	V	35
	THAT DOWN THE ECHOING VALLEYS ROLLED.	84	MAD KING GOLL	V	35
	IN ALL HIS EVENING VAPOURS ROLLED--	86	MAD KING GOLL	V	71
	IS ROLLED AS VERDANT SMOKE! O THOU WHOSE FACE	667	ISLE STAT II 3		35
	HAS ROLLED AWAY THE STARS AND DRIED THE SEA	671	ISLE STAT II 3		146
ROLLING					
	BUT WE, OH ROLLING STARS, ARE FREE.	22	OISIN 1	V	337
	ROLLING HIS FLAGRANT WHEEL OUT OF THE DEEP,	42	OISIN 2		193
	ROLLING HIS WHEEL, WE SANG BESIDE THE DEEP	42	OISIN 2	V	193
	ROLLING ALONG IN DREAMS FROM HILL TO HILL.	68	SAD SHEPHERD		11
	FROM ROLLING VALE AND RIVERY GLEN,	83	MAD KING GOLL		19
	FROM ROLLING VALLEY AND RIVERY GLEN,	83	MAD KING GOLL	V	17
	ON OLD DEEP SILVER ROLLING THERE	271	GREY ROCK		20
	ROLLING A BLIND PEARL EYE,	552	SONGS REWRIT 2		2
	WITH ROLLING FIRE, BEYOND THE HIGH TREES TURBANED	656	ISLE STAT I 3		32
	YOU MUST BE GONE; THE ROLLING GRAINS OF SAND	663	ISLE STAT II 2		34

ROLLING   (CONTINUED)
    OF ASIAN RIVERS, ROLLING ON IN LIGHT. . . . .   682 SEEKER   20
    OF INDIA'S RIVERS, ROLLING ON IN LIGHT. . . . .   682 SEEKER   V 20
    HE RUSHES, ROLLING FROM HIS LIPS A MADMAN'S LAUGH. . . .   715 FERENCZ RENYI   122
ROLLS
    AND ROLLS ALONG THE UNWIELDY SUN, ...   18 OISIN 1   267
    ROUND US, AND ROLLS THE UNWIELDY SUN. . . . .   18 OISIN 1   V 268
    CEASE THE SAILS THEIR FLAPPING UPROAR, AND THE HULL NO   719 PHANTOM SHIP   18
        LONGER ROLLS.
    CEASE THE SAILS, THEIR FLAPPING UPROAR TO THE HULL   719 PHANTOM SHIP V 18
        NO LONGER ROLLS.
    ROLLS ALONG THE SEA SANDS WHITE. . . . .   732 STREET DANCERS   34
    ROLLS ALONG THE SEA-SANDS WHITE. . . . .   732 STREET DANCERS V 34
ROLLY
    IS FOL DE ROL DE ROLLY O. . . . .   592 PILGRIM   5
    BUT FOL DE ROL DE ROLLY O. . . . .   593 PILGRIM   10
    WAS FOL DE ROL DE ROLLY O. . . . .   593 PILGRIM   15
    BUT FOL DE ROL DE ROLLY O. . . . .   593 PILGRIM   20
    IS FOL DE ROL DE ROLLY O. . . . .   593 PILGRIM   25
ROMAN
    A ROMAN CAESAR IS HELD DOWN . . . .   379 SAINT HUNCH   4
    THE ROMAN EMPIRE STOOD APPALLED! . . . .   437 SONGS PLAY 1   13
    ON ROMAN OR ON RUSSIAN . . . .   631 POLITICS   3
ROMANCE
    YET OLD ROMANCE BEING KIND, LET HIM PREVAIL . . . .   258 KING NO KING   5
    ROMANCE IN IRELAND . . . .   289 SEPTEMBER 1913 V T
ROMANTIC
    ROMANTIC IRELAND . . . .   289 SEPTEMBER 1913 V T
    ROMANTIC IRELAND'S DEAD AND GONE, ...   289 SEPTEMBER 1913   7
    ROMANTIC IRELAND'S DEAD AND GONE, ...   289 SEPTEMBER 1913 15
    ROMANTIC IRELAND'S DEAD AND GONE, ...   290 SEPTEMBER 1913 23
    ROMANTIC FISH SWAM IN NETS COMING TO THE HAND! . . .   485 THREE MOVEMENT   2
ROMANTICS
    WE WERE THE LAST ROMANTICS--CHOSE FOR THEME . . . .   491 COOLE BALLYLEE 41
ROME
    THE HAND AND LASH THAT BEAT DOWN FRIGID ROME? . . . .   560 WHENCE COME   10
    EGYPT AND GREECE, GOOD-BYE, AND GOOD-BYE, ROME! . . .   563 MERU   8
    TO MOSCOW OR TO ROME. . . . .   600 THOSE IMAGES   6
ROMP
    WE HUSHED THE SINGING AND THE ROMP, ...   20 OISIN 1   V 296
ROOD
    WORD BE-MOCKERS?--BY THE ROOD, ...   65 HAPPY SHEPHERD 12
    WORD BEMOCKERS?--BY THE ROOD . . . .   65 HAPPY SHEPHERD V 12
    TO THE ROSE UPON THE ROOD OF TIME . . . .   100 ROSE UPON ROOD   T
    SAW THE PIERCED HANDS AND ROOD OF ELDER RISE . . .   169 SECRET ROSE   10
    BUT PURER THAN A TALL CANDLE BEFORE THE HOLY ROOD . . .   208 HANRAHANS SONG 14
    BUT PURER THAN A TALL CANDLE BEFORE THE BLESSED ROOD   208 HANRAHANS SONG V 14
ROOF
    PRESSED ON THE EVER-TREMBLING ROOF . . . .   25 OISIN 1   V 383
    AND THE ROOF FALLS IN OF HIS TUNNELLED HOUSE. . . . .   27 OISIN 1   V 419
    AND THE ROOF FALLS IN OF HIS TUNNELLED HOUSE. . . . .   28 OISIN 1   423
    TWO WALLS, A ROOF, A FLOOD! THERE TREMBLING GREEN . .   31 OISIN 2   V 32
    UNDER THE ROOF, AND WITH A STRAINING THROAT . . . .   36 OISIN 2   106
    UNDER THAT WOVEN CHANGELESS ROOF OF BOUGHS! . . . . .   126 DREAM OF FAERY 11
    AND NOT A ROOF OF IVORY AND GOLD. . . . .   246 SHADOW WATER B 500
    I WOULD GROW JEALOUS OF THE IVORY ROOF, ...   246 SHADOW WATER B 501
    "I BID THEM MAKE HIS BED UNDER THIS ROOF . . . . .   280 TWO KINGS   87
    AT KYLE-NA-NO UNDER THAT ANCIENT ROOF . . . . . .   321 REED WHISPERER   7
    TO KYLE-NA-INO AND TO THAT ANCIENT ROOF . . . . .   321 REED WHISPERER V 7
    STARING UPON A BEDOUIN'S HORSE-HAIR ROOF . . . . .   368 EGO DOMINUS   29
    WHILE MICHAEL ANGELO'S SISTINE ROOF, ...   386 ROBARTES DANCE 32
    THE BROKEN WALL, THE BURNING ROOF AND TOWER . . .   441 LEDA AND SWAN   10
    A ROOF, GOOD CLOTHES, PASSION, LOVE PERHAPS, ...   609 IN TARAS HALLS   8
    LANDOR'S TARPAULIN ON THE ROOF. . . . .   625 NATIVITY   6
    ON THE SISTINE CHAPEL ROOF, ...   638 BEN BULBEN   46
ROOFLESS
    BECOME A ROOFLESS RUIN THAT THE OWL . . . .   423 MY DESCENDANTS 14
ROOF-LEVELLING
    WHEREBY THE HAYSTACK- AND ROOF-LEVELLING WIND, ...   403 FOR DAUGHTER   5
ROOFS
    UNDER THE WOVEN ROOFS OF QUICKEN BOUGHS!-- . . . . . .   126 DREAM OF FAERY V 11
ROOF-TIMBERS
    STAND UNDER THE ROUGH ROOF-TIMBERS OF THE HALL . . .   377 PHASES OF MOON 125
ROOF-TREES
    MEAN ROOF-TREES WERE THE STURDIER FOR ITS FALL, . . .   264 HOUSE SHAKEN   8
ROOK
    SUDDENLY I SAW THE COLD AND ROOK DELIGHTING HEAVEN . .   316 COLD HEAVEN   V 1
ROOK-DELIGHTING
    SUDDENLY I SAW THE COLD AND ROOK-DELIGHTING HEAVEN . .   316 COLD HEAVEN   1
ROOKS
    CAME KEENERS HOARSER THAN ROOKS, ...   92 FATHER OHART   22
ROOM   SEE SLEEPING-ROOM DRAWING-ROOM
    AND LIGHTS THE CURTAINED ROOM, ...   89 ISLE IN WATER   10
    O WHAT TO ME THE LITTLE ROOM . . . .   151 HEART OF WOMAN   1
    "O, WHAT TO ME THE FIRELIT ROOM, ...   151 HEART OF WOMAN V 1
    LIFTED THE CURTAIN OF HER SLEEPING ROOM, ...   182 QUEEN MAEVE   V 63
    IF WE BUT SAW IN DREAMS THAT ROOM, ...   272 GREY ROCK   38
    THAT THERE BE NO FOOT SILENT IN THE ROOM . . . . .   311 MOUNTAIN TOMB   6
    LET THERE BE NO FOOT SILENT IN THE ROOM, ...   311 MOUNTAIN TOMB V 6
    THE ENTIRE COMBUSTIBLE WORLD IN ONE SMALL ROOM . . .   327 ROBERT GREGORY 82
    ALL THE COMBUSTIBLE WORLD IN ONE SMALL ROOM . . . .   327 ROBERT GREGORY V 82

ROOM   (CONTINUED)

AND FLINGS HERSELF OUT OF THE ROOM WHEN JULIET WOULD BE   354 HIS PHOENIX   13
    BRIDE
AND FLINGS HERSELF OUT OF THE ROOM WHEN JULIET WOULD BE   354 HIS PHOENIX   V   13
    A BRIDE
BY MERELY WALKING IN A ROOM. . . . .   356 BROKEN DREAMS   13
HE WALKED THAT ROOM AND ISSUED THENCE . . . .   438 SONGS PLAY 2   2
AND MANY A LESSER BELL SOUND THROUGH THE ROOM; . . . .   470 ALL SOUL NIGHT   2
WINGS BEATING ABOUT THE ROOM; . . . .   499 MOTHER OF GOD   3
GREAT HATRED, LITTLE ROOM, ...   506 REMORSE SPEECH   12
"HAVE NO LIT CANDLES IN YOUR ROOM," . . . .   569 THREE BUSHES   8
AT MIDNIGHT TO MY ROOM, ...   570 THREE BUSHES   39
AND FOUND AN EMPTY ROOM. . . . .   594 COLONEL MARTIN   8
ROOMFUL
BEFORE THAT ROOMFUL OR AS GOOD. . . . .   273 GREY ROCK   52
ROOMS
IN THE OLD ROOMS; NIGHT CAN OUTBALANCE DAY, ...   435 NEW FACES   6
THE GARDEN PATHS, NOR COUNTED UP THE ROOMS, ...   466 HARUN RASHID   119
WHEN ALL THOSE ROOMS AND PASSAGES ARE GONE, ...   489 COOLE PARK 29   26
GREAT ROOMS WHERE TRAVELLED MEN AND CHILDREN FOUND . . .   491 COOLE BALLYLEE   29
ROOT
THE SURETY OF ITS HIDDEN ROOT . . . .   134 TWO TREES   7
AND THAT IS CURED BY A BOILED LIQUORICE ROOT. . . . . .   227 SHADOW WATER B V 116B
THOUGH LEAVES ARE MANY, THE ROOT IS ONE; . . . . . .   261 COMING WISDOM   1
THROUGH BUSH THEY PLUNGED AND OVER IVIED ROOT, ...   278 TWO KINGS   32
WHILE UP FROM MY HEART'S ROOT . . . .   316 FRIENDS   26
I TOOK A BROKEN ROOT TO FLING . . . .   317 APPOINTMENT   2
AT SOME OLD WINDING WHITETHORN ROOT . . . .   342 SHEP GOATHERD   101
AND SAPLINGS ROOT AMONG THE BROKEN STONE, ...   489 COOLE PARK 29   28
SEEMED SPRUNG FROM BUT A SINGLE ROOT . . . .   571 THREE BUSHES   61
OF ROOT, SHOOT, BLOSSOM OR CLAY . . . .   600 SPIRIT MEDIUM   21
FOR IF SEVERED FROM THE ROOT . . . .   668 ISLE STAT II 3   61
AND THEREON GREW A TENDER ROOT, ...   743 DANAAN QUICK   13
ROOTED   SEE GREAT-ROOTED DEEP-ROOTED
ROOTED IN FOAM AND CLOUDS, AND CRIED TO ALL . . . . . .   38 OISIN 2   132
ROOTED IN FOAM AND CLOUDS. THERE MIGHTIER MASTERS MET . .   38 OISIN 2   V   132
AND HAD ROOTED THE SUN AND MOON AND STARS OUT OF THE SKY   153 CHANGE BELOVED   11
AND ROOTED THE SUN AND MOON AND STARS OUT OF THE SKY, . .   153 CHANGE BELOVED V   11
ROOTED IN ONE DEAR PERPETUAL PLACE. . . . .   405 FOR DAUGHTER   48
O CHESTNUT TREE, GREAT ROOTED BLOSSOMER, ...   446 SCHOOL CHILDR V   61
AND HERE'S JOHN SYNGE HIMSELF, THAT ROOTED MAN, ...   603 GALLERY REVIS   48
ROOTS
BY ROOTS THAT JOINED ABOVE OUR PLUMES-- . . . .   16 OISIN 1   V 224C
IN THE ROOTS OF THE GRASSES, THE SORRELS, I LAID MY BODY   52 OISIN 3   73
    AS LOW;
IN THE TREE ROOTS, AND ALL THE SACRED FLOCKS . . . . .   75 ANASHU VIJAYA   88
IN THE TREE ROOTS, AND ALL THY SACRED FLOCKS . . . . .   75 ANASHU VIJAYA V   88
ROOTS HALF HIDDEN UNDER SNOWS, ...   135 TWO TREES   27
AND ROOTS HALF HIDDEN UNDER SNOWS . . . .   135 TWO TREES   V   27
THE ROOTS OF THE WORLD. SHADOWS BEFORE NOW . . . . . .   227 SHADOW WATER B   104
THE ROOTS OF THE WORLD. WHO KNOWS THAT SHADOWS . . . .   227 SHADOW WATER B V 104
I GROPED MY WAY THROUGH BOUGHS, AND OVER ROOTS, ...   283 TWO KINGS   V 139
KNOW WHERE ITS ROOTS BEGAN. . . . .   571 THREE BUSHES   76
WHAT DEEP ROOTS ARE," AND NEVER FORESAW THE END . . . .   603 GALLERY REVIS V   37
THE ROOTS OF THE ROSES. . . . .   672 ISLE STAT II 3   169
ROPE
AND PAID YOU ON THE NAIL. TAKE UP THAT ROPE . . . . .   232 SHADOW WATER B   224
WHILE THERE'S A ROPE TO RUN INTO A NOOSE . . . . . .   238 SHADOW WATER B   347
AND I WILL FOLLOW YOU AND CUT THE ROPE . . . .   250 SHADOW WATER B   586
AND CUT THE ROPE, FOR I GO ON WITH FORGAEL. . . . . .   250 SHADOW WATER B   592
FAREWELL! FAREWELL! THE SWORD IS IN THE ROPE-- . . . .   251 SHADOW WATER B   595
FOR WHOM THE HANGMAN'S ROPE WAS SPUN, ...   289 SEPTEMBER 1913   13
BUT A GOOD STRONG CAUSE"--THE ROPE GAVE A JERK THERE, .   545 TO SAME TUNE 1   23
BUT A GOOD STRONG CAUSE"--THE ROPE GAVE A JERK THERE, .   616 MARCH SONGS 3   23
I HAD THROWN IT DOWN BEHIND THIS COIL OF ROPE. . . . .   759 SHADOW WATER A   245
I HAVE CUT THE ROPE THAT BOUND THIS GALLEY TO OURS, . .   768 SHADOW WATER A   421
ROPE'S
THE ROPE'S IN TWO--IT FALLS INTO THE SEA, ...   251 SHADOW WATER B   596
ROPES
"BRING THE ROPES NOW! STAND YE BY NOW! . . . .   718 PHANTOM SHIP   13
ROSA
ROSA MUNDI . . . .   111 ROSE OF WORLD V   T
ROSARY
OVER THE BEADS OF HIS ROSARY. . . . .   730 PRIEST FAIRY   52
THE FATHER DROPT HIS ROSARY-- . . . .   730 PRIEST FAIRY   57
ROSE (NOUN)   SEE RED-ROSE-BORDERED
BUT NOW THE MOON LIKE A WHITE ROSE SHONE . . . . . .   12 OISIN 1   152
AND THE MOON LIKE A PALE ROSE WITHER AWAY." . . . . .   28 OISIN 1   427
TO THE ROSE UPON THE ROOD OF TIME . . . .   100 ROSE UPON ROOD   T
RED ROSE, PROUD ROSE, SAD ROSE OF ALL MY DAYS! . . . .   100 ROSE UPON ROOD   1
RED ROSE, PROUD ROSE, SAD ROSE OF ALL MY DAYS! . . . .   100 ROSE UPON ROOD   1
RED ROSE, PROUD ROSE, SAD ROSE OF ALL MY DAYS! . . . .   100 ROSE UPON ROOD   1
RED ROSE, PROUD ROSE, SAD ROSE OF ALL MY DAYS. . . . .   101 ROSE UPON ROOD   24
RED ROSE, PROUD ROSE, SAD ROSE OF ALL MY DAYS. . . . .   101 ROSE UPON ROOD   24
RED ROSE, PROUD ROSE, SAD ROSE OF ALL MY DAYS. . . . .   101 ROSE UPON ROOD   24
THE ROSE OF THE WORLD . . . .   111 ROSE OF WORLD   T
THE ROSE OF PEACE . . . .   112 ROSE OF PEACE   T
THE PEACE OF THE ROSE . . . .   112 ROSE OF PEACE V   T
THE ROSE OF BATTLE . . . .   113 ROSE OF BATTLE   T
ROSE OF ALL ROSES, ROSE OF ALL THE WORLD! . . . . . .   113 ROSE OF BATTLE   1
ROSE OF ALL ROSES, ROSE OF ALL THE WORLD! . . . . . .   113 ROSE OF BATTLE   1

		PAGE	TITLE		LINE
ROSE	(CONTINUED)				
ROSE OF ALL ROSES, ROSE OF ALL THE WORLD!		115	ROSE OF BATTLE		25
ROSE OF ALL ROSES, ROSE OF ALL THE WORLD!		115	ROSE OF BATTLE		25
. . . DEW-DABBLED, THE LILY AND ROSE;		122	WHITE BIRDS		5
SOON FAR FROM THE ROSE AND THE LILY .		122	WHITE BIRDS		11
. . . DEW DABBLED, THE LILY AND ROSE;		122	WHITE BIRDS	V	5
AND HOW, WHEN FADES THE SEA-STREWN ROSE OF DAY,		128	DREAM OF FAERY	V	33
BECAUSE THE RED ROSE BORDERED HEM .		137	TO IRELAND	V	6
AFTER THE RED ROSE BORDERED HEM.		139	TO IRELAND	V	30
AFTER THE RED ROSE BORDERED HEM.		139	TO IRELAND	V	48
THE LOVER TELLS OF THE ROSE IN HIS HEART		142	ROSE IN HEART		T
THE ROSE IN MY HEART		142	ROSE IN HEART	V	T
AEDH TELLS OF THE ROSE IN HIS HEART		142	ROSE IN HEART	V	T
ARE WRONGING YOUR IMAGE THAT BLOSSOMS A ROSE		143	ROSE IN HEART		4
FOR MY DREAMS OF YOUR IMAGE THAT BLOSSOMS A ROSE		143	ROSE IN HEART		8
CRUMPLE THE ROSE IN YOUR HAIR;		162	ASKS FORGIVE		4
CRUSH THE ROSE IN YOUR HAIR,		162	ASKS FORGIVE	V	4
THE INCORRUPTIBLE ROSE,		168	BLESSED		36
"THE ROSE THAT MUST DROP, OUT OF SWEET LEAVES,		168	BLESSED	V	37
THE SECRET ROSE		169	SECRET ROSE		T
O'SULLIVAN RUA TO THE SECRET ROSE		169	SECRET ROSE	V	T
TO THE SECRET ROSE		169	SECRET ROSE	V	T
FAR-OFF, MOST SECRET, AND INVIOLATE ROSE,		169	SECRET ROSE		1
FAR OFF, MOST SECRET, AND INVIOLATE ROSE,		169	SECRET ROSE	V	1
FAR-OFF, MOST SECRET, AND INVIOLATE ROSE?		170	SECRET ROSE		32
FAR OFF, MOST SECRET, AND INVIOLATE ROSE?		170	SECRET ROSE	V	32
HAVE PULLED THE IMMORTAL ROSE;		174	ELEMENT POWERS		2
AND STOLE THE CRIMSON ROSE,		174	ELEMENT POWERS	V	2
OF THE ROSE IN ITS DOOM.		175	ELEMENT POWERS	V	12
BRING ROSES IF THE ROSE BE YET IN BLOOM;		311	MOUNTAIN TOMB		2
THE ROSE TREE		396	ROSE TREE		T
HAS WITHERED OUR ROSE TREE;		396	ROSE TREE		4
CAN MAKE A RIGHT ROSE TREE."		396	ROSE TREE		18
HAVE WITHERED OUR ROSE TREE!		396	ROSE TREE	V	4
WHERE THE SYMBOLIC ROSE CAN BREAK IN FLOWER,		419	MY HOUSE		4
WHEN THEY HAVE PLUCKED A ROSE THERE,		571	THREE BUSHES		75
AS THE CANKER-WORM ON A MILK-WHITE ROSE;		673	ISLE STAT II 3		177
WHEN HE GAVE TO THEE THE ROSE,		744	ROSY CROSS		2
WHEN HE GAVE TO THEE THE ROSE,		744	ROSY CROSS		10
ROSE	(VERB)				
AS HER SOFT BOSOM ROSE AND FELL.		4	OISIN 1		30
ROSE EVER OUT OF THE WARM SEA;		13	OISIN 1		172
ROSE EVER FROM THE SEA'S WARM FLOOR,		13	OISIN 1	V	172
AND ROSE FROM ALL THEIR DISTANT PARTS,		16	OISIN 1	V	228
ROSE IN THE DARKNESS, AND THE WHITE SURF GLEAMED		30	OISIN 2		23
IN NIAM'S HAIR--WHEN ROSE A WORLD OF TOWERS		30	OISIN 2	V	22
OUR TREAD, AS ROSE AND FELL THE LIQUID TONES		33	OISIN 2	V	68B
ROSE FROM A LITTLE RUNNEL ON WHOSE EDGE		39	OISIN 2	V	157
KINGFISHER COLOUR GREW WITH RAGE. HE ROSE		40	OISIN 2	V	169
. . . AND I ROSE, AND WALKED ON THE EARTH,		60	OISIN 3		191
WITH EYES OF SADNESS ROSE TO HEAR,		85	MAD KING GOLL	V	62
IN SOLEMN REVERIE ROSE TO HEAR		85	MAD KING GOLL	V	62
WHERE SUCH GREY CLOUDS OF INCENSE ROSE		156	FORGOT BEAUTY		13
WHERE A SO SLEEPY INCENSE ROSE		156	FORGOT BEAUTY	V	13
IT ROSE IN A STRAIGHT BLUE GARMENT,		159	CAP AND BELLS		5
SHE ROSE IN HER PALE NIGHT-GOWN;		159	CAP AND BELLS		10
SHE ROSE IN HER PALE NIGHT GOWN,		159	CAP AND BELLS	V	10
WHEN SHE ROSE UP TO DEPART?		171	MAID QUIET		6
WASHED BY TIME'S WATERS AS THEY ROSE AND FELL		206	ADAMS CURSE		32
WHILE I WAS LOOKING THEY ROSE HURRIEDLY,		223	SHADOW WATER B		25
SHE MOTIONED HIM AFAR, AND ROSE AND SPOKE!		280	TWO KINGS		68
AND AT THOSE WORDS I ROSE AND I WENT OUT		282	TWO KINGS		125
TOLD HIM, THAT WHEN ORION ROSE, AND ALL		282	TWO KINGS	V	132A
ROSE ROUND THE WALLS, AND THROUGH THE BRONZE-RINGED DOOR		286	TWO KINGS		215
SHOULD BE SO SIMPLE--A BAT ROSE FROM THE HAZELS		377	PHASES OF MOON		137
THAT EVERY MORNING ROSE AGAIN		385	ROBARTES DANCE		7
WHILE THAT GREAT QUEEN, THAT ROSE OUT OF THE SPRAY,		404	FOR DAUGHTER		27
ROSE FROM THE TABLE AND DECLARED IT RIGHT		410	TOWER		43
HANRAHAN ROSE IN FRENZY THERE		412	TOWER		71
I ROSE THAT I MIGHT SCREEN IT WITH A CLOTH.		467	HARUN RASHID		131
BUT WOKE AT THE FIRST GLEAM OF DAY, ROSE UP		467	HARUN RASHID		147
SHE ROSE, AND WITH HER EYES SHUT FAST IN SLEEP		468	HARUN RASHID		152
AND ONCE AGAIN SHE ROSE AND SWEPT THE HOUSE		468	HARUN RASHID		159
MANY TIMES ROSE AGAIN.		467	DEATH		6
ROSE OUT OF THE RACE		480	BLOOD AND MOON		4
ROSE LIKE THESE WALLS FROM THESE		480	BLOOD AND MOON		6
ROSE; SOME CONQUEROR DREW REIN		502	VACILLATION		64
HE ROSE THE LATCH AND WENT UPSTAIRS		594	COLONEL MARTIN		7
I ROSE, I ROSE		672	ISLE STAT II 3		161
I ROSE, I ROSE		672	ISLE STAT II 3		161
I ROSE, I ROSE		672	ISLE STAT II 3		163
I ROSE, I ROSE		672	ISLE STAT II 3		163
JUST NOW MY SOUL ROSE UP AND TOUCHED IT, FAR		705	REMEMBRANCE		13
A FULL HOUR LONG, WHEN ROSE A FEATHER		728	PRIEST FAIRY		19
THREE SPANS HIGH AS HE ROSE TO HIS FEET,		729	PRIEST FAIRY		25
AND JOHN ROSE UP AND STOOD,		741	EARL PAUL		54
ROSEATE					
WHAT ROSEATE FINGERS! NO; NOR IS THERE ONE		720	WITCH VIVIEN		5
WHAT ROSEATE FINGERS! HA, HA! HA, HA, HA!		720	WITCH VIVIEN		15
ROSE-BREATH					
A LITTLE SPACE FOR THE ROSE-BREATH TO FILL!		101	ROSE UPON ROOD		14

666

		PAGE	TITLE		LINE
ROSE-HEAVY					
COVER YOUR LIPS WITH ROSE-HEAVY TWILIGHT, AND SAY:		162	ASKS FORGIVE	V	5
THE ROSE-HEAVY TWILIGHT THERE.		163	ASKS FORGIVE	V	24
ROSE'S					
AS WE KISSED EACH ROSE'S HEAD:		21	OISIN 1	V	307
ROSES					
THE DAMASK ROSES, BLOOM ON BLOOM,		21	OISIN 1		305
FALL THE LEAVES OF OTHER ROSES,		21	OISIN 1		311
SHALL FALL THE LEAVES OF DAMASK ROSES.		21	OISIN 1		315
DAMASK ROSES IN THE NIGHT,		21	OISIN 1	V	306A
ROSE OF ALL ROSES, ROSE OF ALL THE WORLD!		113	ROSE OF BATTLE		1
ROSE OF ALL ROSES, ROSE OF ALL THE WORLD!		115	ROSE OF BATTLE		25
THE SOUTH IS POURING DOWN ROSES OF CRIMSON FIRE!		154	BELOVED PEACE		6
THE SOUTH WOULD COVER THEM WITH ROSES OF CRIMSON FIRE!		154	BELOVED PEACE	V	6
THE ROSES THAT OF OLD TIME WERE		156	FORGOT BEAUTY		9
LILIES OF DEATH-PALE HOPE, ROSES OF PASSIONATE DREAM.		172	TRAV PASSION		8
BRING ROSES IF THE ROSE BE YET IN BLOOM:		311	MOUNTAIN TOMB		2
TO TAKE THE ROSES FOR HIS MEAT.		382	SONG OF FOOL		12
SO DID THEIR ROSES MERGE.		571	THREE BUSHES		62
WHERE REVEL OF FOX-GLOVE IS AND REVEL OF ROSES."		669	ISLE STAT II 3		86
WHERE REVEL OF FOXGLOVE IS AND REVEL OF ROSES."		669	ISLE STAT II 3	V	86
THE ROOTS OF THE ROSES.		672	ISLE STAT II 3		169
THREE TIMES THE ROSES HAVE GROWN LESS AND LESS,		690	MOSADA 1		1
TENDING THE ROSES ROUND HIS LATTICE DOOR.		692	MOSADA 1		53
WHERE THE ROSES IN SCARLET ARE HEAVY		707	FAIRY PEDANT		3
THOUGH TENDEREST ROSES WERE ROUND YOU,		708	FAIRY PEDANT		29
ROSE-TREE					
AND SET A ROSE-TREE ON HER GRAVE,		571	THREE BUSHES		73
ROSICROSS					
OUR FATHER ROSICROSS IS IN HIS TOMB.		311	MOUNTAIN TOMB		4
OUR FATHER ROSICROSS IS IN HIS TOMB.		311	MOUNTAIN TOMB		8
OUR FATHER ROSICROSS SLEEPS IN HIS TOMB.		311	MOUNTAIN TOMB		12
ROSNAREE					
MY COUSIN OF ROSNAREE.		178	FIDDLER DOONEY	V	4
MY COUSIN IN ROSNAREE.		178	FIDDLER DOONEY	V	4
ROSSES					
FAR OFF BY FURTHEST ROSSES		87	STOLEN CHILD		15
ROSSES'					
BUT ACTUAL SHELLS OF ROSSES' LEVEL SHORE.		494	AT ALGECIRAS		12
BUT TURN FROM ROSSES' CRAWLING TIDE,		549	SEVERED HEAD		5
ROSY					
AND SOFTLY MAKE A ROSY PEACE,		113	ROSE OF PEACE		15
A SONG OF THE ROSY CROSS		744	ROSY CROSS		T
ROT					
BUT FAME AND VIRTUE ROT.		584	GHOST ROG CASE		36
ROTE					
HE TELLS HIS LIES BY ROTE:		598	STONE CROSS		2
ROTS					
WOULD END THIS PEACEFUL LIFE THAT ROTS THE BONES,		752	SHADOW WATER A		110
ROTTED SEE SEA-ROTTED					
LIKE ROTTED FLESH, AND STONE BY STONE MY HALL		45	OISIN 2	V	236
ROTTING					
--FROM POOLS AND ROTTING LEAVES--ME SING		85	MAD KING GOLL	V	63
LIES TORN AND ROTTING. THE FIERCE KESTREL BIRDS		675	ISLE STAT II 3		234
ROUGE					
PROPPED UPON PILLOWS, ROUGE ON THE PALLOR OF HER FACE.		362	HER COURTESY		3
ROUGH					
WHERE ARE YOU WITH YOUR LONG ROUGH HAIR?		11	OISIN 1		126
WHERE ARE YE WITH YOUR LONG ROUGH HAIR?		11	OISIN 1	V	126
STAND UNDER THE ROUGH ROOF-TIMBERS OF THE HALL		377	PHASES OF MOON		125
AND WHAT ROUGH BEAST, ITS HOUR COME ROUND AT LAST,		402	SECOND COMING		21
ROUGH MEN-AT-ARMS, CROSS-GARTERED TO THE KNEES		412	TOWER		82
ROUGH MEN AT ARMS, CROSS-GARTERED TO THE KNEES		412	TOWER	V	82
HURRIED THROUGH THE SMOOTH AND ROUGH		436	FOR MY SON		29
HAVE BORNE YOU THROUGH THE SMOOTH AND ROUGH		436	FOR MY SON	V	29
"AND THE NIGHT GROWS ROUGH."		526	AM OF IRELAND		13
MARINERS, ROUGH HARVESTERS:		540	FROM ANTIGONE		5
ROUND					
THAN DOVES THAT MOANED ROUND EMAN'S HALL		3	OISIN 1	V	7EE
WHERE ROUND AND ROUND THE RAVENS GO.		5	OISIN 1	V	42
WHERE ROUND AND ROUND THE RAVENS GO.		5	OISIN 1	V	42
AND FAR BEHIND US, SLOWLY ROUND		10	OISIN 1	V	114B
LULLED WEARINESS, AND SOFTLY ROUND		11	OISIN 1		137
LULLED WEARINESS: AND CLOSELY ROUND		11	OISIN 1	V	137
IN SILENCE ROUND HIS CRIMSON BALL.		12	OISIN 1	V	155
WHEN ROUND US SUDDENLY THERE CAME		13	OISIN 1	V	165
OF THE GREAT ROUND SUN, FROM HIS CENTRAL FIRES.		13	OISIN 1	V	168
ROUND EVERY BRANCH THE SONG-BIRDS FLEW,		14	OISIN 1		180
WHILE ROUND THE SHORE A MILLION STOOD		14	OISIN 1		182
FOR ROUND EACH BRANCH THE SONG-BIRDS FLEW,		14	OISIN 1	V	180
TRIMMED ROUND WITH MANY A CRIMSON FEATHER:		15	OISIN 1	V	206
ROUND US, AND ROLLS THE UNWIELDY SUN.		18	OISIN 1	V	268
THE MIST CLOSED ROUND US: PEARLY LIGHT		28	OISIN 1	V	427C
ROLLED ROUND WITH MUSIC OF THE SIGHING SPRAY:		30	OISIN 1		14
AND BLACKNESS IN THE DARK. THE SEA ROLLED ROUND,		30	OISIN 2	V	23
WITH CHAIN SEA-ROTTED, ROUND HER MIDDLE TIED,		34	OISIN 2	V	75
WRAPT ROUND IN SOME DIM MEMORY, IT SEEMED--		36	OISIN 2	V	99
CLOTHING HIM ROUND, I SAW A SEAGULL FLOAT		36	OISIN 2	V	105
WITH A PALE LIGHT, I JOURNEYED ROUND THE HALL		39	OISIN 2		153
OF MISTY DAWN: WHEN, CIRCLING ROUND THE HALL,		39	OISIN 2	V	153
HUNG ROUND WITH SLIME, AND WHISPERING IN HIS HAIR,		43	OISIN 2	V	216

	PAGE	TITLE		LINE

ROUND (CONTINUED)

FLED FOAM UNDERNEATH US, AND ROUND US, A WANDERING AND MILKY SMOKE.	47	OISIN 3		1
FLED FOAM UNDERNEATH US, AND ROUND US, A WANDERING AND MILKY SMOKE.	47	OISIN 3		12
COULD SLEEP ON A COUCH OF RUSHES--ROUND AND ABOUT THEM LAID.	49	OISIN 3	V	32
MOVED ROUND ME, OF SEAMEN OR LANDSMEN, ALL WHO ARE WINTER TALES;	53	OISIN 3		86
FLED FOAM UNDERNEATH ME, AND ROUND ME, A WANDERING AND MILKY SMOKE.	57	OISIN 3		148
AND IN FOLDS ROUND HIS EYES AND HIS MOUTH, ...	59	OISIN 3		174
WEARY, WITH ALL HIS POPPIES GATHERED ROUND HIM.	72	ANASHU VIJAYA		25
WHILE WE ALONE HAVE ROUND US WOVEN WOODS, ...	73	ANASHU VIJAYA		56
OF AWELESS BIRDS, AND ROUND THEIR STIRLESS FEET	74	ANASHU VIJAYA		73
MY SPIRIT ROCKED IN EVENING LIGHT, THE RUSHES ROUND MY KNEES,	76	INDIAN ON GOD		2
EACH OTHER ROUND IN CIRCLES, AND HEARD THE ELDEST SPEAK;	76	INDIAN ON GOD		5
MY SPIRIT ROCKED IN EVENING'S HUSH, THE RUSHES ROUND MY KNEES,	76	INDIAN ON GOD	V	2
EACH OTHER ROUND IN CIRCLES; AND I HEARD THE ELDEST SPEAK!--	76	INDIAN ON GOD	V	5
ONE WITH THE WAVES THAT SOFTLY ROUND US LAUGH AND DART.	78	INDIAN TO LOVE	V	15
THE WOODS WERE ROUND THEM, AND THE YELLOW LEAVES	80	EPHEMERA		13
THEY WILL NOT HUSH, THE LEAVES A-FLUTTER ROUND ME, . . .	82	MAD KING GOLL		12
(THEY WILL NOT HUSH, THE LEAVES THAT ROUND ME FLUTTER-- . . .	82	MAD KING GOLL	V	REF
THEY WILL NOT HUSH, THE LEAVES A-FLUTTER ROUND ME, . . .	83	MAD KING GOLL		24
TO HIS OWN ICE!" I GATHERED ROUND ME, ...	83	MAD KING GOLL	V	18
THEY WILL NOT HUSH, THE LEAVES A-FLUTTER ROUND ME, . . .	84	MAD KING GOLL		36
THEY WILL NOT HUSH, THE LEAVES A-FLUTTER ROUND ME, . . .	84	MAD KING GOLL		48
THEY WILL NOT HUSH, THE LEAVES A-FLUTTER ROUND ME, . . .	85	MAD KING GOLL		60
THEY WILL NOT HUSH, THE LEAVES A-FLUTTER ROUND ME, . . .	86	MAD KING GOLL		72
ROUND AND ROUND THE OATMEAL-CHEST.	88	STOLEN CHILD		49
ROUND AND ROUND THE OATMEAL-CHEST.	88	STOLEN CHILD		49
ROUND AND ROUND THE OATMEAL CHEST.	88	STOLEN CHILD	V	49
ROUND AND ROUND THE OATMEAL CHEST.	88	STOLEN CHILD	V	49
AND THE WORLD ROUND KNOCKNASHEE	93	FATHER OHART		31
COME ROUND ME, LITTLE CHILDER;	94	MOLL MAGEE	.	1
THE LITTLE STRAWS WERE TURNIN' ROUND	95	MOLL MAGEE		31
BUT ALWAYS, AS I'M MOVIN' ROUND, ...	96	MOLL MAGEE		43
POURS ROUND HIS SLEEPY STREAMS.	98	FOXHUNTER	V	16
POURS ROUND IN SLEEPY STREAMS.	98	FOXHUNTER	V	16
HIS LOLLARD LEAD THEY ROUND THE LAWN, ...	98	FOXHUNTER	V	17
SERVANTS ROUND HIS CUSHIONED PLACE	99	FOXHUNTER		37
THE SERVANTS ROUND HIS CUSHIONED PLACE	99	FOXHUNTER	V	37
WHO CAST ROUND FERGUS DREAMS, AND RUIN UNTOLD; . . .	101	ROSE UPON ROOD		5
UNLOOSE THE CORD, AND THEY WILL WRAP YOU ROUND.	104	FERGUS DRUID		30
WHO LOVES YOU, NO WHITE ARMS TO WRAP YOU ROUND, ...	109	CUCHULAIN SEA		59
RANKING HIS DRUIDS ROUND HIM TEN BY TEN, ...	110	CUCHULAIN SEA		76
NEAR TO CUCHULLIN, ROUND A QUICKEN TREE, ...	111	CUCHULAIN SEA	V	81A
MY ARMS ROUND MY OWN!	118	CRADLE SONG	V	10
WITH ARMS ROUND MY OWN, ...	118	CRADLE SONG	V	10
THE FULL ROUND MOON AND THE STAR-LADEN SKY, ...	119	SORROW OF LOVE	V	2
AND PLANTED CYPRESS ROUND;	123	DREAM OF DEATH		8
FOR ROUND ABOUT MY TABLE GO	138	TO IRELAND	V	23
THE WINDS AWAKEN, THE LEAVES WHIRL ROUND, ...	140	HOSTING SIDHE		6
WHEN MY ARMS WRAP YOU ROUND I PRESS	155	FORGOT BEAUTY		1
THAT KEEPS THE STARS IN THEIR ROUND, ...	165	CRY OF SEDGE		5
I KNOW OF THE SLEEPY COUNTRY, WHERE SWANS FLY ROUND . . .	204	WITHER BOUGHS		17
MOVED ROUND ME IN THE SHADOWS, AND AT NIGHT	218	WOODS OF COOLE		19
MOVED ROUND ME IN THE VOICES AND THE FIRES, ...	218	WOODS OF COOLE		23
A GOOD ROUND SUM UPON THIS CRUISE, AND TURN--	222	SHADOW WATER B		5
I SWEAR BEFORE THE DAWN COMES ROUND AGAIN	260	FASC DIFFICULT		12
WHEN CUPS WENT ROUND AT CLOSE OF DAY--	271	GREY ROCK		12
AND PUT HIS PATTERN ROUND THEIR TOPS	272	GREY ROCK	V	24
AND FOR NINE DAYS MY MIND WENT WHIRLING ROUND	282	TWO KINGS		127
ROSE ROUND THE WALLS, AND THROUGH THE BRONZE-RINGED DOOR	286	TWO KINGS		215
ROUND ABOUT HELL'S GATE TO STARE	294	HATED PLAYBOY	V	3
UNDER THE ROUND TOWER	331	ROUND TOWER		T
BELLOWED AND PRANCED IN THE ROUND TOWER;	331	ROUND TOWER		12
BELLOWING UP AND BELLOWING ROUND, ...	331	ROUND TOWER		14
PRANCING ROUND AND PRANCING UP	331	ROUND TOWER		17
WE HAVE GONE ROUND AND ROUND	332	SOLOMON SHEBA		6
WE HAVE GONE ROUND AND ROUND	332	SOLOMON SHEBA		6
THE ROUND GREEN EYES AND THE LONG WAVERING BODIES . . .	343	DEJECTION		2
MANAGE THE TALK UNTIL HER NAME COME ROUND.	351	HER PRAISE		14
MANAGE TO TALK UNTIL HER NAME COME ROUND.	351	HER PRAISE	V	14
HE HAD LEARNT FROM PATER, AND TO ROUND HIS TALE . . .	373	PHASES OF MOON		27
THE FIRST THIN CRESCENT IS WHEELED ROUND ONCE MORE. . . .	377	PHASES OF MOON		116
AND CIRCLED ROUND HIM WITH ITS SQUEAKY CRY, ...	377	PHASES OF MOON		138
AND THE MOON SPUN ROUND LIKE A TOP, ...	378	CAT AND MOON		2
AND THAT FROM ROUND TO CRESCENT, ...	379	CAT AND MOON		23
FROM CRESCENT TO ROUND THEY RANGE?	379	CAT AND MOON		24
AND WHAT ROUGH BEAST, ITS HOUR COME ROUND AT LAST, . . .	402	SECOND COMING		21
AND HAVE NO BUSINESS BUT DISPENSING ROUND	404	FOR DAUGHTER		43
WHAT MORE IS THERE TO SAY? THAT COUNTRY ROUND . . .	430	NINETEEN 19		43
HAD FALLEN AMONG DANCERS, HAD WHIRLED THEM ROUND . . .	430	NINETEEN 19		52
GREEKS WERE BUT LOVERS! ALL THAT COUNTRY ROUND . . .	430	NINETEEN 19	V	43
BUT WEARIED RUNNING ROUND AND ROUND IN THEIR COURSES . .	433	NINETEEN 19		116
BUT WEARIED RUNNING ROUND AND ROUND IN THEIR COURSES . .	433	NINETEEN 19		116

		PAGE	TITLE		LINE
ROUND	(CONTINUED)				
BUT, WEARY RUNNING ROUND AND ROUND IN THEIR COURSES,	• •	433	NINETEEN 19	V	116
BUT, WEARY RUNNING ROUND AND ROUND IN THEIR COURSES,	• •	433	NINETEEN 19	V	116
TILL HIS MORNING MEAL COME ROUND;	• •	435	FOR MY SON		4
FROM SOME COURT-LADY'S DRESS AND ROUND	• •	477	SELF AND SOUL		14
FROM SOME COURT-LADIES' DRESS AND ROUND	• •	477	SELF AND SOUL	V	14
TO ROUND THAT SHELL'S ELABORATE WHORL,	• •	509	JANE REPROVED		8
WHAT SET IT WHIRLING ROUND?	• •	520	HIS BARGAIN		2
AND PRAYER COMES ROUND AGAIN--	• •	553	PRAYER OLD AGE		10
AND MUST THE COMMON ROUND OF DAY RESUME.	• •	557	RIBH ECSTASY		8
THAT DAY BRINGS ROUND THE NIGHT, THAT BEFORE DAWN	• •	563	MERU		13
I TURN ROUND	• •	572	LADYS 1ST SONG		1
DRAW ROUND, BELOVED AND BITTER MEN,	• •	584	GHOST ROG CASE		37
DRAW ROUND AND RAISE A SHOUT;	• •	584	GHOST ROG CASE		38
COME GATHER ROUND ME, PARNELLITES,	• •	586	PARNELLITES		T
COME GATHER ROUND ME, PARNELLITES,	• •	586	PARNELLITES		1
AND PASS THE BOTTLE ROUND.	• •	586	PARNELLITES		8
SO PASS THE BOTTLE ROUND.	• •	587	PARNELLITES		24
FOR PASSING ROUND THE BOTTLE WITH GIRLS IN RAGS OR SILK,	• •	592	PILGRIM		2
FOR PASSING ROUND THE BOTTLE WITH GIRLS IN RAG OR SILK,	• •	592	PILGRIM	V	2
ROUND LOUGH DERG'S HOLY ISLAND I WENT UPON THE STONES,	• •	593	PILGRIM		6
COME GATHER ROUND ME, PLAYERS ALL!	• •	608	SONGS BURDEN 3		1
OR ROUND THE CITY HALL,	• •	608	SONGS BURDEN 3		6
UNDER THE TROPIC SHADE, GREW ROUND AND SLOW,	• •	610	STATUES		18
HUMAN, SUPERHUMAN, A BIRD'S ROUND EYE,	• •	618	BRONZE HEAD		2
HUMAN, SUPER-HUMAN, A BIRD'S ROUND EYE,	• •	618	BRONZE HEAD	V	2
ROUND THE MAREOTIC LAKE	• •	636	BEN BULBEN		2
SLEEPILY CLOSE HER ROUND BRIGHT EYNE;	• •	646	ISLE STAT I 1		35
HANG ON THE SIDE OF THE ROUND GRAPE-CLUSTER;	• •	646	ISLE STAT I 1		45
WITH SINGING SWEET AS E'ER ROUND LAKE-LULLED ISLE	• •	649	ISLE STAT I 1		106
WILL CIRCLE ROUND THE WORLD UPON A QUEST,	• •	651	ISLE STAT I 1		159
AND I SANG ROUND THE TREE	• •	654	ISLE STAT I 2		66
AND I SANG ROUND THE TREE,	• •	654	ISLE STAT I 2		76
AND I SANG ROUND THE TREE,	• •	655	ISLE STAT I 2		80
HERE WHERE THE ROUND WAVES COME, HERE LET THEM BUILD,	• •	663	ISLE STAT II 2		19
THE SPINNING STARS--THE TOILING SEA--WHIRL ROUND	• •	665	ISLE STAT II 2		72
THEY WERE SITTING ROUND A POOL,	• •	667	ISLE STAT II 3		24
AND THEY WERE SITTING ROUND A POOL.	• •	667	ISLE STAT II 3	V	24
HAS FENCED US ROUND FOR ALL ETERNITY.	• •	670	ISLE STAT II 3		95
AND ALL WAS QUIET ROUND ME SPREAD,	• •	670	ISLE STAT II 3		112
MY DREAMS ROUND THOUGHTS OF PLENTY, AS IN GLOOM	• •	681	SEEKER		3
AND ROVE UNCEASING ROUND THEIR DREADFUL BROOD.	• •	681	SEEKER		5
WEARY OF WATCHING ROUND THE FIRE AT NIGHT.	• •	683	SEEKER		42
AS ROUND HER, SLOW ON FEET THAT HAVE NO BLOOD,	• •	687	TWO TITANS		18
FOR EVER ROUND THY WAKING AND THY SLEEP	• •	688	TWO TITANS		57
NOR TREMBLE TO ITS FALL. THE FIRE SWEEPS ROUND	• •	689	NETTLESHIP		11
POURS UP AND FLOATS IN FRAGRANCE ROUND MY HEAD	• •	691	MOSADA 1		40
OF SILVER HANGING ROUND LAME COLA'S NECK--	• •	691	MOSADA 1	V	35
TENDING THE ROSES ROUND HIS LATTICE DOOR.	• •	692	MOSADA 1		53
AND, WHILE THEY GATHER ROUND MY BECKONING ARMS,	• •	694	MOSADA 1		100
FOR YE ARE HID WITH VAPOUR. ROUND THE STAKE	• •	695	MOSADA 1		111
FOR YE ARE HID WITH VAPOURS? ROUND THE STAKE	• •	695	MOSADA 1	V	111
POOR LOVE AND SORROW, WITH THEIR ARMS THROWN ROUND	• •	703	MOSADA 3		119
THOUGH TENDEREST ROSES WERE ROUND YOU,	• •	708	FAIRY PEDANT		29
RINGED ROUND AND FONDLED, A BROWN FARM HOUSE SEES.	• •	710	FERENCZ RENYI	V	23
CLOSELY ROUND US, BODY AND MIND--	• •	717	FAIRY DOCTOR		23
ROUND SHE COMES IN STAYS BEFORE THEM;	• •	719	PHANTOM SHIP		17
FROM WHERE THE OLD IVY CRAWLS ROUND THE OLD STEEPLE,	• •	728	PRIEST FAIRY		6
ROUND US THE WHITE ROADS ARE ENDLESS,	• •	737	IN FIRELIGHT		3
ROUND US HERDS OF SHADOWS STEAL--	• •	737	IN FIRELIGHT		6
AND GATHER ROUND HIM, THAT NO GOD MAY KNOW	• •	758	SHADOW WATER A	V	231
AT THE GREY ROUND OF THE HILL	• •	782	GREY ROUND		1
WHEN MOON'S ROUND IS FINISHED	• •	786	YOUR HEART		33
ROUNDING					
BUT WHILE THE MOON IS ROUNDING TOWARDS THE FULL	• • •	373	PHASES OF MOON		39
ROUNDLY					
'TWAS ROUNDLY SPOKE, BUT WHEN NIGHT CAME	• • •	275	GREY ROCK		95
ROUNDS					
ROUNDS A MIGHTY SCENE,	• •	599	STONE CROSS		22
• • • SEE, SHE ROUNDS THE HARBOUR CLEAR.	• • •	718	PHANTOM SHIP		13
ROUSE					
TO SHAKE HIM OUT OF SLEEP, I COULD NOT ROUSE HIM.	• •	283	TWO KINGS		143
COULD ROUSE MY WHOLE NATURE.	• •	400	DEMON BEAST		32
ROUSED					
THE WAR-SONGS THAT ROUSED THEM OF OLD;	• •	61	OISIN 3		202
HE ROUSED HIS HORSE OUT OF ITS SLEEP,	• •	133	FR GILLIGAN		27
I HAVE ROUSED THEE; FOR THE WEEPING	• •	729	PRIEST FAIRY		40
ROUT					
LIKE TO A MERRY WANDERING ROUT	• •	18	OISIN 1		253
AND THROUGH THE DOORS, A RUSTLING ROUT,	• •	20	OISIN 1	V	290
WHAT ONE IN THE ROUT	• •	142	MOODS		5
BUT, KINDLY OLD ROUT	• •	142	MOODS	V	5
WITH EQUAL COURAGE IN THAT WHIRLING ROUT;	• •	186	QUEEN MAEVE		131
ROVE					
HOW WHEN WE DIE OUR SHADES WILL ROVE,	• • •	78	INDIAN TO LOVE		18
HOW WHEN WE DIE OUR SHADES MAY ROVE,	• • •	78	INDIAN TO LOVE	V	18
IS FROM THE HOLY SHADES THAT ROVE	• •	275	GREY ROCK		110
OUR SHADOWS ROVE THE GARDEN GRAVEL STILL,	• • •	435	NEW FACES		7
FROM WHOSE GREEN BANKS NO LIVING THING MAY ROVE,	• •	664	ISLE STAT II 2		57
DOTH STILL THE WANDERER ROVE? WITH ALL HIS SHIPS	• •	677	ISLE STAT II 3		287
AND THROUGH THE MANSION OF THE SPIRIT ROVE	• • •	681	SEEKER		2

669

		PAGE	TITLE	LINE

ROVE   (CONTINUED)
OF DESERT-CAVES THE RED-EYED PANTHERS ROVE . . . . . .   681 SEEKER   4
AND ROVE UNCEASING ROUND THEIR DREADFUL BROOD. . . . .   681 SEEKER   5
EYED PANTHERS IN THEIR DESERT CAVERNS ROVE . . . . . .   681 SEEKER   V   4
ROVED
AND MANY A POOR MAN THAT HAS ROVED, ...   404 FOR DAUGHTER   38
ROVER
OF MANY A SLAUGHTERED FOREST ROVER. . . . .   17 OISIN 1   V 249A
SAILETH THE ROVER SORROW, ...   70 CLOAK BOAT   9
SAILETH THE ROVER SORROW, ...   666 ISLE STAT II 3   9
A ROVER I, WHO COME FROM WHERE MEN'S EARS . . . . . .   678 ISLE STAT II 3   293
DOTH STILL THE MAN WHOM EACH STERN ROVER FEARS, ... 678 ISLE STAT II 3   295
ROVING   SEE A-ROVING
ROW
IN A LONG AND SHADOWY ROW, ...   20 OISIN 1   V 295
AND LAYS THEM IN A ROW. . . . .   89 ISLE IN WATER   6
THE ARCHANGELS STAND IN A ROW THERE . . . .   774 COME RIDE   9
ROWAN
YELLOW THE LEAVES OF THE ROWAN ABOVE US, ...   79 FALLING LEAVES   3
ROWBOAT
ROWER BENT IN HIS ROWBOAT . . . .   589 OLD WICKED MAN V   50
ROW-BOAT
ROWER BENT IN HIS ROW-BOAT . . . .   589 OLD WICKED MAN   50
ROWED
WHEN WE ROWED NORTH, SINGING ABOVE THE OARS, ... 749 SHADOW WATER A   39
ROWER
ROWER BENT IN HIS ROW-BOAT . . . .   589 OLD WICKED MAN   50
ROWER BENT IN HIS ROWBOAT . . . .   589 OLD WICKED MAN V   50
ROWERS'
UPON THE ROWERS' BENCHES UNDERNEATH, ...   751 SHADOW WATER A   92
ROWS   SEE BEAN-ROWS
NINE BEAN ROWS WILL I HAVE THERE, A HIVE FOR THE HONEY BEE, 117 ISLE INNISFREE V   3
ROXBOROUGH
FROM CASTLE TAYLOR TO THE ROXBOROUGH SIDE . . . . . .   326 ROBERT GREGORY   58
ROYAL
ON MR. NETTLESHIP'S PICTURE AT THE ROYAL HIBERNIAN ACADEMY. 688 NETTLESHIP   T
ROYSTERER   SEE FELLOW-ROYSTERER
TO ABD-AL-RABBAN: FELLOW ROYSTERER ONCE . . . . . .   460 HARUN RASHID   V   2
RUA
WINDLE-STRAWS I. O'SULLIVAN RUA TO THE CURLEW . . . . . 155 REPROVE CURLEW V   T
O'SULLIVAN RUA TO MARY LAVELL . . . .   155 FORGOT BEAUTY V   T
O'SULLIVAN RUA TO THE SECRET ROSE . . . .   169 SECRET ROSE   V   T
RUB
PUSH OUT HIS VIGOROUS LIMBS AND RUB HIS EYES, ... 284 TWO KINGS   162
IF I SHOULD RUB AN EYE, ...   384 VISION ROBART   52
RUBBED
AND RUBBED ALONG THE RAIL HIS NOSE. . . . .   725 LEGEND   28
RUBBING
SCALE RUBBING SCALE WHERE LIGHT IS DIM . . . .   195 BAILE AILLINN   145
RUBBISH
FOR ONLY RUBBISH COMES MY WAY. . . . .   295 THREE BEGGARS   4
AND SEEN THE RUBBISH RUN ABOUT, ...   297 THREE BEGGARS   65
AND SEEN THE RUBBISH RUNABOUT, ...   297 THREE BEGGARS V   65
FAIL, AND THAT HISTORY TURNS INTO RUBBISH, ... 546 TO SAME TUNE 2   21
FAIL, AND THAT HISTORY TURNS INTO RUBBISH, ... 614 MARCH SONGS 1   21
RUBIES
LET'S HOME: I'D GIVE SOME RUBIES TO A WOMAN. . . . . . 248 SHADOW WATER B   537
RUBY
ACROSS YOUR WANDERING RUBY CARS . . . .   22 OISIN 1   330
THE ANCIENT BEARDS, THE HELMS OF RUBY AND GOLD . . . . 169 SECRET ROSE   8
OF OPAL AND RUBY AND PALE CHRYSOLITE . . . .   219 HARP OF AENGUS   6
DRAGONS WITH EYES OF RUBY. THE WHOLE SHIP . . . . . .   248 SHADOW WATER B   535
OF OPAL AND RUBY AND PALE CHRYSOLITE . . . .   762 SHADOW WATER A   301
AND CHRYSOPRASE AND RUBY AND SARDONYX. . . . . . .   765 SHADOW WATER A   358
RUDDY
WITH HOOFS OF THE RUDDY FINDRINNY . . . .   25 OISIN 1   V 383
AS ANY RUDDY MOTH, LOOKED DOWN ON US: . . . . . .   34 OISIN 2   72
AS LIKE A RUDDY MOTH THEY WAVED AND FLUTTERED. . . . .   34 OISIN 2   V   72
TALL, PROUD AND RUDDY, AND LIGHT WINGS . . . . . .   195 BAILE AILLINN   140
ON THE RUDDY RIVER SEDGE, ...   646 ISLE STAT I 1   25
OR LONG ERE THIS HAD LOST THEIR RUDDY STAIN: . . . . . 687 TWO TITANS   8
AND THEREON GREW THE RUDDY FRUIT . . . .   743 DANAAN QUICK   15
RUEFUL
HIS RUEFUL SPIRIT FLUTTERED BY. . . . .   673 ISLE STAT II 3   188
RUFFIAN'S
AND WHEN THAT ANCIENT RUFFIAN'S TURN WAS ON . . . . .   411 TOWER   66
RUFFLED
THERE ONE THAT RUFFLED IN A MANLY POSE . . . .   489 COOLE PARK 29   11
RUFFLES
HE RUFFLES WITH HIS BILL THE MINNOWED STREAMS. . . . .   73 ANASHU VIJAYA   37
RUFFLING
IN MIDST OF AN OLD MAN'S BOSOM: OWLS RUFFLING AND PACING 50 OISIN 3   47
   AROUND
IN THE MIDST OF AN OLD MAN'S BOSOM: OWLS RUFFLING   50 OISIN 3   V   47
   AND PACING AROUND
RUIN
WILL SCATTER IN RUIN THE LEAST OF OUR DAYS, ...   27 OISIN 1   V 419B
SHALL BLOW INTO RUIN OUR MUSICAL DAYS, ...   28 OISIN 1   V 425
WHO CAST ROUND FERGUS DREAMS, AND RUIN UNTOLD: . . . . 101 ROSE UPON ROOD   5
WHEN ALL IS RUIN ONCE AGAIN. . . . .   406 CARVED STONE   6
FROM RUIN OR FROM ANCIENT TREES, ...   410 TOWER   23

670

RUIN   (CONTINUED)
```
    BEFORE THAT RUIN CAME, FOR CENTURIES,                  412 TOWER              81
    BECOME A ROOFLESS RUIN THAT THE OWL                    423 MY DESCENDANTS     14
    MY HEART COULD NEVER TURN FROM DAILY RUIN,             464 HARUN RASHID       83
    MY HEART MUST LOOK UPON A DAILY RUIN                   464 HARUN RASHID    V  83
    RUIN, WRECK AND WRACK!                                 505 RESULT THOUGHT      8
    BUT I WOKE IN AN OLD RUIN THAT THE WINDS HOWLED THROUGH! 581 CURSE CROMWELL   28
    THAT WITH THEIR FIERY RUIN FILL THE HALL,              683 SEEKER             45
    TO PRISONS GO, AND MOSSY RUIN REST                     709 FERENCZ RENYI       2
    TO PRISON GO, AND MOSSY RUIN REST                      709 FERENCZ RENYI   V   2
    RUIN ON A GREAT KING'S HOUSE                           775 AGAINST WITCH       3
    CASTLE DARGAN'S RUIN ALL LIT,                          788 HAWTHORN TREE       3
RUINED
    IN CORMAC'S RUINED HOUSE.                              384 VISION ROBART      68
    EMPTIED, RUINED, WRACKED, AND LOST,                    776 AGAINST WITCH      27
RUINOUS
    TIME OUT OF MIND, BECAME TOO RUINOUS                   264 HOUSE SHAKEN        3
    UNINHABITED, RUINOUS,                                  512 JANE ON GOD        15
    UNTIL ALL BE RUINOUS.                                  775 AGAINST WITCH       4
RULE
    BUT HERE THERE IS NOR LAW NOR RULE,                     19 OISIN 1          282
    WITH HEARTS THAT KNOW NOR LAW NOR RULE,                 22 OISIN 1          339
    OUR LIVES HAVE KNOWN NO LAW NOR RULE!                   22 OISIN 1       V  340
    TO RULE MORE MIGHTY MEN, AND TO THE WORLD               38 OISIN 2       V  133
    "LAST OF MY RACE, THREE THINGS I RULE ALONE--           45 OISIN 2       V  239A
    AND WITH A RULE SERENE AND MILD                         82 MAD KING GOLL  V   6
    "THOUGH LOGIC-CHOPPERS RULE THE TOWN,                  337 TOM OROUGHLEY       1
    "THOUGH LOGIC CHOPPERS RULE THE TOWN,                  337 TOM OROUGHLEY   V   1
    MEN THAT DO ALL BY RULE,                               380 SONGS FOOL 1      14
    CAN RULE BY SUPERNATURAL RIGHT                         386 ROBARTES DANCE    36
    AND PLANNED TO BRING THE WORLD UNDER A RULE,           429 NINETEEN 19       31
    FIT AUDIENCE FOUND, BUT CANNOT RULE                    506 REMORSE SPEECH     4
    AND RULE IN HIS OWN RIGHT!                             538 LAST CONFESS      20
    UNDER A RULE, UNDER THE SEMBLANCE OF PEACE             563 MERU               2
    HE THOUGHT THE SAME AND LIVED BY RULE,                 576 WHAT THEN          3
    THAT RULE BECAUSE A STRONG RIGHT ARM                   597 MODEL LAUREATE    11
    "OBEY OUR ANCIENT RULE AND MAKE A SHROUD!             634 CUCHULAIN COMF    13
    CARES WHAT KING SETS UP HIS RULE.                      635 BLACK TOWER       14
    THE AUSTERE ARTHUR, RULE FROM UTHER'S CHAIR?          678 ISLE STAT II 3   296
    AND RULE THE SHADOWS OF THE EVE AND DAWN?             678 ISLE STAT II 3   304
    "HOW FEW THE MIND'S INTEMPERANCE RULE!                725 LEGEND            10
    THE GREATNESS OF MY LOVE.  DID I NOT RULE             748 SHADOW WATER A V  32
    AND RULE TOGETHER UNDER A CANOPY.                     767 SHADOW WATER A   385
RULED
    I RULED O'ER ALL MY FAIR DOMINIONS,                    82 MAD KING GOLL  V   7
    I RULED AND RULED MY LIFE WITHIN--                      82 MAD KING GOLL  V   7
    I RULED AND RULED MY LIFE WITHIN--                      82 MAD KING GOLL  V   7
    WHEN HER OWN PEOPLE RULED THIS TRAGIC EIRE;            129 BOOK STORIES       2
    WHEN HER OWN PEOPLE RULED IN WAVE-WORN ERI,            129 BOOK STORIES   V   2
    NO OSCAR RULED THE TABLE,                              626 STATES HOLIDAY     5
    HAST THOU NOT RULED AMONG THE GILDED WALLS?           724 KANVA ON SELF      7
RULERS
    GREAT RULERS OF THE STILLNESS, LET HER NO LONGER BE   175 ELEMENT POWERS V  13
    GREAT RULERS OF STILLNESS, LET HER NO LONGER BE       175 ELEMENT POWERS V  13
RULES
    HE RULES YOU WITH AN IRON ROD,                         22 OISIN 1          332
    FOR FERGUS RULES THE BRAZEN CARS,                     126 GOES FERGUS        9
    AND RULES THE SHADOWS OF THE WOOD,                    126 GOES FERGUS       10
    FAMOUS, A MAN OF RULES, A VICTOR.  STANDS             709 FERENCZ RENYI      9
RULETH
    WHO MADE THE WORLD AND RULETH IT, HE HANGETH ON A STALK, 76 INDIAN ON GOD  10
RUMBLE
    ONE HEARS THE RUMBLE OF IT FAR BELOW                  420 MY HOUSE       V  20B
RUMMAGED
    SECOND RUMMAGED FOR A FLEA!                           298 THREE HERMITS      4
    WHILE HE'D RUMMAGED RAGS AND HAIR,                    299 THREE HERMITS     29
RUMOROUS
    WANDERING OF YORE IN FORESTS RUMOROUS,               723 KANVA ON SELF      3
RUMOUR
    A RUMOUR OF DELIGHTED HEARTS.                          16 OISIN 1          230
    VAST GREENNESS, WHERE ETERNAL RUMOUR DWELLS,         657 ISLE STAT I 3    45
RUN
    THAT YOU THROUGH ALL THAT FOAM SHOULD RUN?"            6 OISIN 1           61
    AMONG UNDYING PEOPLE HAS RUN                           6 OISIN 1       V   60
    AND MAKES THE LITTLE PLANETS RUN!                     18 OISIN 1          268
    FOR JOY THE LITTLE PLANETS RUN                        18 OISIN 1       V  267
    THE IMAGED METEORS HAD FLASHED AND RUN                31 OISIN 2           38
    THE IMAGED METEORS HAD SHONE AND RUN,                 31 OISIN 2       V   38
    THE HARES RUN BY ME GROWING BOLD.                     84 MAD KING GOLL     47
    AND HARES RUN NEAR ME GROWING BOLD.                   84 MAD KING GOLL  V  47
    BEFORE MY THOUGHTS BEGIN TO RUN                      189 BAILE AILLINN      3
    I RUN TO BAILE HONEY-MOUTH,                          191 BAILE AILLINN     48
    I RUN TO BAILE HONEY MOUTH                           191 BAILE AILLINN  V  48
    GATHERING HIS CLOAK ABOUT HIM, RUN                   193 BAILE AILLINN    101
    THAT RUN BEFORE THE REAPING-HOOK AND LIE             218 WOODS OF COOLE    32
    THAT RUN BEFORE THE REAPING HOOK AND LIE             218 WOODS OF COOLE V  32
    UPON ITS BANDY LEGS.  RUN AT THEM NOW,               233 SHADOW WATER B   239
    COMES CRYING, "I HAVE RUN UPON THE SWORD.            234 SHADOW WATER B   261
    WHY LINGER?  RUN TO YOUR DESIRE,                     234 SHADOW WATER B   272
    WHY DO YOU NOT RUN TO YOUR DESIRE,                   234 SHADOW WATER B V  272
    WHILE THERE'S A ROPE TO RUN INTO A NOOSE             238 SHADOW WATER B   347
```

	PAGE	TITLE		LINE

RUN (CONTINUED)
BUT IT IS TRUE. WHY DID THEY RUN UPON HIM,	243	SHADOW WATER B		424
HAD RUN INTO ONE FOUNTAIN. SPEAK TO HIM,	249	SHADOW WATER B		561
HOW SHOULD THEIR LUCK RUN HIGH ENOUGH TO REACH	264	HOUSE SHAKEN		9
AND THEREFORE, FRIEND, IF YOUR GREAT RACE WERE RUN	265	THESE CLOUDS		7
TILL THE STARS HAD RUN AWAY	268	BROWN PENNY		13
IS NOT THAT HOW GOOD STORIES RUN?--	271	GREY ROCK		13
AND SEEN THE RUBBISH RUN ABOUT,	297	THREE BEGGARS		65
TREMBLED AND GASPED AND SHOULD HAVE RUN	303	HOUR DAWN	V	22
HE GAVE A GASP AND THOUGHT TO RUN,	303	HOUR DAWN	V	22
OR RUN WHERE LADS REFORM OUR DAYTIME	343	SHEP GOATHERD	V	105
AND I AM AFRAID THAT YOU WILL RUN	356	BROKEN DREAMS		30
I AM AFRAID THAT YOU WILL RUN	356	BROKEN DREAMS	V	30
WHY SHOULD YOU RUN	359	TO A SQUIRREL		2
THE HARE MAY RUN TILL IT'S FOUND	380	SONGS FOOL 1		11
ON LIMBS THAT HAD RUN WILD.	394	EASTER 1916		64
THEY NEVER SAW HOW SEASONS RUN,	432	NINETEEN 19		101
FROM CRADLE RUN TO GRAVE	449	HERO GIRL FOOL		19
FROM GRAVE TO CRADLE RUN INSTEAD:	449	HERO GIRL FOOL		20
"BECAUSE I MADE YOU TURN AWAY AND RUN FROM THAT YOUNG CHILD:	450	OWEN AHERNE		14
AND THEN I LAUGH TILL TEARS RUN DOWN	456	FRIENDS YOUTH		17
UNTIL THAT GLANCE RUN IN THE WORLD'S DESPITE	474	ALL SOUL NIGHT		94
RUN TILL ALL THE SAGES KNOW.	476	EVA GORE-BOOTH		29
RUN FOR A MILE UNDIMMED IN HEAVEN'S FACE	490	COOLE BALLYLEE		3
RUN UNDERGROUND, RISE IN A ROCKY PLACE	490	COOLE BALLYLEE		5
SPREAD TO A LAKE AND RUN INTO A HOLE.	490	COOLE BALLYLEE	V	7
BID IMAGINATION RUN	494	AT ALGECIRAS		15
WHEN THE LAST THREAD HAS RUN,	520	HIS BARGAIN		10
WHEN THE LAZY THREAD HAS RUN--	520	HIS BARGAIN	V	10
ROE COULD RUN OR DOE COULD LEAP	522	LULLABY		10
ROE COULD LEAP OR DOE COULD RUN:	522	LULLABY		12
STAG COULD RUN AND ROE LEAP	522	LULLABY	V	10
STAG COULD LEAP AND ROE COULD RUN.	522	LULLABY	V	12
ALL THAT COULD RUN OR LEAP OR SWIM	528	DANCER CRUACH		6
ALL THAT RUN OR LEAP OR SWIM	528	DANCER CRUACH	V	6
HOW COULD PASSION RUN SO DEEP	534	CONSOLATION		7
WHAT SHUDDERS RUN THROUGH ALL THAT ANIMAL BLOOD?	541	PARN FUNERAL 1		5
MARCH, MARCH--HOW DOES IT RUN?--	548	TO SAME TUNE 3		15
O BUT HEART'S WINE SHALL RUN PURE,	554	CHURCH STATE		5
WINE SHALL RUN THICK TO THE END,	554	CHURCH STATE		11
THAT'S HOW ALL NATURAL OR SUPERNATURAL STORIES RUN.	556	RIBH PATRICK		3
BUT ALL THAT RUN IN COUPLES, ON EARTH, IN FLOOD OR AIR,	556	RIBH PATRICK		11
THE WORKMAN, NOBLE AND SAINT, AND ALL THINGS RUN	565	GYRES		23
FEET TO THE RISING AND SETTING MAY RUN,	591	WHAT WAS LOST		4
THAT OFFICE FOOLS HAVE RUN,	598	MODEL LAUREATE		20
MARCH, MARCH, AND HOW DOES IT RUN?	615	MARCH SONGS 2		26
ON GANGLING STOCKS GROWN GREAT, GREAT STOCKS RUN DRY,	619	BRONZE HEAD		25
MALACHI STILT-JACK AM I, WHATEVER I LEARNED HAS RUN WILD,	623	HIGH TALK		9
THAT HEAVENS HAD OPENED. GYRES RUN ON:	639	BEN BULBEN		62
AND ALL HIS VEINS HAD NEAR RUN DRY,	670	ISLE STAT II 3		119
RUN LIKE THE MARCH WIND:	774	COME RIDE	V	6

RUNABOUT
| AND SEEN THE RUBBISH RUNABOUT, | 297 | THREE BEGGARS | V | 65 |

RUNNEL
| A LITTLE RUNNEL MADE A BUBBLING STRAIN, | 39 | OISIN 2 | | 156 |
| ROSE FROM A LITTLE RUNNEL ON WHOSE EDGE | 39 | OISIN 2 | V | 157 |

RUNNEL'S
| AND ON THE RUNNEL'S STONY AND BARE EDGE | 39 | OISIN 2 | | 157 |
| HIS HAND ALONG THE RUNNEL'S SIDE, AS THOUGH | 39 | OISIN 2 | | 162 |

RUNNER
| THAT RUNNER SAID: "I AM FROM THE SOUTH: | 191 | BAILE AILLINN | | 47 |
| BLUE-EYED, AND A QUICK RUNNER ON BARE FEET, | 242 | SHADOW WATER B | | 416 |

RUNNERS
| HAD SENT NO RUNNERS TO AND FRO | 288 | TO WEALTHY MAN | | 18 |

RUNNING
THE FIELD-MOUSE RUNNING BY ME IN THE GRASS,	101	ROSE UPON ROOD		17
THE FIELD MOUSE RUNNING BY ME IN THE GRASS,	101	ROSE UPON ROOD	V	17
THEY FOUND AN OLD MAN RUNNING THERE:	190	BAILE AILLINN		25
RIVERS ARE RUNNING OVER	214	HAPPY TOWNLAND		7
WHERE RIVERS ARE RUNNING OVER	214	HAPPY TOWNLAND	V	7
WITH SO RED LIPS, AND RUNNING ON SUCH FEET,	231	SHADOW WATER B		199
OUT OF THE RUNNING STREAM, O MORNING STAR,	251	SHADOW WATER B		610
AND AFTER RUNNING AT THE BRIM	254	HIS DREAM		9
AND RUNNING CROWD AND GAUDY SHIP	254	HIS DREAM		15
RUNNING TO PARADISE	300	RUN PARADISE		T
FOR I AM RUNNING TO PARADISE:	300	RUN PARADISE		3
AND I AM RUNNING TO PARADISE:	301	RUN PARADISE		10
AND I AM RUNNING TO PARADISE:	301	RUN PARADISE		17
FOR I AM RUNNING TO PARADISE:	301	RUN PARADISE		24
WHILE I AM RUNNING TO PARADISE.	301	RUN PARADISE	V	REF
THAT SAW THE SURGES RUNNING BY,	338	TOM OROUGHLEY		6
BUT WEARIED RUNNING ROUND AND ROUND IN THEIR COURSES	433	NINETEEN 19		116
BUT, WEARY RUNNING ROUND AND ROUND IN THEIR COURSES,	433	NINETEEN 19	V	116
HALF RUNNING, DROPPED AT THE FIRST RIDGE OF THE DESERT	468	HARUN RASHID		155
A RED HOUND RUNNING FROM A SILVER ARROW.	747	SHADOW WATER A		6
OUT OF A RUNNING STREAM, O MORNING STAR	769	SHADOW WATER A		426
WERE HIS MEASURE RUNNING DRY,	772	SONG DEIRDRE 1		14
WERE HIS MEASURES RUNNING DRY.	772	SONG DEIRDRE 1	V	14
PLANTED IN THE RUNNING WAVE:	775	AGAINST WITCH		13

RUNS
    THE HARE RUNS BY ME GROWING BOLD-- . . . .   84 MAD KING GOLL   V   47
    THAT FROM THOSE FINGERS GLITTERING SUMMER RUNS   . . . .   128 DREAM OF FAERY   44
    IN THE HALF LIGHT, AND RUNS TO ITS OWN DOOR   . . . . .   279 TWO KINGS   V   45C
    AND RUNS OR A WHILE HALF-FLIES . . . .   341 SHEP GOATHERD   64
    AND RUNS FOR A WHILE OR A WHILE HALF-FLIES . . . . . .   341 SHEP GOATHERD   V   64
    MINNALOUSHE RUNS IN THE GRASS . . . .   378 CAT AND MOON   9
    MAN RUNS HIS COURSE: . . . .   499 VACILLATION   2
    AND TIME RUNS ON," CRIED SHE. . . . .   526 AM OF IRELAND   3
    AND TIME RUNS ON," HE SAID, ...   526 AM OF IRELAND   12
    AND TIME RUNS ON," CRIED SHE. . . . .   527 AM OF IRELAND   16
    "BUT TIME RUNS ON, RUNS ON." . . . .   527 AM OF IRELAND   26
    "BUT TIME RUNS ON, RUNS ON." . . . .   527 AM OF IRELAND   26
    AND TIME RUNS ON," CRIED SHE. . . . .   527 AM OF IRELAND   29
    HALF DIZZY WITH THE LIGHTNING THERE RUNS A GATHERING BAND--   718 PHANTOM SHIP   9
    NOW HALF DIZZY WITH THE LIGHTNING THERE RUNS A GATHERING   718 PHANTOM SHIP   V   9
        BAND:
    WHERE THE WORLD ENDS, OR RUNS FROM WIND TO WIND   . . . .   768 SHADOW WATER A   417
    RUNS, RUNS AND IS SUDDENLY STILL. . . . .   783 GREY ROUND   3
    RUNS, RUNS AND IS SUDDENLY STILL. . . . .   783 GREY ROUND   3
RURY'S
    BAILE, THAT WAS OF RURY'S SEED. . . . .   194 BAILE AILLINN   118
RUSH
    I BECAME A RUSH THAT HORSES TREAD: . . . .   177 PAST GREATNESS   6
    NOR THE GREY RUSH WHEN THE WIND IS HIGH, ...   189 BAILE AILLINN   2
    NOR THE GREY RUSH WHEN WIND IS HIGH . . . .   189 BAILE AILLINN   V   2
    BUT THE GREY RUSH UNDER THE WIND . . . .   192 BAILE AILLINN   88
    LET RUSH AND BIRD CRY OUT THEIR FILL . . . .   197 BAILE AILLINN   198
    BUT I'D HAVE BIRD AND RUSH FORGET . . . .   197 BAILE AILLINN   204
    BUT I'D HAVE BIRDS AND RUSH FORGET . . . .   197 BAILE AILLINN   V 204
    TO STAY THE STAG'S NEXT RUSH. WHEN SWORD MET HORN   . . .   277 TWO KINGS   V   15
    OPINION IS NOT WORTH A RUSH: . . . .   385 ROBARTES DANCE   1
    AND HOW CAN BODY, LAID IN THAT WHITE RUSH, ...   441 LEDA AND SWAN   7
    A RUSH, A SUDDEN WHEEL, AND HOVERING STILL . . . . .   441 LEDA AND SWAN   V   1
    ALL THE STRETCHED BODY'S LAID ON THE WHITE RUSH   . . . .   441 LEDA AND SWAN   V   7
    NOW RUSH UPON HER AND FIND OUT WHAT PREY . . . . .   752 SHADOW WATER A   130
    WHAT WERE TRUE-LOVE AMONG THE RUSH OF HIS STREAMS?   . .   764 SHADOW WATER A   338
    WHAT WERE TRUE LOVE AMONG THE RUSH OF HIS STREAMS?   . .   764 SHADOW WATER A V 338
RUSHED
    AND FROM THE WOODS RUSHED OUT A BAND . . . .   15 OISIN 1   201
    AND FROM THE WOODS THERE RUSHED A BAND . . . . . .   15 OISIN 1   V 201
    THE MANY-COLOURED DANCERS RUSHED, ...   21 OISIN 1   V 322
    I PAUSED--AND FAR AWAY RUSHED ON, ...   83 MAD KING GOLL   V   31
    AND WITH LOUD SINGING I RUSHED ON . . . .   83 MAD KING GOLL   V   31
RUSHES
    COULD SLEEP ON A COUCH OF RUSHES, AND ALL INWROUGHT AND   49 OISIN 3   31
        INLAID,
    COULD SLEEP ON A BED OF RUSHES, AND ALL INWROUGHT   49 OISIN 3   V   31
        AND INLAID,
    COULD SLEEP ON A COUCH OF RUSHES--ROUND AND ABOUT THEM   49 OISIN 3   V   32
        LAID.
    BUT TO BE AMID SHOOTING OF FLIES AND FLOWERING OF RUSHES   55 OISIN 3   120
        AND FLAGS."
    . . . AND THE FLOWERING OF RUSHES AND FLAGS." . . . .   55 OISIN 3   V 120
    MY SPIRIT ROCKED IN EVENING LIGHT, THE RUSHES ROUND MY   76 INDIAN ON GOD   2
        KNEES,
    MY SPIRIT ROCKED IN EVENING'S HUSH, THE RUSHES ROUND MY   76 INDIAN ON GOD   V   2
        KNEES,
    AND RUSHES WAVED AND WATERS ROLLED. . . . .   84 MAD KING GOLL   35
    IN POOLS AMONG THE RUSHES . . . .   88 STOLEN CHILD   30
    ALTHOUGH THE RUSHES AND THE FOWL OF THE AIR . . . .   177 PAST GREATNESS V   11
    WHERE THE TIRED HORSE-BOYS LAY UPON THE RUSHES, . . .   180 QUEEN MAEVE   13
    AMONG WHAT RUSHES WILL THEY BUILD, ...   323 SWANS AT COOLE   27
    HE RUSHES, ROLLING FROM HIS LIPS A MADMAN'S LAUGH. . .   715 FERENCZ RENYI   122
    A HOUND THAT HAD LAIN IN THE RED RUSHES . . . . . .   761 SHADOW WATER A   278
RUSHING
    AND IF ANY GAZE ON OUR RUSHING BAND, ...   141 HOSTING SIDHE   10
    THE HOST IS RUSHING 'TWIXT NIGHT AND DAY, ...   141 HOSTING SIDHE   13
    OH, HEART! HER DIRGE! WITH RUSHING ARMS THE WAVES . .   665 ISLE STAT II 2   70
RUSHY
    BY ROCKY SHORE AND RUSHY FEN! . . . .   83 MAD KING GOLL   32
    O WANDERING BIRDS AND RUSHY BEDS, ...   190 BAILE AILLINN   31
    BY HEATH OR HOLLOW OR RUSHY MERE, ...   716 FAIRY DOCTOR   10
RUSSET
    YOUNG MAN, LIFT UP YOUR RUSSET BROW, ...   125 GOES FERGUS   4
    NODDING HER RUSSET HOOD? . . . .   171 MAID QUIET   2
    OF THE DREAD WOODS: ALONG THEIR RUSSET FLOOR . . . .   675 ISLE STAT II 3   243
RUSSIA
    A SAINT OF RUSSIA IN A VISION SAW . . . .   696 MOSADA 2   V   21
RUSSIAN
    ON ROMAN OR ON RUSSIAN . . . .   631 POLITICS   3
    THAT SONG I'VE MADE--IS OF A RUSSIAN TALE . . . . .   696 MOSADA 2   V   19
RUST
    IS NOT THY BODY BUT THE GARNERED RUST . . . . . .   724 KANVA ON SELF   15
    THAT THE RED RUST MAKES DIM." . . . .   740 EARL PAUL   20
RUSTED   SEE WAVE-RUSTED
RUSTLE
    IN RUSTLE OF LACE OR SILKEN STUFF, ...   358 PRESENCES   5
    AMID THE RUSTLE OF HIS PLANTED HILLS, ...   417 ANCEST HOUSES   2
    SOFT AS THE RUSTLE OF A REED FROM CLOYNE . . . . .   487 SEVEN SAGES   22

PAGE TITLE LINE

RUSTLED
  BUT SOMETHING RUSTLED ON THE FLOOR, ... 149 WANDER AENGUS 11
  BUT SOMETHING RUSTLED ON THE STOOL, ... 149 WANDER AENGUS V 11
RUSTLES
  THAT RUSTLES IN THE REEDS WITH PATIENT PUSHES, ... 699 MOSADA 3 4
RUSTLING SEE EVER-RUSTLING
  AND THROUGH THE DOORS, A RUSTLING ROUT, ... 20 OISIN 1 V 290
  BY MIGHTY BRAHMA'S EVER RUSTLING ROBE, ... 71 ANASHU VIJAYA V 14
  SHALL WARM THEIR LIVES AT MANY A RUSTLING FLAME." . . . 80 EPHEMERA V 12B
  I'VE HEARD A RUSTLING OVERHEAD IN THE WIND. . . . . . 223 SHADOW WATER B 28
  THAT'S RUSTLING IN THE REEDS WITH PATIENT PUSHES, . . . 699 MOSADA 3 V 4
  FROM THE RUSTLING OF OUR FEET. . . . . 726 LOVERS QUARREL 8
RUTH
  TILL THEY SHALL SINGING FADE IN RUTH . . . . 66 HAPPY SHEPHERD 41
  FOR RUTH AND JOY HAVE BROTHERHOOD, ... 66 HAPPY SHEPHERD V 42
  AND RUTH ST. DENIS HAD MORE CHARM ALTHOUGH SHE HAD POOR 353 HIS PHOENIX 10
    LUCK;
  ALMINTOR, THOU HAST GROWN SO FULL OF RUTH, ... 652 ISLE STAT I 2 26
  YET EVER MORE, THROUGH ALL THY DAYS OF RUTH, ... 674 ISLE STAT II 3 206
  YET EVERMORE, THROUGH ALL THY DAYS OF RUTH, ... 674 ISLE STAT II 3 V 206
  THEIR PASSION AND THEIR RESTLESSNESS AND RUTH . . . . 687 TWO TITANS 24
  AS THOUGH HIS DAYS WERE FULL OF RUTH. . . . . 731 PRIEST FAIRY 76
RUTHLESS
  MY LOVE HATH MANY A RUTHLESS MOOD, ... 723 GIRLS SONG A V 5
SACK SEE SAND-SACK
  . . . TWO CARRIED A SACK FULL OF SAND, ... 60 OISIN 3 185
  . . . THEY LIFTED AND SHOULDERED A SACK FULL OF SAND, . 60 OISIN 3 V 185
  HAVE CHANGED THEIR SILK FOR SACK. . . . . 458 HIS WILDNESS 6
  THAT SLEPT UPON THE SACK? . . . . 627 STATES HOLIDAY 15
SACKED
  AND TELL HOW MANANAN SACKED MURIAS . . . . 766 SHADOW WATER A 377
SACRED
  . . . AND GUARDLESS THE SACRED CAIRN AND THE RATH, . . . 58 OISIN 3 163
  SEE HOW THE SACRED OLD FLAMINGOES COME, ... 72 ANASHU VIJAYA 29
  DREAD OATH, WHO DWELL ON SACRED HIMALAY, ... 74 ANASHU VIJAYA 67
  IN THE TREE ROOTS, AND ALL THE SACRED FLOCKS . . . . 75 ANASHU VIJAYA 88
  IN THE TREE ROOTS, AND ALL THY SACRED FLOCKS . . . . 75 ANASHU VIJAYA V 88
  THROUGH MANY A SACRED CORRIDOR . . . . 156 FORGOT BEAUTY 12
  TO HOLD THE SACRED STUFF HE BREWS . . . . 272 GREY ROCK 24
  THAT SACRED GOBAN BREWED," HE CRIED . . . . 304 HOUR DAWN V 50
  THE SACRED MOON OVERHEAD . . . . 379 CAT AND MOON 19
  AND ALL HIS SACRED COMPANY . . . . 386 ROBARTES DANCE 27
  IN THE FORBIDDEN SACRED GROVE . . . . 389 SOLOMON WITCH 39
  AT WINE-DARK MIDNIGHT IN THE SACRED WOOD, ... 536 HER VISION 2
  A BEAUTIFUL SEATED BOY; A SACRED BOW; . . . . 541 PARN FUNERAL 1 10
  AS TRIPS THE SACRED MOON . . . . 559 HE AND SHE V 3
  WHAT SACRED DRAMA THROUGH HER BODY HEAVED . . . . . . 560 WHENCE COME 11
  "A LAUGHING, CRYING, SACRED SONG, ... 570 THREE BUSHES 43
  WENT TO THE SACRED HOUSE AND STOOD BETWEEN . . . . . 609 IN TARAS HALLS 11
  PROFFERING ITS SACRED LAUREL CROWNS, ... 612 NEWS ORACLE 23
  FOR GUIDING OF THE GODS. THE SACRED BLOOM . . . . . 656 ISLE STAT I 3 41
  THY SACRED DOOR;" BUT PETER CRIED, ... 697 MOSADA 2 25
SACRIFICE
  TOO LONG A SACRIFICE . . . . 394 EASTER 1916 57
  WHAT IS THIS SACRIFICE? CAN SOMEONE THERE . . . . . 541 PARN FUNERAL 1 6
SAD
  SAD TO REMEMBER, SICK WITH YEARS, ... 2 OISIN 1 5
  'TIS SAD REMEMBERING, SICK WITH YEARS, ... 2 OISIN 1 V 5
  THE STAG WE CHASED WAS NOT MORE SAD, ... 2 OISIN 1 V 7J
  THE HORNLESS DEER IS NOT MORE SAD . . . . 4 OISIN 1 34
  THE STAG YE CHASE IS NOT MORE SAD, ... 4 OISIN 1 V 35
  BUT NIAM, WITH A SAD DISTRESS, ... 15 OISIN 1 V 211
  AND NOW, STILL SAD, WE CAME TO WHERE . . . . 17 OISIN 1 247
  AND NOW STILL SAD OUR TROOP DREW NIGH . . . . 17 OISIN 1 V 247
  THEN, WARRIOR, WHY SO SAD AND STERN, ... 19 OISIN 1 V 286
  AND THINGS THAT HAVE GROWN SAD ARE WICKED, ... 20 OISIN 1 301
  EVERYTHING THAT'S SAD IS WICKED-- . . . . 20 OISIN 1 V 301
  AFORETIME, AND SHALL NOT GROW SAD . . . . 22 OISIN 1 V 340E
  AND A SAD MOUTH, THAT FEAR MADE TREMULOUS . . . . . 34 OISIN 2 71
  IN A SAD REVELRY HE SANG AND SWUNG . . . . 39 OISIN 2 160
  SAD NIAM CAME NEAR ME, AND LAID HER BROWS ON THE MIDST 52 OISIN 3 V 74
    OF MY BREAST
  . . . CAME FERGUS WHO FEASTWARD SAD SLUNK, ... 53 OISIN 3 V 89
  . . . HE SAD AS A CHILD WITHOUT MILK; . . . . 59 OISIN 3 174
  IT WERE SAD TO GAZE ON THE BLESSED AND NO MAN I LOVED OF 63 OISIN 3 221
    OLD THERE;
  IT WAS SAD TO GAZE ON THE BLESSED AND NO MAN I LOVED OF 63 OISIN 3 V 221
    OLD THERE;
  . . . OF BEST ONES A SAD THING WERE-- . . . . 63 OISIN 3 V 222
  THE SAD SHEPHERD . . . . 67 SAD SHEPHERD T
  BUT THE SAD DWELLER BY THE SEA-WAYS LONE . . . . . . 69 SAD SHEPHERD 26
  BUT THE SAD DWELLER BY THE SEAWAYS LONE . . . . . . 69 SAD SHEPHERD V 26
  A SAD, SAD THOUGHT WENT BY ME SLOWLY; . . . . 72 ANASHU VIJAYA 17
  A SAD, SAD THOUGHT WENT BY ME SLOWLY; . . . . 72 ANASHU VIJAYA 17
  THE SAD, SAD THOUGHT HAS GONE FROM ME NOW WHOLLY; . . . 72 ANASHU VIJAYA 19
  THE SAD, SAD THOUGHT HAS GONE FROM ME NOW WHOLLY; . . . 72 ANASHU VIJAYA 19
  CONCEIVE A THING SO SAD AND SOFT, A GENTLE THING LIKE ME? 77 INDIAN ON GOD 16
  AND WEARY AND WORN ARE OUR SAD SOULS NOW; . . . . . 79 FALLING LEAVES 6
  "THOUGH OUR SAD LOVE IS FADING, LET US YET . . . . . 79 EPHEMERA V 4
  CAME FLYING, HEAVY AND SAD; . . . . 93 FATHER OHART 34
  RED ROSE, PROUD ROSE, SAD ROSE OF ALL MY DAYS; . . . . 100 ROSE UPON ROOD 1

674

		PAGE	TITLE		LINE
SAD	**(CONTINUED)**				
	RED ROSE, PROUD ROSE, SAD ROSE OF ALL MY DAYS.	101	ROSE UPON ROOD		24
	"NAY, HE IS OLD AND SAD WITH MANY WARS.	107	CUCHULAIN SEA	V	29
	"BUT HE IS OLD AND SAD WITH MANY WARS."	107	CUCHULAIN SEA	V	30
	OR COMES IN LAUGHTER FROM THE SEA'S SAD LIPS,	114	ROSE OF BATTLE		19
	THE SAD, THE LONELY, THE INSATIABLE,	114	ROSE OF BATTLE		21
	OF THEIR SAD HEARTS, THAT MAY NOT LIVE NOR DIE.	114	ROSE OF BATTLE		24
	BEAUTY GROWN SAD WITH ITS ETERNITY	115	ROSE OF BATTLE		29
	OF OUR SAD HEARTS, THAT MAY NOT LIVE NOR DIE.	115	ROSE OF BATTLE		36
	MURMUR, A LITTLE SAD, "FROM US FLED LOVE,	121	YOU ARE OLD	V	10
	FOR SHE NEEDS NOT HER SAD BEAUTY--	124	CATHLEEN PARA	V	7
	GAY BELLS OR SAD, THEY BRING YOU MEMORIES	130	BOOK STORIES		21
	THE SAD BELLS BOW THE FOREHEAD ON THE HANDS.	130	BOOK STORIES	V	20
	AND NEVER WAS PIPING SO SAD	144	HOST OF AIR		11
	WITH A SAD AND A GAY FACE.	144	HOST OF AIR		16
	AND NEVER WAS PIPING SO SAD	145	HOST OF AIR		43
	CUMHAL THE KING, BEING ANGRY AND SAD,	166	BLESSED	V	1
	THE SAD SHEPHERD	338	SHEP GOATHERD	V	T
	SHE WOULD NOT HAVE US SAD BECAUSE SHE IS LYING THERE,	362	HER COURTESY		4
	FOR THOSE THAT LOVE ARE SAD.	383	VISION ROBART		36
	OF SAD QUEEN DIDO SHONE THE LAPPING FIRE	645	ISLE STAT I 1		9
	NOT A SAD NOTE WILL I SING.	646	ISLE STAT I 1		39
	SAD LADY OF THE DEEP, POURS DOWN HER LIGHT,	650	ISLE STAT I 1		127
	OR SAD SEA-SHELLS WHERE LITTLE ECHOES SIT?	650	ISLE STAT I 1		149
	I COULD NOT GO. LET'S TALK, AND LET'S BE SAD.	651	ISLE STAT I 2		7
	THE BIRDS THAT NESTLE IN THE LEAVES ARE SAD,	652	ISLE STAT I 2		15
	POOR SAD WOOD-RHAPSODISTS. NOT SO! THEY'RE GLAD.	652	ISLE STAT I 2		16
	'TIS BEAUTIFUL, AND THEREFORE IT IS SAD.	652	ISLE STAT I 2		24
	SAD FAERY TONES. 'TIS THUS THEY EVER SEEM,	654	ISLE STAT I 2		58
	SAD HISTORIES ARE LETTERED ON THY CHEEK.	660	ISLE STAT II 1		52
	AND LET THEM TELL SAD HISTORIES, TILL THEIR EYES	663	ISLE STAT II 2		32
	OF MY SAD HUNTER-FRIEND WILL ALL DEPART	668	ISLE STAT II 3		45
	SAD LADY, CEASE!	672	ISLE STAT II 3		160
	I SAW HIM FROM SAD DIDO'S SHORES DEPART,	677	ISLE STAT II 3		288
	THOUGH SAD IS MANY A SPIRIT	680	LOVE AND DEATH		23
	THROUGH HIS SAD SOUL FOR EVER OLD AND YOUNG,	687	TWO TITANS		25
	OF HIS SAD GOD; AND DOWN AMONG THE GRASS	690	MOSADA 1		16
	WHOSE FOOTFALL I HAVE LONGED FOR, THREE SAD SUMMERS.	692	MOSADA 1		45
	TO SAINTED EBREMAR'S SAD EYES. I THINK	696	MOSADA 2		15
	FOR THAT'S THE SWEETEST MUSIC FOR SAD SOULS.	702	MOSADA 3		85
	LIKE HAPPY THOUGHTS GROWN SAD IN EVIL DAYS.	703	MOSADA 3		116
	NOR, GAZING FORTH WHERE LIFE'S SAD SICKLES REAP,	710	FERENCZ RENYI		31
	FULL MOODY IS MY LOVE AND SAD,	723	GIRLS SONG A		1
	AND ALL THE SAD FAY CHIVALRY	730	PRIEST FAIRY		71
	LONG THOU FOR NOTHING, NEITHER SAD NOR GAY;	734	QUATRAIN APHOR		9
	YE BY THE WAVES THAT CLOSE IN OUR SAD NATION,	738	MOURN THEN ON		5
	WHEN YOU ARE SAD.	738	YOU ARE SAD		T
	WHEN YOU ARE SAD.	738	YOU ARE SAD		1
	WHEN YOU ARE SAD,	738	YOU ARE SAD		5
	WHEN YOU ARE SAD,	738	YOU ARE SAD		9
	TILL THEY COME WHERE YOUR SAD, SAD HEART IS,	739	WHERE BOOKS GO		5
	TILL THEY COME WHERE YOUR SAD, SAD HEART IS,	739	WHERE BOOKS GO		5
	FOR GOD GIVES POWER TO THE SAD	741	EARL PAUL		47
	FOR GOD GIVES POWER TO THE SAD	741	EARL PAUL		51
	PLAYED ON HIS HARP. AND I WOULD BE AS SAD	747	SHADOW WATER A		3
SADDEN					
	WHISPER LEST WE TOO MAY SADDEN,	737	IN FIRELIGHT		5
SADDER					
	"A SADDER CREATURE NEVER STEPT	17	OISIN 1		238
	ALAS! I MAKE YOU SADDER, SHEPHERDESS.	659	ISLE STAT II 1		18
SADDEST					
	"O SADDEST HARP IN ALL THE WORLD,	17	OISIN 1		245
	"THE SADDEST HARP IN ALL THE WORLD!"	17	OISIN 1	V	246
	THE SADDEST OF ALL MEN."	33	OISIN 2		68
	AND YET THE SADDEST CHIMES ARE BEST ENJOYED.	130	BOOK STORIES		20
SADDLE					
	ON HORSE AND SEA AND SADDLE SHONE.	28	OISIN 1	V	427D
	HIGH AS THE SADDLE GIRTH, COVERING AWAY FROM OUR GLANCES THE TIDE:	47	OISIN 3	V	2
	"THEN GO THROUGH THE LANDS IN THE SADDLE AND SEE WHAT THE MORTALS DO,	55	OISIN 3		125
	I SAW FROM A DISTANT SADDLE; FROM THE EARTH SHE MADE HER MOAN:	56	OISIN 3		130
	I RODE AWAY ON THE SURGES, WHERE HIGH AS THE SADDLE BOW	57	OISIN 3	V	147
	LEANING DOWN FROM THE GEM-STUDDED SADDLE,	60	OISIN 3		187
	LEANING FORTH FROM THE GEM-STUDDED SADDLE,	60	OISIN 3	V	187
	THOUGH MOUNTED IN THAT SADDLE HOMER RODE	492	COOLE BALLYLEE		47
	SADDLE AND RIDE, I HEARD A MAN SAY,	549	SEVERED HEAD		1
	OUT OF THE GRAVE. SADDLE AND RIDE	549	SEVERED HEAD	V	4
SADDLEBOW					
	I RODE AWAY ON THE SURGES, WHERE, HIGH AS THE SADDLEBOW,	57	OISIN 3	V	147
SADDLE-BOW					
	I RODE AWAY ON THE SURGES, WHERE, HIGH AS THE SADDLE-BOW,	57	OISIN 3		147
SADDLED					
	AND ONCE MORE SADDLED THE WHITE STEED,	25	OISIN 1	V	378
SADDLE-GIRTH					
	HIGH AS THE SADDLE-GIRTH, COVERING AWAY FROM OUR GLANCES THE TIDE:	47	OISIN 3		2
SADLY					
	CAME SWIMMING SADLY DOWN THE MIGHTY STAIR.	32	OISIN 2	V	50B
	HOLDING THAT HORSE, AND SADLY CALLED MY NAME:	44	OISIN 2		230

675

SADLY   (CONTINUED)
HOW THE SLOW, BLUE-EYED OXEN OF FINN LOW SADLY AT EVENING   52 OISIN 3   84
   TIDE.
MURMUR, A LITTLE SADLY, HOW LOVE FLED . . . .   121 YOU ARE OLD   10
COULD BUT AWAKEN SADLY UPON LIPS . . . .   185 QUEEN MAEVE   104
YON WIND GOES SADLY, AND THE GRASS AND TREES . . . . .   652 ISLE STAT I 2   10
THE WHOLE WORLD'S SADLY TALKING TO ITSELF. . . . . . .   652 ISLE STAT I 2   12
BY A PEOPLE SADLY GAY! . . . .   680 LOVE AND DEATH   10
NOW SADLY, NOW UNEARTHLY GAY, ...   716 FAIRY DOCTOR   3
SADNESS
WE RODE IN SADNESS ABOVE LOUGH LAEN, ...   2 OISIN 1   V   7H
MY HUMAN SADNESS FAY ARMS WOUND. . . . .   11 OISIN 1   V 138
THE HUMAN SADNESS DAWNS ONCE MORE!" . . . .   25 OISIN 1   V 381
THAT ONCE MORE MOVED IN MY BOSOM THE ANCIENT SADNESS OF   54 OISIN 3   107
   MAN,
. . . THE FLUTTERING SADNESS OF EARTH. . . . .   55 OISIN 3   124
FOR MOVETH ALIVE IN THY FINGERS THE FLUTTERING SADNESS   55 OISIN 3   V 124
   OF EARTH.
THEIR SADNESS THROUGH A HOLLOW, PEARLY HEART! . . . . .   68 SAD SHEPHERD   21
THEIR SADNESS THROUGH THE HOLLOWS OF ITS HEART, ...   68 SAD SHEPHERD   V   21
FLASHES THE FIRE OF SADNESS, FOR THEY SEE . . . . . .   73 ANASHU VIJAYA   49
WITH EYES OF SADNESS CAME TO HEAR . . . .   85 MAD KING GOLL V   62
WITH EYES OF SADNESS ROSE TO HEAR, ...   85 MAD KING GOLL V   62
AND THINE OWN SADNESS, WHEREOF STARS, GROWN OLD . . . .   101 ROSE UPON ROOD   6
HAS AWAKED IN OUR HEARTS, MY BELOVED, A SADNESS THAT MAY   122 WHITE BIRDS   4
   NOT DIE.
HAS AWAKED IN OUR HEARTS, MY BELOVED, A SADNESS THAT NEVER 122 WHITE BIRDS   V   4
   MAY DIE.
SADNESS, SOUL OF JOY MOST DEEP, ...   647 ISLE STAT I 1   74
SAD'S
FOR, LOOK YOU, SAD'S THE MURMUR OF THE BEES, ...   652 ISLE STAT I 2   9
SAEVA
SAEVA INDIGNATIO AND THE LABOURER'S HIRE, ...   481 BLOOD AND MOON   28
SAFE
THE HOUSE WHERE I WAS SAFE AND WARM! . . . .   151 HEART OF WOMAN   6
THE HOME WHERE I WAS SAFE AND WARM? . . . .   151 HEART OF WOMAN V   6
HANGS ON MY BREAST! LISTEN! WE SHALL BE SAFE. . . . .   701 MOSADA 3   73
SAFE ON THE BREAST OF GOMEZ LIES THY HEAD. . . . . .   703 MOSADA 3   101
SAFE ON THE BREAST OF VALLENCE IS THY HEAD . . . . .   703 MOSADA 3   V 101
SAFE ON THE BREAST OF GOMEZ IS THY HEAD, ...   703 MOSADA 3   V 101
SAFER
AWAY, AWAY! YOU ARE SAFER IN THE TOMB. . . . .   293 TO A SHADE   24
SAFETY
(ALL FIND SAFETY IN THE TOMB.) . . . .   508 JANE BISHOP   3
(ALL FIND SAFETY IN THE TOMB.) . . . .   508 JANE BISHOP   10
(ALL FIND SAFETY IN THE TOMB.) . . . .   508 JANE BISHOP   17
(ALL FIND SAFETY IN THE TOMB.) . . . .   508 JANE BISHOP   24
BECAUSE THERE IS SAFETY IN DERISION . . . .   624 APPARITIONS   1
SAFFRON
THAT FROM THE SAFFRON MORNING CAME, ...   19 OISIN 1   277
WATCHED WHERE THE SUN IN A SAFFRON BLAZE . . . . . .   26 OISIN 1   394
HALF SLUMBERED WITH HIS SAFFRON BLAZE! . . . .   26 OISIN 1   V 395
AND WHEN THE SUN ONCE MORE IN SAFFRON STEPT, ...   41 OISIN 2   192
AND WHEN THE SUN IN ALL HIS FLAGRANT SAFFRON STEPT, . . .   41 OISIN 2   V 192
BUT WHEN THE SUN ONCE MORE IN SAFFRON STEPT, ...   41 OISIN 2   V 192
PROUDLY IN HIS SAFFRON WALKING! . . . .   705 DAWN-SONG   2
SAFFRONS   SEE MEADOW-SAFFRONS
SAGE
THE SAGE, WHO DEEP IN CENTRAL NATURE DELVES, ...   686 LIFE   2
THOUGHTLESS JOY AND SORROW SAGE. . . . .   733 STREET DANCERS   47
THOUGHTLESS JOYS AND SORROWS SAGE. . . . .   733 STREET DANCERS V   47
THE SAGE WHO DEEP IN CENTRAL NATURE DELVES, ...   734 QUATRAIN APHOR   2
SAGES
O SAGES STANDING IN GOD'S HOLY FIRE . . . .   408 SAIL BYZANTIUM   17
RUN TILL ALL THE SAGES KNOW. . . . .   476 EVA GORE-BOOTH   29
THE SEVEN SAGES . . . .   486 SEVEN SAGES   T
OR, AS GREAT SAGES SAY, ...   496 MOHINI CHATTER   27
OLD SAGES WERE NOT DECEIVED! . . . .   504 QUARREL IN AGE   11
IN WHAT THE SAGES SAID! . . . .   534 CONSOLATION   2
TILL I HAVE TOLD THE SAGES . . . .   534 CONSOLATION   5
SWEAR BY WHAT THE SAGES SPOKE . . . .   636 BEN BULBEN   1
SAID
"WHY DO YOU WIND NO HORN?" SHE SAID, ...   4 OISIN 1   32
WHY DO YE SOUND NO HORN?" SHE SAID. . . . .   4 OISIN 1   V   33
WHY DO YOU WIND NO HORN?" SHE SAID. . . . .   4 OISIN 1   V   33
SHE SAID, WITH LAUGHTER TENDER AND SWEET! . . . . . .   6 OISIN 1   V   54
SHE SAID: "FOR HE IS FAIR ABOVE . . . .   7 OISIN 1   V 62A
"VEX THEM NO LONGER," NIAMH SAID, ...   12 OISIN 1   148
"WHO ARE THE RIDING ONES?" I SAID. . . . .   12 OISIN 1   V 146
SAID NIAM, AS SHE LAID THE TIP . . . .   12 OISIN 1   V 150
AND EACH ONE SAID, WITH A LONG, LONG SIGH, ...   17 OISIN 1   244
AND BENDING OVER THEM SOFTLY SAID, ...   21 OISIN 1   307
"GAZE NO MORE ON THE PHANTOMS," NIAMH SAID, ...   29 OISIN 2   5
"I BRING DELIVERANCE," PEARL-PALE NIAMH SAID. . . . .   34 OISIN 2   78
SAID NIAM. "AY, AND HUGE. WHEN YE HAVE LED . . . . .   35 OISIN 2   V   89
TO FLY A SPIRIT," NIAM WEEPING SAID. . . . .   35 OISIN 2   V   92
AND MANY PATER NOSTERS SAID SINCE DAWN. . . . . . .   43 OISIN 2   V 208D
IS THE ISLAND OF CONTENT?" "NONE KNOW," SHE SAID! . .   46 OISIN 2   249
WHICH IS THE ISLE OF YOUTH?" "NONE KNOW," SHE SAID, . .   46 OISIN 2   V 249
BY THE STAMMERING SCHOOLBOY SAID, ...   65 HAPPY SHEPHERD   15

		PAGE	TITLE		LINE

SAID (CONTINUED)

	PAGE	TITLE		LINE
BRIMFUL OF STARLIGHT, AND HE SAID: THE STAMPER OF THE SKIES,	76	INDIAN ON GOD		14
IN BOSOM AND HAIR. "AH, DO NOT MOURN," HE SAID,	80	EPHEMERA		20
AND EVERY ANCIENT OLLAVE SAID,	82	MAD KING GOLL		9
AND EVERY WHISPERING DRUID SAID,	82	MAD KING GOLL	V	9
AND EVERY MUMBLING OLD MAN SAID,	82	MAD KING GOLL	V	9
AND EVERY WHISPERING OLD MAN SAID,	82	MAD KING GOLL	V	9
AND HE SAID WITH A SMILE, "HAVE PEACE NOW":	92	FATHER OHART		19
BUT SEEK ALONE TO HEAR THE STRANGE THINGS SAID	101	ROSE UPON ROOD		19
AND SAID, "I AM THAT SWINEHERD WHOM YOU BID	105	CUCHULAIN SEA		3
AND SAID, CASTING ASIDE HIS DRAGGLED HAIR,	105	CUCHULAIN SEA	V	3
THAT SWINEHERD STARED UPON HER FACE AND SAID,	106	CUCHULAIN SEA		9
LOOKING ON HER, ALEEL, THE SWINEHERD, SAID:	106	CUCHULAIN SEA	V	9
AND MANY A SWEET THING SAID,	144	HOST OF AIR		18
AND CUMHAL SAID, BENDING HIS KNEES,	167	BLESSED		5
"PRAISE GOD AND GOD'S MOTHER," DATHI SAID,	167	BLESSED		17
"AND WHICH IS THE BLESSEDEST," CUMHAL SAID,	167	BLESSED		21
"AND WHO IS THE BLESSEDEST," CUMHAL SAID,	167	BLESSED	V	21
"MY EYES ARE BLINKING," DATHI SAID	168	BLESSED		25
HE SAID, "HIGH QUEEN OF CRUACHAN AND MAGH AI,	183	QUEEN MAEVE		77
HE SAID "QUEEN OF UNSHELTERED CRUACHAN,	183	QUEEN MAEVE	V	77
OR FELL INTO UNHAPPINESS, I'VE SAID,	186	QUEEN MAEVE		137
SAID, "AENGUS AND HIS SWEETHEART GIVE THEIR THANKS	187	QUEEN MAEVE		146
AND THERE, FOR ALL THAT FOOLS HAD SAID,	190	BAILE AILLINN		23
THAT RUNNER SAID: "I AM FROM THE SOUTH:	191	BAILE AILLINN		47
ONE THAT IS EVER KIND SAID YESTERDAY:	199	FOLLY COMFORT		1
OR, IF THERE NEEDS BE MORE, BE NOTHING SAID	201	OLD MEMORY		11
I SAID: "A LINE WILL TAKE US HOURS MAYBE:	204	ADAMS CURSE		4
I SAID: "IT'S CERTAIN THERE IS NO FINE THING	205	ADAMS CURSE		21
WHEN I HAVE SAID FAREWELL TO THIS MAN HERE,	250	SHADOW WATER B		587
THERE WAS NO MOTHER'S SON BUT SAID,	253	HIS DREAM		6
OF SUCH NOBLE LINES," I SAID,	259	PEACE		6
IN PRAISE OF WHAT ANOTHER'S SAID OR SUNG,	262	TO A POET		2
AND TREMBLING WITH HER PASSION SAID,	272	GREY ROCK		31
AND SAID, "IN TWO OR IN THREE YEARS	272	GREY ROCK		46
AND HAVING SAID IT, BURST IN TEARS.	273	GREY ROCK		48
BETWEEN THE DAWN AND DUSK," SHE SAID:	273	GREY ROCK		66
WHO SAID, "BECAUSE SHE HELD ME IN	274	GREY ROCK		86
AND WHEN FOR ALL I'D DONE OR SAID--	275	GREY ROCK		99
KING EOCHAID SAID, AND HE THAT BORE HIS SHIELD	276	TWO KINGS	V	8
AND CARVE HIS NAME IN OGHAM." EOCHAID SAID,	280	TWO KINGS		83
AND SO THE WEEKS PASSED BY. BUT WHEN I SAID,	280	TWO KINGS		89
AND RAISE HIS PILLAR STONE." KING EOCHAID SAID,	280	TWO KINGS	V	83
SAID, "IF A WOMAN HAS PUT THIS ON YOU,	281	TWO KINGS		111
"A WEARY WOOING AND A LONG," HE SAID,	283	TWO KINGS		154
AND TOUCHED HER FOREHEAD WITH HIS LIPS AND SAID:	286	TWO KINGS	V	211B
AND THERE TO THREE OLD BEGGARS SAID,	295	THREE BEGGARS		10
A BEGGAR SAID, "THEY GET THE MOST	295	THREE BEGGARS		15
"AND IF I WIN," ONE BEGGAR SAID,	296	THREE BEGGARS		29
ANOTHER SAID: "AND I WILL TRADE	296	THREE BEGGARS	V	32
NOW THEY ARE SILENT," SAID THE CRANE.	297	THREE BEGGARS		62
BECAUSE AN ANCIENT HISTORY SAID	303	HOUR DAWN		24
FOR ANYTHING YOU DID OR SAID	306	HOUR DAWN		89
HAS NO ONE SAID THOSE DARING	312	TWO YEAR LATER		1
BELIEVING EVERY WORD I SAID,	314	MEMORY YOUTH		8
WE KNEW, THOUGH SHE'D NOT SAID A WORD,	314	MEMORY YOUTH		16
AND KNEW, THOUGH SHE'D NOT SAID A WORD,	314	MEMORY YOUTH	V	16
THAT RAMBLING JAILBIRD BILLY SAID:	332	ROUND TOWER		26
SAID SOLOMON TO SHEBA,	333	SOLOMON SHEBA	V	17
OR SOMETHING OF THAT SORT HE SAID,	338	TOM OROUGHLEY		14
"WHAT HAVE I EARNED FOR ALL THAT WORK," I SAID,	351	PEOPLE		1
SAID I WAS DEAD: AND DEAD I CHOOSE TO BE.	373	PHASES OF MOON		28
SAID I WAS DEAD: AND DEAD I CHOSE TO BE.	373	PHASES OF MOON	V	28
YET BE BUT SINEW. I HAVE HEARD SAID	386	ROBARTES DANCE		37
WHATEVER HAS BEEN SAID, SIGHED, SUNG,	387	SOLOMON WITCH		7
YOU HEARD THAT LABOURING MAN WHO HAD SERVED MY PEOPLE. HE SAID	391	UNDER SATURN		11
NO, NO, NOT SAID, BUT CRIED IT OUT--"YOU HAVE COME AGAIN,	391	UNDER SATURN		13
OR HAVE LINGERED AWHILE AND SAID	392	EASTER 1916		7
FOR ALL THAT IS DONE AND SAID.	394	EASTER 1916		69
FOR ALL SHE HAD DONE AND SAID.	394	EASTER 1916	V	69
SAID PEARSE TO CONNOLLY,	396	ROSE TREE		2
SAID PEARSE TO CONNOLLY,	396	ROSE TREE		14
OF OLD LUKE WADDING'S PORTRAIT SAID	400	DEMON BEAST		10
"YOU HAVE CALLED ME MAD," IT SAID,	450	OWEN AHERNE		13
TOLD ALL THAT HAD BEEN SAID OR DONE	456	SUMMER SPRING		3
HALF DEAD AT THE TOP? NO MATTER WHAT I SAID,	482	BLOOD AND MOON		48
"THOSE PLATONISTS ARE A CURSE," HE SAID,	485	STATISTICS		1
BUT THE BRAHMIN SAID,	495	MOHINI CHATTER		2
THINGS SAID OR DONE LONG YEARS AGO,	501	VACILLATION		51
THE LION AND THE HONEYCOMB, WHAT HAS SCRIPTURE SAID?	503	VACILLATION		88
THE LION AND THE HONEY-COMB, WHAT HAS SCRIPTURE SAID?	503	VACILLATION	V	88
NOTHING SAID OR DONE CAN REACH	506	REMORSE SPEECH		9
COXCOMB WAS THE LEAST HE SAID:	508	JANE BISHOP		6
AND THAT IS WHAT JANE SAID.	510	JANE JUDGMENT		5
"THAT'S CERTAINLY THE CASE," SAID HE.	510	JANE JUDGMENT		10
AND THAT IS WHAT JANE SAID.	510	JANE JUDGMENT		15
"THAT'S CERTAINLY THE CASE," SAID HE.	510	JANE JUDGMENT		20
"THAT'S CERTAINLY THE CASE," SAID SHE.	510	JANE JUDGMENT	V	10
AND MUCH SAID HE AND I.	513	JANE TALK BISH		2

677

<pre>
                                                   PAGE   TITLE   LINE
SAID   (CONTINUED)
      WHEN SHE, AND THOUGH SOME SAID SHE PLAYED . . . . .   514 JANE GROWN OLD   8
      I SAID THAT SHE HAD DANCED HEART'S TRUTH, ...   514 JANE GROWN OLD   9
      FOR NO MATTER WHAT IS SAID . . . .   514 JANE GROWN OLD   12
      AND TIME RUNS ON," HE SAID, ...   526 AM OF IRELAND   12
      IN WHAT THE SAGES SAID; . . . .   534 CONSOLATION   2
      "THAT I HAVE MET WITH SUCH," SAID HE. . . . .   539 MEETING   5
      "LET OTHERS BOAST THEIR FILL," SAID I, ...   539 MEETING   7
      ALL THAT WAS SAID IN IRELAND IS A LIE . . . .   542 PARN FUNERAL 1   26
      GRANDFATHER SAID IN THE GREAT REBELLION; . . . . . .   544 TO SAME TUNE 1 V 1
      HE SAID NO MORE FOR HIS THROAT WAS TOO SMALL. . . .   545 TO SAME TUNE 1 V 24
      "DROWN ALL THE DOGS," SAID THE FIERCE YOUNG WOMAN. .   546 TO SAME TUNE 2   7
      DROWN ALL THE DOGS," SAID THE FIERCE YOUNG WOMAN. .   546 TO SAME TUNE 2   10
      "DROWN ALL THE DOGS," SAID THE FIERCE YOUNG WOMAN. .   546 TO SAME TUNE 2   17
      DROWN ALL THE DOGS," SAID THE FIERCE YOUNG WOMAN. .   546 TO SAME TUNE 2   20
      "DROWN ALL THE DOGS," SAID THE FIERCE YOUNG WOMAN. .   547 TO SAME TUNE 2   27
      DROWN ALL THE DOGS," SAID THE FIERCE YOUNG WOMAN. .   547 TO SAME TUNE 2   30
      "WHO'D CARE TO DIG 'EM," SAID THE OLD, OLD MAN, . .   548 TO SAME TUNE 3   7
      TIME I WERE BURIED," SAID THE OLD, OLD MAN. . . . .   548 TO SAME TUNE 3   10
      "WHO'D CARE TO DIG 'EM," SAID THE OLD, OLD MAN, . .   548 TO SAME TUNE 3   17
      TIME I WERE BURIED," SAID THE OLD, OLD MAN. . . . .   548 TO SAME TUNE 3   20
      "WHO'D CARE TO DIG 'EM," SAID THE OLD, OLD MAN, . .   549 TO SAME TUNE 3   27
      TIME I WERE BURIED," SAID THE OLD, OLD MAN. . . . .   549 TO SAME TUNE 3   30
      FOR THINGS BELOW ARE COPIES, THE GREAT SMARAGDINE TABLET 556 RIBH PATRICK   6
         SAID.
      SAID LADY ONCE TO LOVER, ...   569 THREE BUSHES   1
      THAT LOVELY LADY SAID, ...   569 THREE BUSHES   9
      DEAR CHAMBERMAID," SAID SHE. . . . .   569 THREE BUSHES   16
      "NO, NOT ANOTHER SONG," SAID HE, ...   570 THREE BUSHES   36
      A LECHING SONG," THEY SAID. . . . .   570 THREE BUSHES   44
      SAID THAT WILD OLD WICKED MAN . . . .   587 OLD WICKED MAN   3
      THEN SAID SHE TO THAT WILD OLD MAN, ...   588 OLD WICKED MAN   19
      PARNELL CAME DOWN THE ROAD, HE SAID TO A CHEERING MAN; 590 PARNELL   1
      "O WHAT'S A WIFELESS MAN?" SAID HE. . . . .   594 COLONEL MARTIN   5
      AND THOUGH SHE MAY BE THERE," HE SAID, ...   594 COLONEL MARTIN   12
      FOR WHO CAN SAY?" HE SAID. . . . .   594 COLONEL MARTIN   15
      "I AM SORRY," SAID THE MAID . . . .   595 COLONEL MARTIN   29
      THE COLONEL SAID TO TOM HIS MAN, ...   596 COLONEL MARTIN   50
      YOU HAD THREE KEGS" SAID HE. . . . .   596 COLONEL MARTIN   65
      SAID THE MAN IN THE GOLDEN BREASTPLATE . . . . . .   598 STONE CROSS   7
      SAID THE MAN IN THE GOLDEN BREASTPLATE . . . . . .   599 STONE CROSS   15
      SAID THE MAN IN THE GOLDEN BREASTPLATE . . . . . .   599 STONE CROSS   23
      SAID THE OLD MAN IN THE GOLDEN BREASTPLATE . . . .   599 STONE CROSS   V 23
      ALL THAT WE DID, ALL THAT WE SAID OR SANG . . . .   603 GALLERY REVIS   42
      FOR PATRICK PEARSE HAD SAID . . . .   608 SONGS BURDEN 3   24
      SAID TO THE WOMAN ON HIS KNEES, "LIE STILL. . . . .   609 IN TARAS HALLS   2
      TO MANY WOMEN I HAVE SAID, "LIE STILL," . . . . . .   609 IN TARAS HALLS   6
      BE STILL, BE STILL, WHAT CAN BE SAID? . . . .   613 MARCH SONGS 1   7
      BE STILL, BE STILL, WHAT CAN BE SAID? . . . .   613 MARCH SONGS 1   17
      BE STILL, BE STILL, WHAT CAN BE SAID? . . . .   614 MARCH SONGS 1   27
      ON EVERYTHING SHE SAID. . . . .   621 JOHN KINSELLA   22
      BUT NEVER SAID A THING, ...   627 STATES HOLIDAY   10
      (SAID CRAZY JANE) . . . .   628 JANE MOUNTAIN   2
      (SAID CRAZY JANE) . . . .   628 JANE MOUNTAIN   12
      HEART-MYSTERIES THERE, AND YET WHEN ALL IS SAID . .   630 CIRCUS ANIMALS   27
      HEART-MYSTERIES THERE, AND YET WHEN ALL IS SAID . .   630 CIRCUS ANIMALS V 27
      ALL THAT I HAVE SAID AND DONE, ...   632 MAN AND ECHO   6
      AND THEREUPON THAT LINEN-CARRIER SAID; . . . . . .   634 CUCHULAIN COMF   11
      KNOW THAT WHEN ALL WORDS ARE SAID . . . .   638 BEN BULBEN   27
      THE STAR-TAUGHT MOOR, SAID THUS IT WAS DECREED . .   691 MOSADA 1   25
      THEY SAID I'D BURN IN HELL UNLESS I TOLD. . . . . .   694 MOSADA 1   108
      YE SAID THAT YE WOULD FRIGHT HER FROM HER SIN-- . .   695 MOSADA 1   113
      I ALWAYS SAID YOU COULD NOT TRUST THESE MOORS, . .   704 MOSADA 3   V 134A
      "ON THIS EMBROIDERED CLOUD," THE SUN HATH SAID, . .   712 FERENCZ RENYI   74
      "THE PROPS," SAID HE. "OF STARS AND WORLDS . . . .   725 LEGEND   5
      BECAUSE OF THE THING HIS TONGUE HAD SAID. . . . . .   730 PRIEST FAIRY   60
      AND SAID, "YON BITTERN CRIES, IN TRUTH, ...   731 PRIEST FAIRY   75
      THE EARL OF KINSALE SAID. . . . .   742 EARL PAUL   62
      AND SAID: "SHE HAS FOOLED ME ENOUGH," . . . .   744 GLOVE CLOAK   3
      AND SAID: "I WILL SEE HER NO MORE," . . . .   744 GLOVE CLOAK   6
      WHO SAID WE HAD A SKIN OF YELLOW ALE? . . . .   759 SHADOW WATER A 243
      I SAID THE ALE WAS BROWN. I HAVE FOUND THE ALE. . .   759 SHADOW WATER A 244
      AND SAID IT WAS MIGHTIER THAN THE SUN AND MOON, . .   762 SHADOW WATER A 289
      "WHY IS IT," QUEEN EDAIN SAID. . . . .   771 SONG DEIRDRE 1   1
      A HIGH, GREY CAIRN. WHAT MORE IS TO BE SAID? . . .   778 SONG DEIRDRE 3   5
      "GIVE ME YOUR WIFE," SAID HE. . . . .   779 GOING THE ROAD   5
      HAVE NOT OLD WRITERS SAID . . . .   781 MY HEART BEAT   6
      SAID THE RAMBLING, SHAMBLING TRAVELLING-MAN; . . .   788 HAWTHORN TREE   2
      SAID THE WICKED, CROOKED, HAWTHORN TREE; . . . . .   788 HAWTHORN TREE   6
      SAID THE RAMBLING, SHAMBLING TRAVELLING-MAN; . . .   788 HAWTHORN TREE   10
      SAID THE WICKED, CROOKED, HAWTHORN TREE. . . . . .   788 HAWTHORN TREE   14
      OF ALL THAT LOVERS SAID. . . . .   789 SINGING HEAD   10
      OUTWEIGHED ALL OTHER YEARS, YOU SAID, ...   791 REPRISALS   6
SAIL
      NOR ULADH, WHEN NAOISE HAD THROWN A SAIL UPON THE WIND; 209 UNDER THE MOON   4
      OR ULADH WHEN NAISI HAD HUNG A SAIL UPON THE WIND; .   209 UNDER THE MOON V 4
      AND THEY WERE LISTENING THERE BEYOND THE SAIL. . .   223 SHADOW WATER B   37
      AND YOU HAD SPREAD A SAIL FOR HOME, A WIND . . . .   236 SHADOW WATER B 309
      WOULD I COULD CAST A SAIL ON THE WATER . . . . . .   330 BONE OF A HARE   1
      THEY CAN SPREAD OUT WHAT SAIL THEY PLEASE FOR ALL I HAVE 354 HIS PHOENIX   22
         TO SAY,
</pre>

	PAGE	TITLE	LINE

SAIL   (CONTINUED)
```
O BID ME MOUNT AND SAIL UP THERE . . . . . . . .   458 HIS WILDNESS            1
THINGS OUT OF PERFECTION SAIL. . . . . . . . . .   530 OLD TOM AGAIN           1
TO YONDER ISLE, WHERE NEVER SAIL WAS FURLED, . .   664 ISLE STAT II 2         56
AWAKE, AWAKE, AND WE WILL SAIL AFAR, . . . . . .   702 MOSADA 3               78
NOW FLINGING LOOSE THE SLANTING SAIL, . . . . . .  742 DANAAN QUICK            3
FROM HILLY LOCHLANN; BUT OUR SAIL HAS PASSED . .   749 SHADOW WATER A         44
OUT OF MERE WANTONNESS TO LURE A SAIL . . . . .    750 SHADOW WATER A         79
LOOK! THERE SHE LIES UNDER A FLAPPING SAIL. . .    751 SHADOW WATER A         90
AND BID THEM HIDE IN SHADOW OF THE SAIL, . . . .   751 SHADOW WATER A         93
NODS BY THE HELM, AND NEARER TO THE SAIL . . . .   752 SHADOW WATER A        119
NEAR BY, BUT IN THE SHADOW OF THE SAIL, . . . .    752 SHADOW WATER A        121
BEYOND THE SAIL A MAN WITH A RED CROWN . . . . .   752 SHADOW WATER A        126
BULWARK TO BULWARK, AND SQUARE HER SAIL BY OURS.   752 SHADOW WATER A        129
HAVE BID ME HOPE, SAIL TO THE LOCHLANN SHORE . .   756 SHADOW WATER A V      184
UNDER A SILKEN SAIL AND SILVER YARD, . . . . . .   763 SHADOW WATER A        316
```
SAILED
```
AND THEREFORE I HAVE SAILED THE SEAS AND COME . .  408 SAIL BYZANTIUM         15
AND THEREFORE HAVE I SAILED THE SEAS AND COME .    408 SAIL BYZANTIUM V       15
SWIFT HAS SAILED INTO HIS REST; . . . . . . . .    493 SWIFTS EPITAPH          1
SWIFT HAD SAILED INTO HIS REST; . . . . . . . .    493 SWIFTS EPITAPH V        1
AND EVIL FORTUNE HAVE OVERTHROWN SAILED HITHER .    757 SHADOW WATER A        196
```
SAILETH
```
SAILETH THE ROVER SORROW, . . . . . . . . . . .     70 CLOAK BOAT             9
SAILETH THE ROVER SORROW, . . . . . . . . . . .    666 ISLE STAT II 3         9
```
SAILING
```
THE SAILING SEVEN . . . . . . . . . . . . . . .    118 CRADLE SONG            7
SAILING TO BYZANTIUM . . . . . . . . . . . . . .   407 SAIL BYZANTIUM         T
THOUGH NURTURED LIKE THE SAILING MOON . . . . . .  451 FIRST LOVE             1
THE COLONEL WENT OUT SAILING. . . . . . . . . .    594 COLONEL MARTIN         1
AND HE CAME SAILING HOME. . . . . . . . . . . .    594 COLONEL MARTIN         6
THE COLONEL WENT OUT SAILING. . . . . . . . . .    594 COLONEL MARTIN         9
THE COLONEL WENT OUT SAILING. . . . . . . . . .    594 COLONEL MARTIN        18
THE COLONEL WENT OUT SAILING. . . . . . . . . .    595 COLONEL MARTIN        27
THE COLONEL WENT OUT SAILING. . . . . . . . . .    595 COLONEL MARTIN        36
THE COLONEL WENT OUT SAILING. . . . . . . . . .    596 COLONEL MARTIN        45
THE COLONEL WENT OUT SAILING. . . . . . . . . .    596 COLONEL MARTIN        54
THE COLONEL WENT OUT SAILING. . . . . . . . . .    596 COLONEL MARTIN        63
THE COLONEL WENT OUT SAILING. . . . . . . . . .    597 COLONEL MARTIN        72
AND MANNED AN ARGOSY AND SAILING DIED. . . . . .   693 MOSADA 1              89
```
SAILOR
```
FOR, AS DRIFT FROM A SAILOR SLOW DROWNING . . .     48 OISIN 3               22
BUT WHERE IS LAID THE SAILOR JOHN . . . . . . .    360 ALF POLLEXFEN         17
WHERE HAVE THEY LAID THE SAILOR JOHN? . . . . .    361 ALF POLLEXFEN         23
HE, DISGUISED AS A SAILOR BEFORE THE MAST, . . .   790 DEDICATION             2
```
SAILOR'S
```
SINBAD THE SAILOR'S BROUGHT A PAINTED CHEST, . .   371 ON GOING HOUSE        10
```
SAILORS
```
AND LISTEN TO ME FOR A WHILE.  THE SAILORS . . .   226 SHADOW WATER B        92
AND LISTEN TO ME FOR AWHILE. THE SAILORS . . . .   226 SHADOW WATER B V      92
WITH SAILORS THAT WERE SWORN TO DO YOUR WILL, .    236 SHADOW WATER B       308
I CARE NOT WHAT THE SAILORS SAY! . . . . . . . .   509 JANE REPROVED          1
WE WILL GO CALL THESE SAILORS, AND ESCAPE . . .    766 SHADOW WATER A       382
```
SAILS
```
. . . LOVE-MAKING OR PIERCING THE TEMPEST WITH SAILS. .   53 OISIN 3         88
. . . SAILS TURNING TO THREADBARE RAGS! . . . .     55 OISIN 3              118
. . . SAILS TURNING TO THREAD-BARE RAGS! . . . .    55 OISIN 3            V 118
"WHAT DO YOU BUILD WITH SAILS FOR FLIGHT?" . . .    69 CLOAK BOAT             6
THE TALL THOUGHT-WOVEN SAILS, THAT FLAP UNFURLED   113 ROSE OF BATTLE         2
OUR LONG SHIPS LOOSE THOUGHT-WOVEN SAILS AND WAIT, 115 ROSE OF BATTLE        31
WHERE NO SHIP SAILS, WHERE NOTHING THAT'S ALIVE    226 SHADOW WATER B        98
WHEN THE MOON SAILS OUT. . . . . . . . . . . . .   451 FIRST LOVE            18
AND, LIKE THE SOUL, IT SAILS INTO THE SIGHT . .    490 COOLE BALLYLEE        19
AND FAR AWAY THE HERON SAILS, I WIS. . . . . . .   649 ISLE STAT I 1        116
WHAT DO YOU BUILD WITH SAILS FOR FLIGHT? . . . .   666 ISLE STAT II 3         6
YONDER THE SICKLE OF THE MOON SAILS ON, . . . .    688 NETTLESHIP             1
CEASE THE SAILS THEIR FLAPPING UPROAR, AND THE HULL NO   719 PHANTOM SHIP    18
   LONGER ROLLS.
ON THE DROWNED MEN'S HANDS AND FACES, ON THE SPARS AND   719 PHANTOM SHIP    22
   ON THE SAILS.
CEASE THE SAILS, THEIR FLAPPING UPROAR TO THE HULL   719 PHANTOM SHIP   V  18
   NO LONGER ROLLS.
AND WHEN YOU CAME, THE NORTH UNDER YOUR SAILS, .   749 SHADOW WATER A        34
BUT THESE WASTE WATERS AND WIND-BEATEN SAILS . .   763 SHADOW WATER A       319
```
SAINT
```
SAINT, DO YOU WEEP?  I HEAR AMID THE THUNDER . .    43 OISIN 2              209
SAINT, DOST THOU WEEP? I HEAR AMID THE THUNDER .    43 OISIN 2            V 209
HUNCHBACK AND SAINT AND FOOL ARE THE LAST CRESCENTS.   377 PHASES OF MOON   118
"HUNCHBACK AND SAINT AND FOOL," AND THAT THEY CAME .   377 PHASES OF MOON   132
THE SAINT AND THE HUNCHBACK . . . . . . . . . .    379 SAINT HUNCH            T
THAT NEVER LOOKED OUT OF THE EYE OF A SAINT . .    486 SEVEN SAGES           12
THE BODY OF SAINT TERESA LIES UNDECAYED IN TOMB,   503 VACILLATION           80
ETERNALISED THE BODY OF A MODERN SAINT THAT ONCE   503 VACILLATION           83
SAINT GEORGE OR ELSE A PAGAN PERSEUS! . . . . .    533 HER TRIUMPH           10
THE WORKMAN, NOBLE AND SAINT, AND ALL THINGS RUN   565 GYRES                 23
SAINT JOSEPH THOUGHT THE WORLD WOULD MELT . . .    619 STICK INCENSE          3
ON BACKGROUNDS FOR A GOD OR SAINT . . . . . . .    639 BEN BULBEN            54
A SAINT OF MUNSTER, WHEN MUCH FASTING, SAW . . .   696 MOSADA 2              20
A SAINT OF RUSSIA IN A VISION SAW . . . . . . .    696 MOSADA 2           V  21
```
SAINTED
```
TO SAINTED EBREMAR'S SAD EYES, I THINK . . . . .   696 MOSADA 2              15
```

```
                                                       PAGE    TITLE        LINE
SAINT'S
    I WOULD LEAVE NO SAINT'S HEAD ON HIS BODY . . . . . . .    58 OISIN 3          160
SAINTS
    THINKING OF SAINTS AND OF PETRONIUS ARBITER. . . . . .    362 HER COURTESY       8
    ACCEPT THE MIRACLES OF THE SAINTS AND HONOUR SANCTITY? . .  503 VACILLATION       79
    "THIS LAND OF SAINTS," AND THEN AS THE APPLAUSE DIED OUT,  577 LOFTY THINGS       3
    "OF PLASTER SAINTS"; HIS BEAUTIFUL MISCHIEVOUS HEAD THROWN  577 LOFTY THINGS       4
        BACK.
SAKE
    THAT BEAUTIFUL MILD WOMAN FOR WHOSE SAKE  . . . . . .     205 ADAMS CURSE       15
    MURMURED WITH HER YOUNG VOICE FOR WHOSE MILD SAKE  . . .  205 ADAMS CURSE    V  15
    I'LL DO IT FOR HIS SAKE.  NO.  TAKE THIS SWORD  . . . .   250 SHADOW WATER B   591
    BEING FOR A WOMAN'S SAKE. . . . . . . . . . . . .         259 UNWORTH PRAISE     4
    PARDON THAT FOR A BARREN PASSION'S SAKE,  . . . . . . .   270 PARDON FATHERS    19
    PROMISED THAT FOR A PIN'S SAKE . . . . . . . . . .        274 GREY ROCK         90
    I'D SAVED HIS LIFE, YET FOR THE SAKE . . . . . . . .      275 GREY ROCK        102
    I'D SAVE HIS LIFE, YET FOR THE SAKE . . . . . . . .       275 GREY ROCK     V  102
    BEING WAKEFUL FOR HER SAKE, . . . . . . . . . .          316 FRIENDS           23
    FOR YOUR SOLE SAKE--THAT ALL HEART'S ACHE HAVE KNOWN,     355 BROKEN DREAMS      7
    BUT FOR YOUR SAKE--THAT ALL HEART'S ACHE HAVE KNOWN,      355 BROKEN DREAMS  V   7
    BURDENSOME BEAUTY--FOR YOUR SOLE SAKE  . . . . . . .      356 BROKEN DREAMS     10
    BURDENSOME BEAUTY--BUT FOR YOUR SAKE  . . . . . . .       356 BROKEN DREAMS  V  10
    FOR OLD SAKE'S SAKE. . . . . . . . . . . . . .            357 BROKEN DREAMS     36
    O LET HER CHOOSE A YOUNG MAN NOW AND ALL FOR HIS         450 OWEN AHERNE       24
        WILD SAKE."
    TWO SONGS REWRITTEN FOR THE TUNE'S SAKE  . . . . . .     550 SONGS REWRIT 1     T
    FOR THE SONG'S SAKE A FOOL? . . . . . . . . . . .        553 PRAYER OLD AGE     8
    I, TOO, WILL FOLLOW FOR THIS EVIL-STARRED ONE'S SAKE  . . 655 ISLE STAT I 2     84
    BRAVED LIONS FOR MY SAKE. . . . . . . . . . . .          789 SINGING HEAD       2
SAKE'S
    FOR OLD SAKE'S SAKE. . . . . . . . . . . . . .            357 BROKEN DREAMS     36
SALAD
    A CRAZY SALAD WITH THEIR MEAT . . . . . . . . . .        404 FOR DAUGHTER      31
SALAMIS
    THE MANY-HEADED FOAM AT SALAMIS. . . . . . . . .         610 STATUES           14
SALE
    THAT CARRIED THE FISH FOR THE SALE IN THE FAR-AWAY TOWN,   91 OLD FISHERMAN  V   7
SALIVA
    ABOVE, SALIVA DRIPPING FROM HIS JAWS, . . . . . . .      689 NETTLESHIP         4
SALLEY
    DOWN BY THE SALLEY GARDENS . . . . . . . . . . .          90 SALLEY GARDENS     T
    DOWN BY THE SALLEY GARDENS MY LOVE AND I DID MEET; . . .   90 SALLEY GARDENS     1
    SHE PASSED THE SALLEY GARDENS WITH LITTLE SNOW-WHITE FEET.  90 SALLEY GARDENS     2
SALMON
    HAVE A SPEED LIKE THE SPEED OF THE SALMON HERDS, . . . .    9 OISIN 1           98
    AND SWIFTER THAN THE SALMON HERDS; . . . . . . . .         9 OISIN 1        V  96
    "I CAN BRING YOU SALMON OUT OF THE STREAMS, . . . . .    167 BLESSED            9
    THE SALMON FALLS, THE MACKEREL-CROWDED SEAS, . . . .     407 SAIL BYZANTIUM V   4
    AND THE SALMON BEHOLD, AND THE OUSEL TOO, . . . . .      717 LOVE SONG          3
SALMON-FALLS
    THE SALMON-FALLS, THE MACKEREL-CROWDED SEAS, . . . .     407 SAIL BYZANTIUM     4
SALMON-SHOALED
    AND STREAMS, WIDE-WATERING, SALMON-SHOALED, . . . . .     81 MAD KING GOLL  V   3
SALT
    HAVE FACES ALIVE WITH SUCH BEAUTY BEEN KNOWN TO THE SALT   50 OISIN 3           51
        EYE OF MAN,
    ARE FACES ALIVE WITH SUCH BEAUTY MADE KNOWN TO THE SALT    50 OISIN 3        V  51
        EYE OF MAN,
    TO DRINK OF THAT SALT BREATH OUT OF THE SEA  . . . . .   292 TO A SHADE         5
    THE TIME FOR YOU TO TASTE OF THAT SALT BREATH . . . .    293 TO A SHADE        21
    THAT THE SALT DROPS HAVE WET; . . . . . . . . . .        312 CHILD DANCING      5
    AND THERE IS SALT TO LENGTHEN OUT THE SMART  . . . .     324 ROBERT GREGORY    11
    SALT BLOOD BLOCKS HIS EYES. . . . . . . . . . .          530 DELPHIC ORACLE     5
    THE SALT FLAKES ON HIS BREAST, . . . . . . . . .         612 NEWS ORACLE    V  10
SALTED
    TO THROW ME A BIT OF SALTED FISH; . . . . . . . .        301 RUN PARADISE       6
SALT-FLAKES
    THE SALT-FLAKES ON HIS BREAST, . . . . . . . . .         612 NEWS ORACLE       10
SALTIN'
    MY WORK WAS SALTIN' HERRINGS  . . . . . . . . .           94 MOLL MAGEE         7
    AND SOMETIMES FROM THE SALTIN' SHED . . . . . . .         94 MOLL MAGEE         9
    TIMES FROM THE SALTIN' SHED, . . . . . . . . . .          94 MOLL MAGEE     V   9
SALUTING
    THE SOLDIER TAKES PRIDE IN SALUTING HIS CAPTAIN, . . . . 547 TO SAME TUNE 3     1
    SOLDIERS TAKE PRIDE IN SALUTING THEIR CAPTAIN, . . . .   547 TO SAME TUNE 3 V   1
    SOLDIERS TAKE PRIDE IN SALUTING THEIR CAPTAIN, . . . .   548 TO SAME TUNE 3    21
    THE SOLDIER TAKES PRIDE IN SALUTING HIS CAPTAIN, . . .   614 MARCH SONGS 2      1
SALVATION
    LOOK ON THAT FIRE, SALVATION WALKS WITHIN. . . . . .     502 VACILLATION       76
SAME      SEE SELF-SAME
    AMRITA.  THIS SAME EVE SHE WATCHED ME PASS. . . . .       74 ANASHU VIJAYA  V  64
    SOME FEASTING MAN THAT THE SAME OATH HAS BOUND." . . .   108 CUCHULAIN SEA     38
    SOME FEATING MAN THAT THE SAME OATH HAS BOUND." . . .    108 CUCHULAIN SEA  V  38
    SOME FEASTING MAN THAT THE SAME OATH HAS BOUND. . . .    109 CUCHULAIN SEA     54
    "SOME FEATING MAN THAT THE SAME OATH HAS BOUND." . . .   109 CUCHULAIN SEA  V  54
    THEY HAVE GONE DOWN UNDER THE SAME WHITE STARS, . . .    115 ROSE OF BATTLE    34
    WHILE THOSE SAME HUNDREDS MOCK ANOTHER DAY . . . . .     265 ABBEY THEATRE      4
    TILL DAYTIME, PLAYTIME SEEM THE SAME; . . . . . .        343 SHEP GOATHERD    106
    BUT IS THE SAME FOR ALL . . . . . . . . . . .           452 HUMAN DIGNITY      4
    GAME-BIRD, NOR WOMAN DOES THE SAME THING TWICE; . . .    463 HARUN RASHID      60
    GAME BIRD, OR WOMAN DOES THE SAME THING TWICE; . . .     463 HARUN RASHID   V  60
```

		PAGE	TITLE		LINE

SAME   (CONTINUED)
```
        GAMEBIRD, NOR WOMAN DOES THE SAME THING TWICE!  . . . .   463 HARUN RASHID    V    60
        THAT IN THE SAME CALAMITY  . . . . . . . . . . . . . .    540 FROM ANTIGONE         9
        THREE SONGS TO THE SAME TUNE  . . . . . . . . . . . .     543 TO SAME TUNE 1        T
        THREE SONGS TO THE SAME TUNE   SECOND SONG  . . . . . .   544 TO SAME TUNE 1  V     T
        AND MAYBE WE ARE ALL THE SAME  . . . . . . . . . . . .    570 THREE BUSHES         24
        AND MAYBE WE ARE ALL THE SAME  . . . . . . . . . . . .    570 THREE BUSHES         26
        NOW SINKS THE SAME REST  . . . . . . . . . . . . . . .    574 LOVERS SONG           4
        HE THOUGHT THE SAME AND LIVED BY RULE,  . . . . . . . .   576 WHAT THEN             3
        THEY ALWAYS BEAT ON THE SAME SMALL STONE.  . . . . . .    591 WHAT WAS LOST         5
        AY, BOY. LET'S SEE IF THAT SAME HERON'S DEAD.  . . . .    651 ISLE STAT I 1       169
        IS STONE! OLD SLEEPER! THIS SAME AFTERNOON  . . . . .     657 ISLE STAT I 3        74
        STANDS EACH GREY AND SILENT PHANTOM ON THE SAME REGARDLESS 719 PHANTOM SHIP        25
            SPOT--
SAMUEL
        THE LONELY LIGHT THAT SAMUEL PALMER ENGRAVED,  . . . . .  373 PHASES OF MOON       17
SAN
        FOR THE SAN MARCO LIBRARY,  . . . . . . . . . . . . .     288 TO WEALTHY MAN       24
SANCTITY
        BROODED UPON SANCTITY . . . . . . . . . . . . . . . .     324 ROBERT GREGORY       20
        TRADITIONAL SANCTITY AND LOVELINESS!  . . . . . . . . .   491 COOLE BALLYLEE       42
        ACCEPT THE MIRACLES OF THE SAINTS AND HONOUR SANCTITY? . .  503 VACILLATION        79
        TO LIGHTEST OF LIGHT THINGS ALL SANCTITY.  . . . . . . .  686 DRAWING-ROOM          8
        TO LIGHTEST OF ALL LIGHT THINGS SANCTITY.  . . . . . .    734 QUATRAIN APHOR        8
        TO LIGHTEST OF LIGHT THINGS ALL SANCTITY.  . . . . . .    734 QUATRAIN APHOR  V     8
SAND
        GREY SAND ON THE GREEN OF THE GRASSES AND OVER THE DRIPPING  48 OISIN 3            14
            TREES,
        GREY SAND ON THE GREEN OF THE GRASSES AND OVER THE DRIPPING  57 OISIN 3           142
            TREES,
        . . . THE STRONG HOOFS CRUSHING THE SAND AND THE SHELLS,   58 OISIN 3            157
        . . . TWO CARRIED A SACK FULL OF SAND,  . . . . . . .      60 OISIN 3            185
        . . . THEY LIFTED AND SHOULDERED A SACK FULL OF SAND,  . .  60 OISIN 3          V 185
        AND CANDLE-LIKE FOAM ON THE DIM SAND,  . . . . . . . .    158 BELOVED RHYMES       10
        ON THE GREY SAND BESIDE THE SHALLOW STREAM . . . . . .    367 EGO DOMINUS           1
        AND TRACE THESE CHARACTERS UPON THE SAND?  . . . . . .    370 EGO DOMINUS     V    64
        SHALL WALK THE WET SAND BY THE WATER'S EDGE,  . . . . .   371 EGO DOMINUS     V    71
        TROUBLES MY SIGHT! A WASTE OF DESERT SAND!  . . . . .     402 SECOND COMING   V    13
        AND THERE MARKED OUT THOSE EMBLEMS ON THE SAND  . . . .   468 HARUN RASHID        156
        AND THERE MARKED OUT EMBLEMS ON THE SAND  . . . . . .     468 HARUN RASHID    V   156
        MOULDING IT OF DUST OR SAND,  . . . . . . . . . . . .     600 SPIRIT MEDIUM        14
        BEAT OUT THEIR LIVES LAMENTING O'ER THE SAND!  . . . .    652 ISLE STAT I 2        14
        IT BORE ME SOFTLY WHERE THE SHALLOW SAND  . . . . . .     657 ISLE STAT I 3        58
        THE BOAT'S PROW GRATED ON THE SHALLOW SAND,  . . . . .    659 ISLE STAT II 1       11
        IN SAND HIS NAME AND MINE I'VE ALSO READ.  . . . . . .    662 ISLE STAT II 2       12
        BETWEEN THE LONELY FOREST AND THE SAND.  . . . . . . .    663 ISLE STAT II 2       22
        YOU MUST BE GONE! THE ROLLING GRAINS OF SAND  . . . . .   663 ISLE STAT II 2       34
        LOW BOWED AND DUMB UPON THE SAND.  . . . . . . . . . .    671 ISLE STAT II 3      130
        WITH WONDERFUL WHITE SAND, WHERE NEVER YET  . . . . . .   693 MOSADA 1        V    81
SANDALLED      SEE SILVER-SANDALLED
        IN DANCING SILVER SANDALLED ON THE SEA,  . . . . . . .    101 ROSE UPON ROOD  V     7
SANDALS
        THE SANDALS THESE OF SORROW!  . . . . . . . . . . . .      70 CLOAK BOAT      V    12
        AND LIFE THE SANDALS OF HER FLEETNESS,  . . . . . . . .    77 INDIAN TO LOVE  V    5B
        AND HOW THE WINGED SANDALS DART,  . . . . . . . . . .     135 TWO TREES            18
        THE SANDALS THESE OF SORROW!  . . . . . . . . . . . .     666 ISLE STAT II 3       12
        WITH PURPLE SANDALS SWEEP THE GRAVE-EYED HOURS--  . . .   705 REMEMBRANCE           5
SANDALWOOD
        BUT FOR THE AMBERGRIS AND SANDALWOOD.  . . . . . . . .    232 SHADOW WATER B      221
SANDED
        BEFORE A SANDED PLACE!  . . . . . . . . . . . . . . .     740 EARL PAUL            32
SANDS      SEE SEA-SANDS
        MOURNFUL, AND GATHERED ON THE SANDS!  . . . . . . . .      10 OISIN 1         V 111B
        AT EVENING ON THE GLIMMERING SANDS,  . . . . . . . . .     23 OISIN 1             347
        GREY SANDS ON THE GREEN OF THE GRASSES AND OVER THE        48 OISIN 3         V    14
            DRIPPING TREES,
        AND THE WINDS MADE THE SANDS ON THE SEA'S EDGE . . . .     57 OISIN 3             145
        GREY SANDS ON THE GREEN OF THE GRASSES AND OVER THE        57 OISIN 3         V   142
            DRIPPING TREES,
        . . . THE GOLD HOOVES CRUSHING THE SANDS AND THE SHELLS    58 OISIN 3         V   157
        . . . THE STRONG HOOFS CRUSHING THE SANDS AND THE SHELLS   58 OISIN 3         V   157
        AND HUMMING SANDS, WHERE WINDY SURGES WEND!  . . . . .     68 SAD SHEPHERD          4
        TO MIGHTY BRAHMA, HE WHO MADE YOU MANY AS THE SANDS,  . .   72 ANASHU VIJAYA       21
        TO MIGHTY BRAHMA--HE WHO MADE YE MANY AS THE SANDS,  . .    72 ANASHU VIJAYA   V   21
        TO MIGHTY BRAHMA, WHO HAS MADE YOU MANY AS THE SANDS,  . .  72 ANASHU VIJAYA   V   21
        ALONG THE GRASS, ALONG THE SANDS,  . . . . . . . . . .     78 INDIAN TO LOVE        9
        THE DIM GREY SANDS WITH LIGHT,  . . . . . . . . . . .      87 STOLEN CHILD         14
        AND WENT DOWN TO THE LONG SANDS ALONE,  . . . . . . .     111 CUCHULAIN SEA   V    84
        AND HE WENT DOWN TO THE LONG SANDS ALONE,  . . . . . .    111 CUCHULAIN SEA   V    84
        STOOD UP, AND CAME TO THE LONG SANDS ALONE!  . . . . .    111 CUCHULAIN SEA   V    84
        HE WANDERED BY THE SANDS OF LISSADELL!  . . . . . . .     127 DREAM OF FAERY       13
        AS HE WENT BY THE SANDS OF LISADILL  . . . . . . . . .    127 DREAM OF FAERY  V    13
        AS THE TIDE WEARS THE DOVE-GREY SANDS,  . . . . . . . .   157 POET BELOVED          4
        AS THE TIDE HAS THE DOVE-GREY SANDS,  . . . . . . . .     157 POET BELOVED    V     4
        AND TRACE THESE CHARACTERS UPON THE SANDS?  . . . . . .   370 EGO DOMINUS          64
        SHALL WALK THE WET SANDS BY THE EDGE OF THE STREAM  . . . 371 EGO DOMINUS          71
        TROUBLES MY SIGHT! SOMEWHERE IN SANDS OF THE DESERT  . . 402 SECOND COMING        13
        HE WROTE IT ON THE SANDS (THE OWLS MAY READ  . . . . .    659 ISLE STAT II 1        9
        WITH WONDERFUL WHITE SANDS, WHERE NEVER YET  . . . . .    693 MOSADA 1             81
        ROLLS ALONG THE SEA SANDS WHITE.  . . . . . . . . . .     732 STREET DANCERS       34
        TO THE LOUD SANDS BEFORE DAY HAS BROKEN.  . . . . . . .   784 WOMANS BEAUTY        18
```

		PAGE	TITLE		LINE
SAND-SACK					
. . . THEY LAY 'NEATH THE SAND-SACK AT LENGTH		60	OISIN 3	V	186
HOW THE MEN OF THE SAND-SACK SHOWED ME A CHURCH		61	OISIN 3		193
HOW THE MEN OF THE SAND-SACK LED ME TO SHAUL, ...		61	OISIN 3	V	193
SANDY					
COME, BESIDE A SANDY LAKE, ...		727	LOVERS QUARREL		41
SANDYMOUNT					
SANDYMOUNT CORBETS, THAT NOTABLE MAN		604	YOU CONTENT		13
SANG					
AND NIAMH SANG CONTINUALLY		11	OISIN 1		134
FOR NEAVE SANG CONTINUALLY		11	OISIN 1	V	134
SANG NIAM, AND THEIR DEWY SHOWERS		11	OISIN 1	V	135
FROM ALL THEIR LIPS, AND ONCE THEY SANG		16	OISIN 1		226
AND WHILE THEY SANG, A SINGER LAID		16	OISIN 1	V	231
BUT WHEN I SANG OF HUMAN JOY		17	OISIN 1		234
AND WHEN I SANG OF HUMAN JOY		17	OISIN 1	V	234
SANG, "GOD IS JOY AND JOY IS GOD, ...		20	OISIN 1		300
AND SANG WE LIGHTLY TO EACH BLOOM		21	OISIN 1	V	306B
SANG WE SOFTLY IN THE DANCE, ...		21	OISIN 1	V	308
SANG WE SOFTLY, "ON THE DEAD, ...		21	OISIN 1		310
AND SANG UNTO THE STARRY BROODS.		22	OISIN 1		326
I LOVED AND SANG, AND IN LONG WASSAILS		23	OISIN 1	V	345C
AND SANG, AND WITH A DREAMY GAZE		26	OISIN 1		393
AND, AS THEY SANG, THE PAINTED BIRDS		26	OISIN 1		396
AND HER BRIGHT BODY, SANG OF FAERY AND MAN		29	OISIN 2		7
AND NOW SANG NIAM, SWAYING HER BRIGHT HEAD		29	OISIN 2	V	6
YET SANG NO MORE AS WHEN, LIKE A BROWN BEE		30	OISIN 2		15
SO SANG YOUNG NIAM, SWAYING HER BRIGHT HEAD, ...		30	OISIN 2	V	15
BUT SANG NO MORE, AS WHEN, LIKE A BROWN BEE . . .		30	OISIN 2	V	15
IN A SAD REVELRY HE SANG AND SWUNG		39	OISIN 2		160
WE SANG THE LOVES AND ANGERS WITHOUT SLEEP, . . .		42	OISIN 2		194
ROLLING HIS WHEEL, WE SANG BESIDE THE DEEP . . .		42	OISIN 2	V	193
AND NEVER A SONG SANG NIAMH, AND OVER MY FINGER-TIPS		47	OISIN 3		6
THEN HE SANG SOFTLY NIGH THE PEARLY RIM;		69	SAD SHEPHERD		25
CHANGED ALL HE SANG TO INARTICULATE MOAN		69	SAD SHEPHERD		27
THEN SANG HE SOFTLY NIGH THE PEARLY RIM;		69	SAD SHEPHERD	V	25
I SANG HOW, WHEN DAY'S TOIL IS DONE, ...		85	MAD KING GOLL		61
AND AS I SANG MY SOUL WAS FREE		86	MAD KING GOLL	V	65
MY SINGING SANG ME FEVER FREE, ...		86	MAD KING GOLL	V	65
MY SINGING SANG ME FEVER-FREE;		86	MAD KING GOLL	V	65
AND SANG WHAT GOLD MORNING OR EVENING SHEDS . . .		126	DREAM OF FAERY		7
AND SANG HOW DAY A DRUID TWILIGHT SHEDS		126	DREAM OF FAERY	V	7
SANG THAT SOMEWHERE TO NORTH OR WEST OR SOUTH . .		127	DREAM OF FAERY		19
SANG WHERE--UNNECESSARY CRUEL VOICE--		127	DREAM OF FAERY		30
SANG HOW SOMEWHERE TO NORTH OR EAST OR SOUTH . .		127	DREAM OF FAERY	V	19
SANG HOW SOMEWHERE TO NORTH OR WEST OR SOUTH . .		127	DREAM OF FAERY	V	19
THAT SANG, TO SWEETEN IRELAND'S WRONG, ...		137	TO IRELAND		3
WHO SANG TO SWEETEN IRELAND'S WRONG, ...		137	TO IRELAND	V	3
HE HEARD WHILE HE SANG AND DREAMED		144	HOST OF AIR		9
IT SANG TO HER THROUGH THE DOOR.		160	CAP AND BELLS		16
AND HER RED LIPS SANG THEM A LOVE-SONG		160	CAP AND BELLS		27
HER RED LIPS SANG THEM A LOVE-SONG, ...		160	CAP AND BELLS	V	27
AND HER RED LIPS SANG THEM A LOVE SONG, ...		160	CAP AND BELLS	V	27
TALKED OF HIS COUNTRY AND ITS PEOPLE, SANG . . .		180	QUEEN MAEVE		3
THEY SANG A DROWSY SONG, OR SNORED, ...		271	GREY ROCK		16
AND SANG A DROWSY SONG, OR SNORED, ...		271	GREY ROCK	V	16
SANG THROUGH THEIR TEETH FROM NOON TO NOON; . .		296	THREE BEGGARS		41
SANG UNNOTICED LIKE A BIRD.		298	THREE HERMITS		7
SANG UNNOTICED LIKE A BIRD.		299	THREE HERMITS		32
MY MOTHER DANDLED ME AND SANG, ...		308	PLAYER QUEEN		1
"HE WENT AWAY," MY MOTHER SANG, ...		308	PLAYER QUEEN		5
"WHEN SHE WAS GOT," MY MOTHER SANG, ...		308	PLAYER QUEEN		13
SANG TILL STARS BEGAN TO FADE, ...		332	ROUND TOWER		20
SANG SOLOMON TO SHEBA, ...		332	SOLOMON SHEBA		1
TO SOLOMON SANG SHEBA, ...		333	SOLOMON SHEBA		9
SANG SOLOMON TO SHEBA, ...		333	SOLOMON SHEBA		17
THE POET STUBBORN WITH HIS PASSION SANG US . . .		356	BROKEN DREAMS		18
WHAT A STAR SANG AND CARELESS MUSES HEARD! . . .		445	SCHOOL CHILDR		47
"SPEAK ALL YOUR MIND," MY HEART SANG OUT, . . .		450	OWEN AHERNE		21
AND SWEPT THE HOUSE AND SANG ABOUT HER WORK . .		468	HARUN RASHID		148
OLIVER GOLDSMITH SANG WHAT HE HAD SEEN, ...		487	SEVEN SAGES		17
SANG A BONE UPON THE SHORE:		521	THREE THINGS		2
SANG A BONE UPON THE SHORE;		521	THREE THINGS		8
SANG A BONE UPON THE SHORE.		521	THREE THINGS		14
UPON CRO-PATRICK SANG ALOUD:		528	DANCER CRUACH		5
UPON CROAGH PATRICK SANG IT LOUD:		528	DANCER CRUACH	V	5
SANG OLD TOM THE LUNATIC		528	TOM LUNATIC		1
SANG OF THE BEAST THAT GAVE THE FATAL WOUND. . .		537	HER VISION		16
AND SANG MY MALEDICTION WITH THE REST.		537	HER VISION		24
GRANDFATHER SANG IT UNDER THE GALLOWS!		544	TO SAME TUNE 1		1
HE SANG IT FROM HIS HEART.		544	TO SAME TUNE 1		6
NO MORE SANG HE, FOR HIS THROAT WAS TOO SMALL; .		545	TO SAME TUNE 1		24
DOUBTLESS I SPOKE OR SANG WHAT I HAD HEARD . . .		557	RIBH ECSTASY		2
"WHAT THEN?" SANG PLATO'S GHOST. "WHAT THEN?"		576	WHAT THEN		5
"WHAT THEN?" SANG PLATO'S GHOST. "WHAT THEN?"		577	WHAT THEN		10
"WHAT THEN?" SANG PLATO'S GHOST. "WHAT THEN?"		577	WHAT THEN		15
BUT LOUDER SANG THAT GHOST, "WHAT THEN?" . . .		577	WHAT THEN		20
BUT SANG, "O SEA-STARVED, HUNGRY SEA."		578	CRAZED GIRL		14
ALL THAT WE DID, ALL THAT WE SAID OR SANG . . .		603	GALLERY REVIS		42
MY FATHER SANG THAT SONG, ...		613	MARCH SONGS 1		8
MY FATHER SANG THAT SONG, ...		613	MARCH SONGS 1		18

SANG   (CONTINUED)
```
      MY FATHER SANG THAT SONG,  . . . . . . . . . . .   614 MARCH SONGS 1        28
      GRANDFATHER SANG IT UNDER THE GALLOWS!  . . . . . .   615 MARCH SONGS 3         1
      HE SANG IT FROM HIS HEART.  . . . . . . . . . . .   616 MARCH SONGS 3         6
      NO MORE SANG HE, FOR HIS THROAT WAS TOO SMALL!  . . .   616 MARCH SONGS 3        24
      THEY SANG, BUT HAD NOR HUMAN TUNES NOR WORDS, . . .   635 CUCHULAIN COMF       23
      AND I SANG ROUND THE TREE . . . . . . . . . . .   654 ISLE STAT I 2        66
      AND I SANG ROUND THE TREE,  . . . . . . . . . .   654 ISLE STAT I 2        76
      AND I SANG ROUND THE TREE,  . . . . . . . . . .   655 ISLE STAT I 2        80
      AND, NODDING TO AND FRO, SANG SONGS OF LOVE, . . .   688 TWO TITANS          35
      'TWAS EVENING, AND THE CRICKET NATION SANG . . . .   690 MOSADA 1            18
      A LILY-BLANCHED PLACE, SHE SAT AND SANG, . . . . .   693 MOSADA 1            83
      A LILY BLANCHED PLACE, SHE SAT AND SANG,  . . . .   693 MOSADA 1        V   83
      IN THE FAR ISLE SHE SANG HERSELF ASLEEP,  . . . .   694 MOSADA 1            90
      MY FOSTER-MOTHER SANG IN AN OLD RHYME  . . . . .   763 SHADOW WATER A      314
      MY FOSTER MOTHER SANG IN AN OLD RHYME  . . . . .   763 SHADOW WATER A  V   314
SANK
      FOR THE SPARKLING HOOVES THEY SANK NOT IN!  . . . .    10 OISIN 1         V  114A
      IN THE PALE WEST, AND THE SUN'S RIM SANK; . . . .    12 OISIN 1            153
      NOW IN THE SEA THE SUN'S RIM SANK,  . . . . . . .    12 OISIN 1         V  153
      AND, AS THE SUN SANK EVER LOWER,  . . . . . . . .    13 OISIN 1         V  170A
      AS THOUGH ONE LISTENED THERE, AND HIS VOICE SANK . .   180 QUEEN MAEVE          7
      DO YOU REMEMBER WHEN WE SANK THAT GALLEY  . . . . .   223 SHADOW WATER B       20
      FOR CERTAINLY HE SANK INTO HIS GRAVE . . . . . .   370 EGO DOMINUS         57
      LOCKE SANK INTO A SWOON!  . . . . . . . . . . .   439 FRAGMENTS            1
      FROM THE LIMBS OF LEDA SANK  . . . . . . . . . .   522 LULLABY             17
      FROM THE LIMBS OF HELEN SANK . . . . . . . . . .   522 LULLABY         V   17
      SCARCE SANK HE FROM THE WEST  . . . . . . . . . .   535 CHOSEN               5
      WHEN LOW THE SUN SANK DOWN IN CLOTTED FLAME . . . .   656 ISLE STAT I 3        30
      THE SHEPHERD RAISED HIS ARMS AND SANK, . . . . . .   673 ISLE STAT II 3      187
SAP
      UNTIL THE SAP OF SUMMER HAD GROWN WEARY!  . . . . .   130 BOOK STORIES        14
      HAS DRIED THE SAP OUT OF MY VEINS, AND RENT . . . .   260 FASC DIFFICULT       2
SAPLINGS
      AND SAPLINGS ROOT AMONG THE BROKEN STONE,  . . . .   489 COOLE PARK 29       28
SAPPHO'S
      AT THE GREAT BOOK OF SAPPHO'S SONG; BUT NO, . . . .   461 HARUN RASHID        12
SAPPING
      SORROWS SAPPING BRAIN AND HEART. . . . . . . . .   733 STREET DANCERS      60
SAPPY
      "'TIS JOY MAKES SWIM THE SAPPY TIDE, . . . . . . .    18 OISIN 1         V  261
SARDONYX
      AND CHRYSOPRASE AND RUBY AND SARDONYX. . . . . . .   765 SHADOW WATER A      358
SAT
      OR SAT IN DREAMS ON THE PALE STRAND, . . . . . . .    25 OISIN 1            390
      AND OTHERS SAT THEM BY THE SEA,  . . . . . . . .    25 OISIN 1         V  390
      OF MANY THOUSAND STEPS.  SAT EITHER SIDE, . . . .    31 OISIN 2         V   35
      HE HAD SAT DOWN AND SIGHED WITH CUMBERED HEART, . .    37 OISIN 2            111
      I SAT ON CUSHIONED OTTER-SKIN!  . . . . . . . . .    81 MAD KING GOLL        1
      I SAT ON CUSHIONED OTTER SKIN . . . . . . . . .    81 MAD KING GOLL  V    1
      I SAT AND MUSED AND DRANK SWEET WINE! . . . . . .    82 MAD KING GOLL       13
      YOUNG SUBTLE CONCHUBAR SAT CLOSE BY ME . . . . . .   102 FERGUS DRUID        10
      HE SAT AND PLAYED IN A DREAM . . . . . . . . . .   145 HOST OF AIR         27
      HE SAT DOWN AND PLAYED IN A DREAM . . . . . . . .   145 HOST OF AIR     V   27
      THE PORTER SLEPT, ALTHOUGH HE SAT UPRIGHT . . . .   182 QUEEN MAEVE         45
      WHERE THE HOUND OF ULADH SAT BEFORE . . . . . . .   192 BAILE AILLINN       73
      WE SAT TOGETHER AT ONE SUMMER'S END, . . . . . . .   204 ADAMS CURSE          1
      WE SAT GROWN QUIET AT THE NAME OF LOVE; . . . . .   205 ADAMS CURSE         28
      HE SAT WITH TIGHTENED REIN AND LOOSENED MOUTH . . .   277 TWO KINGS           10
      HE SAT WITH TIGHTENED REIN AMAZED, HIS HORSE . . .   277 TWO KINGS       V   10
      SAT UPRIGHT WITH A SWORD BEFORE HER FEET, . . . .   279 TWO KINGS           62
      "YOU BROUGHT ME WHERE YOUR BROTHER ARDAN SAT . . .   280 TWO KINGS           79
      THEY SAT UPON THEIR HEELS TO RAIL, . . . . . . . .   297 THREE BEGGARS       53
      OR SAT UPON THEIR HEELS TO RAIL  . . . . . . . .   297 THREE BEGGARS   V   53
      WE SAT AS SILENT AS A STONE, . . . . . . . . . .   314 MEMORY YOUTH        15
      I SAT AS SILENT AS A STONE . . . . . . . . . . .   314 MEMORY YOUTH    V   15
      LAST EVENING!  THAT I, WHO HAD SAT . . . . . . . .   349 HAWK                15
      SAT LATE, OR SHELLEY'S VISIONARY PRINCE! . . . . .   373 PHASES OF MOON      16
      WHILE ON THAT OLD GREY STONE I SAT . . . . . . .   406 IN TIME OF WAR       2
      HIS MAJESTIC MOTHER SAT  . . . . . . . . . . . .   440 WISDOM              11
      WE SAT UNDER AN OLD THORN-TREE . . . . . . . . .   456 SUMMER SPRING        1
      SAT DOWN UPON THE FOUNTAIN'S MARBLE EDGE, . . . .   463 HARUN RASHID        43
      I SAT WHERE I COULD WATCH HER SLEEPING FORM, . . .   467 HARUN RASHID       128
      I SAT, A SOLITARY MAN, . . . . . . . . . . . . .   501 VACILLATION         36
      I SAT AND CRIED. . . . . . . . . . . . . . . .   515 GIRLS SONG B         8
      THAT SAT SO STILL AND PLAYED AT THE CHESS? . . . .   550 SEVERED HEAD        12
      I TOLD HIM THAT NIGHTLY FROM SIX TO SEVEN I SAT AT THIS   578 LOFTY THINGS         9
          TABLE,
      ALL SORTS OF KINGS HAVE SAT  . . . . . . . . . .   597 MODEL LAUREATE       2
      ONE IMAGE CROSSED THE MANY-HEADED, SAT . . . . . .   610 STATUES             17
      GREAT-BLADDERED EMER SAT, . . . . . . . . . . .   628 JANE MOUNTAIN       15
      CUCHULAIN SAT AT HER SIDE! . . . . . . . . . . .   628 JANE MOUNTAIN       17
      GREAT BLADDERED EMER SAT, . . . . . . . . . . .   628 JANE MOUNTAIN   V   15
      HE SAT, AND THEN I HEARD THE WHITE LAKE SING, . . .   659 ISLE STAT II 1      15
      FILLED THEM AS THEY SAT TOGETHER! . . . . . . . .   667 ISLE STAT II 3      31
      TO MAKE US GLAD WITH WONDER AS WE SAT . . . . . .   683 SEEKER              41
      WHERE SAT OLD SUMMER FADING INTO SONG, . . . . . .   690 MOSADA 1            18
      A LILY-BLANCHED PLACE, SHE SAT AND SANG, . . . . .   693 MOSADA 1        V   18
      A LILY BLANCHED PLACE, SHE SAT AND SANG, . . . . .   693 MOSADA 1            83
      A LILY BLANCHED PLACE, SHE SAT AND SANG,  . . . .   693 MOSADA 1        V   83
      I SAT ME DOWN BESIDE THEE, AND I KNEW  . . . . . .   713 FERENCZ RENYI       92
      HAST THOU NOT SAT OF YORE UPON THE KNEES . . . . .   724 KANVA ON SELF        9
```

683

	PAGE	TITLE	LINE

SAT (CONTINUED)

		PAGE	TITLE	LINE
SAT UNDERNEATH THE MARKET CROSS,		724	LEGEND	2
AND UNDER A SHADY OAK-TREE SAT,		728	PRIEST FAIRY	7
EARL PAUL CAME WHERE THE KING SAT,		740	EARL PAUL	29
I SAT BESIDE MY FOSTER-MOTHER, AND NOW		762	SHADOW WATER A	292
I SAT BESIDE MY FOSTER MOTHER, AND NOW		762	SHADOW WATER A V	292

SATIN

		PAGE	TITLE	LINE
ALL THAT SILK AND SATIN GEAR;		525	DANCING DAYS	3

SATISFACTION

		PAGE	TITLE	LINE
AND ASK FOR SATISFACTION UPON THESE		235	SHADOW WATER B	281
BRINGS SUCH SATISFACTION		533	FIRST CONFESS	11

SATISFIED

		PAGE	TITLE	LINE
WHAT WOMAN'S SATISFIED,		334	SONG	8
OF LOVELY, SATISFIED, INDIFFERENT EYES.		375	PHASES OF MOON	83
I AM SATISFIED WITH THAT,		430	NINETEEN 19	61
SATISFIED IF A TROUBLED MIRROR SHOW IT,		430	NINETEEN 19	62
AND EVERY BRIDE'S AMBITION SATISFIED.		491	COOLE BALLYLEE	37
THAT THEY BE SATISFIED—		496	MOHINI CHATTER	20
IMAGINATION HAD BEEN SATISFIED,		543	PARN FUNERAL 2	6
NOR SATISFIED CONSCIENCE, BUT THAT GREAT FAMILY		579	DOR WELLESLEY	14
BUT NOTHING SATISFIED THE FOOL,		620	JOHN KINSELLA	7
I MUST BE SATISFIED WITH MY HEART, ALTHOUGH		629	CIRCUS ANIMALS	4
CAN GHOST OR MAN BE SATISFIED?		791	REPRISALS	4

SATISFY

		PAGE	TITLE	LINE
SATISFY AMBITION, ANIMATE		500	VACILLATION	20
SATISFY AMBITION, OR ANIMATE		500	VACILLATION V	20

SATO'S

		PAGE	TITLE	LINE
WHERE SATO'S GIFT, A CHANGELESS SWORD,		421	MY TABLE	2
WHEN IT WAS FORGED. IN SATO'S HOUSE,		421	MY TABLE	9
IS SATO'S ANCIENT BLADE, STILL AS IT WAS,		477	SELF AND SOUL	10
IS SATO'S ANCIENT SWORD, STILL AS IT WAS,		477	SELF AND SOUL V	10

SATURATED SEE BLOOD-SATURATED

		PAGE	TITLE	LINE
THERE, ON BLOOD SATURATED GROUND, HAVE STOOD		482	BLOOD AND MOON V	35

SATURN

		PAGE	TITLE	LINE
UNDER SATURN		390	UNDER SATURN	T
IF JUPITER AND SATURN MEET,		562	CONJUNCTIONS	1

SATURNIAN

		PAGE	TITLE	LINE
STRETCH OUT YOUR LIMBS AND SLEEP A LONG SATURNIAN SLEEP;		442	BLACK CENTAUR	13

SATURNINE

		PAGE	TITLE	LINE
DO NOT BECAUSE THIS DAY I HAVE GROWN SATURNINE		390	UNDER SATURN	1

SATYRS

		PAGE	TITLE	LINE
FLASH FISHLIKE; NYMPHS AND SATYRS		612	NEWS ORACLE	35

SAVAGE

		PAGE	TITLE	LINE
TO MAKE THE SAVAGE HEART OF LOVE		193	BAILE AILLINN	109
SAVAGE INDIGNATION THERE		493	SWIFTS EPITAPH	2
DANCE THE SAVAGE CHILDREN SMALL,		732	STREET DANCERS	29

SAVAGELY

		PAGE	TITLE	LINE
AND HAD BEEN SAVAGELY UNDONE		314	MEMORY YOUTH	18

SAVE

		PAGE	TITLE	LINE
ALL PEARLY WHITE, SAVE ONE RED EAR;		12	OISIN 1	141
SAVE DEER TOWARDS NOON THAT WATER SOUGHT.		17	OISIN 1 V	243
SAVE ONLY MANY TIMES MY NAME,		25	OISIN 1	375
AND LIFE IS OVER SAVE THE MURMUR AND THE SWEETNESS.		77	INDIAN TO LOVE V	5E
AND ALL IS OVER SAVE THE MURMUR AND THE SWEETNESS.		77	INDIAN TO LOVE V	5E
SAVE BY AN EVIL CHANCE,		178	FIDDLER DOONEY	14
I'D SAVE HIS LIFE, YET FOR THE SAKE		275	GREY ROCK V	102
FOR MEN WERE BORN TO PRAY AND SAVE;		289	SEPTEMBER 1913	6
AND WHAT, GOD HELP US, COULD THEY SAVE?		289	SEPTEMBER 1913	14
AND WONDERED WHAT WAS LEFT FOR MASSACRE TO SAVE.		619	BRONZE HEAD	28
BUT MASTERFUL HEAVEN HAD INTERVENED TO SAVE IT.		630	CIRCUS ANIMALS	20
WHO SEEK MAY FIND, SAVE ONLY ONE,		668	ISLE STAT II 3	48
THE FLOWER, SAVE SOME THING BE FOUND		668	ISLE STAT II 3	51
THAT SHE FORSWEAR HER HERESIES AND SAVE		698	MOSADA 2	46
CAST OFF THY HERESIES, AND SAVE THY SOUL		701	MOSADA 3	64
FLINGS HER BEFORE HIM. "SAVE THYSELF AND ME.		713	FERENCZ RENYI	86
"AH, FERENCZ, SPEAK AND SAVE THYSELF AND ME!		713	FERENCZ RENYI V	86
FOR ALL SAVE HIM WHO PINING FELL,		717	FAIRY DOCTOR	19
FOR ALL SAVE HE WHO PINING FELL,		717	FAIRY DOCTOR V	19
SAVE, WITH THE LITTLE GOLDEN GREEDY CARP,		720	WITCH VIVIEN	2

SAVED

		PAGE	TITLE	LINE
BECAUSE YOU SAVED MY RICE. HAVE YOU NO THANKS?		73	ANASHU VIJAYA	40
I'D SAVED HIS LIFE, YET FOR THE SAKE		275	GREY ROCK	102
AND SAVED THE IRISH POOR,		586	PARNELLITES	12

SAVES

		PAGE	TITLE	LINE
BUT SAVES US FROM A DREAM. AND WHAT OF THOSE		376	PHASES OF MOON	102

SAVING

		PAGE	TITLE	LINE
SAVING IN THINE OWN HEART. SEEK, THEN,		66	HAPPY SHEPHERD	27
SAVING THE RHYME RATS HEAR BEFORE THEY DIE.		542	PARN FUNERAL 1	28
SAVING A GREEN FROG DEAD UPON THE GRASS.		676	ISLE STAT II 3	269
MINE HEART-STRINGS ARE ALL BROKEN SAVING ONE,		684	SEEKER V	69B

SAW

		PAGE	TITLE	LINE
NEAR BY, THE FENIANS SAW, AND KNEW		10	OISIN 1 V	111
AND WHEN THEY SAW THE CLOAK I WORE		15	OISIN 1	207
AND WHEN THEY SAW MY EARTHLY DRESS,		15	OISIN 1 V	207
AND WHEN THEY SAW THAT THE BRATTA I WORE		15	OISIN 1 V	207
I SAW NOT WHO; 'NEATH OTHER SKIES		25	OISIN 1 V	381A
AND WHEN THE WHITE STEED SAW WHAT BLACKNESS GLEAMED,		30	OISIN 2 V	24
I SAW A FOAM-WHITE SEAGULL DRIFT AND FLOAT		36	OISIN 2	105
CLOTHING HIM ROUND, I SAW A SEAGULL FLOAT		36	OISIN 2 V	105
WE SAW, SOME NEW, SOME PRINTED WHEN THE PLACE WAS YOUNG,		37	OISIN 2 V	116
TO LIE UNTIL THE FOURTH MORN SAW EMERGE		44	OISIN 2	220

		PAGE	TITLE		LINE
SAW	(CONTINUED)				
TO LIE THERE 'TILL THE FOURTH DAY SAW EMERGE		44	OISIN 2	V	220
THE IMMORTAL DESIRE OF IMMORTALS WE SAW IN THEIR FACES, AND SIGHED.		47	OISIN 3		4
AND WE STOOD ON A SEA'S EDGE WE SAW NOT:		47	OISIN 3		11
I SAW HOW THOSE SLUMBERERS, GROWN WEARY, ...		50	OISIN 3		54
I SAW FROM A DISTANT SADDLE: FROM THE EARTH SHE MADE HER MOAN:		56	OISIN 3		130
TILL I SAW WHERE MAEVE LIES SLEEPING		60	OISIN 3		184
I SAW HER STANDING IN HER DOOR BUT NOW		74	ANASHU VIJAYA		64
MY SPIRIT ROCKED IN SLEEP AND SIGHS: AND SAW THE MOORFOWL PACE		76	INDIAN ON GOD		3
ALL DRIPPING ON A GRASSY SLOPE, AND SAW THEM CEASE TO CHASE		76	INDIAN ON GOD		4
TURNING, HE SAW THAT SHE HAD THRUST DEAD LEAVES		80	EPHEMERA		18
GLIMMERING IN HER DROOPED EYES, SAW HER LIPS MOVE		81	EPHEMERA	V	24D
AND SAW WHERE THIS OLD TYMPAN LAY		85	MAD KING GOLL		55
I SAW THIS HARP ALL SONGLESS LIE		85	MAD KING GOLL	V	55
I SAW A KINDLY NEIGHBOUR		95	MOLL MAGEE		35
I SAW A NEIGHBOUR GOOD.		95	MOLL MAGEE	V	36
AND HE SAW HOW THE REEDS GREW DARK		144	HOST OF AIR		5
AND HE SAW YOUNG MEN AND YOUNG GIRLS		144	HOST OF AIR		13
AND SAW YOUR IMAGE WAS THERE:		152	LOSS OF LOVE		6
THAT SAW YOUNG NIAMH HOVER WITH LOVE-LORN FACE		162	ASKS FORGIVE		13
AND CUMHAL SAW LIKE A DRIFTING SMOKE		167	BLESSED		13
SAW THE PIERCED HANDS AND ROOD OF ELDER RISE		169	SECRET ROSE		10
SHE SAW HER HUSBAND AILELL SLEEPING THERE, ...		183	QUEEN MAEVE		69
WE SAW THE LAST EMBERS OF DAYLIGHT DIE, ...		205	ADAMS CURSE		29
I SAW THEM ON THAT NIGHT AS WELL AS YOU.		223	SHADOW WATER B		29
I SAW THEM, TOO, ONE NIGHT. FORGAEL WAS PLAYING, . . .		223	SHADOW WATER B		36
I SAW A FLAGON OF BROWN ALE ABOARD HER.		240	SHADOW WATER B		388
AND SAW WHEREVER I COULD TURN		253	HIS DREAM		3
IF WE BUT SAW IN DREAMS THAT ROOM, ...		272	GREY ROCK		38
WITH THE GROUND-IVY'S BLUE, HE SAW A STAG		277	TWO KINGS		6
HE THOUGHT TO HAVE GIVEN HIS HORSE THE SPUR, BUT SAW . .		277	TWO KINGS	V	48
AND SAW WHERE IN THE MIDST OF THE GREAT HALL		279	TWO KINGS		60
AND THEREON SAW, WHERE STONES HAD BEEN		302	HOUR DAWN	V	20
AND SAW A FLAKE OF THE YELLOW FOAM		309	PLAYER QUEEN		15
I SAW A FLAKE OF YELLOW FOAM		309	PLAYER QUEEN	V	15
SUDDENLY I SAW THE COLD AND ROOK-DELIGHTING HEAVEN . . .		316	COLD HEAVEN		1
SUDDENLY I SAW THE COLD AND ROOK DELIGHTING HEAVEN . . .		316	COLD HEAVEN	V	1
I SAW, BEFORE I HAD WELL FINISHED, ...		322	SWANS AT COOLE		9
THAT SAW THE SURGES RUNNING BY, ...		338	TOM OROUGHLEY		6
OR ON THE WITHERED MEN THAT SAW		344	DAWN		5
THAT SAW THE WICKS GROW YELLOW IN THE DAWN:		352	PEOPLE		18
ON THE GREY ROCK OF CASHEL I SUDDENLY SAW		383	VISION ROBART		17
ALTHOUGH I SAW IT ALL IN THE MIND'S EYE		383	VISION ROBART		25
I SAW BY THE MOON'S LIGHT		383	VISION ROBART		27
WHEN LONG AGO I SAW HER RIDE		397	POLIT PRISONER		13
I SAW MY FREEDOM WON		400	DEMON BEAST		7
IN REVERIE, OR IN VISION, SAW		420	MY HOUSE	V	20E
THEY NEVER SAW HOW SEASONS RUN, ...		432	NINETEEN 19		101
I SAW A STARING VIRGIN STAND		437	SONGS PLAY 1		1
I SAW THAT STARING, VIRGIN STAND		437	SONGS PLAY 1	V	1
SINCE FIRST WE SAW THE LIGHT, ...		456	SUMMER SPRING		4
AND OFTEN THOSE FIRST DAYS I SAW HER STARE		466	HARUN RASHID		122
AND SAW HER SITTING UPRIGHT ON THE BED:		467	HARUN RASHID		134
I SAW HER SITTING UPRIGHT ON THE BED, ...		467	HARUN RASHID	V	134
BUT MINE SAW STELLA ONCE. WHENCE CAME OUR THOUGHT? . .		486	SEVEN SAGES		6
MINE SAW STELLA ONCE. WHENCE CAME OUR THOUGHT? . . .		486	SEVEN SAGES	V	6
MINE SAW STELLA ONCE. WHEN CAME OUR THOUGHT?		486	SEVEN SAGES	V	6
BUT NEVER SAW THE TREFOIL STAINED WITH BLOOD, ...		487	SEVEN SAGES		19
SAW I AN OLD MAN YOUNG		515	GIRLS SONG B		11
NO WITHERED CRONE I SAW		516	MANS SONG		11
THAT BLINKED AND SAW THEM IN A SHROUD.		529	TOM LUNATIC		12
NOR SAW MY BODY FALL NOR HEARD IT SHRIEK, ...		537	HER VISION		29
TO THOSE THAT NEVER SAW THIS TONSURED HEAD		555	RIBH AT TOMB		4
FOR IF I SAW MYSELF CREEP IN		569	THREE BUSHES		12
HIS LADY SAW IT ALL		571	THREE BUSHES		53
AND WANT HE DID FOR MY GRAND-DAD SAW		596	COLONEL MARTIN	V	68
SAW THE STORY'S END.		597	COLONEL MARTIN		69
SAW THAT THE GRAVE WAS DEEP, THE COFFIN SOUND, ...		609	IN TARAS HALLS		18
I SAW THE WILDNESS IN HER AND I THOUGHT		619	BRONZE HEAD		16
AS ARGIVE CLYTEMNESTRA SAW OUT-BURN		645	ISLE STAT I 1		12
OENONE SAW THE FIRES OF TROIA LEAP, ...		645	ISLE STAT I 1		17
I SENT AN ARROW. AND I SAW YOU MISS:		649	ISLE STAT I 1		115
I SAW HER AS YOU NOW ARISE:		654	ISLE STAT I 2		73
OF THOSE VAST WOODS: AND THEN I SAW THE BOAT, ...		657	ISLE STAT I 3		53
WE SAW THE DOLOROUS LAKE: AND THEN THY NAME		659	ISLE STAT II 1		7
AND, BOY, SAW YOU, WHEN THROUGH THE FOREST WE		662	ISLE STAT II 2		9
I SAW HIM FROM SAD DIDO'S SHORES DEPART, ...		677	ISLE STAT II 3		288
AS HERE I CAME I SAW GOD PAN. HE PLAYED		678	ISLE STAT II 3		300
BEFORE THE WIND. SAW YOU HIS EYES A-GLITTER?		683	SEEKER		35
I SAW HIM STAGGER WITH THE CLANKING CHAIN, ...		687	TWO TITANS		31
ALONG THE VELVET VALE I SAW HIM COME—		690	MOSADA 1		10
I SAW HIM SIGH AND TURN AND PASS AWAY:		690	MOSADA 1		14
I SAW HIS JOVIAL MOOD BRING ONCE A SMILE		696	MOSADA 2		14
A SAINT OF MUNSTER, WHEN MUCH FASTING, SAW		696	MOSADA 2		20
I SAW A STRANGER TAP AND WAIT		696	MOSADA 2		22
A SAINT OF RUSSIA IN A VISION SAW		696	MOSADA 2	V	21
A WEAK, THIN CHILD, WHEN LAST I SAW HIM THERE.		699	MOSADA 3		14
I SAW A GIRL AFRAID TO BE TOO NEAR, ...		712	FERENCZ RENYI		68

685

SAW   (CONTINUED)
    SAW ON THE WOOD'S EDGE GLEAM AN ASH-GREY FEATHER: 715 DWELT SYCAMORE   2
    I SAW HER GLITTER AND GLEAM,   744 GLOVE CLOAK   1
    AND HEARD THE MUSIC IN THE WIND, AND SAW   747 SHADOW WATER A   5
    O, BUT I SAW A SOLEMN SIGHT: 788 HAWTHORN TREE   1
    LIVE, FOR I SAW THEM DANCING THERE.   788 HAWTHORN TREE   12
SAWDUST
    SWEPT THE SAWDUST FROM THE FLOOR   440 WISDOM   6
SAY
    I HEARD ONE SAY, "HIS EYES GROW DIM   25 OISIN 1   380
    I HEARD ONE SAY, "WITHIN HIS EYES   25 OISIN 1   V 380
    AND THE STARS SHALL ARISE AND SAY IN THE MORNING,   28 OISIN 1   V 423G
    SAY HOW HE WEEPS IN ERI."   33 OISIN 2   V   68
    AND THUS, MY LATE-LOST NIAM, DIDST THOU SAY: 34 OISIN 2   V   78
    LOST NIAM MOURN AND SAY, "AH, LOVE, WE GO   46 OISIN 2   V 245B
    YE HAVE NO POWER." "AND, NIAM, SAY, OF THESE   46 OISIN 2   V 248
    I PASSED A LITTLE FURTHER ON AND HEARD A PEACOCK SAY: 77 INDIAN ON GOD   17
    I PACED A LITTLE FURTHER AND I HEARD A PEACOCK SAY:--   77 INDIAN ON GOD   V   17
    I PASSED A LITTLE FURTHER AND I HEARD A PEACOCK SAY:--   77 INDIAN ON GOD   V   17
    WITH SHORE LINES IN THE SAY: 94 MOLL MAGEE   6
    THEY HEAR HIM FEEBLY SAY: 99 FOXHUNTER   32
    THIS WOULD I SAY, MOST WISE OF LIVING SOULS: 102 FERGUS DRUID   9
    AND COVER YOUR LIPS WITH ODOROUS TWILIGHT AND SAY: 162 ASKS FORGIVE   5
    COVER YOUR LIPS WITH ROSE-HEAVY TWILIGHT, AND SAY: 162 ASKS FORGIVE   V   5
    THEIR CHILDREN'S CHILDREN SHALL SAY THEY HAVE LIED.   166 EVIL OF BELOV   6
    AND LEARN THE PRAYERS THAT YOU SAY.   167 BLESSED   8
    AND SHOOK HIM WIDE AWAKE, AND BID HIM SAY   182 QUEEN MAEVE   50
    HAD TROUBLED HIS SLEEP. BUT ALL HE HAD TO SAY   182 QUEEN MAEVE   52
    AND POETS FOUND, OLD WRITERS SAY,   197 BAILE AILLINN   187
    AWAKENS AN OLD MEMORY, AND SAY,   201 OLD MEMORY   2
    FOR THEY, FOR ALL SMOOTH LIPS CAN SAY,   202 NEVER GIVE ALL   9
    AND THROWN THE THUNDER ON THE STONES FOR ALL THAT MAEVE 207 HANRAHANS SONG   7
        CAN SAY.
    I HEARD THE OLD, OLD MEN SAY,   208 OLD MEN ADMIRE   1
    I HEARD THE OLD, OLD MEN SAY,   208 OLD MEN ADMIRE   7
    WHEN FORGAEL'S IN THE OTHER SCALE. I'D SAY IT   225 SHADOW WATER B   V   75
    NO, NO, DO NOT SAY THAT. YOU KNOW RIGHT WELL   227 SHADOW WATER B   107
    YOU SAY THAT ALSO? YOU HAVE HEARD THE VOICES,   228 SHADOW WATER B   136
    FOR THAT IS WHAT THEY SAY--ALL, ALL THE SHADOWS--   228 SHADOW WATER B   137
    BRING MADNESS? QUEEN, I AM NOT MAD. YET SAY   236 SHADOW WATER B   316
    AND YET YOU SAY THE WATER AND THE WIND   236 SHADOW WATER B   317
    BUT WHAT IS IT THAT MADE ME SAY I LOVED HIM?   242 SHADOW WATER B   422
    AND IF YOU SAY THAT SHE CAME WILLINGLY--   244 SHADOW WATER B   460
    AND YOU SAY THAT SHE CAME WILLINGLY--   244 SHADOW WATER B   V 460
    THAT COMING TIME CAN SAY,   255 WOMAN HOMER   12
    THAT HAD SHE DONE SO WHO CAN SAY   256 WORDS   13
    YOU SAY, AS I HAVE OFTEN GIVEN TONGUE   262 TO A POET   1
    WHEN WE ARE HIGH AND AIRY HUNDREDS SAY   265 ABBEY THEATRE   2
    AS THOUGH TO SAY "IT IS THE SWORD ELSEWHERE,"   267 ALL TEMPT ME   V   8
    MY FANCY, AND SET MY BOYISH LIPS TO SAY,   270 PARDON FATHERS   17
    OLD WHOLESOME GOBAN HAD NO SAY: 271 GREY ROCK   10
    THE BOW-LEGGED GOBAN HAD NO SAY: 271 GREY ROCK   V   10
    "SAY WHAT YOU PLEASE, BUT FROM DAYBREAK   304 HOUR DAWN   42
    "SAY WHAT YOU PLEASE, BUT FROM DAY-BREAK   304 HOUR DAWN   V   42
    "I'LL HAVE MY SAY, TILL I AM ABLE   304 HOUR DAWN   51
    "WHY, BEER IS ONLY BEER." "BUT SAY   305 HOUR DAWN   56
    YOU'VE BUT TO DRINK THE BEER AND SAY   305 HOUR DAWN   56
    IF YOU BUT DRINK THAT BEER AND SAY   305 HOUR DAWN   V   56
    AND YET FOR ALL THAT I COULD SAY,   313 MEMORY YOUTH   4
    OUT NAKED ON THE ROADS, AS THE BOOKS SAY, AND STRICKEN 316 COLD HEAVEN   11
    I'LL SAY AND MAYBE DREAM I HAVE DRAWN CONTENT,   333 LIVING BEAUTY   V   1
    LORD, WHAT WOULD THEY SAY   337 SCHOLARS   11
    OR SO DID TOM O'ROUGHLEY SAY   338 TOM OROUGHLEY   5
    THEY SAY THAT ON YOUR BARREN MOUNTAIN RIDGE   342 SHEP GOATHERD   79
    THEY SAY HE COUNTED GRASS,   345 ON WOMAN   14
    THEY CAN SPREAD OUT WHAT SAIL THEY PLEASE FOR ALL I HAVE 354 HIS PHOENIX   22
        TO SAY,
    AND WHO CAN SAY BUT SOME YOUNG BELLE MAY WALK AND TALK 354 HIS PHOENIX   26
        MEN WILD
    WILL SAY TO AN OLD MAN, "TELL ME OF THAT LADY   356 BROKEN DREAMS   17
    THEY HAD A PRIEST SAY MASS, AND EVEN THE JAPANESE,   363 DOLLS FACES   2
    WILL COME FROM THE HOUSE, AND SAY--   364 END OF DAY   6
    THEY SAY SUCH DIFFERENT THINGS AT SCHOOL.   387 ROBARTES DANCE   52
    YOU SAY THAT WE SHOULD STILL THE LAND   395 SIXTEEN DEAD   7
    THERE'S NOT A NEIGHBOUR LEFT TO SAY   412 TOWER   78
    WHAT MORE IS THERE TO SAY? THAT COUNTRY ROUND   430 NINETEEN 19   43
    AND NEEDS NO CRUELTY. I HAVE HEARD ONE SAY   448 HERO GIRL FOOL   13
    AND NOT THEMSELVES. SAY ON AND SAY   448 HERO GIRL FOOL   15
    AND NOT THEMSELVES. SAY ON AND SAY   448 HERO GIRL FOOL   15
    WHAT NO DECEPTION WON. I HAVE HEARD THEM SAY   448 HERO GIRL FOOL   V   13
    IN WHAT I DO OR SAY   455 HIS MEMORIES   8
    OR SAY THE THINGS WE SAY: 458 SECRETS OF OLD   12
    OR SAY THE THINGS WE SAY: 458 SECRETS OF OLD   12
    NEVER TO HAVE LIVED IS BEST, ANCIENT WRITERS SAY: 459 FROM OEDIPUS   10
    AND ALL THE POPULAR STATESMEN SAY   460 THREE MONUMENT   5
    AND PAUSE AT LAST, I WAS ABOUT TO SAY,   461 HARUN RASHID   11
    I SAY THAT A DJINN SPOKE. A LIVELONG HOUR   467 HARUN RASHID   136
    I SAY THAT A DJIN SPOKE. A LIVE LONG HOUR   467 HARUN RASHID   V 136
    I SAY THAT A JINN SPOKE. A LIVE-LONG HOUR   467 HARUN RASHID   V 136
    BECAUSE I HAVE A MARVELLOUS THING TO SAY,   471 ALL SOUL NIGHT   15
    THAT IS TO SAY, ASCENDS TO HEAVEN: 478 SELF AND SOUL   38

		PAGE	TITLE	LINE
SAY (CONTINUED)				
"PRAY FOR NOTHING, SAY		495	MOHINI CHATTER	3
OR, AS GREAT SAGES SAY,		496	MOHINI CHATTER	27
OR THINGS I DID NOT DO OR SAY		501	VACILLATION	52
BUT THOUGHT THAT I MIGHT SAY OR DO,		501	VACILLATION	53
I CARE NOT WHAT THE SAILORS SAY:		509	JANE REPROVED	1
SHE HEARS ME STRIKE THE BOARD AND SAY		531	FATHER CHILD	1
SAY THAT OF LIVING MEN I HATE		539	MEETING	11
SADDLE AND RIDE, I HEARD A MAN SAY,		549	SEVERED HEAD	1
IMAGES RIDE, I HEARD A MAN SAY,		549	SEVERED HEAD V	1
I HAVE HEARD THAT HYSTERICAL WOMEN SAY		565	LAPIS LAZULI	1
TO LEAD HER AWAY, DO NOT SAY		568	SWEET DANCER	9
AND THROUGH THE CHIME SHE'D SAY,		570	THREE BUSHES	30
AND AT NIGHT TIME WOULD SHE SAY,		570	THREE BUSHES V	30
WHAT IS THERE LEFT TO SAY?		580	CURSE CROMWELL	8
WHAT IS THERE LEFT TO SAY?		580	CURSE CROMWELL	16
WHAT IS THERE LEFT TO SAY?		581	CURSE CROMWELL	24
WHAT IS THERE LEFT TO SAY?		581	CURSE CROMWELL	32
I SAY THAT ROGER CASEMENT		581	ROGER CASEMENT	1
FOR HE KNOWS HOW TO SAY,		583	GHOST ROG CASE	14
AND WHAT'S THE GOOD OF WOMEN, FOR ALL THAT THEY CAN SAY		592	PILGRIM	4
AND THAT OLD MAN BESIDE ME, NOTHING WOULD HE SAY		593	PILGRIM	9
I SWEAR TO GOD I QUESTIONED THEM, AND ALL THEY HAD TO SAY		593	PILGRIM	14
BUT I NEVER STOPPED TO QUESTION, WHAT COULD THE BOATMAN SAY		593	PILGRIM	19
FOR I CAN PUT THE WHOLE LOT DOWN, AND ALL I HAVE TO SAY		593	PILGRIM	24
I SWEAR TO GOD I QUESTIONED THEM ALL AND ALL THEY HAD TO SAY		593	PILGRIM V	14
FOR WHO CAN SAY?" HE SAID,		594	COLONEL MARTIN	15
THEY SAY IT IS MORE HUMAN		599	STONE CROSS	19
BLESSING THE TRICOLOUR. "THIS IS NOT," I SAY,		601	GALLERY REVIS	10
AND SAY MY GLORY WAS I HAD SUCH FRIENDS,		604	GALLERY REVIS	55
AND MAYBE WHAT THEY SAY IS TRUE		631	POLITICS	9
SAY THAT THE MEN OF THE OLD BLACK TOWER,		635	BLACK TOWER	1
HAVE DONE THIS PHRASING, AND SAY WHY, IN SOOTH,		652	ISLE STAT I 2	25
SOME SAY THAT ALL WHO TOUCH THE ISLAND LONE		653	ISLE STAT I 2	42
MY PRETTY CHILD, SINCE HE HAS GONE, OH SAY		658	ISLE STAT II 1	3
OF GRIEF. AND IF THEY SAY, "ANTONIO LAUGHED,"		664	ISLE STAT II 2	51
SAY THEN,--"A POPINJAY BEFORE GRIEF'S SHAFT		664	ISLE STAT II 2	52
SHE WILL SAY WITH BATED BREATH,		680	LOVE AND DEATH	30
THEY SAY THE WISH ITSELF IS HALF THE SIN:		692	MOSADA 1	48
THEY SAY I AM ALL UGLINESS: LAME-FOOTED		692	MOSADA 1	60
SO SHE MUST BURN, YOU SAY? SHE MUST IN TRUTH.		696	MOSADA 2	2
LIKE SMALL BROWN MOTHS, A-TREMBLE. "RENYI SAY		713	FERENCZ RENYI	82
SAY WHAT RINGER RINGS AT MIDNIGHT: FOR, IN THE BELFRY HIGH,		718	PHANTOM SHIP	15
THEY SAY YOU ARE A GAMBLER AND A PLAYER		721	WITCH VIVIEN	34
"SAY AND THRICE ANIGH THY DOOR		730	PRIEST FAIRY	54
TO THE EVER-LONGING AND MOURNFUL SPIRIT SAY,		734	QUATRAIN APHOR	12
AND HEARS THE ROAR OF THE STREAMS WHERE, DRUIDS SAY,		749	SHADOW WATER A	46
SHE WILL SAY SOMETHING IN A LITTLE WHILE,		760	SHADOW WATER A	248
WHY DID YOU SAY THAT I HAVE FOLLOWED HIM		761	SHADOW WATER A	267
HITHER AND THITHER AND SAY AT THE HIGH NOON		767	SHADOW WATER A	404
AND ALL MEN LIE THAT SAY THAT I		789	SINGING HEAD	3
THEY LIE THAT SAY, IN MOCKERY		789	SINGING HEAD	9
SOME NINETEEN GERMAN PLANES, THEY SAY,		791	REPRISALS	1
SAYETH				
AND ENTER, AND NONE SAYETH "NO"		62	OISIN 3	210
AND ENTER, AND NONE SAYETH "NAY"		62	OISIN 3 V	210
SAYING				
SAYING ALL THINGS WERE WELL:		113	ROSE OF PEACE	14
BUT YOU WERE SAYING THERE IS SOMEBODY		240	SHADOW WATER B	380
YOU KNOW THE SAYING, "CHANGE THE BRIDE WITH SPRING,"		463	HARUN RASHID	50
SAYING "EARL PAUL IS PARDONED		741	EARL PAUL	55
SAYS				
AND "A WEARINESS SOON IS MY SPEED," SAYS THE MOUSE,		27	OISIN 1 V	417
SHE SAYS MY MAN WILL SURELY COME,		96	MOLL MAGEE	41
SHE SAYS MY HUSBAND SURE WILL COME		96	MOLL MAGEE V	41
NOW I CAN HEAR. THERE'S ONE OF THEM THAT SAYS,		233	SHADOW WATER B	252
AND SAYS, "A SWORD-BLADE PIERCED ME IN MY SLEEP."		234	SHADOW WATER B	257
AND SAYS: "A SWORD BLADE PIERCED ME IN MY SLEEP."		234	SHADOW WATER B V	257
WHAT SAYS THE CLOCK IN THE GREAT CLOCK TOWER?		549	SEVERED HEAD	3
WHAT SAYS THE CLOCK IN THE GREAT CLOCK TOWER?		550	SEVERED HEAD	10
WHAT SAYS THE CLOCK IN THE GREAT CLOCK TOWER?		550	SEVERED HEAD	17
THE PRIESTS HAVE GOT A BOOK THAT SAYS		621	JOHN KINSELLA	25
HE SAYS 'TWAS HE, AND 'TWAS NO OTHER,		656	ISLE STAT I 3	15
THE DARK STILL MAN, HAS COME AND SAYS 'TIS SIN.		692	MOSADA 1	47
TWO HOVER THERE TOGETHER, AND ONE SAYS,		753	SHADOW WATER A	142
AND SAYS, "A SWORD-BLADE PIERCED ME IN MY SLEEP."		753	SHADOW WATER A	147
AND SAYS, "A SWORD BLADE PIERCED ME IN MY SLEEP."		753	SHADOW WATER A V	147
SCABBARD				
IF YOU WILL DRAW THAT SWORD OUT OF ITS SCABBARD		225	SHADOW WATER B	78
THE WOODEN SCABBARD BOUND AND WOUND,		477	SELF AND SOUL	15
SCAFFOLD				
JUSTIFY ALL THAT HAVE DIED ON THE SCAFFOLD,		546	TO SAME TUNE 2	13
REMEMBER ALL THAT HAVE DIED ON THE SCAFFOLD,		613	MARCH SONGS 1	13
SCAFFOLDING				
THERE ON THAT SCAFFOLDING RECLINES		618	LONG-LEG FLY	25
SCALE				
SCALE RUBBING SCALE WHERE LIGHT IS DIM		195	BAILE AILLINN	145
SCALE RUBBING SCALE WHERE LIGHT IS DIM		195	BAILE AILLINN	145
AND FORGAEL IN THE OTHER SCALE: KILL FORGAEL,		225	SHADOW WATER B	76
WHEN FORGAEL'S IN THE OTHER SCALE. I'D SAY IT		225	SHADOW WATER B V	75

SCALE   (CONTINUED)
     THOUGHT, IN THAT SCALE OF HIS! . . . .   267 FRIEND ILLNESS   2
     NOW BATHING LILY LEAF AND FISH'S SCALE, ...   464 HARUN RASHID   65
     NOW BATHING LILY LEAF AND FISHES' SCALE, ...   464 HARUN RASHID   V   65
SCALED   SEE MIRROR-SCALED
     THE MIRROR SCALED SERPENT IS MULTIPLICITY, ...   556 RIBH PATRICK   V   10
SCALES   SEE DRAGON-SCALES
     SHOWED PRINTS OF SEA-BORN SCALES, WHILE DOWN THROUGH IT   37 OISIN 2   115
     THE NETTED MARKS OF CRAWLING SCALES SEA-SPRUNG . . . .   37 OISIN 2   V   115
SCANAVIN
     HE MUSED BESIDE THE WELL OF SCANAVIN. . . . .   127 DREAM OF FAERY   25
SCARCE
     SCARCE WORTHY OF A HOOF GOLD-SHOD. . . . .   2 OISIN 1   V   7Y
     SCARCE LEFT A WHITENING FEATHER, GREY AND SERE! . . . .   34 OISIN 2   V   76A
     THAT SCARCE COULD BATHE A STAR, ...   88 STOLEN CHILD   31
     I SCARCE COULD DRAG MY FEET, ...   94 MOLL MAGEE   10
     THEN SEEING THAT HE SCARCE HAD SPOKE . . . .   194 BAILE AILLINN   126
     WITH SCARCE A PITYING LOOK? . . . .   315 FRIENDS   19
     WHERE MY GOATS BROWSE ON THE SCARCE GRASS OR LEAP . . .   339 SHEP GOATHERD   8
     LIFE SCARCE CAN CAST A FRAGRANCE ON THE WIND, ...   422 MY DESCENDANTS   5
     SCARCE SPREAD A GLORY TO THE MORNING BEAMS, ...   422 MY DESCENDANTS   6
     THAT NEVER KNEW THAT STRAIN WOULD SCARCE SEEM BRIGHT, . .   465 HARUN RASHID   88
     SCARCE DID HE MY BODY TOUCH. . . . .   535 CHOSEN   4
     SCARCE SANK HE FROM THE WEST . . . .   535 CHOSEN   5
     I SLEPT, 'TWAS SULTRY, AND SCARCE CIRCLING SHOOK . . . .   677 ISLE STAT II 3   278
     NEVER STORM AROSE SO SWIFTLY! SCARCE THE CHILDREN WERE   718 PHANTOM SHIP   4
       IN BED,
     SCARCE THE OLD AND WIZEN HOUSES HAD THEIR DOORS AND WINDOWS   718 PHANTOM SHIP   5
       SHUT.
     SCARCE THE OLD AND WIZENED HOUSES HAD THEIR DOORS   718 PHANTOM SHIP   V   5
       AND WINDOWS SHUT.
SCARCELY
     SCARCELY A FEATHER LINGERED, THEN YOU SEEMED . . . . .   102 FERGUS DRUID   4
     HAD SCARCELY ACCUSTOMED OUR EARS . . . .   341 SHEP GOATHERD   67
     HAD SCARCELY ACCUSTOMED OUR EYES . . . .   341 SHEP GOATHERD   69
     WILL SCARCELY FIND FOR HIM A BROKEN CRUST . . . . . .   373 PHASES OF MOON   23
     THAT WILL BE LATER, DAY IS SCARCELY DAWNING. . . . . .   699 MOSADA 3   12
SCARE
     OLD CLOTHES UPON OLD STICKS TO SCARE A BIRD. . . . . .   445 SCHOOL CHILDR   48
SCARECROW
     THERE IS A COMFORTABLE KIND OF OLD SCARECROW. . . . . .   444 SCHOOL CHILDR   32
SCARED
     SCARED OF ITS GLITTERING LIKE A METEOR STAR, ...   38 OISIN 2   V   137
     SCARED BY THE SPLASHING OF A DOZEN COWS! . . . .   419 MY HOUSE   10
     SCARED BY THE SPLASHING OF A HUNDRED COWS. . . . . . .   419 MY HOUSE   V   10
     AS TRIPS THE SCARED MOON . . . .   559 HE AND SHE   3
SCARES
     THAT SCARES WITH HIS BUSTLE THE DELICATE NIGHT, ...   28 OISIN 1   V   423B
SCARLET
     AND THE LIPS MORE SCARLET, ...   532 BEFORE WORLD   3
     A SCARLET BLOOM. WHY RAISEST THOU, PALE ONE, ...   673 ISLE STAT II 3   196
     WHERE THE ROSES IN SCARLET ARE HEAVY . . . .   707 FAIRY PEDANT   3
SCARRED
     AMONG WHIMS NOT IMPOSSIBLE, AND THOUGH SCARRED, ...   374 PHASES OF MOON   41
SCATTER
     WILL SCATTER IN RUIN THE LEAST OF OUR DAYS, ...   27 OISIN 1   V   419B
     LET THE BIRDS SCATTER, FOR THE TREE IS BROKEN, ...   250 SHADOW WATER B   584
     AND SCATTER WHEELING IN GREAT BROKEN RINGS . . . . . .   322 SWANS AT COOLE   11
     TO SCATTER THE ACACIA SPRAY . . . .   360 ALF POLLEXFEN   10
     AS THE LEAVES IN AUTUMN SCATTER. . . . .   648 ISLE STAT I 1   90
     AND AWAY IN THE WOODS WE WILL SCATTER THE DEW! . . . .   717 LOVE SONG   2
SCATTERED   SEE STORM-SCATTERED
     O'DRISCOLL SCATTERED THE CARDS . . . .   145 HOST OF AIR   37
     AND SCATTERED THE CARDS WITH A CRY, ...   145 HOST OF AIR   V   38
     AND ALL THE BIRDS ARE SCATTERED. O! O! O! O! . . . . .   241 SHADOW WATER B   395
     AND ALL THE BIRDS ARE SCATTERED--O! O! O! . . . . . .   251 SHADOW WATER B   594
     SCATTERED ON THE LEVEL GRASS . . . .   530 DELPHIC ORACLE   6
SCENE
     AS THOUGH MY SORROW WERE A SCENE . . . .   452 HUMAN DIGNITY   5
     A SCENE WELL SET AND EXCELLENT COMPANY. . . . . . .   489 COOLE PARK 29   16
     AND HALF IS HALF AND YET IS ALL THE SCENE. . . . . .   500 VACILLATION   14
     WHAT MATTER FOR THE SCENE, THE SCENE ONCE GONE! . . . .   542 PARN FUNERAL 1   19
     WHAT MATTER FOR THE SCENE, THE SCENE ONCE GONE! . . . .   542 PARN FUNERAL 1   19
     YET THEY, SHOULD THE LAST SCENE BE THERE, ...   565 LAPIS LAZULI   12
     ON ALL THE TRAGIC SCENE THEY STARE. . . . .   567 LAPIS LAZULI   52
     ROUNDS A MIGHTY SCENE, ...   599 STONE CROSS   22
     OR FROM THE PAINTED SCENE . . . .   608 SONGS BURDEN 3   4
     BEFORE THE PAINTED SCENE. . . . .   608 SONGS BURDEN 3   17
     WHERE BEN BULBEN SETS THE SCENE. . . . .   637 BEN BULBEN   11
SCENERY
     AND CHOSEN WHAT SCENERY HAD PLEASED ME BEST." . . . . .   352 PEOPLE   21
SCENES   SEE DROP-SCENES
     AND ALL THE DROP SCENES DROP AT ONCE . . . .   566 LAPIS LAZULI   V   22
SCENT
     O SCENT OF THE BROKEN APPLES! . . . .   774 COME RIDE   14
SCENTED
     TO THE SCENTED OAKEN PRESS. . . . .   124 CATHLEEN PARA   8
     NEITHER CATALPA-TREE NOR SCENTED LIME . . . .   435 NEW FACES   2
     NEITHER CATALPA TREE NOR SCENTED LIME . . . .   435 NEW FACES   V   2
SCENTS
     THE SUMMERS FLING THEIR SCENTS? AH, SUBTILE AND SLOW, . .   675 ISLE STAT II 3   231

688

		PAGE	TITLE		LINE

SCEOLAN
WITH BRAN, SCEOLAN, AND LOMAIR, ... 3 OISIN 1 15
AND BRAN, SCEOLAN, AND LOMAIR, ... 11 OISIN 1 125
I MUSED ON THE CHASE WITH THE FENIANS, AND BRAN, SCEOLAN, 47 OISIN 3 5
    LOMAIR,
WHEN THE FENIANS MADE FORAY AT MORNING WITH BRAN, SCEOLAN, 54 OISIN 3 104
    LOMAIR.
WHAT PLACE HAVE CAOILTE AND CONAN, AND BRAN, SCEOLAN, 61 OISIN 3 195
    LOMAIR?
I WILL GO TO CAOILTE, AND CONAN, AND BRAN, SCEOLAN, LOMAIR, 63 OISIN 3 223

SCEPTRE
AND ONE A SCEPTRE FLASHING OUT . . . . 17 OISIN 1 251
AND KISSED THE SCEPTRE WITH RED LIPS, ... 18 OISIN 1 258
HE HELD THAT FLASHING SCEPTRE UP. . . . . 18 OISIN 1 260
AROUND A SCEPTRE OF ALL LIGHTS, ... 18 OISIN 1 V 254
AND KISSED THE SCEPTRE WITH HOT LIPS, ... 18 OISIN 1 V 258

SCHOLAR
OLD COUNTRY SCHOLAR, ROBERT EMMET'S FRIEND, ... 269 PARDON FATHERS 5
MERCHANT AND SCHOLAR WHO HAVE LEFT ME BLOOD . . . . . 269 PARDON FATHERS 7
AND COUNTRY SCHOLAR, ROBERT EMMET'S FRIEND, ... 269 PARDON FATHERS V 5
SOLDIER, SCHOLAR, HORSEMAN, HE, ... 327 ROBERT GREGORY 70
SOLDIER, SCHOLAR, HORSEMAN, HE, ... 327 ROBERT GREGORY 78
SOLDIER, SCHOLAR, HORSEMAN, HE, ... 327 ROBERT GREGORY 86
HERE, TRAVELLER, SCHOLAR, POET, TAKE YOUR STAND . . . . 489 COOLE PARK 29 25

SCHOLARLY
OF ALL THAT SCHOLARLY GENERATIONS HAD HELD DEAR, ... 603 GALLERY REVIS V 37A

SCHOLARS
THE SCHOLARS . . . . 337 SCHOLARS T
A STRING OF SCHOLARS WENT IN FEAR . . . . 381 SONG OF FOOL 7
FOR SCHOLARS AND FOR POETS AFTER US, ... 488 COOLE PARK 29 6

SCHOOL
ALTHOUGH THEY DO NOT TALK OF IT AT SCHOOL-- . . . . . 205 ADAMS CURSE 19
ALTHOUGH WE NEVER HEARD OF IT AT SCHOOL. . . . . . . 205 ADAMS CURSE V 19
THAT GRAMMAR SCHOOL OF COURTESIES . . . . 288 TO WEALTHY MAN 15
THAT TOSSED A BARE HEEL WHEN AT SCHOOL, ... 301 RUN PARADISE 19
YOU MAY, THAT MIRROR FOR A SCHOOL, ... 335 YOUNG BEAUTY 7
THE MALL AND EADES'S GRAMMAR SCHOOL, ... 360 ALF POLLEXFEN 15
I SEE A SCHOOL BOY WHEN I THINK OF HIM . . . . 370 EGO DOMINUS V 55
THEY SAY SUCH DIFFERENT THINGS AT SCHOOL. . . . . . . 387 ROBARTES DANCE 52
THIS MAN HAD KEPT A SCHOOL . . . . 392 EASTER 1916 24
THIS MAN HAD MANAGED A SCHOOL . . . . 392 EASTER 1916 V 24
NOR IS THERE SINGING SCHOOL BUT STUDYING . . . . . . 407 SAIL BYZANTIUM 13
AND THERE'S NO SINGING SCHOOL BUT STUDYING . . . . . 407 SAIL BYZANTIUM V 13
IN A LEARNED SCHOOL . . . . 416 TOWER 183
AMONG SCHOOL CHILDREN . . . . 443 SCHOOL CHILDR T
PREFERRED TO TEACH A SCHOOL . . . . 472 ALL SOUL NIGHT 46
BUT OUTGREW THAT SCHOOL, ... 506 REMORSE SPEECH 2
THEIR SCHOOL A CROWD, HIS MASTER SOLITUDE; . . . . . 543 PARN FUNERAL 2 10
THEIR SCHOOL THE CROWD, HIS MASTER SOLITUDE, ... 543 PARN FUNERAL 2 V 10
THEIR SCHOOL A CROWD, HIS MASTER'S SOLITUDE; . . . . 543 PARN FUNERAL 2 V 10
HIS CHOSEN COMRADES THOUGHT AT SCHOOL . . . . 576 WHAT THEN 1
I CAME THE FIRST TIME TO THY VILLAGE SCHOOL? . . . . . 713 FERENCZ RENYI 90

SCHOOLBOY
BY THE STAMMERING SCHOOLBOY SAID, ... 65 HAPPY SHEPHERD 15
I SEE A SCHOOLBOY WHEN I THINK OF HIM, ... 370 EGO DOMINUS 55

SCHOOLCHILDREN
AMONG SCHOOLCHILDREN . . . . 443 SCHOOL CHILDR V T

SCHOOLING
WHAT SCHOOLING HAD THESE FOUR? THEY WALKED THE ROADS . . 487 SEVEN SAGES 24
THEY HAVE SCHOOLING OF THEIR OWN, BUT I PASS THEIR 580 CURSE CROMWELL 13
    SCHOOLING BY,
THEY HAVE SCHOOLING OF THEIR OWN, BUT I PASS THEIR 580 CURSE CROMWELL 13
    SCHOOLING BY,

SCHOOLMASTER
ONCE HE LIVED A SCHOOLMASTER . . . . 381 SONG OF FOOL 5
SCHOOLMASTER HE, A DREAMER, FIDDLER, FIRST . . . . . . 709 FERENCZ RENYI 11

SCHOOLMASTERS
OF BANKERS, SCHOOLMASTERS, AND CLERGYMEN . . . . . . 205 ADAMS CURSE 13

SCHOOLROOM
I WALK THROUGH THE LONG SCHOOLROOM QUESTIONING; . . . . 443 SCHOOL CHILDR 1

SCOFF
I CAN SCOFF AND LOUR . . . . 510 JANE JUDGMENT 8
HOW SINFULLY THE WICKED SCOFF!" . . . . 725 LEGEND 22
SCOFF THEY AT THE MODERN EARTH-- . . . . 727 LOVERS QUARREL 38

SCOLD
AND SCOLD FOR AN HOUR." . . . . 510 JANE JUDGMENT 9
WHILE WE SHAKE OUR HEADS AND SCOLD . . . . 727 LOVERS QUARREL 54

SCONCE
WHEN EVERY SILVER CANDLESTICK OR SCONCE . . . . . . 410 TOWER 26

SCOOPED
HAD SCOOPED OUT PHARAOH'S MUMMY. I--THOUGH HEART MIGHT 503 VACILLATION 84
    FIND RELIEF

SCORE   SEE FOUR-SCORE
WHEN, WEEPING SCORE BY SCORE, ... 93 FATHER OHART 26
WHEN, WEEPING SCORE BY SCORE, ... 93 FATHER OHART 26
SENT FOR HIS DRUIDS TWENTY SCORE AND TEN, ... 110 CUCHULAIN SEA V 76
THERE'S NOTHING OF HIM LEFT BUT HALF A SCORE . . . . 341 SHEP GOATHERD 56
AND THERE'S A SCORE OF DUCHESSES, SURPASSING WOMANKIND, 353 HIS PHOENIX 5
AND THERE'S A SCORE OF DUCHESSES, SURPASSING WOMAN-KIND, 353 HIS PHOENIX V 5
OR ELSE BY TOASTING HER A SCORE OF TIMES, ... 410 TOWER 42
GATHERED A SCORE OF HORSE AND SPENT HIS DAYS . . . . 420 MY HOUSE 22

689

		PAGE	TITLE		LINE

SCORE   (CONTINUED)
HIS DWINDLING SCORE AND HE SEEMED CASTAWAYS . . . . . . 420 MY HOUSE   25
HIS DWINDLING SCORE AND HE SEEMED CAST--A-WAYS . . . . . 420 MY HOUSE   V   25
AND WRITERS BY THE SCORE. . . . . 582 ROGER CASEMENT   16
SO WHEN I TAKE ON HALF A SCORE . . . . 605 SONGS BURDEN 1   7
MY COUSINS BY THE SCORE, ... 620 JOHN KINSELLA   6
A SCORE OF YARDS OFF 'NEATH A WILLOW, SHOT. . . . . . . 712 FERENCZ RENYI   65
DID I NOT FOLLOW WITH A SCORE OF SHIPS? . . . . 749 SHADOW WATER A   36
SCORES
AND THERE ARE--BUT NO MATTER IF THERE ARE SCORES BESIDE: 354 HIS PHOENIX   15
SCORN
WENT THE LAUGHTER OF SCORN FROM MY MOUTH . . . . 58 OISIN 3   168
WHO WAS IT PUT SO GREAT A SCORN . . . . 190 BAILE AILLINN   41
IN SCORN OF THIS AUDIENCE, ... 348 FISHERMAN   27
IF BUT IMAGINATION SCORN THE EARTH . . . . 478 SELF AND SOUL   21
OR, BY THE MOON EMBITTERED, SCORN ALOUD . . . . 498 BYZANTIUM   21
SCORN THE SORT NOW GROWING UP . . . . 639 BEN BULBEN   70
AND WHEN YOU CAME TO SCORN OUR LITTLE WARS . . . . . 749 SHADOW WATER A   V   34
SCORNIN'
AND STILL, WITH PITYIN', SCORNIN' EYE, ... 96 MOLL MAGEE   39
SCOT-FREE
TO CRAWL IN HER OWN BLOOD, AND GO SCOT-FREE: . . . . 429 NINETEEN 19   28
SCOURGE
OUR HEARTS ENDURE THE SCOURGE, THE PLAITED THORNS, THE WAY 172 TRAV PASSION   3
THE KNOTTED SCOURGE, THE NAIL-PIERCED HANDS, THE WOUNDED   172 TRAV PASSION   V   4
   SIDE,
SCOURING
LIKE THE EYES OF SOME GREAT KITE SCOURING THE WOODS, . . 283 TWO KINGS   150
SCOWL
SHE CAN, THOUGH EVERY FACE SHOULD SCOWL . . . . 405 FOR DAUGHTER   70
SCRATCH
IS TO SCRATCH YOUR HEAD . . . . 359 TO A SQUIRREL   7
SCREAM
JABBER AND SCREAM ABOUT HIM IN THE NIGHT: . . . . . . 34 OISIN 2   82
JABBER AND SCREAM. YET HE, FOR ALL HIS BOLD . . . . . 34 OISIN 2   V   82
OF MY LONG SPEAR, WITH SCREAM AND LAUGH. . . . . 84 MAD KING GOLL   V   34
AND THEREUPON THERE COMES THAT SCREAM . . . . 389 IMAGE PAST   5
AND HEARD THE SEA-WIND SCREAM UPON THE TOWER, ... 403 FOR DAUGHTER   10
AND UNDER THE ARCHES OF THE BRIDGE, AND SCREAM . . . 403 FOR DAUGHTER   11
THE DAWS CHATTER AND SCREAM, ... 415 TOWER   167
AS THOUGH TO STRANGLE HER, NO SCREAM . . . . 514 JANE GROWN OLD   4
CLIMB ON A WAGONETTE TO SCREAM. . . . . 626 OLD MEN BE MAD   8
NOW A SCREAM FROM ALL THOSE FISHERS, FOR THERE ON DECK   719 PHANTOM SHIP   19
   THERE BE
SCREAMED
ABOUT THEM: AND THE HORSE OF FAERY SCREAMED . . . . . 30 OISIN 2   24
HE SHIVERING PAUSED, AND RAISED HIS HEAD AND SCREAMED. . . 30 OISIN 2   V   25
A SQUIRREL WHINNIED AND A BIRD SCREAMED OUT: . . . . 278 TWO KINGS   34
JUNO'S PEACOCK SCREAMED. . . . . 422 MY TABLE   32
SCREAMS   SEE OUT-SCREAMS
SCREEN
I ROSE THAT I MIGHT SCREEN IT WITH A CLOTH. . . . . . 467 HARUN RASHID   131
AS THOUGH UPON A LIGHTED SCREEN, ... 626 OLD MEN BE MAD   12
NOW A NOTABLE MAN ON STAGE AND ON SCREEN: . . . . . . 790 DEDICATION   8
SCRIPTURE
THE LION AND THE HONEYCOMB, WHAT HAS SCRIPTURE SAID? . . 503 VACILLATION   88
THE LION AND THE HONEY-COMB, WHAT HAS SCRIPTURE SAID? . . 503 VACILLATION   V   88
SCRUB
AND THEN I MUST SCRUB AND BAKE AND SWEEP . . . . . . 150 OLD MOTHER   3
AND SCRUB A KITCHEN PAVEMENT, OR BREAK STONES . . . . 204 ADAMS CURSE   8
I SCRUB ITS FLOORS AND MAKE MY BED, ... 607 SONGS BURDEN 2   5
SCULLION
THE SCULLION GONE WILD." . . . . 349 HAWK   6
SCULPTOR
POET AND SCULPTOR, DO THE WORK, ... 638 BEN BULBEN   37
SCYTHE
I DO NOT NEED YOUR SCYTHE. MAY THAT BRING PEACE . . . . 721 WITCH VIVIEN   26
SEA   SEE HUMMING-SEA OVER-SEA
AND FOUND ON THE DOVE-GREY EDGE OF THE SEA . . . . . .   3 OISIN 1   19
THY WANDERING STEPS ACROSS THE SEA? . . . .   5 OISIN 1   V   51
ACROSS THE GLOSSY SEA." "OH, WILD . . . .   6 OISIN 1   V   58
OVER THE GLOSSY SEA." "O, WILD . . . .   6 OISIN 1   V   58
TO MY OWN KINGDOM IN THE SEA-- . . . .   8 OISIN 1   V   80A
WHOSE LONG WOOL WHITER THAN SEA FROTH FLOWS, ...   8 OISIN 1   V   90
AND STOOD BESIDE THE SEA TOGETHER: . . . .   9 OISIN 1   V   101B
WE RODE ACROSS THE OILY SEA, ... 10 OISIN 1   V   114
WE GALLOPED OVER THE GLOSSY SEA: . . . . 11 OISIN 1   132
ON, ON, WE GALLOPED O'ER THE SEA. . . . . 11 OISIN 1   V   132
NOW IN THE SEA THE SUN'S RIM SANK, ... 12 OISIN 1   V   153
WAS NOT MORE LEVEL THAN THE SEA, ... 13 OISIN 1   157
ROSE EVER OUT OF THE WARM SEA: . . . . 13 OISIN 1   172
AND LAUGHED LIKE MURMURS OF THE SEA: . . . . 15 OISIN 1   210
AMONG THE FOAMDROPS OF THE SEA, ... 20 OISIN 1   294
BESIDE THE SEA, WHERE, HUSHED AND SLOW, ... 20 OISIN 1   V   292
WHISPERED TO THE SEA WHOSE FLOW . . . . 20 OISIN 1   V   298
THE EVER-WINDING WAKEFUL SEA, ... 22 OISIN 1   V   338
OVER THE GLIMMERING PURPLE SEA. . . . . 25 OISIN 1   384
AND OTHERS SAT THEM BY THE SEA, ... 25 OISIN 1   V   390
WAS SLUMBERING HALF IN THE SEA WAYS: . . . . 26 OISIN 1   V   395
WHEN GOD SHALL COME FROM THE SEA WITH A SIGH . . . . . 28 OISIN 1   425
ON HORSE AND SEA AND SADDLE SHONE. . . . . 28 OISIN 1   V   427D

	PAGE	TITLE		LINE
SEA (CONTINUED)				
THAT HAS DRUNK FULL, SHE CROSSED THE MISTY SEA • • • •	30	OISIN 2		16
I LAY, AS OVER SEA THE LIGHT HOOVES GLANCED • • • •	30	OISIN 2	V	19A
AND BLACKNESS IN THE DARK. THE SEA ROLLED ROUND, • • • •	30	OISIN 2	V	23
HALF IN THE UNVESSELLED SEA, WE CLIMBED THE STAIR • • •	32	OISIN 2		47
HALF IN THE UNVESSELLED SEA. WE'D MOUNTED FAR; • • •	32	OISIN 2	V	47
HALF IN THE UNVESSELLED SEA, WE CLIMBED THE STAIRS • • •	32	OISIN 2	V	47
FLUTTER ALONG THE FROTH LIPS OF THE SEA. • • • • •	33	OISIN 2		58
FLUTTER ALONG THE FROTH LIPS OF THE SEA • • • • •	33	OISIN 2		64
FLUTTER ALONG THE FROTH-LIPS OF THE SEA • • • • •	33	OISIN 2	V	58
OH MAIDEN." "ARE YE SPIRITS OF THE SEA, • • • •	34	OISIN 2	V	78B
THAT SEA GOD'S NAME, WHO IN A DEEP CONTENT • • • • •	38	OISIN 2	V	129
THEN IN THAT HALL, LIT BY THE DIM SEA SHINE, • • • •	41	OISIN 2	V	187
BREWED BY THE SEA GODS, FROM HUGE CUPS THAT LAY • • •	41	OISIN 2	V	189
I FOUND, DROPPING SEA FOAM ON THE WIDE STAIR, • • • •	43	OISIN 2	V	215
INTO THE CLANGOUR OF THE WIND AND SEA. • • • • •	45	OISIN 2		234
SURLY AND DISTANT, WITH THE WINDS AND SEA;— • • • •	45	OISIN 2	V	234
GATHER SEA SLIME AND FALL THE SEAWARD WAY, • • • • •	45	OISIN 3	V	237
COMING OUT OF THE SEA AS THE DAWN COMES, A CHAUNT OF LOVE ON MY LIPS,	58	OISIN 3		158
COMING FORTH FROM THE SEA LIKE THE MORNING • • • • •	58	OISIN 3	V	158
GO GATHER BY THE HUMMING SEA • • • • •	66	HAPPY SHEPHERD		35
CRIED OUT, DIM SEA, HEAR MY MOST PITEOUS STORY! • • •	68	SAD SHEPHERD		9
THE SEA SWEPT ON AND CRIED HER OLD CRY STILL, • • • •	68	SAD SHEPHERD		10
"OH SEA, OLD SEA, HEAR THOU MY PITEOUS STORY!" • • •	68	SAD SHEPHERD	V	9
"OH SEA, OLD SEA, HEAR THOU MY PITEOUS STORY!" • • •	68	SAD SHEPHERD	V	9
WHO STILL WERE OLD WHEN THE GREAT SEA WAS YOUNG; • • •	74	ANASHU VIJAYA		69
RAGING AT HIS OWN IMAGE IN THE ENAMELLED SEA. • • • •	77	INDIAN TO LOVE		5
RAGES AT HIS OWN IMAGE IN THE ENAMELLED SEA • • • •	77	INDIAN TO LOVE		5
RAGING AT HIS OWN IMAGE IN THE DIM ENAMELLED SEA • • •	77	INDIAN TO LOVE	V	5
WHIPS TO THE SEA THE COWS AND SWINE." • • • •	82	MAD KING GOLL	V	16
AND I MUST WAIL BESIDE THE SEA • • • • •	86	MAD KING GOLL	V	67
I MUST AWAY BY WOOD AND SEA • • • • •	86	MAD KING GOLL	V	67
IN DANCING SILVER-SANDALLED ON THE SEA, • • • • •	101	ROSE UPON ROOD		7
IN DANCING SILVER SANDALLED ON THE SEA, • • • • •	101	ROSE UPON ROOD	V	7
IN THE WHITE BORDER OF THE MURMURING SEA! • • • • •	103	FERGUS DRUID		19
CUCHULAIN'S FIGHT WITH THE SEA • • • • • •	105	CUCHULAIN SEA		T
GO DWELL UPON THE SEA CLIFFS, VAPOUR HID, • • • • •	105	CUCHULAIN SEA		4
GO DWELL UPON THE SEA CLIFFS, VAPOUR-HID • • • • •	105	CUCHULAIN SEA	V	4
AND LOVELIER THAN THE MOON UPON THE SEA; • • • • •	106	CUCHULAIN SEA	V	16A
BETWEEN WOOD'S RIM AND THE HORSES OF THE SEA. • • • •	108	CUCHULAIN SEA		34
BETWEEN THE GAME AND THE HORSES OF THE SEA. • • • •	108	CUCHULAIN SEA	V	34
THAT HE MAY FIGHT THE HORSES OF THE SEA." • • • • •	111	CUCHULAIN SEA		81
STARED ON THE HORSES OF THE SEA, AND HEARD • • • •	111	CUCHULAIN SEA		84
THAT HE MAY FIGHT THE WAVES OF THE LOUD SEA." • • • •	111	CUCHULAIN SEA	V	81
THAT HE MIGHT FIGHT THE WAVES OF THE LOUD SEA." • • •	111	CUCHULAIN SEA	V	81
MADE YOU OF US, AND OF THE DIM GREY SEA. • • • • •	115	ROSE OF BATTLE		30
I WOULD THAT WE WERE, MY BELOVED, WHITE BIRDS ON THE FOAM OF THE SEA!	121	WHITE BIRDS		1
O WOULD THAT WE WERE, MY BELOVED, WHITE BIRDS ON THE FOAM OF THE SEA,	121	WHITE BIRDS	V	1
• • • BUOYED OUT ON THE FOAM OF THE SEA! • • • • •	122	WHITE BIRDS		12
AND THE WHITE BREAST OF THE DIM SEA • • • • •	126	GOES FERGUS		11
DESOLATE WINDS THAT CRY OVER THE WANDERING SEA! • • •	147	UNAPPEAS HOST		7
LIKE THE PALE CUP OF THE SEA, • • • • •	175	ELEMENT POWERS		14
AS THE LIGHT ON THE SEA, • • • • •	175	ELEMENT POWERS	V	14
FOLK DANCE LIKE A WAVE OF THE SEA! • • • • •	178	FIDDLER DOONEY		2
AND DANCE LIKE A WAVE OF THE SEA. • • • • •	179	FIDDLER DOONEY		20
AND DRAGS HIM THROUGH THE SEA. WELL, NET OR NONE, • •	224	SHADOW WATER B		57
WHAT RICHES CAN YOU FIND IN THIS WASTE SEA • • • •	226	SHADOW WATER B		97
WRUNG FROM THE COLD WOMEN OF THE SEA— • • • • •	237	SHADOW WATER B		343
FOR YOU ARE LOOKING AT THE SEA. DO YOU NOT KNOW • •	246	SHADOW WATER B		513
WHY ARE YOU LOOKING AT THE SEA? LOOK THERE! • • • •	246	SHADOW WATER B		516
THE ROPE'S IN TWO—IT FALLS INTO THE SEA, • • • • •	251	SHADOW WATER B		596
CRYING AMID THE GLITTERING SEA, • • • • •	254	HIS DREAM		17
WITH THE LOUD HOST BEFORE THE SEA, • • • • •	276	GREY ROCK		128
WHITER THAN CURDS, ITS EYES THE TINT OF THE SEA. • • •	277	TWO KINGS		7
TO DRINK OF THAT SALT BREATH OUT OF THE SEA • • • •	292	TO A SHADE		5
BY A COLD AND DESOLATE SEA, • • • • •	298	THREE HERMITS		2
AND FIND MY HEALTH AGAIN IN THE SEA AIR," • • • • •	299	BEGGAR CRIED		2
SEA NYMPHS IN THEIR PEARLY WAGGONS • • • • •	309	REALISTS	V	5
AND DIED IN THE GREAT WAR BEYOND THE SEA. • • • •	339	SHEP GOATHERD		22
A VISIONARY WHITE SEA BIRD • • • • •	361	ALF POLLEXFEN	V	37
MANACLE HIS SOUL UPON THE RED SEA BOTTOM. • • • •	372	ON GOING HOUSE		16
ACROSS THE BITTER SEA." • • • • •	396	ROSE TREE		6
CRIED OUT THE HOLLOWS OF THE SEA. • • • • •	397	POLIT PRISONER		24
OR BY THE MAREOTIC SEA. • • • • •	401	DEMON BEAST		45
OUT OF THE MURDEROUS INNOCENCE OF THE SEA. • • • •	403	FOR DAUGHTER		16
OF HORSES AND HORSES OF THE SEA, WHITE HORSES. • • •	447	COLONUS PRAISE		32
SHAKESPEAREAN FISH SWAM THE SEA, FAR AWAY FROM LAND; • •	485	THREE MOVEMENT		1
THAT DOLPHIN-TORN, THAT GONG-TORMENTED SEA. • • • •	498	BYZANTIUM		40
AND NOW WE STARE ASTONISHED AT THE SEA, • • • • •	534	HER TRIUMPH		11
BUT SANG, "O SEA-STARVED, HUNGRY SEA." • • • •	578	CRAZED GIRL		14
"O SEA—STARVED, HUNGRY SEA." • • • • •	578	CRAZED GIRL	V	14
"O SEA—STARVED, HUNGRY SEA." • • • • •	578	CRAZED GIRL	V	14
IT NEVER CROSSED THE SEA BECAUSE • • • • •	583	GHOST ROG CASE		3
JOHN BULL AND THE SEA ARE FRIENDS; • • • • •	583	GHOST ROG CASE		4
BUT THIS IS NOT THE OLD SEA • • • • •	583	GHOST ROG CASE		5
SMILING AT THE SEA, • • • • •	605	YOU CONTENT		20
CUCHULAIN FOUGHT THE UNGOVERNABLE SEA! • • • • •	630	CIRCUS ANIMALS		26
THE WOOD AND THE VALLEY AND SEA • • • • •	646	ISLE STAT I 1		42

SEA   (CONTINUED)

	PAGE	TITLE		LINE
AND THE DESOLATE SHUDDERING SEA.	648	ISLE STAT I 1		85
THE SPINNING STARS--THE TOILING SEA--WHIRL ROUND	665	ISLE STAT II 2		72
TILL THOU REMEMBEREST ONLY HOW THE SEA	670	ISLE STAT II 3		94
FAR FLEETER THAN THE MILLION-FOOTED SEA.	670	ISLE STAT II 3		108
HAS ROLLED AWAY THE STARS AND DRIED THE SEA	671	ISLE STAT II 3		146
ABOUT THE SEA. BEFORE HER LIES THAT YOUTH.	687	TWO TITANS		22
MAKING ALL ONE O'ER ROCK AND SEA AND SKIES:	687	TWO TITANS		28
IN CREVICED ROCKS, AND LAUGHED TO THE OLD SEA,	688	TWO TITANS		34
ALONG THE SEA: AND MANY A MAN GREW HUSHED	693	MOSADA 1		86
AYE AND SHAKES IN SEA GREEN WAVERINGS, ALONG THE FISHERS' STREET.	718	PHANTOM SHIP	V	2
ALL THE DROWNED THAT EVER WERE DROWNED FROM THAT VILLAGE BY THE SEA:	719	PHANTOM SHIP		20
ROLLS ALONG THE SEA SANDS WHITE.	732	STREET DANCERS		34
ON THE CLIFF BY THE SEA,	739	EARL PAUL		4
THEY ARE CHANGED AND AS GREY BIRDS FLY OUT TO SEA,	750	SHADOW WATER A		82
LEANS ON HIS ELBOWS, GAZING AT THE SEA.	752	SHADOW WATER A		127
LET THE SEA BEAR WITNESS.	770	BLOOD BOND		7
SEA-BIRD				
A VISIONARY WHITE SEA-BIRD	361	ALF POLLEXFEN		37
FRAIL BIRD, LIKE A WHITE SEA-BIRD ALONE	784	WOMANS BEAUTY		2
SEA-BORN				
SHOWED PRINTS OF SEA-BORN SCALES, WHILE DOWN THROUGH IT	37	OISIN 2		115
SEA-BORNE				
LIKE ANY ROCK-BRED, SEA-BORNE BIRD:	397	POLIT PRISONER		18
SEA-BORNE, OR BALANCED ON THE AIR	397	POLIT PRISONER		19
SEA-COVERED				
THE MOIL OF MY CENTURIES FILLED ME: AND GONE LIKE A SEA-COVERED STONE	51	OISIN 3		70
SEA-DASHED				
AND SUNKEN SHAPE, A NINE DAYS' CORPSE SEA-DASHED--	40	OISIN 2	V	179
SEAFARER				
SEAFARER, WAKE! WAS MY SLEEP LONG? LONG YEARS.	678	ISLE STAT II 3		292
SEAFARERS				
HE DOES NOT HATE SEAFARERS AS HE HATES	224	SHADOW WATER B		53
SEA-FOAM				
I FOUND, DROPPING SEA-FOAM ON THE WIDE STAIR,	43	OISIN 2		215
SEA-FROTH				
WHOSE LONG WOOL WHITER THAN SEA-FROTH FLOWS,	8	OISIN 1		90
SEAGHAN				
HOW ARE WE BETTER OFF THAN SEAGHAN THE FOOL,	228	SHADOW WATER B		129
WE HAVE BEEN NO BETTER OFF THAN SEAGHAN THE FOOL,	228	SHADOW WATER B	V	129
SEA-GOD				
SEA-GOD, THAT ONCE, TO GIVE HIS SLAVES CONTENT,	38	OISIN 2	V	129
SEA-GOD'S				
THAT SEA-GOD'S NAME, WHO IN A DEEP CONTENT	38	OISIN 2		129
SEA-GODS				
BY MACE AND SPEAR AND SWORD OF SEA-GODS, NAILS	31	OISIN 2	V	30A
BREWED BY THE SEA-GODS, FROM HUGE CUPS THAT LAY	41	OISIN 2		189
UPON THE LIPS OF SEA-GODS IN THEIR DAY!	41	OISIN 2		190
BREWED OF THE SEA-GODS, FROM HUGE CUPS THAT LAY	41	OISIN 2	V	189
SEA-GREEN				
AND STARED INTO THE SEA-GREEN EYE, AND SO	278	TWO KINGS		25
AND STARED INTO THE SEA-GREEN EYES, AND SO	278	TWO KINGS	V	25
WITH OLD MILL BOARDS AND SEA-GREEN SLATES,	406	CARVED STONE		2
AY, AND SHAKES IN SEA-GREEN WAVERINGS ALONG THE FISHERS' STREET:	718	PHANTOM SHIP		2
SEAGULL				
I SAW A FOAM-WHITE SEAGULL DRIFT AND FLOAT	36	OISIN 2		105
CLOTHING HIM ROUND, I SAW A SEAGULL FLOAT	36	OISIN 2	V	105
SEA-HORSES				
THOSE GREAT SEA-HORSES BARE THEIR TEETH AND LAUGH AT THE DAWN.	623	HIGH TALK		14
SEA-KING				
HATH COME A SEA-KING MASTERFUL,	82	MAD KING GOLL	V	15
SOUTHWARD A SEA-KING MASTERFUL	82	MAD KING GOLL	V	15
COMES A SEA-KING MASTERFUL	82	MAD KING GOLL	V	15
SEAL				
THAT WAXEN SEAL, THAT SIGNATURE,	598	MODEL LAUREATE		21
LEST ON THINE HEART THE STONY SEAL	667	ISLE STAT II 3		41
SEALED				
ABOVE THESE MEN WHOSE MOUTHS WERE SEALED	656	ISLE STAT I 3		27
BE ONE? I THINK ALL'S FINISHED NOW AND SEALED.	701	MOSADA 3		62
SEALING				
WITH DEW, AS THOUGH 'TWERE SEALING THEM FOR DEATH.	691	MOSADA 1		22
SEAMAN				
MANY A LANDSMAN, MANY A SEAMAN.	82	MAD KING GOLL	V	4
THESE HANDS SLEW MANY A SEAMAN BOLD.	83	MAD KING GOLL	V	23
SEAMEN				
MOVED ROUND ME, OF SEAMEN OR LANDSMEN, ALL WHO ARE WINTER TALES:	53	OISIN 3		86
THE HEARTS OF THE WORLD-TROUBLING SEAMEN,	82	MAD KING GOLL		4
SEAMEW				
"I HEARD A SEAMEW CRY,	308	PLAYER QUEEN	V	14
SEA-MEW				
"I HEARD A SEA-MEW CRY,	308	PLAYER QUEEN		14
SEAMLESS				
WATCHED HER THOSE SEAMLESS FACES FROM THE VALLEY'S GLIMMERING GIRTH:	55	OISIN 3		122

692

		PAGE	TITLE	LINE

SEAMLESS (CONTINUED)
     WATCHED HER THOSE SEAMLESS FACES FROM THE VALLEY'S MURAL   55 OISIN 3   V 122
       GIRTH
SEA-NYMPHS
     SEA-NYMPHS IN THEIR PEARLY WAGONS . . . .   309 REALISTS   5
SEARCH
     YONDER'S THE ISLE IN SEARCH WHEREOF WE CAME: . . . . .   662 ISLE STAT II 2   13
     REMEMBERING THEE, I SEARCH OUT THESE FAINT FLOWERS . . .   704 REMEMBRANCE   1
SEARCHED
     SEARCHED THE UNSEARCHABLE--WHY GOOD MEN WEEP: . . . . .   710 FERENCZ RENYI   32
SEA-RIDER
     FIRST THAT SEA-RIDER OISIN LED BY THE NOSE . . . . . .   629 CIRCUS ANIMALS   10
SEA-ROTTED
     WITH CHAIN SEA-ROTTED, ROUND HER MIDDLE TIED, ...   34 OISIN 2   V   75
SEA'S
     ROSE EVER FROM THE SEA'S WARM FLOOR, ...   13 OISIN 1   V 172
     THE FLOWERS STILL GREW THERE: FAR ON THE SEA'S WASTE . .   39 OISIN 2   163
     THE FLOWERS STILL GREW THERE. MOVED BEYOND HIM THE SEA'S   39 OISIN 2   V 163
       WASTE:
     AND WE STOOD ON A SEA'S EDGE WE SAW NOT: . . . . . .   47 OISIN 3   11
     AND WE RODE ON THE PLAINS OF THE SEA'S EDGE: . . . . .   48 OISIN 3   13
     . . . THE SEA'S EDGE BARREN AND GREY, ...   48 OISIN 3   13
     . . . THE SOUND OF THE SEA'S VAGUE DRUM? . . . . . .   56 OISIN 3   135
     AND I RODE BY THE PLAINS OF THE SEA'S EDGE, ...   56 OISIN 3   141
     AND THE WINDS MADE THE SANDS ON THE SEA'S EDGE . . . .   57 OISIN 3   145
     I TURNED AND RODE TO THE WESTWARD, AND FOLLOWED THE SEA'S   60 OISIN 3   183
       OLD SHOUT
     AND RODE ON TILL OVER THE WORLD'S RIM FLOATED THE SEA'S   60 OISIN 3   V 183
       OLD SHOUT,
     MORE FLEETING THAN THE SEA'S FOAM-FICKLE FACE, ...   112 ROSE OF WORLD V   8
     MORE FLEETING THAN THE SEA'S FOAM FICKLE FACE, ...   112 ROSE OF WORLD V   8
     OR COMES IN LAUGHTER FROM THE SEA'S SAD LIPS, ...   114 ROSE OF BATTLE   19
     THAT ROAR IN THE SEA'S ROAR? . . . .   583 GHOST ROG CASE   8
     AS THE SEA'S FURROWS ON A SEA-TOST SHELL, ...   660 ISLE STAT II 1   51
     IN THE SOUTH SEA'S AZURE MILES, ...   732 STREET DANCERS   28
SEAS
     AND BIRDS THAT ON THE SEVEN SEAS RANGE. . . . .   4 OISIN 1   V 27A
     AND THE GENTLE WAVES OF THE SUMMER SEAS, ...   27 OISIN 1   418
     FOR HE IS STRONG AND CRAFTY AS THE SEAS . . . . . .   35 OISIN 2   83
     OUT OF THE SEVENFOLD SEAS, BUILT THE DARK HALL . . . .   38 OISIN 2   131
     FROM THE WHOLE SEVEN SEAS, THOSE TOWERS SET . . . . .   38 OISIN 2   V 131
     OUT OF THE SEVEN-FOLD SEAS, BUILT THE DARK HALL . . . .   38 OISIN 2   V 131
     LIKE AN ARMY OF OLD MEN LONGING FOR REST FROM THE MOAN   48 OISIN 3   16
       OF THE SEAS.
     . . . WHEN THE SEVENFOLD SEAS WERE YOUNG. . . . . . .   50 OISIN 3   52
     . . . AND PACING THE SHORES OF THE WANDERING SEAS, . . .   50 OISIN 3   55
     . . . WHEN THE SEVEN-FOLD SEAS WERE YOUNG: . . . . . .   50 OISIN 3   V   52
     . . . AND PACING THE SHORES OF THE SEVEN SEAS, ...   50 OISIN 3   V   55
     NO MORE TO CRAWL ON THE SEAS WITH LONG OARS MILE AFTER   55 OISIN 3   119
       MILE,
     "IN THE ISLES OF THE FARTHEST SEAS WHERE ONLY THE SPIRITS   56 OISIN 3   133
       COME.
     LIKE AN ARMY OF OLD MEN LONGING FOR REST FROM THE MOAN   57 OISIN 3   144
       OF THE SEAS.
     LIKE AN ARMY OF OLD MEN LOUNGING FOR REST FROM THE FOAM   57 OISIN 3   144
       OF THE SEAS.
     O SWIFT ON THE SEAS ALL DAY AND NIGHT . . . .   70 CLOAK BOAT   8
     WHERE PEOPLE LOVE BESIDE THE RAVELLED SEAS: . . . . .   126 DREAM OF FAERY   9
     WHERE PEOPLE LOVE BESIDE STAR-LADEN SEAS: . . . . . .   126 DREAM OF FAERY V   9
     AH, EXILES WANDERING OVER LANDS AND SEAS, ...   129 BOOK STORIES   9
     AH, EXILES, WANDERING OVER MANY SEAS, ...   129 BOOK STORIES V   9
     FOR THE GREY WINDS ARE BLOWING UP, OUT OF THE CLINGING   207 HANRAHANS SONG V   12
       SEAS:
     HAS HE NOT LED US INTO THESE WASTE SEAS . . . . . .   221 SHADOW WATER B   1
     AND BRING US INTO POPULOUS SEAS AGAIN? . . . .   225 SHADOW WATER B   74
     IF HE HAD BROUGHT US AMONG PEOPLED SEAS, ...   225 SHADOW WATER B V 68C
     THAT WEIGH AND MEASURE ALL IN THESE WASTE SEAS-- . . . .   235 SHADOW WATER B   292
     AS NOW. DOES WANDERING IN THESE DESOLATE SEAS . . . .   236 SHADOW WATER B   314
     IS SHAKEN IN THESE SEAS, AND WHAT ONE DOES . . . . .   237 SHADOW WATER B   339
     WHAT MORE HAVE YOU TO LOOK FOR ON THE SEAS? . . . . .   248 SHADOW WATER B   543
     THAT TURNS AND CHANGES LIKE HIS DRAUGHTY SEAS? . . . .   265 ABBEY THEATRE   12
     AND THOUGH THEY HAVE TO CROSS THE LOUGHLAN SEAS . . . .   282 TWO KINGS   V   113
     QUIET LANDS OR UNQUIET SEAS . . . .   360 ALF POLLEXFEN   19
     THAT HAVE THE FRENZY OF OUR WESTERN SEAS, ...   384 VISION ROBART   62
     THE SALMON-FALLS, THE MACKEREL-CROWDED SEAS, ...   407 SAIL BYZANTIUM   4
     THE SALMON FALLS, THE MACKEREL-CROWDED SEAS, ...   407 SAIL BYZANTIUM V   4
     AND THEREFORE I HAVE SAILED THE SEAS AND COME . . . .   408 SAIL BYZANTIUM   15
     AND THEREFORE HAVE I SAILED THE SEAS AND COME . . . .   408 SAIL BYZANTIUM V   15
     TILL THE DAWN BREAK UPON THOSE MINGLED SEAS. . . . . .   494 AT ALGECIRAS   6
     BUFFETED BY SUCH SEAS: . . . .   530 DELPHIC ORACLE   2
     O SWIFT ON THE SEAS ALL DAY AND NIGHT . . . . . .   666 ISLE STAT II 3   8
     WHERE SPICE-ISLES NESTLE ON THE STAR-TROD SEAS, ...   682 SEEKER   17
     FROM WASTE SEAS CROSS'D, YET EVER GARRULOUS) . . . . .   690 MOSADA 1   9
     HER SOUL FROM SEAS OF ENDLESS FLAME IN HELL, ...   698 MOSADA 2   47
     WHERE A SHELL THE SEAS ANOINT, ...   732 STREET DANCERS   32
     AND PRAISED YOUR WAR AMONG THE ENDLESS SEAS, ...   749 SHADOW WATER A   35
     AND PRAISE A WAR AMONG THE ENDLESS SEAS, ...   749 SHADOW WATER A V   35
     A GALLEY FROM THE LOCHLANN SEAS: HER FLAG . . . . . .   751 SHADOW WATER A   98
SEAS'
     IN THE SOUTH SEAS' AZURE MILES, ...   732 STREET DANCERS V   28

```
                                                    PAGE      TITLE        LINE
SEA-SANDS
   ROLLS ALONG THE SEA-SANDS WHITE.  . . . . . . . .   732 STREET DANCERS V   34
SEA-SHELL
   FOR BROOCH 'TWAS BOUND WITH A BRIGHT SEA-SHELL, . . . .     4 OISIN 1     V   28
   AS IF SOME MARVELLOUS EMPTY SEA-SHELL FLUNG  . . . . .   417 ANCEST HOUSES    13
SEA-SHELLS
   OR SAD SEA-SHELLS WHERE LITTLE ECHOES SIT?  . . . . . .   650 ISLE STAT I 1  149
SEASHINE
   THE SEASHINE ON OUR FACES, WE OUR WAY  . . . . . . .    41 OISIN 2      V 184B
SEA-SHINE
   THEN IN THAT HALL, LIT BY THE DIM SEA-SHINE,  . . . . .    41 OISIN 2        187
SEASHORE
   NOR THIS THE OLD SEASHORE.  . . . . . . . . . . .   583 GHOST ROG CASE     6
   GIRLS DOWN ON THE SEASHORE  . . . . . . . . . .   588 OLD WICKED MAN    30
SEA-SLIME
   GATHER SEA-SLIME AND FALL THE SEAWARD WAY,  . . . . .    45 OISIN 2        237
   GATHERS SEA-SLIME AND GOES THE SEAWARD WAY,  . . . . .    45 OISIN 2      V 237
SEASON
   LET US PART, ERE THE SEASON OF PASSION FORGET US,  . . . .    79 FALLING LEAVES     7
   I COULD WEEP THAT THE OLD IS OUT OF SEASON.  . . . . .   199 ARROW              8
   VANISHED, AND LEFT BUT MEMORIES, THAT SHOULD BE OUT OF    316 COLD HEAVEN        5
      SEASON
   "AND YET THE JASMINE SEASON WARMS OUR BLOOD."  . . . . .   464 HARUN RASHID      73
   AS THOUGH THEIR SEASON HAD NO DATE,  . . . . . . .   736 SUMMER EVENING    10
SEASONS
   OH, PATRICK, THERE A HUNDRED SEASONS  . . . . . . .    23 OISIN 1      V 345B
   A HUNDRED SEASONS; FOR A SOUND OF TEARS  . . · . . .    30 OISIN 2      V  18
   THEY NEVER SAW HOW SEASONS RUN,  . . . . . . . .   432 NINETEEN 19      101
   YOU THINK THAT LOVE HAS SEASONS, AND YOU THINK  . . . .   464 HARUN RASHID      75
   HAVE I NOT SEEN A THOUSAND SEASONS EBB AND FLOW  . . . .   675 ISLE STAT II 3   229
SEA-SPRUNG
   OF SEA-SPRUNG PEARL, AND QUEENS OF FAIRY LANDS  . . . . .    29 OISIN 2      V  10A
   THE NETTED MARKS OF CRAWLING SCALES SEA-SPRUNG  . . . .    37 OISIN 2      V 115
SEA-STARVED
   BUT SANG, "O SEA-STARVED, HUNGRY SEA."  . . . . . .   578 CRAZED GIRL       14
SEA-STREWN
   AND HOW, WHEN FADES THE SEA-STREWN ROSE OF DAY,  . . . .   128 DREAM OF FAERY V  33
SEAT
   DESERTED ON A DOORWAY SEAT,  . . . . . . . . . .    85 MAD KING GOLL      56
   DESERTED IN A DOORWAY SEAT,  . . . . . . . . . . .    85 MAD KING GOLL  V  56
   WEARY AND KIND ONE LINGERED BY HIS SEAT;  . . . . . .   112 ROSE OF WORLD     13
   WEARY AND KIND ONE STOOD BESIDE HIS SEAT;  . . . . .   112 ROSE OF WORLD  V  13
   THE HILL SEAT OF LAIGHEN, BECAUSE  . . . . . . . .   194 BAILE AILLINN    130
   ALWAYS IN HIS ONE SEAT, AND BID ME CARE HIM  . . . . .   280 TWO KINGS         80
   THE CRAVEN MAN IN HIS SEAT,  . . . . . . . . . .   347 FISHERMAN         15
   IN DAMASK CLOTHED AND ON A SEAT  . . . . . . . .   440 WISDOM             9
   IN THE LONG GRASS--FOUR EYES DROOP LOW--A SEAT  . . .   716 DWELT SYCAMORE    11
SEATED
   A BEAUTIFUL SEATED BOY; A SACRED BOW;  . . . . . .   541 PARN FUNERAL 1    10
   DELIGHT TO IMAGINE THEM SEATED THERE;  . . . . . .   567 LAPIS LAZULI      50
   AUGUSTA GREGORY SEATED AT HER GREAT ORMOLU TABLE,  . . .   577 LOFTY THINGS       7
   COME HERE.  BE SEATED NOW; I'D BUY OF YOU.  . . . . .   720 WITCH VIVIEN      17
SEA-TOST
   AS THE SEA'S FURROWS ON A SEA-TOST SHELL,  . . . . .   660 ISLE STAT II 1    51
SEATS
   TO BUILD THE CIRCLING SEATS, WHERE HIGH IN AIR  . . . .   699 MOSADA 3          18
   BEFORE WE TAKE OUR SEATS ABOVE THE CROWD.  . . . . .   704 MOSADA 3         134
SEAWARD
   GATHER SEA-SLIME AND FALL THE SEAWARD WAY,  . . . . .    45 OISIN 2        237
   GATHERS SEA-SLIME AND GOES THE SEAWARD WAY,  . . . . .    45 OISIN 2      V 237
   GATHER SEA SLIME AND FALL THE SEAWARD WAY,  . . . . .    45 OISIN 2      V 237
SEAWAYS
   BUT THE SAD DWELLER BY THE SEAWAYS LONE  . . . . .    69 SAD SHEPHERD   V  26
SEA-WAYS
   WAS SLUMBERING HALF IN THE SEA-WAYS;  . . . . . .    26 OISIN 1          395
   WATCHED THE OLD SUN THAT IN SEA-WAYS  . . . . . .    26 OISIN 1      V 394
   BUT THE SAD DWELLER BY THE SEA-WAYS LONE  . . . . .    69 SAD SHEPHERD      26
SEAWEED
   FROM THE SEAWEED ON THE STRAND.  . . . . . . . .   597 COLONEL MARTIN    71
SEA-WEED
   FROM THE SEA-WEED ON THE STRAND.  . . . . . . . .   597 COLONEL MARTIN V  71
SEAWEED-COVERED
   THE SEAWEED-COVERED PILLARS; AND THE GREEN  . . . . .    31 OISIN 2           32
SEA-WEEDY
   THAT OLD, SEA-WEEDY, SQUARED, THREE HUNDRED FEET  . . .    31 OISIN 2      V  30C
SEA-WIND
   AND HEARD THE SEA-WIND SCREAM UPON THE TOWER,  . . . .   403 FOR DAUGHTER      10
   WHEN SEA-WIND SWEPT THE CORNER, STANDS;  . . . . . .   566 LAPIS LAZULI      32
SEA-WORLD
   AND SHAKES O'ER THE WIDTH OF THE SEA-WORLD BORDER  . . .    28 OISIN 1      V 423C
SEA-WORN
   A SEA-WORN WAIF CAME FLOATING BY.  . . . . . . . .    24 OISIN 1      V 365
   "MY FATHER DWELLS AMONG THE SEA-WORN BANDS,  . . . . .   107 CUCHULAIN SEA  V  25
SECOND
   AND CAME AGAIN, HOLDING A SECOND LIGHT  . . . . . .    37 OISIN 2          124
   AWHILE, AND CAME AGAIN, A SECOND LIGHT  . . . . . .    37 OISIN 2      V 124
   NO SECOND TROY  . . . . . . . . . . . . . .   256 NO SECOND TROY     T
   TO A WEALTHY MAN WHO PROMISED A SECOND SUBSCRIPTION . . .   287 TO WEALTHY MAN     T
   THE SECOND; "I SHALL LEARN A TRADE";  . . . . . . .   296 THREE BEGGARS     32
   THE SECOND; "I HAVE THOUGHT AGAIN;  . . . . . . . .   296 THREE BEGGARS     36
   AND WHEN THE SECOND TWILIGHT BROUGHT  . . . . . . .   296 THREE BEGGARS     42
```

SECOND   (CONTINUED)
 ABOUT A FARM," THE SECOND CRIED. . . . .   296 THREE BEGGARS   V   38
 SECOND RUMMAGED FOR A FLEA. . . . .   298 THREE HERMITS   4
 SO THE FIRST, BUT NOW THE SECOND. . . . .   298 THREE HERMITS   13
 BUT THE SECOND MOCKED HIS MOAN. . . . .   299 THREE HERMITS   24
 WHAT'S DYING BUT A SECOND WIND? . . . .   338 TOM OROUGHLEY   11
 "HE GROWS YOUNGER EVERY SECOND. . . . .   342 SHEP GOATHERD   89
 THE SECOND COMING . . . .   401 SECOND COMING   T
 SURELY THE SECOND COMING IS AT HAND. . . . .   402 SECOND COMING   10
 THE SECOND COMING! HARDLY ARE THOSE WORDS OUT . . . .   402 SECOND COMING   11
 THE SECOND BEST'S A GAY GOODNIGHT AND QUICKLY TURN AWAY.   459 FROM OEDIPUS   12
 AND IF IT TAKE THE SECOND MUST REFUSE . . . . . .   491 COOLE BALLYLEE V   40C
 AND IF IT TAKE THE SECOND MUST REFUSE . . . . . .   495 CHOICE   3
 THREE SONGS TO THE SAME TUNE   SECOND SONG . . . .   544 TO SAME TUNE 1 V   T
 THE LADY'S SECOND SONG . . . .   572 LADYS 2ND SONG   T
 THE CHAMBERMAID'S SECOND SONG . . . .   575 MAIDS 2ND SONG   T
 TILL CERTAIN SECOND THOUGHTS HAVE COME . . . . . .   791 REPRISALS   12
SECOND-BEST
 I CHOOSE THE SECOND-BEST. . . . .   590 OLD WICKED MAN   60
SECRET
 SNATCHING THE BIRD IN SECRET! NOR KNEW I, EMBOSOMED APART,   57 OISIN 3   150
 IN MY MOST SECRET SPIRIT GREW . . . .   83 MAD KING GOLL   27
 THE EAST TELLS ALL HER SECRET JOY BEFORE DAYBREAK, . . .   154 BELOVED PEACE V   4
 THE SECRET ROSE . . . .   169 SECRET ROSE   T
 O'SULLIVAN RUA TO THE SECRET ROSE . . . .   169 SECRET ROSE   V   T
 TO THE SECRET ROSE . . . .   169 SECRET ROSE   V   T
 FAR-OFF, MOST SECRET, AND INVIOLATE ROSE, ...   169 SECRET ROSE   1
 FAR OFF, MOST SECRET, AND INVIOLATE ROSE, ...   169 SECRET ROSE   V   1
 FAR-OFF, MOST SECRET, AND INVIOLATE ROSE? . . . . .   170 SECRET ROSE   32
 FAR OFF, MOST SECRET, AND INVIOLATE ROSE? . . . . .   170 SECRET ROSE   V   32
 AND THEIR SECRET SMILE, OUT OF THE DEPTHS OF THE LAKE! . .   203 WITHER BOUGHS   11
 AND THEIR SECRET SMILE, OUT OF THE DEEPS OF THE LAKE! . .   203 WITHER BOUGHS V   11
 THEY'LL FLY UPON THAT SECRET WAY OF THEIRS. . . . .   233 SHADOW WATER B   248
 MADE OF DIM GOLD RAVE OUT IN SECRET TOMBS! . . . . .   235 SHADOW WATER B   295
 A SECRET BETWEEN YOU TWO, ...   259 UNWORTH PRAISE   9
 WE'LL KEEP THE SECRET--A NEW TRICK TO PLEASE. . . . .   265 ABBEY THEATRE   10
 THEN I REPLIED, "ALTHOUGH YOU HIDE A SECRET, ...   281 TWO KINGS   95
 BE SECRET AND TAKE DEFEAT . . . .   290 TO A FRIEND   2
 BE SECRET AND EXULT, ...   291 TO A FRIEND   14
 BUT GUAIRE LAUGHED WITH SECRET THOUGHT, ...   295 THREE BEGGARS   19
 THAT ARE OUR SECRET DISCIPLINE . . . .   326 ROBERT GREGORY   68
 WHETHER IN PUBLIC OR IN SECRET RAGE . . . .   413 TOWER   99
 A MAN IN HIS OWN SECRET MEDITATION . . . .   431 NINETEEN 19   69
 ADORNING EVERY SECRET TRACK . . . .   509 JANE REPROVED   9
 "I LOVE A MAN IN SECRET, ...   569 THREE BUSHES   15
 AND SHOUT A SECRET TO THE STONE. . . . .   632 MAN AND ECHO   5
 BEFORE THE SECRET WORKING MIND! . . . .   639 BEN BULBEN   51
 IN THE DEEP CENTRES OF THE SECRET WOODS. . . . . .   661 ISLE STAT II 1   54
 DEAR HEART, THERE IS A SECRET WAY THAT LEADS . . . .   702 MOSADA 3   75
 HE KNOWS BY SIGNS OF SECRET WIT . . . .   716 FAIRY DOCTOR   5
 OF EQUAL POWER IN SPELLS AND SECRET RITES. . . . . .   720 WITCH VIVIEN   6
 MADE OF DIM GOLD, RAVE OUT IN SECRET TOMBS, ...   765 SHADOW WATER A   345
 INTO THE SECRET WILDERNESS OF THEIR LOVE. . . . . .   778 SONG DEIRDRE 3   4
SECRET'S
 AS THEY HAVE KNOWN IT. NOW THE SECRET'S OUT! . . . .   228 SHADOW WATER B   140
SECRETS
 WITH THE SECRETS OF GOD IN HIS EYES. . . . .   167 BLESSED   12
 "WITH THE SECRETS OF GOD HALF BLIND, ...   168 BLESSED   26
 THE SECRETS OF THE OLD . . . .   457 SECRETS OF OLD   T
 I HAVE OLD WOMEN'S SECRETS NOW . . . .   457 SECRETS OF OLD   1
SECT
 WE IRISH, BORN INTO THAT ANCIENT SECT . . . . . .   611 STATUES   28
SECTION
 FROM THE BOOK OF KAURI THE INDIAN-- SECTION V. ON THE   76 INDIAN ON GOD V   T
  NATURE OF GOD
SEDENTARY
 A STYLE IS FOUND BY SEDENTARY TOIL . . . .   370 EGO DOMINUS   65
 THIS SEDENTARY TRADE. . . . .   416 TOWER   180
 THE SEDENTARY TRADE. . . . .   416 TOWER   V   180
 THE SEDENTARY SOUL . . . .   784 WOMANS BEAUTY   8
SEDGE
 A DUSKY DEMON DRY AS A WITHERED SEDGE . . . . . .   39 OISIN 2   158
 A DUSK DEMON, DRY AS A WITHERED SEDGE, ...   39 OISIN 2   V   158
 A HUSKY DEMON, DRY AS A WITHERED SEDGE . . . . . .   39 OISIN 2   V   158
 HE HEARS THE CRY OF THE SEDGE . . . .   165 CRY OF SEDGE   T
 AEDH HEARS THE CRY OF THE SEDGE . . . .   165 CRY OF SEDGE   V   T
 WHERE WIND CRIES IN THE SEDGE! . . . .   165 CRY OF SEDGE   3
 ON THE RUDDY RIVER SEDGE, ...   646 ISLE STAT I 1   25
SEDGY
 AND SEDGY STREAM, AND IN EACH BABBLING BRAKE . . . .   675 ISLE STAT II 3   225
SEE
 STOOD TIMIDLY. LEST THEY SHOULD SEE SOME SIGHT . . .   38 OISIN 2   V   141
 ALL IS DONE NOW--I SEE THE RAVENS FLOCK-- . . . . .   43 OISIN 2   V   212
 "THEN GO THROUGH THE LANDS IN THE SADDLE AND SEE WHAT THE   55 OISIN 3   125
  MORTALS DO,
 . . . AND SEE WHAT THE MORTAL MEN DO, ...   55 OISIN 3   V   125
 MUCH WONDERING TO SEE UPON ALL HANDS, OF WATTLES   58 OISIN 3   162
  AND WOODWORK MADE,
 MUCH WONDERING TO SEE UPON ALL HANDS, OF WATTLES   58 OISIN 3   V   162
  AND WOOD-WORK MADE,
 O LOVELY TO SEE IN ALL MEN'S SIGHT . . . .   69 CLOAK BOAT   3

		PAGE	TITLE		LINE
SEE	(CONTINUED)				
SEE HOW THE SACRED OLD FLAMINGOES COME,		72	ANASHU VIJAYA		29
FLASHES THE FIRE OF SADNESS, FOR THEY SEE		73	ANASHU VIJAYA		49
THEY SEE IN FLAMING FORESTS COWER THE LION		73	ANASHU VIJAYA	V	52
OR SEE THE BROWN MICE BOB		88	STOLEN CHILD		48
NO NEIGHBOUR COULD I SEE.		95	MOLL MAGEE		28
TO SEE THE WORLD ONCE MORE.		97	FOXHUNTER		4
I SEE MY LIFE GO DRIFTING LIKE A RIVER		104	FERGUS DRUID		31
I SEE MY LIFE GO DRIPPING LIKE A STREAM		104	FERGUS DRUID	V	31
TO SEE YOU SO GOOD!		118	CRADLE SONG		6
WHEN NO ONE TURNED TO SEE		131	OLD PENSIONER	V	2
TO SEE MEN'S SOULS BARTERED AND BOUGHT.		136	TWO TREES	V	36
BUT I CAN SEE WHERE THE WIND GOES		168	BLESSED		27
I SEE THE BLESSEDEST SOUL IN THE WORLD		168	BLESSED		31
BUT WHERE IT COULD SEE HER EVERY DAY.		191	BAILE AILLINN		55
IF HE COULD SEE THE TOWNLAND		214	HAPPY TOWNLAND		3
WHERE THE DEAD DRIFTED, I COULD SEE A BIRD		223	SHADOW WATER B		23
HE COULD NOT SEE THEM, BUT I HELD OUT MY HANDS		223	SHADOW WATER B		38
YOU DO NOT SEE MY PURPOSE. I SHALL HAVE GONE		238	SHADOW WATER B		357
YOU DID NOT SEE MY PURPOSE. I SHALL HAVE GONE		238	SHADOW WATER B	V	357
NO MAN SHOULD SEE TO DO ME HURT!		274	GREY ROCK		91
TO PLOUGH OR PASTURE-LAND, MIGHT SEE ME THERE,		283	TWO KINGS		146
TO PLOUGH OR PASTURE LAND, MIGHT SEE ME THERE .		283	TWO KINGS	V	146
NOW AS AT ALL TIMES I CAN SEE IN THE MIND'S EYE,		318	MAGI		1
ALTHOUGH I CAN SEE HIM STILL,		347	FISHERMAN		1
THE CERTAINTY THAT I SHALL SEE THAT LADY		356	BROKEN DREAMS		22
I SEE A SCHOOLBOY WHEN I THINK OF HIM,		370	EGO DOMINUS		55
I SEE A SCHOOL BOY WHEN I THINK OF HIM		370	EGO DOMINUS	V	55
I SEE PHANTOMS OF HATRED AND OF THE HEART'S		425	PHANTOM HATRED		T
WOULD THINK HER SON, DID SHE BUT SEE THAT SHAPE		444	SCHOOL CHILDR		37
FOR HE CANNOT SEE MY LADY		552	SONGS REWRIT 2		3
"MY MISTRESS CANNOT SEE THESE THINGS,		595	COLONEL MARTIN		30
SEE, I TELL THY BEAUTIES O'ER,		647	ISLE STAT I 1		56
AY, BOY. LET'S SEE IF THAT SAME HERON'S DEAD.		651	ISLE STAT I 1		169
SEE, YONDER SINKS THE SUN, YONDER A SHADE		653	ISLE STAT I 2		52
THERE! THERE! DOST THOU NOT SEE? I SEE THE NIGHT,		653	ISLE STAT I 2		54
THERE! THERE! DOST THOU NOT SEE? I SEE THE NIGHT,		653	ISLE STAT I 2		54
SEE! OH, SEE! THE DEW-DROWNED BUNCHES		655	ISLE STAT I 3		1
SEE! OH, SEE! THE DEW-DROWNED BUNCHES		655	ISLE STAT I 3		1
NO MORE A-ROVING SHALT THOU SEE		658	ISLE STAT I 3		82
CAN ENTER THERE. SEE! SEE! ABOVE YON BROW		659	ISLE STAT II 1		27
CAN ENTER THERE. SEE! SEE! ABOVE YON BROW		659	ISLE STAT II 1		27
WE MUST GET SWORDS. IS'T THE ONLY WAY? OH, SEE,		660	ISLE STAT II 1		34
TO SEE THEM DROWNED BY THOSE VAST SOLITUDES,		661	ISLE STAT II 1		57
AND SEE AGAIN THE HAPPY WOODLAND LIGHT,		664	ISLE STAT II 2		58
OH, LOVELY TO SEE IN ALL MEN'S SIGHT		666	ISLE STAT II 3		3
'TIS BUT TO SEE IF ANYTHING WILL STIR		669	ISLE STAT II 3		75
I SEE WITHIN A CLOVEN ROCK DISPART		673	ISLE STAT II 3		195
I FADE, AND SHALL NOT SEE THE MORNINGS WAKE,		674	ISLE STAT II 3		223
THE SULLEN WOOD. BUT MANY WOODS I SEE		682	SEEKER		24
THEN LET ME SEE THY FACE BEFORE I DIE.		684	SEEKER		66
NO SIN TO SEE IN COIL ON COIL OF AZURE		692	MOSADA 1		43
YOURSELF. NONE BUT THE INNOCENT CAN SEE.		692	MOSADA 1		59
THAT YOU SHALL SEE ON YONDER GLOWING CLOUD		692	MOSADA 1	V	43
I CANNOT SEE. THE BEETLES, AND THE BATS,		693	MOSADA 1		63
I CANNOT SEE! I CANNOT SEE! BUT YOU		693	MOSADA 1		66
I CANNOT SEE! I CANNOT SEE! BUT YOU		693	MOSADA 1		66
SHALL SEE A THING TO TALK ON WHEN YOU'RE OLD,		693	MOSADA 1		67
BE NOT AFRAID, YOU'LL SEE NO FEARFUL THING.		693	MOSADA 1		74
FROM FASTING—SEE, THE RED LIGHT SLANTING DOWN		697	MOSADA 2		36
AND SEE HOW THICK THE DEW LIES ON MY FACE.		703	MOSADA 3		104
I'LL SEE HIM LONGER IF I STAND OUT HERE		703	MOSADA 3		113
'TWILL PASS. I'LL SEE THE OTHER PRISONERS NOW,		704	MOSADA 3		130
YOUR HOOD IS THREADBARE—SEE THAT IT BE CHANGED		704	MOSADA 3		133
SPEAK, FERENCZ, SPEAK. WE LOVE EACH OTHER. SEE,		713	FERENCZ RENYI		87
SEE THE DARKNESS SLOW DISGORGING A VESSEL BLIND WITH SQUALL.		718	PHANTOM SHIP		12
. . . SEE, SHE ROUNDS THE HARBOUR CLEAR.		718	PHANTOM SHIP		13
I'LL PLAY YOU FOR YOUR OLD HOUR-GLASS. YOU SEE		721	WITCH VIVIEN		36
YONDER SEE THE FAIRY GIRLS		726	LOVERS QUARREL		21
SEE YOU, BROTHER, CRANBERRY FRUIT—		727	LOVERS QUARREL		25
"EVERY SUMMER WILT THOU SEE		730	PRIEST FAIRY		55
NOT EVEN "I LONG TO SEE THY LONGING OVER,"		734	QUATRAIN APHOR		11
WHEN HUNDREDS STOOD ABOUT TO SEE		740	EARL PAUL		27
AND SAID! "I WILL SEE HER NO MORE,"		744	GLOVE CLOAK		6
SEED					
AS A GRASS SEED CRUSHED BY A PEBBLE, AS A WOLF SUCKED UNDER A WEIR.		63	OISIN 3	V	220
TILL THE SEED OF THE FIRE FLICKER AND GLOW!		150	OLD MOTHER		2
AND THE SEED OF THE FIRE GETS FEEBLE AND COLD.		151	OLD MOTHER		10
BUT THE SEED OF THE FIRE GETS FEEBLE AND COLD,		151	OLD MOTHER	V	9
BAILE, THAT WAS OF RURY'S SEED.		194	BAILE AILLINN		118
SEED PODS AND FLOWERS THAT ARE NOT ALL WILD POPPY.		342	SHEP GOATHERD	V	88
FOR THE WOMB THE SEED SIGHS.		574	LOVERS SONG		3
FIERCE THRUST! A TARDY BLOSSOM HAD THE SEED,		665	ISLE STAT II 2		65
SEED-PODS					
SEED-PODS AND FLOWERS THAT ARE NOT ALL WILD POPPY.		342	SHEP GOATHERD		88
SEEDS					
AND WAKES THE SLUGGARD SEEDS OF CORN,		18	OISIN 1		263
CRIES TO THE SLUGGARD SEEDS OF CORN,		18	OISIN 1	V	263

	PAGE	TITLE		LINE

SEEING
    AND ALL FOLK SEEING HIM BOW DOWN, ... 113 ROSE OF PEACE 9
    THEN SEEING THAT HE SCARCE HAD SPOKE . . . . 194 BAILE AILLINN 126
    SEEING, KING'S SON, WHAT WOUNDS YOU HAVE." . . . . 275 GREY ROCK 94
    "SEEING THAT WHEN YOU COME TO THE DEATHBED . . . . . 285 TWO KINGS 196
    "SEEING THAT WHEN YOU COME TO THE DEATH-BED . . . . 285 TWO KINGS V 196
    --SEEING THAT FAME HAS PERISHED THIS LONG WHILE, . . 321 REED WHISPERER 11
    I HAD THOUGHT, SEEING HOW BITTER IS THAT WIND . . . 327 ROBERT GREGORY 89
    SEEING THAT TIME HAS FROZEN UP THE BLOOD . . . . . 333 LIVING BEAUTY V 2
    SEEING THAT I, IGNORANT FOR SO LONG, ... 384 VISION ROBART 66
    SEEING THAT LOVE AND FRIENDSHIP ARE ENOUGH, ... 423 MY DESCENDANTS 20
    AND COLA, SEEING, KNOWS THE SIGN AND COMES. . . . . 691 MOSADA 1 38
    AND COLA, SEEING, KNOWS THE SIGN AND RISES. . . . . 691 MOSADA 1 V 38
    BEYOND HEARING OR SEEING, ... 784 WOMANS BEAUTY 11
SEEK
    HOPELESS FOR EVER, THEY ALONE SHALL SEEK . . . . . 42 OISIN 2 V 200
    NOR SEEK, FOR THIS IS ALSO SOOTH, ... 65 HAPPY SHEPHERD 23
    SAVING IN THINE OWN HEART. SEEK, THEN, ... 66 HAPPY SHEPHERD 27
    SEEK, THEN, FOR THIS IS ALSO SOOTH, ... 66 HAPPY SHEPHERD 31
    AGED AND WISE, THEY SEEK THEIR WONTED PERCHES . . . 72 ANASHU VIJAYA 31
    WE SEEK FOR SLUMBERING TROUT . . . . 88 STOLEN CHILD 32
    BUT SEEK ALONE TO HEAR THE STRANGE THINGS SAID . . 101 ROSE UPON ROOD 19
    SEEK OUT WHAT MAN HE IS." ONE WENT AND CAME. . . . 109 CUCHULAIN SEA 51
    THE PARTED LIPS REPLIED, "I SEEK YOUR HELP, ... 183 QUEEN MAEVE 83
    AND NOW THEY WILL NOT FOLLOW, WHILE I SEEK . . . . 226 SHADOW WATER B 95
    BECAUSE I SEEK AN IMAGE, NOT A BOOK. . . . . . . 370 EGO DOMINUS 67
    ALL THAT I SEEK; AND WHISPER IT AS THOUGH . . . . 371 EGO DOMINUS 76
    MANY A TIME I THINK TO SEEK . . . . 475 EVA GORE-BOOTH 14
    SEEK OUT REALITY, LEAVE THINGS THAT SEEM. . . . . 502 VACILLATION 72
    WHY SHOULD I SEEK FOR LOVE OR STUDY IT? . . . . . 558 RIBH CHRISTIAN 1
    AND THAT SHOULD MOTHER SEEK HER SON SHE'D HAVE BUT LITTLE 593 PILGRIM 12
       LUCK
    SEEK THOSE IMAGES . . . . 601 THOSE IMAGES 9
    WILL STRUGGLE. OR HE'LL SEEK ENCHANTER OLD, . . . 651 ISLE STAT I 1 162
    HOW THEY WHO SEEK ARE EVER DOOMED TO FAIL. . . . . 653 ISLE STAT I 2 41
    THAT FLOWER I SEEK. THOU NEVER WILT RETURN. . . . 653 ISLE STAT I 2 44
    TO SEEK NOT HOPELESS HAVE I CROSSED THE GLOOM, . . 656 ISLE STAT I 3 42
    I, AS A SHEPHERD DRESSED, WILL SEEK AND SEEK . . . 658 ISLE STAT II 1 1
    I, AS A SHEPHERD DRESSED, WILL SEEK AND SEEK . . . 658 ISLE STAT II 1 1
    WHO SEEK MAY FIND, SAVE ONLY ONE, ... 668 ISLE STAT II 3 48
    SEEK NOT THAT WOOD, FOR THERE THE GOBLIN SNAKES . . 682 SEEKER 29
    "OR SEEK WHERE SWEETEST WATER BUBBLES, ... 731 PRIEST FAIRY 79
    WALKED ON THE WATERS AND BID FORGAEL SEEK . . . . 747 SHADOW WATER A 12
    FORGAEL, SEEK OUT CONTENT, WHERE OTHER MEN . . . . 750 SHADOW WATER A 71
    SEEK AIBRIC ON THE LOCHLANN GALLEY, AND TELL HIM . . 767 SHADOW WATER A 401
SEEKER
    AN EPILOGUE TO "THE ISLAND OF STATUES" AND "THE SEEKER" 64 HAPPY SHEPHERD V T
    THE SEEKER. . . . . 681 SEEKER T
SEEKING
    FOR IT IS LOVE THAT I AM SEEKING FOR, ... 228 SHADOW WATER B 141
SEEKS
    NO MAIDEN LOVES ME, NO MAN SEEKS MY HELP, ... 103 FERGUS DRUID V 26
    NO WOMAN LOVES ME, NO MAN SEEKS MY HELP, ... 103 FERGUS DRUID V 26
    AND NOW HE SEEKS IN BOOK OR MANUSCRIPT . . . . . 373 PHASES OF MOON 19
SEEM
    HOW FAR AWAY THE STARS SEEM, AND HOW FAR . . . . . 80 EPHEMERA 8
    THOUGH NOW IT SEEM IMPOSSIBLE, AND SO . . . . . . 200 FOLLY COMFORT 5
    WILL HARDLY SEEM WORTH THINKING OF . . . . . . 202 NEVER GIVE ALL 2
    TO PASSIONATE WOMEN IF IT SEEM . . . . 202 NEVER GIVE ALL 3
    YET IF IT DOES NOT SEEM A MOMENT'S THOUGHT, ... 204 ADAMS CURSE 5
    NOR LANDS THAT SEEM TOO DIM TO BE BURDENS ON THE HEART! 209 UNDER THE MOON 5
    THAT LIFE AND LETTERS SEEM . . . . 255 WOMAN HOMER 20
    THAT MADE THE BODY SEEM AS IT WERE A STRING . . . . 284 TWO KINGS 176
    IF BUT I DO NOT SEEM TO CARE." . . . . 297 THREE BEGGARS 68
    AND WE ARE HURT IF EITHER FRIEND SEEM COLD, ... 324 ROBERT GREGORY 10
    AND NOW THEIR BREATHLESS FACES SEEM TO LOOK . . . . 325 ROBERT GREGORY 43
    AND THEIR BREATHLESS FACES SEEM TO LOOK . . . . . 325 ROBERT GREGORY V 43
    TILL DAYTIME, PLAYTIME SEEM THE SAME; . . . . . . 343 SHEP GOATHERD 106
    BEFORE MY TIME, SEEM LIKE A VIVID MEMORY. . . . . 391 UNDER SATURN 10
    THROUGH SUMMER AND WINTER SEEM . . . . 393 EASTER 1916 42
    O MAY THE MOON AND SUNLIGHT SEEM . . . . 411 TOWER 54
    SEEM BUT THE CLOUDS OF THE SKY . . . . 416 TOWER 192
    THE LIVING SEEM MORE SHADOWY THAN THEY, ... 435 NEW FACES 8
    "BUT SUCH AS YOU AND I DO NOT SEEM OLD . . . . . . 463 HARUN RASHID 55
    THAT NEVER KNEW THAT STRAIN WOULD SCARCE SEEM BRIGHT, 465 HARUN RASHID 88
    AND YET HERSELF CAN SEEM YOUTH'S VERY FOUNTAIN, . . 465 HARUN RASHID 89
    AND WHAT IF MIND SEEM CHANGED, ... 473 ALL SOUL NIGHT 66
    AND IT SEEM CHANGED WITH THE MIND, ... 473 ALL SOUL NIGHT 67
    . . . ITS FARROW THAT SO SOLID SEEM, ... 481 BLOOD AND MOON 26
    AND SEEM TO CLING UPON THE MOONLIT SKIES, ... 482 BLOOD AND MOON 44
    OUR HANDS ARE BLENCHED, OUR FINGERS SEEM . . . . . 488 CRAZED MOON 14
    SEEK OUT REALITY, LEAVE THINGS THAT SEEM. . . . . 502 VACILLATION 72
    WHAT MADE ME LIVE LIKE THESE THAT SEEM . . . . . 507 STREAM AND SUN 14
    WHAT BIDS ME LIVE LIKE THESE THAT SEEM . . . . . 507 STREAM AND SUN V 14
    SEEM TO DIE OR DIED THEY BOTH? . . . . 514 JANE GROWN OLD V 16
    AND I SEEM TO KNOW . . . . 523 MAD AS MIST 4
    WHERE HIS HEART MY HEART DID SEEM . . . . 535 CHOSEN 15
    O WHAT AM I THAT I SHOULD NOT SEEM . . . . . . 553 PRAYER OLD AGE 7
    THAT I MAY SEEM, THOUGH I DIE OLD, ... 553 PRAYER OLD AGE 11
    WHERE FOR ITS MOMENT BOTH SEEM LOST, CONSUMED. . . . 555 RIBH AT TOMB 16
    OR SEEM PLAUSIBLE TO A MAN OF SENSE, ... 624 APPARITIONS 4

697

		PAGE	TITLE	LINE

SEEM   (CONTINUED)
```
    ITS JOY OR NIGHT SEEM BUT A DREAM;  . . . . . . .    633 MAN AND ECHO        42
    RESEMBLE FORMS THAT ARE OR SEEM  . . . . . . . . .   639 BEN BULBEN          58
    SAD FAERY TONES.  'TIS THUS THEY EVER SEEM,  . . .   654 ISLE STAT I 2       58
    THEY SEEM TO JOIN HER PRAYER—— . . . . . . . . . .   736 IN CHURCH           12
    OR CROWD BEHIND THE BULWARK, THAT WE SEEM  . . . .   751 SHADOW WATER A      94
    AND ALL SEEM WELL ENOUGH,  . . . . . . . . . . . .   786 YOUR HEART          15
SEEMED
    IT SEEMED TO BLOW FROM THE DYING FLAME,  . . . . .    13 OISIN 1            167
    THEY SEEMED TO SING IN THE SMOULDERING FIRES. . . .   13 OISIN 1            168
    IT SEEMED TO FALL FROM THE VERY FLAME  . . . . . .    13 OISIN 1          V 167
    HE SEEMED THE WATCHER FOR A SIGN.  THE OTHER . . .    31 OISIN 2          V  41
    AND FACE THAT SEEMED WROUGHT OUT OF MOONLIT VAPOURS, . 33 OISIN 2          V  70
    HER FACE SEEMED FASHIONED ALL OF MOONLIT VAPOURS, .   33 OISIN 2            V  70
    WRAPT ROUND IN SOME DIM MEMORY, IT SEEMED—— . . .     36 OISIN 2          V  99
    SCARCELY A FEATHER LINGERED, THEN YOU SEEMED . . .   102 FERGUS DRUID         4
    TO HIM SEEMED EASY, SO I LAID THE CROWN . . . . .    102 FERGUS DRUID        13
    "YOUR HEAD A WHILE SEEMED LIKE A WOMAN'S HEAD . . .  110 CUCHULAIN SEA       63
    AND SEEMED THE GREATNESS OF THE WORLD IN TEARS,  .   120 SORROW OF LOVE       6
    IT SEEMED THEY RAISED THEIR LITTLE SILVER HEADS,  .  126 DREAM OF FAERY       6
    IT SEEMED THE SUN AND MOON WERE IN THE FRUIT;  . .   127 DREAM OF FAERY      23
    REMEMBERING THAT SHE TOO HAD SEEMED DIVINE . . . .   182 QUEEN MAEVE         64
    THAT IT HAD ALL SEEMED HAPPY, AND YET WE'D GROWN .   206 ADAMS CURSE         37
    OR LANDS THAT SEEMED TOO OLD TO BE BURDENS ON THE HEART, 209 UNDER THE MOON V   5
    HAD SEEMED TO BE THE GIVER OF ALL PEACE,  . . . .   228 SHADOW WATER B     149
    HAD THE WORLD'S TOTAL LIFE GATHERED UP, IT SEEMED,   231 SHADOW WATER B     194
    ENOUGH IF THE WORK HAS SEEMED,  . . . . . . . . .   259 UNWORTH PRAISE       5
    BECAUSE IT STOOD UPON HIS PATH AND SEEMED  . . . .  277 TWO KINGS            8
    SO MOURNFUL THAT IT SEEMED THE CRY OF ONE  . . . .  278 TWO KINGS           39
    TILL ALL HAD SEEMED A SHADOW OR A VISION . . . . .  278 TWO KINGS           43
    AND SHE SEEMED HAPPY AS A KING,  . . . . . . . . .  313 MEMORY YOUTH   V     6
    WHEREON A THING ONCE WALKED THAT SEEMED A BURNING CLOUD. 315 FALLEN MAJESTY    8
    ONCE WALKED A THING THAT SEEMED, AS IT WERE, A BURNING   315 FALLEN MAJESTY  V 8
        CLOUD.
    THAT SEEMED AS THOUGH ICE BURNED AND WAS BUT THE MORE ICE, 316 COLD HEAVEN   2
    TILL ALL HIS GREEK AND LATIN LEARNING SEEMED . . .  324 ROBERT GREGORY      21
    THE YEARS TO COME SEEMED WASTE OF BREATH,  . . . .  328 IRISH AIRMAN        14
    MUCH TOO SOLEMN SEEMED;  . . . . . . . . . . . . .  342 SHEP GOATHERD       91
    A MAN—SO VAGUELY THAT HE SEEMED TO DREAM—— . . .    351 HER PRAISE     V     8
    THIS NIGHT HAS BEEN SO STRANGE THAT IT SEEMED . . . 358 PRESENCES            1
    VEHEMENT AND WITTY SHE HAD SEEMED——; THE VENETIAN LADY, 363 DOLLS FACES      5
    WHO HAD SEEMED TO GLIDE TO SOME INTRIGUE IN HER RED SHOES, 363 DOLLS FACES   6
    AND THEN HE LAUGHED TO THINK THAT WHAT SEEMED HARD .  377 PHASES OF MOON    136
    FOR NOW BEING DEAD IT SEEMED . . . . . . . . . . .  383 VISION ROBART       23
    MIND MOVED YET SEEMED TO STOP  . . . . . . . . . .  384 VISION ROBART       43
    SO SENSITIVE HIS NATURE SEEMED,  . . . . . . . . .  392 EASTER 1916         29
    SHE SEEMED TO HAVE GROWN CLEAN AND SWEET . . . . .  397 POLIT PRISONER      17
    HIS DWINDLING SCORE AND HE SEEMED CASTAWAYS  . . .  420 MY HOUSE            25
    HIS DWINDLING SCORE AND HE SEEMED CAST-A-WAYS  . .  420 MY HOUSE       V    25
    AND SEEMED UNCHANGING LIKE THE SWORD. . . . . . .   421 MY TABLE            21
    HAD WAKING WITS; IT SEEMED . . . . . . . . . . . .  422 MY TABLE            31
    THAT SEEMED SHEER MIRACLE TO THE MULTITUDE,  . . .  428 NINETEEN 19          2
    IT SEEMED THAT A DRAGON OF AIR . . . . . . . . . .  430 NINETEEN 19         51
    WHATEVER MISCHIEF SEEMED . . . . . . . . . . . . .  431 NINETEEN 19    V    85
    WHAT EVER MISCHIEF SEEMED  . . . . . . . . . . . .  431 NINETEEN 19         85
    TOLD, AND IT SEEMED THAT OUR TWO NATURES BLENT . .  443 SCHOOL CHILDR       13
    FOR IT SEEMED THAT HE AND SHE  . . . . . . . . . .  457 SUMMER SPRING       10
    SEEMED FOR A WHILE TO HAVE GROWN YOUNG AGAIN; . .   462 HARUN RASHID        36
    SEEMED SO ON PURPOSE; MUTTERED JAFFER'S FRIENDS, .  462 HARUN RASHID        37
    SHE SEEMED THE LEARNED MAN AND I THE CHILD;  . . .  467 HARUN RASHID       137
    IT SEEMED A GOLD-FISH SWIMMING IN A BOWL. . . . .   472 ALL SOUL NIGHT      40
    AND WHAT IF MIND SEEMED CHANGE . . . . . . . . . .  473 ALL SOUL NIGHT V    66
    AND IT SEEMED CHANGED WITH THE MIND, . . . . . . .  473 ALL SOUL NIGHT V    67
    THAT SEEMED TO WHIRL UPON A COMPASS-POINT, . . . .  489 COOLE PARK 29       21
    THAT SEEMED TO WHIRL UPON A COMPASS POINT,  . . .   489 COOLE PARK 29  V    21
    SEEMED ONCE MORE DEAR THAN LIFE; ANCESTRAL TREES,   491 COOLE BALLYLEE      34
    IT SEEMED, SO GREAT MY HAPPINESS . . . . . . . . .  501 VACILLATION         43
    AND ALL MY HEART SEEMED GAY; . . . . . . . . . . .  507 STREAM AND SUN       3
    SEEMED TO DIE OR DIED THEY BOTH?  . . . . . . . .   514 JANE GROWN OLD      16
    AND SEEMED TO STAND ALTHOUGH IN BED I LAY. . . . .  535 CHOSEN               9
    IT SEEMED A QUATTROCENTO PAINTER'S THRONG, . . . .  537 HER VISION          19
    IT SEEMED A QUATTRO-CENTO PAINTER'S THRONG . . . .  537 HER VISION     V    19
    THAT SEEMED BUT A WILD WENCHING MAN; . . . . . . .  550 SEVERED HEAD        16
    MADE DRAPERIES THAT SEEMED TO RISE . . . . . . . .  566 LAPIS LAZULI        31
    SEEMED SPRUNG FROM BUT A SINGLE ROOT . . . . . . .  571 THREE BUSHES        61
    HIS NUMBERS, THOUGH THEY MOVED OR SEEMED TO MOVE .  610 STATUES              2
    A SHROUD THAT SEEMED TO HAVE AUTHORITY . . . . . .  634 CUCHULAIN COMF       7
SEEMING
    THE SEEMING NEEDS OF MY FOOL-DRIVEN LAND;  . . . .  267 ALL TEMPT ME         3
SEEMS
    THOUGH NOW IT SEEMS IMPOSSIBLE, AND SO . . . . . .  200 FOLLY COMFORT  V     5
    YET NOW IT SEEMS AN IDLE TRADE ENOUGH."  . . . . .  205 ADAMS CURSE         27
    "WHO IS THE FRIEND THAT SEEMS BUT AIR  . . . . . .  274 GREY ROCK           83
    "IF THAT BE TRUE AS IT SEEMS TRUE, . . . . . . . .  295 THREE BEGGARS       20
    SO THAT IT SEEMS EVEN I SLEEP LIGHT; . . . . . . .  303 HOUR DAWN      V    34
    IT SEEMS THAT I MUST BID THE MUSE GO PACK, . . . .  409 TOWER               11
    THE ABOUNDING GLITTERING JET; THOUGH NOW IT SEEMS   417 ANCEST HOUSES       12
    AS VIGOROUS OF MIND, AND YET IT SEEMS . . . . . .   422 MY DESCENDANTS       4
    THAT SEEMS UNLIKE ITSELF, THAT SEEMS UNCHANGEABLE,  426 PHANTOM HATRED       4
    THAT SEEMS UNLIKE ITSELF, THAT SEEMS UNCHANGEABLE,  426 PHANTOM HATRED       4
    THAT SEEMS UNNATURAL TO ARABIAN MINDS, . . . . . .  464 HARUN RASHID        79
```

		PAGE	TITLE		LINE

SEEMS   (CONTINUED)
    IT SEEMS ENOUGH THAT I AM THERE; AND YET, ... 468 HARUN RASHID   166
    IT SEEMS I MUST BUY KNOWLEDGE WITH MY PEACE. . . . . . 468 HARUN RASHID   169
    SOME VAGUE UTOPIA--AND SHE SEEMS, ... 475 EVA GORE-BOOTH   11
    BUT SEEMS A CONCENTRATION OF THE SKY; . . . . 490 COOLE BALLYLEE   18
    WHAT SEEMS MOST WELCOME IN THE TOMB--PLAY A PREDESTINED 503 VACILLATION   86
      PART.
    SEEMS A WATER-COURSE OR AN AVALANCHE, ... 567 LAPIS LAZULI   45
    THEMES OF THE EMBITTERED HEART, OR SO IT SEEMS, ... 629 CIRCUS ANIMALS   13
    AND ALL SEEMS EVIL UNTIL I . . . . 632 MAN AND ECHO   17
    ITS JOY OR NIGHT SEEMS BUT A DREAM. . . . . 633 MAN AND ECHO   V 42
    IT SEEMS TO FONDLE, WITH A FINGER BRIGHT . . . . 714 FERENCZ RENYI   114
    MY WAY IS WEST. SHE SEEMS BOTH YOUNG AND SHAPELY; . . 755 SHADOW WATER A   171
    AND MANY A NIGHT IT SEEMS . . . . 781 MY HEART BEAT   9
SEEN
    HOLDING THAT HORSE LONG SEEN NOT, NIAM STOOD. . . . . . 44 OISIN 2   V 230
    O HAD YOU SEEN BEAUTIFUL NIAMH GROW WHITE AS THE WATERS 54 OISIN 3   109
      ARE WHITE,
    OH, HADST THOU SEEN BEAUTIFUL NIAM WAIL TO HERSELF AND   54 OISIN 3   V 109
      BLANCH,
    O, HAD YOU SEEN BEAUTIFUL NEAVE WAIL TO HERSELF AND BLANCH, 54 OISIN 3   V 109
    AND ONE HAS SEEN IN THE REDNESS OF WINE . . . . 168 BLESSED   35
    AND HAVE SEEN THE BLESSEDEST SOUL IN THE WORLD, ... 168 BLESSED   V 31
    I NEVER HAVE SEEN MAID QUIET . . . . 171 MAID QUIET   V   1
    TO SOME STRINGED INSTRUMENT NONE THERE HAD SEEN, . . . 180 QUEEN MAEVE   4
    HAVE SEEN IMMORTAL, MILD, PROUD SHADOWS WALK; . . . . . 217 WOODS OF COOLE   12
    BUT THERE WERE OTHERS. I HAVE SEEN NOTHING PASS. . . . 226 SHADOW WATER B   82
    THAT HAS BEEN PROMISED ME. I HAVE NOT SEEN THEM . . . 226 SHADOW WATER B   88
    HAS SHE NOT SEEN HIM LYING LIKE A LOG. . . . . 230 SHADOW WATER B   173
    NOW I HAVE SEEN IT WEIGHED . . . . 267 FRIEND ILLNESS   6
    WHO HAS SEEN A GARDEN IMAGE OR TWISTED TREE . . . . . . 279 TWO KINGS   V 45B
    AND SEEN THE RUBBISH RUN ABOUT, ... 297 THREE BEGGARS   65
    AND SEEN THE RUBBISH RUNABOUT, ... 297 THREE BEGGARS   V 65
    HE HAD SEEN A RED-HAIRED JOLLY LAD . . . . 303 HOUR DAWN   V 27
    WHO HAD SEEN, BEING KEPT FOR SHOW . . . . 319 DOLLS   5
    BUT SUCH AS I HAVE SEEN UPON HER FACE . . . . 340 SHEP GOATHERD   40
    ARE LEARNED IN WAITING. YOU CANNOT BUT HAVE SEEN . . . 340 SHEP GOATHERD   48
    AND LITTLE SHE BY WHOM HER DANCE WAS SEEN . . . . 383 VISION ROBART   38
    I KNEW THAT I HAD SEEN, HAD SEEN AT LAST . . . . 384 VISION ROBART   49
    I KNEW THAT I HAD SEEN, HAD SEEN AT LAST . . . . 384 VISION ROBART   49
    HAVE I NOT SEEN THE LOVELIEST WOMAN BORN . . . . 405 FOR DAUGHTER   59
    HAVE SEEN HIS MIDNIGHT CANDLE GLIMMERING. . . . . 420 MY HOUSE   20
    HAD SEEN HIS MIDNIGHT CANDLE GLIMMERING . . . . 420 MY HOUSE   20
    IF YOU HAVE SEEN THAT IMAGE AND NOT THE WOMAN. . . . . 448 HERO GIRL FOOL   8
    IF YOU HAVE SEEN THAT IMAGE AND NOT MY WORTH. . . . . . 448 HERO GIRL FOOL V 8
    OLIVER GOLDSMITH SANG WHAT HE HAD SEEN, ... 487 SEVEN SAGES   17
    FIFTEEN APPARITIONS HAVE I SEEN; . . . . 624 APPARITIONS   7
    FIFTEEN APPARITIONS HAVE I SEEN; . . . . 624 APPARITIONS   15
    FIFTEEN APPARITIONS HAVE I SEEN; . . . . 624 APPARITIONS   23
    'TIS CLEAR THAT YOU HAVE SEEN HER NOT. THE CROWN . . . 661 ISLE STAT II 1   70
    HAVE THEY NE'ER SEEN THE EYES OF LYNX OR KINE, ... 672 ISLE STAT II 3   152
    OR HAST THOU NEVER SEEN, WITH VISAGE MEEK, ... 672 ISLE STAT II 3   156
    HAVE I NOT SEEN A THOUSAND SEASONS EBB AND FLOW . . . . 675 ISLE STAT II 3   229
    THE TIDE OF STARS? HAVE I NOT SEEN A THOUSAND YEARS . 675 ISLE STAT II 3   230
    FADED AND VANISHED, NOTHING NOW IS SEEN . . . . 676 ISLE STAT II 3   268
    WE, TOO, HAVE SEEN OUR BRAVEST AND OUR BEST . . . . . . 709 FERENCZ RENYI   1
    AND THEN A POINTED FACE WAS SEEN . . . . 728 PRIEST FAIRY   21
    FOR I HAVE SEEN A SHIP HID IN THE FOG. . . . . 751 SHADOW WATER A   89
    IN ONE ANOTHER'S ARMS. AENGUS HAS SEEN . . . . 763 SHADOW WATER A   321
SEER
    SEER OF VISIONS! NOW EVE FALLS ASLEEP, ... 691 MOSADA 1   36
SEES
    "GOD ONLY SEES WHAT DOOM FOR ME LIES STORED." . . . . . 110 CUCHULAIN SEA   V 62
    FOR ALL THINGS THE DELIGHTED EYE NOW SEES . . . . 326 ROBERT GREGORY   49
    HE NUMBERS. HE A BROWN FARM-HOUSE SEES. . . . . 710 FERENCZ RENYI   22
    RINGED ROUND AND FONDLED, A BROWN FARM HOUSE SEES. . . 710 FERENCZ RENYI   V 23
    HE SEES THE FAIRY HOSTING MOVE . . . . 716 FAIRY DOCTOR   9
SEIZE
    AND SEIZE HER, AND THUS FLOATS HER QUIVERING CRY; . . . 714 FERENCZ RENYI   105
SEIZED
    KING EOCHAID SEIZED THE HORNS IN HIS STRONG HANDS . . 278 TWO KINGS   24
    EOCHAID SEIZED BOTH THE HORNS IN HIS STRONG HANDS . . . 278 TWO KINGS   V 24
    THEREON HE SEIZED ME IN HIS ARMS, BUT I . . . . 285 TWO KINGS   201
SELDOM
    FOR PEACE AND LAUGHTER HAVE BEEN SELDOM FRIENDS. . . . 670 ISLE STAT II 3   103
SELECTED
    THE DEDICATION TO A BOOK OF STORIES SELECTED FROM THE IRISH 129 BOOK STORIES   T
      NOVELISTS
SELF   SEE ANTI-SELF
    FOR BEAUTY'S VERY SELF, HAS CHARM MADE WISE, ... 404 FOR DAUGHTER   37
    THAT OUT OF LIFE'S OWN SELF DELIGHT HAD SPRUNG . . . . 417 ANCEST HOUSES   V 11
    A DIALOGUE OF SELF AND SOUL . . . . 477 SELF AND SOUL   T
    MY BETTER SELF DISOWNS, ... 533 FIRST CONFESS   9
SELF-ACCUSED
    WHO IS SELF-ACCUSED. IF SHE BE INNOCENT . . . . 280 TWO KINGS   72
SELF-AFFRIGHTING
    SELF-APPEASING, SELF-AFFRIGHTING, ... 405 FOR DAUGHTER   68
SELF-APPEASING
    SELF-APPEASING, SELF-AFFRIGHTING, ... 405 FOR DAUGHTER   68
SELF-BEGOTTEN
    THE SELF-SOWN, SELF-BEGOTTEN SHAPE THAT GIVES . . . . . 446 COLONUS PRAISE   10

699

```
                                                        PAGE    TITLE            LINE
SELF-BEGOTTEN   (CONTINUED)
     NOR SHALL THE SELF-BEGOTTEN FAIL  . . . . . . . .   530 OLD TOM AGAIN        3
SELF-BORN
     O SELF-BORN MOCKERS OF MAN'S ENTERPRISE!  . . . . . 445 SCHOOL CHILDR       56
     SELF-BORN, HIGH-BORN, AND SOLITARY TRUTHS, . . . . . 467 HARUN RASHID      141
     BEGOT! SELF-BORN, HIGH-BORN, AND SOLITARY. . . . .  467 HARUN RASHID    V 141
     SELF-BORN, BORN ANEW? . . . . . . . . . . . .       507 STREAM AND SUN      15
SELF-DELIGHT
     THAT OUT OF LIFE'S OWN SELF-DELIGHT HAD SPRUNG  . . . . 417 ANCEST HOUSES    11
SELF-DELIGHTING
     AND LEARNS AT LAST THAT IT IS SELF-DELIGHTING, . . . . 405 FOR DAUGHTER     67
     TO BRAZEN HAWKS. NOR SELF-DELIGHTING REVERIE, . . . . 427 PHANTOM HATRED    29
SELFSAME
     BUT NOT THAT SELFSAME EXCELLENCE AGAIN. . . . . . . . 602 GALLERY REVIS     32
SELF-SAME
     LOOKED DOWN ON ME; AND IN THE SELF-SAME PLACE . . . .  39 OISIN 2         146
     MELTED AND FLOWED; AND IN THE SELF-SAME PLACE . . . .  39 OISIN 2       V 146
     FROM SELF-SAME DOLT AND KNAVE: . . . . . . . . . .   260 UNWORTH PRAISE    17
     HEALING FROM ITS LETTERED SLAB. THOSE SELF-SAME HANDS 503 VACILLATION      82
         PERCHANCE
     NATURAL AND SUPERNATURAL WITH THE SELF-SAME RING ARE WED. 556 RIBH PATRICK   4
     BUT NOT THAT SELF-SAME EXCELLENCE AGAIN. . . . . . .  602 GALLERY REVIS   V 32
     FOUGHT ONCE FOR SELF-SAME REASON ON THE HEM . . . . . 660 ISLE STAT II 1   32
SELF-SOWN
     THE SELF-SOWN, SELF-BEGOTTEN SHAPE THAT GIVES . . . . 446 COLONUS PRAISE   10
SELL
     THE SISTER: "SELL THY COUNTRY, AND THE SHAME . . . .  712 FERENCZ RENYI    60
     I'D BUY YOUR GLASS. MY GLASS I WILL NOT SELL. . . . . 721 WITCH VIVIEN     28
SELLERS       SEE ONION-SELLERS
     WHAT TH' ONION SELLERS THOUGHT OR DID  . . . . . . . 287 TO WEALTHY MAN  V 11
SELLING
     THE FOLK WHO ARE BUYING AND SELLING, . . . . . . . . 119 PITY OF LOVE      3
SELVES
     ON THEIR OWN SELVES IN THE WATERS WHITE,  . . . . .   14 OISIN 1        V 185
     ALL THESE ARE SOULS THAT FLY FROM THEIR DREAD SELVES. . . 686 LIFE          4
     ALL THESE ARE SOULS WHO FLY FROM THEIR DREAD SELVES. . . 734 QUATRAIN APHOR  4
     ALL THESE ARE SOULS THAT FLY FROM THEIR DREAD SELVES. . . 734 QUATRAIN APHOR V 4
SEMBLANCE
     UNDER A RULE, UNDER THE SEMBLANCE OF PEACE . . . . . . 563 MERU             2
SEMELE'S
     SEMELE'S LAD A GAY COMPANION. . . . . . . . . . . .  446 COLONUS PRAISE    8
SEND
     TILL MY OWN WORDS, RE-ECHOING, SHALL SEND . . . . . .  68 SAD SHEPHERD     20
     AND MINE OWN WORDS RE-ECHOING SHALL SEND  . . . . .    68 SAD SHEPHERD   V 20
     SEND PEACE ON ALL THE LANDS AND FLICKERING CORN.-- . . . 71 ANASHU VIJAYA   1
     WHOSE BLADE COMPELS, AND BID THEM SEND YOU ONE . . . . 108 CUCHULAIN SEA  V 37
     "I WILL SEND THEM TO HER AND DIE": . . . . . . . . . 160 CAP AND BELLS    22
     THEY WOULD NOT SEND ME ONE THAT CASTS A SHADOW. . . . 235 SHADOW WATER B  285
     SPEAK IT, THAT I MAY SEND THROUGH THE WIDE WORLD . . . 281 TWO KINGS       97
     AND SEND IMAGINATION FORTH . . . . . . . . . . . .   410 TOWER  .         20
     DID THAT PLAY OF MINE SEND OUT . . . . . . . . . .   632 MAN AND ECHO     11
     "SEND WAR IN OUR TIME, O LORD!" . . . . . . . . . .  638 BEN BULBEN       26
     I'LL SEND MINE ARROW; NOW MY ONE RESOURCE: . . . . . 657 ISLE STAT I 3    64
     THE BLESSED GOD WAS GOOD TO SEND US SUCH, . . . . .  683 SEEKER           40
     NONE SHOULD ESCAPE MY SWORD! I WOULD SEND ALL . . . . 752 SHADOW WATER A  111
     HAS TOLD ME THAT THE UNDYING SEND THEIR EAGLES . . . . 765 SHADOW WATER A  346
     TO GARRET OR CELLAR A WHEEL I SEND, . . . . . . . . . 787 GARRET CELLAR    1
SENNACHIES
     . . . FAR SUNG BY THE SENNACHIES. . . . . . . . . .   50 OISIN 3         53
     . . . FAR SUNG OF THE SENNACHIES. . . . . . . . . .   50 OISIN 3       V 53
SENSE
     AND GET INTO THEIR WORLD THAT TO THE SENSE . . . . . 230 SHADOW WATER B  179
     AND THERE, IN JUGGLERIES OF SIGHT AND SENSE, . . . . 231 SHADOW WATER B  216
     WHAT NEED YOU, BEING CONTENT TO SENSE, . . . . . . . 289 SEPTEMBER 1913    1
     AND I TOOK ALL THE BLAME OUT OF ALL SENSE AND REASON, . . 316 COLD HEAVEN    7
     AND CHILDHOOD A DELIGHT FOR EVERY SENSE, . . . . . . 418 ANCEST HOUSES    31
     SENSE THAN A COMMON MAN? . . . . . . . . . . . . .   507 STREAM AND SUN   10
     OF EVERYTHING THAT IS NOT MIND OR SENSE. . . . . . . 558 RIBH CHRISTIAN    6
     THAT HAD SUCH LITTLE SENSE . . . . . . . . . . . .   585 ORAHILLY         11
     OR SEEM PLAUSIBLE TO A MAN OF SENSE, . . . . . . . . 624 APPARITIONS       4
SENSELESS
     BECAUSE OF ALL THAT SENSELESS TUMULT, ALL BUT CRIED  . . 426 PHANTOM HATRED  15
SENSES
     HIS SENSES AND HIS HEART UNSATISFIED,  . . . . . . . 370 EGO DOMINUS      58
SENSITIVE
     WE HAVE LIT UPON THE GENTLE, SENSITIVE MIND . . . . . 368 EGO DOMINUS      12
     SO SENSITIVE HIS NATURE SEEMED, . . . . . . . . .    392 EASTER 1916      29
     ON DELICATE SENSITIVE EAR OR TOSSING MANE, . . . . . 433 NINETEEN 19     115
     AND BLOOD AND MIRE THE SENSITIVE BODY STAIN? . . . . 564 GYRES            10
SENSUAL
     CAUGHT IN THAT SENSUAL MUSIC ALL NEGLECT . . . . . . 407 SAIL BYZANTIUM    7
SENSUALITY
     AND ALL THE SENSUALITY OF THE SHADE-- . . . . . . .  489 COOLE PARK 29    31
SENSUOUS
     OF THAT MOST SENSUOUS SILENCE OF THE NIGHT . . . . . 579 DOR WELLESLEY     6
SENT
     FOR NEVER MORTAL CRY SO FAR HATH SENT. . . . . . . .  36 OISIN 2       V 108
     SPRANG DRIPPING, AND, WITH CAPTIVE DEMONS SENT . . . . 38 OISIN 2         130
     THEN CONCHUBAR SENT THAT SWEET-THROATED MAID, . . . . 110 CUCHULAIN SEA   72
     THEN CONCOBAR SENT THAT SWEET THROATED MAID . . . . . 110 CUCHULAIN SEA V 72
     SENT FOR HIS DRUIDS TWENTY SCORE AND TEN, . . . . .  110 CUCHULAIN SEA V 76
```

700

SENT   (CONTINUED)
    ANOTHER POOR MAN SENT FOR HIM, ...   132 FR GILLIGAN   7
    SENT ONE OF HIS GREAT ANGELS DOWN . . . .   134 FR GILLIGAN   43
    "FOR GOD AND GOD'S MOTHER HAVE SENT . . . .   167 BLESSED   18
    "I HAVE SENT AMONG THE FIELDS OR TO THE WOODS . . .   280 TWO KINGS   69
    "I HAVE SENT OUT INTO THE FIELDS AND WOODS . . . . .   280 TWO KINGS   V   69
    HAD SENT NO RUNNERS TO AND FRO . . . .   288 TO WEALTHY MAN   18
    CONFUSION OF THE DEATH-BED OVER, IS IT SENT . . . .   316 COLD HEAVEN   10
    THE RED MAN THE JUGGLER SENT . . . .   412 TOWER   92
    THAT IS A LIGHT MY JEALOUS SOUL HAS SENT. . . . . .   558 RIBH CHRISTIAN   8
    SPOILT WHAT OLD LOINS HAVE SENT? . . . .   604 YOU CONTENT   6
    I SENT AN ARROW. AND I SAW YOU MISS, ...   649 ISLE STAT I 1   115
    AND SENT THE OLD MEN ON THEIR WAY. . . . .   725 LEGEND   23
SENTENCE
    THE REST I PASS, ONE SENTENCE I UNSAY. . . . .   542 PARN FUNERAL 2   1
    I PASS THE REST—ONE SENTENCE I UNSAY— . . . .   542 PARN FUNERAL 2 V   1
SENTENCES
    IN BROKEN SENTENCES. MY SOUL HAD FOUND . . . . . .   557 RIBH ECSTASY   3
    SENTENCES THAT HE HAS NEVER THOUGHT, ...   560 WHENCE COME   6
SENTIMENTALIST
    THE SENTIMENTALIST HIMSELF, WHILE ART . . . .   369 EGO DOMINUS   47
SENTINELS
    THE AGELESS SENTINELS WHO HOLD THEIR WATCH . . . . .   664 ISLE STAT II 2   45
SENTRIES
    BEYOND THE GATEWAY—BY THE SENTRIES NOW— . . . . . .   720 WITCH VIVIEN   10
SEPARATE
    FOR SEPARATE, PERFECT, AND IMMOVABLE . . . .   375 PHASES OF MOON   81
    UNDER IT ARMED WISDOM STANDS, A SEPARATE WISDOM . .   469 HARUN RASHID   V 189
    FOR EVERY SEPARATE QUALITY OF LOVE, ...   469 HARUN RASHID   V 189A
SEPTEMBER
    SEPTEMBER [NINETEEN-THIRTEEN] . . . .   289 SEPTEMBER 1913   T
SEPULCHRE
    WHO SOUGHT THEE IN THE HOLY SEPULCHRE, ...   169 SECRET ROSE   3
    WHO SOUGHT THEE AT THE HOLY SEPULCHRE, ...   169 SECRET ROSE   V   3
    FROM MARBLE OF A BROKEN SEPULCHRE, ...   565 GYRES   20
SERAPHS
    OF SERAPHS, BROODING, EACH ALONE, ...   156 FORGOT BEAUTY   V   22
SERE
    SCARCE LEFT A WHITENING FEATHER, GREY AND SERE, . . .   34 OISIN 2   V 76A
    BUT WHENCE, AND WHEN? OVER THE WILLOWS SERE . . . .   652 ISLE STAT I 2   28
SERENE
    AND WITH A RULE SERENE AND MILD . . . .   82 MAD KING GOLL   V   6
    SERENE. THEY'RE LED AWAY, AND WHERE A BAND . . . .   712 FERENCZ RENYI   63
SERPENT   SEE WATER-SERPENT
    THE MIRROR-SCALED SERPENT IS MULTIPLICITY, ...   556 RIBH PATRICK   10
    THE MIRROR SCALED SERPENT IS MULTIPLICITY, ...   556 RIBH PATRICK   V   10
    A CONTRAPUNTAL SERPENT HISS. . . . .   573 LADYS 3RD SONG   10
SERPENT-TAILS
    THERE ALL THE SERPENT-TAILS ARE BIT, ...   557 THERE   2
SERVANT
    HOW HARD A LIFE HER SERVANT LIVES, ...   336 YOUNG BEAUTY   14
    IT WOULD BE THE WORLD'S SERVANT, AND AS IT SERVES, . .   376 PHASES OF MOON   90
    THAT I AM STILL THEIR SERVANT THOUGH ALL ARE UNDERGROUND.   581 CURSE CROMWELL   22
    SOME GOBLIN, MY SERVANT, ON WINGS THAT ARE FLEET, . .   657 ISLE STAT I 3   67
    WHY THESE NEW FEARS? THE SERVANT OF THE LORD, . . .   692 MOSADA 1   V   46
SERVANT'S
    OH! GRACIOUS PAN, TAKE NOW THY SERVANT'S PART. . . .   657 ISLE STAT I 3   77
SERVANTS
    "AND OF MY SERVANTS SOME ONE GO, ...   97 FOXHUNTER   V   5
    SERVANTS ROUND HIS CUSHIONED PLACE . . . .   99 FOXHUNTER   37
    THE SERVANTS BEAR THE BODY IN, ...   99 FOXHUNTER   47
    THE SERVANTS ROUND HIS CUSHIONED PLACE . . . .   99 FOXHUNTER   V   37
    THEN TO HER SERVANTS, "BEAT HIM FROM THE DOOR . . .   106 CUCHULAIN SEA   V 17A
    THE FIGHTING-MEN AND SERVANTS OF THIS HOUSE, ...   280 TWO KINGS   70
    THE FIGHTING MEN AND SERVANTS OF THIS HOUSE, ...   280 TWO KINGS   V   70
    THE SERVANTS OF YOUR ENEMY, ...   436 FOR MY SON   26
    I SPEAK ALONE WITH SERVANTS OF THE CROSS . . . . . .   698 MOSADA 2   48
SERVE
    FOR THOSE THAT LOVE THE WORLD SERVE IT IN ACTION, . .   369 EGO DOMINUS   42
    IF YOU WOULD SERVE ME, AS YOUR WORD AND VOICE . . .   756 SHADOW WATER A V 183
SERVED
    OR THE AMBITIONS THAT HE SERVED, ...   342 SHEP GOATHERD   93
    WHERE WHO HAS SERVED THE MOST IS MOST DEFAMED, . . .   351 PEOPLE   4
    THOSE I HAD SERVED AND SOME THAT I HAD FED, ...   352 PEOPLE   27
    YOU HEARD THAT LABOURING MAN WHO HAD SERVED MY PEOPLE,   391 UNDER SATURN   11
      HE SAID
    SERVED HUMAN LIBERTY. . . . .   493 SWIFTS EPITAPH   6
    HIS FATHERS SERVED THEIR FATHERS BEFORE CHRIST WAS   580 CURSE CROMWELL   6
      CRUCIFIED.
    UPON THE CAUSE YOU SERVED, THAT WE . . . .   791 REPRISALS   13
SERVES
    IT WOULD BE THE WORLD'S SERVANT, AND AS IT SERVES, . .   376 PHASES OF MOON   90
SERVICE
    NOR GAVE LOUD SERVICE TO A CAUSE . . . .   273 GREY ROCK   57
    OR LEAVE SOME SERVICE ALL UNDONE, ...   743 DANAAN QUICK   21
SERVILE
    THAT THE LAST SERVILE CRESCENT HAS SET FREE? . . . .   376 PHASES OF MOON   103
    OR SERVILE SHAPE, AT OTHERS' BECK AND CALL. . . . .   417 ANCEST HOUSES   8
SERVING
    OF YOUR OWN PASSIONATE SERVING KIND WHO HAD BROUGHT . . .   292 TO A SHADE   10
    OF YOUR OWN PASSIONATE SERVING KIND WHO HAS BROUGHT . . .   292 TO A SHADE   V   10

```
                                                        PAGE    TITLE          LINE
SERVING   (CONTINUED)
        A SERVING MAID AND A SERVING MAN,  . . . . . . . . . .   301 RUN PARADISE   V  13
        A SERVING MAID AND A SERVING MAN,  . . . . . . . . . .   301 RUN PARADISE   V  13
        A SERVING MAN THAT COULD DIVINE  . . . . . . . . . .     410 TOWER          V  28
SERVING—MAID
        A SERVING—MAID AND A SERVING—MAN:  . . . . . . . . . .   301 RUN PARADISE      13
SERVING—MAN
        A SERVING—MAID AND A SERVING—MAN:  . . . . . . . . . .   301 RUN PARADISE      13
        A SERVING—MAN, THAT COULD DIVINE  . . . . . . . . . .    410 TOWER             28
        THE THIRD, DOUBTLESS A SERVING—MAN.  . . . . . . . . .   566 LAPIS LAZULI      41
SET
        AND SET YOUR NAME ALL NAMES ABOVE,  . . . . . . . . .      7 OISIN 1          76
        AND THE FIXED STARS HAD DAWNED AND SHONE AND SET,  . . .  31 OISIN 2          40
        FOR CENTURIES, AND STARS HAD DAWNED AND SET.  . . . . .   31 OISIN 2       V  40
        FROM THE WHOLE SEVEN SEAS, THOSE TOWERS SET  . . . . .    38 OISIN 2       V 131
        MAY SET A STONE UPON ANCESTRAL SORROW!  . . . . . . .    130 BOOK STORIES     11
        OF THE PALE TIDE WHEN THE MOON HAS SET,  . . . . . . .   146 FISH              2
        THEY SET UP A NOISE LIKE CRICKETS,  . . . . . . . . .    161 CAP AND BELLS    33
        AND SET THEM DIGGING UNDER BUAL'S HILL.  . . . . . . .   184 QUEEN MAEVE      93
        AND SET THEM DIGGING INTO ANBUAL'S HILL.  . . . . . .    184 QUEEN MAEVE   V  93
        AND SET THEM DIGGING IN THE WEST OF THE HILL.  . . . .   184 QUEEN MAEVE   V  93
        BE THOUGHT AN IDLER BY THE NOISY SET  . . . . . . . .    205 ADAMS CURSE      12
        ANGERS THAT ARE LIKE NOISY CLOUDS HAVE SET OUR HEARTS    207 HANRAHANS SONG    8
            ABEAT:
        ANGERS THAT ARE LIKE BUNDLED CLOUDS HAVE SET OUR HEARTS  207 HANRAHANS SONG V  8
            ABEAT:
        UNTIL THE MOON HAD SET: AND WHEN I LOOKED  . . . . . .   223 SHADOW WATER B   22
        THAT SET HIM TO THE FANCY.  ALL WOULD BE WELL  . . . .   230 SHADOW WATER B  177
        THOUGH IT BUT SET US SIGHING? FELLOW—WANDERER,  . . .    230 SHADOW WATER B  187
        THOUGH IT BUT SET US SIGHING.  FELLOW WANDERER  . . .    230 SHADOW WATER B  187
        AND SET YOU DREAMING.  HOW CAN WE HAVE A WAKE  . . . .   240 SHADOW WATER B  386
        THAT HAVE TO BE SET UP IN FIFTY WAYS,  . . . . . . . .   260 FASC DIFFICULT    9
        AND AFTER SET YOUR HEART TO BEAT,  . . . . . . . . . .   263 MASK              9
        MY FANCY, AND SET MY BOYISH LIPS TO SAY,  . . . . . .    270 PARDON FATHERS   17
        AND CAME INTO A WOOD AS THE SUN SET  . . . . . . . . .   277 TWO KINGS     V   3
        SO THAT HIS PLAUTUS SET THE PACE  . . . . . . . . . .    287 TO WEALTHY MAN   12
        SO THAT HIS PLUTARCH SET THE PACE  . . . . . . . . . .   287 TO WEALTHY MAN V 12
        HE GAVE THE HOURS THEY HAD SET FREE  . . . . . . . . .   288 TO WEALTHY MAN   22
        YOUR ENEMY, AN OLD FOUL MOUTH, HAD SET  . . . . . . .    292 TO A SHADE       17
        AN OLD FOUL MOUTH THAT SLANDERED YOU HAD SET  . . . .    292 TO A SHADE    V  17
        THIS NIGHT CAN SET US QUARRELLING,  . . . . . . . . .    324 ROBERT GREGORY   15
        TOWARDS NIGHTFALL UPON CERTAIN SET APART  . . . . . .    325 ROBERT GREGORY   29
        THE TOWER SET ON THE STREAM'S EDGE  . . . . . . . . .    326 ROBERT GREGORY   52
        THE TOWER SET BY THE STREAM'S EDGE:  . . . . . . . . .   326 ROBERT GREGORY V 52
        SET ALL HER BLOOD ASTIR  . . . . . . . . . . . . . .     336 YOUNG GIRL       10
        SET CARPENTERS TO WORK ON NO WIDE TABLE,  . . . . . .    340 SHEP GOATHERD    50
        CRAWLED FROM OBSCURITY, AND SET UPON ME  . . . . . . .   352 PEOPLE           26
        HAS SET ME MUTTERING LIKE A FOOL.  . . . . . . . . . .   356 BROKEN DREAMS    26
        WE HAVE NO GIFT TO SET A STATESMAN RIGHT:  . . . . . .   359 WAR POEM          3
        HE SET HIS CHISEL TO THE HARDEST STONE.  . . . . . . .   369 EGO DOMINUS      32
        MAY HANDLE NOTHING AND SET EYES ON NOTHING  . . . . .    371 ON GOING HOUSE    6
        THAT THE LAST SERVILE CRESCENT HAS SET FREE?  . . . .    376 PHASES OF MOON  103
        AUSTERITY, A PLACE SET OUT FOR WISDOM  . . . . . . . .   377 PHASES OF MOON  127
        IT HAD SET DOWN AMONG ITS LAWS:  . . . . . . . . . .     399 BREAK OF DAY     16
        OR SET UPON A GOLDEN BOUGH TO SING  . . . . . . . . .    408 SAIL BYZANTIUM   30
        A COMPANY OF FRIENDS, A CONSCIENCE SET AT EASE,  . . .   427 PHANTOM HATRED   37
        ANOTHER TROY MUST RISE AND SET,  . . . . . . . . . .     437 SONGS PLAY 1      9
        AM SET DOWN STANDING IN THE WOOD  . . . . . . . . . .    453 DEATH OF HARE    11
        SET ALL YOUR MIND UPON THE STEEP ASCENT,  . . . . . .    477 SELF AND SOUL     2
        HEART'S PURPLE——AND ALL THESE I SET  . . . . . . . . .   478 SELF AND SOUL    28
        IN MOCKERY I HAVE SET  . . . . . . . . . . . . . . .     480 BLOOD AND MOON    8
        A SCENE WELL SET AND EXCELLENT COMPANY,  . . . . . . .   489 COOLE PARK 29    16
        WHAT KNOWLEDGE OR ITS LACK HAD SET AWRY,  . . . . . .    490 COOLE BALLYLEE   22
        WHAT KNOWLEDGE OR ITS LACK HAS SET AWRY,  . . . . . .    490 COOLE BALLYLEE V 22
        AND SET SUCH COLOUR THERE,  . . . . . . . . . . . . .    492 ANNE GREGORY      8
        THAT HE MIGHT SET AT REST  . . . . . . . . . . . . .     496 MOHINI CHATTER   12
        THINKING TO SET AT REST  . . . . . . . . . . . . . .     496 MOHINI CHATTER V 12
        SET ME BY THAT OAK, FOR HE  . . . . . . . . . . . . .    508 JANE BISHOP   V 22
        WHAT SET IT WHIRLING ROUND?  . . . . . . . . . . . .     520 HIS BARGAIN       2
        AND BROKE THE CHAIN AND SET MY ANKLES FREE,  . . . . .   533 HER TRIUMPH       9
        AND SET A ROSE—TREE ON HER GRAVE,  . . . . . . . . . .   571 THREE BUSHES     73
        SET UP THE OLD STONE CROSS,  . . . . . . . . . . . .     604 YOU CONTENT      10
        A SMALL FORGOTTEN HOUSE THAT'S SET  . . . . . . . . .    606 SONGS BURDEN 2    3
        BUT WHAT CARED I THAT SET HIM ON TO RIDE,  . . . . . .   629 CIRCUS ANIMALS   15
        SPOKE AND SET THE COCKS A—CROW,  . . . . . . . . . .     637 BEN BULBEN        4
        PROOF THAT THERE'S A PURPOSE SET  . . . . . . . . . .    639 BEN BULBEN       50
        AND BLAME THE SNARE THEY SET FOR ME.  . . . . . . . .    743 DANAAN QUICK     23
        THESE ARE THEIR LURES, BUT THEY HAVE SET THEIR HEARTS .  757 SHADOW WATER A  206
        ON NAUGHT HAS SET STORE  . . . . . . . . . . . . . .     780 WELL AND TREE    13
        AND SET IT ON A STAKE.  . . . . . . . . . . . . . .      789 SINGING HEAD      6
SETS
        THE THIRTEENTH MOON BUT SETS THE SOUL AT WAR  . . . . .  374 PHASES OF MOON   50
        AND IS SO LOVELY THAT IT SETS TO RIGHT  . . . . . . .    490 COOLE BALLYLEE   21
        CARES WHAT KING SETS UP HIS RULE.  . . . . . . . . . .   635 BLACK TOWER      14
        WHERE BEN BULBEN SETS THE SCENE.  . . . . . . . . . .    637 BEN BULBEN       11
        ALE SETS THEM QUARRELLING.  GIVE ME YOUR SWORDS.  . .    766 SHADOW WATER A  372
        WHAT SETS IT BEATING SO?  . . . . . . . . . . . . .      781 HEART FRIGHT      2
SETTING
        WHEN WE ARE DEAD, BEYOND THE SETTING SUNS,  . . . . .     71 ANASHU VIJAYA     8
        A MAN CAME SLOWLY FROM THE SETTING SUN,  . . . . . . .   105 CUCHULAIN SEA     1
        THAT SHADES THE ROAD, OR SETTING UP A COTTAGE  . . . .   372 ON GOING HOUSE   14
```

SETTING (CONTINUED)
```
  OR THE UNCERTAINTY OF HIS SETTING FORTH?  . . . . . . .   444 SCHOOL CHILDR       40
  HE HAD MUCH INDUSTRY AT SETTING OUT. . . . . . . . . .    473 ALL SOUL NIGHT      71
  FEET TO THE RISING AND SETTING MAY RUN. . . . . . . . .   591 WHAT WAS LOST        4
SETTLED
  NOW THAT WE'RE ALMOST SETTLED IN OUR HOUSE . . . . . . .  323 ROBERT GREGORY       1
  NOW THAT WE'VE ALMOST SETTLED IN OUR HOUSE . . . . . . .  323 ROBERT GREGORY V     1
  NO SETTLED MAN. AND NOW THAT HE IS GONE  . . . . . . .    341 SHEP GOATHERD       55
  BEFORE SHE HAD SETTLED HER MIND  . . . . . . . . . . .    381 SONGS FOOL 2         8
  IMPROVISATION, OR A SETTLED GAME . . . . . . . . . . .    533 HER TRIUMPH          3
  AND WERE THE LAST TO CHOOSE THE SETTLED GROUND. . . . .   621 HOUND VOICE          2
SETTLES
  BUT NOW WIND DROPS, DUST SETTLES; THEREUPON  . . . . . .  433 NINETEEN 19        125
SEVEN     SEE NINETEEN-SEVEN
  AND BIRDS THAT ON THE SEVEN SEAS RANGE. . . . . . . . .     4 OISIN 1        V   27A
  THAT SPRANG UNDER THE SEVEN HAZEL TREES. . . . . . . .     35 OISIN 2           84
  FROM THE WHOLE SEVEN SEAS, THOSE TOWERS SET  . . . . .    38 OISIN 2        V  131
  . . . AND PACING THE SHORES OF THE SEVEN SEAS. . . . .    50 OISIN 3        V   55
  THE SAILING SEVEN . . . . . . . . . . . . . . . . . .    118 CRADLE SONG          7
  AND THE OLD PLANETS SEVEN . . . . . . . . . . . . . .    118 CRADLE SONG          7
  THE OLD PLANETS SEVEN . . . . . . . . . . . . . . . .    118 CRADLE SONG    V     7
  THE SHINING SEVEN . . . . . . . . . . . . . . . . . .    118 CRADLE SONG    V     7
  'MONG THE FEET OF ANGELS SEVEN . . . . . . . . . . . .   125 CATHLEEN PARA       13
  WITH WHITE FEET OF ANGELS SEVEN  . . . . . . . . . . .   125 CATHLEEN PARA  V    13
  AND HER GUIDES ARE ANGELS SEVEN. . . . . . . . . . . .   125 CATHLEEN PARA  V    15
  AND THOUGH THE SEVEN LIGHTS BOWED IN THEIR DANCE AND WEPT, 174 ELEMENT POWERS      3
  IN THE SEVEN WOODS . . . . . . . . . . . . . . . . .    198 SEVEN WOODS          T
  I HAVE HEARD THE PIGEONS OF THE SEVEN WOODS  . . . . .   198 SEVEN WOODS          1
  SEVEN OLD SISTERS WIND THE THREADS OF THE LONG-LIVED ONES, 209 UNDER THE MOON      7
  SEVEN OLD SISTERS WIND THE THREADS OF THE LONG LIVED ONES, 209 UNDER THE MOON      7
  I WALKED AMONG THE SEVEN WOODS OF COOLE: . . . . . . .   217 WOODS OF COOLE       1
  SEVEN ODOURS, SEVEN MURMURS, SEVEN WOODS. . . . . . .    218 WOODS OF COOLE      16
  SEVEN ODOURS, SEVEN MURMURS, SEVEN WOODS. . . . . . .    218 WOODS OF COOLE      16
  SEVEN ODOURS, SEVEN MURMURS, SEVEN WOODS. . . . . . .    218 WOODS OF COOLE      16
  AWAKE UNSLEEPING FIRES: AND WOVE SEVEN STRINGS. . . . .  219 HARP OF AENGUS       7
  SEVEN POEMS  I  UPON A DYING LADY  . . . . . . . . . .   362 HER COURTESY   V     T
  WE, WHO SEVEN YEARS AGO . . . . . . . . . . . . . .. .   431 NINETEEN 19         89
  WHERE SEVEN EPHESIAN TOPERS SLEPT AND NEVER KNEW . . . . 442 BLACK CENTAUR       11
  EVEN TO-DAY, AFTER SOME SEVEN YEARS  . . . . . . . . .   468 HARUN RASHID       161
  EVEN TODAY, AFTER SOME SEVEN YEARS . . . . . . . . . .   468 HARUN RASHID   V   161
  SEVEN CENTURIES HAVE PASSED AND IT IS PURE. . . . . . .  482 BLOOD AND MOON      33
  THE SEVEN SAGES . . . . . . . . . . . . . . . . . . .    486 SEVEN SAGES          T
  SEVEN POEMS  GIRL'S SONG . . . . . . . . . . . . . . .   515 GIRLS SONG B   V     T
  I TOLD HIM THAT NIGHTLY FROM SIX TO SEVEN I SAT AT THIS   578 LOFTY THINGS         9
    TABLE,
  THROUGH SEVEN HEROIC CENTURIES: . . . . . . . . . . .   640 BEN BULBEN          80
  ARE DYING TOO.  THEY WERE FULL SEVEN STARS: . . . . . .  700 MOSADA 3            48
  AWAKE UNSLEEPING FIRES; AND WOVE SEVEN STRINGS. . . . .  762 SHADOW WATER A     302
  THERE ARE SEVEN THAT PULL THE THREAD. . . . . . . . . .  770 SPINNING SONG        1
  HOLIEST, HOLIEST SEVEN. . . . . . . . . . . . . . . .    771 SPINNING SONG       11
SEVENFOLD
  OUT OF THE SEVENFOLD SEAS, BUILT THE DARK HALL  . . . .   38 OISIN 2            131
  . . . WHEN THE SEVENFOLD SEAS WERE YOUNG. . . . . . . .   50 OISIN 3             52
SEVEN-FOLD
  OUT OF THE SEVEN-FOLD SEAS, BUILT THE DARK HALL  . . .    38 OISIN 2        V  131
  . . . WHEN THE SEVEN-FOLD SEAS WERE YOUNG. . . . . . .    50 OISIN 3        V   52
SEVENTY
  SEVENTY YEARS HAVE I LIVED: . . . . . . . . . . . . .    567 FROM JAPANESE        2
  SEVENTY YEARS HAVE I LIVED  . . . . . . . . . . . . .    567 FROM JAPANESE        5
  SEVENTY YEARS HAVE I LIVED. . . . . . . . . . . . . .    567 FROM JAPANESE        7
  SEVENTY YEARS MAN AND BOY. . . . . . . . . . . . . .     567 FROM JAPANESE        8
SEVERAL
  THOUGH SEVERAL, ARE A SINGLE LIGHT. . . . . . . . . . .  388 SOLOMON WITCH       29
SEVERED
  ALTERNATIVE SONG FOR THE SEVERED HEAD IN . . . . . . .   549 SEVERED HEAD         T
  FOR IF SEVERED FROM THE ROOT . . . . . . . . . . . .    668 ISLE STAT II 3      61
SEW
  TO CUT AND SEW, BE NEAT IN EVERYTHING  . . . . . . . .   443 SCHOOL CHILDR        5
  TOOK UP THE NEAREST AND BEGAN TO SEW. . . . . . . . . .  634 CUCHULAIN COMF      18
SEWED
  AND GRANIA, WALKING AND SMILING, SEWED WITH HER NEEDLE    53 OISIN 3             94
    OF BONE.
SEWN     SEE GOLD-SEWN
SEXUAL
  GODHEAD ON GODHEAD IN SEXUAL SPASM BEGOT  . . . . . . .  557 RIBH ECSTASY         5
  CRY AT THE ONSET OF THEIR SEXUAL JOY . . . . . . . . .   560 WHENCE COME          2
  CRY AT THE ONSET OF THE SEXUAL JOY  . . . . . . . . .    560 WHENCE COME    V     2
SGEOLAN
  BRAN, SGEOLAN, AND LOMAIR. . . . . . . . . . . . . .       2 OISIN 1        V    7D
  AND BRAN, SGEOLAN, AND LOMAIR  . . . . . . . . . . .       2 OISIN 1        V    7R
  WHAT PLACE HAVE CAOLTE AND FIN, AND BRAN, SGEOLAN, LOMAIR?  61 OISIN 3       V  195
  TO FIN, CAOLTE, AND CONAN, AND BRAN, SGEOLAN, LOMAIR. . .  63 OISIN 3       V  224
SHADE
  SIDLED THEIR BODIES AGAINST HIM, FILLING THE SHADE WITH   50 OISIN 3             48
    THEIR EYES.
  HIS EVENING FIRE AMID THE LEAFY SHADE. . . . . . . . .   109 CUCHULAIN SEA       48
  AFTER SHORT FIGHTING IN THE LEAFY SHADE. . . . . . . .   109 CUCHULAIN SEA       57
  BESIDE HER CLEAN-SWEPT HEARTH, HER QUIET SHADE: . . . .  114 ROSE OF BATTLE      11
  BESIDES HER CLEAN SWEPT HEARTH, HER QUIET SHADE: . . .   114 ROSE OF BATTLE V    11
  AND PIERCE THE DEEP WOOD'S WOVEN SHADE. . . . . . . .    125 GOES FERGUS          2
  AND GOD COVERED THE WORLD WITH SHADE. . . . . . . . .    133 FR GILLIGAN         19
```

SHADE   (CONTINUED)
        TO A SHADE . . . .   292 TO A SHADE   T
        IF YOU HAVE REVISITED THE TOWN, THIN SHADE, ...   292 TO A SHADE   1
        AMID THAT FIRST ASTONISHMENT, WITH GRANIA'S SHADE, . . .   366 HER COURAGE   4
        WHILE WONDERING STILL TO BE A SHADE, WITH GRANIA'S SHADE,   366 HER COURAGE   V   4
        WHILE WONDERING STILL TO BE A SHADE, WITH GRANIA'S SHADE,   366 HER COURAGE   V   4
        AND I MERE SHADE AT LAST . . . .   449 HERO GIRL FOOL   25
        UPON THE NORMAN UPLAND OR IN THAT POPLAR SHADE, ...   449 OWEN AHERNE   2
        UPON THE NORTHERN UPLAND OR IN THAT POPLAR SHADE, ...   449 OWEN AHERNE   V   2
        PICK OUT MY FEATURES IN SUCH LIGHT AND SHADE . . . . .   466 HARUN RASHID   116
        AND ALL THE SENSUALITY OF THE SHADE-- . . . .   489 COOLE PARK 29   31
        BEFORE ME FLOATS AN IMAGE, MAN OR SHADE, ...   497 BYZANTIUM   9
        SHADE MORE THAN MAN, MORE IMAGE THAN A SHADE! . . . .   497 BYZANTIUM   10
        SHADE MORE THAN MAN, MORE IMAGE THAN A SHADE! . . . .   497 BYZANTIUM   10
        UNFRIENDLY LAMPLIGHT HID UNDER ITS SHADE, ...   523 LONG SILENCE   3
        UNDER THE TROPIC SHADE, GREW ROUND AND SLOW, ...   610 STATUES   18
        DREAMING THE LIVE-LONG SUMMER IN THE SHADE, ...   650 ISLE STAT I 1   139
        HERE IN THE SHADE. WHY? WHY? FOR WHAT IS GLAD? . . .   652 ISLE STAT I 2   8
        SEE, YONDER SINKS THE SUN, YONDER A SHADE . . . . . .   653 ISLE STAT I 2   52
        AH, WOE IS ME! I GO FROM SUN AND SHADE, ...   674 ISLE STAT II 3   216
        DOTH HE STILL DWELL WITHIN THE WOODY SHADE, ...   678 ISLE STAT II 3   303
        WITH QUIET SHADE ITS EVER DEWY-PLOT. . . . .   714 FERENCZ RENYI   109
        WITH QUIET SHADE ITS EVER DEWY SPOT, ...   714 FERENCZ RENYI   V   109
        WITH QUIET SHADE ITS EVER DEWY PLOT, ...   714 FERENCZ RENYI   V   109
        SO PASSIONATE IS A SHADE, ...   781 MY HEART BEAT   13
SHADED
        FROM THE GREEN SHADED HOLLOW . . . .   655 ISLE STAT I 2   82
SHADES
        AMID THE SHADES OF NIGHT, HE CHANGED AND RAN . . . . .   40 OISIN 2   174
        A LITTLE FROM THE OTHER SHADES APART, ...   71 ANASHU VIJAYA   9
        HOW WHEN WE DIE OUR SHADES WILL ROVE, ...   78 INDIAN TO LOVE   18
        HOW WHEN WE DIE OUR SHADES MAY ROVE, ...   78 INDIAN TO LOVE   V   18
        WHO AMID LEAFY LIGHTS AND SHADES . . . .   193 BAILE AILLINN   103
        IS FROM THE HOLY SHADES THAT ROVE . . . .   275 GREY ROCK   110
        THAT THE SHADES OF HOLY MEN . . . .   298 THREE HERMITS   17
        THAT SHADES THE ROAD, OR SETTING UP A COTTAGE . . . . .   372 ON GOING HOUSE   14
        AMONG THE DEEPENING SHADES. . . . .   416 TOWER   195
SHADING   SEE BROW-SHADING
SHADOW
        HIS SHADOW ALONG IN THE EVENING BLAZE, ...   27 OISIN 1   V   409
        AND IN THE SHADOW OF MY HAIR LIE HID, ...   33 OISIN 2   66
        UNDER THE STARLIGHT AND SHADOW, A MONSTROUS SLUMBERING
            FOLK,   48 OISIN 3   27
        NOW IN A PLACE OF STAR-FIRE, AND NOW IN A SHADOW PLACE
            WIDE!   49 OISIN 3   V   42
        LAY LOOSE IN A PLACE OF SHADOW! WE DREW THE REINS BY HIS
            SIDE.   50 OISIN 3   44
        I CRIED, "COME OUT OF THE SHADOW, KING OF THE NAILS OF
            GOLD!   51 OISIN 3   61
        I CRIED, "COME OUT OF THE SHADOW, CANN OF THE NAILS OF
            GOLD!   51 OISIN 3   V   61
        PAINTING WITH SHADOW ALL THE MARBLE STEPS! . . . . .   72 ANASHU VIJAYA   30
        BODIES OF SHADOW AND BLIND EYES LIKE PEARLS, ...   185 QUEEN MAEVE   116
        THAT HAVE ONE SHADOW ON THE GROUND! . . . . . .   195 BAILE AILLINN   154
        O SHE WAS BUT A SHADOW, AND SLIPPED FROM ME. . . . . .   223 SHADOW WATER B   40
        A SHADOW DOES NOT CARRY SWORD OR SPEAR. . . . . . .   224 SHADOW WATER B   44
        AS A LAMP SHADOW--NO--NO LAMP, THE SUN. . . . . . .   229 SHADOW WATER B   160
        IS SHADOW, AND NOT LINGER WRETCHEDLY . . . .   230 SHADOW WATER B   180
        LET GO MY HANDS! WHY DO YOU CAST A SHADOW? . . . . .   235 SHADOW WATER B   283
        THEY WOULD NOT SEND ME ONE THAT CASTS A SHADOW. . . . .   235 SHADOW WATER B   285
        IT VANISHED LIKE A SHADOW, AND A CRY . . . . . .   278 TWO KINGS   38
        TILL ALL HAD SEEMED A SHADOW OR A VISION . . . . .   278 TWO KINGS   43
        IN THE GREEN SHADOW OF FERRARA WALL! . . . . . .   352 PEOPLE   9
        IN THE GREEN SHADOW ON FERRARA WALL! . . . . . .   352 PEOPLE   V   9
        WE ARE ON THE BRIDGE! THAT SHADOW IS THE TOWER, . . .   372 PHASES OF MOON   10
        A SHADOW OF CLOUD ON THE STREAM . . . .   393 EASTER 1916   49
        UNDER THE SHADOW OF STUPID STRAW-PALE LOCKS, ...   433 NINETEEN 19   127
        THE MOUNTAIN THROWS A SHADOW, ...   519 LOVES LONENESS   7
        GODHEAD. SOME SHADOW FELL. MY SOUL FORGOT . . . . .   557 RIBH ECSTASY   6
        BENEATH THE SHELTERING SHADOW OF THY CHURCH! . . . . .   698 MOSADA 2   58
        WHERE SHADOW OF CHERRY, AND SHADOW OF APPLE TREES, . . .   710 FERENCZ RENYI   23
        WHERE SHADOW OF CHERRY, AND SHADOW OF APPLE TREES, . . .   710 FERENCZ RENYI   23
        AND EVERY FLOWER ABOVE ITS SHADOW SITS. . . . . .   712 FERENCZ RENYI   73
        AND EVERY FLOWER ABOVE A SHADOW SITS. . . . . .   712 FERENCZ RENYI   V   73
        AND BID THEM HIDE IN SHADOW OF THE SAIL, ...   751 SHADOW WATER A   93
        NEAR BY, BUT IN THE SHADOW OF THE SAIL, ...   752 SHADOW WATER A   121
        OR A GOD HID THEM UNDER THE SHADOW OF WINGS. . . . .   752 SHADOW WATER A   125
        WHOSE SHADOW IS THE SLEEP THAT COMES WITH LOVE, ...   754 SHADOW WATER A   162
        THE GRASS AND THE BLUE SHADOW ON THE STREAM . . . . .   761 SHADOW WATER A   280
        DID NOT A SHADOW PASS? . . . .   781 MY HEART BEAT   2
SHADOWED
        "HE SHADOWED IN A GLASS . . . .   255 WOMAN HOMER   13
SHADOWING
        IN SOME LIKE CHAMBER, SHADOWING FORTH . . . . . .   419 MY HOUSE   15
SHADOWLESS
        ALL DAY LONG FROM SHADOWLESS NOON . . . .   332 SOLOMON SHEBA   5
SHADOW-PLACE
        NOW IN A PLACE OF STAR-FIRE, AND NOW IN A SHADOW-PLACE
            WIDE!   49 OISIN 3   42
SHADOWS
        UPON THEIR SHADOWS IN THE TIDE, ...   14 OISIN 1   185

	PAGE	TITLE		LINE

SHADOWS   (CONTINUED)
SOME DANCED LIKE SHADOWS ON THE MOUNTAINS, ... 25 OISIN 1 388
NOW, MAN OF CROZIERS, SHADOWS CALLED OUR NAMES . . . . 29 OISIN 2 1
HALF LOST IN VAPOUR, SHADOWS CALLED OUR NAMES, ... 29 OISIN 2 V 3
UNDER THE DEEPEST SHADOWS OF THE HALL . . . . . . 37 OISIN 2 119
UNDER THE SHADOWS TILL THE TUMULTS DIED . . . . . . 38 OISIN 2 140
YOUR EYES HAD ONCE, AND OF THEIR SHADOWS DEEP: . . . . 121 YOU ARE OLD 4
THE LONG HAIR SHADOWS HER FACE: . . . . 124 CATHLEEN PARA V 10
AND RULES THE SHADOWS OF THE WOOD, ... 126 GOES FERGUS 10
OF THE FAR-WANDERING SHADOWS HAS COME TO ME . . . . 183 QUEEN MAEVE 80
OF THE FAR WANDERING SHADOWS HAS COME TO ME, ... 183 QUEEN MAEVE V 80
WE SHADOWS, WHILE THEY UPROOT HIS EARTHY HOUSE, . . . 184 QUEEN MAEVE 94
WILL OVERTHROW HIS SHADOWS AND CARRY OFF . . . . . 184 QUEEN MAEVE 95
WE SHADOWS, WHILE THEY UPROOT THE EARTHY HOUSE . . . 184 QUEEN MAEVE V 94
WITH HOLY SHADOWS." HER HIGH HEART WAS GLAD, ... 186 QUEEN MAEVE 126
AND LITTLE SHADOWS COME ABOUT HER EYES: . . . . . 199 FOLLY COMFORT 3
HAVE SEEN IMMORTAL, MILD, PROUD SHADOWS WALK: . . . . 217 WOODS OF COOLE 12
MOVED ROUND ME IN THE SHADOWS, AND AT NIGHT . . . . 218 WOODS OF COOLE 19
HOW SHALL I NAME YOU, IMMORTAL, MILD, PROUD SHADOWS? . 218 WOODS OF COOLE 27
THE ROOTS OF THE WORLD. SHADOWS BEFORE NOW . . . . 227 SHADOW WATER B 104
THE ROOTS OF THE WORLD. WHO KNOWS THAT SHADOWS . . . 227 SHADOW WATER B V 104
FOR THAT IS WHAT THEY SAY—ALL, ALL THE SHADOWS— . . 228 SHADOW WATER B 137
THAT I HAVE THE BEST OF PILOTS. SHADOWS, ILLUSIONS, . . 249 SHADOW WATER B 565
AND THE SHADOWS EATEN THE MOON. . . . . 268 BROWN PENNY 14
SHADOWS AND SHOWS THAT CAN BUT TURN THE BRAIN." . . . 281 TWO KINGS 108
THAT CAST THEIR SHADOWS UPON ROAD AND BRIDGE: . . . 326 ROBERT GREGORY 51
OUR SHADOWS ON THE GROUND . . . . 333 SOLOMON SHEBA 14
AMONG THE EVENING SHADOWS. . . . . 341 SHEP GOATHERD 71
TO HIS SHAPE IN THE LENGTHENING SHADOWS, ... 341 SHEP GOATHERD V 70
REEL SHADOWS OF THE INDIGNANT DESERT BIRDS. . . . . 402 SECOND COMING 17
WIND SHADOWS OF THE INDIGNANT DESERT BIRDS. . . . . 402 SECOND COMING V 17
SHADOWS THE INHERITED GLORY OF THE RICH. . . . . . 418 ANCEST HOUSES 16
OUR SHADOWS ROVE THE GARDEN GRAVEL STILL, ... 435 NEW FACES 7
AND TOOK A MESS OF SHADOWS FOR ITS MEAT? . . . . . 444 SCHOOL CHILDR 28
AND TOOK A MASS OF SHADOWS FOR ITS MEAT, ... 444 SCHOOL CHILDR V 28
DEAR SHADOWS, NOW YOU KNOW IT ALL, ... 476 EVA GORE-BOOTH 21
BACK THE SHADOWS CREEP AGHAST— . . . . 648 ISLE STAT I 1 98
THE WARMTH OF LIFE IS CHILLING, AND THE SHADOWS GROW . 675 ISLE STAT II 3 232
AND RULE THE SHADOWS OF THE EVE AND DAWN? . . . . 678 ISLE STAT II 3 304
THE SHADOWS PASS: BUT NOW, I LOVE MY RING. . . . . 700 MOSADA 3 27
ENFOLDEN IN THE SHADOWS OF THE EAST, ... 705 REMEMBRANCE 11
LISTENING, UPON THEIR SHADOWS STOOD. . . . . . . 725 LEGEND 8
ROUND US HERDS OF SHADOWS STEAL— . . . . . . 737 IN FIRELIGHT 6
CARE NOT IF BEYOND THE SHADOWS . . . . 737 IN FIRELIGHT 7
SHADOWY
THEY LED US BY LONG AND SHADOWY WAYS . . . . . . 16 OISIN 1 221
THEY LEAD US BY LONG AND SHADOWY WAYS . . . . . . 16 OISIN 1 V 221
IN A LONG AND SHADOWY ROW, ... 20 OISIN 1 V 295
WARS SHADOWY, VAST, EXULTANT: FAERIES OF OLD . . . . 29 OISIN 2 9
WARS SHADOWY, VAST, EXULTANT: FAIRY KINGS . . . . . 29 OISIN 2 V 9
WHERE SHADOWY FACE FLOWED INTO SHADOWY FACE, ... 39 OISIN 2 145
WHERE SHADOWY FACE FLOWED INTO SHADOWY FACE, ... 39 OISIN 2 145
AND THE SHADOWY HAZEL GROVE . . . . 119 PITY OF LOVE 6
THE SHADOWY BLOSSOM OF MY HAIR . . . . 152 HEART OF WOMAN 7
TWO LOVE POEMS   THE SHADOWY HORSES . . . . . . 154 BELOVED PEACE V T
I HEAR THE SHADOWY HORSES, THEIR LONG MANES A-SHAKE, . 154 BELOVED PEACE 1
IN SHADOWY POOLS, WHEN ARMIES FLED: . . . . . . 155 FORGOT BEAUTY 5
WITH YOUR DIM SHADOWY HAIR, ... 163 ASKS FORGIVE V 22
DEDICATION TO THE "SHADOWY WATERS" . . . . . . 217 WOODS OF COOLE V T
THE SHADOWY WATERS . . . . 221 SHADOW WATER B T
THE LIVING SEEM MORE SHADOWY THAN THEY. . . . . . 435 NEW FACES 8
FROM THE SHADOWY HOLLOW . . . . 654 ISLE STAT I 2 56
FROM THE SHADOWY HOLLOW . . . . 654 ISLE STAT I 2 78
IN SHADOWY DIMNESS. TO BE FAIR AS THEE . . . . . 670 ISLE STAT II 3 106
FROM HERE, ALONG THE SHADOWY WAY THAT WINDS . . . . 703 MOSADA 3 111
THE SHADOWY WATERS . . . . 745 SHADOW WATER A T
SHADY
I FIND NO HAPPINESS IN SHADY BRYCELINDE . . . . . 209 UNDER THE MOON V 1
SHADY KYLE-DORTHA: SUNNIER KYLE-NA-NO, ... 217 WOODS OF COOLE 4
AND UNDER A SHADY OAK-TREE SAT, ... 728 PRIEST FAIRY 7
SHAFT   SEE SPEAR-SHAFT
HAS FLUNG ITS ARROWY SHAFT UPON THE FLOOR. . . . . 482 BLOOD AND MOON 32
HAD FLUNG ITS ARROWY SHAFT UPON THE FLOOR, ... 482 BLOOD AND MOON V 32
AROUND THE FEATHERY TIP. UNTO THE SHAFT . . . . . 657 ISLE STAT I 3 71
SAY THEN,—"A POPINJAY BEFORE GRIEF'S SHAFT . . . . 664 ISLE STAT II 2 52
SHAFTS
SHOOT ON HIM SHAFTS OF QUIETNESS, THAT HE MAY EVER KEEP 75 ANASHU VIJAYA 81
SHOOT ON HIM SHAFTS OF QUIETNESS, AND ORDER HIM TO KEEP 75 ANASHU VIJAYA V 81
SHAGGY
WITH ANTLERS AND THE SHAGGY SKIN . . . . 17 OISIN 1 V 249
SHAKE   SEE A-SHAKE
SHAKE THE LOOSE REINS: YOU SLAVES OF GOD, ... 22 OISIN 1 331
SHAKE THE LOOSE REINS: YE SLAVES OF GOD, ... 22 OISIN 1 V 331
AND SHAKE THEIR COVERLET. . . . . 33 OISIN 2 62
AND SHAKE THEIR COVERLET'S HEM. . . . . 33 OISIN 2 V 62
SIGH, O YOU LITTLE STARS! O SIGH AND SHAKE YOUR 72 ANASHU VIJAYA 18
  BLUE APPAREL!
SIGH, OH YE LITTLE STARS! OH, SIGH AND SHAKE YOUR BLUE 72 ANASHU VIJAYA V 18
  APPAREL!
AND SING, AND SHAKE MY HEAVY LOCKS. . . . . . . 84 MAD KING GOLL 44
WHY MUST YOU BLENCH AND SHAKE FROM FOOT TO CROWN?" . . 106 CUCHULAIN SEA 13

705

		PAGE	TITLE	LINE

SHAKE (CONTINUED)
WHY ARE YOU PALE AND SHAKE FROM FOOT TO CROWN?" • • • • 106 CUCHULAIN SEA V 13
LEAPING TO SHAKE A COBWEB FROM THE RAFTER, • • • • • 130 BOOK STORIES V 19
AND SHAKE A MOULDERING COBWEB FROM THE RAFTER, • • • • 130 BOOK STORIES V 19
AND SHAKE THEIR RAGGED WINGS! ALAS! • • • • • • • 136 TWO TREES 38
AND WHEN THEY SHAKE THEIR WINGS--ALAS! • • • • • • 136 TWO TREES V 38
AND SHAKE DOWN THUNDER ON THE STONES BECAUSE THE RED WINDS 207 HANRAHANS SONG V 7
    RAVE!
TO SHAKE THEIR WICKED SIDES AT YOUTH • • • • • • • 262 STUDENTS AGIT 3
TO SHAKE HIM OUT OF SLEEP, I COULD NOT ROUSE HIM. • • • 283 TWO KINGS 143
I SHAKE FROM HEAD TO FOOT. • • • • • • • • • • 316 FRIENDS 28
AND SHAKE THE BLOSSOM FROM THE BUD • • • • • • • 396 ROSE TREE 11
CAN SHAKE MORE BLOSSOM FROM AUTUMNAL CHILL • • • • • 465 HARUN RASHID 104
WHAT HEADS SHAKE OR NOD? • • • • • • • • • • 505 RESULT THOUGHT 18
WHAT MOST COULD SHAKE HIS SOUL! • • • • • • • • 529 TOM CRUACHAN 3
WHAT MOST CAN SHAKE HIS SOUL! • • • • • • • • • 529 TOM CRUACHAN V 3
SHAKE THE DEAD IN THEIR SHROUDS! • • • • • • • • 576 ACRE OF GRASS 22
THEY SHAKE WHEN THE WINDS ROAR. • • • • • • • • 635 BLACK TOWER 9
OLD BONES UPON THE MOUNTAIN SHAKE. • • • • • • • 635 BLACK TOWER 10
THEY SHAKE WHEN THE WINDS ROAR, • • • • • • • • 636 BLACK TOWER 19
OLD BONES UPON THE MOUNTAIN SHAKE. • • • • • • • 636 BLACK TOWER 20
THEY SHAKE WHEN THE WINDS ROAR, • • • • • • • • 636 BLACK TOWER 29
OLD BONES UPON THE MOUNTAIN SHAKE. • • • • • • • 636 BLACK TOWER 30
OF THE MONK'S-HOOD HOW THEY SHAKE, • • • • • • • 655 ISLE STAT I 3 2
WILL HE HAVE HAPPINESS? GREAT SOBS HER BEING SHAKE. • • 676 ISLE STAT II 3 247
HIS BODY SHAKE? AY, QUIVERING AS YON SMOKE • • • • 683 SEEKER 36
THE HEATHEN. YEA, AND SHAKE THE SULLEN KINGS • • • • 698 MOSADA 2 55
ROASTING BERRIES STEAM AND SHAKE-- • • • • • • • 727 LOVERS QUARREL 43
WHILE WE SHAKE OUR HEADS AND SCOLD • • • • • • • 727 LOVERS QUARREL 54
AND SHAKE THEIR BIRDS UPON THE AIR, • • • • • • • 736 SUMMER EVENING 3
AND SHAKE THEIR BIRDS UPON THE AIR, • • • • • • • 737 SUMMER EVENING 19
SHAKEN
AH ME! TO BE SHAKEN WITH COUGHING AND BROKEN WITH OLD AGE 63 OISIN 3 217
    AND PAIN.
ARE SHAKEN WITH EARTH'S OLD AND WEARY CRY. • • • • • 120 SORROW OF LOVE V 12
REMEMBERING ALL THAT SHAKEN HAIR • • • • • • • 135 TWO TREES 17
WHEN LOOKING ON THEIR SHAKEN HAIR. • • • • • • • 135 TWO TREES V 17
IN SHAKEN BOUGHS, IN TIDE ON THE SHORE? • • • • • 141 EVERLAST VOICE 7
O HEART THE WINDS HAVE SHAKEN, THE UNAPPEASABLE HOST • • 147 UNAPPEAS HOST 11
AND HEART THE WINDS HAVE SHAKEN! THE UNAPPEASABLE HOST • • 147 UNAPPEAS HOST V 11
AND HEAR THE WINDS HAVE SHAKEN, THE UNAPPEASABLE HOST • • 147 UNAPPEAS HOST V 11
THAT WAS SHAKEN OUT OVER MY BREAST! • • • • • • • 155 REPROVE CURLEW 5
IN TWILIGHT SHAKEN WITH LOW SIGHS! • • • • • • • 156 FORGOT BEAUTY V 10B
IS SHAKEN IN THESE SEAS, AND WHAT ONE DOES • • • • 237 SHADOW WATER B 339
WHAT WOULD HAVE SHAKEN FROM THE SIEVE? • • • • • • 256 WORDS 14
UPON A HOUSE SHAKEN BY THE LAND AGITATION • • • • • 264 HOUSE SHAKEN T
SHAKES
AND BENDS TO THE FIRE AND SHAKES WITH THE COLD • • • 26 OISIN 1 405
AND SHAKES O'ER THE WIDTH OF THE SEA-WORLD BORDER • • • 28 OISIN 1 V 423C
GOD SHAKES THE WORLD WITH RESTLESS HANDS. MORE NEAR • • 43 OISIN 2 V 208
ORCHIL SHAKES OUT HER LONG DARK HAIR • • • • • • 85 MAD KING GOLL 62
THAT SHAKES A MOULDERING COBWEB FROM THE RAFTER! • • • 130 BOOK STORIES 19
THAT SHAKES THE SHUTTER, TO HAVE BROUGHT TO MIND • • • 327 ROBERT GREGORY 90
NOT AS HE SHAKES THE FOREST! BUT A CRY • • • • • 689 NETTLESHIP 8
AY, AND SHAKES IN SEA-GREEN WAVERINGS ALONG THE FISHERS' 718 PHANTOM SHIP 2
    STREET!
AYE AND SHAKES IN SEA GREEN WAVERINGS, ALONG THE FISHERS' 718 PHANTOM SHIP V 2
    STREET.
ONE WHOSE BREATHING SHAKES THE AIR, • • • • • • • 727 LOVERS QUARREL 31
ONE WHOSE FOOTFALL SHAKES THE GROUND, • • • • • • 727 LOVERS QUARREL 32
MY LOVE SHAKES OUT HER HAIR UPON THE STREAMS • • • • 768 SHADOW WATER A 416
SHAKESPEAREAN
SHAKESPEAREAN FISH SWAM THE SEA, FAR AWAY FROM LAND! • • 485 THREE MOVEMENT 1
SHAKING SEE EARTH-SHAKING
OF THE LOUD CRASHING AND EARTH SHAKING FIGHT • • • • 38 OISIN 2 V 141
SHAKING AND WAVING, VAPOUR VAPOUR CHASED, • • • • • 39 OISIN 2 164
SHAKING AND WAVING, VAPOURS VAPOURS CHASED! • • • • • 39 OISIN 2 V 164
AND, SHAKING THE PLUMES OF THE GRASSES • • • • • • 49 OISIN 3 35
HE, SHAKING THE FOLD OF HIS LIPS, • • • • • • • 51 OISIN 3 59
HE, SHAKING THE FOLDS OF HIS LIPS • • • • • • • 51 OISIN 3 V 59
HEARING THE SHAKING OF SHIELDS • • • • • • • • 62 OISIN 3 207
THE SHAKING OF ITS LEAFY HEAD • • • • • • • • 134 TWO TREES 9
THROUGH THE SHAKING TREE • • • • • • • • • • 359 TO A SQUIRREL 3
THAT STORMS ARE SHAKING, HEAR THE ARMED MAN SPEAK. • • 470 HARUN RASHID V 193
WHERE THE SHAKING LEAF WITH THE BEAM WAS PLAYING, • • • 728 PRIEST FAIRY 2
SHALLOP
WHERE LIES A SHALLOP IN THE YELLOW REEDS. • • • • • 702 MOSADA 3 77
SHALLOW
ON THE GREY SAND BESIDE THE SHALLOW STREAM • • • • • 367 EGO DOMINUS 1
FROM SHALLOW WITS! WHO KNOWS NO WORK CAN STAND, • • • 429 NINETEEN 19 35
IT BORE ME SOFTLY WHERE THE SHALLOW SAND • • • • • 657 ISLE STAT I 3 58
THE BOAT'S PROW GRATED ON THE SHALLOW SAND, • • • • 659 ISLE STAT II 1 11
WHAT SHALLOW THOUGHTS ABOUT DEEP THINGS! • • • • • 725 LEGEND 11
SHALLOWING
PIERCED WITH SOFT LIGHT THE SHALLOWING DEEPS. • • • • 13 OISIN 1 164
SHAMBLING
SAID THE RAMBLING, SHAMBLING TRAVELLING-MAN! • • • • 788 HAWTHORN TREE 2
SAID THE RAMBLING, SHAMBLING TRAVELLING-MAN! • • • • 788 HAWTHORN TREE 10
SHAME
IT BRINGS NO SHAME UPON A HUMAN HEAD • • • • • • 35 OISIN 2 V 90A
THE FORTUNE THAT HAD BEEN MY SHAME • • • • • • • 274 GREY ROCK 93

706

		PAGE	TITLE		LINE

SHAME   (CONTINUED)
    AND THAT IS MY SHAME. . . . .   572 LADYS 1ST SONG   8
    AND THINK IT IS NO SHAME. . . . .   605 SONGS BURDEN 1   4
    THE SISTER: "SELL THY COUNTRY, AND THE SHAME . . . . .   712 FERENCZ RENYI   60
SHAMED
    WERE NEITHER SHAMED IN HIS OWN . . . .   291 TO A FRIEND   7
SHAMELESS
    WHO LIVED IN SHAMELESS JOY AND LAUGHED INTO THE FACE OF   366 HER COURAGE   V   10
    DEATH.
SHAMMING
    ONE BEGGAR CRIED: "YOU'RE SHAMMING SLEEP," . . . . .   297 THREE BEGGARS   V   45
SHANWALLA
    SHANWALLA, WHERE A WILLOW BORDERED POND . . . . . .   217 WOODS OF COOLE   V   2
SHAN-WALLA
    SHAN-WALLA, WHERE A WILLOW-BORDERED POND . . . . . .   217 WOODS OF COOLE   2
SHAPE
    AND SUNKEN SHAPE, A NINE DAYS' CORPSE SEA-DASHED-- . . .   40 OISIN 2   V   179
    AND SUNKEN SHAPE, AGAINST MY FACE AND BREAST, ...   40 OISIN 2   V   179
    AND DRIPPING AND SUNKEN SHAPE, TO FACE AND BREAST, . . .   40 OISIN 2   V   179
    HIS NEW-HEALED SHAPE: AND FOR A HUNDRED YEARS . . . .   44 OISIN 2   221
    HIS HEALED SHAPE: AND FOR A HUNDRED YEARS . . . . .   44 OISIN 2   V   221
    HIS NEW HEALED SHAPE: AND FOR A HUNDRED YEARS . . . .   44 OISIN 2   V   221
    AND YOU HAVE CHANGED AND FLOWED FROM SHAPE TO SHAPE, . .   102 FERGUS DRUID   2
    AND YOU HAVE CHANGED AND FLOWED FROM SHAPE TO SHAPE, . .   102 FERGUS DRUID   2
    AND NOW AT LAST YOU WEAR A HUMAN SHAPE, ...   102 FERGUS DRUID   6
    AND NOW AT LAST YOU TAKE ON HUMAN SHAPE-- . . . . .   102 FERGUS DRUID   V   6
    THE POWERS WHOSE NAME AND SHAPE NO LIVING CREATURE KNOWS   174 ELEMENT POWERS   1
    LONGING TO KNEAD AND PULL IT INTO SHAPE . . . . . .   246 SHADOW WATER B   510
    FOR WHAT IS DOUBLY BRIEF." AND NOW THE SHAPE . . . . .   285 TWO KINGS   207
    FOR WHAT IS DOUBLY BRIEF." "BUT NOW THE SHAPE, ...   285 TWO KINGS   V   207
    INTO SOME MOST FEARFUL SHAPE." . . . .   299 THREE HERMITS   23
    TO HIS SHAPE AT THE RINSING-POOL . . . .   341 SHEP GOATHERD   70
    TO HIS SHAPE IN THE LENGTHENING SHADOWS, ...   341 SHEP GOATHERD   V   70
    TO HIS SHAPE AT THE RINSING POOL . . . .   341 SHEP GOATHERD   V   70
    THEIR CONNEMARA CLOTH WORN OUT OF SHAPE: . . . . . .   372 PHASES OF MOON   4
    A SHAPE WITH LION BODY AND THE HEAD OF A MAN, ...   402 SECOND COMING   14
    AS THOUGH TO CHOOSE WHATEVER SHAPE IT WILLS . . . . .   417 ANCEST HOUSES   6
    OR SERVILE SHAPE, AT OTHERS' BECK AND CALL. . . . . .   417 ANCEST HOUSES   8
    WHAT YOUTHFUL MOTHER, A SHAPE UPON HER LAP . . . . .   444 SCHOOL CHILDR   33
    WOULD THINK HER SON, DID SHE BUT SEE THAT SHAPE . . . .   444 SCHOOL CHILDR   37
    THE SELF-SOWN, SELF-BEGOTTEN SHAPE THAT GIVES . . . .   446 COLONUS PRAISE   10
    THAT DEFILING AND DISFIGURED SHAPE . . . .   479 SELF AND SOUL   51
    HE THINKS THAT SHAPE MUST BE HIS SHAPE? . . . . . .   479 SELF AND SOUL   54
    HE THINKS THAT SHAPE MUST BE HIS SHAPE? . . . . . .   479 SELF AND SOUL   54
    ALL OUT OF SHAPE FROM TOE TO TOP, ...   639 BEN BULBEN   71
    THE SHAPE CHANGERS THAT CAN PUT . . . .   775 AGAINST WITCH   V   2
SHAPE-CHANGERS
    THAT THE SHAPE-CHANGERS, THE EVER-LAUGHING ONES, . . .   249 SHADOW WATER B   566
    THE SHAPE-CHANGERS THAT CAN PUT . . . .   775 AGAINST WITCH   2
SHAPED
    HIS LONG LAMP-CHIMNEY SHAPED LIKE THE STEM . . . . .   566 LAPIS LAZULI   33
    HIS LONG LAMP CHIMNEY SHAPED LIKE THE STEM . . . . .   566 LAPIS LAZULI   V   33
SHAPELESS
    WHEN NETTLES WAVE UPON A SHAPELESS MOUND . . . . . .   489 COOLE PARK 29   27
SHAPELY
    AND ALL THE SHAPELY BODY NO TITTLE GONE ASTRAY. . . .   354 HIS PHOENIX   30
    TO GREAT SHAPELY KNEES . . . .   355 PROPERTIUS   2
    MY WAY IS WEST. SHE SEEMS BOTH YOUNG AND SHAPELY: . .   755 SHADOW WATER A   171
SHAPES
    THROUGH MANY SHAPES: I LUNGED AT THE SMOOTH THROAT . . .   40 OISIN 2   175
    TO MANY SHAPES: I LUNGED AT THE SMOOTH THROAT . . . .   40 OISIN 2   V   175
    ON THE FAR GOLDEN PEAK: ENORMOUS SHAPES, ...   74 ANASHU VIJAYA   68
    MAGICAL SHAPES. BY THE HELP OF AN IMAGE . . . . . .   367 EGO DOMINUS   7
    PARTICULAR QUALITY. THE SIGNS AND SHAPES: . . . . .   469 HARUN RASHID   181
    BECAUSE THE FIRES OF PURGATORY HAVE ATE THEIR SHAPES AWAY: 593 PILGRIM   13
    OR, FOR MANY SHAPES THEY HAVE, ...   775 AGAINST WITCH   14
SHARE
    BUT HAVE NO SHARE IN LOSS OR VICTORY. . . . .   104 FERGUS DRUID   V   38E
    FOR GOD HAS BID THEM SHARE AN EQUAL FATE: . . . . . .   115 ROSE OF BATTLE   32
    O MY SHARE OF THE WORLD, O YELLOW HAIR! . . . . . .   211 RAGGED WOOD   11
    AND TAKE THE CAPTAIN'S SHARE OF EVERYTHING . . . . .   225 SHADOW WATER B   73
    YOU'LL HAVE THE CAPTAIN'S SHARE OF EVERYTHING. . . . .   225 SHADOW WATER B   V   67A
    A PRETTY GIRL TO SHARE MY BED": . . . .   296 THREE BEGGARS   31
    I HAD MY SHARE OF MOTHER-WIT, ...   313 MEMORY YOUTH   3
    I HAD MY SHARE OF MOTHER WIT: . . . .   313 MEMORY YOUTH   V   3
    COULD SHARE IN THAT DISCOURTESY OF DEATH. . . . . .   325 ROBERT GREGORY   48
    IN SOMETHING THAT ALL OTHERS UNDERSTAND OR SHARE: . . .   427 PHANTOM HATRED   35
    FOR EVEN DAUGHTERS OF THE SWAN CAN SHARE . . . . . .   444 SCHOOL CHILDR   20
    . . . SHARE GOD THAT IS BUT THREE. . . . .   556 RIBH PATRICK   11
    I WILL NOT SHARE YOUR SIN. THIS IS NO SIN. . . . . .   692 MOSADA 1   42
    I WILL NOT SHARE YOUR SIN. IT IS NO SIN. . . . . .   692 MOSADA 1   V   42
SHARED
    IN GRATTAN'S HOUSE. MY GREAT-GRANDFATHER SHARED . . .   486 SEVEN SAGES   2
    NONE SHARED OUR GUILT: NOR DID WE PLAY A PART . . . .   542 PARN FUNERAL 1   22
    SHARED THE BYZANTINE CROWN? . . . .   789 SINGING HEAD   14
SHARES
    HAVE LIT UPON A WOMAN WHO SO SHARES . . . .   465 HARUN RASHID   85
SHARP
    SHARP THEIR SPADES, THEIR MUSCLES STRONG, ...   637 BEN BULBEN   22
    SHARP THEIR SPADES, THEIR MUSCLE STRONG, ...   637 BEN BULBEN   V   22

	PAGE	TITLE	LINE

SHARPENED
    BEING SHARPENED BY HIS DEATH, ...   471 ALL SOUL NIGHT   8
    CAN GIVE HIS SHARPENED PALATE ECSTASY . . . .   474 ALL SOUL NIGHT   84
    GIVE TO HIS SHARPENED PALATE ECSTASY . . . .   474 ALL SOUL NIGHT V   84
SHATTER
    FAR THE MORNING VAPOURS SHATTER, ...   648 ISLE STAT I 1   89
SHATTERED
    HAD SHATTERED HER SOUL. PROPINQUITY HAD BROUGHT . . . .   619 BRONZE HEAD   18
    THE DARKNESS OF THE WHIRLWIND SHATTERED DEEP. . . . . .   688 TWO TITANS   58
SHAUL
    HOW THE MEN OF THE SAND-SACK LED ME TO SHAUL, ...   61 OISIN 3   V   193
SHAVINGS
    DREAM OF SHAVINGS ON A FLOOR . . . .   440 WISDOM   V   6
SHAWE-TAYLOR
    IMPETUOUS MEN, SHAWE-TAYLOR AND HUGH LANE, ...   489 COOLE PARK 29   14
SHAWL
    IN COUNTRY SHAWL OR PARIS CLOAK, HAD PUT MY WITS ASTRAY,   592 PILGRIM   3
    SO COME IN RAGS OR COME IN SILK, IN CLOAK OR COUNTRY SHAWL, 593 PILGRIM   22
    SO COME IN RAG OR COME IN SILK, IN CLOAK OR COUNTRY SHAWL, 593 PILGRIM   V   22
SHEAF
    OR MICE IN THE ONE WHEATEN SHEAF . . . .   195 BAILE AILLINN   147
SHEARS
    RAN AND WITH THE GARDEN SHEARS . . . .   410 TOWER   30
    BUT A RAVING AUTUMN SHEARS . . . .   475 EVA GORE-BOOTH   5
SHEATH
    COVERS ITS WOODEN SHEATH. . . . .   421 MY TABLE   7
    LONG ERE AN ARROW WHIZZED OR SWORD LEFT SHEATH . . . .   650 ISLE STAT I 1   135
SHEAVES
    AND OVER THE MICE IN THE BARLEY SHEAVES: . . . . . .   79 FALLING LEAVES   2
    AND ALL THE SHEAVES TO BIND. . . . .   312 CHILD DANCING   10
SHEBA
    SOLOMON TO SHEBA . . . .   332 SOLOMON SHEBA   T
    SANG SOLOMON TO SHEBA, ...   332 SOLOMON SHEBA   1
    TO SOLOMON SANG SHEBA, ...   333 SOLOMON SHEBA   9
    SANG SOLOMON TO SHEBA, ...   333 SOLOMON SHEBA   17
    SAID SOLOMON TO SHEBA, ...   333 SOLOMON SHEBA   V   17
    WHEN SHEBA WAS HIS LASS, ...   345 ON WOMAN   16
    THAT SHEBA LED A DANCE. . . . .   346 ON WOMAN   43
    GAVE SHEBA TO HER SOLOMON." . . . .   388 SOLOMON WITCH   32
SHED   SEE MILKING-SHED
    AND SOMETIMES FROM THE SALTIN' SHED . . . .   94 MOLL MAGEE   9
    TIMES FROM THE SALTIN' SHED, ...   94 MOLL MAGEE   V   9
    AND THESE IMMORTAL EYES SHED TEARS— . . . .   275 GREY ROCK   100
    FOR THIS THAT ALL THAT BLOOD WAS SHED, ...   290 SEPTEMBER 1913   19
    ON NO LONG BENCH NOR LOFTY MILKING SHED . . . . . .   341 SHEP GOATHERD   V   51
    INTO ITS NARROW SHED. . . . .   358 BALLOON MIND   4
    OR OUT OF ABSTRACT HATRED, AND SHED BLOOD, ...   482 BLOOD AND MOON   38
    AND WE THAT HAVE SHED NONE MUST GATHER THERE . . . .   482 BLOOD AND MOON   41
    MUST IRELAND'S BLOOD BE SHED. . . . .   608 SONGS BURDEN 3   26
    THAT I WOULD SHED LIKE TWILIGHT OVER YOU. . . . . .   765 SHADOW WATER A   352
SHEDS
    AND SHEDS FAINT ODOURS THROUGH THE AIR! . . . . . .   85 MAD KING GOLL   64
    AND SHEDS FAINT ODOUR THROUGH THE AIR! . . . . . .   85 MAD KING GOLL   V   64
    AND SANG WHAT GOLD MORNING OR EVENING SHEDS . . . .   126 DREAM OF FAERY   7
    AND SANG HOW DAY A DRUID TWILIGHT SHEDS . . . . .   126 DREAM OF FAERY V   7
SHEE
    "I AM NEAVE, A CHILD OF THE MIGHTY SHEE, ...   5 OISIN 1   V   48
    AND MEAT TO THE ASLAUGA SHEE. . . . .   743 DANAAN QUICK   17
SHEEN
    SMALL ISLAND, WHERE THE FULL SOFT SHEEN . . . . . .   653 ISLE STAT I 2   36
SHEEP
    AND A HUNDRED CALVES AND A HUNDRED SHEEP . . . . .   8 OISIN 1   89
    A PAIR OF LAPWINGS, ONE OLD SHEEP, ...   302 HOUR DAWN   9
    AND THE SHEEP BLEATING AT THE WIND . . . .   306 HOUR DAWN   78
    FROM STONE TO STONE. I AM LOOKING FOR STRAYED SHEEP! . .   339 SHEP GOATHERD   9
    THE SHEEP HAD GONE FROM THEIRS. I KNOW RIGHT WELL . .   339 SHEP GOATHERD   15
    WHERE THE SHEEP ARE THROWN IN THE POOL, ...   341 SHEP GOATHERD   V   71
    'TIS MORN! THY SHEEP ARE WANDERING DOWN THE VALE— . . .   645 ISLE STAT I 1   3
    NOW HER SHEEP ALL BROWSING MEET . . . .   646 ISLE STAT I 1   22
    THEIR SHEEP IN ARCADY, NASCHINA, HAIL! . . . . . .   649 ISLE STAT I 1   119
    THEIR SHEEP IN ARCADY, NASCHINA, HAIL! . . . . . .   649 ISLE STAT I 1   121
    NASCHINA, HAIL! I'D DRIVE THY WOOLLY SHEEP, ...   649 ISLE STAT I 1   122
    AND ONLY SHEEP HE LOVED OF ALL THE TROOP. . . . . .   661 ISLE STAT II 1   61
    HEAVY WITH WOOL THE SHEEP ARE GATHERED IN, ...   681 SEEKER   1
    ARE ALL THINGS WELL WITH YOU AND WITH YOUR SHEEP? . . .   682 SEEKER   13
    AND TO GIVE WEALTH OF OXEN AND SHEEP TO ALL! . . . .   756 SHADOW WATER A   184
    A HUNDRED OXEN AND A HUNDRED SHEEP, ...   756 SHADOW WATER A V   189
    GIVE ME A HUNDRED SHEEP. GIVE ME A HOUSE . . . . .   758 SHADOW WATER A   220
SHEEP-GUIDING
    SHEEP-GUIDING, OR THE BRINGING SOME STRANGE BIRD, . . .   650 ISLE STAT I 1   147
SHEER
    THAT SEEMED SHEER MIRACLE TO THE MULTITUDE, ...   428 NINETEEN 19   2
    THROUGH SHEER BEWILDERMENT? SHE HAD NOT PACED . . . .   466 HARUN RASHID   118
SHEET   SEE WINDING-SHEET
    I CAN STREW THE SHEET. . . . .   572 LADYS 2ND SONG   6
    THE WHITE WAVES WRAP IT IN A SHEET OF FLAME, ...   662 ISLE STAT II 2   14
SHEETS
    AND I MUST LIE BETWEEN THE SHEETS . . . .   570 THREE BUSHES   40
SHELF
    OUT-SCREAMS THE WHOLE SHELF! "ALTHOUGH . . . .   319 DOLLS   7

		PAGE	TITLE	LINE

SHELL   SEE SEA-SHELL
```
    AND IT WAS BOUND WITH A PEARL-PALE SHELL   • • • • • •      4 OISIN 1              28
    AND IT WAS BOUND WITH A PEARL PALE SHELL   • • • • • •      4 OISIN 1          V   28
    WHERE MANY A TRUMPET-TWISTED SHELL   • • • • • • •         13 OISIN 1             160
    WE RODE ON MURMURING. MANY A SHELL   • • • • • • •         13 OISIN 1          V  159
    OUT OF THE MOON'S PALE TWISTED SHELL:   • • • • • •        19 OISIN 1             279
    • • • WAKING WHITE AS A SHELL   • • • • • • • •            54 OISIN 3             103
    SOME TWISTED, ECHO-HARBOURING SHELL,   • • • • • •         66 HAPPY SHEPHERD       36
    SOUGHT ONCE AGAIN THE SHORE, AND FOUND A SHELL,   • • •    68 SAD SHEPHERD         18
    SOUGHT ONCE AGAIN THE SHORE, AND CHOSE A SHELL   • • •     68 SAD SHEPHERD     V   18
    A MOON, WORN AS IF IT HAD BEEN A SHELL   • • • • •        206 ADAMS CURSE          31
    A MOON--MOON WORN AS IF IT HAD BEEN A SHELL   • • •       206 ADAMS CURSE      V   31
    INTO THE YOLK AND WHITE OF THE ONE SHELL.   • • • •       443 SCHOOL CHILDR        16
    AS THE SEA'S FURROWS ON A SEA-TOST SHELL,   • • • •       660 ISLE STAT II 1       51
    WHERE A SHELL THE SEAS ANOINT,   • • • • • • •           732 STREET DANCERS       32
    A FRAGILE, EXQUISITE, PALE SHELL,   • • • • • • •        784 WOMANS BEAUTY        16
SHELLEY
    AND SHELLEY HAD HIS TOWERS,   • • • • • • • • • •        480 BLOOD AND MOON       15
SHELLEY'S
    SAT LATE, OR SHELLEY'S VISIONARY PRINCE:   • • • • •     373 PHASES OF MOON       16
SHELL'S
    TO ROUND THAT SHELL'S ELABORATE WHORL,   • • • • • •     509 JANE REPROVED         8
SHELLS     SEE SEA-SHELLS
    • • • THE STRONG HOOFS CRUSHING THE SAND AND THE SHELLS,  58 OISIN 3             157
    • • • THE GOLD HOOVES CRUSHING THE SANDS AND THE SHELLS   58 OISIN 3          V  157
    • • • THE STRONG HOOFS CRUSHING THE SANDS AND THE SHELLS  58 OISIN 3          V  157
    BUT ACTUAL SHELLS OF ROSSES' LEVEL SHORE.   • • • • •    494 AT ALGECIRAS         12
    ARE 'NEATH ITS PROW, AND CRUSHING SHELLS.   • • • • •    663 ISLE STAT II 2       35
SHELTER
    BETWEEN THE LAVISH SHELTER OF A WOOD   • • • • • •       108 CUCHULAIN SEA    V 38A
    ALTHOUGH I SHELTER FROM THE RAIN   • • • • • • •         131 OLD PENSIONER         1
    FOR HE WILL SHELTER YOU AND BRING YOU HOME.   • • • •    250 SHADOW WATER B      590
    A SHELTER TILL THE DAYLIGHT BROKE.   • • • • • • •       302 HOUR DAWN            15
    AND THERE IS SHELTER UNDER IT,   • • • • • • • •         509 JANE BISHOP          26
    THEY LEFT THEIR HOMESTEADS TO SHELTER THE FOXES,   • •   546 TO SAME TUNE 2   V    3
SHELTERED     SEE CLIFF-SHELTERED
    THE MILKING-PLACE, THE SHELTERED FARM?   • • • • •       151 HEART OF WOMAN   V    6
    A FARMHOUSE THAT IS SHELTERED BY ITS WALL,   • • • •     419 MY HOUSE              2
    A FARM-HOUSE THAT IS SHELTERED BY ITS WALL,   • • •      419 MY HOUSE         V    2
    FLED TO FAR COUNTRIES, OR SHELTERED THEMSELVES   • •     546 TO SAME TUNE 2        4
    FLED TO FAR COUNTRIES, OR SHELTERED THEMSELVES   • • •   613 MARCH SONGS 1         4
    WELL SHELTERED FROM THE WINDS, AND FRUITFUL FIELDS,   • • 758 SHADOW WATER A      221
SHELTERING
    SOME BEGGAR SHELTERING FROM THE WIND, AND THERE   • • •  351 HER PRAISE           13
    BENEATH THE SHELTERING SHADOW OF THY CHURCH:   • • • •   698 MOSADA 2             58
SHEPHERD
    THE SONG OF THE HAPPY SHEPHERD   • • • • • • • • •        64 HAPPY SHEPHERD        T
    THE SAD SHEPHERD   • • • • • • • • • • • • •              67 SAD SHEPHERD          T
    SHEPHERD AND GOATHERD   • • • • • • • • • • •            338 SHEP GOATHERD         T
    THE SAD SHEPHERD   • • • • • • • • • • • • •             338 SHEP GOATHERD     V   T
    WHAT TURNED SO GOOD A SHEPHERD FROM HIS CHARGE.   • •    339 SHEP GOATHERD        16
    HOW DOES SHE BEAR HER GRIEF?  THERE IS NOT A SHEPHERD  • • 340 SHEP GOATHERD       28
    WATCHING OUR SHEPHERD SPORTS AT HARVEST-TIME   • • •     340 SHEP GOATHERD        41
    COURT HIS SHEPHERD LASS.   • • • • • • • • •             343 SHEP GOATHERD       104
    FOR SHEPHERD LADS IN GALILEE: AND GRANT   • • • • •      371 ON GOING HOUSE        4
    SHEPHERD, TO MAR THE MORNING HAST THOU COME?   • • •     646 ISLE STAT I 1        30
    HEAR ME, AND, SHEPHERD, HEARING ME, GROW DUMB.   • •     646 ISLE STAT I 1        31
    YON SHEPHERD--CAME YOUR SPIRIT TO BEGUILE   • • • •      648 ISLE STAT I 1       105
    SING SUMMER WAVES.  BUT YONDER SHEPHERD VILE,   • • •    649 ISLE STAT I 1       107
    THE SHEPHERD PARIS FOR OENONE MADE,   • • • • • •        650 ISLE STAT I 1       136
    I, AS A SHEPHERD DRESSED, WILL SEEK AND SEEK   • • •     658 ISLE STAT II 1        1
    MY SHEPHERD GARMENTS, AND RETURN ANON.   • • • • •       659 ISLE STAT II 1       29
    IT IS THE SHEPHERD GUARIMOND, WHO LOVETH WELL   • •      661 ISLE STAT II 1       53
    NOW, JUDGE, MUST SHEPHERD THERNOT THERE AND I   • •      661 ISLE STAT II 1       65
    E'EN THEN, BEFORE HER SHEPHERD HAIR   • • • • • •        668 ISLE STAT II 3       54
    FAIR SHEPHERD, AS WE WANDERED HITHER,   • • • • •        669 ISLE STAT II 3       83
    THE SHEPHERD RAISED HIS ARMS AND SANK.   • • • • •       673 ISLE STAT II 3      187
    NO SHEPHERD FOOT HAS EVER DARED ITS DEPTHS.   • • •      682 SEEKER               32
SHEPHERD-BOY
    I LIT BY THE THING, 'TWAS A SHEPHERD-BOY,   • • • •      673 ISLE STAT II 3      180
SHEPHERDESS
    ALAS! I MAKE YOU SADDER, SHEPHERDESS.   • • • • •        659 ISLE STAT II 1       18
    A SHEPHERDESS LONG YEARS FORETOLD:   • • • • • •         668 ISLE STAT II 3       49
    THAT SHEPHERDESS: ARISE, AND BRING TO ME,   • • • •      673 ISLE STAT II 3      191
SHEPHERD'S
    HE'LL PRACTISE ON THE SHEPHERD'S FLUTE,   • • • • •      343 SHEP GOATHERD       102
SHEPHERDS
    FLY! FLY! SO THESE BRAVE SHEPHERDS BOTH ARE GONE!   • •  649 ISLE STAT I 1       112
    OF HILL TWO SHEPHERDS COME.  FAREWELL! I'LL DON   • •    659 ISLE STAT II 1       28
    OF WAR.  OF YORE, TWO SHEPHERDS, WHERE WE PAUSE,   • •   659 ISLE STAT II 1       31
    ONCE MORE THOSE SHEPHERDS COME.  MAYHAP SOME MIRTH   • • 664 ISLE STAT II 2       49
    THE SINGING SHEPHERDS, TOO, HAVE PASSED AWAY.   • • •    676 ISLE STAT II 3      271
    SHEPHERDS, I CAME THIS MORNING TO YOUR LAND   • • • •    682 SEEKER               15
    BETWEEN THE HORNED HILLS--SHEPHERDS, FAREWELL!   • •     682 SEEKER               27
    SHEPHERDS, FAREWELL!  HE SOON WILL BE--ASHES   • • •     682 SEEKER               34
SHEPHERDS'
    THAT HE MIGHT LEARN THE SHEPHERDS' WILL.   • • • • •     288 TO WEALTHY MAN       19
    THE SHEPHERDS' CONTEST OF SONG   • • • • • • • •         646 ISLE STAT I 1     V   T
SHIELD
    AH, FENIANS, WITH THE SHIELD AND BOW?   • • • • • •       10 OISIN 1             116
```

709

		PAGE	TITLE		LINE

SHIELD (CONTINUED)
    AND BY THEM WERE ARROW AND WAR-AXE, ARROW AND SHIELD AND   49 OISIN 3   29
      BLADE!
    WERE ARROW AND SHIELD AND WAR-AXE, ARROW AND SPEAR AND   49 OISIN 3   V 30
      BLADE.
    . . . THE SHIELD OUT OF OSIER AND HIDE! . . . .   52 OISIN 3   82
    AND THROUGH THE OTHER'S SHIELD HIS LONG BLADE BROKE, . . .   110 CUCHULAIN SEA V 66
    KING EOCHAID SAID, AND HE THAT BORE HIS SHIELD . . . . .   276 TWO KINGS   V   8
    THE SKIES MORE DIM, THOUGH BURNING LIKE A SHIELD, ...   656 ISLE STAT I 3   26
    "SHIELD BREAKER, BREAK A SHIELD TO-DAY, ...   739 EARL PAUL   1
    "SHIELD BREAKER, BREAK A SHIELD TO-DAY, ...   739 EARL PAUL   1
    SHIELD-BREAKER, BREAK A SHIELD TO-DAY, ...   739 EARL PAUL   V   1
    MEN CRY "BRING PAUL, SHIELD BREAKER, ...   740 EARL PAUL   11
    "SHIELD BREAKER, GREAT SHIELD BREAKER," . . . . . .   740 EARL PAUL   25
    "SHIELD BREAKER, GREAT SHIELD BREAKER," . . . . . .   740 EARL PAUL   25
    WITH SHIELD AND ARMOUR WROUGHT WITH GOLD, ...   741 EARL PAUL   37
    THE DIM SPEAR BREAKS THE BRIGHT SHIELD . . . .   741 EARL PAUL   49
SHIELD-BREAKER
    SHIELD-BREAKER, BREAK A SHIELD TO-DAY, ...   739 EARL PAUL   V   1
    MEN CRY! "BRING PAUL, SHIELD-BREAKER, ...   740 EARL PAUL   V 11
    THOUGH THE GLAD CRY "SHIELD-BREAKER," . . . .   741 EARL PAUL   35
    THE PEOPLE CRIED "SHIELD-BREAKER!" . . . .   741 EARL PAUL   53
SHIELDS
    HEARING THE SHAKING OF SHIELDS . . . .   62 OISIN 3   207
    THE HORNS AND SHIELDS AND WILD SWAN'S PINIONS! . . . .   82 MAD KING GOLL V   5
    SHOOK THE ALE-HORNS AND SHIELDS UPON THEIR HOOKS! . .   181 QUEEN MAEVE   38
    SHOOK THE ALE HORNS AND SHIELDS UPON THEIR HOOKS! . .   181 QUEEN MAEVE   38
    ARMLETS OF GOLD OR SHIELDS WITH GOLDEN NAILS, ...   749 SHADOW WATER A   43
    AND TO GIVE YOU BESIDES A HUNDRED SHIELDS, ...   756 SHADOW WATER A   185
    A HUNDRED SHIELDS OF BRASS, A HUNDRED SWORDS, ...   756 SHADOW WATER A V 188
SHIFT
    OR THAT THE WIND WOULD SHIFT A POINT, ...   306 HOUR DAWN   92
    WE SHIFT ABOUT--ALL THAT GREAT GLORY SPENT-- . . . .   491 COOLE BALLYLEE   39
    OR SHIFT TIME'S FILTHY LOAD, ...   505 RESULT THOUGHT   15
SHIFTED
    IF HE BUT SHIFTED A FEW STONES, ...   302 HOUR DAWN   14
SHIFTS
    MAN SHIFTS ABOUT--ALL THAT GREAT GLORY SPENT-- . . . .   491 COOLE BALLYLEE V 39
SHIN
    I HAVE A LUCKY WOODEN SHIN . . . .   302 HOUR DAWN   18
    ALONE AND ALONE, WITH A SPECKLED SHIN? . . . . . .   551 SONGS REWRIT 1   8
    DRINKING ALONE WITH A SPECKLED SHIN? . . . .   551 SONGS REWRIT 1 V   8
    LIVE LONE, ALONE WITH A SPECKLED SHIN? . . . . . .   551 SONGS REWRIT 1 V   8
SHINE   SEE SEA-SHINE
    LAID IT AND SIGHED! I HELD A SWORD WHOSE SHINE . . .   37 OISIN 2   126
    LAID IT AND SIGHED--A SWORD WHOSE WIZARD SHINE . . .   37 OISIN 2   V 126
    THEN IN THAT HALL, LIT BY THE DIM SEA SHINE, ...   41 OISIN 2   V 187
    DOWN TO THEIR FEET THE STARS THAT SHINE ALONE, . . .   662 ISLE STAT II 1   80
    SHINE DULL UNMOVING EYES. WHAT THING ART THOU? . . .   685 SEEKER   74
    WAVES OFF THE FLIES, AND WARMS HIM IN THE SHINE. . . .   709 FERENCZ RENYI   7
    AND THAT DREAM ONLY SHINE BEFORE HER FEET. . . . . .   761 SHADOW WATER A   258
SHININ'
    BUT GATHER WITH YOUR SHININ' LOOKS . . . .   96 MOLL MAGEE   55
SHINING   SEE A-SHINING SOFT-SHINING CLEAR-SHINING RE-SHINING
    THE SHINING SEVEN . . . .   118 CRADLE SONG   V   7
    SHINING BRIGHT AS A NEW LANCE! . . . .   125 CATHLEEN PARA V 14
    DEW EVER SHINING AND TWILIGHT GREY! . . . .   148 INTO TWILIGHT   6
    AND STARS LIKE MOTHS WERE SHINING OUT, ...   149 WANDER AENGUS V   6
    A WOMAN OF SO SHINING LOVELINESS . . . .   170 SECRET ROSE   25
    THOUGH YOU ARE IN YOUR SHINING DAYS, ...   172 PLEADS FRIEND   1
    ALTHOUGH YOU ARE IN YOUR SHINING DAYS, ...   172 PLEADS FRIEND V   1
    MORE SHINING WINDS, MORE STAR-GLIMMERING PONDS? . . .   218 WOODS OF COOLE   35
    SHINING ON WATER AND FALLEN AMONG LEAVES, ...   218 WOODS OF COOLE   38
    INTO THEIR SHINING LIMBS--I'VE HAD GREAT TEACHERS. . .   231 SHADOW WATER B   195
    AND HAVING SUCH WIDE-OPEN, SHINING EYES. . . . . .   231 SHADOW WATER B   200
    A SHINING WEB, A FLOATING RIBBON OF CLOTH, ...   430 NINETEEN 19   50
    EACH SHINING CLEAR AS SOME UNBAFFLED STAR! . . . . .   656 ISLE STAT I 3   25
    TRAILING AND SHINING 'NEATH THE FLICKERING GLARE. . .   688 TWO TITANS   32
    SINKS, SHINING ON THE LITTLE CRUCIFIX . . . . . .   691 MOSADA 1   34
    O SHINING ONES, LIGHTLY WITH SONG PASS, ...   708 FAIRY PEDANT   21
SHIP
    HERE WE WILL MOOR OUR LONELY SHIP . . . .   78 INDIAN TO LOVE   6
    THERE WE WILL MOOR OUR LONELY SHIP . . . .   78 INDIAN TO LOVE V   6
    "HE IS THE MIGHTIEST MAN IN SHIP OR DUN." . . . . .   107 CUCHULAIN SEA V 28
    WE HAVE NOT COME UPON A SHORE OR SHIP . . . . . .   222 SHADOW WATER B   3
    WHERE NO SHIP SAILS, WHERE NOTHING THAT'S ALIVE . . .   226 SHADOW WATER B   98
    LOOK THERE! THERE IN THE MIST! A SHIP OF SPICE! . . .   232 SHADOW WATER B   219
    BUT IF I WERE TO PUT YOU ON THAT SHIP, ...   236 SHADOW WATER B   307
    AND BEAT THE BULWARK OF YOUR SHIP ON MINE, ...   236 SHADOW WATER B   312
    UPON THAT OTHER SHIP WE ARE TO WAKE. . . . . . .   240 SHADOW WATER B   381
    WHAT NAME TO CALL HIM BY? COME TO HIS SHIP. . . . .   240 SHADOW WATER B   390
    BUT DESOLATE WATERS AND A BATTERED SHIP. . . . . . .   246 SHADOW WATER B   497
    DRAGONS WITH EYES OF RUBY. THE WHOLE SHIP . . . .   248 SHADOW WATER B   535
    AND THERE'S NO HELP IN WORDS. TO THE OTHER SHIP, . .   250 SHADOW WATER B   585
    AND RUNNING CROWD AND GAUDY SHIP . . . .   254 HIS DREAM   15
    AND FISH AND CROWD AND PAINTED SHIP, ...   254 HIS DREAM   15
    AND FISH AND CROWD AND GAUDY SHIP . . . .   254 HIS DREAM   V 15
    THE FAERY SHIP THAT SWIMS ATHWART THE SKY. . . . .   663 ISLE STAT II 2   16
    THE PHANTOM SHIP. . . . .   718 PHANTOM SHIP   T
    A LEGEND OF THE PHANTOM SHIP. . . . .   718 PHANTOM SHIP   V   T
    FOR I HAVE SEEN A SHIP HID IN THE FOG. . . . . . .   751 SHADOW WATER A   89

SHIP   (CONTINUED)
    THAT MY TRUE-LOVE WOULD COME IN A SHIP OF PEARL . . . .   763 SHADOW WATER A   315
    THAT MY TRUE LOVE WOULD COME IN A SHIP OF PEARL . . . .   763 SHADOW WATER A V   315
    A HOUSE, A SWORD, A SHIP, A MASK. . . . .   788 BRAVEST ASK   2
SHIPBOARD
    ON THEIR OWN FEET THEY CAME, OR ON SHIPBOARD, ...   566 LAPIS LAZULI   25
SHIPS
    A STORMY SUNSET ON DOOMED SHIPS; . . . .   3 OISIN 1   23
    A STORMY SUNSET O'ER DOOMED SHIPS. . . . .   3 OISIN 1   V   23
    . . . FROM RACHLIN TO BERA OF SHIPS. . . . .   58 OISIN 3   160
    AND WAGE GOD'S BATTLES IN THE LONG GREY SHIPS. . . . .   114 ROSE OF BATTLE   20
    "FROM THE GREY SHIPS AND BATTLES NEVER WON. . . . . .   114 ROSE OF BATTLE   8
    OUR LONG SHIPS LOOSE THOUGHT-WOVEN SAILS AND WAIT, . . .   115 ROSE OF BATTLE   31
    DOOMED LIKE ODYSSEUS AND THE LABOURING SHIPS . . . . .   120 SORROW OF LOVE   7
    AND ALL THE SORROWS OF HER LABOURING SHIPS, ...   120 SORROW OF LOVE   V   7
    AND ALL THE TROUBLE OF HER LABOURING SHIPS, ...   120 SORROW OF LOVE   V   7
    WOULD THAT THE STORM THAT OVERTHREW MY SHIPS, ...   235 SHADOW WATER B   286
    UNTO THE WANDERER'S SHIPS, OR AS DAY FILLS . . . . .   645 ISLE STAT I 1   10
    DRIFT AND FLOAT LIKE SILVER SHIPS; . . . . . .   647 ISLE STAT I 1   67
    DOTH STILL THE WANDERER ROVE? WITH ALL HIS SHIPS . . .   677 ISLE STAT II 3   287
    WERE FURLED THE WINGS OF SHIPS. THERE IN A DELL, . . .   693 MOSADA 1   82
    DID I NOT FOLLOW WITH A SCORE OF SHIPS? . . . . . .   749 SHADOW WATER A   36
SHIRK
    LIE DOWN AND DIE. THAT WERE TO SHIRK . . . . . .   632 MAN AND ECHO   19
    AND SHIRK IT IN VAIN. THERE IS NO RELEASE . . . . .   632 MAN AND ECHO   21
    NOR LET THE MODISH PAINTER SHIRK . . . .   638 BEN BULBEN   38
SHIRT
    "EACH ONE A HORSEHAIR SHIRT HATH ON, ...   43 OISIN 2   V 208C
    AND PUSHING IT INTO MY SHIRT. . . . .   274 GREY ROCK   89
    "IF BUT THE SHIRT UPON MY BODY KNEW IT . . . . . .   462 HARUN RASHID   33
SHIVER
    THE CORMORANTS SHIVER ON THEIR ROCKS; . . . . . .   84 MAD KING GOLL   42
    SHIVER UNDER THE LASH, STRAIN, SWEAT AND JOLT . . . .   260 FASC DIFFICULT   7
SHIVERED
    AND SHIVERED, KNOWING THE ISLE OF MANY FEARS, ...   30 OISIN 2   25
    AND LONELY AND LONGING FOR NIAMH, I SHIVERED AND TURNED   60 OISIN 3   181
      ME ABOUT,
SHIVERING
    HE SHIVERING PAUSED, AND RAISED HIS HEAD AND SCREAMED. . .   30 OISIN 2   V   25
    AND SHIVERING AND LONELY, AND LONGING FOR NIAM, I TURNED   60 OISIN 3   V 181
      ME ABOUT,
    OR THAN THE SHIVERING CASTING-NET OF THE STARS, ...   237 SHADOW WATER B   329
    AND PRAYER TO SHIVERING PRAYER, UNTIL . . . . . .   289 SEPTEMBER 1913   4
    AND I LEFT SHIVERING. THE VOICE HAS DRAWN . . . . .   469 HARUN RASHID   179
    SHIVERING CLOSER TO THEIR DAMS . . . .   726 LOVERS QUARREL   7
    OR THAN THE SHIVERING CASTING-NET OF THE STARS. . . . .   762 SHADOW WATER A   290
    OR THAN THE SHIVERING CASTING NET OF THE STARS. . . . .   762 SHADOW WATER A V   290
SHIVERS
    ALL CREATION SHIVERS . . . .   559 HE AND SHE   11
SHOALED   SEE SALMON-SHOALED
SHOCK
    LAUGHTER AND CRIES. THE ARMIES CLASH AND SHOCK, ...   43 OISIN 2   211
    OF ARMOUR--LAUGHTER AND CRIES--THE ARMIES' SHOCK. . . .   43 OISIN 2   V 211
SHOD   SEE GOLD-SHOD
    OR SHOD IN IRON, CLIMBED THE NARROW STAIRS, ...   412 TOWER   83
    TO HIM WITH THUNDER SHOD, ...   735 IN CHURCH   2
    TO HIM WITH THUNDER SHOD, ...   736 IN CHURCH   14
SHOE
    BUT WEEP FOR YOUR NIAMH, O OISIN, WEEP; FOR IF ONLY YOUR   55 OISIN 3   127
      SHOE
    BUT WEEP FOR THY NIAM, OH OISIN, WEEP; FOR IF ONLY THY SHOE 55 OISIN 3   V 127
SHOED   SEE SILVER-SHOED
SHOES
    THE CLOAK, THE BOAT, AND THE SHOES . . . .   69 CLOAK BOAT   T
    "I WEAVE THE SHOES OF SORROW! . . . .   70 CLOAK BOAT   12
    AND HE WORE SMALL HOLES IN HIS SHOES, ...   92 FATHER OHART   11
    HE HAD PUDDLE-WATER IN HIS SHOES; . . . .   190 BAILE AILLINN   28
    HE HAD PUDDLE WATER IN HIS SHOES; . . . .   190 BAILE AILLINN   V   28
    THAT PUT THIS HURRY IN MY SHOES.'" . . . .   194 BAILE AILLINN   125
    OR CREAKY SHOES. AND AT THE END OF ALL . . . . . .   228 SHADOW WATER B   128
    TO RID ME OF THE DEVIL IN MY SHOES," . . . . . .   299 BEGGAR CRIED   6
    ALL WEAR THE CARPET WITH THEIR SHOES; . . . . . .   337 SCHOLARS   8
    WEAR OUT THE CARPET WITH THEIR SHOES . . . . . .   337 SCHOLARS   V   8
    WHO HAD SEEMED TO GLIDE TO SOME INTRIGUE IN HER RED SHOES, 363 DOLLS FACES   6
    WITH OLD PATCHED SHOES, ...   627 STATES HOLIDAY   30
    NOD TO THE IRON SHOES OF TIME, ...   736 SUMMER EVENING   11
    O SHUFFLING OF HOLY SHOES! . . . .   774 COME RIDE   15
SHONE
    BUT NOW THE MOON LIKE A WHITE ROSE SHONE . . . . . .   12 OISIN 1   152
    ON HORSE AND SEA AND SADDLE SHONE. . . . .   28 OISIN 1   V 427D
    SHONE MANY TIMES AMONG THE GLIMMERING FLOWERS . . . .   30 OISIN 2   21
    AND THE FIXED STARS HAD DAWNED AND SHONE AND SET, . . .   31 OISIN 2   40
    AT LAST THE MOON AND STARS SHONE, AND A FLIGHT . . . .   31 OISIN 2   V   34
    THE IMAGED METEORS HAD SHONE AND RUN, ...   31 OISIN 2   V   38
    FEEBLER AND FEEBLER SHONE THE MISTY GLARE. . . . . .   37 OISIN 2   V 121
    WITH BOWED HEAD, TREMBLING WHEN THE WHITE BLADE SHONE, . .   38 OISIN 2   137
    I STOOD: KEEN STARS ABOVE ME SHONE, ...   83 MAD KING GOLL   29
    AROUND ME SHONE KEEN EYES OF MEN; . . . .   83 MAD KING GOLL   30
    I PAUSED--THE STARS ABOVE ME SHONE . . . .   83 MAD KING GOLL   V   29
    AND SHONE AROUND THE EYES OF MEN; . . . .   83 MAD KING GOLL   V   30
    ONE STAR SHONE FAINT AND GREEN, ...   95 MOLL MAGEE   30

		PAGE	TITLE	LINE

SHONE   (CONTINUED)
- THEY MAULED AND BIT TILL THE DAY SHONE؛ . . . . 297 THREE BEGGARS   49
- TRUTH FLOURISHES WHERE THE STUDENT'S LAMP HAS SHONE, . . 398 LEADERS CROWD   8
- THAT SHONE BEFORE THESE EYES . . . . 504 QUARREL IN AGE   15
- BUT THE DARK CHANGED TO RED, AND TORCHES SHONE, ... 537 HER VISION   12
- OF SAD QUEEN DIDO SHONE THE LAPPING FIRE . . . . 645 ISLE STAT I 1   9
- COURAGEOUS MIRACLES! THE SUNLIGHT SHONE . . . . 649 ISLE STAT I 1   113
- OF ALL ON WHOM ARCADIAN SUNS HAVE SHONE . . . . 650 ISLE STAT I 1   143
- OH, ALLAH! IT WAS THUS THEY SHONE THAT NIGHT . . . . . . 701 MOSADA 3   50
- THE FLAME THAT SHONE WITHIN HIS EYES BUT NOW . . . . . . 704 MOSADA 3   128

SHONEEN
- TO A SHONEEN WHO HAD FREE LANDS . . . . 92 FATHER OHART   3
- ALL LOVED HIM, ONLY THE SHONEEN, ... 92 FATHER OHART   13
- TO A SHONEEN IN HIS FREELANDS, ... 92 FATHER OHART   V   3

SHOOK
- HE SHOOK HIMSELF AND NEIGHED THREE TIMES؛ . . . . 10 OISIN 1   110
- HE SHOOK HIMSELF FOR TRAVELLING, ... 10 OISIN 1   V   110
- NOR SHOOK MY FIRM AND SPACIOUS SOUL ONE JOT؛ . . . . . 36 OISIN 2   V   94
- AND SHOOK AT INVER AMERGIN . . . . 81 MAD KING GOLL   3
- THEREON HE SHOOK THE MORE AND CAST HIM DOWN . . . . . . 106 CUCHULAIN SEA   14
- THE SINGING SHOOK HIM OUT OF HIS NEW EASE. . . . . . . 126 DREAM OF FAERY   12
- AND LEAVES SHOOK IN THE WIND؛ . . . . 133 FR GILLIGAN   18
- SHOOK THE ALE-HORNS AND SHIELDS UPON THEIR HOOKS؛ . . . 181 QUEEN MAEVE   38
- SHOOK THE ALE HORNS AND SHIELDS UPON THEIR HOOKS؛ . . . 181 QUEEN MAEVE   V   38
- AND SHOOK HIM WIDE AWAKE, AND BID HIM SAY . . . . 182 QUEEN MAEVE   50
- AND SHOOK WITH HATE AND FEAR. . . . . 254 WOMAN HOMER   4
- SHOOK OFF THE WATER FROM HIS BACK؛ . . . . 400 DEMON BEAST   29
- AND DEAFENING MUSIC SHOOK THE LEAVES؛ A TROOP . . . . . 537 HER VISION   13
- GENTLY SHOOK THEIR MOTH-LIKE WINGS؛ . . . . 667 ISLE STAT II 3   26
- I SLEPT, 'TWAS SULTRY, AND SCARCE CIRCLING SHOOK . . . . 677 ISLE STAT II 3   278
- SHOOK THE PALE APPLE-BLOSSOM OVER IT؛ . . . . 761 SHADOW WATER A   275
- SHOOK THE PALE APPLE BLOSSOM OVER IT؛ . . . . 761 SHADOW WATER A V   275

SHOOT
- SHOOT ON HIM SHAFTS OF QUIETNESS, THAT HE MAY EVER KEEP   75 ANASHU VIJAYA   81
- SHOOT ON HIM SHAFTS OF QUIETNESS, AND ORDER HIM TO KEEP   75 ANASHU VIJAYA V   81
- WHO BUT AWAITS HIS HOUR TO SHOOT, STILL HANGS . . . . . 198 SEVEN WOODS   13
- THE BURNING BOW THAT ONCE COULD SHOOT AN ARROW . . . . . 377 PHASES OF MOON   119
- TO SHOOT THE COLONEL DEAD! . . . . 596 COLONEL MARTIN   58
- THAT THEY COULD NEVER SHOOT A MAN . . . . 596 COLONEL MARTIN   61
- OF ROOT, SHOOT, BLOSSOM OR CLAY . . . . 600 SPIRIT MEDIUM   21
- THAT I MYSELF COULD SHOOT A GREAT GREY LYNX. . . . . . . 650 ISLE STAT I 1   152

SHOOTING
- BUT TO BE AMID SHOOTING OF FLIES AND FLOWERING OF RUSHES 55 OISIN 3   120
  AND FLAGS."
- BUT TO BE 'MID THE SHOOTING OF FLIES . . . . 55 OISIN 3   V   120

SHOOTS
- BRIGHTNESS REMAINS؛ A BRIGHTER STAR SHOOTS DOWN؛ . . . . 541 PARN FUNERAL 1   4
- OF THE BARLEY SHOOTS IN THE SUN. . . . . 643 SONG FAERIES   8
- OF THE BARLEY SHOOTS IN THE SUN. . . . . 676 ISLE STAT II 3   255

SHOP   SEE SWEET-SHOP
- OF OUR OLD PAUDEEN IN HIS SHOP, I STUMBLED BLIND . . . . 291 PAUDEEN   2
- IN A CROWDED LONDON SHOP, ... 501 VACILLATION   37
- WHILE ON THE SHOP AND STREET I GAZED . . . . 501 VACILLATION   40
- IN A GALWAY SHOP, ... 595 COLONEL MARTIN   22
- IN THE FOUL RAG-AND-BONE SHOP OF THE HEART. . . . . . . 630 CIRCUS ANIMALS   40
- IN THE FOUL RAG AND BONE SHOP OF THE HEART. . . . . . . 630 CIRCUS ANIMALS V   40

SHORE
- TO THIS DIM SHORE THOSE GENTLE FEET? . . . .   5 OISIN 1   V   51
- TO THIS DIM SHORE ON FOAM WET FEET? . . . .   5 OISIN 1   V   51
- TO THIS DIM SHORE ON FOAM-WET FEET? . . . .   5 OISIN 1   V   51
- WE CANTERED TO THE SHORE, AND KNEW . . . . 14 OISIN 1   178
- WHILE ROUND THE SHORE A MILLION STOOD . . . . 14 OISIN 1   182
- WAS DIM WITH MIRE OF A MORTAL SHORE, ... 15 OISIN 1   208
- WAS DIM WITH THE MIRE OF A MORTAL SHORE, ... 15 OISIN 1   V   208
- I CHASED UPON THAT WOODY SHORE . . . . 23 OISIN 1   344
- OH, PATRICK, ON THAT WOODY SHORE . . . . 23 OISIN 1   V   343
- WHEN ONCE BESIDE THE SHORE I STOOD؛ . . . . 24 OISIN 1   364
- WHEN ONE DAY BY THE SHORE I STOOD, ... 24 OISIN 1   V   364
- AND RODE AND STOOD BESIDE THE SHORE. . . . . 25 OISIN 1   V 379A
- LATER A SOUND CAME, HALF LOST IN THE SOUND OF A SHORE FAR 57 OISIN 3   155
  AWAY,
- SOUGHT ONCE AGAIN THE SHORE, AND FOUND A SHELL, ... 68 SAD SHEPHERD   18
- SOUGHT ONCE AGAIN THE SHORE, AND CHOSE A SHELL, ... 68 SAD SHEPHERD   V   18
- AND SING FROM SHORE TO SHORE, AND EVERY YEAR . . . . . 81 EPHEMERA   V   24G
- AND SING FROM SHORE TO SHORE, AND EVERY YEAR . . . . . 81 EPHEMERA   V   24G
- BY ROCKY SHORE AND RUSHY FEN؛ . . . . 83 MAD KING GOLL   32
- WHO PACED IN THE EVE BY THE NETS ON THE PEBBLY SHORE, . 91 OLD FISHERMAN   11
- WITH SHORE LINES IN THE SKY؛ . . . . 94 MOLL MAGEE   6
- I HEAR LAKE WATER LAPPING WITH LOW SOUNDS BY THE SHORE؛ 117 ISLE INNISFREE   10
- I HEAR LAKE WATER LAPPING WITH LOW SOUNDS ON THE SHORE؛ 117 ISLE INNISFREE V   10
- I AM HAUNTED BY NUMBERLESS ISLANDS, AND MANY A DANAAN   122 WHITE BIRDS   9
  SHORE,
- AND DANCE UPON THE LEVEL SHORE? . . . . 125 GOES FERGUS   3
- IN SHAKEN BOUGHS, IN TIDE ON THE SHORE? . . . . 141 EVERLAST VOICE   7
- WE WHO STILL LABOUR BY THE CROMLECH ON THE SHORE, . . . 161 BLACK PIG   5
- WE, WHO ARE LABOURING BY THE CROMLECH ON THE SHORE, . . 161 BLACK PIG   V   5
- BY A GREY SHORE WHERE THE WIND NEVER BLEW, ... 170 SECRET ROSE   14
- AND WHETHER I GO IN MY DREAMS BY WOODLAND, OR DUN,   210 UNDER THE MOON   14
  OR SHORE,
- WE HAVE NOT COME UPON A SHORE OR SHIP . . . . 222 SHADOW WATER B   3
- A CROWD UPON A SHORE. . . . . 253 HIS DREAM   4

712

		PAGE	TITLE		LINE

SHORE   (CONTINUED)
```
    MEN RAN UPON THE SHORE.                        253 HIS DREAM          V    4
    I, THOUGH UPRIGHT ON THE SHORE,                298 THREE HERMITS          11
    TO A CHILD DANCING UPON THE SHORE              312 CHILD DANCING     V    T
    DANCE THERE UPON THE SHORE;                    312 CHILD DANCING          1
    THE FIRST TIME ON THIS SHORE;                  323 SWANS AT COOLE         16
    STARVED UPON THE SHORE                         401 DEMON BEAST            48
    BUT TROD THE ROAD, OR SPLASHED ABOUT THE SHORE, 447 COLONUS PRAISE        27
    BUT TROD THE ROAD, OR PADDLED BY THE SHORE,    447 COLONUS PRAISE    V   27
    THE RATTLE OF PEBBLES ON THE SHORE             485 NINETEENTH CEN         3
    BUT ACTUAL SHELLS OF ROSSES' LEVEL SHORE.      494 AT ALGECIRAS          12
    SANG A BONE UPON THE SHORE.                    521 THREE THINGS           2
    SANG A BONE UPON THE SHORE;                    521 THREE THINGS           8
    SANG A BONE UPON THE SHORE;                    521 THREE THINGS          14
    BUILDING-YARD AND STORMY SHORE,                530 OLD TOM AGAIN          5
    BUILDING YARD AND STORMY SHORE,                530 OLD TOM AGAIN     V    5
    HER POETRY, DANCING UPON THE SHORE,            578 CRAZED GIRL            2
    THOUGH RICH ON EVERY SHORE                     606 SONGS BURDEN 1        11
    THEN STUMBLING TO THE KILL BESIDE THE SHORE;   622 HOUND VOICE           19
    THAT STUMBLING TO THE KILL BESIDE THE SHORE;   622 HOUND VOICE       V   19
    BUT WINDS COME UP FROM THE SHORE.              635 BLACK TOWER            8
    BUT WIND COMES UP FROM THE SHORE;              636 BLACK TOWER           18
    BUT WIND COMES UP FROM THE SHORE.              636 BLACK TOWER           28
    BUT WINDS COME UP FROM THE SHORE;              636 BLACK TOWER       V  REF
    THEN BID THEM RAISE MY STATUE ON THE SHORE;    663 ISLE STAT II 2        18
    TO WANDER BY THE BUBBLING SHORE,               668 ISLE STAT II 3        57
    I HURRIED FROM THE WOODY SHORE,                742 DANAAN QUICK           4
    HAVE BID ME HOPE, SAIL TO THE LOCHLANN SHORE   756 SHADOW WATER A    V  184
SHORES
    WASHES THE SHORES WHERE YE ABIDE,                5 OISIN 1           V   47
    YOUR MORTAL SHORES TILL TIME IS DONE!"           6 OISIN 1           V   59
    TO SHORES BY THE WASH OF THE TREMULOUS TIDE,     8 OISIN 1               81
    TO SHORES WHERE DYING HAS NEVER BEEN KNOWN,      8 OISIN 1           V   84
    AND ON THE SHORES WERE MANY BOATS               14 OISIN 1              188
    YET LOVE AND KISS ON DIM SHORES FAR AWAY        29 OISIN 2               13
    BUT LOVE AND KISS ON DIM SHORES FAR AWAY        29 OISIN 2           V   13
    THEY WALK ON SHORES UNSEEN OF OARING GALLEYS,   30 OISIN 2              14D
    AND SHORES THE FROTH LIPS WET;                  33 OISIN 2               59
    . . . AND PACING THE SHORES OF THE WANDERING SEAS, 50 OISIN 3           55
    . . . AND PACING THE SHORES OF THE SEVEN SEAS,  50 OISIN 3           V   55
    I SAW HIM FROM SAD DIDO'S SHORES DEPART,       677 ISLE STAT II 3       288
SHOREWARD
    AND SHOREWARD WAVES, WE NIGH HAVE FOUGHT; WAVES BRING  660 ISLE STAT II 1  44
SHORE-WEEDS
    . . . AND LATER THE SHORE-WEEDS BROWN.          57 OISIN 3              156
SHORN
    THAT I HAD SHORN MY LOCKS AWAY                 519 HER DREAM             3
SHORT
    AFTER SHORT FIGHTING IN THE LEAFY SHADE,       109 CUCHULAIN SEA        57
    I CELEBRATE THE SILENT KISS THAT ENDS SHORT LIFE OR LONG. 459 FROM OEDIPUS  9
SHORTEN
    PLANNED IN A GOVERNMENT OFFICE, SHORTEN HIS LIFE,  372 ON GOING HOUSE   15
SHOT      SEE EAR-SHOT BLOOD-SHOT CANNON-SHOT
    THE SIXTEEN MEN WERE SHOT,                     395 SIXTEEN DEAD          2
    OR EYELID SHOT THE GLEAM                       507 STREAM AND SUN       12
    HURRAH FOR REVOLUTION AND MORE CANNON SHOT;    590 GREAT DAY         V    1
    WHO WAS THE FIRST MAN SHOT THAT DAY?           608 SONGS BURDEN 3       10
    ANOTHER STAR HAS SHOT AN EAR.                  625 NATIVITY              2
    CERTAIN MEN THE ENGLISH SHOT?                  632 MAN AND ECHO         12
    A SCORE OF YARDS OFF 'NEATH A WILLOW, SHOT.    712 FERENCZ RENYI        65
    ARE SHOT AT ON THE OPEN PLAIN.                 791 REPRISALS            18
SHOULDER
    THRUSTING HIS NOSE TO MY SHOULDER; HE KNEW IN HIS BOSOM  54 OISIN 3     106
        DEEP
    AND ON MY LEANING SHOULDER SHE LAID HER SNOW-WHITE HAND.  90 SALLEY GARDENS  6
    HEAD UPON SHOULDER LEANT;                      319 DOLLS                18
    AND CHILDREN WHEN THEY SPRING UP SHOULDER HIGH. 343 SHEP GOATHERD    V  119
    AND START--I AT YOUR SHOULDER--               390 IMAGE PAST           30
    HANDS UPON EITHER SHOULDER MADE HER MOVE,      466 HARUN RASHID      V 125B
    WHAT'S BOWED YOUR SHOULDER AND MADE PALE YOUR CHEEK"; 467 HARUN RASHID  133
    BELLY, SHOULDER, BUM,                          612 NEWS ORACLE          34
    I AM; ONE SHOULDER TURNED AWRY--WHY THEN       692 MOSADA 1             61
    ONE SHOULDER TWISTED, AND THE CHILDREN CRY     695 MOSADA 1            116
SHOULDERED
    . . . THEY LIFTED AND SHOULDERED A SACK FULL OF SAND,  60 OISIN 3    V  185
    NOT DOUBTING TO HAVE SHOULDERED IT AWAY.       277 TWO KINGS         V  11A
    SHOULDERED A LITTER WITH A WOUNDED MAN,        537 HER VISION           14
SHOULDER-HIGH
    AND CHILDREN WHEN THEY SPRING UP SHOULDER-HIGH. 343 SHEP GOATHERD      119
SHOULDERS
    SHE LAID A HAND ON EITHER OF HIS SHOULDERS,    182 QUEEN MAEVE          49
    UPON HIS SHOULDERS. YOU'VE NOTHING BUT WILD WORDS,  235 SHADOW WATER B  300
    ABOVE THE CLOUDY SHOULDERS OF THE HORSES;      344 DAWN                 12
SHOUT
    AMONG THE RINGING HALLS A SHOUT                 20 OISIN 1           V  288
    I TURNED AND RODE TO THE WESTWARD, AND FOLLOWED THE SEA'S  60 OISIN 3  183
        OLD SHOUT
    AND RODE ON TILL OVER THE WORLD'S RIM FLOATED THE SEA'S  60 OISIN 3  V 183
        OLD SHOUT,
    DRAW ROUND AND RAISE A SHOUT;                  584 GHOST ROG CASE       38
    AND SHOUT A SECRET TO THE STONE.               632 MAN AND ECHO          5
```

SHOUT   (CONTINUED)
    AND SHOUT AT THE WISEST OWLS . . . .   644 SONG FAERIES   10
    AND SHOUT AT THE WISEST OWLS . . . .   676 ISLE STAT II 3   257
    A NEIGHBOURING CRICKET LIFTS HIS SHRILLY SHOUT . . . .   711 FERENCZ RENYI   45
SHOUTED
    SHOUTED, AND HAILED HIM! HE HUNG THERE A STAR, ...   36 OISIN 2   107
    SHOUTED AND HAILED HIM. STILL HE HUNG CONTENT, ...   36 OISIN 2   V   107
    SHOUTED. WITH FIRE OF HAIR ABOUT HER SWIRLED, ...   38 OISIN 2   134
    JOSTLED AND SHOUTED THOSE WAR-WASTED MEN, ...   286 TWO KINGS   216
    ALL SHOUTED TILL THEIR ANGER GREW . . . .   297 THREE BEGGARS   46
    THE OTHER SHOUTED, "YOU WOULD ROB . . . .   307 HOUR DAWN   109
    SHOUTED A MOMENT 'TWEEN THE EARTH AND SKY. . . . . .   675 ISLE STAT II 3   237
    THEN HE SHOUTED, "OPEN WIDE . . . .   697 MOSADA 2   24
    AND HE SHOUTED OPEN WIDE . . . .   697 MOSADA 2   V   24
    THE STRANGER SHOUTED, "OPEN WIDE . . . .   697 MOSADA 2   24
SHOUTING
    HEARING HELL LOUD WITH A MURMUR, AS SHOUTING AND MOCKING   62 OISIN 3   208
      WE SWEEP,
    HIS SHOUTING DAYS WITH MIRTH WERE CROWNED! . . . . .   67 HAPPY SHEPHERD   50
    BUT SLOWLY, AS I SHOUTING SLEW . . . .   83 MAD KING GOLL   25
    WITH SHOUTING AND THE CLANG OF UNHOOKED ARMS. . . . .   185 QUEEN MAEVE   111
    THE SHOUTING OF AN UNSEEN MAN! . . . .   274 GREY ROCK   76
    TILL THAT IS THEIR LONG SHOUTING PLAYTIME! . . . . .   343 SHEP GOATHERD V 106
    WITH SHOUTING AND SINGING. . . . .   672 ISLE STAT II 3   173
SHOVE
    ALL HIS BODY CAN BUT SHOVE . . . .   776 AGAINST WITCH   33
SHOW
    WITHOUT LAUGHTER, A SHOW UNTO CHILDREN, ...   63 OISIN 3   218
    AH ME! TO BE OLD WITHOUT SUCCOUR, A SHOW UNTO CHILDREN,   63 OISIN 3   V   217
    A STAIN,
    CASTS UP A SHOW AND THE WINDS ANSWER IT . . . . . .   186 QUEEN MAEVE   125
    I'LL SHOW YOU THAT I AM MADE DIFFERENTLY, ...   227 SHADOW WATER B   119
    THAT COULD SHOW WHAT HOMER'S AGE . . . .   258 PEACE   2
    WHO HAD SEEN, BEING KEPT FOR SHOW, ...   319 DOLLS   5
    IS HOT TO SHOW WHATEVER IT HAS FOUND, ...   340 SHEP GOATHERD   44
    JUST TRUTH ENOUGH TO SHOW THAT HIS WHOLE LIFE . . . .   373 PHASES OF MOON   22
    IS WHAT YOUR LOOKING-GLASS CAN SHOW, ...   385 ROBARTES DANCE   15
    SATISFIED IF A TROUBLED MIRROR SHOW IT, ...   430 NINETEEN 19   62
    CONTENTED THAT A TROUBLED MIRROR SHOW IT, ...   430 NINETEEN 19 V   62
    SHRIEK WITH PLEASURE IF WE SHOW . . . .   431 NINETEEN 19   91
    BETTER TO SMILE ON ALL THAT SMILE, AND SHOW . . . .   444 SCHOOL CHILDR   31
    TO SHOW HOW VIOLENT GREAT HEARTS CAN LOSE . . . . .   463 HARUN RASHID   47
    MY LANTERN IS TOO LOYAL NOT TO SHOW . . . .   464 HARUN RASHID   71
    CAN BUT SHOW THAT HEAVEN YAWNS! . . . .   509 JANE REPROVED   4
    SHE WOULD AS BRAVELY SHOW . . . .   516 MANS SONG   9
    DISCOVER IMPURITIES, CAN SHOW AT LAST . . . .   558 RIBH CHRISTIAN   10
    WHERE CAN SHE LOOK UNTIL HE MAKE THE SHOW! . . . . .   558 RIBH CHRISTIAN   22
    LIKE A DUMB BEAST IN A SHOW, ...   572 LADYS 1ST SONG   2
    BUT WHERE IS THE BRUSH THAT COULD SHOW ANYTHING . . .   602 GALLERY REVIS   28
    MIRROR ON MIRROR MIRRORED IS ALL THE SHOW. . . . . .   610 STATUES   22
    MY CIRCUS ANIMALS WERE ALL ON SHOW, ...   629 CIRCUS ANIMALS   6
SHOWED
    AND SHOWED THEIR EYES WITH TEARDROPS DIM, ...   18 OISIN 1   256
    SHOWED PRINTS OF SEA-BORN· SCALES, WHILE DOWN THROUGH IT   37 OISIN 2   115
    HOW THE MEN OF THE SAND-SACK SHOWED ME A CHURCH . . .   61 OISIN 3   193
    FLICKERING WITH ASH AND HAZEL, BUT HALF SHOWED . . .   180 QUEEN MAEVE   12
    SHOWED THEIR FAINT LIGHT THROUGH THE UNSHUTTERED WINDOWS,   279 TWO KINGS   50
    ALTHOUGH CROWDS GATHERED ONCE IF SHE BUT SHOWED HER FACE,   314 FALLEN MAJESTY   1
SHOWER
    A DANAAN FRUITAGE MAKES A SHOWER OF MOONS, ...   127 DREAM OF FAERY V 22
    OR THAT OF THE SUDDEN SHOWER . . . .   414 TOWER   137
SHOWERED
    SHOWERED AWAY THE KEEN DEW DROPS! . . . .   705 DAWN-SONG   18
SHOWERS
    DANAAN SONGS, AND THEIR DEWY SHOWERS . . . .   11 OISIN 1   135
    SANG NIAM, AND THEIR DEWY SHOWERS . . . .   11 OISIN 1   V   135
    RISES, AND SHOWERS ABROAD HIS FRAGRANT ARROWS, . . .   72 ANASHU VIJAYA   27
    AND CLINGING WITH THE DEW OF ODOROUS SHOWERS, ...   704 REMEMBRANCE   4
SHOWING
    FEATURES, OR MAYBE SHOWING . . . .   363 DOLLS DRAWINGS   4
    FEATURES, OR MAY BE SHOWING . . . .   363 DOLLS DRAWINGS V   4
SHOWN
    AS THOSE THAT CAN OUTLIVE THE MOON HAVE SHOWN IT, . .   230 SHADOW WATER B V 193
    AND SHOWN MY HUSBAND SLEEPING THERE, I HAVE SIGHED, .   285 TWO KINGS   188
    AND FOR THE LOVE THAT YOU HAVE SHOWN YOUR KING, . . .   286 TWO KINGS   V 212A
    THAT COULD HAVE SHOWN HOW PURE-BRED HORSES . . . . .   325 ROBERT GREGORY   36
    THAT COULD HAVE SHOWN HOW PUREBRED HORSES . . . . .   325 ROBERT GREGORY V 36
    "WHAT CAN BE SHOWN? . . . .   510 JANE JUDGMENT   16
    ALL COULD BE KNOWN OR SHOWN . . . .   510 JANE JUDGMENT   18
    WHICH OF HER FORMS HAS SHOWN HER SUBSTANCE RIGHT? . .   618 BRONZE HEAD   11
SHOWS
    SHADOWS AND SHOWS THAT CAN BUT TURN THE BRAIN." . . .   281 TWO KINGS   108
    YOUR OPEN HAND BUT SHOWS OUR LOSS, ...   288 TO WEALTHY MAN   29
    WHAT EAGLE LOOK STILL SHOWS, ...   316 FRIENDS   25
    SHOWS HER THAT SOME ONE SOON . . . .   364 END OF DAY   5
    SHOWS HER THAT SOMEONE SOON . . . .   364 END OF DAY   V   5
    BEING BUT HOLY SHOWS . . . .   454 HIS MEMORIES   2
    SHOWS THROUGH OUR LINEAMENTS. MY CANDLE'S BRIGHT, . .   464 HARUN RASHID   70
    HAD I NOT FOUND CONTENT AMONG THE SHOWS . . . . . .   499 MOTHER OF GOD   6
    BECAUSE PIEBALD PONIES, LED BEARS, CAGED LIONS, MAKE BUT   623 HIGH TALK   5
      POOR SHOWS,

	PAGE	TITLE	LINE

SHOWS   (CONTINUED)
    THAT MIGHT ADORN OLD SONGS OR COURTLY SHOWS; • • • • •   629 CIRCUS ANIMALS   14
SHOWY
    AND A GREAT ARMY BUT A SHOWY THING; • • • • • • • •   429 NINETEEN 19   18
SHRANK
    AND MIND AND BODY SHRANK. • • • • • • • • • • •   626 STATES HOLIDAY   4
    HE SHRANK BEFORE MY VOICE, AND STOOD • • • • • • •   671 ISLE STAT II 3   129
SHRIEK
    SHRIEK WITH PLEASURE IF WE SHOW • • • • • •   431 NINETEEN 19   91
    AND THAT MUST SLEEP, SHRIEK, STRUGGLE TO ESCAPE • • • •   444 SCHOOL CHILDR   35
    I COULD RECOVER IF I SHRIEK • • • • • • • • •   452 HUMAN DIGNITY V   9
    "STRIKE ME IF I SHRIEK." • • • • • • • • • •   455 HIS MEMORIES   18
    REMEMBERING THAT HER SHRIEK WAS LOVE • • • • • •   456 FRIENDS YOUTH   19
    NOR SAW MY BODY FALL NOR HEARD IT SHRIEK, • • • •   537 HER VISION   29
    THAT PATCHING OLD HEELS THEY MAY SHRIEK, I TAKE TO CHISEL   623 HIGH TALK   8
        AND PLANE.
SHRIEKED
    AND DUG ITS CLAWS AND SHRIEKED AND FOUGHT. • • • • •   385 ROBARTES DANCE   8
    WIND SHRIEKED--AND WHERE ARE THEY? • • • • • • •   432 NINETEEN 19   107
    I COULD RECOVER IF I SHRIEKED • • • • • • • •   452 HUMAN DIGNITY   9
SHRIEKS
    SHRIEKS, "I AM KING OF THE PEACOCKS," • • • • •   456 FRIENDS YOUTH   15
    AND THAT HE SHRIEKS FROM PRIDE. • • • • • • •   456 FRIENDS YOUTH   20
    AND A MIRACULOUS STRANGE BIRD SHRIEKS AT US. • • • • •   534 HER TRIUMPH   12
SHRILL
    UNTIL HER VOICE GREW SHRILL. • • • • • •   392 EASTER 1916   20
    THAT WOMAN A WHILE WOULD BE SHRILL • • • • • •   392 EASTER 1916   V   17
    OH, CEASE YOUR SINGING! WILD AND SHRILL AND LOUD, • • •   648 ISLE STAT I 1   99
SHRILLY
    O! LAY THE SHRILLY TRUMPET DOWN, • • • • • • •   212 BLESS PSALTER   4
    A NEIGHBOURING CRICKET LIFTS HIS SHRILLY SHOUT • • •   711 FERENCZ RENYI   45
SHRINE
    THAT FEED WHITE MOTHS BY SOME DE DANAAN SHRINE; • • • •   41 OISIN 2   186
    FEEDING WHITE MOTHS AROUND SOME EASTERN SHRINE, • • • •   41 OISIN 2   V   186
SHROUD
    "WHAT IS THE FIGURE IN A SHROUD • • • • • •   253 HIS DREAM   7
    THAT BLINKED AND SAW THEM IN A SHROUD. • • • • • •   529 TOM LUNATIC   12
    A SHROUD THAT SEEMED TO HAVE AUTHORITY • • • • •   634 CUCHULAIN COMF   7
    "OBEY OUR ANCIENT RULE AND MAKE A SHROUD! • • • • •   634 CUCHULAIN COMF   13
    THEY WILL WRAP THEM IN THE SHROUD, • • • • • •   733 STREET DANCERS   55
SHROUDS
    THEIR SHROUDS ARE BLOODY AND THEIR LIPS ARE WET. • • • •   483 OIL AND BLOOD   6
    SHAKE THE DEAD IN THEIR SHROUDS! • • • • • • •   576 ACRE OF GRASS   22
    THEN CERTAIN SHROUDS THAT MUTTERED HEAD TO HEAD • • • •   634 CUCHULAIN COMF   4
    A BUNDLE OF LINEN. SHROUDS BY TWO AND THREE • • • •   634 CUCHULAIN COMF   9
SHRUNKEN
    AND I AM SHRUNKEN TO SKIN AND BONE. • • • • •   550 SONGS REWRIT 1   2
    YET I AM SHRUNKEN TO SKIN AND BONE • • • • •   550 SONGS REWRIT 1 V   2
    YET AM I SHRUNKEN TO SKIN AND BONE • • • • •   550 SONGS REWRIT 1 V   2
    BUT I AM SHRUNKEN TO SKIN AND BONE, • • • • •   550 SONGS REWRIT 1 V   2
    THOUGH I AM SHRUNKEN TO BONE AND SKIN, • • • • •   551 SONGS REWRIT 1 V   8
SHUDDER
    LEST NIAMH SHUDDER. FULL OF HOPE AND DREAD • • • •   41 OISIN 2   183
    SHUDDER THAT MADE THEM ONE. • • • • • •   346 ON WOMAN   23
    WHO SHUDDER AND HURRY BY! BODY AND SOUL • • • •   375 PHASES OF MOON   77
    A SHUDDER IN THE LOINS ENGENDERS THERE • • • • •   441 LEDA AND SWAN   9
    WHAT MAKES ME SHUDDER SO? • • • • • • • •   524 MAD AS MIST   14
    I SHUDDER AND I SIGH TO THINK • • • • • • •   524 MAD AS MIST   15
SHUDDERED
    IT SHUDDERED IN THE WATER! • • • • • • • •   345 ON WOMAN   19
SHUDDERING   SEE STAR-SHUDDERING
    AND THE DESOLATE SHUDDERING SEA. • • • • • •   648 ISLE STAT I 1   85
    SUCH MAY I LOVE. THE SHUDDERING FOREST LIGHTS • • • •   651 ISLE STAT I 1   165
SHUDDERS
    SHUDDERS IN MANY CRADLES! ALL IS CHANGED, • • • •   375 PHASES OF MOON   89
    WHAT SHUDDERS RUN THROUGH ALL THAT ANIMAL BLOOD? • • •   541 PARN FUNERAL 1   5
SHUFFLE
    ALL SHUFFLE THERE; ALL COUGH IN INK; • • • • •   337 SCHOLARS   7
    TO SHUFFLE, GRUNT AND GROAN, • • • • • • •   599 STONE CROSS   20
    PRACTICE A TINKER SHUFFLE • • • • • • • • •   617 LONG-LEG FLY   17
SHUFFLED
    GOOD FELLOWS SHUFFLED CARDS IN AN OLD BAWN! • • • • •   411 TOWER   65
SHUFFLING
    O SHUFFLING OF HOLY SHOES! • • • • • • • •   774 COME RIDE   15
SHUN
    WHAT CAN THEY DO BUT SHUN ME • • • • • • •   533 FIRST CONFESS   17
SHUT
    HE DROVE ME OUT AND SHUT THE DOOR, • • • • •   95 MOLL MAGEE   25
    THE WINDOWS AND THE DOORS WERE SHUT, • • • • •   95 MOLL MAGEE   29
    HE DROVE ME FORTH AND SHUT THE DOOR, • • • • •   95 MOLL MAGEE   V   25
    PEACEABLE MEN THAT SHUT THE WIND AWAY, • • • • •   224 SHADOW WATER B   54
    ALL WISDOM SHUT INTO HIS ONYX EYES, • • • • •   311 MOUNTAIN TOMB   11
    ALL WISDOM SHUT INTO ITS ONYX EYES. • • • • •   311 MOUNTAIN TOMB V   11
    HAD SHUT THEIR EYES! AND WHERE WAS IT • • • •   326 ROBERT GREGORY   62
    WHEN I HAVE SHUT THESE EWES AND THIS OLD RAM • • • •   343 SHEP GOATHERD   113
    WE POETS KEEP OUR MOUTHS SHUT, FOR IN TRUTH • • • •   359 WAR POEM   V   2
    A POET KEEP HIS MOUTH SHUT, FCR IN TRUTH • • • •   359 WAR POEM   V   2
    SHUT OUT FROM ALL THE LUXURY OF THE WORLD, • • • •   370 EGO DOMINUS   60
    AND WHETHER THE DOOR WERE SHUT. • • • • • •   381 SONGS FOOL 2   5
    I TURN AWAY AND SHUT THE DOOR, AND ON THE STAIR • • • •   427 PHANTOM HATRED   33
    SHE ROSE, AND WITH HER EYES SHUT FAST IN SLEEP • • • •   468 HARUN RASHID   152

		PAGE	TITLE	LINE

SHUT   (CONTINUED)

SHUT THE DOOR OF THE POPE'S CHAPEL, ...   618 LONG-LEG FLY   23
SCARCE THE OLD AND WIZEN HOUSES HAD THEIR DOORS AND WINDOWS   718 PHANTOM SHIP   5
SHUT.
SCARCE THE OLD AND WIZENED HOUSES HAD THEIR DOORS   718 PHANTOM SHIP   V   5
AND WINDOWS SHUT.
THE HARVEST'S IN: THE GRANARY DOORS ARE SHUT: . . . . .   755 SHADOW WATER A   177
ALTHOUGH THE DOOR BE SHUT . . . .   786 YOUR HEART   14

SHUTS

THE MAJESTY THAT SHUTS HIS BURNING EYE: . . . .   265 THESE CLOUDS   2
THE MAJESTY THAT SHUTS HIS BURNING EYE. . . . .   265 THESE CLOUDS   12
WHILE NIGHT SHUTS THE EYES . . . .   535 PARTING   2

SHUTTER

THAT SHAKES THE SHUTTER, TO HAVE BROUGHT TO MIND . . . .   327 ROBERT GREGORY   90
BOLT AND BAR THE SHUTTER, ...   523 MAD AS MIST   1

SHUTTLE

FLAMES THE SHUTTLE OF THE LIGHTNING ACROSS THE DRIVING   718 PHANTOM SHIP   1
SLEET,

SHY

SHY ONE, SHY ONE, ...   89 ISLE IN WATER   1
SHY ONE, SHY ONE, ...   89 ISLE IN WATER   1
SHY ONE OF MY HEART, ...   89 ISLE IN WATER   2
SHY IN THE DOORWAY . . . .   89 ISLE IN WATER   11
AND SHY IN THE GLOOM: . . . .   89 ISLE IN WATER   12
AND SHY AS A RABBIT, ...   89 ISLE IN WATER   13
HELPFUL AND SHY. . . . .   89 ISLE IN WATER   14
HERE GROW THAT SHY, RETIRING SISTERHOOD, ...   651 ISLE STAT I 2   4

SIBYL

SLEW THEE, POOR SIBYL: COMRADES THOU AND I: . . . . .   675 ISLE STAT II 3   235
A SIBYL, WITH FIERCE FACE AS OF A HOUND . . . .   687 TWO TITANS   9

SIBYLLINE

SWIFT BEATING ON HIS BREAST IN SIBYLLINE FRENZY BLIND . .   481 BLOOD AND MOON   19

SIBYL'S

AND IN THE SIBYL'S EYES A LANGUID FLAME . . . .   688 TWO TITANS   41

SICILIAN

STAMPED BOY AND TREE UPON SICILIAN COIN. . . . .   541 PARN FUNERAL 1   15

SICK   SEE LOVE-SICK

SAD TO REMEMBER, SICK WITH YEARS, ...   2 OISIN 1   5
'TIS SAD REMEMBERING, SICK WITH YEARS, ...   2 OISIN 1   V   5
BUT O, SICK CHILDREN OF THE WORLD, ...   65 HAPPY SHEPHERD   6
THE SICK MAN'S WIFE OPENED THE DOOR: . . . .   133 FR GILLIGAN   31
SICK OF HIS GRAVE HAS WAKENED ME? . . . .   303 HOUR DAWN   37
CONSUME MY HEART AWAY: SICK WITH DESIRE . . . .   408 SAIL BYZANTIUM   21
AND SICK OF SOLITUDE . . . .   432 NINETEEN 19   105
THEY ARE SICK OF THE PALETTE AND FIDDLE-BOW, ...   565 LAPIS LAZULI   2

SICKEN

BLENCHING ON HIGH THE DULL STARS SICKEN . . . .   646 ISLE STAT I 1   46

SICKENING

THAT SICKENING NEAR THEIR MOTHERS LIE: . . . .   717 FAIRY DOCTOR   16

SICKLE

THERE DREAMY TIME LETS FALL HIS SICKLE . . . . . .   77 INDIAN TO LOVE V   5A
PASSETH THE MOON WITH HER SICKLE OF LIGHT, ...   648 ISLE STAT I 1   82
YONDER THE SICKLE OF THE MOON SAILS ON, ...   688 NETTLESHIP   1

SICKLES

AND THRICE THE CORN AROUND THE SICKLES FLAMED, ...   690 MOSADA 1   3
NOR, GAZING FORTH WHERE LIFE'S SAD SICKLES REAP, ...   710 FERENCZ RENYI   31

SICKNESS

SICKNESS BROUGHT ME THIS . . . .   267 FRIEND ILLNESS   1
OR SICKNESS BREAK HER WILL . . . .   365 HER RACE   10
A MEDITATION WRITTEN DURING SICKNESS AT ALGECIRAS . . .   493 AT ALGECIRAS   V   T

SIDE   SEE CRADLE-SIDE MOUNTAIN-SIDE COUNTRY-SIDE HILL-SIDE ROAD-SIDE
          RIVER-SIDE WATER-SIDE

AND ONCE A LADY BY MY SIDE . . . .   16 OISIN 1   231
AND ONCE A MAIDEN BY MY SIDE . . . .   16 OISIN 1   V   231
IN HONOUR SOON BY HIS MASTER'S SIDE . . . .   26 OISIN 1   V 399C
OF MANY THOUSAND STEPS. SAT EITHER SIDE, ...   31 OISIN 2   V   35
THAT WITH DIM EYEBALLS STOOD ON EITHER SIDE. . . . . .   34 OISIN 2   75
STOOD LONELY, WITH DIM EYEBALLS ON EACH SIDE, ...   34 OISIN 2   V   74
HIS HAND ALONG THE RUNNEL'S SIDE, AS THOUGH . . . . .   39 OISIN 2   162
AT EMAN, 'NEATH THE BEECH TREES, ON EACH SIDE, ...   44 OISIN 2   V   228
LAY LOOSE IN A PLACE OF SHADOW: WE DREW THE REINS BY HIS   50 OISIN 3   44
SIDE.
. . . YOU WILL COME NO MORE TO MY SIDE. . . . . . .   56 OISIN 3   128
. . . NO MORE SHALT THOU BE BY MY SIDE. . . . . . .   56 OISIN 3   V   128
OF THE CALVES ON THE WARM HILL SIDE, ...   88 STOLEN CHILD V   45
WITH THE FEET LAID SIDE BY SIDE. . . . .   124 CATHLEEN PARA   4
WITH THE FEET LAID SIDE BY SIDE. . . . .   124 CATHLEEN PARA   4
HAD COME THROUGH THE MOUNTAIN SIDE, ...   171 MAID QUIET   V   4B
CROWDED WITH BITTER FACES, THE WOUNDS IN PALM AND SIDE,   172 TRAV PASSION   4
THE KNOTTED SCOURGE, THE NAIL-PIERCED HANDS, THE WOUNDED   172 TRAV PASSION V   4
SIDE,
ABOUT THE WINDY WATER SIDE . . . .   192 BAILE AILLINN V   93
WHO PEERED ABOUT ON EVERY SIDE: . . . .   193 BAILE AILLINN V   112
TO THE OTHER SIDE, AND HIGHER IN THE AIR. . . . . . .   234 SHADOW WATER B   259
THERE IS NONE TO TAKE HIS SIDE. I AM ON HIS SIDE. . . .   239 SHADOW WATER B   364
THERE IS NONE TO TAKE HIS SIDE. I AM ON HIS SIDE. . . .   239 SHADOW WATER B   364
HER HANDS ON EITHER SIDE HAD GRIPPED THE BENCH, ...   279 TWO KINGS   63
FROM WELL SIDE OR FROM PLOUGH LAND, WAS THEIR NOISE: . .   279 TWO KINGS   V   53
THE CATARACT SMOKES UPON THE MOUNTAIN SIDE, ...   311 MOUNTAIN TOMB   3
THE CATARACT SMOKES ON THE MOUNTAIN SIDE. . . . . . .   311 MOUNTAIN TOMB V   3
AND ALL THEIR HELMS OF SILVER HOVERING SIDE BY SIDE, . .   318 MAGI   5

716

SIDE   (CONTINUED)
      AND ALL THEIR HELMS OF SILVER HOVERING SIDE BY SIDE,   . . .   318 MAGI   5
      FROM CASTLE TAYLOR TO THE ROXBOROUGH SIDE   . . . .   326 ROBERT GREGORY   58
      BECAUSE AT HER SIDE? . . . .   335 SONG   10
      TILL, CLAMBERING AT THE CRADLE SIDE, ...   343 SHEP GOATHERD   V   109
      AT PALLAS ATHENE'S SIDE, ...   355 PROPERTIUS   6
      AND SPREAD ON EVERY SIDE, ...   396 ROSE TREE   10
      UPON BEN BULBEN SIDE   . . . .   398 BREAK OF DAY   6
      DROP THEIR CAST AT THE SIDE   . . . .   414 TOWER   125
      THAT CLIMB THE MOUNTAIN SIDE, ...   416 TOWER   V   175
      AND TEAR THE HEART OUT OF HIS SIDE, ...   437 SONGS PLAY 1   3
      OUT OF HIS SIDE. . . . .   439 FRAGMENTS   4
      I RAN, I RAN, FROM MY LOVE'S SIDE BECAUSE MY HEART WENT   450 OWEN AHERNE   12
         MAD.
      I DID NOT FIND IN ANY CAGE THE WOMAN AT MY SIDE. . . . .   450 OWEN AHERNE   19
      AND THE HEART THUMPS AT MY SIDE, ...   456 FRIENDS YOUTH   18
      LIVED AT MY SIDE; THOUGHT TIME'S DISFIGURING TOUCH   . . .   466 HARUN RASHID   110
      LIVED AT MY SIDE; THAT TIME'S DISFIGURING TOUCH   . . . .   466 HARUN RASHID   V   110
      THE HEART IN MY SIDE. . . . .   516 MANS SONG   3
      THE MEET'S UPON THE MOUNTAIN SIDE. . . . .   549 SEVERED HEAD   V   6
      DESERT THE PERJURER'S SIDE; . . . .   582 ROGER CASEMENT   20
      AN AMBUSH; PILGRIMS AT THE WATER SIDE; . . . .   601 GALLERY REVIS   V   2
      WHEN PEARSE SUMMONED CUCHULAIN TO HIS SIDE, ...   611 STATUES   25
      CUCHULAIN SAT AT HER SIDE; . . . .   628 JANE MOUNTAIN   17
      HANG ON THE SIDE OF THE ROUND GRAPE-CLUSTER;   . . . . .   646 ISLE STAT I 1   45
      BRIGHT ON A GRASS BLADE'S UNDER SIDE, MIGHT HEAR,   . . .   689 NETTLESHIP   10
      BUT NOW I WAVE HER HITHER TO MY SIDE. . . . .   694 MOSADA 1   91
      AT LAST.   BUT NOW I WAVE HER TO MY SIDE. . . . .   694 MOSADA 1   V   91
      TWO ONLY NOW THEY ARE, TWO SIDE BY SIDE. . . . .   700 MOSADA 3   49
      TWO ONLY NOW THEY ARE, TWO SIDE BY SIDE. . . . .   700 MOSADA 3   49
      OF OUR NATIVITY HANG SIDE BY SIDE, ...   701 MOSADA 3   53
      OF OUR NATIVITY HANG SIDE BY SIDE, ...   701 MOSADA 3   53
      FOR I AM OLD AND WEAK."" AND AT HER SIDE   . . . .   712 FERENCZ RENYI   59
      SUCH WAR PLOTS, PEACE PLOTS, LOVE PLOTS--EVERY SIDE;   . .   722 WITCH VIVIEN   66
      IF I GO NEARER TO THE WINDWARD SIDE, ...   753 SHADOW WATER A   140
      TO THE OTHER SIDE AND HIGHER IN THE AIR. . . . . . .   753 SHADOW WATER A   149
      IN THE WASTE AIR.   I WILL WANDER BY HIS SIDE   . . . .   754 SHADOW WATER A   152
      TILL THE SIDE OF HATE COMES UP.   . . . .   776 AGAINST WITCH   35
      WHAT MAN IS AT YOUR SIDE?   . . . .   786 YOUR HEART   28
      SOME ONE SHOULD STAY AT HER SIDE. . . . .   786 YOUR HEART   V   28
      IS THERE NO MAN AT YOUR SIDE?   . . . .   786 YOUR HEART   V   28
SIDES   SEE WELL-SIDES
      TO SHAKE THEIR WICKED SIDES AT YOUTH   . . . .   262 STUDENTS AGIT   3
      STRANGE DRAPERIES DID ALL THE SIDES ADORN, ...   657 ISLE STAT I 3   55
SIDHE
      THE HOSTING OF THE SIDHE . . . .   140 HOSTING SIDHE   T
      AND WONDERING WHO OF THE MANY-CHANGING SIDHE   . . . . .   181 QUEEN MAEVE   41
      AND WONDERING WHO OF THE MANY CHANGING SIDHE   . . . . .   181 QUEEN MAEVE   V   41
      WHAT MATTERS WERE AFOOT AMONG THE SIDHE, ...   182 QUEEN MAEVE   61
SIDLE
      MUST SHE SIDLE UP, ...   559 HE AND SHE   2
SIDLED
      SIDLED THEIR BODIES AGAINST HIM, FILLING THE SHADE WITH   50 OISIN 3   48
         THEIR EYES.
SIDLES
      AS THE MOON SIDLES UP . . . .   559 HE AND SHE   1
SIDNEY
      OUR SIDNEY AND OUR PERFECT MAN, ...   325 ROBERT GREGORY   47
SIEVE
      WHAT WOULD HAVE SHAKEN FROM THE SIEVE?   . . . .   256 WORDS   14
SIGH
      AND EACH ONE SAID, WITH A LONG, LONG SIGH, ...   17 OISIN 1   244
      GROWN DESOLATE, WHISPER AND SIGH TO EACH OTHER;   . . . .   26 OISIN 1   403
      GROWN DESOLATE, WHISPER AND SIGH TO EACH OTHER.   . . . .   27 OISIN 1   V   407
      AND THEY CEASE WITH A SIGH OF "UNJUST! UNJUST!"   . . . .   27 OISIN 1   V   416
      WHEN GOD SHALL COME FROM THE SEA WITH A SIGH   . . . . .   28 OISIN 1   425
      O SIGH, O FLUTTERING SIGH, BE KIND TO ME; . . . .   33 OISIN 2   57
      O SIGH, O FLUTTERING SIGH, BE KIND TO ME; . . . .   33 OISIN 2   57
      "OH, SIGH, AWAKE AND GO YOU FORTH FOR ME; . . . .   33 OISIN 2   V   57
      . . . AND GAZED ON THE GRASS WITH A SIGH. . . . .   54 OISIN 3   100
      SIGH, O YOU LITTLE STARS!   O SIGH AND SHAKE YOUR   72 ANASHU VIJAYA   18
         BLUE APPAREL!
      SIGH, O YOU LITTLE STARS!   O SIGH AND SHAKE YOUR   72 ANASHU VIJAYA   18
         BLUE APPAREL!
      SIGH, OH YE LITTLE STARS! OH, SIGH AND SHAKE YOUR BLUE   72 ANASHU VIJAYA   V   18
         APPAREL!
      SIGH, OH YE LITTLE STARS! OH, SIGH AND SHAKE YOUR BLUE   72 ANASHU VIJAYA   V   18
         APPAREL!
      SING, TILL YOU RAISE YOUR HANDS AND SIGH, ...   73 ANASHU VIJAYA   45
      SING, TILL YE RAISE YOUR HANDS AND SIGH, ...   73 ANASHU VIJAYA   V   45
      I CAN BUT WEEP AND SIGH."   . . . .   99 FOXHUNTER   36
      I SIGH THAT KISS YOU, ...   118 CRADLE SONG   9
      WHO SIGH WITH MINGLED SORROW AND CONTENT, ...   136 TO SOME I TALK   7
      SIGH, HEART, AGAIN IN THE DEW OF THE MORN. . . . . . .   147 INTO TWILIGHT   4
      AND THEY SIGH IF THE WIND BUT LIFT A TRESS;   . . . . . .   151 OLD MOTHER   8
      AND THEY SIGH IF THE WIND BUT LIFT UP A TRESS;   . . . . .   151 OLD MOTHER   V   8
      AND WHEN YOU SIGH FROM KISS TO KISS . . . .   156 FORGOT BEAUTY   18
      AND BIND UP YOUR LONG HAIR AND SIGH;   . . . .   158 BELOVED RHYMES   8
      AND TROUBLE WITH A SIGH FOR ALL THINGS LONGING FOR REST   163 ASKS FORGIVE   23
      MAEVE WALKED THROUGH THAT GREAT HALL, AND WITH A SIGH   . .   182 QUEEN MAEVE   62
      THAT THEY WOULD SIGH AND QUOTE WITH LEARNED LOOKS   . . .   205 ADAMS CURSE   25

		PAGE	TITLE		LINE

SIGH (CONTINUED)

	PAGE	TITLE		LINE
THE DELICATE-STEPPING STAG AND HIS LADY SIGH,	210	RAGGED WOOD		2
FOR THERE THE TALL DEER AND HIS LEMAN SIGH	210	RAGGED WOOD	V	2
THE DELICATE STEPPING STAG AND HIS LADY SIGH	210	RAGGED WOOD	V	2
AND THEN SMOOTH OUT WITH IVORY HANDS AND SIGH,	228	SHADOW WATER B		133
I LOOK AT YOU, AND I SIGH.	261	DRINKING SONG		6
ALTHOUGH IT BE FOR CHILDREN THAT YOU SIGH!	265	THESE CLOUDS		10
OR BY A TOUCH OR A SIGH.	413	TOWER		111
THAT THEY TOUCH OR SIGH.	517	HER ANXIETY		9
YOU ASK WHAT MAKES ME SIGH, OLD FRIEND,	524	MAD AS MIST		13
I SHUDDER AND I SIGH TO THINK	524	MAD AS MIST		15
WHAT MATTER? HEAVE NO SIGH, LET NO TEAR DROP,	564	GYRES		11
BUT HEAVED A SIGH IF THE CHAMBERMAID	570	THREE BUSHES		33
ALL THE LABOURING HEAVENS SIGH.	573	LADYS 3RD SONG		12
WHAT'S LEFT TO SIGH FOR?	574	MAIDS 1ST SONG		5
I SAW HIM SIGH AND TURN AND PASS AWAY!	690	MOSADA 1		14
IN SPACE, MADE EQUAL WITH A SIGH, WE MET.	705	REMEMBRANCE		14
AND THEN SMOOTH OUT WITH IVORY HANDS AND SIGH.	750	SHADOW WATER A		70
OR GIVE BUT A SIGH AND A WORD,	786	YOUR HEART		12
OR GIVE BUT A SIGH AND A WORD,	786	YOUR HEART		25
OR GIVE BUT A SIGH AND A WORD,	786	YOUR HEART		38

SIGHED

	PAGE	TITLE		LINE
THEN SHE SIGHED GENTLY, "IT GROWS LATE.	9	OISIN 1		102
THEN SIGHED SHE SOFTLY, "LATE! 'TIS LATE!	9	OISIN 1	V	102
HE HAD SAT DOWN AND SIGHED WITH CUMBERED HEART,	37	OISIN 2		111
LAID IT AND SIGHED! I HELD A SWORD WHOSE SHINE	37	OISIN 2		126
LAID IT AND SIGHED——A SWORD WHOSE WIZARD SHINE	37	OISIN 2	V	126
THE IMMORTAL DESIRE OF IMMORTALS WE SAW IN THEIR FACES, AND SIGHED.	47	OISIN 3		4
SIGHED, "YOU, EVEN YOU YOURSELF, COULD WORK THE CURE!"	282	TWO KINGS		124
AND SHOWN MY HUSBAND SLEEPING THERE, I HAVE SIGHED,	285	TWO KINGS		188
ONE TO ANOTHER SIGHED AND CRIED!	296	THREE BEGGARS		38
HEARING IT NOW HAVE SIGHED FOR THAT YOUNG MAN	342	SHEP GOATHERD		77
WHATEVER HAS BEEN SAID, SIGHED, SUNG,	387	SOLOMON WITCH		7
ON BREAST OF MARS THE GODDESS SIGHED.	562	CONJUNCTIONS		4
IN ANCIENT TOMBS I SIGHED, BUT NOT AGAIN!	564	GYRES		14
AND THE GREAT WATER SIGHED FOR LOVE,	611	NEWS ORACLE		3
AND THE WIND SIGHED TOO.	611	NEWS ORACLE		4
MAN-PICKER NIAMH LEANT AND SIGHED	611	NEWS ORACLE		5
THERE SIGHED AMID HIS CHOIR OF LOVE	611	NEWS ORACLE		7

SIGHING

	PAGE	TITLE		LINE
AND SIGHING BOWED HER GENTLE HEAD,	12	OISIN 1		149
AND SIGHING LAID THE PEARLY TIP	12	OISIN 1		150
ROLLED ROUND WITH MUSIC OF THE SIGHING SPRAY!	30	OISIN 2		14
I HEAR WHITE BEAUTY SIGHING, TOO,	156	FORGOT BEAUTY		19
I HEAR PALE BEAUTY SIGHING TOO,	156	FORGOT BEAUTY	V	19
FOR THAT BRIEF SIGHING. IF YOU HAD LOVED SOME WOMAN——	228	SHADOW WATER B		135
THOUGH IT BUT SET US SIGHING? FELLOW-WANDERER,	230	SHADOW WATER B		187
THOUGH IT BUT SET US SIGHING. FELLOW WANDERER	230	SHADOW WATER B	V	187
SIGHING REPLIED! "WHAT NEED HAVE WE FOR HASTE	276	TWO KINGS	V	C
LAY SIGHING LIKE THE REST.	612	NEWS ORACLE		12

SIGHS

	PAGE	TITLE		LINE
AND NOW THE WARMTH OF SIGHS, AND AFTER THE QUIVER OF LIPS.	47	OISIN 3		8
LONG SIGHS AROSE IN OUR SPIRITS, BENEATH US BUBBLED THE GROUND.	48	OISIN 3		20
IN ONE WAS A BRANCH SOFT-SHINING WITH BELLS MORE MANY THAN SIGHS	50	OISIN 3		46
MY SPIRIT ROCKED IN SLEEP AND SIGHS! AND SAW THE MOORFOWL PACE	76	INDIAN ON GOD		3
THAT MOANS AND SIGHS A HUNDRED DAYS!	78	INDIAN TO LOVE		17
OR SIGHS AMID THE WANDERING, STARRY MIRTH,	114	ROSE OF BATTLE		18
THE WEST WEEPS IN PALE DEW AND SIGHS PASSING AWAY,	154	BELOVED PEACE		5
IN TWILIGHT SHAKEN WITH LOW SIGHS!	156	FORGOT BEAUTY	V	10B
AND TROUBLE WITH SIGHS FOR ALL HEARTS WITHOUT REST	163	ASKS FORGIVE	V	23
I DREAMED THAT I STOOD IN A VALLEY, AND AMID SIGHS,	163	VALLEY LOVERS		1
AND SOULS AS IF THEY WERE BUT SIGHS,	307	HOUR DAWN		102
BIRD SIGHS FOR THE AIR,	574	LOVERS SONG		1
FOR THE WOMB THE SEED SIGHS.	574	LOVERS SONG		3
THE MOTHER OF THE WAVE SIGHS TOO,	738	YOU ARE SAD		10
FROM ITS FIRST SIGHS AND LAUGHTER, BEFORE THE SLEEP,	754	SHADOW WATER A		161

SIGHT

	PAGE	TITLE		LINE
PASSED UNDER THE DIM DOORWAY, OUT OF SIGHT,	37	OISIN 2		123
MAKING A WORLD ABOUT HER, PASSED FROM SIGHT	37	OISIN 2		123
PASSED UNDER A DIM DOORWAY, OUT OF SIGHT,	37	OISIN 2	V	123
LEST THEY SHOULD LOOK UPON SOME DREADFUL SIGHT!	38	OISIN 2		142
STOOD TIMIDLY, LEST THEY SHOULD SEE SOME SIGHT	38	OISIN 2	V	141
O LOVELY TO SEE IN ALL MEN'S SIGHT	69	CLOAK BOAT		3
IN ALL MEN'S SIGHT."	69	CLOAK BOAT		5
UNFOLD YOUR FLAMING WINGS AND COVER OUT OF SIGHT	175	ELEMENT POWERS		11
THAT OUT OF SIGHT IS OUT OF MIND.	192	BAILE AILLINN		87
AND THERE, IN JUGGLERIES OF SIGHT AND SENSE,	231	SHADOW WATER B		216
WHO CANNOT PUT ME FROM HIS SIGHT FOR EVER.	251	SHADOW WATER B		601
WHEN, THE EARS BEING DEAFENED, THE SIGHT OF THE EYES BLIND	257	RECONCILIATION		3
THAT ALL MUST COME TO SIGHT AND TOUCH!	386	ROBARTES DANCE		31
NOR ANY HUMAN SIGHT WITHIN IT	389	SOLOMON WITCH		41
RAN OUT OF MY SIGHT!	399	DEMON BEAST		4
TROUBLES MY SIGHT! SOMEWHERE IN SANDS OF THE DESERT	402	SECOND COMING		13
TROUBLES MY SIGHT! A WASTE OF DESERT SAND!	402	SECOND COMING	V	13
TO TEST THEIR FANCY BY THEIR SIGHT!	410	TOWER		44
OF THE STARK MYSTERY THAT HAS DAZED MY SIGHT,	466	HARUN RASHID		113
AND, LIKE THE SOUL, IT SAILS INTO THE SIGHT	490	COOLE BALLYLEE		19

PAGE   TITLE   LINE

SIGHT   (CONTINUED)
```
    ANOTHER CAME IN SIGHT . . . . .              515 GIRLS SONG B          5
    BUT SOMETHING BORE THEM OUT OF SIGHT . . .   519 HER DREAM             5
    AND EYES THAT HAD SO KEEN A SIGHT?           529 TOM LUNATIC           4
    OUT OF INTELLECT AND SIGHT . . .             633 MAN AND ECHO         35
    OH, LOVELY TO SEE IN ALL MEN'S SIGHT . . .   666 ISLE STAT II 3        3
    IN ALL MEN'S SIGHT. . . . .                  666 ISLE STAT II 3        5
    THE FAIRY VANISHED FROM HIS SIGHT,           730 PRIEST FAIRY         62
    THE STARS ARE OUT OF SIGHT.                  786 YOUR HEART           34
    O, BUT I SAW A SOLEMN SIGHT:                 788 HAWTHORN TREE         1
```
SIGHTS   SEE ELFIN-SIGHTS
```
    WITH ALL THOSE SIGHTS AND ALL THAT CRYING OUT? . . .  249 SHADOW WATER B  573
    THE HEART WELL WORN UPON THE SLEEVE MAY BE THE BEST OF  790 HEART SLEEVE    1
        SIGHTS,
```
SIGN
```
    HE SEEMED THE WATCHER FOR A SIGN.  THE OTHER   31 OISIN 2        V   41
    NOW IT IS OLD AND MOUSE-LIKE.  FOR A SIGN .    36 OISIN 2        V   96
    NOW OLD AND MOUSELIKE.  FOR AN ANSWERING SIGN  36 OISIN 2            96
    AS A TOKEN AND A SIGN,                        648 ISLE STAT I 1      78
    AND COLA, SEEING, KNOWS THE SIGN AND COMES.   691 MOSADA 1           38
    AND COLA, SEEING, KNOWS THE SIGN AND RISES.   691 MOSADA 1       V   38
```
SIGNAL
```
    THE FLAGRANT SIGNAL OF HER LORD'S RETURN,     645 ISLE STAT I 1      13
    HER ARMS AROUND HIS FEET.  THE SIGNAL GOES    714 FERENCZ RENYI     103
```
SIGNATURE
```
    THAT WAXEN SEAL, THAT SIGNATURE,             598 MODEL LAUREATE      21
```
SIGNS
```
    HE WHO CAN READ THE SIGNS NOR SINK UNMANNED  429 NINETEEN 19         33
    PARTICULAR QUALITY.  THE SIGNS AND SHAPES:   469 HARUN RASHID       181
    HE KNOWS BY SIGNS OF SECRET WIT              716 FAIRY DOCTOR        5
```
SILENCE
```
    IN SILENCE ROUND HIS CRIMSON BALL             12 OISIN 1        V  155
    THAT IN IMMORTAL SILENCE SLEEPS               13 OISIN 1           161
    WE PASSED IN SILENCE O'ER THE MEAD,           25 OISIN 1        V 376A
    SOBBED INTO SILENCE.  WE HAD MOUNTED FEET     33 OISIN 2        V  68E
    DROPPING: A MURMUROUS DROPPING: OLD SILENCE AND THAT ONE  48 OISIN 3    18
        SOUND:
    WHERE EVER IS MURMUROUS DROPPING, OLD SILENCE AND THAT  56 OISIN 3     138
        ONE SOUND:
    GATHERED IN SILENCE, DEWY AS HER EYES,        80 EPHEMERA           19
    I WENT AWAY IN SILENCE.                       95 MOLL MAGEE         27
    I WENT AWAY IN SILENCE:                       95 MOLL MAGEE         33
    A WOVEN SILENCE, OR BUT CAME TO CAST         114 ROSE OF BATTLE     13
    SILENCE AND LOVE:                            116 FAERY SONG          6
    OLD SILENCE BIDS ITS CHOSEN RACE REJOICE,    127 DREAM OF FAERY     31
    OLD SILENCE BIDS A LONELY FOLK REJOICE,      127 DREAM OF FAERY V   31
    BUT LET A GENTLE SILENCE WROUGHT WITH MUSIC FLOW  175 ELEMENT POWERS  17
    BUT LET A GENTLE SILENCE ENWROUGHT WITH MUSIC FLOW  175 ELEMENT POWERS V 17
    WHO STOOD AMID A SILENCE BY THE THORN        187 QUEEN MAEVE        142
    HEAVY LIKE STONE, THEIR WISDOM BEING HALF SILENCE.  218 WOODS OF COOLE 26
    SILENCE: FOR YOU HAVE TAKEN FORGAEL'S PAY.   225 SHADOW WATER B V   68
    KNOWING THAT SILENCE BRINGS NO GOOD TO KINGS,  279 TWO KINGS        57
    FOR WHAT BUT EYE AND EAR SILENCE THE MIND    384 VISION ROBART      41
    TO SILENCE THE ENVY IN MY THOUGHT:           424 ROAD AT DOOR       13
    THE POLE-STAR AND THE SILENCE OF THE POLE.   477 SELF AND SOUL  V    8
    AFTER LONG SILENCE .                         523 LONG SILENCE        T
    SPEECH AFTER LONG SILENCE: IT IS RIGHT,      523 LONG SILENCE        1
    OF THAT MOST SENSUOUS SILENCE OF THE NIGHT   579 DOR WELLESLEY       6
    HIS MIND MOVES UPON SILENCE.                 617 LONG-LEG FLY       10
    HER MIND MOVES UPON SILENCE.                 617 LONG-LEG FLY       20
    HIS MIND MOVES UPON SILENCE.                 618 LONG-LEG FLY       30
    I'LL SILENCE THIS DULL SINGER--              647 ISLE STAT I 1      50
    OF EVENING AND GLAD SILENCE DWELLETH AYE,    653 ISLE STAT I 2      37
    IN SILENCE, THAT FAMED FLOWER OF WIZARDRY,   673 ISLE STAT II 3    192
    AMONG THE PLANTS: THE FLOWERY SILENCE FELL   692 MOSADA 1           55
    IN LIST'NING SILENCE GAZING ON OUR GRIEF.    702 MOSADA 3           87
    AND SILENCE HOLDING REVELRY AND FEAST:       705 REMEMBRANCE        12
    SILENCE!  THOU SHALT BE DEAD!" NOW SUDDENLY  710 FERENCZ RENYI      16
    THE HEART OF NOON FOLDS SILENCE AND FOLDS SLEEP,  735 QUATRAIN APHOR 25
    BUT OUR SILENCE HAD BEEN WISE.               773 SONG DEIRDRE 1     22
    YET OUR SILENCE HAD BEEN WISE:               773 SONG DEIRDRE 1 V   22
```
SILENT
```
    WHILE BIRDS GREW SILENT ONE BY ONE.          176 BELOVED DEAD   V   13
    YOU MOST OF ALL, SILENT AND FIERCE OLD MAN,  270 PARDON FATHERS     15
    BUT FINDING HIM STILL SILENT I STOOPED DOWN  281 TWO KINGS         109
    NOW THEY ARE SILENT," SAID THE CRANE.        297 THREE BEGGARS      62
    THAT THERE BE NO FOOT SILENT IN THE ROOM     311 MOUNTAIN TOMB       6
    LET THERE BE NO FOOT SILENT IN THE ROOM,     311 MOUNTAIN TOMB  V    6
    WE SAT AS SILENT AS A STONE                  314 MEMORY YOUTH       15
    I SAT AS SILENT AS A STONE                   314 MEMORY YOUTH   V   15
    A REASON FOR KEEPING SILENT                  359 WAR POEM            T
    A POET'S MOUTH BE SILENT, FOR IN TRUTH       359 WAR POEM            2
    I CELEBRATE THE SILENT KISS THAT ENDS SHORT LIFE OR LONG.  459 FROM OEDIPUS  9
    I AM NOT DUMB:  I'D SOONER SILENT WAIT       646 ISLE STAT I 1      40
    O'ER MUCH I'VE TALKED: I SHALL BE SILENT SOON,  657 ISLE STAT I 3   75
    IF WRONG MY CHOICE, AS SILENT AS THOU ART.   657 ISLE STAT I 3      76
    BUT WHY ART THOU SO SILENT? DID'ST THOU HEAR  670 ISLE STAT II 3    96
    AND WHY SO SILENT? I WOULD HAVE THEE SPEAK.  671 ISLE STAT II 3    140
    TO THEIR FARM WORK: HOW SILENT ALL WILL BE:  699 MOSADA 3            8
    TO THEIR FARM-WORK: HOW SILENT ALL WILL BE.  699 MOSADA 3       V    8
    HOW FERENCZ RENYI KEPT SILENT.               709 FERENCZ RENYI       T
```

		PAGE	TITLE		LINE

SILENT (CONTINUED)
- WHITE, RENYI SILENT STANDS; THAT MAIDEN SWEET . . . . . — 713 FERENCZ RENYI V 84
- I CURSE THEE—CURSE THEE!" RENYI SILENT STANDS, ... — 714 FERENCZ RENYI 107
- STANDS EACH GREY AND SILENT PHANTOM ON THE SAME REGARDLESS SPOT— — 719 PHANTOM SHIP 25
- TO CRY HIS FOLDING CRY! NO, NO, BE SILENT, ... — 760 SHADOW WATER A 253

SILK
- FOR GOLD HIS HOOVES AND SILK HIS REIN, ... — 2 OISIN 1 V 7Z
- AND A HUNDRED ROBES OF MURMURING SILK, ... — 8 OISIN 1 88
- AND A HUNDRED ROBES OF THE SOFTEST SILK, ... — 8 OISIN 1 V 88
- THEIR CLOAKS MADE OUT OF YELLOW SILK . . . . — 15 OISIN 1 205
- THEIR ROBES WERE ALL OF YELLOW SILK . . . . — 15 OISIN 1 V 205
- THEIR BRATTAS MADE OUT OF YELLOW SILK, ... — 15 OISIN 1 V 205
- . . . AND THEIR EYES THAT GLIMMER LIKE SILK. . . . . — 59 OISIN 3 176
- . . . AND THEIR YOUTH, AND THEIR EYES SOFT AS SILK. . . — 59 OISIN 3 V 176
- SHE MAY HAVE WORN SILK CLOTHES, OR WORN A CROWN, . . . — 282 TWO KINGS 117
- HAVE CHANGED THEIR SILK FOR SACK. . . . . — 458 HIS WILDNESS 6
- TWO GIRLS IN SILK KIMONOS, BOTH . . . . — 475 EVA GORE-BOOTH 3
- TWO GIRLS IN SILK KIMONOS, BOTH . . . . — 475 EVA GORE-BOOTH 19
- GOLD-SEWN SILK ON THE SWORD-BLADE . . . . — 484 SYMBOLS 5
- GOLD-SOWN SILK ON THE SWORD BLADE! . . . . — 484 SYMBOLS V 5
- ALL THAT SILK AND SATIN GEAR! . . . . — 525 DANCING DAYS 3
- FOR PASSING ROUND THE BOTTLE WITH GIRLS IN RAGS OR SILK, — 592 PILGRIM 2
- FOR PASSING ROUND THE BOTTLE WITH GIRLS IN RAG OR SILK, — 592 PILGRIM V 2
- SO COME IN RAGS OR COME IN SILK, IN CLOAK OR COUNTRY SHAWL, — 593 PILGRIM 22
- SO COME IN RAG OR COME IN SILK, IN CLOAK OR COUNTRY SHAWL, — 593 PILGRIM V 22

SILKEN
- WERE LOLLING THEIR TONGUES, AND THE SILKEN HAIR . . . . — 2 OISIN 1 V 7S
- HIS HEART HUNG ALL UPON A SILKEN DRESS, ... — 126 DREAM OF FAERY 2
- THE LOVE-TALES WROUGHT WITH SILKEN THREAD . . . . . . — 155 FORGOT BEAUTY 6
- THE LOVE-TALES WOVE WITH SILKEN THREAD . . . . — 155 FORGOT BEAUTY V 6
- IN RUSTLE OF LACE OR SILKEN STUFF, ... — 358 PRESENCES 5
- OVER SOME SILKEN DRESS . . . . — 363 DOLLS DRAWINGS 7
- FOR SILKEN CLOTHES AND STATELY WALK, ... — 422 MY TABLE 30
- THAT FLOWERING, SILKEN, OLD EMBROIDERY, TORN . . . . . — 477 SELF AND SOUL 13
- UNDER A SILKEN SAIL AND SILVER YARD, ... — 763 SHADOW WATER A 316

SILL   SEE WINDOW-SILL
- AND STAND ON HER WINDOW SILL. . . . . — 159 CAP AND BELLS V 4

SILLY
- COWARDICE, SOME SILLY OVER-SUBTLE THOUGHT . . . . . . — 413 TOWER 117
- COWARDICE, OVER SOME SILLY SUBTLE THOUGHT . . . . . . — 413 TOWER V 117

SILVER
- AND GATHERED IN A SILVER CINCTURE! . . . . — 3 OISIN 1 V 24A
- OUT OF A LITTLE SILVER TRUMP! . . . . — 15 OISIN 1 196
- A HARP OF SILVER IN MY HANDS, ... — 16 OISIN 1 V 232
- AND TOUCH THE LAUGHING SILVER STRING! . . . . — 17 OISIN 1 233
- AND CAUGHT THE SILVER HARP AWAY, ... — 17 OISIN 1 240
- THEREIN THE SILVER HARP HE HURLED, ... — 17 OISIN 1 V 244
- OR DROPS OF SILVER JOY THAT FELL . . . . — 19 OISIN 1 278
- . . . WITH BRONZE AND SILVER AND GOLD. . . . . — 49 OISIN 3 32
- MORE COMELY THAN MAN MAY MAKE THEM, INLAID WITH SILVER AND GOLD, — 49 OISIN 3 V 29
- . . . WHEN THE SUN WAS ON SILVER OR GOLD! . . . . . . — 53 OISIN 3 97
- IN DANCING SILVER SANDALLED ON THE SEA, ... — 101 ROSE UPON ROOD V 7
- IT SEEMED THEY RAISED THEIR LITTLE SILVER HEADS, . . . — 126 DREAM OF FAERY 6
- UNDER THE GOLDEN OR THE SILVER SKIES! . . . . — 127 DREAM OF FAERY 21
- OR STORMY SILVER FRET THE GOLD OF DAY, ... — 128 DREAM OF FAERY 33
- OVER THE LITTLE SILVER CORDS, ... — 146 FISH 6
- AND CAUGHT A LITTLE SILVER TROUT. . . . . — 149 WANDER AENGUS 8
- AND HOOKED A LITTLE SILVER TROUT. . . . . — 149 WANDER AENGUS V 8
- THE SILVER APPLES OF THE MOON, ... — 150 WANDER AENGUS 23
- ENWROUGHT WITH GOLDEN AND SILVER LIGHT, ... — 176 CLOTHS HEAVEN 2
- AS MIDDLE NIGHT GREAT CATS WITH SILVER CLAWS, ... — 185 QUEEN MAEVE 115
- A QUEEN-WOMAN DRESSED OUT IN SILVER, CRY . . . . . . — 210 RAGGED WOOD V 2
- IN A GOLDEN AND SILVER WOOD! . . . . — 214 HAPPY TOWNLAND 10
- IN A GOLD AND SILVER WOOD! . . . . — 214 HAPPY TOWNLAND V 10
- FROM GOLDEN AND SILVER BOUGHS! . . . . — 215 HAPPY TOWNLAND 24
- OF HAMMERED SILVER, AND DRINK . . . . — 215 HAPPY TOWNLAND 50
- FROM THE GOLDEN AND SILVER BOUGHS. . . . . — 215 HAPPY TOWNLAND V 24
- AND WHEN ONE CHANGED HER TO A SILVER FLY, ... — 220 HARP OF AENGUS V 10
- CARE MORE ABOUT THE KEGS OF SILVER AND GOLD . . . . . — 232 SHADOW WATER B 234
- O SILVER FISH THAT MY TWO HANDS HAVE TAKEN . . . . . — 251 SHADOW WATER B 609
- ON OLD DEEP SILVER ROLLING THERE . . . . — 271 GREY ROCK 20
- THE HORN RESOUNDED AS THOUGH IT HAD BEEN SILVER, . . . — 277 TWO KINGS 16
- THE GOLD AND SILVER THREAD. . . . . — 308 PLAYER QUEEN 8
- AND ALL THEIR HELMS OF SILVER HOVERING SIDE BY SIDE, . — 318 MAGI 5
- OF GOLDEN KING AND SILVER LADY, ... — 331 ROUND TOWER 13
- WHEN EVERY SILVER CANDLESTICK OR SCONCE . . . . — 410 TOWER 26
- GET ALL THE GOLD AND SILVER THAT YOU CAN, ... — 500 VACILLATION 19
- THE MOON IN A SILVER BAG. . . . . — 525 DANCING DAYS 8
- THE MOON IN A SILVER BAG. . . . . — 525 DANCING DAYS 16
- THE MOON IN A SILVER BAG. . . . . — 525 DANCING DAYS 24
- THERE THE SILVER DEW, ... — 611 NEWS ORACLE 2
- DRIFT AND FLOAT LIKE SILVER SHIPS! . . . . — 647 ISLE STAT I 1 67
- FROM THE WOOD'S WAYS; THEN, LIKE A SILVER FLAME, . . . — 658 ISLE STAT II 1 6
- OF SILVER HANGING ROUND LAME COLA'S NECK— . . . . . . — 691 MOSADA 1 V 35
- AND LIKE A SILVER TRUMPET RING. . . . . — 736 SUMMER EVENING 4
- AND LIKE A SILVER TRUMPET RING. . . . . — 737 SUMMER EVENING 20
- A RED HOUND RUNNING FROM A SILVER ARROW. . . . . . . — 747 SHADOW WATER A 6
- HAD I NOT GOLD AND SILVER, AND ENOUGH . . . . — 748 SHADOW WATER A 32
- TILL HIS EDAINE, NO MORE A SILVER FLY . . . . — 757 SHADOW WATER A V 210

	PAGE	TITLE		LINE

SILVER (CONTINUED)
    A WHITE BIRD HAS TORN ME WITH HIS SILVER CLAWS. . . . . 759 SHADOW WATER A 234
    MY EYES ARE TROUBLED BY THE SILVER ARROWS. . . . . . 761 SHADOW WATER A 269
    UNDER A SILKEN SAIL AND SILVER YARD, ... 763 SHADOW WATER A 316
    AND WHEN ONE CHANGED HER TO A SILVER FLY, ... 763 SHADOW WATER A V 305
    O SILVER FISH THAT MY TWO HANDS HAVE TAKEN . . . . . 769 SHADOW WATER A 425
SILVER-PROUD
    PALE SILVER-PROUD QUEEN-WOMAN OF THE SKY, ... 211 RAGGED WOOD 6
SILVER-SANDALLED
    IN DANCING SILVER-SANDALLED ON THE SEA, ... 101 ROSE UPON ROOD 7
SILVER-SHOED
    OR HAVE YOU HEARD THAT SLIDING SILVER-SHOED . . . . 211 RAGGED WOOD 5
SIMPLE
    THAT NOBLENESS MADE SIMPLE AS A FIRE, ... 256 NO SECOND TROY 7
    PASSIONATE AND SIMPLE LIKE HIS HEART. . . . . 325 ROBERT GREGORY 32
    THIS WISE AND SIMPLE MAN. . . . . 347 FISHERMAN 8
    NO TABLE OR CHAIR OR STOOL NOT SIMPLE ENOUGH . . . . 371 ON GOING HOUSE 3
    SHOULD BE SO SIMPLE--A BAT ROSE FROM THE HAZELS . . . . 377 PHASES OF MOON 137
    GLAD, SIMPLE--NAY, HE SOUGHT NOT MYSTERY, ... 710 FERENCZ RENYI 30
SIMPLEST
    TO TELL YOUR SIMPLEST WANT, AND KNOWN. . . . . . . 436 FOR MY SON 21
    TO TELL YOUR SIMPLEST WANT, AND KNOW, ... 436 FOR MY SON V 21
SIMPLICITY
    BUT NOT THE EXACT LIKENESS, THE SIMPLICITY OF A CHILD, . . 354 HIS PHOENIX 28
    ITS FIRST SIMPLICITY, LOVE, VOICE AND ALL, ... 469 HARUN RASHID 177
    ITS FIRST SIMPLICITY, LOVE AND ALL. . . . . 469 HARUN RASHID V 177
    STRUCK DUMB IN THE SIMPLICITY OF FIRE! . . . . . . 502 VACILLATION 75
SIN
    BEND DOWN AND PRAY FOR ALL THAT SIN I WOVE IN SONG, . . . 173 SPEAKS HEARERS 5
    BEND DOWN AND PRAY FOR THE GREAT SIN I WOVE IN SONG, . . . 173 SPEAKS HEARERS V 5
    COUNT EVERY SIN OF ACTION OR OF THOUGHT! . . . . . . 479 SELF AND SOUL V 66
    WHAT THEME HAD HOMER BUT ORIGINAL SIN? . . . . . . 502 VACILLATION 77
    BUT FOR ADAM'S SIN . . . . 621 JOHN KINSELLA 26
    I WILL NOT SHARE YOUR SIN. THIS IS NO SIN. . . . . 692 MOSADA 1 42
    I WILL NOT SHARE YOUR SIN. THIS IS NO SIN. . . . . 692 MOSADA 1 42
    NO SIN TO SEE IN COIL ON COIL OF AZURE . . . . . . 692 MOSADA 1 43
    THE DARK STILL MAN, HAS COME AND SAYS 'TIS SIN. . . . . 692 MOSADA 1 47
    THEY SAY THE WISH ITSELF IS HALF THE SIN! . . . . . 692 MOSADA 1 48
    YET 'TIS NO SIN! MY FATHER TAUGHT IT ME. . . . . . 692 MOSADA 1 50
    WOULD HE TEACH ANY SIN? GAZE IN THE CLOUD . . . . . 692 MOSADA 1 58
    I WILL NOT SHARE YOUR SIN. IT IS NO SIN. . . . . . 692 MOSADA 1 V 42
    I WILL NOT SHARE YOUR SIN. IT IS NO SIN. . . . . . 692 MOSADA 1 V 42
    YE SAID THAT YE WOULD FRIGHT HER FROM HER SIN-- . . . . 695 MOSADA 1 113
    FRIEND! BUT 'TWERE A DEADLY SIN . . . . 697 MOSADA 2 31
    THE WAGES OF SIN IS DEATH. NO USE. NO GOOD. . . . . 697 MOSADA 2 42
    THE WAGE OF SIN IS DEATH. NO USE. NO USE. . . . . . 697 MOSADA 2 V 42
SINAI'S
    FROM DEATH, AND WOUNDS, OR ON SINAI'S TOP, ... 375 PHASES OF MOON 67
SINBAD
    SINBAD THE SAILOR'S BROUGHT A PAINTED CHEST, ... 371 ON GOING HOUSE 10
SINCE
    SINCE GOD MADE TIME AND DEATH AND SLEEP! THE OTHER . . . 31 OISIN 2 41
    AND MANY A PATER NOSTERS SAID SINCE DAWN. . . . . . 43 OISIN 2 V 208D
    . . . NO, NOT SINCE THE WORLD BEGAN. . . . . . . 50 OISIN 3 49
    SINCE ADAM'S FALL BUT NEEDS MUCH LABOURING. . . . . 205 ADAMS CURSE 22
    FLEW WESTWARD! AND MANY A TIME SINCE THEN . . . . . 223 SHADOW WATER B 27
    BUT, DEAR, CLING CLOSE TO ME! SINCE YOU WERE GONE, . . . 257 RECONCILIATION 11
    SINCE, TAVERN COMRADES, YOU HAVE DIED, ... 273 GREY ROCK 49
    AND THE WORLD'S ALTERED SINCE YOU DIED, ... 276 GREY ROCK 126
    SINCE I FIRST MADE MY COUNT! . . . . 322 SWANS AT COOLE 8
    ALL'S CHANGED SINCE I, HEARING AT TWILIGHT, ... 322 SWANS AT COOLE 15
    MY DAILY THOUGHTS SINCE THE FIRST STUPOR OF YOUTH . . . 342 SHEP GOATHERD 83
    IT'S LONG SINCE I BEGAN . . . . 347 FISHERMAN 6
    MAYBE A TWELVEMONTH SINCE . . . . 348 FISHERMAN 25
    MAYBE A TWELVE-MONTH SINCE . . . . 348 FISHERMAN V 25
    MAY BE A TWELVEMONTH SINCE . . . . 348 FISHERMAN V 25
    SINCE OLD WILLIAM POLLEXFEN . . . . 360 ALF POLLEXFEN 2
    SINCE HE WHO HAD BEEN CONTENTED LONG, ... 361 ALF POLLEXFEN 28
    O NOT SINCE LIFE BEGAN. . . . . 382 VISION ROBART 8
    BUT SINCE I LAID A HAND THEREON . . . . 451 FIRST LOVE 7
    SINCE FIRST WE SAW THE LIGHT, ... 456 SUMMER SPRING 4
    (FOR SINCE THE HORIZON'S BOUGHT STRANGE STRANGE DOGS ARE STILL) 579 DOR WELLESLEY 7
    "GREATEST SINCE REMBRANDT," ACCORDING TO JOHN SYNGE! . . 602 GALLERY REVIS 26
    MY PRETTY CHILD, SINCE HE HAS GONE, OH SAY . . . . . 658 ISLE STAT II 1 3
    SINCE 'MONG MY PEOPLE, TENTED ON THE HILLS, ... 690 MOSADA 1 4
    WITH POISONOUS LIPS, AND HE IS PINING SINCE? . . . . 696 MOSADA 2 7
    HIS FACE HAS NEVER GLADDENED SINCE HE CAME . . . . . 747 SHADOW WATER A 1
    I HAVE BEEN WAITING YOU. A MOMENT SINCE . . . . . 763 SHADOW WATER A 313
SINEW
    HOW SINEW THAT HAS BEEN PULLED TIGHT, ... 386 ROBARTES DANCE 34
    YET BE BUT SINEW. I HAVE HEARD SAID . . . . . . 386 ROBARTES DANCE 37
    BEEN BONE AND SINEW! WHEN SUCH BODIES JOIN . . . . . 555 RIBH AT TOMB 12
SINEWY
    BUT WHEN AT LAST HE FORCED THOSE SINEWY FLANKS . . . . 278 TWO KINGS 35
    STARING UPON HIS SINEWY THIGH. . . . . 294 HATED PLAYBOY 6
    MADDENED BY THAT SINEWY THIGH. . . . . 294 HATED PLAYBOY V 6
    STARING ON HIS SINEWY THIGH. . . . . 294 HATED PLAYBOY V 6
    . . . MOVE HIS MOUTH AND SINEWY TONGUE. . . . . . 560 MAGIC DRUM 5
    WHERE THEIR SINEWY MIGHT IS STRUNG . . . . . . 658 ISLE STAT I 3 88
    WHEN HIS SINEWY WINGS TOGETHER CLOSE. . . . . . . 673 ISLE STAT II 3 179

```
                                                    PAGE      TITLE            LINE
SINFULLY
      HOW SINFULLY THE WICKED SCOFF!"  . . . . . . . . .   725 LEGEND             22
SING
      HAVE KNOWN THREE CENTURIES, POETS SING, . . . . . .     2 OISIN 1            3
      THE BAD OLD DAYS. THOU WERT, MEN SING, . . . . . .      2 OISIN 1        V   3
      THEY SEEMED TO SING IN THE SMOULDERING FIRES. . . . .  13 OISIN 1          168
      GAVE ME A HARP, AND BID ME SING, . . . . . . . . .     16 OISIN 1          232
      GAVE ME A HARP, AND BADE ME SING, . . . . . . . .      16 OISIN 1        V 232
      AND BADE ME SING OF EARTHLY LANDS! . . . . . . . .     17 OISIN 1        V 233
      SING, THEN, FOR THIS IS ALSO SOOTH. . . . . . . .      66 HAPPY SHEPHERD    44
      AMONG THEMSELVES LAUGH ON AND SING ALWAY! . . . . .    68 SAD SHEPHERD       7
      AND MY OWN TALE AGAIN FOR ME SHALL SING, . . . . .     68 SAD SHEPHERD      22
      AND MINE OWN TALE AGAIN FOR ME SHALL SING, . . . .     68 SAD SHEPHERD    V  22
      SING, O YOU LITTLE STARS!  O SING AND RAISE YOUR RAPTUROUS  72 ANASHU VIJAYA   20
            CAROL
      SING, O YOU LITTLE STARS!  O SING AND RAISE YOUR RAPTUROUS  72 ANASHU VIJAYA   20
            CAROL
      SING, OH YE LITTLE STARS! OH, SING, AND RAISE YOUR     72 ANASHU VIJAYA V  20
            RAPTUROUS CAROL
      SING, OH YE LITTLE STARS! OH, SING, AND RAISE YOUR     72 ANASHU VIJAYA V  20
            RAPTUROUS CAROL
      SING YOU OF HER, O FIRST FEW STARS, . . . . . . .      73 ANASHU VIJAYA     41
      SING, TURNING IN YOUR CARS. . . . . . . . . . . .      73 ANASHU VIJAYA     44
      SING, TILL YOU RAISE YOUR HANDS AND SIGH, . . . . .    73 ANASHU VIJAYA     45
      SING YE OF HER, OH FIRST FEW STARS, . . . . . . .      73 ANASHU VIJAYA V  41
      SING, TILL YE RAISE YOUR HANDS AND SIGH, . . . . .     73 ANASHU VIJAYA V  45
      AND SING FROM SHORE TO SHORE, AND EVERY YEAR . . . .   81 EPHEMERA      V 24G
      AND SING, AND SHAKE MY HEAVY LOCKS. . . . . . . .      84 MAD KING GOLL     44
      FROM POND AND FALLEN TREE--ME SING . . . . . . . .     85 MAD KING GOLL V  63
      --FROM POOLS AND ROTTING LEAVES--ME SING . . . . .     85 MAD KING GOLL V  63
      SING PEACE INTO HIS BREAST. . . . . . . . . . . .      88 STOLEN CHILD      47
      COME NEAR ME, WHILE I SING THE ANCIENT WAYS! . . . .  100 ROSE UPON ROOD     2
      SING IN THEIR HIGH AND LONELY MELODY. . . . . . .     101 ROSE UPON ROOD     8
      SING OF OLD EIRE AND THE ANCIENT WAYS! . . . . . .    101 ROSE UPON ROOD    23
      FOR HIM WHO HEARS LOVE SING AND NEVER CEASE, . . . .  114 ROSE OF BATTLE    10
      ENCIRCLE HER I LOVE AND SING HER INTO PEACE, . . . .  174 ELEMENT POWERS     9
      COUPLED WITH GOLDEN CHAINS, AND SING AS THEY FLY. . . 204 WITHER BOUGHS     18
      SING ON! SOMEWHERE AT SOME NEW MOON . . . . . . .     266 GALWAY RACES      10
      SING ON! SOMETIME, AND AT SOME NEW MOON . . . . .     266 GALWAY RACES  V  10
      DID NOT THE POET SING IT WITH SUCH AIRS . . . . . .   267 ALL TEMPT ME       7
      AMONG THOSE MOUTHS THAT SING THEIR SWEETHEARTS' PRAISE,  285 TWO KINGS      185
      COULD LIKE A BRACE OF BLACKBIRDS SING. . . . . . .    332 ROUND TOWER       24
      WHEN HER SON'S TURN WAS OVER, SING YOUR SONG. . . .   340 SHEP GOATHERD     42
      YOU SING AS ALWAYS OF THE NATURAL LIFE. . . . . .     342 SHEP GOATHERD     75
      SING, FOR IT MAY BE THAT YOUR THOUGHTS HAVE PLUCKED   342 SHEP GOATHERD     85
      AND SING WHEN THEY HAVE FOUND IT.  NO, NOT SING, . .  369 EGO DOMINUS       41
      AND SING WHEN THEY HAVE FOUND IT.  NO, NOT SING, . .  369 EGO DOMINUS       41
      SING ME THE CHANGES OF THE MOON ONCE MORE! . . . .    373 PHASES OF MOON    29
      SING OUT THE SONG! SING TO THE END, AND SING . . .    374 PHASES OF MOON    56
      SING OUT THE SONG! SING TO THE END, AND SING . . .    374 PHASES OF MOON    56
      SING OUT THE SONG! SING TO THE END, AND SING . . .    374 PHASES OF MOON    56
      SOUL CLAP ITS HANDS AND SING, AND LOUDER SING . . .   407 SAIL BYZANTIUM    11
      SOUL CLAP ITS HANDS AND SING, AND LOUDER SING . . .   407 SAIL BYZANTIUM    11
      OR SET UPON A GOLDEN BOUGH TO SING . . . . . . . .    408 SAIL BYZANTIUM    30
      AND THERE SING HIS LAST SONG. . . . . . . . . . .     414 TOWER            144
      AND WHEN ABOUNDING HEDGES SING . . . . . . . . . .    434 WHEEL         V   3
      THE MORNING STARS TO SING . . . . . . . . . . . .     436 FOR MY SON        19
      AND THEN DID ALL THE MUSES SING . . . . . . . . .     437 SONGS PLAY 1       6
      THE CHILDREN LEARN TO CIPHER AND TO SING, . . . . .   443 SCHOOL CHILDR      3
      AND SING IT LULLABY. . . . . . . . . . . . . . .      459 HIS WILDNESS      12
      WE MUST LAUGH AND WE MUST SING, . . . . . . . . .     479 SELF AND SOUL     70
      AND SING IT RHYME UPON RHYME . . . . . . . . . .      480 BLOOD AND MOON    10
      TO SING A SONG OR TWO. . . . . . . . . . . . . .      515 GIRLS SONG B       2
      COME, LET ME SING INTO YOUR EAR! . . . . . . . .      524 DANCING DAYS       1
      CURSE AS YOU MAY I SING IT THROUGH! . . . . . . .     525 DANCING DAYS       9
      MAY SING, AND SING UNTIL HE DROP, . . . . . . . .     525 DANCING DAYS      21
      MAY SING, AND SING UNTIL HE DROP, . . . . . . . .     525 DANCING DAYS      21
      OR SING A PENANCE ON THE ROAD! . . . . . . . . .      529 TOM LUNATIC       10
      THAT MUST SING IN A RHYME . . . . . . . . . . . .     529 TOM CRUACHAN       2
      THAT BIRD . . . LET HIM SING ON, . . . . . . . .      536 PARTING           12
      PRAY I WILL AND SING I MUST. . . . . . . . . . .      540 FROM ANTIGONE     14
      HOW COULD YOU SING THOSE SONGS OF LOVE? . . . . .     569 THREE BUSHES       5
      I AM CONTENT TO STAND AND SING . . . . . . . . .      582 ROGER CASEMENT V  21
      SING OF THE O'RAHILLY. . . . . . . . . . . . . .      584 ORAHILLY           1
      SING A "THE" BEFORE HIS NAME! . . . . . . . . . .     584 ORAHILLY           3
      SING OF THE O'RAHILLY. . . . . . . . . . . . . .      585 ORAHILLY          10
      WHAT REMAINS TO SING ABOUT . . . . . . . . . . .      585 ORAHILLY          28
      I SING WHAT WAS LOST AND DREAD WHAT WAS WON, . . .    591 WHAT WAS LOST      1
      THAT MAKE THE MUSES SING. . . . . . . . . . . . .     601 THOSE IMAGES      16
      AND NIGHT AND MORNING SING! . . . . . . . . . . .     627 STATES HOLIDAY    12
      AND I DELIGHT TO SING! . . . . . . . . . . . . .      627 STATES HOLIDAY    25
      "NOW MUST WE SING AND SING THE BEST WE CAN, . . . .   634 CUCHULAIN COMF    19
      "NOW MUST WE SING AND SING THE BEST WE CAN, . . . .   634 CUCHULAIN COMF    19
      SING WHATEVER IS WELL MADE, . . . . . . . . . . .     639 BEN BULBEN        69
      SING THE PEASANTRY, AND THEN . . . . . . . . . .      639 BEN BULBEN        74
      SING THE LORDS AND LADIES GAY . . . . . . . . . .     640 BEN BULBEN        78
      NOT A SAD NOTE WILL I SING. . . . . . . . . . . .     646 ISLE STAT I 1     39
      SING SUMMER WAVES. BUT YONDER SHEPHERD VILE, . . . .  649 ISLE STAT I 1    107
      AS I SING NOW TO THEE! . . . . . . . . . . . . .      654 ISLE STAT I 2     67
      AS I SING NOW TO THEE! . . . . . . . . . . . . .      654 ISLE STAT I 2     77
      AS I SING NOW TO THEE! . . . . . . . . . . . . .      655 ISLE STAT I 2     81
```

		PAGE	TITLE		LINE
SING (CONTINUED)					
HE SAT, AND THEN I HEARD THE WHITE LAKE SING,		659	ISLE STAT II 1		15
GO UP AND DOWN, AND RAISE THEIR HEADS AND SING		682	SEEKER		30
I'LL SING THE SONGS THE DUSKY LOVERS SING,		694	MOSADA 1		101
I'LL SING THE SONGS THE DUSKY LOVERS SING,		694	MOSADA 1		101
CHILDREN SING IN TWOS AND THREES.		732	STREET DANCERS		17
AND SING TO YOU IN THE NIGHT,		739	WHERE BOOKS GO		6
THOUGH WE WERE BIDDEN TO SING, CRY NOTHING LOUD.		778	SONG DEIRDRE 3		2
HE SWORE TO SING MY BEAUTY		789	SINGING HEAD		7
AND HEARD THE DEAD LIPS SING.		790	SINGING HEAD		24
SINGE					
AN AGONY OF FLAME THAT CANNOT SINGE A SLEEVE.		498	BYZANTIUM		32
SINGER SEE BALLAD-SINGER					
AND WHILE THEY SANG, A SINGER LAID		16	OISIN 1	V	231
WHAT, BE A SINGER BORN AND LACK A THEME?		502	VACILLATION		73
AS THOUGH SOME BALLAD SINGER HAD SUNG IT ALL.		602	GALLERY REVIS	V	24
I'LL SILENCE THIS DULL SINGER--		647	ISLE STAT I 1		50
SINGETH					
OF MOSS, A MAIDEN WEAVING. SINGETH SHE!		716	DWELT SYCAMORE		12
SINGING SEE EVER-SINGING					
AND SINGING, SINGING ALL TOGETHER!		15	OISIN 1		203
AND SINGING, SINGING ALL TOGETHER!		15	OISIN 1		203
AND SINGING, SINGING ALTOGETHER!		15	OISIN 1	V	203
AND SINGING, SINGING ALTOGETHER!		15	OISIN 1	V	203
WE HUSHED THE SINGING AND THE ROMP,		20	OISIN 1	V	296
THAT RAISE THEIR HEADS AND WANDER SINGING,		27	OISIN 1		419
THE SINGING MELTED IN THE NIGHT!		28	OISIN 1	V	427A
FLOATED IN ALL HER SINGING. HALF ENTRANCED		30	OISIN 2	V	19
INNUMERABLE, SINGING, EXULTANT. THE CLAY UNDERNEATH THEM SHALL PANT,		61	OISIN 3		203
TILL THEY SHALL SINGING FADE IN RUTH		66	HAPPY SHEPHERD		41
PIERCED BY MY GLAD SINGING THROUGH,		67	HAPPY SHEPHERD		53
AND WITH LOUD SINGING I RUSHED ON		83	MAD KING GOLL	V	31
MY SINGING SANG ME FEVER FREE,		86	MAD KING GOLL	V	65
MY SINGING SANG ME FEVER-FREE!		86	MAD KING GOLL	V	65
MY SINGING FADES, THE STRINGS ARE TORN,		86	MAD KING GOLL	V	66
I HAVE OFTEN HEARD HIM SINGING TO AND FRO,		109	CUCHULAIN SEA		49
I OFTEN HEAR HIM SINGING TO AND FRO,		109	CUCHULAIN SEA	V	49
A SONG INTO THE AIR, AND SINGING PASSED		114	ROSE OF BATTLE		14
A SONG INTO THE AIR, AND SINGING PAST		114	ROSE OF BATTLE	V	14
THE SINGING SHOOK HIM OUT OF HIS NEW EASE.		126	DREAM OF FAERY		12
AND AT THAT SINGING HE WAS NO MORE WISE.		127	DREAM OF FAERY		24
AND WE, OUR SINGING AND OUR LOVE,		139	TO IRELAND		37
ARE SINGING ABOUT THE WOOD?"		167	BLESSED		24
YET SHE, SINGING UPON HER ROAD,		260	UNWORTH PRAISE		19
NOR IS THERE SINGING SCHOOL BUT STUDYING		407	SAIL BYZANTIUM		13
AND THERE'S NO SINGING SCHOOL BUT STUDYING		407	SAIL BYZANTIUM	V	13
AND BE THE SINGING MASTERS OF MY SOUL.		408	SAIL BYZANTIUM	V	20
WITH SINGING HUSH AND HUSH-A-BYE!		456	FRIENDS YOUTH		9
NOR KNEW, DRUNKEN WITH SINGING AS WITH WINE,		537	HER VISION		30
COME MARCH, SINGING THIS SONG,		544	TO SAME TUNE 1	V	REF
SINGING, SINGING A SONG.		546	TO SAME TUNE 2		16
SINGING, SINGING A SONG.		546	TO SAME TUNE 2		16
TO WELCOME THEE, NASCHINA, WITH SWEET SINGING.		645	ISLE STAT I 1		7
BY THE SINGING WATERS' EDGE,		646	ISLE STAT I 1		23
I'LL QUENCH HIS SINGING WITH LOUD SONG--		647	ISLE STAT I 1		63
HUNDRED-THROATED MORN IS SINGING,		647	ISLE STAT I 1		70
SINGING O'ER AND O'ER AND O'ER.		648	ISLE STAT I 1		79
IN THE HEART OF THE DAWN THE RIVERS ARE SINGING,		648	ISLE STAT I 1		91
ALL THE WORLD IS SINGING, SINGING.		648	ISLE STAT I 1		94
ALL THE WORLD IS SINGING, SINGING.		648	ISLE STAT I 1		94
OH, CEASE YOUR SINGING! WILD AND SHRILL AND LOUD,		648	ISLE STAT I 1		99
I FAIN HAD BEEN THE FIRST OF SINGING THINGS		648	ISLE STAT I 1		101
WITH SINGING SWEET AS E'ER ROUND LAKE-LULLED ISLE		649	ISLE STAT I 1		106
SINGING OF ARMS AND BATTLES SOME OLD STAVE.		650	ISLE STAT I 1		137
AS SOME DEAD MAIDEN'S SINGING IN A DREAM.		654	ISLE STAT I 2		59
WITH SHOUTING AND SINGING.		672	ISLE STAT II 3		173
THE SINGING SHEPHERDS, TOO, HAVE PASSED AWAY.		676	ISLE STAT II 3		271
AND IN HER SINGING WOVE AROUND HER HEAD		693	MOSADA 1		84
HEARING THE FAR-OFF SINGING GUILE, AND GROANED,		693	MOSADA 1		88
HEARING THE FAR OFF SINGING GUILE AND GROANED,		693	MOSADA 1	V	88
HE'D SLEPT AMONG THE SINGING TREES,		728	PRIEST FAIRY		17
SINGING IN THIS LONDON STREET,		731	STREET DANCERS		1
SINGING TO THEIR LIGHT FOOTFALL.		732	STREET DANCERS		30
SINGING A LOVE RHYME TO HIMSELF,		741	EARL PAUL		41
WHEN WE ROWED NORTH, SINGING ABOVE THE OARS,		749	SHADOW WATER A		39
THE SINGING HEAD AND THE LADY		789	SINGING HEAD	V	T
SINGING-MASTERS					
AND BE THE SINGING-MASTERS OF MY SOUL.		408	SAIL BYZANTIUM		20
SINGLE					
BUTTED BELOW THE SINGLE AND SO PIERCED		278	TWO KINGS		22
A SINGLE SOUL THAT LACKS A SWEET CRYSTALLINE CRY.		291	PAUDEEN		8
THREE TIMES IN A SINGLE DAY		298	THREE HERMITS		10
I HAD NOT WAKED A SINGLE MINUTE,		305	HOUR DAWN		72
THOUGH SEVERAL, ARE A SINGLE LIGHT,		388	SOLOMON WITCH		29
BUT COULD NOT CAST A SINGLE JET THEREON.		482	BLOOD AND MOON		39
THOUGHTS LONG KNITTED INTO A SINGLE THOUGHT,		488	COOLE PARK 29		7
SEEMED SPRUNG FROM BUT A SINGLE ROOT		571	THREE BUSHES		61
NO SINGLE STORY WOULD THEY FIND		626	OLD MEN BE MAD		13
SINGLED					
KNOWING THAT THOU HADST SINGLED ME WITH WORD		684	SEEKER		57

		PAGE	TITLE	LINE

SINGS
    TO THE CRACKED TUNE THAT CHRONOS SINGS, ...   65 HAPPY SHEPHERD   9
    TO THE OLD CRACKED TUNE THAT CHRONOS SINGS, ...   65 HAPPY SHEPHERD V 9
    DROPPING FROM THE VEILS OF THE MORNING TO WHERE THE CRICKET 117 ISLE INNISFREE   6
      SINGS!
    BUT SINGS ON! . . . . 512 JANE ON GOD   23
    HE THAT SINGS A LASTING SONG . . . . 553 PRAYER OLD AGE   3
    SHE SINGS AS THE MOON SINGS! . . . . 559 HE AND SHE   7
    SHE SINGS AS THE MOON SINGS! . . . . 559 HE AND SHE   7
    A PASSION-DRIVEN EXULTANT MAN SINGS OUT . . . . . . 560 WHENCE COME   5
    EVERY MAN THAT SINGS A SONG . . . . 586 PARNELLITES   19
    BY DAY AND NIGHT A LONELY FOUNTAIN SINGS, ... 650 ISLE STAT I 1 130
    THE WATER-SERPENT SINGS HIS HEART . . . . 673 ISLE STAT II 3 184
    SINGS THE YOUNG WISTFUL SPIRIT OF A STAR . . . . . . 705 REMEMBRANCE   10
SINK
    AFTER NINE YEARS, I SINK MY HEAD ABASHED. . . . . . 353 PEOPLE   37
    HE WHO CAN READ THE SIGNS NOR SINK UNMANNED . . . . 429 NINETEEN 19   33
    AND SINK INTO ITS OWN DELIGHT AT LAST. . . . . . . 473 ALL SOUL NIGHT 60
    OR WINTRY MOONLIGHT SINK THE FIELD . . . . 501 VACILLATION   47
    HEART-SMITTEN WITH EMOTION I SINK DOWN, ... 602 GALLERY REVIS 17
    HEART SMITTEN WITH EMOTION, I SINK DOWN, ... 602 GALLERY REVIS V 17
    THAT CIVILISATION MAY NOT SINK, ... 617 LONG-LEG FLY   1
    SLOW WATERS, AND THE BOAT AND MAIDEN SINK . . . . . 663 ISLE STAT II 2 39
    LOOK ON ME ONCE. WHY SINK YOUR EYELIDS THUS? . . . . 703 MOSADA 3   107
    LOOK ON ME ONCE. WHY SINK YOUR EYELIDS SO? . . . . 703 MOSADA 3   V 107
SINKING
    AND THE EARS OF THE HORSE WENT SINKING AWAY IN THE HOLLOW 48 OISIN 3   21
      NIGHT,
    ABOVE A SINKING FIRE, A TALE THAT SHE . . . . 443 SCHOOL CHILDR 10
    ABOVE A SINKING FIRE, SOME TALE THAT SHE . . . . . . 443 SCHOOL CHILDR 10
    MY SINKING BRAIN!--CEASE!--CEASE! HEARD YE YON SOUND? . . 665 ISLE STAT II 2 73
SINKS
    THE GREY CAIRN ON THE HILL, WHEN DAY SINKS DROWNED IN DEW, 161 BLACK PIG   6
    THE RIVER RISES, AND IT SINKS AGAIN! . . . . 420 MY HOUSE   V 20A
    WHEN THE CONFLAGRATION OF THEIR PASSION SINKS, . . . 556 RIBH PATRICK   8
    NOW SINKS THE SAME REST . . . . 574 LOVERS SONG   4
    AND SINKS AT LAST INTO THE NIGHT. . . . . 633 MAN AND ECHO   36
    SEE, YONDER SINKS THE SUN, YONDER A SHADE . . . . . 653 ISLE STAT I 2 52
    SINKS, SHINING ON THE LITTLE CRUCIFIX . . . . 691 MOSADA 1   34
    SINKS DOWN AT LAST WITH YONDER MINARET, ... 691 MOSADA 1   V 36
    A WOMAN IN MY ARMS, SHE SINKS AWAY . . . . 749 SHADOW WATER A 54
SINNED
    IF THEY HAVE SINNED NOBODY KNOWS! . . . . 337 SCHOLARS   V 10
    "IF LITTLE PLANNED IS LITTLE SINNED . . . . 338 TOM OROUGHLEY   9
    "OH, LITTLE PLANNED IS LITTLE SINNED . . . . 338 TOM OROUGHLEY V 9
    THEN HAS THIS ONE BEEN SINNED FULL MANY TIMES. . . . 692 MOSADA 1   49
SINNING
    I WAS AT HER SINNING. . . . . 654 ISLE STAT I 2 62
    TELLS ALL HIS SINNING IN THEIR EARS. . . . . 655 ISLE STAT I 3 14
    TELLS ALL HER SINNING IN THEIR EARS. . . . . 655 ISLE STAT I 3 V 14
SINS
    BALD HEADS FORGETFUL OF THEIR SINS, ... 337 SCHOLARS   1
SIPPING
    GOLDSMITH DELIBERATELY SIPPING AT THE HONEY-POT OF HIS 481 BLOOD AND MOON 21
      MIND,
    GOLDSMITH DELIBERATELY SIPPING AT THE HONEY POT OF HIS 481 BLOOD AND MOON V 21
      MIND!
SIPS
    O WAKE! WAKE! WAKE! FOR SOFT AS A BEE SIPS . . . . . 677 ISLE STAT II 3 276
    OLD WARRIOR, WAKE! FOR SOFT AS A BEE SIPS, ... 677 ISLE STAT II 3 284
    THOSE TWAIN ARE DUST. WAKE! LIGHT AS A BEE SIPS . . 678 ISLE STAT II 3 290
    HE IS LONG DEAD. WAKE! SOFT AS A BEE SIPS . . . . . 678 ISLE STAT II 3 297
    NAY, HE IS GONE. WAKE! WAKE! AS A BEE SIPS . . . . . 678 ISLE STAT II 3 305
    BEFORE HIS TENT THE GENERAL SIPS HIS WINE, ... 709 FERENCZ RENYI   6
SIR
    "I NEVER THOUGHT OF THAT, SIR." . . . . 596 COLONEL MARTIN 66
    YON IS THE HUNTER'S, SIR ALMINTOR'S, PAGE! . . . . . 660 ISLE STAT II 1 35
    SIR PAGE, ALMINTOR'S FRIEND, AND THEREFORE LEARNED . . 660 ISLE STAT II 1 38
    A LONG, BROWN GRASSHOPPER OF MAIDS! PEACE, SIR! . . . 661 ISLE STAT II 1 69
SIRS
    NO NEED TO BIND MY HANDS. WHERE ARE YE, SIRS? . . . . 695 MOSADA 1   110
    NO MORE! TAKE ME INSTEAD OF HER, GREAT SIRS. . . . . 695 MOSADA 1   114
SISTER
    MY MARRIED SISTER PUT INTO MY CARE . . . . 276 TWO KINGS   V E
    HE MIGHT HAVE HAD MY SISTER, ... 620 JOHN KINSELLA   5
    I HAD A SISTER LIKE HER ONCE, MY FRIEND. . . . . . . 696 MOSADA 2   11
    O SISTER OF SORROWFUL GAZE! . . . . 706 FAIRY PEDANT   2
    THERE LIVE HIS SISTER AND HIS MOTHER. HIGH . . . . . 710 FERENCZ RENYI V 25
    OF MIDDLE AGE. "HIS SISTER HERE AND MOTHER." . . . . 711 FERENCZ RENYI   53
    THE SISTER! "SELL THY COUNTRY, AND THE SHAME . . . . 712 FERENCZ RENYI   60
    WALKS IN THE VESTURE OF HER SISTER SORROW. . . . . . 735 QUATRAIN APHOR 28
SISTERHOOD
    HERE GROW THAT SHY, RETIRING SISTERHOOD, ... 651 ISLE STAT I 2   4
SISTER'S
    AUGUSTA GREGORY'S SON! HER SISTER'S SON, ... 602 GALLERY REVIS 21
SISTERS
    "MY BROTHERS AND MY SISTERS LIVE AND THRIVE, ... 32 OISIN 2   V 50C
    SEVEN OLD SISTERS WIND THE THREADS OF THE LONG-LIVED ONES, 209 UNDER THE MOON   7
    SEVEN OLD SISTERS WIND THE THREADS OF THE LONG LIVED ONES, 209 UNDER THE MOON V 7
SISTINE
    WHILE MICHAEL ANGELO'S SISTINE ROOF, ... 386 ROBARTES DANCE 32

724

SISTINE   (CONTINUED)
   ON THE SISTINE CHAPEL ROOF, ...   638 BEN BULBEN   46
SIT
   I HUNGER TO BUILD THEM ANEW AND SIT ON A GREEN KNOLL APART,   143 ROSE IN HEART   6
   WHERE I CAN SIT UP HALF THE NIGHT . . . .   624 APPARITIONS   11
   OR SAD SEA-SHELLS WHERE LITTLE ECHOES SIT? . . . . .   650 ISLE STAT I 1   149
   AND 'NEATH IT SIT, AND OF THE WOVEN SUM . . . . . .   663 ISLE STAT II 2   30
   AS MOTHS WITH BROKEN WINGS, AND AS WE SIT . . . . .   671 ISLE STAT II 3   142
   BY THOSE WAN STARS THAT SIT IN COMPANY . . . . . .   691 MOSADA 1   26
   COME, FATHER. LADY, I NOR REST NOR SIT. . . . . . .   720 WITCH VIVIEN   18
   WHERE MAY NEW-MARRIED WOMEN SIT . . . .   791 REPRISALS   19
SITS
   SITS A YOUNGER AND A STRONGER. . . . .   26 OISIN 1   V 399D
   WHO SITS IN LONELY SPLENDOUR, MAIL'D IN GOLD, ...   651 ISLE STAT I 1   163
   BUT LOUD THE GRASSHOPPER THAT SITS BENEATH. . . . . .   662 ISLE STAT II 2   8
   AND EVERY FLOWER ABOVE ITS SHADOW SITS. . . . . . .   712 FERENCZ RENYI   73
   AND EVERY FLOWER ABOVE A SHADOW SITS. . . . .   712 FERENCZ RENYI V   73
SITTING
   THERE WAS A WONDROUS YOUNG MAN SITTING. . . . . . .   18 OISIN 1   V 252
   A KING SITTING UPON A CHAIR OF GOLD-- . . . .   104 FERGUS DRUID   36
   TO PETER SITTING IN STATE, ...   178 FIDDLER DOONEY   10
   THE GODS WERE SITTING AT THE BOARD . . . .   271 GREY ROCK   14
   AND SAW HER SITTING UPRIGHT ON THE BED; . . . . . .   467 HARUN RASHID   134
   I SAW HER SITTING UPRIGHT ON THE BED, ...   467 HARUN RASHID   V   134
   THEY WERE SITTING ROUND A POOL, ...   667 ISLE STAT II 3   24
   AND THEY WERE SITTING ROUND A POOL. . . . .   667 ISLE STAT II 3 V   24
   AND ALL THE ELDERS SITTING IN THE SUN . . . .   693 MOSADA 1   69
   SITTING ON A WARM SMOOTH MAT . . . .   726 LOVERS QUARREL   11
   SITTING ON MY RIGHT HAND." . . . .   741 EARL PAUL   60
SIX   SEE FIVE-SIX SIX THREE-SIX
   "THOSE SIX FEET MARKED IN CHALK? . . . .   548 TO SAME TUNE 3   8
   "THOSE SIX FEET MARKED IN CHALK? . . . .   548 TO SAME TUNE 3   18
   "THOSE SIX FEET MARKED IN CHALK? . . . .   549 TO SAME TUNE 3   28
   I TOLD HIM THAT NIGHTLY FROM SIX TO SEVEN I SAT AT THIS   578 LOFTY THINGS   9
      TABLE,
   I SOUGHT IT DAILY FOR SIX WEEKS OR SO. . . . . . .   629 CIRCUS ANIMALS   2
   A MAN THAT HAD SIX MORTAL WOUNDS, A MAN . . . . . .   634 CUCHULAIN COMF   1
   DEEP IN THE WOODLAND PAUSED THEY, THE SIX FEET . . .   716 DWELT SYCAMORE   9
   DEEP IN THE WOODLAND PASSED THEY. THE SIX FEET . . .   716 DWELT SYCAMORE V   9
   WHO IS SIX FEET HIGH IN HIS SOCKS AT LEAST? . . . .   729 PRIEST FAIRY   28
   SIX THAT ARE DEATHLESS, ...   770 BLOOD BOND   13
   SIX HOLY CREATURES, ...   770 BLOOD BOND   14
SIX-AND-TWENTY
   TWENTY-AND-EIGHT, AND YET BUT SIX-AND-TWENTY . . . .   373 PHASES OF MOON   33
SIXES
   DOUBLE SIXES! . . . .   721 WITCH VIVIEN   43
SIXTEEN   SEE NINETEEN-SIXTEEN
   SIXTEEN DEAD MEN . . . .   395 SIXTEEN DEAD   T
   THE SIXTEEN MEN WERE SHOT, ...   395 SIXTEEN DEAD   2
   COME PRAISE NINETEEN SIXTEEN, ...   608 SONGS BURDEN 3 V   2
SIXTY
   A SIXTY YEAR OLD SMILING PUBLIC MAN. . . . .   443 SCHOOL CHILDR V   8
   WITH SIXTY OR MORE WINTERS ON ITS HEAD, ...   444 SCHOOL CHILDR   38
SIXTY-YEAR-OLD
   A SIXTY-YEAR-OLD SMILING PUBLIC MAN. . . . .   443 SCHOOL CHILDR   8
SKEIN
   FOR LOVE IS BUT A SKEIN UNWOUND . . . .   511 JANE AND JACK   5
   I--LOVE'S SKEIN UPON THE GROUND, ...   511 JANE AND JACK   9
   THE SKEIN SO BOUND US GHOST TO GHOST . . . .   511 JANE AND JACK   15
SKELETON-GAUNT
   WHEN WITHERED OLD AND SKELETON-GAUNT, ...   475 EVA GORE-BOOTH   12
SKELPING
   WITH SKELPING HIS BIG BRAWLING LOUT, ...   301 RUN PARADISE   9
SKIES
   I SAW NOT WHO; 'NEATH OTHER SKIES . . . .   25 OISIN 1   V 381A
   ON THE ANVIL OF THE WORLD. BE STILL! THE SKIES . . .   42 OISIN 2   204
   UPON THE ANVIL OF THE WORLD. THE SKIES . . . . . .   42 OISIN 2   V 204
   WAR ON THE MIGHTIEST MEN UNDER THE SKIES, ...   45 OISIN 2   241
   . . . NOR GO FROM HIS DEW-CUMBERED SKIES! . . . . .   49 OISIN 3   38
   BRIMFUL OF STARLIGHT, AND HE SAID; THE STAMPER OF   76 INDIAN ON GOD   14
      THE SKIES,
   EVEN AS SPRING UPON THE ANCIENT SKIES, ...   108 CUCHULAIN SEA   42
   STARED LIKE THE SPRING UPON THE ANCIENT SKIES, . . .   108 CUCHULAIN SEA V   41
   MORE MOURNFUL THAN THE DEPTH OF STARRY SKIES, ...   108 CUCHULAIN SEA V   42
   UNDER THE GOLDEN OR THE SILVER SKIES; . . . . . .   127 DREAM OF FAERY   21
   AND HOW BENEATH THOSE THREE TIMES BLESSED SKIES . . .   127 DREAM OF FAERY V   21
   ON MUNSTER GRASS AND CONNEMARA SKIES. . . . . . .   130 BOOK STORIES   24
   A HONIED RINGING! UNDER THE NEW SKIES . . . . . .   130 BOOK STORIES   V   21
   ON MUNSTER GRASS, OR CONNEMARA SKIES. . . . . . .   130 BOOK STORIES   V   24
   AND BY THE UNLABOURING BROOD OF THE SKIES; . . . .   164 PERFECT BEAUTY   5
   AND HERON OUT OF THE SKIES." . . . .   167 BLESSED   10
   BY THE INJUSTICE OF THE SKIES FOR PUNISHMENT? . . .   316 COLD HEAVEN   12
   BORN UNDER THE SKIES . . . .   333 SOLOMON SHEBA   20
   FAR FROM THE CUSTOMARY SKIES, ...   360 ALF POLLEXFEN   14
   THE RIVER IMAGING THE FLASHING SKIES, ...   390 IMAGE PAST   20
   AND SEEM TO CLING UPON THE MOONLIT SKIES, ...   482 BLOOD AND MOON   44
   FROM THE OLD MAN IN THE SKIES. . . . .   588 OLD WICKED MAN   8
   THAT OLD MAN IN THE SKIES. . . . .   588 OLD WICKED MAN   24
   FROM THE OLD MAN IN THE SKIES . . . .   589 OLD WICKED MAN   56
   THE SKIES MORE DIM, THOUGH BURNING LIKE A SHIELD, . .   656 ISLE STAT I 3   26
   OF THESE STAR-SHUDDERING SKIES, YOU ARE THE QUEEN. . .   679 ISLE STAT II 3   323

SKIES   (CONTINUED)
        MAKING ALL ONE O'ER ROCK AND SEA AND SKIES• • • • • •   687 TWO TITANS   28
        PRAYED THOSE FORGOTTEN FISHERS, TILL IN THE EASTERN SKIES   719 PHANTOM SHIP   32
        ALL THOSE LONG FORGOTTEN FISHERS, TILL IN THE EASTERN SKIES 719 PHANTOM SHIP   V   32
        UNTO THE WHITE SKIES• • • • • • • • • • • • • •   740 EARL PAUL   24
SKILL
        HE LACKED THOSE YEARS THAT GO WITH SKILL, • • • • • •   608 SONGS BURDEN 3   14
        CHANCE, AND NOT SKILL, HAS FAVOURED YOU, OLD FATHER! • •   722 WITCH VIVIEN   60
        CHANCE HATH A SKILL! • • • • • • • • • • • • •   722 WITCH VIVIEN   69
SKIN   SEE OTTER-SKIN
        A HOUSE OF WATTLES, CLAY, AND SKIN• • • • • • • • •   17 OISIN 1   249
        WITH ANTLERS AND THE SHAGGY SKIN • • • • • • • • •   17 OISIN 1   V   249
        THEY HEALED MY WOUNDS• AND ON THE SKIN SUPINE • • • • •   41 OISIN 1   187
        I SAT ON CUSHIONED OTTER SKIN• • • • • • • • • • •   81 MAD KING GOLL V   1
        CHAIRED IN THE CUSHIONED OTTER SKIN, • • • • • • • •   82 MAD KING GOLL V   5
        SUDDENLY DRENCHED HER TO THE SKIN• • • • • • • • • •   275 GREY ROCK   120
        THE BISHOP HAS A SKIN, GOD KNOWS, • • • • • • • • •   508 JANE BISHOP   15
        AND I AM SHRUNKEN TO SKIN AND BONE, • • • • • • • •   550 SONGS REWRIT 1   2
        YET I AM SHRUNKEN TO SKIN AND BONE • • • • • • • • •   550 SONGS REWRIT 1 V 2
        YET AM I SHRUNKEN TO SKIN AND BONE, • • • • • • • •   550 SONGS REWRIT 1 V 2
        BUT I AM SHRUNKEN TO SKIN AND BONE, • • • • • • • •   550 SONGS REWRIT 1 V 2
        THOUGH I AM SHRUNKEN TO BONE AND SKIN, • • • • • • •   551 SONGS REWRIT 1 V 8
        AND BEING OLD SHE PUT A SKIN • • • • • • • • • • •   621 JOHN KINSELLA   21
        AND THE GREAT GREY LYNX'S SKIN! IN SOOTH, METHINKS • • •   650 ISLE STAT I 1   151
        WHO SAID WE HAD A SKIN OF YELLOW ALE? • • • • • • •   759 SHADOW WATER A   243
SKINS
        WE LAY ON SKINS OF OTTERS, AND DRANK WINE, • • • • • •   41 OISIN 2   188
        AND THEN ON HEAPED-UP SKINS OF OTTERS SLEPT• • • • • • •   41 OISIN 2   191
        AND ON THE SKINS OF WOLVES AND BEARS WE SLEPT! • • • • •   41 OISIN 2   V   191
        MINE WAS A CHAIR OF SKINS AND GOLD, • • • • • • • • •   81 MAD KING GOLL V   1
        ON DAPPLED SKINS IN A GLASS BOAT, • • • • • • • • •   196 BAILE AILLINN   180
        AND STRETCHED OUT SLEEPING ON A PILE OF SKINS • • • • •   283 TWO KINGS   141
        AMONG DARK SKINS, AND THERE • • • • • • • • • • •   472 ALL SOUL NIGHT   48
SKIPPER
        OLD MERCHANT SKIPPER THAT LEAPED OVERBOARD • • • • • •   270 PARDON FATHERS   13
        YOU MERCHANT SKIPPER THAT LEAPED OVERBOARD • • • • • •   270 PARDON FATHERS V 13
        AND MERCHANT SKIPPER THAT LEAPED OVERBOARD • • • • • •   270 PARDON FATHERS V 13
SKIRT
        HER DOMINO, HER PANNIERED SKIRT COPIED FROM LONGHI: • • •   363 DOLLS FACES   7
SKY
        THAT KEPT DIM WATERS FROM THE SKY• • • • • • • • • •   17 OISIN 1   243
        AND BID THE STARS DROP DOWN FROM THE SKY, • • • • • • •   28 OISIN 1   426
        IS AN UNDYING MOORFOWL, AND HE LIVES BEYOND THE SKY. • • •   76 INDIAN ON GOD   7
        YOU HAVE THE HEAVIEST ARM UNDER THE SKY." • • • • • • •   107 CUCHULAIN SEA   24
        UNDER THE PASSING STARS, FOAM OF THE SKY• • • • • • • •   112 ROSE OF WORLD   9
        THE BRILLIANT MOON AND ALL THE MILKY SKY• • • • • • • •   119 SORROW OF LOVE   2
        THE FULL ROUND MOON AND THE STAR-LADEN SKY, • • • • • •   119 SORROW OF LOVE V 2
        A CLIMBING MOON UPON AN EMPTY SKY, • • • • • • • • •   120 SORROW OF LOVE   10
        THE CRUMBLING MOON, THE WHITE STARS IN THE SKY, • • • • •   120 SORROW OF LOVE V 10
        THE CURD-PALE MOON, THE WHITE STARS IN THE SKY, • • • • •   120 SORROW OF LOVE V 10
        • • • HUNG LOW ON THE RIM OF THE SKY• • • • • • • • •   122 WHITE BIRDS   3
        THAT GOD HAS LAID HIS FINGERS ON THE SKY, • • • • • • •   128 DREAM OF FAERY   43
        OF HOW GOD LEANS HIS HANDS OUT OF THE SKY, • • • • • • •   128 DREAM OF FAERY V 43
        THAT GOD HAD LEANED HIS HANDS OUT OF THE SKY, • • • • • •   128 DREAM OF FAERY V 43
        THAT GOD HAD LEANT HIS HANDS OUT OF THE SKY, • • • • • •   128 DREAM OF FAERY V 43
        WITH THE EARTH AND THE SKY AND THE WATER. • • • • • • •   143 ROSE IN HEART   7
        AS A CLOUD FADED INTO THE SKY. • • • • • • • • • • •   145 HOST OF AIR   40
        AND HAD ROOTED THE SUN AND MOON AND STARS OUT OF THE SKY   153 CHANGE BELOVED   11
        AND ROOTED THE SUN AND MOON AND STARS OUT OF THE SKY, • • •   153 CHANGE BELOVED V 11
        AND STARS CLIMBING THE DEW-DROPPING SKY, • • • • • • •   158 BELOVED RHYMES   11
        WHEN SHALL THE STARS BE BLOWN ABOUT THE SKY, • • • • • •   170 SECRET ROSE   29
        OF MORNING LIGHT IN A DIM SKY• • • • • • • • • • • •   195 BAILE AILLINN   150
        FAR OUT UNDER A WINDLESS SKY! • • • • • • • • • • •   197 BAILE AILLINN   181
        AND IN THE TREMBLING BLUE-GREEN OF THE SKY • • • • • • •   206 ADAMS CURSE   30
        PALE SILVER-PROUD QUEEN-WOMAN OF THE SKY, • • • • • • •   211 RAGGED WOOD   6
        HE HAS CAUGHT THE CRESCENT MOON OUT OF THE SKY, • • • • •   239 SHADOW WATER B   370
        APPEAR AND DISAPPEAR IN THE BLUE DEPTH OF THE SKY • • • •   318 MAGI   3
        APPEAR AND DISAPPEAR IN THE BLUE DEPTHS OF THE SKY • • • •   318 MAGI   V   3
        MIRRORS A STILL SKY! • • • • • • • • • • • • • •   322 SWANS AT COOLE   4
        THE PURE COLD LIGHT IN THE SKY • • • • • • • • • • •   378 CAT AND MOON   7
        WHEN THE OLD MOON IS VANISHED FROM THE SKY, • • • • • •   382 VISION ROBART   3
        WHEN THE OLD MOON IS VANISHING FROM THE SKY • • • • • •   382 VISION ROBART V   3
        SEEM BUT THE CLOUDS OF THE SKY • • • • • • • • • • •   416 TOWER   192
        HER DESOLATION TO THE DESOLATE SKY. • • • • • • • • •   423 MY DESCENDANTS   16
        LIKE THIS PURE JET, NOW LOST AMID BLUE SKY, • • • • • •   464 HARUN RASHID   64
        THE MOON IS STAGGERING IN THE SKY! • • • • • • • • •   487 CRAZED MOON   2
        BUT SEEMS A CONCENTRATION OF THE SKY! • • • • • • • •   490 COOLE BALLYLEE   18
        CLOUDY LEAFAGE OF THE SKY, • • • • • • • • • • • •   501 VACILLATION   46
        MAY CALL A CURSE OUT OF THE SKY • • • • • • • • • •   508 JANE BISHOP   V   4
        BANNERS CHOKE THE SKY! • • • • • • • • • • • • •   512 JANE ON GOD   7
        ABOUT THE SKY! WHERE THAT IS CLEAR OF CLOUD • • • • • •   541 PARN FUNERAL 1   3
        THERE, ON THE MOUNTAIN AND THE SKY, • • • • • • • • •   567 LAPIS LAZULI   51
        WHAT GREAT TOMB-HAUNTER SWEEPS THE DISTANT SKY • • • • •   618 BRONZE HEAD   4
        DROPPING OUT OF SKY OR ROCK, • • • • • • • • • • •   633 MAN AND ECHO   44
        FLOWERS AND GRASS AND CLOUDLESS SKY, • • • • • • • • •   639 BEN BULBEN   57
        THE BRAZEN SKY, SO BLAZE THE DAFFODILLS! • • • • • • •   645 ISLE STAT I 1   11
        FROM THE DEEP EARTH UNTO THE LURID SKY • • • • • • • •   662 ISLE STAT II 2   5
        THE FAERY SHIP THAT SWIMS ATHWART THE SKY. • • • • • • •   663 ISLE STAT II 2   16
        THE SKY WAS BANDED O'ER WITH WRACK. • • • • • • • • •   667 ISLE STAT II 3   23
        UNTIL THIS MORN. THE SKY WITH WRACK • • • • • • • • •   667 ISLE STAT II 3 V 22
        SHOUTED A MOMENT 'TWEEN THE EARTH AND SKY. • • • • • • •   675 ISLE STAT II 3 237

	PAGE	TITLE		LINE
SKY (CONTINUED)				
MY THOUGHTS, AND YONDER BRIGHTENING PATCH OF SKY	700	MOSADA 3		31
AND WHO FOREGATHER IN THE SKY.	716	FAIRY DOCTOR		8
IN WASTE PLACES OF THE SKY,	772	SONG DEIRDRE 1		6
SKY'S				
I HEAR THE WHOLE SKY'S SORROW IN ONE VOICE.	652	ISLE STAT I 2		22
SLAB				
HEALING FROM ITS LETTERED SLAB. THOSE SELF-SAME HANDS PERCHANCE	503	VACILLATION		82
SLAIN				
AND ON THE HEROES LYING SLAIN	5	OISIN 1		42
BY AGE'S WEARINESS ARE SLAIN,	27	OISIN 1	V	415A
HAS SLAIN SO MIGHTY ARMIES, SO GREAT KINGS,	106	CUCHULAIN SEA	V	10A
ARMED MEN HAVE COME UPON US! O I AM SLAIN!	233	SHADOW WATER B		241
ARMED MEN HAVE COME UPON US! O I AM SLAIN!	233	SHADOW WATER B		243
WHO HAVE SLAIN MY HUSBAND AND LAID HANDS UPON ME.	235	SHADOW WATER B		282
ODOUR OF BLOOD WHEN CHRIST WAS SLAIN	438	SONGS PLAY 2		6
THE LOFTY INNOCENCE THAT IT HAS SLAIN,	614	MARCH SONGS 2		12
CONVICTED COWARDS ALL, BY KINDRED SLAIN	634	CUCHULAIN COMF		21
ARMED MEN HAVE COME UPON US. O! I AM SLAIN!	753	SHADOW WATER A		133
ENDS ALL THINGS. I HAVE SLAIN THE LOCHLANN KING.	754	SHADOW WATER A		163
SLANDER				
EARNED SLANDER, INGRATITUDE,	260	UNWORTH PRAISE		16
SLANDERED				
AN OLD FOUL MOUTH THAT SLANDERED YOU HAD SET	292	TO A SHADE	V	17
SLANDEROUS				
AH, SWEET TO ME NOW WERE EVEN BALD CONAN'S SLANDEROUS TONGUE!	55	OISIN 3		116
BURNING IN FIRES OF A SLANDEROUS TONGUE.	148	INTO TWILIGHT		8
SLANTING				
FROM FASTING--SEE, THE RED LIGHT SLANTING DOWN	697	MOSADA 2		36
NOW FLINGING LOOSE THE SLANTING SAIL,	742	DANAAN QUICK		3
SLATE				
AS THAT WHICH CLEANS MAN'S DIRTY SLATE.	633	MAN AND ECHO		24
SLATE-COLOURED				
LAY HIDDEN IN THE SMALL SLATE-COLOURED THING!	104	FERGUS DRUID		40
TAKE THEN THIS SMALL SLATE-COLOURED BAG OF DREAMS!	104	FERGUS DRUID	V	29
LAY HIDDEN IN THE SMALL SLATE-COLOURED BAG!	104	FERGUS DRUID	V	40
SLATES				
WITH OLD MILL BOARDS AND SEA-GREEN SLATES,	406	CARVED STONE		2
SLAUGHTERED				
OF MANY A SLAUGHTERED FOREST ROVER.	17	OISIN 1	V	249A
SLAVE				
TO ALL THINGS CRIED! "I AM A SLAVE!	19	OISIN 1	V	280
AN OLD SLAVE GRINDING AT A HEAVY QUERN,	104	FERGUS DRUID		35
I HAVE BEEN A SLAVE,	495	MOHINI CHATTER		6
A SLAVE BOWS DOWN TO A SLAVE.	547	TO SAME TUNE 3		6
A SLAVE BOWS DOWN TO A SLAVE.	547	TO SAME TUNE 3		6
A SLAVE BOWS DOWN TO A SLAVE.	614	MARCH SONGS 2		6
A SLAVE BOWS DOWN TO A SLAVE.	614	MARCH SONGS 2		6
AND AS A SLAVE BEEN WAKEFUL IN THE HALLS	724	KANVA ON SELF		5
SLAVES				
BUT NOW HEARTS CRY THAT HEARTS ARE SLAVES,	19	OISIN 1		280
SHAKE THE LOOSE REINS! YOU SLAVES OF GOD,	22	OISIN 1		331
SHAKE THE LOOSE REINS! YE SLAVES OF GOD,	22	OISIN 1	V	331
SEA-GOD, THAT ONCE, TO GIVE HIS SLAVES CONTENT,	38	OISIN 2	V	129
NEITHER TO SLAVES THAT WERE SPAT ON,	414	TOWER		130
AND OUR SLAVES BE AS OF OLD.	727	LOVERS QUARREL		56
SLAY				
AND THEN ARISE, AND RAVING SLAY US ALL.	110	CUCHULAIN SEA		79
SLEEK				
SLEEK AS ANY GRANARY MOUSE	2	OISIN 1	V	7M
MORE SLEEK THAN ANY GRANARY MOUSE,	4	OISIN 1		36
SLEEK AS ANY GRANARY MOUSE,	4	OISIN 1	V	37
AND SLEEK YOUNG JOY IS NO MORE FICKLE,	77	INDIAN TO LOVE	V	5C
BUT EVEN AT THE STARTING-POST, ALL SLEEK AND NEW,	619	BRONZE HEAD		15
SLEEP				
AND SLEEP DROWN SUN AND MOON AND STAR."	5	OISIN 1	V	49
AND ALWAYS NEVER-ANXIOUS SLEEP;	8	OISIN 1		93
MUSIC AND LOVE AND SLEEP AWAIT,	9	OISIN 1		103
THE FENIANS. LET THEIR DEER-HOUNDS SLEEP.	11	OISIN 1	V	131
SLEEP THERE TILL THE MOON AND THE STARS DIE!"	17	OISIN 1		246
O'ER MEN WHO SLEEP, AND WAKE, AND DIE,	22	OISIN 1	V	340B
MAY SLEEP IN THE END WITH THE WHOLE OF HIS FATE DONE,	28	OISIN 1	V	423F
SINCE GOD MADE TIME AND DEATH AND SLEEP: THE OTHER	31	OISIN 2		41
AH, TOUCH THEIR BLUE-VEINED EYELIDS IF THEY SLEEP,	33	OISIN 2		61
AH, TOUCH THEIR BLUE VEINED EYELIDS IF THEY SLEEP,	33	OISIN 2	V	61
WE SANG THE LOVES AND ANGERS WITHOUT SLEEP,	42	OISIN 2		194
THE SPACIOUS LOVES, THE ANGER WITHOUT SLEEP	42	OISIN 2	V	194
COULD SLEEP ON A COUCH OF RUSHES, AND ALL INWROUGHT AND INLAID,	49	OISIN 3		31
COULD SLEEP ON A BED OF RUSHES, AND ALL INWROUGHT AND INLAID,	49	OISIN 3	V	31
COULD SLEEP ON A COUCH OF RUSHES--ROUND AND ABOUT THEM LAID.	49	OISIN 3	V	32
. . . AND FED OF UNHUMAN SLEEP.	51	OISIN 3		56
IN A LONG IRON SLEEP, AS A FISH IN THE WATER GOES DUMB AS A STONE.	53	OISIN 3		96
. . . THEIR DIMNESS, THEIR DEWS DROPPING SLEEP.	54	OISIN 3		108
SO SLEEP THEE BY DAYTIME." A VOICE CRIED,	59	OISIN 3		172
SO SLEEP THEY BY DAYTIME." A VOICE CRIED,	59	OISIN 3	V	172

727

SLEEP (CONTINUED)

	PAGE	TITLE		LINE
A CREEPING OLD MAN, FULL OF SLEEP,	60	OISIN 3		192
A LONELY LAUGHTER, AND MAY KISS HIS HANDS TO ME IN SLEEP.	75	ANASHU VIJAYA		82
PRAYERS FOR THE LAND. O BRAHMA, GUARD IN SLEEP	75	ANASHU VIJAYA		85
AN INNER LAUGHTER, AND MAY KISS HIS HANDS TO ME IN SLEEP.	75	ANASHU VIJAYA	V	82
A LONELY LAUGHTER, THAT HE MAY KISS HANDS TO ME IN SLEEP.	75	ANASHU VIJAYA	V	82
MY SPIRIT ROCKED IN SLEEP AND SIGHS, AND SAW THE MOORFOWL PACE	76	INDIAN ON GOD		3
AND HURLED THEM IN THE GULPH OF SLEEP!	83	MAD KING GOLL		22
AND THEY INHERIT THE GREAT SLEEP.	83	MAD KING GOLL	V	22
AND IS ANXIOUS IN ITS SLEEP.	87	STOLEN CHILD		23
WHEN YOU ARE OLD AND GREY AND FULL OF SLEEP,	120	YOU ARE OLD		1
AND MIGHT HAVE KNOWN AT LAST UNHAUNTED SLEEP	128	DREAM OF FAERY		38
AND HUSHED IN SLEEP THE ROARING RANKS OF BATTLE!	129	BOOK STORIES		7
HE ROUSED HIS HORSE OUT OF ITS SLEEP,	133	FR GILLIGAN		27
THAT GOD GIVES UNTO MAN IN SLEEP.	138	TO IRELAND	V	22
O VANITY OF SLEEP, HOPE, DREAM, ENDLESS DESIRE,	154	BELOVED PEACE		7
THRONE OVER THRONE WHERE IN HALF SLEEP,	156	FORGOT BEAUTY		22
IS DROPPING SLEEP, UNTIL GOD BURN TIME,	164	PERFECT BEAUTY		7
OF YOUR BELOVED IN SLEEP.	165	CRY OF SEDGE		10
AMONG PALE EYELIDS, HEAVY WITH THE SLEEP	169	SECRET ROSE		6
WHEN WILL HE WAKE FROM SLEEP?	174	ELEMENT POWERS		6
IN COMFORTABLE SLEEP! ALL LIVING SLEPT	180	QUEEN MAEVE		15
HAD TROUBLED HIS SLEEP. BUT ALL HE HAD TO SAY	182	QUEEN MAEVE		52
SHE TURNED AWAY! HE TURNED AGAIN TO SLEEP	182	QUEEN MAEVE		59
SUDDENLY AILELL SPOKE OUT OF HIS SLEEP,	183	QUEEN MAEVE		73
THE CHILDREN OF THE MAINES OUT OF SLEEP,	184	QUEEN MAEVE		92
FACE DOWNWARD, TOSSING IN A TROUBLED SLEEP!	185	QUEEN MAEVE		106
THE WATERS OF SLEEP CAN MAKE A CHATTERING TONGUE	218	WOODS OF COOLE		25
IT'S CERTAIN I'D SLEEP EASIER O' NIGHTS	224	SHADOW WATER B		59
YOU'RE CERTAIN OF IT? I NEVER WAKE FROM SLEEP	226	SHADOW WATER B		83
WAKE ALL BELOW! WHY HAVE YOU BROKEN OUR SLEEP?	233	SHADOW WATER B		242
AND SAYS, "A SWORD-BLADE PIERCED ME IN MY SLEEP."	234	SHADOW WATER B		257
AND SAYS! "A SWORD BLADE PIERCED ME IN MY SLEEP."	234	SHADOW WATER B	V	257
TO SHAKE HIM OUT OF SLEEP, I COULD NOT ROUSE HIM.	283	TWO KINGS		143
AND LEFT MERE SLEEP. HE'LL WAKE WHEN THE SUN WAKES,	284	TWO KINGS		161
SLEEP BEFORE THE THIRD NOON SOUNDS."	295	THREE BEGGARS		24
TO KEEP HIS FELLOWS FROM THEIR SLEEP!	297	THREE BEGGARS		45
ONE BEGGAR CRIED! "YOU'RE SHAMMING SLEEP,"	297	THREE BEGGARS	V	45
TILL EVEN I SLEEP LIGHT! BUT WHO	303	HOUR DAWN		34
THAT I MAY FIND THE SLEEP I HAVE LOST."	303	HOUR DAWN		39
SO THAT IT SEEMS EVEN I SLEEP LIGHT!	303	HOUR DAWN	V	34
I HAVE TO FIND THE SLEEP I HAVE LOST."	303	HOUR DAWN	V	39
"WHAT CARE I IF YOU SLEEP OR WAKE?	304	HOUR DAWN		40
I'LL SLEEP ANOTHER CENTURY."	304	HOUR DAWN		43
"AND I WILL TALK BEFORE I SLEEP	304	HOUR DAWN		44
"I'LL SLEEP UNTIL THE WINTER'S GONE,	305	HOUR DAWN		57
AND DRINK, AND YOU WILL SLEEP THAT LENGTH."	305	HOUR DAWN		59
"I'D LIKE TO SLEEP TILL WINTER'S GONE	305	HOUR DAWN		60
YOU WILL SLEEP THAT LENGTH! AND AT THE FIRST	305	HOUR DAWN	V	59
I'LL SLEEP AWAY ALL TIME WITHIN IT!	306	HOUR DAWN		74
MY SLEEP WERE NOW NINE CENTURIES	306	HOUR DAWN		75
AND SLEEP AWAY ALL TIME WITHIN IT.	306	HOUR DAWN	V	74
AND WAIT HIM IN A DRUNKEN SLEEP."	307	HOUR DAWN		106
PLEASURE THAT COMES WITH SLEEP,	345	ON WOMAN		22
SLEEP DRIVEN FROM MY BED,	346	ON WOMAN		36
WHEN I CLAMBER TO THE HEIGHTS OF SLEEP,	357	DEEP-SWORN VOW		4
AND SLEEP THERE!	380	SONGS FOOL 1		3
I START OUT OF MY SLEEP TO THINK	380	SONGS FOOL 1		7
HAD I BUT AWAKENED FROM SLEEP	381	SONGS FOOL 2		10
WHEN SLEEP AT LAST HAS COME	394	EASTER 1916		63
HAD WATCHED IN BITTERER SLEEP	399	BREAK OF DAY		22
THAT TWENTY CENTURIES OF STONY SLEEP	402	SECOND COMING		19
THAT THIRTY CENTURIES OF STONY SLEEP	402	SECOND COMING	V	19
RIDES UPON SLEEP! A DRUNKEN SOLDIERY	429	NINETEEN 19		26
THAT MY MICHAEL MAY SLEEP SOUND,	435	FOR MY SON		2
HER FILL OF SLEEP.	435	FOR MY SON		8
STRETCH OUT YOUR LIMBS AND SLEEP A LONG SATURNIAN SLEEP!	442	BLACK CENTAUR		13
STRETCH OUT YOUR LIMBS AND SLEEP A LONG SATURNIAN SLEEP!	442	BLACK CENTAUR		13
AND THAT MUST SLEEP, SHRIEK, STRUGGLE TO ESCAPE	444	SCHOOL CHILDR		35
AND MY SLEEP IS GONE.	454	EMPTY CUP		10
AND FEARING THAT MY LIGHT DISTURBED HER SLEEP	467	HARUN RASHID		130
A DOZEN NIGHTS OF NATURAL SLEEP, AND THEN	468	HARUN RASHID		150
SHE ROSE, AND WITH HER EYES SHUT FAST IN SLEEP	468	HARUN RASHID		152
BELOVED, MAY YOUR SLEEP BE SOUND	522	LULLABY		1
SLEEP UPON A GOLDEN BED	522	LULLABY		5
SLEEP, BELOVED, SUCH A SLEEP	522	LULLABY		7
SLEEP, BELOVED, SUCH A SLEEP	522	LULLABY		7
SUCH A SLEEP AND SOUND AS FELL	522	LULLABY		13
BELOVED SUCH A SLEEP AS FELL	522	LULLABY	V	13
AND NOW LIES SUNK IN SLEEP. WHAT CLIMBS THE STAIR?	579	DOR WELLESLEY		11
BUT NOW LIES SUNK IN SLEEP. WHAT CLIMBS THE STAIR?	579	DOR WELLESLEY	V	11
WINE OR LOVE DRUG HIM TO SLEEP,	633	MAN AND ECHO		26
WINE OR LOVE DRUGS HIM TO SLEEP,	633	MAN AND ECHO	V	26
OF THE SONGS THAT NEVER SLEEP,	647	ISLE STAT I 1		76
DREAMING IN THEIR SOFT ODOUR-LADEN SLEEP!	650	ISLE STAT I 1		125
SEAFARER, WAKE! WAS MY SLEEP LONG? LONG YEARS.	678	ISLE STAT II 3		292
WAS MY SLEEP LONG, OH, YOUTH? LONG, LONG AND DEEP.	678	ISLE STAT II 3		299
SLEEPER, AWAKE! HOW LONG MY SLEEP? UNNUMBERED	678	ISLE STAT II 3		307
THE YEARS OF GOBLIN SLEEP. AH! WHILE I SLUMBERED	679	ISLE STAT II 3		308
FOR EVER ROUND THY WAKING AND THY SLEEP	688	TWO TITANS		57

```
                                                PAGE    TITLE              LINE
SLEEP    (CONTINUED)
    UPON MY KNEES I PRAY YOU, LET IT SLEEP, . . . . . .   693 MOSADA 1              72
    THE WORLD WERE DREAMING IN ITS SUMMER SLEEP! . . . .  699 MOSADA 3              11
    THIS DEATH IS HEAVY IN MY VEINS LIKE SLEEP. . . . .   701 MOSADA 3              57
    SLEEP IN SOME FAR OTHER FIELD  . . . . . . . . . . .  705 DAWN-SONG              3
    "WAKEN, WAKEN, SLEEPY FISHERS! NO HOUR IS THIS FOR SLEEP,"  718 PHANTOM SHIP     7
    THE HEART OF NOON FOLDS SILENCE AND FOLDS SLEEP, . .  735 QUATRAIN APHOR        25
    AND COMMON MEN THAT SLEEP. . . . . . . . . . . . .    736 IN CHURCH              8
    WHEN AENGUS AND HIS EDAINE WAKE FROM SLEEP . . . .    749 SHADOW WATER A        57
    WAKE ALL BELOW.  WHY HAVE YOU BROKEN OUR SLEEP? . .   753 SHADOW WATER A       132
    AND SAYS, "A SWORD-BLADE PIERCED ME IN MY SLEEP." .   753 SHADOW WATER A       147
    AND SAYS, "A SWORD BLADE PIERCED ME IN MY SLEEP." .   753 SHADOW WATER A  V    147
    FROM ITS FIRST SIGHS AND LAUGHTER, BEFORE THE SLEEP, 754 SHADOW WATER A       161
    WHOSE SHADOW IS THE SLEEP THAT COMES WITH LOVE, . .   754 SHADOW WATER A       162
    I HAD WOVEN OF THE SLEEP THAT IS IN POOLS . . . .     762 SHADOW WATER A       284
    TO DROWN IN ITS OWN IMAGE?  EVEN THAT SLEEP  . . .    765 SHADOW WATER A       364
SLEEPER
    FROM SLEEPER UNTO SLEEPER MURMUR YOU. . . . . . .      33 OISIN 2         V     60
    FROM SLEEPER UNTO SLEEPER MURMUR YOU. . . . . . .      33 OISIN 2         V     60
    THAT PUT A PASSION IN THE SLEEPER THERE, . . . .     284 TWO KINGS            157
    HAD NOT THE SLEEPER STARTED UP. . . . . . . . . .    304 HOUR DAWN             48
    FOR ALL THE SLEEPER KNEW OR CARED! . . . . . . .     307 HOUR DAWN            115
    IS STONE! OLD SLEEPER! THIS SAME AFTERNOON . . . .   657 ISLE STAT I 3         74
    SLEEPER, AWAKE!  HOW LONG MY SLEEP?  UNNUMBERED . .   678 ISLE STAT II 3       307
    ON THE NOSE OF THE SLEEPER HE MADE IT PLAY! . . .    729 PRIEST FAIRY          30
    THE SLEEPER AWOKE WITH A SUDDEN START, . . . . . .   729 PRIEST FAIRY          31
SLEEPER'S
    INTO THE SLEEPER'S TUB OF BEER . . . . . . . . . .   304 HOUR DAWN             47
    TO BREAK UPON A SLEEPER'S REST . . . . . . . . . .   412 TOWER                 87
SLEEPERS
    AND MY GAZE WAS THRONGED WITH THE SLEEPERS! . . . .   50 OISIN 3               49
    CAME SOUND FROM THOSE MONSTROUS SLEEPERS, . . . . .   51 OISIN 3               58
    WHEN SLEEPERS WAKE AND YET STILL DREAM. . . . . .    639 BEN BULBEN            59
    THY PEACE.  AH, NOW I'LL WAKE THESE SLEEPERS, LOST   677 ISLE STAT II 3       274
    BEHOLD THE HAPLESS SLEEPERS STANDING BY. . . . . .   677 ISLE STAT II 3       281
SLEEPILY
    SLEEPILY CLOSE HER ROUND BRIGHT EYNE! . . . . . . .  646 ISLE STAT I 1         35
SLEEPING
    SO LONG WERE THEY SLEEPING, . . . . . . . . . .      49 OISIN 3               39
    TILL I SAW WHERE MAEVE LIES SLEEPING . . . . . .     60 OISIN 3              184
    TROUBLE HIS SLEEPING! GIVE HIM DREAMS OF ME. . . .    75 ANASHU VIJAYA        91
    LIFTED THE CURTAIN OF HER SLEEPING ROOM, . . . .    182 QUEEN MAEVE      V    63
    SHE SAW HER HUSBAND AILELL SLEEPING THERE, . . . .  183 QUEEN MAEVE           69
    TO MAKE AN END WHILE HE IS SLEEPING THERE. . . . .  222 SHADOW WATER B  V     14
    WE'LL LEARN THAT SLEEPING IS NOT DEATH, . . . . .   266 GALWAY RACES          11
    AND STRETCHED OUT SLEEPING ON A PILE OF SKINS . . . 283 TWO KINGS            141
    AND SHOWN MY HUSBAND SLEEPING THERE, I HAVE SIGHED, . 285 TWO KINGS           188
    TO JUDGE IF A LIGHT SLEEPING FOOL . . . . . . . .   304 HOUR DAWN        V    52
    I SAT WHERE I COULD WATCH HER SLEEPING FORM, . . .  467 HARUN RASHID         128
    ARE SOMEWHERE SLEEPING LIKE A TOP . . . . . . . .   525 DANCING DAYS          13
    SLEEPING LORD OF ARCHERY. . . . . . . . . . . .     658 ISLE STAT I 3         81
    SLEEPING LORD OF ARCHERY. . . . . . . . . . . .     658 ISLE STAT I 3         96
    A MOUSE FROM HIS SLEEPING, . . . . . . . . . . .    672 ISLE STAT II 3       172
    AND STRAIGHT BEFORE THE SLEEPING PRIEST . . . . .   729 PRIEST FAIRY          23
    "MAN OF WISDOM, FROM THY SLEEPING . . . . . . . .   729 PRIEST FAIRY          39
SLEEPING-ROOM
    LIFTED THE CURTAIN OF HER SLEEPING-ROOM, . . . . .  182 QUEEN MAEVE           63
SLEEPLESS
    HIS SLEEPLESS CANDLE AND LABORIOUS PEN. . . . . .   375 PHASES OF MOON        86
    SLEEPLESS WOULD LIE DOWN AND DIE. . . . . . . . .   632 MAN AND ECHO          18
SLEEP'S
    AND I GAZED ON THE BELL-BRANCH, SLEEP'S FOREBEAR, . . 50 OISIN 3             53
SLEEPS
    THAT IN IMMORTAL SILENCE SLEEPS  . . . . . . . .     13 OISIN 1             161
    . . . WHO SLEEPS ON HER NEST, . . . . . . . . .      56 OISIN 3             134
    A WEARY WOMAN SLEEPS SO HARD! . . . . . . . . .      95 MOLL MAGEE            21
    TO TAKE HIM WHILE HE SLEEPS AND CARRY HIM . . . .   222 SHADOW WATER B        14
    TO MAKE AN END OF FORGAEL WHILE HE SLEEPS. . . . .  225 SHADOW WATER B        65
    OUR FATHER ROSICROSS SLEEPS IN HIS TOMB. . . . .    311 MOUNTAIN TOMB         12
    MY CHILD SLEEPS ON.  THERE IS NO OBSTACLE . . . .   403 FOR DAUGHTER           3
    THAT SLEEPS UNDER THE CANOPY! . . . . . . . . .     528 TOM LUNATIC            2
    BUT BODY GONE HE SLEEPS NO MORE, . . . . . . . .    633 MAN AND ECHO          29
    SHE SLEEPS WITH OWLETS TWO AND TWO, . . . . . .     646 ISLE STAT I 1         34
    FROM THE UNDYING WORM.  SHE SLEEPS--MOSADA-- . . .  701 MOSADA 3              65
    OH, GOD!--AWAKE! THOU SHALT NOT DIE.  SHE SLEEPS, .  701 MOSADA 3              66
    FROM DATELESS PAIN.  SHE SLEEPS--MOSADA--THOU-- . .  701 MOSADA 3         V    65
SLEEPY
    BURIED UNDER THE SLEEPY GROUND, . . . . . . . .      67 HAPPY SHEPHERD        48
    (WHO'S BURIED IN THE SLEEPY GROUND), . . . . . .     67 HAPPY SHEPHERD V      48
    THE HOUR WHEN KAMA, FULL OF SLEEPY LAUGHTER, . . .   72 ANASHU VIJAYA         26
    A VAPOURY FOOTFALL ON THE OCEAN'S SLEEPY BLAZE. . .  78 INDIAN TO LOVE V      20
    FALLS IN SLEEPY STREAMS. . . . . . . . . . . .       98 FOXHUNTER             16
    POURS ROUND HIS SLEEPY STREAMS. . . . . . . . .      98 FOXHUNTER             16
    POURS ROUND IN SLEEPY STREAMS. . . . . . . . . .     98 FOXHUNTER        V    16
    OR DO YOU LONG FOR THE DIM SLEEPY GROUND, . . . .   109 CUCHULAIN SEA         60
    BEFORE EARTH MADE OF HIM HER SLEEPY CARE! . . . .   126 DREAM OF FAERY V       4
    WHERE A SO SLEEPY INCENSE ROSE . . . . . . . .      156 FORGOT BEAUTY V       13
    UNDER A CAIRN OF SLEEPY STONE . . . . . . . . .     192 BAILE AILLINN         81
    THE HONEY-PALE MOON LAY LOW ON THE SLEEPY HILL, . . 203 WITHER BOUGHS          5
    THE HONEY PALE MOON HUNG LOW ON THE SLEEPY HILL, . . 203 WITHER BOUGHS  V       5
    I KNOW OF THE SLEEPY COUNTRY, WHERE SWANS FLY ROUND . . 204 WITHER BOUGHS     17
```

PAGE   TITLE   LINE

SLEEPY   (CONTINUED)
  AND SLEEPY BOUGHS, AND BOUGHS WHERE APPLES MADE . . . . .   219 HARP OF AENGUS   5
  AND SLEEPY HAVING HAD THEIR MEAL! . . . .   271 GREY ROCK   V   17
  BEFORE THEIR SLEEPY EYELIDS RAN . . . .   272 GREY ROCK   30
  OR A BIRD'S SLEEPY CRY . . . .   416 TOWER   194
  AND FREE--'TWILL THIEVE AWAY WITH SLEEPY MOOD . . . . .   700 MOSADA 3   30
  "WAKEN, WAKEN, SLEEPY FISHERS! NO HOUR IS THIS FOR SLEEP,"   718 PHANTOM SHIP   7
  AND SLEEPY BOUGHS, AND BOUGHS WHERE APPLES MADE . . . .   762 SHADOW WATER A   300
SLEEPY-HEADED
  WAKE, MA CUSHLA, SLEEPY-HEADED. . . . .   705 DAWN-SONG   9
SLEET
  IT DIED AFAR. GREY SLEET THOSE TOWERS HID . . . . . .   46 OISIN 2   V   245
  FLAMES THE SHUTTLE OF THE LIGHTNING ACROSS THE DRIVING   718 PHANTOM SHIP   1
    SLEET,
SLEEVE
  BUT BRIDGET DREW HIM BY THE SLEEVE . . . .   144 HOST OF AIR   21
  AN AGONY OF FLAME THAT CANNOT SINGE A SLEEVE. . . . . .   498 BYZANTIUM   32
  THE HEART WELL WORN UPON THE SLEEVE MAY BE THE BEST OF   790 HEART SLEEVE   1
    SIGHTS,
SLEIVEENS
  SLEIVEENS WERE ALL HIS RACE! . . . .   92 FATHER OHART   6
SLENDER
  A MAIDEN, ON A SLENDER STEED, ...   2 OISIN 1   V   7V
  THEIR LEGS LONG, DELICATE AND SLENDER, AQUAMARINE THEIR   426 PHANTOM HATRED   17
    EYES,
  "I HAVE BROUGHT A SLENDER BRIDE INTO THE HOUSE! . . . .   463 HARUN RASHID   49
  BUT SLENDER NEEDLES OF BONE! . . . .   488 CRAZED MOON   15
  OF A SLENDER PALM, STOOD BUT A DAY! . . . .   566 LAPIS LAZULI   34
SLEPT
  AND THEN ON HEAPED-UP SKINS OF OTTERS SLEPT. . . . . .   41 OISIN 2   191
  AND ON THE SKINS OF WOLVES AND BEARS WE SLEPT! . . . .   41 OISIN 2   V   191
  HE SLEPT UNDER THE HILL OF LUGNAGALL! . . . .   128 DREAM OF FAERY   37
  WHILE I SLEPT ON THE CHAIR"! . . . .   133 FR GILLIGAN   26
  MADE WHEN GOD SLEPT IN TIMES OF OLD. . . . .   135 TWO TREES   32
  THE POLAR DRAGON SLEPT, ...   174 ELEMENT POWERS   4
  IN COMFORTABLE SLEEP! ALL LIVING SLEPT . . . .   180 QUEEN MAEVE   15
  BUT THE HORSE-BOYS SLEPT ON, AS THOUGH SOME POWER . . .   181 QUEEN MAEVE   39
  THE PORTER SLEPT, ALTHOUGH HE SAT UPRIGHT . . . . . .   182 QUEEN MAEVE   45
  WHERE HER GRANDCHILDREN SLEPT, AND CRIED ALOUD, ...   185 QUEEN MAEVE   109
  WHERE HER GRAND-CHILDREN SLEPT, AND CRIED ALOUD . . . .   185 QUEEN MAEVE   V   109
  I BADE HIM GO WHEN ALL HIS HOUSEHOLD SLEPT . . . . . .   282 TWO KINGS   133
  SO SLEPT FOR HALF A YEAR OR SO! . . . .   305 HOUR DAWN   67
  AND SLEPT FOR HALF A YEAR OR SO! . . . .   305 HOUR DAWN   V   67
  I SLEPT ON MY THREE-LEGGED STOOL BY THE FIRE, ...   381 SONGS FOOL 2   1
  THE SPECKLED CAT SLEPT ON MY KNEE! . . . .   381 SONGS FOOL 2   2
  WHERE SEVEN EPHESIAN TOPERS SLEPT AND NEVER KNEW . . .   442 BLACK CENTAUR   11
  WHEN ALEXANDER'S EMPIRE PASSED, THEY SLEPT SO SOUND. . .   442 BLACK CENTAUR   12
  WHEN ALEXANDER'S EMPIRE PAST, THEY SLEPT SO SOUND. . . .   442 BLACK CENTAUR   V   12
  AND SHE LAY DOWN UPON HER BED AND SLEPT, ...   467 HARUN RASHID   146
  ON CRUACHAN'S PLAIN SLEPT HE . . . .   529 TOM CRUACHAN   1
  THAT SLEPT UPON THE SACK? . . . .   627 STATES HOLIDAY   15
  I SLEPT, 'TWAS SULTRY, AND SCARCE CIRCLING SHOOK . . . .   677 ISLE STAT II 3   278
  HAVE I SLEPT LONG? LONG YEARS. WITH HUNGRY HEART . . .   677 ISLE STAT II 3   286
  HE'D SLEPT AMONG THE SINGING TREES, ...   728 PRIEST FAIRY   17
  AH, THEY HAVE PIERCED HIS HEART! I HAVE SLEPT LONG! . .   761 SHADOW WATER A   270
SLEUTH
  OF SLEUTH WOOD IN THE LAKE, ...   86 STOLEN CHILD   2
SLEUTH-HOUNDS
  HIS SLEUTH-HOUNDS FOLLOW EVERY FAERY THING. . . . . .   675 ISLE STAT II 3   244
SLEW
  AND SLEW THE BADGER AND THE DEER, ...   23 OISIN 1   V   345
  BUT SLOWLY, AS I SHOUTING SLEW . . . .   83 MAD KING GOLL   25
  THESE HANDS SLEW MANY WARRIORS BOLD-- . . . .   83 MAD KING GOLL   V   23
  THESE HANDS SLEW MANY ROBBERS BOLD-- . . . .   83 MAD KING GOLL   V   23
  THESE HANDS SLEW MANY A SEAMAN BOLD. . . . .   83 MAD KING GOLL   V   23
  SLEW THEE, POOR SIBYL! COMRADES THOU AND I! . . . . .   675 ISLE STAT II 3   235
SLID
  SPLASHED, OR AN OTTER SLID INTO THE STREAM. . . . . .   372 PHASES OF MOON   9
  SLID CIRCLING DOWN AND SOFTLY TOUCHED MY LIPS . . . . .   690 MOSADA 1   21
SLIDES
  A HORSE-HOOF SLIDES ON THE BRIM, ...   393 EASTER 1916   51
SLIDING
  CAME NOW THE SLIDING OF TEARS AND SWEEPING OF MIST-COLD   47 OISIN 3   7
    HAIR,
  CAME NOW THE SLIDING OF TEARS AND SWEEPING OF MIST-COLD   47 OISIN 3   V   7
    AIR,
  CAME NOW THE SLIDING OF TEARS AND SWEEPING OF MIST COLD   47 OISIN 3   V   7
    HAIR,
  IS BUT A SLIDING DROP OF RAIN BETWEEN HIS PETALS WIDE. . .   76 INDIAN ON GOD   12
  IS BUT A SLIDING DROP OF RAIN WITHIN HIS PETALS WIDE." . .   76 INDIAN ON GOD   V   12
  OR HAVE YOU HEARD THAT SLIDING SILVER-SHOED . . . . .   211 RAGGED WOOD   5
SLIEVENAMON
  IN THEIR GREAT HOUSE AT SLIEVENAMON. . . . .   271 GREY ROCK   15
  IF BOOKS SPEAK TRUTH, IN SLIEVENAMON-- . . . .   271 GREY ROCK   V   15
SLIGHT
  AND THAT A SLIGHT COMPANIONABLE GHOST, ...   472 ALL SOUL NIGHT   35
SLIGO
  THAT CARRIED THE TAKE TO SLIGO TOWN TO BE SOLD, ...   91 OLD FISHERMAN   7
  I BOUGHT AT THE SLIGO FAIR. . . . .   178 FIDDLER DOONEY   8
  UPON THE OPEN ROAD, NEAR TO THE SLIGO QUAY-- . . . . .   391 UNDER SATURN   12
  HE THAT IN SLIGO AT DRUMCLIFF . . . .   604 YOU CONTENT   9

		PAGE	TITLE		LINE

SLIM
    SLIM ADOLESCENCE THAT A NYMPH HAS STRIPPED, • • • • • 612 NEWS ORACLE   25
SLIME   SEE SEA-SLIME
    THAT WAS MOST DISTANT FROM THE DOOR: GREEN SLIME • • • 37 OISIN 2   113
    MOST DISTANT STRODE WE. ON THE FLOOR LAY SLIME, • • • 37 OISIN 2   V 113
    AND HUNG WITH SLIME, AND WHISPERING IN HIS HAIR, • • • 43 OISIN 2   216
    HUNG ROUND WITH SLIME, AND WHISPERING IN HIS HAIR, • • • 43 OISIN 2   V 216
    GATHER SEA SLIME AND FALL THE SEAWARD WAY, • • • • 45 OISIN 2   V 237
SLIMY
    AND THRUST THE TORCH BETWEEN THE SLIMY FLAGS. • • • • 38 OISIN 2   143
SLINGERS   SEE WOMEN-SLINGERS
    THE WOMEN SLINGERS ON THE NARROW BRIDGE, • • • • • • 749 SHADOW WATER A V 41
SLINGS
    AND LEATHER-COATED MEN WITH SLINGS • • • • • • • • 193 BAILE AILLINN V 111
SLIPPED
    O SHE WAS BUT A SHADOW, AND SLIPPED FROM ME. • • • • 223 SHADOW WATER B   40
SLIPPER
    NOR DOOR, NOR MOUTH, NOR SLIPPER MADE A NOISE, • • • 279 TWO KINGS   51
SLIPPERED
    WHERE SLIPPERED CONTEMPLATION FINDS HIS EASE • • • • 418 ANCEST HOUSES   30
SLIPPERS
    FOR HE HIS SLIPPERS WORE. • • • • • • • • • • 595 COLONEL MARTIN 40
    AH! WOE FOR YOUR SLIPPERS OF RED. • • • • • • • • 708 FAIRY PEDANT   36
SLIPPERY
    MADE THE WAY SLIPPERY, AND TIME ON TIME • • • • • 37 OISIN 2   114
    GREENISH AND SLIPPERY. TIME AFTER TIME • • • • 37 OISIN 2   V 114
SLOE-BERRIES
    AND FIGHT FOR THE BLACK SLOE-BERRIES, • • • • • 644 SONG FAERIES   13
    AND FIGHT FOR THE BLACK SLOE-BERRIES, • • • • • 676 ISLE STAT II 3 260
SLOPE
    ALL DRIPPING ON A GRASSY SLOPE, AND SAW THEM CEASE TO CHASE 76 INDIAN ON GOD   4
    OR LOFTY SLOPE WHERE IT STILL SNOWS • • • • • 567 LAPIS LAZULI   46
SLOPES
    IN AUTUMN, WHEN FAR DOWN THE MOUNTAIN SLOPES • • • 690 MOSADA 1   12
SLOPING
    O YOU, WITH WHOM IN SLOPING VALLEYS, • • • • • • • 10 OISIN 1   119
    OH YE WITH WHOM, IN SLOPING VALLEYS • • • • • • 10 OISIN 1   V 119
    THAT SLOPING GREEN DE DANAAN SOD • • • • • • • 20 OISIN 1   299
    EAT AWAY THE SLOPING SOD, • • • • • • • • • 20 OISIN 1   V 299
    OF HOLLIES, AND HAZELS, AND OAK TREES, A VALLEY WAS SLOPING 48 OISIN 3   V 26
       AWAY
SLOUCHES
    SLOUCHES TOWARDS BETHLEHEM TO BE BORN? • • • • • • 402 SECOND COMING   22
SLOW
    BESIDE THE SEA, WHERE, HUSHED AND SLOW, • • • • • 20 OISIN 1   V 292
    HUNG THE FRAIL LOFTIER CLOUDLETS. TURNED HE SLOW-- • • 40 OISIN 2   V 167
    FOR, AS DRIFT FROM A SAILOR SLOW DROWNING • • • • 48 OISIN 3   22
    AND OVER THE LIMBS AND THE VALLEY THE SLOW OWLS WANDERED 49 OISIN 3   41
       AND CAME,
    • • • SLOW DROPPING A SOUND IN FAINT STREAMS • • • • 51 OISIN 3   67
    HOW THE SLOW, BLUE-EYED OXEN OF FINN LOW SADLY AT EVENING 52 OISIN 3   84
       TIDE.
    WENT WALKING WITH SLOW STEPS ALONG THE GLEAMING • • • 68 SAD SHEPHERD   3
    FIELDS FATTENING SLOW, MEN WISE IN JOY, • • • • • 82 MAD KING GOLL V 6
    LIFTS SLOW HIS WINTRY HEAD! • • • • • • • • 99 FOXHUNTER   46
    AND PRESSING ON, OR LINGERING SLOW WITH FEAR, • • • 114 ROSE OF BATTLE V 5
    AND I SHALL HAVE SOME PEACE THERE, FOR PEACE COMES DROPPING 117 ISLE INNISFREE   5
       SLOW,
    MAEVE WALKED, YET WITH SLOW FOOTFALL, BEING OLD, • • • 181 QUEEN MAEVE   43
    BUT MAEVE, AND NOT WITH A SLOW FEEBLE FOOT, • • • 185 QUEEN MAEVE   107
    WITH A SLOW SMILE AND WITHOUT SOUND, • • • • • 275 GREY ROCK   117
    MOST COURTEOUS TO SLOW AGE AND HASTY YOUTH • • • • 339 SHEP GOATHERD   19
    IS MOVING ITS SLOW THIGHS, WHILE ALL ABOUT IT • • • 402 SECOND COMING   16
    SLOW DECAY OF BLOOD, • • • • • • • • • • • 416 TOWER   185
    FOR ALL HIS TIMID HEART, THERE THAT SLOW MAN, • • • 489 COOLE PARK 29   12
    A SLOW LOW NOTE AND AN IRON BELL. • • • • • • • 549 SEVERED HEAD   7
    A SLOW LOW NOTE AND AN IRON BELL. • • • • • • • 550 SEVERED HEAD   14
    A SLOW LOW NOTE AND AN IRON BELL. • • • • • • • 550 SEVERED HEAD   21
    UNDER THE TROPIC SHADE, GREW ROUND AND SLOW, • • • 610 STATUES   18
    THAT DIETH SLOW WITH SUNSICK DOOM. • • • • • • 655 ISLE STAT I 3   12
    SLOW WATERS, AND THE BOAT AND MAIDEN SINK • • • • 663 ISLE STAT II 2   39
    THE SUMMERS FLING THEIR SCENTS? AH, SUBTILE AND SLOW, • 675 ISLE STAT II 3 231
    IN THEIR COILING CALM AND SLOW. • • • • • • • 680 LOVE AND DEATH   8
    AS ROUND HER, SLOW ON FEET THAT HAVE NO BLOOD, • • • 687 TWO TITANS   18
    CLOGGED IN A MARSH WHERE THE SLOW MARSH CLAY CLINGS, • 711 FERENCZ RENYI   35
    DROPS ON HIS BOSOM, SOMBRE, MOIST AND SLOW. • • • 711 FERENCZ RENYI   40
    UPON HIS BOSOM, SOMBRE, MOIST AND SLOW. • • • • 711 FERENCZ RENYI V 40
    SEE THE DARKNESS SLOW DISGORGING A VESSEL BLIND WITH 718 PHANTOM SHIP   12
       SQUALL.
    SLOW THE CHAPEL BELL IS TOLLING AS THOUGH THE DEAD PASSED 718 PHANTOM SHIP   16
       BY.
    BY THE SLOW HEAVING OCEAN--MUMBLING MOTHER OF THE DEAD. 719 PHANTOM SHIP   34
SLOW-FOOTING
    DEEP-EYED, SLOW-FOOTING DOWN THE EMPTY GLADE. • • • • 653 ISLE STAT I 2   55
SLOWLY
    AND FAR BEHIND US, SLOWLY ROUND • • • • • • • 10 OISIN 1   V 114B
    HUNG IN THE PASSIONATE DAWN. HE SLOWLY TURNED! • • • 40 OISIN 2   167
    HIS LIPS MOVED SLOWLY IN ANSWER, NO ANSWER OUT OF THEM 51 OISIN 3   66
       CAME!
    A SAD, SAD THOUGHT WENT BY ME SLOWLY! • • • • • • 72 ANASHU VIJAYA   17
    WHILE SLOWLY HE WHOSE HAND HELD HERS REPLIED! • • • • 80 EPHEMERA   11

```
                                                        PAGE    TITLE         LINE

SLOWLY  (CONTINUED)
    WHILE SLOWLY ANSWERED HE WHOSE HAND HELD HERS--  . . . . .    80 EPHEMERA        V   11
    BUT SLOWLY, AS I SHOUTING SLEW  . . . . . . . . . . .         83 MAD KING GOLL       25
    AND LEAD HIM SLOWLY TO AND FRO,  . . . . . . . . . .          97 FOXHUNTER       V    7
    AND SLOWLY UP AND DOWN.  . . . . . . . . . . . . .            97 FOXHUNTER       V    8
    A MAN CAME SLOWLY FROM THE SETTING SUN,  . . . . . .         105 CUCHULAIN SEA        1
    AND SLOWLY READ, AND DREAM OF THE SOFT LOOK  . . . . .       121 YOU ARE OLD          3
    THEY SLOWLY INTO MILLIONS GREW,  . . . . . . . . . .         133 FR GILLIGAN         17
    THE DEWS DROP SLOWLY AND DREAMS GATHER: UNKNOWN SPEARS  . .  161 BLACK PIG            1
    THE DEW DROPS SLOWLY: THE DREAMS GATHER: UNKNOWN SPEARS      161 BLACK PIG       V    1
    "WE RIDE BUT SLOWLY THOUGH SO NEAR OUR HOME,"  . . . . .     276 TWO KINGS       V    A
    WHAT IS THERE BUT THE SLOWLY FADING WEST,  . . . . . .       390 IMAGE PAST          19
    AND AFTER BAKED IT SLOWLY IN AN OVEN: BUT NOW  . . . .       442 BLACK CENTAUR        9
    SLOWLY, SLOWLY FADETH SHE,  . . . . . . . . . . . .          648 ISLE STAT I 1       83
    SLOWLY, SLOWLY FADETH SHE,  . . . . . . . . . . . .          648 ISLE STAT I 1       83
    TO MINE, AND HE IS SLOWLY SUCKING FORTH  . . . . . .         684 SEEKER          V  63A
    AS SLOWLY AUTUMN CLIMBED THE GOLDEN THRONE  . . . . .        690 MOSADA 1        V   1A
SLOW-MUFFLED
    CARVED: HERE, BEYOND THE LAKE'S SLOW-MUFFLED TREAD,  . . .   662 ISLE STAT II 2      11
SLUGGARD
    AND WAKES THE SLUGGARD SEEDS OF CORN,  . . . . . . . .        18 OISIN 1            263
    CRIES TO THE SLUGGARD SEEDS OF CORN,  . . . . . . . .         18 OISIN 1         V  263
SLUGGISH
    HAVING GROWN SLUGGISH AND CONTEMPLATIVE.  . . . . . .        325 ROBERT GREGORY      40
    A BEARDED WITCH, HER SLUGGISH HEAD LOW BENT  . . . . .       685 SEEKER              72
SLUMBER
    IF THEY STILL SLUMBER, TOUCH THEIR EYELIDS BLUE,  . . . .     33 OISIN 2         V   61
    AT TIMES OUR SLUMBER WAS LIGHTENED. . . . . . . . .           53 OISIN 3             97
    OF TWILIGHT AND SLUMBER WERE GONE, AND THAT HOOFS            54 OISIN 3            112
        IMPATIENTLY STEPT.
    OUR VOICES CARRY: AND THOUGH SLUMBER BOUND,  . . . . .       622 HOUND VOICE     V    5
    WHEN WE HALE MEN LIE STRETCHED IN SLUMBER  . . . . . .       636 BLACK TOWER         23
    NO TASTE HAVE I FOR SLUMBER 'NEATH AN OAK. . . . . . .       721 WITCH VIVIEN        31
    AND HE SHALL SLUMBER ON MY BREAST.  . . . . . . . .          723 GIRLS SONG A         4
    HAST THOU NOT KNOWN A RAJA'S DREAMLESS SLUMBER?  . . . .     724 KANVA ON SELF        8
SLUMBER-BOUND
    OUR VOICES CARRY: AND THOUGH SLUMBER-BOUND,  . . . . .       622 HOUND VOICE          5
SLUMBERED
    HALF SLUMBERED WITH HIS SAFFRON BLAZE:  . . . . . . .         26 OISIN 1         V  395
    THAT SLUMBERED IN THE HARVEST MOON,  . . . . . . . .          85 MAD KING GOLL       50
    THAT SLUMBERED 'NEATH THE HARVEST MOON,  . . . . . . .        85 MAD KING GOLL   V   50
    THE YEARS OF GOBLIN SLEEP. AH! WHILE I SLUMBERED,  . . .     679 ISLE STAT II 3     308
SLUMBERERS
    I SAW HOW THOSE SLUMBERERS, GROWN WEARY, . . . . . .          50 OISIN 3             54
SLUMBERING     SEE NEVER-SLUMBERING
    WAS SLUMBERING HALF IN THE SEA-WAYS:  . . . . . . . .         26 OISIN 1            395
    WAS SLUMBERING HALF IN THE SEA WAYS:  . . . . . . . .         26 OISIN 1         V  395
    AS THOUGH UNTO HIS NEVER SLUMBERING HEART  . . . . . .        32 OISIN 2         V   44
    AS THOUGH HE TOLD HIS NEVER SLUMBERING HEART  . . . . .       32 OISIN 2         V   44
    UNDER THE STARLIGHT AND SHADOW, A MONSTROUS SLUMBERING        48 OISIN 3             27
        FOLK.
    FROM HIS HOOVES IN THE HEAVY GRASSES, WITH MONSTROUS         48 OISIN 3         V   27
        SLUMBERING FOLK,
    WE SEEK FOR SLUMBERING TROUT  . . . . . . . . . . .          88 STOLEN CHILD        32
SLUNK
    CAME BLANAID, MAC NESSA, TALL FERGUS WHO FEASTWARD OF OLD     53 OISIN 3             89
        TIME SLUNK,
    . . . CAME FERGUS WHO FEASTWARD SAD SLUNK,  . . . . . .       53 OISIN 3         V   89
    CAME BLANID, MAC NESSA, AND FERGUS WHO FEASTWARD OF OLD       53 OISIN 3         V   89
        TIME SLUNK,
SLUT
    OLD IRON, OLD BONES, OLD RAGS, THAT RAVING SLUT  . . . .     630 CIRCUS ANIMALS      37
SLY
    WHETHER IT BE BOLD OR SLY.  . . . . . . . . . . . .          624 APPARITIONS          6
SMALL
    LIKE A SMALL RIVER, AND WHERE FEET TOUCHED CAME  . . . .      37 OISIN 2            117
    GREY IN THE MIDST LIKE A SMALL RIVULET'S FLOW,  . . . .       37 OISIN 2         V  117
    "I WOULD DIE LIKE A SMALL WITHERED LEAF IN THE AUTUMN,        56 OISIN 3            131
        . . .
    AND A SMALL AND A FEEBLE POPULACE STOOPING WITH MATTOCK       58 OISIN 3            164
        AND SPADE,
    AND A SMALL AND A FEEBLE RACE STOOPING WITH MATTOCK AND       58 OISIN 3         V  164
        SPADE.
    AND A SMALL AND FEEBLE RACE STOOPING WITH MATTOCK            58 OISIN 3         V  164
        AND SPADE.
    I THROW DOWN THE CHAIN OF SMALL STONES:  . . . . . .         63 OISIN 3            222
    AND HE WORE SMALL HOLES IN HIS SHOES,  . . . . . . .         92 FATHER OHART        11
    THE WEAK WORM HIDING DOWN IN ITS SMALL CAVE,  . . . . .     101 ROSE UPON ROOD      16
    LAY HIDDEN IN THE SMALL SLATE-COLOURED THING!  . . . .      104 FERGUS DRUID        40
    TAKE THEN THIS SMALL SLATE-COLOURED BAG OF DREAMS!  . . .   104 FERGUS DRUID    V   29
    LAY HIDDEN IN THE SMALL SLATE-COLOURED BAG!  . . . . .      104 FERGUS DRUID    V   40
    AND A SMALL CABIN BUILD THERE, OF CLAY AND WATTLES MADE:    117 ISLE INNISFREE       2
    AND A SMALL CABIN BUILT THERE, OF CLAY AND WATTLES MADE:    117 ISLE INNISFREE  V    2
    BUT ONE SMALL KNOT-GRASS GROWING BY THE POOL  . . . . .     127 DREAM OF FAERY      29
    BUT ONE SMALL KNOT-GRASS GROWING BY THE RIM  . . . . .      127 DREAM OF FAERY  V   29
    TO THAT SMALL CHAMBER BY THE OUTER GATE.  . . . . . .       181 QUEEN MAEVE         44
    THE ENTIRE COMBUSTIBLE WORLD IN ONE SMALL ROOM  . . . .     327 ROBERT GREGORY      82
    ALL THE COMBUSTIBLE WORLD IN ONE SMALL ROOM  . . . . .      327 ROBERT GREGORY  V   82
    YOUR SMALL HANDS WERE NOT BEAUTIFUL. . . . . . . . .        356 BROKEN DREAMS       29
    AWAIT THE HOUR OF WAR, ENTER THE SMALL,  . . . . . .        461 HARUN RASHID    V    8
    NO MORE SANG HE, FOR HIS THROAT WAS TOO SMALL:  . . . .     545 TO SAME TUNE 1      24
```

		PAGE	TITLE	LINE

SMALL   (CONTINUED)
HE SAID NO MORE FOR HIS THROAT WAS TOO SMALL. • • • • •   545 TO SAME TUNE 1 V   24
A SMALL OLD HOUSE, WIFE, DAUGHTER, SON, • • • • • • •   577 WHAT THEN   12
THEY ALWAYS BEAT ON THE SAME SMALL STONE. • • • • • •   591 WHAT WAS LOST   5
I HAVE A SMALL DEMESNE, • • • • • • • • • • • • •   606 SONGS BURDEN 2   2
A SMALL FORGOTTEN HOUSE THAT'S SET   • • • • • •   606 SONGS BURDEN 2   3
NO MORE SANG HE, FOR HIS THROAT WAS TOO SMALL; • • • •   616 MARCH SONGS 3   24
CATCHING SMALL BIRDS IN THE DEW OF THE MORN • • • •   636 BLACK TOWER   22
OR SOME SMALL BEAST MOST WONDERFULLY FURR'D, • • • •   650 ISLE STAT I 1   148
SMALL ISLAND, WHERE THE FULL SOFT SHEEN • • • •   653 ISLE STAT I 2   36
A LITTLE MOORISH GIRL? SMALL WORTH, MY SONG-- • • •   696 MOSADA 2   10
AND HASSAN WILL BE WITH THEM--HE WAS SO SMALL, • • •   699 MOSADA 3   13
AND NOT COME THENCE! FOR HERE IN THIS SMALL RING-- • •   699 MOSADA 3   22
HASSAN IS WITH THEM TOO--HE WAS SO SMALL, • • • •   699 MOSADA 3   V   13
SO SMALL MAKES ONE GROW WEAK AND TOTTERING! • • • •   700 MOSADA 3   35
FLOATING FROM YON BARRED WINDOW. SMALL NEW-COMER, • •   700 MOSADA 3   43
TWO WOMEN, WITHERED ONE AND SMALL AND THIN, • • • •   711 FERENCZ RENYI   51
LIKE SMALL BROWN MOTHS, A-TREMBLE. "RENYI SAY • • •   713 FERENCZ RENYI   82
LIKE SMALL BROWN MOTHS, A-TREMBLE CEASELESSLY. • • •   713 FERENCZ RENYI   V   82
AND WE ARE SO VERY SMALL! • • • • • • • • • •   726 LOVERS QUARREL   18
DANCE THE SAVAGE CHILDREN SMALL, • • • • • • • •   732 STREET DANCERS   29
AND PLUCKED SMALL FRUITS ON INNISFREE. • • • • • •   742 DANAAN QUICK   5
WHEN SOMETHING FOLDED AND SMALL • • • • • • • •   744 GLOVE CLOAK   7
SMALLEST
BEYOND THE LAKE, WHOSE SMALLEST WAVE WAS BURDENED • • •   656 ISLE STAT I 3   31
THE BREATHING OF THE SMALLEST BIRD, • • • • • • • •   730 PRIEST FAIRY   68
SMARAGDINE
FOR THINGS BELOW ARE COPIES, THE GREAT SMARAGDINE TABLET   556 RIBH PATRICK   6
SAID.
SMART
AND THERE IS SALT TO LENGTHEN OUT THE SMART   • • • • •   324 ROBERT GREGORY   11
SMELLED
THE NIGHT SMELLED RICH WITH JUNE. • • • • • • • • •   160 CAP AND BELLS   V   28
SMELT
BUT LIKED THE WAY HIS FINGER SMELT. • • • • • • • •   619 STICK INCENSE   4
SMILE
WATCHING THE BLESSED ONES MOVE FAR OFF, AND THE SMILE ON   61 OISIN 3   199
GOD'S FACE.
THE HOUR WHEN KAMA, WITH A SUMPTUOUS SMILE, • • • • •   72 ANASHU VIJAYA   V   26
AND HE SAID WITH A SMILE, "HAVE PEACE NOW"! • • • • •   92 FATHER OHART   19
TO SMILE ON THE PALE DAWN; AND GATHER YOU • • • • •   114 ROSE OF BATTLE   15
TO SMILE UPON HER STARS! AND GATHER YOU, • • • • • •   114 ROSE OF BATTLE   V   15
HE WILL SMILE ON THE THREE OLD SPIRITS, • • • • • •   178 FIDDLER DOONEY   11
AND THEIR SECRET SMILE, OUT OF THE DEPTHS OF THE LAKE!   203 WITHER BOUGHS   11
AND THEIR SECRET SMILE, OUT OF THE DEEPS OF THE LAKE!   203 WITHER BOUGHS   V   11
WITH A SLOW SMILE AND WITHOUT SOUND, • • • • • • •   275 GREY ROCK   117
BETTER TO SMILE ON ALL THAT SMILE, AND SHOW • • • •   444 SCHOOL CHILDR   31
BETTER TO SMILE ON ALL THAT SMILE, AND SHOW • • • •   444 SCHOOL CHILDR   31
SOON WILT THOU SMILE, FOR HERE THE WINDS ARE WEAK • • •   671 ISLE STAT II 3   141
I SAW HIS JOVIAL MOOD BRING ONCE A SMILE • • • • • •   696 MOSADA 2   14
SMILED
BUT DATHI FOLDED HIS HANDS AND SMILED • • • • • • •   167 BLESSED   11
AND EVEN STRAFFORD SMILED AS THOUGH • • • • • • •   400 DEMON BEAST   13
AND EVEN STAFFORD SMILED AS THOUGH • • • • • • • •   400 DEMON BEAST   V   13
SHE SMILED AND THAT TRANSFIGURED ME • • • • • • • •   451 FIRST LOVE   13
SMILES
GOD SMILES IN HIGH HEAVEN • • • • • • • • • • •   118 CRADLE SONG   V   5
IN THE DEEP ALCOVES DIMNESS SMILES AND HIDES. • • • • •   685 DRAWING-ROOM   4
SHE SMILES--IS HAPPY WITH HER WANDERING GRIEFS, • • • •   702 MOSADA 3   95
IN THE DEEP ALCOVE'S DIMNESS SMILES AND HIDES." • • • •   735 QUATRAIN APHOR   24
IN THE DEEP ALCOVES DIMNESS SMILES AND HIDES. • • • •   735 QUATRAIN APHOR   V   24
SMILING
AND GRANIA, WALKING AND SMILING, SEWED WITH HER NEEDLE   53 OISIN 3   94
OF BONE.
"MY FATHER," MADE HE, SMILING, ANSWER THEN, • • • •   107 CUCHULAIN SEA   V   25
A SIXTY-YEAR-OLD SMILING PUBLIC MAN. • • • • • • • •   443 SCHOOL CHILDR   8
A SIXTY YEAR OLD SMILING PUBLIC MAN. • • • • • • •   443 SCHOOL CHILDR   V   8
SMILING AT THE SEA, • • • • • • • • • • • •   605 YOU CONTENT   20
AND SMILING FROM SWEET THOUGHT, • • • • • • • • •   741 EARL PAUL   42
SMITH
YET CHOSE A BANDY-LEGGED SMITH FOR MAN. • • • • • • •   404 FOR DAUGHTER   29
SMITHIES
SPIRIT AFTER SPIRIT! THE SMITHIES BREAK THE FLOOD, • • •   498 BYZANTIUM   34
THE GOLDEN SMITHIES OF THE EMPEROR! • • • • • • •   498 BYZANTIUM   35
SMITHY
LIKE THE SPARKS BLOWN OUT OF A SMITHY, AND DIE? • • • •   170 SECRET ROSE   30
WHEN FROM THE SMITHY FIRE • • • • • • • • • • •   345 ON WOMAN   18
AND SMITHY WORK FROM THE GORT FORGE, • • • • • • •   406 CARVED STONE   3
SMITTEN   SEE SUN-SMITTEN FAIRY-SMITTEN HEART-SMITTEN
AN IMAGE OF MY HEART THAT IS SMITTEN THROUGH • • • •   389 IMAGE PAST   8
AMID MOST LOVELY PLACES! SMITTEN AS THOUGH • • • • •   389 IMAGE PAST   13
HEART SMITTEN WITH EMOTION, I SINK DOWN, • • • • • •   602 GALLERY REVIS   V   17
SMOKE
FLED FOAM UNDERNEATH US, AND ROUND US, A WANDERING AND   47 OISIN 3   1
MILKY SMOKE.
FLED FOAM UNDERNEATH US, AND ROUND US, A WANDERING AND   47 OISIN 3   12
MILKY SMOKE.
FLED FOAM UNDERNEATH US, AND AROUND US, A WANDERING AND   47 OISIN 3   V   1
MILKY SMOKE,
• • • DULL WITH THE SMOKE OF THEIR DREAMS! • • • • • •   51 OISIN 3   65

733

                                                            PAGE   TITLE   LINE

SMOKE   (CONTINUED)
    FLED FOAM UNDERNEATH ME, AND ROUND ME, A WANDERING AND   57 OISIN 3   148
        MILKY SMOKE.
    WERE GONE LIKE A DRIFTING SMOKE! . . . .   145 HOST OF AIR   40
    AND CUMHAL SAW LIKE A DRIFTING SMOKE . . . .   167 BLESSED   13
    AND SMOKE FROM THIS DEAD HEART DRIFTS THROUGH THE VIOLET   173 SPEAKS HEARERS   3
        AIR
    AND COVERS AWAY THE SMOKE OF MYRRH AND FRANKINCENSE!   173 SPEAKS HEARERS   4
    IS ROLLED AS VERDANT SMOKE! O THOU WHOSE FACE . . .   667 ISLE STAT II 3   35
    HIS BODY SHAKE? AY, QUIVERING AS YON SMOKE . . . .   683 SEEKER   36
    THUS DO I BURN THESE PRECIOUS HERBS, WHOSE SMOKE . .   691 MOSADA 1   39
    SO ENDS A BRAIN--A WORLD! THE SMOKE GOES UP, ...   714 FERENCZ RENYI   111
    OF FIRE. SO ENDS A BRAIN--A WORLD! THE SMOKE FLOATS UP,   714 FERENCZ RENYI   V 111
    AS A WREATH OF SMOKE IN WIND-BLOWN FLIGHT . . . . .   730 PRIEST FAIRY   61
SMOKES
    THE CATARACT SMOKES UPON THE MOUNTAIN SIDE, ...   311 MOUNTAIN TOMB   3
    THE CATARACT SMOKES ON THE MOUNTAIN SIDE. . . . . . .   311 MOUNTAIN TOMB   V   3
SMOKING
    AND LEAVE NO SMOKING WICK BEHIND, ...   306 HOUR DAWN   97
    WHAT HAS TURNED TO SMOKING WICK . . . .   529 TOM LUNATIC   5
SMOKY
    THE SMOKY TORCHES MADE A GLARE . . . .   271 GREY ROCK   18
    AND SMOKY TORCHES MADE A GLARE . . . .   271 GREY ROCK   V   18
SMOOTH
    THROUGH MANY SHAPES! I LUNGED AT THE SMOOTH THROAT . .   40 OISIN 2   175
    TO MANY SHAPES! I LUNGED AT THE SMOOTH THROAT . . .   40 OISIN 2   V 175
    I WILL PRAY NO MORE WITH THE SMOOTH STONES . . . . .   63 OISIN 3   V 221
    THE PEAHENS DANCE ON A SMOOTH LAWN, ...   77 INDIAN TO LOVE   3
    AND WHERE HER SON, FINMOLE, ON THE SMOOTH GRASS . .   106 CUCHULAIN SEA   V   18
    FOR THEY, FOR ALL SMOOTH LIPS CAN SAY, ...   202 NEVER GIVE ALL   9
    AND THEN SMOOTH OUT WITH IVORY HANDS AND SIGH, . . .   228 SHADOW WATER B   133
    AND SMOOTH OUT STAIN AND BLEMISH WITH THE ELEGANCE OF HIS   353 HIS PHOENIX   7
        MIND!
    HURRIED THROUGH THE SMOOTH AND ROUGH . . . .   436 FOR MY SON   29
    HAVE BORNE YOU THROUGH THE SMOOTH AND ROUGH . . . .   436 FOR MY SON   V   29
    ON THE LEAF-SOWN, NEW-MOWN, SMOOTH . . . .   568 SWEET DANCER   2
    ON THE LEAF-SOWN, NEW MOWN, SMOOTH . . . .   568 SWEET DANCER   V   2
    SITTING ON A WARM SMOOTH MAT . . . .   726 LOVERS QUARREL   11
    AND THEN SMOOTH OUT WITH IVORY HANDS AND SIGH. . . .   750 SHADOW WATER A   70
SMOOTHS
    HE SMOOTHS THE LONG BROWN NOSE. . . . .   98 FOXHUNTER   20
SMOTE
    SMOTE ON THEIR BRAINS THAT DWELT REMEMBERING AYE. . . .   34 OISIN 2   V 77A
    OF A GREAT EEL! IT CHANGED, AND I BUT SMOTE . . . .   40 OISIN 2   176
    SHE SMOTE WITH RADDLED FIST, AND WHERE HER SON . . .   106 CUCHULAIN SEA   18
    ONCE, WHEN MIDNIGHT SMOTE THE AIR . . . .   294 HATED PLAYBOY   1
    OR SMOTE UPON THE STRING AND TO THE SOUND . . . . .   537 HER VISION   15
SMOTHER
    STRETCHED HIS LONG ARM TO WHERE, A MISTY SMOTHER, . . .   31 OISIN 2   42
SMOULDERING
    THEY SEEMED TO SING IN THE SMOULDERING FIRES. . . . .   13 OISIN 1   168
SMUGGLER
    THE SMUGGLER MIDDLETON, BUTLERS FAR BACK, ...   605 YOU CONTENT   15
SNAKES
    SEEK NOT THAT WOOD, FOR THERE THE GOBLIN SNAKES . . .   682 SEEKER   29
SNAP
    HE'LL SNAP HIS SWORD. RAISED IS THE LION'S PAW. . . .   664 ISLE STAT II 2   63
SNAPS
    AH! THERE HE SNAPS MY RICE. I TOLD YOU SO. . . . .   73 ANASHU VIJAYA   38
SNARE
    AND BLAME THE SNARE THEY SET FOR ME. . . . .   743 DANAAN QUICK   23
    AND MOIDERED IN THAT SNARE . . . .   783 GREY ROUND   8
    IN THAT SWEET WANDERING SNARE. . . . .   783 GREY ROUND   10
SNATCH
    THE STRONGEST OF THE WORLD, TO SNATCH MY PREY, . . .   45 OISIN 2   V 241
    TO SNATCH ALIVE OUT OF THE STREAMS ALL LOVERS . . .   765 SHADOW WATER A   347
SNATCHED
    FROM THEE I SNATCHED IT! E'EN THE FAY THAT TRIPS . . . .   670 ISLE STAT II 3   98
SNATCHES
    AND MURMURED SNATCHES OF DELIGHT! . . . .   14 OISIN 1   187
SNATCHING
    SNATCHING THE HORN OF NIAMH, I BLEW A LONG LINGERING NOTE.   51 OISIN 3   57
    SNATCHING THE HORN OF NIAM, I BLEW FORTH A LINGERING NOTE!   51 OISIN 3   V   57
    SNATCHING THE HORN OF NIAM, I BLEW A LINGERING NOTE! . .   51 OISIN 3   V   57
    SNATCHING THE BIRD IN SECRET! NOR KNEW I, EMBOSOMED APART,   57 OISIN 3   150
SNICKED
    SHE SNICKED THE BRASS BOLTS DOWN. . . . .   159 CAP AND BELLS   V   12
SNIFF
    OR ELSE THEY STAND AND SNIFF THE WIND, ...   136 TWO TREES   37
SNIPE
    AND HIS OWN SNIPE AND TROUT. . . . .   92 FATHER OHART   4
    WITH HIS SNIPE MARSH AND HIS TROUT. . . . .   92 FATHER OHART   V   4
SNORE
    THOUGH DRUNKARDS LIE AND SNORE. . . . .   592 DRUNK SOBRIETY   8
SNORED
    THEY SANG A DROWSY SONG, OR SNORED, ...   271 GREY ROCK   16
    AND SANG A DROWSY SONG, OR SNORED, ...   271 GREY ROCK   V   16
    FELL DOWN UPON THE DUST AND SNORED. . . . .   297 THREE BEGGARS   60
    AND SNORED, NO PHANTOM BY HIS LOOK. . . . .   303 HOUR DAWN   30
SNOW
    OR ARE YOU PHANTOMS WHITE AS SNOW, ...   10 OISIN 1   117

734

SNOW   (CONTINUED)

OR ARE YE PHANTOMS WHITE AS SNOW,   10 OISIN 1   V 117
A DEMON'S LEISURE. EYES FIRST WHITE AS SNOW, 40 OISIN 2   V 168
WHERE MEN LIE FROZEN IN THE GLIMMERING SNOW!   73 ANASHU VIJAYA   51
AND PINCHES AMONG HAIL AND SNOW?   191 BAILE AILLINN   46
A MIST THAT IS LIKE BLOWN SNOW IS SWEEPING OVER ALL, 425 PHANTOM HATRED   2
CRIED, CASTING OFF THE MOUNTAIN SNOW,   502 VACILLATION   60
MAD AS THE MIST AND SNOW   523 MAD AS MIST   T
MAD AS THE MIST AND SNOW.   523 MAD AS MIST   6
MAD AS THE MIST AND SNOW?   524 MAD AS MIST   12
MAD AS THE MIST AND SNOW.   524 MAD AS MIST   18
CAVERNED IN NIGHT UNDER THE DRIFTED SNOW,   563 MERU   10
OR WHERE THAT SNOW AND WINTER'S DREADFUL BLAST 563 MERU   11
THE PASSING OF THOSE LITTLE GRAINS IS SNOW   722 WITCH VIVIEN   48

SNOWFLAKES

SOFTER THAN SNOWFLAKES IN APRIL, AND PIERCING THE MARROW
   LIKE FLAME.   51 OISIN 3   V   68

SNOW-FLAKES

SOFTER THAN SNOW-FLAKES IN APRIL AND PIERCING THE MARROW
   LIKE FLAME.   51 OISIN 3   68

SNOWS

AND WANDER IN THE STORMS AND CLINGING SNOWS,   42 OISIN 2   201
ROOTS HALF HIDDEN UNDER SNOWS,   135 TWO TREES   27
AND ROOTS HALF HIDDEN UNDER SNOWS   135 TWO TREES   V   27
IN THE COLD SNOWS OF A DREAM.   424 ROAD AT DOOR   15
OR LOFTY SLOPE WHERE IT STILL SNOWS   567 LAPIS LAZULI   46

SNOW-WHITE

SHE PASSED THE SALLEY GARDENS WITH LITTLE SNOW-WHITE FEET. 90 SALLEY GARDENS   2
AND ON MY LEANING SHOULDER SHE LAID HER SNOW-WHITE HAND.   90 SALLEY GARDENS   6

SNUG

AND SNUG IT IN A FEATHER BED.   332 ROUND TOWER   28
AND SNUG IT IN A FEATHER-BED,   332 ROUND TOWER V 28

SOB

WITH A SOB FOR MEN WAXING SO WEAKLY,   60 OISIN 3   188
. . . A SOB FOR THE FENIANS' OLD STRENGTH.   60 OISIN 3   188

SOBBED

SOBBED INTO SILENCE. WE HAD MOUNTED FEET   33 OISIN 2   V 68E
AND THEN THE FAY QUEEN SOBBED APART,   730 PRIEST FAIRY   70

SOBER

AND DROVE HIM DRUNK OR SOBER THROUGH THE DAWN 411 TOWER   58
THOUGH NOT FOR SOBER EAR!   471 ALL SOUL NIGHT 18
THOUGH NOT FOR SOBER EAR,   474 ALL SOUL NIGHT 88
THAT I MAY STAY A SOBER MAN   591 DRUNK SOBRIETY 3
AND DRUNK OR SOBER LIVE AT EASE   597 MODEL LAUREATE 13

SOBRIETY

A DRUNKEN MAN'S PRAISE OF SOBRIETY   591 DRUNK SOBRIETY T
SOBRIETY IS A JEWEL   592 DRUNK SOBRIETY 5

SOBS

WILL HE HAVE HAPPINESS? GREAT SOBS HER BEING SHAKE. 676 ISLE STAT II 3 247

SOCIAL

A HELEN OF SOCIAL WELFARE DREAM,   626 OLD MEN BE MAD 7

SOCK

NOW IT HAS FILLED AN OLD SOCK FULL!   301 RUN PARADISE   20

SOCKS

WHO IS SIX FEET HIGH IN HIS SOCKS AT LEAST?   729 PRIEST FAIRY   28

SOD   SEE EDEN-SOD

WHOSE CAREFUL PASTERN PRESSED THE SOD   2 OISIN 1   V 7W
THAT SLOPING GREEN DE DANAAN SOD   20 OISIN 1   299
EAT AWAY THE SLOPING SOD,   20 OISIN 1   V 299
AND YOU HAVE GROWN TO BE A BURNING SOD   245 SHADOW WATER B 487
THIS SOD HAS BOUND US   769 BLOOD BOND   1

SODDEN   SEE BLOOD-SODDEN

SODS

OR UNDER GREEN SODS LAY.   132 FR GILLIGAN   4

SOFT

HER EYES WERE SOFT AS DEWDROPS HANGING   3 OISIN 1   V 7HH
AS HER SOFT BOSOM ROSE AND FELL.   4 OISIN 1   30
PIERCED WITH SOFT LIGHT THE SHALLOWING DEEPS. 13 OISIN 1   164
AND PONDERED IN A SOFT VAIN MOOD   14 OISIN 1   184
"BUT NEVER THE YEARS IN THE ISLE'S SOFT PLACES 27 OISIN 1   V 419A
"BUT NEVER THE YEARS IN OUR ISLE'S SOFT PLACES 28 OISIN 1   \ V 424
A LADY WITH SOFT EYES LIKE FUNERAL TAPERS,   33 OISIN 2   69
A MAIDEN WITH SOFT EYES LIKE FUNERAL TAPERS,   33 OISIN 2   V 69
. . . HIS KNEES IN THE SOFT STAR-FLAME,   50 OISIN 3   43
ARE FACES ALIVE WITH SUCH BEAUTY MADE KNOWN TO THE SOFT
   EYE OF MAN,   50 OISIN 3   V 51
AND BY ME, IN SOFT RED RAIMENT, THE FENIANS MOVED IN LOUD
   STREAMS,   53 OISIN 3   93
WERE THE WINDS LESS SOFT THAN THE BREATH OF A PIGEON 56 OISIN 3 134
. . . AND THEIR YOUTH, AND THEIR EYES SOFT AS SILK.   59 OISIN 3 V 176
FOR LONELY TO MOVE 'MONG THE SOFT EYES   63 OISIN 3   V 222
"WHAT DO YOU WEAVE SO SOFT AND BRIGHT?"   69 CLOAK BOAT   V   1
CONCEIVE A THING SO SAD AND SOFT, A GENTLE THING LIKE ME? 77 INDIAN ON GOD 16
IN VAIN HER ARMS, IN VAIN HER SOFT WHITE BREAST. 110 CUCHULAIN SEA 74
AND SLOWLY READ, AND DREAM OF THE SOFT LOOK   121 YOU ARE OLD   3
WHERE HER SOFT FOOTSTEPS GO.   175 ELEMENT POWERS V 18
BUT SOFT BEAUTY AND INDOLENT DESIRE.   181 QUEEN MAEVE   22
WITH BODIES MADE OUT OF SOFT FIRE. THE ONE, 187 QUEEN MAEVE   144
A MURMUR OF SOFT WORDS AND MEETING LIPS,   187 QUEEN MAEVE   154
FOR PROUD, SOFT, CEREMONIOUS PROOF   386 ROBARTES DANCE 30
SOFT AS THE RUSTLE OF A REED FROM CLOYNE   487 SEVEN SAGES   22

735

		PAGE	TITLE	LINE

SOFT (CONTINUED)
```
    INHABITANT OF THE SOFT CHEEK OF A GIRL--             540 FROM ANTIGONE          2
    DREAMING IN THEIR SOFT ODOUR-LADEN SLEEP!            650 ISLE STAT I 1        125
    SMALL ISLAND, WHERE THE FULL SOFT SHEEN              653 ISLE STAT I 2         36
    O WAKE! WAKE! WAKE! FOR SOFT AS A BEE SIPS,          677 ISLE STAT II 3       276
    OLD WARRIOR, WAKE! FOR SOFT AS A BEE SIPS,           677 ISLE STAT II 3       284
    HE IS LONG DEAD.  WAKE! SOFT AS A BEE SIPS           678 ISLE STAT II 3       297
    I GO AS SOFT AS FOLLY! I AM FATE."                   686 LIFE                  18
    BUT HERE THE LIONESS LICKS HER SOFT CUB              688 NETTLESHIP            2
    SOFT AS THE WHISPERING OF A LONG-LOST FOOTSTEP       699 MOSADA 3              5
    SOFT AS A LONG DEAD FOOTSTEP WHISPERING THROUGH      699 MOSADA 3       V      5
    SOFT AS THE WHISPERING OF A LOST FOOTSTEP            699 MOSADA 3       V      5
    ABOVE, THE WOODS WHERE WITH THE SOFT MILD EYE        710 FERENCZ RENYI        26
    AND SOFT, ONE GLIMMERING STAR.  RENYI HAS CAST       714 FERENCZ RENYI       115
    AND SOFT, ONE GLIMMERING STAR--WITH POWER VAST!      714 FERENCZ RENYI   V   115
    A KID! HELD BY ONE SOFT WHITE EAR FOR TETHER,        715 DWELT SYCAMORE        3
    ILL WORDS FOR ALL THINGS SOFT AND FAIR.              723 GIRLS SONG A          6
    I GO AS SOFT AS FOLLY! I AM FATE."                   735 QUATRAIN APHOR       20
    AND BODILY TENDERNESS TO THE SOFT FIRE               750 SHADOW WATER A       60
SOFTENING
    PLUNGE, LURED BY A SOFTENING EYE,                    413 TOWER               110
SOFTER
    SOFTER THAN SNOW-FLAKES IN APRIL AND PIERCING THE MARROW   51 OISIN 3         68
        LIKE FLAME.
    SOFTER THAN SNOWFLAKES IN APRIL, AND PIERCING THE MARROW   51 OISIN 3    V    68
        LIKE FLAME.
SOFTEST
    AND A HUNDRED ROBES OF THE SOFTEST SILK,              8 OISIN 1        V      88
SOFTLY
    THEN SIGHED SHE SOFTLY, "LATE! 'TIS LATE!             9 OISIN 1        V     102
    LULLED WEARINESS, AND SOFTLY ROUND                   11 OISIN 1              137
    AND BENDING OVER THEM SOFTLY SAID,                   21 OISIN 1              307
    SANG WE SOFTLY IN THE DANCE,                         21 OISIN 1        V     308
    SANG WE SOFTLY, "ON THE DEAD,                        21 OISIN 1        V     310
    THEREON YOUNG NIAMH SOFTLY CAME                      25 OISIN 1              373
    THEN SOFTLY TO ME NIAM CAME,                         25 OISIN 1        V     373
    AND SOFTLY COME TO YOUR NIAMH OVER THE TOPS OF THE TIDE!   55 OISIN 3       126
    AND SOFTLY COME TO THY NIAM OVER THE TOPS OF THE TIDE!     52 OISIN 3   V   126
    THEN HE SANG SOFTLY NIGH THE PEARLY RIM!             69 SAD SHEPHERD         25
    THEN SANG HE SOFTLY NIGH THE PEARLY RIM!             69 SAD SHEPHERD   V     25
    MURMURING SOFTLY LIP TO LIP,                         78 INDIAN TO LOVE        8
    ONE WITH THE WAVES THAT SOFTLY ROUND US LAUGH AND DART.   78 INDIAN TO LOVE V 15
    LEANING SOFTLY OUT                                   88 STOLEN CHILD         35
    AND SOFTLY MAKE A ROSY PEACE,                       113 ROSE OF PEACE        15
    TREAD SOFTLY BECAUSE YOU TREAD ON MY DREAMS.        176 CLOTHS HEAVEN         8
    IT BORE ME SOFTLY WHERE THE SHALLOW SAND            657 ISLE STAT I 3        58
    SLID CIRCLING DOWN AND SOFTLY TOUCHED MY LIPS       690 MOSADA 1             21
    THEN THE STRANGER SOFTLY CREW--                     697 MOSADA 2             28
SOFTNESS
    OR THE SOFTNESS OF YOUTH BE GONE FROM OUR FACES,     27 OISIN 1             410
    WILL THE SOFTNESS OF YOUTH BE GONE FROM OUR FACES,   27 OISIN 1        V    410
    OR THE SOFTNESS OF YOUTH BE GONE FROM OUR FACES,     27 OISIN 1        V  419C
    OR THE SOFTNESS OF YOUTH BE GONE FROM OUR FACES,     28 OISIN 1        V    426
    AND A SOFTNESS CAME FROM THE STARLIGHT               52 OISIN 3              72
    AND FEEL THE SOFTNESS OF EACH OTHER'S HAND,          74 ANASHU VIJAYA        57
    AND FEEL THE SOFTNESS OF EACH OTHER'S HANDS,         74 ANASHU VIJAYA  V     57
SOFT-SHINING
    IN ONE WAS A BRANCH SOFT-SHINING WITH BELLS MORE MANY THAN   50 OISIN 3     46
        SIGHS
SOIL
    MUST COME FROM CONTACT WITH THE SOIL, FROM THAT     603 GALLERY REVIS        43
    DEEP IN HIS SOUL, LIKE RAIN UPON A SOIL             692 MOSADA 1             56
SOILED
    HAD TROD THE UNEVEN ROAD.  THEIR BOOTS WERE SOILED, 372 PHASES OF MOON        3
SOLD
    THAT CARRIED THE TAKE TO SLIGO TOWN TO BE SOLD,      91 OLD FISHERMAN         7
    AND HIM WHO SOLD TILLAGE, AND HOUSE, AND GOODS,     170 SECRET ROSE          22
    A HUSBAND THAT HAD SOLD HIS WIFE                    587 PARNELLITES          27
    A HUSBAND WHO HAD SOLD HIS WIFE                     587 PARNELLITES    V     27
    THOSE CHEERS THAT CAN BE BOUGHT OR SOLD,            598 MODEL LAUREATE       19
    CRAMM'D ALL HER YOUTH! AND HATES HAVE BOUGHT AND SOLD   687 TWO TITANS       13
SOLDERED
    NOR SOLDERED POT OR PAN!                            606 SONGS BURDEN 1       15
SOLDIER
    SOLDIER, SCHOLAR, HORSEMAN, HE,                     327 ROBERT GREGORY       70
    SOLDIER, SCHOLAR, HORSEMAN, HE,                     327 ROBERT GREGORY       78
    SOLDIER, SCHOLAR, HORSEMAN, HE,                     327 ROBERT GREGORY       86
    THAT DEAD YOUNG SOLDIER IN HIS BLOOD!               425 STARES NEST          14
    SOLDIER, ASSASSIN, EXECUTIONER,                     482 BLOOD AND MOON       36
    THE SOLDIER TAKES PRIDE                             547 TO SAME TUNE 3 V      T
    THE SOLDIER TAKES PRIDE IN SALUTING HIS CAPTAIN,    547 TO SAME TUNE 3        1
    A REVOLUTIONARY SOLDIER KNEELING TO BE BLESSED!     601 GALLERY REVIS         8
    THE SOLDIER TAKES PRIDE IN SALUTING HIS CAPTAIN,    614 MARCH SONGS 2         1
    LACK NOTHING THAT A SOLDIER NEEDS,                  635 BLACK TOWER           4
    HE WHISPERS TO A SOLDIER, WHO GOES OUT--            711 FERENCZ RENYI        44
    RETURNS THAT SOLDIER IN THE EVENING RAYS            711 FERENCZ RENYI        49
    THE SOLDIER THUS, AND HAYNAU--"PEASANT, SPEAK       711 FERENCZ RENYI        54
    A SOLDIER ANSWERS! "BY THE CAMP'S FAR END           712 FERENCZ RENYI        67
SOLDIER'S
    THE HERALD'S CRY, THE SOLDIER'S TREAD               438 SONGS PLAY 2         13
    AND CLAIM AS BY A SOLDIER'S RIGHT                   478 SELF AND SOUL        31
```

SOLDIERS
SOLDIERS THAT GAVE, WHATEVER DIE WAS CAST! . . . . . . 269 PARDON FATHERS 9
TRADERS OR SOLDIERS WHO HAVE LEFT ME BLOOD . . . . . 269 PARDON FATHERS V 7
SOLDIERS TAKE PRIDE IN SALUTING THEIR CAPTAIN, ... 547 TO SAME TUNE 3 V 1
SOLDIERS TAKE PRIDE IN SALUTING THEIR CAPTAIN, ... 548 TO SAME TUNE 3 21
MY KING A LOST KING, AND LOST SOLDIERS MY MEN! . . . . 591 WHAT WAS LOST 3
OF SOLDIERS RANKED IS ON A GRASSY SPOT, ... 712 FERENCZ RENYI 64
OF SOLDIERS DRAWN IS ON A GRASSY SPOT, ... 712 FERENCZ RENYI V 64
SOLDIERY
RIDES UPON SLEEP! A DRUNKEN SOLDIERY . . . . 429 NINETEEN 19 26
THE EMPEROR'S DRUNKEN SOLDIERY ARE ABED! . . . . . 497 BYZANTIUM 2
THE EMPEROR'S DRUNKEN SOLDIERY ARE A-BED! . . . . . 497 BYZANTIUM V 2
HALF-DRUNK OR WHOLE-MAD SOLDIERY . . . . 791 REPRISALS 15
SOLE   SEE FOOT-SOLE
FOR YOUR SOLE SAKE--THAT ALL HEART'S ACHE HAVE KNOWN, . . 355 BROKEN DREAMS 7
BURDENSOME BEAUTY--FOR YOUR SOLE SAKE . . . . . . 356 BROKEN DREAMS 10
WHEN UPWARD TURNED, ON ONE SOLE IMAGE FELL! . . . . 471 ALL SOUL NIGHT 34
FOR NOTHING CAN BE SOLE OR WHOLE . . . . 513 JANE TALK BISH 17
O'HIGGINS ITS SOLE STATESMAN HAD NOT DIED. . . . . 543 PARN FUNERAL 2 8
MY PAISTIN FINN IS MY SOLE DESIRE, ... 550 SONGS REWRIT 1 1
EVERYTHING DOWN TO THAT SOLE TEST AGAIN, ... 603 GALLERY REVIS 46
AND ITS OLD SOLE STRING . . . . 627 STATES HOLIDAY 23
SOLEMN
THE MURMURING BIRDS IN SOLEMN POMP . . . . . 20 OISIN 1 V 293
IN SOLEMN REVERIE ROSE TO HEAR . . . . 85 MAD KING GOLL V 62
MUCH TOO SOLEMN SEEMED! . . . . 342 SHEP GOATHERD 91
MUCH TOO SOLEMN AND RESERVED. . . . . 342 SHEP GOATHERD 94
O, BUT I SAW A SOLEMN SIGHT! . . . . 788 HAWTHORN TREE 1
SOLEMN-EYED
THE SOLEMN-EYED! . . . . 88 STOLEN CHILD 43
SOLID
THERE IS A SOLID DIGNITY . . . . 296 THREE BEGGARS V 37
AND SOLID MEN, FOR ALL THEIR PASSION, LIVE . . . . 325 ROBERT GREGORY 37
. . . ITS FARROW THAT SO SOLID SEEM, ... 481 BLOOD AND MOON 26
THE SOLID MAN AND THE COXCOMB. . . . . 508 JANE BISHOP 7
THE SOLID MAN AND THE COXCOMB. . . . . 508 JANE BISHOP 14
THE SOLID MAN AND THE COXCOMB. . . . . 508 JANE BISHOP 21
THE SOLID MAN AND THE COXCOMB. . . . . 509 JANE BISHOP 28
SOLIDER
THERE CAN BE NOTHING SOLIDER TILL I DIE! . . . . 383 VISION ROBART 26
SOLIDER ARISTOTLE PLAYED THE TAWS . . . . . . 445 SCHOOL CHILDR 43
SOLITARY
BEING HIGH AND SOLITARY AND MOST STERN? . . . . 257 NO SECOND TROY 10
COMPARES THE SOLITARY SOUL TO A SWAN! . . . . . 430 NINETEEN 19 60
SELF-BORN, HIGH-BORN, AND SOLITARY TRUTHS, ... 467 HARUN RASHID 141
BEGOT! SELF-BORN, HIGH-BORN, AND SOLITARY. . . . 467 HARUN RASHID V 141
I SAT, A SOLITARY MAN, ... 501 VACILLATION 36
ONE SOLITARY MAN . . . . 526 AM OF IRELAND 8
BY WATER, HERB AND SOLITARY PRAYER . . . . . . 555 RIBH AT TOMB 23
OF SOLITARY BEDS, KNEW WHAT THEY WERE, ... 610 STATUES 5
THE LION, THE WORLD'S GREAT SOLITARY, BENDS . . . 689 NETTLESHIP 5
THE SOLITARY FAIRY . . . . 706 FAIRY PEDANT V T
SOLITUDE
WONDERING TO LAY HER IN THAT SOLITUDE, ... 123 DREAM OF DEATH 5
AND WONDERING PLANTED BY HER SOLITUDE . . . . 123 DREAM OF DEATH V 5
BEING MORE INDIFFERENT TO OUR SOLITUDE . . . . 334 LIVING BEAUTY 7
IMAGES CAN BREAK THE SOLITUDE . . . . . . 375 PHASES OF MOON 82
AND THERE ALONE, THAT HAVE NO SOLITUDE? . . . 398 LEADERS CROWD 9
BUT BREAK UPON HIS GHOSTLY SOLITUDE. . . . . 429 NINETEEN 19 40
FOR TRIUMPH CAN BUT MAR OUR SOLITUDE. . . . . 431 NINETEEN 19 78
AND SICK OF SOLITUDE . . . . 432 NINETEEN 19 105
GROWN TIRED OF THEIR SOLITUDE, ... 432 NINETEEN 19 V 105
WE THREE MAKE UP A SOLITUDE! . . . . 457 SECRETS OF OLD 9
THEIR SCHOOL A CROWD, HIS MASTER SOLITUDE! . . . 543 PARN FUNERAL 2 10
THEIR SCHOOL THE CROWD, HIS MASTER SOLITUDE, . . 543 PARN FUNERAL 2 V 10
THEIR SCHOOL A CROWD, HIS MASTER'S SOLITUDE! . . 543 PARN FUNERAL 2 V 10
AS MY LONG-PLANNED HALF SOLITUDE, ... 624 APPARITIONS 10
AS MY LONG PLANNED HALF SOLITUDE, ... 624 APPARITIONS V 10
A STATUE OF SOLITUDE, ... 785 YOUR HEART 4
SOLITUDES
THE EVER-SUMMERED SOLITUDES! . . . . . . 21 OISIN 1 321
THE EVER SUMMERED SOLITUDES, ... 21 OISIN 1 V 321
OR IN AUTUMNAL SOLITUDES . . . . 84 MAD KING GOLL 39
OR IN THE AUTUMN SOLITUDES . . . . . . 84 MAD KING GOLL V 39
NOURISH THE PANTHERS IN DIM SOLITUDES! . . . 657 ISLE STAT I 3 44
TO SEE THEM DROWNED BY THOSE VAST SOLITUDES, . . 661 ISLE STAT II 1 57
SOLOMON
SOLOMON TO SHEBA . . . . 332 SOLOMON SHEBA T
SANG SOLOMON TO SHEBA, ... 332 SOLOMON SHEBA 1
TO SOLOMON SANG SHEBA, ... 333 SOLOMON SHEBA 9
SANG SOLOMON TO SHEBA, ... 333 SOLOMON SHEBA 17
SAID SOLOMON TO SHEBA, ... 333 SOLOMON SHEBA V 17
THAT SOLOMON GREW WISE . . . . 345 ON WOMAN 11
AND LIVE LIKE SOLOMON . . . . 346 ON WOMAN 42
SOLOMON AND THE WITCH . . . . 387 SOLOMON WITCH T
WITHIN MY ARMS GREAT SOLOMON, ... 387 SOLOMON WITCH 4
GAVE SHEBA TO HER SOLOMON." . . . . . . 388 SOLOMON WITCH 32
O! SOLOMON! LET US TRY AGAIN." . . . . . 389 SOLOMON WITCH 44
SOLSTICE
WORN BY THE SOLSTICE FIERCE, AND MADE IT PURE. . . . 692 MOSADA 1 57

	PAGE	TITLE		LINE
SOMBRE				
DROPS ON HIS BOSOM, SOMBRE, MOIST AND SLOW.	711	FERENCZ RENYI		40
UPON HIS BOSOM, SOMBRE, MOIST AND SLOW.	711	FERENCZ RENYI	V	40
HIS MOODS BOW LOW HIS SOMBRE CREST.	723	GIRLS SONG A		2
SOME				
BLOSSOM IN SOME NEW CRIMSON FLOWER,	16	OISIN 1		224
AND IN SOME GLOOMY BARROW LIE	19	OISIN 1		272
AND IN SOME URN FUNEREAL LIE	19	OISIN 1		272
IN OTHER YEARS FROM SOME OLD STAR	19	OISIN 1	V	277
FROM SOME DEAD WARRIOR'S BROKEN LANCE!	24	OISIN 1		367
IT WAS OF SOME DEAD WARRIOR'S LANCE.	24	OISIN 1	V	367
SOME DANCED LIKE SHADOWS ON THE MOUNTAINS,	25	OISIN 1		388
SOME WANDERED EVER HAND IN HAND!	25	OISIN 1		389
OF SOME FORGOTTEN FIEND. NOW NONE ASSAILS	31	OISIN 2	V	30B
IN SOME DIM MEMORY OR ANCIENT MOOD,	36	OISIN 2		99
WRAPT ROUND IN SOME DIM MEMORY, IT SEEMED--	36	OISIN 2	V	99
WE SAW, SOME NEW, SOME PRINTED WHEN THE PLACE WAS YOUNG,	37	OISIN 2		116
WE SAW, SOME NEW, SOME PRINTED WHEN THE PLACE WAS YOUNG,	37	OISIN 2	V	116
LEST THEY SHOULD LOOK UPON SOME DREADFUL SIGHT!	38	OISIN 2		142
STOOD TIMIDLY. LEST THEY SHOULD SEE SOME SIGHT	38	OISIN 2	V	141
THAT FEED WHITE MOTHS BY SOME DE DANAAN SHRINE!	41	OISIN 2		186
FEEDING WHITE MOTHS AROUND SOME EASTERN SHRINE,	41	OISIN 2	V	186
"LIKE ME WERE SOME GALLEY FORSAKEN FAR OFF IN MERIDIAN ISLE.	55	OISIN 3		117
READING SOME ENTANGLED STORY!	65	HAPPY SHEPHERD		16
SOME TWISTED, ECHO-HARBOURING SHELL,	66	HAPPY SHEPHERD		36
THEIR HEARING, AND SOME COMFORT GIVE, BUT THEY	68	SAD SHEPHERD	V	6
SOME OTHER FILLS YOUR MIND. MY MOTHER'S NAME.	71	ANASHU VIJAYA		16
AND MAY SOME SUDDEN DREADFUL ILL BEFALL HER!	74	ANASHU VIJAYA		59
AND MAY SOME DREADFUL ILL BEFALL HER QUICK!	74	ANASHU VIJAYA	V	59
OF SOME INHUMAN MISERY	85	MAD KING GOLL		58
OF SOME UNHUMAN MISERY	85	MAD KING GOLL	V	58
"AND OF MY SERVANTS SOME ONE GO,	97	FOXHUNTER	V	5
AND SOME ONE FROM THE STABLE BRING	97	FOXHUNTER	V	5
AND SOME ONE FROM THE STABLES BRING	97	FOXHUNTER	V	5
SOME FEASTING MAN THAT THE SAME OATH HAS BOUND."	108	CUCHULAIN SEA		38
SOME FEATING MAN THAT THE SAME OATH HAS BOUND."	108	CUCHULAIN SEA	V	38
AT LAST CUCHULAIN SPAKE, "SOME MAN HAS MADE	109	CUCHULAIN SEA		47
SOME FEASTING MAN THAT THE SAME OATH HAS BOUND."	109	CUCHULAIN SEA		54
"SOME FEATING MAN THAT THE SAME OATH HAS BOUND."	109	CUCHULAIN SEA	V	54
AND I SHALL HAVE SOME PEACE THERE, FOR PEACE COMES DROPPING SLOW,	117	ISLE INNISFREE		5
AND HE HAD KNOWN AT LAST SOME TENDERNESS,	126	DREAM OF FAERY		3
AND HE HAD KNOWN AT LAST SOME PRUDENT YEARS	127	DREAM OF FAERY		15
AND PLANNING, PLOTTING ALWAYS THAT SOME MORROW	129	BOOK STORIES		10
FOR SOME CONSPIRACY,	131	OLD PENSIONER		8
TO SOME I HAVE TALKED WITH BY THE FIRE	136	TO SOME I TALK		T
AND SOME ONE CALLED ME BY MY NAME!	149	WANDER AENGUS		12
GATHERED A CROWD IN SOME BYZANTINE LANE,	180	QUEEN MAEVE		2
TO SOME STRINGED INSTRUMENT NONE THERE HAD SEEN,	180	QUEEN MAEVE		4
WHO HAS BEEN BURIED SOME TWO THOUSAND YEARS?	181	QUEEN MAEVE		35
BUT THE HORSE-BOYS SLEPT ON, AS THOUGH SOME POWER	181	QUEEN MAEVE		39
YOUNG BAILE HONEY-MOUTH, WHOM SOME	189	BAILE AILLINN		16
YOUNG BAILE HONEY MOUTH, WHOM SOME	189	BAILE AILLINN	V	16
THEIR BODICES IN SOME DIM PLACE	193	BAILE AILLINN		105
SOME GOD OR KING HAD MADE THE LAWS	194	BAILE AILLINN		131
THEY COME WHERE SOME HUGE WATCHER IS,	196	BAILE AILLINN		168
FOR THAT BRIEF SIGHING. IF YOU HAD LOVED SOME WOMAN--	228	SHADOW WATER B		135
BELIEVED THERE WAS SOME OTHER NEAR AT HAND,	229	SHADOW WATER B		154
THAT RAISED THEIR HANDS AGAINST HIM. THERE ARE SOME	235	SHADOW WATER B		291
SOME OTHER WOMAN HAS A CLAIM ON YOU,	245	SHADOW WATER B		474
LET'S HOME! I'D GIVE SOME RUBIES TO A WOMAN.	248	SHADOW WATER B		537
BUT IN SOME ISLAND WHERE THE LIFE OF THE WORLD	249	SHADOW WATER B		559
TO SOME SURE COUNTRY, SOME FAMILIAR PLACE.	249	SHADOW WATER B		569
TO SOME SURE COUNTRY, SOME FAMILIAR PLACE.	249	SHADOW WATER B	V	569
SOME MAY HAVE BLAMED YOU THAT YOU TOOK AWAY	257	RECONCILIATION		1
ALL THEIR LIVES THROUGH INTO SOME DRIFT OF WINGS.	265	ABBEY THEATRE		7
SING ON! SOMEWHERE AT SOME NEW MOON	266	GALWAY RACES		10
BUT SOME DAY AND AT SOME NEW MOON	266	GALWAY RACES	V	10
BUT SOME DAY AND AT SOME NEW MOON	266	GALWAY RACES	V	10
SING ON! SOMETIME, AND AT SOME NEW MOON	266	GALWAY RACES	V	10
OR ON SOME STILL UNEMPTIED CUP	271	GREY ROCK		21
SOMEWHERE WITHIN SOME HOLLOW HILL,	271	GREY ROCK	V	14
I NEEDS MUST MARRY SOME POOR LOUT,"	273	GREY ROCK		47
'TWAS WINE OR WOMEN, OR SOME CURSE--	273	GREY ROCK		54
I NEED MUST MARRY SOME POOR LOUT,"	273	GREY ROCK	V	47
WHO HAD LOST SOME UNIMAGINABLE TREASURE	278	TWO KINGS		40
SOME PASSION HAD MADE HER STONE. HEARING A FOOT	279	TWO KINGS		65
THEN FEARING THAT SOME LABOURER, ON HIS WAY	283	TWO KINGS		145
LIKE THE EYES OF SOME GREAT KITE SCOURING THE WOODS,	283	TWO KINGS		150
HAD HALF AWAKENED SOME OLD MEMORY--	284	TWO KINGS		172
HAD HALF WAKENED SOME OLD MEMORY,	284	TWO KINGS	V	172
WHY MUST I LIVE SOME THIRTY, FORTY YEARS,	285	TWO KINGS		199
TO BE "SOME SORT OF EVIDENCE",	287	TO WEALTHY MAN		4
THAT SOME NEW DAY MAY BREED THE BEST	288	TO WEALTHY MAN		34
YOU'D CRY, "SOME WOMAN'S YELLOW HAIR	290	SEPTEMBER 1913		28
FOR SOME TRIVIAL AFFAIR	293	HELEN LIVED		3
INTO SOME MOST FEARFUL SHAPE."	299	THREE HERMITS		23
IN SOME OUTLANDISH COAT BESIDE	303	HOUR DAWN	V	28
LIKE SOME OLD RABBIT TO MY CLEFT	307	HOUR DAWN		105
LIKE SOME LAST COURTIER AT A GYPSY CAMPING-PLACE	314	FALLEN MAJESTY		3

```
                                                          PAGE    TITLE        LINE
SOME  (CONTINUED)
     LIKE SOME LAST COURTIER AT A GYPSY CAMPING PLACE • • • •   314 FALLEN MAJESTY V   3
     DELIGHT MEN'S EYES WHEN I AWAKE SOME DAY • • • • • •       323 SWANS AT COOLE    29
     AND HAVING TALKED TO SOME LATE HOUR • • • • • • • •        324 ROBERT GREGORY     4
     OUT OF SOME OLD PICTURE-BOOK: • • • • • • • • • • •        325 ROBERT GREGORY    44
     OUT OF SOME OLD PICTURE BOOK: • • • • • • • • • • •        325 ROBERT GREGORY V  44
     SOME BURN DAMP FAGGOTS, OTHERS MAY CONSUME • • • •         327 ROBERT GREGORY    81
     WITH SOME APPROPRIATE COMMENTARY ON EACH: • • • • •        328 ROBERT GREGORY    93
     SOME MEDICABLE HERB TO MAKE OUR GRIEF • • • • • •          342 SHEP GOATHERD     86
     AT SOME OLD WINDING WHITETHORN ROOT • • • • • • •          342 SHEP GOATHERD    101
     OR PUT HIS HEART INTO SOME GAME • • • • • • • • •          343 SHEP GOATHERD    105
     AND ALL BECAUSE OF SOME ONE • • • • • • • •               346 ON WOMAN          40
     A WOMAN SPOKE OF SOME NEW TALE SHE HAD READ, • • • • •     350 HER PRAISE         7
     AS THOUGH SOME OTHER NAME RAN IN HIS HEAD. • • • • •       351 HER PRAISE         9
     SOME BEGGAR SHELTERING FROM THE WIND, AND THERE • • • •    351 HER PRAISE        13
     OF SOME STRANGE WOMAN'S NAME THAT RAN IN HIS HEAD. • • •   351 HER PRAISE   V     9
     THOSE I HAD SERVED AND SOME THAT I HAD FED: • • • • • •    352 PEOPLE            27
     AND WHO CAN SAY BUT SOME YOUNG BELLE MAY WALK AND TALK     354 HIS PHOENIX       26
        MEN WILD
     AND MAY BE THERE'LL BE SOME YOUNG BELLE WALK OUT TO MAKE   354 HIS PHOENIX  V    26
        MEN WILD
     AND MAYBE THERE'LL BE SOME YOUNG BELLE WALK OUT TO MAKE    354 HIS PHOENIX  V    26
        MEN WILD
     BUT MAYBE SOME OLD GAFFER MUTTERS A BLESSING • • • • •     355 BROKEN DREAMS      4
     OVER SOME SILKEN DRESS • • • • • • • • • • • • •           363 DOLLS DRAWINGS     7
     BECAUSE TO-DAY IS SOME RELIGIOUS FESTIVAL • • • • • •      363 DOLLS FACES        1
     WHO HAD SEEMED TO GLIDE TO SOME INTRIGUE IN HER RED SHOES, 363 DOLLS FACES        6
     SHOWS HER THAT SOME ONE SOON • • • • • • • • • •           364 END OF DAY         5
     THAT MADE HER DIARMUID DEAR, AND SOME OLD CARDINAL • • •   366 HER COURAGE        6
     AND THAT MADE HER DERMUID DEAR, AND SOME OLD CARDINAL • •  366 HER COURAGE  V     6
     THAT DREAM IS A NORM: AND SHOULD SOME LIMB OF THE DEVIL    372 ON GOING HOUSE    12
     OR FROM SOME BLOODY WHIP IN THEIR OWN HANDS. • • • • •     375 PHASES OF MOON    68
     BUT TAKE ME FOR SOME DRUNKEN COUNTRYMAN: • • • • • •       377 PHASES OF MOON   130
     BUT TAKE ME FOR SOME DRUNKEN COUNTRY MAN: • • • • • •      377 PHASES OF MOON V 130
     SOME DAY I MAY FORGET • • • • • • • • • • •                380 SONGS FOOL 1       8
     OBEDIENT TO SOME HIDDEN MAGICAL BREATH. • • • • • •        382 VISION ROBART     13
     TO FIND OUT SOME APPROPRIATE PAIN-- • • • • • • • •        388 SOLOMON WITCH     20
     WILL FIND OUT SOME APPROPRIATE PAIN, • • • • • • •         388 SOLOMON WITCH V   20
     IMAGINE THAT SOME LOST LOVE, UNASSAILABLE • • • • •        390 UNDER SATURN V     2
     TO SOME WHO ARE NEAR MY HEART, • • • • • • • •             393 EASTER 1916       34
     "SOME POLITICIANS IDLE WORDS • • • • • • • •               396 ROSE TREE    V     3
     HER THOUGHT SOME POPULAR ENMITY: • • • • • • • •           397 POLIT PRISONER    10
     UPON SOME LOFTY ROCK TO STARE • • • • • • • • •            397 POLIT PRISONER    21
     FOR THOUGHT SOME POPULAR ENMITY, • • • • • • • •           397 POLIT PRISONER V  10
     SURELY SOME REVELATION IS AT HAND: • • • • • • •           402 SECOND COMING      9
     O MAY SHE LIVE LIKE SOME GREEN LAUREL • • • • •            405 FOR DAUGHTER      47
     SOME FEW REMEMBERED STILL WHEN I WAS YOUNG • • • •         410 TOWER             33
     COWARDICE, SOME SILLY OVER-SUBTLE THOUGHT • • • •          413 TOWER            117
     FROM SOME GREAT LABYRINTH OUT OF PRIDE, • • • • •          413 TOWER            116
     COWARDICE, OVER SOME SILLY SUBTLE THOUGHT • • • •          413 TOWER        V   117
     AS IF SOME MARVELLOUS EMPTY SEA-SHELL FLUNG • • • •        417 ANCEST HOUSES     13
     SOME VIOLENT BITTER MAN, SOME POWERFUL MAN • • •           418 ANCEST HOUSES     17
     SOME VIOLENT BITTER MAN, SOME POWERFUL MAN • • •           418 ANCEST HOUSES     17
     IN SOME LIKE CHAMBER, SHADOWING FORTH • • • • •            419 MY HOUSE          15
     SOME FOURTEEN DAYS OF CIVIL WAR: • • • • • •               425 STARES NEST       12
     INTO THE HALF-DECEIT OF SOME INTOXICANT • • • •            429 NINETEEN 19       34
     SOME MORALIST OR MYTHOLOGICAL POET • • • • •               430 NINETEEN 19       59
     SOME PLATONIST AFFIRMS THAT IN THE STATION • • • •         431 NINETEEN 19       72
     TO LEAVE SOME MONUMENT BEHIND, • • • • • • •               432 NINETEEN 19       96
     SOME FEW HAVE HANDSOME RIDERS, ARE GARLANDED • • •         432 NINETEEN 19      114
     UPON SOME BRAND-NEW HAPPY DAY: • • • • • • • •             432 NINETEEN 19  V   106
     AND SHOULD SOME CRAZY HAND DARE TOUCH A DAUGHTER • • •     433 NINETEEN 19      122
     SOME THERE ARE, FOR I AVOW • • • • • • • • • •             435 FOR MY SON        10
     OF SOME MOST HAUGHTY DEED OR THOUGHT • • • • • •           436 FOR MY SON        13
     BY SOME PEASANT GOSPELLER: • • • • • • • • •               440 WISDOM             5
     WHEN SOME PEASANT GOSPELLER • • • • • • • •                440 WISDOM       V     5
     BECAUSE OF SOME GREEN WING, GATHERED OLD MUMMY WHEAT • •   442 BLACK CENTAUR      7
     THAT CHANGED SOME CHILDISH DAY TO TRAGEDY-- • • • •        443 SCHOOL CHILDR     12
     ABOVE A SINKING FIRE, SOME TALE THAT SHE • • • •           443 SCHOOL CHILDR V   10
     I WILL FIND OUT SOME CAVERN IN THE HILLS • • • •           448 HERO GIRL FOOL V  11
     ARE GONE AWAY, AND SOME THAT STAY • • • • •                458 HIS WILDNESS       5
     THE PARCHMENT WILL DISCLOSE TO SOME LEARNED MAN • • •      461 HARUN RASHID      20
     OR BRIGHTEN ONLY FOR SOME YOUNGER EYE: • • • • •           464 HARUN RASHID      82
     ITSELF AND NOT SOME OTHER SOUL." "THAT LOVE • • •          465 HARUN RASHID      94
     ITSELF AND NOT SOME OTHER SOUL. "SUCH LOVE • • •           465 HARUN RASHID V    94
     PERCHED IN SOME WINDOW OF HER MOTHER'S HOUSE • • •         466 HARUN RASHID     106
     IMAGINED SOME IMPOSSIBLE HISTORY • • • • • •               466 HARUN RASHID     109
     WERE SOME DEAR CHEEK. UPON A MOONLESS NIGHT • •            466 HARUN RASHID     127
     WERE SOME DEAR FACE. UPON A MOONLESS NIGHT • •             466 HARUN RASHID V   127
     OR WAS IT SHE THAT SPOKE OR SOME GREAT DJINN? • • •        467 HARUN RASHID     135
     EVEN TO-DAY, AFTER SOME SEVEN YEARS • • • • •              468 HARUN RASHID     161
     EVEN TODAY, AFTER SOME SEVEN YEARS • • • • •               468 HARUN RASHID V   161
     I NEED SOME MIND THAT, IF THE CANNON SOUND • • • •         471 ALL SOUL NIGHT    11
     BY SOME LEARNED INDIAN • • • • • • • • •                   472 ALL SOUL NIGHT    53
     SOME VAGUE UTOPIA--AND SHE SEEMS, • • • • • •              475 EVA GORE-BOOTH    11
     FROM SOME COURT-LADY'S DRESS AND ROUND • • • •             477 SELF AND SOUL     14
     FROM SOME COURT-LADIES' DRESS AND ROUND • • • •            477 SELF AND SOUL V   14
     SOME FOUND A DIFFERENT POLE, AND WHERE IT STOOD • • •      483 VERONIC NAPKIN     7
     LIKE SOME POOR ARAB TRIBESMAN AND HIS TENT. • • • •        491 COOLE BALLYLEE    40
     THAT FEED ON SOME FOUL PARASITE • • • • • • •              493 AT ALGECIRAS       2
     THAT FEEDS ON SOME FOUL PARASITE • • • • • • •             493 AT ALGECIRAS V     2
```

		PAGE	TITLE	LINE

SOME   (CONTINUED)
```
    ROSE: SOME CONQUEROR DREW REIN . . . . . . . . . . .   502 VACILLATION        64
    SOME STUPID THING THAT I HAD DONE . . . . . . . . .     507 STREAM AND SUN      4
    NOT IN SOME FOUL STY." . . . . . . . . . . . . . .      513 JANE TALK BISH      6
    WHEN SHE, AND THOUGH SOME SAID SHE PLAYED . . . . .     514 JANE GROWN OLD      8
    INTO SOME LESSER THING. . . . . . . . . . . . . .       517 HER ANXIETY         5
    BY SOME NEW-MARRIED BRIDE, I TAKE . . . . . . . .       535 CHOSEN             13
    BY SOME NEW MARRIED BRIDE I TAKE . . . . . . . .        535 CHOSEN           V 13
    CUT OUT HIS HEART. SOME MASTER OF DESIGN . . . . .      541 PARN FUNERAL 1     14
    SOME BACK A MARE THROWN FROM A THOROUGHBRED, . . . .    547 TO SAME TUNE 3      3
    SOME TAKE DELIGHT IN ADORNING A WOMAN. . . . . . .      547 TO SAME TUNE 3 V    3
    SOME BACK A MARE THROWN FROM A THOROUGH-BRED, . . .     547 TO SAME TUNE 3 V    3
    GODHEAD. SOME SHADOW FELL. MY SOUL FORGOT . . . .       557 RIBH ECSTASY        6
    SOME ANCIENT FAMOUS AUTHORS MISREPRESENT, . . . . .     579 DOR WELLESLEY      15
    THAT SOME AMENDS BE MADE . . . . . . . . . . . .        582 ROGER CASEMENT     22
    BUT FOR WHAT SOME TRAVELLING MAN . . . . . . . . .      585 ORAHILLY           21
    "THAT SOME STREAM OF LIGHTNING . . . . . . . . . .      589 OLD WICKED MAN     55
    I FASTED FOR SOME FORTY DAYS ON BREAD AND BUTTERMILK, . .   592 PILGRIM         1
    SOME TWENTY FEET FROM TIP TO TIP HAD IT STRETCHED RIGHTLY   593 PILGRIM        17
       OUT,
    SOME TWENTY FEET FROM TIP TO TIP HAD ITS WINGS STRETCHED    593 PILGRIM      V 17
       RIGHTLY OUT,
    SOME BOAST OF BEGGAR-KINGS AND KINGS . . . . . . .      597 MODEL LAUREATE      9
    SOME THAT BEING UNBEGOTTEN . . . . . . . . . . .        600 SPIRIT MEDIUM      11
    BUT COPY SOME ONE ACTION, . . . . . . . . . . .         600 SPIRIT MEDIUM      13
    FOR TWENTY MINUTES IN SOME STUDIO. . . . . . . . .      602 GALLERY REVIS      16
    AS THOUGH SOME BALLAD-SINGER HAD SUNG IT ALL: . . .     602 GALLERY REVIS      24
    AS THOUGH SOME BALLAD SINGER HAD SUNG IT ALL. . . .     602 GALLERY REVIS    V 24
    IN SOME GOOD COMPANY, . . . . . . . . . . . . .         605 YOU CONTENT        18
    SOME HAD NO THOUGHT OF VICTORY . . . . . . . . .        608 SONGS BURDEN 3     19
    AND PRESSED AT MIDNIGHT IN SOME PUBLIC PLACE . . . .    610 STATUES             7
    UNTIL, IN SOME CLIFF-SHELTERED BAY . . . . . . .        612 NEWS ORACLE        21
    SOME BACK A MARE THROWN FROM A THOROUGHBRED, . . . .    614 MARCH SONGS 2       3
    SOME FEW HALF WAKE AND HALF RENEW THEIR CHOICE, . . .   622 HOUND VOICE         6
    SOME DAY WE SHALL GET UP BEFORE THE DAWN . . . . .      622 HOUND VOICE        15
    SOME ROGUE OF THE WORLD STOLE THEM TO PATCH UP A FENCE  623 HIGH TALK           4
       OR A FIRE.
    WITH SOME FRIEND THAT HAS THE WIT . . . . . . . .       624 APPARITIONS        12
    WITH SOME FRIEND WHO HAS THE WIT . . . . . . . .        624 APPARITIONS      V 12
    SOME HAVE KNOWN A LIKELY LAD . . . . . . . . . .        625 OLD MEN BE MAD      2
    SOME THINK IT A MATTER OF COURSE THAT CHANCE . . .      626 OLD MEN BE MAD      9
    SOME THINK IT MATTER OF COURSE THAT CHANCE . . . .      626 OLD MEN BE MAD V    9
    SOME KNEW WHAT AILED THE WORLD . . . . . . . . .        627 STATES HOLIDAY      9
    A KING HAD SOME BEAUTIFUL COUSINS, . . . . . . .        628 JANE MOUNTAIN       7
    UP THERE SOME HAWK OR OWL HAS STRUCK, . . . . . .       633 MAN AND ECHO       43
    WITH SOME SORT OF VIOLENCE . . . . . . . . . . .        638 BEN BULBEN         34
    DANCING IN SOME MOONY PLACE, . . . . . . . . . .        647 ISLE STAT I 1      54
    SOME OLD MISER TELLS HIS STORE: . . . . . . . .         647 ISLE STAT I 1      58
    A HORN! SOME TROOP OF ROBBERS WINDING GOES . . . .      649 ISLE STAT I 1     110
    SINGING OF ARMS AND BATTLES SOME OLD STAVE, . . . .     650 ISLE STAT I 1     137
    SHEEP-GUIDING, OR THE BRINGING SOME STRANGE BIRD, . .   650 ISLE STAT I 1     147
    OR SOME SMALL BEAST MOST WONDERFULLY FURR'D, . . .      650 ISLE STAT I 1     148
    SOME SAY THAT ALL WHO TOUCH THE ISLAND LONE . . . .     653 ISLE STAT I 2      42
    AS SOME DEAD MAIDEN'S SINGING IN A DREAM. . . . .       654 ISLE STAT I 2      59
    SOME BARBAROUS, UN-FAERY THING DRAW NEAR. . . . .       656 ISLE STAT I 3      21
    EACH SHINING CLEAR AS SOME UNBAFFLED STAR! . . . .      656 ISLE STAT I 3      25
    UNLESS SOME PITYING GOD SHALL SUCCOUR ME . . . .        656 ISLE STAT I 3      36
    IN THIS MY CHOICE. SOME GOD MIGHT HELP! IF SO . .       656 ISLE STAT I 3      37
    SOME CAST OF DIE, OR LET SOME ARROW GLANCE . . .        656 ISLE STAT I 3      40
    SOME CAST OF DIE, OR LET SOME ARROW GLANCE . . .        656 ISLE STAT I 3      40
    SHALL NOT SO HOPELESS PROVE! SOME GOD MAY REST . .      657 ISLE STAT I 3      61
    SOME GOBLIN, MY SERVANT, ON WINGS THAT ARE FLEET,      657 ISLE STAT I 3      67
    CURVING BENEATH THE PROW: AS SOME WILD DRAKE . .        659 ISLE STAT II 1     16
    ONCE MORE THOSE SHEPHERDS COME. MAYHAP SOME MIRTH . .   664 ISLE STAT II 2     49
    THE FLOWER, SAVE SOME THING BE FOUND . . . . . .        668 ISLE STAT II 3     51
    IT IS MY WHIM! BID SOME ATTENDANT SPRITE . . . . .      669 ISLE STAT II 3     72
    AND CROUCH IN SOME FAR STILLNESS OF THE ISLE, AND DIE. . .  675 ISLE STAT II 3 246
    EVE-SOOTHED IN SOME FAR LEAFY REST, . . . . . . .       686 LIFE               10
    SLEEP IN SOME FAR OTHER FIELD . . . . . . . . .         705 DAWN-SONG           3
    OFTEN HE HAD BENT DOWN SOME BOUGH ALL BRIGHT . . .      710 FERENCZ RENYI      28
    OFTEN HE HAD BENT DOWN SOME BOUGH ALL BRIGHT WITH BERRIES!  710 FERENCZ RENYI V 28
    LEST HE MAY SOME GLAMOUR FOLD . . . . . . . . .         717 FAIRY DOCTOR       22
    LEST SOME GLAMOUR HE MAY FOLD . . . . . . . . .         717 FAIRY DOCTOR     V 22
    THEN EACH WIFE AND MAID AND MOTHER CALLS BY NAME        719 PHANTOM SHIP       24
       SOME DROWNED ONE.
    OBEYS. SOME FIERCE MAGICIAN FLIES OR WALKS . . . .      720 WITCH VIVIEN        9
    SOME GREAT ONE. NO: I HEAR THE WAVERING STEPS . .       720 WITCH VIVIEN       12
    I DREAMT SOME GREAT ONE. AH, MY BEAUTIFUL, . . .        720 WITCH VIVIEN       14
    SOME DAY YOU'LL BUY THEM, MAYBE. NEVER! NEVER? . .      721 WITCH VIVIEN       24
    THERE WAS SOME TALKING OF THE POOR-- . . . . . .        725 LEGEND             14
    THERE WAS SOME TALKING OF MAN'S GOD, . . . . . .        725 LEGEND             19
    HE'D FIND FOR THIS SOME HOLY TEXT. . . . . . . .        728 PRIEST FAIRY       16
    MAYBE NOW IN SOME FAR LANE, . . . . . . . . . .         731 STREET DANCERS     14
    MAYBE IN SOME ISLE OF ISLES, . . . . . . . . . .        732 STREET DANCERS     27
    OR LEAVE SOME SERVICE ALL UNDONE, . . . . . . .         743 DANAAN QUICK       21
    OF SOME MILD WOMAN, OR IN CHILDREN'S WAYS. . . .        750 SHADOW WATER A     74
    AND NO MAN KILL ME: FOR SOME WIND HAS BLOWN . . .       751 SHADOW WATER A     97
    THEIR HAIR MINGLES ON SOME STRINGED INSTRUMENT, . .     752 SHADOW WATER A    123
    WITH SOME YOU HAVE KILLED AND DIE: FOR WHEN I LEFT . .  758 SHADOW WATER A V  226
    TO CRY HIS FOLDING CRY. THERE IS SOME MAN . . . .       760 SHADOW WATER A V  253
    AND, HURRYING HOMEWARD, FALL UPON SOME LAND . . . .     767 SHADOW WATER A    384
```

		PAGE	TITLE		LINE

SOME   (CONTINUED)
    WHERE SOME LAUGHING ELEMENT . . . .   777 SONG DEIRDRE 2   4
    SOME ONE SHOULD STAY AT HER SIDE. . . . .   786 YOUR HEART   V   28
    SOME NINETEEN GERMAN PLANES, THEY SAY, ...   791 REPRISALS   1
SOMEBODY
    FOR SOMEBODY HID HATRED AND HOPE AND DESIRE AND FEAR . .   153 CHANGE BELOVED   4
    WITH SOMEBODY IN YOUR OWN LAND." . . . .   191 BAILE AILLINN   59
    THAT SOMEBODY HAD DRUNK DRY. . . . .   215 HAPPY TOWNLAND   32
    BUT YOU WERE SAYING THERE IS SOMEBODY . . . . . .   240 SHADOW WATER B   380
    THERE'S SOMEBODY I'D GIVE THE AMETHYST EYES TO. . .   248 SHADOW WATER B   538
    AND SOMEBODY PUTS HIS HAND IN THE DISH . . . . . .   301 RUN PARADISE   5
    FROM SOMEBODY THAT TOILS FROM CHAIR TO CHAIR; . . .   491 COOLE BALLYLEE   26
    FOR I AM CERTAIN SOMEBODY IS DEAD. . . . .   760 SHADOW WATER A   254
SOMEHOW
    SOMEWHERE OR SOMEHOW THAT I HAVE FORGOT, ...   258 KING NO KING   6
SOMEONE
    AND SOMEONE CALLED ME BY MY NAME. . . . .   149 WANDER AENGUS V   12
    SHOWS HER THAT SOMEONE SOON . . . .   364 END OF DAY   V   5
    WHAT IS THIS SACRIFICE? CAN SOMEONE THERE . . . .   541 PARN FUNERAL 1   6
SOMETHING
    BUT SOMETHING RUSTLED ON THE FLOOR. . . . .   149 WANDER AENGUS   11
    BUT SOMETHING RUSTLED ON THE STOOL, ...   149 WANDER AENGUS V   11
    BECAUSE OF SOMETHING TOLD UNDER THE FAMISHED HORN . .   210 UNDER THE MOON   17
    BECAUSE OF SOMETHING I HEARD OF UNDER THE THIN HORN . .   210 UNDER THE MOON V   17
    FOR I AM GETTING ON IN LIFE—TO SOMETHING . . . .   222 SHADOW WATER B   6
    IF SOMETHING THAT'S MOST FABULOUS WERE TRUE— . .   245 SHADOW WATER B   489
    OUT OF MY HEART. THERE'S SOMETHING AILS OUR COLT .   260 FASC DIFFICULT   4
    OR SOMETHING OF THAT SORT HE SAID, ...   338 TOM OROUGHLEY   14
    SOMETHING HAS TROUBLED ME AND IN MY TROUBLE . . .   339 SHEP GOATHERD   10
    IN SOMETHING THAT ALL OTHERS UNDERSTAND OR SHARE; .   427 PHANTOM HATRED   35
    SOMETHING OF EVERY PADDLER'S HERITAGE— . . . . .   444 SCHOOL CHILDR   21
    A SOMETHING INCOMPATIBLE WITH LIFE; AND POWER, . .   482 BLOOD AND MOON   50
    BUT SOMETHING IS RECALLED, ...   501 VACILLATION   55
    BUT SOMETHING BORE THEM OUT OF SIGHT . . . .   519 HER DREAM   5
    SOMETHING MADE THESE EYEBALLS WEARY . . . .   529 TOM LUNATIC   11
    SOMETHING TO PERFECTION BROUGHT"; . . . .   577 WHAT THEN   19
    AND THAT IS SOMETHING NEW; . . . .   582 ROGER CASEMENT   12
    THAT SOMETHING IS ABOUT TO HAPPEN, I THINK . . . .   609 IN TARAS HALLS   4
    (SOMETHING MAY LINGER THERE THOUGH ALL ELSE DIE!) .   618 BRONZE HEAD   5
    I HAVE FOUND SOMETHING WORSE . . . .   628 JANE MOUNTAIN   5
    SOMETHING DROPS FROM EYES LONG BLIND, ...   638 BEN BULBEN   29
    WHEN SOMETHING FOLDED AND SMALL . . . .   744 GLOVE CLOAK   7
    WHEN SOMETHING THAT WAS BEARDED LIKE A GOAT . . .   747 SHADOW WATER A   11
    WHEN SOMETHING, HALF A LAMB AND HALF A GOAT, . . .   747 SHADOW WATER A V   11
    SHE WILL SAY SOMETHING IN A LITTLE WHILE, ...   760 SHADOW WATER A   248
    BUT FAITHFUL LOVERS. SOMETHING GLITTERS THERE— .   763 SHADOW WATER A   309
SOMETIME
    SING ON; SOMETIME, AND AT SOME NEW MOON . . . . .   266 GALWAY RACES   V   10
SOMETIMES
    AND SOMETIMES FROM THE SALTIN' SHED . . . .   94 MOLL MAGEE   9
    AND SOMETIMES I AM SURE SHE KNOWS . . . .   96 MOLL MAGEE   49
    WHY THEY WHO WILL THE HIGHEST SOMETIMES BROOD, . .   711 FERENCZ RENYI   34
SOMEWHAT
    THOUGH SOMEWHAT BROKEN BY THE LEAVES, THAT LIGHT .   555 RIBH AT TOMB   25
SOMEWHERE
    "YET SOMEWHERE UNDER STARLIGHT OR THE SUN . . . .   107 CUCHULAIN SEA   28
    "NO, SOMEWHERE UNDER DAYLIGHT OR THE STARS . . . .   107 CUCHULAIN SEA V   25
    SANG THAT SOMEWHERE TO NORTH OR WEST OR SOUTH . .   127 DREAM OF FAERY   19
    SANG HOW SOMEWHERE TO NORTH OR EAST OR SOUTH . . .   127 DREAM OF FAERY V   19
    SANG HOW SOMEWHERE TO NORTH OR WEST OR SOUTH . . .   127 DREAM OF FAERY V   19
    MUST BE SUBSTANTIAL SOMEWHERE. I HAVE HEARD THE DRUIDS   229 SHADOW WATER B   162
    OR SOMEWHERE, I SHALL FIND THE LOVE THEY HAVE PROMISED.   231 SHADOW WATER B   208
    SOMEWHERE OR SOMEHOW THAT I HAVE FORGOT, ...   258 KING NO KING   6
    SING ON! SOMEWHERE AT SOME NEW MOON, ...   266 GALWAY RACES   10
    SOMEWHERE IN EAR-SHOT FOR THE STORY'S END, ...   269 PARDON FATHERS   2
    SOMEWHERE WITHIN SOME HOLLOW HILL, ...   271 GREY ROCK   V   14
    WHO'S BURROWING SOMEWHERE IN THE GROUND, ...   272 GREY ROCK   33
    IT'S CERTAIN THERE ARE TROUT SOMEWHERE . . . . . .   297 THREE BEGGARS   66
    "TIME TO PUT OFF THE WORLD AND GO SOMEWHERE . . .   299 BEGGAR CRIED   1
    SOMEWHERE AMONG THE CLOUDS ABOVE; . . . .   328 IRISH AIRMAN   2
    TROUBLES MY SIGHT; SOMEWHERE IN SANDS OF THE DESERT . .   402 SECOND COMING   13
    WHO'D LIVED SOMEWHERE UPON THAT ROCKY PLACE, . . .   410 TOWER   35
    FROM SOMEWHERE IN THE NEIGHBOURING COTTAGES, . . .   411 TOWER   59
    ON OUR UNCERTAINTY; SOMEWHERE . . . .   425 STARES NEST   7
    SOMEWHERE BEYOND THE CURTAIN . . . .   504 QUARREL IN AGE   12
    ARE SOMEWHERE SLEEPING LIKE A TOP . . . .   525 DANCING DAYS   13
    SOMEWHERE OFF HENRY STREET; . . . .   585 ORAHILLY   31
    YET SOMEWHERE IN THE FOOTSORE WORLD WE MEET, . . .   691 MOSADA 1   23
SON
    THAT I MIGHT HAVE YOUR SON TO KISS." . . . .   6 OISIN 1   59
    "WERE THERE NO BETTER THAN MY SON . . . .   6 OISIN 1   60
    OF OISIN, THE YOUNG MAN, MY SON? . . . .   6 OISIN 1   60
    BY THIS YOUNG MAN, USHEEN MY SON?" . . . .   6 OISIN 1   V   60
    PRINCESS, BY THIS YOUNG MAN, MY SON?" . . . . . .   6 OISIN 1   V   61
    ON THIS YOUNG MAN, OISIN, MY SON?" . . . .   6 OISIN 1   V   61
    SHE SMOTE WITH RADDLED FIST, AND WHERE HER SON . .   106 CUCHULAIN SEA   18
    AND WHERE HER SON, FINMOLE, ON THE SMOOTH GRASS .   106 CUCHULAIN SEA V   18
    AND CRIED OUT TO HIM, "SON IT IS NOT MEET . . . .   107 CUCHULAIN SEA   20
    AND CALLED OUT TO HIM, "SON IT IS NOT MEET . . .   107 CUCHULAIN SEA V   20
    "NAY, YOU ARE TALLER THAN CUCHULAIN, SON." . . .   107 CUCHULAIN SEA V   27
    "CUCHULAIN I, MIGHTY CUCHULAIN'S SON." . . . . .   110 CUCHULAIN SEA   68

SON   (CONTINUED)
"I AM FINMOLE, MIGHTY CUCHULAIN'S SON." . . . .   110 CUCHULAIN SEA V   68
ON THE HEIR OF ULADH, BUAN'S SON, ...   189 BAILE AILLINN   4
THERE WAS NO MOTHER'S SON BUT SAID, ...   253 HIS DREAM   6
MURROUGH, THE KING OF IRELAND'S SON, ...   274 GREY ROCK   71
SEEING, KING'S SON, WHAT WOUNDS YOU HAVE." . . . .   275 GREY ROCK   94
FOR HE AND THE KING'S SON WERE DEAD. . . . .   275 GREY ROCK   97
HAS MADDENED EVERY MOTHER'S SON": . . . .   290 SEPTEMBER 1913   29
BUT NOT THAT MY DEAR FRIEND'S DEAR SON, ...   325 ROBERT GREGORY   46
HIS SON GEORGE, THE ASTROLOGER: . . . .   360 ALF POLLEXFEN   8
MANY A SON AND DAUGHTER LIES . . . .   360 ALF POLLEXFEN   13
AND YESTERDAY THE YOUNGEST SON, ...   361 ALF POLLEXFEN   24
THE COARSE-BRED SON OF A LIVERY-STABLE KEEPER-- . .   370 EGO DOMINUS   61
THE ILL-BRED SON OF A LIVERY STABLE KEEPER-- . . .   370 EGO DOMINUS   V   61
THE ILL-BRED SON OF A LIVERY STABLE-KEEPER-- . . .   370 EGO DOMINUS   V   61
FROM FATHER UNTO SON . . . .   421 MY TABLE   19
A PRAYER FOR MY SON . . . .   435 FOR MY SON   T
WOULD THINK HER SON, DID SHE BUT SEE THAT SHAPE . .   444 SCHOOL CHILDR   37
LIFT, EVERY MOTHER'S SON, ...   548 TO SAME TUNE 3 V   15
 . . . MAN, WOMAN, CHILD (A DAUGHTER OR A SON), . .   556 RIBH PATRICK   2
RECALL HIS TRINITY. A FATHER, MOTHER, CHILD (A DAUGHTER 556 RIBH PATRICK V   2
    OR A SON),
A SMALL OLD HOUSE, WIFE, DAUGHTER, SON, ...   577 WHAT THEN   12
AND THAT SHOULD MOTHER SEEK HER SON SHE'D HAVE BUT LITTLE 593 PILGRIM   12
    LUCK
AUGUSTA GREGORY'S SON: HER SISTER'S SON, ...   602 GALLERY REVIS   21
AUGUSTA GREGORY'S SON: HER SISTER'S SON, ...   602 GALLERY REVIS   21
I CALL ON THOSE THAT CALL ME SON, ...   604 YOU CONTENT   1
NO, NO, MY SON, NOT YET: . . . .   614 MARCH SONGS 2   8
NO, NO, MY SON, NOT YET: . . . .   615 MARCH SONGS 2   18
NO, NO, MY SON, NOT YET: . . . .   615 MARCH SONGS 2   28
THAT ANCIENT MOTHER CRIES, "SPEAK NOT, MY SON. . .   711 FERENCZ RENYI   56
HUSH'D THE FISHERS, TILL A MOTHER CALLS BY NAME HER DROWNED 719 PHANTOM SHIP 23
    SON:
NOT I, NOR MAINE THERE, NOR DUACH'S SON. . . . . .   748 SHADOW WATER A   22
LIKE SON TO FATHER . . . .   769 BLOOD BOND   V   2
LIKE SON TO FATHER. . . . .   770 BLOOD BOND   3
SONG   SEE LOVE-SONG MARRIAGE-SONG DAWN-SONG
I NE'ER LOVED ANY TILL SONG BROUGHT ME . . . . .   7 OISIN 1   V   69
AS THUS OUR SONG AROSE: "YOU STARS, ...   22 OISIN 1   329
AS THUS OUR SONG AROSE: "YE STARS, ...   22 OISIN 1   V   329
TROUBLED HER SONG. I DO NOT KNOW IF DAYS . . . .   30 OISIN 2   19
BUT NOW THE LYING CLERICS MURDER SONG . . . . . .   42 OISIN 2   196
PATRICK, BEFORE THY CRAFT DIES EACH OLD SONG. . . .   42 OISIN 2   V   196
AND NEVER A SONG SANG NIAMH, AND OVER MY FINGER-TIPS   47 OISIN 3   6
 . . . WITH RED LIPS MURMURING A SONG, ...   58 OISIN 3   V   158
THE SONG OF THE HAPPY SHEPHERD . . . .   64 HAPPY SHEPHERD   T
SONG OF THE LAST ARCADIAN . . . .   64 HAPPY SHEPHERD V   T
AN INDIAN SONG . . . .   77 INDIAN TO LOVE V   T
OF MY LONG SPEAR WITH SONG AND LAUGH . . . . . .   84 MAD KING GOLL V   34
AND SONG THAT DOWN THE VALLEYS ROLLED-- . . . . .   84 MAD KING GOLL V   35
AND SONG THAT DOWN THE VALLEY ROLLED-- . . . . .   84 MAD KING GOLL V   35
THE SONG OF OUTLAWS AND THEIR FEAR: . . . .   85 MAD KING GOLL V   64
AN OLD SONG RE-SUNG . . . .   90 SALLEY GARDENS V   T
A SONG INTO THE AIR, AND SINGING PASSED . . . . .   114 ROSE OF BATTLE   14
A SONG INTO THE AIR, AND SINGING PAST . . . . . .   114 ROSE OF BATTLE V   14
A FAERY SONG . . . .   115 FAERY SONG   T
A CRADLE SONG . . . .   118 CRADLE SONG   T
AND THE LOUD SONG OF THE EVER-SINGING LEAVES . . .   120 SORROW OF LOVE V   3
SONG . . . .   124 CATHLEEN PARA V   T
MURMURING A WIZARD SONG FOR THEE. . . . .   134 TWO TREES   12
BALLAD AND STORY, RANN AND SONG: . . . .   137 TO IRELAND   4
O'DRISCOLL DROVE WITH A SONG . . . .   143 HOST OF AIR   1
TWO POEMS CONCERNING PEASANT VISIONARIES A CRADLE SONG 146 UNAPPEAS HOST V   T
THE SONG OF WANDERING AENGUS . . . .   149 WANDER AENGUS   T
A MAD SONG . . . .   149 WANDER AENGUS V   T
THE SONG OF THE OLD MOTHER . . . .   150 OLD MOTHER   T
AND HER RED LIPS SANG THEM A LOVE SONG. . . . . . .   160 CAP AND BELLS V   27
IN A TUMULTUOUS SONG": . . . .   163 ASKS FORGIVE   20
BUT WEIGH THIS SONG WITH THE GREAT AND THEIR PRIDE: 166 EVIL OF BELOV   4
SONG . . . .   172 PLEADS FRIEND V   T
BEND DOWN AND PRAY FOR ALL THAT SIN I WOVE IN SONG,   173 SPEAKS HEARERS   5
WHEN SONG I WOVE FOR MY BELOVED HIDES THE PRAYER,   173 SPEAKS HEARERS V   2
BEND DOWN AND PRAY FOR THE GREAT SIN I WOVE IN SONG,   173 SPEAKS HEARERS V   5
SONG OF MONGAN . . . .   177 PAST GREATNESS V   T
RED HANRAHAN'S SONG ABOUT IRELAND . . . .   206 HANRAHANS SONG   T
THE SONG OF RED HANRAHAN . . . .   206 HANRAHANS SONG V   T
LIKE AN OLD SONG. . . . .   211 O DO NOT LOVE   4
LIKE AN OLD SONG. . . . .   212 O DO NOT LOVE   12
AND ALL THAT MURMURING IS BUT A MARRIAGE SONG: . .   244 SHADOW WATER B V   452
WHAT COULD I BUT TAKE UP THE SONG? . . . .   254 HIS DREAM   14
NOTHING TO MAKE A SONG ABOUT BUT KINGS, ...   257 RECONCILIATION   5
A DRINKING SONG . . . .   261 DRINKING SONG   T
I HAD NOT GIVEN A PENNY FOR A SONG . . . .   267 ALL TEMPT ME   6
THE YOUNG MAN'S SONG . . . .   268 BROWN PENNY   V   T
THEY SANG A DROWSY SONG, OR SNORED, ...   271 GREY ROCK   16
AND SANG A DROWSY SONG, OR SNORED, ...   271 GREY ROCK   V   16
BUT NEVER MADE A POORER SONG . . . .   273 GREY ROCK   55
A SONG FROM "THE PLAYER QUEEN" . . . .   308 PLAYER QUEEN   T
THE PLAYER QUEEN SONG FROM AN UNFINISHED PLAY . .   308 PLAYER QUEEN   V   T
I MADE MY SONG A COAT . . . .   320 COAT   1

	PAGE	TITLE	LINE
SONG (CONTINUED)			
SONG, LET THEM TAKE IT, ...	320	COAT	8
A SONG	334	SONG	T
WHEN HER SON'S TURN WAS OVER. SING YOUR SONG. . . .	340	SHEP GOATHERD	42
LUXURIANT SONG, WHY SHOULD YOU LEAVE THE LAMP . . .	370	EGO DOMINUS	62
TRUE SONG, THOUGH SPEECH: "MINE AUTHOR SUNG IT ME." . .	373	PHASES OF MOON	30
SING OUT THE SONG; SING TO THE END, AND SING	374	PHASES OF MOON	56
HAVE YOU NOT ALWAYS KNOWN IT? THE SONG WILL HAVE IT	374	PHASES OF MOON	65
ANOTHER SONG OF A FOOL	381	SONG OF FOOL	T
AND AFTER THAT ARRANGED IT IN A SONG	384	VISION ROBART	65
YET I NUMBER HIM IN THE SONG;	393	EASTER 1916	35
OR CALUMNY A SONG. HOW CAN THEY KNOW	398	LEADERS CROWD	7
--THOSE DYING GENERATIONS--AT THEIR SONG, ...	407	SAIL BYZANTIUM	3
A PEASANT GIRL COMMENDED BY A SONG, ...	410	TOWER	34
SO GREAT A GLORY DID THE SONG CONFER.	410	TOWER	40
STRANGE, BUT THE MAN WHO MADE THE SONG WAS BLIND; . .	411	TOWER	49
AND THERE SING HIS LAST SONG.	414	TOWER	144
SOUNDS LIKE AN OLD SONG.	457	SECRETS OF OLD	6
. . . THROUGH TORCHLIGHT AND TUMULTUOUS SONG; . .	459	FROM OEDIPUS	8
. . . THROUGH TORCH-LIGHT AND TUMULTUOUS SONG; .	459	FROM OEDIPUS V	8
AT THE GREAT BOOK OF SAPPHO'S SONG; BUT NO, . . .	461	HARUN RASHID	12
MUST KEEP THAT PERFECT, AS THEY KEEP HER SONG, . . .	461	HARUN RASHID	18
THOUGH THE GREAT SONG RETURN NO MORE	485	NINETEENTH CEN	1
NIGHT RESONANCE RECEDES, NIGHT-WALKERS' SONG . . .	497	BYZANTIUM	3
NIGHT'S RESONANCE RECEDES, NIGHT-WALKERS SONG . . .	497	BYZANTIUM V	3
WHAT'S THE MEANING OF ALL SONG?	502	VACILLATION	70
GIRL'S SONG	515	GIRLS SONG B	T
SEVEN POEMS GIRL'S SONG	515	GIRLS SONG B V	T
TO SING A SONG OR TWO, ...	515	GIRLS SONG B	2
AND THAT WAS ALL MY SONG--	515	GIRLS SONG B	9
YOUNG MAN'S SONG	516	MANS SONG	T
UPON THE SUPREME THEME OF ART AND SONG!	523	LONG SILENCE	6
A SONG FOR MUSIC	524	DANCING DAYS V	T
THAT SONG ANNOUNCES DAWN.	536	PARTING	4
WHILE HIS LOUD SONG REPROVES	536	PARTING	7
ALL STATELY WOMEN MOVING TO A SONG	537	HER VISION	17
THREE SONGS TO THE SAME TUNE SECOND SONG	544	TO SAME TUNE 1 V	T
COME MARCH, SINGING THIS SONG, ...	544	TO SAME TUNE 1 V	REF
FIRST SONG	545	TO SAME TUNE 2 V	T
SINGING, SINGING A SONG.	546	TO SAME TUNE 2	16
THIRD SONG	547	TO SAME TUNE 3 V	T
MARCH, MARCH, LIFT UP THE SONG;	549	TO SAME TUNE 3	26
LIFT, LIFT, LIFT UP THE SONG.	549	TO SAME TUNE 3 V	26
ALTERNATIVE SONG FOR THE SEVERED HEAD IN . . .	549	SEVERED HEAD	T
HE THAT SINGS A LASTING SONG	553	PRAYER OLD AGE	3
THAT WERE A COWARDLY SONG, ...	554	CHURCH STATE	7
"NO, NOT ANOTHER SONG," SAID HE, ...	570	THREE BUSHES	36
"A LAUGHING, CRYING, SACRED SONG, ...	570	THREE BUSHES	43
A LECHING SONG," THEY SAID.	570	THREE BUSHES	44
DID EVER MEN HEAR SUCH A SONG?	570	THREE BUSHES	45
THE LADY'S FIRST SONG	572	LADYS 1ST SONG	T
THE LADY'S SECOND SONG	572	LADYS 2ND SONG	T
THE LADY'S THIRD SONG	573	LADYS 3RD SONG	T
THE LOVER'S SONG	574	LOVERS SONG	T
THE CHAMBERMAID'S FIRST SONG	574	MAIDS 1ST SONG	T
THE CHAMBERMAID'S SECOND SONG	575	MAIDS 2ND SONG	T
EVERY MAN THAT SINGS A SONG	586	PARNELLITES	19
WHAT ELSE HAVE I TO SPUR ME INTO SONG?	591	SPUR	4
MY FATHER SANG THAT SONG, ...	613	MARCH SONGS 1	8
MY FATHER SANG THAT SONG, ...	613	MARCH SONGS 1	18
MY FATHER SANG THAT SONG, ...	614	MARCH SONGS 1	28
SONG OF THE FAERIES	643	SONG FAERIES V	T
THE SHEPHERDS' CONTEST OF SONG	646	ISLE STAT I 1 V	T
I'LL QUENCH HIS SINGING WITH LOUD SONG--	647	ISLE STAT I 1	63
WITH FIERY SONG I'LL DROWN YON PUNY VOICE.	648	ISLE STAT I 1	81
YON EAGER LARK, THAT FILLS WITH SONG THE WHOLE . .	652	ISLE STAT I 2	18
IS SORROW IN HIS SONG, OR ANY CARE?	652	ISLE STAT I 2	20
NAY, NAY, ALMINTOR, YONDER SONG IS GLAD.	652	ISLE STAT I 2	23
AND WHEREFORE HAVE WE COME? A SONG TO HEAR. . . .	652	ISLE STAT I 2	27
BEYOND A MORTAL'S YEARS. I WAIT THE SONG	653	ISLE STAT I 2	48
WITH THAT SONG LEADING WHERE HARMONIC WOODS . . .	657	ISLE STAT I 3	43
IN SONG, FROM GOBLIN WATERS SWAYING WHITE, ...	657	ISLE STAT I 3	51
EACH CAME ONE MORN, WITH WELCOMING OF SONG, . . .	660	ISLE STAT II 1	42
HAVE CLOTHED THEIR TONGUES WITH SONG OF SONGLESS DAYS? . .	666	ISLE STAT II 3	17
AND HOLLOW LULLING THE YOUNG WINDS WITH SONG. . . .	675	ISLE STAT II 3	226
WHERE SAT OLD SUMMER FADING INTO SONG, ...	690	MOSADA 1 V	1B
WHITE LILIES, AND HER SONG FLEW FORTH AFAR	693	MOSADA 1	85
WILL YOU NOT HEAR MY LAST NEW SONG? HUSH, HUSH! . .	695	MOSADA 2	1
YOU'RE FULL OF WORDINESS. COME, HEAR MY SONG. . . .	696	MOSADA 2	8
A LITTLE MOORISH GIRL? SMALL WORTH. MY SONG-- . .	696	MOSADA 2	10
THAT SONG I'VE MADE. 'TIS OF AN IRISH TALE. . . .	696	MOSADA 2	19
THAT SONG I'VE MADE--IS OF A RUSSIAN TALE.	696	MOSADA 2 V	19
O SHINING ONES, LIGHTLY WITH SONG PASS, ...	708	FAIRY PEDANT	21
LOVE SONG	717	LOVE SONG	T
GIRL'S SONG	723	GIRLS SONG A V	T
I'D GLAD FOLKS' HEARTS WITH BLITHER SONG."	731	PRIEST FAIRY	82
A SONG OF THE ROSY CROSS	744	ROSY CROSS	T
SPINNING SONG.	770	SPINNING SONG	T
BUT IS EDAIN WORTH A SONG	773	SONG DEIRDRE 1	17
WHEN EVER I REMAKE A SONG, ...	778	FRIENDS WRONG	2

743

		PAGE	TITLE	LINE

SONG-BIRDS
    ROUND EVERY BRANCH THE SONG-BIRDS FLEW, ... 14 OISIN 1   180
    FOR ROUND EACH BRANCH THE SONG-BIRDS FLEW, ... 14 OISIN 1   V 180
SONGLESS
    I SAW THIS HARP ALL SONGLESS LIE, ... 85 MAD KING GOLL V 55
    HAVE CLOTHED THEIR TONGUES WITH SONG OF SONGLESS DAYS? . . 666 ISLE STAT II 3   17
SONG-RAPT
    MID BUBBLING LEAVES A WANDERING SONG-RAPT BIRD . . . . . 672 ISLE STAT II 3   154
    MID BABBLING LEAVES A WANDERING SONG-RAPT BIRD . . . . . 672 ISLE STAT II 3 V 154
SONG'S
    BUT THE ESCAPE, THE SONG'S NOT FINISHED YET, ... 377 PHASES OF MOON   117
    FOR THE SONG'S SAKE A FOOL? . . . . 553 PRAYER OLD AGE   8
SONGS   SEE WAR-SONGS
    "AND I WILL MAKE A THOUSAND SONGS, ... 7 OISIN 1   75
    BELOVED IN A THOUSAND SONGS. . . . . 7 OISIN 1   V 76
    DANAAN SONGS, AND THEIR DEWY SHOWERS . . . . 11 OISIN 1   135
    FOR FAIRY SONGS CONTINUALLY . . . . 11 OISIN 1   V 134
    HELD TO THE TOWERS WITH BOASTING SONGS AND GAY, ... 41 OISIN 2   V 184C
    . . . WITH ROARING OF LAUGHTER AND SONGS, ... 53 OISIN 3   87
    WITH MIRTHFUL SONGS BEFORE THE DAWN, ... 67 HAPPY SHEPHERD   49
    MY SONGS OF OLD EARTH'S DREAMY YOUTH! . . . . 67 HAPPY SHEPHERD   54
    WITH MIRTHFUL SONGS TILL RISE THE DAWN. . . . . 67 HAPPY SHEPHERD V 49
    AODH TO DECTORA   THREE SONGS . . . . 152 LOSS OF LOVE   V T
    THE LOVER SPEAKS TO THE HEARERS OF HIS SONGS IN COMING DAYS 173 SPEAKS HEARERS V T
    HANRAHAN SPEAKS TO THE LOVERS OF HIS SONGS IN COMING DAYS 173 SPEAKS HEARERS V T
    A LOVER SPEAKS TO THE HEARERS OF HIS SONGS IN COMING DAYS 173 SPEAKS HEARERS V T
    WHEN SONGS I WOVE FOR MY BELOVED HIDE THE PRAYER, . . . 173 SPEAKS HEARERS   2
    I READ IN MY BOOK OF SONGS . . . . 178 FIDDLER DOONEY   7
    I READ IN A BOOK OF SONGS . . . . 178 FIDDLER DOONEY V 7
    TWO SONGS OF A FOOL . . . . 380 SONGS FOOL 1   T
    TWO SONGS FROM A PLAY . . . . 437 SONGS PLAY 1   T
    FOUR SONGS FROM THE YOUNG COUNTRYMAN . . . . 451 FIRST LOVE   V T
    TWO SONGS FROM THE OLD COUNTRYMAN . . . . 454 EMPTY CUP   V T
    MORE SONGS OF AN OLD COUNTRYMAN . . . . 454 HIS MEMORIES V T
    THREE SONGS TO THE SAME TUNE . . . . 543 TO SAME TUNE 1   T
    THREE SONGS TO THE SAME TUNE   SECOND SONG . . . . . 544 TO SAME TUNE 1 V T
    TWO SONGS REWRITTEN FOR THE TUNE'S SAKE . . . . 550 SONGS REWRIT 1   T
    SUPERNATURAL SONGS . . . . 554 RIBH AT TOMB   T
    HOW COULD YOU SING THOSE SONGS OF LOVE? . . . . 569 THREE BUSHES   5
    THREE SONGS TO THE ONE BURDEN . . . . 605 SONGS BURDEN 1   T
    THREE MARCHING SONGS . . . . 613 MARCH SONGS 1   T
    THAT MIGHT ADORN OLD SONGS OR COURTLY SHOWS! . . . . . 629 CIRCUS ANIMALS   14
    OF THE SONGS THAT NEVER SLEEP. . . . . 647 ISLE STAT I 1   76
    I WEARY OF YOUR SONGS AND HUNTER'S TOYS. . . . . . . 651 ISLE STAT I 1   157
    NOW THEIR SONGS ARE MOURNFUL WHOLLY . . . . 667 ISLE STAT II 3   32
    WITH LITTLE VOICES SONGS OF FEARFUL THINGS. . . . . . 682 SEEKER   31
    AND, NODDING TO AND FRO, SANG SONGS OF LOVE, ... 688 TWO TITANS   35
    I'LL SING THE SONGS THE DUSKY LOVERS SING, ... 694 MOSADA 1   101
    SONGS FROM DEIRDRE . . . . 771 SONG DEIRDRE 1 V T
SON'S
    WHEN HER SON'S TURN WAS OVER. SING YOUR SONG. . . . . 340 SHEP GOATHERD   42
SONS
    WHAT ONE OF MAEVE'S NINE BRAWLING SONS . . . . 303 HOUR DAWN   36
    HAS ONE OF MAEVE'S NINE BRAWLING SONS . . . . 303 HOUR DAWN   V 36
SOON
    DRIPPED ON THE EARTH, BUT SOON, AH! SOON, ... 19 OISIN 1   V 279
    DRIPPED ON THE EARTH, BUT SOON, AH! SOON, ... 19 OISIN 1   V 279
    IN HONOUR SOON BY HIS MASTER'S SIDE . . . . 26 OISIN 1   V 399C
    AND "A WEARINESS SOON IS MY SPEED," SAYS THE MOUSE, . . . 27 OISIN 1   V 417
    SOON FAR FROM THE ROSE AND THE LILY . . . . 122 WHITE BIRDS   11
    AND AS SOON AS THE MORN HAD WHITENED, ... 160 CAP AND BELLS V 23
    HOW COULD WE BE SO SOON CONTENT, ... 193 BAILE AILLINN   95
    AND AS SOON FINISHED. ALL THAT EVER LOVED . . . . . 229 SHADOW WATER B   151
    ONE CANNOT BEGIN IT TOO SOON. . . . . 268 BROWN PENNY   16
    LOVE LOST AS SOON AS WON, ... 312 CHILD DANCING   8
    SOON TOPPLES DOWN THE HILL. . . . . 335 YOUNG BEAUTY   6
    SHOWS HER THAT SOME ONE SOON . . . . 364 END OF DAY   5
    SHOWS HER THAT SOMEONE SOON . . . . 364 END OF DAY   V 5
    BUT SOON A TEAR-DROP STARTED UP, ... 400 DEMON BEAST   21
    THOSE VEINS MUST SOON BE DRY; . . . . 513 JANE TALK BISH   4
    FOR SOON WE LIE WHERE HE IS LAID, ... 586 PARNELLITES   5
    AND THIS BROUGHT FORTH A DREAM AND SOON ENOUGH . . . . 630 CIRCUS ANIMALS   23
    SOON SHALL OUR WINGS BE STILLED, ... 643 SONG FAERIES   5
    O'ER MUCH I'VE TALKED: I SHALL BE SILENT SOON, ... 657 ISLE STAT I 3   75
    SOON WILT THOU SMILE, FOR HERE THE WINDS ARE WEAK . . . 671 ISLE STAT II 3   141
    SOON SHALL OUR WINGS BE STILLED, ... 676 ISLE STAT II 3   252
    SHEPHERDS, FAREWELL! HE SOON WILL BE--ASHES . . . . . 682 SEEKER   34
    BUT SOON MY WANDERING SHALL BE DONE I KNOW. . . . . . 682 SEEKER   V 21
    QUITE SOON THE CORNFIELD, WHERE THE POPPIES GROW, . . . 699 MOSADA 3   7
    SOON WILL THE CHURCHMEN NOD ABOVE THE CROWD, ... 699 MOSADA 3   19
    THE NOISY WORLD DIVIDES. HOW SOON A DEED . . . . . . 700 MOSADA 3   34
    OF MY DEAD CHILDREN SOON, WHATE'ER BETIDE, ... 712 FERENCZ RENYI   58
    I HAVE FORGOT IT ALL. HOW SOON DREAMS FADE! . . . . . 761 SHADOW WATER A   272
SOONER
    THEY'D SOONER LEAVE THEIR COSSETING . . . . 455 HIS MEMORIES   9
    THE SOONER LOVE IS GONE, ... 511 JANE AND JACK   4
    I AM NOT DUMB! I'D SOONER SILENT WAIT . . . . . . 646 ISLE STAT I 1   40
SOOT
    I COUNT THOSE FEATHERED BALLS OF SOOT . . . . 424 ROAD AT DOOR   11
SOOTH
    NOR SEEK, FOR THIS IS ALSO SOOTH, ... 65 HAPPY SHEPHERD   23

SOOTH   (CONTINUED)
   SEEK, THEN, FOR THIS IS ALSO SOOTH, • • • • • • • •   66 HAPPY SHEPHERD   31
   SING, THEN, FOR THIS IS ALSO SOOTH. • • • • • • • •   66 HAPPY SHEPHERD   44
   DREAM, DREAM, FOR THIS IS ALSO SOOTH. • • • • • • •   67 HAPPY SHEPHERD   57
   AND THE GREAT GREY LYNX'S SKIN! IN SOOTH, METHINKS • • • 650 ISLE STAT I 1   151
   HAVE DONE THIS PHRASING, AND SAY WHY, IN SOOTH, • • • • 652 ISLE STAT I 2   25
   I LIKE YOU, AND, IN SOOTH I KNOW NOT WHY. • • • • • •   661 ISLE STAT II 1   64
SOOTHE
   THAT I MAY SOOTHE THAT HAPLESS FAUN • • • • • • • •   67 HAPPY SHEPHERD V   47
SOOTHED   SEE EVE-SOOTHED
   AND CALLED HIM SWEETEST NAMES AND SOOTHED HIS FEARS. • •   30 OISIN 2   V   27
SOOTY
   LIKE SOOTY FINGERS, MANY A TREE • • • • • • • • •   13 OISIN 1   171
   TREE, LIKE A SOOTY FINGER, STARTS FROM THE EARTH; • • • 410 TOWER   19
SOPHOCLES
   "I LAUGHED UPON THE LIPS OF SOPHOCLES, • • • • • • •   686 LIFE   17
   "I LAUGHED UPON THE LIPS OF SOPHOCLES, • • • • • • •   735 QUATRAIN APHOR   19
SORACA
   OF THE HIGH PEOPLE OF SORACA NOR IN GLAMOUR BY DEMONS   50 OISIN 3   V   50
      FLUNG,
SORDID
   SORDID SORROWS OF THE MART, • • • • • • • • • • •   733 STREET DANCERS   59
SORE
   A BEECH-BOUGH TO ME, AND MY HEART GREW SORE, • • • • •   44 OISIN 2   226
   A BEECH BOUGH TO ME, AND MY HEART GREW SORE, • • • • •   44 OISIN 2   V   226
   AND NOW MY HEART IS SORE. • • • • • • • • • • •   322 SWANS AT COOLE   14
   NINE NIGHTS I LAY IN LONGING SORE • • • • • • • •   551 SONGS REWRIT 1 V   13
   NINE NIGHTS I LAY AND IN LONGING SORE • • • • • • •   551 SONGS REWRIT 1 V   13
   HIS BONDS AWAY, SORE STRUGGLING. NOW AT LAST • • • • • 714 FERENCZ RENYI   116
SORREL-COVERED
   OVER THE SORREL-COVERED WOLD-- • • • • • • • • • •   716 FAIRY DOCTOR   2
SORRELS
   IN THE ROOTS OF THE GRASSES, THE SORRELS, I LAID MY BODY   52 OISIN 3   73
      AS LOW:
SORROW
   WE RODE IN SORROW, WITH STRONG HOUNDS THREE, • • • • •   2 OISIN 1   V   7C
   MY HUMAN SORROW HER WHITE ARMS WOUND. • • • • • • •   11 OISIN 1   138
   A SORROW WRAPPED EACH MERRY FACE, • • • • • • • •   17 OISIN 1   235
   NOR SORROW WITH HER OSPREY CLAW. • • • • • • • •   19 OISIN 1   V   285
   OR THE GREY WANDERING OSPREY SORROW." • • • • • • •   20 OISIN 1   303
   OR THE WILD GREY OSPREY SORROW." • • • • • • • •   20 OISIN 1   V   303
   NOR THE GREY WANDERING OSPREY SORROW." • • • • • • •   21 OISIN 1   319
   OR THE WILD GREY OSPREY SORROW." • • • • • • • •   21 OISIN 1   V   319
   NOR THE GREY WANDERING OSPREY SORROW." • • • • • • •   23 OISIN 1   342
   OR FEAR THE WILD GREY OSPREY SORROW." • • • • • • •   23 OISIN 1   V   342
   WITH ALL THE ANCIENT SORROW OF MEN"; • • • • • • •   25 OISIN 1   381
   THE OSPREY OF SORROW GOES AFTER AND CLUTCHES, • • • •   27 OISIN 1   V 415D
   OF RAVENING SORROW, OR THE HAND OF WRATH? • • • • •   42 OISIN 2   199
   WERE THE MEMORIES OF THE WHOLE OF MY SORROW • • • •   52 OISIN 3   71
   • • • AND I KNEW HOW MEN SORROW AND PASS. • • • •   59 OISIN 3   175
   THERE WAS A MAN WHOM SORROW NAMED HIS FRIEND, • • • •   67 SAD SHEPHERD   1
   AND HE, OF HIS HIGH COMRADE SORROW DREAMING, • • • •   67 SAD SHEPHERD   2
   AND HE, OF HIS HIGH KINSMAN SORROW DREAMING, • • • •   67 SAD SHEPHERD V   2
   AND THEN THE MAN WHOM SORROW NAMED HIS FRIEND • • • •   68 SAD SHEPHERD   8
   AND THEN THE MAN WHOM SORROW NAMED HIS FRIEND • • • •   68 SAD SHEPHERD   17
   THEN CRIED THE MAN WHOM SORROW NAMED HIS FRIEND! • • •   68 SAD SHEPHERD V   8
   "I MAKE THE CLOAK OF SORROW: • • • • • • • • •   69 CLOAK BOAT   2
   SHALL BE THE CLOAK OF SORROW, • • • • • • • • •   69 CLOAK BOAT   4
   THE CLOAK I WEAVE OF SORROW: • • • • • • • • •   69 CLOAK BOAT V   2
   "I BUILD A BOAT FOR SORROW: • • • • • • • • •   70 CLOAK BOAT   7
   SAILETH THE ROVER SORROW. • • • • • • • • • •   70 CLOAK BOAT   9
   "I WEAVE THE SHOES OF SORROW: • • • • • • • • •   70 CLOAK BOAT   12
   IN ALL MEN'S EARS OF SORROW, • • • • • • • • •   70 CLOAK BOAT   14
   A BOAT I BUILD FOR SORROW: • • • • • • • • •   70 CLOAK BOAT V   7
   THE SANDALS THESE OF SORROW: • • • • • • • • •   70 CLOAK BOAT V   12
   IN EACH MAN'S EARS OF SORROW-- • • • • • • • •   70 CLOAK BOAT V   14
   WHO IS AMRITA? SORROW OF ALL SORROWS! • • • • •   71 ANASHU VIJAYA   15
   ARE BOWED IN SORROW UNDER PENDULOUS LIDS, • • • • •   79 EPHEMERA   2
   ARE BOWED IN SORROW UNDER THEIR TREMBLING LIDS, • • •   79 EPHEMERA   V   2
   VEILED IN A DREAMY SORROW FOR THEIR LOVE • • • • •   79 EPHEMERA   V   2A
   MY SORROW! FOR MANY A CREAK GAVE THE CREEL IN THE CART • •   91 OLD FISHERMAN   6
   ARE WITH NEW SORROW WRUNG! • • • • • • • • •   99 FOXHUNTER   38
   UPON HIS HEAD TO CAST AWAY MY SORROW. • • • • • •   102 FERGUS DRUID   14
   AH! DRUID, DRUID, HOW GREAT WEBS OF SORROW • • • •   104 FERGUS DRUID   39
   UPON THE WHARVES OF SORROW, AND HEARD RING • • • •   115 ROSE OF BATTLE   27
   THE SORROW OF LOVE • • • • • • • • • • • •   119 SORROW OF LOVE   T
   WHERE TIME WOULD SURELY FORGET US, AND SORROW COME NEAR   122 WHITE BIRDS   10
      US NO MORE:
   WHERE SURELY TIME WOULD FORGET US AND SORROW COME NEAR   122 WHITE BIRDS V   10
      US NO MORE:
   MAY SET A STONE UPON ANCESTRAL SORROW! • • • • •   130 BOOK STORIES   11
   AH, WORLD-WIDE NATION, ALWAYS GROWING SORROW, • • •   130 BOOK STORIES V   11
   AH, WORLDWIDE NATION, ALWAYS GROWING SORROW! • • •   130 BOOK STORIES V   11
   WHO SIGH WITH MINGLED SORROW AND CONTENT, • • • •   136 TO SOME I TALK   7
   AND SORROW AWAY, AND CALLING BARD AND CLOWN • • •   170 SECRET ROSE   20
   O, WHEN SHALL SORROW WANDER NO MORE IN THE LAND • •   174 ELEMENT POWERS V   5
   AND BLEW ME HITHER TO MY LASTING SORROW, • • • •   235 SHADOW WATER B   288
   YOU HAD ENOUGH OF SORROW BEFORE DEATH-- • • • •   293 TO A SHADE   23
   AS THOUGH MY SORROW WERE A SCENE • • • • • • •   452 HUMAN DIGNITY   5
   STRONG DRINK I HAD, AND IT BROUGHT ME TO SORROW, • • •   544 TO SAME TUNE 1   13
   STRONG DRINK I HAD, AND IT BROUGHT ME TO SORROW, • • •   616 MARCH SONGS 3   13

```
                                              PAGE     TITLE            LINE

SORROW   (CONTINUED)
    LOVE AND SORROW, ONE EXISTENCE,  . . . . . . .    647 ISLE STAT I 1      73
    ALL RHAPSODY HATH SORROW FOR ITS SOUL. . . . . .   652 ISLE STAT I 2      17
    IS SORROW IN HIS SONG, OR ANY CARE?  . . . . . .   652 ISLE STAT I 2      20
    I HEAR THE WHOLE SKY'S SORROW IN ONE VOICE.  . .   652 ISLE STAT I 2      22
    AYE, VERY LATELY, SORROW CAME TO WEEP  . . . . .   659 ISLE STAT II 1     25
    WITHIN MINE HEART; AND NAUGHT BUT SORROW NOW  . .  659 ISLE STAT II 1     26
    OF HUMAN SORROW LET THEM MORALIZE;  . . . . . .    663 ISLE STAT II 2     31
    O'ER GRIEF.  THE WORLD DRINKS SORROW FROM THE BEAMS  664 ISLE STAT II 2   46
    THE CLOAK I WEAVE OF SORROW.  . . . . . . . . .    666 ISLE STAT II 3      2
    SHALL BE THE CLOAK OF SORROW. . . . . . . . . .    666 ISLE STAT II 3      4
    A BOAT I BUILD FOR SORROW.  . . . . . . . . . .    666 ISLE STAT II 3      7
    SAILETH THE ROVER SORROW. . . . . . . . . . . .    666 ISLE STAT II 3      9
    THE SANDALS THESE OF SORROW,  . . . . . . . . .    666 ISLE STAT II 3     12
    IN EACH MAN'S EARS OF SORROW, . . . . . . . . .    666 ISLE STAT II 3     14
    SORROW THAT GIVES FOR GUERDON LIBERTY,  . . . .    686 DRAWING-ROOM        6
    POOR LOVE AND SORROW, WITH THEIR ARMS THROWN ROUND 703 MOSADA 3          119
    HAST THOU NOT KNOWN ALL SORROW AND DELIGHT  . .    723 KANVA ON SELF       2
    THOUGHTLESS JOY AND SORROW SAGE.  . . . . . . .    733 STREET DANCERS     47
    SORROW, THAT GIVES FOR GUERDON LIBERTY, . . . .    734 QUATRAIN APHOR      6
    WALKS IN THE VESTURE OF HER SISTER SORROW.  . .    735 QUATRAIN APHOR     28
    AND ALL HER STARLIGHT IS WITH SORROW MAD, . . .    738 YOU ARE SAD         3
    AND STOOD IN MY SORROW APART. . . . . . . . . .    744 GLOVE CLOAK         2
    WOULD OVERCOME YOUR SORROW AND YOUR DREAMS. . .    749 SHADOW WATER A     52
SORROWED      SEE MANY-SORROWED
SORROWFUL
    EARTH'S ALIENS.  WHY SO SORROWFUL?  OUR SOULS . .   80 EPHEMERA       V  12A
    BUILDING A SORROWFUL LOVELINESS . . . . . . . .    158 BELOVED RHYMES      5
    OF SORROWFUL, AUSTERE, SWEET, LOFTY PIPE TUNES.    341 SHEP GOATHERD      57
    O SISTER OF SORROWFUL GAZE! . . . . . . . . . .    706 FAIRY PEDANT        2
SORROWING
    GROW GENTLE WITHOUT SORROWING, . . . . . . . . .   193 BAILE AILLINN     110
SORROWINGS
    GROW GENTLE WITHOUT SORROWINGS;  . . . . . . . .   193 BAILE AILLINN   V 110
SORROWS
    ON THE OLD SORROWS OF HIS HUMAN DAYS. . . . . .     29 OISIN 2        V  12
    WHO IS AMRITA?  SORROW OF ALL SORROWS!  . . . .     71 ANASHU VIJAYA      15
    THE SORROWS OF THE WORLD BOW DOWN MY HEAD, . . .   104 FERGUS DRUID   V 38A
    AND ALL THE SORROWS OF HER LABOURING SHIPS, . .    120 SORROW OF LOVE V   7
    AND LOVED THE SORROWS OF YOUR CHANGING FACE;  .    121 YOU ARE OLD         8
    WITH THEIR UNHUMAN SORROWS.  CEASE! NO MORE!  .     661 ISLE STAT II 1     58
    BLINDER SORROWS, HARDER WAGE-- . . . . . . . . .   733 STREET DANCERS     58
    SORDID SORROWS OF THE MART. . . . . . . . . . .    733 STREET DANCERS     59
    SORROWS SAPPING BRAIN AND HEART.  . . . . . . .    733 STREET DANCERS     60
    THOUGHTLESS JOYS AND SORROWS SAGE.  . . . . . .    733 STREET DANCERS  V  47
SORROW-WORN
    SORROW-WORN, YET PLACID-BROWED.  . . . . . . . .   733 STREET DANCERS     56
    SORROW-WORN, YET PLACID BROWED. . . . . . . . .    733 STREET DANCERS  V  56
SORRY
    SORRY PLACE, WHERE FOR SWING OF THE WAR-AXE IN MY DIM EYES  61 OISIN 3    194
      . . .
    SHE MAY NOT BE TOO SORRY IN THE END. . . . . . .   232 SHADOW WATER B    232
    THAT MAYBE "I AM SORRY" IN PLAIN PROSE . . . . .   341 SHEP GOATHERD      60
    "I AM SORRY," SAID THE MAID.  . . . . . . . . .    595 COLONEL MARTIN     29
    WITHOUT MY GLASS I'D BE A SORRY CLOWN. . . . . .   721 WITCH VIVIEN       29
SORT
    TO BE "SOME SORT OF EVIDENCE", . . . . . . . . .   287 TO WEALTHY MAN      4
    GENERATIONS OF HIS SORT, . . . . . . . . . . . .   319 DOLLS               6
    WITH EVERY SORT OF COMPANY, . . . . . . . . . .    335 YOUNG BEAUTY        2
    OR SOMETHING OF THAT SORT HE SAID, . . . . . . .   338 TOM OROUGHLEY      14
    THE SORT OF BEAUTY THAT I HAVE APPROVED, . . . .   405 FOR DAUGHTER       50
    A SORT OF BATTERED KETTLE AT THE HEEL. . . . . .   409 TOWER              16
    A LEVELLING, RANCOROUS, RATIONAL SORT OF MIND . .  486 SEVEN SAGES        11
    A SORT OF BESOM THAT CAN CLEAR THE SOUL . . . . .  558 RIBH CHRISTIAN      5
    WHAT SORT OF MAN IS COMING  . . . . . . . . . .    572 LADYS 2ND SONG      1
    AND I BEAT UP THE COMMON SORT  . . . . . . . . .   605 SONGS BURDEN 1      3
    YOUNG MEN KNOW NOTHING OF THIS SORT, . . . . . .   626 OLD MEN BE MAD     16
    WITH ANY SORT OF CLOTHES, . . . . . . . . . . .    627 STATES HOLIDAY     28
    WITH SOME SORT OF VIOLENCE  . . . . . . . . . .    638 BEN BULBEN         34
    SCORN THE SORT NOW GROWING UP . . . . . . . . .    639 BEN BULBEN         70
SORTS
    ALL SORTS OF KINGS HAVE SAT . . . . . . . . . .    597 MODEL LAUREATE      2
    THAT MEN AND WOMEN OF ALL SORTS  . . . . . . . .   597 MODEL LAUREATE      3
SOUGHT
    SAVE DEER TOWARDS NOON THAT WATER SOUGHT. . . . .   17 OISIN 1        V 243
    AS THOUGH HIS HOUR WERE COME.  WE SOUGHT THE PART   37 OISIN 2          112
    SOUGHT ONCE AGAIN THE SHORE, AND FOUND A SHELL, .   68 SAD SHEPHERD       18
    SOUGHT ONCE AGAIN THE SHORE, AND CHOSE A SHELL, .   68 SAD SHEPHERD   V  18
    NO WOMAN'S LOVED ME, NO MAN SOUGHT MY HELP. . .    103 FERGUS DRUID       26
    WHO HAVE SOUGHT MORE THAN IS IN RAIN OR DEW  . .   114 ROSE OF BATTLE     16
    WHO SOUGHT THEE IN THE HOLY SEPULCHRE, . . . . .   169 SECRET ROSE         3
    WHO SOUGHT THEE AT THE HOLY SEPULCHRE, . . . . .   169 SECRET ROSE    V   3
    AND SOUGHT THROUGH LANDS AND ISLANDS NUMBERLESS YEARS, 170 SECRET ROSE    23
    NONE CLOSED HIS BLOOD-SHOT EYES BUT SOUGHT . . .   296 THREE BEGGARS      44
    LIES ONE LONG SOUGHT  . . . . . . . . . . . . .    310 WITCH               7
    IT SOUGHT ITSELF AND AFTERWARDS THE WORLD. . . .   376 PHASES OF MOON     95
    I SOUGHT MY BETTERS; THOUGH IN EACH  . . . . . .   506 REMORSE SPEECH      6
    I SOUGHT A THEME AND SOUGHT FOR IT IN VAIN,  . .   629 CIRCUS ANIMALS      1
    I SOUGHT A THEME AND SOUGHT FOR IT IN VAIN, . .    629 CIRCUS ANIMALS      1
    I SOUGHT IT DAILY FOR SIX WEEKS OR SO. . . . . .   629 CIRCUS ANIMALS      2
    THE PALE ANEMONES.  WE'VE SOUGHT ALL DAY, . . .    651 ISLE STAT I 2       5
```

746

```
                                                          PAGE    TITLE           LINE
SOUGHT  (CONTINUED)
      BY MANY SOUGHT, AND 'TIS A FOREST TALE,              653 ISLE STAT I 2        40
      WHO, SWIMMING, SOUGHT THE ISLAND LONE,               673 ISLE STAT II 3      181
      I SOUGHT THEE NOT.  MEN CALL ME INFAMY,              685 SEEKER               75
      I KNOW NOT WHAT I AM.  I SOUGHT THEE NOT,            685 SEEKER               76
      IN EVERY DANCE, BY CHILDREN SOUGHT.  "ACCURST,       709 FERENCZ RENYI        12
      GLAD, SIMPLE—NAY, HE SOUGHT NOT MYSTERY,             710 FERENCZ RENYI        30
SOUL
      "THE SOUL IS A DROP OF JOY AFAR,                       19 OISIN 1         V  276
      THE SOUL IS FREE, AND FINDS NO FLAW,                   19 OISIN 1         V  284
      MY ANGRY KING—REMEMBERING SOUL ONE JOT.               36 OISIN 2             94
      THERE WAS NO MIGHTIER SOUL OF HEBER'S LINE;            36 OISIN 2             95
      THEY STIRRED MY SPACIOUS SOUL IN ME NO JOT—            36 OISIN 2         V   94
      NOR SHOOK MY FIRM AND SPACIOUS SOUL ONE JOT;          36 OISIN 2         V   94
      MY ANGRY, KING REMEMBERING SOUL ONE JOT;              36 OISIN 2         V   94
      MY SOUL, ONCE GLORY OF ITS ANCIENT LINE,              36 OISIN 2         V   95
      "I HEAR MY SOUL DROP DOWN INTO DECAY.                  45 OISIN 2            235
      "AGE AFTER AGE I FEEL MY SOUL DECAY                    45 OISIN 2         V  235
      MY SOUL, MY PREY, AND THIS MY HEAPED PILE,             45 OISIN 2         V 239B
      BUT KNEEL AND WEAR OUT THE FLAGS AND PRAY FOR YOUR SOUL
         THAT IS LOST                                        63 OISIN 3            215
      . . . FOR THY SOUL THAT IS LOST,                       63 OISIN 3         V  215
      KNEEL, USHEEN, WEAR OUT THE FLAGS AND PRAY FOR YOUR SOUL
         THAT IS LOST                                        63 OISIN 3         V  215
      AND AS I SANG MY SOUL WAS FREE                         86 MAD KING GOLL   V   65
      BUT ONE MAN LOVED THE PILGRIM SOUL ·IN YOU,          121 YOU ARE OLD           7
      HE BADE HIS SOUL RISE UPWARD                         159 CAP AND BELLS         3
      HE MADE HIS SOUL GO UPWARD                           159 CAP AND BELLS    V    3
      AND THE HEART AND THE SOUL CAME THROUGH,             160 CAP AND BELLS        30
      THE HEART AND THE SOUL CAME THROUGH;                 160 CAP AND BELLS    V   30
      I SEE THE BLESSEDEST SOUL IN THE WORLD               168 BLESSED              31
      AND HAVE SEEN THE BLESSEDEST SOUL IN THE WORLD,      168 BLESSED          V   31
      THAT EVERY MAN SHOULD CARRY HIS OWN SOUL             235 SHADOW WATER B      299
      YOUR SOUL SHALL GIVE THE KISS.  I AM NOT AFRAID,     238 SHADOW WATER B      346
      WHEN NEITHER SOUL NOR BODY HAS BEEN CROSSED.         258 KING NO KING         16
      AGAINST A SOUL?                                      267 FRIEND ILLNESS        7
      A SINGLE SOUL THAT LACKS A SWEET CRYSTALLINE CRY.    291 PAUDEEN               8
      "AND MAKE MY SOUL BEFORE MY PATE IS BARE."           299 BEGGAR CRIED          4
      HER SOUL HAD SUCH DESIRE.                            317 NIGHT COME            2
      YOU HAVE MEASURED OUT THE ROAD THAT THE SOUL TREADS  342 SHEP GOATHERD        80
      WHEN HER SOUL FLIES TO THE PREDESTINED DANCING—PLACE 365 HER COURAGE           1
      MANACLE HIS SOUL UPON THE RED SEA BOTTOM.            372 ON GOING HOUSE       16
      THE THIRTEENTH MOON BUT SETS THE SOUL AT WAR         374 PHASES OF MOON       50
      THE SOUL BEGINS TO TREMBLE INTO STILLNESS,           374 PHASES OF MOON       54
      ALL THOUGHT BECOMES AN IMAGE AND THE SOUL            374 PHASES OF MOON       58
      BECOMES A BODY; THAT BODY AND THAT SOUL              374 PHASES OF MOON       59
      BODY AND SOUL CAST OUT AND CAST AWAY                 374 PHASES OF MOON       62
      BEYOND THE VISIBLE WORLD.  ALL DREAMS OF THE SOUL    374 PHASES OF MOON       63
      OF BODY AND SOUL.  THE LOVER'S HEART KNOWS THAT.     375 PHASES OF MOON       71
      WHO SHUDDER AND HURRY BY; BODY AND SOUL              375 PHASES OF MOON       77
      THE SOUL REMEMBERING ITS LONELINESS                 375 PHASES OF MOON       88
      UPON THE BODY AND UPON THE SOUL                      376 PHASES OF MOON       93
      THE SOUL RECOVERS RADICAL INNOCENCE                  405 FOR DAUGHTER         66
      SOUL CLAP ITS HANDS AND SING, AND LOUDER SING        407 SAIL BYZANTIUM       11
      AND BE THE SINGING—MASTERS OF MY SOUL.               408 SAIL BYZANTIUM       20
      AND BE THE SINGING MASTERS OF MY SOUL.               408 SAIL BYZANTIUM   V   20
      OUT OF HIS BITTER SOUL,                              415 TOWER               151
      NOW SHALL I MAKE MY SOUL,                            416 TOWER               181
      SYMBOLS OF THE SOUL,                                 420 MY HOUSE         V  20F
      THROUGH NATURAL DECLENSION OF THE SOUL,              423 MY DESCENDANTS       10
      COMPARES THE SOLITARY SOUL TO A SWAN;                430 NINETEEN 19          60
      I HAVE LOVED YOU BETTER THAN MY SOUL FOR ALL MY WORDS, 442 BLACK CENTAUR      14
      THE BODY IS NOT BRUISED TO PLEASURE SOUL,            445 SCHOOL CHILDR        58
      KNEW THAT WE'D HALVED A SOUL                         457 SUMMER SPRING         6
      THAT MAKE A MAN'S SOUL OR A WOMAN'S SOUL             465 HARUN RASHID         93
      THAT MAKE A MAN'S SOUL OR A WOMAN'S SOUL             465 HARUN RASHID         93
      ITSELF AND NOT SOME OTHER SOUL."  "THAT LOVE         465 HARUN RASHID         94
      IS A MAN'S MOCKERY OF THE CHANGELESS SOUL."          465 HARUN RASHID        102
      ITSELF AND NOT SOME OTHER SOUL.  "SUCH LOVE          465 HARUN RASHID     V   94
      WHEN UPWARD TURNED ON ONE SOUL IMAGE FELL,           471 ALL SOUL NIGHT   V   34
      A DIALOGUE OF SELF AND SOUL                          477 SELF AND SOUL         T
      WHO CAN DISTINGUISH DARKNESS FROM THE SOUL?          477 SELF AND SOUL         8
      A PROUD WOMAN NOT KINDRED OF HIS SOUL,               479 SELF AND SOUL        64
      WHAT'S WATER BUT THE GENERATED SOUL?                 490 COOLE BALLYLEE        8
      AND, LIKE THE SOUL, IT SAILS INTO THE SIGHT          490 COOLE BALLYLEE       19
      BODY AND SOUL";                                      510 JANE JUDGMENT         4
      WHAT MOST COULD SHAKE HIS SOUL;                      529 TOM CRUACHAN          3
      WHAT MOST CAN SHAKE HIS SOUL;                        529 TOM CRUACHAN     V    3
      I ANSWER THAT I GAVE MY SOUL                         538 LAST CONFESS          3
      HE FANCIED THAT I GAVE A SOUL                        538 LAST CONFESS          9
      BUT WHEN THIS SOUL, ITS BODY OFF,                    538 LAST CONFESS         15
      TO THIS BARE SOUL, LET ALL MEN JUDGE THAT CAN        542 PARN FUNERAL 1       30
      DEFENDING IRELAND'S SOUL.                            546 TO SAME TUNE 2        6
      IN BROKEN SENTENCES.  MY SOUL HAD FOUND              557 RIBH ECSTASY          3
      GODHEAD.  SOME SHADOW FELL.  MY SOUL FORGOT          557 RIBH ECSTASY          6
      A SORT OF BESOM THAT CAN CLEAR THE SOUL              558 RIBH CHRISTIAN        5
      THAT IS A LIGHT MY JEALOUS SOUL HAS SENT.            558 RIBH CHRISTIAN        8
      HOW SOUL MAY WALK WHEN ALL SUCH THINGS ARE PAST,     558 RIBH CHRISTIAN       11
      HOW SOUL COULD WALK BEFORE SUCH THINGS BEGAN.        558 RIBH CHRISTIAN       12
      THEN MY DELIVERED SOUL HERSELF SHALL LEARN           558 RIBH CHRISTIAN       13
      HATRED OF GOD MAY BRING THE SOUL TO GOD.             558 RIBH CHRISTIAN       18
```

SOUL   (CONTINUED)
    AT STROKE OF MIDNIGHT SOUL CANNOT ENDURE . . . . . .   558 RIBH CHRISTIAN   19
    HOW SOUL HAS WALKED BEFORE SUCH THINGS BEGAN. . . . .   558 RIBH CHRISTIAN V   12
    CONDUCT AND WORK GROW COARSE, AND COARSE THE SOUL, . . . 564 GYRES   17
    LOVED HIM WITH HER SOUL. . . . .   571 THREE BUSHES   55
    WHAT HURTS THE SOUL . . . .   572 LADYS 1ST SONG   9
    MY SOUL ADORES, ...   572 LADYS 1ST SONG   10
    HE SHALL LOVE MY SOUL AS THOUGH . . . .   572 LADYS 2ND SONG   8
    UNTROUBLED BY THE SOUL, ...   573 LADYS 2ND SONG   11
    SOUL MUST LEARN A LOVE THAT IS . . . .   573 LADYS 2ND SONG   15
    IF SOUL MAY LOOK AND BODY TOUCH, ...   573 LADYS 2ND SONG   19
    SPEAK NO EVIL OF THE SOUL, ...   573 LADYS 3RD SONG   3
    HER SOUL IN DIVISION FROM ITSELF . . . .   578 CRAZED GIRL   3
    THAT COME INTO MY SOUL AND ESCAPE . . . .   599 SPIRIT MEDIUM   3
    A SOUL INCAPABLE OF REMORSE OR REST: . . . .   601 GALLERY REVIS   7
    DEFENDING IRELAND'S SOUL. . . . .   613 MARCH SONGS 1   6
    HAD SHATTERED HER SOUL. PROPINQUITY HAD BROUGHT . . . . 619 BRONZE HEAD   18
    TO KEEP THE SOUL OF MAN ALIVE, ...   620 JOHN KINSELLA   19
    WHAT HOUR OF TERROR COMES TO TEST THE SOUL, ...   622 HOUND VOICE   11
    SHE, PITY-CRAZED, HAD GIVEN HER SOUL AWAY, ...   629 CIRCUS ANIMALS   19
    I THOUGHT MY DEAR MUST HER OWN SOUL DESTROY, ...   630 CIRCUS ANIMALS   21
    THEN STANDS IN JUDGMENT ON HIS SOUL, ...   633 MAN AND ECHO   33
    THAT OF RACE AND THAT OF SOUL, ...   637 BEN BULBEN   15
    BRING THE SOUL OF MAN TO GOD, ...   638 BEN BULBEN   40
    SADNESS, SOUL OF JOY MOST DEEP, ...   647 ISLE STAT I 1   74
    AND MY SOUL IN WAITING DIETH, ...   648 ISLE STAT I 1   87
    LIFT MY SOUL FROM RAYLESS NIGHT-- . . . .   648 ISLE STAT I 1   95
    MUSIC OF MY SOUL AND LIGHT-- . . . .   648 ISLE STAT I 1   97
    SUSTAINS HIS SOUL IN COURAGE OR IN MIGHT. . . . . . .   650 ISLE STAT I 1   144
    ALL RHAPSODY HATH SORROW FOR ITS SOUL. . . . . . .   652 ISLE STAT I 2   17
    THY SOUL SHALL BE, THOUGH PITILESS AND BRIGHT . . . .   674 ISLE STAT II 3   210
    MY SOUL. HIS DARKNESS AND HIS CHILL I FEEL. . . . .   684 SEEKER   V   63B
    THROUGH HIS SAD SOUL FOR EVER OLD AND YOUNG, ...   687 TWO TITANS   25
    DEEP IN HIS SOUL, LIKE RAIN UPON A SOIL . . . . . .   692 MOSADA 1   56
    HER SOUL FROM SEAS OF ENDLESS FLAME IN HELL. . . . .   698 MOSADA 2   47
    MY SOUL SHALL TOUCH WITH HIS, AND THE TWO FLAMES . . .   701 MOSADA 3   61
    CAST OFF THY HERESIES, AND SAVE THY SOUL . . . . .   701 MOSADA 3   64
    JUST NOW MY SOUL ROSE UP AND TOUCHED IT, FAR . . . .   705 REMEMBRANCE   13
    THE SOUL OF THE PITILESS PLACE . . . .   708 FAIRY PEDANT   30
    UPON MY SOUL, OLD TIME. NO: THUS IT STANDS. . . . .   722 WITCH VIVIEN   49
    THE SOUL UPON THE ASHES OF THE HEART." . . . . . .   735 QUATRAIN APHOR   16
    THE SEDENTARY SOUL . . . .   784 WOMANS BEAUTY   8
SOULED   SEE SUBTLE-SOULED
SOULLESS
    BUT SOULLESS A FAIRY DIES, ...   643 SONG FAERIES   2
    FOR SOULLESS A FAIRY DIES, ...   644 SONG FAERIES   14
    BUT SOULLESS A FAERY DIES, ...   676 ISLE STAT II 3   249
    FOR SOULLESS A FAERY DIES, ...   676 ISLE STAT II 3   261
SOUL'S
    THAT WORD OF THE SOUL'S PEACE--"ETERNITY." . . . . .   81 EPHEMERA   V   24B
    SOUL'S BEAUTY BEING MOST ADORED, ...   421 MY TABLE   22
    THE SOUL'S UNCHANGING LOOK: . . . .   422 MY TABLE   24
    THE SOUL'S OWN YOUTH AND NOT THE BODY'S YOUTH . . . .   464 HARUN RASHID   69
    ON THE SOUL'S JOURNEY. HOW IT IS WHIRLED ABOUT, . . .   472 ALL SOUL NIGHT   54
    THOUGHT IS A GARMENT AND THE SOUL'S A BRIDE . . . .   558 RIBH CHRISTIAN   16
    GARDENS WHERE A SOUL'S AT EASE: . . . .   639 BEN BULBEN   55
SOULS
    AND WEARY AND WORN ARE OUR SAD SOULS NOW: . . . . .   79 FALLING LEAVES   6
    EARTH'S ALIENS. WHY SO SORROWFUL? OUR SOULS . . . . .   80 EPHEMERA   V   12A
    BEFORE US LIES ETERNITY: OUR SOULS . . . .   81 EPHEMERA   23
    THIS WOULD I SAY, MOST WISE OF LIVING SOULS: . . . .   102 FERGUS DRUID   9
    AMID MEN'S SOULS, THAT WAVER AND GIVE PLACE . . . .   112 ROSE OF WORLD   7
    AMID MEN'S SOULS THAT DAY BY DAY GIVE PLACE, ...   112 ROSE OF WORLD   7
    THE SOULS OF THE DEAD . . . .   118 CRADLE SONG   V   4
    FOR SOULS WHO TIRE AND BLEED, ...   134 FR GILLIGAN   42
    TO SEE MEN'S SOULS BARTERED AND BOUGHT. . . . . . .   136 TWO TREES   V   36
    AND TALKED OF THE DARK FOLK WHO LIVE IN SOULS . . . .   136 TO SOME I TALK   4
    OF THAT DARK FOLK WHO GATHER IN THE SOULS . . . . .   136 TO SOME I TALK V   4
    ALL MANNER OF BLESSED SOULS, ...   167 BLESSED   14
    THE BLESSEDEST SOULS THAT WALK IN THE WORLD . . . .   167 BLESSED   19
    ALL MANNER OF BLESSEDEST SOULS, ...   167 BLESSED   V   14
    TILL THE ATTORNEY FOR LOST SOULS CRY HER SWEET CRY, . . 173 SPEAKS HEARERS   6
    DARK AND DULL AND EARTHY OUR SOULS AND BODIES BE: . . . 208 HANRAHANS SONG V   13
    AND SOULS AS IF THEY SWAM WITH SIGHS, ...   307 HOUR DAWN   102
    THAT BLEST SOULS ARE NOT COMPOSITE, ...   387 ROBARTES DANCE   44
    BE MIMICRY?" "WHAT MATTER IF OUR SOULS . . . . . .   464 HARUN RASHID   66
    THAN SOULS THAT START NO GAME AND TURN NO RHYME: . . .   464 HARUN RASHID   6a
    CAN BE NO MIMICRY. "WHAT IF OUR SOULS . . . . . .   464 HARUN RASHID   V   66
    ALL THESE ARE SOULS THAT FLY FROM THEIR DREAD SELVES. . 686 LIFE   4
    FOR THAT'S THE SWEETEST MUSIC FOR SAD SOULS, ...   702 MOSADA 3   85
    AND IMPORTUNE THEIR SOULS TO PENITENCE, ...   704 MOSADA 3   131
    "PRAY FOR THE SOULS IN PURGATORY," THE PALE PRIEST   719 PHANTOM SHIP   31
        TREMBLING CRIES.
    WHERE THE SOULS OF FAIRIES GO?" . . . .   729 PRIEST FAIRY   48
    ALL THESE ARE SOULS WHO FLY FROM THEIR DREAD SELVES. . . 734 QUATRAIN APHOR   4
    ALL THESE ARE SOULS THAT FLY FROM THEIR DREAD SELVES. . 734 QUATRAIN APHOR V   4
SOULS'
    ALL SOULS' NIGHT . . . .   470 ALL SOUL NIGHT   T
    AND IT IS ALL SOULS' NIGHT, ...   470 ALL SOUL NIGHT   3
    IT IS ALL SOULS' NIGHT AND THE GREAT CHRIST CHURCH BELL 470 ALL SOUL NIGHT V   1

		PAGE	TITLE	LINE
SOUND	SEE THUNDER-SOUND			
WHY DO YE SOUND NO HORN?" SHE SAID.		4 OISIN 1	V	33
OF PENSIVE LAUGHTER, UNHUMAN SOUND,		11 OISIN 1		136
AND A FAR SOUND OF FEATHERY QUIRES:		13 OISIN 1		166
A FAR VAGUE SOUND OF FEATHERY CHOIRS.		13 OISIN 1	V	166
AND NOW FLED BY, MIST-COVERED, WITHOUT SOUND,		29 OISIN 2		3
A HUNDRED SEASONS: FOR A SOUND OF TEARS		30 OISIN 2	V	18
CRAZED WITH ITS OWN INTERMINABLE SOUND.		30 OISIN 2	V	23A
DROPPING: A MURMUROUS DROPPING: OLD SILENCE AND THAT ONE SOUND:		48 OISIN 3		18
CAME SOUND FROM THOSE MONSTROUS SLEEPERS,		51 OISIN 3		58
. . . A SOUND LIKE THE STIRRING OF FLIES.		51 OISIN 3		58
. . . SLOW DROPPING A SOUND IN FAINT STREAMS		51 OISIN 3		67
. . . THE SOUND OF THE SEA'S VAGUE DRUM?		56 OISIN 3		135
WHERE EVER IS MURMUROUS DROPPING, OLD SILENCE AND THAT ONE SOUND:		56 OISIN 3		138
LATER A SOUND CAME, HALF LOST IN THE SOUND OF A SHORE FAR AWAY,		57 OISIN 3		155
LATER A SOUND CAME, HALF LOST IN THE SOUND OF A SHORE FAR AWAY,		57 OISIN 3		155
AND MIXED WITH THE SOUND OF THAT ROARER		60 OISIN 3	V	184
. . . THE SOUND OF TWO STUMBLING APART.		60 OISIN 3	V	184
THE DEWDROPS, FOR THE SOUND OF THEIR OWN DROPPING.		68 SAD SHEPHERD		16
THE DEW DROPS, FOR THE SOUND OF THEIR OWN DROPPING--		68 SAD SHEPHERD	V	16
IT QUENCHED, WITH SOUND LIKE FALLING DEW,		86 MAD KING GOLL		66
I HAVE OFTEN HEARD THE SWEET SOUND OF HIS BOW.		109 CUCHULAIN SEA		50
I OFTEN HEAR THE SWEET SOUND OF HIS BOW.		109 CUCHULAIN SEA	V	50
A MAN WITH A HAZEL WAND CAME WITHOUT SOUND:		153 CHANGE BELOVED		6
A MAN WITH A WAND OF HAZEL CAME WITHOUT SOUND:		153 CHANGE BELOVED	V	6
WORTH KNITTING TO A MEASURE OF SWEET SOUND?		181 QUEEN MAEVE		33
OR THE TWO STRINGS THAT MADE ONE SOUND		195 BAILE AILLINN		155
A KING AND A QUEEN ARE WANDERING THERE, AND THE SOUND		204 WITHER BOUGHS		19
YOU HAVE A DRUID CRAFT OF WICKED SOUND		237 SHADOW WATER B		342
YOU HAVE A DRUID CRAFT, WICKED SOUND		237 SHADOW WATER B	V	342
WITH A SLOW SMILE AND WITHOUT SOUND,		275 GREY ROCK		117
A SWEET, MIRACULOUS, TERRIFYING SOUND.		277 TWO KINGS		17
AND THERE HAD BEEN NO SOUND OF LIVING THING		279 TWO KINGS	V	54
THERE CANNOT BE, CONFUSION OF OUR SOUND FORGOT,		291 PAUDEEN		7
AND HE, WITH THAT LOW WHINNYING SOUND		318 APPOINTMENT		5
NIGHTLY, AND STARTLED BY THAT SOUND		326 ROBERT GREGORY		54
MOUTH MASTERED A SWEET SOUND,		331 ROUND TOWER		16
WHAT MADE THAT SOUND? A RAT OR WATER-HEN		372 PHASES OF MOON		8
"THE NIGHT HAS FALLEN: NOT A SOUND		389 SOLOMON WITCH		38
THEIR MAGNANIMITIES OF SOUND,		404 FOR DAUGHTER		44
THE SOUND OF THE RAIN OR SOUND		419 MY HOUSE		6
THE SOUND OF THE RAIN OR SOUND,		419 MY HOUSE		6
THAT MY MICHAEL MAY SLEEP SOUND,		435 FOR MY SON		2
WHEN ALEXANDER'S EMPIRE PASSED, THEY SLEPT SO SOUND.		442 BLACK CENTAUR		12
WHEN ALEXANDER'S EMPIRE PAST, THEY SLEPT SO SOUND.		442 BLACK CENTAUR	V	12
DIZZY WITH HARMONIOUS SOUND,		446 COLONUS PRAISE		7
AND MANY A LESSER BELL SOUND THROUGH THE ROOM:		470 ALL SOUL NIGHT		2
I NEED SOME MIND THAT, IF THE CANNON SOUND		471 ALL SOUL NIGHT		11
SOUND OF A STICK UPON THE FLOOR, A SOUND		491 COOLE BALLYLEE		25
SOUND OF A STICK UPON THE FLOOR, A SOUND		491 COOLE BALLYLEE		25
BELOVED, MAY YOUR SLEEP BE SOUND		522 LULLABY		1
SUCH A SLEEP AND SOUND AS FELL		522 LULLABY		13
OR SMOTE UPON THE STRING AND TO THE SOUND		537 HER VISION		15
NO COMMON INTELLIGIBLE SOUND		578 CRAZED GIRL		13
CAN PAY THE POET FOR A VERSE AND HEAR THE FIDDLE SOUND,		581 CURSE CROMWELL		21
SAW THAT THE GRAVE WAS DEEP, THE COFFIN SOUND,		609 IN TARAS HALLS		18
WITH NO MORE SOUND THAN THE MICE MAKE		618 LONG-LEG FLY		27
THAT HAD A SOUND FLY-FISHER'S WRIST		625 OLD MEN BE MAD		3
THAT HAD A SOUND FLY FISHER'S WRIST		625 OLD MEN BE MAD	V	3
CAST ON THE SOUND, ON, ON. THIS NIGHT OF GRAVES,		665 ISLE STAT II 2		71
MY SINKING BRAIN!--CEASE!--CEASE! HEARD YE YON SOUND?		665 ISLE STAT II 2		73
NAY, GIVE IT ME, AND I WILL SOUND A MEASURE:		681 SEEKER		9
DEAFENING US WITH IDLE SOUND--		727 LOVERS QUARREL		30
HOW LITTLE AND REEDY A SOUND AWAKES A GOD		760 SHADOW WATER A		252
AND OVERTURNED THE DEMON WITH A SOUND		762 SHADOW WATER A		283
SOUNDED				
HAD SOUNDED BETTER TO YOUR MOUNTAIN FANCY.		341 SHEP GOATHERD		61
THAT COGNOMEN SOUNDED BEST		440 WISDOM		18
HEARD YOU? YOUR LUTE HUNG IN THE WINDOW SOUNDED!		694 MOSADA 1		95
HEARD YOU? YOUR LUTE UPON THE WALL HAS SOUNDED!		694 MOSADA 1	V	95
SOUNDING	SEE SWEET-SOUNDING			
SOUNDLESS				
SOUNDLESS SHALL BE THE FOOTFALL LIGHT		70 CLOAK BOAT		13
SOUNDLESS SHALL BE THE FOOTFALL LIGHT		666 ISLE STAT II 3		13
SOUNDS				
SO PALE! AND SOUNDS OF WONDER HER LIPS UTTERED,		34 OISIN 2	V	71
DIE OFF THE FEEBLE SOUNDS!		99 FOXHUNTER	V	42
I HEAR LAKE WATER LAPPING WITH LOW SOUNDS BY THE SHORE!		117 ISLE INNISFREE		10
I HEAR LAKE WATER LAPPING WITH LOW SOUNDS ON THE SHORE!		117 ISLE INNISFREE	V	10
FOR TO ARTICULATE SWEET SOUNDS TOGETHER		205 ADAMS CURSE		10
SLEEP BEFORE THE THIRD NOON SOUNDS."		295 THREE BEGGARS		24
ALL SOUNDS BY BIRD OR ANGEL SUNG		387 SOLOMON WITCH	V	7
SOUNDS LIKE AN OLD SONG.		457 SECRETS OF OLD		6
SOUR				
"TAKE THE SOUR		510 JANE JUDGMENT		6
BREAD TASTE SOUR.		554 CHURCH STATE		12
THEIR MONEY SPENT, THEIR WINE GONE SOUR,		635 BLACK TOWER		3

SOURCE
    I AM CONTENT TO FOLLOW TO ITS SOURCE . . . . 479 SELF AND SOUL   65
    CONTENT TO TRACE THAT MISERY TO ITS SOURCE, ... 479 SELF AND SOUL V 65
    OUT OF A DESOLATE SOURCE, ... 518 HIS CONFIDENCE   11
SOURS
    THIS SULLEN PEASANT SOURS THE GOOD RED WINE. . . . . . 711 FERENCZ RENYI V 43
SOUTH
    SANG THAT SOMEWHERE TO NORTH OR WEST OR SOUTH . . . . . 127 DREAM OF FAERY   19
    SANG HOW SOMEWHERE TO NORTH OR EAST OR SOUTH . . . . . 127 DREAM OF FAERY V 19
    SANG HOW SOMEWHERE TO NORTH OR WEST OR SOUTH . . . . . 127 DREAM OF FAERY V 19
    THE SOUTH IS POURING DOWN ROSES OF CRIMSON FIRE! . . . . 154 BELOVED PEACE   6
    THE SOUTH WOULD COVER THEM WITH ROSES OF CRIMSON FIRE! . . 154 BELOVED PEACE V 6
    AND THAT MILD WOMAN OF THE SOUTH, ... 189 BAILE AILLINN   6
    THAT RUNNER SAID! "I AM FROM THE SOUTH! . . . . 191 BAILE AILLINN   47
    AND HURRYING TO THE SOUTH HE CAME . . . . 194 BAILE AILLINN V 128
    STRAYING TOO FAR INTO THE NORTH OR SOUTH, ... 226 SHADOW WATER B   86
    IF BUT THIS WIND WERE IN THE SOUTH." . . . . 306 HOUR DAWN   90
    NEITHER THE SPRING NOR THE SOUTH WIND . . . . 306 HOUR DAWN   95
    HE AND HIS FRIEND, THEIR FACES TO THE SOUTH, ... 372 PHASES OF MOON   2
    THE SOUTH WIND BROUGHT IT LONGING, AND THE EAST WIND   449 OWEN AHERNE   5
        DESPAIR,
    THE SOUTH WIND BROUGHT IT LONGING, AND THE EAST BROUGHT   449 OWEN AHERNE V 5
        IN DESPAIR,
    THE SOUTH WIND BROUGHT IT LONGING, AND THE EAST BROUGHT   449 OWEN AHERNE V 5
        IT DESPAIR,
    GREAT WINDOWS OPEN TO THE SOUTH, ... 475 EVA GORE-BOOTH   2
    THE SOUTH BREEZE NOW IN DYING FEARS . . . . 655 ISLE STAT I 3   13
    IN THE SOUTH SEA'S AZURE MILES, ... 732 STREET DANCERS   28
    IN THE SOUTH SEAS' AZURE MILES, ... 732 STREET DANCERS V 28
    MY FOSTER-MOTHER'S GARDEN IN THE SOUTH . . . . 758 SHADOW WATER A   227
    MY FOSTER MOTHER'S GARDEN IN THE SOUTH . . . . 758 SHADOW WATER A V 227
SOUTHERN
    OH WANDERER IN THE SOUTHERN WEATHER, ... 77 INDIAN TO LOVE V 1
    IN SOUTHERN LOCHLANN. I WOULD NOT OBEY . . . . . . 756 SHADOW WATER A V 191
SOUTHWARD
    SOUTHWARD A SEA-KING MASTERFUL . . . . 82 MAD KING GOLL V 15
SOWN   SEE SELF-SOWN GOLD-SOWN LEAF-SOWN
SPACE
    IN CLANGING SPACE A MOMENT HEARD, ... 65 HAPPY SHEPHERD   20
    'MID CLANGING SPACE A MOMENT HEARD . . . . 65 HAPPY SHEPHERD V 20
    WITH ALL YOUR WHIRLING HAIR, AND DROP THROUGH SPACE AN   73 ANASHU VIJAYA V 46
        AZURE TEAR.
    A LITTLE SPACE FOR THE ROSE-BREATH TO FILL! . . . . . 101 ROSE UPON ROOD   14
    OR BIRDS LOST IN THE ONE CLEAR SPACE . . . . 195 BAILE AILLINN   149
    OR BIRDS LOST IN ONE CLEAR SPACE . . . . 195 BAILE AILLINN V 149
    IS EDEN OUT OF TIME AND OUT OF SPACE? . . . . 218 WOODS OF COOLE   36
    A CLUMP OF BEECH TREES MADE AN EMPTY SPACE . . . . . 277 TWO KINGS V 4A
    IN SPACE, MADE EQUAL WITH A SIGH, WE MET. . . . . . 705 REMEMBRANCE   14
SPACIOUS
    THEY STIRRED MY SPACIOUS SOUL IN ME NO JOT-- . . . . . 36 OISIN 2 V 94
    NOR SHOOK MY FIRM AND SPACIOUS SOUL ONE JOT! . . . . . 36 OISIN 2 V 94
    THE SPACIOUS LOVES, THE ANGER WITHOUT SLEEP . . . . . 42 OISIN 2 V 194
    THE WOOD WAS SO SPACIOUS ABOVE THEM, ... 49 OISIN 3   37
    SO SPACIOUS THE WOOD WAS ABOVE THEM, ... 49 OISIN 3 V 37
    . . . THOUGH SPACIOUS HIS LANDS WERE AND STRONG. . . . . 58 OISIN 3 V 160
SPADE
    AND A SMALL AND A FEEBLE POPULACE STOOPING WITH MATTOCK   58 OISIN 3   164
        AND SPADE,
    AND A SMALL AND A FEEBLE RACE STOOPING WITH MATTOCK AND   58 OISIN 3 V 164
        SPADE.
    AND A SMALL AND FEEBLE RACE STOOPING WITH MATTOCK   58 OISIN 3 V 164
        AND SPADE.
    THAT WOULD LET THE SPADE LIE, ... 215 HAPPY TOWNLAND   30
    I CALL FOR SPADE AND HORSE AND HOUND . . . . 275 GREY ROCK   105
    I BEND MY BODY TO THE SPADE . . . . 599 SPIRIT MEDIUM   7
    I BEND MY BODY TO THE SPADE . . . . 600 SPIRIT MEDIUM   15
    I BEND MY BODY TO THE SPADE . . . . 600 SPIRIT MEDIUM   23
    ITS BOREDOM OF THE DESK OR OF THE SPADE, BECAUSE . . . . 621 HOUND VOICE   3
SPADES
    THE MAINES' CHILDREN DROPPED THEIR SPADES, AND STOOD . . 185 QUEEN MAEVE   120
    THE MAINES' CHILDREN HAVE NOT DROPPED THEIR SPADES . . . 186 QUEEN MAEVE   123
    SHARP THEIR SPADES, THEIR MUSCLES STRONG, ... 637 BEN BULBEN   22
    SHARP THEIR SPADES, THEIR MUSCLE STRONG, ... 637 BEN BULBEN V 22
SPAIN
    OR TRADING OUT OF GALWAY INTO SPAIN! . . . . 269 PARDON FATHERS   4
    THERE IS A QUEEN IN CHINA, OR MAYBE IT'S IN SPAIN, . . . 353 HIS PHOENIX   1
    THERE IS A QUEEN IN CHINA, OR MAY BE IT'S IN SPAIN, . . . 353 HIS PHOENIX V 1
SPAKE
    AND CAUGHT MY HANDS, BUT SPAKE NO WORD . . . . . . 25 OISIN 1   374
    AND CAUGHT MY HANDS AND SPAKE NO WORD . . . . . . 25 OISIN 1 V 374
    HE SPAKE ONCE MORE AND FONDLED WITH HIS LIPS . . . . . 81 EPHEMERA V 24A
    WITH THONGS OF LEATHER." AS SHE SPAKE IT WAS! . . . . 106 CUCHULAIN SEA V 17B
    AT LAST CUCHULAIN SPAKE, "SOME MAN HAS MADE . . . . . 109 CUCHULAIN SEA   47
    HE SPAKE TO THE YOUNG MAN, "IS THERE NO MAID . . . . . 109 CUCHULAIN SEA   58
    AT LAST CUCHULAIN SPAKE, "A YOUNG MAN STRAYS . . . . . 109 CUCHULAIN SEA V 47
    SPAKE THUS! "CUCHULAIN WILL DWELL THERE AND BROOD . . . 110 CUCHULAIN SEA   77
    MY BODY SPAKE, NOT I!" . . . . 132 FR GILLIGAN   12
    FOR ANY GENTLE THING SHE SPAKE, ... 191 BAILE AILLINN   63
    IGNORANT WHAT DRAMATIS PERSONAE SPAKE! . . . . . . 560 WHENCE COME   4
    THE FAIRIES' HERALD SPAKE ONCE MORE! . . . . 730 PRIEST FAIRY   53
    THUS SPAKE THE TOWN JAILOR . . . . 740 EARL PAUL   13

PAGE   TITLE   LINE

SPAN
    ENDURE WHAT LIFE GOD GIVES AND ASK NO LONGER SPAN! . . .   459 FROM OEDIPUS   1
SPANISH
    OR ON SPANISH POLITICS? . . . .   631 POLITICS   4
SPANS
    THREE SPANS HIGH AS HE ROSE TO HIS FEET, ...   729 PRIEST FAIRY   25
SPARE
    WHERE LOVE'S TO GIVE AND TO SPARE! . . . .   214 HAPPY TOWNLAND V   4
    WILL HE NOT SPARE HER LIFE? HOW WOULD ONE MATTER . . .   696 MOSADA 2   3
SPARED
    I WOULD HAVE SPARED HER HANDMAID, BUT SHE CAUGHT . . .   755 SHADOW WATER A   167
    I SPARED HER HANDMAID, TOO! BUT HALF WAY HITHER . . .   755 SHADOW WATER A V 167
SPARKLING
    FOR THE SPARKLING HOOVES THEY SANK NOT IN! . . . . .   10 OISIN 1   V 114A
SPARKS
    LIKE THE SPARKS BLOWN OUT OF A SMITHY, AND DIE? . . .   170 SECRET ROSE   30
SPARROW
    THE BRAWLING OF A SPARROW IN THE EAVES, ...   119 SORROW OF LOVE   1
    UPON THE TIME OF SPARROW CHIRP, ...   133 FR GILLIGAN   V 21
SPARROW-CHIRP
    UPON THE TIME OF SPARROW-CHIRP, ...   133 FR GILLIGAN   21
SPARROWS
    THE QUARREL OF THE SPARROWS IN THE EAVES, ...   119 SORROW OF LOVE V   1
    AND NOW THE SPARROWS WARRING IN THE EAVES, ...   120 SORROW OF LOVE V   9
    LARGER SPARROWS OF THE TOWN, ...   731 STREET DANCERS   5
SPARS
    ON THE DROWNED MEN'S HANDS AND FACES, ON THE SPARS AND   719 PHANTOM SHIP   22
    ON THE SAILS.
SPARTAN
    AS THE FOX IN THE OLD FABLE DESTROYED THE SPARTAN BOY'S,   580 CURSE CROMWELL   18
SPASM
    GODHEAD ON GODHEAD IN SEXUAL SPASM BEGOT . . . . .   557 RIBH ECSTASY   5
SPAT
    NEITHER TO SLAVES THAT WERE SPAT ON, ...   414 TOWER   130
    NOR TO THE TYRANTS THAT SPAT, ...   414 TOWER   131
SPAWN   SEE FROG-SPAWN
SPAWNING
    AND BY ITS FORMLESS SPAWNING FURY WRECKED, ...   611 STATUES   30
SPEAK
    AND NEVER FIND, THOUGH YE IN MUSIC SPEAK. . . . . .   42 OISIN 2   V 201
    SPEAK, YOU TOO ARE OLD WITH YOUR MEMORIES, ...   61 OISIN 3   196
    SPEAK, THOU TOO ART OLD WITH THY MEMORIES, ...   61 OISIN 3   V 196
    EACH OTHER ROUND IN CIRCLES, AND HEARD THE ELDEST SPEAK!   76 INDIAN ON GOD   5
    EACH OTHER ROUND IN CIRCLES! AND I HEARD THE ELDEST   76 INDIAN ON GOD V 5
        SPEAK!--
    AND PIERCED HIM. "SPEAK BEFORE YOUR BREATH IS DONE." . .   110 CUCHULAIN SEA   67
    A KING OF THE GREAT PLAIN WOULD SPEAK WITH YOU." . . .   183 QUEEN MAEVE   78
    THE MOUTHS THAT SPEAK, THE NOTES AND STRINGS, ...   212 BLESS PSALTER   2
    WITH THE EVER-LIVING. WHAT IF HE SPEAK THE TRUTH, . .   229 SHADOW WATER B 170
    SPEAK LOWER, OR THEY'LL HEAR. THEY CANNOT HEAR! . .   232 SHADOW WATER B 228
    NO, NO, NOR HALF A THOUGHT! BUT DO NOT SPEAK. . . .   245 SHADOW WATER B 478
    I WOULD NOT LET YOU SPEAK, FOR I WOULD KNOW . . . .   246 SHADOW WATER B 492
    HAD RUN INTO ONE FOUNTAIN. SPEAK TO HIM. . . . . .   249 SHADOW WATER B 561
    SPEAK--HE WILL NOT DENY IT. IS THAT TRUE? . . . . .   249 SHADOW WATER B 563
    IF BOOKS SPEAK TRUTH, IN SLIEVENAMON-- . . . . . .   271 GREY ROCK   V 15
    SPEAK IT, THAT I MAY SEND THROUGH THE WIDE WORLD . . .   281 TWO KINGS   97
    WHERE I MAY SPEAK TO YOU ALONE, MY CRAFT . . . . .   284 TWO KINGS   159
    SO WE SPEAK A DIFFERENT TONGUE. . . . .   313 TWO YEAR LATER   6
    AND I SPEAK A BARBAROUS TONGUE, ...   313 TWO YEAR LATER 12
    TILL WINTER BLASTS WERE GONE, BUT SPEAK OF HER . . .   340 SHEP GOATHERD   33
    WHO KNOW IT ALL RING AT HIS DOOR, AND SPEAK . . . .   373 PHASES OF MOON 21
    AND YET THEY SPEAK WHAT'S BLOWN INTO THE MIND! . . .   376 PHASES OF MOON 110
    "SPEAK ALL YOUR MIND," MY HEART SANG OUT, ...   450 OWEN AHERNE   21
    . . . "SPEAK ALL YOUR MIND! WHO CARES, ...   450 OWEN AHERNE   21
    IN AFTER TIME THEY WILL SPEAK MUCH OF ME . . . . .   462 HARUN RASHID   29
    AND SPEAK BUT FANTASY. RECALL THE YEAR . . . . .   462 HARUN RASHID   30
    AND SPEAK BUT PHANTASY. RECALL THE YEAR . . . . .   462 HARUN RASHID V 30
    AND SPEAK BUT LIES. CALL UP TO MEMORY . . . . . .   462 HARUN RASHID V 30
    CAN HEAR THE ARMED MAN SPEAK. . . . .   470 HARUN RASHID   193
    THAT STORMS ARE SHAKING, HEAR THE ARMED MAN SPEAK. . .   470 HARUN RASHID V 193
    ONE OR THE OTHER OUT AND SPEAK . . . .   475 EVA GORE-BOOTH 15
    OF BAILE AND AILLINN YOU NEED NOT SPEAK, ...   555 RIBH AT TOMB   6
    SURMOUNT THEIR BONES! BUT SPEAK WHAT NONE HAVE HEARD. .   555 RIBH AT TOMB   9
    SURMOUNTS THEIR BONES! BUT SPEAK WHAT NONE HAVE HEARD. .   555 RIBH AT TOMB V 9
    SPEAK NO EVIL OF THE SOUL. . . . .   573 LADYS 3RD SONG   3
    COME SPEAK YOUR BIT IN PUBLIC . . . .   582 ROGER CASEMENT 21
    HE WAS OUR ANCIENT GOD. IF I SPEAK LOW, ...   658 ISLE STAT I 3   78
    ALMINTOR WITH HER LOVE. WHO ART THOU?--SPEAK, . . .   660 ISLE STAT II 1 50
    AND WHY SO SILENT? I WOULD HAVE THEE SPEAK. . . . .   671 ISLE STAT II 3 140
    I KNOW NOT OF THE THINGS YOU SPEAK. BUT WHAT . . .   675 ISLE STAT II 3 239
    MY ECHOING HEART. NOW RAISE THY VOICE AND SPEAK! . .   683 SEEKER   47
    TO JOYS UNHUMAN, AND TO THEE--SPEAK! SPEAK! . . . .   684 SEEKER   60
    TO JOYS UNHUMAN, AND TO THEE--SPEAK! SPEAK! . . . .   684 SEEKER   60
    THOU WILT NOT SPEAK, AND I WITH AGE AM NEAR . . . .   684 SEEKER   62
    THOU WILT NOT SPEAK, OH CRUEL ART THOU YET! . . . .   684 SEEKER   V 69A
    HE IS NOT FAR. I'D HAVE HIM SPEAK FOR HER. . . . .   696 MOSADA 2   13
    EVER MORE TO SPEAK A WORD . . . .   697 MOSADA 2   32
    I SPEAK ALONE WITH SERVANTS OF THE CROSS . . . . .   698 MOSADA 2   48
    THE SOLDIER THUS, AND HAYNAU--"PEASANT, SPEAK . . .   711 FERENCZ RENYI 54
    THAT ANCIENT MOTHER CRIES, "SPEAK NOT, MY SON. . . .   711 FERENCZ RENYI 56
    SPEAK, FERENCZ, SPEAK. WE LOVE EACH OTHER. SEE, . .   713 FERENCZ RENYI 87

SPEAK   (CONTINUED)
    SPEAK, FERENCZ, SPEAK. WE LOVE EACH OTHER. SEE, ...   713 FERENCZ RENYI   87
    "AH, FERENCZ, SPEAK AND SAVE THYSELF AND ME! . . . . .   713 FERENCZ RENYI V   86
    THEN 'GAN TO SPEAK THAT GOBLIN RARE, ...   729 PRIEST FAIRY   37
    FOR I HAVE ALL HIS GARDEN WISDOM. O SPEAK! . . . . .   756 SHADOW WATER A   180
    ALL THAT TIME KNOWS. SPEAK TO ME, QUEEN. O SPEAK! . . .   756 SHADOW WATER A   180
    ALL THAT TIME KNOWS. SPEAK TO ME, QUEEN. O SPEAK! . . .   756 SHADOW WATER A V   180
SPEAKERS
    AND THEN THE SPEAKERS GOT IT . . . .   582 ROGER CASEMENT   15
SPEAKING
    TOWARDS THE HOUR FOR SPEAKING OF THE DEAD? . . . . .   276 TWO KINGS   V   0
    THE SPEAKING OF IT COULD BE NO GREAT WRONG, ...   281 TWO KINGS   104
    AND SPEAKING WHAT HE WOULD NOT THOUGH HE WOULD, ...   282 TWO KINGS   123
    "SPEAKING OF LOVE THROUGH OTHER LIPS AND LOOKING . . . .   283 TWO KINGS   155
    SPEAKING TO A DRUNKEN AUDIENCE HIGH NONSENSICAL WORDS! . .   577 LOFTY THINGS   6
SPEAKS
    FOR GOD HAS HEARD, AND SPEAKS HIS ANGRY MIND! . . . . .   42 OISIN 2   206
    THE LOVER SPEAKS TO THE HEARERS OF HIS SONGS IN COMING DAYS   173 SPEAKS HEARERS   T
    HANRAHAN SPEAKS TO THE LOVERS OF HIS SONGS IN COMING DAYS   173 SPEAKS HEARERS V   T
    A LOVER SPEAKS TO THE HEARERS OF HIS SONGS IN COMING DAYS   173 SPEAKS HEARERS V   T
    BUT GROWS MORE GENTLE WHEN HE SPEAKS HER NAME, ...   340 SHEP GOATHERD   29
    THE LOVER SPEAKS . . . .   449 OWEN AHERNE   V   T
SPEAR   SEE HUNTING-SPEAR
    WITH WHOM I HURLED THE HURRYING SPEAR, ...   10 OISIN 1   122
    BY MACE AND SPEAR AND SWORD OF SEA-GODS' NAILS . . . .   31 OISIN 2   V 30A
    AN ASHEN HUNTING SPEAR. . . . .   32 OISIN 2   56
    OR CARVE A DREADFUL SPEAR. . . . .   32 OISIN 2   V   56
    A LARCH-WOOD HUNTING SPEAR. . . . .   32 OISIN 2   V   56
    AN ASH-WOOD HUNTING SPEAR. . . . .   32 OISIN 2   V   56
    WERE ARROW AND SHIELD AND WAR-AXE, ARROW AND SPEAR AND   49 OISIN 3   V   30
       BLADE,
    OF MY LONG SPEAR, WITH SCREAM AND LAUGH, ...   84 MAD KING GOLL V   34
    OF MY LONG SPEAR WITH SONG AND LAUGH . . . . . .   84 MAD KING GOLL V   34
    THE PAIN OF WOUNDS, THE LABOUR OF THE SPEAR, ...   104 FERGUS DRUID   V 38D
    CAULDRON AND SPEAR AND STONE AND SWORD, ...   196 BAILE AILLINN   165
    A SHADOW DOES NOT CARRY SWORD OR SPEAR. . . . . .   224 SHADOW WATER B   44
    WHO GRIPS HIS LONG SPEAR SO TO PUSH . . . . . .   385 ROBARTES DANCE   3
    THE DIM SPEAR MET THE BRIGHT SPEAR, ...   741 EARL PAUL   45
    THE DIM SPEAR MET THE BRIGHT SPEAR, ...   741 EARL PAUL   45
    AND MADE THE BRIGHT SPEAR BEND, ...   741 EARL PAUL   46
    THE DIM SPEAR BREAKS THE BRIGHT SHIELD . . . . .   741 EARL PAUL   49
    THE DIM SPEAR MET THE BRIGHT SPEAR . . . . . .   741 EARL PAUL   V   49
    THE DIM SPEAR MET THE BRIGHT SPEAR . . . . . .   741 EARL PAUL   V   49
SPEAR-GRASS
    AS DANCE UPON THE SPEAR-GRASS BRITTLE, ...   731 PRIEST FAIRY   78
SPEARHEAD'S
    HOW THE HAMMERS SPRING ON THE ANVIL, ON THE SPEARHEAD'S   52 OISIN 3   83
       BURNING SPOT!
SPEAR-HEAD'S
    . . . ON THE SPEAR-HEAD'S BURNING SPOT! . . . . .   52 OISIN 3   V   83
SPEARS   SEE HUNTING-SPEARS
    THE SWIFT INNUMERABLE SPEARS, ...   2 OISIN 1   6
    AND A HUNDRED SPEARS AND A HUNDRED BOWS, ...   8 OISIN 1   91
    BESIDE THE PILED-UP HUNTING SPEARS, ...   23 OISIN 1   348
    THE DEWS DROP SLOWLY AND DREAMS GATHER! UNKNOWN SPEARS . .   161 BLACK PIG   1
    THE DEW DROPS SLOWLY! THE DREAMS GATHER! UNKNOWN SPEARS   161 BLACK PIG   V   1
    OR AS THE CHANGING SPEARS FLUNG BY THE GOLDEN STARS . . .   175 ELEMENT POWERS V   15
    PAST THE SPEARS AND PALM-STEMS DRY, ...   733 STREET DANCERS   42
SPEARSHAFT
    THAT THE SPEARSHAFT IS MADE OUT OF ASHWOOD, ...   52 OISIN 3   V   82
SPEAR-SHAFT
    THAT THE SPEAR-SHAFT IS MADE OUT OF ASHWOOD, ...   52 OISIN 3   82
SPECKLED
    "LIKE THE SPECKLED BIRD THAT STEERS . . . . . .   341 SHEP GOATHERD   62
    A SPECKLED CAT AND A TAME HARE . . . .   380 SONGS FOOL 1   1
    THE SPECKLED CAT SLEPT ON MY KNEE! . . . . . .   381 SONGS FOOL 2   2
    ALONE AND ALONE, WITH A SPECKLED SHIN? . . . . .   551 SONGS REWRIT 1   8
    DRINKING ALONE WITH A SPECKLED SHIN? . . . . . .   551 SONGS REWRIT 1   8
    LIVE LONE, ALONE WITH A SPECKLED SHIN? . . . . .   551 SONGS REWRIT 1 V   8
SPECTACLE
    BECAUSE THE DAILY SPECTACLE THAT STIRRED . . . . .   270 PARDON FATHERS   16
    BECAUSE YOU WERE THE SPECTACLE THAT STIRRED . . . .   270 PARDON FATHERS V   16
    HAS FOUND THE LOVELIEST SPECTACLE THERE IS. . . . .   447 COLONUS PRAISE   24
SPECTRAL
    MOST OUT OF REACH? AND IS THAT SPECTRAL IMAGE . . . .   368 EGO DOMINUS   25
SPED
    NO LONGER GLAD AS ON THAT MORNING, SPED . . . . .   30 OISIN 2   V   16
    THAT I LOVED ONCE." AGAIN THE FIGHTING SPED, ...   110 CUCHULAIN SEA   64
    'TIS MORN, AND FROM THE DEW-DRENCH'D WOOD I'VE SPED . .   645 ISLE STAT I 1   6
    HOW SPED THY QUEST? THIS PRELUDE WE'LL NOT HEAR IT. . .   673 ISLE STAT II 3   174
SPEECH
    "FRET NOT WITH SPEECH THE PHANTOMS DREAD," . . . . .   12 OISIN 1   V 148
    "THESE FORMS?" "VEX NOT WITH SPEECH THE PHANTOMS DREAD."   29 OISIN 2   V   5
    AND WITH LOW MURMURING LAUGHING SPEECH . . . . . .   195 BAILE AILLINN   137
    THE HOURLY KINDNESS, THE DAY'S COMMON SPEECH, ...   258 KING NO KING   14
    TO GRADUAL TIME'S LAST GIFT, A WRITTEN SPEECH . . . .   264 HOUSE SHAKEN   11
    "AND CANNOT HAVE A HUMOROUS HAPPY SPEECH." . . . . .   300 BEGGAR CRIED   16
    OF THAT LATE DEATH TOOK ALL MY HEART FOR SPEECH. . . .   328 ROBERT GREGORY   96
    TO HIS SPEECH AT THE BREAK OF DAY, ...   341 SHEP GOATHERD   68
    THE EYE OF THE MIND NOR KEEP MY TONGUE FROM SPEECH." . .   353 PEOPLE   34
    HER SPEECH A WICKED TALE THAT WE MAY VIE WITH HER, . .   362 HER COURTESY   6

```
                                                  PAGE    TITLE            LINE
SPEECH  (CONTINUED)
    (I HAVE NO SPEECH BUT SYMBOL, THE PAGAN SPEECH I MADE  .  .   365  HER COURAGE          2
    (I HAVE NO SPEECH BUT SYMBOL, THE PAGAN SPEECH I MADE  .  .   365  HER COURAGE          2
    TRUE SONG, THOUGH SPEECH! "MINE AUTHOR SUNG IT ME." .  .  .   373  PHASES OF MOON      30
    YOU HAVE LACKED ARTICULATE SPEECH . . . . . . . . . .  .  .   436  FOR MY SON          20
    THAT SPEECH WAS ALL THAT THE TOWN KNEW, BUT HE  .  .  .  .    462  HARUN RASHID        35
    THAT SPEECH WAS ALL THAT THE COURT KNOW, BUT HE  .  .  .  .   462  HARUN RASHID    V   35
    "GREAT PRINCE, FORGIVE THE FREEDOM OF MY SPEECH! .  .  .  .   464  HARUN RASHID        74
    FROM A DISCOURSE IN FIGURATIVE SPEECH  .  .  .  .  .  .  .    472  ALL SOUL NIGHT      52
    REMORSE FOR INTEMPERATE SPEECH  .  .  .  .  .  .  .  .  .     506  REMORSE SPEECH       T
    FINE MANNERS, LIBERAL SPEECH;  .  .  .  .  .  .  .  .  .  .   506  REMORSE SPEECH       7
    SPEECH AFTER LONG SILENCE! IT IS RIGHT, .  .  .  .  .  .  .   523  LONG SILENCE         1
SPEECHLESS
    BUT SPEECHLESS, AND THE MAIDEN WITH LONG WAIL  .  .  .  .  .  713  FERENCZ RENYI       85
SPEED
    HAVE A SPEED LIKE THE SPEED OF THE SALMON HERDS,  .  .  .  .    9  OISIN 1             98
    HAVE A SPEED LIKE THE SPEED OF THE SALMON HERDS, .  .  .  .     9  OISIN 1             98
    AND FOLLOWING HER AT A HEADLONG SPEED  .  .  .  .  .  .  .     12  OISIN 1         V  144
    AND "A WEARINESS SOON IS MY SPEED," SAYS THE MOUSE, .  .  .    27  OISIN 1         V  417
    AND "MY SPEED IS A WEARINESS," FALTERS THE MOUSE, .  .  .  .   28  OISIN 1            421
    AND HOOF AND HORN THAT HAD SUCKED IN THEIR SPEED .  .  .  .   278  TWO KINGS           30
SPEEDS
    IT SPEEDS THE PARTING GUEST. . . . . . . . . . . . . .       434  YOUTH AND AGE        4
SPEEDY
    AND BECAUSE I WENT BY THEM SO HUGH AND SO SPEEDY WITH EYES    59  OISIN 3            169
        SO BRIGHT,
    AND BEFORE I WENT BY THEM SO HUGE AND SO SPEEDY WITH EYES     59  OISIN 3         V  169
        SO BRIGHT,
    WITH SPEEDY FEET AND A MOST THANKFUL HEART!  .  .  .  .  .   185  QUEEN MAEVE        100
SPELL
    HE HAS FLUNG A DRUID SPELL UPON THE AIR,  .  .  .  .  .  .   240  SHADOW WATER B     385
    AND MANY A HERB AND MANY A SPELL .  .  .  .  .  .  .  .  .   717  FAIRY DOCTOR        17
    AND MANY HERBS AND MANY A SPELL .  .  .  .  .  .  .  .  .    717  FAIRY DOCTOR    V   17
    OR THEY'D HURL A SPELL AT HIM, .  .  .  .  .  .  .  .  .  .  775  AGAINST WITCH       18
SPELL-BOUND
    BY THEE SPELL-BOUND? THOU SHALT KNOW MORE!  .  .  .  .  .    675  ISLE STAT II 3     241
SPELLS
    THEY GAVE ME THAT OLD HARP OF THE NINE SPELLS .  .  .  .  .  237  SHADOW WATER B V   327
    FOR ALL HIS SPELLS WILL VANISH WHEN HE DIES, .  .  .  .  .   240  SHADOW WATER B     376
    THROUGH WICKED SPELLS.  THAT IS NOT ALL THE TALE, .  .  .   242  SHADOW WATER B     408
    IF YOU HAD TAKEN ME BY MAGIC SPELLS, .  .  .  .  .  .  .  .  245  SHADOW WATER B     490
    O LET ME PASS! THE SPELLS FROM OFF THE HEART  .  .  .  .  .  668  ISLE STAT II 3      44
    OF EQUAL POWER IN SPELLS AND SECRET RITES. .  .  .  .  .  .  720  WITCH VIVIEN         6
SPEND
    LET'S HOME AND SPEND IT IN OUR VILLAGES. .  .  .  .  .  .   248  SHADOW WATER B V 538A
    AND HAD THE LIVELONG SUMMER DAY TO SPEND. .  .  .  .  .  .   409  TOWER               10
SPENSER
    (AN IMAGE OUT OF SPENSER AND THE COMMON TONGUE). .  .  .  .  603  GALLERY REVIS       40
SPENT
    OR HAPPIER-THOUGHTED WHEN THE DAY IS SPENT .  .  .  .  .  .  292  TO A SHADE           4
    OR HAPPIER THOUGHTED WHEN THE DAY IS SPENT .  .  .  .  .  .  292  TO A SHADE      V    4
    I BADE, BECAUSE THE WICK AND OIL ARE SPENT .  .  .  .  .     333  LIVING BEAUTY        1
    THE WICK OF YOUTH BEING BURNED AND THE OIL SPENT, .  .  .    334  LIVING BEAUTY   V    3
    THAT WOMAN'S DAYS WERE SPENT  .  .  .  .  .  .  .  .  .  .   392  EASTER 1916         17
    ALL THAT SHE GOT SHE SPENT, .  .  .  .  .  .  .  .  .  .  .  392  EASTER 1916     V   20
    GATHERED A SCORE OF HORSE AND SPENT HIS DAYS  .  .  .  .    420  MY HOUSE            22
    WHETHER HEALTH, WEALTH OR PEACE OF MIND WERE SPENT  .  .    429  NINETEEN 19         36
    WE SHIFT ABOUT--ALL THAT GREAT GLORY SPENT--  .  .  .  .    491  COOLE BALLYLEE      39
    MAN SHIFTS ABOUT--ALL THAT GREAT GLORY SPENT--  .  .  .     491  COOLE BALLYLEE V    39
    THEIR MONEY SPENT, THEIR WINE GONE SOUR, .  .  .  .  .  .   635  BLACK TOWER          3
    HOW MANY CENTURIES SPENT .  .  .  .  .  .  .  .  .  .  .  .  784  WOMANS BEAUTY        7
SPHERE
    INTO A SPHERE FROM YOUTHFUL SYMPATHY, .  .  .  .  .  .  .    443  SCHOOL CHILDR       14
    THE ZODIAC IS CHANGED INTO A SPHERE. .  .  .  .  .  .  .  .  535  CHOSEN              18
SPHINX
    A SPHINX WITH WOMAN BREAST AND LION PAW, .  .  .  .  .  .    383  VISION ROBART       18
SPICE
    LOOK THERE! THERE IN THE MIST! A SHIP OF SPICE!  .  .  .  .  232  SHADOW WATER B     ∠19
    TREASURE ON TREASURE.  BOXES OF PRECIOUS SPICE. .  .  .  .   247  SHADOW WATER B     533
    TREASURE AND TREASURE.  BOXES OF PRECIOUS SPICE. .  .  .  .  247  SHADOW WATER B V   533
SPICE-ISLES
    WHERE SPICE-ISLES NESTLE ON THE STAR-TROD SEAS, .  .  .  .   682  SEEKER              17
SPIDER
    NOT THERE, FOR THERE A SPIDER WEAVES HER WEB. .  .  .  .  .  700  MOSADA 3            38
SPIDER'S
    FOR THOUGH LOVE HAS A SPIDER'S EYE  .  .  .  .  .  .  .  .   388  SOLOMON WITCH       19
    A LOVER WITH A SPIDER'S EYE .  .  .  .  .  .  .  .  .  .  .  388  SOLOMON WITCH   V   19
SPIDERS
    AND SPIDERS ARE MY FRIENDS! I'M THEIRS, AND THEY ARE  .  .   693  MOSADA 1            64
SPIES
    OF THE HOUSEHOLD SPIES! .  .  .  .  .  .  .  .  .  .  .  .   536  PARTING              3
SPILLED
    BY A SPILLED WINE-CUP LIE. .  .  .  .  .  .  .  .  .  .  .   168  BLESSED         V   32
SPILLS
    AND RAINS DOWN LIFE UNTIL THE BASIN SPILLS, .  .  .  .  .    417  ANCEST HOUSES        4
SPILT
    SPILT MILK  .  .  .  .  .  .  .  .  .  .  .  .  .  .  .  .   484  SPILT MILK           T
    LIKE MILK SPILT ON A STONE. .  .  .  .  .  .  .  .  .  .  .  484  SPILT MILK           4
SPINDLE
    WHO TALKS OF PLATO'S SPINDLE! .  .  .  .  .  .  .  .  .  .   520  HIS BARGAIN          1
```

753

SPINDLES
WHO COME WITH THEIR CROWNS OF PEARL AND THEIR SPINDLES
OF WOOL, 203 WITHER BOUGHS 10
SPINE
THROUGH HEART AND SPINE; AND CAST HIM IN THE WAVE . . . 41 OISIN 2 182
THROUGH HEART AND DEMON SPINE, AND IN THE WAVE . . . . 41 OISIN 2 V 182
SPINNER
AND ONE SPINNER IS LOST. . . . . 771 SPINNING SONG 10
SPINNING
SPINNING AT ALL TIMES ERI'S GOOD TO-MORROW, ... 129 BOOK STORIES V 10
THE SPINNING STARS--THE TOILING SEA--WHIRL ROUND . . . 665 ISLE STAT II 2 72
SPINNING SONG . . . . 770 SPINNING SONG T
SPINNING-JENNY
GOD TOOK THE SPINNING-JENNY . . . . 439 FRAGMENTS 3
SPINNING-TOP
AS 'TWERE A SPINNING-TOP. . . . . 384 VISION ROBART 44
SPIRAL
AND THEN AWAY, AWAY, LIKE SPIRAL FLAMES; . . . . . . 29 OISIN 2 V 2
SPIRED
DID NOT THE WORMS THAT SPIRED ABOUT HIS BONES . . . . 128 DREAM OF FAERY 41
WERE NOT THE WORMS THAT SPIRED ABOUT HIS BONES . . . 128 DREAM OF FAERY V 41
SPIRING
GYRING, SPIRING TO AND FRO . . . . 135 TWO TREES 15
THIS WINDING, GYRING, SPIRING TREADMILL OF A STAIR . . . 480 BLOOD AND MOON 17
SPIRIT
TO FLY A SPIRIT," NIAM WEEPING SAID. . . . . 35 OISIN 2 V 92
MY SPIRIT ROCKED IN EVENING LIGHT, THE RUSHES ROUND MY
KNEES, 76 INDIAN ON GOD 2
MY SPIRIT ROCKED IN SLEEP AND SIGHS; AND SAW THE MOORFOWL
PACE 76 INDIAN ON GOD 3
MY SPIRIT ROCKED IN EVENING'S HUSH, THE RUSHES ROUND MY
KNEES, 76 INDIAN ON GOD V 2
IN MY MOST SECRET SPIRIT GREW . . . . 83 MAD KING GOLL 27
A DREAM OF A BLESSED SPIRIT . . . . 124 CATHLEEN PARA V T
SPIRIT AFTER SPIRIT! THE SMITHIES BREAK THE FLOOD, . . . 498 BYZANTIUM 34
SPIRIT AFTER SPIRIT! THE SMITHIES BREAK THE FLOOD, . . . 498 BYZANTIUM 34
HIS SPIRIT THAT HAS FLED . . . . 575 MAIDS 2ND SONG 5
THE SPIRIT MEDIUM . . . . 599 SPIRIT MEDIUM T
YON SHEPHERD--CAME YOUR SPIRIT TO BEGUILE . . . . . 648 ISLE STAT I 1 105
I' FAITH THOU EVER WAST A WORDY SPIRIT! . . . . . . 673 ISLE STAT II 3 175
HIS RUEFUL SPIRIT FLUTTERED BY. . . . . 673 ISLE STAT II 3 188
THOUGH SAD IS MANY A SPIRIT . . . . 680 LOVE AND DEATH 23
AND THROUGH THE MANSION OF THE SPIRIT ROVE . . . . 681 SEEKER 2
STAR-ENVIOUS. HE WAS A SPIRIT, BROTHER. . . . . . 683 SEEKER 39
TWO SPIRIT THINGS A MAN HATH FOR HIS FRIENDS! . . . 686 DRAWING-ROOM 5
HER SPIRIT. AS SHE MOVES, THE FOAM-GLOBES BURST . . 687 TWO TITANS 14
SINGS THE YOUNG WISTFUL SPIRIT OF A STAR . . . . . 705 REMEMBRANCE 10
WILD WISDOMS OF SPIRIT AND TONGUE. . . . . 708 FAIRY PEDANT 27
THE SPIRIT OF YOUNG RENYI HAS GROWN OLD. . . . . . 710 FERENCZ RENYI 17
THE PROUDEST OR MOST COY OF SPIRIT THINGS, ... 720 WITCH VIVIEN 7
TO THE EVER-LONGING AND MOURNFUL SPIRIT SAY. . . . 734 QUATRAIN APHOR 12
TWO SPIRIT THINGS A MAN HATH FOR HIS FRIENDS! . . . 734 QUATRAIN APHOR V 5
SPIRITS
OH MAIDEN." "ARE YE SPIRITS OF THE SEA, ... 34 OISIN 2 V 7&8
LONG SIGHS AROSE IN OUR SPIRITS, BENEATH US BUBBLED THE
GROUND, 48 OISIN 3 20
THEIR MOTIONLESS EYEBALLS OF SPIRITS . . . . 55 OISIN 3 121
"IN THE ISLES OF THE FARTHEST SEAS WHERE ONLY THE SPIRITS
COME. 56 OISIN 3 133
. . . AND NO MAN MAY WAR WITH THE STRONG SPIRITS WAGE! . . 62 OISIN 3 V 214
HE WILL SMILE ON THE THREE OLD SPIRITS, ... 178 FIDDLER DOONEY 11
COULD NOT AMEND. I HAVE GOOD SPIRITS ENOUGH. . . . 227 SHADOW WATER B 116
HAS CALLED UP THE COLD SPIRITS THAT ARE BORN . . . 382 VISION ROBART 2
WHERE BLOOD-BEGOTTEN SPIRITS COME . . . . 498 BYZANTIUM 28
WHERE BLOOD BEGOTTEN SPIRITS COME . . . . 498 BYZANTIUM V 28
FORTH! FORTH! O SPIRITS, YE HAVE HEARD YOUR TASK! . . . 669 ISLE STAT II 3 81
TWO LONELY SPIRITS WAIT. . . . . 680 LOVE AND DEATH 18
ARE THE SPIRITS LOVE AND DEATH. . . . . 680 LOVE AND DEATH 32
THE SPIRITS STOLE, AND GAVE HIM IN ITS STEAD . . . 684 SEEKER 55
WILD SPIRITS OF WISDOM AND TONGUE. . . . . 708 FAIRY PEDANT V 27
SPIRIT-THINGS
TWO SPIRIT-THINGS A MAN HATH FOR HIS FRIENDS-- . . . . 734 QUATRAIN APHOR 5
SPIRITUAL
THE SPIRITUAL INTELLECT'S GREAT WORK, ... 632 MAN AND ECHO 20
SPIRITUALISED
EYES SPIRITUALISED BY DEATH CAN JUDGE, ... 604 YOU CONTENT 7
SPIRITUS
WHEN A VAST IMAGE OUT OF SPIRITUS MUNDI . . . . . . 402 SECOND COMING 12
SPIT
I SPIT INTO THE FACE OF TIME . . . . 132 OLD PENSIONER 17
FOR LARDER AND SPIT ARE BARE, ... 349 HAWK 4
BUT SHOULD THAT OTHER COME, I SPIT! . . . . 509 JANE BISHOP 27
SPITE
INDIGNANT AT THE FUMBLING WITS, THE OBSCURE SPITE . . . 291 PAUDEEN 1
THE DAILY SPITE OF THIS UNMANNERLY TOWN, ... 351 PEOPLE 3
GREAT WORKS CONSTRUCTED THERE IN NATURE'S SPITE . . . 488 COOLE PARK 29 5
SPITTLE
. . . THE SPITTLE ON HIS BEARD NEVER DRY, ... 53 OISIN 3 90
. . . WITH THE SPITTLE ON HIS BEARD NEVER DRY. . . . . 60 OISIN 3 192
SPLASH
HOW STILL IT IS! I HEAR THE CARP GO SPLASH, ... 722 WITCH VIVIEN 62

SPLASHED   SEE FROTH-SPLASHED
  SPLASHED ALL WITH CLAY AND JOURNEY DULL,   82 MAD KING GOLL V   13
  SPLASHED, OR AN OTTER SLID INTO THE STREAM.   372 PHASES OF MOON   9
  HE SPLASHED WHERE AN ABSURD   400 DEMON BEAST   27
  BUT TROD THE ROAD, OR SPLASHED ABOUT THE SHORE,   447 COLONUS PRAISE   27
SPLASHING
  THE HEAVY STEPS OF THE PLOUGHMAN, SPLASHING THE WINTRY   143 ROSE IN HEART   3
    MOULD,
  THE HEAVY STEPS OF THE PLOUGHMAN SPLASHING THE WINTER   143 ROSE IN HEART V   3
    MOULD,
  SCARED BY THE SPLASHING OF A DOZEN COWS!   419 MY HOUSE   10
  SCARED BY THE SPLASHING OF A HUNDRED COWS.   419 MY HOUSE V   10
SPLEEN
  DO MOST EXCITE MY SPLEEN,   599 STONE CROSS   18
SPLENDOUR
  AND HORRIBLE SPLENDOUR OF DESIRE!   411 TOWER   63
  WHO SITS IN LONELY SPLENDOUR, MAIL'D IN GOLD,   651 ISLE STAT I 1   163
SPLIT
  BUT IN HONOUR SPLIT HIS LOVE   573 LADYS 3RD SONG   7
SPLITS
  . . . NIGHT SPLITS AND THE DAWN BREAKS LOOSE!   623 HIGH TALK   12
SPOIL
  OR BEEN FIT SPOIL FOR A CENTAUR   355 PROPERTIUS   7
SPOILS
  THIS SULLEN PEASANT SPOILS THE GOOD SUNSHINE,   711 FERENCZ RENYI   42
  THIS SULLEN PEASANT SPOILS THE GOOD RED WINE.   711 FERENCZ RENYI   43
SPOILT
  SPOILT WHAT OLD LOINS HAVE SENT?   604 YOU CONTENT   6
SPOKE
  SUDDENLY AILELL SPOKE OUT OF HIS SLEEP,   183 QUEEN MAEVE   73
  THEN SEEING THAT HE SCARCE HAD SPOKE   194 BAILE AILLINN   126
  HE HAD BUT GAZED ON THORN-TREES, SPOKE,   274 GREY ROCK   82
  HE HAD BUT GAZED ON THORN TREES, SPOKE!   274 GREY ROCK V   82
  'TWAS ROUNDLY SPOKE, BUT WHEN NIGHT CAME   275 GREY ROCK   95
  SHE MOTIONED HIM AFAR, AND ROSE AND SPOKE!   280 TWO KINGS   68
  BUT ASKED THE MORE UNTIL HE SPOKE THESE WORDS,   281 TWO KINGS V   92A
  A WOMAN SPOKE OF SOME NEW TALE SHE HAD READ,   350 HER PRAISE   7
  OR WAS IT SHE THAT SPOKE OR SOME GREAT DJINN?   467 HARUN RASHID   135
  I SAY THAT A DJINN SPOKE. A LIVELONG HOUR   467 HARUN RASHID   136
  I SAY THAT A DJIN SPOKE. A LIVE LONG HOUR   467 HARUN RASHID V   136
  I SAY THAT A JINN SPOKE. A LIVE-LONG HOUR   467 HARUN RASHID V   136
  MY GREAT-GRANDFATHER SPOKE TO EDMUND BURKE   486 SEVEN SAGES   1
  SPOKE THESE, OR WORDS LIKE THESE,   496 MOHINI CHATTER   15
  DOUBTLESS I SPOKE OR SANG WHAT I HAD HEARD   557 RIBH ECSTASY   2
  HE SPOKE WITH TURK AND JEW,   594 COLONEL MARTIN   2
  THE GOLDEN PLOUGH AND HARROW AND SPOKE ALOUD   609 IN TARAS HALLS   12
  THE WOMEN THAT I PICKED SPOKE SWEET AND LOW   622 HOUND VOICE   8
  SWEAR BY WHAT THE SAGES SPOKE   636 BEN BULBEN   1
  SPOKE AND SET THE COCKS A-CROW.   637 BEN BULBEN   4
SPOKEN
  BEEN SPOKEN OF WITH ANY MAN!   6 OISIN 1   56
  BEEN SPOKEN OF WITH ANY ONE,   6 OISIN 1 V   56
  BEEN SPOKEN OF WITH ANYONE!   6 OISIN 1 V   56
  HE THINKS OF THOSE WHO HAVE SPOKEN EVIL OF HIS BELOVED   166 EVIL OF BELOV   T
  AEDH THINKS OF THOSE WHO HAVE SPOKEN EVIL OF HIS BELOVED   166 EVIL OF BELOV V   T
  THEY HAVE SPOKEN AGAINST YOU EVERYWHERE,   166 EVIL OF BELOV   3
  AND WHEN YOU HAVE SPOKEN TAKE THE ROADS AGAIN?   373 PHASES OF MOON   25
  "O WORDS ARE LIGHTLY SPOKEN,"   396 ROSE TREE   1
  HAD SPOKEN OF THEIR CHILDISH DAYS   457 SUMMER SPRING   11
  HAS SPOKEN THE WISDOM OF THE DESERT DJINS,   468 HARUN RASHID V   163
  COULD MY SPOKEN WORDS HAVE CHECKED   632 MAN AND ECHO   15
  AND SPOKEN IN THE COUNCIL, AND HEARD TALES   748 SHADOW WATER A   28
SPONGE
  THE VINEGAR-HEAVY SPONGE, THE FLOWERS BY KEDRON STREAM!   172 TRAV PASSION   5
  THE HISSOP-HEAVY SPONGE, THE FLOWERS BY KIDRON STREAM!   172 TRAV PASSION V   5
SPONGY
  O'ER HILL AND HEATH AND SPONGY FEN,   83 MAD KING GOLL V   32
  OVER THE HEATH AND SPONGY FEN,   83 MAD KING GOLL V   32
SPONTANEOUS
  SPONTANEOUS JOY AND NATURAL CONTENT   260 FASC DIFFICULT   3
SPOOL
  HAS WOUND UPON A SPOOL   449 HERO GIRL FOOL   22
  WHEN CRADLE AND SPOOL ARE PAST   449 HERO GIRL FOOL   24
SPORT
  HAVE DRIVEN TRAVELLERS MAD FOR THEIR OWN SPORT.   227 SHADOW WATER B   105
  MAY NOT HAVE DRIVEN YOU MAD FOR THEIR OWN SPORT?   227 SHADOW WATER B V   105
  OR NOISY, INSOLENT SPORT,   293 HELEN LIVED   4
  HE THAT WAS BEST IN EVERY COUNTRY SPORT   339 SHEP GOATHERD   17
  TURN HATRED INTO SPORT,   506 REMORSE SPEECH   8
SPORTS
  WATCHING OUR SHEPHERD SPORTS AT HARVEST-TIME   340 SHEP GOATHERD   41
SPOT
  HOW THE HAMMERS SPRING ON THE ANVIL, ON THE SPEARHEAD'S   52 OISIN 3   83
    BURNING SPOT!
  . . . ON THE SPEAR-HEAD'S BURNING SPOT!   52 OISIN 3 V   83
  PACING WITH HALF-CLOSED EYELIDS IN A SUNNY SPOT   366 HER COURAGE   7
  IN THIS TUMULTUOUS SPOT,   420 MY HOUSE   23
  IT CAN BE MURDERED WITH A SPOT OF INK.   491 COOLE BALLYLEE   24
  A SPOT WHEREON THE FOUNDERS LIVED AND DIED   491 COOLE BALLYLEE   33
  THAT IS AN AIRY SPOT,   614 MARCH SONGS 2   9
  THAT IS AN AIRY SPOT,   615 MARCH SONGS 2   19

		PAGE	TITLE		LINE

SPOT   (CONTINUED)
THAT IS AN AIRY SPOT, ...   615 MARCH SONGS 2   29
ON LIMESTONE QUARRIED NEAR THE SPOT . . . .   640 BEN BULBEN   90
AND WHEN THE SUMMER'S DEEP, THEN TO THIS SPOT . . . . .   663 ISLE STAT II 2   24
OF HIM ON YONDER BRAZEN-GATED SPOT, ...   675 ISLE STAT II 3   240
OF SOLDIERS RANKED IS ON A GRASSY SPOT, ...   712 FERENCZ RENYI   64
OF SOLDIERS DRAWN IS ON A GRASSY SPOT, ...   712 FERENCZ RENYI   V 64
WITH QUIET SHADE ITS EVER DEWY SPOT, ...   714 FERENCZ RENYI   V 109
STANDS EACH GREY AND SILENT PHANTOM ON THE SAME REGARDLESS   719 PHANTOM SHIP   25
    SPOT--
SPOTS
HIS LANGUID TAIL ABOVE US, LIT WITH MYRIAD SPOTS OF LIGHT.   77 INDIAN ON GOD   20
SPOTTED
OVER HER SPOTTED FLESH AND FLYING HAIR . . . .   687 TWO TITANS   15
SPRANG
AND ONCE A SUDDEN LAUGHTER SPRANG . . . .   16 OISIN 1   225
SPRANG FROM A GATEWAY WALLED AROUND WITH BLACK . . . .   31 OISIN 2   V 29
THAT SPRANG UNDER THE SEVEN HAZEL TREES, ...   35 OISIN 2   84
SPRANG DRIPPING, AND, WITH CAPTIVE DEMONS SENT . . . .   38 OISIN 2   130
THAT IS LIKE LAUGHTER, SPRANG AGAIN . . . .   318 APPOINTMENT   6
WHEN FIRST IT SPRANG OUT OF THE NEST . . . .   397 POLIT PRISONER   20
A FRENZIED CROWD, AND WHERE THE BRANCHES SPRANG . . . .   541 PARN FUNERAL 1   9
SPRAY
ROLLED ROUND WITH MUSIC OF THE SIGHING SPRAY! . . . . .   30 OISIN 2   14
TO SCATTER THE ACACIA SPRAY . . . .   360 ALF POLLEXFEN   10
THE COLD BLOWN SPRAY IN MY NOSTRIL. . . . .   399 BREAK OF DAY   20
WHILE THAT GREAT QUEEN, THAT ROSE OUT OF THE SPRAY, . . .   404 FOR DAUGHTER   27
SPRAY-DABBLED
WITH BLOWN, SPRAY-DABBLED HAIR GATHER AT HAND. . . . .   114 ROSE OF BATTLE   6
SPREAD   SEE OUT-SPREAD
THE LONG-HAIRED WARRIORS, THE SPREAD FEAST! . . . . .   2 OISIN 1   V 7
. . . "WHERE WHITE CLOUDS LIE SPREAD . . . .   59 OISIN 3   178
I WOULD SPREAD THE CLOTHS UNDER YOUR FEET! . . . . . .   176 CLOTHS HEAVEN   5
I HAVE SPREAD MY DREAMS UNDER YOUR FEET! . . . . . .   176 CLOTHS HEAVEN   7
NO WAITING-MAID SHOULD EVER SPREAD . . . .   194 BAILE AILLINN   120
NO WAITING MAID SHOULD EVER SPREAD . . . .   194 BAILE AILLINN V 120
WHEN THE SUPPER HAS BEEN SPREAD. . . . .   215 HAPPY TOWNLAND   44
AND YOU HAD SPREAD A SAIL FOR HOME, A WIND . . . . .   236 SHADOW WATER B   309
IT WAS IN ALL HIS BATTLES. I WILL SPREAD MY HAIR, . . .   242 SHADOW WATER B   413
WAS IT FOR THIS THE WILD GEESE SPREAD . . . .   290 SEPTEMBER 1913   17
HAIR SPREAD ON THE WIND THEY MADE! . . . .   332 ROUND TOWER   22
HAIRS SPREAD ON THE WIND THEY MADE! . . . .   332 ROUND TOWER   V 22
THEY CAN SPREAD OUT WHAT SAIL THEY PLEASE FOR ALL I HAVE   354 HIS PHOENIX   22
    TO SAY,
AND SPREAD ON EVERY SIDE, ...   396 ROSE TREE   10
SCARCE SPREAD A GLORY TO THE MORNING BEAMS, ...   422 MY DESCENDANTS   6
THE WINGS HALF SPREAD FOR FLIGHT, ...   430 NINETEEN 19   65
BEFORE SHE HAD SPREAD A BOOK UPON HER KNEES . . . . .   466 HARUN RASHID   120
THEY ARE SPREAD WIDE THAT EACH . . . .   488 CRAZED MOON   17
THEY ATE SPREAD WIDE THAT EACH . . . .   488 CRAZED MOON   V 17
SPREAD TO A LAKE AND DROP INTO A HOLE. . . . .   490 COOLE BALLYLEE   7
SPREAD TO A LAKE AND RUN INTO A HOLE. . . . . . .   490 COOLE BALLYLEE V 7
A RIVERY FIELD SPREAD OUT BELOW, ...   502 VACILLATION   57
WHERE THE MAPS ARE SPREAD, ...   617 LONG-LEG FLY   6
AND ALL WAS QUIET ROUND ME SPREAD, ...   670 ISLE STAT II 3   112
WHERE THE MOSS WAS SPREAD LIKE HIS OWN DOORMAT. . . . .   728 PRIEST FAIRY   8
MUST SPREAD OUT THEIR WINGS UNTIRING, ...   739 WHERE BOOKS GO   3
SPREADING
AND CUSTOM FOR THE SPREADING LAUREL TREE. . . . . . .   406 FOR DAUGHTER   80
PLUNGES TOWARDS NOTHING, ARMS AND FINGERS SPREADING WIDE   426 PHANTOM HATRED   13
SPRIGHTLY
THAT SHE MIGHT BE THAT SPRIGHTLY GIRL TRODDEN BY A BIRD!   353 HIS PHOENIX   4
THAT SHE MIGHT BE THAT SPRIGHTLY GIRL WHO HAD MARRIED WITH   353 HIS PHOENIX   V 4
    A BIRD!
THAT SHE MIGHT BE THAT SPRIGHTLY GIRL WHO WAS TRODDEN BY   353 HIS PHOENIX   V 4
    A BIRD!
SPRIGHTS
THEY ARE THE FLOWERS' GUARDIAN SPRIGHTS! . . . .   666 ISLE STAT II 3   18
SPRING
THAT SPRING FIVE PACES IN THEIR BOUNDS, ...   8 OISIN 1   V 86A
"MY BROTHERS SPRING OUT OF THEIR BEDS AT MORN, ...   32 OISIN 2   51
HOW THE HAMMERS SPRING ON THE ANVIL, ON THE SPEARHEAD'S   52 OISIN 3   83
    BURNING SPOT
EVEN AS SPRING UPON THE ANCIENT SKIES, ...   108 CUCHULAIN SEA   42
STARED LIKE THE SPRING UPON THE ANCIENT SKIES, ...   108 CUCHULAIN SEA V 41
THEIR RICHNESS THROUGH THE SUMMER AND THE SPRING! . . .   279 TWO KINGS   V 62C
"YOU CRY ALOUD, O WOULD 'TWERE SPRING . . . . . .   306 HOUR DAWN   91
NEITHER THE SPRING NOR THE SOUTH WIND . . . .   306 HOUR DAWN   95
BUT THE OTHER CRIED, "YOU LONG FOR SPRING . . . . .   306 HOUR DAWN   V 91
TAKING DELIGHT THAT HE COULD SPRING! . . . .   317 APPOINTMENT   4
AND CHILDREN WHEN THEY SPRING UP SHOULDER-HIGH. . . . .   343 SHEP GOATHERD   119
AND CHILDREN WHEN THEY SPRING UP SHOULDER HIGH. . . .   343 SHEP GOATHERD V 119
THROUGH WINTER-TIME WE CALL ON SPRING, ...   434 WHEEL   1
AND THROUGH THE SPRING ON SUMMER CALL, ...   434 WHEEL   2
OF MAGNUS ANNUS AT THE SPRING, ...   437 SONGS PLAY 1   7
SUMMER AND SPRING . . . .   456 SUMMER SPRING   T
AND SHE HAD ALL THE SPRING! . . . .   457 SUMMER SPRING   16
YOU KNOW THE SAYING, "CHANGE THE BRIDE WITH SPRING," . . .   463 HARUN RASHID   50
THAT IF THE SPRING BEAR OFF WHAT THE SPRING GAVE . . .   464 HARUN RASHID   76
THAT IF THE SPRING BEAR OFF WHAT THE SPRING GAVE . . .   464 HARUN RASHID   76
THE EXTRAVAGANCE OF SPRING! OR MOVE A HAND . . . . .   466 HARUN RASHID   125

```
                                                      PAGE      TITLE           LINE

SPRING   (CONTINUED)
     THE EXTRAVAGANCE OF SPRING; OR CERTAIN TIMES  . . . . .    466 HARUN RASHID    V  125
     TARGETED, TROD LIKE SPRING. . . . . . . . . . . . . . .    504 QUARREL IN AGE      16
     AWAITS RETURNING SPRING. . . . . . . . . . . . . . . .     517 HER ANXIETY          2
     (HURRAH FOR THE FLOWERS OF SPRING, . . . . . . . . . .     567 FROM JAPANESE        3
     FOR SPRING IS HERE AGAIN.) . . . . . . . . . . . . . .     567 FROM JAPANESE        4
     FOR SPRING RICE HAD TO WHISPER IT, . . . . . . . . . .     582 ROGER CASEMENT      13
     THAT DIZZY DREAMS CAN SPRING  . . . . . . . . . . . .      781 MY HEART BEAT        7
SPRINGING
     GO ASK THE SPRINGING FLOWERS, . . . . . . . . . . . .      680 LOVE AND DEATH      13
SPRINGS
     THAT SPRINGS FROM BODY AND IN BODY FALLS  . . . . . . .    463 HARUN RASHID        63
SPRINGTIME
     THAN ALL MY BURSTING SPRINGTIME KNEW.  A GIRL . . . . .    466 HARUN RASHID       105
     FOR IN MY FIRST HARD SPRINGTIME WE WERE FRIENDS, . . . .   473 ALL SOUL NIGHT      62
SPRING-TIME
     BECAUSE THE SPRING-TIME HAS NOT COME—— . . . . . . . .     434 WHEEL                6
     FOR IN MY FIRST HARD SPRING-TIME WE WERE FRIENDS, . . .    473 ALL SOUL NIGHT V    62
SPRITE
     IT IS MY WHIM! BID SOME ATTENDANT SPRITE . . . . . . .     669 ISLE STAT II 3      72
     WHERE LIES THE LONG-LOST FOREST OF THE SPRITE, . . . . .   682 SEEKER              23
     THERE LIES THE LONG-LOST FOREST OF THE SPRITE, . . . . .   682 SEEKER          V   23
SPRITES
     FIRST DREAMS, AND GOBLINS, AND THE LESSER SPRITES, . . .   722 WITCH VIVIEN        56
SPRUNG      SEE SEA-SPRUNG
     THAT OUT OF LIFE'S OWN SELF-DELIGHT HAD SPRUNG  . . . .    417 ANCEST HOUSES       11
     THAT OUT OF LIFE'S OWN SELF DELIGHT HAD SPRUNG  . . . .    417 ANCEST HOUSES   V   11
     FROM MAN'S BLOOD-SODDEN HEART ARE SPRUNG  . . . . . . .    502 VACILLATION         67
     SEEMED SPRUNG FROM BUT A SINGLE ROOT . . . . . . . . .     571 THREE BUSHES        61
SPUME
     PLATO THOUGHT NATURE BUT A SPUME THAT PLAYS  . . . . .     445 SCHOOL CHILDR       41
SPUN
     WHERE I HAVE LAUGHED AND SPUN AND PLAYED? . . . . . . .    151 HEART OF WOMAN V     2
     FOR WHOM THE HANGMAN'S ROPE WAS SPUN, . . . . . . . . .    289 SEPTEMBER 1913      13
     AND THE MOON SPUN ROUND LIKE A TOP, . . . . . . . . . .    378 CAT AND MOON         2
     I HAVE SPUN IN THE HOUSE THIS NIGHT! . . . . . . . . .     771 SPINNING SONG       13
SPUR
     UPON HIS TREMBLING HORSE, THEN DROVE THE SPUR; . . . .     277 TWO KINGS           11
     HE THOUGHT TO HAVE GIVEN HIS HORSE THE SPUR, BUT SAW  . .  277 TWO KINGS       V   4B
     TREMBLING BENEATH HIM, AND THEN DROVE THE SPUR  . . . .    277 TWO KINGS       V   11
     THE SPUR . . . . . . . . . . . . . . . . . . . . . . .     591 SPUR                 T
     WHAT ELSE HAVE I TO SPUR ME INTO SONG? . . . . . . . .     591 SPUR                 4
SPURRED
     ON A FANTASTIC RIDE, MY HORSE'S FLANKS ARE SPURRED  . . .  391 UNDER SATURN         6
     ON A FANTASTIC RIDE I SWEAR MY HORSE'S FLANKS WERE SPURRED 391 UNDER SATURN    V    6
SPUTTERING
     FOUND THAT OLD HOUSE, A SPUTTERING TORCH WITHIN, . . . .   283 TWO KINGS          140
     AND FOUND THE HOUSE, A SPUTTERING TORCH WITHIN, . . . .    283 TWO KINGS       V  140
SPY
     AND WHEN THE FOLK THERE SPY ME, . . . . . . . . . . .      179 FIDDLER DOONEY      17
     AND THE FOLK THERE WHEN THEY SPY ME . . . . . . . . . .    179 FIDDLER DOONEY V    17
     AND WHEN THE FOLKS THERE SPY ME, . . . . . . . . . . .     179 FIDDLER DOONEY V    17
SPYING
     THAT HIDES US FROM ALL HUMAN SPYING, . . . . . . . . .      22 OISIN 1         V 338A
SQUALL
     THAT NONE MAY FEEL THE POWER OF SQUALL AND WAVE, . . . .   128 DREAM OF FAERY V    45
     SEE THE DARKNESS SLOW DISGORGING A VESSEL BLIND WITH       718 PHANTOM SHIP        12
          SQUALL.
SQUANDERER
     THE WRINKLED SQUANDERER OF HUMAN WEALTH. . . . . . . .     720 WITCH VIVIEN        16
SQUARE
     SQUARE LEAVES OF THE IVY MOVED OVER US, BINDING US DOWN     52 OISIN 3             76
          TO OUR REST.
     BY OPPOSITION, SQUARE AND TRINE; . . . . . . . . . . .     325 ROBERT GREGORY      39
     THE MEN ARE BUSY IN THE GLIMMERING SQUARE. . . . . . .     699 MOSADA 3            16
     ERE LONG SHALL FALTER THROUGH THE NOISY SQUARE, . . . .    699 MOSADA 3            21
     BULWARK TO BULWARK, AND SQUARE HER SAIL BY OURS. . . . .   752 SHADOW WATER A     129
SQUARED
     THAT OLD, SEA-WEEDY, SQUARED, THREE HUNDRED FEET . . . .    31 OISIN 2         V  30C
SQUEAKY
     AND CIRCLED ROUND HIM WITH ITS SQUEAKY CRY, . . . . . .    377 PHASES OF MOON     138
SQUIRREL
     A SQUIRREL WHINNIED AND A BIRD SCREAMED OUT; . . . . . .   278 TWO KINGS           34
     WHERE THE PROUD, WAYWARD SQUIRREL WENT. . . . . . . . .    317 APPOINTMENT          3
     TO A SQUIRREL AT KYLE-NA-NO . . . . . . . . . . . . . .    359 TO A SQUIRREL        T
     THERE WHERE YONDER SQUIRREL CRUNCHES . . . . . . . . .     655 ISLE STAT I 3        4
     THE RED SQUIRREL SHALL REAR HER YOUNG WHERE THOU           674 ISLE STAT II 3     215
          HAST DWELT——
     THE VERY SQUIRREL DIES THAT ENTERS THERE. . . . . . . .    682 SEEKER              33
     THE VERY SQUIRREL DIES THAT ENTERS IT. . . . . . . . .     682 SEEKER          V   33
     THE SQUIRREL YONDER, HUSHED AND WISE, . . . . . . . . .    686 LIFE                 5
SQUIRREL-BROWN
     DULL-WITTED THING, WITH FACE RED SQUIRREL-BROWN. . . . .   661 ISLE STAT II 1      68
SQUIRREL'S
     ALTHOUGH HE HAD A SQUIRREL'S EYE. . . . . . . . . . . .    190 BAILE AILLINN       30
SQUIRRELS
     WHERE MANY HUNDRED SQUIRRELS ARE AS HAPPY  . . . . . . .   217 WOODS OF COOLE       5
ST.
     AND RUTH ST. DENIS HAD MORE CHARM ALTHOUGH SHE HAD POOR    353 HIS PHOENIX         10
          LUCK;
     BECAUSE ST. JOSEPH'S IMAGE HANGETH HERE . . . . . . . .    676 ISLE STAT II 3     266
```

757

STABLE   SEE LIVERY-STABLE
  "TO STABLE AND TO KENNEL GO¡ . . . .   97 FOXHUNTER   5
  AND SOME ONE FROM THE STABLE BRING . . . .   97 FOXHUNTER   V   5
  I'LL FIND THE STABLE AND PULL OUT THE BOLT. . . . .   260 FASC DIFFICULT   13
  THE ILL-BRED SON OF A LIVERY STABLE KEEPER— . . . . . 370 EGO DOMINUS   V 61
STABLE-KEEPER
  THE ILL-BRED SON OF A LIVERY STABLE-KEEPER— . . . . . 370 EGO DOMINUS   V 61
STABLES
  AND SOME ONE FROM THE STABLES BRING . . . .   97 FOXHUNTER   V   5
STABLING
  STABLING HIS UNLOOSED LIGHTNINGS IN THEIR STALL, . . . 36 OISIN 2   110
  AND STABLING TO YOUR MIND. . . . .   774 COME RIDE   8
STAFF
  OF DREAMY FOAM A STAFF OF WOOD . . . .   24 OISIN 1   366
  I DREW IT FORTH¡ THE STAFF OF WOOD, ...   24 OISIN 1   366
  WHITE FLOWERS OF THE FOAM A STAFF OF WOOD . . . . .   24 OISIN 1   V   366
  PUT THE STAFF IN MY HANDS¡ . . . .   61 OISIN 3   201
  AND CRUMPLED IN MY HANDS THE STAFF . . . .   84 MAD KING GOLL V 33
  AND BROKE BETWEEN MY HANDS THE STAFF . . . .   84 MAD KING GOLL V 33
STAFFORD
  AND EVEN STAFFORD SMILED AS THOUGH . . . .   400 DEMON BEAST   V 13
STAG
  THE STAG WE CHASED WAS NOT MORE SAD, ...   2 OISIN 1   V 7J
  THE STAG YE CHASE IS NOT MORE SAD, ...   4 OISIN 1   V 35
  THE DELICATE-STEPPING STAG AND HIS LADY SIGH, . . . 210 RAGGED WOOD   2
  THE DELICATE STEPPING STAG AND HIS LADY SIGH . . .   210 RAGGED WOOD   V   2
  WITH THE GROUND-IVY'S BLUE, HE SAW A STAG . . . .   277 TWO KINGS   6
  MORE HANDS IN HEIGHT THAN ANY STAG IN THE WORLD . . 277 TWO KINGS   9
  BUT THE STAG STOOPED AND RAN AT HIM, AND PASSED, . . 277 TWO KINGS   12
  AGAINST THE STAG. WHEN HORN AND STEEL WERE MET . .   277 TWO KINGS   15
  AS THOUGH A STAG AND UNICORN WERE MET . . . . . .   277 TWO KINGS   19
  AND THE GROUND IVY'S BLUER LIGHT, A STAG . . . . .   277 TWO KINGS   V   6
  BUT THE STAG STOOPED ITS HEAVY BRANCHING HORNS, . . 277 TWO KINGS   V 12
  THE MARVELLOUS STAG OF ARTHUR, ...   399 BREAK OF DAY   23
  THAT LOFTY WHITE STAG, LEAP . . . .   399 BREAK OF DAY   24
  THE WILD STAG AND THE DOE¡ THAT MOUTH TO MOUTH . . . 465 HARUN RASHID   101
  STAG COULD RUN AND ROE LEAP . . . .   522 LULLABY   V 10
  STAG COULD LEAP AND ROE COULD RUN. . . . .   522 LULLABY   V 12
STAGE
  WE LIVED LIKE MEN THAT WATCH A PAINTED STAGE. . . . 542 PARN FUNERAL 1   18
  UPON A PAINTED STAGE WHEN WE DEVOURED HIS HEART, . . 542 PARN FUNERAL 1   23
  THE GREAT STAGE CURTAIN ABOUT TO DROP, ...   565 LAPIS LAZULI   13
  MY FATHER UPON THE ABBEY STAGE, BEFORE HIM A RAGING CROWD¡ 577 LOFTY THINGS 2
  PLAYERS AND PAINTED STAGE TOOK ALL MY LOVE, ... 630 CIRCUS ANIMALS   31
  NOW A NOTABLE MAN ON STAGE AND ON SCREEN¡ . . . .   790 DEDICATION   8
STAGES
  UPON A HUNDRED THOUSAND STAGES, ...   566 LAPIS LAZULI   23
STAGGER
  AND THEN I'D STAGGER OUT. HE'D CRACK HIS WITS . . . 377 PHASES OF MOON 134
  I SAW HIM STAGGER WITH THE CLANKING CHAIN, ...   687 TWO TITANS   31
STAGGERED
  I STAGGERED, BUT A BEECH-TREE STAYED MY FALL, . . . 286 TWO KINGS   209
  I STAGGERED, BUT A BEECH TREE STAYED MY FALL, . . . 286 TWO KINGS   V 209
STAGGERING
  THEY BORE IT WITH STAGGERING AND SWEATING, ...   60 OISIN 3   186
  WITH SWEATING, WITH STAGGERING, ...   60 OISIN 3   V 185
  ABOVE THE STAGGERING GIRL, HER THIGHS CARESSED . .   441 LEDA AND SWAN   2
  THE MOON IS STAGGERING IN THE SKY¡ . . . .   487 CRAZED MOON   2
  STAGGERING WITH LANGUID EYE. . . . .   717 FAIRY DOCTOR V 16
STAG'S
  TO STAY THE STAG'S NEXT RUSH. WHEN SWORD MET HORN . . 277 TWO KINGS   V 15
STAID
  WITH HEAD BOWED ON HIS KNEES, CUCHULLIN STAID, . . . 110 CUCHULAIN SEA V 71
STAIN
  AH ME¡ TO BE OLD WITHOUT SUCCOUR, A SHOW UNTO CHILDREN, 63 OISIN 3   V 217
    A STAIN,
  OF HER UNBLEMISHED LINEAMENTS, A WHITENESS WITH NO STAIN, 353 HIS PHOENIX 3
  AND SMOOTH OUT STAIN AND BLEMISH WITH THE ELEGANCE OF HIS 353 HIS PHOENIX 7
    MIND¡
  WRITTEN IN GOLD UPON A PURPLE STAIN, ...   461 HARUN RASHID   10
  THE BLOOD OF INNOCENCE HAS LEFT NO STAIN. . . . .   482 BLOOD AND MOON   34
  LIKE EVERYTHING THAT HAS THE STAIN OF BLOOD, . . .   482 BLOOD AND MOON   51
  A PROPERTY OF THE LIVING¡ BUT NO STAIN . . . . .   482 BLOOD AND MOON   52
  AND BLOOD AND MIRE THE SENSITIVE BODY STAIN? . . .   564 GYRES   10
  OR LONG ERE THIS HAD LOST THEIR RUDDY STAIN¡ . . .   687 TWO TITANS   8
  DANCING ON THE MOON'S BROAD STAIN, ...   731 STREET DANCERS   15
STAINED   SEE WINE-STAINED
  BUT NEVER SAW THE TREFOIL STAINED WITH BLOOD, . . . 487 SEVEN SAGES   19
  LOVE STORM¡ AND STAINED WITH MIST THE NEW MOONS FLARE. . 678 ISLE STAT II 3 294
  LOVE STORM AND STAINED WITH MIST THE NEW MOON'S FLARE . . 678 ISLE STAT II 3 V 294
STAINING
  IRRATIONAL STREAMS OF BLOOD ARE STAINING EARTH¡ . . 564 GYRES   5
STAINS
  I TURNED IT IN MY HANDS¡ THE STAINS . . . .   24 OISIN 1   368
STAIR
  HALF IN THE UNVESSELLED SEA, WE CLIMBED THE STAIR . . 32 OISIN 2   47
  WE MOUNTED ON THE STAIR, THE WHITE STEED TYING, . .   32 OISIN 2   V   46
  CAME SWIMMING SADLY DOWN THE MIGHTY STAIR. . . . .   32 OISIN 2   V 50B
  AND THEN WE CLIMBED THE STAIR TO A HIGH DOOR¡ . . .   36 OISIN 2   101
  AND UP THE STAIR WE TOILED TO A HIGH DOOR, ...   36 OISIN 2   V 101
  I FOUND, DROPPING SEA-FOAM ON THE WIDE STAIR, . . .   43 OISIN 2   215

STAIR   (CONTINUED)
  I FOUND, FOAM-OOZY ON THE VASTY STAIR, ...   43 OISIN 2   V 215
  I FOUND, DROPPING SEA FOAM ON THE WIDE STAIR, ... 43 OISIN 2   V 215
  I STOOD UPON THE STAIR! THE SURGES BORE . . . . . .   44 OISIN 2   225
  CLIMB UP THE NARROW WINDING STAIR TO BED! . . . . .   324 ROBERT GREGORY   5
  CLIMBED UP MY CREAKING STAIR. THEY HAD READ . . . .   358 PRESENCES   6
  TO CLIMB THAT STAIR AND EAT THAT BITTER BREAD, ... 369 EGO DOMINUS   35
  A WINDING STAIR, A CHAMBER ARCHED WITH STONE, ...   419 MY HOUSE   11
  MAY THIS LABORIOUS STAIR AND THIS STARK TOWER . . . .   423 MY DESCENDANTS   13
  I TURN AWAY AND SHUT THE DOOR, AND ON THE STAIR . . .   427 PHANTOM HATRED   33
  I SUMMON TO THE WINDING ANCIENT STAIR! . . . . . .   477 SELF AND SOUL   1
  I SUMMON TO THE WINDY ANCIENT STAIR! . . . . . .   477 SELF AND SOUL V   1
  THIS WINDING, GYRING, SPIRING TREADMILL OF A STAIR . . 480 BLOOD AND MOON   17
  . . . IS MY ANCESTRAL STAIR! . . . .   480 BLOOD AND MOON   17
  ODOUR OF BLOOD ON THE ANCESTRAL STAIR! . . . . . .   482 BLOOD AND MOON   40
  AND NOW LIES SUNK IN SLEEP. WHAT CLIMBS THE STAIR? . . 579 DOR WELLESLEY   11
  BUT NOW LIES SUNK IN SLEEP. WHAT CLIMBS THE STAIR? . . 579 DOR WELLESLEY V 11
  AND BOTH CLIMBED UP THE STAIR, ...   595 COLONEL MARTIN   38
  AND WHEN THEY CAME TO THE TOP STAIR . . . . . .   595 COLONEL MARTIN   41
  "IF I DO BUT CLIMB THE STAIR . . . .   771 SONG DEIRDRE 1   2
STAIRS
  HALF IN THE UNVESSELLED SEA, WE CLIMBED THE STAIRS . . . 32 OISIN 2   V 47
  LEAP IN THE MEADOW. ON THE MISTY STAIRS . . . . . .   44 OISIN 2   V 229
  OR SHOD IN IRON, CLIMBED THE NARROW STAIRS, ...   412 TOWER   83
STAKE
  FOR YE ARE HID WITH VAPOUR. ROUND THE STAKE . . . .   695 MOSADA 1   111
  THE VAPOUR IS MUCH THICKER. GOD! THE STAKE! . . . .   695 MOSADA 1   112
  FOR YE ARE HID WITH VAPOURS? ROUND THE STAKE . . . .   695 MOSADA 1   V 111
  SHOULD KNOW WHAT ISSUE IS AT STAKE! . . . .   778 FRIENDS WRONG   3
  AND SET IT ON A STAKE. . . . .   789 SINGING HEAD   6
  BUT NEVER STOOD BEFORE A STAKE . . . .   790 SINGING HEAD   23
STAKES
  FOR OTHER STAKES WE PLAY. YOU LOST THE GLASS. . . . . 722 WITCH VIVIEN   50
STALK
  WHO MADE THE WORLD AND RULETH IT, HE HANGETH ON A STALK, 76 INDIAN ON GOD   10
  I, THROUGH THE TERRIBLE NOVELTY OF LIGHT, STALK ON, STALK 623 HIGH TALK   13
    ON!
  I, THROUGH THE TERRIBLE NOVELTY OF LIGHT, STALK ON, STALK 623 HIGH TALK   13
    ON!
  GHOSTS OF HER VANISHED GLORIES, MUSE AND STALK . . . . 687 TWO TITANS   21
STALKED
  WHAT STALKED THROUGH THE POST OFFICE? WHAT INTELLECT, . . 611 STATUES   26
STALKS
  AND MINE WERE BUT FIFTEEN FOOT, NO MODERN STALKS   623 HIGH TALK   3
    UPON HIGHER,
STALL
  STABLING HIS UNLOOSED LIGHTNINGS IN THEIR STALL, ... 36 OISIN 2   110
STALLION
  MARE OR STALLION, COCK OR HEN, ...   529 TOM LUNATIC   15
  "THE STALLION ETERNITY . . . .   529 TOM CRUACHAN   4
STAMMERING
  BY THE STAMMERING SCHOOLBOY SAID, ...   65 HAPPY SHEPHERD   15
STAMP
  WHEN THERE ARE MANY? EBREMAR WILL STAMP . . . . .   696 MOSADA 2   4
STAMPED
  YOUR HOOVES HAVE STAMPED AT THE BLACK MARGIN OF THE WOOD, 442 BLACK CENTAUR   1
  MY WORKS ARE ALL STAMPED DOWN INTO THE SULTRY MUD. . . 442 BLACK CENTAUR   3
  STAMPED BOY AND TREE UPON SICILIAN COIN. . . . . .   541 PARN FUNERAL 1   15
STAMPER
  BRIMFUL OF STARLIGHT, AND HE SAID! THE STAMPER OF   76 INDIAN ON GOD   14
    THE SKIES,
STAND
  WITH WISDOM HOUR BY HOUR.--MAY WE TWO STAND, ...   71 ANASHU VIJAYA   7
  WITH WISDOM HOUR BY HOUR.--MAY WE TOO STAND, ...   71 ANASHU VIJAYA V   7
  STAND YOU. BY BRAHMA'S EVER-RUSTLING ROBE, ...   71 ANASHU VIJAYA V 14
  "ALTHOUGH OUR LOVE IS WANING, LET US STAND . . . . .   79 EPHEMERA   4
  STAND BY THE BORDER OF THE LAKE ONCE MORE, ...   79 EPHEMERA   V   5
  IN A FIELD BY THE RIVER MY LOVE AND I DID STAND, . . . 90 SALLEY GARDENS   5
  WHILE I STAND ON THE ROADWAY, OR ON THE PAVEMENTS GREY, 117 ISLE INNISFREE   11
  WHILE I STAND ON THE ROADWAY, OR ON THE PAVEMENT GREY, . 117 ISLE INNISFREE V 11
  OR ELSE THEY STAND AND SNIFF THE WIND, ...   136 TWO TREES   37
  AND STAND ON HER WINDOW-SILL, ...   159 CAP AND BELLS   4
  AND STAND ON HER WINDOW SILL, ...   159 CAP AND BELLS V   4
  STAND UNDER THE ROUGH ROOF-TIMBERS OF THE HALL . . .   377 PHASES OF MOON   125
  I'D STAND AND MUTTER THERE UNTIL HE CAUGHT . . . .   377 PHASES OF MOON   131
  STAND UP AND LIFT YOUR HAND AND BLESS . . . . . .   379 SAINT HUNCH   1
  STAND AT MY DOOR, AND I COMPLAIN . . . .   424 ROAD AT DOOR   8
  FROM SHALLOW WITS, WHO KNOWS NO WORK CAN STAND, . . . 429 NINETEEN 19   35
  BID A STRONG GHOST STAND AT THE HEAD . . . . . .   435 FOR MY SON   1
  I SAW A STARING VIRGIN STAND . . . .   437 SONGS PLAY 1   1
  I SAW THAT STARING, VIRGIN STAND . . . .   437 SONGS PLAY 1   V   1
  OUR MOST RENOWNED PATRIOTS STAND, ...   460 THREE MONUMENT   2
  HERE, TRAVELLER, SCHOLAR, POET, TAKE YOUR STAND . . . 489 COOLE PARK 29   25
  AND BIDS MY HAIR STAND UP? . . . .   499 MOTHER OF GOD   15
  AND MAKES MY HAIR STAND UP? . . . .   499 MOTHER OF GOD V 15
  AND SEEMED TO STAND ALTHOUGH IN BED I LAY. . . . .   535 CHOSEN   9
  AS THOUGH THAT HAND COULD REACH TO WHERE THEY STAND, . 579 DOR WELLESLEY   2
  I AM CONTENT TO STAND AND SING . . . .   582 ROGER CASEMENT V 21
  STAND UPRIGHT ON YOUR LEGS AWHILE, ...   586 PARNELLITES   3
  STAND UPRIGHT WHILE YOU CAN, ...   586 PARNELLITES   4
  BEFORE A WOMAN'S PORTRAIT SUDDENLY I STAND, ... 602 GALLERY REVIS   13

759

STAND   (CONTINUED)
  THERE IN THE TOMB STAND THE DEAD UPRIGHT, ...   635 BLACK TOWER   7
  STAND WE ON GUARD OATH-BOUND! . . . .   636 BLACK TOWER   26
  A WHITE, DUMB THING OF TEARS, HERE LET IT STAND, ... 663 ISLE STAT II 2   21
  I'LL SEE HIM LONGER IF I STAND OUT HERE . . . .   703 MOSADA 1   113
  "BRING THE ROPES NOW!   STAND YE BY NOW! . . . .   718 PHANTOM SHIP   13
  "MAY STAND BEFORE THY RACE AND THEE . . . .   742 EARL PAUL   63
  THE ARCHANGELS STAND IN A ROW THERE . . . .   774 COME RIDE   9
STANDEST
  NO! THOU STANDEST STILL AND STARK, ...   658 ISLE STAT I 3   90
STANDING
  I SAW HER STANDING IN HER DOOR BUT NOW. . . . .   74 ANASHU VIJAYA   64
  WHY ARE YOU STANDING WITH YOUR EYES UPON ME? . . . . .   234 SHADOW WATER B   276
  LEANING OR STANDING OR WALKING . . . .   356 BROKEN DREAMS   23
  AND, STANDING BY THESE CHARACTERS, DISCLOSE . . . . .   371 EGO DOMINUS   75
  O SAGES STANDING IN GOD'S HOLY FIRE . . . .   408 SAIL BYZANTIUM   17
  AM SET DOWN STANDING IN THE WOOD . . . .   453 DEATH OF HARE   11
  THERE, STANDING ON THE CART, ...   544 TO SAME TUNE 1   5
  THERE, STANDING ON THE CART, ...   616 MARCH SONGS 3   5
  HOW CAN I, THAT GIRL STANDING THERE, ...   631 POLITICS   1
  AS I AM STANDING NOW--AS THOUGH I GAZED, ...   663 ISLE STAT II 2   26
  BEHOLD THE HAPLESS SLEEPERS STANDING BY. . . . .   677 ISLE STAT II 3   281
STANDISH
  STANDISH O'GRADY SUPPORTING HIMSELF BETWEEN THE TABLES . . 577 LOFTY THINGS   5
STANDS
  THE HUNTSMAN NEAR HIM STANDS, ...   98 FOXHUNTER   24
  THE HUNTSMAN NEAR HIM STANDS, ...   98 FOXHUNTER   V   22
  MY FATHER STANDS AMID HIS BATTLE-CARS." . . . .   107 CUCHULAIN SEA   26
  MY FATHER STANDS." "AGED, WORN OUT WITH WARS . . . . .   107 CUCHULAIN SEA   29
  MY FATHER STANDS AMID HIS BATTLE CARS." . . . .   107 CUCHULAIN SEA V   26
  AND GOD STANDS WINDING HIS LONELY HORN. . . . .   148 INTO TWILIGHT   13
  SHE STANDS BEFORE ME AS A LIVING CHILD. . . . .   444 SCHOOL CHILDR   24
  UNDER IT WISDOM STANDS, AND I ALONE-- . . . .   469 HARUN RASHID   189
  UNDER IT ARMED WISDOM STANDS, A SEPARATE WISDOM . . . . 469 HARUN RASHID   V   189
  HORACE THERE BY HOMER STANDS, ...   524 MAD AS MIST   7
  PLATO STANDS BELOW, ...   524 MAD AS MIST   8
  "WHATEVER STANDS IN FIELD OR FLOOD, ...   529 TOM LUNATIC   13
  STANDS IN GOD'S UNCHANGING EYE . . . .   529 TOM LUNATIC   16
  WHEN SEA-WIND SWEPT THE CORNER, STANDS: . . . . . .   566 LAPIS LAZULI   32
  WHAT ON THE THRESHOLD STANDS? . . . .   583 GHOST ROG CASE   2
  THEN STANDS IN JUDGMENT ON HIS SOUL, ...   633 MAN AND ECHO   33
  FOR AN INSTANT STANDS AT EASE, ...   638 BEN BULBEN   31
  LONG YEARS AGO, A CHURCH STANDS NEAR, ...   640 BEN BULBEN   87
  FAMOUS, A MAN OF RULES, A VICTOR. STANDS . . . . . .   709 FERENCZ RENYI   9
  WHITE, RENYI SILENT STANDS: THAT MAIDEN SWEET . . . .   713 FERENCZ RENYI   84
  I CURSE THEE--CURSE THEE! RENYI SILENT STANDS, ... 714 FERENCZ RENYI V   107
  STANDS EACH GREY AND SILENT PHANTOM ON THE SAME REGARDLESS 719 PHANTOM SHIP   25
      SPOT--
  UPON MY SOUL, OLD TIME. NO! THUS IT STANDS. . . . . .   722 WITCH VIVIEN   49
STAR   SEE POLE-STAR
  AND SLEEP DROWN SUN AND MOON AND STAR." . . . .   5 OISIN 1   V   49
  IN OTHER YEARS FROM SOME OLD STAR . . . .   19 OISIN 1   V   277
  EACH FOREHEAD LIKE AN OBSCURE STAR . . . .   26 OISIN 1   391
  HUNG FROM THE MORNING STAR! WHEN THESE MILD WORDS . . .   32 OISIN 2   49
  SO MUCH REMAINED THAT ON THE EVENING STAR . . . . . .   32 OISIN 2   V   48
  WHERE GOES TO GAZE THE RESTLESS-FOOTED STAR . . . . .   32 OISIN 2   V   50G
  WHEN THE EARLIEST DEW-WASHED STAR FROM EVE HATH LEANT, . 32 OISIN 2   V   54
  SHOUTED, AND HAILED HIM! HE HUNG THERE A STAR, ...   36 OISIN 2   107
  SCARED OF ITS GLITTERING LIKE A METEOR STAR, ...   38 OISIN 2   V   137
  I HAVE FORGIVEN, O NEW STAR! . . . .   75 ANASHU VIJAYA   77
  WHILE OUR LOVE GROWS AN INDIAN STAR, ...   78 INDIAN TO LOVE   13
  WHILE GROWS OUR LOVE AN INDIAN STAR, ...   78 INDIAN TO LOVE V   13
  AND UNDER THE BLINK O' THE MORNING STAR, ...   83 MAD KING GOLL V   20
  THAT SCARCE COULD BATHE A STAR, ...   88 STOLEN CHILD   31
  ONE STAR SHONE FAINT AND GREEN, ...   95 MOLL MAGEE   30
  AND THE FLAME OF THE BLUE STAR OF TWILIGHT, . . .   122 WHITE BIRDS   3
  OR THE FLAME OF THE BLUE STAR THAT LINGERS . . . .   122 WHITE BIRDS   7
  FOR THE WINDS THAT AWAKENED THE STAR, ...   171 MAID QUIET   V   3
  THE PILOT STAR AND THE CROOKED PLOUGH . . . . . .   177 PAST GREATNESS   4
  OUT OF THE RUNNING STREAM, O MORNING STAR, ...   251 SHADOW WATER B   610
  AYE, SUN AND MOON AND STAR, ALL, ...   415 TOWER   152
  WHEN THAT FIERCE VIRGIN AND HER STAR . . . .   437 SONGS PLAY 1   15
  WHEN THE FIERCE VIRGIN AND HER STAR . . . .   437 SONGS PLAY 1   V   15
  WHAT A STAR SANG AND CARELESS MUSES HEARD! . . . . .   445 SCHOOL CHILDR   47
  UPON THE STAR THAT MARKS THE HIDDEN POLE: . . . . .   477 SELF AND SOUL   5
  THIS FALLEN STAR MY MILK SUSTAINS, ...   499 MOTHER OF GOD   12
  BRIGHTNESS REMAINS! A BRIGHTER STAR SHOOTS DOWN! . . .   541 PARN FUNERAL 1   4
  RECALL THE CRETAN BARB THAT PIERCED A STAR? . . . .   541 PARN FUNERAL 1   7
  A PIERCED BOY, IMAGE OF A STAR LAID LOW. . . . . .   541 PARN FUNERAL 1   12
  ANOTHER STAR HAS SHOT AN EAR. . . . .   625 NATIVITY   2
  EACH SHINING CLEAR AS SOME UNBAFFLED STAR! . . . . .   656 ISLE STAT I 3   25
  DRAW STAR TO STAR, AS ON THAT EVE HE PASSED . . . .   691 MOSADA 1   29
  DRAW STAR TO STAR, AS ON THAT EVE HE PASSED . . . .   691 MOSADA 1   29
  WE'LL FLY FROM THIS BEFORE THE MORNING STAR. . . . .   702 MOSADA 3   74
  SINGS THE YOUNG WISTFUL SPIRIT OF A STAR . . . . .   705 REMEMBRANCE   10
  WHILE THE MORNING STAR DECAYETH . . . .   706 DAWN-SONG   29
  AND SOFT, ONE GLIMMERING STAR. RENYI HAS CAST . . . .   714 FERENCZ RENYI   115
  AND SOFT, ONE GLIMMERING STAR--WITH POWER VAST! . . .   714 FERENCZ RENYI V   115
  BESIDE THE WILLOW. NAY, TO YONDER STAR, ...   715 FERENCZ RENYI   118
  BENEATH THE WILLOW--NAY, TO YONDER STAR, ...   715 FERENCZ RENYI V   118
  OUT OF A RUNNING STREAM, O MORNING STAR . . . . . .   769 SHADOW WATER A   426

STAR-BANE
    NO WORD OF THEIRS--THE COLD STAR-BANE . . . .   66 HAPPY SHEPHERD   32
STARE
    ON EVERY CROWDED STREET TO STARE . . . .   294 HATED PLAYBOY   3
    ROUND ABOUT HELL'S GATE TO STARE . . . .   294 HATED PLAYBOY V   3
    AND PIERCE IT THROUGH WITH A GIMLET, AND STARE . . . .   330 BONE OF A HARE   12
    UPON SOME LOFTY ROCK TO STARE . . . .   397 POLIT PRISONER   21
    I PACE UPON THE BATTLEMENTS AND STARE . . . . . .   409 TOWER   17
    COME BUILD IN THE EMPTY HOUSE OF THE STARE. . . . . .   424 STARES NEST   5
    COME BUILD IN THE EMPTY HOUSE OF THE STARE. . . . . .   425 STARES NEST   10
    COME BUILD IN THE EMPTY HOUSE OF THE STARE. . . . . .   425 STARES NEST   15
    COME BUILD IN THE EMPTY HOUSE OF THE STARE. . . . . .   425 STARES NEST   20
    IN MOMENTARY WONDER STARE UPON . . . .   443 SCHOOL CHILDR   7
    AND OFTEN THOSE FIRST DAYS I SAW HER STARE . . . . .   466 HARUN RASHID   122
    AND NOW WE STARE ASTONISHED AT THE SEA, ...   534 HER TRIUMPH   11
    THE KING THAT COULD MAKE HIS PEOPLE STARE, ...   550 SEVERED HEAD   19
    ON ALL THE TRAGIC SCENE THEY STARE. . . . .   567 LAPIS LAZULI   52
    PYTHAGORAS PLANNED IT. WHY DID THE PEOPLE STARE? . . .   610 STATUES   1
    AND IN HER EYES A LIGHTLESS STARE, ...   668 ISLE STAT II 3   60
    UNQUENCHABLE STILL GLOWS IN HER DULL STARE, ...   687 TWO TITANS   17
STARED
    THAT SWINEHERD STARED UPON HER FACE AND SAID, ...   106 CUCHULAIN SEA   9
    STARED ON THE MOURNFUL WONDER OF HIS EYES, ...   108 CUCHULAIN SEA   41
    STARED LIKE THE SPRING UPON THE ANCIENT SKIES, ...   108 CUCHULAIN SEA V   41
    STARED ON THE HORSES OF THE SEA, AND HEARD . . . . .   111 CUCHULAIN SEA   84
    STARED AT THE GODS WITH LAUGHING LIP. . . . .   276 GREY ROCK   123
    AND STARED INTO THE SEA-GREEN EYE, AND SO . . . . . .   278 TWO KINGS   25
    AND STARED INTO THE SEA-GREEN EYES, AND SO . . . . .   278 TWO KINGS V   25
    WITH BLOOD-SHOT EYES UPON HIM STARED. . . . .   297 THREE BEGGARS   58
    BLACK MINNALOUSHE STARED AT THE MOON, ...   378 CAT AND MOON   5
    STARED AT THE WINE-DARK NAIL, OR DARK THAT RAN . . . .   537 HER VISION   10
    I STARED UPON HIS BLOOD-BEDABBLED BREAST . . . . . .   537 HER VISION   23
    I STARED UPON MY BLOOD-BEDABBLED BREAST . . . . . .   537 HER VISION V   23
    EYES STARED OUT OF THE BRANCHES AND WERE GONE. . . . .   634 CUCHULAIN COMF   3
STAR-ENVIOUS
    STAR-ENVIOUS. HE WAS A SPIRIT, BROTHER. . . . . . .   683 SEEKER   39
STARE'S
    THE STARE'S NEST BY MY WINDOW . . . .   424 STARES NEST   T
STARES
    THE GREAT GREY-EYED ATHENE STARES THEREON. . . . . .   447 COLONUS PRAISE   16
    PELEUS ON THETIS STARES. . . . .   612 NEWS ORACLE   26
STAR-FIRE
    NOW IN A PLACE OF STAR-FIRE, AND NOW IN A SHADOW-PLACE   49 OISIN 3   42
        WIDE!
    NOW IN A PLACE OF STAR-FIRE, AND NOW IN A SHADOW PLACE   49 OISIN 3 V   42
        WIDE!
STAR-FIRES
    NOR LOST IN THE STAR-FIRES AND ODOURS . . . .   56 OISIN 3   135
STAR-FLAME
    . . . HIS KNEES IN THE SOFT STAR-FLAME, ...   50 OISIN 3   43
STAR-FOUGHT
    WITH CLINGING MIST, EACH STAR-FOUGHT WANDERER CAME . . .   656 ISLE STAT I 3   33
STAR-GLIMMERING
    MORE SHINING WINDS, MORE STAR-GLIMMERING PONDS? . . . .   218 WOODS OF COOLE   35
STARING
    STARING UPON HIS SINEWY THIGH. . . . .   294 HATED PLAYBOY   6
    STARING ON HIS SINEWY THIGH. . . . .   294 HATED PLAYBOY V   6
    STARING UPON A BEDOUIN'S HORSE-HAIR ROOF . . . . . .   368 EGO DOMINUS   29
    I SAW A STARING VIRGIN STAND . . . .   437 SONGS PLAY 1   1
    I SAW THAT STARING VIRGIN STAND . . . .   437 SONGS PLAY 1 V   1
    THAT STARING FURY AND THE BLIND LUSH LEAF . . . . . .   500 VACILLATION   17
    GUARDED! GRIFFITH STARING IN HYSTERICAL PRIDE! . . . .   601 GALLERY REVIS   4
    STILL STARING AT THEIR FLOWERS, ...   680 LOVE AND DEATH   25
STARK
    BESIDE THE CASTLE DOOR, WHERE ALL IS STARK . . . . . .   377 PHASES OF MOON   126
    WITH A STARK, DENYING LOOK! . . . .   381 SONG OF FOOL   6
    MAY THIS LABORIOUS STAIR AND THIS STARK TOWER . . . .   423 MY DESCENDANTS   13
    OF THE STARK MYSTERY THAT HAS DAZED MY SIGHT, ...   466 HARUN RASHID   113
    OF THAT STARK MYSTERY WHERE I AM PLUNGED . . . . . .   466 HARUN RASHID V   113
    FORMS A STARK EGYPTIAN THOUGHT, ...   638 BEN BULBEN   43
    NO! THOU STANDEST STILL AND STARK, ...   658 ISLE STAT I 3   90
STAR-LADEN
    THE FULL ROUND MOON AND THE STAR-LADEN SKY, ...   119 SORROW OF LOVE V   2
    WHERE PEOPLE LOVE BESIDE STAR-LADEN SEAS! . . . . . .   126 DREAM OF FAERY V   9
STARLIGHT
    UNDER THE STARLIGHT AND SHADOW, A MONSTROUS SLUMBERING   48 OISIN 3   27
        FOLK,
    THAT WE MAY MUSE IN THE STARLIGHT AND TALK OF THE BATTLES   51 OISIN 3   63
        OF OLD!
    AND A SOFTNESS CAME FROM THE STARLIGHT . . . .   52 OISIN 3   72
    . . . TILL STARLIGHT AND MIDNIGHT PART, ...   60 OISIN 3   184
    BRIMFUL OF STARLIGHT, AND HE SAID! THE STAMPER OF   76 INDIAN ON GOD   14
        THE SKIES!
    AND STARLIGHT GLEAMED, AND CLOUDS FLEW HIGH, ...   84 MAD KING GOLL   34
    "YET SOMEWHERE UNDER STARLIGHT OR THE SUN . . . . . .   107 CUCHULAIN SEA   28
    THE ELABORATE STARLIGHT THROWS A REFLECTION . . . . .   389 IMAGE PAST   2
    THE BABYLONIAN STARLIGHT BROUGHT . . . .   438 SONGS PLAY 2   4
    A STARLIGHT OR A MOONLIT DOME DISTAINS . . . .   497 BYZANTIUM V   5
    RICH FOLIAGE THAT THE STARLIGHT GLITTERED THROUGH, . . .   541 PARN FUNERAL 1   8
    AND ALL HER STARLIGHT IS WITH SORROW MAD, ...   738 YOU ARE SAD   3

```
                                                          PAGE      TITLE            LINE
STAR-LIGHT
    THE ELABORATE STAR-LIGHT HAS THROWN REFLECTIONS  . . . .    389 IMAGE PAST       V    2
    THE BABYLONIAN STAR-LIGHT BROUGHT  . . . . . . . .         438 SONGS PLAY 2      V    4
STARLING
    A STARLING LIKE THEM THAT FORGATHERED 'NEATH A MOON . . .   54 OISIN 3               103
STARLIT
    UPON THE BREATHLESS STARLIT AIR,  . . . . . . . .          477 SELF AND SOUL          4
    A STARLIT OR A MOONLIT DOME DISDAINS  . . . . . .          497 BYZANTIUM              5
    PLANTED ON THE STARLIT GOLDEN BOUGH,  . . . . . .          497 BYZANTIUM         V   19
STAR-LIT
    PLANTED ON THE STAR-LIT GOLDEN BOUGH,  . . . . . .         497 BYZANTIUM             19
    A STAR-LIT RAPIER, HALF BLOOD-DARK,  . . . . . .           671 ISLE STAT II 3      125
STARN
    ABOUT THE STARN AND BROKE IN DAYS AND YEARS. . . . .       206 ADAMS CURSE       V   33
STARRED      SEE EVIL-STARRED
    THAT CALLS. O EVIL STARRED! IT COMES ALONG  . . . . .      653 ISLE STAT I 2        49
STARRY
    AND SANG UNTO THE STARRY BROODS. . . . . . . . .           22 OISIN 1               326
    NO LEARNING FROM THE STARRY MEN. . . . . . . . .           66 HAPPY SHEPHERD         28
    MORE MOURNFUL THAN THE DEPTH OF STARRY SKIES, . . . .     108 CUCHULAIN SEA     V   42
    OR SIGHS AMID THE WANDERING, STARRY MIRTH, . . . .        114 ROSE OF BATTLE        18
    AND STILL THE STARRY CANDLES FLARE . . . . . . .          138 TO IRELAND        V   13
    AND THE WINDS THAT BLOW THROUGH THE STARRY WAYS, . . . .  158 TO HIS HEART           4
    LET THE STARRY WINDS AND THE FLAME AND THE FLOOD  . . .   158 TO HIS HEART           5
    AND THE WINDS BLOWING THROUGH THE STARRY WAYS, . . . .    158 TO HIS HEART      V    4
    UPON THE STARRY BRINK. . . . . . . . . . . .             216 HAPPY TOWNLAND         52
    AMONG THE STARRY EDDIES OF HER HAIR  . . . . . .          390 IMAGE PAST             27
    IN STARRY TOWERS OF BABYLON  . . . . . . . . .           440 WISDOM                 14
    FOR, AH, OUR LIVES WERE BUT TWO STARRY WORDS  . . . .    675 ISLE STAT II 3        236
    FAR AWAY THE STARRY MIRTH  . . . . . . . . . .           731 STREET DANCERS         7
    OTHERS KNOW THE STARRY MIRTH! . . . . . . . . .          733 STREET DANCERS        54
    STORM DARKENED OR STARRY BRIGHT. . . . . . . . .         739 WHERE BOOKS GO         8
STARS
    WHEN THE STARS ARE TO WANE AND THE WORLD BE DONE. . . .    16 OISIN 1               220
    SLEEP THERE TILL THE MOON AND THE STARS DIE!"  . . . .     17 OISIN 1               246
    AND FILLS WITH STARS NIGHT'S PURPLE CUP, . . . . .         18 OISIN 1               262
    AS THUS OUR SONG AROSE! "YOU STARS,  . . . . . .           22 OISIN 1               329
    AS THUS OUR SONG AROSE! "YE STARS,  . . . . . .            22 OISIN 1           V  329
    BUT WE, OH ROLLING STARS, ARE FREE,  . . . . . .           22 OISIN 1           V  337
    AND BID THE STARS DROP DOWN FROM THE SKY, . . . . .        28 OISIN 1               426
    AND THE STARS SHALL ARISE AND SAY IN THE MORNING, . . .    28 OISIN 1           V 423G
    AND THE FIXED STARS HAD DAWNED AND SHONE AND SET. . . .    31 OISIN 2               40
    AT LAST THE MOON AND STARS SHONE, AND A FLIGHT  . . . .    31 OISIN 2           V   34
    FOR CENTURIES, AND STARS HAD DAWNED AND SET. . . . .       31 OISIN 2           V   40
    AND WHEN THE DEW-DROWNED STARS HANG IN THE AIR  . . . .    32 OISIN 2               54
    AND THE STARS WERE BLOTTED ABOVE US, . . . . . .           48 OISIN 3               24
    . . . THAT HE WHO HAS STARS FOR HIS FLOCKS  . . . .        49 OISIN 3               37
    . . . THAT HE WHO HAD STARS FOR HIS FLOCKS  . . . .        49 OISIN 3           V   37
    THE WHIRLING WAYS OF STARS THAT PASS—  . . . . . .         66 HAPPY SHEPHERD         30
    AND HE CALLED LOUDLY TO THE STARS TO BEND  . . . . .       68 SAD SHEPHERD           5
    HE CALLED ALOUD TO ALL THE STARS TO LEND  . . . . .        68 SAD SHEPHERD      V    5
    SIGH, O YOU LITTLE STARS! O SIGH AND SHAKE YOUR            72 ANASHU VIJAYA         18
        BLUE APPAREL!
    SING, O YOU LITTLE STARS!  O SING AND RAISE YOUR RAPTUROUS 72 ANASHU VIJAYA         20
        CAROL
    SIGH, OH YE LITTLE STARS! OH, SIGH AND SHAKE YOUR BLUE     72 ANASHU VIJAYA     V   18
        APPAREL!
    SING, OH YE LITTLE STARS! OH, SING, AND RAISE YOUR         72 ANASHU VIJAYA     V   20
        RAPTUROUS CAROL
    SING YOU OF HER, O FIRST FEW STARS,  . . . . . .           73 ANASHU VIJAYA         41
    WHAT KNOW THE PILOTS OF THE STARS OF TEARS? . . . .        73 ANASHU VIJAYA         47
    SING YE OF HER, OH FIRST FEW STARS  . . . . . .            73 ANASHU VIJAYA     V   41
    HOW FAR AWAY THE STARS SEEM, AND HOW FAR  . . . . .        80 EPHEMERA               8
    AND UNDER THE BLINKING OF THE STARS  . . . . . .           83 MAD KING GOLL         20
    I STOOD! KEEN STARS ABOVE ME SHONE . . . . . .            83 MAD KING GOLL          29
    I PAUSED—THE STARS ABOVE ME FLASHED, . . . . . .           83 MAD KING GOLL     V   29
    I PAUSED—THE STARS ABOVE ME SHONE  . . . . . .             83 MAD KING GOLL     V   29
    GOD LIGHTS THE STARS, HIS CANDLES, . . . . . .            96 MOLL MAGEE             51
    AND THINE OWN SADNESS, WHEREOF STARS, GROWN OLD  . . .    101 ROSE UPON ROOD         6
    "WHETHER UNDER ITS DAYLIGHT OR ITS STARS  . . . . .       107 CUCHULAIN SEA         25
    "NO, SOMEWHERE UNDER DAYLIGHT OR THE STARS . . . .        107 CUCHULAIN SEA     V   25
    "WHETHER UNDER ITS DAYLIGHT OR THE STARS  . . . . .       107 CUCHULAIN SEA     V   25
    UNDER THE PASSING STARS, FOAM OF THE SKY, . . . . .       112 ROSE OF WORLD          9
    HE WOULD GO WEAVE OUT OF THE STARS . . . . . .           113 ROSE OF PEACE          7
    AND WHITE STARS TELL YOUR PRAISE,  . . . . . . .         113 ROSE OF PEACE         10
    TO SMILE UPON HER STARS! AND GATHER YOU, . . . .         114 ROSE OF BATTLE    V   15
    THEY HAVE GONE DOWN UNDER THE SAME WHITE STARS, . . . .   115 ROSE OF BATTLE        34
    AND THE STARS ABOVE! . . . . . . . . . . . .             116 FAERY SONG             8
    THE STARS OF GOD WHERE THEY MOVE, . . . . . .            119 PITY OF LOVE           4
    THE CRUMBLING MOON, THE WHITE STARS IN THE SKY, . . .    120 SORROW OF LOVE    V   10
    THE CURD-PALE MOON, THE WHITE STARS IN THE SKY, . . .    120 SORROW OF LOVE    V   10
    AND HID HIS FACE AMID A CROWD OF STARS. . . . . .        121 YOU ARE OLD           12
    AND LEFT HER TO THE INDIFFERENT STARS ABOVE  . . . .     123 DREAM OF DEATH         9
    AND GAZED UPON THE MOURNFUL STARS ABOVE . . . .          123 DREAM OF DEATH    V   11
    WHILE YOUNG STARS ABOUT HER DANCE. . . . . . .           125 CATHLEEN PARA     V   16
    AND ALL DISHEVELLED WANDERING STARS. . . . . . .         126 GOES FERGUS           12
    AND STARS BEGAN TO PEEP. . . . . . . . . . .            133 FR GILLIGAN           16
    "HE WHO HATH MADE THE NIGHT OF STARS . . . . . .         134 FR GILLIGAN           41
    HAVE DOWERED THE STARS WITH MERRY LIGHT! . . . . .       134 TWO TREES              6
    AND MOTH-LIKE STARS WERE FLICKERING OUT, . . . . .       149 WANDER AENGUS          6
    AND STARS LIKE MOTHS WERE SHINING OUT, . . . . .         149 WANDER AENGUS     V    6
```

762

		PAGE	TITLE	LINE

STARS (CONTINUED)

TILL STARS ARE BEGINNING TO BLINK AND PEEP,	150	OLD MOTHER	4
AND HAD ROOTED THE SUN AND MOON AND STARS OUT OF THE SKY	153	CHANGE BELOVED	11
AND ROOTED THE SUN AND MOON AND STARS OUT OF THE SKY,	153	CHANGE BELOVED V	11
AND STARS CLIMBING THE DEW-DROPPING SKY,	158	BELOVED RHYMES	11
TILL STARS GREW OUT OF THE AIR.	160	CAP AND BELLS	28
THE STARS GREW OUT OF THE AIR.	160	CAP AND BELLS V	28
MASTER OF THE STILL STARS AND OF THE FLAMING DOOR.	161	BLACK PIG	8
BEFORE THE UNLABOURING STARS AND YOU.	164	PERFECT BEAUTY	8
BEFORE UNLABOURING STARS AND YOU.	164	PERFECT BEAUTY V	8
THAT KEEPS THE STARS IN THEIR ROUND,	165	CRY OF SEDGE	5
WHEN SHALL THE STARS BE BLOWN ABOUT THE SKY,	170	SECRET ROSE	29
THE WINDS THAT AWAKENED THE STARS	171	MAID QUIET	3
FOR THE WINDS THAT AWAKENED THE STARS	171	MAID QUIET V	3
OR AS THE CHANGING SPEARS FLUNG BY THE GOLDEN STARS	175	ELEMENT POWERS V	15
ABOUT THE STARS AND MOON AND SUN!	176	BELOVED DEAD	10
ABOVE THE STARS AND MOON AND SUN!	176	BELOVED DEAD V	10
BUT LIGHT FROM THE PALE STARS, AND GLEAMS	196	BAILE AILLINN	173
ABOUT THE STARS AND BROKE IN DAYS AND YEARS.	206	ADAMS CURSE	33
JUDGE OF THE STARS, AND FIND A COURSE FOR US?	224	SHADOW WATER B	61
FOR HE CAN JUDGE THE STARS AS WELL AS FORGAEL.	225	SHADOW WATER B	63
IT HAD WASHED AMONG THE STARS AND PUT THEM OUT,	236	SHADOW WATER B	311
OR THAN THE SHIVERING CASTING-NET OF THE STARS,	237	SHADOW WATER B	329
MORE MIGHTY THAN THE STARS HALF TROUBLED ME,	237	SHADOW WATER B	332
TILL THE STARS HAD RUN AWAY	268	BROWN PENNY	13
BUT AS THE OUTRAGEOUS STARS INCLINE	325	ROBERT GREGORY	38
SANG TILL STARS BEGAN TO FADE.	332	ROUND TOWER	20
THE STARS FADE OUT WHERE THE MOON COMES,	344	DAWN	8
THE MORNING STARS TO SING,	436	FOR MY SON	19
THAN THE HEAVENLY CIRCUIT OF ITS STARS	451	FIRST LOVE	17
THAN HEAVENLY CIRCUIT OF ITS STARS	451	FIRST LOVE V	17
'TIS MORN! LIKE OLD MEN'S EYES THE STARS ARE PALE,	645	ISLE STAT I 1	4
BLENCHING ON HIGH THE DULL STARS SICKEN	646	ISLE STAT I 1	46
DOWN TO THEIR FEET THE STARS THAT SHINE ALONE,	662	ISLE STAT II 1	80
THE MOBS OF STARS IN GOLD AND GREEN AND BLUE,	663	ISLE STAT II 2	43
THE SPINNING STARS—THE TOILING SEA—WHIRL ROUND	665	ISLE STAT II 2	72
HAS ROLLED AWAY THE STARS AND DRIED THE SEA	671	ISLE STAT II 3	146
THE TIDE OF STARS? HAVE I NOT SEEN A THOUSAND YEARS	675	ISLE STAT II 3	230
BY THOSE WAN STARS THAT SIT IN COMPANY	691	MOSADA 1	26
THAT WHEN THE STARS OF OUR NATIVITY	691	MOSADA 1	28
AND YON FEW STARS GROWN DIM, LIKE EYES OF LOVERS	700	MOSADA 3	33
MY BLOSSOM, I AM DYING, AND THE STARS	700	MOSADA 3	47
ARE DYING TOO. THEY WERE FULL SEVEN STARS!	700	MOSADA 3	48
WE MEET AT LAST, THE MINISTERING STARS	701	MOSADA 3	52
A LITTLE NEARER THOSE BRIGHT STARS. TELL ME,	701	MOSADA 3	59
IS IT YOUR MESSAGE, STARS, THAT WHEN DEATH COMES	701	MOSADA 3	60
GONE THE STARS AND GONE THE WHITE MOON,	718	PHANTOM SHIP	3
THEN THE STARS GROW OUT OF HEAVEN WITH THEIR COUNTENANCES FAIR.	719	PHANTOM SHIP	30
THE MAKER OF THE STARS AND WORLDS	724	LEGEND	1
"THE PROPS," SAID HE, "OF STARS AND WORLDS	725	LEGEND	5
THE MAKER OF THE STARS AND WORLDS	725	LEGEND	29
MOURNFUL UNDER MOURNFUL STARS.	737	IN FIRELIGHT	4
THE MOTHER OF THE STARS WEEPS TOO,	738	YOU ARE SAD	2
AND UNFORGOTTEN NAMES, AND THE COLD STARS	757	SHADOW WATER A	204
THE STARS WOULD HURL THEIR CROWNS AMONG THE FOAM	761	SHADOW WATER A	265
OR THAN THE SHIVERING CASTING-NET OF THE STARS.	762	SHADOW WATER A	290
OR THAN THE SHIVERING CASTING-NET OF THE STARS.	762	SHADOW WATER A V	290
AMID THE DARKNESS, NOW THAT ALL MY STARS	767	SHADOW WATER A V	404
LET THE STARS BEAR WITNESS!	770	BLOOD BOND	12
THE STARS ARE OUT OF SIGHT.	786	YOUR HEART	34

STAR-SHUDDERING

| OF THESE STAR-SHUDDERING SKIES, YOU ARE THE QUEEN. | 679 | ISLE STAT II 3 | 323 |

START

FROM JOY THE HOLY BRANCHES START,	134	TWO TREES	3
I START OUT OF MY SLEEP TO THINK	380	SONGS FOOL 1	7
AND START—I AT YOUR SHOULDER—	390	IMAGE PAST	30
THAN SOULS THAT START NO GAME AND TURN NO RHYME!	464	HARUN RASHID	68
MAIMED US AT THE START.	506	REMORSE SPEECH	13
A FINISH WORTHY OF THE START.	626	OLD MEN BE MAD	15
I MUST LIE DOWN WHERE ALL THE LADDERS START,	630	CIRCUS ANIMALS	39
THE SLEEPER AWOKE WITH A SUDDEN START,	729	PRIEST FAIRY	31
I FELT A SUDDEN TEAR START,	744	GLOVE CLOAK	10

STAR-TAUGHT

| THE STAR-TAUGHT MOOR, SAID THUS IT WAS DECREED | 691 | MOSADA 1 | 25 |

STARTED

SHE STARTED AND THEN KNEW WHOSE FOOT IT WAS!	280	TWO KINGS	66
HAD NOT THE SLEEPER STARTED UP.	304	HOUR DAWN	48
BUT SOON A TEAR-DROP STARTED UP,	400	DEMON BEAST	21

STAR-THROBBING

| THE HEAVENS ALL STAR-THROBBING ARE A-LIT. | 671 | ISLE STAT II 3 | 143 |
| THE HEAVENS ALL STAR-THROBBING ARE ALIT. | 671 | ISLE STAT II 3 V | 143 |

STARTING-POST

| BUT EVEN AT THE STARTING-POST, ALL SLEEK AND NEW, | 619 | BRONZE HEAD | 15 |

STARTLE

| IN THEIR DOWNY CAPS, AND STARTLE THE NAPS | 644 | SONG FAERIES | 11 |
| IN THEIR DOWNY CAPS, AND STARTLE THE NAPS | 676 | ISLE STAT II 3 | 258 |

STARTLED

| A CURLEW ANSWERED, AND I WAS STARTLED BY THE THOUGHT | 291 | PAUDEEN V | 5 |
| NIGHTLY, AND STARTLED BY THAT SOUND | 326 | ROBERT GREGORY | 54 |

STAR-TROD
    WHERE SPICE-ISLES NESTLE ON THE STAR-TROD SEAS, ... 682 SEEKER   17
STARTS
    TREE, LIKE A SOOTY FINGER, STARTS FROM THE EARTH; . . . 410 TOWER   19
STARVE
    SHOULD STARVE GOOD MEN AND BAD ADVANCE, ... 626 OLD MEN BE MAD   10
STARVED   SEE SEA-STARVED
    STARVED UPON THE SHORE . . . . 401 DEMON BEAST   48
    "O SEA--STARVED, HUNGRY SEA." . . . . 578 CRAZED GIRL   V 14
    I, STARVED FOR THE BOSOM OF HIS FAERY BRIDE? . . . . 629 CIRCUS ANIMALS   16
STATE
    MOUNT MY WHITE STEED, FOR THE FAIRY STATE . . . . .   9 OISIN 1   V 103
    AND MANY A MILE IS THE FAERY STATE, ...   9 OISIN 1   V 103
    TO PETER SITTING IN STATE, ... 178 FIDDLER DOONEY   10
    BOUND NEITHER TO CAUSE NOR TO STATE, ... 414 TOWER   129
    THOUGHTS UPON THE PRESENT STATE OF THE WORLD . . . 428 NINETEEN 19   V   T
    AN IMAGE OF ITS STATE; . . . . 430 NINETEEN 19   64
    THAT PURITY BUILT UP THE STATE . . . . 460 THREE MONUMENT   6
    WITH THE GREAT TOIL AND CEREMONY OF STATE, . . . 462 HARUN RASHID V 25
    AND HAUGHTIER-HEADED BURKE THAT PROVED THE STATE A TREE, 481 BLOOD AND MOON   22
    THE STRENGTH THAT GIVES OUR BLOOD AND STATE MAGNANIMITY 481 BLOOD AND MOON   29
    . . .
    AND HAUGHTIER HEADED BURKE THAT PROVED THE STATE A TREE 481 BLOOD AND MOON V 22
    CHURCH AND STATE . . . . 553 CHURCH STATE   T
    MIGHT OF THE CHURCH AND THE STATE, ... 554 CHURCH STATE   3
    WHAT IF THE CHURCH AND THE STATE . . . . . . 554 CHURCH STATE   9
    FOR REASON OF THE STATE . . . . 597 MODEL LAUREATE   6
STATELY
    THE STATELY MIDNIGHT THROUGH UNTIL THEY STOOD . . . . 352 PEOPLE   14
    FOR SILKEN CLOTHES AND STATELY WALK, ... 422 MY TABLE   30
    HAD TURNED HIS STATELY HEAD. . . . . 526 AM OF IRELAND   10
    THERE STATELY PYTHAGORAS . . . . 531 DELPHIC ORACLE   9
    ALL STATELY WOMEN MOVING TO A SONG . . . . . 537 HER VISION   17
STATES
    AND THERE'S A PLAYER IN THE STATES WHO GATHERS UP HER CLOAK 354 HIS PHOENIX   12
    AND THERE'S THE PLAYER IN THE STATES WHO GATHERS UP HER 354 HIS PHOENIX V 12
      CLOAK
STATESMAN
    WE HAVE NO GIFT TO SET A STATESMAN RIGHT; . . . . 359 WAR POEM   3
    REFORMER, MERCHANT, STATESMAN, LEARNED MAN, ... 376 PHASES OF MOON   98
    O'HIGGINS ITS SOLE STATESMAN HAD NOT DIED. . . . 543 PARN FUNERAL 2   8
    A STATESMAN IS AN EASY MAN, ... 598 STONE CROSS   1
STATESMAN'S
    THE STATESMAN'S HOLIDAY . . . . 626 STATES HOLIDAY   T
STATESMEN
    AND ALL THE POPULAR STATESMEN SAY . . . . . . 460 THREE MONUMENT   5
STATION
    SOME PLATONIST AFFIRMS THAT IN THE STATION . . . . 431 NINETEEN 19   72
    THE BLINDS DRAWN UP"; MAUD GONNE AT HOWTH STATION WAITING 578 LOFTY THINGS   10
      A TRAIN,
    THE MAN IS GONE WHO FROM HIS LONELY STATION . . . . 738 MOURN THEN ON   7
STATIONS
    I PRAYED AT ALL THE STATIONS UPON MY MARROW-BONES, . . . 593 PILGRIM   7
    I PRAYED AT ALL THE STATIONS UPON MY MARROW BONES, . . 593 PILGRIM   V   7
STATISTICS
    STATISTICS . . . . 485 STATISTICS   T
STATUARY
    WHEN PAINTED PANEL, STATUARY, ... 440 WISDOM   2
STATUE
    THIS BLOSSOM IS MOST NEAR. STATUE! OH, THOU . . . 657 ISLE STAT I 3   72
    THEN BID THEM RAISE MY STATUE ON THE SHORE; . . . 663 ISLE STAT II 2 18
    A STATUE OF SOLITUDE. . . . . 785 YOUR HEART   4
    MAY TURN FROM A STATUE . . . . 786 YOUR HEART   20
STATUED
    LEAD ME, I PRAY THEE, TO THE STATUED PLACE! . . . . 667 ISLE STAT II 3 37
STATUES
    DARK STATUES GLIMMERED OVER THE PALE TIDE . . . .   31 OISIN 2   36
    AN EPILOGUE TO "THE ISLAND OF STATUES" AND "THE SEEKER"   64 HAPPY SHEPHERD V   T
    THE STATUES . . . . 610 STATUES   T
    THE ISLAND OF STATUES. . . . . 644 ISLE STAT I 1   T
    LYRICS FROM "THE ISLAND OF STATUES" . . . . . 646 ISLE STAT I 1 V T
    ISLAND OF STATUES A FRAGMENT . . . . . . 666 ISLE STAT II 3 V T
STAVE
    SINGING OF ARMS AND BATTLES SOME OLD STAVE, ... 650 ISLE STAT I 1 137
STAY
    AND BID ME STAY, WITH MANY A TEAR; . . . . .   10 OISIN 2   113
    AND STAY A LITTLE WHILE, AND BID THEM WEEP; . . .   33 OISIN 2   60
    THAT YOU STAY IDLING HERE WITH FLOCKS AND HERDS." . . 107 CUCHULAIN SEA V 21
    THAT YOU STAY IDLING HERE WITH FLOCK AND HERDS." . . 107 CUCHULAIN SEA V 21
    TO STAY THE STAG'S NEXT RUSH. WHEN SWORD MET HORN . . 277 TWO KINGS   V 15
    OR IF THEY MADE A MOMENT'S STAY . . . . . . 297 THREE BEGGARS   52
    ARE GONE AWAY, AND SOME THAT STAY . . . . . . 458 HIS WILDNESS   5
    FROM EVERY QUARTER OF THE WORLD, CAN STAY . . . 471 ALL SOUL NIGHT   12
    NOTHING CAN STAY MY GLANCE . . . . 474 ALL SOUL NIGHT   93
    HESITATE OR STAY? . . . . 505 RESULT THOUGHT   17
    I CANNOT STAY FROM THAT . . . . 533 FIRST CONFESS   8
    OR STAY CONTENT ON THE LOW, ... 589 OLD WICKED MAN   49
    THAT I MAY STAY A SOBER MAN . . . . 591 DRUNK SOBRIETY   3
    SO STAY AT HOME AND DRINK YOUR BEER . . . . . 598 STONE CROSS   5
    INFIRM AND AGED I MIGHT STAY . . . . 605 YOU CONTENT   17
    OH STAY, NASCHINA, STAY! . . . . 650 ISLE STAT I 1 153

STAY   (CONTINUED)
        OH STAY, NASCHINA, STAY! . . . .   650 ISLE STAT I 1   153
        I BID THEE STAY, RENOUNCING THY MAD QUEST." . .   669 ISLE STAT II 3   89
        AND THOU WILT STAY. ALL THOUGHT OF WHAT THEY FIND . . 670 ISLE STAT II 3   92
        STAY, STAY, OR I WILL HOLD YOUR WHITE ARMS DOWN. . .   694 MOSADA 1   92
        STAY, STAY, OR I WILL HOLD YOUR WHITE ARMS DOWN. . .   694 MOSADA 1   92
        OR STAY WITH ME BESIDE THE THAMES, ...   741 EARL PAUL   59
        SOME ONE SHOULD STAY AT HER SIDE. . . . .   786 YOUR HEART   V   28
        FLIT TO KILTARTAN CROSS AND STAY . . . .   791 REPRISALS   11
STAYED
        NOR STAYED FOR BITE OR SUP! . . . .   93 FATHER OHART   38
        WITH HEAD BOWED ON HIS KNEES CUCHULAIN STAYED! . .   110 CUCHULAIN SEA   71
        THAT IF A DANCER STAYED HIS HUNGRY FOOT . . . . .   127 DREAM OF FAERY   22
        I STAGGERED, BUT A BEECH-TREE STAYED MY FALL, . . .   286 TWO KINGS   209
        I STAGGERED, BUT A BEECH TREE STAYED MY FALL, . . .   286 TWO KINGS   V 209
        HE STAYED FOR A WHILE! AND WE . . . .   341 SHEP GOATHERD   66
        BRED ON THE ATLANTIC, CAN BE STAYED! . . . . . .   403 FOR DAUGHTER   6
STAYS
        "YET THE WORLD STAYS." "IF THAT BE SO, ...   388 SOLOMON WITCH   33
        ROUND SHE COMES IN STAYS BEFORE THEM! . . .   719 PHANTOM SHIP   17
        "HAS MARRIED AND STAYS . . . .   780 WELL AND TREE   11
STEAD
        THE SPIRITS STOLE, AND GAVE HIM IN ITS STEAD . . . . . 684 SEEKER   55
STEADIED
        AND STEADIED BY A FIN, ...   612 NEWS ORACLE   14
STEADY
        AND COPY THEIR PROUD STEADY GAZE. . . . .   273 GREY ROCK   64
        HER EYES WERE COLD AND STEADY, HER LIPS TIGHT. . . .   279 TWO KINGS   64
        THEY HAD KEPT A STEADY PACE AS THOUGH THEIR BEDS, . . 372 PHASES OF MOON   5
STEAL
        ROUND US HERDS OF SHADOWS STEAL-- . . . . . .   737 IN FIRELIGHT   6
STEALTH
        THE MURDEROUS STEALTH OF DAY. . . . .   536 PARTING   8
STEALTHILY
        AND I DREAMED MY LOST LOVE CAME STEALTHILY OUT OF THE WOOD 163 VALLEY LOVERS   3
STEAM
        ROASTING BERRIES STEAM AND SHAKE-- . . . .   727 LOVERS QUARREL   43
STEAMSHIP
        HIDING AMID THE CARGO OF A STEAMSHIP, ...   578 CRAZED GIRL   5
STEED
        A MAIDEN, ON A SLENDER STEED, ...   2 OISIN 1   V   7V
        MOUNT MY WHITE STEED, FOR THE FAIRY STATE . . . . .   9 OISIN 1   V 103
        AND WHEN THE WHITE STEED FELT MY WEIGHT, ...   9 OISIN 1   V 109
        AND NOW A MAID, ON A SWIFT BROWN STEED . . . . . .   12 OISIN 1   V 142
        THE STEED TOWARDS THE MUSIC RACED, ...   13 OISIN 1   V 169
        AMONG THEM 'LIGHTING FROM OUR STEED, ...   14 OISIN 1   V 193
        AND ONCE MORE SADDLED THE WHITE STEED, ...   25 OISIN 1   V 378
        AND WHEN THE WHITE STEED SAW WHAT BLACKNESS GLEAMED, . . 30 OISIN 2   V   24
        WE MOUNTED ON THE STAIR, THE WHITE STEED TYING, ... 32 OISIN 2   V   46
STEEDS
        OF OUR STRONG STEEDS WAS DARK WITH SWEAT, ...   2 OISIN 1   V   7T
        AND A HUNDRED STEEDS, TUMULTUOUS-FOOTED, ...   8 OISIN 1   V 85A
        NOR TEAR THE FOEMEN FROM THEIR STEEDS. . . . . . .   11 OISIN 1   128
        AND THEIR HOUNDS, AND THEIR STEEDS, AND THEIR LOVES, . . 59 OISIN 3   V 176
STEEL
        LONG WHILE, ARE WHIPS OF STEEL." "IS HE SO DREAD?" . . . 35 OISIN 2   V   88
        AGAINST THE STAG. WHEN HORN AND STEEL WERE MET . . . 277 TWO KINGS   15
        FLAMES THAT NO FAGGOT FEEDS, NOR STEEL HAS LIT, . . . 498 BYZANTIUM   26
        OF THOSE STEEL TONGUES! CRASH, SWORDS! WELL THRUST!   665 ISLE STAT II 2   67
            WELL BENT
        THEN FARRELL, STEEL KING, MASTER OF MEN, ...   790 DEDICATION   5
STEEL-BLUE
        STREWING UPON THE ROCKS THEIR STEEL-BLUE HAIR, . . .   687 TWO TITANS   30
STEEP
        UNDER THAT COLD AND VAPOUR-TURBANED STEEP, ...   128 DREAM OF FAERY   39
        EVENING AND MORNING, THE STEEP STREET OF URBINO . . . 352 PEOPLE   12
        EVENING AND MORN, THE STEEP STREET OF URBINO . . . . 352 PEOPLE   V   12
        FROM MOUNTAIN STEEP TO STEEP. . . . .   399 BREAK OF DAY   25
        FROM MOUNTAIN STEEP TO STEEP. . . . .   399 BREAK OF DAY   25
        SET ALL YOUR MIND UPON THE STEEP ASCENT, ...   477 SELF AND SOUL   2
        AS WHEN UPON HER CLOUD-O'ER-MUFFLED STEEP . . . . .   645 ISLE STAT I 1   16
STEEPLE
        FROM WHERE THE OLD IVY CRAWLS ROUND THE OLD STEEPLE, . . 728 PRIEST FAIRY   6
STEER
        THAT I MAY DROWN MYSELF? BETTER STEER HOME, ...   222 SHADOW WATER B   12
        AND SO WITH WOLF, AND BOAR, AND STEER. . . . . . .   671 ISLE STAT II 3   122
STEERING
        I HELD A PAINTED STEERING OAR, ...   253 HIS DREAM   V   2
        THE BUTT END OF A STEERING OAR, ...   253 HIS DREAM   V   2
STEERING-OAR
        THE BUTT-END OF A STEERING-OAR, ...   253 HIS DREAM   2
STEERS
        "LIKE THE SPECKLED BIRD THAT STEERS . . . .   341 SHEP GOATHERD   62
STELLA
        BUT MINE SAW STELLA ONCE. WHENCE CAME OUR THOUGHT? . . . 486 SEVEN SAGES   6
        MINE SAW STELLA ONCE. WHENCE CAME OUR THOUGHT? . . . . 486 SEVEN SAGES   V   6
        MINE SAW STELLA ONCE. WHEN CAME OUR THOUGHT? . . . . 486 SEVEN SAGES   V   6
STEM   SEE APPLE-STEM
        HIS LONG LAMP-CHIMNEY SHAPED LIKE THE STEM . . . . . 566 LAPIS LAZULI   33
        HIS LONG LAMP CHIMNEY SHAPED LIKE THE STEM . . . . . 566 LAPIS LAZULI   V   33
        AND THEREON GREW A TENDER STEM, ...   743 DANAAN QUICK   14

		PAGE	TITLE		LINE

STEM   (CONTINUED)
    PRAISE THE BLOSSOMING APPLE STEM; • • • • • • • • • • •   773 SONG DEIRDRE 1 V   21
STEMS   SEE PALM-STEMS
    • • • FOR, CUMBROUS WITH STEMS OF THE HAZEL AND OAK, • •   48 OISIN 3   25
    FEED A FIRE WITH STEMS OF GRASS; • • • • • • • • • • 727 LOVERS QUARREL   42
STEP   SEE DOOR-STEP
    BE STILL; I HEAR THE STEP OF EBREMAR. • • • ⸳ • • • • 697 MOSADA 2   34
STEPPED
    THAT STEPPED OUT OF THEIR CLOTHES, • • • • • • • • • 538 LAST CONFESS   14
STEPPING   SEE DELICATE-STEPPING
    THE DELICATE STEPPING STAG AND HIS LADY SIGH • • • • • 210 RAGGED WOOD   V   2
STEPS
    THY WANDERING STEPS ACROSS THE SEA? • • • • • • • • • 5 OISIN 1   V   51
    OF MOONLIT STEPS GLIMMERED; AND LEFT AND RIGHT • • • • 31 OISIN 2   35
    OF MANY THOUSAND STEPS, SAT EITHER SIDE, • • • • • • • 31 OISIN 2   V   35
    AND CLIMBED SO LONG, I THOUGHT THE LAST STEPS WERE • • 32 OISIN 2   48
    WENT WALKING WITH SLOW STEPS ALONG THE GLEAMING • • • • 68 SAD SHEPHERD   3
    PAINTING WITH SHADOW ALL THE MARBLE STEPS; • • • • • • 72 ANASHU VIJAYA   30
    THE HEAVY STEPS OF THE PLOUGHMAN, SPLASHING THE WINTRY 143 ROSE IN HEART   3
        MOULD,
    THE HEAVY STEPS OF THE PLOUGHMAN SPLASHING THE WINTER 143 ROSE IN HEART V   3
        MOULD,
    NOW STEPS DRAW CLOSE, HE HIDES BENEATH A DRUM, • • • • 713 FERENCZ RENYI   78
    SOME GREAT ONE. NO; I HEAR THE WAVERING STEPS • • • • 720 WITCH VIVIEN   12
STEPT
    "A SADDER CREATURE NEVER STEPT • • • • • • • • • • • 17 OISIN 1   238
    REMEMBERING HOW THE FENIANS STEPT • • • • • • • • • 24 OISIN 1   370
    IN WAR, THE NOBLE FENIANS STEPT. • • • • • • • • • 24 OISIN 1   V 372
    AND WHEN THE SUN ONCE MORE IN SAFFRON STEPT, • • • • • 41 OISIN 2   V 192
    AND WHEN THE SUN IN ALL HIS FLAGRANT SAFFRON STEPT, • • 41 OISIN 2   V 192
    BUT WHEN THE SUN ONCE MORE IN SAFFRON STEPT, • • • • • 41 OISIN 2   V 192
    OF TWILIGHT AND SLUMBER WERE GONE, AND THAT HOOFS • • 54 OISIN 3   112
        IMPATIENTLY STEPT.
    • • • BENEATH ME THE HOOVES IMPATIENTLY STEPT. • • • • 54 OISIN 3   V 112
STERN
    THEN, WARRIOR, WHY SO SAD AND STERN, • • • • • • • • 19 OISIN 1   V 286
    I SWAYED UPON THE GAUDY STERN • • • • • • • • • • • 253 HIS DREAM   1
    THERE ON THE HIGH AND PAINTED STERN • • • • • • • • 253 HIS DREAM   V 1
    BEING HIGH AND SOLITARY AND MOST STERN? • • • • • • 257 NO SECOND TROY   10
    TO THAT STERN COLOUR AND THAT DELICATE LINE • • • • • 326 ROBERT GREGORY   67
    DOTH STILL THE MAN WHOM EACH STERN ROVER FEARS, • • • 678 ISLE STAT II 3   295
STERNER
    YOU KEPT THE MUSES' STERNER LAWS, • • • • • • • • • 273 GREY ROCK   59
    A STERNER CONSCIENCE AND A FRIENDLIER HOME, • • • • • 321 REED WHISPERER   8
    AS THOUGH A STERNER EYE LOOKED THROUGH HER EYE • • • • 619 BRONZE HEAD   23
STERNNESS
    ALL THAT STERNNESS AMID CHARM, • • • • • • • • • • 259 PEACE   8
    SO MUCH STERNNESS AND SUCH CHARM." • • • • • • • • 259 PEACE   V   8
STERNS
    WITH BENDING STERNS AND BENDING BOWS, • • • • • • • 14 OISIN 1   189
    WITH BENDING STERNS AND BENDING BOWS, • • • • • • • 23 OISIN 1   353
STICK   SEE FIDDLE-STICK
    A TATTERED COAT UPON A STICK, UNLESS • • • • • • • • 407 SAIL BYZANTIUM   10
    FINGERED UPON A FIDDLE STICK OR STRING • • • • • • • 445 SCHOOL CHILDR V   46
    SOUND OF A STICK UPON THE FLOOR, A SOUND • • • • • • 491 COOLE BALLYLEE   25
    THAT ON A STICK RELIED • • • • • • • • • • • • • 515 GIRLS SONG B   6
    WHO LEANS UPON A STICK, • • • • • • • • • • • • • 525 DANCING DAYS   20
    HIS STOUT STICK UNDER HIS HAND, • • • • • • • • • • 588 OLD WICKED MAN   20
    A STICK OF INCENSE • • • • • • • • • • • • • • • 619 STICK INCENSE   T
STICKS   SEE BROOM-STICKS
    THE ANCIENT HABIT STICKS, • • • • • • • • • • • • 431 NINETEEN 19   74
    OLD CLOTHES UPON OLD STICKS TO SCARE A BIRD. • • • • • 445 SCHOOL CHILDR   48
    NOW ALL DRY STICKS UNDER A WINTRY SUN, • • • • • • • 490 COOLE BALLYLEE   10
STIFF
    IN THEIR STIFF, PAINTED CLOTHES, THE PALE UNSATISFIED ONES 318 MAGI   2
    "A WOMAN CAN BE PROUD AND STIFF • • • • • • • • • • 513 JANE TALK BISH   13
    THOUGH STIFF TO STRIKE A BARGAIN, • • • • • • • • • 620 JOHN KINSELLA   13
    WITH A STIFF STRAIGHT BACK, • • • • • • • • • • • 627 STATES HOLIDAY   33
STILL   SEE STONY-STILL
    WHERE PASSIONATE MAIVE IS STONY STILL; • • • • • • • 3 OISIN 1   V   18
    YOU ARE STILL WRECKED AMONG HEATHEN DREAMS. • • • • • 4 OISIN 1   31
    OISIN, THOU ART HALF HEATHEN STILL; • • • • • • • • 4 OISIN 1   V   31
    AND NOW, STILL SAD, WE CAME TO WHERE • • • • • • • • 17 OISIN 1   247
    AND NOW STILL SAD OUR TROOP DREW NIGH • • • • • • • 17 OISIN 1   V 247
    UNTIL THE TOSSING ARMS GREW STILL • • • • • • • • • 21 OISIN 1   322
    OF THE THINGS THAT HIS HEART STILL KNOWS WERE SWEET-- • 26 OISIN 1   V 402
    WHILE HIS HEART STILL DREAMS OF BATTLE AND LOVE • • • • 27 OISIN 1   406
    AND HAD DISPORTED IN THE EYES STILL JET • • • • • • • 31 OISIN 2   V   39
    IF THEY STILL SLUMBER, TOUCH THEIR EYELIDS BLUE, • • • 33 OISIN 2   V   61
    BUT FLY WHILE STILL YOU MAY." AND THEREON I; • • • • 35 OISIN 2   89
    BUT FLEE WHILE YOU STILL MAY." THEN I; • • • • • • 35 OISIN 2   V   89
    I BURST THE CHAIN; STILL EARLESS, NERVELESS, BLIND; • • 36 OISIN 2   97
    STILL EARLESS, NERVELESS, BLIND, THE EAGLES STOOD. • • 36 OISIN 2   100
    STILL EARLESS, NERVELESS, BLIND, THE EAGLES DREAMED. • • 36 OISIN 2   V 100
    SHOUTED AND HAILED HIM. STILL HE HUNG CONTENT, • • • • 36 OISIN 2   V 107
    THE FLOWERS STILL GREW THERE; FAR ON THE SEA'S WASTE • • 39 OISIN 2   163
    THE FLOWERS STILL GREW THERE. MOVED BEYOND HIM THE SEA'S 39 OISIN 2   V 163
        WASTE;
    ON THE ANVIL OF THE WORLD. BE STILL; THE SKIES • • • • 42 OISIN 2   204
    YET STILL SHE TURNS HER RESTLESS HEAD; • • • • • • • 65 HAPPY SHEPHERD   5
    AND STILL I DREAM HE TREADS THE LAWN, • • • • • • • 67 HAPPY SHEPHERD   51

STILL   (CONTINUED)

```
THE SEA SWEPT ON AND CRIED HER OLD CRY STILL,              68  SAD SHEPHERD      10
HAIL! HAIL, MY ANASHUYA.  NO! BE STILL.                    71  ANASHU VIJAYA     11
HAIL! HAIL, MY ANASHUYA.  NAY! BE STILL.                   71  ANASHU VIJAYA  V  11
WHO STILL WERE OLD WHEN THE GREAT SEA WAS YOUNG!           74  ANASHU VIJAYA     69
FOR THE KIND WIRES ARE TORN AND STILL,                    86  MAD KING GOLL     69
AND STILL, WITH PITYIN', SCORNIN' EYE,                    96  MOLL MAGEE        39
COME NEAR, COME NEAR, COME NEAR--AH, LEAVE ME STILL      101  ROSE UPON ROOD    13
AND STILL I FEEL THE CROWN UPON MY HEAD.                 103  FERGUS DRUID      20
BUT STILL I FEEL THE CROWN UPON MY HEAD.                 103  FERGUS DRUID   V  20
"STILL TREADS THE WORLD AMID HIS ARMED MEN."             107  CUCHULAIN SEA     26
STILL SHE GOES WITH FOOTSTEPS WARY,                      124  CATHLEEN PARA  V  11
AND STILL THE STARRY CANDLES FLARE                       138  TO IRELAND     V  13
AND STILL THE THOUGHTS OF IRELAND BROOD,                 138  TO IRELAND     V  15
WHILE STILL I MAY, I WRITE FOR YOU                       139  TO IRELAND        33
WHILE STILL I MAY I WRITE OUT TRUE                       139  TO IRELAND     V  33
O SWEET EVERLASTING VOICES, BE STILL!                    141  EVERLAST VOICE     1
O SWEET EVERLASTING VOICES, BE STILL.                    141  EVERLAST VOICE     8
PALE BROWS, STILL HANDS AND DIM HAIR,                    152  LOSS OF LOVE       1
PALE BROW, STILL HANDS, AND DIM HAIR,                    152  LOSS OF LOVE   V   1
BE YOU STILL, BE YOU STILL, TREMBLING HEART!             158  TO HIS HEART       1
BE YOU STILL, BE YOU STILL, TREMBLING HEART!             158  TO HIS HEART       1
THE GARDEN HAD FALLEN STILL,                             159  CAP AND BELLS      2
AND ONCE, WHEN THE OWLS GREW STILL,                      159  CAP AND BELLS  V   2
WE WHO STILL LABOUR BY THE CROMLECH ON THE SHORE,        161  BLACK PIG          5
MASTER OF THE STILL STARS AND OF THE FLAMING DOOR.       161  BLACK PIG          8
AND STILL MURMUR AND LONG!                               163  ASKS FORGIVE      18
STILL OVERTHROWN BY A WOMAN'S GAZE,                      164  PERFECT BEAUTY V   4
WITH STILL AND STONY LIMBS AND OPEN EYES,                182  QUEEN MAEVE       46
MORE STILL THAN THEY HAD BEEN FOR A GOOD MONTH,          182  QUEEN MAEVE       54
HAVE SUCH LONG MEMORIES THAT THEY STILL                  192  BAILE AILLINN     90
WHO BUT AWAITS HIS HOUR TO SHOOT, STILL HANGS            198  SEVEN WOODS       13
WHETHER HE WILL OR NO! AND BETTER STILL                  222  SHADOW WATER B    13
BUT WHY ARE THEY STILL WAITING?  WHY ARE THEY            234  SHADOW WATER B   265
BEFORE A HAND CAN TOUCH ME.  MY HANDS ARE STILL!         238  SHADOW WATER B   358
WHAT, STILL YOU WOULD HAVE THEIR PRAISE!                 259  UNWORTH PRAISE    11
PARDON, OLD FATHERS, IF YOU STILL REMAIN                 269  PARDON FATHERS     1
OR ON SOME STILL UNEMPTIED CUP                           271  GREY ROCK         21
BUT LET THAT BE--THE GODS WERE STILL,                    271  GREY ROCK      V  16
"IF HE BE LIVING STILL THE WHOLE WORLD'S MINE,           280  TWO KINGS      V  85
BUT FINDING HIM STILL SILENT I STOOPED DOWN              281  TWO KINGS        109
OUR SUDDEN PALACES IN THE STILL AIR                      284  TWO KINGS        180
THE WIND IS OLD AND STILL AT PLAY                        301  RUN PARADISE      22
AND YET STOOD STILL, BECAUSE INSIDE                      303  HOUR DAWN         26
POUR WINE AND DANCE IF MANHOOD STILL HAVE PRIDE,         311  MOUNTAIN TOMB      1
IN VAIN, IN VAIN! THE CATARACT STILL CRIES!              311  MOUNTAIN TOMB      9
POUR WINE AND DANCE, IF MANKIND STILL HAVE PRIDE,        311  MOUNTAIN TOMB  V   1
WHAT EAGLE LOOK STILL SHOWS,                             316  FRIENDS           25
AND ALL THEIR EYES STILL FIXED, HOPING TO FIND ONCE MORE, 318 MAGI               6
BEN JONSON'S PHRASE--AND STILL MAY TURN MY FEET          321  REED WHISPERER V   6
MIRRORS A STILL SKY!                                     322  SWANS AT COOLE     4
UNWEARIED STILL, LOVER BY LOVER,                         323  SWANS AT COOLE    19
ATTEND UPON THEM STILL.                                  323  SWANS AT COOLE    24
BUT NOW THEY DRIFT ON THE STILL WATER,                   323  SWANS AT COOLE    25
ALTHOUGH I CAN SEE HIM STILL,                            347  FISHERMAN          1
FOR AN EXAMPLE STILL?                                    365  HER RACE          12
WHILE WONDERING STILL TO BE A SHADE, WITH GRANIA'S SHADE, 366 HER COURAGE    V   4
UNDER YOUR OLD WIND-BEATEN TOWER, WHERE STILL            367  EGO DOMINUS        2
AND, THOUGH YOU HAVE PASSED THE BEST OF LIFE, STILL TRACE, 367 EGO DOMINUS      5
AND SHOULD THEY PAINT OR WRITE, STILL IT IS ACTION       369  EGO DOMINUS       44
AND SHOULD THEY PAINT OR WRITE STILL IS IT ACTION,       369  EGO DOMINUS    V  44
WERE DISTANT STILL.  AN OLD MAN COCKED HIS EAR.          372  PHASES OF MOON     7
AND THE LIGHT PROVES THAT HE IS READING STILL.           373  PHASES OF MOON    11
AND THE NEW STILL HIDES HER HORN.                        382  VISION ROBART      4
UNDER BLANK EYES AND FINGERS NEVER STILL                 382  VISION ROBART      5
YOU SAY THAT WE SHOULD STILL THE LAND                    395  SIXTEEN DEAD       7
OR EVERY BELLOWS BURST, BE HAPPY STILL.                  405  FOR DAUGHTER      72
SOME FEW REMEMBERED STILL WHEN I WAS YOUNG               410  TOWER             33
OUR SHADOWS ROVE THE GARDEN GRAVEL STILL,                435  NEW FACES          7
A SUDDEN BLOW! THE GREAT WINGS BEATING STILL             441  LEDA AND SWAN      1
A RUSH, A SUDDEN WHEEL, AND HOVERING STILL               441  LEDA AND SWAN  V   1
MUST DRIVE THE ARABIAN HOST.  THE VOICE GREW STILL,      467  HARUN RASHID     145
MADE DRIVE THE ARABIAN HOST.  THE VOICE GREW STILL,      467  HARUN RASHID   V 145
IS SATO'S ANCIENT BLADE, STILL AS IT WAS,                477  SELF AND SOUL     10
STILL RAZOR-KEEN, STILL LIKE A LOOKING-GLASS             477  SELF AND SOUL     11
STILL RAZOR-KEEN, STILL LIKE A LOOKING-GLASS             477  SELF AND SOUL     11
CAN, TATTERED, STILL PROTECT, FADED ADORN.               477  SELF AND SOUL     16
IS SATO'S ANCIENT SWORD, STILL AS IT WAS,                477  SELF AND SOUL  V  10
STILL RAZOR-KEEN, STILL LIKE A LOOKING GLASS             477  SELF AND SOUL  V  11
STILL RAZOR-KEEN, STILL LIKE A LOOKING GLASS             477  SELF AND SOUL  V  11
MORE BLESSED STILL THIS TOWER!                           480  BLOOD AND MOON     2
ALL-DESTROYING SWORD-BLADE STILL                         484  SYMBOLS            3
THAT SO STILL HAD LAIN,                                  516  MANS SONG          4
WENCHING, DRINKING, STILL REMAIN                         529  TOM LUNATIC        9
THAT SAT SO STILL AND PLAYED AT THE CHESS?               550  SEVERED HEAD      12
FROM NEEDLE'S EYE STILL GOAD IT ON.                      562  NEEDLES EYE        4
OR LOFTY SLOPE WHERE IT STILL SNOWS                      567  LAPIS LAZULI      46
(FOR SINCE THE HORIZON'S BOUGHT STRANGE DOGS ARE STILL)  579  DOR WELLESLEY      7
THAT THE SWORDSMEN AND THE LADIES CAN STILL KEEP COMPANY, 581 CURSE CROMWELL   20
THAT I AM STILL THEIR SERVANT THOUGH ALL ARE UNDERGROUND. 581 CURSE CROMWELL   22
"IRELAND SHALL GET HER FREEDOM AND YOU STILL BREAK STONE." 590 PARNELL          2
```

STILL (CONTINUED)

AND KEEP ME DANCING STILL . . . . 591 DRUNK SOBRIETY 2
BUT SHE IS STILL ABED, ... 595 COLONEL MARTIN 31
BUT SHE IS STILL A-BED . . . . 595 COLONEL MARTIN V 31
SAID TO THE WOMAN ON HIS KNEES, "LIE STILL. . . . . . 609 IN TARAS HALLS 2
TO MANY WOMEN I HAVE SAID, "LIE STILL," . . . . . . 609 IN TARAS HALLS 6
BE STILL, BE STILL, WHAT CAN BE SAID? . . . . 613 MARCH SONGS 1 7
BE STILL, BE STILL, WHAT CAN BE SAID? . . . . 613 MARCH SONGS 1 7
BE STILL, BE STILL, WHAT CAN BE SAID? . . . . 613 MARCH SONGS 1 17
BE STILL, BE STILL, WHAT CAN BE SAID? . . . . 613 MARCH SONGS 1 17
BE STILL, BE STILL, WHAT CAN BE SAID? . . . . 614 MARCH SONGS 1 27
BE STILL, BE STILL, WHAT CAN BE SAID? . . . . 614 MARCH SONGS 1 27
WHILE HIS MAN CAN STILL HIS BODY KEEP . . . . 633 MAN AND ECHO 25
CAME CREEPING UP BECAUSE THE MAN WAS STILL. . . . . 634 CUCHULAIN COMF 10
WHEN SLEEPERS WAKE AND YET STILL DREAM, ... 639 BEN BULBEN 59
AND WHEN IT'S VANISHED STILL DECLARE, ... 639 BEN BULBEN 60
STILL THE INDOMITABLE IRISHRY. . . . . 640 BEN BULBEN 83
NO! THOU STANDEST STILL AND STARK, ... 658 ISLE STAT I 3 90
THE AIR IS STILL ABOVE, AND STILL EACH LEAF, . . . 662 ISLE STAT II 2 7
THE AIR IS STILL ABOVE, AND STILL EACH LEAF, . . . 662 ISLE STAT II 2 7
SO BE THOU STILL, DEAR HEART, A LITTLE WHILE! . . . 677 ISLE STAT II 3 283
DOTH STILL THE WANDERER ROVE? WITH ALL HIS SHIPS . 677 ISLE STAT II 3 287
DOTH STILL THE MAN WHOM EACH STERN ROVER FEARS, . . 678 ISLE STAT II 3 295
DOTH HE STILL DWELL WITHIN THE WOODY SHADE, ... 678 ISLE STAT II 3 303
ARE STILL THE ACHAIANS' TENTED CHIEFS AT BAY? . . . 679 ISLE STAT II 3 310
STILL STARING AT THEIR FLOWERS, ... 680 LOVE AND DEATH 25
UNQUENCHABLE STILL GLOWS IN HER DULL STARE, ... 687 TWO TITANS 17
OR PERCHING ON THE TENTS, A-WEARY STILL . . . . . . 690 MOSADA 1 8
THE DARK STILL MAN, HAS COME AND SAYS 'TIS SIN. . . 692 MOSADA 1 47
BE STILL! I HEAR THE STEP OF EBREMAR. . . . . 697 MOSADA 2 34
I NEVER KNEW AN EVE SO MARVELLOUS STILL. . . . . . 702 MOSADA 3 88
STILL WANDER THROUGH THE WORLD. HE'S GONE, HE'S GONE. . 703 MOSADA 3 121
TO LOVE EACH OTHER. IN MY PRAYER-BOOK STILL . . . . 713 FERENCZ RENYI 94
TO LOVE EACH OTHER. IN MY PRAYER BOOK STILL . . . . 713 FERENCZ RENYI V 94
HOW STILL IT IS! I HEAR THE CARP GO SPLASH, ... 722 WITCH VIVIEN 62
AND EVIL STILL IS ACTION'S CHILD. . . . . 728 PRIEST FAIRY 14
THEY GREW SO VERY STILL, I WIS . . . . 730 PRIEST FAIRY 66
AND NOW THEY ARE ALL GONE; I FOLLOW STILL. . . . . 749 SHADOW WATER A 37
THEY ARE STILL WAITING; AND NOW THE LAGGARD COMES. . 754 SHADOW WATER A 150
THEY ARE STILL WAITING; AND A LAGGARD COMES. . . . 754 SHADOW WATER A 150
OF VOICES AND OF DREAMS. O HEART, BE STILL! . . . . 765 SHADOW WATER A 362
RUNS, RUNS AND IS SUDDENLY STILL. . . . . 783 GREY ROUND 3
CARRY IT! SUDDENLY IT IS STILL. . . . . 783 GREY ROUND 5
O STILL THAT HEART AT LAST. . . . . 785 YOUR HEART 8
STILLED
THE NAMES THAT STILLED YOUR CHILDISH PLAY, ... 289 SEPTEMBER 1913 10
SOON SHALL OUR WINGS BE STILLED, ... 643 SONG FAERIES 5
SOON SHALL OUR WINGS BE STILLED, ... 676 ISLE STAT II 3 252
STILLNESS
GREAT RULERS OF THE STILLNESS, LET HER NO LONGER BE . . . 175 ELEMENT POWERS V 13
GREAT RULERS OF STILLNESS, LET HER NO LONGER BE . . 175 ELEMENT POWERS V 13
THE SOUL BEGINS TO TREMBLE INTO STILLNESS, ... 374 PHASES OF MOON 54
NOTHING BUT STILLNESS CAN REMAIN WHEN HEARTS ARE FULL . . 426 PHANTOM HATRED 23
THAT STILLNESS FOR A THEME . . . . 535 CHOSEN 14
AND CROUCH IN SOME FAR STILLNESS OF THE ISLE, AND DIE. . 675 ISLE STAT II 3 246
IN A FAR STILLNESS OF THE ISLAND DIE. . . . . 675 ISLE STAT II 3 V 246
STILLY
AND HAD DISPORTED IN THE STILLY JET, ... 31 OISIN 2 39
STILT
FROM COLLAR TO COLLAR, FROM STILT TO STILT, FROM FATHER 623 HIGH TALK 10
 TO CHILD.
FROM COLLAR TO COLLAR, FROM STILT TO STILT, FROM FATHER 623 HIGH TALK 10
 TO CHILD.
STILTED
THE STILTED WATER-HEN . . . . 419 MY HOUSE 8
THOSE STILTED BOYS, THAT BURNISHED CHARIOT, ... 629 CIRCUS ANIMALS 7
STILT-JACK
MALACHI STILT-JACK AM I, WHATEVER I LEARNED HAS RUN WILD, 623 HIGH TALK 9
STILTS
PROCESSIONS THAT LACK HIGH STILTS HAVE NOTHING THAT CATCHES 622 HIGH TALK 1
 THE EYE.
ALL METAPHOR, MALACHI, STILTS AND ALL. A BARNACLE GOOSE 623 HIGH TALK 11
STIR
OR IN THE WINE-VAT, DWELL BEYOND THE STIR . . . . . 169 SECRET ROSE 4
OR IN THE WINE VAT, DWELL BEYOND THE STIR . . . . . 169 SECRET ROSE V 4
UNTIL THE PILLARED DARK BEGAN TO STIR . . . . 185 QUEEN MAEVE 110
TO STIR THEIR COVERLET AND THEIR HAIR. . . . . . . 197 BAILE AILLINN 186
THE FORD WHERE DRINKING CATTLE MAKE A STIR . . . . 326 ROBERT GREGORY 53
TO STIR THE BOILING POT? . . . . 395 SIXTEEN DEAD 6
WHAT STIR RAN THROUGH THE COUNTRYSIDE . . . . 488 CRAZED MOON 10
'TIS BUT TO SEE IF ANYTHING WILL STIR . . . . 669 ISLE STAT II 3 75
HAD NOT ALL HIS LIMBS A STIR . . . . 772 SONG DEIRDRE 1 11
STIRLESS
OF AWELESS BIRDS, AND ROUND THEIR STIRLESS FEET . . . . 76 ANASHU VIJAYA 73
STIRRED
THEY STIRRED MY SPACIOUS SOUL IN ME NO JOT— . . . . 36 OISIN 2 V 94
AND CHAUNTED FOR THREE DAYS. CUCHULAIN STIRRED, . . 111 CUCHULAIN SEA 83
AND CHANTED FOR THREE DAYS. CUCHULAIN STIRRED, . . 111 CUCHULAIN SEA V 83
BECAUSE THE DAILY SPECTACLE THAT STIRRED . . . . . 270 PARDON FATHERS 16
BECAUSE YOU WERE THE SPECTACLE THAT STIRRED . . . . 270 PARDON FATHERS V 16
THAT HE, WHEN FRENZY STIRRED HIS THEWS, ... 271 GREY ROCK 22

STIRRED   (CONTINUED)
    IT MAY BE, AND HAD NOT STIRRED, ...   381 SONGS FOOL 2   12
    NEVER UNTIL THIS NIGHT HAVE I BEEN STIRRED. . . . . .   389 IMAGE PAST   1
    WITH ALL YOUTH'S LONELY WILDNESS STIRRED, ...   397 POLIT PRISONER   16
    THAT STIRRED HER FANTASY AND PLANNED HER CARE, ...   466 HARUN RASHID   V 114
STIRRING
    . . . A SOUND LIKE THE STIRRING OF FLIES. . . . . . .   51 OISIN 3   58
STIRS
    AND STIRS THE YOUNG KID'S BUDDING HORN. . . . . . .   18 OISIN 1   264
    "AN OLD MAN STIRS THE FIRE TO A BLAZE, ...   26 OISIN 1   400
    THE FIRE THAT STIRS ABOUT HER, WHEN SHE STIRS, . . .   200 FOLLY COMFORT   10
    THE FIRE THAT STIRS ABOUT HER, WHEN SHE STIRS, . . .   200 FOLLY COMFORT   10
    WHEN EVENING STIRS THE JASMINE BOUGH, AND YET . . . .   463 HARUN RASHID   53
    WHEN EVENING STIRS THE JASMINE, AND YET . . . . .   463 HARUN RASHID   V 53
    LIKE PASSION STIRS THE PEACOCK AND HIS MATE, ...   465 HARUN RASHID   100
    WHERE NOTHING STIRS BUT A MOUSE. . . . .   575 ACRE OF GRASS   6
    BUT BLESSED HE THAT STIRS THEM NOT . . . .   779 ACCURSED WHO   3
STITCHING
    OUR STITCHING AND UNSTITCHING HAS BEEN NAUGHT. . . .   204 ADAMS CURSE   6
    STITCHING AT A PURPLE HOARDED . . . .   440 WISDOM   12
STOATS
    OF BITTERNS, AND FISH-EATING STOATS, ...   14 OISIN 1   191
    OF BITTERNS AND FISH-EATING STOATS. . . . .   23 OISIN 1   355
STOCK
    MADE LOCK, STOCK AND BARREL . . . .   415 TOWER   150
    THE WOMEN TAKE SO LITTLE STOCK . . . .   455 HIS MEMORIES   7
STOCKS
    ON GANGLING STOCKS GROWN GREAT, GREAT STOCKS RUN DRY, . .   619 BRONZE HEAD   25
    ON GANGLING STOCKS GROWN GREAT, GREAT STOCKS RUN DRY, . .   619 BRONZE HEAD   25
STOLE
    AND STOLE THE CRIMSON ROSE, ...   174 ELEMENT POWERS V   2
    SOME ROGUE OF THE WORLD STOLE THEM TO PATCH UP A FENCE   623 HIGH TALK   4
        OR A FIRE.
    AND WHEN THE FOOL AND BLIND MAN STOLE THE BREAD . . . .   630 CIRCUS ANIMALS   25
    THE SPIRITS STOLE, AND GAVE HIM IN ITS STEAD . . . .   684 SEEKER   55
STOLEN
    THE STOLEN CHILD . . . .   86 STOLEN CHILD   T
    AND OF REDDEST STOLEN CHERRIES. . . . .   87 STOLEN CHILD   8
    THE STOLEN BRIDE . . . .   143 HOST OF AIR   V   T
    A LITTLE STOLEN TRESS. I, TOO, AWAIT . . . . . .   170 SECRET ROSE   27
STOLES
    AND OLD MEN WITH CROZIERS AND STOLES. . . . . . .   167 BLESSED   16
STONE   SEE JEWEL-STONE
    HUGE FORMS OF STONE! BETWEEN THE LIDS OF ONE . . . .   31 OISIN 2   V 37
    AND MANANNAN'S DARK TOWER, STONE AFTER STONE, ...   45 OISIN 2   236
    AND MANANNAN'S DARK TOWER, STONE AFTER STONE, ...   45 OISIN 2   236
    LIKE ROTTED FLESH, AND STONE BY STONE MY HALL . . . .   45 OISIN 2   236
    LIKE ROTTED FLESH, AND STONE BY STONE MY HALL . . . .   45 OISIN 2   V 236
    AND MANANAN'S DARK TOWER, STONE BY STONE, ...   45 OISIN 2   V 236
    AND MANANAN'S DARK TOWER, STONE BY STONE, ...   45 OISIN 2   V 236
    THE MOIL OF MY CENTURIES FILLED ME! AND GONE LIKE   51 OISIN 3   70
        A SEA-COVERED STONE
    IN A LONG IRON SLEEP, AS A FISH IN THE WATER GOES DUMB   53 OISIN 3   96
        AS A STONE.
    A WEASEL MOVING ON FROM STONE TO STONE, ...   102 FERGUS DRUID   5
    A WEASEL MOVING ON FROM STONE TO STONE, ...   102 FERGUS DRUID   5
    MAY SET A STONE UPON ANCESTRAL SORROW! . . . . . .   130 BOOK STORIES   11
    UNDER A CAIRN OF SLEEPY STONE . . . .   192 BAILE AILLINN   81
    ALTHOUGH HE IS CARRYING STONE, BUT TWO . . . . . .   192 BAILE AILLINN   83
    CAULDRON AND SPEAR AND STONE AND SWORD, ...   196 BAILE AILLINN   165
    BUT FRUIT THAT IS OF PRECIOUS STONE, ...   196 BAILE AILLINN   175
    HEAVY LIKE STONE, THEIR WISDOM BEING HALF SILENCE. . . .   218 WOODS OF COOLE   26
    A BOY OF TWENTY YEARS!--A MOUND AND STONE . . . . .   276 TWO KINGS   V   F
    AND WHERE THE STONE STRUCK FIRE, WHILE IN THE LEAVES . .   278 TWO KINGS   33
    SOME PASSION HAD MADE HER STONE. HEARING A FOOT . .   279 TWO KINGS   65
    AND RAISE HIS PILLAR STONE." KING EOCHAID SAID, . .   280 TWO KINGS   V 83
    THAT MAKE THE HEART AKIN TO THE DUMB STONE. . . . .   281 TWO KINGS   94
    THAN MOUND AND STONE THAT KEEP ALL VIRTUE IN, . . .   281 TWO KINGS   106
    DEARER THAN ANY THAT THE DUMB STONE HIDES. . . . .   281 TWO KINGS   V 96
    MUST END AT THE DUMB STONE? BUT WHERE WE BUILD . . .   284 TWO KINGS   179
    AMID A PLACE OF STONE, ...   291 TO A FRIEND   13
    I'VE STOOD AS I WERE MADE OF STONE . . . . . .   297 THREE BEGGARS   64
    ON A WINDY STONE, THE THIRD, ...   298 THREE HERMITS   5
    BUT MIGHT HAVE PUMMELLED AT A STONE . . . . . .   307 HOUR DAWN   114
    AND AFTER HEAPED UP STONE ON STONE, ...   307 HOUR DAWN   116
    AND AFTER HEAPED UP STONE ON STONE, ...   307 HOUR DAWN   116
    AND HEAPED UP STONE ON STONE AGAIN, ...   307 HOUR DAWN   118
    AND HEAPED UP STONE ON STONE AGAIN, ...   307 HOUR DAWN   118
    WE SAT AS SILENT AS A STONE, ...   314 MEMORY YOUTH   15
    I SAT AS SILENT AS A STONE . . . .   314 MEMORY YOUTH   V 15
    IN MOULDED PLASTER OR IN CARVEN STONE? . . . . . .   327 ROBERT GREGORY   77
    FROM STONE TO STONE. I AM LOOKING FOR STRAYED SHEEP! . .   339 SHEP GOATHERD   9
    FROM STONE TO STONE. I AM LOOKING FOR STRAYED SHEEP! . .   339 SHEP GOATHERD   9
    THE EXULTATION OF THEIR STONE, THAT CRIED . . . . .   339 SHEP GOATHERD   25
    WHERE STONE IS DARK UNDER FROTH, ...   348 FISHERMAN   32
    WHERE STONE IS DARK WITH FROTH, ...   348 FISHERMAN   V 32
    IN THE GREY STONE TOMB HE MADE. . . . . . .   360 ALF POLLEXFEN   5
    HE SET HIS CHISEL TO THE HARDEST STONE. . . . . .   369 EGO DOMINUS   32
    AND AFTER KISSED A STONE, ...   384 VISION ROBART   64
    ENCHANTED TO A STONE . . . .   393 EASTER 1916   43
    CAN MAKE A STONE OF THE HEART. . . . .   394 EASTER 1916   58

	PAGE	TITLE		LINE

STONE   (CONTINUED)

	PAGE	TITLE		LINE
COLD STONE AND WATER. I GREW WILD,	399	BREAK OF DAY		14
WHILE ON THAT OLD GREY STONE I SAT	406	IN TIME OF WAR		2
TO BE CARVED ON A STONE AT THOOR BALLYLEE	406	CARVED STONE		T
TO BE CARVED ON A STONE AT BALLYLEE	406	CARVED STONE	V	T
OF DRIPPING STONE; I DECLARE	414	TOWER		126
BITTER AND VIOLENT MEN, MIGHT REAR IN STONE	418	ANCEST HOUSES		19
A WINDING STAIR, A CHAMBER ARCHED WITH STONE,	419	MY HOUSE		11
A GREY STONE FIREPLACE WITH AN OPEN HEARTH,	419	MY HOUSE		12
A GREY STONE FIRE-PLACE WITH AN OPEN HEARTH,	419	MY HOUSE	V	12
A BARRICADE OF STONE OR OF WOOD;	425	STARES NEST		11
I CLIMB TO THE TOWER-TOP AND LEAN UPON BROKEN STONE,	425	PHANTOM HATRED		1
I CLIMB TO THE TOWER TOP AND LEAN UPON BROKEN STONE,	425	PHANTOM HATRED	V	1
AMID THE ORNAMENTAL BRONZE AND STONE	428	NINETEEN 19		5
MIRACLE-BRED OUT OF THE LIVING STONE;	446	COLONUS PRAISE		13
AND FOUND A HEART OF STONE	451	FIRST LOVE		8
SO LIKE A BIT OF STONE I LIE	452	HUMAN DIGNITY		7
A STONE UPON HER BREAST,	456	FRIENDS YOUTH		6
AND A CLOAK WRAPPED ABOUT THE STONE,	456	FRIENDS YOUTH		7
AND PERCHES ON A STONE;	456	FRIENDS YOUTH		16
BEING ALL ALONE I'D NURSE A STONE	459	HIS WILDNESS		11
BUT WHEN I THINK OF THAT MY TONGUE'S A STONE.	478	SELF AND SOUL		40
LIKE MILK SPILT ON A STONE.	484	SPILT MILK		2
AND SAPLINGS ROOT AMONG THE BROKEN STONE,	489	COOLE PARK 29		28
CROUCH UPON A STONE,	525	DANCING DAYS		4
EVERY DISCOLORATION OF THE STONE,	567	LAPIS LAZULI		43
"IRELAND SHALL GET HER FREEDOM AND YOU STILL BREAK STONE."	590	PARNELL		2
THEY ALWAYS BEAT ON THE SAME SMALL STONE.	591	WHAT WAS LOST		5
THE OLD STONE CROSS	598	STONE CROSS		T
UNDER THE OLD STONE CROSS.	598	STONE CROSS		8
UNDER THE OLD STONE CROSS.	599	STONE CROSS		16
UNDER THE OLD STONE CROSS.	599	STONE CROSS		24
SET UP THE OLD STONE CROSS,	604	YOU CONTENT		10
I KISSED A STONE;	628	JANE MOUNTAIN		20
UNDER BROKEN STONE I HALT	632	MAN AND ECHO		2
AND SHOUT A SECRET TO THE STONE.	632	MAN AND ECHO		5
ARE CHANGED FOR EVER INTO MOON-WHITE STONE.	653	ISLE STAT I 2		43
LONG YEARS AGO, AND UNTO STONE CONGEALED.	656	ISLE STAT I 3		28
AND THEY ARE ALL NOW STONE, AS I SHALL BE,	656	ISLE STAT I 3		35
I PASSED BY MANY CAVES OF DRIPPING STONE.	657	ISLE STAT I 3		47
IS STONE; OLD SLEEPER; THIS SAME AFTERNOON	657	ISLE STAT I 3		74
THE ARCADIANS BRING, AND BID THE STONE BE RAISED	663	ISLE STAT II 2		25
AND HANG O'ER THE HISTORIED STONE;	707	FAIRY PEDANT		6
THE HISTORY HERE IN THE STONE NOW;	707	FAIRY PEDANT		15
THE HISTORY HERE IN THE STONE--	707	FAIRY PEDANT	V	15
AND THIS HARD FLAG OF STONE,	739	EARL PAUL		6

STONE-GREY

	PAGE	TITLE		LINE
THE WIND-BEATEN, STONE-GREY,	310	PEACOCK		4

STONE'S

	PAGE	TITLE		LINE
THE STONE'S IN THE MIDST OF ALL.	393	EASTER 1916		56
THINKS THAT THE STONE'S A CHILD.	456	FRIENDS YOUTH		12

STONES   SEE THUNDER-STONES

	PAGE	TITLE		LINE
CRASHED ON THE STONES, UPON THE GLIMMERING STONES,	33	OISIN 2	V	68A
CRASHED ON THE STONES, UPON THE GLIMMERING STONES,	33	OISIN 2	V	68A
GO CAST YOUR BODY ON THE STONES AND PRAY,	42	OISIN 2		207
. . . ON THE BURNING STONES IS THEIR PLACE;	61	OISIN 3		197
. . . ON THE BURNING STONES OF WIDE HELL,	61	OISIN 3		198
WE WILL TEAR OUT THE FLAMING STONES, AND BATTER THE GATEWAY OF BRASS	62	OISIN 3		209
ON THE FLAMING STONES, WITHOUT REFUGE,	62	OISIN 3		213
WE WILL TEAR OUT THE RED FLAMING STONES,	62	OISIN 3	V	209
WE WILL TEAR THE RED FLAMING STONES OUT,	62	OISIN 3	V	209
ON THE RED FLAMING STONES WITHOUT REFUGE	62	OISIN 3	V	213
I THROW DOWN THE CHAIN OF SMALL STONES;	63	OISIN 3		222
I WILL PRAY NO MORE WITH THE SMOOTH STONES;	63	OISIN 3	V	221
THERE, DON'T FLING STONES AT ME	94	MOLL MAGEE		2
YE WON'T FLING STONES AT ME;	96	MOLL MAGEE		54
I HAVE BEEN IN THE PATH OF STONES AND THE WOOD OF THORNS,	153	CHANGE BELOVED		3
THEY HAVE HEAPED THE STONES ABOVE HIS GRAVE	193	BAILE AILLINN		115
AND SCRUB A KITCHEN PAVEMENT, OR BREAK STONES	204	ADAMS CURSE		8
AND THROWN THE THUNDER ON THE STONES FOR ALL THAT MAEVE CAN SAY.	207	HANRAHANS SONG		7
AND SHAKE DOWN THUNDER ON THE STONES BECAUSE THE RED WINDS RAVE;	207	HANRAHANS SONG	V	7
AMONG THE STONES AND THORN-TREES, UNDER MORNING LIGHT;	291	PAUDEEN		3
AMONG THE STONES AND THORN TREES, UNDER MORNING LIGHT,	291	PAUDEEN	V	3
OF GREY STONES AND A ROCKY LEDGE	302	HOUR DAWN		12
IF HE BUT SHIFTED A FEW STONES,	302	HOUR DAWN		14
BUT WHILE HE FUMBLED WITH THE STONES	302	HOUR DAWN		16
BEFORE HIS EYES, WHERE STONES HAD BEEN,	302	HOUR DAWN		20
AND THEREON SAW, WHERE STONES HAD BEEN	302	HOUR DAWN	V	20
AND AFTER HEAPED THE STONES AGAIN	307	HOUR DAWN	V	116
WITH ALL THEIR ANCIENT FACES LIKE RAIN-BEATEN STONES,	318	MAGI		4
UPON THE BRIMMING WATER AMONG THE STONES	322	SWANS AT COOLE		5
AND THE PROUD STONES OF GREECE,	415	TOWER		159
THESE STONES REMAIN THEIR MONUMENT AND MINE.	423	MY DESCENDANTS		24
ROUND LOUGH DERG'S HOLY ISLAND I WENT UPON THE STONES,	593	PILGRIM		6
ALL FLAME-LIKE GUSHING FROM THE HOLLOW STONES,	650	ISLE STAT I 1		129
DRY STONES IN A WELL?"	780	WELL AND TREE		8

STONY

	PAGE	TITLE		LINE
WHERE PASSIONATE MAIVE IS STONY STILL;	3	OISIN 1	V	18

770

STONY (CONTINUED)
    AND ON THE RUNNEL'S STONY AND BARE EDGE • • • • • • •   39 OISIN 2   157
    BEFORE EARTH TOOK HIM TO HER STONY CARE: • • • • • • 126 DREAM OF FAERY   4
    WITH STILL AND STONY LIMBS AND OPEN EYES• • • • • • • 182 QUEEN MAEVE   46
    IN A MOST DESOLATE STONY PLACE, • • • • • • • 325 ROBERT GREGORY   30
    AN IMAGE THAT MIGHT HAVE BEEN A STONY FACE • • • • • • 368 EGO DOMINUS   28
    THAT TWENTY CENTURIES OF STONY SLEEP • • • • • • • 402 SECOND COMING   19
    THAT THIRTY CENTURIES OF STONY SLEEP • • • • • • • 402 SECOND COMING V 19
    AN ACRE OF STONY GROUND, • • • • • • • • • • 419 MY HOUSE   3
    LEST ON THINE HEART THE STONY SEAL • • • • • • • 667 ISLE STAT II 3   41
STONY-HEARTED
    AND STONY-HEARTED; NOW THOU HAST GROWN KIND, • • • • • 670 ISLE STAT II 3   91
STONY-STILL
    WHERE PASSIONATE MAEVE IS STONY-STILL: • • • • • • • •   3 OISIN 1   18
STOOD
    AND STOOD BESIDE THE SEA TOGETHER: • • • • • • • •   9 OISIN 1   V 101B
    WHILE ROUND THE SHORE A MILLION STOOD • • • • • • •   14 OISIN 1   182
    WHEN ONE DAY BY THE TIDE I STOOD, • • • • • • • •   24 OISIN 1   364
    WHEN ONCE BESIDE THE SHORE I STOOD, • • • • • • •   24 OISIN 1   V 364
    WHEN ONE DAY BY THE SHORE I STOOD• • • • • • • •   24 OISIN 1   V 364
    AND RODE AND STOOD BESIDE THE SHORE• • • • • • • •   25 OISIN 1   V 379A
    THAT WITH DIM EYEBALLS STOOD ON EITHER SIDE• • • • • •   34 OISIN 2   75
    STOOD LONELY, WITH DIM EYEBALLS ON EACH SIDE, • • • • •   34 OISIN 2   V 74
    STILL EARLESS, NERVELESS, BLIND, THE EAGLES STOOD• • • •   36 OISIN 2   100
    AND STOOD WITHIN: CLOTHED IN A MISTY RAY • • • • • •   36 OISIN 2   104
    AND STOOD WITHIN THE HALL. A MISTY RAY • • • • • •   36 OISIN 2   V 104
    BUT ONLY EXULTANT FACES. NIAMH STOOD • • • • • • •   38 OISIN 2   136
    STOOD TIMIDLY. LEST THEY SHOULD SEE SOME SIGHT • • • • •   38 OISIN 2   141
    I STOOD UPON THE STAIR: THE SURGES BORE • • • • • •   44 OISIN 2   225
    REMEMBERING HOW I HAD STOOD BY WHITE-HAIRED FINN • • • •   44 OISIN 2   227
    REMEMBERING HOW I STOOD BY WHITE-HAIRED FINN • • • • •   44 OISIN 2   V 227
    HOLDING THAT HORSE LONG SEEN NOT, NIAM STOOD• • • • •   44 OISIN 2   V 230
    AND WE STOOD ON A SEA'S EDGE WE SAW NOT: • • • • • •   47 OISIN 3   11
    • • • WITH BODIES UNGLORIOUS, THEIR CHIEFTAINS STOOD, • • •   58 OISIN 3   166
    A WHITEBEARD STOOD HUSHED ON THE PATHWAY• • • • • •   59 OISIN 3   173
    AUTUMN WAS OVER HIM: AND NOW THEY STOOD • • • • • •   80 EPHEMERA   16
    I STOOD: KEEN STARS ABOVE ME SHONE, • • • • • • •   83 MAD KING GOLL   29
    MY HUSBAND STOOD UP PALE, • • • • • • • • • •   95 MOLL MAGEE   V 22
    IN THREE DAYS' TIME HE STOOD UP WITH A MOAN, • • • • • 111 CUCHULAIN SEA   83
    STOOD UP, AND CAME TO THE LONG SANDS ALONE: • • • • • 111 CUCHULAIN SEA   84
    WEARY AND KIND ONE STOOD BESIDE HIS SEAT: • • • • • 112 ROSE OF WORLD V 13
    HE STOOD AMONG A CROWD AT DROMAHAIR• • • • • • • 126 DREAM OF FAERY   1
    STOOD UPRIGHT ON THE FLOOR. • • • • • • • • • 133 FR GILLIGAN   24
    I DREAMED THAT I STOOD IN A VALLEY, AND AMID SIGHS, • • • 163 VALLEY LOVERS   1
    FOR HAPPY LOVERS PASSED TWO BY TWO WHERE I STOOD: • • • 163 VALLEY LOVERS   2
    TILL DATHI CAME AND STOOD, • • • • • • • • • 166 BLESSED   2
    TILL DATHI CAME AND STOOD, • • • • • • • • • 167 BLESSED   V 4B
    THE MAINES' CHILDREN DROPPED THEIR SPADES, AND STOOD • • • 185 QUEEN MAEVE   120
    TILL IT DIED OUT WHERE AN OLD THORN-TREE STOOD. • • • • 186 QUEEN MAEVE   129
    FRIEND OF THESE MANY YEARS, YOU TOO HAD STOOD. • • • • 186 QUEEN MAEVE   130
    TILL IT DIED OUT WHERE AN OLD THORN TREE STOOD. • • • • 186 QUEEN MAEVE   V 129
    FRIEND OF THESE MANY YEARS, YOU TO HAVE STOOD. • • • • 186 QUEEN MAEVE   V 130
    WHO STOOD AMID A SILENCE BY THE THORN • • • • • • 187 QUEEN MAEVE   142
    UNTIL YOU STOOD BEFORE ME ON THE DECK-- • • • • • • 236 SHADOW WATER B   313
    OLD BUTLERS WHEN YOU TOOK TO HORSE AND STOOD • • • • • 270 PARDON FATHERS V 10
    MAYBE YOUR IMAGES HAVE STOOD, • • • • • • • • • 273 GREY ROCK   50
    WHERE BY OLD THORN-TREES THAT MAN STOOD: • • • • • • 274 GREY ROCK   80
    WHERE BY OLD THORN TREES THAT MAN STOOD: • • • • • • 274 GREY ROCK   V 80
    BUT THEREON EVERY GOD STOOD UP • • • • • • • • 275 GREY ROCK   116
    BECAUSE IT STOOD UPON HIS PATH AND SEEMED • • • • • • 277 TWO KINGS   8
    TOWARD PEOPLED TARA, NOR STOOD TO DRAW HIS BREATH • • • • 279 TWO KINGS   46
    ON PEOPLED TARA, NOR STOOD TO DRAW HIS BREATH • • • • • 279 TWO KINGS   V 46
    TOWARDS PEOPLED TARA, NOR STOOD TO DRAW HIS BREATH • • • 279 TWO KINGS   V 46
    BUT WHEN NINE DAYS HAD GONE I STOOD AGAIN • • • • • • 282 TWO KINGS   131
    STOOD ON MY PATH. TREMBLING FROM HEAD TO FOOT • • • • 283 TWO KINGS   151
    STOOD ON MY PATH. TREMBLING FROM HAND TO FOOT • • • • 283 TWO KINGS   V 151
    AND IN THE MIDST KING EOCHAID'S BROTHER STOOD, • • • • 286 TWO KINGS   217
    I HAVE STOOD HERE FROM BREAK OF DAY, • • • • • • • 294 THREE BEGGARS   2
    AND WHEN OLD GUAIRE CAME AND STOOD • • • • • • • 297 THREE BEGGARS   54
    I'VE STOOD AS I WERE MADE OF STONE • • • • • • • 297 THREE BEGGARS   64
    AND YET STOOD STILL, BECAUSE INSIDE • • • • • • • 303 HOUR DAWN   26
    THAT MERELY STOOD, ROCKING THE GLITTERING COACH • • • • 344 DAWN   11
    THE STATELY MIDNIGHT THROUGH UNTIL THEY STOOD • • • • • 352 PEOPLE   14
    AS IF THE HAIR STOOD UP ON MY HEAD. • • • • • • • 358 PRESENCES   2
    THEY STOOD IN THE DOOR AND STOOD BETWEEN • • • • • • 358 PRESENCES   9
    THEY STOOD IN THE DOOR AND STOOD BETWEEN • • • • • • 358 PRESENCES   9
    TO ALL THAT IN YOUR FLESH HAVE STOOD. • • • • • • 380 SAINT HUNCH   13
    THAT PITCHES COMMON THINGS ABOUT. THERE STOOD • • • • • 428 NINETEEN 19   4
    OR ALL THAT WAYWARD EBB AND FLOW. THERE STOOD • • • • 428 NINETEEN 19   V 4
    ON ALL THAT WAYWARD EBB AND FLOW. THERE STOOD • • • • 428 NINETEEN 19   V 4
    THE ROMAN EMPIRE STOOD APPALLED: • • • • • • • 437 SONGS PLAY 1   13
    AND WONDER IF SHE STOOD SO AT THAT AGE-- • • • • • • 444 SCHOOL CHILDR   19
    AND ON MY PATHWAY STOOD • • • • • • • • • • 451 FIRST LOVE   4
    THERE, ON BLOOD-SATURATED GROUND, HAVE STOOD • • • • • 482 BLOOD AND MOON   35
    THERE, ON BLOOD SATURATED GROUND, HAVE STOOD • • • • • 482 BLOOD AND MOON V 35
    STOOD IN THE CIRCUIT OF A NEEDLE'S EYE• • • • • • • 483 VERONIC NAPKIN   6
    SOME FOUND A DIFFERENT POLE, AND WHERE IT STOOD • • • • 483 VERONIC NAPKIN   7
    AND IN A COPSE OF BEECHES THERE I STOOD, • • • • • • 490 COOLE BALLYLEE   11
    BUT A BIRCH-TREE STOOD MY JACK: • • • • • • • • 508 JANE BISHOP   20
    BUT A BIRCH TREE STOOD MY JACK: • • • • • • • • 508 JANE BISHOP   V 20
    THAT FROM CHILDHOOD STOOD • • • • • • • • • • 512 JANE ON GOD   14

STOOD   (CONTINUED)
    CAME WHERE YOU STOOD, ...   518 LOVES LONENESS   4
    AND THEN YOU STOOD AMONG THE DRAGON-RINGS. . . . . . . 533 HER TRIUMPH   7
    AND THEN YOU STOOD AMONG THE DRAGON RINGS. . . . . . . 533 HER TRIUMPH   V   7
    TOO OLD FOR A MAN'S LOVE I STOOD IN RAGE . . . . .   536 HER VISION   3
    TOO OLD FOR A MAN'S LOVE I STOOD AND RAGED . . . . .   536 HER VISION   V   1
    FACE TO FACE WE STOOD: . . . .   539 MEETING   4
    JUSTIFY ALL THAT HAVE FLED, THAT HAVE STOOD, . . .   546 TO SAME TUNE 2   14
    STOOD OR HAVE MARCHED THE NIGHT LONG . . . .   546 TO SAME TUNE 2   15
    JUSTIFY ALL THAT HAVE FLED OR HAVE STOOD, ...   546 TO SAME TUNE 2 V   14
    OF A SLENDER PALM, STOOD BUT A DAY. . . . .   566 LAPIS LAZULI   34
    SHE STOOD IN DESPERATE MUSIC WOUND, ...   578 CRAZED GIRL   10
    A PERJURER STOOD READY . . . .   582 ROGER CASEMENT   9
    JOHN BULL HAS STOOD FOR PARLIAMENT, ...   583 GHOST ROG CASE   11
    A MAN WITH A PISTOL STOOD, ...   596 COLONEL MARTIN   56
    WENT TO THE SACRED HOUSE AND STOOD BETWEEN . . . .   609 IN TARAS HALLS   11
    REMEMBER ALL THAT HAVE FLED, THAT HAVE STOOD, . . .   613 MARCH SONGS 1   14
    STOOD, TOOK DEATH LIKE A TUNE . . . .   613 MARCH SONGS 1   15
    A MAN WHO BY A DEAD MAN STOOD. . . . .   671 ISLE STAT II 3   124
    HE SHRANK BEFORE MY VOICE, AND STOOD . . . . . .   671 ISLE STAT II 3   129
    HE STOOD A MESSENGER. IN APRIL'S PRIME . . . .   690 MOSADA 1   6
    AND ON TIPTOE THE WINDS A-WHISPERING STOOD. . . .   715 DWELT SYCAMORE   8
    AND ON TIP-TOE THE WINDS A-WHISPERING STOOD. . . .   715 DWELT SYCAMORE V   8
    LISTENING, UPON THEIR SHADOWS STOOD. . . . . .   725 LEGEND   8
    THERE STOOD A MAN, OF MEN THE LEAST-- . . . . .   729 PRIEST FAIRY   24
    AND CAME TO WHERE HIS BRETHREN STOOD, ...   730 PRIEST FAIRY   63
    EARL PAUL STOOD ON THE BED OF STRAW, ...   740 EARL PAUL   17
    WHEN HUNDREDS STOOD ABOUT TO SEE . . . . . .   740 EARL PAUL   27
    AND STOOD IN HIS DIM ARMOUR, ...   741 EARL PAUL   33
    STOOD THERE THE NORMAN KNIGHT. . . . .   741 EARL PAUL   40
    AND JOHN ROSE UP AND STOOD, ...   741 EARL PAUL   54
    AND STOOD IN MY SORROW APART. . . . .   744 GLOVE CLOAK   2
    I STOOD WITH HER CLOAK ON MY ARM . . . . . .   744 GLOVE CLOAK   5
    I HAVE STOOD SO LONG BY A GAP IN THE WALL . . . .   788 HAWTHORN TREE   15
    BUT NEVER STOOD BEFORE A STAKE . . . .   790 SINGING HEAD   23
STOOL
    WHEN I HAD LAIN IT ON A STOOL, ...   149 WANDER AENGUS V   9
    WHEN I HAD LAID IT ON A STOOL . . . .   149 WANDER AENGUS V   9
    BUT SOMETHING RUSTLED ON THE STOOL, ...   149 WANDER AENGUS V   11
    NO TABLE OR CHAIR OR STOOL NOT SIMPLE ENOUGH . . .   371 ON GOING HOUSE   3
    I SLEPT ON MY THREE-LEGGED STOOL BY THE FIRE, . . .   381 SONGS FOOL 2   1
    THOU HAST FORGOTTEN. ON THE OAKEN STOOL . . . .   713 FERENCZ RENYI   91
STOOP
    AND NEVER STOOP TO A MECHANICAL . . . .   417 ANCEST HOUSES   7
    MORE GRIEF IS MINE. NO MAN SHALL EVER STOOP . . .   661 ISLE STAT II 1   62
STOOPED
    WHEN I HAD STOOPED AND TENDERLY . . . . . .   10 OISIN 1   V 112A
    I STOOPED TO BLOW THE FIRE AFLAME, ...   149 WANDER AENGUS V   10
    HE HAS STOOPED DOWN AND KISSED HER ON THE LIPS. . .   232 SHADOW WATER B   230
    BUT THE STAG STOOPED AND RAN AT HIM, AND PASSED, . .   277 TWO KINGS   12
    BUT THE STAG STOOPED ITS HEAVY BRANCHING HORNS, . .   277 TWO KINGS   V   12
    BUT FINDING HIM STILL SILENT I STOOPED DOWN . . .   281 TWO KINGS   109
STOOPING
    AND A SMALL AND A FEEBLE POPULACE STOOPING WITH MATTOCK   58 OISIN 3   164
       AND SPADE,
    AND A SMALL AND A FEEBLE RACE STOOPING WITH MATTOCK AND   58 OISIN 3   V 164
       SPADE.
    AND A SMALL AND FEEBLE RACE STOOPING WITH MATTOCK   58 OISIN 3   V 164
       AND SPADE.
    THE ANGELS ARE STOOPING . . . .   118 CRADLE SONG   1
STOP
    MIND MOVED YET SEEMED TO STOP . . . .   384 VISION ROBART   43
    FOR AIMLESS JOY HAD MADE ME STOP . . . . . .   400 DEMON BEAST   22
    THIS LOVE THAT MAKES MY HEART'S BLOOD STOP . . . .   499 MOTHER OF GOD   13
    DARED I STOP". . . . .   559 HE AND SHE   6
    IF HE STOP LOVING ME, ...   569 THREE BUSHES   18
STOPPED
    BUT I NEVER STOPPED TO QUESTION, WHAT COULD THE BOATMAN SAY   593 PILGRIM   19
    LAY IN THE COFFIN, STOPPED HIS BREATH AND DIED. . . . 609 IN TARAS HALLS   20
    I HAVE STOPPED SO LONG A GAP IN THE WALL . . . .   788 HAWTHORN TREE V   15
STOPPING
    AND, IN A FAR-OFF, GENTLE VALLEY STOPPING, ...   68 SAD SHEPHERD   13
    HE FLED, AND IN A FAR-OFF VALLEY STOPPING, ...   68 SAD SHEPHERD   V   13
STOPS
    ABOUT YOUR HEAD TILL THE DUST STOPS YOUR EAR, . . .   293 TO A SHADE   20
    HE HOLDS HIM FROM DESIRE, ALL BUT STOPS HIS BREATHING LEST   559 MAGIC DRUM   1
STORE
    SOME OLD MISER TELLS HIS STORE: . . . .   647 ISLE STAT I 1   58
    ON NAUGHT HAS SET STORE . . . .   780 WELL AND TREE   13
STORED
    "GOD ONLY SEES WHAT DOOM FOR ME LIES STORED." . . .   110 CUCHULAIN SEA V   62
    WHOSE IMAGES, IN THE GREAT MEMORY STORED, ...   412 TOWER   85
STOREYS
    BECAUSE WOMEN IN THE UPPER STOREYS DEMAND A FACE AT THE   623 HIGH TALK   7
       PANE,
STORIES
    OF STORIES BUILDED BY HIS WORDS . . . .   7 OISIN 1   68
    THE DEDICATION TO A BOOK OF STORIES SELECTED FROM THE IRISH   129 BOOK STORIES   T
       NOVELISTS
    ALL THE LOVE STORIES THAT THEY KNEW. . . . . .   197 BAILE AILLINN   197
    YOUR EARS THAN STORIES NOW IN FASHION, ...   271 GREY ROCK   5

	PAGE	TITLE	LINE

STORIES   (CONTINUED)
IS NOT THAT HOW GOOD STORIES RUN?-- . . . .   271 GREY ROCK   13
CAN KNOW THE STORIES THAT WE KNOW . . . .   458 SECRETS OF OLD   11
STORIES OF THE BED OF STRAW . . . .   458 SECRETS OF OLD   17
THAT'S HOW ALL NATURAL OR SUPERNATURAL STORIES RUN. . . .   556 RIBH PATRICK   3
BUT STORIES THAT LIVE LONGEST . . . .   587 PARNELLITES   29
AND O! BUT SHE HAD STORIES. . . . .   620 JOHN KINSELLA   17
STORM
HE HEARS THE STORM IN THE CHIMNEY ABOVE. . . . . . .   26 OISIN 1   404
A STORM OF BIRDS IN THE ASIAN TREES . . . .   27 OISIN 1   416
DRIVEN BY A STORM THAT EVER GRIEVES. . . . .   135 TWO TREES   V 28
AND, LIKE A STORM, CRY THE INEFFABLE NAME, ...   137 TO SOME I TALK   12
WILL HIDE US FROM THE BITTER STORM. . . . .   152 HEART OF WOMAN   8
SHALL HIDE US FROM THE BITTER STORM. . . . .   152 HEART OF WOMAN V 8
WOULD THAT THE STORM THAT OVERTHREW MY SHIPS, . . .   235 SHADOW WATER B   286
"WERE NOT ALL HER LIFE BUT STORM, ...   259 PEACE   4
BECAUSE THERE IS SUCH A STORM AMID MY THOUGHTS . . .   281 TWO KINGS   100
SHE LIVED IN STORM AND STRIFE. . . . .   317 NIGHT COME   1
ONCE MORE THE STORM IS HOWLING, AND HALF HID . . . .   403 FOR DAUGHTER   1
A PEAR-TREE BROKEN BY THE STORM. . . . .   424 ROAD AT DOOR   10
A PEAR TREE BROKEN BY THE STORM. . . . .   424 ROAD AT DOOR   V 10
TO BAR THAT FOUL STORM OUT, FOR WE . . . .   432 NINETEEN 19   111
NOR STORM DISTURBS, FLAMES BEGOTTEN OF FLAME, . . .   498 BYZANTIUM   27
ALL THAT STORM THAT BLOTS THE DAY . . . .   509 JANE REPROVED   3
LOVE STORM: AND STAINED WITH MIST THE NEW MOONS FLARE. . .   678 ISLE STAT II 3   294
LOVE STORM AND STAINED WITH MIST THE NEW MOON'S FLARE . .   678 ISLE STAT II 3 V 294
NEVER STORM AROSE SO SWIFTLY: SCARCE THE CHILDREN WERE
   IN BED,   718 PHANTOM SHIP   4
STORM DARKENED OR STARRY BRIGHT. . . . .   739 WHERE BOOKS GO   8
A SUDDEN STORM, AND IT WAS THROWN . . . .   784 WOMANS BEAUTY   5
THE STORM AROSE AND SUDDENLY FELL . . . .   784 WOMANS BEAUTY   19
STORMBEATEN
STORMBEATEN COTTAGES. . . . .   480 BLOOD AND MOON V 7
STORM-BEATEN
WHILE UNDER ITS STORM-BEATEN BREAST . . . .   397 POLIT PRISONER   23
STORM-BEATEN COTTAGES-- . . . .   480 BLOOD AND MOON   7
A STORM-BEATEN OLD WATCH-TOWER, ...   484 SYMBOLS   1
A STORM-BEATEN OLD WATCH TOWER, ...   484 SYMBOLS   V 1
STORM-BITTEN
ON A STORM-BITTEN GREEN. . . . .   606 SONGS BURDEN 2   4
STORM-BROKEN
WERE LOVED BY HIM: THE OLD STORM-BROKEN TREES . . .   326 ROBERT GREGORY   50
STORMS
AND WANDER IN THE STORMS AND CLINGING SNOWS, ...   42 OISIN 2   201
I BELLOW TO THE WINDS WHEN STORMS MAKE MOAN, ...   45 OISIN 2   V 239D
THAT UNIMAGINABLE STORMS OF WIND AND WAVE . . . . .   236 SHADOW WATER B   317
THAT STORMS ARE SHAKING, HEAR THE ARMED MAN SPEAK. .   470 HARUN RASHID   V 193
ALL THOSE STORMS THAT BLOT THE DAY . . . .   509 JANE REPROVED V 3
STORM-SCATTERED
IN STORM-SCATTERED INTRICACY. . . . .   501 VACILLATION   48
STORM-TOSSED
A WOMAN'S BEAUTY IS A STORM-TOSSED BANNER: . . . . .   469 HARUN RASHID   188
STORMY
A STORMY SUNSET ON DOOMED SHIPS: . . . .   3 OISIN 1   23
A STORMY SUNSET O'ER DOOMED SHIPS. . . . .   3 OISIN 1   V 23
OR STORMY SILVER FRET THE GOLD OF DAY, ...   128 DREAM OF FAERY   33
THAT THE STORMY NIGHT RECEIVES, ...   135 TWO TREES   26
ANOTHER EMBLEM THERE!   THAT STORMY WHITE . . . . .   490 COOLE BALLYLEE   17
BUILDING-YARD AND STORMY SHORE, ...   530 OLD TOM AGAIN   5
BUILDING YARD AND STORMY SHORE, ...   530 OLD TOM AGAIN V 5
AT DAYBREAK AFTER STORMY NIGHT . . . .   784 WOMANS BEAUTY   3
STORY   SEE LOVE-STORY
OISIN, TELL ME THE FAMOUS STORY . . . .   2 OISIN 1   V 1
READING SOME ENTANGLED STORY: . . . .   65 HAPPY SHEPHERD   16
IN THE VERSE OF ATTIC STORY . . . .   65 HAPPY SHEPHERD V 16
AND TO ITS LIPS THY STORY TELL, ...   66 HAPPY SHEPHERD   37
CRIED OUT, DIM SEA, HEAR MY MOST PITEOUS STORY! . .   68 SAD SHEPHERD   9
CRIED ALL HIS STORY TO THE DEWDROPS GLISTENING. . .   68 SAD SHEPHERD   14
AND THOUGHT, I WILL MY HEAVY STORY TELL . . . . . .   68 SAD SHEPHERD   19
"OH SEA, OLD SEA, HEAR THOU MY PITEOUS STORY!" . . .   68 SAD SHEPHERD   V 9
AND THOUGHT, "TO THIS WILL I MY STORY TELL, ...   68 SAD SHEPHERD   V 19
SHE DREW FROM ME MY STORY-- . . . .   96 MOLL MAGEE   37
BALLAD AND STORY, RANN AND SONG: . . . .   137 TO IRELAND   4
FOR THERE IS NO HIGH STORY ABOUT QUEENS . . . . . .   186 QUEEN MAEVE   134
EVEN IN AN OLD STORY, IS A BURDEN NOT TO BE BORNE. .   210 UNDER THE MOON   20
BECAUSE OF A STORY I HEARD UNDER THE THIN HORN . . .   210 UNDER THE MOON V 17
BECAUSE OF A STORY I HEARD UNDER A THIN HORN . . . .   210 UNDER THE MOON   17
IT IS LUCKY THAT THEIR STORY . . . .   215 HAPPY TOWNLAND   27
AND THE IMAGES I HAVE WOVEN IN THIS STORY . . . . .   218 WOODS OF COOLE   21
TO TELL THEM A PLAIN STORY.   THAT'S NOT THE STORY: .   245 SHADOW WATER B   482
TO TELL THEM A PLAIN STORY.   THAT'S NOT THE STORY: .   245 SHADOW WATER B   482
HERE'S AN OLD STORY I'VE REMADE, ...   270 GREY ROCK   3
HERE'S AN OLD STORY I'VE RE-MADE, ...   270 GREY ROCK   V 3
HAD RAVELLED HER OWN STORY OUT, ...   272 GREY ROCK   45
THAT TRAGIC STORY MADE. . . . .   587 PARNELLITES   26
WHEN HE HEARD THAT STORY TOLD, ...   596 COLONEL MARTIN   47
WHEN HE HAD HEARD THAT STORY TOLD . . . .   596 COLONEL MARTIN V 47
NO SINGLE STORY WOULD THEY FIND . . . .   626 OLD MEN BE MAD   13
THEY HEAR THE STORY OF THE WIND, ...   655 ISLE STAT I 3   11
AND TELL ME A LOVE STORY WHILE I DRINK. . . . . . .   760 SHADOW WATER A V 250
AND TELL ITS STORY OVER THEIR BROWN ALE. . . . . . .   767 SHADOW WATER A 393

	PAGE	TITLE	LINE

STORY'S
SOMEWHERE IN EAR-SHOT FOR THE STORY'S END, ... 269 PARDON FATHERS 2
AND WHEN THE STORY'S FINISHED, WHAT'S THE NEWS? . . . 491 COOLE BALLYLEE V 40E
WHEN ALL THAT STORY'S FINISHED, WHAT'S THE NEWS? . . . . 495 CHOICE 5
SAW THE STORY'S END, ... 597 COLONEL MARTIN 69
STOUT
HIS STOUT STICK UNDER HIS HAND, ... 588 OLD WICKED MAN 20
STRADDLE
A STRADDLE ON THE DOLPHIN'S MIRE AND BLOOD . . . . . 498 BYZANTIUM V 33
STRADDLING
STRADDLING EACH A DOLPHIN'S BACK . . . . 612 NEWS ORACLE 13
STRAFFORD
AND EVEN STRAFFORD SMILED AS THOUGH . . . . 400 DEMON BEAST 13
STRAIGHT
IT ROSE IN A STRAIGHT BLUE GARMENT, ... 159 CAP AND BELLS 5
IN A LONG AND STRAIGHT BLUE GARMENT . . . . 159 CAP AND BELLS V 5
AND THOUGHT OF DAYS WHEN HE'D HAD A STRAIGHT BODY, . . 183 QUEEN MAEVE 70
THAT HAD SO STRAIGHT A BACK, ... 458 HIS WILDNESS 4
THOSE TERRIBLE IMPLACABLE STRAIGHT LINES . . . . . . 467 HARUN RASHID 142
PALLAS ATHENE IN THAT STRAIGHT BACK AND ARROGANT HEAD! 578 LOFTY THINGS 11
HOW CAN THE YOUNG GO STRAIGHT? . . . . 607 SONGS BURDEN 2 17
WITH A STIFF STRAIGHT BACK, ... 627 STATES HOLIDAY 33
AND STRAIGHT BEFORE THE SLEEPING PRIEST . . . . . . 729 PRIEST FAIRY 23
STRAIGHTEN
STRAIGHTEN AGED KNEES, ... 505 RESULT THOUGHT 16
STRAIGHTENED
STRAIGHTENED ALL THAT WENT AWRY . . . . . . 440 WISDOM V 4
BUT I HAVE STRAIGHTENED OUT . . . . 505 RESULT THOUGHT 7
STRAIN
A LITTLE RUNNEL MADE A BUBBLING STRAIN, ... 39 OISIN 2 156
DUSKY AND HERBLESS, WHERE A BUBBLING STRAIN . . . 39 OISIN 2 V 156
SHIVER UNDER THE LASH, STRAIN, SWEAT AND JOLT . . . . 260 FASC DIFFICULT 7
THAT NEVER KNEW THAT STRAIN WOULD SCARCE SEEM BRIGHT, . 465 HARUN RASHID 88
DID WORDS OF MINE PUT TOO GREAT STRAIN . . . . . 632 MAN AND ECHO 13
STRAINING
UNDER THE ROOF, AND WITH A STRAINING THROAT . . . . 36 OISIN 2 106
DRIFTING ON HIGH, AND WITH A STRAINING THROAT . . . . 36 OISIN 2 V 106
NOR STRAINING JOY, BUT WHOLE IS JOINED TO WHOLE! . . . 555 RIBH AT TOMB 14
ON STRAINING THIGHS, ... 574 LOVERS SONG 6
STRAINS
SO STRAINS TO LOOK BEYOND OUR LIFE, AN EYE . . . . . 465 HARUN RASHID 87
STRAIT
YOUR WEEPING FITS! LOOK YOU, SO VERY STRAIT . . . . 659 ISLE STAT II 1 22
STRAITS
CROSS THE NARROW STRAITS TO LIGHT . . . . 494 AT ALGECIRAS 4
CROSSES THE NARROW STRAITS TO LIGHT . . . . . . 494 AT ALGECIRAS V 4
CROSS THOSE NARROW STRAITS TO LIGHT . . . . . . 494 AT ALGECIRAS V 4
STRAND
OR SAT IN DREAMS ON THE PALE STRAND, ... 25 OISIN 1 390
THE OLD BROWN THORN-TREES BREAK IN TWO HIGH OVER CUMMEN 206 HANRAHANS SONG 1
STRAND,
THE OLD BROWN THORN TREES BREAK IN TWO HIGH OVER CUMANN'S 206 HANRAHANS SONG V 1
STRAND,
WEAK AND WORN AND WEARY THE WAVES OF CUMMEN STRAND, . . 207 HANRAHANS SONG V 6
WHAT ARE ALL THOSE FISH THAT LIE GASPING ON THE STRAND? 485 THREE MOVEMENT 3
FROM THE SEAWEED ON THE STRAND, ... 597 COLONEL MARTIN 71
FROM THE SEA-WEED ON THE STRAND, ... 597 COLONEL MARTIN V 71
STRANDS
OR WHEN ALONG THE WINTRY STRANDS . . . . 84 MAD KING GOLL 41
OR WHERE ALONG THE WINTRY STRANDS . . . . 84 MAD KING GOLL V 41
STRANGE
OF MANY A FIGURED CREATURE STRANGE, ... 4 OISIN 1 V 27
THAN THIS STRANGE HUMAN BARD," HE CRIED; . . . . . 17 OISIN 1 239
THAN THIS STRANGE BARD," HE CRIED, AND CAUGHT . . . . 17 OISIN 1 V 239
LIAR AND FLATTERER OF THE WEAK, IN WHAT STRANGE CLIME . . 42 OISIN 2 V 198
I AWOKE! THE STRANGE HORSE WITHOUT SUMMONS OUT OF 54 OISIN 3 105
THE DISTANCE RAN,
AND I ON THIS STRANGE ROAD WILL PASS . . . . . . 97 FOXHUNTER V 11
BUT SEEK ALONE TO HEAR THE STRANGE THINGS SAID . . . 101 ROSE UPON ROOD 19
I DREAMED THAT ONE HAD DIED IN A STRANGE PLACE . . . 123 DREAM OF DEATH 1
STRANGE CREATURES FLUTTER UP BEFORE ONE'S EYES, . . . 222 SHADOW WATER B 18
AND AFTER CIRCLING WITH STRANGE CRIES AWHILE . . . 223 SHADOW WATER B 26
THROUGH THAT STRANGE ILLNESS THAT HAD FIXED HIM THERE, . 280 TWO KINGS 81
EARNING RESPECT: HAVE NO STRANGE FRIEND; . . . . . 337 SCHOLARS V 9
OF SOME STRANGE WOMAN'S NAME THAT RAN IN HIS HEAD, . . 351 HER PRAISE V 9
THIS NIGHT HAS BEEN SO STRANGE THAT IT SEEMED . . . 358 PRESENCES 1
THE STRANGE REWARD OF ALL THAT DISCIPLINE, ... 374 PHASES OF MOON 57
I SUDDENLY CRIED OUT IN A STRANGE TONGUE . . . . 387 SOLOMON WITCH 5
STRANGE, BUT THE MAN WHO MADE THE SONG WAS BLIND; . . 411 TOWER 49
THAT NOTHING STRANGE; THE TRAGEDY BEGAN . . . . . 411 TOWER 51
BUT FEEL THE STRANGE HEART BEATING WHERE IT LIES? . . 441 LEDA AND SWAN 8
AND FEELS THE STRANGE HEART BEATING WHERE IT LIES! . . 441 LEDA AND SWAN V 8
A STRANGE THING SURELY THAT MY HEART, WHEN LOVE HAD COME 449 OWEN AHERNE 1
UNSOUGHT
THAT FIRST STRANGE INTEREST IN MY BOOKS AND STUDIES. . . 468 HARUN RASHID V 165
HORTON'S THE FIRST I CALL. HE LOVED STRANGE THOUGHT . 471 ALL SOUL NIGHT 21
AND A MIRACULOUS STRANGE BIRD SHRIEKS AT US. . . . . 534 HER TRIUMPH 12
IF STRANGE MEN COME FROM THE HOUSE . . . . . . 568 SWEET DANCER 8
STRANGE NIGHT HAS COME! . . . . 574 MAIDS 1ST SONG 6
(FOR SINCE THE HORIZON'S BOUGHT STRANGE DOGS ARE STILL) 579 DOR WELLESLEY 7
THEIR CRIES ARE SWEET AND STRANGE, ... 612 NEWS ORACLE 18

		PAGE	TITLE	LINE
STRANGE	(CONTINUED)			
SHEEP-GUIDING, OR THE BRINGING SOME STRANGE BIRD,	. . .	650	ISLE STAT I 1	147
STRANGE DRAPERIES DID ALL THE SIDES ADORN, . .	. . .	657	ISLE STAT I 3	55
AND THAT WAS STRANGE! BUT THIS IS MANY A WORLD	. . .	664	ISLE STAT II 2	60
BUT WHY THIS WHIM OF THINE? A STRANGE UNREST,	. . .	671	ISLE STAT II 3	137
HAVE NOT A MYRIAD SWAYED BELOW STRANGE TREES .	. . .	724	KANVA ON SELF	11
A STRANGE, UNSERVICEABLE THING, ...	. . .	784	WOMANS BEAUTY	15
ITS STRANGE HEART BEATING FAST	. . .	785	YOUR HEART	6
STRANGENESS				
THAT HER OWN STRANGENESS PERPLEXED!	. . .	260	UNWORTH PRAISE	14
ESTRANGED AMID THE STRANGENESS OF THEMSELVES, .	. . .	375	PHASES OF MOON	78
NOR HAD FORGOT THE STRANGENESS OF MY PRESENCE .	. . .	466	HARUN RASHID V	119A
STRANGER				
THE STRANGER WATCHED THE SWORD! BUT NIAM FAR, .	. . .	38	OISIN 2 V	136
STRANGER WITH STRANGER, ...	. . .	574	MAIDS 1ST SONG	3
STRANGER WITH STRANGER, ...	. . .	574	MAIDS 1ST SONG	3
I SAW A STRANGER TAP AND WAIT	. . .	696	MOSADA 2	22
A STRANGER NEW ARISEN WAIT	. . .	696	MOSADA 2 V	22
THEN THE STRANGER SOFTLY CREW--	. . .	697	MOSADA 2	28
THE STRANGER SHOUTED, "OPEN WIDE	. . .	697	MOSADA 2 V	24
STRANGER'S				
BEAUTY TO MAKE A STRANGER'S EYE DISTRAUGHT, .	. . .	403	FOR DAUGHTER	18
BECOME A STRANGER'S LEMAN! AND THAT YOU, .	. . .	757	SHADOW WATER A	215
STRANGERS				
WHEN STRANGERS MURDERED EMMET, FITZGERALD, TONE,	. . .	541	PARN FUNERAL 1	17
STRANGLE				
AS THOUGH TO STRANGLE HER, NO SCREAM . . .	. . .	514	JANE GROWN OLD	4
STRAW				
AS THOUGH DRIED STRAW, AND IF WE TURN ABOUT .	. . .	327	ROBERT GREGORY	83
I WOULD BE--FOR NO KNOWLEDGE IS WORTH A STRAW--	. . .	344	DAWN	13
STORIES OF THE BED OF STRAW	. . .	458	SECRETS OF OLD	17
"NOT TO DIE ON THE STRAW AT HOME	. . .	587	OLD WICKED MAN	5
"AND HALF FORGET THIS BED OF STRAW	. . .	739	EARL PAUL	5
EARL PAUL STOOD ON THE BED OF STRAW, . . .	. . .	740	EARL PAUL	17
STRAWBERRY SEE WILD-STRAWBERRY				
STRAW-DEATH				
AWAITING IN PATIENCE THE STRAW-DEATH, . . .	. . .	58	OISIN 3	167
STRAW-PALE				
UNDER THE SHADOW OF STUPID STRAW-PALE LOCKS, .	. . .	433	NINETEEN 19	127
STRAWS SEE WINDLE-STRAWS				
THE LITTLE STRAWS WERE TURNIN' ROUND . . .	. . .	95	MOLL MAGEE	31
STRAY				
I LET THEM STRAY. I THOUGHT OF RHYME ALONE, .	. . .	339	SHEP GOATHERD	11
MADE MY ATTENTION STRAY.	. . .	507	STREAM AND SUN	5
STRAYED				
THAT WOULD BE HARSH FOR CHILDREN THAT HAVE STRAYED.	. .	201	OLD MEMORY	12
THAT HAD BEEN HARSH FOR CHILDREN THAT HAVE STRAYED.	. .	201	OLD MEMORY V	12
FROM STONE TO STONE. I AM LOOKING FOR STRAYED SHEEP!	.	339	SHEP GOATHERD	9
O WHAT A SWEETNESS STRAYED	. . .	401	DEMON BEAST	43
STRAYETH				
STRAYING AS THE HERON STRAYETH, ...	. . .	706	DAWN-SONG	27
STRAYING				
STRAYING TOO FAR INTO THE NORTH OR SOUTH, .	. . .	226	SHADOW WATER B	86
STRAYING AS THE HERON STRAYETH, ...	. . .	706	DAWN-SONG	27
UNTO THE HEART OF THE WOODLAND STRAYING, .	. . .	728	PRIEST FAIRY	1
STRAYS				
AT LAST CUCHULAIN SPAKE, "A YOUNG MAN STRAYS .	. . .	109	CUCHULAIN SEA V	47
O WHAT IF GARDENS WHERE THE PEACOCK STRAYS .	. . .	418	ANCEST HOUSES	25
STREAM				
THE STREAM CHURNED, CHURNED, AND CHURNED--HIS LIPS APART,		31	OISIN 2	43
THE STREAM CHURNED, CHURNED, ...	. .	31	OISIN 2 V	43
I SEE MY LIFE GO DRIPPING LIKE A STREAM . .	. . .	104	FERGUS DRUID V	31
AND RIVER AND STREAM WORK OUT THEIR WILL! .	. . .	148	INTO TWILIGHT	12
I DROPPED THE BERRY IN A STREAM	. . .	149	WANDER AENGUS	7
THE VINEGAR-HEAVY SPONGE, THE FLOWERS BY KEDRON STREAM!		172	TRAV PASSION	5
THE HISSOP-HEAVY SPONGE, THE FLOWERS BY KIDRON STREAM!		172	TRAV PASSION V	5
DARK AND DULL AND EARTHY THE STREAM OF DRUMAHAIR	. .	207	HANRAHANS SONG V	11
OUT OF THE RUNNING STREAM, O MORNING STAR, .	. .	251	SHADOW WATER B	610
IN GLENDALOUGH BESIDE THE STREAM, ...	. . .	331	ROUND TOWER	8
WHEN THE FLIES DROP IN THE STREAM!	. . .	348	FISHERMAN	34
ON THE GREY SAND BESIDE THE SHALLOW STREAM .	. . .	367	EGO DOMINUS	1
SHALL WALK THE WET SANDS BY THE EDGE OF THE STREAM	. .	371	EGO DOMINUS	71
SPLASHED, OR AN OTTER SLID INTO THE STREAM. .	. .	372	PHASES OF MOON	9
ON THE DARK STREAM, ...	. . .	389	IMAGE PAST	3
TO TROUBLE THE LIVING STREAM.	. . .	393	EASTER 1916	44
A SHADOW OF CLOUD ON THE STREAM	. . .	393	EASTER 1916	49
IN THE ELMS ABOVE THE FLOODED STREAM! . . .	. . .	403	FOR DAUGHTER	12
LAST REACH OF GLITTERING STREAM	. . .	414	TOWER	143
CROSSING STREAM AGAIN	. . .	419	MY HOUSE	9
THAT PLUNGED IN STREAM AGAIN	. . .	419	MY HOUSE V	9
THE MOOR-HEN GUIDES UPON THE STREAM, . . .	. . .	424	ROAD AT DOOR	12
STREAM AND SUN AT GLENDALOUGH	. . .	506	STREAM AND SUN	T
STREAM AND GLIDING SUN	. . .	506	STREAM AND SUN	2
WHAT MOTION OF THE SUN OR STREAM	. . .	507	STREAM AND SUN	11
AND BOTH ADRIFT ON THE MIRACULOUS STREAM . .	. . .	535	CHOSEN	16
ALL THE STREAM THAT'S ROARING BY	. . .	562	NEEDLES EYE	1
"THAT SOME STREAM OF LIGHTNING	. . .	589	OLD WICKED MAN	55
LIKE A LONG-LEGGED FLY UPON THE STREAM . . .	. . .	617	LONG-LEG FLY	9
LIKE A LONG-LEGGED FLY UPON THE STREAM . . .	. . .	617	LONG-LEG FLY	19
LIKE A LONG-LEGGED FLY UPON THE STREAM . . .	. . .	618	LONG-LEG FLY	29
AND SEDGY STREAM, AND IN EACH BABBLING BRAKE .	. . .	675	ISLE STAT II 3	225

	PAGE	TITLE	LINE
STREAM (CONTINUED)			
I WILL DRINK OUT OF THE STREAM. THE STREAM IS GONE!	761	SHADOW WATER A	273
I WILL DRINK OUT OF THE STREAM. THE STREAM IS GONE!	761	SHADOW WATER A	273
THE GRASS AND THE BLUE SHADOW ON THE STREAM	761	SHADOW WATER A	280
A STREAM HAS TOLD ME THEY ARE BEAUTIFUL.	767	SHADOW WATER A	398
OUT OF A RUNNING STREAM, O MORNING STAR	769	SHADOW WATER A	426
STREAMING			
WITH STREAMING HAIR AS WANDERING LIGHTS	667	ISLE STAT II 3	19
STREAM'S			
THE TOWER SET ON THE STREAM'S EDGE!	326	ROBERT GREGORY	52
THE TOWER SET BY THE STREAM'S EDGE!	326	ROBERT GREGORY V	52
STREAMS			
THAT WAVERED LIKE THE SUMMER STREAMS.	4	OISIN 1	29
. . . SLOW DROPPING A SOUND IN FAINT STREAMS	51	OISIN 3	67
AND BY ME, IN SOFT RED RAIMENT, THE FENIANS MOVED IN LOUD STREAMS,	53	OISIN 3	93
HE RUFFLES WITH HIS BILL THE MINNOWED STREAMS.	73	ANASHU VIJAYA	37
AND STREAMS, WIDE-WATERING, SALMON-SHOALED,	81	MAD KING GOLL V	3
OVER THE YOUNG STREAMS.	88	STOLEN CHILD	37
OF DEW ON THE YOUNG STREAMS.	88	STOLEN CHILD V	37
FALLS IN SLEEPY STREAMS.	98	FOXHUNTER	16
POURS ROUND HIS SLEEPY STREAMS.	98	FOXHUNTER V	16
POURS ROUND IN SLEEPY STREAMS.	98	FOXHUNTER V	16
"I CAN BRING YOU SALMON OUT OF THE STREAMS	167	BLESSED	9
MIRRORED IN STREAMS THAT NEITHER HAIL NOR RAIN	184	QUEEN MAEVE	89
THOUGH NOTHING TROUBLES THE GREAT STREAMS	196	BAILE AILLINN	172
ECHTGE OF STREAMS	203	WITHER BOUGHS V	T
AND I FELL ASLEEP UPON LONELY ECHTGE OF STREAMS.	203	WITHER BOUGHS	6
I KNOW, AND THE CURLEW AND PEEWIT ON ECHTGE OF STREAMS.	204	WITHER BOUGHS	22
AND THE CURLEW AND PEEWIT KNOW ON ECHTGE OF STREAMS.	204	WITHER BOUGHS V	22
LEAPS UPWARD, AS IF ALL THE STREAMS O' THE WORLD	249	SHADOW WATER B	560
COMPANIONABLE STREAMS OR CLIMB THE AIR:	323	SWANS AT COOLE	21
AMONG THE STREAMS:	329	MEN IMPROVE	3
AMONG THE STREAMS.	329	MEN IMPROVE	18
THAT HER HAIR STREAMS UPON THE WIND,	390	IMAGE PAST	40
THAT CLIMB THE STREAMS UNTIL	414	TOWER	123
WHEN ALL STREAMS ARE DRY,	414	TOWER	138
OUT OF THE OBSCURE DARK OF THE RICH STREAMS,	417	ANCEST HOUSES	14
THE SUBTERRANEAN STREAMS,	420	MY HOUSE V	20H
IRRATIONAL STREAMS OF BLOOD ARE STAINING EARTH:	564	GYRES	5
AND THE JOY OF THE STREAMS WHERE LONG-LIMBED HERONS WADE!	674	ISLE STAT II 3	217
AND HEARS THE ROAR OF THE STREAMS WHERE, DRUIDS SAY,	749	SHADOW WATER A	46
AMONG THOSE STREAMS, OR ON THEIR CLOUDY EDGE.	750	SHADOW WATER A	63
IN THE COLD STREAMS, AND WAKE TO THEIR DESIRE,	750	SHADOW WATER A	85
THEY LURE US TO THE STREAMS WHERE THE WORLD ENDS.	764	SHADOW WATER A	334
ALL DIES AMONG THOSE STREAMS. THE FOOL HAS MADE .	764	SHADOW WATER A	335
WHAT WERE TRUE-LOVE AMONG THE RUSH OF HIS STREAMS?	764	SHADOW WATER A	338
WHAT WERE TRUE LOVE AMONG THE RUSH OF HIS STREAMS?	764	SHADOW WATER A V	338
TO SNATCH ALIVE OUT OF THE STREAMS ALL LOVERS .	765	SHADOW WATER A	347
THAT HAVE GONE THITHER TO LOOK FOR THE LOUD STREAMS,	765	SHADOW WATER A	348
TO LEAD US TO THE STREAMS WHERE THE WORLD ENDS.	765	SHADOW WATER A	369
MY LOVE SHAKES OUT HER HAIR UPON THE STREAMS	768	SHADOW WATER A	416
STREET			
ALONG THE PEBBLY STREET.	94	MOLL MAGEE	12
WANDERING FROM BROKEN STREET TO STREET	196	BAILE AILLINN	167
WANDERING FROM BROKEN STREET TO STREET	196	BAILE AILLINN	167
ON EVERY CROWDED STREET TO STARE	294	HATED PLAYBOY	3
WILL GATHER, AND NOT KNOW IT WALKS THE VERY STREET	315	FALLEN MAJESTY	7
WILL GATHER AND NOT KNOW THAT THROUGH ITS VERY STREET	315	FALLEN MAJESTY V	7
EVENING AND MORNING, THE STEEP STREET OF URBINO	352	PEOPLE	12
EVENING AND MORN, THE STEEP STREET OF URBINO	352	PEOPLE V	12
IN THE LONG ECHOING STREET THE LAUGHING DANCERS THRONG,	459	FROM OEDIPUS	7
AND FOLLOWED THROUGH THE EMPTY STREET, AND SHE,	468	HARUN RASHID V	154A
WHILE ON THE SHOP AND STREET I GAZED	501	VACILLATION	40
SOMEWHERE OFF HENRY STREET:	585	ORAHILLY	31
AND THERE AT ALL STREET CORNERS	596	COLONEL MARTIN V	55
PICKED UP ON A STREET.	617	LONG-LEG FLY	18
PICKED UP ON THE STREET.	617	LONG-LEG FLY V	18
A MOUND OF REFUSE OR THE SWEEPINGS OF A STREET,	630	CIRCUS ANIMALS	35
A MOUND OF REFUSE OR THE SWEEPINGS OF THE STREET,	630	CIRCUS ANIMALS V	35
AY, AND SHAKES IN SEA-GREEN WAVERINGS ALONG THE FISHERS' STREET:	718	PHANTOM SHIP	2
AYE AND SHAKES IN SEA GREEN WAVERINGS, ALONG THE FISHERS' STREET.	718	PHANTOM SHIP V	2
STREET DANCERS	731	STREET DANCERS	T
SINGING IN THIS LONDON STREET,	731	STREET DANCERS	1
WAS CRIED IN STREET AND LANE	740	EARL PAUL	26
STREET-CORNERS			
AND THERE AT ALL STREET-CORNERS	596	COLONEL MARTIN	55
STREETS			
UPON THE THRONE AND CRYING ABOUT THE STREETS	198	SEVEN WOODS	7
OR HURLED THE LITTLE STREETS UPON THE GREAT,	256	NO SECOND TROY	4
IN THE LONG ECHOING STREETS THE LAUGHING DANCERS THRONG,	459	FROM OEDIPUS V	7
LONDON STREETS HAVE HERITAGE,	733	STREET DANCERS	57
STRENGTH			
AND FLOWING STRENGTH, WITH AGE IS SUBTLE-SOULED.	35	OISIN 2 V	83
. . . THE STRENGTH OF THE BELL-BRANCH IS NAUGHT,	55	OISIN 3	123
. . . A SOB FOR THE FENIANS' OLD STRENGTH.	60	OISIN 3	188
"YOUR STRENGTH, THAT IS SO LOFTY AND FIERCE AND KIND,	201	OLD MEMORY	3
BECAUSE I HAVE COME INTO MY STRENGTH,	256	WORDS	11
ALL THAT SWEETNESS AMID STRENGTH?"	259	PEACE	9

776

	PAGE	TITLE		LINE

STRENGTH (CONTINUED)
TILL THEY HAD CHANGED US TO LIKE STRENGTH?" . . . . . . 259 PEACE V 9
SO DID SHE YOUR STRENGTH RENEW, ... 259 UNWORTH PRAISE 6
"YOUR STRENGTH AND NOBLENESS WILL PASS AWAY"? . . . . 285 TWO KINGS 189
OR TILL THE SUN IS IN HIS STRENGTH. . . . . 305 HOUR DAWN 61
HAD STRENGTH THAT COULD UNBIND . . . . 315 FRIENDS 11
I HAVE RAGED AT MY OWN STRENGTH BECAUSE YOU HAVE LOVED IT. 448 HERO GIRL FOOL 9
IF YOU ARE NO MORE STRENGTH THAN I AM BEAUTY . . . . . 448 HERO GIRL FOOL 10
ALL MEN HAVE PRAISED MY STRENGTH BUT NOT MY WORTH. . . 448 HERO GIRL FOOL V 9
THE STRENGTH THAT GIVES OUR BLOOD AND STATE MAGNANIMITY 481 BLOOD AND MOON 29
ALL THEIR WHOLESOME STRENGTH. . . . . 505 RESULT THOUGHT 12
NOW STRENGTH OF BODY GOES! . . . . 575 ACRE OF GRASS 4
BUT HE HAS NEED OF ALL THAT STRENGTH . . . . 624 APPARITIONS 20
STRETCH
HEARING HIM GROAN AND STRETCH . . . . 319 DOLLS 13
"STRETCH BONES TILL THE DAYLIGHT COME . . . . 331 ROUND TOWER 5
THAT MADE THEM STRETCH AND YAWN, ... 345 ON WOMAN 21
STRETCH OUT YOUR LIMBS AND SLEEP A LONG SATURNIAN SLEEP! 442 BLACK CENTAUR 13
AND DID AFTER STRETCH AND YAWN"! . . . . 521 THREE THINGS 17
BUT STRETCH THAT BODY FOR A WHILE . . . . 534 CONSOLATION 3
STRETCH TOWARDS THE MOONLESS MIDNIGHT OF THE TREES, . . 579 DOR WELLESLEY 1
STRETCH NECK AND CLAP THE WING, ... 783 GREY ROUND 27
STRETCHED
STRETCHED HIS LONG ARM TO WHERE, A MISTY SMOTHER, . . . 31 OISIN 2 42
. . . AND THE QUIVER OF STRETCHED BOWSTRINGS, ... 62 OISIN 3 207
AND STRETCHED OUT SLEEPING ON A PILE OF SKINS . . . . . 283 TWO KINGS 141
YOUNG RED-HEAD STRETCHED HIMSELF TO YAWN . . . . . 303 HOUR DAWN V 32A
AND DRANK AND YAWNED AND STRETCHED HIM OUT, ... 307 HOUR DAWN 108
HE STRETCHED HIS BONES AND FELL IN A DREAM . . . . . . 331 ROUND TOWER 10
STRETCHED UP ON TWO LEGS FROM THE MAT, ... 381 SONGS FOOL 2 7
UPON A MOMENT, AND SO STRETCHED IT OUT . . . . 384 VISION ROBART 46
ALL THE STRETCHED BODY'S LAID ON THE WHITE RUSH . . . . 441 LEDA AND SWAN V 7
STRETCHED UNDER A DOORWAY . . . . 585 ORAHILLY 30
SOME TWENTY FEET FROM TIP TO TIP HAD IT STRETCHED RIGHTLY 593 PILGRIM 17
OUT,
SOME TWENTY FEET FROM TIP TO TIP HAD ITS WINGS STRETCHED 593 PILGRIM V 17
RIGHTLY OUT,
AND HAVING STRETCHED AND YAWNED AWHILE . . . . . . 612 NEWS ORACLE 11
I LAY STRETCHED OUT IN THE DIRT . . . . 628 JANE MOUNTAIN 21
WHEN WE HALE MEN LIE STRETCHED IN SLUMBER . . . . . 636 BLACK TOWER 23
STRETCHES
FAR UP IN THE STRETCHES OF NIGHT! . . . . 623 HIGH TALK 12
STRETCHING
AND STRETCHING OUT HER ARMS, RED WITH THE DYE, ... 105 CUCHULAIN SEA V 7
AND STRETCHING FORTH HIS ARM AND CUP . . . . 275 GREY ROCK 118
STREW
BUT THE TORN PETALS STREW THE GARDEN PLOT! . . . . . 422 MY DESCENDANTS 7
WHEN THE TORN PETALS STREW THE GARDEN PLOT! . . . . 422 MY DESCENDANTS V 7
I CAN STREW THE SHEET. . . . . 572 LADYS 2ND SONG 6
STREWING
STREWING UPON THE ROCKS THEIR STEEL-BLUE HAIR, ... 687 TWO TITANS 30
STREWN   SEE SEA-STREWN
LIE STREWN THE YELLOW LEAVES—THE CLOTTED LEAVES. . . . 684 SEEKER 69
LIE STREWN THE CLOTTED LEAVES—THE DEAD OLD LEAVES. . . 684 SEEKER V 69
STRICKEN   SEE TERROR-STRICKEN
AT THE MOST QUIET MIDNIGHT IS TO BE STRICKEN. . . . . . 236 SHADOW WATER B 321
STRICKEN WITH PANIC FROM THE ATTACK, ... 274 GREY ROCK 75
OUT NAKED ON THE ROADS, AS THE BOOKS SAY, AND STRICKEN . 316 COLD HEAVEN 11
THOUGH MARGERY IS STRICKEN DUMB . . . . 457 SECRETS OF OLD 7
THAT MAN IS STRICKEN DEAF AND DUMB AND BLIND, ... 478 SELF AND SOUL 35
A STRICKEN RABBIT IS CRYING OUT, ... 633 MAN AND ECHO 45
STRICKEN ALL THE NIGHT IS PAST— . . . . 648 ISLE STAT I 1 96
STRIFE
BY KNOWING NOR TUMULT NOR HATE NOR STRIFE, ... 9 OISIN 1 95
AND FLOATING-HAIRED AND PROUD IN STRIFE! . . . . . . 9 OISIN 1 V 99
WINGED LOVES BORNE ON IN GENTLE STRIFE, ... 135 TWO TREES V 14
SHE LIVED IN STORM AND STRIFE, ... 317 NIGHT COME 1
OF LOVE FROM OUT A DREAMLESS RACE FOR STRIFE, ... 684 SEEKER 58
STRIKE
A HUSH! AH, ME! IT HANGS TO STRIKE US DEAD. . . . . . 43 OISIN 2 V 208B
I'LL STRIKE A BLOW FOR HIM TO GIVE HIM TIME . . . . . . 239 SHADOW WATER B 365
TO HIM THAT STRIKES HIM FIRST! I WILL STRIKE HIM FIRST. . . 239 SHADOW WATER B 369
TO BURN US TO THE MARROW IF WE STRIKE. . . . . 239 SHADOW WATER B 372
I WILL STRIKE AT HIM. AND I! AND I! AND I! . . . . . . 240 SHADOW WATER B 379
AND STRIKE THE GOLDEN PILLARS WITH MY HANDS. . . . . 246 SHADOW WATER B 502
TO STRIKE YOU DEAD? . . . . 359 TO A SQUIRREL 5
"STRIKE ME IF I SHRIEK." . . . . 455 HIS MEMORIES 18
ARISE AND BID ME STRIKE A MATCH . . . . 476 EVA GORE-BOOTH 26
AND STRIKE ANOTHER TILL TIME CATCH! . . . . 476 EVA GORE-BOOTH 27
BID ME STRIKE A MATCH AND BLOW. . . . . 476 EVA GORE-BOOTH 32
DREW A KNIFE TO STRIKE HIM DEAD, ... 514 JANE GROWN OLD 10
SHE HEARS ME STRIKE THE BOARD AND SAY . . . . 531 FATHER CHILD 1
I COME TO HEAR IT STRIKE." . . . . 585 ORAHILLY 26
THOUGH STIFF TO STRIKE A BARGAIN, ... 620 JOHN KINSELLA 13
STRIKE QUICKLY! IT WILL FADE OUT WHEN YOU STRIKE. . . . 759 SHADOW WATER A 238
STRIKE QUICKLY! IT WILL FADE OUT WHEN YOU STRIKE. . . . 759 SHADOW WATER A 238
STRIKES
TO HIM THAT STRIKES HIM FIRST! I WILL STRIKE HIM FIRST. . . 239 SHADOW WATER B 369
OR STRIKES A SUDDEN CHILL INTO MY BONES . . . . . . 499 MOTHER OF GOD 14

STRING   SEE HARP-STRING FIDDLE-STRING
    AND TOUCH THE LAUGHING SILVER STRING! . . . . .   17 OISIN 1   233
    AND ALL AROUND THE HARP STRING TOLD HIS PRAISE. . . . .   109 CUCHULAIN SEA V   44
    I HEAR THE HARP STRING PRAISE THEM OR HEAR THEIR MOURNFUL   210 UNDER THE MOON V   16
      TALK.
    LISTEN TO THAT LOW-LAUGHING STRING OF THE MOON . . . .   243 SHADOW WATER B   432
    THAT MADE THE BODY SEEM AS IT WERE A STRING . . . . .   284 TWO KINGS   176
    AND LIKE A LAUGHING STRING . . . .   291 TO A FRIEND   11
    A STRING OF SCHOLARS WENT IN FEAR . . . .   381 SONG OF FOOL   7
    FINGERED UPON A FIDDLE STICK OR STRING . . . . . .   445 SCHOOL CHILDR V   46
    OR THE FIDDLE STRING ACCURSED. . . . .   527 AM OF IRELAND V   20
    OR SMOTE UPON THE STRING AND TO THE SOUND . . . . . .   537 HER VISION   15
    A WOMAN, AND AN ARROW ON A STRING! . . . . . .   541 PARN FUNERAL 1   11
    AND ITS OLD SOLE STRING . . . .   627 STATES HOLIDAY   23
    COME THOU, COME, AND TO THIS STRING-- . . . . . .   646 ISLE STAT I 1   37
    AND A STRING MURMURS AS THOUGH TIME WERE DEAD . . . .   752 SHADOW WATER A   124
STRINGED
    TO SOME STRINGED INSTRUMENT NONE THERE HAD SEEN, ...   180 QUEEN MAEVE   4
    OF OLD STRINGED INSTRUMENTS, HUNG THERE . . . . . .   271 GREY ROCK   V   20
    THEIR HAIR MINGLES ON SOME STRINGED INSTRUMENT, ...   752 SHADOW WATER A   123
STRING'S   SEE BOW-STRING'S
STRINGS   SEE HARP-STRINGS HEART-STRINGS
    AND, WEEPING OVER THE WHITE STRINGS, HURLED . . . . . .   17 OISIN 1   241
    HEARING AEDH TOUCH THE MOURNFUL STRINGS OF GOLD." . . .   35 OISIN 2   87
    OF FEVER. NOW THE STRINGS ARE TORN . . . .   86 MAD KING GOLL V   66
    MY SINGING FADES, THE STRINGS ARE TORN, ...   86 MAD KING GOLL V   66
    WITH HIS OWN FINGERS TOUCHED THE BRAZEN STRINGS. . . . .   109 CUCHULAIN SEA   46
    WITH HIS OWN FINGER TOUCHED THE BRAZEN STRINGS. . . . .   109 CUCHULAIN SEA V   46
    OR LET ITS MEANING MIX INTO THE STRINGS. . . . . .   180 QUEEN MAEVE   8
    AWOKE THE HARP STRINGS LONG AGO. . . . .   190 BAILE AILLINN V   37
    OR THE TWO STRINGS THAT MADE ONE SOUND . . . .   195 BAILE AILLINN   155
    WERE HOVERING OVER THE HARP STRINGS . . . .   195 BAILE AILLINN V 141
    I HEAR THE HARP STRINGS PRAISE THEM, OR HEAR THEIR MOURNFUL 210 UNDER THE MOON V   16
      TALK.
    THE MOUTHS THAT SPEAK, THE NOTES AND STRINGS, ...   212 BLESS PSALTER   2
    AWAKE UNSLEEPING FIRES! AND WOVE SEVEN STRINGS, ...   219 HARP OF AENGUS   7
    BY MAGIC STRINGS, I'LL MAKE THIS ANSWER TO IT! . . . .   243 SHADOW WATER B   440
    MY MAGIC STRINGS, I'LL MAKE THIS ANSWER TO IT! . . . .   243 SHADOW WATER B V   440
    FINGERED UPON A FIDDLE-STICK OR STRINGS . . . . . .   445 SCHOOL CHILDR   46
    AWAKE UNSLEEPING FIRES! AND WOVE SEVEN STRINGS, ...   762 SHADOW WATER A   302
STRIP
    THAT STRIP THE BODY BARE." . . . .   570 THREE BUSHES   27
STRIPPED
    SLIM ADOLESCENCE THAT A NYMPH HAS STRIPPED, ...   612 NEWS ORACLE   25
STRIPS
    CUT OUT OUR RHYMES ON STRIPS OF NEW-TORN BARK . . . . .   343 SHEP GOATHERD   115
STRIVE
    IN TRUTH, AN EVIL RACE. WHY STRIVE FOR HER, ...   696 MOSADA 2   9
STRIVING
    UNTUNED BY THEIR OWN STRIVING. IF ONE SUCH . . . . .   711 FERENCZ RENYI   37
STRODE
    MOST DISTANT STRODE WE. ON THE FLOOR LAY SLIME, ...   37 OISIN 2   V 113
    VIOLENT AND FAMOUS, STRODE AMONG THE DEAD! . . . . .   634 CUCHULAIN COMF   2
STROKE
    AND YET COULD GIVE SO FINE A STROKE?" . . . .   274 GREY ROCK   84
    HEAVEN HAS PUT AWAY THE STROKE OF HER DOOM, ...   356 BROKEN DREAMS   11
    THE LAST STROKE OF MIDNIGHT DIES. . . . .   357 BROKEN DREAMS   37
    THAT I, MIDNIGHT UPON THE STROKE, ...   507 JANE BISHOP   2
    AT STROKE OF MIDNIGHT SOUL CANNOT ENDURE . . . . . .   558 RIBH CHRISTIAN   19
    AT STROKE OF MIDNIGHT GOD SHALL WIN. . . . . . .   561 FOUR AGES MAN   8
STROKED
    STROKED THE YOUNG WINDS AS THEY ROLLED ON THE PLAIN, . .   27 OISIN 2   V 415C
    NOR CEASED UNTIL WHITE NIAMH STROKED HIS EARS . . . .   30 OISIN 2   26
STROKES   SEE SWORD-STROKES
    THAT THINK SWORD STROKES WERE BETTER MEANT . . . . .   276 GREY ROCK   V 129
STRONG
    WE RODE IN SORROW, WITH STRONG HOUNDS THREE, ...   2 OISIN 1   V   7C
    OF OUR STRONG STEEDS WAS DARK WITH SWEAT, ...   2 OISIN 1   V   7T
    FOR HE IS STRONG AND CRAFTY AS THE SEAS . . . .   35 OISIN 2   83
    AND ALL THE EXULTANT LABOURS OF THE STRONG. . . . . .   42 OISIN 2   195
    OF ANCIENT WARRIORS, THE LABOURS OF THE STRONG. . . .   42 OISIN 2   V 195
    . . . THE STRONG HOOFS CRUSHING THE SAND AND THE SHELLS,   58 OISIN 3   157
    . . . THE STRONG HOOFS CRUSHING THE SANDS AND THE SHELLS   58 OISIN 3   V 157
    . . . THOUGH SPACIOUS THEIR LANDS WERE AND STRONG. . .   58 OISIN 3   V 160
    . . . AND NO MAN MAY WAR WITH THE STRONG SPIRITS WAGE! .   62 OISIN 3   V 214
    WHO HOLDS THE WORLD BETWEEN HIS BILL AND MADE US STRONG   76 INDIAN ON GOD   6
      OR WEAK
    WHO HOLDS THE WORLD BETWEEN HIS BILL AND MAKES US STRONG   76 INDIAN ON GOD V   6
      OR WEAK
    FASHIONED TO BE THE MOTHER OF STRONG CHILDREN! . . . .   181 QUEEN MAEVE   26
    THERE'S MANY A STRONG FARMER . . . .   213 HAPPY TOWNLAND   1
    FOR O, THE STRONG FARMERS . . . .   215 HAPPY TOWNLAND   29
    THAN A STRONG BODY AND A READY HAND. . . . . . .   232 SHADOW WATER B   236
    THE WEAK LAY HAND ON WHAT THE STRONG HAS DONE, ...   265 THESE CLOUDS   3
    KING EOCHAID SEIZED THE HORNS IN HIS STRONG HANDS . .   278 TWO KINGS   24
    THE STRONG THIGH AND THE AGILE THIGH WERE MET, ...   278 TWO KINGS   28
    EOCHAID SEIZED BOTH THE HORNS IN HIS STRONG HANDS . .   278 TWO KINGS   V   24
    LAID HIS STRONG BONES DOWN IN DEATH . . . .   360 ALF POLLEXFEN   3
    LAID HIS STRONG BONES IN DEATH . . . .   360 ALF POLLEXFEN V   3
    MAYBE AN IMAGE IS TOO STRONG . . . .   388 SOLOMON WITCH   36
    OR MAYBE IS NOT STRONG ENOUGH." . . . .   388 SOLOMON WITCH   37

778

	PAGE	TITLE		LINE
STRONG (CONTINUED)				
BID A STRONG GHOST STAND AT THE HEAD	435	FOR MY SON		1
WHEN MY BLOOD WAS STRONG, ...	457	SECRETS OF OLD		4
BUT GOOD STRONG BLOWS ARE DELIGHTS TO THE MIND."	544	TO SAME TUNE 1		4
STRONG DRINK I HAD, AND IT BROUGHT ME TO SORROW, ...	544	TO SAME TUNE 1		13
BUT A GOOD STRONG CAUSE AND BLOWS ARE DELIGHT." . . .	545	TO SAME TUNE 1		14
BUT A GOOD STRONG CAUSE"--THE ROPE GAVE A JERK THERE, . .	545	TO SAME TUNE 1		23
BUT A GOOD STRONG CAUSE AND THE BLOWS ARE DELIGHT." . .	545	TO SAME TUNE 1	V	14
WHEN ORDER HAS WEAKENED OR FACTION IS STRONG, . . .	548	TO SAME TUNE 3		12
THAT RULE BECAUSE A STRONG RIGHT ARM	597	MODEL LAUREATE		11
CONTACT EVERYTHING ANTAEUS-LIKE GREW STRONG.	603	GALLERY REVIS		44
CONTACT ALL THINGS ANTAEUS-LIKE GREW STRONG!	603	GALLERY REVIS	V	44
BRACE ME AND MAKE ME STRONG!	607	SONGS BURDEN 2		24
BUT GOOD STRONG BLOWS ARE DELIGHTS TO THE MIND." . . .	616	MARCH SONGS 3		4
STRONG DRINK I HAD, AND IT BROUGHT ME TO SORROW, . . .	616	MARCH SONGS 3		13
BUT A GOOD STRONG CAUSE AND BLOWS ARE DELIGHT." . . .	616	MARCH SONGS 3		14
BUT A GOOD STRONG CAUSE"--THE ROPE GAVE A JERK THERE, .	616	MARCH SONGS 3		23
SHARP THEIR SPADES, THEIR MUSCLES STRONG, ...	637	BEN BULBEN		22
SHARP THEIR SPADES, THEIR MUSCLE STRONG, ...	637	BEN BULBEN	V	22
AND A STRONG GALLEY. I GIVE YOU ALL AS MUCH.	758	SHADOW WATER A		222
PRAISE THE BEAUTIFUL AND STRONG!	773	SONG DEIRDRE 1		19
THE STRONG MARCH BIRDS A-CROW.	783	GREY ROUND		26
STRONGER				
ALL MEN, AND STRONGER OF HIS HANDS, ...	7	OISIN 1	V	63
SITS A YOUNGER AND A STRONGER.	26	OISIN 1	V	399D
IT MAKES MY PASSION STRONGER BUT TO THINK	465	HARUN RASHID		99
STRONGEST				
THE STRONGEST OF THE WORLD, TO SNATCH MY PREY, ...	45	OISIN 2	V	241
STRONGLY				
. . . WHEN THERE ENTERS THE STRONGLY ARMED GUEST! . . .	62	OISIN 3		210
STROVE				
THAT YOU WERE BEAUTIFUL, AND THAT I STROVE	206	ADAMS CURSE		35
STRUCK SEE FRENZY-STRUCK TERROR-STRUCK MOON-STRUCK CONSCIENCE-STRUCK				
IMAGINED, AS THEY STRUCK THE WAY	189	BAILE AILLINN		20
FOR THAT WAS IN THE BARGAIN WHEN WE STRUCK IT.	225	SHADOW WATER B	V	68D
WE SHOULD BE DAZED AND TERROR STRUCK	272	GREY ROCK	V	37
AND WHERE THE STONE STRUCK FIRE, WHILE IN THE LEAVES . .	278	TWO KINGS		33
THAT NONE MIGHT KNOW THAT HE WAS CONSCIENCE STRUCK, . . .	462	HARUN RASHID	V	38
STRUCK DUMB IN THE SIMPLICITY OF FIRE!	502	VACILLATION		75
SO HARD I STRUCK.	518	HIS CONFIDENCE		8
"HIS LIGHT HAD STRUCK ME BLIND	559	HE AND SHE		5
HER BARGAIN STRUCK WE LAUGHED AND TALKED	620	JOHN KINSELLA		15
UP THERE SOME HAWK OR OWL HAS STRUCK, ...	633	MAN AND ECHO		43
STRUCKEN SEE TERROR-STRUCKEN				
WITH QUAKING JOINTS AND TERROR STRUCKEN FACES, ...	185	QUEEN MAEVE	V	121
STRUGGLE				
THE STRUGGLE OF THE FLY IN MARMALADE.	369	EGO DOMINUS		45
AND THAT MUST SLEEP, SHRIEK, STRUGGLE TO ESCAPE . . .	444	SCHOOL CHILDR		35
WILL STRUGGLE. OR HE'LL SEEK ENCHANTER OLD, ...	651	ISLE STAT I 1		162
STRUGGLED				
HORN LOCKED IN SWORD, THEY TUGGED AND STRUGGLED THERE . .	277	TWO KINGS		18
I STRUGGLED WITH THE HORROR OF DAYBREAK, ...	535	CHOSEN		10
THEN HE STRUGGLED WITH THE HEART!	561	FOUR AGES MAN		3
THEN HE STRUGGLED WITH THE MIND!	561	FOUR AGES MAN		5
STRUGGLES				
WORN WITH LONG STRUGGLES! AND THE WAVES HAVE SUNG . . .	687	TWO TITANS		23
STRUGGLING				
BUT PRONE ON THE PATHWAY, PRONE STRUGGLING, ...	60	OISIN 3	V	186
STRUGGLING FOR AN IMAGE ON THE TRACK	534	CHOSEN		2
HIS BONDS AWAY, SORE STRUGGLING. NOW AT LAST	714	FERENCZ RENYI		116
STRUNG				
AND A HUNDRED YOUTHS, WHOSE LIMBS ARE STRUNG	9	OISIN 1	- V	97
WHERE THEIR SINEWY MIGHT IS STRUNG	658	ISLE STAT I 3		88
STRUTS				
THERE STRUTS HAMLET, THERE IS LEAR, ...	565	LAPIS LAZULI		10
STRUTTING				
WITH A STRUTTING TURKEY WALK, ...	627	STATES HOLIDAY		34
STUB				
AND I, THAT I MIGHT FIND AND STUB IT OUT, ...	281	TWO KINGS	V	92
STUBBORN				
THE POET STUBBORN WITH HIS PASSION SANG US	356	BROKEN DREAMS		18
STUBBORN-HEARTED				
WOMEN ARE HARD AND PROUD AND STUBBORN-HEARTED, ...	245	SHADOW WATER B		479
STUCK				
HE HAD KNEES THAT STUCK OUT OF HIS HOSE!	190	BAILE AILLINN		27
ALL KNOW THAT ALL THE DEAD IN THE WORLD ABOUT THAT PLACE	593	PILGRIM		11
ARE STUCK,				
AND HE STUCK TO HIS THRONE.	628	JANE MOUNTAIN		10
STUDDED SEE GEM-STUDDED				
STUDENT SEE FELLOW-STUDENT				
OLD FELLOW STUDENT, WHOSE MOST PATIENT EAR	468	HARUN RASHID	V	167
STUDENT'S				
TRUTH FLOURISHES WHERE THE STUDENT'S LAMP HAS SHONE, . .	398	LEADERS CROWD		8
STUDENTS				
ON HEARING THAT THE STUDENTS OF OUR NEW UNIVERSITY . . .	262	STUDENTS AGIT		T
STUDIES				
THAT FIRST STRANGE INTEREST IN MY BOOKS AND STUDIES. . .	468	HARUN RASHID	V	165
STUDIO				
FOR TWENTY MINUTES IN SOME STUDIO.	602	GALLERY REVIS		16
STUDY				
COMPELLING IT TO STUDY	416	TOWER		182

PAGE TITLE LINE

STUDY (CONTINUED)
 TO STUDY READING-BOOKS AND HISTORY, ... 443 SCHOOL CHILDR 4
 TO STUDY READING BOOKS AND HISTORY . . . . 443 SCHOOL CHILDR V 4
 TO STUDY READING BOOKS AND HISTORIES, ... 443 SCHOOL CHILDR V 4
 THAT DAY BY DAY I STUDY AND MARVEL AT, ... 468 HARUN RASHID 157
 WHY SHOULD I SEEK FOR LOVE OR STUDY IT? . . . . 558 RIBH CHRISTIAN 1
 I STUDY HATRED WITH GREAT DILIGENCE, ... 558 RIBH CHRISTIAN 3
STUDYING
 NOR IS THERE SINGING SCHOOL BUT STUDYING . . . . . . 407 SAIL BYZANTIUM 13
 AND THERE'S NO SINGING SCHOOL BUT STUDYING . . . . . 407 SAIL BYZANTIUM V 13
STUFF
 TO HOLD THE SACRED STUFF HE BREWS . . . . 272 GREY ROCK 24
 IN RUSTLE OF LACE OR SILKEN STUFF, ... 358 PRESENCES 5
 COAGULATE OF STUFF . . . . 449 HERO GIRL FOOL 26
 NOT KNOWING WHAT UNEARTHLY STUFF . . . . 599 STONE CROSS 21
STUFFED
 AND STUFFED WITH ALL THAT'S OLD AND BAD! . . . . . . 303 HOUR DAWN V 25
 THAT'S STUFFED WITH ALL THAT'S OLD AND BAD! . . . . . 303 HOUR DAWN V 25
STUMBLED
 OF OUR OLD PAUDEEN IN HIS SHOP, I STUMBLED BLIND . . . 291 PAUDEEN 2
 STUMBLED UPON THAT WINDY PLACE . . . . 302 HOUR DAWN 3
 STUMBLED ON WINDY CRUACHAN . . . . 302 HOUR DAWN V 3
 BECAUSE HE HAS STUMBLED ON THIS HOLE . . . . 304 HOUR DAWN V 54
 HE STUMBLED, TUMBLED, FUMBLED TO AND FRO . . . . . . 411 TOWER 61
STUMBLING
 . . . THE SOUND OF TWO STUMBLING APART. . . . . 60 OISIN 3 V 184
 HERDED THE CATTLE CAME WITH STUMBLING FEET, ... 106 CUCHULAIN SEA 19
 MERELY FOR STUMBLING ON THIS HOLE . . . . 304 HOUR DAWN 54
 STUMBLING UPON THE BLOOD-DARK TRACK ONCE MORE, ... 622 HOUND VOICE 18
 THEN STUMBLING TO THE KILL BESIDE THE SHORE; . . . . . 622 HOUND VOICE 19
 THAT STUMBLING TO THE KILL BESIDE THE SHORE; . . . . . 622 HOUND VOICE V 19
STUMP
 TO BURN THAT STUMP ON THE ACROPOLIS, ... 430 NINETEEN 19 46
STUMPIER
 A STUMPIER ON EITHER HAND! . . . . 460 THREE MONUMENT 4
STUMPS
 E'EN THOUGH HIS WINGS WERE PLUMELESS STUMPS, ... 670 ISLE STAT II 3 118
STUNTED
 BECAUSE WE LOVE BARE HILLS AND STUNTED TREES . . . . . 621 HOUND VOICE 1
 AND 'MONG THE STUNTED ASH-TREES' DROOPING RINGS, . . . 650 ISLE STAT I 1 128
STUPEFIED
 OWN NOTHING BUT THEIR BLIND, STUPEFIED HEARTS. . . . . 370 EGO DOMINUS 69
STUPID
 A STUPID HAPPY CREATURE . . . . 400 DEMON BEAST 31
 UNDER THE SHADOW OF STUPID STRAW-PALE LOCKS, ... 433 NINETEEN 19 127
 SOME STUPID THING THAT I HAD DONE . . . . 507 STREAM AND SUN 4
STUPIDITY
 BUT THE STUPIDITY . . . . 600 SPIRIT MEDIUM 20
 HAS BODY AND ITS STUPIDITY, ... 633 MAN AND ECHO 28
STUPOR
 MY DAILY THOUGHTS SINCE THE FIRST STUPOR OF YOUTH . . . 342 SHEP GOATHERD 83
 HIS GOD OF STUPOR AND OF WRATH. . . . . 725 LEGEND 20
STURDIER
 MEAN ROOF-TREES WERE THE STURDIER FOR ITS FALL, ... 264 HOUSE SHAKEN 8
STURDY
 AS THE ONE STURDY LEG COULD DO . . . . 302 HOUR DAWN 5
STY
 NOT IN SOME FOUL STY." . . . . 513 JANE TALK BISH 6
 ANCESTRAL PEARLS ALL PITCHED INTO A STY, ... 619 BRONZE HEAD 26
STYLE
 A STYLE IS FOUND BY SEDENTARY TOIL . . . . 370 EGO DOMINUS 65
 HE WROTE OF ME IN THAT EXTRAVAGANT STYLE . . . . 373 PHASES OF MOON 26
SUBMISSIVE
 THE FLAGELLANT LASHES THOSE SUBMISSIVE LOINS . . . . . 560 WHENCE COME 7
SUBSCRIPTION
 TO A WEALTHY MAN WHO PROMISED A SECOND SUBSCRIPTION . . . 287 TO WEALTHY MAN T
SUBSTANCE
 BUT THAT HE FOUND MORE SUBSTANCE THERE THAN DREAMS, . . . 417 ANCEST HOUSES V 10
 MORE SUBSTANCE IN OUR ENMITIES . . . . 425 STARES NEST 18
 TRANSFIGURED TO PURE SUBSTANCE WHAT HAD ONCE . . . . . 555 RIBH AT TOMB 11
 YET KEEP HIS SUBSTANCE WHOLE. . . . . 573 LADYS 2ND SONG 13
 WHICH OF HER FORMS HAS SHOWN HER SUBSTANCE RIGHT? . . . 618 BRONZE HEAD 11
 OR MAYBE SUBSTANCE CAN BE COMPOSITE, ... 619 BRONZE HEAD 12
 OR MAY BE SUBSTANCE CAN BE COMPOSITE, ... 619 BRONZE HEAD V 12
SUBSTANTIAL
 MUST BE SUBSTANTIAL SOMEWHERE. I HAVE HEARD THE DRUIDS 229 SHADOW WATER B 162
 AMONG SUBSTANTIAL THINGS! FOR IT IS DREAMS . . . . . . 230 SHADOW WATER B 181
 I MIGHT HAVE USED THE ONE SUBSTANTIAL RIGHT . . . . . . 352 PEOPLE 19
 HOPING MORE SUBSTANTIAL JOY . . . . 494 AT ALGECIRAS 9
 HOPING A MORE SUBSTANTIAL JOY . . . . 494 AT ALGECIRAS V 9
SUBTERRANEAN
 THE SUBTERRANEAN STREAMS, ... 420 MY HOUSE V 20H
 OR FOUND A SUBTERRANEAN REST . . . . 535 CHOSEN 6
SUBTILE
 THE SUMMERS FLING THEIR SCENTS? AH, SUBTILE AND SLOW, . . 675 ISLE STAT II 3 231
SUBTLE SEE OVER-SUBTLE
 YOUNG SUBTLE CONCHUBAR SAT CLOSE BY ME . . . . 102 FERGUS DRUID 10
 AND FOUND HER DYEING CLOTH WITH SUBTLE CARE . . . . . . 105 CUCHULAIN SEA V 2A
 THE DEMONS, WITH THEIR SUBTLE GUILE, ... 135 TWO TREES 22
 COWARDICE, OVER SOME SILLY SUBTLE THOUGHT . . . . 413 TOWER V 117
 ALONG THE WOOD WITH SUBTLE TREAD AND BENDED BOWS. . . . 649 ISLE STAT I 1 111

	PAGE	TITLE		LINE

SUBTLE-SOULED
  AND FLOWING STRENGTH, WITH AGE IS SUBTLE-SOULED. . . . .   35 OISIN 2   V   83
SUBTLEST
  THEN CONCHUBAR, THE SUBTLEST OF ALL MEN, ... 110 CUCHULAIN SEA   75
SUCCOUR
  AH ME! TO BE OLD WITHOUT SUCCOUR, A SHOW UNTO CHILDREN,   63 OISIN 3   V 217
    A STAIN,
  UNLESS SOME PITYING GOD SHALL SUCCOUR ME . . . . . .   656 ISLE STAT I 3   36
SUCH
  HOW SUCH A WARRIOR NEVER TURNED HIS GAZE . . . . . .   29 OISIN 2   V   11
  HAVE FACES ALIVE WITH SUCH BEAUTY BEEN KNOWN TO THE SALT   50 OISIN 3   51
    EYE OF MAN,
  ARE FACES ALIVE WITH SUCH BEAUTY MADE KNOWN TO THE SALT   50 OISIN 3   V   51
    EYE OF MAN,
  ARE FACES ALIVE WITH SUCH BEAUTY MADE KNOWN TO THE SOFT   50 OISIN 3   V   51
    EYE OF MAN.
  WHERE SUCH GREY CLOUDS OF INCENSE ROSE . . . .   156 FORGOT BEAUTY   13
  YOU PUT SUCH FOLLY IN OUR HEADS . . . .   190 BAILE AILLINN   32
  HAVE SUCH LONG MEMORIES THAT THEY STILL . . . .   192 BAILE AILLINN   90
  MUTTER SUCH THINGS AS THEY AWAKE FROM TRANCE. . . . .   229 SHADOW WATER B   163
  WITH SO RED LIPS, AND RUNNING ON SUCH FEET, ...   231 SHADOW WATER B   199
  AND HAVING SUCH WIDE-OPEN, SHINING EYES. . . . . . .   231 SHADOW WATER B   200
  IF THERE BE SUCH A COUNTRY. NO, NOT THERE, ...   249 SHADOW WATER B   558
  --IT HAD SUCH DIGNITY OF LIMB-- . . . .   254 HIS DREAM   11
  BECAUSE IT HAD SUCH DIGNITY. . . . .   254 HIS DREAM   19
  TO SUCH A PITCH MY THOUGHT . . . .   255 WOMAN HOMER   11
  OF SUCH NOBLE LINES," I SAID, ...   259 PEACE   6
  "SUCH A DELICATE HIGH HEAD, ...   259 PEACE   7
  SO MUCH STERNNESS AND SUCH CHARM." . . . .   259 PEACE   V   8
  DID NOT THE POET SING IT WITH SUCH AIRS . . . . . .   267 ALL TEMPT ME   7
  BECAUSE THERE IS SUCH A STORM AMID MY THOUGHTS . . . .   281 TWO KINGS   100
  GAVE ME SUCH PLEASURE I'D FORGO . . . .   305 HOUR DAWN   69
  HER SOUL HAD SUCH DESIRE . . . .   317 NIGHT COME   2
  BUT SUCH AS I HAVE SEEN UPON HER FACE . . . .   340 SHEP GOATHERD   40
  AND BIRTHDAYS AND HOLIDAYS SUCH PRAISES CAN BE HEARD . . 353 HIS PHOENIX   2
  TO SUCH A PITCH OF FOLLY I AM BROUGHT. . . . . . .   384 VISION ROBART   58
  THEY SAY SUCH DIFFERENT THINGS AT SCHOOL. . . . . .   387 ROBARTES DANCE   52
  OR HERS BEFORE A LOOKING-GLASS, FOR SUCH, ...   403 FOR DAUGHTER   19
  BUT SUCH A FORM AS GRECIAN GOLDSMITHS MAKE . . . . .   408 SAIL BYZANTIUM   27
  HAD SUCH AN ACHING HEART . . . .   422 MY TABLE   28
  BUT O! AMBITIOUS HEART, HAD SUCH A PROOF DRAWN FORTH   427 PHANTOM HATRED   36
  NONE DARED ADMIT, IF SUCH A THOUGHT WERE HIS, ...   430 NINETEEN 19   44
  THAT HAD SUCH BURDENS ON THE MIND . . . .   432 NINETEEN 19   94
  SUCH DEVILISH THINGS EXIST, ...   436 FOR MY SON   11
  AND DID SUCH PLEASURE TAKE-- . . . .   455 HIS MEMORIES   14
  HOW SUCH A MAN PLEASED WOMEN MOST . . . .   458 SECRETS OF OLD   13
  HOW SUCH A PAIR LOVED MANY YEARS . . . .   458 SECRETS OF OLD   15
  AND SUCH A PAIR BUT ONE, ...   458 SECRETS OF OLD   16
  HOW SUCH A MAN HAD PLEASURED MOST . . . .   458 SECRETS OF OLD V   13
  "BUT SUCH AS YOU AND I DO NOT SEEM OLD . . . . . .   463 HARUN RASHID   55
  ITSELF AND NOT SOME OTHER SOUL. "SUCH LOVE . . . . .   465 HARUN RASHID V   94
  PICK OUT MY FEATURES IN SUCH LIGHT AND SHADE . . . .   466 HARUN RASHID   116
  AND THAT TO SUCH A PITCH OF PASSION WROUGHT . . . .   471 ALL SOUL NIGHT   24
  SUCH THOUGHT--SUCH THOUGHT HAVE I THAT HOLD IT TIGHT   474 ALL SOUL NIGHT   91
  SUCH THOUGHT--SUCH THOUGHT HAVE I THAT HOLD IT TIGHT   474 ALL SOUL NIGHT   91
  SUCH THOUGHT, THAT IN IT BOUND . . . .   474 ALL SOUL NIGHT   97
  AN IMAGE OF SUCH POLITICS. . . . .   475 EVA GORE-BOOTH   13
  SUCH FULLNESS IN THAT QUARTER OVERFLOWS . . . . . .   478 SELF AND SOUL   33
  WHEN SUCH AS I CAST OUT REMORSE . . . .   479 SELF AND SOUL   68
  AND SET SUCH COLOUR THERE, ...   492 ANNE GREGORY   8
  NOT SUCH AS ARE IN NEWTON'S METAPHOR, ...   494 AT ALGECIRAS   11
  THAT SUCH CANNONADE . . . .   496 MOHINI CHATTER   24
  THAT ARE NOT SUITED FOR SUCH MEN AS COME . . . . .   501 VACILLATION   33
  SUCH A DANCE AS THERE WAS DANCED-- . . . .   515 JANE GROWN OLD   20
  SUCH BODY LOVERS HAVE, ...   517 HER ANXIETY   7
  SUCH EXACTING BREATH, ...   517 HER ANXIETY   8
  SLEEP, BELOVED, SUCH A SLEEP . . . .   522 LULLABY   7
  SUCH A SLEEP AND SOUND AS FELL . . . .   522 LULLABY   13
  BELOVED SUCH A SLEEP AS FELL . . . .   522 LULLABY   V   13
  BUFFETED BY SUCH SEAS! . . . .   530 DELPHIC ORACLE   2
  BRINGS SUCH SATISFACTION . . . .   533 FIRST CONFESS   11
  TO THINK HIS PASSION SUCH . . . .   538 LAST CONFESS   8
  "THAT I HAVE MET WITH SUCH," SAID HE, ...   539 MEETING   5
  THAT SUCH AS I HAD SUCH A MAN . . . .   539 MEETING   9
  THAT SUCH AS I HAD SUCH A MAN . . . .   539 MEETING   9
  SUCH A MAN THE MOST." . . . .   539 MEETING   12
  "A LOONY'D BOAST OF SUCH A LOVE," . . . .   539 MEETING   13
  BUT SUCH AS HE FOR SUCH AS ME-- . . . .   539 MEETING   15
  BUT SUCH AS HE FOR SUCH AS ME-- . . . .   539 MEETING   15
  OR LACKING THAT, GOVERNMENT IN SUCH HANDS, ...   543 PARN FUNERAL 2   7
  THE MIRACLE THAT GAVE THEM SUCH A DEATH . . . . .   555 RIBH AT TOMB   10
  BEEN BONE AND SINEW! WHEN SUCH BODIES JOIN . . . .   555 RIBH AT TOMB   12
  HOW SOUL MAY WALK WHEN ALL SUCH THINGS ARE PAST, . .   558 RIBH CHRISTIAN   11
  HOW SOUL COULD WALK BEFORE SUCH THINGS BEGAN, . . .   558 RIBH CHRISTIAN   12
  HOW SOUL HAS WALKED BEFORE SUCH THINGS BEGAN. . . .   558 RIBH CHRISTIAN V   12
  DID EVER MEN HEAR SUCH A SONG? . . . .   570 THREE BUSHES   45
  DID EVER MAN RIDE SUCH A RACE? . . . .   570 THREE BUSHES   47
  OR SUCKED SUCH MILK AS HE. . . . .   584 GHOST ROG CASE   26
  THAT HAD SUCH LITTLE SENSE . . . .   585 ORAHILLY   11
  "AM I SUCH A CRAVEN THAT . . . .   585 ORAHILLY   19
  HE WAS OF SUCH A KIND . . . .   586 PARNELLITES   18

781

<pre>
                                                        PAGE   TITLE   LINE
SUCH   (CONTINUED)
    THEY WERE NOT SUCH A PLAGUE WHEN I WAS YOUNG,   591 SPUR   3
    AND WHAT'S THE ODDS IF SUCH AS THESE   597 MODEL LAUREATE   5
    AND SAY MY GLORY WAS I HAD SUCH FRIENDS.   604 GALLERY REVIS   55
    HE HAD SUCH CHARACTER,   606 SONGS BURDEN 1   13
    SUCH QUESTS AS THESE, I TROW, NEED LITTLE WIT.   650 ISLE STAT I 1   150
    SUCH MAY I LOVE. THE SHUDDERING FOREST LIGHTS   651 ISLE STAT I 1   165
    SUCH MEN, SUCH HEARTS. BUT, UNCOUTH HUNTER, THOU   651 ISLE STAT I 1   167
    SUCH MEN, SUCH HEARTS. BUT, UNCOUTH HUNTER, THOU   651 ISLE STAT I 1   167
    IN ALL SUCH THINGS, PRAY LET THINE EARS BE TURNED,   660 ISLE STAT II 1   39
    TO US. OH WISE ART THOU IN SUCH A THING,   660 ISLE STAT II 1   46
    AND NONE THERE IS, IF SUCH THERE WERE,   668 ISLE STAT II 3   53
    FOR SUCH A CALL. LET THE WILD WORD BE CRIED   669 ISLE STAT II 3   76
    THE BLESSED GOD WAS GOOD TO SEND US SUCH,   683 SEEKER   40
    UNTUNED BY THEIR OWN STRIVING. IF ONE SUCH   711 FERENCZ RENYI   37
    GOD! THEY'RE MAD TO FLY SUCH CANVAS!"   718 PHANTOM SHIP   14
    I KEEP SUCH THINGS ABOUT ME, THEY ARE FOOD   721 WITCH VIVIEN   37
    I MUST BE CAREFUL NOW. I HAVE SUCH PLOTS--   722 WITCH VIVIEN   65
    SUCH WAR PLOTS, PEACE PLOTS, LOVE PLOTS--EVERY SIDE, 722 WITCH VIVIEN   66
    IMAGINED SUCH A FINE AFFAIR!   791 REPRISALS   14
SUCKED
    AS A HAY-COCK OUT ON THE FLOOD, OR A WOLF SUCKED UNDER 63 OISIN 3   220
      A WEIR.
    AS A GRASS SEED CRUSHED BY A PEBBLE, AS A WOLF SUCKED UNDER 63 OISIN 3   V 220
      A WEIR.
    AND HOOF AND HORN THAT HAD SUCKED IN THEIR SPEED   278 TWO KINGS   30
    SUCKED UP THE PASSION OUT OF HIM AGAIN   284 TWO KINGS   160
    OR SUCKED SUCH MILK AS HE,   584 GHOST ROG CASE   26
SUCKING
    BY SUCKING AT THE DUGS OF GREECE.   288 TO WEALTHY MAN   28
    TO MINE, AND HE IS SLOWLY SUCKING FORTH   684 SEEKER   V 63A
SUCKLE
    AND SUCKLE CHILDREN NOW? ARMED MEN   791 REPRISALS   20
SUDDEN
    AND ONCE A SUDDEN LAUGHTER SPRANG   16 OISIN 1   225
    WHERE TREES MADE SUDDEN CAVERN-GLOOMS   16 OISIN 1   V 224B
    AND IN A WILD AND SUDDEN DANCE   20 OISIN 1   290
    IMMEDIATE, MOURNFUL, WHITE WITH SUDDEN CARES,   44 OISIN 2   V 229A
    ONLY A SUDDEN FLAMING WORD,   65 HAPPY SHEPHERD   19
    SUDDEN AND LIGHT."   70 CLOAK BOAT   15
    AND MAY SOME SUDDEN DREADFUL ILL BEFALL HER!   74 ANASHU VIJAYA   59
    PARTED HER LIPS WITH A LOUD SUDDEN CRY,   105 CUCHULAIN SEA   8
    HIS SUDDEN VENGEANCE WERE A COUNTRY TALE,   127 DREAM OF FAERY   27
    SUDDEN AND LAUGHING. O UNQUIET HEART,   181 QUEEN MAEVE   30
    THEIR SUDDEN FRAGRANCES ON THE GREEN AIR,   217 WOODS OF COOLE   10
    WOULD RISE OF A SUDDEN, OR A WAVE SO HUGE   236 SHADOW WATER B   310
    HE HAS PUT A SUDDEN DARKNESS OVER THE MOON.   239 SHADOW WATER B   367
    BUT IT WAS SUDDEN. YOU ARE IN THE RIGHT!   240 SHADOW WATER B   383
    WHY ARE THEY ALL A-FLUTTER OF A SUDDEN?   243 SHADOW WATER B   436
    OUR SUDDEN PALACES IN THE STILL AIR   284 TWO KINGS   180
    OR THAT OF THE SUDDEN SHOWER   414 TOWER   137
    WHERE THROUGH LONG WARS AND SUDDEN NIGHT ALARMS   420 MY HOUSE   24
    WHERE THROUGH LONG WARS AND SUDDEN NIGHT ALARUMS   420 MY HOUSE   V   24
    A SUDDEN BLAST OF DUSTY WIND AND AFTER   433 NINETEEN 19   119
    A SUDDEN BLOW: THE GREAT WINGS BEATING STILL   441 LEDA AND SWAN   1
    A RUSH, A SUDDEN WHEEL, AND HOVERING STILL   441 LEDA AND SWAN   V   1
    AT SUDDEN THUNDER OF THE MOUNTING SWAN   490 COOLE BALLYLEE   14
    OR STRIKES A SUDDEN CHILL INTO MY BONES   499 MOTHER OF GOD   14
    MY BODY OF A SUDDEN BLAZED,   501 VACILLATION   41
    O WHAT HAS MADE THAT SUDDEN NOISE?   583 GHOST ROG CASE   1
    A BLOODY AND A SUDDEN END,   620 JOHN KINSELLA   1
    SUDDEN AND LIGHT.   666 ISLE STAT II 3   15
    BUT A SUDDEN MELANCHOLY   667 ISLE STAT II 3   30
    THE SLEEPER AWOKE WITH A SUDDEN START,   729 PRIEST FAIRY   31
    BE FULL OF SUDDEN FEARS,   738 MOURN THEN ON   6
    I FELT A SUDDEN TEAR START,   744 GLOVE CLOAK   10
    FOR THERE ARE SUDDEN VOICES IN MY EARS.   753 SHADOW WATER A   141
    THIS BLADE OUT OF MY HAND AND DIED OF A SUDDEN.   755 SHADOW WATER A   168
    I AND THAT MIGHTY KING A SUDDEN BLOW   757 SHADOW WATER A   195
    A MAN IS LOST OF A SUDDEN,   783 GREY ROUND   9
    A SUDDEN STORM, AND IT WAS THROWN   784 WOMANS BEAUTY   5
SUDDENLY
    WHEN ROUND US SUDDENLY THERE CAME   13 OISIN 1   V 165
    HE CHANGED ME SUDDENLY, I WAS LOOKING ANOTHER WAY! 153 CHANGE BELOVED   7
    SUDDENLY HURTLE BEFORE MY DREAM-AWAKENED EYES,   161 BLACK PIG   2
    SUDDENLY AILELL SPOKE OUT OF HIS SLEEP,   183 QUEEN MAEVE   73
    SUDDENLY, AND RAN AT THEM AND HARRIED THEM.   185 QUEEN MAEVE   119
    AND NOW THEY ALL WHEEL SUDDENLY AND FLY   234 SHADOW WATER B   258
    SUDDENLY DRENCHED HER TO THE SKIN,   275 GREY ROCK   120
    MY HANDS WERE PRESSED TO VANISHED SUDDENLY.   286 TWO KINGS   208
    A CURLEW ANSWERED, AND SUDDENLY THEREUPON I THOUGHT 291 PAUDEEN   5
    SUDDENLY HID LOVE'S MOON AWAY.   313 MEMORY YOUTH   7
    SUDDENLY I SAW THE COLD AND ROOK-DELIGHTING HEAVEN 316 COLD HEAVEN   1
    SUDDENLY I SAW THE COLD AND ROOK DELIGHTING HEAVEN 316 COLD HEAVEN   V   1
    ALL SUDDENLY MOUNT   322 SWANS AT COOLE   10
    SUDDENLY I BEGAN,   348 FISHERMAN   26
    YOUNG MEN NO LONGER SUDDENLY CATCH THEIR BREATH   355 BROKEN DREAMS   2
    SUDDENLY I MEET YOUR FACE.   357 DEEP-SWORN VOW   6
    ON THE GREY ROCK OF CASHEL I SUDDENLY SAW   383 VISION ROBART   17
    I SUDDENLY CRIED OUT IN A STRANGE TONGUE   387 SOLOMON WITCH   5
    WHAT CAN HAVE SUDDENLY ALARMED YOU   389 IMAGE PAST   16
</pre>

	PAGE	TITLE	LINE

SUDDENLY   (CONTINUED)
BUT WHY SHOULD YOU GROW SUDDENLY AFRAID . . . . 390 IMAGE PAST 29
THEN SUDDENLY MY HEART IS WRUNG . . . . 453 DEATH OF HARE 7
SUDDENLY LIT UP . . . . 512 JANE ON GOD 16
TILL SUDDENLY IN GRIEF'S CONTAGION CAUGHT, ... 537 HER VISION 22
BEFORE A WOMAN'S PORTRAIT SUDDENLY I STAND, ... 602 GALLERY REVIS 13
AND FLOWERS AND LITTLE CHILDREN.   SUDDENLY . . . . . . 688 TWO TITANS 36
SILENCE!   THOU SHALT BE DEAD!"   NOW SUDDENLY . . . . 710 FERENCZ RENYI 16
WITH CRIES AND MURMURS.   SUDDENLY HE FLINGS . . . . . 714 FERENCZ RENYI 101
AND NOW THEY ALL WHEEL SUDDENLY AND FLY . . . . 753 SHADOW WATER A 148
RUNS, RUNS AND IS SUDDENLY STILL. . . . . 783 GREY ROUND 3
CARRY IT!   SUDDENLY IT IS STILL. . . . . 783 GREY ROUND 5
THE STORM AROSE AND SUDDENLY FELL . . . . 784 WOMANS BEAUTY 19

SUFFER
SUFFER AS YOUR MOTHER SUFFERED, ... 313 TWO YEAR LATER 9
THE HEART NEED SUFFER NO DEFEAT!   BUT I . . . . 464 HARUN RASHID 77
OR MUST SUFFER, IF HE WOOS . . . . 479 SELF AND SOUL 63

SUFFERED
SUFFER AS YOUR MOTHER SUFFERED, ... 313 TWO YEAR LATER 9

SUFFERING
A SUFFERING PASSION AND A LABOURING THOUGHT? . . . . . 420 MY HOUSE V 20J
"ALL MEN LIVE IN SUFFERING, ... 589 OLD WICKED MAN 46
CAN BURN OUT THAT SUFFERING . . . . 589 OLD WICKED MAN 57

SUFFICE
O WHEN MAY IT SUFFICE? . . . . 394 EASTER 1916 59
SUFFICE THE AGEING MAN AS ONCE THE GROWING BOY. . . . . 427 PHANTOM HATRED 40

SUFFICIENT
THAT OUR SUFFICIENT PORTION OF THE WORLD . . . . 282 TWO KINGS 119
CONSIDER BEAUTY A SUFFICIENT END, ... 403 FOR DAUGHTER 21
SUFFICIENT MONEY FOR HIS NEED, ... 577 WHAT THEN 8

SUGGESTED
SUGGESTED BY A PICTURE OF A BLACK CENTAUR . . . . . . 442 BLACK CENTAUR V T

SUIT
AS WITH AN AUREOLE.   MY SUIT TO YOU-- . . . . 697 MOSADA 2 38

SUITED
THAT ARE NOT SUITED FOR SUCH MEN AS COME . . . . 501 VACILLATION 33

SULLEN
ON THE LONE BORDER OF THE SULLEN LAKE. . . . . 80 EPHEMERA V 17
THE SULLEN WOOD.   BUT MANY WOODS I SEE . . . . 682 SEEKER 24
THE HEATHEN.   YEA, AND SHAKE THE SULLEN KINGS . . . . 698 MOSADA 2 55
THIS SULLEN PEASANT SPOILS THE GOOD SUNSHINE, ... 711 FERENCZ RENYI 42
THIS SULLEN PEASANT SPOILS THE GOOD RED WINE, ... 711 FERENCZ RENYI 43
THIS SULLEN PEASANT CHILLS THE GOOD SUNSHINE. . . . . . 711 FERENCZ RENYI V 42
THIS SULLEN PEASANT SOURS THE GOOD RED WINE. . . . . . 711 FERENCZ RENYI V 43

SULPHUROUS
HAS NO WORD OF THE SULPHUROUS END. . . . . 736 SUMMER EVENING 8

SULTRY
MY WORKS ARE ALL STAMPED DOWN INTO THE SULTRY MUD. . . . 442 BLACK CENTAUR 3
I SLEPT, 'TWAS SULTRY, AND SCARCE CIRCLING SHOOK . . . . 677 ISLE STAT II 3 278
WANDERING IN SULTRY PALACES OF IND, ... 694 MOSADA 1 102

SUM
A GOOD ROUND SUM UPON THIS CRUISE, AND TURN-- . . . . . 222 SHADOW WATER B 5
AND 'NEATH IT SIT, AND OF THE WOVEN SUM . . . . 663 ISLE STAT II 2 30

SUMMER
THAT WAVERED LIKE THE SUMMER STREAMS, ... 4 OISIN 1 29
AND WAVERED LIKE A SUMMER RILL, ... 4 OISIN 1 V 29
AND THE GENTLE WAVES OF THE SUMMER SEAS. . . . . . . 27 OISIN 1 418
I FELL ON THE PATH, AND THE HORSE WENT AWAY LIKE A SUMMER 60 OISIN 3 190
FLY!
WHEN SUMMER GLUTS THE GOLDEN BEES, ... 84 MAD KING GOLL 38
WHERE SUMMER GLUTS THE GOLDEN BEES, ... 84 MAD KING GOLL V 38
THAT FROM THOSE FINGERS GLITTERING SUMMER RUNS . . . . . 128 DREAM OF FAERY 44
UNTIL THE SAP OF SUMMER HAD GROWN WEARY! . . . . . . 130 BOOK STORIES 14
AND WALK AND WALK THROUGH SUMMER GRASS, ... 150 WANDER AENGUS V 21
WHEN ALL THE WILD SUMMER WAS IN HER GAZE." . . . . . . 200 FOLLY COMFORT 12
THEIR RICHNESS THROUGH THE SUMMER AND THE SPRING; . . . 279 TWO KINGS V 62C
THROUGH SUMMER AND WINTER SEEM . . . . 393 EASTER 1916 42
FISH, FLESH, OR FOWL, COMMEND ALL SUMMER LONG . . . . . 407 SAIL BYZANTIUM 5
AND HAD THE LIVELONG SUMMER DAY TO SPEND. . . . . . . 409 TOWER 10
AND THROUGH THE SPRING ON SUMMER CALL, ... 434 WHEEL 2
SUMMER AND WINTER, DAY AND NIGHT, ... 447 COLONUS PRAISE 31
SUMMER AND SPRING . . . . 456 SUMMER SPRING T
WHEN WE HAD ALL THE SUMMER TIME . . . . 457 SUMMER SPRING V 15
THAT IN THE EARLY SUMMER OF THE YEAR . . . . 462 HARUN RASHID 40
THAT IN THE EARLY SUMMER OF THAT YEAR . . . . 462 HARUN RASHID V 40
ALTHOUGH THE SUMMER SUNLIGHT GILD . . . . 501 VACILLATION 45
WINTER AND SUMMER TILL OLD AGE BEGAN . . . . 629 CIRCUS ANIMALS 5
SING SUMMER WAVES.   BUT YONDER SHEPHERD VILE, ... 649 ISLE STAT I 1 107
DREAMING THE LIVE-LONG SUMMER IN THE SHADE, ... 650 ISLE STAT I 1 139
THE FEET OF SUMMER DABBLE . . . . 680 LOVE AND DEATH 7
WHERE THEY ALL SUMMER FEED THEIR WANDERING FLOCKS, . . . 690 MOSADA 1 5
WHERE SAT OLD SUMMER FADING INTO SONG, ... 690 MOSADA 1 V 1B
THE WORLD WERE DREAMING IN ITS SUMMER SLEEP; . . . . . 699 MOSADA 3 11
AS THE SUMMER VOICE OF THE DAYTIME CEASED, ... 728 PRIEST FAIRY 4
"EVERY SUMMER WILT THOU SEE . . . . 730 PRIEST FAIRY 55
A SUMMER EVENING . . . . 736 SUMMER EVENING T

SUMMERED   SEE EVER-SUMMERED
THE EVER SUMMERED SOLITUDES, ... 21 OISIN 1 V 321

SUMMER'S
THROUGH SUMMER'S HEAT AND WINTER'S COLD. . . . . . . 86 MAD KING GOLL 71
WE SAT TOGETHER AT ONE SUMMER'S END, ... 204 ADAMS CURSE 1

783

		PAGE	TITLE	LINE

SUMMER'S (CONTINUED)
```
    BLOSSOM FROM THE SUMMER'S WREATH:  . . . . . . . .   475 EVA GORE-BOOTH       6
    AND WHEN THE SUMMER'S DEEP, THEN TO THIS SPOT . . .   663 ISLE STAT II 2      24
SUMMERS
    THE SUMMERS FLING THEIR SCENTS?  AH, SUBTILE AND SLOW, .  675 ISLE STAT II 3   231
    WHOSE FOOTFALL I HAVE LONGED FOR, THREE SAD SUMMERS. . .  692 MOSADA 1          45
SUMMER-TIME
    WHEN WE HAD ALL THE SUMMER-TIME  . . . . . . . .     457 SUMMER SPRING       15
SUMMON
    I CALL TO MY OWN OPPOSITE, SUMMON ALL  . . . . . .   367 EGO DOMINUS          8
    I SUMMON TO THE WINDING ANCIENT STAIR:  . . . . .    477 SELF AND SOUL        1
    I SUMMON TO THE WINDY ANCIENT STAIR:  . . . . . .    477 SELF AND SOUL  V     1
    BREATHLESS MOUTHS MAY SUMMON:  . . . . . . . . .     497 BYZANTIUM           14
    I CAN SUMMON BACK . . . . . . . . . . . . . .       505 RESULT THOUGHT      11
    I COULD SUMMON BACK  . . . . . . . . . . . . .       505 RESULT THOUGHT V    11
SUMMONED
    SUMMONED THE GENERATIONS OF HIS HOUSE,  . . . . .    609 IN TARAS HALLS      19
    WHEN PEARSE SUMMONED CUCHULAIN TO HIS SIDE,  . . .   611 STATUES             25
    LOVER, THE VOICE THAT SUMMONED THEE WAS MINE. . . .  685 SEEKER              77
SUMMONS
    I AWOKE: THE STRANGE HORSE WITHOUT SUMMONS OUT OF
         THE DISTANCE RAN,                                54 OISIN 3            105
    BUT SUMMONS TO ADVENTURE AND THE MAN . . . . . . .   373 PHASES OF MOON      37
SUMPTUOUS
    THE HOUR WHEN KAMA, WITH A SUMPTUOUS SMILE,  . . .    72 ANASHU VIJAYA V     26
SUMS
    AND TOOK THEIR TABLETS AND DID SUMS:  . . . . . .    344 DAWN                 9
    AND TOOK THEIR TABLETS AND MADE SUMS—  . . . . .     344 DAWN           V     9
SUN
    AND WAS BORN WHERE THE SUN DROPS DOWN IN THE TIDE, . .    5 OISIN 1       V    49
    AND SLEEP DROWN SUN AND MOON AND STAR."  . . . . .      5 OISIN 1       V    49
    THE RED SUN FALLS AND THE WORLD GROWS DIM."  . . .      9 OISIN 1           105
    OF THE GREAT ROUND SUN, FROM HIS CENTRAL FIRES. . .    13 OISIN 1       V   168
    AND, AS THE SUN SANK EVER LOWER,  . . . . . . .        13 OISIN 1       V 170A
    UPON THE CENTRE OF THE SUN.  . . . . . . . . .         14 OISIN 1           175
    WHERE AENGUS DREAMS, FROM SUN TO SUN,  . . . . .       16 OISIN 1           218
    WHERE AENGUS DREAMS, FROM SUN TO SUN,  . . . . .       16 OISIN 1           218
    AND ROLLS ALONG THE UNWIELDY SUN, . . . . . . .        18 OISIN 1           267
    ROUND US, AND ROLLS THE UNWIELDY SUN. . . . . .        18 OISIN 1       V   268
    WATCHED WHERE THE SUN IN A SAFFRON BLAZE  . . . .      26 OISIN 1           394
    WATCHED THE OLD SUN THAT IN SEA-WAYS  . . . . .        26 OISIN 1       V   394
    THE HARE GROWS OLD AS SHE PLAYS IN THE SUN  . . .      27 OISIN 1           412
    "OLD GROWS THE HARE AS SHE PLAYS IN THE SUN,  . .      28 OISIN 1       V   420
    AND EVEN THE SUN, THE DAY CASTLE'S WARDER,  . . .      28 OISIN 1       V 423A
    BUT WHEN AT WITHERING OF THE SUN HE KNEW  . . . .      40 OISIN 2       V   173
    AND WHEN AT WITHERING OF THE SUN HE KNEW,  . . .       40 OISIN 2       V   173
    AND WHEN THE SUN ONCE MORE IN SAFFRON STEPT,  . .      41 OISIN 2           192
    AND WHEN THE SUN IN ALL HIS FLAGRANT SAFFRON STEPT, . . 41 OISIN 2       V   192
    BUT WHEN THE SUN ONCE MORE IN SAFFRON STEPT,  . .      41 OISIN 2       V   192
    TO LIE UNTIL THE FOURTH MORN SUN EMERGE  . . . .       44 OISIN 2       V   220
    . . . THE GLEAMS OF THE WORLD AND THE SUN.  . . .      48 OISIN 3            22
    . . . WHEN THE SUN WAS ON SILVER OR GOLD:  . . .       53 OISIN 3            97
    THE SUN HAS LAID HIS CHIN ON THE GREY WOOD,  . . .     72 ANASHU VIJAYA      24
    THE SUN HATH LAID HIS CHIN ON THE GREY WOOD,  . .      72 ANASHU VIJAYA V    24
    THAT HIDES AWAY THE DYING SUN  . . . . . . . .         85 MAD KING GOLL      63
    OR FLING MY LAUGHTER TO THE SUN  . . . . . . .         86 MAD KING GOLL V    69
    AND FLING MY LAUGHTER TO THE SUN  . . . . . . .        86 MAD KING GOLL V    69
    THE SUN UPON ALL THINGS THAT GROW  . . . . . . .       98 FOXHUNTER          15
    A MAN CAME SLOWLY FROM THE SETTING SUN, . . . . .     105 CUCHULAIN SEA       1
    "YET SOMEWHERE UNDER STARLIGHT OR THE SUN  . . .      107 CUCHULAIN SEA      28
    WHERE THE SUN FALLS INTO THE WESTERN DEEP. . . .      108 CUCHULAIN SEA V    34
    OR IN THE SUN AND MOON, OR ON THE EARTH,  . . . .     114 ROSE OF BATTLE     17
    IT SEEMED THE SUN AND MOON WERE IN THE FRUIT:  . .    127 DREAM OF FAERY     23
    OF SUN AND MOON AND HOLLOW AND WOOD  . . . . . .      148 INTO TWILIGHT      11
    THE GOLDEN APPLES OF THE SUN.  . . . . . . . .        150 WANDER AENGUS      24
    AND HAD ROOTED THE SUN AND MOON AND STARS OUT OF THE SKY  153 CHANGE BELOVED  11
    AND ROOTED THE SUN AND MOON AND STARS OUT OF THE SKY, .  153 CHANGE BELOVED V 11
    WHEN WINDS HAVE GATHERED AND SUN AND MOON BURNED DIM  .  175 ELEMENT POWERS  15
    ABOUT THE STARS AND MOON AND SUN:  . . . . . . .      176 BELOVED DEAD       10
    ABOVE THE STARS AND MOON AND SUN:  . . . . . . .      176 BELOVED DEAD  V    10
    OR APPLES OF THE SUN AND MOON. . . . . . . . .        196 BAILE AILLINN     176
    WHEN THE SUN LOOKED OUT OF HIS GOLDEN HOOD,  . . .    210 RAGGED WOOD   V     3
    WHEN THE SUN LOOKED OUT OF HIS GOLDEN HOOD?—  . .     211 RAGGED WOOD        7
    THE SUN WAS LAUGHING SWEETLY,  . . . . . . . . .      214 HAPPY TOWNLAND     15
    THE SUN WAS LAUGHING SWEETLY,  . . . . . . . . .      215 HAPPY TOWNLAND     35
    THE SUN WAS LAUGHING SWEETLY,  . . . . . . . . .      216 HAPPY TOWNLAND     55
    AS A LAMP SHADOW—NO—NO LAMP, THE SUN. . . . . .       229 SHADOW WATER B    160
    THAT IS MORE MIGHTY THAN THE SUN AND MOON, . . . .    237 SHADOW WATER B    328
    AND I GREW WEARY OF THE SUN  . . . . . . . . .        256 WORDS               5
    I SWAYED MY LEAVES AND FLOWERS IN THE SUN:  . . .     261 COMING WISDOM       3
    TO BREED THE LIDLESS EYE THAT LOVES THE SUN?  . .     264 HOUSE SHAKEN        4
    THESE ARE THE CLOUDS ABOUT THE FALLEN SUN  . . . .    265 THESE CLOUDS        1
    THESE ARE THE CLOUDS ABOUT THE FALLEN SUN,  . . .     265 THESE CLOUDS       11
    "ONLY THE WASTEFUL VIRTUES EARN THE SUN":  . . .      270 PARDON FATHERS     18
    AND CAME INTO A WOOD AS THE SUN SET . . . . . . .     277 TWO KINGS     V     3
    AND LEFT MERE SLEEP.  HE'LL WAKE WHEN THE SUN WAKES, .   284 TWO KINGS       161
    OR TILL THE SUN IS IN HIS STRENGTH.  . . . . . .      305 HOUR DAWN          61
    OF SUN AND MOON THAT A GOOD HOUR  . . . . . . .       331 ROUND TOWER        11
    YOU HAD BEFORE THE SUN HAD THROWN  . . . . . . .      333 SOLOMON SHEBA      13
    I HAVE NOTHING BUT THE EMBITTERED SUN:  . . . . .     344 DEJECTION           8
    I MUST ENDURE THE TIMID SUN. . . . . . . . . .        344 DEJECTION          11
```

```
                                                         PAGE    TITLE          LINE
SUN    (CONTINUED)
     AND I HAVE NOTHING BUT HARSH SUN•  •  •  •  •  •  •    344 DEJECTION     V    8
     AND THAT PROUD LOOK AS THOUGH SHE HAD GAZED INTO       354 HIS PHOENIX       29
        THE BURNING SUN,
     FROM GOING-DOWN OF THE SUN I HAVE DREAMED  •  •  •  •   358 PRESENCES          3
     FROM GOING DOWN OF THE SUN I HAVE DREAMED  •  •  •  •   358 PRESENCES     V    3
     AND ALL LAUGH IN THE SUN•  •  •  •  •  •  •  •  •  •    400 DEMON BEAST        8
     A GAZE BLANK AND PITILESS AS THE SUN,  •  •  •  •  •    402 SECOND COMING     15
     AYE, SUN AND MOON AND STAR, ALL,  •  •  •  •  •  •  •   415 TOWER            152
     THE FINEST PLAY UNDER THE SUN•  •  •  •  •  •  •  •     424 ROAD AT DOOR       5
     AND NOW BUT GAPE AT THE SUN•  •  •  •  •  •  •  •  •    432 NINETEEN 19      102
     WHAT WHOLESOME SUN HAS RIPENED IS WHOLESOME FOOD TO EAT, 442 BLACK CENTAUR     5
     UNVISITED BY TEMPEST OR BY SUN,  •  •  •  •  •  •  •    446 COLONUS PRAISE     5
     UNTIL IT PLUNGE INTO THE SUN•  •  •  •  •  •  •  •  •   472 ALL SOUL NIGHT    56
     UNTIL IT PLUNGED INTO THE SUN•  •  •  •  •  •  •  •     472 ALL SOUL NIGHT V  56
     BACK TURNED UPON THE BRIGHTNESS OF THE SUN •  •  •  •   489 COOLE PARK 29     30
     NOW ALL DRY STICKS UNDER A WINTRY SUN,  •  •  •  •  •   490 COOLE BALLYLEE    10
     GREATER GLORY IN THE SUN,  •  •  •  •  •  •  •  •  •    494 AT ALGECIRAS      13
     THE TRIVIAL DAYS AND RAM THEM WITH THE SUN,  •  •  •    500 VACILLATION       21
     STREAM AND SUN AT GLENDALOUGH  •  •  •  •  •  •  •  •    506 STREAM AND SUN     T
     STREAM AND GLIDING SUN  •  •  •  •  •  •  •  •  •  •     506 STREAM AND SUN     2
     WHAT MOTION OF THE SUN OR STREAM  •  •  •  •  •  •  •    507 STREAM AND SUN    11
     I CARRY THE SUN IN A GOLDEN CUP,  •  •  •  •  •  •  •    525 DANCING DAYS       7
     I CARRY THE SUN IN A GOLDEN CUP,  •  •  •  •  •  •  •    525 DANCING DAYS      15
     I CARRY THE SUN IN A GOLDEN CUP,  •  •  •  •  •  •  •    525 DANCING DAYS      23
     THERE ALL THE PLANETS DROP IN THE SUN•  •  •  •  •  •   557 THERE              4
     OF THE BARLEY SHOOTS IN THE SUN•  •  •  •  •  •  •  •    643 SONG FAERIES       8
     OUT OF THE AIR•  AND WHEN?  WHEN THE SUN GOES DOWN  •   652 ISLE STAT I 2     29
     THE WIND AT EVENING WHEN THE SUN GOES DOWN  •  •  •  •  653 ISLE STAT I 2     50
     SEE, YONDER SINKS THE SUN, YONDER A SHADE  •  •  •  •   653 ISLE STAT I 2     52
     WHEN LOW THE SUN SANK DOWN IN CLOTTED FLAME  •  •  •    656 ISLE STAT I 3     30
     PIERCED THROUGH, CHATTERING FROM HABIT IN THE SUN,     664 ISLE STAT II 2    53
     OH FAMOUS DYING MINION OF THE SUN,  •  •  •  •  •  •    673 ISLE STAT II 3   197
     AH, WOE IS ME!  I GO FROM SUN AND SHADE,  •  •  •  •    674 ISLE STAT II 3   216
     OF THE BARLEY SHOOTS IN THE SUN•  •  •  •  •  •  •  •    676 ISLE STAT II 3   255
     AWAY FROM ALL THE OTHERS•  NOW THE SUN  •  •  •  •  •   691 MOSADA 1          33
     AND ALL THE ELDERS SITTING IN THE SUN  •  •  •  •  •    693 MOSADA 1          69
     FROM THE WAVES THE SUN HATH REELED•  •  •  •  •  •  •   705 DAWN-SONG          1
     "ON THIS EMBROIDERED CLOUD," THE SUN HATH SAID,  •  •   712 FERENCZ RENYI     74
     I WILL SWEAR BY SUN AND MOON TO PARDON ALL •  •  •  •   756 SHADOW WATER A   183
     BY SUN AND MOON AND A HUNDRED GODS AS WELL,  •  •  •    756 SHADOW WATER A   189
     AND WILL YOU SWEAR IT BY THE SUN AND MOON?  •  •  •     758 SHADOW WATER A   229
     AND SAID IT WAS MIGHTIER THAN THE SUN AND MOON,  •  •   762 SHADOW WATER A   289
     THE LOVE OF ALL UNDER THE LIGHT OF THE SUN •  •  •  •   765 SHADOW WATER A   353
     HAVE FALLEN AND MY SUN AND MOON GONE OUT•  •  •  •  •   767 SHADOW WATER A V 405
     ONE LIVES IN THE HOUSE OF THE SUN,  •  •  •  •  •  •    771 SPINNING SONG      6
     "TILL THE SUN GOES DOWN AND AN HOUR OF THE CLOCK"  •    779 GOING THE ROAD     7
     "FOR A YEAR AND A DAY BY THE CLOCK OF THE SUN"  •  •    779 GOING THE ROAD    11
     THEY DREAM THAT LAUGHED IN THE SUN•  •  •  •  •  •  •    783 GREY ROUND        13
     THEY DREAM AND DARKEN OUR SUN•  •  •  •  •  •  •  •      783 GREY ROUND        15
     THEY DREAMED THAT LAUGHED IN THE SUN•  •  •  •  •  •     783 GREY ROUND    V   13
SUNDAY
     WHEN EVERY SUNDAY AFTERNOON •  •  •  •  •  •  •  •  •    607 SONGS BURDEN 2    19
SUNDOWN
     AND AT THE SUNDOWN THREW HIM IN THE SURGE,  •  •  •  •   44 OISIN 2          219
     AND HALF THE KINGS, BEFORE SUNDOWN  •  •  •  •  •  •    273 GREY ROCK         69
     AND HALF HIS KINGS, BEFORE SUNDOWN  •  •  •  •  •  •    273 GREY ROCK     V   69
     KING EOCHAID CAME AT SUNDOWN TO A WOOD  •  •  •  •  •   276 TWO KINGS          1
SUN-DRY
     HE CARVED ON TREES, AND WITH A SUN-DRY WEED  •  •  •    659 ISLE STAT II 1     8
SUNFLOWERS
     THE SUNFLOWERS WEAVE A GOLDEN CLIME,  •  •  •  •  •  •   736 SUMMER EVENING     9
SUN-FLUSHED
     ABOUT A SUN-FLUSHED DOVE-COT, COOING, CLING  •  •  •    710 FERENCZ RENYI     20
SUN-FRECKLED
     AND HIS SUN-FRECKLED FACE,  •  •  •  •  •  •  •  •  •    348 FISHERMAN         29
SUN    SEE RE-SUNG
     SUNG OF THE BIRDS•  OUR TOIL WAS DONE!  •  •  •  •  •     14 OISIN 1       V  177
     •  •  • FAR SUNG BY THE SENNACHIES•  •  •  •  •  •  •     50 OISIN 3           53
     •  •  • FAR SUNG OF THE SENNACHIES•  •  •  •  •  •  •     50 OISIN 3       V   53
     A WOMAN HOMER SUNG •  •  •  •  •  •  •  •  •  •  •  •    254 WOMAN HOMER        T
     A WOMAN HOMER SUNG,  •  •  •  •  •  •  •  •  •  •  •     255 WOMAN HOMER       19
     IN PRAISE OF WHAT ANOTHER'S SAID OR SUNG, •  •  •  •    262 TO A POET          2
     TRUE SONG, THOUGH SPEECH: "MINE AUTHOR SUNG IT ME•"  • 373 PHASES OF MOON    30
     WHATEVER HAS BEEN SAID, SIGHED, SUNG,  •  •  •  •  •    387 SOLOMON WITCH      7
     ALL SOUNDS BY BIRD OR ANGEL SUNG  •  •  •  •  •  •  •    387 SOLOMON WITCH V    7
     MERE DREAMS, MERE DREAMS!  YET HOMER HAD NOT SUNG  •    417 ANCEST HOUSES      9
     HAS PLUCKED A FLOWER AND SUNG HER LOSS!  •  •  •  •     447 COLONUS PRAISE    22
     I THIRST FOR ACCUSATION•  ALL THAT WAS SUNG,  •  •  •   542 PARN FUNERAL 1    25
     ARE SUNG ABOVE THE GLASS,  •  •  •  •  •  •  •  •  •     587 PARNELLITES       30
     ARE SUNG ABOVE A GLASS!  •  •  •  •  •  •  •  •  •  •    587 PARNELLITES   V   30
     AS THOUGH SOME BALLAD-SINGER HAD SUNG IT ALL!  •  •  •  602 GALLERY REVIS     24
     AS THOUGH SOME BALLAD SINGER HAD SUNG IT ALL•  •  •  •  602 GALLERY REVIS V   24
     ALL CLAMOUR-CLOTHED---WAS'T CLAMOUR WHEN I SUNG,  •  •  649 ISLE STAT I 1    108
     WORN WITH LONG STRUGGLES: AND THE WAVES HAVE SUNG  •    687 TWO TITANS        23
     OF THE GREAT WARRIORS WHOSE NAMES HAVE SUNG  •  •  •    698 MOSADA 2          60
     AND CRADLED ME HERE WHERE ARE SUNG,  •  •  •  •  •  •    708 FAIRY PEDANT      25
SUNK
     DARK BALOR, AS OLD AS A FOREST, CAR-BORNE, HIS MIGHTY HEAD  53 OISIN 3        91
        SUNK
```

	PAGE	TITLE		LINE

SUNK (CONTINUED)

CAME CAR-BORNE BALOR, AS OLD AS A FOREST, HIS VAST FACE   53 OISIN 3   V 91
SUNK

CAME BALOR, AS OLD AS A FOREST, CAR BORNE, HIS MIGHTY HEAD   53 OISIN 3   V 91
SUNK

AND SHE AND I, BEING SUNK IN HAPPINESS, ...   463 HARUN RASHID   51
JUSTIFY ALL THAT HAVE SUNK IN THEIR BLOOD, ...   546 TO SAME TUNE 2   12
NOW SUNK IN REST, ...   574 MAIDS 1ST SONG   2
AND NOW LIES SUNK IN SLEEP. WHAT CLIMBS THE STAIR? . . .   579 DOR WELLESLEY   11
BUT NOW LIES SUNK IN SLEEP. WHAT CLIMBS THE STAIR? . . .   579 DOR WELLESLEY   V 11
REMEMBER ALL THAT HAVE SUNK IN THEIR BLOOD, ...   613 MARCH SONGS 1   12

SUNKEN   SEE DEEP-SUNKEN

DEEP SUNKEN ON THE BLADE'S LENGTH, "MANANAN!" . . . . .   38 OISIN 2   V 128
AND FOUND A DOOR DEEP SUNKEN IN THE WALL, ...   39 OISIN 2   154
AND SUNKEN SHAPE, A NINE DAYS' CORPSE SEA-DASHED-- . . .   40 OISIN 2   V 179
AND SUNKEN SHAPE, AGAINST MY FACE AND BREAST, ...   40 OISIN 2   V 179
AND DRIPPING AND SUNKEN SHAPE, TO FACE AND BREAST, . . .   40 OISIN 2   V 179

SUNLESS

MAKE MOAN AND CRY. WITHIN YON SUNLESS VALLEY, ...   682 SEEKER   26

SUNLIGHT

O MAY THE MOON AND SUNLIGHT SEEM . . . .   411 TOWER   54
ALTHOUGH THE SUMMER SUNLIGHT GILD . . . .   501 VACILLATION   45
IN THE SUNLIGHT AND WIND. . . . .   600 THOSE IMAGES   4
COURAGEOUS MIRACLES! THE SUNLIGHT SHONE . . . . . .   649 ISLE STAT I 1   113
THE SUNLIGHT FLICKERING ON THE PEWS, ...   736 IN CHURCH   9
THE SUNLIGHT IN THE AIR, ...   736 IN CHURCH   10

SUNNIER

SHADY KYLE-DORTHA; SUNNIER KYLE-NA-NO, ...   217 WOODS OF COOLE   4

SUNNY

PACING WITH HALF-CLOSED EYELIDS IN A SUNNY SPOT . . . .   366 HER COURAGE   7
WHISPERING ALONG THE SUNNY PATH; . . . .   725 LEGEND   18

SUN'S

IN THE PALE WEST, AND THE SUN'S RIM SANK, ...   12 OISIN 1   153
NOW IN THE SEA THE SUN'S RIM SANK, ...   12 OISIN 1   V 153
LAND-UNDER-WAVE, WHERE OUT OF THE MOON'S LIGHT AND THE   209 UNDER THE MOON   6
SUN'S

LOOK UP IN THE SUN'S EYE AND GIVE . . . .   288 TO WEALTHY MAN   32
AND THAT IF MEMORY RECUR, THE SUN'S . . . .   414 TOWER   119
MELT DOWN, AS IT WERE WAX IN THE SUN'S RAYS; . . . .   428 NINETEEN 19   12
. . . A LOG-BOOK OF THE SUN'S JOURNEY AND THE MOON'S;   480 BLOOD AND MOON   14
. . . A LOG BOOK OF THE SUN'S JOURNEY AND THE MOON'S,   480 BLOOD AND MOON   V 14

SUNS

WHEN WE ARE DEAD, BEYOND THE SETTING SUNS, ...   71 ANASHU VIJAYA   8
OF ALL ON WHOM ARCADIAN SUNS HAVE SHONE . . . . . .   650 ISLE STAT I 1   143

SUNSET

AND LIKE A SUNSET WERE HER LIPS, ...   3 OISIN 1   22
A STORMY SUNSET ON DOOMED SHIPS; . . . .   3 OISIN 1   23
A STORMY SUNSET O'ER DOOMED SHIPS. . . . .   3 OISIN 1   V 23

SUNSHINE

THIS SULLEN PEASANT SPOILS THE GOOD SUNSHINE, ...   711 FERENCZ RENYI   42
THIS SULLEN PEASANT CHILLS THE GOOD SUNSHINE. . . . .   711 FERENCZ RENYI   V 42

SUNSICK

THAT DIETH SLOW WITH SUNSICK DOOM. . . . .   655 ISLE STAT I 3   12

SUN-SMITTEN

ON THE SUN-SMITTEN GRASS; . . . .   99 FOXHUNTER   42

SUP

NOR STAYED FOR BITE OR SUP; . . . .   93 FATHER OHART   38
SHE GIVES ME BITE AND SUP. . . . .   96 MOLL MAGEE   40
I'LL NAME THE FRIENDS THAT CANNOT SUP WITH US . . . .   323 ROBERT GREGORY   2

SUPERHUMAN

MAN MAKES A SUPERHUMAN . . . .   415 TOWER   164
I HAIL THE SUPERHUMAN; . . . .   497 BYZANTIUM   15
HUMAN, SUPERHUMAN, A BIRD'S ROUND EYE, ...   618 BRONZE HEAD   2
COMPLEXION AND FORM PROVE SUPERHUMAN, ...   637 BEN BULBEN   6

SUPER-HUMAN

HUMAN, SUPER-HUMAN, A BIRD'S ROUND EYE, ...   618 BRONZE HEAD   V 2

SUPERMAN

MAN MAKES A SUPERMAN, ...   415 TOWER   V 164

SUPERNATURAL

CAN RULE BY SUPERNATURAL RIGHT . . . .   386 ROBARTES DANCE   36
SUPERNATURAL SONGS . . . .   554 RIBH AT TOMB   T
THAT'S HOW ALL NATURAL OR SUPERNATURAL STORIES RUN. . .   556 RIBH PATRICK   3
NATURAL AND SUPERNATURAL WITH THE SELF-SAME RING ARE WED.   556 RIBH PATRICK   4
OR ELSE I THOUGHT HER SUPERNATURAL; . . . .   619 BRONZE HEAD   22

SUPERSESSION

SUPERSESSION OF BREATH; . . . .   476 DEATH   10

SUPINE

THEY HEALED MY WOUNDS; AND ON THE SKIN SUPINE . . . .   41 OISIN 2   V 187

SUPPER

YON TALL ONE EYES MY SUPPER; CHASE HIM AWAY, ...   72 ANASHU VIJAYA   34
YON TALL ONE EYES MY SUPPER; SWIFTLY CHASE HIM . . .   72 ANASHU VIJAYA   V 34
WHEN THE SUPPER HAS BEEN SPREAD. . . . .   215 HAPPY TOWNLAND   44

SUPPLER

IF TIME WERE SUPPLER IN THE JOINT, ...   306 HOUR DAWN   94

SUPPLIANT

THAT WATCH ME WITH THEIR SUPPLIANT LIGHT-- . . . . .   723 GIRLS SONG A   10

SUPPORTING

STANDISH O'GRADY SUPPORTING HIMSELF BETWEEN THE TABLES .   577 LOFTY THINGS   5

SUPPOSE

THOUGH FANTASTIC MEN SUPPOSE . . . .   530 OLD TOM AGAIN   4

786

	PAGE	TITLE		LINE

SUPREME
    UPON THE SUPREME THEME OF ART AND SONG! • • • • • • •   523 LONG SILENCE   6
SURE
    AND SOMETIMES I AM SURE SHE KNOWS • • • • • • • • •   96 MOLL MAGEE   49
    SHE SAYS MY HUSBAND SURE WILL COME • • • • • • • • •   96 MOLL MAGEE   V   41
    TO SOME SURE COUNTRY, SOME FAMILIAR PLACE. • • • • • •   249 SHADOW WATER B   569
    AND TILL HIS INTELLECT GROWS SURE • • • • • • • • • •   633 MAN AND ECHO   30
SURELY
    I CRIED, "THOU ART SURELY A WARRIOR, FORGETTING HIS FAMOUS   51 OISIN 3   V   61
      LINE,
    A GOOD NAME IS GOODLY TO HEAR OF, AND A GOOD NAME SURELY   51 OISIN 3   V   63
      IS THINE.
    SHE SAYS MY MAN WILL SURELY COME, • • • • • • • • • •   96 MOLL MAGEE   41
    WHERE TIME WOULD SURELY FORGET US, AND SORROW COME NEAR   122 WHITE BIRDS   10
      US NO MORE:
    WHERE SURELY TIME WOULD FORGET US AND SORROW COME NEAR   122 WHITE BIRDS   V   10
      US NO MORE:
    MAY SURELY BARTER GAZE FOR GAZE. • • • • • • • • • •   139 TO IRELAND   28
    MAY SURELY MEET THEIR ANCIENT GAZE. • • • • • • • • •   139 TO IRELAND   V   28
    SURELY THINE HOUR HAS COME, THY GREAT WIND BLOWS, • • •   170 SECRET ROSE   31
    YET SURELY THERE ARE MEN WHO HAVE MADE THEIR ART • • •   369 EGO DOMINUS   38
    AND SURELY AFTER TWENTY YEARS IT WAS TIME TO COME." • • •   391 UNDER SATURN   14
    SURELY SOME REVELATION IS AT HAND! • • • • • • • • • •   402 SECOND COMING   9
    SURELY THE SECOND COMING IS AT HAND. • • • • • • • • •   402 SECOND COMING   10
    SURELY AMONG A RICH MAN'S FLOWERING LAWNS, • • • • • •   417 ANCEST HOUSES   1
    A STRANGE THING SURELY THAT MY HEART, WHEN LOVE HAD COME   449 OWEN AHERNE   1
      UNSOUGHT
SURETY
    THE SURETY OF ITS HIDDEN ROOT • • • • • • • • • • • •   134 TWO TREES   7
SURF
    ROSE IN THE DARKNESS, AND THE WHITE SURF GLEAMED • • • •   30 OISIN 2   23
SURFACE
    ARE NEARER TO THE SURFACE OF THE BODY • • • • • • • •   464 HARUN RASHID   67
SURGE
    WHITENED AFAR WITH SURGE, FAN-FORMED AND WIDE, • • • •   31 OISIN 2   28
    WHITENING THE SURGE AFAR, FAN-FORMED AND WIDE, • • • •   31 OISIN 2   V   28
    WITH SURGE OF PLUMY FIRE, LUNGING I DRAVE • • • • • •   41 OISIN 2   V   181
    AND AT THE SUNDOWN THREW HIM IN THE SURGE, • • • • • •   44 OISIN 2   219
    AND IN THE EVE I THREW HIM IN THE SURGE, • • • • • • •   44 OISIN 2   V   219
    A GREEN DROP IN THE SURGE, A GLEAM OF LIGHT • • • • •   104 FERGUS DRUID   33
SURGED
    HAD SURGED UP IN A PLUMY FIRE, I DRAVE • • • • • • • •   41 OISIN 2   181
    SURGED UP IN PLUMY FIRE, I LUNGED AND DRAVE • • • • • •   41 OISIN 2   V   181
SURGES
    WHOSE HOOVES THE TOPS OF THE SURGES GRAZED, • • • • • •   12 OISIN 1   V 142A
    I STOOD UPON THE STAIR! THE SURGES BORE • • • • • • •   44 OISIN 2   225
    I RODE AWAY ON THE SURGES, WHERE, HIGH AS THE SADDLE-BOW,   57 OISIN 3   147
    I RODE AWAY ON THE SURGES, WHERE HIGH AS THE SADDLE BOW   57 OISIN 3   V   147
    I RODE AWAY ON THE SURGES, WHERE, HIGH AS THE SADDLEBOW,   57 OISIN 3   V   147
    MAKING WAY FROM THE KINDLING SURGES, I RODE ON A   58 OISIN 3   161
      BRIDLE-PATH
    AND HUMMING SANDS, WHERE WINDY SURGES WEND! • • • • •   68 SAD SHEPHERD   4
    THAT SAW THE SURGES RUNNING BY, • • • • • • • • • • •   338 TOM OROUGHLEY   6
SURGING
    AND SURGING PHOSPHORUS ALONE GAVE LIGHT • • • • • • • •   31 OISIN 2   33
    OF SURGING PHOSPHORUS ALONE GAVE LIGHT. • • • • • • • •   31 OISIN 2   V   33
SURLY
    SURLY AND DISTANT, MIXED INSEPARABLY • • • • • • • • •   45 OISIN 2   233
    SURLY AND DISTANT, WITH THE WINDS AND SEA!-- • • • • •   45 OISIN 2   V   234
SURMISE
    BUT INWARDLY, SURMISE COMPANIONS • • • • • • • • • • •   320 REED WHISPERER   4
SURMOUNT
    SURMOUNT THEIR BONES! BUT SPEAK WHAT NONE HAVE HEARD. • •   555 RIBH AT TOMB   9
SURMOUNTS
    SURMOUNTS THEIR BONES! BUT SPEAK WHAT NONE HAVE HEARD. • •   555 RIBH AT TOMB   V   9
SURPASSING
    AND THERE'S A SCORE OF DUCHESSES, SURPASSING WOMANKIND,   353 HIS PHOENIX   5
    AND THERE'S A SCORE OF DUCHESSES, SURPASSING WOMAN-KIND,   353 HIS PHOENIX   V   5
SURROUNDED
    • • • AN OLD MAN SURROUNDED WITH DREAMS. • • • • • • •   61 OISIN 3   196
SUSTAINS
    THIS FALLEN STAR MY MILK SUSTAINS, • • • • • • • • • •   499 MOTHER OF GOD   12
    SUSTAINS HIS SOUL IN COURAGE OR IN MIGHT. • • • • • • •   650 ISLE STAT I 1   144
SWADDLING
    WINDING-SHEET AND SWADDLING CLOTHES. • • • • • • • • •   530 OLD TOM AGAIN   V   6
SWADDLING-CLOTHES
    WINDING-SHEET AND SWADDLING-CLOTHES. • • • • • • • • •   530 OLD TOM AGAIN   6
SWALLOW
    COULD KEEP A SWALLOW TO ITS FIRST INTENT! • • • • • • •   489 COOLE PARK 29   19
SWALLOW'S
    I MEDITATE UPON A SWALLOW'S FLIGHT, • • • • • • • • •   488 COOLE PARK 29   1
SWALLOWS
    THEY CAME LIKE SWALLOWS AND LIKE SWALLOWS WENT, • • • •   489 COOLE PARK 29   17
    THEY CAME LIKE SWALLOWS AND LIKE SWALLOWS WENT, • • • •   489 COOLE PARK 29   17
    (SWALLOWS WERE FLASHING THEIR WHITE BREASTS ABOVE • • •   690 MOSADA 1   7
    OH, SWALLOWS, SWALLOWS, SWALLOWS, WILL YE FLY • • • • •   699 MOSADA 3   1
    OH, SWALLOWS, SWALLOWS, SWALLOWS, WILL YE FLY • • • • •   699 MOSADA 3   1
    OH, SWALLOWS, SWALLOWS, SWALLOWS, WILL YE FLY • • • • •   699 MOSADA 3   1
    HEARKEN, YE SWALLOWS!--I HAVE HOARDED UP • • • • • • •   699 MOSADA 3   23
SWAM
    WHEN THE FULL MOON SWAM TO ITS GREATEST HEIGHT • • • •   468 HARUN RASHID   151

		PAGE	TITLE	LINE

SWAM   (CONTINUED)
SHAKESPEAREAN FISH SWAM THE SEA, FAR AWAY FROM LAND;   • • • 485 THREE MOVEMENT   1
ROMANTIC FISH SWAM IN NETS COMING TO THE HAND;   • • • • 485 THREE MOVEMENT   2
AND NOT THE BANKS OF OARS THAT SWAM UPON   • • • • • • 610 STATUES   13
SWAN
WHEN THE SWAN MUST FIX HIS EYE • • • • • • • • 414 TOWER   140
COMPARES THE SOLITARY SOUL TO A SWAN;   • • • • • • 430 NINETEEN 19   60
THE SWAN HAS LEAPED INTO THE DESOLATE HEAVEN;   • • • • • 431 NINETEEN 19   79
LEDA AND THE SWAN • • • • • • • • • • • 441 LEDA AND SWAN   T
BOOK III   DOVE OR SWAN I. LEDA • • • • • • • • 441 LEDA AND SWAN   V   T
BOOK V: DOVE OR SWAN I   LEDA • • • • • • • • • 441 LEDA AND SWAN   V   T
FOR EVEN DAUGHTERS OF THE SWAN CAN SHARE   • • • • 444 SCHOOL CHILDR   20
AT SUDDEN THUNDER OF THE MOUNTING SWAN   • • • • • • 490 COOLE BALLYLEE   14
WHERE THE SWAN DRIFTS UPON A DARKENING FLOOD• • • • • 492 COOLE BALLYLEE   48
SWAN'S
THE HORNS AND SHIELDS AND WILD SWAN'S PINIONS;   • • • • • 82 MAD KING GOLL   V   5
SWANS
AND SWANS WITH THEIR EXULTANT THROATS;   • • • • • • • 14 OISIN 1   192
TWO SWANS CAME FLYING UP TO HIM,   • • • • • • • 194 BAILE AILLINN   135
I KNOW OF THE SLEEPY COUNTRY, WHERE SWANS FLY ROUND   • • 204 WITHER BOUGHS   17
THE WILD SWANS AT COOLE • • • • • • • • • • 322 SWANS AT COOLE   T
ARE NINE-AND-FIFTY SWANS. • • • • • • • • • 322 SWANS AT COOLE   6
ARE NINE AND FIFTY SWANS. • • • • • • • • • 322 SWANS AT COOLE   V   6
SWARD
AND UNTO IT WE'LL DANCE UPON THE SWARD• • • • • • • 681 SEEKER   10
SWARM
BEHOLD, HOW LIKE A SWARM OF FIERY BEES   • • • • • • 662 ISLE STAT II 2   1
HIDING THE REBELS SWARM IN YONDER WOOD   • • • • • • 709 FERENCZ RENYI   V   14
SWARMING
OR CLUNG THEREON LIKE SWARMING BEES;   • • • • • • • 14 OISIN 1   181
LIKE SWARMING BEES, ONE WITH THE DOVE   • • • • • • 78 INDIAN TO LOVE   V   16
SWARMS
OR CLUNG AS CLOSE AS SWARMS OF BEES,   • • • • • • • 14 OISIN 1   V   181
SWAY
'TIS OVER; FAR WITH MEMORY I SWAY AND ROCK.   • • • • • 43 OISIN 2   V   212
HIS FINGERS MOVE AND SWAY,   • • • • • • • • • 98 FOXHUNTER   30
THOUGH DRUNKEN WITH THE FLAGS THAT SWAY   • • • • • • 212 BLESS PSALTER   5
SWAYED
SWAYED, CROONING TO HIMSELF AN UNKNOWN TONGUE;   • • • • • 39 OISIN 2   159
LAID HANDS ON THE BELL-BRANCH AND SWAYED IT, • • • • • • 51 OISIN 3   56
THEN HE SWAYED IN HIS FINGERS THE BELL-BRANCH, • • • • • 51 OISIN 3   67
IN GRIEF SWAYED TO AND FRO• • • • • • • • • 133 FR GILLIGAN   36
I SWAYED UPON THE GAUDY STERN • • • • • • • • 253 HIS DREAM   1
I SWAYED MY LEAVES AND FLOWERS IN THE SUN;   • • • • • 261 COMING WISDOM   3
O BODY SWAYED TO MUSIC, O BRIGHTENING GLANCE, • • • • • 446 SCHOOL CHILDR   63
O BODY SWAYED TO MUSIC BRIGHTENING GLANCE   • • • • 446 SCHOOL CHILDR   V   63
HAVE NOT A MYRIAD SWAYED BELOW STRANGE TREES   • • • • • 724 KANVA ON SELF   11
SWAYING
BENT ALL OUR SWAYING BODIES DOWN, • • • • • • • 20 OISIN 1   297
AND KISSED MY EYES, AND, SWAYING HER BRIGHT HEAD   • • • • 29 OISIN 2   6
AND NOW SANG NIAM, SWAYING HER BRIGHT HEAD   • • • • • 29 OISIN 2   V   6
SO SANG YOUNG NIAM, SWAYING HER BRIGHT HEAD, • • • • • 30 OISIN 2   V   15
A PARROT SWAYING ON A TREE • • • • • • • • 77 INDIAN TO LOVE   V   4
THE DRUIDS CHANTED, SWAYING IN THEIR HANDS   • • • • • 111 CUCHULAIN SEA   V   82
THE DRUIDS CHAUNTED, SWAYING IN THEIR HANDS   • • • • • 111 CUCHULAIN SEA   V   82
IN SONG, FROM GOBLIN WATERS SWAYING WHITE, • • • • • • 657 ISLE STAT I 3   51
ON THEIR SWAYING BLADES OF GRASS, • • • • • • • 705 DAWN-SONG   14
SWAYS
A PARROT SWAYS UPON A TREE, • • • • • • • • 77 INDIAN TO LOVE   4
SWEAR
VIJAYA, SWEAR TO HER LOVE NEVER MORE• • • • • • • 74 ANASHU VIJAYA   65
AY, AY.   SWEAR BY THE PARENTS OF THE GODS, • • • • • 74 ANASHU VIJAYA   66
SWEAR!   BY THE PARENTS OF THE GODS, I SWEAR. • • • • • 75 ANASHU VIJAYA   76
SWEAR!   BY THE PARENTS OF THE GODS, I SWEAR• • • • • • 75 ANASHU VIJAYA   76
PROTECT ME NOW, GODS THAT MY PEOPLE SWEAR BY• • • • • • 241 SHADOW WATER B   396
I SWEAR BEFORE THE DAWN COMES ROUND AGAIN • • • • • • 260 FASC DIFFICULT   12
ON A FANTASTIC RIDE I SWEAR MY HORSE'S FLANKS WERE SPURRED   391 UNDER SATURN   V   6
I SWEAR TO GOD I QUESTIONED THEM, AND ALL THEY HAD TO SAY   593 PILGRIM   14
I SWEAR TO GOD I QUESTIONED THEM ALL AND ALL THEY HAD TO   593 PILGRIM   V   14
SAY
AND ALL MEN HEARD THEM SWEAR   • • • • • • • • 596 COLONEL MARTIN   60
SWEAR BY WHAT THE SAGES SPOKE   • • • • • • • • 636 BEN BULBEN   1
SWEAR BY THOSE HORSEMEN, BY THOSE WOMEN • • • • • • 637 BEN BULBEN   5
GRIEF NEEDS MUCH FEEDING THEN.   OF HIM I SWEAR   • • • • 659 ISLE STAT II 1   20
BY BOSKY JUNE I SWEAR, AND BY THE BEE, HER MINISTER. • • • 661 ISLE STAT II 1   74
I WILL SWEAR BY SUN AND MOON TO PARDON ALL • • • • • 756 SHADOW WATER A   183
AND WILL YOU SWEAR NEVER TO BE AVENGED   • • • • • • 758 SHADOW WATER A   223
I SWEAR IT, THOUGH I GLADLY WOULD LIE DOWN • • • • • 758 SHADOW WATER A   225
AND WILL YOU SWEAR IT BY THE SUN AND MOON?   • • • • • 758 SHADOW WATER A   229
I SWEAR IT.   LET EVERY MAN DRAW OUT HIS SWORD• • • • • 758 SHADOW WATER A   230
SWEARS
SWEARS THAT HE HEARS THE KING'S GREAT HORN. • • • • • • 636 BLACK TOWER   24
SWEAT
OF OUR STRONG STEEDS WAS DARK WITH SWEAT, • • • • • 2 OISIN 1   V   7T
SHIVER UNDER THE LASH, STRAIN, SWEAT AND JOLT • • • • • 260 FASC DIFFICULT   7
EVEN LIKE THESE TO RAIL AND SWEAT • • • • • • • 294 HATED PLAYBOY   5
AND LIKE THESE TO RAIL AND SWEAT • • • • • • • 294 HATED PLAYBOY   V   5
A DEAL I'D SWEAT AND LITTLE EARN • • • • • • • 331 ROUND TOWER   2
THE NIGHT CAN SWEAT WITH TERROR AS BEFORE   • • • • • 429 NINETEEN 19   29
SWEATING
THEY BORE IT WITH STAGGERING AND SWEATING, • • • • • • 60 OISIN 3   186

788

		PAGE	TITLE		LINE
SWEATING (CONTINUED)					
WITH SWEATING, WITH STAGGERING, ...		60	OISIN 3	V	185
SWEEP					
HEARING HELL LOUD WITH A MURMUR, AS SHOUTING AND MOCKING WE SWEEP.		62	OISIN 3		208
AND THEN I MUST SCRUB AND BAKE AND SWEEP		150	OLD MOTHER		3
AND THEN I MUST MEND AND BAKE AND SWEEP		150	OLD MOTHER	V	3
AND THOSE WHITE GLIMMERING FRAGMENTS OF THE MIST SWEEP BY.		426	PHANTOM HATRED		6
WITH PURPLE SANDALS SWEEP THE GRAVE-EYED HOURS--		705	REMEMBRANCE		5
SWEEPING					
CAME NOW THE SLIDING OF TEARS AND SWEEPING OF MIST-COLD HAIR,		47	OISIN 3		7
CAME NOW THE SLIDING OF TEARS AND SWEEPING OF MIST-COLD AIR,		47	OISIN 3	V	7
CAME NOW THE SLIDING OF TEARS AND SWEEPING OF MIST COLD HAIR,		47	OISIN 3	V	7
A MIST THAT IS LIKE BLOWN SNOW IS SWEEPING OVER ALL, . .		425	PHANTOM HATRED		2
SWEEPINGS					
A MOUND OF REFUSE OR THE SWEEPINGS OF A STREET, ...		630	CIRCUS ANIMALS		35
A MOUND OF REFUSE OR THE SWEEPINGS OF THE STREET, . . .		630	CIRCUS ANIMALS	V	35
SWEEPS					
WHAT GREAT TOMB-HAUNTER SWEEPS THE DISTANT SKY		618	BRONZE HEAD		4
NOR TREMBLE TO ITS FALL. THE FIRE SWEEPS ROUND		689	NETTLESHIP		11
SWEET **SEE HONEY-SWEET BITTER-SWEET**					
THEREON DID SHE LOOK HAUGHTY AND SWEET!		6	OISIN 1		54
WITH LAUGHTER LOW, AND TENDER, AND SWEET!		6	OISIN 1	V	54
SHE SAID, WITH LAUGHTER TENDER AND SWEET!		6	OISIN 1	V	54
AMONG THE WOODLAND GRASSES SWEET, ...		15	OISIN 1	V	199
THUS ON THE WATERS, FAR AND SWEET, ...		26	OISIN 1	V	398A
OF THE THINGS THAT HIS HEART STILL KNOWS WERE SWEET-- . .		26	OISIN 1	V	402
AND NAMED HIM BY SWEET NAMES. A FOAMING TIDE		30	OISIN 2		27
FULL MANY MORE, WHEN PEERED A MAIDEN SWEET		33	OISIN 2	V	68F
AH, SWEET TO ME NOW WERE EVEN BALD CONAN'S SLANDEROUS TONGUE!		55	OISIN 3		116
I SAT AND MUSED AND DRANK SWEET WINE!		82	MAD KING GOLL		13
"WITH HIM IS ONE SWEET THROATED LIKE A BIRD, ...		106	CUCHULAIN SEA	V	16
I HAVE OFTEN HEARD THE SWEET SOUND OF HIS BOW.		109	CUCHULAIN SEA		50
I OFTEN HEAR THE SWEET SOUND OF HIS BOW.		109	CUCHULAIN SEA	V	50
THEN CONCOBAR SENT THAT SWEET THROATED MAID		110	CUCHULAIN SEA	V	72
THE BELL THAT CALLS US ON! THE SWEET FAR THING.		115	ROSE OF BATTLE		28
GROW SWEET WITH HIS MOOD.		118	CRADLE SONG	V	8
O SWEET EVERLASTING VOICES, BE STILL!		141	EVERLAST VOICE		1
O SWEET EVERLASTING VOICES, BE STILL.		141	EVERLAST VOICE		8
AND MANY A SWEET THING SAID, ...		144	HOST OF AIR		18
THE TONGUE OF IT SWEET WITH DREAMING		160	CAP AND BELLS	V	17
A CHATTERING WISE AND SWEET, ...		161	CAP AND BELLS		34
"THE ROSE THAT MUST DROP, OUT OF SWEET LEAVES, ...		168	BLESSED		37
TILL THE ATTORNEY FOR LOST SOULS CRY HER SWEET CRY, . . .		173	SPEAKS HEARERS		6
TILL MAURYA OF THE WOUNDED HEART CRY A SWEET CRY, . . .		173	SPEAKS HEARERS	V	6
WORTH KNITTING TO A MEASURE OF SWEET SOUND?		181	QUEEN MAEVE		33
OR TWO SWEET BLOSSOMING APPLE-BOUGHS		195	BAILE AILLINN		153
OR TWO SWEET BLOSSOMING APPLE BOUGHS		195	BAILE AILLINN	V	153
WITH ITS SWEET BLOSSOM WHERE HERS WAS!		197	BAILE AILLINN		190
FOR TO ARTICULATE SWEET SOUNDS TOGETHER		205	ADAMS CURSE		10
ON FINDING THAT HER VOICE IS SWEET AND LOW		205	ADAMS CURSE		17
SWEET WITH ALL MUSIC, OUT OF HIS LONG HAIR, ...		219	HARP OF AENGUS		8
BY THE SWEET NAME OF DEATH.		254	HIS DREAM		12
BY THE SWEET NAME OF DEATH.		254	HIS DREAM		20
TO HAVE LIT UPON AS CLEAN AND SWEET A TALE		258	KING NO KING		8
AND THE SWEET LAUGHING EAGLE THOUGHTS THAT GROW		264	HOUSE SHAKEN		5
A SWEET, MIRACULOUS, TERRIFYING SOUND.		277	TWO KINGS		17
A SINGLE SOUL THAT LACKS A SWEET CRYSTALLINE CRY. . . .		291	PAUDEEN		8
THE LINEAMENTS, A HEART THAT LAUGHTER HAS MADE SWEET, . .		315	FALLEN MAJESTY		5
THE LINEAMENTS, THE HEART THAT LAUGHTER HAS MADE SWEET,		315	FALLEN MAJESTY	V	5
TILL TOES MASTERED A SWEET MEASURE, ...		331	ROUND TOWER		15
MOUTH MASTERED A SWEET SOUND, ...		331	ROUND TOWER		16
AND MAKE THE DAYLIGHT SWEET ONCE MORE! BUT WHEN		339	SHEP GOATHERD		13
OF SORROWFUL, AUSTERE, SWEET, LOFTY PIPE TUNES.		341	SHEP GOATHERD		57
THE HORN'S SWEET NOTE AND THE TOOTH OF THE HOUND. . . .		380	SONGS FOOL 1		12
THE HORN'S SWEET NOTE AND THE TOOTH OF THE HOUND. . . .		381	SONGS FOOL 2		14
SWEET AND HARSH, HARSH AND SWEET, ...		382	SONG OF FOOL		10
SWEET AND HARSH, HARSH AND SWEET, ...		382	SONG OF FOOL		10
WHAT VOICE MORE SWEET THAN HERS		392	EASTER 1916		21
SWEET VOICED AND BEAUTIFUL, ...		392	EASTER 1916	V	22
SO DARING AND SWEET HIS THOUGHT.		393	EASTER 1916		30
SHE SEEMED TO HAVE GROWN CLEAN AND SWEET		397	POLIT PRISONER		17
BUT BECKONED TO SWEET COMPANY.		400	DEMON BEAST		18
AND THAT ITS OWN SWEET WILL IS HEAVEN'S WILL!		405	FOR DAUGHTER		69
AND KNEW THAT SWEET EXTREMITY OF PRIDE		471	ALL SOUL NIGHT		22
BATHED IN MIRACULOUS OIL, SWEET ODOURS FROM IT COME, . .		503	VACILLATION		81
MIND'S BREAD GROW SWEET.		554	CHURCH STATE		6
WITH THAT SWEET CRY.		559	HE AND SHE		12
SWEET DANCER		568	SWEET DANCER		T
AH, DANCER, AH, SWEET DANCER!		568	SWEET DANCER		7
AH, DANCER, AH, SWEET DANCER!		568	SWEET DANCER		14
WASH! MAKE YOUR BODY SWEET!		572	LADYS 2ND SONG		4
THEIR CRIES ARE SWEET AND STRANGE, ...		612	NEWS ORACLE		18
THE WOMEN THAT I PICKED SPOKE SWEET AND LOW		622	HOUND VOICE		8
MAKES ME SWEET MUSIC		627	STATES HOLIDAY		24
TO WELCOME THEE, NASCHINA, WITH SWEET SINGING.		645	ISLE STAT I 1		7
WITH SINGING SWEET AS E'ER ROUND LAKE-LULLED ISLE . . .		649	ISLE STAT I 1		106

```
                                                           PAGE     TITLE            LINE
SWEET    (CONTINUED)
    WILD CRIES, GROWN SWEET WITH LULLS AND LINGERINGS LONG.    674  ISLE STAT II 3      222
    I NEVER KNEW A NIGHT SO HONEY SWEET. . . . . . . . .       702  MOSADA 3      V      99
    WHITE, RENYI SILENT STANDS; THAT MAIDEN SWEET . . . .      713  FERENCZ RENYI V      84
    "I AM LONE LADY QUIETNESS, MY SWEET, . . . . . . . .       716  DWELT SYCAMORE       13
    AND SMILING FROM SWEET THOUGHT, . . . . . . . . . .        741  EARL PAUL            42
    DARK JOAN CALL THE BERRIES SWEET, . . . . . . . . .        743  DANAAN QUICK         28
    SWEET WITH ALL MUSIC, OUT OF HIS LONG HAIR, . . . .        762  SHADOW WATER A      303
    HATRED MAY BE SWEET TO THE TASTE." . . . . . . . .         776  AGAINST WITCH        31
    HATRED MAY BE SWEET IN THE TASTE." . . . . . . . .         776  AGAINST WITCH V      31
    IN THAT SWEET WANDERING SNARE. . . . . . . . . . .         783  GREY ROUND           10
SWEETEN
    THAT SANG, TO SWEETEN IRELAND'S WRONG, . . . . . . .       137  TO IRELAND            3
    WHO SANG TO SWEETEN IRELAND'S WRONG, . . . . . . . .       137  TO IRELAND    V       3
    SWEETEN THE LITTLE HALFWAY HOUSE . . . . . . . . .         567  LAPIS LAZULI  V      48
SWEETENED
    SWEETENED BY DEATH, BUT IF I COULD BELIEVE, . . . . .      285  TWO KINGS           205
SWEETENS
    SWEETENS THE LITTLE HALF-WAY HOUSE . . . . . . . .         567  LAPIS LAZULI         48
SWEETER
    AND SWEETER OF VOICE THAN THE PLEASANT BIRDS, . . . .        9  OISIN 1       V      95
    AND FIND THEIR LAUGHTER SWEETER TO THE TASTE . . . .      228  SHADOW WATER B      134
    SWEETER EMOTION, WORKING IN THEIR VEINS . . . . . .       292  TO A SHADE           13
    OF SWEETER IGNORANCE." . . . . . . . . . . . .           343  SHEP GOATHERD       112
    HAD FOUND A SWEETER WORD. . . . . . . . . . . .          539  MEETING              18
    "YOUR LIFE CAN GROW MUCH SWEETER IF YOU WILL . . . .     634  CUCHULAIN COMF       12
SWEETEST
    AND CALLED HIM SWEETEST NAMES AND SOOTHED HIS FEARS. .     30  OISIN 2       V      27
    WHOM MEN HAVE NAMED ARCADIA'S SWEETEST TONGUE. . . .     649  ISLE STAT I 1       109
    FOR THAT'S THE SWEETEST MUSIC FOR SAD SOULS. . . . .     702  MOSADA 3             85
    "OR SEEK WHERE SWEETEST WATER BUBBLES. . . . . . .       731  PRIEST FAIRY         79
SWEETHEART
    AND HIS YOUNG SWEETHEART CLOSE BESIDE HIM KNELT, . . .   108  CUCHULAIN SEA        40
    SAID, "AENGUS AND HIS SWEETHEART GIVE THEIR THANKS . .   187  QUEEN MAEVE         146
    SWEETHEART, DO NOT LOVE TOO LONG: . . . . . . . .        211  O DO NOT LOVE         1
    A SWEETHEART FROM ANOTHER LIFE FLOATS THERE . . . .      390  IMAGE PAST           22
SWEETHEARTS'
    AMONG THOSE MOUTHS THAT SING THEIR SWEETHEARTS' PRAISE,  285  TWO KINGS           185
SWEETLY
    THE SUN WAS LAUGHING SWEETLY, . . . . . . . . . .        214  HAPPY TOWNLAND       15
    THE SUN WAS LAUGHING SWEETLY, . . . . . . . . . .        215  HAPPY TOWNLAND       35
    THE SUN WAS LAUGHING SWEETLY, . . . . . . . . . .        216  HAPPY TOWNLAND       55
    AND TROD SO SWEETLY PROUD . . . . . . . . . . .          255  WOMAN HOMER          17
SWEETNESS    SEE BITTER-SWEETNESS
    WE SHALL MINGLE NO MORE, NOR OUR GAZES EMPTY THEIR         56  OISIN 3            132
        SWEETNESS LONE
    AND LIFE IS OVER SAVE THE MURMUR AND THE SWEETNESS. . .    77  INDIAN TO LOVE V     5E
    AND ALL IS OVER SAVE THE MURMUR AND THE SWEETNESS. . .     77  INDIAN TO LOVE V     5E
    AND THE SWEETNESS OF DESIRE. . . . . . . . . . .         168  BLESSED              38
    ALL THAT SWEETNESS AMID STRENGTH?" . . . . . . . .       259  PEACE                 9
    THE BITTER SWEETNESS OF FALSE FACES? . . . . . . .       275  GREY ROCK           113
    SO GREAT A SWEETNESS FLOWS . . . . . . . . . .           316  FRIENDS              27
    CHILLED BLOOD, THIS SWEETNESS BROUGHT; . . . . . .       401  DEMON BEAST          39
    O WHAT A SWEETNESS STRAYED . . . . . . . . . .           401  DEMON BEAST          43
    THE SWEETNESS THAT ALL LONGED FOR NIGHT AND DAY, . .     418  ANCEST HOUSES        20
    OF THEIR OWN SWEETNESS, BODIES OF THEIR LOVELINESS. . .  426  PHANTOM HATRED       24
    DRUNK WITH THE BITTER SWEETNESS OF HER YOUTH. . . . .    469  HARUN RASHID        186
    SO GREAT A SWEETNESS FLOWS INTO THE BREAST . . . .       479  SELF AND SOUL        69
    THE INTELLECTUAL SWEETNESS OF THOSE LINES . . . . .      489  COOLE PARK 29        23
    WHERE HAD HER SWEETNESS GONE? . . . . . . . . .          503  QUARREL IN AGE        1
    OVERCOME--O BITTER SWEETNESS. . . . . . . . . .          540  FROM ANTIGONE         1
    THE BITTER SWEETNESS OF THE NIGHT . . . . . . . .        781  HEART FRIGHT          3
SWEETSHOP
    WITH FACE AND NOSE PRESSED TO A SWEETSHOP WINDOW. . . .  370  EGO DOMINUS   V      56
SWEET-SHOP
    WITH FACE AND NOSE PRESSED TO A SWEET-SHOP WINDOW, . .   370  EGO DOMINUS          56
SWEET-SOUNDING
    BUT THAT SWEET-SOUNDING VOICE RAN ON: "WOMAN, . . . .    284  TWO KINGS           165
SWEET-THROATED
    "WITH HIM IS ONE SWEET-THROATED LIKE A BIRD." . . . .    106  CUCHULAIN SEA        16
    THEN CONCHUBAR SENT THAT SWEET-THROATED MAID, . . . .    110  CUCHULAIN SEA        72
SWEET-TONGUED
    IT HAD GROWN SWEET-TONGUED BY DREAMING . . . . . . .     160  CAP AND BELLS        17
SWELLING
    AND ALL THEIR SWELLING CANVAS WEAR, . . . . . . . .      530  OLD TOM AGAIN         2
SWEPT    SEE CLEAN-SWEPT
    AND SWEPT OUT OF THE WATTLED HALL . . . . . . . .         20  OISIN 1            292
    SWEPT ON THE DANCE'S LINKED FLOW, . . . . . . . .         20  OISIN 1       V    291
    THE SEA SWEPT ON AND CRIED HER OLD CRY STILL. . . . .     68  SAD SHEPHERD         10
    BESIDES HER CLEAN SWEPT HEARTH, HER QUIET SHADE: . .     114  ROSE OF BATTLE V     11
    SWEPT THE SAWDUST FROM THE FLOOR . . . . . . . .         440  WISDOM                6
    AND AFTER, SWEPT FROM THERE, . . . . . . . . . .         453  DEATH OF HARE        10
    AND SWEPT THE HOUSE AND SANG ABOUT HER WORK . . . .      468  HARUN RASHID        148
    AND ONCE AGAIN SHE ROSE AND SWEPT THE HOUSE . . . .      468  HARUN RASHID        159
    WHEN SEA-WIND SWEPT THE CORNER, STANDS: . . . . . .      566  LAPIS LAZULI         32
    NO FOX CAN FOUL THE LAIR THE BADGER SWEPT-- . . . .      603  GALLERY REVIS        39
SWERVED
    LET THE FOOLS RAGE, I SWERVED IN NAUGHT, . . . . . .     577  WHAT THEN            18
SWIFT
    THE SWIFT INNUMERABLE SPEARS, . . . . . . . . . .          2  OISIN 1               6
    AND NOW A MAID, ON A SWIFT BROWN STEED . . . . . . .      12  OISIN 1       V    142
```

	PAGE	TITLE	LINE
SWIFT (CONTINUED)			
BUT NIAMH WITH A SWIFT DISTRESS	15	OISIN 1	211
WITH A SWIFT AND FRIENDLY GLANCE	21	OISIN 1	309
"SWIFT ARE THE YEARS OF A WARRIOR'S PRIDE:	26	OISIN 1 V	399A
BEFORE THE SWIFT THINGS THAT SHE DREAMED OF WERE DONE	27	OISIN 1	414
ERE HALF THE SWIFT THINGS THAT SHE DREAMT ON WERE DONE,	28	OISIN 1 V	422
O SWIFT ON THE SEAS ALL DAY AND NIGHT	70	CLOAK BOAT	8
WAS DRIVING CATTLE CAME SHE WITH SWIFT FEET,	106	CUCHULAIN SEA V	19
OF THEIR LONG WINGS, THE FLASH OF THEIR SWIFT FEET.	137	TO SOME I TALK V	16
THE RIDERS UPON THE SWIFT HORSES	266	GALWAY RACES V	3
RIDERS UPON THE SWIFT HORSES,	266	GALWAY RACES V	3
SWIFT BEATING ON HIS BREAST IN SIBYLLINE FRENZY BLIND	481	BLOOD AND MOON	19
GOLDSMITH AND BURKE, SWIFT AND THE BISHOP OF CLOYNE	486	SEVEN SAGES	9
THE TOMB OF SWIFT WEARS IT AWAY. A VOICE	487	SEVEN SAGES	21
SWIFT HAS SAILED INTO HIS REST:	493	SWIFTS EPITAPH	1
SWIFT HAD SAILED INTO HIS REST:	493	SWIFTS EPITAPH V	1
BUT HEAVY FRUIT. HOW SWIFT THE ARGUMENT	665	ISLE STAT II 2	66
O SWIFT ON THE SEAS ALL DAY AND NIGHT	666	ISLE STAT II 3	8
SWIFT LAKE. A VERY LITTLE THING THAT IS,	669	ISLE STAT II 3	78
CHECK. AH! HOW BRIGHT YOUR EYES. HOW SWIFT YOUR MOVES.	722	WITCH VIVIEN	61
SWIFTER			
A SWIFTER CREATURE NEVER WAS BORN,	2	OISIN 1 V	7Q
AND SWIFTER THAN THE SALMON HERDS:	9	OISIN 1 V	96
SWIFTEST			
"THE SWIFTEST HE TO DANCE OR FLY,	729	PRIEST FAIRY	45
SWIFTLY			
YON TALL ONE EYES MY SUPPER: SWIFTLY CHASE HIM	72	ANASHU VIJAYA V	34
NEVER STORM AROSE SO SWIFTLY: SCARCE THE CHILDREN WERE IN BED,	718	PHANTOM SHIP	4
TALKING HOURS SWIFTLY PASS!	727	LOVERS QUARREL	44
SWIFT'S			
SWIFT'S EPITAPH	493	SWIFTS EPITAPH	T
"JONATHAN SWIFT'S AT REST:	493	SWIFTS EPITAPH V	1
THROUGH JONATHAN SWIFT'S DARK GROVE HE PASSED, AND THERE	543	PARN FUNERAL 2	11
SWIM			
"'TIS JOY MAKES SWIM THE SAPPY TIDE,	18	OISIN 1 V	261
WHAT SHALL I CALL THEM? FISH THAT SWIM,	195	BAILE AILLINN	144
MONSTROUS FAMILIAR IMAGES SWIM TO THE MIND'S EYE.	426	PHANTOM HATRED	8
ALL THAT COULD RUN OR LEAP OR SWIM	528	DANCER CRUACH	6
ALL THAT RUN OR LEAP OR SWIM	528	DANCER CRUACH V	6
BEHOLD THAT GREAT PLOTINUS SWIM,	530	DELPHIC ORACLE	1
ALL SWIM WITH TEARS. THE FAERY BOAT'S AT HAND!	663	ISLE STAT II 2	33
SWIMMING			
CAME SWIMMING SADLY DOWN THE MIGHTY STAIR.	32	OISIN 2 V	50B
A MERMAID FOUND A SWIMMING LAD,	452	MERMAID	1
IT SEEMED A GOLD-FISH SWIMMING IN A BOWL.	472	ALL SOUL NIGHT	40
WHO, SWIMMING, SOUGHT THE ISLAND LONE:	673	ISLE STAT II 3	181
SWIMS			
THE FAERY SHIP THAT SWIMS ATHWART THE SKY.	663	ISLE STAT II 2	16
SWINE			
CRYING, THE PIRATES DROVE HIS SWINE	82	MAD KING GOLL	15
WHIPS TO THE SEA THE COWS AND SWINE."	82	MAD KING GOLL V	16
TO MIND HIS COWS AND SWINE BY THE RED LAKE.	752	SHADOW WATER A	112
SWINEHERD			
AND SAID, "I AM THAT SWINEHERD WHOM YOU BID	105	CUCHULAIN SEA	3
"I AM ALEEL, THE SWINEHERD, WHOM YOU BID	105	CUCHULAIN SEA V	3A
THAT SWINEHERD STARED UPON HER FACE AND SAID,	106	CUCHULAIN SEA	9
LOOKING ON HER, ALEEL, THE SWINEHERD, SAID:	106	CUCHULAIN SEA V	9
ALEEL, THE SWINEHERD, WEPT AND CAST HIM DOWN	106	CUCHULAIN SEA V	14
SWING			
SORRY PLACE, WHERE FOR SWING OF THE WAR-AXE IN MY DIM EYES	61	OISIN 3	194
EVEN WHERE HORRIBLE GREEN PARROTS CALL AND SWING.	442	BLACK CENTAUR	2
EVEN WHERE THE HORRIBLE GREEN PARROTS CALL AND SWING.	442	BLACK CENTAUR V	2
SWINGING			
SWINGING, SWINGING ALONG.	544	TO SAME TUNE 1 V	REF
SWINGING, SWINGING ALONG.	544	TO SAME TUNE 1 V	REF
SWIRLED			
SHOUTED. WITH FIRE OF HAIR ABOUT HER SWIRLED,	38	OISIN 2 V	134
SWISH			
COME SWISH AROUND, MY PRETTY PUNK,	591	DRUNK SOBRIETY	1
SWOLLEN			
O HEAVY SWOLLEN WATERS, BRIM THE FALL OF THE OAK TREES,	207	HANRAHANS SONG V	11
LIKE HEAVY SWOLLEN WATERS ARE OUR BODIES AND OUR BLOOD:	208	HANRAHANS SONG V	13
SWOON			
HE FELL INTO A DRUID SWOON.	20	OISIN 1	289
LOCKE SANK INTO A SWOON:	439	FRAGMENTS	1
SWOONING			
HURLS THEIR SWOONING LUSTRE UP.	647	ISLE STAT I 1	49
SWOOPS			
AND DOWN I CAME AS A FALCON SWOOPS	673	ISLE STAT II 3	178
SWOP			
AGREED THEIR CLOTHES TO SWOP,	595	COLONEL MARTIN	20
SWORD			
FROM MACE AND SWORD AND POLE-AXE, LONG AGO	31	OISIN 2	30
BY MACE AND SPEAR AND SWORD OF SEA-GODS, NAILS	31	OISIN 2 V	30A
LAID IT AND SIGHED! I HELD A SWORD WHOSE SHINE	37	OISIN 2	126
LAID IT AND SIGHED--A SWORD WHOSE WIZARD SHINE	37	OISIN 2 V	126
THE STRANGER WATCHED THE SWORD: BUT NIAM FAR,	38	OISIN 2 V	136
OF SWORD AND BRAZEN BATTLE-AXE, WHILE DAY	40	OISIN 2	171
AND WHEN HE KNEW THE SWORD OF MANANNAN	40	OISIN 2	173

791

```
                                                          PAGE    TITLE           LINE
SWORD  (CONTINUED)
    MINGLING OF SWORD AND WAR-AXE, WHILE THE DAY  . . . . . .   40  OISIN 2      V  171
    THE DRUID SWORD OF MANANAN, HE GREW  . . . . . . . . . .   40  OISIN 2      V  174
    THE DEAD GOD'S SWORD, TO MANY FORMS HE GREW, . . . . . .   40  OISIN 2      V  175
    AND ON THESE HANDS THAT MAY NOT LIFT THE SWORD, . . . .   103  FERGUS DRUID     24
    UPON A SWORD, A FIR-TREE ON A HILL, . . . . . . . . .    104  FERGUS DRUID     34
    UPON A SWORD, A FIR TREE ON A HILL, . . . . . . . . .    104  FERGUS DRUID  V  34
    AT THE SWORD POINT, AND BADE ME BRING HIM ONE . . . . .   109  CUCHULAIN SEA V  53
    AT THE SWORD POINT, AND WAITS TILL WE HAVE FOUND . . .    109  CUCHULAIN SEA V  53
    THAT YOU COME HERE TO MEET THIS ANCIENT SWORD?" . . . .   109  CUCHULAIN SEA V  61
    AND WITH THE CLASHING OF THEIR SWORD BLADES MAKE . . .    137  TO SOME I TALK V  13
    A SWORD UPON HIS IRON KNEES . . . . . . . . . . . . .    156  FORGOT BEAUTY V  23
    CAULDRON AND SPEAR AND STONE AND SWORD, . . . . . . .    196  BAILE AILLINN   165
    A SHADOW DOES NOT CARRY SWORD OR SPEAR. . . . . . . .    224  SHADOW WATER B   44
    IF YOU WILL DRAW THAT SWORD OUT OF ITS SCABBARD . . .    225  SHADOW WATER B   78
    COMES CRYING, "I HAVE RUN UPON THE SWORD. . . . . . .    234  SHADOW WATER B  261
    AND SAYS: "A SWORD BLADE PIERCED ME IN MY SLEEP." . .    234  SHADOW WATER B V 257
    WHERE IS MY SWORD THAT FELL OUT OF MY HAND . . . . .     241  SHADOW WATER B  397
    WHY DO YOU NEED A SWORD?  BUT YOU MAY KEEP IT. . . .     241  SHADOW WATER B  400
    THIS SWORD IS TO LIE BESIDE HIM IN THE GRAVE. . . .     242  SHADOW WATER B  412
    I'LL DO IT FOR HIS SAKE.  NO.  TAKE THIS SWORD . . .     250  SHADOW WATER B  591
    FAREWELL! FAREWELL!  THE SWORD IS IN THE ROPE-- . . .    251  SHADOW WATER B  595
    THAT ONE BELIEVED HE HAD A SWORD UPSTAIRS! . . . . .     267  ALL TEMPT ME      8
    AS THOUGH TO SAY "IT IS THE SWORD ELSEWHERE," . . . .    267  ALL TEMPT ME  V   8
    THAT THINK SWORD STROKES WERE BETTER MEANT . . . . .     276  GREY ROCK     V 129
    THEN DREW HIS SWORD TO HOLD ITS LEVELLED POINT . . .     277  TWO KINGS        14
    HORN LOCKED IN SWORD, THEY TUGGED AND STRUGGLED THERE    277  TWO KINGS        18
    BUT DREW HIS SWORD, AND THOUGHT WITH LEVELLED POINT .    277  TWO KINGS     V  14
    TO STAY THE STAG'S NEXT RUSH.  WHEN SWORD MET HORN .     277  TWO KINGS     V  15
    THE ENTRAILS OF THE HORSE.  DROPPING HIS SWORD . . .     278  TWO KINGS        23
    THROUGH THE ENTRAILS OF THE HORSE.  DROPPING HIS SWORD   278  TWO KINGS     V  23
    SAT UPRIGHT WITH A SWORD BEFORE HER FEET. . . . . .      279  TWO KINGS        62
    AS ON THE BLUE LIGHT OF A SWORD, A MAN . . . . . . .     283  TWO KINGS       148
    WHERE SATO'S GIFT, A CHANGELESS SWORD, . . . . . . .     421  MY TABLE          2
    AND SEEMED UNCHANGING LIKE THE SWORD. . . . . . . .      421  MY TABLE         21
    A GLITTERING SWORD OUT OF THE EAST.  A PUFF OF WIND .    426  PHANTOM HATRED    5
    BID THE GHOST HAVE SWORD IN FIST! . . . . . . . . .      435  FOR MY SON        9
    BID THE GHOST HAVE SWORD IN HAND! . . . . . . . . .      435  FOR MY SON    V   9
    THE CONSECRATED SWORD UPON MY KNEES . . . . . . . .      477  SELF AND SOUL V   9
    IS SATO'S ANCIENT SWORD, STILL AS IT WAS, . . . . .      477  SELF AND SOUL V  10
    GOLD-SOWN SILK ON THE SWORD BLADE . . . . . . . . .      484  SYMBOLS       V   5
    OLD CIVILISATIONS PUT TO THE SWORD. . . . . . . . .      566  LAPIS LAZULI     27
    LONG ERE AN ARROW WHIZZED OR SWORD LEFT SHEATH . .       650  ISLE STAT I 1   135
    THE BROWN WEED BURDEN, SO THE SWORD BRINGS FEAR . .      660  ISLE STAT II 1   45
    HE'LL SNAP HIS SWORD.  RAISED IS THE LION'S PAW. .       664  ISLE STAT II 2   63
    WITHIN HIS CLENCHED TEETH A SWORD. . . . . . . . .       673  ISLE STAT II 3  182
    I FLING AWAY MY SWORD, BLOOD DIM, . . . . . . . . .      743  DANAAN QUICK     20
    I DREW MY SWORD TO FLING IT IN A POOL,-- . . . . .       747  SHADOW WATER A    7
    NONE SHOULD ESCAPE MY SWORD!  I WOULD SEND ALL . .       752  SHADOW WATER A  111
    I PROMISED HIM THAT NONE SHOULD ESCAPE MY SWORD . .      752  SHADOW WATER A  114
    AND SAYS, "A SWORD BLADE PIERCED ME IN MY SLEEP." .      753  SHADOW WATER A V 147
    I SWEAR IT.  LET EVERY MAN DRAW OUT HIS SWORD. . .       758  SHADOW WATER A  230
    MAY THE SWORD BLADES DRINK THEIR FILL . . . . . .        776  AGAINST WITCH V  37
    A HOUSE, A SWORD, A SHIP, A MASK. . . . . . . . .        788  BRAVEST ASK       2
SWORD-BLADE
    . . . MADE CONCHUBAR'S SWORD-BLADE OF OLD. . . . .        52  OISIN 3          80
    AND SAYS, "A SWORD-BLADE PIERCED ME IN MY SLEEP." .      234  SHADOW WATER B  257
    ALL-DESTROYING SWORD-BLADE STILL . . . . . . . . .       484  SYMBOLS           3
    GOLD-SEWN SILK ON THE SWORD-BLADE, . . . . . . . .       484  SYMBOLS           5
    AND SAYS, "A SWORD-BLADE PIERCED ME IN MY SLEEP." .      753  SHADOW WATER A  147
SWORD-BLADES
    AND WITH THE CLASHING OF THEIR SWORD-BLADES MAKE .       137  TO SOME I TALK   13
    AND WITH THE CLANGING OF THEIR SWORD-BLADES MAKE .       137  TO SOME I TALK V 13
    MAY THE SWORD-BLADES DRINK THEIR FILL . . . . . .        776  AGAINST WITCH    37
SWORD-BLUE
    OF SWORD-BLUE WAVES OF CALM; WHILE O'ER HEAD BLINK .     663  ISLE STAT II 2   42
SWORD-POINT
    AT THE SWORD-POINT, AND WAITS TILL WE HAVE FOUND . .     109  CUCHULAIN SEA    53
SWORD'S
    THE SWORD'S A CROSS! THEREON HE DIED! . . . . . . .      562  CONJUNCTIONS      3
SWORDS
    AND A HUNDRED SWORDS AND A HUNDRED BOWS! . . . . .         8  OISIN 1       V  91
    THEIR SWORDS UPON THEIR IRON KNEES, . . . . . . .       156  FORGOT BEAUTY    23
    THEY UNHOOK THEIR HEAVY SWORDS . . . . . . . . . .      215  HAPPY TOWNLAND   23
    NINE SWORDS WITH HANDLES OF RHINOCEROS HORN . . .       239  SHADOW WATER B  368
    AND BEAT THE GOLDEN HELMET WITH THEIR SWORDS? . .       243  SHADOW WATER B  425
    HELMETS, AND SWORDS, AND HALF-FORGOTTEN THINGS . .      257  RECONCILIATION    6
    HURL HELMETS, CROWNS, AND SWORDS INTO THE PIT . .       257  RECONCILIATION   10
    WE MUST GET SWORDS.  IS'T THE ONLY WAY?  OH, SEE,       660  ISLE STAT II 1   34
    THEY GET THEM SWORDS, AND BOTH OR EITHER FALL? . .      662  ISLE STAT II 1   78
    MORE WONDERFUL!  AND WE HAVE SWORDS.  O NIGHT . .       664  ISLE STAT II 2   61
    OF THOSE STEEL TONGUES!  CRASH, SWORDS!  WELL THRUST!   665  ISLE STAT II 2   67
      WELL BENT
    A HUNDRED SWORDS, A HUNDRED DRINKING-BOWLS, . . .       756  SHADOW WATER A  186
    A HUNDRED SHIELDS OF BRASS, A HUNDRED SWORDS, . .       756  SHADOW WATER A V 188
    THEY ARE ALWAYS QUARRELLING.  GIVE ME YOUR SWORDS.      766  SHADOW WATER A  370
    ALE SETS THEM QUARRELLING.  GIVE ME YOUR SWORDS. .      766  SHADOW WATER A  372
    GIVE ME YOUR SWORDS.  THEY ARE ALWAYS QUARRELLING.      766  SHADOW WATER A V 370
    IT IS THE BROWN ALE DOES IT.  GIVE ME YOUR SWORDS.      766  SHADOW WATER A V 372
SWORDSMAN
    BADE THAT SWORDSMAN TAKE . . . . . . . . . . . .        789  SINGING HEAD      4
```

SWORDSMEN
  AND THE TALL MEN AND THE SWORDSMEN AND THE HORSEMEN, WHERE ARE THEY?   580 CURSE CROMWELL   4
  THAT THE SWORDSMEN AND THE LADIES CAN STILL KEEP COMPANY,   581 CURSE CROMWELL   20
SWORD-STROKES
  THAT THINK SWORD-STROKES WERE BETTER MEANT . . . . . .   276 GREY ROCK   129
SWORE
  I SWORE BUT YESTERDAY IF THE RED GOD . . . .   751 SHADOW WATER A   109
  HE SWORE TO SING MY BEAUTY . . . .   789 SINGING HEAD   7
SWORN   SEE DEEP-SWORN
  WITH SAILORS THAT WERE SWORN TO DO YOUR WILL, ...   236 SHADOW WATER B   308
  A DEEP SWORN VOW . . . .   357 DEEP-SWORN VOW V   T
  THAT DEEP SWORN VOW, HAVE BEEN FRIENDS OF MINE, ...   357 DEEP-SWORN VOW V   2
  I AM THINKING OF A CHILD'S VOW SWORN IN VAIN . . . . .   391 UNDER SATURN   15
  BESIDE A LOCHLANN WHARF, AND THOUGH SHE HAD SWORN . . .   756 SHADOW WATER A   188
SWUNG
  IN A SAD REVELRY HE SANG AND SWUNG . . . .   39 OISIN 2   160
  THAT ON A WILLOW SWUNG. . . . .   308 PLAYER QUEEN   4
SYCAMORE
  A SYCAMORE AND LIME-TREE LOST IN NIGHT . . . .   488 COOLE PARK 29   3
  A SYCAMORE AND LIME TREE LOST IN NIGHT . . . .   488 COOLE PARK 29 V   3
  A LITTLE BOY OUTSIDE THE SYCAMORE WOOD . . . .   715 DWELT SYCAMORE   1
  A LITTLE BOY INSIDE THE SYCAMORE WOOD . . . .   715 DWELT SYCAMORE   5
SYCAMORES
  SHE WHO DWELT AMONG THE SYCAMORES. . . . .   715 DWELT SYCAMORE   T
  SHE DWELT AMONG THE SYCAMORES. . . . .   715 DWELT SYCAMORE V   T
SYMBOL
  (I HAVE NO SPEECH BUT SYMBOL, THE PAGAN SPEECH I MADE . .   365 HER COURAGE   2
  AND NOT A FOUNTAIN, WERE THE SYMBOL WHICH . . . . . .   418 ANCEST HOUSES   15
  I DECLARE THIS TOWER IS MY SYMBOL; I DECLARE . . . . .   480 BLOOD AND MOON   16
  THAT THEY HAD BROUGHT NO FABULOUS SYMBOL THERE . . . .   537 HER VISION   31
  A SYMBOL OF LONGEVITY; . . . .   566 LAPIS LAZULI   40
SYMBOLIC
  WHERE THE SYMBOLIC ROSE CAN BREAK IN FLOWER, ...   419 MY HOUSE   4
SYMBOLICAL
  SYMBOLICAL GLORY OF THE EARTH AND AIR! . . . .   483 VERONIC NAPKIN   3
SYMBOLISE
  AND THAT ALL HEAVENLY GLORY SYMBOLISE-- . . . .   445 SCHOOL CHILDR   55
SYMBOLS
  SYMBOLS OF THE SOUL, ...   420 MY HOUSE   V 20F
  SYMBOLS . . . .   484 SYMBOLS   T
SYMPATHY
  INTO A SPHERE FROM YOUTHFUL SYMPATHY, ...   443 SCHOOL CHILDR   14
SYNGE
  AND THAT ENQUIRING MAN JOHN SYNGE COMES NEXT, ...   324 ROBERT GREGORY   25
  THAT MEDITATIVE MAN, JOHN SYNGE, AND THOSE . . . . . .   489 COOLE PARK 29   13
  "GREATEST SINCE REMBRANDT," ACCORDING TO JOHN SYNGE; . .   602 GALLERY REVIS   26
  JOHN SYNGE, I AND AUGUSTA GREGORY, THOUGHT . . . . . .   603 GALLERY REVIS   41
  AND HERE'S JOHN SYNGE HIMSELF, THAT ROOTED MAN, ...   603 GALLERY REVIS   48
  AND HERE'S JOHN SYNGE, A MEDITATIVE MAN, ...   603 GALLERY REVIS V   48
SYSTEM
  HAYNAU, THE MAN OF SYSTEM, LIFTS HIS HAND . . . . . .   712 FERENCZ RENYI   62
TABLE
  ABOUT MY TABLE TO AND FRO, ...   138 TO IRELAND   24
  FOR ROUND ABOUT MY TABLE GO . . . .   138 TO IRELAND V   23
  ABOUT MY TABLE TO AND FRO, ...   139 TO IRELAND   40
  BUT SHE TOOK UP HER FAN FROM THE TABLE . . . .   160 CAP AND BELLS   19
  BUT SHE TOOK HER FAN FROM THE TABLE, ...   160 CAP AND BELLS V   19
  SET CARPENTERS TO WORK ON NO WIDE TABLE, ...   340 SHEP GOATHERD   50
  NO TABLE OR CHAIR OR STOOL NOT SIMPLE ENOUGH . . . . .   371 ON GOING HOUSE   3
  ROSE FROM THE TABLE AND DECLARED IT RIGHT . . . . . .   410 TOWER   43
  MY TABLE . . . .   421 MY TABLE   T
  BUBBLE UPON THE TABLE. A GHOST MAY COME; . . . . . .   470 ALL SOUL NIGHT   5
  THAT TABLE AND THE TALK OF YOUTH, ...   475 EVA GORE-BOOTH   18
  AUGUSTA GREGORY SEATED AT HER GREAT ORMOLU TABLE, . . .   577 LOFTY THINGS   7
  I TOLD HIM THAT NIGHTLY FROM SIX TO SEVEN I SAT AT THIS TABLE,   578 LOFTY THINGS   9
  AT TABLE OR IN BED. . . . .   620 JOHN KINSELLA   10
  NO OSCAR RULED THE TABLE, ...   626 STATES HOLIDAY   5
TABLES
  STANDISH O'GRADY SUPPORTING HIMSELF BETWEEN THE TABLES . .   577 LOFTY THINGS   5
  BY TABLES THAT WERE FALLEN INTO DUST . . . .   724 KANVA ON SELF   13
TABLET
  FOR THINGS BELOW ARE COPIES, THE GREAT SMARAGDINE TABLET SAID.   556 RIBH PATRICK   6
TABLE-TOP
  ON THE MARBLE TABLE-TOP. . . . .   501 VACILLATION   39
TABLETS
  THEY WROTE ON TABLETS OF THIN BOARD, ...   197 BAILE AILLINN   195
  AND TOOK THEIR TABLETS AND DID SUMS; . . . .   344 DAWN   9
  AND TOOK THEIR TABLETS AND MADE SUMS-- . . . .   344 DAWN   V 9
TABORS
  FROM MARBLE CITIES LOUD WITH TABORS OF OLD . . . . . .   162 ASKS FORGIVE   9
TAFFRAIL
  AND THE GHASTLY GHOST-FLAMES GLIMMER ALL ALONG THE TAFFRAIL RAILS   719 PHANTOM SHIP   21
TAFFREL
  AND THE GHASTLY GHOST FLAMES GLIMMER ALONG THE TAFFREL RAILS,   719 PHANTOM SHIP   V 21
TAIL   SEE FISH-TAIL
  HIS LANGUID TAIL ABOVE US, LIT WITH MYRIAD SPOTS OF LIGHT.   77 INDIAN ON GOD   20

TAIL   (CONTINUED)
    WITH A FISH TAIL, AND TALK . . . .   215 HAPPY TOWNLAND V   46
    ONE LASHED HER TAIL, HER EYES LIT BY THE MOON . . . . .   383 VISION ROBART   29
    AS TO A DOG'S TAIL? NEVER HAD I MORE . . . .   409 TOWER   4
    AS UPON A DOG'S TAIL. NEVER HAD I MORE . . . . . .   409 TOWER   V   4
TAILS   SEE CAT-O'-NINE-TAILS SERPENT-TAILS
TAKE
    SHE BID ME TAKE LOVE EASY, AS THE LEAVES GROW ON THE TREE!   90 SALLEY GARDENS   3
    SHE BID ME TAKE LIFE EASY, AS THE GRASS GROWS ON THE WEIRS!   90 SALLEY GARDENS   7
    SHE BID ME TAKE LOVE EASY, AS THE LEAVES GROW ON THE TREES!   90 SALLEY GARDENS V   3
    THAT CARRIED THE TAKE TO SLIGO TOWN TO BE SOLD,   91 OLD FISHERMAN   7
    AND NOW AT LAST YOU TAKE ON HUMAN SHAPE-- . . . . . .   102 FERGUS DRUID   V   6
    TAKE, IF YOU MUST, THIS LITTLE BAG OF DREAMS! . . . .   104 FERGUS DRUID   29
    TAKE THEN THIS SMALL SLATE-COLOURED BAG OF DREAMS! . .   104 FERGUS DRUID   V   29
    AND NODDING BY THE FIRE, TAKE DOWN THIS BOOK, ...   120 YOU ARE OLD   2
    AND KISS HER LIPS AND TAKE HER HANDS! . . . .   150 WANDER AENGUS   20
    AND KISS HER LIPS AND TAKE HER HAND, ...   150 WANDER AENGUS V   20
    I KNOW OF THE LEAFY PATHS THAT THE WITCHES TAKE . . .   203 WITHER BOUGHS   9
    I KNOW OF THE LEAFY PATH THAT THE WITCHES TAKE, . . .   203 WITHER BOUGHS V   9
    I SAID: "A LINE WILL TAKE US HOURS MAYBE! . . . . .   204 ADAMS CURSE   4
    TO TAKE HIM WHILE HE SLEEPS AND CARRY HIM . . . . .   222 SHADOW WATER B   14
    AND TAKE THE CAPTAIN'S SHARE OF EVERYTHING . . . . .   225 SHADOW WATER B   73
    THEY TAKE A KISS FOR WHAT A KISS IS WORTH, ...   229 SHADOW WATER B   157
    AND PAID YOU ON THE NAIL. TAKE UP THAT ROPE . . . .   232 SHADOW WATER B   224
    AND DID THOSE WATCHERS BID YOU TAKE ME CAPTIVE? . . .   236 SHADOW WATER B   322
    THAT NONE MIGHT TAKE YOU FROM ME. FOR A MOMENT . . .   237 SHADOW WATER B   330
    THERE IS NONE TO TAKE HIS SIDE. I AM ON HIS SIDE.   239 SHADOW WATER B   364
    I'LL DO IT FOR HIS SAKE. NO. TAKE THIS SWORD . . .   250 SHADOW WATER B   591
    WHAT COULD I BUT TAKE UP THE SONG? . . . .   254 HIS DREAM   14
    BUT THERE IT'S GONE! I WILL NOT TAKE . . . .   274 GREY ROCK   92
    BUT WHEN HE THOUGHT TO TAKE HER IN HIS ARMS . . . .   280 TWO KINGS   67
    AND TAKE HER IN THE MIDDLE OF ARMED MEN, ...   282 TWO KINGS   114
    BE SECRET AND TAKE DEFEAT . . . .   290 TO A FRIEND   2
    AND MAYBE I SHALL TAKE A TROUT . . . .   297 THREE BEGGARS   67
    TO TAKE MY FANCY LIKE THE WIND . . . .   301 RUN PARADISE   26
    AND SO TAKE THAT AND THAT." THEREON . . . .   307 HOUR DAWN   112
    O YOU WILL TAKE WHATEVER'S OFFERED . . . .   313 TWO YEAR LATER   7
    SONG, LET THEM TAKE IT, ...   320 COAT   8
    AS OTHERS WILL, WHEN FIRST THEY TAKE POSSESSION, . .   341 SHEP GOATHERD   52
    WE TAKE IT FOR THE NORM! YET SHOULD I DREAM . . . .   371 ON GOING HOUSE   9
    AND WHEN YOU HAVE SPOKEN TAKE THE ROADS AGAIN? . . .   373 PHASES OF MOON   25
    THAT IT CAN TAKE WHAT FORM COOK NATURE FANCIES . . .   377 PHASES OF MOON   115
    BUT TAKE ME FOR SOME DRUNKEN COUNTRYMAN! . . . . .   377 PHASES OF MOON   130
    THAT IT CAN TAKE WHAT FORM COOK NATURE FANCY . . . .   377 PHASES OF MOON V   115
    BUT TAKE ME FOR SOME DRUNKEN COUNTRY MAN! . . . . .   377 PHASES OF MOON V   130
    TO TAKE THE ROSES FOR HIS MEAT. . . . .   382 SONG OF FOOL   12
    AND MAY THE DEVIL TAKE THE REST. . . . .   386 ROBARTES DANCE   24
    BUT WHO CAN TALK OF GIVE AND TAKE, ...   395 SIXTEEN DEAD   3
    OR MEDDLE WITH OUR GIVE AND TAKE . . . .   395 SIXTEEN DEAD   17
    TO WATCH A WHITE GULL TAKE . . . .   400 DEMON BEAST   24
    FROM A GLAD KINDNESS CANNOT TAKE HIS EYES. . . . . .   404 FOR ANNE   40
    ONCE OUT OF NATURE I SHALL NEVER TAKE . . . .   408 SAIL BYZANTIUM   25
    BUT TAKE OUR GREATNESS WITH OUR VIOLENCE? . . . . .   418 ANCEST HOUSES   32
    BUT TAKE OUR GREATNESS WITH OUR BITTERNESS? . . . .   418 ANCEST HOUSES   40
    THE WOMEN TAKE SO LITTLE STOCK . . . .   455 HIS MEMORIES   7
    AND DID SUCH PLEASURE TAKE-- . . . .   455 HIS MEMORIES   14
    TAKE THIS LIGHT PARCHMENT, PASS THROUGH THE GREAT CHAMBER   461 HARUN RASHID   V   5
    HERE, TRAVELLER, SCHOLAR, POET, TAKE YOUR STAND . .   489 COOLE PARK 29   25
    AND IF IT TAKE THE SECOND MUST REFUSE . . . .   491 COOLE BALLYLEE V   40C
    AND IF IT TAKE THE SECOND MUST REFUSE . . . .   495 CHOICE   3
    THAT CANNOT TAKE THE WHOLE . . . .   510 JANE JUDGMENT   3
    "TAKE THE SOUR . . . .   510 JANE JUDGMENT   6
    IF YOU TAKE ME, ...   510 JANE JUDGMENT   7
    HOWEVER THEY MAY TAKE IT, ...   520 HIS BARGAIN   7
    BY SOME NEW-MARRIED BRIDE, I TAKE . . . .   535 CHOSEN   13
    BY SOME NEW MARRIED BRIDE I TAKE . . . .   535 CHOSEN   V   13
    AND GIVE HIS OWN AND TAKE HIS OWN . . . .   538 LAST CONFESS   19
    SOLDIERS TAKE PRIDE IN SALUTING THEIR CAPTAIN, . . .   547 TO SAME TUNE 3 V   1
    SOME TAKE DELIGHT IN ADORNING A WOMAN. . . . . . .   547 TO SAME TUNE 3 V   3
    TAKE TO THE ROADS AND GO MARCHING ALONG. . . . . .   548 TO SAME TUNE 3   14
    SOLDIERS TAKE PRIDE IN SALUTING THEIR CAPTAIN, . . .   548 TO SAME TUNE 3   21
    WHAT CAN SHE TAKE UNTIL HER MASTER GIVE! . . . . .   558 RIBH CHRISTIAN   21
    HE BADE THEM TAKE AND BURY HER . . . .   571 THREE BUSHES   71
    WHETHER THEY TAKE THE UPPER ROAD . . . .   589 OLD WICKED MAN   48
    "TAKE ALL TO YOUR MISTRESS!" . . . .   595 COLONEL MARTIN   34
    SO WHEN I TAKE ON HALF A SCORE . . . .   605 SONGS BURDEN 1   7
    THAT PATCHING OLD HEELS THEY MAY SHRIEK, I TAKE TO CHISEL   623 HIGH TALK   8
        AND PLANE.
    THE NIGHEST BLOSSOM WHERE IT FALLS I'LL TAKE. . . .   657 ISLE STAT I 3   65
    OH! GRACIOUS PAN, TAKE NOW THY SERVANT'S PART. . .   657 ISLE STAT I 3   77
    DID HER LONELY WATCHING TAKE . . . .   658 ISLE STAT I 3   94
    NO MORE! TAKE ME INSTEAD OF HER, GREAT SIRS. . . .   695 MOSADA 1   114
    BEFORE WE TAKE OUR SEATS ABOVE THE CROWD. . . . .   704 MOSADA 3   134
    SHE WOULD WEAVE A NET TO TAKE US. SHE MIGHT KEEP FAITH!   756 SHADOW WATER A   190
    THE GODS WEAVE NETS, AND TAKE US IN THEIR NETS, . .   764 SHADOW WATER A   339
    AND LETS THE KIND WORM TAKE THE LOT! . . . .   779 ACCURSED WHO   4
    WHY SHOULD THE HEART TAKE FRIGHT? . . . .   781 HEART FRIGHT   1
    BADE THAT SWORDSMAN TAKE . . . .   789 SINGING HEAD   4
    NOR LAW NOR PARLIAMENT TAKE HEED. . . . .   791 REPRISALS   22
TAKEN
    "BUT TILL THE MOON HAS TAKEN ALL, I WAGE . . . . .   45 OISIN 2   240

TAKEN   (CONTINUED)

TILL THE MOON HAS TAKEN FLIGHT; . . . .   87 STOLEN CHILD   19
NOW THAT THE EARTH HAD TAKEN MAN AND ALL; . . . . . .   128 DREAM OF FAERY   40
NOW THAT OLD EARTH HAD TAKEN MAN AND ALL; . . . . . .   128 DREAM OF FAERY V   40
YOU HAVE TAKEN PAY AND MADE YOUR BARGAIN FOR IT. . . .   225 SHADOW WATER B   68
SILENCE; FOR YOU HAVE TAKEN FORGAEL'S PAY. . . . . . .   225 SHADOW WATER B V   68
BOTH YOU AND I ARE TAKEN IN THE NET. . . . .   237 SHADOW WATER B   323
IF YOU HAD TAKEN ME BY MAGIC SPELLS, ...   245 SHADOW WATER B   490
BUT NOW THAT THEY HAVE TAKEN TO THE ROAD . . . . . .   247 SHADOW WATER B   526
O SILVER FISH THAT MY TWO HANDS HAVE TAKEN . . . . .   251 SHADOW WATER B   609
HAS TAKEN A NEW PHASE. . . . .   379 CAT AND MOON   20
ROBBERS HAD TAKEN HIS OLD TAMBOURINE, ...   616 MARCH SONGS 3   7
ROBBERS HAD TAKEN HIS OLD TAMBOURINE, ...   616 MARCH SONGS 3   10
ROBBERS HAD TAKEN HIS OLD TAMBOURINE, ...   616 MARCH SONGS 3   17
ROBBERS HAD TAKEN HIS OLD TAMBOURINE, ...   616 MARCH SONGS 3   20
ROBBERS HAD TAKEN HIS OLD TAMBOURINE, ...   616 MARCH SONGS 3   27
ROBBERS HAD TAKEN HIS OLD TAMBOURINE, ...   616 MARCH SONGS 3   30
TAKEN IN MAGIC, IN THE CHURCH'S NAME . . . .   694 MOSADA 1   104
BELIEVE THAT GOLD AND WOMEN TAKEN IN WAR . . . . . .   754 SHADOW WATER A   159
O SILVER FISH THAT MY TWO HANDS HAVE TAKEN . . . . .   769 SHADOW WATER A   425

TAKES

ATHENE TAKES ACHILLES BY THE HAIR, ...   374 PHASES OF MOON   45
AMONG TASKS NOT IMPOSSIBLE, IT TAKES . . . .   376 PHASES OF MOON   92
NO MATTER WHAT HAPPENS AND WHO TAKES THE FALL, . . .   545 TO SAME TUNE 1   22
NO MATTER WHAT HAPPENS OR WHO TAKES THE FALL, ...   545 TO SAME TUNE 1 V   22
THE SOLDIER TAKES PRIDE . . . .   547 TO SAME TUNE 3 V   T
THE SOLDIER TAKES PRIDE IN SALUTING HIS CAPTAIN, . . .   547 TO SAME TUNE 3   1
HE TAKES THE DEVIL'S PAY. . . . .   582 ROGER CASEMENT V   20
AND TAKES YOU BY THE THROAT; . . . .   598 STONE CROSS   4
THE SOLDIER TAKES PRIDE IN SALUTING HIS CAPTAIN, . . .   614 MARCH SONGS 2   1
NO MATTER WHAT HAPPENS AND WHO TAKES THE FALL, . . .   616 MARCH SONGS 3   22
FOR DEATH WHO TAKES WHAT MAN WOULD KEEP, ...   620 JOHN KINSELLA   3

TAKING   SEE LEAVE-TAKING

TAKING THE MORTAL WARRIORS BY THE HANDS; . . . . . .   29 OISIN 2   V 10B
HE KNOWS THAT HE IS TAKING YOU TO DEATH; . . . . . .   249 SHADOW WATER B   562
TAKING DELIGHT THAT HE COULD SPRING; . . . .   317 APPOINTMENT   4
THERE IS NO LEAVE TAKING. I GO NO MORE. . . . . . .   702 MOSADA 3   V 100

TALE

BUT THE TALE, THOUGH WORDS BE LIGHTER THAN AIR, . . .   3 OISIN 1   11
AND MY OWN TALE AGAIN FOR ME SHALL SING, ...   68 SAD SHEPHERD   22
AND MINE OWN TALE AGAIN FOR ME SHALL SING, ...   68 SAD SHEPHERD   V   22
HIS SUDDEN VENGEANCE WERE A COUNTRY TALE, ...   127 DREAM OF FAERY   27
THE TALE DROVE HIS FINE ANGRY MOOD AWAY. . . . . . .   128 DREAM OF FAERY   36
AS IF THERE WERE NO TALE BUT YOUR OWN TALE . . . . .   181 QUEEN MAEVE   32
AS IF THERE WERE NO TALE BUT YOUR OWN TALE . . . . .   181 QUEEN MAEVE   32
THROUGH WICKED SPELLS. THAT IS NOT ALL THE TALE, . . .   242 SHADOW WATER B   408
TO HAVE LIT UPON AS CLEAN AND SWEET A TALE . . . . .   258 KING NO KING   8
BEFORE THE THREE TO END THIS TALE, ...   297 THREE BEGGARS   55
A WOMAN SPOKE OF SOME NEW TALE SHE HAD READ, ...   350 HER PRAISE   7
HER SPEECH A WICKED TALE THAT WE MAY VIE WITH HER, . .   362 HER COURTESY   6
HE HAD LEARNT FROM PATER, AND TO ROUND HIS TALE . . .   373 PHASES OF MOON   27
OF A MOCKING TALE OR A GIBE . . . .   392 EASTER 1916   10
ABOVE A SINKING FIRE, A TALE THAT SHE . . . .   443 SCHOOL CHILDR   10
ABOVE A SINKING FIRE, SOME TALE THAT SHE . . . . . .   443 SCHOOL CHILDR V   10
MARK AND DIGEST MY TALE, CARRY IT AFAR . . . .   554 RIBH AT TOMB   3
ALL KNOW THEIR TALE, ALL KNOW WHAT LEAF AND TWIG, . .   555 RIBH AT TOMB   7
HAZEL LAVERY LIVING AND DYING, THAT TALE . . . . . .   602 GALLERY REVIS   23
BY MANY SOUGHT, AND 'TIS A FOREST TALE. . . . . . .   653 ISLE STAT I 2   40
AND LET THE TALE BE MOURNFUL EACH ONE TELLS. . . . .   663 ISLE STAT II 2   36
WILL WONDERING LISTEN, AND THIS TALE SHALL EASE . . .   693 MOSADA 1   70
THAT SONG I'VE MADE. 'TIS OF AN IRISH TALE. . . . .   696 MOSADA 2   19
THAT SONG I'VE MADE--IS OF A RUSSIAN TALE . . . . .   696 MOSADA 2   V   19
OH, I AM WEARY OF THAT FOOLISH TALE. . . . .   721 WITCH VIVIEN   33
AND WHEN THEY HEARD THAT TALE OF HIS . . . .   730 PRIEST FAIRY   65
BELOVED; HEAR MY BITTER TALE!-- . . . .   742 DANAAN QUICK   1
AND WE GO HOME. COME, AIBRIC; END YOUR TALE . . . .   766 SHADOW WATER A   374

TALE'S

BUT WHEN, IF THE TALE'S TRUE, ...   346 ON WOMAN   29

TALES   SEE LOVE-TALES

MOVED ROUND ME, OF SEAMEN OR LANDSMEN, ALL WHO ARE WINTER 53 OISIN 3   86
    TALES;
DEDICATION OF "IRISH TALES" . . . .   129 BOOK STORIES   V   T
AND SPOKEN IN THE COUNCIL, AND HEARD TALES . . . . .   748 SHADOW WATER A   28

TALK

THAT WE MAY MUSE IN THE STARLIGHT AND TALK OF THE BATTLES   51 OISIN 3   63
    OF OLD;
I PASSED A LITTLE FURTHER ON AND HEARD A LOTUS TALK; . .   76 INDIAN ON GOD   9
I PACED A LITTLE FURTHER ON AND HEARD A LOTUS TALK;-- . . 76 INDIAN ON GOD V   9
A THOUSAND YEARS AGO YOU HELD HIGH TALK . . . . . .   187 QUEEN MAEVE   150
ALTHOUGH THEY DO NOT TALK OF IT AT SCHOOL-- . . . . .   205 ADAMS CURSE   19
I HEAR THE HARP-STRING PRAISE THEM, OR HEAR THEIR MOURNFUL 210 UNDER THE MOON   16
    TALK.
I HEAR THE HARP STRINGS PRAISE THEM, OR HEAR THEIR MOURNFUL 210 UNDER THE MOON V   16
    TALK.
I HEAR THE HARPSTRING PRAISE THEM OR HEAR THEIR MOURNFUL 210 UNDER THE MOON V   16
    TALK.
I HEAR THE HARP STRING PRAISE THEM OR HEAR THEIR MOURNFUL 210 UNDER THE MOON V   16
    TALK.
WITH A FISH-TAIL, AND TALK . . . .   215 HAPPY TOWNLAND   46
WITH A FISH TAIL, AND TALK . . . .   215 HAPPY TOWNLAND V   46
AND YET YOU TALK OF LOVE. THE MOVEMENT OF TIME . . .   237 SHADOW WATER B   338

		PAGE	TITLE	LINE
TALK	(CONTINUED)			
"AND I WILL TALK BEFORE I SLEEP		304	HOUR DAWN	44
AND DRINK BEFORE I TALK." AND HE		304	HOUR DAWN	45
AND THOUGH I HAVE TURNED THE TALK BY HOOK OR CROOK		350	HER PRAISE	5
I WILL TALK NO MORE OF BOOKS OR THE LONG WAR		351	HER PRAISE	11
MANAGE THE TALK UNTIL HER NAME COME ROUND		351	HER PRAISE	14
MANAGE TO TALK UNTIL HER NAME COME ROUND.		351	HER PRAISE V	14
AND WHO CAN SAY BUT SOME YOUNG BELLE MAY WALK AND TALK MEN WILD		354	HIS PHOENIX	26
IN RAMBLING TALK WITH AN IMAGE OF AIR!		357	BROKEN DREAMS	40
BUT WHO CAN TALK OF GIVE AND TAKE,		395	SIXTEEN DEAD	3
THAT HE, ALTHOUGH A COUNTRY'S TALK		422	MY TABLE	29
THAT TABLE AND THE TALK OF YOUTH,		475	EVA GORE-BOOTH	18
AND GATHER ALL THE TALK?		499	MOTHER OF GOD	10
MUCH I TALK, MORE I WALK!		548	TO SAME TUNE 3	9
MUCH I TALK, MORE I WALK!		548	TO SAME TUNE 3	19
MUCH I TALK, MORE I WALK!		549	TO SAME TUNE 3	29
ALL NEIGHBOURLY CONTENT AND EASY TALK ARE GONE,		580	CURSE CROMWELL	9
AMONG THE DOGS AND HORSES THAT UNDERSTAND MY TALK.		581	CURSE CROMWELL	30
BAWDY TALK FOR THE FISHERMEN!		588	OLD WICKED MAN	32
MEMORIES OF THE TALK		607	SONGS BURDEN 2	22
HIGH TALK		622	HIGH TALK	T
THAT KNOWING BETTER TALK HAD GONE		627	STATES HOLIDAY	7
I COULD NOT GO. LET'S TALK, AND LET'S BE SAD,		651	ISLE STAT I 2	7
SHALL SEE A THING TO TALK ON WHEN YOU'RE OLD,		693	MOSADA 1	67
AND HEAVEN, AND HOLINESS. LET'S TALK AND GRIEVE,		702	MOSADA 3	84
TALKED				
THAT TALKED OF LOVE OR POLITICS,		131	OLD PENSIONER	5
TO SOME I HAVE TALKED WITH BY THE FIRE		136	TO SOME I TALK	T
AND TALKED OF THE DARK FOLK WHO LIVE IN SOULS		136	TO SOME I TALK	4
TO THOSE WITH WHOM I HAVE TALKED MANY TIMES,		136	TO SOME I TALK V	2
IT TALKED, ERE THE MORN GREW WHITE.		159	CAP AND BELLS V	6
IT TALKED BEFORE MORN WAS WHITE,		159	CAP AND BELLS V	6
TALKED OF HIS COUNTRY AND ITS PEOPLE, SANG		180	QUEEN MAEVE	3
AND YOU AND I, AND TALKED OF POETRY.		204	ADAMS CURSE	3
AND HAVING TALKED TO SOME LATE HOUR		324	ROBERT GREGORY	4
WE HAVE TALKED IN THE ONE PLACE,		332	SOLOMON SHEBA	4
THAT YOU HAVE TALKED WITH APPARITIONS. INDEED		342	SHEP GOATHERD	82
TO WHERE THE DUCHESS AND HER PEOPLE TALKED		352	PEOPLE	13
O BUT WE TALKED AT LARGE BEFORE		395	SIXTEEN DEAD	1
TALKED OF HONOUR AND OF TRUTH,		431	NINETEEN 19	90
AND TALKED AWAY THE NIGHT,		456	SUMMER SPRING	2
AND WHEN WE TALKED OF GROWING UP		456	SUMMER SPRING	5
MY GREAT-GRANDFATHER'S FATHER TALKED OF MUSIC,		486	SEVEN SAGES	4
MY GREAT-GRANDFATHER'S FATHER TALKED OF MUSIC AND PAINTING,		486	SEVEN SAGES V	4
HER BARGAIN STRUCK WE LAUGHED AND TALKED		620	JOHN KINSELLA	15
I TALKED ABOUT AN APPARITION.		624	APPARITIONS	2
TALKED OF ODDS AND ENDS.		627	STATES HOLIDAY	8
O'ER MUCH I'VE TALKED! I SHALL BE SILENT SOON,		657	ISLE STAT I 3	75
WE'VE TALKED AND TALKED! AND NOT A WHIT MORE RARE		659	ISLE STAT II 1	21
WE'VE TALKED AND TALKED! AND NOT A WHIT MORE RARE		659	ISLE STAT II 1	21
TALKING				
AND I WILL HEAR THEM TALKING IN A MINUTE.		233	SHADOW WATER B	250
WHILE TALKING WITH HIS QUEENS,		345	ON WOMAN	12
A YOUNG MAN WHEN THE OLD MEN ARE DONE TALKING		356	BROKEN DREAMS	16
BY AN OLD HUNTER TALKING WITH GODS!		605	YOU CONTENT	23
THE WHOLE WORLD'S SADLY TALKING TO ITSELF.		652	ISLE STAT I 2	12
THE TALKING WINDS HAVE FOUND THEIR HOME,		686	LIFE	9
FOR LONG THE BURTHEN OF THEIR TALKING GRIEFS,		693	MOSADA 1	71
HER DREAMS ARE TALKING WITH OLD YEARS. AWAKE,		702	MOSADA 3	89
MURMURS OF HER CHILDREN TALKING—		705	DAWN-SONG	6
THERE WAS SOME TALKING OF THE POOR—		725	LEGEND	14
THERE WAS SOME TALKING OF MAN'S GOD,		725	LEGEND	19
TALKING HOURS SWIFTLY PASS!		727	LOVERS QUARREL	44
FOR ALL OUR TALKING.		785	YOUR HEART	7
TALKS				
CRAZY JANE TALKS WITH THE BISHOP		513	JANE TALK BISH	T
WHO TALKS OF PLATO'S SPINDLE!		520	HIS BARGAIN	1
WHAT HE TALKS ABOUT.		631	POLITICS	6
TALL				
CAME BLANAID, MAC NESSA, TALL FERGUS WHO FEASTWARD OF OLD TIME SLUNK,		53	OISIN 3	89
YON TALL ONE EYES MY SUPPER! CHASE HIM AWAY,		72	ANASHU VIJAYA	34
YON TALL ONE EYES MY SUPPER! SWIFTLY CHASE HIM		72	ANASHU VIJAYA V	34
TALL WANDS OF ALDER AND WHITE QUICKEN WANDS.		111	CUCHULAIN SEA V	82A
THE TALL THOUGHT-WOVEN SAILS, THAT FLAP UNFURLED		113	ROSE OF BATTLE	2
FROM THE TALL AND THE TUFTED REEDS		143	HOST OF AIR	3
TALL, PROUD AND RUDDY, AND LIGHT WINGS		195	BAILE AILLINN	140
TALL AND NOBLE BUT WITH FACE AND BOSOM		199	ARROW	5
BUT PURER THAN A TALL CANDLE BEFORE THE HOLY ROOD		208	HANRAHANS SONG	14
BUT PURE AS A TALL CANDLE BEFORE THE TRINITY		208	HANRAHANS SONG V	14
BUT PURER THAN A TALL CANDLE BEFORE THE BLESSED ROOD		208	HANRAHANS SONG V	14
FOR THERE THE TALL DEER AND HIS LEMAN SIGH		210	RAGGED WOOD V	2
FOR THERE THE TALL DEER AND HIS LEMAN CRY		211	RAGGED WOOD V	6
AND THE TALL MEN AND THE SWORDSMEN AND THE HORSEMEN, WHERE ARE THEY?		580	CURSE CROMWELL	4
TALL PYTHAGORAS.		611	NEWS ORACLE	8
TALL DAMES GO WALKING IN GRASS-GREEN AVALON.		627	STATES HOLIDAY	13
TALL DAMES GO WALKING IN GRASS-GREEN AVALON.		627	STATES HOLIDAY	26
TALL DAMES GO WALKING IN GRASS-GREEN AVALON.		627	STATES HOLIDAY	39
TALL DAMES GO WALKING IN GRASS GREEN AVALON.		627	STATES HOLIDAY V	REF

		PAGE	TITLE		LINE

TALL   (CONTINUED)
THAT MAIDEN BRING THEY. WHEN THE TALL RED DEER . . . . . 713 FERENCZ RENYI   79
OF THEIR TALL, NEW-FANGLED QUEEN. . . . . 727 LOVERS QUARREL   48
HIS MEMORY NOW IS A TALL PILLAR, BURNING . . . . . . 738 MOURN THEN ON   15
TALLER
BUT THE TREES GREW TALLER AND CLOSER, ... 48 OISIN 3   17
BUT TALLER THE TREES GREW AND CLOSER, ... 48 OISIN 3   V   17
"BUT YOU HAVE GROWN TO BE THE TALLER MAN." . . . . . 107 CUCHULAIN SEA   27
"NAY, YOU ARE TALLER THAN CUCHULAIN, SON." . . . . . 107 CUCHULAIN SEA   V   27
HE WILL BE TALLER NOW--'TWAS LONG AGO. . . . . 699 MOSADA 3   15
TALMA
TALMA AND HIS THUNDERBOLT. . . . . 625 NATIVITY   10
TAMBOURINE
ON AN OLD TAMBOURINE. . . . . 613 MARCH SONGS 1   16
ROBBERS HAD TAKEN HIS OLD TAMBOURINE, ... 616 MARCH SONGS 3   7
ROBBERS HAD TAKEN HIS OLD TAMBOURINE. . . . . 616 MARCH SONGS 3   10
ROBBERS HAD TAKEN HIS OLD TAMBOURINE, ... 616 MARCH SONGS 3   17
ROBBERS HAD TAKEN HIS OLD TAMBOURINE, ... 616 MARCH SONGS 3   20
ROBBERS HAD TAKEN HIS OLD TAMBOURINE, ... 616 MARCH SONGS 3   27
ROBBERS HAD TAKEN HIS OLD TAMBOURINE. . . . . 616 MARCH SONGS 3   30
TAME
NOR THE TAME WILL, NOR TIMID BRAIN, ... 318 APPOINTMENT   8
A SPECKLED CAT AND A TAME HARE . . . . 380 SONGS FOOL 1   1
TANGLED
AND TANGLED CREEPERS EVERY HOUR . . . . 16 OISIN 1   223
THE TANGLED THOUGHTS OF THE FINISHED DAY . . . . . . 728 PRIEST FAIRY   9
TANGLING
WHERE TANGLING CREEPERS EVERY HOUR . . . . 16 OISIN 1   V   223
TAP
I SAW A STRANGER TAP AND WAIT . . . . 696 MOSADA 2   22
TAPER
THE EVERLASTING TAPER LIGHTS THE GLOOM; . . . . . . 311 MOUNTAIN TOMB   10
TAPERS
A LADY WITH SOFT EYES LIKE FUNERAL TAPERS, ... 33 OISIN 2   69
DOWN ON US WITH HER EYES LIKE FUNERAL TAPERS, ... 33 OISIN 2   V   69
A MAIDEN WITH SOFT EYES LIKE FUNERAL TAPERS, ... 33 OISIN 2   V   69
HAVE LIT LONE TAPERS. NOW THE NIGHT WAS CAST, ... 687 TWO TITANS   27
TAPPING
"CHOOSE!" RESTLESS HAYNAU'S FINGERS TAPPING GO. . . . 711 FERENCZ RENYI   41
TARA
TARA UPROOTED, AND NEW COMMONNESS . . . . 198 SEVEN WOODS   6
WESTWARD OF TARA. HURRYING TO HIS QUEEN . . . . . . 276 TWO KINGS   2
WESTWARD OF TARA. WHERE IN THE MIDDLE WOOD . . . . . 277 TWO KINGS   V   4
TOWARD PEOPLED TARA, NOR STOOD TO DRAW HIS BREATH . . . 279 TWO KINGS   46
ON PEOPLED TARA, NOR STOOD TO DRAW HIS BREATH . . . . 279 TWO KINGS   V   46
TOWARDS PEOPLED TARA, NOR STOOD TO DRAW HIS BREATH . . 279 TWO KINGS   V   46
WESTWARD OF TARA, AMONG THE HAZEL-TREES-- . . . . . . 283 TWO KINGS   135
WESTWARD OF TARA, AMONG THE HAZEL TREES-- . . . . . . 283 TWO KINGS   V   135
WESTWARD OF TARA, THERE TO AWAIT A FRIEND . . . . . . 283 TWO KINGS   V   136
CROW UPON TARA." KING EOCHAID BOWED HIS HEAD . . . . 286 TWO KINGS   211
CROW UPON TARA." SHE HAD FIXED HER EYES . . . . . . 286 TWO KINGS   V   211
TARA'S
IN TARA'S HALLS . . . . 609 IN TARAS HALLS   T
A MAN I PRAISE THAT ONCE IN TARA'S HALLS . . . . . . 609 IN TARAS HALLS   1
TARAV   SEE PAIRC-NA-TARAV
TARDY
FIERCE THRUST! A TARDY BLOSSOM HAD THE SEED, ... 665 ISLE STAT II 2   65
TARGETED
TARGETED, TROD LIKE SPRING. . . . . 504 QUARREL IN AGE   16
TARN
OF THE TARN WHERE YOUNG WAVES QUICKEN . . . . 647 ISLE STAT I 1   48
TARPAULIN
LANDOR'S TARPAULIN ON THE ROOF. . . . . 625 NATIVITY   6
TAR-WATER
DRANK TAR-WATER WITH THE BISHOP OF CLOYNE. . . . . . 486 SEVEN SAGES   5
TASK
FORTH! FORTH! O SPIRITS, YE HAVE HEARD YOUR TASK! . . . 669 ISLE STAT II 3   81
TASK'S
CHOOSING WHATEVER TASK'S MOST DIFFICULT . . . . . . 376 PHASES OF MOON   91
TASKS
AMONG TASKS NOT IMPOSSIBLE, IT TAKES . . . . 376 PHASES OF MOON   92
TASTE
AND FIND THEIR LAUGHTER SWEETER TO THE TASTE . . . . 228 SHADOW WATER B   134
THE TIME FOR YOU TO TASTE OF THAT SALT BREATH . . . . 293 TO A SHADE   21
BREAD TASTE SOUR. . . . . 554 CHURCH STATE   12
NO TASTE HAVE I FOR SLUMBER 'NEATH AN OAK. . . . . . 721 WITCH VIVIEN   31
AND TASTE WITH ME THE FAERIES' MEAT. . . . . 743 DANAAN QUICK   26
HATRED MAY BE SWEET TO THE TASTE." . . . . 776 AGAINST WITCH   31
HATRED MAY BE SWEET IN THE TASTE." . . . . 776 AGAINST WITCH   V   31
TASTING
IS NO MORE THAN A WINE-CUP IN THE TASTING, ... 229 SHADOW WATER B   150
IS NO MORE THAN A WINE CUP IN THE TASTING, ... 229 SHADOW WATER B   V   150
TATTER
FOR EVERY TATTER IN ITS MORTAL DRESS, ... 407 SAIL BYZANTIUM   12
TATTERED
O TATTERED CLOUDS OF THE WORLD, CALL FROM THE HIGH CAIRN   207 HANRAHANS SONG   V   6
   OF MAIVE,
LIKE TATTERED CLOUDS OF THE WORLD, PASSIONS CALL AND OUR   207 HANRAHANS SONG   V   8
   HEARTS BEAT!
A TATTERED COAT UPON A STICK, UNLESS . . . . 407 SAIL BYZANTIUM   10
CAN, TATTERED, STILL PROTECT, FADED ADORN. . . . . . 477 SELF AND SOUL   16

797

```
                                                    PAGE    TITLE          LINE
TAUGHT      SEE STAR-TAUGHT RIGHT-TAUGHT
    HAVE TAUGHT TO IGNORANT MEN MOST VIOLENT WAYS,    . . . .   256 NO SECOND TROY       3
    NO RIGHT TAUGHT MAN DENIES. . . . . . . . . . .   590 OLD WICKED MAN V     58
    YET 'TIS NO SIN; MY FATHER TAUGHT IT ME.  . . .   692 MOSADA 1            50
    TAUGHT ME WISE MUSIC, AND GAVE ME THIS OLD HARP;  . . . .   750 SHADOW WATER A      76
TAUT
    AND WHAT COULD MAKE THEIR MUSCLES TAUT  . . . . . . .   295 THREE BEGGARS       17
TAVERN
    SINCE, TAVERN COMRADES, YOU HAVE DIED,  . . . . .   273 GREY ROCK           49
    NOW I AM IN THE TAVERN AND LEAN AGAINST THE WALL,  . . .   593 PILGRIM        V    21
TAWS
    I LAY ABOUT ME WITH THE TAWS  . . . . . . . . . .   379 SAINT HUNCH          8
    SOLIDER ARISTOTLE PLAYED THE TAWS  . . . . . . .   445 SCHOOL CHILDR       43
TAYLOR      SEE SHAWE-TAYLOR
    FROM CASTLE TAYLOR TO THE ROXBOROUGH SIDE  . . . . . .   326 ROBERT GREGORY      58
TE
    AND HAS NOT HEARD ABSOLVO TE. . . . . . . . . . .   656 ISLE STAT I 3       19
TEACH
    FROM NOTHING EVERY DAY, AND TEACH  . . . . . . .   436 FOR MY SON          18
    PREFERRED TO TEACH A SCHOOL . . . . . . . . . . .   472 ALL SOUL NIGHT      46
    THOU'LT TEACH ME LAUGHING, AND I'LL TEACH THEE PEACE,  . .   670 ISLE STAT II 3     101
    THOU'LT TEACH ME LAUGHING, AND I'LL TEACH THEE PEACE,  . .   670 ISLE STAT II 3     101
    WOULD HE TEACH ANY SIN?  GAZE IN THE CLOUD  . . . . .   692 MOSADA 1            58
TEACHERS
    INTO THEIR SHINING LIMBS--I'VE HAD GREAT TEACHERS.  . . .   231 SHADOW WATER B     195
    FOR HOLIEST TEACHERS OF HIS WILL,  . . . . . . .   736 IN CHURCH            7
TEAR
    AND BID ME STAY, WITH MANY A TEAR;  . . . . . . .    10 OISIN 1            113
    NOR TEAR THE FOEMEN FROM THEIR STEEDS. . . . . . . .    11 OISIN 1            128
    WE WILL TEAR OUT THE FLAMING STONES, AND BATTER THE GATEWAY    62 OISIN 3           209
        OF BRASS
    WE WILL TEAR OUT THE RED FLAMING STONES, . . . . . .    62 OISIN 3        V   209
    WE WILL TEAR THE RED FLAMING STONES OUT, . . . . . .    62 OISIN 3        V   209
    WITH ALL YOUR WHIRLING HAIR, AND DROP MANY AN AZURE TEAR.    73 ANASHU VIJAYA      46
    WITH ALL YOUR WHIRLING HAIR, AND DROP THROUGH SPACE AN       73 ANASHU VIJAYA  V   46
        AZURE TEAR.
    WITH ALL YOUR WHIRLING HAIR, AND DROP TEAR UPON AZURE TEAR.    73 ANASHU VIJAYA  V   46
    WITH ALL YOUR WHIRLING HAIR, AND DROP TEAR UPON AZURE TEAR.    73 ANASHU VIJAYA  V   46
    WITH ALL OUR WHIRLING HAIR, AND DROP MANY AN AZURE TEAR.    73 ANASHU VIJAYA  V   46
    WITH A KISS AND A TEAR ON THY DROOPING BROW. . . . . .    79 FALLING LEAVES       8
    FROM FERNS THAT DROP THEIR TEAR . . . . . . . .    88 STOLEN CHILD   V    36
    CAN NEVER TEAR THE LINNET FROM THE LEAF. . . . . .   405 FOR DAUGHTER        56
    AND TEAR THE HEART OUT OF HIS SIDE, . . . . . . .   437 SONGS PLAY 1         3
    I'D TEAR IT OFF AND THROW IT IN THE FIRE."  . . . .   462 HARUN RASHID        34
    WHAT MATTER?  HEAVE NO SIGH, LET NO TEAR DROP, . . . .   564 GYRES              11
    AND ON THAT CITY DROPPED A TEAR, . . . . . . . .   725 LEGEND             31
    SHE PRAYS FOR EVERY FALLING TEAR . . . . . . . .   735 IN CHURCH            3
    A PRAYER FOR EVERY FALLING TEAR  . . . . . . . .   736 IN CHURCH           15
    I FELT A SUDDEN TEAR START, . . . . . . . . . .   744 GLOVE CLOAK         10
TEAR-DROP
    BUT SOON A TEAR-DROP STARTED UP, . . . . . . . .   400 DEMON BEAST         21
TEARDROPS
    AND SHOWED THEIR EYES WITH TEARDROPS DIM, . . . . .    18 OISIN 1            256
TEARFUL
    UNTIL ONE CAME, A TEARFUL BOY; . . . . . . . . .    17 OISIN 1            237
    AND ONE CAME CLOSE, A TEARFUL BOY. . . . . . . .    17 OISIN 1        V   237
TEARING
    THE HORSES OF THE FENIANS--TEARING ASUNDER . . . . .    43 OISIN 2        V   210
TEARS
    BEFORE THIS DAY; FOR NOW THE FALL OF TEARS . . . . .    30 OISIN 2            18
    A HUNDRED SEASONS; FOR A SOUND OF TEARS . . . . .    30 OISIN 2        V   18
    AND TELL ME HOW MY KINDRED'S TEARS ARE WELLING, . . . .    33 OISIN 2        V   66
    CAME NOW THE SLIDING OF TEARS AND SWEEPING OF MIST-COLD     47 OISIN 3             7
        HAIR,
    CAME NOW THE SLIDING OF TEARS AND SWEEPING OF MIST-COLD     47 OISIN 3        V    7
        AIR,
    CAME NOW THE SLIDING OF TEARS AND SWEEPING OF MIST COLD     47 OISIN 3        V    7
        HAIR,
    CAME, AND MY FOREHEAD FELL LOW, AND MY TEARS LIKE BERRIES   57 OISIN 3           154
        FELL DOWN!
    AND MY TEARS WERE LARGER THAN BERRIES, AND I MURMURED,   59 OISIN 3           178
        . . .
    AND MY TEARS WERE LARGE LIKE TO BERRIES, AND I MURMURED,   59 OISIN 3        V   178
        . . .
    WHAT KNOW THE PILOTS OF THE STARS OF TEARS?  . . . . .    73 ANASHU VIJAYA      47
    THE PHANTOM, BEAUTY, IN A MIST OF TEARS; . . . . .    73 ANASHU VIJAYA      55
    FROM FERNS THAT DROP THEIR TEARS . . . . . . . .    88 STOLEN CHILD        36
    BUT I WAS YOUNG AND FOOLISH, AND NOW AM FULL OF TEARS. .    90 SALLEY GARDENS       8
    AND SEEMED THE GREATNESS OF THE WORLD IN TEARS, . . .   120 SORROW OF LOVE       6
    AND WITH YOU CAME THE WHOLE OF THE WORLD'S TEARS. . . .   120 SORROW OF LOVE V     6
    UNTIL HE FOUND, WITH LAUGHTER AND WITH TEARS, . . . .   170 SECRET ROSE         24
    BEFORE HIS EYES, HE HAS TEARS FOR NONE, . . . . .   192 BAILE AILLINN       82
    BUT LAUGHTER AND TEARS--LAUGHTER, LAUGHTER, AND TEARS!  .   235 SHADOW WATER B     298
    BUT LAUGHTER AND TEARS--LAUGHTER, LAUGHTER, AND TEARS!  .   235 SHADOW WATER B     298
    AND HAVING SAID IT, BURST IN TEARS. . . . . . .   273 GREY ROCK           48
    AND THESE IMMORTAL EYES SHED TEARS-- . . . . . .   275 GREY ROCK          100
    WE CANNOT PAY ITS TRIBUTE OF WILD TEARS. . . . . .   334 LIVING BEAUTY       10
    FOR ALL THEIR BROOM-STICKS AND THEIR TEARS, . . . .   343 DEJECTION            5
    THEIR ANGRY TEARS, ARE GONE. . . . . . . . . .   344 DEJECTION            6
    AND THEN I LAUGH TILL TEARS RUN DOWN . . . . . .   456 FRIENDS YOUTH       17
    LOVE HAS BLINDED HIM WITH TEARS! . . . . . . . .   612 NEWS ORACLE         28
```

798

TEARS   (CONTINUED)
WHAT TEARS DOWN A TREE THAT HAS NOTHING WITHIN IT? . . .   615 MARCH SONGS 2   23
WHAT TEARS DOWN A TREE HAS NOTHING WITHIN IT? . . . . .   615 MARCH SONGS 2 V   23
AND I CRIED TEARS DOWN. . . . .   628 JANE MOUNTAIN   22
WITH TEARS? I WEARY OF YE. THERE IS NONE . . . .   650 ISLE STAT I 1   142
A WHITE, DUMB THING OF TEARS, HERE LET IT STAND, ...   663 ISLE STAT II 2   21
ALL SWIM WITH TEARS. THE FAERY BOAT'S AT HAND! . . . .   663 ISLE STAT II 2   33
WHOSE INSOLENT EYES UNUSED TO TEARS WOULD WEEP. . . . . .   678 ISLE STAT II 3   302
NOW WHEREFORE HAST THOU TEARS INNUMEROUS? . . . .   723 KANVA ON SELF   1
AND TEARS OF FIRE FALL GENTLY IN THE DEW. . . . .   738 YOU ARE SAD   4
ON TEARS AND LAUGHTER! THEY HAVE LURED YOU HITHER . . .   757 SHADOW WATER A   207
I HAVE WET THIS BRAID OF HAIR WITH TEARS WHILE ASLEEP. . .   762 SHADOW WATER A   294
TEASE
COME AND TEASE THEM TILL THE DAY. . . . .   727 LOVERS QUARREL   36
TEASING
TEASING EVERY WILFUL MAID. . . . .   727 LOVERS QUARREL   28
TEETH
YOU ARE NOT ITS CORE. MY TEETH ARE IN THE WORLD, . . .   235 SHADOW WATER B   279
SANG THROUGH THEIR TEETH FROM NOON TO NOON! . . . . . .   296 THREE BEGGARS   41
GNASHING OF TEETH, DESPAIR! . . . .   346 ON WOMAN   39
AND CRY IN PLATO'S TEETH. . . . .   415 TOWER   147
ALL TEETH WERE DRAWN, ALL ANCIENT TRICKS UNLEARNED, . .   429 NINETEEN 19   17
WHERE WE WROUGHT THAT SHALL BREAK THE TEETH OF TIME. . .   435 NEW FACES   4
THOSE GREAT SEA-HORSES BARE THEIR TEETH AND LAUGH AT THE   623 HIGH TALK   14
   DAWN.
WITHIN HIS CLENCHED TEETH A SWORD. . . . .   673 ISLE STAT II 3   182
TELL
OISIN, TELL ME THE FAMOUS STORY . . . .   2 OISIN 1   V   1
NOW, PLEASANT MAIDEN, TELL TO ME . . . .   5 OISIN 1   V   43
TELL ON, NOR BOW THY HEATHEN CREST . . . .   11 OISIN 1   V 131A
FASTING AND PRAYERS. TELL ON. YES, YES, ...   24 OISIN 1   360
FASTING AND PRAYERS. TELL ON. AY, AY! . . . .   24 OISIN 1   V   360
AND TELL ME THAT YOU FOUND A MAN UNBID, ...   33 OISIN 2   67
"AND TELL THEM HOW I WEEP, UNTIL THEY WEEP! . . . . .   33 OISIN 2   V   63
AND TELL ME HOW MY KINDRED'S TEARS ARE WELLING, . . .   33 OISIN 2   V   66
AND TELL ME HOW YOU CAME TO ONE UNBID, ...   33 OISIN 2   V   67
AND TELL OF YOUR GOODLY HOUSEHOLD AND THE GOODLY WORKS   51 OISIN 3   62
   OF YOUR HANDS,
AND TO ITS LIPS THY STORY TELL, ...   66 HAPPY SHEPHERD   37
AND THOUGHT, I WILL MY HEAVY STORY TELL . . . .   68 SAD SHEPHERD   19
AND THOUGHT, "TO THIS WILL I MY STORY TELL? . . . . .   68 SAD SHEPHERD   V   19
"WHO BADE YOU TELL THESE THINGS UPON MY FLOOR?" . . .   106 CUCHULAIN SEA   V   17
"WHO BADE YOU TELL THESE THINGS?" AND THEN SHE CRIED . .   106 CUCHULAIN SEA   17
BUT TELL YOUR NAME AND LINEAGE TO HIM . . . .   108 CUCHULAIN SEA   36
BUT TELL ALONE YOUR NAME AND HOUSE TO HIM . . . . . .   108 CUCHULAIN SEA   V   36
AND WHITE STARS TELL YOUR PRAISE, ...   113 ROSE OF PEACE   10
TO THESE OLD NIGHT SHALL ALL HER MYSTERY TELL! . . . .   114 ROSE OF BATTLE   22
TELL US IT THEN! . . . .   116 FAERY SONG   12
TELL IT US THEN! . . . .   116 FAERY SONG   V   12
MY RHYMES MORE THAN THEIR RHYMING TELL . . . .   138 TO IRELAND   20
HAVE I NOT BID YOU TELL OF THAT GREAT QUEEN . . . . .   181 QUEEN MAEVE   34
OUTRUN THE MEASURE. I'D TELL OF THAT GREAT QUEEN . .   187 QUEEN MAEVE   141
TO TELL HIM HOW THE GIRL AILLINN . . . .   191 BAILE AILLINN   49
THE CRAZY HERDSMAN THAT WILL TELL HIS FELLOWS . . . .   229 SHADOW WATER B   167
AND TELL ME WHO IT IS THAT WE ARE WAKING. . . . . . .   241 SHADOW WATER B   403
TO TELL THEM A PLAIN STORY. THAT'S NOT THE STORY! . .   245 SHADOW WATER B   482
WILL SAY TO AN OLD MAN, "TELL ME OF THAT LADY . . . .   356 BROKEN DREAMS   17
AND HAVING NO DESIRE THEY CANNOT TELL . . . .   376 PHASES OF MOON   107
BUT HAVING NO DESIRE THEY CANNOT TELL . . . .   376 PHASES OF MOON V   107
AND SO FORGET THE COMFORT THAT NO WORDS CAN TELL . . .   391 UNDER SATURN   V   4
TO TELL YOUR SIMPLEST WANT, AND KNOWN, ...   436 FOR MY SON   21
TO TELL YOUR SIMPLEST WANT, AND KNOW, ...   436 FOR MY SON   V   21
TWO THOUGHTS WERE SO MIXED UP I COULD NOT TELL . . . .   471 ALL SOUL NIGHT   31
I HAVE MUMMY TRUTHS TO TELL . . . .   474 ALL SOUL NIGHT   86
YET A MOST GENTLE WOMAN! WHO CAN TELL . . . .   618 BRONZE HEAD   10
NOT TO ALLOW HIS LOOKS TO TELL, ...   624 APPARITIONS   13
AND WHEN THEY KNOW WHAT OLD BOOKS TELL, ...   626 OLD MEN BE MAD   18
SEE, I TELL THY BEAUTIES O'ER, ...   647 ISLE STAT I 1   56
OLD MISER HOARDS OF GRIEF TO TELL AND TELL! . . . . .   661 ISLE STAT II 1   55
OLD MISER HOARDS OF GRIEF TO TELL AND TELL! . . . . .   661 ISLE STAT II 1   55
AYE, FIGHT WE MUST. TELL ME, ANTONIO, MIGHT . . . .   662 ISLE STAT II 1   77
AND LET THEM TELL SAD HISTORIES, TILL THEIR EYES . .   663 ISLE STAT II 2   32
AND OF NASCHINA'S NOW THEY TELL--REND! REND! . . . .   665 ISLE STAT II 2   69
A LITTLE NEARER THOSE BRIGHT STARS. TELL ME, ...   701 MOSADA 3   59
AND TELL ME A LOVE-STORY WHILE I DRINK. . . . .   760 SHADOW WATER A   250
AND TELL ME A LOVE STORY WHILE I DRINK. . . . .   760 SHADOW WATER A V   250
AND TELL HOW MANANAN SACKED MURIAS . . . .   766 SHADOW WATER A   377
AND TELL ITS STORY OVER THEIR BROWN ALE. . . . . . .   767 SHADOW WATER A   393
SEEK AIBRIC ON THE LOCHLANN GALLEY, AND TELL HIM . .   767 SHADOW WATER A   401
TELLER   SEE FORTUNE-TELLER
TELLING   SEE A-TELLING
AND ONE WHOM YOU WILL GO TO WITHOUT TELLING, ...   33 OISIN 2   V   67
A PITY BEYOND ALL TELLING . . . .   119 PITY OF LOVE   1
TELLS
THE LOVER TELLS OF THE ROSE IN HIS HEART . . . . . .   142 ROSE IN HEART   T
AEDH TELLS OF THE ROSE IN HIS HEART . . . .   142 ROSE IN HEART   V   T
THE EAST TELLS ALL HER SECRET JOY BEFORE DAYBREAK, . .   154 BELOVED PEACE   V   4
HE TELLS OF A VALLEY FULL OF LOVERS . . . .   163 VALLEY LOVERS   T
AEDH TELLS OF A VALLEY FULL OF LOVERS . . . .   163 VALLEY LOVERS   V   T
HE TELLS OF THE PERFECT BEAUTY . . . .   164 PERFECT BEAUTY   T
AEDH TELLS OF THE PERFECT BEAUTY . . . .   164 PERFECT BEAUTY V   T

TELLS   (CONTINUED)
    IN ANY ANCIENT BOOK BUT TELLS OF YOU • • • • • • • 186 QUEEN MAEVE   135
    MADGE TELLS ME WHAT I DARED NOT THINK • • • • • • • 457 SECRETS OF OLD   3
    HE TELLS HIS LIES BY ROTE • • • • • • • • 598 STONE CROSS   2
    SOME OLD MISER TELLS HIS STORE • • • • • • • 647 ISLE STAT I 1   58
    TELLS ALL HIS SINNING IN THEIR EARS• • • • • • • 655 ISLE STAT I 3   14
    TELLS ALL HER SINNING IN THEIR EARS• • • • • • • 655 ISLE STAT I 3 V 14
    YOUNG GUARIMOND HE TELLS THEM O'ER AND O'ER• • • • 661 ISLE STAT II 1   56
    AND LET THE TALE BE MOURNFUL EACH ONE TELLS• • • • • 663 ISLE STAT II 2   36
TEMPEST
    • • • LOVE-MAKING OR PIERCING THE TEMPEST WITH SAILS• • • 53 OISIN 3   88
    UNVISITED BY TEMPEST OR BY SUN, • • • • • • • • 446 COLONUS PRAISE   5
    IT FEARED TO GIVE ITS LOVE A HURT WITH ALL THE TEMPEST 450 OWEN AHERNE   7
        THERE
TEMPESTS
    HAVE BORNE ME WHERE THE TEMPESTS BLIND • • • • • • 6 OISIN 1 V 58
TEMPESTUOUS
    A BUNDLE OF TEMPESTUOUS CLOUD IS BLOWN • • • • • • • 541 PARN FUNERAL 1   2
TEMPLE
    I, PRIESTESS OF THIS TEMPLE, OFFER UP • • • • • • • 71 ANASHU VIJAYA   12
    WITHIN THE TEMPLE, DEVIOUS WALKING, MADE • • • • • • 72 ANASHU VIJAYA   32
    I, PRIESTESS OF THIS TEMPLE, OFFER UP • • • • • • • 75 ANASHU VIJAYA   84
    HIS TEMPLE AND HIS BANQUET HALL • • • • • • • • 671 ISLE STAT II 3   134
TEMPT
    ALL THINGS CAN TEMPT ME • • • • • • • • • • 267 ALL TEMPT ME   T
    ALL THINGS CAN TEMPT ME FROM THIS CRAFT OF VERSE • • • 267 ALL TEMPT ME   1
TEMPTATION
    MY TEMPTATION IS QUIET• • • • • • • • • • • 575 ACRE OF GRASS   7
TEN
    RANKING HIS DRUIDS ROUND HIM TEN BY TEN, • • • • • • 110 CUCHULAIN SEA   76
    RANKING HIS DRUIDS ROUND HIM TEN BY TEN, • • • • • • 110 CUCHULAIN SEA   76
    SENT FOR HIS DRUIDS TWENTY SCORE AND TEN, • • • • • • 110 CUCHULAIN SEA V 76
    AND TEN BY TEN UNDER A QUICKEN TREE, • • • • • • • 111 CUCHULAIN SEA V 81A
    AND TEN BY TEN UNDER A QUICKEN TREE," • • • • • • 111 CUCHULAIN SEA V 81A
    OLD DUBLIN MERCHANT "FREE OF TEN AND FOUR" • • • • • 269 PARDON FATHERS   3
    OLD DUBLIN MERCHANT "FREE OF THE TEN AND FOUR" • • • • 269 PARDON FATHERS V 3
    FROM NINETEEN HUNDRED NINE OR TEN, PAVLOVA'S HAD THE CRY, 354 HIS PHOENIX   11
    AND I ALONE, ONE IN TEN THOUSAND YEARS, • • • • • • 470 HARUN RASHID V 190
    OUT OF TEN THOUSAND WINTERS, I ALONE— • • • • • • 470 HARUN RASHID V 190
TENANTS
    ARE MURDERING YOUR TENANTS THERE• • • • • • • • 791 REPRISALS   16
TENDER
    WITH LAUGHTER LOW, AND TENDER, AND SWEET • • • • • • 6 OISIN 1 V 54
    SHE SAID, WITH LAUGHTER TENDER AND SWEET • • • • • • 6 OISIN 1 V 54
    AND LIFT YOUR TENDER EYELIDS, MAID, • • • • • • • 125 GOES FERGUS   5
    THINE EYES GROW FULL OF TENDER CARE • • • • • • • 135 TWO TREES   19
    THY TENDER EYES GROW ALL UNKIND• • • • • • • • • 136 TWO TREES   39
    AND YOU WOULD MURMUR TENDER WORDS, • • • • • • • 175 BELOVED DEAD   5
    I LONG FOR YOUR MERRY AND TENDER AND PITIFUL WORDS, • • 203 WITHER BOUGHS   3
    TENDER AND FEARLESS ON HER FUNERAL PYRE • • • • • • 688 NETTLESHIP   3
    NO TENDER WISDOM FLOODS THE EYES • • • • • • • • 723 GIRLS SONG A   9
    AND THEREON GREW A TENDER ROOT, • • • • • • • • 743 DANAAN QUICK   13
    AND THEREON GREW A TENDER STEM, • • • • • • • • 743 DANAAN QUICK   14
TENDEREST
    AND THE LONG GREY GRASSES, WHOSE TENDEREST TOUCHES • • • 27 OISIN 1 V 415B
    THOUGH TENDEREST ROSES WERE ROUND YOU, • • • • • • • 708 FAIRY PEDANT   29
TENDERLY
    WHEN I HAD STOOPED AND TENDERLY • • • • • • • • 10 OISIN 1 V 112A
TENDERNESS
    OR LOVE'S FIRST TENDERNESS DIE IN OUR GAZE• • • • • • 27 OISIN 1   411
    OR LOVE'S FIRST TENDERNESS DIE IN OUR GAZE• • • • • • 27 OISIN 1 V 419D
    OR LOVE'S FIRST TENDERNESS DIE IN OUR GAZE•" • • • • • 28 OISIN 1 V 427
    BUT SHE WHOSE HOURS OF TENDERNESS WERE GONE • • • • • 38 OISIN 2   138
    AND HE HAD KNOWN AT LAST SOME TENDERNESS, • • • • • • 126 DREAM OF FAERY   3
    AND BODILY TENDERNESS, AND FINDS THAT EVEN • • • • • 228 SHADOW WATER B 147
    BY TENDERNESS AND CARE, • • • • • • • • • • 346 ON WOMAN   37
    AND BODILY TENDERNESS TO THE SOFT FIRE • • • • • • 750 SHADOW WATER A 60
    AND BODILY TENDERNESS; AND HE WHO LONGS • • • • • • 750 SHADOW WATER A 66
    AND BODILY TENDERNESS; BUT LOVE IS MADE • • • • • • 765 SHADOW WATER A 355
TENDING
    THEY WEARY OF TENDING • • • • • • • • • • • 118 CRADLE SONG V 3
    TENDING THE ROSES ROUND HIS LATTICE DOOR• • • • • • • 692 MOSADA 1   53
TENSE
    EVEN THE WISEST MAN GROWS TENSE • • • • • • • • 638 BEN BULBEN   33
TENT
    TENT POLE OF EDEN; THE TENT'S DRAPERY; • • • • • • 483 VERONIC NAPKIN V 2
    LIKE SOME POOR ARAB TRIBESMAN AND HIS TENT• • • • • • 491 COOLE BALLYLEE 40
    OUR MASTER CAESAR IS IN THE TENT • • • • • • • • 617 LONG-LEG FLY   5
    BEFORE HIS TENT THE GENERAL SIPS HIS WINE, • • • • • 709 FERENCZ RENYI   6
    REITERANT. A BIRD GOES BY THE TENT, • • • • • • • 711 FERENCZ RENYI   46
    REITERANT. A BOY GOES BY THE TENT, • • • • • • • 711 FERENCZ RENYI V, 46
TENTED
    ARE STILL THE ACHAIANS' TENTED CHIEFS AT BAY? • • • • 679 ISLE STAT II 3   310
    SINCE 'MONG MY PEOPLE, TENTED ON THE HILLS, • • • • • 690 MOSADA 1   4
TENTH
    YESTERDAY IN THE TENTH YEAR • • • • • • • • • • 361 ALF POLLEXFEN   27
    AND ARE WE NOW IN THE TENTH YEAR? • • • • • • • • 361 ALF POLLEXFEN V 27
TENT-POLE
    TENT-POLE OF EDEN; THE TENT'S DRAPERY; • • • • • • 483 VERONIC NAPKIN   2
TENT'S
    TENT-POLE OF EDEN; THE TENT'S DRAPERY; • • • • • • 483 VERONIC NAPKIN   2

			PAGE	TITLE		LINE

TENT'S (CONTINUED)
TENT POLE OF EDEN; THE TENT'S DRAPERY; • • • • • • • 483 VERONIC NAPKIN V 2
TENTS
THOSE WANDERERS THAT WELCOMED IN THEIR TENTS • • • • 462 HARUN RASHID 23
THAT THEY HAVE WELCOMED IN THEIR TENTS THE DREAM • • • • 462 HARUN RASHID V 23
OR PERCHING ON THE TENTS; A-WEARY STILL • • • • • • 690 MOSADA 1 8
DOWN THE LONG VALLEYS FROM MY PEOPLE'S TENTS; • • • • 691 MOSADA 1 30
ALONG THE TENTS, THE FIELDS, THE VILLAGE WALLS. • • • • 712 FERENCZ RENYI 71
ALONG THE TENTS, FIELD, THE VILLAGE WALLS. • • • • • • 712 FERENCZ RENYI V 71
TERESA
THE BODY OF SAINT TERESA LIES UNDECAYED IN TOMB, • • • • 503 VACILLATION 80
TERRACES
WITH DELICATE FEET UPON OLD TERRACES, • • • • • • • 418 ANCEST HOUSES 26
TERRIBLE
HOPELESS AND DEAR, OR TERRIBLE TO THINK ON, • • • • • 281 TWO KINGS 96
A TERRIBLE BEAUTY IS BORN. • • • • • • • • • • 392 EASTER 1916 16
A TERRIBLE BEAUTY IS BORN. • • • • • • • • • • 393 EASTER 1916 40
A TERRIBLE BEAUTY IS BORN. • • • • • • • • • • 394 EASTER 1916 80
THOSE TERRIBLE IMPLACABLE STRAIGHT LINES • • • • • • 467 HARUN RASHID 142
THE POETS HAVE IMAGINED, TERRIBLE AND GAY." • • • • • 602 GALLERY REVIS 12
I, THROUGH THE TERRIBLE NOVELTY OF LIGHT, STALK ON, STALK 623 HIGH TALK 13
ON;
TERRIFIED
I WAS NO LONGER TERRIFIED--HIS VOICE • • • • • • • 284 TWO KINGS 171
FROM TERRIFIED, INVISIBLE BEAST OR BIRD; • • • • • • 389 IMAGE PAST 6
HOW CAN THOSE TERRIFIED VAGUE FINGERS PUSH • • • • • 441 LEDA AND SWAN 5
TERRIFYING
A SWEET, MIRACULOUS, TERRIFYING SOUND. • • • • • • 277 TWO KINGS 17
TERROR
WITH QUAKING JOINTS AND TERROR STRUCKEN FACES, • • • • 185 QUEEN MAEVE V 121
WE SHOULD BE DAZED AND TERROR STRUCK • • • • • • • 272 GREY ROCK V 37
ITS TERROR GROWING WILDER AT EVERY FOOT-FALL, • • • • 279 TWO KINGS V 45D
ITS TERROR GROWING WILDER AT EVERY FOOTFALL • • • • • 279 TWO KINGS V 45D
I COWERED BACK UPON THE WALL IN TERROR, • • • • • • 284 TWO KINGS 164
IT MUST BE THAT THE TERROR IN THEIR EYES • • • • • • 375 PHASES OF MOON 72
THE NIGHT CAN SWEAT WITH TERROR AS BEFORE • • • • • 429 NINETEEN 19 29
THE THREEFOLD TERROR OF LOVE; A FALLEN FLARE • • • • 499 MOTHER OF GOD 1
THE TERROR OF ALL TERRORS THAT I BORE • • • • • • 499 MOTHER OF GOD 4
THE THREE-FOLD TERROR OF LOVE; A FALLEN FLARE • • • • 499 MOTHER OF GOD V 1
FROM TERROR AND DECEPTION FREED IT CAN • • • • • • 558 RIBH CHRISTIAN 9
AND HE, DESPITE HIS TERROR, CANNOT CEASE • • • • • • 563 MERU 4
AND FINDS THERE NOTHING TO MAKE ITS TERROR LESS • • • • 618 BRONZE HEAD 6
A VISION OF TERROR THAT IT MUST LIVE THROUGH • • • • 619 BRONZE HEAD 17
WHAT HOUR OF TERROR COMES TO TEST THE SOUL, • • • • 622 HOUND VOICE 11
IN TERROR FLINGS HER AT HER LOVER'S FEET. • • • • • 713 FERENCZ RENYI V 85
TERROR'S
AND IN THAT TERROR'S NAME OBEYED THE CALL, • • • • • 622 HOUND VOICE 12
TERRORS
ALL BUT THE TERRORS OF THE WOODLAND FLIGHT FORGOT • • • 366 HER COURAGE 5
THE TERROR OF ALL TERRORS THAT I BORE • • • • • • 499 MOTHER OF GOD 4
TERROR-STRICKEN
WITH QUAKING JOINTS AND TERROR-STRICKEN FACES, • • • • 185 QUEEN MAEVE 121
AND THEN; AS TERROR-STRICKEN AS A CHILD • • • • • • 279 TWO KINGS V 45A
TERROR-STRUCK
WE SHOULD BE DAZED AND TERROR-STRUCK, • • • • • • 272 GREY ROCK 37
WHY IS THE WOMAN TERROR-STRUCK? • • • • • • • • 625 NATIVITY 11
TERROR-STRUCKEN
WITH QUAKING JOINTS AND TERROR-STRUCKEN FACES, • • • • 185 QUEEN MAEVE V 121
TEST
TO TEST THEIR FANCY BY THEIR SIGHT; • • • • • • • 410 TOWER 44
TEST EVERY WORK OF INTELLECT OR FAITH, • • • • • • 501 VACILLATION 30
EVERYTHING DOWN TO THAT SOLE TEST AGAIN, • • • • • 603 GALLERY REVIS 46
ALL THINGS DOWN TO THAT COMMON TEST AGAIN, • • • • • 603 GALLERY REVIS V 46
WHAT HOUR OF TERROR COMES TO TEST THE SOUL, • • • • • 622 HOUND VOICE 11
TESTS
FOR EVERY NERVE, AND TESTS A LOVER • • • • • • • 388 SOLOMON WITCH 22
FOR EVERY NERVE; LOVER TESTS LOVER • • • • • • • 388 SOLOMON WITCH V 22
TESTY
TESTY DELIRIUM • • • • • • • • • • • • • • 416 TOWER 186
TETHER
QUIET THE DOG, TETHER THE PONY • • • • • • • • 617 LONG-LEG FLY 3
A KID, HELD BY ONE SOFT WHITE EAR FOR TETHER, • • • • 715 DWELT SYCAMORE 3
TEXT
BUT HERE'S A HAUGHTIER TEXT, • • • • • • • • • 259 UNWORTH PRAISE 12
THAT DYING CHOSE THE LIVING WORLD FOR TEXT • • • • • 324 ROBERT GREGORY 26
IT FOLLOWS FROM THIS LATIN TEXT • • • • • • • • 386 ROBARTES DANCE 43
AND ASKED ABOUT THE PICTURES OR THE TEXT; • • • • • 466 HARUN RASHID 121
THAT HE HAD FOUND A TEXT TO PROVE • • • • • • • 492 ANNE GREGORY 15
HE'D FIND FOR THIS SOME HOLY TEXT. • • • • • • • 728 PRIEST FAIRY 16
THAMES
OR STAY WITH ME BESIDE THE THAMES, • • • • • • • 741 EARL PAUL 59
THAN
THAN THE HORNLESS DEER WE CHASED THAT MORN, • • • • 2 OISIN 1 V 7P
BUT THE TALE, THOUGH WORDS BE LIGHTER THAN AIR, • • • • 3 OISIN 1 11
THAN DOVES THAT MOANED ROUND EMAN'S HALL • • • • • 3 OISIN 1 V 7EE
MORE SLEEK THAN ANY GRANARY MOUSE, • • • • • • • 4 OISIN 1 36
"WERE THERE NO BETTER THAN MY SON • • • • • • • 6 OISIN 1 60
WHOSE LONG WOOL WHITER THAN SEA-FROTH FLOWS, • • • • 8 OISIN 1 90
WHOSE LONG WOOL WHITER THAN SEA FROTH FLOWS, • • • • 8 OISIN 1 V 90
AND SWEETER OF VOICE THAN THE PLEASANT BIRDS, • • • • 9 OISIN 1 V 95
AND SWIFTER THAN THE SALMON HERDS; • • • • • • • 9 OISIN 1 V 96

		PAGE	TITLE		LINE

THAN (CONTINUED)

	PAGE	TITLE	V	LINE
IN A VIGOUR MORE THAN MORTAL MEASURE, ...	9	OISIN 1	V	98
WAS NOT MORE LEVEL THAN THE SEA, ...	13	OISIN 1		157
THAN THIS STRANGE HUMAN BARD," HE CRIED:	17	OISIN 1		239
THAN THIS STRANGE BARD," HE CRIED, AND CAUGHT	17	OISIN 1	V	239
BUT FAINTER THAN A YOUNG LAMB'S BLEAT.	26	OISIN 1		399
AND FAINTER THAN A YOUNG LAMB'S BLEAT.	26	OISIN 1	V	399
. . . FOR WHITER THAN NEW-WASHED FLEECE	47	OISIN 3		11
AND MORE COMELY THAN MAN CAN MAKE THEM	49	OISIN 3		32
AND EACH OF THE HUGE WHITE CREATURES WAS HUGER THAN FOURSCORE MEN:	49	OISIN 3		33
. . . LONG WARLESS, GROWN WHITER THAN CURDS.	49	OISIN 3		36
MORE COMELY THAN MAN MAY MAKE THEM, INLAID WITH SILVER AND GOLD,	49	OISIN 3	V	29
AND EACH OF THE HUGE WHITE CREATURES WAS HUGER THAN FOUR-SCORE MEN:	49	OISIN 3	V	33
. . . LONG-WARLESS, GROWN WHITER THAN CURDS.	49	OISIN 3	V	36
IN ONE WAS A BRANCH SOFT-SHINING WITH BELLS MORE MANY THAN SIGHS	50	OISIN 3		46
SOFTER THAN SNOW-FLAKES IN APRIL AND PIERCING THE MARROW LIKE FLAME.	51	OISIN 3		68
WRAPT IN THE WAVE OF THAT MUSIC, WITH WEARINESS MORE THAN OF EARTH,	51	OISIN 3		69
SOFTER THAN SNOWFLAKES IN APRIL, AND PIERCING THE MARROW LIKE FLAME.	51	OISIN 3	V	68
WERE THE WINDS LESS SOFT THAN THE BREATH OF A PIGEON . . .	56	OISIN 3		134
AND MY TEARS WERE LARGER THAN BERRIES, AND I MURMURED,	59	OISIN 3		178
. . .				
FOR THE WORLD'S MORE FULL OF WEEPING THAN YOU CAN UNDERSTAND.	87	STOLEN CHILD		12
FOR THE WORLD'S MORE FULL OF WEEPING THAN YOU CAN UNDERSTAND.	87	STOLEN CHILD		27
FOR THE WORLD'S MORE FULL OF WEEPING THAN YOU CAN UNDERSTAND.	88	STOLEN CHILD		41
FROM A WORLD MORE FULL OF WEEPING THAN HE CAN UNDERSTAND.	89	STOLEN CHILD		53
FOR THE WORLD'S MORE FULL OF WEEPING THAN HE CAN UNDERSTAND	89	STOLEN CHILD	V	53
IN THE JUNES THAT WERE WARMER THAN THESE ARE, ...	91	OLD FISHERMAN		3
CAME KEENERS HOARSER THAN ROOKS, ...	92	FATHER OHART		22
AND LOVELIER THAN THE MOON UPON THE SEA:	106	CUCHULAIN SEA	V	16A
"NAY, YOU ARE TALLER THAN CUCHULAIN, SON."	107	CUCHULAIN SEA	V	27
MORE MOURNFUL THAN THE DEPTH OF STARRY SKIES, ...	108	CUCHULAIN SEA	V	42
MORE FLEETING THAN THE SEA'S FOAM-FICKLE FACE, ...	112	ROSE OF WORLD	V	8
MORE FLEETING THAN THE SEA'S FOAM FICKLE FACE, ...	112	ROSE OF WORLD	V	8
WHO HAVE SOUGHT MORE THAN IS IN RAIN OR DEW	114	ROSE OF BATTLE		16
SHE WAS MORE BEAUTIFUL THAN THY FIRST LOVE, ...	123	DREAM OF DEATH		11
MY RHYMES MORE THAN THEIR RHYMING TELL	138	TO IRELAND		20
IS COMELIER THAN CANDLES AT MOTHER MARY'S FEET.	147	UNAPPEAS HOST		12
IS COMELIER THAN CANDLES BEFORE MAURYA'S FEET.	147	UNAPPEAS HOST	V	12
AND LOVE IS LESS KIND THAN THE GREY TWILIGHT, ...	148	INTO TWILIGHT		15
AND HOPE IS LESS DEAR THAN THE DEW OF THE MORN.	148	INTO TWILIGHT		16
A MORE DREAM-HEAVY HOUR THAN THIS:	156	FORGOT BEAUTY		17
AND WITH HEART MORE OLD THAN THE HORN	157	POET BELOVED		5
AND WITH THE HEART MORE OLD THAN THE HORN	157	POET BELOVED	V	5
WITH WORDS LIGHTER THAN AIR, ...	162	ASKS FORGIVE		2
O WINDS, OLDER THAN CHANGING OF NIGHT AND DAY, ...	162	ASKS FORGIVE		7
O WINDS, ELDER THAN CHANGING OF NIGHT AND DAY, ...	162	ASKS FORGIVE	V	7
BUT THAT GREAT QUEEN, WHO MORE THAN HALF THE NIGHT . . .	180	QUEEN MAEVE		16
MORE STILL THAN THEY HAD BEEN FOR A GOOD MONTH, ...	182	QUEEN MAEVE		54
THAN ANY WHOSE UNHAPPINESS	190	BAILE AILLINN		36
AND YOU ARE MORE HIGH OF HEART THAN SHE, ...	197	BAILE AILLINN		202
IT ALL, AND MORE THAN IT ALL, WOULD COME TO NAUGHT, . . .	201	OLD MEMORY		8
IT ALL, MORE THAN IT ALL, WOULD COME TO NAUGHT, ...	201	OLD MEMORY	V	8
IS TO WORK HARDER THAN ALL THESE, AND YET	205	ADAMS CURSE		11
BUT PURER THAN A TALL CANDLE BEFORE THE HOLY ROOD . . .	208	HANRAHANS SONG		14
BUT PURER THAN A TALL CANDLE BEFORE THE BLESSED ROOD . . .	208	HANRAHANS SONG	V	14
YET DREAMED THAT BEINGS HAPPIER THAN MEN	218	WOODS OF COOLE		18
THAT HAS LESS UPS AND DOWNS THAN ROBBERY.	222	SHADOW WATER B		7
AND KISS MORE LIPS THAN LASTING PEACEABLE MEN	225	SHADOW WATER B		71
MORE RICHES THAN THEY EVER HOPED TO FIND?	226	SHADOW WATER B		94
WHY SHOULD YOU BE MORE FAITHFUL THAN THE REST, ...	227	SHADOW WATER B		109
HOW ARE WE BETTER OFF THAN SEAGHAN THE FOOL, ...	228	SHADOW WATER B		129
WE HAVE BEEN NO BETTER OFF THAN SEAGHAN THE FOOL, ...	228	SHADOW WATER B	V	129
IS NO MORE THAN A WINE-CUP IN THE TASTING, ...	229	SHADOW WATER B		150
IS NO MORE THAN A WINE CUP IN THE TASTING, ...	229	SHADOW WATER B	V	150
TO MAKE LOW LAUGHTER MORE THAN MEAT AND DRINK, ...	230	SHADOW WATER B		186
THAN A STRONG BODY AND A READY HAND.	232	SHADOW WATER B		236
WHAT POWER THAT IS MORE MIGHTY THAN DESIRE	234	SHADOW WATER B		267
ALTHOUGH YOU ARE MORE BEAUTIFUL THAN ANY, ...	236	SHADOW WATER B		305
THAT IS MORE MIGHTY THAN THE SUN AND MOON, ...	237	SHADOW WATER B		328
OR THAN THE SHIVERING CASTING-NET OF THE STARS, ...	237	SHADOW WATER B		329
MORE MIGHTY THAN THE STARS HALF TROUBLED ME, ...	237	SHADOW WATER B		332
BETTER THAN MY OWN HANDS. I HAVE DECEIVED YOU	244	SHADOW WATER B		466
AND IF THAT HAPPINESS BE MORE THAN DREAMS, ...	248	SHADOW WATER B		554
MORE THAN THE FROTH, THE FEATHER, THE DUST-WHIRL, ...	248	SHADOW WATER B		555
MORE THAN THE FROTH, THE FEATHER, THE DUSTWHIRL, ...	248	SHADOW WATER B	V	555
THAT BALANCED WITH A WORD IS MORE THAN NOISE:	258	KING NO KING		4
AYE, AND WORSE WRONG THAN THESE.	260	UNWORTH PRAISE		18
THAN THIS ACCUSTOMED TOIL. WHEN I WAS YOUNG, ...	267	ALL TEMPT ME		5
COLDER AND DUMBER AND DEAFER THAN A FISH.	267	ALL TEMPT ME		10
YOUR EARS THAN STORIES NOW IN FASHION, ...	271	GREY ROCK		5
THAT HAS MORE LIFE IN IT THAN DEATH, ...	271	GREY ROCK		8

	PAGE	TITLE	LINE
THAN (CONTINUED)			
THAN LOVER'S MUSIC--LET THAT BE,	276	GREY ROCK	130
WHITER THAN CURDS, ITS EYES THE TINT OF THE SEA.	277	TWO KINGS	7
MORE HANDS IN HEIGHT THAN ANY STAG IN THE WORLD	277	TWO KINGS	9
THAN MOUND AND STONE THAT KEEP ALL VIRTUE IN,	281	TWO KINGS	106
DEARER THAN ANY THAT THE DUMB STONE HIDES,	281	TWO KINGS V	96
THAN TRIUMPH, TURN AWAY	291	TO A FRIEND	10
THAT LOVED HIS LEARNING BETTER THAN MANKIND,	324	ROBERT GREGORY	18
OR LEAVE THEM HAPPIER THAN BEFORE.	328	IRISH AIRMAN	8
THAN 'TWERE AN APPARITION. O HEART, WE ARE OLD!	334	LIVING BEAUTY	8
THAN DUMB-BELL AND FOIL	334	SONG	3
THAN DUMB BELL AND FOIL	334	SONG V	3
MORE THAN ANOTHER	336	YOUNG GIRL	2
YOU ARE MORE BEAUTIFUL THAN ANY ONE,	356	BROKEN DREAMS	27
YOU WERE MORE BEAUTIFUL THAN ANY ONE,	356	BROKEN DREAMS V	27
YOU ARE MORE BEAUTIFUL THAN ANYONE	356	BROKEN DREAMS V	27
MORE PLAIN TO THE MIND'S EYE THAN ANY FACE	368	EGO DOMINUS	21
WHAT BETTER THAN CALL A DANCE?	378	CAT AND MOON	13
WHAT VOICE MORE SWEET THAN HERS	392	EASTER 1916	21
THAN THAT I MAY FIND OUT A WAY	401	DEMON BEAST	41
BUT THAT HE FOUND MORE SUBSTANCE THERE THAN DREAMS,	417	ANCEST HOUSES V	10
THAN IN OUR LOVE! O HONEY-BEES,	425	STARES NEST	19
THAN IN OUR LOVES: OH, HONEY-BEES,	425	STARES NEST V	19
THE LIVING SEEM MORE SHADOWY THAN THEY.	435	NEW FACES	8
I HAVE LOVED YOU BETTER THAN MY SOUL FOR ALL MY WORDS,	442	BLACK CENTAUR	14
IF YOU ARE NO MORE STRENGTH THAN I AM BEAUTY	448	HERO GIRL FOOL	10
THAN THE HEAVENLY CIRCUIT OF ITS STARS	451	FIRST LOVE	17
THAN HEAVENLY CIRCUIT OF ITS STARS	451	FIRST LOVE V	17
THAN SOULS THAT START NO GAME AND TURN NO RHYME!	464	HARUN RASHID	68
THAN ALL MY BURSTING SPRINGTIME KNEW. A GIRL	466	HARUN RASHID	105
MORE WOMEN BORN THAN MEN."	485	STATISTICS	4
SEEMED ONCE MORE DEAR THAN LIFE! ANCESTRAL TREES,	491	COOLE BALLYLEE	34
SHADE MORE THAN MAN, MORE IMAGE THAN A SHADE!	497	BYZANTIUM	10
SHADE MORE THAN MAN, MORE IMAGE THAN A SHADE!	497	BYZANTIUM	10
MORE MIRACLE THAN BIRD OR HANDIWORK,	497	BYZANTIUM	18
MORE MIRACLE THAN BIRD OR HANDY-WORK	497	BYZANTIUM V	18
SENSE THAN A COMMON MAN?	507	STREAM AND SUN	10
NO BETTER THAN A BEAST	572	LADYS 1ST SONG	11
NO! GREATER THAN PYTHAGORAS, FOR THE MEN	610	STATUES	9
WITH NO MORE SOUND THAN THE MICE MAKE	618	LONG-LEG FLY	27
THAN THE PEEPING PANSY'S FACE,	647	ISLE STAT I 1	52
AND THINE EYES MORE BRIGHT THAN FAERY'S,	647	ISLE STAT I 1	53
BENEATH THE WEIGHT OF GREATER GRIEF THAN I!	661	ISLE STAT II 1	63
IS NOT MORE FAIR AND JOYOUS THAN SHE IS	661	ISLE STAT II 1	71
FAR FLEETER THAN THE MILLION-FOOTED SEA.	670	ISLE STAT II 3	108
TO WATCH THEE PASS? YET DEEPER THAN MEN KNOW	672	ISLE STAT II 3	158
FOR I AM MIGHTIER NOW BY FAR THAN THEE,	673	ISLE STAT II 3	193
DEEPER THAN THE DEEPEST WELL."	697	MOSADA 2	27
YET WHITER BEARD HAVE YOU THAN MERLIN HAD.	721	WITCH VIVIEN	30
THAN OLD MEN'S ANY DAY, AS MERLIN FOUND.	721	WITCH VIVIEN	47
I HOLD HIM DEARER THAN THE GLAD,	723	GIRLS SONG A	3
I HOLD HIM DEARER THAN THE GOOD,	723	GIRLS SONG A	7
I HOLD HIM DEARER THAN THE WISE,	723	GIRLS SONG A	11
THAN IN BRIEF LONGING AND DECEIVING HOPE	750	SHADOW WATER A	65
ARE BETTER THAN THE WOODS WHERE NO LOVE FADES	754	SHADOW WATER A	160
AND SAID IT WAS MIGHTIER THAN THE SUN AND MOON,	762	SHADOW WATER A	289
OR THAN THE SHIVERING CASTING-NET OF THE STARS.	762	SHADOW WATER A	290
OR THAN THE SHIVERING CASTING NET OF THE STARS.	762	SHADOW WATER A V	290
THANK			
"I THANK YOU FOR YOUR KINDNESS TO MY BROTHER,	286	TWO KINGS V	212
THANKED			
AND THANKED HER FOR HER KINDNESS TO HIS BROTHER,	286	TWO KINGS	212
THANKFUL			
WITH SPEEDY FEET AND A MOST THANKFUL HEART!	185	QUEEN MAEVE	100
AND BEING THANKFUL MURROUGH FOUND,	274	GREY ROCK	77
THANKS			
BECAUSE YOU SAVED MY RICE. HAVE YOU NO THANKS?	73	ANASHU VIJAYA	40
SAID, "AENGUS AND HIS SWEETHEART GIVE THEIR THANKS	187	QUEEN MAEVE	146
NOR GAVE GOD THANKS TILL OVERHEAD	307	HOUR DAWN	121
AND GAVE GOD THANKS THAT OVERHEAD	307	HOUR DAWN V	121
WAKING HE THANKS THE LORD THAT HE	633	MAN AND ECHO	27
THEATRE			
THEATRE BUSINESS, MANAGEMENT OF MEN.	260	FASC DIFFICULT	11
AT THE ABBEY THEATRE	264	ABBEY THEATRE	T
THEBAID			
THROUGH BARREN THEBAID,	401	DEMON BEAST	44
THEME			
IN THE NARROW THEME OF LOVE	333	SOLOMON SHEBA	7
IN THE ONE NARROW THEME OF LOVE	333	SOLOMON SHEBA V	7
UNTIL HER PRAISE SHOULD BE THE UPPERMOST THEME,	350	HER PRAISE	6
TWO CONTEMPLATING PASSIONS CHOSE ONE THEME	466	HARUN RASHID	117
MUST VANISH ON THE INSTANT IF THE MIND BUT CHANGE ITS THEME;	481	BLOOD AND MOON	27
WE WERE THE LAST ROMANTICS--CHOSE FOR THEME	491	COOLE BALLYLEE	41
WHAT, BE A SINGER BORN AND LACK A THEME?	502	VACILLATION	73
WHAT THEME HAD HOMER BUT ORIGINAL SIN?	502	VACILLATION	77
UPON THE SUPREME THEME OF ART AND SONG!	523	LONG SILENCE	6
THAT STILLNESS FOR A THEME	535	CHOSEN	14
I SOUGHT A THEME AND SOUGHT FOR IT IN VAIN,	629	CIRCUS ANIMALS	1
BUT HUSH, FOR I HAVE LOST THE THEME,	633	MAN AND ECHO	41

	PAGE	TITLE	LINE

THEMES
    WHAT CAN I BUT ENUMERATE OLD THEMES? . . . .   629 CIRCUS ANIMALS   9
    THEMES OF THE EMBITTERED HEART, OR SO IT SEEMS, ...   629 CIRCUS ANIMALS   13
THENCE
    BURIED AND MIGHTY. THENCE I JOURNEYED NOT . . . . . .   39 OISIN 2   V 151
    HE WALKED THAT ROOM AND ISSUED THENCE . . . .   438 SONGS PLAY 2   2
    THENCE HAVE I COME WINGING; . . . .   672 ISLE STAT II 3   170
    AND NOT COME THENCE; FOR HERE IN THIS SMALL RING-- . . .   699 MOSADA 3   22
THEOLOGY
    RIBH PREFERS AN OLDER THEOLOGY . . . .   556 RIBH PATRICK   V T
THEREBY
    AND THESE THINGS CAME, SO MUCH THE MORE THEREBY . . . .   265 THESE CLOUDS   8
THEREIN
    THEREIN THE SILVER HARP HE HURLED, ...   17 OISIN 1   V 244
    THEREIN ARE MANY QUEENS LIKE BRANWEN AND GUINEVERE; . . .   209 UNDER THE MOON   11
    HE IT HAS FOUND SHALL FIND THEREIN . . . .   538 LAST CONFESS   17
    LIES IN A CIRCLE ON THE GRASS; THEREIN . . . .   555 RIBH AT TOMB   26
THEREON
    THEREON DID SHE LOOK HAUGHTY AND SWEET . . . .   6 OISIN 1   54
    OR CLUNG THEREON LIKE SWARMING BEES; . . . .   14 OISIN 1   181
    THEREON YOUNG NIAMH SOFTLY CAME . . . .   25 OISIN 1   373
    BUT FLY WHILE STILL YOU MAY." AND THEREON I . . . . .   35 OISIN 2   89
    THEREON IN OGHAM LETTERS, "MANANNAN"; . . . .   38 OISIN 2   128
    THEREON HE SHOOK THE MORE AND CAST HIM DOWN . . . . .   106 CUCHULAIN SEA   14
    THEREON A YOUNG MAN MET HIS EYE, ...   274 GREY ROCK   85
    THAT WE MAY HARRY HIM." THEREON . . . .   275 GREY ROCK   106
    BUT THEREON EVERY GOD STOOD UP . . . .   275 GREY ROCK   116
    THEREON SHE CAST HERSELF UPON THE GROUND, ...   275 GREY ROCK   V 107
    FOR MEDICINE." THEREON HE CRIED ALOUD, ...   281 TWO KINGS   98
    THEREON HE SEIZED ME IN HIS ARMS, BUT I . . . . . .   285 TWO KINGS   201
    THEREON THE BELLOWING OF THE EMPOUNDED HERDS . . . . .   286 TWO KINGS   214
    AND THEREON, MERRY AS A BIRD . . . .   296 THREE BEGGARS   25
    AND THEREON SAW, WHERE STONES HAD BEEN . . . .   302 HOUR DAWN   V 20
    AND SO TAKE THAT AND THAT." THEREON . . . .   307 HOUR DAWN   112
    THEREON MY PHOENIX ANSWERED IN REPROOF, ...   352 PEOPLE   22
    THEREON I MADE MY MOAN, ...   384 VISION ROBART   63
    THEREON REPLIED; "A COCKEREL . . . .   387 SOLOMON WITCH   9
    THEREON EXPLAINED; "A COCKEREL . . . .   387 SOLOMON WITCH   V 9
    THE GREAT GREY-EYED ATHENE STARES THEREON. . . . . .   447 COLONUS PRAISE   16
    BUT SINCE I LAID A HAND THEREON . . . .   451 FIRST LOVE   7
    BUT COULD NOT CAST A SINGLE JET THEREON. . . . . . .   482 BLOOD AND MOON   39
    I CANNOT LOOK THEREON, ...   501 VACILLATION   49
    THE SWORD'S A CROSS; THEREON HE DIED; . . . .   562 CONJUNCTIONS   3
    AND DROPPED AND DIED THEREON, FOR SHE . . . .   571 THREE BUSHES   54
    WHERE MY FRIENDS' PORTRAITS HANG AND LOOK THEREON; . . .   604 GALLERY REVIS   52
    I SHALL BE OLD INDEED." THEREON THE MAN . . . . . .   609 IN TARAS HALLS   10
    AND THEREON GREW A TENDER ROOT, ...   743 DANAAN QUICK   13
    AND THEREON GREW A TENDER STEM, ...   743 DANAAN QUICK   14
    AND THEREON GREW THE RUDDY FRUIT . . . .   743 DANAAN QUICK   15
THEREUPON
    AND THEREUPON I DREW THE LIVID CHOP . . . .   40 OISIN 2   178
    "YOU DARE ME TO MY FACE," AND THEREUPON . . . .   106 CUCHULAIN SEA   17
    THE MARTYRS CALL THE WORLD." AND THEREUPON . . . . .   205 ADAMS CURSE   14
    A CURLEW ANSWERED; AND SUDDENLY THEREUPON I THOUGHT . . .   291 PAUDEEN   5
    AND THEREUPON THEIR ANGER GREW, ...   297 THREE BEGGARS   V 46
    AND THEREUPON IMAGINATION AND HEART WERE DRIVEN . . . .   316 COLD HEAVEN   3
    AND THEREUPON WITH AGED, HIGH-PITCHED VOICE . . . . .   375 PHASES OF MOON   84
    AND THEREUPON THERE COMES THAT SCREAM . . . .   389 IMAGE PAST   5
    BUT NOW WIND DROPS, DUST SETTLES; THEREUPON . . . . .   433 NINETEEN 19   125
    AND THEREUPON MY HEART IS DRIVEN WILD; . . . .   444 SCHOOL CHILDR   23
    AND THEREUPON A COLLOQUY TOOK PLACE . . . .   463 HARUN RASHID   45
    THAT THEREUPON A COLLOQUY TOOK PLACE . . . .   463 HARUN RASHID   V 45
    AND THEREUPON HIS BOUNTY GAVE WHAT NOW . . . .   465 HARUN RASHID   103
    AND THEREUPON REPLIES . . . .   531 FATHER CHILD   6
    THEREUPON, ...   628 JANE MOUNTAIN   18
    AND THEREUPON THAT LINEN-CARRIER SAID; . . . .   634 CUCHULAIN COMF   11
THERNOT
    NOW, JUDGE, MUST SHEPHERD THERNOT THERE AND I . . . . .   661 ISLE STAT II 1   65
THERNOT'S
    CEASE! THERNOT'S WOUNDED, CEASE! THEY WILL NOT HEED. . .   665 ISLE STAT II 2   64
THETIS
    PELEUS ON THETIS STARES. . . . .   612 NEWS ORACLE   26
THETIS'
    BUT THETIS' BELLY LISTENS. . . . .   612 NEWS ORACLE   29
THEWS
    THAT HE, WHEN FRENZY STIRRED HIS THEWS, ...   271 GREY ROCK   22
THICK
    WINE SHALL RUN THICK TO THE END, ...   554 CHURCH STATE   11
    AND SEE HOW THICK THE DEW LIES ON MY FACE. . . . . .   703 MOSADA 3   104
THICKENED   SEE HONEY-THICKENED
    AND THICKENED ALL THE WHIRLING AIR. THEN DID . . . .   46 OISIN 2   V 245A
THICKENS
    WHO WHEN NIGHT THICKENS ARE AFLOAT . . . .   196 BAILE AILLINN   179
THICKER
    THE VAPOUR IS MUCH THICKER. GOD! THE STAKE! . . . . .   695 MOSADA 1   112
THICKET
    WE DANCED TO WHERE IN THE WINDING THICKET . . . . . .   20 OISIN 1   304
    THEN ONWARD IN THE WINDING THICKET . . . .   20 OISIN 1   V 304
THIEVE
    AND FREE--'TWILL THIEVE AWAY WITH SLEEPY MOOD . . . . .   700 MOSADA 3   30

THIEVING
   BUT A THIEVING RASCALLY CUR— . . . .   552 SONGS REWRIT 2   7
   THEIR THIEVING WINGS THAT WE MIGHT NEVER PART. . . . .   702 MOSADA 3   98
THIGH
   THE STRONG THIGH AND THE AGILE THIGH WERE MET, ...   278 TWO KINGS   28
   THE STRONG THIGH AND THE AGILE THIGH WERE MET, ...   278 TWO KINGS   28
   STARING UPON HIS SINEWY THIGH. . . . .   294 HATED PLAYBOY   6
   MADDENED BY THAT SINEWY THIGH. . . . .   294 HATED PLAYBOY V   6
   STARING ON HIS SINEWY THIGH. . . . .   294 HATED PLAYBOY V   6
   THAT DROPPED UPON MY THIGH." . . . .   309 PLAYER QUEEN   16
   THAT VIGOROUS THIGH, THAT DREAMING EYE? . . . . . .   386 ROBARTES DANCE   23
   YOU, SHOULD HAND EXPLORE A THIGH, ...   573 LADYS 3RD SONG   11
THIGHED   SEE GOLDEN-THIGHED
   WORLD-FAMOUS GOLDEN THIGHED PYTHAGORAS . . . .   445 SCHOOL CHILDR V   45
THIGHS
   "AND THE WORSE DEVIL THAT IS BETWEEN MY THIGHS." . . .   300 BEGGAR CRIED   8
   IS MOVING ITS SLOW THIGHS, WHILE ALL ABOUT IT . . . .   402 SECOND COMING   16
   ABOVE THE STAGGERING GIRL, HER THIGHS CARESSED . . . .   441 LEDA AND SWAN   2
   THE FEATHERED GLORY FROM HER LOOSENING THIGHS? . . . .   441 LEDA AND SWAN   6
   THE BIRD DESCENDS, AND HER FRAIL THIGHS ARE PRESSED . .   441 LEDA AND SWAN V   2
   ON STRAINING THIGHS. . . . .   574 LOVERS SONG   6
THIN
   AND THE THIN CRESCENT OF THE MOON, ...   20 OISIN 1   V   288
   UNDER A BEECH AT ALMHUIN AND HEARD THE THIN . . . . .   44 OISIN 2   228
   A THIN GREY MAN HALF LOST IN GATHERING NIGHT. . . . .   102 FERGUS DRUID   7
   A THIN, GREY MAN, HALF-LOST IN GATHERING NIGHT, . . .   102 FERGUS DRUID   V   7
   LOOK ON MY THIN GREY HAIR AND HOLLOW CHEEKS . . . . .   103 FERGUS DRUID   23
   THEY WROTE ON TABLETS OF THIN BOARD, ...   197 BAILE AILLINN   195
   BECAUSE OF SOMETHING I HEARD OF UNDER THE THIN HORN . .   210 UNDER THE MOON V   17
   BECAUSE OF A STORY I HEARD UNDER THE THIN HORN . . . .   210 UNDER THE MOON V   17
   BECAUSE OF A STORY I HEARD UNDER A THIN HORN . . . . .   210 UNDER THE MOON V   17
   IF YOU HAVE REVISITED THE TOWN, THIN SHADE, ...   292 TO A SHADE   1
   WORN THIN BY THE LAPPING OF WATER, ...   330 BONE OF A HARE   11
   THROUGH THE WHITE THIN BONE OF A HARE. . . . . . .   330 BONE OF A HARE   16
   THE FIRST THIN CRESCENT IS WHEELED ROUND ONCE MORE. . .   377 PHASES OF MOON   116
   MUST RAMBLE, AND THIN OUT . . . .   484 SPILT MILK   3
   THIN IS THE MOON'S HORN! . . . .   519 LOVES LONENESS   8
   NO HAMLET THIN FROM EATING FLIES, A FAT . . . . . .   610 STATUES   19
   A WEAK, THIN CHILD, WHEN LAST I SAW HIM THERE. . . . .   699 MOSADA 1   14
   TWO WOMEN, WITHERED ONE AND SMALL AND THIN, ...   711 FERENCZ RENYI   51
   UPON THIN BOARDS OF YEW AND APPLE WOOD, ...   764 SHADOW WATER A   343
   UPON THIN BOARDS OF YEW AND APPLE-WOOD, ...   764 SHADOW WATER A V   343
THING
   OF DALLIANCE WITH A DEMON THING. . . . .   2 OISIN 1   4
   TRAPPED OF AN AMOROUS DEMON THING. . . . .   2 OISIN 1   V   4
   FOR BATTLE." "FLY YE FROM A THING SO DREAD. . . . . .   35 OISIN 2   V   90
   . . . OF BEST ONES A SAD THING WERE— . . . .   63 OISIN 3   V   222
   CONCEIVE A THING SO SAD AND SOFT, A GENTLE THING LIKE ME?   77 INDIAN ON GOD   16
   CONCEIVE A THING SO SAD AND SOFT, A GENTLE THING LIKE ME?   77 INDIAN ON GOD   16
   AND TOADS AND EVERY OUTLAWED THING . . . .   85 MAD KING GOLL V   61
   LAY HIDDEN IN THE SMALL SLATE-COLOURED THING! . . . .   104 FERGUS DRUID   40
   THE BELL THAT CALLS US ON, THE SWEET FAR THING. . . .   115 ROSE OF BATTLE   28
   AND MANY A SWEET THING SAID, ...   144 HOST OF AIR   18
   OF THIS OR THAT THING, NOR GREW COLD . . . .   189 BAILE AILLINN   9
   OF THIS OR THAT THING, OR GREW COLD . . . .   189 BAILE AILLINN   V   9
   FOR ANY GENTLE THING SHE SPAKE. . . . .   191 BAILE AILLINN   63
   SO FULL OF THAT THING AND OF THIS, ...   192 BAILE AILLINN   86
   I SAID, "IT'S CERTAIN THERE IS NO FINE THING . . . .   205 ADAMS CURSE   21
   "THERE IS ONE THING THAT ALL WE WOMEN KNOW . . . . .   205 ADAMS CURSE   V   18
   WHERE PASSION GROWS TO BE A CHANGELESS THING, ...   231 SHADOW WATER B   213
   CRIED OUT UPON THAT THING BENEATH . . . .   254 HIS DREAM   10
   WHAT THING HER BODY WAS." . . . .   255 WOMAN HOMER   14
   WE'LL FIND SO GOOD A THING AS THAT WE HAVE LOST? . . .   258 KING NO KING   13
   O LOVE IS THE CROOKED THING, ...   268 BROWN PENNY   9
   NOR HAD THERE BEEN THE NOISE OF LIVING THING . . . . .   279 TWO KINGS   54
   AND THERE HAD BEEN NO SOUND OF LIVING THING . . . . .   279 TWO KINGS   V   54
   "ALTHOUGH THE THING THAT YOU HAVE HID WERE EVIL, . . .   281 TWO KINGS   103
   BRED TO A HARDER THING . . . .   291 TO A FRIEND   9
   I HAVE NOT FOUND A THING TO EAT, ...   294 THREE BEGGARS   3
   AND EVERY COMFORTABLE THING, ...   307 HOUR DAWN   111
   WHEREON A THING ONCE WALKED THAT SEEMED A BURNING CLOUD.   315 FALLEN MAJESTY   8
   ONCE WALKED A THING THAT SEEMED, AS IT WERE, A BURNING
      CLOUD.   315 FALLEN MAJESTY V   8
   A NOISY AND FILTHY THING." . . . .   319 DOLLS   12
   AND LEARN THAT THE BEST THING IS . . . .   330 BONE OF A HARE   6
   THERE'S NOT A THING BUT LOVE CAN MAKE . . . .   333 SOLOMON SHEBA   23
   I HAD WISHED A DEAR THING ON THAT DAY . . . .   341 SHEP GOATHERD V   73
   TO HOPE A THING SO DEAR . . . .   346 ON WOMAN   27
   I MOURN FOR THAT MOST LONELY THING! AND YET GOD'S WILL
      BE DONE!   354 HIS PHOENIX   31
   ALL I HAD RHYMED OF THAT MONSTROUS THING . . . . . .   358 PRESENCES   7
   ALL I HAVE RHYMED OF THAT MONSTROUS THING . . . . . .   358 PRESENCES   V   7
   OF THE HOVERING THING NIGHT BROUGHT ME. . . . . . .   390 IMAGE PAST   42
   BECAME A BITTER, AN ABSTRACT THING, ...   397 POLIT PRISONER   9
   I COULD NOT FIND A THING SO DEAR." . . . .   398 BREAK OF DAY   9
   AN AGED MAN IS BUT A PALTRY THING, ...   407 SAIL BYZANTIUM   9
   MY BODILY FORM FROM ANY NATURAL THING, ...   408 SAIL BYZANTIUM   26
   AND A GREAT ARMY BUT A SHOWY THING, ...   429 NINETEEN 19   18
   I KNEW THAT HORSE-PLAY, KNEW IT FOR A MURDEROUS THING. .   442 BLACK CENTAUR   4
   I KNEW THAT HORSE PLAY, KNEW IT FOR A MURDEROUS THING. .   442 BLACK CENTAUR V   4

	PAGE	TITLE	LINE

THING   (CONTINUED)
A STRANGE THING SURELY THAT MY HEART, WHEN LOVE HAD COME   449 OWEN AHERNE   1
     UNSOUGHT
AND NOT A THING IS DONE,   451 FIRST LOVE   10
GAME-BIRD, NOR WOMAN DOES THE SAME THING TWICE!   463 HARUN RASHID   60
GAME BIRD, OR WOMAN DOES THE SAME THING TWICE!   463 HARUN RASHID   V   60
GAMEBIRD, NOR WOMAN DOES THE SAME THING TWICE!   463 HARUN RASHID   V   60
BECAUSE I HAVE A MARVELLOUS THING TO SAY,   471 ALL SOUL NIGHT   15
A CERTAIN MARVELLOUS THING   471 ALL SOUL NIGHT   16
I NEED NO OTHER THING,   474 ALL SOUL NIGHT   98
TO THIS AND THAT AND T'OTHER THING,   478 SELF AND SOUL   23
LIVES THAT LONELY THING   504 QUARREL IN AGE   14
EVERY THING THAT HAS LIVED   504 QUARREL IN AGE V   9
SOME STUPID THING THAT I HAD DONE   507 STREAM AND SUN   4
INTO SOME LESSER THING,   517 HER ANXIETY   5
"THE THIRD THING THAT I THINK OF YET,"   521 THREE THINGS   13
I'D HAVE HIM LOVE THE THING THAT WAS   532 BEFORE WORLD   15
THAT THING ALL BLOOD AND MIRE, THAT BEAST-TORN WRECK,   537 HER VISION   25
WITHOUT A THING IN HIS HEAD   552 SONGS REWRIT 2   10
A MOST ASTONISHING THING--   567 FROM JAPANESE   1
ALL THE OLYMPIANS, A THING NEVER KNOWN AGAIN.   578 LOFTY THINGS   12
A BEAUTIFUL LOFTY THING, OR A THING   578 CRAZED GIRL   7
A BEAUTIFUL LOFTY THING, OR A THING   578 CRAZED GIRL   7
BUT NEVER SAID A THING,   627 STATES HOLIDAY   10
BUT YONDER THING, YON IDLE NOISE, YON CROW,   648 ISLE STAT I 1   104
SOME BARBAROUS, UN-FAERY THING DRAW NEAR.   656 ISLE STAT I 3   21
AND, OH! THE WONDER OF THE THING! EACH CAME   656 ISLE STAT I 3   29
THIS THING WE ASK; MUST WE TWO FIGHT?--JUDGE THOU.   660 ISLE STAT II 1   41
TO US. OH WISE ART THOU IN SUCH A THING,   660 ISLE STAT II 1   46
FOR THIS THING FIGHT--WE LOVE ONE MAID? HER NAME?   661 ISLE STAT II 1   66
DULL-WITTED THING, WITH FACE RED SQUIRREL-BROWN,   661 ISLE STAT II 1   68
A WHITE, DUMB THING OF TEARS, HERE LET IT STAND,   663 ISLE STAT II 2   21
THE FAERY THING FLEW WITH HER O'ER THE GRAY   663 ISLE STAT II 2   38
FROM WHOSE GREEN BANKS NO LIVING THING MAY ROVE,   664 ISLE STAT II 2   57
THE FLOWER, SAVE SOME THING BE FOUND   668 ISLE STAT II 3   51
SWIFT LAKE. A VERY LITTLE THING THAT IS,   669 ISLE STAT II 3   78
I LAUGHED? AND WHY IS THAT A THING SO DEAR?   670 ISLE STAT II 3   97
I CRIED THE THING YOU BADE ME CRY,   670 ISLE STAT II 3   114
A WRIGGLING THING ON THE WHITE LAKE MOVED,   673 ISLE STAT II 3   176
I LIT BY THE THING, 'TWAS A SHEPHERD-BOY,   673 ISLE STAT II 3   180
HIS SLEUTH-HOUNDS FOLLOW EVERY FAERY THING.   675 ISLE STAT II 3   244
SHINE DULL UNMOVING EYES. WHAT THING ART THOU?   685 SEEKER   74
SHALL SEE A THING TO TALK ON WHEN YOU'RE OLD,   693 MOSADA 1   67
BE NOT AFRAID, YOU'LL SEE NO FEARFUL THING.   693 MOSADA 1   74
BECAUSE OF THE THING HIS TONGUE HAD SAID.   730 PRIEST FAIRY   60
"LOVE WOULD BE A THING OF NAUGHT   772 SONG DEIRDRE 1   10
LOVE IS AN IMMODERATE THING   777 SONG DEIRDRE 2   1
HAS MADE IT BUT A LONELY THING.   781 HEART FRIGHT   4
A STRANGE, UNSERVICEABLE THING,   784 WOMANS BEAUTY   15
THINGS   SEE SPIRIT-THINGS
TO ALL THINGS CRIED: "I AM A SLAVE!   19 OISIN 1   V 280
AND THINGS THAT HAVE GROWN SAD ARE WICKED,   20 OISIN 1   301
AND THINGS THAT FEAR THE DAWN OF THE MORROW   20 OISIN 1   302
BUT NOW TWO THINGS DEVOUR MY LIFE;   24 OISIN 1   358
THE THINGS THAT MOST OF ALL I HATE: 24 OISIN 1   359
TWO THINGS THAT 'FORE ALL ELSE I HATE,   24 OISIN 1   V 359
OF THE THINGS THAT HIS HEART STILL KNOWS WERE SWEET--   26 OISIN 1   V 402
BEFORE THE SWIFT THINGS THAT SHE DREAMED OF WERE DONE   27 OISIN 1   414
ERE HALF THE SWIFT THINGS THAT SHE DREAMT ON WERE DONE,   28 OISIN 1   V 422
THINGS DONE ERE GOD FIRST WAS OR MY OLD LINE BEGAN: 29 OISIN 2   V   8
FOR THEIR DIM MINDS WERE WITH THE ANCIENT THINGS.   34 OISIN 2   77
WRAPPED IN THE THINGS OF THE UNHUMAN MIND,   36 OISIN 2   98
ROLLED IN THE THINGS OF THE UNHUMAN MIND,   36 OISIN 2   V   98
"LAST OF MY RACE, THREE THINGS I RULE ALONE--   45 OISIN 2   V 239A
IN A REVERIE FORGETFUL OF ALL THINGS, OVER THE BUBBLING   56 OISIN 3   140
     GROUND.
IN REVERIE FORGETFUL OF ALL THINGS, OVER THE BUBBLING   56 OISIN 3   V 140
     GROUND.
OF ALL THE MANY CHANGING THINGS   65 HAPPY SHEPHERD   7
AND, EVER PACING ON THE VERGE OF THINGS,   73 ANASHU VIJAYA   54
THE SUN UPON ALL THINGS THAT GROW   98 FOXHUNTER   15
IN ALL POOR FOOLISH THINGS THAT LIVE A DAY,   101 ROSE UPON ROOD   11
LEST I NO MORE HEAR COMMON THINGS THAT CRAVE: 101 ROSE UPON ROOD   15
BUT SEEK ALONE TO HEAR THE STRANGE THINGS SAID   101 ROSE UPON ROOD   15
BECAUSE I BE NOT OF THE THINGS I DREAM.   103 FERGUS DRUID   V 26A
FROM CHANGE TO CHANGE: I HAVE BEEN MANY THINGS--   104 FERGUS DRUID   32
AND ALL THESE THINGS WERE WONDERFUL AND GREAT: 104 FERGUS DRUID   37
"WHO BADE YOU TELL THESE THINGS UPON MY FLOOR?"   106 CUCHULAIN SEA   V   17
"WHO BADE YOU TELL THESE THINGS?" AND THEN SHE CRIED   106 CUCHULAIN SEA   V   17
SAYING ALL THINGS WERE WELL!   113 ROSE OF PEACE   14
HAD PITY ON THE LEAST OF THINGS   134 FR GILLIGAN   47
FOR ALL THINGS TURN TO BARRENNESS   135 TWO TREES   29
ALL THINGS TURN TO BARRENNESS   135 TWO TREES   V   29
AND THE WHITE HUSH END ALL THINGS BUT THE BEAT   137 TO SOME I TALK V   15
OF THINGS DISCOVERED IN THE DEEP,   138 TO IRELAND   21
AND ALL BENIGHTED THINGS THAT GO   139 TO IRELAND   39
AND ALL THE WIZARD THINGS THAT GO   139 TO IRELAND   V   39
ALL THINGS UNCOMELY AND BROKEN, ALL THINGS WORN OUT AND   142 ROSE IN HEART   1
     OLD,
ALL THINGS UNCOMELY AND BROKEN, ALL THINGS WORN OUT AND   142 ROSE IN HEART   1
     OLD,

806

		PAGE	TITLE		LINE

THINGS (CONTINUED)

	PAGE	TITLE		LINE
ALL THINGS UNCOMELY AND BROKEN, ALL THINGS WORN AND OLD,	142	ROSE IN HEART	V	1
ALL THINGS UNCOMELY AND BROKEN, ALL THINGS WORN AND OLD,	142	ROSE IN HEART	V	1
THE WRONG OF UNSHAPELY THINGS IS A WRONG TOO GREAT TO BE TOLD:	143	ROSE IN HEART		5
THE WRONG OF THE THINGS MISSHAPEN IS WRONG TOO GREAT TO BE TOLD:	143	ROSE IN HEART	V	5
AND TROUBLE WITH A SIGH FOR ALL THINGS LONGING FOR REST	163	ASKS FORGIVE		23
AND WEEP BECAUSE I KNOW ALL THINGS NOW:	177	PAST GREATNESS		2
KNOWING ONE, OUT OF ALL THINGS, ALONE, THAT HIS HEAD	177	PAST GREATNESS		8
THAT ALL THINGS FELL OUT HAPPILY,	189	BAILE AILLINN		22
YET THEY THAT KNOW ALL THINGS BUT KNOW	190	BAILE AILLINN		38
OF THE EBB OF ALL THINGS TO MAKE LOVE	193	BAILE AILLINN	V	109
THEY KNOW UNDYING THINGS, FOR THEY	196	BAILE AILLINN		170
BECAUSE IT IS ALONE OF ALL THINGS HAPPY.	198	SEVEN WOODS		9
MUTTER SUCH THINGS AS THEY AWAKE FROM TRANCE.	229	SHADOW WATER B		163
AMONG SUBSTANTIAL THINGS: FOR IT IS DREAMS	230	SHADOW WATER B		181
HELMETS, AND SWORDS, AND HALF-FORGOTTEN THINGS	257	RECONCILIATION		6
BECAUSE WE HAVE MADE OUR ART OF COMMON THINGS,	265	ABBEY THEATRE		5
AND ALL THINGS AT ONE COMMON LEVEL LIE,	265	THESE CLOUDS		6
AND THESE THINGS CAME, SO MUCH THE MORE THEREBY	265	THESE CLOUDS		8
ALL THINGS CAN TEMPT ME	267	ALL TEMPT ME		T
ALL THINGS CAN TEMPT ME FROM THIS CRAFT OF VERSE:	267	ALL TEMPT ME		1
WEARY OF MANY QUESTIONS: "THERE ARE THINGS	281	TWO KINGS		93
THAT THINGS IT WERE A PRIDE TO GIVE	287	TO WEALTHY MAN		6
BECAUSE OF ALL THINGS KNOWN	291	TO A FRIEND		15
NOTORIOUS, TILL ALL MY PRICELESS THINGS	321	REED WHISPERER		13
FOR ALL THINGS THE DELIGHTED EYE NOW SEES	326	ROBERT GREGORY		49
ON PRETTY THINGS THAT MAY	366	HER CHRIS TREE		7
AND PROVE OF ALL IMAGINABLE THINGS	371	EGO DOMINUS		73
AND PROVE IF ALL IMAGINABLE THINGS	371	EGO DOMINUS	V	73
GAZED UPON ALL THINGS KNOWN, ALL THINGS UNKNOWN,	383	VISION ROBART		30
GAZED UPON ALL THINGS KNOWN, ALL THINGS UNKNOWN,	383	VISION ROBART		30
BEING FIXED ON ALL THINGS LOVED, ALL THINGS UNLOVED,	383	VISION ROBART		34
BEING FIXED ON ALL THINGS LOVED, ALL THINGS UNLOVED,	383	VISION ROBART		34
THEY SAY SUCH DIFFERENT THINGS AT SCHOOL.	387	ROBARTES DANCE		52
YET THE WORLD ENDS WHEN THESE TWO THINGS,	388	SOLOMON WITCH		28
RIGHT MASTERY OF NATURAL THINGS.	401	DEMON BEAST		37
THINGS FALL APART: THE CENTRE CANNOT HOLD:	402	SECOND COMING		3
THINGS FALL APART: THE CENTRE CAN NOT HOLD,	402	SECOND COMING	V	3
IN ABSTRACT THINGS: OR BE DERIDED BY	409	TOWER		15
WITH LEARNED ITALIAN THINGS	415	TOWER		158
ALL THOSE THINGS WHEREOF	415	TOWER		163
WHAT IF THOSE THINGS THE GREATEST OF MANKIND	418	ANCEST HOUSES		38
MANY INGENIOUS LOVELY THINGS ARE GONE	428	NINETEEN 19		1
THAT PITCHES COMMON THINGS ABOUT. THERE STOOD	428	NINETEEN 19		4
MANY INGENUOUS LOVELY THINGS ARE GONE	428	NINETEEN 19	V	1
TO END ALL THINGS, TO END	431	NINETEEN 19	V	81
THERE ARE MALICIOUS THINGS, ALTHOUGH	435	FOR MY SON	V	10
SUCH DEVILISH THINGS EXIST,	436	FOR MY SON		11
UPON A GHOSTLY PARADIGM OF THINGS:	445	SCHOOL CHILDR		42
UPON THE GHOSTLY IMAGES OF THINGS	445	SCHOOL CHILDR	V	42
I HAVE ATTEMPTED MANY THINGS	451	FIRST LOVE		9
OR SAY THE THINGS WE SAY:	458	SECRETS OF OLD		12
COMPANIONSHIP IN THOSE MYSTERIOUS THINGS	465	HARUN RASHID		92
ALL, ALL THOSE GYRES AND CUBES AND MIDNIGHT THINGS	469	HARUN RASHID		184
THOSE CONES AND CUBES AND GYRES, THOSE MIDNIGHT THINGS,	469	HARUN RASHID	V	184
ON GENEROUS THINGS THAT HE DID	473	ALL SOUL NIGHT		69
LONG PAST HIS PRIME REMEMBER THINGS THAT ARE	477	SELF AND SOUL		18
AND GOD-APPOINTED BERKELEY THAT PROVED ALL THINGS A DREAM,	481	BLOOD AND MOON		25
THINGS SAID OR DONE LONG YEARS AGO,	501	VACILLATION		51
OR THINGS I DID NOT DO OR SAY	501	VACILLATION		52
"LET ALL THINGS PASS AWAY."	502	VACILLATION		61
"LET ALL THINGS PASS AWAY."	502	VACILLATION		66
"LET ALL THINGS PASS AWAY."	502	VACILLATION		71
SEEK OUT REALITY, LEAVE THINGS THAT SEEM.	502	VACILLATION		72
ALL THINGS HANG LIKE A DROP OF DEW	505	GRAT INSTRUCT		3
ALL THINGS REMAIN IN GOD.	512	JANE ON GOD		6
ALL THINGS REMAIN IN GOD.	512	JANE ON GOD		12
ALL THINGS REMAIN IN GOD.	512	JANE ON GOD		18
ALL THINGS REMAIN IN GOD.	512	JANE ON GOD		24
THREE THINGS	521	THREE THINGS		T
"O CRUEL DEATH, GIVE THREE THINGS BACK,"	521	THREE THINGS		1
"THREE DEAR THINGS THAT WOMEN KNOW,"	521	THREE THINGS		7
THINGS OUT OF PERFECTION SAIL,	530	OLD TOM AGAIN		1
FOR THINGS BELOW ARE COPIES, THE GREAT SMARAGDINE TABLET SAID.	556	RIBH PATRICK		6
HOW SOUL MAY WALK WHEN ALL SUCH THINGS ARE PAST,	558	RIBH CHRISTIAN		11
HOW SOUL COULD WALK BEFORE SUCH THINGS BEGAN.	558	RIBH CHRISTIAN		12
HOW SOUL HAS WALKED BEFORE SUCH THINGS BEGAN.	558	RIBH CHRISTIAN	V	12
THINGS UNBORN, THINGS THAT ARE GONE,	562	NEEDLES EYE		3
THINGS UNBORN, THINGS THAT ARE GONE,	562	NEEDLES EYE		3
THINGS THOUGHT TOO LONG CAN BE NO LONGER THOUGHT,	564	GYRES		2
EMPEDOCLES HAS THROWN ALL THINGS ABOUT:	564	GYRES		6
THE WORKMAN, NOBLE AND SAINT, AND ALL THINGS RUN	565	GYRES		23
ALL THINGS FALL AND ARE BUILT AGAIN,	566	LAPIS LAZULI		35
BEAUTIFUL LOFTY THINGS	577	LOFTY THINGS		T
BEAUTIFUL LOFTY THINGS: O'LEARY'S NOBLE HEAD:	577	LOFTY THINGS		1
AND WE AND ALL THE MUSES ARE THINGS OF NO ACCOUNT.	580	CURSE CROMWELL		12
BECAUSE IT PROVES THAT THINGS BOTH CAN AND CANNOT BE:	580	CURSE CROMWELL		19
THINGS HID IN THEIR MARROW-BONES	589	OLD WICKED MAN		41

THINGS   (CONTINUED)

THINGS HID IN THEIR MARROWBONES	589	OLD WICKED MAN V	41
THINGS HID IN THEIR MARROW BONES	589	OLD WICKED MAN V	41
"MY MISTRESS CANNOT SEE THESE THINGS,	595	COLONEL MARTIN	30
FOR THINGS LIKE THESE WHAT DECENT MAN	598	MODEL LAUREATE	22
DEEP-ROOTED THINGS," BUT NEVER FORESAW ITS END,	603	GALLERY REVIS	37
CONTACT ALL THINGS ANTAEUS-LIKE GREW STRONG;	603	GALLERY REVIS V	44
ALL THINGS DOWN TO THAT COMMON TEST AGAIN,	603	GALLERY REVIS V	46
AND NOT THOSE THINGS THAT THEY WERE EMBLEMS OF.	630	CIRCUS ANIMALS	32
AMONG THOSE BIRD-LIKE THINGS CAME, AND LET FALL	634	CUCHULAIN COMF	8
I FAIN HAD BEEN THE FIRST OF SINGING THINGS	648	ISLE STAT I 1	101
TO PROVE WHAT CAN YE DO? WHAT THINGS ABOVE	650	ISLE STAT I 1	146
IN ALL SUCH THINGS, PRAY LET THINE EARS BE TURNED,	660	ISLE STAT II 1	39
ALL THINGS ARE QUIET IN THE EVE'S WIDE EYE.	662	ISLE STAT II 2	6
AND WHEN THOU HAST THESE THINGS FOR MANY AGES FELT,	674	ISLE STAT II 3	214
AND WHEN THOU HAST THESE THINGS FOR AGES FELT,	674	ISLE STAT II 3	214
I KNOW NOT OF THE THINGS YOU SPEAK. BUT WHAT	675	ISLE STAT II 3	239
ARE ALL THINGS WELL WITH YOU AND WITH YOUR SHEEP?	682	SEEKER	13
WITH LITTLE VOICES SONGS OF FEARFUL THINGS.	682	SEEKER	31
TWO SPIRIT THINGS A MAN HATH FOR HIS FRIENDS:	686	DRAWING-ROOM	5
TO LIGHTEST OF LIGHT THINGS ALL SANCTITY.	686	DRAWING-ROOM	8
ABOLISHED BY A MIRE OF LITTLE THINGS,	711	FERENCZ RENYI	36
THE PROUDEST OR MOST COY OF SPIRIT THINGS,	720	WITCH VIVIEN	7
I KEEP SUCH THINGS ABOUT ME: THEY ARE FOOD	721	WITCH VIVIEN	37
THUS PLAY WE FIRST WITH PAWNS, POOR THINGS AND WEAK:	722	WITCH VIVIEN	53
ILL WORDS FOR ALL THINGS SOFT AND FAIR,	723	GIRLS SONG A	6
FOR AS THINGS WERE SO SHALL THINGS EVER BE.	724	KANVA ON SELF	20
FOR AS THINGS WERE SO SHALL THINGS EVER BE.	724	KANVA ON SELF	20
WHAT SHALLOW THOUGHTS ABOUT DEEP THINGS:	725	LEGEND	11
HE THOUGHT WISE THINGS AS HIS GREY HEAD NODDED.	728	PRIEST FAIRY	12
TO LIGHTEST OF ALL LIGHT THINGS SANCTITY.	734	QUATRAIN APHOR	8
TWO SPIRIT THINGS A MAN HATH FOR HIS FRIENDS:	734	QUATRAIN APHOR V	5
TO LIGHTEST OF LIGHT THINGS ALL SANCTITY.	734	QUATRAIN APHOR V	8
TILL ALL THINGS ARE AT REST.	741	EARL PAUL	52
TIME AND THE WORLD AND ALL THINGS DWINDLE OUT.	749	SHADOW WATER A	47
ENDS ALL THINGS. I HAVE SLAIN THE LOCHLANN KING.	754	SHADOW WATER A	163
FOR THE THINGS COME AFTER DEATH?	777	SONG DEIRDRE 2	12
YET ALL THE LOVELY THINGS THAT WERE	788	HAWTHORN TREE	11

THINK

"WE THINK ON OSCAR'S PENCILLED URN.	5	OISIN 1	41
AND THINK THAT YOU WERE HARD AND UNKIND;	146	FISH	7
BUT THINK ABOUT OLD FRIENDS THE MOST:	173	PLEADS FRIEND	5
BUT THINK OF YOUR OLD FRIENDS THE MOST:	173	PLEADS FRIEND V	5
I THINK THAT HE HAS FORGAEL IN HIS NET.	224	SHADOW WATER B	56
AND YET I CANNOT THINK THEY'RE LEADING ME	230	SHADOW WATER B	191
ONE OF THE EVER-LIVING, AS I THINK—	231	SHADOW WATER B	210
AS FOR THIS WOMAN, I THINK SHE IS COMING WITH ME.	248	SHADOW WATER B	545
THE CRAZY NOTHING THAT I THINK IT IS,	248	SHADOW WATER B	556
THOUGH YOU MAY THINK I WASTE MY BREATH	271	GREY ROCK	6
THAT THINK SWORD-STROKES WERE BETTER MEANT	276	GREY ROCK	129
THAT THINK SWORD STROKES WERE BETTER MEANT	276	GREY ROCK V	129
HOPELESS AND DEAR, OR TERRIBLE TO THINK ON,	281	TWO KINGS	96
AND THEN I THINK OF OLD GEORGE POLLEXFEN,	325	ROBERT GREGORY	33
ALL THINK WHAT OTHER PEOPLE THINK:	337	SCHOLARS	9
ALL THINK WHAT OTHER PEOPLE THINK:	337	SCHOLARS	9
I THINK IT BETTER THAT IN TIMES LIKE THESE	359	WAR POEM	1
I THINK IT BETTER THAT AT TIMES LIKE THESE	359	WAR POEM V	1
I THINK HE FASHIONED FROM HIS OPPOSITE	368	EGO DOMINUS	27
I SEE A SCHOOLBOY WHEN I THINK OF HIM,	370	EGO DOMINUS	55
I SEE A SCHOOL BOY WHEN I THINK OF HIM	370	EGO DOMINUS V	55
AND THEN HE LAUGHED TO THINK THAT WHAT SEEMED HARD	377	PHASES OF MOON	136
I START OUT OF MY SLEEP TO THINK	380	SONGS FOOL 1	7
EVEN FROM THE FOOT-SOLE THINK IT TOO.	387	ROBARTES DANCE	51
SO LET HER THINK OPINIONS ARE ACCURSED.	405	FOR DAUGHTER	58
WOULD THINK HER SON, DID SHE BUT SEE THAT SHAPE	444	SCHOOL CHILDR	37
I THINK THAT I MAY FIND	449	HERO GIRL FOOL	28
TO THINK OF BURIED HECTOR	455	HIS MEMORIES	5
MADGE TELLS ME WHAT I DARED NOT THINK	457	SECRETS OF OLD	3
CANNOT ENDURE TO THINK YOU TREAD THESE PATHS,	463	HARUN RASHID	52
YOU THINK THAT LOVE HAS SEASONS, AND YOU THINK	464	HARUN RASHID	75
YOU THINK THAT LOVE HAS SEASONS, AND YOU THINK	464	HARUN RASHID	75
THINK WHEN I CHOOSE A BRIDE I CHOOSE FOR EVER:	464	HARUN RASHID	80
IT MAKES MY PASSION STRONGER BUT TO THINK	465	HARUN RASHID	99
BUT THINK THAT HIS MIND'S EYE	471	ALL SOUL NIGHT	33
MANY A TIME I THINK TO SEEK	475	EVA GORE-BOOTH	14
THINK OF ANCESTRAL NIGHT THAT CAN,	478	SELF AND SOUL	20
BUT WHEN I THINK OF THAT MY TONGUE'S A STONE.	478	SELF AND SOUL	40
SO ARROGANTLY PURE, A CHILD MIGHT THINK	491	COOLE BALLYLEE	23
"THE THIRD THING THAT I THINK OF YET,"	521	THREE THINGS	13
I SHUDDER AND I SIGH TO THINK	524	MAD AS MIST	15
WHY SHOULD HE THINK ME CRUEL	532	BEFORE WORLD	13
WHY SHOULD THEY THINK THAT ARE FOR EVER YOUNG?	537	HER VISION	21
TO THINK HIS PASSION SUCH	538	LAST CONFESS	8
AND LAUGHED UPON HIS BREAST TO THINK	538	LAST CONFESS	11
OH I WOULD THINK THAT I HAD MY FEE,	551	SONGS REWRIT 1 V	7
GOD GUARD ME FROM THOSE THOUGHTS MEN THINK	553	PRAYER OLD AGE	1
I THINK I SHOULD DROP DEAD."	569	THREE BUSHES	13
AND LET HIM THINK ME THERE,	570	THREE BUSHES	23
NOR THINK THAT BODY IS THE WHOLE,	573	LADYS 3RD SONG	4
YOU THINK IT HORRIBLE THAT LUST AND RAGE	591	SPUR	1
"I THINK THAT I SHALL FIND HER	594	COLONEL MARTIN	16

```
                                                            PAGE    TITLE            LINE
THINK   (CONTINUED)
     THINK WHERE MAN'S GLORY MOST BEGINS AND ENDS,  .  .  .  .  .   604  GALLERY REVIS        54
     AND THINK IT IS NO SHAME.  .  .  .  .  .  .  .  .  .  .  .  .  605  SONGS BURDEN 1        4
     MY HUNDREDTH YEAR IS AT AN END.  I THINK   .  .  .  .  .  .  . 609  IN TARAS HALLS        3
     THAT SOMETHING IS ABOUT TO HAPPEN, I THINK .  .  .  .  .  .  . 609  IN TARAS HALLS        4
     SOME THINK IT A MATTER OF COURSE THAT CHANCE .  .  .  .  .  .  626  OLD MEN BE MAD        9
     SOME THINK IT MATTER OF COURSE THAT CHANCE .  .  .  .  .  .  . 626  OLD MEN BE MAD   V    9
     BOTH DEAD!--NO TIME TO THINK.  I AM SHE,  .  .  .  .  .  .  .  673  ISLE STAT II 3      190
     TO SAINTED EBREMAR'S SAD EYES.  I THINK  .  .  .  .  .  .  .   696  MOSADA 2             15
     BE ONE?  I THINK ALL'S FINISHED NOW AND SEALED.  .  .  .  .  . 701  MOSADA 3             62
     FOR AN IMMORTAL WOMAN, AS I THINK.  .  .  .  .  .  .  .  .  .  755  SHADOW WATER A      173
     I THINK HE LIVES IN LOCHLANN.  NO, NOT THERE!  .  .  .  .  .   760  SHADOW WATER A   V 254A
     I THINK THAT THERE IS LOVE IN AIBRIC'S EYES.  .  .  .  .  .  . 768  SHADOW WATER A      407
     THERE'S SO MUCH TO THINK ABOUT .  .  .  .  .  .  .  .  .  .  . 772  SONG DEIRDRE 1        7
THINKIN'
     I'M THINKIN' OF MY BABY .  .  .  .  .  .  .  .  .  .  .  .  .   96  MOLL MAGEE           47
THINKING
     IT HAD GROWN WISE-TONGUED BY THINKING   .  .  .  .  .  .  .  . 159  CAP AND BELLS         7
     IT HAD GROWN MOST WISE WITH THINKING  .  .  .  .  .  .  .  .   159  CAP AND BELLS    V    7
     AND IT HAD GROWN WISE BY THINKING .  .  .  .  .  .  .  .  .  . 159  CAP AND BELLS    V    7
     WILL HARDLY SEEM WORTH THINKING OF  .  .  .  .  .  .  .  .  .  202  NEVER GIVE ALL        2
     FOR HE WOULD BE THINKING OF LOVE  .  .  .  .  .  .  .  .  .  . 268  BROWN PENNY          12
     THINKING OF SAINTS AND OF PETRONIUS ARBITER.  .  .  .  .  .  . 362  HER COURTESY          8
     AHERNE LAUGHED, THINKING OF THE MAN WITHIN,  .  .  .  .  .  .  375  PHASES OF MOON       85
     IN THINKING OF HIS LOST RENOWN.  .  .  .  .  .  .  .  .  .  .  379  SAINT HUNCH           3
     I AM THINKING OF A CHILD'S VOW SWORN IN VAIN .  .  .  .  .  .  391  UNDER SATURN         15
     AND THINKING OF THAT FIT OF GRIEF OR RAGE .  .  .  .  .  .  .  443  SCHOOL CHILDR        17
     THINKING TO SET AT REST .  .  .  .  .  .  .  .  .  .  .  .  .  496  MOHINI CHATTER   V   12
     NOT WORTH THINKING OF,  .  .  .  .  .  .  .  .  .  .  .  .  .  504  QUARREL IN AGE        5
     THINKING TO MEET MY LOVE ONCE MORE  .  .  .  .  .  .  .  .  .  551  SONGS REWRIT 1   V   15
     BOTH DEAD!--NO TIME FOR THINKING.  I AM SHE,  .  .  .  .  .  . 673  ISLE STAT II 3   V  190
     I LEFT HER LIVING, THINKING THAT I HAD FOUND .  .  .  .  .  .  755  SHADOW WATER A      174
THINKS
     HE THINKS OF THOSE WHO HAVE SPOKEN EVIL OF HIS BELOVED .  .   166  EVIL OF BELOV         T
     AEDH THINKS OF THOSE WHO HAVE SPOKEN EVIL OF HIS BELOVED     166  EVIL OF BELOV    V    T
     HE THINKS OF HIS PAST GREATNESS .  .  .  .  .  .  .  .  .  .   177  PAST GREATNESS        T
     MONGAN THINKS OF HIS PAST GREATNESS .  .  .  .  .  .  .  .  .  177  PAST GREATNESS   V    T
     THINKS THAT THE STONE'S A CHILD.  .  .  .  .  .  .  .  .  .  . 456  FRIENDS YOUTH        12
     HE THINKS THAT SHAPE MUST BE HIS SHAPE?  .  .  .  .  .  .  .   479  SELF AND SOUL        54
     THINKS IN A MARROW-BONE!  .  .  .  .  .  .  .  .  .  .  .  .   553  PRAYER OLD AGE        4
     THINKS IN A MARROW BONE!  .  .  .  .  .  .  .  .  .  .  .  .   553  PRAYER OLD AGE   V    4
     THE COUNTRY THINKS NO END OF HIM,  .  .  .  .  .  .  .  .  .   583  GHOST ROG CASE       13
     SHE THINKS, PART WOMAN, THREE PARTS A CHILD,  .  .  .  .  .  . 617  LONG-LEG FLY         15
THIRD
     OF THE THIRD MOON, THAT HUNG BETWEEN THE NIGHT AND THE DAY,  210  UNDER THE MOON   V   18
     SLEEP BEFORE THE THIRD NOON SOUNDS."  .  .  .  .  .  .  .  .   295  THREE BEGGARS        24
     THE THIRD!  "I'LL HURRY TO THE COURSE .  .  .  .  .  .  .  .   296  THREE BEGGARS        33
     BUT THE THIRD CRIED!  "I'LL TO THE COURSE .  .  .  .  .  .  .  296  THREE BEGGARS    V   33
     ON A WINDY STONE, THE THIRD,  .  .  .  .  .  .  .  .  .  .  .  298  THREE HERMITS         5
     CAUGHT AND CRACKED HIS FLEA, THE THIRD,  .  .  .  .  .  .  .   299  THREE HERMITS        30
     MONTASHIGI, THIRD OF HIS FAMILY, FASHIONED IT .  .  .  .  .   478  SELF AND SOUL        25
     "THE THIRD THING THAT I THINK OF YET,"  .  .  .  .  .  .  .   521  THREE THINGS         13
     THIRD SONG .  .  .  .  .  .  .  .  .  .  .  .  .  .  .  .  .   547  TO SAME TUNE 3   V    T
     TWO CHINAMEN, BEHIND THEM A THIRD,  .  .  .  .  .  .  .  .  .  566  LAPIS LAZULI         37
     THE THIRD, DOUBTLESS A SERVING-MAN,  .  .  .  .  .  .  .  .   566  LAPIS LAZULI         41
     THE LADY'S THIRD SONG .  .  .  .  .  .  .  .  .  .  .  .  .   573  LADYS 3RD SONG        T
THIRST
     WHEN ALL BUT DEAD OF THIRST.  .  .  .  .  .  .  .  .  .  .  .  454  EMPTY CUP             2
     WHEN ALL BUT DEAD WITH THIRST,  .  .  .  .  .  .  .  .  .  .  454  EMPTY CUP        V    2
     YOUR THIRST FOR THOSE OLD CRABBED MYSTERIES,  .  .  .  .  .   465  HARUN RASHID         86
     I THIRST FOR ACCUSATION.  ALL THAT WAS SUNG,  .  .  .  .  .   542  PARN FUNERAL 1       25
     TO EASE THEIR WORLD-OLD THIRST ALONG THE BRINK .  .  .  .  .  663  ISLE STAT II 2       41
     NASCHINA'S GONE, DRAWN BY A THIRST OF LOVE,  .  .  .  .  .  . 664  ISLE STAT II 2       59
     AND HER GIGANTIC LIMBS.  THE WEARY THIRST .  .  .  .  .  .  . 687  TWO TITANS           16
THIRSTING
     WHAT THE WORLD'S MILLION LIPS ARE THIRSTING FOR .  .  .  .   229  SHADOW WATER B      161
THIRTEEN        SEE NINETEEN-THIRTEEN
THIRTEENTH
     THE THIRTEENTH MOON BUT SETS THE SOUL AT WAR .  .  .  .  .   374  PHASES OF MOON       50
THIRTY          SEE NINETEEN-THIRTY-TWO NINETEEN-THIRTY-ONE
     WHY MUST I LIVE SOME THIRTY, FORTY YEARS,  .  .  .  .  .  .   285  TWO KINGS           199
     THAT THIRTY CENTURIES OF STONY SLEEP .  .  .  .  .  .  .  .   402  SECOND COMING    V   19
     AROUND ME THE IMAGES OF THIRTY YEARS!  .  .  .  .  .  .  .    601  GALLERY REVIS         1
THITHER
     NO LIVE MAN GOES THITHER,  .  .  .  .  .  .  .  .  .  .  .  .   62  OISIN 3          V  214
     HITHER AND THITHER TO AND FRO THEY TROD .  .  .  .  .  .  .   278  TWO KINGS            26
     THITHER THY DUST, AND KNEAD IT WITH A CRY,  .  .  .  .  .  .  688  TWO TITANS           52
     THAT HAVE GONE THITHER TO LOOK FOR THE LOUD STREAMS,  .  .   765  SHADOW WATER A      348
     HITHER AND THITHER AND SAY AT THE HIGH NOON  .  .  .  .  .   767  SHADOW WATER A      404
THONG
     BOUND A THONG ABOUT HIS HAND,  .  .  .  .  .  .  .  .  .  .   595  COLONEL MARTIN       25
THONGS
     AND CAPTIVES BOUND WITH LEATHERN THONGS .  .  .  .  .  .  .     7  OISIN 1              77
     MY CAPTIVES, BOUND IN LEATHERN THONGS,  .  .  .  .  .  .  .     8  OISIN 1          V   78
     TO THOSE ABOUT, "BEAT HIM WITH THONGS OF HIDE .  .  .  .  .   106  CUCHULAIN SEA    V  17A
     WITH THONGS OF LEATHER."  AS SHE SPAKE IT WAS!  .  .  .  .   106  CUCHULAIN SEA    V  17B
THOOR
     TO BE CARVED ON A STONE AT THOOR BALLYLEE .  .  .  .  .  .   406  CARVED STONE          T
THORN
     OUR HEARTS ENDURE THE PLAITED THORN, THE CROWDED WAY,  .  .  172  TRAV PASSION     V    3
     TILL IT DIED OUT WHERE AN OLD THORN TREE STOOD.  .  .  .  .  186  QUEEN MAEVE      V  129
```

		PAGE	TITLE		LINE
THORN	(CONTINUED)				
	WHO STOOD AMID A SILENCE BY THE THORN	187	QUEEN MAEVE		142
	THE OLD BROWN THORN TREES BREAK IN TWO HIGH OVER CUMANN'S	206	HANRAHANS SONG	V	1
	STRAND,				
	WERE TWISTED LIKE THE OLD THORN TREES	208	OLD MEN ADMIRE	V	5
	WHERE BY OLD THORN TREES THAT MAN STOOD:	274	GREY ROCK	V	80
	HE HAD BUT GAZED ON THORN TREES, SPOKE!	274	GREY ROCK	V	82
	AMONG THE STONES AND THORN TREES, UNDER MORNING LIGHT, .	291	PAUDEEN	V	3
	TO COLD CLARE ROCK AND GALWAY ROCK AND THORN, ...	326	ROBERT GREGORY		66
	THE THORN TREE	350	HER PRAISE	V	T
	BUT WALK BY THE DRY THORN UNTIL I HAVE FOUND	351	HER PRAISE		12
	AND BODIES BROKEN LIKE A THORN	454	HIS MEMORIES		3
	MY ARMS ARE LIKE THE TWISTED THORN	455	HIS MEMORIES		11
	UNDER THE RAGGED THORN?	519	LOVES LONENESS		10
THORNS					
	UNDER A CROWN OF THORNS AND DARK WITH BLOOD, ...	38	OISIN 2		135
	I HAVE BEEN IN THE PATH OF STONES AND THE WOOD OF THORNS,	153	CHANGE BELOVED		3
	OUR HEARTS ENDURE THE SCOURGE, THE PLAITED THORNS, THE WAY	172	TRAV PASSION		3
	OLD RAGGED ELMS, OLD THORNS INNUMERABLE, ...	419	MY HOUSE		5
THORN-TREE					
	TILL IT DIED OUT WHERE AN OLD THORN-TREE STOOD.	186	QUEEN MAEVE		129
	WE SAT UNDER AN OLD THORN-TREE	456	SUMMER SPRING		1
THORN-TREES					
	THE OLD BROWN THORN-TREES BREAK IN TWO HIGH OVER CUMMEN	206	HANRAHANS SONG		1
	STRAND,				
	WERE TWISTED LIKE THE OLD THORN-TREES	208	OLD MEN ADMIRE		5
	WHERE BY OLD THORN-TREES THAT MAN STOOD:	274	GREY ROCK		80
	HE HAD BUT GAZED ON THORN-TREES, SPOKE, ...	274	GREY ROCK		82
	AMONG THE STONES AND THORN-TREES, UNDER MORNING LIGHT: .	291	PAUDEEN		3
THOROUGHBRED					
	SOME BACK A MARE THROWN FROM A THOROUGHBRED, ...	547	TO SAME TUNE 3		3
	SOME BACK A MARE THROWN FROM A THOROUGHBRED, ...	614	MARCH SONGS 2		3
THOROUGH-BRED					
	SOME BACK A MARE THROWN FROM A THOROUGH-BRED, ...	547	TO SAME TUNE 3	V	3
THOROUGHFARE					
	FROM THOROUGHFARE TO THOROUGHFARE, ...	294	HATED PLAYBOY	V	3
	FROM THOROUGHFARE TO THOROUGHFARE, ...	294	HATED PLAYBOY	V	3
THOROUGHFARES					
	PEDDLED IN THE THOROUGHFARES.	406	FOR DAUGHTER		76
THOUGHT					
	WE THOUGHT ON OSCAR'S PENCILLED URN.	2	OISIN 1	V	70
	AND NOW I AM DIZZY WITH THE THOUGHT	7	OISIN 1		65
	BRINGING ME HONEYED, WANDERING THOUGHT	7	OISIN 1	V	65
	NO CREATURE HAD FAMILIAR THOUGHT	17	OISIN 1	V	242
	AND CLIMBED SO LONG, I THOUGHT THE LAST STEPS WERE . .	32	OISIN 2		48
	I THOUGHT THE END HAD RESTED, WHEN THESE WORDS	32	OISIN 2	V	49
	. . . GROWN MILD WITH MYSTERIOUS THOUGHT, ...	55	OISIN 3		121
	AND THOUGHT, I WILL MY HEAVY STORY TELL	68	SAD SHEPHERD		19
	AND THOUGHT, "TO THIS WILL I MY STORY TELL, ...	68	SAD SHEPHERD	V	19
	A SAD, SAD THOUGHT WENT BY ME SLOWLY!	72	ANASHU VIJAYA		17
	THE SAD, SAD THOUGHT HAS GONE FROM ME NOW WHOLLY! . . .	72	ANASHU VIJAYA		19
	THE RAVENS OF UNRESTING THOUGHT, ...	136	TWO TREES		34
	AND THOUGHT NOT OF EVIL CHANCE, ...	145	HOST OF AIR		30
	DIM POWERS OF DROWSY THOUGHT, LET HER NO LONGER BE . .	175	ELEMENT POWERS		13
	AND THOUGHT OF DAYS WHEN HE'D HAD A STRAIGHT BODY, . .	183	QUEEN MAEVE		70
	HALF CRAZY WITH THE THOUGHT, SHE TOO HAS WEPT!	186	QUEEN MAEVE		140
	A MUSIC THAT HAD THOUGHT ENOUGH	193	BAILE AILLINN	V	108
	I THOUGHT OF YOUR BEAUTY, AND THIS ARROW, ...	199	ARROW		1
	MADE OUT OF A WILD THOUGHT, IS IN MY MARROW.	199	ARROW		2
	O THOUGHT, FLY TO HER WHEN THE END OF DAY	201	OLD MEMORY		1
	THROUGH THE LONG YEARS OF YOUTH, AND WHO WOULD HAVE THOUGHT	201	OLD MEMORY		7
	I THOUGHT TO FLY TO HER WHEN THE END OF DAY	201	OLD MEMORY	V	1
	THOUGHT FLY TO HER WHEN THE END OF DAY	201	OLD MEMORY	V	1
	THROUGH THE LONG DAYS OF YOUTH, AND WHO WOULD HAVE THOUGHT	201	OLD MEMORY	V	7
	YET IF IT DOES NOT SEEM A MOMENT'S THOUGHT, ...	204	ADAMS CURSE		5
	BE THOUGHT AN IDLER BY THE NOISY SET	205	ADAMS CURSE		12
	THERE HAVE BEEN LOVERS WHO THOUGHT LOVE SHOULD BE . . .	205	ADAMS CURSE		23
	I HAD A THOUGHT FOR NO ONE'S BUT YOUR EARS:	206	ADAMS CURSE		34
	I HAD A THOUGHT FOR NO ONE BUT YOUR EARS!	206	ADAMS CURSE	V	34
	THEIR OWN THOUGHT FROM THE OTHER'S, ...	212	O DO NOT LOVE		7
	FROM HUMAN THOUGHT, AS HARES AND MICE AND CONEYS . . .	218	WOODS OF COOLE		31
	THESE DOZEN WEEKS. AND I HAD THOUGHT TO MAKE	222	SHADOW WATER B		4
	I'VE THOUGHT OF THAT. WE MUST HAVE AIBRIC WITH US, . .	225	SHADOW WATER B		62
	I HAVE GOOD REASON FOR THAT THOUGHT. AND NOW	238	SHADOW WATER B		354
	I'LL NEVER GIVE ANOTHER THOUGHT TO IT:	245	SHADOW WATER B		477
	NO, NO, NOR HALF A THOUGHT! BUT DO NOT SPEAK.	245	SHADOW WATER B		478
	HOW GREAT A WRONG IT IS TO LET ONE'S THOUGHT	246	SHADOW WATER B		514
	I THOUGHT, "HE HOLDS HER DEAR,"	254	WOMAN HOMER		3
	TO SUCH A PITCH MY THOUGHT	255	WOMAN HOMER		11
	I HAD THIS THOUGHT A WHILE AGO, ...	255	WORDS		1
	I HAD THIS THOUGHT AWHILE AGO, ...	255	WORDS	V	1
	THOUGH HE'D BUT CANNON--WHEREAS WE THAT HAD THOUGHT . .	258	KING NO KING		7
	THOUGHT, IN THAT SCALE OF HIS!	267	FRIEND ILLNESS		2
	HAVING NO THOUGHT BUT FOR HIS QUEEN EDAIN, ...	276	TWO KINGS	V	1
	HE THOUGHT TO HAVE GIVEN HIS HORSE THE SPUR, BUT SAW .	277	TWO KINGS	V	48
	BUT DREW HIS SWORD, AND THOUGHT WITH LEVELLED POINT . .	277	TWO KINGS	V	14
	BUT WHEN HE THOUGHT TO TAKE HER IN HIS ARMS	280	TWO KINGS		67
	THEN HE, DRIVEN BY HIS THOUGHT BEYOND HIS THOUGHT, . .	282	TWO KINGS		122
	THEN HE, DRIVEN BY HIS THOUGHT BEYOND HIS THOUGHT, . .	282	TWO KINGS		122
	THEN HE, DRIVEN BY THIS THOUGHT BEYOND HIS THOUGHT, . .	282	TWO KINGS	V	122
	THEN HE, DRIVEN BY THIS THOUGHT BEYOND HIS THOUGHT, . .	282	TWO KINGS	V	122

810

THOUGHT (CONTINUED)

		PAGE	TITLE		LINE
WHAT TH' ONION-SELLERS THOUGHT OR DID		287	TO WEALTHY MAN		11
WHAT TH' ONION SELLERS THOUGHT OR DID		287	TO WEALTHY MAN	V	11
A CURLEW ANSWERED; AND SUDDENLY THEREUPON I THOUGHT		291	PAUDEEN		5
A CURLEW ANSWERED, AND I WAS STARTLED BY THE THOUGHT		291	PAUDEEN	V	5
HAD GIVEN THEIR CHILDREN'S CHILDREN LOFTIER THOUGHT,		292	TO A SHADE		12
BUT GUAIRE LAUGHED WITH SECRET THOUGHT,		295	THREE BEGGARS		19
THE SECOND: "I HAVE THOUGHT AGAIN;		296	THREE BEGGARS		36
"BUT NOW THAT I HAVE THOUGHT AGAIN,		296	THREE BEGGARS	V	36
I HAD BEEN HURT," THE OLD BEGGAR THOUGHT		302	HOUR DAWN	V	19
HE GAVE A GASP AND THOUGHT TO HAVE FLED,		303	HOUR DAWN		22
HE GAVE A GASP AND THOUGHT TO RUN,		303	HOUR DAWN	V	22
I THOUGHT TO WAIT FOR THAT OR THIS;		305	HOUR DAWN		64
MY LIFE OF EVERY PLEASANT THOUGHT		307	HOUR DAWN		110
ONE BECAUSE NO THOUGHT,		315	FRIENDS		4
ONE THAT NO PASSING THOUGHT,		315	FRIENDS	V	4
SO WILD THAT EVERY CASUAL THOUGHT OF THAT AND THIS		316	COLD HEAVEN		4
A LITTLE NEARER TO HIS THOUGHT		324	ROBERT GREGORY		23
I HAD THOUGHT, SEEING HOW BITTER IS THAT WIND		327	ROBERT GREGORY		89
A FITTER WELCOME; BUT A THOUGHT		328	ROBERT GREGORY		95
I THOUGHT NO MORE WAS NEEDED		334	SONG		1
I THOUGHT 'TWOULD BURN MY BODY		335	SONG		15
WHEN THE WILD THOUGHT,		336	YOUNG GIRL		7
I LET THEM STRAY. I THOUGHT OF RHYME ALONE,		339	SHEP GOATHERD		11
YOU HAVE PUT THE THOUGHT IN RHYME. I WORKED ALL DAY,		341	SHEP GOATHERD		58
MAY BE A QUIET THOUGHT TO WIFE AND MOTHER,		343	SHEP GOATHERD		118
NOR QUARRELS WITH A THOUGHT		345	ON WOMAN		7
WAS: "YOU, THAT HAVE NOT LIVED IN THOUGHT BUT DEED,		353	PEOPLE		30
A THOUGHT FROM PROPERTIUS		355	PROPERTIUS		T
HAPPIER DAYS THOUGHT GOOD;		365	HER RACE		4
WITHOUT AN ANGRY THOUGHT		366	HER CHRIS TREE		2
ALL THOUGHT BECOMES AN IMAGE AND THE SOUL		374	PHASES OF MOON		58
FIXED UPON IMAGES THAT ONCE WERE THOUGHT;		375	PHASES OF MOON		80
AND NEVER WROTE A BOOK, YOUR THOUGHT IS CLEAR.		376	PHASES OF MOON		97
WE NEVER THOUGHT TO ENQUIRE.		381	SONGS FOOL 2		3
SO SHE HAD OUTDANCED THOUGHT.		383	VISION ROBART		39
SO THAT SHE DANCED. NO THOUGHT,		383	VISION ROBART	V	39
WHO NEVER GAVE THE BURNING TOWN A THOUGHT;		384	VISION ROBART		57
THE COMMONNESS OF THOUGHT AND IMAGES		384	VISION ROBART		61
THE HALF-DEAD DRAGON WAS HER THOUGHT,		385	ROBARTES DANCE		6
HER LOVER THOUGHT, UPON THE GLASS		385	ROBARTES DANCE		11
GIVE MAN HIS THOUGHT OR HIS MERE BODY?		386	ROBARTES DANCE		40
WILL BANISH EVERY THOUGHT, UNLESS		387	ROBARTES DANCE		48
AND WOULD NOT NOW BUT THAT HE THOUGHT,		388	SOLOMON WITCH		13
THOUGHT TO HAVE CROWED IT IN AGAIN.		388	SOLOMON WITCH		18
ALTHOUGH HE THOUGHT IT WORTH A CROW.		388	SOLOMON WITCH		35
I HAD THOUGHT THAT ALL MY DAYS WERE CAST		389	IMAGE PAST		12
IMAGINE THAT LOST LOVE, INSEPARABLE FROM MY THOUGHT		390	UNDER SATURN		2
AND THOUGHT BEFORE I HAD DONE		392	EASTER 1916		9
SO DARING AND SWEET HIS THOUGHT.		393	EASTER 1916		30
HER THOUGHT SOME POPULAR ENMITY;		397	POLIT PRISONER		10
FOR THOUGHT SOME POPULAR ENMITY		397	POLIT PRISONER	V	10
I THOUGHT; "THERE IS A WATERFALL		398	BREAK OF DAY		5
FOR ALL MEN'S THOUGHT GREW CLEAR		400	DEMON BEAST	V	5
YET HAVE NO DEARER THOUGHT		401	DEMON BEAST		40
LOVED AND THOUGHT HIMSELF BELOVED,		404	FOR DAUGHTER		39
I THOUGHT IT ALL OUT TWENTY YEARS AGO;		411	TOWER		64
COWARDICE, SOME SILLY OVER-SUBTLE THOUGHT		413	TOWER		117
COWARDICE, OVER SOME SILLY SUBTLE THOUGHT		413	TOWER	V	117
I MOCK PLOTINUS' THOUGHT		415	TOWER		146
A SUFFERING PASSION AND A LABOURING THOUGHT?		420	MY HOUSE		20J
TO SILENCE THE ENVY IN MY THOUGHT;		424	ROAD AT DOOR		13
WE THOUGHT IT WOULD OUTLIVE ALL FUTURE DAYS.		428	NINETEEN 19		14
O WHAT FINE THOUGHT WE HAD BECAUSE WE THOUGHT		428	NINETEEN 19		15
O WHAT FINE THOUGHT WE HAD BECAUSE WE THOUGHT		428	NINETEEN 19		15
O WHAT FINE THOUGHTS WE HAD BECAUSE WE THOUGHT		428	NINETEEN 19	V	15
THOUGHT THAT UNLESS A LITTLE POWDER BURNED		429	NINETEEN 19		21
NONE DARED ADMIT, IF SUCH A THOUGHT WERE HIS,		430	NINETEEN 19		44
NOR THOUGHT OF THE LEVELLING WIND.		432	NINETEEN 19		97
THERE LURCHES PAST; HIS GREAT EYES WITHOUT THOUGHT		433	NINETEEN 19		126
OF SOME MOST HAUGHTY DEED OR THOUGHT		436	FOR MY SON		13
IN PITY FOR MAN'S DARKENING THOUGHT		438	SONGS PLAY 2		1
PLATO THOUGHT NATURE BUT A SPUME THAT PLAYS		445	SCHOOL CHILDR		41
UNTIL I THOUGHT HER BODY BORE		451	FIRST LOVE		5
EMPTIER OF THOUGHT		451	FIRST LOVE		16
BUT THAT'S A TRAITOR'S THOUGHT. ENOUGH FOR ME		462	HARUN RASHID		39
A MIMICRY OF YOUTH. CAN POET'S THOUGHT		463	HARUN RASHID		62
A MIMICRY OF YOUTH. AN ARTIST'S THOUGHT,		463	HARUN RASHID	V	62
LIVED AT MY SIDE; THOUGHT TIME'S DISFIGURING TOUCH		466	HARUN RASHID		110
NOR THOUGHT OUT OF HER MIND OR MINE BEGOT,		467	HARUN RASHID		140
NOR THOUGHT OUT OF HER MIND OR OUT OF MINE		467	HARUN RASHID	V	140
HORTON'S THE FIRST I CALL. HE LOVED STRANGE THOUGHT		471	ALL SOUL NIGHT		21
WHETHER OF HER OR GOD HE THOUGHT THE MOST,		471	ALL SOUL NIGHT		32
I THOUGHT HIM HALF A LUNATIC, HALF KNAVE,		473	ALL SOUL NIGHT		64
FOR MEDITATIONS UPON UNKNOWN THOUGHT		473	ALL SOUL NIGHT		74
SUCH THOUGHT--SUCH THOUGHT HAVE I THAT HOLD IT TIGHT		474	ALL SOUL NIGHT		91
SUCH THOUGHT--SUCH THOUGHT HAVE I THAT HOLD IT TIGHT		474	ALL SOUL NIGHT		91
SUCH THOUGHT, THAT IN IT BOUND		474	ALL SOUL NIGHT		97
FIX EVERY WANDERING THOUGHT UPON		477	SELF AND SOUL		6
THAT QUARTER WHERE ALL THOUGHT IS DONE;		477	SELF AND SOUL		7
EVERY EVENT IN ACTION OR IN THOUGHT;		479	SELF AND SOUL		66

<table>
<thead>
<tr><th></th><th>PAGE</th><th>TITLE</th><th></th><th>LINE</th></tr>
</thead>
</table>

THOUGHT   (CONTINUED)

```
      COUNT EVERY SIN OF ACTION OR OF THOUGHT;  . . . . . .    479 SELF AND SOUL   V   66
      WE THAT HAVE DONE AND THOUGHT, . . . . . . . . . .       484 SPILT MILK          1
      THAT HAVE THOUGHT AND DONE. . . . . . . . . . . .        484 SPILT MILK          2
      BUT MINE SAW STELLA ONCE.  WHENCE CAME OUR THOUGHT? . .  486 SEVEN SAGES         6
      MINE SAW STELLA ONCE.  WHENCE CAME OUR THOUGHT? . . . .  486 SEVEN SAGES     V   6
      MINE SAW STELLA ONCE.  WHEN CAME OUR THOUGHT? . . . .    486 SEVEN SAGES     V   6
      THOUGHTS LONG KNITTED INTO A SINGLE THOUGHT, . . . . .   488 COOLE PARK 29       7
      AND FROM THE FORTIETH WINTER BY THAT THOUGHT . . . . .   501 VACILLATION        29
      BUT THOUGHT THAT I MIGHT SAY OR DO, . . . . . . .        501 VACILLATION        53
      THE RESULTS OF THOUGHT . . . . . . . . . . . . .         504 RESULT THOUGHT      T
      CAME TO SO DEEP A THOUGHT  . . . . . . . . . . .         505 RESULT THOUGHT     10
      I THOUGHT IT OUT THIS VERY DAY, . . . . . . . . .        525 DANCING DAYS       17
      HAD I NEVER THOUGHT  . . . . . . . . . . . . . .         534 CONSOLATION         8
      A THOUGHTLESS IMAGE OF MANTEGNA'S THOUGHT-- . . . . .    537 HER VISION         20
      I THOUGHT TO HAVE WHISTLED HER DOWN THAT WAY, . . . .    551 SONGS REWRIT 1     15
      I HAD THOUGHT TO HAVE CALLED HER OUT TO THE DOOR, . . .  551 SONGS REWRIT 1  V  15
      FROM EVERY THOUGHT OF GOD MANKIND HAS HAD. . . . . .     558 RIBH CHRISTIAN     15
      THOUGHT IS A GARMENT AND THE SOUL'S A BRIDE . . . . .    558 RIBH CHRISTIAN     16
      SENTENCES THAT HE HAS NEVER THOUGHT; . . . . . . .       560 WHENCE COME         6
      BY MANIFOLD ILLUSION; BUT MAN'S LIFE IS THOUGHT, . . .   563 MERU                3
      THINGS THOUGHT TOO LONG CAN BE NO LONGER THOUGHT, . . .  564 GYRES               2
      THINGS THOUGHT TOO LONG CAN BE NO LONGER THOUGHT, . . .  564 GYRES               2
      "THAT WAS A LUCKY THOUGHT OF MINE, . . . . . . . .       570 THREE BUSHES       31
      THOUGHT FOR I KNOW NOT WHERE, . . . . . . . . . .        574 LOVERS SONG         2
      HIS CHOSEN COMRADES THOUGHT AT SCHOOL . . . . . . .      576 WHAT THEN           1
      HE THOUGHT THE SAME AND LIVED BY RULE. . . . . . .       576 WHAT THEN           3
      "THE WORK IS DONE," GROWN OLD HE THOUGHT, . . . . .      577 WHAT THEN          16
      "I NEVER THOUGHT OF THAT, SIR." . . . . . . . . .        596 COLONEL MARTIN     66
      CHILDLESS I THOUGHT, "MY CHILDREN MAY FIND HERE . . .    603 GALLERY REVIS      36
      JOHN SYNGE, I AND AUGUSTA GREGORY, THOUGHT . . . . .     603 GALLERY REVIS      41
      CHILDLESS, I THOUGHT, "MY CHILDREN MAY LEARN HERE . . .  603 GALLERY REVIS   V  36
      SOME HAD NO THOUGHT OF VICTORY . . . . . . . . .         608 SONGS BURDEN 3     19
      THE FIRST ADAM IN THEIR THOUGHT, . . . . . . . . .       617 LONG-LEG FLY       22
      PROFOUND MCTAGGART THOUGHT SO, AND IN A BREATH  . . .    619 BRONZE HEAD        13
      I SAW THE WILDNESS IN HER AND I THOUGHT . . . . . .      619 BRONZE HEAD        16
      OR ELSE I THOUGHT HER SUPERNATURAL; . . . . . . .        619 BRONZE HEAD        22
      SAINT JOSEPH THOUGHT THE WORLD WOULD MELT . . . . .      619 STICK INCENSE       3
      I THOUGHT MY DEAR MUST HER OWN SOUL DESTROY, . . . .     630 CIRCUS ANIMALS     21
      THIS DREAM ITSELF HAD ALL MY THOUGHT AND LOVE. . . .     630 CIRCUS ANIMALS     24
      THAT HAS READ AND THOUGHT, . . . . . . . . . . .         631 POLITICS            8
      THAT HAS BOTH READ AND THOUGHT, . . . . . . . . .        631 POLITICS        V   8
      AND ITS CRY DISTRACTS MY THOUGHT. . . . . . . . .        633 MAN AND ECHO       46
      FORMS A STARK EGYPTIAN THOUGHT. . . . . . . . . .        638 BEN BULBEN         43
      CONFUSION FELL UPON OUR THOUGHT. . . . . . . . .         639 BEN BULBEN         67
      AND THOU WILT STAY.  ALL THOUGHT OF WHAT THEY FIND  . .  670 ISLE STAT II 3     92
      HE THOUGHT WISE THINGS AS HIS GREY HEAD NODDED. . . .    728 PRIEST FAIRY       12
      AND SMILING FROM SWEET THOUGHT, . . . . . . . . .        741 EARL PAUL          42
      AND THOUGHT THAT SHE HAD NO HEART. . . . . . . . .       744 GLOVE CLOAK         4
      I THOUGHT SHE LOVED YOU, AND I THOUGHT HER LOVE . . .    749 SHADOW WATER A     51
      I THOUGHT SHE LOVED YOU, AND I THOUGHT HER LOVE . . .    749 SHADOW WATER A     51
      BORN OUT OF IMMODERATE THOUGHT; . . . . . . . . .        772 SONG DEIRDRE 1     12
      YOUR OWN THOUGHT WILL HAVE DIED . . . . . . . . .        786 YOUR HEART         30
      HER OWN THOUGHT WILL HAVE DIED . . . . . . . . . .       786 YOUR HEART      V  30
      HARD-LIVING MEN AND MEN OF THOUGHT . . . . . . . .       787 HUDDON DUDDON      13
      IT CHASES OTHER THOUGHT AWAY, . . . . . . . . . .        791 REPRISALS           9
THOUGHTED      SEE HAPPIER-THOUGHTED
      OR HAPPIER THOUGHTED WHEN THE DAY IS SPENT . . . . .     292 TO A SHADE      V   4
THOUGHTLESS
      A THOUGHTLESS IMAGE OF MANTEGNA'S THOUGHT--  . . . . .   537 HER VISION         20
      THOUGHTLESS JOY AND SORROW SAGE. . . . . . . . .         733 STREET DANCERS     47
      THOUGHTLESS JOYS AND SORROWS SAGE. . . . . . . .         733 STREET DANCERS  V  47
THOUGHT'S
      . . . THOUGHT'S CROWNED POWERS HE CALLED THEM ONCE. . .  480 BLOOD AND MOON     15
THOUGHTS
      AND MAY THE THOUGHTS OF IRELAND BROOD . . . . . . .      138 TO IRELAND         15
      AND STILL THE THOUGHTS OF IRELAND BROOD, . . . . .       138 TO IRELAND      V  15
      BEFORE MY THOUGHTS BEGIN TO RUN . . . . . . . . .        189 BAILE AILLINN       3
      AND FLYING TOWARDS THEIR PEACE.  PUT BY THESE THOUGHTS,  226 SHADOW WATER B     91
      HIS NAME WILL COME INTO OUR THOUGHTS IN A MINUTE. . . .  241 SHADOW WATER B    391
      IT WAS THAT HARPER PUT IT IN MY THOUGHTS, . . . . .      243 SHADOW WATER B    423
      BUT NOW IT IS YOUR THOUGHTS THAT WANDER AWAY, . . . .    246 SHADOW WATER B    512
      UNTIL MY THOUGHTS CLEARED UP AGAIN, . . . . . . .        256 WORDS               6
      MY BARREN THOUGHTS HAVE CHILLED ME TO THE BONE. . . .    257 RECONCILIATION     12
      MOMENTARY THOUGHTS  . . . . . . . . . . . . . .          260 FASC DIFFICULT  V   T
      AND THE SWEET LAUGHING EAGLE THOUGHTS THAT GROW  . . .   264 HOUSE SHAKEN        5
      BECAUSE THERE IS SUCH A STORM AMID MY THOUGHTS . . .     281 TWO KINGS         100
      WITH HIS OLD THOUGHTS, YOUNG GUAIRE WENT. . . . . .      296 THREE BEGGARS      26
      WHEN ALL THOUGHTS AND DEEDS ARE RECKONED, . . . . .      298 THREE HERMITS      15
      ALL, ALL ARE IN MY THOUGHTS TO-NIGHT BEING DEAD. . . .   324 ROBERT GREGORY      8
      DISCOVERED THAT MY THOUGHTS, NOT IT, . . . . . . .       333 SOLOMON SHEBA      15
      MY DAILY THOUGHTS SINCE THE FIRST STUPOR OF YOUTH  . .   342 SHEP GOATHERD      83
      SING; FOR IT MAY BE THAT YOUR THOUGHTS HAVE PLUCKED . .  342 SHEP GOATHERD      85
      FOR ALL MEN'S THOUGHTS GREW CLEAR . . . . . . . .        400 DEMON BEAST        19
      THAT ALL HER THOUGHTS MAY LIKE THE LINNET BE, . . . .    404 FOR DAUGHTER       42
      THOUGHTS UPON THE PRESENT STATE OF THE WORLD . . . .     428 NINETEEN 19     V   T
      O WHAT FINE THOUGHTS WE HAD BECAUSE WE THOUGHT  . . .    428 NINETEEN 19     V  15
      WE PIECED OUR THOUGHTS INTO PHILOSOPHY, . . . . . .      429 NINETEEN 19        30
      WHEN THOUGHTS THAT A FOOL . . . . . . . . . . .          449 HERO GIRL FOOL     21
      O BUT HER HEART WOULD BREAK TO LEARN MY THOUGHTS ARE FAR 450 OWEN AHERNE        20
        AWAY."
```

		PAGE	TITLE	LINE
THOUGHTS	(CONTINUED)			
	TWO THOUGHTS WERE SO MIXED UP I COULD NOT TELL	471	ALL SOUL NIGHT	31
	WHEN THOUGHTS RISE UP UNBID	473	ALL SOUL NIGHT	68
	THOUGHTS LONG KNITTED INTO A SINGLE THOUGHT,	488	COOLE PARK 29	7
	"WHAT CHANGE HAS PUT MY THOUGHTS ASTRAY	529	TOM LUNATIC	3
	GOD GUARD ME FROM THOSE THOUGHTS MEN THINK	553	PRAYER OLD AGE	1
	AN OLD GHOST'S THOUGHTS ARE LIGHTNING,	600	SPIRIT MEDIUM	17
	PURSUES THE THOUGHTS THAT I PURSUE,	633	MAN AND ECHO	32
	AND ITS CRY DISTRACTS MY THOUGHTS.	633	MAN AND ECHO	V 46
	MY DREAMS ROUND THOUGHTS OF PLENTY, AS IN GLOOM	681	SEEKER	3
	MY DREAMS O'ER THOUGHTS OF PLENTY, AS THE RED—	681	SEEKER	V 3
	MY THOUGHTS, AND YONDER BRIGHTENING PATCH OF SKY	700	MOSADA 3	31
	WAS EBREMAR, WHOSE THOUGHTS WERE FIXED ON GOD,	702	MOSADA 3	83
	LIKE HAPPY THOUGHTS GROWN SAD IN EVIL DAYS.	703	MOSADA 3	116
	MANSIONS OF MEMORIES AND MELLOW THOUGHTS	721	WITCH VIVIEN	21
	WHAT SHALLOW THOUGHTS ABOUT DEEP THINGS!	725	LEGEND	11
	THE TANGLED THOUGHTS OF THE FINISHED DAY	728	PRIEST FAIRY	9
	TILL CERTAIN SECOND THOUGHTS HAVE COME	791	REPRISALS	12
THOUGHT-WOVEN				
	THE TALL THOUGHT-WOVEN SAILS, THAT FLAP UNFURLED	113	ROSE OF BATTLE	2
	OUR LONG SHIPS LOOSE THOUGHT-WOVEN SAILS AND WAIT,	115	ROSE OF BATTLE	31
THOUSAND				
	"AND I WILL MAKE A THOUSAND SONGS,	7	OISIN 1	75
	BELOVED IN A THOUSAND SONGS.	7	OISIN 1	V 76
	OF MANY THOUSAND STEPS. SAT EITHER SIDE,	31	OISIN 2	V 35
	WHO HAS BEEN BURIED SOME TWO THOUSAND YEARS?	181	QUEEN MAEVE	35
	TO MANY THOUSAND EYES, AND TO HER OWN	182	QUEEN MAEVE	65
	A THOUSAND YEARS AGO YOU HELD HIGH TALK	187	QUEEN MAEVE	150
	I KNOW THAT HE DIED A THOUSAND YEARS AGO,	241	SHADOW WATER B	392
	AND THAT HE DIED A THOUSAND YEARS AGO.	242	SHADOW WATER B	417
	THESE THOUSAND YEARS. WHAT ARE THE BIRDS AT THERE?	243	SHADOW WATER B	435
	HAVE I NOT LOVED YOU FOR A THOUSAND YEARS?	244	SHADOW WATER B	463
	THAT YOU WERE BORN A THOUSAND YEARS AGO,	245	SHADOW WATER B	468
	FOR HE SHALL HAVE A THOUSAND POUNDS	295	THREE BEGGARS	22
	AND TWICE A THOUSAND MORE	401	DEMON BEAST	47
	AND I ALONE, ONE IN TEN THOUSAND YEARS,	470	HARUN RASHID	V 190
	OUT OF TEN THOUSAND WINTERS, I ALONE—	470	HARUN RASHID	V 190
	UPON A HUNDRED THOUSAND STAGES,	566	LAPIS LAZULI	23
	COME FORTH, FOR IN A THOUSAND BOWERS	647	ISLE STAT I 1	64
	HAVE I NOT SEEN A THOUSAND SEASONS EBB AND FLOW	675	ISLE STAT II 3	229
	THE TIDE OF STARS? HAVE I NOT SEEN A THOUSAND YEARS	675	ISLE STAT II 3	230
	ERE YONDER PALM COMMENCED HIS THOUSAND YEARS?	724	KANVA ON SELF	14
	UNDER THE WAVES, AND TOOK A THOUSAND WOMEN	766	SHADOW WATER A	378
THOUSANDS				
	THOUSANDS OF YEARS, THOUSANDS OF YEARS,	116	FAERY SONG	3
	THOUSANDS OF YEARS, THOUSANDS OF YEARS,	116	FAERY SONG	3
	THOUSANDS OF YEARS, THOUSANDS OF YEARS,	116	FAERY SONG	15
	THOUSANDS OF YEARS, THOUSANDS OF YEARS,	116	FAERY SONG	15
	THOUSANDS OF LEAGUES OVERSEA,	341	SHEP GOATHERD	63
	AND FLOWERS AROUND IN CLUSTERING THOUSANDS ARE,	656	ISLE STAT I 3	24
THRALLS				
	WHO MIGHT HAVE FLOCKS AND HERDS AND MANY THRALLS,	757	SHADOW WATER A	216
THRANEEN				
	CARED NOT A THRANEEN FOR WHAT CHANCED	514	JANE GROWN OLD	18
	CARE NOT A THRANEEN FOR WHAT CHANCED	514	JANE GROWN OLD	V 18
THRASH				
	THAT NIGHT AND MORNING I MAY THRASH	379	SAINT HUNCH	9
THREAD				
	AND HOOKED A BERRY TO A THREAD;	149	WANDER AENGUS	4
	AND PUT A BERRY ON A THREAD;	149	WANDER AENGUS	V 4
	THE LOVE-TALES WROUGHT WITH SILKEN THREAD	155	FORGOT BEAUTY	6
	THE LOVE-TALES WOVE WITH SILKEN THREAD	155	FORGOT BEAUTY	V 6
	"YOUR WELL-BELOVED'S HAIR HAS A THREAD OF GREY,	199	FOLLY COMFORT	V 2
	THE GOLD AND SILVER THREAD.	308	PLAYER QUEEN	8
	SHE PULLED THE THREAD AND BIT THE THREAD	308	PLAYER QUEEN	9
	SHE PULLED THE THREAD AND BIT THE THREAD	308	PLAYER QUEEN	9
	ARE BUT LOOSE THREAD, ARE BUT LOOSE THREAD;	449	HERO GIRL FOOL	23
	ARE BUT LOOSE THREAD, ARE BUT LOOSE THREAD;	449	HERO GIRL FOOL	23
	BEFORE THE THREAD BEGAN	520	HIS BARGAIN	8
	WHEN THE LAST THREAD HAS RUN,	520	HIS BARGAIN	10
	WHEN THE LAZY THREAD HAS RUN—	520	HIS BARGAIN	V 10
	INSTEAD OF THREAD AND NEEDLE	595	COLONEL MARTIN	23
	"WE THREAD THE NEEDLES' EYES, AND ALL WE DO	634	CUCHULAIN COMF	16
	THERE ARE SEVEN THAT PULL THE THREAD.	770	SPINNING SONG	1
	PUT ALL YOUR POWER ON THE THREAD	771	SPINNING SONG	12
THREADBARE				
	. . . SAILS TURNING TO THREADBARE RAGS!	55	OISIN 3	118
	YOUR HOOD IS THREADBARE—SEE THAT IT BE CHANGED	704	MOSADA 3	133
THREAD-BARE				
	. . . SAILS TURNING TO THREAD-BARE RAGS!	55	OISIN 3	V 118
THREADED				
	WITH THEIR MUSHROOMS LIGHTLY THREADED	705	DAWN-SONG	13
THREADS	SEE MIST-THREADS			
	"YOUR WELL-BELOVED'S HAIR HAS THREADS OF GREY,	199	FOLLY COMFORT	2
	"YOUR WELL BELOVED'S HAIR HAS THREADS OF GREY,	199	FOLLY COMFORT	V 2
	SEVEN OLD SISTERS WIND THE THREADS OF THE LONG-LIVED ONES,	209	UNDER THE MOON	7
	SEVEN OLD SISTERS WIND THE THREADS OF THE LONG LIVED ONES,	209	UNDER THE MOON	V 7
	HANG THE MIST THREADS FOR A LITTLE WHILE LIKE COBWEBS IN THE AIR,	719	PHANTOM SHIP	V 29
	BUT WEAVING IT OUT OF THREADS	743	WISDOM DREAMS	3

		PAGE	TITLE		LINE

THREAT
TO BRIBE OR THREAT: HABITS THAT MADE OLD WRONG . . . . 428 NINETEEN 19 11
THREATEN
THREATEN THE HEAD THAT I LOVE. . . . . 119 PITY OF LOVE 8
ALL THREATEN THE HEAD THAT I LOVE. . . . . 119 PITY OF LOVE V 8
THOSE BANNERS COME TO BRIBE OR THREATEN, ... 635 BLACK TOWER 11
THREATENED
UPON A THREATENED HOUSE . . . . 264 HOUSE SHAKEN V T
HER EIGHTIETH WINTER APPROACHING: "YESTERDAY HE THREATENED 578 LOFTY THINGS 8
    MY LIFE.
THREE
HAVE KNOWN THREE CENTURIES, POETS SING, ... 2 OISIN 1 3
WE RODE IN SORROW, WITH STRONG HOUNDS THREE, ... 2 OISIN 1 V 7C
HE SHOOK HIMSELF AND NEIGHED THREE TIMES! . . . . . . 10 OISIN 1 110
AND NEIGHED THREE TIMES. WHEN, WONDERING . . . . . . 10 OISIN 1 V 110A
AND NIAMH BLEW THREE MERRY NOTES . . . . 14 OISIN 1 195
THAT OLD, SEA-WEEDY, SQUARED, THREE HUNDRED FEET . . . 31 OISIN 2 V 30C
WE FEASTED FOR THREE DAYS. ON THE FOURTH MORN . . . . 43 OISIN 2 214
THREE DAYS WE FEASTED, WHEN ON THE FOURTH MORN . . . . 43 OISIN 2 V 214
"LAST OF MY RACE, THREE THINGS I RULE ALONE— . . . . 45 OISIN 2 V 239A
AND DEW-BLANCHED HORNS, IN WHOSE HOLLOW A CHILD OF THREE 49 OISIN 3 30
    YEARS OLD
AND DEW-BLANCHED HORNS, IN WHOSE HOLLOWS A CHILD OF THREE 49 OISIN 3 V 31
    YEARS OLD
AND MY YEARS THREE HUNDRED FELL ON ME. . . . . 60 OISIN 3 191
FOR THREE DAYS MORE IN DREADFUL QUIETUDE, ... 110 CUCHULAIN SEA 78
AND CHAUNTED FOR THREE DAYS. CUCHULAIN STIRRED, . . . 111 CUCHULAIN SEA 83
IN THREE DAYS' TIME HE STOOD UP WITH A MOAN, ... 111 CUCHULAIN SEA 83
IN THREE DAYS' TIME, CUCHULAIN WITH A MOAN . . . . . 111 CUCHULAIN SEA V 83
AND CHANTED FOR THREE DAYS. CUCHULAIN STIRRED, . . . 111 CUCHULAIN SEA V 83
AND HOW BENEATH THOSE THREE TIMES BLESSED SKIES . . . 127 DREAM OF FAERY V 21
AODH TO DECTORA   THREE SONGS . . . . 152 LOSS OF LOVE V T
HE WILL SMILE ON THE THREE OLD SPIRITS, ... 178 FIDDLER DOONEY 11
O KINSMEN OF THE THREE IN ONE, ... 213 BLESS PSALTER 14
AND SAID, "IN TWO OR IN THREE YEARS . . . . 272 GREY ROCK 46
THE THREE BEGGARS . . . . 294 THREE BEGGARS T
AND THERE TO THREE OLD BEGGARS SAID, ... 295 THREE BEGGARS 10
ONE OF YOU THREE IS A RICH MAN, ... 295 THREE BEGGARS 21
BEFORE THE THREE TO END THIS TALE, ... 297 THREE BEGGARS 55
"TIME'S UP," HE CRIED, AND ALL THE THREE . . . . . . 297 THREE BEGGARS 57
"TIME'S UP," HE CRIED, AND ALL THE THREE . . . . . . 297 THREE BEGGARS 59
THE THREE HERMITS . . . . 298 THREE HERMITS T
THREE OLD HERMITS TOOK THE AIR . . . . 298 THREE HERMITS 1
THREE TIMES IN A SINGLE DAY . . . . 298 THREE HERMITS 10
AND DESOLATE THREE ROCK . . . . 310 PEACOCK 5
NOW MUST I THESE THREE PRAISE— . . . . 315 FRIENDS 1
THREE WOMEN THAT HAVE WROUGHT . . . . 315 FRIENDS 2
AND TWO OR THREE HAD CHARM, ... 350 MEMORY 2
ANOTHER BOASTS, "I PICK AND CHOOSE AND HAVE BUT TWO OR 354 HIS PHOENIX 20
    THREE."
UNDER THE THREE LAST CRESCENTS OF THE MOON, ... 377 PHASES OF MOON 133
IN CONTEMPLATION HAD THOSE THREE SO WROUGHT . . . . . 384 VISION ROBART 45
THREE HUNDRED YEARS BEFORE THE FALL, ... 388 SOLOMON WITCH 11
WE THREE MAKE UP A SOLITUDE! . . . . 457 SECRETS OF OLD 9
THE THREE MONUMENTS . . . . 460 THREE MONUMENT T
THE THREE OLD RASCALS LAUGH ALOUD. . . . . 460 THREE MONUMENT 12
THREE MOVEMENTS . . . . 485 THREE MOVEMENT T
THREE THINGS . . . . 521 THREE THINGS T
"O CRUEL DEATH, GIVE THREE THINGS BACK," . . . . . . 521 THREE THINGS 1
"THREE DEAR THINGS THAT WOMEN KNOW," . . . . 521 THREE THINGS 7
THREE SONGS TO THE SAME TUNE . . . . 543 TO SAME TUNE 1 T
THREE SONGS TO THE SAME TUNE   SECOND SONG . . . . . 544 TO SAME TUNE 1 V T
. . . SHARE GOD THAT IS BUT THREE, ... 556 RIBH PATRICK 11
THE THREE BUSHES . . . . 569 THREE BUSHES T
THREE KEGS OF GOLD. . . . . 596 COLONEL MARTIN 49
YOU HAD THREE KEGS" SAID HE. . . . . 596 COLONEL MARTIN 65
WE THREE ALONE IN MODERN TIMES HAD BROUGHT . . . . . 603 GALLERY REVIS 45
THREE SONGS TO THE ONE BURDEN . . . . 605 SONGS BURDEN 1 T
THREE MARCHING SONGS . . . . 613 MARCH SONGS 1 T
SHE THINKS, PART WOMAN, THREE PARTS A CHILD, ... 617 LONG-LEG FLY 15
THROUGH THREE ENCHANTED ISLANDS, ALLEGORICAL DREAMS, . 629 CIRCUS ANIMALS 11
A BUNDLE OF LINEN. SHROUDS BY TWO AND THREE . . . . 634 CUCHULAIN COMF 9
THREE TIMES THE ROSES HAVE GROWN LESS AND LESS, . . . 690 MOSADA 1 1
WHOSE FOOTFALL I HAVE LONGED FOR, THREE SAD SUMMERS, . 692 MOSADA 1 45
WITH THREE BARS CROSSED, AND THESE FOUR WALLS MY WORLD, 700 MOSADA 3 : 32
WE THROW THREE TIMES. . . . . 721 WITCH VIVIEN 39
THREE SPANS HIGH AS HE ROSE TO HIS FEET, ... 729 PRIEST FAIRY 25
THREE MOONS. IT WERE BEST TO KILL HIM, AND CHOOSE OUT . 748 SHADOW WATER A 15
DIMMED AT THREE QUARTER LIGHT . . . . 786 YOUR HEART V 32
I PUT THREE PERSONS IN THEIR PLACE . . . . 787 HUDDON DUDDON 8
THREEFOLD
THE THREEFOLD TERROR OF LOVE: A FALLEN FLARE . . . . 499 MOTHER OF GOD 1
THREE-FOLD
THE THREE-FOLD TERROR OF LOVE: A FALLEN FLARE . . . . 499 MOTHER OF GOD V 1
THREE-LEGGED
I SLEPT ON MY THREE-LEGGED STOOL BY THE FIRE, ... 381 SONGS FOOL 2 1
THREE-QUARTER
DIMMED AT THREE-QUARTER LIGHT, ... 786 YOUR HEART 32
THREE-ROCK
AND DESOLATE THREE-ROCK . . . . 310 PEACOCK V 5

THREES
    CHILDREN SING IN TWOS AND THREES. . . . .   732 STREET DANCERS   17
    THE FLIES THAT DANCE IN THREES, IN TWOS, ...   736 IN CHURCH   11
THREESCORE
    FROM THREESCORE YEARS OF DREAM-LED WANDERING . . . . .   682 SEEKER   16
THREE-SIX
    THREE-SIX. . . . .   721 WITCH VIVIEN   40
THRESHED
    THAT MEN THRESHED CORN AT MIDNIGHT BY A TRESS, ...   170 SECRET ROSE   26
THRESHING
    FORGOTTEN AT THE THRESHING PLACE: . . . .   195 BAILE AILLINN V 148
THRESHING-PLACE
    FORGOTTEN AT THE THRESHING-PLACE: . . . .   195 BAILE AILLINN   148
THRESHOLD
    ABOUT MY THRESHOLD TO COUNSEL AND TO HELP?" . . . .   183 QUEEN MAEVE   82
    CAME TO THE THRESHOLD OF THE PAINTED HOUSE . . . .   185 QUEEN MAEVE   108
    WHAT ON THE THRESHOLD STANDS? . . . .   583 GHOST ROG CASE   2
    BE DRIVEN FROM THE THRESHOLD . . . .   770 BLOOD BOND   5
    THE THRESHOLD AND THE HEARTHSTONE, ...   775 AGAINST WITCH   6
    BUT THE THRESHOLD AND HEARTHSTONE. . . . .   776 AGAINST WITCH   40
THRESHOLDS
    BE DRIVEN FROM THE THRESHOLDS . . . .   770 BLOOD BOND   V   4
THREW
    AND AT THE SUNDOWN THREW HIM IN THE SURGE, ...   44 OISIN 2   219
    AND IN THE EVE I THREW HIM IN THE SURGE, ...   44 OISIN 2   V   219
    WHEREFORE I THREW A PENNY . . . .   268 BROWN PENNY   3
    AGAINST A BEECH-BOLE, HE THREW DOWN THE BEAST . . . .   278 TWO KINGS   36
    AGAINST A BEECH BOLE, HE THREW DOWN THE BEAST . . . .   278 TWO KINGS   V   36
    THEY THREW A HALFPENNY INTO MY CAP, ...   300 RUN PARADISE   2
    THREW UP IN THE AIR HIS MARVELLOUS MOON, ...   314 MEMORY YOUTH V   21
    AND THREW HIM UP TO LAUGH ON THE BOUGH: . . . . .   318 APPOINTMENT   11
    WHETHER SHE THREW THEM UP TO FLOUT ME, ...   390 IMAGE PAST   37
    BUT THEY THREW DOWN THEIR PISTOLS . . . .   596 COLONEL MARTIN   59
    A BERRY THREW FOR ME--OR THEE. . . . .   743 DANAAN QUICK   11
THRICE
    WHEN MAYBE THRICE IN EVERY MOON HER MOUTH . . . . .   468 HARUN RASHID   162
    AND THRICE THE PEACHES FLUSHED UPON THE WALLS, ...   690 MOSADA 1   2
    AND THRICE THE CORN AROUND THE SICKLES FLAMED, ...   690 MOSADA 1   3
    "SAY AND THRICE ANIGH THY DOOR . . . .   730 PRIEST FAIRY   54
    BUT THE MAN IS THRICE FORLORN, ...   776 AGAINST WITCH   26
THRIVE
    "MY BROTHERS AND MY SISTERS LIVE AND THRIVE, ...   32 OISIN 2   V   50C
    IMAGINES BEST TO MAKE IT THRIVE. . . . .   287 TO WEALTHY MAN   8
    WHAT NONE CAN HAVE AND THRIVE, ...   315 FRIENDS   13
    THE WOMEN NONE CAN KISS AND THRIVE, ...   775 AGAINST WITCH   8
    WOMEN, THAT NONE CAN KISS AND THRIVE, ...   775 AGAINST WITCH V   8
THRIVES
    AND YONDER IN THE GYMNASTS' GARDEN THRIVES . . . . .   446 COLONUS PRAISE   9
THROAT   SEE CUT-THROAT
    UNDER THE ROOF, AND WITH A STRAINING THROAT . . . . .   36 OISIN 2   106
    DRIFTING ON HIGH, AND WITH A STRAINING THROAT . . .   36 OISIN 2   V   106
    THROUGH MANY SHAPES: I LUNGED AT THE SMOOTH THROAT . . .   40 OISIN 2   175
    TO MANY SHAPES; I LUNGED AT THE SMOOTH THROAT . . . .   40 OISIN 2   V   175
    . . . AND HEAVING THE PILLAR OF HIS THROAT, ...   51 OISIN 3   59
    CRUEL CLAW AND HUNGRY THROAT, ...   136 TWO TREES   36
    FROM ANY BRAZEN THROAT, ...   291 TO A FRIEND   3
    FROM HEEL TO THROAT: . . . .   320 COAT   4
    NO MORE SANG HE, FOR HIS THROAT WAS TOO SMALL: . . . .   545 TO SAME TUNE 1   24
    HE SAID NO MORE FOR HIS THROAT WAS TOO SMALL. . . . .   545 TO SAME TUNE 1 V 24
    AND TAKES YOU BY THE THROAT: . . . .   598 STONE CROSS   4
    NO MORE SANG HE, FOR HIS THROAT WAS TOO SMALL: . . . .   616 MARCH SONGS 3   24
    CURES FOR CALVES WITH 'PLAINING THROAT, ...   717 FAIRY DOCTOR   15
    CURES FOR CALF WITH 'PLAINING THROAT, ...   717 FAIRY DOCTOR V   15
THROATED   SEE REED-THROATED SWEET-THROATED HUNDRED-THROATED
    "WITH HIM IS ONE SWEET THROATED LIKE A BIRD, ...   106 CUCHULAIN SEA V 16
    THEN CONCOBAR SENT THAT SWEET THROATED MAID . . .   110 CUCHULAIN SEA V   72
THROATS
    AND SWANS WITH THEIR EXULTANT THROATS: . . . . . .   14 OISIN 1   192
    THEY HAD CHANGED THEIR THROATS AND HAD THE THROATS   635 CUCHULAIN COMF   25
        OF BIRDS.
    THEY HAD CHANGED THEIR THROATS AND HAD THE THROATS   635 CUCHULAIN COMF   25
        OF BIRDS.
THROB
    FOR ONE THROB OF THE ARTERY, ...   406 IN TIME OF WAR   1
    AND THROB WITHIN THE CIRCLES OF GREEN DAWN. . . . . .   701 MOSADA 3   54
THROBBING   SEE STAR-THROBBING
THRONE
    I PACE REMEMBERING. FROM MY MISTY THRONE . . . . .   45 OISIN 2   V 239C
    MINE WAS THE THRONE IN EMAN'S HALL, ...   81 MAD KING GOLL V   2
    THRONE OVER THRONE WHERE IN HALF SLEEP, ...   156 FORGOT BEAUTY   22
    THRONE OVER THRONE WHERE IN HALF SLEEP, ...   156 FORGOT BEAUTY   22
    TILL THERE BE NAUGHT BUT THRONE ON THRONE . . . . .   156 FORGOT BEAUTY   21
    TILL THERE BE NAUGHT BUT THRONE ON THRONE . . . . .   156 FORGOT BEAUTY V 21
    UPON THE THRONE AND CRYING ABOUT THE STREETS . . . .   198 SEVEN WOODS   7
    APPLAUD A MODERN THRONE: . . . .   597 MODEL LAUREATE   18
    AND HE STUCK TO HIS THRONE. . . . .   628 JANE MOUNTAIN   10
    AND HEARD EACH UNSEEN ECHO ON HER THRONE, ...   657 ISLE STAT I 3   48
    EACH ONE AT GAZE FOR AYE UPON HIS WHIRLING THRONE. . . .   662 ISLE STAT II 1   81
    AS SLOWLY AUTUMN CLIMBED THE GOLDEN THRONE . . .   690 MOSADA 1   V   1A
THRONES
    UPON DARK THRONES. BETWEEN THE LIDS OF ONE . . . . .   31 OISIN 2   37

THRONES (CONTINUED)
  FROM THEIR PALE THRONES AND COMFORT HIM, BUT THEY . . . 68 SAD SHEPHERD 6
  WHAT HAD THE CAESARS BUT THEIR THRONES? . . . . . 401 DEMON BEAST 50
  ON THRONES FROM CHINA TO PERU . . . . 597 MODEL LAUREATE 1
  ABOVE THE ALPUJARRAS ON THEIR THRONES! . . . . 691 MOSADA 1 27
  UPON THEIR THRONES. THE LIVES OF MEN SHALL FLOW . . . 698 MOSADA 2 56
THRONG
  AMID THE HOVERING, PITEOUS, PENITENTIAL THRONG." . . 173 SPEAKS HEARERS 8
  A NOBODY IN A GREAT THRONG, ... 361 ALF POLLEXFEN 29
  IN THE LONG ECHOING STREET THE LAUGHING DANCERS THRONG, 459 FROM OEDIPUS 7
  IN THE LONG ECHOING STREETS THE LAUGHING DANCERS THRONG, 459 FROM OEDIPUS V 7
  IT SEEMED A QUATTROCENTO PAINTER'S THRONG, . . . 537 HER VISION 19
  IT SEEMED A QUATTRO-CENTO PAINTER'S THRONG . . . 537 HER VISION V 19
  BRED OUT OF THE CONTAGION OF THE THRONG, . . . 542 PARN FUNERAL 1 27
THRONGED SEE LUTE-THRONGED
  AND MY GAZE WAS THRONGED WITH THE SLEEPERS! . . . 50 OISIN 3 49
THRONGS
  . . . DRIVING THE DUST WITH THEIR THRONGS, . . . 53 OISIN 3 85
  THE THRONGS WITH BLOWN WET HAIR ARE GATHERING NEAR. . . 114 ROSE OF BATTLE V 6
THROUGHOUT
  THROUGHOUT SO MANY VARYING CENTURIES . . . . . . 371 ON GOING HOUSE 8
THROW
  I THROW DOWN THE CHAIN OF SMALL STONES! . . . . 63 OISIN 3 222
  TO THROW ME A BIT OF SALTED FISH! . . . . . 301 RUN PARADISE 6
  I'D TEAR IT OFF AND THROW IT IN THE FIRE." . . . 462 HARUN RASHID 34
  "UPLIFT THOSE EYES AND THROW . . . . 516 MANS SONG 7
  THROW IT IN EVERY PART." . . . . 596 COLONEL MARTIN 53
  THROW LIKELY COUPLES INTO BED . . . . . . 606 SONGS BURDEN 1 25
  MAYHAP 'TWERE BETTER THAT ASIDE I THROW . . . 656 ISLE STAT 1 3 38
  AND WHO WILL THROW HIS MANSION DOWN . . . . 671 ISLE STAT II 3 135
  WE THROW THREE TIMES. . . . . 721 WITCH VIVIEN 39
  TO THROW THE NORMAN KNIGHT." " . . . . . 740 EARL PAUL 12
THROWN
  AND HIS LOOSE BULK BE THROWN IN THE LOUD TIDE." . . . 35 OISIN 2 91
  NOT EVEN YOUR GOD COULD HAVE THROWN DOWN THAT HALL! . . 36 OISIN 2 109
  NOT E'EN THY GOD COULD HAVE THROWN DOWN THAT HALL! . . 36 OISIN 2 V 109
  AND THROWN THE THUNDER ON THE STONES FOR ALL THAT MAEVE 207 HANRAHANS SONG 7
   CAN SAY.
  NOR ULADH, WHEN NAOISE HAD THROWN A SAIL UPON THE WIND! 209 UNDER THE MOON 4
  LAND-OF-THE-TOWER, WHERE AENGUS HAS THROWN THE GATES APART, 209 UNDER THE MOON 8
  LAND OF THE TOWER, WHEN AENGUS HAS THROWN THE GATES APART, 209 UNDER THE MOON V 8
  I MIGHT HAVE THROWN POOR WORDS AWAY . . . . . 256 WORDS 15
  MERE BONE AND MUSCLE THROWN ASIDE, ... 273 GREY ROCK 51
  MOANED THE OTHER, "THEY ARE THROWN . . . . . 299 THREE HERMITS 22
  YOU HAD BEFORE THE SUN HAD THROWN . . . . . 333 SOLOMON SHEBA 13
  BROUGHT THE BARE NEWS. HE HAD THROWN THE CROOK AWAY . 339 SHEP GOATHERD 21
  WHERE THE SHEEP ARE THROWN IN THE POOL, . . . 341 SHEP GOATHERD V 71
  THE ELABORATE STAR-LIGHT HAS THROWN REFLECTIONS . . 389 IMAGE PAST V 2
  NOW SHE HAS THROWN HER ARMS ABOVE HER HEAD! . . . 390 IMAGE PAST 36
  A BIT OF BREAD THROWN UP INTO THE AIR! . . . . 400 DEMON BEAST 25
  IF THROWN IN MADGE'S WAY, ... 457 SECRETS OF OLD 8
  THROWN INTO DESPAIR . . . . 492 ANNE GREGORY 2
  SOME BACK A MARE THROWN FROM A THOROUGHBRED, . . . 547 TO SAME TUNE 3 3
  SOME BACK A MARE THROWN FROM A THOROUGH-BRED, . . . 547 TO SAME TUNE 3 V 3
  EMPEDOCLES HAS THROWN ALL THINGS ABOUT! . . . . 564 GYRES 6
  "OF PLASTER SAINTS"; HIS BEAUTIFUL MISCHIEVOUS HEAD THROWN 577 LOFTY THINGS 4
   BACK.
  BUT THROWN UPON THIS FILTHY MODERN TIDE . . . . 611 STATUES 29
  SOME BACK A MARE THROWN FROM A THOROUGHBRED, . . . 614 MARCH SONGS 2 3
  POOR LOVE AND SORROW, WITH THEIR ARMS THROWN ROUND . . 703 MOSADA 3 119
  HE HAS THROWN A DRUID DREAM UPON THE AIR. . . . 759 SHADOW WATER A 237
  I HAD THROWN IT DOWN BEHIND THIS COIL OF ROPE. . . 759 SHADOW WATER A 245
  A SUDDEN STORM, AND IT WAS THROWN . . . . . 784 WOMANS BEAUTY 5
THROWS
  THE ELABORATE STARLIGHT THROWS A REFLECTION . . . 389 IMAGE PAST 2
  THE MOUNTAIN THROWS A SHADOW. . . . . . . 519 LOVES LONENESS 7
  AWAY HER CLINGING HANDS, AND TURNS. SHE THROWS . . . 714 FERENCZ RENYI 102
  HER OFF AND TURNS AWAY. SHE THROWS . . . . 714 FERENCZ RENYI V 102
THRUST
  AND THRUST THE TORCH BETWEEN THE SLIMY FLAGS. . . . 38 OISIN 2 143
  TURNING, HE SAW THAT SHE HAD THRUST DEAD LEAVES . . 80 EPHEMERA 18
  THRUST HIM AWAY WITH BOTH MY HANDS AND CRIED, . . . 285 TWO KINGS 202
  THE BREAST THRUST OUT IN PRIDE . . . . . . 430 NINETEEN 19 66
  THEY BUT THRUST THEIR BURIED MEN . . . . . 637 BEN BULBEN 23
  FIERCE THRUST! A TARDY BLOSSOM HAD THE SEED, . . . 665 ISLE STAT II 2 65
  OF THOSE STEEL TONGUES! CRASH, SWORDS! WELL THRUST! 665 ISLE STAT II 2 67
   WELL BENT
  AND FLY AMONG THE FOAM. THRUST DOWN THE HELM, . . . 750 SHADOW WATER A 88
THRUSTING
  THRUSTING HIS NOSE TO MY SHOULDER! HE KNEW IN HIS BOSOM 54 OISIN 3 106
   DEEP
THUMB
  MACDONAGH'S BONY THUMB? . . . . 395 SIXTEEN DEAD 12
  HE SO BEWITCHED THE CARDS UNDER HIS THUMB . . . 411 TOWER 67
THUMBS
  "THE FIDDLERS ARE ALL THUMBS, ... 527 AM OF IRELAND 19
THUMPS
  AND THE HEART THUMPS AT MY SIDE, ... 456 FRIENDS YOUTH 18
THUNDER
  ARE CHOKED WITH THUNDER, LIGHTNING, AND FIERCE WIND, . . 42 OISIN 2 205
  SAINT, DO YOU WEEP? I HEAR AMID THE THUNDER . . . . 43 OISIN 2 209

		PAGE	TITLE		LINE
THUNDER (CONTINUED)					
SAINT, DOST THOU WEEP? I HEAR AMID THE THUNDER		43	OISIN 2	V	209
MAKE THEIR FAINT THUNDER, AND THE GARDEN BEES		198	SEVEN WOODS		2
AND THROWN THE THUNDER ON THE STONES FOR ALL THAT MAEVE CAN SAY.		207	HANRAHANS SONG		7
AND SHAKE DOWN THUNDER ON THE STONES BECAUSE THE RED WINDS RAVE!		207	HANRAHANS SONG	V	7
THUNDER OF FEET, TUMULT OF IMAGES, ...		433	NINETEEN 19		120
THAT GATHERS VOLUME: NOW A THUNDER CLAP.		487	SEVEN SAGES	V	23
AT SUDDEN THUNDER OF THE MOUNTING SWAN		490	COOLE BALLYLEE		14
MAY THUNDER TIME AWAY, ...		496	MOHINI CHATTER		25
TO HIM WITH THUNDER SHOD, ...		735	IN CHURCH		2
TO HIM WITH THUNDER SHOD, ...		736	IN CHURCH		14
THUNDER-BALL					
FEARFUL OF THE THUNDER-BALL, ...		43	OISIN 2	V	208F
THUNDERBOLT					
TALMA AND HIS THUNDERBOLT.		625	NATIVITY		10
THUNDER-CLAP					
THAT GATHERS VOLUME: NOW A THUNDER-CLAP.		487	SEVEN SAGES		23
THUNDERING					
THUNDERING, AND THE WIDE USELESS WATERS FRAY		45	OISIN 2	V	238
THUNDER-SOUND					
WILL BE THE FAINT FAR THUNDER-SOUND, AS THOUGH		699	MOSADA 3		10
WILL MOVE THE FAINT FAR THUNDER-SOUND, AS THOUGH		699	MOSADA 3	V	10
THUNDERSTONES					
ALL THOSE DREADFUL THUNDERSTONES, ...		509	JANE REPROVED	V	2
THUNDER-STONES					
ALL THOSE DREADFUL THUNDER-STONES, ...		509	JANE REPROVED		2
THURIBLES					
IS IT THESE THAT WITH GOLDEN THURIBLES		167	BLESSED		23
IS IT THOSE THAT WITH GOLDEN THURIBLES		167	BLESSED	V	23
TIDE SEE NOON-TIDE NIGHT-TIDE					
BEYOND THE TUMBLING OF THIS TIDE."		5	OISIN 1		49
THROUGH BITTER TIDE ON FOAM-WET FEET?		5	OISIN 1		51
MY HOME IS FAR FROM WHERE THE TIDE		5	OISIN 1	V	46
IS NIAMH, AND MY LAND WHERE TIDE		5	OISIN 1	V	48
AND WAS BORN WHERE THE SUN DROPS DOWN IN THE TIDE, . . .		5	OISIN 1	V	49
TO SHORES BY THE WASH OF THE TREMULOUS TIDE, ...		8	OISIN 1		81
UPON THEIR SHADOWS IN THE TIDE, ...		14	OISIN 1		185
"'TIS JOY MAKES SWIM THE SAPPY TIDE, ...		18	OISIN 1	V	261
UNCHAINABLE AS THE DIM TIDE.		22	OISIN 1		338
WHEN ONE DAY BY THE TIDE I STOOD, ...		24	OISIN 1		364
AND NAMED HIM BY SWEET NAMES. A FOAMING TIDE		30	OISIN 2		27
DARK STATUES GLIMMERED OVER THE PALE TIDE		31	OISIN 2		36
NEARER THE CASTLE CAME WE. A VAST TIDE		31	OISIN 2	V	27A
FOG-DRIPPING, PEDESTALLED ABOVE THE TIDE, ...		31	OISIN 2		36
AND HIS LOOSE BULK BE THROWN IN THE LOUD TIDE."		35	OISIN 2		91
FIN, CONAN, OSCAR, MANY MORE, THE TIDE		44	OISIN 2	V	228A
HIGH AS THE SADDLE-GIRTH, COVERING AWAY FROM OUR GLANCES THE TIDE:		47	OISIN 3		2
HIGH AS THE SADDLE GIRTH, COVERING AWAY FROM OUR GLANCES THE TIDE:		47	OISIN 3	V	2
HOW THE SLOW, BLUE-EYED OXEN OF FINN LOW SADLY AT EVENING TIDE.		52	OISIN 3		84
AND SOFTLY COME TO YOUR NIAMH OVER THE TOPS OF THE TIDE:		55	OISIN 3		126
AND SOFTLY COME TO THY NIAM OVER THE TOPS OF THE TIDE:		52	OISIN 3	V	126
FOR I AM IN HIS IMAGE MADE, AND ALL THIS TINKLING TIDE . .		76	INDIAN ON GOD		11
ONE WITH THE TIDE THAT GLEAMS, THE WINGS THAT GLEAM AND DART,		78	INDIAN TO LOVE		15
ONE WITH THE GLIMMERING TIDE, ...		78	INDIAN TO LOVE	V	15
CUCHULAIN BATTLING WITH THE BITTER TIDE:		100	ROSE UPON ROOD		3
GO WATCH THE ROAD BETWEEN THE WOOD AND TIDE, ...		105	CUCHULAIN SEA		4
GO DWELL UPON THE CLIFFS AND WATCH THE TIDE:		105	CUCHULAIN SEA	V	4
AND THE GREY TIDE, THE RED BRANCH MULTITUDE		108	CUCHULAIN SEA	V	38B
AND FOUGHT WITH THE INVULNERABLE TIDE.		111	CUCHULAIN SEA		86
FOR FOUR DAYS WARRED HE WITH THE BITTER TIDE, ...		111	CUCHULAIN SEA	V	85
ABOVE THE TIDE OF HOURS, TROUBLE THE AIR, ...		114	ROSE OF BATTLE		3
ABOVE THE TIDE OF HOURS, RISE ON THE AIR, ...		114	ROSE OF BATTLE	V	3
IN SHAKEN BOUGHS, IN TIDE ON THE SHORE?		141	EVERLAST VOICE		7
AT THE COMING OF NIGHT TIDE, ...		144	HOST OF AIR	V	6
OF THE PALE TIDE WHEN THE MOON HAS SET, ...		146	FISH		2
AS THE TIDE WEARS THE DOVE-GREY SANDS, ...		157	POET BELOVED		4
AS THE TIDE HAS THE DOVE-GREY SANDS, ...		157	POET BELOVED	V	4
ABOVE THE WANDERING TIDE:		162	ASKS FORGIVE		14
AND DRUNK UP THE MURMURING TIDE!		171	MAID QUIET	V	4D
THE GREY WING UPON EVERY TIDE;		290	SEPTEMBER 1913		18
OUT OF THAT RAVING TIDE--IS DRAWN BETWIXT		377	PHASES OF MOON		122
THE BLOOD-DIMMED TIDE IS LOOSED, AND EVERYWHERE		402	SECOND COMING		5
BUT TURN FROM ROSSES' CRAWLING TIDE, ...		549	SEVERED HEAD		5
BUT THROWN UPON THIS FILTHY MODERN TIDE		611	STATUES		29
THE TIDE OF STARS? HAVE I NOT SEEN A THOUSAND YEARS . .		675	ISLE STAT II 3		230
THE TIDE NARROWS BETWEEN, AND ONE OLD MAN		752	SHADOW WATER A		118
TIDE'S					
DROPPING A VAPOURY FOOTSOLE ON THE TIDE'S DROWSY BLAZE.		78	INDIAN TO LOVE	V	20
TIDES					
THE HERRING ARE NOT IN THE TIDES AS THEY WERE OF OLD: . .		91	OLD FISHERMAN		5
YOU, TOO, HAVE COME WHERE THE DIM TIDES ARE HURLED . .		115	ROSE OF BATTLE		26
TIED					
WE TIED THE HORSE IN A LEAFY CLUMP, ...		14	OISIN 1		194
AND SHE WITH A WAVE-RUSTED CHAIN WAS TIED		34	OISIN 2		73
WITH CHAIN SEA-ROTTED, ROUND HER MIDDLE TIED, ...		34	OISIN 2	V	75

			PAGE	TITLE		LINE

TIED   (CONTINUED)
```
      DECREPIT AGE THAT HAS BEEN TIED TO ME . . . . . . .     409 TOWER              3
      DECREPIT AGE THAT HAS BEEN TIED UPON ME . . . . . .     409 TOWER          V   3
TIGHT
      HER EYES WERE COLD AND STEADY, HER LIPS TIGHT.  . . .   279 TWO KINGS          64
      HOW SINEW THAT HAS BEEN PULLED TIGHT, . . . . . .  .   386 ROBARTES DANCE     34
      SUCH THOUGHT--SUCH THOUGHT HAVE I THAT HOLD IT TIGHT  .  474 ALL SOUL NIGHT     91
      CLOSE AND CLING SO TIGHT, . . . . . . . . . .  . .     538 LAST CONFESS       22
TIGHTEN
      DELIGHTFUL TO THE TOUCH; TIGHTEN THAT HAND . . . . .   579 DOR WELLESLEY       4
TIGHTENED
      WITH BEAUTY LIKE A TIGHTENED BOW, A KIND  . . . . .    256 NO SECOND TROY      8
      HE SAT WITH TIGHTENED REIN AND LOOSENED MOUTH . . . .  277 TWO KINGS          10
      HE SAT WITH TIGHTENED REIN AMAZED, HIS HORSE . . . .   277 TWO KINGS      V   10
TILL
      YOUR MORTAL SHORES TILL TIME IS DONE!" . . . . . .  .     6 OISIN 1       V   59
      LOVE, TILL THE DANAAN POETS BROUGHT . . . . . . . .      7 OISIN 1       V   63
      I NE'ER LOVED ANY TILL SONG BROUGHT ME . . . . . .  .    7 OISIN 1       V   69
      SLEEP THERE TILL THE MOON AND THE STARS DIE!" . . . .   17 OISIN 1          246
      TILL ON THE CENTRAL HILL WE HUSHED . . . . . . . .      22 OISIN 1       V  323
      BUT THE LOVE-DEW DIMS OUR EYES TILL THE DAY . . . .     28 OISIN 1          424
      ON OUR DARK PATHWAY, TILL A COUNTLESS FLIGHT . . . .    31 OISIN 2           34
      "THIS DEMON SHALL BE BATTERED TILL HE DIE, . . . . .    35 OISIN 2           90
      UNDER THE SHADOWS TILL THE TUMULTS DIED . . . . . .     38 OISIN 2          140
      TILL THE FAR DOORWAY GREW A BURNING BLOT . . . . . .    39 OISIN 2       V  152
      "BUT TILL THE MOON HAS TAKEN ALL, I WAGE . . . . . .    45 OISIN 2          240
      TILL THE HORSE GAVE A WHINNY! . . . . . . . . . . .     48 OISIN 3           25
      TILL, FATTENING THE WINDS OF THE MORNING, AN ODOUR      57 OISIN 3          153
         OF NEW-MOWN HAY
      TILL I SAW WHERE MAEVE LIES SLEEPING . . . . . . . .    60 OISIN 3          184
      . . . TILL STARLIGHT AND MIDNIGHT PART. . . . . . .     60 OISIN 3          184
      AND RODE ON TILL OVER THE WORLD'S RIM FLOATED THE SEA'S 60 OISIN 3       V  183
         OLD SHOUT,
      TILL THEY SHALL SINGING FADE IN RUTH . . . . . . .     66 HAPPY SHEPHERD     41
      WITH MIRTHFUL SONGS TILL RISE THE DAWN. . . . . . .     67 HAPPY SHEPHERD     49
      TILL MY OWN WORDS, RE-ECHOING, SHALL SEND . . . . .     68 SAD SHEPHERD       20
      SING, TILL YOU RAISE YOUR HANDS AND SIGH, . . . . .     73 ANASHU VIJAYA      45
      SING, TILL YE RAISE YOUR HANDS AND SIGH, . . . . .      73 ANASHU VIJAYA  V   45
      TILL THE MOON HAS TAKEN FLIGHT! . . . . . . . . . .     87 STOLEN CHILD       19
      I MINDED HER TILL MORN. . . . . . . . . . . . .  .      94 MOLL MAGEE         16
      WHOSE BLADE COMPELS, AND WAIT TILL THEY HAVE FOUND . .  108 CUCHULAIN SEA      37
      AT THE SWORD-POINT, AND WAITS TILL WE HAVE FOUND . .   109 CUCHULAIN SEA      53
      AT THE SWORD POINT, AND WAITS TILL WE HAVE FOUND . .   109 CUCHULAIN SEA  V   53
      A RAPTUROUS MUSIC, TILL THE MORNING BREAK . . . . .    137 TO SOME I TALK     14
      CONTINUAL MUSIC TILL THE MORNING BREAK, . . . . . .    137 TO SOME I TALK     14
      FLAME UNDER FLAME, TILL TIME BE NO MORE! . . . . . .   141 EVERLAST VOICE      4
      AND PLUCK TILL TIME AND TIMES ARE DONE . . . . . .     150 WANDER AENGUS      22
      TILL THE SEED OF THE FIRE FLICKER AND GLOW; . . . .    150 OLD MOTHER          2
      TILL STARS ARE BEGINNING TO BLINK AND PEEP! . . . .    150 OLD MOTHER          4
      TILL THERE BE NAUGHT BUT THRONE ON THRONE . . . . .    156 FORGOT BEAUTY  V   21
      TILL STARS GREW OUT OF THE AIR. . . . . . . . . . .    160 CAP AND BELLS      28
      O PITEOUS HEARTS, CHANGING TILL CHANGE BE DEAD . . .   163 ASKS FORGIVE       19
      TILL ALL THE VALLEYS OF THE WORLD HAVE BEEN WITHERED AWAY. 163 VALLEY LOVERS    8
      TILL THE VALLEYS OF THE WORLD HAVE BEEN WITHERED AWAY." 163 VALLEY LOVERS      8
      AT HUSH OF EVENING TILL GOD BURNS TIME . . . . . .     164 PERFECT BEAUTY V    7
      AT HUSH OF EVENING TILL GOD BURN TIME . . . . . . .    164 PERFECT BEAUTY V    7
      TILL DATHI CAME AND STOOD, . . . . . . . . . . . .     166 BLESSED             2
      TILL DATHI CAME AND STOOD, . . . . . . . . . . . .     167 BLESSED        V   4B
      TILL VAIN FRENZY AWOKE AND HE DIED; AND HIM . . . .    169 SECRET ROSE        12
      AND TILL A HUNDRED MORNS HAD FLOWERED RED . . . . .    170 SECRET ROSE        17
      TILL THE ATTORNEY FOR LOST SOULS CRY HER SWEET CRY, .  173 SPEAKS HEARERS      6
      TILL MAURYA OF THE WOUNDED HEART CRY A SWEET CRY, . .  173 SPEAKS HEARERS V    6
      TILL MAEVE CALLED OUT, "THESE ARE BUT COMMON MEN, . .  186 QUEEN MAEVE       122
      TILL IT DIED OUT WHERE AN OLD THORN-TREE STOOD. . . .  186 QUEEN MAEVE       129
      TILL IT DIED OUT WHERE AN OLD THORN TREE STOOD. . . .  186 QUEEN MAEVE    V  129
      THOUGH NOW IT'S HARD, TILL TROUBLE IS AT AN END; . .  200 FOLLY COMFORT  V    5
      WITH WISDOM, THEY WANDER TILL ALL THE YEARS HAVE GONE BY! 204 WITHER BOUGHS   21
      TILL HE HAS FALLEN ASLEEP . . . . . . . . . . . .     216 HAPPY TOWNLAND     51
      TILL THEY HAD CHANGED US TO LIKE STRENGTH?" . . . .    259 PEACE          V    9
      TILL THE WILDERNESS CRIED ALOUD, . . . . . . . . .    259 UNWORTH PRAISE      8
      TILL THAT BE TUMBLED THAT WAS LIFTED HIGH . . . . .    265 THESE CLOUDS        4
      TILL THE STARS HAD RUN AWAY . . . . . . . . . . .     268 BROWN PENNY        13
      TILL YOUR BAD MASTER BLENCHED AND ALL WAS LOST! . . .  270 PARDON FATHERS V   12
      TILL ALL THE PLACE WAS BEATEN INTO MIRE. . . . . .    278 TWO KINGS          27
      TILL ALL HAD SEEMED A SHADOW OR A VISION . . . . .    278 TWO KINGS          43
      TILL JUDGMENT HAS BEEN GIVEN, AND IF GUILTY, . . . .   280 TWO KINGS          74
      AND I BUT ASKED THE MORE, TILL HE CRIED OUT, . . . .   281 TWO KINGS          92
      I WAITED TILL THE NIGHT WAS ON THE TURN, . . . . .    283 TWO KINGS         144
      TILL OAK AND HAZEL CEASED AND BEECH BEGAN, . . . .    283 TWO KINGS      V 139A
      BUT FUMBLE IN A GREASY TILL . . . . . . . . . . .     289 SEPTEMBER 1913      2
      ABOUT YOUR HEAD TILL THE DUST STOPS YOUR EAR, . . .    293 TO A SHADE         20
      ALL SHOUTED TILL THEIR ANGER GREW . . . . . . . .     297 THREE BEGGARS      46
      THEY MAULED AND BIT TILL THE DAY SHONE! . . . . . .    297 THREE BEGGARS      49
      AND TILL ANOTHER NIGHT HAD GONE, . . . . . . . .      297 THREE BEGGARS      51
      TILL THEY WERE WHIRLING IN A HEAP. . . . . . . . .    297 THREE BEGGARS  V   47
      A SHELTER TILL THE DAYLIGHT BROKE. . . . . . . . .    302 HOUR DAWN          15
      TILL EVEN I SLEEP LIGHT! BUT WHO . . . . . . . . .    303 HOUR DAWN          34
      "I'LL HAVE MY SAY, TILL I AM ABLE . . . . . . . .     304 HOUR DAWN      V   51
      "I'D LIKE TO SLEEP TILL WINTER'S GONE . . . . . .     305 HOUR DAWN          60
      OR TILL THE SUN IS IN HIS STRENGTH. . . . . . . .     305 HOUR DAWN          61
      NOR GAVE GOD THANKS TILL OVERHEAD . . . . . . . .     307 HOUR DAWN         121
```

TILL   (CONTINUED)
    TILL PRIDE HAD MADE HER EYES GROW BRIGHT, ... 314 MEMORY YOUTH   10
    YOUTH'S DREAMY LOAD, TILL SHE . . . . . 315 FRIENDS   14
    ALL TILL MY YOUTH WAS GONE . . . . . 315 FRIENDS   18
    NOTORIOUS, TILL ALL MY PRICELESS THINGS . . . 321 REED WHISPERER 13
    TILL ALL HIS GREEK AND LATIN LEARNING SEEMED . . 324 ROBERT GREGORY 21
    "STRETCH BONES TILL THE DAYLIGHT COME . . . . 331 ROUND TOWER   5
    TILL TOES MASTERED A SWEET MEASURE, ... 331 ROUND TOWER   15
    SANG TILL STARS BEGAN TO FADE, ... 332 ROUND TOWER   20
    TILL WINTER BLASTS WERE GONE, BUT SPEAK OF HER . 340 SHEP GOATHERD 33
    AND TILL THAT'S DONE CAN NEITHER WORK NOR WAIT. 340 SHEP GOATHERD 45
    TILL DAYTIME, PLAYTIME SEEM THE SAME, ... 343 SHEP GOATHERD 106
    TILL, CLAMBERING AT THE CRADLE-SIDE, ... 343 SHEP GOATHERD 109
    TILL THAT IS THEIR LONG SHOUTING PLAYTIME! . . 343 SHEP GOATHERD V 106
    TILL, CLAMBERING AT THE CRADLE SIDE, ... 343 SHEP GOATHERD V 109
    TILL THE YELLOW EYE HAS GROWN MILD, ... 349 HAWK   3
    TILL I COULD HEAR THEIR HEARTS BEATING! . . . 358 PRESENCES   11
    TILL ALL THE BOUGHS ARE GAY, ... 366 HER CHRIS TREE 5
    THEY RAN FROM CRADLE TO CRADLE TILL AT LAST . 375 PHASES OF MOON 69
    THE HARE MAY RUN TILL IT'S FOUND . . . . . 380 SONGS FOOL 1   11
    THE PARTICULAR IS POUNDED TILL IT IS MAN. . . 382 VISION ROBART   6
    THERE CAN BE NOTHING SOLIDER TILL I DIE! . . 383 VISION ROBART   26
    AND NEVER CREW AGAIN TILL NOW, ... 388 SOLOMON WITCH 12
    TILL ALL THE EDDIES GLEAM! . . . . . 389 IMAGE PAST   4
    BEWILDERED THEM TILL THEY DIED? . . . . 394 EASTER 1916   73
    TILL GERMANY'S OVERCOME! . . . . . 395 SIXTEEN DEAD   8
    TILL MAN MADE UP THE WHOLE, ... 415 TOWER   149
    TILL IT WAS BROKEN BY . . . . . . 416 TOWER   179
    TILL THE WRECK OF BODY, ... 416 TOWER   184
    TILL HIS MORNING MEAL COME ROUND, ... 435 FOR MY SON   4
    ALL DREAD AFAR TILL MORNING'S BACK, ... 435 FOR MY SON   6
    PROTECTING, TILL THE DANGER PAST, ... 436 FOR MY SON   31
    NOW THAT YOUR TONGUE CANNOT PERSUADE THE CHILD TILL SHE 450 OWEN AHERNE 22
      MISTAKE
    AND THEN I LAUGH TILL TEARS RUN DOWN . . . . 456 FRIENDS YOUTH 17
    TILL MEDITATION MASTER ALL ITS PARTS, . . . 474 ALL SOUL NIGHT 92
    AND STRIKE ANOTHER TILL TIME CATCH! . . . . 476 EVA GORE-BOOTH 27
    RUN TILL ALL THE SAGES KNOW. . . . . 476 EVA GORE-BOOTH 29
    TILL THE DAWN BREAK UPON THOSE MINGLED SEAS. . 494 AT ALGECIRAS   6
    TILL I HAVE TOLD THE SAGES . . . . . 534 CONSOLATION   5
    TILL SUDDENLY IN GRIEF'S CONTAGION CAUGHT, . . 537 HER VISION   22
    HOW CAN SHE LIVE TILL IN HER BLOOD HE LIVE! . 558 RIBH CHRISTIAN 24
    TILL EITHER NEITHER HAVE ENOUGH. . . . . 573 LADYS 3RD SONG 8
    TILL I AM TIMON AND LEAR . . . . . 576 ACRE OF GRASS 15
    TILL TRUTH OBEYED HIS CALL! . . . . . 576 ACRE OF GRASS 18
    WINTER AND SUMMER TILL OLD AGE BEGAN . . . 629 CIRCUS ANIMALS 5
    WHO KEEPS THE TILL. NOW THAT MY LADDER'S GONE, 630 CIRCUS ANIMALS 38
    TURNS INTO A QUESTION TILL . . . . . 632 MAN AND ECHO   8
    AND TILL HIS INTELLECT GROWS SURE . . . . 633 MAN AND ECHO   30
    TILL HER BOWELS ARE IN HEAT, ... 638 BEN BULBEN   49
    TILL ALL ELSE IS EMPTY CHAFF, ... 647 ISLE STAT I 1   60
    TILL I LAUGH WHEN OTHERS WEEP, ... 647 ISLE STAT I 1   61
    AND LET THEM TELL SAD HISTORIES, TILL THEIR EYES . . 663 ISLE STAT II 2 32
    TILL HIS LAST WRETCHEDNESS WAS O'ER AND DONE." 664 ISLE STAT II 2 54
    TILL THOU REMEMBEREST ONLY HOW THE SEA . . . 670 ISLE STAT II 3 94
    AT ARM'S LENGTH, THUS TILL DUMB ETERNITY . . 671 ISLE STAT II 3 145
    GAZE ON TILL RAGGED TIME HIMSELF DECAY. . . . 672 ISLE STAT II 3 148
    TILL THEIR FIERCE MISERIES WITHIN HIS EYES . . 687 TWO TITANS   26
    AND ALL WAS DIMNESS, TILL A DYING LEAF . . . 690 MOSADA 1   20
    HUSH'D THE FISHERS, TILL A MOTHER CALLS BY NAME HER DROWNED 719 PHANTOM SHIP 23
      SON!
    PRAYED THOSE FORGOTTEN FISHERS, TILL IN THE EASTERN SKIES 719 PHANTOM SHIP 32
    ALL THOSE LONG FORGOTTEN FISHERS, TILL IN THE EASTERN SKIES 719 PHANTOM SHIP V 32
    COME AND TEASE THEM TILL THE DAY, ... 727 LOVERS QUARREL 36
    TILL THEY COME WHERE YOUR SAD, SAD HEART IS, . . 739 WHERE BOOKS GO 5
    TILL DAY AND NIGHT TIME END. . . . . 741 EARL PAUL   48
    TILL ALL THINGS ARE AT REST. . . . . 741 EARL PAUL   52
    AND NEED NO MORE OF LIFE TILL THE WHITE WINGS . 751 SHADOW WATER A 102
    TILL HIS EDAINE, NO LONGER A GOLDEN FLY . . . 757 SHADOW WATER A 210
    TILL HIS EDAINE, NO MORE A SILVER FLY . . . 757 SHADOW WATER A V 210
    TILL THE SIDE OF HATE COMES UP. . . . . 776 AGAINST WITCH 35
    TILL IT DIP AN AGEING WING . . . . . 777 SONG DEIRDRE 2 3
    "TILL THE SUN GOES DOWN AND AN HOUR OF THE CLOCK" . . 779 GOING THE ROAD 7
    TILL CERTAIN SECOND THOUGHTS HAVE COME . . . 791 REPRISALS   12
'TILL
    TO LIE THERE 'TILL THE FOURTH DAY SAW EMERGE . . . . . 44 OISIN 2 V 220
TILLAGE
    AND HIM WHO SOLD TILLAGE, AND HOUSE, AND GOODS, ... 170 SECRET ROSE 22
    AND OVER TILLAGE FIELDS AND PASTURE LANDS . . . . . 715 FERENCZ RENYI 120
TILLER
    AND OVER THE TILLER AND THE PROW, ... 197 BAILE AILLINN 183
TIMBER
    DRY TIMBER UNDER THAT RICH FOLIAGE, ... 536 HER VISION   1
    BECAUSE CHILDREN DEMAND DADDY-LONG-LEGS UPON HIS TIMBER 623 HIGH TALK   6
      TOES.
TIMBERS   SEE ROOF-TIMBERS
TIME   SEE WINTER-TIME HARVEST-TIME SUMMER-TIME SPRING-TIME FLOOD-TIME
    YOUR MORTAL SHORES TILL TIME IS DONE!" . . . . . 6 OISIN 1 V 59
    AS THOUGH THEY ALL WERE BEATING TIME, ... 13 OISIN 1 174
    THEN MOCK AT DEATH AND TIME WITH GLANCES . . . 19 OISIN 1 274
    WE MOCKED AT TIME AND FATE AND CHANCE . . . . 20 OISIN 1 291

TIME   (CONTINUED)

		PAGE	TITLE		LINE

OF GRIEVOUS TIME ON HIS OLD CRUTCHES, ... 23 OISIN 1   V 341B
KEPT TIME WITH THEIR BRIGHT WINGS AND FEET;   . . . . . . 26 OISIN 1   397
BEAT TIME WITH THEIR BRIGHT WINGS AND FEET.   . . . . . . 26 OISIN 1   V 397
SINCE GOD MADE TIME AND DEATH AND SLEEP; THE OTHER   . . . 31 OISIN 2   41
MADE THE WAY SLIPPERY, AND TIME ON TIME . . . . 37 OISIN 2   114
MADE THE WAY SLIPPERY, AND TIME ON TIME . . . . 37 OISIN 2   114
GREENISH AND SLIPPERY.   TIME AFTER TIME . . . . 37 OISIN 2   114
GREENISH AND SLIPPERY.   TIME AFTER TIME . . . . 37 OISIN 2   V 114
SHALL THEY TURN WROTH OR PLUCK THE WINGS OF TIME?   . . . 42 OISIN 2   V 199
CAME BLANAID, MAC NESSA, TALL FERGUS WHO FEASTWARD OF OLD   53 OISIN 3   89
  TIME SLUNK,
CAME BLANID, MAC NESSA, AND FERGUS WHO FEASTWARD OF OLD   53 OISIN 3   V 89
  TIME SLUNK,
. . . "THE FENIANS A LONG TIME ARE DEAD." . . . . 59 OISIN 3   172
. . . HE CRIED, "NO, THE GODS A LONG TIME ARE DEAD." . . 59 OISIN 3   180
. . . HE CRIED, "NAY, THE GODS A LONG TIME ARE DEAD." . . 59 OISIN 3   V 180
THE KINGS OF THE OLD TIME ARE DEAD. . . . . 65 HAPPY SHEPHERD   17
THE KINGS OF THE OLD TIME ARE FLED. . . . . 65 HAPPY SHEPHERD V 17
THERE DREAMY TIME LETS FALL HIS SICKLE . . . . 77 INDIAN TO LOVE V 5A
TIME WAS, AS IN A LITTLE TOWN, ... 85 MAD KING GOLL V 49
TO THE ROSE UPON THE ROOD OF TIME . . . . 100 ROSE UPON ROOD   T
COME NEAR; I WOULD, BEFORE MY TIME TO GO, ... 101 ROSE UPON ROOD   22
IN THREE DAYS' TIME HE STOOD UP WITH A MOAN, ... 111 CUCHULAIN SEA V 83
IN THREE DAYS' TIME, CUCHULAIN WITH A MOAN . . . . 111 CUCHULAIN SEA V 83
WHERE TIME WOULD SURELY FORGET US, AND SORROW COME NEAR   122 WHITE BIRDS   10
  US NO MORE;
WHERE SURELY TIME WOULD FORGET US AND SORROW COME NEAR   122 WHITE BIRDS   V 10
  US NO MORE;
THAT TIME CAN NEVER MAR A LOVER'S VOWS . . . . 126 DREAM OF FAERY   10
HOW TIME MAY NEVER MAR THEIR FAERY VOWS . . . . 126 DREAM OF FAERY V 10
ERE TIME TRANSFIGURED ME. . . . . 131 OLD PENSIONER   6
MY CONTEMPLATIONS ARE OF TIME . . . . 131 OLD PENSIONER   11
I SPIT INTO THE FACE OF TIME . . . . 132 OLD PENSIONER   17
UPON THE TIME OF SPARROW-CHIRP . . . . 133 FR GILLIGAN   21
UPON THE TIME OF SPARROW CHIRP, ... 133 FR GILLIGAN   V 21
WHEN TIME BEGAN TO RANT AND RAGE . . . . 138 TO IRELAND   10
AND TIME BADE ALL HIS CANDLES FLARE . . . . 138 TO IRELAND   13
WHAT MEASURER TIME HAS LIT ABOVE, ... 139 TO IRELAND   38
FLAME UNDER FLAME, TILL TIME BE NO MORE; . . . . 141 EVERLAST VOICE   4
TIME DROPS IN DECAY. . . . . 142 MOODS   1
OUT-WORN HEART, IN A TIME OUT-WORN, ... 147 INTO TWILIGHT   1
OUTWORN HEART IN A TIME OUTWORN, ... 147 INTO TWILIGHT V 1
AND TIME AND THE WORLD ARE EVER IN FLIGHT; . . . . 148 INTO TWILIGHT   14
AND PLUCK TILL TIME AND TIMES ARE DONE . . . . 150 WANDER AENGUS   22
AND TIME AND BIRTH AND CHANGE ARE HURRYING BY. . . . . . 153 CHANGE BELOVED   9
THE ROSES THAT OF OLD TIME WERE . . . . 156 FORGOT BEAUTY   9
THAT IS BRIMMED FROM THE PALE FIRE OF TIME; . . . . . . 157 POET BELOVED   6
IS DROPPING SLEEP, UNTIL GOD BURN TIME . . . . 164 PERFECT BEAUTY   7
AT HUSH OF EVENING TILL GOD BURNS TIME . . . . 164 PERFECT BEAUTY V 7
AT HUSH OF EVENING TILL GOD BURN TIME . . . . 164 PERFECT BEAUTY V 7
WHILE TIME AND THE WORLD ARE EBBING AWAY . . . . 168 BLESSED   39
UNTIL TIME AND THE WORLD HAVE EBBED AWAY . . . . 168 BLESSED   V 39
WHEN WE COME AT THE END OF TIME . . . . 178 FIDDLER DOONEY   9
WHEN WE COME AT THE CLOSE OF TIME . . . . 178 FIDDLER DOONEY V 9
IT WAS BEFORE THE TIME OF THE GREAT WAR . . . . 182 QUEEN MAEVE   57
AND WITH GLAD VOICE MAEVE ANSWERED "MANY A TIME . . . . . 183 QUEEN MAEVE   V 79
ABOUT THE TIME WHEN CHRIST WAS BORN, ... 189 BAILE AILLINN   13
A BETTER TIME HAD COME AGAIN . . . . 197 BAILE AILLINN   192
TIME CAN BUT MAKE IT EASIER TO BE WISE . . . . 200 FOLLY COMFORT   4
TIME CAN BUT MAKE HER BEAUTY OVER AGAIN; . . . . 200 FOLLY COMFORT   8
IS EDEN OUT OF TIME AND OUT OF SPACE? . . . . 218 WOODS OF COOLE   36
WHERE TIME IS DROWNED IN ODOUR-LADEN WINDS . . . . 219 HARP OF AENGUS   3
AND NOW THAT TIME PUTS WATER IN MY BLOOD, ... 222 SHADOW WATER B V 11A
FLEW WESTWARD; AND MANY A TIME SINCE THEN . . . . 223 SHADOW WATER B   27
AND YET YOU TALK OF LOVE. THE MOVEMENT OF TIME . . . . . 237 SHADOW WATER B   338
I'LL STRIKE A BLOW FOR HIM TO GIVE HIM TIME . . . . . . 239 SHADOW WATER B   365
THAT COMING TIME CAN SAY. . . . . 255 WOMAN HOMER   12
AH, THAT TIME COULD TOUCH A FORM . . . . 258 PEACE   1
AH, BUT TIME HAS TOUCHED A FORM . . . . 258 PEACE   V 1
CAME WHEN TIME HAD TOUCHED HER FORM. . . . . 259 PEACE   11
THE COMING OF WISDOM WITH TIME . . . . 261 COMING WISDOM   T
TO A CERTAIN COUNTRY HOUSE IN TIME OF CHANGE . . . . . . 264 HOUSE SHAKEN   V T
TIME OUT OF MIND, BECAME TOO RUINOUS . . . . 264 HOUSE SHAKEN   T
ONE TIME IT WAS A WOMAN'S FACE, OR WORSE-- . . . . 267 ALL TEMPT ME   2
NOR CAN TIME WASTE THE CHEEK, NOR IS THERE FOOT . . . . . 284 TWO KINGS   182
BUT LITTLE TIME HAD THEY TO PRAY . . . . 289 SEPTEMBER 1913   12
THE TIME FOR YOU TO TASTE OF THAT SALT BREATH . . . . . . 293 TO A SHADE   21
"TIME TO PUT OFF THE WORLD AND GO SOMEWHERE . . . . . . 299 BEGGAR CRIED   1
I'LL SLEEP AWAY ALL TIME WITHIN IT; . . . . 306 HOUR DAWN   74
IF TIME WERE SUPPLER IN THE JOINT, ... 306 HOUR DAWN   94
AND SLEEP AWAY ALL TIME WITHIN IT. . . . . 306 HOUR DAWN   V 74
TO BUNDLE TIME AWAY . . . . 317 NIGHT COME   11
THE FIRST TIME ON THIS SHORE, ... 323 SWANS AT COOLE   16
SEEING THAT TIME HAS FROZEN UP THE BLOOD . . . . 333 LIVING BEAUTY V 2
BUT LEFT THE HOUSE AS IN HIS FATHER'S TIME . . . . 341 SHEP GOATHERD   53
YET NEVER HAVE I, NOW NOR ANY TIME, ... 352 PEOPLE   28
THAT THEY, TIME OVERTHROWN, ... 384 VISION ROBART   47
SHE WOULD HAVE TIME TO TURN HER EYES, ... 385 ROBARTES DANCE   10
BEFORE MY TIME, SEEM LIKE A VIVID MEMORY. . . . . 391 UNDER SATURN   10
AND SURELY AFTER TWENTY YEARS IT WAS TIME TO COME." . . . 391 UNDER SATURN   14

		PAGE	TITLE	LINE

TIME   (CONTINUED)

	PAGE	TITLE		LINE
NOW AND IN TIME TO BE,	394	EASTER 1916		77
A MEDITATION IN TIME OF WAR	406	IN TIME OF WAR		T
A MEDIATION IN TIME OF WAR	406	IN TIME OF WAR	V	T
IT IS TIME THAT I WROTE MY WILL;	414	TOWER		121
MEDITATIONS IN TIME OF CIVIL WAR ANCESTRAL HOUSES	417	ANCEST HOUSES	V	T
WHERE WE WROUGHT THAT SHALL BREAK THE TEETH OF TIME.	435	NEW FACES		4
LAUGHTER NOT TIME DESTROYED MY VOICE	455	FRIENDS YOUTH		1
WHEN WE HAD ALL THE SUMMER TIME	457	SUMMER SPRING	V	15
SO GREAT ITS FAME. WHEN FITTING TIME HAS PASSED	461	HARUN RASHID		19
IN AFTER TIME THEY WILL SPEAK MUCH OF ME	462	HARUN RASHID		29
MANY A TIME I THINK TO SEEK	475	EVA GORE-BOOTH		14
HAVE NO ENEMY BUT TIME;	476	EVA GORE-BOOTH		25
AND STRIKE ANOTHER TILL TIME CATCH;	476	EVA GORE-BOOTH		27
IN MOCKERY OF A TIME	480	BLOOD AND MOON		11
THAT CUT THROUGH TIME OR CROSS IT WITHERSHINS.	489	COOLE PARK 29		24
THAT CAN CROSS TIME AND CUT IT WITHERSHINS.	489	COOLE PARK 29	V	24
THAT CUT THROUGH TIME AND CUT IT WITHERSHINS	489	COOLE PARK 29	V	24
ALL THAT TIME DENIED--	496	MOHINI CHATTER		18
MAY THUNDER TIME AWAY,	496	MOHINI CHATTER		25
IF TIME WERE BUT GONE."	510	JANE JUDGMENT		19
TIME IS UNWOUND,	520	HIS BARGAIN		4
AND TIME RUNS ON," CRIED SHE.	526	AM OF IRELAND		3
AND TIME RUNS ON," HE SAID,	526	AM OF IRELAND		12
AND TIME RUNS ON," CRIED SHE.	527	AM OF IRELAND		16
"BUT TIME RUNS ON, RUNS ON."	527	AM OF IRELAND		26
AND TIME RUNS ON," CRIED SHE.	527	AM OF IRELAND		29
MOUNTED THE MARE OF TIME,	529	TOM CRUACHAN		5
TIME I WERE BURIED," SAID THE OLD, OLD MAN.	548	TO SAME TUNE 3		10
TIME FOR US ALL TO PICK OUT A GOOD TUNE.	548	TO SAME TUNE 3		13
TIME I WERE BURIED," SAID THE OLD, OLD MAN.	548	TO SAME TUNE 3		20
TIME FOR US ALL BOYS, TO HIT ON A TUNE BOYS,	548	TO SAME TUNE 3	V	13
TIME I WERE BURIED," SAID THE OLD, OLD MAN.	549	TO SAME TUNE 3		30
A GREATER, A MORE GRACIOUS TIME HAS GONE;	564	GYRES		12
A YEAR AGO FOR THE FIRST TIME	570	THREE BUSHES		38
AND AT NIGHT TIME WOULD SHE SAY,	570	THREE BUSHES	V	30
WHAT CAN THEY KNOW THAT WE KNOW THAT KNOW THE TIME TO DIE?	580	CURSE CROMWELL		14
BEFORE THE BENCH OF TIME,	582	ROGER CASEMENT		6
FROM TIME LONG PASSED AWAY,	589	OLD WICKED MAN		42
AND I AM IN DESPAIR THAT TIME MAY BRING	602	GALLERY REVIS		30
AND RANTING TIME RENEW,	606	SONGS BURDEN 1		20
OF GOD OR WOMAN, THE TIME WERE COME TO DIE."	609	IN TARAS HALLS		15
BUT TIME AMENDS OLD WRONG,	613	MARCH SONGS 1		9
BUT TIME AMENDS OLD WRONG,	613	MARCH SONGS 1		19
BUT TIME AMENDS OLD WRONG,	614	MARCH SONGS 1		29
"SEND WAR IN OUR TIME, O LORD!"	638	BEN BULBEN		26
GAZE ON TILL RAGGED TIME HIMSELF DECAY.	672	ISLE STAT II 3		148
BOTH DEAD!--NO TIME TO THINK. I AM SHE,	673	ISLE STAT II 3		190
BOTH DEAD!--NO TIME FOR THINKING. I AM SHE,	673	ISLE STAT II 3	V	190
THOU SHALT OUTLIVE THINE AMOROUS HAPPY TIME,	674	ISLE STAT II 3		203
TIME GOES. THE FLAKED FIRE OF EVENING CRAWLS	712	FERENCZ RENYI		70
TIME GOES. THE FLICKED FIRE OF EVENING CRAWLS	712	FERENCZ RENYI	V	70
I CAME THE FIRST TIME TO THY VILLAGE SCHOOL?	713	FERENCZ RENYI		90
TIME AND THE WITCH VIVIEN	720	WITCH VIVIEN		T
FIVE-SIX. HA, TIME!	721	WITCH VIVIEN		42
I LOSE! THEY'RE LOADED DICE. TIME ALWAYS PLAYS	721	WITCH VIVIEN		44
UPON MY SOUL, OLD TIME. NO; THUS IT STANDS.	722	WITCH VIVIEN		49
AND NOW WITH FATHER TIME I'M FACE TO FACE.	722	WITCH VIVIEN		57
THEN WHEREFORE FEAR THE USURY OF TIME,	724	KANVA ON SELF		17
AND AS THE TIME TO DARKNESS PLODDED	728	PRIEST FAIRY		11
NOD TO THE IRON SHOES OF TIME,	736	SUMMER EVENING		11
TILL DAY AND NIGHT TIME END.	741	EARL PAUL		48
TIME AND THE WORLD AND ALL THINGS DWINDLE OUT.	749	SHADOW WATER A		47
THAT SHALL BURN TIME WHEN TIMES HAVE EBBED AWAY.	750	SHADOW WATER A		61
AND A STRING MURMURS AS THOUGH TIME WERE DEAD	752	SHADOW WATER A		124
AND I MUST LOSE MORE TIME BECAUSE THESE FOOLS	754	SHADOW WATER A		158
ENDS TIME AND CHANGE.	754	SHADOW WATER A	V	163
THE TOPMOST BLOSSOM ON THE BOUGHS OF TIME	756	SHADOW WATER A		178
HAS BLOSSOMED, AND I GROW AS OLD AS TIME.	756	SHADOW WATER A		179
AND I AM OLD AS TIME, BECAUSE I KNOW	756	SHADOW WATER A	V	179
ALL THAT TIME KNOWS. SPEAK TO ME, QUEEN. O SPEAK!	756	SHADOW WATER A	V	180
I GREW AS OLD AS TIME, AND SHE GROWS YOUNG	761	SHADOW WATER A		259
WHERE TIME IS DROWNED IN ODOUR-LADEN WINDS	762	SHADOW WATER A		298

TIME'S

	PAGE	TITLE		LINE
TIME'S BITTER FLOOD WILL RISE,	173	PLEADS FRIEND		6
WASHED BY TIME'S WATERS AS THEY ROSE AND FELL	206	ADAMS CURSE		32
TO GRADUAL TIME'S LAST GIFT, A WRITTEN SPEECH	264	HOUSE SHAKEN		11
"TIME'S UP," HE CRIED, AND ALL THE THREE	297	THREE BEGGARS		57
"TIME'S UP," HE CRIED, AND ALL THE THREE	297	THREE BEGGARS		59
LIVED AT MY SIDE; THOUGHT TIME'S DISFIGURING TOUCH	466	HARUN RASHID		110
LIVED AT MY SIDE; THAT TIME'S DISFIGURING TOUCH	466	HARUN RASHID	V	110
OR SHIFT TIME'S FILTHY LOAD,	505	RESULT THOUGHT		15
LEAPS AND TIME'S OLD LANTHORN DIMS.	777	SONG DEIRDRE 2		5

TIMES   SEE MANY-TIMES-TROUBLED

	PAGE	TITLE		LINE
HE SHOOK HIMSELF AND NEIGHED THREE TIMES;	10	OISIN 1		110
AND NEIGHED THREE TIMES. WHEN, WONDERING	10	OISIN 1	V	110A
I LAUGHED AT TIMES UNNUMBERED TREASONS,	23	OISIN 1	V	345D
SAVE ONLY MANY TIMES MY NAME,	25	OISIN 1		375
SHONE MANY TIMES AMONG THE GLIMMERING FLOWERS	30	OISIN 2		21
AT TIMES OUR SLUMBER WAS LIGHTENED.	53	OISIN 3		97
TIMES FROM THE SALTIN' SHED,	94	MOLL MAGEE	V	9

TIMES   (CONTINUED)
          AND HOW BENEATH THOSE THREE TIMES BLESSED SKIES . . . .   127 DREAM OF FAERY V   21
          SPINNING AT ALL TIMES ERI'S GOOD TO-MORROW, ...   129 BOOK STORIES   V   10
          MADE WHEN GOD SLEPT IN TIMES OF OLD. . . . .   135 TWO TREES   32
          MY HEART WOULD BRIM WITH DREAMS ABOUT THE TIMES . . . .   136 TO SOME I TALK   2
          TO THOSE WITH WHOM I HAVE TALKED MANY TIMES, ...   136 TO SOME I TALK V   2
          TO IRELAND IN THE COMING TIMES . . . .   137 TO IRELAND   T
          THAT YOU, IN THE DIM COMING TIMES, ...   139 TO IRELAND   46
          AND HOW YOU HAVE LEAPED TIMES OUT OF MIND . . . .   146 FISH   5
          AND PLUCK TILL TIME AND TIMES ARE DONE . . . .   150 WANDER AENGUS   22
          OUT OF THE BATTLES OF OLD TIMES. . . . .   158 BELOVED RHYMES   6
          AMONG MY LEAVES IN TIMES OUT OF MIND! . . . .   177 PAST GREATNESS   5
          A LATTICED WINDOW. HIS GLANCE WENT UP AT TIMES . . . .   180 QUEEN MAEVE   6
          HAD COME AS IN THE OLD TIMES TO COUNSEL HER, ...   181 QUEEN MAEVE   42
          HAD COME, AS IN OLD TIMES, TO COUNSEL HER, ...   181 QUEEN MAEVE   V   42
          IN OLD TIMES AMONG THE CLOUDS OF THE AIR. . . . . . .   194 BAILE AILLINN   133
          AT ALL TIMES OF THE YEAR! . . . .   214 HAPPY TOWNLAND   6
          AS MEN IN THE OLD TIMES, BEFORE THE HARPS BEGAN, . . .   219 WOODS OF COOLE   43
          AS MEN IN THE OLD TIMES, BEFORE THE HARP BEGAN, ...   219 WOODS OF COOLE V   43
          THREE TIMES IN A SINGLE DAY . . . .   298 THREE HERMITS   10
          MANY TIMES TROUBLED YEARS. . . . .   315 FRIENDS   V   7
          NOW AS AT ALL TIMES I CAN SEE IN THE MIND'S EYE, . . .   318 MAGI   1
          I THINK IT BETTER THAT IN TIMES LIKE THESE . . . . . .   359 WAR POEM   1
          I THINK IT BETTER THAT AT TIMES LIKE THESE . . . . . .   359 WAR POEM   V   1
          SO MANY TIMES CHILDISH DELIGHT. . . . .   399 BREAK OF DAY   11
          OR ELSE BY TOASTING HER A SCORE OF TIMES, ...   410 TOWER   42
          WONDER HOW MANY TIMES I COULD HAVE PROVED MY WORTH . .   427 PHANTOM HATRED   34
          THE EXTRAVAGANCE OF SPRING! OR CERTAIN TIMES . . . . .   466 HARUN RASHID   V   125
          MANY TIMES HE DIED, ...   476 DEATH   5
          MANY TIMES ROSE AGAIN. . . . .   476 DEATH   6
          GOD BE WITH THE TIMES WHEN I . . . .   514 JANE GROWN OLD   17
          WE THREE ALONE IN MODERN TIMES HAD BROUGHT . . . . . .   603 GALLERY REVIS   45
          MANY TIMES MAN LIVES AND DIES . . . .   637 BEN BULBEN   13
          THREE TIMES THE ROSES HAVE GROWN LESS AND LESS, ...   690 MOSADA 1   1
          THEN HAS THIS ONE BEEN SINNED FULL MANY TIMES. . . . .   692 MOSADA 1   49
          WE THROW THREE TIMES. . . . .   721 WITCH VIVIEN   39
          THAT SHALL BURN TIME WHEN TIMES HAVE EBBED AWAY. . . .   750 SHADOW WATER A   61
TIMID
          FULL OF EARTH'S OLD TIMID GRACE. . . . .   124 CATHLEEN PARA   12
          BREATHED ON THE WORLD WITH TIMID BREATH. . . . .   266 GALWAY RACES   9
          NOR THE TAME WILL, NOR TIMID BRAIN, ...   318 APPOINTMENT   8
          I MUST ENDURE THE TIMID SUN. . . . .   344 DEJECTION   11
          THAT WOMEN LAUGHING, OR TIMID OR WILD, ...   358 PRESENCES   4
          TIMID, ENTANGLED, EMPTY AND ABASHED, ...   368 EGO DOMINUS   16
          FOR ALL HIS TIMID HEART, THERE THAT SLOW MAN, ...   489 COOLE PARK 29   12
TIMIDLY
          STOOD TIMIDLY. LEST THEY SHOULD SEE SOME SIGHT . . . .   38 OISIN 2   V   141
TIMON
          TILL I AM TIMON AND LEAR . . . .   576 ACRE OF GRASS   15
TIMOR
          AYE, AND ACHILLES, TIMOR, BABAR, BARHAIM, ALL . . . . .   366 HER COURAGE   9
TINCTURE
          HER HAIR WAS OF A CITRON TINCTURE, ...   3 OISIN 1   V   24
TINKER
          THE ROARING TINKER IF YOU LIKE, ...   605 SONGS BURDEN 1   1
          PRACTICE A TINKER SHUFFLE . . . .   617 LONG-LEG FLY   17
TINKLING
          FOR I AM IN HIS IMAGE MADE, AND ALL THIS TINKLING TIDE . .   76 INDIAN ON GOD   11
TINSEL
          THAT CANNOT IN THAT TRASH AND TINSEL HIDE! . . . . . .   558 RIBH CHRISTIAN   17
TINT
          WHITER THAN CURDS, ITS EYES THE TINT OF THE SEA. . . .   277 TWO KINGS   7
TINTED   SEE LEMON-TINTED
TIP   SEE FINGER-TIP A-TIP-TOE
          AND SIGHING LAID THE PEARLY TIP . . . .   12 OISIN 1   150
          SAID NIAM, AS SHE LAID THE TIP . . . .   12 OISIN 1   V   150
          SOME TWENTY FEET FROM TIP TO TIP HAD IT STRETCHED RIGHTLY   593 PILGRIM   17
            OUT,
          SOME TWENTY FEET FROM TIP TO TIP HAD IT STRETCHED RIGHTLY   593 PILGRIM   17
            OUT,
          SOME TWENTY FEET FROM TIP TO TIP HAD ITS WINGS STRETCHED   593 PILGRIM   V   17
            RIGHTLY OUT,
          SOME TWENTY FEET FROM TIP TO TIP HAD ITS WINGS STRETCHED   593 PILGRIM   V   17
            RIGHTLY OUT,
          AROUND THE FEATHERY TIP. UNTO THE SHAFT . . . .   657 ISLE STAT I 3   71
          LIES A CHILLY FINGER TIP, ...   732 STREET DANCERS   19
TIPS   SEE FINGER-TIPS
          UPON THE GRASS-BLADES' BENDING TIPS, ...   3 OISIN 1   V   7II
TIPTOE   SEE A-TIPTOE
          AND ON TIPTOE THE WINDS A-WHISPERING STOOD. . . . . .   715 DWELT SYCAMORE   8
TIP-TOE
          I PASSED A TIP-TOE UP AND DOWN, ...   85 MAD KING GOLL   V   51
          AND ON TIP-TOE THE WINDS A-WHISPERING STOOD. . . . . .   715 DWELT SYCAMORE V   8
TIRARAGH
          KEENING IN FROM TIRARAGH, ...   93 FATHER OHART   35
TIRE
          WE TIRE OF THE FLAME OF THE METEOR, BEFORE IT CAN FADE   122 WHITE BIRDS   2
            AND FLEE;
          FOR WE TIRE OF THE FLAME OF THE METEOR BEFORE IT CAN PASS   122 WHITE BIRDS   V   2
            BY AND FLEE

TIRE   (CONTINUED)
```
    WE TIRE OF THE FLAME OF THE METEOR, BEFORE IT CAN PASS        122 WHITE BIRDS      V    2
       BY AND FLEE;
    FOR SOULS WHO TIRE AND BLEED,   . . . . . . . . . . .         134 FR GILLIGAN          42
    WHOM MAN OR DEVIL CANNOT TIRE,  . . . . . . . . . . .         295 THREE BEGGARS        16
    YONDER FOOLISH ONES WILL TIRE   . . . . . . . . . . .         727 LOVERS QUARREL       47
    BODIES THAT CAN NEVER TIRE  . . . . . . . . . . . .           776 AGAINST WITCH        20
TIRED
    OR TIRED ON ANY DAWNING MORROW,   . . . . . . . . .            23 OISIN 1         V  341
    WHEN THE POOR TIRED CHILD, PASSION, FALLS ASLEEP. . .          80 EPHEMERA             7
    "THAT WE ARE TIRED, FOR OTHER LOVES AWAIT US; . . . .          80 EPHEMERA            21
    WHERE THE TIRED HORSE-BOYS LAY UPON THE RUSHES,  . .          180 QUEEN MAEVE         13
    I AM SO TIRED OF BEING BACHELOR   . . . . . . . . . .         222 SHADOW WATER B       8
    HAS TIRED OF HIS OWN COMPANY?   . . . . . . . . . . .         303 HOUR DAWN           35
    GROWN TIRED OF HIS OWN COMPANY?   . . . . . . . . . .         303 HOUR DAWN       V   37
    TIRED OF THAT COURTLY FASHION,  . . . . . . . . . . .         378 CAT AND MOON        15
    TIRED OF HER COURTLY FASHION,   . . . . . . . . . . .         378 CAT AND MOON    V   15
    GROWN TIRED OF THEIR SOLITUDE,  . . . . . . . . . . .         432 NINETEEN 19     V  105
    I AM TIRED OF CURSING THE BISHOP,   . . . . . . . . .         628 JANE MOUNTAIN        1
TIRELESS
    "THE RED BRANCH KINGS A TIRELESS BANQUET KEEP,   . . .        108 CUCHULAIN SEA   V   33
TITAN
    A TITAN, WITH LOUD LAUGHTER,  . . . . . . . . . . .           680 LOVE AND DEATH      11
TITANS
    THE TWO TITANS.  . . . . . . . . . . . . . . .               687 TWO TITANS           T
TITTLE
    AND ALL THE SHAPELY BODY NO TITTLE GONE ASTRAY. . . .        354 HIS PHOENIX         30
TOADS
    AND TOADS AND EVERY OUTLAWED THING   . . . . . . . .          85 MAD KING GOLL   V   61
TOASTING
    OR ELSE BY TOASTING HER A SCORE OF TIMES,   . . . . .        410 TOWER               42
TODAY
    FOR NONE ALIVE TODAY   . . . . . . . . . . . . .             458 SECRETS OF OLD  V   10
    EVEN TODAY, AFTER SOME SEVEN YEARS   . . . . . . . .         468 HARUN RASHID    V  161
    WE CALLED IT A GOOD DEATH.  TODAY   . . . . . . . .          791 REPRISALS            3
TO-DAY
    THAT IT WAS YESTERDAY AND NOT TO-DAY   . . . . . . .         246 SHADOW WATER B     493
    BECAUSE TO-DAY IS SOME RELIGIOUS FESTIVAL   . . . . .        363 DOLLS FACES          1
    FOR NONE ALIVE TO-DAY . . . . . . . . . . . . .             458 SECRETS OF OLD      10
    EVEN TO-DAY, AFTER SOME SEVEN YEARS   . . . . . . .          468 HARUN RASHID       161
    I AM DULL TO-DAY, OR YOU WERE NOW ALL LOST. . . . .          722 WITCH VIVIEN        59
    "SHIELD BREAKER, BREAK A SHIELD TO-DAY,   . . . . . .        739 EARL PAUL            1
    SHIELD-BREAKER, BREAK A SHIELD TO-DAY,   . . . . . .         739 EARL PAUL       V    1
TOE      SEE TIP-TOE A-TIP-TOE
    HEEL UP AND WEIGHT ON TOE, MUST FACE THE WALL   . . .        363 DOLLS FACES          3
    ALL OUT OF SHAPE FROM TOE TO TOP,   . . . . . . . .          639 BEN BULBEN          71
TOES
    TO ONE VAST FOOT, FROTH-SPLASHED, WITH CURVED TOES LYING      32 OISIN 2         V  46A
    TILL TOES MASTERED A SWEET MEASURE,   . . . . . . .          331 ROUND TOWER         15
    HANDS GRIPPED IN HANDS, TOES CLOSE TOGETHER,  . . . .        332 ROUND TOWER         21
    THE MEDITATIVE CRITIC; ALL ARE ON THEIR TOES,   . . .        363 DOLLS FACES          8
    BY THE WEBBED TOES, AND THAT ALL-POWERFUL BILL  . . .        441 LEDA AND SWAN   V    3
    BY THE WEBBED TOES, AND THAT ALL POWERFUL BILL  . . .        441 LEDA AND SWAN   V    3
    BECAUSE CHILDREN DEMAND DADDY-LONG-LEGS UPON HIS TIMBER      623 HIGH TALK            6
       TOES,
    A COCK CAME BY UPON HIS TOES;   . . . . . . . . . .          725 LEGEND              26
TOGETHER
    AND STOOD BESIDE THE SEA TOGETHER;   . . . . . . .             9 OISIN 1         V 101B
    AND SINGING, SINGING ALL TOGETHER;   . . . . . . .            15 OISIN 1            203
    TOGETHER, WHILE THE DARK WOODS RANG,   . . . . . . .          16 OISIN 1            227
    TOGETHER IN THAT HOUR OF GENTLENESS   . . . . . . .           80 EPHEMERA             6
    AND CLAP THEIR HANDS TOGETHER, AND HALF CLOSE THEIR EYES,    146 UNAPPEAS HOST        2
    THAT HELD THE LAND TOGETHER THERE,   . . . . . . .           194 BAILE AILLINN      132
    WE SAT TOGETHER AT ONE SUMMER'S END,   . . . . . .           204 ADAMS CURSE          1
    FOR TO ARTICULATE SWEET SOUNDS TOGETHER   . . . . .          205 ADAMS CURSE         10
    BUT WE BEND TOGETHER AND KISS THE QUIET FEET  . . .          207 HANRAHANS SONG V     4
    ONE--AND ONE--A COUPLE--FIVE TOGETHER;   . . . . .           233 SHADOW WATER B     249
    HANDS GRIPPED IN HANDS, TOES CLOSE TOGETHER,  . . .          332 ROUND TOWER         21
    BEAUTY AND FOOL TOGETHER LAID,  . . . . . . . . .            484 SYMBOLS              6
    CIVILIZATION IS HOOPED TOGETHER, BROUGHT   . . . .           563 MERU                 1
    ALL MUST TOGETHER DO." THAT DONE, THE MAN  . . . .           634 CUCHULAIN COMF      17
    FILLED THEM AS THEY SAT TOGETHER;   . . . . . . .            667 ISLE STAT II 3      31
    IS IN THY FACE, AND LIPS TOGETHER PRESSED;   . . .           671 ISLE STAT II 3     139
    WHEN HIS SINEWY WINGS TOGETHER CLOSE.   . . . . .            673 ISLE STAT II 3     179
    NOW FOUR TOGETHER;  I SHALL HEAR THEIR WORDS  . . .          753 SHADOW WATER A     139
    TWO HOVER THERE TOGETHER, AND ONE SAYS,   . . . .           753 SHADOW WATER A     142
    THEY HAVE FLOWN AWAY TOGETHER.  WE ARE NEARLY  . .          754 SHADOW WATER A     154
    AND RULE TOGETHER UNDER A CANOPY.   . . . . . . .           767 SHADOW WATER A     385
TOIL     SEE MUCH-TOIL
    SUNG OF THE BIRDS.  OUR TOIL WAS DONE;   . . . . .            14 OISIN 1         V  177
    IN PINCHING WAYS I TOIL AND TURN."   . . . . . . .            19 OISIN 1         V  282
    I SANG HOW, WHEN DAY'S TOIL IS DONE,   . . . . . .            85 MAD KING GOLL       61
    AND HEAVY MORTAL HOPES THAT TOIL AND PASS;   . . .           101 ROSE UPON ROOD      18
    THAN THIS ACCUSTOMED TOIL.  WHEN I WAS YOUNG,  . .           267 ALL TEMPT ME         5
    TOIL AND GROW RICH,   . . . . . . . . . . . . .             310 WITCH                1
    A STYLE IS FOUND BY SEDENTARY TOIL   . . . . . . .          370 EGO DOMINUS         65
    AN IMAGE OF MYSTERIOUS WISDOM WON BY TOIL;   . . .          373 PHASES OF MOON      18
    WITH THE GREAT TOIL AND CEREMONY OF STATE,   . . .          462 HARUN RASHID    V   25
    ENDURE THAT TOIL OF GROWING UP;   . . . . . . . .           478 SELF AND SOUL       44
    IN LUCK OR OUT THE TOIL HAS LEFT ITS MARK;   . . .          491 COOLE BALLYLEE  V  40F
    IN LUCK OR OUT THE TOIL HAS LEFT ITS MARK;   . . .          495 CHOICE               6
```

		PAGE	TITLE		LINE

TOIL   (CONTINUED)

	PAGE	TITLE		LINE
FOR ALL MY TOIL HAS HAD FOR ITS HIRE	551	SONGS REWRIT 1	V	3
ALL HIS TWENTIES CRAMMED WITH TOIL;	576	WHAT THEN		4
THOUGH GRAVE-DIGGERS' TOIL IS LONG,	637	BEN BULBEN		21
BENT LOW WITH TOIL AND HOARIEST YEARS. THE OTHER	711	FERENCZ RENYI		52
IN TOIL OF MEASUREMENT	784	WOMANS BEAUTY	V	9

TOILED

	PAGE	TITLE		LINE
AND UP THE STAIR WE TOILED TO A HIGH DOOR,	36	OISIN 2	V	101
TOILED WITH EMPOUNDED CATTLE THROUGH THE MIRE,	276	TWO KINGS	V	2
IL PENSEROSO'S PLATONIST TOILED ON	419	MY HOUSE		14
AND TOILED SO HARD AND LATE	432	NINETEEN 19		95
I TOILED LONG YEARS AND AT LENGTH	505	RESULT THOUGHT		9
TOILED LONG YEARS AND AT LENGTH	505	RESULT THOUGHT	V	9

TOILING

	PAGE	TITLE		LINE
LEST ALL THY TOILING ONLY BREEDS	66	HAPPY SHEPHERD		25
THE SPINNING STARS--THE TOILING SEA--WHIRL ROUND	665	ISLE STAT II 2		72

TOILS

	PAGE	TITLE		LINE
FROM SOMEBODY THAT TOILS FROM CHAIR TO CHAIR;	491	COOLE BALLYLEE		26
IN TOILS OF MEASUREMENT	784	WOMANS BEAUTY		9

TOKEN

	PAGE	TITLE		LINE
AS A TOKEN AND A SIGN,	648	ISLE STAT I 1		78

TOLD

	PAGE	TITLE		LINE
AND TOLD THE PURPLE DEEPS THEIR PRIDE,	14	OISIN 1		186
AS THOUGH HE TOLD HIS NEVER-SLUMBERING HEART	32	OISIN 2		44
AS THOUGH HE TOLD HIS NEVER SLUMBERING HEART	32	OISIN 2	V	44
HE TOLD OF EVERY FROTH-DROP HISSING, FLYING,	32	OISIN 2	V	45
WHEN YOU HAVE TOLD HOW I WEEP ENDLESSLY,	33	OISIN 2		63
AH! THERE HE SNAPS MY RICE. I TOLD YOU SO.	73	ANASHU VIJAYA		38
AND ALL AROUND THE HARP-STRING TOLD HIS PRAISE,	109	CUCHULAIN SEA		44
AND ALL AROUND THE HARPSTRING TOLD HIS PRAISE,	109	CUCHULAIN SEA	V	44
AND ALL AROUND THE HARP STRING TOLD HIS PRAISE,	109	CUCHULAIN SEA	V	44
IF ALL WERE TOLD:	116	FAERY SONG		4
IF ALL WERE TOLD,	116	FAERY SONG		16
TOLD WHERE--AH, LITTLE, ALL-UNNEEDED VOICE!--	127	DREAM OF FAERY	V	30
THE WRONG OF UNSHAPELY THINGS IS A WRONG TOO GREAT TO BE TOLD:	143	ROSE IN HEART		5
THE WRONG OF THE THINGS MISSHAPEN IS WRONG TOO GREAT TO BE TOLD:	143	ROSE IN HEART	V	5
SHE TOLD THEM OF THE MANY-CHANGING ONES:	185	QUEEN MAEVE		112
THE BOUGHS HAVE WITHERED BECAUSE I HAVE TOLD THEM MY DREAMS.	203	WITHER BOUGHS		8
THE BOUGHS HAVE WITHERED BECAUSE I HAVE TOLD THEM MY DREAMS.	203	WITHER BOUGHS		16
THE BOUGHS HAVE WITHERED BECAUSE I HAVE TOLD THEM MY DREAMS.	204	WITHER BOUGHS		24
BECAUSE OF SOMETHING TOLD UNDER THE FAMISHED HORN	210	UNDER THE MOON		17
MY MOTHER TOLD ME THAT THERE IS NOT ONE	224	SHADOW WATER B		45
AND YOU HAVE TOLD ME THAT THEIR JOURNEY LIES	231	SHADOW WATER B		205
TOLD HIM, THAT WHEN ORION ROSE, AND ALL	282	TWO KINGS	V	132A
A FRIEND THAT COULD, HE HAD TOLD HER, WORK HIS CURE	283	TWO KINGS		137
THAT COULD, AS HE HAD TOLD HER, WORK HIS CURE,	283	TWO KINGS	V	137
AMENDED WHAT WAS TOLD AWRY	440	WISDOM		4
TOLD OF A HARSH REPROOF, OR TRIVIAL EVENT	443	SCHOOL CHILDR		11
TOLD, AND IT SEEMED THAT OUR TWO NATURES BLENT	443	SCHOOL CHILDR		13
TOLD ALL THAT HAD BEEN SAID OR DONE	456	SUMMER SPRING		3
AND TOLD HIM SO, BUT FRIENDSHIP NEVER ENDS:	473	ALL SOUL NIGHT		65
WHEN EVERYTHING IS TOLD,	515	GIRLS SONG B		10
TILL I HAVE TOLD THE SAGES	534	CONSOLATION		5
I TOLD HIM THAT NIGHTLY FROM SIX TO SEVEN I SAT AT THIS TABLE,	578	LOFTY THINGS		9
HE TOLD PEARSE AND CONNOLLY	585	ORAHILLY		12
WHEN HE HEARD THAT STORY TOLD,	596	COLONEL MARTIN		47
WHEN HE HAD HEARD THAT STORY TOLD	596	COLONEL MARTIN	V	47
BUT FIRST YOU MUST BE TOLD OUR CHARACTER:	634	CUCHULAIN COMF		20
ASIDE!--THE WILD HORNS TOLD ALMINTOR'S END,	665	ISLE STAT II 2		68
A VOICE HAS TOLD ME HOW WITHIN THIS LAND	682	SEEKER	V	22
FORGIVE! FOR I HAVE TOLD THEM EVERYTHING.	694	MOSADA 1		107
THEY SAID I'D BURN IN HELL UNLESS I TOLD.	694	MOSADA 1		108
HAS TOLD ME THAT THE UNDYING SEND THEIR EAGLES	765	SHADOW WATER A		346
A STREAM HAS TOLD ME THEY ARE BEAUTIFUL.	767	SHADOW WATER A		398

TOLERANCE

	PAGE	TITLE		LINE
MADE ALL PLATONIC TOLERANCE VAIN	438	SONGS PLAY 2		7
MADE PLATO'S TOLERANCE IN VAIN,	438	SONGS PLAY 2	V	7

TOLLING

	PAGE	TITLE		LINE
SLOW THE CHAPEL BELL IS TOLLING AS THOUGH THE DEAD PASSED BY.	718	PHANTOM SHIP		16

TOM

	PAGE	TITLE		LINE
TOM O'ROUGHLEY	337	TOM OROUGHLEY		T
OR SO DID TOM O'ROUGHLEY SAY	338	TOM OROUGHLEY		5
TOM THE LUNATIC	528	TOM LUNATIC		T
SANG OLD TOM THE LUNATIC	528	TOM LUNATIC		1
TOM AT CRUACHAN	529	TOM CRUACHAN		T
OLD TOM AT CRUACHAN	529	TOM CRUACHAN	V	T
OLD TOM AGAIN	530	OLD TOM AGAIN		T
COME TOM AND DICK, COME ALL THE TROOP	582	ROGER CASEMENT		17
THE COLONEL SAID TO TOM HIS MAN,	596	COLONEL MARTIN		50
"AND DID YOU KEEP NO GOLD, TOM?	596	COLONEL MARTIN		64
AND TOM MAKE OUT A LIVING	597	COLONEL MARTIN		70
WHEN TOM MADE OUT A LIVING	597	COLONEL MARTIN	V	70

TOMB

	PAGE	TITLE		LINE
AWAY, AWAY! YOU ARE SAFER IN THE TOMB.	293	TO A SHADE		24

824

TOMB   (CONTINUED)
    THE MOUNTAIN TOMB . . . .   311 MOUNTAIN TOMB   T
    OUR FATHER ROSICROSS IS IN HIS TOMB. . . . . .   311 MOUNTAIN TOMB   4
    OUR FATHER ROSICROSS IS IN HIS TOMB. . . . . .   311 MOUNTAIN TOMB   8
    OUR FATHER ROSICROSS SLEEPS IN HIS TOMB. . . . . 311 MOUNTAIN TOMB   12
    AND NEVER COULD HAVE RESTED IN THE TOMB . . . .   325 ROBERT GREGORY   27
    ON GREAT-GRANDFATHER'S BATTERED TOMB." . . . .   331 ROUND TOWER   6
    ON GREAT-GRANDFATHER'S BATTERED TOMB." . . . .   332 ROUND TOWER   30
    ON GREAT GRANDFATHER'S BATTERED TOMB." . . . .   332 ROUND TOWER   V   30
    IN THE GREY STONE TOMB HE MADE. . . . . . .   360 ALF POLLEXFEN   5
    IN THAT TOMB BY HIM AND HER . . . .   360 ALF POLLEXFEN   7
    AND HEARTIER LOVES! THAT LAMP IS FROM THE TOMB.   398 LEADERS CROWD   12
    IS BUT ITS LONGING FOR THE TOMB. . . . , . .   434 WHEEL   8
    THE TOMB OF SWIFT WEARS IT AWAY.   A VOICE   487 SEVEN SAGES   21
    PROUD, OPEN-EYED AND LAUGHING TO THE TOMB. . .   501 VACILLATION   34
    THE BODY OF SAINT TERESA LIES UNDECAYED IN TOMB, 503 VACILLATION   80
    WHAT SEEMS MOST WELCOME IN THE TOMB--PLAY A PREDESTINED 503 VACILLATION   86
        PART.
    (ALL FIND SAFETY IN THE TOMB.) . . . .   508 JANE BISHOP   3
    (ALL FIND SAFETY IN THE TOMB.) . . . .   508 JANE BISHOP   10
    (ALL FIND SAFETY IN THE TOMB.) . . . .   508 JANE BISHOP   17
    (ALL FIND SAFETY IN THE TOMB.) . . . .   508 JANE BISHOP   24
    MY BODY IN THE TOMB-- . . . .   511 JANE AND JACK   10
    AND LAID THEM ON LOVE'S LETTERED TOMB! . . . .   519 HER DREAM   4
    UNDER THE GREAT COMEDIAN'S TOMB THE CROWD. . .   541 PARN FUNERAL 1   1
    RIBH AT THE TOMB OF BAILE AND AILLINN . . . .   554 RIBH AT TOMB   T
    AND FOUND HIS FAMILY TOMB . . . .   584 GHOST ROG CASE   32
    FROM EMPTY TOMB OR VIRGIN WOMB? . . . . . .   619 STICK INCENSE   2
    THERE IN THE TOMB STAND THE DEAD UPRIGHT, . .   635 BLACK TOWER   7
    THERE IN THE TOMB DROPS THE FAINT MOONLIGHT, .   636 BLACK TOWER   17
    THERE IN THE TOMB THE DARK GROWS BLACKER . .   636 BLACK TOWER   27
    HE GUIDES YE FROM THE TOMB! . . . .   738 MOURN THEN ON   14
    OF MANY A TRAGIC TOMB! . . . .   785 YOUR HEART   10
    OF MANY A TRAGIC TOMB! . . . .   786 YOUR HEART   23
    OF MANY A TRAGIC TOMB! . . . .   786 YOUR HEART   36
    YET RISE FROM YOUR ITALIAN TOMB, ...   791 REPRISALS   10
TOMB-HAUNTER
    WHAT GREAT TOMB-HAUNTER SWEEPS THE DISTANT SKY . 618 BRONZE HEAD   4
    NO DARK TOMB-HAUNTER ONCE! HER FORM ALL FULL . . 618 BRONZE HEAD   8
TOMBS
    MADE OF DIM GOLD RAVE OUT IN SECRET TOMBS! . .   235 SHADOW WATER B   295
    IN TOMBS OF GOLD AND LAPIS LAZULI . . . . . .   483 OIL AND BLOOD   1
    IN TOMBS OF GOLD AND LAPIS-LAZULI . . . . . .   483 OIL AND BLOOD   V   1
    IN ANCIENT TOMBS I SIGHED, BUT NOT AGAIN! . . .   564 GYRES   14
    MADE OF DIM GOLD, RAVE OUT IN SECRET TOMBS, .   765 SHADOW WATER A   345
TOMBSTONE
    UPON A GREY OLD BATTERED TOMBSTONE . . . . .   331 ROUND TOWER   7
    UPON THE GREY OLD BATTERED TOMBSTONE . . . .   331 ROUND TOWER   V   7
TOMORROW
    TOMORROW NIGHT I WILL BREAK DOWN THE DOOR. .   551 SONGS REWRIT 1   V   REF
TO-MORROW
    EVERYTHING THAT FEARS TO-MORROW . . . . . .   20 OISIN 1   V   302
    SPINNING AT ALL TIMES ERI'S GOOD TO-MORROW, .   129 BOOK STORIES   V   10
    TO-MORROW NIGHT I WILL BREAK DOWN THE DOOR. .   551 SONGS REWRIT 1   6
    TO-MORROW NIGHT I WILL BREAK DOWN THE DOOR. .   551 SONGS REWRIT 1   12
    TO-MORROW NIGHT I WILL BREAK DOWN THE DOOR. .   551 SONGS REWRIT 1   18
    TO-MORROW NIGHT I WILL BREAK IN THE DOOR. .   551 SONGS REWRIT 1   V   REF
    THIS EVE, TO-MORROW, OR TO-MORROW NIGHT . . .   699 MOSADA 3   2
    THIS EVE, TO-MORROW, OR TO-MORROW NIGHT . . .   699 MOSADA 3   2
    FORGAEL CAN DIE TO-MORROW.   COME TO THE ALE.   759 SHADOW WATER A   246
    COME TO THE ALE! FOR HE CAN DIE TO-MORROW. .   760 SHADOW WATER A   247
TONE
    AND ROBERT EMMET AND WOLFE TONE, ...   290 SEPTEMBER 1913   21
    LORD EDWARD AND WOLFE TONE, ...   395 SIXTEEN DEAD   16
    WHEN STRANGERS MURDERED EMMET, FITZGERALD, TONE, 541 PARN FUNERAL 1   17
TONES
    OUR TREAD, AS ROSE AND FELL THE LIQUID TONES .   33 OISIN 2   V   68B
    TO BLESS THAT ISLE WITH HONEY IN HIS TONES, .   128 DREAM OF FAERY   V   44
    SAD FAERY TONES. 'TIS THUS THEY EVER SEEM, . .   654 ISLE STAT I 2   58
TONGUE
    SWAYED, CROONING TO HIMSELF AN UNKNOWN TONGUE! .   39 OISIN 2   159
    AH, SWEET TO ME NOW WERE EVEN BALD CONAN'S SLANDEROUS   55 OISIN 3   116
        TONGUE!
    AND NOW MOVES MANY A PLEASANT TONGUE . . . . .   98 FOXHUNTER   21
    AND MOVES THERE MANY A PLEASANT TONGUE, ...   98 FOXHUNTER   V   23
    AND LEARN TO CHAUNT A TONGUE MEN DO NOT KNOW. .   101 ROSE UPON ROOD   21
    AND LEARN TO CHANT A TONGUE MEN DO NOT KNOW. .   101 ROSE UPON ROOD   V   21
    BURNING IN FIRES OF A SLANDEROUS TONGUE. . . .   148 INTO TWILIGHT   8
    THE TONGUE OF IT SWEET WITH DREAMING . . . .   160 CAP AND BELLS   V   17
    THE WATERS OF SLEEP CAN MAKE A CHATTERING TONGUE 218 WOODS OF COOLE   25
    YOU SAY, AS I HAVE OFTEN GIVEN TONGUE . . . . .   262 TO A POET   1
    SO WE SPEAK A DIFFERENT TONGUE. . . . . . .   313 TWO YEAR LATER   6
    AND I SPEAK A BARBAROUS TONGUE. . . . . . .   313 TWO YEAR LATER   12
    THE EYE OF THE MIND NOR KEEP MY TONGUE FROM SPEECH." 353 PEOPLE   34
    I SUDDENLY CRIED OUT IN A STRANGE TONGUE . . .   387 SOLOMON WITCH   5
    BUT NOW WITH FLATTERING TONGUE . . . .   434 YOUTH AND AGE   3
    NOW THAT YOUR TONGUE CANNOT PERSUADE THE CHILD TILL SHE 450 OWEN AHERNE   22
        MISTAKE
    ON OLD DRY WRITING IN A LEARNED TONGUE, ...   466 HARUN RASHID   123
    . . . MOVE HIS MOUTH AND SINEWY TONGUE. . . . . . . 560 MAGIC DRUM   5
    (AN IMAGE OUT OF SPENSER AND THE COMMON TONGUE). . . . 603 GALLERY REVIS   40

825

	PAGE	TITLE		LINE

TONGUE   (CONTINUED)
    GIVE TONGUE, PROCLAIM THEIR HIDDEN NAME--"HOUND VOICE."   622 HOUND VOICE   7
    AND YET GAVE TONGUE. "HOUND VOICES" WERE THEY ALL. . . . . 622 HOUND VOICE   9
    WHOM MEN HAVE NAMED ARCADIA'S SWEETEST TONGUE.   649 ISLE STAT I 1   109
    THOU HAST AN OVER-NIMBLE TONGUE. THY GRIEF, ... 661 ISLE STAT II 1   59
    WILD WISDOMS OF SPIRIT AND TONGUE. . . . . 708 FAIRY PEDANT   27
    WILD SPIRITS OF WISDOM AND TONGUE.   708 FAIRY PEDANT   V 27
    BECAUSE OF THE THING HIS TONGUE HAD SAID. . . . . . . 730 PRIEST FAIRY   60
TONGUED   SEE SWEET-TONGUED WISE-TONGUED DEWY-TONGUED
TONGUE'S
    BUT WHEN I THINK OF THAT MY TONGUE'S A STONE. . . . . 478 SELF AND SOUL   40
TONGUES
    WERE LOLLING THEIR TONGUES, AND THE SILKEN HAIR . . . . 2 OISIN 1   V 75
    AND THE TONGUES OF THE CROWD . . . . 172 PLEADS FRIEND   V   2
    FOR ALL TONGUES HE KNEW. . . . . 594 COLONEL MARTIN   4
    OF THOSE STEEL TONGUES! CRASH, SWORDS! WELL THRUST!   665 ISLE STAT II 2   67
       WELL BENT
    HAVE CLOTHED THEIR TONGUES WITH SONG OF SONGLESS DAYS? . . 666 ISLE STAT II 3   17
TO-NIGHT
    ALL, ALL ARE IN MY THOUGHTS TO-NIGHT BEING DEAD. . . . . 324 ROBERT GREGORY   8
TONSURED
    CHILDREN AND WOMEN AND TONSURED YOUNG MEN, ... 167 BLESSED   V 15
    TO THOSE THAT NEVER SAW THIS TONSURED HEAD . . . . . . 555 RIBH AT TOMB   4
TOOK
    IN TRUST TOOK HE JOHN'S LANDS! . . . . 92 FATHER OHART   5
    THE DRUIDS TOOK THEM TO THEIR MYSTERY, ... 111 CUCHULAIN SEA   82
    BEFORE EARTH TOOK HIM TO HER STONY CARE! . . . . . . 126 DREAM OF FAERY   4
    BUT SHE TOOK UP HER FAN FROM THE TABLE . . . . 160 CAP AND BELLS   19
    BUT SHE TOOK HER FAN FROM THE TABLE, ... 160 CAP AND BELLS   V 19
    SHE TOOK THEM INTO HER BOSOM, ... 160 CAP AND BELLS   V 25
    SOME MAY HAVE BLAMED YOU THAT YOU TOOK AWAY . . . . . 257 RECONCILIATION   1
    OLD BUTLERS WHEN YOU TOOK TO HORSE AND STOOD . . . . . 270 PARDON FATHERS   V 10
    ROCK-NURTURED AOIFE TOOK A PIN, ... 274 GREY ROCK   88
    THREE OLD HERMITS TOOK THE AIR . . . . 298 THREE HERMITS   1
    "I TOOK YOU FOR A BRAWLING GHOST, ... 304 HOUR DAWN   V 41
    AND TOOK THE WOODEN LADLE UP . . . . 304 HOUR DAWN   V 46
    AND WHAT OF HER THAT TOOK . . . . 315 FRIENDS   17
    AND I TOOK ALL THE BLAME OUT OF ALL SENSE AND REASON, . . 316 COLD HEAVEN   7
    I TOOK A BROKEN ROOT TO FLING . . . . 317 APPOINTMENT   2
    OF THAT LATE DEATH TOOK ALL MY HEART FOR SPEECH. . . . . 328 ROBERT GREGORY   96
    AND TOOK THEIR TABLETS AND DID SUMS! . . . . 344 DAWN   9
    AND TOOK THEIR TABLETS AND MADE SUMS-- . . . . 344 DAWN   V   9
    MEN AND THEIR BUSINESS TOOK . . . . 421 MY TABLE   23
    GOD TOOK THE SPINNING-JENNY . . . . 439 FRAGMENTS   3
    AND TOOK A MESS OF SHADOWS FOR ITS MEAT? . . . . . . 444 SCHOOL CHILDR   28
    AND TOOK A MASS OF SHADOWS FOR ITS MEAT, ... 444 SCHOOL CHILDR   V 28
    AND THEREUPON A COLLOQUY TOOK PLACE . . . . 463 HARUN RASHID   45
    THAT THEREUPON A COLLOQUY TOOK PLACE . . . . 463 HARUN RASHID   V 45
    THE CHAMBERMAID LIVED LONG, AND TOOK . . . . 571 THREE BUSHES   57
    STOOD, TOOK DEATH LIKE A TUNE . . . . 613 MARCH SONGS 1   15
    BUT HE TOOK DOWN THE MOON . . . . 616 MARCH SONGS 3   8
    BUT HE TOOK DOWN THE MOON . . . . 616 MARCH SONGS 3   18
    BUT HE TOOK DOWN THE MOON . . . . 616 MARCH SONGS 3   28
    I TOOK NO TROUBLE TO CONVINCE, ... 624 APPARITIONS   3
    PLAYERS AND PAINTED STAGE TOOK ALL MY LOVE, ... 630 CIRCUS ANIMALS   31
    TOOK UP THE NEAREST AND BEGAN TO SEW. . . . . 634 CUCHULAIN COMF   18
    AND PASSED THE OUTER HEBRIDES, AND TOOK . . . . . . 749 SHADOW WATER A   42
    AND PASSED THE NORTHERN HEBRIDES, AND TOOK . . . . . 749 SHADOW WATER A   V 42
    UNDER THE WAVES, AND TOOK A THOUSAND WOMEN . . . . . . 766 SHADOW WATER A   378
    AN ANCIENT LECHER TOOK TO GEESE . . . . 792 GEORGE MOORE   3
TOOL
    NOR HAVE HANDS HELD A WEARY TOOL! . . . . 19 OISIN 1   283
    AND HANDS THAT HOLD NO WEARISOME TOOL, ... 22 OISIN 1   340
    OUR HANDS HAVE KNOWN NO WEARYING TOOL, ... 22 OISIN 1   V 339
TOOTH
    BRED THAT FIERCE TOOTH AND CLEANLY LIMB . . . . . . 318 APPOINTMENT   10
    THE HORN'S SWEET NOTE AND THE TOOTH OF THE HOUND. . . . 380 SONGS FOOL 1   12
    THE HORN'S SWEET NOTE AND THE TOOTH OF THE HOUND. . . . 381 SONGS FOOL 2   14
    THE WEASEL'S TWIST, THE WEASEL'S TOOTH. . . . . . . 431 NINETEEN 19   92
    LOVE IS LIKE THE LION'S TOOTH. . . . . 514 JANE GROWN OLD   7
    LOVE IS LIKE THE LION'S TOOTH. . . . . 514 JANE GROWN OLD   14
    LOVE IS LIKE THE LION'S TOOTH. . . . . 515 JANE GROWN OLD   21
TOOTHLESS
    HIS TOOTHLESS HOUND AT HIS NERVELESS FEET, ... 26 OISIN 1   V 400
TOP   SEE MOUNTAIN-TOP SPINNING-TOP TOWER-TOP TABLE-TOP
    A FIR-TREE ROARING IN ITS LEAFLESS TOP! . . . . . . 40 OISIN 2   177
    A FIR TREE ROARING IN ITS LEAFLESS TOP, ... 40 OISIN 2   V 177
    HAD HAMMERED OUT ON MOUNTAIN TOP . . . . 271 GREY ROCK   23
    THE GOLDEN TOP OF CARE? . . . . 309 PLAYER QUEEN   20
    UNTIL THEY PRANCED UPON THE TOP. . . . . 331 ROUND TOWER   18
    FROM DEATH, AND WOUNDS, OR ON SINAI'S TOP, ... 375 PHASES OF MOON   67
    AND THE MOON SPUN ROUND LIKE A TOP, ... 378 CAT AND MOON   2
    ON THEIR HOLLOW TOP. . . . . 415 TOWER   171
    I CLIMB TO THE TOWER TOP AND LEAN UPON BROKEN STONE, . . 425 PHANTOM HATRED   V   1
    HALF DEAD AT THE TOP. . . . . 480 BLOOD AND MOON   12
    HALF DEAD AT THE TOP? NO MATTER WHAT I SAID, ... 482 BLOOD AND MOON   48
    OTTERS BELOW AND MOOR-HENS ON THE TOP, ... 490 COOLE BALLYLEE   2
    OTTERS BELOW AND MOOR HENS ON THE TOP, ... 490 COOLE BALLYLEE   V   2
    FROM DOOR TO TOP! . . . . 512 JANE ON GOD   17
    ARE SOMEWHERE SLEEPING LIKE A TOP . . . . 525 DANCING DAYS   13
    DOWN EVERY WITHERED FINGER FROM THE TOP! . . . . . . 537 HER VISION   11

		PAGE	TITLE	LINE

TOP   (CONTINUED)
WHEN NATIONS ARE EMPTY UP THERE AT THE TOP, ... 548 TO SAME TUNE 3   11
WHAT MATTER THOUGH NUMB NIGHTMARE RIDE ON TOP, ... 564 GYRES   9
AND WHEN THEY CAME TO THE TOP STAIR . . . . . . 595 COLONEL MARTIN   41
WHAT IF THERE'S NOTHING UP THERE AT THE TOP? . . . . . . 615 MARCH SONGS 2   21
ALL OUT OF SHAPE FROM TOE TO TOP, ... 639 BEN BULBEN   71
LIKE WINE THAT FILLS TO THE TOP . . . . 781 MY HEART BEAT   14

TOPERS
WHERE SEVEN EPHESIAN TOPERS SLEPT AND NEVER KNEW . . . . 442 BLACK CENTAUR   11

TOPLESS
THOSE TOPLESS TOWERS . . . . 293 HELEN LIVED   8
THAT THE TOPLESS TOWERS BE BURNT . . . . 617 LONG-LEG FLY   11

TOPMOST
A TREE THERE IS THAT FROM ITS TOPMOST BOUGH . . . . . 500 VACILLATION   11
THE TOPMOST BLOSSOM ON THE BOUGHS OF TIME . . . . . . 756 SHADOW WATER A   178

TOPPLED
THEY TOPPLED OVER, "WERE IT NOT . . . . . . 302 HOUR DAWN   17

TOPPLES
SOON TOPPLES DOWN THE HILL. . . . . 335 YOUNG BEAUTY   6

TOPPLING
I HAD BEEN HURT"! AND TOPPLING BROUGHT . . . . . . 302 HOUR DAWN   19

TOPS
WHOSE HOOVES THE TOPS OF THE SURGES GRAZED, ... 12 OISIN 1   V 142A
THE TOPS OF THEIR EARS WERE FEATHERED, ... 49 OISIN 3   34
AND SOFTLY COME TO YOUR NIAMH OVER THE TOPS OF THE TIDE! . 55 OISIN 3   126
AND SOFTLY COME TO THY NIAM OVER THE TOPS OF THE TIDE! . . 52 OISIN 3   V 126
AND PUT HIS PATTERN ROUND THEIR TOPS . . . . 272 GREY ROCK   V 24
DEWY-TONGUED, THE DAISY TOPS— . . . . 706 DAWN-SONG   22

TORCH
AND IN THE RING A TORCH, AND WITH ITS FLARE . . . . 37 OISIN 2   121
WHO BROUGHT US FOUND A TORCH, AND, WITH ITS FLARE . . . 37 OISIN 2   V 122
AND THRUST THE TORCH BETWEEN THE SLIMY FLAGS. . . . . . 38 OISIN 2   143
ANOINTING, TORCH JAMMED DOWN BETWEEN THE FLAGS, ... 38 OISIN 2   V 143
FOUND THAT OLD HOUSE, A SPUTTERING TORCH WITHIN, ... 283 TWO KINGS   140
AND FOUND THE HOUSE, A SPUTTERING TORCH WITHIN, ... 283 TWO KINGS   V 140
OR DID THE TORCH LIGHT OF THAT MYSTERY . . . . . 466 HARUN RASHID V 115
THE PROUD FURIES EACH WITH HER TORCH ON HIGH. . . . . . 579 DOR WELLESLEY   16
COMPANIONING THE RIVER'S PILGRIM TORCH. . . . . . . 703 MOSADA 3   112

TORCHES
IN DRUID VAPOUR AND MAKE THE TORCHES DIM! . . . . . . 169 SECRET ROSE   11
THE SMOKY TORCHES MADE A GLARE . . . . 271 GREY ROCK   18
AND SMOKY TORCHES MADE A GLARE . . . . 271 GREY ROCK   V 18
BUT THE DARK CHANGED TO RED, AND TORCHES SHONE, ... 537 HER VISION   12

TORCHLIGHT
. . . THROUGH TORCHLIGHT AND TUMULTUOUS SONG! . . . . 459 FROM OEDIPUS   8
OR DID THE TORCHLIGHT OF THAT MYSTERY . . . . . . 466 HARUN RASHID   115

TORCH-LIGHT
. . . THROUGH TORCH-LIGHT AND TUMULTUOUS SONG! . . . . 459 FROM OEDIPUS   V 8
OR DID THE TORCH-LIGHT OF THAT MYSTERY . . . . . 466 HARUN RASHID V 115

TORE
WHEN I TORE DOWN THE TREE! BUT WHEN THE WEST . . . . 41 OISIN 2   V 180
WHEN I'D TORE DOWN THAT TREE! BUT WHEN THE WEST . . . 41 OISIN 2   V 180
WHEN I TORE DOWN THAT TREE! BUT WHEN THE WEST . . . . 41 OISIN 2   V 180
I TORE IT FROM GREEN BOUGHS WINDS TORE AND TOSSED . . . 130 BOOK STORIES   13
I TORE IT FROM GREEN BOUGHS WINDS TORE AND TOSSED . . . 130 BOOK STORIES   13
I TORE IT FROM THE BARREN BOUGHS OF EIRE, ... 130 BOOK STORIES   15
I TORE IT FROM GREEN BOUGHS WINDS TOSSED AND HURLED, . . 130 BOOK STORIES   V 13
I TORE IT FROM THE GREEN BOUGHS OF OLD ERI, ... 130 BOOK STORIES   V 15
TORE FROM THE CLOUDS HIS MARVELLOUS MOON. . . . . . . 314 MEMORY YOUTH   21
I TORE MY BODY THAT ITS WINE MIGHT COVER . . . . . 537 HER VISION   7
COMMANDING OFFICER THAT TORE . . . . 627 STATES HOLIDAY   16

TORMENTED   SEE RAGE-TORMENTED GONG-TORMENTED
THE RAGE DRIVEN, RAGE TORMENTED, AND RAGE HUNGRY TROOP, 426 PHANTOM HATRED V 11

TORN   SEE NEW-TORN DOLPHIN-TORN BEAST-TORN
WHEN I HAD TORN IT DOWN! BUT WHEN THE WEST . . . . . 41 OISIN 2   V 180
THE FENIAN HORSES! ARMOUR TORN ASUNDER! . . . . . . 43 OISIN 2   210
HAS TORN AND RENT THEIR HEARTS IN TWAIN, ... 66 HAPPY SHEPHERD V 33
FOR THE KIND WIRES ARE TORN AND STILL, ... 86 MAD KING GOLL   V 69
OF FEVER. NOW THE STRINGS ARE TORN . . . . . . 86 MAD KING GOLL   V 66
MY SINGING FADES, THE STRINGS ARE TORN, ... 86 MAD KING GOLL   V 66
UNTIL AT LAST THE UNLOCKED HORN HAD TORN ! . . . . . 278 TWO KINGS   V 21
BUT THE TORN PETALS STREW THE GARDEN PLOT! . . . . . 422 MY DESCENDANTS   7
WHEN THE TORN PETALS STREW THE GARDEN PLOT! . . . . . 422 MY DESCENDANTS V 7
THAT FLOWERING, SILKEN, OLD EMBROIDERY, TORN . . . . 477 SELF AND SOUL   13
AND OUR HEARTS ARE TORN. . . . . 519 LOVES LONENESS   12
NO CIVIL RANCOUR TORN THE LAND APART. . . . . . . 542 PARN FUNERAL 2   4
LIES TORN AND ROTTING. THE FIERCE KESTREL BIRDS . . . 675 ISLE STAT II 3   234
A WHITE BIRD HAS TORN ME WITH HIS SILVER CLAWS. . . . . 759 SHADOW WATER A   234

TORQUE
THESE HANDS WON MANY A TORQUE OF GOLD. . . . . 83 MAD KING GOLL   23

TORTOISESHELL
TORTOISESHELL BUTTERFLIES, PEACOCK BUTTERFLIES, ... 482 BLOOD AND MOON   45

TORTURER
BUT MY HEART'S VICTIM AND ITS TORTURER. . . . . . . 537 HER VISION   32

TOSS   SEE PITCH-AND-TOSS
AND TOSS AND TURN IN NARROW CAVES! . . . . 19 OISIN 1   281
LET PAUDEENS PLAY AT PITCH AND TOSS, ... 288 TO WEALTHY MAN   31
LEAVE PAUDEENS TO THEIR PITCH AND TOSS! . . . . . . 288 TO WEALTHY MAN V 31
THEIR DRINK, THEIR PITCH AND TOSS BY DAY, ... 607 SONGS BURDEN 2 V 14
AND LITTLE BOYS PLAYED PITCH AND TOSS. . . . . . . 725 LEGEND   4
LIFT THEIR CHINS AND TOSS THEIR CURLS, ... 726 LOVERS QUARREL   23

```
                                                         PAGE    TITLE          LINE

TOSS   (CONTINUED)
    MINE WHERE WATERS BROOD AND TOSS:  . . . . .  . .  .   744 ROSY CROSS          7
TOSSED     SEE STORM-TOSSED
    I TORE IT FROM GREEN BOUGHS WINDS TORE AND TOSSED  . . .   130 BOOK STORIES      13
    I TORE IT FROM GREEN BOUGHS WINDS TOSSED AND HURLED,  . .   130 BOOK STORIES   V 13
    THAT TOSSED A BARE HEEL WHEN AT SCHOOL,  . . . . .  .  301 RUN PARADISE       19
TOSSING
    WITH AN APPLE OF GOLD IN HER TOSSING HAND:  . . . .  . .    12 OISIN 1         143
    AN APPLE OF GOLD IN HER TOSSING HAND:  . . . . . . .  .    12 OISIN 1       V 143
    UNTIL THE TOSSING ARMS GREW STILL:  . . . . . .  . .  .    21 OISIN 1         322
    GREEN BOUGHS OF TOSSING ALWAYS, WEARY, WEARY,  . . . .    130 BOOK STORIES   V 14
    TOSSING AND TOSSING TO AND FRO . . . . . . .  . . .  .    135 TWO TREES      V 15
    TOSSING AND TOSSING TO AND FRO . . . . . . .  . . .  .    135 TWO TREES      V 15
    CAOILTE TOSSING HIS BURNING HAIR,  . . . . . . .  . .     140 HOSTING SIDHE    3
    CAOILTE TOSSING HIS BURNING HAIR,  . . . . . . .  . .     141 HOSTING SIDHE   15
    AND HIDING THEIR TOSSING MANES AND THEIR TUMULTUOUS FEET.   154 BELOVED PEACE   12
    AND HIDE THEIR TOSSING MANES AND THEIR TUMULTUOUS FEET.     154 BELOVED PEACE  V 12
    FACE DOWNWARD, TOSSING IN A TROUBLED SLEEP:  . . . .  .    185 QUEEN MAEVE     106
    AND ALL THAT TOSSING OF YOUR WINGS IS JOY,  . . . . .     244 SHADOW WATER B  451
    THAT YOUNG MEN, TOSSING ON THEIR BEDS,  . . . . . .      337 SCHOLARS          4
    ON DELICATE SENSITIVE EAR OR TOSSING MANE,  . . . . .     433 NINETEEN 19     115
    A TOSSING LAUGH BETWEEN THEIR REDNESS 'BIDES--  . . . .    685 DRAWING-ROOM      2
    A TOSSING LAUGH BETWEEN THEIR RED ABIDES:  . . . . .      735 QUATRAIN APHOR   22
    A TOSSING LAUGH BETWEEN THEIR REDNESS 'BIDES--  . . . .    735 QUATRAIN APHOR  V 22
TOST     SEE SEA-TOST
    . . . THE LIMBS OF THE FENIANS ARE TOST:  . . . . .  .     62 OISIN 3         213
TOTAL
    HAD THE WORLD'S TOTAL LIFE GATHERED UP, IT SEEMED,  . . .   231 SHADOW WATER B  194
TOTTERING
    SO SMALL MAKES ONE GROW WEAK AND TOTTERING:  . . . . .    700 MOSADA 3         35
TOTTERS
    AND THAT IS WHY THE WORLD TOTTERS ABOUT . . . . . .  .    233 SHADOW WATER B  238
TOUCH
    AND TOUCH THE LAUGHING SILVER STRING:  . . . . . .  . .     17 OISIN 1         233
    AH, TOUCH THEIR BLUE-VEINED EYELIDS IF THEY SLEEP,  . . .    33 OISIN 2          61
    IF THEY STILL SLUMBER, TOUCH THEIR EYELIDS BLUE,  . . .     33 OISIN 2        V 61
    AH, TOUCH THE BLUE VEINED EYELIDS IF THEY SLEEP,  . . .     33 OISIN 2        V 61
    HEARING AEDH TOUCH THE MOURNFUL STRINGS OF GOLD."  . . .     35 OISIN 2          87
    TO GRASP THE WOMAN.  YOU HAVE DARED TO TOUCH HER?  . . .   223 SHADOW WATER B   39
    BEFORE A HAND CAN TOUCH ME.  MY HANDS ARE STILL:  . . .   238 SHADOW WATER B  358
    AH, THAT TIME COULD TOUCH A FORM . . . . . . .  . .      258 PEACE             1
    THAT ALL MUST COME TO SIGHT AND TOUCH:  . . . . . .  .    386 ROBARTES DANCE   31
    AND THERE ENDURED HER FINGERS' TOUCH . . . . . . .  .    397 POLIT PRISONER    5
    AND THERE ENDURED HER FINGER'S TOUCH . . . . . . .  .    397 POLIT PRISONER  V  5
    IS PONDERABLE TO OUR TOUCH.  . . . . . . . . .  . .      399 BREAK OF DAY     18
    OR BY A TOUCH OR A SIGH,  . . . . . . . . . .  . .       413 TOWER           111
    AND SHOULD SOME CRAZY HAND DARE TOUCH A DAUGHTER  . . .    433 NINETEEN 19     122
    LIVED AT MY SIDE: THOUGHT TIME'S DISFIGURING TOUCH  . .    466 HARUN RASHID    110
    LIVED AT MY SIDE: THAT TIME'S DISFIGURING TOUCH  . . .    466 HARUN RASHID   V 110
    AND THAT SHE DREAMED AWAKE CONTENT TO TOUCH  . . . .     466 HARUN RASHID   V 125C
    THAT THEY TOUCH OR SIGH.  . . . . . . . . . .  . .       517 HER ANXIETY       9
    EVERY TOUCH THEY GIVE,  . . . . . . . . . . .  . .       517 HER ANXIETY      10
    SCARCE DID HE MY BODY TOUCH,  . . . . . . . . . .  .     535 CHOSEN            4
    DID BUT OUR BODIES TOUCH,  . . . . . . . . . . .  .      538 LAST CONFESS     10
    IF SOUL MAY LOOK AND BODY TOUCH,  . . . . . . . .  .     573 LADYS 2ND SONG   19
    DELIGHTFUL TO THE TOUCH: TIGHTEN THAT HAND  . . . .      579 DOR WELLESLEY     4
    BUT WHAT CAN HE DO BUT TOUCH?"  . . . . . . . . .  .     588 OLD WICKED MAN   17
    CAN TOUCH BY MOTHER WIT  . . . . . . . . . . .  . .      589 OLD WICKED MAN   40
    SOME SAY THAT ALL WHO TOUCH THE ISLAND LONE  . . . .     653 ISLE STAT I 2    42
    I'M DYING!  OH, FORGIVE ME IF I TOUCH  . . . . . .  .    684 SEEKER           70
    TO DEATH.  HIS LIPS ARE GLUED, WITH QUIVERING TOUCH,  . .   684 SEEKER         V 63
    AND ROARS, MAD WITH THE TOUCH OF THE UNKNOWN,  . . .  .    689 NETTLESHIP        7
    TOUCH NOT THIS BOY, FOR HE IS INNOCENT.  . . . . .  .     694 MOSADA 1        106
    MY SOUL SHALL TOUCH WITH HIS, AND THE TWO FLAMES  . . .    701 MOSADA 3         61
TOUCHED
    AND TOUCHED IT WITH THEIR FINGER-TIPS.  . . . . . .  .     18 OISIN 1         259
    AND TOUCHED IT WITH HIS FINGER-TIPS.  . . . . . . .  .     18 OISIN 1        V 259
    LIKE A SMALL RIVER, AND WHERE FEET TOUCHED CAME  . . .     37 OISIN 2         117
    WITH HIS OWN FINGERS TOUCHED THE BRAZEN STRINGS.  . . .    109 CUCHULAIN SEA    46
    WITH HIS OWN FINGER TOUCHED THE BRAZEN STRINGS.  . . .    109 CUCHULAIN SEA  V 46
    AH, BUT TIME HAS TOUCHED A FORM . . . . . . . .  . .     258 PEACE          V  1
    CAME WHEN TIME HAD TOUCHED HER FORM,  . . . . . . .  .    259 PEACE            11
    AND TOUCHED HER FOREHEAD WITH HIS LIPS AND SAID:  . . .    286 TWO KINGS      V 211B
    I WOULD HAVE TOUCHED IT LIKE A CHILD . . . . . . .  .    399 BREAK OF DAY     12
    BUT KNEW MY FINGER COULD BUT HAVE TOUCHED  . . . . .     399 BREAK OF DAY     13
    BUT KNEW MY FINGER WOULD HAVE TOUCHED  . . . . . .  .    399 BREAK OF DAY   V 13
    IT HAD NOT TOUCHED OUR LIVES.  BUT POPULAR RAGE,  . . .    542 PARN FUNERAL 1   20
    SLID CIRCLING DOWN AND SOFTLY TOUCHED MY LIPS  . . . .    690 MOSADA 1         21
    JUST NOW MY SOUL ROSE UP AND TOUCHED IT, FAR  . . . .     705 REMEMBRANCE      13
TOUCHES
    AND THE LONG GREY GRASSES, WHOSE TENDEREST TOUCHES  . .     27 OISIN 1        V 415B
TOUCHING
    WHOM BRAHMA, TOUCHING WITH HIS FINGER, PRAISES, FOR YOU     73 ANASHU VIJAYA    42
        HOLD
    WHOM BRAHMA, TOUCHING WITH HIS FINGER, PRAISES, FOR YE HOLD  73 ANASHU VIJAYA  V 42
    DID SHE IN TOUCHING THAT LONE WING . . . . . . .  . .    397 POLIT PRISONER    7
    THERE IS NO TOUCHING HERE, NOR TOUCHING THERE,  . . . .    555 RIBH AT TOMB     13
    THERE IS NO TOUCHING HERE, NOR TOUCHING THERE,  . . . .    555 RIBH AT TOMB     13
    AND JOY, THE TOUCHING OF WHOSE FINGER LENDS  . . . .     686 DRAWING-ROOM      7
    AND JOY, THE TOUCHING OF WHOSE FINGER LENDS  . . . . .    734 QUATRAIN APHOR    7
```

		PAGE	TITLE		LINE

TOUT
DAN AND JERRY TOUT, ... 520 HIS BARGAIN V 5
TOWARD
TOWARD PEOPLED TARA, NOR STOOD TO DRAW HIS BREATH . . . 279 TWO KINGS 46
TOWARDS
THE HORSE TOWARDS THE MUSIC RACED, ... 13 OISIN 1 169
THE STEED TOWARDS THE MUSIC RACED, ... 13 OISIN 1 V 169
SAVE DEER TOWARDS NOON THAT WATER SOUGHT. . . . . . 17 OISIN 1 V 243
MY PILLARS TOWARDS THEIR FALL. . . . . 44 OISIN 2 V 239
AND FLYING TOWARDS THEIR PEACE. PUT BY THESE THOUGHTS, 226 SHADOW WATER B 91
TOWARDS THE COUNTRY OF THE DEAD. WHAT MATTER . . . . 231 SHADOW WATER B 206
TOWARDS THE HOUR FOR SPEAKING OF THE DEAD? . . . . . 276 TWO KINGS V D
HE RAN TOWARDS THE HOUSE HIS FATHERS BUILT . . . . . 279 TWO KINGS V 45E
TOWARDS PEOPLED TARA, NOR STOOD TO DRAW HIS BREATH . . 279 TWO KINGS V 46
AND RIDDEN TOWARDS IT, BEING IGNORANT. . . . . . . 286 TWO KINGS V 218
TOWARDS NIGHTFALL UPON CERTAIN SET APART . . . . . . 325 ROBERT GREGORY 29
TOWARDS NIGHTFALL UPON A RACE . . . . 325 ROBERT GREGORY 31
TOWARDS NIGHTFALL UPON A PLACE . . . . 325 ROBERT GREGORY V 31
BUT WHILE THE MOON IS ROUNDING TOWARDS THE FULL . . . 373 PHASES OF MOON 39
TOWARDS BREAK OF DAY . . . . 398 BREAK OF DAY T
I DREAMED TOWARDS BREAK OF DAY, ... 399 BREAK OF DAY 19
SLOUCHES TOWARDS BETHLEHEM TO BE BORN? . . . . . . 402 SECOND COMING 22
AND FOLLOWED UP THOSE BAYING CREATURES TOWARDS-- . . . 412 TOWER 72
O TOWARDS I HAVE FORGOTTEN WHAT--ENOUGH! . . . . . 412 TOWER 73
AND TURN TOWARDS MY CHAMBER, CAUGHT . . . . 424 ROAD AT DOOR 14
PLUNGES TOWARDS NOTHING, ARMS AND FINGERS SPREADING WIDE 426 PHANTOM HATRED 13
AND WHEN I WAKE TOWARDS MORN I DREAD MYSELF, ... 448 HERO GIRL FOOL 5
THOSE CHINAMEN CLIMB TOWARDS, AND I . . . . 567 LAPIS LAZULI 49
STRETCH TOWARDS THE MOONLESS MIDNIGHT OF THE TREES, . . 579 DOR WELLESLEY 1
ITS PAVEN LENGTH TOWARDS THE RIVER'S MARGE . . . . . 702 MOSADA 3 76
TOWARDS A COUNTRY WHERE THERE ARE NO KINGS. . . . . 755 SHADOW WATER A 165
TOWER   SEE LAND-OF-THE-TOWER WATCH-TOWER
AND MANANNAN'S DARK TOWER, STONE AFTER STONE, ... 45 OISIN 2 236
AND MANANAN'S DARK TOWER, STONE BY STONE, ... 45 OISIN 2 V 236
CAME TO MY TOWER AS AGE DRAGGED AFTER AGE . . . . . 45 OISIN 2 V 242
LAND OF THE TOWER, WHEN AENGUS HAS THROWN THE GATES APART, 209 UNDER THE MOON V 8
BESIDE YOUNG AENGUS IN HIS TOWER OF GLASS, ... 219 HARP OF AENGUS 2
AND IN A TOWER OF GLASS, AND FROM THAT DAY . . . . . 224 SHADOW WATER B 50
BESIDE A FIRE OF TURF IN TH' ANCIENT TOWER, ... 324 ROBERT GREGORY 3
THE TOWER SET ON THE STREAM'S EDGE; . . . . 326 ROBERT GREGORY 52
THE TOWER SET BY THE STREAM'S EDGE; . . . . 326 ROBERT GREGORY V 52
UNDER THE ROUND TOWER . . . . 331 ROUND TOWER T
BELLOWED AND PRANCED IN THE ROUND TOWER; . . . . . 331 ROUND TOWER 12
UNDER YOUR OLD WIND-BEATEN TOWER, WHERE STILL . . . . 367 EGO' DOMINUS 2
GOD GRANT A BLESSING ON THIS TOWER AND COTTAGE . . . 371 ON GOING HOUSE 1
WE ARE ON THE BRIDGE; THAT SHADOW IS THE TOWER, . . . 372 PHASES OF MOON 10
FROM THE FAR TOWER WHERE MILTON'S PLATONIST . . . . 373 PHASES OF MOON 15
THE LIGHT IN THE TOWER WINDOW WAS PUT OUT. . . . . . 377 PHASES OF MOON 139
AND HEARD THE SEA-WIND SCREAM UPON THE TOWER, ... 403 FOR DAUGHTER 10
RESTORED THIS TOWER FOR MY WIFE GEORGE; . . . . . . 406 CARVED STONE 4
THE TOWER . . . . 409 TOWER T
AN ANCIENT BRIDGE, AND A MORE ANCIENT TOWER, ... 419 MY HOUSE 1
TOWER WHERE A CANDLE GLEAMS, ... 420 MY HOUSE V 20I
MAY THIS LABORIOUS STAIR AND THIS STARK TOWER . . . . 423 MY DESCENDANTS 13
AND FIND A COMFORT IN IT? MAY THIS TOWER . . . . . 423 MY DESCENDANTS V 13
I CLIMB TO THE TOWER TOP AND LEAN UPON BROKEN STONE, . 425 PHANTOM HATRED V 1
THE BROKEN WALL, THE BURNING ROOF AND TOWER . . . . 441 LEDA AND SWAN 10
FOR EMBLEMS OF THE DAY AGAINST THE TOWER . . . . . 478 SELF AND SOUL 29
MORE BLESSED STILL THIS TOWER; . . . . 480 BLOOD AND MOON 2
ALEXANDRIA'S WAS A BEACON TOWER, AND BABYLON'S . . . 480 BLOOD AND MOON 13
I DECLARE THIS TOWER IS MY SYMBOL; I DECLARE . . . . 480 BLOOD AND MOON 16
IS EVERY MODERN NATION LIKE THE TOWER, ... 482 BLOOD AND MOON 47
IS EVERY NATION LIKE THE TOWER . . . . 482 BLOOD AND MOON V 47
A STORM-BEATEN OLD WATCH TOWER, ... 484 SYMBOLS V 1
. . . . "THE KING OF THE GREAT CLOCK TOWER" . . . . 549 SEVERED HEAD T
WHAT SAYS THE CLOCK IN THE GREAT CLOCK TOWER? . . . . 549 SEVERED HEAD 3
WHAT SAYS THE CLOCK IN THE GREAT CLOCK TOWER? . . . . 550 SEVERED HEAD 10
WHAT SAYS THE CLOCK IN THE GREAT CLOCK TOWER? . . . . 550 SEVERED HEAD 17
THE BLACK TOWER . . . . 635 BLACK TOWER T
SAY THAT THE MEN OF THE OLD BLACK TOWER, ... 635 BLACK TOWER 1
BESIDE YOUNG AENGUS IN HIS TOWER OF GLASS, ... 762 SHADOW WATER A 297
TO THE TOWER OVERHEAD, ... 772 SONG DEIRDRE 1 3
IN THE TOWER OVER HEAD, ... 772 SONG DEIRDRE 1 V 3
TO THE TOWER OVER HEAD, ... 772 SONG DEIRDRE 1 V 3
TOWER'S
THE TOWER'S OLD COOK THAT MUST CLIMB AND CLAMBER . . . 636 BLACK TOWER 21
TOWERS
WOVEN INTO HER HAIR, BEFORE DARK TOWERS . . . . . 30 OISIN 2 22
IN NIAM'S HAIR--WHEN ROSE A WORLD OF TOWERS . . . . 30 OISIN 2 V 22
WOVE IN HER FLOWER-LIKE HAIR, BEFORE DARK TOWERS . . . 30 OISIN 2 V 22
FROM THE WHOLE SEVEN SEAS, THOSE TOWERS SET . . . . 38 OISIN 2 V 131
HELD TO THE TOWERS WITH BOASTING SONGS AND GAY. . . . 41 OISIN 2 V 184C
IT DIED AFAR. GREY SLEET THOSE TOWERS HID . . . . 46 OISIN 2 V 245
OVER THE RAMPARTS AND THE TOWERS, ... 212 BLESS PSALTER 6
THOSE TOPLESS TOWERS . . . . 293 HELEN LIVED 8
IN STARRY TOWERS OF BABYLON . . . . 440 WISDOM 14
AND SHELLEY HAD HIS TOWERS, ... 480 BLOOD AND MOON 15
THAT THE TOPLESS TOWERS BE BURNT . . . . 617 LONG-LEG FLY 11
TOWER-TOP
I CLIMB TO THE TOWER-TOP AND LEAN UPON BROKEN STONE, . . . 425 PHANTOM HATRED 1

829

	PAGE	TITLE	LINE

TOWERY
THE TOWERY GATES OF GORIAS, ... 196 BAILE AILLINN   161
TOWN
I CAME UPON A LITTLE TOWN . . . . 85 MAD KING GOLL   49
AS ONCE WITHIN A LITTLE TOWN, ... 85 MAD KING GOLL   V 49
TIME WAS, AS IN A LITTLE TOWN, ... 85 MAD KING GOLL   V 49
ONCE, WHILE WITHIN A LITTLE TOWN . . . . 85 MAD KING GOLL   V 49
THAT CARRIED THE TAKE TO SLIGO TOWN TO BE SOLD, ... 91 OLD FISHERMAN   7
THAT CARRIED THE FISH FOR THE SALE IN THE FAR-AWAY TOWN, 91 OLD FISHERMAN   V   7
WOULD COME AT LAST TO GOD'S GREAT TOWN, ... 113 ROSE OF PEACE   11
O MASTERS OF THE GLITTERING TOWN! . . . . 212 BLESS PSALTER   3
ARE WHAT THE BLIND AND IGNORANT TOWN . . . . 287 TO WEALTHY MAN   7
IF YOU HAVE REVISITED THE TOWN, THIN SHADE, ... 292 TO A SHADE   1
"THOUGH LOGIC-CHOPPERS RULE THE TOWN, ... 337 TOM OROUGHLEY   1
"THOUGH LOGIC CHOPPERS RULE THE TOWN, ... 337 TOM OROUGHLEY   V 1
ON THAT OLD QUEEN MEASURING A TOWN . . . . 344 DAWN   3
ON THE OLD QUEEN MEASURING A TOWN . . . . 344 DAWN   V   3
THE DAILY SPITE OF THIS UNMANNERLY TOWN, ... 351 PEOPLE   3
WHO NEVER GAVE THE BURNING TOWN A THOUGHT; . . . . 384 VISION ROBART   57
AND WHEN THROUGH ALL THE TOWN THERE RAN . . . . . 436 FOR MY SON   25
THAT SPEECH WAS ALL THAT THE TOWN KNEW, BUT HE . . 462 HARUN RASHID   35
IN THIS BLIND BITTER TOWN, ... 504 QUARREL IN AGE   3
UNTIL THE TOWN LIE BEATEN FLAT. . . . . 565 LAPIS LAZULI   8
"SHE MAY BE IN THE TOWN, ... 594 COLONEL MARTIN   13
CARRY THE GOLD ABOUT THE TOWN, ... 596 COLONEL MARTIN   52
ON COUNTRY AND ON TOWN, ... 606 SONGS BURDEN 1   24
LARGER SPARROWS OF THE TOWN, ... 731 STREET DANCERS   5
THUS SPAKE THE TOWN JAILOR . . . . 740 EARL PAUL   13
WHEN PAUL RODE FROM THE TOWN . . . . 740 EARL PAUL   21
TOWNLAND
THE HAPPY TOWNLAND . . . . 213 HAPPY TOWNLAND   T
IF HE COULD SEE THE TOWNLAND . . . . 214 HAPPY TOWNLAND   3
HE IS RIDING TO THE TOWNLAND . . . . 214 HAPPY TOWNLAND   19
IN THE HIGH HOLLOW TOWNLAND . . . . 214 HAPPY TOWNLAND   V 3
HE IS RIDING TO THE TOWNLAND . . . . 215 HAPPY TOWNLAND   39
HE IS RIDING TO THE TOWNLAND . . . . 216 HAPPY TOWNLAND   59
TOWNS
AND HARRIED ALBAN TOWNS, AND OVERTHREW . . . . . . 749 SHADOW WATER A   40
TOY
GREY TRUTH IS NOW HER PAINTED TOY; . . . . 65 HAPPY SHEPHERD   4
A POISON DROP. A TOY, A FANCY ONCE, ... 700 MOSADA 3   24
A POISON DROP. THE TOY OF FANCY ONCE, ... 700 MOSADA 3   V 24
TOYS
WE HAVE NAUGHT FOR DEATH BUT TOYS . . . . 363 DOLLS DRAWINGS   11
WE TOO HAD MANY PRETTY TOYS WHEN YOUNG! . . . . . 428 NINETEEN 19   9
FORGET ITS BROKEN TOYS . . . . 473 ALL SOUL NIGHT   59
I WEARY OF YOUR SONGS AND HUNTER'S TOYS. . . . . . 651 ISLE STAT I 1   157
TRACE
AND, THOUGH YOU HAVE PASSED THE BEST OF LIFE, STILL TRACE, 367 EGO DOMINUS   5
AND TRACE THESE CHARACTERS UPON THE SANDS? . . . . 370 EGO DOMINUS   64
AND TRACE THESE CHARACTERS UPON THE SAND? . . . . 370 EGO DOMINUS   V 64
CONTENT TO TRACE THAT MISERY TO ITS SOURCE, . . . 479 SELF AND SOUL   V 65
IRELAND'S HISTORY IN THEIR LINEAMENTS TRACE; . . . 604 GALLERY REVIS   53
CLIMB TO OUR PROPER DARK, THAT WE MAY TRACE . . . 611 STATUES   31
TRACES
WE AND OUR BITTERNESS HAVE LEFT NO TRACES . . . . 130 BOOK STORIES   23
TRACK
ADORNING EVERY SECRET TRACK . . . . 509 JANE REPROVED   9
STRUGGLING FOR AN IMAGE ON THE TRACK . . . . . . 534 CHOSEN   2
STUMBLING UPON THE BLOOD-DARK TRACK ONCE MORE, . . 622 HOUND VOICE   18
TRADE
YET NOW IT SEEMS AN IDLE TRADE ENOUGH." . . . . . 205 ADAMS CURSE   27
POETS WITH WHOM I LEARNED MY TRADE, ... 270 GREY ROCK   1
WHERE WIT AND BEAUTY LEARNED THEIR TRADE . . . . 288 TO WEALTHY MAN   16
THE SECOND: "I SHALL LEARN A TRADE"; . . . . 296 THREE BEGGARS   32
ANOTHER SAID: "AND I WILL TRADE . . . . 296 THREE BEGGARS   V 32
AS THOUGH HE HAD BUT THAT ONE TRADE ALONE. . . . . 327 ROBERT GREGORY   80
MY TRADE ALLOWS! CHOSEN MY COMPANY. . . . . 352 PEOPLE   20
WHERE THE INDIANS TRADE OR JAPANESE? . . . . 361 ALF POLLEXFEN   20
THIS SEDENTARY TRADE. . . . . 416 TOWER   180
THE SEDENTARY TRADE. . . . . 416 TOWER   V 180
WHERE WE SHOULD CAST OFF BODY AND TRADE . . . . . 431 NINETEEN 19   73
I KNOW WHAT DEVIL'S TRADE THEY LEARN . . . . . . 607 SONGS BURDEN 2   12
SO I HAVE PICKED A BETTER TRADE . . . . 627 STATES HOLIDAY   11
IRISH POETS, LEARN YOUR TRADE. . . . . 639 BEN BULBEN   68
TRADERS
TRADERS OR SOLDIERS WHO HAVE LEFT ME BLOOD . . . . 269 PARDON FATHERS   V   7
TRADING
OR TRADING OUT OF GALWAY INTO SPAIN; . . . . 269 PARDON FATHERS   4
A TRADING GALLEY IN HER HELMSMAN'S EYES. . . . . . 751 SHADOW WATER A   95
TRADITIONAL
TRADITIONAL SANCTITY AND LOVELINESS; . . . . 491 COOLE BALLYLEE   42
TRAFFIC
TOO LONELY FOR THE TRAFFIC OF THE WORLD! . . . . . 374 PHASES OF MOON   61
OR TRAFFIC IN THE GRASSHOPPERS OR BEES. . . . . . 430 NINETEEN 19   48
OR TRAFFIC IN THE GRASSHOPPERS AND BEES? . . . . . 430 NINETEEN 19   V 48
TRAFFIC IN MOCKERY. . . . . 432 NINETEEN 19   112
TRAGEDY
THAT NOTHING STRANGE! THE TRAGEDY BEGAN . . . . . 411 TOWER   51
THAT CHANGED SOME CHILDISH DAY TO TRAGEDY-- . . . 443 SCHOOL CHILDR   12
THOSE LOVERS, PURIFIED BY TRAGEDY, ... 555 RIBH AT TOMB   21

	PAGE	TITLE	LINE

TRAGEDY   (CONTINUED)
TRAGEDY WROUGHT TO ITS UTTERMOST. . . . .   566 LAPIS LAZULI   20
TRAGIC
WHEN HER OWN PEOPLE RULED THIS TRAGIC EIRE: 129 BOOK STORIES   2
OUT OF NO TRAGIC WAR, LOVERS OF LIFE, ...   369 EGO DOMINUS   39
FOR NATURE'S PULLED HER TRAGIC BUSKIN ON . . . . .   490 COOLE BALLYLEE   12
FOR NATURE'S PULLED HER TRAGIC BUCKSKIN ON . . . . .   490 COOLE BALLYLEE V   12
FOR NATURE'D PULLED HER TRAGIC BUSKIN ON . . . . .   490 COOLE BALLYLEE V   12
ALL THOSE TRAGIC CHARACTERS RIDE . . . .   549 SEVERED HEAD   4
WE THAT LOOK ON BUT LAUGH IN TRAGIC JOY. . . . . .   564 GYRES   8
ALL PERFORM THEIR TRAGIC PLAY, ...   565 LAPIS LAZULI   9
ON ALL THE TRAGIC SCENE THEY STARE. . . . .   567 LAPIS LAZULI   52
THAT TRAGIC STORY MADE, ...   587 PARNELLITES   26
OF MANY A TRAGIC TOMB! . . . .   785 YOUR HEART   10
OF MANY A TRAGIC TOMB! . . . .   786 YOUR HEART   23
OF MANY A TRAGIC TOMB! . . . .   786 YOUR HEART   36
TRAILING
AND TRAILING CRIMSON VANS, A MUMBLING BROOD, ...   687 TWO TITANS   20
TRAILING AND SHINING 'NEATH THE FLICKERING GLARE. . . .   688 TWO TITANS   32
TRAILS
TRAILS ALL ABOUT THE WRITTEN PAGE. . . . .   138 TO IRELAND   9
TRAIN
THE BLINDS DRAWN UP": MAUD GONNE AT HOWTH STATION WAITING   578 LOFTY THINGS   10
A TRAIN,
TRAITOR
COOK BARACH, THE TRAITOR: AND WARWARD, ...   53 OISIN 3   90
OF TRAITOR EVERMORE IS ON OUR NAME." . . . .   712 FERENCZ RENYI   61
OF TRAITOR EVER MORE IS ON OUR NAME." . . . .   712 FERENCZ RENYI   V   61
TRAITOR'S
BUT THAT'S A TRAITOR'S THOUGHT. ENOUGH FOR ME . . . .   462 HARUN RASHID   39
TRAMPING
A TRAMPING OF TREMENDOUS FEET, ...   85 MAD KING GOLL   54
THE TRAMPING OF TREMENDOUS FEET, ...   85 MAD KING GOLL   V   54
TRAMPLE
AND TRAMPLE MY DARK ISLE. . . . .   45 OISIN 2   V 239E
TRAMPLED
BARKING. WE TRAMPLED UP AND DOWN WITH BLOWS . . . . .   40 OISIN 2   170
WE TRAMPLED TO AND FRO. WHEN HIS MIND KNEW . . . . .   40 OISIN 2   V 173
AND DEMONS BE BROKEN IN PIECES, AND TRAMPLED BENEATH THEM   61 OISIN 3   204
IN DEATH.
AND DEMONS, ALL BROKEN IN PIECES, BE TRAMPLED BENEATH THEM   61 OISIN 3   V 204
IN DEATH.
AND TRAMPLED IN THE BUBBLING MIRE, ...   83 MAD KING GOLL   26
AND TRAMPLED ON THE BUBBLING MIRE, ...   83 MAD KING GOLL   V   26
AND TRAMPLED THE MOUNTAINS AWAY, ...   171 MAID QUIET   V   4C
AND TRAMPLED THE MOUNTAIN AWAY, ...   171 MAID QUIET   V   4C
BUT UNDER HEAVY LOADS OF TRAMPLED CLAY . . . .   483 OIL AND BLOOD   4
TRANCE
MUTTER SUCH THINGS AS THEY AWAKE FROM TRANCE. . . . . .   229 SHADOW WATER B   163
ALL KNOWLEDGE LOST IN TRANCE . . . .   343 SHEP GOATHERD   111
AN AGONY OF TRANCE, ...   498 BYZANTIUM   31
TRANQUILLITY
O MAY TRANQUILLITY WALK BY HIS ELBOW . . . .   71 ANASHU VIJAYA   2
OH, MAY TRANQUILLITY BESIDE HIM GO, ...   71 ANASHU VIJAYA   V   2
AND GREAT BOUGHS DROP TRANQUILLITY: . . . .   77 INDIAN TO LOVE   2
TRANSFIGURED
ERE TIME TRANSFIGURED ME. . . . .   131 OLD PENSIONER   6
THAT HAS TRANSFIGURED ME. . . . .   131 OLD PENSIONER   12
THAT HAS TRANSFIGURED ME. . . . .   132 OLD PENSIONER   18
SHE SMILED AND THAT TRANSFIGURED ME . . . .   451 FIRST LOVE   13
TRANSFIGURED TO PURE SUBSTANCE WHAT HAD ONCE . . . . .   555 RIBH AT TOMB   11
TRANSFIGURING
GAIETY TRANSFIGURING ALL THAT DREAD. . . . .   565 LAPIS LAZULI   17
TRANSFORM
TRANSFORM THESE RASCAL BILLOWS INTO WOMEN . . . . . .   222 SHADOW WATER B   11
WOULD TRANSFORM THE PART, ...   506 REMORSE SPEECH   3
TRANSFORMED
TRANSFORMED UTTERLY! . . . .   393 EASTER 1916   39
TRANSFORMING   SEE WORLD-TRANSFORMING
TRANSLUNAR
TRANSLUNAR PARADISE. . . . .   415 TOWER   156
TRANSPARENT
TRANSPARENT LIKE THE WIND, ...   449 HERO GIRL FOOL   27
TRAP
I TRAP YOU. CHECK. I DO MISCALCULATE. . . . . . .   722 WITCH VIVIEN   58
TRAPPED
THE WANDERINGS OF OISIN AND HOW A DEMON TRAPPED HIM . . .   1 OISIN 1   V   T
TRAPPED OF AN AMOROUS DEMON THING. . . . .   2 OISIN 1   V   4
TRASH
THAT CANNOT IN THAT TRASH AND TINSEL HIDE! . . . . . .   558 RIBH CHRISTIAN   17
TRAVAIL
THE TRAVAIL OF PASSION . . . .   172 TRAV PASSION   T
TRAVEL
WERE I TO TRAVEL FAR AND WIDE . . . .   398 BREAK OF DAY   8
TRAVELLED
. . . BERKELEY AND BURKE HAVE TRAVELLED THERE. . . . .   481 BLOOD AND MOON   18
GREAT ROOMS WHERE TRAVELLED MEN AND CHILDREN FOUND . . .   491 COOLE BALLYLEE   29
HAD TRAVELLED HALF THE NIGHT. . . . .   585 ORAHILLY   17
YET HERE'S A TRAVELLED MAN THAT KNOWS . . . .   631 POLITICS   5
TRAVELLED TO AND FRO ACROSS THE ATLANTIC, ...   790 DEDICATION   3

```
                                                     PAGE    TITLE          LINE

TRAVELLER
    HERE, TRAVELLER, SCHOLAR, POET, TAKE YOUR STAND     489  COOLE PARK 29        25
    WORLD-BESOTTED TRAVELLER: HE  . . . . . . . . .     493  SWIFTS EPITAPH        5
    WORLD BESOTTED TRAVELLER: HE  . . . . . . . . .     493  SWIFTS EPITAPH  V     5
TRAVELLERS
    HAVE DRIVEN TRAVELLERS MAD FOR THEIR OWN SPORT.     227  SHADOW WATER B      105
    BENIGHTED TRAVELLERS . . . . . . . . . . . . .      419  MY HOUSE             18
TRAVELLING
    HE SHOOK HIMSELF FOR TRAVELLING,                     10  OISIN 1         V   110
    BUT THAT, LONG TRAVELLING, HE HAD COME . . . .      325  ROBERT GREGORY       28
    BUT FOR WHAT SOME TRAVELLING MAN . . . . . . .      585  ORAHILLY             21
TRAVELLING-MAN
    SAID THE RAMBLING, SHAMBLING TRAVELLING-MAN;        788  HAWTHORN TREE         2
    SAID THE RAMBLING, SHAMBLING TRAVELLING-MAN;        788  HAWTHORN TREE        10
TRAVELS
    THAT TRAVELS ON THE MOON. . . . . . . . . . .       451  FIRST LOVE           12
    WHO TRAVELS WHERE GOD WILLS. . . . . . . . . .      587  OLD WICKED MAN        4
TRAVEL-WEARIED
    CEASE TO REMEMBER THE DELIGHTS OF YOUTH, TRAVEL-WEARIED   459  FROM OEDIPUS    2
        AGED MAN:
TREACHERY
    ABOVE THE MURDEROUS TREACHERY OF THE MOON, . . .    428  NINETEEN 19     V     3
    THIS THEIR WANTON TREACHERY, . . . . . . . . .      727  LOVERS QUARREL       55
TREAD
    OUR TREAD, AS ROSE AND FELL THE LIQUID TONES . .     33  OISIN 2         V   68B
    TREAD SOFTLY BECAUSE YOU TREAD ON MY DREAMS. . .    176  CLOTHS HEAVEN         8
    TREAD SOFTLY BECAUSE YOU TREAD ON MY DREAMS. . .    176  CLOTHS HEAVEN         8
    I BECAME A RUSH THAT HORSES TREAD: . . . . . .      177  PAST GREATNESS        6
    TROD WITH A LIGHTER TREAD. . . . . . . . . . .      323  SWANS AT COOLE       18
    ALL MEN ARE DANCERS AND THEIR TREAD . . . . .      430  NINETEEN 19          57
    SHOULD HEAR MY LIVING FEET, NOR WOULD I TREAD .     435  NEW FACES             3
    THE HERALD'S CRY, THE SOLDIER'S TREAD . . . . .     438  SONGS PLAY 2         13
    IMMORTAL LADIES TREAD THE GROUND . . . . . . .      446  COLONUS PRAISE        6
    CANNOT ENDURE TO THINK YOU TREAD THESE PATHS, .     463  HARUN RASHID         52
    OR ROCKY CISTERN WHERE WE TREAD THE CLOTHES . .     499  MOTHER OF GOD         9
    MEN-AT-ARMS TREAD: . . . . . . . . . . . .          512  JANE ON GOD           8
    TREAD AND TREAD THEIR CLOVEN FEET . . . . . .       646  ISLE STAT I 1        24
    TREAD AND TREAD THEIR CLOVEN FEET . . . . . .       646  ISLE STAT I 1        24
    ALONG THE WOOD WITH SUBTLE TREAD AND BENDED BOWS.   649  ISLE STAT I 1       111
    CARVED: HERE, BEYOND THE LAKE'S SLOW-MUFFLED TREAD,  662  ISLE STAT II 2      11
TREADMILL
    THIS WINDING, GYRING, SPIRING TREADMILL OF A STAIR . . .  480  BLOOD AND MOON  17
TREADS
    AND STILL I DREAM HE TREADS THE LAWN,               67  HAPPY SHEPHERD       51
    BROWN LOLLARD TREADS UPON THE LAWN, . . . . . .     98  FOXHUNTER            17
    BROWN DERMOT TREADS UPON THE LAWN, . . . . . .      98  FOXHUNTER       V    17
    "STILL TREADS THE WORLD AMID HIS ARMED MEN."       107  CUCHULAIN SEA   V    26
    YET HE WHO TREADS IN MEASURED WAYS . . . . . .     138  TO IRELAND           27
    YET HE WHO TREADS IN AUSTERE WAYS . . . . . .      138  TO IRELAND      V    27
    YOU HAVE MEASURED OUT THE ROAD THAT THE SOUL TREADS . .  342  SHEP GOATHERD   80
    AND NO MAN KNOWS WHAT TREADS THE GRASS. . . . .    614  MARCH SONGS 2        10
    AND NO MAN KNOWS WHAT TREADS THE GRASS. . . . .    615  MARCH SONGS 2        20
    AND NO MAN KNOWS WHAT TREADS THE GRASS. . . . .    615  MARCH SONGS 2        30
    UPON THE MOUNTAIN'S BROW. YONDER HE TREADS . . .   703  MOSADA 3            114
TREASONS
    I LAUGHED AT TIMES UNNUMBERED TREASONS, . . . .     23  OISIN 1         V 345D
TREASURE       SEE MAY-TREASURE
    THE HOLD IS FULL OF TREASURE. FULL TO THE HATCHES.  247  SHADOW WATER B     532
    TREASURE ON TREASURE. BOXES OF PRECIOUS SPICE. . .  247  SHADOW WATER B     533
    TREASURE ON TREASURE. BOXES OF PRECIOUS SPICE. . .  247  SHADOW WATER B     533
    TREASURE AND TREASURE. BOXES OF PRECIOUS SPICE. .   247  SHADOW WATER B  V  533
    TREASURE AND TREASURE. BOXES OF PRECIOUS SPICE. .   247  SHADOW WATER B  V  533
    FOR WE HAVE FOUND A TREASURE THAT'S SO GREAT . .    248  SHADOW WATER B     540
    WHO HAD LOST SOME UNIMAGINABLE TREASURE . . . .     278  TWO KINGS           40
    THROUGH THE GREAT GALLERY OF THE TREASURE HOUSE .   461  HARUN RASHID         5
    ALL THE HEALING EARTH MAY TREASURE . . . . . .     733  STREET DANCERS  V   63
TREASURER
    FOR THE GREAT CALIF'S TREASURER AND MY FRIEND, . .  460  HARUN RASHID    V    2
    NOW THE GOOD CALIPH'S LEARNED TREASURER, . . . .    461  HARUN RASHID         3
TREASURES
    AND DROWNED THE TREASURES OF NINE CONQUERED NATIONS, . .  235  SHADOW WATER B  287
    EVEN FROM THAT DELIGHT MEMORY TREASURES SO, . . .   459  FROM OEDIPUS         4
TREATISE
    PAUSE AT THE TREATISE OF PARMENIDES . . . . . .     461  HARUN RASHID        16
    FROM THE GREAT TREATISE OF PARMENIDES: . . . . .    469  HARUN RASHID       183
TREE       SEE OLIVE-TREE CATALPA-TREE THORN-TREE CHESTNUT-TREE CHRISTMAS-TREE PEAR-TREE
           FIR-TREE YEW-TREE LIME-TREE HAZEL-TREE BEECH-TREE OAK-TREE ROSE-TREE
    LIKE SOOTY FINGERS, MANY A TREE . . . . . . .       13  OISIN 1            171
    A FIR TREE ROARING IN ITS LEAFLESS TOP, . . . .     40  OISIN 2         V  177
    WHEN I TORE DOWN THE TREE: BUT WHEN THE WEST . .     41  OISIN 2         V  180
    WHEN I'D TORE DOWN THAT TREE: BUT WHEN THE WEST .    41  OISIN 2         V  180
    WHEN I TORE DOWN THAT TREE: BUT WHEN THE WEST . .    41  OISIN 2         V  180
    IN THE TREE ROOTS, AND ALL THE SACRED FLOCKS . .     75  ANASHU VIJAYA       88
    IN THE TREE ROOTS, AND ALL THY SACRED FLOCKS . .     75  ANASHU VIJAYA   V   88
    A PARROT SWAYS UPON A TREE, . . . . . . . . .       77  INDIAN TO LOVE       4
    A PARROT SWAYING ON A TREE . . . . . . . . .        77  INDIAN TO LOVE  V    4
    FROM POND AND FALLEN TREE--ME SING . . . . . .      85  MAD KING GOLL   V   63
    SHE BID ME TAKE LOVE EASY, AS THE LEAVES GROW ON THE TREE:  90  SALLEY GARDENS  3
    UPON A SWORD, A FIR TREE ON A HILL, . . . . . .    104  FERGUS DRUID    V   34
    NEAR TO CUCHULLIN, ROUND A QUICKEN TREE, . . . .    111  CUCHULAIN SEA   V  81A
    AND TEN BY TEN UNDER A QUICKEN TREE, . . . . .      111  CUCHULAIN SEA   V  81A
```

TREE   (CONTINUED)
    UNDER A BROKEN TREE . . . .   131 OLD PENSIONER   2
    UPON A BROKEN TREE, ...   131 OLD PENSIONER   14
    GREEN OAK AND POPLAR TREE! . . . .   132 OLD PENSIONER   V 16
    THE HOLY TREE IS GROWING THERE: . . . .   134 TWO TREES   2
    I HAVE BEEN A HAZEL TREE, AND THEY HUNG . . . . . 177 PAST GREATNESS V   3
    TILL IT DIED OUT WHERE AN OLD THORN TREE STOOD. . .186 QUEEN MAEVE   V 129
    A YEW TREE WHERE HIS BODY LAY, ...   197 BAILE AILLINN   V 188
    HUM IN THE LIME TREE FLOWERS: AND PUT AWAY . . . . 198 SEVEN WOODS   V   3
    OUR COURAGE BREAKS LIKE AN OLD TREE IN A BLACK,WIND AND 207 HANRAHANS SONG   3
        DIES,
    LET THE BIRDS SCATTER, FOR THE TREE IS BROKEN,   250 SHADOW WATER B 584
    WHO HAS SEEN A GARDEN IMAGE OR TWISTED TREE . . . .   279 TWO KINGS   V 45B
    I STAGGERED, BUT A BEECH TREE STAYED MY FALL, . . .   286 TWO KINGS   V 209
    AND SO TO THE OTHER TREE AT A BOUND. . . . . . .   318 APPOINTMENT   7
    THE THORN TREE . . . .   350 HER PRAISE   V T
    THROUGH THE SHAKING TREE . . . .   359 TO A SQUIRREL   3
    HER FRIENDS BRING HER A CHRISTMAS TREE . . . . .   366 HER CHRIS TREE   T
    WE'VE CARRIED IN OUR TREE, ...   366 HER CHRIS TREE   3
    THE ROSE TREE . . . .   396 ROSE TREE   T
    HAS WITHERED OUR ROSE TREE! . . . .   396 ROSE TREE   4
    CAN MAKE A RIGHT ROSE TREE." . . . .   396 ROSE TREE   18
    HAVE WITHERED OUR ROSE TREE! . . . .   396 ROSE TREE   V 4
    MAY SHE BECOME A FLOURISHING HIDDEN TREE . . . .   404 FOR DAUGHTER   41
    AND CUSTOM FOR THE SPREADING LAUREL TREE. . . . .   406 FOR DAUGHTER   80
    UNDER THE OLD WIND-BROKEN TREE, ...   406 IN TIME OF WAR   3
    TREE, LIKE A SOOTY FINGER, STARTS FROM THE EARTH: 410 TOWER   19
    A PEAR TREE BROKEN BY THE STORM. . . . .   424 ROAD AT DOOR   V 10
    NEITHER CATALPA TREE NOR SCENTED LIME . . . . .   435 NEW FACES   V 2
    O CHESTNUT TREE, GREAT ROOTED BLOSSOMER, ...   446 SCHOOL CHILDR V 61
    EVEN THE GREY-LEAVED OLIVE TREE . . . .   446 COLONUS PRAISE V 12
    UNDER A BROKEN TREE. . . . .   452 HUMAN DIGNITY   8
    UNDER THAT VERY TREE. . . . .   457 SUMMER SPRING   12
    AND HAUGHTIER-HEADED BURKE THAT PROVED THE STATE A TREE, 481 BLOOD AND MOON 22
    AND HAUGHTIER HEADED BURKE THAT PROVED THE STATE A TREE 481 BLOOD AND MOON V 22
    A SYCAMORE AND LIME TREE LOST IN NIGHT . . . . .   488 COOLE PARK 29 V 3
    IN THE RICH MIDNIGHT OF THE GARDEN TREE . . . . .   494 AT ALGECIRAS   V 5
    THE BURNING TREE . . . .   499 VACILLATION   V T
    A TREE THERE IS THAT FROM ITS TOPMOST BOUGH . . .   500 VACILLATION   11
    BUT A BIRCH TREE STOOD MY JACK! . . . .   508 JANE BISHOP   V 20
    STAMPED BOY AND TREE UPON SICILIAN COIN. . . . .   541 PARN FUNERAL 1   15
    WHAT HAPPENS A TREE THAT HAS NOTHING WITHIN IT? . . 548 SAME TUNE 3   23
    WHAT HAPPENS TO A TREE THAT HAS NOTHING WITHIN IT? . 548 SAME TUNE 3   V 23
    WHAT TEARS DOWN A TREE THAT HAS NOTHING WITHIN IT? . 615 MARCH SONGS 2   23
    WHAT TEARS DOWN A TREE HAS NOTHING WITHIN IT? . . . 615 MARCH SONGS 2 V 23
    CAME AND WERE GONE. HE LEANT UPON A TREE . . . .   634 CUCHULAIN COMF   5
    WHEN THE TREE WAS O'ER-APPLED . . . .   654 ISLE STAT I 2   60
    AND I SANG ROUND THE TREE . . . .   654 ISLE STAT I 2   66
    AND I SANG ROUND THE TREE, ...   654 ISLE STAT I 2   76
    AND I SANG ROUND THE TREE, ...   655 ISLE STAT I 2   80
    TWO CAME, HIS NAME AND MINE ON MANY A TREE . . .   662 ISLE STAT II 2   10
    AN OWL, WHO IN AN ALDER TREE . . . .   670 ISLE STAT II 3 115
    UNDER A LEMON TREE BESIDE YOUR DOOR: . . . . . .   693 MOSADA 1   68
    PUFFED LIKE PUFF-BALLS ON A TREE, ...   727 LOVERS QUARREL   37
    THE DANAAN QUICKEN TREE . . . .   742 DANAAN QUICK   T
    (AH, MOURNFUL DANAAN QUICKEN TREE!) . . . . . .   742 DANAAN QUICK   6
    (AH, MOURNFUL DANAAN QUICKEN TREE!) . . . . . .   743 DANAAN QUICK   12
    (AH, MOURNFUL DANAAN QUICKEN TREE!) . . . . . .   743 DANAAN QUICK   18
    (AH, MOURNFUL DANAAN QUICKEN TREE!) . . . . . .   743 DANAAN QUICK   24
    (AH, MOURNFUL DANAAN QUICKEN TREE!) . . . . . .   743 DANAAN QUICK   30
    OF THE GOLDEN APPLE TREE! . . . .   771 SPINNING SONG   9
    THE WELL AND THE TREE . . . .   780 WELL AND TREE V T
    CRIES OUT THE LEAFLESS TREE, ...   780 WELL AND TREE   10
    A WITHERED TREE?" . . . .   780 WELL AND TREE   16
    THE WICKED HAWTHORN TREE. . . . .   788 HAWTHORN TREE V T
    SAID THE WICKED, CROOKED, HAWTHORN TREE! . . . .   788 HAWTHORN TREE   6
    SAID THE WICKED, CROOKED, HAWTHORN TREE. . . . .   788 HAWTHORN TREE   14
TREES   SEE OLIVE-TREES THORN-TREES BEECH-TREES HAZEL-TREES ROOF-TREES POPLAR-TREES
          ASH-TREES
    THE MIST-DROPS HUNG ON THE FRAGRANT TREES, ...   2 OISIN 1   V 7F
    THE REASON OF THE TREMBLING TREES: . . . .   14 OISIN 1   179
    WHERE TREES MADE SUDDEN CAVERN-GLOOMS . . . . . .   16 OISIN 1   V 224B
    A STORM OF BIRDS IN THE ASIAN TREES . . . . . .   27 OISIN 1   416
    THAT SPRANG UNDER THE SEVEN HAZEL TREES, ...   35 OISIN 2   84
    AT EMAN, 'NEATH THE BEECH TREES, ON EACH SIDE, . . . 44 OISIN 2   V 228
    GREY SAND ON THE GREEN OF THE GRASSES AND OVER THE DRIPPING 48 OISIN 3   14
        TREES,
    BUT THE TREES GREW TALLER AND CLOSER, ...   48 OISIN 3   17
    GREY SANDS ON THE GREEN OF THE GRASSES AND OVER THE   48 OISIN 3   V 14
        DRIPPING TREES,
    BUT TALLER THE TREES GREW AND CLOSER, ...   48 OISIN 3   V 17
    OF HOLLIES, AND HAZELS, AND OAK TREES, A VALLEY WAS SLOPING 48 OISIN 3   26
        AWAY
    GREY SAND ON THE GREEN OF THE GRASSES AND OVER THE DRIPPING 57 OISIN 3   142
        TREES,
    GREY SANDS ON THE GREEN OF THE GRASSES AND OVER THE   57 OISIN 3   V 142
        DRIPPING TREES,
    I PASSED ALONG THE WATER'S EDGE BELOW THE HUMID TREES, . . 76 INDIAN ON GOD 1
    ARISE THE LEOPARD-COLOURED TREES! . . . .   84 MAD KING GOLL   40
    SHE BID ME TAKE LOVE EASY, AS THE LEAVES GROW ON THE TREES! 90 SALLEY GARDENS V 3
    THIS LADY BY THE TREES": . . . .   123 DREAM OF DEATH V 10

833

TREES   (CONTINUED)
THE ROAD-SIDE TREES KEEP MURMURING-- . . . . 131 OLD PENSIONER V 13
THE TWO TREES . . . . 134 TWO TREES T
OF PASSIONATE MEN, LIKE BATS IN THE DEAD TREES: . . . . 136 TO SOME I TALK 5
THE OLD BROWN THORN TREES BREAK IN TWO HIGH OVER CUMANN'S 206 HANRAHANS SONG V 1
    STRAND,
O HEAVY SWOLLEN WATERS, BRIM THE FALL OF THE OAK TREES, 207 HANRAHANS SONG 11
WERE TWISTED LIKE THE OLD THORN TREES . . . . 208 OLD MEN ADMIRE V 5
O HURRY WHERE BY WATER AMONG THE TREES . . . . . . 210 RAGGED WOOD 1
O HURRY TO THE WATER AMID THE TREES, ... 210 RAGGED WOOD V 1
O HURRY WHERE BY WATER AMONG TREES, ... 210 RAGGED WOOD V 1
O HURRY TO THE WATER AMID THE TREES, ... 211 RAGGED WOOD V 5
WHERE BY OLD THORN TREES THAT MAN STOOD: . . . . . 274 GREY ROCK V 80
HE HAD BUT GAZED ON THORN TREES, SPOKE: . . . . . . 274 GREY ROCK V 82
A CLUMP OF BEECH TREES MADE AN EMPTY SPACE . . . . 277 TWO KINGS V 4A
AND WHERE BEECH TREES HAD MIXED A PALE GREEN LIGHT . . . 277 TWO KINGS V 5
CLOSE TO A CLUMP OF BEECH TREES IN THE WOOD . . . . 283 TWO KINGS V 135
WESTWARD OF TARA, AMONG THE HAZEL TREES-- . . . . . 283 TWO KINGS V 135
AMONG THE STONES AND THORN TREES, UNDER MORNING LIGHT, . . 291 PAUDEEN V 3
THE TREES ARE IN THEIR AUTUMN BEAUTY, ... 322 SWANS AT COOLE 1
WERE LOVED BY HIM: THE OLD STORM-BROKEN TREES . . . . 326 ROBERT GREGORY 50
AND ALIGHT AT THE COMELY TREES AND THE LAWN, ... 330 BONE OF A HARE 4
IN ONE ANOTHER'S ARMS, BIRDS IN THE TREES . . . . . 407 SAIL BYZANTIUM 2
FROM RUIN OR FROM ANCIENT TREES, ... 410 TOWER 23
GLITTERING AMONG GREY-LEAVED OLIVE TREES, ... 447 COLONUS PRAISE V 21
SEEMED ONCE MORE DEAR THAN LIFE: ANCESTRAL TREES, . . . 491 COOLE BALLYLEE 34
IN THE RICH MIDNIGHT OF THE GARDEN TREES . . . . . 494 AT ALGECIRAS 5
STRETCH TOWARDS THE MOONLESS MIDNIGHT OF THE TREES, . . . 579 DOR WELLESLEY 1
THAT PLUCKS THE TREES FOR BREAD? . . . . 621 JOHN KINSELLA 34
BECAUSE WE LOVE BARE HILLS AND STUNTED TREES . . . . 621 HOUND VOICE 1
YON WIND GOES SADLY, AND THE GRASS AND TREES . . . . 652 ISLE STAT I 2 10
WITH ROLLING FIRE, BEYOND THE HIGH TREES TURBANED . . . 656 ISLE STAT I 3 32
HE CARVED ON TREES, AND WITH A SUN-DRY WEED . . . . 659 ISLE STAT II 1 8
THE LIGHT IS DANCING O'ER THE KNOTTED TREES, ... 662 ISLE STAT II 2 2
THIS HEARD I WHERE AMONG THE APPLE TREES, ... 686 LIFE 19
WHERE SHADOW OF CHERRY, AND SHADOW OF APPLE TREES, . . . 710 FERENCZ RENYI 23
HE NUMBERS. HE, WITH FLOWERING CURRANT TREES, ... 710 FERENCZ RENYI V 22
NOON WRAPT THE TREES IN VEILS OF VIOLET WEATHER, . . . 715 DWELT SYCAMORE 7
HAVE NOT A MYRIAD SWAYED BELOW STRANGE TREES . . . . 724 KANVA ON SELF 11
HE'D SLEPT AMONG THE SINGING TREES, ... 728 PRIEST FAIRY 17
WATCHED OF PLACID POPLAR TREES, ... 732 STREET DANCERS V 16
THIS HEARD I WHERE, AMID THE APPLE TREES, ... 735 QUATRAIN APHOR 17
THIS HEARD I WHERE AMONG THE APPLE TREES, ... 735 QUATRAIN APHOR V 19
AMONG GREAT TREES, AND IN THE WINGS OF OWLS, ... 762 SHADOW WATER A 285
TREE-WRAPT
WHOSE DWELLING WAS A TREE-WRAPT ISLAND, LULLED . . . . 693 MOSADA 1 79
TREFOIL
BUT NEVER SAW THE TREFOIL STAINED WITH BLOOD, ... 487 SEVEN SAGES 19
TREMBLE   SEE A-TREMBLE
"WHY DO YOU TREMBLE THUS FROM FEET TO CROWN?" . . . . 106 CUCHULAIN SEA V 13
AND TREMBLE WITH THEIR LOVE AND KISS. . . . . . . 196 BAILE AILLINN 169
THE SOUL BEGINS TO TREMBLE INTO STILLNESS, ... 374 PHASES OF MOON 54
I TREMBLE TO THE BONE, ... 511 JANE AND JACK 2
NOR TREMBLE TO ITS FALL. THE FIRE SWEEPS ROUND . . . 689 NETTLESHIP 11
HER EYELIDS TREMBLE AND THE WHITE FOAM FADES: . . . . 761 SHADOW WATER A 264
TREMBLED
TREMBLED AND GASPED AND SHOULD HAVE RUN . . . . . . 303 HOUR DAWN V 22
UNTIL I CRIED AND TREMBLED AND ROCKED TO AND FRO, . . . 316 COLD HEAVEN 8
TREMBLES
HIM WHO TREMBLES BEFORE THE FLAME AND THE FLOOD, . . . 158 TO HIS HEART 3
WHO TREMBLES BEFORE THE FLAME AND THE FLOOD, ... 158 TO HIS HEART V 3
THAT TREMBLES AND RESOUNDS WITH HYMNS TO THEE, ... 684 SEEKER V 69C
TREMBLES AS A BELL OF GLASS . . . . 705 DAWN-SONG 10
TREMBLING   SEE EVER-TREMBLING
AND THEY WERE TREMBLING CEASELESSLY, ... 13 OISIN 1 173
THE REASON OF THE TREMBLING TREES: . . . . 14 OISIN 1 179
TWO WALLS, A ROOF, A FLOOD: THERE TREMBLING GREEN . . . 31 OISIN 2 V 32
WITH BOWED HEAD, TREMBLING WHEN THE WHITE BLADE SHONE, . 38 OISIN 2 137
TREMBLING, ON THE FLAGS WE FALL, ... 43 OISIN 2 V 208E
ARE BOWED IN SORROW UNDER THEIR TREMBLING LIDS, . . . 79 EPHEMERA V 2
THIS BODY TREMBLING LIKE A WIND-BLOWN REED. . . . . 103 FERGUS DRUID 25
AND ALL THE TREMBLING FLOWERS THEY BEAR. . . . . . 134 TWO TREES 4
BE YOU STILL, BE YOU STILL, TREMBLING HEART: . . . . 158 TO HIS HEART 1
AND IN THE TREMBLING BLUE-GREEN OF THE SKY . . . . 206 ADAMS CURSE 30
TREMBLING IN THE BLUE HEAVENS LIKE A WHITE FAWN . . . 251 SHADOW WATER B 611
AND TREMBLING WITH HER PASSION SAID, ... 272 GREY ROCK 31
UPON HIS TREMBLING HORSE, THEN DROVE THE SPUR: . . . 277 TWO KINGS 11
TREMBLING BENEATH HIM, AND THEN DROVE THE SPUR . . . 277 TWO KINGS V 11
STOOD ON MY PATH. TREMBLING FROM HEAD TO FOOT . . . 283 TWO KINGS 151
STOOD ON MY PATH. TREMBLING FROM HAND TO FOOT . . . 283 TWO KINGS V 151
MY BLENCHING AND TREMBLING, ... 532 FIRST CONFESS 4
THE TREMBLING OF THE APPLE AND THE YEW, ... 555 RIBH AT TOMB 18
"PRAY FOR THE SOULS IN PURGATORY," THE PALE PRIEST 719 PHANTOM SHIP 31
    TREMBLING CRIES.
TREMBLING IN THE BLUE HEAVENS LIKE A WHITE FAWN . . . 769 SHADOW WATER A 427
TREMENDOUS
A TRAMPING OF TREMENDOUS FEET, ... 85 MAD KING GOLL 54
THE TRAMPING OF TREMENDOUS FEET, ... 85 MAD KING GOLL V 54
TREMULOUS
TO SHORES BY THE WASH OF THE TREMULOUS TIDE, ... 8 OISIN 1 81
AND A SAD MOUTH, THAT FEAR MADE TREMULOUS . . . . . 34 OISIN 2 71

		PAGE	TITLE		LINE

TRESS
```
    AND THEY SIGH IF THE WIND BUT LIFT A TRESS!            151 OLD MOTHER            8
    AND THEY SIGH IF THE WIND BUT LIFT UP A TRESS!         151 OLD MOTHER        V   8
    AND BIND UP EVERY WANDERING TRESS!                     157 BELOVED RHYMES        2
    THAT MEN THRESHED CORN AT MIDNIGHT BY A TRESS,         170 SECRET ROSE          26
    A LITTLE STOLEN TRESS. I, TOO, AWAIT                   170 SECRET ROSE          27
    HER FEATURES WHEN A TRESS                              363 DOLLS DRAWINGS        5
    MERELY TO LOOSEN OUT A TRESS                           390 IMAGE PAST           26
```
TRESTLES
```
    TWO HEAVY TRESTLES, AND A BOARD                        421 MY TABLE             1
```
TRIAL
```
    CASEMENT UPON TRIAL, HALF HIDDEN BY THE BARS,          601 GALLERY REVIS        3
```
TRIBE
```
    THE FIRST OF ALL THE TRIBE LAY THERE                   455 HIS MEMORIES        13
```
TRIBES
```
    MINE WERE CLAN MORNA'S TRIBES UNTOLD,                   81 MAD KING GOLL    V   3
```
TRIBESMAN
```
    LIKE SOME POOR ARAB TRIBESMAN AND HIS TENT.            491 COOLE BALLYLEE      40
```
TRIBUTE
```
    WE CANNOT PAY ITS TRIBUTE OF WILD TEARS.               334 LIVING BEAUTY       10
```
TRICK
```
    WE'LL KEEP THE SECRET--A NEW TRICK TO PLEASE.          265 ABBEY THEATRE       10
    THEY TURNED A TRICK BY FORGERY                         582 ROGER CASEMENT       7
    THEY TURNED A TRICK OF FORGERY                         582 ROGER CASEMENT   V   7
```
TRICKLING
```
    TRICKLING ALONG THE EARTH, I RAVE!                      19 OISIN 1          V 281
```
TRICKS
```
    FOR THEY ARE AT THEIR OLD TRICKS YET.  A MAN           292 TO A SHADE           9
    ALL TEETH WERE DRAWN, ALL ANCIENT TRICKS UNLEARNED,    429 NINETEEN 19         17
    LET THE NEW FACES PLAY WHAT TRICKS THEY WILL           435 NEW FACES            5
```
TRICOLOUR
```
    BLESSING THE TRICOLOUR. "THIS IS NOT," I SAY,         601 GALLERY REVIS       10
```
TRIED
```
    I HAVE KEPT MY FAITH, THOUGH FAITH WAS TRIED,          276 GREY ROCK          124
    ARDAN, AND THOUGH I CALLED TO HIM AND TRIED            283 TWO KINGS          142
    ALL THOSE THAT MANHOOD TRIED, OR CHILDHOOD LOVED       327 ROBERT GREGORY      91
```
TRIES
```
    UNDER THIS HUMP.  GOD TRIES EACH MAN                   379 SAINT HUNCH          5
```
TRIM
```
    WHO WERE NOT BORN TO KEEP IN TRIM                      336 YOUNG BEAUTY        10
```
TRIMMED
```
    AND TRIMMED WITH MANY A CRIMSON FEATHER!                15 OISIN 1            206
    TRIMMED ROUND WITH MANY A CRIMSON FEATHER!              15 OISIN 1          V 206
```
TRINE
```
    BY OPPOSITION, SQUARE AND TRINE!                       325 ROBERT GREGORY      39
```
TRINITY
```
    BUT PURE AS A TALL CANDLE BEFORE THE TRINITY           208 HANRAHANS SONG   V  14
    RECALL THAT MASCULINE TRINITY.                         556 RIBH PATRICK         2
    RECALL HIS TRINITY.  A FATHER, MOTHER, CHILD (A DAUGHTER  556 RIBH PATRICK  V   2
        OR A SON),
```
TRIP
```
    AWAY MUST SHE TRIP!                                    559 HE AND SHE           4
```
TRIPLE
```
    WHO HAS A LIKE VOW FROM THEIR TRIPLE DUN."             108 CUCHULAIN SEA    V  38
    WHO HAD A LIKE VOW FROM OUR TRIPLE DUN."               109 CUCHULAIN SEA    V  54
```
TRIPS
```
    AS TRIPS THE SCARED MOON                               559 HE AND SHE           3
    AS TRIPS THE SACRED MOON                               559 HE AND SHE       V   3
    FROM THEE I SNATCHED IT; E'EN THE FAY THAT TRIPS       670 ISLE STAT II 3      98
```
TRISTRAM
```
    AS DID THAT WILD TRISTRAM KNOW                         522 LULLABY              8
```
TRITON
```
    A WEATHER-WORN, MARBLE TRITON                          329 MEN IMPROVE          2
    A WEATHER-WORN, MARBLE TRITON                          329 MEN IMPROVE         17
```
TRIUMPH
```
    IN TRIUMPH WITH HER ARMS AROUND ME,                      9 OISIN 1          V 107
    THAN TRIUMPH, TURN AWAY                                291 TO A FRIEND         10
    THE FOOL'S TRIUMPH, NOR YET                            312 CHILD DANCING        7
    WHAT'S GOOD OR BAD, OR WHAT IT IS TO TRIUMPH           376 PHASES OF MOON     108
    TRIUMPH THAT WE OBEY.                                  382 VISION ROBART       16
    IN TRIUMPH OF INTELLECT                                383 VISION ROBART       31
    FOR IF I TRIUMPH I MUST MAKE MEN MAD.                  411 TOWER               56
    HAS BUT ONE COMFORT LEFT: ALL TRIUMPH WOULD            429 NINETEEN 19         39
    FOR TRIUMPH CAN BUT MAR OUR SOLITUDE.                  431 NINETEEN 19         78
    HER TRIUMPH                                            533 HER TRIUMPH          T
    WOUND, WOUND, AND SHE MADE IN HER TRIUMPH              578 CRAZED GIRL         11
    AS LIGHT OF TRIUMPH IN THY GOBLIN EYES--               674 ISLE STAT II 3     199
    THEN GIVE ME TRIUMPH IN MY MANY PLOTS.                 722 WITCH VIVIEN        51
```
TRIUMPHING
```
    WITH HER TRIUMPHING ARMS AROUND ME,                      9 OISIN 1            107
    "BUT IF YOUR MASTER COMES HOME TRIUMPHING              106 CUCHULAIN SEA       12
```
TRIVIAL
```
    FOR SOME TRIVIAL AFFAIR                                293 HELEN LIVED          3
    TOLD OF A HARSH REPROOF, OR TRIVIAL EVENT              443 SCHOOL CHILDR       11
    THE TRIVIAL DAYS AND RAM THEM WITH THE SUN,            500 VACILLATION         21
```
TROD   SEE STAR-TROD
```
    AND TROD SO SWEETLY PROUD                              255 WOMAN HOMER         17
    THAT WITH EMPOUNDED CATTLE TROD THE MIRE,              277 TWO KINGS            4
    HITHER AND THITHER TO AND FRO THEY TROD                278 TWO KINGS           26
    TROD WITH A LIGHTER TREAD.                             323 SWANS AT COOLE      18
    HAD TROD THE UNEVEN ROAD.  THEIR BOOTS WERE SOILED,    372 PHASES OF MOON       3
```

TROD   (CONTINUED)
    WHO TROD UPON THESE ROCKS OR PASSED THIS DOOR, ...   413 TOWER   98
    BUT TROD THE ROAD, OR SPLASHED ABOUT THE SHORE, ...   447 COLONUS PRAISE   27
    BUT TROD THE ROAD, OR PADDLED BY THE SHORE, ...   447 COLONUS PRAISE   V   27
    FIRST TROD ON THE MOUNTAIN'S HEAD . . . .   488 CRAZED MOON   9
    TARGETED, TROD LIKE SPRING. . . . .   504 QUARREL IN AGE   16
    NO PROUDER TROD THE GROUND, ...   587 PARNELLITES   22
    I WANDERED AND TROD, ...   654 ISLE STAT I 2   64
    BEFORE HER I TROD . . . .   654 ISLE STAT I 2   74
    WHO CAN HAVE TROD IN THE GRASS?   . . . .   781 MY HEART BEAT   4
TRODDEN
    ARE TRODDEN AND BROKEN BY THE HERDS, ...   190 BAILE AILLINN   43
    BUT FOR THE TRODDEN MIRE, THE POOL OF BLOOD, ...   278 TWO KINGS   44
    THAT SHE MIGHT BE THAT SPRIGHTLY GIRL TRODDEN BY A BIRD,   353 HIS PHOENIX   4
    THAT SHE MIGHT BE THAT SPRIGHTLY GIRL WHO WAS TRODDEN BY   353 HIS PHOENIX   V   4
        A BIRD,
TROIA
    OENONE SAW THE FIRES OF TROIA LEAP, ...   645 ISLE STAT I 1   17
    HOW HAVE THE YEARS IN TROIA FLOWN AWAY? . . . . . .   679 ISLE STAT II 3   309
TROLLED
    OUR MARRIED VOICES WILDLY TROLLED. . . . .   85 MAD KING GOLL   59
    OUR MARRIED VOICE WILDLY TROLLED.   . . . .   85 MAD KING GOLL   V   59
TROMBONE
    AND THE TROMBONE," CRIED HE, ...   527 AM OF IRELAND   23
    "THE TRUMPET AND TROMBONE," . . . .   527 AM OF IRELAND   24
TROOP
    AND NOW STILL SAD OUR TROOP DREW NIGH . . . . .   17 OISIN 1   V 247
    IN THEIR LONG LIVES? WILL YOU BE OF OUR TROOP . . . .   225 SHADOW WATER B   72
    BE OF YOUR TROOP! AIBRIC BE ONE OF YOU . . . . .   225 SHADOW WATER B   75
    IN THEIR LONG LIVES? IF YOU'LL BE OF OUR TROOP . . . .   225 SHADOW WATER B V   72
    YOU'LL BE AS GOOD A LEADER. BE OF YOUR TROOP! . . . .   225 SHADOW WATER B V   73
    WHAT IS THERE BUT A TROOP OF ASH-GREY BIRDS . . . .   247 SHADOW WATER B   517
    THAT YOU MIGHT HAVE A TROOP OF FRIENDS. . . . . .   273 GREY ROCK   58
    TO TROOP WITH THOSE THE WORLD'S FORGOT, ...   273 GREY ROCK   63
    "THE DANISH TROOP WAS DRIVEN OUT . . . .   273 GREY ROCK   65
    OUTRODE HIS TROOP THAT AFTER TWELVE MONTHS' WAR . . . .   276 TWO KINGS   V   1
    THE RAGE-DRIVEN, RAGE-TORMENTED, AND RAGE-HUNGRY TROOP,   426 PHANTOM HATRED   11
    THE RAGE DRIVEN, RAGE TORMENTED, AND RAGE HUNGRY TROOP,   426 PHANTOM HATRED V   11
    AND DEAFENING MUSIC SHOOK THE LEAVES: A TROOP . . . .   537 HER VISION   13
    COME TOM AND DICK, COME ALL THE TROOP . . . . . .   582 ROGER CASEMENT   17
    BUT I'D A TROOP OF FRIENDS . . . .   626 STATES HOLIDAY   6
    A NEW DAY'S TROOP OF WASP AND BEE . . . .   646 ISLE STAT I 1   44
    A HORN! SOME TROOP OF ROBBERS WINDING GOES . . . .   649 ISLE STAT I 1   110
    AND ONLY SHEEP HE LOVED OF ALL THE TROOP. . . . .   661 ISLE STAT II 1   61
TROOPER
    TROOPER BELABOURING TROOPER, BITING AT ARM OR AT FACE, . . 426 PHANTOM HATRED   12
    TROOPER BELABOURING TROOPER, BITING AT ARM OR AT FACE, . . 426 PHANTOM HATRED   12
TROOPING
    THEY WEARY OF TROOPING . . . .   118 CRADLE SONG   3
TROOPS
    HE AND HIS BEST TROOPS BACK TO BACK . . . .   274 GREY ROCK   73
    THE OLD TROOPS PARADE, ...   496 MOHINI CHATTER   22
TROPHIED
    AND MINE WAS EVERY TROPHIED WALL, ...   82 MAD KING GOLL   V   4
TROPIC
    UNDER THE TROPIC SHADE, GREW ROUND AND SLOW, ...   610 STATUES   18
TROTTED
    TROTTED BESIDE HIM IN A PLAYFUL MOOD. . . . . . .   715 DWELT SYCAMORE   4
TROTTING   SEE GLOBE-TROTTING
TROUBLE
    WHERE CARE CANNOT TROUBLE THE LEAST OF OUR DAYS, ...   27 OISIN 1   409
    TROUBLE HIS SLEEPING! GIVE HIM DREAMS OF ME. . . . .   75 ANASHU VIJAYA   91
    ABOVE THE TIDE OF HOURS, TROUBLE THE AIR, ...   114 ROSE OF BATTLE   3
    AND ALL THE TROUBLE OF HER LABOURING SHIPS, ...   120 SORROW OF LOVE   V   7
    AND ALL THE TROUBLE OF HER MYRIAD YEARS. . . . .   120 SORROW OF LOVE   8
    AND ALL THEIR TROUBLE DIES INTO ITS PEACE:— . . . .   128 DREAM OF FAERY   V   35
    IF THIS IMPORTUNATE HEART TROUBLE YOUR PEACE . . . .   162 ASKS FORGIVE   1
    AND TROUBLE WITH A SIGH FOR ALL THINGS LONGING FOR REST   163 ASKS FORGIVE   23
    AND TROUBLE WITH SIGHS FOR ALL HEARTS WITHOUT REST . . .   163 ASKS FORGIVE   V   23
    THOUGH NOW IT'S HARD, TILL TROUBLE IS AT AN END; . . .   200 FOLLY COMFORT   V   5
    "WHAT IS THIS TROUBLE?" HE WOULD ANSWER NOTHING, . . .   281 TWO KINGS   90
    THOUGH ALWAYS AT MY WORDS HIS TROUBLE GREW; . . . .   281 TWO KINGS   91
    SOMETHING HAS TROUBLED ME AND IN MY TROUBLE . . . .   339 SHEP GOATHERD   10
    FOR RHYME CAN BEAT A MEASURE OUT OF TROUBLE . . . .   339 SHEP GOATHERD   12
    TO TROUBLE THE LIVING STREAM. . . . .   393 EASTER 1916   44
    AND LATER HAD MUCH TROUBLE FROM A FOOL, ...   404 FOR DAUGHTER   26
    ALL THAT GREAT PAST TO A TROUBLE OF FOOLS! . . . .   546 TO SAME TUNE 2   22
    ALL THAT GREAT PAST TO A TROUBLE OF FOOLS! . . . .   614 MARCH SONGS 1   22
    I TOOK NO TROUBLE TO CONVINCE, ...   624 APPARITIONS   3
    IN TROUBLE IS, THE DOE WILL LINGER NEAR. . . . .   713 FERENCZ RENYI   80
    AND THEN THE WHOLE WORLD'S TROUBLE WEEPS WITH YOU. . . .   738 YOU ARE SAD   12
    YOUR HEART'S DESIRE AND THE END OF ALL OUR TROUBLE; . . . 755 SHADOW WATER A   175
TROUBLED   SEE MANY-TIMES-TROUBLED
    TROUBLED HER SONG. I DO NOT KNOW IF DAYS . . . . .   30 OISIN 2   19
    TO HIDE FROM THE TROUBLED DAY. . . . .   166 BLESSED   V   4
    HAD TROUBLED HIS SLEEP. BUT ALL HE HAD TO SAY . . . .   182 QUEEN MAEVE   52
    THAT NO GOD TROUBLED NOW; AND, WONDERING . . . .   182 QUEEN MAEVE   60
    NOR THE COLD NORTH HAS TROUBLED?" HE REPLIED; . . . .   184 QUEEN MAEVE   90
    FACE DOWNWARD, TOSSING IN A TROUBLED SLEEP; . . . .   185 QUEEN MAEVE   106
    MORE MIGHTY THAN THE STARS HALF TROUBLED ME, ...   237 SHADOW WATER B   332
    MANY TIMES TROUBLED YEARS, ...   315 FRIENDS   V   7

```
                                                     PAGE    TITLE           LINE
TROUBLED   (CONTINUED)
      SOMETHING HAS TROUBLED ME AND IN MY TROUBLE     339  SHEP GOATHERD       10
      TROUBLED HIS ANIMAL BLOOD.                      378  CAT AND MOON         8
      O HEART, O TROUBLED HEART--THIS CARICATURE,     409  TOWER                2
      SATISFIED IF A TROUBLED MIRROR SHOW IT,         430  NINETEEN 19         62
      CONTENTED THAT A TROUBLED MIRROR SHOW IT,       430  NINETEEN 19    V    62
      AND TROUBLED EYES CAME MORNING'S FIRST-BORN GLOW;  648  ISLE STAT I 1   103
      MY EYES ARE TROUBLED BY THE SILVER ARROWS;      761  SHADOW WATER A     269
      THAT THE VAST TROUBLED WATERS BRING             784  WOMANS BEAUTY       17
TROUBLES
      WHILE THE WORLD IS FULL OF TROUBLES              87  STOLEN CHILD        22
      THOUGH NOTHING TROUBLES THE GREAT STREAMS       196  BAILE AILLINN      172
      TROUBLES MY SIGHT; SOMEWHERE IN SANDS OF THE DESERT  402  SECOND COMING  13
      TROUBLES MY SIGHT;  A WASTE OF DESERT SAND;     402  SECOND COMING  V    13
      REMOTE FROM ALL THE HARD EARTH TROUBLES,        731  PRIEST FAIRY        80
TROUBLING    SEE WORLD-TROUBLING
      TROUBLING THE ENDLESS REVERIE.                   65  HAPPY SHEPHERD      21
TROUP
      COME ALFRED NOYES AND ALL THE TROUP            582  ROGER CASEMENT V     17
TROUSERS
      EVEN OUR BEAUTY WITH HER TURKISH TROUSERS ON.   364  DOLLS FACES          9
TROUT
      WE SEEK FOR SLUMBERING TROUT                     88  STOLEN CHILD        32
      AND HIS OWN SNIPE AND TROUT.                     92  FATHER OHART         4
      WITH HIS SNIPE MARSH AND HIS TROUT.              92  FATHER OHART   V     4
      AND CAUGHT A LITTLE SILVER TROUT.               149  WANDER AENGUS        8
      AND HOOKED A LITTLE SILVER TROUT.               149  WANDER AENGUS  V     8
      IT'S CERTAIN THERE ARE TROUT SOMEWHERE          297  THREE BEGGARS       66
      AND MAYBE I SHALL TAKE A TROUT                  297  THREE BEGGARS       67
TROW
      SUCH QUESTS AS THESE, I TROW, NEED LITTLE WIT.  650  ISLE STAT I 1      150
      OF GREEN ARCADIA DO NOT HIDE, I TROW,          651  ISLE STAT I 1      166
TROY
      TROY PASSED AWAY IN ONE HIGH FUNERAL GLEAM,    111  ROSE OF WORLD        4
      NO SECOND TROY                                 256  NO SECOND TROY       T
      WAS THERE ANOTHER TROY FOR HER TO BURN?        257  NO SECOND TROY      12
      OF THE MEN AND WOMEN OF TROY,                  293  HELEN LIVED         11
      ANOTHER TROY MUST RISE AND SET,                437  SONGS PLAY 1         9
      AND PUT ALL TROY TO WRECK--                    455  HIS MEMORIES        16
      AND PUT ALL TROY TO WRACK--                    455  HIS MEMORIES   V    16
      TROY BACKED ITS HELEN; TROY DIED AND ADORED;   547  TO SAME TUNE 3       4
      TROY BACKED ITS HELEN; TROY DIED AND ADORED;   547  TO SAME TUNE 3       4
      TROY LOOKED ON HELEN, IT DIED AND ADORED;      547  TO SAME TUNE 3 V     4
      HECTOR IS DEAD AND THERE'S A LIGHT IN TROY;    564  GYRES                7
      TROY BACKED ITS HELEN; TROY DIED AND ADORED;   614  MARCH SONGS 2        4
      TROY BACKED ITS HELEN; TROY DIED AND ADORED;   614  MARCH SONGS 2        4
TRUE
      AND LOVED YOUR BEAUTY WITH LOVE FALSE OR TRUE, 121  YOU ARE OLD          6
      AND LOVED YOUR BEAUTY WILL LOVE FALSE OR TRUE; 121  YOU ARE OLD    V     6
      TRUE BROTHER OF A COMPANY                      137  TO IRELAND           2
      TRUE BROTHER OF THAT COMPANY                   137  TO IRELAND     V     2
      WHILE STILL I MAY I WRITE OUT TRUE             139  TO IRELAND     V    33
      THAT IS BAD ENOUGH TO BE TRUE, IS TRUE,        191  BAILE AILLINN       69
      THAT IS BAD ENOUGH TO BE TRUE, IS TRUE,        191  BAILE AILLINN       69
      BUT IT IS TRUE.  WHY DID THEY RUN UPON HIM,    243  SHADOW WATER B     424
      OUT OF ALL RECKONING.  IS IT NOT TRUE          244  SHADOW WATER B     467
      IF SOMETHING THAT'S MOST FABULOUS WERE TRUE--  245  SHADOW WATER B     489
      THAT IS NOT TRUE, FOR HE HAS PROMISED ME       248  SHADOW WATER B     552
      SPEAK--HE WILL NOT DENY IT.  IS THAT TRUE?     249  SHADOW WATER B     563
      HE CANNOT CONTRADICT ME.  IS THAT TRUE?        249  SHADOW WATER B V   563
      "IF THAT BE TRUE AS IT SEEMS TRUE,             295  THREE BEGGARS       20
      "IF THAT BE TRUE AS IT SEEMS TRUE,             295  THREE BEGGARS       20
      BUT WHEN, IF THE TALE'S TRUE,                  346  ON WOMAN            29
      TRUE SONG, THOUGH SPEECH; "MINE AUTHOR SUNG IT ME."  373  PHASES OF MOON  30
      THE TRUE FAITH DISCOVERED WAS                  440  WISDOM               1
      BEING ALL BRIMMED WITH LIFE?" "WERE IT BUT TRUE 465  HARUN RASHID       90
      WHAT TRUE LOVE BE?                             510  JANE JUDGMENT       17
      ALL TRUE LOVE MUST DIE;                        517  HER ANXIETY          3
      BIDS ALL TRUE LOVERS REST;                     536  PARTING              6
      WHEN YOU AND MY TRUE LOVER MEET                573  LADYS 3RD SONG       1
      ALL HIS HAPPIER DREAMS CAME TRUE--             577  WHAT THEN           11
      TO PROVE THEIR FORGERY TRUE;                   582  ROGER CASEMENT      10
      THOSE WORDS COME TRUE IN THE END               597  COLONEL MARTIN V    69
      AND MAYBE WHAT THEY SAY IS TRUE                631  POLITICS             9
      WANDERS AND WAILS BEFORE MY HEART MOST TRUE    738  YOU ARE SAD          8
      THAT MY TRUE LOVE WOULD COME IN A SHIP OF PEARL  763  SHADOW WATER A V  315
      WHERE TRUE LOVE WANDERS AMONG THE HOLY WOODS.  764  SHADOW WATER A V   337
      WHAT WERE TRUE LOVE AMONG THE RUSH OF HIS STREAMS?  764  SHADOW WATER A V  338
TRUE-LOVE
      THAT MY TRUE-LOVE WOULD COME IN A SHIP OF PEARL  763  SHADOW WATER A    315
      WHERE TRUE-LOVE WANDERS AMONG THE HOLY WOODS.  764  SHADOW WATER A     337
      WHAT WERE TRUE-LOVE AMONG THE RUSH OF HIS STREAMS?  764  SHADOW WATER A  338
TRULY
      AH, YOU WILL KNOW MY LOVED ONE BY HIS HUNTER'S ARROWS   75  ANASHU VIJAYA  80
         TRULY,
TRUMP
      MAID NIAM FROM A LITTLE TRUMP                   14  OISIN 1        V   194
      OUT OF A LITTLE SILVER TRUMP;                   15  OISIN 1            196
TRUMPET
      O! LAY THE SHRILLY TRUMPET DOWN,               212  BLESS PSALTER        4
      MICHAEL WILL UNHOOK HIS TRUMPET                215  HAPPY TOWNLAND      41
```

		PAGE	TITLE	LINE

TRUMPET   (CONTINUED)
TO KNOW WHEN MICHAEL'S TRUMPET CRIES . . . . 307 HOUR DAWN 100
TRUMPET AND KETTLEDRUM, ... 317 NIGHT COME 9
"THE TRUMPET AND TROMBONE," . . . . 527 AM OF IRELAND 24
AND LIKE A SILVER TRUMPET RING. . . . . 736 SUMMER EVENING 4
AND LIKE A SILVER TRUMPET RING. . . . . 737 SUMMER EVENING 20
TRUMPETER
COULD TRUMPETER MICHAEL BE SO BRAVE?" . . . . 338 TOM OROUGHLEY 13
TRUMPETERS
THE TRUMPETERS MIGHT BURST WITH TRUMPETING . . . . . . 429 NINETEEN 19 22
TRUMPETING
THE TRUMPETERS MIGHT BURST WITH TRUMPETING . . . . . . 429 NINETEEN 19 22
TRUMPETS
AND THE TRUMPETS ALL ARE BURST, ... 527 AM OF IRELAND 22
TRUMPET-TWISTED
WHERE MANY A TRUMPET-TWISTED SHELL . . . . 13 OISIN 1 160
TRUNDLED
LAST NIGHT THEY TRUNDLED DOWN THE ROAD . . . . 425 STARES NEST 13
TRUNK
FORTH FROM THE HOLLOW ALDER TRUNK . . . . 670 ISLE STAT II 3 120
TRUST
IN TRUST TOOK HE JOHN'S LANDS, ... 92 FATHER OHART 5
THAT ALL MUST HANG THEIR TRUST . . . . 583 GHOST ROG CASE 16
FROM POISON, FOR YOU CANNOT TRUST THESE MOORS. . . . . 704 MOSADA 3 126
I ALWAYS SAID YOU COULD NOT TRUST THESE MOORS. . . . . 704 MOSADA 3 V 134A
TRUTH   SEE COUNTER-TRUTH
GREY TRUTH IS NOW HER PAINTED TOY, ... 65 HAPPY SHEPHERD 4
TO HUNGER FIERCELY AFTER TRUTH, ... 66 HAPPY SHEPHERD 24
NEW DREAMS, NEW DREAMS, THERE IS NO TRUTH . . . . . 66 HAPPY SHEPHERD 26
AND DEAD IS ALL THEIR HUMAN TRUTH. . . . . 66 HAPPY SHEPHERD 34
WITH THE EVER-LIVING. WHAT IF HE SPEAK THE TRUTH, . . . 229 SHADOW WATER B 170
THAT'S ALL WE SHALL KNOW FOR TRUTH . . . . 261 DRINKING SONG 3
NOW I MAY WITHER INTO THE TRUTH. . . . . 261 COMING WISDOM 4
WHERE, WHERE BUT HERE HAVE PRIDE AND TRUTH, ... 262 STUDENTS AGIT 1
IF BOOKS SPEAK TRUTH, IN SLIEVENAMON-- . . . . . . 271 GREY ROCK V 15
NOW ALL THE TRUTH IS OUT, ... 290 TO A FRIEND 1
DISCOVERERS OF FORGOTTEN TRUTH . . . . 324 ROBERT GREGORY 6
IS THIS MY DREAM, OR THE TRUTH? . . . . 329 MEN IMPROVE 13
A POET'S MOUTH BE SILENT, FOR IN TRUTH . . . . . . 359 WAR POEM 2
WE POETS KEEP OUR MOUTHS SHUT, FOR IN TRUTH . . . . . 359 WAR POEM V 2
A POET KEEP HIS MOUTH SHUT, FOR IN TRUTH . . . . . . 359 WAR POEM V 2
JUST TRUTH ENOUGH TO SHOW THAT HIS WHOLE LIFE . . . . 373 PHASES OF MOON 22
TRUTH FLOURISHES WHERE THE STUDENT'S LAMP HAS SHONE, . . . 398 LEADERS CROWD 8
TALKED OF HONOUR AND OF TRUTH, ... 431 NINETEEN 19 90
WHERE GOT I THAT TRUTH? . . . . 439 FRAGMENTS 5
MUST NEEDS NEGLECT, I CANNOT HIDE THE TRUTH, ... 462 HARUN RASHID 26
MUST NEEDS NEGLECT, BUT CANNOT HIDE THE TRUTH, ... 462 HARUN RASHID V 26
"MY FRIENDS ARE GONE, BUT THAT'S A TRUTH . . . . . 513 JANE TALK BISH 9
I SAID THAT SHE HAD DANCED HEART'S TRUTH, ... 514 JANE GROWN OLD 9
I LONG FOR TRUTH, AND YET . . . . 533 FIRST CONFESS 7
CAN MAKE THE TRUTH KNOWN. . . . . 575 ACRE OF GRASS 12
TILL TRUTH OBEYED HIS CALL, ... 576 ACRE OF GRASS 18
HER LOVE, TO HER WHO WEARS THAT BLOOM COMES TRUTH. . . . 653 ISLE STAT I 2 46
WITH YOU I AM ALL GENTLENESS, IN TRUTH, ... 669 ISLE STAT II 3 70
SHALL GROW THY BEAUTY AND THY DREAMLESS TRUTH, ... 674 ISLE STAT II 3 207
SO SHE MUST BURN, YOU SAY? SHE MUST IN TRUTH. . . . . 696 MOSADA 2 2
IN TRUTH, AN EVIL RACE. WHY STRIVE FOR HER, ... 696 MOSADA 2 9
THE BURTHEN OF THY TRUTH. REACH DOWN THY HANDS . . . . 698 MOSADA 2 53
AND SAID, "YON BITTERN CRIES, IN TRUTH, ... 731 PRIEST FAIRY 75
TRUTH'S
IN TRUTH'S CONSUMING ECSTASY, ... 139 TO IRELAND 42
TRUTHS
OF ALL THOSE TRUTHS THAT ARE YOUR DAILY BREAD, ... 373 PHASES OF MOON 24
TRUTHS WITHOUT FATHER CAME, TRUTHS THAT NO BOOK . . . . 467 HARUN RASHID 138
TRUTHS WITHOUT FATHER CAME, TRUTHS THAT NO BOOK . . . . 467 HARUN RASHID 138
SELF-BORN, HIGH-BORN, AND SOLITARY TRUTHS, ... 467 HARUN RASHID 141
EVEN THOSE TRUTHS THAT WHEN MY BONES ARE DUST . . . . 467 HARUN RASHID 144
TRUTHS THAT WHEN MY VERY BONES ARE DUST . . . . . . 467 HARUN RASHID V 144
I HAVE MUMMY TRUTHS TO TELL . . . . 474 ALL SOUL NIGHT 86
TRY
I BEAR A BURDEN THAT MIGHT WELL TRY . . . . . . 380 SONGS FOOL 1 13
O, SOLOMON, LET US TRY AGAIN." . . . . 389 SOLOMON WITCH 44
SO THAT I HAD THE LIMBS TO TRY . . . . 515 JANE GROWN OLD 19
I TRY TO LIFT MINE ARMS--THEY FALL AGAIN. . . . . . 701 MOSADA 3 56
TUB
A LADLE AND A TUB OF BEER, ... 303 HOUR DAWN 29
INTO THE SLEEPER'S TUB OF BEER . . . . 304 HOUR DAWN 47
HE DIPPED HIS LADLE IN THE TUB . . . . 307 HOUR DAWN 107
TUCKED
HAD TUCKED HIMSELF AWAY BESIDE . . . . 303 HOUR DAWN 28
TUFTED
FROM THE TALL AND THE TUFTED REEDS . . . . 143 HOST OF AIR 3
O TUFTED REEDS, BEND LOW AND LOW IN POOLS ON THE GREEN 206 HANRAHANS SONG V 1
LAND,
LIKE TUFTED REEDS OUR COURAGE DROOPS IN A BLACK WIND AND 207 HANRAHANS SONG V 3
DIES,
TUGGED
HORN LOCKED IN SWORD, THEY TUGGED AND STRUGGLED THERE . . 277 TWO KINGS 18
TULIPS
LIKE TULIPS IN THE AIR A-WINGING, ... 27 OISIN 1 417

838

		PAGE	TITLE	LINE

TULLY'S
   AND HERE IS TULLY'S OPEN PAGE. . . . . 524 MAD AS MIST 9
TUMBLE
   AND TUMBLE OUT YOUR HAIR . . . . 312 CHILD DANCING 4
TUMBLED
   BEING TUMBLED AND BLOWN ABOUT . . . . 191 BAILE AILLINN 66
   TILL THAT BE TUMBLED THAT WAS LIFTED HIGH . . . . . . 265 THESE CLOUDS 4
   HE STUMBLED, TUMBLED, FUMBLED TO AND FRO . . . . 411 TOWER 61
TUMBLES
   THE NORTH WIND TUMBLES TO AND FRO . . . . 191 BAILE AILLINN 45
   THAT NORTH WIND TUMBLES TO AND FRO . . . . . . 191 BAILE AILLINN V 45
TUMBLING
   BEYOND THE TUMBLING OF THIS TIDE." . . . . 5 OISIN 1 49
   OR TUMBLING CLOUD." . . . . 349 HAWK 12
   "WHAT TUMBLING CLOUD DID YOU CLEAVE. . . . . . . 349 HAWK 13
   FROM CLOUD TO TUMBLING CLOUD, ... 393 EASTER 1916 47
TUMULT
   BY KNOWING NOR TUMULT NOR HATE NOR STRIFE, ... 9 OISIN 1 95
   AND DROVE TUMULT AND WAR AWAY . . . . 82 MAD KING GOLL 5
   THEIR HOOFS HEAVY WITH TUMULT, THEIR EYES GLIMMERING WHITE: 154 BELOVED PEACE 2
   AND TUMULT OF DEFEATED DREAMS; AND DEEP . . . . . . 169 SECRET ROSE 5
   DROVE TO THIS TUMULT IN THE CLOUDS; . . . . 328 IRISH AIRMAN 12
   BECAUSE OF ALL THAT SENSELESS TUMULT, ALL BUT CRIED . . . 426 PHANTOM HATRED 15
   THUNDER OF FEET, TUMULT OF IMAGES, ... 433 NINETEEN 19 120
   IN A GREAT TUMULT OF THE AIR, ... 519 HER DREAM 6
   IN THE TUMULT OF THE LIMBS . . . . 777 SONG DEIRDRE 2 7
TUMULTS
   UNDER THE SHADOWS TILL THE TUMULTS DIED . . . . . 38 OISIN 2 140
   ON MY POOR BRAIN YOUR BUSY TUMULTS CROWD. . . . . . . 648 ISLE STAT I 1 100
TUMULTUOUS
   AND WHEN TUMULTUOUS FEET ENWOUND ME . . . . 83 MAD KING GOLL V 20
   AND HIDING THEIR TOSSING MANES AND THEIR TUMULTUOUS FEET. 154 BELOVED PEACE 12
   AND HIDE THEIR TOSSING MANES AND THEIR TUMULTUOUS FEET. 154 BELOVED PEACE V 12
   IN A TUMULTUOUS SONG"! . . . . 163 ASKS FORGIVE 20
   IN THIS TUMULTUOUS SPOT. . . . . 420 MY HOUSE 23
   . . . THROUGH TORCHLIGHT AND TUMULTUOUS SONG! . . . . 459 FROM OEDIPUS 8
   . . . THROUGH TORCH-LIGHT AND TUMULTUOUS SONG! . . . . 459 FROM OEDIPUS V 8
TUMULTUOUS-FOOTED
   AND A HUNDRED STEEDS, TUMULTUOUS-FOOTED, ... 8 OISIN 1 V 85A
TUNE
   THOSE MERRY COUPLES DANCING IN TUNE, ... 3 OISIN 1 9
   AND FEET OF MAIDENS DANCING IN TUNE. . . . . . . 3 OISIN 1 V 9
   AND THE DAYS PASS BY LIKE A WAYWARD TUNE, ... 8 OISIN 1 83
   WHERE THE VOICE OF CHANGE IS THE VOICE OF A TUNE, . . . 8 OISIN 1 V 82
   TO THE CRACKED TUNE THAT CHRONOS SINGS, ... 65 HAPPY SHEPHERD 9
   TO THE OLD CRACKED TUNE THAT CHRONOS SINGS, ... 65 HAPPY SHEPHERD V 9
   MURMURING, TO A FITFUL TUNE. . . . . 85 MAD KING GOLL 52
   A MURMURING A MOUNTAIN TUNE, ... 85 MAD KING GOLL V 52
   MURMURING A MOUNTAIN TUNE, ... 85 MAD KING GOLL V 52
   A DRUID LAND, A DRUID TUNE! . . . . 139 TO IRELAND 32
   IN HER HEART SHE FOUND A TUNE, ... 160 CAP AND BELLS V 26
   HEARING THE WHOLE EARTH CHANGE ITS TUNE, ... 266 GALWAY RACES 12
   A NEW DANCE TUNE. . . . . 378 CAT AND MOON V 16
   THREE SONGS TO THE SAME TUNE . . . . 543 TO SAME TUNE 1 T
   THREE SONGS TO THE SAME TUNE SECOND SONG . . . . 544 TO SAME TUNE 1 V T
   DOWN TO THE TUNE OF O'DONNELL ABU. . . . . . . 544 TO SAME TUNE 1 10
   ALL THERE CAUGHT UP THE TUNE! . . . . 545 TO SAME TUNE 1 15
   DOWN TO THE TUNE OF O'DONNELL ABU. . . . . . . 545 TO SAME TUNE 1 20
   DOWN TO THE TUNE OF O'DONNELL ABU. . . . . . . 545 TO SAME TUNE 1 30
   DOWN TO THE TUNE OF O'DONNELL ABU. . . . . . . 546 TO SAME TUNE 2 V REF
   TIME FOR US ALL TO PICK OUT A GOOD TUNE, ... 548 TO SAME TUNE 3 13
   O ANY OLD WORDS TO A TUNE. . . . . 548 TO SAME TUNE 3 16
   DOWN TO THE TUNE OF O'DONNELL ABU. . . . . . . 548 TO SAME TUNE 3 V REF
   TIME FOR US ALL BOYS, TO HIT ON A TUNE BOYS, . . . 548 TO SAME TUNE 3 V 13
   LIFT, LIFT, LIFT UP THE TUNE. . . . . 548 TO SAME TUNE 3 V 16
   STOOD, TOOK DEATH LIKE A TUNE . . . . 613 MARCH SONGS 1 15
   MARCH WIND, AND ANY OLD TUNE, ... 615 MARCH SONGS 2 25
   AND RATTLED OUT A TUNE! . . . . 616 MARCH SONGS 3 9
   ALL THERE CAUGHT UP THE TUNE! . . . . 616 MARCH SONGS 3 15
   AND RATTLED OUT A TUNE! . . . . 616 MARCH SONGS 3 19
   AND RATTLED OUT A TUNE! . . . . 616 MARCH SONGS 3 29
   WITH AN OLD FOUL TUNE. . . . . 627 STATES HOLIDAY 38
   IN ALL ITS HONEY-THICKENED TUNE . . . . 736 SUMMER EVENING 7
   AN INTELLECTUAL TUNE, ... 743 WISDOM DREAMS 2
TUNE'S
   TWO SONGS REWRITTEN FOR THE TUNE'S SAKE . . . . . 550 SONGS REWRIT 1 T
TUNES
   AND AS IT FALLS AWAKENS LEAFY TUNES!-- . . . . . 127 DREAM OF FAERY V 23
   OF SORROWFUL, AUSTERE, SWEET, LOFTY PIPE TUNES. . . . 341 SHEP GOATHERD 57
   AND HE PLAYS TUNES BETWEEN YOUR FEET. . . . . . 573 LADYS 3RD SONG 2
   THEY SANG, BUT HAD NOR HUMAN TUNES NOR WORDS, . . . 635 CUCHULAIN COMF 23
TUNNELLED
   AND THE ROOF FALLS IN OF HIS TUNNELLED HOUSE. . . . . 27 OISIN 1 V 419
   AND THE ROOF FALLS IN OF HIS TUNNELLED HOUSE. . . . 28 OISIN 1 423
TURBANED   SEE VAPOUR-TURBANED
   WITH ROLLING FIRE, BEYOND THE HIGH TREES TURBANED . . . 656 ISLE STAT I 3 32
TURBULENCE
   BEING BY CALVARY'S TURBULENCE UNSATISFIED, ... 318 MAGI 7
   IN GALILEAN TURBULENCE! . . . . 438 SONGS PLAY 2 3
TURBULENT
   WHENCE TURBULENT ITALY SHOULD DRAW . . . . 288 TO WEALTHY MAN 25

TURBULENT   (CONTINUED)
    A BOY'S TURBULENT DAYS . . . .   496 MOHINI CHATTER   13
TURF
    PILIN' THE WOOD OR PILIN' THE TURF, ...   96 MOLL MAGEE   45
    A-PILIN' WOOD OR PILIN' TURF, ...   96 MOLL MAGEE   V 45
    BESIDE A FIRE OF TURF IN TH' ANCIENT TOWER, ... 324 ROBERT GREGORY   3
TURK
    HE SPOKE WITH TURK AND JEW, ...   594 COLONEL MARTIN   2
TURKEY
    WITH A STRUTTING TURKEY WALK, ...   627 STATES HOLIDAY   34
TURKISH
    CUT IN THE TURKISH FASHION, ...   363 DOLLS DRAWINGS   8
    EVEN OUR BEAUTY WITH HER TURKISH TROUSERS ON. . . . 364 DOLLS FACES   9
TURN   SEE DOWN-TURN
    AND TOSS AND TURN IN NARROW CAVES! . . . .   19 OISIN 1   281
    IN PINCHING WAYS I TOIL AND TURN." . . . .   19 OISIN 1   V 282
    AND HOW THOSE LOVERS NEVER TURN THEIR EYES . . . .   29 OISIN 2   11
    IN WHAT LAND DO THE POWERLESS TURN THE BEAK . . .   42 OISIN 2   198
    SHALL THEY TURN WROTH OR PLUCK THE WINGS OF TIME? . . 42 OISIN 2   V 199
    "O FLAMING LION OF THE WORLD, O WHEN WILL YOU TURN TO YOUR 56 OISIN 3   129
        REST?"
    O FLAMING LION OF THE WORLD, O WHEN WILL YOU TURN TO YOUR   56 OISIN 3   136
        REST?"
    "OH, FLAMING LION OF THE WORLD, OH, WHEN WILT THOU TURN   56 OISIN 3   V 129
        TO THY REST?"
    . . . AND OF OLD WOUNDS, AND TURN TO OUR REST. . . . 62 OISIN 3   212
    TURN IF YOU MAY FROM BATTLES NEVER DONE, ... 114 ROSE OF BATTLE   7
    "TURN IF YE MAY," I CALL OUT TO EACH ONE, ...   114 ROSE OF BATTLE V   7
    AND NO MORE TURN ASIDE AND BROOD . . . .   125 GOES FERGUS   7
    FOR ALL THINGS TURN TO BARRENNESS . . . .   135 TWO TREES   29
    ALL THINGS TURN TO BARRENNESS . . . .   135 TWO TREES   V 29
    O HEART! O HEART! IF SHE'D BUT TURN HER HEAD, . .   200 FOLLY COMFORT   13
    A GOOD ROUND SUM UPON THIS CRUISE, AND TURN-- . .   222 SHADOW WATER B   5
    IT WOULD BE BETTER TO TURN HOME AGAIN, ...   222 SHADOW WATER B V 12
    THAT NEVER DID A HAND'S TURN? AIBRIC! AIBRIC! . .   228 SHADOW WATER B   130
    WHY DO YOU TURN AWAY AND HIDE YOUR FACE, ...   244 SHADOW WATER B   461
    YOU TURN AWAY. WHY DO YOU TURN AWAY? . . . . .   246 SHADOW WATER B   507
    YOU TURN AWAY. WHY DO YOU TURN AWAY? . . . . .   246 SHADOW WATER B   507
    AND SAW WHEREVER I COULD TURN . . . .   253 HIS DREAM   3
    AND EVERYWHERE THAT I COULD TURN . . . .   253 HIS DREAM   V 3
    SHADOWS AND SHOWS THAT CAN BUT TURN THE BRAIN." . . 281 TWO KINGS   108
    I WAITED TILL THE NIGHT WAS ON THE TURN, ...   283 TWO KINGS   144
    YET COULD WE TURN THE YEARS AGAIN, ...   290 SEPTEMBER 1913   25
    THAN TRIUMPH, TURN AWAY . . . .   291 TO A FRIEND   10
    BEN JONSON'S PHRASE--AND STILL MAY TURN MY FEET . . 321 REED WHISPERER V   6
    AS THOUGH DRIED STRAW, AND IF WE TURN ABOUT . . .   327 ROBERT GREGORY   83
    WHEN HER SON'S TURN WAS OVER. SING YOUR SONG. .   340 SHEP GOATHERD   42
    AND THE DOWN TURN OF HIS WRIST . . . .   348 FISHERMAN   V 33
    DUTIFUL HUSBAND, HONEST WIFE BY TURN, ...   376 PHASES OF MOON   99
    A NEW DANCE TURN. . . . .   378 CAT AND MOON   16
    AND NEW DANCE TURN. . . . .   378 CAT AND MOON   V 16
    SHE WOULD HAVE TIME TO TURN HER EYES, ...   385 ROBARTES DANCE   10
    AND THAT HE WILL TURN GREEN WITH RAGE . . . . .   385 ROBARTES DANCE   16
    HE, TOO, HAS BEEN CHANGED IN HIS TURN, ...   393 EASTER 1916   38
    AND WHEN THAT ANCIENT RUFFIAN'S TURN WAS ON . . .   411 TOWER   66
    AND TURN TOWARDS MY CHAMBER, CAUGHT . . . . . .   424 ROAD AT DOOR   14
    I TURN AWAY AND SHUT THE DOOR, AND ON THE STAIR . . 427 PHANTOM HATRED   33
    ALL TURN WITH AMOROUS CRIES, OR ANGRY CRIES, . .   433 NINETEEN 19   123
    NOR CRY, NOR TURN IN THE BED . . . .   435 FOR MY SON   3
    I AM JEALOUS OF THE LOOK MEN TURN ON YOU . . . .   447 HERO GIRL FOOL V   A
    I HAD BETTER FIND A CONVENT AND TURN NUN! . . . .   448 HERO GIRL FOOL   11
    "BECAUSE I MADE YOU TURN AWAY AND RUN FROM THAT YOUNG   450 OWEN AHERNE   14
        CHILD!
    THE SECOND BEST'S A GAY GOODNIGHT AND QUICKLY TURN AWAY.   459 FROM OEDIPUS 12
    THAN SOULS THAT START NO GAME AND TURN NO RHYME! . . 464 HARUN RASHID   68
    MY HEART COULD NEVER TURN FROM DAILY RUIN, . . .   464 HARUN RASHID   83
    I HEARD HER VOICE, "TURN THAT I MAY EXPOUND . . .   467 HARUN RASHID   132
    THAT TURN DULL-EYED AWAY, ...   505 RESULT THOUGHT   14
    TURN HATRED INTO SPORT, ...   506 REMORSE SPEECH   8
    BUT TURN FROM ROSSES' CRAWLING TIDE, ...   549 SEVERED HEAD   5
    I TURN THE PAGES OF MY HOLY BOOK. . . . .   555 RIBH AT TOMB   27
    A DARKER KNOWLEDGE AND IN HATRED TURN . . . . .   558 RIBH CHRISTIAN   14
    I TURN ROUND . . . .   572 LADYS 1ST SONG   1
    THEY TURN DOWN THEIR BEDS. . . . .   589 OLD WICKED MAN   35
    TURN TO A DRUNKEN JOURNALIST! . . . .   626 OLD MEN BE MAD   4
    I SAW HIM SIGH AND TURN AND PASS AWAY! . . . . .   690 MOSADA 1   14
    WERE HERE, HE WOULD TURN DEATH INTO A CRUTCH! . .   711 FERENCZ RENYI   38
    LIFT THEIR CHINS AND TURN AWAY. . . . .   726 LOVERS QUARREL   24
    ANOTHER LEADER, AND TURN HOME AGAIN. . . . . . .   748 SHADOW WATER A   16
    BUT WOULD TURN HOME AGAIN. NO MAN HAD DOUBTS . .   749 SHADOW WATER A   38
    AND TURN BRIEF LONGING AND DECEIVING HOPE . . . .   750 SHADOW WATER A   59
    AND TURN HIS GALLEY ABOUT AND BRING ME HOME. . .   751 SHADOW WATER A   108
    SHE OFFERS GREAT REWARDS IF WE TURN EAST . . . .   755 SHADOW WATER A   169
    MAY TURN FROM A STATUE . . . .   786 YOUR HEART   20
TURNED
    I TURNED IT IN MY HANDS! THE STAINS . . . . . .   24 OISIN 1   368
    HOW SUCH A WARRIOR NEVER TURNED HIS GAZE! . . . .   29 OISIN 2   V 11
    HUNG IN THE PASSIONATE DAWN. HE SLOWLY TURNED! . . 40 OISIN 2   167
    HUNG THE FRAIL LOFTIER CLOUDLETS. TURNED HE SLOW-- . . 40 OISIN 2   V 167
    AND LONELY AND LONGING FOR NIAMH, I SHIVERED AND TURNED   60 OISIN 3   181
        ME ABOUT,

	PAGE	TITLE	LINE

TURNED (CONTINUED)
    I TURNED AND RODE TO THE WESTWARD, AND FOLLOWED THE SEA'S   60 OISIN 3   183
        OLD SHOUT
    AND SHIVERING AND LONELY, AND LONGING FOR NIAM, I TURNED   60 OISIN 3   V 181
        ME ABOUT,
    AND TURNED THE FARMER'S MEMORY FROM HIS CATTLE, • • • •   129 BOOK STORIES   6
    WHEN NO ONE TURNED TO SEE • • • • • • • •   131 OLD PENSIONER   V   2
    "WHEN YOU WERE GONE, HE TURNED AND DIED. • • • •   133 FR GILLIGAN   37
    SHE TURNED AWAY; HE TURNED AGAIN TO SLEEP • • • •   182 QUEEN MAEVE   59
    SHE TURNED AWAY; HE TURNED AGAIN TO SLEEP • • • •   182 QUEEN MAEVE   59
    THAT HAPPIER BREATH HAD MOVED, HER HUSBAND TURNED • •   185 QUEEN MAEVE   105
    THIS LONG WHILE NOW; WE HAD NOT TURNED AGAINST HIM • •   225 SHADOW WATER B V 68B
    THEIR HEADS BEING TURNED WITH PRAISE AND FLATTERY; • •   245 SHADOW WATER B   480
    OF A NEW FRIEND HE HAS TURNED A GHOST. • • • • •   275 GREY ROCK   103
    WHAT TURNED SO GOOD A SHEPHERD FROM HIS CHARGE. • •   339 SHEP GOATHERD   16
    AND THOUGH I HAVE TURNED THE TALK BY HOOK OR CROOK • •   350 HER PRAISE   5
    IF ON THE LOST, ADMIT YOU TURNED ASIDE • • • • •   413 TOWER   115
    WE ARE CLOSED IN, AND THE KEY IS TURNED • • • • •   425 STARES NEST   6
    WE ARE CLOSED IN, AND THE KEY TURNED. • • • • •   425 STARES NEST   V   6
    WHAT MATTER THAT NO CANNON HAD BEEN TURNED • • •   429 NINETEEN 19   19
    WHEN UPWARD TURNED, ON ONE SOLE IMAGE FELL; • • •   471 ALL SOUL NIGHT   34
    WHEN UPWARD TURNED ON ONE SOUL IMAGE FELL, • • •   471 ALL SOUL NIGHT V 34
    BACK TURNED UPON THE BRIGHTNESS OF THE SUN • •   489 COOLE PARK 29   30
    I TURNED ABOUT AND LOOKED WHERE BRANCHES BREAK • •   490 COOLE BALLYLEE   15
    I TURNED ABOUT AND LOOKED WHERE BRANCHES BROKE • •   490 COOLE BALLYLEE V 15
    WHEN HE TURNED HIS HEAD • • • • • • • • •   511 JANE AND JACK   16
    WHEN YOU TURNED YOUR HEAD • • • • • • •   511 JANE AND JACK V 16
    HAD TURNED HIS STATELY HEAD. • • • • • • •   526 AM OF IRELAND   10
    WHAT HAS TURNED TO SMOKING WICK • • • • •   529 TOM LUNATIC   5
    HALF TURNED AND FIXED A GLAZING EYE ON MINE, • • •   537 HER VISION   26
    THEY TURNED A TRICK BY FORGERY • • • • • •   582 ROGER CASEMENT   7
    THEY TURNED A TRICK OF FORGERY • • • • • •   582 ROGER CASEMENT V   7
    IN ALL SUCH THINGS, PRAY LET THINE EARS BE TURNED, •   660 ISLE STAT II 1   39
    WE TURNED AROUND THE PLACE ALWAY, • • • • •   667 ISLE STAT II 3   40
    I AM; ONE SHOULDER TURNED AWRY—WHY THEN • • •   692 MOSADA 1   61
    THEN TURNED HE FROM THE KING'S COURT, • • • •   742 EARL PAUL   65
    YOU HAVE DONE WELL, BECAUSE MY BOWS ARE TURNED • •   755 SHADOW WATER A   164
    I HAVE TURNED HOMEWARDS. IN THE EYES OF THE GODS, •   757 SHADOW WATER A   202
TURNIN'
    THE LITTLE STRAWS WERE TURNIN' ROUND • • • • • • •   95 MOLL MAGEE   31
TURNING
    EVADING, TURNING; ONCE DID I HEW AND HEW • • • •   40 QISIN 2   V 176
    . . . SAILS TURNING TO THREADBARE RAGS; • • • •   55 OISIN 3   118
    . . . SAILS TURNING TO THREAD-BARE RAGS; • • • •   55 OISIN 3   V 118
    . . . TURNING AND TURNING GO, • • • • • • •   57 OISIN 3   145
    . . . TURNING AND TURNING GO, • • • • • • •   57 OISIN 3   145
    SING, TURNING IN YOUR CARS, • • • • • • •   73 ANASHU VIJAYA   44
    TURNING, HE SAW THAT SHE HAD THRUST DEAD LEAVES • •   80 EPHEMERA   18
    AND LAY IN THE DARKNESS, GRUNTING, AND TURNING TO HIS REST.   153 CHANGE BELOVED 12
    TURNING AND TURNING IN THE WIDENING GYRE • • • •   401 SECOND COMING   1
    TURNING AND TURNING IN THE WIDENING GYRE • • • •   401 SECOND COMING   1
TURNS
    AND THE KINGFISHER TURNS TO A BALL OF DUST, • • • •   27 OISIN 1   V 418
    AND THE KINGFISHER TURNS TO A BALL OF DUST, • • • •   28 OISIN 1   V 422
    YET STILL SHE TURNS HER RESTLESS HEAD; • • • • •   65 HAPPY SHEPHERD   5
    THERE'S NOT A WOMAN TURNS HER FACE • • • • •   131 OLD PENSIONER   13
    THAT TURNS AND CHANGES LIKE HIS DRAUGHTY SEAS? • •   265 ABBEY THEATRE   12
    SHE TURNS THE DOLLS' FACES TO THE WALL • • • •   363 DOLLS FACES   T
    FAIL, AND THAT HISTORY TURNS INTO RUBBISH, • • • •   546 TO SAME TUNE 2   21
    FAIL, AND THAT HISTORY TURNS INTO RUBBISH, • • • •   614 MARCH SONGS 1   21
    TURNS INTO A QUESTION TILL • • • • • • •   632 MAN AND ECHO   8
    HE TURNS WHERE, HUNG LIKE DROPS OF DRIPPING GOLD, •   710 FERENCZ RENYI   18
    HE TURNS WHERE, HUNG LIKE DROPS OF LIQUID GOLD, • •   710 FERENCZ RENYI V 18
    AWAY HER CLINGING HANDS, AND TURNS. SHE THROWS •   714 FERENCZ RENYI   102
    HER OFF AND TURNS AWAY. SHE THROWS • • • • •   714 FERENCZ RENYI V 102
TUUS
    EGO DOMINUS TUUS • • • • • • • • • • •   367 EGO DOMINUS   T
TWAIN
    TO EAGLES TWAIN THAT, FULL OF ANCIENT PRIDE, • • •   34 OISIN 2   V 73
    HAS CLOVEN AND RENT THEIR HEARTS IN TWAIN, • • •   66 HAPPY SHEPHERD   33
    HAS TORN AND RENT THEIR HEARTS IN TWAIN, • • • •   66 HAPPY SHEPHERD V 33
    FROM MORN THE TWAIN UNTIL THE EVENING PALES • • •   651 ISLE STAT I 1   161
    THOSE TWAIN ARE DUST. WAKE! LIGHT AS A BEE SIPS • •   678 ISLE STAT II 3 290
TWANGING
    AND FEARED ALWAYS THE BOW-STRING'S TWANGING. • • •   3 OISIN 1   V 7GG
'TWEEN
    AND 'TWEEN HIS EARS, ABOVE HIS MANE, • • • • •   2 OISIN 1   V 7AA
    SHOUTED A MOMENT 'TWEEN THE EARTH AND SKY. • • •   675 ISLE STAT II 3 237
TWELFTH
    BECAUSE THE HERO'S CRESCENT IS THE TWELFTH. • • •   374 PHASES OF MOON   47
    BECAUSE THE HEROES' CRESCENT IS THE TWELFTH. • • •   374 PHASES OF MOON V 47
TWELVE
    OUTRODE HIS TROOP THAT AFTER TWELVE MONTHS' WAR • •   276 TWO KINGS   V   1
    AND WONDER WHAT HAS AILED HIM THESE TWELVE MONTHS." •   284 TWO KINGS   163
    HAS TWELVE KNIGHTS OVERTHROWN! • • • • • • •   740 EARL PAUL   8
    FOR HE HAD OVERTHROWN TWELVE KNIGHTS • • • • •   741 EARL PAUL   43
    OF THE TWELVE KINGS OF THE WORLD TO BE MY KING, • •   757 SHADOW WATER A   214
    AND HAVE BEEN WOOED BY THE TWELVE KINGS OF THE EARTH, •   757 SHADOW WATER A V 214
    I FOUGHT TWELVE BATTLES DRESSED IN GOLDEN ARMOUR. •   761 SHADOW WATER A   271
TWELVE-HOURED
    I CRIED, "O NIAMH! O WHITE ONE! IF ONLY A TWELVE-HOURED   55 OISIN 3   113
        DAY,

		PAGE	TITLE		LINE

TWELVEMONTH
    MAYBE A TWELVEMONTH SINCE • • • • • • • • • • •   348 FISHERMAN   25
    MAY BE A TWELVEMONTH SINCE • • • • • • • • • •   348 FISHERMAN   V   25
TWELVE—MONTH
    MAYBE A TWELVE—MONTH SINCE • • • • • • • • •   348 FISHERMAN   V   25
TWENTIES
    ALL HIS TWENTIES CRAMMED WITH TOIL: • • • • • • •   576 WHAT THEN   4
TWENTY   SEE SIX—AND—TWENTY FIVE—AND—TWENTY NINETEEN—TWENTY—NINE
    SENT FOR HIS DRUIDS TWENTY SCORE AND TEN, • • • •   110 CUCHULAIN SEA V 76
    WHEN THEY HAVE TWENTY YEARS: IN MIDDLE LIFE • • • • 229 SHADOW WATER B   156
    A BOY OF TWENTY YEARS:——A MOUND AND STONE • • • • • 276 TWO KINGS   V   F
    AND AFTER TWENTY YEARS THEY LAID • • • • • • • •   360 ALF POLLEXFEN   6
    FIVE AND TWENTY YEARS HAVE GONE • • • • • • • • •   360 ALF POLLEXFEN V   1
    AND SURELY AFTER TWENTY YEARS IT WAS TIME TO COME." • • • 391 UNDER SATURN   14
    THAT TWENTY CENTURIES OF STONY SLEEP • • • • • • •   402 SECOND COMING   19
    I THOUGHT IT ALL OUT TWENTY YEARS AGO: • • • • • •   411 TOWER   64
    AND TWENTY MINUTES MORE OR LESS • • • • • • • • •   501 VACILLATION   42
    SOME TWENTY FEET FROM TIP TO TIP HAD IT STRETCHED RIGHTLY 593 PILGRIM   17
        OUT,
    SOME TWENTY FEET FROM TIP TO TIP HAD ITS WINGS STRETCHED   593 PILGRIM V 17
        RIGHTLY OUT,
    FOR TWENTY MINUTES IN SOME STUDIO. • • • • • • •   602 GALLERY REVIS   16
    WHAT IF MY GREAT—GRANDDAD HAD A PAIR THAT WERE TWENTY FOOT 622 HIGH TALK   2
        HIGH,
TWENTY—AND—EIGHT
    TWENTY—AND—EIGHT THE PHASES OF THE MOON, • • • • • 373 PHASES OF MOON   31
    TWENTY—AND—EIGHT, AND YET BUT SIX—AND—TWENTY • • • • 373 PHASES OF MOON 33
TWICE
    AND TWICE A HUNDRED WERE THE VASSALS • • • • • • •   23 OISIN 1   V 345E
    AND YET, TWICE BORN, TWICE BURIED, GROW HE MUST, • • • • 374 PHASES OF MOON 48
    AND YET, TWICE BORN, TWICE BURIED, GROW HE MUST, • • • • 374 PHASES OF MOON 48
    AND TWICE A THOUSAND MORE • • • • • • • • • • •   401 DEMON BEAST   47
    GAME—BIRD, NOR WOMAN DOES THE SAME THING TWICE: • • • 463 HARUN RASHID   60
    GAME BIRD, OR WOMAN DOES THE SAME THING TWICE: • • • 463 HARUN RASHID V   60
    GAMEBIRD, NOR WOMAN DOES THE SAME THING TWICE: • • • 463 HARUN RASHID V   60
    AND LOUDLY TWICE THE LIVING WINGS FLAPT WIDE, • • •   659 ISLE STAT II 1   12
    BUT THE MAN IS TWICE FORLORN, • • • • • • • • • • 776 AGAINST WITCH V   26
TWIG
    ALL KNOW THEIR TALE, ALL KNOW WHAT LEAF AND TWIG, • • • 555 RIBH AT TOMB   7
TWIGS
    BUT THE RIGHT TWIGS FOR AN EAGLE'S NEST: • • • • •   288 TO WEALTHY MAN   36
    AND DROP TWIGS LAYER UPON LAYER. • • • • • • • •   415 TOWER   168
TWILIGHT
    IN THE POPPY—HUNG HOUSE OF THE TWILIGHT FLUTED: • • •   8 OISIN 1   V   83
    "JOY DROWNS THE TWILIGHT IN THE DEW, • • • • • • •   18 OISIN 1   261
    OF TWILIGHT WHEN HE'S WEARY. • • • • • • • • • •   32 OISIN 2   V 50H
    OF TWILIGHT AND SLUMBER WERE GONE, AND THAT HOOFS 54 OISIN 3   112
        IMPATIENTLY STEPT.
    PIERCING THE TWILIGHT WITH THEIR MURMURING BARBS. • • •   72 ANASHU VIJAYA   28
    AND THE FLAME OF THE BLUE STAR OF TWILIGHT, • • • • 122 WHITE BIRDS   3
    AND SANG HOW DAY A DRUID TWILIGHT SHEDS • • • • •   126 DREAM OF FAERY V 7
    AND OF THE WAYWARD TWILIGHT COMPANIES • • • • •   136 TO SOME I TALK   6
    AND OF THE WANDERING TWILIGHT COMPANIES • • • • •   136 TO SOME I TALK V 6
    AWAY, COME AWAY, TO THE DIM TWILIGHT. • • • • • •   140 HOSTING SIDHE   8
    INTO THE TWILIGHT • • • • • • • • • • • • •   147 INTO TWILIGHT   T
    THE CELTIC TWILIGHT • • • • • • • • • • • •   147 INTO TWILIGHT   T
    LAUGH, HEART, AGAIN IN THE GREY TWILIGHT, • • • •   147 INTO TWILIGHT   3
    DEW EVER SHINING AND TWILIGHT GREY: • • • • • •   148 INTO TWILIGHT   6
    AND LOVE IS LESS KIND THAN THE GREY TWILIGHT, • • • 148 INTO TWILIGHT   15
    DROWNING LOVE'S LONELY HOUR IN DEEP TWILIGHT OF REST, • • • 154 BELOVED PEACE 11
    IN TWILIGHT SHAKEN WITH LOW SIGHS: • • • • • • •   156 FORGOT BEAUTY V 10B
    THE TWILIGHT OF FORGIVENESS • • • • • • • • • •   162 ASKS FORGIVE   T
    AND COVER YOUR LIPS WITH ODOROUS TWILIGHT AND SAY: • • • 162 ASKS FORGIVE   5
    COVER YOUR LIPS WITH ROSE—HEAVY TWILIGHT, AND SAY: • • • 162 ASKS FORGIVE V 5
    THE ODOROUS TWILIGHT THERE. • • • • • • • • • •   163 ASKS FORGIVE   24
    THE ROSE—HEAVY TWILIGHT THERE. • • • • • • • • •   163 ASKS FORGIVE V   24
    AND WHEN THE SECOND TWILIGHT BROUGHT • • • • • •   296 THREE BEGGARS   42
    UNDER THE OCTOBER TWILIGHT THE WATER • • • • • •   322 SWANS AT COOLE   3
    ALL'S CHANGED SINCE I, HEARING AT TWILIGHT, • • • • 322 SWANS AT COOLE   15
    AND MAY DEPARTING TWILIGHT KEEP • • • • • • • •   435 FOR MY SON   5
    AH! IT DWELT WITHIN THE TWILIGHT AS THE WORM WITHIN THE   718 PHANTOM SHIP   6
        NUT.
    THAT I WOULD SHED LIKE TWILIGHT OVER YOU. • • • • • 765 SHADOW WATER A 352
TWILIGHTS
    IN TWILIGHTS OF DEW AND OF FIRE." • • • • • • •   168 BLESSED   40
    IN TWILIGHTS OF DEW AND FIRE!" • • • • • • • •   168 BLESSED   V   40
TWIN—BORN
    WHAT ARE THE TWIN—BORN WATERS, • • • • • • • • •   680 LOVE AND DEATH   15
TWINE
    UNMINDFUL OF ITS WOES, WOULD TWINE A WREATH • • • • 650 ISLE STAT I 1   133
TWINED
    THAT JUGGLING NATURE MOUNTS, HER COIL IN THEIR EMBRACES   556 RIBH PATRICK   9
        TWINED.
TWINKLING
    WITH A TWINKLING OF ANCIENT HANDS. • • • • • • •   144 HOST OF AIR   24
    GROWS YOUNG AND A MAN'S HEART GROWS OLD IN A TWINKLING.   761 SHADOW WATER A 263
TWIST
    THE WEASEL'S TWIST, THE WEASEL'S TOOTH. • • • • • • 431 NINETEEN 19   92
TWISTED   SEE TRUMPET—TWISTED
    OUT OF THE MOON'S PALE TWISTED SHELL: • • • • • •   19 OISIN 1   279
    IT FELL, OR FROM THE TWISTED MOON • • • • • • •   19 OISIN 1   V 278

842

	PAGE	TITLE		LINE

TWISTED (CONTINUED)
SOME TWISTED, ECHO-HARBOURING SHELL, ... 66 HAPPY SHEPHERD   36
WERE TWISTED LIKE THE OLD THORN-TREES . . . . 208 OLD MEN ADMIRE   5
WERE TWISTED LIKE THE OLD THORN TREES . . . . 208 OLD MEN ADMIRE V   5
WHO HAS SEEN A GARDEN IMAGE OR TWISTED TREE . . . . . 279 TWO KINGS   V   45B
MY ARMS ARE LIKE THE TWISTED THORN . . . . 455 HIS MEMORIES   11
UNTIL MY BEARD IS IN THE TWISTED LEAVES . . . . 683 SEEKER   44
ONE SHOULDER TWISTED, AND THE CHILDREN CRY . . . . . 695 MOSADA 1   116
TWITTER
AROUND THE TWITTER OF THE LIPS OF DUST . . . . 685 DRAWING-ROOM   1
"AROUND, THE TWITTER OF THE LIPS OF DUST . . . . . . 735 QUATRAIN APHOR   21
'TWIXT
THE HOST IS RUSHING 'TWIXT NIGHT AND DAY, ... 141 HOSTING SIDHE   13
TWO   SEE NINETEEN-THIRTY-TWO
"WERE THESE TWO BORN IN THE DANAAN LAND, ...   12 OISIN 1   146
BUT NOW TWO THINGS DEVOUR MY LIFE; . . . .   24 OISIN 1   358
TWO THINGS THAT 'FORE ALL ELSE I HATE, ...   24 OISIN 1   V 359
TWO WALLS, A ROOF, A FLOOD: THERE TREMBLING GREEN . .   31 OISIN 2   V   32
TO TWO OLD EAGLES, FULL OF ANCIENT PRIDE, ...   34 OISIN 2   74
THOSE TWO CAME CARRYING WINE AND MEAT AND BREAD, . .   41 OISIN 2   184
. . . TWO CARRIED A SACK FULL OF SAND, ...   60 OISIN 3   185
. . . THE SOUND OF TWO STUMBLING APART. . . . .   60 OISIN 3   V 184
WITH WISDOM HOUR BY HOUR.--MAY WE TWO STAND, ...   71 ANASHU VIJAYA   7
A CROSS THEY HAD MADE OUT OF TWO BITS OF WOOD, . . . 123 DREAM OF DEATH   7
THE TWO TREES . . . . 134 TWO TREES   T
TWO POEMS CONCERNING PEASANT VISIONARIES A CRADLE SONG 146 UNAPPEAS HOST V   T
TWO LOVE POEMS THE SHADOWY HORSES . . . . 154 BELOVED PEACE V   T
TWO POEMS BY O'SULLIVAN THE RED CONCERNING MARY LAVELL. 157 POET BELOVED   V   T
FOR HAPPY LOVERS PASSED TWO BY TWO WHERE I STOOD; . . 163 VALLEY LOVERS   2
FOR HAPPY LOVERS PASSED TWO BY TWO WHERE I STOOD; . . 163 VALLEY LOVERS   2
WHO HAS BEEN BURIED SOME TWO THOUSAND YEARS? . . . . 181 QUEEN MAEVE   35
UNTIL TWO LOVERS CAME OUT OF THE AIR . . . . 187 QUEEN MAEVE   143
BAILE'S HEART WAS BROKEN IN TWO; . . . . 192 BAILE AILLINN   70
ALTHOUGH HE IS CARRYING STONE, BUT TWO . . . . 192 BAILE AILLINN   83
TWO SWANS CAME FLYING UP TO HIM, ... 194 BAILE AILLINN   135
OR TWO SWEET BLOSSOMING APPLE-BOUGHS . . . . 195 BAILE AILLINN   153
OR THE TWO STRINGS THAT MADE ONE SOUND . . . . 195 BAILE AILLINN   155
OR TWO SWEET BLOSSOMING APPLE BOUGHS . . . . 195 BAILE AILLINN V 153
THOSE OTHER TWO; FOR NEVER YET . . . . 197 BAILE AILLINN   205
THE OLD BROWN THORN-TREES BREAK IN TWO HIGH OVER CUMMEN 206 HANRAHANS SONG   1
   STRAND,
THE OLD BROWN THORN TREES BREAK IN TWO HIGH OVER CUMANN'S 206 HANRAHANS SONG V 1
   STRAND,
WHOSE HEART WOULD BREAK IN TWO, ... 213 HAPPY TOWNLAND   2
YET NEVER HAVE TWO LOVERS KISSED BUT THEY . . . . . . 229 SHADOW WATER B   153
THE YEW-BOUGH HAS BEEN BROKEN INTO TWO, ... 241 SHADOW WATER B   394
THE YEW BOUGH HAS BEEN BROKEN INTO TWO, ... 241 SHADOW WATER B   394
THE YEW-BOUGH HAS BEEN BROKEN INTO TWO, ... 251 SHADOW WATER B   593
THE ROPE'S IN TWO--IT FALLS INTO THE SEA, ... 251 SHADOW WATER B   596
SHALL BE ALONE FOR EVER. WE TWO--THIS CROWN-- . . . 251 SHADOW WATER B   605
O SILVER FISH THAT MY TWO HANDS HAVE TAKEN . . . . . 251 SHADOW WATER B   609
THE YEW BOUGH HAS BEEN BROKEN INTO TWO, ... 251 SHADOW WATER B V 593
THE YEW BOUGH HAS BEEN BROKEN IN TWO, ... 251 SHADOW WATER B V 593
A SECRET BETWEEN YOU TWO, ... 259 UNWORTH PRAISE   9
AND SAID, "IN TWO OR IN THREE YEARS . . . . 272 GREY ROCK   46
I'D PROMISED HIM TWO HUNDRED YEARS, ... 275 GREY ROCK   98
THE TWO KINGS . . . . 276 TWO KINGS   T
TWO YEARS LATER . . . . 312 TWO YEAR LATER   T
DARE MATCH IN LEARNING WITH US TWO, ... 333 SOLOMON SHEBA   21
AND TWO OR THREE HAD CHARM, ... 350 MEMORY   2
ANOTHER BOASTS, "I PICK AND CHOOSE AND HAVE BUT TWO OR 354 HIS PHOENIX   20
   THREE."
WHEN TWO CLOSE KINDRED MEET, ... 378 CAT AND MOON   12
TWO SONGS OF A FOOL . . . . 380 SONGS FOOL 1   T
STRETCHED UP ON TWO LEGS FROM THE MAT, ... 381 SONGS FOOL 2   7
AND RIGHT BETWEEN THESE TWO A GIRL AT PLAY . . . . . 383 VISION ROBART   21
YET THE WORLD ENDS WHEN THESE TWO THINGS, ... 388 SOLOMON WITCH   28
TWO MEN HAVE FOUNDED HERE. A MAN-AT-ARMS . . . . . . 420 MY HOUSE   21
TWO MEN HAVE FOUND IT HERE. A MAN-AT-ARMS . . . . . 420 MY HOUSE   V   21
TWO HEAVY TRESTLES, AND A BOARD . . . . 421 MY TABLE   1
TWO SONGS FROM A PLAY . . . . 437 SONGS PLAY 1   T
TOLD, AND IT SEEMED THAT OUR TWO NATURES BLENT . . . 443 SCHOOL CHILDR   13
TWO SONGS FROM THE OLD COUNTRYMAN . . . . 454 EMPTY CUP   V   T
TWO CONTEMPLATING PASSIONS CHOSE ONE THEME . . . . . 466 HARUN RASHID   117
AND TWO LONG GLASSES BRIMMED WITH MUSCATEL . . . . . 470 ALL SOUL NIGHT   4
TWO THOUGHTS WERE SO MIXED UP I COULD NOT TELL . . . 471 ALL SOUL NIGHT   31
TWO GIRLS IN SILK KIMONOS, BOTH . . . . 475 EVA GORE-BOOTH   3
TWO GIRLS IN SILK KIMONOS, BOTH . . . . 475 EVA GORE-BOOTH   19
TO SING A SONG OR TWO, ... 515 GIRLS SONG B   2
I BROKE MY HEART IN TWO . . . . 518 HIS CONFIDENCE   7
TWO SONGS REWRITTEN FOR THE TUNE'S SAKE . . . . 550 SONGS REWRIT 1   T
BETWEEN TWO BARRELS AT THE INN. . . . . 551 SONGS REWRIT 1   10
BETWEEN TWO BUSHES UNDER THE RAIN; . . . . 551 SONGS REWRIT 1   14
TWO CHINAMEN, BEHIND THEM A THIRD, ... 566 LAPIS LAZULI   37
AND THERE TWO BUSHES PLANTED . . . . 571 THREE BUSHES   59
LOVE CRAM LOVE'S TWO DIVISIONS . . . . 573 LADYS 2ND SONG   12
WE'D DRINK A CAN OR TWO, ... 606 SONGS BURDEN 1   22
THAT ON TWO WHEELS RAN . . . . 628 JANE MOUNTAIN   14
PROPPED UPON MY TWO KNEES, ... 628 JANE MOUNTAIN   19
THERE IN A TWO HORSED CARRIAGE . . . . 628 JANE MOUNTAIN V   13
A BUNDLE OF LINEN. SHROUDS BY TWO AND THREE . . . . 634 CUCHULAIN COMF   9

843

		PAGE	TITLE	LINE

TWO   (CONTINUED)

BETWEEN HIS TWO ETERNITIES, ... 637 BEN BULBEN   14
SHE SLEEPS WITH OWLETS TWO AND TWO, ... 646 ISLE STAT I 1   34
SHE SLEEPS WITH OWLETS TWO AND TWO, ... 646 ISLE STAT I 1   34
I'D BE ALONE. WE TWO, BY THAT PALE FOUNT, ... 650 ISLE STAT I 1   132
BUT WIDE AWAKE HIS TWO EYES WERE. . . . . 655 ISLE STAT I 3   7
HE PASSED ACROSS THE LAKE. WHEN WE TWO CAME . . 658 ISLE STAT II 1   5
OF HILL TWO SHEPHERDS COME. FAREWELL! I'LL DON   659 ISLE STAT II 1   28
TWO MEN WHO LOVE ONE MAID HAVE AMPLE CAUSE . . . . 659 ISLE STAT II 1   30
OF WAR. OF YORE, TWO SHEPHERDS, WHERE WE PAUSE, 659 ISLE STAT II 1   31
THIS THING WE ASK! MUST WE TWO FIGHT?--JUDGE THOU. 660 ISLE STAT II 1   41
TWO CAME, HIS NAME AND MINE ON MANY A TREE . . . . 662 ISLE STAT II 2   10
FOR, AH, OUR LIVES WERE BUT TWO STARRY WORDS . . 675 ISLE STAT II 3   236
TWO LONELY SPIRITS WAIT, ... 680 LOVE AND DEATH   18
TWO SPIRIT THINGS A MAN HATH FOR HIS FRIENDS! . . 686 DRAWING-ROOM   5
THE TWO TITANS, ... 687 TWO TITANS   T
TWO FIGURES CROUCHING ON THE BLACK ROCK, BOUND   687 TWO TITANS   5
WE TWO, BEFORE WE DIE! FOR AZOLAR, ... 691 MOSADA 1   24
WE MEET--WE TWO. HOW MERRY ALL THESE ARE . . . 691 MOSADA 1   31
TWO ONLY NOW THEY ARE, TWO SIDE BY SIDE. . . . . 700 MOSADA 3   49
TWO ONLY NOW THEY ARE, TWO SIDE BY SIDE. . . . . 700 MOSADA 3   49
MY SOUL SHALL TOUCH WITH HIS, AND THE TWO FLAMES 701 MOSADA 3   61
MY COMPANIONS, TWO AND TWO, ... 705 DAWN-SONG   7
MY COMPANIONS, TWO AND TWO, ... 705 DAWN-SONG   7
LADS AND LASSES, TWO AND TWO, ... 705 DAWN-SONG   15
LADS AND LASSES, TWO AND TWO, ... 705 DAWN-SONG   15
A LIZARD CRAWLS--THE TWO MEN GAZE INTENT, ... 711 FERENCZ RENYI   47
TWO WOMEN, WITHERED ONE AND SMALL AND THIN, . . . 711 FERENCZ RENYI   51
BELOVED, HOW TWO LITTLE YEARS AGO . . . . 713 FERENCZ RENYI   89
THERE FAR AWAY FROM ALL WE TWO WILL GO, ... 714 FERENCZ RENYI   99
FROM HAYNAU'S LIFTED FINGERS--TWO DRAW NIGH . . 714 FERENCZ RENYI   104
ARE TWO RAGGED CHILDREN BRIGHT-- . . . . 731 STREET DANCERS   4
TWO SPIRIT-THINGS A MAN HATH FOR HIS FRIENDS-- . 734 QUATRAIN APHOR   5
TWO SPIRIT THINGS A MAN HATH FOR HIS FRIENDS! . . 734 QUATRAIN APHOR V   5
AMONG THESE MISTY WATERS. TWO! NOW FOUR! . . . . 753 SHADOW WATER A   138
TWO HOVER THERE TOGETHER, AND ONE SAYS, ... 753 SHADOW WATER A   142
O SILVER FISH THAT MY TWO HANDS HAVE TAKEN . . . 769 SHADOW WATER A   425
BETWEEN TWO FURROWS UPON THE PLOUGHED LAND! . . . 784 WOMANS BEAUTY   4

TWO-HORSED

THERE IN A TWO-HORSED CARRIAGE . . . . 628 JANE MOUNTAIN   13

TWOS

CHILDREN SING IN TWOS AND THREES. . . . . 732 STREET DANCERS   17
THE FLIES THAT DANCE IN THREES, IN TWOS, ... 736 IN CHURCH   11

TYING

TYING THE HORSE TO HIS VAST FOOT THAT LAY . . . . 32 OISIN 2   46
WE MOUNTED ON THE STAIR, THE WHITE STEED TYING, . 32 OISIN 2   V 46

TYMPAN

AND SAW WHERE THIS OLD TYMPAN LAY . . . . 85 MAD KING GOLL   55

TYRANNY

AT HUMAN TYRANNY, ... 131 OLD PENSIONER   10

TYRANT

AND MADE THE TYRANT BOW. . . . . 738 MOURN THEN ON   12

TYRANTS

NOR TO THE TYRANTS THAT SPAT, ... 414 TOWER   131

UDDERS

WITH FAIRY-SMITTEN UDDERS DRY-- . . . . 716 FAIRY DOCTOR   14

UGLINESS

THEY SAY I AM ALL UGLINESS! LAME-FOOTED . . . . . 692 MOSADA 1   60

ULADH

ON THE HEIR OF ULADH, BUAN'S SON, ... 189 BAILE AILLINN   4
WHERE THE HOUND OF ULADH SAT BEFORE . . . . 192 BAILE AILLINN   73
NOR ULADH, WHEN NAOISE HAD THROWN A SAIL UPON THE WIND! 209 UNDER THE MOON 4
OR ULADH WHEN NAISI HAD HUNG A SAIL UPON THE WIND! . 209 UNDER THE MOON V 4

ULALU

BUT LIFT A MOURNFUL ULALU, ... 86 MAD KING GOLL   68

ULULU

AND LIFT AN ULULU FORLORN, ... 86 MAD KING GOLL   V 68

UNAFRAID

THOSE GLANCES UNAFRAID! . . . . 516 MANS SONG   8

UNAGEING

MONUMENTS OF UNAGEING INTELLECT. . . . . 407 SAIL BYZANTIUM   8

UNAMBITIOUS

A HUMOROUS, UNAMBITIOUS MAN, ... 361 ALF POLLEXFEN   25
BECAUSE THE UNAMBITIOUS THAT HATE THE GODS . . . 754 SHADOW WATER A V 158

UNAPPEASABLE

THE UNAPPEASABLE HOST . . . . 146 UNAPPEAS HOST   T
O HEART THE WINDS HAVE SHAKEN, THE UNAPPEASABLE HOST . 147 UNAPPEAS HOST   11
AND HEART THE WINDS HAVE SHAKEN! THE UNAPPEASABLE HOST . 147 UNAPPEAS HOST V 11
AND HEAR THE WINDS HAVE SHAKEN, THE UNAPPEASABLE HOST 147 UNAPPEAS HOST V 11
THE MOUNTAIN OF THE GODS, THE UNAPPEASABLE GODS 764 SHADOW WATER A   332

UNASSAILABLE

IMAGINE THAT SOME LOST LOVE, UNASSAILABLE . . . . 390 UNDER SATURN   V   2

UNAVAILING

THE UNAVAILING OUTCRIES AND THE OLD BITTERNESS . . 198 SEVEN WOODS   4

UNBAFFLED

EACH SHINING CLEAR AS SOME UNBAFFLED STAR! . . . 656 ISLE STAT I 3   25

UNBEGOTTEN

OR THOSE BEGOTTEN OR UNBEGOTTEN . . . . 599 SPIRIT MEDIUM   5
OR THOSE BEGOTTEN OR UNBEGOTTEN, ... 599 SPIRIT MEDIUM   9
SOME THAT BEING UNBEGOTTEN . . . . 600 SPIRIT MEDIUM   11

844

	PAGE	TITLE	LINE

UNBENT
    CONSTRAINED, ARRAIGNED, BAFFLED, BENT AND UNBENT • • • • 382 VISION ROBART 9
UNBID
    AND TELL ME THAT YOU FOUND A MAN UNBID, • • • • • • • 33 OISIN 2 67
    AND TELL ME HOW YOU CAME TO ONE UNBID, • • • • • • • 33 OISIN 2 V 67
    WHEN THOUGHTS RISE UP UNBID • • • • • • • • • • • 473 ALL SOUL NIGHT 68
UNBIND
    HAD STRENGTH THAT COULD UNBIND • • • • • • • • • • 315 FRIENDS 11
    WHAT BONDS NO MAN COULD UNBIND, • • • • • • • • • 785 WOMANS BEAUTY 22
UNBLEMISHED
    OF HER UNBLEMISHED LINEAMENTS, A WHITENESS WITH NO STAIN, 353 HIS PHOENIX 3
UNBLESSED
    OF ANY UNBLESSED EARTHLY BIRD." • • • • • • • • • 697 MOSADA 2 33
UNBLEST
    BUT THOU WOULDST NOT, FOR THEN THOU WERT UNBLEST • • • 669 ISLE STAT II 3 90
UNBORN
    THINGS UNBORN, THINGS THAT ARE GONE, • • • • • • • • 562 NEEDLES EYE 3
UNBOUND
    OUR CHEEKS ARE PALE, OUR HAIR IS UNBOUND, • • • • • • 140 HOSTING SIDHE 7
    AND THE GIRDLE OF LIGHT IS UNBOUND, • • • • • • • • 165 CRY OF SEDGE 8
UNBROKEN
    OF AN UNBROKEN HAPPY MIND, • • • • • • • • • • • 626 OLD MEN BE MAD 14
UNCEASING
    AND ROVE UNCEASING ROUND THEIR DREADFUL BROOD. • • • • 681 SEEKER 5
UNCERTAINTY
    ON OUR UNCERTAINTY! SOMEWHERE • • • • • • • • • • 425 STARES NEST 7
    OR THE UNCERTAINTY OF HIS SETTING FORTH? • • • • • • 444 SCHOOL CHILDR 40
UNCHAINABLE
    UNCHAINABLE AS THE DIM TIDE, • • • • • • • • • • • 22 OISIN 1 338
UNCHANGEABLE
    THAT SEEMS UNLIKE ITSELF, THAT SEEMS UNCHANGEABLE, • • • 426 PHANTOM HATRED 4
UNCHANGED
    PADDLE AND ARE PERFECT. LEAVE UNCHANGED • • • • • • 357 BROKEN DREAMS 34
UNCHANGING
    THE MIND IS MADE UNCHANGING, FOR IT FINDS • • • • • • 227 SHADOW WATER B 101
    AND SEEMED UNCHANGING LIKE THE SWORD. • • • • • • • 421 MY TABLE 21
    THE SOUL'S UNCHANGING LOOK! • • • • • • • • • • • 422 MY TABLE 24
    UNCHANGING AND AT PEACE, AND IT IS RIGHT • • • • • • 465 HARUN RASHID 96
    NATURE'S PURE UNCHANGING LIGHT? • • • • • • • • • 529 TOM LUNATIC 6
    STANDS IN GOD'S UNCHANGING EYE • • • • • • • • • • 529 TOM LUNATIC 16
UNCHRISTENED
    HOMER IS MY EXAMPLE AND HIS UNCHRISTENED HEART. • • • • 503 VACILLATION 87
UNCIVIL
    SHE HAS NOT GROWN UNCIVIL • • • • • • • • • • • 365 HER RACE 1
UNCLES   SEE GREAT-UNCLES
    ON UNCLES, AUNTS, GREAT-UNCLES OR GREAT-AUNTS, • • • • 604 YOU CONTENT 3
UNCLOUDED
    THE PURITY OF THE UNCLOUDED MOON • • • • • • • • • 482 BLOOD AND MOON 31
UNCOILED
    HIS HEAVY RINGS UNCOILED FROM GLIMMERING DEEP TO DEEP! • • 174 ELEMENT POWERS 5
UNCOMELY
    ALL THINGS UNCOMELY AND BROKEN, ALL THINGS WORN OUT AND 142 ROSE IN HEART 1
        OLD,
    ALL THINGS UNCOMELY AND BROKEN, ALL THINGS WORN AND OLD, 142 ROSE IN HEART V 1
UNCOMPOSITE
    LIVE IN UNCOMPOSITE BLESSEDNESS, • • • • • • • • • 387 ROBARTES DANCE 46
UNCONQUERABLE
    ENTHRALLED BY THE UNCONQUERABLE DELUSION, • • • • • • 367 EGO DOMINUS 6
    THAT THIS UNCONQUERABLE LABYRINTH OF THE BIRDS, • • • • 481 BLOOD AND MOON 23
UNCONTROLLABLE
    THE UNCONTROLLABLE MYSTERY ON THE BESTIAL FLOOR. • • • • 318 MAGI 8
UNCOUNTED
    OF ALL THE UNCOUNTED BOOKS THAT I HAVE READ, • • • • • 467 HARUN RASHID 139
UNCOUTH
    SUCH MEN, SUCH HEARTS. BUT, UNCOUTH HUNTER, THOU • • • 651 ISLE STAT I 1 167
    KNOW'ST NAUGHT OF THIS. AND, UNCOUTH HUNTER, NOW-- • • • 651 ISLE STAT I 1 168
    AND WHITHER, UNCOUTH HUNTER? WHY SO FAST? • • • • • • 651 ISLE STAT I 2 1
UNDECAYED
    THE BODY OF SAINT TERESA LIES UNDECAYED IN TOMB, • • • • 503 VACILLATION 80
UNDER   SEE LAND-UNDER-WAVE
    UNDER THE GOLDEN EVENING LIGHT, • • • • • • • • • 25 OISIN 1 385
    THAT SPRANG UNDER THE SEVEN HAZEL TREES, • • • • • • 35 OISIN 2 84
    UNDER THE ROOF, AND WITH A STRAINING THROAT • • • • • 36 OISIN 2 106
    UNDER THE DEEPEST SHADOWS OF THE HALL • • • • • • • 37 OISIN 2 119
    PASSED UNDER THE DIM DOORWAY, OUT OF SIGHT, • • • • • 37 OISIN 2 123
    PASSED UNDER A DIM DOORWAY, OUT OF SIGHT, • • • • • • 37 OISIN 2 V 123
    UNDER A CROWN OF THORNS AND DARK WITH BLOOD, • • • • • 38 OISIN 2 135
    UNDER THE SHADOWS TILL THE TUMULTS DIED • • • • • • • 38 OISIN 2 140
    UNDER A BEECH AT ALMHUIN AND HEARD THE THIN • • • • • 44 OISIN 2 228
    WAR ON THE MIGHTIEST MEN UNDER THE SKIES, • • • • • • 45 OISIN 2 241
    UNDER THE STARLIGHT AND SHADOW, A MONSTROUS SLUMBERING 48 OISIN 3 27
        FOLK.
    AS A HAY-COCK OUT ON THE FLOOD, OR A WOLF SUCKED UNDER 63 OISIN 3 220
        A WEIR.
    AS A GRASS SEED CRUSHED BY A PEBBLE, AS A WOLF SUCKED UNDER 63 OISIN 3 V 220
        A WEIR.
    BURIED UNDER THE SLEEPY GROUND, • • • • • • • • • 67 HAPPY SHEPHERD 48
    THE ISLAND DREAMS UNDER THE DAWN • • • • • • • • • 77 INDIAN TO LOVE 1
    HID UNDER QUIET BOUGHS APART, • • • • • • • • • • 78 INDIAN TO LOVE 12
    HID UNDER QUIET BOWS APART, • • • • • • • • • • • 78 INDIAN TO LOVE V 12
    ARE BOWED IN SORROW UNDER PENDULOUS LIDS, • • • • • • 79 EPHEMERA 2

845

UNDER   (CONTINUED)
LIE NOW HALF HIDDEN UNDER PENDULOUS LIDS, ...   79 EPHEMERA   V   2
ARE BOWED IN SORROW UNDER THEIR TREMBLING LIDS, ...   79 EPHEMERA   V   2
AND UNDER THE BLINKING OF THE STARS . . . . . .   83 MAD KING GOLL   20
AND UNDER THE BLINK O' THE MORNING STAR, ...   83 MAD KING GOLL   V   20
UNDER THE BLESSED MOONLIGHT, ...   94 MOLL MAGEE   11
I FIND UNDER THE BOUGHS OF LOVE AND HATE, ...   101 ROSE UPON ROOD   10
YOU HAVE THE HEAVIEST ARM UNDER THE SKY." . . . . . .   107 CUCHULAIN SEA   24
"WHETHER UNDER ITS DAYLIGHT OR ITS STARS . . . . . .   107 CUCHULAIN SEA   25
"YET SOMEWHERE UNDER STARLIGHT OR THE SUN . . . . . .   107 CUCHULAIN SEA   28
"NO, SOMEWHERE UNDER DAYLIGHT OR THE STARS . . . . . .   107 CUCHULAIN SEA   V   25
"WHETHER UNDER ITS DAYLIGHT OR THE STARS . . . . . .   107 CUCHULAIN SEA   V   25
AND TEN BY TEN UNDER A QUICKEN TREE, ...   111 CUCHULAIN SEA   V 81A
UNDER THE PASSING STARS, FOAM OF THE SKY, ...   112 ROSE OF WORLD   9
THEY HAVE GONE DOWN UNDER THE SAME WHITE STARS, ...   115 ROSE OF BATTLE   34
BUT NOW LIES UNDER BOARDS. . . . .   123 DREAM OF DEATH   12
UNDER THAT WOVEN CHANGELESS ROOF OF BOUGHS! . . . .   126 DREAM OF FAERY   11
UNDER THE WOVEN ROOFS OF QUICKEN BOUGHS!— . . . . .   126 DREAM OF FAERY   V   11
BEFORE THEY HEAPED HIS GRAVE UNDER THE HILL! . . . . .   127 DREAM OF FAERY   16
UNDER THE GOLDEN OR THE SILVER SKIES! . . . . . .   127 DREAM OF FAERY   21
HE SLEPT UNDER THE HILL OF LUGNAGALL! . . . . . .   128 DREAM OF FAERY   37
UNDER THAT COLD AND VAPOUR-TURBANED STEEP, ...   128 DREAM OF FAERY   39
A HONIED RINGING! UNDER THE NEW SKIES . . . . . .   130 BOOK STORIES   V   21
UNDER A BROKEN TREE . . . .   131 OLD PENSIONER   2
OR UNDER GREEN SODS LAY. . . . .   132 FR GILLIGAN   4
ROOTS HALF HIDDEN UNDER SNOWS, ...   135 TWO TREES   27
AND ROOTS HALF HIDDEN UNDER SNOWS . . . .   135 TWO TREES   V   27
UNDER THE FRUIT OF EVIL AND OF GOOD! . . . . . .   137 TO SOME I TALK   9
AH, FAERIES, DANCING UNDER THE MOON, ...   139 TO IRELAND   31
FLAME UNDER FLAME, TILL TIME BE NO MORE! . . . . .   141 EVERLAST VOICE   4
UNDER MY FEET THAT THEY FOLLOW YOU NIGHT AND DAY, . .   153 CHANGE BELOVED   5
UNDER MY FEET, THAT I FOLLOW YOU, NIGHT AND DAY. . . .   153 CHANGE BELOVED   V   5
BUT FLAME ON FLAME, DEEP UNDER DEEP, ...   156 FORGOT BEAUTY   V   21
UNDER A CLOUD OF HER HAIR, ...   160 CAP AND BELLS   26
UNDER HER PURPLE HOOD. . . . .   171 MAID QUIET   V   8
UNDER THE DOCK-LEAVES IN THE GROUND, ...   176 BELOVED DEAD   12
I WOULD SPREAD THE CLOTHS UNDER YOUR FEET! . . . .   176 CLOTHS HEAVEN   5
I HAVE SPREAD MY DREAMS UNDER YOUR FEET! . . . . .   176 CLOTHS HEAVEN   7
AND SET THEM DIGGING UNDER BUAL'S HILL. . . . . .   184 QUEEN MAEVE   93
UNDER A CAIRN OF SLEEPY STONE . . . .   192 BAILE AILLINN   81
BUT THE GREY RUSH UNDER THE WIND . . . .   192 BAILE AILLINN   88
FAR OUT UNDER A WINDLESS SKY! . . . .   197 BAILE AILLINN   181
UNDER A BITTER BLACK WIND THAT BLOWS FROM THE LEFT HAND!   206 HANRAHANS SONG   2
UNDER THE BITTER BLACK WINDS BLOWING OUT OF THE LEFT HAND! 206 HANRAHANS SONG   V   2
UNDER THE MOON . . . .   209 UNDER THE MOON   T
BECAUSE OF SOMETHING TOLD UNDER THE FAMISHED HORN . .   210 UNDER THE MOON   17
BECAUSE OF SOMETHING I HEARD OF UNDER THE THIN HORN . .   210 UNDER THE MOON   V   17
BECAUSE OF A STORY I HEARD UNDER THE THIN HORN . . .   210 UNDER THE MOON   V   17
BECAUSE OF A STORY I HEARD UNDER A THIN HORN . . . .   210 UNDER THE MOON   V   17
I HEARD UNDER A RAGGED HOLLOW WOOD, ...   210 RAGGED WOOD   V   1
THE FLAGSTONE UNDER ALL, THE FIRE OF FIRES, ...   227 SHADOW WATER B   103
BECAUSE OF THAT OLD DRAUGHT UNDER THE DOOR, ...   228 SHADOW WATER B   127
IN HAPPY DANCES UNDER A WINDY MOON, ...   245 SHADOW WATER B   470
SHIVER UNDER THE LASH, STRAIN, SWEAT AND JOLT . . . .   260 FASC DIFFICULT   7
"I BID THEM MAKE HIS BED UNDER THIS ROOF . . . .   280 TWO KINGS   87
UNDER THE EYELIDS OF ANOTHER, FOR IT WAS MY CRAFT . .   284 TWO KINGS   156
UNDER A BOW, HE CRIED, "WHAT HAPPINESS . . . . .   284 TWO KINGS   177
UNDER AN ALIEN EYELID, FOR IT WAS MY CRAFT . . . .   284 TWO KINGS   V 156
AMONG THE STONES AND THORN-TREES, UNDER MORNING LIGHT; .   291 PAUDEEN   3
AMONG THE STONES AND THORN TREES, UNDER MORNING LIGHT, .   291 PAUDEEN   V   3
I CHOSE THIS BURROW UNDER GROUND, ...   305 HOUR DAWN   73
AT KYLE-NA-NO UNDER THAT ANCIENT ROOF . . . . .   321 REED WHISPERER   7
UNDER THE OCTOBER TWILIGHT THE WATER . . . . . .   322 SWANS AT COOLE   3
UNDER THE ROUND TOWER . . . .   331 ROUND TOWER   T
BORN UNDER THE SKIES . . . .   333 SOLOMON SHEBA   20
UNDER HIS FINGERS. I HAD IT FROM HIS MOTHER, . . .   339 SHEP GOATHERD   26
WHERE STONE IS DARK UNDER FROTH, ...   348 FISHERMAN   32
UNDER YOUR OLD WIND-BEATEN TOWER, WHERE STILL . . .   367 EGO DOMINUS   2
UNDER THE FRENZY OF THE FOURTEENTH MOON, ...   374 PHASES OF MOON   53
STAND UNDER THE ROUGH ROOF-TIMBERS OF THE HALL . . .   377 PHASES OF MOON   125
UNDER THE THREE LAST CRESCENTS OF THE MOON, ...   377 PHASES OF MOON   133
UNDER THIS HUMP. GOD TRIES EACH MAN . . . . . .   379 SAINT HUNCH   5
UNDER BLANK EYES AND FINGERS NEVER STILL . . . . .   382 VISION ROBART   5
"LAST NIGHT, WHERE UNDER THE WILD MOON . . . . .   387 SOLOMON WITCH   2
UNDER SATURN . . . .   390 UNDER SATURN   T
UNDER BEN BULBEN TO THE MEET, ...   397 POLIT PRISONER   14
WHILE UNDER ITS STORM-BEATEN BREAST . . . . . .   397 POLIT PRISONER   23
UNDER THE FIRST COLD GLEAM OF DAY? . . . . . .   398 BREAK OF DAY   4
UNDER THIS CRADLE-HOOD AND COVERLID . . . . . .   403 FOR DAUGHTER   2
AND UNDER THE ARCHES OF THE BRIDGE, AND SCREAM . . .   403 FOR DAUGHTER   11
UNDER THE OLD WIND-BROKEN TREE, ...   406 IN TIME OF WAR   3
UNDER THE DAY'S DECLINING BEAM, AND CALL . . . . .   410 TOWER   21
HE SO BEWITCHED THE CARDS UNDER HIS THUMB . . . . .   411 TOWER   67
UNDER ECLIPSE AND THE DAY BLOTTED OUT. . . . . .   414 TOWER   120
THAT UNDER BURSTING DAWN . . . .   416 TOWER   176
UNDER ITS ROCKY HOLE. . . . .   420 MY HOUSE   V 20C
THE FINEST PLAY UNDER THE SUN. . . . .   424 ROAD AT DOOR   5
VALLEY, RIVER, AND ELMS, UNDER THE LIGHT OF A MOON . .   426 PHANTOM HATRED   3
WHERE EVEN LONGING DROWNS UNDER ITS OWN EXCESS! . . .   426 PHANTOM HATRED   22
VALLEY, RIVER, ELMS, UNDER THE LIGHT OF A MOON . . .   426 PHANTOM HATRED   V   3
AND PLANNED TO BRING THE WORLD UNDER A RULE, ...   429 NINETEEN 19   31

UNDER (CONTINUED)

	PAGE	TITLE		LINE
UNDER THE SHADOW OF STUPID STRAW-PALE LOCKS,	433	NINETEEN 19		127
UNDER A BROKEN TREE.	452	HUMAN DIGNITY		8
WE SAT UNDER AN OLD THORN-TREE	456	SUMMER SPRING		1
UNDER THAT VERY TREE.	457	SUMMER SPRING		12
AS AIR UNDER A WING, CAN GIVE BIRDS' WIT.	462	HARUN RASHID		28
AS AIR UNDER A WING, CAN GIVE BIRD'S WIT.	462	HARUN RASHID	V	28
UNDER IT WISDOM STANDS, AND I ALONE--	469	HARUN RASHID		189
UNDER IT ARMED WISDOM STANDS, A SEPARATE WISDOM	469	HARUN RASHID	V	189
BUT UNDER HEAVY LOADS OF TRAMPLED CLAY	483	OIL AND BLOOD		4
UNDER THE RECEDING WAVE.	485	NINETEENTH CEN		4
UNDER MY WINDOW-LEDGE THE WATERS RACE,	490	COOLE BALLYLEE		1
NOW ALL DRY STICKS UNDER A WINTRY SUN,	490	COOLE BALLYLEE		10
AND THERE IS SHELTER UNDER IT,	509	JANE BISHOP		26
EYES UNDER EYELIDS DID SO GLEAM:	514	JANE GROWN OLD		6
UNDER THE RAGGED THORN?	519	LOVES LONENESS		10
UNDER OAK AND BEECHEN BOUGH,	522	LULLABY		11
UNDER OAK AND BEECHES BOUGH,	522	LULLABY	V	11
UNFRIENDLY LAMPLIGHT HID UNDER ITS SHADE,	523	LONG SILENCE		3
UNDER A MARBLE FLAG?	525	DANCING DAYS		14
THAT SLEEPS UNDER THE CANOPY:	528	TOM LUNATIC		2
THAT SHE IS UNDER BAN	531	FATHER CHILD		2
DRY TIMBER UNDER THAT RICH FOLIAGE,	536	HER VISION		1
UNDER THE GREAT COMEDIAN'S TOMB THE CROWD.	541	PARN FUNERAL 1		1
GRANDFATHER SANG IT UNDER THE GALLOWS!	544	TO SAME TUNE 1		1
BETWEEN TWO BUSHES UNDER THE RAIN:	551	SONGS REWRIT 1		14
THEIR MOBS PUT UNDER THEIR FEET.	554	CHURCH STATE		4
UNDER A RULE, UNDER THE SEMBLANCE OF PEACE	563	MERU		2
UNDER A RULE, UNDER THE SEMBLANCE OF PEACE	563	MERU		2
CAVERNED IN NIGHT UNDER THE DRIFTED SNOW,	563	MERU		10
STRETCHED UNDER A DOORWAY	585	ORAHILLY		30
HIS STOUT STICK UNDER HIS HAND,	588	OLD WICKED MAN		20
AND UNDER EVERY DANCER	592	DRUNK SOBRIETY		11
UNDER THE OLD STONE CROSS.	598	STONE CROSS		8
UNDER THE OLD STONE CROSS.	599	STONE CROSS		16
UNDER THE OLD STONE CROSS.	599	STONE CROSS		24
UNDER THE TROPIC SHADE, GREW ROUND AND SLOW,	610	STATUES		18
GRANDFATHER SANG IT UNDER THE GALLOWS!	615	MARCH SONGS 3		1
A HAND UNDER HIS HEAD.	617	LONG-LEG FLY		8
UNDER BROKEN STONE I HALT	632	MAN AND ECHO		2
UNDER BEN BULBEN	636	BEN BULBEN		T
UNDER BARE BEN BULBEN'S HEAD	640	BEN BULBEN		84
FLICKERING UNDER THE WHITE MOONSHINE?	646	ISLE STAT I 1		33
BRIGHT ON A GRASS BLADE'S UNDER SIDE, MIGHT HEAR,	689	NETTLESHIP		10
UNDER A LEMON TREE BESIDE YOUR DOOR:	693	MOSADA 1		68
AND WHO WILL MOAN IN THE UNDER PIT,	716	FAIRY DOCTOR		7
AND UNDER A SHADY OAK-TREE SAT,	728	PRIEST FAIRY		7
AND UNDER HER HOOFS THE MARIGOLDS BEATEN.	729	PRIEST FAIRY		36
MOURNFUL UNDER MOURNFUL STARS.	737	IN FIRELIGHT		4
A FRUITFUL LAND UNDER THE AIBHLIN HILLS?	748	SHADOW WATER A	V	33
AND WHEN YOU CAME, THE NORTH UNDER YOUR SAILS,	749	SHADOW WATER A		34
LOOK! THERE SHE LIES UNDER A FLAPPING SAIL.	751	SHADOW WATER A		90
OR A GOD HID THEM UNDER THE SHADOW OF WINGS.	752	SHADOW WATER A		125
AMONG THE WINDS, LOOKS UNDER YOUR PALE EYELIDS.	757	SHADOW WATER A		211
AND UNDER LOVERS' EYELIDS. BEND YOUR HEAD	762	SHADOW WATER A		286
UNDER A SILKEN SAIL AND SILVER YARD.	763	SHADOW WATER A		316
IN HAPPY DANCES, UNDER A WINDY MOON:	763	SHADOW WATER A		318
THE LOVE OF ALL UNDER THE LIGHT OF THE SUN	765	SHADOW WATER A		353
IMPERISHABLE FIRE UNDER THE BOUGHS	765	SHADOW WATER A		356
UNDER THE WAVES, AND TOOK A THOUSAND WOMEN	766	SHADOW WATER A		378
AND RULE TOGETHER UNDER A CANOPY.	767	SHADOW WATER A		385
ONE LIVES UNDER THE WAVES,	770	SPINNING SONG		2
AND ONE LIVES UNDER THE BOUGHS	771	SPINNING SONG		8

UNDERGROUND

	PAGE	TITLE	LINE
RUN UNDERGROUND, RISE IN A ROCKY PLACE	490	COOLE BALLYLEE	5
THAT I AM STILL THEIR SERVANT THOUGH ALL ARE UNDERGROUND.	581	CURSE CROMWELL	22
AND HE IS UNDERGROUND!	586	PARNELLITES	6

UNDERNEATH

	PAGE	TITLE		LINE
FLED FOAM UNDERNEATH US, AND ROUND US, A WANDERING AND MILKY SMOKE,	47	OISIN 3		1
FLED FOAM UNDERNEATH US, AND ROUND US, A WANDERING AND MILKY SMOKE,	47	OISIN 3		12
FLED FOAM UNDERNEATH US, AND AROUND US, A WANDERING AND MILKY SMOKE,	47	OISIN 3	V	1
FLED FOAM UNDERNEATH ME, AND ROUND ME, A WANDERING AND MILKY SMOKE.	57	OISIN 3		148
INNUMERABLE, SINGING, EXULTANT: THE CLAY UNDERNEATH THEM SHALL PANT,	61	OISIN 3		203
UNDERNEATH THE GRASS AND CLOVER,	124	CATHLEEN PARA		3
OR ON THE BENCHES UNDERNEATH THE WALLS,	180	QUEEN MAEVE		14
SAT UNDERNEATH THE MARKET CROSS,	724	LEGEND		2
UPON THE ROWERS' BENCHES UNDERNEATH,	751	SHADOW WATER A		92

UNDERSTAND

	PAGE	TITLE		LINE
FOR THE WORLD'S MORE FULL OF WEEPING THAN YOU CAN UNDERSTAND.	87	STOLEN CHILD		12
FOR THE WORLD'S MORE FULL OF WEEPING THAN YOU CAN UNDERSTAND.	87	STOLEN CHILD		27
FOR THE WORLD'S MORE FULL OF WEEPING THAN YOU CAN UNDERSTAND.	88	STOLEN CHILD		41
FROM A WORLD MORE FULL OF WEEPING THAN HE CAN UNDERSTAND.	89	STOLEN CHILD		53
FOR THE WORLD'S MORE FULL OF WEEPING THAN HE CAN UNDERSTAND	89	STOLEN CHILD	V	53

	PAGE	TITLE	LINE

UNDERSTAND (CONTINUED)
    THAT FOLLOWS AFTER. I UNDERSTAND YOU NOW. . . . . 237 SHADOW WATER B   341
    I DO NOT UNDERSTAND. I KNOW YOUR FACE . . . . 244 SHADOW WATER B   465
    "MY DARLING CANNOT UNDERSTAND . . . . 255 WORDS   2
    HOPE THAT YOU MAY UNDERSTAND! . . . . 309 REALISTS   1
    WHAT NONE CAN UNDERSTAND, ... 315 FRIENDS   12
    IN SOMETHING THAT ALL OTHERS UNDERSTAND OR SHARE! . . . 427 PHANTOM HATRED   35
    AMONG THE DOGS AND HORSES THAT UNDERSTAND MY TALK. . . . 581 CURSE CROMWELL   30
    WHO UNDERSTAND THE DARK! . . . . 588 OLD WICKED MAN   31
UNDERSTANDS
    MY DARLING UNDERSTANDS IT ALL, ... 256 WORDS   10
    NOT A POOR FOOL UNDERSTANDS. . . . . 381 SONG OF FOOL   4
UNDERSTOOD
    AS HE THAT PRACTISED OR THAT UNDERSTOOD . . . . . . 327 ROBERT GREGORY   75
    NOT HIS, NOT MINE." WHO UNDERSTOOD . . . . 387 SOLOMON WITCH   6
    I UNDERSTOOD HIS PLAN. . . . . 400 DEMON BEAST   15
    BY QUIET NATURES UNDERSTOOD . . . . 405 FOR DAUGHTER   63
    THEY UNDERSTOOD THAT WISDOM COMES OF BEGGARY. . . . . 487 SEVEN SAGES   26
    WHAT MATTER THAT YOU UNDERSTOOD NO WORD! . . . . . 557 RIBH ECSTASY   1
    AND UNDERSTOOD HER CASE. . . . . 571 THREE BUSHES   69
    AND UNDERSTOOD, WHAT NONE HAVE UNDERSTOOD, ... 622 HOUND VOICE   13
    AND UNDERSTOOD, WHAT NONE HAVE UNDERSTOOD, ... 622 HOUND VOICE   13
    PLAIN TO BE UNDERSTOOD, ... 785 YOUR HEART   2
UNDERTOOK
    WHAT THEY UNDERTOOK TO DO . . . . 505 GRAT INSTRUCT   1
UNDIMMED
    "I COME FROM THE UNDIMMED RIVERS TO BID YOU CALL . . . . 184 QUEEN MAEVE V 91
    "I AM FROM THE UNDIMMED RIVERS. I BID YOU CALL . . . 184 QUEEN MAEVE V 91
    RUN FOR A MILE UNDIMMED IN HEAVEN'S FACE . . . . . 490 COOLE BALLYLEE   3
UNDO
    THOSE FANATICS ALL THAT WE DO WOULD UNDO! . . . . . 544 TO SAME TUNE 1   7
    THOSE FANATICS ALL THAT WE DO WOULD UNDO! . . . . . 545 TO SAME TUNE 1   17
    THOSE FANATICS ALL THAT WE DO WOULD UNDO! . . . . . 545 TO SAME TUNE 1   27
    THOSE FANATICS ALL THAT WE DO WOULD UNDO! . . . . . 546 TO SAME TUNE 2 V REF
    THOSE FANATICS ALL THAT WE DO WOULD UNDO! . . . . . 548 TO SAME TUNE 3 V REF
UNDONE
    AND HAD BEEN SAVAGELY UNDONE . . . . 314 MEMORY YOUTH   18
    AS THOUGH I HAD BEEN UNDONE . . . . 384 VISION ROBART   55
    WHEREBY THE HORN OF PLENTY IS UNDONE. . . . . . . 404 FOR DAUGHTER   32
    ALL BY THEIR YOUTH UNDONE, ... 504 RESULT THOUGHT   4
    OR LEAVE SOME SERVICE ALL UNDONE, ... 743 DANAAN QUICK   21
UNDREAMT
    THOSE UNDREAMT ACCIDENTS THAT HAVE MADE ME . . . . . 321 REED WHISPERER   10
UNDULANT   SEE EVER-UNDULANT
    FLASHING AND FLICKERING, WITH EVER UNDULANT WING, . . . 710 FERENCZ RENYI V 19
UNDYING
    AMONG UNDYING PEOPLE HAS RUN . . . . 6 OISIN 1 V 60
    IS AN UNDYING MOORFOWL, AND HE LIVES BEYOND THE SKY. . . 76 INDIAN ON GOD   7
    THEY KNOW UNDYING THINGS, FOR THEY . . . . 196 BAILE AILLINN   170
    UNDYING LOVE TO BUY . . . . 517 HIS CONFIDENCE   1
    FOR UNDYING LOVE? . . . . 518 HIS CONFIDENCE   6
    FROM THE UNDYING WORM. SHE SLEEPS---MOSADA--- . . . 701 MOSADA 3   65
    HAS TOLD ME THAT THE UNDYING SEND THEIR EAGLES . . . . 765 SHADOW WATER A   346
UNEARTHLY
    NOT KNOWING WHAT UNEARTHLY STUFF . . . . 599 STONE CROSS   21
    NOW SADLY, NOW UNEARTHLY GAY, ... 716 FAIRY DOCTOR   3
UNEASY
    "NIGHT GROWS UNEASY NEAR THE DAWN . . . . 303 HOUR DAWN   33
    THAT'S GROWN UNEASY NEAR THE DAWN . . . . 303 HOUR DAWN V 33
UNEMPTIED
    OR ON SOME STILL UNEMPTIED CUP . . . . 271 GREY ROCK   21
UNENDING
    FOR THE ROADS ARE UNENDING, AND THERE IS NO PLACE TO MY 203 WITHER BOUGHS   4
      MIND."
UNEVEN
    HAD TROD THE UNEVEN ROAD. THEIR BOOTS WERE SOILED, . . . 372 PHASES OF MOON   3
UNFAERY
    I HURL AWAY THESE ALL UNFAERY FEARS. . . . . 675 ISLE STAT II 3   228
UN-FAERY
    SOME BARBAROUS, UN-FAERY THING DRAW NEAR. . . . . . 656 ISLE STAT I 3   21
UNFALTERING
    WITH UNFALTERING PERSISTENCE, ... 647 ISLE STAT I 1   69
UNFASHIONABLE
    ON THAT UNFASHIONABLE GYRE AGAIN. . . . . 565 GYRES   24
UNFELT
    WALKED THROUGH THE HOUSE. UNNOTICED AND UNFELT . . . . 468 HARUN RASHID   153
UNFINISHED
    THE PLAYER QUEEN SONG FROM AN UNFINISHED PLAY . . . . 308 PLAYER QUEEN V T
    THE UNFINISHED MAN AND HIS PAIN . . . . 479 SELF AND SOUL   47
UNFOLD
    UNFOLD YOUR FLAMING WINGS AND COVER OUT OF SIGHT . . . 175 ELEMENT POWERS   11
UNFOLDING
    IS FOLDING AND UNFOLDING, AND IN ITS FOLDS . . . . . 751 SHADOW WATER A   99
UNFOLDS
    THE NORTH UNFOLDS ABOVE THEM CLINGING, CREEPING NIGHT, . . 154 BELOVED PEACE   3
UNFOREKNOWN
    RECKONED UP EVERY UNFOREKNOWN, UNSEEING . . . . . . 413 TOWER   109
UNFORGIVING
    WHO NEVER HEAR THE UNFORGIVING HOUND. . . . . . . 75 ANASHU VIJAYA   75
    WHO NEVER HEARD THE UNFORGIVING HOUND. . . . . . . 75 ANASHU VIJAYA V 75

			PAGE	TITLE		LINE

UNFORGOTTEN
    AND UNFORGOTTEN NAMES, AND THE COLD STARS • • • • • • 757 SHADOW WATER A 204
UNFORMED
    DEFORMED BEYOND DEFORMITY, UNFORMED, • • • • • • • • 376 PHASES OF MOON 111
UNFRIENDLY
    UNFRIENDLY LAMPLIGHT HID UNDER ITS SHADE, • • • • • • 523 LONG SILENCE 3
    THE CURTAINS DRAWN UPON UNFRIENDLY NIGHT, • • • • • • 523 LONG SILENCE 4
UNFURLED
    THE TALL THOUGHT-WOVEN SAILS, THAT FLAP UNFURLED • • • • 113 ROSE OF BATTLE 2
UNGLORIOUS
    • • • WITH BODIES UNGLORIOUS, THEIR CHIEFTAINS STOOD, • • 58 OISIN 3 166
UNGOVERNABLE
    CUCHULAIN FOUGHT THE UNGOVERNABLE SEA; • • • • • • • 630 CIRCUS ANIMALS 26
UNGOVERNED
    OF THE UNGOVERNED UNICORN. • • • • • • • • • • • 776 AGAINST WITCH 25
UNGUENTS
    AND HEALED MY WOUNDS WITH UNGUENTS OUT OF FLOWERS • • • 41 OISIN 2 185
    WITH WITCHERY AND UNGUENTS FROM THE FLOWERS • • • • • 41 OISIN 2 V 185
UNHAPPINESS
    OR FELL INTO UNHAPPINESS, I'VE SAID, • • • • • • • • 186 QUEEN MAEVE 137
    THAN ANY WHOSE UNHAPPINESS • • • • • • • • • • • 190 BAILE AILLINN 36
    FOR HAPPIER LOVE BUT FINDS UNHAPPINESS, • • • • • • • 750 SHADOW WATER A 67
UNHAPPY
    UNHAPPY ONE. GO NOT, GO NOT, GO NOT; • • • • • • • 703 MOSADA 3 102
UNHAUNTED
    AND MIGHT HAVE KNOWN AT LAST UNHAUNTED SLEEP • • • • • 128 DREAM OF FAERY 38
UNHEARD-OF
    BUT OF A BEAUTIFUL, UNHEARD-OF KIND • • • • • • • • 228 SHADOW WATER B 142
UNHOOK
    THEY UNHOOK THEIR HEAVY SWORDS • • • • • • • • • • 215 HAPPY TOWNLAND 23
    MICHAEL WILL UNHOOK HIS TRUMPET • • • • • • • • • • 215 HAPPY TOWNLAND 41
UNHOOKED
    WITH SHOUTING AND THE CLANG OF UNHOOKED ARMS. • • • • • 185 QUEEN MAEVE 111
UNHUMAN
    OF PENSIVE LAUGHTER, UNHUMAN SOUND, • • • • • • • • 11 OISIN 1 136
    WRAPPED IN THE THINGS OF THE UNHUMAN MIND, • • • • • • 36 OISIN 2 98
    ROLLED IN THE THINGS OF THE UNHUMAN MIND, • • • • • • 36 OISIN 2 V 98
    • • • AND FED OF UNHUMAN SLEEP. • • • • • • • • • 51 OISIN 3 56
    OF SOME UNHUMAN MISERY • • • • • • • • • • • • 85 MAD KING GOLL V 58
    WITH THEIR UNHUMAN SORROWS. CEASE! NO MORE! • • • • • 661 ISLE STAT II 1 58
    THROUGH MISERIES UNHUMAN EVER ON • • • • • • • • • 684 SEEKER 59
    TO JOYS UNHUMAN, AND TO THEE--SPEAK! SPEAK! • • • • • 684 SEEKER 60
UNICORN
    AS THOUGH A STAG AND UNICORN WERE MET • • • • • • • 277 TWO KINGS 19
    OF THE UNGOVERNED UNICORN. • • • • • • • • • • • 776 AGAINST WITCH 25
UNICORNS
    MAGICAL UNICORNS BEAR LADIES ON THEIR BACKS. • • • • • 426 PHANTOM HATRED 18
    THE CLOUD-PALE UNICORNS, THE EYES OF AQUAMARINE, • • • • 427 PHANTOM HATRED 25
    THE CLOUD PALE UNICORNS, THE EYES OF AQUAMARINE, • • • • 427 PHANTOM HATRED V 25
UNIFORM
    HALF DRESSED IN NATIONAL UNIFORM, • • • • • • • • • 424 ROAD AT DOOR 7
UNIMAGINABLE
    THAT UNIMAGINABLE STORMS OF WIND AND WAVE • • • • • • 236 SHADOW WATER B 317
    TO UNIMAGINABLE HAPPINESS. • • • • • • • • • • • 247 SHADOW WATER B 524
    AN UNIMAGINABLE HAPPINESS. • • • • • • • • • • • 248 SHADOW WATER B 553
    WHO HAD LOST SOME UNIMAGINABLE TREASURE • • • • • • • 278 TWO KINGS 40
UNINHABITED
    UNINHABITED, RUINOUS, • • • • • • • • • • • • • 512 JANE ON GOD 15
UNINTELLIGIBLE
    WHEN I AM UNINTELLIGIBLE. • • • • • • • • • • • 624 APPARITIONS 14
UNISON
    AND DISCORD FOLLOW UPON UNISON, • • • • • • • • • 265 THESE CLOUDS 5
UNIVERSE
    THE UNIVERSE HERSELF WOULD DIE, • • • • • • • • • 19 OISIN 1 V 271
UNIVERSE'S
    IN THE UNIVERSE'S REVERIE. • • • • • • • • • • • 65 HAPPY SHEPHERD V 21
UNIVERSITY
    ON HEARING THAT THE STUDENTS OF OUR NEW UNIVERSITY • • • 262 STUDENTS AGIT T
UNJUST
    AND THEY CEASE WITH A SIGH OF "UNJUST! UNJUST!" • • • • 27 OISIN 1 V 416
    AND THEY CEASE WITH A SIGH OF "UNJUST! UNJUST!" • • • • 27 OISIN 1 V 416
    MUST MURMUR AT LAST, "UNJUST, UNJUST"; • • • • • • • 28 OISIN 1 420
    MUST MURMUR AT LAST, "UNJUST, UNJUST"; • • • • • • • 28 OISIN 1 420
UNKIND
    THY TENDER EYES GROW ALL UNKIND! • • • • • • • • • 136 TWO TREES 39
    AND THINK THAT YOU WERE HARD AND UNKIND, • • • • • • 146 FISH 7
    BE NOT UNKIND OR PROUD, • • • • • • • • • • • • 173 PLEADS FRIEND 4
UNKNOWN
    WAS A BEAUTIFUL YOUTH FROM AN UNKNOWN LAND. • • • • • 12 OISIN 1 V 145
    SWAYED, CROONING TO HIMSELF AN UNKNOWN TONGUE; • • • • 39 OISIN 2 159
    THE DEWS DROP SLOWLY AND DREAMS GATHER: UNKNOWN SPEARS • • 161 BLACK PIG 1
    OF UNKNOWN PERISHING ARMIES BEAT ABOUT MY EARS. • • • • 161 BLACK PIG 4
    THE DEW DROPS SLOWLY: THE DREAMS GATHER: UNKNOWN SPEARS 161 BLACK PIG V 1
    GAZED UPON ALL THINGS KNOWN, ALL THINGS UNKNOWN, • • • • 383 VISION ROBART 30
    HIS VIZIR JAFFER FOR AN UNKNOWN REASON; • • • • • • • 462 HARUN RASHID 32
    FOR MEDITATIONS UPON UNKNOWN THOUGHT • • • • • • • • 473 ALL SOUL NIGHT 74
    GRATITUDE TO THE UNKNOWN INSTRUCTORS • • • • • • • • 505 GRAT INSTRUCT T
    GRATITUDE TO THE UNKNOWN POWERS • • • • • • • • • 505 GRAT INSTRUCT V T
    AND ROARS, MAD WITH THE TOUCH OF THE UNKNOWN, • • • • • 689 NETTLESHIP 7
UNLABOURING
    "NEITHER THE LIVING, NOR THE UNLABOURING DEAD, • • • • 34 OISIN 2 79

		PAGE	TITLE	LINE
UNLABOURING	(CONTINUED)			
AND BY THE UNLABOURING BROOD OF THE SKIES!	• • • • • •	164	PERFECT BEAUTY	5
BEFORE THE UNLABOURING STARS AND YOU.	• • • • • •	164	PERFECT BEAUTY	8
BEFORE UNLABOURING STARS AND YOU.	• • • • • • •	164	PERFECT BEAUTY V	8
UN-LABOURING				
AND BY THE HEAVEN'S UN-LABOURING BROODS!	• • • • • •	164	PERFECT BEAUTY V	5
UNLACE				
DREAMED OF THE HANDS THAT WOULD UNLACE	• • • • • •	193	BAILE AILLINN	104
UNLANGUID				
UNLANGUID AS THE BIRDS, IN PROUD COMPANIONSHIPS!	• • • •	30	OISIN 2 V	14C
UNLATCHED				
THE MORE I LEAVE THE DOOR UNLATCHED	• • • • • • •	511	JANE AND JACK	3
UNLAUGHING				
NOR AN UNLAUGHING MOUTH, BUT MINE THAT MOURNS,	• • • •	285	TWO KINGS	184
UNLEARNED				
ALL TEETH WERE DRAWN, ALL ANCIENT TRICKS UNLEARNED,	• • •	429	NINETEEN 19	17
UNLESS				
UNLESS WE DRAIN MORE FLAGONS IN A YEAR	• • • • • •	225	SHADOW WATER B	70
UNLESS DESIRE HAD MADE THEM SO?"	• • • • • • •	295	THREE BEGGARS	18
WILL BANISH EVERY THOUGHT, UNLESS	• • • • • • •	387	ROBARTES DANCE	48
UNLESS A PETAL HIT THE GROUND,	• • • • • • • •	389	SOLOMON WITCH	40
A TATTERED COAT UPON A STICK, UNLESS	• • • • • •	407	SAIL BYZANTIUM	10
THOUGHT THAT UNLESS A LITTLE POWDER BURNED	• • • • •	429	NINETEEN 19	21
UNLESS THE HOLY WRITINGS LIE,	• • • • • • • •	436	FOR MY SON	28
UNLESS SOME PITYING GOD SHALL SUCCOUR ME	• • • • •	656	ISLE STAT I 3	36
THAT ONE SHALL DIE, UNLESS ONE DIE FOR HER.	• • • •	669	ISLE STAT II 3	74
THEY SAID I'D BURN IN HELL UNLESS I TOLD.	• • • • •	694	MOSADA 1	108
UNLETTERED				
WERE YOU AND I UNLETTERED LADS	• • • • • • • •	524	MAD AS MIST	11
UNLIKE				
THE MOST UNLIKE, BEING MY ANTI-SELF,	• • • • • •	371	EGO DOMINUS	74
THAT SEEMS UNLIKE ITSELF, THAT SEEMS UNCHANGEABLE,	• • •	426	PHANTOM HATRED	4
THAT'S SO UNLIKE MYSELF THAT WHEN YOU PRAISE IT	• • •	447	HERO GIRL FOOL	2
UNLOCKED				
UNTIL AT LAST THE UNLOCKED HORN HAD TORN	• • • • ' • •	278	TWO KINGS V	21
UNLOCKS				
WAS MOVING. BLEEDING NOW, HIS GRASP UNLOCKS,	• • • •	688	TWO TITANS	42
UNLOOSE				
UNLOOSE THE CORD, AND THEY WILL WRAP YOU ROUND.	• • •	104	FERGUS DRUID	30
UNLOOSED				
STABLING HIS UNLOOSED LIGHTNINGS IN THEIR STALL,	• • •	36	OISIN 2	110
HER HEAD CAST BACKWARD IN HER UNLOOSED HAIR.	• • • •	701	MOSADA 3	67
UNLOVED				
BEING FIXED ON ALL THINGS LOVED, ALL THINGS UNLOVED,	• •	383	VISION ROBART	34
UNMANNED				
HE WHO CAN READ THE SIGNS NOR SINK UNMANNED	• • • •	429	NINETEEN 19	33
UNMANNERLY				
THE DAILY SPITE OF THIS UNMANNERLY TOWN,	• • • • •	351	PEOPLE	3
UNMEASURED				
THAT HURRY FROM UNMEASURED MIND	• • • • • • •	138	TO IRELAND	25
UNMINDFUL				
UNMINDFUL OF ITS WOES, WOULD TWINE A WREATH	• • • •	650	ISLE STAT I 1	133
UNMIXED				
DRUNK WITH THE UNMIXED WINE.	• • • • • • • •	355	PROPERTIUS	8
UN-MIXED				
DRUNK WITH THE UN-MIXED WINE.	• • • • • • • •	355	PROPERTIUS V	8
UNMOVED				
AND MY HEART UNMOVED?	• • • • • • • • • •	532	BEFORE WORLD	12
UNMOVING				
SHINE DULL UNMOVING EYES. WHAT THING ART THOU?	• • •	685	SEEKER	74
UNNATURAL				
WHO HAD UNNATURAL MAJESTY, AND EYES	• • • • • •	283	TWO KINGS	149
BUT WITH A VOICE THAT HAD UNNATURAL MUSIC,	• • • •	283	TWO KINGS	153
THAT SEEMS UNNATURAL TO ARABIAN MINDS,	• • • • •	464	HARUN RASHID	79
THAT FIRST UNNATURAL INTEREST IN MY BOOKS.	• • • •	468	HARUN RASHID	165
UNNECESSARY				
SANG WHERE--UNNECESSARY CRUEL VOICE--	• • • • •	127	DREAM OF FAERY	30
UNNEEDED SEE ALL-UNNEEDED				
UNNOTICED				
SANG UNNOTICED LIKE A BIRD!	• • • • • • • •	298	THREE HERMITS	7
SANG UNNOTICED LIKE A BIRD.	• • • • • • • •	299	THREE HERMITS	32
AND LET IT FALL UNNOTICED TO THE FLOOR.	• • • • •	461	HARUN RASHID	15
AND IT WOULD FALL UNNOTICED ON THE FLOOR.	• • • •	461	HARUN RASHID V	15
WALKED THROUGH THE HOUSE. UNNOTICED AND UNFELT	• • •	468	HARUN RASHID	153
HIDDEN FROM EYESIGHT TO THE UNNOTICED END.	• • • •	472	ALL SOUL NIGHT	50
UNNUMBERED				
I LAUGHED AT TIMES UNNUMBERED TREASONS,	• • • • •	23	OISIN 1 V	345D
FROM YEAR TO YEAR BY THE UNNUMBERED NESTS	• • • •	74	ANASHU VIJAYA	72
SLEEPER, AWAKE! HOW LONG MY SLEEP? UNNUMBERED	• • •	678	ISLE STAT II 3	307
UNPACKS				
HE UNPACKS THE LOADED PERN	• • • • • • • • •	342	SHEP GOATHERD	97
UNPASSING				
NOR THOSE UNPASSING CARES,	• • • • • • • • •	315	FRIENDS	5
UNPEOPLED				
OR ON THE UNPEOPLED WAVES WITH KINGS TO PULL AT THE OAR,		210	UNDER THE MOON	15
UNPERSUADABLE				
HE FOUND THE UNPERSUADABLE JUSTICE, HE FOUND	• • • •	369	EGO DOMINUS	36
UNPERTURBED				
THE UNPERTURBED AND COURTLY IMAGES--	• • • • • •	352	PEOPLE	11
UNPRUNED				
UNPRUNED IS YOUR BEAUTIFUL PINION	• • • • • • •	707	FAIRY PEDANT	7

		PAGE	TITLE	LINE

UNPUBLISHED
A LYRIC FROM AN UNPUBLISHED PLAY • • • • • • • • • 263 MASK V T
UNPURGED
THE UNPURGED IMAGES OF DAY RECEDE; • • • • • • • • 497 BYZANTIUM 1
UNQUENCHABLE
UNQUENCHABLE STILL GLOWS IN HER DULL STARE, • • • • • 687 TWO TITANS 17
UNQUIET
MURMURING HOW FAR AWAY ARE THE UNQUIET LANDS; • • • • • • 78 INDIAN TO LOVE 10
MURMURING GENTLY HOW FAR OFF ARE THE UNQUIET LANDS; • • • 78 INDIAN TO LOVE V 10
GIVE THEM UNQUIET DREAMS; • • • • • • • • • • • 88 STOLEN CHILD 34
AND THE LOUD CHANTING OF THE UNQUIET LEAVES, • • • • • 120 SORROW OF LOVE V 11
AND THE LOUD CHAUNTING OF THE UNQUIET LEAVES, • • • • • 120 SORROW OF LOVE V 11
SUDDEN AND LAUGHING. O UNQUIET HEART, • • • • • • • 181 QUEEN MAEVE 30
THE PACK UPON HIM. GO, UNQUIET WANDERER, • • • • • • 292 TO A SHADE 18
HERDING THE PACK. UNQUIET WANDERER • • • • • • • • 292 TO A SHADE V 18
QUIET LANDS OR UNQUIET SEAS • • • • • • • • • • 360 ALF POLLEXFEN 19
UNREALITY
THAT KNOWLEDGE INCREASES UNREALITY, THAT • • • • • • 610 STATUES 21
UNRECKONABLE
UNRECKONABLE RACE; • • • • • • • • • • • • • 365 HER RACE 8
UNREMEMBERING
THAT GIRL MY UNREMEMBERING NIGHTS HOLD FAST • • • • • 384 VISION ROBART 50
THEIR UNREMEMBERING HEARTS AND HEADS • • • • • • • 639 BEN BULBEN 72
UNREPENTING
AND UNREPENTING FACED YOUR ENDS, • • • • • • • • • 273 GREY ROCK 60
UNREPINING
HATE ON AND LOVE THROUGH UNREPINING HOURS. • • • • • • 80 EPHEMERA 22
UNREPROVED
THE INSOLENT UNREPROVED, • • • • • • • • • • • 347 FISHERMAN 16
UNREQUITED
RETURNED AND YET UNREQUITED LOVE. • • • • • • • • • 358 PRESENCES 8
UNREST
BUT WHY THIS WHIM OF THINE? A STRANGE UNREST, • • • • 671 ISLE STAT II 3 137
UNRESTING
THE RAVENS OF UNRESTING THOUGHT; • • • • • • • • • 136 TWO TREES 34
UNROLLS
THE NORTH UNROLLS ABOVE THEM CLINGING, CREEPING NIGHT, • • 154 BELOVED PEACE V 3
UNSATISFIED
IN THEIR STIFF, PAINTED CLOTHES, THE PALE UNSATISFIED ONES 318 MAGI 2
BEING BY CALVARY'S TURBULENCE UNSATISFIED, • • • • • • 318 MAGI 7
HIS SENSES AND HIS HEART UNSATISFIED, • • • • • • • 370 EGO DOMINUS 58
UNSATISFIED • • • • • • • • • • • • • • • • 510 JANE JUDGMENT 2
UNSAY
THE REST I PASS, ONE SENTENCE I UNSAY. • • • • • • • 542 PARN FUNERAL 2 1
I PASS THE REST—ONE SENTENCE I UNSAY— • • • • • • 542 PARN FUNERAL 2 V 1
UNSEARCHABLE
SEARCHED THE UNSEARCHABLE—WHY GOOD MEN WEEP; • • • • 710 FERENCZ RENYI 32
UNSEEING
RECKONED UP EVERY UNFOREKNOWN, UNSEEING • • • • • • • 413 TOWER 109
UNSEEN
THEY WALK ON SHORES UNSEEN OF OARING GALLEYS, • • • • • 30 OISIN 2 V 14D
THE SHOUTING OF AN UNSEEN MAN; • • • • • • • • • 274 GREY ROCK 76
AS I WANDERED UNSEEN; • • • • • • • • • • • • 654 ISLE STAT I 2 71
AND HEARD EACH UNSEEN ECHO ON HER THRONE, • • • • • • 657 ISLE STAT I 3 48
AND THE CUCKOO UNSEEN IN HIS FESTIVAL MOOD; • • • • • 717 LOVE SONG 7
UNSERVICEABLE
A STRANGE, UNSERVICEABLE THING, • • • • • • • • • 784 WOMANS BEAUTY 15
UNSHAKEN
BUT WITH THE BURNING, LIVE, UNSHAKEN VOICE • • • • • 183 QUEEN MAEVE 75
UNSHAPELY
THE WRONG OF UNSHAPELY THINGS IS A WRONG TOO GREAT TO BE 143 ROSE IN HEART 5
TOLD;
UNSHELTERED
HE SAID "QUEEN OF UNSHELTERED CRUACHAN, • • • • • • 183 QUEEN MAEVE V 77
UNSHUT
OR, THE HOUSE DOOR LEFT UNSHUT, • • • • • • • • • 380 SONGS FOOL 1 10
UNSHUTTERED
SHOWED THEIR FAINT LIGHT THROUGH THE UNSHUTTERED WINDOWS, 279 TWO KINGS 50
UNSLEEPING
AWAKE UNSLEEPING FIRES; AND WOVE SEVEN STRINGS, • • • • 219 HARP OF AENGUS 7
AWAKE UNSLEEPING FIRES; AND WOVE SEVEN STRINGS, • • • • 762 SHADOW WATER A 302
UNSOUGHT
A STRANGE THING SURELY THAT MY HEART, WHEN LOVE HAD COME 449 OWEN AHERNE 1
UNSOUGHT
UNSPOILED
AND ON MY HEIRS, IF ALL REMAIN UNSPOILED, • • • • • • 371 ON GOING HOUSE 2
UNSPOTTED
UNSPOTTED BY THE CENTURIES; • • • • • • • • • • 477 SELF AND SOUL 12
UNSTEADY
HAS MADE MY FEET UNSTEADY, AND BLINDED ME. • • • • • • 767 SHADOW WATER A 406
UNSTITCHING
OUR STITCHING AND UNSTITCHING HAS BEEN NAUGHT. • • • • 204 ADAMS CURSE 6
UNSUBDUABLE
THAT DEMON DULL AND UNSUBDUABLE; • • • • • • • • • 43 OISIN 2 217
UNTIL
UNTIL THE DANAAN POETS BROUGHT • • • • • • • • • • 7 OISIN 1 63
UNTIL THE DANAAN POETS CAME, • • • • • • • • • • 7 OISIN 1 V 64
UNTIL ONE CAME, A TEARFUL BOY; • • • • • • • • • 17 OISIN 1 237
UNTIL THE TOSSING ARMS GREW STILL • • • • • • • • 21 OISIN 1 322
NOR CEASED UNTIL WHITE NIAMH STROKED HIS EARS • • • • • 30 OISIN 2 26
"AND TELL THEM HOW I WEEP, UNTIL THEY WEEP; • • • • • 33 OISIN 2 V 63

851

UNTIL   (CONTINUED)
     UNTIL THE GODS AND DEMONS DROP ASLEEP, ...   35 OISIN 2   86
     TO LIE UNTIL THE FOURTH MORN SAW EMERGE . . . . . .   44 OISIN 2   220
     TO LIE UNTIL THE FOURTH MORN SUN EMERGE . . . . . .   44 OISIN 2   V 220
     UNTIL I CARVED THESE WORDS! . . . .   123 DREAM OF DEATH   10
     DREAM, UNTIL GOD BURN NATURE WITH A KISS? . . . . .   128 DREAM OF FAERY   47
     UNTIL HE BURN UP NATURE WITH A KISS!--   . . . . . .   128 DREAM OF FAERY   V 47
     UNTIL THE SAP OF SUMMER HAD GROWN WEARY! . . . . . .   130 BOOK STORIES   14
     FROM OUR BIRTHDAY, UNTIL WE DIE, ...   139 TO IRELAND   35
     UNTIL ONE BORE BRIDGET HIS BRIDE   . . . .   145 HOST OF AIR   31
     IS DROPPING SLEEP, UNTIL GOD BURN TIME, ...   164 PERFECT BEAUTY   7
     UNTIL THE AXLE BREAK   . . . .   165 CRY OF SEDGE   4
     UNTIL TIME AND THE WORLD HAVE EBBED AWAY . . . . . .   168 BLESSED   V 39
     UNTIL HE FOUND, WITH LAUGHTER AND WITH TEARS, ...   170 SECRET ROSE   24
     OF THE WOMAN THAT HE LOVES, UNTIL HE DIES. . . . . .   177 PAST GREATNESS   10
     UNTIL THE PILLARED DARK BEGAN TO STIR   . . . . . .   185 QUEEN MAEVE   110
     UNTIL TWO LOVERS CAME OUT OF THE AIR   . . . .   187 QUEEN MAEVE   143
     HE RAN AND LAUGHED UNTIL HE CAME   . . . .   194 BAILE AILLINN   128
     UNTIL THE MOON HAD SET, AND WHEN I LOOKED . . . . . .   223 SHADOW WATER B   22
     UNTIL THE OVERBURTHENED MOON IS DEAD. . . . .   231 SHADOW WATER B   218
     UNTIL YOU STOOD BEFORE ME ON THE DECK--   . . . . . .   236 SHADOW WATER B   313
     TO BE HIS BEDFELLOW? UNTIL YOUR LIPS . . . .   237 SHADOW WATER B   335
     UNTIL MY BODY GIVE YOU KISS FOR KISS. . . . .   238 SHADOW WATER B   345
     UNTIL MY THOUGHTS CLEARED UP AGAIN, ...   256 WORDS   6
     UNTIL AT LAST THE DOUBLE HORNS, DRAWN BACKWARD,   . . .   278 TWO KINGS   21
     UNTIL AT LAST THE UNLOCKED HORN HAD TORN . . . . . .   278 TWO KINGS   V 21
     UNTIL HE CAME BEFORE THE PAINTED WALL, ...   279 TWO KINGS   47
     BUT ASKED THE MORE UNTIL HE SPOKE THESE WORDS,   . . .   281 TWO KINGS   V 92A
     UNTIL ENOUGH OF PAUDEEN'S PENCE   . . . .   287 TO WEALTHY MAN   2
     AND PRAYER TO SHIVERING PRAYER, UNTIL . . . .   289 SEPTEMBER 1913   4
     UNTIL A CURLEW CRIED AND IN THE LUMINOUS WIND . . . .   291 PAUDEEN   4
     AND ARE PLAGUED BY CROWDS, UNTIL   . . . .   298 THREE HERMITS   20
     "I'LL SLEEP UNTIL THE WINTER'S GONE, ...   305 HOUR DAWN   57
     UNTIL I CRIED AND TREMBLED AND ROCKED TO AND FRO,   . .   316 COLD HEAVEN   8
     UNTIL IMAGINATION BROUGHT   . . . .   328 ROBERT GREGORY   94
     UNTIL THEY PRANCED UPON THE TOP.   . . . .   331 ROUND TOWER   18
     NEVER UNTIL THIS MOMENT HAVE WE MET   . . . .   339 SHEP GOATHERD   7
     UNTIL I AM DRIVEN MAD, ...   346 ON WOMAN   35
     UNTIL HER PRAISE SHOULD BE THE UPPERMOST THEME,   . . .   350 HER PRAISE   6
     BUT WALK BY THE DRY THORN UNTIL I HAVE FOUND   . . . .   351 HER PRAISE   12
     MANAGE THE TALK UNTIL HER NAME COME ROUND. . . . . .   351 HER PRAISE   14
     MANAGE TO TALK UNTIL HER NAME COME ROUND. . . . . .   351 HER PRAISE   V 14
     THE STATELY MIDNIGHT THROUGH UNTIL THEY STOOD . . . .   352 PEOPLE   14
     I'D STAND AND MUTTER THERE UNTIL HE CAUGHT . . . . .   377 PHASES OF MOON   131
     NEVER UNTIL THIS NIGHT HAVE I BEEN STIRRED. . . . . .   389 IMAGE PAST   1
     UNTIL HER VOICE GREW SHRILL. . . . .   392 EASTER 1916   20
     UNTIL IMAGINATION, EAR AND EYE, ...   409 TOWER   13
     THAT CLIMB THE STREAMS UNTIL   . . . .   414 TOWER   123
     AND RAINS DOWN LIFE UNTIL THE BASIN SPILLS, ...   417 ANCEST HOUSES   4
     UNTIL I THOUGHT HER BODY BORE . . . .   451 FIRST LOVE   5
     UNTIL IT PLUNGE INTO THE SUN! . . . .   472 ALL SOUL NIGHT   56
     UNTIL IT PLUNGED INTO THE SUN!   . . . .   472 ALL SOUL NIGHT   V 56
     UNTIL THAT GLANCE RUN IN THE WORLD'S DESPITE   . . . .   474 ALL SOUL NIGHT   94
     CASTS UPON HIS EYES UNTIL AT LAST . . . .   479 SELF AND SOUL   53
     UNTIL THE MORNING BREAK AS ON A DARK BREAST. . . . .   494 AT ALGECIRAS   V   6
     UNTIL IT PARDON ME.   . . . .   516 MANS SONG   18
     MAY SING, AND SING UNTIL HE DROP. . . . .   525 DANCING DAYS   21
     I DID THE DRAGON'S WILL UNTIL YOU CAME   . . . . . .   533 HER TRIUMPH   1
     WHAT CAN SHE TAKE UNTIL HER MASTER GIVE! . . . . . .   558 RIBH CHRISTIAN   21
     WHERE CAN SHE LOOK UNTIL HE MAKE THE SHOW! . . . . .   558 RIBH CHRISTIAN   22
     WHAT CAN SHE KNOW UNTIL HE BID HER KNOW! . . . . . .   558 RIBH CHRISTIAN   23
     UNTIL THE TOWN LIE BEATEN FLAT.   . . . .   565 LAPIS LAZULI   8
     NO, NOT UNTIL HE RODE.   . . . .   571 THREE BUSHES   48
     MY MEDIAEVAL KNEES LACK HEALTH UNTIL THEY BEND,   . . .   603 GALLERY REVIS   33
     UNTIL, IN SOME CLIFF-SHELTERED BAY . . . .   612 NEWS ORACLE   21
     AND ALL SEEMS EVIL UNTIL I   . . . .   632 MAN AND ECHO   17
     UNTIL AFAR APPEAR THE GLEAMING DRAGON-SCALES! . . . .   651 ISLE STAT I 1   160
     FROM MORN THE TWAIN UNTIL THE EVENING PALES   . . . .   651 ISLE STAT I 1   161
     UNTIL I FIND HIM. WHAT A WEARY WEEK, ...   658 ISLE STAT II 1   2
     UNTIL THIS MORN. AS ADDER'S BACK . . . .   667 ISLE STAT II 3   22
     UNTIL THIS MORN. THE SKY WITH WRACK   . . . .   667 ISLE STAT II 3 V   22
     UNTIL WE DIE WITHIN THE CHARMED RING   . . . .   679 ISLE STAT II 3   322
     UNTIL MY BEARD IS IN THE TWISTED LEAVES   . . . . . .   683 SEEKER   44
     BE PULLERS OF THE OAR UNTIL YOU DIE?   . . . .   757 SHADOW WATER A   217
     UNTIL ALL BE RUINOUS.   . . . .   775 AGAINST WITCH   4
     UNTIL HE HAD DIED OF HIS WOUNDS, ...   775 AGAINST WITCH   16
     OF THE HOME-BREW THERE, UNTIL . . . .   776 AGAINST WITCH   38
     OF THE HOMEBREW THERE, UNTIL   . . . .   776 AGAINST WITCH   V 38
UNTIRING
     MUST SPREAD OUT THEIR WINGS UNTIRING, ...   739 WHERE BOOKS GO   3
UNTO
     AND NIGH UNTO HIM EACH ONE DREW, ...   18 OISIN 1   V 257
     AND SANG UNTO THE STARRY BROODS.   . . . .   22 OISIN 1   326
     AS THOUGH UNTO HIS NEVER SLUMBERING HEART . . . . .   32 OISIN 2   V 44
     FROM SLEEPER UNTO SLEEPER MURMUR YOU. . . . .   33 OISIN 2   V 60
     ONCE MORE UNTO YOUR FLOWERS, FOR NONE MAY FIGHT, . . .   34 OISIN 2   V 80
     DARKEN! HEAVEN IS ANGRY. CEASE! UNTO MY MIND,   . . .   42 OISIN 2   V 205
     AND WE ONCE MORE UNTO OUR FIGHTING FELL. . . . . . .   43 OISIN 2   V 218
     . . . FOR BREAST UNTO BREAST   . . . .   56 OISIN 3   131
     WITHOUT LAUGHTER, A SHOW UNTO CHILDREN, ...   63 OISIN 3   218

	PAGE	TITLE		LINE
UNTO (CONTINUED)				
AH ME! TO BE OLD WITHOUT SUCCOUR, A SHOW UNTO CHILDREN, A STAIN,	63	OISIN 3	V	217
THAT GOD GIVES UNTO MAN IN SLEEP.	138	TO IRELAND	V	22
WHAT ARE THEY? UNTO WHAT COUNTRY DO THEY FLY?	247	SHADOW WATER B		523
FROM FATHER UNTO SON	421	MY TABLE		19
UNTO THE WANDERER'S SHIPS, OR AS DAY FILLS	645	ISLE STAT I 1		10
UNTO THE DOLOROUS BORDER OF THE FAIRY LAKE.	655	ISLE STAT I 2		85
LONG YEARS AGO, AND UNTO STONE CONGEALED.	656	ISLE STAT I 3		28
AROUND THE FEATHERY TIP, UNTO THE SHAFT	657	ISLE STAT I 3		71
UNTO HER DOOR: FOR THIS, WHERE NOD THE LONG	660	ISLE STAT II 1		43
FROM THE DEEP EARTH UNTO THE LURID SKY	662	ISLE STAT II 2		5
AN OATEN PIPE UNTO A LISTENING FAWN,	678	ISLE STAT II 3		301
AN OATEN PIPE UNTO A LISTENING FAUN,	678	ISLE STAT II 3	V	301
AND UNTO IT WE'LL DANCE UPON THE SWARD.	681	SEEKER		10
GOLD UNTO GOLD, A GLEAM IN ITS LONG HAIR,	720	WITCH VIVIEN		3
UNTO THE HEART OF THE WOODLAND STRAYING,	728	PRIEST FAIRY		1
AND ANSWERED UNTO HIM!	740	EARL PAUL		18
UNTO THE WHITE SKIES.	740	EARL PAUL		24
SHOULD LOOK UPON HIS EYES WITH LOVE UNTO THE END	768	SHADOW WATER A	V	409
UNTOLD				
MINE WERE CLAN MORNA'S TRIBES UNTOLD,	81	MAD KING GOLL	V	3
WHO CAST ROUND FERGUS DREAMS, AND RUIN UNTOLD:	101	ROSE UPON ROOD		5
UNTOUCHED				
UNTOUCHED OF HUMAN JOY OR HUMAN LOVE?	684	SEEKER		65
UNTROUBLED				
AND LAUGH OVER THE UNTROUBLED WATER	330	BONE OF A HARE		14
UNTROUBLED BY THE SOUL,	573	LADYS 2ND SONG		11
UNTUNED				
UNTUNED BY THEIR OWN STRIVING. IF ONE SUCH	711	FERENCZ RENYI		37
UNUSED				
WHOSE INSOLENT EYES UNUSED TO TEARS WOULD WEEP.	678	ISLE STAT II 3		302
UNVESSELLED				
HALF IN THE UNVESSELLED SEA, WE CLIMBED THE STAIR	32	OISIN 2		47
HALF IN THE UNVESSELLED SEA, WE'D MOUNTED FAR!	32	OISIN 2	V	47
HALF IN THE UNVESSELLED SEA, WE CLIMBED THE STAIRS	32	OISIN 2	V	47
UNVISITED				
UNVISITED BY TEMPEST OR BY SUN,	446	COLONUS PRAISE		5
UNWEARIED				
PROCLAIM WITH THAT UNWEARIED, REEDY CRY	128	DREAM OF FAERY		42
UNWEARIED STILL, LOVER BY LOVER,	323	SWANS AT COOLE		19
UNWEARIED EYES UPON THOSE HORRIBLE GREEN BIRDS.	442	BLACK CENTAUR		16
UNWEARY				
THE MAN IS GONE WHO GUIDED YE, UNWEARY,	738	MOURN THEN ON		3
UNWET				
NOR MOUTH FROM KISSING, NOR FROM WINE UNWET:	311	MOUNTAIN TOMB		7
NOR MOUTH WITH KISSING NOR WITH WINE UNWET.	311	MOUNTAIN TOMB	V	7
NOR MOUTH WITH KISSING NOR WITH THE WINE UNWET.	311	MOUNTAIN TOMB	V	7
UNWIELDY				
AND ROLLS ALONG THE UNWIELDY SUN,	18	OISIN 1		267
ROUND US, AND ROLLS THE UNWIELDY SUN.	18	OISIN 1	V	268
UNWIND				
WIND AND UNWIND THEIR DANCES WHEN THE LIGHT GROWS COOL	203	WITHER BOUGHS		13
WIND AND UNWIND DANCING WHEN THE LIGHT GROWS COOL	203	WITHER BOUGHS	V	13
KNOWLEDGE HE SHALL UNWIND	343	SHEP GOATHERD		107
MAY UNWIND THE WINDING PATH!	497	BYZANTIUM		12
UNWITHERING				
HAPPY AS CHILDREN WITH UNWITHERING LIPS,	30	OISIN 2	V	148
HELP THEM THAT PACE, HAND IN UNWITHERING HAND,	184	QUEEN MAEVE	V	86
UNWORTHY				
AGAINST UNWORTHY PRAISE	259	UNWORTH PRAISE		T
UNWOUND				
FOR LOVE IS BUT A SKEIN UNWOUND	511	JANE AND JACK		5
TIME IS UNWOUND,	520	HIS BARGAIN		4
UNWRAP				
AND MAKES THE INFANT FERNS UNWRAP,	18	OISIN 1		265
UP SEE PILED-UP HEAPED-UP MAKE-UP				
HE HELD THAT FLASHING SCEPTRE UP.	18	OISIN 1		260
PASSED A-TIPTOE UP AND DOWN	20	OISIN 1	V	294
AND UP THE STAIR WE TOILED TO A HIGH DOOR,	36	OISIN 2	V	101
BARKING. WE TRAMPLED UP AND DOWN WITH BLOWS	40	OISIN 2		170
HAD SURGED UP IN A PLUMY FIRE, I DRAVE	41	OISIN 2		181
SURGED UP IN PLUMY FIRE, I LUNGED AND DRAVE	41	OISIN 2	V	181
. . . SHALL LISTEN AND RISE UP AND WEEP!	62	OISIN 3		206
. . . WHO COULD BREAK UP THE WORLD IN THEIR RAGE!	62	OISIN 3		214
I, PRIESTESS OF THIS TEMPLE, OFFER UP	71	ANASHU VIJAYA		12
I, PRIESTESS OF THIS TEMPLE, OFFER UP	75	ANASHU VIJAYA		84
AND PASSED A-TIPTOE UP AND DOWN,	85	MAD KING GOLL		51
I PASSED A TIP-TOE UP AND DOWN,	85	MAD KING GOLL	V	51
I PASSED A-TIPTOE UP AND DOWN,	85	MAD KING GOLL	V	51
BUT FATHER JOHN WENT UP,	92	FATHER OHART		9
AS HE WENT UP AND DOWN!	92	FATHER OHART		18
WHO DIG OLD CUSTOMS UP.	93	FATHER OHART		40
MY HUSBAND STOOD UP PALE,	95	MOLL MAGEE	V	22
MY MONEY'S ALL USED UP,	96	MOLL MAGEE		38
AND SLOWLY UP AND DOWN.	97	FOXHUNTER	V	8
AND GENTLY UP AND DOWN.	97	FOXHUNTER	V	8
IN THREE DAYS' TIME HE STOOD UP WITH A MOAN,	111	CUCHULAIN SEA	V	83
STOOD UP, AND CAME TO THE LONG SANDS ALONE!	111	CUCHULAIN SEA	V	84
YOUNG MAN, LIFT UP YOUR RUSSET BROW,	125	GOES FERGUS		4
UNTIL HE BURN UP NATURE WITH A KISS:—	128	DREAM OF FAERY	V	47

		PAGE	TITLE		LINE

UP   (CONTINUED)

LIFT UP BEFORE US WHEN THEY PASS,	135	TWO TREES		23
LIFT UP BEFORE US AS THEY PASS,	135	TWO TREES	V	23
BUT HE HEARD HIGH UP IN THE AIR	145	HOST OF AIR		41
O'DRISCOLL GOT UP FROM THE GRASS,	145	HOST OF AIR	V	37
AND THEY SIGH IF THE WIND BUT LIFT UP A TRESS;	151	OLD MOTHER	V	8
THAT WAS BRIMMED UP WITH PRAYER AND REST;	151	HEART OF WOMAN		2
AND BIND UP EVERY WANDERING TRESS;	157	BELOVED RHYMES		2
AND BIND UP YOUR LONG HAIR AND SIGH;	158	BELOVED RHYMES		8
BUT SHE TOOK UP HER FAN FROM THE TABLE	160	CAP AND BELLS		19
THEY SET UP A NOISE LIKE CRICKETS,	161	CAP AND BELLS		33
WHEN SHE ROSE UP TO DEPART?	171	MAID QUIET		6
NOW WORDS THAT CALLED UP THE LIGHTNING	171	MAID QUIET		7
AND DRUNK UP THE MURMURING TIDE;	171	MAID QUIET	V	4D
FOR THE WORDS THAT CALLED UP THE LIGHTNING	171	MAID QUIET	V	7
THEY WILL ALL COME UP TO ME,	179	FIDDLER DOONEY		18
WILL ALL COME UP TO ME,	179	FIDDLER DOONEY	V	18
A LATTICED WINDOW. HIS GLANCE WENT UP AT TIMES	180	QUEEN MAEVE		6
MIGHT BE ACCOMPLISHED. BUNCHING THE CURTAIN UP	183	QUEEN MAEVE		68
CAME UP OUT OF THE HOLE, AND RED-EARED HOUNDS	185	QUEEN MAEVE		117
CASTS UP A SHOW AND THE WINDS ANSWER IT	186	QUEEN MAEVE		125
TWO SWANS CAME FLYING UP TO HIM,	194	BAILE AILLINN		135
IT MIGHT CALL UP A NEW AGE, CALLING TO MIND	201	OLD MEMORY		4
HAVE GIVEN THEIR HEARTS UP TO THE PLAY.	202	NEVER GIVE ALL		10
THE WIND HAS BUNDLED UP THE CLOUDS HIGH OVER KNOCKNAREA,	207	HANRAHANS SONG		6
THE YELLOW POOL HAS OVERFLOWED HIGH UP ON CLOOTH-NA-BARE,	207	HANRAHANS SONG		11
THE WINDS HAVE BUNDLED UP THE CLOUDS HIGH OVER KNOCKNAREA	207	HANRAHANS SONG	V	6
FOR THE GREY WINDS ARE BLOWING UP, OUT OF THE CLINGING	207	HANRAHANS SONG	V	12
SEAS;				
ONE GATHERS UP HIS PURPLE GOWN;	212	BLESS PSALTER		9
AND LIFT UP AN OLD HORN	215	HAPPY TOWNLAND		49
STRANGE CREATURES FLUTTER UP BEFORE ONE'S EYES,	222	SHADOW WATER B		18
A BEAUTIFUL YOUNG MAN AND GIRL CAME UP	223	SHADOW WATER B		33
AND HE MY MASTER FROM MY CHILDHOOD UP!	225	SHADOW WATER B		77
HAD THE WORLD'S TOTAL LIFE GATHERED UP, IT SEEMED,	231	SHADOW WATER B		194
AENGUS AND EDAIN RAN UP OUT OF THE WAVE—	231	SHADOW WATER B		196
AND PAID YOU ON THE NAIL. TAKE UP THAT ROPE	232	SHADOW WATER B		224
A MAGIC THAT CAN CALL A DEMON UP,	238	SHADOW WATER B		344
THAT HE IS HOLDING UP BETWEEN US THERE,	240	SHADOW WATER B		378
I LOVED HIM; I WOULD COVER UP MY EARS,	246	SHADOW WATER B		494
BUT I WILL COVER UP YOUR EYES AND EARS,	250	SHADOW WATER B		574
WHAT COULD I BUT TAKE UP THE SONG?	254	HIS DREAM		14
UNTIL MY THOUGHTS CLEARED UP AGAIN,	256	WORDS		6
THAT HAVE TO BE SET UP IN FIFTY WAYS,	260	FASC DIFFICULT		9
ALL THOSE HAD LIFTED UP THE DIM	272	GREY ROCK		27
BUT THEREON EVERY GOD STOOD UP	275	GREY ROCK		116
THE HANDS THAT GATHERED UP THE MIGHT OF THE WORLD,	278	TWO KINGS		29
SUCKED UP THE PASSION OUT OF HIM AGAIN	284	TWO KINGS		160
LOOK UP IN THE SUN'S EYE AND GIVE	288	TO WEALTHY MAN		32
"TIME'S UP," HE CRIED, AND ALL THE THREE	297	THREE BEGGARS		57
"TIME'S UP," HE CRIED, AND ALL THE THREE	297	THREE BEGGARS		59
HAD NOT THE SLEEPER STARTED UP.	304	HOUR DAWN		48
AND TOOK THE WOODEN LADLE UP	304	HOUR DAWN	V	46
AND AFTER HEAPED UP STONE ON STONE,	307	HOUR DAWN		116
AND HEAPED UP STONE ON STONE AGAIN,	307	HOUR DAWN		118
THREW UP IN THE AIR HIS MARVELLOUS MOON.	314	MEMORY YOUTH	V	21
WHILE UP FROM MY HEART'S ROOT	316	FRIENDS		26
AND THREW HIM UP TO LAUGH ON THE BOUGH;	318	APPOINTMENT		11
CLIMB UP THE NARROW WINDING STAIR TO BED!	324	ROBERT GREGORY		5
AND QUARRELS ARE BLOWN UP UPON THAT HEAD;	324	ROBERT GREGORY		13
"ALTHOUGH I'D LIE LAPPED UP IN LINEN	331	ROUND TOWER		1
BELLOWING UP AND BELLOWING ROUND,	331	ROUND TOWER		14
PRANCING ROUND AND PRANCING UP	331	ROUND TOWER		17
SEEING THAT TIME HAS FROZEN UP THE BLOOD	333	LIVING BEAUTY	V	2
THAT HE ALONE HAD GATHERED UP NO GEAR,	340	SHEP GOATHERD		49
AND CHILDREN WHEN THEY SPRING UP SHOULDER-HIGH.	343	SHEP GOATHERD		119
AND CHILDREN WHEN THEY SPRING UP SHOULDER HIGH.	343	SHEP GOATHERD	V	119
THAT GIVES UP ALL HER MIND,	345	ON WOMAN		2
THAT POUNDS UP ALL ANEW	346	ON WOMAN		31
TO CALL UP TO THE EYES	347	FISHERMAN		7
CLIMBING UP TO A PLACE	348	FISHERMAN		31
I HAVE GONE ABOUT THE HOUSE, GONE UP AND DOWN	350	HER PRAISE		2
AND THERE'S A PLAYER IN THE STATES WHO GATHERS UP HER CLOAK	354	HIS PHOENIX		12
AND THERE'S THE PLAYER IN THE STATES WHO GATHERS UP HER	354	HIS PHOENIX	V	12
CLOAK				
AS IF THE HAIR STOOD UP ON MY HEAD.	358	PRESENCES		2
CLIMBED UP MY CREAKING STAIR. THEY HAD READ	358	PRESENCES		6
HEEL UP AND WEIGHT ON TOE, MUST FACE THE WALL	363	DOLLS FACES		3
THAT SHADES THE ROAD, OR SETTING UP A COTTAGE	372	ON GOING HOUSE		14
CAUGHT UP IN CONTEMPLATION, THE MIND'S EYE	375	PHASES OF MOON		79
WHEN ALL THE DOUGH HAS BEEN SO KNEADED UP	377	PHASES OF MOON		114
OUT OF THE UP AND DOWN, THE WAGON-WHEEL	377	PHASES OF MOON		120
OUT OF THE UP AND DOWN, THE WAGON WHEEL	377	PHASES OF MOON	V	120
THE CREEPING CAT, LOOKED UP.	378	CAT AND MOON		4
STAND UP AND LIFT YOUR HAND AND BLESS	379	SAINT HUNCH		1
AND BOTH LOOK UP TO ME ALONE	380	SONGS FOOL 1		4
AS I LOOK UP TO PROVIDENCE.	380	SONGS FOOL 1		6
STRETCHED UP ON TWO LEGS FROM THE MAT,	381	SONGS FOOL 2		7
HAS CALLED UP THE COLD SPIRITS THAT ARE BORN	382	VISION ROBART		2
HAND LIFTED UP THAT BLEST!	383	VISION ROBART		20
AN IMAGE UP, OR ANYTHING	390	IMAGE PAST		33

	PAGE	TITLE		LINE
WHETHER SHE THREW THEM UP TO FLOUT ME,	390	IMAGE PAST		37
BUT SOON A TEAR-DROP STARTED UP,	400	DEMON BEAST		21
A BIT OF BREAD THROWN UP INTO THE AIR:	400	DEMON BEAST		25
PROSPER BUT LITTLE, HAS DRIED UP OF LATE,	405	FOR DAUGHTER		51
LIT UP THE DARK MAHOGANY AND THE WINE,	410	TOWER		27
AND FOLLOWED UP THOSE BAYING CREATURES TOWARDS--	412	TOWER		72
BRING UP OUT OF THAT DEEP CONSIDERING MIND	413	TOWER		106
RECKONED UP EVERY UNFOREKNOWN, UNSEEING	413	TOWER		109
TILL MAN MADE UP THE WHOLE,	415	TOWER		149
WHEN THEY HAVE MOUNTED UP,	415	TOWER		169
"VENGEANCE UPON THE MURDERERS," THE CRY GOES UP,	426	PHANTOM HATRED		9
AND AGAMEMNON DEAD. BEING SO CAUGHT UP,	441	LEDA AND SWAN		11
AND WHEN WE TALKED OF GROWING UP	456	SUMMER SPRING		5
WE THREE MAKE UP A SOLITUDE:	457	SECRETS OF OLD		9
O BID ME MOUNT AND SAIL UP THERE	458	HIS WILDNESS		1
THAT PURITY BUILT UP THE STATE	460	THREE MONUMENT		6
AND SPEAK BUT LIES. CALL UP TO MEMORY	462	HARUN RASHID	V	30
THE GARDEN PATHS, NOR COUNTED UP THE ROOMS,	466	HARUN RASHID		119
BUT WOKE AT THE FIRST GLEAM OF DAY, ROSE UP	467	HARUN RASHID		147
TWO THOUGHTS WERE SO MIXED UP I COULD NOT TELL	471	ALL SOUL NIGHT		31
HAD SO LIT UP THE WHOLE	472	ALL SOUL NIGHT		37
AND I CALL UP MACGREGOR FROM THE GRAVE,	473	ALL SOUL NIGHT		61
WHEN THOUGHTS RISE UP UNBID	473	ALL SOUL NIGHT		68
ENDURE THAT TOIL OF GROWING UP:	478	SELF AND SOUL		44
A POWERFUL EMBLEM UP,	480	BLOOD AND MOON		9
THE AVENGING LEAF THOSE FIELDS RAISED UP AGAINST IT.	487	SEVEN SAGES		20
IN COOLE DEMESNE, AND THERE TO FINISH UP	490	COOLE BALLYLEE		6
AND BIDS MY HAIR STAND UP?	499	MOTHER OF GOD		15
AND MAKES MY HAIR STAND UP?	499	MOTHER OF GOD	V	15
SUDDENLY LIT UP	512	JANE ON GOD		16
WRAPPING THAT FOUL BODY UP	525	DANCING DAYS		5
AND AFTER THAT I HELD MY FINGERS UP,	537	HER VISION		9
ALL THERE CAUGHT UP THE TUNE:	545	TO SAME TUNE 1		15
WHEN NATIONS ARE EMPTY UP THERE AT THE TOP,	548	TO SAME TUNE 3		11
LIFT, LIFT, LIFT UP THE TUNE.	548	TO SAME TUNE 3	V	16
MARCH, MARCH, LIFT UP THE SONG:	549	TO SAME TUNE 3		26
LIFT, LIFT, LIFT UP THE SONG.	549	TO SAME TUNE 3	V	26
AS THE MOON SIDLES UP	559	HE AND SHE		1
MUST SHE SIDLE UP,	559	HE AND SHE		2
DO NOT BREAK UP THEIR LINES TO WEEP.	565	LAPIS LAZULI		15
THE BLINDS DRAWN UP": MAUD GONNE AT HOWTH STATION WAITING A TRAIN,	578	LOFTY THINGS		10
HE THAT'S MOUNTING UP MUST ON HIS NEIGHBOUR MOUNT,	580	CURSE CROMWELL		11
COME FILL UP ALL THOSE GLASSES	586	PARNELLITES		7
AND BOTH CLIMBED UP THE STAIR,	595	COLONEL MARTIN		38
A JOURNALIST MAKES UP HIS LIES	598	STONE CROSS		3
SET UP THE OLD STONE CROSS,	604	YOU CONTENT		10
AND I BEAT UP THE COMMON SORT	605	SONGS BURDEN 1		3
COULD THAT OLD GOD RISE UP AGAIN	606	SONGS BURDEN 1		21
HER HEART MOUNT UP ON HIGH:	608	SONGS BURDEN 3		22
WHAT IF THERE'S NOTHING UP THERE AT THE TOP?	615	MARCH SONGS 2		21
ALL THERE CAUGHT UP THE TUNE:	616	MARCH SONGS 3		15
PICKED UP ON A STREET.	617	LONG-LEG FLY		18
PICKED UP ON THE STREET.	617	LONG-LEG FLY	V	18
SOME DAY WE SHALL GET UP BEFORE THE DAWN	622	HOUND VOICE		15
SOME ROGUE OF THE WORLD STOLE THEM TO PATCH UP A FENCE OR A FIRE.	623	HIGH TALK		4
FAR UP IN THE STRETCHES OF NIGHT:	623	HIGH TALK		12
WHERE I CAN SIT UP HALF THE NIGHT	624	APPARITIONS		11
UP THERE SOME HAWK OR OWL HAS STRUCK,	633	MAN AND ECHO		43
CAME CREEPING UP BECAUSE THE MAN WAS STILL.	634	CUCHULAIN COMF		10
TOOK UP THE NEAREST AND BEGAN TO SEW.	634	CUCHULAIN COMF		18
BUT WINDS COME UP FROM THE SHORE:	635	BLACK TOWER		8
CARES WHAT KING SETS UP HIS RULE.	635	BLACK TOWER		14
BUT WIND COMES UP FROM THE SHORE:	636	BLACK TOWER		18
BUT WIND COMES UP FROM THE SHORE:	636	BLACK TOWER		28
BUT WINDS COME UP FROM THE SHORE:	636	BLACK TOWER	V	REF
SCORN THE SORT NOW GROWING UP	639	BEN BULBEN		70
HURLS THEIR SWOONING LUSTRE UP.	647	ISLE STAT I 1		49
GO UP AND DOWN, AND RAISE THEIR HEADS AND SING	682	SEEKER		30
THAT FROM THE FIRE IS EVER POURING UP	683	SEEKER		37
POURS UP AND FLOATS IN FRAGRANCE ROUND MY HEAD	691	MOSADA 1		40
POURS UP AND FLOATS IN FRAGRANCE O'ER MY HEAD	691	MOSADA 1	V	40
HEARKEN, YE SWALLOWS!--I HAVE HOARDED UP	699	MOSADA 3		23
LOOK UP, LOOK UP, THY GOMEZ IS BY THEE.	701	MOSADA 3		68
LOOK UP, LOOK UP, THY GOMEZ IS BY THEE.	701	MOSADA 3		68
LOOK UP, LOOK UP, THY VALLENCE IS BY THEE.	701	MOSADA 3	V	68
LOOK UP, LOOK UP, THY VALLENCE IS BY THEE.	701	MOSADA 3	V	68
I KNEEL BY THEE--NO PARTING NOW--LOOK UP.	702	MOSADA 3		94
OH, WOULD THE BUSY MINUTES MIGHT FOLD UP	702	MOSADA 3		97
JUST NOW MY SOUL ROSE UP AND TOUCHED IT, FAR	705	REMEMBRANCE		13
SO ENDS A BRAIN--A WORLD! THE SMOKE GOES UP,	714	FERENCZ RENYI		111
OF FIRE. SO ENDS A BRAIN--A WORLD! THE SMOKE FLOATS UP,	714	FERENCZ RENYI	V	111
LEAPED UP INTO THE AIR.	741	EARL PAUL		36
AND JOHN ROSE UP AND STOOD,	741	EARL PAUL		54
AND, THOUGH YOU LOVED HER, GAVE HER UP TO ME?	749	SHADOW WATER A		50
AS THOUGH THE WATERS HAD FLOWED UP BETWEEN:	749	SHADOW WATER A		55
WERE THEY BUT LIFTED UP. THE RED HOUND IS FLED.	761	SHADOW WATER A		266
WHEN EARTH AND HEAVEN HAVE BEEN FOLDED UP:	765	SHADOW WATER A		366
TILL THE SIDE OF HATE COMES UP.	776	AGAINST WITCH		35

		PAGE	TITLE	LINE

UP   (CONTINUED)
         UP WITH THE NECK AND CLAP THE WING, ...   782 HEART FRIGHT   6
         UP WITH THE NECK AND CLAP THE WING, ...   782 HEART FRIGHT   13
         UP WITH THE NECK AND CLAP THE WING, ...   782 HEART FRIGHT   20
         BURN THEIR BODIES UP FOR NOUGHT, ...   787 HUDDON DUDDON   14
UPHELD
         ONE HAND UPHELD HIS BEARDLESS CHIN, ...   17 OISIN 1   250
UPHOLSTERIES
         AND THEY BUT FAMOUS OLD UPHOLSTERIES   . . . .   579 DOR WELLESLEY   3
UPLAND
         UPON THE NORMAN UPLAND OR IN THAT POPLAR SHADE, ... 449 OWEN AHERNE   2
         UPON THE NORTHERN UPLAND OR IN THAT POPLAR SHADE,   . . .   449 OWEN AHERNE   V   2
         BUT O! MY HEART COULD BEAR NO MORE WHEN THE UPLAND CAUGHT   450 OWEN AHERNE   11
            THE WIND!
UPLIFT
         "UPLIFT THOSE EYES AND THROW   . . . .   516 MANS SONG   7
UPLIFTED
         UPLIFTED GATEWAY. WITH THE FLASHING BEAT   . . . . . .   31 OISIN 2   V   30D
         AND THE GREEN QUIET, HAVE UPLIFTED THE HEART?   . . . . .   219 WOODS OF COOLE   40
UPPER
         WHETHER THEY TAKE THE UPPER ROAD   . . . .   589 OLD WICKED MAN   48
         BECAUSE WOMEN IN THE UPPER STOREYS DEMAND A FACE AT THE   623 HIGH TALK   7
            PANE,
         UPON CLEAR NIGHTS THEY LEAVE THE UPPER AIR   . . . . . .   750 SHADOW WATER A   87
UPPERMOST
         UNTIL HER PRAISE SHOULD BE THE UPPERMOST THEME, ... 350 HER PRAISE   6
UPRAISED
         AN ABBOT OR ARCHBISHOP WITH AN UPRAISED HAND   . . . . . 601 GALLERY REVIS   9
         UPRAISED HIS VOICE, AND HOOTED ME.   . . . .   670 ISLE STAT II 3 V   117
         UPRAISED THEIR VOICES BITTERLY.   . . . .   730 PRIEST FAIRY   72
UP-RAISED
         UP-RAISED HIS VOICE, AND HOOTED ME.   . . . .   670 ISLE STAT II 3   117
UPRIGHT
         STOOD UPRIGHT ON THE FLOOR.   . . . .   133 FR GILLIGAN   24
         THE PORTER SLEPT, ALTHOUGH HE SAT UPRIGHT   . . . . . .   182 QUEEN MAEVE   45
         SAT UPRIGHT WITH A SWORD BEFORE HER FEET.   . . . . . .   279 TWO KINGS   62
         I, THOUGH UPRIGHT ON THE SHORE, ...   298 THREE HERMITS   11
         TO KEEP HIM UPRIGHT WHILE HE CURSED.   . . . .   302 HOUR DAWN   6
         AND SAW HER SITTING UPRIGHT ON THE BED!   . . . . . .   467 HARUN RASHID   134
         I SAW HER SITTING UPRIGHT ON THE BED, ...   467 HARUN RASHID   V   134
         TO HOLD HIMSELF UPRIGHT!   . . . .   515 GIRLS SONG B   7
         BUT BODY WON! IT WALKS UPRIGHT.   . . . .   561 FOUR AGES MAN   2
         STAND UPRIGHT ON YOUR LEGS AWHILE, ...   586 PARNELLITES   3
         STAND UPRIGHT WHILE YOU CAN, ...   586 PARNELLITES   4
         THERE IN THE TOMB STAND THE DEAD UPRIGHT.   . . . . .   635 BLACK TOWER   7
UPROAR
         AND WHEN THE UPROAR RAN ALONG THE GRASS   . . . . . .   186 QUEEN MAEVE   127
         NOISE! UPROAR! AND A MOMENTARY BLOT.   . . . .   714 FERENCZ RENYI V   110
         CEASE THE SAILS THEIR FLAPPING UPROAR, AND THE HULL NO   719 PHANTOM SHIP   18
            LONGER ROLLS.
         CEASE THE SAILS, THEIR FLAPPING UPROAR TO THE HULL   719 PHANTOM SHIP   V   18
            NO LONGER ROLLS.
UPROOT
         WE SHADOWS, WHILE THEY UPROOT HIS EARTHY HOUSE, ... 184 QUEEN MAEVE   94
         WE SHADOWS, WHILE THEY UPROOT THE EARTHY HOUSE   . . . . 184 QUEEN MAEVE   V   94
UPROOTED
         TARA UPROOTED, AND NEW COMMONNESS   . . . .   198 SEVEN WOODS   6
UPROOTING
         RAVENING, RAGING, AND UPROOTING THAT HE MAY COME   . . . 563 MERU   6
UPS
         THAT HAS LESS UPS AND DOWNS THAN ROBBERY.   . . . . . . 222 SHADOW WATER B   7
         NO UPS AND DOWNS, MY PRETTY, ...   592 DRUNK SOBRIETY   13
UPSPRINGING
         WHEN THEY AWAKE UPSPRINGING! WITH LOUD HORN   . . . . .   32 OISIN 2   V   52
UPSTAIRS
         THAT ONE BELIEVED HE HAD A SWORD UPSTAIRS!   . . . . .   267 ALL TEMPT ME   8
         HE ROSE THE LATCH AND WENT UPSTAIRS   . . . .   594 COLONEL MARTIN   7
UPSTANDING
         I CHOOSE UPSTANDING MEN   . . . .   414 TOWER   122
         TO YOUNG UPSTANDING MEN   . . . .   416 TOWER   174
UPTURNED
         FROM DOORED AND WINDOWED CLIFF, OR HALF UPTURNED   . . . 368 EGO DOMINUS   30
UPWARD
         HE BADE HIS SOUL RISE UPWARD   . . . .   159 CAP AND BELLS   3
         HE MADE HIS SOUL GO UPWARD   . . . .   159 CAP AND BELLS V   3
         LEAPS UPWARD, AS IF ALL THE STREAMS O' THE WORLD   . . . 249 SHADOW WATER B   560
         WHEN UPWARD TURNED, ON ONE SOLE IMAGE FELL!   . . . . .   471 ALL SOUL NIGHT   34
         WHEN UPWARD TURNED ON ONE SOUL IMAGE FELL, ...   471 ALL SOUL NIGHT V   34
         A GREY BIRD HAS FLOWN BY. HE HAS FLOWN UPWARD.   . . . 753 SHADOW WATER A   134
URBINO
         EVENING AND MORNING, THE STEEP STREET OF URBINO   . . . 352 PEOPLE   12
         EVENING AND MORN, THE STEEP STREET OF URBINO   . . . .   352 PEOPLE   V   12
URBINO'S
         UPON URBINO'S WINDY HILL, ...   288 TO WEALTHY MAN   17
URGED
         OF DANAAN HOOVES WE URGED OUR WAY BETWEEN   . . . . . .   31 OISIN 2   V   31
         OUR LEARNED MEN HAVE URGED   . . . .   421 MY TABLE   15
URN
         WE THOUGHT ON OSCAR'S PENCILLED URN.   . . . .   2 OISIN 1   V   70
         "WE THINK ON OSCAR'S PENCILLED URN, ...   5 OISIN 1   41
         AND IN SOME URN FUNEREAL LIE   . . . .   19 OISIN 1   V   272

	PAGE	TITLE		LINE

URN   (CONTINUED)
OR ELSE ALL JUNO FROM AN URN DISPLAYS   •   •   •   •   •   •   •   418 ANCEST HOUSES   27
USE
THE WAGES OF SIN IS DEATH. NO USE. NO GOOD. •   •   •   •   697 MOSADA 2   42
THE WAGE OF SIN IS DEATH. NO USE. NO USE. •   •   •   •   •   697 MOSADA 2   V   42
THE WAGE OF SIN IS DEATH. NO USE. NO USE. •   •   •   •   •   697 MOSADA 2   V   42
NO USE. AWAY! HEAR, THOU ENDURING GOD,   •   •   •   •   •   698 MOSADA 2   50
NO USE. AWAY! HEAR OH! THOU ENDURING GOD,   •   •   •   •   698 MOSADA 2   V   50
USED
MY MONEY'S ALL USED UP,   •   •   •   •   •   •   •   •   •   •   96 MOLL MAGEE   38
I MIGHT HAVE USED THE ONE SUBSTANTIAL RIGHT   •   •   •   •   352 PEOPLE   19
BUT WHAT THE GREAT AND PASSIONATE HAVE USED   •   •   •   •   371 ON GOING HOUSE   7
AH! HOW LARGE MICE USED TO BE   •   •   •   •   •   •   •   •   727 LOVERS QUARREL   39
USELESS
THUNDERING, AND THE WIDE USELESS WATERS FRAY   •   •   •   •   45 OISIN 2   V   238
ALONE WITH ALL THIS USELESS HAPPINESS?"   •   •   •   •   •   285 TWO KINGS   200
USHEEN
FOR LOVE OF USHEEN MY FEET RAN   •   •   •   •   •   •   •   •   6 OISIN 1   V   57
BY THIS YOUNG MAN, USHEEN MY SON?"   •   •   •   •   •   •   •   6 OISIN 1   V   60
KNEEL, USHEEN, WEAR OUT THE FLAGS AND PRAY FOR YOUR SOUL   63 OISIN 3   V   215
   THAT IS LOST
USHEEN'S
"RHYME, THAT RHYMED TO USHEEN'S NAME,   •   •   •   •   •   •   7 OISIN 1   V   64
USNA'S
AND USNA'S CHILDREN DIED.   •   •   •   •   •   •   •   •   •   111 ROSE OF WORLD   5
USURY
THEN WHEREFORE FEAR THE USURY OF TIME,   •   •   •   •   •   •   724 KANVA ON SELF   17
UTHER'S
THE AUSTERE ARTHUR, RULE FROM UTHER'S CHAIR?   •   •   •   •   678 ISLE STAT II 3   296
UTMOST
AND NOW MY UTMOST MYSTERY IS OUT.   •   •   •   •   •   •   •   469 HARUN RASHID   187
MY UTMOST PLEASURE WITH A MAN   •   •   •   •   •   •   •   •   535 CHOSEN   12
UTOPIA
SOME VAGUE UTOPIA--AND SHE SEEMS,   •   •   •   •   •   •   •   475 EVA GORE-BOOTH   11
UTTERED
SO PALE! AND SOUNDS OF WONDER HER LIPS UTTERED,   •   •   •   34 OISIN 2   V   71
UTTERING
UTTERING, MASTERING IT,   •   •   •   •   •   •   •   •   •   480 BLOOD AND MOON   5
AND THEN NEW MURMURS CAME NEW UTTERING   •   •   •   •   •   657 ISLE STAT I 3   50
UTTERLY
I HAVE DECEIVED YOU UTTERLY. HOW CAN THAT BE?   •   •   •   245 SHADOW WATER B   472
DANTE ALIGHIERI, SO UTTERLY FOUND HIMSELF   •   •   •   •   •   368 EGO DOMINUS   19
ALL CHANGED, CHANGED UTTERLY!   •   •   •   •   •   •   •   •   392 EASTER 1916   15
TRANSFORMED UTTERLY!   •   •   •   •   •   •   •   •   •   •   393 EASTER 1916   39
ARE CHANGED, CHANGED UTTERLY!   •   •   •   •   •   •   •   •   394 EASTER 1916   79
UTTERMOST
TRAGEDY WROUGHT TO ITS UTTERMOST.   •   •   •   •   •   •   •   566 LAPIS LAZULI   20
VACILLATION
VACILLATION   •   •   •   •   •   •   •   •   •   •   •   •   •   499 VACILLATION   T
VAGUE
A FAR VAGUE SOUND OF FEATHERY CHOIRS.   •   •   •   •   •   •   13 OISIN 1   V   166
A MOMENTARY GLIMMER OF VAGUE PHOSPHORUS FLAME.   •   •   •   37 OISIN 2   V   120
•   •   •   THE SOUND OF THE SEA'S VAGUE DRUM?   •   •   •   •   56 OISIN 3   135
VAGUE MEMORIES, NOTHING BUT MEMORIES.   •   •   •   •   •   •   356 BROKEN DREAMS   15
VAGUE MEMORIES, NOTHING BUT MEMORIES.   •   •   •   •   •   •   356 BROKEN DREAMS   20
VAGUE MEMORIES, NOTHING BUT MEMORIES.   •   •   •   •   •   •   357 BROKEN DREAMS   41
FROM VAGUE DISTRESS   •   •   •   •   •   •   •   •   •   •   •   390 IMAGE PAST   24
HOW CAN THOSE TERRIFIED VAGUE FINGERS PUSH   •   •   •   •   •   441 LEDA AND SWAN   5
SOME VAGUE UTOPIA--AND SHE SEEMS,   •   •   •   •   •   •   •   475 EVA GORE-BOOTH   11
ALL ASIATIC VAGUE IMMENSITIES,   •   •   •   •   •   •   •   •   610 STATUES   12
VAGUELY
A MAN--SO VAGUELY THAT HE SEEMED TO DREAM--   •   •   •   •   351 HER PRAISE   V   8
VAIN
AND PONDERED IN A SOFT VAIN MOOD   •   •   •   •   •   •   •   14 OISIN 1   184
IN VAIN HER ARMS, IN VAIN HER SOFT WHITE BREAST.   •   •   •   110 CUCHULAIN SEA   74
IN VAIN HER ARMS, IN VAIN HER SOFT WHITE BREAST.   •   •   •   110 CUCHULAIN SEA   74
TILL VAIN FRENZY AWOKE AND HE DIED; AND HIM   •   •   •   •   169 SECRET ROSE   12
IN VAIN, IN VAIN! THE CATARACT STILL CRIES;   •   •   •   •   311 MOUNTAIN TOMB   9
IN VAIN, IN VAIN! THE CATARACT STILL CRIES;   •   •   •   •   311 MOUNTAIN TOMB   9
BUT CHARM AND FACE WERE IN VAIN   •   •   •   •   •   •   •   •   350 MEMORY   3
I AM THINKING OF A CHILD'S VOW SWORN IN VAIN   •   •   •   •   391 UNDER SATURN   15
MADE ALL PLATONIC TOLERANCE VAIN   •   •   •   •   •   •   •   438 SONGS PLAY 2   7
AND VAIN ALL DORIC DISCIPLINE.   •   •   •   •   •   •   •   •   438 SONGS PLAY 2   8
MADE PLATO'S TOLERANCE IN VAIN,   •   •   •   •   •   •   •   •   438 SONGS PLAY 2   V   7
AND VAIN THE DORIC DISCIPLINE.   •   •   •   •   •   •   •   •   438 SONGS PLAY 2   V   8
IN VAIN THE DORIC DISCIPLINE.   •   •   •   •   •   •   •   •   438 SONGS PLAY 2   V   8
DELIGHT BECOMES DEATH-LONGING IF ALL LONGING ELSE BE VAIN.   459 FROM OEDIPUS   3
WE GROPE, AND GROPE IN VAIN,   •   •   •   •   •   •   •   •   487 CRAZED MOON   5
I WHISTLED AND WHISTLED AND WHISTLED IN VAIN.   •   •   •   •   551 SONGS REWRIT 1   16
I CRIED AND WHISTLED BUT VAIN, ALL VAIN.   •   •   •   •   •   551 SONGS REWRIT 1 V   16
I CRIED AND WHISTLED BUT VAIN, ALL VAIN.   •   •   •   •   •   551 SONGS REWRIT 1 V   16
BUT THERE I LAY AND I WHISTLED IN VAIN.   •   •   •   •   •   551 SONGS REWRIT 1 V   16
A VAIN HOPE   •   •   •   •   •   •   •   •   •   •   •   •   •   553 CHURCH STATE   V   T
I SOUGHT A THEME AND SOUGHT FOR IT IN VAIN,   •   •   •   •   629 CIRCUS ANIMALS   1
VAIN GAIETY, VAIN BATTLE, VAIN REPOSE.   •   •   •   •   •   •   629 CIRCUS ANIMALS   12
VAIN GAIETY, VAIN BATTLE, VAIN REPOSE,   •   •   •   •   •   •   629 CIRCUS ANIMALS   12
VAIN GAIETY, VAIN BATTLE, VAIN REPOSE,   •   •   •   •   •   •   629 CIRCUS ANIMALS   12
AND SHIRK IT IN VAIN. THERE IS NO RELEASE   •   •   •   •   •   632 MAN AND ECHO   21
VAINGLORIOUS
A DRUNKEN, VAINGLORIOUS LOUT.   •   •   •   •   •   •   •   •   393 EASTER 1916   32

857

VAIN-GLORIOUS
    A DRUNKEN, VAIN-GLORIOUS LOUT. . . . . 393 EASTER 1916 V 32
VALE
    WHEN AMBLING DOWN THE VALE WE MET . . . .   2 OISIN 1 V 7U
    FROM ROLLING VALE AND RIVERY GLEN: . . . .   83 MAD KING GOLL 19
    'TIS MORN: THY SHEEP ARE WANDERING DOWN THE VALE-- 645 ISLE STAT I 1 3
    IN VALE AND DELL SO BLAZE THE DAFFODILLS: . . . . . 645 ISLE STAT I 1 15
    IF SO I MIGHT, ALONG A DEWY VALE, ... 649 ISLE STAT I 1 123
    OF THIS WIDE VALE, EMBOSOMED IN THE AIR, ... 652 ISLE STAT I 2 19
    ALONG THE VELVET VALE I SAW HIM COME-- . . . . . . 690 MOSADA 1 10
    WHERE HOMES ONCE WHITENED VALE AND MOUNTAIN CREST: . . . 709 FERENCZ RENYI 3
VALERA
    HAD DE VALERA EATEN PARNELL'S HEART . . . . 542 PARN FUNERAL 2 2
    OR AM I DE VALERA, ... 627 STATES HOLIDAY 18
VALLENCE
    WHEN MY LOST LOVER LEFT THESE ARMS, MY VALLENCE, . . . 701 MOSADA 3 V 51
    LOOK UP, LOOK UP, THY VALLENCE IS BY THEE. . . . . 701 MOSADA 3 V 68
    GRIEVE NOT, FOR VALLENCE KNEELS BESIDE THEE--VALLENCE, . 702 MOSADA 3 V 90
    GRIEVE NOT, FOR VALLENCE KNEELS BESIDE THEE--VALLENCE, . 702 MOSADA 3 V 90
    SAFE ON THE BREAST OF VALLENCE IS THY HEAD . . . . . 703 MOSADA 3 V 101
    GIVE TO THY VALLENCE. VALLENCE--HE HAS GONE . . . . 703 MOSADA 3 V 110
    GIVE TO THY VALLENCE. VALLENCE--HE HAS GONE . . . . 703 MOSADA 3 V 110
VALLEY
    A VALLEY FLOWED DOWN FROM HIS HOOFS, AND THERE IN THE LONG 48 OISIN 3 26
        GRASS LAY,
    OF HOLLIES, AND HAZELS, AND OAK TREES, A VALLEY WAS SLOPING 48 OISIN 3 V 26
        AWAY
    AND OVER THE LIMBS AND THE VALLEY THE SLOW OWLS WANDERED 49 OISIN 3 41
        AND CAME,
    AND, IN A FAR-OFF, GENTLE VALLEY STOPPING, ... 68 SAD SHEPHERD 13
    HE FLED, AND IN A FAR-OFF VALLEY STOPPING, ... 68 SAD SHEPHERD V 13
    FROM ROLLING VALLEY AND RIVERY GLEN, ... 83 MAD KING GOLL V 17
    AND SONG THAT DOWN THE VALLEY ROLLED-- . . . . 84 MAD KING GOLL V 35
    THE VALLEY OF THE BLACK PIG . . . . 161 BLACK PIG T
    HE TELLS OF A VALLEY FULL OF LOVERS . . . . 163 VALLEY LOVERS T
    THE VALLEY OF LOVERS . . . . 163 VALLEY LOVERS V T
    AEDH TELLS OF A VALLEY FULL OF LOVERS . . . . 163 VALLEY LOVERS V T
    I DREAMED THAT I STOOD IN A VALLEY, AND AMID SIGHS, . . . 163 VALLEY LOVERS 1
    TO KNOW THE MOUNTAIN AND THE VALLEY HAVE GRIEVED . . . . 343 SHEP GOATHERD 117
    TO KNOW THE MOUNTAIN AND THE VALLEY GRIEVE . . . . . . 343 SHEP GOATHERD V 117
    NEVER TO LEAVE THAT VALLEY HIS FATHERS CALLED THEIR HOME. 391 UNDER SATURN 16
    VALLEY, RIVER, AND ELMS, UNDER THE LIGHT OF A MOON . . . 426 PHANTOM HATRED 3
    VALLEY, RIVER, ELMS, UNDER THE LIGHT OF A MOON . . . . 426 PHANTOM HATRED V 3
    THE WOOD AND THE VALLEY AND SEA . . . . 646 ISLE STAT I 1 42
    MAKE MOAN AND CRY, WITHIN YON SUNLESS VALLEY, ... 682 SEEKER 26
    THAT ALL THE VALLEY FILLS . . . . 781 MY HEART BEAT 10
VALLEY'S
    WATCHED HER THOSE SEAMLESS FACES FROM THE VALLEY'S 55 OISIN 3 122
        GLIMMERING GIRTH:
    WATCHED HER THOSE SEAMLESS FACES FROM THE VALLEY'S MURAL 55 OISIN 3 V 122
        GIRTH
VALLEYS
    O YOU, WITH WHOM IN SLOPING VALLEYS, ... 10 OISIN 1 119
    OH YE WITH WHOM, IN SLOPING VALLEYS . . . . 10 OISIN 1 V 119
    OR WRESTLE WITH THEIR PEERS IN DEWY VALLEYS. . . . . . 30 OISIN 2 V 14E
    A HERDSMAN CAME FROM INLAND VALLEYS, ... 82 MAD KING GOLL 14
    THERE CRIED A HERALD, "TO OUR VALLEYS . . . . 82 MAD KING GOLL V 14
    CRIED A HERALD, "TO OUR VALLEYS . . . . 82 MAD KING GOLL V 14
    AND SONG THAT DOWN THE VALLEYS ROLLED-- . . . . . . 84 MAD KING GOLL V 35
    THAT DOWN THE ECHOING VALLEYS ROLLED. . . . . 84 MAD KING GOLL V 35
    TILL ALL THE VALLEYS OF THE WORLD HAVE BEEN WITHERED AWAY. 163 VALLEY LOVERS 8
    TILL THE VALLEYS OF THE WORLD HAVE BEEN WITHERED AWAY." 163 VALLEY LOVERS V 8
    FAR OFF IN DROWSY VALLEYS . . . . 680 LOVE AND DEATH 5
    DOWN THE LONG VALLEYS FROM MY PEOPLE'S TENTS, ... 691 MOSADA 1 30
    WE WILL FIND OUT VALLEYS AND WOODS AND MEADOWS . . . . 767 SHADOW WATER A 388
VALOUR
    WITH HER DEAD BROTHER'S VALOUR . . . . 365 HER RACE 11
VALUE
    TO VALUE BEER: NO HALF-LEGGED FOOL . . . . 304 HOUR DAWN 52
    TO VALUE BEER--I WILL HAVE NO FOOL . . . . 304 HOUR DAWN V 52
VAMPIRES
    LIE BODIES OF THE VAMPIRES FULL OF BLOOD: . . . . . 483 OIL AND BLOOD 5
VAN
    THE VAN OF WANDERING QUIET: ERE YOU BE TOO CALM AND OLD, 73 ANASHU VIJAYA 43
    THE VAN OF WANDERING QUIET: ERE YE BE TOO CALM AND OLD, 73 ANASHU VIJAYA V 43
VANISH
    FOR ALL HIS SPELLS WILL VANISH WHEN HE DIES, ... 240 SHADOW WATER B 376
    BUT VANISH WITH OUR BREATH . . . . 431 NINETEEN 19 76
    ALL BREAK AND VANISH, AND EVIL GATHERS HEAD: . . . . 433 NINETEEN 19 117
    MUST VANISH ON THE INSTANT IF THE MIND BUT CHANGE 481 BLOOD AND MOON 27
        ITS THEME:
    IN THE FAR WORLD WILL VANISH FROM THY MIND, ... 670 ISLE STAT II 3 93
    HAVE COVERED THEM. WHERE DID THEY VANISH AWAY? . . . 764 SHADOW WATER A 328
VANISHED
    O WHEN WILL YOU GROW WEARY?" THEY HAD VANISHED: . . . 187 QUEEN MAEVE 152
    IT VANISHED LIKE A SHADOW, AND A CRY . . . . 278 TWO KINGS 38
    MY HANDS WERE PRESSED TO VANISHED SUDDENLY. . . . . . 286 TWO KINGS 208
    VANISHED, AND LEFT BUT MEMORIES, THAT SHOULD BE OUT OF 316 COLD HEAVEN 5
        SEASON
    WHEN HE VANISHED FROM EARS AND EYES. . . . . 341 SHEP GOATHERD 72
    WHEN IT HAS VANISHED FROM OUR NATURAL EYES: . . . . . 342 SHEP GOATHERD 81

		PAGE	TITLE	LINE

VANISHED   (CONTINUED)
THE HOLY CENTAURS OF THE HILLS ARE VANISHED! . . . . .   344 DEJECTION   7
BANISHED HEROIC MOTHER MOON AND VANISHED, ...   344 DEJECTION   9
HEROIC MOTHER MOON HAS VANISHED, ...   344 DEJECTION   V   9
WHEN THE OLD MOON IS VANISHED FROM THE SKY . . . . . .   382 VISION ROBART   3
AND WHEN IT'S VANISHED STILL DECLARE, ...   639 BEN BULBEN   60
FADED AND VANISHED, NOTHING NOW IS SEEN, ...   676 ISLE STAT II 3   268
GHOSTS OF HER VANISHED GLORIES, MUSE AND STALK . . . .   687 TWO TITANS   21
THE FAIRY VANISHED FROM HIS SIGHT, ...   730 PRIEST FAIRY   62

VANISHES
MAN IS IN LOVE AND LOVES WHAT VANISHES, ...   429 NINETEEN 19   42
TO BE IN LOVE AND LOVE WHAT VANISHES. . . . .   429 NINETEEN 19   V   42

VANISHING
WHEN THE OLD MOON IS VANISHING FROM THE SKY . . . . .   382 VISION ROBART V   3

VANITY
O VANITY OF SLEEP, HOPE, DREAM, ENDLESS DESIRE, ...   154 BELOVED PEACE   7
AND VANITY HER FOOTFALL LIGHT, ...   314 MEMORY YOUTH   12
OR THE DAY'S VANITY, THE NIGHT'S REMORSE. . . . . . .   491 COOLE BALLYLEE V 40H
OR THE DAY'S VANITY, THE NIGHT'S REMORSE. . . . . . .   495 CHOICE   8
MY CONSCIENCE OR MY VANITY APPALLED. . . . .   501 VACILLATION   56

VANITY'S
NO VANITY'S DISPLAYED! . . . .   532 BEFORE WORLD   6

VANS
AND TRAILING CRIMSON VANS, A MUMBLING BROOD, ...   687 TWO TITANS   20

VAPOUR
HALF LOST IN VAPOUR, SHADOWS CALLED OUR NAMES, ...   29 OISIN 2   V   3
NOT LOADED CENTURIES MIGHT VAPOUR. RAN . . . .   38 OISIN 2   V 127
SHAKING AND WAVING, VAPOUR VAPOUR CHASED, ...   39 OISIN 2   164
SHAKING AND WAVING, VAPOUR VAPOUR CHASED, ...   39 OISIN 2   164
GO DWELL UPON THE SEA CLIFFS, VAPOUR HID, ...   105 CUCHULAIN SEA V   4
IN DRUID VAPOUR AND MAKE THE TORCHES DIM! . . . . . .   169 SECRET ROSE   11
WHEN IN RAGGED VAPOUR THEY MUTTER NIGHT AND DAY, . . .   206 HANRAHANS SONG V   2
DARTING YOU WAVE THEM, DARTING IN THE VAPOUR. . . . .   694 MOSADA 1   94
THEM ALL, AND LET THEM FIND YOU IN THE VAPOUR. . . . .   694 MOSADA 1   V 108A
FOR YE ARE HID WITH VAPOUR. ROUND THE STAKE . . . .   695 MOSADA 1   111
THE VAPOUR IS MUCH THICKER. GOD! THE STAKE! . . . .   695 MOSADA 1   112
BREATHED OUT A DRUID VAPOUR, AND CRUMBLED AWAY . . . .   761 SHADOW WATER A   279

VAPOUR-HID
GO DWELL UPON THE SEA CLIFFS, VAPOUR-HID . . . . . .   105 CUCHULAIN SEA V   4

VAPOURS
AND FACE THAT SEEMED WROUGHT OUT OF MOONLIT VAPOURS, . .   33 OISIN 2   70
HER FACE SEEMED FASHIONED ALL OF MOONLIT VAPOURS, . .   33 OISIN 2   V   70
SHAKING AND WAVING, VAPOURS VAPOURS CHASED! . . . . .   39 OISIN 2   164
SHAKING AND WAVING, VAPOURS VAPOURS CHASED! . . . . .   39 OISIN 2   V 164
IN ALL HIS EVENING VAPOURS ROLLED-- . . . .   86 MAD KING GOLL V   71
WHEN THE WINTRY VAPOURS RISE. . . . .   643 SONG FAERIES   4
WHEN THE WINTRY VAPOURS RISE. . . . .   644 SONG FAERIES   16
FAR THE MORNING VAPOURS SHATTER, ...   648 ISLE STAT I 1   89
OVER THEM CRIMSON VAPOURS WINGING. . . . .   648 ISLE STAT I 1   92
WHEN THE WINTRY VAPOURS RISE. . . . .   676 ISLE STAT II 3   251
WHEN THE WINTRY VAPOURS RISE. . . . .   676 ISLE STAT II 3   263
FOR YE ARE HID WITH VAPOURS? ROUND THE STAKE . . . .   695 MOSADA 1   V 111
ALL HEAVEN'S FLOOR, WITH VAPOURS BEDDED-- . . . . .   705 DAWN-SONG   11
DOWN THE VAPOURS FALL AND HIDE THEM FROM THE CHILDREN OF   719 PHANTOM SHIP   27
    A DAY,
AND THE WINDS COME DOWN AND BLOW THEM WITH THE VAPOURS   719 PHANTOM SHIP   28
    FAR AWAY.
NESTED 'MONG THE VAPOURS BROWN. . . . .   731 STREET DANCERS   6

VAPOUR-TURBANED
UNDER THAT COLD AND VAPOUR-TURBANED STEEP, ...   128 DREAM OF FAERY   39

VAPOURY
WITH VAPOURY FOOTSOLE BY THE WATER'S DROWSY BLAZE. . .   78 INDIAN TO LOVE   20
A VAPOURY FOOTFALL ON THE OCEAN'S SLEEPY BLAZE. . . .   78 INDIAN TO LOVE V 20
AND DROP A VAPOURY FOOTFALL IN THE WATER'S DROWSY BLAZE.   78 INDIAN TO LOVE V 20
WITH VAPOURY FOOTSOLE AMONG THE WATER'S DROWSY BLAZE. .   78 INDIAN TO LOVE V 20
DROPPING A VAPOURY FOOTSOLE ON THE TIDE'S DROWSY BLAZE.   78 INDIAN TO LOVE V 20

VARYING
THROUGHOUT SO MANY VARYING CENTURIES . . . .   371 ON GOING HOUSE   8

VASSALS
AND TWICE A HUNDRED WERE THE VASSALS . . . .   23 OISIN 1   V 345E

VAST
WARS SHADOWY, VAST, EXULTANT! FAERIES OF OLD . . . . .   29 OISIN 2   9
WARS SHADOWY, VAST, EXULTANT! FAIRY KINGS . . . . . .   29 OISIN 2   V   9
NEARER THE CASTLE CAME WE. A VAST TIDE. . . . . . .   31 OISIN 2   V 27A
TYING THE HORSE TO HIS VAST FOOT THAT LAY . . . . . .   32 OISIN 2   46
TO ONE VAST FOOT, FROTH-SPLASHED, WITH CURVED TOES LYING   32 OISIN 2   V 46A
CAME CAR-BORNE BALOR, AS OLD AS A FOREST, HIS VAST FACE   53 OISIN 3   V   91
    SUNK
LONG FLED THE FOAM-FLAKES AROUND ME, THE WINDS FLED OUT   57 OISIN 3   149
    OF THE VAST,
ON THEIR VAST FACES MYSTERY AND DREAMS! . . . . . .   74 ANASHU VIJAYA   70
WHEN A VAST IMAGE OUT OF SPIRITUS MUNDI . . . .   402 SECOND COMING   12
VAST GREENNESS, WHERE ETERNAL RUMOUR DWELLS, ...   657 ISLE STAT I 3   45
OF THOSE VAST WOODS! AND THEN I SAW THE BOAT, ...   657 ISLE STAT I 3   53
TO SEE THEM DROWNED BY THOSE VAST SOLITUDES, ...   661 ISLE STAT II 1   57
AND SOFT, ONE GLIMMERING STAR--WITH POWER VAST! . . .   714 FERENCZ RENYI V 115
THAT THE VAST TROUBLED WATERS BRING . . . .   784 WOMANS BEAUTY   17

VASTY
I FOUND, FOAM-OOZY ON THE VASTY STAIR, ...   43 OISIN 2   V 215

VAT   SEE WINE-VAT
OR IN THE WINE VAT, DWELL BEYOND THE STIR . . . . . .   169 SECRET ROSE   V   4

859

		PAGE	TITLE	LINE

VATS
    THERE WE'VE HID OUR FAERY VATS, ... 87 STOLEN CHILD 6
VEERING
    VEERING, FLEETING, FICKLE, THE WINDS OF KNOCKNAREA, . . . 206 HANRAHANS SONG V 1
    VEERING, FLEETING, FICKLE, OUR LOVES AND ANGERS MEET! . . 207 HANRAHANS SONG V 3
VEGETATIVE
    DRAWN THROUGH THE WANDERING VEGETATIVE DREAM, ... 467 HARUN RASHID 143
VEHEMENT
    VEHEMENT AND WITTY SHE HAD SEEMED--: THE VENETIAN LADY . . 363 DOLLS FACES 5
VEILED
    VEILED IN A DREAMY SORROW FOR THEIR LOVE . . . . . . 79 EPHEMERA V 2A
VEILS
    DROPPING FROM THE VEILS OF THE MORNING TO WHERE THE CRICKET 117 ISLE INNISFREE 6
        SINGS!
    NOON WRAPT THE TREES IN VEILS OF VIOLET WEATHER, ... 715 DWELT SYCAMORE 7
    NOON WRAPPED THE WOODS IN VEILS OF VIOLET WEATHER! . . . 715 DWELT SYCAMORE V 7
VEIN
    OR BUT TO FIND IF WITHERED VEIN RAN BLOOD, ... 537 HER VISION 6
VEINED   SEE BLUE-VEINED
    AH, TOUCH THEIR BLUE VEINED EYELIDS IF THEY SLEEP, . . . 33 OISIN 2 V 61
VEINS
    HAS DRIED THE SAP OUT OF MY VEINS, AND RENT . . . . . 260 FASC DIFFICULT 2
    SWEETER EMOTION, WORKING IN THEIR VEINS . . . . 292 TO A SHADE 13
    THE FURY AND THE MIRE OF HUMAN VEINS. . . . . 497 BYZANTIUM 8
    THOSE VEINS MUST SOON BE DRY! . . . . 513 JANE TALK BISH 4
    AND ALL HIS VEINS HAD NEAR RUN DRY, ... 670 ISLE STAT II 3 119
    THIS DEATH IS HEAVY IN MY VEINS LIKE SLEEP. . . . . . 701 MOSADA 3 57
VELVET
    DROPT DOWN THE VELVET DARKNESS FROM ABOVE, ... 688 TWO TITANS 37
    ALONG THE VELVET VALE I SAW HIM COME-- . . . . 690 MOSADA 1 10
VENETIAN
    VEHEMENT AND WITTY SHE HAD SEEMED--: THE VENETIAN LADY . . 363 DOLLS FACES 5
    BEAUTIFUL AND GENTLE IN HER VENETIAN WAY. . . . . . . 602 GALLERY REVIS 14
    BEAUTIFUL, GRACIOUS, IN HER VENETIAN WAY, ... 602 GALLERY REVIS V 14
VENGEANCE
    HIS SUDDEN VENGEANCE WERE A COUNTRY TALE, ... 127 DREAM OF FAERY 27
    AND I WOULD KNOW IF YOU WILL GIVE ME VENGEANCE. . . . . 235 SHADOW WATER B 301
    IT WAS THIS WOMAN IN HER WOMAN'S VENGEANCE . . . . . 248 SHADOW WATER B 547
    "VENGEANCE UPON THE MURDERERS," THE CRY GOES UP, ... 426 PHANTOM HATRED 9
    "VENGEANCE FOR JACQUES MOLAY." IN CLOUD-PALE RAGS, OR 426 PHANTOM HATRED 10
        IN LACE,
    FOR VENGEANCE ON THE MURDERERS OF JACQUES MOLAY. . . . . 426 PHANTOM HATRED 16
VENGENCE
    "VENGENCE FOR JACQUES MOLAY." IN CLOUD PALE RAGS, OR IN 426 PHANTOM HATRED V 10
        LACE,
VERDANT
    IS ROLLED AS VERDANT SMOKE! O THOU WHOSE FACE . . . . 667 ISLE STAT II 3 35
VERGE
    AND, EVER PACING ON THE VERGE OF THINGS, ... 73 ANASHU VIJAYA 54
    THEY ARE CAST BEYOND THE VERGE, AND IN A CLOUD, ... 376 PHASES OF MOON 105
VERONESE
    LEARNED LIKE A MAN? PAUL VERONESE . . . . 386 ROBARTES DANCE 26
VERONICA'S
    VERONICA'S NAPKIN . . . . 483 VERONIC NAPKIN T
VERSE
    IN THE VERSE OF ATTIC STORY . . . . 65 HAPPY SHEPHERD V 16
    ALL THINGS CAN TEMPT ME FROM THIS CRAFT OF VERSE! . . . 267 ALL TEMPT ME 1
    I WRITE IT OUT IN A VERSE-- . . . . 394 EASTER 1916 74
    CAN PAY THE POET FOR A VERSE AND HEAR THE FIDDLE SOUND, 581 CURSE CROMWELL 21
VERSES
    THE VERSES THAT COULD MOVE THEM ON THE DAY . . . . . 257 RECONCILIATION 2
    THE VERSES THAT THEY CARED FOR ON THE DAY . . . . . . 257 RECONCILIATION V 2
VERY
    IT SEEMED TO FALL FROM THE VERY FLAME . . . . 13 OISIN 1 V 167
    THE VERY WORLD ITSELF MAY BE . . . . 65 HAPPY SHEPHERD V 18
    ALL, ALL, THE VERY BOTTOM OF THE BOWL-- . . . . . . 227 SHADOW WATER B 118
    WILL GATHER, AND NOT KNOW IT WALKS THE VERY STREET . . . 315 FALLEN MAJESTY 7
    WILL GATHER AND NOT KNOW THAT THROUGH ITS VERY STREET . . 315 FALLEN MAJESTY V 7
    FOR BEAUTY'S VERY SELF, HAS CHARM MADE WISE, ... 404 FOR DAUGHTER 37
    HAS MADE THE VERY OWLS IN CIRCLES MOVE! . . . . . . 423 MY DESCENDANTS 18
    UNDER THAT VERY TREE. . . . . 457 SUMMER SPRING 12
    AND YET HERSELF CAN SEEM YOUTH'S VERY FOUNTAIN, ... 465 HARUN RASHID 89
    TRUTHS THAT WHEN MY VERY BONES ARE DUST . . . . . . 467 HARUN RASHID V 144
    WHERE VERY FOOT OBEYED HER GLANCE! . . . . 488 CRAZED MOON V 11
    I THOUGHT IT OUT THIS VERY DAY, ... 525 DANCING DAYS 17
    O'ER THE LAKE THIS VERY DAY. . . . . 656 ISLE STAT I 3 17
    YOUR WEEPING FITS! LOOK YOU, SO VERY STRAIT . . . . . 659 ISLE STAT II 1 22
    AYE, VERY LATELY, SORROW CAME TO WEEP . . . . 659 ISLE STAT II 1 25
    SWIFT LAKE. A VERY LITTLE THING THAT IS, ... 669 ISLE STAT II 3 78
    YES, ALL IS VERY WELL. WHENCE COMEST THOU? . . . . . 682 SEEKER 14
    THE VERY SQUIRREL DIES THAT ENTERS THERE. . . . . . . 682 SEEKER 33
    THE VERY SQUIRREL DIES THAT ENTERS IT. . . . . 682 SEEKER V 33
    I'M WEARY--WEARY, AND 'TIS VERY COLD. . . . . 703 MOSADA 3 122
    AH! IT IS SO VERY BIG, ... 726 LOVERS QUARREL 17
    AND WE ARE SO VERY SMALL! . . . . 726 LOVERS QUARREL 18
    THEY GREW SO VERY STILL, I WIS . . . . 730 PRIEST FAIRY 66
VESSEL
    SEE THE DARKNESS SLOW DISGORGING A VESSEL BLIND WITH 718 PHANTOM SHIP 12
        SQUALL.
VESTED   SEE NIGHT-VESTED

VESTITURE
   O, LADY, THOU WHOSE VESTITURE OF GREEN • • • • • • • 667 ISLE STAT II 3   34
VESTURE
   BUT DOWN TO HER FEET WHITE VESTURE FLOWED, • • • • • 3 OISIN 1   25
   DOWN TO HER FEET WHITE VESTURE FLOWED, • • • • • • 3 OISIN 1   V   25
   WALKS IN THE VESTURE OF HER SISTER SORROW. • • • • • 735 QUATRAIN APHOR   28
VEX
   "VEX THEM NO LONGER," NIAMH SAID, • • • • • • • • 12 OISIN 1   148
   "THESE FORMS?" "VEX NOT WITH SPEECH THE PHANTOMS DREAD." 29 OISIN 2   V   5
VEXED
   WERE VEXED TO NIGHTMARE BY A ROCKING CRADLE, • • • • 402 SECOND COMING   20
   AND KNOWING THAT THE FUTURE WOULD BE VEXED • • • • • 472 ALL SOUL NIGHT   44
   AND BY FOREKNOWLEDGE OF THE FUTURE VEXED; • • • • • 472 ALL SOUL NIGHT V   44
   "WITH ACTION ALL THE WORLD IS VEXED," • • • • • • 728 PRIEST FAIRY   15
VICTIM
   BUT MY HEART'S VICTIM AND ITS TORTURER. • • • • • • 537 HER VISION   32
VICTOR
   FAMOUS, A MAN OF RULES, A VICTOR. STANDS • • • • • 709 FERENCZ RENYI   9
   THE ARCHANGEL AXEL, VICTOR THE ANGEL • • • • • • • 774 COME RIDE   11
VICTORIES
   THE ISLAND OF VICTORIES • • • • • • • • • • • 29 OISIN 2   V   T
   THE ISLANDS OF DANCING AND OF VICTORIES • • • • • • 46 OISIN 2   247
   ISLES OF THE LIVING AND OF VICTORIES • • • • • • • 46 OISIN 2   V   247
   PRAISED THEIR GREAT VICTORIES AND GAVE THEM JOY • • • 286 TWO KINGS   V 218B
   THROUGH VICTORIES OF THE MIND, • • • • • • • • • 343 SHEP GOATHERD   108
VICTORY
   BUT HAVE NO SHARE IN LOSS OR VICTORY. • • • • • • 104 FERGUS DRUID   V 38E
   AND MOCKS RETURNING VICTORY, HE PASSED • • • • • • 279 TWO KINGS   58
   THAT EVERY NATURAL VICTORY • • • • • • • • • • 401 DEMON BEAST   34
   SOME HAD NO THOUGHT OF VICTORY • • • • • • • • • 608 SONGS BURDEN 3   19
   AND CHANTS OF VICTORY AMID THE ENCIRCLING HOUNDS. • • 622 HOUND VOICE   21
VIE
   HER SPEECH A WICKED TALE THAT WE MAY VIE WITH HER, • • 362 HER COURTESY   6
VIEW
   DESTROY THE VIEW BY CUTTING DOWN AN ASH • • • • • • 372 ON GOING HOUSE   13
   THE LINEAMENTS THAT PLEASE THEIR VIEW • • • • • • • 387 ROBARTES DANCE   49
   THAT ALL'S ARRANGED IN ONE CLEAR VIEW, • • • • • • 633 MAN AND ECHO   31
VIEWLESS
   THUS, THUS I BECKON FROM HER VIEWLESS FIELDS-- • • • • 693 MOSADA 1   75
VIGOROUS
   PUSH OUT HIS VIGOROUS LIMBS AND RUB HIS EYES, • • • • 284 TWO KINGS   162
   THAT VIGOROUS THIGH, THAT DREAMING EYE? • • • • • • 386 ROBARTES DANCE   23
   HAVING INHERITED A VIGOROUS MIND • • • • • • • 422 MY DESCENDANTS   1
   AS VIGOROUS OF MIND, AND YET IT SEEMS • • • • • • 422 MY DESCENDANTS   4
VIGOUR
   IN A VIGOUR MORE THAN MORTAL MEASURE, • • • • • • • 9 OISIN 1   V   98
   IN ALL THE VIGOUR OF ITS BLOOD; • • • • • • • • 529 TOM LUNATIC   17
VIJAYA
   ANASHUYA AND VIJAYA • • • • • • • • • • • • 70 ANASHU VIJAYA   T
   VIJAYA, I HAVE BROUGHT YOU MY EVENING RICE; • • • • • 72 ANASHU VIJAYA   23
   VIJAYA, SWEAR TO HER LOVE NEVER MORE. • • • • • • 74 ANASHU VIJAYA   65
   FAREWELL, VIJAYA. NAY, NO WORD, NO WORD; • • • • • 75 ANASHU VIJAYA   83
   OF RED FLAMINGOES; AND MY LOVE, VIJAYA; • • • • • • 75 ANASHU VIJAYA   89
   OF RED FLAMINGO; AND MY LOVE, VIJAYA, • • • • • • 75 ANASHU VIJAYA   V   89
VILE
   SING SUMMER WAVES. BUT YONDER SHEPHERD VILE, • • • • 649 ISLE STAT I 1   107
VILLAGE
   YOU LIVE, AND ON THE VILLAGE BORDER SHE, • • • • • 74 ANASHU VIJAYA   62
   YOU LIVE, AND ON THE BORDER OF THE VILLAGE SHE, • • • 74 ANASHU VIJAYA   V   62
   THEY BRING YOU MEMORIES OF OLD VILLAGE FACES, • • • • 130 BOOK STORIES   V   22
   I POKED ABOUT A VILLAGE CHURCH • • • • • • • • 584 GHOST ROG CASE   31
   THY NAME IS?" "RENYI." "OF?" "THIS VILLAGE." "GOOD! 709 FERENCZ RENYI   13
   THY NAME IS?" "FERENCZ RENYI." "OF?" "THIS VILLAGE." 709 FERENCZ RENYI   13
      "GOOD!
   ALONG THE TENTS, THE FIELDS, THE VILLAGE WALLS. • • • • 712 FERENCZ RENYI   71
   ALONG THE TENTS, FIELD, THE VILLAGE WALLS. • • • • • 712 FERENCZ RENYI   V   71
   I CAME THE FIRST TIME TO THY VILLAGE SCHOOL? • • • • 713 FERENCZ RENYI   90
   I AM TO BE YOUR WIFE. A VILLAGE HIGH • • • • • • 713 FERENCZ RENYI   97
   I WAS TO BE YOUR WIFE. A VILLAGE HIGH • • • • • • • 713 FERENCZ RENYI   V   97
   ALL THE DROWNED THAT EVER WERE DROWNED FROM THAT VILLAGE 719 PHANTOM SHIP   20
      BY THE SEA;
   MUSINGLY WANDERED THE VILLAGE PRIEST. • • • • • • 728 PRIEST FAIRY   3
VILLAGES
   LET'S HOME AND SPEND IT IN OUR VILLAGES. • • • • • 248 SHADOW WATER B V 538A
VINCI'
   DA VINCI' FINGER SO HAD FASHIONED IT • • • • • • 444 SCHOOL CHILDR   V   26
VINEGAR-HEAVY
   THE VINEGAR-HEAVY SPONGE, THE FLOWERS BY KEDRON STREAM; 172 TRAV PASSION   5
VIOLENCE
   BUT TAKE OUR GREATNESS WITH OUR VIOLENCE? • • • • • 418 ANCEST HOUSES   32
   VIOLENCE UPON THE ROADS; VIOLENCE OF HORSES; • • • • 432 NINETEEN 19   113
   VIOLENCE UPON THE ROADS; VIOLENCE OF HORSES; • • • • 432 NINETEEN 19   113
   WITH SOME SORT OF VIOLENCE • • • • • • • • • 638 BEN BULBEN   34
VIOLENT
   HAVE TAUGHT TO IGNORANT MEN MOST VIOLENT WAYS, • • • • 256 NO SECOND TROY   3
   SOME VIOLENT BITTER MAN, SOME POWERFUL MAN • • • • • 418 ANCEST HOUSES   17
   BITTER AND VIOLENT MEN, MIGHT REAR IN STONE • • • • • 418 ANCEST HOUSES   19
   TO SHOW HOW VIOLENT GREAT HEARTS CAN LOSE • • • • • 463 HARUN RASHID   47
   HER VIOLENT MAN • • • • • • • • • • • • 628 JANE MOUNTAIN   16
   VIOLENT AND FAMOUS, STRODE AMONG THE DEAD; • • • • • 634 CUCHULAIN COMF   2

VIOLET
    AND SMOKE FROM THIS DEAD HEART DRIFTS THROUGH THE VIOLET   173 SPEAKS HEARERS   3
        AIR
    MIRACULOUS OIL, ODOUR OF VIOLET. . . . . 483 OIL AND BLOOD   3
    NOON WRAPT THE TREES IN VEILS OF VIOLET WEATHER, . . . 715 DWELT SYCAMORE   7
    NOON WRAPPED THE WOODS IN VEILS OF VIOLET WEATHER; . . 715 DWELT SYCAMORE V 7
VIOLETS
    THE VIOLETS ARE THAT ON THE WOODED HILL . . . . . . 713 FERENCZ RENYI   95
VIRGIN
    I SAW A STARING VIRGIN STAND . . . . . . 437 SONGS PLAY 1   1
    WHEN THAT FIERCE VIRGIN AND HER STAR . . . . . 437 SONGS PLAY 1   15
    I SAW THAT STARING, VIRGIN STAND . . . . . . 437 SONGS PLAY 1 V 1
    WHEN THE FIERCE VIRGIN AND HER STAR . . . . 437 SONGS PLAY 1 V 15
    THE LION AND THE VIRGIN, ... 601 THOSE IMAGES   11
    FROM EMPTY TOMB OR VIRGIN WOMB? . . . . . . 619 STICK INCENSE   2
VIRGINAL
    WHEN SHE IN ALL HER VIRGINAL PRIDE . . . . 488 CRAZED MOON   8
VIRGINITY
    JACK HAD MY VIRGINITY, ... 508 JANE BISHOP   22
    THAT HAD MY VIRGINITY . . . . 508 JANE BISHOP V 23
VIRTUE
    THAN MOUND AND STONE THAT KEEP ALL VIRTUE IN, . . . 281 TWO KINGS   106
    BUT FAME AND VIRTUE ROT. . . . . 584 GHOST ROG CASE   36
VIRTUES
    "ONLY THE WASTEFUL VIRTUES EARN THE SUN"; . . . 270 PARDON FATHERS   18
    BUT I, WHOSE VIRTUES ARE THE DEFINITIONS . . . . 353 PEOPLE   32
VISAGE
    AND GAZING ON HIS VISAGE WORN, ... 99 FOXHUNTER V 43
    CAN COME UPON THE VISAGE OF THE MOON . . . . 482 BLOOD AND MOON   53
    OR HAST THOU NEVER SEEN, WITH VISAGE MEEK, . . . 672 ISLE STAT II 3   156
VISAGED   SEE LONG-VISAGED
    THAT PALE, LONG VISAGED COMPANY . . . . 637 BEN BULBEN V 7
VISIBLE
    BEYOND THE VISIBLE WORLD. ALL DREAMS OF THE SOUL . . 374 PHASES OF MOON   63
VISION
    TILL ALL HAD SEEMED A SHADOW OR A VISION . . . . 278 TWO KINGS   43
    IS BUT A VISION OF REALITY. . . . . 369 EGO DOMINUS   48
    THE DOUBLE VISION OF MICHAEL ROBARTES . . . . 382 VISION ROBART   T
    IN REVERIE, OR IN VISION, SAW . . . . . . 420 MY HOUSE V 20E
    HER VISION IN THE WOOD . . . . 536 HER VISION   T
    A VISION OF TERROR THAT IT MUST LIVE THROUGH . . 619 BRONZE HEAD   17
    THE VISION OF A ROCK WHERE LIGHTNINGS WHIRL'D . . 687 TWO TITANS   1
    THE VISION. YOU ARE PALE AND WEEPING. CHILD, . . 693 MOSADA 1   73
    THIS VISION OF PETER AND THE BURNING GATE. . . . 696 MOSADA 2   21
    A SAINT OF RUSSIA IN A VISION SAW . . . . . 696 MOSADA 2 V 21
VISIONARIES
    TWO POEMS CONCERNING PEASANT VISIONARIES A CRADLE SONG 146 UNAPPEAS HOST V T
VISIONARY
    A VISIONARY WHITE SEA-BIRD . . . . 361 ALF POLLEXFEN   37
    A VISIONARY WHITE SEA BIRD . . . . 361 ALF POLLEXFEN V 37
    SAT LATE, OR SHELLEY'S VISIONARY PRINCE; . . . . 373 PHASES OF MOON   16
    THY GARMENTS' HEM, THOU VISIONARY ONE! . . . . 684 SEEKER   71
    THY GARMENT'S HEM, THOU VISIONARY ONE! . . . . 684 SEEKER V 71
VISIONS
    SEER OF VISIONS! NOW EVE FALLS ASLEEP, ... 691 MOSADA 1   36
VISIT
    IF DAYLIGHT EVER VISIT WHERE, ... 446 COLONUS PRAISE   4
VISITED   SEE RE-VISITED
VISITS
    MOORE ONCE HAD VISITS FROM THE MUSE . . . . . . 792 GEORGE MOORE   1
VIVID
    BEFORE MY TIME, SEEM LIKE A VIVID MEMORY. . . . . 391 UNDER SATURN   10
    COMING WITH VIVID FACES . . . . 391 EASTER 1916   2
VIVIEN
    TIME AND THE WITCH VIVIEN. . . . . 720 WITCH VIVIEN   T
VIZIR
    HIS VIZIR JAFFER FOR AN UNKNOWN REASON; . . . . 462 HARUN RASHID   32
VOICE
    WHERE THE VOICE OF CHANGE IS THE VOICE OF A TUNE, . . . 8 OISIN 1 V 82
    WHERE THE VOICE OF CHANGE IS THE VOICE OF A TUNE, . . . 8 OISIN 1 V 82
    AND SWEETER OF VOICE THAN THE PLEASANT BIRDS, . . . 9 OISIN 1 V 95
    AND WHEN THEY HEARD HER VOICE THEY RAN . . . . 15 OISIN 1 V 213
    WITH A CLEAR VOICE THE YOUNG MAN CRIED, ... 18 OISIN 1 V 260
    SO SLEEP THEE BY DAYTIME." A VOICE CRIED, ... 59 OISIN 3   172
    SO SLEEP THEY BY DAYTIME." A VOICE CRIED, ... 59 OISIN 3 V 172
    THAT WANES." "AH, WISTFUL VOICE," REPLIED THE OTHER, . . 79 EPHEMERA V 3
    OUR MARRIED VOICE WILDLY TROLLED. . . . . . 85 MAD KING GOLL V 29
    AND CRIED WITH ANGRY VOICE, "IT IS NOT MEET . . 107 CUCHULAIN SEA   20
    SANG WHERE—UNNECESSARY CRUEL VOICE—— . . . 127 DREAM OF FAERY   30
    TOLD WHERE——AH, LITTLE, ALL-UNNEEDED VOICE!—— . . 127 DREAM OF FAERY V 30
    AS THOUGH ONE LISTENED THERE, AND HIS VOICE SANK . . 180 QUEEN MAEVE   7
    AND NOT WITH HIS OWN VOICE OR A MAN'S VOICE, . . . 183 QUEEN MAEVE   74
    AND NOT WITH HIS OWN VOICE OR A MAN'S VOICE, . . . 183 QUEEN MAEVE   74
    BUT WITH THE BURNING, LIVE, UNSHAKEN VOICE . . . 183 QUEEN MAEVE   75
    AND WITH GLAD VOICE MAEVE ANSWERED HIM, "WHAT KING . 183 QUEEN MAEVE   79
    AND WITH GLAD VOICE MAEVE ANSWERED "MANY A TIME . . 183 QUEEN MAEVE V 79
    ON FINDING THAT HER VOICE IS SWEET AND LOW . . . 205 ADAMS CURSE   17
    MURMURED WITH HER YOUNG VOICE FOR WHOSE MILD SAKE . 205 ADAMS CURSE V 15
    HAVE THE BIRDS PASSED US? I COULD HEAR YOUR VOICE, . . 226 SHADOW WATER B   81
    THEY CANNOT HEAR MY VOICE! BUT WHAT'S THE MEANING? . . 234 SHADOW WATER B   275
    AND YOU WILL RECOLLECT MY FACE AND VOICE, ... 243 SHADOW WATER B   433

```
                                                      PAGE    TITLE            LINE
VOICE  (CONTINUED)
    "WOULD IT WERE ANYTHING BUT MERELY VOICE!" . . . . . .   258 KING NO KING       1
    BUT WITH A VOICE THAT HAD UNNATURAL MUSIC, . . . . . .   283 TWO KINGS        153
    BUT THAT SWEET-SOUNDING VOICE RAN ON! "WOMAN, . . . .    284 TWO KINGS        165
    I WAS NO LONGER TERRIFIED--HIS VOICE . . . . . . .       284 TWO KINGS        171
    WOMEN CAN FIND." WITH A MOST MASTERFUL VOICE, . . . .    284 TWO KINGS        175
    WOMEN CAN FIND." WITH A MOST BURNING VOICE  . . . .      284 TWO KINGS      V 175
    AND THEREUPON WITH AGED, HIGH-PITCHED VOICE  . . . .     375 PHASES OF MOON    84
    UNTIL HER VOICE GREW SHRILL. . . . . . . . . .          392 EASTER 1916       20
    WHAT VOICE MORE SWEET THAN HERS  . . . . . . . .        392 EASTER 1916       21
    LAUGHTER NOT TIME DESTROYED MY VOICE . . . . . . .       455 FRIENDS YOUTH      1
    I HEARD HER VOICE, "TURN THAT I MAY EXPOUND  . . . .     467 HARUN RASHID     132
    MUST DRIVE THE ARABIAN HOST. THE VOICE GREW STILL, . .   467 HARUN RASHID     145
    MADE DRIVE THE ARABIAN HOST. THE VOICE GREW STILL, . .   467 HARUN RASHID   V 145
    DREAM THAT I LOVE HER ONLY FOR THE VOICE, . . . . .     469 HARUN RASHID     171
    IS BUT A PAYMENT FOR THAT MIDNIGHT VOICE . . . . .       469 HARUN RASHID     173
    ITS FIRST SIMPLICITY, LOVE, VOICE AND ALL, . . . . .     469 HARUN RASHID     177
    AND I LEFT SHIVERING. THE VOICE HAS DRAWN  . . . . .     469 HARUN RASHID     179
    DREAM THAT I LOVE HER ONLY FOR THAT VOICE, . . . . .     469 HARUN RASHID   V 171
    THE TOMB OF SWIFT WEARS IT AWAY. A VOICE  . . . . . .    487 SEVEN SAGES       21
    NOR HEARD THIS VOICE THAT NINETY YEARS HAVE CRACKED. .   555 RIBH AT TOMB       5
    WHAT MATTER? OUT OF CAVERN COMES A VOICE, . . . . .      564 GYRES             15
    WHAT MATTER? OUT OF CAVERN COME A VOICE  . . . . . .     564 GYRES          V 15
    CARRIAGE AND VOICE HAD HE! . . . . . . . . . .          608 SONGS BURDEN 3    13
    HOUND VOICE . . . . . . . . . . . . . . . .             621 HOUND VOICE        T
    GIVE TONGUE, PROCLAIM THEIR HIDDEN NAME--"HOUND VOICE."  622 HOUND VOICE        7
    INTO THE NIGHT. O ROCKY VOICE, . . . . . . . . .         633 MAN AND ECHO      37
    WITH FIERY SONG I'LL DROWN YON PUNY VOICE. . . . . .     648 ISLE STAT I 1     81
    I HEAR THE WHOLE SKY'S SORROW IN ONE VOICE. . . . .      652 ISLE STAT I 2     22
    UP-RAISED HIS VOICE, AND HOOTED ME. . . . . . . .        670 ISLE STAT II 3   117
    UPRAISED HIS VOICE, AND HOOTED ME. . . . . . . . .       670 ISLE STAT II 3 V 117
    HE SHRANK BEFORE MY VOICE, AND STOOD . . . . . . .       671 ISLE STAT II 3   129
    IT IS THE VOICE OF ALL OUR HEARTS THAT LAUGH. . . . .    681 SEEKER             7
    IT IS POSSESSED. A PROPHESYING VOICE. . . . . . .        681 SEEKER             8
    A VOICE CAME CALLING ME TO THIS YOUR LAND, . . . .       682 SEEKER            22
    A VOICE HAS TOLD ME HOW WITHIN THIS LAND  . . . . .      682 SEEKER         V 22
    MY ECHOING HEART. NOW RAISE THY VOICE AND SPEAK! . .     683 SEEKER            47
    LOVER, THE VOICE THAT SUMMONED THEE WAS MINE. . . .      685 SEEKER            77
    FOR ALL I GAVE THE VOICE, FOR ALL MY YOUTH, . . . .      685 SEEKER            78
    AGAIN, THE VOICE! THE VOICE! . . . . . . . . . .         685 SEEKER            81
    AGAIN, THE VOICE! THE VOICE! . . . . . . . . . .         685 SEEKER            81
    CRIES A VOICE AT ROARING MIDNIGHT BESIDE THE MOONLESS DEEP.  718 PHANTOM SHIP   8
    AS THE SUMMER VOICE OF THE DAYTIME CEASED, . . . . .     728 PRIEST FAIRY       4
    HEARD THE VOICE OF THEIR DISMAY, . . . . . . . .        730 PRIEST FAIRY      74
    IF YOU WOULD SERVE ME, AS YOUR WORD AND VOICE . . . .    756 SHADOW WATER A   183
VOICED
    SWEET VOICED AND BEAUTIFUL, . . . . . . . . . . .       392 EASTER 1916    V 22
VOICES
    VOICES . . . . . . . . . . . . . . . . . . .            69 CLOAK BOAT      V  T
    OUR MARRIED VOICES WILDLY TROLLED. . . . . . . . .       85 MAD KING GOLL      59
    THE EVERLASTING VOICES  . . . . . . . . . . . .         141 EVERLAST VOICE     T
    EVERLASTING VOICES . . . . . . . . . . . . . .          141 EVERLAST VOICE     T
    O SWEET EVERLASTING VOICES, BE STILL! . . . . . .        141 EVERLAST VOICE     1
    O SWEET EVERLASTING VOICES, BE STILL. . . . . . .        141 EVERLAST VOICE     8
    VOICES AMONG THE CROWD  . . . . . . . . . . . .         172 PLEADS FRIEND      2
    OUR HEARTS CAN HEAR THE VOICES CHIDE. . . . . . .        192 BAILE AILLINN     94
    OUR HEART CAN HEAR THE VOICES CHIDE. . . . . . . .       192 BAILE AILLINN  V 94
    MY DREAMS WERE CLOVEN BY VOICES AND BY FIRES! . . .      218 WOODS OF COOLE    20
    MOVED ROUND ME IN THE VOICES AND THE FIRES, . . . .      218 WOODS OF COOLE    23
    YOU SAY THAT ALSO? YOU HAVE HEARD THE VOICES, . . .      228 SHADOW WATER B   136
    YES, VOICES! BUT I DO NOT CATCH THE WORDS. . . . .       233 SHADOW WATER B   251
    BEING DRIVEN ON BY VOICES AND BY DREAMS . . . . .        243 SHADOW WATER B   441
    WITH HUMAN VOICES. O I CAN HEAR THEM NOW. . . . .        247 SHADOW WATER B   522
    OUR VOICES CARRY! AND THOUGH SLUMBER-BOUND, . . . .      622 HOUND VOICE        5
    AND YET GAVE TONGUE. "HOUND VOICES" WERE THEY ALL. . .   622 HOUND VOICE        9
    OUR VOICES CARRY! AND THOUGH SLUMBER BOUND, . . . .      622 HOUND VOICE     V  5
    THE FAIRY VOICES . . . . . . . . . . . . . . .          655 ISLE STAT I 3   V  T
    WHAT ARE THE VOICES THAT IN FLOWERY WAYS  . . . . .      666 ISLE STAT II 3    16
    WITH LITTLE VOICES SONGS OF FEARFUL THINGS. . . . .      682 SEEKER            31
    UPRAISED THEIR VOICES BITTERLY. . . . . . . . . .        730 PRIEST FAIRY      72
    FOR THERE ARE SUDDEN VOICES IN MY EARS. . . . . . .      753 SHADOW WATER A   141
    OF VOICES AND OF DREAMS. O HEART, BE STILL! . . . .      765 SHADOW WATER A   362
VOLUME
    THAT GATHERS VOLUME! NOW A THUNDER-CLAP. . . . . .       487 SEVEN SAGES       23
    THAT GATHERS VOLUME! NOW A THUNDER CLAP. . . . . .       487 SEVEN SAGES    V 23
VON
    VON HUEGEL  . . . . . . . . . . . . . . . . .           499 VACILLATION     V  T
    MUST WE PART, VON HUEGEL, THOUGH MUCH ALIKE, FOR WE . .  503 VACILLATION       78
    SO GET YOU GONE, VON HUEGEL, THOUGH WITH BLESSINGS ON YOUR  503 VACILLATION    89
        HEAD.
VOTE
    AND LET THE NEIGHBOURS VOTE, . . . . . . . . . .        598 STONE CROSS        6
VOW
    WHO HAS A LIKE VOW FROM THEIR TRIPLE DUN." . . . . .     108 CUCHULAIN SEA  V 38
    WHO HAD A LIKE VOW FROM OUR TRIPLE DUN." . . . . .       109 CUCHULAIN SEA  V 54
    CUCHULAIN CRIED, "HAVE MADE AND KEEP THAT VOW." . . .    109 CUCHULAIN SEA  V 56
    A DEEP-SWORN VOW . . . . . . . . . . . . . .            357 DEEP-SWORN VOW     T
    A DEEP SWORN VOW . . . . . . . . . . . . . .            357 DEEP-SWORN VOW  V  T
    THAT DEEP-SWORN VOW HAVE BEEN FRIENDS OF MINE! . . .     357 DEEP-SWORN VOW     2
    THAT DEEP SWORN VOW, HAVE BEEN FRIENDS OF MINE, . . .    357 DEEP-SWORN VOW  V  2
    I AM THINKING OF A CHILD'S VOW SWORN IN VAIN  . . . .    391 UNDER SATURN      15
```

VOWED
AS THOUGH THEY'D VOWED TO MEASURE ALL ITS WAYS. . . . . 711 FERENCZ RENYI 48
VOWS
THAT TIME CAN NEVER MAR A LOVER'S VOWS . . . . 126 DREAM OF FAERY 10
HOW TIME MAY NEVER MAR THEIR FAERY VOWS . . . . 126 DREAM OF FAERY V 10
VOYAGE
MOPING FOR ONE VOYAGE MORE. . . . . 361 ALF POLLEXFEN 22
VOYAGES
I'D GIVE THE PROFIT OF NINE VOYAGES . . . . 222 SHADOW WATER B V 9
WADDING'S
OF OLD LUKE WADDING'S PORTRAIT SAID . . . . 400 DEMON BEAST 10
WADE
WHERE WADE THE CHOIR OF LOVE . . . . 612 NEWS ORACLE V 22
AND THE JOY OF THE STREAMS WHERE LONG-LIMBED HERONS WADE; 674 ISLE STAT II 3 217
WADES
WHERE WADES THE CHOIR OF LOVE . . . . 612 NEWS ORACLE 22
WAGE
"BUT TILL THE MOON HAS TAKEN ALL, I WAGE . . . . 45 OISIN 2 240
"WITH ALL IN ALL THE WORLD I BATTLE WAGE. . . . . . . 45 OISIN 2 V 240
. . . AND NO MAN MAY WAR WITH THE STRONG SPIRITS WAGE; . . 62 OISIN 3 V 214
WAGE AN ETERNAL BATTLE, AND I FEEL . . . . 104 FERGUS DRUID V 38C
AND WAGE GOD'S BATTLES IN THE LONG GREY SHIPS. . . . . 114 ROSE OF BATTLE 20
BRED TO BE A HERO'S WAGE. . . . . 258 PEACE 3
THAT LONG TO GIVE THEMSELVES FOR WAGE, ... 262 STUDENTS AGIT 2
BUT BEAR IN MIND YOUR LOVER'S WAGE . . . . 385 ROBARTES DANCE 14
THE WAGE OF SIN IS DEATH. NO USE. NO USE. . . . . . 697 MOSADA 2 V 42
BLINDER SORROWS, HARDER WAGE-- . . . . 733 STREET DANCERS 58
WAGED
HE WITH BODY WAGED A FIGHT, ... 561 FOUR AGES MAN 1
WAGER
YOU'VE NEVER KNOWN, I'D LAY A WAGER ON IT, ... 227 SHADOW WATER B 113
WAGES
I KNOW WHAT WAGES BEAUTY GIVES, ... 336 YOUNG BEAUTY 13
THE WAGES OF SIN IS DEATH. NO USE. NO GOOD. . . . . 697 MOSADA 2 42
WAGGED
ABOUT WHOSE FACE BIRDS WAGGED THEIR FIERY WINGS, ... 187 QUEEN MAEVE 145
WAGGONS
SEA NYMPHS IN THEIR PEARLY WAGGONS, ... 309 REALISTS V 5
WAGON
OUT OF THE UP AND DOWN, THE WAGON WHEEL . . . . . . 377 PHASES OF MOON V 120
WAGONETTE
CLIMB ON A WAGONETTE TO SCREAM. . . . . 626 OLD MEN BE MAD 8
WAGONS
SEA-NYMPHS IN THEIR PEARLY WAGONS . . . . 309 REALISTS 5
WAGON-WHEEL
OUT OF THE UP AND DOWN, THE WAGON-WHEEL . . . . . . 377 PHASES OF MOON 120
WAIF
A SEA-WORN WAIF CAME FLOATING BY. . . . . 24 OISIN 1 V 365
WAIL
OH, HADST THOU SEEN BEAUTIFUL NIAM WAIL TO HERSELF AND 54 OISIN 3 V 109
BLANCH,
O, HAD YOU SEEN BEAUTIFUL NEAVE WAIL TO HERSELF AND BLANCH, 54 OISIN 3 V 109
AND I MUST WAIL BESIDE THE SEA . . . . 86 MAD KING GOLL V 67
THE HOUNDS WAIL FOR THE DEAD. . . . . 99 FOXHUNTER 48
AND WRING MY HANDS, AND WAIL HIM BITTERLY, ... 242 SHADOW WATER B 414
FOR, WANDER AND WAIL AS HE WOULD, ... 378 CAT AND MOON 6
BUT SPEECHLESS, AND THE MAIDEN WITH LONG WAIL . . . . 713 FERENCZ RENYI 85
WAILING
THE WAILING GREW DISTANT; I RODE BY THE WOODS OF 56 OISIN 3 137
THE WRINKLING BARK,
I KISS MY WAILING CHILD AND PRESS IT TO MY BREAST, . . . 147 UNAPPEAS HOST 5
WAILING UPON A WOMAN'S KNEE, ... 436 FOR MY SON 22
WAILS
WANDERS AND WAILS BEFORE MY HEART MOST TRUE . . . . . 738 YOU ARE SAD 8
WAIT
FOR HIS LAST DAYS TO LIE IN WAIT. . . . . 24 OISIN 1 363
PRAYERS FOR THE LAND. I WILL WAIT HERE, AMRITA. . . . 71 ANASHU VIJAYA 13
PRAYERS FOR THE LAND. PRAY ON, AND I WILL WAIT YOU, . . 71 ANASHU VIJAYA V 13
WHOSE BLADE COMPELS, AND WAIT TILL THEY HAVE FOUND . . . 108 CUCHULAIN SEA 37
OUR LONG SHIPS LOOSE THOUGHT-WOVEN SAILS AND WAIT, . . . 115 ROSE OF BATTLE 31
TO WAIT THEIR FRIENDS; BUT WHEN THEIR FRIENDS HAVE COME 233 SHADOW WATER B 247
I THOUGHT TO WAIT FOR THAT OR THIS; . . . . 305 HOUR DAWN 64
AND WAIT HIM IN A DRUNKEN SLEEP." . . . . 307 HOUR DAWN 106
AND TILL THAT'S DONE CAN NEITHER WORK NOR WAIT. . . . . 340 SHEP GOATHERD 45
AND WAIT WAR'S MUSIC; PASS THE LITTLE GALLERY; . . . . 461 HARUN RASHID 8
CLIMB TO YOUR CHAMBER FULL OF BOOKS AND WAIT, ... 579 DOR WELLESLEY 8
I AM NOT DUMB; I'D SOONER SILENT WAIT . . . . 646 ISLE STAT I 1 40
BEYOND A MORTAL'S YEARS. I WAIT THE SONG . . . . . 653 ISLE STAT I 2 48
TWO LONELY SPIRITS WAIT, ... 680 LOVE AND DEATH 18
I SAW A STRANGER TAP AND WAIT . . . . 696 MOSADA 2 22
A STRANGER NEW ARISEN WAIT . . . . 696 MOSADA 2 V 22
'TIS LATE, WAIT ONE MORE DAY; BELOW THE HILLS . . . . 702 MOSADA 3 91
GIVE HER TO AIBRIC, IF HE WILL. I WAIT . . . . . . 755 SHADOW WATER A 172
I WAIT YOUR WORDS AS THE DEAD WAIT THE LIVING. . . . . 756 SHADOW WATER A V 182
I WAIT YOUR WORDS AS THE DEAD WAIT THE LIVING. . . . . 756 SHADOW WATER A V 182
WAITED
WAITED. ABOVE, IN ENDLESS CARVEN JAGS, ... 38 OISIN 2 V 144
I WAITED HOUR BY HOUR, AND THE HIGH DOME, ... 39 OISIN 2 147
OF FACES, WAITED; AND THE LEISURED GAZE . . . . . . 39 OISIN 2 149
HOUR AFTER HOUR I WAITED, AND THE DOME . . . . . . 39 OISIN 2 V 147
"I HAVE LONG WAITED, MOTHER, FOR THAT WORD; . . . . . 107 CUCHULAIN SEA 22

WAITED   (CONTINUED)
    "LONG HAVE I WAITED, MOTHER, FOR THOSE WORDS, ...   107 CUCHULAIN SEA V   22
    "I HAVE LONG WAITED, MOTHER, FOR THOSE WORDS! . . . . .   107 CUCHULAIN SEA V   22
    MAEVE WAITED, AND WHEN THAT EAR-PIERCING NOISE . . . .   182 QUEEN MAEVE   47
    ONE THAT THE GENERATIONS HAD LONG WAITED . . . .   182 QUEEN MAEVE   66
    I WAITED TILL THE NIGHT WAS ON THE TURN, ...   283 TWO KINGS   144
    I WAITED SO FOR THAT OR THIS-- . . . .   305 HOUR DAWN   V   64
WAITING
    WHERE AILLINN RODE WITH WAITING MAIDS . . . .   193 BAILE AILLINN V 102
    NO WAITING MAID SHOULD EVER SPREAD . . . .   194 BAILE AILLINN V 120
    BUT WHY ARE THEY STILL WAITING? WHY ARE THEY . . . . .   234 SHADOW WATER B   265
    ARE LEARNED IN WAITING. YOU CANNOT BUT HAVE SEEN . . .   340 SHEP GOATHERD   48
    THE BLINDS DRAWN UP"! MAUD GONNE AT HOWTH STATION WAITING 578 LOFTY THINGS   10
        A TRAIN,
    SHOULD KEEP THEIR LOVERS WAITING, ...   597 MODEL LAUREATE   7
    KEEP THEIR LOVERS WAITING? . . . .   597 MODEL LAUREATE   8
    AND KEEP THEIR LOVERS WAITING, ...   597 MODEL LAUREATE   15
    KEEP THEIR LOVERS WAITING. . . . .   597 MODEL LAUREATE   16
    WOULD KEEP HIS LOVER WAITING, ...   598 MODEL LAUREATE   23
    KEEP HIS LOVER WAITING? . . . .   598 MODEL LAUREATE   24
    AND MY SOUL IN WAITING DIETH, ...   648 ISLE STAT I 1   87
    THEY ARE STILL WAITING! AND NOW THE LAGGARD COMES, . . .   754 SHADOW WATER A   150
    THEY ARE STILL WAITING! AND A LAGGARD COMES, ...   754 SHADOW WATER A V 150
    SHE WILL ANSWER NOW LIKE ANY WAITING WOMAN . . . . . .   757 SHADOW WATER A   193
    I HAVE BEEN WAITING YOU. A MOMENT SINCE . . . .   763 SHADOW WATER A   313
WAITING-MAID
    NO WAITING-MAID SHOULD EVER SPREAD . . . .   194 BAILE AILLINN   120
WAITING-MAIDS
    WHERE AILLINN RODE WITH WAITING-MAIDS, ...   193 BAILE AILLINN   102
WAITS
    AT THE SWORD-POINT, AND WAITS TILL WE HAVE FOUND . . . .   109 CUCHULAIN SEA   53
    AT THE SWORD POINT, AND WAITS TILL WE HAVE FOUND . . . .   109 CUCHULAIN SEA V   53
    AND WHAT WAITS BEHIND THE DOOR, ...   298 THREE HERMITS   9
    THAT WAITS UPON HIS FUTURE DAYS, ...   436 FOR MY SON   14
    HE HOVERS ABOVE THE MAST AND WAITS HIS KIND! . . . . .   753 SHADOW WATER A   135
    AENGUS LOOKS ON YOU WHEN I LOOK! HE WAITS . . . . . .   757 SHADOW WATER A V 209
WAKE
    O'ER MEN WHO SLEEP, AND WAKE, AND DIE, ...   22 OISIN 1   V 340B
    WHERE FLAPPING HERONS WAKE . . . .   86 STOLEN CHILD   4
    WHEN WILL HE WAKE FROM SLEEP? . . . .   174 ELEMENT POWERS   6
    YOU'RE CERTAIN OF IT? I NEVER WAKE FROM SLEEP . . . .   226 SHADOW WATER B   83
    WAKE ALL BELOW! WHY HAVE YOU BROKEN OUR SLEEP? . . . .   233 SHADOW WATER B   242
    UPON THAT OTHER SHIP WE ARE TO WAKE. . . . .   240 SHADOW WATER B   381
    I HAD FORGOTTEN THAT WE MUST GO WAKE HIM. . . . .   240 SHADOW WATER B   384
    AND SET YOU DREAMING. HOW CAN WE HAVE A WAKE . . . . .   240 SHADOW WATER B   386
    AND LEFT MERE SLEEP. HE'LL WAKE WHEN THE SUN WAKES, .   284 TWO KINGS   161
    "WHAT CARE I IF YOU SLEEP OR WAKE? . . . .   304 HOUR DAWN   40
    DO BUT WAKE THE HOPE TO LIVE . . . .   309 REALISTS   V   6
    AND WHEN I WAKE TOWARDS MORN I DREAD MYSELF, ...   448 HERO GIRL FOOL   5
    SOME FEW HALF WAKE AND HALF RENEW THEIR CHOICE, ...   622 HOUND VOICE   6
    WHEN SLEEPERS WAKE AND YET STILL DREAM, ...   639 BEN BULBEN   59
    AS I MY WATCHING LEST YOU WAKE, ...   658 ISLE STAT I 3   95
    I FADE, AND SHALL NOT SEE THE MORNINGS WAKE, ...   674 ISLE STAT II 3   223
    THY PEACE. AH, NOW I'LL WAKE THESE SLEEPERS, LOST . .   677 ISLE STAT II 3   274
    O WAKE! WAKE! WAKE! FOR SOFT AS A BEE SIPS . . . . . .   677 ISLE STAT II 3   276
    O WAKE! WAKE! WAKE! FOR SOFT AS A BEE SIPS . . . . . .   677 ISLE STAT II 3   276
    O WAKE! WAKE! WAKE! FOR SOFT AS A BEE SIPS . . . . . .   677 ISLE STAT II 3   276
    OLD WARRIOR, WAKE! FOR SOFT AS A BEE SIPS, ...   677 ISLE STAT II 3   284
    THOSE TWAIN ARE DUST. WAKE! LIGHT AS A BEE SIPS . .   678 ISLE STAT II 3   290
    SEAFARER, WAKE! WAS MY SLEEP LONG? LONG YEARS. . . .   678 ISLE STAT II 3   292
    HE IS LONG DEAD. WAKE! SOFT AS A BEE SIPS . . . . . .   678 ISLE STAT II 3   297
    NAY, HE IS GONE. WAKE! WAKE! AS A BEE SIPS . . . . . .   678 ISLE STAT II 3   305
    NAY, HE IS GONE. WAKE! WAKE! AS A BEE SIPS . . . . . .   678 ISLE STAT II 3   305
    WAKE, MA CUSHLA, SLEEPY-HEADED! . . . .   705 DAWN-SONG   9
    WAKE! THE HERON, RISING, HATH . . . .   705 DAWN-SONG   17
    WAKE THE LARKS UPON THE GREEN. . . . .   727 LOVERS QUARREL   46
    HE CANNOT WAKE THE GOD THAT HIDES IN IT. . . . .   748 SHADOW WATER A   19
    WHEN AENGUS AND HIS EDAINE WAKE FROM SLEEP . . . . . .   749 SHADOW WATER A   57
    IN THE COLD STREAMS, AND WAKE TO THEIR DESIRE, ...   750 SHADOW WATER A   85
    WAKE ALL BELOW. WHY HAVE YOU BROKEN OUR SLEEP? . . . .   753 SHADOW WATER A   132
WAKED
    AND HAS NOT YET BEEN WAKED. OHONE! O! O! O! . . . . .   241 SHADOW WATER B   393
    I HAD NOT WAKED A SINGLE MINUTE, ...   305 HOUR DAWN   72
    IT MAY BE, BEFORE THE WINDS OF BIRTH HAVE WAKED! . . .   750 SHADOW WATER A   86
WAKEFUL
    THE EVER-WINDING WAKEFUL SEA, ...   22 OISIN 1   V 338
    BEING WAKEFUL FOR HER SAKE, ...   316 FRIENDS   23
    AND AS A SLAVE BEEN WAKEFUL IN THE HALLS . . . .   724 KANVA ON SELF   5
WAKEN
    AND "WAKEN, COURTIERS OF THE MORN!" . . . .   18 OISIN 1   V 262
    THE NOTES THEY WAKEN SHALL LIVE ON . . . .   213 BLESS PSALTER   16
    THOSE IMAGES THAT WAKEN IN THE BLOOD. . . . .   622 HOUND VOICE   14
    "WAKEN, WAKEN, SLEEPY FISHERS! NO HOUR IS THIS FOR SLEEP," 718 PHANTOM SHIP   7
    "WAKEN, WAKEN, SLEEPY FISHERS! NO HOUR IS THIS FOR SLEEP," 718 PHANTOM SHIP   7
WAKENED
    HAD HALF WAKENED SOME OLD MEMORY, ...   284 TWO KINGS   V 172
    SICK OF HIS GRAVE HAS WAKENED ME? . . . .   303 HOUR DAWN   37
WAKENING   SEE HALF-WAKENING
    HALF WAKENING, WE LIFTED OUR EYELIDS, ...   54 OISIN 3   100
WAKENS
    AND WHO ARE YOU THAT WAKENS ME? . . . .   303 HOUR DAWN   V   35

WAKES
    AND WAKES THE SLUGGARD SEEDS OF CORN, • • • • • •   18 OISIN 1   263
    AND LEFT MERE SLEEP. HE'LL WAKE WHEN THE SUN WAKES, • • 284 TWO KINGS   161
    SHE HAS BEGUN FORGETTING. WHEN SHE WAKES, • • • • • 760 SHADOW WATER A   255
WAKING
    • • WAKING WHITE AS A SHELL   54 OISIN 3   103
    AND TELL ME WHO IT IS THAT WE ARE WAKING. • • • • • • 241 SHADOW WATER B   403
    HAD WAKING WITS; IT SEEMED • • • • • • • • • 422 MY TABLE   31
    WAKING HE THANKS THE LORD THAT HE • • • • • • 633 MAN AND ECHO   27
    FOR EVER ROUND THY WAKING AND THY SLEEP • • • • • 688 TWO TITANS   57
WALK
    THEY WALK ON SHORES UNSEEN OF OARING GALLEYS, • • • • 30 OISIN 2   V 140
    O MAY TRANQUILLITY WALK BY HIS ELBOW • • • • • • 71 ANASHU VIJAYA   2
    AND WALK AMONG LONG DAPPLED GRASS, • • • • • • 150 WANDER AENGUS   21
    AND WALK AND WALK THROUGH SUMMER GRASS, • • • • • 150 WANDER AENGUS V 21
    AND WALK AND WALK THROUGH SUMMER GRASS, • • • • • 150 WANDER AENGUS V 21
    THE BLESSEDEST SOULS THAT WALK IN THE WORLD • • • • 167 BLESSED   19
    AND WHEN WE WALK WITH KATE OR NAN • • • • • • • 192 BAILE AILLINN   92
    ON WET ROADS WHERE MEN WALK • • • • • • • • 215 HAPPY TOWNLAND   48
    HAVE SEEN IMMORTAL, MILD, PROUD SHADOWS WALK; • • 217 WOODS OF COOLE   12
    DID THEIR CATULLUS WALK THAT WAY? • • • • • • 337 SCHOLARS   12
    SHOULD THEIR CATULLUS WALK THAT WAY! • • • • • 337 SCHOLARS   V 12
    BUT WALK BY THE DRY THORN UNTIL I HAVE FOUND • • • 351 HER PRAISE   12
    AND WHO CAN SAY BUT SOME YOUNG BELLE MAY WALK AND TALK 354 HIS PHOENIX   26
        MEN WILD
    AND MAY BE THERE'LL BE SOME YOUNG BELLE WALK OUT TO MAKE 354 HIS PHOENIX V 26
        MEN WILD
    AND MAYBE THERE'LL BE SOME YOUNG BELLE WALK OUT TO MAKE 354 HIS PHOENIX V 26
        MEN WILD
    THAT MICHAEL ROBARTES LEFT, YOU WALK IN THE MOON, • • 367 EGO DOMINUS   4
    SHALL WALK THE WET SANDS BY THE EDGE OF THE STREAM • • 371 EGO DOMINUS   71
    SHALL WALK THE WET SAND BY THE WATER'S EDGE, • • • 371 EGO DOMINUS V 71
    FOR SILKEN CLOTHES AND STATELY WALK, • • • • • 422 MY TABLE   30
    I WALK THROUGH THE LONG SCHOOLROOM QUESTIONING; • 443 SCHOOL CHILDR   1
    CHIMNEY CORNER, GARDEN WALK, • • • • • • • • 499 MOTHER OF GOD   8
    MINE MUST WALK WHEN DEAD. • • • • • • • • • 511 JANE AND JACK   18
    MINE WOULD WALK, BEING DEAD. • • • • • • • • 511 JANE AND JACK V 18
    MUCH I TALK, MORE I WALK; • • • • • • • • • 548 TO SAME TUNE 3   9
    MUCH I TALK, MORE I WALK; • • • • • • • • • 548 TO SAME TUNE 3   19
    MUCH I TALK, MORE I WALK; • • • • • • • • • 549 TO SAME TUNE 3   29
    HOW SOUL MAY WALK WHEN ALL SUCH THINGS ARE PAST, • • 558 RIBH CHRISTIAN   11
    HOW SOUL COULD WALK BEFORE SUCH THINGS BEGAN. • • • 558 RIBH CHRISTIAN   12
    AND WHEN I PAY ATTENTION I MUST OUT AND WALK • • • 581 CURSE CROMWELL   29
    I WALK IN A BATTLE FOUGHT OVER AGAIN, • • • • • 591 WHAT WAS LOST   2
    ON THE GREEN LANDS I WALK • • • • • • • • • 607 SONGS BURDEN 2   20
    BUT FRIENDS WALK BY FRIENDS. • • • • • • • • 621 JOHN KINSELLA   32
    WITH A STRUTTING TURKEY WALK, • • • • • • • 627 STATES HOLIDAY   34
    THE PHANTOMS OF HER FADED PLEASURES WALK; • • • 687 TWO TITANS   19
    A BIRD WALK ON THE DOORSTEP. CHECK ONCE MORE. • 722 WITCH VIVIEN   64
WALKED
    • • AND I ROSE, AND WALKED ON THE EARTH, • • • • 60 OISIN 3   191
    THE LITTLE WAVES THAT WALKED IN EVENING WHITENESS, • • 81 EPHEMERA   V 240
    THE JESTER WALKED IN THE GARDEN! • • • • • • • 159 CAP AND BELLS   1
    MAEVE WALKED, YET WITH SLOW FOOTFALL, BEING OLD, • • 181 QUEEN MAEVE   43
    MAEVE WALKED THROUGH THAT GREAT HALL, AND WITH A SIGH • 182 QUEEN MAEVE   62
    I WALKED AMONG THE SEVEN WOODS OF COOLE! • • • • 217 WOODS OF COOLE   1
    YET WE, HAD WE WALKED WITHIN • • • • • • • • 293 HELEN LIVED   7
    WHERE HELEN WALKED WITH HER BOY, • • • • • • • 293 HELEN LIVED   9
    KING GUAIRE WALKED AMID HIS COURT • • • • • • • 295 THREE BEGGARS   8
    WHEREON A THING ONCE WALKED THAT SEEMED A BURNING CLOUD. 315 FALLEN MAJESTY   8
    ONCE WALKED A THING THAT SEEMED, AS IT WERE, A BURNING 315 FALLEN MAJESTY V   8
        CLOUD.
    HAVE WALKED TO THE ALTAR • • • • • • • • • • 355 PROPERTIUS   4
    AND FOR AN HOUR I HAVE WALKED AND PRAYED • • • • 403 FOR DAUGHTER   7
    I HAVE WALKED AND PRAYED FOR THIS YOUNG CHILD AN HOUR • 403 FOR DAUGHTER   9
    REMEMBERING THAT, IF WALKED SHE THERE, • • • • • 410 TOWER   38
    HE WALKED THAT ROOM AND ISSUED THENCE • • • • • 438 SONGS PLAY 2   2
    SHE WALKED AWHILE AND BLUSHED AWHILE • • • • • 451 FIRST LOVE   3
    WALKED THROUGH THE HOUSE. UNNOTICED AND UNFELT • • 468 HARUN RASHID   153
    WHAT SCHOOLING HAD THESE FOUR? THEY WALKED THE ROADS • 487 SEVEN SAGES   24
    HOW SOUL HAS WALKED BEFORE SUCH THINGS BEGAN. • • 558 RIBH CHRISTIAN V 12
    WALKED ON THE WATERS AND BID FORGAEL SEEK • • • • 747 SHADOW WATER A   12
WALKERS   SEE NIGHT-WALKERS
WALKERS'   SEE NIGHT-WALKERS'
WALKING
    AND GRANIA, WALKING AND SMILING, SEWED WITH HER NEEDLE 53 OISIN 3   94
        OF BONE.
    WALKING GHOSTLY IN THE DEW. • • • • • • • • • 67 HAPPY SHEPHERD   52
    WALKING GHOSTLY 'MONG THE DEW, • • • • • • • • 67 HAPPY SHEPHERD V 52
    WENT WALKING WITH SLOW STEPS ALONG THE GLEAMING • • 68 SAD SHEPHERD   3
    WITHIN THE TEMPLE, DEVIOUS WALKING, MADE • • • • 72 ANASHU VIJAYA   32
    WHO MET FAND WALKING AMONG FLAMING DEW • • • • 169 SECRET ROSE   13
    IN WALKING NAKED. • • • • • • • • • • • • 320 COAT   10
    BY MERELY WALKING IN A ROOM. • • • • • • • • 356 BROKEN DREAMS   13
    LEANING OR STANDING OR WALKING. • • • • • • • 356 BROKEN DREAMS   23
    TALL DAMES GO WALKING IN GRASS-GREEN AVALON. • 627 STATES HOLIDAY   13
    TALL DAMES GO WALKING IN GRASS-GREEN AVALON. • 627 STATES HOLIDAY   26
    TALL DAMES GO WALKING IN GRASS-GREEN AVALON. • 627 STATES HOLIDAY   39
    TALL DAMES GO WALKING IN GRASS GREEN AVALON. • 627 STATES HOLIDAY V REF
    PROUDLY IN HIS SAFFRON WALKING; • • • • • • • 705 DAWN-SONG   2
    AND THE OLD MEN WERE WALKING, WALKING, • • • • • 725 LEGEND   3

	PAGE	TITLE	LINE

WALKING   (CONTINUED)
```
    AND THE OLD MEN WERE WALKING, WALKING,  . . . . . .  .  .    725 LEGEND               3
    FOR GOD IS WALKING IN THE DEW, . . . . . . . . . .  .  .    736 SUMMER EVENING      15
    MOVING THERE AND WALKING: . . . . . . . . . . .  .  .    785 YOUR HEART           5
WALKS
    WILL GATHER, AND NOT KNOW IT WALKS THE VERY STREET  .  .  .    315 FALLEN MAJESTY       7
    LOOK ON THAT FIRE, SALVATION WALKS WITHIN. . . . .  .  .    502 VACILATION          76
    BUT BODY WON: IT WALKS UPRIGHT. . . . . . . .  .  .    561 FOUR AGES MAN        2
    OBEYS.  SOME FIERCE MAGICIAN FLIES OR WALKS  . . .  .  .    720 WITCH VIVIEN         9
    WALKS IN THE VESTURE OF HER SISTER SORROW. . . . .  .  .    735 QUATRAIN APHOR      28
WALL
    AMONG THE LEAVES OF THE LAUREL WALL . . . . . .  .  .      3 OISIN 1       V   7FF
    THAT WOMAN FOUND A RING HUNG ON THE WALL, . . . .  .  .     37 OISIN 2          120
    THAT MAIDEN FOUND A RING HUNG ON THE WALL, . . . .  .  .     37 OISIN 2       V  120
    AND FOUND A DOOR DEEP SUNKEN IN THE WALL, . . . .  .  .     39 OISIN 2          154
    I FOUND A DOOR DEEP-SUNKEN IN THE WALL, . . . . .  .  .     39 OISIN 2       V  154
    AND MINE WAS EVERY TROPHIED WALL, . . . . . . .  .  .     82 MAD KING GOLL  V    4
    A WALL BEHIND HIS BACK, OVER HIS HEAD  . . . . .  .  .    180 QUEEN MAEVE          5
    ONE LEANS AND MUTTERS BY THE WALL-- . . . . . .  .  .    212 BLESS PSALTER       10
    UNTIL HE CAME BEFORE THE PAINTED WALL, . . . . .  .  .    279 TWO KINGS           47
    I COWERED BACK UPON THE WALL IN TERROR, . . . . .  .  .    284 TWO KINGS          164
    IN THE GREEN SHADOW OF FERRARA WALL: . . . . . .  .  .    352 PEOPLE               9
    IN THE GREEN SHADOW ON FERRARA WALL: . . . . . .  .  .    352 PEOPLE        V      9
    SHE TURNS THE DOLLS' FACES TO THE WALL  . . . .  .  .    363 DOLLS FACES          T
    HEEL UP AND WEIGHT ON TOE, MUST FACE THE WALL . .  .  .    363 DOLLS FACES          3
    NODDED UPON THE WALL, . . . . . . . . . . . .  .  .    400 DEMON BEAST         12
    AS IN THE GOLD MOSAIC OF A WALL, . . . . . . .  .  .    408 SAIL BYZANTIUM      18
    A FARMHOUSE THAT IS SHELTERED BY ITS WALL, . . .  .  .    419 MY HOUSE             2
    A FARM-HOUSE THAT IS SHELTERED BY ITS WALL, . . .  .  .    419 MY HOUSE      V      2
    MY WALL IS LOOSENING: HONEY-BEES, . . . . . . .  .  .    424 STARES NEST          4
    MY WALL IS LOOSENING: HONEY BEES  . . . . . . .  .  .    424 STARES NEST   V      4
    THE BROKEN WALL, THE BURNING ROOF AND TOWER . .  .  .    441 LEDA AND SWAN       10
    UPON A PAINTED WALL. . . . . . . . . . . . .  .  .    452 HUMAN DIGNITY        6
    WHO BEAT UPON THE WALL  . . . . . . . . . .  .  .    576 ACRE OF GRASS       17
    NOW I AM IN THE PUBLIC-HOUSE AND LEAN UPON THE WALL,  .  .    593 PILGRIM             21
    NOW I AM IN THE TAVERN AND LEAN AGAINST THE WALL,  .  .    593 PILGRIM             21
    NOW I AM IN THE PUBLIC HOUSE AND LEAN UPON THE WALL,  .  .    593 PILGRIM       V    21
    HEARD YOU?  YOUR LUTE UPON THE WALL HAS SOUNDED! .  .  .    694 MOSADA 1      V    95
    AND THE FISHER MEN AND WOMEN FROM THE DRIPPING HARBOUR WALL    718 PHANTOM SHIP        11
    I HAVE STOOD SO LONG BY A GAP IN THE WALL . . .  .  .    788 HAWTHORN TREE       15
    I HAVE STOPPED SO LONG A GAP IN THE WALL  . . .  .  .    788 HAWTHORN TREE V    15
WALLA        SEE SHAN-WALLA
WALLED
    SPRANG FROM A GATEWAY WALLED AROUND WITH BLACK  . . .  .     31 OISIN 2       V   29
WALLS
    TWO WALLS, A ROOF, A FLOOD: THERE TREMBLING GREEN . .  .     31 OISIN 2       V   32
    BETWEEN THE WALLS COVERED WITH BEATEN BRONZE, . . .  .    180 QUEEN MAEVE         10
    OR ON THE BENCHES UNDERNEATH THE WALLS, . . . .  .  .    180 QUEEN MAEVE         14
    I HELPED YOUR FATHERS WHEN THEY BUILT THESE WALLS,  .  .    184 QUEEN MAEVE         97
    ROSE ROUND THE WALLS, AND THROUGH THE BRONZE-RINGED DOOR    286 TWO KINGS          215
    ROSE LIKE THESE WALLS FROM THESE  . . . . . . .  .  .    480 BLOOD AND MOON       6
    A DANCE-LIKE GLORY THAT THOSE WALLS BEGOT. . . .  .  .    488 COOLE PARK 29        8
    HE NEVER LAY BEHIND FOUR WALLS . . . . . . . .  .  .    606 SONGS BURDEN 1      12
    DOWN THE MOUNTAIN WALLS . . . . . . . . . . .  .  .    612 NEWS ORACLE         30
    WHERE RISE THE WALLS MAJESTICAL ABOVE . . . . .  .  .    679 ISLE STAT II 3     311
    AND THRICE THE PEACHES FLUSHED UPON THE WALLS,  .  .  .    690 MOSADA 1             2
    WITH THREE BARS CROSSED, AND THESE FOUR WALLS MY WORLD,    700 MOSADA 3            32
    ALONG THE TENTS, THE FIELDS, THE VILLAGE WALLS. .  .  .    712 FERENCZ RENYI       71
    ALONG THE TENTS, FIELD, THE VILLAGE WALLS. . . .  .  .    712 FERENCZ RENYI V    71
    HAST THOU NOT RULED AMONG THE GILDED WALLS? . .  .  .    724 KANVA ON SELF        7
WAN
    AND THE WAN WAVE THAT LINGERS  . . . . . . .  .  .    672 ISLE STAT II 3     166
    IN THY WAN FACE?  HEAR THOU, O DAUGHTER OF THE DAYS,  .  .    674 ISLE STAT II 3     200
    IN THY WAN FACE?  HEAR, DAUGHTER OF THE DAYS. .  .  .    674 ISLE STAT II 3 V  200
    BY THOSE WAN STARS THAT SIT IN COMPANY  . . . .  .  .    691 MOSADA 1            26
WAND
    AND CUT AND PEELED A HAZEL WAND, . . . . . . .  .  .    149 WANDER AENGUS        3
    A MAN WITH A HAZEL WAND CAME WITHOUT SOUND: . .  .  .    153 CHANGE BELOVED       6
    A MAN WITH A WAND OF HAZEL CAME WITHOUT SOUND: .  .  .    153 CHANGE BELOVED V    6
WANDER
    DID YOUR COMPANION WANDER AWAY . . . . . . . .  .  .      6 OISIN 1             52
    THAT RAISE THEIR HEADS AND WANDER SINGING, . . .  .  .     27 OISIN 1            419
    AND WANDER IN THE STORMS AND CLINGING SNOWS, . .  .  .     42 OISIN 2            201
    TO WANDER BY THEIR MELANCHOLY MINDS. . . . . .  .  .     72 ANASHU VIJAYA       33
    AND WANDER EVER WITH WOVEN HANDS, . . . . . . .  .  .     78 INDIAN TO LOVE       7
    AND NOW I WANDER IN THE WOODS  . . . . . . . .  .  .     84 MAD KING GOLL       37
    I WANDER ON, AND WAVE MY HANDS, . . . . . . .  .  .     84 MAD KING GOLL       43
    AND I MUST WANDER WOOD AND HILL  . . . . . . .  .  .     86 MAD KING GOLL       70
    AND THEREFORE DO I WANDER ON, . . . . . . . .  .  .    131 OLD PENSIONER  V    5
    AND THEREFORE DO I WANDER NOW, . . . . . . . .  .  .    131 OLD PENSIONER  V    5
    AND BID THEM WANDER OBEYING YOUR WILL, . . . . .  .  .    141 EVERLAST VOICE       3
    I WANDER BY THE EDGE  . . . . . . . . . . . .  .  .    165 CRY OF SEDGE         1
    O, WHEN SHALL SORROW WANDER NO MORE IN THE LAND . .  .    174 ELEMENT POWERS V    5
    HELP THEM THAT WANDER WITH HAND CLASPING HAND, .  .  .    184 QUEEN MAEVE         86
    WANDER WHERE EARTH WITHERS AWAY. . . . . . . .  .  .    196 BAILE AILLINN      171
    WITH WISDOM, THEY WANDER TILL ALL THE YEARS HAVE GONE BY:    204 WITHER BOUGHS       21
    IN THE WASTE OF THE HIGH AIR, THAT WE MAY WANDER . .  .    234 SHADOW WATER B     263
    BUT NOW IT IS YOUR THOUGHTS THAT WANDER AWAY, . .  .  .    246 SHADOW WATER B     512
    WANDER A MOMENT WHEN ONE IS IN LOVE? . . . . .  .  .    246 SHADOW WATER B     515
    PASSION OR CONQUEST, WANDER WHERE THEY WILL, . .  .  .    323 SWANS AT COOLE      23
    FOR, WANDER AND WAIL AS HE WOULD, . . . . . .  .  .    378 CAT AND MOON         6
```

PAGE   TITLE   LINE

WANDER   (CONTINUED)
    WANDER IN DREAMS NO MORE; . . . .   554 CHURCH STATE   8
    TO WANDER BY THE BUBBLING SHORE. . . . .   668 ISLE STAT II 3   57
    WANDER AWAY FROM MINE? . . . .   686 LIFE   8
    FEET OF DARK GOMEZ, WHERE NOW WANDER YE? . . . . . .   690 MOSADA 1   11
    PICTURED, WHERE WANDER THE BELOVED FEET? . . . . . .   692 MOSADA 1   44
    STILL WANDER THROUGH THE WORLD. HE'S GONE, HE'S GONE. . .   703 MOSADA 3   121
    WE WILL WANDER, I AND YOU; . . . .   706 DAWN-SONG   23
    WHO WANDER AND WHISPER ALONE. . . . .   707 FAIRY PEDANT   8
    THEN AWAY AND AWAY WILL I WANDER, ...   707 FAIRY PEDANT   16
    IN THE WASTE AIR. I WILL WANDER BY HIS SIDE . . . . .   754 SHADOW WATER A   152
    THE PALE HOUND AND THE DEER WANDER FOR EVER . . . . .   764 SHADOW WATER A   330
    THE PALE HOUND AND THE DEER WANDER FOREVER . . . . .   764 SHADOW WATER A V   330
    TO WANDER IN; YOU HAVE LOVED MANY WOMEN, ...   767 SHADOW WATER A   389
    AND BID HIM TO YOUR COUNTRY. I SHOULD WANDER . . . .   767 SHADOW WATER A   403
WANDERED
    SOME WANDERED EVER HAND IN HAND; . . . .   25 OISIN 1   389
    AND OVER THE LIMBS AND THE VALLEY THE SLOW OWLS WANDERED   49 OISIN 3   41
      AND CAME,
    HE WANDERED BY THE SANDS OF LISSADELL; . . . . . .   127 DREAM OF FAERY   13
    WANDERED BETWEEN THE BLUE AND THE GREEN LEAF . . . .   278 TWO KINGS   41
    "YOU THAT HAVE WANDERED FAR AND WIDE, ...   295 THREE BEGGARS   11
    "YOU HAVE WANDERED FAR AND WIDE, ...   295 THREE BEGGARS V   11
    AND WANDERED MURMURING EVERYWHERE, "MY CHILD, MY CHILD!"   619 BRONZE HEAD   21
    I WANDERED AND TROD, ...   654 ISLE STAT I 2   64
    AS I WANDERED UNSEEN, ...   654 ISLE STAT I 2   71
    FAIR SHEPHERD, AS WE WANDERED HITHER, ...   669 ISLE STAT II 3   83
    HE HOOTED AS I WANDERED BY. . . . .   670 ISLE STAT II 3   121
    MUSINGLY WANDERED THE VILLAGE PRIEST. . . . . . .   728 PRIEST FAIRY   3
WANDERER   SEE FELLOW-WANDERER
    OH WANDERER IN THE SOUTHERN WEATHER, ...   77 INDIAN TO LOVE V   1
    THOUGH IT BUT SET US SIGHING. FELLOW WANDERER . . .   230 SHADOW WATER B V   187
    THE PACK UPON HIM. GO, UNQUIET WANDERER. . . . . .   292 TO A SHADE   18
    HERDING THE PACK. UNQUIET WANDERER . . . . . .   292 TO A SHADE V   18
    WITH CLINGING MIST, EACH STAR-FOUGHT WANDERER CAME .   656 ISLE STAT I 3   33
    DOTH STILL THE WANDERER ROVE? WITH ALL HIS SHIPS .   677 ISLE STAT II 3   287
WANDERER'S
    UNTO THE WANDERER'S SHIPS, OR AS DAY FILLS . . . . .   645 ISLE STAT I 1   10
WANDERERS
    DWELT AMONG WINE-STAINED WANDERERS IN DEEP WOODS; . .   170 SECRET ROSE   21
    AENGUS AND EDAIN, THOSE PASSIONATE WANDERERS, . . .   228 SHADOW WATER B   138
    THOSE WANDERERS THAT WELCOMED IN THEIR TENTS . . . .   462 HARUN RASHID   23
    THE WAVES, ENORMOUS WANDERERS OF THE WORLD, ...   687 TWO TITANS   3
    GAYEST WANDERERS, I AND YOU, ...   706 DAWN-SONG   31
WANDERING   SEE ROCK-WANDERING FAR-WANDERING NIGHT-WANDERING
    WITH A HEAVY HEART AND A WANDERING MIND, ...   2 OISIN 1   2
    MUST LIVE TO BE OLD LIKE THE WANDERING MOON. . . . .   3 OISIN 1   12
    THY WANDERING STEPS ACROSS THE SEA? . . . .   5 OISIN 1 V   51
    BRINGING ME HONEYED, WANDERING THOUGHT . . . . . .   7 OISIN 1 V   65
    BUT NOW A WANDERING LAND BREEZE CAME . . . .   13 OISIN 1   165
    AND, NOW OUR WANDERING HOURS WERE DONE, ...   14 OISIN 1   177
    LIKE TO A MERRY WANDERING ROUT . . . .   18 OISIN 1   253
    AND WAVERING ARMS AND WANDERING DANCES. . . . . . .   19 OISIN 1   275
    AND WAVING ARMS AND WANDERING DANCES. . . . . . .   19 OISIN 1 V   275
    OR THE GREY WANDERING OSPREY SORROW." . . . . . .   20 OISIN 1   303
    NOR THE GREY WANDERING OSPREY SORROW." . . . . . .   21 OISIN 1   319
    ACROSS YOUR WANDERING RUBY CARS . . . .   22 OISIN 1   330
    NOR THE GREY WANDERING OSPREY SORROW." . . . . . .   23 OISIN 1   342
    FLED FOAM UNDERNEATH US, AND ROUND US, A WANDERING AND   47 OISIN 3   1
      MILKY SMOKE,
    FLED FOAM UNDERNEATH US, AND ROUND US, A WANDERING AND   47 OISIN 3   12
      MILKY SMOKE.
    FLED FOAM UNDERNEATH US, AND AROUND US, A WANDERING AND   47 OISIN 3 V   1
      MILKY SMOKE,
    . . . AND PACING THE SHORES OF THE WANDERING SEAS, . . .   50 OISIN 3   55
    AS SHE MURMURED, "O WANDERING OISIN, ...   55 OISIN 3   123
    FLED FOAM UNDERNEATH ME, AND ROUND ME, A WANDERING AND   57 OISIN 3   148
      MILKY SMOKE.
    THE WANDERING EARTH HERSELF MAY BE . . . .   65 HAPPY SHEPHERD   18
    WHEN WANDERING IN THE FOREST, IF HE LOVE . . . . .   71 ANASHU VIJAYA   3
    THE VAN OF WANDERING QUIET; ERE YOU BE TOO CALM AND OLD,   73 ANASHU VIJAYA   43
    THE VAN OF WANDERING QUIET; ERE YE BE TOO CALM AND OLD,   73 ANASHU VIJAYA V   43
    "PASSION HAS OFTEN WORN OUR WANDERING HEARTS." . . .   80 EPHEMERA   12
    "OFTEN HAS PASSION WORN OUR WANDERING HEARTS, . . .   80 EPHEMERA V   12
    A WHIRLING AND A WANDERING FIRE! . . . .   83 MAD KING GOLL   28
    THE WHIRLING AND THE WANDERING FIRE; . . . .   86 MAD KING GOLL   67
    WHERE THE WANDERING WATER GUSHES . . . .   88 STOLEN CHILD   28
    A GAY WANDERING CRY. . . . .   98 FOXHUNTER   28
    A GAY AND WANDERING CRY. . . . .   98 FOXHUNTER V   28
    AND WHEN THE WANDERING MUSIC DIES . . . .   99 FOXHUNTER   31
    ETERNAL BEAUTY WANDERING ON HER WAY. . . . . . .   101 ROSE UPON ROOD   12
    BEFORE HER WANDERING FEET. . . . .   112 ROSE OF WORLD   15
    OR SIGHS AMID THE WANDERING, STARRY MIRTH, ...   114 ROSE OF BATTLE   18
    . . . ON THE WANDERING FOAM; I AND YOU; . . . . .   122 WHITE BIRDS   8
    AND ALL DISHEVELLED WANDERING STARS. . . . . . .   126 GOES FERGUS   12
    AH, EXILES WANDERING OVER LANDS AND SEAS, ...   129 BOOK STORIES   9
    AH, EXILES, WANDERING OVER MANY SEAS, ...   129 BOOK STORIES V   9
    AH, EXILES, WANDERING OVER MANY LANDS, ...   130 BOOK STORIES V   17
    AND OF THE WANDERING TWILIGHT COMPANIES . . . . . .   136 TO SOME I TALK V   6
    DESOLATE WINDS THAT CRY OVER THE WANDERING SEA; . . .   147 UNAPPEAS HOST   7
    THE SONG OF WANDERING AENGUS . . . .   149 WANDER AENGUS   T

```
                                                      PAGE    TITLE            LINE
WANDERING  (CONTINUED)
     THOUGH I AM OLD WITH WANDERING . . . . . . . . . .     150 WANDER AENGUS        17
     AND BIND UP EVERY WANDERING TRESS: . . . . . . . .     157 BELOVED RHYMES        2
     ABOVE THE WANDERING TIDE: . . . . . . . . . . . .      162 ASKS FORGIVE         14
     AND SHE FORGET THE WANDERING AND ALL THE CRIMSON GLOOM . .  175 ELEMENT POWERS V  11
     AND SHE FORGET THE WANDERING AND THE CRIMSON GLOOM . .      175 ELEMENT POWERS V  11
     WHO OF THE WANDERING MANY-CHANGING ONES . . . . .      182 QUEEN MAEVE          51
     OF THE FAR WANDERING SHADOWS HAS COME TO ME, . . .     183 QUEEN MAEVE      V   80
     FOR YOU, ALTHOUGH YOU'VE NOT HER WANDERING HEART, .    186 QUEEN MAEVE         132
     O WANDERING BIRDS AND RUSHY BEDS, . . . . . . . .      190 BAILE AILLINN        31
     WANDERING FROM BROKEN STREET TO STREET . . . . . .     196 BAILE AILLINN       167
     A KING AND A QUEEN ARE WANDERING THERE, AND THE SOUND     204 WITHER BOUGHS     19
     'TWAS AENGUS AND EDAIN, THE WANDERING LOVERS . . .     224 SHADOW WATER B       42
     AS NOW.  DOES WANDERING IN THESE DESOLATE SEAS . .     236 SHADOW WATER B      314
     SO THAT THE WANDERING FOOT'S CONTENT. . . . . . .      276 GREY ROCK           131
     THAT HAS GROWN WEARY OF THE WANDERING DANCE, . . .     285 TWO KINGS           183
     THAT AM A WANDERING WITTED FOOL . . . . . . . . .      380 SONGS FOOL 1     V   16
     AS THAT OLD WANDERING BEGGAR AND THESE GOD-HATED CHILDREN  459 FROM OEDIPUS      6
       KNOW.
     THAT WANDERING IN A DESERT, FEATURELESS . . . . .      462 HARUN RASHID         27
     BUT WANDERING ARABS.  I COMMEND THE ARABS . . . .      462 HARUN RASHID     V   22
     WANDERING IN A DESERT FEATURELESS . . . . . . . .      462 HARUN RASHID     V   27
     DRAWN THROUGH THE WANDERING VEGETATIVE DREAM, . .      467 HARUN RASHID        143
     WOUND IN MIND'S WANDERING . . . . . . . . . . . .      474 ALL SOUL NIGHT       99
     FIX EVERY WANDERING THOUGHT UPON . . . . . . . .       477 SELF AND SOUL         6
     AND INTELLECT ITS WANDERING . . . . . . . . . . .      478 SELF AND SOUL        22
     CARRIED BY THE WANDERING FOOL. . . . . . . . . . .     484 SYMBOLS               4
     GLANCES OF HER WANDERING EYE . . . . . . . . . . .     487 CRAZED MOON           4
     AND THERE IS AN OLD BEGGAR WANDERING IN HIS PRIDE-- . .    580 CURSE CROMWELL    5
     BEST PLEASE A WANDERING MAN. . . . . . . . . . . .     606 SONGS BURDEN 1       17
     'TIS MORN: THY SHEEP ARE WANDERING DOWN THE VALE--     645 ISLE STAT I 1         3
     WITH STREAMING HAIR AS WANDERING LIGHTS . . . . .      667 ISLE STAT II 3       19
     FAIR YOUTH, ALONG A WANDERING WAY . . . . . . . .      667 ISLE STAT II 3       38
     MID BUBBLING LEAVES A WANDERING SONG-RAPT BIRD . .     672 ISLE STAT II 3      154
     MID BABBLING LEAVES A WANDERING SONG-RAPT BIRD . .     672 ISLE STAT II 3 V    154
     FROM THREESCORE YEARS OF DREAM-LED WANDERING . . .     682 SEEKER               16
     BUT NOW MY WANDERING SHALL BE DONE, I KNOW. . . .      682 SEEKER               21
     BUT SOON MY WANDERING SHALL BE DONE I KNOW. . . .      682 SEEKER           V   21
     WERE ALL MY WANDERING DAYS OF NO AVAIL, . . . . .      684 SEEKER               64
     FORSWEARS HIS WANDERING 'MONG THE PINE, . . . . .      686 LIFE                  6
     WHERE THEY ALL SUMMER FEED THEIR WANDERING FLOCKS,     690 MOSADA 1              5
     WANDERING IN SULTRY PALACES OF IND, . . . . . . .      694 MOSADA 1            102
     SHE SMILES--IS HAPPY WITH HER WANDERING GRIEFS. .      702 MOSADA 3             95
     OH, HUSH THE WANDERING MUSIC OF THY MIND. . . . .      703 MOSADA 3            106
     WANDERING OF YORE IN FORESTS RUMOROUS, . . . . . .     723 KANVA ON SELF         3
     THERE THY WANDERING PATHWAY GOES, . . . . . . . .      744 ROSY CROSS            6
     EVEN THE WANDERING ISLANDS OF THE GODS, . . . . .      749 SHADOW WATER A       45
     A WANDERING AIRY MUSIC: . . . . . . . . . . . . .      783 GREY ROUND            7
     IN THAT SWEET WANDERING SNARE. . . . . . . . . . .     783 GREY ROUND           10
     A WANDERING AIRY MUSIC: . . . . . . . . . . . . .      783 GREY ROUND           17
WANDERINGS
     THE WANDERINGS OF OISIN . . . . . . . . . . . . .        1 OISIN 1             T
     THE WANDERINGS OF OISIN AND HOW A DEMON TRAPPED HIM . .     1 OISIN 1       V   T
     O'SULLIVAN THE RED UPON HIS WANDERINGS . . . . . .     171 MAID QUIET       V   T
     HANRAHAN LAMENTS BECAUSE OF HIS WANDERINGS . . . .     171 MAID QUIET       V   T
     THE LOVER MOURNS BECAUSE OF HIS WANDERINGS . . . .     171 MAID QUIET       V   T
     AWAKEN WANDERINGS OF LIGHT AIR . . . . . . . . . .     197 BAILE AILLINN       185
     FOR ALL HER WANDERINGS OVER-SEA: . . . . . . . . .     197 BAILE AILLINN       203
     AND AIMLESS WANDERINGS THE WOODLANDS LONE, . . . .     674 ISLE STAT II 3      209
WANDERING-WITTED
     THAT AM A WANDERING-WITTED FOOL . . . . . . . . .      380 SONGS FOOL 1         16
WANDERS
     AS IN THE WOODS HE WANDERS, IF HE LOVE . . . . .•  .    71 ANASHU VIJAYA V      3
     WANDERS LAUGHING AND EATING HER WILD HEART . . . .     198 SEVEN WOODS          11
     WANDERS OUT INTO THE NIGHT . . . . . . . . . . . .     508 JANE BISHOP          25
     WANDERS AND WAILS BEFORE MY HEART MOST TRUE . . .      738 YOU ARE SAD           8
     WHERE TRUE-LOVE WANDERS AMONG THE HOLY WOODS. . .      764 SHADOW WATER A      337
     WHERE TRUE LOVE WANDERS AMONG THE HOLY WOODS. . .      764 SHADOW WATER A      337
WANDS
     TALL WANDS OF ALDER AND WHITE QUICKEN WANDS. . . .     111 CUCHULAIN SEA V     82A
     TALL WANDS OF ALDER AND WHITE QUICKEN WANDS. . . .     111 CUCHULAIN SEA V     82A
WANE
     WHEN THE STARS ARE TO WANE AND THE WORLD BE DONE.      16 OISIN 1             220
     "GOD'S FIRE UPON THE WANE. . . . . . . . . . . . .     485 STATISTICS            2
     MY WORDS WERE ALL:  "HERE NO LOVES WANE AND WITHER,    669 ISLE STAT II 3       84
WANES
     THAT WANES."  "AH, WISTFUL VOICE," REPLIED THE OTHER,   79 EPHEMERA        V    3
WANING
     THE HOUR OF THE WANING OF LOVE HAS BESET US, . . .      79 FALLING LEAVES       5
     BECAUSE OUR LOVE IS WANING."  AND THEN SHE: . . .       79 EPHEMERA             3
     "ALTHOUGH OUR LOVE IS WANING, LET US STAND . . . .      79 EPHEMERA             4
WANT
     TO TELL YOUR SIMPLEST WANT, AND KNOWN, . . . . .       436 FOR MY SON           21
     TO TELL YOUR SIMPLEST WANT, AND KNOW, . . . . . .      436 FOR MY SON       V   21
     "THEN WANT BEFORE YOU DIE." . . . . . . . . . .        596 COLONEL MARTIN       67
     AND WANT HE DID: FOR MY OWN GRAND-DAD . . . . . .      596 COLONEL MARTIN       68
     AND WANT HE DID FOR MY GRAND-DAD SAW . . . . . .       596 COLONEL MARTIN V     68
WANTED
     . . . THE PEOPLE WANTED PICTURES . . . . . . . .       287 TO WEALTHY MAN       T
WANTING
     LONE, AND WANTING THEE, I WEEP: . . . . . . . . .      647 ISLE STAT I 1        72
```

PAGE   TITLE   LINE

WANTON
   IGNORANT AND WANTON AS THE DAWN. . . . . 344 DAWN   14
   THIS THEIR WANTON TREACHERY, ... 727 LOVERS QUARREL   55
WANTONNESS
   HOW BUT IN ZIG-ZAG WANTONNESS . . . . 338 TOM OROUGHLEY   12
   HOW BUT IN ZIGZAG WANTONNESS . . . . 338 TOM OROUGHLEY V 12
   WHAT BUT HEROIC WANTONNESS? . . . . 550 SEVERED HEAD   13
   OUT OF MERE WANTONNESS TO LURE A SAIL . . . . 750 SHADOW WATER A   79
WAR
   OF WAR WERE ON IT, AND I WEPT, ... 24 OISIN 1   369
   IN WAR, THE NOBLE FENIANS STEPT. . . . . 24 OISIN 1   V 372
   OF WAR, AND THE CHASE, AND HUNTING, AND PLEASURE; . . . 26 OISIN 1   V 403
   AN ENDLESS WAR. THE HUNDRED YEARS HAD CEASED; . . . 44 OISIN 2   224
   AN ENDLESS WAR. THE HUNDREDTH YEAR HAD CEASED. . . . 44 OISIN 2   V 224
   WAR ON THE MIGHTIEST MEN UNDER THE SKIES, ... 45 OISIN 2   241
   NONE WAR ON THE MASTERS OF HELL, ... 62 OISIN 3   214
   . . . AND NO MAN MAY WAR WITH THE STRONG SPIRITS WAGE; . . 62 OISIN 3   V 214
   AND DROVE TUMULT AND WAR AWAY . . . . 82 MAD KING GOLL   5
   BUT NOW THE WAR RAGE IN CUCHULAIN WOKE, ... 110 CUCHULAIN SEA V 65
   WHEN THEY FOR WAR ARE MET, ... 112 ROSE OF PEACE V   2
   DANGER NO REFUGE HOLDS, AND WAR NO PEACE, ... 114 ROSE OF BATTLE   9
   IT WAS BEFORE THE TIME OF THE GREAT WAR . . . . 182 QUEEN MAEVE   57
   FOR LOVE IS WAR, AND THERE IS HATRED IN IT; . . . . . . 244 SHADOW WATER B 459
   ON THE DAY'S WAR WITH EVERY KNAVE AND DOLT, ... 260 FASC DIFFICULT   10
   OUTRODE HIS TROOP THAT AFTER TWELVE MONTHS' WAR . . . 276 TWO KINGS   V   1
   AND DIED IN THE GREAT WAR BEYOND THE SEA. . . . . . . 339 SHEP GOATHERD   22
   THE OUTRAGEOUS WAR SHALL FADE; . . . . 342 SHEP GOATHERD 100
   I WILL TALK NO MORE OF BOOKS OR THE LONG WAR . . . . . 351 HER PRAISE   11
   ON BEING ASKED FOR A WAR POEM . . . . 359 WAR POEM   T
   OUT OF NO TRAGIC WAR, LOVERS OF LIFE, ... 369 EGO DOMINUS   39
   THE THIRTEENTH MOON BUT SETS THE SOUL AT WAR . . . . . 374 PHASES OF MOON   50
   A MEDITATION IN TIME OF WAR . . . . 406 IN TIME OF WAR   T
   A MEDITATION IN TIME OF WAR . . . . 406 IN TIME OF WAR V T
   MEDITATIONS IN TIME OF CIVIL WAR ANCESTRAL HOUSES . . . 417 ANCEST HOUSES V T
   COMES CRACKING JOKES OF CIVIL WAR . . . . 423 ROAD AT DOOR   3
   SOME FOURTEEN DAYS OF CIVIL WAR; . . . . 425 STARES NEST   12
   IT DROPPED THE REINS OF PEACE AND WAR . . . . 437 SONGS PLAY 1   14
   NOR ACCIDENT OF PEACE NOR WAR . . . . 446 COLONUS PRAISE   14
   AWAIT THE HOUR OF WAR, ENTER THE SMALL, ... 461 HARUN RASHID V   8
   WITH PERSIAN EMBASSY OR GRECIAN WAR, ... 462 HARUN RASHID   25
   EMBLEMATICAL OF LOVE AND WAR? . . . . 477 SELF AND SOUL   19
   OF WAR AND WAR'S ALARMS, ... 631 POLITICS   10
   "SEND WAR IN OUR TIME, O LORD!" . . . . 638 BEN BULBEN   26
   AND THEY WILL WAR, 'MID WONDROUS ELFIN-SIGHTS; . . . . 651 ISLE STAT I 1 164
   OF WAR. OF YORE, TWO SHEPHERDS, WHERE WE PAUSE, . . . 659 ISLE STAT II 1   31
   SUCH WAR PLOTS, PEACE PLOTS, LOVE PLOTS--EVERY SIDE; . . 722 WITCH VIVIEN   66
   AND PRAISED YOUR WAR AMONG THE ENDLESS SEAS, ... 749 SHADOW WATER A   35
   AND PRAISE A WAR AMONG THE ENDLESS SEAS, ... 749 SHADOW WATER A V 35
   BELIEVE THAT GOLD AND WOMEN TAKEN IN WAR . . . . . . 754 SHADOW WATER A 159
   AND MORE, IF YOU WILL WAR AGAINST THE DANES . . . . . 756 SHADOW WATER A V 190
   WAR LADEN GALLEYS, AND ARMIES ON WHITE ROADS, ... 757 SHADOW WATER A V 203
WAR-AXE
   MINGLING OF SWORD AND WAR-AXE, WHILE THE DAY . . . . . 40 OISIN 2   V 171
   AND BY THEM WERE ARROW AND WAR-AXE, ARROW AND SHIELD AND
      BLADE; . . . . 49 OISIN 3   29
   WERE ARROW AND SHIELD AND WAR-AXE, ARROW AND SPEAR AND
      BLADE, ... 49 OISIN 3   V 30
   SORRY PLACE, WHERE FOR SWING OF THE WAR-AXE IN MY DIM EYES . 61 OISIN 3   194
     . . .
WARDER
   AND EVEN THE SUN, THE DAY CASTLE'S WARDER, ... 28 OISIN 1   V 423A
WARES
   FOR ARROGANCE AND HATRED ARE THE WARES . . . . 406 FOR DAUGHTER   75
   TO THOSE YOUR "MELLOW" WARES HAVE WEARIED OUT. . . . . 721 WITCH VIVIEN   27
WARFARE
   AND GOD WOULD BID HIS WARFARE CEASE, ... 113 ROSE OF PEACE   13
   AND GOD WOULD BID MAN'S WARFARE CEASE, ... 113 ROSE OF PEACE V 13
WAR-LADEN
   WAR-LADEN GALLEYS, AND ARMIES ON WHITE ROADS, ... 757 SHADOW WATER A 203
WARLESS   SEE LONG-WARLESS
   . . . LONG WARLESS, GROWN WHITER THAN CURDS. . . . . . 49 OISIN 3   36
WARM
   ROSE EVER OUT OF THE WARM SEA; . . . . 13 OISIN 1   172
   ROSE EVER FROM THE SEA'S WARM FLOOR, ... 13 OISIN 1   V 172
   AND BLOWS ON HIS HANDS IN THE FIRE'S WARM BLAZE; . . . . 26 OISIN 1   V 404
   SHALL WARM THEIR LIVES AT MANY A RUSTLING FLAME." . . . 80 EPHEMERA   V 128
   OF THE CALVES ON THE WARM HILLSIDE . . . . 88 STOLEN CHILD   45
   OF THE CALVES ON THE WARM HILL SIDE, ... 88 STOLEN CHILD V 45
   OF THE CALVES ON THE WARM HILL-SIDE. . . . . 88 STOLEN CHILD V 45
   THE HOUSE WHERE I WAS SAFE AND WARM; . . . . 151 HEART OF WOMAN   6
   THE HOME WHERE I WAS SAFE AND WARM? . . . . 151 HEART OF WOMAN V 6
   MY HEART UPON HIS WARM HEART LIES, ... 152 HEART OF WOMAN   11
   AND SO WARM HER WILD NEST. . . . . 415 TOWER   172
   BUT NO, IN THIS WARM WEATHER, 'MONG THE HILLS, ... 699 MOSADA 3   9
   SITTING ON A WARM SMOOTH MAT . . . . 726 LOVERS QUARREL   11
WARMER
   IN THE JUNES THAT WERE WARMER THAN THESE ARE, ... 91 OLD FISHERMAN   3
WARMS
   "AND YET THE JASMINE SEASON WARMS OUR BLOOD." . . . . . 464 HARUN RASHID   73
   WEASEL WARMS HIM ON THE PATH, ... 705 DAWN-SONG   19
   WAVES OFF THE FLIES, AND WARMS HIM IN THE SHINE. . . . . 709 FERENCZ RENYI   7

		PAGE	TITLE		LINE

WARMTH
 AND NOW THE WARMTH OF SIGHS, AND AFTER THE QUIVER OF LIPS,   47 OISIN 3   8
 THE WARMTH OF LIFE IS CHILLING, AND THE SHADOWS GROW   • •   675 ISLE STAT II 3   232
WARNED
 OR WARNED YOU HOW DESPAIRING   313 TWO YEAR LATER   3
 I COULD HAVE WARNED YOU; BUT YOU ARE YOUNG,   • • • •   313 TWO YEAR LATER   5
 CRUELTY MUST KEEP; THEREFORE BE WARNED AND GO •   • • •   448 HERO GIRL FOOL   7
WAR-RAGE
 BUT NOW THE WAR-RAGE IN CUCHULAIN WOKE, • • • • • • • •   110 CUCHULAIN SEA   65
WARRED
 WHEN GODS AND GIANTS WARRED. WE RODE BETWEEN • •   • • •   31 OISIN 2   31
 SO WARRED, SO FEASTED, WITH NOR DREAMS NOR FEARS,   • • •   44 OISIN 2   222
 SO WARRED, SO FEASTED WE. NO DREAMS, NO FEARS,   • • •   44 OISIN 2   V 222
 FOR FOUR DAYS WARRED HE WITH THE BITTER TIDE, • • • •   111 CUCHULAIN SEA   V 85
WARRING
 WHERE ARE NOW THE WARRING KINGS, • • • • • • • •   65 HAPPY SHEPHERD   11
 WHERE ARE NOW THE WARRING KINGS? • • • • • • • •   65 HAPPY SHEPHERD   13
 AND NOW THE SPARROWS WARRING IN THE EAVES, • • • • •   120 SORROW OF LOVE   V 9
WARRIOR
 BUT, WARRIOR, HERE THERE IS NO LAW; • • • • • • •   19 OISIN 1   V 283
 THEN, WARRIOR, WHY SO SAD AND STERN, • • • • • • •   19 OISIN 1   V 286
 THE WARRIOR DREAMS IN AN AGED LEISURE • • • • • •   26 OISIN 1   V 401
 HOW SUCH A WARRIOR NEVER TURNED HIS GAZE • • • • •   29 OISIN 2   V 11
 YOUNG WARRIOR." "NAY," I ANSWERED; "MY HANDS BURN • • •   35 OISIN 2   V 89B
 I CRIED, "THOU ART SURELY A WARRIOR, FORGETTING HIS FAMOUS   51 OISIN 3   V 61
  LINE,
 AND HE, THE BEST WARRIOR, DEAD • • • • • • • •   312 CHILD DANCING   V 9
 OLD WARRIOR, WAKE! FOR SOFT AS A BEE SIPS, • • • • •   677 ISLE STAT II 3   284
WARRIOR'S
 FROM SOME DEAD WARRIOR'S BROKEN LANCE; • • • • • •   24 OISIN 1   367
 IT WAS OF SOME DEAD WARRIOR'S LANCE. • • • • • • •   24 OISIN 1   V 367
 "SWIFT ARE THE YEARS OF A WARRIOR'S PRIDE; • • • • •   26 OISIN 1   V 399A
WARRIORS
 THE LONG-HAIRED WARRIORS, THE SPREAD FEAST; • • • • •   2 OISIN 1   V 7
 TAKING THE MORTAL WARRIORS BY THE HANDS; • • • • •   29 OISIN 2   V 10B
 THOSE WARRIORS OF A LONG-FORGOTTEN DAY, • • • • •   30 OISIN 2   V 14A
 OF ANCIENT WARRIORS, THE LABOURS OF THE STRONG. • • • •   42 OISIN 2   V 195
 THESE HANDS SLEW MANY WARRIORS BOLD-- • • • • •   83 MAD KING GOLL   V 23
 OF THE GREAT WARRIORS WHOSE NAMES HAVE SUNG • • • •   698 MOSADA 2   60
WAR'S
 IN ITS OWN BEING, AND WHEN THAT WAR'S BEGUN • • • •   374 PHASES OF MOON   51
 AND WAIT WAR'S MUSIC; PASS THE LITTLE GALLERY; • • • •   461 HARUN RASHID   8
 OF WAR AND WAR'S ALARMS, • • • • • • • • • •   631 POLITICS   10
WARS
 WARS SHADOWY, VAST, EXULTANT; FAERIES OF OLD • • • • •   29 OISIN 2   9
 WARS SHADOWY, VAST, EXULTANT; FAIRY KINGS • • • • •   29 OISIN 2   V 9
 OF WARS WITH THE WIDE WORLD • • • • • • • • •   50 OISIN 3   55
 THEN FEAST, MAKING CONVERSE OF WARS, • • • • • •   62 OISIN 3   212
 THEN FEAST, MAKING CONVERSE OF EIRE, OF WARS, • • • • •   62 OISIN 3   V 212
 MY FATHER STANDS." "AGED, WORN OUT WITH WARS • • • •   107 CUCHULAIN SEA   29
 "NAY, HE IS OLD AND SAD WITH MANY WARS, • • • • • •   107 CUCHULAIN SEA   V 29
 "BUT HE IS OLD AND SAD WITH MANY WARS." • • • • •   107 CUCHULAIN SEA   V 30
 BROODING NO MORE UPON GOD'S WARS • • • • • • • •   113 ROSE OF PEACE   5
 AND WHEN AT LAST, DEFEATED IN HIS WARS, • • • • •   115 ROSE OF BATTLE   33
 WHEN THE LONG WARS FOR THE WHITE HORN • • • • •   189 BAILE AILLINN   14
 WHERE THROUGH LONG WARS AND SUDDEN NIGHT ALARMS • • •   420 MY HOUSE   24
 WHERE THROUGH LONG WARS AND SUDDEN NIGHT ALARUMS • • •   420 MY HOUSE   V 24
 WITH PERSIAN WARS OR GREEK AMBASSADORS • • • • •   462 HARUN RASHID   V 25
 NOW HIS WARS ON GOD BEGIN; • • • • • • • • •   561 FOUR AGES MAN   7
 BOWING NATIONS, PLUMED WARS-- • • • • • • • •   737 IN FIRELIGHT   10
 AND WHEN YOU CAME TO SCORN OUR LITTLE WARS • • • •   749 SHADOW WATER A   V 34
 OR GO BESIDE HIM TO HIS MOUNTAIN WARS. • • • • •   768 SHADOW WATER A   414
WAR-SONGS
 THE WAR-SONGS THAT ROUSED THEM OF OLD; • • • • • •   61 OISIN 3   202
WARTY
 HID FROM ALL THOSE WARTY LADS • • • • • • • • •   589 OLD WICKED MAN   43
WARWARD
 COOK BARACH, THE TRAITOR; AND WARWARD, • • • • • •   53 OISIN 3   90
WAR-WASTED
 HE HAD OUTRIDDEN HIS WAR-WASTED MEN • • • • • • •   277 TWO KINGS   3
 HE HAD OUT-RIDDEN HIS WAR-WASTED MEN • • • • • •   277 TWO KINGS   V 3
 JOSTLED AND SHOUTED THOSE WAR-WASTED MEN, • • • • •   286 TWO KINGS   216
WAR-WEARY
 "I HAVE NOT YET, WAR-WEARY KING, • • • • • • • •   6 OISIN 1   55
WARY
 YET SHE GOES WITH FOOTSTEP WARY, • • • • • • • •   124 CATHLEEN PARA   11
 STILL SHE GOES WITH FOOTSTEPS WARY, • • • • • • •   124 CATHLEEN PARA   V 11
 AND GAZE ON THE MEADOW-MICE WARY, • • • • • • •   707 FAIRY PEDANT   18
WASH
 TO SHORES BY THE WASH OF THE TREMULOUS TIDE, • • • • •   8 OISIN 1   81
 WASH! MAKE YOUR BODY SWEET; • • • • • • • • •   572 LADYS 2ND SONG   4
WASHED   SEE NEW-WASHED DEW-WASHED
 WASHED BY TIME'S WATERS AS THEY ROSE AND FELL • • • •   206 ADAMS CURSE   32
 IT HAD WASHED AMONG THE STARS AND PUT THEM OUT, • • • •   236 SHADOW WATER B   311
WASHES
 WASHES THE SHORES WHERE YE ABIDE, • • • • • • • •   5 OISIN 1   V 47
WASP
 A NEW DAY'S TROOP OF WASP AND BEE • • • • • • • •   646 ISLE STAT I 1   44
WASSAILS
 I LOVED AND SANG, AND IN LONG WASSAILS • • • • • •   23 OISIN 1   V 345C

WASTE
        NEIGHING ALONG THE LIFELESS WASTE!   .   .   .   .   .   .   13 OISIN 1   170
        THE FLOWERS STILL GREW THERE! FAR ON THE SEA'S WASTE . .   39 OISIN 2   163
        THE FLOWERS STILL GREW THERE. MOVED BEYOND HIM THE SEA'S   39 OISIN 2   V 163
           WASTE!
        HAS HE NOT LED US INTO THESE WASTE SEAS . . . . . .   221 SHADOW WATER B   1
        WHAT RICHES CAN YOU FIND IN THIS WASTE SEA . . . . .   226 SHADOW WATER B   97
        IN THE WASTE OF THE HIGH AIR, THAT WE MAY WANDER . . .   234 SHADOW WATER B   263
        THAT WEIGH AND MEASURE ALL IN THESE WASTE SEAS-- . . .   235 SHADOW WATER B   292
        THOUGH YOU MAY THINK I WASTE MY BREATH . . . . . .   271 GREY ROCK   6
        FORBID, BESEECH AND WASTE MY BREATH." THEN I! . . . .   281 TWO KINGS   102
        AND LOOSEN ON US DREAMS THAT WASTE OUR LIFE, ...   281 TWO KINGS   107
        NOR CAN TIME WASTE THE CHEEK, NOR IS THERE FOOT . . .   284 TWO KINGS   182
        THE YEARS TO COME SEEMED WASTE OF BREATH, ...   328 IRISH AIRMAN   14
        A WASTE OF BREATH THE YEARS BEHIND . . . .   328 IRISH AIRMAN   15
        ARE MET ON THE WASTE HILLS BY COUNTRYMEN . . . . .   375 PHASES OF MOON   76
        ARE MET ON THE WASTE HILLS BY COUNTRY MEN . . . . .   375 PHASES OF MOON   V 76
        TROUBLES MY SIGHT! A WASTE OF DESERT SAND! . . . .   402 SECOND COMING   V 13
        AND THROUGH THE FERTILE AND WASTE, ...   436 FOR MY SON   30
        BY WOOD ANTIQUE, BY WAVE AND WASTE, ...   670 ISLE STAT II 3   109
        FROM WASTE SEAS CROSS'D, YET EVER GARRULOUS) . . . .   690 MOSADA 1   9
        IN THE WASTE AIR. I WILL WANDER BY HIS SIDE . . . .   754 SHADOW WATER A   152
        BUT THESE WASTE WATERS AND WIND-BEATEN SAILS . . . .   763 SHADOW WATER A   319
        IN WASTE PLACES OF THE SKY, ...   772 SONG DEIRDRE 1   6
WASTED   SEE WAR-WASTED
        UPON HIS WASTED HANDS, ...   98 FOXHUNTER   22
        UPON HIS WASTED HANDS. . . . .   98 FOXHUNTER   V 24
        WORDS WERE BUT WASTED BREATH! . . . .   471 ALL SOUL NIGHT   27
WASTEFUL
        "ONLY THE WASTEFUL VIRTUES EARN THE SUN"! . . . . .   270 PARDON FATHERS   18
WASTES
        WHO WASTES HIS BLOOD TO BE ANOTHER'S DREAM. . . . .   103 FERGUS DRUID   28
WASTING
        YOU ARE WASTING AWAY, LITTLE FAIRY. . . . .   707 FAIRY PEDANT   12
        YOU ARE WASTING AWAY, LITTLE FAIRY. . . . .   707 FAIRY PEDANT   20
        YOU ARE WASTING AWAY, LITTLE FAIRY. . . . .   708 FAIRY PEDANT   28
        SHE IS WASTING AWAY, LITTLE FAIRY. . . . .   708 FAIRY PEDANT   40
WATCH
        GO WATCH THE ROAD BETWEEN THE WOOD AND TIDE, ...   105 CUCHULAIN SEA   4
        BUT NOW I HAVE NO NEED TO WATCH IT MORE." . . . . .   105 CUCHULAIN SEA   5
        GO DWELL UPON THE CLIFFS AND WATCH THE TIDE! . . . .   105 CUCHULAIN SEA   V   4
        TO WATCH A WHITE GULL TAKE . . . .   400 DEMON BEAST   24
        AND THERE IS NONE SO FIT TO KEEP A WATCH AND KEEP . .   442 BLACK CENTAUR   15
        I SAT WHERE I COULD WATCH HER SLEEPING FORM, ...   467 HARUN RASHID   128
        A STORM-BEATEN OLD WATCH TOWER, ...   484 SYMBOLS   V   1
        WE LIVED LIKE MEN THAT WATCH A PAINTED STAGE. . . . .   542 PARN FUNERAL 1   18
        MAIDEN, COME FORTH! THE WOODS KEEP WATCH FOR THEE! . .   645 ISLE STAT I 1   1
        THE AGELESS SENTINELS WHO HOLD THEIR WATCH . . . .   664 ISLE STAT II 2   45
        TO WATCH THEE PASS? YET DEEPER THAN MEN KNOW . . .   672 ISLE STAT II 3   158
        NAY HERE, I'LL LAY ME DOWN WHERE I CAN WATCH . . . .   700 MOSADA 3   39
        THAT WATCH ME WITH THEIR SUPPLIANT LIGHT-- . . . .   723 GIRLS SONG A   10
        THE GODS HOLD WATCH ABOUT THE WORDS OF A QUEEN. . . .   756 SHADOW WATER A   191
        O, AENGUS OF THE HERDS, WATCH OVER ME! . . . . . .   762 SHADOW WATER A   291
WATCHED
        WATCHED WHERE THE SUN IN A SAFFRON BLAZE . . . . .   26 OISIN 1   394
        WATCHED THE OLD SUN THAT IN SEA-WAYS . . . .   26 OISIN 1   V 394
        THE STRANGER WATCHED THE SWORD! BUT NIAM FAR, ...   38 OISIN 2   V 136
        OF FACES, WATCHED ME, AND THE LEISURED GAZE . . . .   39 OISIN 2   V 149
        WATCHED ME WITH MOURNFUL WONDER OUT OF THE WELLS OF HIS   51 OISIN 3   60
           EYES.
        SO WATCHED I WHEN, MAN OF THE CROZIERS, ...   54 OISIN 3   101
        WATCHED HER THOSE SEAMLESS FACES FROM THE VALLEY'S   55 OISIN 3   122
           GLIMMERING GIRTH!
        WATCHED HER THOSE SEAMLESS FACES FROM THE VALLEY'S MURAL   55 OISIN 3   V 122
           GIRTH
        AMRITA. THIS SAME EVE SHE WATCHED ME PASS. . . . .   74 ANASHU VIJAYA   V 64
        AND FROM THAT HOUR HE HAS WATCHED OVER NONE . . . .   220 HARP OF AENGUS   13
        HAD WATCHED IN BITTERER SLEEP . . . .   399 BREAK OF DAY   22
        HAD WATCHED MY DAILY PASSAGE TO AND FRO! . . . . .   466 HARUN RASHID   107
        THE DOVES WHOSE GROWING FORMS HE'D WATCHED. NOT THESE .   710 FERENCZ RENYI   21
        THE DOVES WHOSE GROWING FORM HE'D WATCHED. NOT THESE .   710 FERENCZ RENYI   V 21
        WATCHED OF PLACID POPLAR-TREES . . . .   732 STREET DANCERS   16
        WATCHED OF PLACID POPLAR TREES, ...   732 STREET DANCERS   V 16
        AND FROM THAT HOUR HE HAS WATCHED OVER NONE . . . .   763 SHADOW WATER A   308
WATCHER
        HE SEEMED THE WATCHER FOR A SIGN. THE OTHER . . . .   31 OISIN 2   V 41
        THEY COME WHERE SOME HUGE WATCHER IS, ...   196 BAILE AILLINN   168
        "WATCHER, WHEREFORE HAVE YE CALLED US?" EYES GO AFTER   718 PHANTOM SHIP   10
           HIS LEAN HAND,
WATCHERS
        FROM LASTING WATCHERS, THAT OUTLIVE THE MOON, ...   236 SHADOW WATER B   320
        AND DID THOSE WATCHERS BID YOU TAKE ME CAPTIVE? . . .   236 SHADOW WATER B   322
WATCHES
        BENDING HER FACE O'ER HIS, SHE WATCHES MEET . . . .   688 TWO TITANS   45
        HE WATCHES OVER NONE BUT FAITHFUL LOVERS. . . . . .   762 SHADOW WATER A   295
WATCHING
        OF PLANETS WATCHING, WATCHING THE RACE OF HARES . . .   44 OISIN 2   V 228B
        OF PLANETS WATCHING, WATCHING THE RACE OF HARES . . .   44 OISIN 2   V 228B
        WATCHING THE BLESSED ONES MOVE FAR OFF, AND THE SMILE ON   61 OISIN 3   199
           GOD'S FACE,
        BUT NOW MY YEARS OF WATCHING ARE NO MORE." . . . . .   105 CUCHULAIN SEA   V   5

```
                                              PAGE     TITLE          LINE
WATCHING   (CONTINUED)
      WATCHING OUR SHEPHERD SPORTS AT HARVEST-TIME  . . . . .  340 SHEP GOATHERD      41
      WATCHING O'ER HER AWFUL YOUNG, . . . . . . . . . . .  658 ISLE STAT I 3     87
      DID HER LONELY WATCHING TAKE  . . . . . . . . . . .  658 ISLE STAT I 3     94
      AS I MY WATCHING LEST YOU WAKE, . . . . . . . . . .  658 ISLE STAT I 3     95
      WEARY OF WATCHING ROUND THE FIRE AT NIGHT. . . . . .  683 SEEKER            42
      THE PREACHER WATCHING FOR THE EVIL HOUR TO PASS, . . . .  686 LIFE              3
      OF DREAMING AND OF WATCHING BY THE DOOR  . . . . . .  700 MOSADA 3          26
      THE PREACHER WATCHING FOR THE ILL HOUR TO PASS-- . . . .  734 QUATRAIN APHOR    3
      THE PREACHER WATCHING FOR THE EVIL HOUR TO PASS, . .  .  734 QUATRAIN APHOR V  3
WATCH-TOWER
      A STORM-BEATEN OLD WATCH-TOWER,  . . . . . . . . .  484 SYMBOLS           1
WATER       SEE PUDDLE-WATER TAR-WATER
      SAVE DEER TOWARDS NOON THAT WATER SOUGHT. . . . . .  .   17 OISIN 1       V 243
      IN A LONG IRON SLEEP, AS A FISH IN THE WATER GOES DUMB    53 OISIN 3          96
          AS A STONE.
      THE DROWSY WATER RATS: . . . . . . . . . . . . .   87 STOLEN CHILD   V   5
      WHERE THE WANDERING WATER GUSHES . . . . . . . . .   88 STOLEN CHILD      28
      TO AN ISLE IN THE WATER. . . . . . . . . . . . .   89 ISLE IN WATER     T
      TO AN ISLE IN THE WATER. . . . . . . . . . . . .   89 ISLE IN WATER     7
      TO AN ISLE IN THE WATER. . . . . . . . . . . . .   89 ISLE IN WATER     15
      IS HEARD ON THE WATER, AS THEY WERE, THE PROUD AND APART,   91 OLD FISHERMAN    10
      I HEAR LAKE WATER LAPPING WITH LOW SOUNDS BY THE SHORE:  117 ISLE INNISFREE    10
      I HEAR LAKE WATER LAPPING WITH LOW SOUNDS ON THE SHORE:  117 ISLE INNISFREE V  10
      WITH THE EARTH AND THE SKY AND THE WATER, . . . . .  143 ROSE IN HEART     7
      OR ONLY TO THE WATER IN THE WEST: . . . . . . . . .  155 REPROVE CURLEW    2
      HE HAD PUDDLE WATER IN HIS SHOES: . . . . . . . . .  190 BAILE AILLINN  V  28
      ABOUT THE WINDY WATER SIDE . . . . . . . . . . . .  192 BAILE AILLINN  V  93
      THE OLD MEN ADMIRING THEMSELVES IN THE WATER . . . .  208 OLD MEN ADMIRE    T
      O HURRY WHERE BY WATER AMONG THE TREES . . . . . . .  210 RAGGED WOOD       1
      O HURRY TO THE WATER AMID THE TREES. . . . . . . .  210 RAGGED WOOD       1
      O HURRY WHERE BY WATER AMONG THE TREES, . . . . . .  210 RAGGED WOOD    V  1
      O HURRY TO THE WATER AMID THE TREES, . . . . . . .  211 RAGGED WOOD    V  5
      GABRIEL WILL COME FROM THE WATER . . . . . . . . .  215 HAPPY TOWNLAND    45
      SHINING ON WATER AND FALLEN AMONG LEAVES. . . . . .  218 WOODS OF COOLE    38
      AND NOW THAT TIME PUTS WATER IN MY BLOOD, . . . . .  222 SHADOW WATER B V 11A
      AND YET YOU SAY THE WATER AND THE WIND . . . . . . .  236 SHADOW WATER B V 317
      UNDER THE OCTOBER TWILIGHT THE WATER . . . . . . . .  322 SWANS AT COOLE    3
      UPON THE BRIMMING WATER AMONG THE STONES . . . . . .  322 SWANS AT COOLE    5
      BUT NOW THEY DRIFT ON THE STILL WATER, . . . . . . .  323 SWANS AT COOLE    25
      WOULD I COULD CAST A SAIL ON THE WATER . . . . . . .  330 BONE OF A HARE    1
      I WOULD FIND BY THE EDGE OF THAT WATER . . . . . . .  330 BONE OF A HARE    9
      WORN THIN BY THE LAPPING OF WATER, . . . . . . . .  330 BONE OF A HARE    11
      AND LAUGH OVER THE UNTROUBLED WATER . . . . . . . .  330 BONE OF A HARE    14
      IT SHUDDERED IN THE WATER: . . . . . . . . . . .  345 ON WOMAN          19
      "BUT WHERE CAN WE DRAW WATER?" . . . . . . . . . .  396 ROSE TREE         13
      COLD STONE AND WATER.  I GREW WILD, . . . . . . . .  399 BREAK OF DAY      14
      SHOOK OFF THE WATER FROM HIS BACK: . . . . . . . .  400 DEMON BEAST       29
      AND BEAUTY-DRUNKEN BY THE WATER . . . . . . . . . .  447 COLONUS PRAISE    20
      WHAT'S WATER BUT THE GENERATED SOUL? . . . . . . . .  490 COOLE BALLYLEE    8
      WHETHER IN WOOD, WATER OR CLOUD, . . . . . . . . .  528 DANCER CRUACH     7
      DROWN, DROWN IN THE WATER BUTT, . . . . . . . . .  546 TO SAME TUNE 2 V REF
      BY WATER, HERB AND SOLITARY PRAYER . . . . . . . .  555 RIBH AT TOMB      23
      WHEN DARK HANGS UPON THE WATER . . . . . . . . . .  589 OLD WICKED MAN    34
      AN AMBUSH: PILGRIMS AT THE WATER SIDE: . . . . . .  601 GALLERY REVIS  V  2
      AND THE GREAT WATER SIGHED FOR LOVE, . . . . . . .  611 NEWS ORACLE       3
      AS LIES DARK WATER IN A MURMUROUS GLADE, . . . . . .  650 ISLE STAT I 1   138
      OF LILAC O'ER THE PULSING WATER GLEAMS, . . . . . .  664 ISLE STAT II 2   48
      OF THINE CRY OVER WOLD AND WATER WHITE, . . . . . .  669 ISLE STAT II 3   73
      FAR OUT UPON THE WATER WORLD AND RINGED . . . . . .  693 MOSADA 1          80
      "OR SEEK WHERE SWEETEST WATER BUBBLES, . . . . . . .  731 PRIEST FAIRY      79
      THERE'S BARLEY THERE, AND WATER THERE, . . . . . .  774 COME RIDE         7
WATER-BUTT
      DROWN, DROWN IN THE WATER-BUTT,  . . . . . . . . .  546 TO SAME TUNE 2    9
      DROWN, DROWN IN THE WATER-BUTT,  . . . . . . . . .  546 TO SAME TUNE 2    19
      DROWN, DROWN IN THE WATER-BUTT,  . . . . . . . . .  547 TO SAME TUNE 2    29
WATER-COURSE
      SEEMS A WATER-COURSE OR AN AVALANCHE,  . . . . . . .  567 LAPIS LAZULI      45
WATERED
      "IT NEEDS TO BE BUT WATERED," . . . . . . . . . .  396 ROSE TREE         7
WATERFALL
      I THOUGHT: "THERE IS A WATERFALL . . . . . . . . .  398 BREAK OF DAY      5
      THAT WAS BESIDE THE WATERFALL, THY WORDS . . . . .  .  683 SEEKER            49
      "BEHOLD THE KNIGHT OF THE WATERFALL, WHOSE HEART . . . .  684 SEEKER            54
WATER-FLOWERS
      OVER THE LAKE THE WATER-FLOWERS  . . . . . . . . .  647 ISLE STAT I 1     66
WATER-FOWLS
      OF THE DREAMING WATER-FOWLS, . . . . . . . . . . .  644 SONG FAERIES      12
      OF THE DREAMING WATER-FOWLS, . . . . . . . . . . .  676 ISLE STAT II 3   259
WATERHEN
      THE WATERHEN MUST CHANGE HER GROUND: . . . . . . .  326 ROBERT GREGORY V  55
WATER-HEN
      THE WATER-HEN MUST CHANGE HER GROUND: . . . . . .  .  326 ROBERT GREGORY    55
      WHAT MADE THAT SOUND?  A RAT OR WATER-HEN . . . . .  372 PHASES OF MOON    8
      THE STILTED WATER-HEN . . . . . . . . . . . . .  419 MY HOUSE          8
WATERING      SEE WIDE-WATERING
WATER-LILY
      BY A BROAD WATER-LILY LEAF: . . . . . . . . . . .  195 BAILE AILLINN    146
WATERPROOF
      WHAT MADE THE CEILING WATERPROOF? . . . . . . . . .  625 NATIVITY          5
```

	PAGE	TITLE	LINE

WATER-RATS
    THE DROWSY WATER-RATS: . . . . 87 STOLEN CHILD   5
WATER'S
    I PASSED ALONG THE WATER'S EDGE BELOW THE HUMID TREES, . . . 76 INDIAN ON GOD   1
    WITH VAPOURY FOOTSOLE BY THE WATER'S DROWSY BLAZE. . . . 78 INDIAN TO LOVE   20
    AND DROP A VAPOURY FOOTFALL IN THE WATER'S DROWSY BLAZE. 78 INDIAN TO LOVE V   20
    WITH VAPOURY FOOTSOLE AMONG THE WATER'S DROWSY BLAZE. . . 78 INDIAN TO LOVE V   20
    AND GOD'S BELL BUOYED TO BE THE WATER'S CARE: . . . . 114 ROSE OF BATTLE   4
    FOR WIND OR WATER'S ROAR? . . . . 312 CHILD DANCING   3
    SHALL WALK THE WET SAND BY THE WATER'S EDGE, ... 371 EGO DOMINUS   V 71
    I RIDE WITH FALCON TO THE WATER'S EDGE . . . . 463 HARUN RASHID   V 57
WATERS
    AND WHERE THE WOOD AND WATERS MEET . . . . 14 OISIN 1   193
    ON THEIR OWN SELVES IN THE WATERS WHITE, ... 14 OISIN 1   V 185
    AND WHERE THE WOODS AND WATERS MEET . . . . 14 OISIN 1   V 193
    THAT KEPT DIM WATERS FROM THE SKY: . . . . 17 OISIN 1   243
    THUS ON THE WATERS, FAR AND SWEET, ... 26 OISIN 1   V 398A
    AND THE MOON GOAD THE WATERS NIGHT AND DAY, ... 45 OISIN 2   238
    THUNDERING, AND THE WIDE USELESS WATERS FRAY . . . . 45 OISIN 2   V 238
    O HAD YOU SEEN BEAUTIFUL NIAMH GROW WHITE AS THE WATERS 54 OISIN 3   109
        ARE WHITE,
    AND RUSHES WAVED AND WATERS ROLLED. . . . . 84 MAD KING GOLL   35
    TO THE WATERS AND THE WILD . . . . 87 STOLEN CHILD   10
    TO THE WATERS AND THE WILD . . . . 87 STOLEN CHILD   25
    TO THE WOODS AND WATERS WILD . . . . 87 STOLEN CHILD   V REF
    TO THE WATERS AND THE WILD . . . . 88 STOLEN CHILD   39
    TO THE WATERS AND THE WILD . . . . 88 STOLEN CHILD   51
    LIKE THE PALE WATERS IN THEIR WINTRY RACE, ... 112 ROSE OF WORLD   8
    WHERE MOUSE-GREY WATERS ARE FLOWING, ... 119 PITY OF LOVE   7
    THE MOUSE-GREY WATERS ON FLOWING, ... 119 PITY OF LOVE   V 5
    WHATEVER RAVELLED WATERS RISE AND FALL . . . . 127 DREAM OF FAERY   32
    OR ONLY TO WATERS IN THE WEST: . . . . 155 REPROVE CURLEW V   2
    OR ONLY TO THE WATERS IN THE WEST: . . . . 155 REPROVE CURLEW V   2
    MIRRORED IN WATERS THAT NOR HAIL NOR RAIN . . . . . . 184 QUEEN MAEVE   V 89
    WASHED BY TIME'S WATERS AS THEY ROSE AND FELL . . . . 206 ADAMS CURSE   32
    O HEAVY SWOLLEN WATERS, BRIM THE FALL OF THE OAK TREES, 207 HANRAHANS SONG V 11
    LIKE HEAVY FLOODED WATERS OUR BODIES AND OUR BLOOD: . . 208 HANRAHANS SONG V 13
    LIKE HEAVY SWOLLEN WATERS ARE OUR BODIES AND OUR BLOOD: 208 HANRAHANS SONG V 13
    BY THE WATERS. . . . . 208 OLD MEN ADMIRE   6
    LIKE THE WATERS." . . . . 208 OLD MEN ADMIRE   9
    DEDICATION TO THE "SHADOWY WATERS" . . . . 217 WOODS OF COOLE V   T
    OF FORGAEL AND DECTORA AND THE EMPTY WATERS . . . . . 218 WOODS OF COOLE   22
    THE WATERS OF SLEEP CAN MAKE A CHATTERING TONGUE . . . 218 WOODS OF COOLE   25
    THE SHADOWY WATERS . . . . 221 SHADOW WATER B   T
    THAT NOTHING CAN AMEND IT BUT THESE WATERS, ... 227 SHADOW WATER B   120
    BUT DESOLATE WATERS AND A BATTERED SHIP. . . . . . . 246 SHADOW WATER B   497
    BESIDE THE BRACKISH WATERS OF THE BOYNE . . . . . . 270 PARDON FATHERS   11
    AND THOUGH THEY HAVE TO CROSS THE LOUGHLAN WATERS . . . 282 TWO KINGS   113
    UNDER MY WINDOW-LEDGE THE WATERS RACE, ... 490 COOLE BALLYLEE   1
    THE ECSTATIC WATERS LAUGH BECAUSE . . . . 612 NEWS ORACLE   17
    THE POPLARS GAZE ACROSS THE WATERS GREY. . . . . . . 653 ISLE STAT I 2   34
    IN SONG, FROM GOBLIN WATERS SWAYING WHITE, ... 657 ISLE STAT I 3   51
    LIVING, WIDE WINGED, ON THE WATERS FLOAT. . . . . . 657 ISLE STAT I 3   54
    SLOW WATERS, AND THE BOAT AND MAIDEN SINK . . . . . . 663 ISLE STAT II 2   39
    PIERCING THE QUIVERING WATERS THROUGH AND THROUGH, . . 664 ISLE STAT II 2   44
    BEHOLD THE FLASHING WATERS. . . . . 680 LOVE AND DEATH   1
    WHAT ARE THE TWIN-BORN WATERS, ... 680 LOVE AND DEATH   15
    AND WHERE THE POLAR WINDS AND WATERS WRESTLE . . . . . 682 SEEKER   18
    BEYOND WHERE THE WATERS ARE MOVING, ... 739 WHERE BOOKS GO   7
    MINE WHERE WATERS BROOD AND TOSS: . . . . 744 ROSY CROSS   7
    THE SHADOWY WATERS . . . . 745 SHADOW WATER A   T
    WALKED ON THE WATERS AND BID FORGAEL SEEK . . . . . . 747 SHADOW WATER A   12
    AS THOUGH THE WATERS HAD FLOWED UP BETWEEN: . . . . . 749 SHADOW WATER A   55
    AMONG THE WATERS THAT NO PILOT KNOWS. . . . . 750 SHADOW WATER A   80
    AMONG THESE MISTY WATERS. TWO! NOW FOUR! . . . . . . 753 SHADOW WATER A   138
    HAVE THE WINDS BLOWN YOU AMONG THESE EMPTY WATERS? . . 756 SHADOW WATER A   192
    BECAUSE THESE WATERS MAKE ALL WOMEN ONE. . . . . . . 757 SHADOW WATER A   194
    I HAVE FOUND NOTHING BUT THESE EMPTY WATERS: . . . . . 757 SHADOW WATER A   201
    THE WINDS AND WATERS TO BE YOUR HOME FOR EVER: . . . . 762 SHADOW WATER A   282
    THE WINDS AND WATERS TO BE YOUR HOME FOREVER: . . . . 762 SHADOW WATER A V   282
    BUT THESE WASTE WATERS AND WIND-BEATEN SAILS . . . . . 763 SHADOW WATER A   319
    THE CLOUDY WATERS AND THE GLIMMERING WINDS . . . . . 764 SHADOW WATER A   327
    AMONG THE WINDS AND WATERS: AND WHEN THEY PASS . . . . 764 SHADOW WATER A   331
    THAT THE VAST TROUBLED WATERS BRING . . . . 784 WOMANS BEAUTY   17
WATERS'
    BY THE SINGING WATERS' EDGE, ... 646 ISLE STAT I 1   23
WATER-SERPENT
    THE WATER-SERPENT SINGS HIS HEART . . . . 673 ISLE STAT II 3   184
WATER-SIDE
    ABOUT THE WINDY WATER-SIDE, ... 192 BAILE AILLINN   93
    AN AMBUSH: PILGRIMS AT THE WATER-SIDE: . . . . 601 GALLERY REVIS   2
WATTLE
    IN THE FENIANS' DWELLINGS OF WATTLE LEAN ON THE CHESSBOARDS 55 OISIN 3   115
        AND PLAY,
WATTLED
    AND SWEPT OUT OF THE WATTLED HALL . . . . 20 OISIN 1   292
WATTLES
    A HOUSE OF WATTLES, CLAY, AND SKIN: . . . . 17 OISIN 1   249
    MUCH WONDERING TO SEE UPON ALL HANDS, OF WATTLES . . . 58 OISIN 3   162
        AND WOODWORK MADE,

		PAGE	TITLE		LINE
WATTLES	(CONTINUED)				
	MUCH WONDERING TO SEE UPON ALL HANDS, OF WATTLES AND WOOD-WORK MADE,	58	OISIN 3	V	162
	AND A SMALL CABIN BUILD THERE, OF CLAY AND WATTLES MADE!	117	ISLE INNISFREE		2
	AND A SMALL CABIN BUILT THERE, OF CLAY AND WATTLES MADE!	117	ISLE INNISFREE	V	2
WAVE	SEE LAND-UNDER-WAVE				
	THROUGH HEART AND SPINE! AND CAST HIM IN THE WAVE	41	OISIN 2		182
	THROUGH HEART AND DEMON SPINE, AND IN THE WAVE	41	OISIN 2	V	182
	WRAPT IN THE WAVE OF THAT MUSIC, WITH WEARINESS MORE THAN OF EARTH,	51	OISIN 3		69
	WHERE DAFFODIL AND LILY WAVE,	67	HAPPY SHEPHERD		46
	I WANDER ON, AND WAVE MY HANDS,	84	MAD KING GOLL		43
	WHERE THE WAVE OF MOONLIGHT GLOSSES	87	STOLEN CHILD		13
	UPON THE DANCER BY THE DREAMLESS WAVE.	128	DREAM OF FAERY		45
	THAT NONE MAY FEEL THE POWER OF SQUALL AND WAVE,	128	DREAM OF FAERY	V	45
	GREAT POWERS OF FALLING WAVE AND WIND AND WINDY FIRE,	174	ELEMENT POWERS		7
	YOU GREAT ANGELIC POWERS OF WIND, AND WAVE, AND FIRE,	174	ELEMENT POWERS	V	7
	GREAT ELEMENTAL POWERS OF WIND, AND WAVE, AND FIRE,	174	ELEMENT POWERS	V	7
	FOLK DANCE LIKE A WAVE OF THE SEA!	178	FIDDLER DOONEY		2
	AND DANCE LIKE A WAVE OF THE SEA.	179	FIDDLER DOONEY		20
	"FROM HEAT AND COLD AND WIND AND WAVE!	193	BAILE AILLINN		114
	"HE IS WELL OUT OF WIND AND WAVE,	193	BAILE AILLINN	V	114
	IN A WHITE BREAKING WAVE! THEY HAD THE LOOK	223	SHADOW WATER B		34
	AENGUS AND EDAIN RAN UP OUT OF THE WAVE--	231	SHADOW WATER B		196
	WOULD RISE OF A SUDDEN, OR A WAVE SO HUGE	236	SHADOW WATER B		310
	AND LISTENING TO THE CRY OF WIND AND WAVE	236	SHADOW WATER B		315
	THAT UNIMAGINABLE STORMS OF WIND AND WAVE	236	SHADOW WATER B		317
	AND LISTENING TO THE CRY OF THE WIND AND WAVE	236	SHADOW WATER B	V	315
	OR WAVE TO DROWN. BUT I HAVE DONE WITH WORDS,	238	SHADOW WATER B		348
	AND BARREN AS A BREAKING WAVE	456	FRIENDS YOUTH		11
	UNDER THE RECEDING WAVE.	485	NINETEENTH CEN		4
	WHEN NETTLES WAVE UPON A SHAPELESS MOUND	489	COOLE PARK 29		27
	KEEP DANCING LIKE A WAVE,	592	DRUNK SOBRIETY		10
	DREAMING OF FLASHING FLIGHT AND OF THE PLUMED WAVE.	650	ISLE STAT I 1		140
	BEYOND THE LAKE, WHOSE SMALLEST WAVE WAS BURDENED	656	ISLE STAT I 3		31
	BY WOOD ANTIQUE, BY WAVE AND WASTE.	670	ISLE STAT II 3		109
	AND THE WAN WAVE THAT LINGERS	672	ISLE STAT II 3		166
	BEFORE A DEATH. O'ER WAVE AND BANK	673	ISLE STAT II 3		185
	BUT NOW I WAVE HER HITHER TO MY SIDE.	694	MOSADA 1		91
	DARTING YOU WAVE THEM, DARTING IN THE VAPOUR.	694	MOSADA 1		94
	I WAVE THEM HITHER, MY BREAST HEAVES WITH JOY.	694	MOSADA 1		98
	AT LAST. BUT NOW I WAVE HER TO MY SIDE.	694	MOSADA 1	V	91
	HIDE WHERE HE WILL, IN WAVE OR WRINKLED MOON,	720	WITCH VIVIEN		8
	THE MOTHER OF THE WAVE SIGHS TOO,	738	YOU ARE SAD		10
	AND HER DIM WAVE BIDS MAN BE NO MORE GLAD,	738	YOU ARE SAD		11
	PLANTED IN THE RUNNING WAVE!	775	AGAINST WITCH		13
WAVED					
	AS LIKE A RUDDY MOTH THEY WAVED AND FLUTTERED.	34	OISIN 2	V	72
	AND RUSHES WAVED AND WATERS ROLLED.	84	MAD KING GOLL		35
	AND WAVED IT OFF ON THE AIR.	160	CAP AND BELLS		20
	AND WAVED IT OUT ON THE AIR.	160	CAP AND BELLS	V	20
WAVER					
	AMID MEN'S SOULS, THAT WAVER AND GIVE PLACE	112	ROSE OF WORLD		7
WAVERED					
	THAT WAVERED LIKE THE SUMMER STREAMS,	4	OISIN 1		29
	AND WAVERED LIKE A SUMMER RILL.	4	OISIN 1	V	29
WAVERING					
	AND WAVERING ARMS AND WANDERING DANCES.	19	OISIN 1		275
	THE ROUND GREEN EYES AND THE LONG WAVERING BODIES	343	DEJECTION		2
	SOME GREAT ONE. NO! I HEAR THE WAVERING STEPS	720	WITCH VIVIEN		12
WAVERINGS					
	AY, AND SHAKES IN SEA-GREEN WAVERINGS ALONG THE FISHERS' STREET!	718	PHANTOM SHIP		2
	AYE AND SHAKES IN SEA GREEN WAVERINGS, ALONG THE FISHERS' STREET.	718	PHANTOM SHIP	V	2
WAVE-RUSTED					
	AND SHE WITH A WAVE-RUSTED CHAIN WAS TIED	34	OISIN 2		73
WAVES					
	AND TO THE WAVES THAT GLIMMER BY	20	OISIN 1		298
	HEAPED BESIDE THE GLIMMERING WAVES,	21	OISIN 1		314
	HEAVED BESIDE THE GLIMMERING WAVES,	21	OISIN 1	V	314
	AND THE GENTLE WAVES OF THE SUMMER SEAS,	27	OISIN 1		418
	ONE WITH THE WAVES THAT SOFTLY ROUND US LAUGH AND DART.	78	INDIAN TO LOVE	V	15
	THE LITTLE WAVES THAT WALKED IN EVENING WHITENESS,	81	EPHEMERA	V	24C
	YOU WAVES, THOUGH YOU DANCE BY MY FEET LIKE CHILDREN AT PLAY,	90	OLD FISHERMAN		1
	YE WAVES, THOUGH YE DANCE 'FORE MY FEET LIKE CHILDREN AT PLAY,	90	OLD FISHERMAN	V	1
	. . . THE WAVES WERE MORE GAY,	91	OLD FISHERMAN		3
	THAT HE MAY FIGHT THE WAVES OF THE LOUD SEA."	111	CUCHULAIN SEA	V	81
	THAT HE MIGHT FIGHT THE WAVES OF THE LOUD SEA."	111	CUCHULAIN SEA	V	81
	AND THE WAVES FLOWED ABOVE HIM AND HE DIED.	111	CUCHULAIN SEA	V	86
	HAS GIVEN THE WAVES THEIR MELODY,	134	TWO TREES		10
	WEAK AND WORN AND WEARY THE WAVES OF CUMMEN STRAND,	207	HANRAHANS SONG	V	6
	OR ON THE UNPEOPLED WAVES WITH KINGS TO PULL AT THE OAR,	210	UNDER THE MOON		15
	AM I TO FEAR THE WAVES, OR IS THE MOON	246	SHADOW WATER B		508
	SO LET US DANCE ON FRINGED WAVES,	644	SONG FAERIES		9
	AND THE WAVES ARE LEAPING WHITE,	646	ISLE STAT I 1		27
	OF THE TARN WHERE YOUNG WAVES QUICKEN	647	ISLE STAT I 1		48
	SING SUMMER WAVES. BUT YONDER SHEPHERD VILE,	649	ISLE STAT I 1		107
	THE WAVES IN YONDER LAKE WHERE POINTS MY HAND	652	ISLE STAT I 2		13

		PAGE	TITLE	LINE

WAVES (CONTINUED)
AND THE WAVES BOWED BEFORE IT LIKE MOWN CORN, ... 657 ISLE STAT I 3   56
AND SHOREWARD WAVES, WE NIGH HAVE FOUGHT! WAVES BRING . . 660 ISLE STAT II 1   44
AND SHOREWARD WAVES, WE NIGH HAVE FOUGHT! WAVES BRING . . 660 ISLE STAT II 1   44
THE WHITE WAVES WRAP IT IN A SHEET OF FLAME, ... 662 ISLE STAT II 2   14
HERE WHERE THE ROUND WAVES COME, HERE LET THEM BUILD, . . 663 ISLE STAT II 2   19
OF SWORD-BLUE WAVES OF CALM! WHILE O'ER HEAD BLINK . . . 663 ISLE STAT II 2   42
OH, HEART! HER DIRGE! WITH RUSHING ARMS THE WAVES . . 665 ISLE STAT II 2   70
AT THEIR FEET THE WAVES IN RINGS . . . . 667 ISLE STAT II 3   25
SO LET US DANCE ON THE FRINGED WAVES, ... 676 ISLE STAT II 3 256
THE WAVES, ENORMOUS WANDERERS OF THE WORLD, ... 687 TWO TITANS   3
WORN WITH LONG STRUGGLES! AND THE WAVES HAVE SUNG . . . 687 TWO TITANS   23
FROM THE WAVES THE SUN HATH REELED, ... 705 DAWN-SONG   1
WAVES OFF THE FLIES, AND WARMS HIM IN THE SHINE. . . . . 709 FERENCZ RENYI   7
YE BY THE WAVES THAT CLOSE IN OUR SAD NATION, ... 738 MOURN THEN ON   5
A PATH AMONG THESE WAVES AND WEIGH THE WIND? . . . . . 748 SHADOW WATER A   21
AND NOW THE WAVES ARE CRYING IN MY EARS, ... 761 SHADOW WATER A 276
UNDER THE WAVES, AND TOOK A THOUSAND WOMEN . . . . . . 766 SHADOW WATER A 378
ONE LIVES UNDER THE WAVES, ... 770 SPINNING SONG   2
WAVES'
ENAMOURED OF THE WAVES' IMPETUOUS LIPS. . . . . 677 ISLE STAT II 3 289
WAVETH
HE IS A MONSTROUS PEACOCK, AND HE WAVETH ALL THE NIGHT . . 77 INDIAN ON GOD   19
WAVE-WHITENED
A BONE WAVE-WHITENED AND DRIED IN THE WIND. . . . . . 521 THREE THINGS   6
A BONE WAVE-WHITENED AND DRIED IN THE WIND. . . . . . 521 THREE THINGS   12
A BONE WAVE-WHITENED AND DRIED IN THE WIND. . . . . . 521 THREE THINGS   18
WAVE-WORN
WHEN HER OWN PEOPLE RULED IN WAVE-WORN ERI, ... 129 BOOK STORIES   V 2
WAVING   SEE A-WAVING
AMONG THE FIELDS OF WAVING FERN. . . . . 2 OISIN 1   V 7N
AMONG THE WAVING FIELDS OF FERN! . . . . 4 OISIN 1   38
AND WAVING ARMS AND WANDERING DANCES. . . . . 19 OISIN 1   V 275
WE FLUNG ON HIGH EACH WAVING HAND, ... 22 OISIN 1   325
FLUNG ON HIGH EACH WAVING HAND, ... 22 OISIN 1   V 325
SHAKING AND WAVING, VAPOUR VAPOUR CHASED, ... 39 OISIN 2   164
SHAKING AND WAVING, VAPOURS VAPOURS CHASED! . . . . . . 39 OISIN 2   V 164
OUR ARMS ARE WAVING, OUR LIPS ARE APART! . . . . . . 140 HOSTING SIDHE   9
AND WAVING WHITE WINGS TO AND FRO . . . . 197 BAILE AILLINN   184
AND WITH THE WAVING OF YOUR WINGS. . . . . 212 BLESS PSALTER   7
AND HIS HAIR WAS AS YELLOW AS WAVING WHEAT. . . . . . 729 PRIEST FAIRY   26
WAX
MELT DOWN, AS IT WERE WAX IN THE SUN'S RAYS; . . . . . 428 NINETEEN 19   12
WAXEN
THAT WAXEN SEAL, THAT SIGNATURE, ... 598 MODEL LAUREATE   21
WAXING
WITH A SOB FOR MEN WAXING SO WEAKLY, ... 60 OISIN 3   188
WAY   SEE HALF-WAY
OF DANAAN HOOVES WE URGED OUR WAY BETWEEN . . . . . . 31 OISIN 2   V 31
OF EVERY FOAMDROP ON ITS MISTY WAY. . . . . 32 OISIN 2   45
BENEATH HAD PACED CONTENT! WE HELD OUR WAY . . . . . . 36 OISIN 2   103
BASALTIC, MIGHT HAVE PACED. WE HELD OUR WAY . . . . . 36 OISIN 2   V 103
MADE THE WAY SLIPPERY, AND TIME ON TIME . . . . 37 OISIN 2   114
GAVE TO HIGH NOON AND NOON TO NIGHT GAVE WAY; . . . . . 40 OISIN 2   172
GAVE TO THE NOON, AND NOON TO EVE GAVE WAY, ... 40 OISIN 2   V 172
THE SEASHINE ON OUR FACES, WE OUR WAY . . . . 41 OISIN 2   V 184B
GATHER SEA-SLIME AND FALL THE SEAWARD WAY, ... 45 OISIN 2   237
GATHERS SEA-SLIME AND GOES THE SEAWARD WAY, ... 45 OISIN 2   V 237
GATHER SEA SLIME AND FALL THE SEAWARD WAY, ... 45 OISIN 2   V 237
THEIR NAKED AND GLEAMING BODIES POURED OUT AND HEAPED IN   48 OISIN 3   28
    THE WAY.
MAKING WAY FROM THE KINDLING SURGES, I RODE ON A   58 OISIN 3   161
    BRIDLE-PATH
A LITTLE WAY WITHIN THE GLOOM A ROEBUCK RAISED HIS EYES   76 INDIAN ON GOD   13
AND HE WENT HIS WAY WITH A FROWN. . . . . 92 FATHER OHART   20
AND WENT ON HIS WAY WITH A FROWN. . . . . 92 FATHER OHART   V 20
AND WENT HIS WAY WITH A FROWN. . . . . 92 FATHER OHART   V 20
THIS WAY WERE ALL REPROVED . . . . 93 FATHER OHART   39
ETERNAL BEAUTY WANDERING ON HER WAY. . . . . 101 ROSE UPON ROOD   12
"I ONLY ASK WHAT WAY MY JOURNEY LIES, ... 108 CUCHULAIN SEA   31
HE CHANGED ME SUDDENLY! I WAS LOOKING ANOTHER WAY! . . . 153 CHANGE BELOVED   7
CAME BY THE WOODY WAY . . . . 166 BLESSED   V 2
"I HAVE COME BY THE WINDY WAY . . . . 167 BLESSED   6
"I COME BY THE WINDY WAY . . . . 167 BLESSED   V 6
AND FOLLOW THE WAY OF THE WIND! . . . . 168 BLESSED   28
OUR HEARTS ENDURE THE SCOURGE, THE PLAITED THORNS, THE WAY 172 TRAV PASSION   3
OUR HEARTS ENDURE THE PLAITED THORN, THE CROWDED WAY, . . 172 TRAV PASSION   V 3
SHE HAD BEEN BEAUTIFUL IN THAT OLD WAY . . . . 180 QUEEN MAEVE   19
IMAGINED, AS THEY STRUCK THE WAY . . . . 189 BAILE AILLINN   20
WHEN THEY HAD RIDDEN A LITTLE WAY . . . . 191 BAILE AILLINN   56
WHO KNOW THE WAY THAT NAOISE WENT? . . . . 193 BAILE AILLINN   96
TO LOVE YOU IN THE OLD HIGH WAY OF LOVE! . . . . . . 206 ADAMS CURSE   36
MAYBE THEY LINGER BY THE WAY. . . . . 212 BLESS PSALTER   8
WHAT GOOD IS THERE IN THIS HARD WAY OF LIVING, ... 225 SHADOW WATER B   69
HAVE LOVED THAT WAY—THERE IS NO OTHER WAY. . . . . . 229 SHADOW WATER B 152
HAVE LOVED THAT WAY—THERE IS NO OTHER WAY. . . . . . 229 SHADOW WATER B 152
THEY'LL FLY UPON THAT SECRET WAY OF THEIRS. . . . . . 233 SHADOW WATER B 248
FOOT AFTER FOOT WAS GIVING WAY, ... 274 GREY ROCK   72
I GROPED MY WAY FROM BEECH TO HAZEL WOOD, ... 283 TWO KINGS   139
THEN FEARING THAT SOME LABOURER, ON HIS WAY . . . . . 283 TWO KINGS   145
I GROPED MY WAY THROUGH BOUGHS, AND OVER ROOTS, ... 283 TWO KINGS   V 139

```
                                                    PAGE    TITLE          LINE
WAY  (CONTINUED)
    FOR ONLY RUBBISH COMES MY WAY.  . . . . . . . .  295 THREE BEGGARS        4
    WHILE I MUST HURRY UPON MY WAY.  . . . . . . .   301 RUN PARADISE        23
    DID THEIR CATULLUS WALK THAT WAY?  . . . . . .   337 SCHOLARS            12
    SHOULD THEIR CATULLUS WALK THAT WAY!  . . . . .  337 SCHOLARS          V 12
    WITH ALL A WOMAN'S PASSION, A CHILD'S IMPERIOUS WAY .  354 HIS PHOENIX    14
    THAN THAT I MAY FIND OUT A WAY .  . . . . . . .  401 DEMON BEAST         41
    BEING FATHERLESS COULD HAVE HER WAY  . . . . .   404 FOR DAUGHTER        28
    IN THE BEST MODERN WAY--THE CHILDREN'S EYES  . .  443 SCHOOL CHILDR       6
    IF THROWN IN MADGE'S WAY.  . . . . . . . . .     457 SECRETS OF OLD       8
    "THAT IS A LONG WAY OFF,  . . . . . . . . .      526 AM OF IRELAND       11
    BEFORE I HAD MARKED HIM ON HIS NORTHERN WAY,  .  535 CHOSEN               8
    I THOUGHT TO HAVE WHISTLED HER DOWN THAT WAY,  .  551 SONGS REWRIT 1      15
    BEAUTIFUL AND GENTLE IN HER VENETIAN WAY.  . .   602 GALLERY REVIS       14
    BEAUTIFUL, GRACIOUS, IN HER VENETIAN WAY,  . .   602 GALLERY REVIS    V  14
    BUT LIKED THE WAY HIS FINGER SMELT.  . . . .     619 STICK INCENSE        4
    JOY'S BROTHER, FEAR, LURKS IN EACH LEAFY WAY.  .  651 ISLE STAT I 1     156
    AND FOUND.  'TIS WELL!--ANOTHER MILE OF WAY  . .  651 ISLE STAT I 2       6
    WE MUST GET SWORDS.  IS'T THE ONLY WAY?  OH, SEE,  660 ISLE STAT II 1     34
    THERE IS NO WAY BUT THAT YE FIGHT I WIS,  . .    662 ISLE STAT II 1      75
    FAIR YOUTH, ALONG A WANDERING WAY  . . . . .     667 ISLE STAT II 3      38
    DEAR HEART, THERE IS A SECRET WAY THAT LEADS  .  702 MOSADA 3            75
    THE FOOT-WORN WAY IS LONG, AND IT GROWS DARK.  .  702 MOSADA 3           92
    THE FOOTWORN WAY IS LONG, AND IT GROWS DARK.  .  702 MOSADA 3         V  92
    FROM HERE, ALONG THE SHADOWY WAY THAT WINDS  . .  703 MOSADA 3          111
    THE FAIRY DOCTOR COMES OUR WAY .  . . . . . .    716 FAIRY DOCTOR         1
    AND SENT THE OLD MEN ON THEIR WAY,  . . . . .    725 LEGEND              23
    A WOODMAN ON HIS HOMEWARD WAY  . . . . . . .     730 PRIEST FAIRY        73
    THROUGH THE LONG BITTER WAY.  . . . . . . .      738 MOURN THEN ON        4
    IT MAY BE NOW THAT I CAN GO MY WAY .  . . . .    751 SHADOW WATER A      96
    WHEN ALL GATHER THEY WILL FLY UPON THEIR WAY.  .  753 SHADOW WATER A     136
    I SHALL FIND OUT IF I HAVE LOST MY WAY  . . .    753 SHADOW WATER A     137
    I SHALL FIND OUT IF I HAVE LOST THE WAY  . . .   753 SHADOW WATER A   V 137
    A QUARTER OF THE HEAVENS FROM OUR RIGHT WAY.  .  754 SHADOW WATER A     155
    MY WAY IS WEST.  SHE SEEMS BOTH YOUNG AND SHAPELY!  755 SHADOW WATER A   171
    I SPARED HER HANDMAID, TOO; BUT HALF WAY HITHER  .  755 SHADOW WATER A V 167
WAYS      SEE CAST-A-WAYS SEA-WAYS
    THEY LED US BY LONG AND SHADOWY WAYS .  . . .     16 OISIN 1           221
    THEY LEAD US BY LONG AND SHADOWY WAYS  . . .      16 OISIN 1         V 221
    IN PINCHING WAYS I TOIL AND TURN."  . . . . .     19 OISIN 1         V 282
    WAS SLUMBERING HALF IN THE SEA WAYS!  . . . .     26 OISIN 1         V 395
    THE WHIRLING WAYS OF STARS THAT PASS--  . . .     66 HAPPY SHEPHERD     30
    WHEN EVE HAS HUSHED THE FEATHERED WAYS,  . . .    78 INDIAN TO LOVE     19
    WHERE EVE HAS HUSHED THE FEATHERED WAYS,  . .     78 INDIAN TO LOVE  V  19
    COME NEAR ME, WHILE I SING THE ANCIENT WAYS!  .  100 ROSE UPON ROOD      2
    SING OF OLD EIRE AND THE ANCIENT WAYS!  . . .    101 ROSE UPON ROOD     23
    DRIVING THE DEER ALONG THE WOODY WAYS.  . . .    109 CUCHULAIN SEA   V  48
    LED ON BY GENTLE WAYS!  . . . . . . . . . .      113 ROSE OF PEACE      12
    IN THOSE GREAT IGNORANT LEAFY WAYS!  . . . . .   135 TWO TREES          16
    YET HE WHO TREADS IN MEASURED WAYS  . . . . .    138 TO IRELAND         27
    YET HE WHO TREADS IN AUSTERE WAYS  . . . . .     138 TO IRELAND      V  27
    AND THE WINDS THAT BLOW THROUGH THE STARRY WAYS,  158 TO HIS HEART        4
    AND THE WINDS BLOWING THROUGH THE STARRY WAYS,  .  158 TO HIS HEART    V  4
    BURNS BUT MORE CLEARLY.  O SHE HAD NOT THESE WAYS  200 FOLLY COMFORT      11
    HAVE TAUGHT TO IGNORANT MEN MOST VIOLENT WAYS,  .  256 NO SECOND TROY     3
    THAT HAVE TO BE SET UP IN FIFTY WAYS,  . . . .   260 FASC DIFFICULT      9
    O WHAT IF LEVELLED LAWNS AND GRAVELLED WAYS  . .  418 ANCEST HOUSES     29
    "GO YOUR WAYS, O GO YOUR WAYS,  . . . . . . .    588 OLD WICKED MAN     28
    "GO YOUR WAYS, O GO YOUR WAYS,  . . . . . . .    588 OLD WICKED MAN     28
    FROM THE WOOD'S WAYS, THEN, LIKE A SILVER FLAME,  .  658 ISLE STAT II 1   6
    AND MEASURE OUT THE WAYS OF CHIVALRY.  . . . .   660 ISLE STAT II 1      37
    WHAT ARE THE VOICES THAT IN FLOWERY WAYS  . .    666 ISLE STAT II 3      16
    BEHOLD THE LOVING LOVELESS FLOWER OF LONE WAYS,  .  674 ISLE STAT II 3  201
    AS THOUGH THEY'D VOWED TO MEASURE ALL ITS WAYS,  .  711 FERENCZ RENYI    48
    OF SOME MILD WOMAN, OR IN CHILDREN'S WAYS.  . .  750 SHADOW WATER A     74
WAYWARD
    AND THE DAYS PASS BY LIKE A WAYWARD TUNE,  . .     8 OISIN 1            83
    AND OF THE WAYWARD TWILIGHT COMPANIES  . . . .   136 TO SOME I TALK      6
    WHERE THE PROUD, WAYWARD SQUIRREL WENT,  . . .   317 APPOINTMENT         3
    OR ALL THAT WAYWARD EBB AND FLOW.  THERE STOOD  .  428 NINETEEN 19      4
    ON ALL THAT WAYWARD EBB AND FLOW.  THERE STOOD  .  428 NINETEEN 19    V  4
WEAK
    WITH BARREN WORDS AND FLATTERIES OF THE WEAK.  .  42 OISIN 2          197
    FOR HE IS WEAK AND POOR AND BLIND, AND LIES  .    42 OISIN 2          203
    LIAR AND FLATTERER OF THE WEAK, IN WHAT STRANGE CLIME  .  42 OISIN 2      198
    AY, OISIN KNOWS, FOR HE IS OF THE WEAK,  . . .    42 OISIN 2        V 202
    WEAK, IN THE MIDST OF THE MEADOW.  . . . . .      54 OISIN 3          102
    WHO HOLDS THE WORLD BETWEEN HIS BILL AND MADE US STRONG
        OR WEAK                                       76 INDIAN ON GOD       6
    WHO HOLDS THE WORLD BETWEEN HIS BILL AND MAKES US STRONG
        OR WEAK                                       76 INDIAN ON GOD   V   6
    THE WEAK WORM HIDING DOWN IN ITS SMALL CAVE,  .  101 ROSE UPON ROOD     16
    WEAK AND WORN AND WEARY THE WAVES OF CUMMEN STRAND,  .  207 HANRAHANS SONG V  6
    WEAK AND WORN AND WEARY OUR COURAGE DROOPS AND DIES  .  207 HANRAHANS SONG V  8
    THE WEAK LAY HAND ON WHAT THE STRONG HAS DONE,  .  265 THESE CLOUDS      3
    WHO HAVE FAILED, BEING WEAK OF WILL,  . . . .    298 THREE HERMITS      18
    WEAK AS A WORM.  . . . . . . . . . . . . .       574 MAIDS 1ST SONG     10
    SOON WILT THOU SMILE, FOR HERE THE WINDS ARE WEAK  671 ISLE STAT II 3   141
    GOING THE FOREST THROUGH, WITH FLUTINGS WEAK!  .  672 ISLE STAT II 3   155
    BEFORE I AM TOO WEAK, FIERCE MORTAL, LET ME FLY,  .  675 ISLE STAT II 3  245
    BEFORE I AM TOO WEAK, OH LET ME FLY,  . . . .    675 ISLE STAT II 3 V 245
```

WEAK   (CONTINUED)
```
    A WEAK, THIN CHILD, WHEN LAST I SAW HIM THERE.  .   .   .   .    699 MOSADA 3            14
    SO SMALL MAKES ONE GROW WEAK AND TOTTERING!     .   .   .   .    700 MOSADA 3            35
    IF THESE BE PRECIOUS."  "I AM OLD AND WEAK,"    .   .   .   .    711 FERENCZ RENYI       55
    I'M WEAK, AND BY THE HANDS SHALL HOLD EACH ONE  .   .   .   .    712 FERENCZ RENYI       57
    FOR I AM OLD AND WEAK."  AND AT HER SIDE        .   .   .   .    712 FERENCZ RENYI       59
    I'M WEAK, AND BY THE HAND SHALL HOLD EACH ONE   .   .   .   .    712 FERENCZ RENYI    V  57
    THUS PLAY WE FIRST WITH PAWNS, POOR THINGS AND WEAK!  .   .      722 WITCH VIVIEN        53
WEAKENED
    WHEN ORDER HAS WEAKENED OR FACTION IS STRONG,   .   .   .   .    548 TO SAME TUNE 3      12
WEAKLY
    WITH A SOB FOR MEN WAXING SO WEAKLY, .   .   .   .   .   .   .     60 OISIN 3           188
    I'D ALWAYS BEEN BUT WEAKLY, .   .   .   .   .   .   .   .   .      94 MOLL MAGEE          13
WEALTH
    ARE DRIVEN BY WEALTH AS BEGGARS BY THE ITCH,"   .   .   .   .    300 BEGGAR CRIED        14
    WHETHER HEALTH, WEALTH OR PEACE OF MIND WERE SPENT  .   .   .    429 NINETEEN 19         36
    AND PEACE BE WITH YOU, PEACE AND WEALTH OF DAYS. .   .   .   .    682 SEEKER             28
    THE WRINKLED SQUANDERER OF HUMAN WEALTH.    .   .   .   .   .    720 WITCH VIVIEN        16
    AND TO GIVE WEALTH OF OXEN AND SHEEP TO ALL!    .   .   .   .    756 SHADOW WATER A     184
    SO MUCH OF WEALTH AS MAY BEFIT THEIR RANK!  .   .   .   .   .    756 SHADOW WATER A     186
WEALTHY
    TO A WEALTHY MAN WHO PROMISED A SECOND SUBSCRIPTION .   .   .    287 TO WEALTHY MAN       T
WEAR
    BUT KNEEL AND WEAR OUT THE FLAGS AND PRAY FOR YOUR SOUL          63 OISIN 3            215
        THAT IS LOST
    BUT WEEP THOU, AND WEAR THOU THE FLAGS WITH THY KNEES,           63 OISIN 3         V 215
        .  .  .
    BUT WEEP YOU, AND WEAR YOU THE FLAGS WITH YOUR KNEES,  .  .  .   63 OISIN 3         V 215
    BUT WEEP YOU AND KNEEL! WEAR OUT THE FLAGS! .   .   .   .   .     63 OISIN 3         V 215
    KNEEL, USHEEN, WEAR OUT THE FLAGS AND PRAY FOR YOUR SOUL         63 OISIN 3         V 215
        THAT IS LOST
    THEY PINE AWAY AND YELLOW AND WEAR OUT,  .   .   .   .   .   .    81 EPHEMERA        V 24H
    AND NOW AT LAST YOU WEAR A HUMAN SHAPE,  .   .   .   .   .   .   102 FERGUS DRUID        6
    WAS BORN TO WEAR A CROWN.   .   .   .   .   .   .   .   .   .    308 PLAYER QUEEN        12
    ALL WEAR OUT THE CARPET WITH THEIR SHOES!   .   .   .   .   .    337 SCHOLARS            8
    WEAR OUT THE CARPET WITH THEIR SHOES.    .   .   .   .   .   .    337 SCHOLARS            8
    PERMIT FOUL YEARS TO WEAR   .   .   .   .   .   .   .   .   .    472 ALL SOUL NIGHT      49
    AND ALL THEIR SWELLING CANVAS WEAR, .   .   .   .   .   .   .    530 OLD TOM AGAIN        2
    AND ALL THEIR YELLOW CANVAS WEAR,   .   .   .   .   .   .   .    530 OLD TOM AGAIN    V   2
    NO MATTER WHAT THE NAMES THEY WEAR! .   .   .   .   .   .   .    582 ROGER CASEMENT   V   1
    AND WEAR A COAT IN FASHION, .   .   .   .   .   .   .   .   .    607 SONGS BURDEN 2      21
WEARIED    SEE TRAVEL-WEARIED
    BEING WEARIED OUT, I LOVE IN MAN THE CHILD? .   .   .   .   .    285 TWO KINGS          192
    BUT WEARIED RUNNING ROUND AND ROUND IN THEIR COURSES  .   .     433 NINETEEN 19        116
    TO THOSE YOUR "MELLOW" WARES HAVE WEARIED OUT.  .   .   .   .    721 WITCH VIVIEN        27
WEARINESS
    LULLED WEARINESS, AND SOFTLY ROUND  .   .   .   .   .   .   .     11 OISIN 1           137
    LULLED WEARINESS! AND CLOSELY ROUND .   .   .   .   .   .   .     11 OISIN 1        V 137
    BY AGE'S WEARINESS ARE SLAIN,   .   .   .   .   .   .   .   .     27 OISIN 1        V 415A
    AND "A WEARINESS SOON IS MY SPEED," SAYS THE MOUSE,   .   .      27 OISIN 1        V 417
    AND "MY SPEED IS A WEARINESS," FALTERS THE MOUSE,  .   .   .     28 OISIN 1           421
    WRAPT IN THE WAVE OF THAT MUSIC, WITH WEARINESS MORE THAN        51 OISIN 3            69
        OF EARTH,
    A WEARINESS COMES FROM THOSE DREAMERS,  .   .   .   .   .   .    122 WHITE BIRDS          5
    AND A WEARINESS COMES FROM THOSE DREAMERS  .   .   .   .   .     122 WHITE BIRDS      V   5
    THE GLASS OF OUTER WEARINESS,   .   .   .   .   .   .   .   .    135 TWO TREES           31
    PLEASURE ITSELF CAN BRING NO WEARINESS, .   .   .   .   .   .    284 TWO KINGS          181
WEARISOME
    AND HANDS THAT HOLD NO WEARISOME TOOL,   .   .   .   .   .   .    22 OISIN 1           340
WEARS
    AS THE TIDE WEARS THE DOVE-GREY SANDS,   .   .   .   .   .   .   157 POET BELOVED         4
    THE TOMB OF SWIFT WEARS IT AWAY.  A VOICE   .   .   .   .   .    487 SEVEN SAGES         21
    KEVIN O'HIGGINS' COUNTENANCE THAT WEARS  .   .   .   .   .   .   601 GALLERY REVIS        5
    KEVIN O'HIGGINS, AND THAT LOOK HE WEARS, .   .   .   .   .   .   601 GALLERY REVIS    V   5
    HER LOVE! TO HER WHO WEARS THAT BLOOM COMES TRUTH.  .   .   .    653 ISLE STAT I 2       46
WEARY    SEE WAR-WEARY A-WEARY BATTLE-WEARY
    NOR HAVE HANDS HELD A WEARY TOOL!   .   .   .   .   .   .   .     19 OISIN 1           283
    OF TWILIGHT WHEN HE'S WEARY, .   .   .   .   .   .   .   .   .     32 OISIN 2        V 50H
    RETURN WHEN YOU ARE WEARY,   .   .   .   .   .   .   .   .   .     33 OISIN 2        V  65
    YET WEARY WITH PASSIONS THAT FADED  .   .   .   .   .   .   .     50 OISIN 3            52
    I SAW HOW THOSE SLUMBERERS, GROWN WEARY, .   .   .   .   .       50 OISIN 3            54
    HELPLESS, MEN LIFTING THE LIDS OF HIS WEARY                      53 OISIN 3            92
        AND DEATH-MAKING EYE.
    HELPLESS, MEN LIFTING THE LIDS OF HIS WEARY                      53 OISIN 3        V  92
        AND DEATH-POURING EYE.
    WEARY, WITH ALL HIS POPPIES GATHERED ROUND HIM. .   .   .   .     72 ANASHU VIJAYA      25
    AND WEARY AND WORN ARE OUR SAD SOULS NOW! .   .   .   .   .       79 FALLING LEAVES      6
    "YOUR EYES THAT ONCE WERE NEVER WEARY OF MINE . .   .   .   .     79 EPHEMERA            1
    A WEARY WOMAN SLEEPS SO HARD!   .   .   .   .   .   .   .   .      95 MOLL MAGEE         21
    AND WEARY OF THE CRASH OF BATTLE CARS."  .   .   .   .   .   .    107 CUCHULAIN SEA   V  30
    WEARY AND KIND ONE LINGERED BY HIS SEAT! .   .   .   .   .   .    112 ROSE OF WORLD      13
    WEARY AND KIND ONE STOOD BESIDE HIS SEAT! .  .   .   .   .   .    112 ROSE OF WORLD   V  13
    THEY WEARY OF TROOPING  .   .   .   .   .   .   .   .   .   .     118 CRADLE SONG          3
    THEY WEARY OF TENDING.  .   .   .   .   .   .   .   .   .   .     118 CRADLE SONG      V   3
    HAD HID AWAY EARTH'S OLD AND WEARY CRY.  .   .   .   .   .   .    120 SORROW OF LOVE   V   4
    ARE SHAKEN WITH EARTH'S OLD AND WEARY CRY.  .   .   .   .   .    120 SORROW OF LOVE   V  12
    UNTIL THE SAP OF SUMMER HAD GROWN WEARY! .   .   .   .   .   .    130 BOOK STORIES       14
    GREEN BOUGHS OF TOSSING ALWAYS, WEARY, WEARY,  .   .   .   .     130 BOOK STORIES       14
    GREEN BOUGHS OF TOSSING ALWAYS, WEARY, WEARY,  .   .   .   .     130 BOOK STORIES     V  14
    WAS WEARY NIGHT AND DAY!  .   .   .   .   .   .   .   .   .   .    132 FR GILLIGAN         2
    BEING WEARY OF THE WORLD'S EMPIRES, BOW DOWN TO YOU, .   .       161 BLACK PIG            7
```

WEARY   (CONTINUED)
   O WHEN WILL YOU GROW WEARY?" THEY HAD VANISHED, ... 187 QUEEN MAEVE   152
   AS WEARY HEARTED AS THAT HOLLOW MOON. . . . .   206 ADAMS CURSE   V   38
   WEAK AND WORN AND WEARY THE WAVES OF CUMMEN STRAND, . . . 207 HANRAHANS SONG V   6
   WEAK AND WORN AND WEARY OUR COURAGE DROOPS AND DIES . . . 207 HANRAHANS SONG V   8
   AND KEEP TO THE ONE WEARY MARRIAGE-BED. . . . . . .   224 SHADOW WATER B   55
   AND KEEP TO THE ONE WEARY MARRIAGE BED. . . . . . .   224 SHADOW WATER B V   55
   AND I GREW WEARY OF THE SUN . . . .   256 WORDS   5
   WEARY OF MANY QUESTIONS, "THERE ARE THINGS . . . . .   281 TWO KINGS   93
   "A WEARY WOOING AND A LONG," HE SAID, ...   283 TWO KINGS   154
   THAT HAS GROWN WEARY OF THE WANDERING DANCE, ...   285 TWO KINGS   183
   THAT HAS GROWN WEARY OF THE WHIRLING DANCE, ...   285 TWO KINGS   V   183
   AND THEN, GROWN WEARY, PRAYED AND CURSED , ...   307 HOUR DAWN   117
   BUT, WEARY RUNNING ROUND AND ROUND IN THEIR COURSES, . . 433 NINETEEN 19   V   116
   SOMETHING MADE THESE EYEBALLS WEARY . . . .   529 TOM LUNATIC   11
   WEARY OF REAPING THE BARREN NIGHT . . . .   648 ISLE STAT I 1   84
   WITH TEARS? I WEARY OF YE. THERE IS NONE . . . . .   650 ISLE STAT I 1   142
   I WEARY OF YOUR SONGS AND HUNTER'S TOYS. . . . . .   651 ISLE STAT I 1   157
   UNTIL I FIND HIM. WHAT A WEARY WEEK, ...   658 ISLE STAT II 1   2
   WEARY OF WATCHING ROUND THE FIRE AT NIGHT. . . . .   683 SEEKER   42
   AND HER GIGANTIC LIMBS. THE WEARY THIRST . . . . .   687 TWO TITANS   16
   I'M WEARY--WEARY, AND 'TIS VERY COLD. . . . . . .   703 MOSADA 3   122
   I'M WEARY--WEARY, AND 'TIS VERY COLD. . . . . . .   703 MOSADA 3   122
   "A LITTLE WILL I LAY MY WEARY HEAD, ...   712 FERENCZ RENYI   75
   OH, I AM WEARY OF THAT FOOLISH TALE. . . . .   721 WITCH VIVIEN   33
   AT THE HOUSE OF WEARY MEN . . . .   727 LOVERS QUARREL   51
   BUT YOU GREW WEARY OF HER. WHEN I HOLD . . . . . .   749 SHADOW WATER A   53
   SHE BIDS US FOLLOW HER. I HAVE GROWN WEARY . . . .   758 SHADOW WATER A   218
   IT MAY BE, AND HAVE GROWN WEARY OF LOVE. . . . . .   767 SHADOW WATER A   390
WEARY-HEARTED
   AS WEARY-HEARTED AS THAT HOLLOW MOON. . . . .   206 ADAMS CURSE   38
WEARYING
   OUR HANDS HAVE KNOWN NO WEARYING TOOL, ...   22 OISIN 1   V   339
WEASEL
   A WEASEL MOVING ON FROM STONE TO STONE, ...   102 FERGUS DRUID   5
   WEASEL WARMS HIM ON THE PATH, ...   705 DAWN-SONG   19
WEASEL'S
   THE WEASEL'S TWIST, THE WEASEL'S TOOTH. . . . . . .   431 NINETEEN 19   92
   THE WEASEL'S TWIST, THE WEASEL'S TOOTH. . . . . . .   431 NINETEEN 19   92
WEASELS
   FOR NO LIVE CREATURES LIVED THERE, NO WEASELS MOVED IN   48 OISIN 3   19
     THE DARK,
   FOR NO LIVE CREATURES LIVE THERE, NO WEASELS MOVE IN THE 56 OISIN 3   139
     DARK,
   WHO ARE BUT WEASELS FIGHTING IN A HOLE. . . . . . .   429 NINETEEN 19   32
WEATHER
   OH WANDERER IN THE SOUTHERN WEATHER, ...   77 INDIAN TO LOVE V   1
   LIKE AN OLD PAUPER, IN ALL KINDS OF WEATHER, ...   205 ADAMS CURSE   9
   MAYBE THE WEATHER WAS ACCURSED . . . .   305 HOUR DAWN   65
   BECAUSE THE WEATHER WAS A-CURSED . . . .   305 HOUR DAWN   V   65
   OF THE FOUL WEATHER, HAIL AND RAIN, ...   424 ROAD AT DOOR   9
   HOW GOES THE WEATHER? . . . .   585 ORAHILLY   9
   HOW GOES THE WEATHER? . . . .   585 ORAHILLY   18
   HOW GOES THE WEATHER? . . . .   585 ORAHILLY   27
   HOW GOES THE WEATHER? . . . .   585 ORAHILLY   36
   BUT NO, IN THIS WARM WEATHER, 'MONG THE HILLS, . . .   699 MOSADA 3   9
   NOON WRAPT THE TREES IN VEILS OF VIOLET WEATHER, . . .   715 DWELT SYCAMORE   7
   NOON WRAPPED THE WOODS IN VEILS OF VIOLET WEATHER, . .   715 DWELT SYCAMORE V   7
WEATHER-WORN
   A WEATHER-WORN, MARBLE TRITON . . . .   329 MEN IMPROVE   2
   A WEATHER-WORN, MARBLE TRITON . . . .   329 MEN IMPROVE   17
WEAVE
   "WHAT DO YOU WEAVE SO SOFT AND BRIGHT?" . . . . . .   69 CLOAK BOAT   V   1
   "WHAT DO YOU WEAVE SO FAIR AND BRIGHT?" . . . . . .   69 CLOAK BOAT   V   1
   THE CLOAK I WEAVE OF SORROW, ...   69 CLOAK BOAT   V   2
   "WHAT DO YOU WEAVE WITH WOOL SO WHITE?" . . . . . .   70 CLOAK BOAT   11
   "I WEAVE THE SHOES OF SORROW, ...   70 CLOAK BOAT   12
   HE WOULD GO WEAVE OUT OF THE STARS . . . . . .   113 ROSE OF PEACE   7
   WHAT DO YOU WEAVE SO FAIR AND BRIGHT? . . . . . .   666 ISLE STAT II 3   1
   THE CLOAK I WEAVE OF SORROW. . . . .   666 ISLE STAT II 3   2
   WHAT DO YOU WEAVE WITH WOOL SO WHITE? . . . . . .   666 ISLE STAT II 3   11
   AND ON THIS LOOM I WEAVE THY DESTINY." . . . . . .   716 DWELT SYCAMORE   14
   THE SUNFLOWERS WEAVE A GOLDEN CLIME, ...   736 SUMMER EVENING   9
   SHE WOULD WEAVE A NET TO TAKE US. SHE MIGHT KEEP FAITH, 756 SHADOW WATER A   190
   THE GODS WEAVE NETS, AND TAKE US IN THEIR NETS, . . .   764 SHADOW WATER A   339
   THE GODS HATE HAPPINESS, AND WEAVE THEIR NETS . . . .   767 SHADOW WATER A   399
WEAVER
   OR WEAVER BENT AT HIS LOOM, ...   589 OLD WICKED MAN   51
WEAVES
   NOT THERE, FOR THERE A SPIDER WEAVES HER WEB. . . . .   700 MOSADA 3   38
WEAVING   SEE A-WEAVING
   WEAVING OLDEN DANCES, ...   87 STOLEN CHILD   17
   OUR ARMS ARE WEAVING, OUR LIPS ARE APART, ...   140 HOSTING SIDHE   V   9
   OF MOSS, A MAIDEN WEAVING. SINGETH SHE, ...   716 DWELT SYCAMORE   12
   I PRAY THAT I EVER BE WEAVING . . . .   743 WISDOM DREAMS   1
   BUT WEAVING IT OUT OF THREADS . . . .   743 WISDOM DREAMS   3
WEB
   THEN EMER CAST THE WEB UPON THE FLOOR, ...   105 CUCHULAIN SEA   6
   A SHINING WEB, A FLOATING RIBBON OF CLOTH, ...   430 NINETEEN 19   50
   NOT THERE, FOR THERE A SPIDER WEAVES HER WEB. . . . .   700 MOSADA 3   38

	PAGE	TITLE	LINE

WEBBED
```
    BY THE WEBBED TOES, AND THAT ALL-POWERFUL BILL   . . . .   441 LEDA AND SWAN   V    3
    BY THE WEBBED TOES, AND THAT ALL POWERFUL BILL   . . . .   441 LEDA AND SWAN   V    3
```
WEB-HEAPED
```
    UPON THE WEB-HEAPED FLOOR, AND CRIED HIS WORD!         106 CUCHULAIN SEA        15
    UPON THE WEB-HEAPED FLOOR, AND THUS HIS WORD, . . . . . 106 CUCHULAIN SEA   V    15
```
WEBS
```
    AH! DRUID, DRUID, HOW GREAT WEBS OF SORROW . . . . . . . 104 FERGUS DRUID         39
    BY THE DARK WEBS, HER NAPE CAUGHT IN HIS BILL, . . . .   441 LEDA AND SWAN         3
```
WED
```
    "YOU ONLY WILL I WED," I CRIED, . . . . . . . . . . .    7 OISIN 1              74
    IN LOVE.  I CRIED, "THEE WILL I WED, . . . . . . . . .   7 OISIN 1         V    74
    AND MADE MY LIPS AND MUSIC WED, . . . . . . . . . . .    134 TWO TREES            11
    BAILE AND AILLINN WOULD BE WED. . . . . . . . . . . .    190 BAILE AILLINN        24
    WITH! "YOU MUST HOME AGAIN, AND WED . . . . . . . . .    191 BAILE AILLINN        58
    "O LADY, WED WITH ONE OF US"! . . . . . . . . . . . .    191 BAILE AILLINN        61
    NATURAL AND SUPERNATURAL WITH THE SELF-SAME RING ARE WED. 556 RIBH PATRICK         4
```
WEDDED
```
    WHO WEDDED MEN WITH RINGS OF DRUID GOLD! . . . . . . .   29 OISIN 2              10
```
WEDDING
```
    WEDDING THE QUEENS OF EARTHLY LANDS WITH RINGS . . . .   29 OISIN 2         V    10
```
WEED   SEE SEA-WEED
```
    HE CARVED ON TREES, AND WITH A SUN-DRY WEED . . . . .    659 ISLE STAT II 1        8
    THE BROWN WEED BURDEN, SO THE SWORD BRINGS FEAR . . . .  660 ISLE STAT II 1       45
```
WEEDING
```
    OR WEEDING OR PLOUGHING WITH FACES A-SHINING WITH MUCH-TOIL 58 OISIN 3           165
    WET!
```
WEEDS   SEE SHORE-WEEDS
```
    HOW THE FALCONER FOLLOWS THE FALCON IN THE WEEDS OF THE  52 OISIN 3              79
    HERON'S PLOT,
```
WEEDY   SEE SEA-WEEDY
```
    IN ENDLESS DARK, AND BY THE WEEDY MARGE . . . . . . . . 682 SEEKER               19
```
WEEK
```
    UNTIL I FIND HIM.  WHAT A WEARY WEEK, . . . . . . . . . 658 ISLE STAT II 1        2
```
WEEKS
```
    THESE DOZEN WEEKS.  AND I HAD THOUGHT TO MAKE . . . . .  222 SHADOW WATER B        4
    AND SO THE WEEKS PASSED BY.  BUT WHEN I SAID, . . . . .  280 TWO KINGS            89
    I SOUGHT IT DAILY FOR SIX WEEKS OR SO. . . . . . . . .   629 CIRCUS ANIMALS        2
```
WEEP
```
    IN BROODING MEMORY, NOR WEEP. . . . . . . . . . . .      11 OISIN 1         V 131B
    AND STAY A LITTLE WHILE, AND BID THEM WEEP! . . . . .    33 OISIN 2              60
    WHEN YOU HAVE TOLD HOW I WEEP ENDLESSLY, . . . . . .     33 OISIN 2              63
    "AND TELL THEM HOW I WEEP, UNTIL THEY WEEP! . . . . .    33 OISIN 2              63
    "AND TELL THEM HOW I WEEP, UNTIL THEY WEEP! . . . . .    33 OISIN 2         V    63
    AND I MUST NEEDS ENDURE AND HATE AND WEEP, . . . . .     35 OISIN 2              85
    SAINT, DO YOU WEEP?  I HEAR AMID THE THUNDER . . . . .   43 OISIN 2             209
    SAINT, DOST THOU WEEP?  I HEAR AMID THE THUNDER . . . .  43 OISIN 2         V   209
    BUT WEEP FOR YOUR NIAMH, O OISIN, WEEP! FOR IF ONLY YOUR 55 OISIN 3             127
    SHOE
    BUT WEEP FOR YOUR NIAMH, O OISIN, WEEP! FOR IF ONLY YOUR 55 OISIN 3             127
    SHOE
    BUT WEEP FOR THY NIAM, OH OISIN, WEEP! FOR IF ONLY THY SHOE 55 OISIN 3      V   127
    BUT WEEP FOR THY NIAM, OH OISIN, WEEP! FOR IF ONLY THY SHOE 55 OISIN 3      V   127
    . . . SHALL LISTEN AND RISE UP AND WEEP! . . . . . .    62 OISIN 3             206
    BUT WEEP THOU, AND WEAR THOU THE FLAGS WITH THY KNEES,   63 OISIN 3         V   215
    . . .
    BUT WEEP YOU, AND WEAR YOU THE FLAGS WITH YOUR KNEES, . . 63 OISIN 3            215
    BUT WEEP YOU AND KNEEL! WEAR OUT THE FLAGS! . . . . .    63 OISIN 3         V   215
    OR PACE AND WEEP IN WOODS FORLORN, . . . . . . . . .     86 MAD KING GOLL   V    68
    I CAN BUT WEEP AND SIGH." . . . . . . . . . . . . .      99 FOXHUNTER            36
    AND WEEP BECAUSE I KNOW ALL THINGS NOW! . . . . . . .    177 PAST GREATNESS        2
    HIS FACE BOWED LOW TO WEEP THE END . . . . . . . . .     192 BAILE AILLINN        75
    I COULD WEEP THAT THE OLD IS OUT OF SEASON. . . . . .    199 ARROW                 8
    AS I AM DOING NOW.  WHY DO YOU WEEP? . . . . . . . .     246 SHADOW WATER B      495
    I WEEP BECAUSE I'VE NOTHING FOR YOUR EYES . . . . .      246 SHADOW WATER B      496
    I WEEP--I WEEP BECAUSE BARE NIGHT'S ABOVE, . . . . .     246 SHADOW WATER B      499
    I WEEP--I WEEP BECAUSE BARE NIGHT'S ABOVE, . . . . .     246 SHADOW WATER B      499
    SHOULD LAUGH AND WEEP AN HOUR UPON THE CLOCK. . . . .    471 ALL SOUL NIGHT       20
    SHOULD LAUGH AND WEEP AN HOUR UPON THE CLOCK. . . . .    474 ALL SOUL NIGHT       90
    SHOULD WEEP AND LAUGH AN HOUR UPON THE CLOCK. . . . .    474 ALL SOUL NIGHT  V    90
    AND YET I WEEP--OEDIPUS' CHILD . . . . . . . . . . .     540 FROM ANTIGONE        15
    DO NOT BREAK UP THEIR LINES TO WEEP. . . . . . . . .     565 LAPIS LAZULI         15
    TILL I LAUGH WHEN OTHERS WEEP, . . . . . . . . . . .     647 ISLE STAT I 1        61
    LONE, AND WANTING THEE, I WEEP! . . . . . . . . . .      647 ISLE STAT I 1        72
    WHERE ALL NIGHT LONG THE HEAVENS WEEP AND WEEP, . . .    649 ISLE STAT I 1       124
    WHERE ALL NIGHT LONG THE HEAVENS WEEP AND WEEP, . . .    649 ISLE STAT I 1       124
    AYE, VERY LATELY, SORROW CAME TO WEEP . . . . . . .      659 ISLE STAT II 1       25
    WHOSE INSOLENT EYES UNUSED TO TEARS WOULD WEEP. . . .    678 ISLE STAT II 3      302
    SEARCHED THE UNSEARCHABLE--WHY GOOD MEN WEEP! . . . .    710 FERENCZ RENYI        32
    FOR MERRY MEN THAT WEEP, . . . . . . . . . . . . .       736 IN CHURCH             6
    COVER THEIR FACES WITH THEIR HAIR AND WEEP. . . . .      764 SHADOW WATER A      333
```
WEEPING
```
    AND, WEEPING OVER THE WHITE STRINGS, HURLED . . . .      17 OISIN 1             241
    "FLEE FROM HIM," PEARL-PALE NIAMH WEEPING CRIED, . . .   35 OISIN 2              92
    TO FLY A SPIRIT," NIAM WEEPING SAID. . . . . . . . .     35 OISIN 2         V    92
    AND ON MY BOSOM LAID HER WEEPING HEAD. . . . . . . .     46 OISIN 2             250
    FOR THE WORLD'S MORE FULL OF WEEPING THAN YOU CAN        87 STOLEN CHILD         12
    UNDERSTAND.
    FOR THE WORLD'S MORE FULL OF WEEPING THAN YOU CAN        87 STOLEN CHILD         27
    UNDERSTAND.
```

		PAGE	TITLE		LINE

WEEPING   (CONTINUED)
    FOR THE WORLD'S MORE FULL OF WEEPING THAN YOU CAN   88 STOLEN CHILD   41
        UNDERSTAND.
    FROM A WORLD MORE FULL OF WEEPING THAN HE CAN UNDERSTAND.   89 STOLEN CHILD   53
    FOR THE WORLD'S MORE FULL OF WEEPING THAN HE CAN UNDERSTAND   89 STOLEN CHILD V 53
    WHEN, WEEPING SCORE BY SCORE,   93 FATHER OHART   26
    HE CAUGHT HIS BREATH AND CAST HIM WEEPING DOWN   106 CUCHULAIN SEA V 14
    SHE HAS GONE WEEPING AWAY.   152 LOSS OF LOVE   7
    THAT YOU ARE WEEPING FOR. NO, FOR HE IS DEAD.   243 SHADOW WATER B   427
    AND WHILE WE'RE IN OUR LAUGHING, WEEPING FIT,   257 RECONCILIATION   9
    WEEPING WHEN ALL OTHERS LAUGH.   647 ISLE STAT I 1   62
    YOUR WEEPING FITS! LOOK YOU, SO VERY STRAIT   659 ISLE STAT II 1   22
    AH! YOU ARE WEEPING! HERE SHOULD ALL GRIEF CEASE.   672 ISLE STAT II 3   149
    THE VISION. YOU ARE PALE AND WEEPING. CHILD,   693 MOSADA 1   73
    I HAVE ROUSED THEE! FOR THE WEEPING   729 PRIEST FAIRY   40
    PITY THESE WEEPING EYES! I WILL FOLLOW YOU.   768 SHADOW WATER A   420
WEEPS
    SAY HOW HE WEEPS IN ERI."   33 OISIN 2 V 68
    THE WEST WEEPS IN PALE DEW AND SIGHS PASSING AWAY,   154 BELOVED PEACE   5
    THE MOTHER OF THE STARS WEEPS TOO,   738 YOU ARE SAD   2
    AND THEN THE WHOLE WORLD'S TROUBLE WEEPS WITH YOU.   738 YOU ARE SAD   12
WEIGH
    BUT WEIGH THIS SONG WITH THE GREAT AND THEIR PRIDE!   166 EVIL OF BELOV   4
    THAT WEIGH AND MEASURE ALL IN THESE WASTE SEAS——   235 SHADOW WATER B   292
    PARDON, AND YOU THAT DID NOT WEIGH THE COST,   269 PARDON FATHERS V 9
    WEIGH ME DOWN, AND NOT A DAY   501 VACILLATION   54
    WEIGH THEM IN AN HOUR OF DREAMING,   737 IN FIRELIGHT   11
    A PATH AMONG THESE WAVES AND WEIGH THE WIND?   748 SHADOW WATER A   21
    AND WERE ALL DREAMS, IT WOULD NOT WEIGH IN THE HAND.   750 SHADOW WATER A   77
WEIGHED
    NOW I HAVE SEEN IT WEIGHED   267 FRIEND ILLNESS   6
    THEY WEIGHED SO LIGHTLY WHAT THEY GAVE.   290 SEPTEMBER 1913   30
WEIGHS
    AND THE WHOLE WORLD WEIGHS DOWN UPON MY HEART——   104 FERGUS DRUID V 38A
    RESPONSIBILITY SO WEIGHS ME DOWN.   501 VACILLATION   50
WEIGHT
    BUT WHEN THE HORSE HAD FELT MY WEIGHT,   9 OISIN 1   109
    AND WHEN THE WHITE STEED FELT MY WEIGHT,   9 OISIN 1 V 109
    THE ODOROUS WEIGHT OF HIS CURLS OF LIGHT,   28 OISIN 1 V 423D
    HE DREADS THE WEIGHT OF MORTAL HOURS.   212 BLESS PSALTER   11
    HEEL UP AND WEIGHT ON TOE, MUST FACE THE WALL   363 DOLLS FACES   3
    BENEATH THE WEIGHT OF GREATER GRIEF THAN I!   661 ISLE STAT II 1   63
WEIGHTY
    AND IMPORTUNE WITH WEIGHTY WORDS THIS MOOR,   698 MOSADA 2   45
    A WEIGHTY QUESTION, FOR IT IS THE LAST.   700 MOSADA 3   37
WEIR
    AS A HAY-COCK OUT ON THE FLOOD, OR A WOLF SUCKED UNDER   63 OISIN 3   220
        A WEIR.
    AS A GRASS SEED CRUSHED BY A PEBBLE, AS A WOLF SUCKED UNDER   63 OISIN 3 V 220
        A WEIR.
WEIRS
    SHE BID ME TAKE LIFE EASY, AS THE GRASS GROWS ON THE WEIRS!   90 SALLEY GARDENS   7
WELCOME
    HE HAS OVER-LINGERED HIS WELCOME! THE DAYS,   26 OISIN 1   402
    HE HATH OVER LINGERED HIS WELCOME! THE DAYS,   27 OISIN 1 V 406
    AND BADE ALL WELCOME, BEING IGNORANT.   286 TWO KINGS   218
    AND RIDDEN OUT TO WELCOME THEM, AND NOW,   286 TWO KINGS V 218
    A FITTER WELCOME! BUT A THOUGHT   328 ROBERT GREGORY   95
    NEW WELCOME AND OLD WISDOM AT HER FIRE   340 SHEP GOATHERD   32
    WELCOME, AND THE ORMONDES ALL   400 DEMON BEAST   11
    WHAT SEEMS MOST WELCOME IN THE TOMB——PLAY A PREDESTINED   503 VACILLATION   86
        PART.
    AND ALL MY FRIENDS WERE THERE AND MADE ME WELCOME TOO!   581 CURSE CROMWELL   27
    TO WELCOME THEE, NASCHINA, WITH SWEET SINGING.   645 ISLE STAT I 1   7
    TO WELCOME THEE, WHEN O'ER THE OWLET'S WINGS   648 ISLE STAT I 1   102
    THOU'RT WELCOME. LIE THERE CLOSE AGAINST MY FINGERS.   700 MOSADA 3   44
WELCOMED
    THOSE WANDERERS THAT WELCOMED IN THEIR TENTS   462 HARUN RASHID   23
    THAT THEY HAVE WELCOMED IN THEIR TENTS THE DREAM   462 HARUN RASHID V 23
WELCOMER
    HE MIGHT HAVE BEEN YOUR HEARTIEST WELCOMER.   326 ROBERT GREGORY   56
WELCOMING
    EACH CAME ONE MORN, WITH WELCOMING OF SONG,   660 ISLE STAT II 1   42
WELFARE
    A HELEN OF SOCIAL WELFARE DREAM,   626 OLD MEN BE MAD   7
WELL
    FOR WE KNEW WELL THE OLD WAS OVER.   25 OISIN 1   379
    FOR WELL WE KNEW THE OLD WAS OVER,   25 OISIN 1 V 379
    OR GOIN' TO THE WELL,   96 MOLL MAGEE   46
    SAYING ALL THINGS WERE WELL!   113 ROSE OF PEACE   14
    HE MUSED BESIDE THE WELL OF SCANAVIN,   127 DREAM OF FAERY   25
    BECAUSE, TO HIM WHO PONDERS WELL,   138 TO IRELAND   19
    AH! WISE, MY HEART KNOWS WELL HOW WISE.   193 BAILE AILLINN   99
    "HE IS WELL OUT OF WIND AND WAVE,   193 BAILE AILLINN V 114
    "YOUR WELL BELOVED'S HAIR HAS THREADS OF GREY,   199 FOLLY COMFORT V 2
    AND WHO COULD PLAY IT WELL ENOUGH   202 NEVER GIVE ALL   11
    AND WHO CAN PLAY IT WELL ENOUGH   202 NEVER GIVE ALL V 11
    I SAW THEM ON THAT NIGHT AS WELL AS YOU.   223 SHADOW WATER B   29
    AND DRAGS HIM THROUGH THE SEA. WELL, NET OR NONE,   224 SHADOW WATER B   57
    FOR HE CAN JUDGE THE STARS AS WELL AS FORGAEL.   225 SHADOW WATER B   63
    NO, NO, DO NOT SAY THAT. YOU KNOW RIGHT WELL   227 SHADOW WATER B   107

WELL   (CONTINUED)
       THAT SET HIM TO THE FANCY. ALL WOULD BE WELL • • • •   230 SHADOW WATER B   177
       I KNEW HIM WELL, AND WHILE I HEARD HIM LAUGHING • • • •   242 SHADOW WATER B   419
       FROM WELL SIDE OR FROM PLOUGH LAND, WAS THEIR NOISE; • • 279 TWO KINGS   V   53
       I SAW, BEFORE I HAD WELL FINISHED. • • • • • • • •   322 SWANS AT COOLE   9
       IN MUSCULAR YOUTH WELL KNOWN TO MAYO MEN • • • • •   325 ROBERT GREGORY   34
       WELL KNOWN FOR HORSEMANSHIP TO CONNACHT MEN • • • •   325 ROBERT GREGORY   V   34
       WHAT OTHER COULD SO WELL HAVE COUNSELLED US • • • • •   327 ROBERT GREGORY   73
       THE SHEEP HAD GONE FROM THEIRS. I KNOW RIGHT WELL • • •   339 SHEP GOATHERD   15
       AND BE WELL PLEASED REMEMBERING IT, FOR IN THE OLD DAYS,   351 HER PRAISE   16
       AND YOU KNOW WELL HOW GREAT THE LONGING HAS BEEN, • • •   352 PEOPLE   7
       WHEN AGE MIGHT WELL HAVE CHILLED HIS BLOOD." • • • •   356 BROKEN DREAMS   19
       I BEAR A BURDEN THAT MIGHT WELL TRY • • • • • • •   380 SONGS FOOL 1   13
       THAT IS HOW HE LEARNT SO WELL • • • • • • • • •   382 SONG OF FOOL   11
       SHE HAD RIDDEN WELL TO HOUNDS. • • • • • • • • •   392 EASTER 1916   V   23
       MAY WELL BE OF ALL EVIL CHANCES CHIEF. • • • • • •   405 FOR DAUGHTER   53
       A SCENE WELL SET AND EXCELLENT COMPANY. • • • • • •   489 COOLE PARK 29   16
       AND THE RICH MAN HAD PAID THEM WELL • • • • • • •   596 COLONEL MARTIN   57
       OBSERVANT OLD MEN KNOW IT WELL; • • • • • • • •   626 OLD MEN BE MAD   17
       SING WHATEVER IS WELL MADE, • • • • • • • • •   639 BEN BULBEN   69
       AND FOUND. 'TIS WELL!--ANOTHER MILE OF WAY • • • •   651 ISLE STAT I 2   6
       NO OTHER BIRD MAY ENTER IN. WELL? LATE-- • • • •   659 ISLE STAT II 1   24
       IT IS THE SHEPHERD GUARIMOND, WHO LOVETH WELL • • •   661 ISLE STAT II 1   53
       NASCHINA. OH, I KNOW HER WELL--A LAME, • • • • • •   661 ISLE STAT II 1   67
       OF THOSE STEEL TONGUES! CRASH, SWORDS! WELL THRUST!   665 ISLE STAT II 2   67
          WELL BENT
       OF THOSE STEEL TONGUES! CRASH, SWORDS! WELL THRUST!   665 ISLE STAT II 2   67
          WELL BENT
       WELL NIGH IMMORTAL IN THIS CHARMED CLIME, • • • • •   674 ISLE STAT II 3   202
       ARE ALL THINGS WELL WITH YOU AND WITH YOUR SHEEP? • •   682 SEEKER   13
       YES, ALL IS VERY WELL. WHENCE COMEST THOU? • • • •   682 SEEKER   14
       DEEPER THAN THE DEEPEST WELL." • • • • • • • •   697 MOSADA 2   27
       AND POUR UPON THE WORLD! AH! WELL A DAY! • • • • •   703 MOSADA 3   V 118
       HAS FLICKERED AND GONE OUT. I AM NOT WELL. • • • •   704 MOSADA 3   129
       BEFORE HIM ONE WELL GUARDED, WITH BOUND HANDS; • • •   709 FERENCZ RENYI   10
       WELL THEN, TO BUSINESS! WHAT IS IN YOUR BAG? • • • •   720 WITCH VIVIEN   19
       A FAIRY WHOM WE LOVED FULL WELL: • • • • • • •   729 PRIEST FAIRY   44
       YOU HAVE DONE WELL, BECAUSE MY BOWS ARE TURNED • • •   755 SHADOW WATER A   164
       BY SUN AND MOON AND A HUNDRED GODS AS WELL, • • • •   756 SHADOW WATER A   189
       WELL SHELTERED FROM THE WINDS, AND FRUITFUL FIELDS, •   758 SHADOW WATER A   221
       AH, WELL! THEY ARE CALLING ME--THEY ARE CALLING ME.   760 SHADOW WATER A   251
       WE WILL NOT QUARREL, NOW THAT ALL IS WELL, • • • •   766 SHADOW WATER A   373
       THE WELL AND THE TREE • • • • • • • • • •   780 WELL AND TREE   V   T
       CRIES OUT THE EMPTY WELL, • • • • • • • • •   780 WELL AND TREE   2
       DRY STONES IN A WELL?" • • • • • • • • • •   780 WELL AND TREE   8
       AND ALL SEEM WELL ENOUGH, • • • • • • • • •   786 YOUR HEART   15
       THE HEART WELL WORN UPON THE SLEEVE MAY BE THE BEST OF   790 HEART SLEEVE   1
          SIGHTS,
WELL-A-DAY
       AND POUR UPON THE WORLD! AH! WELL-A-DAY! • • • • •   703 MOSADA 3   118
WELL-BELOVED
       THROUGH ALL THE WELL-BELOVED GLADE. • • • • • •   67 HAPPY SHEPHERD   V 46C
       UPON A DIM, GREEN, WELL-BELOVED ISLE, • • • • • •   126 DREAM OF FAERY   V   8
       HIS WELL-BELOVED THROUGH A MORTAL'S EYES: • • • •   763 SHADOW WATER A   322
WELL-BELOVED'S
       "YOUR WELL-BELOVED'S HAIR HAS THREADS OF GREY, • • •   199 FOLLY COMFORT   2
       "YOUR WELL-BELOVED'S HAIR HAS A THREAD OF GREY, • • •   199 FOLLY COMFORT   2
WELLESLEY
       TO DOROTHY WELLESLEY • • • • • • • • • •   579 DOR WELLESLEY   T
WELL-GROOMED
       AND PEARLY WHITE HIS WELL-GROOMED HAIR. • • • • • •   3 OISIN 1   V 7CC
WELLING
       AND TELL ME HOW MY KINDRED'S TEARS ARE WELLING, • • •   33 OISIN 2   V   66
WELLKNOWN
       IN MUSCULAR YOUTH WELLKNOWN TO MAYO MEN • • • • •   324 ROBERT GREGORY   V   34
WELL-KNOWN
       THE WELL-KNOWN FACES ARE ALL GONE, • • • • • • •   132 OLD PENSIONER   V   17
WELL-NIGH
       WELL-NIGH IMMORTAL IN THIS CHARMED CLIME: • • • • •   674 ISLE STAT II 3   V 202
       AND THEN HIS HEART GREW WELL-NIGH DEAD • • • • • •   730 PRIEST FAIRY   59
WELLS
       WATCHED ME WITH MOURNFUL WONDER OUT OF THE WELLS OF HIS   51 OISIN 3   60
          EYES.
       "WHEN ALL THE WELLS ARE PARCHED AWAY? • • • • • •   396 ROSE TREE   15
WELLSIDE
       FROM WELLSIDE OR FROM PLOUGHLAND, WAS THERE NOISE; • •   279 TWO KINGS   V   53
WELL-SIDE
       FROM WELL-SIDE OR FROM PLOUGH-LAND, WAS THERE NOISE; • • 279 TWO KINGS   53
WELL-SIDES
       CABINS GONE NOW, OLD WELL-SIDES, OLD DEAR PLACES, • • •   130 BOOK STORIES   V   23
WENCH
       WHEN MOCKING MUSES CHOSE THE COUNTRY WENCH. • • • •   413 TOWER   96
       AND LOVE WENCH WISDOM'S CRUEL FACE. • • • • • • •   787 HUDDON DUDDON   10
WENCHING
       WENCHING, DRINKING, STILL REMAIN • • • • • • •   529 TOM LUNATIC   9
       THAT SEEMED BUT A WILD WENCHING MAN: • • • • • •   550 SEVERED HEAD   16
WENCH-WISDOM'S
       AND LOVE WENCH-WISDOM'S CRUEL FACE. • • • • • • •   787 HUDDON DUDDON   V   10
WEND
       AND HUMMING SANDS, WHERE WINDY SURGES WEND: • • • •   68 SAD SHEPHERD   4

	PAGE	TITLE		LINE
WENT				
WENT WE TO FIND THEIR PRINCE'S HALL-- • • • • • • •	16	OISIN 1	V	217
WE WENT A-FISHING IN LONG BOATS • • • • • • • •	23	OISIN 1		352
AND THE EARS OF THE HORSE WENT SINKING AWAY IN THE HOLLOW NIGHT,	48	OISIN 3		21
WENT THE LAUGHTER OF SCORN FROM MY MOUTH • • • • • •	58	OISIN 3		168
AND BECAUSE I WENT BY THEM SO HUGH AND SO SPEEDY WITH EYES SO BRIGHT,	59	OISIN 3		169
AND BEFORE I WENT BY THEM SO HUGE AND SO SPEEDY WITH EYES SO BRIGHT,	59	OISIN 3	V	169
AND THE DREAMS OF THE ISLANDS WENT OUT OF ME, • • • • •	59	OISIN 3	V	175
I FELL ON THE PATH, AND THE HORSE WENT AWAY LIKE A SUMMER FLY,	60	OISIN 3		190
WENT WALKING WITH SLOW STEPS ALONG THE GLEAMING • • • • •	68	SAD SHEPHERD		3
A SAD, SAD THOUGHT WENT BY ME SLOWLY! • • • • • • •	72	ANASHU VIJAYA		17
BUT FATHER JOHN WENT UP, • • • • • • • • • • •	92	FATHER OHART		9
AND FATHER JOHN WENT DOWN! • • • • • • • • • •	92	FATHER OHART		10
AS HE WENT UP AND DOWN! • • • • • • • • • • •	92	FATHER OHART		18
AND HE WENT HIS WAY WITH A FROWN. • • • • • • • •	92	FATHER OHART		20
AND WENT ON HIS WAY WITH A FROWN. • • • • • • • •	92	FATHER OHART	V	20
AND WENT HIS WAY WITH A FROWN. • • • • • • • • •	92	FATHER OHART	V	20
I WENT AWAY IN SILENCE, • • • • • • • • • • •	95	MOLL MAGEE		27
I WENT AWAY IN SILENCE! • • • • • • • • • • •	95	MOLL MAGEE		33
SEEK OUT WHAT MAN HE IS.» ONE WENT AND CAME. • • • • •	109	CUCHULAIN SEA		51
AND WENT DOWN TO THE LONG SANDS ALONE, • • • • • • •	111	CUCHULAIN SEA	V	84
AND HE WENT DOWN TO THE LONG SANDS ALONE, • • • • • •	111	CUCHULAIN SEA	V	84
THEY WENT FORTH TO THE BATTLE, BUT THEY ALWAYS FELL • • •	113	ROSE OF BATTLE	V	T
AS HE WENT BY THE SANDS OF LISADILL • • • • • • • •	127	DREAM OF FAERY	V	13
AND THE MOTH-HOUR WENT FROM THE FIELDS, • • • • • • •	133	FR GILLIGAN		15
MAY KNOW HOW MY HEART WENT WITH THEM • • • • • • •	139	TO IRELAND		47
I WENT OUT TO THE HAZEL WOOD, • • • • • • • • •	149	WANDER AENGUS		1
I WENT TO BLOW THE FIRE AFLAME, • • • • • • • • •	149	WANDER AENGUS		10
I WENT TO BLOW THE FIRE A-FLAME, • • • • • • • • •	149	WANDER AENGUS	V	10
HE LEFT THEM WHERE SHE WENT BY. • • • • • • • • •	160	CAP AND BELLS		24
A LATTICED WINDOW. HIS GLANCE WENT UP AT TIMES • • • •	180	QUEEN MAEVE		6
WHO KNOW THE WAY THAT NAOISE WENT? • • • • • • • •	193	BAILE AILLINN		96
WITH LIGHTNING, YOU WENT FROM ME, AND I COULD FIND • • •	257	RECONCILIATION		4
WHEN CUPS WENT ROUND AT CLOSE OF DAY-- • • • • • • •	271	GREY ROCK		12
AND AT THOSE WORDS I ROSE AND I WENT OUT • • • • • •	282	TWO KINGS		125
AND FOR NINE DAYS MY MIND WENT WHIRLING ROUND • • • • •	282	TWO KINGS		127
WENT OUT. AMONG THE IVY-COVERED ROCKS. • • • • • • •	283	TWO KINGS		147
WITH HIS OLD THOUGHTS, KING GUAIRE WENT • • • • • • •	296	THREE BEGGARS		26
WENT DOWN UPON A HAND AND KNEE. • • • • • • • • •	304	HOUR DAWN	V	45
"HE WENT AWAY," MY MOTHER SANG, • • • • • • • • •	308	PLAYER QUEEN		5
WHERE THE PROUD, WAYWARD SQUIRREL WENT, • • • • • • •	317	APPOINTMENT		3
THE CAT WENT HERE AND THERE • • • • • • • • • •	378	CAT AND MOON		1
A STRING OF SCHOLARS WENT IN FEAR • • • • • • • •	381	SONG OF FOOL		7
IN PAINTING OR IN POTTERY, WENT • • • • • • • • •	421	MY TABLE		18
STRAIGHTENED ALL THAT WENT AWRY • • • • • • • • •	440	WISDOM	V	4
IT COULD NOT BEAR THAT BURDEN AND THEREFORE IT WENT MAD.	449	OWEN AHERNE		4
IT FEARED THE HURT THAT SHE COULD GIVE AND THEREFORE IT WENT MAD.	450	OWEN AHERNE		8
I RAN, I RAN, FROM MY LOVE'S SIDE BECAUSE MY HEART WENT MAD.	450	OWEN AHERNE		12
THEY CAME LIKE SWALLOWS AND LIKE SWALLOWS WENT, • • • •	489	COOLE PARK 29		17
WENT IN THE DAWNING LIGHT • • • • • • • • • •	512	JANE ON GOD		3
I WENT OUT ALONE • • • • • • • • • • • • •	515	GIRLS SONG B		1
MONEY I HAD, AND IT WENT IN THE NIGHT, • • • • • • •	544	TO SAME TUNE 1		12
THEN THEY AND THEIR WISDOM WENT TO RACK! • • • • • •	566	LAPIS LAZULI		28
ROUND LOUGH DERG'S HOLY ISLAND I WENT UPON THE STONES, • •	593	PILGRIM		6
THE COLONEL WENT OUT SAILING, • • • • • • • • •	594	COLONEL MARTIN		1
HE ROSE THE LATCH AND WENT UPSTAIRS • • • • • • • •	594	COLONEL MARTIN		7
THE COLONEL WENT OUT SAILING. • • • • • • • • •	594	COLONEL MARTIN		9
THE COLONEL WENT OUT SAILING. • • • • • • • • •	594	COLONEL MARTIN		18
THE COLONEL WENT OUT SAILING. • • • • • • • • •	595	COLONEL MARTIN		27
THE COLONEL WENT OUT SAILING. • • • • • • • • •	595	COLONEL MARTIN		36
AND HE WENT IN AND SHE WENT ON • • • • • • • • •	595	COLONEL MARTIN		37
AND HE WENT IN AND SHE WENT ON • • • • • • • • •	595	COLONEL MARTIN		37
THE COLONEL WENT OUT SAILING. • • • • • • • • •	596	COLONEL MARTIN		45
THE COLONEL WENT OUT SAILING. • • • • • • • • •	596	COLONEL MARTIN		54
THE COLONEL WENT OUT SAILING. • • • • • • • • •	596	COLONEL MARTIN		63
THE COLONEL WENT OUT SAILING. • • • • • • • • •	597	COLONEL MARTIN		72
WENT TO THE SACRED HOUSE AND STOOD BETWEEN • • • • • •	609	IN TARAS HALLS		11
MONEY I HAD, AND IT WENT IN THE NIGHT, • • • • • • •	616	MARCH SONGS 3		12
THE GHOSTS WENT BY ME WITH THEIR LIPS APART • • • • •	734	QUATRAIN APHOR		13
HE, THOUGH BUT A LANDSMAN, WENT TO THE MAST-HEAD! • • •	790	DEDICATION		4
WEPT				
AND WEPT, AND RAISED THEIR LAMENTING HANDS, • • • • •	10	OISIN 1		112
THEY WEPT, AND RAISED LAMENTING HANDS. • • • • • • •	10	OISIN 1	V	112
AND THE FENIANS ALL HAD WEPT WITH ME, • • • • • • •	10	OISIN 1	V	113
AND, PATRICK! BY YOUR BEARD, THEY WEPT, • • • • • • •	17	OISIN 1		236
OH, PATRICK, BY THY BEARD, THEY WEPT, • • • • • • •	17	OISIN 1	V	236
OF WAR WERE ON IT, AND I WEPT, • • • • • • • • •	24	OISIN 1		369
LORD OF THE CROZIERS, YOU EVEN HAD LIFTED YOUR HANDS AND WEPT!	54	OISIN 3		110
LORD OF THE CROSIERS, THOU EVEN HADST LIFTED THY HANDS AND WEPT!	54	OISIN 3	V	110
ALEEL, THE SWINEHERD, WEPT AND CAST HIM DOWN • • • • •	106	CUCHULAIN SEA	V	14
FEASTED, AND WEPT THE BARROWS OF HIS DEAD! • • • • • •	170	SECRET ROSE		18
AND THOUGH THE SEVEN LIGHTS BOWED IN THEIR DANCE AND WEPT,	174	ELEMENT POWERS		3
"SHE WILL GROW OLD AND DIE, AND SHE HAS WEPT!" • • • •	186	QUEEN MAEVE		138

```
                                                          PAGE     TITLE          LINE
WEPT   (CONTINUED)
     HALF CRAZY WITH THE THOUGHT, SHE TOO HAS WEPT!  .  .  .  .  .   186 QUEEN MAEVE       140
     HE ALWAYS WEPT THEM ON THAT DAY,  .  .  .  .  .  .  .  .  .  .  192 BAILE AILLINN      78
     THAT SHE AMONG HER WINDS MIGHT KNOW HE WEPT!  .  .  .  .  .  .  220 HARP OF AENGUS     12
     THAT SHE AMONG HER WOODS MIGHT KNOW HE WEPT!  .  .  .  .  .  .  220 HARP OF AENGUS  V  12
     AND ALMOST WEPT BECAUSE THEY COULD NOT FIND IT.  .  .  .  .  .  229 SHADOW WATER B    155
     AND WEPT BECAUSE SHE HAD DREAMT THAT I  .  .  .  .  .  .  .  .  308 PLAYER QUEEN       11
     AND NOW THAT END HAS COME I HAVE NOT WEPT!  .  .  .  .  .  .  .  603 GALLERY REVIS      38
     BUT NOW THAT END HAS COME I HAVE NOT WEPT!  .  .  .  .  .  .  .  603 GALLERY REVIS   V  38
     THAT SHE AMONG HER WINDS MIGHT KNOW HE WEPT!  .  .  .  .  .  .  763 SHADOW WATER A    307
WEST
     IN THE PALE WEST, AND THE SUN'S RIM SANK,  .  .  .  .  .  .  .   12 OISIN 1          153
     HORROR FROM HORROR GREW! BUT WHEN THE WEST  .  .  .  .  .  .  .  41 OISIN 2          180
     FORMS WITHOUT NUMBER!  WHEN THE LIVE WEST FLASHED  .  .  .  .    41 OISIN 2          180
     WHEN I HAD TORN IT DOWN! BUT WHEN THE WEST  .  .  .  .  .  .  .  41 OISIN 2       V  180
     WHEN I TORE DOWN THE TREE! BUT WHEN THE WEST  .  .  .  .  .  .   41 OISIN 2       V  180
     WHEN I'D TORE DOWN THAT TREE! BUT WHEN THE WEST  .  .  .  .  .   41 OISIN 2       V  180
     WHEN I TORE DOWN THAT TREE! BUT WHEN THE WEST  .  .  .  .  .  .  41 OISIN 2       V  180
     SANG THAT SOMEWHERE TO NORTH OR WEST OR SOUTH  .  .  .  .  .    127 DREAM OF FAERY     19
     SANG HOW SOMEWHERE TO NORTH OR WEST OR SOUTH  .  .  .  .  .     127 DREAM OF FAERY  V  19
     DESOLATE WINDS THAT HOVER IN THE FLAMING WEST!  .  .  .  .  .   147 UNAPPEAS HOST       8
     I WOULD THAT THE BOAR WITHOUT BRISTLES HAD COME FROM THE       153 CHANGE BELOVED     10
        WEST
     THE WEST WEEPS IN PALE DEW AND SIGHS PASSING AWAY,  .  .  .    154 BELOVED PEACE       5
     OR ONLY TO THE WATER IN THE WEST!  .  .  .  .  .  .  .  .  .    155 REPROVE CURLEW      2
     OR ONLY TO WATERS IN THE WEST!  .  .  .  .  .  .  .  .  .  .    155 REPROVE CURLEW  V   2
     OR ONLY TO THE WATERS IN THE WEST!  .  .  .  .  .  .  .  .  .   155 REPROVE CURLEW  V   2
     THE BANNERS OF EAST AND WEST,  .  .  .  .  .  .  .  .  .  .  .  165 CRY OF SEDGE        7
     AND LIGHTS WERE PALING OUT OF THE WEST,  .  .  .  .  .  .  .    175 BELOVED DEAD        2
     AND LIGHT WERE PALING OUT OF THE WEST,  .  .  .  .  .  .  .  .  175 BELOVED DEAD    V   2
     AND SET THEM DIGGING IN THE WEST OF THE HILL.  .  .  .  .  .    184 QUEEN MAEVE     V  93
     THAT FLY INTO THE WEST? BUT LISTEN, LISTEN!  .  .  .  .  .  .   247 SHADOW WATER B    518
     WHAT IS THERE BUT THE SLOWLY FADING WEST,  .  .  .  .  .  .  .  390 IMAGE PAST         19
     THE WEST WIND MADE IT PITIFUL, AND THE NORTH WIND AFRAID.      449 OWEN AHERNE         6
     SCARCE SANK HE FROM THE WEST  .  .  .  .  .  .  .  .  .  .  .   535 CHOSEN              5
     LIBATIONS, FROM THE HUNGARY OF THE WEST.  .  .  .  .  .  .  .   709 FERENCZ RENYI       5
     MY WAY IS WEST.  SHE SEEMS BOTH YOUNG AND SHAPELY!  .  .  .    755 SHADOW WATER A    171
WESTERN
     AT EVENING IN MY WESTERN DUN."  .  .  .  .  .  .  .  .  .  .  .   8 OISIN 1           79
     AND PRAISE THEE IN MY WESTERN HALL."  .  .  .  .  .  .  .  .  .   8 OISIN 1        V  79
     WHERE THE SUN FALLS INTO THE WESTERN DEEP.  .  .  .  .  .  .   108 CUCHULAIN SEA   V  34
     .  .  .  OF THE WESTERN WORLD", [NINETEEN-SEVEN]  .  .  .  .    294 HATED PLAYBOY       T
     THE ATTACK ON "THE PLAYBOY OF THE WESTERN WORLD"  .  .  .  .    294 HATED PLAYBOY   V   T
     THAT HAVE THE FRENZY OF OUR WESTERN SEAS,  .  .  .  .  .  .  .  384 VISION ROBART      62
     ALTHOUGH THAT WESTERN CLOUD IS LUMINOUS,  .  .  .  .  .  .  .   488 COOLE PARK 29       4
WESTWARD
     I TURNED AND RODE TO THE WESTWARD, AND FOLLOWED THE SEA'S       60 OISIN 3          183
        OLD SHOUT
     FLEW WESTWARD! AND MANY A TIME SINCE THEN  .  .  .  .  .  .  .  223 SHADOW WATER B     27
     WESTWARD OF TARA.  HURRYING TO HIS QUEEN  .  .  .  .  .  .  .   276 TWO KINGS           2
     WESTWARD OF TARA.  WHERE IN THE MIDDLE WOOD  .  .  .  .  .  .   277 TWO KINGS       V   4
     WESTWARD OF TARA, AMONG THE HAZEL-TREES—  .  .  .  .  .  .  .   283 TWO KINGS         135
     WESTWARD OF TARA, AMONG THE HAZEL TREES—  .  .  .  .  .  .  .   283 TWO KINGS       V 135
     WESTWARD OF TARA, THERE TO AWAIT A FRIEND  .  .  .  .  .  .  .  283 TWO KINGS       V 136
WET     SEE FOAM-WET
     TO THIS DIM SHORE ON FOAM WET FEET?  .  .  .  .  .  .  .  .  .    5 OISIN 1        V  51
     FOR LOVE OF OISIN FOAM WET FEET  .  .  .  .  .  .  .  .  .  .     6 OISIN 1        V  57
     AND SHORES THE FROTH LIPS WET!  .  .  .  .  .  .  .  .  .  .  .   33 OISIN 2           59
     OR WEEDING OR PLOUGHING WITH FACES A-SHINING WITH MUCH-TOIL     58 OISIN 3          165
        WET!
     AND YELLOW THE WET WILD-STRAWBERRY LEAVES.  .  .  .  .  .  .     79 FALLING LEAVES      4
     THE THRONGS WITH BLOWN WET HAIR ARE GATHERING NEAR.  .  .  .    114 ROSE OF BATTLE  V   6
     THE COLD WET WINDS EVER BLOWING,  .  .  .  .  .  .  .  .  .  .   119 PITY OF LOVE        5
     AND THE COLD WET WINDS EVER BLOWING,  .  .  .  .  .  .  .  .  .  119 PITY OF LOVE    V   7
     FOR THE WET WINDS ARE BLOWING OUT OF THE CLINGING AIR!  .  .    207 HANRAHANS SONG     12
     ON WET ROADS WHERE MEN WALK,  .  .  .  .  .  .  .  .  .  .  .    215 HAPPY TOWNLAND     48
     "THOUGH TO MY FEATHERS IN THE WET,  .  .  .  .  .  .  .  .  .    294 THREE BEGGARS       1
     "THOUGH TO MY FEATHERS IN THE WET  .  .  .  .  .  .  .  .  .  .  297 THREE BEGGARS      63
     AMID WET ROCKS AND HEATHER,  .  .  .  .  .  .  .  .  .  .  .  .  311 PEACOCK             8
     BETWEEN ROCK AND WET HEATHER,  .  .  .  .  .  .  .  .  .  .  .   311 PEACOCK         V   8
     THAT THE SALT DROPS HAVE WET!  .  .  .  .  .  .  .  .  .  .  .   312 CHILD DANCING       5
     SHALL WALK THE WET SANDS BY THE EDGE OF THE STREAM  .  .  .     371 EGO DOMINUS        71
     SHALL WALK THE WET SAND BY THE WATER'S EDGE,  .  .  .  .  .  .  371 EGO DOMINUS     V  71
     HARDLY DARED TO WET HIS MOUTH  .  .  .  .  .  .  .  .  .  .  .   454 EMPTY CUP           3
     THEIR SHROUDS ARE BLOODY AND THEIR LIPS ARE WET.  .  .  .  .    483 OIL AND BLOOD       6
     I HAVE WET THIS BRAID OF HAIR WITH TEARS WHILE ASLEEP.  .  .    762 SHADOW WATER A    294
WHARF
     BESIDE A LOCHLANN WHARF, AND THOUGH SHE HAD SWORN  .  .  .      756 SHADOW WATER A    188
WHARVES
     UPON THE WHARVES OF SORROW, AND HEARD RING  .  .  .  .  .  .    115 ROSE OF BATTLE     27
WHEAT
     WAS ROBBED BEFORE EARTH GAVE THE WHEAT!  .  .  .  .  .  .  .    196 BAILE AILLINN     166
     BECAUSE OF SOME GREEN WING, GATHERED OLD MUMMY WHEAT  .  .      442 BLACK CENTAUR       7
     WHAT A CROP OF MUMMY WHEAT!  .  .  .  .  .  .  .  .  .  .  .  .  562 CONJUNCTIONS        2
     AND HIS HAIR WAS AS YELLOW AS WAVING WHEAT.  .  .  .  .  .  .   729 PRIEST FAIRY       26
     AND WHEAT IN THE WHEAT-EAR WITHERED,  .  .  .  .  .  .  .  .  .  783 GREY ROUND         19
WHEAT-EAR
     AND WHEAT IN THE WHEAT-EAR WITHERED,  .  .  .  .  .  .  .  .  .  783 GREY ROUND         19
WHEATEN
     OR MICE IN THE ONE WHEATEN SHEAF  .  .  .  .  .  .  .  .  .  .   195 BAILE AILLINN     147
```

		PAGE	TITLE		LINE

WHEEL   SEE WAGON-WHEEL
ROLLING HIS FLAGRANT WHEEL OUT OF THE DEEP, ... 42 OISIN 2   193
ROLLING HIS WHEEL, WE SANG BESIDE THE DEEP . . . . . . 42 OISIN 2   V 193
AND NOW THEY ALL WHEEL SUDDENLY AND FLY . . . . . . 234 SHADOW WATER B 258
. . . I.   THE WHEEL AND THE PHASES OF THE MOON . . . . 372 PHASES OF MOON V T
OUT OF THE UP AND DOWN, THE WAGON WHEEL . . . . . . 377 PHASES OF MOON V 120
THE WHEEL . . . . 434 WHEEL   T
A RUSH, A SUDDEN WHEEL, AND HOVERING STILL . . . . 441 LEDA AND SWAN V 1
I'VE LED THEE HERE, AND AS A WHEEL . . . . 667 ISLE STAT II 3 39
FLIETH FORTUNE'S FURIOUS WHEEL. . . . . 737 IN FIRELIGHT   8
AND NOW THEY ALL WHEEL SUDDENLY AND FLY . . . . . 753 SHADOW WATER A 148
AT THE BURNING WHEEL OF LOVE . . . . 776 AGAINST WITCH   34
TO GARRET OR CELLAR A WHEEL I SEND, ... 787 GARRET CELLAR   1
WHEELED
THE FIRST THIN CRESCENT IS WHEELED ROUND ONCE MORE. . . . 377 PHASES OF MOON 116
WHEELING
AND SCATTER WHEELING IN GREAT BROKEN RINGS . . . . . 322 SWANS AT COOLE   11
WHEELS   SEE CHARIOT-WHEELS
AND PACE THE WOODS, AND DRIVE MY CHARIOT WHEELS . . . 103 FERGUS DRUID   V 18
WHEELS BY MILK-WHITE ASSES DRAWN . . . . 502 VACILLATION   62
THAT ON TWO WHEELS RAN . . . . 628 JANE MOUNTAIN   14
WHENCE
WHENCE TURBULENT ITALY SHOULD DRAW . . . . 288 TO WEALTHY MAN   25
BUT MINE SAW STELLA ONCE. WHENCE CAME OUR THOUGHT? . . 486 SEVEN SAGES   6
MINE SAW STELLA ONCE. WHENCE CAME OUR THOUGHT? . . . 486 SEVEN SAGES   V 6
WHENCE HAD THEY COME? . . . . 560 WHENCE COME   T
WHAT MASTER MADE THE LASH. WHENCE HAD THEY COME, . . 560 WHENCE COME   9
WHENCE DID ALL THAT FURY COME? . . . . 619 STICK INCENSE   1
BUT WHENCE, AND WHEN? OVER THE WILLOWS SERE . . . 652 ISLE STAT I 2   28
YES, ALL IS VERY WELL. WHENCE COMEST THOU? . . . . 682 SEEKER   14
WHEREAS
THOUGH HE'D BUT CANNON--WHEREAS WE THAT HAD THOUGHT . . 258 KING NO KING   7
WHEREAT
WHEREAT THE LIVING MOCK, ... 474 ALL SOUL NIGHT   87
WHEREBY
WHEREBY THE HAYSTACK- AND ROOF-LEVELLING WIND, . . . 403 FOR DAUGHTER   5
WHEREBY THE HORN OF PLENTY IS UNDONE. . . . . . . 404 FOR DAUGHTER   32
THAT WHEREBY A HOUSE LAY WRECKED? . . . . 632 MAN AND ECHO   16
THAT WHEREBY A HOUSE WAS WRECKED? . . . . 632 MAN AND ECHO   V 16
NAMES WHEREBY A MAN HAS KNOWN . . . . 775 AGAINST WITCH   5
WHEREFORE
BUT WHEREFORE NOW?" "THERE IS A MAN TO DIE! . . . 107 CUCHULAIN SEA   23
AH, WHEREFORE MURMUR YE . . . . 131 OLD PENSIONER V 14
WHEREFORE I THREW A PENNY . . . . 268 BROWN PENNY   3
NASCHINA, WHEREFORE ARE YOUR EYES SO BRIGHT . . . 650 ISLE STAT I 1   141
AND WHEREFORE HAVE WE COME? A SONG TO HEAR. . . . 652 ISLE STAT I 2   27
AND WHEREFORE, THEN, SHOULD THY GREY EYES . . . . 686 LIFE   7
AND WHEREFORE SHOULD THY BRIGHT BROW ROAM . . . 686 LIFE   11
"WATCHER, WHEREFORE HAVE YE CALLED US?" EYES GO AFTER 718 PHANTOM SHIP   10
    HIS LEAN HAND,
NOW WHEREFORE HAST THOU TEARS INNUMEROUS? . . . . 723 KANVA ON SELF   1
THEN WHEREFORE FEAR THE USURY OF TIME, ... 724 KANVA ON SELF   17
I HAVE FORGOTTEN WHEREFORE. THE RED HOUND . . . 747 SHADOW WATER A   8
AND NONE KNOWS WHEREFORE! BUT THE HEART'S DESIRE . . 764 SHADOW WATER A 340
WHEREIN
WHEREIN THE GAZING HEART DOUBLES HER MIGHT. . . . . 326 ROBERT GREGORY 69
WHEREOF
AND THINE OWN SADNESS, WHEREOF STARS, GROWN OLD . . 101 ROSE UPON ROOD   6
ALL THOSE THINGS WHEREOF . . . . 415 TOWER   163
YONDER'S THE ISLE IN SEARCH WHEREOF WE CAME! . . . 662 ISLE STAT II 2 13
WHEREON
WHEREON I WROTE AND WROUGHT, ... 255 WOMAN HOMER   8
WHEREON MAD FINGERS PLAY . . . . 291 TO A FRIEND   12
WHEREON A THING ONCE WALKED THAT SEEMED A BURNING CLOUD. 315 FALLEN MAJESTY   8
WHEREON 'TWERE BEST . . . . 389 IMAGE PAST   17
WITH ALL THOSE CALENDARS WHEREON . . . . 432 NINETEEN 19   99
WHEREON THE BLEAK NORTH BLOWS, ... 454 HIS MEMORIES   4
A SPOT WHEREON THE FOUNDERS LIVED AND DIED . . . 491 COOLE BALLYLEE 33
WHERETHROUGH
WHERETHROUGH A HUNDRED HORSEMEN ON THE FLOOR . . . 36 OISIN 2   V 102
WHIG
BURKE WAS A WHIG. WHETHER THEY KNEW OR NOT, . . . 486 SEVEN SAGES   8
WHIGGERY
FROM FOUR GREAT MINDS THAT HATED WHIGGERY. . . . 486 SEVEN SAGES   7
ALL HATED WHIGGERY! BUT WHAT IS WHIGGERY? . . . . 486 SEVEN SAGES   10
ALL HATED WHIGGERY! BUT WHAT IS WHIGGERY? . . . . 486 SEVEN SAGES   10
OR OUT OF DRUNKARD'S EYE. ALL'S WHIGGERY NOW, . . 486 SEVEN SAGES   13
OR DRUNKARD'S EYE. ALL'S WHIGGERY NOW, ... 486 SEVEN SAGES   V 13
OR OUT OF A DRUNKARD'S EYE. ALL'S WHIGGERY NOW, . . 486 SEVEN SAGES   V 13
WHILE
WHILE A HUNDRED YOUTHS, MIGHTY OF LIMB, ... 8 OISIN 1   94
WHILE ROUND THE SHORE A MILLION STOOD . . . . . 14 OISIN 1   182
TOGETHER, WHILE THE DARK WOODS RANG, ... 16 OISIN 1   227
AND WHILE THEY SANG, A SINGER LAID . . . . . . 16 OISIN 1   V 231
WHILE HIS HEART STILL DREAMS OF BATTLE AND LOVE . . 27 OISIN 1   406
AND STAY A LITTLE WHILE, AND BID THEM WEEP! . . . 33 OISIN 2   60
BUT FLY WHILE STILL YOU MAY." AND THEREON I! . . . 35 OISIN 2   89
LONG WHILE, ARE WHIPS OF STEEL." "IS HE SO DREAD?" . 35 OISIN 2   88
BUT FLEE WHILE YOU STILL MAY." THEN I! . . . . 35 OISIN 2   V 89
BUT FLEE WHILE YOU MAY FLEE FROM HIM." THEN I! . . 35 OISIN 2   V 89
SHOWED PRINTS OF SEA-BORN SCALES, WHILE DOWN THROUGH IT 37 OISIN 2   115

                                          PAGE   TITLE   LINE

WHILE   (CONTINUED)
    WHILE HIGH FRAIL CLOUDLETS, FED WITH A GREEN LIGHT, . . .   40 OISIN 2   165
    OF SWORD AND BRAZEN BATTLE-AXE, WHILE DAY . . . . . .   40 OISIN 2   171
    MINGLING OF SWORD AND WAR-AXE, WHILE THE DAY . . . .   40 OISIN 2   V   171
    WHILE THE WOOD-PECKER MADE A MERRY DIN, ...   44 OISIN 2   V   228
    AND DRIFTING GREYNESS, WHILE THIS MONOTONE, ...   45 OISIN 2   232
    WHILE IN THIS PLACE AND THAT PLACE, ...   58 OISIN 3   166
    THY FRETFUL WORDS A LITTLE WHILE, ...   66 HAPPY SHEPHERD   40
    WHILE WE ALONE HAVE ROUND US WOVEN WOODS, ...   73 ANASHU VIJAYA   56
    AMRITA, WHILE--AH ME! YOU LOVE ANOTHER, ...   74 ANASHU VIJAYA   58
    WHILE OUR LOVE GROWS AN INDIAN STAR, ...   78 INDIAN TO LOVE   13
    WHILE GROWS OUR LOVE AN INDIAN STAR, ...   78 INDIAN TO LOVE V   13
    WHILE SLOWLY HE WHOSE HAND HELD HERS REPLIED! . . .   80 EPHEMERA   11
    WHILE SLOWLY ANSWERED HE WHOSE HAND HELD HERS-- . .   80 EPHEMERA   V   11
    WHILE HE BENT DOWN HIS FADING HEAD, ...   82 MAD KING GOLL   10
    ONCE, WHILE WITHIN A LITTLE TOWN . . . .   85 MAD KING GOLL   V   49
    WHILE THE WORLD IS FULL OF TROUBLES . . . .   87 STOLEN CHILD   22
    COME NEAR ME, WHILE I SING THE ANCIENT WAYS! . . .   100 ROSE UPON ROOD   2
    "YOUR HEAD A WHILE SEEMED LIKE A WOMAN'S HEAD . . .   110 CUCHULAIN SEA   63
    WHILE DAY ITS BURDEN ON TO EVENING BORE, ...   110 CUCHULAIN SEA   70
    WHILE HUSHED FROM FEAR, OR LOUD WITH HOPE, A BAND .   114 ROSE OF BATTLE   5
    WHILE I STAND ON THE ROADWAY, OR ON THE PAVEMENTS GREY, 117 ISLE INNISFREE   11
    WHILE I STAND ON THE ROADWAY, OR ON THE PAVEMENT GREY, . 117 ISLE INNISFREE   11
    WHILE YOUNG STARS ABOUT HER DANCE. . . . .   125 CATHLEEN PARA   V   16
    BUT WHILE HE PASSED BEFORE A PLASHY PLACE, ...   127 DREAM OF FAERY   17
    AND ALL GREW FRIENDLY FOR A LITTLE WHILE. . . . .   129 BOOK STORIES   8
    FOR ALL WHO HEARD IT DREAMED A LITTLE WHILE. . . .   129 BOOK STORIES   V   8
    AND ALL WHO HEARD GREW FRIENDLY FOR A WHILE. . . .   129 BOOK STORIES   V   8
    ONCE, WHILE HE NODDED ON A CHAIR, ...   132 FR GILLIGAN   5
    WHILE I SLEPT ON THE CHAIR"! . . . .   133 FR GILLIGAN   26
    OR ONLY GAZE A LITTLE WHILE! . . . .   135 TWO TREES   24
    WHILE I WROUGHT OUT THESE FITFUL DANAAN RHYMES, . .   136 TO SOME I TALK   1
    WHILE THE NIGHT GREW, ABOVE THE FADING COALS, . . .   136 TO SOME I TALK V   3
    WHILE STILL I MAY, I WRITE FOR YOU . . . .   139 TO IRELAND   33
    WHILE STILL I MAY I WRITE OUT TRUE . . . .   139 TO IRELAND   V   33
    HE HEARD WHILE HE SANG AND DREAMED . . . .   144 HOST OF AIR   9
    WHILE THE YOUNG LIE LONG AND DREAM IN THEIR BED . .   150 OLD MOTHER   V   5
    WHILE I MUST WORK BECAUSE I AM OLD, ...   151 OLD MOTHER   9
    WHILE TIME AND THE WORLD ARE EBBING AWAY . . . . .   168 BLESSED   39
    WHILE LIGHTS WERE PALING ONE BY ONE. . . . .   176 BELOVED DEAD   13
    WHILE BIRDS GREW SILENT ONE BY ONE. . . . .   176 BELOVED DEAD   V   13
    WE SHADOWS, WHILE THEY UPROOT HIS EARTHY HOUSE, . .   184 QUEEN MAEVE   94
    WE SHADOWS, WHILE THEY UPROOT THE EARTHY HOUSE . .   184 QUEEN MAEVE   V   94
    WHILE OVER THEM BIRDS OF AENGUS FLY, ...   197 BAILE AILLINN   182
    AMONG PIGEONS AND BEES, WHILE THAT GREAT ARCHER, .   198 SEVEN WOODS   12
    WHERE ONE FOUND LANCELOT CRAZED AND HID HIM FOR A WHILE! 209 UNDER THE MOON   3
    TO TAKE HIM WHILE HE SLEEPS AND CARRY HIM . . . .   222 SHADOW WATER B   14
    TO MAKE AN END WHILE HE IS SLEEPING THERE. . . . .   222 SHADOW WATER B V   14
    WHILE I WAS LOOKING THEY ROSE HURRIEDLY, ...   223 SHADOW WATER B   25
    THE OTHER NIGHT, WHILE HE WAS PLAYING IT, ...   223 SHADOW WATER B   32
    I'D DROWN HIM WHILE WE HAVE THE CHANCE TO DO IT. .   224 SHADOW WATER B   58
    I'D KILL HIM WHILE WE HAVE THE CHANCE TO DO IT. .   224 SHADOW WATER B V   58
    TO MAKE AN END OF FORGAEL WHILE HE SLEEPS. . . . .   225 SHADOW WATER B   65
    THIS LONG WHILE NOW! WE HAD NOT TURNED AGAINST HIM .   225 SHADOW WATER B V 68B
    AND LISTEN TO ME FOR A WHILE. THE SAILORS . . . .   226 SHADOW WATER B   92
    AND NOW THEY WILL NOT FOLLOW, WHILE I SEEK . . . .   226 SHADOW WATER B   95
    NOT IN ITS IMAGE ON THE MIRROR! WHILE . . . . . .   230 SHADOW WATER B   189
    TO MAKE HER FAST WHILE WE ARE PLUNDERING HER. . .   232 SHADOW WATER B   225
    AND OVERPOWER THE CREW WHILE YET ASLEEP! . . . . .   233 SHADOW WATER B   240
    WHILE THERE'S A ROPE TO RUN INTO A NOOSE . . . . .   238 SHADOW WATER B   347
    I KNEW HIM WELL, AND WHILE I HEARD HIM LAUGHING . .   242 SHADOW WATER B   419
    I HAD THIS THOUGHT A WHILE AGO, ...   255 WORDS   1
    AND WHILE WE'RE IN OUR LAUGHING, WEEPING FIT, . . .   257 RECONCILIATION   9
    WHILE THOSE SAME HUNDREDS MOCK ANOTHER DAY . . . .   265 ABBEY THEATRE   4
    AND WHERE THE STONE STRUCK FIRE, WHILE IN THE LEAVES   278 TWO KINGS   33
    "WHILE I HAVE HIM AND YOU IT MATTERS LITTLE . . . .   280 TWO KINGS   85
    WHILE THAT GREAT JUAN GALLOPED BY! . . . .   294 HATED PLAYBOY   V   4
    WHILE HE'D RUMMAGED RAGS AND HAIR, ...   299 THREE HERMITS   29
    WHILE I MUST HURRY UPON MY WAY, ...   301 RUN PARADISE   23
    WHILE I AM RUNNING TO PARADISE. . . . .   301 RUN PARADISE   V REF
    TO KEEP HIM UPRIGHT WHILE HE CURSED. . . . .   302 HOUR DAWN   6
    BUT WHILE HE FUMBLED WITH THE STONES . . . .   302 HOUR DAWN   16
    AND ALL THE WHILE HER NEEDLE PULLED . . . .   308 PLAYER QUEEN   7
    WHILE UP FROM MY HEART'S ROOT . . . .   316 FRIENDS   26
    WHILE I, FROM THAT REED-THROATED WHISPERER . . . .   320 REED WHISPERER   1
    --SEEING THAT FAME HAS PERISHED THIS LONG WHILE, . .   321 REED WHISPERER   11
    TO CHANGE MY LOVES WHILE DANCING . . . .   330 BONE OF A HARE   7
    AND RUNS OR A WHILE HALF-FLIES . . . .   341 SHEP GOATHERD   64
    HE STAYED FOR A WHILE! AND WE . . . .   341 SHEP GOATHERD   66
    AND RUNS FOR A WHILE OR A WHILE HALF-FLIES . . . .   341 SHEP GOATHERD   V   64
    AND RUNS FOR A WHILE OR A WHILE HALF-FLIES . . . .   341 SHEP GOATHERD   V   64
    WHILE TALKING WITH HIS QUEENS, ...   345 ON WOMAN   12
    WHILE WONDERING STILL TO BE A SHADE, WITH GRANIA'S SHADE, 366 HER COURAGE   V   4
    THE SENTIMENTALIST HIMSELF! WHILE ART . . . . . .   369 EGO DOMINICUS   47
    BUT WHILE THE MOON IS ROUNDING TOWARDS THE FULL . .   373 PHASES OF MOON   39
    WHILE MICHAEL ANGELO'S SISTINE ROOF, ...   386 ROBARTES DANCE   32
    THAT WOMAN A WHILE WOULD BE SHRILL . . . .   392 EASTER 1916   V   17
    WHILE THOSE DEAD MEN ARE LOITERING THERE . . . . .   395 SIXTEEN DEAD   5
    WHILE UNDER ITS STORM-BEATEN BREAST . . . .   397 POLIT PRISONER   23
    THE BEST LACK ALL CONVICTION, WHILE THE WORST . . .   402 SECOND COMING   7
    IS MOVING ITS SLOW THIGHS, WHILE ALL ABOUT IT . . .   402 SECOND COMING   16

```
                                                          PAGE    TITLE           LINE
WHILE  (CONTINUED)
    THE BEST LACK CONVICTION, WHILE THE WORST  . . . .     402  SECOND COMING   V    7
    WHILE THAT GREAT QUEEN, THAT ROSE OUT OF THE SPRAY, .  404  FOR DAUGHTER        27
    WHILE ON THAT OLD GREY STONE I SAT  . . . . . . .      406  IN TIME OF WAR       2
    WHILE THEIR GREAT WOODEN DICE BEAT ON THE BOARD. . .   412  TOWER               88
    SEEMED FOR A WHILE TO HAVE GROWN YOUNG AGAIN! . . .    462  HARUN RASHID        36
    WHILE OUR GROSS PALATES DRINK FROM THE WHOLE WINE, .   471  ALL SOUL NIGHT      10
    WHILE ON THE SHOP AND STREET I GAZED  . . . . . .      501  VACILLATION         40
    AND MY BLOOD BE COLD THE WHILE . . . . . . . . .       532  BEFORE WORLD        11
    BUT STRETCH THAT BODY FOR A WHILE . . . . . . . .      534  CONSOLATION          3
    WHILE NIGHT SHUTS THE EYES . . . . . . . . . . .       535  PARTING              2
    WHILE HIS LOUD SONG REPROVES . . . . . . . . . .       536  PARTING              7
    STAND UPRIGHT WHILE YOU CAN, . . . . . . . . . .       586  PARNELLITES          4
    WHILE MAN CAN STILL HIS BODY KEEP . . . . . . . .      633  MAN AND ECHO        25
    WHILE THE WORLD IS ROLL'D IN LIGHT. . . . . . . .      646  ISLE STAT I 1       29
    OF SWORD-BLUE WAVES OF CALM: WHILE O'ER HEAD BLINK .   663  ISLE STAT II 2      42
    SO BE THOU STILL, DEAR HEART, A LITTLE WHILE! . . .    677  ISLE STAT II 3     283
    THE YEARS OF GOBLIN SLEEP.  AH! WHILE I SLUMBERED, .   679  ISLE STAT II 3     308
    A LITTLE WHILE AND--RED EVE DIES-- . . . . . . .       686  LIFE                13
    AND, WHILE THEY GATHER ROUND MY BECKONING ARMS, . .    694  MOSADA 1           100
    WHILE O'ER THE BUDS, AND O'ER THE GRASS-BLADES, BRIGHT 704  REMEMBRANCE          3
    REMEMBERING THEE, I MUSE, WHILE FADES IN FLIGHT . .    705  REMEMBRANCE          6
    WHILE THE MORNING STAR DECAYETH . . . . . . . .        706  DAWN-SONG           29
    COME AWAY WHILE THE MOON'S IN THE WOODLAND, . . . .    707  FAIRY PEDANT         9
    WHILE I MURMUR A LITTLE AND PONDER . . . . . . .       707  FAIRY PEDANT        14
    COME AWAY WHILE THE MOON'S IN THE WOODLAND, . . . .    708  FAIRY PEDANT        37
    HANG THE MIST-THREADS FOR A LITTLE WHILE LIKE COBWEBS IN
        THE AIR:                                           719  PHANTOM SHIP        29
    HANG THE MIST THREADS FOR A LITTLE WHILE LIKE COBWEBS IN
        THE AIR,                                           719  PHANTOM SHIP    V   29
    WHILE WE SHAKE OUR HEADS AND SCOLD . . . . . . .       727  LOVERS QUARREL      54
    FOR WHILE I BLAMED THEM I COULD HEAR . . . . . .       743  DANAAN QUICK        27
    BE PATIENT YET A WHILE: FOR THIS NINTH MOON, . . .     748  SHADOW WATER A      23
    SO THESE WOULD HAVE KILLED FORGAEL WHILE ASLEEP . .    748  SHADOW WATER A      25
    BUT WILL IT HOLD WHILE WE ARE EMPTYING HER? . . . .    754  SHADOW WATER A     156
    WHILE THE WIND IS LIGHT.  THE OAR CAN HARDLY MOVE HER, 754  SHADOW WATER A     157
    I LINGER WHILE THE BIRDS ARE ON THE WING, . . . .      754  SHADOW WATER A  V  157
    I SHALL BE HOME NOW IN A LITTLE WHILE, . . . . .       759  SHADOW WATER A     240
    SHE WILL SAY SOMETHING IN A LITTLE WHILE. . . . .      760  SHADOW WATER A     248
    AND TELL ME A LOVE-STORY WHILE I DRINK. . . . . .      760  SHADOW WATER A     250
    AND TELL ME A LOVE STORY WHILE I DRINK. . . . . .      760  SHADOW WATER A  V  250
    I HAVE WET THIS BRAID OF HAIR WITH TEARS WHILE ASLEEP. 762  SHADOW WATER A     294
    AND WHILE SHE FADES AND LIFE WITHERS AWAY, . . . .     768  SHADOW WATER A     422
    WHILE THEY MURMUR, "AFTER THIS . . . . . . . .         776  AGAINST WITCH       30
WHIM
    SHALL FOLLOW YOUR HORN AND OBEY YOUR WHIM, . . . .       9  OISIN 1            99
    WOULD NOURISH HIS WHIM. . . . . . . . . . . . .        310  PEACOCK              6
    IT IS MY WHIM! BID SOME ATTENDANT SPRITE . . . .       669  ISLE STAT II 3      72
    BUT WHY THIS WHIM OF THINE?  A STRANGE UNREST, . .     671  ISLE STAT II 3     137
    BELOVED, BLAME THE DANAAN WHIM, . . . . . . . .        743  DANAAN QUICK        22
    THOUGH THE CHANGE WERE BUT A WHIM; . . . . . . .       775  AGAINST WITCH       17
    THOUGH THEIR CHANGE WERE BUT A WHIM; . . . . . .       775  AGAINST WITCH   V   17
WHIMPERING
    AND LIONESS, WITH ALL THEIR WHIMPERING CUBS: . . .     73  ANASHU VIJAYA       53
    WITH THE WHIMPERING DEAD. . . . . . . . . . . .        118  CRADLE SONG          4
    THE DOORS OF HELL AND BLOW THERE MANY A WHIMPERING GHOST! 147 UNAPPEAS HOST     10
    AMONG THE WHIMPERING GHOSTS. MATE THUS.  ALREADY? . .  722  WITCH VIVIEN        68
WHIM'S
    HE FOLLOWS WHATEVER WHIM'S MOST DIFFICULT . . . . .    374  PHASES OF MOON      40
WHIMS
    AMONG WHIMS NOT IMPOSSIBLE, AND THOUGH SCARRED, . .    374  PHASES OF MOON      41
WHIMSEY
    AND LAUGH OUT THEIR WHIMSEY AND WORK OUT THEIR WILL. . 148  INTO TWILIGHT   V   12
    LAUGH OUT THEIR WHIMSEY AND WORK OUT THEIR WILL. . . . 148  INTO TWILIGHT   V   12
WHINNIED
    A SQUIRREL WHINNIED AND A BIRD SCREAMED OUT: . . . .   278  TWO KINGS           34
WHINNY
    TILL THE HORSE GAVE A WHINNY: . . . . . . . . .        48  OISIN 3             25
WHINNYING
    AND HE, WITH THAT LOW WHINNYING SOUND . . . . . .      318  APPOINTMENT          5
WHIP
    WHERE THE DEMONS WHIP THEM WITH WIRES . . .            61  OISIN 3            198
    OR FROM SOME BLOODY WHIP IN THEIR OWN HANDS. . . . .   375  PHASES OF MOON      68
WHIPS
    LONG WHILE, ARE WHIPS OF STEEL."  "IS HE SO DREAD?" .   35  OISIN 2         V   88
    WHIPS TO THE SEA THE COWS AND SWINE." . . . . . .      82  MAD KING GOLL   V   16
WHIRL      SEE DUST-WHIRL
    THE WINDS AWAKEN, THE LEAVES WHIRL ROUND, . . . .     140  HOSTING SIDHE        6
    THAT SEEMED TO WHIRL UPON A COMPASS-POINT, . . . .    489  COOLE PARK 29       21
    THAT SEEMED TO WHIRL UPON A COMPASS POINT, . . . .    489  COOLE PARK 29   V   21
    THE SPINNING STARS--THE TOILING SEA--WHIRL ROUND . .  665  ISLE STAT II 2      72
WHIRL'D
    THE VISION OF A ROCK WHERE LIGHTNINGS WHIRL'D . . .   687  TWO TITANS           1
WHIRLED
    IN DREARY DANCING PAST US WHIRLED, . . . . . . .      65  HAPPY SHEPHERD       8
    HAD FALLEN AMONG DANCERS, HAD WHIRLED THEM ROUND . .  430  NINETEEN 19         52
    ON THE SOUL'S JOURNEY.  HOW IT IS WHIRLED ABOUT, . .  472  ALL SOUL NIGHT      54
WHIRLING
    AND THEN AWAY, AWAY, LIKE WHIRLING FLAMES: . . . .     29  OISIN 2              2
    AND THICKENED ALL THE WHIRLING AIR.  THEN DID . . .    46  OISIN 2         V 245A
    THE WHIRLING WAYS OF STARS THAT PASS-- . . . . .       66  HAPPY SHEPHERD      30
```

WHIRLING   (CONTINUED)
  WITH ALL YOUR WHIRLING HAIR, AND DROP MANY AN AZURE TEAR.   73 ANASHU VIJAYA   46
  WITH ALL YOUR WHIRLING HAIR, AND DROP THROUGH SPACE AN   73 ANASHU VIJAYA   V   46
    AZURE TEAR.
  WITH ALL YOUR WHIRLING HAIR, AND DROP TEAR UPON AZURE TEAR.   73 ANASHU VIJAYA   V   46
  WITH ALL OUR WHIRLING HAIR, AND DROP MANY AN AZURE TEAR.   73 ANASHU VIJAYA   V   46
  A WHIRLING AND A WANDERING FIRE!   . . . .   83 MAD KING GOLL   28
  A FEVER AND A WHIRLING FIRE!   . . . .   83 MAD KING GOLL   28
  THE WHIRLING AND THE WANDERING FIRE!   . . . .   86 MAD KING GOLL   67
  OUT OF THEIR WHIRLING CARS, ...   175 ELEMENT POWERS   V   16
  WITH EQUAL COURAGE IN THAT WHIRLING ROUT!   . . . . .   186 QUEEN MAEVE   131
  AND FOR NINE DAYS MY MIND WENT WHIRLING ROUND . . . .   282 TWO KINGS   127
  DANCED IN THE WHIRLING FOAM AND IN THE DUST, ...   284 TWO KINGS   167
  THAT HAS GROWN WEARY OF THE WHIRLING DANCE. . . . .   285 TWO KINGS   V   183
  AND THEY WERE WHIRLING IN A HEAP. . . . .   297 THREE BEGGARS   47
  TILL THEY WERE WHIRLING IN A HEAP. . . . .   297 THREE BEGGARS   V   47
  WHAT SET IT WHIRLING ROUND? . . . .   520 HIS BARGAIN   2
  OF THE WHIRLING ZODIAC. . . . .   535 CHOSEN   3
  EACH ONE AT GAZE FOR AYE UPON HIS WHIRLING THRONE. . .   662 ISLE STAT II 1   81
  FOR THEY ARE BUT WHIRLING WIND, ...   775 AGAINST WITCH   9
WHIRLS
  AMONG HER WILDERING WHIRLS, FORGETTING HIM. . . . .   69 SAD SHEPHERD   28
  WITHIN HER WILDERING WHIRLS--FORGETTING HIM. . . . .   69 SAD SHEPHERD   V   28
  IT WHIRLS INTO THE FOAM. O ANCIENT WORM. . . . . .   251 SHADOW WATER B   597
  WHIRLS OUT NEW RIGHT AND WRONG, ...   430 NINETEEN 19   55
  WHIRLS IN THE OLD INSTEAD! . . . .   430 NINETEEN 19   56
WHIRLWIND
  THE DARKNESS OF THE WHIRLWIND SHATTERED DEEP. . . . .   688 TWO TITANS   58
WHIRR
  AND WINDS BLOWING FROM FLOWERS, AND WHIRR OF FEATHERS . .   219 WOODS OF COOLE   39
WHISPER
  A WHISPER OF IMPETUOUS FEET, ...   15 OISIN 1   199
  ERE LONG AN ANSWERING WHISPER FLEW, ...   15 OISIN 1   V   197
  AND THEN AN ANSWERING WHISPER FLEW . . . .   15 OISIN 1   V   197
  GROWN DESOLATE, WHISPER AND SIGH TO EACH OTHER! . . .   26 OISIN 1   403
  GROWN DESOLATE, WHISPER AND SIGH TO EACH OTHER. . . .   27 OISIN 1   V   407
  AND WHISPER, "THE INNUMERABLE REEDS . . . .   81 EPHEMERA   V 24E
  ALL THAT I SEEK: AND WHISPER IT AS THOUGH . . . . .   371 EGO DOMINUS   76
  FOR SPRING RICE HAD TO WHISPER IT, ...   582 ROGER CASEMENT   13
  OR WHISPER THAT A MAN'S A FOOL . . . .   635 BLACK TOWER   12
  WHO WANDER AND WHISPER ALONE. . . . .   707 FAIRY PEDANT   8
  WHISPER LEST WE TOO MAY SADDEN, ...   737 IN FIRELIGHT   5
  THE HANDMAIDS LAUGH AND WHISPER IN THE DOOR. . . . .   759 SHADOW WATER A   242
WHISPERED
  WHISPERED TO THE SEA WHOSE FLOW . . . .   20 OISIN 1   V   298
  AND WHISPERED TO MANKIND. . . . .   133 FR GILLIGAN   20
  I WHISPERED, "I AM TOO YOUNG." . . . .   268 BROWN PENNY   1
WHISPERER
  WHILE I, FROM THAT REED-THROATED WHISPERER . . . . .   320 REED WHISPERER   1
WHISPERING   SEE A-WHISPERING
  AND WHISPERING TO HERSELF ENWOUND ME! . . . . . .   9 OISIN 1   108
  AND THEN AN ANSWERING WHISPERING FLEW . . . . . .   15 OISIN 1   197
  HE HAD GONE WHISPERING FORTH WITH CUMBERED HEART, . . .   37 OISIN 2   V   111
  AND HUNG WITH SLIME, AND WHISPERING IN HIS HAIR, . . .   43 OISIN 2   216
  HUNG ROUND WITH SLIME, AND WHISPERING IN HIS HAIR, . .   43 OISIN 2   V   216
  AND MY OWN WHISPERING WORDS BE COMFORTING, ...   68 SAD SHEPHERD   23
  AND MINE OWN WHISPERING WORDS BE COMFORTING, ...   68 SAD SHEPHERD   V   23
  AND EVERY WHISPERING DRUID SAID, ...   82 MAD KING GOLL   V   9
  AND EVERY WHISPERING OLD MAN SAID, ...   82 MAD KING GOLL   V   9
  AND WHISPERING IN THEIR EARS . . . .   88 STOLEN CHILD   33
  THE COZENING FORTUNE-TELLER THAT COMES WHISPERING, . .   228 SHADOW WATER B   123
  AND WHISPERING THAT NONE BUT HE SHOULD HEAR, ...   281 TWO KINGS   110
  SOFT AS THE WHISPERING OF A LONG-LOST FOOTSTEP . . .   699 MOSADA 3   5
  SOFT AS A LONG DEAD FOOTSTEP WHISPERING THROUGH . . .   699 MOSADA 3   V   5
  SOFT AS THE WHISPERING OF A LOST FOOTSTEP . . . . .   699 MOSADA 3   V   5
  EACH OTHER'S NECKS, AND WHISPERING AS THEY GO, . . .   703 MOSADA 3   120
  WHISPERING ALONG THE SUNNY PATH! . . . .   725 LEGEND   18
  THEY ARE GONE, THEY ARE GONE. WHISPERING WERE ENOUGH. . .   778 SONG DEIRDRE 3   3
WHISPERS
  ALONE WITH OUR OWN WHISPERS AND REPLIES-- . . . . .   702 MOSADA 3   80
  HE WHISPERS TO A SOLDIER, WHO GOES OUT-- . . . . .   711 FERENCZ RENYI   44
WHISTLE
  IS WHAT I CAN WHISTLE ALONE AND ALONE. . . . . . .   551 SONGS REWRIT 1   4
WHISTLED
  I THOUGHT TO HAVE WHISTLED HER DOWN THAT WAY, ...   551 SONGS REWRIT 1   15
  I WHISTLED AND WHISTLED AND WHISTLED IN VAIN. . . . .   551 SONGS REWRIT 1   16
  I WHISTLED AND WHISTLED AND WHISTLED IN VAIN. . . . .   551 SONGS REWRIT 1   16
  I WHISTLED AND WHISTLED AND WHISTLED IN VAIN. . . . .   551 SONGS REWRIT 1   16
  I CRIED AND WHISTLED BUT VAIN, ALL VAIN. . . . . .   551 SONGS REWRIT 1 V   16
  BUT THERE I LAY AND I WHISTLED IN VAIN. . . . . .   551 SONGS REWRIT 1 V   16
WHISTLING
  THAT NESTLES ALONE IN THE WHISTLING WIND, ...   657 ISLE STAT I 3   68
WHIT
  WE'VE TALKED AND TALKED, AND NOT A WHIT MORE RARE . .   659 ISLE STAT II 1   21
  SHE CARES NO WHIT FOR EITHER, BUT HAS BLEST . . . .   660 ISLE STAT II 1   49
WHITE   SEE FOAM-WHITE SNOW-WHITE MILK-WHITE MOON-WHITE
  AND THE WHITE BODY THAT LAY BY MINE! . . . .   3 OISIN 1   10
  BUT DOWN TO HER FEET WHITE VESTURE FLOWED, ...   3 OISIN 1   25
  AND PEARLY WHITE HIS WELL-GROOMED HAIR. . . . . . .   3 OISIN 1   V 7CC
  DOWN TO HER FEET WHITE VESTURE FLOWED, ...   3 OISIN 1   V   25
  WHERE I WOULD BE WHEN THE WHITE MOON CLIMBS, ...   9 OISIN 1   104

	PAGE	TITLE		LINE

WHITE   (CONTINUED)

	PAGE	TITLE		LINE
MOUNT MY WHITE STEED, FOR THE FAIRY STATE	9	OISIN 1	V	103
AND WHEN THE WHITE STEED FELT MY WEIGHT,	9	OISIN 1	V	109
OR ARE YOU PHANTOMS WHITE AS SNOW,	10	OISIN 1		117
OR ARE YE PHANTOMS WHITE AS SNOW,	10	OISIN 1	V	117
MY HUMAN SORROW HER WHITE ARMS WOUND.	11	OISIN 1		138
ALL PEARLY WHITE, SAVE ONE RED EAR:	12	OISIN 1		141
BUT NOW THE MOON LIKE A WHITE ROSE SHONE	12	OISIN 1		152
ON THEIR OWN SELVES IN THE WATERS WHITE,	14	OISIN 1	V	185
THEIR BROWS WERE WHITE AS FRAGRANT MILK	15	OISIN 1		204
THEIR BROWS WERE WHITE AS THE FRAGRANT MILK	15	OISIN 1	V	204
WHERE WHITE DEWDROPS IN MILLIONS FALL:	16	OISIN 1	V	222
AND, WEEPING OVER THE WHITE STRINGS, HURLED	17	OISIN 1		241
WHITE FLOWERS OF THE FOAM A STAFF OF WOOD	24	OISIN 1	V	366
AND ONCE MORE SADDLED THE WHITE STEED	25	OISIN 1	V	378
WITH ME IN HER WHITE ARMS A HUNDRED YEARS	30	OISIN 2		17
ROSE IN THE DARKNESS, AND THE WHITE SURF GLEAMED	30	OISIN 2		23
NOR CEASED UNTIL WHITE NIAMH STROKED HIS EARS	30	OISIN 2		26
AND WHEN THE WHITE STEED SAW WHAT BLACKNESS GLEAMED,	30	OISIN 2	V	24
WE MOUNTED ON THE STAIR, THE WHITE STEED TYING,	32	OISIN 2	V	46
WITH BOWED HEAD, TREMBLING WHEN THE WHITE BLADE SHONE,	38	OISIN 2		137
A DEMON'S LEISURE: EYES, FIRST WHITE, NOW BURNED	40	OISIN 2		168
A DEMON'S LEISURE. EYES FIRST WHITE AS SNOW,	40	OISIN 2	V	168
THAT FEED WHITE MOTHS BY SOME DE DANAAN SHRINE:	41	OISIN 2		186
FEEDING WHITE MOTHS AROUND SOME EASTERN SHRINE,	41	OISIN 2	V	186
IMMEDIATE, MOURNFUL, WHITE WITH SUDDEN CARES,	44	OISIN 2	V	229A
AND EACH OF THE HUGE WHITE CREATURES WAS HUGER THAN FOURSCORE MEN:	49	OISIN 3		33
AND EACH OF THE HUGE WHITE CREATURES WAS HUGER THAN FOUR-SCORE MEN:	49	OISIN 3	V	33
AND THE CHIEF OF THE HUGE WHITE CREATURES,	50	OISIN 3		43
AND, MAN OF THE MANY WHITE CROZIERS, A CENTURY THERE I FORGOT	52	OISIN 3		77
AND, MAN OF THE MANY WHITE CROZIERS, A CENTURY THERE I FORGOT	52	OISIN 3		81
. . . WAKING WHITE AS A SHELL	54	OISIN 3		103
O HAD YOU SEEN BEAUTIFUL NIAMH GROW WHITE AS THE WATERS ARE WHITE,	54	OISIN 3		109
O HAD YOU SEEN BEAUTIFUL NIAMH GROW WHITE AS THE WATERS ARE WHITE,	54	OISIN 3		109
I CRIED, "O NIAMH! O WHITE ONE! IF ONLY A TWELVE-HOURED DAY,	55	OISIN 3		113
. . . "WHERE WHITE CLOUDS LIE SPREAD	59	OISIN 3		178
"WHAT DO YOU WEAVE WITH WOOL SO WHITE?"	70	CLOAK BOAT		11
TO THE BIRDS IN THE WHITE OF THE AIR.	92	FATHER OHART		16
IN THE WHITE BORDER OF THE MURMURING SEA:	103	FERGUS DRUID		19
WHO LOVES YOU, NO WHITE ARMS TO WRAP YOU ROUND,	109	CUCHULAIN SEA		59
IN VAIN HER ARMS, IN VAIN HER SOFT WHITE BREAST.	110	CUCHULAIN SEA		74
TALL WANDS OF ALDER AND WHITE QUICKEN WANDS.	111	CUCHULAIN SEA	V	82A
AND WHITE STARS TELL YOUR PRAISE.	113	ROSE OF PEACE		10
THEY HAVE GONE DOWN UNDER THE SAME WHITE STARS,	115	ROSE OF BATTLE		34
ABOVE YOUR WHITE BED.	118	CRADLE SONG	V	2
THE CRUMBLING MOON, THE WHITE STARS IN THE SKY,	120	SORROW OF LOVE	V	10
THE CURD-PALE MOON, THE WHITE STARS IN THE SKY,	120	SORROW OF LOVE	V	10
THE WHITE BIRDS	121	WHITE BIRDS		T
I WOULD THAT WE WERE, MY BELOVED, WHITE BIRDS ON THE FOAM OF THE SEA!	121	WHITE BIRDS		1
O WOULD THAT WE WERE, MY BELOVED, WHITE BIRDS ON THE FOAM OF THE SEA,	121	WHITE BIRDS	V	1
FOR I WOULD WE WERE CHANGED TO WHITE BIRDS	122	WHITE BIRDS		8
WERE WE ONLY WHITE BIRDS, MY BELOVED,	122	WHITE BIRDS		12
WITH WHITE FEET OF ANGELS SEVEN	125	CATHLEEN PARA	V	13
HER WHITE FEET GO GLIMMERING:	125	CATHLEEN PARA	V	14
AND THE WHITE BREAST OF THE DIM SEA	126	GOES FERGUS		11
AND THE WHITE HUSH END ALL BUT THE LOUD BEAT	137	TO SOME I TALK		15
OF THEIR LONG WINGS, THE FLASH OF THEIR WHITE FEET.	137	TO SOME I TALK		16
AND THE WHITE HUSH END ALL THINGS BUT THE BEAT	137	TO SOME I TALK	V	15
FOR GOD GOES BY WITH WHITE FOOTFALL.	139	TO IRELAND		44
FOR GOD GOES BY WITH WHITE FOOT-FALL.	139	TO IRELAND	V	44
AND A YOUNG GIRL WHITE BREAD.	144	HOST OF AIR		20
AND WHEN WHITE MOTHS WERE ON THE WING,	149	WANDER AENGUS		5
AND MY WHITE BREAST ON HIS HE LAID.	151	HEART OF WOMAN	V	4
DO YOU NOT HEAR ME CALLING, WHITE DEER WITH NO HORNS?	153	CHANGE BELOVED		1
THEIR HOOFS HEAVY WITH TUMULT, THEIR EYES GLIMMERING WHITE!	154	BELOVED PEACE		2
I HEAR WHITE BEAUTY SIGHING, TOO,	156	FORGOT BEAUTY		19
WHITE WOMAN THAT PASSION HAS WORN	157	POET BELOVED		3
WHITE WOMAN WITH NUMBERLESS DREAMS,	157	POET BELOVED		7
IT TALKED, ERE THE MORN GREW WHITE.	159	CAP AND BELLS	V	6
IT TALKED BEFORE MORN WAS WHITE,	159	CAP AND BELLS	V	6
AND HURLED IT FROM ITS PLACE BEFORE HIS FOOTSTOOL WHITE,	174	ELEMENT POWERS	V	3
WITH LONG WHITE BODIES CAME OUT OF THE AIR	185	QUEEN MAEVE		118
WHEN THE LONG WARS FOR THE WHITE HORN	189	BAILE AILLINN		14
AND WAVING WHITE WINGS TO AND FRO	197	BAILE AILLINN		184
IN A WHITE BREAKING WAVE: THEY HAD THE LOOK	223	SHADOW WATER B		34
TREMBLING IN THE BLUE HEAVENS LIKE A WHITE FAWN	251	SHADOW WATER B		611
THROUGH THE WHITE THIN BONE OF A HARE.	330	BONE OF A HARE		16
A VISIONARY WHITE SEA-BIRD	361	ALF POLLEXFEN		37
A VISIONARY WHITE SEA BIRD	361	ALF POLLEXFEN	V	37
NO RED AND WHITE OF A FACE,	365	HER RACE		6
THAT LOFTY WHITE STAG, LEAP	399	BREAK OF DAY		24
TO WATCH A WHITE GULL TAKE	400	DEMON BEAST		24

WHITE   (CONTINUED)
```
    AND THOSE WHITE GLIMMERING FRAGMENTS OF THE MIST SWEEP BY.        426  PHANTOM HATRED         6
    AND HOW CAN BODY, LAID IN THAT WHITE RUSH,       .    .    .      441  LEDA AND SWAN          7
    ALL THE STRETCHED BODY'S LAID ON THE WHITE RUSH  .    .    .      441  LEDA AND SWAN    V     7
    A KIND OLD NUN IN A WHITE HOOD REPLIES:    .    .    .    .    .   443  SCHOOL CHILDR          2
    INTO THE YOLK AND WHITE OF THE ONE SHELL.  .    .    .    .       443  SCHOOL CHILDR         16
    OF HORSES AND HORSES OF THE SEA, WHITE HORSES.   .    .    .      447  COLONUS PRAISE        32
    WITH HER WHITE FINGER.  I LED HER HOME ASLEEP    .    .    .      468  HARUN RASHID         158
    ANOTHER EMBLEM THERE!  THAT STORMY WHITE    .    .    .    .      490  COOLE BALLYLEE        17
    OF RASCALS BLACK AND WHITE    .    .    .    .    .    .    .      597  MODEL LAUREATE        10
    AND THE WAVES ARE LEAPING WHITE,     .    .    .    .    .    .   646  ISLE STAT I 1         27
    FLICKERING UNDER THE WHITE MOONSHINE?      .    .    .    .       646  ISLE STAT I 1         33
    WHERE ALL NIGHT LONG THE LONELY MOON, THE WHITE  .    .    .      650  ISLE STAT I 1        126
    IN SONG, FROM GOBLIN WATERS SWAYING WHITE,  .    .    .    .      657  ISLE STAT I 3         51
    HE SAT, AND THEN I HEARD THE WHITE LAKE SING,    .    .    .      659  ISLE STAT II 1        15
    THE WHITE WAVES WRAP IT IN A SHEET OF FLAME,     .    .    .      662  ISLE STAT II 2        14
    A WHITE, DUMB THING OF TEARS, HERE LET IT STAND, .    .    .      663  ISLE STAT II 2        21
    AND ONE ARM POINTING THUS, IN MARBLE WHITE.      .    .    .      663  ISLE STAT II 2        28
    WHAT DO YOU WEAVE WITH WOOL SO WHITE?      .    .    .    .       666  ISLE STAT II 3        11
    OF THINE CRY OVER WOLD AND WATER WHITE,    .    .    .    .       669  ISLE STAT II 3        73
    WHERE IN WHITE EXULTATION     .    .    .    .    .    .    .      672  ISLE STAT II 3       164
    A WRIGGLING THING ON THE WHITE LAKE MOVED, .    .    .    .       673  ISLE STAT II 3       176
    (SWALLOWS WERE FLASHING THEIR WHITE BREASTS ABOVE     .    .      690  MOSADA 1               7
    AND CALM, ROBED ALL IN RAIMENT MOONY WHITE.      .    .    .      693  MOSADA 1              77
    WITH WONDERFUL WHITE SANDS, WHERE NEVER YET      .    .    .      693  MOSADA 1              81
    WHITE LILIES, AND HER SONG FLEW FORTH AFAR .    .    .    .       693  MOSADA 1              85
    WITH WONDERFUL WHITE SAND, WHERE NEVER YET .    .    .    .       693  MOSADA 1         V    81
    STAY, STAY, OR I WILL HOLD YOUR WHITE ARMS DOWN. .    .    .      694  MOSADA 1              92
    AFAR ALONG THE FLEET WHITE RIVER'S FACE--  .    .    .    .       702  MOSADA 3              79
    WHITE, RENYI SILENT STANDS: THAT MAIDEN SWEET    .    .    .      713  FERENCZ RENYI    V    84
    A KID, HELD BY ONE SOFT WHITE EAR FOR TETHER,    .    .    .      715  DWELT SYCAMORE         3
    GONE THE STARS AND GONE THE WHITE MOON,    .    .    .    .       718  PHANTOM SHIP           3
    NOW THY GREAT WHITE DOLL TO HOLD--    .    .    .    .    .       726  LOVERS QUARREL        15
    ROLLS ALONG THE SEA SANDS WHITE.     .    .    .    .    .    .   732  STREET DANCERS        34
    ROLLS ALONG THE SEA-SANDS WHITE,     .    .    .    .    .    .   732  STREET DANCERS   V    34
    ROUND US THE WHITE ROADS ARE ENDLESS,      .    .    .    .       737  IN FIRELIGHT           3
    UNTO THE WHITE SKIES.    .    .    .    .    .    .    .    .      740  EARL PAUL             24
    AND NEED NO MORE OF LIFE TILL THE WHITE WINGS    .    .    .      751  SHADOW WATER A       102
    WAR-LADEN GALLEYS, AND ARMIES ON WHITE ROADS,    .    .    .      757  SHADOW WATER A       203
    WAR LADEN GALLEYS, AND ARMIES ON WHITE ROADS,    .    .    .      757  SHADOW WATER A   V   203
    THE HAND THAT WOUNDS.  A WHITE BIRD BEATS HIS WINGS   .    .      758  SHADOW WATER A       232
    A WHITE BIRD BEATS HIS WINGS UPON MY FACE. .    .    .    .       759  SHADOW WATER A       233
    A WHITE BIRD HAS TORN ME WITH HIS SILVER CLAWS.  .    .    .      759  SHADOW WATER A       234
    I AM BLIND AND DEAF BECAUSE OF THE WHITE WINGS.  .    .    .      759  SHADOW WATER A       235
    THE WHITE FOOL MAKES AT MORNING OUT OF FOAM.     .    .    .      761  SHADOW WATER A       261
    HER EYELIDS TREMBLE AND THE WHITE FOAM FADES!    .    .    .      761  SHADOW WATER A       264
    TREMBLING IN THE BLUE HEAVENS LIKE A WHITE FAWN  .    .    .      769  SHADOW WATER A       427
    A WOMAN'S BEAUTY IS LIKE A WHITE      .    .    .    .    .       784  WOMANS BEAUTY          1
    FRAIL BIRD, LIKE A WHITE SEA-BIRD ALONE    .    .    .    .       784  WOMANS BEAUTY          2
WHITEBEARD
    A WHITEBEARD STOOD HUSHED ON THE PATHWAY,  .    .    .    .        59  OISIN 3              173
WHITE-HAIRED
    REMEMBERING HOW I HAD STOOD BY WHITE-HAIRED FINN .    .    .       44  OISIN 2              227
    REMEMBERING HOW I STOOD BY WHITE-HAIRED FINN     .    .    .       44  OISIN 2          V   227
WHITE-HORNED
    OVER THE WHITE-HORNED BULL AND THE BROWN BULL.   .    .    .      182  QUEEN MAEVE           58
WHITENED          SEE WAVE-WHITENED
    WHITENED AFAR WITH SURGE, FAN-FORMED AND WIDE,   .    .    .       31  OISIN 2               28
    AND WHEN THE MORNING WHITENED    .    .    .    .    .    .       160  CAP AND BELLS         23
    AND AS SOON AS THE MORN HAD WHITENED,      .    .    .    .       160  CAP AND BELLS    V    23
    WHERE HOMES ONCE WHITENED VALE AND MOUNTAIN CREST!    .    .      709  FERENCZ RENYI          3
WHITENESS
    SHE LIMPS ALONG IN AN AGED WHITENESS:      .    .    .    .        27  OISIN 1              415
    SHE LIMPS ALONG IN AN AGED WHITENESS.      .    .    .    .        28  OISIN 1          V   423
    THE LITTLE WAVES THAT WALKED IN EVENING WHITENESS,   .    .       81  EPHEMERA         V   24C
    OF HER UNBLEMISHED LINEAMENTS, A WHITENESS WITH NO STAIN,        353  HIS PHOENIX            3
WHITENING
    WHITENING THE SURGE AFAR, FAN-FORMED AND WIDE,   .    .    .       31  OISIN 2          V    28
    SCARCE LEFT A WHITENING FEATHER, GREY AND SERE!  .    .    .       34  OISIN 2          V   76A
    WITH HEAVY WHITENING WINGS, AND A HEART FALLEN COLD!  .    .      147  UNAPPEAS HOST          4
    BOWS THE BEDOUIN'S WHITENING HAIR--   .    .    .    .    .       733  STREET DANCERS        45
WHITER
    WHOSE LONG WOOL WHITER THAN SEA-FROTH FLOWS,     .    .    .        8  OISIN 1               90
    WHOSE LONG WOOL WHITER THAN SEA FROTH FLOWS,     .    .    .        8  OISIN 1          V    90
    .  .  .  FOR WHITER THAN NEW-WASHED FLEECE  .    .    .    .       47  OISIN 3               11
    .  .  .  LONG WARLESS, GROWN WHITER THAN CURDS.  .    .    .       49  OISIN 3               36
    .  .  .  LONG-WARLESS, GROWN WHITER THAN CURDS.  .    .    .       49  OISIN 3          V    36
    WHITER THAN CURDS, ITS EYES THE TINT OF THE SEA. .    .    .      277  TWO KINGS              7
    YET WHITER BEARD HAVE YOU THAN MERLIN HAD. .    .    .    .       721  WITCH VIVIEN          30
WHITES
    WILD FLAMES OF RED AND CREAMY WHITES, .    .    .    .    .        18  OISIN 1          V   255
WHITEST
    I WONDER WHICH IS WHITEST, THEY OR THOU.   .    .    .    .       700  MOSADA 3              45
WHITETHORN
    AT SOME OLD WINDING WHITETHORN ROOT  .    .    .    .    .       342  SHEP GOATHERD        101
WHITHER
    AND WHITHER THE WISE HEART KNOWS!     .    .    .    .    .       168  BLESSED               34
    WHITHER HER FOOTSTEPS GO.     .    .    .    .    .    .    .      175  ELEMENT POWERS        18
    AND WHITHER, UNCOUTH HUNTER?  WHY SO FAST? .    .    .    .       651  ISLE STAT I 2          1
    MY WORDS WERE ALL:  "O WHITHER, WHITHER, WHITHER .    .    .      669  ISLE STAT II 3        87
    MY WORDS WERE ALL:  "O WHITHER, WHITHER, WHITHER .    .    .      669  ISLE STAT II 3        87
```

	PAGE	TITLE	LINE

WHITHER   (CONTINUED)
```
      MY WORDS WERE ALL: "O WHITHER, WHITHER, WHITHER . . . .    669 ISLE STAT II 3      87
      BUT FAITHFUL LOVERS. WHITHER HAVE YOU COME, . . . . .      763 SHADOW WATER A V   309
WHIZZED
      LONG ERE AN ARROW WHIZZED OR SWORD LEFT SHEATH . . . .     650 ISLE STAT I 1      135
WHOLE
      MAY SLEEP IN THE END WITH THE WHOLE OF HIS FATE DONE,  . .   28 OISIN 1         V 423F
      FROM THE WHOLE SEVEN SEAS, THOSE TOWERS SET . . . . . .     38 OISIN 2         V 131
      . . . AND THE WHOLE OF THE WORLD WAS ONE. . . . . . .       48 OISIN 3           24
      WERE THE MEMORIES OF THE WHOLE OF MY SORROW . . . . .       52 OISIN 3           71
      . . . AND THE MEMORIES OF THE WHOLE OF MY MIRTH, . . . .    52 OISIN 3           71
      THE WHOLE OF THE LONG DAY. . . . . . . . . . . .           94 MOLL MAGEE         8
      THIS WHOLE DAY HAVE I FOLLOWED IN THE ROCKS, . . . . .    102 FERGUS DRUID        1
      THE WHOLE DAY HAVE I FOLLOWED IN THE ROCKS, . . . . .     102 FERGUS DRUID    V   1
      AND THE WHOLE WORLD WEIGHS DOWN UPON MY HEART-- . . . .   104 FERGUS DRUID    V  38A
      AND WITH YOU CAME THE WHOLE OF THE WORLD'S TEARS, . . .   120 SORROW OF LOVE V    6
      DRAGONS WITH EYES OF RUBY. THE WHOLE SHIP . . . . . .     248 SHADOW WATER B    535
      CRIED OUT THE WHOLE NIGHT LONG, . . . . . . . . .         254 HIS DREAM          16
      HEARING THE WHOLE EARTH CHANGE ITS TUNE, . . . . . .      266 GALWAY RACES       12
      THOUGH FLAME HAD BURNED THE WHOLE . . . . . . . .         267 FRIEND ILLNESS      4
      "IF HE BE LIVING STILL THE WHOLE WORLD'S MINE, . . . .    280 TWO KINGS       V  85
      THEY MAULED AND BIT THE WHOLE NIGHT THROUGH; . . . . .    297 THREE BEGGARS      48
      OUT-SCREAMS THE WHOLE SHELF: "ALTHOUGH . . . . . . .      319 DOLLS               7
      JUST TRUTH ENOUGH TO SHOW THAT HIS WHOLE LIFE . . . .     373 PHASES OF MOON     22
      COULD ROUSE MY WHOLE NATURE. . . . . . . . . . .          400 DEMON BEAST        32
      TILL MAN MADE UP THE WHOLE, . . . . . . . . . .           415 TOWER             149
      THAT WE MIGHT MAKE IT WHOLE: . . . . . . . . . .          457 SUMMER SPRING       8
      WHILE OUR GROSS PALATES DRINK FROM THE WHOLE WINE, . .    471 ALL SOUL NIGHT     10
      HAD SO LIT UP THE WHOLE . . . . . . . . . . . .           472 ALL SOUL NIGHT     37
      NO LIVING MAN CAN DRINK FROM THE WHOLE WINE. . . . .      474 ALL SOUL NIGHT     85
      THAT CANNOT TAKE THE WHOLE . . . . . . . . . . .          510 JANE JUDGMENT       3
      FOR NOTHING CAN BE SOLE OR WHOLE . . . . . . . .          513 JANE TALK BISH     17
      NOR STRAINING JOY, BUT WHOLE IS JOINED TO WHOLE: . . .    555 RIBH AT TOMB       14
      NOR STRAINING JOY, BUT WHOLE IS JOINED TO WHOLE: . . .    555 RIBH AT TOMB       14
      YET KEEP HIS SUBSTANCE WHOLE. . . . . . . . . .           573 LADYS 2ND SONG     13
      NOR THINK THAT BODY IS THE WHOLE, . . . . . . . .         573 LADYS 3RD SONG      4
      FOR I CAN PUT THE WHOLE LOT DOWN, AND ALL I HAVE TO SAY   593 PILGRIM            24
      THE WHOLE WORLD'S SADLY TALKING TO ITSELF. . . . . .      652 ISLE STAT I 2      12
      YON EAGER LARK, THAT FILLS WITH SONG THE WHOLE . . . .    652 ISLE STAT I 2      18
      I HEAR THE WHOLE SKY'S SORROW IN ONE VOICE. . . . .       652 ISLE STAT I 2      22
      "AND CUT NO WOOD THE WHOLE DAY LONG, . . . . . . .        731 PRIEST FAIRY       81
      AND THEN THE WHOLE WORLD'S TROUBLE WEEPS WITH YOU. . .    738 YOU ARE SAD        12
      I'D LET THE WHOLE WORLD GO: . . . . . . . . . .           782 HEART FRIGHT        9
WHOLE-MAD
      HALF-DRUNK OR WHOLE-MAD SOLDIERY . . . . . . . . .        791 REPRISALS          15
WHOLESOME
      OLD WHOLESOME GOBAN HAD NO SAY: . . . . . . . . .         271 GREY ROCK          10
      WHAT WHOLESOME SUN HAS RIPENED IS WHOLESOME FOOD TO EAT,  442 BLACK CENTAUR       5
      WHAT WHOLESOME SUN HAS RIPENED IS WHOLESOME FOOD TO EAT,  442 BLACK CENTAUR       5
      ALL THEIR WHOLESOME STRENGTH. . . . . . . . . .           505 RESULT THOUGHT     12
WHOLLY
      THE SAD, SAD THOUGHT HAS GONE FROM ME NOW WHOLLY: . . .    72 ANASHU VIJAYA      19
      COULD WE BUT GIVE US WHOLLY TO THE DREAMS, . . . .        230 SHADOW WATER B    178
      NOW THEIR SONGS ARE MOURNFUL WHOLLY . . . . . . .         667 ISLE STAT II 3     32
WHORL
      TO ROUND THAT SHELL'S ELABORATE WHORL, . . . . . .        509 JANE REPROVED       8
WICK
      AND LEAVE NO SMOKING WICK BEHIND, . . . . . . . .         306 HOUR DAWN          97
      I BADE, BECAUSE THE WICK AND OIL ARE SPENT . . . . .      333 LIVING BEAUTY       1
      THE WICK OF YOUTH BEING BURNED AND THE OIL SPENT, . . .   334 LIVING BEAUTY   V   3
      WHEN OIL AND WICK ARE BURNED IN ONE: . . . . . .          388 SOLOMON WITCH      30
      WHAT HAS TURNED TO SMOKING WICK . . . . . . . .           529 TOM LUNATIC         5
WICKED
      AND THINGS THAT HAVE GROWN SAD ARE WICKED, . . . .        20 OISIN 1           301
      EVERYTHING THAT'S SAD IS WICKED-- . . . . . . . .         20 OISIN 1         V 301
      WISE BIDDY EARLY CALLED THE WICKED WOOD: . . . . .       218 WOODS OF COOLE     15
      YOU HAVE A DRUID CRAFT OF WICKED SOUND . . . . . .       237 SHADOW WATER B    342
      YOU HAVE A DRUID CRAFT, WICKED SOUND . . . . . .         237 SHADOW WATER B V  342
      THROUGH WICKED SPELLS. THAT IS NOT ALL THE TALE, . .     242 SHADOW WATER B    408
      TO SHAKE THEIR WICKED SIDES AT YOUTH . . . . . .         262 STUDENTS AGIT       3
      HER SPEECH A WICKED TALE THAT WE MAY VIE WITH HER, . .   362 HER COURTESY        6
      THE WILD OLD WICKED MAN . . . . . . . . . . .           587 OLD WICKED MAN      T
      SAID THAT WILD OLD WICKED MAN . . . . . . . . .         587 OLD WICKED MAN      3
      HOW SINFULLY THE WICKED SCOFF!" . . . . . . . .         725 LEGEND             22
      THE WICKED HAWTHORN TREE . . . . . . . . . .           788 HAWTHORN TREE   V   T
      SAID THE WICKED, CROOKED, HAWTHORN TREE: . . . . .      788 HAWTHORN TREE       6
      SAID THE WICKED, CROOKED, HAWTHORN TREE. . . . . .      788 HAWTHORN TREE      14
WICKS
      THAT SAW THE WICKS GROW YELLOW IN THE DAWN: . . . .     352 PEOPLE             18
WIDE        SEE WORLD-WIDE
      WHITENED AFAR WITH SURGE, FAN-FORMED AND WIDE, . . .     31 OISIN 2            28
      WHITENING THE SURGE AFAR, FAN-FORMED AND WIDE, . . .     31 OISIN 2         V  28
      I FOUND, DROPPING SEA-FOAM ON THE WIDE STAIR, . . .      43 OISIN 2           215
      I FOUND, DROPPING SEA FOAM ON THE WIDE STAIR, . . .      43 OISIN 2         V 215
      THUNDERING, AND THE WIDE USELESS WATERS FRAY . . . .     45 OISIN 2         V 238
      NOW IN A PLACE OF STAR-FIRE, AND NOW IN A SHADOW-PLACE    49 OISIN 3            42
         WIDE:
      NOW IN A PLACE OF STAR-FIRE, AND NOW IN A SHADOW PLACE    49 OISIN 3         V  42
         WIDE:
      OF WARS WITH THE WIDE WORLD . . . . . . . . . .          50 OISIN 3            55
      . . . ON THE BURNING STONES OF WIDE HELL, . . . . .      61 OISIN 3           198
```

```
                                                      PAGE     TITLE          LINE
WIDE   (CONTINUED)
        IS BUT A SLIDING DROP OF RAIN BETWEEN HIS PETALS WIDE. .      76  INDIAN ON GOD        12
        IS BUT A SLIDING DROP OF RAIN WITHIN HIS PETALS WIDE." .      76  INDIAN ON GOD    V   12
        WHEN, OPENIN' WIDE HIS DOOR, . . . . . . . . . .              96  MOLL MAGEE           50
        WHEN THE FLAMING LUTE-THRONGED ANGELIC DOOR IS WIDE! . .     172  TRAV PASSION          1
        AND SHOOK HIM WIDE AWAKE, AND BID HIM SAY . . . . .          182  QUEEN MAEVE          50
        SPEAK IT, THAT I MAY SEND THROUGH THE WIDE WORLD . .         281  TWO KINGS            97
        "YOU THAT HAVE WANDERED FAR AND WIDE . . . . . . .           295  THREE BEGGARS        11
        "YOU HAVE WANDERED FAR AND WIDE, . . . . . . . . .           295  THREE BEGGARS    V   11
        AND THEN AT LAST BEING WIDE AWAKE . . . . . . . .            304  HOUR DAWN        V   40
        SET CARPENTERS TO WORK ON NO WIDE TABLE, . . . . .           340  SHEP GOATHERD        50
        WERE I TO TRAVEL FAR AND WIDE . . . . . . . . . .            398  BREAK OF DAY          8
        PLUNGES TOWARDS NOTHING, ARMS AND FINGERS SPREADING WIDE     426  PHANTOM HATRED       13
        THEY ARE SPREAD WIDE THAT EACH . . . . . . . . .            488  CRAZED MOON          17
        THEY ATE SPREAD WIDE THAT EACH . . . . . . . . .            488  CRAZED MOON      V   17
        YOU ASK WHAT I HAVE FOUND, AND FAR AND WIDE I GO! . . .     580  CURSE CROMWELL        1
        THAT CRIED IT FAR AND WIDE, . . . . . . . . . .            582  ROGER CASEMENT       18
        AND WIDE AWAKE KNOW THAT THE HUNT IS ON! . . . . .         622  HOUND VOICE          17
        OF THIS WIDE VALE, EMBOSOMED IN THE AIR, . . . . .         652  ISLE STAT I 2        19
        BUT WIDE AWAKE HIS TWO EYES WERE. . . . . . . . .          655  ISLE STAT I 3         7
        LIVING, WIDE WINGED, ON THE WATERS FLOAT. . . . . .        657  ISLE STAT I 3        54
        AND LOUDLY TWICE THE LIVING WINGS FLAPT WIDE, . . .        659  ISLE STAT II 1       12
        OF THE WIDE WOODS.  AND THE DEEP EARTH GATHERED THEM.      660  ISLE STAT II 1       33
        ALL THINGS ARE QUIET IN THE EVE'S WIDE EYE. . . . .        662  ISLE STAT II 2        6
        AS THOUGH SHE WHOM YOU FEAR HAD CROSSED THE WIDE . .       669  ISLE STAT II 3       77
        THEN HE SHOUTED, "OPEN WIDE . . . . . . . . . .            697  MOSADA 2             24
        AND HE SHOUTED OPEN WIDE . . . . . . . . . . .            697  MOSADA 2         V   24
        THE STRANGER SHOUTED, "OPEN WIDE . . . . . . . .          697  MOSADA 2         V   24
        OF A WIDE WOOD'S LEAFY LEISURE, . . . . . . . .           731  STREET DANCERS       11
        ALTHOUGH WIDE WORLD HOLD NOT . . . . . . . . . .          786  YOUR HEART           16
WIDE-EYED
        AND NEVER ANY MORE THE WIDE-EYED BANDS . . . . . .        674  ISLE STAT II 3      218
WIDENING
        TURNING AND TURNING IN THE WIDENING GYRE . . . . .        401  SECOND COMING         1
WIDE-OPEN
        AND HAVING SUCH WIDE-OPEN, SHINING EYES. . . . . .        231  SHADOW WATER B      200
WIDE-WATERING
        AND STREAMS, WIDE-WATERING, SALMON-SHOALED, . . . .        81  MAD KING GOLL    V    3
WIDTH
        AND SHAKES O'ER THE WIDTH OF THE SEA-WORLD BORDER . . .     28  OISIN 1          V 423C
WIFE
        AND NIAMH BE WITH YOU FOR A WIFE." . . . . . . .             9  OISIN 1             101
        AND I BE WITH THEE AS THY WIFE." . . . . . . . .             9  OISIN 1          V  101
        THE GENTLE NIAMH WAS MY WIFE! . . . . . . . . .             24  OISIN 1             357
        THE SICK MAN'S WIFE OPENED THE DOOR! . . . . . .           133  FR GILLIGAN          31
        THAT EDAIN, MIDHIR'S WIFE, HAD WOVE . . . . . . .          195  BAILE AILLINN       142
        WHEN MIDHIR'S WIFE HAD CHANGED HER TO A FLY, . . . .       220  HARP OF AENGUS       10
        OF THAT MORE POWERFUL LIFE? HIS WIFE KNOWS BETTER. . .     230  SHADOW WATER B      172
        RAYMOND LULLY AND HIS WIFE PERNELLA . . . . . . .         253  HIS DREAM        V    T
        PALE-FACED, ALONE UPON A BENCH, HIS WIFE . . . . .        279  TWO KINGS        V   61
        THAT I MAY CLAIM YOU AS MY WIFE AGAIN." . . . . . .       284  TWO KINGS           170
        YET ANSWERED HIM, "I AM KING EOCHAID'S WIFE . . . .       284  TWO KINGS           173
        "AND GET A COMFORTABLE WIFE AND HOUSE . . . . . .         299  BEGGAR CRIED          5
        THE DOLL-MAKER'S WIFE IS AWARE . . . . . . . . .         319  DOLLS                14
        EVEN BEFORE HIS CHILDREN AND HIS WIFE? . . . . . .        340  SHEP GOATHERD        34
        MAY BE A QUIET THOUGHT TO WIFE AND MOTHER, . . . .        343  SHEP GOATHERD       118
        BY HIS WIFE ELIZABETH . . . . . . . . . . .             360  ALF POLLEXFEN         4
        DUTIFUL HUSBAND, HONEST WIFE BY TURN, . . . . . .         376  PHASES OF MOON       99
        RESTORED THIS TOWER FOR MY WIFE GEORGE! . . . . .         406  CARVED STONE          4
        A SMALL OLD HOUSE, WIFE, DAUGHTER, SON, . . . . .         577  WHAT THEN            12
        A HUSBAND THAT HAD SOLD HIS WIFE . . . . . . . .         587  PARNELLITES          27
        A HUSBAND WHO HAD SOLD HIS WIFE . . . . . . . .          587  PARNELLITES      V   27
        HIS WIFE HE FOUND AND THE RICH MAN . . . . . . .         595  COLONEL MARTIN       43
        I AM TO BE YOUR WIFE.  A VILLAGE HIGH . . . . . .        713  FERENCZ RENYI        97
        I WAS TO BE YOUR WIFE.  A VILLAGE HIGH . . . . . .       713  FERENCZ RENYI    V   97
        THEN EACH WIFE AND MAID AND MOTHER CALLS BY NAME         719  PHANTOM SHIP         24
            SOME DROWNED ONE.
        WHEN MIDHER'S WIFE HAD CHANGED HER TO A FLY . . . .       763  SHADOW WATER A      305
        "GIVE ME YOUR WIFE," SAID HE, . . . . . . . . .          779  GOING THE ROAD        5
WIFELESS
        "O WHAT'S A WIFELESS MAN?" SAID HE, . . . . . . .         594  COLONEL MARTIN        5
WIGHT
        TO THE GREEN ISLE OF WIGHT . . . . . . . . . .           740  EARL PAUL            10
WILD
        ACROSS THE GLOSSY SEA." "OH, WILD . . . . . . .             6  OISIN 1          V   58
        OVER THE GLOSSY SEA." "O, WILD . . . . . . . .             6  OISIN 1          V   58
        WILD FLAMES OF RED AND GOLD AND BLUE, . . . . . .          18  OISIN 1             252
        WILD FLAMES OF RED AND CREAMY WHITES, . . . . . .          18  OISIN 1          V  255
        AND IN A WILD AND SUDDEN DANCE . . . . . . . .            20  OISIN 1             290
        OR THE WILD GREY OSPREY SORROW," . . . . . . .            20  OISIN 1          V  303
        OR THE WILD GREY OSPREY SORROW." . . . . . . .            21  OISIN 1          V  319
        OR FEAR THE WILD GREY OSPREY SORROW." . . . . .            23  OISIN 1          V  342
        "BUT NEVER WITH US WHERE THE WILD FOWL CHASES . . .        27  OISIN 1          V  408
        AND CHASE THE WILD BEE HOMEWARD TO HIS HIVE . . .          32  OISIN 2          V  50D
        THE WILD FOWL OF THE AIR INCREASED! . . . . . .           82  MAD KING GOLL         8
        THE HORNS AND SHIELDS AND WILD SWAN'S PINIONS! . .         82  MAD KING GOLL    V    5
        THE WILD BOAR KNOWS ME, BY ONE EAR . . . . . . .          84  MAD KING GOLL    V   45
        TO THE WATERS AND THE WILD . . . . . . . . . .           87  STOLEN CHILD         10
        TO THE WATERS AND THE WILD . . . . . . . . . .           87  STOLEN CHILD         25
        TO THE WOODS AND WATERS WILD . . . . . . . . .           87  STOLEN CHILD     V  REF
        TO THE WATERS AND THE WILD . . . . . . . . . .           88  STOLEN CHILD         39
```

WILD (CONTINUED)

	PAGE	TITLE		LINE
TO THE WATERS AND THE WILD	88	STOLEN CHILD		51
A WILD AND FOOLISH LABOURER IS A KING	103	FERGUS DRUID	V	27
THE WILD DUCK AND THE DRAKE	143	HOST OF AIR		2
THOUGH YOU HAVE THE WILL OF THE WILD BIRDS,	176	BELOVED DEAD		8
WHEN NIGHT WAS AT ITS DEEPEST, A WILD GOOSE	181	QUEEN MAEVE		36
WHERE WILD BEES HIVE ON THE GREAT PLAIN.	194	BAILE AILLINN		123
QUIET'S WILD HEART, LIKE DAILY MEAT;	196	BAILE AILLINN		178
BUT A WILD APPLE HID THE GRASS	197	BAILE AILLINN		189
WANDERS LAUGHING AND EATING HER WILD HEART	198	SEVEN WOODS		11
MADE OUT OF A WILD THOUGHT, IS IN MY MARROW.	199	ARROW		2
WHEN ALL THE WILD SUMMER WAS IN HER GAZE."	200	FOLLY COMFORT		12
GATHERS THE WILD DUCK FROM THE WINTER DAWN;	217	WOODS OF COOLE		3
DIM PAIRC-NA-CARRAIG, WHERE THE WILD BEES FLING	217	WOODS OF COOLE		9
BECAUSE HER HANDS HAD BEEN MADE WILD BY LOVE.	219	HARP OF AENGUS		9
AS THAT WILD AENGUS. LONG BEFORE HER DAY	224	SHADOW WATER B		47
AND IF SHE HEAR HIM MUTTER OF WILD RIDERS,	230	SHADOW WATER B		175
SHE WILL BE LIKE A WILD CAT; FOR THESE QUEENS	232	SHADOW WATER B		233
UPON HIS SHOULDERS. YOU'VE NOTHING BUT WILD WORDS,	235	SHADOW WATER B		300
BUT WHERE'S THE WILD DOG THAT HAS PRAISED HIS FLEAS?	262	TO A POET	V	4
TO FIND IF HEARTS BE WILD AND WISE,	263	MASK		4
ITS FLESH BEING WILD, AND IT AGAIN	266	GALWAY RACES		13
FLESH WILD AGAIN, AND IT AGAIN	266	GALWAY RACES	V	13
AND AFTER, WHEN HER BLOOD RAN WILD,	272	GREY ROCK		44
WAS IT FOR THIS THE WILD GEESE SPREAD	290	SEPTEMBER 1913		17
SO WILD THAT EVERY CASUAL THOUGHT OF THAT AND THIS	316	COLD HEAVEN		4
THE WILD SWANS AT COOLE	322	SWANS AT COOLE		T
THAT GOLDEN KING AND THAT WILD LADY	332	ROUND TOWER		19
WE CANNOT PAY ITS TRIBUTE OF WILD TEARS.	334	LIVING BEAUTY		10
WHEN THE WILD THOUGHT,	336	YOUNG GIRL		7
SEED-PODS AND FLOWERS THAT ARE NOT ALL WILD POPPY.	342	SHEP GOATHERD		88
SEED PODS AND FLOWERS THAT ARE NOT ALL WILD POPPY.	342	SHEP GOATHERD	V	88
ALL THE WILD WITCHES, THOSE MOST NOBLE LADIES,	343	DEJECTION		4
THE SCULLION GONE WILD."	349	HAWK		6
AND WHO CAN SAY BUT SOME YOUNG BELLE MAY WALK AND TALK MEN WILD	354	HIS PHOENIX		26
THERE'LL BE THAT CROWD TO MAKE MEN WILD THROUGH ALL THE CENTURIES,	354	HIS PHOENIX	V	25
AND MAY BE THERE'LL BE SOME YOUNG BELLE WALK OUT TO MAKE MEN WILD	354	HIS PHOENIX	V	26
AND MAYBE THERE'LL BE SOME YOUNG BELLE WALK OUT TO MAKE MEN WILD	354	HIS PHOENIX	V	26
THAT WOMEN LAUGHING, OR TIMID OR WILD,	358	PRESENCES		4
FANTASTICAL AND WILD	364	END OF DAY		3
"LAST NIGHT, WHERE UNDER THE WILD MOON	387	SOLOMON WITCH		2
ON LIMBS THAT HAD RUN WILD.	394	EASTER 1916		64
COLD STONE AND WATER. I GREW WILD,	399	BREAK OF DAY		14
AND SO WARM HER WILD NEST.	415	TOWER		172
CONSIDERING WHAT WILD INFANCY	440	WISDOM		19
AND THEREUPON MY HEART IS DRIVEN WILD;	444	SCHOOL CHILDR		23
. . . AND THE WILD BIRD MATE IN THE WILD."	450	OWEN AHERNE		16
. . . AND THE WILD BIRD MATE IN THE WILD."	450	OWEN AHERNE		16
O LET HER CHOOSE A YOUNG MAN NOW AND ALL FOR HIS WILD SAKE."	450	OWEN AHERNE		24
SHE THAT HAS BEEN WILD	456	FRIENDS YOUTH		10
BUT THE WILD BEDOUIN. THOUGH I APPROVE	462	HARUN RASHID		22
THE WILD STAG AND THE DOE; THAT MOUTH TO MOUTH	465	HARUN RASHID		101
WILD WITH DIVINITY;	472	ALL SOUL NIGHT		36
I HAD WILD JACK FOR A LOVER;	512	JANE ON GOD		19
AS DID THAT WILD TRISTRAM KNOW	522	LULLABY		8
BY THAT GREAT GLORY DRIVEN WILD.	540	FROM ANTIGONE		13
MARINERS, WILD HARVESTERS;	540	FROM ANTIGONE	V	5
THAT SEEMED BUT A WILD WENCHING MAN;	550	SEVERED HEAD		16
THE WILD OLD WICKED MAN	587	OLD WICKED MAN		T
SAID THAT WILD OLD WICKED MAN	587	OLD WICKED MAN		3
THEN SAID SHE TO THAT WILD OLD MAN,	588	OLD WICKED MAN		19
BUT A WILD OLD MAN IN THE LIGHT,	589	OLD WICKED MAN		38
THAT CONSTITUTE THE WILD,	601	THOSE IMAGES		10
ALL THAT IS NOT ITSELF; I HAD GROWN WILD	619	BRONZE HEAD		20
MALACHI STILT-JACK AM I, WHATEVER I LEARNED HAS RUN WILD,	623	HIGH TALK		9
OH, CEASE YOUR SINGING! WILD AND SHRILL AND LOUD,	648	ISLE STAT I 1		99
CURVING BENEATH THE PROW; AS SOME WILD DRAKE	659	ISLE STAT II 1		16
ASIDE!--THE WILD HORNS TOLD ALMINTOR'S END!	665	ISLE STAT II 2		68
FOR SUCH A CALL. LET THE WILD WORD BE CRIED	669	ISLE STAT II 3		76
WILD CRIES, GROWN SWEET WITH LULLS AND LINGERINGS LONG.	674	ISLE STAT II 3		222
WILD INDOLENCE AND MUSIC HAVE NO DATE.	686	LIFE		20
WILD WISDOMS OF SPIRIT AND TONGUE.	708	FAIRY PEDANT		27
WILD SPIRITS OF WISDOM AND TONGUE.	708	FAIRY PEDANT	V	27
WILD BEES' HONEY LAID FOR THEE."	730	PRIEST FAIRY		56
WILD INDOLENCE AND MUSIC HAVE NO DATE,	735	QUATRAIN APHOR		18
BECAUSE HER HANDS HAD BEEN MADE WILD BY LOVE;	762	SHADOW WATER A		304
THOSE WILD HANDS THAT HAVE EMBRACED	776	AGAINST WITCH		32
MY HEART RAN WILD WHEN IT HEARD	783	GREY ROUND		21

WILDER

	PAGE	TITLE		LINE
ITS TERROR GROWING WILDER AT EVERY FOOT-FALL,	279	TWO KINGS	V	45D
ITS TERROR GROWING WILDER AT EVERY FOOTFALL	279	TWO KINGS	V	45D
AND THE MOON IS WILDER EVERY MINUTE.	389	SOLOMON WITCH		43

WILDERING

	PAGE	TITLE		LINE
AMONG HER WILDERING WHIRLS, FORGETTING HIM.	69	SAD SHEPHERD		28
WITHIN HER WILDERING WHIRLS--FORGETTING HIM.	69	SAD SHEPHERD	V	28

	PAGE	TITLE	LINE
WILDERNESS			
O BEAST OF THE WILDERNESS, BIRD OF THE AIR,	177	PAST GREATNESS	11
TILL THE WILDERNESS CRIED ALOUD,	259	UNWORTH PRAISE	8
AMID THE ELABORATE WILDERNESS OF THE AIR.	278	TWO KINGS	31
INTO THE SECRET WILDERNESS OF THEIR LOVE.	778	SONG DEIRDRE 3	4
HE HAD FAMISHED IN A WILDERNESS.	789	SINGING HEAD	1
WILDEST			
LAUGHING GOES IN WILDEST MOOD,	732	STREET DANCERS	41
WILDLY			
OUR MARRIED VOICES WILDLY TROLLED.	85	MAD KING GOLL	59
OUR MARRIED VOICE WILDLY TROLLED.	85	MAD KING GOLL V	59
HOW COULD SHE MATE WITH FIFTY YEARS THAT WAS SO WILDLY BRED?	450	OWEN AHERNE	15
WILDNESS			
WITH ALL YOUTH'S LONELY WILDNESS STIRRED,	397	POLIT PRISONER	16
THAT IMAGE CAN BRING WILDNESS, BRING A RAGE	431	NINETEEN 19	80
AND I REMEMBER WILDNESS LOST	453	DEATH OF HARE	9
HIS WILDNESS	458	HIS WILDNESS	T
I SAW THE WILDNESS IN HER AND I THOUGHT	619	BRONZE HEAD	16
WILDS			
THE DEMONS OF THE WILDS AND WINDS FOR FRIGHT	34	OISIN 2 V	81B
WILD-STRAWBERRY			
AND YELLOW THE WET WILD-STRAWBERRY LEAVES.	79	FALLING LEAVES	4
WILFUL			
TEASING EVERY WILFUL MAID.	727	LOVERS QUARREL	28
WILL SEE GOOD-WILL			
AND BID THEM WANDER OBEYING YOUR WILL,	141	EVERLAST VOICE	3
AND RIVER AND STREAM WORK OUT THEIR WILL;	148	INTO TWILIGHT	12
AND LAUGH OUT THEIR WHIMSEY AND WORK OUT THEIR WILL.	148	INTO TWILIGHT	12
LAUGH OUT THEIR WHIMSEY AND WORK OUT THEIR WILL.	148	INTO TWILIGHT V	12
AND THE CHANGING MOON WORK OUT THEIR WILL.	148	INTO TWILIGHT V	12
THOUGH YOU HAVE THE WILL OF THE WILD BIRDS,	176	BELOVED DEAD	8
QUEEN OF HIGH CRUACHAN." "I OBEY YOUR WILL	184	QUEEN MAEVE	99
WITH SAILORS THAT WERE SWORN TO DO YOUR WILL,	236	SHADOW WATER B	308
I'D DO YOUR WILL, BUT THEY ARE TOO HIGH—TOO HIGH.	250	SHADOW WATER B	577
AND WHEN I HAD GOT MY WILL AND DRAWN YOU HERE,	284	TWO KINGS	158
THAT HE MIGHT LEARN THE SHEPHERDS' WILL.	288	TO WEALTHY MAN	19
WHO HAVE FAILED, BEING WEAK OF WILL,	298	THREE HERMITS	18
NOR THE TAME WILL, NOR TIMID BRAIN,	318	APPOINTMENT	8
I MOURN FOR THAT MOST LONELY THING; AND YET GOD'S WILL BE DONE!	354	HIS PHOENIX	31
OR SICKNESS BREAK HER WILL	365	HER RACE	10
WHEN HAD I MY OWN WILL?	382	VISION ROBART	7
IN IGNORANT GOOD WILL,	392	EASTER 1916 V	18
HAD IGNORANT GOOD WILL;	392	EASTER 1916 V	19
AND THAT ITS OWN SWEET WILL IS HEAVEN'S WILL;	405	FOR DAUGHTER	69
AND THAT ITS OWN SWEET WILL IS HEAVEN'S WILL;	405	FOR DAUGHTER	69
IT IS TIME THAT I WROTE MY WILL;	414	TOWER	121
ACCOMPLISHED HIS PREDESTINED WILL,	522	LULLABY	16
I DID THE DRAGON'S WILL UNTIL YOU CAME	533	HER TRIUMPH	1
GIVES FORTH. HE, THE ETERNAL, WORKS HIS WILL.	689	NETTLESHIP	16
I HERE ARREST THEE. IT WAS ALLAH'S WILL.	694	MOSADA 1	105
I HERE ARREST THEE. IT IS ALLAH'S WILL.	694	MOSADA 1 V	105
FORGIVE ME! IT WAS ALLAH'S WILL. THE CORDS.	695	MOSADA 1	109
FORGIVE, OR I WILL DIE. 'TWAS ALLAH'S WILL.	695	MOSADA 1	118
FORGIVE ME! IT WAS ALLAH'S WILL. NOW CORDS.	695	MOSADA 1 V	109
FOR HOLIEST TEACHERS OF HIS WILL,	736	IN CHURCH	7
IS IT YOUR WILL THAT I, WHO AM A QUEEN	757	SHADOW WATER A	212
COME RIDE AND RIDE WITH A WILL!	773	COME RIDE	2
WILLED			
FOR SO SHE WILLED—THOU HEARD'ST? UPON THE BREAST	653	ISLE STAT I 2	32
WILLIAM			
SINCE OLD WILLIAM POLLEXFEN	360	ALF POLLEXFEN	2
I, THE POET WILLIAM YEATS,	406	CARVED STONE	1
OR THAT WILLIAM BLAKE	576	ACRE OF GRASS	16
OLD WILLIAM POLLEXFEN,	604	YOU CONTENT	14
WILLINGLY			
AND IF YOU SAY THAT SHE CAME WILLINGLY—	244	SHADOW WATER B	460
AND YOU SAY THAT SHE CAME WILLINGLY—	244	SHADOW WATER B V	460
WILLOW			
THE WILLOW OF THE MANY-SORROWED WORLD.	130	BOOK STORIES V	16
SHANWALLA, WHERE A WILLOW BORDERED POND	217	WOODS OF COOLE V	2
THAT ON A WILLOW SWUNG.	308	PLAYER QUEEN	4
AND HANGING O'ER THE HUSH OF WILLOW BOWERS,	705	REMEMBRANCE	8
A SCORE OF YARDS OFF 'NEATH A WILLOW, SHOT.	712	FERENCZ RENYI	65
AND SHE IS DRAGGED TO WHERE THE WILLOW BANDS	714	FERENCZ RENYI	108
BESIDE THE WILLOW. NAY, TO YONDER STAR,	715	FERENCZ RENYI	118
BENEATH THE WILLOW—NAY, TO YONDER STAR,	715	FERENCZ RENYI V	118
WILLOW-BORDERED			
SHAN-WALLA, WHERE A WILLOW-BORDERED POND	217	WOODS OF COOLE	2
WILLOW-GLADE			
SO! MID THE WILLOW-GLADE YOU PAUSE AT LAST.	651	ISLE STAT I 2	2
WILLOWS			
BUT WHENCE, AND WHEN? OVER THE WILLOWS SERE	652	ISLE STAT I 2	28
OVER THE CROWN OF THE WILLOWS BROWN.	653	ISLE STAT I 2	30
OVER THE CROWN OF THE WILLOWS BROWN.	653	ISLE STAT I 2	51
BY THE WILLOWS IN THE GLADE,	726	LOVERS QUARREL	3
WILLS			
AS THOUGH TO CHOOSE WHATEVER SHAPE IT WILLS	417	ANCEST HOUSES	6
WHO TRAVELS WHERE GOD WILLS.	587	OLD WICKED MAN	4

	PAGE	TITLE		LINE
WILSON				
CALVERT AND WILSON, BLAKE AND CLAUDE,	639	BEN BULBEN		64
AND WILSON, BLAKE AND CALVERT, CLAUDE,	639	BEN BULBEN	V	64
WIN				
AND SHE, TO WIN HIM, HIS GREY HAIR CARESSED;	110	CUCHULAIN SEA		73
TO WIN A WOMAN IN HER OWN DESPITE,	244	SHADOW WATER B		458
TO WIN A WOMAN IS IN HER OWN DESPITE,	244	SHADOW WATER B	V	458
"AND IF I WIN," ONE BEGGAR SAID,	296	THREE BEGGARS		29
AT STROKE OF MIDNIGHT GOD SHALL WIN.	561	FOUR AGES MAN		8
THAT MURMURS WITH HOLY WOODS, AND WIN THEIR HELP	757	SHADOW WATER A		199
WIND SEE SEA-WIND				
"WHY DO YOU WIND NO HORN?" SHE SAID,	4	OISIN 1		32
WHY DO YOU WIND NO HORN? SHE SAID,	4	OISIN 1	V	33
AND NOW A LADY RODE LIKE THE WIND	12	OISIN 1		142
AND NOW A MAIDEN RODE LIKE THE WIND	12	OISIN 1	V	142
ARE CHOKED WITH THUNDER, LIGHTNING, AND FIERCE WIND,	42	OISIN 2		205
OLD AND REMEMBERING, WHAT AVAILS THE WIND	42	OISIN 2	V	206
INTO THE CLANGOUR OF THE WIND AND SEA.	45	OISIN 2		234
. . . LIKE THE ROARING OF WIND IN A WOOD.	58	OISIN 3		168
AND LEAVES SHOOK IN THE WIND;	133	FR GILLIGAN		18
OR ELSE THEY STAND AND SNIFF THE WIND;	136	TWO TREES		37
WHEN THEY ARE HEARD UPON THE WIND;	136	TWO TREES	V	37
TO RANT AND RAGE IN FLOOD AND WIND;	138	TO IRELAND		26
IN FLOOD AND FIRE AND CLAY AND WIND,	138	TO IRELAND	V	25
THAT YOU CALL IN BIRDS, IN WIND ON THE HILL,	141	EVERLAST VOICE		6
AND THEY SIGH IF THE WIND BUT LIFT A TRESS;	151	OLD MOTHER		8
AND THEY SIGH IF THE WIND BUT LIFT UP A TRESS;	151	OLD MOTHER	V	8
THERE IS ENOUGH EVIL IN THE CRYING OF WIND,	155	REPROVE CURLEW		6
WHERE WIND CRIES IN THE SEDGE;	165	CRY OF SEDGE		3
BETWEEN THE WIND AND THE WOOD	166	BLESSED		4
BETWEEN THE WIND AND THE WOOD.	167	BLESSED	V	4D
BUT I CAN SEE WHERE THE WIND GOES	168	BLESSED		27
AND FOLLOW THE WAY OF THE WIND;	168	BLESSED		28
"AND BLESSEDNESS GOES WHERE THE WIND GOES,	168	BLESSED		29
BUT I HAVE FOUND WHERE THE WIND GOES .	168	BLESSED	V	27
BY A GREY SHORE WHERE THE WIND NEVER BLEW,	170	SECRET ROSE		14
THE HOUR OF THY GREAT WIND OF LOVE AND HATE.	170	SECRET ROSE		28
SURELY THINE HOUR HAS COME, THY GREAT WIND BLOWS,	170	SECRET ROSE		31
GREAT POWERS OF FALLING WAVE AND WIND AND WINDY FIRE,	174	ELEMENT POWERS		7
YOU GREAT ANGELIC POWERS OF WIND, AND WAVE, AND FIRE,	174	ELEMENT POWERS	V	7
GREAT ELEMENTAL POWERS OF WIND, AND WAVE, AND FIRE,	174	ELEMENT POWERS	V	7
I BECAME A MAN, A HATER OF THE WIND,	177	PAST GREATNESS		7
NOR THE GREY RUSH WHEN THE WIND IS HIGH,	189	BAILE AILLINN		2
NOR THE GREY RUSH WHEN WIND IS HIGH	189	BAILE AILLINN	V	2
WITH ALL THIS CRYING IN THE WIND,	190	BAILE AILLINN		33
THE NORTH WIND TUMBLES TO AND FRO	191	BAILE AILLINN		45
THAT NORTH WIND TUMBLES TO AND FRO	191	BAILE AILLINN	V	45
BUT THE GREY RUSH UNDER THE WIND,	192	BAILE AILLINN		88
"FROM HEAT AND COLD AND WIND AND WAVE;	193	BAILE AILLINN		114
"HE IS WELL OUT OF WIND AND WAVE,	193	BAILE AILLINN	V	114
FOR WHEN WE HAVE BLAMED THE WIND WE CAN BLAME LOVE;	201	OLD MEMORY		10
NO BOUGHS HAVE WITHERED BECAUSE OF THE WINTRY WIND;	203	WITHER BOUGHS		7
WIND AND UNWIND THEIR DANCES WHEN THE LIGHT GROWS COOL	203	WITHER BOUGHS		13
NO BOUGHS HAVE WITHERED BECAUSE OF THE WINTRY WIND;	203	WITHER BOUGHS		15
WIND AND UNWIND DANCING WHEN THE LIGHT GROWS COOL	203	WITHER BOUGHS	V	13
NO BOUGHS HAVE WITHERED BECAUSE OF THE WINTRY WIND;	204	WITHER BOUGHS		23
UNDER A BITTER BLACK WIND THAT BLOWS FROM THE LEFT HAND;	206	HANRAHANS SONG		2
OUR COURAGE BREAKS LIKE AN OLD TREE IN A BLACK WIND AND DIES,	207	HANRAHANS SONG		3
THE WIND HAS BUNDLED UP THE CLOUDS HIGH OVER KNOCKNAREA,	207	HANRAHANS SONG		6
LIKE TUFTED REEDS OUR COURAGE DROOPS IN A BLACK WIND AND DIES;	207	HANRAHANS SONG	V	3
WHEN THE WIND COMES BLOWING ACROSS THE HILLY LAND;	207	HANRAHANS SONG	V	7
NOR ULADH, WHEN NAOISE HAD THROWN A SAIL UPON THE WIND;	209	UNDER THE MOON		4
SEVEN OLD SISTERS WIND THE THREADS OF THE LONG-LIVED ONES;	209	UNDER THE MOON		7
OR ULADH WHEN NAISI HAD HUNG A SAIL UPON THE WIND;	209	UNDER THE MOON	V	4
SEVEN OLD SISTERS WIND THE THREADS OF THE LONG LIVED ONES,	209	UNDER THE MOON	V	7
I'VE HEARD A RUSTLING OVERHEAD IN THE WIND.	223	SHADOW WATER B		28
PEACEABLE MEN THAT SHUT THE WIND AWAY.	224	SHADOW WATER B		54
AND YOU HAD SPREAD A SAIL FOR HOME, A WIND	236	SHADOW WATER B		309
AND LISTENING TO THE CRY OF WIND AND WAVE	236	SHADOW WATER B		315
THAT UNIMAGINABLE STORMS OF WIND AND WAVE	236	SHADOW WATER B		317
AND LISTENING TO THE CRY OF THE WIND AND WAVE	236	SHADOW WATER B	V	315
AND YET YOU SAY THE WATER AND THE WIND	236	SHADOW WATER B	V	317
IN ISLANDS WHERE THE CHILDREN OF AENGUS WIND	245	SHADOW WATER B		469
THEY HAVE GONE ABOUT LIKE WIND,	289	SEPTEMBER 1913		11
UNTIL A CURLEW CRIED AND IN THE LUMINOUS WIND	291	PAUDEEN		4
THE WIND IS OLD AND STILL AT PLAY	301	RUN PARADISE		22
TO TAKE MY FANCY LIKE THE WIND	301	RUN PARADISE		26
CURSING THE WIND. IT WAS AS MUCH	302	HOUR DAWN	V	4
AND THE SHEEP BLEATING AT THE WIND	306	HOUR DAWN		78
IF A GOOD EASTER WIND WERE BLOWING,	306	HOUR DAWN		86
AND THOUGH THE WINTER WIND IS BAD	306	HOUR DAWN		87
IF BUT THIS WIND WERE IN THE SOUTH."	306	HOUR DAWN		90
OR THAT THE WIND WOULD SHIFT A POINT,	306	HOUR DAWN		92
NEITHER THE SPRING NOR THE SOUTH WIND	306	HOUR DAWN		95
TO A CHILD DANCING IN THE WIND	312	CHILD DANCING		T
FOR WIND OR WATER'S ROAR?	312	CHILD DANCING		3
THE MONSTROUS CRYING OF WIND?	312	CHILD DANCING		12
I HAD THOUGHT, SEEING HOW BITTER IS THAT WIND	327	ROBERT GREGORY		89
HAIR SPREAD ON THE WIND THEY MADE;	332	ROUND TOWER		22

WIND (CONTINUED)

		PAGE	TITLE		LINE
HAIRS SPREAD ON THE WIND THEY MADE;		332	ROUND TOWER	V	22
WHAT'S DYING BUT A SECOND WIND?		338	TOM OROUGHLEY		11
SOME BEGGAR SHELTERING FROM THE WIND, AND THERE		351	HER PRAISE		13
THAT BELLIES AND DRAGS IN THE WIND		358	BALLOON MIND		3
WHO KNOWS HOW SHE DRANK THE WIND		381	SONGS FOOL 2		6
THAT HER HAIR STREAMS UPON THE WIND,		390	IMAGE PAST		40
OR MAYBE BUT A WIND THAT BLOWS		396	ROSE TREE		5
WIND SHADOWS OF THE INDIGNANT DESERT BIRDS.		402	SECOND COMING	V	17
WHEREBY THE HAYSTACK- AND ROOF-LEVELLING WIND,		403	FOR DAUGHTER		5
ASSAULT AND BATTERY OF THE WIND		405	FOR DAUGHTER		55
FOR AN OLD BELLOWS FULL OF ANGRY WIND?		405	FOR DAUGHTER		64
OLD LECHER WITH A LOVE ON EVERY WIND,		413	TOWER		105
OF EVERY WIND THAT BLOWS!		419	MY HOUSE		7
LIFE SCARCE CAN CAST A FRAGRANCE ON THE WIND,		422	MY DESCENDANTS		5
A GLITTERING SWORD OUT OF THE EAST. A PUFF OF WIND		426	PHANTOM HATRED		5
NOR THOUGHT OF THE LEVELLING WIND.		432	NINETEEN 19		97
WIND SHRIEKED--AND WHERE ARE THEY?		432	NINETEEN 19		107
A SUDDEN BLAST OF DUSTY WIND AND AFTER		433	NINETEEN 19		119
THEIR PURPOSE IN THE LABYRINTH OF THE WIND;		433	NINETEEN 19		121
ACCORDING TO THE WIND, FOR ALL ARE BLIND.		433	NINETEEN 19		124
BUT NOW WIND DROPS, DUST SETTLES; THEREUPON		433	NINETEEN 19		125
HOLLOW OF CHEEK AS THOUGH IT DRANK THE WIND		444	SCHOOL CHILDR		27
TRANSPARENT LIKE THE WIND,		449	HERO GIRL FOOL		27
THE SOUTH WIND BROUGHT IT LONGING, AND THE EAST WIND DESPAIR,		449	OWEN AHERNE		5
THE SOUTH WIND BROUGHT IT LONGING, AND THE EAST WIND DESPAIR,		449	OWEN AHERNE		5
THE WEST WIND MADE IT PITIFUL, AND THE NORTH WIND AFRAID.		449	OWEN AHERNE		6
THE WEST WIND MADE IT PITIFUL, AND THE NORTH WIND AFRAID.		449	OWEN AHERNE		6
THE SOUTH WIND BROUGHT IT LONGING, AND THE EAST BROUGHT IN DESPAIR,		449	OWEN AHERNE	V	5
THE SOUTH WIND BROUGHT IT LONGING, AND THE EAST BROUGHT IT DESPAIR,		449	OWEN AHERNE	V	5
BUT O! MY HEART COULD BEAR NO MORE WHEN THE UPLAND CAUGHT THE WIND;		450	OWEN AHERNE		11
A BONE WAVE-WHITENED AND DRIED IN THE WIND.		521	THREE THINGS		6
A BONE WAVE-WHITENED AND DRIED IN THE WIND.		521	THREE THINGS		12
A BONE WAVE-WHITENED AND DRIED IN THE WIND.		521	THREE THINGS		18
COLD AS THE MARCH WIND HIS EYES.		531	FATHER CHILD		8
O MARCHING WIND, O A BLAST OF THE WIND,		548	TO SAME TUNE 3		24
O MARCHING WIND, O A BLAST OF THE WIND,		548	TO SAME TUNE 3		24
"BECAUSE I HELPED TO WIND THE CLOCK		585	ORAHILLY		25
IN THE SUNLIGHT AND WIND.		600	THOSE IMAGES		4
AND THE WIND SIGHED TOO.		611	NEWS ORACLE		4
A BLAST OF THE WIND, O A MARCHING WIND,		615	MARCH SONGS 2		24
A BLAST OF THE WIND, O A MARCHING WIND,		615	MARCH SONGS 2		24
MARCH WIND, AND ANY OLD TUNE.		615	MARCH SONGS 2		25
A BLAST OF WIND, O A MARCHING WIND,		615	MARCH SONGS 2	V	24
A BLAST OF WIND, O A MARCHING WIND,		615	MARCH SONGS 2	V	24
BUT WIND COMES UP FROM THE SHORE!		636	BLACK TOWER		18
BUT WIND COMES UP FROM THE SHORE!		636	BLACK TOWER		28
YON WIND GOES SADLY, AND THE GRASS AND TREES		652	ISLE STAT I 2		10
THE WIND AT EVENING WHEN THE SUN GOES DOWN		653	ISLE STAT I 2		50
THEY HEAR THE STORY OF THE WIND,		655	ISLE STAT I 3		11
UPON THE WIND, AND GUIDE MINE ARROW'S COURSE.		657	ISLE STAT I 3		62
THAT NESTLES ALONE IN THE WHISTLING WIND,		657	ISLE STAT I 3		68
BEFORE THE WIND. SAW YOU HIS EYES A-GLITTER?		683	SEEKER		35
THE MOTHER OF THE WIND MOURNS TOO,		738	YOU ARE SAD		6
AND HER OLD WIND THAT NO MIRTH EVER HAD,		738	YOU ARE SAD		7
BUT THAT THE WIND CHANGED; FOR I FOLLOWED HIM		747	SHADOW WATER A		4
AND HEARD THE MUSIC IN THE WIND, AND SAW		747	SHADOW WATER A		5
A PATH AMONG THESE WAVES AND WEIGH THE WIND?		748	SHADOW WATER A		21
AND I HAVE HEARD THEM CALL FROM WIND TO WIND		750	SHADOW WATER A		83
AND I HAVE HEARD THEM CALL FROM WIND TO WIND		750	SHADOW WATER A		83
AND NO MAN KILL ME; FOR SOME WIND HAS BLOWN		751	SHADOW WATER A		97
MAKE GALLEYS OUT OF WIND THAT CHANGE TO WIND		751	SHADOW WATER A		105
MAKE GALLEYS OUT OF WIND THAT CHANGE TO WIND		751	SHADOW WATER A		105
WHILE THE WIND IS LIGHT. THE OAR CAN HARDLY MOVE HER,		754	SHADOW WATER A		157
OF FOLLOWING FORGAEL'S DREAM FROM WIND TO WIND.		758	SHADOW WATER A		219
OF FOLLOWING FORGAEL'S DREAM FROM WIND TO WIND.		758	SHADOW WATER A		219
AND A COLD WIND IS BLOWING IN MY HAIR.		761	SHADOW WATER A		277
AND BRING ME WHERE THE CHILDREN OF AENGUS WHERE THE WORLD ENDS, OR RUNS FROM WIND TO WIND		763	SHADOW WATER A		317
WHERE THE WORLD ENDS, OR RUNS FROM WIND TO WIND		768	SHADOW WATER A		417
WHERE THE WORLD ENDS, OR RUNS FROM WIND TO WIND		768	SHADOW WATER A		417
HAD WOVEN HER OF WIND. LIFE WITHERS OUT		768	SHADOW WATER A	V	423
LET THE WIND BEAR WITNESS.		770	BLOOD BOND		8
COME RIDE LIKE THE MARCH WIND;		774	COME RIDE		6
RUN LIKE THE MARCH WIND;		774	COME RIDE	V	6
GATHER ON THE WIND AND DRIVE		775	AGAINST WITCH		7
FOR THEY ARE BUT WHIRLING WIND,		775	AGAINST WITCH		9
AND THE WIND BLOWS IT AWAY.		783	GREY ROUND		20

WIND-BEATEN

THE WIND-BEATEN, STONE-GREY,		310	PEACOCK		4
UNDER YOUR OLD WIND-BEATEN TOWER, WHERE STILL		367	EGO DOMINUS		2
BUT THESE WASTE WATERS AND WIND-BEATEN SAILS		763	SHADOW WATER A		319

WIND-BLOWN

THIS BODY TREMBLING LIKE A WIND-BLOWN REED.		103	FERGUS DRUID		25
"O HEARTS OF WIND-BLOWN FLAME!		162	ASKS FORGIVE		6
"THE WIND-BLOWN CLAMOUR OF THE BARNACLE-GEESE."		300	BEGGAR CRIED		20
AS A WREATH OF SMOKE IN WIND-BLOWN FLIGHT		730	PRIEST FAIRY		61

896

```
                                                              PAGE    TITLE              LINE
WIND-BROKEN
     UNDER THE OLD WIND-BROKEN TREE,  . . . . . . . . . . .   406  IN TIME OF WAR          3
WINDING       SEE EVER-WINDING
     WE DANCED TO WHERE IN THE WINDING THICKET . . . . . .     20  OISIN 1               304
     THEN ONWARD IN THE WINDING THICKET  . . . . . . . . .     20  OISIN 1          V    304
     AND GOD STANDS WINDING HIS LONELY HORN, . . . . . . .    148  INTO TWILIGHT          13
     CLIMB UP THE NARROW WINDING STAIR TO BED: . . . . . .    324  ROBERT GREGORY          5
     AT SOME OLD WINDING WHITETHORN ROOT . . . . . . . . .    342  SHEP GOATHERD         101
     A WINDING STAIR, A CHAMBER ARCHED WITH STONE, . . . .    419  MY HOUSE               11
     I SUMMON TO THE WINDING ANCIENT STAIR: . . . . . . .     477  SELF AND SOUL           1
     THIS WINDING, GYRING, SPIRING TREADMILL OF A STAIR . . . 480  BLOOD AND MOON         17
     MAY UNWIND THE WINDING PATH: . . . . . . . . . . . .     497  BYZANTIUM              12
     OR WINDING THROUGH THE GROVE  . . . . . . . . . . . .    530  DELPHIC ORACLE          7
     A HORN! SOME TROOP OF ROBBERS WINDING GOES . . . . . .   649  ISLE STAT I 1         110
WINDINGS
     AND ALL THE WINDINGS THERE. . . . . . . . . . . . . .    520  HIS BARGAIN            12
WINDING-SHEET
     WINDING-SHEET AND SWADDLING-CLOTHES. . . . . . . . . .   530  OLD TOM AGAIN           6
     WINDING-SHEET AND SWADDLING-CLOTHES. . . . . . . . . .   530  OLD TOM AGAIN    V      6
WINDLESS
     THE DANCE WOUND THROUGH THE WINDLESS WOODS: . . . . .     21  OISIN 1               320
     THEN ON AMONG THE WINDLESS WOODS, . . . . . . . . . .     21  OISIN 1          V    320
     FAR OUT UNDER A WINDLESS SKY: . . . . . . . . . . . .    197  BAILE AILLINN         181
WINDLE-STRAWS
     WINDLE-STRAWS I.  O'SULLIVAN RUA TO THE CURLEW . . . .   155  REPROVE CURLEW   V      T
WINDOW
     AND STAND ON HER WINDOW SILL. . . . . . . . . . . . .    159  CAP AND BELLS    V      4
     SHE OPENED HER DOOR AND HER WINDOW, . . . . . . . . .    160  CAP AND BELLS          29
     A LATTICED WINDOW.  HIS GLANCE WENT UP AT TIMES . . .    180  QUEEN MAEVE             6
     IN THEIR GREAT WINDOW LOOKING AT THE DAWN: . . . . .     352  PEOPLE                 15
     WITH FACE AND NOSE PRESSED TO A SWEET-SHOP WINDOW, . .   370  EGO DOMINUS            56
     WITH FACE AND NOSE PRESSED TO A SWEETSHOP WINDOW. . .    370  EGO DOMINUS      V     56
     THE LIGHT IN THE TOWER WINDOW WAS PUT OUT. . . . . . .   377  PHASES OF MOON        139
     THE STARE'S NEST BY MY WINDOW . . . . . . . . . . . .    424  STARES NEST            T
     THE JAY'S NEST BY MY WINDOW . . . . . . . . . . . . .    424  STARES NEST      V      T
     PERCHED IN SOME WINDOW OF HER MOTHER'S HOUSE . . . . .   466  HARUN RASHID          106
     HEARD YOU?  YOUR LUTE HUNG IN THE WINDOW SOUNDED! . .    694  MOSADA 1               95
     FROM THE GREAT PAINTED WINDOW WRAPS HIS BROW, . . . .    697  MOSADA 2               37
     FLOATING FROM YON BARRED WINDOW.  SMALL NEW-COMER, . .   700  MOSADA 3               43
     FLOATING FROM YON BARRED WINDOW.  NEW COMER, . . . . .   700  MOSADA 3         V     43
WINDOWED
     FROM DOORED AND WINDOWED CLIFF, OR HALF UPTURNED . . .   368  EGO DOMINUS            30
WINDOW-GLASS
     GLASS-MOSAIC, WINDOW-GLASS, . . . . . . . . . . . . .    440  WISDOM                  3
WINDOW-LEDGE
     UNDER MY WINDOW-LEDGE THE WATERS RACE, . . . . . . .     490  COOLE BALLYLEE          1
WINDOWLESS
     WINDOWLESS, PILLARLESS, MULTITUDINOUS HOME . . . . . .    39  OISIN 2               148
WINDOW'S
     BY A WINDOW'S FEEBLE LIGHT . . . . . . . . . . . . .     731  STREET DANCERS          3
WINDOWS
     THE WINDOWS AND THE DOORS WERE SHUT, . . . . . . . .      95  MOLL MAGEE             29
     SHOWED THEIR FAINT LIGHT THROUGH THE UNSHUTTERED WINDOWS, 279  TWO KINGS             50
     GREAT WINDOWS OPEN TO THE SOUTH, . . . . . . . . . .     475  EVA GORE-BOOTH          2
     UPON THE DUSTY, GLITTERING WINDOWS CLING, . . . . . .    482  BLOOD AND MOON         43
     ITS OPEN LIGHTED DOORWAY AND ITS WINDOWS ALL ALIGHT, .   581  CURSE CROMWELL         26
     SCARCE THE OLD AND WIZEN HOUSES HAD THEIR DOORS AND WINDOWS 718  PHANTOM SHIP          5
        SHUT.
     SCARCE THE OLD AND WIZENED HOUSES HAD THEIR DOORS        718  PHANTOM SHIP     V      5
        AND WINDOWS SHUT.
WINDOW-SILL
     AND STAND ON HER WINDOW-SILL. . . . . . . . . . . .     159  CAP AND BELLS           4
WINDS
     STROKED THE YOUNG WINDS AS THEY ROLLED ON THE PLAIN, . .  27  OISIN 1          V 415C
     THE DEMONS OF THE WILDS AND WINDS FOR FRIGHT . . . . .    34  OISIN 2          V  81B
     SURLY AND DISTANT, WITH THE WINDS AND SEA:—  . . . . .    45  OISIN 2          V  234
     I BELLOW TO THE WINDS WHEN STORMS MAKE MOAN, . . . . .    45  OISIN 2          V 239D
     WERE THE WINDS LESS SOFT THAN THE BREATH OF A PIGEON . .  56  OISIN 3               134
     AND THE WINDS MADE THE SANDS ON THE SEA'S EDGE . . . .    57  OISIN 3               145
     LONG FLED THE FOAM-FLAKES AROUND ME, THE WINDS FLED OUT   57  OISIN 3               149
        OF THE VAST,
     TILL, FATTENING THE WINDS OF THE MORNING, AN ODOUR       57  OISIN 3               153
        OF NEW-MOWN HAY
     THE COLD WET WINDS EVER BLOWING, . . . . . . . . . .     119  PITY OF LOVE            5
     AND THE COLD WET WINDS EVER BLOWING, . . . . . . . .     119  PITY OF LOVE     V      7
     I TORE IT FROM GREEN BOUGHS WINDS TORE AND TOSSED . . .  130  BOOK STORIES          13
     I TORE IT FROM GREEN BOUGHS WINDS TOSSED AND HURLED, .   130  BOOK STORIES     V     13
     THE WINDS AWAKEN, THE LEAVES WHIRL ROUND, . . . . . .    140  HOSTING SIDHE          6
     FOR WINDS WILL BEAR THEM GENTLY WHEN THE EAGLE FLIES, .  146  UNAPPEAS HOST    V      3
     FOR THEY WILL RIDE THE WINDS WHEN THE GIER-EAGLE FLIES . 146  UNAPPEAS HOST          3
     DESOLATE WINDS THAT CRY OVER THE WANDERING SEA: . . . .  147  UNAPPEAS HOST          7
     DESOLATE WINDS THAT HOVER IN THE FLAMING WEST: . . . .   147  UNAPPEAS HOST          8
     DESOLATE WINDS THAT BEAT THE DOORS OF HEAVEN, AND BEAT . 147  UNAPPEAS HOST          9
     O HEART THE WINDS HAVE SHAKEN, THE UNAPPEASABLE HOST . . 147  UNAPPEAS HOST         11
     AND HEART THE WINDS HAVE SHAKEN: THE UNAPPEASABLE HOST . 147  UNAPPEAS HOST    V     11
     AND HEAR THE WINDS HAVE SHAKEN, THE UNAPPEASABLE HOST . . 147  UNAPPEAS HOST    V     11
     AND THE WINDS THAT BLOW THROUGH THE STARRY WAYS, . . . . 158  TO HIS HEART           4
     LET THE STARRY WINDS AND THE FLAME AND THE FLOOD . . . . 158  TO HIS HEART           5
     AND THE WINDS BLOWING THROUGH THE STARRY WAYS, . . . .   158  TO HIS HEART     V      4
     O WINDS, OLDER THAN CHANGING OF NIGHT AND DAY, . . . .   162  ASKS FORGIVE           7
     O WINDS, ELDER THAN CHANGING OF NIGHT AND DAY, . . . .   162  ASKS FORGIVE     V      7
                              897
```

PAGE   TITLE   LINE

WINDS   (CONTINUED)

	PAGE	TITLE		LINE
THE WINDS THAT AWAKENED THE STARS	171	MAID QUIET		3
FOR THE WINDS THAT AWAKENED THE STAR,	171	MAID QUIET	V	3
FOR THE WINDS THAT AWAKENED THE STARS	171	MAID QUIET	V	3
WHEN WINDS HAVE GATHERED AND SUN AND MOON BURNED DIM	175	ELEMENT POWERS		15
CASTS UP A SHOW AND THE WINDS ANSWER IT	186	QUEEN MAEVE		125
VEERING, FLEETING, FICKLE, THE WINDS OF KNOCKNAREA,	206	HANRAHANS SONG	V	1
UNDER THE BITTER BLACK WINDS BLOWING OUT OF THE LEFT HAND!	206	HANRAHANS SONG	V	2
FOR THE WET WINDS ARE BLOWING OUT OF THE CLINGING AIR!	207	HANRAHANS SONG		12
THE WINDS HAVE BUNDLED UP THE CLOUDS HIGH OVER KNOCKNAREA	207	HANRAHANS SONG	V	6
AND SHAKE DOWN THUNDER ON THE STONES BECAUSE THE RED WINDS RAVE!	207	HANRAHANS SONG	V	7
FOR THE GREY WINDS ARE BLOWING UP, OUT OF THE CLINGING SEAS!	207	HANRAHANS SONG	V	12
AND WINDS AND PONDS COVER MORE QUIET WOODS,	218	WOODS OF COOLE		34
MORE SHINING WINDS, MORE STAR-GLIMMERING PONDS?	218	WOODS OF COOLE		35
AND WINDS BLOWING FROM FLOWERS, AND WHIRR OF FEATHERS	219	WOODS OF COOLE		39
WHERE TIME IS DROWNED IN ODOUR-LADEN WINDS	219	HARP OF AENGUS		3
THAT SHE AMONG HER WINDS MIGHT KNOW HE WEPT!	220	HARP OF AENGUS		12
IT WAS THEIR HANDS THAT PLUCKED THE WINDS AWAKE	237	SHADOW WATER B		324
THOSE WINDS THAT CLAMOUR OF APPROACHING NIGHT.	431	NINETEEN 19		68
THAT WINDS OF WINTER BLOW	431	NINETEEN 19		87
FOR THE FOUL WINDS BLOW!	523	MAD AS MIST		2
BUT I WOKE IN AN OLD RUIN THAT THE WINDS HOWLED THROUGH!	581	CURSE CROMWELL		28
BUT WINDS COME UP FROM THE SHORE!	635	BLACK TOWER		8
THEY SHAKE WHEN THE WINDS ROAR,	635	BLACK TOWER		9
THEY SHAKE WHEN THE WINDS ROAR,	636	BLACK TOWER		19
THEY SHAKE WHEN THE WINDS ROAR,	636	BLACK TOWER		29
BUT WINDS COME UP FROM THE SHORE!	636	BLACK TOWER	V	REF
AS BLOSSOMS, WHEN THE WINDS OF MARCH	671	ISLE STAT II 3		127
SOON WILT THOU SMILE, FOR HERE THE WINDS ARE WEAK	671	ISLE STAT II 3		141
AND HOLLOW LULLING THE YOUNG WINDS WITH SONG.	675	ISLE STAT II 3		226
AND WHERE THE POLAR WINDS AND WATERS WRESTLE	682	SEEKER		18
THE TALKING WINDS HAVE FOUND THEIR HOME,	686	LIFE		9
FROM HERE, ALONG THE SHADOWY WAY THAT WINDS	703	MOSADA 3		111
AND ON TIPTOE THE WINDS A-WHISPERING STOOD.	715	DWELT SYCAMORE		8
AND ON TIP-TOE THE WINDS A-WHISPERING STOOD.	715	DWELT SYCAMORE	V	8
. . . CEASE THE WINDS, AND ON THEIR POLES . .	719	PHANTOM SHIP		17
AND THE WINDS COME DOWN AND BLOW THEM WITH THE VAPOURS FAR AWAY.	719	PHANTOM SHIP		28
IT MAY BE, BEFORE THE WINDS OF BIRTH HAVE WAKED!	750	SHADOW WATER A		86
HAVE THE WINDS BLOWN YOU AMONG THESE EMPTY WATERS?	756	SHADOW WATER A		192
AMONG THE WINDS, LOOKS UNDER YOUR PALE EYELIDS.	757	SHADOW WATER A		211
WELL SHELTERED FROM THE WINDS, AND FRUITFUL FIELDS,	758	SHADOW WATER A		221
THE WINDS AND WATERS TO BE YOUR HOME FOR EVER!	762	SHADOW WATER A		282
WHERE TIME IS DROWNED IN ODOUR-LADEN WINDS	762	SHADOW WATER A		298
THE WINDS AND WATERS TO BE YOUR HOME FOREVER!	762	SHADOW WATER A		282
THAT SHE AMONG HER WINDS MIGHT KNOW HE WEPT!	763	SHADOW WATER A		307
AND SHE, NO LONGER BLOWN AMONG THE WINDS,	763	SHADOW WATER A		323
THE CLOUDY WATERS AND THE GLIMMERING WINDS	764	SHADOW WATER A		327
AMONG THE WINDS AND WATERS: AND WHEN THEY PASS	764	SHADOW WATER A		331
ALL THAT KNOW LOVE AMONG THE WINDS OF THE WORLD	767	SHADOW WATER A		386
THAT HAVE KNOWN LOVE AMONG THE WINDS OF THE WORLD	767	SHADOW WATER A		392
LOVE WAS NOT MADE FOR DARKNESS AND THE WINDS	767	SHADOW WATER A		394
WHETHER AMONG THE COLD WINDS OF THE DEAD.	768	SHADOW WATER A	V	413
OR AMONG WINDS THAT MOVE IN THE MEADOWS AND WOODS.	768	SHADOW WATER A	V	413
AND ONE WHERE THE WINDS ARE WOVE,	771	SPINNING SONG		3
WHEN THE WINDS ARE CALLING THERE,	772	SONG DEIRDRE 1		4
BECAUSE THE NIGHT WINDS BLOW	782	HEART FRIGHT		16
THE WINDS OUT OF CLARE-GALWAY	783	GREY ROUND		4

WINDWARD

	PAGE	TITLE		LINE
IF I GO NEARER TO THE WINDWARD SIDE,	753	SHADOW WATER A		140

WINDY

	PAGE	TITLE		LINE
AND HUMMING SANDS, WHERE WINDY SURGES WEND!	68	SAD SHEPHERD		4
"I HAVE COME BY THE WINDY WAY	167	BLESSED		6
"I COME BY THE WINDY WAY	167	BLESSED	V	6
GREAT POWERS OF FALLING WAVE AND WIND AND WINDY FIRE,	174	ELEMENT POWERS		7
ABOUT THE WINDY WATER-SIDE,	192	BAILE AILLINN		93
ABOUT THE WINDY WATER SIDE	192	BAILE AILLINN	V	93
ALIGHTED ON THE WINDY GRASS.	195	BAILE AILLINN		138
AMONG THE WINDY MEADOWS OF THE DAWN."	234	SHADOW WATER B		264
IN HAPPY DANCES UNDER A WINDY MOON,	245	SHADOW WATER B		470
THE GREY ROCK AND THE WINDY LIGHT?	275	GREY ROCK		111
ABOVE A WINDY PRECIPICE?" THEN HE:	285	TWO KINGS		195
UPON URBINO'S WINDY HILL,	288	TO WEALTHY MAN		17
ON A WINDY STONE, THE THIRD,	298	THREE HERMITS		5
AS I CAME OVER WINDY GAP	300	RUN PARADISE		1
STUMBLED UPON THAT WINDY PLACE	302	HOUR DAWN		3
STUMBLED ON WINDY CRUACHAN	302	HOUR DAWN	V	3
AND EVERY WINDY QUARTER HOWL	405	FOR DAUGHTER		71
I SUMMON TO THE WINDY ANCIENT STAIR!	477	SELF AND SOUL	V	1
DANCED ON CRUACHAN'S WINDY PLAIN,	528	DANCER CRUACH		4
DANCED IT ON CRUACHAN'S WINDY PLAIN,	528	DANCER CRUACH	V	4
AMONG THE WINDY MEADOWS OF THE DAWN."	754	SHADOW WATER A		153
IN HAPPY DANCES, UNDER A WINDY MOON,	763	SHADOW WATER A		318

WINE

	PAGE	TITLE		LINE
AND BOWLS OF BARLEY, HONEY, AND WINE,	3	OISIN 1		8
AND OIL AND WINE AND HONEY AND MILK,	8	OISIN 1		92
AND HONEY, AND WINE, AND OIL, AND MILK,	8	OISIN 1	V	92
THOSE TWO CAME CARRYING WINE AND MEAT AND BREAD,	41	OISIN 2		184
WE LAY ON SKINS OF OTTERS, AND DRANK WINE,	41	OISIN 2		188

898

WINE (CONTINUED)

	PAGE	TITLE		LINE
HOPING AND FEARING, BROUGHT ME WINE AND BREAD.	41	OISIN 2	V	184A
OF WOLVES, OF BOREAL BEARS, WE QUAFFED THE WINE	41	OISIN 2	V	188
I SAT AND MUSED AND DRANK SWEET WINE;	82	MAD KING GOLL		13
AND A YOUNG MAN BROUGHT HIM RED WINE	144	HOST OF AIR		19
THE BREAD AND THE WINE HAD A DOOM,	144	HOST OF AIR		25
AND ONE HAS SEEN IN THE REDNESS OF WINE	168	BLESSED		35
OR IN THE WINE VAT, DWELL BEYOND THE STIR	169	SECRET ROSE	V	4
POURED OUT WINE FOR THE HIGH INVISIBLE ONES.	219	WOODS OF COOLE		44
A MELANCHOLY THAT A CUP OF WINE,	227	SHADOW WATER B		114
IS NO MORE THAN A WINE CUP IN THE TASTING,	229	SHADOW WATER B		150
THAT HAS THE HEADY FLAVOUR OF NEW WINE,	240	SHADOW WATER B		374
WINE COMES IN AT THE MOUTH	261	DRINKING SONG		1
AND THOUGH AT BOTTLING OF YOUR WINE	271	GREY ROCK		9
FOR ALL WERE FULL OF WINE AND MEAT.	271	GREY ROCK		17
THOUGH AT THE BOTTLING OF YOUR WINE	271	GREY ROCK	V	9
TO HOLD THE WINE THEY BUY OF HIM.	272	GREY ROCK	V	25
'TWAS WINE OR WOMEN, OR SOME CURSE--	273	GREY ROCK		54
AND SHE WITH GOBAN'S WINE ADRIP,	276	GREY ROCK		121
POUR WINE AND DANCE IF MANHOOD STILL HAVE PRIDE,	311	MOUNTAIN TOMB		1
NOR MOUTH FROM KISSING, NOR FROM WINE UNWET;	311	MOUNTAIN TOMB		7
POUR WINE AND DANCE, IF MANKIND STILL HAVE PRIDE,	311	MOUNTAIN TOMB	V	1
NOR MOUTH WITH KISSING NOR WITH WINE UNWET.	311	MOUNTAIN TOMB	V	7
NOR MOUTH WITH KISSING NOR WITH THE WINE UNWET.	311	MOUNTAIN TOMB	V	7
DRUNK WITH THE UNMIXED WINE.	355	PROPERTIUS		8
DRUNK WITH THE UN-MIXED WINE.	355	PROPERTIUS		8
OR WHEN I GROW EXCITED WITH WINE,	357	DEEP-SWORN VOW		5
DID GOD IN PORTIONING WINE AND BREAD	386	ROBARTES DANCE		39
LIT UP THE DARK MAHOGANY AND THE WINE,	410	TOWER		27
I BRING FULL-FLAVOURED WINE OUT OF A BARREL FOUND	442	BLACK CENTAUR		10
I BRING FULL FLAVOURED WINE OUT OF A BARREL FOUND	442	BLACK CENTAUR	V	10
THE WINE DARK OF THE WOOD'S INTRICACIES,	446	COLONUS PRAISE	V	2
WHILE OUR GROSS PALATES DRINK FROM THE WHOLE WINE,	471	ALL SOUL NIGHT		10
NO LIVING MAN CAN DRINK FROM THE WHOLE WINE.	474	ALL SOUL NIGHT		85
I TORE MY BODY THAT ITS WINE MIGHT COVER	537	HER VISION		7
NOR KNEW, DRUNKEN WITH SINGING AS WITH WINE,	537	HER VISION		30
O BUT HEART'S WINE SHALL RUN PURE,	554	CHURCH STATE		5
WINE SHALL RUN THICK TO THE END,	554	CHURCH STATE		11
WINE OR LOVE DRUG HIM TO SLEEP,	633	MAN AND ECHO		26
WINE OR LOVE DRUGS HIM TO SLEEP,	633	MAN AND ECHO	V	26
THEIR MONEY SPENT, THEIR WINE GONE SOUR,	635	BLACK TOWER		3
BEFORE HIS TENT THE GENERAL SIPS HIS WINE.	709	FERENCZ RENYI		6
THIS SULLEN PEASANT SPOILS THE GOOD RED WINE.	711	FERENCZ RENYI		43
THIS SULLEN PEASANT SOURS THE GOOD RED WINE.	711	FERENCZ RENYI	V	43
IN OTHER LIVES? HAST THOU NOT QUAFFED OLD WINE	724	KANVA ON SELF		12
LIKE WINE THAT FILLS TO THE TOP	781	MY HEART BEAT		14

WINE-BREATH

	PAGE	TITLE		LINE
TO DRINK FROM THE WINE-BREATH	471	ALL SOUL NIGHT		9

WINE-CUP

	PAGE	TITLE		LINE
BY A SPILLED WINE-CUP LIE.	168	BLESSED	V	32
IS NO MORE THAN A WINE-CUP IN THE TASTING,	229	SHADOW WATER B		150

WINE-DARK

	PAGE	TITLE		LINE
THE WINE-DARK OF THE WOOD'S INTRICACIES,	446	COLONUS PRAISE		2
AT WINE-DARK MIDNIGHT IN THE SACRED WOOD,	536	HER VISION		2
STARED AT THE WINE-DARK NAIL, OR DARK THAT RAN	537	HER VISION		10

WINE-DRENCHED

	PAGE	TITLE		LINE
THOSE WINE-DRENCHED EYES, AND CURSE OUR LUCK	272	GREY ROCK		39

WINE-STAINED

	PAGE	TITLE		LINE
DWELT AMONG WINE-STAINED WANDERERS IN DEEP WOODS;	170	SECRET ROSE		21

WINE-VAT

	PAGE	TITLE		LINE
OR IN THE WINE-VAT, DWELL BEYOND THE STIR	169	SECRET ROSE		4

WING

	PAGE	TITLE		LINE
FROM WHERE THE BIRDS OF AENGUS WING?"	6	OISIN 1		53
THE RAINS ARE FROM HIS DRIPPING WING, THE MOONBEAMS FROM HIS EYE.	76	INDIAN ON GOD		8
FLAME TO FLAME AND WING TO WING.	125	CATHLEEN PARA		16
FLAME TO FLAME AND WING TO WING.	125	CATHLEEN PARA		16
FLAME ON FLAME AND WING ON WING.	125	CATHLEEN PARA		16
FLAME ON FLAME AND WING ON WING.	125	CATHLEEN PARA	V	16
WHO RISE, WING ABOVE WING, FLAME ABOVE FLAME,	137	TO SOME I TALK		11
WHO RISE, WING ABOVE WING, FLAME ABOVE FLAME,	137	TO SOME I TALK		11
AND WHEN WHITE MOTHS WERE ON THE WING,	149	WANDER AENGUS		5
ARE DUST ON THE MOTH'S WING; THAT NOTHING MATTERS	235	SHADOW WATER B		297
THE GREY WING UPON EVERY TIDE;	290	SEPTEMBER 1913		18
DID SHE IN TOUCHING THAT LONE WING	397	POLIT PRISONER		7
BECAUSE OF SOME GREEN WING, GATHERED OLD MUMMY WHEAT	442	BLACK CENTAUR		7
AS AIR UNDER A WING, CAN GIVE BIRDS' WIT.	462	HARUN RASHID		28
AS AIR UNDER A WING, CAN GIVE BIRD'S WIT.	462	HARUN RASHID	V	28
A COUPLE OF NIGHT-MOTHS ARE ON THE WING.	482	BLOOD AND MOON		46
A COUPLE OF NIGHT MOTHS ARE ON THE WING,	482	BLOOD AND MOON	V	46
AN EAGLE ON THE WING,	601	THOSE IMAGES		14
EACH OTHER ANSWERING. THEN BETWEEN EACH WING	659	ISLE STAT II 1		14
YON ARCHER, HE WHO HATH THE HALCYON'S WING	679	ISLE STAT II 3		316
AMONG THE BOUGHS, BLUE AS THE HALCYON'S WING,	683	SEEKER		38
WITHIN THE WOODWAYS, BLUE AS THE HALCYON'S WING,	683	SEEKER	V	38
THY WITHERED FOE, AND WITH THE PURPLE WING	688	TWO TITANS		55
FLASHING AND FLICKERING WITH EVER-UNDULANT WING,	710	FERENCZ RENYI		19
FLASHING AND FLICKERING, WITH EVER UNDULANT WING,	710	FERENCZ RENYI	V	19
THEIR DREAD OF AUTUMN'S MORTAL WING,	736	SUMMER EVENING		2
AND DREAD NO MORE FOUL AUTUMN'S WING,	737	SUMMER EVENING		18
I LINGER WHILE THE BIRDS ARE ON THE WING,	754	SHADOW WATER A	V	157

	PAGE	TITLE		LINE
WING (CONTINUED)				
THAT HAVE BUILT ALL ARE DUST ON A MOTH'S WING.	757	SHADOW WATER A		205
TILL IT DIP AN AGEING WING	777	SONG DEIRDRE 2		3
UP WITH THE NECK AND CLAP THE WING,	782	HEART FRIGHT		6
UP WITH THE NECK AND CLAP THE WING,	782	HEART FRIGHT		13
UP WITH THE NECK AND CLAP THE WING,	782	HEART FRIGHT		20
STRETCH NECK AND CLAP THE WING,	783	GREY ROUND		27
WINGED				
AND HOW THE WINGED SANDALS DART,	135	TWO TREES		18
WINGED LOVES BORNE ON IN GENTLE STRIFE.	135	TWO TREES	V	14
WITH THE LONELY, PROUD, WINGED MULTITUDE.	158	TO HIS HEART	V	7
ARE YOU NOT HAPPY WINGED BODIES NOW?	234	SHADOW WATER B		273
NOW THAT YOU HAVE HAPPY WINGED BODIES?	234	SHADOW WATER B	V	273
ALONE AND WINGED. OUR LOVE SHALL BE LIKE THEIRS	250	SHADOW WATER B		581
AND RODE OUR WINGED HORSE!	392	EASTER 1916		25
AND OUR WINGED METTLESOME HORSE.	392	EASTER 1916	V	25
LIVING, WIDE WINGED, ON THE WATERS FLOAT.	657	ISLE STAT I 3		54
THE WINGED WONDER OF ALL FAERY LAND.	657	ISLE STAT I 3		57
AND THE HAPPY WINGED DAY.	668	ISLE STAT II 3		64
WINGING SEE A-WINGING				
AND THRO' THE ODOROUS AIR LOVE-DREAMS ARE WINGING—	645	ISLE STAT I 1		5
OVER THEM CRIMSON VAPOURS WINGING.	648	ISLE STAT I 1		92
THENCE HAVE I COME WINGING.	672	ISLE STAT II 3		170
NOW HERE I COME WINGING!	672	ISLE STAT II 3	V	170
WINGS				
KEPT TIME WITH THEIR BRIGHT WINGS AND FEET!	26	OISIN 1		397
BEAT TIME WITH THEIR BRIGHT WINGS AND FEET.	26	OISIN 1	V	397
FANNED THE DELIGHTED AIR LIKE WINGS OF BIRDS!	32	OISIN 2		50
FEW FEATHERS WERE ON THEIR DISHEVELLED WINGS.	34	OISIN 2		76
CHAINED WAS SHE. ON THEIR WINGS THE HUNDREDTH YEAR	34	OISIN 2	V	76
LIKE WINGS OF KINGFISHERS! AND HE AROSE.	40	OISIN 2		169
SHALL THEY TURN WROTH OR PLUCK THE WINGS OF TIME?	42	OISIN 2	V	199
WHEN BRUSHED WITH THE WINGS OF THE OWLS!	53	OISIN 3		98
. . . DEEP HORROR OF EYES AND OF WINGS,	62	OISIN 3		205
ONE WITH THE TIDE THAT GLEAMS, THE WINGS THAT GLEAM AND DART.	78	INDIAN TO LOVE		15
. . . THE WINGS THAT GLIMMER AND GLEAM AND DART!	78	INDIAN TO LOVE	V	15
. . . AND WINGS, THAT GLIMMER AND GLEAM AND DART,	78	INDIAN TO LOVE	V	15
FIRST AS A RAVEN ON WHOSE ANCIENT WINGS	102	FERGUS DRUID		3
AND EVENING FULL OF THE LINNET'S WINGS.	117	ISLE INNISFREE		8
AND EVENING FULL OF THE LINNETS' WINGS.	117	ISLE INNISFREE		8
AND SHAKE THEIR RAGGED WINGS! ALAS!	136	TWO TREES		38
AND WHEN THEY SHAKE THEIR WINGS—ALAS!	136	TWO TREES	V	38
OF THEIR LONG WINGS, THE FLASH OF THEIR WHITE FEET.	137	TO SOME I TALK		16
OF THEIR LONG WINGS, THE FLASH OF THEIR SWIFT FEET.	137	TO SOME I TALK	V	16
WITH HEAVY WHITENING WINGS, AND A HEART FALLEN COLD!	147	UNAPPEAS HOST		4
UNFOLD YOUR FLAMING WINGS AND COVER OUT OF SIGHT	175	ELEMENT POWERS		11
ABOUT WHOSE FACE BIRDS WAGGED THEIR FIERY WINGS,	187	QUEEN MAEVE		145
TALL, PROUD AND RUDDY, AND LIGHT WINGS	195	BAILE AILLINN		140
AND WAVING WHITE WINGS TO AND FRO	197	BAILE AILLINN		184
AND WITH THE WAVING OF YOUR WINGS.	212	BLESS PSALTER		7
AND ALL THAT TOSSING OF YOUR WINGS IS JOY,	244	SHADOW WATER B		451
WHERE WINGS HAVE MEMORY OF WINGS, AND ALL	264	HOUSE SHAKEN		6
WHERE WINGS HAVE MEMORY OF WINGS, AND ALL	264	HOUSE SHAKEN		6
ALL THEIR LIVES THROUGH INTO SOME DRIFT OF WINGS.	265	ABBEY THEATRE		7
UPON THEIR CLAMOROUS WINGS.	322	SWANS AT COOLE		12
THE BELL-BEAT OF THEIR WINGS ABOVE MY HEAD,	323	SWANS AT COOLE		17
THE INNUMERABLE CLANGING WINGS THAT HAVE PUT OUT THE MOON.	427	PHANTOM HATRED		32
THE WINGS HALF SPREAD FOR FLIGHT,	430	NINETEEN 19		65
A SUDDEN BLOW! THE GREAT WINGS BEATING STILL	441	LEDA AND SWAN		1
WINGS BEATING ABOUT THE ROOM!	499	MOTHER OF GOD		3
THOSE DEEDS WERE BEST THAT GAVE THE MINUTE WINGS	533	HER TRIUMPH		5
SOME TWENTY FEET FROM TIP TO TIP HAD ITS WINGS STRETCHED RIGHTLY OUT,	593	PILGRIM	V	17
SOON SHALL OUR WINGS BE STILLED,	643	SONG FAERIES		5
TO WELCOME THEE, WHEN O'ER THE OWLET'S WINGS	648	ISLE STAT I 1		102
UPON HIS WINGS. THRO' YONDER GREEN ABYSS	649	ISLE STAT I 1		114
SOME GOBLIN, MY SERVANT, ON WINGS THAT ARE FLEET,	657	ISLE STAT I 3		67
AND LOUDLY TWICE THE LIVING WINGS FLAPT WIDE,	659	ISLE STAT II 1		12
HALF LIT, SO FLAPT THE WINGS ACROSS THE LAKE—	659	ISLE STAT II 1		17
GENTLY SHOOK THEIR MOTH-LIKE WINGS!	667	ISLE STAT II 3		26
E'EN THOUGH HIS WINGS WERE PLUMELESS STUMPS,	670	ISLE STAT II 3		118
AS MOTHS WITH BROKEN WINGS, AND AS WE SIT	671	ISLE STAT II 3		142
WHEN HIS SINEWY WINGS TOGETHER CLOSE,	673	ISLE STAT II 3		179
SOON SHALL OUR WINGS BE STILLED,	676	ISLE STAT II 3		252
WERE FURLED THE WINGS OF SHIPS. THERE IN A DELL,	693	MOSADA 1		82
THEIR THIEVING WINGS THAT WE MIGHT NEVER PART.	702	MOSADA 3		98
AH! WOE FOR YOUR WINGS AND YOUR HEAD—	708	FAIRY PEDANT		34
MUST SPREAD OUT THEIR WINGS UNTIRING,	739	WHERE BOOKS GO		3
OR BE HIS FOOD, I FOLLOW THE GREY WINGS,	751	SHADOW WATER A		101
AND NEED NO MORE OF LIFE TILL THE WHITE WINGS	751	SHADOW WATER A		102
OR A GOD HID THEM UNDER THE SHADOW OF WINGS.	752	SHADOW WATER A		125
THE HAND THAT WOUNDS. A WHITE BIRD BEATS HIS WINGS	758	SHADOW WATER A	V	232
A WHITE BIRD BEATS HIS WINGS UPON MY FACE.	759	SHADOW WATER A		233
I AM BLIND AND DEAF BECAUSE OF THE WHITE WINGS.	759	SHADOW WATER A		235
I AM AFRAID OF THE HARP. O! WINGS ON WINGS!	759	SHADOW WATER A		236
I AM AFRAID OF THE HARP. O! WINGS ON WINGS!	759	SHADOW WATER A		236
AMONG GREAT TREES, AND IN THE WINGS OF OWLS,	762	SHADOW WATER A		285
WINKING				
IS BUT THE WINKING OF AN EYE!	139	TO IRELAND		36

	PAGE	TITLE	LINE
WINNING			
FOR MOTHER EVE'S WINNING • • • • • • • • • •	654	ISLE STAT I 2	61
WINS			
FOR THE HEART CRIES THAT WHAT DECEPTION WINS • • • • •	448	HERO GIRL FOOL	6
WINTER			
MOVED ROUND ME, OF SEAMEN OR LANDSMEN, ALL WHO ARE WINTER TALES:	53	OISIN 3	86
THE HEAVY STEPS OF THE PLOUGHMAN SPLASHING THE WINTER MOULD,	143	ROSE IN HEART V	3
GATHERS THE WILD DUCK FROM THE WINTER DAWN: • • • • •	217	WOODS OF COOLE	3
AND THOUGH THE WINTER WIND IS BAD • • • • • • • •	306	HOUR DAWN	87
TILL WINTER BLASTS WERE GONE, BUT SPEAK OF HER • • •	340	SHEP GOATHERD	33
THROUGH SUMMER AND WINTER SEEM • • • • • • • • •	393	EASTER 1916	42
THAT WINDS OF WINTER BLOW • • • • • • • • • • •	431	NINETEEN 19	87
SUMMER AND WINTER, DAY AND NIGHT, • • • • • • •	447	COLONUS PRAISE	31
OF THAT OR THE NEXT WINTER WOULD BE DEATH. • • • • •	471	ALL SOUL NIGHT	30
AND FROM THE FORTIETH WINTER BY THAT THOUGHT • • • •	501	VACILLATION	29
HER EIGHTIETH WINTER APPROACHING: "YESTERDAY HE THREATENED MY LIFE.	578	LOFTY THINGS	8
WINTER AND SUMMER TILL OLD AGE BEGAN • • • • • • •	629	CIRCUS ANIMALS	5
WINTER'S			
THROUGH SUMMER'S HEAT AND WINTER'S COLD. • • • • • •	86	MAD KING GOLL	71
"I'LL SLEEP UNTIL THE WINTER'S GONE, • • • • • • •	305	HOUR DAWN	57
"I'D LIKE TO SLEEP TILL WINTER'S GONE • • • • • •	305	HOUR DAWN	60
OR AN OLD MAN UPON A WINTER'S NIGHT. • • • • • • •	359	WAR POEM	6
DECLARE THAT WINTER'S BEST OF ALL: • • • • • • •	434	WHEEL	4
OR WHERE THAT SNOW AND WINTER'S DREADFUL BLAST • • • •	563	MERU	11
WINTERS			
YET PRAISE THE WINTERS GONE: • • • • • • • • •	336	YOUNG BEAUTY	15
WITH SIXTY OR MORE WINTERS ON ITS HEAD, • • • • • •	444	SCHOOL CHILDR	38
OUT OF TEN THOUSAND WINTERS, I ALONE-- • • • • • •	470	HARUN RASHID V	190
WINTER-TIME			
THROUGH WINTER-TIME WE CALL ON SPRING, • • • • • •	434	WHEEL	1
WINTRY			
OR WHEN ALONG THE WINTRY STRANDS • • • • • • • •	84	MAD KING GOLL	41
OR WHERE ALONG THE WINTRY STRANDS • • • • • • •	84	MAD KING GOLL V	41
LIFTS SLOW HIS WINTRY HEAD: • • • • • • • • •	99	FOXHUNTER	46
LIKE THE PALE WATERS IN THEIR WINTRY RACE. • • • • •	112	ROSE OF WORLD	8
THE HEAVY STEPS OF THE PLOUGHMAN, SPLASHING THE WINTRY MOULD,	143	ROSE IN HEART	3
NO BOUGHS HAVE WITHERED BECAUSE OF THE WINTRY WIND: • • •	203	WITHER BOUGHS	7
NO BOUGHS HAVE WITHERED BECAUSE OF THE WINTRY WIND: • • •	203	WITHER BOUGHS	15
NO BOUGHS HAVE WITHERED BECAUSE OF THE WINTRY WIND: • • •	204	WITHER BOUGHS	23
WHEN THE RAIN IS PELTING OUT OF THE WINTRY AIR: • • •	207	HANRAHANS SONG V	12
IF HONOUR FIND HIM IN THE WINTRY BLAST? • • • • • •	479	SELF AND SOUL	56
NOW ALL DRY STICKS UNDER A WINTRY SUN, • • • • • •	490	COOLE BALLYLEE	10
OR WINTRY MOONLIGHT SINK THE FIELD • • • • • • •	501	VACILLATION	47
NOW THEY RIDE THE WINTRY DAWN • • • • • • • • •	637	BEN BULBEN	10
WHEN THE WINTRY VAPOURS RISE. • • • • • • • • •	643	SONG FAERIES	4
WHEN THE WINTRY VAPOURS RISE. • • • • • • • • •	644	SONG FAERIES	16
WHEN THE WINTRY VAPOURS RISE. • • • • • • • • •	676	ISLE STAT II 3	251
WHEN THE WINTRY VAPOURS RISE. • • • • • • • • •	676	ISLE STAT II 3	263
THE FOOL THAT CAME OUT OF THE WINTRY WOOD • • • • • •	750	SHADOW WATER A	75
WIRE			
WHEN MY HAND PASSED FROM WIRE TO WIRE • • • • • • •	86	MAD KING GOLL	65
WHEN MY HAND PASSED FROM WIRE TO WIRE • • • • • • •	86	MAD KING GOLL	65
WIRE-JOINTED			
BY THESE WIRE-JOINTED JAWS AND LIMBS OF WOOD, • • • • •	382	VISION ROBART	10
WIRES			
WHERE THE DEMONS WHIP THEM WITH WIRES • • • • • • •	61	OISIN 3	198
FOR THE KIND WIRES ARE TORN AND STILL. • • • • • •	86	MAD KING GOLL	69
WIS SEE I-WIS			
AND FAR AWAY THE HERON SAILS, I WIS. • • • • • • •	649	ISLE STAT I 1	116
THERE IS NO WAY BUT THAT YE FIGHT I WIS, • • • • • •	662	ISLE STAT II 1	75
THEY GREW SO VERY STILL, I WIS • • • • • • • • •	730	PRIEST FAIRY	66
WISDOM			
OF ALL THAT WISDOM AND THE FAME • • • • • • • • •	7	OISIN 1	66
WITH WISDOM HOUR BY HOUR.--MAY WE TWO STAND, • • • • •	71	ANASHU VIJAYA	7
WITH WISDOM HOUR BY HOUR.--MAY WE TOO STAND, • • • • •	71	ANASHU VIJAYA V	7
BUT LEARN THE DREAMING WISDOM THAT IS YOURS. • • • • •	103	FERGUS DRUID	22
AND GAZED UPON THE WISDOM OF HIS EYES. • • • • • •	108	CUCHULAIN SEA V	41
REMEMBER THE WISDOM OUT OF THE OLD DAYS: • • • • • •	158	TO HIS HEART	2
AND WISDOM THAT CAUGHT FIRE LIKE THE DRIED FLAX, • • • •	181	QUEEN MAEVE	28
WITH WISDOM, THEY WANDER TILL ALL THE YEARS HAVE GONE BY:	204	WITHER BOUGHS	21
HEAVY LIKE STONE, THEIR WISDOM BEING HALF SILENCE. • • • •	218	WOODS OF COOLE	26
THEY THAT HAVE ALL THE WISDOM THAT'S IN LIFE, • • • • •	235	SHADOW WATER B	293
THE COMING OF WISDOM WITH TIME • • • • • • • • •	261	COMING WISDOM	T
ALL WISDOM SHUT INTO HIS ONYX EYES, • • • • • • •	311	MOUNTAIN TOMB	11
ALL WISDOM SHUT INTO ITS ONYX EYES, • • • • • • •	311	MOUNTAIN TOMB V	11
I HAD THE WISDOM LOVE BRINGS FORTH: • • • • • • •	313	MEMORY YOUTH	2
I HAD THE WISDOM LOVE CAN BRING, • • • • • • • •	313	MEMORY YOUTH V	2
"AND WISDOM IS A BUTTERFLY • • • • • • • • • •	338	TOM OROUGHLEY	7
NEW WELCOME AND OLD WISDOM AT HER FIRE • • • • • • •	340	SHEP GOATHERD	32
AN IMAGE OF MYSTERIOUS WISDOM WON BY TOIL: • • • • •	373	PHASES OF MOON	18
AUSTERITY, A PLACE SET OUT FOR WISDOM • • • • • •	377	PHASES OF MOON	127
FOR HOW SHOULD I FORGET THE WISDOM THAT YOU BROUGHT. • • •	391	UNDER SATURN	4
THE HALF-READ WISDOM OF DAEMONIC IMAGES, • • • • •	427	PHANTOM HATRED	39
THE HALF-READ WISDOM OF DEMONIC IMAGES, • • • • • •	427	PHANTOM HATRED V	39
THE HALF READ WISDOM OF DAEMONIC IMAGES, • • • • • •	427	PHANTOM HATRED V	39
WISDOM • • • • • • • • • • • • • • • • •	440	WISDOM	T
INNOCENCE: AND WISDOM HE. • • • • • • • • • •	440	WISDOM	17

```
                                                     PAGE   TITLE         LINE

WISDOM  (CONTINUED)
    NOR BLEAR-EYED WISDOM OUT OF MIDNIGHT OIL. . . . . . . .   446 SCHOOL CHILDR      60
    MURMURED THE WISDOM OF THE DESERT DJINNS, . . . . . . .   468 HARUN RASHID      163
    HAS SPOKEN THE WISDOM OF THE DESERT DJINNS, . . . . . .   468 HARUN RASHID    V 163
    HAS MURMURED WISDOM OF THE DESERT DJINNS, . . . . . . .   468 HARUN RASHID    V 163
    A QUALITY OF WISDOM FROM HER LOVE'S . . . . . . . . . .   469 HARUN RASHID      180
    UNDER IT WISDOM STANDS, AND I ALONE-- . . . . . . . . .   469 HARUN RASHID      189
    QUALITY OF WISDOM FROM LOVE'S QUALITY. . . . . . . . .   469 HARUN RASHID    V 180
    UNDER IT ARMED WISDOM STANDS, A SEPARATE WISDOM . . . .   469 HARUN RASHID    V 189
    UNDER IT ARMED WISDOM STANDS, A SEPARATE WISDOM . . . .   469 HARUN RASHID    V 189
    FOR WISDOM IS THE PROPERTY OF THE DEAD, . . . . . . .   482 BLOOD AND MOON     49
    THEY UNDERSTOOD THAT WISDOM COMES OF BEGGARY. . . . .   487 SEVEN SAGES        26
    ALL NIGHT'S FATHOMLESS WISDOM COME, . . . . . . . . .   519 HER DREAM           2
    BODILY DECREPITUDE IS WISDOM; YOUNG . . . . . . . . .   523 LONG SILENCE        7
    O BUT THERE IS WISDOM . . . . . . . . . . . . . . .   534 CONSOLATION         1
    PLUCKED BITTER WISDOM THAT ENRICHED HIS BLOOD. . . .   543 PARN FUNERAL 2     12
    THEN THEY AND THEIR WISDOM WENT TO RACK; . . . . . .   566 LAPIS LAZULI       28
    THE WISDOM OF THE PEOPLE'S GONE. . . . . . . . . . .   607 SONGS BURDEN 2     16
    AND ELVISH WISDOM, AND LONG YEARS OF YOUTH . . . . .   653 ISLE STAT I 2      47
    AND FULL OF WISDOM IS EACH BLOOM, . . . . . . . . .   655 ISLE STAT I 3       9
    WILD SPIRITS OF WISDOM AND TONGUE. . . . . . . . . .   708 FAIRY PEDANT    V  27
    NO TENDER WISDOM FLOODS THE EYES . . . . . . . . . .   723 GIRLS SONG A        9
    "MAN OF WISDOM, FROM THY SLEEPING . . . . . . . . . .   729 PRIEST FAIRY       39
    "MAN OF WISDOM, DOST THOU KNOW . . . . . . . . . . .   729 PRIEST FAIRY       47
    WISDOM AND DREAMS . . . . . . . . . . . . . . . . .   743 WISDOM DREAMS       T
    WISDOM AND DREAMS ARE ONE, . . . . . . . . . . . . .   743 WISDOM DREAMS       5
    AND WISDOM THE FRUIT OF THE GARDEN; . . . . . . . . .   743 WISDOM DREAMS       7
    I DOUBT YOUR WISDOM, BUT DO NOT DOUBT MY LOVE. . . .   748 SHADOW WATER A     31
    ALTHOUGH I DOUBT YOUR WISDOM, DO NOT DOUBT . . . . .   748 SHADOW WATER A V   31
    FOR I HAVE ALL HIS GARDEN WISDOM. O SPEAK! . . . . .   756 SHADOW WATER A    180
    THE FOOL, WHO HAS MADE THE WISDOM THAT MEN WRITE . .   764 SHADOW WATER A    342
    AND ALL THE WISDOM THAT OLD IMAGES, . . . . . . . .   764 SHADOW WATER A    344
WISDOM'S        SEE WENCH-WISDOM'S
    OF BEAUTY'S CRUELTY AND WISDOM'S CHATTER-- . . . . .   377 PHASES OF MOON    121
    AND LOVE WENCH WISDOM'S CRUEL FACE. . . . . . . . .   787 HUDDON DUDDON      10
WISDOMS
    OF THE DIM WISDOMS OLD AND DEEP, . . . . . . . . . .   138 TO IRELAND      V  21
    WILD WISDOMS OF SPIRIT AND TONGUE. . . . . . . . . .   708 FAIRY PEDANT       27
WISE
    AND A HUNDRED MAIDENS WISE AND YOUNG, . . . . . . . .     8 OISIN 1         V  94
    THEN NO WISE WORSHIP DUSTY DEEDS, . . . . . . . . . .    65 HAPPY SHEPHERD  V  22
    AGED AND WISE, THEY SEEK THEIR WONTED PERCHES . . . .    72 ANASHU VIJAYA      31
    I WAS A WISE YOUNG KING OF OLD; . . . . . . . . . . .    81 MAD KING GOLL   V   1
    FIELDS FATTENING SLOW, MEN WISE IN JOY. . . . . . . .    82 MAD KING GOLL   V   6
    THIS WOULD I SAY, MOST WISE OF LIVING SOULS: . . . .   102 FERGUS DRUID        9
    WHEN I GAVE JUDGMENT, AND HIS WORDS WERE WISE, . . .   102 FERGUS DRUID       11
    FOR HE WHO MADE YOU BITTER MADE YOU WISE." . . . . .   108 CUCHULAIN SEA      32
    FOR GOD WHO MADE YOU BITTER MADE YOU WISE." . . . .   108 CUCHULAIN SEA   V  32
    AND AT THAT SINGING HE WAS NO MORE WISE. . . . . . .   127 DREAM OF FAERY     24
    IT HAD GROWN MOST WISE WITH THINKING . . . . . . . .   159 CAP AND BELLS       7
    AND IT HAD GROWN WISE BY THINKING . . . . . . . . .   159 CAP AND BELLS   V   7
    A CHATTERING WISE AND SWEET. . . . . . . . . . . .   161 CAP AND BELLS      34
    AND WHITHER THE WISE HEART KNOWS; . . . . . . . . .   168 BLESSED            34
    WHO BEING LOVELY WAS SO WISE-- . . . . . . . . . . .   193 BAILE AILLINN      98
    AH! WISE, MY HEART KNOWS WELL HOW WISE. . . . . . .   193 BAILE AILLINN      99
    AH! WISE, MY HEART KNOWS WELL HOW WISE. . . . . . .   193 BAILE AILLINN      99
    WHERE THAT WISE HARPER'S FINGER RAN. . . . . . . . .   195 BAILE AILLINN     156
    WHERE THAT WISE HARPER'S FINGERS RAN. . . . . . . .   195 BAILE AILLINN   V 156
    TIME CAN BUT MAKE IT EASIER TO BE WISE . . . . . . .   200 FOLLY COMFORT       4
    AND SO BE PATIENT; BE WISE AND PATIENT FRIEND." . .   200 FOLLY COMFORT   V   6
    WISE BIDDY EARLY CALLED THE WICKED WOOD! . . . . . .   218 WOODS OF COOLE     15
    TO FIND IF HEARTS BE WILD AND WISE, . . . . . . . .   263 MASK                4
    THERE IS NOBODY WISE ENOUGH . . . . . . . . . . . .   268 BROWN PENNY        10
    NOW FROM THAT JUICE THAT MADE THEM WISE . . . . . .   272 GREY ROCK          26
    BUT FROM THE JUICE THAT MADE THEM WISE . . . . . . .   272 GREY ROCK       V  26
    DELIGHTED TO BE BUT WISE. . . . . . . . . . . . . .   329 MEN IMPROVE        10
    THAT SOLOMON GREW WISE . . . . . . . . . . . . . .   345 ON WOMAN           11
    THIS WISE AND SIMPLE MAN. . . . . . . . . . . . . .   347 FISHERMAN           8
    THE BEATING DOWN OF THE WISE . . . . . . . . . . .   348 FISHERMAN          23
    THOSE MEN THAT IN THEIR WRITINGS ARE MOST WISE . .   370 EGO DOMINUS        68
    ALONE, IMPORTANT AND WISE, . . . . . . . . . . . .   379 CAT AND MOON       26
    AND ON THE INSTANT WOULD GROW WISE. . . . . . . . .   385 ROBARTES DANCE     12
    FOR BEAUTY'S VERY SELF, HAS CHARM MADE WISE, . . .   404 FOR DAUGHTER       37
    COME LET US MOCK AT THE WISE! . . . . . . . . . . .   432 NINETEEN 19        98
    TO HELP GOOD, WISE OR GREAT . . . . . . . . . . . .   432 NINETEEN 19       110
    FROM ALL THAT MAKES A WISE OLD MAN . . . . . . . .   553 PRAYER OLD AGE      5
    TO US. OH WISE ART THOU IN SUCH A THING, . . . . .   660 ISLE STAT II 1     46
    THE SQUIRREL YONDER, HUSHED AND WISE, . . . . . . .   686 LIFE                5
    I HOLD HIM DEARER THAN THE WISE, . . . . . . . . .   723 GIRLS SONG A       11
    AND FOR HIM MAKE ME WISE AND BRIGHT. . . . . . . .   723 GIRLS SONG A       12
    HE THOUGHT WISE THINGS AS HIS GREY HEAD NODDED. . .   728 PRIEST FAIRY       12
    BECAUSE A GOD HAS MADE HIM WISE WITH DREAMS; . . .   748 SHADOW WATER A     26
    TAUGHT ME WISE MUSIC, AND GAVE ME THIS OLD HARP; .   750 SHADOW WATER A     76
    BUT OUR SILENCE HAD BEEN WISE. . . . . . . . . . .   773 SONG DEIRDRE 1     22
    YET OUR SILENCE HAD BEEN WISE; . . . . . . . . . .   773 SONG DEIRDRE 1 V   22
WISER
    SHE IS NOT WISER NOR LOVELIER, . . . . . . . . . .   197 BAILE AILLINN     201
    ARE WISER WITCHCRAFT, FOR OUR PEACE AWAKES . . . .   763 SHADOW WATER A    320
WISEST
    EVEN THE WISEST MAN GROWS TENSE . . . . . . . . . .   638 BEN BULBEN         33
    AND SHOUT AT THE WISEST OWLS . . . . . . . . . . .   644 SONG FAERIES       10
```

		PAGE	TITLE		LINE

WISEST   (CONTINUED)
    AND SHOUT AT THE WISEST OWLS . . . .   676 ISLE STAT II 3   257
WISE-TONGUED
    IT HAD GROWN WISE-TONGUED BY THINKING . . . .   159 CAP AND BELLS   7
WISH
    YET WOULD BE NOW, COULD I BUT HAVE MY WISH, ...   267 ALL TEMPT ME   9
    I WOULD BE NOW, COULD I BUT HAVE MY WISH, ...   267 ALL TEMPT ME   V   9
    AND ALL THAT I NEED DO IS TO WISH . . . .   300 RUN PARADISE   4
    COULD MAKE ME WISH FOR ANYTHING THIS DAY, ...   338 SHEP GOATHERD   3
    LET THE YOUNG WISH. BUT WHAT HAS BROUGHT YOU HERE? . . .   339 SHEP GOATHERD   6
    THAT MOST RESPECTED LADY'S EVERY WISH, ...   410 TOWER   29
    THEY SAY THE WISH ITSELF IS HALF THE SIN: . . . . . .   692 MOSADA 1   48
WISHED
    "YOU WILL HAVE ALL YOU HAVE WISHED FOR WHEN YOU HAVE EARNED   228 SHADOW WATER B   124
    I WISHED BEFORE IT CEASED. NOR BIRD NOR BEAST . . . .   338 SHEP GOATHERD   2
    YEAR. I WISHED BEFORE IT CEASED. NOR BIRD NOR BEAST . .   338 SHEP GOATHERD V   2
    I MIGHT HAVE WISHED ON THE DAY . . . .   341 SHEP GOATHERD V   73
    I HAD WISHED A DEAR THING ON THAT DAY . . . .   341 SHEP GOATHERD V   73
WISHES
    HE WISHES HIS BELOVED WERE DEAD . . . .   175 BELOVED DEAD   T
    AEDH WISHES HIS BELOVED WERE DEAD . . . .   175 BELOVED DEAD   V   T
    HE WISHES FOR THE CLOTHS OF HEAVEN . . . .   176 CLOTHS HEAVEN   T
    AEDH WISHES FOR THE CLOTHS OF HEAVEN . . . .   176 CLOTHS HEAVEN V   T
WISTFUL
    THAT WANES." "AH, WISTFUL VOICE," REPLIED THE OTHER, . .   79 EPHEMERA   V   3
    SINGS THE YOUNG WISTFUL SPIRIT OF A STAR . . . . . .   705 REMEMBRANCE   10
WIT   SEE MOTHER-WIT
    WHERE WIT AND BEAUTY LEARNED THEIR TRADE . . . . . .   288 TO WEALTHY MAN   16
    I HAD MY SHARE OF MOTHER WIT: . . . .   313 MEMORY YOUTH   V   3
    A PRETENCE OF WIT." . . . .   349 HAWK   18
    MATCHING OUR BROKEN-HEARTED WIT AGAINST HER WIT, ...   362 HER COURTESY   7
    MATCHING OUR BROKEN-HEARTED WIT AGAINST HER WIT, ...   362 HER COURTESY   7
    AS AIR UNDER A WING, CAN GIVE BIRDS' WIT . . . .   462 HARUN RASHID   28
    AS AIR UNDER A WING, CAN GIVE BIRD'S WIT . . . .   462 HARUN RASHID   V   28
    AND HEAVENLY MUSIC IF THEY GAVE IT WIT: . . . .   533 HER TRIUMPH   6
    IT IS OF GOD AND PASSES HUMAN WIT . . . .   558 RIBH CHRISTIAN   2
    CAN TOUCH BY MOTHER WIT . . . .   589 OLD WICKED MAN   40
    WITH SOME FRIEND THAT HAS THE WIT . . . .   624 APPARITIONS   12
    WITH SOME FRIEND WHO HAS THE WIT . . . .   624 APPARITIONS   V   12
    SUCH QUESTS AS THESE, I TROW, NEED LITTLE WIT. . . . .   650 ISLE STAT I 1   150
    HE KNOWS BY SIGNS OF SECRET WIT . . . .   716 FAIRY DOCTOR   5
WITCH
    THE WITCH . . . .   310 WITCH   T
    WITH A FOUL WITCH . . . .   310 WITCH   3
    SOLOMON AND THE WITCH . . . .   387 SOLOMON WITCH   T
    THAT THE WITCH OF ATLAS KNEW, ...   637 BEN BULBEN   3
    A BEARDED WITCH, HER SLUGGISH HEAD LOW BENT . . . . . .   685 SEEKER   72
    TIME AND THE WITCH VIVIEN. . . . .   720 WITCH VIVIEN   T
WITCHCRAFT
    ARE WISER WITCHCRAFT, FOR OUR PEACE AWAKES . . . . . .   763 SHADOW WATER A   320
    AGAINST WITCHCRAFT . . . .   775 AGAINST WITCH V   T
WITCHERY
    WITH WITCHERY AND UNGUENTS FROM THE FLOWERS . . . . .   41 OISIN 2   V 185
WITCHES
    I KNOW OF THE LEAFY PATHS THAT THE WITCHES TAKE . . . .   203 WITHER BOUGHS   9
    I KNOW OF THE LEAFY PATH THAT THE WITCHES TAKE, ...   203 WITHER BOUGHS V   9
    ALL THE WILD WITCHES, THOSE MOST NOBLE LADIES, ...   343 DEJECTION   4
WITHER
    AND THE MOON LIKE A PALE ROSE WITHER AWAY." . . . . .   28 OISIN 1   427
    THEIR HAUGHTY IMAGES THAT CANNOT WITHER, ...   184 QUEEN MAEVE   87
    NOW I MAY WITHER INTO THE TRUTH. . . . .   261 COMING WISDOM   4
    SHALL WITHER THAT OLD MARVEL, FOR . . . .   447 COLONUS PRAISE   15
    MY WORDS WERE ALL: "HERE NO LOVES WANE AND WITHER, . . .   669 ISLE STAT II 3   84
WITHERED
    THESE NOW OUTWORN AND WITHERED HANDS. . . . .   23 OISIN 1   349
    THESE NOW O'ERWORN AND WITHERED HANDS, ...   23 OISIN 1   V 348
    A DUSKY DEMON DRY AS A WITHERED SEDGE . . . .   39 OISIN 2   158
    A DUSK DEMON, DRY AS A WITHERED SEDGE, ...   39 OISIN 2   V 158
    A HUSKY DEMON, DRY AS A WITHERED SEDGE . . . .   39 OISIN 2   V 158
    BLIND AND NIGH DEAF, WITH WITHERED ARMS HE LIES . . . .   42 OISIN 2   V 203
    "I WOULD DIE LIKE A SMALL WITHERED LEAF IN THE AUTUMN,
      . . .   56 OISIN 3   131
    TILL ALL THE VALLEYS OF THE WORLD HAVE BEEN WITHERED AWAY.   163 VALLEY LOVERS   8
    TILL THE VALLEYS OF THE WORLD HAVE BEEN WITHERED AWAY."   163 VALLEY LOVERS V   8
    NO BOUGHS HAVE WITHERED BECAUSE OF THE WINTRY WIND: . .   203 WITHER BOUGHS   7
    THE BOUGHS HAVE WITHERED BECAUSE I HAVE TOLD THEM   203 WITHER BOUGHS   8
      MY DREAMS.
    NO BOUGHS HAVE WITHERED BECAUSE OF THE WINTRY WIND: . .   203 WITHER BOUGHS   15
    THE BOUGHS HAVE WITHERED BECAUSE I HAVE TOLD THEM   203 WITHER BOUGHS   16
      MY DREAMS.
    NO BOUGHS HAVE WITHERED BECAUSE OF THE WINTRY WIND: . .   204 WITHER BOUGHS   23
    THE BOUGHS HAVE WITHERED BECAUSE I HAVE TOLD THEM   204 WITHER BOUGHS   24
      MY DREAMS.
    OR ON THE WITHERED MEN THAT SAW . . . .   344 DAWN   5
    HAS WITHERED OUR ROSE TREE: . . . .   396 ROSE TREE   4
    HAVE WITHERED OUR ROSE TREE: . . . .   396 ROSE TREE   V   4
    AND WITHERED TO A BAG OF BONES: . . . .   401 DEMON BEAST   49
    WHEN WITHERED OLD AND SKELETON-GAUNT, ...   475 EVA GORE-BOOTH   12
    "INTO A WITHERED CRONE." . . . .   516 MANS SONG   2
    NO WITHERED CRONE I SAW . . . .   516 MANS SONG   11
    OR BUT TO FIND IF WITHERED VEIN RAN BLOOD, ...   537 HER VISION   6

WITHERED   (CONTINUED)
    DOWN EVERY WITHERED FINGER FROM THE TOP,   537 HER VISION   11
    EVERYTHING ELSE WITHERED AND MUMMY-DEAD.   618 BRONZE HEAD   3
    AS A LEAF THAT IS OLD, AND WITHERED, AND COLD, 643 SONG FAERIES   3
    AS A LEAF THAT IS OLD, AND WITHERED, AND COLD, 644 SONG FAERIES   15
    AS A LEAF THAT IS OLD, AND WITHERED, AND COLD, 676 ISLE STAT II 3   250
    AS A LEAF THAT IS OLD, AND WITHERED, AND COLD, 676 ISLE STAT II 3   262
    WITH WREATHS OF WITHERED FLOWERS   680 LOVE AND DEATH   17
    WITH WREATHS OF WITHERED FLOWERS,   680 LOVE AND DEATH   19
    ON HER BROAD BREAST! BENEATH HER WITHERED BROWS 685 SEEKER   73
    THY WITHERED FOE, AND WITH THE PURPLE WING   688 TWO TITANS   55
    TWO WOMEN, WITHERED ONE AND SMALL AND THIN,   711 FERENCZ RENYI   51
    A LITTLE WITHERED MAN, AND OLD.   716 FAIRY DOCTOR   4
    THE LITTLE WITHERED MAN, AND OLD.   717 FAIRY DOCTOR   24
    A WITHERED TREE?"   780 WELL AND TREE   16
    OUR LUCK IS WITHERED AWAY,   783 GREY ROUND   18
    AND WHEAT IN THE WHEAT-EAR WITHERED,   783 GREY ROUND   19
WITHERING
    BUT WHEN AT WITHERING OF THE SUN HE KNEW   40 OISIN 2   V   173
    AND WHEN AT WITHERING OF THE SUN HE KNEW   40 OISIN 2   V   173
    THE WITHERING OF THE BOUGHS   203 WITHER BOUGHS   T
    LOVE'S MOON WAS WITHERING AWAY.   313 MEMORY YOUTH   V   7
    THAT BLOW WHEN HEAVEN AND EARTH ARE WITHERING, 767 SHADOW WATER A   395
WITHERS
    WANDER WHERE EARTH WITHERS AWAY,   196 BAILE AILLINN   171
    AND WHILE SHE FADES AND LIFE WITHERS AWAY,   768 SHADOW WATER A   422
    HAD WOVEN HER OF WIND. LIFE WITHERS OUT   768 SHADOW WATER A V 423
WITHERSHINS
    THAT CUT THROUGH TIME OR CROSS IT WITHERSHINS. 489 COOLE PARK 29   24
    THAT CAN CROSS TIME AND CUT IT WITHERSHINS.   489 COOLE PARK 29 V   24
    THAT CUT THROUGH TIME AND CUT IT WITHERSHINS   489 COOLE PARK 29 V   24
WITHHOLD
    DO NOT THE REST WITHHOLD.   588 OLD WICKED MAN   11
    "LOVE TO GIVE OR TO WITHHOLD   588 OLD WICKED MAN   21
WITHHOLDS
    WITHHOLDS THEM NOW? HAVE THE EVER-LIVING ONES 234 SHADOW WATER B   269
WITHIN
    A BEAUTIFUL YOUNG MAN DREAMED WITHIN   17 OISIN 1   248
    WE PASSED THE PORTALS, AND WITHIN,   17 OISIN 1   V 250
    WITHIN HIS OTHER HAND WERE FLITTING   18 OISIN 1   V 253
    WE DANCED TO WHERE WITHIN THE GLOOM   21 OISIN 1   V 305
    I HEARD ONE SAY, "WITHIN HIS EYES   25 OISIN 1   V 380
    AND STOOD WITHIN, CLOTHED IN A MISTY RAY   36 OISIN 2   104
    AND STOOD WITHIN THE HALL. A MISTY RAY   36 OISIN 2   V 104
    WITHIN HER WILDERING WHIRLS—FORGETTING HIM.   69 SAD SHEPHERD   V   28
    WITHIN THE TEMPLE, DEVIOUS WALKING, MADE   72 ANASHU VIJAYA   32
    A LITTLE WAY WITHIN THE GLOOM A ROEBUCK RAISED HIS EYES 76 INDIAN ON GOD 13
    IS BUT A SLIDING DROP OF RAIN WITHIN HIS PETALS WIDE."   76 INDIAN ON GOD V 12
    I RULED AND RULED MY LIFE WITHIN——   82 MAD KING GOLL V   7
    AS ONCE WITHIN A LITTLE TOWN   85 MAD KING GOLL V   49
    ONCE, WHILE WITHIN A LITTLE TOWN   85 MAD KING GOLL V   49
    WITHOUT DOORS OR WITHIN,   96 MOLL MAGEE   44
    SOMEWHERE WITHIN SOME HOLLOW HILL,   271 GREY ROCK   V   14
    SHE'LL NOT BE PROUD, KNOWING WITHIN HER HEART, 282 TWO KINGS   118
    FOUND THAT OLD HOUSE, A SPUTTERING TORCH WITHIN, 283 TWO KINGS   140
    AND FOUND THE HOUSE, A SPUTTERING TORCH WITHIN, 283 TWO KINGS   V 140
    THAT WHEN HE HAS FALLEN ASLEEP WITHIN MY ARMS, 285 TWO KINGS   191
    YET WE, HAD WE WALKED WITHIN   293 HELEN LIVED   7
    I'LL SLEEP AWAY ALL TIME WITHIN IT,   306 HOUR DAWN   74
    AND SLEEP AWAY ALL TIME WITHIN IT.   306 HOUR DAWN   V   74
    HIS BODY MOULDED FROM WITHIN HIS BODY   374 PHASES OF MOON   43
    AHERNE LAUGHED, THINKING OF THE MAN WITHIN,   375 PHASES OF MOON   85
    WITHIN MY ARMS GREAT SOLOMON,   387 SOLOMON WITCH   4
    NOR ANY HUMAN SIGHT WITHIN IT   389 SOLOMON WITCH   41
    AND A HORSE PLASHES WITHIN IT;   393 EASTER 1916   52
    THOUGH BUT A FEW LEARNED MEN SHALL LOOK WITHIN, 461 HARUN RASHID V 18A
    LOOK ON THAT FIRE, SALVATION WALKS WITHIN.   502 VACILLATION   76
    WHAT HAPPENS A TREE THAT HAS NOTHING WITHIN IT? 548 TO SAME TUNE 3   23
    WHAT HAPPENS TO A TREE THAT HAS NOTHING WITHIN IT? 548 TO SAME TUNE 3 V 23
    WHAT TEARS DOWN A TREE THAT HAS NOTHING WITHIN IT? 615 MARCH SONGS 2   23
    WHAT TEARS DOWN A TREE HAS NOTHING WITHIN IT?   615 MARCH SONGS 2 V   23
    AND I THERE WITHIN.   621 JOHN KINSELLA   28
    WITHIN THE DROWSY BLOSSOM HANGS THE BEE   645 ISLE STAT I 1   2
    WITHIN THE FOLD TO HEAR THE CREAKING GATE——   646 ISLE STAT I 1   41
    AS WITHIN A CELLAR CHILLY   647 ISLE STAT I 1   57
    BINDS, AS WITHIN A GIRDLE OR A RING,   657 ISLE STAT I 3   59
    WITHIN MINE HEART; AND NAUGHT BUT SORROW NOW   659 ISLE STAT II 1   26
    FOR EACH WITHIN HIMSELF HATH ALL   671 ISLE STAT II 3   132
    THE WORLD, WITHIN HIS FOLDED HEART,   671 ISLE STAT II 3   133
    WITHIN HIS CLENCHED TEETH A SWORD.   673 ISLE STAT II 3   182
    I SEE WITHIN A CLOVEN ROCK DISPART   673 ISLE STAT II 3   195
    DOTH HE STILL DWELL WITHIN THE WOODY SHADE.   678 ISLE STAT II 3   303
    UNTIL WE DIE WITHIN THE CHARMED RING   679 ISLE STAT II 3   322
    MAKE MOAN AND CRY. WITHIN YON SUNLESS VALLEY, 682 SEEKER   26
    A VOICE HAS TOLD ME HOW WITHIN THIS LAND   682 SEEKER   V 22
    WITHIN THE WOODWAYS, BLUE AS THE HALCYON'S WING, 683 SEEKER   V 38
    TILL THEIR FIERCE MISERIES WITHIN HIS EYES   687 TWO TITANS   26
    AND THROB WITHIN THE CIRCLES OF GREEN DAWN.   701 MOSADA 3   54
    THE FLAME THAT SHONE WITHIN HIS EYES BUT NOW   704 MOSADA 3   128
    AH! IT DWELT WITHIN THE TWILIGHT AS THE WORM WITHIN THE 718 PHANTOM SHIP 6
       NUT.

```
                                                            PAGE     TITLE          LINE
WITHIN   (CONTINUED)
     AH! IT DWELT WITHIN THE TWILIGHT AS THE WORM WITHIN THE   718 PHANTOM SHIP        6
        NUT.
     HE HAD DREAMED THE COW HAD GOT WITHIN  . . . . . . . .    729 PRIEST FAIRY       33
     ON BRAHMA'S GATEWAY, "THEY WITHIN HAVE FED  . . . . . .   735 QUATRAIN APHOR     15
     BEING IMAGINED WITHIN . . . . . . . . . . . . . . . .     785 WOMANS BEAUTY      23
WITHOUT
     AND NOW FLED BY, MIST-COVERED, WITHOUT SOUND, . . . . .    29 OISIN 2             3
     AND ONE WHOM YOU WILL GO TO WITHOUT TELLING, . . . . .     33 OISIN 2        V   67
     FORMS WITHOUT NUMBER!  WHEN THE LIVE WEST FLASHED . . .    41 OISIN 2        V  180
     WE SANG THE LOVES AND ANGERS WITHOUT SLEEP  . . . . .      42 OISIN 2           194
     THE SPACIOUS LOVES, THE ANGER WITHOUT SLEEP  . . . . .     42 OISIN 2        V  194
     I AWOKE! THE STRANGE HORSE WITHOUT SUMMONS OUT OF         54 OISIN 3           105
        THE DISTANCE RAN,
     . . . HE SAD AS A CHILD WITHOUT MILK!  . . . . . . .      59 OISIN 3           174
     ON THE FLAMING STONES, WITHOUT REFUGE, . . . . . . . .    62 OISIN 3           213
     ON THE RED FLAMING STONES WITHOUT REFUGE . . . . . . .    62 OISIN 3        V  213
     WITHOUT LAUGHTER, A SHOW UNTO CHILDREN, . . . . . . . .   63 OISIN 3           218
     FOR THY YOUTH WITHOUT PEACE, AND THY YEARS WITH THE DEMONS, 63 OISIN 3       V  216
        . . .
     AH ME! TO BE OLD WITHOUT SUCCOUR, A SHOW UNTO CHILDREN,   63 OISIN 3        V  217
        A STAIN,
     WITHOUT LAUGHTER, A COUGHING, ALONE WITH REMEMBRANCE AND  63 OISIN 3        V  218
        FEAR!
     WITHOUT DOORS OR WITHIN, . . . . . . . . . . . . . . .    96 MOLL MAGEE         44
     AND WHAT TO ME WAS BURDEN WITHOUT END, . . . . . . . .   102 FERGUS DRUID       12
     HE MUSED UPON HIS MOCKERS! WITHOUT FAIL . . . . . . .    127 DREAM OF FAERY     26
     A MAN WITH A HAZEL WAND CAME WITHOUT SOUND! . . . . .    153 CHANGE BELOVED      6
     I WOULD THAT THE BOAR WITHOUT BRISTLES HAD COME FROM THE 153 CHANGE BELOVED     10
        WEST
     A MAN WITH A WAND OF HAZEL CAME WITHOUT SOUND! . . . .   153 CHANGE BELOVED V    6
     AND TROUBLE WITH SIGHS FOR ALL HEARTS WITHOUT REST . .   163 ASKS FORGIVE   V   23
     GROW GENTLE WITHOUT SORROWING, . . . . . . . . . . .    193 BAILE AILLINN     110
     GROW GENTLE WITHOUT SORROWINGS! . . . . . . . . . . .    193 BAILE AILLINN  V  110
     HAVE HAPPINESS WITHOUT AN END, . . . . . . . . . . .    195 BAILE AILLINN     158
     WITH A SLOW SMILE AND WITHOUT SOUND, . . . . . . . .    275 GREY ROCK         117
     HE RODE A RACE WITHOUT A BIT? . . . . . . . . . . .     326 ROBERT GREGORY     63
     WITHOUT AN ANGRY THOUGHT . . . . . . . . . . . . . .    366 HER CHRIS TREE      2
     LIFE OVERFLOWS WITHOUT AMBITIOUS PAINS! . . . . . . .   417 ANCEST HOUSES       3
     THERE LURCHES PAST, HIS GREAT EYES WITHOUT THOUGHT . .   433 NINETEEN 19       126
     TRUTHS WITHOUT FATHER CAME, TRUTHS THAT NO BOOK . . .   467 HARUN RASHID      138
     WITHOUT A FRIEND ON THE EARTH . . . . . . . . . . .     552 SONGS REWRIT 2      6
     WITHOUT A THING IN HIS HEAD . . . . . . . . . . . .     552 SONGS REWRIT 2     10
     WITHOUT A FRIEND ON THIS EARTH . . . . . . . . . . .    552 SONGS REWRIT 2 V    6
     WITHOUT THERE OF A LITTLE, LIGHT OLD MAN! . . . . . .   720 WITCH VIVIEN       13
     WITHOUT MY GLASS I'D BE A SORRY CLOWN. . . . . . . .    721 WITCH VIVIEN       29
WITHSTOOD
     A BUTLER OR AN ARMSTRONG THAT WITHSTOOD . . . . . . .   270 PARDON FATHERS     10
WITNESS
     LET THE SEA BEAR WITNESS,  . . . . . . . . . . . . .    770 BLOOD BOND          7
     LET THE WIND BEAR WITNESS, . . . . . . . . . . . . .    770 BLOOD BOND          8
     LET THE EARTH BEAR WITNESS, . . . . . . . . . . . . .   770 BLOOD BOND          9
     LET THE FIRE BEAR WITNESS, . . . . . . . . . . . . .    770 BLOOD BOND         10
     LET THE DEW BEAR WITNESS, . . . . . . . . . . . . . .   770 BLOOD BOND         11
     LET THE STARS BEAR WITNESS! . . . . . . . . . . . .     770 BLOOD BOND         12
WITNESSED
     HAVE WITNESSED THE BINDING. . . . . . . . . . . . .     770 BLOOD BOND         15
WIT'S
     AND MANY A DARLING WIT'S GROWN DULL . . . . . . . . .   301 RUN PARADISE       18
WITS
     INDIGNANT AT THE FUMBLING WITS, THE OBSCURE SPITE . .   291 PAUDEEN             1
     AND THEN I'D STAGGER OUT. HE'D CRACK HIS WITS . . . .   377 PHASES OF MOON    134
     THE COMFORT THAT YOU MADE? ALTHOUGH MY WITS HAVE GONE   391 UNDER SATURN        5
     MUSIC HAD DRIVEN THEIR WITS ASTRAY— . . . . . . . .     411 TOWER              47
     HAD WAKING WITS! IT SEEMED . . . . . . . . . . . .      422 MY TABLE           31
     FOR THE EMBRACE OF NOTHING! AND I, MY WITS ASTRAY . .   426 PHANTOM HATRED     14
     FROM SHALLOW WITS! WHO KNOWS NO WORK CAN STAND, . . .   429 NINETEEN 19        35
     POETS AND WITS ABOUT HIM DREW! . . . . . . . . . . .    577 WHAT THEN          14
     IN COUNTRY SHAWL OR PARIS CLOAK, HAD PUT MY WITS ASTRAY, 592 PILGRIM            3
     THE HARE HATH LAID ASLEEP HER FROLIC WITS, . . . . .    712 FERENCZ RENYI      72
     COME TO THE CHESS, FOR YOUNG GIRLS' WITS ARE BETTER .   721 WITCH VIVIEN       46
     NIGH OF HIS WITS BY FEAR BEREFT. . . . . . . . . .      730 PRIEST FAIRY       50
WITTED     SEE WANDERING-WITTED DULL-WITTED
     THAT AM A WANDERING WITTED FOOL . . . . . . . . . .     380 SONGS FOOL 1   V   16
WITTY
     OR A WITTY LOVELY LADY." . . . . . . . . . . . . .      299 THREE HERMITS      28
     THE WITTY MAN AND HIS JOKE . . . . . . . . . . . .      347 FISHERMAN          19
     VEHEMENT AND WITTY SHE HAD SEEMED—! THE VENETIAN LADY .  363 DOLLS FACES         5
WIVE
     HAS LOVER LIVED, BUT LONGED TO WIVE . . . . . . . .     197 BAILE AILLINN     206
     WHAT CAN BOOKS OF MEN THAT WIVE  . . . . . . . . .      309 REALISTS            2
WIVES
     FROM THE WIVES, AND THE CATS, AND THE CHILDREN, . . .    92 FATHER OHART       15
     FROM THEIR WIVES, AND THEIR CATS, AND THEIR CHILDREN, .  92 FATHER OHART   V   15
     OF HEN WIVES AND OF QUEER OLD MEN . . . . . . . . .     607 SONGS BURDEN 2 V   23
WIZARD
     IN EVERY BRAIN A WIZARD GLOW. . . . . . . . . . . .      20 OISIN 1        V 291A
     LAID IT AND SIGHED—A SWORD WHOSE WIZARD SHINE . . . .    37 OISIN 2        V  126
     MURMURING A WIZARD SONG FOR THEE! . . . . . . . . .     134 TWO TREES          12
     AND ALL THE WIZARD THINGS THAT GO . . . . . . . . .     139 TO IRELAND     V   39
     FROM MY WIZARD ISLAND LAIR, . . . . . . . . . . . .     668 ISLE STAT II 3     63

                              905
```

WIZARDRY
    IN SILENCE, THAT FAMED FLOWER OF WIZARDRY, ...   673 ISLE STAT II 3   192
WIZEN
    SCARCE THE OLD AND WIZEN HOUSES HAD THEIR DOORS AND WINDOWS   718 PHANTOM SHIP   5
       SHUT.
WIZENED
    SCARCE THE OLD AND WIZENED HOUSES HAD THEIR DOORS   718 PHANTOM SHIP   V   5
       AND WINDOWS SHUT.
WOE
    WHO IS AMRITA? WOE! AH, WOE IS ME! . . . . . .   71 ANASHU VIJAYA V   15
    WHO IS AMRITA? WOE! AH, WOE IS ME! . . . . . .   71 ANASHU VIJAYA V   15
    AH WOE! FULL MANY A CREAK GAVE THE CREEL IN THE CART . .   91 OLD FISHERMAN V   6
    AH, WOE! WOE IS ME! I GO FROM SUN AND SHADE, ...   674 ISLE STAT II 3   216
    SHE IS LONG AGES DUST. AH, WOE IS ME! . . . . . .   679 ISLE STAT II 3   313
    FOR ALL MY JOY--AH, WOE! . . . .   685 SEEKER   79
    AH! WOE FOR THE LOSS OF YOUR FACE, ...   708 FAIRY PEDANT   32
    AH! WOE FOR YOUR WINGS AND YOUR HEAD-- . . . . . .   708 FAIRY PEDANT   34
    AH! WOE FOR YOUR EYES AND THEIR BRIGHTNESS-- . . . .   708 FAIRY PEDANT   35
    AH! WOE FOR YOUR SLIPPERS OF RED. . . . .   708 FAIRY PEDANT   36
WOE-BEGONE
    AND WOE-BEGONE, FOR THEM NO EVIL DAY! . . . . . .   677 ISLE STAT II 3   275
WOES
    UNMINDFUL OF ITS WOES, WOULD TWINE A WREATH . . . . .   650 ISLE STAT I 1   133
WOKE
    BUT NOW THE WAR-RAGE IN CUCHULAIN WOKE, ...   110 CUCHULAIN SEA   65
    BUT NOW THE WAR RAGE IN CUCHULAIN WOKE, ...   110 CUCHULAIN SEA V   65
    BUT WOKE AT THE FIRST GLEAM OF DAY, ROSE UP . . . .   467 HARUN RASHID   147
    BUT I WOKE IN AN OLD RUIN THAT THE WINDS HOWLED THROUGH; 581 CURSE CROMWELL   28
    AND THE PALE BLOSSOM; BUT I WOKE INSTEAD . . . . .   761 SHADOW WATER A   281
WOLD
    OF THINE CRY OVER WOLD AND WATER WHITE, ...   669 ISLE STAT II 3   73
    OVER THE SORREL-COVERED WOLD-- . . . .   716 FAIRY DOCTOR   2
WOLF
    AS A HAY-COCK OUT ON THE FLOOD, OR A WOLF SUCKED UNDER   63 OISIN 3   220
       A WEIR.
    AS A GRASS SEED CRUSHED BY A PEBBLE, AS A WOLF SUCKED UNDER 63 OISIN 3   V 220
       A WEIR.
    THE GREY WOLF KNOWS ME; BY ONE EAR . . . . . .   84 MAD KING GOLL   45
    AND SO WITH WOLF, AND BOAR, AND STEER. . . . . .   671 ISLE STAT II 3   122
WOLF-BREEDING
    WOLF-BREEDING MOUNTAINS, GALLERIED EMAN, ...   81 MAD KING GOLL V   2
WOLFE
    AND ROBERT EMMET AND WOLFE TONE, ...   290 SEPTEMBER 1913   21
    LORD EDWARD AND WOLFE TONE, ...   395 SIXTEEN DEAD   16
WOLVES
    OF WOLVES, OF BOREAL BEARS, WE QUAFFED THE WINE . . .   41 OISIN 2   V 188
    AND ON THE SKINS OF WOLVES AND BEARS WE SLEPT; . . .   41 OISIN 2   V 191
    . . . "THE FENIANS HUNT WOLVES IN THE NIGHT, ...   59 OISIN 3   171
    THEY LEFT THEIR BODIES TO FATTEN THE WOLVES, ...   545 TO SAME TUNE 2   2
    THEY LEFT THEIR BODIES TO FATTEN THE WOLVES. . . . .   613 MARCH SONGS 1   2
WOMAN   SEE WOOD-WOMAN QUEEN-WOMAN
    "O PLEASANT WOMAN," ANSWERED FINN. . . . . . .   5 OISIN 1   40
    THAT WOMAN FOUND A RING HUNG ON THE WALL, ...   37 OISIN 2   120
    A WEARY WOMAN SLEEPS SO HARD! . . . .   95 MOLL MAGEE   21
    NO WOMAN LOVES ME, NO MAN SEEKS MY HELP, ...   103 FERGUS DRUID   V   26
    THERE'S NOT A WOMAN TURNS HER FACE . . . . . .   131 OLD PENSIONER   13
    THE HEART OF THE WOMAN . . . .   151 HEART OF WOMAN   T
    THE DESIRE OF MAN AND OF WOMAN . . . . . .   153 CHANGE BELOVED V   T
    WHITE WOMAN THAT PASSION HAS WORN . . . . .   157 POET BELOVED   3
    WHITE WOMAN WITH NUMBERLESS DREAMS, ...   157 POET BELOVED   7
    A WOMAN OF SO SHINING LOVELINESS . . . . .   170 SECRET ROSE   25
    OF THE WOMAN THAT HE LOVES, UNTIL HE DIES. . . .   177 PAST GREATNESS   10
    AND THAT MILD WOMAN OF THE SOUTH, ...   189 BAILE AILLINN   6
    AS WHEN NEWLY GROWN TO BE A WOMAN, ...   199 ARROW   4
    THAT BEAUTIFUL MILD WOMAN, YOUR CLOSE FRIEND, . . .   204 ADAMS CURSE   2
    THAT BEAUTIFUL MILD WOMAN FOR WHOSE SAKE . . . .   205 ADAMS CURSE   15
    REPLIED! "TO BE BORN WOMAN IS TO KNOW-- . . . .   205 ADAMS CURSE   18
    THE MARTYRS CALL THE WORLD." THAT WOMAN THEN . . .   205 ADAMS CURSE   V   14
    AND THE WOOD WOMAN, WHOSE LOVER WAS CHANGED TO A BLUE-EYED 209 UNDER THE MOON V 13
       HAWK;
    TO GRASP THE WOMAN. YOU HAVE DARED TO TOUCH HER? . . .   223 SHADOW WATER B   39
    FOR THAT BRIEF SIGHING. IF YOU HAD LOVED SOME WOMAN-- .   228 SHADOW WATER B   135
    THAT MUCH IS CERTAIN. I SHALL FIND A WOMAN, . . .   231 SHADOW WATER B   209
    AND WHERE THERE IS ONE WOMAN THERE'LL BE OTHERS. . . .   232 SHADOW WATER B   227
    TO WIN A WOMAN IN HER OWN DESPITE, ...   244 SHADOW WATER B   458
    TO WIN A WOMAN IS IN HER OWN DESPITE, ...   244 SHADOW WATER B V 458
    SOME OTHER WOMAN HAS A CLAIM ON YOU, ...   245 SHADOW WATER B   474
    LET'S HOME! I'D GIVE SOME RUBIES TO A WOMAN. . . .   248 SHADOW WATER B   537
    AND HAVING LIT UPON THIS WOMAN THERE, ...   248 SHADOW WATER B   542
    AS FOR THIS WOMAN, I THINK SHE IS COMING WITH ME. . .   248 SHADOW WATER B   545
    IT WAS THIS WOMAN IN HER WOMAN'S VENGEANCE . . . .   248 SHADOW WATER B   547
    AND HAVING LIT UPON THIS WOMAN HERE, ...   248 SHADOW WATER B   542
    I AM A WOMAN, I DIE AT EVERY BREATH. . . . .   250 SHADOW WATER B   583
    A WOMAN HOMER SUNG . . . .   254 WOMAN HOMER   T
    A WOMAN HOMER SUNG, ...   255 WOMAN HOMER   19
    FOR ONE THAT WAS LIKE WOMAN MADE . . . . .   272 GREY ROCK   29
    I KNEW A WOMAN NONE COULD PLEASE, ...   272 GREY ROCK   41
    I KNOW A WOMAN NONE COULD PLEASE, ...   272 GREY ROCK   V   41
    A KIND MILD WOMAN HAD SHE BEEN, WHO POURED . . . .   279 TWO KINGS   62A
    SAID, "IF A WOMAN HAS PUT THIS ON YOU, ...   281 TWO KINGS   111
    BUT THAT SWEET-SOUNDING VOICE RAN ON: "WOMAN, ...   284 TWO KINGS   165

		PAGE	TITLE	LINE
WOMAN	(CONTINUED)			
OR I HAD NO WOMAN THERE TO KISS:		305	HOUR DAWN	66
THE MAN AND THE WOMAN BRING		319	DOLLS	10
"THERE'S NOT A MAN OR WOMAN		333	SOLOMON SHEBA	19
ON WOMAN		345	ON WOMAN	T
MAY GOD BE PRAISED FOR WOMAN		345	ON WOMAN	1
A WOMAN SPOKE OF SOME NEW TALE SHE HAD READ,		350	HER PRAISE	7
SHE KNOWS HERSELF A WOMAN,		365	HER RACE	5
A SPHINX WITH WOMAN BREAST AND LION PAW,		383	VISION ROBART	18
AND MUST NO BEAUTIFUL WOMAN BE		386	ROBARTES DANCE	25
THAT WOMAN A WHILE WOULD BE SHRILL		392	EASTER 1916 V	17
THE WOMAN THAT BY ME LAY		398	BREAK OF DAY	2
HAVE I NOT SEEN THE LOVELIEST WOMAN BORN		405	FOR DAUGHTER	59
UPON A WOMAN WON OR WOMAN LOST?		413	TOWER	114
UPON A WOMAN WON OR WOMAN LOST?		413	TOWER	114
AND LEAVE A WOMAN AND A MAN BEHIND		422	MY DESCENDANTS	3
TO LEAVE A WOMAN AND A MAN BEHIND		422	MY DESCENDANTS V	3
A WOMAN AND A MAN,		436	FOR MY SON	27
IF YOU HAVE SEEN THAT IMAGE AND NOT THE WOMAN.		448	HERO GIRL FOOL	8
I DID NOT FIND IN ANY CAGE THE WOMAN AT MY SIDE.		450	OWEN AHERNE	19
OR COURT A WOMAN: NEITHER ENEMY.		463	HARUN RASHID	59
GAME-BIRD, NOR WOMAN DOES THE SAME THING TWICE:		463	HARUN RASHID	60
GAME BIRD, OR WOMAN DOES THE SAME THING TWICE:		463	HARUN RASHID V	60
GAMEBIRD, NOR WOMAN DOES THE SAME THING TWICE:		463	HARUN RASHID V	60
HAVE LIT UPON A WOMAN WHO SO SHARES		465	HARUN RASHID	85
A PROUD WOMAN NOT KINDRED OF HIS SOUL.		479	SELF AND SOUL	64
UPON AN AGED WOMAN AND HER HOUSE,		488	COOLE PARK 29	2
EVERY COMMON WOMAN KNOWS,		499	MOTHER OF GOD	7
ONE DEAR BRILLIANT WOMAN:		504	RESULT THOUGHT	2
"A WOMAN CAN BE PROUD AND STIFF		513	JANE TALK BISH	13
A WOMAN YOUNG AND OLD I FATHER AND CHILD		531	FATHER CHILD V	T
A WOMAN, AND AN ARROW ON A STRING:		541	PARN FUNERAL 1	11
THAT WOMAN, THE GREAT MOTHER IMAGING,		541	PARN FUNERAL 1	13
"DROWN ALL THE DOGS," SAID THE FIERCE YOUNG WOMAN,		546	TO SAME TUNE 2	7
DROWN ALL THE DOGS," SAID THE FIERCE YOUNG WOMAN.		546	TO SAME TUNE 2	10
"DROWN ALL THE DOGS," SAID THE FIERCE YOUNG WOMAN,		546	TO SAME TUNE 2	17
DROWN ALL THE DOGS," SAID THE FIERCE YOUNG WOMAN,		546	TO SAME TUNE 2	20
"DROWN ALL THE DOGS," SAID THE FIERCE YOUNG WOMAN,		547	TO SAME TUNE 2	27
DROWN ALL THE DOGS," SAID THE FIERCE YOUNG WOMAN.		547	TO SAME TUNE 2	30
SOME TAKE DELIGHT IN ADORNING A WOMAN.		547	TO SAME TUNE 3 V	3
. . . MAN, WOMAN, CHILD (A DAUGHTER OR A SON),		556	RIBH PATRICK	2
WHY DO I HATE MAN, WOMAN OR EVENT?		558	RIBH CHRISTIAN	7
BUT IN THAT WOMAN, IN THAT HOUSEHOLD WHERE		603	GALLERY REVIS	34
SAID TO THE WOMAN ON HIS KNEES, "LIE STILL.		609	IN TARAS HALLS	2
AND GIVEN EVERYTHING A WOMAN NEEDS,		609	IN TARAS HALLS	7
OF GOD OR WOMAN, THE TIME WERE COME TO DIE."		609	IN TARAS HALLS	15
SHE THINKS, PART WOMAN, THREE PARTS A CHILD,		617	LONG-LEG FLY	15
YET A MOST GENTLE WOMAN: WHO CAN TELL		618	BRONZE HEAD	10
WHAT WOMAN HUGS HER INFANT THERE?		625	NATIVITY	1
WHY IS THE WOMAN TERROR-STRUCK?		625	NATIVITY	11
LION AND WOMAN AND THE LORD KNOWS WHAT.		629	CIRCUS ANIMALS	8
A CAPTIVE WOMAN FROM THE NARROW BRIDGE,		749	SHADOW WATER A	49
A WOMAN IN MY ARMS, SHE SINKS AWAY		749	SHADOW WATER A	54
NO MAN NOR WOMAN HAS LOVED OTHERWISE		750	SHADOW WATER A	64
OF SOME MILD WOMAN, OR IN CHILDREN'S WAYS.		750	SHADOW WATER A	74
NO MAN OR WOMAN HAS LOVED OTHERWISE		750	SHADOW WATER A V	64
A WOMAN LIES AMONG EMBROIDERIES.		752	SHADOW WATER A	120
FOR AN IMMORTAL WOMAN, AS I THINK.		755	SHADOW WATER A	173
SHE WILL ANSWER NOW LIKE ANY WAITING WOMAN		757	SHADOW WATER A	193
I CEASED TO BE A WOMAN, BEING A QUEEN.		758	SHADOW WATER A	228
WOMANHOOD				
IN THE FIRST LOVELINESS OF WOMANHOOD,		356	BROKEN DREAMS	24
WOMANKIND				
AND THERE'S A SCORE OF DUCHESSES, SURPASSING WOMANKIND,		353	HIS PHOENIX	5
WOMAN-KIND				
AND THERE'S A SCORE OF DUCHESSES, SURPASSING WOMAN-KIND,		353	HIS PHOENIX V	5
WOMAN'S				
NO WOMAN'S LOVED ME, NO MAN SOUGHT MY HELP.		103	FERGUS DRUID	26
"YOUR HEAD A WHILE SEEMED LIKE A WOMAN'S HEAD		110	CUCHULAIN SEA	63
ARE OVERTHROWN BY A WOMAN'S GAZE		164	PERFECT BEAUTY	4
STILL OVERTHROWN BY A WOMAN'S GAZE,		164	PERFECT BEAUTY V	4
WHATEVER WOMAN'S LOVER HAD HIT HER FANCY,		181	QUEEN MAEVE	24
A CHILD'S LAUGHTER, A WOMAN'S KISS.		190	BAILE AILLINN	40
A LUCKY BATTLE, OR A WOMAN'S KISS		227	SHADOW WATER B	115
BUT WITH A MAN'S HEAD, OR A FAIR WOMAN'S,		233	SHADOW WATER B	245
AND NOW A LAGGARD WITH A WOMAN'S HEAD		234	SHADOW WATER B	260
IT WAS THIS WOMAN IN HER WOMAN'S VENGEANCE		248	SHADOW WATER B	547
BEING FOR A WOMAN'S SAKE.		259	UNWORTH PRAISE	4
ONE TIME IT WAS A WOMAN'S FACE, OR WORSE—		267	ALL TEMPT ME	2
YOU'D CRY, "SOME WOMAN'S YELLOW HAIR		290	SEPTEMBER 1913	28
WHAT WOMAN'S SATISFIED,		334	SONG	8
OF SOME STRANGE WOMAN'S NAME THAT RAN IN HIS HEAD.		351	HER PRAISE V	9
WITH ALL A WOMAN'S PASSION, A CHILD'S IMPERIOUS WAY,		354	HIS PHOENIX	14
END IN A BEAUTIFUL MAN'S OR WOMAN'S BODY.		374	PHASES OF MOON	64
THAT WOMAN'S DAYS WERE SPENT		392	EASTER 1916	17
WAILING UPON A WOMAN'S KNEE,		436	FOR MY SON	22
THAT MAKE A MAN'S SOUL OR A WOMAN'S SOUL		465	HARUN RASHID	93
GAVE BUT MORE REASON FOR A WOMAN'S CARE.		466	HARUN RASHID	111
A WOMAN'S BEAUTY IS A STORM-TOSSED BANNER:		469	HARUN RASHID	188
THE BEAUTY OF A WOMAN'S MIND OR BODY		469	HARUN RASHID V	187
AND YET A WOMAN'S POWERFUL CHARACTER		489	COOLE PARK 29	18

907

		PAGE	TITLE	LINE

WOMAN'S (CONTINUED)
OF CHILDREN'S GRATITUDE OR WOMAN'S LOVE. • • • • • • 500 VACILLATION 26
REMEMBERING A WOMAN'S BEAUTY. • • • • • • • • 552 SONGS REWRIT 2 V 11
UPON A WOMAN'S BREAST." • • • • • • • • • 590 OLD WICKED MAN 62
BEFORE A WOMAN'S PORTRAIT SUDDENLY I STAND, • • • • • 602 GALLERY REVIS 13
ON THAT WOMAN'S REELING BRAIN? • • • • • • • 632 MAN AND ECHO 14
FOR LOVE IS A-WEAVING WHEN A WOMAN'S HEART • • • • 761 SHADOW WATER A 262
A WOMAN'S BEAUTY IS LIKE A WHITE • • • • • • • 784 WOMANS BEAUTY 1
OR IN MERE WOMAN'S CRUELTY • • • • • • • • 789 SINGING HEAD 11

WOMB
THE HEAVENS IN MY WOMB. • • • • • • • • • 499 MOTHER OF GOD 5
I CARRY FROM MY MOTHER'S WOMB • • • • • • • • 506 REMORSE SPEECH 14
IN MY MOTHER'S WOMB. • • • • • • • • • • 511 JANE AND JACK 12
FOR THE WOMB THE SEED SIGHS. • • • • • • • 574 LOVERS SONG 3
OR CHILD HID IN THE WOMB. • • • • • • • • 589 OLD WICKED MAN 53
FROM EMPTY TOMB OR VIRGIN WOMB? • • • • • • • 619 STICK INCENSE 2

WOMEN
OLD WOMEN WERE KEENING THE DEAD; • • • • • • • 145 HOST OF AIR V 40D
I CRIED IN MY DREAM, O WOMEN, BID THE YOUNG MEN LAY • • 163 VALLEY LOVERS 5
AND I CRIED IN MY DREAM "O WOMEN, BID THE YOUNG MEN LAY 163 VALLEY LOVERS V 5
WOMEN AND CHILDREN, YOUNG MEN WITH BOOKS, • • • • • 167 BLESSED 15
CHILDREN AND WOMEN AND TONSURED YOUNG MEN, • • • • 167 BLESSED V 15
O WOMEN, KNEELING BY YOUR ALTAR-RAILS LONG HENCE, • • • 173 SPEAKS HEARERS 1
O, WOMEN, KNEELING BY YOUR ALTAR RAILS LONG HENCE, • • 173 SPEAKS HEARERS V 1
TO PASSIONATE WOMEN IF IT SEEM • • • • • • • 202 NEVER GIVE ALL 3
"THERE IS ONE THING THAT ALL WE WOMEN KNOW • • • • 205 ADAMS CURSE V 18
TO DREAM OF WOMEN WHOSE BEAUTY WAS FOLDED IN DISMAY, • • 210 UNDER THE MOON 19
TRANSFORM THESE RASCAL BILLOWS INTO WOMEN • • • • • 222 SHADOW WATER B 11
HAS BEAUTIFUL WOMEN TO PLEASE EVERY MAN. • • • • • 228 SHADOW WATER B 144
WRUNG FROM THE COLD WOMEN OF THE SEA— • • • • • 237 SHADOW WATER B 343
WOMEN ARE HARD AND PROUD AND STUBBORN-HEARTED, • • • 245 SHADOW WATER B 479
OF MEN AND WOMEN MADE LIKE THESE; • • • • • • 272 GREY ROCK 43
'TWAS WINE OR WOMEN, OR SOME CURSE— • • • • • 273 GREY ROCK 54
THE WOMEN OF HIS HOUSEHOLD WERE ASLEEP, • • • • • 282 TWO KINGS V 133
WOMEN CAN FIND." WITH A MOST MASTERFUL VOICE, • • • 284 TWO KINGS 175
WOMEN CAN FIND." WITH A MOST BURNING VOICE • • • • 284 TWO KINGS V 175
OF THE MEN AND WOMEN OF TROY, • • • • • • • 293 HELEN LIVED 11
THREE WOMEN THAT HAVE WROUGHT • • • • • • • 315 FRIENDS 2
THAT WOMEN LAUGHING, OR TIMID OR WILD, • • • • • 358 PRESENCES 4
AT ALL THESE DEATH-BEDS WOMEN HEARD • • • • • • 361 ALF POLLEXFEN 36
AT ALL THESE DEATHBEDS WOMEN HEARD • • • • • • 361 ALF POLLEXFEN V 36
AND THAT ALL BEAUTIFUL WOMEN MAY • • • • • • 387 ROBARTES DANCE 45
IT'S CERTAIN THAT FINE WOMEN EAT • • • • • • 404 FOR DAUGHTER 30
DID ALL OLD MEN AND WOMEN, RICH AND POOR, • • • • 413 TOWER 97
MEMORIES OF THE WORDS OF WOMEN• • • • • • • 415 TOWER 162
THE WOMEN TAKE SO LITTLE STOCK • • • • • • • 455 HIS MEMORIES 7
HOW SUCH A MAN PLEASED WOMEN MOST • • • • • • 458 SECRETS OF OLD 13
BODIES OF HOLY MEN AND WOMEN EXUDE • • • • • • 483 OIL AND BLOOD 2
MORE WOMEN BORN THAN MEN." • • • • • • • 485 STATISTICS 4
ALL WOMEN DOTE UPON AN IDLE MAN • • • • • • 500 VACILLATION 23
"THREE DEAR THINGS THAT WOMEN KNOW," • • • • • 521 THREE THINGS 7
OF ALL GOOD MEN AND WOMEN, • • • • • • • 531 FATHER CHILD 3
ALL STATELY WOMEN MOVING TO A SONG • • • • • • 537 HER VISION 17
I GAVE WHAT OTHER WOMEN GAVE • • • • • • • 538 LAST CONFESS 13
LOVERS OF HORSES AND OF WOMEN, SHALL, • • • • • 564 GYRES 19
I HAVE HEARD THAT HYSTERICAL WOMEN SAY • • • • • 565 LAPIS LAZULI 1
WHAT MATTER, WE ARE BUT WOMEN• • • • • • • 572 LADYS 2ND SONG 3
NOTHING THAT COMMON WOMEN PONDER ON • • • • • • 579 DOR WELLESLEY 12
"BECAUSE I AM MAD ABOUT WOMEN • • • • • • • 587 OLD WICKED MAN 1
AND WHAT'S THE GOOD OF WOMEN, FOR ALL THAT THEY CAN SAY 592 PILGRIM 4
THAT MEN AND WOMEN OF ALL SORTS • • • • • • 597 MODEL LAUREATE 3
APPROVED PATTERNS OF WOMEN OR OF MEN • • • • • 602 GALLERY REVIS 31
TO MANY WOMEN I HAVE SAID, "LIE STILL," • • • • • 609 IN TARAS HALLS 6
GAVE WOMEN DREAMS AND DREAMS THEIR LOOKING-GLASS. • • 610 STATUES 16
GAVE WOMEN DREAMS AND DREAMS THEIR LOOKING GLASS. • • • 610 STATUES V 16
THE WOMEN THAT I PICKED SPOKE SWEET AND LOW • • • • 622 HOUND VOICE 8
BECAUSE WOMEN IN THE UPPER STOREYS DEMAND A FACE AT THE 623 HIGH TALK 7
PANE,
SWEAR BY THOSE HORSEMEN, BY THOSE WOMEN • • • • • 637 BEN BULBEN 5
TWO WOMEN, WITHERED ONE AND SMALL AND THIN, • • • • 711 FERENCZ RENYI 51
AND THE FISHER MEN AND WOMEN FROM THE DRIPPING HARBOUR WALL 718 PHANTOM SHIP 11
THE BOYS, THE WOMEN, AND OLD MEN, • • • • • • 725 LEGEND 7
AND DROVE THE BOYS AND WOMEN OFF. • • • • • • 725 LEGEND 24
THE WOMEN SLINGERS ON THE NARROW BRIDGE, • • • • • 749 SHADOW WATER A V 41
BUT WOMEN AND JUGGLERS AND PLAYERS ON THE HARP. • • • 752 SHADOW WATER A 115
BELIEVE THAT GOLD AND WOMEN TAKEN IN WAR • • • • 754 SHADOW WATER A 159
BECAUSE THESE WATERS MAKE ALL WOMEN ONE. • • • • 757 SHADOW WATER A 194
UNDER THE WAVES, AND TOOK A THOUSAND WOMEN • • • • 766 SHADOW WATER A 378
TO WANDER IN; YOU HAVE LOVED MANY WOMEN, • • • • 767 SHADOW WATER A 389
THE WOMEN NONE CAN KISS AND THRIVE, • • • • • 775 AGAINST WITCH 8
WOMEN, THAT NONE CAN KISS AND THRIVE, • • • • • 775 AGAINST WITCH V 8
GAVE ALL THE LOVE THAT WOMEN KNOW! • • • • • 789 SINGING HEAD 21
WHERE MAY NEW-MARRIED WOMEN SIT • • • • • • 791 REPRISALS 19

WOMEN'S
I HAVE OLD WOMEN'S SECRETS NOW • • • • • • • 457 SECRETS OF OLD 1

WOMEN-SLINGERS
THE WOMEN-SLINGERS ON THE NARROW BRIDGE, • • • • • 749 SHADOW WATER A 41

WON
THESE HANDS WON MANY A TORQUE OF GOLD. • • • • 83 MAD KING GOLL 23
HAS WON THE GOLD HIS CARS OF BATTLE BRING." • • • • 106 CUCHULAIN SEA 11
NOR WON THE GOLD THAT NOW CUCHULAIN BRINGS." • • • • 106 CUCHULAIN SEA V 11

PAGE   TITLE   LINE

WON   (CONTINUED)

"FROM THE GREY SHIPS AND BATTLES NEVER WON. . . . . . . 114 ROSE OF BATTLE V   8
BEAUTY THAT WE HAVE WON . . . . 293 HELEN LIVED   5
LOVE LOST AS SOON AS WON, ... 312 CHILD DANCING   8
WHO HAS WON A DRUNKEN CHEER, ... 347 FISHERMAN   18
AN IMAGE OF MYSTERIOUS WISDOM WON BY TOIL! . . . . . . 373 PHASES OF MOON   18
HE MIGHT HAVE WON FAME IN THE END, ... 392 EASTER 1916   28
I SAW MY FREEDOM WON . . . . 400 DEMON BEAST   7
UPON A WOMAN WON OR WOMAN LOST? . . . . 413 TOWER   114
WHAT NO DECEPTION WON. I HAVE HEARD THEM SAY . . . . . 448 HERO GIRL FOOL V 13
NO LOOSE-LIPPED DEMAGOGUE HAD WON THE DAY, ... 542 PARN FUNERAL 2   3
NO LOOSE LIPPED DEMAGOGUE HAD WON THE DAY, ... 542 PARN FUNERAL 2 V   3
BUT BODY WON! IT WALKS UPRIGHT. . . . . 561 FOUR AGES MAN   2
AFTER CERTAIN YEARS HE WON . . . . 577 WHAT THEN   7
I SING WHAT WAS LOST AND DREAD WHAT WAS WON, ... 591 WHAT WAS LOST   1
COMPLETENESS OF THEIR PASSIONS WON! . . . . 637 BEN BULBEN   9
IF WHEN THE BATTLE IS HALF WON, ... 743 DANAAN QUICK   19

WONDER

SO PALE! AND SOUNDS OF WONDER HER LIPS UTTERED, . . .   34 OISIN 2   V   71
WATCHED ME WITH MOURNFUL WONDER OUT OF THE WELLS OF HIS
    EYES. . . . .   51 OISIN 3   60
STARED ON THE MOURNFUL WONDER OF HIS EYES, ... 108 CUCHULAIN SEA   41
UPON THE MOURNFUL WONDER OF HIS EYES, ... 108 CUCHULAIN SEA V   42
AND PONDERED ON THE WONDER OF HIS DAYS, ... 108 CUCHULAIN SEA V   43
MOURNFUL THAT NO NEW WONDER MAY BETIDE, ... 111 ROSE OF WORLD   3
WHY, IT'S A WONDER OUT OF RECKONING . . . . 243 SHADOW WATER B   445
AND WONDER WHAT HAS AILED HIM THESE TWELVE MONTHS." . . 284 TWO KINGS   163
(I WONDER IF THE BUILDER HAS BEEN PAID) . . . . 292 TO A SHADE   3
WONDER HOW MANY TIMES I COULD HAVE PROVED MY WORTH . . 427 PHANTOM HATRED   34
IN MOMENTARY WONDER STARE UPON . . . . 443 SCHOOL CHILDR   7
AND WONDER IF SHE STOOD SO AT THAT AGE-- . . . . . . 444 SCHOOL CHILDR   19
AND, OH! THE WONDER OF THE THING! EACH CAME . . . . . 656 ISLE STAT I 3   29
THE WINGED WONDER OF ALL FAERY LAND. . . . . 657 ISLE STAT I 3   57
TO MAKE US GLAD WITH WONDER AS WE SAT . . . . 683 SEEKER   41
I WONDER WHICH IS WHITEST, THEY OR THOU. . . . . . . 700 MOSADA 3   45

WONDERED

AND WONDERED WHAT WAS LEFT FOR MASSACRE TO SAVE. . . . . 619 BRONZE HEAD   28

WONDERFUL

AND ALL THESE THINGS WERE WONDERFUL AND GREAT! . . . . 104 FERGUS DRUID   37
MORE WONDERFUL! AND WE HAVE SWORDS. O NIGHT . . . . . 664 ISLE STAT II 2   61
WITH WONDERFUL WHITE SANDS, WHERE NEVER YET . . . . . 693 MOSADA 1   81
WITH WONDERFUL WHITE SAND, WHERE NEVER YET . . . . . . 693 MOSADA 1   V   81

WONDERFULLY

OR SOME SMALL BEAST MOST WONDERFULLY FURR'D, ... 650 ISLE STAT I 1   148

WONDERING

AND NEIGHED THREE TIMES. WHEN, WONDERING . . . . . .   10 OISIN 1   V 110A
MUCH WONDERING TO SEE UPON ALL HANDS, OF WATTLES
    AND WOODWORK MADE, ...   58 OISIN 3   162
MUCH WONDERING TO SEE UPON ALL HANDS, OF WATTLES
    AND WOOD-WORK MADE, ...   58 OISIN 3   V 162
WONDERING TO LAY HER IN THAT SOLITUDE, ... 123 DREAM OF DEATH   5
AND WONDERING PLANTED BY HER SOLITUDE . . . . 123 DREAM OF DEATH V   5
AND WONDERING WHO OF THE MANY-CHANGING SIDHE . . . . . 181 QUEEN MAEVE   41
AND WONDERING WHO OF THE MANY CHANGING SIDHE . . . . . 181 QUEEN MAEVE   V   41
THAT NO GOD TROUBLED NOW, AND, WONDERING . . . . . . 182 QUEEN MAEVE   60
WHILE WONDERING STILL TO BE A SHADE, WITH GRANIA'S SHADE, 366 HER COURAGE   V   4
WILL WONDERING LISTEN, AND THIS TALE SHALL EASE . . . . 693 MOSADA 1   70

WONDERS   SEE WOOD-OF-WONDERS

THEY KNOW ALL WONDERS, FOR THEY PASS . . . . 196 BAILE AILLINN   160
OF WONDERS THAT HAVE HAPPENED . . . . 215 HAPPY TOWNLAND   47
OF WONDERS! EVE OF PRODIGIES! DRAW! DRAW! . . . . . . 664 ISLE STAT II 2   62

WONDROUS

THERE WAS A WONDROUS YOUNG MAN SITTING. . . . .   18 OISIN 1   V 252
AND THEY WILL WAR, 'MID WONDROUS ELFIN-SIGHTS! . . . . 651 ISLE STAT I 1   164
AND FADED NOW IS ALL THY WONDROUS ART. . . . . 673 ISLE STAT II 3   194
WHO, DREAMING TO A WONDROUS AGE, LIVED ON, ... 692 MOSADA 1   52

WONTED

AGED AND WISE, THEY SEEK THEIR WONTED PERCHES . . . . .   72 ANASHU VIJAYA   31

WOOD   SEE LARCH-WOOD ASH-WOOD APPLE-WOOD PINE-WOOD

AND WHERE THE WOOD AND WATERS MEET . . . .   14 OISIN 1   193
OF DREAMY FOAM A STAFF OF WOOD . . . .   24 OISIN 1   366
I DREW IT FORTH: THE STAFF OF WOOD, ...   24 OISIN 1   366
WHITE FLOWERS OF THE FOAM A STAFF OF WOOD . . . . . .   24 OISIN 1   V 366
THE WOOD WAS SO SPACIOUS ABOVE THEM, ...   49 OISIN 3   37
SO SPACIOUS THE WOOD WAS ABOVE THEM, ...   49 OISIN 3   V   37
. . . LIKE THE ROARING OF WIND IN A WOOD. . . . . .   58 OISIN 3   168
THE SUN HAS LAID HIS CHIN ON THE GREY WOOD, ...   72 ANASHU VIJAYA   24
THE SUN HATH LAID HIS CHIN ON THE GREY WOOD, ...   72 ANASHU VIJAYA V   24
AND I MUST WANDER WOOD AND HILL . . . .   86 MAD KING GOLL   70
I MUST AWAY BY WOOD AND SEA . . . .   86 MAD KING GOLL V   67
OF SLEUTH WOOD IN THE LAKE, ...   86 STOLEN CHILD   2
BEYOND OLD MARTIN'S WOOD, ...   95 MOLL MAGEE   V   34
PILIN' THE WOOD OR PILIN' THE TURF, ...   96 MOLL MAGEE   45
A-PILIN' WOOD OR PILIN' TURF, ...   96 MOLL MAGEE   V   45
THE DRUID, GREY, WOOD NURTURED, QUIET EYED, ... 101 ROSE UPON ROOD V   4
GO WATCH THE ROAD BETWEEN THE WOOD AND TIDE, ... 105 CUCHULAIN SEA   4
BETWEEN THE LAVISH SHELTER OF A WOOD . . . . 108 CUCHULAIN SEA V 38A
A CROSS THEY HAD MADE OUT OF TWO BITS OF WOOD, ... 123 DREAM OF DEATH   7
I CAME AND WROTE UPON A CROSS OF WOOD-- . . . . 123 DREAM OF DEATH V   7
AND RULES THE SHADOWS OF THE WOOD, ... 126 GOES FERGUS   10
OF SUN AND MOON AND HOLLOW AND WOOD . . . . 148 INTO TWILIGHT   11

909

		PAGE	TITLE		LINE
WOOD	(CONTINUED)				
	OF THE FLOOD AND FLAME, OF THE HEIGHT AND WOOD, ...	148	INTO TWILIGHT	V	11
	OF HOLLOW WOOD AND THE HILLY WOOD	148	INTO TWILIGHT	V	11
	OF HOLLOW WOOD AND THE HILLY WOOD	148	INTO TWILIGHT	V	11
	I WENT OUT TO THE HAZEL WOOD, ...	149	WANDER AENGUS		1
	I HAVE BEEN IN THE PATH OF STONES AND THE WOOD OF THORNS,	153	CHANGE BELOVED		3
	AND I DREAMED MY LOST LOVE CAME STEALTHILY OUT OF THE WOOD	163	VALLEY LOVERS		3
	BETWEEN THE WIND AND THE WOOD.	166	BLESSED		4
	ARE SINGING ABOUT THE WOOD?"	167	BLESSED		24
	BETWEEN THE WIND AND THE WOOD.	167	BLESSED	V	4D
	AND THE WOOD WOMAN, WHOSE LOVER WAS CHANGED TO A BLUE-EYED	209	UNDER THE MOON	V	13
	HAWK;				
	THE RAGGED WOOD	210	RAGGED WOOD		T
	THE HOLLOW WOOD	210	RAGGED WOOD	V	T
	I HEARD UNDER A RAGGED HOLLOW WOOD, ...	210	RAGGED WOOD	V	1
	O HURRY TO THE RAGGED WOOD, FOR THERE	211	RAGGED WOOD		9
	O HURRY TO THE HOLLOW WOOD, FOR THERE	211	RAGGED WOOD	V	9
	IN A GOLDEN AND SILVER WOOD;	214	HAPPY TOWNLAND		10
	IN A GOLD AND SILVER WOOD;	214	HAPPY TOWNLAND	V	10
	DIM INCHY WOOD, THAT HIDES BADGER AND FOX	218	WOODS OF COOLE		13
	AND MARTEN-CAT, AND BORDERS THAT OLD WOOD	218	WOODS OF COOLE		14
	WISE BIDDY EARLY CALLED THE WICKED WOOD;	218	WOODS OF COOLE		15
	AND MARTIN CAT, AND BORDERS THAT OLD WOOD	218	WOODS OF COOLE	V	14
	HE MADE A HARP WITH DRUID APPLE WOOD	220	HARP OF AENGUS	V	11
	UPON THE MISTY BORDER OF THE WOOD, ...	251	SHADOW WATER B		612
	KING EOCHAID CAME AT SUNDOWN TO A WOOD	276	TWO KINGS		1
	BETWEEN THE WOOD OF DURAS AND MAGAI	276	TWO KINGS	V	G
	AND CAME INTO A WOOD AS THE SUN SET	277	TWO KINGS	V	3
	WESTWARD OF TARA. WHERE IN THE MIDDLE WOOD	277	TWO KINGS	V	4
	I GROPED MY WAY FROM BEECH TO HAZEL WOOD, ...	283	TWO KINGS		139
	CLOSE TO A CLUMP OF BEECH TREES IN THE WOOD	283	TWO KINGS	V	135
	ALL WORK IN METAL OR IN WOOD, ...	327	ROBERT GREGORY		76
	HOVERING OVER THE WOOD	349	HAWK		10
	MY GREAT WOOD LECTERN AND THE FIRE	358	PRESENCES		10
	BY THESE WIRE-JOINTED JAWS AND LIMBS OF WOOD, ...	382	VISION ROBART		10
	BUT GREGORY'S WOOD AND ONE BARE HILL	403	FOR DAUGHTER		4
	A BARRICADE OF STONE OR OF WOOD;	425	STARES NEST		11
	AN ANCIENT IMAGE MADE OF OLIVE WOOD--	428	NINETEEN 19		6
	YOUR HOOVES HAVE STAMPED AT THE BLACK MARGIN OF THE WOOD,	442	BLACK CENTAUR		1
	THE HARE LEAP TO THE WOOD, ...	453	DEATH OF HARE		2
	AM SET DOWN STANDING IN THE WOOD	453	DEATH OF HARE		11
	UPON THE BORDER OF THAT LAKE'S A WOOD	490	COOLE BALLYLEE		9
	WHETHER IN WOOD, WATER OR CLOUD, ...	528	DANCER CRUACH		7
	HER VISION IN THE WOOD	536	HER VISION		T
	AT WINE-DARK MIDNIGHT IN THE SACRED WOOD, ...	536	HER VISION		2
	'TIS MORN, AND FROM THE DEW-DRENCH'D WOOD I'VE SPED . .	645	ISLE STAT I 1		6
	THE WOOD AND THE VALLEY AND SEA	646	ISLE STAT I 1		42
	ALONG THE WOOD WITH SUBTLE TREAD AND BENDED BOWS. . . .	649	ISLE STAT I 1		111
	HERE IS THE PLACE, THE CLIFF-ENCIRCLED WOOD;	651	ISLE STAT I 2		3
	BY WOOD ANTIQUE, BY WAVE AND WASTE, ...	670	ISLE STAT II 3		109
	THE SULLEN WOOD. BUT MANY WOODS I SEE	682	SEEKER		24
	SEEK NOT THAT WOOD; FOR THERE THE GOBLIN SNAKES	682	SEEKER		29
	HIDING THE REBELS WORM IN YONDER WOOD	709	FERENCZ RENYI		14
	HIDING THE REBELS SWARM IN YONDER WOOD	709	FERENCZ RENYI	V	14
	HIDING THE REBEL WORMS IN YONDER WOOD, ...	709	FERENCZ RENYI	V	14
	A LITTLE BOY OUTSIDE THE SYCAMORE WOOD	715	DWELT SYCAMORE		1
	A LITTLE BOY INSIDE THE SYCAMORE WOOD	715	DWELT SYCAMORE		5
	IN THE BOSOM AFAR OF THE FRAGRANT WOOD.	717	LOVE SONG		9
	AWAY IN THE HEART OF THE ANTIQUE WOOD	730	PRIEST FAIRY		64
	"AND CUT NO WOOD THE WHOLE DAY LONG, ...	731	PRIEST FAIRY		81
	FROM PLAYING HURLEY IN THE WOOD	743	DANAAN QUICK		9
	IN A WOOD OF DEW AND MOSS, ...	744	ROSY CROSS		5
	OUT OF THAT ISLAND WHERE THE FOOL OF THE WOOD	747	SHADOW WATER A		2
	THAT DRUIDS WRITE ON YEW AND APPLE WOOD, ...	748	SHADOW WATER A		29
	THE FOOL THAT CAME OUT OF THE WINTRY WOOD	750	SHADOW WATER A		75
	HEARING THE HARPERS PLAY, THE PINE WOOD CRACKLE, . . .	759	SHADOW WATER A	V	241
	HE MADE A HARP WITH DRUID APPLE WOOD	763	SHADOW WATER A		306
	UPON THIN APPLE BOARDS OF YEW AND APPLE WOOD, ...	764	SHADOW WATER A		343
	UPON THE MISTY BORDER OF THE WOOD,--	769	SHADOW WATER A		428
WOOD-CUTTER					
	WITH HER OLD FATHER THE BLIND WOOD-CUTTER;	74	ANASHU VIJAYA		63
	THE DAUGHTER OF THE GREY OLD WOOD-CUTTER, ...	74	ANASHU VIJAYA	V	63
WOODED					
	THE VIOLETS ARE THAT ON THE WOODED HILL	713	FERENCZ RENYI		95
	HANGS O'ER ALL THE WOODED EARTH.	731	STREET DANCERS		8
WOODEN					
	I HAVE A LUCKY WOODEN SHIN	302	HOUR DAWN		18
	HAD DIPPED THE WOODEN LADLE DEEP	304	HOUR DAWN		46
	AND TOOK THE WOODEN LADLE UP	304	HOUR DAWN	V	46
	WHILE THEIR GREAT WOODEN DICE BEAT ON THE BOARD. . . .	412	TOWER		88
	COVERS ITS WOODEN SHEATH.	421	MY TABLE		7
	THE WOODEN SCABBARD BOUND AND WOUND, ...	477	SELF AND SOUL		15
WOODLAND					
	TO THAT LOW LAUGHING WOODLAND RHYME.	14	OISIN 1		176
	AMONG THE WOODLAND GRASSES SWEET.	15	OISIN 1	V	199
	I LEAD ALONG THE WOODLAND DEER;	84	MAD KING GOLL		46
	AND WHETHER I GO IN MY DREAMS BY WOODLAND, OR DUN, . .	210	UNDER THE MOON		14
	OR SHORE,				
	THE WOODLAND PATHS ARE DRY.	322	SWANS AT COOLE		2
	ALL BUT THE TERRORS OF THE WOODLAND FLIGHT FORGOT . . .	366	HER COURAGE		5
	ALL BUT THE PERILS OF THE WOODLAND FLIGHT FORGOT, . . .	366	HER COURAGE	V	5

		PAGE	TITLE	LINE
WOODLAND (CONTINUED)				
HERE, WHERE MEN KNOW THE GRACIOUS WOODLAND JOYS,	• • • •	651	ISLE STAT I 1	154
AND SEE AGAIN THE HAPPY WOODLAND LIGHT,	• • • • • •	664	ISLE STAT II 2	58
AGAIN THE WOODLAND LAUGHTER, AND THE CLEAR	• • • •	674	ISLE STAT II 3	221
COME AWAY WHILE THE MOON'S IN THE WOODLAND,	• • • •	707	FAIRY PEDANT	9
COME AWAY WHILE THE MOON'S IN THE WOODLAND,	• • • •	708	FAIRY PEDANT	37
DEEP IN THE WOODLAND PAUSED THEY, THE SIX FEET	• • •	716	DWELT SYCAMORE	9
DEEP IN THE WOODLAND PASSED THEY. THE SIX FEET	• •	716	DWELT SYCAMORE V	9
UNTO THE HEART OF THE WOODLAND STRAYING,	• • • •	728	PRIEST FAIRY	1
WOODLANDS				
AND AIMLESS WANDERINGS THE WOODLANDS LONE,	• • • •	674	ISLE STAT II 3	209
THE HOLLOW WOODLANDS FEEL HIM THERE,	• • • • • •	737	SUMMER EVENING	17
WOODMAN				
A WOODMAN ON HIS HOMEWARD WAY	• • • • • • • •	730	PRIEST FAIRY	73
WOODMAN'S				
TO AN OLD EMPTY WOODMAN'S HOUSE THAT'S HIDDEN	• • • •	282	TWO KINGS	134
WOOD-NURTURED				
THE DRUID, GREY, WOOD-NURTURED, QUIET-EYED,	• • • •	101	ROSE UPON ROOD	4
WOOD-OF-WONDERS				
AND WOOD-OF-WONDERS, WHERE ONE KILLS AN OX AT DAWN,	• •	209	UNDER THE MOON	9
WOOD-PECKER				
WHILE THE WOOD-PECKER MADE A MERRY DIN,	• • • • • •	44	OISIN 2	V 228
WOODPECKER'S				
THE BARRED WOODPECKER'S MANSION IS AND DEEP,	• • • •	659	ISLE STAT II 1	23
WOOD-RHAPSODISTS				
POOR SAD WOOD-RHAPSODISTS. NOT SO! THEY'RE GLAD.	• • •	652	ISLE STAT I 2	16
WOOD'S				
THE RIVERS, AND THE WOOD'S OLD NIGHT.	• • • • •	25	OISIN 1	V 387
BETWEEN WOOD'S RIM AND THE HORSES OF THE SEA.	• • •	108	CUCHULAIN SEA	34
GO THERE, AND LIGHT A CAMP-FIRE AT WOOD'S RIM!	• • •	108	CUCHULAIN SEA	35
GO THERE, AND LIGHT A CAMP FIRE AT WOOD'S RIM!	• • •	108	CUCHULAIN SEA	V 35
AND PIERCE THE DEEP WOOD'S WOVEN SHADE,	• • • • •	125	GOES FERGUS	2
BY THE WOOD'S EDGE WHERE ONLY EQUALS MEET,	• • • •	321	REED WHISPERER V	8
THE WINE-DARK OF THE WOOD'S INTRICACIES,	• • • •	446	COLONUS PRAISE	2
THE WINE DARK OF THE WOOD'S INTRICACIES,	• • • •	446	COLONUS PRAISE	V 2
FROM THE WOOD'S WAYS, THEN, LIKE A SILVER FLAME,	• • •	658	ISLE STAT II 1	6
FROM THE DIM WOOD'S FOUNDATION--	• • • • • •	672	ISLE STAT II 3	162
SAW ON THE WOOD'S EDGE GLEAM AN ASH-GREY FEATHER!	• • •	715	DWELT SYCAMORE	2
OF A WIDE WOOD'S LEAFY LEISURE,	• • • • • • • •	731	STREET DANCERS	11
WOODS				
AND WHERE THE WOODS AND WATERS MEET	• • • • • •	14	OISIN 1	V 193
AND FROM THE WOODS RUSHED OUT A BAND	• • • • • •	15	OISIN 1	201
AND FROM THE WOODS THERE RUSHED A BAND	• • • • •	15	OISIN 1	V 201
TOGETHER, WHILE THE DARK WOODS RANG,	• • • • • •	16	OISIN 1	227
NOW IN THE WOODS, AWAY WITH THEM	• • • • • • •	16	OISIN 1	V 216A
ON IN THE WOODS, AWAY WITH THEM,	• • • • • • •	16	OISIN 1	V 222A
THE DANCE WOUND THROUGH THE WINDLESS WOODS!	• • • •	21	OISIN 1	320
THEN ON AMONG THE WINDLESS WOODS,	• • • • • •	21	OISIN 1	V 320
WE PASSED BY WOODS, AND LAWNS OF CLOVER,	• • • •	25	OISIN 1	377
BY WOODS OF MOSS, BY LAWNS OF CLOVER,	• • • • •	25	OISIN 1	V 377
THE WAILING GREW DISTANT! I RODE BY THE WOODS OF		56	OISIN 3	137
THE WRINKLING BARK,				
THE WOODS OF ARCADY ARE DEAD,	• • • • • • •	64	HAPPY SHEPHERD	1
AS IN THE WOODS HE WANDERS, IF HE LOVE	• • • • •	71	ANASHU VIJAYA	V 3
WHILE WE ALONE HAVE ROUND US WOVEN WOODS,	• • • •	73	ANASHU VIJAYA	56
AMONG THE MOULDERING OF ANCIENT WOODS	• • • • •	74	ANASHU VIJAYA	61
THE WOODS WERE ROUND THEM, AND THE YELLOW LEAVES	• • •	80	EPHEMERA	13
AND NOW I WANDER IN THE WOODS	• • • • • • • •	84	MAD KING GOLL	37
AND BORE IT TO THE WOODS WITH ME!	• • • • • •	85	MAD KING GOLL	57
OR PACE AND WEEP IN WOODS FORLORN,	• • • • • •	86	MAD KING GOLL	V 68
TO THE WOODS AND WATERS WILD	• • • • • • • •	87	STOLEN CHILD	V REF
AND PACE THE WOODS, AND DRIVE MY CHARIOT-WHEELS	• • •	103	FERGUS DRUID	18
AND PACE THE WOODS, AND DRIVE MY CHARIOT WHEELS	• • •	103	FERGUS DRUID	V 18
AND THE MOUNTAINS AND WOODS	• • • • • • • •	142	MOODS	3
THE MOUNTAINS AND WOODS	• • • • • • • • •	142	MOODS	V 3
O DAUGHTER OF THE ISLAND OF WOODS!	• • • • • •	164	PERFECT BEAUTY V	1
DWELT AMONG WINE-STAINED WANDERERS IN DEEP WOODS!	• • •	170	SECRET ROSE	21
IN THE SEVEN WOODS	• • • • • • • • • • •	198	SEVEN WOODS	T
I HAVE HEARD THE PIGEONS OF THE SEVEN WOODS	• • • •	198	SEVEN WOODS	1
I WALKED AMONG THE SEVEN WOODS OF COOLE!	• • • •	217	WOODS OF COOLE	1
SEVEN ODOURS, SEVEN MURMURS, SEVEN WOODS.	• • • •	218	WOODS OF COOLE	16
IN THE LAST RIDGE OF THE BARLEY? DO OUR WOODS	• • •	218	WOODS OF COOLE	33
AND WINDS AND PONDS COVER MORE QUIET WOODS,	• • • •	218	WOODS OF COOLE	34
THAT SHE AMONG HER WOODS MIGHT KNOW HE WEPT!	• • • •	220	HARP OF AENGUS V	12
"I HAVE SENT AMONG THE FIELDS OR TO THE WOODS	• • •	280	TWO KINGS	69
"I HAVE SENT OUT INTO THE FIELDS AND WOODS	• • • •	280	TWO KINGS	V 69
LIKE THE EYES OF SOME GREAT KITE SCOURING THE WOODS,	• •	283	TWO KINGS	150
INTO THE FOLD, WE'LL TO THE WOODS AND THERE	• • •	343	SHEP GOATHERD	114
BUT GREGORY'S WOODS AND ONE BARE HILL	• • • • • •	403	FOR DAUGHTER V	4
MAIDEN, COME FORTH! THE WOODS KEEP WATCH FOR THEE!	• •	645	ISLE STAT I 1	1
WITH THAT SONG LEADING WHERE HARMONIC WOODS	• • • •	657	ISLE STAT I 3	43
LONE REGENT OF THE WOODS, DEEP MUTTERING	• • • •	657	ISLE STAT I 3	49
OF THOSE VAST WOODS! AND THEN I SAW THE BOAT,	• • • •	657	ISLE STAT I 3	53
OF THE WIDE WOODS. AND THE DEEP EARTH GATHERED THEM.	• •	660	ISLE STAT II 1	33
IN THE DEEP CENTRES OF THE SECRET WOODS.	• • • •	661	ISLE STAT II 1	54
WHAT IS IT, FRIEND? HE LOST I! THE WOODS THE CHIEF	• •	661	ISLE STAT II 1	60
OF THE DREAD WOODS! ALONG THEIR RUSSET FLOOR	• • •	675	ISLE STAT II 3	243
THE SULLEN WOOD. BUT MANY WOODS I SEE	• • • • •	682	SEEKER	24
ABOVE, THE WOODS WHERE WITH THE SOFT MILD EYE	• • •	710	FERENCZ RENYI	26
WHERE IN THE WOODS OR HILLS THE REBELS BE?"	• • •	713	FERENCZ RENYI	V 83A
NOON WRAPPED THE WOODS IN VEILS OF VIOLET WEATHER!	• •	715	DWELT SYCAMORE V	7

911

```
                                                      PAGE    TITLE           LINE
WOODS   (CONTINUED)
        AND AWAY IN THE WOODS WE WILL SCATTER THE DEW:  • • •   717 LOVE SONG           2
        THE LIVING WOODS FOREGO THEIR CARE,  • • • •   736 SUMMER EVENING      1
        ARE BETTER THAN THE WOODS WHERE NO LOVE FADES • • • •   754 SHADOW WATER A    160
        THAT MURMURS WITH HOLY WOODS, AND WIN THEIR HELP • •   757 SHADOW WATER A    199
        WHERE TRUE-LOVE WANDERS AMONG THE HOLY WOODS.  • • •   764 SHADOW WATER A    337
        WHERE TRUE LOVE WANDERS AMONG THE HOLY WOODS.  • • •   764 SHADOW WATER A V  337
        WHERE ARE THESE BOUGHS?  WHERE ARE THE HOLY WOODS • •   765 SHADOW WATER A    359
        THAT LIVES AMONG THE WOODS OF THE DARK HOUNDS.  • • •   766 SHADOW WATER A    376
        WE WILL FIND OUT VALLEYS AND WOODS AND MEADOWS.  • •   767 SHADOW WATER A    388
        OR AMONG WINDS THAT MOVE IN THE MEADOWS AND WOODS.  • •  768 SHADOW WATER A V  413
WOODS'
        BY RIVERS AND THE WOODS' OLD NIGHT:  • • • • • •   25 OISIN 1           387
WOODWAYS
        WITHIN THE WOODWAYS, BLUE AS THE HALCYON'S WING,  • • •   683 SEEKER        V  38
WOOD-WOMAN
        AND THE WOOD-WOMAN, WHOSE LOVER WAS CHANGED TO A BLUE-EYED   209 UNDER THE MOON     13
            HAWK:
WOODWORK
        MUCH WONDERING TO SEE UPON ALL HANDS, OF WATTLES   58 OISIN 3          162
            AND WOODWORK MADE,
WOOD-WORK
        MUCH WONDERING TO SEE UPON ALL HANDS, OF WATTLES   58 OISIN 3        V 162
            AND WOOD-WORK MADE,
WOODY
        OVER THE BARE AND WOODY LAND,  • • • • • • • • •   15 OISIN 1           198
        UPON THE WOODY CENTRAL HILL:  • • • • • • • • •   22 OISIN 1           323
        I CHASED UPON THAT WOODY SHORE  • • • • • • • •   23 OISIN 1           344
        OH, PATRICK, ON THAT WOODY SHORE  • • • • • • •   23 OISIN 1         V 343
        DRIVING THE DEER ALONG THE WOODY WAYS.  • • • • •   109 CUCHULAIN SEA  V  48
        CAME BY THE WOODY WAY • • • • • • • • • •   166 BLESSED         V   2
        DOTH HE STILL DWELL WITHIN THE WOODY SHADE,  • • •   678 ISLE STAT II 3    303
        I HURRIED FROM THE WOODY SHORE,  • • • • • • •   742 DANAAN QUICK       4
WOOED
        AND HAVE BEEN WOOED BY THE TWELVE KINGS OF THE EARTH, • •   757 SHADOW WATER A V  214
WOOING
        "A WEARY WOOING AND A LONG," HE SAID,  • • • • • •   283 TWO KINGS        154
WOOL
        WHOSE LONG WOOL WHITER THAN SEA-FROTH FLOWS,  • • • •   8 OISIN 1            90
        WHOSE LONG WOOL WHITER THAN SEA FROTH FLOWS,  • • • •   8 OISIN 1         V  90
        THEN MUSE THEY ON THE HOUSEHOLD WOOL INTENT,  • • • •   32 OISIN 2        V  55
        "WHAT DO YOU WEAVE WITH WOOL SO WHITE?"  • • • • •   70 CLOAK BOAT         11
        WHO COME WITH THEIR CROWNS OF PEARL AND THEIR SPINDLES   203 WITHER BOUGHS      10
            OF WOOL,
        WHAT DO YOU WEAVE WITH WOOL SO WHITE?  • • • • • •   666 ISLE STAT II 3     11
        HEAVY WITH WOOL THE SHEEP ARE GATHERED IN,  • • • • •   681 SEEKER             1
WOOLLY
        NASCHINA, HAIL! I'D DRIVE THY WOOLLY SHEEP,  • • • •   649 ISLE STAT I 1     122
WOOS
        OR MUST SUFFER, IF HE WOOS • • • • • • • •   479 SELF AND SOUL      63
WORD      SEE MINSTREL-WORD
        AND CAUGHT MY HANDS, BUT SPAKE NO WORD  • • • • •   25 OISIN 1           374
        AND CAUGHT MY HANDS AND SPAKE NO WORD  • • • • •   25 OISIN 1         V 374
        NO CENTURIES COULD DIM, AND A WORD RAN • • • • •   38 OISIN 2           127
        WORD BE-MOCKERS?--BY THE ROOD,  • • • • • • •   65 HAPPY SHEPHERD     12
        AN IDLE WORD IS NOW THEIR GLORY,  • • • • • • •   65 HAPPY SHEPHERD     14
        ONLY A SUDDEN FLAMING WORD,  • • • • • • • •   65 HAPPY SHEPHERD     19
        WORD BEMOCKERS?--BY THE ROOD,  • • • • • • •   65 HAPPY SHEPHERD   V  12
        NO WORD OF THEIRS--THE COLD STAR-BANE  • • • •   66 HAPPY SHEPHERD     32
        FAREWELL, VIJAYA.  NAY, NO WORD, NO WORD!  • • •   75 ANASHU VIJAYA      83
        FAREWELL, VIJAYA.  NAY, NO WORD, NO WORD!  • • •   75 ANASHU VIJAYA      83
        THAT WORD OF THE SOUL'S PEACE--"ETERNITY."  • • •   81 EPHEMERA        V 24B
        I KNOW THE WORD THEY CRY, "ETERNITY!"  • • • • •   81 EPHEMERA        V 24F
        MY WORD WAS LAW FROM ITH TO EMAIN,  • • • • • •   81 MAD KING GOLL      2
        UPON THE WEB-HEAPED FLOOR, AND CRIED HIS WORD:  • •   106 CUCHULAIN SEA     15
        UPON THE WEB-HEAPED FLOOR, AND THUS HIS WORD,  • •   106 CUCHULAIN SEA  V  15
        "I HAVE LONG WAITED, MOTHER, FOR THAT WORD:  • • •   107 CUCHULAIN SEA     22
        HE KNELT HIM AT THAT WORD.  • • • • • • • •   133 FR GILLIGAN       40
        THAT BALANCED WITH A WORD IS MORE THAN NOISE:  • •   258 KING NO KING       4
        A WORD AND A JEST.  • • • • • • • • • •   293 HELEN LIVED       12
        BELIEVING EVERY WORD I SAID,  • • • • • • •   314 MEMORY YOUTH       8
        WE KNEW, THOUGH SHE'D NOT SAID A WORD,  • • • •   314 MEMORY YOUTH      16
        AND KNEW, THOUGH SHE'D NOT SAID A WORD,  • • • •   314 MEMORY YOUTH   V  16
        THEY CHANGE THEIR BODIES AT A WORD.  AND THEN?  •   376 PHASES OF MOON   113
        THAT EVERY GIFT AND EVERY WORD OF PRAISE  • • • •   469 HARUN RASHID     172
        HAD FOUND A SWEETER WORD.  • • • • • • • •   539 MEETING           18
        I PRAY--FOR FASHION'S WORD IS OUT • • • • • •   553 PRAYER OLD AGE     9
        WHAT MATTER THAT YOU UNDERSTOOD NO WORD!  • • • •   557 RIBH ECSTASY       1
        AND ALL IT KNOWS IS THAT ONE WORD "REJOICE!"  • • •   564 GYRES             16
        HE WROTE OUT THAT WORD HIMSELF,  • • • • • •   585 ORAHILLY           7
        I SHOULD NOT GET THE WORD  • • • • • • • •   585 ORAHILLY          20
        FOR SUCH A CALL.  LET THE WILD WORD BE CRIED  • •   669 ISLE STAT II 3    76
        A FOOLISH WORD THOU GAVEST ME!  • • • • • • •   671 ISLE STAT II 3   131
        KNOWING THAT THOU HADST SINGLED ME WITH WORD  • •   684 SEEKER            57
        EVER MORE TO SPEAK A WORD • • • • • • • •   697 MOSADA 2          32
        HAS NO WORD OF THE SULPHUROUS END.  • • • • •   736 SUMMER EVENING     8
        IF YOU WOULD SERVE ME, AS YOUR WORD AND VOICE  • •   756 SHADOW WATER A V  183
        OR GIVE BUT A SIGH AND A WORD,  • • • • • • •   786 YOUR HEART        12
        A PASSING WORD.  • • • • • • • • • • •   786 YOUR HEART        13
        OR GIVE BUT A SIGH AND A WORD,  • • • • • • •   786 YOUR HEART        25
        A PASSING WORD.  • • • • • • • • • • •   786 YOUR HEART        26
```

		PAGE	TITLE	LINE
WORD (CONTINUED)				
OR GIVE BUT A SIGH AND A WORD,		786	YOUR HEART	38
A PASSING WORD.		786	YOUR HEART	39
WORDINESS				
YOU'RE FULL OF WORDINESS. COME, HEAR MY SONG.		696	MOSADA 2	8
WORDLESS				
WITH NO RETURNING GLANCE, IN WORDLESS MOOD		44	OISIN 2	V 230A
WORDS				
BUT THE TALE, THOUGH WORDS BE LIGHTER THAN AIR,		3	OISIN 1	11
OF STORIES BUILDED BY HIS WORDS		7	OISIN 1	68
AND DROPS OF HONEY ARE HIS WORDS,		7	OISIN 1	V 64
LIKE DROPS OF HONEY CAME THEIR WORDS,		26	OISIN 1	398
HUNG FROM THE MORNING STAR; WHEN THESE MILD WORDS		32	OISIN 2	49
I THOUGHT THE END HAD RESTED, WHEN THESE WORDS		32	OISIN 2	V 49
WITH BARREN WORDS AND FLATTERIES OF THE WEAK,		42	OISIN 2	197
WORDS ALONE ARE CERTAIN GOOD.		65	HAPPY SHEPHERD	10
THY FRETFUL WORDS A LITTLE WHILE,		66	HAPPY SHEPHERD	40
FOR WORDS ALONE ARE CERTAIN GOOD!		66	HAPPY SHEPHERD	43
AND WORDS ALONE ARE CERTAIN GOOD.		66	HAPPY SHEPHERD	V 43
TILL MY OWN WORDS, RE-ECHOING, SHALL SEND		68	SAD SHEPHERD	20
AND MY OWN WHISPERING WORDS BE COMFORTING,		68	SAD SHEPHERD	23
AND MINE OWN WORDS RE-ECHOING SHALL SEND		68	SAD SHEPHERD	V 20
AND MINE OWN WHISPERING WORDS BE COMFORTING,		68	SAD SHEPHERD	V 23
CHANGED ALL HIS WORDS TO INARTICULATE MOAN		69	SAD SHEPHERD	V 27
WHEN I GAVE JUDGMENT, AND HIS WORDS WERE WISE,		102	FERGUS DRUID	11
"LONG HAVE I WAITED, MOTHER, FOR THOSE WORDS,		107	CUCHULAIN SEA	V 22
"I HAVE LONG WAITED, MOTHER, FOR THOSE WORDS!		107	CUCHULAIN SEA	V 22
UNTIL I CARVED THESE WORDS!		123	DREAM OF DEATH	10
AND BLAME YOU WITH MANY BITTER WORDS.		146	FISH	8
WITH WORDS LIGHTER THAN AIR,		162	ASKS FORGIVE	2
NOW WORDS THAT CALLED UP THE LIGHTNING		171	MAID QUIET	7
FOR THE WORDS THAT CALLED UP THE LIGHTNING		171	MAID QUIET	V 7
AND YOU WOULD MURMUR TENDER WORDS,		175	BELOVED DEAD	5
AND WHEN I'D WRITE IT OUT ANEW, THE WORDS,		186	QUEEN MAEVE	139
A MURMUR OF SOFT WORDS AND MEETING LIPS.		187	QUEEN MAEVE	154
AND THAT DEAR WORDS MEANT NOTHING?" BUT ENOUGH,		201	OLD MEMORY	9
I LONG FOR YOUR MERRY AND TENDER AND PITIFUL WORDS,		203	WITHER BOUGHS	3
YES, VOICES! BUT I DO NOT CATCH THE WORDS.		233	SHADOW WATER B	251
UPON HIS SHOULDERS. YOU'VE NOTHING BUT WILD WORDS,		235	SHADOW WATER B	300
OR WAVE TO DROWN. BUT I HAVE DONE WITH WORDS.		238	SHADOW WATER B	348
THEY'RE CRYING OUT, COULD YOU BUT HEAR THEIR WORDS,		247	SHADOW WATER B	529
AND THERE'S NO HELP IN WORDS. TO THE OTHER SHIP,		250	SHADOW WATER B	585
WORDS		255	WORDS	T
AND WORDS OBEY MY CALL"!		256	WORDS	12
I MIGHT HAVE THROWN POOR WORDS AWAY		256	WORDS	15
AND AT THESE WORDS HE PALED, AS SHE HAD PALED,		280	TWO KINGS	76
THOUGH ALWAYS AT MY WORDS HIS TROUBLE GREW;		281	TWO KINGS	91
BUT ASKED THE MORE UNTIL HE SPOKE THESE WORDS;		281	TWO KINGS	V 92A
AND AT THOSE WORDS I ROSE AND I WENT OUT		282	TWO KINGS	125
THOUGH I HAVE MANY WORDS,		334	SONG	7
AND YET, BECAUSE MY HEART LEAPED AT HER WORDS,		353	PEOPLE	35
AND SO FORGET THE COMFORT THAT NO WORDS CAN TELL		391	UNDER SATURN	V 4
OR POLITE MEANINGLESS WORDS,		392	EASTER 1916	6
POLITE MEANINGLESS WORDS,		392	EASTER 1916	8
"O WORDS ARE LIGHTLY SPOKEN,"		396	ROSE TREE	1
"MAYBE A BREATH OF POLITIC WORDS		396	ROSE TREE	3
"SOME POLITICIANS IDLE WORDS		396	ROSE TREE	V 3
THE SECOND COMING! HARDLY ARE THOSE WORDS OUT		402	SECOND COMING	11
MEMORIES OF THE WORDS OF WOMEN,		415	TOWER	162
I HAVE LOVED YOU BETTER THAN MY SOUL FOR ALL MY WORDS,		442	BLACK CENTAUR	14
WORDS WERE BUT WASTED BREATH!		471	ALL SOUL NIGHT	27
SPOKE THESE, OR WORDS LIKE THESE.		496	MOHINI CHATTER	15
WORDS FOR MUSIC PERHAPS		507	JANE BISHOP	V T
O ANY OLD WORDS TO A TUNE.		548	TO SAME TUNE 3	16
SPEAKING TO A DRUNKEN AUDIENCE HIGH NONSENSICAL WORDS!		577	LOFTY THINGS	6
"KIND ARE ALL YOUR WORDS, MY DEAR,		588	OLD WICKED MAN	10
WORDS I HAVE THAT CAN PIERCE THE HEART,		588	OLD WICKED MAN	16
THOSE WORDS COME TRUE IN THE END		597	COLONEL MARTIN	V 69
"FORGETTING HUMAN WORDS," A GRAVE DEEP FACE.		603	GALLERY REVIS	49
HAVE I, THAT PUT IT INTO WORDS,		604	YOU CONTENT	5
DID WORDS OF MINE PUT TOO GREAT STRAIN		632	MAN AND ECHO	13
COULD MY SPOKEN WORDS HAVE CHECKED		632	MAN AND ECHO	15
THEY SANG, BUT HAD NOR HUMAN TUNES NOR WORDS,		635	CUCHULAIN COMF	23
KNOW THAT WHEN ALL WORDS ARE SAID		638	BEN BULBEN	27
BY HIS COMMAND THESE WORDS ARE CUT!		640	BEN BULBEN	91
MY WORDS WERE ALL! "HERE NO LOVES WANE AND WITHER,		669	ISLE STAT II 3	84
MY WORDS WERE ALL! "O WHITHER, WHITHER, WHITHER		669	ISLE STAT II 3	87
I CRIED THE WORDS YOU BID ME CRY.		673	ISLE STAT II 3	186
FOR, AH, OUR LIVES WERE BUT TWO STARRY WORDS		675	ISLE STAT II 3	236
AS WORDS OF THINE THROUGH FOURSCORE YEARS HAVE FILLED		683	SEEKER	46
THAT WAS BESIDE THE WATERFALL, THY WORDS		683	SEEKER	49
AND IMPORTUNE WITH WEIGHTY WORDS THIS MOOR,		698	MOSADA 2	45
ILL WORDS FOR ALL THINGS SOFT AND FAIR,		723	GIRLS SONG A	6
ALL THE WORDS THAT I GATHER,		739	WHERE BOOKS GO	1
AND ALL THE WORDS THAT I WRITE,		739	WHERE BOOKS GO	2
NOW FOUR TOGETHER! I SHALL HEAR THEIR WORDS		753	SHADOW WATER A	139
I AWAIT YOUR WORDS AS THE BLIND GRASS AWAITS		756	SHADOW WATER A	181
THE GODS HOLD WATCH ABOUT THE WORDS OF A QUEEN.		756	SHADOW WATER A	191
I WAIT YOUR WORDS AS THE DEAD WAIT THE LIVING.		756	SHADOW WATER A	V 182
WORDY				
THEY WERE OF NO WORDY MOOD;		65	HAPPY SHEPHERD	V 13A

913

WORDY   (CONTINUED)
    I' FAITH THOU EVER WAST A WORDY SPIRIT! • • • • • • •   673 ISLE STAT II 3   175
WORE
    AND WHEN THEY SAW THE CLOAK I WORE • • • • • • • • •   15 OISIN 1   207
    AND WHEN THEY SAW THAT THE BRATTA I WORE • • • • • • •   15 OISIN 1   V 207
    AND HE WORE SMALL HOLES IN HIS SHOES, • • • • • • • •   92 FATHER OHART   11
    AND HE WORE LARGE HOLES IN HIS GOWN. • • • • • • • • •   92 FATHER OHART   12
    WORE IT IN THE WORLD'S EYES • • • • • • • • • • • • •   320 COAT   6
    WORE IT IN THE WORLD'S EYE • • • • • • • • • • • • •   320 COAT   V   6
    FOR HE HIS SLIPPERS WORE. • • • • • • • • • • • • • •   595 COLONEL MARTIN   40
WORK   SEE MASTER-WORK WOOD-WORK FARM-WORK HANDY-WORK
    MY WORK WAS SALTIN' HERRINGS • • • • • • • • • • • •   94 MOLL MAGEE   7
    AND RIVER AND STREAM WORK OUT THEIR WILL! • • • • • •   148 INTO TWILIGHT   12
    AND LAUGH OUT THEIR WHIMSEY AND WORK OUT THEIR WILL. • •   148 INTO TWILIGHT V 12
    LAUGH OUT THEIR WHIMSEY AND WORK OUT THEIR WILL. • • •   148 INTO TWILIGHT V 12
    AND THE CHANGING MOON WORK OUT THEIR WILL. • • • • • •   148 INTO TWILIGHT V 12
    WHILE I MUST WORK BECAUSE I AM OLD, • • • • • • • • •   151 OLD MOTHER   9
    AND I MUST WORK BECAUSE I AM OLD. • • • • • • • • • •   151 OLD MOTHER V 10
    THAT WORK TOO DIFFICULT FOR MORTAL HANDS • • • • • • •   182 QUEEN MAEVE   67
    IS TO WORK HARDER THAN ALL THESE, AND YET • • • • • •   205 ADAMS CURSE   11
    ENOUGH IF THE WORK HAS SEEMED, • • • • • • • • • • • •   259 UNWORTH PRAISE   5
    HEARERS AND HEARTENERS OF THE WORK! • • • • • • • • •   266 GALWAY RACES   6
    HEARERS, HEARTENERS OF THE WORK, • • • • • • • • • • •   266 GALWAY RACES V 6
    SIGHED, "YOU, EVEN YOU YOURSELF, COULD WORK THE CURE!" • •   282 TWO KINGS   124
    A FRIEND THAT COULD, HE HAD TOLD HER, WORK HIS CURE • •   283 TWO KINGS   137
    THAT COULD, AS HE HAD TOLD HER, WORK HIS CURE, • • • •   283 TWO KINGS V 137
    TO A FRIEND WHOSE WORK HAS COME TO NOTHING • • • • • •   290 TO A FRIEND   T
    ALL WORK IN METAL OR IN WOOD, • • • • • • • • • • • •   327 ROBERT GREGORY 76
    BECAUSE THE WORK HAD FINISHED IN THAT FLARE. • • • • •   327 ROBERT GREGORY 85
    AND TILL THAT'S DONE CAN NEITHER WORK NOR WAIT. • • • •   340 SHEP GOATHERD   45
    SET CARPENTERS TO WORK ON NO WIDE TABLE, • • • • • • •   340 SHEP GOATHERD   50
    "WHAT HAVE I EARNED FOR ALL THAT WORK," I SAID, • • • •   351 PEOPLE   1
    AND SMITHY WORK FROM THE GORT FORGE, • • • • • • • • •   406 CARVED STONE   3
    CONCEIVES A CHANGELESS WORK OF ART. • • • • • • • • •   421 MY TABLE   14
    FROM SHALLOW WITS! WHO KNOWS NO WORK CAN STAND, • • • •   429 NINETEEN 19   35
    ON MASTER WORK OF INTELLECT OR HAND, • • • • • • • • •   429 NINETEEN 19 V 37
    AND SWEPT THE HOUSE AND SANG ABOUT HER WORK • • • • • •   468 HARUN RASHID   148
    PERFECTION OF THE LIFE, OR OF THE WORK, • • • • • • •   491 COOLE BALLYLEE V 40B
    PERFECTION OF THE LIFE, OR OF THE WORK. • • • • • • •   495 CHOICE   2
    TEST EVERY WORK OF INTELLECT OR FAITH, • • • • • • • •   501 VACILLATION   30
    WHEN, THE POTION'S WORK BEING DONE, • • • • • • • • •   522 LULLABY   9
    CONDUCT AND WORK GROW COARSE, AND COARSE THE SOUL, • •   564 GYRES   17
    "THE WORK IS DONE," GROWN OLD HE THOUGHT, • • • • • • •   577 WHAT THEN   16
    I WHO HAVE ALWAYS HATED WORK, • • • • • • • • • • • •   605 YOU CONTENT   19
    THE SPIRITUAL INTELLECT'S GREAT WORK, • • • • • • • •   632 MAN AND ECHO   20
    NOR CAN THERE BE WORK SO GREAT • • • • • • • • • • •   632 MAN AND ECHO   23
    NOR CAN THERE BE A WORK SO GREAT • • • • • • • • • • •   632 MAN AND ECHO V 23
    AND, ALL WORK DONE, DISMISSES ALL • • • • • • • • • •   633 MAN AND ECHO   34
    KNOW HIS WORK OR CHOOSE HIS MATE. • • • • • • • • • •   638 BEN BULBEN   36
    POET AND SCULPTOR, DO THE WORK, • • • • • • • • • • •   638 BEN BULBEN   37
    TO THEIR FARM WORK! HOW SILENT ALL WILL BE! • • • • •   699 MOSADA 3   8
    WORK AT THE CIDER PRESS. • • • • • • • • • • • • • •   774 COME RIDE   12
WORKED
    IT WORKED AT THEM, DAY OUT, DAY IN, • • • • • • • • •   158 BELOVED RHYMES 4
    YOU HAVE PUT THE THOUGHT IN RHYME. I WORKED ALL DAY, • •   341 SHEP GOATHERD   58
WORKING   SEE MIRACLE-WORKING
    SWEETER EMOTION, WORKING IN THEIR VEINS • • • • • • •   292 TO A SHADE   13
    BEFORE THE SECRET WORKING MIND! • • • • • • • • • • •   639 BEN BULBEN   51
WORKING-CARPENTER
    OF THAT WORKING-CARPENTER. • • • • • • • • • • • • • •   440 WISDOM   7
    OF A WORKING-CARPENTER. • • • • • • • • • • • • • • •   440 WISDOM   V   7
WORKMAN
    THE WORKMAN, NOBLE AND SAINT, AND ALL THINGS RUN • • • •   565 GYRES   23
WORKS
    AND TELL OF YOUR GOODLY HOUSEHOLD AND THE GOODLY WORKS   51 OISIN 3   62
       OF YOUR HANDS,
    AND EVEN THE NAMES OF HIS FATHERS, AND EVEN THE WORKS OF   51 OISIN 3 V 62
       HIS HANDS?
    AND THESE WERE THE WORKS OF JOHN, • • • • • • • • • •   93 FATHER OHART   25
    AND THAT IF OUR WORKS COULD • • • • • • • • • • • • •   431 NINETEEN 19   75
    MY WORKS ARE ALL STAMPED DOWN INTO THE SULTRY MUD. • • •   442 BLACK CENTAUR   3
    WHEN ALL WORKS THAT HAVE • • • • • • • • • • • • • •   449 HERO GIRL FOOL 18
    GREAT WORKS CONSTRUCTED THERE IN NATURE'S SPITE • • • •   488 COOLE PARK 29   5
    AND CALL THOSE WORKS EXTRAVAGANCE OF BREATH • • • • • •   501 VACILLATION   32
    GIVES FORTH. HE, THE ETERNAL, WORKS HIS WILL. • • • •   689 NETTLESHIP   16
WORLD   SEE SEA-WORLD
    THE RED SUN FALLS AND THE WORLD GROWS DIM." • • • • • •   9 OISIN 1   105
    WHEN THE STARS ARE TO WANE AND THE WORLD BE DONE. • • •   16 OISIN 1   220
    "O SADDEST HARP IN ALL THE WORLD, • • • • • • • • • •   17 OISIN 1   245
    "THE SADDEST HARP IN ALL THE WORLD!" • • • • • • • • •   17 OISIN 1 V 246
    IN NIAM'S HAIR--WHEN ROSE A WORLD OF TOWERS • • • • • •   30 OISIN 2 V 22
    MAKING A WORLD ABOUT HER IN THE AIR, • • • • • • • • •   37 OISIN 2   122
    MAKING A WORLD ABOUT HER, PASSED FROM SIGHT • • • • • •   37 OISIN 2 V 123
    TO RULE MORE MIGHTY MEN, AND TO THE WORLD . • • • • • •   38 OISIN 2 V 133
    ON THE ANVIL OF THE WORLD. BE STILL! THE SKIES • • • •   42 OISIN 2   204
    UPON THE ANVIL OF THE WORLD. THE SKIES • • • • • • • •   42 OISIN 2 V 204
    GOD SHAKES THE WORLD WITH RESTLESS HANDS. MORE NEAR • •   43 OISIN 2 V 208
    "WITH ALL IN ALL THE WORLD I BATTLE WAGE. • • • • • • •   45 OISIN 2 V 240
    THE STRONGEST OF THE WORLD, TO SNATCH MY PREY, • • • •   45 OISIN 2 V 241
    • • • THE GLEAMS OF THE WORLD AND THE SUN, • • • • • •   48 OISIN 3   22
    • • • AND THE WHOLE OF THE WORLD WAS ONE. • • • • • • •   48 OISIN 3   24

	PAGE	TITLE		LINE
WORLD (CONTINUED)

. . . NO, NOT SINCE THE WORLD BEGAN, ...	50	OISIN 3		49
OF WARS WITH THE WIDE WORLD	50	OISIN 3		55
"O FLAMING LION OF THE WORLD, O WHEN WILL YOU TURN TO YOUR REST?"	56	OISIN 3		129
O FLAMING LION OF THE WORLD, O WHEN WILL YOU TURN TO YOUR REST?"	56	OISIN 3		136
"OH, FLAMING LION OF THE WORLD, OH, WHEN WILT THOU TURN TO THY REST?"	56	OISIN 3	V	129
. . . WHO COULD BREAK UP THE WORLD IN THEIR RAGE! . . .	62	OISIN 3		214
OF OLD THE WORLD ON DREAMING FED!	64	HAPPY SHEPHERD		3
BUT O, SICK CHILDREN OF THE WORLD, ...	65	HAPPY SHEPHERD		6
THE VERY WORLD ITSELF MAY BE	65	HAPPY SHEPHERD	V	18
WHO HOLDS THE WORLD BETWEEN HIS BILL AND MADE US STRONG OR WEAK	76	INDIAN ON GOD		6
WHO MADE THE WORLD AND RULETH IT, HE HANGETH ON A STALK,	76	INDIAN ON GOD		10
WHO HOLDS THE WORLD BETWEEN HIS BILL AND MAKES US STRONG OR WEAK	76	INDIAN ON GOD	V	6
WHILE THE WORLD IS FULL OF TROUBLES	87	STOLEN CHILD		22
FROM A WORLD MORE FULL OF WEEPING THAN HE CAN UNDERSTAND.	89	STOLEN CHILD		53
AND THE WORLD ROUND KNOCKNASHEE	93	FATHER OHART		31
TO SEE THE WORLD ONCE MORE.	97	FOXHUNTER		4
THE SORROWS OF THE WORLD BOW DOWN MY HEAD, ...	104	FERGUS DRUID	V	38A
AND THE WHOLE WORLD WEIGHS DOWN UPON MY HEART-- . . .	104	FERGUS DRUID	V	38A
"STILL TREADS THE WORLD AMID HIS ARMED MEN."	107	CUCHULAIN SEA	V	26
THE ROSE OF THE WORLD	111	ROSE OF WORLD		T
WE AND THE LABOURING WORLD ARE PASSING BY!	112	ROSE OF WORLD		6
HE MADE THE WORLD TO BE A GRASSY ROAD	112	ROSE OF WORLD		14
ROSE OF ALL ROSES, ROSE OF ALL THE WORLD!	113	ROSE OF BATTLE		1
ROSE OF ALL ROSES, ROSE OF ALL THE WORLD!	115	ROSE OF BATTLE		25
GIVE TO THESE CHILDREN, NEW FROM THE WORLD, ...	116	FAERY SONG		5
GIVE TO THESE CHILDREN, NEW FROM THE WORLD, ...	116	FAERY SONG		9
AND SEEMED THE GREATNESS OF THE WORLD IN TEARS, ...	120	SORROW OF LOVE		6
THE WILLOW OF THE MANY-SORROWED WORLD.	130	BOOK STORIES	V	16
AND GOD COVERED THE WORLD WITH SHADE, ...	133	FR GILLIGAN		19
AND TIME AND THE WORLD ARE EVER IN FLIGHT!	148	INTO TWILIGHT		14
. . . AND HIS BELOVED, AND LONGS FOR THE END OF THE WORLD	153	CHANGE BELOVED		T
THAT HAS LONG FADED FROM THE WORLD!	155	FORGOT BEAUTY		3
THAT HAS LONG FADED IN THE WORLD!	155	FORGOT BEAUTY	V	3
TILL ALL THE VALLEYS OF THE WORLD HAVE BEEN WITHERED AWAY.	163	VALLEY LOVERS		8
TILL THE VALLEYS OF THE WORLD HAVE BEEN WITHERED AWAY."	163	VALLEY LOVERS	V	8
THE BLESSEDEST SOULS THAT WALK IN THE WORLD	167	BLESSED		19
I SEE THE BLESSEDEST SOUL IN THE WORLD	168	BLESSED		31
WHILE TIME AND THE WORLD ARE EBBING AWAY	168	BLESSED		39
AND HAVE SEEN THE BLESSEDEST SOUL IN THE WORLD, ...	168	BLESSED	V	31
UNTIL TIME AND THE WORLD HAVE EBBED AWAY	168	BLESSED	V	39
AND LOST THE WORLD AND EMER FOR A KISS!	170	SECRET ROSE		15
SHE COULD HAVE CALLED OVER THE RIM OF THE WORLD	181	QUEEN MAEVE		23
THE MARTYRS CALL THE WORLD." AND THEREUPON	205	ADAMS CURSE		14
THE MARTYRS CALL THE WORLD." THAT WOMAN THEN	205	ADAMS CURSE	V	14
O TATTERED CLOUDS OF THE WORLD, CALL FROM THE HIGH CAIRN OF MAIVE,	207	HANRAHANS SONG	V	6
LIKE TATTERED CLOUDS OF THE WORLD, PASSIONS CALL AND OUR HEARTS BEAT!	207	HANRAHANS SONG	V	8
O MY SHARE OF THE WORLD, O YELLOW HAIR!	211	RAGGED WOOD		11
DYING AT EVERY MOMENT IN THE WORLD, ...	226	SHADOW WATER B		90
KNOWING IT FOR THE WORLD'S END? WHERE THE WORLD ENDS . .	226	SHADOW WATER B		100
THE ROOTS OF THE WORLD. SHADOWS BEFORE NOW	227	SHADOW WATER B		104
WHERE I AM RID OF LIFE--THE EVENTS OF THE WORLD-- . . .	227	SHADOW WATER B		121
THE ROOTS OF THE WORLD. WHO KNOWS THAT SHADOWS	227	SHADOW WATER B	V	104
BREATHE ON THE BURNISHED MIRROR OF THE WORLD	228	SHADOW WATER B		132
THAT IS NOT IN THE WORLD. AND YET THE WORLD	228	SHADOW WATER B		143
THAT IS NOT IN THE WORLD. AND YET THE WORLD	228	SHADOW WATER B		143
AND GET INTO THEIR WORLD THAT TO THE SENSE	230	SHADOW WATER B		179
THAT LIFT US TO THE FLOWING, CHANGING WORLD	230	SHADOW WATER B		182
BUT DREAMS THAT HURRY FROM BEYOND THE WORLD	230	SHADOW WATER B		185
AND THAT IS WHY THE WORLD TOTTERS ABOUT	233	SHADOW WATER B		238
YOU ARE NOT ITS CORE. MY TEETH ARE IN THE WORLD . . .	235	SHADOW WATER B		279
THERE'S NOTHING IN THE WORLD THAT'S WORTH A FEAR. . . .	238	SHADOW WATER B		353
I WOULD THAT THERE WAS NOTHING IN THE WORLD	246	SHADOW WATER B		503
"THERE IS A COUNTRY AT THE END OF THE WORLD	247	SHADOW WATER B		530
BUT IN SOME ISLAND WHERE THE LIFE OF THE WORLD	249	SHADOW WATER B		559
LEAPS UPWARD, AS IF ALL THE STREAMS O' THE WORLD . . .	249	SHADOW WATER B		560
DRAGON THAT LOVED THE WORLD AND HELD US TO IT, ...	251	SHADOW WATER B		598
YOU ARE BROKEN, YOU ARE BROKEN. THE WORLD DRIFTS AWAY,	251	SHADOW WATER B		599
FOR WE WILL GAZE UPON THIS WORLD NO LONGER.	251	SHADOW WATER B		614
FOR HE WILL GAZE UPON THIS WORLD NO LONGER.	251	SHADOW WATER B	V	614
FOR WE WILL GAZE UPON THE WORLD NO LONGER.	251	SHADOW WATER B	V	614
WE'LL OUT, FOR THE WORLD LIVES AS LONG AGO!	257	RECONCILIATION		8
HOW SHOULD THE WORLD BE LUCKIER IF THIS HOUSE, ...	264	HOUSE SHAKEN		1
BREATHED ON THE WORLD WITH TIMID BREATH.	266	GALWAY RACES		9
WORLD, AS IT WERE A COAL, ...	267	FRIEND ILLNESS		5
MORE HANDS IN HEIGHT THAN ANY STAG IN THE WORLD	277	TWO KINGS		9
THE HANDS THAT GATHERED UP THE MIGHT OF THE WORLD, . . .	278	TWO KINGS		29
BUT IF NOT LIVING, HALF THE WORLD IS LOST."	280	TWO KINGS	V	86
SPEAK IT, THAT I MAY SEND THROUGH THE WIDE WORLD . . .	281	TWO KINGS		97
THAT OUR SUFFICIENT PORTION OF THE WORLD	282	TWO KINGS		119
THEY HAVE GONE ABOUT THE WORLD LIKE WIND, ...	289	SEPTEMBER 1913		11
. . . OF THE WESTERN WORLD", [NINETEEN-SEVEN]	294	HATED PLAYBOY		T
THE ATTACK ON "THE PLAYBOY OF THE WESTERN WORLD" . . .	294	HATED PLAYBOY	V	T
"TIME TO PUT OFF THE WORLD AND GO SOMEWHERE	299	BEGGAR CRIED		1

915

		PAGE	TITLE	LINE
WORLD (CONTINUED)				
THAT DYING CHOSE THE LIVING WORLD FOR TEXT		324	ROBERT GREGORY	26
THE ENTIRE COMBUSTIBLE WORLD IN ONE SMALL ROOM		327	ROBERT GREGORY	82
ALL THE COMBUSTIBLE WORLD IN ONE SMALL ROOM		327	ROBERT GREGORY V	82
AT THE OLD BITTER WORLD WHERE THEY MARRY IN CHURCHES, . .		330	BONE OF A HARE	13
THE WORLD A NARROW POUND."		333	SOLOMON SHEBA	24
WE HAVE GIVEN THE WORLD OUR PASSION, ...		363	DOLLS DRAWINGS	10
WE AND OUR DOLLS BEING BUT THE WORLD WERE BEST AWAY. . .		364	DOLLS FACES	12
FOR THOSE THAT LOVE THE WORLD SERVE IT IN ACTION, . . .		369	EGO DOMINUS	42
WHAT PORTION IN THE WORLD CAN THE ARTIST HAVE		369	EGO DOMINUS	49
NO ONE DENIES TO KEATS LOVE OF THE WORLD:		370	EGO DOMINUS	52
SHUT OUT FROM ALL THE LUXURY OF THE WORLD, ...		370	EGO DOMINUS	60
TOO LONELY FOR THE TRAFFIC OF THE WORLD:		374	PHASES OF MOON	61
BEYOND THE VISIBLE WORLD. ALL DREAMS OF THE SOUL . . .		374	PHASES OF MOON	63
IT SOUGHT ITSELF AND AFTERWARDS THE WORLD.		376	PHASES OF MOON	95
AND THIS FOUL WORLD WERE DEAD AT LAST.		388	SOLOMON WITCH	16
YET THE WORLD ENDS WHEN THESE TWO THINGS, ...		388	SOLOMON WITCH	28
"YET THE WORLD STAYS." "IF THAT BE SO, ...		388	SOLOMON WITCH	33
MERE ANARCHY IS LOOSED UPON THE WORLD, ...		402	SECOND COMING	4
THOUGHTS UPON THE PRESENT STATE OF THE WORLD		428	NINETEEN 19 V	T
AND PLANNED TO BRING THE WORLD UNDER A RULE, ...		429	NINETEEN 19	31
BEING BY THE WORLD OPPRESSED, ...		434	YOUTH AND AGE	2
THE MIGHTIEST OF THE PRINCES OF THE WORLD		462	HARUN RASHID	41
FROM EVERY QUARTER OF THE WORLD, CAN STAY		471	ALL SOUL NIGHT	12
THAT THIS PRAGMATICAL, PREPOSTEROUS PIG OF A WORLD, . . .		481	BLOOD AND MOON	26
BUT WE OLD MEN ARE MASSED AGAINST THE WORLD.		486	SEVEN SAGES	14
BUT WE OLD MEN ARE OUT AGAINST THE WORLD.		486	SEVEN SAGES V	14
WORLD BESOTTED TRAVELLER: HE		493	SWIFTS EPITAPH V	5
BEFORE THE WORLD WAS MADE."		516	MANS SONG	12
'GAT THE FOAL OF THE WORLD."		529	TOM CRUACHAN	6
BEFORE THE WORLD WAS MADE		531	BEFORE WORLD	T
BEFORE THE WORLD WAS MADE.		532	BEFORE WORLD	8
BEFORE THE WORLD WAS MADE.		532	BEFORE WORLD	16
THEY GAVE IT OUT TO ALL THE WORLD, ...		582	ROGER CASEMENT	11
ALL KNOW THAT ALL THE DEAD IN THE WORLD ABOUT THAT PLACE		593	PILGRIM	11
ARE STUCK,				
ON THIS FOUL WORLD IN ITS DECLINE AND FALL:		619	BRONZE HEAD	24
SAINT JOSEPH THOUGHT THE WORLD WOULD MELT		619	STICK INCENSE	3
SOME ROGUE OF THE WORLD STOLE THEM TO PATCH UP A FENCE		623	HIGH TALK	4
OR A FIRE.				
SOME KNEW WHAT AILED THE WORLD		627	STATES HOLIDAY	9
WHILE THE WORLD IS ROLL'D IN LIGHT.		646	ISLE STAT I 1	29
ALL THE WORLD IS RINGING, RINGING:		648	ISLE STAT I 1	93
ALL THE WORLD IS SINGING, SINGING.		648	ISLE STAT I 1	94
WILL CIRCLE ROUND THE WORLD UPON A QUEST, ...		651	ISLE STAT I 1	159
O'ER GRIEF. THE WORLD DRINKS SORROW FROM THE BEAMS . .		664	ISLE STAT II 2	46
AND THAT WAS STRANGE: BUT THIS IS MANY A WORLD . . .		664	ISLE STAT II 2	60
IN THE FAR WORLD WILL VANISH FROM THY MIND, ...		670	ISLE STAT II 3	93
THE WORLD, WITHIN HIS FOLDED HEART, ...		671	ISLE STAT II 3	133
THE WAVES, ENORMOUS WANDERERS OF THE WORLD, ...		687	TWO TITANS	3
YET SOMEWHERE IN THE FOOTSORE WORLD WE MEET, ...		691	MOSADA 1	23
FAR OUT UPON THE WATER WORLD AND RINGED		693	MOSADA 1	80
AND—MERCY IS THE MANNA OF THE WORLD.		697	MOSADA 2	41
THE WORLD TO ITS FIERCE INFANCY AGAIN.		698	MOSADA 2	61
THE WORLD WERE DREAMING IN ITS SUMMER SLEEP:		699	MOSADA 3	11
FOR IT ALONE OF ALL THE WORLD WILL DO		700	MOSADA 3	28
WITH THREE BARS CROSSED, AND THESE FOUR WALLS MY WORLD,		700	MOSADA 3	32
THE NOISY WORLD DIVIDES. HOW SOON A DEED		700	MOSADA 3	34
AND POUR UPON THE WORLD: AH: WELL-A-DAY!		703	MOSADA 3	118
AND POUR UPON THE WORLD: AH! WELL A DAY!		703	MOSADA 3 V	118
STILL WANDER THROUGH THE WORLD. HE'S GONE, HE'S GONE. . .		703	MOSADA 3	121
SO ENDS A BRAIN—A WORLD! THE SMOKE GOES UP, ...		714	FERENCZ RENYI	111
OF FIRE. SO ENDS A BRAIN—A WORLD! THE SMOKE FLOATS UP,		714	FERENCZ RENYI V	111
THE WORLD GROWS OLD AND PLAYS THE FOOL."		725	LEGEND	12
"WITH ACTION ALL THE WORLD IS VEXED,"		728	PRIEST FAIRY	15
HIS HEART'S DESIRE WHERE THE WORLD DWINDLES OUT?		747	SHADOW WATER A	13
TIME AND THE WORLD AND ALL THINGS DWINDLE OUT.		749	SHADOW WATER A	47
BREATHE ON THE BURNISHED MIRROR OF THE WORLD		750	SHADOW WATER A	69
HOW ALL THAT DIE ARE BORNE ABOUT THE WORLD		750	SHADOW WATER A	84
OF THE TWELVE KINGS OF THE WORLD TO BE MY KING, . . .		757	SHADOW WATER A	214
THEY LURE US TO THE STREAMS WHERE THE WORLD ENDS. . . .		764	SHADOW WATER A	334
TO LEAD US TO THE STREAMS WHERE THE WORLD ENDS.		765	SHADOW WATER A	369
ALL THAT KNOW LOVE AMONG THE WINDS OF THE WORLD . . .		767	SHADOW WATER A	386
THAT HAVE KNOWN LOVE AMONG THE WINDS OF THE WORLD . . .		767	SHADOW WATER A	392
WHERE THE WORLD ENDS, OR RUNS FROM WIND TO WIND . . .		768	SHADOW WATER A	417
FOR WE WILL GAZE UPON THIS WORLD NO LONGER.		769	SHADOW WATER A	430
UPON THIS WORLD NO LONGER. THE HARP CRIES OUT. . . .		769	SHADOW WATER A V	430
I'D LET THE WHOLE WORLD GO:		782	HEART FRIGHT	9
ALTHOUGH WIDE WORLD HOLD NOT		786	YOUR HEART	16
WORLD-BESOTTED				
WORLD-BESOTTED TRAVELLER: HE		493	SWIFTS EPITAPH	5
WORLD-FAMOUS				
WORLD-FAMOUS GOLDEN-THIGHED PYTHAGORAS		445	SCHOOL CHILDR	45
WORLD-FAMOUS GOLDEN THIGHED PYTHAGORAS		445	SCHOOL CHILDR V	45
WORLD-FORGOTTEN				
UPON A WOVEN WORLD-FORGOTTEN ISLE		126	DREAM OF FAERY	8
WORLD-OLD				
TO EASE THEIR WORLD-OLD THIRST ALONG THE BRINK		663	ISLE STAT II 2	41
WORLD'S				
AND RODE ON TILL OVER THE WORLD'S RIM FLOATED THE SEA'S		60	OISIN 3 V	183
OLD SHOUT,				

	PAGE	TITLE	LINE

WORLD'S   (CONTINUED)
FOR THE WORLD'S MORE FULL OF WEEPING THAN YOU CAN   87 STOLEN CHILD   12
    UNDERSTAND.
FOR THE WORLD'S MORE FULL OF WEEPING THAN YOU CAN   87 STOLEN CHILD   27
    UNDERSTAND.
FOR THE WORLD'S MORE FULL OF WEEPING THAN YOU CAN   88 STOLEN CHILD   41
    UNDERSTAND.
FOR THE WORLD'S MORE FULL OF WEEPING THAN HE CAN UNDERSTAND   89 STOLEN CHILD   V   53
AND WITH YOU CAME THE WHOLE OF THE WORLD'S TEARS,   . . .   120 SORROW OF LOVE V   6
FOR IN THE WORLD'S FIRST BLOSSOMING AGE . . . . . .   138 TO IRELAND   V   10
BEING WEARY OF THE WORLD'S EMPIRES, BOW DOWN TO YOU, . .   161 BLACK PIG   7
"O WHAT OF THE WORLD'S BANE?" . . . .   214 HAPPY TOWNLAND   14
THAT IS THE WORLD'S BANE." . . . .   214 HAPPY TOWNLAND   20
O WHAT IS THE WORLD'S BANE?, ...   214 HAPPY TOWNLAND V   REF
"O WHAT OF THE WORLD'S BANE?" . . . .   215 HAPPY TOWNLAND   34
THAT IS THE WORLD'S BANE." . . . .   215 HAPPY TOWNLAND   40
"O WHAT OF THE WORLD'S BANE?" . . . .   216 HAPPY TOWNLAND   54
THAT IS THE WORLD'S BANE." . . . .   216 HAPPY TOWNLAND   60
KNOWING IT FOR THE WORLD'S END? WHERE THE WORLD ENDS . .   226 SHADOW WATER B   100
WHAT THE WORLD'S MILLION LIPS ARE THIRSTING FOR . . .   229 SHADOW WATER B   161
HAD THE WORLD'S TOTAL LIFE GATHERED UP, IT SEEMED, . . .   231 SHADOW WATER B   194
SHALL LIGHT UPON A PLACE IN THE WORLD'S CORE, ...   231 SHADOW WATER B   212
YOU ARE NOT THE WORLD'S CORE. O NO, NO, NO! . . . .   234 SHADOW WATER B   277
TO TROOP WITH THOSE THE WORLD'S FORGOT, ...   273 GREY ROCK   63
AND THE WORLD'S ALTERED SINCE YOU DIED, ...   276 GREY ROCK   126
"IF HE BE LIVING STILL THE WHOLE WORLD'S MINE, . . .   280 TWO KINGS   V   85
AND DREAM THAT ALL THE WORLD'S A FRIEND, ...   313 TWO YEAR LATER   8
WORE IT IN THE WORLD'S EYES . . . .   320 COAT   6
WORE IT IN THE WORLD'S EYE . . . .   320 COAT   V   6
TO HAVE PUBLISHED ALL TO BE A WORLD'S DELIGHT. . . .   327 ROBERT GREGORY   72
THEY'LL COUGH IN THE INK TO THE WORLD'S END; . . . .   337 SCHOLARS   V   7
IT WOULD BE THE WORLD'S SERVANT, AND AS IT SERVES, . .   376 PHASES OF MOON   90
AND HIDE IT THERE, FOR CALIPHS TO WORLD'S END . . . .   461 HARUN RASHID   17
UNTIL THAT GLANCE RUN IN THE WORLD'S DESPITE . . . .   474 ALL SOUL NIGHT   94
WHAT WERE ALL THE WORLD'S ALARMS . . . .   522 LULLABY   3
WHAT ARE ALL THE WORLD'S ALARMS? . . . .   522 LULLABY   V   3
THE WHOLE WORLD'S SADLY TALKING TO ITSELF. . . . .   652 ISLE STAT I 2   12
THE LION, THE WORLD'S GREAT SOLITARY, BENDS . . . .   689 NETTLESHIP   5
AND THEN THE WHOLE WORLD'S TROUBLE WEEPS WITH YOU. . .   738 YOU ARE SAD   12
WORLDS
THE MAKER OF THE STARS AND WORLDS . . . .   724 LEGEND   1
"THE PROPS," SAID HE, "OF STARS AND WORLDS . . . . .   725 LEGEND   5
THE MAKER OF THE STARS AND WORLDS . . . .   725 LEGEND   29
WORLD-TRANSFORMING
WHEN WORLD-TRANSFORMING CHARLEMAGNE WAS CONCEIVED? . . .   560 WHENCE COME   12
WORLD-TROUBLING
THE HEARTS OF THE WORLD-TROUBLING SEAMEN, ...   82 MAD KING GOLL   4
WORLDWIDE
AH, WORLDWIDE NATION, ALWAYS GROWING SORROW! . . . .   130 BOOK STORIES   V   11
WORLD-WIDE
AH, WORLD-WIDE NATION, ALWAYS GROWING SORROW, ...   130 BOOK STORIES   V   11
WORM   SEE LUG-WORM GLOW-WORM CANKER-WORM
THE WEAK WORM HIDING DOWN IN ITS SMALL CAVE, ...   101 ROSE UPON ROOD   16
IT WHIRLS INTO THE FOAM. O ANCIENT WORM, ...   251 SHADOW WATER B   597
BEFORE THE FULL MOON, HELPLESS AS A WORM. . . . . .   374 PHASES OF MOON   49
OR THE HUMBLER WORM, I CLIMBED BEN BULBEN'S BACK . . .   409 TOWER   9
WEAK AS A WORM. . . . .   574 MAIDS 1ST SONG   10
DULL AS A WORM, ...   575 MAIDS 2ND SONG   2
LIMP AS A WORM. . . . .   575 MAIDS 2ND SONG   4
BLIND AS A WORM. . . . .   575 MAIDS 2ND SONG   6
ARISE, WORM, AND FOLLOW! . . . .   655 ISLE STAT I 2   83
FROM THE UNDYING WORM. SHE SLEEPS--MOSADA-- . . . .   701 MOSADA 3   65
HIDING THE REBELS WORM IN YONDER WOOD . . . . . .   709 FERENCZ RENYI   14
WHERE WORM THE REBELS, OR MY BULLETS LAY . . . . .   713 FERENCZ RENYI   83
AH! IT DWELT WITHIN THE TWILIGHT AS THE WORM WITHIN THE   718 PHANTOM SHIP   6
    NUT.
AND LETS THE KIND WORM TAKE THE LOT! . . . .   779 ACCURSED WHO   4
WORMS
WHO MADE THE GRASS AND MADE THE WORMS AND MADE MY FEATHERS   77 INDIAN ON GOD   18
    GAY,
DID NOT THE WORMS THAT SPIRED ABOUT HIS BONES . . . .   128 DREAM OF FAERY   41
WERE NOT THE WORMS THAT SPIRED ABOUT HIS BONES . . .   128 DREAM OF FAERY   41
HIDING THE REBEL WORMS IN YONDER WOOD, ...   709 FERENCZ RENYI V   14
WORN   SEE WEATHER-WORN WAVE-WORN SEA-WORN OUT-WORN LOVE-WORN FOOT-WORN SORROW-WORN
YE WORN DEED-DOERS, AND MY NAME . . . .   5 OISIN 1   V   48
O WORN DEED-DOER." "WHAT MAY BRING . . . . . .   5 OISIN 1   V   50
THAT LACKEY THE WORN MOON IN MIDNIGHT HOURS, ...   41 OISIN 2   V 185A
THEIR FACES ARE ALL WORN, AND IN THEIR EYES . . . .   73 ANASHU VIJAYA   48
AND WEARY AND WORN ARE OUR SAD SOULS NOW: . . . .   79 FALLING LEAVES   6
"PASSION HAS OFTEN WORN OUR WANDERING HEARTS." . . .   80 EPHEMERA   12
"OFTEN HAS PASSION WORN OUR WANDERING HEARTS, . . .   80 EPHEMERA   V   12
AND GAZING ON HIS VISAGE WORN, ...   99 FOXHUNTER   V   43
MY FATHER STANDS." "AGED, WORN OUT WITH WARS . . . .   107 CUCHULAIN SEA   29
ALL THINGS UNCOMELY AND BROKEN, ALL THINGS WORN OUT AND   142 ROSE IN HEART   1
    OLD,
ALL THINGS UNCOMELY AND BROKEN, ALL THINGS WORN AND OLD,   142 ROSE IN HEART V   1
WHITE WOMAN THAT PASSION HAS WORN . . . .   157 POET BELOVED   3
BECAUSE A LOVER'S HEART'S WORN OUT, ...   191 BAILE AILLINN   65
A MOON, WORN AS IF IT HAD BEEN A SHELL . . . . .   206 ADAMS CURSE   31
A MOON--MOON WORN AS IF IT HAD BEEN A SHELL . . .   206 ADAMS CURSE   V   31
WEAK AND WORN AND WEARY THE WAVES OF CUMMEN STRAND, . .   207 HANRAHANS SONG V   6

PAGE   TITLE   LINE

WORN (CONTINUED)
    WEAK AND WORN AND WEARY OUR COURAGE DROOPS AND DIES . . .   207 HANRAHANS SONG V   8
    SHE MAY HAVE WORN SILK CLOTHES, OR WORN A CROWN, ...   282 TWO KINGS   117
    SHE MAY HAVE WORN SILK CLOTHES, OR WORN A CROWN,   282 TWO KINGS   117
    MY BROTHER MOURTEEN IS WORN OUT . . . .   301 RUN PARADISE   8
    I AM WORN OUT WITH DREAMS; . . . .   329 MEN IMPROVE   1
    WORN THIN BY THE LAPPING OF WATER, ...   330 BONE OF A HARE   11
    THEIR CONNEMARA CLOTH WORN OUT OF SHAPE; . . . . . .   372 PHASES OF MOON   4
    BUT LIVED WHERE MOTLEY IS WORN; . . . .   392 EASTER 1916   14
    WHEREVER GREEN IS WORN, ...   394 EASTER 1916   78
    SHOULD FIND NO BURDEN BUT ITSELF AND YET SHOULD BE WORN   449 OWEN AHERNE   3
        OUT.
    IS WORN AS THOUGH WITH FIRE. OH, GOBLIN QUEEN, ...   667 ISLE STAT II 3   36
    THE BANKS ARE WORN FOR EVER . . . .   680 LOVE AND DEATH   9
    WORN WITH LONG STRUGGLES; AND THE WAVES HAVE SUNG . . .   687 TWO TITANS   23
    WORN BY THE SOLSTICE FIERCE, AND MADE IT PURE. . . . .   692 MOSADA 1   57
    THE HEART WELL WORN UPON THE SLEEVE MAY BE THE BEST OF   790 HEART SLEEVE   1
        SIGHTS,
WORSE
    AYE, AND WORSE WRONG THAN THESE. . . . .   260 UNWORTH PRAISE   18
    ONE TIME IT WAS A WOMAN'S FACE, OR WORSE-- . . . . .   267 ALL TEMPT ME   2
    AND EVIL MUST IT BE, IF DONE 'TWERE WORSE . . . . .   281 TWO KINGS   105
    "AND THE WORSE DEVIL THAT IS BETWEEN MY THIGHS." . . .   300 BEGGAR CRIED   8
    OR WHAT WORSE EVIL COME-- . . . .   416 TOWER   188
    KNOW WORSE EVIL OF THE BODY; . . . .   573 LADYS 3RD SONG   6
    I HAVE FOUND SOMETHING WORSE . . . .   628 JANE MOUNTAIN   5
    MOSADA, IT IS THEN SO MUCH THE WORSE; . . . . . .   692 MOSADA 1   V 41A
WORSHIP
    THEN NOWISE WORSHIP DUSTY DEEDS, ...   65 HAPPY SHEPHERD   22
    THEN NO WISE WORSHIP DUSTY DEEDS, ...   65 HAPPY SHEPHERD V   22
    BOTH NUNS AND MOTHERS WORSHIP IMAGES, ...   445 SCHOOL CHILDR   49
WORST
    FOR HE IS THE WORST OF ALL DEAD MEN." . . . .   272 GREY ROCK   36
    THOUGH COURTEOUS TO THE WORST; MUCH FALLING HE . . . .   324 ROBERT GREGORY   19
    THE BEST LACK ALL CONVICTION, WHILE THE WORST . . . .   402 SECOND COMING   7
    THE BEST LACK CONVICTION, WHILE THE WORST . . . . .   402 SECOND COMING V   7
    AN INTELLECTUAL HATRED IS THE WORST, ...   405 FOR DAUGHTER   57
    THAT THE WORST ROGUES AND RASCALS HAD DIED OUT. . . . .   428 NINETEEN 19   16
    ALL OF THAT WORST IGNOMINY . . . .   436 FOR MY SON   23
    THAT HAS THE WORST OF ALL BAD NAMES; . . . .   531 FATHER CHILD   5
    THE WORST A COAT UPON A COAT-HANGER. . . . .   624 APPARITIONS   8
    THE WORST A COAT UPON A COAT-HANGER. . . . .   624 APPARITIONS   16
    THE WORST A COAT UPON A COAT-HANGER. . . . .   624 APPARITIONS   24
    IS THE WORST MAN HAS TO FEAR. . . . .   637 BEN BULBEN   20
WORTH
    WORTH KNITTING TO A MEASURE OF SWEET SOUND? . . . . .   181 QUEEN MAEVE   33
    WILL HARDLY SEEM WORTH THINKING OF . . . . . .   202 NEVER GIVE ALL   2
    THEY TAKE A KISS FOR WHAT A KISS IS WORTH, ...   229 SHADOW WATER B   157
    THERE'S NOTHING IN THE WORLD THAT'S WORTH A FEAR. . . .   238 SHADOW WATER B   353
    OR HOW SHOULD LOVE BE WORTH ITS PAINS WERE IT NOT . . .   285 TWO KINGS   190
    AS IF IT WERE NOT WORTH THE DOING. . . . . . .   306 HOUR DAWN   84
    I WOULD BE--FOR NO KNOWLEDGE IS WORTH A STRAW-- . . . .   344 DAWN   13
    OPINION IS NOT WORTH A RUSH; . . . .   385 ROBARTES DANCE   1
    ALTHOUGH HE THOUGHT IT WORTH A CROW. . . . .   388 SOLOMON WITCH   35
    WONDER HOW MANY TIMES I COULD HAVE PROVED MY WORTH . . .   427 PHANTOM HATRED   34
    FOR ALL MEN LOVE YOUR WORTH; AND I MUST RAGE . . . .   447 HERO GIRL FOOL V   8
    IF YOU HAVE SEEN THAT IMAGE AND NOT MY WORTH. . . . .   448 HERO GIRL FOOL V   8
    ALL MEN HAVE PRAISED MY STRENGTH BUT NOT MY WORTH. . . .   448 HERO GIRL FOOL V   9
    AND NOT THEIR WORTH. GOD LOVES US FOR OUR WORTH; . . .   448 HERO GIRL FOOL V   15
    AND NOT THEIR WORTH. GOD LOVES US FOR OUR WORTH; . . .   448 HERO GIRL FOOL V   15
    NOT WORTH THINKING OF, ...   504 QUARREL IN AGE   5
    FOR BEAUTY DIES OF BEAUTY, WORTH OF WORTH, ...   564 GYRES   3
    FOR BEAUTY DIES OF BEAUTY, WORTH OF WORTH, ...   564 GYRES   3
    IF YOU ARE WORTH MY HOPE! NEITHER CONTENT . . . . .   579 DOR WELLESLEY   13
    A LITTLE MOORISH GIRL? SMALL WORTH. MY SONG-- . . . .   696 MOSADA 2   10
    BUT IS EDAIN WORTH A SONG . . . .   773 SONG DEIRDRE 1   17
WORTHY
    SCARCE WORTHY OF A HOOF GOLD-SHOD. . . . .   2 OISIN 1   V 7Y
    YOUR QUESTIONER, OISIN, IS WORTHY, HE COMES FROM THE FENIAN   51 OISIN 3   64
        LANDS."
    IF WORTHY THEIR PROMINENT PART IN THE PLAY, ...   565 LAPIS LAZULI   14
    A FINISH WORTHY OF THE START. . . . .   626 OLD MEN BE MAD   15
    SO WORTHY AMONG MEN. I FOLLOW YOU, ...   768 SHADOW WATER A V   412
WORTHY'S
    WORTHY'S THY QUESTIONER, OISIN, HE FROM THE FENIAN LANDS."   51 OISIN 3   V 64
WOUND
    MY HUMAN SORROW HER WHITE ARMS WOUND. . . . . . .   11 OISIN 1   138
    MY HUMAN SADNESS FAY ARMS WOUND. . . . .   11 OISIN 1   V 138
    THE DANCE WOUND THROUGH THE WINDLESS WOODS; . . . . .   21 OISIN 1   320
    BUT KNOW YOUR HAIR WAS BOUND AND WOUND . . . . . .   176 BELOVED DEAD   9
    NOR ON THE ANCIENT BEATEN PATHS, THAT WOUND . . . . .   279 TWO KINGS   52
    AND OTHER COMFORT WERE A BITTER WOUND; . . . . . .   429 NINETEEN 19   V 41
    HAS WOUND UPON A SPOOL . . . .   449 HERO GIRL FOOL   22
    WOUND IN MIND'S PONDERING . . . .   471 ALL SOUL NIGHT   13
    AS MUMMIES IN THE MUMMY-CLOTH ARE WOUND; . . . . .   471 ALL SOUL NIGHT   14
    AS MUMMIES IN THE MUMMY CLOTH ARE WOUND; . . . . .   471 ALL SOUL NIGHT V   14
    WOUND IN MIND'S WANDERING . . . .   474 ALL SOUL NIGHT   99
    AS MUMMIES IN THE MUMMY-CLOTH ARE WOUND. . . . . .   474 ALL SOUL NIGHT   100
    AS MUMMIES IN THE MUMMY CLOTH ARE WOUND. . . . . .   474 ALL SOUL NIGHT V   100
    THE WOODEN SCABBARD BOUND AND WOUND, ...   477 SELF AND SOUL   15
    BUT WHEN HE WOUND HER COAL-BLACK HAIR . . . . . .   514 JANE GROWN OLD   3

918

WOUND   (CONTINUED)
    SANG OF THE BEAST THAT GAVE THE FATAL WOUND. . . . . .   537 HER VISION   16
    SHE STOOD IN DESPERATE MUSIC WOUND, ...   578 CRAZED GIRL   10
    WOUND, WOUND, AND SHE MADE IN HER TRIUMPH . . . . . .   578 CRAZED GIRL   11
    WOUND, WOUND, AND SHE MADE IN HER TRIUMPH . . . . . .   578 CRAZED GIRL   11
WOUNDED
    THE KNOTTED SCOURGE, THE NAIL-PIERCED HANDS, THE WOUNDED   172 TRAV PASSION   V   4
      SIDE.
    TILL MAURYA OF THE WOUNDED HEART CRY A SWEET CRY, . . .   173 SPEAKS HEARERS V   6
    SHOULDERED A LITTER WITH A WOUNDED MAN, ...   537 HER VISION   14
    CEASE! THERNOT'S WOUNDED, CEASE!   THEY WILL NOT HEED. . .   665 ISLE STAT II 2   64
WOUND'S
    THAT THE IMMEDICABLE WOUND'S BEYOND . . . .   282 TWO KINGS   V 129
WOUNDS
    AND HEALED MY WOUNDS WITH UNGUENTS OUT OF FLOWERS . . .   41 OISIN 2   185
    THEY HEALED MY WOUNDS; AND ON THE SKIN SUPINE . . . . .   41 OISIN 3   V 187
    . . . AND OF OLD WOUNDS, AND TURN TO OUR REST. . . . .   62 OISIN 3   212
    . . . AND OF OLD WOUNDS AND REST. . . . .   62 OISIN 3   V 212
    THE PAIN OF WOUNDS, THE LABOUR OF THE SPEAR, ...   104 FERGUS DRUID   V 38D
    CROWDED WITH BITTER FACES, THE WOUNDS IN PALM AND SIDE,   172 TRAV PASSION   4
    TO HIM THAT WOUNDS HIM TO THE DEATH. I'LL DO IT. . . .   240 SHADOW WATER B   375
    SEEING, KING'S SON, WHAT WOUNDS YOU HAVE." . . . . .   275 GREY ROCK   94
    FROM DEATH, AND WOUNDS, OR ON SINAI'S TOP, ...   375 PHASES OF MOON   67
    THEIR WOUNDS OPEN AGAIN. . . . .   612 NEWS ORACLE   16
    THEN CLEANING OUT AND BANDAGING OF WOUNDS, ...   622 HOUND VOICE   20
    A MAN THAT HAD SIX MORTAL WOUNDS, A MAN . . . .   634 CUCHULAIN COMF   1
    AS THOUGH TO MEDITATE ON WOUNDS AND BLOOD. . . . . . .   634 CUCHULAIN COMF   6
    THE HAND THAT WOUNDS HIM, BECAUSE THE GODS ARE HIS FRIENDS.   758 SHADOW WATER A   232
    THE HAND THAT WOUNDS. A WHITE BIRD BEATS HIS WINGS . .   758 SHADOW WATER A V 232
    UNTIL HE HAD DIED OF HIS WOUNDS, ...   775 AGAINST WITCH   16
    WHAT WOUNDS, WHAT BLOODY PRESS, ...   785 WOMANS BEAUTY   26
WOVE
    WOVE IN HER FLOWER-LIKE HAIR, BEFORE DARK TOWERS . . . .   30 OISIN 2   V   22
    THE LOVE-TALES WOVE WITH SILKEN THREAD . . . .   155 FORGOT BEAUTY V   6
    WHEN SONGS I WOVE FOR MY BELOVED HIDE THE PRAYER, . . .   173 SPEAKS HEARERS   2
    BEND DOWN AND PRAY FOR ALL THAT SIN I WOVE IN SONG, . .   173 SPEAKS HEARERS   5
    WHEN SONG I WOVE FOR MY BELOVED HIDES THE PRAYER, . . .   173 SPEAKS HEARERS V   2
    BEND DOWN AND PRAY FOR THE GREAT SIN I WOVE IN SONG, . .   173 SPEAKS HEARERS V   5
    THAT EDAIN, MIDHIR'S WIFE, HAD WOVE . . . .   195 BAILE AILLINN   142
    AWAKE UNSLEEPING FIRES! AND WOVE SEVEN STRINGS, ...   219 HARP OF AENGUS   7
    AND IN HER SINGING WOVE AROUND HER HEAD . . . .   693 MOSADA 1   84
    AWAKE UNSLEEPING FIRES! AND WOVE SEVEN STRINGS, ...   762 SHADOW WATER A   302
    AND ONE WHERE THE WINDS ARE WOVE, ...   771 SPINNING SONG   3
WOVEN   SEE THOUGHT-WOVEN
    AND WITH THE WOVEN CRIMSON GLOWED . . . .   3 OISIN 1   V   26
    EACH ONE WOVEN TO THE OTHER, ...   22 OISIN 1   334
    EACH ONE WOVEN TO HIS BROTHER . . . .   22 OISIN 1   335
    WOVEN INTO HER HAIR, BEFORE DARK TOWERS . . . .   30 OISIN 2   22
    WHILE WE ALONE HAVE ROUND US WOVEN WOODS, ...   73 ANASHU VIJAYA   56
    AND WANDER EVER WITH WOVEN HANDS, ...   78 INDIAN TO LOVE   7
    A WOVEN SILENCE, OR BUT CAME TO CAST . . . .   114 ROSE OF BATTLE   13
    AND PIERCE THE DEEP WOOD'S WOVEN SHADE, ...   125 GOES FERGUS   2
    UPON A WOVEN WORLD-FORGOTTEN ISLE . . . .   126 DREAM OF FAERY   8
    UNDER THAT WOVEN CHANGELESS ROOF OF BOUGHS! . . . . .   126 DREAM OF FAERY   11
    UNDER THE WOVEN ROOFS OF QUICKEN BOUGHS!— . . . . .   126 DREAM OF FAERY V   11
    WOVEN BY LADIES IN THEIR HAIR, ...   156 FORGOT BEAUTY   10
    AND THE IMAGES I HAVE WOVEN IN THIS STORY . . . . . .   218 WOODS OF COOLE   21
    AND 'NEATH IT SIT, AND OF THE WOVEN SUM . . . .   663 ISLE STAT II 2   30
    I HAD WOVEN OF THE SLEEP THAT IS IN POOLS . . . . . .   762 SHADOW WATER A   284
    I AM CAUGHT IN WOVEN NETS OF ENCHANTMENT. LOOK! . . .   762 SHADOW WATER A   293
    O! I WOULD BREAK THIS NET THE GODS HAVE WOVEN . . . .   765 SHADOW WATER A   361
    THE NETS THE GODS HAVE WOVEN AND OUR OWN HEARTS, . . .   766 SHADOW WATER A   383
    HAD WOVEN HER OF WIND. LIFE WITHERS OUT . . . . . .   768 SHADOW WATER A V 423
WRACK
    AND PUT ALL TROY TO WRACK—— . . . .   455 HIS MEMORIES   V   16
    AMID THE CLOUDY WRACK, ...   458 HIS WILDNESS   2
    RUIN, WRECK AND WRACK! . . . .   505 RESULT THOUGHT   8
    ALL THE WRECK AND WRACK! . . . .   505 RESULT THOUGHT V   8
    THE SKY WAS BANDED O'ER WITH WRACK. . . . .   667 ISLE STAT II 3   23
    UNTIL THIS MORN. THE SKY WITH WRACK . . . .   667 ISLE STAT II 3 V   22
WRACKED
    EMPTIED, RUINED, WRACKED, AND LOST, ...   776 AGAINST WITCH   27
WRAP
    UNLOOSE THE CORD, AND THEY WILL WRAP YOU ROUND. . . . .   104 FERGUS DRUID   30
    WHO LOVES YOU, NO WHITE ARMS TO WRAP YOU ROUND, ...   109 CUCHULAIN SEA   59
    WHEN MY ARMS WRAP YOU ROUND I PRESS . . . .   155 FORGOT BEAUTY   1
    THE WHITE WAVES WRAP IT IN A SHEET OF FLAME, ...   662 ISLE STAT II 2   14
    THEY WILL WRAP THEM IN THE SHROUD, ...   733 STREET DANCERS   55
WRAPPED
    A SORROW WRAPPED EACH MERRY FACE, ...   17 OISIN 1   235
    AND WRAPPED IN DREAMS RODE OUT AGAIN . . . .   25 OISIN 1   382
    WRAPPED IN THE THINGS OF THE UNHUMAN MIND, ...   36 OISIN 2   98
    "HE WHO IS WRAPPED IN PURPLE ROBES, ...   134 FR GILLIGAN   45
    AND WRAPPED THE FLAMES ABOVE HIS HOLY HEAD! . . . . .   162 ASKS FORGIVE   17
    AND A CLOAK WRAPPED ABOUT THE STONE, ...   456 FRIENDS YOUTH   7
    I WRAPPED HER IN A HOODED CLOAK, AND SHE, ...   468 HARUN RASHID   154
    I WRAPPED HER IN A HEAVY HOODED CLOAK, ...   468 HARUN RASHID   V 154
    I WRAPPED HER IN A HEAVY HOODED CLOAK, AND SHE . . . .   468 HARUN RASHID   V 154
    NOON WRAPPED THE WOODS IN VEILS OF VIOLET WEATHER! . .   715 DWELT SYCAMORE V   7
WRAPPING
    AND WRAPPING MY FACE IN MY HAIR, ...   59 OISIN 3   177

919

		PAGE	TITLE	LINE

WRAPPING   (CONTINUED)
    WRAPPING THAT FOUL BODY UP . . . .   525 DANCING DAYS   5
WRAPS
    A GENTLE FEELING WRAPS THEM LIKE A FLEECE, ...   128 DREAM OF FAERY V   34
    FROM THE GREAT PAINTED WINDOW WRAPS HIS BROW, ... 697 MOSADA 2   37
WRAPT   SEE TREE-WRAPT
    WRAPT ROUND IN SOME DIM MEMORY, IT SEEMED-- . . . . .   36 OISIN 2   V   99
    WRAPT IN THE WAVE OF THAT MUSIC, WITH WEARINESS MORE THAN 51 OISIN 3   69
        OF EARTH,
    NOON WRAPT THE TREES IN VEILS OF VIOLET WEATHER, ... 715 DWELT SYCAMORE   7
WRATH
    OF RAVENING SORROW, OR THE HAND OF WRATH? . . . . . .   42 OISIN 2   199
    HIS GOD OF STUPOR AND OF WRATH. . . . .   725 LEGEND   20
WREATH
    BLOSSOM FROM THE SUMMER'S WREATH: . . . .   475 EVA GORE-BOOTH   6
    UNMINDFUL OF ITS WOES, WOULD TWINE A WREATH . . . . .   650 ISLE STAT I 1   133
    AS A WREATH OF SMOKE IN WIND-BLOWN FLIGHT . . . . . .   730 PRIEST FAIRY   61
WREATHS
    WITH WREATHS OF WITHERED FLOWERS, ...   680 LOVE AND DEATH   17
    WITH WREATHS OF WITHERED FLOWERS, ...   680 LOVE AND DEATH   19
WRECK
    TILL THE WRECK OF BODY, ...   416 TOWER   184
    AND PUT ALL TROY TO WRECK-- . . . .   455 HIS MEMORIES   16
    RUIN, WRECK AND WRACK: . . . .   505 RESULT THOUGHT   8
    ALL THE WRECK AND WRACK: . . . .   505 RESULT THOUGHT V   8
    THAT THING ALL BLOOD AND MIRE, THAT BEAST-TORN WRECK, . . 537 HER VISION   25
WRECKED
    YOU ARE STILL WRECKED AMONG HEATHEN DREAMS. . . . . .   4 OISIN 1   31
    BITTER GLORY WRECKED. . . . .   504 RESULT THOUGHT   6
    AND BY ITS FORMLESS SPAWNING FURY WRECKED, ...   611 STATUES   30
    THAT WHEREBY A HOUSE LAY WRECKED? . . . .   632 MAN AND ECHO   16
    THAT WHEREBY A HOUSE WAS WRECKED? . . . .   632 MAN AND ECHO   V   16
WREN
    WHO GIVETH TO THE GOLDEN-CRESTED WREN . . . .   698 MOSADA 2   51
WRESTLE
    OR WRESTLE WITH THEIR PEERS IN DEWY VALLEYS. . . . . .   30 OISIN 2   V 14E
    AND WHERE THE POLAR WINDS AND WATERS WRESTLE . . . . .   682 SEEKER   18
WRESTLED
    WRESTLED AMONG THE ISLAND BANDS. . . . .   23 OISIN 1   350
WRETCH
    HER HUSBAND HAS HEARD THE WRETCH, ...   319 DOLLS   15
    FROM ANY PASSING WRETCH: . . . .   598 STONE CROSS   12
WRETCHED
    MY WRETCHED DRAGON IS PERPLEXED. . . . .   386 ROBARTES DANCE   41
WRETCHEDLY
    IS SHADOW, AND NOT LINGER WRETCHEDLY . . . .   230 SHADOW WATER B   180
WRETCHEDNESS
    TILL HIS LAST WRETCHEDNESS WAS O'ER AND DONE." . . . . 664 ISLE STAT II 2   54
WRETCHES
    "AND ALL THOSE LIES HAVE BUT ONE END, POOR WRETCHES TO 450 OWEN AHERNE   18
        BETRAY:
WRIGGLING
    A WRIGGLING THING ON THE WHITE LAKE MOVED, ... 673 ISLE STAT II 3   176
WRING
    AND WRING MY HANDS, AND WAIL HIM BITTERLY, ... 242 SHADOW WATER B   414
WRINKLED
    WRINKLED LIKE THE FOOT OF A GOOSE, ...   508 JANE BISHOP   16
    HIDE WHERE HE WILL, IN WAVE OR WRINKLED MOON, ... 720 WITCH VIVIEN   8
    THE WRINKLED SQUANDERER OF HUMAN WEALTH. . . . . . .   720 WITCH VIVIEN   16
WRINKLES
    WHO FINDING THE FIRST WRINKLES ON A FACE . . . . . .   472 ALL SOUL NIGHT   42
    THEIR EYES MID MANY WRINKLES, THEIR EYES, ...   567 LAPIS LAZULI   55
    AND--NO: I'LL NONE OF THESE, OLD FATHER WRINKLES. . . . 721 WITCH VIVIEN   23
WRINKLING
    . . . IMMENSE IN THEIR WRINKLING BARK: . . . .   48 OISIN 3   17
    THE WAILING GREW DISTANT: I RODE BY THE WOODS OF   56 OISIN 3   137
        THE WRINKLING BARK,
WRIST
    AND THE DOWN-TURN OF HIS WRIST . . . .   348 FISHERMAN   33
    AND THE DOWN TURN OF HIS WRIST . . . .   348 FISHERMAN   V   33
    NOR A CAGE, NOR ALIGHT UPON WRIST, ...   349 HAWK   8
    AND PADDLE TO THE WRIST . . . .   356 BROKEN DREAMS   31
    THAT HAD A SOUND FLY-FISHER'S WRIST . . . .   625 OLD MEN BE MAD   3
    THAT HAD A SOUND FLY FISHER'S WRIST . . . .   625 OLD MEN BE MAD V   3
WRIT
    THE CAPTIVE'S JOURNEYS TO AND FRO WERE WRIT . . . . .   37 OISIN 2   116
    THE CAPTIVES' JOURNEYS TO AND FRO WERE WRIT . . . . .   37 OISIN 2   V 116
    IN CHANGELESS OGHAM LETTERS WRIT-- . . . .   194 BAILE AILLINN   117
    R.I.P." WRIT IN BLOOD. . . . .   585 ORAHILLY   35
WRITE
    WHILE STILL I MAY, I WRITE FOR YOU . . . .   139 TO IRELAND   33
    WHILE STILL I MAY I WRITE OUT TRUE . . . .   139 TO IRELAND   V   33
    AND WHEN I'D WRITE IT OUT ANEW, THE WORDS, ...   186 QUEEN MAEVE   139
    AND MORE I MAY NOT WRITE OF, FOR THEY THAT CLEAVE . . . 218 WOODS OF COOLE   24
    AND MORE I MAY NOT WRITE OF, FOR THEM THAT CLEAVE . . . 218 WOODS OF COOLE V   24
    TO WRITE FOR MY OWN RACE . . . .   347 FISHERMAN   11
    AND SHOULD THEY PAINT OR WRITE, STILL IT IS ACTION: . . 369 EGO DOMINUS   44
    AND SHOULD THEY PAINT OR WRITE STILL IS IT ACTION, . . 369 EGO DOMINUS   V   44
    I WRITE IT OUT IN A VERSE-- . . . .   394 EASTER 1916   74
    KUSTA BEN LUKA IS MY NAME, I WRITE . . . .   460 HARUN RASHID   1
    AND ALL THE WORDS THAT I WRITE, ...   739 WHERE BOOKS GO   2

```
                                                        PAGE    TITLE            LINE
WRITE   (CONTINUED)
      THAT DRUIDS WRITE ON YEW AND APPLE WOOD,  . . . . .     748 SHADOW WATER A      29
      THE FOOL, WHO HAS MADE THE WISDOM THAT MEN WRITE . . .  764 SHADOW WATER A     342
WRITERS
      AND POETS FOUND, OLD WRITERS SAY. . . . . . . . .       197 BAILE AILLINN      187
      NEVER TO HAVE LIVED IS BEST, ANCIENT WRITERS SAY,  . .  459 FROM OEDIPUS        10
      AND WRITERS BY THE SCORE. . . . . . . . . . .          582 ROGER CASEMENT      16
      HAVE NOT OLD WRITERS SAID . . . . . . . . . .          781 MY HEART BEAT        6
WRITING
      ON OLD DRY WRITING IN A LEARNED TONGUE, . . . . . .     466 HARUN RASHID       123
      AS IF THAT WRITING OR THE FIGURED PAGE  . . . . . .     466 HARUN RASHID       126
WRITINGS
      THOSE MEN THAT IN THEIR WRITINGS ARE MOST WISE  . . .   370 EGO DOMINUS         68
      UNLESS THE HOLY WRITINGS LIE, . . . . . . . . .        436 FOR MY SON          28
      THE WRITINGS I HAVE CAST AWAY! . . . . . . . . .       779 ACCURSED WHO         2
WRITTEN    SEE HALF-WRITTEN RE-WRITTEN
      THE CAPTIVES' FOOTSTEPS WRITTEN TO AND FRO! . . . .      37 OISIN 2         V 118
      TRAILS ALL ABOUT THE WRITTEN PAGE. . . . . . . .       138 TO IRELAND           9
      TO GRADUAL TIME'S LAST GIFT, A WRITTEN SPEECH . . .    264 HOUSE SHAKEN        11
      LINES WRITTEN IN DEJECTION  . . . . . . . . . .        343 DEJECTION            T
      I SHALL HAVE WRITTEN HIM ONE  . . . . . . . . .        348 FISHERMAN           38
      A CANDLE AND WRITTEN PAGE. . . . . . . . . . .         419 MY HOUSE            13
      THE HALF IMAGINED, THE HALF WRITTEN PAGE. . . . .      431 NINETEEN 19     V  83
      WRITTEN IN GOLD UPON A PURPLE STAIN, . . . . . .       461 HARUN RASHID        10
      AS THOUGH THE WRITTEN OR THE PICTURED PAGE  . . . .    466 HARUN RASHID     V 126
      WHATEVER'S WRITTEN IN WHAT POETS NAME . . . . . .      492 COOLE BALLYLEE      43
      ALL THAT IS WRITTEN IN WHAT POETS NAME  . . . . .      492 COOLE BALLYLEE V   43
      A MEDITATION WRITTEN DURING SICKNESS AT ALGECIRAS . .  493 AT ALGECIRAS    V   T
WRONG
      THAT SANG, TO SWEETEN IRELAND'S WRONG, . . . . . .     137 TO IRELAND           3
      WHO SANG TO SWEETEN IRELAND'S WRONG, . . . . . .       137 TO IRELAND      V    3
      THE WRONG OF UNSHAPELY THINGS IS A WRONG TOO GREAT TO BE 143 ROSE IN HEART      5
        TOLD!
      THE WRONG OF UNSHAPELY THINGS IS A WRONG TOO GREAT TO BE 143 ROSE IN HEART      5
        TOLD!
      THE WRONG OF THE THINGS MISSHAPEN IS WRONG TOO GREAT TO 143 ROSE IN HEART   V  5
        BE TOLD!
      THE WRONG OF THE THINGS MISSHAPEN IS WRONG TOO GREAT TO 143 ROSE IN HEART   V  5
        BE TOLD!
      COME CLEAR OF THE NETS OF WRONG AND RIGHT! . . . . .   147 INTO TWILIGHT        2
      COME CLEAR OFF THE NETS OF WRONG AND RIGHT! . . . .    147 INTO TWILIGHT   V    2
      BUT I HAVE DONE SO GREAT A WRONG AGAINST YOU, . . .    245 SHADOW WATER B     483
      HOW GREAT A WRONG IT IS TO LET ONE'S THOUGHT  . . .    246 SHADOW WATER B     514
      BUT O! 'TWAS BITTER WRONG . . . . . . . . . .         255 WOMAN HOMER          5
      AYE, AND WORSE WRONG THAN THESE. . . . . . . . .       260 UNWORTH PRAISE      18
      THE SPEAKING OF IT COULD BE NO GREAT WRONG, . . . .    281 TWO KINGS          104
      I CAN FORGIVE EVEN THAT WRONG OF WRONGS, . . . . .     321 REED WHISPERER       9
      YOUR COCKEREL FOUND US IN THE WRONG . . . . . .       388 SOLOMON WITCH       34
      HE HAD DONE MOST BITTER WRONG . . . . . . . .         393 EASTER 1916         33
      TO BRIBE OR THREAT! HABITS THAT MADE OLD WRONG  . .    428 NINETEEN 19         11
      WHIRLS OUT NEW RIGHT AND WRONG, . . . . . . . .       430 NINETEEN 19         55
      HAVE WRONG TO BROOD UPON—ENOUGH OF THAT, . . . .      444 SCHOOL CHILDR   V  30
      WITH A COMMON WRONG OR RIGHT. . . . . . . . .         476 EVA GORE-BOOTH      23
      BUT TIME AMENDS OLD WRONG, . . . . . . . . . .        613 MARCH SONGS 1        9
      BUT TIME AMENDS OLD WRONG, . . . . . . . . . .        613 MARCH SONGS 1       19
      BUT TIME AMENDS OLD WRONG, . . . . . . . . . .        614 MARCH SONGS 1       29
      IF WRONG MY CHOICE, AS SILENT AS THOU ART. . . . .    657 ISLE STAT I 3       76
      THE FRIENDS THAT HAVE IT I DO WRONG . . . . . . .     778 FRIENDS WRONG        1
WRONGED
      HOW HAVE I WRONGED HER NOW THAT SHE IS MERRY? . . . .  244 SHADOW WATER B     448
WRONGING
      ARE WRONGING YOUR IMAGE THAT BLOSSOMS A ROSE . . . .   143 ROSE IN HEART        4
WRONGS
      I CAN FORGIVE EVEN THAT WRONG OF WRONGS, . . . . .     321 REED WHISPERER       9
      ALL WRONGS DONE. . . . . . . . . . . . . . .          518 HIS CONFIDENCE       4
WROTE
      I CAME AND WROTE UPON A CROSS OF WOOD— . . . . .      123 DREAM OF DEATH V     7
      THEY WROTE ON TABLETS OF THIN BOARD, . . . . . . .    197 BAILE AILLINN      195
      WHEREON I WROTE AND WROUGHT, . . . . . . . . .        255 WOMAN HOMER          8
      HE WROTE OF ME IN THAT EXTRAVAGANT STYLE  . . . .     373 PHASES OF MOON      26
      AND NEVER WROTE A BOOK, YOUR THOUGHT IS CLEAR. . . .   376 PHASES OF MOON      97
      IT IS TIME THAT I WROTE MY WILL! . . . . . . . .      414 TOWER              121
      AND WROTE BY CANDLE-LIGHT! BUT HER FORM MOVED, . .    467 HARUN RASHID       129
      AND WROTE BY CANDLE LIGHT! BUT HER FORM MOVED . . .   467 HARUN RASHID    V 129
      I WROTE UPON . . . . . . . . . . . . . . . .         517 HIS CONFIDENCE       2
      WHERE—WROTE A LEARNED ASTROLOGER— . . . . . .       535 CHOSEN              17
      EVERYTHING HE WROTE WAS READ, . . . . . . . . .       577 WHAT THEN            6
      HE WROTE OUT THAT WORD HIMSELF, . . . . . . . .       585 ORAHILLY             7
      HE WROTE IT ON THE SANDS (THE OWLS MAY READ . . . .   659 ISLE STAT II 1       9
WROTH
      SHALL THEY TURN WROTH OR PLUCK THE WINGS OF TIME? . .   42 OISIN 2        V 199
      . . . AND PRAYING, AND WROTH WITH THE BELLS, . . . .    58 OISIN 3            159
WROUGHT
      AND FACE THAT SEEMED WROUGHT OUT OF MOONLIT VAPOURS, . . 33 OISIN 2            70
      FOR HE HAS WROUGHT MIDNIGHT AND DAWN AND DAY. . . . .   43 OISIN 2            208
      SO LIVED I AND LIVED NOT, SO WROUGHT I AND WROUGHT NOT,  53 OISIN 3            95
        . . .
      SO LIVED I AND LIVED NOT, SO WROUGHT I AND WROUGHT NOT,  53 OISIN 3            95

      WHILE I WROUGHT OUT THESE FITFUL DANAAN RHYMES, . . . . 136 TO SOME I TALK      1
      THE DANAAN CHILDREN LAUGH, IN CRADLES OF WROUGHT GOLD, . 146 UNAPPEAS HOST      1
```

WROUGHT   (CONTINUED)
THE FAERY CHILDREN LAUGH IN CRADLES OF WROUGHT GOLD,   • •   146   UNAPPEAS HOST   V   1
THE LOVE-TALES WROUGHT WITH SILKEN THREAD   • • • • •   155   FORGOT BEAUTY   6
QUEENS WROUGHT WITH GLIMMERING HANDS: •   •   • •   162   ASKS FORGIVE   12
BUT LET A GENTLE SILENCE WROUGHT WITH MUSIC FLOW   • • •   175   ELEMENT POWERS   17
WHEREON I WROTE AND WROUGHT,   •   •   •   •   •   •   •   255   WOMAN HOMER   8
WROUGHT OF HIGH LAUGHTER, LOVELINESS AND EASE?   • • •   264   HOUSE SHAKEN   12
OLD GOBAN HAMMERED THEM AND WROUGHT THEM,   • • • •   271   GREY ROCK   V   23
THREE WOMEN THAT HAVE WROUGHT   •   •   •   •   •   •   •   315   FRIENDS   2
AS THOUGH THEY'D WROUGHT IT.   •   •   •   •   •   •   •   320   COAT   7
WHEN SHE THE IRON WROUGHT, OR   •   •   •   •   •   •   345   ON WOMAN   17
IN CONTEMPLATION HAD THOSE THREE SO WROUGHT   • • •   384   VISION ROBART   45
WHERE WE WROUGHT THAT SHALL BREAK THE TEETH OF TIME.   •   435   NEW FACES   4
AND THAT TO SUCH A PITCH OF PASSION WROUGHT   • • •   471   ALL SOUL NIGHT   24
AND EVERYTHING THAT YOUR OWN HANDS HAVE WROUGHT,   • • •   501   VACILLATION   31
TRAGEDY WROUGHT TO ITS UTTERMOST.   •   •   •   •   •   •   566   LAPIS LAZULI   20
FORMS THAT GENTLER PHIDIAS WROUGHT.   •   •   •   •   •   638   BEN BULBEN   44
WITH SHIELD AND ARMOUR WROUGHT WITH GOLD,   •   •   •   •   741   EARL PAUL   37
WRUNG
ARE WITH NEW SORROW WRUNG: •   •   •   •   •   •   •   99   FOXHUNTER   38
WRUNG FROM THE COLD WOMEN OF THE SEA—   •   •   •   •   237   SHADOW WATER B   343
THEN SUDDENLY MY HEART IS WRUNG   •   •   •   •   •   453   DEATH OF HARE   7
YARD   SEE PALACE-YARD BUILDING-YARD
BUILDING YARD AND STORMY SHORE,   •   •   •   •   •   530   OLD TOM AGAIN   V   5
WHAT'S EQUALITY?—MUCK IN THE YARD: •   •   •   •   •   547   TO SAME TUNE 3 V   4
UNDER A SILKEN SAIL AND SILVER YARD,   •   •   •   •   763   SHADOW WATER A   316
YARDS
• • • I FLUNG IT FIVE YARDS WITH MY HAND,   •   •   •   60   OISIN 3   187
A SCORE OF YARDS OFF 'NEATH A WILLOW, SHOT.   •   •   •   712   FERENCZ RENYI   65
YAWN
YOUNG RED-HEAD STRETCHED HIMSELF TO YAWN   •   •   •   303   HOUR DAWN   V   32A
THAT MADE THEM STRETCH AND YAWN,   •   •   •   •   •   345   ON WOMAN   21
AND DID AFTER STRETCH AND YAWN":   •   •   •   •   •   521   THREE THINGS   17
YAWNED
AND DRANK AND YAWNED AND STRETCHED HIM OUT,   •   •   •   307   HOUR DAWN   108
AND HAVING STRETCHED AND YAWNED AWHILE   •   •   •   •   612   NEWS ORACLE   11
YAWNS
CAN BUT SHOW THAT HEAVEN YAWNS: •   •   •   •   •   •   509   JANE REPROVED   4
YEA
YEA, NOBLE AND MOST KNIGHTLY HATH IT BEEN.   •   •   •   679   ISLE STAT II 3   320
THE HEATHEN.   YEA, AND SHAKE THE SULLEN KINGS   •   •   698   MOSADA 2   55
YEAR   SEE SIXTY-YEAR-OLD HUNDRED-YEAR-OLD A-YEAR
CHAINED WAS SHE.   ON THEIR WINGS THE HUNDREDTH YEAR   •   •   34   OISIN 2   V   76
AN ENDLESS WAR.   THE HUNDREDTH YEAR HAD CEASED.   •   •   •   44   OISIN 2   V 224
FROM YEAR TO YEAR BY THE UNNUMBERED NESTS   •   •   •   74   ANASHU VIJAYA   72
FROM YEAR TO YEAR BY THE UNNUMBERED NESTS   •   •   •   74   ANASHU VIJAYA   72
AND SING FROM SHORE TO SHORE, AND EVERY YEAR   •   •   81   EPHEMERA   V   24G
AT ALL TIMES OF THE YEAR: •   •   •   •   •   •   •   214   HAPPY TOWNLAND   6
UNLESS WE DRAIN MORE FLAGONS IN A YEAR   •   •   •   •   225   SHADOW WATER B   70
THAT EVERY YEAR I HAVE CRIED, "AT LENGTH   •   •   •   256   WORDS   9
GIDDY WITH HIS HUNDREDTH YEAR,   •   •   •   •   •   •   298   THREE HERMITS   6
GIDDY WITH HIS HUNDREDTH YEAR,   •   •   •   •   •   •   299   THREE HERMITS   31
SO SLEPT FOR HALF A YEAR OR SO: •   •   •   •   •   305   HOUR DAWN   67
BUT YEAR BY YEAR I FOUND THAT LESS   •   •   •   •   305   HOUR DAWN   68
BUT YEAR BY YEAR I FOUND THAT LESS   •   •   •   •   305   HOUR DAWN   68
AND SLEPT FOR HALF A YEAR OR SO: •   •   •   •   •   305   HOUR DAWN   V   67
THEY WERE MY CLOSE COMPANIONS MANY A YEAR,   •   •   •   325   ROBERT GREGORY   41
THAT CRY'S FROM THE FIRST CUCKOO OF THE YEAR.   •   •   338   SHEP GOATHERD   1
YEAR.   I WISHED BEFORE IT CEASED.   NOR BIRD NOR BEAST   •   338   SHEP GOATHERD   V   2
YESTERDAY IN THE TENTH YEAR   •   •   •   •   •   •   •   361   ALF POLLEXFEN   27
NOW THAT HIS FIFTIETH YEAR HAD COME,   •   •   •   •   361   ALF POLLEXFEN   31
AND ARE WE NOW IN THE TENTH YEAR?   •   •   •   •   •   361   ALF POLLEXFEN   V   27
THAT I MYSELF FOR PORTIONS OF THE YEAR   •   •   •   •   371   ON GOING HOUSE   5
SO THE PLATONIC YEAR   •   •   •   •   •   •   •   •   430   NINETEEN 19   54
A SIXTY YEAR OLD SMILING PUBLIC MAN.   •   •   •   •   443   SCHOOL CHILDR   V   8
AND SPEAK BUT FANTASY.   RECALL THE YEAR   •   •   •   462   HARUN RASHID   30
AND SPEAK BUT PHANTASY.   RECALL THE YEAR   •   •   •   462   HARUN RASHID   V   30
THAT IN THE EARLY SUMMER OF THE YEAR   •   •   •   •   462   HARUN RASHID   40
THAT YEAR WHEN GREAT HAROUN EL RASHID KILLED   •   •   462   HARUN RASHID   31
THAT IN THE EARLY SUMMER OF THAT YEAR   •   •   •   •   462   HARUN RASHID   V   40
MY FIFTIETH YEAR HAD COME AND GONE,   •   •   •   •   501   VACILLATION   35
A YEAR AGO FOR THE FIRST TIME   •   •   •   •   •   •   570   THREE BUSHES   38
WHO CAN KNOW THE YEAR, MY DEAR,   •   •   •   •   •   588   OLD WICKED MAN   12
MY HUNDREDTH YEAR IS AT AN END.   I THINK   •   •   •   609   IN TARAS HALLS   3
HE BADE, HIS HUNDRED AND FIRST YEAR AT END,   •   •   609   IN TARAS HALLS   16
"FOR A YEAR AND A DAY BY THE CLOCK OF THE SUN"   •   •   779   GOING THE ROAD   11
ALTHOUGH YOUR LAST EXCITING YEAR   •   •   •   •   •   791   REPRISALS   5
YEAR'S
AND WHEN AT ONE YEAR'S END I FOUND   •   •   •   •   •   305   HOUR DAWN   71
YEARS
SAD TO REMEMBER, SICK WITH YEARS,   •   •   •   •   •   2   OISIN 1   5
'TIS SAD REMEMBERING, SICK WITH YEARS,   •   •   •   •   2   OISIN 1   V   5
IN OTHER YEARS FROM SOME OLD STAR   •   •   •   •   •   19   OISIN 1   V 277
AFAR FROM WHERE THE YEARS ARE FLYING   •   •   •   •   •   22   OISIN 1   V 340A
O PATRICK! FOR A HUNDRED YEARS   •   •   •   •   •   •   23   OISIN 1   343
O PATRICK! FOR A HUNDRED YEARS   •   •   •   •   •   •   23   OISIN 1   346
O PATRICK! FOR A HUNDRED YEARS   •   •   •   •   •   •   23   OISIN 1   351
O PATRICK! FOR A HUNDRED YEARS   •   •   •   •   •   •   23   OISIN 1   356
A HUNDRED YEARS I CHASED THE BOAR,   •   •   •   •   •   23   OISIN 1   V 344
OH, PATRICK, THERE A HUNDRED YEARS,   •   •   •   •   •   23   OISIN 1   V 346
"SWIFT ARE THE YEARS OF A WARRIOR'S PRIDE: •   •   •   26   OISIN 1   V 399A

	PAGE	TITLE		LINE
YEARS (CONTINUED)				
"BUT NEVER THE YEARS IN THE ISLE'S SOFT PLACES	27	OISIN 1	V	419A
"BUT NEVER THE YEARS IN OUR ISLE'S SOFT PLACES	28	OISIN 1	V	424
WITH ME IN HER WHITE ARMS A HUNDRED YEARS	30	OISIN 2		17
TO JOIN HIS BROTHERS IN THE HOME OF YEARS	30	OISIN 2	V	17
HIS NEW-HEALED SHAPE: AND FOR A HUNDRED YEARS	44	OISIN 2		221
AN ENDLESS WAR. THE HUNDRED YEARS HAD CEASED:	44	OISIN 2		224
HIS HEALED SHAPE: AND FOR A HUNDRED YEARS	44	OISIN 2	V	221
HIS NEW HEALED SHAPE: AND FOR A HUNDRED YEARS	44	OISIN 2	V	221
AND DEW-BLANCHED HORNS, IN WHOSE HOLLOW A CHILD OF THREE YEARS OLD	49	OISIN 3		30
AND DEW-BLANCHED HORNS, IN WHOSE HOLLOWS A CHILD OF THREE YEARS OLD	49	OISIN 3	V	31
. . . AND YEARS AFTER YEARS 'GAN FLOW:	52	OISIN 3		75
. . . AND YEARS AFTER YEARS 'GAN FLOW:	52	OISIN 3		75
. . . AND YEARS AFTER YEARS 'GAN THEIR FLOW:	52	OISIN 3	V	75
. . . AND YEARS AFTER YEARS 'GAN THEIR FLOW:	52	OISIN 3	V	75
AND MY YEARS THREE HUNDRED FELL ON ME, ...	60	OISIN 3		191
FOR THY YOUTH WITHOUT PEACE, AND THY YEARS WITH THE DEMONS, . . .	63	OISIN 3	V	216
BUT NOW MY YEARS OF WATCHING ARE NO MORE."	105	CUCHULAIN SEA	V	5
THOUSANDS OF YEARS, THOUSANDS OF YEARS, ...	116	FAERY SONG		3
THOUSANDS OF YEARS, THOUSANDS OF YEARS, ...	116	FAERY SONG		3
THOUSANDS OF YEARS, THOUSANDS OF YEARS, ...	116	FAERY SONG		15
THOUSANDS OF YEARS, THOUSANDS OF YEARS, ...	116	FAERY SONG		15
AND ALL THE BURDEN OF HER MYRIAD YEARS.	120	SORROW OF LOVE	V	8
AND ALL THE TROUBLE OF HER MYRIAD YEARS.	120	SORROW OF LOVE	V	8
AND HE HAD KNOWN AT LAST SOME PRUDENT YEARS	127	DREAM OF FAERY		15
AND SOUGHT THROUGH LANDS AND ISLANDS NUMBERLESS YEARS, . .	170	SECRET ROSE		23
WHO HAS BEEN BURIED SOME TWO THOUSAND YEARS?	181	QUEEN MAEVE		35
FRIEND OF THESE MANY YEARS, YOU TOO HAD STOOD	186	QUEEN MAEVE		130
FRIEND OF THESE MANY YEARS, YOU TO HAVE STOOD	186	QUEEN MAEVE	V	130
A THOUSAND YEARS AGO YOU HELD HIGH TALK	187	QUEEN MAEVE		150
FOR ALTHOUGH YEARS HAD PASSED AWAY	192	BAILE AILLINN		77
THROUGH THE LONG YEARS OF YOUTH, AND WHO WOULD HAVE THOUGHT	201	OLD MEMORY		7
WITH WISDOM, THEY WANDER TILL ALL THE YEARS HAVE GONE BY:	204	WITHER BOUGHS		21
ABOUT THE STARS AND BROKE IN DAYS AND YEARS.	206	ADAMS CURSE		33
ABOUT THE STARN AND BROKE IN DAYS AND YEARS.	206	ADAMS CURSE	V	33
ALL THROUGH THE YEARS OF OUR YOUTH	211	O DO NOT LOVE		5
TOO MANY YEARS TO LIFT A HAND AGAINST YOU.	227	SHADOW WATER B		111
WHEN THEY HAVE TWENTY YEARS: IN MIDDLE LIFE	229	SHADOW WATER B		156
I KNOW THAT HE DIED A THOUSAND YEARS AGO	241	SHADOW WATER B		392
AND THAT HE DIED A THOUSAND YEARS AGO.	242	SHADOW WATER B		417
THESE THOUSAND YEARS. WHAT ARE THE BIRDS AT THERE? . .	243	SHADOW WATER B		435
HAVE I NOT LOVED YOU FOR A THOUSAND YEARS?	244	SHADOW WATER B		463
THAT YOU WERE BORN A THOUSAND YEARS AGO, ...	245	SHADOW WATER B		468
AND SAID, "IN TWO OR IN THREE YEARS	272	GREY ROCK		46
I'D PROMISED HIM TWO HUNDRED YEARS, ...	275	GREY ROCK		98
A BOY OF TWENTY YEARS:—A MOUND AND STONE	276	TWO KINGS	V	F
WHY MUST I LIVE SOME THIRTY, FORTY YEARS, ...	285	TWO KINGS		199
YET COULD WE TURN THE YEARS AGAIN, ...	290	SEPTEMBER 1913		25
HE HAD COUNTED, WHERE LONG YEARS AGO	302	HOUR DAWN		7
HE COUNTED, WHERE LONG YEARS AGO	302	HOUR DAWN	V	7
TWO YEARS LATER	312	TWO YEAR LATER		T
MANY-TIMES-TROUBLED YEARS, ...	315	FRIENDS		7
MANY TIMES TROUBLED YEARS, ...	315	FRIENDS	V	7
THE YEARS TO COME SEEMED WASTE OF BREATH, ...	328	IRISH AIRMAN		14
A WASTE OF BREATH THE YEARS BEHIND	328	IRISH AIRMAN		15
MEN IMPROVE WITH THE YEARS	329	MEN IMPROVE		T
FOR MEN IMPROVE WITH THE YEARS:	329	MEN IMPROVE		11
AND NOW THAT I HAVE COME TO FIFTY YEARS	344	DEJECTION		10
AFTER NINE YEARS, I SINK MY HEAD ABASHED.	353	PEOPLE		37
FIVE-AND-TWENTY YEARS HAVE GONE	360	ALF POLLEXFEN		1
AND AFTER TWENTY YEARS THEY LAID	360	ALF POLLEXFEN		6
FIVE AND TWENTY YEARS HAVE GONE	360	ALF POLLEXFEN	V	1
HE WOULD NEVER KNOW ME AFTER ALL THESE YEARS	377	PHASES OF MOON		129
THREE HUNDRED YEARS BEFORE THE FALL, ...	388	SOLOMON WITCH		11
AND SURELY AFTER TWENTY YEARS IT WAS TIME TO COME." . .	391	UNDER SATURN		14
RECALL THE YEARS BEFORE HER MIND	397	POLIT PRISONER		8
THAT THE FUTURE YEARS HAD COME, ...	403	FOR DAUGHTER		14
I THOUGHT IT ALL OUT TWENTY YEARS AGO:	411	TOWER		64
IT LAY FIVE HUNDRED YEARS.	421	MY TABLE		11
WE, WHO SEVEN YEARS AGO	431	NINETEEN 19		89
HOW COULD SHE MATE WITH FIFTY YEARS THAT WAS SO WILDLY BRED?	450	OWEN AHERNE		15
HER CHILDISH GRATITUDE FOR LOVE AND MATCH YOUR FIFTY YEARS?	450	OWEN AHERNE		23
HOW SUCH A PAIR LOVED MANY YEARS	458	SECRETS OF OLD		15
ARE BRIDELESS." "I AM FALLING INTO YEARS."	463	HARUN RASHID		54
EVEN TO-DAY, AFTER SOME SEVEN YEARS	468	HARUN RASHID		161
EVEN TODAY, AFTER SOME SEVEN YEARS	468	HARUN RASHID	V	161
AND I ALONE, ONE IN TEN THOUSAND YEARS, ...	470	HARUN RASHID	V	190
PERMIT FOUL YEARS TO WEAR	472	ALL SOUL NIGHT		49
PARDONED, DRAGS OUT LONELY YEARS	475	EVA GORE-BOOTH		8
FIVE HUNDRED YEARS AGO, ABOUT IT LIE	478	SELF AND SOUL		26
THINGS SAID OR DONE LONG YEARS AGO, ...	501	VACILLATION		51
I TOILED LONG YEARS AND AT LENGTH	505	RESULT THOUGHT		9
TOILED LONG YEARS AND AT LENGTH	505	RESULT THOUGHT	V	9
HOW MANY YEARS AGO	524	MAD AS MIST		10
FORTY YEARS LATER	542	PARN FUNERAL 2	V	T
NOR HEARD THIS VOICE THAT NINETY YEARS HAVE CRACKED. .	555	RIBH AT TOMB		5
SEVENTY YEARS HAVE I LIVED:	567	FROM JAPANESE		2

YEARS   (CONTINUED)
    SEVENTY YEARS HAVE I LIVED . . . .   567 FROM JAPANESE   5
    SEVENTY YEARS HAVE I LIVED, ...   567 FROM JAPANESE   7
    SEVENTY YEARS MAN AND BOY, ...   567 FROM JAPANESE   8
    AFTER CERTAIN YEARS HE WON . . . .   577 WHAT THEN   7
    AROUND ME THE IMAGES OF THIRTY YEARS! . . . . .   601 GALLERY REVIS   1
    I MET HER ALL BUT FIFTY YEARS AGO . . . .   602 GALLERY REVIS   15
    HE LACKED THOSE YEARS THAT GO WITH SKILL, . . .   608 SONGS BURDEN 3   14
    SO MANY YEARS COMPANIONED BY A HOUND, ...   621 HOUND VOICE   4
    LONG YEARS AGO, A CHURCH STANDS NEAR, ...   640 BEN BULBEN   87
    AND ELVISH WISDOM, AND LONG YEARS OF YOUTH . .   653 ISLE STAT I 2   47
    BEYOND A MORTAL'S YEARS. I WAIT THE SONG . . .   653 ISLE STAT I 2   48
    LONG YEARS AGO, AND UNTO STONE CONGEALED. . . .   656 ISLE STAT I 3   28
    A SHEPHERDESS LONG YEARS FORETOLD: . . . . . .   668 ISLE STAT II 3   49
    HAD HOOTED FOR AN HUNDRED YEARS, ...   670 ISLE STAT II 3   116
    IN THOSE FAR YEARS, O DAUGHTER OF THE DAYS. . .   674 ISLE STAT II 3   213
    IN THOSE FAIR YEARS, O DAUGHTER OF THE DAYS. .   674 ISLE STAT II 3 V   213
    THE TIDE OF STARS? HAVE I NOT SEEN A THOUSAND YEARS . .   675 ISLE STAT II 3   230
    HAVE I SLEPT LONG? LONG YEARS. WITH HUNGRY HEART . .   677 ISLE STAT II 3   286
    SEAFARER, WAKE! WAS MY SLEEP LONG? LONG YEARS. . .   678 ISLE STAT II 3   292
    THE YEARS OF GOBLIN SLEEP. AH! WHILE I SLUMBERED, . .   679 ISLE STAT II 3   308
    HOW HAVE THE YEARS IN TROIA FLOWN AWAY? . . . .   679 ISLE STAT II 3   309
    FROM THREESCORE YEARS OF DREAM-LED WANDERING . . . .   682 SEEKER   16
    AS WORDS OF THINE THROUGH FOURSCORE YEARS HAVE FILLED . .   683 SEEKER   46
    FOR YEARS HIS DAYS HAD DAWNED AND FADED THUS . .   692 MOSADA 1   54
    HER DREAMS ARE TALKING WITH OLD YEARS. AWAKE, .   702 MOSADA 3   89
    BENT LOW WITH TOIL AND HOARIEST YEARS. THE OTHER . .   711 FERENCZ RENYI   52
    BELOVED, HOW TWO LITTLE YEARS AGO . . . .   713 FERENCZ RENYI   89
    ERE YONDER PALM COMMENCED HIS THOUSAND YEARS? .   724 KANVA ON SELF   14
    HAS MOULDED THE HARD YEARS. . . . .   738 MOURN THEN ON   8
    THE YEARS THAT HAVE GONE OVER HER FROM THE HOUR   760 SHADOW WATER A   256
    FOR THESE NINE YEARS? O ARROW UPON ARROW! . . .   761 SHADOW WATER A   268
    OUTWEIGHED ALL OTHER YEARS, YOU SAID, ...   791 REPRISALS   6
YEATS
    AND OF A RED-HAIRED YEATS WHOSE LOOKS, ALTHOUGH HE DIED   391 UNDER SATURN   9
    I, THE POET WILLIAM YEATS, ...   406 CARVED STONE   1
    IN DRUMCLIFF CHURCHYARD YEATS IS LAID. . . . . .   640 BEN BULBEN   85
YELLED
    HOWLED, MIAU-D, BARKED, BRAYED, BELLED, YELLED, CRIED,   387 SOLOMON WITCH   8
        CROWED,
YELLING
    I HAVE POINTED OUT THE YELLING PACK, ...   453 DEATH OF HARE   1
YELLOW   SEE GRASS-YELLOW
    THEIR CLOAKS MADE OUT OF YELLOW SILK, ...   15 OISIN 1   205
    THEIR ROBES WERE ALL OF YELLOW SILK . . . . . .   15 OISIN 1   V 205
    THEIR BRATTAS MADE OUT OF YELLOW SILK, ...   15 OISIN 1   V 205
    YELLOW THE LEAVES OF THE ROWAN ABOVE US, ...   79 FALLING LEAVES   3
    AND YELLOW THE WET WILD-STRAWBERRY LEAVES. . . .   79 FALLING LEAVES   4
    THE WOODS WERE ROUND THEM, AND THE YELLOW LEAVES   80 EPHEMERA   13
    THEY PINE AWAY AND YELLOW AND WEAR OUT, ...   81 EPHEMERA   V 24H
    THE YELLOW POOL HAS OVERFLOWED HIGH UP ON CLOOTH-NA-BARE,   207 HANRAHANS SONG   11
    THE YELLOW POOL HAS OVERFLOWED HIGH UPON CLOOTH-NA-BARE,   207 HANRAHANS SONG V   11
    O MY SHARE OF THE WORLD, O YELLOW HAIR! . . . .   211 RAGGED WOOD   11
    WHEN WE HAVE NEITHER BROWN NOR YELLOW ALE? . . .   240 SHADOW WATER B   387
    YOU'D CRY, "SOME WOMAN'S YELLOW HAIR . . . . . .   290 SEPTEMBER 1913   28
    AND SAW A FLAKE OF THE YELLOW FOAM . . . .   309 PLAYER QUEEN   15
    I SAW A FLAKE OF YELLOW FOAM . . . .   309 PLAYER QUEEN   V 15
    ON HIS YELLOW LEGS THROUGH OUR MEADOWS, ...   341 SHEP GOATHERD   65
    UPON HIS YELLOW LEGS THROUGH OUR MEADOWS, . . .   341 SHEP GOATHERD   V 65
    TILL THE YELLOW EYE HAS GROWN MILD, ...   349 HAWK   3
    THAT SAW THE WICKS GROW YELLOW IN THE DAWN! . .   352 PEOPLE   18
    AND NOT YOUR YELLOW HAIR." . . . .   492 ANNE GREGORY   6
    AND NOT MY YELLOW HAIR." . . . .   492 ANNE GREGORY   12
    AND NOT YOUR YELLOW HAIR." . . . .   492 ANNE GREGORY   18
    AND ALL THEIR YELLOW CANVAS WEAR, ...   530 OLD TOM AGAIN   V   2
    SO LET US DANCE WHERE THE YELLOW LANCE . . . . .   643 SONG FAERIES   7
    THE PANTHER WITH HER YELLOW HIDE, ...   658 ISLE STAT I 3   83
    SO LET US DANCE WHERE THE YELLOW LANCE . . . . .   676 ISLE STAT II 3   254
    LIE STREWN THE YELLOW LEAVES--THE CLOTTED LEAVES. . . .   684 SEEKER   69
    WHERE LIES A SHALLOP IN THE YELLOW REEDS. . . .   702 MOSADA 3   77
    AND HIS HAIR WAS AS YELLOW AS WAVING WHEAT. . .   729 PRIEST FAIRY   26
    BRUSHING BACK HIS YELLOW HAIR! . . . .   729 PRIEST FAIRY   38
    WHO SAID WE HAD A SKIN OF YELLOW ALE? . . . . .   759 SHADOW WATER A   243
    (O THE BROWN AND THE YELLOW BEER!) . . . . . .   779 GOING THE ROAD   2
    (O THE BROWN AND THE YELLOW BEER!) . . . . . .   779 GOING THE ROAD   6
    (O THE BROWN AND THE YELLOW BEER!) . . . . . .   779 GOING THE ROAD   10
YELLOW-EYED
    YELLOW-EYED HAWK OF THE MIND, ...   349 HAWK   14
YELPING
    HIDING AWAY THE OCEAN'S YELPING FLOCKS. . . . .   688 TWO TITANS   38
YES
    FASTING AND PRAYERS. TELL ON. YES, YES, . . .   24 OISIN 1   360
    FASTING AND PRAYERS. TELL ON. YES, YES, . . .   24 OISIN 1   360
    NO MORTAL CAN. YES! IF THEY GIVE US HELP. . . .   229 SHADOW WATER B   165
    YES, VOICES! BUT I DO NOT CATCH THE WORDS. . . .   233 SHADOW WATER B   251
    YES, ALL IS VERY WELL. WHENCE COMEST THOU? . .   682 SEEKER   14
YESTERDAY
    ONE THAT IS EVER KIND SAID YESTERDAY! . . . . .   199 FOLLY COMFORT   1
    THAT IT WAS YESTERDAY AND NOT TO-DAY. . . . . .   246 SHADOW WATER B   493
    AND YESTERDAY THE YOUNGEST SON, ...   361 ALF POLLEXFEN   24
    YESTERDAY IN THE TENTH YEAR . . . .   361 ALF POLLEXFEN   27

YESTERDAY   (CONTINUED)
     HER EIGHTIETH WINTER APPROACHING: "YESTERDAY HE THREATENED   578 LOFTY THINGS   8
       MY LIFE.
     OUR LOVE SHALL BE OF YESTERDAY, ...   686 LIFE   14
     I SWORE BUT YESTERDAY IF THE RED GOD . . . .   751 SHADOW WATER A   109
YESTERNIGHT
     BUT YESTERNIGHT DECLARE . . . .   492 ANNE GREGORY   14
YET
     YET WILL I MAKE ALL PLAIN FOR THEE.   . . . .   2 OISIN 1   V   7B
     AND YET, OF YORE, MUCH PEACE HE HAD . . . .   2 OISIN 1   V   7K
     AND YET, OF YORE, MUCH PEACE HE HAD, ...   4 OISIN 1   V   36
     "I HAVE NOT YET, WAR-WEARY KING, ...   6 OISIN 1   55
     YET NOW I CHOOSE, FOR THESE FOUR FEET . . . . . .   6 OISIN 1   57
     YET LOVE AND KISS ON DIM SHORES FAR AWAY . . . . .   29 OISIN 2   13
     YET SANG NO MORE AS WHEN, LIKE A BROWN BEE . . . .   30 OISIN 2   15
     OR HOURS PASSED BY, YET HOLD THE MORNING RAYS . . .   30 OISIN 2   20
     YET DIMLY DEEM I THAT THE MORNING RAYS . . . . . .   30 OISIN 2   V   20
     JABBER AND SCREAM. YET HE, FOR ALL HIS BOLD . . .   34 OISIN 2   V   82
     YET DO WITH US WHATE'ER THOU WILT, ...   43 OISIN 2   V 208G
     YET WEARY WITH PASSIONS THAT FADED . . . .   50 OISIN 3   52
     YET STILL SHE TURNS HER RESTLESS HEAD! . . . . . .   65 HAPPY SHEPHERD   5
     "THOUGH OUR SAD LOVE IS FADING, LET US YET . . . .   79 EPHEMERA   V   4
     A GENTLE YET A KINGLY CHILD! . . . .   82 MAD KING GOLL V   8
     "YET SOMEWHERE UNDER STARLIGHT OR THE SUN . . . . 107 CUCHULAIN SEA   28
     YET SHE GOES WITH FOOTSTEP WARY. . . . . 124 CATHLEEN PARA   11
     AND YET THE SADDEST CHIMES ARE BEST ENJOYED. . . . 130 BOOK STORIES   20
     AND YET THE BEAUTIES THAT I LOVED . . . . 131 OLD PENSIONER   15
     YET HE WHO TREADS IN MEASURED WAYS . . . . 138 TO IRELAND   27
     YET HE WHO TREADS IN AUSTERE WAYS . . . . 138 TO IRELAND   V   27
     AND YET HAD BEEN GREAT-BODIED AND GREAT-LIMBED, . 181 QUEEN MAEVE   25
     MAEVE WALKED, YET WITH SLOW FOOTFALL, BEING OLD, . 181 QUEEN MAEVE   43
     AND YET HAD BEEN GREAT BODIED AND GREAT LIMBED, .   181 QUEEN MAEVE   V   25
     AND THE BROWN BULL HAD NOT YET COME . . . . 189 BAILE AILLINN   15
     YET THEY THAT KNOW ALL THINGS BUT KNOW . . . . . . 190 BAILE AILLINN   38
     THOSE OTHER TWO: FOR NEVER YET . . . . 197 BAILE AILLINN   205
     THIS BEAUTY'S KINDER, YET FOR A REASON . . . . . . 199 ARROW   7
     YET IF IT DOES NOT SEEM A MOMENT'S THOUGHT, ... 204 ADAMS CURSE   5
     IS TO WORK HARDER THAN ALL THESE, AND YET . . . . 205 ADAMS CURSE   11
     YET NOW IT SEEMS AN IDLE TRADE ENOUGH." . . . . . . 205 ADAMS CURSE   27
     THAT IT HAD ALL SEEMED HAPPY, AND YET WE'D GROWN . 206 ADAMS CURSE   37
     YET DREAMED THAT BEINGS HAPPIER THAN MEN . . . . . 218 WOODS OF COOLE   18
     THESE MANY DAYS: AND YET THERE MUST BE MANY . . . 226 SHADOW WATER B   89
     THAT IS NOT IN THE WORLD. AND YET THE WORLD . . . 228 SHADOW WATER B   143
     YET NEVER HAVE TWO LOVERS KISSED BUT THEY . . . . 229 SHADOW WATER B   153
     AND YET I CANNOT THINK THEY'RE LEADING ME . . . . 230 SHADOW WATER B   191
     AND OVERPOWER THE CREW WHILE YET ASLEEP! . . . . . 233 SHADOW WATER B   240
     BUT HAVE NOT BITTEN YET. I AM A QUEEN, ... 235 SHADOW WATER B   280
     HAD DROWNED ME ALSO. BUT, BEING YET ALIVE, ... 235 SHADOW WATER B   289
     BRING MADNESS? QUEEN, I AM NOT MAD. YET SAY . . . 236 SHADOW WATER B   316
     AND YET YOU SAY THE WATER AND THE WIND . . . . . . 236 SHADOW WATER B V 317
     AND YET YOU TALK OF LOVE. THE MOVEMENT OF TIME . . 237 SHADOW WATER B   338
     AND HAS NOT YET BEEN WAKED. OHONE! O! O! O! . . . . 241 SHADOW WATER B   393
     AND YET YOU MAKE A CLAMOUR OF REPROACH. . . . . . . 243 SHADOW WATER B   444
     YET OLD ROMANCE BEING KIND, LET HIM PREVAIL . . . 258 KING NO KING   5
     YET SHE, SINGING UPON HER ROAD, ... 260 UNWORTH PRAISE   19
     AND YET NOT COLD." . . . . 263 MASK   5
     YET WOULD BE NOW, COULD I BUT HAVE MY WISH, ... 267 ALL TEMPT ME   9
     AND THEREFORE EARNED THE RIGHT--AND YET . . . . . . 273 GREY ROCK   61
     AND YET COULD GIVE SO FINE A STROKE?" . . . . 274 GREY ROCK   84
     I'D SAVED HIS LIFE, YET FOR THE SAKE . . . . 275 GREY ROCK   102
     I'D SAVE HIS LIFE, YET FOR THE SAKE . . . . 275 GREY ROCK   V   102
     YET ANSWERED HIM, "I AM KING EOCHAID'S WIFE . . . 284 TWO KINGS   173
     YET THEY WERE OF A DIFFERENT KIND, ... 289 SEPTEMBER 1913   9
     YET COULD WE TURN THE YEARS AGAIN, ... 290 SEPTEMBER 1913   25
     FOR THEY ARE AT THEIR OLD TRICKS YET. A MAN . . . 292 TO A SHADE   9
     YET WE, HAD WE WALKED WITHIN . . . . 293 HELEN LIVED   7
     "MAYBE I SHALL BE LUCKY YET," . . . . 297 THREE BEGGARS   61
     YET NEVER HAVE I LIT ON A FRIEND . . . . 301 RUN PARADISE   25
     AND YET STOOD STILL, BECAUSE INSIDE . . . . 303 HOUR DAWN   26
     BRING ROSES IF THE ROSE BE YET IN BLOOM: . . . . . 311 MOUNTAIN TOMB   2
     THE FOOL'S TRIUMPH, NOR YET . . . . 312 CHILD DANCING   7
     AND YET FOR ALL THAT I COULD SAY, ... 313 MEMORY YOUTH   4
     YET WE, FOR ALL THAT PRAISE, COULD FIND . . . . . 314 MEMORY YOUTH   13
     AND YET HIS MIND OUTRAN THE HORSES' FEET. . . . . . 326 ROBERT GREGORY   64
     AND YET HE HAD THE INTENSITY . . . . 327 ROBERT GREGORY   71
     AND YET, AND YET, ... 329 MEN IMPROVE   12
     AND YET, AND YET, ... 329 MEN IMPROVE   12
     YET PRAISE THE WINTERS GONE! . . . . 336 YOUNG BEAUTY   15
     YET DID BUT LOOK, ROCKING THE GLITTERING COACH . . 344 DAWN   V   11
     YET NEVER COULD, ALTHOUGH . . . . 345 ON WOMAN   13
     YET NEVER HAVE I, NOW NOR ANY TIME, ... 352 PEOPLE   28
     AND YET, BECAUSE MY HEART LEAPED AT HER WORDS, . . . 353 PEOPLE   35
     I MOURN FOR THAT MOST LONELY THING: AND YET GOD'S WILL   354 HIS PHOENIX   31
      BE DONE!
     AND YET YOUR BODY HAD A FLAW! . . . . 356 BROKEN DREAMS   28
     AND YET YOUR BEAUTY HAD A FLAW! . . . . 356 BROKEN DREAMS V   28
     YET ALWAYS WHEN I LOOK DEATH IN THE FACE, ... 357 DEEP-SWORN VOW   3
     RETURNED AND YET UNREQUITED LOVE. . . . . 358 PRESENCES   8
     LACKING THE COUNTENANCE OF OUR FRIENDS. AND YET . 368 EGO DOMINUS   17
     YET SURELY THERE ARE MEN WHO HAVE MADE THEIR ART . . . 369 EGO DOMINUS   38
     BUT DISSIPATION AND DESPAIR? AND YET . . . . . . 369 EGO DOMINUS   51

YET   (CONTINUED)

		PAGE	TITLE		LINE
I CALL TO THE MYSTERIOUS ONE WHO YET		371	EGO DOMINUS		70
WE TAKE IT FOR THE NORM; YET SHOULD I DREAM		371	ON GOING HOUSE		9
TWENTY-AND-EIGHT, AND YET BUT SIX-AND-TWENTY		373	PHASES OF MOON		33
AND YET, TWICE BORN, TWICE BURIED, GROW HE MUST,		374	PHASES OF MOON		48
AND YET THEY SPEAK WHAT'S BLOWN INTO THE MIND;		376	PHASES OF MOON		110
BUT THE ESCAPE; THE SONG'S NOT FINISHED YET.		377	PHASES OF MOON		117
DAY AFTER DAY, YET NEVER FIND THE MEANING.		377	PHASES OF MOON		135
YET LITTLE PEACE HE HAD,		383	VISION ROBART		35
MIND MOVED YET SEEMED TO STOP		384	VISION ROBART		43
WERE DEAD YET FLESH AND BONE.		384	VISION ROBART		48
AND YET IN FLYING FLING INTO MY MEAT		384	VISION ROBART		53
YET BE BUT SINEW. I HAVE HEARD SAID		386	ROBARTES DANCE		37
YET THE WORLD ENDS WHEN THESE TWO THINGS,		388	SOLOMON WITCH		28
"YET THE WORLD STAYS." "IF THAT BE SO,		388	SOLOMON WITCH		33
YET I NUMBER HIM IN THE SONG;		393	EASTER 1916		35
YET I AM CERTAIN AS CAN BE		401	DEMON BEAST		33
THAT NEVER YET HAD FREEMAN		401	DEMON BEAST		36
YET HAVE NO DEARER THOUGHT		401	DEMON BEAST		40
MAY SHE BE GRANTED BEAUTY AND YET NOT		403	FOR DAUGHTER		17
YET CHOSE A BANDY-LEGGED SMITH FOR MAN.		404	FOR DAUGHTER		29
YET MANY, THAT HAVE PLAYED THE FOOL		404	FOR DAUGHTER		36
YET KNOWS THAT TO BE CHOKED WITH HATE		405	FOR DAUGHTER		52
YET, NOW I HAVE CONSIDERED IT, I FIND		411	TOWER		50
MERE DREAMS, MERE DREAMS! YET HOMER HAD NOT SUNG		417	ANCEST HOUSES		9
YET IF NO CHANGE APPEARS		421	MY TABLE		12
AS VIGOROUS OF MIND, AND YET IT SEEMS		422	MY DESCENDANTS		4
YET NO CLEAR FACT TO BE DISCERNED;		425	STARES NEST		9
AND YET IT LACK ALL GLORY; AND PERCHANCE		429	NINETEEN 19		23
DRIVE TO A FLASHIER BAUBLE YET.		437	SONGS PLAY 1		12
AND THAT ALONE; YET I, BEING DRIVEN HALF INSANE		442	BLACK CENTAUR		6
AND YET THEY TOO BREAK HEARTS—O PRESENCES		445	SCHOOL CHILDR		53
SHOULD FIND NO BURDEN BUT ITSELF AND YET SHOULD BE WORN OUT.		449	OWEN AHERNE		3
AND YET THERE BEAUTY LAY;		455	HIS MEMORIES		12
WHEN EVENING STIRS THE JASMINE BOUGH, AND YET		463	HARUN RASHID		53
WHEN EVENING STIRS THE JASMINE, AND YET		463	HARUN RASHID	V	53
"AND YET THE JASMINE SEASON WARMS OUR BLOOD."		464	HARUN RASHID		73
AND YET HERSELF CAN SEEM YOUTH'S VERY FOUNTAIN,		465	HARUN RASHID		89
YET WAS IT LOVE OF ME, OR WAS IT LOVE		466	HARUN RASHID		112
IT SEEMS ENOUGH THAT I AM THERE; AND YET,		468	HARUN RASHID		166
AND THERE, FREE AND YET FAST,		472	ALL SOUL NIGHT		57
AND YET AGAIN, IF IT BE LIFE TO PITCH		479	SELF AND SOUL		58
AND YET A WOMAN'S POWERFUL CHARACTER		489	COOLE PARK 29		18
AND YET UPON MY BREAST		496	MOHINI CHATTER		10
"OLD LOVERS YET MAY HAVE		496	MOHINI CHATTER		17
OLD LOVERS YET SHALL HAVE		496	MOHINI CHATTER	V	17
THOSE IMAGES THAT YET		498	BYZANTIUM		38
AND HALF IS HALF AND YET IS ALL THE SCENE;		500	VACILLATION		14
AND YET UPON THESE MAXIMS MEDITATE;		500	VACILLATION		22
YET HE, AN OLD BOOK IN HIS FIST;		508	JANE BISHOP		12
"THE THIRD THING THAT I THINK OF YET,"		521	THREE THINGS		13
THAT WE DESCANT AND YET AGAIN DESCANT		523	LONG SILENCE		5
I LONG FOR TRUTH, AND YET		533	FIRST CONFESS		7
AND YET I WEEP—OEDIPUS' CHILD		540	FROM ANTIGONE		15
YET I AM SHRUNKEN TO SKIN AND BONE		550	SONGS REWRIT 1	V	2
YET AM I SHRUNKEN TO SKIN AND BONE,		550	SONGS REWRIT 1	V	2
YET ALL MUST COPY COPIES, ALL INCREASE THEIR KIND;		556	RIBH PATRICK		7
YET THEY, SHOULD THE LAST SCENE BE THERE,		565	LAPIS LAZULI		12
YET WHAT COULD I BUT DROP DOWN DEAD		569	THREE BUSHES		19
YET KEEP HIS SUBSTANCE WHOLE.		573	LADYS 2ND SONG		13
AS THOUGH TO DRAW THEM CLOSER YET. RAMMED FULL		579	DOR WELLESLEY		5
POETRY, MUSIC, I HAVE LOVED, AND YET		599	SPIRIT MEDIUM		1
AND YET WHO KNOWS WHAT'S YET TO COME?		608	SONGS BURDEN 3		23
AND YET WHO KNOWS WHAT'S YET TO COME?		608	SONGS BURDEN 3		23
NO, NO, MY SON, NOT YET;		614	MARCH SONGS 2		8
NO, NO, MY SON, NOT YET;		615	MARCH SONGS 2		18
NO, NO, MY SON, NOT YET;		615	MARCH SONGS 2		28
YET A MOST GENTLE WOMAN; WHO CAN TELL		618	BRONZE HEAD		10
AND YET GAVE TONGUE. "HOUND VOICES" WERE THEY ALL.		622	HOUND VOICE		9
HEART-MYSTERIES THERE, AND YET WHEN ALL IS SAID		630	CIRCUS ANIMALS		27
HEART MYSTERIES THERE, AND YET WHEN ALL IS SAID		630	CIRCUS ANIMALS	V	27
YET HERE'S A TRAVELLED MAN THAT KNOWS		631	POLITICS		5
WHEN SLEEPERS WAKE AND YET STILL DREAM,		639	BEN BULBEN		59
TO WATCH THEE PASS? YET DEEPER THAN MEN KNOW		672	ISLE STAT II 3		158
YET EVER MORE, THROUGH ALL THY DAYS OF RUTH,		674	ISLE STAT II 3		206
IT IS, YET SHALL IT FAIL THEE DAY AND NIGHT		674	ISLE STAT II 3		211
YET EVERMORE, THROUGH ALL THY DAYS OF RUTH,		674	ISLE STAT II 3	V	206
A PEERING HARE'S!" AND YET I MURMURED NOT,		684	SEEKER		56
THOU WILT NOT SPEAK, OH CRUEL ART THOU YET!		684	SEEKER	V	69A
FROM WASTE SEAS CROSS'D, YET EVER GARRULOUS)		690	MOSADA 1		9
YET SOMEWHERE IN THE FOOTSORE WORLD WE MEET,		691	MOSADA 1		23
YET 'TIS NO SIN; MY FATHER TAUGHT IT ME.		692	MOSADA 1		50
WITH WONDERFUL WHITE SANDS, WHERE NEVER YET		693	MOSADA 1		81
WITH WONDERFUL WHITE SAND, WHERE NEVER YET		693	MOSADA 1	V	81
AND DYING MEN—AND YET—BUT NO, FAREWELL.		698	MOSADA 2		49
YET WHITER BEARD HAVE YOU THAN MERLIN HAD.		721	WITCH VIVIEN		30
SORROW-WORN, YET PLACID-BROWED.		733	STREET DANCERS		56
SORROW-WORN, YET PLACID BROWED.		733	STREET DANCERS	V	56
YET ONE JOY HAVE I; HID CLOSE,		744	ROSY CROSS		8
BE PATIENT YET A WHILE; FOR THIS NINTH MOON,		748	SHADOW WATER A		23

926

	PAGE	TITLE	LINE
YET (CONTINUED)			
BE PATIENT YET AWHILE: FOR THIS NINTH MOON,	748	SHADOW WATER A V	23
AND YET, THERE IS A LOVE THAT THE GODS GIVE,	749	SHADOW WATER A V	56
YET OUR SILENCE HAD BEEN WISE:	773	SONG DEIRDRE 1 V	22
YET ALL THE LOVELY THINGS THAT WERE	788	HAWTHORN TREE	11
YET RISE FROM YOUR ITALIAN TOMB,	791	REPRISALS	10
MEN THAT REVERE YOUR FATHER YET	791	REPRISALS	17
YEW			
A CYPRESS AND A YEW.	123	DREAM OF DEATH V	6
MADE OF THE APPLE AND THE YEW,	197	BAILE AILLINN	196
A YEW TREE WHERE HIS BODY LAY,	197	BAILE AILLINN V	188
THE YEW BOUGH HAS BEEN BROKEN INTO TWO,	241	SHADOW WATER B V	394
THE YEW BOUGH HAS BEEN BROKEN INTO TWO,	251	SHADOW WATER B V	593
THE YEW BOUGH HAS BEEN BROKEN IN TWO,	251	SHADOW WATER B V	593
THE POSTS OF POLISHED YEW, CIRCLED WITH BRONZE,	279	TWO KINGS	48
WHAT JUNCTURE OF THE APPLE AND THE YEW,	555	RIBH AT TOMB	8
THE TREMBLING OF THE APPLE AND THE YEW,	555	RIBH AT TOMB	18
THAT DRUIDS WRITE ON YEW AND APPLE WOOD,	748	SHADOW WATER A	29
UPON THIN BOARDS OF YEW AND APPLE WOOD,	764	SHADOW WATER A	343
UPON THIN BOARDS OF YEW AND APPLE-WOOD,	764	SHADOW WATER A V	343
PRAISE THE REDNESS OF THE YEW:	773	SONG DEIRDRE 1	20
YEW-BOUGH			
THE YEW-BOUGH HAS BEEN BROKEN INTO TWO,	241	SHADOW WATER B	394
THE YEW-BOUGH HAS BEEN BROKEN INTO TWO,	251	SHADOW WATER B	593
YEW-TREE			
A YEW-TREE WHERE HIS BODY LAY:	197	BAILE AILLINN	188
YOLK			
INTO THE YOLK AND WHITE OF THE ONE SHELL.	443	SCHOOL CHILDR	16
YON			
AMRITA. DRAW YOU NEAR, AND 'NEATH YON PILLAR	71	ANASHU VIJAYA V	13A
YON TALL ONE EYES MY SUPPER: CHASE HIM AWAY,	72	ANASHU VIJAYA	34
YON TALL ONE EYES MY SUPPER: SWIFTLY CHASE HIM	72	ANASHU VIJAYA V	34
WITH FIERY SONG I'LL DROWN YON PUNY VOICE.	648	ISLE STAT I 1	81
BUT YONDER THING, YON IDLE NOISE, YON CROW,	648	ISLE STAT I 1	104
BUT YONDER THING, YON IDLE NOISE, YON CROW,	648	ISLE STAT I 1	104
YON SHEPHERD--CAME YOUR SPIRIT TO BEGUILE	648	ISLE STAT I 1	105
YON WIND GOES SADLY, AND THE GRASS AND TREES	652	ISLE STAT I 2	10
YON EAGER LARK, THAT FILLS WITH SONG THE WHOLE	652	ISLE STAT I 2	18
DOTH NOT YON BIRD, YON QUIVERING BIRD, REJOICE?	652	ISLE STAT I 2	21
DOTH NOT YON BIRD, YON QUIVERING BIRD, REJOICE?	652	ISLE STAT I 2	21
CAN ENTER THERE. SEE: SEE: ABOVE YON BROW	659	ISLE STAT II 1	27
YON IS THE HUNTER'S, SIR ALMINTOR'S, PAGE:	660	ISLE STAT II 1	35
OF BEAMS A-FLICKER ON YON LONELY FIR,	661	ISLE STAT II 1	72
MY SINKING BRAIN!--CEASE!--CEASE! HEARD YE YON SOUND?	665	ISLE STAT II 2	73
MORE DARK BENEATH THE POPLARS, WHERE YON OWL	675	ISLE STAT II 3	233
YON ARCHER, HE WHO HATH THE HALCYON'S WING	679	ISLE STAT II 3	316
MAKE MOAN AND CRY. WITHIN YON SUNLESS VALLEY,	682	SEEKER	26
HIS BODY SHAKE? AY, QUIVERING AS YON SMOKE	683	SEEKER	36
AMONG THE FRUIT. BUT YON, LAME COLA CROUCHES	691	MOSADA 1 V	32
AND YON FEW STARS GROWN DIM, LIKE EYES OF LOVERS	700	MOSADA 3	33
FLOATING FROM YON BARRED WINDOW. SMALL NEW-COMER,	700	MOSADA 3	43
FLOATING FROM YON BARRED WINDOW. NEW COMER,	700	MOSADA 3 V	43
YON BAUBLE OF THE HEAVENS, HE LIFTS HIS HANDS,	715	FERENCZ RENYI	119
HUGS AND PETS AND PATS YON NEWT,	727	LOVERS QUARREL	27
AND SAID, "YON BITTERN CRIES, IN TRUTH.	731	PRIEST FAIRY	75
YONDER			
OUT YONDER, WHERE THE RACE COURSE IS,	266	GALWAY RACES V	1
AND YONDER IN THE GYMNASTS' GARDEN THRIVES,	446	COLONUS PRAISE	9
BUT YONDER THING, YON IDLE NOISE, YON CROW,	648	ISLE STAT I 1	104
SING SUMMER WAVES. BUT YONDER SHEPHERD VILE,	649	ISLE STAT I 1	107
UPON HIS WINGS. THRO' YONDER GREEN ABYSS	649	ISLE STAT I 1	114
THE WAVES IN YONDER LAKE WHERE POINTS MY HAND	652	ISLE STAT I 2	13
NAY, NAY, ALMINTOR, YONDER SONG IS GLAD.	652	ISLE STAT I 2	23
OF YONDER LAKE, FROM WHOSE GREEN BANKS ALWAY	653	ISLE STAT I 2	33
SEE, YONDER SINKS THE SUN, YONDER A SHADE	653	ISLE STAT I 2	52
SEE, YONDER SINKS THE SUN, YONDER A SHADE	653	ISLE STAT I 2	52
THERE WHERE YONDER SQUIRREL CRUNCHES	655	ISLE STAT I 3	4
FROM YONDER PINNACLE ABOVE THE LAKE	657	ISLE STAT I 3	63
AND YONDER HUDDLING BLACKNESS DRAWETH NIGH--	663	ISLE STAT II 2	15
AND PENETRATION OF THEIR EYES. WHERE YONDER BLOTCH	664	ISLE STAT II 2	47
TO YONDER ISLE, WHERE NEVER SAIL WAS FURLED,	664	ISLE STAT II 2	56
OF HIM ON YONDER BRAZEN-GATED SPOT.	675	ISLE STAT II 3	240
WITH PATIENT BEAUTY YONDER ATTIC BUST	685	DRAWING-ROOM	3
THE SQUIRREL YONDER, HUSHED AND WISE,	686	LIFE	5
YONDER THE SICKLE OF THE MOON SAILS ON,	688	NETTLESHIP	1
SINKS DOWN AT LAST WITH YONDER MINARET,	691	MOSADA 1 V	36
THAT YOU SHALL SEE ON YONDER GLOWING CLOUD	692	MOSADA 1 V	43
YONDER HE COMES: BRIGHT-EYED, AND HOLLOW-CHEEKED	697	MOSADA 2	35
MY THOUGHTS, AND YONDER BRIGHTENING PATCH OF SKY	700	MOSADA 3	31
YONDER A LEAF	700	MOSADA 3	41
UPON THE MOUNTAIN'S BROW. YONDER HE TREADS	703	MOSADA 3	114
HIDING THE REBELS WORM IN YONDER WOOD	709	FERENCZ RENYI	14
HIDING THE REBELS SWARM IN YONDER WOOD	709	FERENCZ RENYI V	14
HIDING THE REBEL WORMS IN YONDER WOOD	709	FERENCZ RENYI V	14
OR YONDER MOUNTAINS. WHERE? THOU SHALT BE FREE--	710	FERENCZ RENYI	15
OR YONDER MOUNTAIN. WHERE? THOU SHALT BE FREE--	710	FERENCZ RENYI V	15
AND LOST AND FAR IN YONDER HILLS I KNOW:	713	FERENCZ RENYI	98
BESIDE THE WILLOW. NAY, TO YONDER STAR,	715	FERENCZ RENYI	118
BENEATH THE WILLOW--NAY, TO YONDER STAR,	715	FERENCZ RENYI V	118
MY IMAGE YONDER? AH, MY BEAUTIFUL,	720	WITCH VIVIEN	4
ERE YONDER PALM COMMENCED HIS THOUSAND YEARS?	724	KANVA ON SELF	14

		PAGE	TITLE		LINE
YONDER	(CONTINUED)				
	YONDER SEE THE FAIRY GIRLS • • • • • •	726	LOVERS QUARREL		21
	YONDER FOOLISH ONES WILL TIRE • • • • • • •	727	LOVERS QUARREL		47
	WITH PATIENT BEAUTY YONDER ATTIC BUST • • • • • •	735	QUATRAIN APHOR		23
YONDER'S					
	YONDER'S THE ISLE IN SEARCH WHEREOF WE CAME: • • • • •	662	ISLE STAT II 2		13
YORE					
	AND YET, OF YORE, MUCH PEACE HE HAD • • • • • • • •	2	OISIN 1	V	7K
	AND YET, OF YORE, MUCH PEACE HE HAD, • • • • • • • •	4	OISIN 1	V	36
	LOVE FROM HEAVEN CAME OF YORE. • • • • • • • •	648	ISLE STAT I 1		77
	OF WAR. OF YORE, TWO SHEPHERDS, WHERE WE PAUSE, • • • •	659	ISLE STAT II 1		31
	SHE WAS A GREAT ENCHANTRESS ONCE OF YORE, • • • • • • •	693	MOSADA 1		78
	WANDERING OF YORE IN FORESTS RUMOROUS, • • • • • • •	723	KANVA ON SELF		3
	HAST THOU NOT SAT OF YORE UPON THE KNEES • • • • •	724	KANVA ON SELF		9
YOUNG					
	OF THE YOUNG. "YOUNG MAIDEN, WHAT MAY BRING • • • • •	5	OISIN 1	V	50
	OF THE YOUNG. "YOUNG MAIDEN, WHAT MAY BRING • • • • •	5	OISIN 1		50
	YOUNG PRINCESS, WHY WERT THOU BEGUILED • • • • • • •	6	OISIN 1	V	59
	YOUNG PRINCESS, WHEN WERE YOU BEGUILED • • • • • •	6	OISIN 1		59
	OF OISIN, THE YOUNG MAN, MY SON? • • • • • • •	6	OISIN 1	V	60
	BY THIS YOUNG MAN, USHEEN MY SON?" • • • • • • • •	6	OISIN 1		60
	PRINCESS, BY THIS YOUNG MAN, MY SON?" • • • • • • •	6	OISIN 1	V	61
	ON THIS YOUNG MAN, OISIN, MY SON?" • • • • • • •	6	OISIN 1		61
	YOUNG NIAM, AND THOU SHALT BE CALLEN • • • • • •	7	OISIN 1	V	75
	AND A HUNDRED MAIDENS WISE AND YOUNG, • • • • • • •	8	OISIN 1	V	94
	AND A BEAUTIFUL YOUNG MAN FOLLOWED BEHIND • • • • • •	12	OISIN 1		144
	A BEAUTIFUL YOUNG MAN FOLLOWED BEHIND. • • • • • • •	12	OISIN 1	V	145
	A BEAUTIFUL YOUNG MAN DREAMED WITHIN • • • • • • •	17	OISIN 1		248
	AND STIRS THE YOUNG KID'S BUDDING HORN, • • • • • •	18	OISIN 1		264
	THERE WAS A WONDROUS YOUNG MAN SITTING, • • • • • •	18	OISIN 1	V	252
	WITH A CLEAR VOICE THE YOUNG MAN CRIED, • • • • • •	18	OISIN 1	V	260
	THEREON YOUNG NIAMH SOFTLY CAME • • • • • • • •	25	OISIN 1		373
	BUT FAINTER THAN A YOUNG LAMB'S BLEAT. • • • • • •	26	OISIN 1		399
	AND FAINTER THAN A YOUNG LAMB'S BLEAT. • • • • • • •	26	OISIN 1	V	399
	STROKED THE YOUNG WINDS AS THEY ROLLED ON THE PLAIN, • •	27	OISIN 1	V	415C
	SO SANG YOUNG NIAM, SWAYING HER BRIGHT HEAD, • • • • •	30	OISIN 2	V	15
	A—MURMUR LIKE YOUNG PARTRIDGE: WITH LOUD HORN • • • •	32	OISIN 2		52
	FROM HIGH ABOVE, LIKE FEATHERS OF YOUNG BIRDS • • • •	32	OISIN 2	V	50
	"THEY MURMUR LIKE YOUNG PARTRIDGE IN THE MORN, • • • •	32	OISIN 2	V	51
	YOUNG WARRIOR." "NAY," I ANSWERED: "MY HANDS BURN • • •	35	OISIN 2	V	89B
	WE SAW, SOME NEW, SOME PRINTED WHEN THE PLACE WAS YOUNG, • •	37	OISIN 2	V	116
	OUTCRY OF BATS. AND THEN YOUNG NIAMH CAME • • • • •	44	OISIN 2		229
	THE HARE LEAPED IN THE GRASS. YOUNG NIAMH CAME • • • •	44	OISIN 2	V	229
	• • • WHEN THE SEVENFOLD SEAS WERE YOUNG. • • • • • •	50	OISIN 3		52
	• • • WHEN THE SEVEN—FOLD SEAS WERE YOUNG: • • • • • •	50	OISIN 3	V	52
	• • • AND MOVE WHERE THE OLD MEN AND YOUNG • • • • •	55	OISIN 3		114
	• • • AND MARCH ON AS OXEN MOVE OVER YOUNG GRASS: • • • •	62	OISIN 3		211
	WHO STILL WERE OLD WHEN THE GREAT SEA WAS YOUNG: • • • •	74	ANASHU VIJAYA		69
	THE FLIES BELOW THE LEAVES, AND THE YOUNG MICE • • • •	75	ANASHU VIJAYA		87
	AND SLEEK YOUNG JOY IS NO MORE FICKLE. • • • • • • •	77	INDIAN TO LOVE	V	5C
	I WAS A WISE YOUNG KING OF OLD: • • • • • • •	81	MAD KING GOLL	V	1
	"THIS YOUNG MAN BRINGS THE AGE OF GOLD." • • • • •	82	MAD KING GOLL	V	11
	AND YOUNG HARES BROOK MY HARMLESS HOLD—— • • • • • •	84	MAD KING GOLL	V	47
	OVER THE YOUNG STREAMS. • • • • • • • • •	88	STOLEN CHILD		37
	OF DEW ON THE YOUNG STREAMS. • • • • • • • • •	88	STOLEN CHILD	V	37
	BUT I, BEING YOUNG AND FOOLISH, WITH HER WOULD NOT AGREE. • •	90	SALLEY GARDENS		4
	BUT I WAS YOUNG AND FOOLISH, AND NOW AM FULL OF TEARS. • •	90	SALLEY GARDENS		8
	THE YOUNG BIRDS AND OLD BIRDS • • • • • • • •	93	FATHER OHART		33
	FOR LEADING AGED HOUNDS AND YOUNG • • • • • • •	98	FOXHUNTER		23
	AND NOW WITH AGED HOUNDS AND YOUNG • • • • • •	98	FOXHUNTER	V	21
	AGED HOUNDS AND YOUNG. • • • • • • • • • •	99	FOXHUNTER		40
	THE OLD HOUNDS AND THE YOUNG. • • • • • • • •	99	FOXHUNTER	V	40
	BOTH AGED HOUNDS AND YOUNG. • • • • • • • •	99	FOXHUNTER	V	40
	YOUNG SUBTLE CONCHUBAR SAT CLOSE BY ME • • • • • •	102	FERGUS DRUID		10
	AND HIS YOUNG SWEETHEART CLOSE BESIDE HIM KNELT, • • •	108	CUCHULAIN SEA		40
	AND HIS YOUNG DEAR ONE CLOSE BESIDE HIM KNELT, • • •	108	CUCHULAIN SEA	V	40
	HE SPAKE TO THE YOUNG MAN, "IS THERE NO MAID • • •	109	CUCHULAIN SEA		58
	AT LAST CUCHULAIN SPAKE: "A YOUNG MAN STRAYS • • •	109	CUCHULAIN SEA	V	47
	WHILE YOUNG STARS ABOUT HER DANCE. • • • • • • •	125	CATHLEEN PARA	V	16
	YOUNG MAN, LIFT UP YOUR RUSSET BROW, • • • • • • •	125	GOES FERGUS		4
	AND HE SAW YOUNG MEN AND YOUNG GIRLS • • • • • •	144	HOST OF AIR		13
	AND HE SAW YOUNG MEN AND YOUNG GIRLS • • • • • •	144	HOST OF AIR	V	13
	AND A YOUNG MAN BROUGHT HIM RED WINE • • • • • •	144	HOST OF AIR		19
	AND A YOUNG GIRL WHITE BREAD. • • • • • • • •	144	HOST OF AIR		20
	THE HANDSOMEST YOUNG MAN THERE, • • • • • • • •	145	HOST OF AIR		34
	OLD MEN AND YOUNG MEN AND YOUNG GIRLS • • • • • •	145	HOST OF AIR		39
	OLD MEN AND YOUNG MEN AND YOUNG GIRLS • • • • • •	145	HOST OF AIR	V	39
	YOUR MOTHER EIRE IS ALWAYS YOUNG, • • • • • • •	148	INTO TWILIGHT		5
	THY MOTHER ERI IS ALWAYS YOUNG, • • • • • • •	148	INTO TWILIGHT	V	5
	AND THE YOUNG LIE LONG AND DREAM IN THEIR BED • • •	150	OLD MOTHER		5
	WHILE THE YOUNG LIE LONG AND DREAM IN THEIR BED • • • •	150	OLD MOTHER	V	5
	BUT THE YOUNG LIE LONG AND DREAM IN THEIR BED • • • •	150	OLD MOTHER	V	5
	BUT THE YOUNG QUEEN WOULD NOT LISTEN: • • • • • •	159	CAP AND BELLS		9
	THAT SAW YOUNG NIAMH HOVER WITH LOVE—LORN FACE • • •	162	ASKS FORGIVE		13
	I CRIED IN MY DREAM, O WOMEN, BID THE YOUNG MEN LAY • •	163	VALLEY LOVERS		5
	AND I CRIED IN MY DREAM "O WOMEN, BID THE YOUNG MEN LAY	163	VALLEY LOVERS	V	5
	WOMEN AND CHILDREN, YOUNG MEN WITH BOOKS, • • • • •	167	BLESSED		15
	CHILDREN AND WOMEN AND TONSURED YOUNG MEN, • • • • •	167	BLESSED	V	15
	I HAVE DRUNK ALE FROM THE COUNTRY OF THE YOUNG • • •	177	PAST GREATNESS		1
	THOUGH NOW IN HER OLD AGE, IN HER YOUNG AGE • • • • •	180	QUEEN MAEVE		18
	YOUNG BAILE HONEY—MOUTH, WHOM SOME • • • • • • •	189	BAILE AILLINN		16

		PAGE	TITLE		LINE
YOUNG (CONTINUED)					
OF HARPERS AND YOUNG MEN; AND THEY	• • • • • • •	189	BAILE AILLINN		19
YOUNG BAILE HONEY MOUTH, WHOM SOME	• • •	189	BAILE AILLINN	V	16
AND OLD AND YOUNG MEN RODE WITH HER;	• • •	191	BAILE AILLINN		51
A YOUNG MAN CRIED AND KISSED HER HAND;	• • •	191	BAILE AILLINN		60
FOR THIS YOUNG GIRL AND THIS YOUNG MAN	• • •	195	BAILE AILLINN		157
FOR THIS YOUNG GIRL AND THIS YOUNG MAN	• • •	195	BAILE AILLINN		157
MURMURED WITH HER YOUNG VOICE FOR WHOSE MILD SAKE	• •	205	ADAMS CURSE	V	15
IN FINDING THAT IT'S YOUNG AND MILD AND LOW.	• • •	205	ADAMS CURSE	V	17
BESIDE YOUNG AENGUS IN HIS TOWER OF GLASS;	• •	219	HARP OF AENGUS		2
A BEAUTIFUL YOUNG MAN AND GIRL CAME UP	• • • •	223	SHADOW WATER B		33
WHEN I WAS YOUNG,	• • • • • • • • •	254	WOMAN HOMER		2
WHEN I WAS YOUNG,	• • • • • • • • •	255	WOMAN HOMER		16
THAN THIS ACCUSTOMED TOIL. WHEN I WAS YOUNG,	• • •	267	ALL TEMPT ME		5
THE YOUNG MAN'S SONG	• • • • • • •	268	BROWN PENNY	V	T
I WHISPERED, "I AM TOO YOUNG."	• • •	268	BROWN PENNY		1
"GO AND LOVE, GO AND LOVE, YOUNG MAN,	• • •	268	BROWN PENNY		5
IF THE LADY BE YOUNG AND FAIR."	• • •	268	BROWN PENNY		6
YOU HAD TO FACE YOUR ENDS WHEN YOUNG—	• •	273	GREY ROCK		53
THEREON A YOUNG MAN MET HIS EYE,	• • •	274	GREY ROCK		85
YOUNG RED-HEAD STRETCHED HIMSELF TO YAWN	• •	303	HOUR DAWN	V	32A
"HOW YOUNG IT IS, HOW YOUNG!"	• • • •	308	PLAYER QUEEN		2
"HOW YOUNG IT IS, HOW YOUNG!"	• • • •	308	PLAYER QUEEN		2
BEING YOUNG YOU HAVE NOT KNOWN	• • • •	312	CHILD DANCING		6
I COULD HAVE WARNED YOU; BUT YOU ARE YOUNG,	• •	313	TWO YEAR LATER		5
BUT I AM OLD AND YOU ARE YOUNG,	• • •	313	TWO YEAR LATER		11
TO KEEP THE BODY YOUNG.	• • • • •	334	SONG		4
TO A YOUNG BEAUTY	• • • • • • •	335	YOUNG BEAUTY		T
TO A YOUNG GIRL	• • • • • •	336	YOUNG GIRL		T
THAT YOUNG MEN, TOSSING ON THEIR BEDS,	• • •	337	SCHOLARS		4
LET THE YOUNG WISH. BUT WHAT HAS BROUGHT YOU HERE?	• •	339	SHEP GOATHERD		6
HEARING IT NOW HAVE SIGHED FOR THAT YOUNG MAN	•	342	SHEP GOATHERD		77
OR A YOUNG GIRL DRESSED OUT IN HER NEW GOWN,	• • •	350	HER PRAISE		4
THOUGH SHE HAD YOUNG MEN'S PRAISE AND OLD MEN'S BLAME,	•	351	HER PRAISE		17
AMONG THE POOR BOTH OLD AND YOUNG GAVE HER PRAISE.	•	351	HER PRAISE		18
THE YOUNG MEN EVERY NIGHT APPLAUD THEIR GABY'S LAUGHING EYE,		353	HIS PHOENIX		9
AND WHO CAN SAY BUT SOME YOUNG BELLE MAY WALK AND TALK MEN WILD		354	HIS PHOENIX		26
AND MAY BE THERE'LL BE SOME YOUNG BELLE WALK OUT TO MAKE MEN WILD		354	HIS PHOENIX	V	26
AND MAYBE THERE'LL BE SOME YOUNG BELLE WALK OUT TO MAKE MEN WILD		354	HIS PHOENIX	V	26
YOUNG MEN NO LONGER SUDDENLY CATCH THEIR BREATH	• • •	355	BROKEN DREAMS		2
A YOUNG MAN WHEN THE OLD MEN ARE DONE TALKING	• • •	356	BROKEN DREAMS		16
A YOUNG GIRL IN THE INDOLENCE OF HER YOUTH,	• •	359	WAR POEM		5
WHEN, YOUNG AND BEAUTIFUL,	• • • •	392	EASTER 1916		22
I HAVE WALKED AND PRAYED FOR THIS YOUNG CHILD AN HOUR	•	403	FOR DAUGHTER		9
THAT IS NO COUNTRY FOR OLD MEN. THE YOUNG	• • •	407	SAIL BYZANTIUM		1
SOME FEW REMEMBERED STILL WHEN I WAS YOUNG	• • •	410	TOWER		33
TO YOUNG UPSTANDING MEN	• • • • • •	416	TOWER		174
THAT DEAD YOUNG SOLDIER IN HIS BLOOD;	• • •	425	STARES NEST		14
WE TOO HAD MANY PRETTY TOYS WHEN YOUNG;	• • •	428	NINETEEN 19		9
MUCH DID I RAGE WHEN YOUNG,	• • • • • •	434	YOUTH AND AGE		1
"BECAUSE I MADE YOU TURN AWAY AND RUN FROM THAT YOUNG CHILD;		450	OWEN AHERNE		14
O LET HER CHOOSE A YOUNG MAN NOW AND ALL FOR HIS WILD SAKE."		450	OWEN AHERNE		24
FOUR SONGS FROM THE YOUNG COUNTRYMAN	• • • • • • •	451	FIRST LOVE	V	T
THE YOUNG COUNTRYMAN	• • • • • • •	451	FIRST LOVE	V	T
A MAN YOUNG AND OLD FIRST LOVE	• • • • • •	451	FIRST LOVE	V	T
THAT HAD THOSE OF THE YOUNG;	• • • • • •	457	SECRETS OF OLD		2
SEEMED FOR A WHILE TO HAVE GROWN YOUNG AGAIN;	• • •	462	HARUN RASHID		36
"NEVER SHALL A YOUNG MAN,	• • • • •	492	ANNE GREGORY		1
THAT YOUNG MEN IN DESPAIR	• • • • •	492	ANNE GREGORY		10
SAW I AN OLD MAN YOUNG	• • • • • •	515	GIRLS SONG B		11
OR YOUNG MAN OLD?	• • • • • • • •	515	GIRLS SONG B		12
OR A YOUNG MAN OLD?	• • • • • • •	515	GIRLS SONG B	V	12
YOUNG MAN'S SONG	• • • • • • •	516	MANS SONG		T
BODILY DECREPITUDE IS WISDOM; YOUNG	• • • •	523	LONG SILENCE		7
A WOMAN YOUNG AND OLD I FATHER AND CHILD	• • •	531	FATHER CHILD	V	T
WHY SHOULD THEY THINK THAT ARE FOR EVER YOUNG?	• • •	537	HER VISION		21
"DROWN ALL THE DOGS," SAID THE FIERCE YOUNG WOMAN,	• •	546	TO SAME TUNE 2		7
DROWN ALL THE DOGS," SAID THE FIERCE YOUNG WOMAN.	• •	546	TO SAME TUNE 2		10
"DROWN ALL THE DOGS," SAID THE FIERCE YOUNG WOMAN,	• •	546	TO SAME TUNE 2		17
DROWN ALL THE DOGS," SAID THE FIERCE YOUNG WOMAN.	• •	546	TO SAME TUNE 2		20
"DROWN ALL THE DOGS," SAID THE FIERCE YOUNG WOMAN.	• •	547	TO SAME TUNE 2		27
DROWN ALL THE DOGS," SAID THE FIERCE YOUNG WOMAN.	• •	547	TO SAME TUNE 2		30
WHAT FROM THE FOREST CAME? WHAT BEAST HAS LICKED ITS YOUNG?		560	MAGIC DRUM		6
I SHOULD BE BLAMED, YOUNG MAN.	• • • • • •	569	THREE BUSHES		6
I HAVE WHAT NO YOUNG MAN CAN HAVE	• • • • •	588	OLD WICKED MAN		14
"A YOUNG MAN IN THE DARK AM I;	• • • • •	589	OLD WICKED MAN		37
THEY WERE NOT SUCH A PLAGUE WHEN I WAS YOUNG;	• • •	591	SPUR		3
IN A YOUNG MAN'S BED."	• • • • • •	594	COLONEL MARTIN		17
I PITY ALL THE YOUNG,	• • • • • • •	607	SONGS BURDEN 2		11
HOW CAN THE YOUNG GO STRAIGHT?	• • • • •	607	SONGS BURDEN 2		17
YOUNG MEN KNOW NOTHING OF THIS SORT,	• • • • •	626	OLD MEN BE MAD		16
BUT O THAT I WERE YOUNG AGAIN	• • • • • •	631	POLITICS		11
OF THE TARN WHERE YOUNG WAVES QUICKEN	• • • • •	647	ISLE STAT I 1		48
WATCHING O'ER HER AWFUL YOUNG,	• • • • • • • •	658	ISLE STAT I 3		87

929

YOUNG   (CONTINUED)
    O'ER HER YOUNG SO EAGERLY . . . .   658 ISLE STAT I 3   93
    YOUNG GUARIMOND HE TELLS THEM O'ER AND O'ER, ...   661 ISLE STAT II 1   56
    THE RED SQUIRREL SHALL REAR HER YOUNG WHERE THOU   674 ISLE STAT II 3   215
        HAST DWELT--
    AND HOLLOW LULLING THE YOUNG WINDS WITH SONG. . . . . .   675 ISLE STAT II 3   226
    THROUGH HIS SAD SOUL FOR EVER OLD AND YOUNG, ...   687 TWO TITANS   25
    A LOTUS IN THEIR HANDS--YOUNG MOORISH GIRL . . . . . .   694 MOSADA 1   103
    YOUNG MOORISH GIRL, THY FINAL HOUR IS HERE! . . . . .   701 MOSADA 3   63
    SINGS THE YOUNG WISTFUL SPIRIT OF A STAR . . . . . .   705 REMEMBRANCE   10
    THE SPIRIT OF YOUNG RENYI HAS GROWN OLD. . . . . . .   710 FERENCZ RENYI   17
    THE YOUNG ONE WITH THE OTHERS." RENYI'S PALE . . . .   713 FERENCZ RENYI   84
    I AM SO YOUNG. DOST THOU NO LONGER KNOW, ...   713 FERENCZ RENYI   88
    A PEASANT YOUNG AND FAIR, HER EYES FOR FEAR . . . .   713 FERENCZ RENYI V 81
    YOUNG FERENCZ RENYI BURSTS HIS BONDS--AT LAST, . . .   714 FERENCZ RENYI V 116
    COME TO THE CHESS, FOR YOUNG GIRLS' WITS ARE BETTER . .   721 WITCH VIVIEN   46
    MY WAY IS WEST. SHE SEEMS BOTH YOUNG AND SHAPELY! . .   755 SHADOW WATER A   171
    I GREW AS OLD AS TIME, AND SHE GROWS YOUNG . . . . .   761 SHADOW WATER A   259
    GROWS YOUNG AND A MAN'S HEART GROWS OLD IN A TWINKLING.   761 SHADOW WATER A   263
    BESIDE YOUNG AENGUS IN HIS TOWER OF GLASS, ...   762 SHADOW WATER A   297
YOUNGER
    SITS A YOUNGER AND A STRONGER. . . . .   26 OISIN 1   V 399D
    THE LIVING BEAUTY IS FOR YOUNGER MEN! . . . .   334 LIVING BEAUTY   9
    "HE GROWS YOUNGER EVERY SECOND . . . .   342 SHEP GOATHERD   89
    OR BRIGHTEN ONLY FOR SOME YOUNGER EYE, ...   464 HARUN RASHID   82
    I KNOW NOT WHAT THE YOUNGER DREAMS-- . . . .   475 EVA GORE-BOOTH   10
YOUNGEST
    AND YESTERDAY THE YOUNGEST SON, ...   361 ALF POLLEXFEN   24
    GO ASK THE YOUNGEST ANGEL, ...   680 LOVE AND DEATH   29
    THOUGH YOUNGEST OF ALL IN OUR GOOD BAND, ...   707 FAIRY PEDANT   11
    THOUGH YOUNGEST OF ALL IN OUR GOOD BAND, ...   708 FAIRY PEDANT   39
YOUTH
    AND LOVE, IN THE HOURS WHEN YOUTH HAS CEASED! . . . . .   2 OISIN 1   V 7A
    WAS A BEAUTIFUL YOUTH FROM AN UNKNOWN LAND, ...   12 OISIN 1   V 145
    OR THE SOFTNESS OF YOUTH BE GONE FROM OUR FACES, . . .   27 OISIN 1   410
    WILL THE SOFTNESS OF YOUTH BE GONE FROM OUR FACES, . .   27 OISIN 1   V 410
    OR THE SOFTNESS OF YOUTH BE GONE FROM OUR FACES, . . .   27 OISIN 1   V 419C
    OR THE SOFTNESS OF YOUTH BE GONE FROM OUR FACES, . . .   28 OISIN 1   V 426
    THE YOUTH AND LADY AND THE DEER AND HOUND! . . . . .   29 OISIN 2   4
    ONCE MORE--THE YOUTH AND LADY, DEER AND HOUND! . . .   29 OISIN 2   V 2
    WHICH IS THE ISLE OF YOUTH?" "NONE KNOW," SHE SAID, . .   46 OISIN 2   V 249
    THE DEER AND THE HOUND, AND THE LADY AND YOUTH, ...   47 OISIN 3   V 3
    CAME AFTER THE HARD GAZE OF YOUTH, OR AN OLD MAN LIFTED   59 OISIN 3   170
        HIS HEAD!
    . . . AND THEIR YOUTH, AND THEIR EYES SOFT AS SILK. . . .   59 OISIN 3   V 176
    THROUGH THE DEMON LOVE OF ITS YOUTH . . . .   63 OISIN 3   216
    FOR THY YOUTH WITHOUT PEACE, AND THY YEARS WITH THE DEMONS,   63 OISIN 3   V 216
        . . .
    MY SONGS OF OLD EARTH'S DREAMY YOUTH! . . . .   67 HAPPY SHEPHERD   54
    THROUGH THE LONG YEARS OF YOUTH, AND WHO WOULD HAVE THOUGHT   201 OLD MEMORY   7
    THROUGH THE LONG DAYS OF YOUTH, AND WHO WOULD HAVE THOUGHT   201 OLD MEMORY   V 7
    ALL THROUGH THE YEARS OF OUR YOUTH . . . .   211 O DO NOT LOVE   5
    YOUTH AND AGE . . . .   261 COMING WISDOM V T
    THROUGH ALL THE LYING DAYS OF MY YOUTH . . . . . .   261 COMING WISDOM   2
    TO SHAKE THEIR WICKED SIDES AT YOUTH . . . .   262 STUDENTS AGIT   3
    A MEMORY OF YOUTH . . . .   313 MEMORY YOUTH   T
    ALL TILL MY YOUTH WAS GONE . . . .   315 FRIENDS   18
    WITH THE HOT BLOOD OF YOUTH, OF LOVE CROSSED LONG AGO! . .   316 COLD HEAVEN   6
    OR MERE COMPANIONS OF MY YOUTH, ...   324 ROBERT GREGORY   7
    IN MUSCULAR YOUTH WELL KNOWN TO MAYO MEN . . . . . .   325 ROBERT GREGORY   34
    IN MUSCULAR YOUTH WELLKNOWN TO MAYO MEN . . . . . .   325 ROBERT GREGORY V 34
    IN MUSCULAR YOUTH, AT MEETS OR AT RACECOURSES, ...   325 ROBERT GREGORY V 35
    WHEN I HAD MY BURNING YOUTH! . . . .   329 MEN IMPROVE   15
    THE WICK OF YOUTH BEING BURNED AND THE OIL SPENT, . . .   334 LIVING BEAUTY V 3
    YOUTH TO PROLONG . . . .   334 SONG   2
    MOST COURTEOUS TO SLOW AGE AND HASTY YOUTH, ...   339 SHEP GOATHERD   19
    I TOO HAVE RHYMED MY REVERIES, BUT YOUTH . . . . . .   340 SHEP GOATHERD   43
    YOUTH CAN EXCEL THEM IN ACCOMPLISHMENT, ...   340 SHEP GOATHERD   47
    AND I THAT MADE LIKE MUSIC IN MY YOUTH . . . . . .   342 SHEP GOATHERD   76
    MY DAILY THOUGHTS SINCE THE FIRST STUPOR OF YOUTH . . .   342 SHEP GOATHERD   83
    I KNEW A PHOENIX IN MY YOUTH, SO LET THEM HAVE THEIR DAY.   353 HIS PHOENIX   8
    I KNEW A PHOENIX IN MY YOUTH, SO LET THEM HAVE THEIR DAY.   354 HIS PHOENIX   16
    I KNEW A PHOENIX IN MY YOUTH, SO LET THEM HAVE THEIR DAY.   354 HIS PHOENIX   24
    I KNEW A PHOENIX IN MY YOUTH, SO LET THEM HAVE THEIR DAY.   354 HIS PHOENIX   32
    A YOUNG GIRL IN THE INDOLENCE OF HER YOUTH, ...   359 WAR POEM   5
    AMID THE DREAMS OF YOUTH! LET HER COME FACE TO FACE, . .   366 HER COURAGE   3
    BECAUSE I HAVE NO OTHER YOUTH, CAN MAKE ME PINE! . . .   391 UNDER SATURN   3
    BEING A PORTION OF MY YOUTH, CAN MAKE ME PINE . . . .   391 UNDER SATURN V 3
    YOUTH AND AGE . . . .   434 YOUTH AND AGE   T
    THE FRIENDS OF HIS YOUTH . . . .   455 FRIENDS YOUTH   T
    CEASE TO REMEMBER THE DELIGHTS OF YOUTH, TRAVEL-WEARIED   459 FROM OEDIPUS   2
        AGED MAN!
    A MIMICRY OF YOUTH. CAN POET'S THOUGHT . . . . . .   463 HARUN RASHID   62
    A MIMICRY OF YOUTH. AN ARTIST'S THOUGHT, ...   463 HARUN RASHID V 62
    THE SOUL'S OWN YOUTH AND NOT THE BODY'S YOUTH . . . .   464 HARUN RASHID   69
    THE SOUL'S OWN YOUTH AND NOT THE BODY'S YOUTH . . . .   464 HARUN RASHID   69
    HEARD ALL THE ANXIETY OF MY PASSIONATE YOUTH, ...   468 HARUN RASHID   168
    DRUNK WITH THE BITTER SWEETNESS OF HER YOUTH. . . . .   469 HARUN RASHID   186
    DRUNK WITH THE BITTER-SWEETNESS OF HER YOUTH. . . . .   469 HARUN RASHID V 186
    THAT TABLE AND THE TALK OF YOUTH, ...   475 EVA GORE-BOOTH   18
    ALL BY THEIR YOUTH UNDONE, ...   504 RESULT THOUGHT   4

930

		PAGE	TITLE	LINE
YOUTH	(CONTINUED)			
DANCING WITH HER CHOSEN YOUTH,	• • • • • • • • •	514	JANE GROWN OLD	2
ESCAPED FROM BITTER YOUTH,	• • • • • • • • •	568	SWEET DANCER	4
"THE DEAD IRELAND OF MY YOUTH, BUT AN IRELAND	• • • • •	602	GALLERY REVIS	11
AND ELVISH WISDOM, AND LONG YEARS OF YOUTH	• • • • • •	653	ISLE STAT I 2	47
FAIR YOUTH, ALONG A WANDERING WAY	• • • • • •	667	ISLE STAT II 3	38
THERE'S LITTLE I'D REFUSE THEE, DEAREST YOUTH.	• • • •	669	ISLE STAT II 3	71
MY LIPS, FAIR YOUTH. IT SHALL BE AS YOU ASK.	• • • •	669	ISLE STAT II 3	80
BUT ART THOU HAPPY? YOUTH, I AM AT PEACE.	• • • • •	672	ISLE STAT II 3	150
SHALL BE THE HUNTER—LOVER OF THY YOUTH.	• • • • • •	674	ISLE STAT II 3	205
WAS MY SLEEP LONG, OH, YOUTH? LONG, LONG AND DEEP.	• • •	678	ISLE STAT II 3	299
YOUTH, HERE WILL WE ABIDE, AND BE THOU KING	• • • •	679	ISLE STAT II 3	314
FOR ALL I GAVE THE VOICE, FOR ALL MY YOUTH,	• • • •	685	SEEKER	78
A GREY—HAIRED YOUTH, WHOSE CHEEKS HAD NEVER FOUND,	• • •	687	TWO TITANS	7
CRAMM'D ALL HER YOUTH; AND HATES HAVE BOUGHT AND SOLD	• •	687	TWO TITANS	13
ABOUT THE SEA. BEFORE HER LIES THAT YOUTH,	• • • • •	687	TWO TITANS	22
THE YOUTH HAD FLUNG HIS ARMS AROUND THE ROCKS,	• • • •	688	TWO TITANS	40
GATHERED ON HER OWN LIPS, OH YOUTH, AND FLING	• • • •	688	TWO TITANS	53
PEACE OF YOUTH AND PEACE OF AGE,	• • • • • • • •	733	STREET DANCERS	46
YOUTHFUL				
AND WITH THE FERVOUR OF MY YOUTHFUL EYES,	• • • • • •	356	BROKEN DREAMS	25
INTO A SPHERE FROM YOUTHFUL SYMPATHY,	• • • • • •	443	SCHOOL CHILDR	14
WHAT YOUTHFUL MOTHER, A SHAPE UPON HER LAP	• • • • •	444	SCHOOL CHILDR	33
IN THEIR DAYS OF YOUTHFUL MIRTH!	• • • • • • • •	727	LOVERS QUARREL	40
YOUTH'S				
YOUTH'S DREAMY LOAD, TILL SHE	• • • • • • • •	315	FRIENDS	14
YOUTH'S BITTERNESS BEING PAST,	• • • • • • • •	389	IMAGE PAST	11
WITH ALL YOUTH'S LONELY WILDNESS STIRRED,	• • • • •	397	POLIT PRISONER	16
AND YET HERSELF CAN SEEM YOUTH'S VERY FOUNTAIN,	• • • •	465	HARUN RASHID	89
YOUTHS				
WHILE A HUNDRED YOUTHS, MIGHTY OF LIMB,	• • • • • •	8	OISIN 1	94
AND A HUNDRED YOUTHS, WHOSE LIMBS ARE STRUNG	• • • •	9	OISIN 1	V 97
OF YOUTHS AND MAIDENS HAND IN HAND,	• • • • • •	15	OISIN 1	V 202
ZAG	SEE ZIG—ZAG			
ZEPPELIN				
AEROPLANE AND ZEPPELIN WILL COME OUT,	• • • • • • •	565	LAPIS LAZULI	6
ZIGZAG				
HOW BUT IN ZIGZAG WANTONNESS	• • • • • • • • •	338	TOM OROUGHLEY	V 12
ZIG—ZAG				
HOW BUT IN ZIG—ZAG WANTONNESS	• • • • • • • •	338	TOM OROUGHLEY	12
ZODIAC				
THE ONE DISASTROUS ZODIAC, MUTTERING	• • • • • • •	282	TWO KINGS	128
FROM THE ZODIAC,	• • • • • • • • • • • •	533	FIRST CONFESS	14
OF THE WHIRLING ZODIAC.	• • • • • • • • •	535	CHOSEN	3
THE ZODIAC IS CHANGED INTO A SPHERE.	• • • • • • •	535	CHOSEN	18

APPENDIX

22 (cont.)
MOVED
NAY
PAINTED
SHEPHERD
SHONE
STORM
STREET
TALL
TOP
TROUBLE
WASTE
WINDY

21
AFAR
AFRAID
BELL
BLESSED
BOOKS
BUILD
CRYING
CUP
DREW
DROPS
FOREST
HATE
HELP
LIMBS
MERE
MOVE
OISIN
ONES
PAST
PRAYER
SAIL
SAND
SCHOOL
SHADOWY
SLEEPY
SLOWLY
SOUTH
SPEECH
SWIFT
THOUSAND
TOGETHER
WALKED
WEPT
WHIRLING
WORTH

20
BEATING
BENT
BRINGS
CHOOSE
DRAW
DRIPPING
DUMB
FORGAEL
GATHERED
GLEAM
HAZEL
LEAF
LEARN
LONE
LORD

LOVELY
LOVE'S
MAIDEN
MURMURED
NAMES
PASSIONATE
PURPLE
ROSES
SACRED
SAVE
SPOKE
SUNG
TAKEN
TEAR
THIN
TREMBLING
VALLEY
WAIT
WEEPING
WET

19
BLOWS
BOUGH
BRANCH
CHANCE
COMPANY
DROPPING
DROWNED
FENIANS
FILL
GRIEF
GROWING
HATRED
HAVING
HEADS
HONEY
HURRY
IGNORANT
MANKIND
PLEASURE
READ
REMEMBER
ROOM
SAKE
SHUT
SILK
SOFTLY
SPEAR
SWEAR
WON
WOUND
WOVEN

18
ACROSS
BARE
BOSOM
BURN
CALLING
CENTURIES
DESOLATE
DRAWN
DROVE
DULL
EVE
FISH

FLAMES
FLESH
GLOOM
JOHN
MASTER
MOMENT
MURMUR
NARROW
NOON
NORTH
PLEASE
POETS
PRIEST
ROCK
RUNS
SIN
STRENGTH
TROOP
WALKING
WARS
WHISPERING
WINTRY

17
ALOUD
ARROW
BEECH
BENDING
BLADE
BROOD
CRIMSON
DANCED
DEMON
DESPAIR
DRUNK
FADE
FALLS
FAMOUS
FEARS
FEATHER
FIELDS
FLIES
FLIGHT
FORGOTTEN
FOUR
GET
GIVES
GLITTERING
HARE
HEARING
HITHER
HORSEMEN
HOST
HUSBAND
IMMORTAL
KISSED
LATE
LEAFY
LEAP
LOOSE
MARBLE
MARCH
MIST
MOAN
MOOD
NATURAL
NOBLE

PATH
ROOF
SAILS
SEA'S
SENT
SHEEP
SHOOK
SIGHED
SLEEPING
STARE
STRIKE
STRINGS
SWEETNESS
SWORDS
THREAD
TOIL
TOSSING
WATCHED
WOUNDS

16
ALE
ALIVE
ANSWER
ANSWERED
ANYTHING
AWHILE
BEER
BEHOLD
BLOWN
BROKE
BURIED
CLAY
CLOCK
CUT
DEMONS
DRUNKEN
ENDS
FEEL
FLUNG
FOOTFALL
FORGOT
HEAPED
IMAGINATION
INTELLECT
KNOWING
LADIES
LESS
MICHAEL
MIRE
MIRROR
NEEDS
OAK
PIERCED
PLAYED
POET
POWER
RAGGED
RING
RUIN
SCARCE
SHINING
SOLITUDE
SPOT
STAG
TERROR
THEREUPON

TREAD
TROUBLED
VAPOURS
WAITING
WONDER

15
AGED
AYE
BEE
BELOW
BIT
BRIDE
BROW
COLONEL
COVER
CRADLE
CREATURES
DANCERS
DROWSY
FAINT
FEW
FLYING
FORM
GAZED
GIRLS
GIVEN
GLANCE
HARD
HELL
HUSHED
JANE
KEPT
KILLED
KNEE
LEAST
LEST
LIFTED
MAEVE
MINUTE
NAUGHT
PATRICK
PROMISED
RAIN
RAISE
RAISED
REASON
ROLLED
RUSH
SADNESS
SAYS
SCORE
SEND
SHELL
SHIELD
SHIPS
SIGHS
SKIN
SMOKE
SPIRITS
STARRY
STATE
STRETCHED
TABLE
TELLS
THINKING
WALLS

Index Words in Order of Frequency

101
DAYS
GOOD

100
DREAM
FIND

99
CRY
RED

98
SUCH
WOMAN

97
SANG

94
MAKE
PLACE
WILD

93
KING
MOST
SING

92
ALONE
HIGH
THING

91
DEAR
DIE
EVER
GIVE
STONE

90
WANDERING

89
WOOD

88
ABOVE
AFTER
LIPS

86
EYE
SAD

85
LOOK

84
FULL

83
FIRE
UNTIL

82
BRING

NOTHING
WINDS

81
DIM
FIRST
TAKE
WORDS

80
BIRDS
END
SEE

79
BEAUTY
DARK
DOOR
LAY
TREE

78
BIRD
BLOOD

77
NAME
SORROW

76
BREAST
GAVE
LAST
LOST
SWEET
WAY

75
GREEN
LEAVES

74
PALE
YOUTH

73
NONE

72
LOVED

69
PASS
RUN
WENT

68
DEEP
KNEW
SEEMED

67
CALL
DONE
PEACE
SET
VOICE

66
BETWEEN
GRASS
JOY
SIDE
THREE
TURN

65
ANCIENT
CHILD
GOLD
HOUR
PUT
THINK
WOMEN

64
BROUGHT
GOLDEN
PRAISE
SOUND

63
DIED
NEW
PASSED

62
GROWN
LIE

61
DANCE
GREW
KEEP
LIVE
WATERS
WINGS

60
BROKEN
COMES
EVEN
SWORD
WOODS

59
FRIEND
HUNDRED
TREES
WELL

58
ARMS
BESIDE
CHILDREN
KNOWS
MOTHER
REST
SHORE

57
MOUNTAIN
SPEAK
WITHIN

56
ALONG
ANY
DAWN
HEARTS
MUSIC
SINGING
WISDOM

55
BEAUTIFUL
LAID
MINE

54
COLD
IMAGE
MAN'S
ONLY
SKY

53
AGE
EARTH
ROSE (Noun)
SILVER

52
BED
BLIND
LOW
PLAY

51
FLY
GROW
LEFT
MUCH
SAT
TELL
WEARY

50
BELOVED
GAZE
LIES
WINE

49
AMID
GOES
KISS
LAND
NEAR
QUEEN

48
BID
FALL
FOOL
LOVERS
PROUD
WATER

47
BEYOND
CHANGED

FELL
GIRL
HEAVY
RAN
RIGHT

46
BITTER
FATHER
O'ER
ROSE (Verb)
SEAS
SIGH
TIDE
WISE

45
BOUGHS
COUNTRY
EVENING
FEAR
FLAME
HOLY
HORN
LIVING
PRIDE
SON

44
BETTER
BREAK
CALLED
CARE
CAST
HUMAN
MAYBE
MORNING
SHADOWS
SMALL
STRONG

43
BREATH
BRIGHT
DROP
HOME
KNOWN
LADY
LOOKED
RIDE
TIMES

42
BOOK
CERTAIN
CHANGE
ENOUGH
LIVED
RODE
SEEM
SEEN
SOFT
THOUGHTS
TOLD
TOWER
WAR
WORD

41
BROWN
HILL
LAKE
LAUGHTER
LONELY
MEMORY
OFF
STAR
WORK

40
DESIRE
DEW
GODS
HOLLOW
IMAGES
KINGS
LEAVE
LOVER
POOR
TURNED

39
CLOSE
FRIENDS
HORSE
MOUTH
STREAMS
WAVE
WAVES
WEEP
WITHERED

38
BEST
GROWS
HOPE
LAUGH
MOURNFUL
NEED
PASSION
SILENCE
WIDE
YONDER

37
FAIR
GROUND
HARP
HEAVEN
HOLD
KIND
QUIET
SHAKE
STREAM
SUDDEN
TEARS
WHOLE

36
AGO
BEGGAR
FACES
SHADOW
SONGS
STAND

TALK
TOOK
WORLD'S

35
AROUND
BONE
BORN
DREAMED
FOAM
HAPPY
PEOPLE
SEVEN
STRANGE
TOMB
WALK
WANDER
YEAR

34
BEAT
BODIES
BOY
BURNING
DANCING
EAR
EMPTY
FOOT
FORTH
HOUND
STONES
TUNE
WING
WITHOUT

33
BLOSSOM
CEASE
CONTENT
DEER
FINGERS
GAY
GRAVE
LANDS
LAUGHING
LOUD
MATTER
MIDNIGHT
SECRET
SLOW
TRUTH
WAKE
YELLOW

32
AGAINST
ALWAYS
BOUND
CLOUD
CROWD
FIERCE
FLED
FLOOR
FRO
HID
MORN
NIAMH
REMEMBERING

RISE
WILL
WOMAN'S

31
BACK
CAUGHT
CRIES
DRIVEN
EVIL
FOLLOW
GATHER
HUNG
KNEES
LIFT
MERRY
SHADE
SUDDENLY
SUMMER
THEREON
TOUCH
TRUE
WORN

30
APPLE
EARS
FAERY
GARDEN
LEARNED
LIVES
MAD
MAKES
RAGE
SHAPE
SKIES
WALL

29
COMMON
DREAMING
EVERYTHING
FALLEN
FLOWERS
HILLS
MEET
MET
MURMURING
PLAIN
RICH
SEEK
SIGHT
STORY

28
BADE
BEGAN
BLUE
CRAZY
GLORY
HALL
HOUNDS
HUSH
ISLE
PRAY
RACE
RHYME
SOON

SOULS
SPRING
TALE
THROWN
TWILIGHT
WAYS

27
AENGUS
BEND
BLOW
DELIGHT
DRINK
DRUID
EDGE
FOUL
GHOST
HELD
HIDDEN
HIDE
HORSES
LAUGHED
LONGER
NIAM
SANDS
SINCE
UNTO
WIFE

26
BATTLE
BROTHER
CLOUDS
DAUGHTER
DRY
FINGER
GLAD
HOURS
IRELAND
ISLAND
LIT
MAID
MIGHTY
SLEPT
SOMETHING
SPREAD
TONGUE
TOWARDS
TOWN
YON

25
APART
ASLEEP
AWAKE
BEAST
BLACK
CARRY
CLEAR
CLOAK
CROWN
CUCHULAIN
DIES
FAIRY
GLASS
GLIMMERING
GOD'S

LONGING
MOCK
MORTAL
NINE
PASSING
STAIR
VAIN
WEST
WRONG

24
BEES
BONES
COMING
DANAAN
EYELIDS
FLAMING
GENTLE
MEASURE
MEMORIES
OPEN
PART
ROAD
RUNNING
SPIRIT
STAY
TALKED
VOICES
WEAK

23
ASK
BEAR
BOW
CROSS
DARKNESS
DREAD
DROWN
DUST
DYING
FOLLOWED
LOVES
MEN'S
RULE
SAME
SECOND
SEEMS
SHIP
SHOW
SILENT
SOMEWHERE
SOUGHT
STANDS
VERY
WROUGHT

22
BEHIND
BENEATH
CHAIR
ELSE
FIGHT
FLOWER
FREE
HAPPINESS
HEART'S
MILD

15 (cont.)

WATCH
WEAR
WOODLAND

14

AIBRIC
BAILE
BRAIN
CLIMB
CURSE
DESERT
DWELL
EASE
ENDLESS
ERE
FALLING
FASHION
FED
FEEBLE
FINISHED
FLING
FLOCKS
FORGET
FRUIT
GLOW
HAIL
HANG
HEAVEN'S
HOLE
JUDGE
LEAD
LED
LION
LOOKS
MISTY
MOON'S
MURMURS
MYSTERY
NET
OWLS
PACE
PETER
PITCH
PRAISED
PRAYED
PROVE
RIM
RUSHES
SAILING
SAINT
SHARE
SHOES
SMOOTH
SNOW
SOLDIER
SORT
STRING
SURELY
THORN
THROAT
TORN
TOUCHED
TRADE
TROD
VANISHED
VAST

WEAVE
WICKED
WINDOW
WIT
WORM

13

BAD
BLAZE
BORE
BOWED
BREAD
BURDEN
CANDLE
CHANGING
CHURCH
CLOTHES
COURSE
CROW
CRUACHAN
DANCER
DAYBREAK
DISTANT
DOGS
FAITH
FANCY
FEAST
FINE
FIXED
FLOOD
FLOW
FOLK
GALLEY
HEAVENS
IMAGINED
IRELAND'S
IRON
LACK
LIGHTS
LOFTY
LUCK
MIRTH
MOTHER'S
MOUNTAINS
MOUNTED
'NEATH
NIGH
NOISE
OAR
OFTEN
PEASANT
POOL
PRETTY
PUBLIC
RHYMES
RIVERS
ROLLING
SANK
SEEING
SHAKEN
SLEEPS
SMILE
SPAKE
STARED
TALKING
TRAGIC
TRIUMPH

TROY
TURNS
TWENTY
UNDERSTAND
VALLEYS
VILLAGE
WARM
WATCHING
WRITE
WROTE
YEW

12

ANGRY
ARMED
ART
AY
BAND
BEATEN
BIRTH
BISHOP
BLOWING
BORDER
BRIEF
CEASED
CHASE
CHOSEN
CLIMBED
CLOWN
COMFORT
CRAZED
CROSSED
CURLEW
DELICATE
DEWY
DRESS
EDAIN
EOCHAID
EVER-LIVING
FADED
FINDS
FIRES
FLAGS
FOLD
FOLLY
FOOLISH
FORGIVE
FRENZY
GATE
GATHERING
GOT
HEM
HERDS
LABOURING
LAW
LENGTH
LIGHTNING
LISTEN
LOOKING
MAGIC
MIDST
MIGHT
MOVES
NAMED
NATURE
PAIN
PATIENT

PEACOCK
PITY
QUICKEN
REMAIN
REPLIED
RIDING
ROARING
ROOT
ROOTS
SHAKES
SHORES
SINGS
SPENT
SPOKEN
STARLIGHT
THEME
THIRD
THRONE
THUNDER
TOM
UPRIGHT
VAPOUR
WANDERED
WEATHER
WELCOME
WHEEL
WHEREFORE
WHISPER
WINTER
WITS
WOOD'S
WORST
WRITTEN

11

ARISE
ARMOUR
BARREN
BEDS
BIDS
BLESS
BLOSSOMING
BODILY
BOLD
BOWS
BRONZE
CARRIED
CAT
CAUSE
CHOSE
CIRCLING
CLOUDY
COMPANIONS
CRESCENT
DAYLIGHT
DOORS
DREADFUL
DRIED
DRIFTS
DRIVE
DROPPED
DWELT
ETERNITY
FADING
FAREWELL
FILLED
FILLS

FLEW
FLICKERING
FOUGHT
GENERATIONS
GOBLIN
GRASSES
HIDES
HISTORY
HUGE
INDIFFERENT
KNAVE
KNELT
KNOWLEDGE
LEAPED
LINES
MARY
MEAT
MIDDLE
MILK
MIND'S
MONEY
MOTHS
MOUNT
NEST
NETS
PACED
PEARLY
PLUCKED
POWERS
PURE
QUEENS
QUESTION
QUIVERING
RAGS
RECALL
RETURN
RIVER
ROADS
ROCKY
SATISFIED
SCENE
SHAKING
SITTING
SIX
SLAIN
SOLOMON
STANDING
TAKES
TARA
TENDER
THREW
TIRED
TORE
TOWERS
TREADS
UNKNOWN
WAITED
WAVING
WINDING
WINGED
WOVE

10

AEDH
ANCESTRAL
ANEW
ARM

8 (cont.)

PULL
PULLED
PURPOSE
ROAR
RUTH
SAGES
SALT
SEED
SHEBA
SHEPHERDS
SHIVERING
SHOOT
SHOT
SHOUT
SHOWN
SHY
SICK
SISTER
SIT
SLAVE
SLUMBER
SOLE
SOMEBODY
SOUNDS
SQUIRREL
STARING
STEPT
STORMY
STRETCH
SUN'S
SURGES
TEETH
THIGH
THRUST
TIP
TOES
UNHUMAN
VALE
VOW
WANDERINGS
WARRIOR
WATER'S
WHENCE
WILLOW
WOODY
WORSE

7

ABSTRACT
ACTION
A-FLUTTER
ALL'S
APPLES
ASKED
AWAIT
BANE
BARGAIN
BEGINS
BENCH
BILL
BOARD
BORNE
BOUGHT
BRED
BRILLIANT
BROAD

BULL
BURKE
CANDLE-END
CART
CARVEN
CHRIST
CIRCLE
CIRCLES
CITY
CLAMOUR
CLAP
CONNOLLY
CONSCIENCE
CRACK
CREATURE
CREEPING
CREW
CUMHAL
DARLING
DESPITE
DIPPED
DOUBLE
DOVE
DRANK
EARTHLY
EAT
EBB
EMER
ENCHANTED
ERI
EYEBALLS
FAITHFUL
FAR-OFF
FAY
FEED
FERENCZ
FIFTY
FIGHTING
FIVE
FLASH
FLEET
FLOCK
FLOWING
FLOWN
FLUTTER
FOLIAGE
FORETOLD
FUNERAL
FURTHER
GALLERY
GALLEYS
GARDENS
GATES
GATEWAY
GREGORY
GUILE
GYRES
HARSH
HATED
HEARTH
HOPING
HOUSES
HOVERING
HURL
HURRIED
KEENING
LADLE

LADS
LANE
LAWN
LEADER
LEARNING
LEISURE
LIDS
LIGHTLY
LIP
LONG-LEGGED
LOOKING-GLASS
LOT
LUCKY
MAIDENS
MARCHING
MARKED
MARRIAGE
MARRIED
MEADOWS
MEDITATION
MIGHTIER
MINGLING
MOCKERY
MOONLIGHT
MOONS
MOUND
MUMMY
MUSE
MUSES
NAILS
NEXT
NOBODY
ONE'S
OVERTHROWN
OWL
PACK
PERFECTION
PLAINS
PLATO'S
POEMS
POPULAR
POST
PRAYERS
RANK
REFUSE
REPLY
RINGING
ROBERT
ROGER
ROOTED
RUDDY
RULED
SAFFRON
SCALE
SCHOLAR
SCORN
SEDGE
SELF-SAME
SERVED
SHAPES
SHIELDS
SHINE
SHOUTING
SHRIEK
SINEWY
SKINS
SLUMBERING

SOFTNESS
SOLDIERS
SOLID
SOOTH
SOUL'S
SPEARS
SPRANG
STARK
STAYED
STEEP
STICK
STILLNESS
STRAND
STRANGER
STRICKEN
STUDY
SUBSTANCE
SULLEN
SWALLOWS
SWIM
TAMBOURINE
TASTE
TERRIBLE
THIRST
THRONG
TIMID
TIRE
TO-DAY
TOOTH
TOSS
TOUCHING
TRESS
TROUT
TRUMPET
TRUTHS
TUMULTUOUS
TWELVE
UNDYING
VALLENCE
WAIL
WED
WEIGH
WESTERN
WESTWARD
WHEREON
WHIM
WHITER
WHITHER
WINDOWS
WISH
WOOL
WORE
YESTERDAY
YORE

6

ABOUNDING
ACCURSED
ACCUSTOMED
AIRY
AMRITA
ANIMAL
ARCADY
ARMIES
ASTRAY
A-TIPTOE
AWAITS

AWAKEN
AWOKE
BARLEY
BEGOTTEN
BEGUN
BIND
BITTERNESS
BLESSEDEST
BLEST
BLOT
BOAST
BRAHMA
BRASS
BRIGHTENING
BROTHERS
BURNISHED
CALLS
CANNON
CAOILTE
CAPTAIN
CARDS
CARES
CARVED
CASTS
CERTAINLY
CHARACTER
CHARM
CHARMED
CHILL
CHURNED
CLING
CLOTHS
CLOVEN
COCKS
COIL
COMELY
COMPANION
CONAN
COOK
CORN
COUNT
COUNTED
COUNTRYMAN
COURT
COWS
CREST
CROWDS
CROWNS
CRUELTY
CUCKOO
CURSED
DANCES
DATHI
DEED
DEEDS
DENIES
DEPART
DEVIL
DIFFERENT
DIFFICULT
DIGNITY
DISCIPLINE
DISTRESS
DIZZY
DOME
DRESSED
DRIFTING

6 (cont.)

DRUM
EAGLE
EARL
EARNED
EASY
EATEN
ECSTASY
EMBROIDERED
ENTER
ETERNAL
FABULOUS
FALCON
FAMILY
FANATICS
FEARFUL
FEASTED
FELT
FENIAN
FIDDLE
FIERY
FIN
FIT
FLAPPING
FOLDS
FOLLOWS
FOOLS
FOOTSOLE
FORGETTING
FRIGHT
FROZEN
FURY
GALWAY
GILLIGAN
GLADE
GLANCES
GOLDEN-ARMED
GOLDSMITH
GOOSE
GOVERNMENT
HAMMER
HANGING
HAUGHTY
HEAVING
HEEL
HEROIC
HOPELESS
HOPES
HORRIBLE
HORROR
HUNGER
HUNGRY
HURRYING
ILL
INNUMERABLE
INSTANT
IVORY
JET
JOINED
JOYOUS
JUSTIFY
KINGDOM
KNIGHT
KNOCKNAREA
LADY'S
LAME
LANCE

LAWNS
LEGS
LET'S
LIFE'S
LIFTS
LINGERING
LONGS
MAGICAL
MAJESTY
MARRY
MASTERFUL
MATE
MEETS
METEOR
MILKY
MINNALOUSHE
MIRACULOUS
MISERY
MISS
MOCKED
MORROW
MOSADA
MOUTHS
MYSTERIOUS
NATIONS
NECK
NOD
NODDING
NOISY
ODOUR
ORO
O'SULLIVAN
OTTERS
OUTLIVE
PASSIONS
PATHS
PAUSE
PAUSED
PEARL
PICKED
PICTURE
PIERCING
PILOTS
PIPING
PITEOUS
PLAYER
PLOT
PLOTS
PLUCK
POEM
PORTRAIT
PROVED
PYTHAGORAS
QUARTER
QUEST
RAGING
RAVING
REJOICE
REMORSE
RENOWNED
RESTLESS
RHYMED
RIDERS
RIDGE
ROBARTES
ROLLS
ROOD

RUBY
RUSTLING
SAFE
SANCTITY
SCATTER
SCEOLAN
SETS
SETTING
SETTLED
SHELTER
SHELTERED
SHOP
SHOWED
SHUDDER
SIGN
SIMPLE
SIPS
SLAVES
SLEW
SLIDING
SMILING
SOLD
SOLITUDES
SORE
SPACIOUS
SPEAKS
SPECKLED
SPEED
SPELLS
STAFF
STAGE
STAKE
STATUES
STERN
STOOL
STOOPED
STRAW
STROKE
STUMBLING
SUMMON
SUNLIGHT
SURGE
SWANS
SWEAT
SWEETER
SYNGE
TENT
TENTS
TEXT
THIGHS
THOUSANDS
THREADS
THRESHOLD
THRONES
TOILED
TOPS
TOWNLAND
TRACE
TREMBLE
UNCHANGING
UNNOTICED
UPWARD
VANISH
VEINS
VENGEANCE
VIJAYA
VIOLENT

VIRGIN
WAITS
WANDERER
WANDERS
WARRIORS
WEALTH
WEIGHT
WHIGGERY
WHISTLED
WIN
WINTER'S
WITCH
WITNESS
WOMB
WOODEN
WRACK
WRIST

5

ABU
AGES
ALLAH'S
ALMOST
AMOROUS
ANSWERING
APPARITIONS
ARGUMENT
ARMY
ASKS
ASTONISHED
ATTENTION
AVALON
AWRY
BALLYLEE
BANDS
BARBAROUS
BARS
BATS
BAY
BEAMS
BECAME
BEGGARS
BEGOT
BELL-BRANCH
BLACKENED
BLESSING
BLINDED
BLINK
BLOODY
BLOTTED
BLUE-EYED
BOAR
BOARDS
BOTTOM
BOY'S
BRAWLING
BREAKS
BREASTS
BREEZE
BRIM
BRIMMED
BRUSH
BULBEN
BURTHEN
BUSINESS
BYZANTIUM
CAIRN

CALVES
CARED
CARRIES
CASE
CASUAL
CATCH
CATHLEEN
CENTRAL
CHARACTERS
CHEER
CHILDREN'S
CHOIR
CHRYSOLITE
CLAWS
CLIMBING
CLOUD-PALE
COARSE
COCK
COMFORTABLE
CONFUSION
CONNEMARA
CONTENTED
COOL
COUNSEL
COXCOMB
CRADLES
CRAWLS
CROOKED
CROWDED
CROWNED
CUPS
CURTAIN
DAWNING
DAYTIME
DEARER
DEDICATION
DEEPS
DEWDROPS
DIETH
DIG
DIRTY
DISTANCE
DOE
DOOM
DOZEN
DRIFT
DROOPING
DWELLS
EARTHY
EDAINE
EDEN
EIRE
ELEMENTAL
EMBLEMS
EMBROIDERY
EMPTIED
ENFOLD
EVERLASTING
FANCIED
FANTASTIC
FARM
FAWN
FEATHERED
FEEDS
FELLOW
FICKLE
FIFTEEN

4 (cont.)

BROTHERHOOD	DEIRDRE	GALLOPED	KINDRED	MUMMIES
BULWARK	DIMMED	GENTLEMEN	KINGFISHER	MURDERED
BUNDLE	DIN	GENTLENESS	LABOURER	MUSED
BURDENS	DISCOVERED	GETS	LACE	MUTTERED
BURNS	DITCH	GIRTH	LACKED	MYSTERIES
BUSHES	DIVINE	GLARE	LACKING	NATURE'S
CAGE	DOLLS	GOAT	LAMENTING	NEAVE
CAPTIVE	DOLT	GOBAN	LANGUOR	NEEDLE'S
CASTING	DOOMED	GONG	LAPPING	NEIGHBOURING
CASTLE	DOVE-GREY	GOOD-BYE	LASHES	NERVELESS
CELLAR	DREAMLESS	GOODLY	LEADING	NIGHTMARE
CEREMONY	DREAMT	GRACE	LEANS	NORTHERN
CHARITY	DRIVING	GRAIN	LEAPING	NOTES
CHAUNT	DROOPS	GRANARY	LEAR	OARS
CHEEKS	DUDDON	GRASSHOPPERS	LEARNT	OCEAN
CHIEF	DUSKY	GREAT-	LEDA	ODOURS
CHILD'S	DUSTY	GRANDFATHER'S	LESSER	OFFICE
CHILLED	DWINDLING	GREY-LEAVED	LIFTING	OPENED
CHIMNEY	EAVES	GROVE	LIGHTER	O'RAHILLY
CHIN	EBREMAR	GUAIRE	LIGHTEST	OUTER
CHINA	ECHOING	GUILT	LIME	OXEN
CHISEL	ECHTGE	GULL	LION'S	PANTHERS
CHOP	E'EN	GYRE	LIVID	PARIS
CHURCHES	ELABORATE	HABIT	LOCKS	PARK
CIRCUIT	ELMS	HALLS	LOLLARD	PARNELL'S
CIVIL	EMMET	HAMLET	LONDON	PARTING
CLANGING	EMPIRE	HANDIWORK	LONGED	PARTS
CLANGOUR	EMPTINESS	HANDSOME	LOOSED	PASTURE
CLEAN	ENCLOSES	HARPER'S	LOOSEN	PATIENCE
CLIME	ENDURING	HAWTHORN	LOOSENED	PEACEFUL
CLOSER	EVENT	HAYNAU	LOOSENING	PEEWIT
CLOTHED	EVERMORE	HEALED	LUNATIC	PEOPLED
CLUMP	EXILES	HEALING	LURED	PERPLEXED
COBWEB	FAERIES	HEARTENERS	MAEVE'S	PETALS
COCKED	FAIRIES	HEATHER	MAGI	PHANTASY
COCKEREL	FAN	HECTOR	MALICIOUS	PHOSPHORUS
COLA	FASTING	HEED	MAR	PHRASE
COMFORTED	FATTEN	HEIGHT	MARK	PICK
COMMEND	FEARING	HEROES	MASK	PICTURED
COMRADES	FEASTING	HISTORIES	MASTERED	PIERCE
CONCHUBAR	FEATURES	HIT	MATCH	PILLAR
CORDS	FEN	HIVE	MAULED	PILOT
CORE	FIGURED	HOLINESS	MEADOW	PIT
COUGHING	FIGURES	HOLLOWS	MEAN	PLACID
COURTEOUS	FINDING	HOODED	MEANT	PLATO
COURTESY	FINGERED	HOOKED	MEASUREMENT	PLEADS
COURTLY	FINISH	HOOTED	MEDITATE	PLEASED
COUSIN	FISHERMAN	HOPED	MEETING	PLENTY
COVERLET	FITFUL	HORSEBACK	MELANCHOLY	PLOTINUS
COW	FIX	HOSTING	MELODY	PLUNGED
CREAK	FLANKS	HOVER	MID	POETRY
CREEP	FLASHED	HUDDON	'MID	POISON
CRIME	FLEECE	HUNTER'S	MIGHTIEST	POLE
CRUMBLING	FLEETING	HURRAH	MILES	POND
CRUSHING	FOLDING	ICE	MIMICRY	PONDERING
DAFFODILS	FOOT-FALL	IMAGINE	MINUTES	POPLAR
DAMASK	FOOTSTEP	IMMOVABLE	MIRRORED	POT
DAMES	FOOTSTEPS	INDEED	MIRTHFUL	POURED
DANGER	FORCED	INTELLECTUAL	MOANED	PRAISES
DANIEL	FORESTS	INTRODUCTORY	MOCKERS	PREY
DAZED	FORGAEL'S	INVIOLATE	MOCKING	PRINCE
DEAL	FORGIVEN	ISLES	MOMENTS	PRINCESS
DECEIVED	FORLORN	JOINTS	MONUMENT	PROTECT
DECEIVING	FOWL	JOT	MONUMENTS	QUARRELS
DECTORA	FRAGRANCE	JOYS	MOORE	QUESTIONING
DEEPEST	FRAIL	JUICE	MOSS	RAILS
	FRIENDSHIP	JUNE	MUMBLING	RANT

4 (cont.)

RASCAL
RASCALS
RATTLE
RAVE
RAVELLED
RAVENS
RAYS
READING
REBELS
REDNESS
REEDY
REFUSED
REINS
REMAKE
REMEMBRANCE
RENEW
RETURNING
REVEL
REVELRY
REVOLUTION
REWARD
RICE
RINGED
RISING
RIVER'S
ROBES
ROD
ROE
ROGUE
ROOMS
RULES
SACK
SADDEST
SAGE
SAILOR
SAINTS
SALUTING
SATO'S
SAVING
SAYING
SCARED
SCREAMED
SEA-GODS
SEA-GREEN
SEATED
SECRETS
SEDENTARY
SELF
SELF-BORN
SELVES
SENSITIVE
SEVENTY
SGEOLAN
SHAFT
SHEDS
SHIELD-BREAKER
SHIN
SHOWERS
SHROUDS
SIDHE
SIMPLICITY
SINGER
SINKING
SINNED
SIR
SLIGO

SLUMBERED
SMILED
SNATCHING
SNORED
SOLDIERY
SORROWFUL
SOULLES
SOUNDED
SPADES
SPED
SPELL
SPLASHED
SPLASHING
SPRAY
SPRUNG
SPUN
STABLE
STALK
STATESMAN
STATUE
STEEDS
STEM
STIFF
STOLE
STOLEN
STOOPING
STORM-BEATEN
STORY'S
STRAINING
STRAYED
STREETS
STRUGGLED
STUFF
SUMMER'S
SUNDOWN
SUPERHUMAN
SURE
SWAM
SWEEPING
SWEETEST
SWEETHEART
SWEETLY
SWIMMING
SYCAMORE
TAKING
TAPERS
TATTERED
TAUGHT
TEMPLE
THENCE
THEREIN
THONGS
THORNS
THROWS
TIGHT
TORCHES
TOYS
TRAFFIC
TRAGEDY
TREMBLES
TRODDEN
TRUST
TRY
TUMBLING
TUNES
ULADH
UNIMAGINABLE

UNJUST
UNLABOURING
UNNATURAL
UNSATISFIED
UNWIND
UPROAR
URN
USED
VERSE
VEXED
VIGOROUS
VIOLENCE
VIOLET
WAN
WANTONESS
WAR-AXE
WARRED
WASTING
WAVED
WEEPS
WHIMPERING
WHIRL
WHITENED
WHITENESS
WHITENING
WHOLESOME
WILLIAM
WILLOWS
WIND-BLOWN
WINGING
WISHES
WOLF
WONDERFUL
WONDROUS
WORMS
WOUNDED
WRIT
WRITERS
YOUNGEST
YOUTHFUL
YOUTH'S
ZODIAC

3

ABBEY
ABIDE
ABLE
ABOARD
ABSTRACTIONS
ACCURST
ACHE
ACRE
ADAM'S
ADD
ADMIT
ADORN
ADORNING
AFLAME
AGITATION
AGONY
AIRS
ALAS
ALDER
ALFRED
ALGECIRAS
ALIEN
ALIGHT

ALTAR
ALWAY
AMBER
ANASHUYA
ANGEL
ANGELO
ANTIQUE
ANVIL
ANYONE
AODH
APPLE-BLOSSOM
APPLE-WOOD
APPROVED
AQUAMARINE
ARAB
ARABIAN
ARROWS
ARTIST
ASSASSIN
ASTIR
ASTROLOGER
ATE
ATTACK
ATTIC
AUDIENCE
AUSTERE
AUTUMNAL
AWAKED
BABBLING
BABYLON
BALANCED
BALOR
BANDED
BARK
BARKED
BARRED
BARREL
BATTLE-CARS
BAWD
BAYING
BEARS
BEAUTIES
BECOMES
BEDOUIN'S
BEECHES
BEFALL
BEGETS
BEGGAR-MAN
BEGUILED
BELLE
BELLOWING
BERYL
BESOUGHT
BEWILDERED
BIDDING
BILLY
BLACKNESS
BLADE'S
BLADES
BLAKE
BLEAT
BLENCHED
BLINKED
BLINKING
BLOOD-
  BEDABBLED
BLOOD-SHOT

BOLT
BOND
BONDS
BOUNDS
BOWING
BOXES
BOYISH
BRAVE
BREATHED
BREED
BRUTAL
BUBBLES
BUNDLED
BURIAL
BURSTING
BUTTERFLIES
BUTTERFLY
BYZANTINE
CAESAR
CALAMITY
CALIPH
CAMP
CANOPY
CANVAS
CAOLTE
CAREFUL
CARELESS
CARESSED
CARPENTERS
CARRIAGE
CATARACT
CATS
CAVE
CEASELESS
CENTAUR
CENTRE
CERTAINTY
CHALK
CHAMBERMAID
CHANGES
CHAPEL
CHAPLET
CHARGE
CHASES
CHATTERING
CHECK
CHEERING
CHEST
CHILDER
CHRISTIAN
CHRYSOBERYL
CIRCUS
CITIES
CITRON
CLAIM
CLASHING
CLAW
CLEAVE
CLIFF
CLIFFS
CLIMBS
CLINGS
CLOOTH-NA-
  BARE
CLOSELY
CLOTTED
CLOVER

3 (cont.)

CLOYNE
COAL
COAT-HANGER
COFFIN
COMELIER
COMMAND
COMPLACENT
COMPLEXITIES
COMPOSITE
CONFESSION
CONFIDENCE
CONSIDERING
CONSUME
CONTACT
CONTEMPLA-
TION
CONTINUALLY
CONVERSE
COPY
CORNERS
CORPSE
COTTAGES
COUNTESS
COUNTRIES
COUPLE
COUPLES
COURSES
COVERING
COVERS
CRAFTY
CRANE
CRAWL
CREEL
CREEPS
CRESCENTS
CREVICE
CRICKET
CROWED
CROZIERED
CRUACHAN'S
CRUTCHES
CUCHULAIN'S
CUCHULLIN
CURDS
CURE
CURES
CURSING
CURVED
CYPRESS
DAEMONIC
DARKENING
DATE
DAUGHTERS
DAWNED
DAYS'
DEATH-BED
DEATH'S
DECEIT
DECEPTION
DECK
DECLARED
DEEPER
DEFEAT
DEFEATED
DEFORMITY
DELIGHTS

DELL
DEMAND
DEPTHS
DERIDED
DESK
DESPAIRING
DESTROY
DESTROYED
DICE
DIGGING
DISAPPEAR
DISASTER
DISCLOSE
DISPLAY
DOG'S
DOLL
DOLOROUS
DOLPHIN'S
DOONEY
DORIC
DOUBTLESS
DOUGH
DOVES
DOWNY
DRAGS
DRAPERY
DRAVE
DRAWS
DREAMER
DROOP
DRUMS
DRUNKARD'S
DUBLIN
DUTY
EARLESS
EARLY
EARN
EASTERN
ECHO
ELEGANCE
EMAN'S
EMBITTERED
EMERGE
EMOTION
EMPEROR'S
EMPOUNDED
ENAMELLED
ENTANGLED
ENTERS
ENWOUND
EOCHAID'S
EQUALITY
ERECT
ESTABLISHED
ESTRANGED
EXCITED
EXIST
EXTRAVAGANCE
EYELID
FALCONER
FALSE
FAMILIAR
FAND
FARMER'S
FARM-HOUSE
FAT
FATHER'S

FATIGUE
FAUN
FEARED
FEASTWARD
FEATHERY
FEEDING
FELLOWS
FERN
FERNS
FESTIVAL
FEVER
FIDDLER
FIDGET
FIGURE
FILLING
FILTHY
FINAL
FINDRINNY
FINGER-TIPS
FIR
FIST
FITTING
FLAG
FLAGRANT
FLAT
FLAW
FLEAS
FLIT
FLOODED
FLOORS
FLOWER-LIKE
FLOWERY
FLUTTERED
FOAM-WET
FOLLOWING
'FORE
FORGERY
FORGETFUL
FORGETFULNESS
FORGIVENESS
FORTY
FOSTER
FOXES
FRAGMENTS
FREEDOM
FRIENDLY
FRIEND'S
FURROWS
GAIN
GALLANT
GALLOWS
'GAN
GAP
GAZES
GEAR
GHOSTS
GIDDY
GIVING
GLAMOUR
GLEAMED
GLEN
GLIMMERED
GLOSSY
GOVERN
GRANDFATHER
GRASSHOPPER
GREATEST

GREENNESS
GREET
GREGORY'S
GROAN
GUERDON
GUIDES
GUIDING
GYRING
HAIRS
HALCYON'S
HAMMERS
HAPLESS
HARDER
HARMONIOUS
HARP-STRINGS
HARRY
HARUN
HASTEN
HAUGHTIER
HAY
HEARTHSTONE
HEAT
HEATH
HEAVED
HEBRIDES
HEELS
HELM
HERB
HERDSMAN
HERMITS
HERON-BILLED
HERON'S
HEW
HIGH-BORN
HO
HOARY
HOLIEST
HOMESTEADS
HONEY-BEES
HONEY-MOUTH
HORSEMANSHIP
HOT
HOULIHAN
HOWLED
HUEGEL
HUGH
HUNCHBACK
HUNDREDS
HUNT
IMMORTALITY
IMMORTALS
IMPERISHABLE
IMPETUOUS
INCENSE
INDIGNANT
INDOLENCE
INK
INLAID
INNISFREE
INSTRUMENT
INTRICACIES
INVENT
ITALIAN
IVORIES
JACQUES
JAPANESE
JASMINE

JEALOUS
JESTER
JEWELRY
JOIN
JOINT
JOSTLED
JOURNEYMAN
JOURNEYS
JUAN
JUST
KEEPING
KEGS
KETTLE
KINDLY
KINE
KINGDOMS
KINGLY
KISSING
KNITTED
KNITTING
KNOCK
KYLE-NA-NO
LABORIOUS
LAGGARD
LAKE'S
LAMBS
LAMENTS
LAPIS
LAVELL
LAWS
LAZULI
LEAFAGE
LEAFLESS
LEAPS
LEMAN
LETTER
LETTERED
LETTERS
LEVELLED
LIBERTY
LIGHTED
LIGHTNINGS
LIKELY
LILIES
LINEN
LINKED
LIQUID
LIZARDS
LO
LOAD
LOGIC
LOINS
LONG-LOST
LOTUS
LOVELESS
LOVE-LORN
LOVING
LULLED
LUMINOUS
LUNGED
LURE
MAC
MADDENED
MAGEE
MAGNIFICENCE
MAIDS
MAIL

3 (cont.)

MAJESTICAL
MANANAN
MANANNAN
MANES
MAN-HEADED
MANHOOD
MANNER
MANY-CHANGING
MARCHES
MARINERS
MARRIAGE-BED
MARROW-BONES
MARSH
MAST
MASTER'S
MATCHING
MATTERS
MATTOCK
MEASURED
MEASURES
MEDITATIONS
MEDITATIVE
MEN-AT-ARMS
MERMAID
MIDDLETON
MIDHIR'S
MILK-WHITE
MISTRESS
MOLAY
MOMENT'S
MONGAN
MONOTONE
MOORFOWL
MOOR-HENS
MORNIN'
MORNING'S
MORTAL'S
MOULDED
MOULDERING
MOVEMENT
MRS
MUIRTHEMNE
MUMMY-CLOTH
MUNICIPAL
MUNSTER
MURDER
MURIAS
MURMUROUS
MUSCLE
MUSCULAR
MUSICAL
NAN
NATIVITY
NATURES
NEAREST
NEEDLE
NE'ER
NEGLECT
NESSA
NEW-MOWN
NIGHTLY
NOBLENESS
NODDED
NORMAN
NOURISH
NUMBERS

NUN
OBSCURE
ODOUR-LADEN
O'DRISCOLL
OFFER
OGHAM
O'HART
OISIN'S
ONWARD
OPINION
ORDER
OUTLANDISH
OUTRAGEOUS
OUTWORN
OVERBOARD
PADDLE
PAINTER
PAINTER'S
PAINTING
PALING
PALM
PAN
PARCHMENT
PARLIAMENT
PARTED
PASSES
PAVEMENT
PEAK
PEASANT'S
PEBBLES
PEN
PERISHED
PERSIAN
PHASES
PILE
PILGRIM
PILIN'
PIN
PINING
PINIONS
PIOUS
PIPE
PIRATES
PITIFUL
PLATONIC
PLATONIST
PLAYBOY
PLAYTIME
PLEASURES
PLUMED
PLUMY
POET'S
POINTED
PONDER
POUND
PREACHER
PREDESTINED
PRESENT
PRINCES
PROCLAIM
PROCLAIMING
PROPER
PROPHESYING
PURITY
PURSE
PURSUING
PUSH

PUSHED
PUTS
QUAKING
QUATTROCENTO
QUENCHLESS
QUESTIONER
QUICKLY
QUIETNESS
QUIETUDE
QUIVER
RAFTER
RAIMENT
RAINS
RANGE
RAPTUROUS
RARE
RATTLED
RAVENING
READY
RECKONED
RED-ROSE-
    BORDERED
REED
REELED
REFUGE
RELIGIOUS
REMEMBERS
REND
RENOWN
REPOSE
REPROACH
REPROVED
REPROVES
REVERENCE
REVERIES
RISES
RIVERY
ROADWAY
ROBE
ROCKING
ROMAN
ROME
ROSICROSS
ROUSED
ROW
RUA
RUINOUS
RUSHING
RUSHY
RUSSET
RUSTLE
SALLEY
SALTIN'
SAND-SACK
SAVAGE
SAVED
SCARLET
SCENTED
SCHOLARS
SCHOOLING
SCOFF
SCREEN
SCRUB
SEA-KING
SEAWARD
SEA-WAYS
SEEKS

SEIZED
SEPARATE
SEPULCHRE
SERPENT
SERVING-MAN
SEXUAL
SHADY
SHAPELY
SHARED
SHARPENED
SHAWL
SHEPHERDESS
SHIFT
SHIRK
SHIRT
SHOD
SHONEEN
SHOOTS
SHOULDERED
SHOULDERS
SHRIEKED
SHRIEKS
SHRILL
SHUFFLE
SHUTS
SICKLE
SICKNESS
SIGNS
SINEW
SINNING
SISTERS
SIXTEEN
SKEIN
SKILL
SKIPPER
SLATE-COLOURED
SLEEVE
SLUNK
SMITHY
SMITTEN
SNARE
SOMBRE
SOMEONE
SOMETIMES
SOONER
SOULS'
SOUR
SOURCE
SPAIN
SPARROWS
SPECTACLE
SPEEDY
SPICE
SPINNING
SPIT
SPITE
SPRIGHTLY
SPRITE
SPY
STAINED
STAIRS
STAMPED
STARLIT
STARTED
STARVED
STATION
STAYS

STEADY
STELLA
STERNER
STICKS
STILLED
STOPPED
STRAITS
STRANGENESS
STRAYING
STREW
STRINGED
STRONGER
STRUGGLE
STRUGGLING
STUCK
STUPID
SUFFER
SUFFERING
SUFFICIENT
SULTRY
SUMMONED
SUNSET
SUP
SUPPER
SWAY
SWEETEN
SWIFTLY
SWIFT'S
SWINE
SWING
SWORD-BLADES
TABLETS
TALES
TALKS
TEMPEST
TERRIFIED
THIRTY
THOUGHTLESS
THREATEN
THROATS
TIGHTENED
TODAY
TONE
TONES
TOOL
TOSSED
TOY
TRACK
TRAITOR
TRANCE
TRANQUILLITY
TRAVELLER
TRAVELLING
TRICK
TRICKS
TRIED
TRINITY
TRIPS
TRIVIAL
TRUE-LOVE
TUB
TUFTED
TUMBLED
TURF
UNBEGOTTEN
UNBID
UNCOUTH

2 (cont.)

FOAMING
FOIL
FONDLE
FONDLED
FOOT-SOLE
FOOTSTOOL
FORBID
FORCE
FORD
FOREHEADS
FOREKNOWLEDGE
FOREMOST
FORESAW
FOREVER
FORGED
FORMLESS
FORTUNE
FOSTER-MOTHER
FOUNTAINS
FOURSCORE
FOXHUNTER
FRANCE
FRENCH
FRENZIED
FRESH
FRINGED
FROSTY
FRUITFUL
FRUITS
FULLNESS
FUMBLED
FUMBLING
FURIES
FURIOUS
FURLED
GABRIEL
GAIETY
GALLOPING
GARDEN'S
GARMENTS'
GASP
GAUNT
GAZELLE
GEESE
GEM-STUDDED
GENERATION
GHASTLY
GHOST'S
GILD
GILDED
GIRDLE
GIVER
GLAMOURS
GLASNEVIN
GLASSES
GLENDALOUGH
GLITTERED
GLOOMY
GLOVE
GLOWED
GLOWING
GLOW-WORM
GLUTS
GOAD
GOATHERD
GOATS

GOBAN'S
GODLESS
GODS'
GOLD-
  EMBROIDERED
GOLDS
GORT
GOSPELLER
GRAINS
GRAMMAR
GRANDCHILDREN
GRAND-DAD
GRANDDAUGHTER
GRANDSON
GRANIA'S
GRASP
GRAY
GRAZE
GRAZING
GREAT-
  GRANDFATHER
GREAT-GRANDSON
GRECIAN
GREYNESS
GRIEF'S
GRIEFS
GRIEVOUS
GRIPPED
GROANED
GROPED
GUARDED
GUARIMOND
GUEST
GUIDO
GUINEAS
GULLS
GULPH
GUN
GUNSHOT
GYPSY
HADES'
HAILED
HALE
HALF-CLOSED
HALF-FLIES
HALF-FORGOTTEN
HALFPENNIES
HALF-PENNIES
HALF-READ
HANDLED
HANDMAID
HANDY-WORK
HANGETH
HAPPIEST
HARBOUR
HARK
HARLOT
HAROUN
HARPSTRING
HARP-STRING
HARVEST
HARVESTERS
HASSAN
HASTE
HAT
HATES
HATING

HAYNAU'S
HAZELS
HEADLONG
HEADY
HEALTHY
HEARTS'
HEAVENS'
HEAVILY
HEAVINESS
HEDGES
HEIR
HEIRS
HELEN'S
HELMETS
HELMS
HELPED
HEN
HENRY
HENS
HERBLESS
HERBS
HERD
HERESIES
HERITAGE
HERO
HEROICALLY
HERONS
HERO'S
HERRINGS
HIVES
HOARD
HOARDED
HOLES
HOLIDAY
HOLLO
HOMER'S
HONEYCOMB
HOOK
HOOKS
HORIZON
HORIZON'S
HORN'S
HORSE-BOYS
HOWL
HUES
HUGER
HUGS
HULL
HUM
HUMBLY
HUMILITY
HUMMING
HUMOROUS
HURLEY
HURTING
HURTS
HYSTERICA
HYSTERICAL
IDIOT
IDLENESS
IDLING
IGNOBLE
IGNOMINY
ILL-BRED
ILLNESS
IMAGED
IMAGINABLE

IMAGING
IMITATORS
IMMEDICABLE
IMMENSE
IMMODERATE
IMMORAL
IMPATIENTLY
IMPORTUNE
IMPROVE
IMPURE
INANIMATE
INARTICULATE
INDIA
INDOLENT
INFANCY
INFANT
INFERIOR
INFINITE
INHERIT
INHERITED
INHERITOR
INHUMAN
INNER
INNOCENTS
INSEPARABLY
INSIDE
INSULT
INTENSITY
INTERCOURSE
INTEREST
INVISIBLE
INWROUGHT
ISLE'S
IVY
JABBER
JAGS
JAMES
JAWS
JEALOUSY
JERK
JERRY
JEW
JOHNSON
JONATHAN
JONSON'S
JOURNALIST
JOURNEYED
JOURNEY'S
JOY'S
JUGGLERIES
JUGGLING
JULIET
KAMA
KANVA
KATE
KATHLEEN-
  NY-HOOLIHAN
KEEPER
KEVIN
KEY
KICKED
KILTARTAN
KILVARNET
KIMONOS
KINSMEN
KITE
KITH

KNEAD
KNEADED
KNEELS
KNIFE
KNIGHTS
KNIT
KNOCKED
KNOCKFEFIN
KNOT-GRASS
KNOTTED
LABAN
LABOURS
LACKS
LAMB'S
LAMENTATION
LANCELOT
LANDSMAN
LANDWARD
LAPPED
LARGER
LATELY
LATEST
LATIN
LAUGHS
LAYER
LEAF-SOWN
LEATHERN
LEBEEN-LONE
LECHER
LECHEROUS
LEDAEAN
LEDGE
LEGEND
LEISURED
LEMON
LENDS
LEOPARD
LETS
LEVELLING
LIME-TREE
LIMPS
LINEAGE
LINGERS
LINNET
LIONESS
LIONS
LISSADELL
LISTENED
LITERATURE
LIVELONG
LIVE-LONG
LIVERY
LOCKED
LOFTIER
LOG
LONG-FORGOTTEN
LOOM
LOOPHOLE
LORDS
LORE
LOUDER
LOUDLY
LOUGH
LOUGHLAN
LOVELIER
LOVELIEST
LOVERS'

2 (cont.)
LOVE-SONG
LOVE-TALES
LOW-LAUGHING
LULLABULLOO
LULLABY
LUSTRE
LYNX
MACE
MACGREGOR
MACKEREL-
 CROWDED
MADGE
MADNESS
MAGNANIMITY
MAILED
MAINE
MAINES
MAINES'
MAIVE
MAKER
MALACHI
MANAGE
MAN-AT-ARMS
MANE
MANTLING
MANY-HEADED
MARCHED
MAREOTIC
MARGE
MARGERY
MARKET
MARKS
MARRED
MARTIN
MARTIN'S
MARTS
MARTYRS
MARVEL
MARY'S
MASONRY
MASS
MASTERY
MASTHEAD
MAT
MATHEMATICAL
MAUNDERING
MAVRONE
MAYHAP
MAYO
MEAD
MEAL
MEANINGLESS
MEANS
MEASURING
MEET'S
MELLOW
MELODIOUS
MELT
MELTED
MELTING
MEND
MERIT
MERLIN
MERRIMENT
MERU
MESSAGE

MESSAGES
MESSENGERS
METAPHOR
MIDHER'S
MIDNIGHTS
MILL
MILLION
MILLIONS
MINDED
MINGLED
MIRACLES
MISCHIEF
MISER
MISERIES
MIST-COLD
MISTS
MOANS
MOBS
MODELLED
MOHINI
MOIST
MONEY'S
MONKS
MONTASHIGI
MONTHS
MOONY
MOORS
MORNINGS
MOROCCAN
MORTALS
MOSSY
MOTHERS
MOTH-HOUR
MOTH-LIKE
MOTH'S
MOTIONLESS
MOUNDS
MOUNTAIN'S
MOUNTAIN-SIDE
MOUNTING
MOUNTS
MOUSE-GREY
MOVETH
MOWN
MR
MULTIPLICITY
MULTIPLIED
MUMMERS
MUNDI
MURAL
MURDERERS
MURDERING
MURROUGH
MUSCATEL
MUSCLES
MUSING
MUTE
MUTTERS
MYRIADS
MYSTICAL
NAIL
NAILED
NAOISE
NAPKIN
NAPS
NASCHINA'S
NEIGHED

NERVE
NESTLE
NESTS
NEWLY
NEW-MARRIED
NINETEEN-
 SIXTEEN
NINETEENTH
NINETEEN-
 THIRTY-ONE
NINEVEH
NINTH
NODS
NOOSE
NORM
NOTABLE
NOTHINGNESS
NOUGHT
NOWHERE
NUMB
NURTURED
NYMPHS
OAKEN
OATEN
OATH-BOUND
OBEDIENT
OBJECT
OCCUPIED
OCEAN'S
OCHONE
OCTOBER
ODDS
OENONE
OFT
O'HIGGINS
OLDEST
OLIVER
OLYMPUS
OMEN
O'NEILLS
ONSET
ONYX
OPAL
ORACLE
O'ROUGHLEY
OSCAR
OSCAR'S
OTHERWISE
OTTER-SKIN
OUTSIDE
OUT-WORN
OVERFLOWED
OVERFLOWS
OVERTHREW
OWING
PACKED
PAGAN
PAINTINGS
PAIRC-NA-LEE
PAISTIN
PALACES
PALACE-YARD
PALATE
PALED
PALE-FACED
PALENESS
PALLAS

PANG
PANIC
PANTHER
PANTING
PANTRY
PAPER
PARASITE
PARDONED
PARENTS
PARMENIDES
PARNELLITES
PARROT
PARROTS
PARTICULAR
PARTRIDGE
PASSETH
PASSIO
PASSION'S
PASTURE-LAND
PATCH
PATER
PATTERN
PATTERNS
PAUDEEN
PAUDEENS
PAW
PAYMENT
PEACEABLE
PEARLS
PEBBLY
PEDANT
PEELED
PFFP
PEER
PEERED
PEERING
PEERS
PENANCE
PENCE
PENCILLED
PENDULOUS
PENSIONER
PENSIVE
PERCHANCE
PERCHES
PERHAPS
PERISH
PERNING
PERPLEXITY
PERSECUTION
PERSISTENCE
PERSUADE
PETAL
PETER'S
PHIDIAS
PHIDIAS'
PHILOSOPHY
PIECES
PIG
PIGEON
PIGEONS
PILED-UP
PILGRIMS
PILLARED
PIPER
PIPES
PITCH-DARK

PITCHED
PITYING
PLAGUE
'PLAINING
PLAITED
PLASTER
PLEASURED
PLOTTING
PLOUGHED
PLOUGH-LAND
PLOUGHMAN
PLUM
PLUMES
PLUMMET-
 MEASURED
POLAR
POLISHED
POLITE
POLITIC
PONDS
POPINJAY
POPLARS
POPPY
POPULACE
PORTRAITS
POUNDS
POURING
PRAISING
PRANCED
PRANCING
PRAYS
PREPARED
PRESENCE
PRESENCES
PRETENCE
PRIESTESS
PRIME
PRINTS
PRISON
PROCLAIMED
PROFFERS
PROFOUND
PROMISE
PRONE
PROPERTY
PROPHECIES
PROPPED
PROSE
PROSPEROUS
PROTECTING
PROVES
PROVIDENCE
PROWS
PSALTERIES
PUBLISHED
PUFFED
PULLERS
PULSES
PUNISHMENT
PUNK
PURER
PURGATORY
PURR
PUSHES
PUSHING
PYRE
QUAFFED

2 (cont.)

TARA'S
TASTING
TAVERN
TAWS
TEACHERS
TEARFUL
TELLING
TEMPT
TENDEREST
TENDING
TENTED
TENTH
TENT'S
TERRORS
TERROR-STRICKEN
TERROR-STRUCK
TESTS
TETHER
THANKFUL
THEATRE
THEMES
THICK
THICKET
THIEVING
THORN-TREE
THOROUGHBRED
THOROUGHFARE
THOUGHT-WOVEN
THRANEEN
THREADBARE
THREATENED
THREES
THROATED
THROB
THRONGS
THUMB
THUNDER-SOUND
THURIBLES
TIDES
TILLAGE
TIMBER
TINKER
TIP-TOE
TOE
TOILING
TOILS
TOLERANCE
TOMB-HAUNTER
TOMBSTONE
TONSURED
TOPLESS
TOPMOST
TORCHLIGHT
TORCH-LIGHT
TRADING
TRAILING
TRAMPING
TRANSFORM
TRAPPED
TRAVELLERS
TRAVELLING-MAN
TRAVELS

TREACHERY
TREASURER
TREASURES
TREATISE
TREMBLED
TREMENDOUS
TREMULOUS
TRIMMED
TRIPLE
TRITON
TRIUMPHING
TROIA
TROLLED
TROMBONE
TROOPER
TROOPS
TROW
TRUMP
TUMBLES
TUMULTS
TUNNELLED
TURBULENCE
TURBULENT
TURKISH
'TWEEN
TWELFTH
TWELVEMONTH
TWENTY-AND-EIGHT
TWIGS
TWILIGHTS
TWINKLING
TWITTER
TWOS
TYING
UNAMBITIOUS
UNBIND
UNBOUND
UNCERTAINTY
UNCOMELY
UNCONQUER-ABLE
UNDERSTANDS
UNEARTHLY
UNEASY
UNFINISHED
UNFORGIVING
UNFRIENDLY
UNGUENTS
UNHOOK
UNICORN
UNLOOSED
UNREMEMBERING
UNSAY
UNSLEEPING
UNTOLD
UNTROUBLED
UNWIELDY
UNWITHERING
UNWOUND
UPLIFTED
UPROOT
UPS
UPSTAIRS
UPSTANDING
URBINO
URGED

USELESS
UTMOST
UTTERING
VALERA
VALLEY'S
VALUE
VAN
VANISHES
VEERING
VELVET
VERGE
VERSES
VEX
VICTOR
VIGOUR
VIRGINITY
VIRTUE
VIRTUES
VIVID
VOLUME
VOWS.
WADE
WAGES
WAKENED
WANDS
WANTON
WARES
WARFARE
WARMTH
WASH
WASHED
WATCHERS
WATCHES
WATER-FOWLS
WATER-SIDE
WAVERED
WAVERINGS
WEAKLY
WEASEL
WEASEL'S
WEATHER-WORN
WEBBED
WEB-HEAPED
WEBS
WEED
WEIGHED
WEIGHS
WEIGHTY
WEIR
WELCOMED
WELL-BELOVED'S
WELL-NIGH
WELLS
WENCH
WENCHING
WHIMSEY
WHIP
WHIPS
WHISPERS
WHIT
WHITE-HAIRED
WILDERING
WILLINGLY
WILLS
WILSON
WINDING-SHEET
WINE-CUP

WIRE
WIRES
WISDOM'S
WISDOMS
WISER
WISTFUL
WITCHCRAFT
WITHHOLD
WIVE
WOLD
WOLFE
WOOD-CUTTER
WOODED
WOODLANDS
WORDY
WORKED
WORKING
WORKING-CARPENTER
WORLD-FAMOUS
WRAPPING
WRAPS
WRATH
WREATHS
WRESTLE
WRETCH
WRINKLING
WRITING
WRONGS
WROTH
YARDS
YAWNED
YEA
YEW-BOUGH

1

ABBOT
ABD
ABD-AL-RABBAN
ABIDES
ABLOW
A-BLOWIN'
ABOLISHED
ABROAD
ABSENT
ABSOLVO
ABSTINENCE
ABSURD
ABYSS
ACACIA
ACADEMY
ACCEPT
ACCEPTED
ACCIDENTAL
ACCIDENTS
ACCLAIMING
ACCOMPLISH
ACCOUNT
ACCOUNTED
ACCUSATION
ACCUSE
ACH
ACHAIANS'
ACKNOWLEDGE
ACORNS
ACQUAINTANCE
ACROPOLIS

ACTION'S
ACTOR
ACTORS
ACTUAL
A-CURSED
ADDERS
ADDING
ADDRESSED
ADMIRED
ADMIRING
ADMONISH
ADOLESCENCE
ADORE
ADORES
ADRIFT
ADRIP
ADVANCE
ADVERSITY
AEROPLANE
AERY
AFFABLE
AFFECTION
AFFECTIONS
AFFIRMS
AFFLICT
A-FISHING
A-FLAME
AFLASH
A-FLASH
A-FLICKER
AFLOAT
A-FLUTTERING
AFOOT
AFORETIME
AFRICA
AFRICAN
AFTERWARDS
AGAMEMNON
AGATE
AGE'S
AGHAST
AGILE
AGIN
AGLEAM
A-GLITTER
AGREE
AGREED
A-HAWKING
AHEAD
AI
AIBHLIN
AIBRIC'S
AID
AILING
AIMLESSNESS
AIR-BREATH
AIRMAN
AKIN
ALARM
ALARMED
ALARUMS
ALBAN
ALCOVE'S
ALE-HORNS
ALEXANDER
ALEXANDRIA'S
ALHAMBRA

1 (cont.)

ALIENS
ALIGHIERI
ALIGHTED
ALIKE
A-LIT
ALLAH
ALL-DESTROYING
ALLEGORICAL
ALLEN'S
ALLIANCES
ALL-LABOURING
ALLOWS
ALL-POWERFUL
ALL-UNNEEDED
ALMANACS
ALMHUIN
ALMHUIN'S
ALPUJARRAS
AL-RABBAN
AL-RASCHID
ALT
ALTAR-PIECE
ALTAR-RAILS
ALTERNATIVE
ALTERS
ALTOGETHER
AMAZED
AMBASSADOR
AMBASSADORS
AMBERGRIS
AMBERS
AMBITIONS
AMBLING
AMBUSCADE
AMENDED
AMERGIN
AMERICAN
AMPLE
A-MURMUR
ANALYTIC
ANARCHY
ANBUAL'S
ANCESTOR
ANCESTORS
ANEMONES
ANGELO'S
ANIGH
ANIMAL'S
ANIMALS
ANIMALS'
ANKLES
ANNOTATE
ANNOUNCES
ANNUS
ANODYNE
ANOINTING
ANON
ANTELOPE
ANTELOPES
ANTHONY
ANTIGONE
ANTINOMIES
ANTIQUARIAN
ANTI-SELF
ANTLERS
ANXIOUS

ANYBODY
ANYWHERE
AOIBHIN
AOIFE
AOLAN
APHORISMS
A-PILIN'
APOLOGIA
APPLE-BOUGHS
APPLE-STEM
APPOINTED
APPROVE
APRIL'S
A-QUAKE
AQUILINE
ARABIA'S
ARBITER
ARCADIA
ARCADIA'S
ARCHANGEL
ARCHBISHOP
ARCHED
ARCHES
ARCHIMEDES'
ARCHITECT
ARGIVE
ARGO'S
ARGOSY
ARGUE
ARGUED
ARISEN
ARISTOTLE
ARMCHAIR
ARMIES'
ARMLETS
ARMOURED
ARM'S
ARMSTRONG
A-ROVING
ARRAIGNED
ARROGANCE
ARROGANTLY
ARTERY
ARTICULATION
ARTIFICE
ARTISSON
ARTIST'S
ARTISTS
ASCENDS
ASCENT
A-SHAKE
ASHEN
ASHORE
ASH-TREES'
ASH-WOOD
ASIATIC
ASLAUGA
ASS
ASSAILS
ASSAULT
ASS-BACK
ASSES
ASSIZE
ASS'S
ASSUAGE
ASTONISHING
ASTONISHMENT

ASTRADDLE
A-TELLING
ATHEIST
ATHENE'S
ATHENIAN
ATLAS
ATTEMPTED
ATTENDANT
ATTENDANTS
ATTIS'
ATTORNEY
AUGHT
AUGUSTUS
AUNTS
AUREOLE
AUSTERITY
AUSTRIAN
AUTHOR
AUTHORITY
AUTHORS
AVAIL
AVAILS
AVALANCHE
AVALLON
AVE
AVENGED
AVENGING
AVOW
AWAITING
AWARDED
AWARE
A-WAVING
A-WEARY
A-WEAVING
AWELESS
AWFUL
A-WINGING
AXEL
AXES
AXLE
A-YEAR
AZOLAR
AZURES
BABAR
BABYLON'S
BACCHANT
BACHELOR
BACKGROUNDS
BACKS
BACKWARDS
BADGERED
BAFFLED
BAGPIPES
BAILE'S
BALANCE
BALES
BALLAD-SINGER
BALLINAFAD
BALLS
BANDAGING
BANDIT
BANDY
BANDY-LEGGED
BANKERS
BANKRUPT
BANNERET
BANSHEE

BARACH
BARB
BARBS
BARCELONA
BARHAIM
BARNACLE
BARNACLE-GEESE
BARREL-HOOPS
BARRELS
BARRICADE
BARROW
BARROWS
BARTERED
BASALT
BASE-BORN
BASKETS
BAT
BATHE
BATTERING
BATTERY
BATTLE-AXE
BATTLE-AXES
BATTLE-BANNERS
BATTLE-
   BREAKING
BATTLE-HOST
BATTLEMENT
BATTLEMENTS
BATTLE-WEARY
BATTLING
BAWDY
BAWLS
BAWN
BEACON
BEAN
BEANFEAST
BEANFEST
BEAN-ROWS
BEARDS
BEASTS
BEAST-TORN
BEAUJOLET
BEAUTY-
   DRUNKEN
BEAUVARLET
BECK
BECKONED
BECKONING
BECKONS
BEDFELLOW
BEDOUIN
BEDSTEAD
BEECH-BOLE
BEECH-BOUGH
BEECHEN
BEECH-LEAVES
BEECH-TREE
BEECH-TREES
BEE-LOUD
BEERY
BEE'S
BEES'
BEETLES
BEFIT
BEFITTING
BEG
BEGETTER

BEGGAR-KINGS
BEGGARLY
BEGGARMAN
BEGGARS'
BEGONE
BELABOURING
BELIEF
BELIEVING
BELL-BEAT
BELLED
BELLIES
BELL-NOTES
BELLOW
BELLYFUL
BELONG
BELONGS
BELOVED'S
BELOVEDS
BELT
BEMOCKERS
BE-MOCKERS
BENDED
BERA
BEREFT
BESEECH
BESET
BESOM
BESOT
BESOTTED
BESOTTING
BEST-ENDOWED
BESTIAL
BESTIR
BEST'S
BETAKE
BETHLEHEM
BETRAY
BETTERS
BEWILDER
BEWILDERMENT
BEWITCHED
BEWITCHMENT
BIDDEN
BIDDY
BIER
BIGOT
BILLOWS
BINDS
BIRCH-TREE
BIRD-CLAWS
BIRD-LIKE
BIRDLY
BIRDS'
BIRTHDAY
BIRTH-HOUR
BISCAY
BISHOPS
BITING
BITTERER
BITTEREST
BITTERN
BITTER-SWEET
BITTER-
   SWEETNESS
BLACKBIRDS
BLACKENS
BLACKER

1 (cont.)
BLADDERED
BLANAID
BLANCHED
BLAND
BLASPHEMOUS
BLASTED
BLASTS
BLAZED
BLEAK
BLEAR-EYED
BLEATING
BLEED
BLEMISH
BLENCH
BLENDING
BLENT
BLESSINGS
BLINDER
BLITHER
BLOCKS
BLONDE
BLOOD-BEGOTTEN
BLOOD-DIMMED
BLOODLESS
BLOOD-RED
BLOOD-
  SATURATED
BLOTCH
BLOTS
BLOWIN'
BLUE-GREEN
BLUER
BLUE-VEINED
BLUSHED
BLUSHES
BOARDED
BOASTING
BOASTS
BOATMAN
BOB
BODES
BODICES
BODIED
BODKIN
BOG
BOG'S
BOILED
BOILING
BOISTEROUS
BOLTS
BOMB-BALLS
BOOTS
BORDA
BOREAL
BOREDOM
BOREEN
BORROW
BOSKY
BOTTLES
BOUNTIFUL
BOWELS
BOW-LEGGED
BOW-STRING'S
BOWSTRINGS
BOX-BORDERED
BOYNE

BRACKISH
BRAHMIN
BRAINS
BRAKE
BRANCHING
BRAND
BRAND-NEW
BRANWEN
BRATTA
BRATTAS
BRAVED
BRAVELY
BRAY
BRAYED
BREAKERS
BREATHES
BREECHED
BREEZES
BRESSEL
BRETHREN
BREWS
BRIAR
BRIDEGROOM
BRIDE-GROOM
BRIDEGROOM'S
BRIDELESS
BRIDE'S
BRIDLED
BRIDLE-PATH
BRIGAND
BRIGHTEN
BRIGHTER
BRIGHT-EYED
BRIMFUL
BRISTLES
BRITAIN
BRITISH
BRITTLE
BROACHED
BROKENHEARTED
BRONZED
BRONZE-RINGED
BROODED
BROOM
BROOM-STICKS
BROTHER'S
BROWED
BROWNING
BROWSE
BROW-SHADING
BRUISE
BRUISED
BRUISING
BRUSHED
BRUSHES
BRUSHING
BUAL'S
BUAN'S
BUBBLED
BUCKET
BUCKLED
BUCKSKIN
BUD
BUDDHA
BUDDHA'S
BUDDING
BUDS

BUFFETED
BUGLE
BUILDER
BUILDINGS
BUILDING-YARD
BUILDS
BULLETS
BULLO
BUM
BUNCH
BUNCHES
BUNCHING
BURDENED
BURGHERS
BURIAL-MOUND
BURKE'S
BURROW
BURROWING
BURSTS
BURY
BUSH
BUSTLE
BUTLER
BUTTED
BUTT-END
BUTTERMILK
BUTTING
BUYING
BYRE
BYRNE
BYRNES
CABBAGE
CABBAGES
CABINS
CAESARS
CAGES
CAIRN-HEAPED
CAIRN'S
CAKE
CALCULATION
CALCULATIONS
CALENDARS
CALIPH'S
CALLED'ST
CALLEN
CALLIMACHUS
CALUMNY
CALVARY'S
CAMEL
CAMEL-BACK
CAMEL-DUNG
CAMEL'S
CAMP-FIRE
CAMPING-PLACE
CAMP'S
CANDLE-LIKE
CANDLE'S
CANDLESTICK
CANKER-WORM
CANNONADE
CANNON-SHOT
CANTERED
CAPTIVE'S
CARD
CARGO
CARHEADS
CARICATURE

CARROT
CART-HORSE
CASTAWAYS
CAST-A-WAYS
CASTLE'S
CATALPA
CATALPA-TREE
CATCH-CRIES
CATCHES
CATCHING
CAT-HEADED
CATHEDRAL
CAT-O'-NINE-
  TAILS
CATTLE-BIRDS
CAULDRON
CAVE-MOUTH
CAVERNED
CAVERN-GLOOMS
CAVERNS
CAVE'S
CEDAR
CEDAR-BOARDED
CEILING
CELEBRANT
CELEBRATE
CELL
CELTIC
CENTRES
CEPHISUS
CEREMONIAL
CEREMONY'S
CHAFF
CHAINED
CHAINS
CHAMBERS
CHANCELLOR
CHANGERS
CHANNELS
CHANTING
CHANTS
CHARGERS
CHARIOT-WHEELS
CHARLEMAGNE
CHARTER
CHASTITY
CHAT
CHAUCER
CHAUNTING
CHEATED
CHECKED
CHEERS
CHEESE
CHERRIES
CHERRY
CHERRY-BRANCH
CHERUBIM
CHESHIRE
CHESSBOARDS
CHESTNUT
CHESTNUT-TREE
CHIEFLY
CHIEFS
CHIEFTAINS
CHILD-BEARING
CHILLING
CHILLS

CHIMAERAS
CHIMES
CHINESE
CHIRP
CHOIRS
CHOKE
CHOOSES
CHOOSING
CHOPPERS
CHORUS
CHOU
CHRISTENDOM
CHRISTMAS
CHRISTMAS-TREE
CHRONICLER
CHRONICLERS
CHRONICLING
CHUBBY
CHURCHMEN
CHURCH'S
CHURCHYARD
CICERO
CIDER
CINCTURE
CINNAMON
CIPHER
CISTERN
CIVILISATION
CIVILISATIONS
CIVILIZATION
CLAMOUR-
  CLOTHED
CLANKING
CLANN
CLAPPED
CLARE
CLARE-GALWAY
CLARIONET
CLASPING
CLATTER
CLAY-COLD
CLAY-PILED
CLEANING
CLEANLY
CLEAN-SWEPT
CLEARED
CLEARLY
CLEAR-SHINING
CLENCHED
CLERGYMEN
CLERICS
CLERK
CLIFF-ENCIRCLED
CLIFF-SHELTERED
CLOAKS
CLOGGED
CLOONE
CLOSE-CROPPED
CLOTHING
CLOUDLESS
CLOUD-O'ER-
  MUFFLED
CLUB
CLUMSINESS
CLUSTERING
CLUSTERS
CLYTEMNESTRA

1 (cont.)
COAGULATE
COAL-BLACK
COARSE-BRED
COARSENESS
COAST
COCK-A-DOODLE-
DOODLE-DO
COCK'S
CODGERS
COGENT
COGNOMEN
COILS
COLA'S
COLDER
COLIN
COLLEENS
COLLEGE
COLONIES
COLOONEY
COLOONY
COLT
COLTSFOOT
COMB
COMBS
COMEDIAN'S
COMEDIES
COMEDY
COMER
COMEST
COMETH
COMFORTERS
COMMANDED
COMMANDING
COMMENCED
COMMENDED
COMMINGLING
COMMIT
COMMITTED
COMMONEST
COMMUNE
COMMUNIST
COMPANIONED
COMPANIONING
COMPANIONSHIP
COMPANION-
SHIPS
COMPARES
COMPASS
COMPASS-POINT
COMPEL
COMPELLING
COMPENSATION
COMPETE
COMPLACENCY
COMPLAINED
COMPLAINING
COMPLETED
COMPLETENESS
COMPLETES
COMPLEXION
COMPLEXITY
COMPLIMENT
COMPOSE
COMPOUNDED
COMRADE
CON

CONAN'S
CONCEIVE
CONCEIVED
CONCEIVES
CONCENTRATION
CONCH
CONCHUBAR'S
CONCOBAR
CONDEMNED
CONES
CONEYS
CONFER
CONFESS
CONFRONTING
CONGEALED
CONHOR
CONJUNCTIONS
CONNACHT
CONOR
CONQUER
CONQUERED
CONQUEROR
CONQUERORS
CONQUEST
CONSCIENCE-
STRUCK
CONSIDERATION
CONSIDERS
CONSPIRACY
CONSPIRING
CONSTITUTE
CONSTRAINED
CONSTRUCTED
CONSUMES
CONSUMMATION
CONTEMPLATING
CONTEMPLATIONS
CONTEMPLATIVE
CONTEND
CONTEST
CONTRADICT
CONTRAPUNTAL
CONTROL
CONVENT
CONVENTIONAL
CONVERGE
CONVINCE
COOING
COPSE
COPULATE
COQUETRY
CORAL
CORBETS
CORD
CORDELIA
CORMAC'S
CORMORANTS
CORRIDOR
COSGRAVE
COSIMO
COSSETING
COUNCIL
COUNCILS
COUNSELLED
COUNSELS
COUNTENANCES
COUNTER

COUNTER-TRUTH
COUNTING-HOUSE
COUNTLESS
COUNTRYSIDE
COUNTRY-SIDE
COUNTY
COUPLED
COURAGEOUS
COURT-LADIES'
COURT-LADY'S
COVERLET'S
COVERLID
COWARD
COWARDLY
COWARDS
COWERED
COY
COZENING
CRABBED
CRACKING
CRACKLING
CRACK-PATED
CRADLED
CRADLE-HOOD
CRADLE-SIDE
CRAM
CRAMM'D
CRAMMED
CRANBERRY
CRAOIBHIN
CRASHED
CRASHING
CRAVE
CRAVING
CREAKY
CREAMY
CREASES
CREATION
CRESTED
CRETAN
CREVICED
CREVICES
CRICKETS
CRIETH
CRIME'S
CRITIC
CRITICS
CROACH
CROCUS
CROMWELL
CROON
CROONING
CROP
CROPS
CROSS'D
CROSSES
CROSSING
CROWNLESS
CRUCIFIED
CRUELTIES
CRUISE
CRUMBLED
CRUMPLE
CRUMPLED
CRUNCHES
CRUSH
CRUST

CRYSTALLINE
CU
CUB
CUBS
CUCHULIN
CUFF
CUMANN'S
CUMBROUS
CUPBOARDS
CUR
CURD-PALE
CURED
CURRANT-BUSHES
CURSES
CURTAINED
CURTAINS
CURVING
CUSHLA
CUSTOMARY
CUSTOMS
CUT-THROAT
CUTTING
DA
DABBLE
DABBLED
DADDY-LONG-
LEGS
DAEMONS
DAFFODIL
DAISY
DALLIANCE
DAMAGES
DAMNED
DAMP
DAMPED
DAMS
DANCE-LIKE
DANCING-PLACE
DANE
DANGLING
DANISH
DAPHNE
DARGAN'S
DARK-BEAKED
DARKENED
DARKER
DARKEST
DASHED
DATELESS
DAVIS
DAWNS
DAWN-SONG
DAWS
DAYLIGHT-
DARKENING
DAY-LONG
DAYSPRING
DAZZLING
DEADLY
DEAFENED
DEAFENS
DEAFER
DEAN
DEARTH
DEATHBED
DEATHBEDS
DEATH-BEDS

DEATHFUL
DEATH-HOUR
DEATH-IN-LIFE
DEATH-LONGING
DEATH-MAKING
DEATH-POURING
DEATHS
DECAYETH
DECEITLESS
DECEIVE
DECENT
DECIDE
DECKED
DECLAIMING
DECLENSION
DECLIVITIES
DECREES
DEED-DOER
DEED-DOERS
DEEM
DEEPENED
DEEPENING
DEEP-EYED
DEEP-SUNKEN
DEER-HOUNDS
DEFAMED
DEFENCE
DEFILE
DEFILED
DEFILING
DEFINITIONS
DEGREES
DEIGN
DEIRDRE'S
DEITIES
DEJECTION
DELACROIX
DELIBERATE
DELICATE-
STEPPING
DELIGHTFUL
DELIGHTING
DELIVER
DELIVERANCE
DELIVERED
DELIVERER
DELLS
DELUSION
DEMONIAC
DEMONSTRATE
DENIS
DENOUNCES
DENT
DENYING
DEPARTING
DERG'S
DERIDING
DERMUID
DESCEND
DESERT-CAVES
DESIGN
DESIGNED
DESISTED
DESTINY
DESTROYS
DEVILISH
DEVILS

1 (cont.)

DEVIOUS
DEVOUR
DEVOURED
DEVOUTLY
DEW-
  BEDROWNED
DEW-COLD
DEW-CUMBERED
DEW-DABBLED
DEW-DRENCH'D
DEW-DROP
DEW-WASHED
DEWY-PLOT
DEWY-TONGUED
DIAGRAM
DIARMUID
DICK
DIDO
DIDO'S
DIFFERENTLY
DIGEST
DIGGERS
DIGGES
DIGS
DILIGENCE
DIMLY
DIONYSUS
DIPPING
DIPS
DISASTROUS
DISCARD
DISCERNING
DISCOLORATION
DISCONTENTED
DISCORD
DISCOURSE
DISCOURSES
DISCOURTESY
DISCOVER
DISCOVERERS
DISDAINS
DISEASE
DISFIGURED
DISGORGING
DISGUISED
DISHES
DISHONEST
DISINTER
DISK
DISLIKE
DISMAYED
DISMISSES
DISOWNS
DISPART
DISPENSING
DISPLAYED
DISPLAYS
DISPLEASE
DISSEMBLING
DISSIPATION
DISSOLVE
DISTAFF
DISTAINS
DISTINGUISH
DISTINGUISHED
DISTORTING

DISTRACTION
DISTRUSTFUL
DISTURB
DISTURBED
DITCHES
DIVER
DIVIDED
DIVIDES
DIVINITY
DIVISIONS
DJIN
DJINS
DOCK-LEAVES
DOLLS'
DOLPHIN
DOLPHIN-DRAWN
DOLPHINS
DOLPHIN-TORN
DOMINATE
DOMINION
DOMINIONS
DOMINO
DOMINUS
DON
DONNE
DOORED
DOORMAT
DOOR-PILLARS
DOOR-PIN
DOOR-POST
DOOR-POSTS
DOORSTEP
DOOR-STEP
DOTE
DOUBLES
DOUBLET
DOUBTING
DOUBTS
DOVE-COT
DOWERED
DOWERS
DOWN-TURN
DOWNWARD
DOWSON
DRAG
DRAGGLED
DRAGON-
  GUARDED
DRAGON-RIDDEN
DRAGON-RINGS
DRAGON'S
DRAGON-SCALES
DRAIN
DRAINED
DRAMA
DRAMATIC
DRAMATIS
DRAMATIST
DRAUGHT
DRAUGHTY
DRAWETH
DRAWING
DRAWINGS
DREADING
DREADS
DREAM-
  AWAKENED

DREAM-FED
DREAM-LED
DREAR
DREEPY
DRINKING-BOWLS
DRIP
DRIPPED
DROMAHAIR
DROOPED
DROOPETH
DROP-SCENES
DROUGHT
DROUTH
DROWSILY
DRUDGE
DRUDGERY
DRUGS
DRUMAHAIR
DRUNKARD
DUACH'S
DUCHESS
DUDLEY
DUE
DUGS
DUKE
DULAC
DULL-EYED
DULL-WITTED
DUMB-BELL
DUMBER
DUMBFOUNDED
DUNCE
DUNG
DUNGEON
DURAS
DURING
DUSTWHIRL
DUST-WHIRL
DUTCHMAN
DUTIFUL
DWELLETH
DWELLING
DWELLINGS
DWINDLES
DYEING
EADES'S
EAGERLY
EAGLE'S
EARNING
EAR-PIERCING
EAR-SHOT
EARTH-
  ENKINDLED
EARTH-SHAKING
EASTERN-HEARTED
EBBING
EBREMAR'S
ECHO-
  HARBOURING
ECLIPSE
ECSTACY
EDDYING
EDEN'S
EDIT
EEL
E'ER
EGG

EGGED
EGO
EGYPT
EGYPTIAN
EIGHT
EIGHTEENTH-
  CENTURY
EIGHTIETH
ELBOW
ELBOWS
ELDERS
ELEVATE
ELEVEN
ELF
ELFIN-SIGHTS
ELIZABETH
ELSEWHERE
ELVISH
EMBASSY
EMBERS
EMBRACED
EMBRACES
EMEN'S
EMERALD
EMERY
EMPEDOCLES
EMPIRES
EMPTIER
EMPTYING
EMPYREAN
ENAMELLING
ENAMOURED
ENCHANTER
ENCHANTMENT
ENCIRCLE
ENCIRCLING
ENCLOSE
ENDED
ENDLESSLY
ENDOWED
ENDURES
ENEMIES
ENERGY
ENFOLDEN
ENGAGED
ENGENDER
ENGENDERS
ENGINES
ENGLISH
ENGRAVED
ENGROSS
ENJOINS
ENJOYED
ENMITIES
ENQUIRING
ENRAGED
ENRICHED
ENSLAVE
ENTANGLEMENTS
ENTHRALLED
ENTIRE
ENTIRELY
ENTRANCED
ENTWINED
ENUMERATE
ENVY
EOCHA

EPHEMERA
EPHEMERAL
EPHESIAN
EPILOGUE
EPITOME
EQUALS
ERCOLE
ERI'S
ERROR
ESCUTCHEONED
ESSERKELLY
ESTATE
ESTEEMS
ETERNALISED
ETERNITIES
EUNUCHS
EUROPA
EUROPE
EUROTAS'
EVA
EVADING
EVENING'S
EVENINGS
EVENTS
EVEREST
EVER-LAUGHING
EVER-LONGING
EVER-MOVING
EVER-SINGING
EVER-SUMMERED
EVER-TREMBLING
EVER-UNDULANT
EVER-WINDING
EVERYBODY
EVE-SOOTHED
EVIDENCE
EVIL-STARRED
EWES
EXACT
EXACTING
EXALT
EXALTED
EXCEL
EXCELLENT
EXCHANGE
EXCITE
EXCITING
EXCREMENT
EXECUTIONER
EXHAUST
EXORBITANT
EXPECTATION
EXPECTED
EXPENSE
EXPLAINED
EXPLORE
EXPOUND
EXPRESSION
EXQUISITE
EXTINGUISH
EXTRAVAGANT
EXTREMITIES
EXTREMITY
EXUDE
EXULT
EXULTING
EYE-BALLS

1 (cont.)

EYE'S
EYES'
EYESIGHT
EYNE
FABLE
FABRIC
FACED
FACING
FACT
FACTION
FADETH
FAERYLAND
FAERY'S
FAGGOT
FAILED
FAILS
FAIN
FAIRIES'
FAIRS
FAIRY-HAUNTED
FAIRYLAND
FAIRY'S
FAIRY-SMITTEN
FAITHFULLEST
FAITHLESS
FALIAS
FALSTAFFAN
FALSTAFFIAN
FALTER
FALTERS
FAMED
FAMISH
FANATICISM
FANCIES
FANCY-MAN
FANNED
FAR-AWAY
FARISTAH
FARMHOUSE
FARM-WORK
FARRELL
FARROW
FARTHEST
FAR-WANDERING
FASTED
FASTEN
FATED
FATHERLESS
FATHOMLESS
FATNESS
FATTER
FAVOURED
FAVOURITE
FEACRA
FEATHER-BED
FECUND
FEE
FEEBLY
FEELS
FELLOW-ARTIST
FELLOW-
  ROYSTERER
FELLOW-STUDENT
FELLOW-
  WANDERER

FENCED
FERGUSON
FERTILE
FERVOUR
FETLOCKS
FEVER-FREE
FEVERISH
FIBROUS
FIDDLE-BOW
FIDDLERS
FIDDLE'S
FIDDLES
FIDDLE-STICK
FIDDLE-STRING
FIELDS'
FIERCELY
FIFTEENTH
FIGHTING-MEN
FIGURATIVE
FINDRIAS
FINEST
FINGER'S
FINGERS'
FINGER-TIP
FINVARRA
FIRE-BORN
FIRED
FIRELIT
FIREPLACE
FIRE-PLACE
FIRE'S
FIRM
FIRST-BORN
FIRWOOD
FISHER-LADS
FISHERMEN
FISHER'S
FISHES
FISHES'
FISHING-LINES
FISHLIKE
FISH'S
FISH-TAIL
FITS
FITTER
FIVE-AND-TWENTY
FIVE-SIX
FLAGELLANT
FLAGON
FLAGONS
FLAGSTONE
FLAME-
  BEWILDERED
FLAMED
FLAME-LIKE
FLAMINGO
FLANK
FLAP
FLASHIER
FLATTERER
FLATTERIES
FLATTERING
FLAVOUR
FLAVOURED
FLAX
FLEEING

FLEETER
FLICKED
FLICKERED
FLICKERS
FLIETH
FLITTING
FLOATING-HAIRED
FLOODS
FLOOD-TIME
FLORENCE
FLOURISH
FLOURISHES
FLOURISHING
FLOUT
FLOWERED
FLOWERS'
FLUSH
FLUSHED
FLUSHES
FLUTES
FLUTINGS
FLUTTERS
FLY-CATCHERS
FLY-FISHER'S
FOAL
FOAMDROP
FOAMDROPS
FOAM-FICKLE
FOAM-FLAKES
FOAM-GLOBES
FOAM-OOZY
FOAM-PALE
FOAM-WHITE
FOE
FOEMAN'S
FOEMEN
FOEMEN'S
FOG
FOG-DRIPPING
FOILED
FOLKS
FOLKS'
FOLLOWERS
FOND
FONDER
FOOL-DRIVEN
FOOLED
FOOL'S
FOOT'S
FOOTSORE
FOOTWORN
FOOT-WORN
FORAY
FORBADE
FORBIDDEN
FOREBEAR
FOREFATHERS
FOREGATHER
FOREGO
FORESEES
FOREST'S
FORGAIL'S
FORGATHERED
FORGE
FORGER
FORGIVING

FORGO
FORMATION
FORSAKE
FORSAKEN
FORSWEAR
FORSWEARS
FORTIETH
FORTUNE'S
FORTUNE-TELLER
FORTY-NINE
FOSTER-MOTHER'S
FOUNDATION
FOUNDATIONS
FOUNDED
FOUNDERS
FOUNT
FOUNTAIN'S
FOUNTS
FOURS
FOUR-SCORE
FOUR-SIX
FOURTEEN
FOURTEENTH
FOXGLOVE
FOX-GLOVE
FOXHOUNDS
FOX-HUNTER
FRAGILE
FRAGMENT
FRAGRANCES
FRANKINCENSE
FRAY
FRECKLED
FREED
FREELANDS
FREEMAN
FRENZIES
FRESHET
FRETFUL
FRIENDLIER
FRIENDS'
FRIGHTED
FRIGID
FROG
FROG-SPAWN
FROLIC
FROTH-DROP
FROTH-LIPS
FROTH-SPLASHED
FROTHY
FROZE
FRUITAGE
FULLER'S
FULL-FLAVOURED
FUMBLE
FUME
FUNDS
FUNEREAL
FURNITURE
FURR'D
FURTHEST
FURZE
GABHRA'S
GABY'S
GAFFER
GAINSAY

GALILEAN
GALILEE
GALLERIED
GALLERIES
GALLIVANTING
GAMBLER
GAMEBIRD
GAME-BIRD
GANGLING
GANNET
GANNETS
GAPE
GARDEN-BOY
GARLANDED
GARMENT'S
GARMENTS
GARNERED
GARRET
GARRULOUS
GASPED
GASPING
'GAT
GAUGE
GAVEST
GAVRA
GAVRA'S
GAYEST
GAZEBO
GENERAL
GENERATED
GENEROSITY
GENEROUS
GENII
GENTLEMAN
GENTLER
GEOMETRY
GEORGIAN
GER-EAGLE
GERMAN
GERMANY'S
GETTING
GHOST-FLAMES
GHOST-LOVER
GIANT
GIANTS
GIBE
GIER-EAGLE
GIFTED
GIFTS
GIGANTIC
GILLYFLOWER
GIMLET
GIORGIONE
GIRLHOOD'S
GIRLS'
GIST
GIVETH
GLADDENED
GLADLY
GLAMOURED
GLANCED
GLASS-MOSAIC
GLAZING
GLEN-CAR
GLIDE
GLIDING

1 (cont.)

GLISTEN
GLISTENING
GLITTER
GLITTERS
GLOBE-TROTTING
GLOOMED
GLORIES
GLORIFIED
GLORIOUS
GLOSSES
GLOWS
GLUED
GNASHING
GOAT-HEAD
GOATHERDS
GOAT'S
GOATS'
GOBAN'D
GOBLINS
GOD-APPOINTED
GODDESS
GOD-FORSAKEN
GOD-HATED
GOD-KIND
GOIN'
GOING-DOWN
GOLDEN-CRESTED
GOLDEN-THIGHED
GOLDFISH
GOLD-FISH
GOLD-SEWN
GOLD-SHOD
GOLDSMITHS
GOLD-SOWN
GOLL
GONG-
  TORMENTED
GONNE
GOODMAN
GOODNESS
GOODNIGHT
GOODS
GOOD-WILL
GORE-BOOTH
GORIAS
GORSE
GOSPELLERS'
GOVERNED
GRADUAL
GRAND
GRANDAM
GRAND-CHILDREN
GRANDEST
GRANDFATHER'S
GRANDFATHERS
GRANIA
GRANTED
GRAPE-CLUSTER
GRAPES
GRASS-BARNACLE
GRASS-BLADES
GRASS-BLADES'
GRASS-COLOURED
GRASS-LEAF
GRASS-YELLOW
GRATED

GRATTAN
GRATTAN'S
GRAVE-DIGGERS
GRAVE-DIGGERS'
GRAVE-EYED
GRAVEL
GRAVELLED
GRAVITY
GRAZED
GREASE
GREASY
GREAT-AUNTS
GREAT-
  BLADDERED
GREAT-BODIED
GREAT-
  GRANDCHILDREN
GREAT-
  GRANDDAD
GREAT-
  GRANDFATHERS
GREAT-LIMBED
GREAT-ROOTED
GREAT-UNCLES
GREEDY
GREEKS
GREENISH
GREEN-PATED
GREY-EYED
GREY-GREEN
GREY-HAIRED
GRIDDLE
GRIDDLE-CAKE
GRIEF-
  DISTRAUGHT
GRIEVED
GRIEVES
GRIEVING
GRIFFITH
GRIMALKIN
GRINDING
GRIP
GRIPS
GRISLY
GROSS
GROUND-IVY'S
GROUNDS
GROUSE
GROWETH
GRUBS
GRUMBLE
GRUNT
GRUNTING
GUARD-HOUSE
GUARDIAN
GUARDLESS
GUARDS
GUARDSMEN'S
GUESS
GUIDE
GUIDED
GUIDOBALDO
GUILTY
GUINEVERE
GULLEON'S
GUNNEL
GUSHES

GUSHING
GUST
GUTTER
GUTTERS
GYMNASTS'
HABILIMENT
HABITS
HABITUAL
HACK
HADES
HAG
HAIR-DYE
HALF-AWAKENED
HALF-DEAD
HALF-DECEIT
HALF-DONE
HALF-DRUNK
HALF-HOUR'S
HALF-IMAGINED
HALF-LEGENDARY
HALF-LEGGED
HALF-LIGHT
HALF-LOST
HALF-LYING
HALF-MOUNTED
HALFPENCE
HALFPENNY
HALF-WAKENING
HALFWAY
HALF-WAY
HALF-WRITTEN
HALLOWED
HALT
HALVE
HALVED
HANDLE
HANDLES
HANDMAIDS
HAND'S
HANDSOMEST
HANGMAN'S
HANRAHAN'S
HAPPEN
HAPPENED
HAPPIER-
  THOUGHTED
HAPPILY
HARDEST
HARDIHOOD
HARD-LIVING
HARD-RIDING
HARE'S
HARM
HARMLESS
HARMONIC
HARMONY
HARNESS
HARPER
HARPING
HARPS
HARRIERS
HARROW
HARSHNESS
HART
HARVEST'S
HARVEST-TIME
HASTY

HATCHES
HATER
HATS
HAUGHTIER-
  HEADED
HAUNTED
HAUNTS
HAWKS
HAY-COCK
HAYMOUSE
HAYSTACK
HAZEL-TREE
HAZEL-TREES
HEADED
HEAPED-UP
HEARD'ST
HEARKEN
HEARTACHE
HEART-BREAK
HEARTBURN
HEARTED
HEARTIER
HEARTIEST
HEART-MYSTERIES
HEART-REVEALING
HEART-SMITTEN
HEART-STRINGS
HEARTY
HEAVE
HEAVES
HEAVIER
HEAVIEST
HEAVILY-BUILT
HEBER'S
HEEDS
HEIGHTS
HELICON
HELL'S
HELMET
HELMSMAN'S
HELPER
HELPFUL
HENWIVES
HERALD'S
HERDED
HERDING
HERDSMEN
HERESY
HERMIT
HERODIAS'
HEROES'
HERRING
HESITATE
HIBERNIAN
HIBERNIANS
HIERARCHY
HIGHEST
HIGH-HORSE
HIGHLAND
HIGH-PITCHED
HIGHWAY
HILL-HEADS
HILL'S
HILLSIDE
HILL-SIDE
HIMALAY
HISS

HISSING
HISSOP-HEAVY
HISTORIANS
HISTORIC
HISTORIED
HISTORY'S
HITCHED
HOARDS
HOARIEST
HOARSER
HOB
HOISTING
HOLIDAYS
HOLLIES
HOLLOW-CHEEKED
HOMEBREW
HOME-BREW
HOMES
HOMESTEAD
HOMEWARDS
HONEST
HONESTY
HONEY-BEE
HONEY-
  COLOURED
HONEY-COMB
HONEYED
HONEY-HEART
HONEY-HEARTED
HONEY-MARTS
HONEY-PALE
HONEY-POT
HONEY-SWEET
HONEY-
  THICKENED
HONIED
HONOURED
HOOPED
HORACE
HORDE
HORNED
HORSE-BACK
HORSED
HORSEHAIR
HORSE-HAIR
HORSE-HOOF
HORSE-PLAY
HORSES'
HORTON'S
HOSE
HOSTED
HOSTS
HOUR-GLASS
HOURLY
HOUR'S
HOVERS
HOWEVER
HOWLING
HOWLS
HOWTH
HUCKSTER'S
HUDDLE
HUDDLING
HUMBLER
HUMID
HUMMING-SEA
HUMP

1 (cont.)
HUNCH
HUNDRED-
 THROATED
HUNDRED-YEAR-
 OLD
HUNGARY
HUNKERS
HUNTER-FRIEND
HUNTER-LOVER
HUNTING-CALL
HUNTING-SPEAR
HUNTING-SPEARS
HURLS
HURRIEDLY
HURRIES
HURTLE
HURTLING
HUSH-A-BYE
HUSH'D
HUSKY
HYDE
HYMNS
HYSTERICO-
 PASSIO
ICICLES
IDA'S
IDLER
IL
ILLUSION
ILLUSIONS
IMAGINATIONS
IMAGINES
IMAGININGS
IMITATE
IMITATED
IMITATION
IMMEDIATE
IMMENSITIES
IMMORTALS'
IMPART
IMPASSIONED
IMPATIENT
IMPERIOUS
IMPERMANENT
IMPLACABLE
IMPORTANT
IMPORTUNATE
IMPRISONED
IMPROVISATION
IMPROVISING
IMPULSE
IMPULSIVE
IMPURITIES
IMPURITY
INCANTATION
INCAPABLE
INCENDIARY
INCH
INCHY
INCIDENT
INCLEMENCY
INCLINE
INCOMPATIBLE
INCORRUPTIBLE
INCREASE
INCREASED

INCREASES
INCREASING
IND
INDIANS
INDIA'S
INDIGNATIO
INDIGNATION
INDIVIDUAL
INDOMITABLE
INDUSTRY
INEFFABLE
INEXTRICABLE
INFAMY
INFANTINE
INFIDEL
INFIRM
INFLUENCE
INGENIOUS
INGENUOUS
INGRATITUDE
INHABITANT
INHERITANCE
INISHMURRAY
INJURE
INJUSTICE
INLAND
INMOST
INN
INNKEEPER'S
INNUMEROUS
INSANE
INSATIABLE
INSEPARABLE
INSIPID
INSPIRED
INSTEP'S
INSTRUCTORS
INSTRUMENTS
INSUFFICIENT
INTELLECT'S
INTELLIGIBLE
INTEMPERANCE
INTEMPERATE
INTERMINABLE
INTERVENED
INTIMACY
INTOLERABLE
INTOXICANT
INTRICACY
INTRICATE
INTRIGUE
INTRODUCTION
INVER
INVULNERABLE
INWARDLY
IOLAN
IRISHRY
IRRATIONAL
IRREGULAR
IRVING
ISAIAH'S
ISOLATED
ISSUE
ISSUED
ITALY
ITCH
ITERATION

ITH
IVIED
IVY-COVERED
IVY'S
I-WIS
JACKASS
JADE
JAFFER
JAFFER'S
JAILBIRD
JAILOR
JAMMED
JAUNTING
JAY'S
JESSAMINE
JEST
JEWEL
JEWELLED
JEWELS
JEWEL-STONE
JIG
JILL
JINN
JOAN
JOE
JOHN'S
JOKE
JOKES
JOLLY
JOLT
JOSEPH
JOSEPH'S
JOURNEY-DULL
JOURNEYING
JOURNEY-MAN
JOVIAL
JUBILANT
JUGGLER
JUGGLERS
JUNCTURE
JUNES
JUNO
JUNO'S
JUPITER
JUSTICE
KATHLEEN
KAURI
KEATS
KEDRON
KEENED
KEENERS
KEENIN'
KENNEL
KERCHIEF
KERRY
KESTREL
KETTLEDRUM
KETTLEDRUMS
KETTLES
KEYS
KHAKI
KID
KIDRON
KID'S
KILBARNET
KILLS
KILTARTAN'S

KINDER
KINDLING
KINDRED'S
KINDS
KINGFISHERS
KING-
 REMEMBERING
KINSELLA'S
KINSMAN
KISSES
KITCHEN
KNEE-CAP
KNIGHTLY
KNOCKNASHEE
KNOCKS
KNOLL
KNOWER
KNOWEST
KNOWETH
KNOW'ST
KUSTA
KYLE-DORTHA
KYLE-NA-INO
KYTELER
LABOURED
LABOURER'S
LABURNUM
LACERATE
LACKEY
LADDER'S
LADDERS
LADEN
LADIES'
LAEN
LAGOON
LAIGHEN
LAKE-
 ENBOSOMED
LAKE-LULLED
LAKE-NURTURED
LAKES
LAMB
LAME-FOOTED
LAMENT
LAMP-CHIMNEY
LAMPLIGHT
LAMPS
LAND-OF-THE-
 TOWER
LANDOR
LANDOR'S
LAND'S
LANDSMEN
LAND-UNDER-
 WAVE
LANGUAGE
LANGUORS
LANTERN
LANTHORN
LAP
LAPIS-LAZULI
LAPO
LAPWING
LAPWINGS
LARCH-WOOD
LARDER
LARGELY

LARK
LARKS
LASHED
LASSES
LATCH
LATCHES
LATE-LOST
LATE-RISEN
LATTICE
LATTICED
LAUGH'D
LAUGHTER-LIPPED
LAUGHTER-LIT
LAUNCH
LAUREATE
LAURELLED
LAVERY
LAVISH
LAYS
LAZY
LEA
LEADERS
LEADERSHIP
LEADS
LEAF-CROWNED
LEAF-HID
LEAGUES
LEANED
LEANNESS
LEAPT
LEARN'D
LEARNS
LEATHER
LEATHER-COATED
LEAVE-TAKING
LECHING
LECTERN
LEG
LEGENDARY
LEMON-TINTED
LEND
LENGTHEN
LENGTHENING
LEOPARD-
 COLOURED
LEOPARDS
LESSON
LETHEAN
LET'ST
LEVEE
LEV'RET'S
LIAR
LIBATIONS
LIBERAL
LIBRARY
LICE
LICKED
LICKS
LIDLESS
LIED
LIETH
LIEUTENANT
LIFE-IN-DEATH
LIFE-KEY
LIFELESS
LIFETIME
'LIGHTED

LIGHT-
 ENDAPPLED
LIGHTENED
'LIGHTING
LIGHTLESS
LIGHTNESS
LIGHT-
 OBLITERATING
LIKED
LIKELIHOOD
LIKENESS
LILAC
LILY-BLANCHED
LIMBED
LIMESTONE
LIMP
LIMPED
LINED
LINEN-CARRIER
LINEN-CHEST
LINGERETH
LINGERINGS
LINK
LINKS
LINNET'S
LINNETS'
LIONEL
LIPPED
LIQUORICE
LISADILL
LISS
LISTENS
LISTLESS
LIST'NING
LITTER
LITTLE-LAND
LIVELY
LIVER
LIVERPOOL
LIVERY-STABLE
LIZARD
LOADS
LOADSTONE
LOAM
LOCK
LOCKE
LODGE
LOG-BOOK
LOGIC-
 CHOPPERS
LOIE
LOIN
LOITERING
LOLLING
LONG-ARMED
LONGEST
LONGEVITY
LONG-HAIRED
LONGHI
LONGINGS
LONG-LIMBED
LONG-LIVED
LONG-OARED
LONG-PLANNED
LONG-VISAGED
LONG-WARLESS

LOOMED
LOONY'D
LOOPED
LOOPS
LOOSE-LIPPED
LOOSELY
LOOSENS
LORD'S
LOUD-CRASHING
LOUNGING
LOUR
LOVE-DEW
LOVE-DREAMS
LOVE-LONGING
LOVELORN
LOVE-MAKING
LOVE-PLAY
LOVE-SICK
LOVE-STORY
LOVETH
LOVE-WORN
LOWERED
LOWING
LOWLIER
LOWLINESS
LOWLY
LOYAL
LUCKIER
LUGAIDH'S
LUGNAGALL
LUG-WORM
LUKA
LUKE
LULLING
LULLS
LULLY
LUMBERING
LUNGING
LURCHES
LURES
LURID
LURKS
LUSH
LUST
LUTE-THRONGED
LUXURIANT
LUXURY
LYNX'S
LYRIC
LYRICS
MA
MACBRIDE
MACCARTAN
MACDONAGH
MACDONAGH'S
MADAM
MADEST
MADGE'S
MADMAN'S
MADONNA
MAGAI
MAGH
MAGICIAN
MAGNANIMITIES
MAGNIFIED
MAGNIFY
MAGNITUDE

MAGNUS
MAHOGANY
MAHRAJAS
MAIDEN'S
MAIL'D
MAIMED
MAINLY
MAJESTIC
MAJOR
MAKE-UP
MALEDICTION
MALIGN
MALL
MALLET
MANACLE
MANAGED
MANAGEMENT
MANANAN'S
MANANNAN'S
MANCINI'S
MANGAN
MANIFOLD
MAN-KIND
MANLY
MANNA
MANNED
MANNERS
MANNION
MANNIONS
MAN-PICKER
MANSIONS
MANTEGNA'S
MANUSCRIPT
MANY-
 COLOURED
MANY-FOLDED
MANY-MINDED
MANY-
 PASTURED
MANY-PILLARED
MANY-
 SORROWED
MANY-TIMES-
 TROUBLED
MAPS
MARBLES
MARCO
MARGARET
MARGIN
MARIE
MARIGOLDS
MARJORIE
MARKET-PLACE
MARKETS
MARKIEWICZ
MARMALADE
MARRIAGE-DAY
MARRIAGES
MARRIAGE-SONG
MARROW-BONE
MARROWBONES
MARS
MARSHY
MART
MARTEN-CAT
MASCULINE
MASKER'S

MASONS
MASSACRE
MASSED
MASTERING
MASTER-WORK
MAST-HEAD
MATERNAL
MATHERS
MATTRESS
MAUD
MAURYA
MAURYA'S
MAXIMS
MAYOR
MAY-TREASURE
MCTAGGART
MEADOW-MICE
MEADOW-
 SAFFRONS
MEAGRE
MEASURELESS
MEASURER
MECHANICAL
MEDDLE
MEDDLING
MEDIAEVAL
MEDIAN
MEDIATION
MEDICABLE
MEDICINE
MEDIUM
MEDIUM'S
MEEK
MEETINGS
MEG
MELODIES
MEMORIAM
MENTAL
MENTIONED
MERCHANTS
MERGE
MERIDIAN
MESS
MESSENGER
METHINKS
METTLESOME
MIAU-D
MICHAELANGELO
MICHAEL'S
MICHELOZZO'S
MIDDAY
MID-DAY
MIDDLE-AGE
MIDDLE-AGES
MIDHIR
MIDNIGHT'S
MIDSUMMER
MIEN
MILCH
MILCH-COWS
MILKING
MILKING-PLACE
MILKING-SHED
MILK-PALE
MILLION-FOOTED
MILTON'S
MIMIC

MIMICKING
MINARET
MINDFUL
MINGLE
MINGLES
MINION
MINIONS
'MINISHED
MINISTER
MINISTERING
MINNOWED
MINOS
MINSTREL-WORD
MIRACLE-BRED
MIRACLE-
 WORKING
MIRROR-
 RESEMBLING
MIRRORS
MIRROR-SCALED
MISCALCULATE
MISCHIEVOUS
MISERABLE
MISERRIMUS
MISREPRESENT
MISS'D
MISSHAPEN
MISTAKE
MIST-COVERED
MIST-DROPS
MISTOOK
MIST-THREADS
MITCHEL'S
MOANING
MOB
MOBILE
MOCHARABUIEE
MOCKS
MODEL
MODISH
MOIDERED
MOIL
MOISTENED
MOISTURE
MOLE
MONK
MONKEY
MONK'S-HOOD
MONK'S-HOOD'S
MONTENEGRIN
MONTH
MONTH'S
MOODY
MOON-
 ACCURSED
MOONBEAMS
MOONEEN
MOON-
 LUMINOUS
MOONSHINE
MOON-STRUCK
MOON-WHITE
MOOR-COCKS
MOORED
MOOR-HEN
MOPING
MORALISE

963

1 (cont.)
RENOUNCE
RENOUNCING
RENYI'S
REPENTANCE
REPINING
REPRISALS
REPUTATION
REPUTE
RESEMBLE
RESEMBLING
RESERVED
RESIGNED
RESINOUS
RESOUNDED
RESOUNDING
RESOUNDS
RESOURCE
RESPECT
RESPECTABLE
RESPONSIBILITIES
RESPONSIBILITY
RESTLESS-FOOTED
RESTLESSNESS
RESTORED
RESTRAINING
RESULTS
RESUME
RE-SUNG
RETIRING
RETURNS
REVELATION
REVERBERATED
REVERE
REVERENT
REVERSAL
RE-VISITED
REWARDED
REWARDING
REWARDS
REWORDING
REWRITTEN
RE-WRITTEN
RHADAMANTHUS
RHAPSODY
RHETORICIAN
RHINOCEROS
RHYMER
RHYMER'S
RHYTHM
RIB
RIBBON
RICHNESS
RICK
RIDDLED
RIDES
RIDICULOUS
RIGHTFUL
RIGHT-TAUGHT
RILL
RILLS
RIME
RINGDOVE'S
RING-DOVE'S
RINGER
RINSING
RINSING-POOL

R.I.P.
RIPENED
RIPENING
RIPPED
RISEN
RITES
RIVETED
RIVULET'S
RIVULETS
ROAD-METAL
ROADSIDE
ROAD-SIDE
ROARER
ROARS
ROASTING
ROBBED
ROBBER
ROBED
ROCK-BORN
ROCK-BRED
ROCK-NURTURED
ROCK'S
ROCK-
  WANDERING
ROGUES
ROLL'D
ROMANTICS
ROMP
ROOFLESS
ROOF-LEVELLING
ROOFS
ROOF-TIMBERS
ROOF-TREES
ROOK
ROOK-
  DELIGHTING
ROOKS
ROOMFUL
ROPE'S
ROPES
ROSA
ROSE-BREATH
ROSE'S
ROSE-TREE
ROSSES
ROT
ROTE
ROTS
ROTTED
ROUGE
ROUNDING
ROUNDLY
ROVED
ROWAN
ROWBOAT
ROW-BOAT
ROWED
ROWERS'
ROWS
ROXBOROUGH
ROYAL
ROYSTERER
RUBBED
RUBBING
RUBIES
RUEFUL
RUFFIAN'S

RUFFLED
RUFFLES
RULETH
RUMBLE
RUMOROUS
RUNABOUT
RUNNERS
RURY'S
RUSSIA
RUSTLES
RUTHLESS
SACKED
SADDEN
SADDLEBOW
SADDLE-BOW
SADDLED
SADDLE-GIRTH
SAD'S
SAEVA
SAFER
SAILOR'S
SAINTED
SAINT'S
SAKE'S
SALAD
SALAMIS
SALE
SALIVA
SALMON-FALLS
SALMON-
  SHOALED
SALTED
SALT-FLAKES
SALVATION
SAMUEL
SAN
SANDALLED
SANDALWOOD
SANDED
SANDY
SANDYMOUNT
SAPLINGS
SAPPHO'S
SAPPING
SAPPY
SARDONYX
SATIN
SATURATED
SATURNIAN
SATURNINE
SATYRS
SAVAGELY
SAVES
SAWDUST
SCAFFOLDING
SCALED
SCANAVIN
SCARE
SCARECROW
SCARES
SCARRED
SCENERY
SCENES
SCENT
SCENTS
SCHOLARLY
SCHOOLCHILDREN

SCHOOLMASTERS
SCHOOLROOM
SCONCE
SCOOPED
SCORES
SCORNIN'
SCOT-FREE
SCOURING
SCOWL
SCRATCH
SCULLION
SCULPTOR
SCYTHE
SEA-BORN
SEA-COVERED
SEA-DASHED
SEAFARER
SEAFARERS
SEA-FOAM
SEA-FROTH
SEA-GOD
SEA-GOD'S
SEA-HORSES
SEALING
SEAMEW
SEA-MEW
SEA-NYMPHS
SEARCHED
SEA-RIDER
SEA-ROTTED
SEAS'
SEA-SANDS
SEA-SHELLS
SEASHINE
SEA-SHINE
SEA-STARVED
SEA-STREWN
SEA-TOST
SEAWAYS
SEAWEED
SEA-WEED
SEAWEED-
  COVERED
SEA-WEEDY
SEA-WORLD
SECOND-BEST
SECRET'S
SECT
SECTION
SEDGY
SEED-PODS
SEEKING
SEEMING
SEER
SEIZE
SELDOM
SELECTED
SELF-ACCUSED
SELF-
  AFFRIGHTING
SELF-APPEASING
SELF-DELIGHT
SELFSAME
SELF-SOWN
SELLERS
SELLING
SEMBLANCE

SEMELE'S
SENSELESS
SENSES
SENSUAL
SENSUALITY
SENSUOUS
SENTIMENTALIST
SENTINELS
SENTRIES
SEPTEMBER
SERAPHS
SERPENT-TAILS
SERVANT'S
SERVES
SERVING-MAID
SETTLES
SEVERAL
SEWED
SHADED
SHADOWED
SHADOWING
SHADOWLESS
SHADOW-PLACE
SHAGGY
SHAKESPEAREAN
SHALLOP
SHALLOWING
SHAMED
SHAMELESS
SHAMMING
SHANWALLA
SHAN-WALLA
SHAPELESS
SHARES
SHATTER
SHAUL
SHAVINGS
SHAWE-TAYLOR
SHEAF
SHEEN
SHEEP-GUIDING
SHEETS
SHELF
SHELLEY
SHELLEY'S
SHELL'S
SHEPHERD-BOY
SHEPHERD'S
SHIFTED
SHIFTS
SHININ'
SHIPBOARD
SHIVERS
SHOREWARD
SHORE-WEEDS
SHORN
SHORTEN
SHOULDER-HIGH
SHOVE
SHOWERED
SHOWY
SHUDDERED
SHUFFLED
SHUFFLING
SHUN
SHUTTLE
SIBYLLINE

SIBYL'S
SICILIAN
SICKEN
SICKENING
SIDLE
SIDLED
SIDLES
SIDNEY
SIEVE
SIGNATURE
SILL
SILVER-PROUD
SILVER-
  SANDALLED
SILVER-SHOED
SINAI'S
SINBAD
SINFULLY
SINGE
SINGETH
SINGING-
  MASTERS
SINGLED
SINS
SISTERHOOD
SISTER'S
SIX-AND-TWENTY
SIXES
SIXTY-YEAR-OLD
SKELETON-GAUNT
SKELPING
SKIRT
SKY'S
SLAB
SLANDER
SLANDERED
SLATE
SLATES
SLAUGHTERED
SLAY
SLEEPILY
SLEEPING-ROOM
SLEEP'S
SLEEPY-HEADED
SLEIVEENS
SLEUTH
SLEUTH-HOUNDS
SLIDES
SLIGHT
SLIM
SLIMY
SLINGERS
SLINGS
SLIPPED
SLIPPER
SLIPPERED
SLOPES
SLOUCHES
SLOW-FOOTING
SLOW-MUFFLED
SLUMBER-BOUND
SLUMBERERS
SLUT
SLY
SMARAGDINE
SMART

SMELLED
SMELT
SMITH
SMOOTHS
SMOTHER
SMOULDERING
SMUGGLER
SNAKES
SNAP
SNAPS
SNATCHED
SNATCHES
SNICKED
SNIFF
SNORE
SNOWFLAKES
SNOW-FLAKES
SOBS
SOCIAL
SOCK
SOCKS
SODS
SOFTENING
SOFTEST
SOFT-SHINING
SOILED
SOLDERED
SOLEMN-EYED
SOLSTICE
SOMEHOW
SOMETIME
SOMEWHAT
SON'S
SOOT
SOOTHE
SOOTHED
SORACA
SORDID
SORREL-COVERED
SORRELS
SORROWING
SORROWINGS
SOURS
SOUTHWARD
SPAN
SPANISH
SPANS
SPARKLING
SPARKS
SPARROW-CHIRP
SPARS
SPARTAN
SPASM
SPAWNING
SPEAKERS
SPEAR-GRASS
SPEARHEAD'S
SPEAR-HEAD'S
SPEARSHAFT
SPEAR-SHAFT
SPECTRAL
SPEECHLESS
SPEEDS
SPELL-BOUND
SPENSER
SPHINX
SPICE-ISLES

SPIDER
SPIDERS
SPIES
SPILLED
SPILLS
SPINDLE
SPINDLES
SPINNER
SPINNING-JENNY
SPINNING-TOP
SPIRAL
SPIRIT-THINGS
SPIRITUAL
SPIRITUALISED
SPIRITUS
SPLASH
SPLEEN
SPLIT
SPLITS
SPOIL
SPOILT
SPONTANEOUS
SPORTS
SPOTS
SPOTTED
SPRAY-DABBLED
SPRIGHTS
SPRINGING
SPRINGS
SPRITES
SPUME
SPYING
SQUANDERER
SQUARED
SQUEAKY
SQUIRREL-BROWN
SQUIRREL'S
SQUIRRELS
STABLE-KEEPER
STABLES
STAFFORD
STAGES
STAG'S
STAID
STAINING
STAINS
STAKES
STALKED
STALKS
STALL
STAMMERING
STAMP
STAMPER
STANDEST
STANDISH
STAR-BANE
STAR-ENVIOUS
STARE'S
STAR-FIRES
STAR-FLAME
STAR-FOUGHT
STAR-
  GLIMMERING
STARLING
STARN
STARRED
STAR-

SHUDDERING
STAR-TAUGHT
STARTING-POST
STAR-TROD
STARTS
STARVE
STATESMAN'S
STATESMEN
STATISTICS
STATUARY
STATUED
STAVE
STEAD
STEADIED
STEAL
STEALTH
STEALTHILY
STEAM
STEAMSHIP
STEEL-BLUE
STEEPLE
STEERING-OAR
STEERS
STEP
STEPPED
STEPPING
STILLY
STILT-JACK
STIRLESS
STIRRING
STOLES
STONE-GREY
STONY-HEARTED
STONY-STILL
STOREYS
STORMBEATEN
STORM-BITTEN
STORM-BROKEN
STORM-
  SCATTERED
STORM-TOSSED
STOUT
STRADDLE
STRADDLING
STRAFFORD
STRAIGHTEN
STRAINS
STRAIT
STRANGERS
STRANGLE
STRAW-DEATH
STRAW-PALE
STRAWS
STRAYETH
STREAMING
STREET-CORNERS
STRETCHES
STREWING
STRIP
STRIPPED
STRIPS
STRIVE
STRIVING
STROKES
STRONGEST
STRONGLY
STROVE

STRUCKEN
STRUGGLES
STRUTS
STRUTTING
STUB
STUBBORN
STUBBORN-
  HEARTED
STUDENT
STUDENT'S
STUDENTS
STUDIES
STUDIO
STUMP
STUMPIER
STUMPS
STUPEFIED
STURDIER
STURDY
SUBMISSIVE
SUBSCRIPTION
SUBTILE
SUBTLE-SOULED
SUBTLEST
SUCKLE
SUFFERED
SUGGESTED
SUIT
SUITED
SULPHUROUS
SUMMERED
SUMMER-TIME
SUMPTUOUS
SUNDAY
SUN-DRY
SUNFLOWERS
SUN-FLUSHED
SUN-FRECKLED
SUNLESS
SUNNIER
SUNSICK
SUN-SMITTEN
SUPER-HUMAN
SUPERMAN
SUPERSESSION
SUPINE
SUPPLER
SUPPLIANT
SUPPORTING
SUPPOSE
SUPREME
SURETY
SURF
SURFACE
SURMISE
SURMOUNT
SURMOUNTS
SURROUNDED
SWADDLING
SWADDLING-
  CLOTHES
SWALLOW
SWALLOW'S
SWAN'S
SWARD
SWARMS
SWAYS